DATE DUE

DE 3 02			

DEMCO 38-296

THE
ELECTION DATA BOOK

THE
ELECTION DATA BOOK

A Statistical Portrait of Voting in America

1992

Compiled and Edited by Kimball W. Brace
and the staff of Election Data Services, Inc.

≋BERNAN PRESS

Lanham, MD

Printed in the United States of America

94 93   4 3 2 1

∞ ™

Bernan Press
An Imprint of Bernan Associates
4611-F Assembly Drive
Lanham, MD 20706-4391
(301) 459-7666

ISBN: 0-89059-011-7

CONTENTS

ACKNOWLEDGEMENTS

This volume was prepared under the direction of Kimball W. Brace, president of Election Data Services, as well as the daily guidance of Dale Tibbitts, director of computer operations.

A special acknowledgement goes to Election Data Services' Robert Grundstad, who has been this volume's constant companion since Election Day, 1992—proposing table ideas, formatting data, and generating copy to explain the inner workings of the election process. Robert also kept track of the many changes that accompanied this book's production.

In addition, other members of Election Data Services have devoted considerable time and their varied talents to different aspects of this effort. Dean Plotnick supervised the initial collection and subsequent entry of the mountains of data that went into the book; he also lent his encyclopedic knowledge of politics to make certain that these vast fields of numbers were grounded in political reality. Justin Shriver wrote most of the programs to generate thousands of percentages, pluralities, and rankings (with the assistance of Jane Waliszewski and Phil Bender). The hundreds of maps were prepared by our talented cartographic staff, including Joe Pindell (who composed the black and white maps), Jeff Macintire (who supervised the creation of the intricate color maps), and Karl Phillips. Doug Chapin contributed both his talents as "wordsmith" and, more importantly, his considerable patience in dealing with constant revisions to the text. The state historical pages (both tables and charts) were assembled from Election Data Services archives and checked and double-checked by Molly Kelly. Dr. Lisa Handley, Dwight Wilson, and Lisa Phillips provided further assistance to this project. Their excellent work is evident throughout the pages of this publication, and they deserve much recognition.

Thanks are also due to the thousands of individuals in state, city, county, and town election offices nationwide for their assistance in collecting the data which is the heart of the book.

I would also like to acknowledge personally a friend and long-time mentor, Richard Scammon, for his immense contribution to the field of election analysis, especially as creator (and current co-editor) of the *America Votes* series. Dick has always been an important force in my life, from his early helping hand when I was a fledgling researcher at the NBC News Election Unit in 1972, to his offer of office space to help start Election Data Services in 1977. His trailblazing work in the organization and publication of election statistics paved the way for volumes like this one. The graphics in this publication, especially the thematic maps, are the product of my personal, twenty-year obsession inspired by his work in *America Votes*. While Dick's eyesight may have faded (an occupational hazard for those of us who work with "the numbers" of elections), his passion for reporting election results in a clear, concise, and comprehensive manner lives on as the creative spark behind this volume.

I would also like to acknowledge Alice McGillivray, co-editor of *America Votes*, and Curt Gans of the Committee for the Study of the American Electorate, for insuring both accurate and uniform data. Both individuals have been extremely cooperative in sharing data and comparing notes on problems over the past six months as both this volume and their own publications were compiled. I am grateful to these friends and colleagues for their assistance.

Finally, this book is dedicated to the thousands of candidates for elective office, as well as the more than one hundred million voters across the country who came together in 1992 to produce the largest voter turnout in United States history. Without them this book would be a collection of blank pages. But because of their faith in the workings of our democracy, this profile will provide scholars and interested observers with a snapshot of the **vox populi** (voice of the people) for years to come.

Kimball Brace
June 1993

INTRODUCTION

The Election Data Book is a biennial publication containing maps, charts, and tables which show the results of the most recent primary, general, and special elections. It includes the vote for major party candidates for the offices of president of the United States, U.S. senator, U.S. representative in Congress, and governor; plus information on voter registration and voter turnout. Data are presented for states, counties, and congressional districts. Finally, because of the essential role of the 1990 decennial census in the analysis of election statistics, a selection of demographic data from the census is also included.

This edition provides the results of the November 3, 1992, general elections; presidential primaries that occurred in the spring of that year; the November 1991 general elections for governor in Kentucky, Louisiana, and Mississippi; and various special elections held in 1991 and 1992 to fill U.S. Senate vacancies. Special elections that occurred in 1991 or 1992 for members of the U.S. House of Representatives are not included in this edition because the elections were held within boundaries that existed before the 1991 reapportionment and redistricting of the U.S. House of Representatives. The extensive reapportionment and redistricting process that occurred in 1991 and 1992 produced the new districts that were used for the first time in the November 3, 1992, general elections and are reported in this edition. Results from any subsequent special elections held to fill congressional vacancies will be included in future editions.

Book Organization

The body of this book is divided into individual state chapters organized around a series of 10 tables. The tables, by their abbreviated titles, are:

A. 1990 Population
B. 1990 Voting Age Population (VAP)
C. Voter Participation
D. Voter Registration, by Political Party Affiliation
E. Vote for President
F. Vote for U.S. Senator
G. Vote for Governor
H. Vote for U.S. Representative in Congress
I. Vote for President, Democratic Primaries
J. Vote for President, Republican Primaries

Every state chapter contains the population and voter participation tables (Tables A, B, and C), as well as tables for the presidential and congressional elections (Tables E and H). Additional tables are included if a state reported voter registration statistics by political party affiliation (Table D), if the state conducted any senatorial or gubernatorial elections—whether regularly scheduled or special (Tables F and G), or if presidential primaries were held in that state (Tables I and J).

Chapters begin with a one-page abstract of the electoral process within each state, including population statistics, information on congressional districts, and a summary of voting equipment usage. This abstract is followed by a profile of the individual candidates for each office. This profile lists the name of each candidate, the total number of votes he or she received, any affiliation between the candidate and a political party, and the candidate's status as incumbent or challenger. Next are a chart and table that show statewide voter registration and turnout trends between 1948 and 1992, followed by a reference map that depicts the geographic areas (the state, counties, and congressional districts) covered in that chapter. All tables appropriate to the given state appear next, with thematic maps showing results of presidential, senatorial, and gubernatorial elections (if applicable) concluding the chapter.

There are three additional parts to the book. A United States chapter precedes the individual state chapters and provides a summary of the statewide data from each of the tables. Tables in the U.S. chapter are similar to the tables in the state chapters, although certain items have been omitted where appropriate. The U.S. chapter also contains a profile of the presidential candidates; included are candidate names, their total nationwide vote, their percentage of the vote, as well as any party affiliation.

A second supplemental chapter abstracts data from the population, voter participation, and presidential election tables for the 70 counties in the U.S. with the largest population. This chapter presents a composite view of a significant section of the country, since these 70 counties account for more than one third of the national population. Also included in this section are tables listing the 70 counties and the 70 congressional districts with the highest and lowest percentage values for a portion of the data items presented in this volume. For example, one table shows which counties gave George Bush the highest share of their vote, while another shows which counties had the lowest voter turnout.

The third featured section is a series of one- and two-page color maps (collected at the back of the book) that show election and demographic data for the entire country at the state and county levels. The color maps also show types of voting equipment used in each county, counties covered by the Voting Rights Act (42 U.S.C. § 1973), and control of state legislatures by political parties.

Geographic Areas

The tables, which form the core of *The Election Data Book,* present data for states, counties, and (in New England) townships. In addition, various totals and subtotals in the tables present data for congressional districts and the country as a whole.

Although it is a unique geographic entity, the District of Columbia has its own "state" chapter, which has been placed after the other state chapters. The maps and tables for the District of Columbia present data by wards. Within the U.S. chapter, data for the District of Columbia appears following the states.

Geographic codes for states and counties are presented in the left-hand column of Table A. For states and the District of Columbia, the two-digit state code is that assigned for Federal Information Processing Standards (FIPS) use. For each county or county equivalent the assigned five-digit code includes the two-digit FIPS state code, plus a three-digit census code unique to each component county.

Counties and County Equivalents

In most states, the county is the primary political subdivision as well as the political unit responsible for administering elections. In Louisiana, subdivisions of the state are called "parishes" and perform functions similar to the counties of other states. In Alaska, which is not divided into counties, elections are administered and tallied by the state government, using boundaries that correspond to state house districts. Geographic codes are provided in Table A for Alaskan county equivalents (boroughs and census areas), but not for Alaskan election districts.

In four states, one or more cities are considered the political equivalent of counties. These "independent cities"—Baltimore, Maryland; St. Louis, Missouri; Carson City, Nevada; and the 41 independent cities in Virginia—also administer elections. The tables for these four states first present data for their counties, then for their independent city or cities. Geographic codes listed for independent cities in Table A correspond to the codes used by the U.S. Census Bureau. Several cities in Illinois and Missouri also administer elections independently, but since they are not Census county equivalents, their demographic and election data are included in data for the counties in which they are located. The entire District of Columbia and the part of Yellowstone National Park in Montana are also considered counties for statistical purposes.

Two counties—Kalawao County in Hawaii and Yellowstone National Park in Montana—have been merged with adjacent counties for election administration purposes. Consequently, Kalawao and Yellowstone National Park counties are listed separately only in Tables A and B. Counties exist in the six New England states (Connecticut, Maine, Massachusetts, New Hampshire, Rhode Island, and Vermont), but their officials do not administer elections. Instead, that function is assumed by approximately 1,500 cities and towns which subdivide the counties. In order to limit the size of this book, data are reported only for the 412 cities and towns of New England that have more than one voting precinct.

A voting precinct is a subdivision of a county, city, or town established for the purpose of administering elections, and is usually created around a polling place. This book does not present data for voting precincts, although the number of precincts within each state is noted in the statistical abstracts.

Demographic Data

Demographic data are relevant to the analysis of voting statistics in a number of ways. First, the U.S. House of Representatives is reapportioned every 10 years based on the census count of each state's population. Likewise, electoral voting districts, including congressional and state legislative districts, are periodically redrawn on the basis of their total population. The racial and ethnic composition of a given area is considered during the process of redrawing districts, since federal laws such as the Voting Rights Act (42 U.S.C. § 1973) require that the voting strength of minority group populations not be diluted during redistricting. Finally, voting age population is often paired with voter registration and turnout data to measure election participation rates.

Most of the demographic data in *The Election Data Book* is presented in the first three tables. Table A shows the total 1990 population of the given areas, and breaks down this total by race and ethnic origin. Table B is similar, but presents 1990 data for only those persons of voting age (18 years of age or older). Table C, which focuses on voter participation, presents updated 1992 estimates of the voting age population (VAP); these estimated figures are used to calculate various voter participation statistics relative to the November 1992 general election.

The primary source of the demographic data presented in this book is the 1990 Census of Population and Housing, conducted by the U.S. Census Bureau. Most of the data for counties and their subdivisions (such as the New England cities and towns), come directly from this source. The Bureau is also the original source of demographic data for legislative and congressional districts, but such data has been aggregated from a lower level of geography (for instance, the census block level) by Election Data Services or by various state agencies.

Racial and ethnic characteristics The tables generally follow Census Bureau categories for subdividing the population on the basis of race and ethnic origin. On its questionnaires, the Bureau asks two basic questions, both of which rely upon the self-identification of the respondent. The first question asks the respondent's race, and provides only the following categories: white, black, native American, Asian and Pacific Islander, and other. "Hispanic" is not a possible answer to this question, but all respondents are asked in a separate question to identify whether they are of Hispanic origin. As a result, respondents could state that they were both black and Hispanic or both Asian and non-Hispanic. Because of this potential for overlap, it would be incorrect for researchers to simply add the Hispanic data to the racial data in order to arrive at a total minority population. The Census Bureau, however, has cross-tabulated the results of these two questions and provided counts by which users can generate cleaner data in order to merge race and ethnicity. Election Data Services has utilized such cross-tabulated counts so that *The Election Data Book* reports non-Hispanic racial counts (i.e., non-Hispanic whites, non-Hispanic blacks, etc.) and a separate, complete count of the Hispanic population.

Voting Age Population (VAP) The state-level VAP estimates for the years 1948 to 1992, and the 1990 county-level VAP figures were obtained from the Census Bureau. Donnelley Marketing Information Services provided updated estimates for 1992, but these county-by-county estimates were for July 1992—four months prior to the election. Therefore, Election Data Services modified the Donnelley figures by aging the data on a straight-line projection method. In this process, the average monthly increase between the 1990 VAP and the July 1992 estimates was added for each month from July to November 1992.

In addition, the data were normalized to conform to the Census Bureau's 1992 state-level VAP estimates. (In other words, each of the aged county estimates for November 1992 was adjusted upwards or downwards to account for state-level differences between the Census Bureau figures and Donnelley estimates.) The VAP estimates for 1992 are available only for counties and county equivalents recognized by Donnelley; therefore, no 1992 VAP estimates are presented for Alaska's election districts, wards in the District of Columbia, and New England cities and towns.

Voter Registration

Most state and/or local governments maintain a roster of eligible voters. However, state voter registration requirements and procedures—minimum residency requirements, registration deadlines, allowances for declarations of political party affiliation, and voter roll purges due to death, relocation, or failure to vote—vary widely across the country.

There are four states that do not require persons to register prior to election day. North Dakota has no voter registration requirement whatsoever, while the three other states—Maine, Minnesota, and Wisconsin—allow election day registration. Wisconsin requires registration only in municipalities with a population of 5,000 or more. In Table C (Voter Participation), no voter registration data are reported for North Dakota or Wisconsin due to the lack of statewide reporting. Only statewide data could be presented for Vermont since officially certified county-level voter registration data were not available from the Vermont Secretary of State at the time of publication.

In 25 states and the District of Columbia, persons registering to vote may declare their affiliation with a political party. Table D (Voter Registration by Political Party Affiliation) shows the number of persons registered as Democrats, Republicans, and independents. This third category includes persons who declared their status as "independent" or "unaffiliated"; persons who declined to affiliate with either of the two major parties in states where only three categories of registrants were reported (Democratic, Republican, or Other); or residents of other states who declined affiliation with any political party, including any minor party. In cases within Table D where the number of registered Democrats, Republicans, and independents does not equal total voter registration, footnotes to the statewide totals provide a breakdown of registration counts for minor parties.

Several states provided data on voter registration by party in a separate report, and in a few instances the total number of registrants on that report differs slightly from total registration and turnout reported on returns from the general election. Instances where the sum of registrants by party differs from total voter registration reported on election returns are documented in footnotes to the tables.

In some states (Alabama, Arkansas, Florida, Georgia, Kentucky, Louisiana, North Carolina, and South Carolina), persons who register to vote are requested to identify themselves by race. Statewide data on voter registration by race are included in footnotes to Table C (Voter Participation).

Additional information on the regulation of voter registration is provided in the statistical abstracts. In particular, the abstracts list the various methods of voter registration offered as alternatives to traditional, in-person registration. These alternatives include: (1) voter registration by mail, (2) voter registration on election day, (3) voter registration forms and services provided by governmental agencies with extensive dealings with the public, such as welfare offices (agency-based voter registration), (4) voter registration forms and services provided by public offices of motor vehicle departments ("motor-voter" registration), and (5) voter registration performed by persons who have been deputized as registrars by local elections officials. State deadlines for registration prior to elections are also included in the abstracts. Deadlines range from five to 30 days before an election, excluding the three states previously noted as allowing registration on election day itself. This information pertains to general elections, unless otherwise indicated.

The sources of the voter registration data were secretaries of state, city and county clerks, and registrars of voters. The information on voter registration regulations appearing in the statistical abstracts and illustrated in the color map section was obtained from the National Clearinghouse on Election Administration of the Federal Election Commission in Washington, DC.

Voter Turnout

Voter turnout is the primary means for measuring voter participation at the polls. In 1992, 35 states and the District of Columbia reported the actual number of voters who turned out by tabulating the number of persons who requested a ballot on election day, or who previously obtained an absentee ballot. Such persons were counted in voter turnout, regardless of whether they cast a vote for any candidate. While each election has seen more states report this data, there are still states which do not report actual voter turnout.

Actual voter turnout data are presented for Iowa but the data were not officially certified by the Iowa Secretary of State at time of publication. Only certified state-level data were available for Vermont.

For states that do not report actual voter turnout, an approximate measure of turnout can be devised by adding the total vote received by every candidate for each individual office, and selecting the office with the highest number of votes. The resulting figure can be used in place of an actual turnout statistic. These turnout approximations appear in the column labelled "highest office turnout" in Table C, and are included for even those states that do report the actual turnout. "Highest office" data are calculated at the county level for the office with highest turnout within that county, based upon an analysis of votes for president, U.S. senator, U.S. representative, or governor. In the chart and table presenting 1948-1992 voter registration and turnout trends, highest office turnout is calculated at the state level, using statewide vote totals to determine which office received the highest number of votes.

Table C also contains an item labelled "maximum vote turnout", which is either actual voter turnout or highest office voter turnout, whichever is greater. Maximum vote turnout can be used for comparisons among jurisdictions, such as between the states in Table C of the U.S. chapter.

Like the voter registration data, the sources for voter turnout data are the secretaries of state, city and county clerks, and registrars of voters. Voter turnout rates shown in the tables include voter turnout as a percentage of both voter registration and the voting age population . (For a more extensive discussion of voter turnout rates and use of this data, see the preface "LIES, DAMNED LIES, AND STATISTICS.")

Two states—Louisiana and South Carolina—report voter turnout by race, and three states—Louisiana, Maryland, and Oregon—report voter turnout by political party affiliation. These data are included in footnotes to Table C (Voter Participation).

Vote for Candidates

The votes obtained by candidates are shown in the candidate profiles, in the statistical tables, and on various maps. The candidate profiles present nationwide, statewide, or district-wide vote totals for all candidates on the ballot in that respective jurisdiction. Generally, the county-wide tables show the votes for candidates of the two major parties, with the votes for candidates who ran as independent or minor party candidates combined under a single, "Other" category. Votes for a minor party or independent candidate are shown separately when such candidates placed first or second or were nationally prominent, such as presidential candidate Ross Perot. In several states where candidates ran as the nominee of more than one political party, vote totals in the candidate profiles are presented both by individual parties and for all parties combined under each candidate's name. In the tables, however, the combined vote for candidates running under multiple parties is shown under the candidate's name and a major party designation. In a few states, certain write-in votes or votes cast by residents overseas are not reported by county and are reflected only in the tables' statewide totals; these instances are indicated by footnotes wherever they apply.

In the presidential primary tables, the number of candidates for which votes are presented is limited to eight in the Democratic primaries, and four in the Republican primaries. If there were candidates beyond these set limits, then the last column contains a sum of votes for all other candidates. Votes for "uncommitted" are included in these tables.

In several instances, data from primary elections for senatorial, gubernatorial, and congressional races are included in the tables when candidates were elected to office directly from the primaries. In Louisiana, where all candidates (regardless of party) appear on the same ballot in an open primary, a candidate may be elected to office from the primary election if he or she obtains a majority of the vote. In Florida, the name of the winner of a Republican primary election for a congressional seat did not appear on the general election ballot since there was neither a Democratic primary nor a qualified write-in candidate.

The black and white thematic maps for each state show vote percentages obtained in each county by the candidate who won statewide; these percentages are divided into quartiles for graphics presentation. The quartiles, which vary for each electoral race and each state, were determined by considering the minimum and maximum data values for each contest and distributing the units of data so that each quartile contains approximately the same number of units. Frames placed around the labels of individual geographic areas (e.g., counties) indicate those areas carried by the statewide winner.

The sources of the officially certified election results used in the tables and maps are secretaries of state, and city and county clerks.

Other Data

The Election Data Book presents several other data items in the statistical abstracts and color maps; one such item is the various types of voting systems used by counties. The statistical abstracts show the number of counties using each type of system from the following categories: paper ballots, Datavote punch cards, all other punch cards, mechanical lever voting machines, optical scanners, and combinations of systems (referred to as mixed systems).

Reports on voting equipment use are collected by Election Data Services on a regular basis from secretaries of state, and city and county clerks, and are current as of the spring of 1992. The total number of jurisdictions using the various systems may exceed the number of counties or county equivalents in a few states where other jurisdictions administer elections in addition to or instead of counties (e.g., the New England states).

The statistical abstracts show data on straight ticket voting, which refers to the process that allows voters to cast votes for all candidates of a particular political party simply by marking their ballots for the party instead of for individual candidates. Twenty states permit straight ticket voting. In most of these states, a person may vote for one or more candidates of another party (including independent or write-in candidates) as exceptions to their otherwise straight ticket. In the statistical abstracts, this procedure is referred to as ticket splitting by "exception". In several states with straight ticket voting , voters who desire to split a ticket must vote separately for each and every office. In the statistical abstracts, this procedure is referred to as ticket splitting by "separate" voting. The source of the data on straight ticket voting is the National Clearinghouse on Election Administration of the Federal Election Commission.

The statistical abstracts also show data concerning control of state legislative houses by political parties, both before and after the November 1992 general election. Data are not provided for Nebraska or the District of Columbia, which have unicameral legislatures to which members are elected on a non-partisan basis. The source of this information is the National Conference of State Legislatures.

Other data included on the statistical abstracts are the number of legislative and congressional districts in each state, average district populations, and current state officials and members of Congress.

Math Calculations

Most of math calculations in the tables consist of simple percentages and rankings. Percentages are used in two ways: either by row or by column. The first shows the subsets of data that make up the reported total for a given geographic area and the second shows an area's share of the sum total of data for all areas combined in a state (also referred to as contribution to sum total).

In the tables, math calculations of a similar type have been grouped together whenever possible and follow the items containing whole numbers of raw data in the following order: (1) row percentages, (2) rankings, and (3) percent contribution calculations (column percentages). Except in the candidate profile, all percentages are rounded to one decimal place. Due to rounding, column percentages do not always total 100 percent. Vote percentages in the presidential tables have been calculated based on (1) all candidates in the race and (2) the major party (Democrat and Republican) candidates' share of the vote.

Entries where data are missing or cases where entries would be inappropriate are indicated as follows:

Blank — Inappropriate entry (e.g., on a statewide totals' row under an item ranking geographic areas)

Dash (-) — No data (e.g., no contest in 1992, statistic not reported or not available at the time of publication, or an entry requiring a calculation based on an unreported statistic)

"0" — Data value is zero (e.g., for a candidate on ballot who received no votes)

"<0.1" — Data value is not zero, but the value reported would be zero if rounded

Missing data, particularly in voter registration and turnout, are responsible for gaps that appear in certain maps, charts, and tables.

"Drop-off" refers to a tendency among some voters to show up at the polls but not vote for all offices on the ballot. Prior research done by Election Data Services and the Congressional Research Service shows some degree of drop-off occurs even for the office at the top of the ballot. Generally, drop-off is derived by subtracting the total combined vote for all candidates for a particular office from the actual turnout; the difference is then divided by the turnout to obtain the drop-off percentage. In the 15 states that do not compile or report actual turnout, drop-off is instead derived from highest office turnout. In those instances where highest office turnout is used to determine the drop-off percentage, drop-off for the office generating the turnout figure will be zero.

The tables presenting election results for candidates also calculate plurality, which is the excess number of votes obtained by the winning candidate over and above the number of votes for the candidate who received the second highest number of votes. Table D (Voter Registration by Party) also calculates plurality for the party with the largest number of registrants.

ABOUT ELECTION DATA SERVICES

Election Data Services, Incorporated, is a leading authority in the field of election data collection and analysis, and one of the foremost experts in redistricting and reapportionment. In the course of its redistricting work, Election Data Services has developed census and election return databases, analyzed current district boundaries, and assisted in the drawing of new district lines. Representatives of Election Data Services have testified as expert witnesses in court hearings involving redistricting plans in over half of the nation. Election Data Services has also assisted local election administrators with the implementation of redistricting plans into their office operations.

Election Data Services maintains an extensive collection of state, county, congressional district, and precinct-level election returns. At the state and county level, Election Data Services has automated returns for presidential, gubernatorial, and U.S. senatorial elections dating back to 1948; at the congressional district level, Election Data Services has computer files of returns for the same offices dating back to 1972. At the precinct level, Election Data Services has collected returns in both computer and paper form, as well as maintained an archive of precinct maps, dating back to 1984 for nearly all areas of the country. (Additional information is available for selected areas dating back to 1976.) All of these election returns, including the 1992 returns printed in this volume, may be purchased from Election Data Services.

Since its creation in 1977, Election Data Services has distinguished itself as a leading firm in the development of political graphics. This process places census and political data onto maps so that higher-level trends and special cases can be more readily identified.

Election Data Services also offers a number of products that are designed to explain the reapportionment of congressional and state legislative districts that followed the 1990 Census. Among these are **ZIP+DISTRICT**, a nationwide file linking five- and nine-digit postal ZIP codes to congressional and state legislative districts, and a series of electronic files showing the boundaries for the new congressional districts and selected state legislative districts. Election Data Services also develops custom reports illustrating district- and precinct-level demographics and political data.

Kimball W. Brace, the founder and president of Election Data Services, is a nationally recognized expert on election matters. Over the years, Mr. Brace has travelled across the country advising, teaching, and acting as a consultant to public officials on all aspects of the electoral process. Mr. Brace has lectured on redistricting and election topics in a number of distinguished forums, and is often quoted in magazines and newspapers. His apportionment estimates are a standard for reporters and analysts in the field. Mr. Brace is a graduate of The American University in Washington, DC.

"LIES, DAMNED LIES, AND STATISTICS"

Observations on using election data

by Kimball Brace, Doug Chapin,
and the staff of Election Data Services, Incorporated

The title quote, alternately attributed to Benjamin Disraeli or to Mark Twain, reflects many individuals' contempt for the gathering, the reporting, and the analysis of statistics. However, the critics' scorn is no match for the insatiable hunger for statistics demonstrated by both the business world and the public at large, as evidenced by the proliferation of daily polls, census data, and economic indicators (as well as the sports page of USA Today). As contributors to the deluge, the editor acknowledges this skepticism, but seeks to demonstrate that a proper reading of the tables and graphs in this book is possible using only common sense and a little caution.

There is a certain delicate balance involved in compiling and editing a volume of data this size. The editor is torn between a desire to offer as comprehensive a set of information as possible, while at the same time offering enough context to allow readers a meaningful understanding of the items or trends to be illustrated.

In assembling this profile of the 1992 elections, we at Election Data Services have been fortunate enough to rely on the excellent work of federal, state, and local election officials. An accurate count is vitally important to everyone in the wee hours of election night; however, long after most of us have forgotten all but the most significant results, the smallest details of voter statistics remain part of these professionals' daily lives.

We have also had the opportunity to take advantage of the huge quantity of information compiled by the Census Bureau, whose personnel invest thousands of hours of effort in making data available to the American public.

But despite the work of these skilled professionals, the world of voting analysis and election administration is sufficiently full of twists, turns, and quirks that a short primer on the potential "lies" involved in interpreting the tables and graphs is presented in this preface. For each of the "lies", we offer the countervailing "truth" and a short explanation of the reasons for the confusion. The goal is to provide the reader with the "know-how" to navigate the potential traps found in the data.

"LIE"

Census estimates accurately portray the pool of persons eligible to register to vote on election day.

TRUTH

Estimates are just that ... educated guesses. In fact, some apparent anomalies in the statistics contained in this volume are partly a function of the inaccuracy of the voting age population estimates.

The statewide November 1992 voting age population projections contained in this volume were actually created by the Census Bureau in the fall of 1991 and released in the spring of 1992. These projected data actually have a greater potential for error (contrary to the presumption of greater accuracy given their proximity to the 1990 Census) because final Census counts had just been released to the estimators. As a result, there was not enough time for a thorough study of population changes at the state and county level.

But as time passes and more information is collected on these local-level changes (via birth and death records, migration studies, etc.), better projections will be possible. The Census Bureau's practice of revising past projections as it releases new ones is a tacit admission that its own estimates improve with time. The 1992 data, for example, contained revised population estimates dating back to 1982.

Estimates and projections usually have a higher geographic level that acts as a control; in other words, national estimates control state estimates, which control county estimates, and so on. As a result, relatively less-populated areas are subject to disproportionate rounding error in the estimation process. The reader will note, for example, that in a few cases states and counties are shown with more than 100% of their voting age population registered to vote. A review of such apparently erroneous figures by the staff at Election Data Services revealed that most of these jurisdictions had relatively small numbers of inhabitants. Checks with state and local election officials confirmed the accuracy of the registration numbers (but note the caveat on registration which follows). Whatever their flaws, the estimates are included because they are helpful in bringing voting age population data into line with the changes in overall population that occur over time.

"LIE"

Everyone in the voting age population (reported by the Census Bureau for individuals 18 years old and older) is eligible to vote.

TRUTH

Many members of the voting age population are ineligible to vote because of residency, citizenship, criminal record, or mental health.

The Constitution of the United States requires that a census of "persons" be taken every ten years. The census asks respondents to indicate where they *resided* on Census Day (April 1, 1990); these figures are then reported by the Census Bureau and used for redistricting congressional and state legislative boundaries. By their nature, however, census figures have less meaning when applied to election administration, since a person's census residence and legal residence (which is usually the basis for voter qualification) are not always the same. Still other individuals who legally reside in a given jurisdiction lose the right to vote because of their criminal record or mental health.

One resulting limitation on using the census voting age population data to analyze voting statistics is that voting age population includes some persons not qualified to vote. Among these persons are resident and illegal aliens (the Census questionnaire does not, in fact, ask directly about citizenship), felons, and persons in mental institutions.

Another limitation on the "fit" between voting age population and actual voters is the local nature of elections. Many temporary residents (e.g., college students) maintain their permanent residence and voter registration elsewhere. As a result, differences between a given area's voting age population and voter registration may arise.

"LIE"
Everyone who is registered to vote is a potential voter.

TRUTH
Some voters on a jurisdiction's voter list are no longer eligible to vote because they have died, moved, or failed to vote.

Like the voting age population data, there are also limitations on the use of voter registration data to represent the potential number of eligible voters. As noted above, most states require resident citizens to meet certain qualifications to be eligible to vote. Obviously, death disqualifies a voter; a move to a location outside of the jurisdiction ends the fulfillment of the residency requirement, and likewise disqualifies a voter. Finally, many states have laws which revoke the registration of those who have failed to vote in a certain consecutive number of elections. These names are removed from the voter rolls in order to ensure that registration lists are "clean" and largely populated with voters who not only meet the qualifications for registration, but who also have demonstrated a willingness to exercise their right to vote.

To be accurate, rolls of registered voters must be purged periodically to remove what is known in the field as "deadwood" —the names of persons who are deceased or who have relocated outside of the jurisdiction. Laws and practices regarding the frequency and rationale of such purges vary from state to state. As a result, the voter registration rolls in some jurisdictions may contain greater shares of persons no longer eligible to vote. In fact, in at least one case (the state of Maine), voter registration totals exceed voting age population totals—a registration of 103.2% of the voting age population, to be exact! This apparent error is actually the result of counting "deadwood" among registered voters, or occurs because of inaccuracies in the estimating process used to produce voting age population in small jurisdictions.

"LIE"
Turnout is the actual measure of both the number of voters who came to vote and the number of votes that were cast on election day.

TRUTH
For a variety of reasons, no one measure of turnout gives an accurate picture of voter participation on election day.

There are generally two sources for measuring voter participation. "Actual" turnout, which is reported by some jurisdictions (35 states and the District of Columbia), is calculated by totalling the number of voters who requested a ballot on election day and adding the number who obtained an absentee ballot. "Highest office turnout," on the other hand, is calculated by totalling all the candidates' votes in each contest and then choosing the contest with the highest total.

Neither of these methods offers a complete picture of turnout on election day. "Actual" turnout is a better measure of the number of *voters* on election day, and therefore overstates the total number of *votes*. This discrepancy is because of voters who request a ballot but fail to cast a vote due to an error on their part (often known as a "spoiled ballot"), because of administrative errors which sometimes occur in tabulating the ballots, or simply because of a voter's decision not to vote on a certain contest (this phenomenon, known as "drop-off," is described in greater detail below).

Tabulating actual turnout can be difficult in some states where the state keeps a central computer file based on county-level voting rolls. Voters whose addresses do not match the state voter file (because of relocation, death, etc.) after election day are, therefore, not counted; as a result a state's reported "actual turnout" may understate the "real" turnout on election day 1992. The problem evolves thus:

Election Day
Voter goes to polls, casts vote

Later
Voter relocates or dies

Still later
State or county removes voter from voter file

Finally
State or county attempts to update voter history from precinct registers and fails to find voter whose record has been removed. (In one state this problem resulted in an actual turnout figure which is less than the total votes cast for President.)

"Highest office turnout" is a better measure of *votes;* however, it usually underestimates the actual number of *voters* who participated on election day. For example:

Peoria County, Illinois (Table C):

Actual turnout for 1992 election:
82,242

Highest office turnout:
81,328

In fact, in any state that reports actual turnout, a comparison between this figure and highest office turnout reveals a difference. In almost every case, the highest office turnout is less than the actual turnout. This is the voter/votes difference described above, the result of void or spoiled ballots, or the result of voters who cast a ballot, but who did not vote in the election which received the highest total number of votes (drop-off).

"LIE"
Since only registered voters can vote in an election, the only measure of voter participation is the percentage of registered voters who voted on election day.

TRUTH
The nature of voter registration rolls is such that the turnout vs. registration figure measures just one aspect of voter participation. Other useful voter participation measures compare registration to voting age population and turnout to voting age population.

Assessing voter participation is an elusive quest which has spawned three different measures: turnout of registered voters, registration of voting age population, and turnout of voting age population. Each of these has a unique focus and usefulness, and because of this all three measures are presented in Table C.

•**Registration of voting age population** measures how well a jurisdiction has performed the limited task of registering voters from the overall eligible base before the date for "closing" the voter rolls (typically 30 days before election day). Comparisons between jurisdictions offer insight into the effectiveness of different states and counties in bringing eligible voters into the process via registration.

•**Turnout of registered voters** is valuable to election administrators because it gives them a sense of how well they—in concert with candidates, campaigns, and other organizations—have motivated *their* base of registered voters to get out and vote. This reflects upon the specific act of voting, as opposed to registering, since in most states the number of potential voters is finite once registration deadlines are past. Until something like election day registration is enacted nationwide (effectively eliminating the registration process), not everyone is eligible to vote on election day.

•**Turnout of voting age population** measures the same "get out the vote" effects as the turnout of registered voters, but uses *potential* voters as the base. Academics and some practitioners prefer this figure since it is comparable across jurisdictions, because (1) all voting age counts usually come from a single source (however flawed, as discussed above) and (2) registration counts

differ by jurisdiction due to registration practices and variable purging of "deadwood". This measure also approximates a *combined* measure of a jurisdiction's registration efficiency and efficiency in "getting out the vote." As a result, it provides ammunition for advocates who point to the difference between turnout rates of registered voters and the total voting age population as evidence of the need to remove or reduce the barriers to voting posed by registration requirements. For example:

Will County, Illinois (Table C):

Actual turnout: 156,597
1992 registration: 219,528
1992 voting age population: 261,641

Registration of voting age population: 83.9%
(measuring registration efficiency—how well county registers potential voters)

Turnout % of registration: 71.3%
(measuring "get out the vote" efficiency—how well county "turns out" registered voters)

Turnout % of voting age population: 59.9%
(providing a combined measure—how well county encourages participation of all persons eligible to register and vote)

Table C presents all three of these measures, enabling the reader to make comparisons and related judgments about the quality of various jurisdictions' data, as well as their effort to encourage their citizens to participate in the electoral process.

"LIE"
Turnout is the same as voter participation; therefore, states with relatively high turnout have better voter participation than states that do not.

TRUTH
Accurate comparisons between state voter participation levels are complicated by varying registration practices as well as by difficulties in measuring voter participation.

One of the last great bastions of state autonomy can be found in the diversity of practices relating to voter eligibility and registration. State voter registration requirements and procedures vary widely across the country with respect to minimum residency requirements, deadlines for closing voter registration before election day, declarations of affiliation with political parties, and the purging of names from the voter rolls due to death, relocation, or failure to vote. Deadlines for registration range from five to 30 days before an election, excluding the three states (Maine, Minnesota, and Wisconsin) that allow registration on election day itself. One other state, North Dakota, requires no registration at all.

In addition, some states offer alternatives to traditional, in-person registration. These alternatives include registration by mail, voter registration forms and services provided by public offices of motor vehicle departments ("motor-voter" registration), and the distribution of voter registration forms by public assistance agencies ("agency-based" voter registration). Some states have flexible requirements for the appointment of "deputy registrars" who register voters at locations like libraries, shopping malls, and subway stations.

This variety of practices, when combined with the degree of uncertainty inherent in any turnout calculation (as discussed above), means that simple comparisons of turnout between states may not offer an accurate picture of interstate differences in voter participation. Turnout in any given state may also be affected by the personalities of the candidates involved, the volatility of issues on the ballot, the level of demographic heterogeneity of the electorate, or even the weather; all of these factors make comparisons difficult.

Consider the following rankings from 1992 (REG=registration, VAP=voting age population, TO=turnout):

State	Rank REG÷ VAP	TO÷ REG	TO÷ VAP
Maine	1	45	2
Minnesota	3	33	1
Wyoming	31	1	18

States with high rates of registration or turnout compared to voting age population (Maine and Minnesota) fare rather poorly on the measure of turnout against registration. In Maine, this is largely a function of the huge registration base (as already noted, Maine reports that 103.2% of its voting age population is registered to vote); in Minnesota, it is the result of liberal registration policies, including election day registration. Yet Maine and Minnesota both rank extremely high in turnout of voting age population, suggesting that whatever their registration practices, these are two states with high degrees of voter participation. By comparison, Wyoming, which ranks further down the list on registration (*31st* of 49!) and turnout of voting age population (a likely pattern given traditional registration practices and typical levels of participation) still ranks at the top in turnout of registered voters because of the state's ability to keep its voter lists free of "deadwood" and to encourage voters on the rolls to vote. (Similar comparative differences occur within states with rankings for individual counties.) Therefore, anyone using registration or turnout statistics should check the rankings to ensure that conclusions drawn from the data are valid and consistent with other information available about the state(s) and county(ies) in question.

In addition, there is some debate in the field about how, if at all, alternative registration systems affect turnout. Some advocates of such procedures see traditional registration practices as barriers to participation. Skeptics, on the other hand, observe that alternative methods are likely to result in significant turnout differences only in those areas where other conditions for increased participation are present.

When using Table C to compare states or counties, readers should understand the differences between the measures (outlined above) and draw their conclusions accordingly.

"LIE"
Turnout measures voter participation all the way down the ballot (i.e., shows how people voted in every contest in the election).

TRUTH
Contrary to popular belief, "top of the ticket" races do not always drive turnout; for that reason "drop-off" statistics compare turnout in a given race to that of the electorate as a whole.

Another common error in calculating turnout by the "highest office" method is assuming that the office at the top of the ballot (in 1992, president of the United States) is also the office with the highest turnout. While this is often the case, other statewide elections, local issues, referenda, or controversial campaigns (for mayor, city council, etc.) will sometimes bring out a larger number of voters.

To measure this phenomenon, election observers calculate "drop-off" figures which show the extent to which voters fail to cast a ballot in certain races. These figures may be found at the far right of Table C, and can be used to compare the number of votes in individual races versus the number of votes as a whole.

For this reason, when calculating turnout down the ballot from the total turnout, readers should make sure to verify calculations with the highest office percentage found for each state and county in Table C.

"LIE"
Subtracting "drop-off" from total turnout will provide the percentage of the electorate that voted in a certain contest.

TRUTH
The drop-off figures in Table C are percentages of percentages; as a result, it is necessary to multiply turnout by drop-off or risk understating turnout for a given race.

When using the drop-off figures at the far right of Table C, readers should be careful not to *subtract* the drop-off percentages for each office from total turnout (whether actual, or highest office percentages). These figures are "percentages of percentages", derived by dividing total votes for an office by total turnout and then subtracting the result from 100%. The proper way to use the Table C drop-off figures is to multiply total turnout by a reduced percentage to yield the turnout for each office. For example:

Cook County, Illinois (Table C):
Actual turnout: 57.3% of voting age population
Presidential drop-off: 2.4%

"Lie"
Presidential turnout:
Actual turnout minus drop-off
57.3% - 2.4% =
<u>54.9%</u>

Truth
Presidential turnout %:
Actual turnout adjusted for drop-off
57.3% x (100% - 2.4%) =
97.6% of 57.3% =
<u>55.9%</u>

To "double check" with raw numbers:
Actual total turnout: 2,199,608
Presidential total turnout: 2,146,655
Voting age population: 3,840,168
Presidential turnout % =
(2,146,655 ÷ 3,840,168) * 100 =
<u>55.9%</u>!

Note that merely *subtracting* the drop-off percentage from the total turnout percentage understates turnout for that office.

"LIE"
The composition of the electorate reflects that of society at large.

TRUTH
The demographic composition of the electorate on election day is the result of a variety of influences, all of which force changes in its size and complexion.

One of the most interesting areas of focus in election analysis is the effect of demographics on past, present, and future voting patterns. This volume contains several items of information which are and will be useful in spotting voting trends:

· Voting age population and total population by race Tables A and B list total and voting age population by race. As a result, it is possible to see in Table A that 13.5% of Arlington County, Virginia's total population is of Hispanic origin, yet Hispanics represent just 12.0% of Arlington's voting age population (Table B). Why the discrepancy? Table B suggests the answer.

The far-right column of Table B shows that just 75.7% of Arlington's Hispanic population is of voting age, compared to 88.0% of the non-Hispanic white population and 84.9% of the county's entire population. This suggests that Arlington's Hispanic population is younger on average, and as a result, Hispanic influence on the electorate is not in proportion to its share of the county's population as a whole.

· Differential participation/contribution rates by jurisdiction Also note that a jurisdiction's impact on elections is not merely a function of its size. Participation is affected by registration and turnout, with the result that a significant geographic area may see its eventual impact on elections increase or decrease by the time the votes are counted. For example:

<u>Cook County, Illinois</u>
Share of state's total population:
44.7% (Table A)

Share of state's total voting age population:
45.1% (Table B)

Share of state's total registered voters:
44.3% (Table C)

Share of 1992 voter turnout:
42.6% (Table C)

Share of state's 1992 presidential vote:
42.5% (Table E)

Share of state's Democratic presidential vote:
50.9% (Table E)

These figures suggest several conclusions about the partisan tendencies of Cook County compared to counties statewide. Information of this sort is available throughout this volume, and is a veritable "gold mine" for spotting differential behavior by race or partisan affiliation across states and counties. (For ideas about areas of particular interest, consult the maps throughout the volume.)

In summary, this volume offers a wealth of statistics, tables, and graphs about election day 1992. Keeping in mind the limitations and strengths of the data, it is possible for even the most inexperienced "election analyst" to separate the statistics from the "lies".

And the "damned lies"? Perhaps they can wait until the next campaign.

Table Outlines and Explanations
STATE NAME

Congressional Districts ....
    Average Population ....
State Senate Districts ....
    Average Population ....
State House Districts ....
    Average Population ....

Electoral College Votes[1] ....
Counties[2] ....
Voting Precincts ....

Alternative Registration Methods:[3]

....

Registration Deadline (Days before Election)[4] ....

Voting Equipment Use (Counties)[5]

Datavote Punch Card	Paper Ballot
Electronic	Other Punch Card
Lever Machine	Mixed Systems
Optical Scanner	

Party Control[6]	DEM	REP	IND	VAC
1993 State Senate				
1992 State Senate				
1993 State House				
1992 State House				

Population Statistics 1990[7]					
Race/ Ethnicity	Total Population		Voting Age Population		Voting Age Population % of total population
	Number	%	Number	%	
Non-Hispanic White					
Black					
Asian/Pacific Islander					
Native American					
Other					
All Hispanic					
TOTAL					

Estimated Voting Age Population 1992 (VAP)[8] ....
Number of Registered Voters[9] ....
    % of estimated VAP ....
Voter Turnout[10] ....
    % of VAP ....
    % of Registration ....
Persons Not Voting—of Voting Age[11] ....
    % of VAP ....
Persons Not Voting—of Registered[12] ....
    % of Registration ....
Straight Ticket Voting[13] ....

---

[1] Electoral college votes equal the congressional districts in a given state plus two (one vote per U.S. Senate seat). The District of Columbia is an exception, with three electoral votes.

[2] County equivalents include election districts in Alaska and parishes in Louisiana, as well as independent cities in Maryland, Missouri, Nevada, and Virginia.

[3] Source: National Clearinghouse on Election Administration, Federal Election Commission, *Fast Facts on State Registration and Election Procedures*, Technical Report 2, compiled by Brian Hancock (Washington, DC: Government Printing Office, February 1992). Alternatives to traditional, in-person registration are: (1) registration by mail, (2) election day registration, (3) agency-based registration (registration forms and services provided by government public assistance agencies, such as welfare offices), (4) "motor-voter" registration (registration forms and services provided by motor vehicle departments), and (5) deputized registrars (people deputized as registrars by local election officials).

[4] Source: National Clearinghouse on Election Administration, Federal Election Commission, *Fast Facts on State Registration and Election Procedures*, Technical Report 2, compiled by Brian Hancock (Washington, DC: Government Printing Office, February 1992).

[5] Source: Reports from secretaries of state, and city and county clerks collected by Election Data Services in spring of 1992. Types reported may exceed number of counties in states where cities administer elections. "Datavote punch card" is a punch card system with candidates' names printed directly on the card; voters mark ballots using a hole-punching device. "Other punch card systems" print a code for each candidate on the ballot card; this code must be matched against a master list of candidate names and codes. "Lever machine systems" are older systems; voters cast their votes by pulling selected levers on a large machine. "Optical scanners" typically require voters to use a device

such as a No. 2 pencil to mark paper ballots, which are then tallied by an optical scanning device. Newer "Electronic systems" record votes cast by touching a pressure-sensitive surface next to each candidate's name. "Mixed systems" denotes a combination of these systems, and usually occur in counties where local cities and townships administer elections.

[6]Source: National Conference of State Legislatures, *Partisan Composition of the State Legislatures, 1993 Legislative Session*, April 1993 and *State Legislative Election Results, 1992 Session Strength*, November 1992. Nebraska and the District of Columbia have unicameral legislatures with members elected on a nonpartisan basis.

[7]Source: 1990 Census of Population and Housing, U.S. Census Bureau.

[8]Source: U.S. Department of Commerce, Bureau of the Census, *Projections of the Voting-Age Population, for States: November 1992*, Series P-25, No. 1085 (Washington, DC: Government Printing Office, April 1992). Includes only persons age 18 or older. May include persons not eligible to vote, such as felons, persons in mental institutions, and resident or illegal aliens.

[9]Source: Secretaries of state, city and county clerks, and registrars of voters; provided at the close of registration for November 1992 general election. Voter registration rolls may be inflated when deceased or ineligible voters are not purged from the records through regular updating.

[10]Source: Secretaries of state, city and county clerks, and registrars of voters. Reported as either *actual* turnout (as in 35 states and the District of Columbia), *highest office* turnout, the total number of votes cast for every candidate for the office which received the highest number of votes, or as *maximum vote* turnout, where county-level votes for candidates exceed reported actual turnout. This voter turnout data comes from the sum of the combined county-level maximum vote turnout data presented in Table C and may differ from the 1992 highest office turnout on the 1948–1992 voter registration and turnout trends page, which is computed from statewide data.

[11]Difference between estimated Voting Age Population (VAP) and voter turnout.

[12]Difference between number of registered voters and voter turnout.

[13]Source: National Clearinghouse on Election Administration, Federal Election Commission, *Fast Facts on State Registration and Election Procedures*, Technical Report 2, compiled by Brian Hancock (Washington, DC: Government Printing Office, February 1992). Refers to laws allowing voters to select every candidate of a particular political party by marking a ballot for that party (single mark) as opposed to each individual candidate running under that party's label. If straight ticket voting is provided for on the ballot, there are two possibilities for voters who wish to split their votes between parties. "Yes, exception" indicates that splitting a ticket is accomplished by marking a ballot for the party as well as the names of individual candidates of other parties (including independent or write-in candidates). "Yes, separate" indicates that separate voting for each and every office is required to split a ticket.

ABBREVIATIONS: DEM = Democratic. IND = Independent. REP = Republican. VAC = Vacancy.

Chart: Voter Registration and Turnout, 1948–1992 Elections

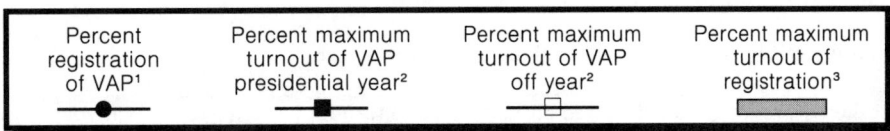

Percent registration of VAP[1]	Percent maximum turnout of VAP presidential year[2]	Percent maximum turnout of VAP off year[2]	Percent maximum turnout of registration[3]
●—	■—	□—	▬

[1]Equal to **Item 4** in the following table.　[2]Equal to **Item 16** in the following table. Presidential election years are 1948, 1952, 1956, 1960, 1964, 1968, 1972, 1976, 1980, 1984, 1988, and 1992. Off year refers to non-presidential elections in even numbered years.　[3]Equal to **Item 14** in the following table. In several states' charts, gaps between bars and lines appear because of missing data.

Year	Estimated Voting Age Population (VAP)	Voter registration (REG)			Voter turnout											
						Highest office						Maximum vote				
		Total	Percent of VAP	Rank by percent of VAP	Actual	Total	Office	Percent total REG	Rank by percent of REG	Percent of VAP	Rank by percent of VAP	Total	Percent total REG	Rank by percent of REG	Percent total VAP	Rank by percent of VAP
1	2	3	4	5	6	7	8	9	10	11	12	13	14	15	16	17

Item 1 Prior to 1980, the number of states that reported voter registration and turnout statistics decreases considerably. Furthermore, Alaska and Hawaii did not become states until 1959, and District of Columbia residents did not vote in presidential elections until 1964.

Item 2 Source: U.S. Department of Commerce, Economics and Statistics Administration, Bureau of the Census, *Projections of the Voting-Age Population, for States: November 1992*, Series P-25, No. 1085 (Washington, DC: Government Printing Office, April 1992). Prior to 1992, sources are similar Census Bureau publications in the P-25 series. (In this series, data from previous years are sometimes updated in subsequent reports. All updates have been applied to this data.) Includes only persons age 18 or older and may include persons not eligible to vote, such as felons, persons in mental institutions, and resident or illegal aliens.

Item 3 Source: Secretaries of state, city and county clerks, and registrars of voters. May include names of nonresidents and deceased persons if roll of registered voters has not recently been purged or updated.

Item 4 Total voter registration divided by VAP for respective year. May exceed 100 percent if roll of registered voters has not been updated recently, or if VAP estimate is not accurate.

Item 5 Rank of states and the District of Columbia based on registration percentages of VAP reported in item 4.

Item 6 Source: Secretaries of state, city and county clerks, and registrars of voters. Number of persons who requested a ballot on election day or who previously obtained an absentee ballot, regardless of whether they cast a vote for any candidate. Only 35 states and the District of Columbia reported this statistic in 1992.

Item 7 Source: Secretaries of state, city and county clerks, and registrars of voters. *Statewide* highest office turnout in presidential election years is the vote for president; in off years, this is the total number of votes cast for every candidate in the office which received the highest number of votes (based on *statewide* results); an approximate, substitute measure of voter turnout for states not reporting actual turnout. This statewide uniform office data may differ from statewide highest office turnout found in Table C, which is the sum of county-level data.

Item 8 Denotes office for which highest number of votes were cast: P = president, S = U.S. senator, G = governor, C = U.S. representative in Congress, M = mayor, and O = other (e.g., local office or referendum).

Item 9 Highest office turnout divided by total voter registration for respective year.

Item 10 Rank of states and the District of Columbia based on highest office turnout percentages of total voter registration reported in item 9. Rankings for earlier years may not be based on data from all 50 states and the District of Columbia.

Item 11 Highest office turnout divided by VAP for respective year.

Item 12 Rank of states and the District of Columbia based on highest office turnout percentages of VAP reported in item 11.

Item 13 Either actual voter turnout from **Item 6** or highest office voter turnout from **Item 7**, whichever is greater. Used to compare voter turnout among all jurisdictions.

Item 14 Maximum vote turnout divided by total voter registration for respective year.

Item 15 Rank of states and the District of Columbia based on maximum vote turnout percentages of total voter registration reported in item 14.

Item 16 Maximum vote turnout divided by VAP for respective year.

Item 17 Rank of states and the District of Columbia based on maximum vote turnout percentages of VAP reported in item 16.

Statistical Tables A–J

Table A. — 1990 Population by Race and Ethnic Origin

State/ county code	County	Total persons	Percent of total persons						Rank				Percent contribution to state population			
			White	Black	Asian and Pacific Islander	Native American	Other	Hispanic	Total	White	Black	Hispanic	Total	White	Black	Hispanic
					Non-Hispanic					Percent of total persons				Non-Hispanic		
											Non-Hispanic					
1	2	3	4	5	6	7	8	9	10	11	12	13	14	15	16	17

Item 1 The first column of Table A contains the two-digit Federal Information Processing Standards (FIPS) code for each state and the District of Columbia, and a three-digit census code for each county or county equivalent. No codes are provided for election districts in Alaska, cities and towns in New England states, or wards in the District of Columbia.

Item 3 Source: 1990 Census of Population and Housing, U.S. Census Bureau. Includes persons of all ages.

Items 4–9 Racial and ethnic populations of a given area divided by its total population.

Item 10 Rank of geographic area based on raw number of total persons reported in item 3. In state chapters, Table A contains two sets of rankings, (1) counties and county equivalents, and (2) congressional districts.

Items 11–13 Rank based on each racial and ethnic group's percentage of the total population of a county or jurisdiction reported in items 4, 5, and 9. In state chapters, Table A contains two sets of rankings, (1) counties and county equivalents, and (2) congressional districts.

Items 14–17 Racial and ethnic populations of a given area divided by total population of the state (nation). Due to single-digit rounding, column percentages do not always total the 100 percent figure indicated.

Table B. — 1990 Voting Age Population (VAP) by Race and Ethnic Origin

County	Total Voting Age Population (VAP)	Percent of total VAP						Rank				Percent contribution to state VAP				VAP percent of total population						
		White	Black	Asian and Pacific Islander	Native American	Other	Hispanic	Total	White	Black	Hispanic	Total	White	Black	Hispanic	Total	White	Black	Asian and Pacific Islander	Native American	Other	Hispanic
				Non-Hispanic					Non-Hispanic				Non-Hispanic					Non-Hispanic			
1	2	3	4	5	6	7	8	9	10	11	12	13	14	15	16	17	18	19	20	21	22	23

Item 2 Source: 1990 Census of Population and Housing, U.S. Census Bureau. Includes only persons age 18 or older and may include persons not eligible to vote, such as felons, persons in mental institutions, and resident or illegal aliens.

Items 3–8 VAP of racial and ethnic groups of a given geographic area divided by total VAP of that area.

Item 9 Rank of geographic area based on raw number of total VAP reported in item 2. In state chapters, Table B contains two sets of rankings, (1) counties and county equivalents, and (2) congressional districts.

Items 10–12 Rank of geographic area based on each racial and ethnic group's percentage of total VAP for that county or jurisdiction reported in items 3, 4, and 8. In state chapters, Table B contains two sets of rankings, (1) counties and county equivalents, and (2) congressional districts.

Items 13–16 VAP of racial and ethnic groups in a given area divided by total VAP for the state (nation). Due to single-digit rounding, column percentages do not always total the 100 percent figure indicated.

Items 17–23 Total VAP and VAP of racial and ethnic groups of a given area divided by respective populations (from Table A) of that area.

Table C. — Voter Participation: November 3, 1992, General Election

County	Estimated Voting Age Population (VAP), 1992	Voter registration (REG)				Voter turnout														
							Highest office			Maximum vote										
																Percent drop-off, by office			
		Total	% contri-bution to state REG	% of 1992 VAP	Rank by % of 1992 VAP	Actual	Total	Office	% of 1992 VAP	Total	% contri-bution to state turnout	% of REG	Rank by % of REG	% of 1992 VAP	Rank by % 1992 VAP	Pres-ident	Sen-ator	Gov-ernor	Repre-sent-ative
1	2	3	4	5	6	7	8	9	10	11	12	13	14	15	16	17	18	19	20

Item 2 Sources: State-level VAP — U.S. Department of Commerce, Bureau of the Census, *Projections of the Voting-Age Population, for States: November 1992*, Series P-25, No. 1085 (Washington, DC: Government Printing Office, April 1992); county-level VAP — Donnelley Marketing Information Services (Stamford, CT), as adjusted by Election Data Services. (See explanation of the adjustment process on pages xiii and ix of the Introduction.) Includes only persons age 18 or older and may include persons not eligible to vote, such as felons, persons in mental institutions, and resident or illegal aliens.

Item 3 Source: Secretaries of state, city and county clerks, and registrars of voters; provided at the close of registration for November 1992 general election. May include names of nonresidents and deceased persons if roll of registered voters has not recently been purged or updated. In cases where states report voter registration by race or by party, footnotes to statewide voter registration totals provide a breakdown of registration for racial groups and political parties.

Item 4 Total voter registration of a given geographic area divided by total voter registration for the state (nation). Due to single-digit rounding, column percentages do not always total the 100 percent figure indicated.

Item 5 Total voter registration divided by estimated 1992 VAP. May exceed 100 percent if roll of registered voters has not recently been updated, or if VAP estimate is not accurate.

Item 6 Rank of geographic areas based on voter registration percentages of estimated 1992 VAP reported in item 5.

Item 7 Source: Secretaries of state, city and county clerks, and registrars of voters. Number of persons who requested a ballot on election day or who previously obtained an absentee ballot, regardless of whether they cast a vote for any candidate. Only 35 states and the District of Columbia reported this statistic in 1992. In cases where states report voter turnout by race or by political party, footnotes to statewide voter turnout totals provide a breakdown of turnout for racial groups and political parties.

Item 8 Source: Secretaries of state, city and county clerks, and registrars of voters. Total number of votes cast for every candidate for the office which received the highest number of votes for a given geographic area; approximate measure of voter turnout for states not reporting actual turnout. In some cases, highest number of votes for an office exceeds what was reported as actual voter turnout, but in each instance data was verified with state and local election officials.

Item 9 Denotes office for which highest number of votes were cast: P = president, S = U.S. senator, G = governor, C = U.S. representative in Congress, M = mayor, and O = other (e.g., local office or referendum).

Item 10 Highest office turnout divided by estimated 1992 VAP.

Item 11 Either actual voter turnout from **Item 7** or highest office voter turnout from **Item 8**, whichever is greater. Used to compare voter turnout among various jurisdictions. This voter turnout data comes from the sum of the combined maximum county-level data presented in Table C and may differ from the 1992 highest office turnout on the 1948–1992 voter registration and turnout trends page, which is computed from statewide data.

Item 12 Maximum vote turnout of a given area divided by total maximum vote turnout for the state (nation). Due to single-digit rounding, column percentages do not always total the 100 percent figure indicated.

Item 13 Maximum vote turnout divided by total voter registration.

Item 14 Rank of geographic areas based on maximum vote turnout percentages of total voter registration reported in item 13.

Item 15 Maximum vote turnout divided by estimated 1992 VAP.

xxii Table Outlines and Explanations

Item 16 Rank of geographic areas based on maximum vote turnout percentages of estimated 1992 VAP reported in item 15.

Item 17–20 "Drop-off" is the difference between maximum voter turnout and total number of votes for all candidates for a particular office. Obtained by subtracting a given geographic area's total vote for all candidates for the offices of president, U.S. senator, governor, and U.S. representative in Congress (from Tables E-H) from the area's maximum vote turnout and dividing respective differences by the area's maximum vote turnout. If highest office turnout is used as maximum vote turnout, drop-off for the office generating the highest office turnout figure will be zero.

Table D. — Voter Registration by Political Party Affiliation: November 3, 1992, General Election

County	Total voter registration	Political party affiliation					Percent of total registration						Percent contribution to state registration			
		Democrat (DEM)	Republican (REP)	Independent (IND)	Plurality		DEM	REP	IND	Rank			Total	DEM	REP	IND
					Total	Party				DEM	REP	IND				
1	2	3	4	5	6	7	8	9	10	11	12	13	14	15	16	17

Table D has been compiled for the 25 states and the District of Columbia that report voter registration by political party.

Items 2–5 Source: Secretaries of state, city and county clerks, and registrars of voters. Independent refers to persons who (1) declared their status as "independent" or "unaffiliated"; (2) declined to affiliate with either of the two major parties in states where only three categories of registrants (Democratic, Republican, or Other) were reported; or (3) declined to affiliate with any political party, including any minor party. In cases where the number of registered Democrats, Republicans, and Independents does not equal total voter registration, footnotes to statewide voter registration totals provide a breakdown of registration for minor parties or document discrepancies from conflicting reports.

Item 6 Excess number of registrants of the party with the largest number of affiliates over the party with the next highest number of affiliates.

Item 7 Denotes party holding plurality of registrants: D = Democratic, R = Republican, I = Independent.

Items 8–10 Number of Democratic, Republican, and Independent registrants of a given geographic area divided by total voter registration of that area.

Items 11–13 Rank of geographic areas based on respective party percentages of total voter registration reported in items 8–10.

Items 14–17 Total, Democratic, Republican, and Independent registrants of a given area divided by respective totals of that registrant category for all areas. Due to single-digit rounding, column percentages do not always total the 100 percent figure indicated.

Table E. — Vote for President: November 3, 1992, General Election

County	All candidates																			Major party	
	Total	Clinton (DEM)	Bush (REP)	Perot (IND)	Other	Plurality		Percent of total vote				Rank			Percent contribution to state vote				Percent of vote	
						Total	Party	DEM	REP	IND	Other	DEM	REP	IND	Total	DEM	REP	IND	DEM	REP
1	2	3	4	5	6	7	8	9	10	11	12	13	14	15	16	17	18	19	20	21

Items 2–6 Source: Official vote from November 3, 1992, general election, as certified by secretaries of state, and city and county clerks. In Connecticut and New York, where candidates ran under multiple parties, the vote shown under a candidate's name is the combined vote for all parties. In several states, the sum of county vote totals for all candidates and for other candidates does not equal statewide totals because of write-in votes reported only at the state level. Footnotes to the statewide totals provide a count of those write-in votes.

Item 7 Excess number of votes obtained by winning candidate over those obtained by candidate receiving next highest amount.

Item 8 Denotes political party of candidate holding plurality of vote: D = Democratic, R = Republican, I = Independent, and O = Other.

Items 9–12 Vote obtained by each candidate in a given geographic area divided by total vote for all candidates in that area.

Items 13–15 Rank of geographic areas based on candidates' vote as a percentage of total vote reported in items 9–11.

Items 16–19 Vote for each candidate in a given area divided by total vote for each candidate in the state (nation). Due to single-digit rounding, column percentages do not always total the 100 percent figure indicated.

Items 20–21 Vote for each Democratic or Republican candidate in a given area divided by the sum of Democratic and Republican vote in that area.

Table F. — **Vote for U.S. Senator: November 3, 1992, General Election**

County					Plurality		Percent of total vote						Percent contribution to state vote			
										Rank						
	Total	(DEM)	(REP)	Other	Total	Party	DEM	REP	Other	DEM	REP	Other	Total	DEM	REP	Other
1	2	3	4	5	6	7	8	9	10	11	12	13	14	15	16	17

Items 2–5 Source: Official vote as certified by secretaries of state, and city and county clerks. In Connecticut and New York, where candidates ran under multiple parties, the vote shown under a candidate's name is the combined vote for all parties. In several states, the sum of county vote totals for all candidates and for other candidates does not equal statewide totals because of write-in votes reported only at the state level. Footnotes to the statewide totals provide a count of those write-in votes.

Item 6 Excess number of votes obtained by winning candidate over those obtained by candidate receiving next highest amount.

Item 7 Denotes party of candidate holding plurality of vote: D = Democratic, R = Republican, and O = Other.

Items 8–10 Vote obtained by each candidate in a given geographic area divided by total vote for all candidates in that area.

Items 11–13 Rank of geographic areas based on candidates' vote as a percentage of total vote reported in items 8–10.

Items 14–17 Vote for each candidate in a given area divided by respective statewide vote total for each candidate. Due to single-digit rounding, column percentages do not always total the 100 percent figure indicated.

Table G. — **Vote for Governor: November 3, 1992, General Election**

County					Plurality		Percent of total vote						Percent contribution to state vote			
										Rank						
	Total	(DEM)	(REP)	Other	Total	Party	DEM	REP	Other	DEM	REP	Other	Total	DEM	REP	Other
1	2	3	4	5	6	7	8	9	10	11	12	13	14	15	16	17

Items 2–5 Source: Official vote as certified by secretaries of state, and city and county clerks. In several states, the sum of county vote totals for all candidates and for other candidates does not equal statewide totals because of write-in votes reported only at the state level. Footnotes to the statewide totals provide a count of those write-in votes. In Utah, where an independent candidate for governor placed second, the column for other candidates includes only the vote for that independent candidate; and the statewide vote for other candidates is documented in a footnote.

Item 6 Excess number of votes obtained by winning candidate over those obtained by candidate receiving next highest amount.

Item 7 Denotes political party of candidate holding plurality of vote: D = Democratic, R = Republican, and O = Other.

Items 8–10 Vote obtained by each candidate in a given geographic area divided by total vote for all candidates in that area.

Items 11–13 Rank of geographic areas based on candidates' vote as a percentage of total vote reported in items 8–10.

Items 14–17 Vote for each candidate in a given area divided by respective statewide vote total for each candidate. Due to single-digit rounding, column percentages do not always total the 100 percent figure indicated.

Table H. — Vote for U.S. Representative in Congress: November 3, 1992, General Election

Congressional district and county	Total	Democrat (DEM)	Republican (REP)	Other	Plurality		Percent of total vote			Rank within district			Percent contribution to district vote			
					Total	Party	DEM	REP	Other	DEM	REP	Other	Total	DEM	REP	Other
1	2	3	4	5	6	7	8	9	10	11	12	13	14	15	16	17

Table H presents the results of the vote for U.S. representative in Congress for geographic areas grouped by congressional district.

Item 1 Districts and their components. The abbreviation "(pt)" indicates that only part of a geographic area is included in the district.

Items 2–5 Source: Official vote as certified by secretaries of state, and city and county clerks. In Connecticut and New York, where candidates ran under multiple parties, the vote shown under a candidate's name is the combined vote for all parties. In several cases, the sum of county vote totals for all candidates and for other candidates does not equal district-wide totals because of write-in votes reported only at the district level. Footnotes to the district-wide totals provide a count of those write-in votes. In Vermont, where an independent congressional candidate was elected, the column for other candidates includes only the vote for that independent candidate; and the district-wide vote for other candidates is documented in a footnote.

Item 6 Excess number of votes obtained by winning candidate over those obtained by candidate receiving next highest amount.

Item 7 Denotes political party of candidate holding plurality of vote: D = Democratic, R = Republican, and O = Other.

Items 8–10 Vote obtained by each candidate in a geographic area divided by total vote for all candidates in that area.

Items 11–13 Rank of geographic areas within each congressional district based on candidates' vote as a percentage of total vote reported in items 8–10.

Items 14–17 Vote for each candidate in a given area divided by respective district-wide total for each candidate. Due to single-digit rounding, column percentages do not always total the 100 percent figure indicated.

Table I. — Vote for Presidential Preference: Democratic Primary Election

County	Top candidates									Top three candidates (state vote)						Percent contribution to state vote			
										Percent of total vote			Rank						
	Total	Candi-date 1	Candi-date 2	Candi-date 3	Candi-date 4	Candi-date 5	Candi-date 6	Candi-date 7	Candi-date 8	Candi-date 1	Candi-date 2	Candi-date 3	Candi-date 1	Candi-date 2	Candi-date 3	Total	Candi-date 1	Candi-date 2	Candi-date 3
1	2	3	4	5	6	7	8	9	10	11	12	13	14	15	16	17	18	19	20

Table I presents the vote for up to eight candidates who received the highest number of votes. If there were more than eight candidates, the eighth item shows the combined vote for all other candidates. Votes for uncommitted delegates are included.

Items 2–10 Source: Official vote as certified by secretaries of state, and city and county clerks.

Items 11–13 Vote obtained by each candidate in a given geographic area divided by total vote for all candidates in same area. Shown only for the three candidates who received the highest number of votes.

Items 14–16 Rank of geographic areas based on candidates' vote as a percentage of total vote reported in items 11–13. Shown only for the three candidates who received the highest number of votes.

Items 17–20 Vote for each candidate in a given area divided by respective statewide total for each candidate. Shown only for the three candidates who received the highest number of votes. Due to single-digit rounding, column percentages do not always total the 100 percent figure indicated.

Table J. – **Vote for Presidential Preference: Republican Primary Election**

County	Top candidates					Top four candidates (state vote)												
						Percent of total vote								Percent contribution to state vote				
										Rank								
	Total	Candi-date 1	Candi-date 2	Candi-date 3	Candi-date 4	Candi-date 1	Candi-date 2	Candi-date 3	Candi-date 4	Candi-date 1	Candi-date 2	Candi-date 3	Candi-date 4	Total	Candi-date 1	Candi-date 2	Candi-date 3	Candi-date 4
1	2	3	4	5	6	7	8	9	10	11	12	13	14	15	16	17	18	19

Table J presents the vote for up to four candidates who received the highest number of votes. If there were more than four candidates, the fourth item shows the combined vote for all other candidates. Votes for uncommitted delegates are included.

Items 2–6 Source: Official vote as certified by secretaries of state, and city and county clerks.

Items 7–10 Vote obtained by each candidate in a geographic area divided by total vote for all candidates in that area.

Items 11–14 Rank of geographic areas based on candidates' vote as a percentage of total vote reported in items 7–10.

Items 15–19 Vote for each candidate in a given area divided by respective statewide vote total for each candidate. Due to single-digit rounding, column percentages do not always total the 100 percent figure indicated.

UNITED STATES

UNITED STATES

Congressional Districts[1] 435
   Average Population[1] 570,352
State Senate Districts[2] 1,984
   Average Population[2] 125,052
State House Districts[3] 5,440
   Average Population[3] 45,317

Electoral College Votes[4] 538
Counties[5] 3,156
Voting Precincts 182,140

Alternative Registration Methods:
.... N/A

Registration Deadline (Days before Election) .... N/A

Population Statistics 1990

Race/Ethnicity	Total Population		Voting Age Population		Voting Age Population % of total population
	Number	%	Number	%	
Non-Hispanic					
White	188,128,296	75.6	144,320,985	78.0	76.7
Black	29,216,293	11.7	19,897,893	10.7	68.1
Asian/Pacific Islander	6,968,359	2.8	4,993,126	2.7	71.7
Native American	1,793,773	0.7	1,166,165	0.6	65.0
Other	249,093	0.1	130,713	<.1	52.5
All Hispanic	22,354,059	9.0	14,596,559	7.9	65.3
TOTAL	248,709,873	100.0	185,105,441	100.0	74.4

Voting Equipment Use (Counties)[6]

Datavote Punch Card	84	Paper Ballot	662
Electronic	117	Other Punch Card	651
Lever Machine	795	Mixed Systems	189
Optical Scanner	627		

Party Control[7]	DEM	REP	IND[8]	VAC
1993 State Senate	1,132	797	3	3
1992 State Senate	1,183	758	2	3
1993 State House	3,197	2,214	20	9
1992 State House	3,236	2,208	9	13

Estimated Voting Age Population 1992 (VAP) .. 189,044,000
Number of Registered Voters[9] 133,809,723
   % of estimated VAP[10] 72.4
Voter Turnout (Maximum Vote)[11] 105,867,768
   % of VAP[12] 56.0
   % of Registration[13] 77.0
Persons Not Voting—of Voting Age 83,176,232
   % of VAP[12] 44.0
Persons Not Voting—of Registered[13] 30,789,131
   % of Registration[13] 23.0
Straight Ticket Voting .... N/A

[1]District of Columbia not included. Average district population based on total population of 248,102,973 for 50 states. [2]Includes Nebraska (unicameral); District of Columbia not included. [3]Nebraska and the District of Columbia not included (Nebraska's unicameral included in senate districts). [4]The number of electors allocated to a given state is equivalent to the number of senators and representatives that state has in the U.S. Congress. The District of Columbia has three electors. [5]Includes 3,006 counties; the District of Columbia; 40 election districts in Alaska; 64 parishes in Louisiana; Yellowstone National Park (part) in Montana; Baltimore (city), MD; St. Louis (city), MO; Carson City (city), NV; and 41 independent cities in Virginia (e.g., jurisdictions appearing on maps and for which population data are presented in Tables A and B.). [6]Includes Alaska as a single unit (no subdivisions); New England counties (no cities and towns); and independent city-county equivalents in Maryland, Missouri, Nevada, and Virginia; and several additional cities that administer elections independently-Kansas City, MO, and nine cities in Illinois. Kalawao county in Hawaii and Yellowstone National Park in Montana not included. [7]Does not include Nebraska or the District of Columbia, where members of unicameral legislatures are elected on a nonpartisan basis. [8]1993 State House includes six members of minor political parties. [9]Total voter registration for 48 states and the District of Columbia. (North Dakota and Wisconsin have no statewide voter registration requirement.) [10]Based on estimated voting age population (VAP) of 184,917,000 for 48 states and the District of Columbia. (North Dakota and Wisconsin not included.) [11]Actual or highest office voter turnout, whichever is greater, for all 50 states and the District of Columbia. Actual voter turnout data for Iowa was not officially certified by Iowa Secretary of State at time of publication. [12]Based on estimated voting age population (VAP) for all 50 states and the District of Columbia. [13]Based on maximum vote turnout of 103,020,592 for 48 states and the District of Columbia. (North Dakota and Wisconsin not included.) Actual voter turnout data for Iowa was not officially certified by Iowa Secretary of State at time of publication.

Candidates: General Election, November 3, 1992

Candidate(s)	Total vote	Percent	Party	Status	First elected
President/Vice President					
Clinton/Gore	44,909,326	43.01%	Democrat[1]	Challenger	1992
Bush/Quayle	39,103,882	37.45%	Republican[2]	Incumbent	1988
Perot/Stockdale	19,741,657	18.91%	Independent[3]	Challenger	
Marrou/Lord	291,627	0.28%	Libertarian[3]	Challenger	
Gritz/Minett	106,401	0.10%	Populist[3]	Challenger	
Fulani/Munoz or Mulholland[4]	73,709	0.07%	New Alliance[3]	Challenger	
Phillips/Knight or Graves[4]	43,396	0.04%	Taxpayers[3]	Challenger	
Hagelin/Tompkins	39,115	0.04%	Natural Law[3]	Challenger	
Daniels/Tupahache	27,960	0.03%	Independent[3]	Challenger	
LaRouche/Bevel or Greenspan[4]	26,309	0.03%	Independent[3]	Challenger	
Warren/Debates or Reid[4]	23,087	0.02%	Socialist Workers[3]	Challenger	
Write ins	7,723	<.01%	Write in	Challenger	
Drew Bradford	4,749	<.01%	Independent	Challenger	
Herer/Grimmer	3,875	<.01%	Grassroots	Challenger	
Others	3,297	<.01%	Write in	Challenger	
Halyard/Mazelis	3,050	<.01%	Worker's League	Challenger	
Brisben/Garson or Edwards[4]	3,020	<.01%	Socialist[3]	Challenger	
Miscellaneous	2,609	<.01%	Write in	Challenger	
None of these Candidates	2,537	<.01%	No Party	Challenger	
Yiamouyiannis/McCone	2,199	<.01%	Independent	Challenger	
Ehlers/Wendt	1,149	<.01%	Independent	Challenger	
Dodge/Ormsby	961	<.01%	Prohibition[3]	Challenger	
Honest Jim Boren	956	<.01%	Apathy	Challenger	
Scattering	730	<.01%	Write in	Challenger	
Hem/Roland	405	<.01%	Third Party	Challenger	
Isabell Masters	339	<.01%	Looking Back Group	Challenger	
Smith/Smith or Feimer[4]	311	<.01%	American	Challenger	
La Riva/Holmes	181	<.01%	Workers World	Challenger	
Jack Kemp	168	<.01%	Write in	Challenger	
Carter/Aschenbach	131	<.01%	Write in	Challenger	
Paul Tsongas	129	<.01%	Write in	Challenger	
Wright/Cunningham	23	<.01%	Write in	Challenger	
King	10	<.01%	Write in	Challenger	
Kim Peterson	2	<.01%	Write in	Challenger	
Scott	1	<.01%	Write in	Challenger	
George Muzyk	1	<.01%	Write in	Challenger	
Messiah	1	<.01%	Write in	Challenger	
Don Allensworth	1	<.01%	Write in	Challenger	

[1]Includes votes cast for Clinton-Gore as nominees of the Liberal party in New York. [2]Includes votes cast for Bush-Quayle as nominees of the Conservative and Right to Life parties in New York. [3]Party designation varies in different states. [4]Presidential candidate's running mate varies in different states.

Candidates: 1992 Presidental Preference Primary Elections

Candidate	Total vote	Percent	Candidate	Total vote	Percent
Presidential Preference, Democratic			**Presidential Preference, Republican**		
Bill Clinton	10,495,008	51.85%	George Bush	9,199,463	72.57%
Jerry Brown	4,071,210	20.12%	Patrick Buchanan	2,899,488	22.87%
Paul Tsongas	3,656,104	18.06%	Uncommitted	174,643	1.38%
Uncommitted	565,626	2.79%	David Duke	119,115	0.94%
Bob Kerrey	318,460	1.57%	None of the Above	62,488	0.49%
Tom Harkin	280,304	1.38%	No Preference	52,994	0.42%
Lyndon LaRouche, Jr.	154,484	0.76%	Miscellaneous	35,805	0.28%
No Preference	147,059	0.73%	Ross Perot	29,275	0.23%
Eugene McCarthy	108,467	0.54%	Scattering	12,801	0.10%
Charles Woods	88,948	0.44%	Write ins	12,674	0.10%
Larry Agran	58,279	0.29%	Pat Paulsen	10,384	0.08%
None of the Above	38,188	0.19%	Maurice Horton	9,637	0.08%
Ross Perot	37,827	0.19%	Harold Stassen	7,893	0.06%
Ralph Nader	35,935	0.18%	Others	7,699	0.06%
Miscellaneous	33,540	0.17%	Jack Fellure	6,260	0.05%
Louis Stokes	29,983	0.15%	George Zimmermann	5,629	0.04%
Others	15,575	0.08%	Tennie Rogers	4,160	0.03%
Scattering	13,886	0.07%	Paul Tsongas	3,677	0.03%
Angus McDonald	9,900	0.05%	Ralph Nader	3,257	0.03%
Write ins	8,597	0.04%	Isabell Masters	3,133	0.02%
J. Louis McAlpine	7,911	0.04%	Stephen Michael	2,619	0.02%
George Benns	7,876	0.04%	Bill Clinton	1,696	0.01%
Rufus Higginbotham	7,674	0.04%	Jim Lennane	1,684	0.01%
Tom Hawks	7,434	0.04%	Paul Jensen	1,332	0.01%
Mario Cuomo	6,577	0.03%	Philip Skow	1,105	<.01%
Stephen Burke	5,222	0.03%	Emmanuel Branch	1,013	<.01%
Tom Laughlin	5,202	0.03%	Stephen Koczak	921	<.01%
Tom Shiekman	4,942	0.02%	Mario Cuomo	798	<.01%
Jeffrey Marsh	2,445	0.01%	Jerry Brown	772	<.01%
George Ballard	2,067	0.01%	Bob Kerrey	735	<.01%
Ralph Spelbring	1,626	<.01%	Jack Beemont	735	<.01%
Robert Hanson	1,473	<.01%	Terrance Scott	719	<.01%
George Bush	1,433	<.01%	Paul Daugherty	718	<.01%
Bob Cunningham	1,369	<.01%	Tom Harkin	542	<.01%
Gary Hauptli	1,303	<.01%	Charles Doty	417	<.01%
Patrick Buchanan	1,248	<.01%	Billy Clegg	408	<.01%
Ray Rollinson	1,206	<.01%	Sharon Anderson	300	<.01%
Don Beamgard	1,009	<.01%	Beatrice Mooney	196	<.01%
John Barnes	892	<.01%	Thomas Fabish	158	<.01%
Mary Rachner	620	<.01%	Hubert Patty	62	<.01%
Raymond Vanskiver	*510	<.01%			
William Pawley	364	<.01%			
William Kreml	336	<.01%			
Susan Fey	308	<.01%			
Jim Hayes	279	<.01%			
Leonard Talbow	202	<.01%			
John Staradumsky	168	<.01%			
Lawrence Wilder	137	<.01%			
Nathan Averick	105	<.01%			
Curly Thornton	52	<.01%			

Table A. — 1990 Population by Race and Ethnic Origin

State code	State	Total persons	Percent of total persons — Non-Hispanic White	Black	Asian and Pacific Islander	Native American	Other	Hispanic	Rank — Percent of total persons Total	Non-Hispanic White	Black	Hispanic	Percent contribution to national population Total	Non-Hispanic White	Black	Hispanic
01	Alabama	4,040,587	73.3	25.2	0.5	0.4	<.1	0.6	22	38	6	48	1.6	1.6	3.5	0.1
02	Alaska	550,043	73.9	4.0	3.4	15.4	<.1	3.2	50	37	31	22	0.2	0.2	<.1	<.1
04	Arizona	3,665,228	71.7	2.9	1.4	5.2	0.1	18.8	24	40	37	4	1.5	1.4	0.4	3.1
05	Arkansas	2,350,725	82.2	15.9	0.5	0.5	<.1	0.8	33	28	12	42	0.9	1.0	1.3	<.1
06	California	29,760,021	57.2	7.0	9.1	0.6	0.2	25.8	1	48	26	2	12.0	9.1	7.2	34.4
08	Colorado	3,294,394	80.7	3.9	1.7	0.7	0.1	12.9	26	30	32	5	1.3	1.4	0.4	1.9
09	Connecticut	3,287,116	83.8	7.9	1.5	0.2	0.1	6.5	27	25	22	12	1.3	1.5	0.9	1.0
10	Delaware	666,168	79.3	16.7	1.3	0.3	<.1	2.4	46	31	10	26	0.3	0.3	0.4	<.1
12	Florida	12,937,926	73.2	13.1	1.1	0.3	<.1	12.2	4	39	16	7	5.2	5.0	5.8	7.0
13	Georgia	6,478,216	70.1	26.8	1.1	0.2	<.1	1.7	11	41	5	33	2.6	2.4	5.9	0.5
15	Hawaii	1,108,229	31.4	2.3	58.3	0.4	0.3	7.3	41	50	38	11	0.4	0.2	<.1	0.4
16	Idaho	1,006,749	92.2	0.3	0.9	1.2	<.1	5.3	42	9	50	15	0.4	0.5	<.1	0.2
17	Illinois	11,430,602	74.8	14.6	2.4	0.2	<.1	7.9	6	35	13	10	4.6	4.5	5.7	4.0
18	Indiana	5,544,159	89.6	7.7	0.7	0.2	<.1	1.8	14	17	23	32	2.2	2.6	1.5	0.4
19	Iowa	2,776,755	95.9	1.7	0.9	0.2	<.1	1.2	30	4	41	38	1.1	1.4	0.2	0.1
20	Kansas	2,477,574	88.4	5.7	1.2	0.8	<.1	3.8	32	19	28	21	1.0	1.2	0.5	0.4
21	Kentucky	3,685,296	91.7	7.1	0.5	0.1	<.1	0.6	23	11	25	49	1.5	1.8	0.9	<.1
22	Louisiana	4,219,973	65.8	30.6	0.9	0.4	<.1	2.2	21	45	3	28	1.7	1.5	4.4	0.4
23	Maine	1,227,928	98.0	0.4	0.5	0.5	<.1	0.6	38	2	48	50	0.5	0.6	<.1	<.1
24	Maryland	4,781,468	69.6	24.6	2.9	0.3	<.1	2.6	19	42	7	24	1.9	1.8	4.0	0.6
25	Massachusetts	6,016,425	87.8	4.6	2.3	0.2	0.4	4.8	13	20	30	17	2.4	2.8	0.9	1.3
26	Michigan	9,295,297	82.3	13.8	1.1	0.6	<.1	2.2	8	27	15	29	3.7	4.1	4.4	0.9
27	Minnesota	4,375,099	93.7	2.1	1.7	1.1	<.1	1.2	20	7	39	36	1.8	2.2	0.3	0.2
28	Mississippi	2,573,216	63.1	35.4	0.5	0.3	<.1	0.6	31	46	2	47	1.0	0.9	3.1	<.1
29	Missouri	5,117,073	86.9	10.7	0.8	0.4	<.1	1.2	15	23	19	37	2.1	2.4	1.9	0.3
30	Montana	799,065	91.8	0.3	0.5	5.8	<.1	1.5	44	10	51	34	0.3	0.4	<.1	<.1
31	Nebraska	1,578,385	92.5	3.6	0.8	0.7	<.1	2.3	36	8	33	27	0.6	0.8	0.2	0.2
32	Nevada	1,201,833	78.7	6.4	3.0	1.5	<.1	10.4	39	32	27	8	0.5	0.5	0.3	0.6
33	New Hampshire	1,109,252	97.3	0.6	0.8	0.2	<.1	1.0	40	3	45	40	0.4	0.6	<.1	<.1
34	New Jersey	7,730,188	74.0	12.7	3.4	0.2	0.1	9.6	9	36	17	9	3.1	3.0	3.4	3.3
35	New Mexico	1,515,069	50.4	1.8	0.8	8.5	0.2	38.2	37	49	40	1	0.6	0.4	<.1	2.6
36	New York	17,990,455	69.3	14.3	3.7	0.3	0.2	12.3	2	43	14	6	7.2	6.6	8.8	9.9
37	North Carolina	6,628,637	75.0	21.9	0.8	1.2	<.1	1.2	10	34	8	39	2.7	2.6	5.0	0.3
38	North Dakota	638,800	94.2	0.5	0.5	4.0	<.1	0.7	47	6	46	44	0.3	0.3	<.1	<.1
39	Ohio	10,847,115	87.1	10.6	0.8	0.2	<.1	1.3	7	22	20	35	4.4	5.0	3.9	0.6
40	Oklahoma	3,145,585	81.0	7.4	1.0	7.8	<.1	2.7	28	29	24	23	1.3	1.4	0.8	0.4
41	Oregon	2,842,321	90.8	1.6	2.4	1.3	<.1	4.0	29	16	42	20	1.1	1.4	0.2	0.5
42	Pennsylvania	11,881,643	87.7	9.0	1.1	0.1	<.1	2.0	5	21	21	30	4.8	5.5	3.7	1.0
44	Rhode Island	1,003,464	89.3	3.4	1.8	0.4	0.6	4.6	43	18	34	18	0.4	0.5	0.1	0.2
45	South Carolina	3,486,703	68.5	29.7	0.6	0.2	<.1	0.9	25	44	4	41	1.4	1.3	3.5	0.1
46	South Dakota	696,004	91.2	0.5	0.4	7.1	<.1	0.8	45	13	47	43	0.3	0.3	<.1	<.1
47	Tennessee	4,877,185	82.6	15.9	0.6	0.2	<.1	0.7	17	26	11	45	2.0	2.1	2.7	0.1
48	Texas	16,986,510	60.6	11.6	1.8	0.3	0.1	25.5	3	47	18	3	6.8	5.5	6.8	19.4
49	Utah	1,722,850	91.2	0.6	1.9	1.3	<.1	4.9	35	14	44	16	0.7	0.8	<.1	0.4
50	Vermont	562,758	98.1	0.3	0.6	0.3	<.1	0.7	49	1	49	46	0.2	0.3	<.1	<.1
51	Virginia	6,187,358	76.0	18.6	2.5	0.2	<.1	2.6	12	33	9	25	2.5	2.5	3.9	0.7
53	Washington	4,866,692	86.7	3.0	4.2	1.6	<.1	4.4	18	24	36	19	2.0	2.2	0.5	1.0
54	West Virginia	1,793,477	95.8	3.1	0.4	0.1	<.1	0.5	34	5	35	51	0.7	0.9	0.2	<.1
55	Wisconsin	4,891,769	91.3	4.9	1.1	0.8	<.1	1.9	16	12	29	31	2.0	2.4	0.8	0.4
56	Wyoming	453,588	91.0	0.8	0.6	2.0	<.1	5.7	51	15	43	13	0.2	0.2	<.1	0.1
11	District of Columbia	606,900	27.4	65.1	1.8	0.2	0.1	5.4	48	51	1	14	0.2	<.1	1.4	0.1
	UNITED STATES	**248,709,873**	**75.6**	**11.7**	**2.8**	**0.7**	**0.1**	**9.0**					**100.0**	**100.0**	**100.0**	**100.0**

Table B. — 1990 Voting Age Population (VAP) by Race and Ethnic Origin

State	Total Voting Age Population	Percent of total VAP — Non-Hispanic White	Black	Asian and Pacific Islander	Native American	Other	Hispanic	Rank — Percent of total VAP Total	Non-Hispanic White	Black	Hispanic	Percent contribution to national VAP Total	Non-Hispanic White	Black	Hispanic	VAP percent of total population Total	Non-Hispanic White	Black	Asian and Pacific Islander	Native American	Other	Hispanic
Alabama	2,981,799	75.9	22.7	0.5	0.4	<.1	0.6	22	40	7	47	1.6	1.6	3.4	0.1	73.8	76.5	66.4	71.4	65.6	52.5	67.8
Alaska	377,699	76.5	3.8	3.4	13.4	<.1	2.9	50	36	31	22	0.2	0.2	<.1	<.1	68.7	71.1	65.1	68.6	59.6	47.3	62.1
Arizona	2,684,109	76.0	2.6	1.4	4.2	<.1	15.8	24	38	37	4	1.5	1.4	0.3	2.9	73.2	77.7	66.4	72.6	58.6	56.4	61.4
Arkansas	1,729,594	84.6	13.7	0.5	0.5	<.1	0.7	33	26	12	42	0.9	1.0	1.2	<.1	73.6	75.7	63.5	68.1	71.4	46.6	62.5
California	22,009,296	61.2	6.7	8.9	0.6	0.2	22.5	1	48	24	2	11.9	9.3	7.4	33.9	74.0	79.1	70.3	71.9	72.0	59.6	64.5
Colorado	2,433,128	82.9	3.6	1.6	0.6	<.1	11.2	27	30	32	7	1.3	1.4	0.4	1.9	73.9	75.8	68.6	70.1	68.6	55.9	64.0
Connecticut	2,537,535	85.9	7.1	1.4	0.2	<.1	5.4	26	25	22	12	1.4	1.5	0.9	0.9	77.2	79.1	69.3	70.8	75.2	54.3	63.7
Delaware	502,827	81.2	15.1	1.3	0.3	<.1	2.0	45	31	10	27	0.3	0.3	0.4	<.1	75.5	77.4	68.5	71.2	75.7	55.6	64.7
Florida	10,071,689	75.9	11.0	1.0	0.2	<.1	11.7	4	39	17	5	5.4	5.3	5.6	8.1	77.8	80.7	65.2	72.0	74.6	48.1	75.1
Georgia	4,750,913	72.6	24.5	1.1	0.2	<.1	1.6	11	41	5	31	2.6	2.4	5.8	0.5	73.3	75.9	66.9	70.3	74.7	43.5	70.0
Hawaii	828,103	32.7	2.2	58.5	0.3	0.2	6.1	41	50	38	11	0.4	0.2	<.1	0.3	74.7	77.8	70.2	75.0	71.8	52.3	61.7
Idaho	698,344	93.3	0.3	0.9	1.1	<.1	4.4	43	10	49	16	0.4	0.5	<.1	0.2	69.4	70.1	64.0	68.5	64.3	48.9	57.5
Illinois	8,484,236	77.4	13.3	2.3	0.2	<.1	6.8	6	34	13	10	4.6	4.6	5.7	3.9	74.2	76.8	67.4	71.7	73.6	46.7	63.4
Indiana	4,088,195	90.6	7.0	0.7	0.2	<.1	1.5	14	18	23	32	2.2	2.6	1.4	0.4	73.7	74.6	66.8	73.0	71.9	31.2	62.9
Iowa	2,057,875	96.6	1.5	0.8	0.2	<.1	1.0	30	4	41	39	1.1	1.4	0.2	0.1	74.1	74.6	63.4	65.9	63.1	28.3	60.6
Kansas	1,815,960	89.8	5.1	1.2	0.8	<.1	3.1	32	19	28	21	1.0	1.1	0.5	0.4	73.3	74.4	66.2	68.1	67.8	43.0	60.8
Kentucky	2,731,202	92.3	6.6	0.4	0.2	<.1	0.5	23	13	26	49	1.5	1.7	0.9	0.1	74.1	74.6	68.5	70.0	75.6	22.7	67.7
Louisiana	2,992,704	68.8	27.7	0.9	0.4	<.1	2.2	21	45	3	26	1.6	1.4	4.2	0.5	70.9	74.2	64.2	65.5	64.9	65.9	71.2
Maine	918,926	98.3	0.4	0.5	0.4	<.1	0.5	38	2	48	50	0.5	0.6	<.1	0.1	74.8	75.0	67.1	66.6	64.6	32.8	63.1
Maryland	3,619,227	71.3	23.2	2.7	0.2	<.1	2.5	17	44	6	23	2.0	1.8	4.2	0.6	75.7	77.6	71.4	72.5	74.3	44.3	71.0
Massachusetts	4,663,350	89.4	4.1	2.1	0.2	0.3	3.9	13	20	29	17	2.5	2.9	1.0	1.2	77.5	79.0	69.6	71.3	72.6	64.0	62.7
Michigan	6,836,532	83.9	12.7	1.0	0.5	<.1	1.8	8	28	15	29	3.7	4.0	4.4	0.9	73.5	75.0	67.6	67.0	66.5	37.5	61.7
Minnesota	3,208,316	95.0	1.8	1.3	0.9	<.1	1.0	20	7	39	38	1.7	2.1	0.3	0.2	73.3	74.3	61.0	54.9	59.5	29.5	58.2
Mississippi	1,826,455	67.1	31.5	0.5	0.3	<.1	0.6	31	46	2	46	1.0	0.8	2.9	<.1	71.0	75.5	63.1	67.2	61.4	50.1	66.9
Missouri	3,802,247	88.1	9.7	0.8	0.4	<.1	1.1	15	24	20	36	2.1	2.3	1.8	0.3	74.3	75.3	67.4	71.3	72.2	32.8	65.5
Montana	576,961	93.3	0.2	0.5	4.7	<.1	1.2	44	9	51	34	0.3	0.4	<.1	<.1	72.2	73.4	64.1	65.9	58.6	46.2	58.0
Nebraska	1,149,373	93.6	3.1	0.7	0.6	<.1	1.9	35	8	33	28	0.6	0.7	0.2	0.2	72.8	73.7	63.6	67.6	58.6	29.8	60.2
Nevada	904,885	80.9	5.6	3.0	1.3	<.1	9.1	39	32	27	8	0.5	0.5	0.3	0.6	75.3	77.4	66.4	74.7	69.2	51.8	66.0
New Hampshire	830,497	97.6	0.6	0.8	0.2	<.1	0.9	40	3	45	40	0.4	0.6	<.1	<.1	74.9	75.1	68.5	70.6	74.7	36.7	65.2
New Jersey	5,930,726	76.1	11.8	3.1	0.2	<.1	8.7	9	37	16	9	3.2	3.1	3.5	3.5	76.7	78.9	70.9	70.6	74.9	51.9	69.9
New Mexico	1,068,328	54.9	1.7	0.8	7.2	0.2	35.2	37	49	40	1	0.6	0.4	<.1	2.6	70.5	76.7	67.3	70.2	59.9	65.8	64.9
New York	13,730,906	71.5	13.3	3.7	0.3	0.1	11.2	2	43	14	6	7.4	6.8	9.2	10.5	76.3	78.8	71.0	75.2	70.5	51.6	69.5
North Carolina	5,022,488	77.2	20.0	0.7	1.1	<.1	1.1	10	35	8	37	2.7	2.7	5.0	0.4	75.8	78.0	69.2	70.7	67.1	40.4	68.8
North Dakota	463,415	95.4	0.5	0.5	3.1	<.1	0.6	48	6	46	48	0.3	0.3	<.1	<.1	72.5	73.5	62.9	69.2	55.4	39.5	55.2
Ohio	8,047,371	88.2	9.7	0.8	0.2	<.1	1.1	7	23	19	35	4.3	4.9	3.9	0.6	74.2	75.2	68.1	71.2	74.2	29.7	62.4
Oklahoma	2,308,578	83.4	6.6	1.0	6.7	<.1	2.2	28	29	25	25	1.2	1.3	0.8	0.5	73.4	75.6	65.8	71.3	63.1	48.1	59.8
Oregon	2,118,191	92.0	1.4	2.2	1.1	<.1	3.3	29	15	42	20	1.1	1.3	0.1	0.5	74.5	75.5	65.1	70.3	66.3	43.6	61.2
Pennsylvania	9,086,833	88.9	8.4	1.0	0.1	<.1	1.6	5	21	21	30	4.9	5.6	3.8	0.4	76.5	77.5	70.8	69.6	74.9	34.8	62.9
Rhode Island	777,774	90.9	2.9	1.5	0.3	0.5	3.8	42	17	35	18	0.4	0.5	0.1	0.2	77.5	78.9	66.8	65.7	67.8	64.4	64.8
South Carolina	2,566,496	71.5	26.8	0.6	0.2	<.1	0.8	25	42	4	41	1.4	1.3	3.5	0.1	73.6	76.8	66.5	70.9	71.8	42.0	68.1
South Dakota	497,542	93.2	0.4	0.4	5.4	<.1	0.6	46	11	47	45	0.3	0.3	<.1	<.1	71.5	73.1	62.3	64.3	53.8	37.0	55.9
Tennessee	3,660,581	84.3	14.3	0.6	0.2	<.1	0.6	16	27	11	43	2.0	2.1	2.6	0.2	75.1	76.6	67.6	69.9	75.6	37.0	68.6
Texas	12,150,671	64.4	11.0	1.8	0.3	0.1	22.4	3	47	18	3	6.6	5.4	6.7	18.6	71.5	76.1	67.6	70.2	74.5	61.2	62.7
Utah	1,095,406	91.7	0.6	1.9	1.2	<.1	4.5	36	16	44	15	0.6	0.7	<.1	0.3	63.6	63.9	65.0	65.0	55.6	52.0	58.5
Vermont	419,675	98.3	0.5	0.5	0.3	<.1	0.6	49	1	50	44	0.2	0.3	<.1	<.1	74.6	74.7	64.7	67.5	68.7	45.1	69.9
Virginia	4,682,620	77.5	17.4	2.4	0.2	<.1	2.4	12	33	9	24	2.5	2.5	4.1	0.8	75.7	77.2	70.8	71.7	77.1	41.3	70.7
Washington	3,605,305	88.4	2.7	3.9	1.4	<.1	3.6	18	22	36	19	1.9	2.2	0.5	0.9	74.1	75.5	66.7	69.6	64.8	43.4	59.8
West Virginia	1,349,900	96.1	2.9	0.4	0.1	<.1	0.4	34	5	34	51	0.7	0.9	0.2	<.1	75.3	75.5	71.0	70.7	76.2	23.6	69.5
Wisconsin	3,602,787	93.0	4.0	0.8	0.7	<.1	1.5	19	12	30	33	1.9	2.3	0.7	0.4	73.7	75.0	60.0	57.2	62.4	25.8	57.8
Wyoming	318,063	92.2	0.7	0.6	1.7	<.1	4.8	51	14	43	14	0.2	0.2	<.1	0.1	70.1	71.0	66.2	71.7	59.5	56.6	59.7
District of Columbia	489,808	30.9	61.7	1.9	0.2	0.1	5.2	47	51	1	13	0.3	0.1	1.5	0.2	80.7	91.0	76.5	86.1	84.3	68.4	77.8
UNITED STATES	185,105,441	78.0	10.7	2.7	0.6	<.1	7.9					100.0	100.0	100.0	100.0	74.4	76.7	68.1	71.7	65.0	52.5	65.3

Table C. — **Voter Participation: November 3, 1992, General Election**

State	Estimated Voting Age Population (VAP), 1992	Voter registration (REG) Total	REG % contribution to national REG	REG % of 1992 VAP	REG Rank by % of 1992 VAP	Voter turnout — Highest office Actual	Highest office Total	Office	Highest office % of 1992 VAP	Maximum vote Total	Max % contribution to national turnout	Max % of REG	Max Rank by % of REG	Max % of 1992 VAP	Max Rank by % 1992 VAP	Drop-off President	Drop-off Senator	Drop-off Governor	Drop-off Representative
Alabama[2]	3,056,000	2,367,972	1.8	77.5	19	-	1,688,933		55.3	1,688,933	1.6	71.3	43	55.3	31	0.1	6.6	-	5.1
Alaska	395,000	315,058	0.2	79.8	15	261,427	258,448		65.4	261,427	0.2	83.0	10	66.2	12	1.1	8.3	-	8.5
Arizona	2,749,000	1,964,949	1.5	71.5	33	1,516,276	1,487,003		54.1	1,516,276	1.4	77.2	29	55.2	32	1.9	8.9	-	7.1
Arkansas[2]	1,768,000	1,317,944	1.0	74.5	25	-	956,978		54.1	956,978	0.9	72.6	40	54.1	35	0.7	3.9	-	7.2
California[3]	22,668,000	15,101,473	11.3	66.6	39	11,374,565	11,136,462		49.1	11,374,565	10.7	75.3	33	50.2	47	2.1	5.1	-	7.4
Colorado	2,501,000	2,003,375	1.5	80.1	14	1,597,166	1,571,927		62.9	1,597,166	1.5	79.7	22	63.9	15	1.8	2.8	-	7.4
Connecticut	2,535,000	1,961,503	1.5	77.4	20	1,645,609	1,616,156		63.8	1,645,609	1.6	83.9	6	64.9	13	1.8	8.8	-	12.8
Delaware	525,000	342,088	0.3	65.2	42	290,836	289,735		55.2	290,836	0.3	85.0	3	55.4	30	0.4	-	4.7	5.1
Florida[2,4]	10,586,000	6,541,825	4.9	61.8	47	5,438,612	5,326,061		50.3	5,438,617	5.1	83.1	9	51.4	42	2.3	8.8	-	9.6
Georgia[2]	4,950,000	3,177,061	2.4	64.2	43	-	2,325,470		47.0	2,325,470	2.2	73.2	37	47.0	49	0.2	3.2	-	4.8
Hawaii	889,000	464,495	0.3	52.2	49	382,882	372,842		41.9	382,882	0.4	82.4	15	43.1	51	2.6	5.0	-	6.4
Idaho	740,000	611,121	0.5	82.6	10	491,725	483,135		65.3	491,725	0.5	80.5	20	66.4	10	1.9	2.7	-	3.9
Illinois	8,568,000	6,600,358	4.9	77.0	21	5,164,357	5,050,157		58.9	5,164,357	4.9	78.2	27	60.3	25	2.2	4.4	-	6.5
Indiana	4,176,000	3,180,157	2.4	76.2	23	2,347,912	2,305,871		55.2	2,348,650	2.2	73.9	36	56.2	29	1.8	5.8	5.1	5.7
Iowa[5]	2,075,000	1,703,532	1.3	82.1	11	1,374,111	1,360,856		65.6	1,375,751	1.3	80.8	19	66.3	11	1.5	6.1	-	9.7
Kansas	1,836,000	1,365,849	1.0	74.4	26	1,161,044	1,157,353		63.0	1,167,216	1.1	85.5	2	63.6	17	0.8	3.5	-	3.6
Kentucky[2]	2,779,000	2,076,263	1.6	74.7	24	-	1,492,900		53.7	1,492,900	1.4	71.9	41	53.7	37	0.0	10.9	-	8.8
Louisiana[4,6,7]	2,992,000	2,292,129	1.7	76.6	22	1,799,596	1,790,017		59.8	1,800,641	1.7	78.6	25	60.2	26	0.6	-	-	62.0
Maine	944,000	974,605	0.7	103.2	1	-	679,499		72.0	679,499	0.6	69.7	45	72.0	2	0.0	-	-	1.5
Maryland[6]	3,719,000	2,463,010	1.8	66.2	40	1,999,486	1,985,046		53.4	1,999,503	1.9	81.2	18	53.8	36	0.7	7.9	-	9.6
Massachusetts	4,607,000	3,351,918	2.5	72.8	30	2,822,962	2,773,700		60.2	2,822,962	2.7	84.2	5	61.3	23	1.7	-	-	7.4
Michigan	6,923,000	6,147,083	4.6	88.8	7	4,341,909	4,274,673		61.7	4,341,909	4.1	70.6	44	62.7	19	1.5	-	-	10.5
Minnesota	3,278,000	3,138,901	2.3	95.8	3	2,355,796	2,347,948		71.6	2,362,280	2.2	75.3	34	72.1	1	0.6	-	-	3.7
Mississippi	1,861,000	1,640,150	1.2	88.1	8	1,008,019	1,005,349		54.0	1,026,251	1.0	62.6	49	55.1	33	4.3	-	-	5.9
Missouri	3,858,000	3,067,955	2.3	79.5	17	-	2,391,568		62.0	2,391,568	2.3	78.0	28	62.0	21	0.0	1.5	2.0	1.8
Montana	586,000	529,822	0.4	90.4	4	417,564	411,205		70.2	417,564	0.4	78.8	24	71.3	3	1.7	-	2.3	3.3
Nebraska	1,167,000	951,395	0.7	81.5	12	744,548	737,546		63.2	744,548	0.7	78.3	26	63.8	16	0.9	-	-	4.5
Nevada	1,013,000	649,913	0.5	64.2	44	513,387	507,614		50.1	513,387	0.5	79.0	23	50.7	43	1.4	3.4	-	4.2
New Hampshire	852,000	660,985	0.5	77.6	18	545,197	537,943		63.1	545,197	0.5	82.5	14	64.0	14	1.3	4.9	5.3	6.3
New Jersey	5,943,000	4,059,472	3.0	68.3	36	3,348,312	3,343,594		56.3	3,366,794	3.2	82.9	11	56.7	28	0.7	-	-	11.1
New Mexico	1,104,000	706,966	0.5	64.0	45	590,901	569,986		51.6	590,901	0.6	83.6	8	53.5	38	3.5	-	-	6.0
New York	13,609,000	9,193,391	6.9	67.6	37	7,068,630	6,926,925		50.9	7,068,630	6.7	76.9	31	51.9	41	2.0	8.6	-	16.2
North Carolina[2]	5,217,000	3,817,380	2.9	73.2	29	-	2,625,045		50.3	2,625,045	2.5	68.8	46	50.3	46	0.5	1.8	1.1	3.7
North Dakota[8]	458,000	-	-	-	-	315,199	308,664		67.4	315,199	0.3	-	-	68.8	5	2.2	3.6	3.3	5.5
Ohio	8,146,000	6,542,931	4.9	80.3	13	5,043,094	4,940,173		60.6	5,043,094	4.8	77.1	30	61.9	22	2.0	4.9	-	9.2
Oklahoma	2,328,000	2,302,279	1.7	98.9	2	1,455,635	1,390,359		59.7	1,455,635	1.4	63.2	48	62.5	20	4.5	11.1	-	12.4
Oregon[6]	2,226,000	1,775,416	1.3	79.8	16	1,498,959	1,464,759		65.8	1,498,959	1.4	84.4	4	67.3	8	2.4	8.2	-	7.2
Pennsylvania	9,129,000	5,993,002	4.5	65.6	41	-	4,960,233		54.3	4,960,233	4.7	82.8	12	54.3	34	0.0	3.2	-	7.5
Rhode Island	776,000	554,664	0.4	71.5	34	-	453,471		58.4	453,471	0.4	81.8	16	58.4	27	0.0	-	6.3	12.1
South Carolina[2,7]	2,672,000	1,537,140	1.1	57.5	48	1,234,712	1,207,387		45.2	1,235,798	1.2	80.4	21	46.2	50	2.7	4.5	-	9.7
South Dakota	502,000	448,292	0.3	89.3	6	-	336,409		67.0	336,409	0.3	75.0	35	67.0	9	0.0	0.6	-	1.0
Tennessee	3,783,000	2,726,649	2.0	72.1	32	-	1,986,635		52.5	1,986,635	1.9	72.9	38	52.5	40	0.2	-	-	13.1
Texas	12,524,000	8,440,143	6.3	67.4	38	-	6,154,088		49.1	6,154,088	5.8	72.9	39	49.1	48	0.0	-	-	8.6
Utah	1,142,000	965,211	0.7	84.5	9	784,988	763,184		66.8	784,988	0.7	81.3	17	68.7	6	5.2	3.4	2.9	7.4
Vermont	429,000	383,371	0.3	89.4	5	292,797	289,701		67.5	292,797	0.3	76.4	32	68.3	7	1.1	2.5	2.5	3.9
Virginia	4,842,000	3,054,662	2.3	63.1	46	-	2,558,665		52.8	2,558,665	2.4	83.8	7	52.8	39	0.0	-	-	7.4
Washington	3,818,000	2,814,680	2.1	73.7	28	2,324,907	2,294,519		60.1	2,324,974	2.2	82.6	13	60.9	24	1.6	4.6	2.3	4.4
West Virginia	1,350,000	956,172	0.7	70.8	35	-	683,762		50.6	683,762	0.6	71.5	42	50.6	44	0.0	-	3.9	17.8
Wisconsin[8]	3,669,000	-	-	-	-	-	2,531,977		69.0	2,531,977	2.4	-	-	69.0	4	0.0	3.0	-	5.7
Wyoming	322,000	234,260	0.2	72.8	31	203,602	200,651		62.3	203,602	0.2	86.9	1	63.2	18	1.5	-	-	3.3
District of Columbia	459,000	340,953	0.3	74.3	27	231,445	227,137		49.5	231,445	0.2	67.9	47	50.4	45	1.7	-	-	15.0
UNITED STATES	**189,044,000**	-	-	-		-	104,539,719		55.3	105,867,768	100.0	-		56.0		1.4	5.5	3.0	9.1
US (48 states DC w/REG)[9]	184,917,000	133,809,723	100.0	72.4		-	101,699,078		55.0	103,020,592	100.0	77.0		55.7					
US (35 states DC w/TO[10])	129,897,000	-	-	-		73,988,167	72,714,086		56.0	74,042,135	100.0	-		57.0		2.3			

[1]Percent drop-off is based on the statewide total of county-level data and is zero or slightly greater than zero for states without actual voter turnout and where the vote for President was used as highest office turnout. Percentages only slightly higher than zero occur when the office of President was not the highest office in all counties. [2]Also reports voter registration by race; see individual state pages for data. [3]California has two U.S. Senate races; drop-off is for six-year term. [4]Drop-off for U.S. Representative does not include all congressional districts (Florida No. 21, and Louisiana No. 1, 2, 3, and 7 not included. [5]Actual voter turnout data for Iowa was not officially certified by the Iowa Secretary of State at the time of publication. [6]Also reports voter turnout by political party; see individual state pages for data. [7]Also reports voter turnout by race; see individual state pages for data. [8]No statewide voter registration requirement (registration in Wisconsin required only for municipalities over 5,000 population). [9]Does not include North Dakota and Wisconsin. [10]Includes Alaska, Arizona, California, Colorado, Connecticut, Delaware, Florida, Hawaii, Idaho, Illinois, Indiana, Iowa, Kansas, Louisiana, Maryland, Massachusetts, Michigan, Minnesota, Mississippi, Montana, Nebraska, Nevada, New Hampshire, New Jersey, New Mexico, New York, North Dakota, Ohio, Oklahoma, Oregon, South Carolina, Utah, Vermont, Washington, Wyoming, and the District of Columbia.

Table D. — Voter Registration by Political Party Affiliation: November 3, 1992, General Election

State	Total voter registration	Political party affiliation Democrat (DEM)	Republican (REP)	Independent (IND)	Plurality Total	Party	Percent of total registration DEM	REP	IND	Rank[1] DEM	REP	IND	Percent contribution to national registration[1] Total	DEM	REP	IND
Alabama	-	-	-	-	-	-	-	-	-	-	-	-	-	-	-	-
Alaska[2,3]	315,058	59,938	70,739	191,381	120,642	I	18.6	22.0	59.4	26	23	1	0.5	0.2	0.3	2.2
Arizona[2,3]	1,964,949	833,997	889,644	232,712	55,647	R	42.6	45.5	11.9	16	4	12	3.1	2.7	4.1	2.7
Arkansas	-	-	-	-	-	-	-	-	-	-	-	-	-	-	-	-
California[2]	15,101,473	7,410,914	5,593,355	1,557,255	1,817,559	D	50.9	38.4	10.7	10	11	14	23.5	23.6	25.7	18.2
Colorado[2]	2,003,375	680,773	668,051	647,906	12,722	D	34.1	33.5	32.4	23	16	4	3.1	2.2	3.1	7.6
Connecticut[2,3]	1,961,503	736,914	506,115	708,584	28,330	D	37.8	25.9	36.3	20	22	3	3.0	2.3	2.3	8.3
Delaware	342,088	148,542	125,829	67,717	22,713	D	43.4	36.8	19.8	15	12	8	0.5	0.5	0.6	0.8
Florida[2]	6,541,825	3,318,565	2,672,968	546,058	645,597	D	50.8	40.9	8.4	11	7	19	10.2	10.6	12.3	6.4
Georgia	-	-	-	-	-	-	-	-	-	-	-	-	-	-	-	-
Hawaii	-	-	-	-	-	-	-	-	-	-	-	-	-	-	-	-
Idaho	-	-	-	-	-	-	-	-	-	-	-	-	-	-	-	-
Illinois	-	-	-	-	-	-	-	-	-	-	-	-	-	-	-	-
Indiana	-	-	-	-	-	-	-	-	-	-	-	-	-	-	-	-
Iowa	1,703,532	636,528	532,202	534,802	101,726	D	37.4	31.2	31.4	21	18	5	2.6	2.0	2.4	6.3
Kansas[2,3]	1,365,849	424,478	587,303	349,864	162,825	R	31.2	43.1	25.7	25	5	7	2.1	1.4	2.7	4.1
Kentucky[2]	2,076,263	1,374,459	615,732	61,972	758,727	D	67.0	30.0	3.0	3	20	25	3.2	4.4	2.8	0.7
Louisiana	2,292,129	1,634,832	437,660	219,637	1,197,172	D	71.3	19.1	9.6	2	24	16	3.6	5.2	2.0	2.6
Maine	-	-	-	-	-	-	-	-	-	-	-	-	-	-	-	-
Maryland[2]	2,463,010	1,506,184	717,963	236,113	788,221	D	61.2	29.2	9.6	6	21	17	3.8	4.8	3.3	2.8
Massachusetts	3,351,918	1,346,097	447,181	1,548,618	202,521	I	40.3	13.4	46.3	19	25	2	5.2	4.3	2.1	18.1
Michigan	-	-	-	-	-	-	-	-	-	-	-	-	-	-	-	-
Minnesota	-	-	-	-	-	-	-	-	-	-	-	-	-	-	-	-
Mississippi	-	-	-	-	-	-	-	-	-	-	-	-	-	-	-	-
Missouri	-	-	-	-	-	-	-	-	-	-	-	-	-	-	-	-
Montana	-	-	-	-	-	-	-	-	-	-	-	-	-	-	-	-
Nebraska[2]	951,395	389,102	464,955	97,144	75,853	R	40.9	48.9	10.2	18	2	15	1.5	1.2	2.1	1.1
Nevada[2,3]	649,913	295,111	255,897	95,888	39,214	D	45.6	39.6	14.8	13	9	10	1.0	0.9	1.2	1.1
New Hampshire[2]	660,985	219,769	257,312	180,267	37,543	R	33.4	39.1	27.4	24	10	6	1.0	0.7	1.2	2.1
New Jersey[2,3]	4,059,472	1,175,041	817,837	6,470	357,204	D	58.8	40.9	0.3	9	8	26	6.3	3.7	3.8	<.1
New Mexico[2]	706,966	411,263	239,473	47,645	171,790	D	58.9	34.3	6.8	8	14	21	1.1	1.3	1.1	0.6
New York	-	-	-	-	-	-	-	-	-	-	-	-	-	-	-	-
North Carolina[2]	3,817,380	2,313,520	1,217,114	286,069	1,096,406	D	60.6	31.9	7.5	7	17	20	5.9	7.4	5.6	3.3
North Dakota	-	-	-	-	-	-	-	-	-	-	-	-	-	-	-	-
Ohio	-	-	-	-	-	-	-	-	-	-	-	-	-	-	-	-
Oklahoma	2,302,279	1,452,949	775,754	73,576	677,195	D	63.1	33.7	3.2	5	15	24	3.6	4.6	3.6	0.9
Oregon[2]	1,775,416	792,551	642,206	321,532	150,345	D	45.1	36.6	18.3	14	13	9	2.8	2.5	3.0	3.8
Pennsylvania	5,993,002	3,043,757	2,567,643	381,602	476,114	D	50.8	42.8	6.4	12	6	22	9.3	9.7	11.8	4.5
Rhode Island	-	-	-	-	-	-	-	-	-	-	-	-	-	-	-	-
South Carolina	-	-	-	-	-	-	-	-	-	-	-	-	-	-	-	-
South Dakota[2]	448,292	189,935	215,285	42,726	25,350	R	42.4	48.1	9.5	17	3	18	0.7	0.6	1.0	0.5
Tennessee	-	-	-	-	-	-	-	-	-	-	-	-	-	-	-	-
Texas	-	-	-	-	-	-	-	-	-	-	-	-	-	-	-	-
Utah	-	-	-	-	-	-	-	-	-	-	-	-	-	-	-	-
Vermont	-	-	-	-	-	-	-	-	-	-	-	-	-	-	-	-
Virginia	-	-	-	-	-	-	-	-	-	-	-	-	-	-	-	-
Washington	-	-	-	-	-	-	-	-	-	-	-	-	-	-	-	-
West Virginia	956,172	627,836	291,253	37,083	336,583	D	65.7	30.5	3.9	4	19	23	1.5	2.0	1.3	0.4
Wisconsin	-	-	-	-	-	-	-	-	-	-	-	-	-	-	-	-
Wyoming[2]	234,260	83,091	125,363	25,728	42,272	R	35.5	53.5	11.0	22	1	13	0.4	0.3	0.6	0.3
District of Columbia[2]	340,953	263,574	28,544	44,925	218,649	D	78.2	8.5	13.3	1	26	11	0.5	0.8	0.1	0.5
UNITED STATES	64,379,457	31,369,720	21,763,378	8,543,274	9,606,342	D	48.7	33.8	13.3				100.0	100.0	100.0	100.0

[1]Limited to the 25 states and the District of Columbia with voter registration by political party affiliation. [2]Total voter registration also includes registrants of minor political parties; see individual state pages for data. [3]Sum of registrants by party from separate report differs slightly from total voter registration reported with November 1992 general election returns.

Table E. — Vote for President: November 3, 1992, General Election

State	All candidates — Total	Clinton (DEM)	Bush (REP)	Perot (IND)	Other	Plurality Total	Party	Pct DEM	Pct REP	Pct IND	Pct Other	Rank DEM	Rank REP	Rank IND	Contrib Total	Contrib DEM	Contrib REP	Contrib IND	Major DEM	Major REP
Alabama	1,688,060	690,080	804,283	183,109	10,588	114,203	R	40.9	47.6	10.8	0.6	29	3	47	1.6	1.5	2.1	0.9	46.2	53.8
Alaska	258,506	78,294	102,000	73,481	4,731	23,706	R	30.3	39.5	28.4	1.8	48	21	2	0.2	0.2	0.3	0.4	43.4	56.6
Arizona	1,486,975	543,050	572,086	353,741	18,098	29,036	R	36.5	38.5	23.8	1.2	43	23	11	1.4	1.2	1.5	1.8	48.7	51.3
Arkansas	950,653	505,823	337,324	99,132	8,374	168,499	D	53.2	35.5	10.4	0.9	2	35	48	0.9	1.1	0.9	0.5	60.0	40.0
California	11,131,721	5,121,325	3,630,574	2,296,006	83,816	1,490,751	D	46.0	32.6	20.6	0.8	12	43	27	10.7	11.4	9.3	11.6	58.5	41.5
Colorado	1,569,180	629,681	562,850	366,010	10,639	66,831	D	40.1	35.9	23.3	0.7	33	32	14	1.5	1.4	1.4	1.9	52.8	47.2
Connecticut	1,616,332	682,318	578,313	348,771	6,930	104,005	D	42.2	35.8	21.6	0.4	27	33	24	1.5	1.5	1.5	1.8	54.1	45.9
Delaware	289,735	126,054	102,313	59,213	2,155	23,741	D	43.5	35.3	20.4	0.7	19	37	28	0.3	0.3	0.3	0.3	55.2	44.8
Florida	5,314,392	2,072,698	2,173,310	1,053,067	15,317	100,612	R	39.0	40.9	19.8	0.3	35	16	29	5.1	4.6	5.6	5.3	48.8	51.2
Georgia	2,321,125	1,008,966	995,252	309,657	7,250	13,714	D	43.5	42.9	13.3	0.3	20	9	44	2.2	2.2	2.5	1.6	50.3	49.7
Hawaii	372,842	179,310	136,822	53,003	3,707	42,488	D	48.1	36.7	14.2	1.0	7	29	39	0.4	0.4	0.3	0.3	56.7	43.3
Idaho	482,142	137,013	202,645	130,395	12,089	65,632	R	28.4	42.0	27.0	2.5	50	13	4	0.5	0.3	0.5	0.7	40.3	59.7
Illinois	5,050,157	2,453,350	1,734,096	840,515	22,196	719,254	D	48.6	34.3	16.6	0.4	5	40	34	4.8	5.5	4.4	4.3	58.6	41.4
Indiana	2,305,871	848,420	989,375	455,934	12,142	140,955	R	36.8	42.9	19.8	0.5	42	10	30	2.2	1.9	2.5	2.3	46.2	53.8
Iowa	1,354,607	586,353	504,891	253,468	9,895	81,462	D	43.3	37.3	18.7	0.7	23	26	32	1.3	1.3	1.3	1.3	53.7	46.3
Kansas	1,157,335	390,434	449,951	312,358	4,592	59,517	R	33.7	38.9	27.0	0.4	46	22	5	1.1	0.9	1.2	1.6	46.5	53.5
Kentucky	1,492,900	665,104	617,178	203,944	6,674	47,926	D	44.6	41.3	13.7	0.4	16	14	41	1.4	1.5	1.6	1.0	51.9	48.1
Louisiana	1,790,017	815,971	733,386	211,478	29,182	82,585	D	45.6	41.0	11.8	1.6	14	15	45	1.7	1.8	1.9	1.1	52.7	47.3
Maine	679,499	263,420	206,504	206,820	2,755	56,600	D	38.8	30.4	30.4	0.4	37	47	1	0.7	0.6	0.5	1.0	56.1	43.9
Maryland	1,985,046	988,571	707,094	281,414	7,967	281,477	D	49.8	35.6	14.2	0.4	3	34	40	1.9	2.2	1.8	1.4	58.3	41.7
Massachusetts	2,773,700	1,318,662	805,049	630,731	19,258	513,613	D	47.5	29.0	22.7	0.7	8	49	19	2.7	2.9	2.1	3.2	62.1	37.9
Michigan	4,274,673	1,871,182	1,554,940	824,813	23,738	316,242	D	43.8	36.4	19.3	0.6	18	30	31	4.1	4.2	4.0	4.2	54.6	45.4
Minnesota	2,347,948	1,020,997	747,841	562,506	16,604	273,156	D	43.5	31.9	24.0	0.7	21	46	10	2.2	2.3	1.9	2.8	57.7	42.3
Mississippi	981,793	400,258	487,793	85,626	8,116	87,535	R	40.8	49.7	8.7	0.8	30	1	50	0.9	0.9	1.2	0.4	45.1	54.9
Missouri	2,391,565	1,053,873	811,159	518,741	7,792	242,714	D	44.1	33.9	21.7	0.3	17	41	23	2.3	2.3	2.1	2.6	56.5	43.5
Montana	410,611	154,507	144,207	107,225	4,672	10,300	D	37.6	35.1	26.1	1.1	38	38	7	0.4	0.3	0.4	0.5	51.7	48.3
Nebraska	737,546	216,864	343,678	174,104	2,900	126,814	R	29.4	46.6	23.6	0.4	49	4	13	0.7	0.5	0.9	0.9	38.7	61.3
Nevada	506,318	189,148	175,828	132,580	8,762	13,320	D	37.4	34.7	26.2	1.7	39	39	6	0.5	0.4	0.4	0.7	51.8	48.2
New Hampshire	537,943	209,040	202,484	121,337	5,082	6,556	D	38.9	37.6	22.6	0.9	36	25	20	0.5	0.5	0.5	0.6	50.8	49.2
New Jersey	3,343,594	1,436,206	1,356,865	521,829	28,694	79,341	D	43.0	40.6	15.6	0.9	24	18	38	3.2	3.2	3.5	2.6	51.4	48.6
New Mexico	569,986	261,617	212,824	91,895	3,650	48,793	D	45.9	37.3	16.1	0.6	13	27	35	0.5	0.6	0.5	0.5	55.1	44.9
New York[1]	6,926,925	3,444,450	2,346,649	1,090,721	45,105	1,097,801	D	49.7	33.9	15.7	0.7	4	42	37	6.6	7.7	6.0	5.5	59.5	40.5
North Carolina	2,611,850	1,114,042	1,134,661	357,864	5,283	20,619	R	42.7	43.4	13.7	0.2	25	7	42	2.5	2.5	2.9	1.8	49.5	50.5
North Dakota	308,133	99,168	136,244	71,084	1,637	37,076	R	32.2	44.2	23.1	0.5	47	6	16	0.3	0.2	0.3	0.4	42.1	57.9
Ohio	4,939,967	1,984,942	1,894,310	1,036,426	24,289	90,632	D	40.2	38.3	21.0	0.5	32	24	26	4.7	4.4	4.8	5.2	51.2	48.8
Oklahoma	1,390,359	473,066	592,929	319,878	4,486	119,863	R	34.0	42.6	23.0	0.3	44	11	17	1.3	1.1	1.5	1.6	44.4	55.6
Oregon	1,462,643	621,314	475,757	354,091	11,481	145,557	D	42.5	32.5	24.2	0.8	26	44	9	1.4	1.4	1.2	1.8	56.6	43.4
Pennsylvania	4,959,810	2,239,164	1,791,841	902,667	26,138	447,323	D	45.1	36.1	18.2	0.5	15	31	33	4.7	5.0	4.6	4.6	55.5	44.5
Rhode Island	453,471	213,299	131,601	105,045	3,526	81,698	D	47.0	29.0	23.2	0.8	10	50	15	0.4	0.5	0.3	0.5	61.8	38.2
South Carolina	1,202,527	479,514	577,507	138,872	6,634	97,993	R	39.9	48.0	11.5	0.6	34	2	46	1.2	1.1	1.5	0.7	45.4	54.6
South Dakota	336,254	124,888	136,718	73,295	1,353	11,830	R	37.1	40.7	21.8	0.4	40	17	22	0.3	0.3	0.3	0.4	47.7	52.3
Tennessee	1,982,638	933,521	841,300	199,968	7,849	92,221	D	47.1	42.4	10.1	0.4	9	12	49	1.9	2.1	2.2	1.0	52.6	47.4
Texas	6,154,018	2,281,815	2,496,071	1,354,781	21,351	214,256	R	37.1	40.6	22.0	0.3	41	19	21	5.9	5.1	6.4	6.9	47.8	52.2
Utah	743,999	183,429	322,632	203,400	34,538	119,232	R	24.7	43.4	27.3	4.6	51	8	3	0.7	0.4	0.8	1.0	36.2	63.8
Vermont	289,701	133,592	88,122	65,991	1,996	45,470	D	46.1	30.4	22.8	0.7	11	48	18	0.3	0.3	0.2	0.3	60.3	39.7
Virginia	2,558,665	1,038,650	1,150,517	348,639	20,859	111,867	R	40.6	45.0	13.6	0.8	31	5	43	2.5	2.3	2.9	1.8	47.4	52.6
Washington	2,288,230	993,037	731,234	541,780	22,179	261,803	D	43.4	32.0	23.7	1.0	22	45	12	2.2	2.2	1.9	2.7	57.6	42.4
West Virginia	683,762	331,001	241,974	108,829	1,958	89,027	D	48.4	35.4	15.9	0.3	6	36	36	0.7	0.7	0.6	0.6	57.8	42.2
Wisconsin	2,531,114	1,041,066	930,855	544,479	14,714	110,211	D	41.1	36.8	21.5	0.6	28	28	25	2.4	2.3	2.4	2.8	52.8	47.2
Wyoming	200,617	68,160	79,347	51,263	1,847	11,187	R	34.0	39.6	25.6	0.9	45	20	8	0.2	0.2	0.2	0.3	46.2	53.8
District of Columbia	227,572	192,619	20,698	9,681	4,574	171,921	D	84.6	9.1	4.3	2.0	1	51	51	0.2	0.4	<.1	<.1	90.3	9.7
UNITED STATES	104,425,027	44,909,326	39,103,882	19,741,657	670,162	5,805,444	D	43.0	37.4	18.9	0.6				100.0	100.0	100.0	100.0	53.5	46.5

[1]Democratic vote also includes ballots cast for Clinton-Gore as nominees of the Liberal party; Republican vote also includes ballots for Bush-Quayle as nominees of Conservative and Right to Life parties.

Table F. — Vote for U.S. Senator: November 3, 1992, General Election

State	Total	Democrat (DEM)	Republican (REP)	Other	Plurality Total	Plurality Party	DEM	REP	Other	Rank DEM	Rank REP	Rank Other	Total	DEM	REP	Other
Alabama	1,577,799	1,022,698	522,015	33,086	500,683	D	64.8	33.1	2.1	4	30	23	2.2	2.9	1.6	1.1
Alaska	239,714	92,065	127,163	20,486	35,098	R	38.4	53.0	8.5	29	8	5	0.3	0.3	0.4	0.7
Arizona	1,382,051	436,321	771,395	174,335	335,074	R	31.6	55.8	12.6	31	6	2	1.9	1.2	2.4	5.8
Arkansas	920,008	553,635	366,373	-	187,262	D	60.2	39.8	-	6	25	-	1.3	1.6	1.1	-
California²	10,799,703	5,173,467	4,644,182	982,054	529,285	D	47.9	43.0	9.1	19	21	3	15.2	14.5	14.4	32.7
Colorado	1,552,289	803,725	662,893	85,671	140,832	D	51.8	42.7	5.5	14	22	9	2.2	2.3	2.1	2.9
Connecticut³	1,500,709	882,569	572,036	46,104	310,533	D	58.8	38.1	3.1	8	27	18	2.1	2.5	1.8	1.5
Delaware	-	-	-	-	-	-	-	-	-	-	-	-	-	-	-	-
Florida	4,962,290	3,245,565	1,716,505	220	1,529,060	D	65.4	34.6	<.1	2	29	29	7.0	9.1	5.3	<.1
Georgia⁴	2,251,587	1,108,416	1,073,282	69,889	35,134	D	49.2	47.7	3.1	18	15	19	3.2	3.1	3.3	2.3
Hawaii	363,662	208,266	97,928	57,468	110,338	D	57.3	26.9	15.8	9	33	1	0.5	0.6	0.3	1.9
Idaho⁵	478,504	208,036	270,468	-	62,432	R	43.5	56.5	-	26	5	-	0.7	0.6	0.8	-
Illinois	4,939,558	2,631,229	2,126,833	181,496	504,396	D	53.3	43.1	3.7	12	20	12	7.0	7.4	6.6	6.1
Indiana	2,211,423	900,148	1,267,972	43,303	367,824	R	40.7	57.3	2.0	27	4	25	3.1	2.5	3.9	1.4
Iowa	1,292,494	351,561	899,761	41,172	548,200	R	27.2	69.6	3.2	33	1	15	1.8	1.0	2.8	1.4
Kansas	1,126,447	349,525	706,246	70,676	356,721	R	31.0	62.7	6.3	32	2	8	1.6	1.0	2.2	2.4
Kentucky	1,330,858	836,888	476,604	17,366	360,284	D	62.9	35.8	1.3	5	28	28	1.9	2.3	1.5	0.6
Louisiana	-	-	-	-	-	-	-	-	-	-	-	-	-	-	-	-
Maine	-	-	-	-	-	-	-	-	-	-	-	-	-	-	-	-
Maryland	1,841,735	1,307,610	533,688	437	773,922	D	71.0	29.0	<.1	1	32	30	2.6	3.7	1.7	<.1
Massachusetts	-	-	-	-	-	-	-	-	-	-	-	-	-	-	-	-
Michigan	-	-	-	-	-	-	-	-	-	-	-	-	-	-	-	-
Minnesota	-	-	-	-	-	-	-	-	-	-	-	-	-	-	-	-
Mississippi	-	-	-	-	-	-	-	-	-	-	-	-	-	-	-	-
Missouri	2,354,925	1,057,967	1,221,901	75,057	163,934	R	44.9	51.9	3.2	25	10	16	3.3	3.0	3.8	2.5
Montana	-	-	-	-	-	-	-	-	-	-	-	-	-	-	-	-
Nebraska	-	-	-	-	-	-	-	-	-	-	-	-	-	-	-	-
Nevada	495,887	253,150	199,413	43,324	53,737	D	51.0	40.2	8.7	15	24	4	0.7	0.7	0.6	1.4
New Hampshire	518,416	234,982	249,591	33,843	14,609	R	45.3	48.1	6.5	24	14	7	0.7	0.7	0.8	1.1
New Jersey	-	-	-	-	-	-	-	-	-	-	-	-	-	-	-	-
New Mexico	-	-	-	-	-	-	-	-	-	-	-	-	-	-	-	-
New York³	6,458,826	3,086,200	3,166,994	205,632	80,794	R	47.8	49.0	3.2	20	13	17	9.1	8.7	9.8	6.9
North Carolina	2,577,891	1,194,015	1,297,892	85,984	103,877	R	46.3	50.3	3.3	22	11	13	3.6	3.3	4.0	2.9
North Dakota	303,957	179,347	118,162	6,448	61,185	D	59.0	38.9	2.1	7	26	24	0.4	0.5	0.4	0.2
Ohio	4,793,953	2,444,419	2,028,300	321,234	416,119	D	51.0	42.3	6.7	16	23	6	6.8	6.9	6.3	10.7
Oklahoma	1,294,423	494,350	757,876	42,197	263,526	R	38.2	58.5	3.3	30	3	14	1.8	1.4	2.3	1.4
Oregon	1,376,033	639,851	717,455	18,727	77,604	R	46.5	52.1	1.4	21	9	26	1.9	1.8	2.2	0.6
Pennsylvania	4,802,410	2,224,966	2,358,125	219,319	133,159	R	46.3	49.1	4.6	23	12	11	6.8	6.2	7.3	7.3
Rhode Island	-	-	-	-	-	-	-	-	-	-	-	-	-	-	-	-
South Carolina	1,180,438	591,030	554,175	35,233	36,855	D	50.1	46.9	3.0	17	16	20	1.7	1.7	1.7	1.2
South Dakota	334,495	217,095	108,733	8,667	108,362	D	64.9	32.5	2.6	3	31	21	0.5	0.6	0.3	0.3
Tennessee	-	-	-	-	-	-	-	-	-	-	-	-	-	-	-	-
Texas	-	-	-	-	-	-	-	-	-	-	-	-	-	-	-	-
Utah	758,479	301,228	420,069	37,182	118,841	R	39.7	55.4	4.9	28	7	10	1.1	0.8	1.3	1.2
Vermont	285,739	154,762	123,854	7,123	30,908	D	54.2	43.3	2.5	10	19	22	0.4	0.4	0.4	0.2
Virginia	-	-	-	-	-	-	-	-	-	-	-	-	-	-	-	-
Washington	2,219,162	1,197,973	1,020,829	360	177,144	D	54.0	46.0	<.1	11	17	31	3.1	3.4	3.2	<.1
West Virginia	-	-	-	-	-	-	-	-	-	-	-	-	-	-	-	-
Wisconsin	2,455,124	1,290,662	1,129,599	34,863	161,063	D	52.6	46.0	1.4	13	18	27	3.5	3.6	3.5	1.2
Wyoming	-	-	-	-	-	-	-	-	-	-	-	-	-	-	-	-
District of Columbia	-	-	-	-	-	-	-	-	-	-	-	-	-	-	-	-
UNITED STATES	70,980,989	35,673,721	32,308,312	2,998,956	3,365,409	D	50.3	45.5	4.2				100.0	100.0	100.0	100.0
California⁶	10,782,690	5,853,621	4,093,488	835,581	1,760,133	D	54.3	38.0	7.7							
Georgia⁴	1,253,991	618,877	635,114	-	16,237	R	49.4	50.6	-							
Louisiana⁷	843,037	661,860	106,392	74,785	555,468	D	78.5	12.6	8.9							
North Dakota⁸	163,311	103,246	55,194	4,871	48,052	D	63.2	33.8	3.0							
Pennsylvania⁹	3,382,746	1,860,760	1,521,986	-	338,774	D	55.0	45.0	-							

[1]Limited to the 33 states with regularly scheduled senate contests in 1992, but not including Louisiana where the senator was elected from the primary. [2]Six-year term. [3]Democratic vote and Republican vote also include ballots cast for candidates as nominees of minor political parties. [4]Senator elected from November 24, 1992, runoff election because no candidate received a majority of votes in the November 3, 1992, general election. [5]Does not include 18 write-in votes for independent candidate. [6]For remaining two years of term vacated by Pete Wilson (R), who was elected governor of California in 1990. [7]Senator elected from October 3, 1992, primary election received more than 50 percent of vote. Democratic vote includes 616,021 votes for winning candidate John Breaux. [8]December 4, 1992, special election for remaining two years of term of the late Senator Quentin Burdick (D). [9]November 5, 1991, special election for remaining three years of term of the late Senator John Heinz (R).

Table G. — Vote for Governor: November 3, 1992, General Election

State	Total	Democrat (DEM)	Republican (REP)	Other	Plurality Total	Plurality Party	Percent of total vote DEM	REP	Other	Rank[1] DEM	REP	Other	Percent contribution to national vote[2] Total	DEM	REP	Other
Alabama	-	-	-	-	-	-	-	-	-	-	-	-	-	-	-	-
Alaska	-	-	-	-	-	-	-	-	-	-	-	-	-	-	-	-
Arizona	-	-	-	-	-	-	-	-	-	-	-	-	-	-	-	-
Arkansas	-	-	-	-	-	-	-	-	-	-	-	-	-	-	-	-
California	-	-	-	-	-	-	-	-	-	-	-	-	-	-	-	-
Colorado	-	-	-	-	-	-	-	-	-	-	-	-	-	-	-	-
Connecticut	-	-	-	-	-	-	-	-	-	-	-	-	-	-	-	-
Delaware	277,034	179,365	90,725	6,944	88,640	D	64.7	32.7	2.5	2	11	6	2.1	2.5	1.6	1.4
Florida	-	-	-	-	-	-	-	-	-	-	-	-	-	-	-	-
Georgia	-	-	-	-	-	-	-	-	-	-	-	-	-	-	-	-
Hawaii	-	-	-	-	-	-	-	-	-	-	-	-	-	-	-	-
Idaho	-	-	-	-	-	-	-	-	-	-	-	-	-	-	-	-
Illinois	-	-	-	-	-	-	-	-	-	-	-	-	-	-	-	-
Indiana	2,229,116	1,382,151	822,533	24,432	559,618	D	62.0	36.9	1.1	3	8	9	17.0	19.6	14.9	4.9
Iowa	-	-	-	-	-	-	-	-	-	-	-	-	-	-	-
Kansas	-	-	-	-	-	-	-	-	-	-	-	-	-	-	-	-
Kentucky	-	-	-	-	-	-	-	-	-	-	-	-	-	-	-	-
Louisiana	-	-	-	-	-	-	-	-	-	-	-	-	-	-	-	-
Maine	-	-	-	-	-	-	-	-	-	-	-	-	-	-	-	-
Maryland	-	-	-	-	-	-	-	-	-	-	-	-	-	-	-	-
Massachusetts	-	-	-	-	-	-	-	-	-	-	-	-	-	-	-	-
Michigan	-	-	-	-	-	-	-	-	-	-	-	-	-	-	-	-
Minnesota	-	-	-	-	-	-	-	-	-	-	-	-	-	-	-	-
Mississippi	-	-	-	-	-	-	-	-	-	-	-	-	-	-	-	-
Missouri	2,344,121	1,375,425	968,574	122	406,851	D	58.7	41.3	<.1	5	7	10	17.9	19.5	17.5	<.1
Montana	407,822	198,421	209,401	-	10,980	R	48.7	51.3	-	9	3	-	3.1	2.8	3.8	-
Nebraska	-	-	-	-	-	-	-	-	-	-	-	-	-	-	-
Nevada	-	-	-	-	-	-	-	-	-	-	-	-	-	-	-
New Hampshire	516,170	206,232	289,170	20,768	82,938	R	40.0	56.0	4.0	11	2	4	3.9	2.9	5.2	4.2
New Jersey	-	-	-	-	-	-	-	-	-	-	-	-	-	-	-
New Mexico	-	-	-	-	-	-	-	-	-	-	-	-	-	-	-
New York	-	-	-	-	-	-	-	-	-	-	-	-	-	-	-
North Carolina	2,595,184	1,368,246	1,121,955	104,983	246,291	D	52.7	43.2	4.0	7	5	5	19.8	19.4	20.3	21.1
North Dakota	304,861	123,845	176,398	4,618	52,553	R	40.6	57.9	1.5	10	1	8	2.3	1.8	3.2	0.9
Ohio	-	-	-	-	-	-	-	-	-	-	-	-	-	-	-
Oklahoma	-	-	-	-	-	-	-	-	-	-	-	-	-	-	-
Oregon	-	-	-	-	-	-	-	-	-	-	-	-	-	-	-
Pennsylvania	-	-	-	-	-	-	-	-	-	-	-	-	-	-	-
Rhode Island	424,818	261,484	145,590	17,744	115,894	D	61.6	34.3	4.2	4	10	3	3.2	3.7	2.6	3.6
South Carolina	-	-	-	-	-	-	-	-	-	-	-	-	-	-	-
South Dakota	-	-	-	-	-	-	-	-	-	-	-	-	-	-	-
Tennessee	-	-	-	-	-	-	-	-	-	-	-	-	-	-	-
Texas	-	-	-	-	-	-	-	-	-	-	-	-	-	-	-
Utah	762,536	177,181	321,713	263,642	58,071	R	23.2	42.2	34.6	12	6	1	5.8	2.5	5.8	52.9
Vermont	285,728	213,523	65,837	6,368	147,686	D	74.7	23.0	2.2	1	12	7	2.2	3.0	1.2	1.3
Virginia	-	-	-	-	-	-	-	-	-	-	-	-	-	-	-
Washington	2,270,826	1,184,315	1,086,216	295	98,099	D	52.2	47.8	<.1	8	4	11	17.4	16.8	19.6	<.1
West Virginia	657,193	368,302	240,390	48,501	127,912	D	56.0	36.6	7.4	6	9	2	5.0	5.2	4.3	9.7
Wisconsin	-	-	-	-	-	-	-	-	-	-	-	-	-	-	-
Wyoming	-	-	-	-	-	-	-	-	-	-	-	-	-	-	-
District of Columbia	-	-	-	-	-	-	-	-	-	-	-	-	-	-	-
UNITED STATES	13,075,409	7,038,490	5,538,502	498,417	1,499,988	D	53.8	42.4	3.8				100.0	100.0	100.0	100.0
Kentucky (Off-year)[2]	834,920	540,468	294,452	-	246,010	D	64.7	35.3	-							
Louisiana (Off-year)[3]	1,728,040	1,057,031	671,009	-	386,022	D	61.2	38.8	-							
Mississippi (Off-year)[4]	711,212	338,459	361,500	11,253	23,041	R	47.6	50.8	1.6							

[1]Limited to the 12 states with regularly scheduled gubernatorial contests in 1992. [2]November 5, 1991, general election. [3]November 16, 1991, general election. [4]November 5, 1991, general election.

Table H. — Vote for U.S. Representative in Congress: November 3, 1992, General Election

State	Total	Democrat (DEM)	Republican (REP)	Other	Plurality Total	Plurality Party	DEM	REP	Other	Rank DEM	Rank REP	Rank Other	Total	DEM	REP	Other
Alabama	1,602,536	895,601	643,150	63,785	252,451	D	55.9	40.1	4.0	11	41	18	1.7	1.8	1.5	1.9
Alaska	239,116	102,378	111,849	24,889	9,471	R	42.8	46.8	10.4	44	25	2	0.2	0.2	0.3	0.7
Arizona	1,408,921	582,317	740,047	86,557	157,730	R	41.3	52.5	6.1	47	7	8	1.5	1.2	1.7	2.5
Arkansas	888,521	525,197	356,900	6,424	168,297	D	59.1	40.2	0.7	8	40	43	0.9	1.1	0.8	0.2
California	10,535,065	5,446,966	4,365,155	722,944	1,081,811	D	51.7	41.4	6.9	22	37	5	10.9	11.1	10.0	21.0
Colorado	1,479,209	691,479	757,666	30,064	66,187	R	46.7	51.2	2.0	37	9	34	1.5	1.4	1.7	0.9
Connecticut[1]	1,435,163	644,424	699,155	91,584	54,731	R	44.9	48.7	6.4	42	17	7	1.5	1.3	1.6	2.7
Delaware	276,124	117,426	153,037	5,661	35,611	R	42.5	55.4	2.1	45	5	33	0.3	0.2	0.3	0.2
Florida[2]	4,914,833	2,256,681	2,510,725	147,427	254,044	R	45.9	51.1	3.0	38	10	26	5.1	4.6	5.7	4.3
Georgia	2,213,987	1,214,792	999,182	13	215,610	D	54.9	45.1	<.1	14	29	47	2.3	2.5	2.3	<.1
Hawaii	358,431	260,786	81,645	16,000	179,141	D	72.8	22.8	4.5	3	49	14	0.4	0.5	0.2	0.5
Idaho	472,747	222,435	230,766	19,546	8,331	R	47.1	48.8	4.1	35	16	17	0.5	0.5	0.5	0.6
Illinois	4,830,941	2,677,685	2,096,717	56,539	580,968	D	55.4	43.4	1.2	13	34	39	5.0	5.5	4.8	1.6
Indiana	2,214,836	1,203,105	996,958	14,773	206,147	D	54.3	45.0	0.7	15	30	44	2.3	2.5	2.3	0.4
Iowa	1,242,436	492,843	729,496	20,097	236,653	R	39.7	58.7	1.6	49	2	37	1.3	1.0	1.7	0.6
Kansas	1,124,915	488,386	591,712	44,817	103,326	R	43.4	52.6	4.0	43	6	19	1.2	1.0	1.4	1.3
Kentucky	1,360,911	721,747	638,166	998	83,581	D	53.0	46.9	<.1	18	24	48	1.4	1.5	1.5	<.1
Louisiana[3]	683,589	284,910	398,679	-	113,769	R	41.7	58.3	-	46	3	-	0.7	0.6	0.9	0.0
Maine	669,581	363,520	278,258	27,803	85,262	D	54.3	41.6	4.2	16	36	16	0.7	0.7	0.6	0.8
Maryland	1,807,507	955,952	842,789	8,766	113,163	D	52.9	46.6	0.5	19	27	46	1.9	2.0	1.9	0.3
Massachusetts[4]	2,614,249	1,518,218	856,576	239,455	661,642	D	58.1	32.8	9.2	9	45	3	2.7	3.1	2.0	7.0
Michigan	3,884,403	1,913,175	1,855,241	115,987	57,934	D	49.3	47.8	3.0	29	19	27	4.0	3.9	4.2	3.4
Minnesota[5]	2,275,192	1,178,072	930,814	166,306	247,258	D	51.8	40.9	7.3	21	39	4	2.4	2.4	2.1	4.8
Mississippi	965,401	669,582	273,234	22,585	396,348	D	69.4	28.3	2.3	4	47	31	1.0	1.4	0.6	0.7
Missouri	2,348,560	1,269,486	1,036,268	42,806	233,218	D	54.1	44.1	1.8	17	32	36	2.4	2.6	2.4	1.2
Montana	403,735	203,711	189,570	10,454	14,141	D	50.5	47.0	2.6	26	23	29	0.4	0.4	0.4	0.3
Nebraska	710,835	283,278	427,398	159	144,120	R	39.9	60.1	<.1	48	1	49	0.7	0.6	1.0	<.1
Nevada	491,949	245,477	213,792	32,680	31,685	D	49.9	43.5	6.6	27	33	6	0.5	0.5	0.5	0.9
New Hampshire	511,038	265,906	227,062	18,070	38,844	D	52.0	44.4	3.5	20	31	22	0.5	0.5	0.5	0.5
New Jersey	2,991,739	1,354,915	1,503,145	133,679	148,230	R	45.3	50.2	4.5	41	13	15	3.1	2.8	3.4	3.9
New Mexico	555,601	272,607	277,833	5,161	5,226	R	49.1	50.0	0.9	30	14	41	0.6	0.6	0.6	0.1
New York[1]	5,924,853	3,050,738	2,686,620	187,495	364,118	D	51.5	45.3	3.2	23	28	24	6.2	6.2	6.1	5.4
North Carolina	2,527,019	1,282,474	1,203,949	40,596	78,525	D	50.8	47.6	1.6	25	21	38	2.6	2.6	2.7	1.2
North Dakota	297,898	169,273	117,442	11,183	51,831	D	56.8	39.4	3.8	10	44	21	0.3	0.3	0.3	0.3
Ohio	4,576,934	2,198,039	2,154,080	224,815	43,959	D	48.0	47.1	4.9	34	22	12	4.8	4.5	4.9	6.5
Oklahoma	1,275,696	764,249	504,133	7,314	260,116	D	59.9	39.5	0.6	6	43	45	1.3	1.6	1.2	0.2
Oregon	1,390,754	824,796	553,101	12,857	271,695	D	59.3	39.8	0.9	7	42	42	1.4	1.7	1.3	0.4
Pennsylvania	4,590,519	2,154,372	2,347,441	88,706	193,069	R	46.9	51.1	1.9	36	11	35	4.8	4.4	5.4	2.6
Rhode Island	398,502	192,542	185,980	19,980	6,562	D	48.3	46.7	5.0	32	26	11	0.4	0.4	0.4	0.6
South Carolina	1,115,450	505,887	581,159	28,404	75,272	R	45.4	52.1	2.5	40	8	30	1.2	1.0	1.3	0.8
South Dakota	332,902	230,070	89,375	13,457	140,695	D	69.1	26.8	4.0	5	48	20	0.3	0.5	0.2	0.4
Tennessee	1,725,674	882,973	737,690	105,011	145,283	D	51.2	42.7	6.1	24	35	9	1.8	1.8	1.7	3.1
Texas	5,622,472	2,806,044	2,685,973	130,455	120,071	D	49.9	47.8	2.3	28	20	32	5.8	5.7	6.1	3.8
Utah	727,284	331,479	362,363	33,442	30,884	R	45.6	49.8	4.6	39	15	13	0.8	0.7	0.8	1.0
Vermont[6]	281,626	22,279	86,901	172,446	85,545	I	7.9	30.9	61.2	51	46	1	0.3	<.1	0.2	5.0
Virginia	2,368,047	1,148,570	1,142,649	76,828	5,921	D	48.5	48.3	3.2	31	18	25	2.5	2.3	2.6	2.2
Washington	2,223,158	1,236,665	911,913	74,580	324,752	D	55.6	41.0	3.4	12	38	23	2.3	2.5	2.1	2.2
West Virginia	562,305	439,191	123,114	-	316,077	D	78.1	21.9	-	2	50	-	0.6	0.9	0.3	0.0
Wisconsin	2,387,930	1,153,862	1,210,827	23,241	56,965	R	48.3	50.7	1.0	33	12	40	2.5	2.4	2.8	0.7
Wyoming	196,977	77,418	113,882	5,677	36,464	R	39.3	57.8	2.9	50	4	28	0.2	0.2	0.3	0.2
District of Columbia	196,754	166,808	20,108	9,838	146,700	D	84.8	10.2	5.0	1	51	10	0.2	0.3	<.1	0.3
UNITED STATES	**96,234,825**	**48,960,786**	**43,831,685**	**3,442,354**	**5,129,101**	**D**	**50.9**	**45.5**	**3.6**				**100.0**	**100.0**	**100.0**	**100.0**

[1]Democratic vote and Republican vote also include ballots cast for candidates as nominees of minor political parties. [2]Does not include congressional district No. 21, where representative was elected from Republican primary (no Democratic primary). [3]Includes votes from congressional districts No. 4, 5 and 6 only; representatives in districts No. 1, 2, 3 and 7 were elected by receiving vote majorities in open primary elections. [4]Does not include corrected vote for independent candidates in congressional district No. 2, which would reduce the vote for other candidates and the state total vote to 239,443 and 2,614,237, respectively. [5]Does not include corrected vote for independent candidate in congressional district No. 2, which would reduce the vote for other candidates and the state total vote to 166,206 and 2,275,092, respectively. [6]Other vote includes 162,724 votes for an independent candidate (Bernie Sanders) who was elected.

Table I. — Vote for Presidential Preference: Democratic Primary Election 1992

State	Total	Clinton	Brown	Tsongas	Uncommitted	Kerrey	Harkin	LaRouche	Others	Clinton	Brown	Tsongas	Rank[1] Clinton	Rank[1] Brown	Rank[1] Tsongas	Total	Clinton	Brown	Tsongas
Alabama	450,899	307,621	30,626	-	90,863	-	-	6,542	15,247	68.2	6.8	-	6	35	-	2.2	2.9	0.8	-
Alaska	-	-	-	-	-	-	-	-	-	-	-	-	-	-	-	-	-	-	-
Arizona	-	-	-	-	-	-	-	-	-	-	-	-	-	-	-	-	-	-	-
Arkansas	502,617	342,017	55,234	-	90,710	-	-	14,656	-	68.0	11.0	-	7	25	-	2.5	3.3	1.4	-
California	2,863,419	1,359,112	1,150,460	212,522	-	33,935	-	21,971	85,419	47.5	40.2	7.4	24	1	30	14.1	13.0	28.3	5.8
Colorado	239,643	64,470	69,073	61,360	-	29,572	5,866	328	8,974	26.9	28.8	25.6	34	6	8	1.2	0.6	1.7	1.7
Connecticut	173,119	61,698	64,472	33,811	5,430	1,169	1,919	896	3,724	35.6	37.2	19.5	31	2	12	0.9	0.6	1.6	0.9
Delaware	-	-	-	-	-	-	-	-	-	-	-	-	-	-	-	-	-	-	-
Florida	1,123,857	570,566	139,569	388,124	-	12,011	13,587	-	-	50.8	12.4	34.5	21	23	4	5.6	5.4	3.4	10.6
Georgia	454,631	259,907	36,808	109,148	17,256	22,033	9,479	-	-	57.2	8.1	24.0	15	31	9	2.2	2.5	0.9	3.0
Hawaii	-	-	-	-	-	-	-	-	-	-	-	-	-	-	-	-	-	-	-
Idaho	55,124	27,004	9,212	-	-	-	-	-	2,011	16,897	49.0	16.7	-	23	19	-	0.3	0.3	0.2	-
Illinois	1,504,130	776,829	220,346	387,891	67,612	10,916	30,710	6,599	3,227	51.6	14.6	25.8	19	20	7	7.4	7.4	5.4	10.6
Indiana	476,850	301,905	102,377	58,215	-	14,353	-	-	-	63.3	21.5	12.2	12	11	20	2.4	2.9	2.5	1.6
Iowa	-	-	-	-	-	-	-	-	-	-	-	-	-	-	-	-	-	-	-
Kansas	160,251	82,145	20,811	24,413	-	2,215	940	631	29,096	51.3	13.0	15.2	20	22	17	0.8	0.8	0.5	0.7
Kentucky	370,578	207,804	30,709	18,097	103,590	3,242	7,136	-	-	56.1	8.3	4.9	17	28	34	1.8	2.0	0.8	0.5
Louisiana	384,397	267,002	25,480	42,508	-	2,984	4,033	3,082	39,308	69.5	6.6	11.1	5	36	22	1.9	2.5	0.6	1.2
Maine	-	-	-	-	-	-	-	-	-	-	-	-	-	-	-	-	-	-	-
Maryland	567,224	189,906	46,480	230,490	36,155	27,035	32,899	4,259	-	33.5	8.2	40.6	32	29	3	2.8	1.8	1.1	6.3
Massachusetts[2]	792,885	86,817	115,746	526,297	-	5,409	3,764	2,167	52,685	10.9	14.6	66.4	39	21	1	3.9	0.8	2.8	14.4
Michigan	585,972	297,280	151,400	97,017	27,836	3,219	6,265	2,049	906	50.7	25.8	16.6	22	8	16	2.9	2.8	3.7	2.7
Minnesota	204,170	63,584	62,474	43,588	11,366	1,191	4,077	532	17,358	31.1	30.6	21.3	33	5	11	1.0	0.6	1.5	1.2
Mississippi	191,357	139,893	18,396	15,538	11,796	1,660	2,509	1,394	171	73.1	9.6	8.1	3	27	29	0.9	1.3	0.5	0.4
Missouri	-	-	-	-	-	-	-	-	-	-	-	-	-	-	-	-	-	-	-
Montana	117,471	54,989	21,704	12,614	-	-	-	-	28,164	46.8	18.5	10.7	25	16	23	0.6	0.5	0.5	0.3
Nebraska	150,587	68,562	31,673	10,707	24,714	-	4,239	1,148	9,544	45.5	21.0	7.1	26	12	31	0.7	0.7	0.8	0.3
Nevada	-	-	-	-	-	-	-	-	-	-	-	-	-	-	-	-	-	-	-
New Hampshire	167,800	41,522	13,654	55,638	-	18,575	17,057	-	21,354	24.7	8.1	33.2	35	30	5	0.8	0.4	0.3	1.5
New Jersey	392,744	256,337	79,877	45,191	-	-	-	7,799	3,540	65.3	20.3	11.5	10	13	21	1.9	2.4	2.0	1.2
New Mexico	181,537	95,933	30,705	11,409	35,269	-	3,233	2,415	2,573	52.8	16.9	6.3	18	17	33	0.9	0.9	0.8	0.3
New York	1,007,726	412,349	264,278	288,330	-	11,147	11,535	-	20,087	40.9	26.2	28.6	29	7	6	5.0	3.9	6.5	7.9
North Carolina	691,875	443,498	71,984	57,589	-	6,216	5,891	-	106,697	64.1	10.4	8.3	11	26	28	3.4	4.2	1.8	1.6
North Dakota	32,786	4,760	-	-	-	-	-	7,003	21,023	14.5	-	-	38	-	-	0.2	<.1	-	-
Ohio	1,042,335	638,347	197,449	110,773	-	22,976	25,395	17,412	29,983	61.2	18.9	10.6	14	14	24	5.2	6.1	4.8	3.0
Oklahoma	416,129	293,266	69,624	-	-	13,252	14,015	6,474	19,498	70.5	16.7	-	4	18	-	2.1	2.8	1.7	-
Oregon	354,332	159,802	110,494	37,139	-	-	-	3,096	43,801	45.1	31.2	10.5	27	4	25	1.8	1.5	2.7	1.0
Pennsylvania	1,265,495	715,031	325,543	161,572	-	20,802	21,013	21,534	-	56.5	25.7	12.8	16	9	19	6.3	6.8	8.0	4.4
Rhode Island	50,709	10,762	9,541	26,825	703	469	319	300	1,790	21.2	18.8	52.9	36	15	2	0.3	0.1	0.2	0.7
South Carolina	116,414	73,221	6,961	21,338	3,640	566	7,657	204	2,827	62.9	6.0	18.3	13	37	15	0.6	0.7	0.2	0.6
South Dakota	59,503	11,375	2,300	5,729	-	23,892	15,023	441	743	19.1	3.9	9.6	37	38	27	0.3	0.1	<.1	0.2
Tennessee	318,482	214,485	25,560	61,717	12,551	1,638	2,099	-	432	67.3	8.0	19.4	8	32	13	1.6	2.0	0.6	1.7
Texas	1,482,975	972,151	118,923	285,191	-	20,298	19,617	12,220	54,575	65.6	8.0	19.2	9	33	14	7.3	9.3	2.9	7.8
Utah	-	-	-	-	-	-	-	-	-	-	-	-	-	-	-	-	-	-	-
Vermont	-	-	-	-	-	-	-	-	-	-	-	-	-	-	-	-	-	-	-
Virginia	-	-	-	-	-	-	-	-	-	-	-	-	-	-	-	-	-	-	-
Washington	147,981	62,171	34,111	18,981	-	1,489	1,858	1,060	28,311	42.0	23.1	12.8	28	10	18	0.7	0.6	0.8	0.5
West Virginia	306,866	227,815	36,505	21,271	-	3,152	2,774	3,141	12,208	74.2	11.9	6.9	1	24	32	1.5	2.2	0.9	0.6
Wisconsin	772,596	287,356	266,207	168,619	15,487	3,044	5,395	3,120	23,368	37.2	34.5	21.8	30	3	10	3.8	2.7	6.5	4.6
Wyoming	-	-	-	-	-	-	-	-	-	-	-	-	-	-	-	-	-	-	-
District of Columbia	61,904	45,716	4,444	6,452	5,292	-	-	-	-	73.8	7.2	10.4	2	34	26	0.3	0.4	0.1	0.2
UNITED STATES	20,239,370	10,495,008	4,071,210	3,656,104	560,270	318,460	280,304	154,484	703,530	51.9	20.1	18.1				100.0	100.0	100.0	100.0

[1]Limited to the 38 states and the District of Columbia that held Democratic presidential primaries. [2]Does not include corrected vote for the Massachusetts categories "no preference" and "all others", which would increase the vote for other candidates to 53,915 and the state total vote to 794,115.

Table J. — Vote for Presidential Preference: Republican Primary Election 1992

State	Top candidates — Total	Bush	Buchanan	Uncommitted	Others	Percent of total vote — Bush	Buchanan	Uncommitted	Other	Rank[1] — Bush	Buchanan	Uncommitted	Other	Pct contribution to national vote — Total	Bush	Buchanan	Uncommitted	Other
Alabama	165,121	122,703	12,588	29,830	-	74.3	7.6	18.1	-	13	35	4	-	1.3	1.3	0.4	17.1	-
Alaska	-	-	-	-	-	-	-	-	-	-	-	-	-	-	-	-	-	-
Arizona	-	-	-	-	-	-	-	-	-	-	-	-	-	-	-	-	-	-
Arkansas	54,883	45,590	6,551	2,742	-	83.1	11.9	5.0	-	3	31	7	-	0.4	0.5	0.2	1.6	-
California	2,156,261	1,587,369	568,892	-	4,837	73.6	26.4	-	2.5	14	10	-	21	17.0	17.3	19.6	-	1.2
Colorado	195,690	132,100	58,753	-	4,837	67.5	30.0	-	2.5	24	5	-	21	1.5	1.4	2.0	-	1.2
Connecticut	99,473	66,356	21,815	9,008	2,294	66.7	21.9	9.1	2.3	29	18	5	23	0.8	0.7	0.8	5.2	0.6
Delaware	-	-	-	-	-	-	-	-	-	-	-	-	-	-	-	-	-	-
Florida	893,463	608,077	285,386	-	-	68.1	31.9	-	-	23	3	-	-	7.0	6.6	9.8	-	-
Georgia	453,990	291,905	162,085	-	-	64.3	35.7	-	-	31	2	-	-	3.6	3.2	5.6	-	-
Hawaii	-	-	-	-	-	-	-	-	-	-	-	-	-	-	-	-	-	-
Idaho	115,502	73,297	15,167	-	27,038	63.5	13.1	-	23.4	34	30	-	1	0.9	0.8	0.5	-	6.7
Illinois	831,140	634,588	186,915	-	9,637	76.4	22.5	-	1.2	10	16	-	24	6.6	6.9	6.4	-	2.4
Indiana	467,615	374,666	92,949	-	-	80.1	19.9	-	-	8	19	-	-	3.7	4.1	3.2	-	-
Iowa	-	-	-	-	-	-	-	-	-	-	-	-	-	-	-	-	-	-
Kansas	213,196	132,131	31,494	-	49,571	62.0	14.8	-	23.3	37	27	-	2	1.7	1.4	1.1	-	12.3
Kentucky	101,119	75,371	-	25,748	-	74.5	-	25.5	-	12	-	3	-	0.8	0.8	-	14.7	-
Louisiana	135,109	83,744	36,525	-	14,840	62.0	27.0	-	11.0	36	8	-	8	1.1	0.9	1.3	-	3.7
Maine	-	-	-	-	-	-	-	-	-	-	-	-	-	-	-	-	-	-
Maryland	240,021	168,374	71,647	-	-	70.1	29.9	-	-	19	6	-	-	1.9	1.8	2.5	-	-
Massachusetts[2]	269,701	176,868	74,797	-	18,036	65.6	27.7	-	6.7	30	7	-	13	2.1	1.9	2.6	-	4.5
Michigan	449,133	301,948	112,122	23,809	11,254	67.2	25.0	5.3	2.5	25	12	6	20	3.5	3.3	3.9	13.6	2.8
Minnesota	132,756	84,841	32,094	4,098	11,723	63.9	24.2	3.1	8.8	32	13	9	11	1.0	0.9	1.1	2.3	2.9
Mississippi	154,708	111,794	25,891	-	17,023	72.3	16.7	-	11.0	16	23	-	7	1.2	1.2	0.9	-	4.2
Missouri	-	-	-	-	-	-	-	-	-	-	-	-	-	-	-	-	-	-
Montana	90,975	65,176	10,701	-	15,098	71.6	11.8	-	16.6	17	32	-	5	0.7	0.7	0.4	-	3.7
Nebraska	192,098	156,346	25,847	-	9,905	81.4	13.5	-	5.2	5	29	-	15	1.5	1.7	0.9	-	2.5
Nevada	-	-	-	-	-	-	-	-	-	-	-	-	-	-	-	-	-	-
New Hampshire	174,167	92,233	65,087	-	16,847	53.0	37.4	-	9.7	38	1	-	10	1.4	1.0	2.2	-	4.2
New Jersey	286,967	240,535	46,432	-	-	83.8	16.2	-	-	1	26	-	-	2.3	2.6	1.6	-	-
New Mexico	86,967	55,522	7,871	23,574	-	63.8	9.1	27.1	-	33	34	2	-	0.7	0.6	0.3	13.5	-
New York	-	-	-	-	-	-	-	-	-	-	-	-	-	-	-	-	-	-
North Carolina	283,571	200,387	55,420	-	27,764	70.7	19.5	-	9.8	18	20	-	9	2.2	2.2	1.9	-	6.9
North Dakota	49,428	39,863	-	-	9,565	80.6	-	-	19.4	6	-	-	4	0.4	0.4	-	-	2.4
Ohio	860,453	716,766	143,687	-	-	83.3	16.7	-	-	2	24	-	-	6.8	7.8	5.0	-	-
Oklahoma	217,721	151,612	57,933	-	8,176	69.6	26.6	-	3.8	21	9	-	17	1.7	1.6	2.0	-	2.0
Oregon	304,159	203,957	57,730	-	42,472	67.1	19.0	-	14.0	26	21	-	6	2.4	2.2	2.0	-	10.5
Pennsylvania	1,008,777	774,865	233,912	-	-	76.8	23.2	-	-	9	15	-	-	8.0	8.4	8.1	-	-
Rhode Island	15,636	9,853	4,967	444	372	63.0	31.8	2.8	2.4	35	4	10	22	0.1	0.1	0.2	0.3	<.1
South Carolina	148,840	99,558	38,247	-	11,035	66.9	25.7	-	7.4	28	11	-	12	1.2	1.1	1.3	-	2.7
South Dakota	44,671	30,964	-	13,707	-	69.3	-	30.7	-	22	-	1	-	0.4	0.3	-	7.8	-
Tennessee	245,653	178,219	54,585	5,022	7,827	72.5	22.2	2.0	3.2	15	17	11	18	1.9	1.9	1.9	2.9	1.9
Texas	797,146	556,280	190,572	27,936	22,358	69.8	23.9	3.5	2.8	20	14	8	19	6.3	6.0	6.6	16.0	5.5
Utah	-	-	-	-	-	-	-	-	-	-	-	-	-	-	-	-	-	-
Vermont	-	-	-	-	-	-	-	-	-	-	-	-	-	-	-	-	-	-
Virginia	-	-	-	-	-	-	-	-	-	-	-	-	-	-	-	-	-	-	-
Washington	129,655	86,839	13,273	-	29,543	67.0	10.2	-	22.8	27	33	-	3	1.0	0.9	0.5	-	7.3
West Virginia	124,157	99,994	18,067	-	6,096	80.5	14.6	-	4.9	7	28	-	16	1.0	1.1	0.6	-	1.5
Wisconsin	482,248	364,507	78,516	8,725	30,500	75.6	16.3	1.8	6.3	11	25	12	14	3.8	4.0	2.7	5.0	7.6
Wyoming	-	-	-	-	-	-	-	-	-	-	-	-	-	-	-	-	-	-
District of Columbia	5,235	4,265	970	-	-	81.5	18.5	-	-	4	22	-	-	<.1	<.1	<.1	-	-
UNITED STATES	12,677,405	9,199,463	2,899,488	174,643	403,811	72.6	22.9	1.4	3.2					100.0	100.0	100.0	100.0	100.0

[1]Limited to the 37 states and the District of Columbia that held Republican presidential primaries. [2]Does not include corrected vote for the Massachusetts category "all others", which would increase the vote for other candidates to 18,037 and the state total vote to 269,702.

COUNTY RANKINGS

Table A. — 70 Largest Counties, 1990 Population by Race and Ethnic Origin

State & county code	County	Total persons	Percent of total persons — Non-Hispanic White	Black	Asian and Pacific Islander	Native American	Other	Hispanic	Rank Total	Rank % Non-Hispanic White	Black	Hispanic	Pct contribution Total	Non-Hispanic White	Black	Hispanic
06 037	Los Angeles	8,863,164	40.8	10.5	10.2	0.3	0.2	37.8	1	65	36	4	3.6	1.9	3.2	15.0
17 031	Cook (Chicago)............	5,105,067	57.1	25.5	3.6	0.2	<.1	13.6	2	52	9	21	2.1	1.5	4.5	3.1
48 201	Harris (Houston)	2,818,199	54.2	18.7	3.8	0.2	0.2	22.9	3	55	19	12	1.1	0.8	1.8	2.9
06 073	San Diego	2,498,016	65.4	6.0	7.4	0.6	0.2	20.4	4	45	51	14	1.0	0.9	0.5	2.3
06 059	Orange (Anaheim)	2,410,556	64.5	1.6	10.0	0.4	0.1	23.4	5	46	67	11	1.0	0.8	0.1	2.5
36 047	Kings (NYC-Brooklyn)	2,300,664	40.1	34.7	4.6	0.2	0.3	20.1	6	66	7	15	0.9	0.5	2.7	2.1
04 013	Maricopa (Phoenix)	2,122,101	77.1	3.3	1.6	1.5	0.1	16.3	7	28	60	18	0.9	0.9	0.2	1.5
26 163	Wayne (Detroit)............	2,111,687	56.1	40.0	1.0	0.4	<.1	2.4	8	53	4	55	0.8	0.6	2.9	0.2
36 081	Queens (New York City)	1,951,598	48.0	20.0	11.8	0.3	0.3	19.5	9	60	16	16	0.8	0.5	1.3	1.7
12 025	Dade (Miami)	1,937,094	30.2	19.1	1.2	0.1	0.1	49.2	10	68	18	2	0.8	0.3	1.3	4.3
48 113	Dallas	1,852,810	60.2	19.5	2.7	0.4	0.1	17.0	11	50	17	17	0.7	0.6	1.2	1.4
42 101	Philadelphia	1,585,577	52.1	39.3	2.7	0.2	0.1	5.6	12	57	5	46	0.6	0.4	2.1	0.4
53 033	King (Seattle)	1,507,319	83.3	5.0	7.7	1.1	0.1	2.9	13	16	56	53	0.6	0.7	0.3	0.2
06 085	Santa Clara (San Jose) ..	1,497,577	58.1	3.5	16.8	0.4	0.2	21.0	14	51	59	13	0.6	0.5	0.2	1.4
36 061	New York (NYC-Manhattan)	1,487,536	48.9	17.6	7.1	0.2	0.3	26.0	15	59	20	9	0.6	0.4	0.9	1.7
06 071	San Bernardino	1,418,380	60.8	7.7	3.9	0.7	0.2	26.7	16	49	45	6	0.6	0.5	0.4	1.7
39 035	Cuyahoga (Cleveland)	1,412,140	71.6	24.7	1.3	0.2	<.1	2.2	17	39	10	58	0.6	0.5	1.2	0.1
25 017	Middlesex (Boston suburb)	1,398,468	90.0	2.7	3.7	0.1	0.1	3.4	18	4	63	52	0.6	0.7	0.1	0.2
42 003	Allegheny (Pittsburg)	1,336,449	87.0	11.1	1.0	<.1	<.1	0.7	19	11	35	70	0.5	0.6	0.5	<.1
36 103	Suffolk (NYC suburbs)	1,321,864	85.5	5.8	1.7	0.2	<.1	6.6	20	12	52	40	0.5	0.6	0.3	0.4
36 059	Nassau (NYC suburbs)....	1,287,348	82.6	8.2	3.0	<.1	<.1	6.0	21	18	44	45	0.5	0.6	0.4	0.3
06 001	Alameda (Oakland)	1,279,182	53.2	17.4	14.4	0.5	0.2	14.2	22	56	21	19	0.5	0.4	0.8	0.8
12 011	Broward (Fort Lauderdale)..................	1,255,488	74.9	14.9	1.3	0.2	<.1	8.6	23	32	24	32	0.5	0.5	0.6	0.5
36 005	Bronx (New York City)	1,203,789	22.6	30.7	2.6	0.3	0.4	43.5	24	70	8	3	0.5	0.1	1.3	2.3
48 029	Bexar (San Antonio)........	1,185,394	41.9	6.9	1.2	0.2	0.2	49.7	25	63	50	1	0.5	0.3	0.3	2.6
06 065	Riverside.....................	1,170,413	64.4	5.1	3.3	0.7	0.2	26.3	26	47	55	8	0.5	0.4	0.2	1.4
48 439	Tarrant (Fort Worth)	1,170,103	73.3	11.8	2.5	0.4	<.1	12.0	27	34	31	24	0.5	0.5	0.5	0.6
26 125	Oakland (Detroit suburbs)	1,083,592	88.4	7.1	2.3	0.3	<.1	1.8	28	10	49	59	0.4	0.5	0.3	<.1
06 067	Sacramento..................	1,041,219	69.3	9.0	8.8	0.9	0.2	11.7	29	42	43	25	0.4	0.4	0.3	0.5
27 053	Hennepin (Minneapolis)..	1,032,431	88.6	5.7	2.8	1.4	0.1	1.4	30	8	53	60	0.4	0.5	0.2	<.1
29 189	St. Louis Co. (suburbs) ..	993,529	83.4	14.0	1.4	0.1	<.1	1.0	31	15	26	66	0.4	0.4	0.5	<.1
36 029	Erie (Buffalo)	968,532	84.9	11.2	1.0	0.6	<.1	2.3	32	13	34	57	0.4	0.4	0.4	<.1
39 049	Franklin (Columbus)........	961,437	80.9	15.8	2.0	0.2	0.1	1.0	33	22	23	67	0.4	0.4	0.5	<.1
55 079	Milwaukee...................	959,275	72.9	20.2	1.6	0.7	0.1	4.7	34	36	15	47	0.4	0.4	0.7	0.2
36 119	Westchester (NYC suburbs)	874,866	73.2	13.1	3.6	0.1	0.1	9.9	35	35	27	29	0.4	0.3	0.4	0.4
39 061	Hamilton (Cincinnati)	866,228	77.3	20.8	1.0	0.1	<.1	0.6	36	27	14	71	0.3	0.4	0.6	<.1
12 099	Palm Beach	863,518	79.1	12.0	1.0	0.1	<.1	7.7	37	25	30	36	0.3	0.4	0.4	0.3
09 003	Hartford	851,783	80.2	9.6	1.5	0.1	0.1	8.4	38	23	39	35	0.3	0.4	0.3	0.3
12 103	Pinellas (St. Petersburg)	851,659	88.6	7.6	1.1	0.2	<.1	2.4	39	7	46	56	0.3	0.4	0.2	<.1
15 003	Honolulu	836,231	29.9	3.0	59.8	0.3	0.3	6.8	40	69	61	39	0.3	0.1	<.1	0.3
12 057	Hillsborough (Tampa)	834,054	72.7	12.8	1.3	0.3	<.1	12.8	41	37	28	22	0.3	0.3	0.4	0.5
09 001	Fairfield (Bridgeport)	827,645	79.8	9.4	2.0	0.1	0.1	8.6	42	24	40	33	0.3	0.4	0.3	0.3
47 157	Shelby (Memphis)	826,330	54.6	43.4	0.9	0.2	<.1	0.9	43	54	3	68	0.3	0.2	1.2	<.1
34 003	Bergen (NYC suburbs)	825,380	82.7	4.6	6.5	0.1	<.1	6.0	44	17	58	43	0.3	0.4	0.1	0.2
51 059	Fairfax (DC suburbs)	818,584	77.4	7.6	8.3	0.2	0.1	6.3	45	26	47	42	0.3	0.3	0.2	0.2
09 009	New Haven (NYC suburbs)	804,219	82.3	9.8	1.3	0.2	0.1	6.3	46	20	38	41	0.3	0.4	0.3	0.2
06 013	Contra Costa (SF suburbs)	803,732	69.7	9.1	9.2	0.6	0.2	11.4	47	41	42	26	0.3	0.3	0.2	0.4
18 097	Marion (Indianapolis)......	797,159	76.5	21.2	0.9	0.2	<.1	1.1	48	30	12	64	0.3	0.3	0.6	<.1
17 043	DuPage (Chicago suburbs)	781,666	88.5	1.9	5.0	0.1	<.1	4.4	49	9	65	49	0.3	0.4	<.1	0.2
34 013	Essex (Newark)	778,206	45.1	39.3	2.6	0.2	0.2	12.6	50	62	6	23	0.3	0.2	1.0	0.4
24 031	Montgomery (DC suburbs)	757,027	72.4	11.8	8.1	0.2	0.1	7.4	51	38	32	37	0.3	0.3	0.3	0.2
32 003	Clark (Las Vegas)...........	741,459	75.4	9.3	3.3	0.7	0.1	11.2	52	31	41	27	0.3	0.3	0.2	0.4
24 510	Baltimore City...............	736,014	38.6	58.9	1.0	0.3	<.1	1.0	53	67	1	65	0.3	0.2	1.5	<.1
24 033	Pr. George's (DC suburbs)	729,268	41.6	50.1	3.7	0.3	0.1	4.1	54	64	2	50	0.3	0.2	1.3	0.1
49 035	Salt Lake	725,956	89.8	0.7	2.7	0.8	<.1	6.0	55	5	70	44	0.3	0.3	<.1	0.2
06 075	San Francisco...............	723,959	46.6	10.5	28.4	0.4	0.2	13.9	56	61	37	20	0.3	0.2	0.3	0.5
26 099	Macomb (Detroit suburbs)	717,400	95.8	1.4	1.2	0.4	<.1	1.1	57	1	69	63	0.3	0.4	<.1	<.1
36 055	Monroe (Rochester)	713,968	82.6	11.6	1.7	0.3	<.1	3.7	58	19	33	51	0.3	0.3	0.3	0.1
25 027	Worcester	709,705	91.6	1.9	1.6	0.2	<.1	4.6	59	2	66	48	0.3	0.3	<.1	0.1

Table A. — 70 Largest Counties, 1990 Population by Race and Ethnic Origin (cont)

State & county code	County	Total persons	Percent of total persons Non-Hispanic White	Black	Asian and Pacific Islander	Native American	Other	Hispanic	Rank Total	Rank Non-Hispanic White	Black	Hispanic	Percent contribution to national population Total	Non-Hispanic White	Black	Hispanic
24 005	Baltimore Co. (suburbs)	692,134	84.1	12.2	2.2	0.2	<.1	1.2	60	14	29	62	0.3	0.3	0.3	<.1
42 091	Montgomery (Phil suburbs)	678,111	90.6	5.6	2.3	<.1	<.1	1.2	61	3	54	61	0.3	0.3	0.1	<.1
12 095	Orange (Orlando)	677,491	73.3	14.8	2.0	0.3	<.1	9.6	62	33	25	30	0.3	0.3	0.3	0.3
12 031	Duval (Jacksonville)	672,971	71.2	24.1	1.8	0.3	<.1	2.6	63	40	11	54	0.3	0.3	0.6	<.1
34 023	Middlesex (New Brunswick)	671,780	77.0	7.4	6.5	0.1	0.1	8.9	64	29	48	31	0.3	0.3	0.2	0.3
25 009	Essex (Boston suburbs)	670,080	89.6	1.5	1.4	0.1	0.1	7.2	65	6	68	38	0.3	0.3	<.1	0.2
06 111	Ventura	669,016	65.9	2.2	4.9	0.5	0.1	26.4	66	44	64	7	0.3	0.2	<.1	0.8
06 019	Fresno	667,490	50.7	4.7	8.1	0.8	0.3	35.5	67	58	57	5	0.3	0.2	0.1	1.1
04 019	Pima (Tucson)	666,880	68.2	2.9	1.7	2.5	0.2	24.5	68	43	62	10	0.3	0.2	<.1	0.7
21 111	Jefferson (Louisville)	664,937	81.5	17.0	0.7	0.2	<.1	0.7	69	21	22	69	0.3	0.3	0.4	<.1
25 025	Suffolk (Boston)	663,906	62.1	20.9	4.9	0.3	0.9	11.0	70	48	13	28	0.3	0.2	0.5	0.3
	Top 70 (Subtotal)	89,718,810	63.8	14.8	5.4	0.4	0.1	15.6					36.1	30.4	45.4	62.4
	UNITED STATES	248,709,873	75.6	11.7	2.8	0.7	0.1	9.0					100.0	100.0	100.0	100.0

County	Total Voting Age Population	Percent of total VAP Non-Hispanic White	Black	Asian and Pacific Islander	Native American	Other	Hispanic	Rank Total	Rank Non-Hispanic White	Black	Hispanic	Contribution Total	Contribution Non-Hispanic White	Black	Hispanic	VAP% Total	VAP% Non-Hispanic White	Black	Asian and Pacific Islander	Native American	Other	Hispanic
Los Angeles	6,537,054	45.6	10.2	10.3	0.3	0.2	33.3	1	64	32	4	3.5	2.1	3.4	14.9	73.8	82.4	71.5	74.4	76.7	59.8	65.0
Cook (Chicago)	3,825,022	61.6	23.2	3.5	0.1	<.1	11.5	2	52	9	22	2.1	1.6	4.5	3.0	74.9	80.8	68.2	73.2	73.7	55.2	63.6
Harris (Houston)	2,013,190	57.9	17.8	3.7	0.2	0.1	20.2	3	55	17	12	1.1	0.8	1.8	2.8	71.4	76.3	68.0	69.9	76.3	62.1	62.9
San Diego	1,887,070	69.2	5.5	6.9	0.6	0.1	17.6	4	45	51	16	1.0	0.9	0.5	2.3	75.5	80.0	69.5	70.5	73.2	56.3	65.1
Orange (Anaheim)	1,821,253	68.0	1.5	9.4	0.4	<.1	20.6	5	47	67	11	1.0	0.9	0.1	2.6	75.6	79.7	70.4	71.1	77.3	61.4	66.4
Kings (NYC-Brooklyn)	1,695,110	43.8	32.8	4.7	0.2	0.2	18.2	6	66	7	14	0.9	0.6	2.8	2.1	73.7	80.5	69.7	75.6	71.5	57.9	66.8
Maricopa (Phoenix)	1,566,310	80.7	2.9	1.6	1.3	<.1	13.4	7	26	60	18	0.8	0.9	0.2	1.4	73.8	77.3	65.2	71.8	63.6	55.9	60.5
Wayne (Detroit)	1,541,050	59.1	37.5	0.9	0.3	<.1	2.1	9	53	4	55	0.8	0.6	2.9	0.2	73.0	76.8	68.3	67.0	71.6	43.1	64.3
Queens (New York City)	1,542,971	51.4	18.5	11.3	0.3	0.3	18.2	8	60	14	15	0.8	0.6	1.4	1.9	79.1	84.7	72.9	76.2	74.6	59.9	73.8
Dade (Miami)	1,469,084	31.8	16.3	1.2	<.1	<.1	50.5	10	68	18	1	0.8	0.3	1.2	5.1	75.8	79.7	64.9	75.3	72.7	48.7	77.8
Dallas	1,357,162	64.3	18.0	2.6	0.4	0.1	14.7	11	50	16	17	0.7	0.6	1.2	1.4	73.2	78.2	67.4	69.7	74.1	60.5	63.0
Philadelphia	1,206,156	55.6	36.9	2.5	0.2	<.1	4.6	13	58	6	45	0.7	0.5	2.2	0.4	76.1	81.3	71.5	71.4	76.2	55.5	62.7
King (Seattle)	1,166,248	84.9	4.4	7.2	1.0	<.1	2.6	14	17	57	52	0.6	0.7	0.3	0.2	77.4	78.9	68.4	72.2	70.6	44.1	67.4
Santa Clara (San Jose)	1,138,370	61.7	3.3	16.0	0.4	0.1	18.5	15	51	59	13	0.6	0.5	0.2	1.4	76.0	80.7	71.6	72.4	76.1	61.3	66.9
New York (NYC-Manhattan)	1,240,709	53.7	16.2	7.2	0.2	0.2	22.6	12	59	20	8	0.7	0.5	1.0	1.9	83.4	91.7	77.1	83.6	79.8	52.6	72.4
San Bernardino	979,157	64.7	7.1	3.8	0.7	0.2	23.5	22	49	46	6	0.5	0.4	0.4	1.6	69.0	73.4	63.8	68.0	69.5	57.2	60.7
Cuyahoga (Cleveland)	1,073,957	74.2	22.6	1.2	0.2	<.1	1.8	17	38	10	57	0.6	0.6	1.2	0.1	76.1	78.8	69.6	71.9	72.1	38.2	62.7
Middlesex (Boston suburb)	1,107,476	91.0	2.5	3.3	0.1	0.1	2.9	16	6	63	51	0.6	0.7	0.1	0.2	79.2	80.1	73.6	71.3	78.7	64.3	68.8
Allegheny (Pittsburg)	1,054,266	88.4	9.9	0.9	<.1	<.1	0.6	18	11	34	68	0.6	0.6	0.5	<.1	78.9	80.1	70.3	73.8	74.6	22.8	72.4
Suffolk (NYC suburbs)	995,276	86.8	5.3	1.6	0.2	<.1	6.1	21	12	53	37	0.5	0.6	0.3	0.4	75.3	76.4	68.6	70.3	70.8	49.0	68.9
Nassau (NYC suburbs)	1,006,650	84.0	7.6	2.6	<.1	<.1	5.6	19	20	44	41	0.5	0.6	0.4	0.4	78.2	79.5	72.3	68.3	76.1	47.8	73.4
Alameda (Oakland)	975,777	56.4	16.3	13.9	0.5	0.2	12.7	23	57	19	19	0.5	0.4	0.8	0.9	76.3	80.9	71.4	73.2	76.4	60.9	68.3
Broward (Fort Lauderdale)	998,870	78.5	12.1	1.2	0.2	<.1	8.0	20	31	27	31	0.5	0.5	0.6	0.5	79.6	83.4	64.7	71.5	73.7	53.7	73.6
Bronx (New York City)	872,141	27.0	29.9	2.6	0.3	0.3	40.0	24	70	8	3	0.5	0.2	1.3	2.4	72.4	86.4	70.6	73.4	68.8	51.4	66.6
Bexar (San Antonio)	839,453	46.0	6.8	1.2	0.2	0.2	45.6	26	63	48	2	0.5	0.3	0.3	2.6	70.8	77.8	69.8	75.1	77.3	63.4	65.0
Riverside	837,152	68.7	4.8	3.1	0.7	0.1	22.5	27	46	54	9	0.5	0.4	0.2	1.3	71.5	76.3	67.0	68.7	69.5	59.1	61.3
Tarrant (Fort Worth)	852,582	76.1	10.8	2.3	0.4	<.1	10.3	25	35	31	24	0.5	0.4	0.5	0.6	72.9	75.6	66.8	68.0	75.9	56.3	62.9
Oakland (Detroit suburbs)	815,534	89.6	6.5	2.0	0.3	<.1	1.5	28	10	49	58	0.4	0.5	0.3	<.1	75.3	76.3	68.9	66.5	70.5	34.0	64.4
Sacramento	766,240	72.6	8.1	8.0	0.9	0.1	10.2	30	42	43	25	0.4	0.4	0.3	0.5	73.6	77.1	65.9	66.8	71.5	55.0	64.3
Hennepin (Minneapolis)	793,622	91.1	4.5	2.2	1.1	<.1	1.1	29	5	55	60	0.4	0.5	0.2	<.1	76.9	79.0	60.6	59.5	59.3	26.9	63.7
St. Louis Co. (suburbs)	749,134	85.1	12.5	1.3	0.1	<.1	0.9	31	16	25	66	0.4	0.4	0.5	<.1	75.4	76.9	67.6	70.4	77.0	29.5	67.6
Erie (Buffalo)	743,065	86.6	10.1	1.0	0.5	<.1	1.9	32	13	33	56	0.4	0.4	0.4	<.1	76.7	78.2	69.2	72.9	66.5	45.3	62.1
Franklin (Columbus)	724,671	82.8	14.2	1.9	0.2	<.1	0.9	33	23	23	65	0.4	0.4	0.5	<.1	75.4	77.1	67.6	71.8	75.9	30.9	70.8
Milwaukee	712,973	78.3	16.2	1.3	0.6	<.1	3.6	34	32	21	49	0.4	0.4	0.6	0.2	74.3	79.9	59.7	61.3	65.0	24.5	57.4
Westchester (NYC suburbs)	684,597	75.5	12.1	3.2	0.1	<.1	9.0	37	36	26	29	0.4	0.4	0.4	0.4	78.3	80.7	72.7	68.9	78.9	52.3	71.2
Hamilton (Cincinnati)	641,298	79.5	18.8	1.0	0.1	<.1	0.5	40	27	13	70	0.3	0.4	0.6	<.1	74.0	76.1	66.6	73.1	76.4	25.3	67.6
Palm Beach	693,965	82.5	9.6	0.9	0.1	<.1	6.9	36	24	36	35	0.4	0.4	0.3	0.3	80.4	83.7	64.4	72.9	78.2	51.5	71.7
Hartford	659,440	83.0	8.7	1.4	0.1	0.1	6.6	38	22	38	36	0.4	0.4	0.3	0.3	77.4	80.2	70.2	69.9	78.1	60.4	61.1
Pinellas (St. Petersburg)	700,203	90.6	6.1	0.9	0.2	<.1	2.1	35	7	50	54	0.4	0.4	0.2	0.1	82.2	84.0	65.7	68.9	77.0	44.5	74.6
Honolulu	631,618	30.9	2.7	60.2	0.3	0.2	5.7	43	69	61	40	0.3	0.1	<.1	0.2	75.5	78.2	70.2	76.0	72.6	52.6	62.9
Hillsborough (Tampa)	631,780	75.2	10.9	1.3	0.3	<.1	12.4	42	37	30	21	0.3	0.3	0.3	0.5	75.7	78.3	64.5	72.7	77.6	45.4	73.1
Fairfield (Bridgeport)	640,520	82.2	8.4	1.8	0.1	0.1	7.4	41	25	40	33	0.3	0.4	0.3	0.3	77.4	79.8	69.1	69.0	77.8	56.1	66.8
Shelby (Memphis)	600,023	58.5	39.5	0.9	0.2	<.1	0.9	48	54	3	67	0.3	0.2	1.2	<.1	72.6	77.8	66.1	70.5	75.4	36.3	73.1
Bergen (NYC suburbs)	657,012	84.1	4.4	5.6	0.1	<.1	5.7	39	19	56	39	0.4	0.4	0.1	0.3	79.6	81.0	76.8	68.6	72.1	48.2	75.4
Fairfax (DC suburbs)	618,516	78.7	7.2	7.8	0.2	<.1	6.0	45	30	45	38	0.3	0.3	0.2	0.3	75.6	76.8	71.6	70.9	75.5	49.2	71.6
New Haven (NYC suburbs)	621,601	84.7	8.6	1.2	0.2	<.1	5.2	44	18	39	44	0.3	0.4	0.3	0.2	77.3	79.6	68.0	74.4	72.9	52.4	63.1
Contra Costa (SF suburbs)	601,644	72.5	8.3	8.6	0.6	0.1	9.9	47	43	41	26	0.3	0.3	0.2	0.4	74.9	77.9	68.3	69.9	75.6	55.0	65.5
Marion (Indianapolis)	593,974	78.7	19.2	0.9	0.2	<.1	0.9	49	29	12	64	0.3	0.3	0.6	<.1	74.5	76.6	67.6	72.9	75.5	23.8	65.8
DuPage (Chicago suburbs)	575,250	89.7	1.7	4.5	0.1	<.1	4.0	52	9	65	46	0.3	0.4	<.1	0.2	73.6	74.5	66.1	66.6	74.1	42.7	66.0
Essex (Newark)	589,569	48.8	37.0	2.5	0.2	0.2	11.3	50	62	5	23	0.3	0.2	1.1	0.5	75.8	81.9	71.4	72.3	75.5	64.3	68.2
Montgomery (DC suburbs)	578,783	74.1	11.1	7.6	0.2	<.1	6.9	51	39	28	34	0.3	0.3	0.3	0.3	76.5	78.2	72.3	72.0	76.9	47.6	71.9
Clark (Las Vegas)	559,650	78.0	8.1	3.3	0.7	<.1	9.9	53	33	42	27	0.3	0.3	0.3	0.4	75.5	78.1	65.7	74.9	73.5	49.7	66.7
Baltimore City	556,145	42.0	55.5	1.1	0.3	<.1	1.0	54	67	1	62	0.3	0.2	1.6	<.1	75.6	82.2	71.2	80.2	69.7	53.1	73.5
Pr. George's (DC suburbs)	551,323	44.7	47.2	3.7	0.3	<.1	3.9	55	65	2	47	0.3	0.2	1.3	0.1	75.6	81.4	71.2	75.4	75.9	46.3	71.9
Salt Lake	473,539	90.3	0.7	2.6	0.7	<.1	5.6	69	8	70	42	0.3	0.3	<.1	0.2	65.2	65.7	65.0	63.9	59.6	53.5	60.2
San Francisco	607,076	50.7	9.5	26.7	0.4	0.2	12.6	46	61	37	20	0.3	0.2	0.3	0.5	83.9	91.2	75.5	78.9	84.4	66.2	75.9
Macomb (Detroit suburbs)	545,747	96.3	1.3	1.1	0.3	<.1	1.0	56	1	69	63	0.3	0.4	<.1	<.1	76.1	76.4	68.6	66.1	70.4	30.2	67.9
Monroe (Rochester)	538,518	85.5	9.7	1.5	0.3	<.1	3.0	58	15	35	50	0.3	0.3	0.3	0.1	75.4	78.0	63.3	66.9	71.6	34.0	60.3
Worcester	536,506	93.1	1.7	1.3	0.2	<.1	3.6	59	2	66	48	0.3	0.3	<.1	0.1	75.6	76.8	67.1	64.9	70.2	42.0	58.8

Table B. — 70 Largest Counties, 1990 Voting Age Population (VAP) by Race and Ethnic Origin (cont)

County	Total Voting Age Population	Percent of total VAP						Rank				Percent contribution to national VAP				VAP percent of total population						
		Non-Hispanic						Percent of total VAP				Non-Hispanic				Non-Hispanic						
									Non-Hispanic													
		White	Black	Asian and Pacific Islander	Native American	Other	Hispanic	Total	White	Black	Hispanic	Total	White	Black	Hispanic	Total	White	Black	Asian and Pacific Islander	Native American	Other	Hispanic
Baltimore Co. (suburbs)	540,972	85.6	11.1	2.0	0.2	<.1	1.1	57	14	29	61	0.3	0.3	0.3	<.1	78.2	79.5	71.2	71.4	74.2	44.2	71.8
Montgomery (Phil suburbs)........................	525,206	91.2	5.4	2.1	0.1	<.1	1.1	62	4	52	59	0.3	0.3	0.1	<.1	77.5	78.0	74.3	68.8	81.6	41.9	71.5
Orange (Orlando)	516,005	76.4	12.6	1.9	0.3	<.1	8.8	63	34	24	30	0.3	0.3	0.3	0.3	76.2	79.4	64.9	71.7	77.7	48.1	69.9
Duval (Jacksonville)	498,625	73.8	21.7	1.7	0.3	<.1	2.4	67	40	11	53	0.3	0.3	0.5	<.1	74.1	76.8	66.8	69.7	75.7	39.7	70.4
Middlesex (New Brunswick)......................	527,149	78.9	7.0	5.9	0.1	<.1	7.9	61	28	47	32	0.3	0.3	0.2	0.3	78.5	80.5	74.2	71.4	75.4	53.9	70.0
Essex (Boston suburbs)	511,503	91.9	1.3	1.2	0.1	<.1	5.5	64	3	68	43	0.3	0.3	<.1	0.2	76.3	78.3	65.2	62.5	70.6	34.1	57.9
Ventura	486,030	69.3	2.1	4.7	0.5	0.1	23.2	68	44	64	7	0.3	0.2	<.1	0.8	72.6	76.5	69.4	70.5	74.1	60.2	63.8
Fresno	458,454	56.8	4.3	6.4	0.8	0.2	31.5	70	56	58	5	0.2	0.2	<.1	1.0	68.7	76.9	63.1	54.3	68.5	61.1	61.1
Pima (Tucson)	500,682	72.8	2.7	1.7	2.1	0.1	20.7	66	41	62	10	0.3	0.3	<.1	0.7	75.1	80.1	68.9	75.5	61.5	58.6	63.4
Jefferson (Louisville)	502,361	83.4	15.2	0.6	0.2	<.1	0.6	65	21	22	69	0.3	0.3	0.4	<.1	75.6	77.4	67.5	69.7	77.5	20.0	69.0
Suffolk (Boston).................	535,721	67.1	18.1	4.7	0.2	0.7	9.2	60	48	15	28	0.3	0.2	0.5	0.3	80.7	87.2	70.0	76.6	72.7	63.9	67.4
Top 70 (Subtotal)	67,595,760	67.1	13.6	5.2	0.4	0.1	13.7					36.5	31.4	46.1	63.5	75.3	79.3	69.1	72.9	71.2	54.8	66.4
UNITED STATES	185,105,441	78.0	10.7	2.7	0.6	<.1	7.9					100.0	100.0	100.0	100.0	74.4	76.7	68.1	71.7	65.0	52.5	65.3

Table C. — 70 Largest Counties, Voter Participation: November 3, 1992, General Election

County	Estimated Voting Age Population (VAP), 1992	Voter registration (REG) Total	% contribution to national REG	% of 1992 VAP	Rank by % of 1992 VAP	Voter turnout — Highest office Actual	Total	Office	% of 1992 VAP	Max vote Total	% contribution to national turnout	% of REG	Rank by % of REG	% of 1992 VAP	Rank by % 1992 VAP	Drop-off President	Senator	Governor	Representative
Los Angeles	6,616,370	3,744,096	2.8	56.6	64	2,831,077	2,753,403	P	41.6	2,831,077	2.7	75.6	42	42.8	65	2.7	5.2	-	8.3
Cook (Chicago)	3,840,168	2,924,493	2.2	76.2	21	2,199,608	2,146,655	P	55.9	2,199,608	2.1	75.2	43	57.3	35	2.4	4.3	-	7.1
Harris (Houston)	2,057,565	1,315,010	1.0	63.9	53	-	942,947	P	45.8	942,947	0.9	71.7	57	45.8	58	0.0	-	-	11.6
San Diego	1,961,574	1,382,383	1.0	70.5	38	1,002,914	986,646	P	50.3	1,002,914	0.9	72.5	55	51.1	49	1.6	5.6	-	7.0
Orange (Anaheim)	1,869,133	1,240,778	0.9	66.4	48	979,024	972,549	P	52.0	979,024	0.9	78.9	32	52.4	47	0.7	2.9	-	9.7
Kings (NYC-Brooklyn)	1,695,073	967,539	0.7	57.1	62	607,629	581,594	P	34.3	607,629	0.6	62.8	68	35.8	70	4.3	11.7	-	31.6
Maricopa (Phoenix)	1,623,488	1,147,672	0.9	70.7	37	890,680	876,832	P	54.0	890,680	0.8	77.6	34	54.9	41	1.6	11.2	-	5.9
Wayne (Detroit)	1,532,918	1,296,934	1.0	84.6	6	857,484	841,965	P	54.9	857,484	0.8	66.1	66	55.9	37	1.8	-	-	7.5
Queens (New York City)	1,536,113	821,019	0.6	53.4	66	575,104	555,956	P	36.2	575,104	0.5	70.0	62	37.4	67	3.3	9.0	-	27.2
Dade (Miami)[2]	1,510,041	675,286	0.5	44.7	69	557,909	544,841	P	36.1	557,909	0.5	82.6	21	36.9	68	2.3	6.4	-	37.8
Dallas	1,389,477	879,137	0.7	63.3	55	-	661,252	P	47.6	661,252	0.6	75.2	44	47.6	55	0.0	-	-	9.1
Philadelphia	1,192,586	874,181	0.7	73.3	30	-	638,058	P	53.5	638,058	0.6	73.0	53	53.5	44	0.0	4.1	-	8.7
King (Seattle)	1,229,788	943,396	0.7	76.7	18	788,511	778,593	P	63.3	788,511	0.7	83.6	19	64.1	11	1.3	2.6	2.1	5.2
Santa Clara (San Jose)	1,145,351	820,028	0.6	71.6	33	610,002	602,055	P	52.6	610,002	0.6	74.4	46	53.3	45	1.3	4.6	-	6.5
New York (NYC-Manhattan)	1,233,244	859,861	0.6	69.7	41	550,085	532,118	P	43.1	550,085	0.5	64.0	67	44.6	61	3.3	8.8	-	20.6
San Bernardino	1,092,014	682,980	0.5	62.5	57	482,162	474,070	P	43.4	482,162	0.5	70.6	60	44.2	62	1.7	7.5	-	8.7
Cuyahoga (Cleveland)	1,069,718	932,611	0.7	87.2	3	656,034	640,241	P	59.9	656,034	0.6	70.3	61	61.3	20	2.4	5.4	-	9.1
Middlesex (Boston suburb)	1,085,272	815,979	0.6	75.2	24	699,754	689,452	P	63.5	699,754	0.7	85.8	4	64.5	9	1.5	-	-	8.2
Allegheny (Pittsburgh)	1,037,739	730,613	0.5	70.4	39	-	614,187	P	59.2	614,187	0.6	84.1	16	59.2	27	0.0	3.3	-	6.9
Suffolk (NYC suburbs)	990,909	730,094	0.5	73.7	28	573,006	567,955	P	57.3	573,006	0.5	78.5	33	57.8	31	0.9	5.6	-	12.0
Nassau (NYC suburbs)	990,390	760,028	0.6	76.7	19	618,369	609,326	P	61.5	618,369	0.6	81.4	26	62.4	18	1.5	5.1	-	14.9
Alameda (Oakland)	976,370	758,435	0.5	77.7	15	541,928	530,145	P	54.3	541,928	0.5	71.5	58	55.5	38	2.2	5.5	4.7	7.4
Broward (Fort Lauderdale)	1,031,106	657,548	0.5	63.8	54	542,547	533,050	P	51.7	542,547	0.5	82.5	23	52.6	46	1.8	17.6	-	5.4
Bronx (New York City)	868,620	521,102	0.4	60.0	60	319,771	305,460	P	35.2	319,771	0.3	61.4	69	36.8	69	4.5	13.4	-	28.4
Bexar (San Antonio)	863,383	584,335	0.4	67.7	46	-	415,276	P	48.1	415,276	0.4	71.1	59	48.1	51	0.0	-	-	23.2
Riverside	947,935	597,020	0.4	63.0	56	434,316	430,275	P	45.4	434,316	0.4	72.7	54	45.8	59	0.9	2.8	-	6.6
Tarrant (Fort Worth)	905,365	596,958	0.4	65.9	50	-	471,396	P	52.1	471,396	0.4	79.0	31	52.1	48	0.0	-	-	3.9
Oakland (Detroit suburbs)	841,454	761,611	0.6	90.5	2	562,691	555,760	P	66.0	562,691	0.5	73.9	47	66.9	4	1.2	-	-	9.1
Sacramento	799,059	629,200	0.5	78.7	12	461,887	453,512	P	56.8	461,887	0.4	73.4	50	57.8	30	1.8	4.8	-	5.1
Hennepin (Minneapolis)	809,508	790,678	0.6	97.7	1	588,335	586,619	P	72.5	588,335	0.6	74.4	45	72.7	1	0.3	-	-	4.2
St. Louis Co. (suburbs)	754,002	637,685	0.5	84.6	5	-	534,763	P	70.9	534,763	0.5	83.9	18	70.9	2	0.0	0.7	1.6	1.1
Erie (Buffalo)	723,152	540,215	0.4	74.7	26	455,943	451,496	P	62.4	455,943	0.4	84.4	15	63.0	16	1.0	10.3	-	9.1
Franklin (Columbus)	744,450	582,202	0.4	78.2	14	450,833	444,801	P	59.7	450,833	0.4	77.4	36	60.6	22	1.3	6.8	-	10.1
Milwaukee[3]	716,406	-	-	-	-	-	465,496	P	65.0	465,496	0.4	-	-	65.0	6	0.0	2.2	-	7.5
Westchester (NYC suburbs)	674,399	479,127	0.4	71.0	35	389,129	378,840	P	56.2	389,129	0.4	81.2	28	57.7	33	2.6	6.9	-	13.0
Hamilton (Cincinnati)	644,767	536,386	0.4	83.2	7	413,357	403,420	P	62.6	413,357	0.4	77.1	38	64.1	10	2.4	4.7	-	8.0
Palm Beach	739,125	484,440	0.4	65.5	51	414,050	405,251	P	54.8	414,050	0.4	85.5	7	56.0	36	2.1	14.2	-	7.3
Hartford	658,792	509,750	0.4	77.4	16	421,126	414,804	P	63.0	421,126	0.4	82.6	22	63.9	13	1.5	7.3	-	12.7
Pinellas (St. Petersburg)	712,416	504,465	0.4	70.8	36	429,674	422,851	P	59.4	429,674	0.4	85.2	12	60.3	23	1.6	12.3	-	3.3
Honolulu	667,642	328,463	0.2	49.2	67	272,081	265,841	P	39.8	272,081	0.3	82.8	20	40.8	66	2.3	5.0	-	6.0
Hillsborough (Tampa)	659,808	372,439	0.3	56.4	65	316,006	310,502	P	47.1	316,006	0.3	84.8	13	47.9	54	1.7	3.5	-	8.4
Fairfield (Bridgeport)	637,065	488,559	0.4	76.6	20	416,238	409,410	P	64.2	416,238	0.4	85.2	10	65.3	5	1.6	9.8	-	15.1
Shelby (Memphis)	618,812	498,719	0.4	80.6	10	-	366,110	P	59.2	366,110	0.3	73.4	51	59.2	28	0.0	-	-	8.9
Bergen (NYC suburbs)	646,293	475,151	0.4	73.5	29	406,143	403,137	P	62.4	406,143	0.4	85.5	6	62.8	17	0.7	-	-	7.3
Fairfax (DC suburbs)	669,856	459,102	0.3	68.5	45	-	385,280	P	57.5	385,280	0.4	83.9	17	57.5	34	0.0	-	-	6.0
New Haven (NYC suburbs)	619,311	485,083	0.4	78.3	13	395,583	385,132	P	62.2	395,583	0.4	81.5	25	63.9	14	2.6	10.3	-	12.0
Contra Costa (SF suburbs)	613,606	507,451	0.4	82.7	8	389,391	382,823	P	62.4	389,391	0.4	76.7	40	63.5	15	1.7	5.2	-	8.6
Marion (Indianapolis)	609,995	468,408	0.4	76.8	17	327,043	323,790	P	53.1	327,043	0.3	69.8	63	53.6	42	1.0	7.0	5.7	7.0
DuPage (Chicago suburbs)	604,559	431,876	0.3	71.4	34	376,837	370,987	P	61.4	376,837	0.4	87.3	3	62.3	19	1.6	3.3	-	5.7
Essex (Newark)	575,211	357,544	0.3	62.2	58	267,483	276,858	P	48.1	276,858	0.3	77.4	35	48.1	52	0.0	-	-	14.5
Montgomery (DC suburbs)	618,021	428,740	0.3	69.4	43	365,128	362,613	P	58.7	365,128	0.3	85.2	11	59.1	29	0.7	3.1	-	6.0
Clark (Las Vegas)	639,285	396,628	0.3	62.0	59	306,387	302,782	P	47.4	306,387	0.3	77.2	37	47.9	53	1.2	3.8	-	4.6
Baltimore City	543,202	360,405	0.3	66.3	49	247,310	245,091	P	45.1	247,310	0.2	68.6	65	45.5	60	0.9	8.6	-	14.6
Pr. George's (DC suburbs)	558,117	318,524	0.2	57.1	63	258,699	256,859	P	46.0	258,699	0.2	81.2	27	46.4	57	0.7	11.8	-	10.3
Salt Lake	491,386	397,534	0.3	80.9	9	336,195	326,308	G	66.4	336,195	0.3	84.6	14	68.4	3	5.2	3.1	2.9	8.9
San Francisco	597,642	477,740	0.4	79.9	11	329,695	322,207	P	53.9	329,695	0.3	69.0	64	55.2	39	2.3	7.7	-	10.2
Macomb (Detroit suburbs)	552,775	481,886	0.4	87.2	4	353,851	349,238	P	63.2	353,851	0.3	73.4	49	64.0	12	1.3	-	-	9.2
Monroe (Rochester)	529,254	386,876	0.3	73.1	31	343,347	340,369	P	64.3	343,347	0.3	88.7	2	64.9	7	0.9	9.8	-	8.5
Worcester	535,865	374,554	0.3	69.9	40	319,936	315,782	P	58.9	319,936	0.3	85.4	9	59.7	26	1.3	-	-	6.6

[1]Percent drop-off is zero for any office used as highest office turnout. [2]Does not include congressional district 21 where representative was elected from Republican primary (no Democratic Primary). [3]No voter registration data since Wisconsin has no statewide voter registration requirement.

22 County Rankings

Table C. — 70 Largest Counties, Voter Participation: November 3, 1992, General Election (cont)

County	Estimated Voting Age Population (VAP), 1992	Voter registration (REG)				Voter turnout													
						Highest office				Maximum vote						Percent drop-off, by office[1]			
		Total	% contribution to national REG	% of 1992 VAP	Rank by % of 1992 VAP	Actual	Total	Office	% of 1992 VAP	Total	% contribution to national turnout	% of REG	Rank by % of REG	% of 1992 VAP	Rank by % 1992 VAP	President	Senator	Governor	Representative
Baltimore Co. (suburbs)	540,797	401,278	0.3	74.2	27	324,870	323,220	P	59.8	324,870	0.3	81.0	29	60.1	24	0.5	9.6	-	11.7
Montgomery (Phil suburbs)	533,160	371,118	0.3	69.6	42	-	318,576	P	59.8	318,576	0.3	85.8	5	59.8	25	0.0	2.9	-	7.2
Orange (Orlando)	553,274	267,878	0.2	48.4	68	238,650	237,011	P	42.8	238,650	0.2	89.1	1	43.1	63	0.7	2.4	-	4.0
Duval (Jacksonville)	506,780	349,984	0.3	69.1	44	255,683	249,926	P	49.3	255,683	0.2	73.1	52	50.5	50	2.3	15.3	-	6.3
Middlesex (New Brunswick)	532,156	360,115	0.3	67.7	47	278,199	285,271	P	53.6	285,271	0.3	79.2	30	53.6	43	0.0	-	-	13.1
Essex (Boston suburbs)	508,203	384,383	0.3	75.6	22	328,180	322,328	P	63.4	328,180	0.3	85.4	8	64.6	8	1.8	-	-	7.4
Ventura	501,210	359,236	0.3	71.7	32	276,404	267,647	P	53.4	276,404	0.3	76.9	39	55.1	40	3.2	4.7	-	5.2
Fresno	477,250	311,952	0.2	65.4	52	224,241	219,161	P	45.9	224,241	0.2	71.9	56	47.0	56	2.3	5.4	-	6.7
Pima (Tucson)	498,571	375,942	0.3	75.4	23	287,718	281,484	P	56.5	287,718	0.3	76.5	41	57.7	32	2.2	7.1	-	10.0
Jefferson (Louisville)	505,110	379,521	0.3	75.1	25	-	309,793	P	61.3	309,793	0.3	81.6	24	61.3	21	0.0	3.0	-	2.4
Suffolk (Boston)	521,766	303,727	0.2	58.2	61	224,223	219,273	P	42.0	224,223	0.2	73.8	48	43.0	64	2.2	-	-	12.1
Top 70 (Subtotal)[2]	**68,775,666**	**47,076,091**	**35.3**	**69.2**		**30,370,460**	**35,948,719**		**52.3**	**36,510,041**	**34.5**	**77.6**		**53.1**					
UNITED STATES	**189,026,699**	**133,531,306**	**100.0**	**70.6**		**73,695,312**	**104,541,053**		**55.3**	**105,865,513**	**100.0**	**79.3**		**56.0**					

[1]Percent drop-off is zero for any office used as highest office turnout. [2]Registration percent of VAP based on VAP of 68,059,260 (Milwaukee, WI not included).

Table E. — 70 Largest Counties, Vote for President: November 3, 1992, General Election

County	Total	Clinton (DEM)	Bush (REP)	Perot (IND)	Other	Plurality Total	Party	DEM	REP	IND	Other	Rank DEM	Rank REP	Rank IND	Total	DEM	REP	IND	DEM	REP
Los Angeles	2,753,403	1,446,529	799,607	488,624	18,643	646,922	D	52.5	29.0	17.7	0.7	17	54	36	2.6	3.2	2.0	2.5	64.4	35.6
Cook (Chicago)	2,146,655	1,249,533	605,300	281,999	9,823	644,233	D	58.2	28.2	13.1	0.5	12	58	53	2.1	2.8	1.5	1.4	67.4	32.6
Harris (Houston)	942,947	360,171	406,778	172,922	3,076	46,607	R	38.2	43.1	18.3	0.3	55	11	32	0.9	0.8	1.0	0.9	47.0	53.0
San Diego	986,646	367,397	352,125	259,249	7,875	15,272	D	37.2	35.7	26.3	0.8	59	36	5	0.9	0.8	0.9	1.3	51.1	48.9
Orange (Anaheim)	972,549	306,930	426,613	232,394	6,612	119,683	R	31.6	43.9	23.9	0.7	68	7	10	0.9	0.7	1.1	1.2	41.8	58.2
Kings (NYC-Brooklyn)[1]	581,594	411,183	133,344	33,014	4,053	277,839	D	70.7	22.9	5.7	0.7	5	64	67	0.6	0.9	0.3	0.2	75.5	24.5
Maricopa (Phoenix)	876,832	285,457	360,049	221,475	9,851	74,592	R	32.6	41.1	25.3	1.1	67	17	7	0.8	0.6	0.9	1.1	44.2	55.8
Wayne (Detroit)	841,965	508,464	227,002	102,074	4,425	281,462	D	60.4	27.0	12.1	0.5	11	61	57	0.8	1.1	0.6	0.5	69.1	30.9
Queens (New York City)[1]	555,956	349,520	157,561	46,014	2,861	191,959	D	62.9	28.3	8.3	0.5	9	57	65	0.5	0.8	0.4	0.2	68.9	31.1
Dade (Miami)	544,841	254,607	235,313	54,003	918	19,294	D	46.7	43.2	9.9	0.2	29	10	61	0.5	0.6	0.6	0.3	52.0	48.0
Dallas	661,252	231,412	256,007	170,571	3,262	24,595	R	35.0	38.7	25.8	0.5	64	28	6	0.6	0.5	0.7	0.9	47.5	52.5
Philadelphia	638,058	434,904	133,328	65,455	4,371	301,576	D	68.2	20.9	10.3	0.7	6	65	60	0.6	1.0	0.3	0.3	76.5	23.5
King (Seattle)	778,593	391,050	212,986	167,216	7,341	178,064	D	50.2	27.4	21.5	0.9	22	60	15	0.7	0.9	0.5	0.8	64.7	35.3
Santa Clara (San Jose)	602,055	296,265	170,870	128,895	6,025	125,395	D	49.2	28.4	21.4	1.0	25	56	16	0.6	0.7	0.4	0.7	63.4	36.6
New York (NYC-Manhattan)[1]	532,118	416,142	84,501	27,689	3,786	331,641	D	78.2	15.9	5.2	0.7	1	70	69	0.5	0.9	0.2	0.1	83.1	16.9
San Bernardino	474,070	183,634	176,563	109,183	4,690	7,071	D	38.7	37.2	23.0	1.0	52	32	14	0.5	0.4	0.5	0.6	51.0	49.0
Cuyahoga (Cleveland)	640,241	337,548	187,186	112,352	3,155	150,362	D	52.7	29.2	17.5	0.5	16	53	37	0.6	0.7	0.5	0.6	64.3	35.7
Middlesex (Boston suburb)	689,452	343,994	193,703	146,831	4,924	150,291	D	49.9	28.1	21.3	0.7	23	59	17	0.7	0.8	0.5	0.7	64.0	36.0
Allegheny (Pittsburg)	614,187	324,004	183,035	103,470	3,678	140,969	D	52.8	29.8	16.8	0.6	15	51	42	0.6	0.7	0.5	0.5	63.9	36.1
Suffolk (NYC suburbs)[1]	567,955	220,811	229,467	112,973	4,704	8,656	R	38.9	40.4	19.9	0.8	51	21	25	0.5	0.5	0.6	0.6	49.1	51.0
Nassau (NYC suburbs)[1]	609,326	282,593	246,881	77,097	2,755	35,712	D	46.4	40.5	12.7	0.5	31	20	56	0.6	0.6	0.6	0.4	53.4	46.6
Alameda (Oakland)	530,145	334,224	109,292	81,643	4,986	224,932	D	63.0	20.6	15.4	0.9	8	67	47	0.5	0.7	0.3	0.4	75.4	24.6
Broward (Fort Lauderdale)	533,050	276,361	164,832	90,937	920	111,529	D	51.8	30.9	17.1	0.2	19	49	39	0.5	0.6	0.4	0.5	62.6	37.4
Bronx (New York City)[1]	305,460	225,038	63,310	15,115	1,997	161,728	D	73.7	20.7	4.9	0.7	3	66	70	0.3	0.5	0.2	< .1	78.0	22.0
Bexar (San Antonio)	415,276	172,513	168,816	72,110	1,837	3,697	D	41.5	40.7	17.4	0.4	47	18	38	0.4	0.4	0.4	0.4	50.5	49.5
Riverside	430,275	166,241	159,457	102,233	2,344	6,784	D	38.6	37.1	23.8	0.5	54	33	12	0.4	0.4	0.4	0.5	51.0	49.0
Tarrant (Fort Worth)	471,396	156,230	183,387	129,998	1,781	27,157	R	33.1	38.9	27.6	0.4	66	27	2	0.5	0.3	0.5	0.7	46.0	54.0
Oakland (Detroit suburbs)	555,760	214,733	242,160	94,911	3,956	27,427	R	38.6	43.6	17.1	0.7	53	9	40	0.5	0.5	0.6	0.5	47.0	53.0
Sacramento	453,512	197,540	160,366	91,412	4,194	37,174	D	43.6	35.4	20.2	0.9	39	38	24	0.4	0.4	0.4	0.5	55.2	44.8
Hennepin (Minneapolis)	586,619	278,648	179,581	123,659	4,731	99,067	D	47.5	30.6	21.1	0.8	27	50	18	0.6	0.6	0.5	0.6	60.8	39.2
St. Louis Co. (suburbs)	534,763	235,760	188,285	109,099	1,619	47,475	D	44.1	35.2	20.4	0.3	36	39	22	0.5	0.5	0.5	0.6	55.6	44.4
Erie (Buffalo)[1]	451,496	196,233	129,444	123,358	2,461	66,789	D	43.5	28.7	27.3	0.5	40	55	3	0.4	0.4	0.3	0.6	60.3	39.7
Franklin (Columbus)	444,801	176,656	186,324	79,049	2,772	9,668	R	39.7	41.9	17.8	0.6	49	15	34	0.4	0.4	0.5	0.4	48.7	51.3
Milwaukee	465,496	235,521	151,314	76,039	2,622	84,207	D	50.6	32.5	16.3	0.6	21	43	44	0.4	0.5	0.4	0.4	60.9	39.1
Westchester (NYC suburbs)[1]	378,840	184,300	151,990	39,933	2,617	32,310	D	48.6	40.1	10.5	0.7	26	22	59	0.4	0.4	0.4	0.2	54.8	45.2
Hamilton (Cincinnati)	403,420	148,409	192,447	60,145	2,419	44,038	R	36.8	47.7	14.9	0.6	63	3	49	0.4	0.3	0.5	0.3	43.5	56.5
Palm Beach	405,251	187,869	140,350	76,243	789	47,519	D	46.4	34.6	18.8	0.2	32	40	30	0.4	0.4	0.4	0.4	57.2	42.8
Hartford	414,804	195,495	132,591	85,005	1,713	62,904	D	47.1	32.0	20.5	0.4	28	47	21	0.4	0.4	0.3	0.4	59.6	40.4
Pinellas (St. Petersburg)	422,851	160,528	159,121	101,257	1,945	1,407	D	38.0	37.6	23.9	0.5	56	31	11	0.4	0.4	0.4	0.5	50.2	49.8
Honolulu	265,841	123,908	103,937	35,728	2,268	19,971	D	46.6	39.1	13.4	0.9	30	26	52	0.3	0.3	0.3	0.2	54.4	45.6
Hillsborough (Tampa)	310,502	115,282	130,643	63,054	1,523	15,361	R	37.1	42.1	20.3	0.5	60	14	23	0.3	0.3	0.3	0.3	46.9	53.1
Fairfield (Bridgeport)	409,410	160,202	175,158	72,532	1,518	14,956	R	39.1	42.8	17.7	0.4	50	12	35	0.4	0.4	0.4	0.4	47.8	52.2
Shelby (Memphis)	366,110	191,322	153,310	20,223	1,255	38,012	D	52.3	41.9	5.5	0.3	18	16	68	0.4	0.4	0.4	0.1	55.5	44.5
Bergen (NYC suburbs)	403,137	171,104	178,223	52,082	1,728	7,119	R	42.4	44.2	12.9	0.4	42	6	54	0.4	0.4	0.5	0.3	49.0	51.0
Fairfax (DC suburbs)	385,280	160,186	170,488	53,012	1,594	10,302	R	41.6	44.3	13.8	0.4	45	5	50	0.4	0.4	0.4	0.3	48.4	51.6
New Haven (NYC suburbs)	385,132	161,374	141,264	80,817	1,677	20,110	D	41.9	36.7	21.0	0.4	44	35	19	0.4	0.4	0.4	0.4	53.3	46.7
Contra Costa (SF suburbs)	382,823	194,960	112,965	72,518	2,380	81,995	D	50.9	29.5	18.9	0.6	20	52	28	0.4	0.4	0.3	0.4	63.3	36.7
Marion (Indianapolis)	323,790	122,234	141,369	57,878	2,309	19,135	R	37.8	43.7	17.9	0.7	57	8	33	0.3	0.3	0.4	0.3	46.4	53.6
DuPage (Chicago suburbs)	370,987	114,564	178,271	76,839	1,313	63,707	R	30.9	48.1	20.7	0.4	70	2	20	0.4	0.3	0.5	0.4	39.1	60.9
Essex (Newark)	276,858	158,130	89,146	26,961	2,621	68,984	D	57.1	32.2	9.7	0.9	13	46	62	0.3	0.4	0.2	0.1	63.9	36.1
Montgomery (DC suburbs)	362,613	199,757	119,705	41,971	1,180	80,052	D	55.1	33.0	11.6	0.3	14	42	58	0.3	0.4	0.3	0.2	62.5	37.5
Clark (Las Vegas)	302,782	124,586	97,403	75,364	5,429	27,183	D	41.1	32.2	24.9	1.8	48	45	8	0.3	0.3	0.2	0.4	56.1	43.9
Baltimore City	245,091	185,753	40,725	17,381	1,232	145,028	D	75.8	16.6	7.1	0.5	2	69	66	0.2	0.4	0.1	< .1	82.0	18.0
Pr. George's (DC suburbs)	256,859	168,691	62,955	23,355	1,858	105,736	D	65.7	24.5	9.1	0.7	7	62	63	0.2	0.4	0.2	0.1	72.8	27.2
Salt Lake	318,661	100,082	117,247	91,968	9,364	17,165	R	31.4	36.8	28.9	2.9	69	34	1	0.3	0.2	0.3	0.5	46.1	53.9
San Francisco	322,207	233,263	57,352	29,018	2,574	175,911	D	72.4	17.8	9.0	0.8	4	68	64	0.5	0.5	0.1	0.1	80.3	19.7
Macomb (Detroit suburbs)	349,238	130,732	147,795	67,954	2,757	17,063	R	37.4	42.3	19.5	0.8	58	13	26	0.3	0.3	0.4	0.3	46.9	53.1
Monroe (Rochester)[1]	340,369	141,502	134,021	63,229	1,617	7,481	D	41.6	39.4	18.6	0.5	46	24	31	0.3	0.3	0.3	0.3	51.4	48.6
Worcester	315,782	138,122	101,984	74,051	1,625	36,138	D	43.7	32.3	23.5	0.5	37	44	13	0.3	0.3	0.3	0.4	57.5	42.5

[1]Democratic vote also includes ballots cast for Clinton-Gore as the nominees of Liberal party; Republican vote also includes ballots for Bush-Quayle as the nominees of Conservative and Right to Life parties.

County	All candidates					Plurality		Percent of total vote				Rank			Percent contribution to national vote				Major party Percent of vote	
	Total	Clinton (DEM)	Bush (REP)	Perot (IND)	Other	Total	Party	DEM	REP	IND	Other	DEM	REP	IND	Total	DEM	REP	IND	DEM	REP
Baltimore Co. (suburbs)	323,220	143,498	126,728	51,757	1,237	16,770	D	44.4	39.2	16.0	0.4	35	25	45	0.3	0.3	0.3	0.3	53.1	46.9
Montgomery (Phil suburbs)	318,576	136,572	125,704	53,738	2,562	10,868	D	42.9	39.5	16.9	0.8	41	23	41	0.3	0.3	0.3	0.3	52.1	47.9
Orange (Orlando)	237,011	82,683	108,788	44,844	696	26,105	R	34.9	45.9	18.9	0.3	65	4	29	0.2	0.2	0.3	0.2	43.2	56.8
Duval (Jacksonville)	249,926	92,098	123,631	33,388	809	31,533	R	36.9	49.5	13.4	0.3	62	1	51	0.2	0.2	0.3	0.2	42.7	57.3
Middlesex (New Brunswick)	285,271	128,824	108,701	45,055	2,691	20,123	D	45.2	38.1	15.8	0.9	34	29	46	0.3	0.3	0.3	0.2	54.2	45.8
Essex (Boston suburbs)..	322,328	140,593	102,212	77,459	2,064	38,381	D	43.6	31.7	24.0	0.6	38	48	9	0.3	0.3	0.3	0.4	57.9	42.1
Ventura	267,647	99,011	94,911	71,844	1,881	4,100	D	37.0	35.5	26.8	0.7	61	37	4	0.3	0.2	0.2	0.4	51.1	48.9
Fresno	219,161	92,418	89,137	36,299	1,307	3,281	D	42.2	40.7	16.6	0.6	43	19	43	0.2	0.2	0.2	0.2	50.9	49.1
Pima (Tucson).................	281,484	128,569	97,036	53,925	1,954	31,533	D	45.7	34.5	19.2	0.7	33	41	27	0.3	0.3	0.2	0.3	57.0	43.0
Jefferson (Louisville)	309,793	152,728	116,566	39,822	677	36,162	D	49.3	37.6	12.9	0.2	24	30	55	0.3	0.3	0.3	0.2	56.7	43.3
Suffolk (Boston)	219,273	132,921	51,378	32,914	2,060	81,543	D	60.6	23.4	15.0	0.9	10	63	48	0.2	0.3	0.1	0.2	72.1	27.9
Top 70 (Subtotal)	**35,941,072**	**17,170,116**	**12,240,039**	**6,302,626**	**228,291**	**4,930,077**	**D**	**47.8**	**34.1**	**17.5**	**0.6**				**34.4**	**38.2**	**31.3**	**31.9**	**58.4**	**41.6**
UNITED STATES.............	**104,425,026**	**44,909,326**	**39,103,882**	**19,741,657**	**670,161**	**5,805,444**	**D**	**43.0**	**37.4**	**18.9**	**0.6**				**100.0**	**100.0**	**100.0**	**100.0**	**53.5**	**46.5**

Top/Bottom 70 Counties: 1990 Population by Race and Ethnic Origin (Table A)

Counties lowest percent Non-Hispanic White	%	Counties highest percent Non-Hispanic Black	%	Counties highest percent Non-Hispanic Asian & Pacific Islander	%	Counties highest percent Non-Hispanic Native American	%	Counties highest percent Hispanic	%
TX Starr	2.5	MS Jefferson	85.9	HI Kalawao	73.1	SD Shannon	93.1	TX Starr	97.2
TX Maverick	4.3	AL Macon	85.4	HI Honolulu	59.8	WI Menominee	88.0	TX Webb	93.9
SD Shannon	5.0	MS Claiborne	81.8	HI Kauai	56.5	AK 38 Nome-Yukon River¹	82.4	TX Maverick	93.5
TX Webb	5.6	AL Greene	80.4	HI Maui	54.0	SD Todd	81.3	TX Jim Hogg	91.2
TX Zavala	7.8	GA Hancock	79.0	HI Hawaii	52.5	AK 37 Northwest Alaska¹	79.7	TX Zavala	89.4
TX Jim Hogg	8.3	MS Holmes	75.6	CA San Francisco	28.4	AK 39 Bethel-Dillingham¹	78.2	TX Brooks	89.4
TX Brooks	10.0	MS Tunica	74.6	CA Santa Clara	16.8	SD Buffalo	77.5	TX Duval	87.2
WI Menominee	10.6	AL Lowndes	74.3	CA San Mateo	16.2	AZ Apache	77.0	TX Hidalgo	85.3
TX Duval	12.4	AL Bullock	72.0	CA Alameda	14.4	ND Sioux	74.8	TX Willacy	85.0
NM Rio Arriba	12.7	VA Petersburg City	71.6	CA Solano	11.9	NM McKinley	70.4	TX Willacy	84.4
MS Jefferson	13.6	AL Sumter	69.9	NY Queens	11.8	ND Rolette	66.2	NM Guadalupe	84.3
AL Macon	13.8	AL Wilcox	68.8	CA San Joaquin	11.6	SD Dewey	66.0	TX Dimmit	83.3
TX Hidalgo	14.1	MS Noxubee	68.0	AK 06 Kodiak Island¹	10.3	SD Ziebach	62.8	TX Cameron	81.9
NM Guadalupe	14.4	SC Allendale	67.7	CA Los Angeles	10.2	AK 36 Rural Interior¹	61.4	TX Presidio	81.6
NM Mora	14.4	MS Humphreys	67.4	CA Orange	10.0	MT Glacier	55.9	TX Zapata	81.0
TX Willacy	15.0	MS Wilkinson	67.3	CA Contra Costa	9.2	MT Big Horn	54.5	NM San Miguel	79.6
NM McKinley	15.8	MS Sharkey	65.9	AK 40 Aleutians¹	9.0	UT San Juan	53.7	TX Kenedy	78.7
TX Dimmit	15.9	DC District of Columbia	65.1	CA Sutter	8.9	AZ Navajo	51.2	AZ Santa Cruz	78.2
AK 38 Nome-Yukon River¹	16.1	LA East Carroll	64.6	CA Sacramento	8.8	MT Roosevelt	48.1	TX La Salle	77.4
AK 37 Northwest Alaska¹	16.3	MS Coahoma	64.2	VA Fairfax	8.3	SD Corson	47.7	CO Costilla	76.9
SD Todd	17.0	AL Perry	64.2	MD Montgomery	8.1	SD Mellette	46.4	TX Reeves	72.8
MS Claiborne	17.4	SC Williamsburg	64.0	CA Yolo	8.1	SD Bennett	45.6	NM Rio Arriba	72.6
TX Cameron	17.4	MS Sunflower	63.9	CA Fresno	8.1	OK Adair	43.3	TX Frio	72.4
TX Presidio	18.0	VA Charles City	63.1	CA Yuba	7.9	NE Thurston	43.3	TX Jim Wells	72.2
NM San Miguel	18.2	GA Stewart	63.1	CA Merced	7.9	SD Jackson	42.0	TX Culberson	71.0
AZ Apache	18.4	MS Bolivar	62.6	WA King	7.7	MT Blaine	39.2	TX Val Verde	70.5
HI Kalawao	18.5	SC Lee	62.3	AK 13 Coastal Trail¹	7.5	ND Benson	38.3	TX El Paso	69.6
TX Zapata	18.6	GA Talbot	62.0	CA San Diego	7.4	NC Robeson	38.3	TX Hudspeth	66.4
AL Greene	19.4	NC Bertie	61.4	AK 15 Spenard-Downtown¹	7.2	NM Cibola	37.6	CA Imperial	65.8
AK 39 Bethel-Dillingham¹	19.6	LA Orleans	61.4	NY New York	7.1	NM San Juan	36.1	NM Taos	64.9
GA Hancock	20.1	SC Bamberg	61.3	CA Monterey	7.1	AK 05 Southeast Islands¹	35.4	TX Kleberg	61.2
TX Kenedy	20.2	MS Leflore	60.4	CA Fairfax City	7.0	OK Cherokee	33.0	TX Uvalde	60.4
AZ Santa Cruz	20.8	GA Clay	60.4	AK 16 Fairview-Mt. View¹	7.0	AZ Coconino	28.7	CO Conejos	59.9
TX La Salle	21.0	GA Warren	60.2	AK 12 Sand Lake¹	6.9	SD Lyman	28.6	TX Pecos	56.8
CO Costilla	21.6	GA Taliaferro	60.2	VA Arlington	6.5	NC Swain	27.0	NM Dona Ana	56.4
SD Buffalo	22.3	GA Terrell	59.7	NJ Middlesex	6.5	MT Rosebud	26.0	TX Terrell	53.3
NY Bronx	22.6	LA Madison	59.3	NJ Bergen	6.5	AK 40 Aleutians¹	25.9	TX Atascosa	52.6
MS Holmes	23.9	AL Hale	59.2	TX Fort Bend	6.2	OK Delaware	25.1	TX Nueces	52.2
ND Sioux	24.1	MS Quitman	59.0	AK 20 Midtown¹	5.5	MN Mahnomen	23.5	TX Edwards	52.2
MS Tunica	24.3	NC Northampton	58.9	WA Whitman	5.4	CA Alpine	23.1	TX Bee	51.4
TX Reeves	24.7	MD Baltimore City	58.9	OR Benton	5.4	SD Roberts	22.9	NM Grant	50.8
AL Lowndes	25.1	GA Calhoun	58.7	NY Tompkins	5.4	SD Charles Mix	21.7	TX San Patricio	50.7
TX El Paso	25.6	GA Macon	58.5	AK 11 West Anchorage¹	5.3	OK Caddo	21.2	TX Kinney	50.3
TX Frio	26.0	SC McCormick	58.4	MN Ramsey	5.0	OK Sequoyah	20.5	NM Valencia	50.3
VA Petersburg City	26.2	VA Brunswick	58.3	IL DuPage	5.0	MT Lake	20.5	NM Hidalgo	50.1
TX Jim Wells	26.8	VA Sussex	58.1	AK 14 Elmendorf¹	5.0	OK Okfuskee	20.0	TX Bexar	49.7
TX Val Verde	26.9	SC Fairfield	58.1	MA Suffolk	4.9	ND Mountrail	19.8	TX Crockett	49.6
AL Bullock	27.3	MS Tallahatchie	58.1	CA Ventura	4.9	AK 16 Fairview-Mt. View¹	19.3	NM Santa Fe	49.5
NM Cibola	27.3	SC Orangeburg	57.9	CA Stanislaus	4.9	NM Sandoval	19.2	FL Dade	49.2
DC District of Columbia	27.4	GA Randolph	57.7	AK 19 Lake Otis & Tudor¹	4.9	OK Craig	19.0	TX Deaf Smith	48.8
NM Taos	27.7	AL Dallas	57.7	AK 17 Dimond-Campbell¹	4.8	OR Jefferson	18.7	NM Colfax	47.9
TX Culberson	27.9	NC Hertford	57.5	WA Pierce	4.7	OK McIntosh	18.1	NM Socorro	47.8
VA Charles City	28.6	MS Washington	57.5	VA Falls Church City	4.7	OK Ottawa	18.0	NM Luna	47.6
CA Imperial	29.0	FL Gadsden	57.5	OR Multnomah	4.6	OK Mayes	17.9	TX Karnes	47.5
AL Sumter	29.3	SC Jasper	57.3	NY Kings	4.6	WA Ferry	17.8	NM Harding	46.7
HI Honolulu	29.9	AR Lee	57.1	IA Story	4.6	AK 02 Sitka-Wrangell¹	17.6	TX Castro	46.2
FL Dade	30.2	NC Warren	56.9	IL Champaign	4.6	WY Fremont	17.5	CA San Benito	45.6
SC Allendale	30.7	SC Clarendon	56.3	AK 21 East Anchorage¹	4.6	OK Hughes	16.9	CO Saguache	45.6
AL Wilcox	30.8	AR Chicot	56.1	NY Richmond	4.3	OK Seminole	16.7	TX Sutton	45.1
MS Noxubee	31.4	NC Edgecombe	55.8	NJ Somerset	4.3	OK Coal	16.3	TX Medina	44.4
MS Humphreys	31.6	MS Issaquena	55.8	MD Howard	4.3	MN Beltrami	16.3	CO Las Animas	44.2
HI Kauai	31.7	GA Jefferson	55.7	OR Washington	4.2	AK 03 Downtown Juneau¹	16.3	NY Bronx	43.5
MS Wilkinson	32.1	VA Surry	55.5	AK 03 Downtown Juneau¹	4.2	OK Nowata	16.2	AZ Greenlee	43.2
TX Hudspeth	32.8	MS Kemper	55.2	VA Virginia Beach City	4.1	MI Mackinac	15.8	TX Reagan	43.0
ND Rolette	32.9	VA Richmond City	55.0	VA Alexandria City	4.1	OK Johnston	15.5	TX Dawson	42.7
SD Dewey	32.9	VA Greensville	55.0	MI Washtenaw	4.1	MT Hill	15.4	TX Crosby	42.6
LA Orleans	33.1	LA West Feliciana	54.9	CA Santa Barbara	4.1	OK Latimer	15.1	TX Brewster	42.6
MS Sharkey	33.1	SC Marion	54.5	WA Kitsap	4.0	OK Pushmataha	15.0	TX Cochran	42.4
LA East Carroll	33.9	AR Phillips	54.5	WA Island	4.0	WI Sawyer	14.9	TX Lynn	41.7
TX Kleberg	34.0	MS Jefferson Davis	54.4					TX Hale	41.6
UNITED STATES	75.6	UNITED STATES	11.7	UNITED STATES	2.8	UNITED STATES	0.7	UNITED STATES	9.0

¹Election district (not borough or Census area).

Top/Bottom 70 Counties: Voter Participation, November 3, 1992, General Election (Table C)

Counties lowest percent Voter Registration of 92 VAP	%	Counties highest percent Voter Turnout of 92 VAP	%	Counties lowest percent Voter Turnout of 92 VAP	%	Counties highest percent Voter Turnout of 92 REG	%	Counties lowest percent Voter Turnout of 92 REG	%
GA Chattahoochee	18.4	OK Washington	134.7	GA Chattahoochee	11.0	OK Washington	136.7	MS Tunica	36.0
GA Liberty	28.4	CO Hinsdale	125.8	GA Liberty	20.3	AL DeKalb	101.7	SD Shannon	37.5
NC Onslow	31.2	TX Loving	124.7	NC Onslow	20.5	AL Choctaw	98.9	MS Leflore	41.3
TX Coryell	42.1	CO Mineral	115.5	TX Webb	27.4	FL Collier	96.0	MS Sunflower	42.4
GA Camden	42.6	UT Daggett	99.8	GA Camden	29.6	KS Atchison	93.1	GA Wheeler	45.9
VA Manassas Park City	43.2	NM Harding	97.8	SD Shannon	30.6	AL Colbert	92.8	OK McCurtain	46.4
VA Harrisonburg City	44.5	WY Teton	95.4	TX Coryell	30.8	VA Falls Church City	92.7	MS Choctaw	47.6
FL Dade	44.7	NY Hamilton	93.6	TX Maverick	30.9	NM Los Alamos	92.5	TX Webb	47.7
VA Radford City	44.9	NE Blaine	93.6	KY Christian	31.7	KS Kingman	92.5	MS Jones	47.8
LA Vernon	46.1	CO Custer	93.0	TX El Paso	32.4	UT Morgan	91.3	SD Todd	47.8
MO Pulaski	46.1	CO San Miguel	92.5	NC Cumberland	32.9	NM Lincoln	91.2	GA Clinch	48.3
KY Christian	46.3	ID Camas	92.4	TX Cameron	33.1	VA Hanover	91.1	KY Breathitt	48.4
VA Williamsburg City	46.5	TX Real	91.3	TX Starr	33.1	AL Russell	91.1	SD Buffalo	48.8
KS Geary	46.6	ND Billings	90.7	TX Hidalgo	33.4	NY Schuyler	90.9	TN Hancock	48.9
SC Berkeley	46.8	ID Valley	90.4	SD Todd	33.5	IL Effingham	90.8	TX Culberson	49.0
VA Norfolk City	47.7	MN Cook	89.8	LA Vernon	33.6	KS Republic	90.6	AL Wilcox	49.1
FL Orange	48.4	MI Keweenaw	89.3	NC Wayne	34.5	KS Haskell	90.6	MS Montgomery	49.4
IN Lagrange	48.5	AK 18 Hillside¹	89.3	MO Pulaski	34.6	KS Sheridan	90.5	MS Tippah	49.8
SC Sumter	48.5	MT Prairie	89.0	CA Kings	35.2	VA Roanoke	90.4	KY Martin	50.1
SC Laurens	48.9	CO San Juan	89.0	VA Norfolk City	35.7	VA Goochland	90.4	AL Covington	50.6
CA Kings	49.1	SD Sully	88.8	GA Murray	35.8	NJ Warren	90.4	NC Swain	50.7
HI Honolulu	49.2	CO Ouray	88.6	NY Kings	35.8	KS Chase	90.4	TN Marion	51.3
AL Russell	49.4	UT Rich	88.3	KS Geary	35.9	AK 26 Wasilla-Chugiak²	90.4	MS Lafayette	51.5
VA Lexington City	49.5	TX Roberts	88.1	VA Manassas Park City	36.6	NE Blaine	90.3	MO Pemiscot	51.8
PA Mifflin	50.2	MT Judith Basin	87.4	AK 40 Aleutians¹	36.7	WY Sheridan	90.2	NC Scotland	52.0
VA Montgomery	50.2	MA Nantucket	87.3	NY Bronx	36.8	KS Lane	90.1	OK Adair	52.8
GA Baldwin	50.3	ND Slope	87.2	FL Dade	36.9	AK 28 Rural Mat-Su²	89.9	AL Chambers	53.0
AK 40 Aleutians¹	50.4	CO Kiowa	87.2	VA Harrisonburg City	36.9	CT Tolland	89.8	MS Scott	53.1
TX El Paso	50.4	OK Pittsburg	87.1	AZ Yuma	37.1	WA San Juan	89.7	MS Tate	53.2
SC Spartanburg	50.5	NM Catron	86.7	CA Imperial	37.2	VA Powhatan	89.7	AL Dallas	53.4
TN Montgomery	50.6	UT Piute	86.5	IN Lagrange	37.3	KS Barton	89.7	MO Dent	53.4
GA Tift	50.7	OK Coal	86.0	NY Queens	37.4	AL Lauderdale	89.7	OK Haskell	53.4
AL DeKalb	50.8	NE Keya Paha	86.0	SC Sumter	37.4	OR Wheeler	89.5	OK Payne	53.4
KS Riley	51.0	UT Wayne	85.9	VA Radford City	37.6	KS Wichita	89.5	TX Frio	53.4
PA Union	51.1	AZ Greenlee	85.7	NC Scotland	37.8	AK 09 Kenai²	89.5	OK Choctaw	53.5
SC Pickens	51.1	MT Treasure	85.5	TX Culberson	37.9	VA Fauquier	89.4	MS Warren	53.8
NM Cibola	51.2	ID Boise	85.5	TX Anderson	38.0	KS Ness	89.4	MS Yazoo	53.8
VA Prince William	51.2	KS Wallace	84.9	GA Baldwin	38.2	KS Morton	89.4	OK Johnston	53.8
SC Chesterfield	51.5	CO Jackson	84.8	NC Hoke	38.2	MO Platte	89.3	MS Humphreys	53.9
MD Caroline	51.6	MN Lake	84.7	SC Berkeley	38.2	KS Clark	89.2	KY Wolfe	54.3
NC Cumberland	51.6	UT Morgan	84.6	GA Tift	38.3	NY Delaware	89.1	TX Zavala	54.3
SC York	51.7	NE Grant	84.4	SC Laurens	38.3	KS Sherman	89.1	TX Starr	54.4
AZ Yuma	51.8	AK 33 Northeast Fairbanks¹	84.4	GA Bartow	38.8	KS Leavenworth	89.1	GA Seminole	54.5
MD Somerset	52.1	MA Dukes	84.3	TX Walker	38.8	FL Orange	89.1	KY Knox	54.5
SC Anderson	52.2	MT McCone	84.1	GA Chattooga	38.9	WA Thurston	89.0	MS Stone	54.5
VA Winchester City	52.3	MT Daniels	84.0	GA Colquitt	38.9	IL Boone	89.0	MS Covington	54.6
GA Bartow	52.4	IL Hardin	84.0	GA Ben Hill	39.0	VA Henrico	88.7	MS Marion	54.6
TX Walker	52.5	UT Summit	83.8	GA Spalding	39.0	RI Bristol	88.7	MS Neshoba	54.6
KS Leavenworth	52.8	NM Mora	83.8	KY Lincoln	39.1	NY Seneca	88.7	MS Holmes	54.7
NM Curry	52.9	NE McPherson	83.6	GA Bulloch	39.2	NY Monroe	88.7	NC Hertford	54.7
PA Snyder	52.9	OR Gilliam	83.5	GA Muscogee	39.2	IA Audubon³	88.7	MS Hancock	54.8
SC Greenwood	52.9	MT Chouteau	83.5	VA Williamsburg City	39.3	UT Garfield	88.6	OK Oklahoma	54.9
TX Bell	53.2	VT Grand Isle	83.4	GA Coffee	39.4	NY Livingston	88.6	TX Duval	54.9
NY Queens	53.4	SD Hand	83.4	TX Presidio	39.4	VA Fairfax City	88.5	KY Clay	55.0
VA Charlottesville City	53.4	LA St. Helena	83.4	GA Cook	39.5	VA Prince William	88.5	NC Robeson	55.0
VA Fredericksburg City	53.4	TX Kent	83.3	SC Pickens	39.5	KS Johnson	88.5	TX Maverick	55.0
GA Whitfield	53.5	AK 34 North Pole-Denali¹	83.0	TX Bell	39.6	VA Augusta	88.4	WV Lincoln	55.0
NC Wayne	53.5	WA San Juan	82.9	GA Cherokee	39.9	KS Hodgeman	88.4	MS Perry	55.1
VA Prince George	53.5	SD Jones	82.9	GA Jackson	40.0	FL Lee	88.4	MS Greene	55.6
GA Walker	53.6	SD Jerauld	82.8	NC Harnett	40.0	CO Sedgwick	88.4	KY Jackson	55.7
NM Otero	53.6	CO Grand	82.7	AZ Santa Cruz	40.1	AK 18 Hillside²	88.4	MS Quitman	55.8
TX Potter	53.6	NE Hooker	82.4	AR Mississippi	40.1	PA Lebanon	88.3	OK Pushmataha	56.0
CA Imperial	53.7	ND Steele	82.2	GA Brooks	40.1	NY Broome	88.3	IL Alexander	56.1
PA Clinton	53.8	NE Loup	82.2	GA Walker	40.1	MD Howard	88.3	KY Elliott	56.2
VA Virginia Beach City	54.0	SD Stanley	81.9	GA Lowndes	40.2	AK 29 University²	88.3	KY Leslie	56.3
AZ Santa Cruz	54.1	KS Rawlins	81.9	TN Montgomery	40.2	WY Platte	88.2	SD Dewey	56.3
FL Hendry	54.2	MN Grant	81.8	WV McDowell	40.2	VA Rockingham	88.2	WV Mingo	56.4
FL Polk	54.2	ID Clark	81.8	GA Crisp	40.3	VA New Kent	88.2	KY Johnson	56.5
GA Muscogee	54.4	MT Carter	81.6	CA Merced	40.4	PA Schuylkill	88.2	TX Jim Hogg	56.5
LA West Feliciana	54.4	ID Oneida	81.4	KY Hardin	40.4	PA Adams	88.2	GA Atkinson	56.6
UNITED STATES	70.6	UNITED STATES	56.0	UNITED STATES	56.0	UNITED STATES	79.3	UNITED STATES	79.3

¹Election district (not borough or Census area); percentages of Voting Age Population (VAP) based on 1990, rather than 1992 VAP data.   ²Election district (not borough or Census area).   ³Voter turnout not officially certified by Iowa Secretary of State at time of publication.

Top/Bottom 70 Counties: Vote for President, November 3, 1992 General Election (Table E)

Counties highest percent Vote for Clinton (DEM)	%	Counties lowest percent Vote for Clinton (DEM)	%	Counties highest percent Vote for Bush (REP)	%	Counties lowest percent Vote for Bush (REP)	%
DC District of Columbia	84.6	NE Arthur	6.8	KY Jackson	75.0	DC District of Columbia	9.1
TX Starr	82.8	ID Madison	9.5	IA Sioux	72.2	AL Macon	12.9
AL Macon	82.8	ID Franklin	12.9	TX Hansford	69.1	TX Starr	13.1
TX Duval	79.6	NE Hayes	13.0	TX Ochiltree	68.1	SD Shannon	13.6
MS Jefferson	79.4	UT Utah	13.0	AL Shelby	68.0	TX Duval	13.9
AL Greene	79.2	UT Kane	13.6	MS Rankin	67.8	TX Zavala	14.8
TX Zavala	79.1	ID Jefferson	13.7	KY Rockcastle	67.1	TX Brooks	15.5
NY New York¹	78.2	NE Blaine	14.1	TX Glasscock	66.0	MT Deer Lodge	15.8
GA Hancock	78.0	UT Box Elder	14.1	NE McPherson	66.0	NY New York²	15.9
SD Shannon	76.7	NE Banner	14.2	MS Newton	65.7	GA Hancock	16.0
TX Brooks	75.9	TX Hansford	14.4	SD Haakon	65.3	MS Jefferson	16.0
MD Baltimore City	75.8	NE Holt	14.6	KY Monroe	65.1	AL Greene	16.5
TN Jackson	75.3	NE Thomas	14.7	WV Grant	64.3	MD Baltimore City	16.6
KY Knott	75.1	NE Loup	14.9	KY Clay	63.9	TN Jackson	16.6
MS Claiborne	74.8	NE McPherson	14.9	KY Clinton	63.8	KY Knott	17.0
AR Woodruff	74.1	IA Sioux	15.1	KY Russell	63.7	MO St. Louis City	17.3
NY Bronx¹	73.7	MT Garfield	15.3	KS Wallace	63.7	KY Elliott	17.6
TX Dimmit	72.4	KS Wallace	15.4	TX Roberts	63.4	CA San Francisco	17.8
CA San Francisco	72.4	NE Hooker	15.4	MS Lamar	63.4	KY Floyd	19.0
TX Jim Hogg	72.0	UT Garfield	15.6	VA Colonial Heights City	63.1	MT Silver Bow	19.2
WV McDowell	71.8	UT Millard	15.6	NC Mitchell	62.8	AR Woodruff	19.3
TN Smith	71.8	KS Stevens	15.7	KY Casey	62.6	TX Dimmit	19.3
KY Floyd	71.5	TX Ochiltree	15.7	IN Hamilton	62.5	WV McDowell	19.8
KY Elliott	71.1	UT Washington	15.7	UT Garfield	62.3	WV Logan	20.5
NY Kings¹	70.7	SD Harding	15.8	MS Lauderdale	62.3	CA Alameda	20.6
MO St. Louis City	69.4	SD Haakon	15.9	TX Sherman	62.2	CO Lake	20.7
TN Trousdale	69.3	UT Cache	16.2	NE Hooker	62.2	NY Bronx²	20.7
AR Jefferson	68.8	NE Garden	16.3	TX McMullen	61.9	CO Costilla	20.9
AR Chicot	68.7	NE Rock	16.4	VA Poquoson City	61.7	PA Philadelphia	20.9
AR Clay	68.5	UT Iron	16.4	TX Randall	61.6	WV Boone	20.9
AL Sumter	68.5	NE Keya Paha	16.6	KY Owsley	61.4	TN Smith	21.0
TN Grundy	68.3	UT Sevier	16.6	MS Neshoba	61.1	WI Menominee	21.0
GA Taliaferro	68.3	NE Grant	16.7	KY Cumberland	61.0	KS Wyandotte	21.1
VA Petersburg City	68.2	NE Brown	16.8	MS Clarke	60.7	MS Claiborne	21.2
TN Houston	68.2	NE Phelps	16.9	VA Rockingham	60.6	NM Taos	21.2
PA Philadelphia	68.2	UT Duchesne	16.9	SC Lexington	60.5	TN Trousdale	21.2
WV Logan	68.1	KY Jackson	17.1	NE Thomas	60.5	TX Presidio	21.2
WV Boone	68.1	NE Madison	17.1	MS Smith	60.5	TX Stonewall	21.5
MS Holmes	68.0	NE Antelope	17.2	TX Parmer	60.3	MA Berkshire	21.7
AL Lowndes	68.0	NE Pierce	17.2	TX Hartley	60.2	CA Mendocino	21.8
NM Rio Arriba	67.9	ID Caribou	17.4	NE Logan	60.1	CA Santa Cruz	21.9
AR Desha	67.9	NE Platte	17.4	UT Rich	59.9	ID Shoshone	22.0
AR Lee	67.8	TX Glasscock	17.4	UT Iron	59.9	TN Houston	22.0
AL Bullock	67.7	MT Carter	17.6	NE Loup	59.9	TX Newton	22.0
WV Mingo	67.5	NE Cuming	17.6	TX Hale	59.6	GA Clay	22.1
TN Overton	67.5	TX McMullen	17.6	OK Beaver	59.6	OK Jefferson	22.2
LA Orleans	67.5	UT Rich	17.6	NE Rock	59.6	MA Hampshire	22.4
CO Costilla	67.3	ID Cassia	17.7	VA Hanover	59.4	CO Pitkin	22.6
VA Charles City	66.7	NE Logan	17.7	OK Cimarron	59.4	MN St. Louis	22.6
NM Taos	66.0	UT Morgan	17.7	NE Banner	59.2	NM Santa Fe	22.6
NM San Miguel	65.9	UT Uintah	17.7	TX Oldham	59.1	TX Jim Hogg	22.7
GA Webster	65.9	NE Sheridan	17.9	MI Ottawa	59.1	WV Webster	22.7
GA Talbot	65.9	NE Perkins	18.0	ID Madison	59.1	AR Desha	22.8
MD Prince George's	65.7	ND Billings	18.1	GA Columbia	59.1	GA Webster	22.8
AR Jackson	65.7	TX Rockwall	18.1	VA Augusta	59.0	NY Kings²	22.9
TX La Salle	65.6	ID Fremont	18.2	TX Lubbock	59.0	TN Grundy	22.9
AR Phillips	65.6	UT Davis	18.3	TX Gray	58.9	GA Calhoun	23.0
KY Breathitt	65.5	IN Hamilton	18.4	KY Pulaski	58.8	MN Lake	23.0
GA Macon	65.4	KS Haskell	18.4	SD Harding	58.5	PA Greene	23.0
NC Warren	65.3	NE Sioux	18.5	TX Midland	58.4	UT Carbon	23.1
TN DeKalb	65.2	NE Cherry	18.7	MS DeSoto	58.4	MA Dukes	23.2
NC Northampton	65.2	NV Eureka	18.7	SD Jones	58.3	NM Rio Arriba	23.2
NC Bertie	65.0	TX Kendall	18.7	NE Keya Paha	58.3	NC Northampton	23.2
GA Clay	65.0	ID Oneida	18.8	KY Leslie	58.3	AR Clay	23.3
WV Webster	64.9	KS Kiowa	18.8	AL Houston	58.3	CA Marin	23.3
MS Wilkinson	64.9	NE Keith	18.8	TX Hemphill	58.2	MO Reynolds	23.3
AL Wilcox	64.8	KS Scott	18.9	OK Texas	58.2	NM San Miguel	23.3
TN Perry	64.7	NE Wheeler	19.0	KY Adair	58.2	MA Suffolk	23.4
MS Tunica	64.7	TX Collin	19.0	FL Clay	58.0	CO San Miguel	23.6
AR Clark	64.6	NE Boone	19.1	KY McCreary	57.8	AR Jefferson	23.7
UNITED STATES	43.0	UNITED STATES	43.0	UNITED STATES	37.4	UNITED STATES	37.4

¹Also includes votes for Clinton-Gore as nominees of the Liberal party. ²Also includes votes for Bush-Quayle as nominees of the Conservative and Right to Life parties.

Top/Bottom 70 Counties: Vote for President and Drop-Off, November 3, 1992 General Election (Tables E and C)

Counties highest percent Vote for Perot (IND)	%	Counties lowest percent Vote for Perot (IND)	%	Counties highest percent Presidential Drop-off	%	Counties highest percent Senatorial Drop-off	%	Counties highest percent Gubernatorial Drop-off	%
TX Loving	46.9	AL Macon	3.2	OK Washington	50.6	OK Washington	54.7	IN Spencer	19.5
CO San Juan	40.4	AL Wilcox	3.3	MS Carroll	32.2	GA Stewart	37.8	IN Gibson	15.9
AK 28 Rural Mat-Su¹	40.2	MS Holmes	3.4	OK Pittsburg	29.6	KY McCreary	37.2	IN Scott	15.8
ND Billings	39.8	MS Claiborne	3.6	CO Huerfano	25.5	OK Pittsburg	33.7	WV Summers	13.3
ME Somerset	39.0	AL Perry	3.7	CO Sedgwick	25.2	WI Menominee	32.5	MT Powder River	12.6
NV Esmeralda	37.7	TX Starr	3.7	NV Humboldt	24.9	GA Charlton	32.5	IN Dearborn	11.9
KS Wabaunsee	37.2	AL Greene	4.0	MS Holmes	24.6	KY Owsley	32.1	IN Crawford	10.7
NE Arthur	36.9	MS Noxubee	4.0	MS Tallahatchie	24.4	OK Coal	30.7	IN Switzerland	10.6
AK 09 Kenai¹	36.9	MS Washington	4.0	OK Coal	24.3	GA Quitman	29.2	RI Newport	9.7
ME Piscataquis	36.8	MS Bolivar	4.2	OK Logan	17.1	KY Monroe	28.8	IN Clark	9.2
CO Moffat	36.8	DC District of Columbia	4.3	IN Spencer	16.8	KY Todd	28.2	UT San Juan	8.2
NV Storey	36.2	MS Copiah	4.3	CO Alamosa	16.8	GA Talbot	27.7	IN Washington	8.1
MT Phillips	36.2	MS Tunica	4.3	OH Holmes	16.3	KY Bell	27.3	ND Burleigh	8.0
ME Waldo	36.2	MS Jefferson	4.4	OR Umatilla	16.0	CO Sedgwick	26.9	IN De Kalb	8.0
AK 26 Wasilla-Chugiak¹	36.2	MS Coahoma	4.6	FL Hernando	15.8	KY Letcher	26.8	IN Warrick	7.9
AK 08 Seward-Soldotna¹	36.1	MS Leflore	4.9	MS Amite	14.6	AL Henry	26.8	IN Lake	7.8
ID Adams	35.9	NY Bronx	4.9	MS Monroe	13.8	KY Clay	25.8	IN Franklin	7.6
TX Cooke	35.6	AR Crittenden	5.0	OK Kay	13.6	OR Jackson	25.2	NH Coos	7.5
ND Bowman	35.6	MS Quitman	5.1	MS Panola	12.5	KY Whitley	24.8	MT Valley	7.0
KS Chase	35.6	TN Pickett	5.1	OK Woods	12.3	GA Clinch	24.7	IN Starke	7.0
ID Blaine	35.3	TX Jim Hogg	5.1	KS Kingman	12.2	AL Conecuh	24.6	IN Jennings	6.9
TX Somervell	35.2	NY New York	5.2	IN Gibson	12.0	GA Echols	24.3	IN Fayette	6.9
CO Eagle	35.2	TN Haywood	5.2	WA Yakima	11.9	GA Hancock	24.1	IN Dubois	6.8
TX Irion	34.9	MS Sharkey	5.3	WA Franklin	11.8	KY Powell	24.0	RI Bristol	6.7
TX Grayson	34.8	AL Bullock	5.5	MS Jefferson Davis	11.8	GA Atkinson	23.8	NC Madison	6.7
KS Anderson	34.8	AL Lowndes	5.5	MS Harrison	11.8	GA Webster	23.5	WV Logan	6.6
KS Russell	34.7	AL Sumter	5.5	MS Yalobusha	11.7	KY Nicholas	23.2	WV Hancock	6.6
KS Jackson	34.7	LA Orleans	5.5	NV Lander	11.6	AL Barbour	23.2	NC Bertie	6.5
CA Trinity	34.7	MS Humphreys	5.5	MI Menominee	11.6	AL Cleburne	23.0	IN Cass	6.5
KS Rooks	34.4	MS Marshall	5.5	FL Baker	11.5	KY Pendleton	22.6	WV Raleigh	6.4
KS Pottawatomie	34.4	TN Shelby	5.5	MS Newton	11.4	AR Stone	22.5	IN Lawrence	6.4
KS Morris	34.4	MS Hinds	5.6	CA Trinity	11.4	FL Sarasota	22.0	IN Jasper	6.4
AK 27 Palmer¹	34.4	AL Dallas	5.7	FL Santa Rosa	11.3	AL Covington	21.9	WV Wayne	6.3
MT Garfield	34.3	NY Kings	5.7	MS Tate	10.6	OK Logan	21.7	RI Providence	6.3
ME Hancock	34.2	GA Hancock	6.0	FL Dixie	10.6	AL Geneva	21.6	NH Merrimack	6.3
KS Osage	34.1	GA Stewart	6.0	OK Grady	10.1	AL Clay	21.6	IN Wabash	6.3
KS Harper	34.1	MS Lauderdale	6.0	MS Stone	9.7	KY Perry	21.5	MO Newton	6.2
TX Denton	34.0	AR Lee	6.1	MS Kemper	9.7	GA Dade	21.0	IN Grant	6.2
KS Jefferson	34.0	AR Mississippi	6.1	MS Copiah	9.7	GA Telfair	20.9	DE Sussex	6.2
KS Barton	33.7	SC Allendale	6.1	GA Seminole	9.7	GA Screven	20.9	NH Strafford	6.1
ID Custer	33.7	SC Williamsburg	6.1	MS Lowndes	9.5	GA Lanier	20.9	IN Union	6.1
CO Jackson	33.7	TX Zavala	6.1	FL Gilchrist	9.5	KY Jackson	20.8	IN Jackson	6.1
CO Dolores	33.7	MS Madison	6.2	OH Greene	9.4	OH Holmes	20.7	IN Brown	6.1
TX Collin	33.6	MS Wilkinson	6.2	MS Walthall	9.2	AL Randolph	20.5	RI Washington	6.0
ME Androscoggin	33.6	MS Yazoo	6.2	TN Polk	8.6	GA Treutlen	20.3	NH Hillsborough	6.0
KS Coffey	33.6	TN Hancock	6.2	MS Franklin	8.6	MD Garrett	20.1	MO Scotland	6.0
ID Caribou	33.6	MS Newton	6.3	MS Lincoln	8.5	IN Spencer	19.9	IN Sullivan	6.0
ID Bonner	33.6	SC Bamberg	6.3	MS Jasper	8.5	KY Leslie	19.8	IN Ripley	6.0
MN Sibley	33.5	AR Phillips	6.4	CA Imperial	8.3	KY Clinton	19.7	IN Jefferson	6.0
ME Kennebec	33.5	AR Pulaski	6.4	OK Major	8.2	KY Bath	19.7	WV Jefferson	5.9
KS Sumner	33.5	MS Grenada	6.4	MS Greene	8.1	KY Mercer	19.6	IN Floyd	5.9
AK 07 Homer¹	33.5	MS Kemper	6.4	MS Lawrence	8.0	GA Chattahoochee	19.4	ND Dickey	5.8
NE Cedar	33.4	MS Leake	6.4	SC Sumter	7.9	GA Warren	19.3	NC Mecklenburg	5.8
ME Oxford	33.4	MS Panola	6.4	UT Wasatch	7.8	WA Whitman	19.2	NH Carroll	5.8
KS Sheridan	33.4	MS Sunflower	6.4	MS Pike	7.7	GA Glascock	19.1	IN Miami	5.8
KS Miami	33.4	AL Choctaw	6.5	IA Wapello²	7.7	KY Pulaski	19.0	IN Putnam	5.7
TX Parker	33.3	AR Jefferson	6.5	IA Cass²	7.6	KY Gallatin	18.9	IN Marion	5.7
AK 35 PWS-Delta¹	33.3	AR Woodruff	6.5	OK Alfalfa	7.5	GA Bacon	18.9	IN Knox	5.7
ND Burke	33.2	MS Carroll	6.5	MS Wayne	7.4	KY Magoffin	18.8	WV Berkeley	5.6
MT Toole	33.2	MS Clarke	6.5	MS Scott	7.4	GA Camden	18.8	IN Owen	5.6
MT Mineral	33.2	TN Lake	6.5	AR Saline	7.3	AK 23 Northeast Anchorage¹	18.8	IN Monroe	5.6
ME Washington	33.2	TX Duval	6.5	MS DeSoto	7.2	KY Morgan	18.7	IN Martin	5.6
TX Wise	33.1	VA Petersburg City	6.6	MS Calhoun	7.2	OK Kay	18.6	IN Howard	5.6
TX Rockwall	33.1	AR Chicot	6.8	IN Warrick	7.2	KY Bracken	18.6	NC Scotland	5.5
ND Oliver	33.1	MS Jefferson Davis	6.8	FL DeSoto	7.2	GA Hart	18.6	IN White	5.4
KS Stafford	33.0	SC Clarendon	6.8	UT Weber	7.1	AL Escambia	18.6	MO Putnam	5.3
ME Penobscot	32.9	VA Emporia City	6.8	UT Sanpete	7.1	MD Somerset	18.5	WV Mercer	5.2
KS Kingman	32.9	MS Tallahatchie	6.9	UT Beaver	7.1	MD Kent	18.4	WA Skamania	5.2
NE Howard	32.8	TN Clay	6.9	IA Monroe²	7.1	OH Shelby	18.3	WA Klickitat	5.2
KS Linn	32.8	TN Hardeman	6.9	CA San Joaquin	7.1	KY Wayne	18.3	ND Benson	5.2
UNITED STATES	18.9	UNITED STATES	18.9	UNITED STATES	0.0	UNITED STATES	0.0	UNITED STATES	0.0

¹Election district (not borough or Census area). ²Voter turnout not officially certified by Iowa Secretary of State at time of publication.

Top/Bottom 70 Congressional Districts: 1990 Population by Race and Ethnic Origin (Table A)

Districts lowest percent Non-Hispanic White	%	Districts highest percent Non-Hispanic Black	%	Districts highest percent Non-Hispanic Asian & Pacific Islander	%	Districts highest percent Non-Hispanic Native American	%	Districts highest percent Hispanic	%
NY District 16	4.2	MD District 7	70.6	HI District 1	64.0	AZ District 6	21.1	CA District 33	83.7
CA District 33	8.1	MI District 15	69.7	HI District 2	52.7	NM District 3	19.6	TX District 15	74.5
CA District 35	10.4	NY District 11	69.4	CA District 8	27.0	OK District 2	17.0	TX District 16	70.4
CA District 37	12.0	IL District 1	69.3	CA District 12	25.0	AK District 1	15.4	FL District 21	69.6
NY District 12	14.0	MI District 14	68.8	CA District 31	22.1	OK District 3	11.3	FL District 18	66.7
NY District 15	14.0	IL District 2	68.0	CA District 16	20.1	NC District 7	7.2	TX District 27	66.2
CA District 30	15.2	AL District 7	67.4	CA District 30	19.8	SD District 1	7.1	IL District 4	65.0
NY District 11	15.8	LA District 4	66.2	NY District 12	18.7	MT District 1	5.8	TX District 23	62.5
CA District 31	17.5	IL District 7	65.2	CA District 13	18.5	OK District 1	5.0	CA District 34	62.3
FL District 17	19.8	GA District 11	63.8	CA District 9	15.1	OK District 6	4.7	CA District 30	61.5
NY District 10	21.0	VA District 3	63.7	CA District 50	13.7	OK District 4	4.6	TX District 20	60.7
NY District 6	22.8	MS District 2	62.7	CA District 7	13.6	OK District 5	4.5	TX District 29	60.6
CA District 32	23.6	GA District 5	62.0	CA District 39	13.3	ND District 1	4.0	TX District 28	60.4
TX District 15	23.9	SC District 6	61.9	CA District 28	12.6	AZ District 2	3.7	NY District 16	60.2
IL District 2	24.6	PA District 2	61.8	CA District 5	12.6	NM District 2	3.5	CA District 31	58.5
MI District 15	24.9	LA District 2	60.4	CA District 36	12.2	AZ District 3	3.0	NY District 12	57.9
TX District 16	25.0	TN District 9	59.0	CA District 14	11.9	WI District 8	2.6	CA District 20	55.4
FL District 21	25.5	NJ District 10	58.6	CA District 46	11.7	WA District 4	2.6	CA District 26	52.7
IL District 1	25.9	OH District 11	58.3	WA District 7	11.3	UT District 3	2.5	AZ District 2	50.5
NJ District 10	26.4	MD District 4	57.7	NY District 7	11.1	NC District 8	2.5	CA District 46	50.0
CA District 34	26.7	NC District 1	57.1	CA District 15	10.9	MI District 1	2.4	NY District 15	46.4
IL District 4	26.8	NY District 10	56.6	CA District 11	10.8	CA District 1	2.4	CA District 37	45.1
MD District 7	26.9	NC District 12	56.4	CA District 45	10.7	NM District 1	2.3	CA District 35	43.1
IL District 7	27.2	GA District 2	56.3	NY District 5	10.5	MN District 5	2.3	NM District 2	42.1
HI District 1	27.6	FL District 17	55.7	CA District 27	10.2	WA District 6	2.2	NJ District 13	41.5
TX District 29	27.8	FL District 3	54.5	CA District 37	10.1	NV District 2	2.2	CA District 50	40.6
MI District 14	28.8	NY District 6	53.3	IL District 9	9.8	MN District 7	2.2	NM District 1	38.1
NY District 17	29.1	MO District 1	52.2	CA District 41	9.7	CA District 2	2.2	CA District 16	36.8
FL District 18	29.2	PA District 1	51.5	CA District 47	9.4	OR District 2	2.1	NM District 3	34.6
TX District 28	30.4	TX District 18	50.2	CA District 34	8.7	MN District 8	2.1	CA District 42	34.3
TX District 27	30.7	FL District 23	50.2	CA District 38	8.6	WY District 1	2.0	CA District 17	31.6
MD District 4	31.1	TX District 30	49.2	NY District 18	8.0	WA District 2	1.9	CA District 41	31.5
TX District 18	31.3	MS District 4	40.6	VA District 11	7.9	WI District 7	1.7	CA District 32	30.2
TX District 30	31.4	CA District 35	40.4	MD District 8	7.9	WI District 1	1.5	CA District 23	30.0
CA District 50	31.5	CA District 32	38.2	CA District 51	7.8	LA District 3	1.5	NY District 17	29.1
AL District 7	32.0	NY District 17	37.8	CA District 32	7.4	AZ District 1	1.5	CA District 44	28.1
TX District 20	32.2	NY District 15	36.8	CA District 29	7.4	WA District 9	1.4	CA District 18	26.0
LA District 4	32.4	WI District 5	34.9	CA District 19	7.0	NC District 11	1.4	CA District 38	25.7
CA District 20	32.6	NY District 16	33.2	TX District 22	6.8	WA District 7	1.3	CA District 43	25.0
VA District 3	33.4	CA District 37	32.2	CA District 26	6.8	OR District 4	1.3	CA District 28	24.1
LA District 2	33.5	VA District 4	31.9	VA District 8	6.5	ID District 1	1.3	TX District 14	23.6
TX District 23	33.6	MS District 3	31.3	NJ District 9	6.4	WA District 3	1.2	CA District 19	23.6
GA District 11	34.1	CA District 9	31.0	CA District 25	6.3	ID District 2	1.2	FL District 17	23.0
PA District 2	34.1	SC District 5	30.7	CA District 24	6.3	CA District 40	1.2	CA District 39	22.8
CA District 26	34.2	OH District 1	30.0	CA District 49	6.2	CA District 21	1.2	CA District 52	22.6
GA District 5	34.9	IN District 10	29.7	NY District 9	6.1	CA District 3	1.2	CO District 1	21.9
HI District 2	35.1	AL District 1	28.4	NY District 8	6.1	OR District 5	1.1	TX District 24	21.8
CA District 46	35.6	AR District 4	26.5	CA District 10	6.1	OR District 3	1.1	TX District 10	21.4
PA District 1	36.0	TX District 25	26.3	NY District 6	6.0	MS District 3	1.1	NY District 7	21.3
MS District 2	36.4	AL District 3	25.9	WA District 9	5.9	KS District 4	1.1	CA District 22	21.3
SC District 6	37.1	SC District 2	25.2	CA District 18	5.7	KS District 2	1.1	CA District 11	21.1
CA District 16	37.5	VA District 5	24.7	CA District 17	5.7	CO District 3	1.1	CA District 27	20.6
AZ District 2	38.2	AL District 2	24.0	IL District 5	5.6	CA District 4	1.1	CA District 21	20.3
FL District 23	39.3	MO District 5	23.5	CA District 35	5.5	AR District 3	1.1	NY District 10	19.7
OH District 11	39.3	OH District 12	23.1	TX District 7	5.4	AZ District 4	1.1	TX District 19	19.6
TN District 9	39.3	NC District 8	23.1	NY District 14	5.4	NE District 1	1.0	CA District 13	18.4
CA District 9	41.1	FL District 2	23.0	NY District 13	5.4	MO District 7	1.0	TX District 5	17.9
GA District 2	41.3	TN District 5	22.7	MA District 8	5.4	CA District 19	1.0	NJ District 8	17.8
NC District 1	41.4	MS District 1	22.7	WA District 1	5.2	WA District 8	0.9	CO District 3	17.4
NC District 12	41.4	GA District 1	22.5	CA District 3	5.2	WA District 1	0.9		
FL District 3	41.7	LA District 5	22.0	CA District 20	5.0	FL District 1	0.9	TX District 17	17.2
NJ District 13	42.3	NC District 2	21.8	CA District 23	4.9	CA District 52	0.9	CA District 48	17.2
NM District 3	44.0	MA District 8	21.8	IL District 6	4.8	CA District 5	0.9	TX District 30	17.1
CA District 8	44.3	LA District 3	21.7	NJ District 6	4.6	WI District 4	0.8	NY District 6	16.9
MO District 1	45.8	TX District 9	21.4	MN District 4	4.6	UT District 1	0.8	TX District 25	16.7
CA District 42	50.5	NC District 3	21.4	WA District 8	4.5	NY District 24	0.8	AZ District 5	16.5
NM District 2	51.7	GA District 8	20.9	NJ District 7	4.5	MN District 4	0.8	CA District 25	16.4
CA District 41	51.9	IN District 1	20.8	OR District 3	4.4	CO District 1	0.8	TX District 12	16.3
TX District 25	53.0	SC District 3	20.7	NJ District 5	4.4	CA District 48	0.8	TX District 22	16.1
CA District 13	55.2	SC District 1	20.0	MD District 4	4.4	CA District 44	0.8	CA District 40	16.1
UNITED STATES	75.6	UNITED STATES	11.7	UNITED STATES	2.8	UNITED STATES	0.7	UNITED STATES	9.0

Top/Bottom 70 Congressional Districts: Vote for Congress, November 3, 1992, General Election (Table H)

Districts highest percent for Winning Democrat	%	Districts lowest percent for Winning Democrat	%	Districts highest percent for Winning Republican	%	Districts lowest percent for Winning Republican	%
WV 1 Mollohan (D)	100.0	CA 19 Lehman (D)	46.9	TX 7 Archer (R)	100.0	CT 5 Franks (R)	43.7
TX 20 Gonzalez (D)	100.0	NJ 8 Klein (D)	47.0	PA 9 Shuster (R)	100.0	OH 15 Pryce (R)	44.1
TX 1 Chapman (D)	100.0	CA 1 Hamburg (D)	47.6	PA 5 Clinger (R)	100.0	MN 6 Grams (R)	44.4
PA 12 Murtha (D)	100.0	MI 8 Carr (D)	47.6	OH 5 Gillmor (R)	100.0	PA 19 Goodling (R)	45.3
FL 17 Meek (D)	100.0	MO 9 Volkmer (D)	47.7	IA 5 Grandy (R)	99.3	CA 43 Calvert (R)	46.7
NY 10 Towns (D)[1]	95.8	MN 2 Minge (D)	47.8	PA 10 McDade (R)	90.4	AK 1 Young (R)	46.8
NY 15 Rangel (D)[1]	94.9	CA 36 Harman (D)	48.4	SC 2 Spence (R)	87.6	CA 11 Pombo (R)	47.6
NY 11 Owens (D)[1]	93.6	TN 3 Llody (D)	48.8	MI 7 Smith (R)	87.6	NV 2 Vucanovich (R)	47.9
NY 16 Serrano (D)[1]	91.4	FL 5 Thurman (D)	49.2	TX 3 Johnson (R)	86.1	CA 38 Horn (R)	48.6
NY 9 Schumer (D)[1]	88.6	VA 11 Byrne (D)	50.0	VA 7 Bliley (R)	82.9	IA 3 Lightfoot (R)	48.9
CA 32 Dixon (D)	87.2	PA 13 Margolies-Mezvinsky	50.3	FL 14 Goss (R)	82.1	ME 2 Snowe (R)	49.1
TX 28 Tejeda (D)	87.1	MN 7 Peterson (D)	50.4	TX 19 Combest (R)	77.4	AL 2 Everett (R)	49.5
CA 37 Tucker (D)	85.7	NY 14 Maloney (D)[1]	50.4	TX 8 Fields (R)	77.0	NY 3 King (R)[7]	49.6
MD 7 Mfume (D)	85.3	NY 26 Hinchey (D)[1]	50.4	OH 8 Boehner (R)	74.0	CA 27 Moorhead (R)	49.7
DC 1 Holmes (D)	84.8	MT 1 Williams (D)	50.5	TX 26 Armey (R)	73.1	CA 4 Doolittle (R)	49.8
CA 18 Condit (D)	84.7	UT 2 Shepherd (D)	50.5	MD 8 Morella (R)	72.5	AR 3 Hutchinson (R)	50.2
OH 17 Traficant (D)	84.2	CA 42 Brown (D)	50.7	TX 21 Smith (R)	72.2	CA 46 Dornan (R)	50.2
TN 8 Tanner (D)	83.7	FL 15 Bacchus (D)	50.7	TN 2 Duncan (R)	72.2	IA 2 Nussle (R)	50.2
MA 8 Kennedy (D)	83.1	OH 6 Strickland (D)	50.7	IN 6 Burton (R)	72.2	NY 4 Levy (R)[7]	50.2
IL 1 Rush (D)	82.8	PA 20 Murphy (D)	50.7	TX 6 Barton (R)	71.9	SC 4 Inglis (R)	50.3
CA 35 Waters (D)	82.5	CT 2 Gejdenson (D)[5]	50.8	NE 3 Barrett (R)	71.7	MA 3 Blute (R)	50.4
CA 8 Pelosi (D)	82.5	WA 4 Inslee (D)	50.8	NJ 5 Roukema (R)	71.5	MO 2 Talent (R)	50.4
MI 14 Conyers (D)	82.4	CA 49 Schenk (D)	51.1	OH 7 Hobson (R)	71.3	GA 4 Linder (R)	50.5
NY 8 Nadler (D)[1]	81.2	CA 3 Fazio (D)	51.2	OH 12 Kasich (R)	71.2	MD 1 Gilchrest (R)	51.3
MS 3 Montgomery (D)	81.2	NE 2 Hoagland (D)	51.2	CO 5 Hefley (R)	71.1	IN 5 Buyer (R)	51.4
IL 7 Collins (D)	81.1	AZ 1 Coopersmith (D)	51.3	NC 6 Coble (R)	70.8	NY 30 Quinn (R)[10]	51.7
NY 6 Flake (D)	81.0	OH 1 Mann (D)	51.3	NY 31 Houghton (R)[7]	70.6	CA 25 McKeon (R)	51.9
PA 1 Foglietta (D)	80.9	MA 1 Olver (D)	51.5	WI 8 Roth (R)	70.1	PA 8 Greenwood (R)	51.9
MI 15 Collins (D)	80.5	KS 4 Glickman (D)	51.7	RI 1 Machtley (R)	70.1	CA 10 Baker (R)	52.0
NY 17 Engel (D)[1]	80.1	NY 1 Hochbrueckner (D)[6]	51.7	OH 2 Gradison (R)[8]	70.1	FL 22 Shaw (R)	52.0
VA 3 Scott (D)	78.6	MI 13 Ford (D)	51.9	NJ 11 Gallo (R)	70.1	FL 12 Canady (R)	52.1
PA 4 Klink (D)	78.5	TX 16 Coleman (D)	51.9	WI 9 Sensenbrenner (R)	69.7	AL 6 Bachus (R)	52.3
WA 7 McDermott (D)	78.4	FL 1 Hutto (D)	52.0	CT 6 Johnson (R)	69.7	AR 4 Dickey (R)	52.3
NJ 10 Payne (D)	78.4	OR 1 Furse (D)	52.0	PA 17 Gekas (R)	69.5	CA 22 Huffington (R)	52.5
IL 2 Reynolds (D)	78.1	WA 2 Swift (D)	52.0	TX 22 DeLay (R)	68.9	OK 1 Inhofe (R)	52.8
IL 4 Gutierrez (D)	77.6	PA 6 Holden (D)	52.1	FL 8 McCollum (R)	68.5	CA 52 Hunter (R)	52.9
OR 3 Wyden (D)	77.1	WA 9 Kreidler (D)	52.1	IL 13 Fawell (R)	68.4	WI 6 Petri (R)	52.9
PA 2 Blackwell (D)	76.8	MA 5 Meehan (D)	52.2	KS 1 Roberts (R)	68.3	NH 1 Zeliff (R)	53.1
NY 12 Velazquez (D)	76.5	PA 15 McHale (D)	52.2	IA 1 Leach (R)	68.1	NY 2 Lazio (R)[7]	53.2
MS 2 Espy (D)[2]	76.4	NJ 6 Pallone (D)	52.3	PA 21 Ridge (R)	68.0	NJ 7 Franks (R)	53.3
OK 3 Brewster (D)	75.1	NY 5 Ackerman (D)[1]	52.4	TN 1 Quillen (R)	67.5	OK 5 Istook (R)	53.4
MD 4 Wynn (D)	75.1	IN 8 McCloskey (D)	52.5	NC 9 McMillan (R)	67.3	MD 6 Bartlett (R)	54.1
AR 2 Thornton (D)	74.2	MI 12 Levin (D)	52.6	IL 14 Hastert (R)	67.3	CA 44 McCandless (R)	54.2
LA 4 Fields (D)[3]	73.9	OH 19 Fingerhut (D)	52.6	CT 4 Shays (R)	67.3	CA 23 Gallegly (R)	54.3
MN 1 Penny (D)	73.9	KY 3 Mazzoli (D)	52.7	OR 2 Smith (R)	67.1	CA 45 Rohrabacher (R)	54.5
OH 9 Kaptur (D)	73.6	NC 5 Neal (D)	52.7	FL 18 Ros-Lehtinen (R)	66.8	KY 5 Rogers (R)	54.6
MD 3 Cardin (D)	73.5	FL 11 Gibbons (D)	52.8	AZ 5 Kolbe (R)	66.5	CO 3 McInnis (R)	54.7
FL 2 Peterson (D)	73.4	AZ 6 English (D)	53.0	SC 1 Ravenel (R)	66.1	NC 11 Taylor (R)	54.7
GA 11 McKinney (D)	73.1	MD 5 Hoyer (D)	53.0	NY 20 Gilman (R)	66.1	GA 3 Collins (R)	54.8
HI 1 Abercrombie (D)	72.9	MA 2 Neal (D)	53.1	PA 7 Weldon (R)	66.0	MA 6 Torkildsen (R)	54.8
HI 2 Mink (D)	72.6	MI 10 Bonior (D)	53.1	IL 6 Hyde (R)	65.5	DE 1 Castle (R)	55.4
PA 14 Coyne (D)	72.3	OH 13 Brown (D)	53.3	NY 22 Solomon (R)[9]	65.4	IL 16 Manzullo (R)	55.6
GA 5 Lewis (D)	72.1	TX 9 Brooks (D)	53.6	FL 6 Stearns (R)	65.4	IL 8 Crane (R)	55.7
CA 17 Panetta (D)[4]	72.0	MI 9 Kildee (D)	53.7	UT 1 Hansen (R)	65.3	NY 25 Walsh (R)[7]	55.7
CA 9 Dellums (D)	71.9	NC 2 Valentine (D)	53.7	CA 21 Thomas (R)	65.2	CA 51 Cunningham (R)	56.1
TX 30 Johnson (D)	71.5	GA 10 Johnson (D)	53.8	CA 2 Herger (R)	65.2	NY 13 Molinari (R)[7]	56.1
OR 4 DeFazio (D)	71.4	MI 1 Stupak (D)	53.9	MD 2 Bentley (R)	65.1	FL 7 Mica (R)	56.4
IL 12 Costello (D)	71.2	NC 3 Lancaster (D)	54.4	CA 47 Cox (R)	64.9	NM 2 Skeen (R)	56.4
WV 2 Wise (D)	70.9	NY 29 LaFalce (D)[1]	54.5	PA 16 Walker (R)	64.8	WI 3 Gunderson (R)	56.4
RI 2 Reed (D)	70.7	WA 1 Cantwell (D)	54.9	IL 10 Porter (R)	64.5	FL 10 Young (R)	56.6
OK 4 McCurdy (D)	70.7	FL 20 Deutsch (D)	55.1	NJ 12 Zimmer (R)	63.9	FL 4 Fowler (R)	56.7
NC 12 Watt (D)	70.4	NY 28 Slaughter (D)	55.2	OH 16 Regula (R)	63.7	OH 10 Hoke (R)	56.8
MO 4 Skelton (D)	70.4	WA 5 Foley (D)	55.2	VA 10 Wolf (R)	63.6	CA 39 Royce (R)	57.3
CA 7 Miller (D)	70.3	MO 6 Danner (D)	55.4	NY 23 Boehlert (R)	63.6	VA 1 Bateman (R)	57.5
AR 1 Lambert (D)	69.8	CA 24 Beilenson (D)	55.5	MN 3 Ramstad (R)	63.6	MI 11 Knollenberg (R)	57.6
IN 9 Hamilton (D)	69.7	OK 2 Synar (D)	55.5	NY 27 Paxon (R)[9]	63.5	GA 6 Gingrich (R)	57.7
AL 7 Hilliard (D)	69.5	TX 27 Ortiz (D)	55.5	NC 10 Ballenger (R)	63.4	CO 4 Allard (R)	57.8
IN 1 Visclosky (D)	69.4	NY 18 Lowey (D)	55.6	CA 40 Lewis (R)	63.1	FL 13 Miller (R)	57.8
WI 5 Barrett (D)	69.3	GA 8 Rowland (D)	55.7	MI 2 Hoekstra (R)	63.0	GA 1 Kingston (R)	57.8
OH 11 Stokes (D)	69.2	IL 11 Sangmeister (D)	55.7	LA 5 McCrery (R)	63.0	IL 18 Michel (R)	57.8
UNITED STATES	50.9	UNITED STATES	50.9	UNITED STATES	45.6	UNITED STATES	45.6

[1]Also includes votes for candidate as the nominee of the Liberal party. [2]Resigned to become U.S. Secretary of Agriculture. [3]Candidate's opponent on November 3, 1992, was another Democrat, due to Lousiana's open primary law where the top two candidates regardless of party affiliation run in the general election if no one received a majority of the vote in the primary. [4]Resigned to become Director of the Office of Management and Budget (OMB). [5]Also includes votes for candidate as the nominee of A Connecticut Party (ACP). [6]Also includes votes for candidate as the nominee of Long Island First party. [7]Also includes votes for candidate as the nominee of the Conservative party. [8]Resigned. [9]Also includes votes for candidate as the nominee of the Conservative and Right to Life parties. [10]Also includes votes for candidate as the nominee of the Change Congress party.

STATES AND DISTRICT OF COLUMBIA

Alabama	35	Nebraska	571
Alaska	53	Nevada	593
Arizona	69	New Hampshire	603
Arkansas	79	New Jersey	617
California	101	New Mexico	633
Colorado	129	New York	647
Connecticut	147	North Carolina	669
Delaware	171	North Dakota	699
Florida	181	Ohio	717
Georgia	203	Oklahoma	741
Hawaii	239	Oregon	767
Idaho	247	Pennsylvania	783
Illinois	261	Rhode Island	805
Indiana	287	South Carolina	819
Iowa	313	South Dakota	835
Kansas	333	Tennessee	851
Kentucky	359	Texas	871
Louisiana	387	Utah	911
Maine	409	Vermont	925
Maryland	419	Virginia	939
Massachusetts	433	Washington	959
Michigan	469	West Virginia	977
Minnesota	491	Wisconsin	993
Mississippi	511	Wyoming	1011
Missouri	535		
Montana	557	District of Columbia	1019

ALABAMA

Congressional Districts 7
   Average Population 577,227
State Senate Districts 35
   Average Population 115,445
State House Districts 105
   Average Population 38,482

Electoral College Votes..9
Counties 67
Voting Precincts 2,135

Alternative Registration Methods:
.... None

Registration Deadline (Days before Election) 10

Population Statistics 1990

Race/ Ethnicity	Total Population		Voting Age Population		Voting Age Population % of total population
	Number	%	Number	%	
Non-Hispanic					
White	2,960,167	73.3	2,263,288	75.9	76.5
Black	1,017,713	25.2	675,707	22.7	66.4
Asian/Pacific Islander	21,217	0.5	15,144	0.5	71.4
Native American	16,221	0.4	10,635	0.4	65.6
Other	640	<.1	336	<.1	52.5
All Hispanic	24,629	0.6	16,689	0.6	67.8
TOTAL	4,040,587	100.0	2,981,799	100.0	73.8

Voting Equipment Use (Counties)

Datavote Punch Card	0	Paper Ballot	4
Electronic	4	Other Punch Card	0
Lever Machine	42	Mixed Systems	0
Optical Scanner	17		

Party Control	DEM	REP	IND	VAC
1993 State Senate	27	8	0	0
1992 State Senate	28	7	0	0
1993 State House	81	23	0	1
1992 State House	82	23	0	0

Estimated Voting Age Population 1992 (VAP) 3,056,000
Number of Registered Voters................................. 2,367,972
   % of estimated VAP 77.5
Voter Turnout (Highest Office) 1,688,933
   % of VAP 55.3
   % of Registration 71.3
Persons Not Voting—of Voting Age 1,367,067
   % of VAP 44.7
Persons Not Voting—of Registered 679,039
   % of Registration 28.7
Straight Ticket Voting ....Yes, Separate

State Officials and Members of Congress

Governor:
Jim Folsom (D) 1993, succeeded to office for remainder of term expiring 1995.

U.S. Senators:
Howell Heflin (D) 1978, elected to a six-year term in 1990.
Richard Shelby (D) 1986, elected to a six-year term in 1992.

U.S. Representative in Congress:
(District, Name, Party, Date first elected)

1. Callahan (R) 1984
2. Everett (R) 1992
3. Browder (D) 1989
4. Bevill (D) 1966
5. Cramer (D) 1990
6. Bachus (R) 1992
7. Hilliard (D) 1992

Candidates: General Election, November 3, 1992

Candidate(s)	Total vote	Percent	Party	Status	First elected
President/Vice President					
Bush/Quayle	804,283	47.65%	Republican	Incumbent	1988
Clinton/Gore	690,080	40.88%	Democrat	Challenger	1992
Perot/Stockdale	183,109	10.85%	Independent	Challenger	
Marrou/Lord	5,737	0.34%	Libertarian	Challenger	
Fulani/Munoz	2,161	0.13%	Independent	Challenger	
Warren/Debates	831	0.05%	Independent	Challenger	
Write ins	723	0.04%	Unknown	Challenger	
LaRouche/Bevel	641	0.04%	Independent	Challenger	
Hagelin/Tompkins	495	0.03%	Independent	Challenger	
U.S. Senator					
Richard Shelby	1,022,698	64.82%	Democrat	Incumbent	1986
Richard Sellers	522,015	33.09%	Republican	Challenger	
Jerome Shockley	31,811	2.02%	Libertarian	Challenger	
Write ins	1,275	0.08%	Write in	Challenger	
Governor (No Contest)					
U.S. Representative in Congress					
District 1					
Sonny Callahan	128,874	60.16%	Republican	Incumbent	1984
William Brewer	78,742	36.76%	Democrat	Challenger	
John Garrett	6,548	3.06%	Libertarian	Challenger	
Write ins	40	0.02%	Write in	Challenger	
District 2					
Terry Everett	112,906	49.49%	Republican	Challenger	1992
George Wallace Jr.	109,335	47.92%	Democrat	Challenger	
Glynn Reeves	3,150	1.38%	Libertarian	Challenger	
Malcolm Brassell	1,426	0.63%	Independent	Challenger	
Richard Boone	1,330	0.58%	Independent	Challenger	
Write ins	13	<.01%	Write in	Challenger	
District 3					
Glen Browder	119,175	60.31%	Democrat	Incumbent	1989
Don Sledge	73,800	37.35%	Republican	Challenger	
Rodric Templeton	4,570	2.31%	Libertarian	Challenger	
Write ins	59	0.03%	Write in	Challenger	
District 4					
Tom Bevill	157,907	68.50%	Democrat	Incumbent	1966
Mickey Strickland	66,934	29.04%	Republican	Challenger	
Robert King	5,646	2.45%	Libertarian	Challenger	
Write ins	36	0.02%	Write in	Challenger	
District 5					
Bud Cramer	160,060	65.56%	Democrat	Incumbent	1990
Terry Smith	77,951	31.93%	Republican	Challenger	
C Michael Seibert	6,006	2.46%	Libertarian	Challenger	
Write ins	116	0.05%	Write in	Challenger	
District 6					
Spencer Bachus	146,599	52.33%	Republican	Challenger	1992
Ben Erdreich	126,062	45.00%	Democrat	Incumbent	1982
Carla Cloum	4,521	1.61%	Independent	Challenger	
Mark Bodenhausen	2,836	1.01%	Libertarian	Challenger	
Write ins	121	0.04%	Write in	Challenger	

Candidate(s)	Total vote	Percent	Party	Status	First elected
U.S. Representative in Congress (cont)					
District 7					
Earl Hilliard	144,320	69.46%	Democrat	Challenger	1992
Kervin Jones	36,086	17.37%	Republican	Challenger	
James Lewis	12,461	6.00%	Independent	Challenger	
James Chambliss	11,466	5.52%	Independent	Challenger	
Michael Mayer	2,135	1.03%	Libertarian	Challenger	
John Hawkins	1,165	0.56%	Socialist Worker	Challenger	
Write ins	140	0.07%	Write in	Challenger	

Candidates: June 2, 1992, Primary Election

Candidate	Total vote	Percent	Candidate	Total vote	Percent
Presidential Preference, Democratic			**Presidential Preference, Republican**		
Bill Clinton	307,621	68.22%	George Bush	122,703	74.31%
Uncommitted	90,863	20.15%	Uncommitted	29,830	18.07%
Jerry Brown	30,626	6.79%	Patrick Buchanan	12,588	7.62%
Charles Woods	15,247	3.38%			
Lyndon LaRouche	6,542	1.45%			

Voter Registration and Turnout, 1948-1992 Elections

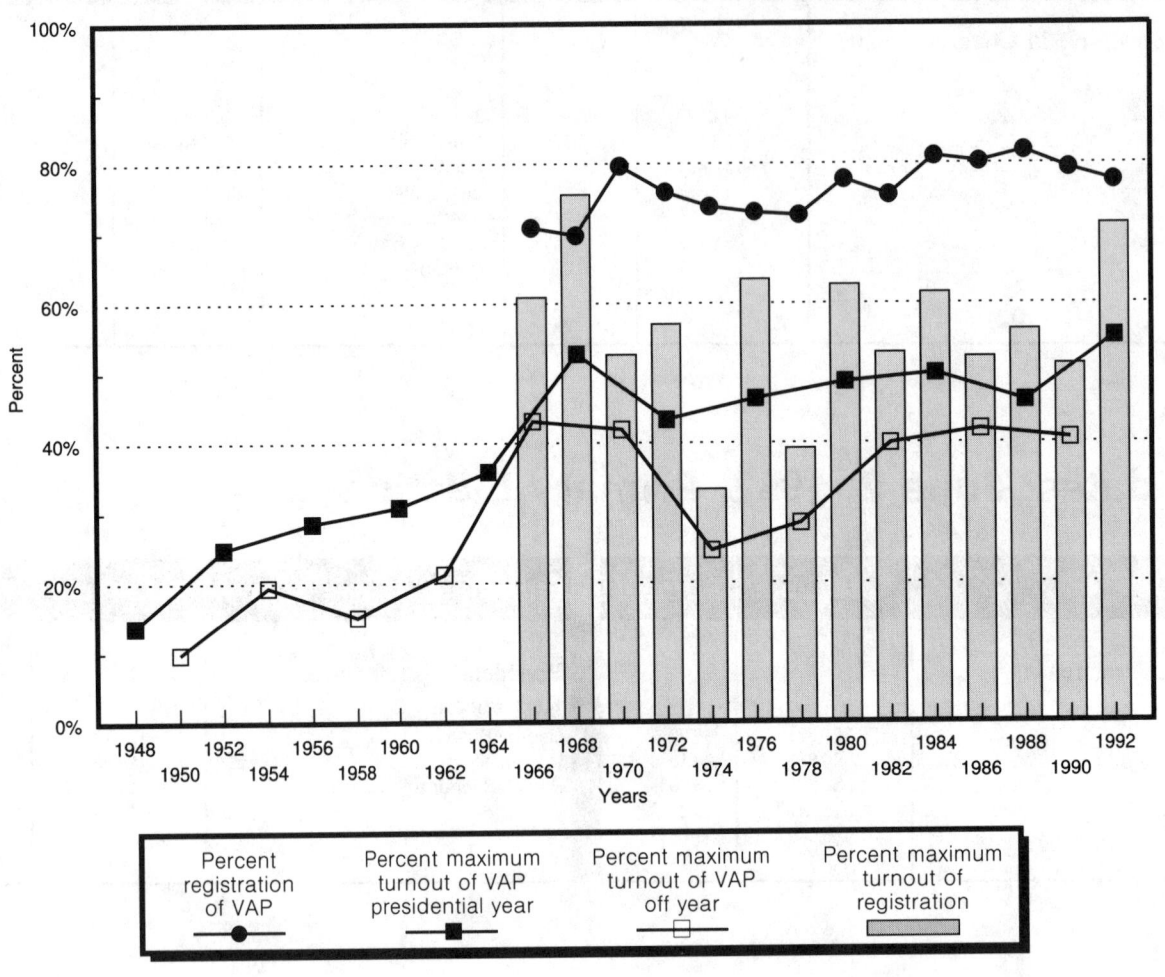

		Voter registration (REG)				Voter turnout										
							Highest office					Maximum vote				
Year	Estimated Voting Age Population (VAP)	Total	Percent of VAP	Rank by percent of VAP	Actual	Total	Office	Percent total REG	Rank by percent of REG	Percent of VAP	Rank by percent of VAP	Total	Percent total REG	Rank by percent of REG	Percent total VAP	Rank by percent of VAP
1992	3,056,000	2,367,972	77.5	19	-	1,688,060	P	71.3	43	55.2	29	1,688,060	71.3	43	55.2	31
1990	2,995,000	2,374,824	79.3	9	-	1,215,889	G	51.2	38	40.6	22	1,215,889	51.2	39	40.6	23
1988	2,997,000	2,451,494	81.8	11	-	1,378,476	P	56.2	48	46.0	42	1,378,476	56.2	48	46.0	42
1986	2,947,000	2,362,361	80.2	9	-	1,236,230	G	52.3	35	41.9	19	1,236,230	52.3	36	41.9	22
1984	2,892,000	2,343,448	81.0	13	-	1,441,713	P	61.5	48	49.9	40	1,441,713	61.5	48	49.9	41
1982	2,827,000	2,135,704	75.5	12	-	1,128,725	G	52.9	41	39.9	34	1,128,725	52.9	41	39.9	35
1980	2,757,000	2,142,139	77.7	15	-	1,341,929	P	62.6	46	48.7	39	1,341,929	62.6	47	48.7	41
1978	2,669,000	1,938,231	72.6	18	-	760,474	G	39.2	46	28.5	45	760,474	39.2	46	28.5	45
1976	2,554,000	1,864,947	73.0	23	-	1,182,850	P	63.4	48	46.3	44	1,182,850	63.4	48	46.3	45
1974	2,429,000	1,792,686	73.8	17	-	598,305	G	33.4	45	24.6	47	598,305	33.4	45	24.6	47
1972	2,325,000	1,763,845	75.9	21	-	1,006,111	P	57.0	45	43.3	47	1,006,111	57.0	45	43.3	45
1970	2,042,000	1,625,912	79.6	11	-	854,952	G	52.6	40	41.9	38	854,952	52.6	40	41.9	38
1968	1,993,000	1,389,198	69.7	33	-	1,049,922	P	75.6	35	52.7	43	1,049,922	75.6	35	52.7	43
1966	1,968,000	1,392,755	70.8	28	-	848,101	G	60.9	28	43.1	36	848,101	60.9	28	43.1	36
1964	1,919,000	-	-	-	-	689,818	P	-	-	35.9	50	689,818	-	-	35.9	50
1962	1,874,000	-	-	-	-	397,079	S	-	-	21.2	47	397,079	-	-	21.2	47
1960	1,850,000	-	-	-	-	570,225	P	-	-	30.8	47	570,225	-	-	30.8	47
1958	1,800,000	-	-	-	-	270,952	G	-	-	15.1	43	270,952	-	-	15.1	43
1956	1,742,000	-	-	-	-	496,861	P	-	-	28.5	46	496,861	-	-	28.5	46
1954	1,747,000	-	-	-	-	339,090	G	-	-	19.4	41	339,090	-	-	19.4	41
1952	1,720,000	-	-	-	-	426,120	P	-	-	24.8	47	426,120	-	-	24.8	47
1950	1,742,000	-	-	-	-	170,541	G	-	-	9.8	45	170,541	-	-	9.8	45
1948	1,570,000	-	-	-	-	214,980	P	-	-	13.7	46	214,980	-	-	13.7	46

ALABAMA

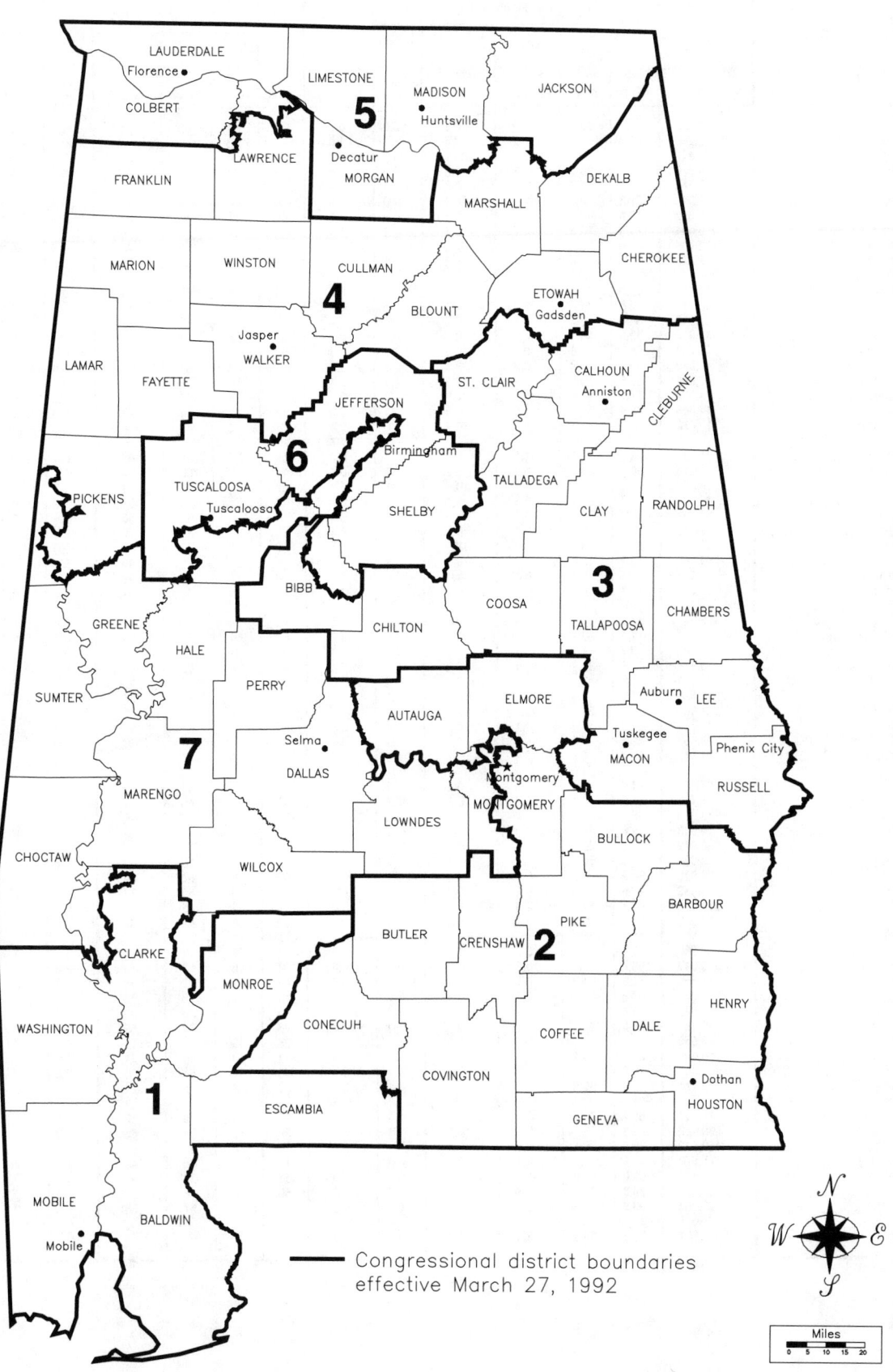

Congressional district boundaries
effective March 27, 1992

Alabama 39

Table A. — 1990 Population by Race and Ethnic Origin

State/county code	County	Total persons	Percent of total persons — Non-Hispanic — White	Black	Asian and Pacific Islander	Native American	Other	Hispanic	Rank — Percent of total persons — Total	Non-Hispanic White	Black	Hispanic	Percent contribution to state population — Total	Non-Hispanic White	Black	Hispanic
01 001	Autauga	34,222	78.9	19.9	0.3	0.2	0.0	0.7	33	28	38	9	0.8	0.9	0.7	0.9
01 003	Baldwin	98,280	85.3	12.8	0.2	0.6	<.1	1.0	10	22	48	5	2.4	2.8	1.2	4.1
01 005	Barbour	25,417	55.3	43.9	0.2	0.2	0.0	0.5	40	57	12	22	0.6	0.5	1.1	0.5
01 007	Bibb	16,576	78.6	20.9	<.1	0.2	0.0	0.2	52	29	36	62	0.4	0.4	0.3	0.2
01 009	Blount	39,248	97.5	1.3	<.1	0.3	<.1	0.7	28	4	65	8	1.0	1.3	<.1	1.2
01 011	Bullock	11,042	27.3	72.0	<.1	<.1	0.0	0.6	66	64	4	15	0.3	0.1	0.8	0.3
01 013	Butler	21,892	59.4	40.1	<.1	0.1	0.0	0.3	46	51	17	53	0.5	0.4	0.9	0.3
01 015	Calhoun	116,034	79.4	18.5	0.7	0.3	<.1	1.1	6	27	39	4	2.9	3.1	2.1	5.2
01 017	Chambers	36,876	63.8	35.8	<.1	<.1	<.1	0.3	30	48	20	45	0.9	0.8	1.3	0.5
01 019	Cherokee	19,543	92.7	6.6	0.1	0.3	<.1	0.3	49	11	57	55	0.5	0.6	0.1	0.2
01 021	Chilton	32,458	88.0	11.3	0.1	0.2	<.1	0.4	34	16	52	43	0.8	1.0	0.4	0.5
01 023	Choctaw	16,018	55.5	44.0	<.1	<.1	<.1	0.3	54	56	11	47	0.4	0.3	0.7	0.2
01 025	Clarke	27,240	56.8	42.5	0.1	0.2	<.1	0.4	39	54	13	39	0.7	0.5	1.1	0.4
01 027	Clay	13,252	83.2	16.3	<.1	0.2	<.1	0.2	61	24	43	65	0.3	0.4	0.2	0.1
01 029	Cleburne	12,730	94.8	4.6	0.1	0.2	0.0	0.3	63	7	59	52	0.3	0.4	<.1	0.2
01 031	Coffee	40,240	80.5	17.2	0.8	0.4	<.1	1.2	27	26	41	3	1.0	1.1	0.7	1.9
01 033	Colbert	51,666	82.6	16.5	0.2	0.3	<.1	0.4	20	25	42	42	1.3	1.4	0.8	0.8
01 035	Conecuh	14,054	57.1	41.9	<.1	0.3	<.1	0.6	58	53	14	17	0.3	0.3	0.6	0.3
01 037	Coosa	11,063	65.4	34.1	<.1	0.3	<.1	0.2	65	44	24	67	0.3	0.2	0.4	<.1
01 039	Covington	36,478	86.2	13.1	0.1	0.2	0.0	0.4	31	20	47	44	0.9	1.1	0.5	0.5
01 041	Crenshaw	13,635	73.5	26.0	<.1	0.2	<.1	0.2	59	37	31	63	0.3	0.3	0.3	0.1
01 043	Cullman	67,613	98.4	0.8	0.2	0.2	<.1	0.4	17	2	66	34	1.7	2.2	<.1	1.1
01 045	Dale	49,633	78.0	17.7	1.4	0.5	<.1	2.4	22	30	40	1	1.2	1.3	0.9	4.9
01 047	Dallas	48,130	41.7	57.7	0.3	<.1	<.1	0.3	24	59	9	57	1.2	0.7	2.7	0.5
01 049	DeKalb	54,651	96.7	1.9	0.1	0.9	<.1	0.4	18	5	63	35	1.4	1.8	0.1	0.8
01 051	Elmore	49,210	76.6	22.3	0.3	0.3	<.1	0.5	23	32	35	19	1.2	1.3	1.1	1.1
01 053	Escambia	35,518	68.2	28.2	0.2	2.9	<.1	0.5	32	41	27	25	0.9	0.8	1.0	0.7
01 055	Etowah	99,840	85.2	13.8	0.4	0.2	<.1	0.3	8	23	45	46	2.5	2.9	1.4	1.3
01 057	Fayette	17,962	87.2	12.2	0.1	<.1	0.0	0.4	50	18	49	29	0.4	0.5	0.2	0.3
01 059	Franklin	27,814	94.8	4.5	0.1	0.2	0.0	0.4	37	8	60	41	0.7	0.9	0.1	0.4
01 061	Geneva	23,647	87.1	11.9	<.1	0.4	<.1	0.5	43	19	50	21	0.6	0.7	0.3	0.5
01 063	Greene	10,153	19.4	80.4	0.0	<.1	0.0	0.2	67	66	2	61	0.3	<.1	0.8	<.1
01 065	Hale	15,498	40.3	59.2	<.1	0.1	0.0	0.4	56	60	8	40	0.4	0.2	0.9	0.2
01 067	Henry	15,374	64.3	34.9	<.1	0.2	<.1	0.6	57	46	22	14	0.4	0.3	0.5	0.4
01 069	Houston	81,331	75.3	23.2	0.5	0.3	<.1	0.6	12	35	34	18	2.0	2.1	1.9	1.9
01 071	Jackson	47,796	93.2	4.1	0.2	2.1	<.1	0.4	25	9	61	28	1.2	1.5	0.2	0.8
01 073	Jefferson	651,525	63.9	35.0	0.5	0.1	<.1	0.4	1	47	21	30	16.1	14.1	22.4	11.1
01 075	Lamar	15,715	87.5	11.8	<.1	0.2	<.1	0.5	55	17	51	27	0.4	0.5	0.2	0.3
01 077	Lauderdale	79,661	89.5	9.6	0.2	0.2	<.1	0.4	13	14	54	36	2.0	2.4	0.8	1.3
01 079	Lawrence	31,513	77.7	15.2	<.1	6.7	<.1	0.3	35	31	44	50	0.8	0.8	0.5	0.4
01 081	Lee	87,146	74.0	23.4	1.8	0.1	<.1	0.6	11	36	33	12	2.2	2.2	2.0	2.2
01 083	Limestone	54,135	85.8	13.1	0.3	0.3	<.1	0.5	19	21	46	23	1.3	1.6	0.7	1.1
01 085	Lowndes	12,658	25.1	74.3	<.1	<.1	0.0	0.5	64	65	3	26	0.3	0.1	0.9	0.2
01 087	Macon	24,928	13.8	85.4	0.3	<.1	<.1	0.4	41	67	1	32	0.6	0.1	2.1	0.4
01 089	Madison	238,912	76.3	20.0	1.7	0.7	<.1	1.2	3	33	37	2	5.9	6.2	4.7	12.1
01 091	Marengo	23,084	48.9	50.7	<.1	<.1	<.1	0.3	44	58	10	49	0.6	0.4	1.2	0.3
01 093	Marion	29,830	96.2	3.2	0.1	0.2	<.1	0.2	36	6	62	64	0.7	1.0	<.1	0.3
01 095	Marshall	70,832	97.6	1.5	0.2	0.3	<.1	0.4	15	3	64	33	1.8	2.3	0.1	1.2
01 097	Mobile	378,643	66.7	31.0	0.9	0.5	<.1	0.8	2	42	25	6	9.4	8.5	11.5	12.8
01 099	Monroe	23,968	59.5	39.0	0.2	0.9	<.1	0.4	42	50	18	37	0.6	0.5	0.9	0.4
01 101	Montgomery	209,085	56.7	41.6	0.7	0.2	<.1	0.8	4	55	16	7	5.2	4.0	8.6	6.6
01 103	Morgan	100,043	88.7	10.0	0.4	0.3	<.1	0.6	7	15	53	16	2.5	3.0	1.0	2.4
01 105	Perry	12,759	35.2	64.2	0.1	0.1	<.1	0.3	62	61	7	56	0.3	0.2	0.8	0.1
01 107	Pickens	20,699	57.8	41.7	0.1	0.1	0.0	0.2	47	52	15	60	0.5	0.4	0.8	0.2
01 109	Pike	27,595	64.4	34.5	0.2	0.5	<.1	0.4	38	45	23	38	0.7	0.6	0.9	0.4
01 111	Randolph	19,881	76.0	23.5	0.1	0.1	<.1	0.3	48	34	32	59	0.5	0.5	0.5	0.2
01 113	Russell	46,860	60.4	38.5	0.2	0.2	<.1	0.6	26	49	19	11	1.2	1.0	1.8	1.2
01 115	St. Clair	50,009	90.1	9.1	0.2	0.3	<.1	0.4	21	13	55	31	1.2	1.5	0.4	0.8
01 117	Shelby	99,358	90.9	7.7	0.6	0.3	<.1	0.5	9	12	56	20	2.5	3.1	0.8	2.1
01 119	Sumter	16,174	29.3	69.9	0.2	<.1	<.1	0.5	53	63	5	24	0.4	0.2	1.1	0.3
01 121	Talladega	74,107	68.4	30.5	0.2	0.2	<.1	0.7	14	40	26	10	1.8	1.7	2.2	2.0
01 123	Tallapoosa	38,826	73.3	26.2	<.1	0.2	<.1	0.2	29	38	29	66	1.0	1.0	1.0	0.3
01 125	Tuscaloosa	150,522	72.3	26.1	0.8	0.2	<.1	0.6	5	39	30	13	3.7	3.7	3.9	3.8
01 127	Walker	67,670	92.9	6.5	0.1	0.1	<.1	0.3	16	10	58	48	1.7	2.1	0.4	0.9
01 129	Washington	16,694	65.6	27.6	<.1	6.3	<.1	0.3	51	43	28	51	0.4	0.4	0.5	0.2
01 131	Wilcox	13,568	30.8	68.8	<.1	<.1	0.0	0.3	60	62	6	54	0.3	0.1	0.9	0.2
01 133	Winston	22,053	99.2	0.3	0.1	0.2	0.0	0.3	45	1	67	58	0.5	0.7	<.1	0.2
01	**ALABAMA**	4,040,587	73.3	25.2	0.5	0.4	<.1	0.6					100.0	100.0	100.0	100.0

Table A. – 1990 Population by Race and Ethnic Origin (cont)

State/county code	County	Total persons	Percent of total persons						Rank				Percent contribution to state population			
			Non-Hispanic					Hispanic	Total	Percent of total persons		Hispanic	Total	Non-Hispanic		Hispanic
			White	Black	Asian and Pacific Islander	Native American	Other			Non-Hispanic				White	Black	
										White	Black					
	CONGRESSIONAL															
	District 1.........................	577,226	69.3	28.4	0.6	0.8	<.1	0.8	6	6	2	2	14.3	13.5	16.1	18.6
	District 2.........................	577,227	74.3	24.0	0.6	0.3	<.1	0.8	1	4	4	1	14.3	14.5	13.6	19.3
	District 3.........................	577,227	72.8	25.9	0.5	0.2	<.1	0.6	2	5	3	4	14.3	14.2	14.7	13.9
	District 4.........................	577,227	92.3	6.6	0.2	0.6	<.1	0.4	3	1	7	6	14.3	18.0	3.7	8.9
	District 5.........................	577,227	82.9	14.8	0.9	0.6	<.1	0.8	4	3	5	3	14.3	16.2	8.4	18.5
	District 6.........................	577,226	89.3	9.2	0.8	0.2	<.1	0.6	7	2	6	5	14.3	17.4	5.2	13.0
	District 7.........................	577,227	32.0	67.4	0.2	0.1	<.1	0.3	5	7	1	7	14.3	6.2	38.2	7.8

Alabama 41

Table B. — 1990 Voting Age Population (VAP) by Race and Ethnic Origin

County	Total Voting Age Population	Percent of total VAP – Non-Hispanic White	Black	Asian and Pacific Islander	Native American	Other	Hispanic	Rank Total	Rank Non-Hisp White	Rank Non-Hisp Black	Rank Hispanic	Pct contribution to state VAP Total	Non-Hisp White	Non-Hisp Black	Hispanic	VAP pct of total pop Total	Non-Hisp White	Black	Asian and Pacific Islander	Native American	Other	Hispanic
Autauga	24,124	80.8	18.0	0.4	0.2	0.0	0.6	33	30	38	12	0.8	0.9	0.6	0.9	70.5	72.2	63.8	75.4	67.6	0.0	63.5
Baldwin	72,747	87.4	10.9	0.2	0.6	<.1	0.9	9	21	49	5	2.4	2.8	1.2	3.9	74.0	75.8	62.8	71.3	72.9	44.8	64.0
Barbour	17,953	59.6	39.6	0.2	0.2	0.0	0.4	41	56	12	28	0.6	0.5	1.1	0.5	70.6	76.2	63.7	67.4	82.5	0.0	61.3
Bibb	11,783	81.5	18.1	<.1	0.1	0.0	0.2	51	28	37	60	0.4	0.4	0.3	0.2	71.1	73.7	61.4	72.7	64.0	0.0	69.2
Blount	29,212	97.7	1.2	<.1	0.3	<.1	0.7	28	4	65	9	1.0	1.3	<.1	1.2	74.4	74.5	70.1	72.7	72.1	66.7	68.9
Bullock	7,661	32.6	66.7	0.1	<.1	0.0	0.5	66	64	4	15	0.3	0.1	0.8	0.3	69.4	82.9	64.3	80.0	87.5	0.0	64.6
Butler	15,301	64.6	35.0	<.1	<.1	0.0	0.3	46	49	18	52	0.5	0.4	0.8	0.3	69.9	76.0	60.9	47.4	62.5	0.0	64.6
Calhoun	87,056	81.3	16.8	0.7	0.3	<.1	1.0	6	29	39	4	2.9	3.1	2.2	5.0	75.0	76.8	68.1	70.6	81.8	41.2	64.6
Chambers	27,244	67.8	31.8	<.1	<.1	<.1	0.3	30	46	21	50	0.9	0.8	1.3	0.4	73.9	78.5	65.7	75.0	77.8	50.0	59.1
Cherokee	14,851	93.3	6.0	0.1	0.3	<.1	0.3	47	11	57	56	0.5	0.6	0.1	0.2	76.0	76.5	69.6	75.0	76.5	50.0	68.4
Chilton	23,771	89.5	9.9	<.1	0.2	<.1	0.3	34	16	52	53	0.8	0.9	0.3	0.4	73.2	74.5	64.3	62.2	74.6	100.0	55.2
Choctaw	11,310	59.1	40.5	<.1	<.1	<.1	0.3	54	57	11	43	0.4	0.3	0.7	0.2	70.6	75.2	64.9	70.0	70.0	50.0	69.8
Clarke	19,085	61.0	38.3	0.1	0.2	<.1	0.4	39	54	13	32	0.6	0.5	1.1	0.4	70.1	75.3	63.2	62.9	64.4	25.0	68.9
Clay	9,934	85.4	14.2	0.1	0.2	0.0	0.2	60	24	43	63	0.3	0.4	0.2	0.1	75.0	77.0	65.0	76.9	69.6	0.0	66.7
Cleburne	9,418	95.3	4.1	0.1	0.2	0.0	0.3	61	7	60	55	0.3	0.4	<.1	0.1	74.0	74.4	66.1	84.6	75.0	0.0	65.8
Coffee	29,913	82.6	15.3	0.8	0.4	<.1	1.0	27	26	41	3	1.0	1.1	0.7	1.8	74.3	76.2	66.2	74.8	72.3	50.0	64.1
Colbert	39,118	84.4	14.9	0.1	0.1	<.1	0.3	20	25	42	45	1.3	1.5	0.9	0.7	75.7	77.4	68.0	58.1	69.6	80.0	65.8
Conecuh	10,136	61.7	37.4	0.1	0.2	<.1	0.5	58	53	15	19	0.3	0.3	0.6	0.3	72.1	78.0	64.4	84.6	60.0	40.0	59.8
Coosa	8,181	68.1	31.5	<.1	0.3	<.1	<.1	65	45	22	67	0.3	0.2	0.4	<.1	73.9	77.1	68.1	100.0	61.8	100.0	44.4
Covington	27,241	88.0	11.3	0.1	0.2	0.0	0.3	31	20	48	35	0.9	1.1	0.5	0.6	74.7	76.2	64.6	66.7	78.6	0.0	73.1
Crenshaw	9,991	76.0	23.5	<.1	0.2	0.0	0.2	59	38	29	59	0.3	0.3	0.3	0.1	73.3	75.8	66.1	60.0	80.0	0.0	80.0
Cullman	50,601	98.5	0.8	0.2	0.2	<.1	0.3	16	2	66	37	1.7	2.2	<.1	1.1	74.8	74.9	68.9	70.0	73.8	50.0	64.7
Dale	35,757	80.6	15.3	1.4	0.5	<.1	2.1	23	31	40	1	1.2	1.3	0.8	4.4	72.0	74.5	62.6	72.5	77.0	50.0	61.1
Dallas	33,025	46.6	52.7	0.3	<.1	<.1	0.3	26	59	9	54	1.1	0.7	2.6	0.5	68.6	76.8	62.7	70.5	78.0	28.6	67.9
DeKalb	40,744	97.2	1.7	0.1	0.7	<.1	0.3	18	5	63	44	1.4	1.7	0.1	0.8	74.6	74.9	67.7	56.6	59.2	50.0	61.4
Elmore	36,418	78.0	21.1	0.2	0.3	<.1	0.5	22	35	32	22	1.2	1.3	1.1	1.0	74.0	75.3	69.7	66.4	76.6	80.0	63.3
Escambia	26,051	70.6	26.2	0.1	2.7	<.1	0.4	32	41	27	26	0.9	0.8	1.0	0.7	73.3	75.9	68.0	55.2	67.3	69.2	66.3
Etowah	75,251	86.7	12.3	0.5	0.2	<.1	0.3	7	22	46	48	2.5	2.9	1.4	1.2	75.4	76.7	67.4	84.8	73.6	83.3	62.8
Fayette	13,360	88.1	11.4	<.1	<.1	0.0	0.4	50	19	47	33	0.4	0.5	0.2	0.3	74.4	75.1	69.5	57.9	66.7	0.0	61.5
Franklin	20,910	95.2	4.1	<.1	0.2	0.0	0.3	37	8	59	36	0.7	0.9	0.1	0.4	75.2	75.5	69.4	52.9	68.4	0.0	72.3
Geneva	17,757	88.9	10.3	<.1	0.4	0.0	0.4	42	17	51	31	0.6	0.7	0.3	0.4	75.1	76.6	65.0	84.6	77.8	0.0	55.4
Greene	6,811	24.1	75.7	0.0	<.1	0.0	0.1	67	66	2	66	0.2	<.1	0.8	<.1	67.1	83.5	63.2	0.0	100.0	0.0	37.5
Hale	10,616	44.9	54.7	<.1	0.1	0.0	0.3	57	60	8	40	0.4	0.2	0.9	0.2	68.5	76.3	63.3	50.0	55.0	0.0	63.2
Henry	11,273	67.8	31.4	<.1	0.2	0.0	0.6	55	47	23	14	0.4	0.3	0.5	0.4	73.3	77.3	66.0	100.0	76.7	0.0	69.6
Houston	58,858	78.2	20.4	0.5	0.4	<.1	0.5	13	33	34	17	2.0	2.0	1.8	1.8	72.4	75.2	63.6	62.1	74.6	40.0	64.9
Jackson	35,482	94.1	3.8	0.2	1.6	<.1	0.4	24	9	61	30	1.2	1.5	0.2	0.8	74.2	75.0	68.2	62.9	55.2	66.7	67.3
Jefferson	488,937	66.9	32.1	0.5	0.1	<.1	0.4	1	48	20	29	16.4	14.4	23.2	11.8	75.0	78.5	68.8	73.3	78.9	52.9	71.8
Lamar	11,725	88.6	10.7	<.1	0.1	<.1	0.4	52	18	50	24	0.4	0.5	0.2	0.3	74.6	75.6	67.3	100.0	70.8	100.0	73.2
Lauderdale	60,580	90.5	8.7	0.2	0.2	<.1	0.3	12	13	55	39	2.0	2.4	0.8	1.2	76.0	76.9	68.6	70.5	77.3	20.0	66.1
Lawrence	22,874	81.5	13.5	<.1	4.6	0.0	0.3	35	27	44	47	0.8	0.8	0.5	0.4	72.6	76.2	64.5	63.2	49.9	0.0	63.7
Lee	68,058	77.1	20.3	1.8	0.2	<.1	0.6	11	36	35	10	2.3	2.3	2.0	2.6	78.1	81.3	67.8	77.3	81.3	86.7	78.8
Limestone	40,529	86.3	12.8	0.2	0.3	<.1	0.4	19	23	45	25	1.4	1.5	0.8	1.1	74.9	75.2	72.8	64.3	75.7	50.0	68.6
Lowndes	8,263	30.4	69.1	<.1	<.1	0.0	0.5	64	65	3	18	0.3	0.1	0.8	0.2	65.3	79.0	60.7	75.0	44.4	0.0	66.7
Macon	18,286	15.1	84.0	0.3	<.1	<.1	0.5	40	67	1	21	0.6	0.1	2.3	0.5	73.4	80.7	72.1	71.8	73.9	40.0	84.5
Madison	180,157	78.2	18.5	1.6	0.5	<.1	1.1	3	34	36	2	6.0	6.2	4.9	11.8	75.4	77.3	69.7	70.8	59.3	51.6	66.1
Marengo	16,091	52.9	46.8	<.1	<.1	0.0	0.2	45	58	10	58	0.5	0.4	1.1	0.2	69.7	75.4	64.3	63.6	90.0	0.0	53.3
Marion	22,508	96.4	3.2	<.1	0.1	<.1	0.2	36	6	62	65	0.8	1.0	0.1	0.2	75.5	75.6	73.6	66.7	57.9	50.0	60.0
Marshall	53,366	97.8	1.4	0.1	0.3	<.1	0.3	15	3	64	41	1.8	2.3	0.1	1.1	75.3	75.5	70.4	68.8	69.6	33.3	62.3
Mobile	270,610	70.0	27.9	0.8	0.5	<.1	0.8	2	42	25	6	9.1	8.4	11.2	13.3	71.5	74.9	64.3	67.0	66.4	56.3	70.3
Monroe	16,590	63.6	34.9	0.2	0.9	0.0	0.3	44	50	19	38	0.6	0.5	0.9	0.3	69.2	74.1	62.0	56.6	70.7	0.0	60.6
Montgomery	151,701	60.6	37.8	0.7	0.2	<.1	0.7	4	55	14	8	5.1	4.1	8.5	6.8	72.6	77.6	65.8	69.9	73.0	45.1	70.0
Morgan	74,027	90.1	8.8	0.3	0.3	<.1	0.5	8	15	53	16	2.5	2.9	1.0	2.3	74.0	75.1	64.8	66.1	67.4	44.4	65.6
Perry	8,757	42.4	57.0	0.2	0.1	<.1	0.3	63	61	7	46	0.3	0.2	0.7	0.1	68.6	82.6	60.9	100.0	56.3	100.0	69.4
Pickens	14,805	63.1	36.4	0.1	0.1	0.0	0.2	48	51	16	61	0.5	0.4	0.8	0.2	71.5	78.1	62.5	63.0	70.8	0.0	66.0
Pike	20,729	68.3	30.5	0.3	0.4	<.1	0.4	38	44	24	27	0.7	0.6	0.9	0.5	75.1	79.7	66.5	92.6	63.2	50.0	82.4
Randolph	14,696	79.1	20.4	<.1	0.1	0.0	0.3	49	43	33	57	0.5	0.5	0.4	0.2	73.9	77.0	64.2	57.1	65.5	0.0	69.8
Russell	34,380	63.0	36.0	0.3	0.2	<.1	0.6	25	52	17	13	1.2	1.0	1.8	1.2	73.4	76.5	68.5	81.1	73.3	50.0	66.1
St. Clair	36,699	90.4	8.8	0.1	0.3	<.1	0.4	21	14	54	34	1.2	1.5	0.5	0.8	73.4	73.7	70.8	65.8	77.6	42.9	62.7
Shelby	72,167	91.6	7.1	0.5	0.3	<.1	0.4	10	12	56	23	2.4	2.9	0.8	2.0	72.6	73.2	66.8	66.0	67.7	42.9	64.2
Sumter	11,202	34.5	64.8	0.2	<.1	<.1	0.5	56	63	5	20	0.4	0.2	1.1	0.2	69.3	81.3	64.1	93.1	83.3	66.7	69.2
Talladega	53,614	71.5	27.4	0.1	0.2	<.1	0.8	14	40	26	7	1.8	1.7	2.2	2.5	72.3	75.6	64.8	69.9	73.8	37.5	84.9
Tallapoosa	28,899	76.4	23.2	<.1	0.1	<.1	0.2	29	37	30	64	1.0	1.0	1.0	0.3	74.4	77.6	65.8	67.6	66.1	62.5	73.2
Tuscaloosa	114,857	75.2	23.1	0.9	0.2	<.1	0.6	5	39	31	11	3.9	3.8	3.9	4.2	76.3	79.4	67.6	81.3	77.2	78.1	74.3
Walker	50,560	93.8	5.6	0.1	0.1	0.0	0.3	17	10	58	51	1.7	2.1	0.4	0.8	74.7	75.4	67.4	73.3	79.5	0.0	62.1
Washington	11,611	69.0	25.1	0.1	5.5	<.1	0.3	53	43	28	49	0.4	0.4	0.4	0.2	69.6	73.1	63.1	85.7	60.7	100.0	62.7
Wilcox	8,956	36.7	62.9	<.1	<.1	0.0	0.3	62	62	6	42	0.3	0.1	0.8	0.2	66.0	78.4	60.4	60.0	100.0	0.0	75.0
Winston	16,621	99.3	0.2	0.1	0.2	0.0	0.2	43	1	67	62	0.6	0.7	<.1	0.2	75.4	75.4	66.7	70.8	73.8	0.0	62.7
ALABAMA	**2,981,799**	**75.9**	**22.7**	**0.5**	**0.4**	**<.1**	**0.6**					**100.0**	**100.0**	**100.0**	**100.0**	**73.8**	**76.5**	**66.4**	**71.4**	**65.6**	**52.5**	**67.8**

County	Total Voting Age Population	Percent of total VAP						Rank				Percent contribution to state VAP				VAP percent of total population						
		Non-Hispanic							Percent of total VAP					Non-Hispanic				Non-Hispanic				
		White	Black	Asian and Pacific Islander	Native American	Other	Hispanic	Total	Non-Hispanic		Hispanic	Total	White	Black	Hispanic	Total	White	Black	Asian and Pacific Islander	Native American	Other	Hispanic
									White	Black												
CONGRESSIONAL																						
District 1	414,476	72.5	25.4	0.6	0.8	<.1	0.8	6	6	2	1	13.9	13.3	15.6	18.8	71.8	75.1	64.2	66.9	66.4	54.5	68.3
District 2	423,324	77.1	21.3	0.5	0.3	<.1	0.7	5	4	4	2	14.2	14.4	13.3	18.8	73.3	76.1	65.0	70.2	73.0	48.1	65.8
District 3	429,511	75.2	23.5	0.5	0.2	<.1	0.6	4	5	3	4	14.4	14.3	14.9	14.4	74.4	76.9	67.5	74.4	76.3	51.1	70.1
District 4	432,149	93.2	5.9	0.2	0.5	<.1	0.3	3	1	7	6	14.5	17.8	3.8	8.5	74.9	75.6	66.9	74.5	58.0	54.3	64.5
District 5	433,310	84.4	13.6	0.8	0.5	<.1	0.7	2	3	5	3	14.5	16.2	8.7	18.0	75.1	76.4	68.9	69.8	60.3	50.5	66.1
District 6	441,662	90.2	8.4	0.7	0.2	<.1	0.5	1	2	6	5	14.8	17.6	5.5	13.8	76.5	77.3	69.5	74.7	76.5	58.7	71.6
District 7	407,367	36.0	63.4	0.2	0.1	<.1	0.3	7	7	1	7	13.7	6.5	38.2	7.8	70.6	79.4	66.4	73.0	75.5	48.9	68.5

Table C. — Voter Participation: November 3, 1992, General Election

County	Estimated Voting Age Population (VAP) 1992	Voter registration (REG) Total	% contribution to state REG	% of 1992 VAP	Rank by % of 1992 VAP	Highest office Actual	Highest office Total	Office	% of 1992 VAP	Maximum vote Total	% contribution to state turnout	% of REG	Rank by % of REG	% of 1992 VAP	Rank by % 1992 VAP	Drop-off President	Drop-off Senator	Drop-off Governor	Drop-off Representative
Autauga	25,065	21,157	0.9	84.4	27	-	15,585	P	62.2	15,585	0.9	73.7	18	62.2	8	0.0	13.2	-	1.9
Baldwin	78,220	66,931	2.8	85.6	25	-	46,479	P	59.4	46,479	2.8	69.4	31	59.4	15	0.0	11.0	-	7.3
Barbour	18,530	17,239	0.7	93.0	11	-	10,431	P	56.3	10,431	0.6	60.5	60	56.3	30	0.0	23.2	-	6.1
Bibb	12,268	8,477	0.4	69.1	56	-	6,720	P	54.8	6,720	0.4	79.3	11	54.8	40	0.0	1.0	-	4.3
Blount	30,217	24,865	1.1	82.3	34	-	16,505	P	54.6	16,505	1.0	66.4	40	54.6	41	0.0	10.9	-	7.9
Bullock	7,844	6,517	0.3	83.1	32	-	4,816	P	61.4	4,816	0.3	73.9	17	61.4	10	0.0	15.1	-	2.8
Butler	15,754	10,767	0.5	68.3	58	-	8,481	P	53.8	8,481	0.5	78.8	13	53.8	45	0.0	16.8	-	6.1
Calhoun	86,983	64,999	2.7	74.7	49	-	42,800	P	49.2	42,800	2.5	65.8	41	49.2	59	0.0	11.3	-	9.4
Chambers	27,302	24,696	1.0	90.5	15	-	13,099	P	48.0	13,099	0.8	53.0	65	48.0	64	0.0	5.3	-	5.2
Cherokee	15,226	12,413	0.5	81.5	36	-	7,876	P	51.7	7,876	0.5	63.4	45	51.7	52	0.0	16.9	-	10.5
Chilton	24,678	22,536	1.0	91.3	14	-	14,468	P	58.6	14,468	0.9	64.2	44	58.6	18	0.0	1.7	-	7.8
Choctaw	11,600	7,643	0.3	65.9	59	-	7,560	P	65.2	7,560	0.4	98.9	2	65.2	5	0.0	16.7	-	22.7
Clarke	19,545	16,423	0.7	84.0	28	-	11,717	P	59.9	11,717	0.7	71.3	24	59.9	13	0.0	14.4	-	13.2
Clay	10,065	7,817	0.3	77.7	45	-	5,755	P	57.2	5,755	0.3	73.6	19	57.2	26	0.0	21.6	-	22.7
Cleburne	9,620	8,821	0.4	91.7	13	-	5,237	P	54.4	5,237	0.3	59.4	62	54.4	43	0.0	23.0	-	22.8
Coffee	30,846	25,137	1.1	81.5	37	-	15,534	P	50.4	15,534	0.9	61.8	52	50.4	56	0.0	10.7	-	2.7
Colbert	39,077	24,187	1.0	61.9	61	-	22,451	P	57.5	22,451	1.3	92.8	3	57.5	25	0.0	2.4	-	2.4
Conecuh	10,086	10,199	0.4	101.1	5	-	6,307	P	62.5	6,307	0.4	61.8	51	62.5	7	0.0	24.6	-	13.7
Coosa	8,267	6,908	0.3	83.6	31	-	4,798	P	58.0	4,798	0.3	69.5	30	58.0	22	0.0	1.7	-	4.0
Covington	27,645	27,572	1.2	99.7	6	-	13,962	P	50.5	13,962	0.8	50.6	66	50.5	54	0.0	21.9	-	7.3
Crenshaw	10,165	8,645	0.4	85.0	26	-	5,290	P	52.0	5,290	0.3	61.2	57	52.0	49	0.0	17.8	-	4.6
Cullman	52,428	41,430	1.7	79.0	42	-	29,050	P	55.4	29,050	1.7	70.1	27	55.4	35	0.0	2.2	-	1.9
Dale	36,444	25,664	1.1	70.4	54	-	15,787	P	43.3	15,787	0.9	61.5	55	43.3	67	0.0	13.3	-	3.4
Dallas	33,032	36,708	1.6	111.1	3	-	19,604	P	59.3	19,604	1.2	53.4	64	59.3	16	0.0	3.5	-	3.6
DeKalb	41,812	21,224	0.9	50.8	66	-	21,588	P	51.6	21,588	1.3	101.7	1	51.6	53	0.0	11.2	-	9.1
Elmore	38,268	30,153	1.3	78.8	43	-	20,389	P	53.3	20,389	1.2	67.6	38	53.3	46	0.0	3.1	-	1.5
Escambia	26,179	16,082	0.7	61.4	63	-	12,824	P	49.0	12,824	0.8	79.7	10	49.0	61	0.0	18.6	-	18.9
Etowah	76,183	61,342	2.6	80.5	39	-	42,451	P	55.7	42,451	2.5	69.2	34	55.7	32	0.0	2.7	-	2.0
Fayette	13,470	11,834	0.5	87.9	21	-	8,472	P	62.9	8,472	0.5	71.6	23	62.9	6	0.0	2.5	-	1.6
Franklin	21,134	19,026	0.8	90.0	16	-	11,858	P	56.1	11,858	0.7	62.3	47	56.1	31	0.0	3.5	-	3.0
Geneva	17,894	15,905	0.7	88.9	19	-	9,867	P	55.1	9,867	0.6	62.0	49	55.1	36	0.0	21.6	-	4.1
Greene	6,895	6,854	0.3	99.4	7	-	4,881	P	70.8	4,881	0.3	71.2	25	70.8	1	0.0	6.9	-	5.8
Hale	10,934	9,768	0.4	89.3	18	-	6,023	P	55.1	6,023	0.4	61.7	53	55.1	38	0.0	14.5	-	12.6
Henry	11,516	9,280	0.4	80.6	38	-	6,499	P	56.4	6,499	0.4	70.0	28	56.4	28	0.0	26.5	-	3.0
Houston	61,251	36,922	1.6	60.3	65	-	29,760	P	48.6	29,760	1.8	80.6	8	48.6	62	0.0	2.7	-	0.8
Jackson	35,776	22,939	1.0	64.1	60	-	18,916	P	52.9	18,916	1.1	82.5	7	52.9	47	0.0	16.9	-	14.2
Jefferson	491,909	386,343	16.3	78.5	44	-	299,096	P	60.8	299,096	17.7	77.4	14	60.8	11	0.0	1.9	-	1.8
Lamar	11,846	11,198	0.5	94.5	10	-	6,901	P	58.3	6,901	0.4	61.6	54	58.3	19	0.0	6.2	-	4.6
Lauderdale	60,899	37,662	1.6	61.8	62	-	33,782	P	55.5	33,782	2.0	89.7	5	55.5	33	0.0	3.3	-	3.2
Lawrence	23,650	18,026	0.8	76.2	47	-	11,589	P	49.0	11,589	0.7	64.3	43	49.0	60	0.0	2.9	-	4.7
Lee	68,285	57,270	2.4	83.9	29	-	35,490	P	52.0	35,490	2.1	62.0	50	52.0	50	0.0	13.8	-	15.2
Limestone	42,857	30,542	1.3	71.3	52	-	21,606	P	50.4	21,606	1.3	70.7	26	50.4	55	0.0	3.4	-	3.2
Lowndes	8,486	8,375	0.4	98.7	8	-	5,148	P	60.7	5,148	0.3	61.5	56	60.7	12	0.0	14.5	-	11.6
Macon	17,671	12,544	0.5	71.0	53	-	8,764	P	49.6	8,764	0.5	69.9	29	49.6	58	0.0	10.3	-	11.5
Madison	189,682	139,594	5.9	73.6	50	-	107,834	P	56.8	107,834	6.4	77.2	15	56.8	27	0.0	2.7	-	1.8
Marengo	16,254	18,619	0.8	114.6	2	-	11,246	P	69.2	11,246	0.7	60.4	61	69.2	2	0.0	12.4	-	9.4
Marion	22,828	19,119	0.8	83.8	30	-	13,270	P	58.1	13,270	0.8	69.4	32	58.1	20	0.0	3.3	-	4.1
Marshall	55,164	43,977	1.9	79.7	40	-	26,747	P	48.5	26,747	1.6	60.8	58	48.5	63	0.0	13.7	-	9.4
Mobile	277,892	212,076	9.0	76.3	46	-	144,038	P	51.8	144,038	8.5	67.9	36	51.8	51	0.0	6.7	-	6.2
Monroe	17,306	14,377	0.6	83.1	33	-	9,745	P	56.3	9,745	0.6	67.8	37	56.3	29	0.0	12.8	-	12.7
Montgomery	155,509	107,041	4.5	68.8	57	-	86,188	P	55.4	86,188	5.1	80.5	9	55.4	34	0.0	7.5	-	5.6
Morgan	77,242	61,419	2.6	79.5	41	-	44,864	C	58.1	44,864	2.7	73.0	20	58.1	21	1.9	4.5	-	0.0
Perry	8,556	8,947	0.4	104.6	4	-	5,813	P	67.9	5,813	0.3	65.0	42	67.9	4	0.0	9.3	-	10.6
Pickens	15,000	12,969	0.5	86.5	23	-	8,146	P	54.3	8,146	0.5	62.8	46	54.3	44	0.0	4.0	-	3.8
Pike	20,384	18,024	0.8	88.4	20	-	11,193	P	54.9	11,193	0.7	62.1	48	54.9	39	0.0	15.5	-	0.9
Randolph	14,933	11,319	0.5	75.8	48	-	8,153	P	54.6	8,153	0.5	72.0	21	54.6	42	0.0	20.5	-	20.1
Russell	34,834	17,224	0.7	49.4	67	-	15,690	P	45.0	15,690	0.9	91.1	4	45.0	66	0.0	16.0	-	17.9
St. Clair	39,221	28,538	1.2	72.8	51	-	21,624	P	55.1	21,624	1.3	75.8	16	55.1	37	0.0	1.7	-	4.1
Shelby	81,868	70,167	3.0	85.7	24	-	48,165	P	58.8	48,165	2.9	68.6	35	58.8	17	0.0	1.7	-	1.5
Sumter	11,306	10,127	0.4	89.6	17	-	7,025	P	62.1	7,025	0.4	69.4	33	62.1	9	0.0	3.0	-	4.8
Talladega	54,856	33,338	1.4	60.8	64	-	26,264	P	47.9	26,264	1.6	78.8	12	47.9	65	0.0	14.8	-	15.9
Tallapoosa	29,575	27,268	1.2	92.2	12	-	15,508	P	52.4	15,508	0.9	56.9	63	52.4	48	0.0	2.4	-	4.3
Tuscaloosa	116,399	81,087	3.4	69.7	55	-	58,114	P	49.9	58,114	3.4	71.7	22	49.9	57	0.0	1.6	-	3.5
Walker	51,357	44,427	1.9	86.5	22	-	29,534	P	57.5	29,534	1.7	66.5	39	57.5	24	0.0	2.5	-	1.3
Washington	11,946	9,812	0.4	82.1	35	-	8,162	P	68.3	8,162	0.5	83.2	6	68.3	3	0.0	3.5	-	3.2
Wilcox	9,175	10,811	0.5	117.8	1	-	5,305	P	57.8	5,305	0.3	49.1	67	57.8	23	0.0	3.2	-	7.7
Winston	16,891	16,650	0.7	98.6	9	-	10,089	P	59.7	10,089	0.6	60.6	59	59.7	14	0.0	3.2	-	2.6
ALABAMA[2]	**3,056,000**	**2,367,972**	**100.0**	**77.5**		**-**	**1,688,933**		**55.3**	**1,688,933**	**100.0**	**71.3**		**55.3**		**0.1**	**6.6**	**-**	**5.1**

[1]Percent drop-off is zero for any office used as highest office turnout. [2]Alabama does not report voter registration by political party affiliation, but does report registration by race. State voter registration by race is 1,667,342 (78.1%) for white, 443,809 (20.8%) for black, and 24,164 (1.1%) for other. Three counties—Hale, Mobile, and Wilcox—did not report the racial registration data.

Vote for President: November 3, 1992, General Election

County	Total	Clinton (DEM)	Bush (REP)	Perot (IND)	Other	Plurality Total	Party	DEM	REP	IND	Other	Rank DEM	Rank REP	Rank IND	Total	DEM	REP	IND	DEM	REP
Autauga	15,585	4,819	8,715	1,916	135	3,896	R	30.9	55.9	12.3	0.9	62	6	17	0.9	0.7	1.1	1.0	35.6	64.4
Baldwin	46,479	12,195	26,270	7,656	358	14,075	R	26.2	56.5	16.5	0.8	66	4	3	2.8	1.8	3.3	4.2	31.7	68.3
Barbour	10,431	4,836	4,475	1,020	100	361	D	46.4	42.9	9.8	1.0	27	41	44	0.6	0.7	0.6	0.6	51.9	48.1
Bibb	6,720	2,900	3,124	686	10	224	R	43.2	46.5	10.2	0.1	32	32	38	0.4	0.4	0.4	0.4	48.1	51.9
Blount	16,505	5,433	8,882	1,949	241	3,449	R	32.9	53.8	11.8	1.5	60	9	23	1.0	0.8	1.1	1.1	38.0	62.0
Bullock	4,816	3,259	1,253	266	38	2,006	D	67.7	26.0	5.5	0.8	5	63	61	0.3	0.5	0.2	0.1	72.2	27.8
Butler	8,481	4,021	3,494	867	99	527	D	47.4	41.2	10.2	1.2	23	44	37	0.5	0.6	0.4	0.5	53.5	46.5
Calhoun	42,800	16,453	20,623	4,717	1,007	4,170	R	38.4	48.2	11.0	2.4	45	23	29	2.5	2.4	2.6	2.6	44.4	55.6
Chambers	13,099	5,938	5,682	1,427	52	256	D	45.3	43.4	10.9	0.4	29	40	31	0.8	0.9	0.7	0.8	51.1	48.9
Cherokee	7,876	4,222	2,745	846	63	1,477	D	53.6	34.9	10.7	0.8	14	57	32	0.5	0.6	0.3	0.5	60.6	39.4
Chilton	14,468	4,946	8,126	1,363	33	3,180	R	34.2	56.2	9.4	0.2	58	5	45	0.9	0.7	1.0	0.7	37.8	62.2
Choctaw	7,560	3,941	3,069	489	61	872	D	52.1	40.6	6.5	0.8	15	48	59	0.4	0.6	0.4	0.3	56.2	43.8
Clarke	11,717	5,023	5,495	872	327	472	R	42.9	46.9	7.4	2.8	34	30	57	0.7	0.7	0.7	0.5	47.8	52.2
Clay	5,755	2,073	2,859	652	171	786	R	36.0	49.7	11.3	3.0	54	15	25	0.3	0.3	0.4	0.4	42.0	58.0
Cleburne	5,237	2,144	2,425	630	38	281	R	40.9	46.3	12.0	0.7	38	34	20	0.3	0.3	0.3	0.3	46.9	53.1
Coffee	15,534	5,776	7,591	2,021	146	1,815	R	37.2	48.9	13.0	0.9	50	19	13	0.9	0.8	0.9	1.1	43.2	56.8
Colbert	22,451	12,206	8,073	2,098	74	4,133	D	54.4	36.0	9.3	0.3	13	55	46	1.3	1.8	1.0	1.1	60.2	39.8
Conecuh	6,307	3,155	2,463	552	137	692	D	50.0	39.1	8.8	2.2	19	52	51	0.4	0.5	0.3	0.3	56.2	43.8
Coosa	4,798	2,330	1,973	476	19	357	D	48.6	41.1	9.9	0.4	21	46	43	0.3	0.3	0.2	0.3	54.1	45.9
Covington	13,962	5,004	6,840	1,880	238	1,836	R	35.8	49.0	13.5	1.7	56	18	10	0.8	0.7	0.9	1.0	42.2	57.8
Crenshaw	5,290	2,404	2,339	485	62	65	D	45.4	44.2	9.2	1.2	28	39	47	0.3	0.3	0.3	0.3	50.7	49.3
Cullman	29,050	10,451	14,411	4,113	75	3,960	R	36.0	49.6	14.2	0.3	55	16	7	1.7	1.5	1.8	2.2	42.0	58.0
Dale	15,787	5,098	8,123	2,423	143	3,025	R	32.3	51.5	15.3	0.9	61	11	5	0.9	0.7	1.0	1.3	38.6	61.4
Dallas	19,604	11,053	7,394	1,110	47	3,659	D	56.4	37.7	5.7	0.2	9	54	60	1.2	1.6	0.9	0.6	59.9	40.1
DeKalb	21,588	8,245	10,519	2,741	83	2,274	R	38.2	48.7	12.7	0.4	46	20	15	1.3	1.2	1.3	1.5	43.9	56.1
Elmore	20,389	6,223	11,356	2,765	45	5,133	R	30.5	55.7	13.6	0.2	63	7	9	1.2	0.9	1.4	1.5	35.4	64.6
Escambia	12,824	4,809	5,955	1,616	444	1,146	R	37.5	46.4	12.6	3.5	48	33	16	0.8	0.7	0.7	0.9	44.7	55.3
Etowah	42,451	20,558	17,467	4,277	149	3,091	D	48.4	41.1	10.1	0.4	22	45	40	2.5	3.0	2.2	2.3	54.1	45.9
Fayette	8,472	3,830	3,604	1,012	26	226	D	45.2	42.5	11.9	0.3	30	43	21	0.5	0.6	0.4	0.6	51.5	48.5
Franklin	11,858	5,953	4,794	1,075	36	1,159	D	50.2	40.4	9.1	0.3	17	49	49	0.7	0.9	0.6	0.6	55.4	44.6
Geneva	9,867	3,622	4,843	1,323	79	1,221	R	36.7	49.1	13.4	0.8	52	17	11	0.6	0.5	0.6	0.7	42.8	57.2
Greene	4,881	3,865	805	194	17	3,060	D	79.2	16.5	4.0	0.3	2	66	64	0.3	0.6	0.1	0.1	82.8	17.2
Hale	6,023	3,481	2,001	486	55	1,480	D	57.8	33.2	8.1	0.9	8	58	55	0.4	0.5	0.2	0.3	63.5	36.5
Henry	6,499	2,804	2,970	667	58	166	R	43.1	45.7	10.3	0.9	33	36	36	0.4	0.4	0.4	0.4	48.6	51.4
Houston	29,760	8,857	17,360	3,492	51	8,503	R	29.8	58.3	11.7	0.2	65	2	24	1.8	1.3	2.2	1.9	33.8	66.2
Jackson	18,916	10,628	5,711	2,462	115	4,917	D	56.2	30.2	13.0	0.6	10	62	12	1.1	1.5	0.7	1.3	65.0	35.0
Jefferson	299,096	125,889	149,832	22,191	1,184	23,943	R	42.1	50.1	7.4	0.4	35	14	58	17.7	18.2	18.6	12.1	45.7	54.3
Lamar	6,901	2,849	3,262	763	27	413	R	41.3	47.3	11.1	0.4	37	28	28	0.4	0.4	0.4	0.4	46.6	53.4
Lauderdale	33,782	15,936	13,728	4,009	109	2,208	D	47.2	40.6	11.9	0.3	24	47	22	2.0	2.3	1.7	2.2	53.7	46.3
Lawrence	11,589	6,364	3,576	1,624	25	2,788	D	54.9	30.9	14.0	0.2	12	61	8	0.7	0.9	0.4	0.9	64.0	36.0
Lee	35,490	13,770	16,885	4,572	263	3,115	R	38.8	47.6	12.9	0.7	44	26	14	2.1	2.0	2.1	2.5	44.9	55.1
Limestone	21,606	8,087	9,862	3,584	73	1,775	R	37.4	45.6	16.6	0.3	49	37	2	1.3	1.2	1.2	2.0	45.1	54.9
Lowndes	5,148	3,500	1,328	284	36	2,172	D	68.0	25.8	5.5	0.7	4	64	63	0.3	0.5	0.2	0.2	72.5	27.5
Macon	8,764	7,253	1,134	283	94	6,119	D	82.8	12.9	3.2	1.1	1	67	67	0.5	1.1	0.1	0.2	86.5	13.5
Madison	107,834	38,974	51,444	16,989	427	12,470	R	36.1	47.7	15.8	0.4	53	25	4	6.4	5.6	6.4	9.3	43.1	56.9
Marengo	11,246	5,632	4,470	919	225	1,162	D	50.1	39.7	8.2	2.0	18	51	52	0.7	0.8	0.6	0.5	55.8	44.2
Marion	13,270	6,167	5,692	1,389	22	475	D	46.5	42.9	10.5	0.2	25	42	34	0.8	0.9	0.7	0.8	52.0	48.0
Marshall	26,747	10,421	12,249	3,795	282	1,828	R	39.0	45.8	14.2	1.1	43	35	6	1.6	1.5	1.5	2.1	46.0	54.0
Mobile	144,038	54,962	72,935	15,105	1,036	17,973	R	38.2	50.6	10.5	0.7	47	12	33	8.5	8.0	9.1	8.2	43.0	57.0
Monroe	9,745	3,872	4,919	759	195	1,047	R	39.7	50.5	7.8	2.0	42	13	56	0.6	0.6	0.6	0.4	44.0	56.0
Montgomery	86,188	37,342	40,742	7,647	457	3,400	R	43.3	47.3	8.9	0.5	31	27	50	5.1	5.4	5.1	4.2	47.8	52.2
Morgan	43,991	15,091	21,073	7,683	144	5,982	R	34.3	47.9	17.5	0.3	57	24	1	2.6	2.2	2.6	4.2	41.7	58.3
Perry	5,813	3,712	1,829	213	59	1,883	D	63.9	31.5	3.7	1.0	7	60	65	0.3	0.5	0.2	0.1	67.0	33.0
Pickens	8,146	3,783	3,634	690	39	149	D	46.4	44.6	8.5	0.5	26	38	53	0.5	0.5	0.5	0.4	51.0	49.0
Pike	11,193	4,688	5,423	1,024	58	735	R	41.9	48.4	9.1	0.5	36	21	48	0.7	0.7	0.7	0.6	46.4	53.6
Randolph	8,153	3,318	3,813	919	103	495	R	40.7	46.8	11.3	1.3	40	31	27	0.5	0.5	0.5	0.5	46.5	53.5
Russell	15,690	8,647	5,587	1,360	96	3,060	D	55.1	35.6	8.7	0.6	11	56	52	0.9	1.3	0.7	0.7	60.7	39.3
St. Clair	21,624	6,517	12,447	2,614	46	5,930	R	30.1	57.6	12.1	0.2	64	3	18	1.3	0.9	1.5	1.4	34.4	65.6
Shelby	48,165	10,317	32,736	5,022	90	22,419	R	21.4	68.0	10.4	0.2	67	1	35	2.9	1.5	4.1	2.7	24.0	76.0
Sumter	7,025	4,810	1,807	388	20	3,003	D	68.5	25.7	5.5	0.3	3	65	62	0.4	0.7	0.2	0.2	72.7	27.3
Talladega	26,264	10,695	12,661	2,629	279	1,966	R	40.7	48.2	10.0	1.1	39	22	41	1.6	1.5	1.6	1.4	45.8	54.2
Tallapoosa	15,508	5,703	8,140	1,562	103	2,437	R	36.8	52.5	10.1	0.7	51	10	41	0.9	0.8	1.0	0.9	41.2	58.8
Tuscaloosa	58,114	23,495	27,454	7,011	154	3,959	R	40.4	47.2	12.1	0.3	41	29	19	3.4	3.4	3.4	3.8	46.1	53.9
Walker	29,534	14,831	11,301	3,344	58	3,530	D	50.2	38.3	11.3	0.2	16	53	26	1.7	2.1	1.4	1.8	56.8	43.2
Washington	8,162	4,046	3,270	829	17	776	D	49.6	40.1	10.2	0.2	20	50	39	0.5	0.6	0.4	0.5	55.3	44.7
Wilcox	5,305	3,439	1,671	174	21	1,768	D	64.8	31.5	3.3	0.4	6	59	66	0.3	0.5	0.2	< .1	67.3	32.7
Winston	10,089	3,415	5,550	1,110	14	2,135	R	33.8	55.0	11.0	0.1	59	8	30	0.6	0.5	0.7	0.6	38.1	61.9
ALABAMA	1,688,060	690,080	804,283	183,109	10,588	114,203	R	40.9	47.6	10.8	0.6				100.0	100.0	100.0	100.0	46.2	53.8

Table F. — Vote for U.S. Senator: November 3, 1992, General Election

County	Total	Shelby (DEM)	Sellers (REP)	Other	Plurality Total	Party	DEM	REP	Other	Rank DEM	Rank REP	Rank Other	Total	DEM	REP	Other
Autauga	13,534	9,012	4,279	243	4,733	D	66.6	31.6	1.8	42	26	41	0.9	0.9	0.8	0.7
Baldwin	41,388	21,036	19,258	1,094	1,778	D	50.8	46.5	2.6	66	2	14	2.6	2.1	3.7	3.3
Barbour	8,015	5,783	2,087	145	3,696	D	72.2	26.0	1.8	28	38	40	0.5	0.6	0.4	0.4
Bibb	6,653	4,877	1,698	78	3,179	D	73.3	25.5	1.2	24	39	58	0.4	0.5	0.3	0.2
Blount	14,706	8,311	5,974	421	2,337	D	56.5	40.6	2.9	62	6	11	0.9	0.8	1.1	1.3
Bullock	4,087	3,564	480	43	3,084	D	87.2	11.7	1.1	3	64	61	0.3	0.3	<.1	0.1
Butler	7,059	5,305	1,655	99	3,650	D	75.2	23.4	1.4	19	48	52	0.4	0.5	0.3	0.3
Calhoun	37,958	22,735	14,190	1,033	8,545	D	59.9	37.4	2.7	60	9	13	2.4	2.2	2.7	3.1
Chambers	12,406	8,187	3,942	277	4,245	D	66.0	31.8	2.2	46	24	23	0.8	0.8	0.8	0.8
Cherokee	6,542	5,004	1,372	166	3,632	D	76.5	21.0	2.5	17	52	17	0.4	0.5	0.3	0.5
Chilton	14,219	9,636	4,409	174	5,227	D	67.8	31.0	1.2	39	28	55	0.9	0.9	0.8	0.5
Choctaw	6,294	5,069	1,195	30	3,874	D	80.5	19.0	0.5	11	55	65	0.4	0.5	0.2	<.1
Clarke	10,030	6,655	3,260	115	3,395	D	66.4	32.5	1.1	44	21	59	0.6	0.7	0.6	0.3
Clay	4,512	3,061	1,309	142	1,752	D	67.8	29.0	3.1	38	31	4	0.3	0.3	0.3	0.4
Cleburne	4,033	2,560	1,354	119	1,206	D	63.5	33.6	3.0	50	19	6	0.3	0.3	0.3	0.4
Coffee	13,879	10,222	3,420	237	6,802	D	73.7	24.6	1.7	23	43	43	0.9	1.0	0.7	0.7
Colbert	21,913	16,589	4,965	359	11,624	D	75.7	22.7	1.6	18	50	47	1.4	1.6	1.0	1.1
Conecuh	4,755	3,679	980	96	2,699	D	77.4	20.6	2.0	15	53	29	0.3	0.4	0.2	0.3
Coosa	4,716	3,452	1,142	122	2,310	D	73.2	24.2	2.6	25	46	16	0.3	0.3	0.2	0.4
Covington	10,906	7,835	2,703	368	5,132	D	71.8	24.8	3.4	30	42	3	0.7	0.8	0.5	1.1
Crenshaw	4,350	3,484	777	89	2,707	D	80.1	17.9	2.0	12	57	28	0.3	0.3	0.1	0.3
Cullman	28,405	17,366	10,380	659	6,986	D	61.1	36.5	2.3	54	13	21	1.8	1.7	2.0	2.0
Dale	13,686	9,096	4,341	249	4,755	D	66.5	31.7	1.8	43	25	37	0.9	0.9	0.8	0.8
Dallas	18,915	15,493	3,275	147	12,218	D	81.9	17.3	0.8	8	60	63	1.2	1.5	0.6	0.4
DeKalb	19,168	11,176	7,515	477	3,661	D	58.3	39.2	2.5	61	7	19	1.2	1.1	1.4	1.4
Elmore	19,762	13,288	6,078	396	7,210	D	67.2	30.8	2.0	40	29	30	1.3	1.3	1.2	1.2
Escambia	10,442	6,268	3,874	300	2,394	D	60.0	37.1	2.9	58	12	10	0.7	0.6	0.7	0.9
Etowah	41,323	29,183	11,289	851	17,894	D	70.6	27.3	2.1	34	34	27	2.6	2.9	2.2	2.6
Fayette	8,260	6,184	1,960	116	4,224	D	74.9	23.7	1.4	20	47	51	0.5	0.6	0.4	0.4
Franklin	11,444	8,215	3,021	208	5,194	D	71.8	26.4	1.8	32	36	38	0.7	0.8	0.6	0.6
Geneva	7,735	5,629	1,802	304	3,827	D	72.8	23.3	3.9	26	49	2	0.5	0.6	0.3	0.9
Greene	4,546	4,155	371	20	3,784	D	91.4	8.2	0.4	1	67	67	0.3	0.4	<.1	<.1
Hale	5,151	4,227	861	63	3,366	D	82.1	16.7	1.2	7	61	56	0.3	0.4	0.2	0.2
Henry	4,775	3,533	1,162	80	2,371	D	74.0	24.3	1.7	21	45	45	0.3	0.3	0.2	0.2
Houston	28,953	18,918	9,651	384	9,267	D	65.3	33.3	1.3	48	20	53	1.8	1.8	1.8	1.2
Jackson	15,726	11,396	3,973	357	7,423	D	72.5	25.3	2.3	27	41	22	1.0	1.1	0.8	1.1
Jefferson	293,280	178,070	109,615	5,595	68,455	D	60.7	37.4	1.9	57	10	35	18.6	17.4	21.0	16.9
Lamar	6,476	4,318	2,015	143	2,303	D	66.7	31.1	2.2	41	27	24	0.4	0.4	0.4	0.4
Lauderdale	32,677	23,521	8,509	647	15,012	D	72.0	26.0	2.0	29	37	31	2.1	2.3	1.6	2.0
Lawrence	11,248	9,103	1,971	174	7,132	D	80.9	17.5	1.5	10	59	50	0.7	0.9	0.4	0.5
Lee	30,592	15,983	13,684	925	2,299	D	52.2	44.7	3.0	65	3	5	1.9	1.6	2.6	2.8
Limestone	20,882	13,703	6,657	522	7,046	D	65.6	31.9	2.5	47	23	18	1.3	1.3	1.3	1.6
Lowndes	4,400	3,748	597	55	3,151	D	85.2	13.6	1.3	5	63	54	0.3	0.4	0.1	0.2
Macon	7,865	6,818	700	347	6,118	D	86.7	8.9	4.4	4	66	1	0.5	0.7	0.1	1.0
Madison	104,925	66,537	35,311	3,077	31,226	D	63.4	33.7	2.9	51	18	7	6.7	6.5	6.8	9.3
Marengo	9,850	8,019	1,747	84	6,272	D	81.4	17.7	0.9	9	58	62	0.6	0.8	0.3	0.3
Marion	12,837	8,946	3,650	241	5,296	D	69.7	28.4	1.9	35	33	36	0.8	0.9	0.7	0.7
Marshall	23,092	14,665	7,790	637	6,875	D	63.5	33.7	2.8	49	17	12	1.5	1.4	1.5	1.9
Mobile	134,451	80,566	50,731	3,154	29,835	D	59.9	37.7	2.3	59	8	20	8.5	7.9	9.7	9.5
Monroe	8,500	5,276	3,084	140	2,192	D	62.1	36.3	1.6	53	15	46	0.5	0.5	0.6	0.4
Montgomery	79,724	55,442	22,838	1,444	32,604	D	69.5	28.6	1.8	36	32	39	5.1	5.4	4.4	4.4
Morgan	42,865	26,110	15,645	1,110	10,465	D	60.9	36.5	2.6	55	14	15	2.7	2.6	3.0	3.4
Perry	5,270	4,215	992	63	3,223	D	80.0	18.8	1.2	13	56	57	0.3	0.4	0.2	0.2
Pickens	7,822	5,616	1,980	226	3,636	D	71.8	25.3	2.9	31	40	8	0.5	0.5	0.4	0.7
Pike	9,456	7,278	2,073	105	5,205	D	77.0	21.9	1.1	16	51	60	0.6	0.7	0.4	0.3
Randolph	6,485	4,079	2,219	187	1,860	D	62.9	34.2	2.9	52	16	9	0.4	0.4	0.4	0.6
Russell	13,180	9,066	3,831	283	5,235	D	68.8	29.1	2.1	37	30	25	0.8	0.9	0.7	0.9
St. Clair	21,255	11,528	9,318	409	2,210	D	54.2	43.8	1.9	64	4	33	1.3	1.1	1.8	1.2
Shelby	47,343	22,118	24,470	755	2,352	R	46.7	51.7	1.6	67	1	49	3.0	2.2	4.7	2.3
Sumter	6,812	5,980	785	47	5,195	D	87.8	11.5	0.7	2	65	64	0.4	0.6	0.2	0.1
Talladega	22,379	13,594	8,319	466	5,275	D	60.7	37.2	2.1	56	11	26	1.4	1.3	1.6	1.4
Tallapoosa	15,142	10,042	4,839	261	5,203	D	66.3	32.0	1.7	45	22	42	1.0	1.0	0.9	0.8
Tuscaloosa	57,170	40,937	15,136	1,097	25,801	D	71.6	26.5	1.9	33	35	34	3.6	4.0	2.9	3.3
Walker	28,789	21,262	7,037	490	14,225	D	73.9	24.4	1.7	22	44	44	1.8	2.1	1.3	1.5
Washington	7,879	6,209	1,541	129	4,668	D	78.8	19.6	1.6	14	54	48	0.5	0.6	0.3	0.4
Wilcox	5,136	4,269	844	23	3,425	D	83.1	16.4	0.4	6	62	66	0.3	0.4	0.2	<.1
Winston	9,771	5,497	4,085	189	1,412	D	56.3	41.8	1.9	63	5	32	0.6	0.5	0.8	0.6
ALABAMA	**1,577,799**	**1,022,698**	**522,015**	**33,086**	**500,683**	**D**	**64.8**	**33.1**	**2.1**				**100.0**	**100.0**	**100.0**	**100.0**

Table H. — Vote for U.S. Representative in Congress: November 3, 1992, General Election

Congressional district and county	Total	Democrat (DEM)	Republican (REP)	Other	Plurality Total	Plurality Party	Percent of total vote DEM	REP	Other	Rank within district DEM	REP	Other	Percent contribution to district vote Total	DEM	REP	Other
District 1	214,204	78,742	128,874	6,588	50,132	R	36.8	60.2	3.1				100.0	100.0	100.0	100.0
Baldwin	43,101	11,951	29,426	1,724	17,475	R	27.7	68.3	4.0	6	1	1	20.1	15.2	22.8	26.2
Clarke (pt)	9,230	3,784	5,214	232	1,430	R	41.0	56.5	2.5	2	5	4	4.3	4.8	4.0	3.5
Escambia	10,396	3,976	6,134	286	2,158	R	38.2	59.0	2.8	4	3	3	4.9	5.0	4.8	4.3
Mobile	135,075	52,356	78,674	4,045	26,318	R	38.8	58.2	3.0	3	4	2	63.1	66.5	61.0	61.4
Monroe	8,503	3,242	5,123	138	1,881	R	38.1	60.2	1.6	5	2	6	4.0	4.1	4.0	2.1
Washington	7,899	3,433	4,303	163	870	R	43.5	54.5	2.1	1	6	5	3.7	4.4	3.3	2.5
District 2	228,160	109,335	112,906	5,919	3,571	R	47.9	49.5	2.6				100.0	100.0	100.0	100.0
Autauga	15,289	7,716	7,104	469	612	D	50.5	46.5	3.1	10	6	4	6.7	7.1	6.3	7.9
Barbour	9,791	6,427	3,144	220	3,283	D	65.6	32.1	2.2	3	13	10	4.3	5.9	2.8	3.7
Bullock	4,683	3,618	974	91	2,644	D	77.3	20.8	1.9	1	15	12	2.1	3.3	0.9	1.5
Butler	7,962	4,985	2,793	184	2,192	D	62.6	35.1	2.3	5	11	9	3.5	4.6	2.5	3.1
Coffee	15,118	6,617	8,151	350	1,534	R	43.8	53.9	2.3	12	4	8	6.6	6.1	7.2	5.9
Conecuh	5,446	3,732	1,508	206	2,224	D	68.5	27.7	3.8	2	14	1	2.4	3.4	1.3	3.5
Covington	12,945	6,747	5,719	479	1,028	D	52.1	44.2	3.7	8	8	2	5.7	6.2	5.1	8.1
Crenshaw	5,046	3,230	1,705	111	1,525	D	64.0	33.8	2.2	4	12	11	2.2	3.0	1.5	1.9
Dale	15,249	6,470	8,364	415	1,894	R	42.4	54.8	2.7	13	3	7	6.7	5.9	7.4	7.0
Elmore	20,089	9,572	9,936	581	364	R	47.6	49.5	2.9	11	5	6	8.8	8.8	8.8	9.8
Geneva	9,458	4,906	4,229	323	677	D	51.9	44.7	3.4	9	7	3	4.1	4.5	3.7	5.5
Henry	6,301	3,694	2,512	95	1,182	D	58.6	39.9	1.5	7	9	14	2.8	3.4	2.2	1.6
Houston	29,531	11,561	17,539	431	5,978	R	39.1	59.4	1.5	14	1	15	12.9	10.6	15.5	7.3
Montgomery (pt)	60,159	23,415	34,993	1,751	11,578	R	38.9	58.2	2.9	15	2	5	26.4	21.4	31.0	29.6
Pike	11,093	6,645	4,235	213	2,410	D	59.9	38.2	1.9	6	10	13	4.9	6.1	3.8	3.6
District 3	197,604	119,175	73,800	4,629	45,375	D	60.3	37.3	2.3				100.0	100.0	100.0	100.0
Bibb (pt)	5,032	3,103	1,851	78	1,252	D	61.7	36.8	1.6	8	5	14	2.5	2.6	2.5	1.7
Calhoun	38,791	26,060	11,779	952	14,281	D	67.2	30.4	2.5	4	11	6	19.6	21.9	16.0	20.6
Chambers	12,420	6,565	5,661	194	904	D	52.9	45.6	1.6	12	3	13	6.3	5.5	7.7	4.2
Chilton	13,342	7,608	5,459	275	2,149	D	57.0	40.9	2.1	11	4	9	6.8	6.4	7.4	5.9
Clay	4,448	2,927	1,381	140	1,546	D	65.8	31.0	3.1	5	10	1	2.3	2.5	1.9	3.0
Cleburne	4,044	2,636	1,305	103	1,331	D	65.2	32.3	2.5	6	9	4	2.0	2.2	1.8	2.2
Coosa	4,608	3,222	1,256	130	1,966	D	69.9	27.3	2.8	2	13	3	2.3	2.7	1.7	2.8
Lee	30,103	15,009	14,231	863	778	D	49.9	47.3	2.9	13	2	2	15.2	12.6	19.3	18.6
Macon	7,754	6,916	683	155	6,233	D	89.2	8.8	2.0	1	14	11	3.9	5.8	0.9	3.3
Randolph	6,517	3,989	2,372	156	1,617	D	61.2	36.4	2.4	9	7	8	3.3	3.3	3.2	3.4
Russell	12,879	8,887	3,727	265	5,160	D	69.0	28.9	2.1	3	12	10	6.5	7.5	5.1	5.7
St. Clair	20,731	9,372	10,840	519	1,468	R	45.2	52.3	2.5	14	1	5	10.5	7.9	14.7	11.2
Talladega	22,087	13,449	8,102	536	5,347	D	60.9	36.7	2.4	10	6	7	11.2	11.3	11.0	11.6
Tallapoosa	14,848	9,432	5,153	263	4,279	D	63.5	34.7	1.8	7	8	12	7.5	7.9	7.0	5.7
District 4	230,523	157,907	66,934	5,682	90,973	D	68.5	29.0	2.5				100.0	100.0	100.0	100.0
Blount	15,194	8,852	5,582	760	3,270	D	58.3	36.7	5.0	12	3	1	6.6	5.6	8.3	13.4
Cherokee	7,049	5,237	1,614	198	3,623	D	74.3	22.9	2.8	6	11	3	3.1	3.3	2.4	3.5
Cullman	28,490	18,449	9,394	647	9,055	D	64.8	33.0	2.3	10	4	6	12.4	11.7	14.0	11.4
DeKalb	19,618	10,726	8,356	536	2,370	D	54.7	42.6	2.7	14	1	4	8.5	6.8	12.5	9.4
Etowah	41,599	29,436	11,275	888	18,161	D	70.8	27.1	2.1	9	6	7	18.0	18.6	16.8	15.6
Fayette	8,333	6,571	1,652	110	4,919	D	78.9	19.8	1.3	2	13	14	3.6	4.2	2.5	1.9
Franklin	11,502	8,470	2,847	185	5,623	D	73.6	24.8	1.6	7	8	13	5.0	5.4	4.3	3.3
Lamar	6,587	4,693	1,742	152	2,951	D	71.2	26.4	2.3	8	7	5	2.9	3.0	2.6	2.7
Lawrence (pt)	9,407	7,742	1,480	185	6,262	D	82.3	15.7	2.0	1	14	9	4.1	4.9	2.2	3.3
Marion	12,726	9,510	2,981	235	6,529	D	74.7	23.4	1.8	5	9	11	5.5	6.0	4.5	4.1
Marshall	24,229	15,527	7,819	883	7,708	D	64.1	32.3	3.6	11	5	2	10.5	9.8	11.7	15.5
Pickens (pt)	6,806	5,130	1,552	124	3,578	D	75.4	22.8	1.8	3	12	12	3.0	3.2	2.3	2.2
Walker	29,161	21,865	6,699	597	15,166	D	75.0	23.0	2.0	4	10	8	12.6	13.8	10.0	10.5
Winston	9,822	5,699	3,941	182	1,758	D	58.0	40.1	1.9	13	2	10	4.3	3.6	5.9	3.2
District 5	244,133	160,060	77,951	6,122	82,109	D	65.6	31.9	2.5				100.0	100.0	100.0	100.0
Colbert	21,909	16,502	5,065	342	11,437	D	75.3	23.1	1.6	2	6	6	9.0	10.3	6.5	5.6
Jackson	16,221	11,815	4,028	378	7,787	D	72.8	24.8	2.3	3	5	4	6.6	7.4	5.2	6.2
Lauderdale	32,702	23,126	8,978	598	14,148	D	70.7	27.5	1.8	4	4	5	13.4	14.4	11.5	9.8
Lawrence (pt)	1,635	1,374	242	19	1,132	D	84.0	14.8	1.2	1	7	7	0.7	0.9	0.3	0.3
Limestone	20,917	12,627	7,722	568	4,905	D	60.4	36.9	2.7	6	2	2	8.6	7.9	9.9	9.3
Madison	105,885	67,997	34,866	3,022	33,131	D	64.2	32.9	2.9	5	3	1	43.4	42.5	44.7	49.4
Morgan	44,864	26,619	17,050	1,195	9,569	D	59.3	38.0	2.7	7	1	3	18.4	16.6	21.9	19.5
District 6	280,139	126,062	146,599	7,478	20,537	R	45.0	52.3	2.7				100.0	100.0	100.0	100.0
Bibb (pt)	1,398	943	417	38	526	D	67.5	29.8	2.7	1	4	3	0.5	0.7	0.3	0.5
Jefferson (pt)	199,493	88,591	105,910	4,992	17,319	R	44.4	53.1	2.5	3	2	4	71.2	70.3	72.2	66.8
Shelby	47,432	17,259	28,733	1,440	11,474	R	36.4	60.6	3.0	4	1	2	16.9	13.7	19.6	19.3
Tuscaloosa (pt)	31,816	19,269	11,539	1,008	7,730	D	60.6	36.3	3.2	2	3	1	11.4	15.3	7.9	13.5

Congressional district and county	Total	Democrat (DEM)	Republican (REP)	Other	Plurality		Percent of total vote			Rank within district			Percent contribution to district vote			
					Total	Party	DEM	REP	Other	DEM	REP	Other	Total	DEM	REP	Other
District 7	**207,773**	**144,320**	**36,086**	**27,367**	**108,234**	**D**	**69.5**	**17.4**	**13.2**				**100.0**	**100.0**	**100.0**	**100.0**
Choctaw	5,844	3,815	1,270	759	2,545	D	65.3	21.7	13.0	10	3	7	2.8	2.6	3.5	2.8
Clarke (pt)	939	647	201	91	446	D	68.9	21.4	9.7	7	4	10	0.5	0.4	0.6	0.3
Dallas	18,904	10,906	3,034	4,964	5,942	D	57.7	16.0	26.3	12	7	2	9.1	7.6	8.4	18.1
Greene	4,596	3,778	550	268	3,228	D	82.2	12.0	5.8	1	13	14	2.2	2.6	1.5	1.0
Hale	5,265	3,276	1,164	825	2,112	D	62.2	22.1	15.7	11	2	5	2.5	2.3	3.2	3.0
Jefferson (pt)	94,242	70,667	13,473	10,102	57,194	D	75.0	14.3	10.7	3	9	9	45.4	49.0	37.3	36.9
Lowndes	4,552	3,062	597	893	2,169	D	67.3	13.1	19.6	9	12	3	2.2	2.1	1.7	3.3
Marengo	10,191	5,701	1,591	2,899	2,802	D	55.9	15.6	28.4	13	8	1	4.9	4.0	4.4	10.6
Montgomery (pt)	21,173	16,979	2,283	1,911	14,696	D	80.2	10.8	9.0	2	14	11	10.2	11.8	6.3	7.0
Perry	5,195	3,694	923	578	2,771	D	71.1	17.8	11.1	6	6	8	2.5	2.6	2.6	2.1
Pickens (pt)	1,030	755	202	73	553	D	73.3	19.6	7.1	4	5	13	0.5	0.5	0.6	0.3
Sumter	6,686	4,805	927	954	3,851	D	71.9	13.9	14.3	5	11	6	3.2	3.3	2.6	3.5
Tuscaloosa (pt)	24,257	12,935	9,174	2,148	3,761	D	53.3	37.8	8.9	14	1	12	11.7	9.0	25.4	7.8
Wilcox	4,899	3,300	697	902	2,398	D	67.4	14.2	18.4	8	10	4	2.4	2.3	1.9	3.3
ALABAMA	**1,602,536**	**895,601**	**643,150**	**63,785**	**252,451**	**D**	**55.9**	**40.1**	**4.0**							

Table I. — Vote for Presidential Preference: June 2, 1992, Democratic Primary Election

County	Top candidates									Top three candidates (state vote)									
										Percent of total vote			Rank			Percent contribution to state vote			
	Total	Clinton	Uncom-mitted	Brown	Woods	LaRouche				Clinton	Uncom-mitted	Brown	Clinton	Uncom-mitted	Brown	Total	Clinton	Uncom-mitted	Brown
Autauga	3,249	1,938	501	516	215	79	-	-	-	59.6	15.4	15.9	60	40	2	0.7	0.6	0.6	1.7
Baldwin	3,334	2,076	541	529	104	84	-	-	-	62.3	16.2	15.9	56	36	3	0.7	0.7	0.6	1.7
Barbour	2,623	1,668	425	321	147	62	-	-	-	63.6	16.2	12.2	53	37	9	0.6	0.5	0.5	1.0
Bibb	3,037	1,935	756	144	172	30	-	-	-	63.7	24.9	4.7	52	12	52	0.7	0.6	0.8	0.5
Blount	3,410	2,313	745	196	114	42	-	-	-	67.8	21.8	5.7	37	19	43	0.8	0.8	0.8	0.6
Bullock	1,888	1,454	118	183	71	62	-	-	-	77.0	6.3	9.7	7	64	18	0.4	0.5	0.1	0.6
Butler	2,421	1,730	213	274	140	64	-	-	-	71.5	8.8	11.3	23	58	12	0.5	0.6	0.2	0.9
Calhoun	6,102	4,291	995	489	216	111	-	-	-	70.3	16.3	8.0	28	34	29	1.4	1.4	1.1	1.6
Chambers	3,507	2,419	752	163	116	57	-	-	-	69.0	21.4	4.6	32	21	54	0.8	0.8	0.8	0.5
Cherokee	2,314	1,596	429	199	48	42	-	-	-	69.0	18.5	8.6	33	29	25	0.5	0.5	0.5	0.6
Chilton	5,830	3,945	1,365	261	189	70	-	-	-	67.7	23.4	4.5	38	16	58	1.3	1.3	1.5	0.9
Choctaw	3,825	2,884	579	170	144	48	-	-	-	75.4	15.1	4.4	9	42	59	0.8	0.9	0.6	0.6
Clarke	2,845	1,931	411	325	129	49	-	-	-	67.9	14.4	11.4	36	45	10	0.6	0.6	0.5	1.1
Clay	1,932	1,238	266	147	108	173	-	-	-	64.1	13.8	7.6	49	48	31	0.4	0.4	0.3	0.5
Cleburne	2,107	1,392	459	132	93	31	-	-	-	66.1	21.8	6.3	44	20	38	0.5	0.5	0.5	0.4
Coffee	3,562	2,562	433	301	218	48	-	-	-	71.9	12.2	8.5	21	52	26	0.8	0.8	0.5	1.0
Colbert	10,459	7,012	2,525	488	289	145	-	-	-	67.0	24.1	4.7	40	13	53	2.3	2.3	2.8	1.6
Conecuh	1,671	1,252	89	160	113	57	-	-	-	74.9	5.3	9.6	11	65	20	0.4	0.4	< .1	0.5
Coosa	1,187	839	237	52	46	13	-	-	-	70.7	20.0	4.4	25	23	60	0.3	0.3	0.3	0.2
Covington	3,721	2,630	74	421	432	164	-	-	-	70.7	2.0	11.3	26	67	13	0.8	0.9	< .1	1.4
Crenshaw	1,012	751	109	75	51	26	-	-	-	74.2	10.8	7.4	15	55	33	0.2	0.2	0.1	0.2
Cullman	9,113	5,610	2,543	486	341	133	-	-	-	61.6	27.9	5.3	59	7	46	2.0	1.8	2.8	1.6
Dale	3,275	2,105	570	314	225	61	-	-	-	64.3	17.4	9.6	48	32	19	0.7	0.7	0.6	1.0
Dallas	7,073	5,217	896	611	227	122	-	-	-	73.8	12.7	8.6	17	49	23	1.6	1.7	1.0	2.0
DeKalb	4,291	3,013	917	198	78	85	-	-	-	70.2	21.4	4.6	29	22	56	1.0	1.0	1.0	0.6
Elmore	3,457	2,049	561	496	239	112	-	-	-	59.3	16.2	14.3	62	35	4	0.8	0.7	0.6	1.6
Escambia	3,227	2,008	581	363	161	114	-	-	-	62.2	18.0	11.2	57	30	14	0.7	0.7	0.6	1.2
Etowah	10,812	7,909	2,027	451	303	122	-	-	-	73.2	18.7	4.2	20	27	61	2.4	2.6	2.2	1.5
Fayette	3,705	2,328	1,002	172	138	65	-	-	-	62.8	27.0	4.6	55	9	55	0.8	0.8	1.1	0.6
Franklin	4,946	3,639	882	202	141	82	-	-	-	73.6	17.8	4.1	19	31	62	1.1	1.2	1.0	0.7
Geneva	2,825	1,881	429	182	257	76	-	-	-	66.6	15.2	6.4	42	41	36	0.6	0.6	0.5	0.6
Greene	3,769	3,214	277	153	77	48	-	-	-	85.3	7.3	4.1	1	62	63	0.8	1.0	0.3	0.5
Hale	1,830	1,361	226	159	58	26	-	-	-	74.4	12.3	8.7	13	51	22	0.4	0.4	0.2	0.5
Henry	2,583	1,652	481	148	271	31	-	-	-	64.0	18.6	5.7	50	28	44	0.6	0.5	0.5	0.5
Houston	8,292	4,595	2,471	450	665	111	-	-	-	55.4	29.8	5.4	67	5	45	1.8	1.5	2.7	1.5
Jackson	4,974	3,743	701	374	79	77	-	-	-	75.3	14.1	7.5	10	47	32	1.1	1.2	0.8	1.2
Jefferson	94,673	70,779	16,364	4,979	1,889	662	-	-	-	74.8	17.3	5.3	12	33	47	21.0	23.0	18.0	16.3
Lamar	3,649	2,256	1,027	182	142	42	-	-	-	61.8	28.1	5.0	58	6	49	0.8	0.7	1.1	0.6
Lauderdale	14,966	9,509	4,121	752	394	190	-	-	-	63.5	27.5	5.0	54	8	48	3.3	3.1	4.5	2.5
Lawrence	2,049	1,637	154	127	72	59	-	-	-	79.9	7.5	6.2	4	61	40	0.5	0.5	0.2	0.4
Lee	4,207	2,685	618	707	125	72	-	-	-	63.8	14.7	16.8	51	43	1	0.9	0.9	0.7	2.3
Limestone	6,457	3,832	1,947	388	213	77	-	-	-	59.3	30.2	6.0	61	4	42	1.4	1.2	2.1	1.3
Lowndes	2,013	1,551	131	208	74	49	-	-	-	77.0	6.5	10.3	6	63	16	0.4	0.5	0.1	0.7
Macon	2,630	2,035	107	329	68	91	-	-	-	77.4	4.1	12.5	5	66	8	0.6	0.7	0.1	1.1
Madison	25,083	13,979	8,198	1,960	635	311	-	-	-	55.7	32.7	7.8	66	1	30	5.6	4.5	9.0	6.4
Marengo	3,559	2,624	445	300	120	70	-	-	-	73.7	12.5	8.4	18	50	27	0.8	0.9	0.5	1.0
Marion	4,942	3,418	1,137	178	146	63	-	-	-	69.2	23.0	3.6	31	17	66	1.1	1.1	1.3	0.6
Marshall	3,879	2,288	871	491	154	75	-	-	-	59.0	22.5	12.7	63	18	5	0.9	0.7	1.0	1.6
Mobile	25,050	18,612	3,571	2,062	522	283	-	-	-	74.3	14.3	8.2	14	46	28	5.6	6.1	3.9	6.7
Monroe	2,123	1,513	186	268	94	62	-	-	-	71.3	8.8	12.6	24	59	6	0.5	0.5	0.2	0.9
Montgomery	20,661	13,509	4,095	1,777	936	344	-	-	-	65.4	19.8	8.6	45	24	24	4.6	4.4	4.5	5.8
Morgan	11,898	6,682	3,758	792	510	156	-	-	-	56.2	31.6	6.7	65	2	35	2.6	2.2	4.1	2.6
Perry	2,883	2,339	237	181	85	41	-	-	-	81.1	8.2	6.3	3	60	37	0.6	0.8	0.3	0.6
Pickens	2,215	1,521	416	158	88	32	-	-	-	68.7	18.8	7.1	35	26	34	0.5	0.5	0.5	0.5
Pike	2,338	1,676	241	239	114	68	-	-	-	71.7	10.3	10.2	22	56	17	0.5	0.5	0.3	0.8
Randolph	2,400	1,596	351	302	90	61	-	-	-	66.5	14.6	12.6	43	44	7	0.5	0.5	0.4	1.0
Russell	3,249	2,403	371	311	109	55	-	-	-	74.0	11.4	9.6	16	53	21	0.7	0.8	0.4	1.0
St. Clair	3,588	2,332	927	171	111	47	-	-	-	65.0	25.8	4.8	46	10	51	0.8	0.8	1.0	0.6
Shelby	4,310	2,903	1,010	268	103	26	-	-	-	67.4	23.4	6.2	39	15	39	1.0	0.9	1.1	0.9
Sumter	4,514	3,440	710	179	125	60	-	-	-	76.2	15.7	4.0	8	39	64	1.0	1.1	0.8	0.6
Talladega	4,910	3,179	795	528	215	193	-	-	-	64.7	16.2	10.8	47	38	15	1.1	1.0	0.9	1.7
Tallapoosa	2,101	1,482	231	239	84	65	-	-	-	70.5	11.0	11.4	27	54	11	0.5	0.5	0.3	0.8
Tuscaloosa	21,774	12,705	6,815	1,341	737	176	-	-	-	58.3	31.3	6.2	64	3	41	4.8	4.1	7.5	4.4
Walker	14,824	9,873	3,742	453	507	249	-	-	-	66.6	25.2	3.1	41	11	67	3.3	3.2	4.1	1.5
Washington	5,149	3,567	986	256	254	86	-	-	-	69.3	19.1	5.0	30	25	50	1.1	1.2	1.1	0.8
Wilcox	2,546	2,107	228	116	69	26	-	-	-	82.8	9.0	4.6	2	57	57	0.6	0.7	0.3	0.4
Winston	2,051	1,409	487	79	47	29	-	-	-	68.7	23.7	3.9	34	14	65	0.5	0.5	0.5	0.3
ALABAMA	**450,899**	**307,621**	**90,863**	**30,626**	**15,247**	**6,542**	**-**	**-**	**-**	**68.2**	**20.2**	**6.8**				**100.0**	**100.0**	**100.0**	**100.0**

Table J. — Vote for Presidential Preference: June 2, 1992, Republican Primary Election

County	Total	Bush	Uncom-mitted	Bu-chanan		Bush	Uncom-mitted	Bu-chanan		Bush	Uncom-mitted	Bu-chanan		Total	Bush	Uncom-mitted	Bu-chanan	
		Top candidates				Top four candidates (state vote) — Percent of total vote				Rank				Percent contribution to state vote				
Autauga	1,243	910	185	148	-	73.2	14.9	11.9	-	52	27	14	-	0.8	0.7	0.6	1.2	-
Baldwin	7,888	5,470	1,655	763	-	69.3	21.0	9.7	-	63	4	29	-	4.8	4.5	5.5	6.1	-
Barbour	139	92	22	25	-	66.2	15.8	18.0	-	65	22	2	-	<.1	<.1	<.1	0.2	-
Bibb	304	251	30	23	-	82.6	9.9	7.6	-	14	49	45	-	0.2	0.2	0.1	0.2	-
Blount	1,363	1,037	223	103	-	76.1	16.4	7.6	-	40	19	46	-	0.8	0.8	0.7	0.8	-
Bullock	35	27	6	2	-	77.1	17.1	5.7	-	33	17	58	-	<.1	<.1	<.1	<.1	-
Butler	182	145	16	21	-	79.7	8.8	11.5	-	17	54	19	-	0.1	0.1	<.1	0.2	-
Calhoun	2,461	1,881	375	205	-	76.4	15.2	8.3	-	37	24	36	-	1.5	1.5	1.3	1.6	-
Chambers	586	461	77	48	-	78.7	13.1	8.2	-	24	39	37	-	0.4	0.4	0.3	0.4	-
Cherokee	106	82	13	11	-	77.4	12.3	10.4	-	32	42	25	-	<.1	<.1	<.1	<.1	-
Chilton	1,484	1,149	268	67	-	77.4	18.1	4.5	-	31	10	64	-	0.9	0.9	0.9	0.5	-
Choctaw	62	53	4	5	-	85.5	6.5	8.1	-	9	59	41	-	<.1	<.1	<.1	<.1	-
Clarke	117	92	10	15	-	78.6	8.5	12.8	-	26	55	10	-	<.1	<.1	<.1	0.1	-
Clay	60	55	0	5	-	91.7	0.0	8.3	-	2	65	35	-	<.1	<.1	0.0	<.1	-
Cleburne	72	57	4	11	-	79.2	5.6	15.3	-	22	61	6	-	<.1	<.1	<.1	<.1	-
Coffee	1,518	1,138	234	146	-	75.0	15.4	9.6	-	46	23	30	-	0.9	0.9	0.8	1.2	-
Colbert	211	167	25	19	-	79.1	11.8	9.0	-	23	43	33	-	0.1	0.1	<.1	0.2	-
Conecuh	95	77	3	15	-	81.1	3.2	15.8	-	16	62	5	-	<.1	<.1	<.1	0.1	-
Coosa	239	188	42	9	-	78.7	17.6	3.8	-	25	14	66	-	0.1	0.2	0.1	<.1	-
Covington	233	208	1	24	-	89.3	0.4	10.3	-	5	64	26	-	0.1	0.2	<.1	0.2	-
Crenshaw	160	143	5	12	-	89.4	3.1	7.5	-	4	63	47	-	<.1	0.1	<.1	<.1	-
Cullman	1,286	999	206	81	-	77.7	16.0	6.3	-	29	21	56	-	0.8	0.8	0.7	0.6	-
Dale	1,103	979	0	124	-	88.8	0.0	11.2	-	6	66	22	-	0.7	0.8	0.0	1.0	-
Dallas	303	240	27	36	-	79.2	8.9	11.9	-	21	51	15	-	0.2	0.2	<.1	0.3	-
DeKalb	517	427	65	25	-	82.6	12.6	4.8	-	13	41	62	-	0.3	0.3	0.2	0.2	-
Elmore	1,642	1,210	247	185	-	73.7	15.0	11.3	-	51	25	21	-	1.0	1.0	0.8	1.5	-
Escambia	99	74	17	8	-	74.7	17.2	8.1	-	47	16	40	-	<.1	<.1	<.1	<.1	-
Etowah	2,346	1,787	381	178	-	76.2	16.2	7.6	-	39	20	44	-	1.4	1.5	1.3	1.4	-
Fayette	202	168	22	12	-	83.2	10.9	5.9	-	12	46	57	-	0.1	0.1	<.1	<.1	-
Franklin	103	76	15	12	-	73.8	14.6	11.7	-	50	29	18	-	<.1	<.1	<.1	<.1	-
Geneva	438	343	60	35	-	78.3	13.7	8.0	-	27	35	42	-	0.3	0.3	0.2	0.3	-
Greene	12	8	1	3	-	66.7	8.3	25.0	-	64	56	1	-	<.1	<.1	<.1	<.1	-
Hale	67	52	10	5	-	77.6	14.9	7.5	-	30	26	48	-	<.1	<.1	<.1	<.1	-
Henry	155	112	28	15	-	72.3	18.1	9.7	-	57	9	28	-	<.1	<.1	<.1	0.1	-
Houston	2,965	2,273	504	188	-	76.7	17.0	6.3	-	36	18	55	-	1.8	1.9	1.7	1.5	-
Jackson	125	90	22	13	-	72.0	17.6	10.4	-	58	13	24	-	<.1	<.1	<.1	0.1	-
Jefferson	71,481	53,670	13,232	4,579	-	75.1	18.5	6.4	-	43	7	54	-	43.3	43.7	44.4	36.4	-
Lamar	21	16	3	2	-	76.2	14.3	9.5	-	38	31	31	-	<.1	<.1	<.1	<.1	-
Lauderdale	540	394	75	71	-	73.0	13.9	13.1	-	54	33	8	-	0.3	0.3	0.3	0.6	-
Lawrence	122	89	13	20	-	73.0	10.7	16.4	-	55	47	4	-	<.1	<.1	<.1	0.2	-
Lee	1,686	1,233	245	208	-	73.1	14.5	12.3	-	53	30	12	-	1.0	1.0	0.8	1.7	-
Limestone	586	381	129	76	-	65.0	22.0	13.0	-	66	3	9	-	0.4	0.3	0.4	0.6	-
Lowndes	90	75	8	7	-	83.3	8.9	7.8	-	11	53	43	-	<.1	<.1	<.1	<.1	-
Macon	52	47	3	2	-	90.4	5.8	3.8	-	3	60	65	-	<.1	<.1	<.1	<.1	-
Madison	8,643	5,572	2,199	872	-	64.5	25.4	10.1	-	67	1	27	-	5.2	4.5	7.4	6.9	-
Marengo	129	92	23	14	-	71.3	17.8	10.9	-	60	11	23	-	<.1	<.1	<.1	0.1	-
Marion	279	222	38	19	-	79.6	13.6	6.8	-	19	36	52	-	0.2	0.2	0.1	0.2	-
Marshall	607	426	105	76	-	70.2	17.3	12.5	-	61	15	11	-	0.4	0.3	0.4	0.6	-
Mobile	18,529	14,257	2,755	1,517	-	76.9	14.9	8.2	-	34	28	38	-	11.2	11.6	9.2	12.1	-
Monroe	478	420	34	24	-	87.9	7.1	5.0	-	7	58	60	-	0.3	0.3	0.1	0.2	-
Montgomery	4,913	3,826	685	402	-	77.9	13.9	8.2	-	28	32	39	-	3.0	3.1	2.3	3.2	-
Morgan	2,267	1,642	412	213	-	72.4	18.2	9.4	-	56	8	32	-	1.4	1.3	1.4	1.7	-
Perry	12	9	1	2	-	75.0	8.3	16.7	-	45	57	3	-	<.1	<.1	<.1	<.1	-
Pickens	623	507	83	33	-	81.4	13.3	5.3	-	15	37	59	-	0.4	0.4	0.3	0.3	-
Pike	506	401	45	60	-	79.2	8.9	11.9	-	20	52	16	-	0.3	0.3	0.2	0.5	-
Randolph	141	107	18	16	-	75.9	12.8	11.3	-	41	40	20	-	<.1	<.1	<.1	0.1	-
Russell	374	281	42	51	-	75.1	11.2	13.6	-	42	45	7	-	0.2	0.2	0.1	0.4	-
St. Clair	1,838	1,358	347	133	-	73.9	18.9	7.2	-	49	6	49	-	1.1	1.1	1.2	1.1	-
Shelby	13,994	9,713	3,325	956	-	69.4	23.8	6.8	-	62	2	51	-	8.5	7.9	11.1	7.6	-
Sumter	20	17	2	1	-	85.0	10.0	5.0	-	10	48	61	-	<.1	<.1	<.1	<.1	-
Talladega	1,277	954	168	155	-	74.7	13.2	12.1	-	48	38	13	-	0.8	0.8	0.6	1.2	-
Tallapoosa	601	462	68	71	-	76.9	11.3	11.8	-	35	44	17	-	0.4	0.4	0.2	0.6	-
Tuscaloosa	2,359	1,691	465	203	-	71.7	19.7	8.6	-	59	5	34	-	1.4	1.4	1.6	1.6	-
Walker	671	534	93	44	-	79.6	13.9	6.6	-	18	34	53	-	0.4	0.4	0.3	0.3	-
Washington	21	18	2	1	-	85.7	9.5	4.8	-	8	50	63	-	<.1	<.1	<.1	<.1	-
Wilcox	45	45	0	0	-	100.0	0.0	0.0	-	1	67	67	-	<.1	<.1	0.0	0.0	-
Winston	2,295	1,723	409	163	-	75.1	17.8	7.1	-	44	12	50	-	1.4	1.4	1.4	1.3	-
ALABAMA	**165,121**	**122,703**	**29,830**	**12,588**	-	**74.3**	**18.1**	**7.6**	-				-	**100.0**	**100.0**	**100.0**	**100.0**	-

1992 Vote for President
Percent for Bush (R), by County

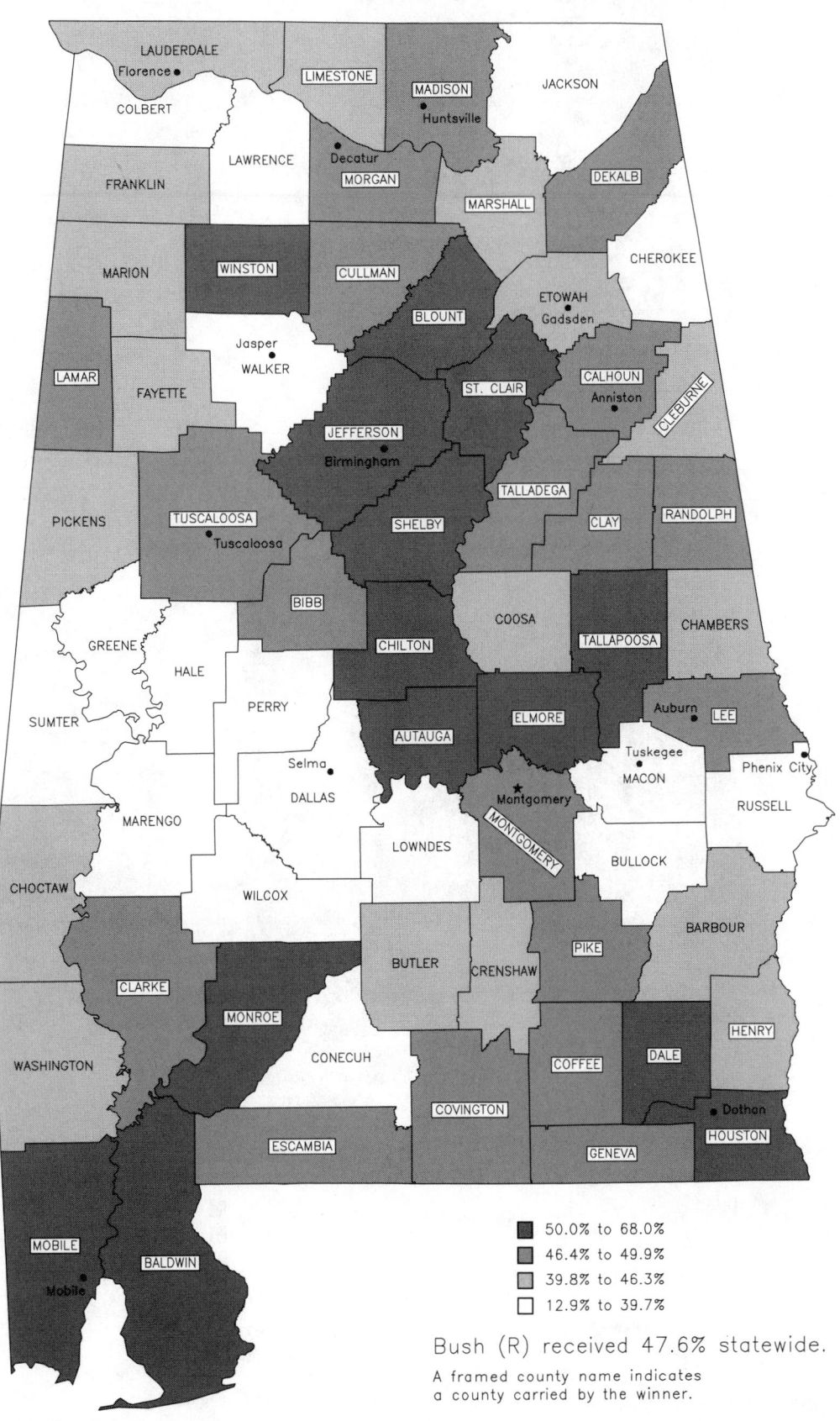

LAUDERDALE
Florence •
LIMESTONE
MADISON
Huntsville •
JACKSON
COLBERT
LAWRENCE
Decatur •
MORGAN
MARSHALL
DEKALB
FRANKLIN
CHEROKEE
MARION
WINSTON
CULLMAN
ETOWAH
Gadsden •
BLOUNT
Jasper •
WALKER
ST. CLAIR
CALHOUN
Anniston •
CLEBURNE
LAMAR
FAYETTE
JEFFERSON
Birmingham •
TALLADEGA
PICKENS
TUSCALOOSA
Tuscaloosa •
SHELBY
CLAY
RANDOLPH
BIBB
COOSA
TALLAPOOSA
CHAMBERS
GREENE
HALE
CHILTON
Auburn •
LEE
SUMTER
PERRY
ELMORE
Tuskegee •
MACON
Phenix City •
RUSSELL
AUTAUGA
Selma •
DALLAS
★
Montgomery
MONTGOMERY
MARENGO
LOWNDES
BULLOCK
CHOCTAW
WILCOX
BUTLER
CRENSHAW
PIKE
BARBOUR
CLARKE
MONROE
HENRY
WASHINGTON
CONECUH
COFFEE
DALE
Dothan •
HOUSTON
ESCAMBIA
COVINGTON
GENEVA
MOBILE
BALDWIN
Mobile •

■ 50.0% to 68.0%
▨ 46.4% to 49.9%
▨ 39.8% to 46.3%
□ 12.9% to 39.7%

Bush (R) received 47.6% statewide.

A framed county name indicates
a county carried by the winner.

Alabama 51

1992 Vote for U.S. Senator
Percent for Shelby (D), by County

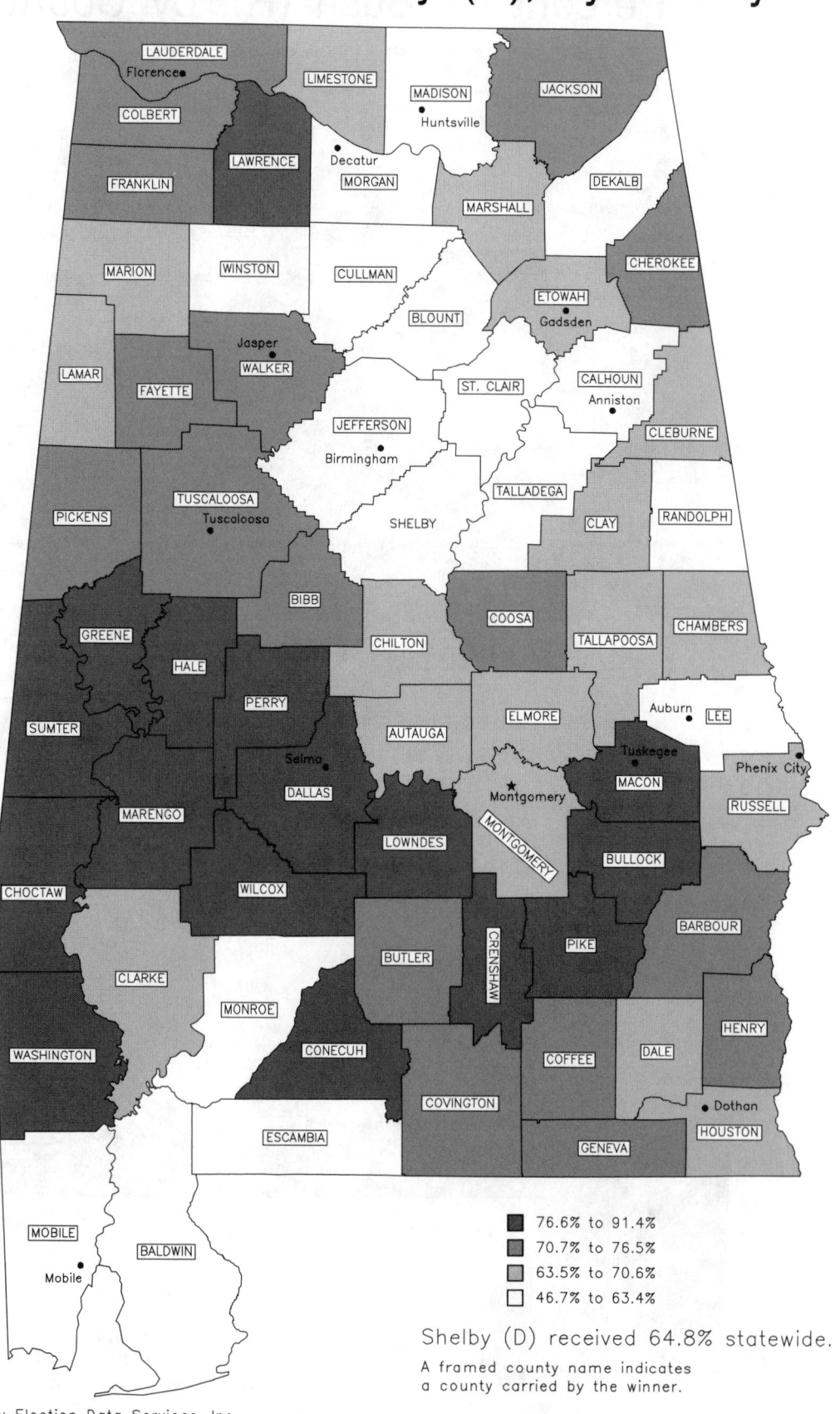

76.6% to 91.4%
70.7% to 76.5%
63.5% to 70.6%
46.7% to 63.4%

Shelby (D) received 64.8% statewide.

A framed county name indicates
a county carried by the winner.

ALASKA

Congressional Districts 1
    Average Population 550,043
State Senate Districts 20
    Average Population 27,502
State House Districts 40
    Average Population 13,751

Electoral College Votes 3
Election Districts[1] 40
Voting Precincts 469

Alternative Registration Methods:
    Agency-based, Deputized Registrars, Mail-in, Motor-voter

Registration Deadline (Days before Election) 30

Voting Equipment Use (Election Districts)

Datavote Punch Card	40	Paper Ballot	0
Electronic	0	Other Punch Card	0
Lever Machine	0	Mixed Systems	0
Optical Scanner	0		

Party Control	DEM	REP	IND	VAC
1993 State Senate	9	10	1	0
1992 State Senate	10	10	0	0
1993 State House	20	18	2	0
1992 State House	23	17	0	0

Population Statistics 1990

Race/ Ethnicity	Total Population		Voting Age Population		Voting Age Population % of total population
	Number	%	Number	%	
Non-Hispanic					
White	406,722	73.9	288,976	76.5	71.1
Black	21,799	4.0	14,200	3.8	65.1
Asian/Pacific Islander	18,730	3.4	12,853	3.4	68.6
Native American	84,594	15.4	50,435	13.4	59.6
Other	395	<.1	187	<.1	47.3
All Hispanic	17,803	3.2	11,048	2.9	62.1
TOTAL	550,043	100.0	377,699	100.0	68.7

Estimated Voting Age Population 1992 (VAP) 395,000
Number of Registered Voters 315,058
    % of estimated VAP 79.8
Voter Turnout (Actual) 261,427
    % of VAP 66.2
    % of Registration 83.0
Persons Not Voting—of Voting Age 133,573
    % of VAP 33.8
Persons Not Voting—of Registered 53,631
    % of Registration 17.0
Straight Ticket Voting .... No

State Officials and Members of Congress

Governor:
Walter Hickel (I) 1966, elected to a four-year term in 1990.

U.S. Senators:
Ted Stevens (R) 1968, elected to a six-year term in 1988.
Frank Murkowski (R) 1980, elected to a six-year term in 1992.

U.S. Representative in Congress:
(District, Name, Party, Date first elected)

At-Large. Young (R) 1973

---

[1]Also divided into 25 boroughs and census areas which are considered county equivalents by the Census Bureau for demographic purposes (e.g., population data, Tables A and B).

Candidates: General Election, November 3, 1992

Candidate(s)	Total vote	Percent	Party	Status	First elected
President/Vice President					
Bush/Quayle	102,000	39.46%	Republican	Incumbent	1988
Clinton/Gore	78,294	30.29%	Democrat	Challenger	1992
Perot/Stockdale	73,481	28.43%	Independent	Challenger	
Gritz/Minett	1,379	0.53%	America First	Challenger	
Marrou/Lord	1,378	0.53%	Libertarian	Challenger	
LaRouche/Bevel	469	0.18%	Ind. Econ. Recovery	Challenger	
Hagelin/Tompkins	433	0.17%	Natural Law	Challenger	
Phillips/Knight	377	0.15%	Taxpayers	Challenger	
Write ins	365	0.14%	Write in	Challenger	
Fulani/Munoz	330	0.13%	New Alliance	Challenger	
U.S. Senator					
Frank Murkowski	127,163	53.05%	Republican	Incumbent	1980
Tony Smith	92,065	38.41%	Democrat	Challenger	
Mary Jordan	20,019	8.35%	Green	Challenger	
Write ins	467	0.19%	Write in	Challenger	
Governor (No Contest)					
U.S. Representative in Congress					
District At-Large					
Don Young	111,849	46.78%	Republican	Incumbent	1973
John Devens	102,378	42.82%	Democrat	Challenger	
Michael States	15,049	6.29%	Alaskan Independence	Challenger	
Mike Milligan	9,529	3.99%	Green	Challenger	
Write ins	311	0.13%	Write in	Challenger	

Voter Registration and Turnout, 1948-1992 Elections

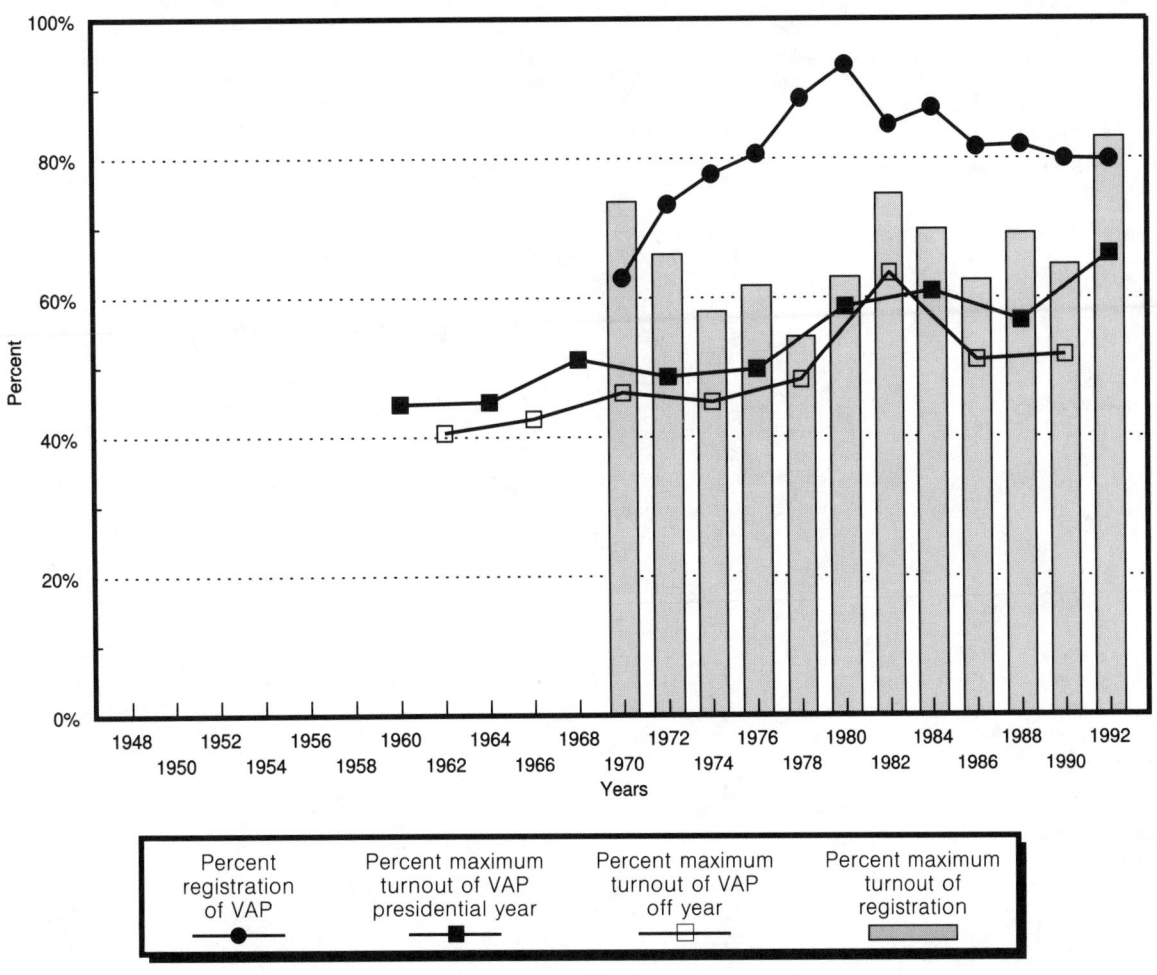

Percent registration of VAP	Percent maximum turnout of VAP presidential year	Percent maximum turnout of VAP off year	Percent maximum turnout of registration

		Voter registration (REG)			Voter turnout												
						Highest office						Maximum vote					
Year	Estimated Voting Age Population (VAP)	Total	Percent of VAP	Rank by percent of VAP	Actual	Total	Office	Percent total REG	Rank by percent of REG	Percent of VAP	Rank by percent of VAP	Total	Percent total REG	Rank by percent of REG	Percent total VAP	Rank by percent of VAP
1992	395,000	315,058	79.8	15	261,427	258,506	P	82.1	10	65.4	9	261,427	83.0	10	66.2	12
1990	382,000	305,268	79.9	8	197,540	194,750	G	63.8	11	51.0	7	197,540	64.7	12	51.7	9
1988	359,000	293,871	81.9	10	203,433	200,116	P	68.1	34	55.7	16	203,433	69.2	35	56.7	16
1986	358,000	292,274	81.6	7	182,526	180,801	S	61.9	12	50.5	6	182,526	62.5	13	51.0	7
1984	350,000	305,262	87.2	6	213,173	207,605	P	68.0	41	59.3	13	213,173	69.8	39	60.9	12
1982	314,000	266,224	84.8	6	199,458	194,885	G	73.2	4	62.1	1	199,458	74.9	3	63.5	1
1980	277,000	258,742	93.4	3	162,653	158,445	P	61.2	47	57.2	20	162,653	62.9	46	58.7	17
1978	269,000	238,434	88.6	2	129,705	126,910	G	53.2	35	47.2	7	129,705	54.4	33	48.2	8
1976	257,190	207,190	80.6	13	127,877	123,574	P	59.6	49	48.0	39	127,877	61.7	49	49.7	35
1974	219,000	170,055	77.7	9	98,557	96,163	G	56.5	27	43.9	20	98,557	58.0	26	45.0	19
1972	203,000	148,960	73.4	25	98,581	95,219	P	63.9	41	46.9	41	98,581	66.2	40	48.6	38
1970	178,000	111,734	62.8	37	82,405	80,779	G	72.3	10	45.4	35	82,405	73.8	12	46.3	33
1968	166,000	-	-	-	84,902	83,035	P	-	-	50.0	46	84,902	-	-	51.1	46
1966	158,000	-	-	-	67,361	66,294	G	-	-	42.0	38	67,361	-	-	42.6	37
1964	153,000	-	-	-	68,858	67,259	P	-	-	44.0	45	68,858	-	-	45.0	44
1962	148,000	-	-	-	60,084	58,181	S	-	-	39.3	39	60,084	-	-	40.6	38
1960	139,000	-	-	-	62,177	60,762	P	-	-	43.7	43	62,177	-	-	44.7	42
1958	-	-	-	-	-	-	-	-	-	-	-	-	-	-	-	-
1956	-	-	-	-	-	-	-	-	-	-	-	-	-	-	-	-
1954	-	-	-	-	-	-	-	-	-	-	-	-	-	-	-	-
1952	-	-	-	-	-	-	-	-	-	-	-	-	-	-	-	-
1950	-	-	-	-	-	-	-	-	-	-	-	-	-	-	-	-
1948	-	-	-	-	-	-	-	-	-	-	-	-	-	-	-	-

Alaska 55

ALASKA

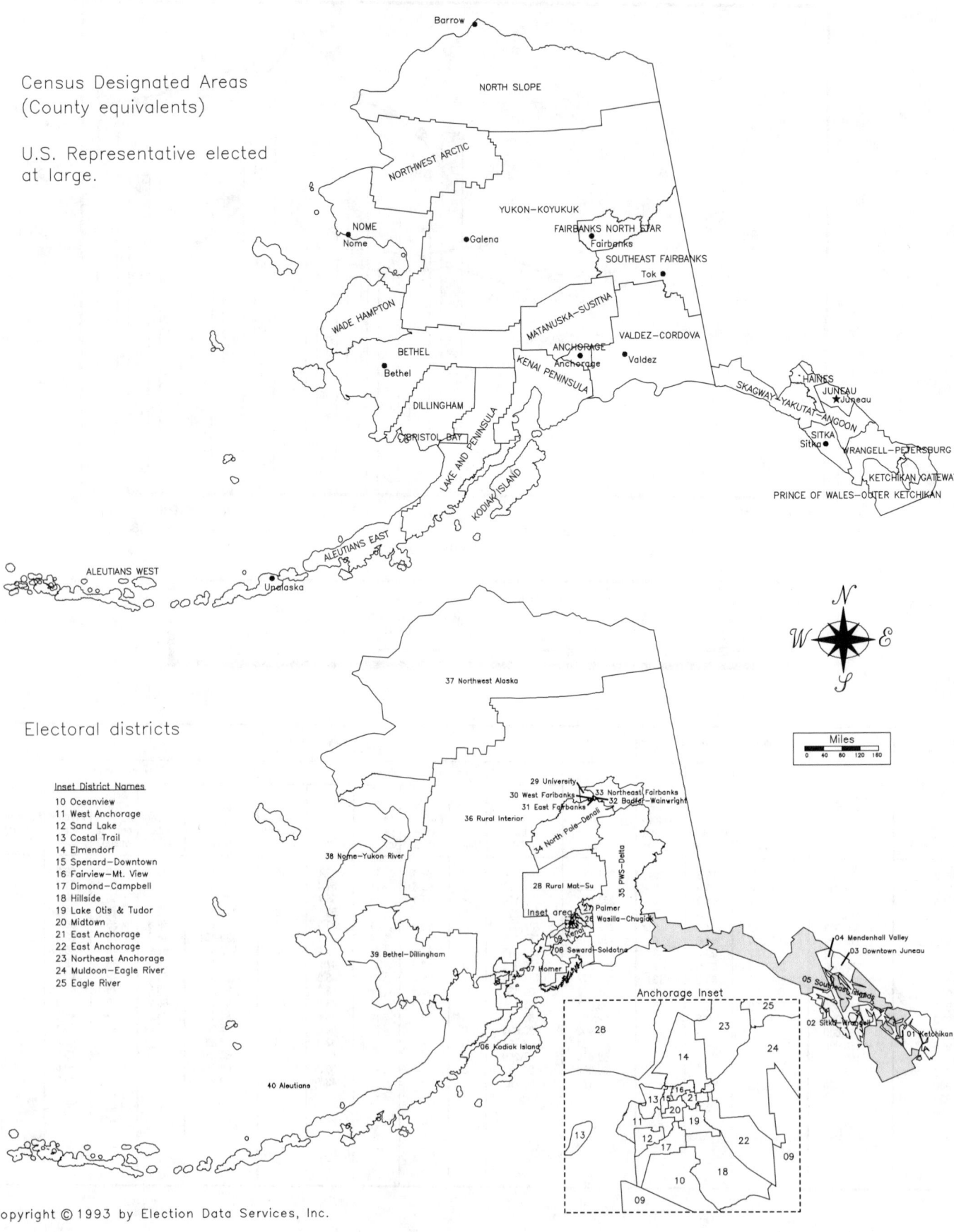

Census Designated Areas
(County equivalents)

U.S. Representative elected
at large.

Electoral districts

Inset District Names
10 Oceanview
11 West Anchorage
12 Sand Lake
13 Costal Trail
14 Elmendorf
15 Spenard—Downtown
16 Fairview—Mt. View
17 Dimond—Campbell
18 Hillside
19 Lake Otis & Tudor
20 Midtown
21 East Anchorage
22 East Anchorage
23 Northeast Anchorage
24 Muldoon—Eagle River
25 Eagle River

56 Alaska

Table A. — 1990 Population by Race and Ethnic Origin

State/ county code	Election district	Total persons	Percent of total persons						Rank				Percent contribution to state population			
			Non-Hispanic					Hispanic	Percent of total persons				Non-Hispanic			
			White	Black	Asian and Pacific Islander	Native American	Other		Total	Non-Hispanic		Native American[1]	Total	White	Black	Native American[1]
										White	Black					
	01 Ketchikan	13,985	81.0	0.4	3.3	13.2	<.1	2.0	4	19	35	12	2.5	2.8	0.3	2.2
	02 Sitka-Wrangell	14,622	77.1	0.3	2.8	17.6	0.0	2.2	2	25	37	8	2.7	2.8	0.2	3.0
	03 Downtown Juneau	13,595	75.5	0.9	4.2	16.3	<.1	3.1	29	26	27	10	2.5	2.5	0.6	2.6
	04 Mendenhall Valley	13,324	83.7	1.2	4.0	8.7	<.1	2.4	35	14	25	14	2.4	2.7	0.7	1.4
	05 Southeast Islands	13,483	62.3	0.1	0.6	35.4	<.1	1.6	31	34	40	5	2.5	2.1	<.1	5.6
	06 Kodiak Island	13,664	66.4	1.0	10.3	17.5	<.1	4.9	26	33	26	9	2.5	2.2	0.6	2.8
	07 Homer	13,941	92.9	0.2	0.9	4.6	<.1	1.4	9	1	38	30	2.5	3.2	0.1	0.8
	08 Seward-Soldotna	13,793	90.2	0.6	1.0	6.4	<.1	1.8	24	8	32	22	2.5	3.1	0.4	1.0
	09 Kenai	13,810	89.4	0.6	1.1	6.8	<.1	2.1	21	9	30	18	2.5	3.0	0.4	1.1
	10 Oceanview	13,966	88.8	2.1	3.2	3.1	0.1	2.8	7	10	19	39	2.5	3.0	1.3	0.5
	11 West Anchorage	13,981	81.1	3.8	5.3	6.1	<.1	3.7	5	18	16	24	2.5	2.8	2.4	1.0
	12 Sand Lake	13,807	82.1	3.4	6.9	4.3	<.1	3.2	22	17	17	32	2.5	2.8	2.2	0.7
	13 Coastal Trail	13,876	82.3	2.1	7.5	4.8	<.1	3.3	17	16	20	27	2.5	2.8	1.3	0.8
	14 Elmendorf	13,863	71.9	12.4	5.0	5.3	0.1	5.3	18	29	4	25	2.5	2.5	7.9	0.9
	15 Spenard-Downtown	13,859	70.0	4.8	7.2	12.2	0.2	5.8	19	30	14	13	2.5	2.4	3.0	2.0
	16 Fairview-Mt. View	13,915	52.2	13.4	7.0	19.3	0.2	7.9	15	36	3	7	2.5	1.8	8.6	3.2
	17 Dimond-Campbell	13,964	80.5	4.8	4.8	6.2	<.1	3.5	8	20	13	23	2.5	2.8	3.1	1.0
	18 Hillside	13,925	92.6	1.4	1.9	2.2	<.1	1.9	13	3	24	40	2.5	3.2	0.9	0.4
	19 Lake Otis & Tudor	13,919	77.8	6.5	4.9	6.5	0.2	4.2	14	23	9	20	2.5	2.7	4.1	1.1
	20 Midtown	13,751	80.0	5.0	5.5	6.4	0.1	2.9	25	21	12	21	2.5	2.7	3.2	1.0
	21 East Anchorage	13,928	74.7	8.3	4.6	8.3	0.1	4.0	12	27	7	16	2.5	2.6	5.3	1.4
	22 East Anchorage	13,933	78.6	8.4	3.9	4.7	0.1	4.3	11	22	6	28	2.5	2.7	5.4	0.8
	23 Northeast Anchorage	13,898	68.5	17.4	3.2	3.9	0.1	6.8	16	32	1	36	2.5	2.3	11.1	0.6
	24 Muldoon-Eagle River	13,805	84.1	5.8	2.0	4.2	<.1	3.8	23	12	11	33	2.5	2.9	3.7	0.7
	25 Eagle River	13,934	90.3	2.0	1.8	3.4	<.1	2.4	10	7	22	37	2.5	3.1	1.2	0.6
	26 Wasilla-Chugiak	13,628	91.1	0.8	0.9	4.8	<.1	2.3	28	5	29	26	2.5	3.1	0.5	0.8
	27 Palmer	13,970	92.2	0.9	0.6	4.5	<.1	1.7	6	4	28	31	2.5	3.2	0.6	0.7
	28 Rural Matanuska-Susitna	13,537	92.8	0.4	0.8	4.1	<.1	1.8	30	2	33	34	2.5	3.1	0.3	0.7
	29 University	13,257	86.5	1.9	3.1	6.5	0.1	1.9	36	11	23	19	2.4	2.8	1.1	1.0
	30 West Fairbanks	13,247	77.2	7.5	2.6	8.6	0.1	4.0	37	24	8	15	2.4	2.5	4.5	1.3
	31 East Fairbanks	13,390	69.5	9.1	2.7	14.5	0.1	4.0	32	31	5	11	2.4	2.3	5.6	2.3
	32 Badger-Wainwright	13,643	74.3	13.6	2.7	3.2	<.1	6.0	27	28	2	38	2.5	2.5	8.5	0.5
	33 Northeast Fairbanks	13,226	90.5	2.0	1.4	4.1	<.1	2.0	38	6	21	35	2.4	2.9	1.2	0.6
	34 North Pole-Denali	13,359	83.2	6.3	1.9	4.6	0.1	3.9	33	15	10	29	2.4	2.7	3.9	0.7
	35 PWS-Delta	13,215	83.7	2.8	2.9	7.6	<.1	3.0	39	13	18	17	2.4	2.7	1.7	1.2
	36 Rural Interior	12,741	36.6	0.6	0.4	61.4	<.1	1.1	40	37	31	4	2.3	1.1	0.4	9.2
	37 Northwest Alaska	13,346	16.3	0.4	2.3	79.7	<.1	1.2	34	39	36	2	2.4	0.5	0.2	12.6
	38 Nome-Yukon River	14,098	16.1	0.1	0.5	82.4	<.1	0.9	3	40	39	1	2.6	0.6	<.1	13.7
	39 Bethel-Dillingham	13,858	19.6	0.4	0.8	78.2	<.1	0.9	20	38	34	3	2.5	0.7	0.3	12.8
	40 Aleutians	14,987	54.0	4.6	9.0	25.9	<.1	6.5	1	35	15	6	2.7	2.0	3.2	4.6
	02 ALASKA	**550,043**	**73.9**	**4.0**	**3.4**	**15.4**	**<.1**	**3.2**					**100.0**	**100.0**	**100.0**	**100.0**
	CONGRESSIONAL District At-Large	550,043	73.9	4.0	3.4	15.4	<.1	3.2								
	BOROUGHS AND CENSUS AREAS															
02 013	Aleutians East	2,464	32.5	0.6	17.2	42.2	0.2	7.3	22	18	11	9	0.4	0.2	<.1	1.2
02 016	Aleutians West	9,478	64.7	6.7	9.5	11.2	<.1	7.8	10	13	2	21	1.7	1.5	2.9	1.3
02 020	Anchorage	226,338	78.7	6.2	4.6	6.2	0.1	4.1	1	8	3	24	41.1	43.8	64.8	16.7
02 050	Bethel	13,656	15.2	0.5	0.7	83.0	<.1	0.6	7	23	14	3	2.5	0.5	0.3	13.4
02 060	Bristol Bay	1,410	62.5	2.7	0.9	31.6	0.0	2.3	25	14	5	12	0.3	0.2	0.2	0.5
02 070	Dillingham	4,012	25.1	0.2	0.6	72.7	0.1	1.2	21	19	18	6	0.7	0.2	<.1	3.4
02 090	Fairbanks North Star	77,720	80.0	6.9	2.5	6.7	<.1	3.7	2	6	1	23	14.1	15.3	24.7	6.2
02 100	Haines	2,117	84.7	<.1	0.8	13.2	0.0	1.3	23	3	24	17	0.4	0.3	<.1	0.3
02 110	Juneau	26,751	79.5	1.0	4.1	12.6	<.1	2.8	5	7	6	19	4.9	5.2	1.3	4.0
02 122	Kenai Peninsula	40,802	89.7	0.5	1.0	7.1	<.1	1.8	3	2	13	22	7.4	9.0	0.9	3.4
02 130	Ketchikan Gateway	13,828	80.9	0.4	3.3	13.3	<.1	2.1	6	5	16	16	2.5	2.7	0.3	2.2
02 150	Kodiak Island	13,309	67.7	1.0	10.5	15.8	<.1	5.0	8	12	8	15	2.4	2.2	0.6	2.5
02 164	Lake and Peninsula	1,668	22.7	0.0	0.7	74.6	0.0	1.9	24	21	25	4	0.3	<.1	0.0	1.5
02 170	Matanuska-Susitna	39,683	91.9	0.7	0.7	4.8	<.1	1.9	4	1	9	25	7.2	9.0	1.3	2.2
02 180	Nome	8,288	24.0	0.1	0.6	74.0	<.1	1.3	13	20	23	5	1.5	0.5	<.1	7.2
02 185	North Slope	5,979	20.9	0.6	4.4	72.0	<.1	2.1	17	22	10	7	1.1	0.3	0.2	5.1
02 188	Northwest Arctic	6,113	13.5	0.2	0.8	84.9	<.1	0.6	16	24	19	2	1.1	0.2	<.1	6.1
02 201	Prince of Wales Outer Ketchikan	6,278	60.5	0.1	0.4	37.0	<.1	1.9	15	15	21	11	1.1	0.9	<.1	2.7
02 220	Sitka	8,588	73.0	0.5	3.6	20.5	0.0	2.4	11	11	15	13	1.6	1.5	0.2	2.1
02 231	Skagway-Yakutat-Angoon	4,385	59.8	0.1	0.7	37.8	<.1	1.5	20	16	22	10	0.8	0.6	<.1	2.0

[1] Non-Hispanic Native American.

Table A. — **1990 Population by Race and Ethnic Origin (cont)**

State/ county code	Election district	Total persons	Percent of total persons						Rank				Percent contribution to state population			
			Non-Hispanic							Percent of total persons				Non-Hispanic		
			White	Black	Asian and Pacific Islander	Native American	Other	Hispanic	Total	Non-Hispanic		Native American[1]	Total	White	Black	Native American[1]
										White	Black					
02 240	Southeast Fairbanks	5,913	78.0	4.8	1.3	12.9	< .1	3.0	18	9	4	18	1.1	1.1	1.3	0.9
02 261	Valdez–Cordova	9,952	81.4	0.6	3.1	12.2	< .1	2.7	9	4	12	20	1.8	2.0	0.3	1.4
02 270	Wade Hampton	5,791	5.9	0.2	0.4	93.2	< .1	0.3	19	25	17	1	1.1	< .1	< .1	6.4
02 280	Wrangell–Petersburg	7,042	77.7	0.2	1.3	19.1	< .1	1.7	14	10	20	14	1.3	1.3	< .1	1.6
02 290	Yukon–Koyukuk................	8,478	41.7	1.0	0.6	55.7	< .1	1.0	12	17	7	8	1.5	0.9	0.4	5.6

[1]Non-Hispanic Native American.

58 Alaska

Table B. — 1990 Voting Age Population (VAP) by Race and Ethnic Origin

Election district	Total Voting Age Population	Percent of total VAP Non-Hispanic White	Black	Asian and Pacific Islander	Native American	Other	Hispanic	Rank Percent of total VAP Total	Non-Hispanic White	Black	Native American[1]	Percent contribution to state VAP Total	White	Black	Native American[1]	VAP percent of total population Total	White	Black	Asian and Pacific Islander	Native American	Other	Hispanic
01 Ketchikan	9,831	83.0	0.5	3.1	11.8	<.1	1.6	10	19	34	12	2.6	2.8	0.3	2.3	70.3	72.0	85.5	65.2	63.0	33.3	55.6
02 Sitka-Wrangell	10,165	79.2	0.3	2.7	15.7	0.0	2.0	7	25	37	9	2.7	2.8	0.2	3.2	69.5	71.5	66.0	67.5	61.9	0.0	64.4
03 Downtown Juneau	10,062	78.6	0.9	4.0	14.1	<.1	2.5	8	26	27	10	2.7	2.7	0.7	2.8	74.0	77.0	76.9	70.6	63.9	50.0	58.5
04 Mendenhall Valley	8,957	86.0	1.0	3.6	7.2	<.1	2.1	32	12	25	16	2.4	2.7	0.7	1.3	67.2	69.1	58.9	61.2	55.7	57.1	57.1
05 Southeast Islands	9,157	66.4	<.1	0.5	31.5	<.1	1.4	28	34	40	5	2.4	2.1	<.1	5.7	67.9	72.4	50.0	64.0	60.5	66.7	58.3
06 Kodiak Island	9,399	68.2	1.0	10.5	15.8	<.1	4.5	19	33	26	8	2.5	2.2	0.7	2.9	68.8	70.7	71.4	70.3	62.0	28.6	63.9
07 Homer	9,194	93.5	0.2	0.7	4.3	<.1	1.3	26	3	38	27	2.4	3.0	0.1	0.8	65.9	66.4	57.1	55.8	61.8	100.0	60.0
08 Seward-Soldotna	9,436	90.5	0.7	0.9	6.4	<.1	1.5	17	8	29	19	2.5	3.0	0.5	1.2	68.4	68.7	82.9	57.0	68.8	33.3	55.8
09 Kenai	9,382	90.2	0.6	1.0	6.4	<.1	1.8	21	9	32	18	2.5	2.9	0.4	1.2	67.9	68.5	67.4	63.0	64.1	66.7	57.2
10 Oceanview	9,383	89.7	1.9	3.0	2.8	<.1	2.5	20	10	19	39	2.5	2.9	1.2	0.5	67.2	67.8	61.0	64.1	61.3	47.4	61.5
11 West Anchorage	10,286	83.4	3.4	4.9	5.2	<.1	3.1	5	18	16	24	2.7	3.0	2.4	1.1	73.6	75.6	65.8	68.2	62.5	55.6	62.8
12 Sand Lake	9,615	83.7	3.1	6.5	3.7	<.1	3.1	14	17	17	34	2.5	2.8	2.1	0.7	69.6	71.0	62.5	65.2	59.4	27.3	66.4
13 Coastal Trail	10,549	84.4	1.8	6.7	4.1	<.1	2.9	3	16	21	30	2.8	3.1	1.3	0.9	76.0	78.0	65.2	68.4	65.5	38.5	67.7
14 Elmendorf	9,166	73.6	11.8	5.2	4.7	<.1	4.6	27	30	4	25	2.4	2.3	7.6	0.9	66.1	67.7	63.0	68.8	59.6	53.3	56.5
15 Spenard-Downtown	11,230	73.6	4.3	6.4	10.6	0.1	5.0	2	29	14	13	3.0	2.9	3.4	2.4	81.0	85.3	73.3	71.6	70.9	59.1	69.9
16 Fairview-Mt. View	10,167	56.9	12.2	6.5	17.4	<.1	6.9	6	35	3	7	2.7	2.0	8.8	3.5	73.1	79.7	66.7	67.3	66.0	26.1	63.4
17 Dimond-Campbell	9,778	82.9	4.0	4.5	5.5	<.1	2.9	11	20	15	23	2.6	2.8	2.8	1.1	70.0	72.1	58.7	65.2	62.2	66.7	58.3
18 Hillside	9,402	93.7	1.2	1.5	1.8	<.1	1.8	18	2	24	40	2.5	3.0	0.8	0.3	67.5	68.3	59.6	55.0	53.8	100.0	62.9
19 Lake Otis & Tudor	9,604	80.4	5.7	4.6	5.7	<.1	3.6	15	23	10	22	2.5	2.7	3.8	1.1	69.0	71.3	60.5	64.8	60.2	30.4	65.1
20 Midtown	10,419	82.0	4.5	5.2	5.8	<.1	2.5	4	21	13	21	2.8	3.0	3.3	1.2	75.8	77.6	68.0	70.9	68.3	43.8	65.1
21 East Anchorage	9,865	77.9	7.6	4.3	6.7	<.1	3.3	9	27	6	17	2.6	2.7	5.3	1.3	70.8	73.9	65.2	67.5	57.2	31.3	58.5
22 East Anchorage	9,704	80.9	7.4	3.9	4.0	<.1	3.7	12	22	7	31	2.6	2.7	5.0	0.8	69.6	71.7	61.0	70.6	59.8	44.4	59.4
23 Northeast Anchorage	9,323	70.4	16.7	3.2	3.5	<.1	6.2	23	32	1	35	2.5	2.3	10.9	0.7	67.1	69.0	64.2	66.2	60.3	33.3	60.6
24 Muldoon-Eagle River	9,248	84.9	5.6	2.0	4.2	<.1	3.3	24	13	11	28	2.4	2.7	3.7	0.8	67.0	67.6	65.3	66.0	66.6	33.3	57.8
25 Eagle River	9,153	91.4	1.7	1.7	3.2	<.1	2.0	29	7	22	37	2.4	2.9	1.1	0.6	65.7	66.4	56.3	62.1	60.8	28.6	55.9
26 Wasilla-Chugiak	8,669	92.0	0.7	0.8	4.5	<.1	1.9	35	5	30	26	2.3	2.8	0.4	0.8	63.6	64.2	58.5	54.0	58.9	85.7	54.2
27 Palmer	9,000	93.4	0.7	0.6	3.9	<.1	1.4	31	4	31	32	2.4	2.9	0.4	0.7	64.4	65.2	51.2	64.4	55.0	100.0	52.0
28 Rural Matanuska-Susitna	8,810	93.8	0.4	0.7	3.7	0.0	1.5	33	1	35	33	2.3	2.9	0.3	0.6	65.1	65.7	63.3	55.2	59.0	0.0	51.4
29 University	9,519	87.4	1.6	3.3	5.8	0.1	1.8	16	11	23	20	2.5	2.9	1.1	1.1	71.8	72.6	62.2	76.9	64.3	71.4	64.7
30 West Fairbanks	9,379	79.8	6.8	2.4	7.5	<.1	3.4	22	24	8	14	2.5	2.6	4.5	1.4	70.8	73.2	64.7	66.0	61.6	40.0	60.0
31 East Fairbanks	9,670	72.7	8.1	2.6	12.9	<.1	3.6	13	31	5	11	2.6	2.4	5.5	2.5	72.2	75.5	63.9	70.3	64.4	42.1	65.7
32 Badger-Wainwright	9,106	74.9	13.9	2.7	2.8	<.1	5.6	30	28	2	38	2.4	2.4	8.9	0.6	66.7	67.3	68.1	65.6	58.0	85.7	62.2
33 Northeast Fairbanks	8,658	91.8	1.9	1.3	3.3	0.0	1.7	36	6	20	36	2.3	2.8	1.1	0.6	65.5	66.4	60.8	61.0	52.8	0.0	56.0
34 North Pole-Denali	8,727	84.7	6.0	1.8	4.1	<.1	3.2	34	14	9	29	2.3	2.6	3.7	0.7	65.3	66.5	61.7	63.5	59.0	53.3	54.0
35 PWS-Delta	9,197	84.5	2.7	2.7	7.3	<.1	2.7	25	15	18	15	2.4	2.7	1.7	1.3	69.6	70.3	66.7	66.7	67.0	66.7	62.2
36 Rural Interior	8,127	42.5	0.7	0.4	55.5	<.1	0.8	39	37	28	4	2.2	1.2	0.4	8.9	63.8	74.1	76.9	67.4	57.7	100.0	50.0
37 Northwest Alaska	7,953	21.9	0.5	2.8	73.6	<.1	1.2	40	39	33	3	2.1	0.6	0.3	11.6	59.6	79.9	83.7	70.0	55.0	42.9	58.9
38 Nome-Yukon River	8,289	20.0	0.2	0.6	78.4	<.1	0.8	38	40	39	1	2.2	0.6	<.1	12.9	58.8	73.2	66.7	65.3	56.0	50.0	55.8
39 Bethel-Dillingham	8,566	23.7	0.4	0.8	74.2	<.1	0.9	37	38	36	2	2.3	0.7	0.2	12.6	61.8	74.6	58.6	65.1	58.6	38.5	61.5
40 Aleutians	11,554	56.6	5.0	10.2	20.7	0.1	7.4	1	36	12	6	3.1	2.3	4.0	4.8	77.1	80.9	83.3	88.1	61.7	100.0	87.6
ALASKA	**377,699**	**76.5**	**3.8**	**3.4**	**13.4**	**<.1**	**2.9**					**100.0**	**100.0**	**100.0**	**100.0**	**68.7**	**71.1**	**65.1**	**68.6**	**59.6**	**47.3**	**62.1**
CONGRESSIONAL District At-Large	377,699	76.5	3.8	3.4	13.4	<.1	2.9									68.7	71.1	65.1	68.6	59.6	47.3	62.1
BOROUGHS AND CENSUS AREAS																						
Aleutians East	1,917	35.3	0.7	21.8	33.0	0.3	8.9	22	18	10	11	0.5	0.2	<.1	1.3	77.8	84.5	93.3	98.6	60.9	100.0	95.0
Aleutians West	7,595	65.6	6.9	9.9	9.1	<.1	8.5	9	14	1	21	2.0	1.7	3.7	1.4	70.5	80.1	81.3	83.4	63.5	100.0	86.5
Anchorage	159,650	80.7	5.7	4.4	5.6	<.1	3.6	1	8	3	24	42.3	44.6	63.8	17.8	70.5	72.3	64.1	67.2	63.5	42.5	61.7
Bethel	8,324	18.7	0.4	0.8	79.4	<.1	2.2	8	23	16	3	2.2	0.5	0.2	13.1	61.0	75.2	56.5	72.2	58.3	45.5	62.5
Bristol Bay	1,028	67.1	3.7	0.7	25.9	0.0	2.6	25	13	5	12	0.3	0.2	0.3	0.5	62.5	78.3	100.0	58.3	59.6	0.0	81.8
Dillingham	2,508	29.8	0.2	0.4	68.4	0.1	1.1	21	19	19	6	0.7	0.3	<.1	3.4	62.5	74.3	50.0	44.0	58.8	50.0	55.1
Fairbanks North Star	53,383	81.6	6.5	2.4	6.0	<.1	3.3	2	7	2	23	14.1	15.1	24.6	6.4	68.7	70.0	64.8	68.2	61.6	51.4	60.6
Haines	1,525	86.5	<.1	0.6	11.9	0.0	1.0	23	3	24	17	0.4	0.5	<.1	0.4	72.0	73.6	100.0	52.9	64.9	0.0	55.6
Juneau	18,901	82.0	1.0	3.8	10.9	<.1	2.3	5	6	8	20	5.0	5.4	1.3	4.1	70.7	72.9	66.7	66.1	61.1	55.6	57.8
Kenai Peninsula	27,406	90.3	0.5	0.8	6.8	<.1	1.5	3	2	12	22	7.3	8.6	1.0	3.7	67.7	67.6	74.0	58.3	64.5	50.0	57.2
Ketchikan Gateway	9,706	82.8	0.5	3.1	11.9	<.1	1.6	6	5	14	16	2.6	2.8	0.3	2.3	70.2	71.9	85.5	65.2	63.0	33.3	55.8
Kodiak Island	9,178	69.3	1.0	10.7	14.3	<.1	4.6	7	12	7	15	2.4	2.2	0.7	2.6	69.0	70.6	71.4	70.2	62.6	28.6	63.8
Lake and Peninsula	1,034	25.1	0.0	1.0	72.2	0.0	1.6	24	22	25	4	0.3	<.1	0.0	1.5	62.0	68.6	0.0	83.3	60.0	0.0	53.1
Matanuska-Susitna	25,670	92.7	0.7	0.7	4.4	<.1	1.6	4	1	11	25	6.8	8.2	1.3	2.2	64.7	65.3	60.5	61.0	59.1	62.5	53.2
Nome	5,113	28.2	0.2	0.7	69.9	0.0	1.1	13	20	20	5	1.4	0.5	<.1	7.1	61.7	72.5	88.9	70.6	58.3	0.0	52.8
North Slope	3,741	27.2	0.9	5.2	64.7	<.1	2.0	17	21	9	7	1.0	0.4	0.2	4.8	62.6	81.7	86.5	73.1	56.3	50.0	59.7
Northwest Arctic	3,481	18.3	0.3	0.7	80.1	<.1	0.6	18	24	17	2	0.9	0.2	<.1	5.5	56.9	77.2	75.0	52.1	53.7	66.7	55.6
Prince of Wales-Outer Ketchikan	4,250	64.8	<.1	0.3	33.2	<.1	1.5	15	15	23	10	1.1	1.0	<.1	2.8	67.7	72.5	44.4	58.3	60.8	100.0	53.7
Sitka	5,953	75.2	0.5	3.5	18.5	0.0	2.3	11	11	15	13	1.6	1.5	0.2	2.2	69.3	71.4	71.8	67.6	62.7	0.0	65.1
Skagway-Yakutat-Angoon	2,951	64.1	0.1	0.8	33.4	<.1	1.5	20	16	22	9	0.8	0.7	<.1	2.0	67.3	72.2	50.0	77.4	59.6	33.3	64.2

[1] Non-Hispanic Native American.

Table B. — 1990 Voting Age Population (VAP) by Race and Ethnic Origin (cont)

Election district	Total Voting Age Population	Percent of total VAP						Rank				Percent contribution to state VAP				VAP percent of total population						
		Non-Hispanic							Percent of total VAP				Non-Hispanic				Non-Hispanic					
		White	Black	Asian and Pacific Islander	Native American	Other	Hispanic	Total	Non-Hispanic		Native American[1]	Total	White	Black	Native American[1]	Total	White	Black	Asian and Pacific Islander	Native American	Other	Hispanic
									White	Black												
Southeast Fairbanks	3,805	80.2	4.6	1.3	11.3	0.0	2.5	16	10	4	19	1.0	1.1	1.2	0.9	64.3	66.2	62.0	66.2	56.3	0.0	54.2
Valdez-Cordova	7,048	82.9	0.5	3.0	11.3	<.1	2.3	10	4	13	18	1.9	2.0	0.2	1.6	70.8	72.2	63.6	67.1	65.3	100.0	61.1
Wade Hampton	3,137	8.7	0.2	0.4	90.3	<.1	0.4	19	25	18	1	0.8	<.1	<.1	5.6	54.2	79.8	50.0	50.0	52.5	100.0	76.5
Wrangell-Petersburg	4,870	80.4	0.1	1.3	16.7	<.1	1.6	14	9	21	14	1.3	1.4	<.1	1.6	69.2	71.5	45.5	67.0	60.2	100.0	64.7
Yukon-Koyukuk	5,525	47.6	1.4	0.6	49.4	<.1	1.0	12	17	6	8	1.5	0.9	0.6	5.4	65.2	74.3	89.8	66.0	57.8	100.0	65.9

[1]Non-Hispanic Native American.

Table C. — Voter Participation: November 3, 1992, General Election

Election district	Voting Age Population (VAP) 1990	Voter registration (REG) Total	% contribution to state REG	% of 1990 VAP	Rank by % of 1990 VAP	Voter turnout — Highest office Actual	Total	Office	% of 1990 VAP	Voter turnout — Maximum vote Total	% contribution to state turnout	% of REG	Rank by % of REG	% of 1990 VAP	Rank by % 1990 VAP	Percent drop-off, by office President	Senator	Governor	Representative
01 Ketchikan	9,831	8,454	2.7	86.0	18	6,849	6,760	P	68.8	6,849	2.6	81.0	28	69.7	20	1.3	9.1	-	9.5
02 Sitka-Wrangell	10,165	9,298	3.0	91.5	8	7,800	7,719	P	75.9	7,800	3.0	83.9	20	76.7	12	1.0	8.1	-	8.6
03 Downtown Juneau	10,062	9,490	3.0	94.3	4	8,128	8,042	P	79.9	8,128	3.1	85.6	14	80.8	5	1.1	5.2	-	5.5
04 Mendenhall Valley	8,957	8,416	2.7	94.0	5	7,282	7,238	P	80.8	7,282	2.8	86.5	11	81.3	4	0.6	5.0	-	5.4
05 Southeast Islands	9,157	7,948	2.5	86.8	17	5,867	5,742	P	62.7	5,867	2.2	73.8	36	64.1	31	2.1	8.3	-	8.1
06 Kodiak Island	9,399	7,148	2.3	76.1	34	5,827	5,711	P	60.8	5,827	2.2	81.5	26	62.0	32	2.0	12.0	-	11.9
07 Homer	9,194	7,858	2.5	85.5	20	6,774	6,704	P	72.9	6,774	2.6	86.2	12	73.7	16	1.0	8.4	-	8.2
08 Seward-Soldotna	9,436	7,420	2.4	78.6	32	6,514	6,449	P	68.3	6,514	2.5	87.8	6	69.0	21	1.0	10.1	-	9.8
09 Kenai	9,382	7,224	2.3	77.0	33	6,467	6,414	P	68.4	6,467	2.5	89.5	3	68.9	22	0.8	10.7	-	11.0
10 Oceanview	9,383	8,698	2.8	92.7	7	7,544	7,493	P	79.9	7,544	2.9	86.7	10	80.4	8	0.7	5.7	-	5.9
11 West Anchorage	10,286	8,274	2.6	80.4	28	6,971	6,920	P	67.3	6,971	2.7	84.3	19	67.8	24	0.7	8.2	-	8.4
12 Sand Lake	9,615	7,978	2.5	83.0	22	6,996	6,963	P	72.4	6,996	2.7	87.7	7	72.8	17	0.5	7.6	-	8.0
13 Coastal Trail	10,549	9,454	3.0	89.6	11	8,058	7,989	P	75.7	8,058	3.1	85.2	17	76.4	13	0.9	6.1	-	6.4
14 Elmendorf	9,166	7,600	2.4	82.9	23	6,172	6,124	P	66.8	6,172	2.4	81.2	27	67.3	26	0.8	11.3	-	11.8
15 Spenard-Downtown	11,230	7,642	2.4	68.0	37	6,017	5,941	P	52.9	6,017	2.3	78.7	32	53.6	37	1.3	10.0	-	10.2
16 Fairview-Mt. View	10,167	6,599	2.1	64.9	39	4,734	4,633	P	45.6	4,734	1.8	71.7	39	46.6	39	2.1	13.9	-	14.0
17 Dimond-Campbell	9,778	7,807	2.5	79.8	29	6,469	6,423	P	65.7	6,469	2.5	82.9	25	66.2	30	0.7	8.4	-	8.8
18 Hillside	9,402	9,495	3.0	101.0	2	8,394	8,357	P	88.9	8,394	3.2	88.4	4	89.3	1	0.4	4.6	-	4.9
19 Lake Otis & Tudor	9,604	7,562	2.4	78.7	31	6,460	6,419	P	66.8	6,460	2.5	85.4	16	67.3	27	0.6	8.9	-	9.3
20 Midtown	10,419	8,677	2.8	83.3	21	7,276	7,225	P	69.3	7,276	2.8	83.9	21	69.8	19	0.7	7.2	-	7.6
21 East Anchorage	9,865	8,002	2.5	81.1	26	6,678	6,632	P	67.2	6,678	2.6	83.5	22	67.7	25	0.7	8.3	-	8.7
22 East Anchorage	9,704	8,649	2.7	89.1	14	7,290	7,233	P	74.5	7,290	2.8	84.3	18	75.1	15	0.8	6.3	-	6.3
23 Northeast Anchorage	9,323	6,287	2.0	67.4	38	4,621	4,550	P	48.8	4,621	1.8	73.5	37	49.6	38	1.5	18.8	-	19.1
24 Muldoon-Eagle River	9,248	8,626	2.7	93.3	6	7,377	7,338	P	79.3	7,377	2.8	85.5	15	79.8	9	0.5	8.2	-	8.3
25 Eagle River	9,153	8,020	2.5	87.6	16	6,980	6,927	P	75.7	6,980	2.7	87.0	9	76.3	14	0.8	8.6	-	9.1
26 Wasilla-Chugiak	8,669	7,442	2.4	85.8	19	6,729	6,686	P	77.1	6,729	2.6	90.4	1	77.6	11	0.6	8.6	-	9.1
27 Palmer	9,000	8,050	2.6	89.4	13	7,018	6,970	P	77.4	7,018	2.7	87.2	8	78.0	10	0.7	7.0	-	6.8
28 Rural Matanuska-Susitna	8,810	7,901	2.5	89.7	10	7,102	7,034	P	79.8	7,102	2.7	89.9	2	80.6	6	1.0	10.0	-	10.3
29 University	9,519	8,674	2.8	91.1	9	7,657	7,623	P	80.1	7,657	2.9	88.3	5	80.4	7	0.4	6.0	-	6.4
30 West Fairbanks	9,379	7,682	2.4	81.9	25	6,406	6,333	P	67.5	6,406	2.5	83.4	24	68.3	23	1.1	7.6	-	7.9
31 East Fairbanks	9,670	7,720	2.5	79.8	30	6,442	6,340	P	65.6	6,442	2.5	83.4	23	66.6	29	1.6	7.9	-	8.2
32 Badger-Wainwright	9,106	6,660	2.1	73.1	35	5,350	5,293	P	58.1	5,350	2.0	80.3	29	58.8	35	1.1	13.7	-	14.1
33 Northeast Fairbanks	8,658	8,524	2.7	98.5	3	7,311	7,252	P	83.8	7,311	2.8	85.8	13	84.4	2	0.8	5.9	-	6.1
34 North Pole-Denali	8,727	9,037	2.9	103.6	1	7,246	7,183	P	82.3	7,246	2.8	80.2	30	83.0	3	0.9	7.9	-	8.1
35 PWS-Delta	9,197	8,152	2.6	88.6	15	6,473	6,415	P	69.8	6,473	2.5	79.4	31	70.4	18	0.9	6.1	-	6.1
36 Rural Interior	8,127	7,280	2.3	89.6	12	5,452	5,284	P	65.0	5,452	2.1	74.9	34	67.1	28	3.1	7.9	-	7.8
37 Northwest Alaska	7,953	6,564	2.1	82.5	24	4,685	4,543	P	57.1	4,685	1.8	71.4	40	58.9	34	3.0	7.4	-	7.9
38 Nome-Yukon River	8,289	6,705	2.1	80.9	27	5,003	4,864	P	58.7	5,003	1.9	74.6	35	60.4	33	2.8	7.2	-	7.4
39 Bethel-Dillingham	8,566	6,221	2.0	72.6	36	4,712	4,516	P	52.7	4,712	1.8	75.7	33	55.0	36	4.2	9.4	-	10.2
40 Aleutians	11,554	5,820	1.8	50.4	40	4,238	4,166	P	36.1	4,238	1.6	72.8	38	36.7	40	1.7	11.7	-	11.5
ALASKA[1]	**395,000**	**315,058**	**100.0**	**79.8**		**261,427**	**258,448**		**65.4**	**261,427**	**100.0**	**83.0**		**66.2**		**1.1**	**8.3**	**-**	**8.5**

[1]Actual turnout includes 58 federal absentee ballots cast by residents overseas and reported only at the state level. Statewide VAP (395,000) is 1992 estimate; sum of 1990 VAP by district is 377,699.

Alaska 61

Election district	Total voter registration	Political party affiliation			Plurality		Percent of total registration			Rank			Percent contribution to state registration			
		Democrat[1] (DEM)	Republican[1] (REP)	Independent[1] (IND)	Total	Party	DEM	REP	IND	DEM	REP	IND	Total	DEM	REP	IND
01 Ketchikan	8,454	1,559	1,658	2,514	856	I	27.2	28.9	43.9	19	29	19	2.7	2.6	2.3	1.3
02 Sitka-Wrangell	9,298	1,794	1,753	2,955	1,161	I	27.6	27.0	45.4	15	30	13	3.0	3.0	2.5	1.5
03 Downtown Juneau	9,490	2,520	1,361	3,043	523	I	36.4	19.7	43.9	4	36	10	3.0	4.2	1.9	1.6
04 Mendenhall Valley......	8,416	1,609	1,659	2,858	1,199	I	26.3	27.1	46.7	17	28	2	2.7	2.7	2.3	1.5
05 Southeast Islands	7,948	1,907	1,063	2,482	575	I	35.0	19.5	45.5	6	37	15	2.5	3.2	1.5	1.3
06 Kodiak Island.............	7,148	1,440	1,603	1,980	377	I	28.7	31.9	39.4	12	20	26	2.3	2.4	2.3	1.0
07 Homer	7,858	1,168	1,673	2,679	1,006	I	21.2	30.3	48.5	34	25	1	2.5	1.9	2.4	1.4
08 Seward-Soldotna........	7,420	1,092	1,604	2,423	819	I	21.3	31.3	47.3	36	24	6	2.4	1.8	2.3	1.3
09 Kenai	7,224	1,195	1,612	2,337	725	I	23.2	31.3	45.4	28	21	8	2.3	2.0	2.3	1.2
10 Oceanview	8,698	1,232	2,632	2,791	159	I	18.5	39.5	41.9	37	2	9	2.8	2.1	3.7	1.5
11 West Anchorage	8,274	1,491	2,076	2,444	368	I	24.8	34.5	40.7	22	14	20	2.6	2.5	2.9	1.3
12 Sand Lake	7,978	1,235	2,142	2,487	345	I	21.1	36.5	42.4	30	11	16	2.5	2.1	3.0	1.3
13 Coastal Trail	9,454	1,832	2,343	2,864	521	I	26.0	33.3	40.7	14	16	18	3.0	3.1	3.3	1.5
14 Elmendorf..................	7,600	1,331	2,403	1,291	1,072	R	26.5	47.8	25.7	23	1	40	2.4	2.2	3.4	0.7
15 Spenard-Downtown	7,642	1,766	1,406	2,074	308	I	33.7	26.8	39.5	7	31	29	2.4	2.9	2.0	1.1
16 Fairview-Mt. View	6,599	1,714	974	1,610	104	D	39.9	22.7	37.5	5	35	34	2.1	2.9	1.4	0.8
17 Dimond-Campbell	7,807	1,305	2,106	2,108	2	I	23.6	38.2	38.2	26	10	30	2.5	2.2	3.0	1.1
18 Hillside.....................	9,495	1,432	2,677	3,116	439	I	19.8	37.1	43.1	33	5	5	3.0	2.4	3.8	1.6
19 Lake Otis & Tudor	7,562	1,255	1,960	2,028	68	I	23.9	37.4	38.7	27	13	31	2.4	2.1	2.8	1.1
20 Midtown	8,677	1,584	2,125	2,659	534	I	24.9	33.4	41.8	21	17	17	2.8	2.6	3.0	1.4
21 East Anchorage	8,002	1,731	1,771	2,198	427	R	30.4	31.1	38.6	9	23	27	2.5	2.9	2.5	1.1
22 East Anchorage	8,649	1,506	2,372	2,358	14	R	24.2	38.0	37.8	24	7	28	2.7	2.5	3.4	1.2
23 Northeast Anchorage ...	6,287	1,205	1,751	1,082	546	R	29.8	43.4	26.8	16	6	39	2.0	2.0	2.5	0.6
24 Muldoon-Eagle River ...	8,626	1,442	2,589	2,119	470	R	23.4	42.1	34.5	25	3	33	2.7	2.4	3.7	1.1
25 Eagle River	8,020	1,126	2,188	2,335	147	I	19.9	38.7	41.3	40	8	22	2.5	1.9	3.1	1.2
26 Wasilla-Chugiak.........	7,442	1,046	1,850	2,363	513	I	19.9	35.2	44.9	39	15	14	2.4	1.7	2.6	1.2
27 Palmer	8,050	1,220	1,932	2,702	770	I	20.8	33.0	46.2	32	18	3	2.6	2.0	2.7	1.4
28 Rural																
Matanuska-Susitna	7,901	1,209	1,785	2,560	775	I	21.8	32.1	46.1	31	19	7	2.5	2.0	2.5	1.3
29 University..................	8,674	1,614	1,576	2,869	1,255	I	26.6	26.0	47.4	18	32	4	2.8	2.7	2.2	1.5
30 West Fairbanks	7,682	1,497	1,704	2,162	458	I	27.9	31.8	40.3	13	22	25	2.4	2.5	2.4	1.1
31 East Fairbanks...........	7,720	1,638	1,549	2,200	562	I	30.4	28.8	40.8	10	27	24	2.5	2.7	2.2	1.1
32 Badger-Wainwright	6,660	1,216	1,798	1,378	420	R	27.7	40.9	31.4	20	9	38	2.1	2.0	2.5	0.7
33 Northeast Fairbanks ..	8,524	1,205	2,255	2,502	247	I	20.2	37.8	42.0	38	12	21	2.7	2.0	3.2	1.3
34 North Pole-Denali	9,037	1,334	2,649	1,955	694	R	22.5	44.6	32.9	35	4	37	2.9	2.2	3.7	1.0
35 PWS-Delta	8,152	1,273	1,650	2,607	957	I	23.0	29.8	47.1	29	26	11	2.6	2.1	2.3	1.4
36 Rural Interior	7,280	1,667	1,149	2,315	648	I	32.5	22.4	45.1	8	34	12	2.3	2.8	1.6	1.2
37 Northwest Alaska	6,564	2,054	772	1,501	553	D	47.5	17.8	34.7	3	39	36	2.1	3.4	1.1	0.8
38 Nome-Yukon River	6,705	2,229	863	1,762	467	D	45.9	17.8	36.3	2	38	32	2.1	3.7	1.2	0.9
39 Bethel-Dillingham	6,221	2,079	656	1,807	272	D	45.8	14.4	39.8	1	40	23	2.0	3.5	0.9	0.9
40 Aleutians	5,820	1,186	1,050	1,387	201	I	32.7	29.0	38.3	11	33	35	1.8	2.0	1.5	0.7
ALASKA[2].........................	**315,058**	**59,938**	**70,739**	**191,381**	**120,642**	**I**	**18.6**	**22.0**	**59.4**				**100.0**	**100.0**	**100.0**	**100.0**

[1]Data from report dated December 7, 1992; sum of registrants by party differs from total voter registration reported with November 1992 general election returns. [2]Total voter registration also includes 9,871 for Alaska Independent party, 2,114 for Green party, 5,554 for other, and 82,937 undeclared.

Table E. — Vote for President: November 3, 1992, General Election

Election district	Total	Clinton (DEM)	Bush (REP)	Perot (IND)	Other	Plurality Total	Party	DEM	REP	IND	Other	Rank DEM	Rank REP	Rank IND	Total	DEM	REP	IND	DEM	REP
01 Ketchikan	6,760	2,055	2,495	2,120	90	375	R	30.4	36.9	31.4	1.3	18	30	11	2.6	2.6	2.4	2.9	45.2	54.8
02 Sitka-Wrangell	7,719	2,565	2,916	2,137	101	351	R	33.2	37.8	27.7	1.3	12	27	22	3.0	3.3	2.9	2.9	46.8	53.2
03 Downtown Juneau	8,042	4,064	2,447	1,424	107	1,617	D	50.5	30.4	17.7	1.3	1	38	39	3.1	5.2	2.4	1.9	62.4	37.6
04 Mendenhall Valley	7,238	2,688	2,894	1,561	95	206	R	37.1	40.0	21.6	1.3	9	18	36	2.8	3.4	2.8	2.1	48.2	51.8
05 Southeast Islands	5,742	2,095	1,844	1,684	119	251	D	36.5	32.1	29.3	2.1	10	36	18	2.2	2.7	1.8	2.3	53.2	46.8
06 Kodiak Island	5,711	1,546	2,345	1,748	72	597	R	27.1	41.1	30.6	1.3	25	14	14	2.2	2.0	2.3	2.4	39.7	60.3
07 Homer	6,704	2,088	2,173	2,244	199	71	I	31.1	32.4	33.5	3.0	16	35	6	2.6	2.7	2.1	3.1	49.0	51.0
08 Seward-Soldotna	6,449	1,509	2,499	2,325	116	174	R	23.4	38.8	36.1	1.8	33	25	4	2.5	1.9	2.5	3.2	37.6	62.4
09 Kenai	6,414	1,540	2,349	2,368	157	19	I	24.0	36.6	36.9	2.4	31	32	2	2.5	2.0	2.3	3.2	39.6	60.4
10 Oceanview	7,493	1,947	3,548	1,899	99	1,601	R	26.0	47.4	25.3	1.3	27	3	31	2.9	2.5	3.5	2.6	35.4	64.6
11 West Anchorage	6,920	2,009	2,730	2,081	100	649	R	29.0	39.5	30.1	1.4	23	21	17	2.7	2.6	2.7	2.8	42.4	57.6
12 Sand Lake	6,963	1,831	2,999	2,039	94	960	R	26.3	43.1	29.3	1.4	26	10	19	2.7	2.3	2.9	2.8	37.9	62.1
13 Coastal Trail	7,989	3,001	2,963	1,907	118	38	D	37.6	37.1	23.9	1.5	8	29	34	3.1	3.8	2.9	2.6	50.3	49.7
14 Elmendorf	6,124	1,423	3,013	1,599	89	1,414	R	23.2	49.2	26.1	1.5	35	1	28	2.4	1.8	3.0	2.2	32.1	67.9
15 Spenard-Downtown	5,941	2,389	1,842	1,591	119	547	D	40.2	31.0	26.8	2.0	3	37	24	2.3	3.1	1.8	2.2	56.5	43.5
16 Fairview-Mt. View	4,633	1,814	1,375	1,320	124	439	D	39.2	29.7	28.5	2.7	6	39	21	1.8	2.3	1.3	1.8	56.9	43.1
17 Dimond-Campbell	6,423	1,749	2,623	1,958	93	665	R	27.2	40.8	30.5	1.4	24	15	15	2.5	2.2	2.6	2.7	40.0	60.0
18 Hillside	8,357	2,483	3,629	2,134	111	1,146	R	29.7	43.4	25.5	1.3	20	9	29	3.2	3.2	3.6	2.9	40.6	59.4
19 Lake Otis & Tudor	6,419	1,931	2,539	1,840	109	608	R	30.1	39.6	28.7	1.7	19	20	20	2.5	2.5	2.5	2.5	43.2	56.8
20 Midtown	7,225	2,383	2,914	1,823	105	531	R	33.0	40.3	25.2	1.5	14	16	32	2.8	3.0	2.9	2.5	45.0	55.0
21 East Anchorage	6,632	2,386	2,437	1,693	116	51	R	36.0	36.7	25.5	1.7	11	31	30	2.6	3.0	2.4	2.3	49.5	50.5
22 East Anchorage	7,233	2,253	3,164	1,713	103	911	R	31.1	43.7	23.7	1.4	15	8	35	2.8	2.9	3.1	2.3	41.6	58.4
23 Northeast Anchorage	4,550	1,139	2,127	1,217	67	910	R	25.0	46.7	26.7	1.5	29	5	25	1.8	1.5	2.1	1.7	34.9	65.1
24 Muldoon-Eagle River	7,338	1,876	3,441	1,930	91	1,511	R	25.6	46.9	26.3	1.2	28	4	27	2.8	2.4	3.4	2.6	35.3	64.7
25 Eagle River	6,927	1,513	3,197	2,122	95	1,075	R	21.8	46.2	30.6	1.4	36	6	13	2.7	1.9	3.1	2.9	32.1	67.9
26 Wasilla-Chugiak	6,686	1,439	2,675	2,419	153	256	R	21.5	40.0	36.2	2.3	39	17	3	2.6	1.8	2.6	3.3	35.0	65.0
27 Palmer	6,970	1,625	2,757	2,401	187	356	R	23.3	39.6	34.4	2.7	34	19	5	2.7	2.1	2.7	3.3	37.1	62.9
28 Rural Matanuska-Susitna	7,034	1,522	2,459	2,825	228	366	I	21.6	35.0	40.2	3.2	38	34	1	2.7	1.9	2.4	3.8	38.2	61.8
29 University	7,623	3,216	2,205	2,026	176	1,011	D	42.2	28.9	26.6	2.3	2	40	26	2.9	4.1	2.2	2.8	59.3	40.7
30 West Fairbanks	6,333	1,860	2,434	1,912	127	522	R	29.4	38.4	30.2	2.0	21	26	16	2.4	2.4	2.4	2.6	43.3	56.7
31 East Fairbanks	6,340	1,969	2,223	1,992	156	231	R	31.1	35.1	31.4	2.5	17	33	9	2.5	2.5	2.2	2.7	47.0	53.0
32 Badger-Wainwright	5,293	1,150	2,339	1,724	80	615	R	21.7	44.2	32.6	1.5	37	7	8	2.0	1.5	2.3	2.3	33.0	67.0
33 Northeast Fairbanks	7,252	1,712	3,100	2,278	162	822	R	23.6	42.7	31.4	2.2	32	12	10	2.8	2.2	3.0	3.1	35.6	64.4
34 North Pole-Denali	7,183	1,455	3,408	2,201	119	1,207	R	20.3	47.4	30.6	1.7	40	2	12	2.8	1.9	3.3	3.0	29.9	70.1
35 PWS-Delta	6,415	1,572	2,525	2,139	179	386	R	24.5	39.4	33.3	2.8	30	23	7	2.5	2.0	2.5	2.9	38.4	61.6
36 Rural Interior	5,284	1,748	2,081	1,322	133	333	R	33.1	39.4	25.0	2.5	13	22	33	2.0	2.2	2.0	1.8	45.7	54.3
37 Northwest Alaska	4,543	1,822	1,689	925	107	133	D	40.1	37.2	20.4	2.4	4	28	37	1.8	2.3	1.7	1.3	51.9	48.1
38 Nome-Yukon River	4,864	1,897	2,011	850	106	114	R	39.0	41.3	17.5	2.2	7	13	40	1.9	2.4	2.0	1.2	48.5	51.5
39 Bethel-Dillingham	4,516	1,797	1,777	860	82	20	D	39.8	39.3	19.0	1.8	5	24	38	1.7	2.3	1.7	1.2	50.3	49.7
40 Aleutians	4,166	1,211	1,786	1,122	47	575	R	29.1	42.9	26.9	1.1	22	11	23	1.6	1.5	1.8	1.5	40.4	59.6
ALASKA[1]	258,506	78,294	102,000	73,481	4,731	23,706	R	30.3	39.5	28.4	1.8				100.0	100.0	100.0	100.0	43.4	56.6

[1]Includes the following absentee votes cast by residents overseas and reported only at the state level: 22 for Clinton (DEM), 28 for Bush (REP), and 8 for Perot (IND); total of 58.

Alaska 63

Election district	Total	Smith (DEM)	Murkowski (REP)	Other	Plurality Total	Plurality Party	Percent of total vote DEM	REP	Other	Rank DEM	REP	Other	Percent contribution to state vote Total	DEM	REP	Other
01 Ketchikan	6,227	2,233	3,576	418	1,343	R	35.9	57.4	6.7	25	10	32	2.6	2.4	2.8	2.0
02 Sitka-Wrangell	7,168	2,642	3,990	536	1,348	R	36.9	55.7	7.5	22	16	29	3.0	2.9	3.1	2.6
03 Downtown Juneau	7,704	3,805	3,143	756	662	D	49.4	40.8	9.8	3	40	6	3.2	4.1	2.5	3.7
04 Mendenhall Valley.....	6,915	2,929	3,485	501	556	R	42.4	50.4	7.2	11	29	31	2.9	3.2	2.7	2.4
05 Southeast Islands	5,379	2,483	2,461	435	22	D	46.2	45.8	8.1	6	34	25	2.2	2.7	1.9	2.1
06 Kodiak Island..............	5,125	2,204	2,426	495	222	R	43.0	47.3	9.7	10	32	8	2.1	2.4	1.9	2.4
07 Homer	6,207	2,298	2,964	945	666	R	37.0	47.8	15.2	20	31	1	2.6	2.5	2.3	4.6
08 Seward-Soldotna	5,859	2,157	3,189	513	1,032	R	36.8	54.4	8.8	23	18	19	2.4	2.3	2.5	2.5
09 Kenai	5,773	2,215	3,013	545	798	R	38.4	52.2	9.4	17	25	11	2.4	2.4	2.4	2.7
10 Oceanview	7,116	2,217	4,358	541	2,141	R	31.2	61.2	7.6	40	1	27	3.0	2.4	3.4	2.6
11 West Anchorage	6,397	2,409	3,441	547	1,032	R	37.7	53.8	8.6	19	20	21	2.7	2.6	2.7	2.7
12 Sand Lake	6,466	2,188	3,743	535	1,555	R	33.8	57.9	8.3	32	8	23	2.7	2.4	2.9	2.6
13 Coastal Trail	7,567	2,951	3,849	767	898	R	39.0	50.9	10.1	16	28	5	3.2	3.2	3.0	3.7
14 Elmendorf..................	5,475	1,727	3,268	480	1,541	R	31.5	59.7	8.8	38	5	18	2.3	1.9	2.6	2.3
15 Spenard-Downtown	5,414	2,332	2,416	666	84	R	43.1	44.6	12.3	9	35	2	2.3	2.5	1.9	3.3
16 Fairview-Mt. View	4,075	1,860	1,753	462	107	D	45.6	43.0	11.3	7	38	4	1.7	2.0	1.4	2.3
17 Dimond-Campbell	5,928	2,070	3,365	493	1,295	R	34.9	56.8	8.3	30	13	22	2.5	2.2	2.6	2.4
18 Hillside	8,008	2,696	4,596	716	1,900	R	33.7	57.4	8.9	34	11	15	3.3	2.9	3.6	3.5
19 Lake Otis & Tudor	5,885	2,165	3,206	514	1,041	R	36.8	54.5	8.7	24	17	20	2.5	2.4	2.5	2.5
20 Midtown	6,754	2,498	3,645	611	1,147	R	37.0	54.0	9.0	21	19	13	2.8	2.7	2.9	3.0
21 East Anchorage.........	6,127	2,402	3,129	596	727	R	39.2	51.1	9.7	14	27	7	2.6	2.6	2.5	2.9
22 East Anchorage.........	6,833	2,390	3,944	499	1,554	R	35.0	57.7	7.3	28	9	30	2.9	2.6	3.1	2.4
23 Northeast Anchorage	3,753	1,296	2,126	331	830	R	34.5	56.6	8.8	31	14	17	1.6	1.4	1.7	1.6
24 Muldoon-Eagle River	6,775	2,176	4,048	551	1,872	R	32.1	59.7	8.1	37	4	24	2.8	2.4	3.2	2.7
25 Eagle River	6,377	1,997	3,816	564	1,819	R	31.3	59.8	8.8	39	2	16	2.7	2.2	3.0	2.8
26 Wasilla-Chugiak.........	6,148	2,063	3,494	591	1,431	R	33.6	56.8	9.6	35	12	9	2.6	2.2	2.7	2.9
27 Palmer	6,524	2,285	3,653	586	1,368	R	35.0	56.0	9.0	27	15	14	2.7	2.5	2.9	2.9
28 Rural Matanuska-Susitna	6,391	2,234	3,393	764	1,159	R	35.0	53.1	12.0	29	22	3	2.7	2.4	2.7	3.7
29 University..................	7,198	3,428	3,090	680	338	D	47.6	42.9	9.4	5	39	10	3.0	3.7	2.4	3.3
30 West Fairbanks	5,916	2,476	3,080	360	604	R	41.9	52.1	6.1	12	26	37	2.5	2.7	2.4	1.8
31 East Fairbanks...........	5,932	2,624	2,953	355	329	R	44.2	49.8	6.0	8	30	38	2.5	2.9	2.3	1.7
32 Badger-Wainwright	4,619	1,562	2,750	307	1,188	R	33.8	59.5	6.6	33	6	34	1.9	1.7	2.2	1.5
33 Northeast Fairbanks ..	6,880	2,422	4,039	419	1,617	R	35.2	58.7	6.1	26	7	36	2.9	2.6	3.2	2.0
34 North Pole-Denali	6,671	2,182	3,988	501	1,806	R	32.7	59.8	7.5	36	3	28	2.8	2.4	3.1	2.4
35 PWS-Delta	6,081	2,296	3,213	572	917	R	37.8	52.8	9.4	18	23	12	2.5	2.5	2.5	2.8
36 Rural Interior	5,020	2,056	2,628	336	572	R	41.0	52.4	6.7	13	24	33	2.1	2.2	2.1	1.6
37 Northwest Alaska	4,336	2,214	1,918	204	296	D	51.1	44.2	4.7	1	36	40	1.8	2.4	1.5	1.0
38 Nome-Yukon River	4,644	2,272	2,137	235	135	D	48.9	46.0	5.1	4	33	39	1.9	2.5	1.7	1.1
39 Bethel-Dillingham	4,268	2,131	1,872	265	259	D	49.9	43.9	6.2	2	37	35	1.8	2.3	1.5	1.3
40 Aleutians	3,743	1,462	1,992	289	530	R	39.1	53.2	7.7	15	21	26	1.6	1.6	1.6	1.4
ALASKA[1]......................	**239,714**	**92,065**	**127,163**	**20,486**	**35,098**	**R**	**38.4**	**53.0**	**8.5**				**100.0**	**100.0**	**100.0**	**100.0**

[1]Includes the following absentee votes cast by residents overseas and reported only at the state level: 18 for Smith (DEM), 13 for Murkowski (REP), and 5 for Other; total of 36.

Table H. — Vote for U.S. Representative in Congress: November 3, 1992, General Election

Congressional and election district	Total	Democrat (DEM)	Republican (REP)	Other	Plurality Total	Plurality Party	Percent of total vote DEM	Percent of total vote REP	Percent of total vote Other	Rank within district DEM	Rank within district REP	Rank within district Other	Percent contribution to district vote Total	Percent contribution to district vote DEM	Percent contribution to district vote REP	Percent contribution to district vote Other
District At-Large[1]	**239,116**	**102,378**	**111,849**	**24,889**	**9,471**	**R**	**42.8**	**46.8**	**10.4**				**100.0**	**100.0**	**100.0**	**100.0**
01 Ketchikan	6,197	2,367	3,265	565	898	R	38.2	52.7	9.1	30	7	23	2.6	2.3	2.9	2.3
02 Sitka-Wrangell	7,126	2,698	3,703	725	1,005	R	37.9	52.0	10.2	31	9	20	3.0	2.6	3.3	2.9
03 Downtown Juneau	7,683	4,521	2,557	605	1,964	D	58.8	33.3	7.9	1	39	32	3.2	4.4	2.3	2.4
04 Mendenhall Valley	6,891	3,393	2,903	595	490	D	49.2	42.1	8.6	5	34	30	2.9	3.3	2.6	2.4
05 Southeast Islands	5,394	2,272	2,424	698	152	R	42.1	44.9	12.9	22	27	12	2.3	2.2	2.2	2.8
06 Kodiak Island	5,136	1,772	2,531	833	759	R	34.5	49.3	16.2	36	16	1	2.1	1.7	2.3	3.3
07 Homer	6,217	2,865	2,501	851	364	D	46.1	40.2	13.7	10	37	8	2.6	2.8	2.2	3.4
08 Seward-Soldotna	5,874	2,565	2,619	690	54	R	43.7	44.6	11.7	15	28	13	2.5	2.5	2.3	2.8
09 Kenai	5,757	2,477	2,533	747	56	R	43.0	44.0	13.0	19	29	11	2.4	2.4	2.3	3.0
10 Oceanview	7,102	3,026	3,573	503	547	R	42.6	50.3	7.1	20	12	35	3.0	3.0	3.2	2.0
11 West Anchorage	6,384	2,878	2,938	568	60	R	45.1	46.0	8.9	11	25	25	2.7	2.8	2.6	2.3
12 Sand Lake	6,439	2,797	3,117	525	320	R	43.4	48.4	8.2	16	19	31	2.7	2.7	2.8	2.1
13 Coastal Trail	7,546	3,848	3,180	518	668	D	51.0	42.1	6.9	4	33	38	3.2	3.8	2.8	2.1
14 Elmendorf	5,446	1,815	3,156	475	1,341	R	33.3	58.0	8.7	39	1	28	2.3	1.8	2.8	1.9
15 Spenard-Downtown	5,404	2,772	2,108	524	664	D	51.3	39.0	9.7	3	38	21	2.3	2.7	1.9	2.1
16 Fairview-Mt. View	4,069	1,953	1,685	431	268	D	48.0	41.4	10.6	6	36	17	1.7	1.9	1.5	1.7
17 Dimond-Campbell	5,899	2,475	2,905	519	430	R	42.0	49.2	8.8	23	17	27	2.5	2.4	2.6	2.1
18 Hillside	7,985	3,696	3,721	568	25	R	46.3	46.6	7.1	9	22	34	3.3	3.6	3.3	2.3
19 Lake Otis & Tudor	5,858	2,623	2,697	538	74	R	44.8	46.0	9.2	12	24	22	2.4	2.6	2.4	2.2
20 Midtown	6,725	3,180	3,070	475	110	D	47.3	45.7	7.1	8	26	36	2.8	3.1	2.7	1.9
21 East Anchorage	6,095	2,899	2,658	538	241	D	47.6	43.6	8.8	7	30	26	2.5	2.8	2.4	2.2
22 East Anchorage	6,830	3,032	3,316	482	284	R	44.4	48.6	7.1	14	18	37	2.9	3.0	3.0	1.9
23 Northeast Anchorage	3,738	1,363	2,040	335	677	R	36.5	54.6	9.0	35	3	24	1.6	1.3	1.8	1.3
24 Muldoon-Eagle River	6,768	2,782	3,398	588	616	R	41.1	50.2	8.7	25	13	29	2.8	2.7	3.0	2.4
25 Eagle River	6,345	2,402	3,272	671	870	R	37.9	51.6	10.6	32	11	19	2.7	2.3	2.9	2.7
26 Wasilla-Chugiak	6,120	2,374	3,050	696	676	R	38.8	49.8	11.4	28	15	14	2.6	2.3	2.7	2.8
27 Palmer	6,538	2,699	3,139	700	440	R	41.3	48.0	10.7	24	21	16	2.7	2.6	2.8	2.8
28 Rural Matanuska-Susitna	6,373	2,473	2,964	936	491	R	38.8	46.5	14.7	27	23	4	2.7	2.4	2.7	3.8
29 University	7,168	3,936	2,254	978	1,682	D	54.9	31.4	13.6	2	40	9	3.0	3.8	2.0	3.9
30 West Fairbanks	5,898	2,559	2,526	813	33	D	43.4	42.8	13.8	17	32	7	2.5	2.5	2.3	3.3
31 East Fairbanks	5,913	2,638	2,474	801	164	D	44.6	41.8	13.5	13	35	10	2.5	2.6	2.2	3.2
32 Badger-Wainwright	4,596	1,538	2,412	646	874	R	33.5	52.5	14.1	38	8	5	1.9	1.5	2.2	2.6
33 Northeast Fairbanks	6,868	2,516	3,316	1,036	800	R	36.6	48.3	15.1	34	20	2	2.9	2.5	3.0	4.2
34 North Pole-Denali	6,660	2,039	3,632	989	1,593	R	30.6	54.5	14.8	40	4	3	2.8	2.0	3.2	4.0
35 PWS-Delta	6,079	2,619	2,615	845	4	D	43.1	43.0	13.9	18	31	6	2.5	2.6	2.3	3.4
36 Rural Interior	5,028	1,898	2,598	532	700	R	37.7	51.7	10.6	33	10	18	2.1	1.9	2.3	2.1
37 Northwest Alaska	4,314	1,672	2,351	291	679	R	38.8	54.5	6.7	29	5	39	1.8	1.6	2.1	1.2
38 Nome-Yukon River	4,635	1,878	2,446	311	568	R	40.5	52.8	6.7	26	6	40	1.9	1.8	2.2	1.2
39 Bethel-Dillingham	4,231	1,789	2,122	320	333	R	42.3	50.2	7.6	21	14	33	1.8	1.7	1.9	1.3
40 Aleutians	3,751	1,260	2,066	425	806	R	33.6	55.1	11.3	37	2	15	1.6	1.2	1.8	1.7
ALASKA[1]	**239,116**	**102,378**	**111,849**	**24,889**	**9,471**	**R**	**42.8**	**46.8**	**10.4**							

[1]Includes the following absentee votes cast by residents overseas and reported only at the state level: 19 for Devens (DEM), 14 for Young (REP), and 3 for Other; total of 36.

1992 Vote for President
Percent for Bush (R), by Electoral District

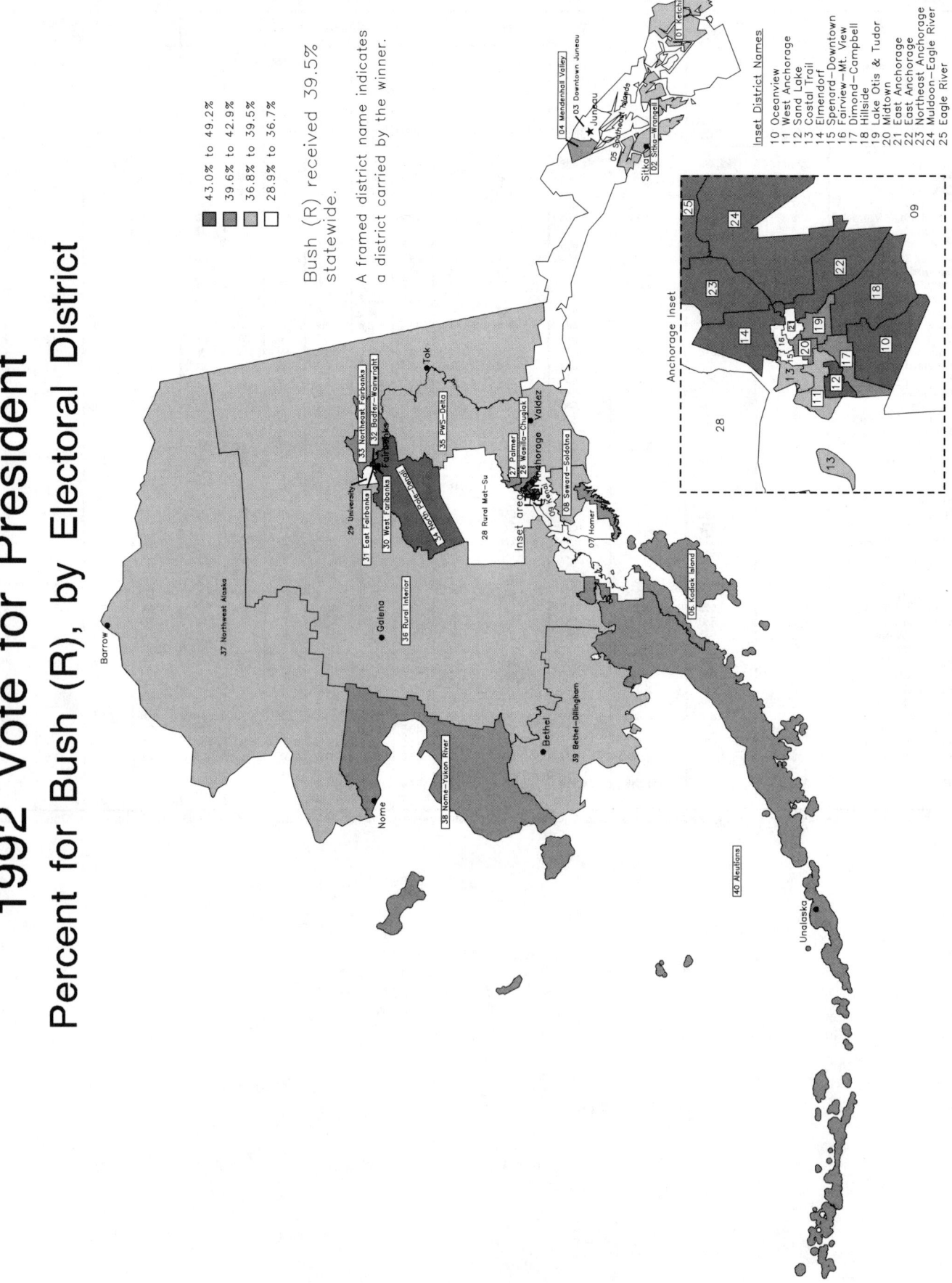

43.0% to 49.2%
39.6% to 42.9%
36.8% to 39.5%
28.9% to 36.7%

Bush (R) received 39.5% statewide.

A framed district name indicates a district carried by the winner.

Inset District Names
10 Oceanview
11 West Anchorage
12 Sand Lake
13 Costal Trail
14 Elmendorf
15 Spenard—Downtown
16 Fairview—Mt. View
17 Dimond—Campbell
18 Hillside
19 Lake Otis & Tudor
20 Midtown
21 East Anchorage
22 East Anchorage
23 Northeast Anchorage
24 Muldoon—Eagle River
25 Eagle River

Anchorage Inset

01 Ketchikan
02 Sitka—Wrangell
03 Downtown Juneau
04 Mendenhall Valley
05 Southeast Islands
06 Kodiak Island
07 Homer
08 Seward—Soldotna
26 Wasilla—Chugiak
27 Palmer
28 Rural Mat-Su
29 University
30 West Fairbanks
31 East Fairbanks
32 Northeast Fairbanks
33 Barrow—Wainwright
34 North Pole—Valdez
35 PWS—Delta
36 Rural Interior
37 Northwest Alaska
38 Nome—Yukon River
39 Bethel—Dillingham
40 Aleutions

Barrow
Nome
Bethel
Galena
Tok
Fairbanks
Valdez
Juneau
Unalaska

1992 Vote for U.S. Senator

Percent for Murkowski (R), by Electoral District

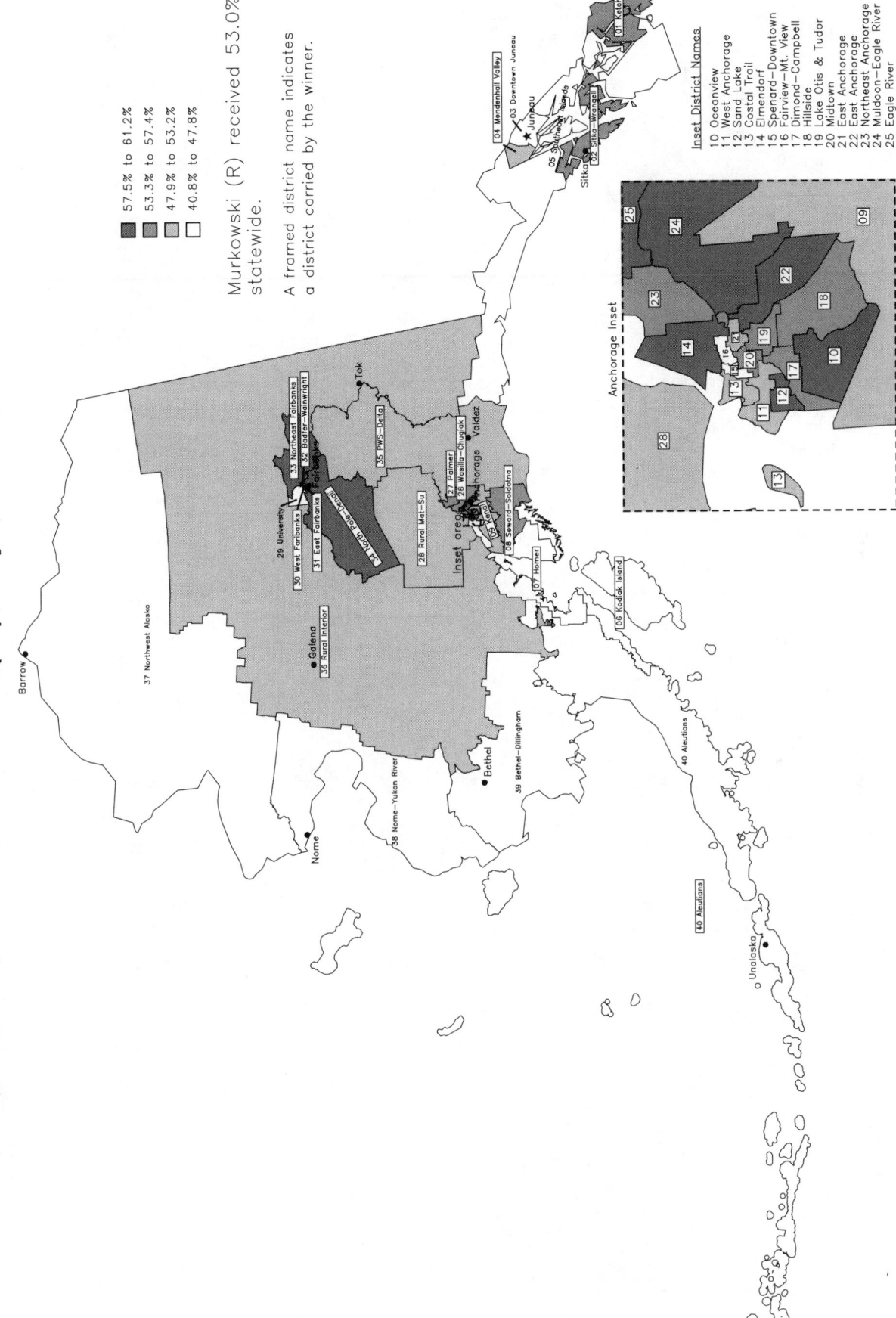

57.5% to 61.2%
53.3% to 57.4%
47.9% to 53.2%
40.8% to 47.8%

Murkowski (R) received 53.0% statewide.

A framed district name indicates a district carried by the winner.

Inset District Names:
10 Oceanview
11 West Anchorage
12 Sand Lake
13 Costal Trail
14 Elmendorf
15 Spenard–Downtown
16 Fairview–Mt. View
17 Dimond–Campbell
18 Hillside
19 Lake Otis & Tudor
20 Midtown
21 East Anchorage
22 East Anchorage
23 Northeast Anchorage
24 Muldoon–Eagle River
25 Eagle River

Anchorage Inset

01 Ketchikan
03 Downtown Juneau
04 Mendenhall Valley
05 Southeast Islands
02 Sitka–Wrangell
Juneau
Sitka

37 Northwest Alaska
Barrow
38 Nome–Yukon River
Nome
39 Bethel–Dillingham
Bethel
36 Rural Interior
Galena
Tok
33 Northeast Fairbanks
32 Badger–Wainwright
29 University
30 West Fairbanks
31 East Fairbanks
35 PWS–Delta
28 Rural Mat–Su
27 Palmer
26 Wasilla–Chugiak
Valdez
Anchorage
09 Kenai
08 Seward–Soldotna
07 Homer
06 Kodiak Island
40 Aleutians
Unalaska
Inset area

Alaska 67

ARIZONA

Congressional Districts 6
   Average Population 610,871
State Senate Districts 30
   Average Population 122,174
State House Districts 60
   Average Population 61,087

Electoral College Votes..8
Counties 15
Voting Precincts 1,843

Alternative Registration Methods:
......................Deputized Registrars, Mail-in, Motor-voter

Registration Deadline (Days before Election) 29

Voting Equipment Use (Counties)

Datavote Punch Card	0	Paper Ballot	0
Electronic	0	Other Punch Card	15
Lever Machine	0	Mixed Systems	0
Optical Scanner	0		

Party Control	DEM	REP	IND	VAC
1993 State Senate	12	18	0	0
1992 State Senate	17	13	0	0
1993 State House	25	35	0	0
1992 State House	27	33	0	0

Population Statistics 1990

Race/ Ethnicity	Total Population		Voting Age Population		Voting Age Population % of total population
	Number	%	Number	%	
Non-Hispanic					
White	2,626,185	71.7	2,040,355	76.0	77.7
Black	104,809	2.9	69,553	2.6	66.4
Asian/Pacific Islander	51,530	1.4	37,402	1.4	72.6
Native American	190,091	5.2	111,426	4.2	58.6
Other	4,275	<.1	2,409	<.1	56.4
All Hispanic	688,338	18.8	422,964	15.8	61.4
TOTAL	3,665,228	100.0	2,684,109	100.0	73.2

Estimated Voting Age Population 1992 (VAP) 2,749,000
Number of Registered Voters................................. 1,964,949
   % of estimated VAP 71.5
Voter Turnout (Actual) 1,516,276
   % of VAP 55.2
   % of Registration 77.2
Persons Not Voting—of Voting Age 1,232,724
   % of VAP 44.8
Persons Not Voting—of Registered 448,673
   % of Registration 22.8
Straight Ticket Voting .... No

State Officials and Members of Congress

Governor:
Fife Symington (R) 1991, elected to a four-year term in 1991
(special election).

U.S. Senators:
Dennis DeConcini (D) 1976, elected to a six-year term in 1988.
John McCain (R) 1986, elected to a six-year term in 1992.

U.S. Representative in Congress:
(District, Name, Party, Date first elected)

1. Coppersmith (D) 1992
2. Pastor (D) 1991
3. Stump (R) 1976
4. Kyl (R) 1986
5. Kolbe (R) 1984
6. English (D) 1992

Candidates: General Election, November 3, 1992

Candidate(s)	Total vote	Percent	Party	Status	First elected
President/Vice President					
Bush/Quayle	572,086	38.47%	Republican	Incumbent	1988
Clinton/Gore	543,050	36.52%	Democrat	Challenger	1992
Perot/Stockdale	353,741	23.79%	Independent	Challenger	
Gritz/Minett	8,141	0.55%	Independent	Challenger	
Marrou/Lord	6,759	0.45%	Libertarian	Challenger	
Hagelin/Tompkins	2,267	0.15%	Natural Law	Challenger	
Fulani/Munoz	923	0.06%	New Alliance	Challenger	
LaRouche/Bevel	8	<.01%	Independent	Challenger	
U.S. Senator					
John McCain	771,395	55.82%	Republican	Incumbent	1986
Claire Sargent	436,321	31.57%	Democrat	Challenger	
Evan Mecham	145,361	10.52%	Independent	Challenger	
Kiana Delamare	22,613	1.64%	Libertarian	Challenger	
Ed Finkelstein	6,335	0.46%	New Alliance	Challenger	
Robert Winn	26	<.01%	Write in	Challenger	
Governor (No Contest)					
U.S. Representative in Congress					
District 1					
Sam Coppersmith	130,715	51.30%	Democrat	Challenger	1992
John Rhodes III	113,613	44.59%	Republican	Incumbent	1986
Ted Goldstein	10,461	4.11%	Natural Law	Challenger	
District 2					
Ed Pastor	90,693	66.02%	Democrat	Incumbent	1991
Don Shooter	41,257	30.03%	Republican	Challenger	
Dan Detaranto	5,423	3.95%	Libertarian	Challenger	
Robert Brown	5	<.01%	Write in	Challenger	
District 3					
Bob Stump	158,906	61.47%	Republican	Incumbent	1976
Roger Hartstone	88,830	34.36%	Democrat	Challenger	
Pamela Volponi	10,767	4.17%	Natural Law	Challenger	
District 4					
Jon Kyl	156,330	59.20%	Republican	Incumbent	1986
Walter Mybeck II	70,572	26.73%	Democrat	Challenger	
Debbie Collings	25,553	9.68%	Independent	Challenger	
Tim McDermott	11,611	4.40%	Libertarian	Challenger	
District 5					
Jim Kolbe	172,867	66.54%	Republican	Incumbent	1984
Jim Toevs	77,256	29.74%	Democrat	Challenger	
Perry Willis	9,690	3.73%	Libertarian	Challenger	
District 6					
Karan English	124,251	53.01%	Democrat	Challenger	1992
Doug Wead	97,074	41.42%	Republican	Challenger	
Sarah Stannard	13,047	5.57%	Independent	Challenger	

Voter Registration and Turnout, 1948-1992 Elections

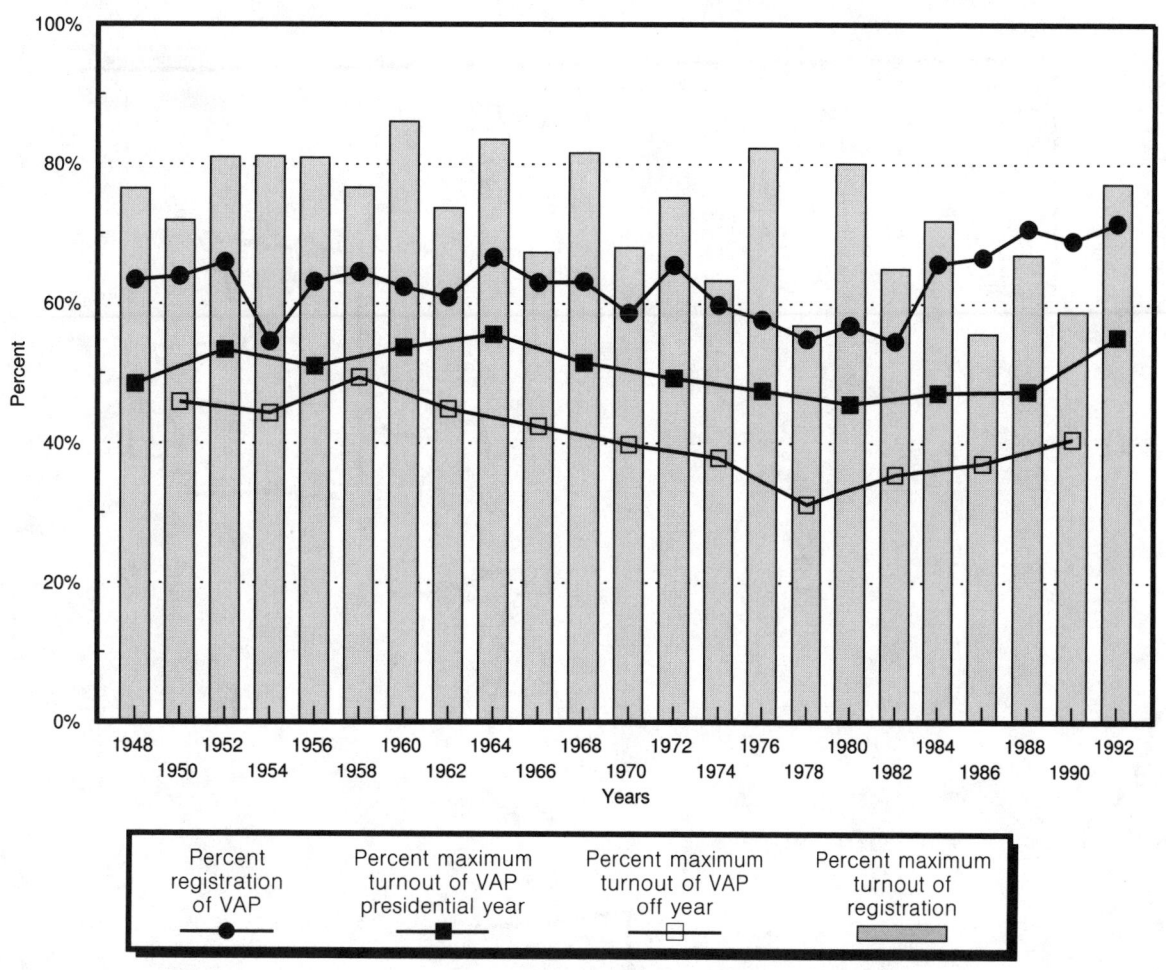

		Voter registration (REG)			Voter turnout											
						Highest office						Maximum vote				
Year	Estimated Voting Age Population (VAP)	Total	Percent of VAP	Rank by percent of VAP	Actual	Total	Office	Percent total REG	Rank by percent of REG	Percent of VAP	Rank by percent of VAP	Total	Percent total REG	Rank by percent of REG	Percent total VAP	Rank by percent of VAP
1992	2,749,000	1,964,949	71.5	33	1,516,276	1,486,975	P	75.7	29	54.1	33	1,516,276	77.2	29	55.2	32
1990	2,696,000	1,858,941	69.0	24	1,094,735	1,055,406	G	56.8	27	39.1	26	1,094,735	58.9	25	40.6	24
1988	2,543,000	1,797,714	70.7	27	1,204,169	1,171,873	P	65.2	41	46.1	41	1,204,169	67.0	39	47.4	39
1986	2,400,000	1,597,934	66.6	32	889,668	866,984	G	54.3	26	36.1	34	889,668	55.7	29	37.1	34
1984	2,226,000	1,462,818	65.7	41	1,051,339	1,025,897	P	70.1	37	46.1	46	1,051,339	71.9	34	47.2	46
1982	2,092,000	1,142,159	54.6	47	742,923	726,364	G	63.6	23	34.7	42	742,923	65.0	22	35.5	42
1980	1,970,000	1,121,169	56.9	47	898,183	873,945	P	77.9	12	44.4	45	898,183	80.1	8	45.6	45
1978	1,766,000	969,430	54.9	45	551,169	538,556	G	55.6	26	30.5	43	551,169	56.9	30	31.2	43
1976	1,611,000	929,654	57.7	46	764,886	742,719	P	79.9	10	46.1	46	764,886	82.3	6	47.5	43
1974	1,490,000	890,833	59.8	43	563,991	552,202	G	62.0	19	37.1	36	563,991	63.3	17	37.9	36
1972	1,315,000	861,809	65.5	40	648,061	622,926	P	72.3	29	47.4	40	648,061	75.2	25	49.3	37
1970	1,056,000	618,451	58.6	45	420,269	411,409	G	66.5	25	39.0	41	420,269	68.0	21	39.8	41
1968	975,000	614,763	63.1	40	501,832	486,936	P	79.2	25	49.9	47	501,832	81.6	23	51.5	44
1966	917,000	577,671	63.0	37	388,783	378,342	G	65.5	21	41.3	39	388,783	67.3	20	42.4	38
1964	878,000	584,337	66.6	30	488,081	480,770	P	82.3	19	54.8	34	488,081	83.5	17	55.6	34
1962	836,000	509,446	60.9	26	375,435	365,841	G	71.8	14	43.8	35	375,435	73.7	13	44.9	34
1960	760,000	474,124	62.4	28	408,137	398,491	P	84.0	19	52.4	38	408,137	86.1	16	53.7	37
1958	607,000	391,511	64.5	23	300,004	293,623	S	75.0	10	48.4	32	300,004	76.6	8	49.4	32
1956	583,000	367,661	63.1	24	297,552	290,173	P	78.9	20	49.8	37	297,552	80.9	18	51.0	37
1954	563,000	307,545	54.6	22	249,482	243,970	G	79.3	4	43.3	37	249,482	81.1	4	44.3	34
1952	501,000	330,083	65.9	18	267,325	260,570	P	78.9	19	52.0	38	267,325	81.0	18	53.4	37
1950	437,000	279,164	63.9	15	200,767	195,227	G	69.9	10	44.7	33	200,767	71.9	10	45.9	32
1948	380,000	240,998	63.4	16	184,323	177,065	P	73.5	13	46.6	35	184,323	76.5	11	48.5	34

ARIZONA

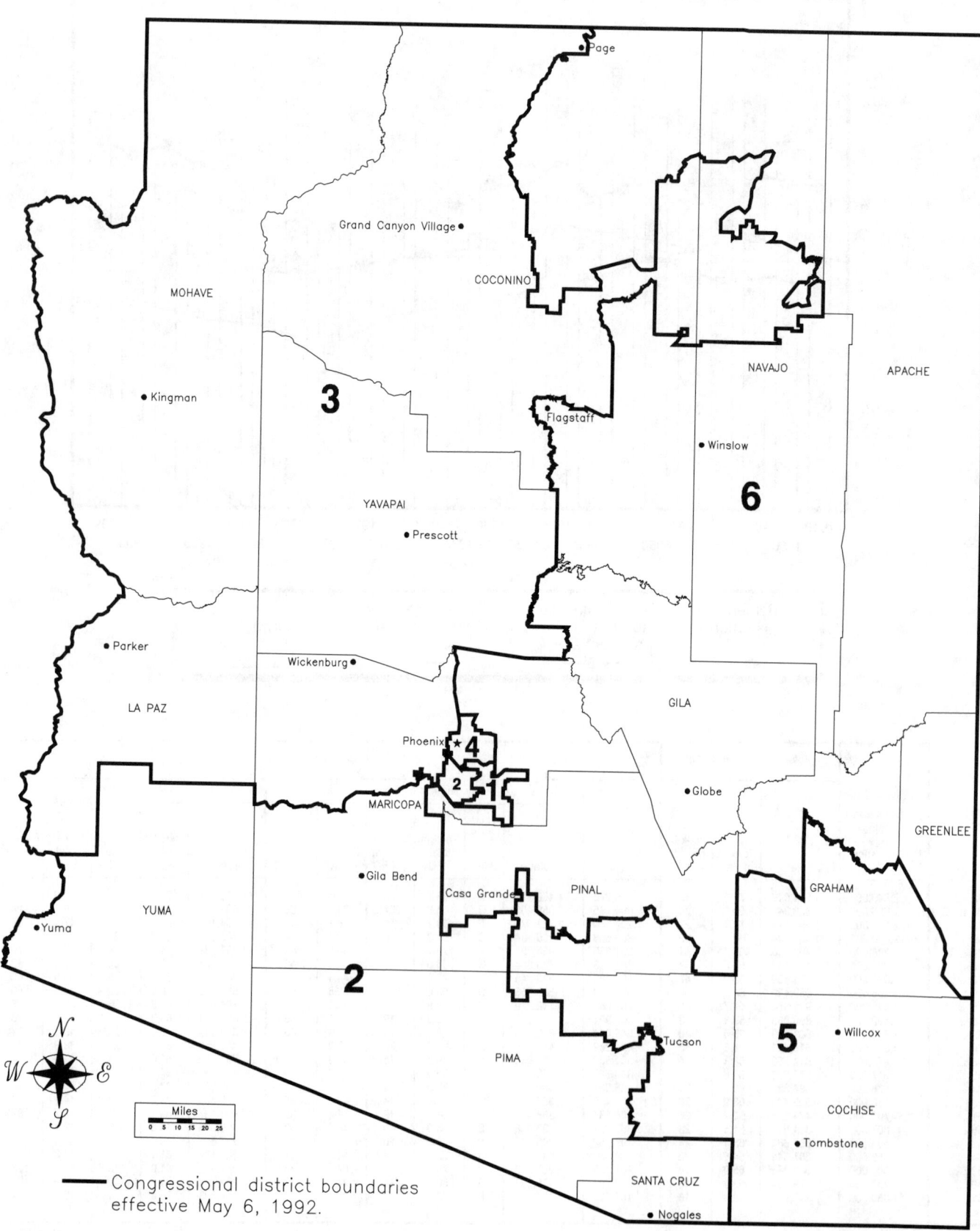

Congressional district boundaries
effective May 6, 1992.

Copyright © 1993 by Election Data Services, Inc.

72 Arizona

Table A. — 1990 Population by Race and Ethnic Origin

State/ county code	County	Total persons	White	Black	Asian and Pacific Islander	Native American	Other	Hispanic	Total	White	Black	Hispanic	Total	White	Black	Hispanic
			Percent of total persons — Non-Hispanic						Rank — Total / Percent of total persons Non-Hispanic				Percent contribution to state population — Total / Non-Hispanic			
04 001	Apache	61,591	18.4	0.2	0.1	77.0	<.1	4.2	10	15	15	15	1.7	0.4	<.1	0.4
04 003	Cochise	97,624	63.0	4.9	2.2	0.7	0.1	29.1	6	6	1	5	2.7	2.3	4.6	4.1
04 005	Coconino	96,591	58.9	1.4	0.9	28.7	<.1	10.0	7	9	7	11	2.6	2.2	1.3	1.4
04 007	Gila	40,216	68.1	0.2	0.3	12.7	<.1	18.6	11	5	13	9	1.1	1.0	<.1	1.1
04 009	Graham	26,554	58.1	1.8	0.4	14.5	<.1	25.2	13	10	6	6	0.7	0.6	0.4	1.0
04 011	Greenlee	8,008	54.6	0.3	0.2	1.6	0.1	43.2	15	11	10	2	0.2	0.2	<.1	0.5
04 012	La Paz	13,844	61.4	0.7	0.6	14.5	0.1	22.7	14	7	9	8	0.4	0.3	<.1	0.5
04 013	Maricopa	2,122,101	77.1	3.3	1.6	1.5	0.1	16.3	1	3	2	10	57.9	62.3	67.6	50.2
04 015	Mohave	93,497	91.8	0.3	0.5	2.1	<.1	5.3	8	1	11	14	2.6	3.3	0.3	0.7
04 017	Navajo	77,658	40.2	0.9	0.3	51.2	<.1	7.3	9	13	8	12	2.1	1.2	0.6	0.8
04 019	Pima	666,880	68.2	2.9	1.7	2.5	0.2	24.5	2	4	4	7	18.2	17.3	18.6	23.7
04 021	Pinal	116,379	59.2	3.0	0.4	8.1	<.1	29.3	3	8	3	4	3.2	2.6	3.3	4.9
04 023	Santa Cruz	29,676	20.8	0.2	0.4	<.1	0.2	78.2	12	14	14	1	0.8	0.2	<.1	3.4
04 025	Yavapai	107,714	91.3	0.3	0.4	1.5	<.1	6.4	4	2	12	13	2.9	3.7	0.3	1.0
04 027	Yuma	106,895	54.4	2.6	1.1	1.1	0.2	40.6	5	12	5	3	2.9	2.2	2.6	6.3
04	ARIZONA	3,665,228	71.7	2.9	1.4	5.2	<.1	18.8					100.0	100.0	100.0	100.0
	CONGRESSIONAL															
	District 1	610,872	80.0	3.0	2.2	1.5	<.1	13.2	1	3	2	3	16.7	18.6	17.7	11.7
	District 2	610,871	38.2	6.4	1.1	3.7	0.3	50.5	3	6	1	1	16.7	8.9	37.1	44.8
	District 3	610,871	82.2	1.9	1.0	3.0	0.1	11.8	4	2	4	5	16.7	19.1	10.8	10.5
	District 4	610,871	87.5	1.8	1.7	1.1	<.1	7.8	5	1	5	6	16.7	20.4	10.5	6.9
	District 5	610,871	78.0	2.8	1.8	0.7	<.1	16.5	6	4	3	2	16.7	18.2	16.5	14.7
	District 6	610,872	64.0	1.3	0.6	21.1	<.1	13.0	2	5	6	4	16.7	14.9	7.5	11.5

Table B. — 1990 Voting Age Population (VAP) by Race and Ethnic Origin

County	Total Voting Age Population	White	Black	Asian and Pacific Islander	Native American	Other	Hispanic	Total	White	Black	Hispanic	Total	White	Black	Hispanic	Total	White	Black	Asian and Pacific Islander	Native American	Other	Hispanic
		Percent of total VAP — Non-Hispanic						Rank — Total / Percent of total VAP Non-Hispanic				Percent contribution to state VAP — Total / Non-Hispanic				VAP percent of total population — Total / Non-Hispanic						
Apache	35,927	20.4	0.2	0.2	75.1	<.1	4.1	10	15	13	15	1.3	0.4	<.1	0.3	58.3	64.6	70.4	64.0	56.9	31.0	56.7
Cochise	70,057	66.9	4.6	2.1	0.7	<.1	25.6	7	7	1	4	2.6	2.3	4.6	4.2	71.8	76.1	67.0	70.4	74.9	43.2	63.3
Coconino	66,682	65.0	1.5	0.9	23.1	<.1	9.5	8	8	7	11	2.5	2.1	1.4	1.5	73.3	78.5	75.2	74.3	55.5	60.0	65.2
Gila	29,489	72.9	0.2	0.3	10.4	<.1	16.3	11	4	15	9	1.1	1.1	<.1	1.1	73.3	78.5	47.4	74.3	59.7	71.4	64.1
Graham	17,752	61.4	2.2	0.4	11.7	<.1	24.3	13	10	6	6	0.7	0.5	0.5	1.0	66.9	70.6	81.6	75.3	54.0	23.1	64.5
Greenlee	5,269	58.0	0.4	0.2	1.4	<.1	40.0	15	12	10	2	0.2	0.1	<.1	0.5	73.5	83.0	69.9	73.5	57.4	52.6	57.2
La Paz	10,175	69.3	0.7	0.6	11.6	<.1	17.6	14	6	9	8	0.4	0.3	0.1	0.4	73.5	83.0	69.9	73.5	59.1	52.6	57.2
Maricopa	1,566,310	80.7	2.9	1.6	1.3	<.1	13.4	1	3	2	10	58.4	62.0	66.4	49.4	73.8	77.3	65.2	71.8	63.6	55.9	60.5
Mohave	72,372	93.1	0.3	0.5	1.7	<.1	4.4	6	1	11	14	2.7	3.3	0.3	0.8	77.4	78.5	79.7	70.6	63.0	52.2	64.8
Navajo	47,826	44.7	1.0	0.3	46.7	<.1	7.2	9	13	8	12	1.8	1.0	0.7	0.8	61.6	68.4	74.8	62.0	56.1	61.2	60.8
Pima	500,682	72.8	2.7	1.7	2.1	0.1	20.7	2	5	4	7	18.7	17.9	19.3	24.5	75.1	80.1	68.9	75.5	61.5	58.6	63.4
Pinal	82,281	64.9	2.8	0.4	7.1	<.1	24.8	4	9	3	5	3.1	2.6	3.3	4.8	70.7	77.5	65.9	73.6	62.0	72.0	59.9
Santa Cruz	19,471	25.2	0.2	0.5	0.1	0.2	73.8	12	14	14	1	0.7	0.2	<.1	3.4	65.6	79.6	66.1	68.7	86.2	54.9	61.9
Yavapai	84,530	92.8	0.3	0.4	1.2	<.1	5.3	3	2	12	13	3.1	3.8	0.3	1.1	78.5	79.7	71.8	72.3	65.2	49.3	64.4
Yuma	75,286	60.9	2.6	1.2	1.0	0.2	34.2	5	11	5	3	2.8	2.2	2.8	6.1	70.4	78.9	69.6	73.3	65.3	56.1	59.3
ARIZONA	2,684,109	76.0	2.6	1.4	4.2	<.1	15.8					100.0	100.0	100.0	100.0	73.2	77.7	66.4	72.6	58.6	56.4	61.4
CONGRESSIONAL																						
District 1	457,975	82.7	2.7	2.2	1.3	<.1	11.1	3	3	2	4	17.1	18.6	17.8	12.0	75.0	77.5	74.2	74.2	65.4	58.0	63.1
District 2	414,281	44.4	6.2	1.2	3.3	0.2	44.8	6	6	1	1	15.4	9.0	36.8	43.8	67.8	78.9	65.8	75.1	60.2	61.2	60.2
District 3	457,293	85.6	1.0	2.5	1.6	<.1	9.4	4	2	4	5	17.0	19.2	10.4	10.1	74.9	77.9	64.1	69.2	60.6	50.2	59.4
District 4	464,379	89.2	1.6	1.6	1.0	<.1	6.6	2	1	5	6	17.3	20.3	10.5	7.3	76.0	77.4	66.2	71.2	66.7	51.0	64.9
District 5	465,370	81.0	2.5	1.7	0.7	<.1	14.0	1	4	3	2	17.3	18.5	16.9	15.4	76.2	79.1	68.1	73.8	72.1	49.8	64.6
District 6	424,811	69.6	1.2	0.6	17.2	<.1	11.3	5	5	6	3	15.8	14.5	7.6	11.4	69.5	75.7	67.4	68.6	56.7	59.5	60.6

Table C. – Voter Participation: November 3, 1992, General Election

County	Estimated Voting Age Population (VAP) 1992	Voter registration (REG)				Voter turnout													
						Highest office				Maximum vote						Percent drop-off, by office			
		Total	% contribution to state REG	% of 1992 VAP	Rank by % of 1992 VAP	Actual	Total	Office	% of 1992 VAP	Total	% contribution to state turnout	% of REG	Rank by % REG	% of 1992 VAP	Rank by % 1992 VAP	President	Senator	Governor	Representative
Apache	36,072	28,397	1.4	78.7	5	18,973	18,258	P	50.6	18,973	1.3	66.8	15	52.6	10	3.8	4.7	-	6.4
Cochise	68,934	44,985	2.3	65.3	12	34,012	33,150	P	48.1	34,012	2.2	75.6	10	49.3	12	2.5	3.4	-	6.2
Coconino	66,615	54,649	2.8	82.0	3	43,501	42,618	P	64.0	43,501	2.9	79.6	3	65.3	4	2.0	3.9	-	6.3
Gila	28,526	24,311	1.2	85.2	2	19,026	18,478	P	64.8	19,026	1.3	78.3	4	66.7	3	2.9	3.6	-	7.0
Graham	17,411	12,883	0.7	74.0	8	10,077	9,727	S	55.9	10,077	0.7	78.2	5	57.9	5	3.8	3.5	-	7.9
Greenlee	4,798	5,108	0.3	106.5	1	4,111	3,962	P	82.6	4,111	0.3	80.5	2	85.7	1	3.6	3.7	-	8.8
La Paz	9,910	6,557	0.3	66.2	11	5,109	4,961	P	50.1	5,109	0.3	77.9	6	51.6	11	2.9	3.9	-	7.4
Maricopa	1,623,488	1,147,672	58.4	70.7	10	890,680	876,832	P	54.0	890,680	58.7	77.6	7	54.9	7	1.6	11.2	-	5.9
Mohave	76,863	55,009	2.8	71.6	9	41,732	40,616	P	52.8	41,732	2.8	75.9	9	54.3	8	2.7	4.7	-	9.6
Navajo	47,593	36,431	1.9	76.5	6	25,432	24,638	P	51.8	25,432	1.7	69.8	14	53.4	9	3.1	3.7	-	6.6
Pima	498,571	375,942	19.1	75.4	7	287,718	281,484	P	56.5	287,718	19.0	76.5	8	57.7	6	2.2	7.1	-	10.0
Pinal	83,272	51,143	2.6	61.4	13	38,230	36,739	P	44.1	38,230	2.5	74.8	11	45.9	13	3.9	4.5	-	7.9
Santa Cruz	20,812	11,268	0.6	54.1	14	8,355	8,080	P	38.8	8,355	0.6	74.1	12	40.1	14	3.3	7.0	-	9.4
Yavapai	88,126	70,202	3.6	79.7	4	60,356	59,415	P	67.4	60,356	4.0	86.0	1	68.5	2	1.6	3.0	-	8.7
Yuma	78,009	40,392	2.1	51.8	15	28,964	28,045	P	36.0	28,964	1.9	71.7	13	37.1	15	3.2	5.2	-	7.4
ARIZONA	2,749,000	1,964,949	100.0	71.5		1,516,276	1,487,003		54.1	1,516,276	100.0	77.2		55.2		1.9	8.9	-	7.1

Table D. – Voter Registration by Political Party Affiliation: November 3, 1992, General Election

County	Total voter registration	Political party affiliation					Percent of total registration						Percent contribution to state registration			
		Democrat (DEM)[1]	Republican (REP)[1]	Independent (IND)[1]	Plurality					Rank						
					Total	Party	DEM	REP	IND	DEM	REP	IND	Total	DEM	REP	IND
Apache	28,397	20,726	5,531	2,070	15,195	D	73.2	19.5	7.3	2	14	11	1.4	2.5	0.6	0.9
Cochise	44,985	22,772	15,967	4,608	6,805	D	52.5	36.8	10.6	10	8	6	2.3	2.7	1.8	2.0
Coconino	54,649	26,603	20,217	7,383	6,386	D	49.1	37.3	13.6	11	7	1	2.8	3.2	2.3	3.2
Gila	24,311	15,632	7,379	1,265	8,253	D	64.4	30.4	5.2	5	11	13	1.2	1.9	0.8	0.5
Graham	12,883	8,395	3,913	569	4,482	D	65.2	30.4	4.4	4	10	14	0.7	1.0	0.4	0.2
Greenlee	5,108	4,233	743	131	3,490	D	82.9	14.5	2.6	1	15	15	0.3	0.5	<.1	<.1
La Paz	6,557	3,321	2,643	579	678	D	50.8	40.4	8.8	9	4	8	0.3	0.4	0.3	0.2
Maricopa	1,147,672	422,309	577,911	143,275	155,602	R	36.9	50.5	12.5	14	2	2	58.4	50.6	65.0	61.6
Mohave	55,009	22,272	25,971	6,657	3,699	R	40.6	47.3	12.1	13	3	4	2.8	2.7	2.9	2.9
Navajo	36,431	21,699	12,510	2,310	9,189	D	59.4	34.3	6.3	7	9	12	1.9	2.6	1.4	1.0
Pima	375,942	181,395	146,252	46,661	35,143	D	48.5	39.1	12.5	12	5	3	19.1	21.8	16.4	20.1
Pinal	51,143	31,888	15,071	3,982	16,817	D	62.6	29.6	7.8	6	12	10	2.6	3.8	1.7	1.7
Santa Cruz	11,268	7,514	2,846	894	4,668	D	66.8	25.3	7.9	3	13	9	0.6	0.9	0.3	0.4
Yavapai	70,202	24,470	37,091	8,377	12,621	R	35.0	53.0	12.0	15	1	5	3.6	2.9	4.2	3.6
Yuma	40,392	20,768	15,599	3,951	5,169	D	51.5	38.7	9.8	8	6	7	2.1	2.5	1.8	1.7
ARIZONA[2]	1,964,949	833,997	889,644	232,712	55,647	R	42.6	45.5	11.9				100.0	100.0	100.0	100.0

[1]Data from report dated October 1992; sum of registrants by party differs slightly from total voter registration reported with November 1992 general election returns. [2]Total voter registration also includes 5,299 for Libertarian party, 1,561 for Green party, and 279 for New Alliance party (as reported October 1992).

Table E. — Vote for President: November 3, 1992, General Election

County	Total	Clinton (DEM)	Bush (REP)	Perot (IND)	Other	Plurality Total	Party	\%DEM	\%REP	\%IND	\%Other	Rank DEM	Rank REP	Rank IND	%contrib Total	%contrib DEM	%contrib REP	%contrib IND	Major DEM	Major REP
Apache	18,258	11,218	4,588	1,979	473	6,630	D	61.4	25.1	10.8	2.6	1	15	15	1.2	2.1	0.8	0.6	71.0	29.0
Cochise	33,150	12,701	12,202	7,857	390	499	D	38.3	36.8	23.7	1.2	9	6	7	2.2	2.3	2.1	2.2	51.0	49.0
Coconino	42,618	18,888	13,769	9,363	598	5,119	D	44.3	32.3	22.0	1.4	3	11	8	2.9	3.5	2.4	2.6	57.8	42.2
Gila	18,478	7,571	5,781	4,694	432	1,790	D	41.0	31.3	25.4	2.3	8	14	4	1.2	1.4	1.0	1.3	56.7	43.3
Graham	9,699	3,391	4,169	1,860	279	778	R	35.0	43.0	19.2	2.9	12	1	12	0.7	0.6	0.7	0.5	44.9	55.1
Greenlee	3,962	1,695	1,451	794	22	244	D	42.8	36.6	20.0	0.6	6	7	10	0.3	0.3	0.3	0.2	53.9	46.1
La Paz	4,961	1,808	1,599	1,488	66	209	D	36.4	32.2	30.0	1.3	11	12	2	0.3	0.3	0.3	0.4	53.1	46.9
Maricopa	876,832	285,457	360,049	221,475	9,851	74,592	R	32.6	41.1	25.3	1.1	14	3	5	59.0	52.6	62.9	62.6	44.2	55.8
Mohave	40,616	13,255	13,684	12,706	971	429	R	32.6	33.7	31.3	2.4	13	9	1	2.7	2.4	2.4	3.6	49.2	50.8
Navajo	24,638	10,882	7,994	4,787	975	2,888	D	44.2	32.4	19.4	4.0	4	10	11	1.7	2.0	1.4	1.4	57.6	42.4
Pima	281,484	128,569	97,036	53,925	1,954	31,533	D	45.7	34.5	19.2	0.7	2	8	13	18.9	23.7	17.0	15.2	57.0	43.0
Pinal	36,739	15,468	11,669	9,231	371	3,799	D	42.1	31.8	25.1	1.0	7	13	6	2.5	2.8	2.0	2.6	57.0	43.0
Santa Cruz	8,080	3,512	3,024	1,447	97	488	D	43.5	37.4	17.9	1.2	5	5	14	0.5	0.6	0.5	0.4	53.7	46.3
Yavapai	59,415	18,268	23,419	16,409	1,319	5,151	R	30.7	39.4	27.6	2.2	15	4	3	4.0	3.4	4.1	4.6	43.8	56.2
Yuma	28,045	10,367	11,652	5,726	300	1,285	R	37.0	41.5	20.4	1.1	10	2	9	1.9	1.9	2.0	1.6	47.1	52.9
ARIZONA	1,486,975	543,050	572,086	353,741	18,098	29,036	R	36.5	38.5	23.8	1.2				100.0	100.0	100.0	100.0	48.7	51.3

Table F. — Vote for U.S. Senator: November 3, 1992, General Election

County	Total	Sargent (DEM)	McCain (REP)	Other	Plurality Total	Party	\%DEM	\%REP	\%Other	Rank DEM	Rank REP	Rank Other	%contrib Total	%contrib DEM	%contrib REP	%contrib Other
Apache	18,081	8,543	7,564	1,974	979	D	47.2	41.8	10.9	1	15	10	1.3	2.0	1.0	1.1
Cochise	32,857	10,304	19,166	3,387	8,862	R	31.4	58.3	10.3	11	3	11	2.4	2.4	2.5	1.9
Coconino	41,797	14,414	23,766	3,617	9,352	R	34.5	56.9	8.7	4	5	12	3.0	3.3	3.1	2.1
Gila	18,346	6,011	9,007	3,328	2,996	R	32.8	49.1	18.1	8	13	2	1.3	1.4	1.2	1.9
Graham	9,727	2,659	4,766	2,302	2,107	R	27.3	49.0	23.7	15	14	1	0.7	0.6	0.6	1.3
Greenlee	3,957	1,375	2,086	496	711	R	34.7	52.7	12.5	3	10	9	0.3	0.3	0.3	0.3
La Paz	4,910	1,465	2,641	804	1,176	R	29.8	53.8	16.4	12	8	3	0.4	0.3	0.3	0.5
Maricopa	790,649	234,584	443,607	112,458	209,023	R	29.7	56.1	14.2	13	6	8	57.2	53.8	57.5	64.5
Mohave	39,771	12,513	21,190	6,068	8,677	R	31.5	53.3	15.3	10	9	6	2.9	2.9	2.7	3.5
Navajo	24,498	7,949	12,601	3,948	4,652	R	32.4	51.4	16.1	9	12	4	1.8	1.8	1.6	2.3
Pima	267,194	95,789	153,015	18,390	57,226	R	35.9	57.3	6.9	2	4	15	19.3	22.0	19.8	10.5
Pinal	36,505	12,011	19,095	5,399	7,084	R	32.9	52.3	14.8	6	11	7	2.6	2.8	2.5	3.1
Santa Cruz	7,770	2,614	4,591	565	1,977	R	33.6	59.1	7.3	5	2	14	0.6	0.6	0.6	0.3
Yavapai	58,525	17,073	32,053	9,399	14,980	R	29.2	54.8	16.1	14	7	5	4.2	3.9	4.2	5.4
Yuma	27,464	9,017	16,247	2,200	7,230	R	32.8	59.2	8.0	7	1	13	2.0	2.1	2.1	1.3
ARIZONA	1,382,051	436,321	771,395	174,335	335,074	R	31.6	55.8	12.6				100.0	100.0	100.0	100.0

Table H. — Vote for U.S. Representative in Congress: November 3, 1992, General Election

Congressional district and county	Total	Democrat (DEM)	Republican (REP)	Other	Plurality Total	Party	DEM	REP	Other	Rank within district DEM	REP	Other	Total	DEM	REP	Other
District 1	**254,789**	**130,715**	**113,613**	**10,461**	**17,102**	**D**	**51.3**	**44.6**	**4.1**				**100.0**	**100.0**	**100.0**	**100.0**
Maricopa (pt)	254,789	130,715	113,613	10,461	17,102	D	51.3	44.6	4.1	1	1	1	100.0	100.0	100.0	100.0
District 2	**137,378**	**90,693**	**41,257**	**5,428**	**49,436**	**D**	**66.0**	**30.0**	**4.0**				**100.0**	**100.0**	**100.0**	**100.0**
Maricopa (pt)	54,757	37,605	14,858	2,294	22,747	D	68.7	27.1	4.2	4	3	2	39.9	41.5	36.0	42.3
Pima (pt)	48,143	35,026	10,844	2,273	24,182	D	72.8	22.5	4.7	2	4	1	35.0	38.6	26.3	41.9
Pinal (pt)	99	87	10	2	77	D	87.9	10.1	2.0	1	5	5	0.1	0.1	0.0	0.0
Santa Cruz	7,570	5,294	2,056	220	3,238	D	69.9	27.2	2.9	3	2	3	5.5	5.8	5.0	4.1
Yuma	26,809	12,681	13,489	639	808	R	47.3	50.3	2.4	5	1	4	19.5	14.0	32.7	11.8
District 3	**258,503**	**88,830**	**158,906**	**10,767**	**70,076**	**R**	**34.4**	**61.5**	**4.2**				**100.0**	**100.0**	**100.0**	**100.0**
Coconino (pt)	12,558	4,680	7,329	549	2,649	R	37.3	58.4	4.4	2	5	4	4.9	5.3	4.6	5.1
La Paz	4,732	1,567	3,023	142	1,456	R	33.1	63.9	3.0	5	1	6	1.8	1.8	1.9	1.3
Maricopa (pt)	147,615	50,867	90,997	5,751	40,130	R	34.5	61.6	3.9	4	3	5	57.1	57.3	57.3	53.4
Mohave	37,743	13,375	22,662	1,706	9,287	R	35.4	60.0	4.5	3	4	3	14.6	15.1	14.3	15.8
Navajo (pt)	729	432	262	35	170	D	59.3	35.9	4.8	1	6	1	0.3	0.5	0.2	0.3
Yavapai	55,126	17,909	34,633	2,584	16,724	R	32.5	62.8	4.7	6	2	2	21.3	20.2	21.8	24.0
District 4	**264,066**	**70,572**	**156,330**	**37,164**	**85,758**	**R**	**26.7**	**59.2**	**14.1**				**100.0**	**100.0**	**100.0**	**100.0**
Maricopa (pt)	264,066	70,572	156,330	37,164	85,758	R	26.7	59.2	14.1	1	1	1	100.0	100.0	100.0	100.0
District 5	**259,813**	**77,256**	**172,867**	**9,690**	**95,611**	**R**	**29.7**	**66.5**	**3.7**				**100.0**	**100.0**	**100.0**	**100.0**
Cochise	31,894	9,288	21,261	1,345	11,973	R	29.1	66.7	4.2	3	1	3	12.3	12.0	12.3	13.9
Graham (pt)	8,820	2,540	5,751	529	3,211	R	28.8	65.2	6.0	4	3	1	3.4	3.3	3.3	5.5
Pima (pt)	210,808	62,946	140,497	7,365	77,551	R	29.9	66.6	3.5	2	2	4	81.1	81.5	81.3	76.0
Pinal (pt)	8,291	2,482	5,358	451	2,876	R	29.9	64.6	5.4	1	4	2	3.2	3.2	3.1	4.7
District 6	**234,372**	**124,251**	**97,074**	**13,047**	**27,177**	**D**	**53.0**	**41.4**	**5.6**				**100.0**	**100.0**	**100.0**	**100.0**
Apache	17,768	11,340	5,728	700	5,612	D	63.8	32.2	3.9	2	7	7	7.6	9.1	5.9	5.4
Coconino (pt)	28,221	17,001	9,714	1,506	7,287	D	60.2	34.4	5.3	3	6	4	12.0	13.7	10.0	11.5
Gila	17,688	9,253	7,340	1,095	1,913	D	52.3	41.5	6.2	6	3	1	7.5	7.4	7.6	8.4
Graham (pt)	461	397	44	20	353	D	86.1	9.5	4.3	1	8	6	0.2	0.3	0.0	0.2
Greenlee	3,749	2,097	1,530	122	567	D	55.9	40.8	3.3	4	4	8	1.6	1.7	1.6	0.9
Maricopa (pt)	116,637	57,308	52,391	6,938	4,917	D	49.1	44.9	5.9	8	1	2	49.8	46.1	54.0	53.2
Navajo (pt)	23,023	12,009	9,907	1,107	2,102	D	52.2	43.0	4.8	7	2	5	9.8	9.7	10.2	8.5
Pinal (pt)	26,825	14,846	10,420	1,559	4,426	D	55.3	38.8	5.8	5	5	3	11.4	11.9	10.7	11.9
ARIZONA	**1,408,921**	**582,317**	**740,047**	**86,557**	**157,730**	**R**	**41.3**	**52.5**	**6.1**							

1992 Vote for President
Percent for Bush (R), by County

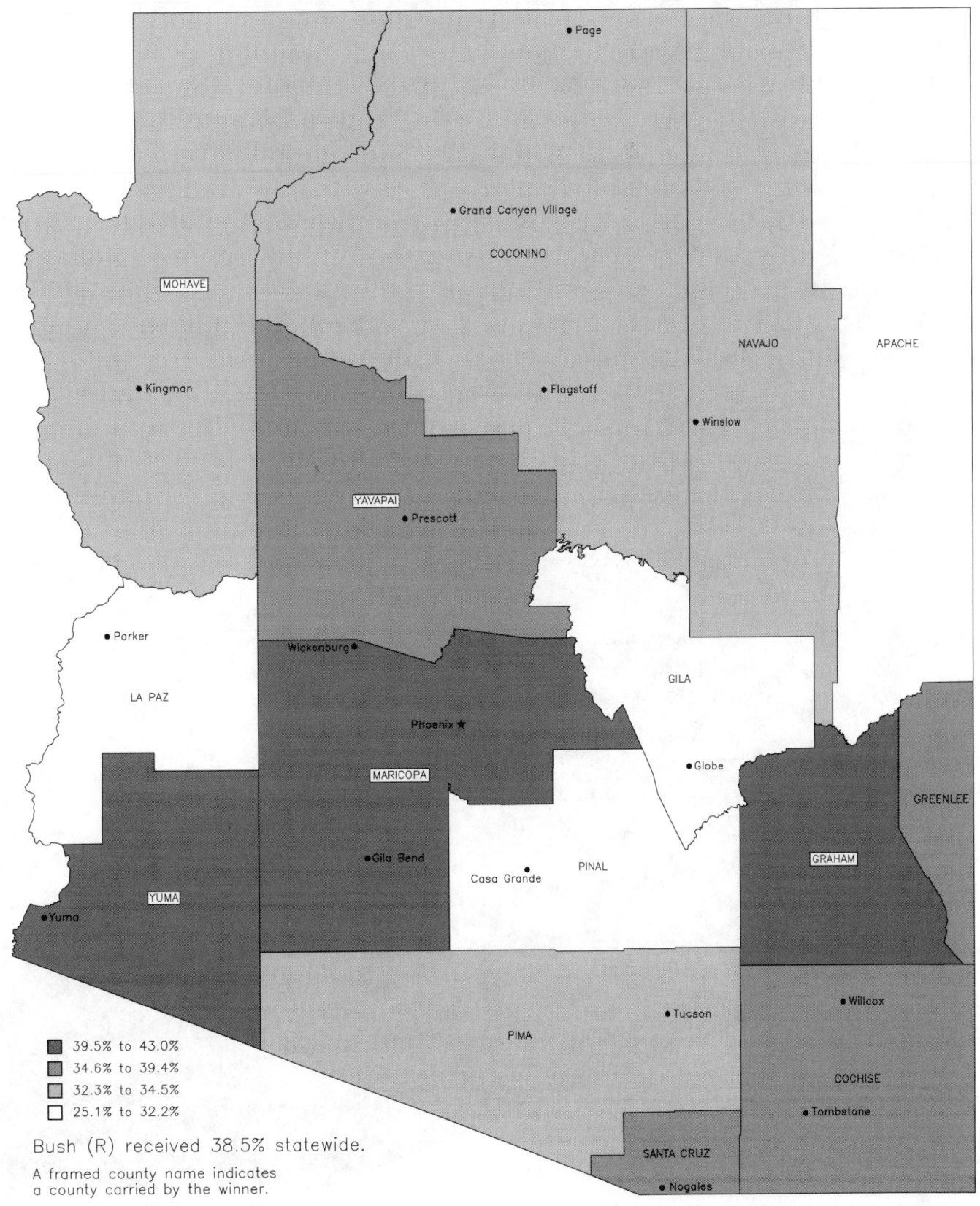

Page

Grand Canyon Village

COCONINO

MOHAVE

NAVAJO   APACHE

Kingman   Flagstaff

Winslow

Prescott

YAVAPAI

Parker

Wickenburg

LA PAZ   GILA

Phoenix ★

MARICOPA   Globe   GREENLEE

GRAHAM

Gila Bend

YUMA   Casa Grande   PINAL

Yuma

Willcox

Tucson

PIMA

COCHISE

Tombstone

SANTA CRUZ

Nogales

Bush (R) received 38.5% statewide.

A framed county name indicates
a county carried by the winner.

- 39.5% to 43.0%
- 34.6% to 39.4%
- 32.3% to 34.5%
- 25.1% to 32.2%

Arizona 77

1992 Vote for U.S. Senator
Percent for McCain (R), by County

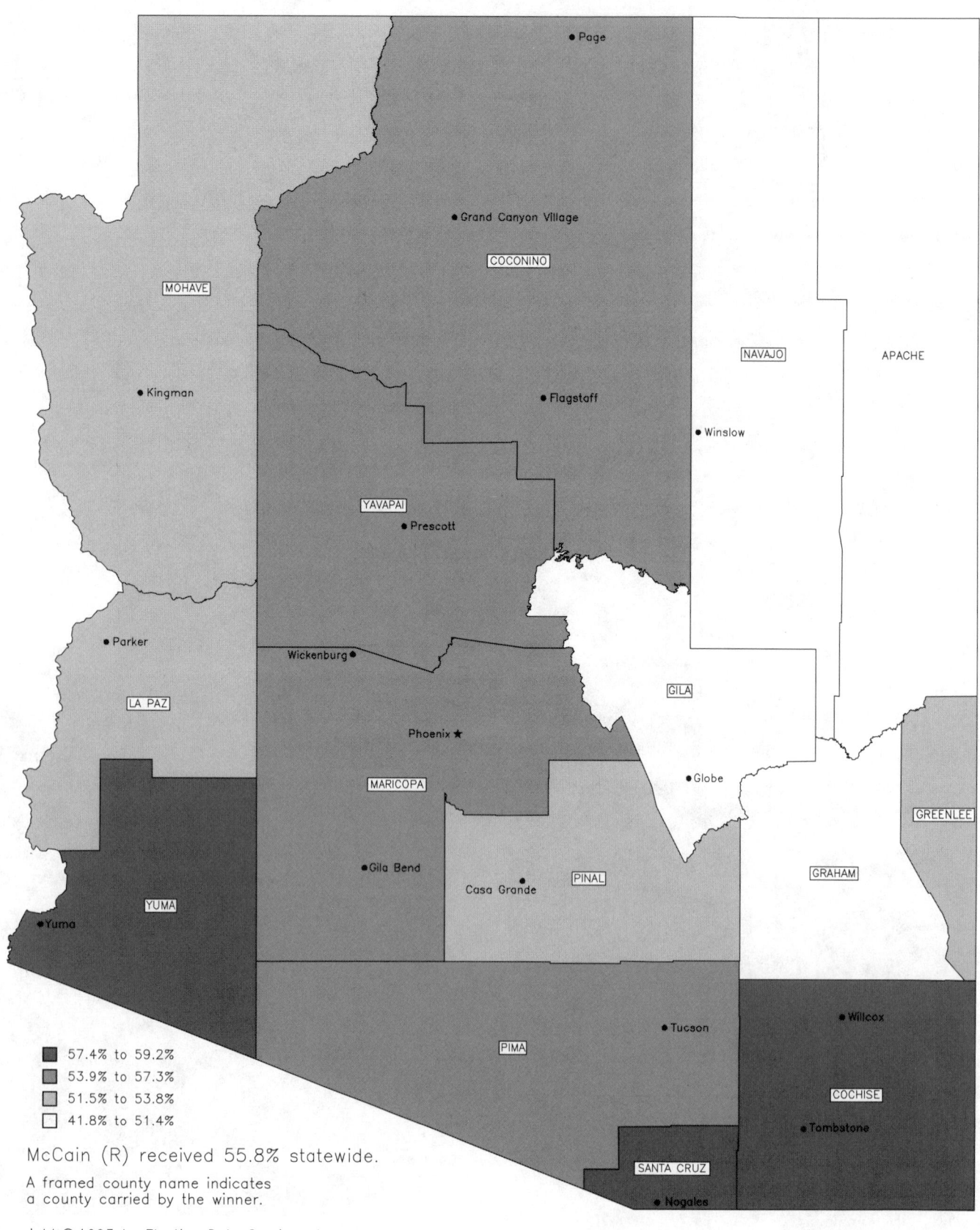

Page

● Grand Canyon Village

COCONINO

MOHAVE

● Kingman

● Flagstaff

NAVAJO

APACHE

● Winslow

YAVAPAI

● Prescott

● Parker

Wickenburg ●

LA PAZ

GILA

Phoenix ★

● Globe

MARICOPA

GREENLEE

● Gila Bend

PINAL

GRAHAM

Casa Grande ●

YUMA

● Yuma

● Willcox

● Tucson

PIMA

COCHISE

● Tombstone

SANTA CRUZ

● Nogales

■	57.4% to 59.2%
▨	53.9% to 57.3%
▨	51.5% to 53.8%
□	41.8% to 51.4%

McCain (R) received 55.8% statewide.

A framed county name indicates
a county carried by the winner.

78 Arizona

ARKANSAS

Congressional Districts 4
  Average Population 587,681
State Senate Districts 35
  Average Population 67,164
State House Districts 100
  Average Population 23,507

Electoral College Votes..6
Counties 75
Voting Precincts 2,720

Alternative Registration Methods:
  ....Deputized Registrars

Registration Deadline (Days before Election) 20

Voting Equipment Use (Counties)

Datavote Punch Card	0	Paper Ballot	34
Electronic	3	Other Punch Card	10
Lever Machine	11	Mixed Systems	0
Optical Scanner	17		

Party Control	DEM	REP	IND	VAC
1993 State Senate	30	5	0	0
1992 State Senate	31	4	0	0
1993 State House	89	10	1	0
1992 State House	91	9	0	0

Population Statistics 1990

Race/Ethnicity	Total Population		Voting Age Population		Voting Age Population % of total population
	Number	%	Number	%	
Non-Hispanic					
White	1,933,082	82.2	1,463,022	84.6	75.7
Black	372,762	15.9	236,805	13.7	63.5
Asian/Pacific Islander	12,144	0.5	8,264	0.5	68.1
Native American	12,393	0.5	8,854	0.5	71.4
Other	468	<.1	218	<.1	46.6
All Hispanic	19,876	0.8	12,431	0.7	62.5
TOTAL	2,350,725	100.0	1,729,594	100.0	73.6

Estimated Voting Age Population 1992 (VAP) 1,768,000
Number of Registered Voters................................... 1,317,944
  % of estimated VAP 74.5
Voter Turnout (Highest Office) 956,978
  % of VAP 54.1
  % of Registration 72.6
Persons Not Voting—of Voting Age 811,022
  % of VAP 45.9
Persons Not Voting—of Registered 360,966
  % of Registration 27.4
Straight Ticket Voting .... No

State Officials and Members of Congress

Governor:
Jim Guy Tucker (D) 1992, succeeded to office for remainder of term expiring in 1995.

U.S. Senators:
Dale Bumpers (D) 1974, elected to a six-year term in 1992.
David Pryor (D) 1978, elected to a six-year term in 1990.

U.S. Representative in Congress:
(District, Name, Party, Date first elected)

1. Lambert (D) 1992   2. Thornton (D) 1990   3. Hutchinson (R) 1992   4. Dickey (R) 1992

Candidates: General Election, November 3, 1992

Candidate(s)	Total vote	Percent	Party	Status	First elected
President/Vice President					
Clinton/Gore	505,823	53.21%	Democrat	Challenger	1992
Bush/Quayle	337,324	35.48%	Republican	Incumbent	1988
Perot/Stockdale	99,132	10.43%	Independent	Challenger	
Phillips/Knight	1,437	0.15%	Independent	Challenger	
Marrou/Lord	1,261	0.13%	Independent	Challenger	
Fulani/Munoz	1,022	0.11%	Independent	Challenger	
Boren, Honest Jim	956	0.10%	Independent	Challenger	
Gritz/Minett	819	0.09%	Independent	Challenger	
Hagelin/Tompkins	764	0.08%	Independent	Challenger	
LaRouche/Bevel	762	0.08%	Independent	Challenger	
Yiamouyiannis/McCone	554	0.06%	Independent	Challenger	
Dodge, Earl	472	0.05%	Independent	Challenger	
Masters, Isabell	327	0.03%	Independent	Challenger	
U.S. Senator					
Dale Bumpers	553,635	60.18%	Democrat	Incumbent	1974
Mike Huckabee	366,373	39.82%	Republican	Challenger	
Governor (No Contest)					
U.S. Representative in Congress					
District 1					
Blanche Lambert	149,558	69.83%	Democrat	Challenger	1992
Terry Hayes	64,618	30.17%	Republican	Challenger	
District 2					
Ray Thornton	154,946	74.16%	Democrat	Incumbent	1990
Dennis Scott	53,978	25.84%	Republican	Challenger	
District 3					
Tim Hutchinson	125,295	50.22%	Republican	Challenger	1992
John Vanwinkle	117,775	47.21%	Democrat	Challenger	
Ralph Forbes	6,329	2.54%	Independent	Challenger	
Rex Petty	95	0.04%	Write in	Challenger	
District 4					
Jay Dickey	113,009	52.34%	Republican	Challenger	1992
William McCuen	102,918	47.66%	Democrat	Challenger	

Candidates: May 26, 1992, Primary Election

Candidate	Total vote	Percent	Candidate	Total vote	Percent
Presidential Preference, Democratic			**Presidential Preference, Republican**		
Bill Clinton	342,017	68.05%	George Bush	45,590	83.07%
Uncommitted	90,710	18.05%	Patrick Buchanan	6,551	11.94%
Jerry Brown	55,234	10.99%	Uncommitted	2,742	5.00%
Lyndon LaRouche, Jr.	14,656	2.92%			

80 Arkansas

Voter Registration and Turnout, 1948-1992 Elections

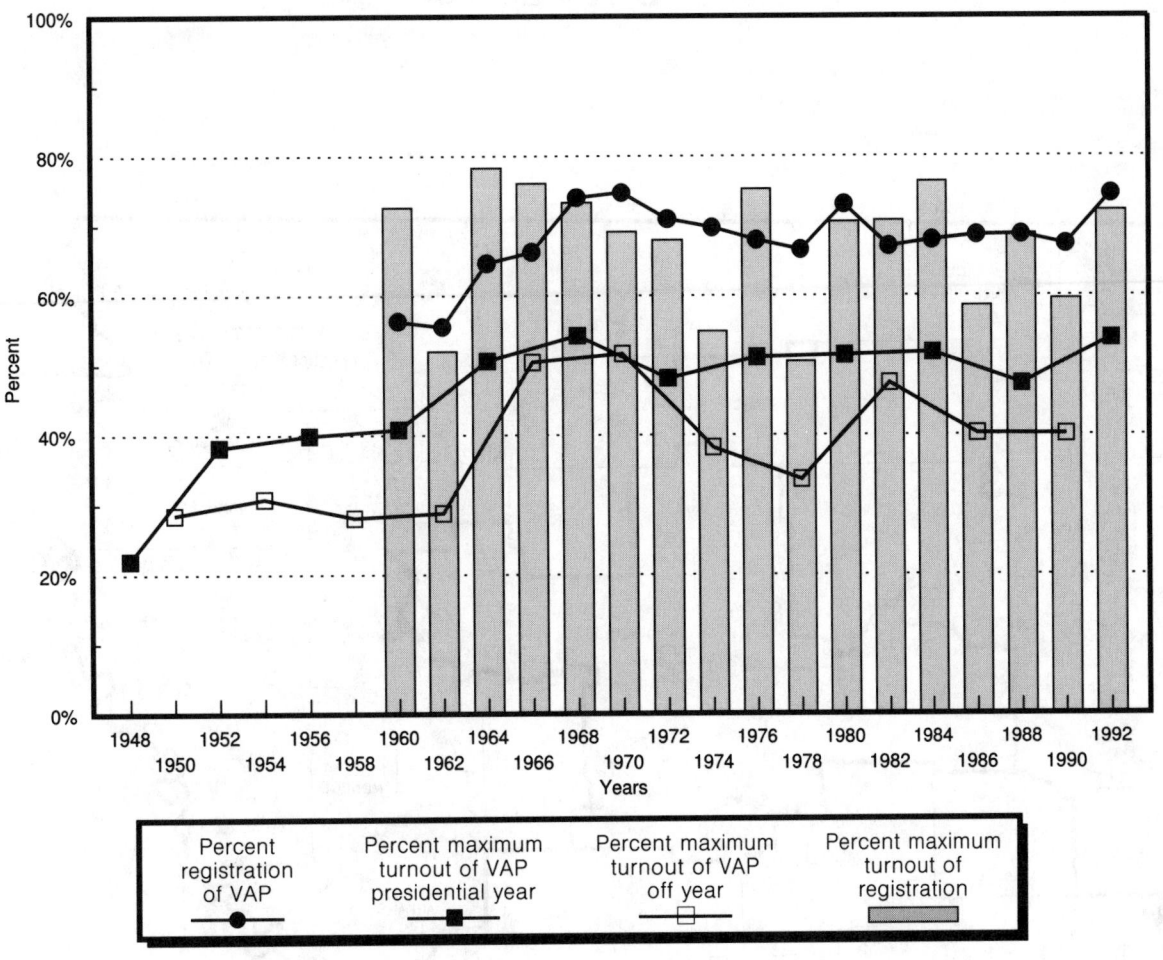

| Percent registration of VAP ——●—— | Percent maximum turnout of VAP presidential year ——■—— | Percent maximum turnout of VAP off year ——□—— | Percent maximum turnout of registration (shaded bar) |

Year	Estimated Voting Age Population (VAP)	Voter registration (REG)				Voter turnout											
							Highest office						Maximum vote				
		Total	Percent of VAP	Rank by percent of VAP	Actual	Total	Office	Percent total REG	Rank by percent of REG	Percent of VAP	Rank by percent of VAP	Total	Percent total REG	Rank by percent of REG	Percent total VAP	Rank by percent of VAP
1992	1,768,000	1,317,944	74.5	25	-	950,653	P	72.1	40	53.8	34	950,653	72.1	40	53.8	35
1990	1,737,000	1,169,835	67.3	28	-	696,209	G	59.5	22	40.1	23	696,209	59.5	24	40.1	27
1988	1,750,000	1,203,016	68.7	32	-	827,738	P	68.8	33	47.3	38	827,738	68.8	36	47.3	40
1986	1,732,000	1,188,831	68.6	26	-	695,487	S	58.5	19	40.2	22	695,487	58.5	23	40.2	24
1984	1,707,000	1,159,588	67.9	38	-	884,406	P	76.3	15	51.8	33	884,406	76.3	21	51.8	36
1982	1,667,000	1,116,082	67.0	27	-	789,351	G	70.7	7	47.4	13	789,351	70.7	10	47.4	16
1980	1,628,000	1,188,902	73.0	26	-	837,582	P	70.5	36	51.4	34	837,582	70.5	38	51.4	35
1978	1,575,000	1,047,453	66.5	32	-	528,912	G	50.5	39	33.6	40	528,912	50.5	39	33.6	40
1976	1,502,000	1,020,533	67.9	34	-	767,535	P	75.2	26	51.1	32	767,535	75.2	27	51.1	34
1974	1,431,000	996,985	69.7	27	-	545,974	G	54.8	30	38.2	34	545,974	54.8	32	38.2	35
1972	1,354,000	959,871	70.9	31	-	651,320	P	67.9	36	48.1	38	651,320	67.9	36	48.1	40
1970	1,180,000	881,403	74.7	21	-	609,198	G	69.1	14	51.6	19	609,198	69.1	17	51.6	23
1968	1,143,000	845,759	74.0	26	-	619,969	P	73.3	39	54.2	38	619,969	73.3	40	54.2	39
1966	1,119,000	740,609	66.2	31	-	563,527	G	76.1	6	50.4	28	563,527	76.1	7	50.4	30
1964	1,108,000	715,528	64.6	31	-	560,426	P	78.3	28	50.6	42	560,426	78.3	29	50.6	42
1962	1,085,000	601,991	55.5	32	-	312,880	S	52.0	31	28.8	41	312,880	52.0	31	28.8	41
1960	1,049,000	590,501	56.3	30	-	428,509	P	72.6	31	40.8	45	428,509	72.6	31	40.8	45
1958	1,021,000	-	-	-	-	286,886	G	-	-	28.1	37	286,886	-	-	28.1	37
1956	1,019,000	-	-	-	-	406,572	P	-	-	39.9	41	406,572	-	-	39.9	41
1954	1,090,000	-	-	-	-	335,176	G	-	-	30.8	38	335,176	-	-	30.8	38
1952	1,061,000	-	-	-	-	404,800	P	-	-	38.2	43	404,800	-	-	38.2	43
1950	1,112,000	-	-	-	-	317,087	G	-	-	28.5	38	317,087	-	-	28.5	38
1948	1,101,000	-	-	-	-	242,475	P	-	-	22.0	44	242,475	-	-	22.0	44

Arkansas 81

ARKANSAS

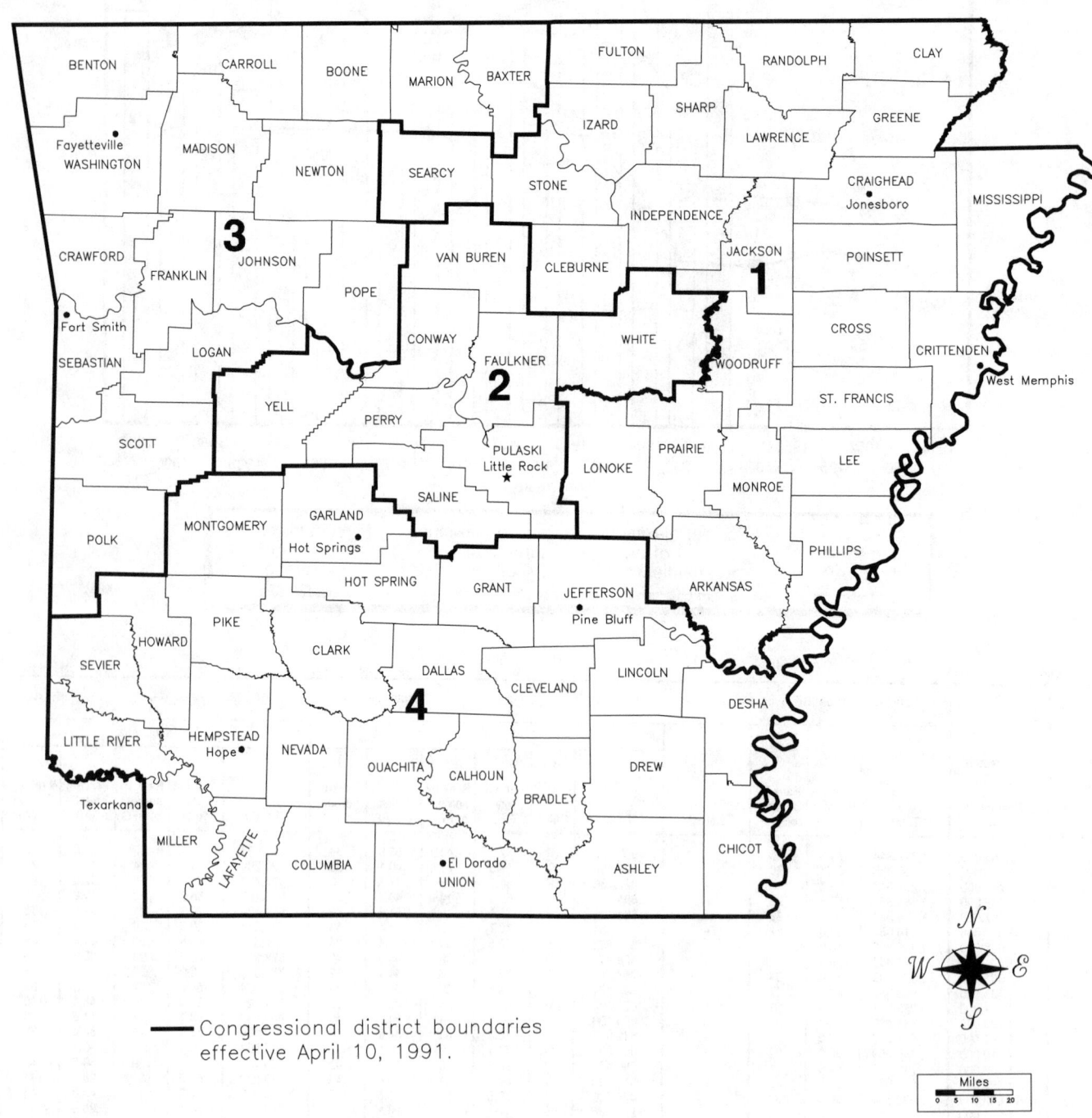

— Congressional district boundaries
effective April 10, 1991.

Table A. — 1990 Population by Race and Ethnic Origin

State/county code	County	Total persons	Percent of total persons						Rank				Percent contribution to state population			
			Non-Hispanic					Hispanic	Percent of total persons					Non-Hispanic		Hispanic
			White	Black	Asian and Pacific Islander	Native American	Other		Total	Non-Hispanic		Hispanic	Total	White	Black	
										White	Black					
05 001	Arkansas	21,653	77.5	21.8	0.2	0.2	<.1	0.3	29	47	27	72	0.9	0.9	1.3	0.3
05 003	Ashley	24,319	71.6	27.2	0.2	0.2	0.0	0.9	28	56	21	22	1.0	0.9	1.8	1.1
05 005	Baxter	31,186	98.8	<.1	0.2	0.4	<.1	0.5	20	6	72	49	1.3	1.6	<.1	0.9
05 007	Benton	97,499	96.6	0.1	0.5	1.4	<.1	1.4	4	25	59	4	4.1	4.9	<.1	6.8
05 009	Boone	28,297	98.6	<.1	0.1	0.6	<.1	0.6	24	9	71	37	1.2	1.4	<.1	0.9
05 011	Bradley	11,793	67.3	30.9	<.1	<.1	0.1	1.6	57	62	16	3	0.5	0.4	1.0	1.0
05 013	Calhoun	5,826	74.6	24.7	0.1	<.1	0.0	0.5	75	52	24	51	0.2	0.2	0.4	0.2
05 015	Carroll	18,654	97.9	<.1	0.3	0.8	<.1	1.0	37	17	70	16	0.8	0.9	<.1	1.0
05 017	Chicot	15,713	42.4	56.1	0.3	0.1	<.1	1.0	46	74	2	17	0.7	0.3	2.4	0.8
05 019	Clark	21,437	75.9	22.8	0.4	0.3	<.1	0.6	31	51	25	39	0.9	0.8	1.3	0.6
05 021	Clay	18,107	99.3	<.1	<.1	0.2	0.0	0.4	39	1	67	67	0.8	0.9	<.1	0.4
05 023	Cleburne	19,411	99.0	<.1	0.1	0.3	0.0	0.5	33	4	66	50	0.8	1.0	<.1	0.5
05 025	Cleveland	7,781	85.5	13.5	0.2	0.2	<.1	0.6	73	44	33	38	0.3	0.3	0.3	0.2
05 027	Columbia	25,691	64.3	35.0	0.2	0.2	<.1	0.3	26	63	13	71	1.1	0.9	2.4	0.4
05 029	Conway	19,151	83.9	14.9	0.2	0.4	<.1	0.6	35	46	30	36	0.8	0.8	0.8	0.6
05 031	Craighead	68,956	93.1	5.5	0.6	0.3	<.1	0.6	7	35	41	46	2.9	3.3	1.0	1.9
05 033	Crawford	42,493	95.7	0.8	0.9	1.5	<.1	1.1	15	30	54	14	1.8	2.1	<.1	2.3
05 035	Crittenden	49,939	56.0	42.7	0.4	0.2	<.1	0.7	12	70	6	32	2.1	1.4	5.7	1.7
05 037	Cross	19,225	74.3	24.7	0.2	0.2	<.1	0.6	34	53	23	44	0.8	0.7	1.3	0.5
05 039	Dallas	9,614	61.0	38.4	0.1	0.2	<.1	0.3	67	69	7	70	0.4	0.3	1.0	0.2
05 041	Desha	16,798	56.2	42.3	0.2	0.3	<.1	0.9	44	69	7	23	0.7	0.5	1.9	0.8
05 043	Drew	17,369	71.9	27.3	0.1	0.1	<.1	0.5	42	54	20	52	0.7	0.6	1.3	0.5
05 045	Faulkner	60,006	90.7	8.0	0.4	0.4	<.1	0.6	9	37	36	43	2.6	2.8	1.3	1.7
05 047	Franklin	14,897	97.4	0.7	0.2	0.6	<.1	1.2	47	20	55	11	0.6	0.8	<.1	0.9
05 049	Fulton	10,037	99.1	<.1	<.1	0.5	<.1	0.3	64	2	62	74	0.4	0.5	<.1	0.1
05 051	Garland	73,397	90.3	7.6	0.3	0.6	<.1	1.1	6	38	37	15	3.1	3.4	1.5	3.9
05 053	Grant	13,948	96.3	2.7	0.1	0.3	0.0	0.6	51	27	44	42	0.6	0.7	0.1	0.4
05 055	Greene	31,804	99.0	<.1	0.1	0.2	<.1	0.5	18	3	64	53	1.4	1.6	<.1	0.8
05 057	Hempstead	21,621	68.4	29.8	<.1	0.3	<.1	1.3	30	59	18	6	0.9	0.8	1.7	1.5
05 059	Hot Spring	26,115	88.0	11.0	0.1	0.5	<.1	0.4	25	41	34	58	1.1	1.2	0.8	0.6
05 061	Howard	13,569	77.1	21.4	0.4	0.4	<.1	0.7	54	48	28	30	0.6	0.5	0.8	0.5
05 063	Independence	31,192	96.9	1.9	0.3	0.2	<.1	0.6	19	24	48	48	1.3	1.6	0.2	0.9
05 065	Izard	11,364	98.7	<.1	0.1	0.5	0.0	0.6	59	8	61	35	0.5	0.6	<.1	0.4
05 067	Jackson	18,944	84.7	14.5	0.1	0.3	<.1	0.3	36	45	31	68	0.8	0.8	0.7	0.3
05 069	Jefferson	85,487	55.8	43.0	0.4	0.3	<.1	0.5	5	71	5	55	3.6	2.5	9.9	2.1
05 071	Johnson	18,221	96.1	1.7	0.4	0.6	<.1	1.2	38	28	49	10	0.8	0.9	<.1	1.1
05 073	Lafayette	9,643	60.8	38.4	0.2	0.2	<.1	0.4	66	67	10	61	0.4	0.3	1.0	0.2
05 075	Lawrence	17,457	98.3	0.5	<.1	0.7	<.1	0.3	41	12	56	69	0.7	0.9	<.1	0.3
05 077	Lee	13,053	41.2	57.1	0.4	<.1	0.0	1.3	55	75	1	8	0.6	0.3	2.0	0.9
05 079	Lincoln	13,690	62.5	35.8	0.1	0.5	<.1	1.1	52	65	11	13	0.6	0.4	1.3	0.8
05 081	Little River	13,966	77.0	20.9	<.1	0.8	0.0	1.1	50	49	29	12	0.6	0.6	0.8	0.8
05 083	Logan	20,557	97.2	1.3	0.1	0.6	<.1	0.7	32	21	52	29	0.9	1.0	<.1	0.7
05 085	Lonoke	39,268	89.7	9.0	0.3	0.4	<.1	0.6	16	39	35	34	1.7	1.8	0.9	1.2
05 087	Madison	11,618	97.7	<.1	0.1	1.2	0.0	1.0	58	19	68	19	0.5	0.6	<.1	0.6
05 089	Marion	12,001	98.9	<.1	0.2	0.4	<.1	0.4	56	5	65	65	0.5	0.6	<.1	0.2
05 091	Miller	38,467	76.1	22.4	0.4	0.3	<.1	0.8	17	50	26	25	1.6	1.5	2.3	1.6
05 093	Mississippi	57,525	70.1	27.8	0.6	0.3	<.1	1.3	10	57	19	9	2.4	2.1	4.3	3.7
05 095	Monroe	11,333	60.5	38.9	0.2	0.2	0.0	0.3	60	68	8	73	0.5	0.4	1.2	0.2
05 097	Montgomery	7,841	97.9	0.1	0.1	1.2	0.0	0.7	71	18	60	26	0.3	0.4	<.1	0.3
05 099	Nevada	10,101	67.5	31.6	<.1	0.3	0.0	0.6	62	61	14	33	0.4	0.4	0.9	0.3
05 101	Newton	7,666	98.6	0.0	0.2	0.7	<.1	0.6	74	10	74	45	0.3	0.4	0.0	0.2
05 103	Ouachita	30,574	64.2	35.0	0.2	0.1	<.1	0.4	21	64	12	59	1.3	1.0	2.9	0.7
05 105	Perry	7,969	97.2	1.5	0.2	0.5	0.0	0.6	70	22	50	40	0.3	0.4	<.1	0.2
05 107	Phillips	28,838	44.4	54.5	0.2	0.1	<.1	0.8	22	73	3	24	1.2	0.7	4.2	1.2
05 109	Pike	10,086	95.2	3.7	<.1	0.5	0.0	0.6	63	33	42	47	0.4	0.5	0.1	0.3
05 111	Poinsett	24,664	92.0	7.2	<.1	0.2	<.1	0.5	27	36	38	54	1.0	1.2	0.5	0.6
05 113	Polk	17,347	97.0	0.0	0.2	1.0	<.1	1.7	43	23	75	2	0.7	0.9	0.0	1.5
05 115	Pope	45,883	95.5	2.4	0.4	0.7	<.1	0.9	14	32	45	20	2.0	2.3	0.3	2.1
05 117	Prairie	9,518	85.6	13.6	<.1	0.3	<.1	0.4	69	43	32	66	0.4	0.4	0.3	0.2
05 119	Pulaski	349,660	71.7	26.3	0.8	0.3	<.1	0.9	1	55	22	21	14.9	13.0	24.7	16.1
05 121	Randolph	16,558	98.2	0.9	0.1	0.3	<.1	0.5	45	15	53	57	0.7	0.8	<.1	0.4
05 123	St. Francis	28,497	51.4	47.3	0.4	0.2	<.1	0.7	23	72	4	27	1.2	0.8	3.6	1.0
05 125	Saline	64,183	96.5	2.1	0.4	0.4	<.1	0.6	8	26	46	41	2.7	3.2	0.4	1.9
05 127	Scott	10,205	98.0	<.1	0.5	1.0	<.1	0.4	61	16	73	62	0.4	0.5	<.1	0.2
05 129	Searcy	7,841	98.5	<.1	0.2	0.8	0.0	0.4	72	11	69	63	0.3	0.4	<.1	0.2
05 131	Sebastian	99,590	88.4	5.6	3.2	1.4	<.1	1.4	3	40	40	5	4.2	4.6	1.5	6.9
05 133	Sevier	13,637	88.0	5.7	0.1	1.5	<.1	4.6	53	42	39	1	0.6	0.6	0.2	3.2
05 135	Sharp	14,109	98.3	0.5	0.1	0.7	0.0	0.4	48	14	57	64	0.6	0.7	<.1	0.3
05 137	Stone	9,775	98.7	<.1	0.2	0.5	0.0	0.4	65	7	63	60	0.4	0.5	<.1	0.2
05 139	Union	46,719	69.1	30.0	0.2	0.2	<.1	0.5	13	58	17	56	2.0	1.7	3.8	1.1

State/ county code	County	Total persons	Percent of total persons						Rank				Percent contribution to state population			
			Non-Hispanic					Hispanic	Total	Percent of total persons			Total	Non-Hispanic		Hispanic
										Non-Hispanic						
			White	Black	Asian and Pacific Islander	Native American	Other			White	Black	Hispanic		White	Black	
05 141	Van Buren	14,008	98.3	0.3	0.1	0.5	0.0	0.7	49	13	58	28	0.6	0.7	<.1	0.5
05 143	Washington	113,409	95.0	1.5	0.9	1.3	<.1	1.3	2	34	51	7	4.8	5.6	0.4	7.7
05 145	White	54,676	95.6	3.1	0.2	0.4	<.1	0.7	11	31	43	31	2.3	2.7	0.5	1.9
05 147	Woodruff.................	9,520	68.2	31.3	0.1	0.1	<.1	0.2	68	60	15	75	0.4	0.3	0.8	<.1
05 149	Yell.................	17,759	96.1	2.1	0.4	0.4	<.1	1.0	40	29	47	18	0.8	0.9	<.1	0.9
05	**ARKANSAS**	**2,350,725**	**82.2**	**15.9**	**0.5**	**0.5**	**<.1**	**0.8**					**100.0**	**100.0**	**100.0**	**100.0**
	CONGRESSIONAL															
	District 1.........................	588,588	81.0	17.8	0.3	0.3	<.1	0.6	2	2	2	4	25.0	24.7	28.1	18.4
	District 2.........................	587,412	80.7	17.6	0.6	0.4	<.1	0.8	3	3	3	3	25.0	24.5	27.7	23.8
	District 3.........................	589,523	95.2	1.6	1.0	1.1	<.1	1.1	1	1	4	1	25.1	29.0	2.6	34.0
	District 4.........................	585,202	72.1	26.5	0.2	0.4	<.1	0.8	4	4	1	2	24.9	21.8	41.6	23.8

Table B. — 1990 Voting Age Population (VAP) by Race and Ethnic Origin

County	Total Voting Age Population	Percent of total VAP Non-Hispanic White	Black	Asian and Pacific Islander	Native American	Other	Hispanic	Rank Total	Rank White (NH)	Rank Black (NH)	Rank Hispanic	Percent contribution to state VAP Total	White (NH)	Black (NH)	Hispanic	VAP percent of total population Total	White (NH)	Black (NH)	Asian and Pacific Islander (NH)	Native American (NH)	Other (NH)	Hispanic
Arkansas	15,711	80.7	18.6	0.2	0.2	0.0	0.2	30	47	29	73	0.9	0.9	1.2	0.3	72.6	75.6	62.0	74.3	73.6	0.0	63.9
Ashley	17,468	74.7	24.3	0.2	0.2	0.0	0.7	28	55	20	24	1.0	0.9	1.8	1.0	71.8	75.0	64.1	63.6	78.6	0.0	54.1
Baxter	25,119	99.0	<.1	0.2	0.4	<.1	0.4	18	5	72	48	1.5	1.7	<.1	0.9	80.5	80.7	25.0	68.3	78.3	50.0	64.3
Benton	73,315	97.0	<.1	0.4	1.3	<.1	1.2	4	25	60	5	4.2	4.9	<.1	7.0	75.2	75.5	61.0	68.7	66.5	72.7	63.6
Boone	21,281	98.8	<.1	0.1	0.6	<.1	0.5	22	11	69	36	1.2	1.4	<.1	0.9	75.2	75.3	60.0	69.2	71.2	100.0	63.2
Bradley	8,746	71.1	27.6	<.1	0.1	<.1	1.2	57	60	15	6	0.5	0.4	1.0	0.8	74.2	78.3	66.2	100.0	81.8	41.7	53.9
Calhoun	4,258	76.6	22.8	0.1	0.1	0.0	0.4	75	53	22	61	0.2	0.2	0.4	0.1	73.1	75.1	67.4	85.7	100.0	0.0	48.4
Carroll	14,133	98.1	<.1	0.3	0.8	<.1	0.8	34	18	71	20	0.8	0.9	<.1	0.9	75.8	76.0	25.0	66.7	79.3	100.0	58.8
Chicot	10,627	47.6	50.9	0.4	0.2	<.1	0.9	49	74	2	14	0.6	0.3	2.3	0.8	67.6	75.9	61.4	77.8	72.7	100.0	61.6
Clark	16,648	78.4	20.6	0.3	0.3	<.1	0.5	29	51	25	40	1.0	0.9	1.4	0.6	77.7	80.2	69.9	68.4	77.8	26.7	61.4
Clay	13,934	99.3	<.1	<.1	0.2	0.0	0.4	37	1	70	62	0.8	0.9	<.1	0.4	77.0	77.0	40.0	57.1	76.2	0.0	70.0
Cleburne	15,193	99.1	<.1	<.1	0.3	0.0	0.4	32	2	64	50	0.9	1.0	<.1	0.5	78.3	78.4	100.0	54.5	76.9	0.0	60.0
Cleveland	5,735	86.9	12.2	0.2	0.2	<.1	0.6	73	45	32	32	0.3	0.3	0.3	0.3	73.7	74.9	66.3	69.2	84.6	100.0	68.1
Columbia	18,958	67.7	31.6	0.2	0.2	<.1	0.3	26	63	13	67	1.1	0.9	2.5	0.4	72.8	77.7	66.7	71.0	64.2	100.0	59.7
Conway	13,945	85.4	13.6	0.2	0.3	0.0	0.5	36	46	30	35	0.8	0.8	0.8	0.6	72.8	74.1	66.3	76.7	64.3	0.0	59.7
Craighead	51,922	93.8	4.9	0.6	0.3	<.1	0.5	7	35	41	46	3.0	3.3	1.1	1.9	75.3	75.8	67.0	82.7	77.2	25.0	60.6
Crawford	30,153	96.3	0.8	0.7	1.4	<.1	0.9	15	30	54	17	1.7	2.0	0.1	2.1	71.0	71.4	66.8	57.4	64.6	33.3	56.0
Crittenden	34,014	61.0	37.7	0.4	0.2	<.1	0.7	12	69	7	25	2.0	1.4	5.4	1.8	68.1	74.1	60.1	75.6	71.9	50.0	67.3
Cross	13,408	78.1	21.1	0.2	0.2	<.1	0.4	39	52	24	47	0.8	0.7	1.2	0.5	69.7	73.3	59.5	63.2	72.5	100.0	54.1
Dallas	7,060	64.1	35.4	<.1	0.2	<.1	0.3	66	68	8	71	0.4	0.3	1.1	0.1	73.4	77.2	67.7	50.0	68.8	100.0	56.3
Desha	11,474	60.8	37.8	0.2	0.3	<.1	0.8	45	70	6	18	0.7	0.5	1.8	0.8	68.3	73.9	61.0	59.5	72.9	100.0	61.8
Drew	12,540	74.6	24.7	0.1	0.2	<.1	0.4	43	57	19	52	0.7	0.6	1.3	0.4	72.2	74.9	65.4	68.2	80.8	50.0	55.4
Faulkner	44,661	91.3	7.5	0.4	0.4	<.1	0.5	9	38	36	45	2.6	2.8	1.4	1.6	74.4	74.9	70.0	72.6	75.7	40.0	59.2
Franklin	10,986	97.5	0.6	0.1	0.6	<.1	1.0	47	20	55	13	0.6	0.7	<.1	0.9	73.7	73.9	71.4	60.9	78.7	100.0	63.7
Fulton	7,672	99.0	<.1	0.1	0.5	<.1	0.3	61	7	62	69	0.4	0.5	<.1	0.2	76.4	76.4	55.6	100.0	89.4	100.0	75.0
Garland	57,580	91.8	6.5	0.3	0.6	<.1	0.9	6	37	37	16	3.3	3.6	1.6	3.9	78.5	79.7	66.8	70.4	71.8	65.0	63.2
Grant	10,204	96.4	2.7	0.2	0.3	0.0	0.5	51	29	44	34	0.6	0.7	0.1	0.4	73.2	73.2	71.9	80.0	70.3	0.0	64.6
Greene	23,789	99.1	<.1	0.1	0.3	<.1	0.4	19	3	63	51	1.4	1.6	<.1	0.8	74.8	74.9	75.0	66.7	84.8	75.0	58.7
Hempstead	15,636	71.0	27.3	0.1	0.4	<.1	1.2	31	61	17	3	0.9	0.8	1.8	1.5	72.3	75.1	66.2	80.0	74.3	71.4	64.9
Hot Spring	19,358	89.4	9.7	0.1	0.5	<.1	0.3	23	41	34	68	1.1	1.2	0.8	0.4	74.1	75.3	65.7	81.3	77.0	100.0	47.0
Howard	9,818	80.0	18.8	0.3	0.3	0.0	0.5	54	48	28	33	0.6	0.5	0.8	0.4	72.4	75.1	63.6	57.1	66.7	0.0	56.4
Independence	22,999	97.2	1.7	0.3	0.3	<.1	0.5	20	24	48	41	1.3	1.5	0.2	0.9	73.7	73.9	67.6	64.8	79.2	100.0	61.6
Izard	8,916	98.9	<.1	<.1	0.4	0.0	0.5	56	8	61	37	0.5	0.6	<.1	0.4	78.5	78.7	63.6	57.1	66.1	0.0	62.0
Jackson	14,080	87.0	12.2	0.1	0.3	<.1	0.3	35	44	31	64	0.8	0.8	0.7	0.4	74.3	76.4	62.7	82.6	67.2	28.6	69.7
Jefferson	61,332	59.7	39.1	0.4	0.3	<.1	0.4	5	71	5	49	3.5	2.5	10.1	2.1	71.7	76.8	65.3	72.6	80.9	25.0	61.1
Johnson	13,712	96.4	1.4	0.4	0.5	<.1	1.1	38	28	50	8	0.8	0.9	<.1	1.3	75.3	75.5	63.7	79.5	69.9	88.9	71.0
Lafayette	6,976	64.3	35.0	0.2	0.2	<.1	0.4	68	66	9	60	0.4	0.3	1.0	0.2	72.3	76.4	66.0	64.7	81.3	66.7	61.0
Lawrence	13,157	98.4	0.5	0.1	0.7	<.1	0.3	41	15	56	65	0.8	0.9	<.1	0.3	75.4	75.7	72.7	87.5	73.4	100.0	68.3
Lee	8,661	47.2	51.2	0.4	0.1	0.0	1.1	58	75	1	12	0.5	0.3	1.9	0.8	66.4	76.0	59.5	78.3	100.0	0.0	55.2
Lincoln	10,506	64.1	34.0	0.1	0.5	<.1	1.2	50	67	10	4	0.6	0.5	1.5	1.0	76.7	78.7	73.0	68.4	90.5	100.0	82.2
Little River	10,037	79.1	18.9	<.1	0.7	0.0	1.2	53	49	27	7	0.6	0.5	0.8	0.9	71.9	73.8	64.9	76.9	63.2	0.0	73.8
Logan	15,006	97.5	1.2	<.1	0.6	<.1	0.6	33	21	52	29	0.9	1.0	<.1	0.7	73.0	73.2	67.3	58.3	68.3	60.0	61.5
Lonoke	27,702	90.7	8.1	0.3	0.4	<.1	0.6	16	39	35	30	1.6	1.7	0.9	1.3	70.5	71.3	63.3	65.7	71.9	33.3	65.4
Madison	8,503	98.2	<.1	<.1	1.1	0.0	0.6	59	17	65	26	0.5	0.6	<.1	0.4	73.2	73.6	100.0	53.8	66.4	0.0	45.9
Marion	9,366	99.0	<.1	0.2	0.4	<.1	0.3	55	6	68	66	0.5	0.6	<.1	0.2	78.0	78.1	33.3	95.8	73.1	66.7	56.3
Miller	27,540	78.7	19.9	0.3	0.4	<.1	0.7	17	50	26	23	1.6	1.5	2.3	1.6	71.6	74.0	63.8	60.7	73.6	54.5	62.6
Mississippi	39,523	74.6	23.4	0.6	0.3	<.1	1.1	11	56	21	10	2.3	2.0	3.9	3.6	68.7	73.2	57.8	70.0	72.5	41.7	59.5
Monroe	7,992	65.4	33.9	0.2	0.3	0.0	0.2	60	65	11	74	0.5	0.4	1.1	0.2	70.5	76.3	61.5	77.8	80.0	0.0	59.4
Montgomery	6,030	98.1	0.1	<.1	1.1	0.0	0.6	70	19	57	31	0.3	0.4	<.1	0.3	76.9	77.1	87.5	54.5	72.0	0.0	60.7
Nevada	7,361	70.2	29.0	<.1	0.3	0.0	0.5	65	62	14	38	0.4	0.4	0.9	0.3	72.9	75.8	66.9	40.0	80.8	0.0	56.3
Newton	5,523	98.8	0.0	0.1	0.6	<.1	0.4	74	9	73	57	0.3	0.4	0.0	0.2	72.0	72.2	0.0	53.8	64.7	100.0	48.8
Ouachita	22,316	67.0	32.2	0.2	0.2	<.1	0.4	21	64	12	54	1.3	1.0	3.0	0.7	73.0	76.2	67.1	65.2	81.4	100.0	63.9
Perry	5,949	97.4	1.6	0.1	0.4	0.0	0.5	71	23	49	44	0.3	0.4	<.1	0.2	74.7	74.8	79.0	47.1	63.2	0.0	57.4
Phillips	18,969	50.5	48.3	0.2	0.2	<.1	0.8	25	73	3	22	1.1	0.7	3.9	1.2	65.8	74.9	58.3	70.8	88.9	100.0	60.8
Pike	7,453	96.0	3.1	<.1	0.5	0.0	0.5	63	31	42	43	0.4	0.5	<.1	0.3	73.9	74.5	61.5	50.0	64.8	0.0	60.7
Poinsett	18,088	93.2	6.1	<.1	0.2	<.1	0.4	27	36	38	55	1.0	1.2	0.5	0.6	73.3	74.3	62.1	78.3	97.7	25.0	55.6
Polk	12,886	97.4	0.0	0.2	0.9	<.1	1.5	42	22	74	2	0.7	0.9	0.0	1.5	74.3	74.6	0.0	66.7	66.3	100.0	62.5
Pope	33,806	95.9	2.2	0.4	0.7	<.1	0.8	14	32	45	21	2.0	2.2	0.3	2.2	73.7	74.0	67.3	62.9	72.4	33.3	63.4
Prairie	7,055	87.9	11.4	<.1	0.3	<.1	0.4	67	43	33	59	0.4	0.4	0.3	0.2	74.1	76.1	62.1	50.0	73.3	100.0	68.4
Pulaski	257,917	75.5	22.5	0.7	0.3	<.1	0.8	1	54	23	19	14.9	13.3	24.6	17.0	73.8	77.8	63.2	70.1	78.2	33.6	66.0
Randolph	12,310	98.4	0.9	0.1	0.3	<.1	0.4	44	16	53	58	0.7	0.8	<.1	0.4	74.3	74.4	72.4	68.4	74.0	25.0	61.3
St. Francis	19,103	57.2	41.5	0.5	0.2	<.1	0.6	24	72	4	27	1.1	0.7	3.3	0.9	67.0	74.6	58.8	80.2	85.1	83.3	55.9
Saline	46,655	96.8	1.9	0.3	0.4	<.1	0.5	8	26	46	39	2.7	3.1	0.4	1.8	72.7	72.9	67.2	66.1	72.6	46.2	58.7
Scott	7,605	98.4	0.0	0.3	0.8	<.1	0.4	62	14	75	56	0.4	0.5	0.0	0.2	74.5	74.8	0.0	49.0	59.4	75.0	69.0
Searcy	5,933	98.8	<.1	0.2	0.7	0.0	0.3	72	10	66	72	0.3	0.4	<.1	0.1	75.7	75.9	100.0	60.0	65.2	0.0	46.9
Sebastian	73,640	90.0	4.9	2.6	1.3	<.1	1.1	3	40	40	9	4.3	4.5	1.5	6.7	73.9	75.3	64.4	60.6	69.1	35.7	61.5
Sevier	10,072	88.8	5.5	0.1	1.3	<.1	4.2	52	42	39	1	0.6	0.6	0.2	3.4	73.9	74.6	70.5	93.8	66.8	75.0	66.1
Sharp	11,054	98.7	0.3	<.1	0.6	0.0	0.3	46	13	58	63	0.6	0.7	<.1	0.3	78.3	78.6	51.6	58.8	65.3	0.0	64.9
Stone	7,407	99.0	<.1	0.1	0.5	0.0	0.3	64	4	67	70	0.4	0.5	<.1	0.2	75.8	76.0	25.0	45.0	75.5	0.0	47.6
Union	33,905	72.4	26.8	0.2	0.2	<.1	0.5	13	58	18	42	2.0	1.7	3.8	1.3	72.6	76.0	64.7	72.4	77.3	100.0	70.3

Table B. – 1990 Voting Age Population (VAP) by Race and Ethnic Origin (cont)

County	Total Voting Age Population	Percent of total VAP Non-Hispanic White	Black	Asian and Pacific Islander	Native American	Other	Hispanic	Rank Percent of total VAP Total	Non-Hispanic White	Black	Hispanic	Percent contribution to state VAP Total	Non-Hispanic White	Black	Hispanic	VAP percent of total population Total	Non-Hispanic White	Black	Asian and Pacific Islander	Native American	Other	Hispanic
Van Buren	10,877	98.7	0.3	0.1	0.4	0.0	0.4	48	12	57	53	0.6	0.7	<.1	0.4	77.6	78.0	82.9	73.7	61.8	0.0	44.9
Washington	85,369	95.4	1.4	0.9	1.2	<.1	1.1	2	34	51	11	4.9	5.6	0.5	7.7	75.3	75.6	73.2	78.3	68.3	41.7	62.3
White	40,977	95.9	2.9	0.2	0.4	<.1	0.6	10	33	43	28	2.4	2.7	0.5	1.9	74.9	75.2	68.9	84.6	75.2	42.9	65.1
Woodruff	6,777	72.1	27.5	<.1	0.2	0.0	0.2	69	59	16	75	0.4	0.3	0.8	<.1	71.2	75.2	62.4	45.5	84.6	0.0	70.6
Yell	13,203	96.5	1.8	0.4	0.4	<.1	0.9	40	27	47	15	0.8	0.9	<.1	0.9	74.3	74.7	64.3	65.8	79.7	16.7	64.4
ARKANSAS	**1,729,594**	**84.6**	**13.7**	**0.5**	**0.5**	**<.1**	**0.7**					**100.0**	**100.0**	**100.0**	**100.0**	**73.6**	**75.7**	**63.5**	**68.1**	**71.4**	**46.6**	**62.5**
CONGRESSIONAL																						
District 1	425,369	84.1	14.8	0.3	0.3	<.1	0.5	4	2	3	4	24.6	24.4	26.6	17.9	72.3	75.0	60.0	73.3	75.4	48.6	61.0
District 2	434,184	83.2	15.2	0.6	0.4	<.1	0.7	2	3	2	2	25.1	24.7	27.8	24.4	73.9	76.2	63.8	70.3	75.6	34.8	64.1
District 3	440,403	95.8	1.4	0.8	1.0	<.1	1.0	1	1	4	1	25.5	28.8	2.7	33.7	74.7	75.2	66.4	64.8	68.3	52.8	62.0
District 4	429,638	75.0	23.7	0.2	0.4	<.1	0.7	3	4	1	3	24.8	22.0	42.9	24.0	73.4	76.4	65.5	69.5	73.6	55.0	63.0

Table C. — Voter Participation: November 3, 1992, General Election

County	Estimated Voting Age Population (VAP) 1992	Voter registration (REG) Total	% contribution to state REG	% of 1992 VAP	Rank by % of 1992 VAP	Highest office Actual	Highest office Total	Office	% of 1992 VAP	Maximum vote Total	% contribution to state turnout	% of REG	Rank by % of REG	% of 1992 VAP	Rank by % 1992 VAP	Pres-ident	Sen-ator	Gov-ernor	Repre-sent-ative
Arkansas	15,610	10,650	0.8	68.2	66	-	7,980	P	51.1	7,980	0.8	74.9	24	51.1	63	0.0	13.3	-	19.1
Ashley	17,468	13,105	1.0	75.0	42	-	9,567	P	54.8	9,567	1.0	73.0	41	54.8	43	0.0	10.1	-	13.4
Baxter	26,130	21,472	1.6	82.2	24	-	15,732	S	60.2	15,732	1.6	73.3	38	60.2	15	0.0	4.8	-	13.2
Benton	78,288	55,984	4.2	71.5	53	-	43,541	S	55.6	43,541	4.5	77.8	5	55.6	35	0.6	0.0	-	0.5
Boone	21,950	18,674	1.4	85.1	19	-	14,437	P	65.8	14,437	1.5	77.3	6	65.8	4	0.0	7.6	-	8.1
Bradley	8,598	6,542	0.5	76.1	39	-	4,897	S	57.0	4,897	0.5	74.9	25	57.0	26	1.2	0.0	-	2.7
Calhoun	4,297	3,914	0.3	91.1	6	-	2,713	S	63.1	2,713	0.3	69.3	60	63.1	9	0.4	0.0	-	3.0
Carroll	14,898	11,784	0.9	79.1	28	-	8,878	S	59.6	8,878	0.9	75.3	17	59.6	18	0.2	0.0	-	1.5
Chicot	10,626	8,170	0.6	76.9	33	-	5,155	S	48.5	5,155	0.5	63.1	71	48.5	72	1.1	0.0	-	0.4
Clark	15,925	11,783	0.9	74.0	46	-	8,964	S	56.3	8,964	0.9	76.1	12	56.3	33	0.5	0.0	-	3.2
Clay	13,688	9,952	0.8	72.7	48	-	7,080	P	51.7	7,080	0.7	71.1	52	51.7	59	0.0	1.0	-	2.4
Cleburne	15,913	12,907	1.0	81.1	26	-	10,098	S	63.5	10,098	1.1	78.2	2	63.5	8	1.2	0.0	-	1.7
Cleveland	5,837	5,115	0.4	87.6	11	-	3,450	S	59.1	3,450	0.4	67.4	64	59.1	21	2.1	0.0	-	3.0
Columbia	18,890	12,884	1.0	68.2	67	-	9,819	P	52.0	9,819	0.9	76.2	11	52.0	58	0.0	10.1	-	18.1
Conway	14,123	12,882	1.0	91.2	5	-	8,481	P	60.1	8,481	0.9	65.8	67	60.1	16	0.0	1.8	-	5.9
Craighead	52,889	34,014	2.6	64.3	74	-	25,596	P	48.4	25,596	2.7	75.3	19	48.4	73	0.0	4.6	-	8.7
Crawford	31,975	21,350	1.6	66.8	71	-	16,165	P	50.6	16,165	1.7	75.7	15	50.6	65	0.0	2.0	-	2.0
Crittenden	34,855	25,110	1.9	72.0	52	-	17,108	P	49.1	17,108	1.8	68.1	62	49.1	70	0.0	16.1	-	17.5
Cross	13,596	9,445	0.7	69.5	63	-	6,986	P	51.4	6,986	0.7	74.0	34	51.4	62	0.0	1.5	-	0.3
Dallas	7,061	6,057	0.5	85.8	16	-	4,179	S	59.2	4,179	0.4	69.0	61	59.2	19	6.1	0.0	-	6.2
Desha	11,350	8,080	0.6	71.2	57	-	5,621	P	49.5	5,621	0.6	69.6	59	49.5	69	0.0	6.4	-	17.5
Drew	12,575	8,975	0.7	71.4	55	-	6,298	P	50.1	6,298	0.7	70.2	56	50.1	66	0.0	0.9	-	1.6
Faulkner	47,450	33,860	2.6	71.4	56	-	25,215	P	53.1	25,215	2.6	74.5	28	53.1	50	0.0	4.6	-	15.3
Franklin	11,250	10,210	0.8	90.8	7	-	6,739	S	59.9	6,739	0.7	66.0	66	59.9	17	0.0	0.0	-	0.4
Fulton	7,786	7,631	0.6	98.0	2	-	4,736	P	60.8	4,736	0.5	62.1	72	60.8	13	0.0	2.1	-	3.3
Garland	58,600	48,900	3.7	83.4	21	-	35,995	P	61.4	35,995	3.8	73.6	37	61.4	10	0.0	13.4	-	17.0
Grant	10,625	8,122	0.6	76.4	36	-	6,230	S	58.6	6,230	0.7	76.7	7	58.6	23	0.5	0.0	-	1.9
Greene	24,334	16,962	1.3	69.7	62	-	12,764	P	52.5	12,764	1.3	75.3	20	52.5	54	3.5	0.0	-	1.1
Hempstead	15,674	12,005	0.9	76.6	35	-	8,922	P	56.9	8,922	0.9	74.3	30	56.9	27	0.0	2.2	-	4.5
Hot Spring	19,598	15,266	1.2	77.9	30	-	11,290	S	57.6	11,290	1.2	74.0	35	57.6	24	6.0	0.0	-	3.2
Howard	10,022	6,697	0.5	66.8	70	-	4,975	P	49.6	4,975	0.5	74.3	32	49.6	67	0.0	4.5	-	7.8
Independence	23,621	16,588	1.3	70.2	58	-	12,935	S	54.8	12,935	1.4	78.0	3	54.8	44	0.7	0.0	-	1.5
Izard	9,171	7,567	0.6	82.5	23	-	5,628	S	61.4	5,628	0.6	74.4	29	61.4	11	0.7	0.0	-	2.2
Jackson	13,886	10,594	0.8	76.3	38	-	7,524	S	54.2	7,524	0.8	71.0	53	54.2	47	0.0	0.4	-	2.8
Jefferson	61,372	44,526	3.4	72.6	49	-	31,692	P	51.6	31,692	3.3	71.2	51	51.6	61	0.0	7.7	-	15.5
Johnson	14,037	10,397	0.8	74.1	45	-	7,747	S	55.2	7,747	0.8	74.5	27	55.2	38	2.2	0.0	-	1.8
Lafayette	7,041	5,257	0.4	74.7	44	-	3,979	P	56.5	3,979	0.4	75.7	16	56.5	29	0.0	0.6	-	2.6
Lawrence	13,107	9,553	0.7	72.9	47	-	6,929	P	52.9	6,929	0.7	72.5	43	52.9	51	0.0	1.1	-	2.9
Lee	8,607	7,809	0.6	90.7	8	-	5,066	P	58.9	5,066	0.5	64.9	69	58.9	22	0.0	1.4	-	2.8
Lincoln	10,720	6,122	0.5	57.1	75	-	4,347	P	40.6	4,347	0.5	71.0	54	40.6	74	0.0	0.4	-	1.9
Little River	10,273	7,938	0.6	77.3	32	-	5,718	P	55.7	5,718	0.6	72.0	46	55.7	34	0.0	0.7	-	2.5
Logan	15,402	11,651	0.9	75.6	40	-	8,687	P	56.4	8,687	0.9	74.6	26	56.4	31	0.0	2.2	-	4.0
Lonoke	29,350	19,225	1.5	65.5	73	-	15,824	P	53.9	15,824	1.7	82.3	1	53.9	48	0.0	1.3	-	1.5
Madison	8,726	7,328	0.6	84.0	20	-	5,279	C	60.5	5,279	0.6	72.0	45	60.5	14	0.0	0.3	-	0.0
Marion	9,592	8,293	0.6	86.5	14	-	6,245	P	65.1	6,245	0.7	75.3	18	65.1	6	0.0	13.1	-	14.4
Miller	28,176	19,543	1.5	69.4	64	-	14,663	S	52.0	14,663	1.5	75.0	22	52.0	57	0.3	0.0	-	1.5
Mississippi	40,153	26,675	2.0	66.4	72	-	16,089	C	40.1	16,089	1.7	60.3	73	40.1	75	0.8	14.2	-	0.0
Monroe	7,797	5,959	0.5	76.4	37	-	4,305	S	55.2	4,305	0.4	72.2	44	55.2	37	0.8	0.0	-	2.8
Montgomery	6,139	5,252	0.4	85.6	17	-	3,745	S	61.0	3,745	0.4	71.3	50	61.0	12	0.9	0.0	-	2.9
Nevada	7,386	6,827	0.5	92.4	4	-	4,058	S	54.9	4,058	0.4	59.4	74	54.9	42	2.7	0.0	-	0.6
Newton	5,657	5,775	0.4	102.1	1	-	4,144	P	73.3	4,144	0.4	71.8	48	73.3	1	0.0	2.5	-	5.8
Ouachita	22,758	19,550	1.5	85.9	15	-	12,523	S	55.0	12,523	1.3	64.1	70	55.0	40	0.9	0.0	-	2.6
Perry	6,210	5,401	0.4	87.0	13	-	3,504	P	56.4	3,504	0.4	64.9	68	56.4	30	0.0	1.0	-	3.7
Phillips	18,715	16,732	1.3	89.4	9	-	9,837	P	52.6	9,837	1.0	58.8	75	52.6	53	0.0	4.2	-	9.9
Pike	7,548	6,014	0.5	79.7	27	-	4,254	S	56.4	4,254	0.4	70.7	55	56.4	32	0.5	0.0	-	3.5
Poinsett	17,901	12,520	1.0	69.9	60	-	8,740	S	48.8	8,740	0.9	69.8	57	48.8	71	1.9	0.0	-	0.4
Polk	13,155	9,905	0.8	75.3	41	-	7,232	S	55.0	7,232	0.8	73.0	40	55.0	41	0.2	0.0	-	0.9
Pope	35,412	24,173	1.8	68.3	65	-	18,845	S	53.2	18,845	2.0	78.0	4	53.2	49	5.2	0.0	-	2.2
Prairie	7,054	5,418	0.4	76.8	34	-	4,025	S	57.1	4,025	0.4	74.3	31	57.1	25	1.7	0.0	-	2.8
Pulaski	262,564	196,596	14.9	74.9	43	-	136,957	P	52.2	136,957	14.3	69.7	58	52.2	56	0.0	2.7	-	15.0
Randolph	12,470	8,426	0.6	67.6	69	-	6,314	P	50.6	6,314	0.7	74.9	23	50.6	64	0.0	5.0	-	6.4
St. Francis	19,307	16,040	1.2	83.1	22	-	10,635	P	55.1	10,635	1.1	66.3	65	55.1	39	0.0	1.1	-	2.7
Saline	50,135	36,252	2.8	72.3	50	-	27,688	S	55.2	27,688	2.9	76.4	10	55.2	36	7.3	0.0	-	3.8
Scott	7,786	6,394	0.5	82.1	25	-	4,603	C	59.1	4,603	0.5	72.0	47	59.1	20	0.9	1.0	-	0.0
Searcy	5,843	5,455	0.4	93.4	3	-	3,984	P	68.2	3,984	0.4	73.0	39	68.2	2	0.0	8.2	-	23.3
Sebastian	75,259	52,500	4.0	69.8	61	-	39,764	C	52.8	39,764	4.2	75.7	14	52.8	52	0.3	9.8	-	0.0
Sevier	10,158	6,926	0.5	68.2	68	-	5,036	S	49.6	5,036	0.5	72.7	42	49.6	68	0.5	0.0	-	5.7
Sharp	11,172	9,550	0.7	85.5	18	-	7,246	S	64.9	7,246	0.8	75.9	13	64.9	7	0.7	0.0	-	1.0
Stone	7,666	6,789	0.5	88.6	10	-	5,039	P	65.7	5,039	0.5	74.2	33	65.7	5	0.0	22.5	-	4.1
Union	34,254	24,734	1.9	72.2	51	-	18,580	P	54.2	18,580	1.9	75.1	21	54.2	46	0.0	5.2	-	10.7

[1] Percent drop-off is zero for any office used as highest office turnout.

Table C. — **Voter Participation: November 3, 1992, General Election (cont)**

County	Estimated Voting Age Population (VAP) 1992	Voter registration (REG)					Voter turnout												
							Highest office			Maximum vote							Percent drop-off, by office[1]			
		Total	% contribution to state REG	% of 1992 VAP	Rank by % of 1992 VAP	Actual	Total	Office	% of 1992 VAP	Total	% contribution to state turnout	% of REG	Rank by % of REG	% of 1992 VAP	Rank by % 1992 VAP	President	Senator	Governor	Representative
Van Buren	11,072	9,630	0.7	87.0	12	-	7,361	P	66.5	7,361	0.8	76.4	9	66.5	3	0.0	2.3	-	5.1
Washington....................	87,538	62,508	4.7	71.4	54	-	47,880	P	54.7	47,880	5.0	76.6	8	54.7	45	0.0	0.7	-	0.8
White............................	41,719	29,195	2.2	70.0	59	-	21,563	P	51.7	21,563	2.3	73.9	36	51.7	60	0.0	11.2	-	13.6
Woodruff......................	6,668	5,174	0.4	77.6	31	-	3,495	P	52.4	3,495	0.4	67.5	63	52.4	55	0.0	12.8	-	3.7
Yell	13,542	10,681	0.8	78.9	29	-	7,658	S	56.6	7,658	0.8	71.7	49	56.6	28	0.2	0.0	-	1.2
ARKANSAS²	**1,768,000**	**1,317,944**	**100.0**	**74.5**		**-**	**956,978**		**54.1**	**956,978**	**100.0**	**72.6**		**54.1**		**0.7**	**3.9**	**-**	**7.2**

¹Percent drop-off is zero for any office used as highest office turnout. ²Arkansas does not report voter registration by political party affiliation, but does report registration by race. State voter registration by race as of May 1, 1992, is 1,944,744 (82.7%) for white, 373,912 (15.9%) for black, and 32,069 (1.4%) for other.

Table E. — Vote for President: November 3, 1992, General Election

County	Total	Clinton (DEM)	Bush (REP)	Perot (IND)	Other	Plurality Total	Party	DEM	REP	IND	Other	Rank DEM	Rank REP	Rank IND	Total	DEM	REP	IND	DEM	REP
Arkansas	7,980	4,709	2,594	639	38	2,115	D	59.0	32.5	8.0	0.5	27	42	64	0.8	0.9	0.8	0.6	64.5	35.5
Ashley	9,567	5,876	2,686	931	74	3,190	D	61.4	28.1	9.7	0.8	15	60	46	1.0	1.2	0.8	0.9	68.6	31.4
Baxter	15,732	6,991	5,640	2,938	163	1,351	D	44.4	35.9	18.7	1.0	65	27	2	1.7	1.4	1.7	3.0	55.3	44.7
Benton	43,279	15,774	21,126	6,128	251	5,352	R	36.4	48.8	14.2	0.6	75	1	13	4.6	3.1	6.3	6.2	42.7	57.3
Boone	14,437	6,128	6,094	2,079	136	34	D	42.4	42.2	14.4	0.9	71	8	12	1.5	1.2	1.8	2.1	50.1	49.9
Bradley	4,837	2,954	1,482	391	10	1,472	D	61.1	30.6	8.1	0.2	19	52	62	0.5	0.6	0.4	0.4	66.6	33.4
Calhoun	2,702	1,389	1,047	257	9	342	D	51.4	38.7	9.5	0.3	49	16	49	0.3	0.3	0.3	0.3	57.0	43.0
Carroll	8,857	3,769	3,535	1,500	53	234	D	42.6	39.9	16.9	0.6	70	10	4	0.9	0.7	1.0	1.5	51.6	48.4
Chicot	5,099	3,504	1,242	347	6	2,262	D	68.7	24.4	6.8	0.1	3	71	68	0.5	0.7	0.4	0.4	73.8	26.2
Clark	8,922	5,767	2,403	714	38	3,364	D	64.6	26.9	8.0	0.4	9	64	65	0.9	1.1	0.7	0.7	70.6	29.4
Clay	7,080	4,848	1,647	568	17	3,201	D	68.5	23.3	8.0	0.2	4	73	63	0.7	1.0	0.5	0.6	74.6	25.4
Cleburne	9,980	5,090	3,580	1,263	47	1,510	D	51.0	35.9	12.7	0.5	53	26	22	1.0	1.0	1.1	1.3	58.7	41.3
Cleveland	3,378	1,893	1,127	337	21	766	D	56.0	33.4	10.0	0.6	35	36	42	0.4	0.4	0.3	0.3	62.7	37.3
Columbia	9,819	4,747	3,702	1,090	280	1,045	D	48.3	37.7	11.1	2.9	58	18	35	1.0	0.9	1.1	1.1	56.2	43.8
Conway	8,481	4,898	2,719	803	61	2,179	D	57.8	32.1	9.5	0.7	31	45	50	0.9	1.0	0.8	0.8	64.3	35.7
Craighead	25,596	13,931	9,104	2,274	287	4,827	D	54.4	35.6	8.9	1.1	39	29	57	2.7	2.8	2.7	2.3	60.5	39.5
Crawford	16,165	6,656	6,882	2,442	185	226	R	41.2	42.6	15.1	1.1	74	4	9	1.7	1.3	2.0	2.5	49.2	50.8
Crittenden	17,108	9,683	5,910	848	667	3,773	D	56.6	34.5	5.0	3.9	34	34	75	1.8	1.9	1.8	0.9	62.1	37.9
Cross	6,986	4,058	2,303	602	23	1,755	D	58.1	33.0	8.6	0.3	29	39	60	0.7	0.8	0.7	0.6	63.8	36.2
Dallas	3,925	2,107	1,458	345	15	649	D	53.7	37.1	8.8	0.4	41	22	59	0.4	0.4	0.4	0.3	59.1	40.9
Desha	5,621	3,815	1,279	392	135	2,536	D	67.9	22.8	7.0	2.4	5	74	67	0.6	0.8	0.4	0.4	74.9	25.1
Drew	6,298	3,748	1,938	596	16	1,810	D	59.5	30.8	9.5	0.3	25	50	51	0.7	0.7	0.6	0.6	65.9	34.1
Faulkner	25,215	13,000	9,491	2,437	287	3,509	D	51.6	37.6	9.7	1.1	47	19	47	2.7	2.6	2.8	2.5	57.8	42.2
Franklin	6,736	3,217	2,495	987	37	722	D	47.8	37.0	14.7	0.5	60	23	11	0.7	0.6	0.7	1.0	56.3	43.7
Fulton	4,736	2,827	1,258	631	20	1,569	D	59.7	26.6	13.3	0.4	24	66	14	0.5	0.6	0.4	0.6	69.2	30.8
Garland	35,995	18,811	12,886	3,475	823	5,925	D	52.3	35.8	9.7	2.3	43	28	48	3.8	3.7	3.8	3.5	59.3	40.7
Grant	6,198	3,190	2,272	702	34	918	D	51.5	36.7	11.3	0.5	48	24	31	0.7	0.6	0.7	0.7	58.4	41.6
Greene	12,322	7,541	3,510	1,213	58	4,031	D	61.2	28.5	9.8	0.5	17	58	44	1.3	1.5	1.0	1.2	68.2	31.8
Hempstead	8,922	5,476	2,387	1,022	37	3,089	D	61.4	26.8	11.5	0.4	16	65	28	0.9	1.1	0.7	1.0	69.6	30.4
Hot Spring	10,616	6,308	3,036	1,209	63	3,272	D	59.4	28.6	11.4	0.6	26	57	29	1.1	1.2	0.9	1.2	67.5	32.5
Howard	4,975	2,764	1,728	466	17	1,036	D	55.6	34.7	9.4	0.3	36	32	52	0.5	0.5	0.5	0.5	61.5	38.5
Independence	12,840	7,083	4,232	1,444	81	2,851	D	55.2	33.0	11.2	0.6	37	40	32	1.4	1.4	1.3	1.5	62.6	37.4
Izard	5,588	3,419	1,532	606	31	1,887	D	61.2	27.4	10.8	0.6	18	62	39	0.6	0.7	0.5	0.6	69.1	30.9
Jackson	7,524	4,944	1,864	673	43	3,080	D	65.7	24.8	8.9	0.6	7	70	56	0.8	1.0	0.6	0.7	72.6	27.4
Jefferson	31,692	21,819	7,525	2,067	281	14,294	D	68.8	23.7	6.5	0.9	2	74	64	3.3	4.3	2.2	2.1	74.4	25.6
Johnson	7,578	3,951	2,563	1,013	51	1,388	D	52.1	33.8	13.4	0.7	44	35	17	0.8	0.8	0.8	1.0	60.7	39.3
Lafayette	3,979	2,273	1,188	504	14	1,085	D	57.1	29.9	12.7	0.4	32	54	21	0.4	0.4	0.4	0.5	65.7	34.3
Lawrence	6,929	4,146	2,124	636	23	2,022	D	59.8	30.7	9.2	0.3	21	51	53	0.7	0.8	0.6	0.6	66.1	33.9
Lee	5,066	3,436	1,293	308	29	2,143	D	67.8	25.5	6.1	0.6	6	69	74	0.5	0.7	0.4	0.3	72.7	27.3
Lincoln	4,347	2,805	1,142	390	10	1,663	D	64.5	26.3	9.0	0.2	10	67	55	0.5	0.6	0.3	0.4	71.1	28.9
Little River	5,718	3,327	1,483	890	18	1,844	D	58.2	25.9	15.6	0.3	28	68	5	0.6	0.7	0.4	0.9	69.2	30.8
Logan	8,687	3,995	3,408	1,220	64	587	D	46.0	39.2	14.0	0.7	63	15	14	0.9	0.8	1.0	1.2	54.0	46.0
Lonoke	15,824	7,963	6,253	1,554	54	1,710	D	50.3	39.5	9.8	0.3	54	12	45	1.7	1.6	1.9	1.6	56.0	44.0
Madison	5,277	2,415	2,238	598	26	177	D	45.8	42.4	11.3	0.5	64	5	30	0.6	0.5	0.7	0.6	51.9	48.1
Marion	6,245	2,757	2,023	1,327	138	734	D	44.1	32.4	21.2	2.2	66	44	1	0.7	0.5	0.6	1.3	57.7	42.3
Miller	14,623	7,050	5,273	2,249	51	1,777	D	48.2	36.1	15.4	0.3	59	25	7	1.5	1.4	1.6	2.3	57.2	42.8
Mississippi	15,962	10,046	4,697	981	238	5,349	D	62.9	29.4	6.1	1.5	11	55	73	1.7	2.0	1.4	1.0	68.1	31.9
Monroe	4,272	2,578	1,324	355	15	1,254	D	60.3	31.0	8.3	0.4	20	47	61	0.4	0.5	0.4	0.4	66.1	33.9
Montgomery	3,712	1,904	1,205	576	27	699	D	51.3	32.5	15.5	0.7	50	43	6	0.4	0.4	0.4	0.6	61.2	38.8
Nevada	3,948	2,242	1,217	455	34	1,025	D	56.8	30.8	11.5	0.9	33	49	27	0.4	0.4	0.4	0.5	64.8	35.2
Newton	4,144	1,765	1,730	608	41	35	D	42.6	41.7	14.7	1.0	69	9	10	0.4	0.3	0.5	0.6	50.5	49.5
Ouachita	12,415	7,411	3,711	1,238	55	3,700	D	59.7	29.9	10.0	0.4	23	53	43	1.3	1.5	1.1	1.2	66.6	33.4
Perry	3,504	1,906	1,162	412	24	744	D	54.4	33.2	11.8	0.7	40	38	26	0.4	0.4	0.3	0.4	62.1	37.9
Phillips	9,837	6,456	2,695	634	52	3,761	D	65.6	27.4	6.4	0.5	8	63	71	1.0	1.3	0.8	0.6	70.5	29.5
Pike	4,232	2,168	1,577	472	15	591	D	51.2	37.3	11.2	0.4	51	20	33	0.4	0.4	0.5	0.5	57.9	42.1
Poinsett	8,571	5,341	2,425	761	44	2,916	D	62.3	28.3	8.9	0.5	12	59	58	0.9	1.1	0.7	0.8	68.8	31.2
Polk	7,217	3,162	2,757	1,225	73	405	D	43.8	38.2	17.0	1.0	67	17	3	0.8	0.6	0.8	1.2	53.4	46.6
Pope	17,862	7,704	8,056	1,989	113	352	R	43.1	45.1	11.1	0.6	68	2	34	1.9	1.5	2.4	2.0	48.9	51.1
Prairie	3,956	2,366	1,154	434	2	1,212	D	59.8	29.2	11.0	< .1	22	56	38	0.4	0.5	0.3	0.4	67.2	32.8
Pulaski	136,957	79,482	47,789	8,751	935	31,693	D	58.0	34.9	6.4	0.7	30	31	72	14.4	15.7	14.2	8.8	62.5	37.5
Randolph	6,314	3,921	1,766	578	49	2,155	D	62.1	28.0	9.2	0.8	13	61	54	0.7	0.8	0.5	0.6	68.9	31.1
St. Francis	10,635	6,548	3,289	766	32	3,259	D	61.6	30.9	7.2	0.3	14	48	66	1.1	1.3	1.0	0.8	66.6	33.4
Saline	25,661	12,671	10,105	2,751	134	2,566	D	49.4	39.4	10.7	0.5	55	13	40	2.7	2.5	3.0	2.8	55.6	44.4
Scott	4,562	2,228	1,695	610	29	533	D	48.8	37.2	13.4	0.6	56	21	16	0.5	0.4	0.5	0.6	56.8	43.2
Searcy	3,984	1,679	1,772	503	30	93	R	42.1	44.5	12.6	0.8	72	3	23	0.4	0.3	0.5	0.5	48.7	51.3
Sebastian	39,659	16,570	16,817	6,023	249	247	R	41.8	42.4	15.2	0.6	73	6	8	4.2	3.3	5.0	6.1	49.6	50.4
Sevier	5,011	2,558	1,592	643	218	966	D	51.0	31.8	12.8	4.4	52	46	19	0.5	0.5	0.5	0.6	61.6	38.4
Sharp	7,196	3,761	2,486	921	28	1,275	D	52.3	34.5	12.8	0.4	42	33	20	0.8	0.7	0.7	0.9	60.2	39.8
Stone	5,039	2,622	1,672	697	48	950	D	52.0	33.2	13.8	1.0	45	37	15	0.5	0.5	0.5	0.7	61.1	38.9
Union	18,580	8,786	7,305	1,919	570	1,481	D	47.3	39.3	10.3	3.1	61	14	41	2.0	1.7	2.2	1.9	54.6	45.4

County	All candidates					Plurality		Percent of total vote				Rank			Percent contribution to state vote				Major party Percent of vote	
	Total	Clinton (DEM)	Bush (REP)	Perot (IND)	Other	Total	Party	DEM	REP	IND	Other	DEM	REP	IND	Total	DEM	REP	IND	DEM	REP
Van Buren	7,361	3,819	2,612	888	42	1,207	D	51.9	35.5	12.1	0.6	46	30	25	0.8	0.8	0.8	0.9	59.4	40.6
Washington	47,880	22,029	20,292	5,304	255	1,737	D	46.0	42.4	11.1	0.5	62	7	36	5.0	4.4	6.0	5.4	52.1	47.9
White	21,563	10,494	8,538	2,366	165	1,956	D	48.7	39.6	11.0	0.8	57	11	37	2.3	2.1	2.5	2.4	55.1	44.9
Woodruff	3,495	2,589	676	227	3	1,913	D	74.1	19.3	6.5	<.1	1	75	70	0.4	0.5	0.2	0.2	79.3	20.7
Yell	7,643	4,165	2,506	940	32	1,659	D	54.5	32.8	12.3	0.4	38	41	24	0.8	0.8	0.7	0.9	62.4	37.6
ARKANSAS	**950,653**	**505,823**	**337,324**	**99,132**	**8,374**	**168,499**	**D**	**53.2**	**35.5**	**10.4**	**0.9**				**100.0**	**100.0**	**100.0**	**100.0**	**60.0**	**40.0**

Table F. — Vote for U.S. Senator: November 3, 1992, General Election

County	Total	Bumpers (DEM)	Huckabee (REP)		Plurality Total	Party	DEM	REP		Rank DEM	Rank REP		Total	DEM	REP	
Arkansas	6,922	5,063	1,859	-	3,204	D	73.1	26.9	-	10	66	-	0.8	0.9	0.5	-
Ashley	8,604	5,418	3,186	-	2,232	D	63.0	37.0	-	35	41	-	0.9	1.0	0.9	-
Baxter	14,978	7,907	7,071	-	836	D	52.8	47.2	-	62	14	-	1.6	1.4	1.9	-
Benton	43,541	18,944	24,597	-	5,653	R	43.5	56.5	-	75	1	-	4.7	3.4	6.7	-
Boone	13,335	6,971	6,364	-	607	D	52.3	47.7	-	64	12	-	1.4	1.3	1.7	-
Bradley	4,897	3,364	1,533	-	1,831	D	68.7	31.3	-	21	55	-	0.5	0.6	0.4	-
Calhoun	2,713	1,658	1,055	-	603	D	61.1	38.9	-	42	34	-	0.3	0.3	0.3	-
Carroll	8,878	4,441	4,437	-	4	D	50.0	50.0	-	69	7	-	1.0	0.8	1.2	-
Chicot	5,155	3,927	1,228	-	2,699	D	76.2	23.8	-	4	72	-	0.6	0.7	0.3	-
Clark	8,964	6,312	2,652	-	3,660	D	70.4	29.6	-	15	61	-	1.0	1.1	0.7	-
Clay	7,009	5,285	1,724	-	3,561	D	75.4	24.6	-	6	70	-	0.8	1.0	0.5	-
Cleburne	10,098	6,231	3,867	-	2,364	D	61.7	38.3	-	39	37	-	1.1	1.1	1.1	-
Cleveland	3,450	2,286	1,164	-	1,122	D	66.3	33.7	-	27	49	-	0.4	0.4	0.3	-
Columbia	8,828	3,976	4,852	-	876	R	45.0	55.0	-	74	2	-	1.0	0.7	1.3	-
Conway	8,332	5,418	2,914	-	2,504	D	65.0	35.0	-	31	45	-	0.9	1.0	0.8	-
Craighead	24,408	15,291	9,117	-	6,174	D	62.6	37.4	-	36	40	-	2.7	2.8	2.5	-
Crawford	15,844	7,473	8,371	-	898	R	47.2	52.8	-	71	5	-	1.7	1.3	2.3	-
Crittenden	14,355	8,759	5,596	-	3,163	D	61.0	39.0	-	43	33	-	1.6	1.6	1.5	-
Cross	6,880	4,612	2,268	-	2,344	D	67.0	33.0	-	26	50	-	0.7	0.8	0.6	-
Dallas	4,179	2,828	1,351	-	1,477	D	67.7	32.3	-	25	51	-	0.5	0.5	0.4	-
Desha	5,263	3,986	1,277	-	2,709	D	75.7	24.3	-	5	71	-	0.6	0.7	0.3	-
Drew	6,241	4,361	1,880	-	2,481	D	69.9	30.1	-	16	60	-	0.7	0.8	0.5	-
Faulkner	24,064	14,463	9,601	-	4,862	D	60.1	39.9	-	45	31	-	2.6	2.6	2.6	-
Franklin	6,739	4,000	2,739	-	1,261	D	59.4	40.6	-	47	29	-	0.7	0.7	0.7	-
Fulton	4,638	3,186	1,452	-	1,734	D	68.7	31.3	-	22	54	-	0.5	0.6	0.4	-
Garland	31,163	16,253	14,910	-	1,343	D	52.2	47.8	-	66	10	-	3.4	2.9	4.1	-
Grant	6,230	3,868	2,362	-	1,506	D	62.1	37.9	-	38	38	-	0.7	0.7	0.6	-
Greene	12,764	8,904	3,860	-	5,044	D	69.8	30.2	-	18	58	-	1.4	1.6	1.1	-
Hempstead	8,727	4,557	4,170	-	387	D	52.2	47.8	-	65	11	-	0.9	0.8	1.1	-
Hot Spring	11,290	7,648	3,642	-	4,006	D	67.7	32.3	-	24	52	-	1.2	1.4	1.0	-
Howard	4,752	2,666	2,086	-	580	D	56.1	43.9	-	56	20	-	0.5	0.5	0.6	-
Independence	12,935	8,515	4,420	-	4,095	D	65.8	34.2	-	28	48	-	1.4	1.5	1.2	-
Izard	5,628	3,865	1,763	-	2,102	D	68.7	31.3	-	23	53	-	0.6	0.7	0.5	-
Jackson	7,495	5,575	1,920	-	3,655	D	74.4	25.6	-	8	68	-	0.8	1.0	0.5	-
Jefferson	29,248	20,880	8,368	-	12,512	D	71.4	28.6	-	13	63	-	3.2	3.8	2.3	-
Johnson	7,747	4,736	3,011	-	1,725	D	61.1	38.9	-	41	35	-	0.8	0.9	0.8	-
Lafayette	3,955	2,315	1,640	-	675	D	58.5	41.5	-	51	25	-	0.4	0.4	0.4	-
Lawrence	6,854	4,899	1,955	-	2,944	D	71.5	28.5	-	12	64	-	0.7	0.9	0.5	-
Lee	4,995	3,977	1,018	-	2,959	D	79.6	20.4	-	2	74	-	0.5	0.7	0.3	-
Lincoln	4,330	3,170	1,160	-	2,010	D	73.2	26.8	-	9	67	-	0.5	0.6	0.3	-
Little River	5,677	3,332	2,345	-	987	D	58.7	41.3	-	49	27	-	0.6	0.6	0.6	-
Logan	8,494	4,809	3,685	-	1,124	D	56.6	43.4	-	55	21	-	0.9	0.9	1.0	-
Lonoke	15,612	9,594	6,018	-	3,576	D	61.5	38.5	-	40	36	-	1.7	1.7	1.6	-
Madison	5,261	2,842	2,419	-	423	D	54.0	46.0	-	59	17	-	0.6	0.5	0.7	-
Marion	5,429	2,860	2,569	-	291	D	52.7	47.3	-	63	13	-	0.6	0.5	0.7	-
Miller	14,663	6,718	7,945	-	1,227	R	45.8	54.2	-	73	3	-	1.6	1.2	2.2	-
Mississippi	13,805	9,494	4,311	-	5,183	D	68.8	31.2	-	20	56	-	1.5	1.7	1.2	-
Monroe	4,305	3,216	1,089	-	2,127	D	74.7	25.3	-	7	69	-	0.5	0.6	0.3	-
Montgomery	3,745	2,223	1,522	-	701	D	59.4	40.6	-	46	30	-	0.4	0.4	0.4	-
Nevada	4,058	2,531	1,527	-	1,004	D	62.4	37.6	-	37	39	-	0.4	0.5	0.4	-
Newton	4,040	2,082	1,958	-	124	D	51.5	48.5	-	68	8	-	0.4	0.4	0.5	-
Ouachita	12,523	8,048	4,475	-	3,573	D	64.3	35.7	-	33	43	-	1.4	1.5	1.2	-
Perry	3,470	2,230	1,240	-	990	D	64.3	35.7	-	34	42	-	0.4	0.4	0.3	-
Phillips	9,426	7,276	2,150	-	5,126	D	77.2	22.8	-	3	73	-	1.0	1.3	0.6	-
Pike	4,254	2,424	1,830	-	594	D	57.0	43.0	-	54	22	-	0.5	0.4	0.5	-
Poinsett	8,740	6,178	2,562	-	3,616	D	70.7	29.3	-	14	62	-	1.0	1.1	0.7	-
Polk	7,232	3,519	3,713	-	194	R	48.7	51.3	-	70	6	-	0.8	0.6	1.0	-
Pope	18,845	9,816	9,029	-	787	D	52.1	47.9	-	67	9	-	2.0	1.8	2.5	-
Prairie	4,025	2,934	1,091	-	1,843	D	72.9	27.1	-	11	65	-	0.4	0.5	0.3	-
Pulaski	133,285	86,421	46,864	-	39,557	D	64.8	35.2	-	32	44	-	14.5	15.6	12.8	-
Randolph	6,001	4,188	1,813	-	2,375	D	69.8	30.2	-	17	59	-	0.7	0.8	0.5	-
St. Francis	10,516	7,282	3,234	-	4,048	D	69.2	30.8	-	19	57	-	1.1	1.3	0.9	-
Saline	27,688	16,214	11,474	-	4,740	D	58.6	41.4	-	50	26	-	3.0	2.9	3.1	-
Scott	4,558	2,482	2,076	-	406	D	54.5	45.5	-	58	18	-	0.5	0.4	0.6	-
Searcy	3,658	1,942	1,716	-	226	D	53.1	46.9	-	61	15	-	0.4	0.4	0.5	-
Sebastian	35,871	16,897	18,974	-	2,077	R	47.1	52.9	-	72	4	-	3.9	3.1	5.2	-
Sevier	5,036	2,927	2,109	-	818	D	58.1	41.9	-	52	24	-	0.5	0.5	0.6	-
Sharp	7,246	4,415	2,831	-	1,584	D	60.9	39.1	-	44	32	-	0.8	0.8	0.8	-
Stone	3,903	2,552	1,351	-	1,201	D	65.4	34.6	-	29	47	-	0.4	0.5	0.4	-
Union	17,611	9,373	8,238	-	1,135	D	53.2	46.8	-	60	16	-	1.9	1.7	2.2	-

Table F. — Vote for U.S. Senator: November 3, 1992, General Election (cont)

County	Total	Bumpers (DEM)	Huckabee (REP)		Plurality Total	Party	Percent of total vote DEM	REP		Rank DEM	Rank REP		Percent contribution to state vote Total	DEM	REP	
Van Buren	7,192	4,238	2,954	-	1,284	D	58.9	41.1	-	48	28	-	0.8	0.8	0.8	-
Washington	47,562	26,088	21,474	-	4,614	D	54.9	45.1	-	57	19	-	5.2	4.7	5.9	-
White	19,143	11,019	8,124	-	2,895	D	57.6	42.4	-	53	23	-	2.1	2.0	2.2	-
Woodruff	3,048	2,500	548	-	1,952	D	82.0	18.0	-	1	75	-	0.3	0.5	0.1	-
Yell	7,658	4,983	2,675	-	2,308	D	65.1	34.9	-	30	46	-	0.8	0.9	0.7	-
ARKANSAS	**920,008**	**553,635**	**366,373**	**-**	**187,262**	**D**	**60.2**	**39.8**	**-**				**100.0**	**100.0**	**100.0**	**-**

92 Arkansas

Congressional district and county	Total	Democrat (DEM)	Republican (REP)	Other	Plurality Total	Plurality Party	Percent of total vote DEM	REP	Other	Rank within district DEM	REP	Other	Percent contribution to district vote Total	DEM	REP	Other
District 1	214,176	149,558	64,618	-	84,940	D	69.8	30.2	-				100.0	100.0	100.0	-
Arkansas	6,455	4,748	1,707	-	3,041	D	73.6	26.4	-	8	18	-	3.0	3.2	2.6	-
Clay	6,908	5,102	1,806	-	3,296	D	73.9	26.1	-	6	20	-	3.2	3.4	2.8	-
Cleburne	9,927	6,989	2,938	-	4,051	D	70.4	29.6	-	16	10	-	4.6	4.7	4.5	-
Craighead	23,361	13,773	9,588	-	4,185	D	59.0	41.0	-	24	2	-	10.9	9.2	14.8	-
Crittenden	14,115	10,121	3,994	-	6,127	D	71.7	28.3	-	11	15	-	6.6	6.8	6.2	-
Cross	6,966	4,577	2,389	-	2,188	D	65.7	34.3	-	21	5	-	3.3	3.1	3.7	-
Fulton	4,578	3,283	1,295	-	1,988	D	71.7	28.3	-	10	16	-	2.1	2.2	2.0	-
Greene	12,626	8,483	4,143	-	4,340	D	67.2	32.8	-	18	8	-	5.9	5.7	6.4	-
Independence	12,747	8,558	4,189	-	4,369	D	67.1	32.9	-	19	7	-	6.0	5.7	6.5	-
Izard	5,507	3,881	1,626	-	2,255	D	70.5	29.5	-	15	11	-	2.6	2.6	2.5	-
Jackson	7,317	5,393	1,924	-	3,469	D	73.7	26.3	-	7	19	-	3.4	3.6	3.0	-
Lawrence	6,727	4,351	2,376	-	1,975	D	64.7	35.3	-	23	3	-	3.1	2.9	3.7	-
Lee	4,923	4,150	773	-	3,377	D	84.3	15.7	-	1	25	-	2.3	2.8	1.2	-
Lonoke	15,581	11,090	4,491	-	6,599	D	71.2	28.8	-	13	13	-	7.3	7.4	7.0	-
Mississippi	16,089	11,491	4,598	-	6,893	D	71.4	28.6	-	12	14	-	7.5	7.7	7.1	-
Monroe	4,184	3,197	987	-	2,210	D	76.4	23.6	-	5	21	-	2.0	2.1	1.5	-
Phillips	8,866	7,422	1,444	-	5,978	D	83.7	16.3	-	2	24	-	4.1	5.0	2.2	-
Poinsett	8,705	6,003	2,702	-	3,301	D	69.0	31.0	-	17	9	-	4.1	4.0	4.2	-
Prairie	3,914	3,014	900	-	2,114	D	77.0	23.0	-	4	22	-	1.8	2.0	1.4	-
Randolph	5,908	4,165	1,743	-	2,422	D	70.5	29.5	-	14	12	-	2.8	2.8	2.7	-
St. Francis	10,349	7,461	2,888	-	4,573	D	72.1	27.9	-	9	17	-	4.8	5.0	4.5	-
Searcy	3,056	1,769	1,287	-	482	D	57.9	42.1	-	25	1	-	1.4	1.2	2.0	-
Sharp	7,173	4,644	2,529	-	2,115	D	64.7	35.3	-	22	4	-	3.3	3.1	3.9	-
Stone	4,830	3,191	1,639	-	1,552	D	66.1	33.9	-	20	6	-	2.3	2.1	2.5	-
Woodruff	3,364	2,702	662	-	2,040	D	80.3	19.7	-	3	23	-	1.6	1.8	1.0	-
District 2	208,924	154,946	53,978	-	100,968	D	74.2	25.8	-				100.0	100.0	100.0	-
Conway	7,977	6,314	1,663	-	4,651	D	79.2	20.8	-	1	8	-	3.8	4.1	3.1	-
Faulkner	21,355	15,728	5,627	-	10,101	D	73.7	26.3	-	6	3	-	10.2	10.2	10.4	-
Perry	3,375	2,605	770	-	1,835	D	77.2	22.8	-	3	6	-	1.6	1.7	1.4	-
Pulaski	116,408	87,371	29,037	-	58,334	D	75.1	24.9	-	4	5	-	55.7	56.4	53.8	-
Saline	26,625	18,206	8,419	-	9,787	D	68.4	31.6	-	8	1	-	12.7	11.7	15.6	-
Van Buren	6,986	5,006	1,980	-	3,026	D	71.7	28.3	-	7	2	-	3.3	3.2	3.7	-
White	18,633	13,733	4,900	-	8,833	D	73.7	26.3	-	5	4	-	8.9	8.9	9.1	-
Yell	7,565	5,983	1,582	-	4,401	D	79.1	20.9	-	2	7	-	3.6	3.9	2.9	-
District 3	249,494	117,775	125,295	6,424	7,520	R	47.2	50.2	2.6				100.0	100.0	100.0	100.0
Baxter	13,650	6,504	6,416	730	88	D	47.6	47.0	5.3	12	8	2	5.5	5.5	5.1	11.4
Benton	43,337	16,131	26,101	1,105	9,970	R	37.2	60.2	2.5	16	1	9	17.4	13.7	20.8	17.2
Boone	13,271	6,120	6,793	358	673	R	46.1	51.2	2.7	15	2	7	5.3	5.2	5.4	5.6
Carroll	8,746	4,247	4,218	281	29	D	48.6	48.2	3.2	11	7	4	3.5	3.6	3.4	4.4
Crawford	15,843	7,419	7,968	456	549	R	46.8	50.3	2.9	14	4	5	6.4	6.3	6.4	7.1
Franklin	6,715	3,956	2,637	122	1,319	D	58.9	39.3	1.8	1	16	15	2.7	3.4	2.1	1.9
Johnson	7,611	4,322	3,103	186	1,219	D	56.8	40.8	2.4	3	14	10	3.1	3.7	2.5	2.9
Logan	8,336	4,381	3,732	223	649	D	52.6	44.8	2.7	5	12	8	3.3	3.7	3.0	3.5
Madison	5,279	2,815	2,372	92	443	D	53.3	44.9	1.7	4	11	16	2.1	2.4	1.9	1.4
Marion	5,348	2,623	2,410	315	213	D	49.0	45.1	5.9	8	10	1	2.1	2.2	1.9	4.9
Newton	3,905	2,014	1,760	131	254	D	51.6	45.1	3.4	7	9	3	1.6	1.7	1.4	2.0
Polk	7,168	3,761	3,206	201	555	D	52.5	44.7	2.8	6	13	6	2.9	3.2	2.6	3.1
Pope	18,425	8,954	9,021	450	67	R	48.6	49.0	2.4	10	6	11	7.4	7.6	7.2	7.0
Scott	4,603	2,645	1,865	93	780	D	57.5	40.5	2.0	2	15	12	1.8	2.2	1.5	1.4
Sebastian	39,764	18,740	20,225	799	1,485	R	47.1	50.9	2.0	13	3	13	15.9	15.9	16.1	12.4
Washington	47,493	23,143	23,468	882	325	R	48.7	49.4	1.9	9	5	14	19.0	19.7	18.7	13.7
District 4	215,927	102,918	113,009	-	10,091	R	47.7	52.3	-				100.0	100.0	100.0	-
Ashley	8,284	4,103	4,181	-	78	R	49.5	50.5	-	16	11	-	3.8	4.0	3.7	-
Bradley	4,767	2,228	2,539	-	311	R	46.7	53.3	-	20	7	-	2.2	2.2	2.2	-
Calhoun	2,632	1,168	1,464	-	296	R	44.4	55.6	-	22	5	-	1.2	1.1	1.3	-
Chicot	5,132	3,094	2,038	-	1,056	D	60.3	39.7	-	2	25	-	2.4	3.0	1.8	-
Clark	8,673	4,687	3,986	-	701	D	54.0	46.0	-	7	20	-	4.0	4.6	3.5	-
Cleveland	3,345	1,748	1,597	-	151	D	52.3	47.7	-	10	17	-	1.5	1.7	1.4	-
Columbia	8,037	3,186	4,851	-	1,665	R	39.6	60.4	-	24	3	-	3.7	3.1	4.3	-
Dallas	3,919	1,991	1,928	-	63	D	50.8	49.2	-	12	15	-	1.8	1.9	1.7	-
Desha	4,640	2,316	2,324	-	8	R	49.9	50.1	-	15	12	-	2.1	2.3	2.1	-
Drew	6,198	3,035	3,163	-	128	R	49.0	51.0	-	18	9	-	2.9	2.9	2.8	-
Garland	29,891	10,812	19,079	-	8,267	R	36.2	63.8	-	26	1	-	13.8	10.5	16.9	-
Grant	6,112	3,089	3,023	-	66	D	50.5	49.5	-	13	14	-	2.8	3.0	2.7	-
Hempstead	8,523	4,526	3,997	-	529	D	53.1	46.9	-	8	19	-	3.9	4.4	3.5	-
Hot Spring	10,924	5,934	4,990	-	944	D	54.3	45.7	-	5	22	-	5.1	5.8	4.4	-
Howard	4,588	2,037	2,551	-	514	R	44.4	55.6	-	21	6	-	2.1	2.0	2.3	-
Jefferson	26,777	13,174	13,603	-	429	R	49.2	50.8	-	17	10	-	12.4	12.8	12.0	-
Lafayette	3,877	2,103	1,774	-	329	D	54.2	45.8	-	6	21	-	1.8	2.0	1.6	-
Lincoln	4,266	2,378	1,888	-	490	D	55.7	44.3	-	3	24	-	2.0	2.3	1.7	-
Little River	5,576	3,385	2,191	-	1,194	D	60.7	39.3	-	1	26	-	2.6	3.3	1.9	-
Miller	14,444	7,218	7,226	-	8	R	50.0	50.0	-	14	13	-	6.7	7.0	6.4	-

Arkansas 93

Congressional district and county	Total	Democrat (DEM)	Republican (REP)	Other	Plurality		Percent of total vote				Rank within district			Percent contribution to district vote			
					Total	Party	DEM	REP	Other	DEM	REP	Other	Total	DEM	REP	Other
District 4 (cont)																
Montgomery	3,637	1,706	1,931	-	225	R	46.9	53.1	-	19	8	-	1.7	1.7	1.7	-
Nevada	4,032	2,229	1,803	-	426	D	55.3	44.7	-	4	23	-	1.9	2.2	1.6	-
Ouachita	12,201	6,381	5,820	-	561	D	52.3	47.7	-	9	18	-	5.7	6.2	5.2	-
Pike	4,103	1,792	2,311	-	519	R	43.7	56.3	-	23	4	-	1.9	1.7	2.0	-
Sevier	4,751	2,479	2,272	-	207	D	52.2	47.8	-	11	16	-	2.2	2.4	2.0	-
Union..........................	16,598	6,119	10,479	-	4,360	R	36.9	63.1	-	25	2	-	7.7	5.9	9.3	-
ARKANSAS....................	**888,521**	**525,197**	**356,900**	**6,424**	**168,297**	**D**	**59.1**	**40.2**	**0.7**							

Table I. — Vote for Presidential Preference: May 26, 1992, Democratic Primary Election

| County | Top candidates | | | | | | | | | Top three candidates (state vote) | | | | | | | | | |
| | | | | | | | | | | Percent of total vote | | | Rank | | | Percent contribution to state vote | | | |
	Total	Clinton	Uncom-mitted	Brown	LaRouche					Clinton	Uncom-mitted	Brown	Clinton	Uncom-mitted	Brown	Total	Clinton	Uncom-mitted	Brown
Arkansas	5,752	3,733	1,222	696	101	-	-	-	-	64.9	21.2	12.1	49	36	25	1.1	1.1	1.3	1.3
Ashley	6,412	4,511	1,192	520	189	-	-	-	-	70.4	18.6	8.1	29	43	58	1.3	1.3	1.3	0.9
Baxter	3,637	2,955	0	544	138	-	-	-	-	81.2	0.0	15.0	1	69	11	0.7	0.9	0.0	1.0
Benton	6,627	5,372	804	364	87	-	-	-	-	81.1	12.1	5.5	2	64	72	1.3	1.6	0.9	0.7
Boone	3,370	2,268	618	405	79	-	-	-	-	67.3	18.3	12.0	38	45	26	0.7	0.7	0.7	0.7
Bradley	4,131	2,728	899	406	98	-	-	-	-	66.0	21.8	9.8	46	30	40	0.8	0.8	1.0	0.7
Calhoun	1,833	1,386	0	361	86	-	-	-	-	75.6	0.0	19.7	14	70	3	0.4	0.4	0.0	0.7
Carroll	3,015	1,795	782	337	101	-	-	-	-	59.5	25.9	11.2	60	14	32	0.6	0.5	0.9	0.6
Chicot	3,751	2,915	557	211	68	-	-	-	-	77.7	14.8	5.6	8	56	70	0.7	0.9	0.6	0.4
Clark	6,492	4,750	1,110	544	88	-	-	-	-	73.2	17.1	8.4	23	48	53	1.3	1.4	1.2	1.0
Clay	3,953	3,021	603	221	108	-	-	-	-	76.4	15.3	5.6	13	53	71	0.8	0.9	0.7	0.4
Cleburne	6,865	3,918	1,835	965	147	-	-	-	-	57.1	26.7	14.1	67	9	17	1.4	1.1	2.0	1.7
Cleveland	2,538	1,365	825	260	88	-	-	-	-	53.8	32.5	10.2	72	2	38	0.5	0.4	0.9	0.5
Columbia	5,425	4,001	0	935	489	-	-	-	-	73.8	0.0	17.2	19	71	7	1.1	1.2	0.0	1.7
Conway	6,648	4,246	1,192	962	248	-	-	-	-	63.9	17.9	14.5	51	46	14	1.3	1.2	1.3	1.7
Craighead	11,446	8,118	1,688	577	1,063	-	-	-	-	70.9	14.7	5.0	26	57	74	2.3	2.4	1.9	1.0
Crawford	8,194	4,580	2,438	953	223	-	-	-	-	55.9	29.8	11.6	69	6	28	1.6	1.3	2.7	1.7
Crittenden	9,006	6,884	1,042	850	230	-	-	-	-	76.4	11.6	9.4	12	65	44	1.8	2.0	1.1	1.5
Cross	4,629	3,250	902	336	141	-	-	-	-	70.2	19.5	7.3	30	40	62	0.9	1.0	1.0	0.6
Dallas	3,565	2,151	823	493	98	-	-	-	-	60.3	23.1	13.8	57	25	19	0.7	0.6	0.9	0.9
Desha	4,137	3,087	620	328	102	-	-	-	-	74.6	15.0	7.9	16	55	60	0.8	0.9	0.7	0.6
Drew	4,401	2,927	954	408	112	-	-	-	-	66.5	21.7	9.3	43	31	45	0.9	0.9	1.1	0.7
Faulkner	12,456	8,233	1,610	2,184	429	-	-	-	-	66.1	12.9	17.5	45	61	6	2.5	2.4	1.8	4.0
Franklin	4,263	2,455	1,153	465	190	-	-	-	-	57.6	27.0	10.9	65	8	34	0.8	0.7	1.3	0.8
Fulton	3,472	2,318	768	291	95	-	-	-	-	66.8	22.1	8.4	41	29	52	0.7	0.7	0.8	0.5
Garland	16,240	11,636	2,587	1,768	249	-	-	-	-	71.7	15.9	10.9	25	50	35	3.2	3.4	2.9	3.2
Grant	3,704	2,107	900	559	138	-	-	-	-	56.9	24.3	15.1	68	20	10	0.7	0.6	1.0	1.0
Greene	8,709	6,162	1,736	557	254	-	-	-	-	70.8	19.9	6.4	27	39	65	1.7	1.8	1.9	1.0
Hempstead	5,923	4,628	0	921	374	-	-	-	-	78.1	0.0	15.5	7	72	8	1.2	1.4	0.0	1.7
Hot Spring	7,933	4,690	1,796	1,207	240	-	-	-	-	59.1	22.6	15.2	61	27	9	1.6	1.4	2.0	2.2
Howard	3,484	2,324	890	201	69	-	-	-	-	66.7	25.5	5.8	42	16	69	0.7	0.7	1.0	0.4
Independence	8,973	5,857	1,848	998	270	-	-	-	-	65.3	20.6	11.1	48	38	33	1.8	1.7	2.0	1.8
Izard	3,277	2,273	624	279	101	-	-	-	-	69.4	19.0	8.5	33	41	50	0.7	0.7	0.7	0.5
Jackson	4,594	3,329	809	351	105	-	-	-	-	72.5	17.6	7.6	24	47	61	0.9	1.0	0.9	0.6
Jefferson	18,591	14,256	2,373	1,598	364	-	-	-	-	76.7	12.8	8.6	9	62	49	3.7	4.2	2.6	2.9
Johnson	5,108	3,004	1,337	586	181	-	-	-	-	58.8	26.2	11.5	62	11	30	1.0	0.9	1.5	1.1
Lafayette	3,188	2,143	741	192	112	-	-	-	-	67.2	23.2	6.0	39	22	68	0.6	0.6	0.8	0.3
Lawrence	3,838	2,671	707	341	119	-	-	-	-	69.6	18.4	8.9	32	●44	47	0.8	0.8	0.8	0.6
Lee	4,256	3,180	699	274	103	-	-	-	-	74.7	16.4	6.4	15	49	64	0.8	0.9	0.8	0.5
Lincoln	3,588	2,406	766	285	131	-	-	-	-	67.1	21.3	7.9	40	35	59	0.7	0.7	0.8	0.5
Little River	3,968	2,768	921	203	76	-	-	-	-	69.8	23.2	5.1	31	23	73	0.8	0.8	1.0	0.4
Logan	5,521	3,035	1,403	811	272	-	-	-	-	55.0	25.4	14.7	70	17	13	1.1	0.9	1.5	1.5
Lonoke	9,759	5,849	2,537	1,128	245	-	-	-	-	59.9	26.0	11.6	59	13	29	1.9	1.7	2.8	2.0
Madison	1,694	1,297	212	141	44	-	-	-	-	76.6	12.5	8.3	10	63	55	0.3	0.4	0.2	0.3
Marion	2,744	2,025	0	552	167	-	-	-	-	73.8	0.0	20.1	18	73	2	0.5	0.6	0.0	1.0
Miller	8,389	5,683	2,295	322	89	-	-	-	-	67.7	27.4	3.8	36	7	75	1.7	1.7	2.5	0.6
Mississippi	9,868	7,257	1,527	688	396	-	-	-	-	73.5	15.5	7.0	21	52	63	2.0	2.1	1.7	1.2
Monroe	3,076	2,288	0	601	187	-	-	-	-	74.4	0.0	19.5	17	74	4	0.6	0.7	0.0	1.1
Montgomery	3,060	1,680	914	360	106	-	-	-	-	54.9	29.9	11.8	71	5	27	0.6	0.5	1.0	0.7
Nevada	3,490	2,281	747	377	85	-	-	-	-	65.4	21.4	10.8	47	34	36	0.7	0.7	0.8	0.7
Newton	785	617	78	75	15	-	-	-	-	78.6	9.9	9.6	4	66	43	0.2	0.2	<.1	0.1
Ouachita	9,286	6,291	2,004	779	212	-	-	-	-	67.7	21.6	8.4	35	32	51	1.8	1.8	2.2	1.4
Perry	1,988	1,237	308	355	88	-	-	-	-	62.2	15.5	17.9	55	51	5	0.4	0.4	0.3	0.6
Phillips	6,104	4,483	926	529	166	-	-	-	-	73.4	15.2	8.7	22	54	48	1.2	1.3	1.0	1.0
Pike	3,324	2,032	828	372	92	-	-	-	-	61.1	24.9	11.2	56	18	31	0.7	0.6	0.9	0.7
Poinsett	5,377	4,295	457	439	186	-	-	-	-	79.9	8.5	8.2	3	67	57	1.1	1.3	0.5	0.8
Polk	4,677	2,493	1,591	449	144	-	-	-	-	53.3	34.0	9.6	74	1	41	0.9	0.7	1.8	0.8
Pope	10,040	5,383	3,019	1,411	227	-	-	-	-	53.6	30.1	14.1	73	4	18	2.0	1.6	3.3	2.6
Prairie	2,939	1,884	686	298	71	-	-	-	-	64.1	23.3	10.1	50	21	39	0.6	0.6	0.8	0.5
Pulaski	62,358	45,875	8,166	7,646	671	-	-	-	-	73.6	13.1	12.3	20	60	24	12.4	13.4	9.0	13.8
Randolph	4,687	3,225	886	448	128	-	-	-	-	68.8	18.9	9.6	34	42	42	0.9	0.9	1.0	0.8
St. Francis	6,651	4,491	1,429	556	175	-	-	-	-	67.5	21.5	8.4	37	33	54	1.3	1.3	1.6	1.0
Saline	14,415	9,046	3,223	1,851	295	-	-	-	-	62.8	22.4	12.8	54	28	22	2.9	2.6	3.6	3.4
Scott	3,077	1,601	969	399	108	-	-	-	-	52.0	31.5	13.0	75	3	21	0.6	0.5	1.1	0.7
Searcy	981	768	55	135	23	-	-	-	-	78.3	5.6	13.8	5	68	20	0.2	0.2	<.1	0.2
Sebastian	13,354	8,389	3,504	1,238	223	-	-	-	-	62.8	26.2	9.3	53	10	46	2.7	2.5	3.9	2.2
Sevier	3,617	2,395	932	230	60	-	-	-	-	66.2	25.8	6.4	44	15	66	0.7	0.7	1.0	0.4
Sharp	4,775	3,019	1,105	492	159	-	-	-	-	63.2	23.1	10.3	52	24	37	1.0	0.9	1.2	0.9
Stone	4,268	2,448	979	630	211	-	-	-	-	57.4	22.9	14.8	66	26	12	0.8	0.7	1.1	1.1
Union	11,898	7,146	2,467	1,702	583	-	-	-	-	60.1	20.7	14.3	58	37	16	2.4	2.1	2.7	3.1

County	Top candidates								Top three candidates(state vote)									
									Percent of total vote			Rank			Percent contribution to state vote			
	Total	Clinton	Uncom-mitted	Brown	LaRouche				Clinton	Uncom-mitted	Brown	Clinton	Uncom-mitted	Brown	Total	Clinton	Uncom-mitted	Brown
Van Buren	5,470	3,157	1,343	788	182	-	-	-	57.7	24.6	14.4	64	19	15	1.1	0.9	1.5	1.4
Washington...................	13,518	10,341	1,845	1,105	227	-	-	-	76.5	13.6	8.2	11	58	56	2.7	3.0	2.0	2.0
White.................	11,330	7,994	0	2,479	857	-	-	-	70.6	0.0	21.9	28	75	1	2.3	2.3	0.0	4.5
Woodruff.....................	2,786	2,179	365	172	70	-	-	-	78.2	13.1	6.2	6	59	67	0.6	0.6	0.4	0.3
Yell	5,919	3,432	1,539	740	208	-	-	-	58.0	26.0	12.5	63	12	23	1.2	1.0	1.7	1.3
ARKANSAS...................	**502,617**	**342,017**	**90,710**	**55,234**	**14,656**	-	-	-	**68.0**	**18.0**	**11.0**				**100.0**	**100.0**	**100.0**	**100.0**

Table J. — Vote for Presidential Preference: May 26, 1992, Republican Primary Election

County	Top candidates					Top four candidates (state vote)								Percent contribution to state vote				
						Percent of total vote				Rank								
	Total	Bush	Bu-chanan	Uncom-mitted		Bush	Bu-chanan	Uncom-mitted		Bush	Bu-chanan	Uncom-mitted		Total	Bush	Bu-chanan	Uncom-mitted	
Arkansas	59	53	6	0	-	89.8	10.2	0.0	-	14	60	5	-	0.1	0.1	<.1	0.0	-
Ashley	34	30	4	0	-	88.2	11.8	0.0	-	25	47	6	-	<.1	<.1	<.1	0.0	-
Baxter	1,849	1,506	343	0	-	81.4	18.6	0.0	-	53	19	7	-	3.4	3.3	5.2	0.0	-
Benton	12,317	8,801	957	2,559	-	71.5	7.8	20.8	-	73	70	1	-	22.4	19.3	14.6	93.3	-
Boone	736	598	138	0	-	81.3	18.8	0.0	-	54	17	8	-	1.3	1.3	2.1	0.0	-
Bradley	19	15	4	0	-	78.9	21.1	0.0	-	63	11	9	-	<.1	<.1	<.1	0.0	-
Calhoun	12	11	1	0	-	91.7	8.3	0.0	-	7	67	10	-	<.1	<.1	<.1	0.0	-
Carroll	642	528	114	0	-	82.2	17.8	0.0	-	51	21	11	-	1.2	1.2	1.7	0.0	-
Chicot	19	19	0	0	-	100.0	0.0	0.0	-	1	73	12	-	<.1	<.1	0.0	0.0	-
Clark	134	114	20	0	-	85.1	14.9	0.0	-	42	31	13	-	0.2	0.3	0.3	0.0	-
Clay	20	18	2	0	-	90.0	10.0	0.0	-	12	62	14	-	<.1	<.1	<.1	0.0	-
Cleburne	213	189	24	0	-	88.7	11.3	0.0	-	23	51	15	-	0.4	0.4	0.4	0.0	-
Cleveland	21	18	3	0	-	85.7	14.3	0.0	-	41	32	16	-	<.1	<.1	<.1	0.0	-
Columbia	385	353	32	0	-	91.7	8.3	0.0	-	6	69	17	-	0.7	0.8	0.5	0.0	-
Conway	23	20	3	0	-	87.0	13.0	0.0	-	34	39	18	-	<.1	<.1	<.1	0.0	-
Craighead	609	514	95	0	-	84.4	15.6	0.0	-	45	28	19	-	1.1	1.1	1.5	0.0	-
Crawford	998	844	154	0	-	84.6	15.4	0.0	-	44	29	20	-	1.8	1.9	2.4	0.0	-
Crittenden	83	68	15	0	-	81.9	18.1	0.0	-	52	20	21	-	0.2	0.1	0.2	0.0	-
Cross	42	41	1	0	-	97.6	2.4	0.0	-	4	72	22	-	<.1	<.1	<.1	0.0	-
Dallas	4	2	2	0	-	50.0	50.0	0.0	-	74	2	23	-	<.1	<.1	<.1	0.0	-
Desha	12	11	1	0	-	91.7	8.3	0.0	-	8	68	24	-	<.1	<.1	<.1	0.0	-
Drew	71	59	12	0	-	83.1	16.9	0.0	-	48	25	25	-	0.1	0.1	0.2	0.0	-
Faulkner	1,254	1,017	142	95	-	81.1	11.3	7.6	-	56	50	3	-	2.3	2.2	2.2	3.5	-
Franklin	215	178	37	0	-	82.8	17.2	0.0	-	50	23	26	-	0.4	0.4	0.6	0.0	-
Fulton	57	51	6	0	-	89.5	10.5	0.0	-	19	55	27	-	0.1	0.1	<.1	0.0	-
Garland	2,875	2,511	364	0	-	87.3	12.7	0.0	-	31	42	28	-	5.2	5.5	5.6	0.0	-
Grant	68	49	19	0	-	72.1	27.9	0.0	-	72	3	29	-	0.1	0.1	0.3	0.0	-
Greene	63	50	13	0	-	79.4	20.6	0.0	-	62	12	30	-	0.1	0.1	0.2	0.0	-
Hempstead	181	157	24	0	-	86.7	13.3	0.0	-	36	37	31	-	0.3	0.3	0.4	0.0	-
Hot Spring	87	73	14	0	-	83.9	16.1	0.0	-	46	27	32	-	0.2	0.2	0.2	0.0	-
Howard	40	37	3	0	-	92.5	7.5	0.0	-	5	71	33	-	<.1	<.1	<.1	0.0	-
Independence	158	137	21	0	-	86.7	13.3	0.0	-	37	36	34	-	0.3	0.3	0.3	0.0	-
Izard	170	133	30	7	-	78.2	17.6	4.1	-	65	22	4	-	0.3	0.3	0.5	0.3	-
Jackson	68	61	7	0	-	89.7	10.3	0.0	-	16	58	35	-	0.1	0.1	0.1	0.0	-
Jefferson	917	743	93	81	-	81.0	10.1	8.8	-	58	61	2	-	1.7	1.6	1.4	3.0	-
Johnson	323	283	40	0	-	87.6	12.4	0.0	-	29	44	36	-	0.6	0.6	0.6	0.0	-
Lafayette	29	22	7	0	-	75.9	24.1	0.0	-	69	6	37	-	<.1	<.1	0.1	0.0	-
Lawrence	62	48	14	0	-	77.4	22.6	0.0	-	66	9	38	-	0.1	0.1	0.2	0.0	-
Lee	1	0	1	0	-	0.0	100.0	0.0	-	75	1	39	-	<.1	0.0	<.1	0.0	-
Lincoln	16	14	2	0	-	87.5	12.5	0.0	-	30	43	40	-	<.1	<.1	<.1	0.0	-
Little River	31	28	3	0	-	90.3	9.7	0.0	-	11	64	41	-	<.1	<.1	<.1	0.0	-
Logan	221	183	38	0	-	82.8	17.2	0.0	-	49	24	42	-	0.4	0.4	0.6	0.0	-
Lonoke	368	298	70	0	-	81.0	19.0	0.0	-	59	15	43	-	0.7	0.7	1.1	0.0	-
Madison	511	459	52	0	-	89.8	10.2	0.0	-	15	59	44	-	0.9	1.0	0.8	0.0	-
Marion	327	272	55	0	-	83.2	16.8	0.0	-	47	26	45	-	0.6	0.6	0.8	0.0	-
Miller	811	706	105	0	-	87.1	12.9	0.0	-	32	41	46	-	1.5	1.5	1.6	0.0	-
Mississippi	144	129	15	0	-	89.6	10.4	0.0	-	18	56	47	-	0.3	0.3	0.2	0.0	-
Monroe	31	25	6	0	-	80.6	19.4	0.0	-	61	13	48	-	<.1	<.1	<.1	0.0	-
Montgomery	14	11	3	0	-	78.6	21.4	0.0	-	64	10	49	-	<.1	<.1	<.1	0.0	-
Nevada	14	14	0	0	-	100.0	0.0	0.0	-	2	74	50	-	<.1	<.1	0.0	0.0	-
Newton	119	105	14	0	-	88.2	11.8	0.0	-	26	48	51	-	0.2	0.2	0.2	0.0	-
Ouachita	159	122	37	0	-	76.7	23.3	0.0	-	67	8	52	-	0.3	0.3	0.6	0.0	-
Perry	49	43	6	0	-	87.8	12.2	0.0	-	28	45	53	-	<.1	<.1	<.1	0.0	-
Phillips	16	16	0	0	-	100.0	0.0	0.0	-	3	75	54	-	<.1	<.1	0.0	0.0	-
Pike	33	29	4	0	-	87.9	12.1	0.0	-	27	46	55	-	<.1	<.1	<.1	0.0	-
Poinsett	60	46	14	0	-	76.7	23.3	0.0	-	68	7	56	-	0.1	0.1	0.2	0.0	-
Polk	149	128	21	0	-	85.9	14.1	0.0	-	40	33	57	-	0.3	0.3	0.3	0.0	-
Pope	843	751	92	0	-	89.1	10.9	0.0	-	20	54	58	-	1.5	1.6	1.4	0.0	-
Prairie	77	69	8	0	-	89.6	10.4	0.0	-	17	57	59	-	0.1	0.2	0.1	0.0	-
Pulaski	8,961	7,976	985	0	-	89.0	11.0	0.0	-	21	53	60	-	16.3	17.5	15.0	0.0	-
Randolph	42	34	8	0	-	81.0	19.0	0.0	-	60	14	61	-	<.1	<.1	0.1	0.0	-
St. Francis	43	39	4	0	-	90.7	9.3	0.0	-	9	66	68	-	<.1	<.1	<.1	0.0	-
Saline	1,552	1,370	182	0	-	88.3	11.7	0.0	-	24	49	62	-	2.8	3.0	2.8	0.0	-
Scott	64	52	12	0	-	81.3	18.8	0.0	-	55	18	63	-	0.1	0.1	0.2	0.0	-
Searcy	647	561	86	0	-	86.7	13.3	0.0	-	38	35	64	-	1.2	1.2	1.3	0.0	-
Sebastian	5,952	5,172	780	0	-	86.9	13.1	0.0	-	35	38	65	-	10.8	11.3	11.9	0.0	-
Sevier	81	72	9	0	-	88.9	11.1	0.0	-	22	52	66	-	0.1	0.2	0.1	0.0	-
Sharp	323	279	44	0	-	86.4	13.6	0.0	-	39	34	67	-	0.6	0.6	0.7	0.0	-
Stone	40	30	10	0	-	75.0	25.0	0.0	-	70	5	69	-	<.1	<.1	0.2	0.0	-
Union	178	129	49	0	-	72.5	27.5	0.0	-	71	4	70	-	0.3	0.3	0.7	0.0	-

Table J. – **Vote for Presidential Preference: May 26, 1992, Republican Primary Election (cont)**

County	Top candidates					Top four candidates (state vote)												
						Percent of total vote				Rank				Percent contribution to state vote				
	Total	Bush	Bu-chanan	Uncom-mitted		Bush	Bu-chanan	Uncom-mitted		Bush	Bu-chanan	Uncom-mitted		Total	Bush	Bu-chanan	Uncom-mitted	
Van Buren	167	151	16	0	-	90.4	9.6	0.0	-	10	65	71	-	0.3	0.3	0.2	0.0	-
Washington....................	7,148	6,221	927	0	-	87.0	13.0	0.0	-	33	40	72	-	13.0	13.6	14.2	0.0	-
White...........................	738	625	113	0	-	84.7	15.3	0.0	-	43	30	73	-	1.3	1.4	1.7	0.0	-
Woodruff......................	10	9	1	0	-	90.0	10.0	0.0	-	13	63	74	-	<.1	<.1	<.1	0.0	-
Yell	74	60	14	0	-	81.1	18.9	0.0	-	57	16	75	-	0.1	0.1	0.2	0.0	-
**ARKANSAS.................... **	**54,883**	**45,590**	**6,551**	**2,742**	**-**	**83.1**	**11.9**	**5.0**	**-**					**100.0**	**100.0**	**100.0**	**100.0**	**-**

1992 Vote for President
Percent for Clinton (D), by County

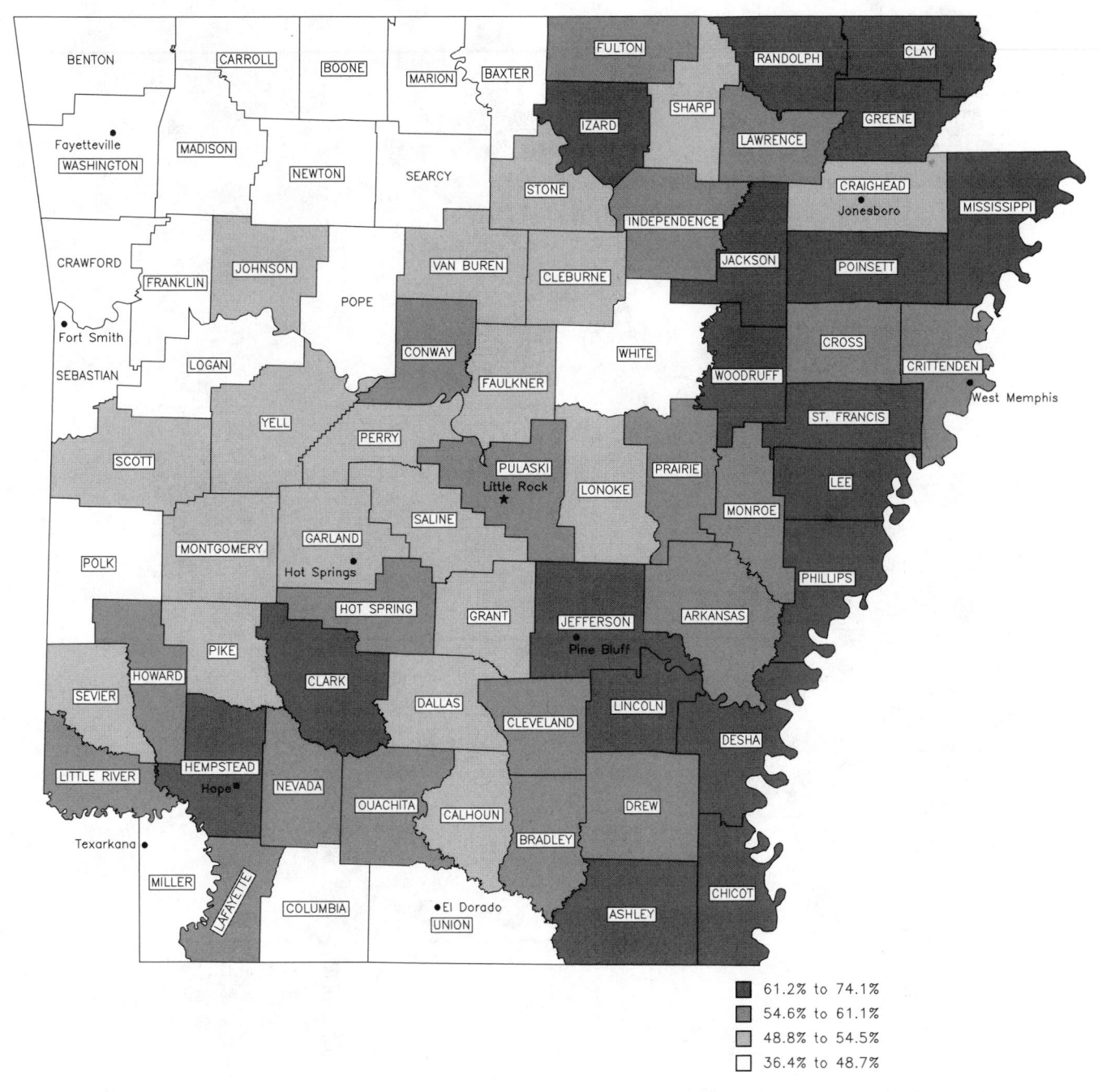

■ 61.2% to 74.1%

▨ 54.6% to 61.1%

▧ 48.8% to 54.5%

□ 36.4% to 48.7%

Clinton (D) received 53.2% statewide.

A framed county name indicates
a county carried by the winner.

Copyright © 1993 by Election Data Services, Inc.

Arkansas 99

1992 Vote for U.S. Senator
Percent for Bumpers (D), by County

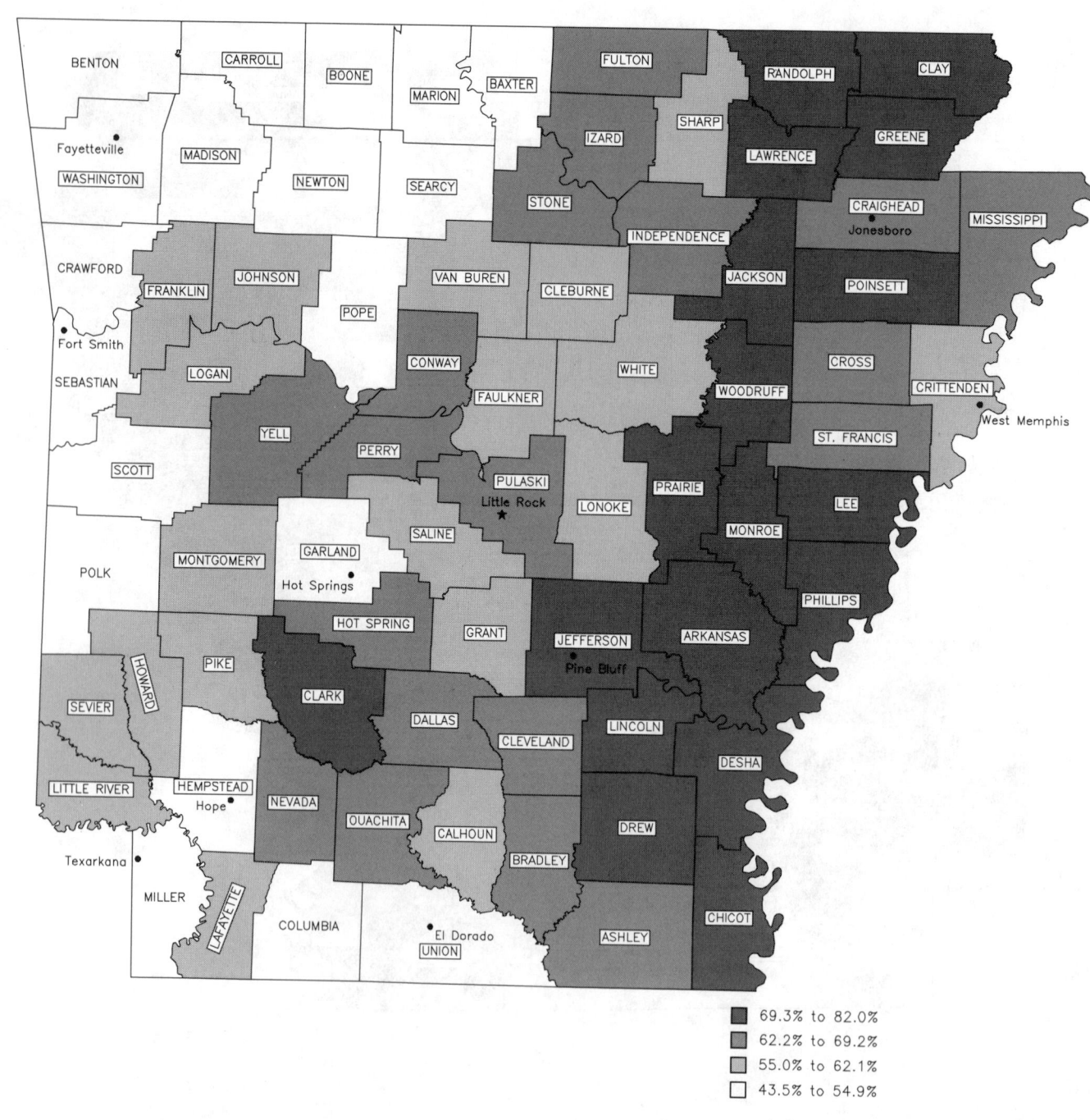

69.3% to 82.0%
62.2% to 69.2%
55.0% to 62.1%
43.5% to 54.9%

Bumpers (D) received 60.2% statewide.

A framed county name indicates
a county carried by the winner.

CALIFORNIA

Congressional Districts 52
   Average Population 572,308
State Senate Districts 40
   Average Population 744,001
State House Districts 80
   Average Population 372,000

Electoral College Votes...54
Counties 58
Voting Precincts 25,942

Alternative Registration Methods:
   ....Deputized Registrars, Mail-in

Registration Deadline (Days before Election) 29

Population Statistics 1990

Race/ Ethnicity	Total Population		Voting Age Population		Voting Age Population % of total population
	Number	%	Number	%	
Non-Hispanic					
White	17,029,126	57.2	13,469,917	61.2	79.1
Black	2,092,446	7.0	1,470,259	6.7	70.3
Asian/Pacific Islander	2,710,353	9.1	1,948,236	8.9	71.9
Native American	184,065	0.6	132,571	0.6	72.0
Other	56,093	0.2	33,438	0.2	59.6
All Hispanic	7,687,938	25.8	4,954,875	22.5	64.5
TOTAL	29,760,021	100.0	22,009,296	100.0	74.0

Voting Equipment Use (Counties)

Datavote Punch Card	30	Paper Ballot	0
Electronic	0	Other Punch Card	17
Lever Machine	2	Mixed Systems	0
Optical Scanner	9		

Party Control	DEM	REP	IND	VAC
1993 State Senate	22	14	2	2
1992 State Senate	25	13	2	0
1993 State House	47	31	0	2
1992 State House	47	33	0	0

Estimated Voting Age Population 1992 (VAP) 22,668,000
Number of Registered Voters................................. 15,101,473
   % of estimated VAP... 66.6
Voter Turnout (Actual) 11,374,565
   % of VAP 50.2
   % of Registration 75.3
Persons Not Voting—of Voting Age 11,293,435
   % of VAP 49.8
Persons Not Voting—of Registered 3,726,908
   % of Registration 24.7
Straight Ticket Voting .... No

State Officials and Members of Congress

Governor:
Pete Wilson (R) 1990, elected to a four-year term in 1990.

U.S. Senators:
Dianne Feinstein (D) 1992, elected to a two-year term in 1992.
Barbara Boxer (D) 1992, elected to a six-year term in 1992.

U.S. Representative in Congress:
(District, Name, Party, Date first elected)

1. Hamburg (D) 1992
2. Herger (R) 1986
3. Fazio (D) 1978
4. Doolittle (R) 1990
5. Matsui (D) 1978
6. Woolsey (D) 1992
7. Miller (D) 1974
8. Pelosi (D) 1987
9. Dellums (D) 1970
10. Baker (R) 1992
11. Pombo (R) 1992
12. Lantos (D) 1980
13. Stark (D) 1972

14. Eshoo (D) 1992
15. Mineta (D) 1974
16. Edwards (D) 1962
17. Farr (D) 1993[1]
18. Condit (D) 1989
19. Lehman (D) 1982
20. Dooley (D) 1990
21. Thomas (R) 1978
22. Huffington (R) 1992
23. Gallegly (R) 1986
24. Beilenson (D) 1976
25. McKeon (R) 1992
26. Berman (D) 1982

27. Moorhead (R) 1972
28. Dreier (R) 1980
29. Waxman (D) 1974
30. Becerra (D) 1992
31. Martinez (D) 1982
32. Dixon (D) 1978
33. Roybal-Allard (D) 1992
34. Torres (D) 1982
35. Waters (D) 1990
36. Harman (D) 1992
37. Tucker (D) 1992
38. Horn (R) 1992
39. Royce (R) 1992

40. Lewis (R) 1978
41. Kim (R) 1992
42. Brown (D) 1972
43. Calvert (R) 1992
44. McCandless (R) 1982
45. Rohrabacher (R) 1988
46. Dornan (R) 1984
47. Cox (R) 1988
48. Packard (R) 1982
49. Schenk (D) 1992
50. Filner (D) 1992
51. Cunningham (R) 1990
52. Hunter (R) 1980

[1]Elected from the June 8, 1993, runoff election to replace Leon Panetta, who resigned upon appointment as Director of the Office of Management and Budget (OMB).

Candidates: General Election, November 3, 1992

Candidate(s)	Total vote	Percent	Party	Status	First elected
President/Vice President					
Clinton/Gore	5,121,325	46.01%	Democrat	Challenger	1992
Bush/Quayle	3,630,574	32.61%	Republican	Incumbent	1988
Perot/Stockdale	2,296,006	20.63%	Independent	Challenger	
Marrou/Lord	48,139	0.43%	Libertarian	Challenger	
Daniels/Tupahache	18,597	0.17%	Peace and Freedom	Challenger	
Phillips/Knight	12,711	0.11%	American Independent	Challenger	
Gritz/Minett	3,077	0.03%	Write in	Challenger	
Hagelin/Tompkins	836	<.01%	Write in	Challenger	
LaRouche/Bevel	180	<.01%	Write in	Challenger	
Carter/Aschenbach	131	<.01%	Write in	Challenger	
Warren/Bates	115	<.01%	Write in	Challenger	
Smith/Smith	18	<.01%	Write in	Challenger	
Masters/Masters	12	<.01%	Write in	Challenger	
U.S. Senator (six-year term)					
Barbara Boxer	5,173,467	47.90%	Democrat	Challenger	1992
Bruce Herschensohn	4,644,182	43.00%	Republican	Challenger	
Genevieve Torres	372,817	3.45%	Peace and Freedom	Challenger	
Jerome McCready	373,051	3.45%	American Independent	Challenger	
June Genis	235,919	2.18%	Libertarian	Challenger	
Joel Britton	110	<.01%	Write in	Challenger	
John Cortese	101	<.01%	Write in	Challenger	
Robert Bell	56	<.01%	Write in	Challenger	
U.S. Senator (two-year term)[1]					
Dianne Feinstein	5,853,651	54.29%	Democrat	Challenger	1992
John Seymour	4,093,501	37.96%	Republican	Incumbent	
Gerald Horne	305,697	2.84%	Peace and Freedom	Challenger	
Paul Meeuwenberg	281,973	2.62%	American Independent	Challenger	
Richard Boddie	247,799	2.30%	Libertarian	Challenger	
Joe Swanson	85	<.01%	Write in	Challenger	
Jerry Carroll	37	<.01%	Write in	Challenger	
Governor (No contest)					
U.S. Representative in Congress					
District 1					
Dan Hamburg	119,676	47.64%	Democrat	Challenger	1992
Frank Riggs	113,266	45.09%	Republican	Incumbent	1990
Phil Baldwin	10,764	4.28%	Peace and Freedom	Challenger	
Matthew Howard	7,500	2.99%	Libertarian	Challenger	
District 2					
Wally Herger	167,247	65.19%	Republican	Incumbent	1986
Elliot Roy Freedman	71,780	27.98%	Democrat	Challenger	
Harry H. Pendery	17,529	6.83%	Libertarian	Challenger	
District 3					
Vic Fazio	122,149	51.18%	Democrat	Incumbent	1978
Bill Richardson	96,092	40.26%	Republican	Challenger	
Ross Crain	20,444	8.57%	Libertarian	Challenger	
District 4					
John Doolittle	141,155	49.81%	Republican	Incumbent	1990
Patricia Malberg	129,489	45.70%	Democrat	Challenger	
Patrick McHargue	12,705	4.48%	Libertarian	Challenger	
Don Brooksher	16	<.01%	Write in	Challenger	

[1]For remaining two years of term vacated by Pete Wilson (R), who was elected governor of California in 1990. Incumbent John Seymour (R) appointed as interim senator in January 1991.

Candidate(s)	Total vote	Percent	Party	Status	First elected
U.S. Representative in Congress (cont)					
District 5					
Robert Matsui	158,250	68.64%	Democrat	Incumbent	1978
Robert Dinsmore	58,698	25.46%	Republican	Challenger	
Gordon Mors	4,745	2.06%	American Independent	Challenger	
Chris Rufer	4,547	1.97%	Libertarian	Challenger	
Tian Harter	4,316	1.87%	Green	Challenger	
Jan Bergeron	4	<.01%	Write in	Challenger	
District 6					
Lynn Woolsey	190,322	65.23%	Democrat	Challenger	1992
Bill Filante	98,171	33.64%	Republican	Challenger	
Claude Heater	3,141	1.08%	Write in	Challenger	
Louis Beary	152	0.05%	Write in	Challenger	
District 7					
George Miller	153,320	70.34%	Democrat	Incumbent	1974
Dave Scholl	54,822	25.15%	Republican	Challenger	
David Franklin	9,840	4.51%	Peace and Freedom	Challenger	
District 8					
Nancy Pelosi	191,906	82.47%	Democrat	Incumbent	1987
Marc Wolin	25,693	11.04%	Republican	Challenger	
Cesar Cadabes	7,572	3.25%	Peace and Freedom	Challenger	
James Elwood	7,511	3.23%	Libertarian	Challenger	
Michael Goldwater	9	<.01%	Write in	Challenger	
District 9					
Ronald Dellums	164,265	71.90%	Democrat	Incumbent	1970
William Hunter	53,707	23.51%	Republican	Challenger	
Dave Linn	10,472	4.58%	Peace and Freedom	Challenger	
Omari Musa	23	0.01%	Write in	Challenger	
District 10					
Bill Baker	145,702	51.96%	Republican	Challenger	1992
Wendell Williams	134,635	48.01%	Democrat	Challenger	
Dave Williams	55	0.02%	Write in	Challenger	
Valerie Janlois	37	0.01%	Write in	Challenger	
District 11					
Richard Pombo	94,453	47.59%	Republican	Challenger	1992
Patricia Garamendi	90,539	45.61%	Democrat	Challenger	
Christine Roberts	13,498	6.80%	Libertarian	Challenger	
District 12					
Tom Lantos	157,205	68.83%	Democrat	Incumbent	1980
Jim Tomlin	53,278	23.33%	Republican	Challenger	
Mary Weldon	10,142	4.44%	Peace and Freedom	Challenger	
George O'Brien	7,782	3.41%	Libertarian	Challenger	
District 13					
Fortney 'Pete' Stark	123,795	60.24%	Democrat	Incumbent	1972
Verne Teyler	64,953	31.60%	Republican	Challenger	
Roslyn Allen	16,768	8.16%	Peace and Freedom	Challenger	
District 14					
Anna G. Eshoo	146,873	56.66%	Democrat	Challenger	1992
Tom Huening	101,202	39.04%	Republican	Challenger	
Chuck Olson	7,220	2.79%	Libertarian	Challenger	
David Wald	3,912	1.51%	Peace and Freedom	Challenger	
Richard Sims	12	<.01%	Write in	Challenger	
Dave Maginnis	3	<.01%	Write in	Challenger	
District 15					
Norm Mineta	168,617	63.54%	Democrat	Incumbent	1974
Robert Wick	82,875	31.23%	Republican	Challenger	
Duggan Dieterly	13,293	5.01%	Libertarian	Challenger	
Bill Futrell	585	0.22%	Write in	Challenger	

Candidate(s)	Total vote	Percent	Party	Status	First elected
U.S. Representative in Congress (cont)					
District 16					
Don Edwards	96,661	62.01%	Democrat	Incumbent	1962
Ted Bundesen	49,843	31.97%	Republican	Challenger	
Amani Kuumba	9,370	6.01%	Peace and Freedom	Challenger	
Andrew Hunt	5	<.01%	Write in	Challenger	
Carl Loeber	3	<.01%	Write in	Challenger	
Peter James	1	<.01%	Write in	Challenger	
District 17					
Leon Panetta[2]	151,565	72.05%	Democrat	Incumbent	1976
Bill McCampbell	49,947	23.74%	Republican	Challenger	
Maureen Smith	4,804	2.28%	Peace and Freedom	Challenger	
John Wilkes	4,051	1.93%	Libertarian	Challenger	
District 18					
Gary Condit	139,704	84.66%	Democrat	Incumbent	1989
Kim Almstrom	25,307	15.34%	Libertarian	Challenger	
District 19					
Richard Lehman	101,620	46.91%	Democrat	Incumbent	1982
Tal Cloud	100,590	46.43%	Republican	Challenger	
Dorothy Wells	13,334	6.15%	Peace and Freedom	Challenger	
James Williams	1,098	0.51%	Write in	Challenger	
District 20					
Calvin Dooley	72,679	64.85%	Democrat	Incumbent	1990
Ed Hunt	39,388	35.15%	Republican	Challenger	
District 21					
Bill Thomas	127,758	65.19%	Republican	Incumbent	1978
Deborah Vollmer	68,058	34.73%	Democrat	Challenger	
Michael Hodges	149	0.08%	Write in	Challenger	
District 22					
Michael Huffington	131,242	52.51%	Republican	Challenger	1992
Gloria Ochoa	87,328	34.94%	Democrat	Challenger	
Mindy Lorenz	23,699	9.48%	Green	Challenger	
W. Howard Dilbeck	7,553	3.02%	Libertarian	Challenger	
Richard Bialosky	102	0.04%	Write in	Challenger	
District 23					
Elton Gallegly	115,504	54.26%	Republican	Incumbent	1986
Anita Perez Ferguson	88,225	41.44%	Democrat	Challenger	
Jay Wood	9,091	4.27%	Libertarian	Challenger	
Edward Dunbar, Jr.	61	0.03%	Write in	Challenger	
District 24					
Anthony Beilenson	141,742	55.53%	Democrat	Incumbent	1976
Tom McClintock	99,835	39.11%	Republican	Challenger	
John Lindblad	13,690	5.36%	Peace and Freedom	Challenger	
District 25					
Howard McKeon	113,611	51.94%	Republican	Challenger	1992
James Gilmartin	72,233	33.03%	Democrat	Challenger	
Rick Pamplin	13,930	6.37%	Independent	Challenger	
Peggy Christensen	6,932	3.17%	Libertarian	Challenger	
Charles Wilken	6,919	3.16%	Green	Challenger	
Nancy Lawrence	5,090	2.33%	Peace and Freedom	Challenger	
District 26					
Howard L. Berman	73,807	61.04%	Democrat	Incumbent	1982
Gary Forsch	36,453	30.15%	Republican	Challenger	
Margery Hinds	7,180	5.94%	Peace and Freedom	Challenger	
Bernard Zimring	3,468	2.87%	Libertarian	Challenger	

[2]Resigned upon appointment as Director of the Office of Management and Budget (OMB). Sam Farr (D) elected at June 8, 1993, runoff election to fill vacancy.

Candidate(s)	Total vote	Percent	Party	Status	First elected
U.S. Representative in Congress (cont)					
District 27					
Carlos Moorhead	105,521	49.67%	Republican	Incumbent	1972
Doug Kahn	83,805	39.45%	Democrat	Challenger	
Jesse Moorman	11,003	5.18%	Green	Challenger	
Margaret Edwards	7,329	3.45%	Peace and Freedom	Challenger	
Dennis Decherd	4,790	2.25%	Libertarian	Challenger	
Peter Ballantyne	2	<.01%	Write in	Challenger	
District 28					
David Dreier	122,353	58.44%	Republican	Incumbent	1980
Al Wachtel	76,525	36.55%	Democrat	Challenger	
Walter Sheasby	6,233	2.98%	Green	Challenger	
Thomas Dominy	4,271	2.04%	Libertarian	Challenger	
District 29					
Henry Waxman	160,312	61.31%	Democrat	Incumbent	1974
Mark Robbins	67,141	25.68%	Republican	Challenger	
David Davis	15,445	5.91%	Independent	Challenger	
Susan Davies	13,888	5.31%	Peace and Freedom	Challenger	
Felix Rogin	4,699	1.80%	Libertarian	Challenger	
Yaakov Vann	1	<.01%	Write in	Challenger	
District 30					
Xavier Becerra	48,800	58.41%	Democrat	Challenger	1992
Morry Waksberg	20,034	23.98%	Republican	Challenger	
Blase Bonpane	6,315	7.56%	Green	Challenger	
Elizabeth Nakano	6,173	7.39%	Peace and Freedom	Challenger	
Andrew Consalvo	2,221	2.66%	Libertarian	Challenger	
District 31					
Matthew G. Martinez	68,324	62.57%	Democrat	Incumbent	1982
Reuben Franco	40,873	37.43%	Republican	Challenger	
District 32					
Julian Dixon	150,644	87.17%	Democrat	Incumbent	1978
Bob Weber	12,384	7.17%	Libertarian	Challenger	
William R. Williams	9,782	5.66%	Peace and Freedom	Challenger	
Carole Lesnick-Beltran	2	<.01%	Write in	Challenger	
District 33					
Lucille Roybal-Allard	32,010	63.04%	Democrat	Challenger	1992
Robert Guzman	15,428	30.38%	Republican	Challenger	
Tim Delia	2,135	4.20%	Peace and Freedom	Challenger	
Dale Olvera	1,206	2.38%	Libertarian	Challenger	
District 34					
Esteban Torres	91,738	61.27%	Democrat	Incumbent	1982
Jay Hernandez	50,907	34.00%	Republican	Challenger	
Carl Swinney	7,072	4.72%	Libertarian	Challenger	
M V Paul Worland	1	<.01%	Write in	Challenger	
District 35					
Maxine Waters	102,941	82.50%	Democrat	Incumbent	1990
Nate Truman	17,417	13.96%	Republican	Challenger	
Alice Miles	2,797	2.24%	Peace and Freedom	Challenger	
Carin Rogers	1,618	1.30%	Libertarian	Challenger	
Gordon Mego	3	<.01%	Write in	Challenger	
District 36					
Jane Harman	125,751	48.41%	Democrat	Challenger	
Joan Milke Flores	109,684	42.23%	Republican	Challenger	
Richard Greene	13,297	5.12%	Green	Challenger	
Owen Staley	5,519	2.12%	Peace and Freedom	Challenger	
Marc Denny	5,504	2.12%	Libertarian	Challenger	
Larry Martz	2	<.01%	Write in	Challenger	
District 37					
Walter Tucker	97,159	85.73%	Democrat	Challenger	1992
B Kwaku Duren	16,178	14.27%	Peace and Freedom	Challenger	

Candidate(s)	Total vote	Percent	Party	Status	First elected
U.S. Representative in Congress (cont)					
District 38					
Steve Horn	92,038	48.61%	Republican	Challenger	1992
Evan Braude	82,108	43.37%	Democrat	Challenger	
Paul Burton	8,391	4.43%	Peace and Freedom	Challenger	
Blake Ashley	6,756	3.57%	Libertarian	Challenger	
James Brown	14	<.01%	Write in	Challenger	
Roy Venable, Jr.	14	<.01%	Write in	Challenger	
District 39					
Ed Royce	122,472	57.31%	Republican	Challenger	1992
Molly McClanahan	81,728	38.25%	Democrat	Challenger	
Jack Dean	9,484	4.44%	Libertarian	Challenger	
District 40					
Jerry Lewis	129,563	63.11%	Republican	Incumbent	1978
Donald Rusk	63,881	31.12%	Democrat	Challenger	
Margie Akin	11,839	5.77%	Peace and Freedom	Challenger	
District 41					
Jay Kim	101,753	59.62%	Republican	Challenger	1992
Bob Baker	58,777	34.44%	Democrat	Challenger	
Mike Noonan	10,136	5.94%	Peace and Freedom	Challenger	
District 42					
George Brown, Jr.	79,780	50.67%	Democrat	Incumbent	1972
Dick Rutan	69,251	43.98%	Republican	Challenger	
Fritz Ward	8,424	5.35%	Libertarian	Challenger	
District 43					
Ken Calvert	88,987	46.68%	Republican	Challenger	1992
Mark Takano	88,468	46.41%	Democrat	Challenger	
Gary Odom	6,095	3.20%	American Independent	Challenger	
Gene Berkman	4,989	2.62%	Libertarian	Challenger	
John Schwab	2,100	1.10%	Write in	Challenger	
District 44					
Al McCandless	110,333	54.21%	Republican	Incumbent	1982
Georgia Smith	81,693	40.14%	Democrat	Challenger	
Phil Turner	11,515	5.66%	Libertarian	Challenger	
District 45					
Dana Rohrabacher	123,731	54.50%	Republican	Incumbent	1988
Patricia McCabe	88,508	38.99%	Democrat	Challenger	
Gary Copeland	14,777	6.51%	Libertarian	Challenger	
District 46					
Robert Dornan	55,659	50.23%	Republican	Incumbent	1984
Robert Banuelos	45,435	41.00%	Democrat	Challenger	
Richard Newhouse	9,712	8.76%	Libertarian	Challenger	
District 47					
Christopher Cox	165,004	64.90%	Republican	Incumbent	1988
John Anwiler	76,924	30.25%	Democrat	Challenger	
Maxine Quirk	12,297	4.84%	Peace and Freedom	Challenger	
Barry Charles	32	0.01%	Write in	Challenger	
District 48					
Ron Packard	140,935	61.14%	Republican	Incumbent	1982
Michael Farber	67,415	29.25%	Democrat	Challenger	
Donna White	13,396	5.81%	Peace and Freedom	Challenger	
Ted Lowe	8,749	3.80%	Libertarian	Challenger	
District 49					
Lynn Schenk	127,280	51.14%	Democrat	Challenger	1992
Judy Jarvis	106,170	42.66%	Republican	Challenger	
John Wallner	10,706	4.30%	Libertarian	Challenger	
Milton Zaslow	4,738	1.90%	Peace and Freedom	Challenger	
Perry Thompson	4	<.01%	Write in	Challenger	

Candidate(s)	Total vote	Percent	Party	Status	First elected
U.S. Representative in Congress (cont)					
District 50					
Bob Filner	77,293	56.57%	Democrat	Challenger	1992
Tony Valencia	39,531	28.93%	Republican	Challenger	
Barbara Hutchinson	15,489	11.34%	Libertarian	Challenger	
Roger Batchelder	4,250	3.11%	Peace and Freedom	Challenger	
Lincoln Pickard	63	0.05%	Write in	Challenger	
District 51					
Randy Cunningham	141,890	56.08%	Republican	Incumbent	1990
Bea Herbert	85,148	33.66%	Democrat	Challenger	
Bill Holmes	10,309	4.07%	Libertarian	Challenger	
Miriam Clark	10,307	4.07%	Peace and Freedom	Challenger	
Richard Roe	5,328	2.11%	Green	Challenger	
Kathleen Johnson	13	<.01%	Write in	Challenger	
District 52					
Duncan Hunter	112,995	52.85%	Republican	Incumbent	1980
Janet Gastil	88,076	41.20%	Democrat	Challenger	
Joe Shea	6,977	3.26%	Libertarian	Challenger	
Dennis Gretsinger	5,734	2.68%	Peace and Freedom	Challenger	
David Marmon	2	<.01%	Write in	Challenger	

Candidates: June 2, 1992, Primary Election

Candidate	Total vote	Percent	Candidate	Total vote	Percent
Presidential Preference, Democratic			**Presidential Preference, Republican**		
Bill Clinton	1,359,112	47.46%	George Bush	1,587,369	73.62%
Jerry Brown	1,150,460	40.18%	Patrick Buchanan	568,892	26.38%
Paul Tsongas	212,522	7.42%			
Eugene McCarthy	60,635	2.12%			
Bob Kerrey	33,935	1.19%			
Larry Agran	24,784	0.87%			
Lyndon LaRouche, Jr.	21,971	0.77%			

Voter Registration and Turnout, 1948-1992 Elections

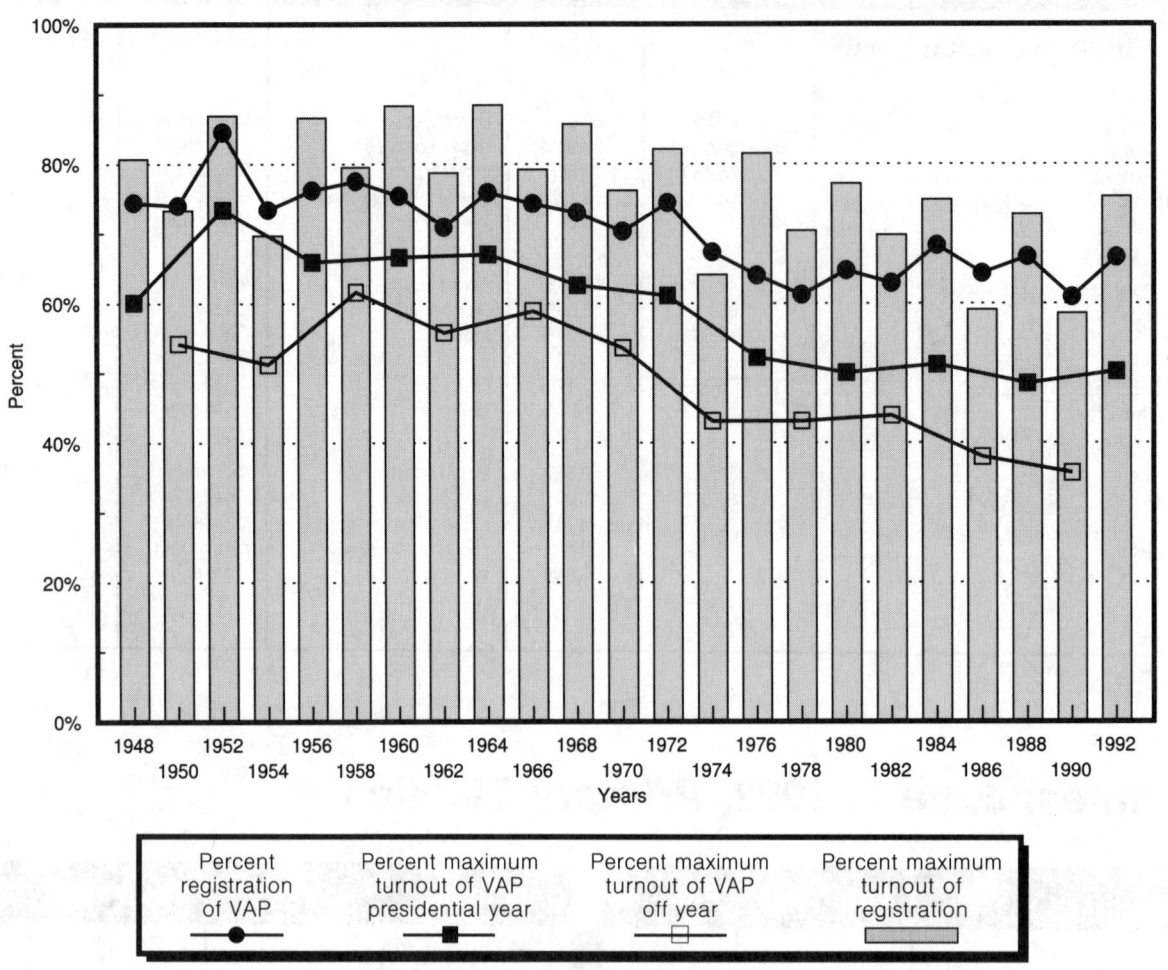

| | Percent registration of VAP ● | Percent maximum turnout of VAP presidential year ■ | Percent maximum turnout of VAP off year ☐ | Percent maximum turnout of registration ▒ |

Year	Estimated Voting Age Population (VAP)	Voter registration (REG)			Voter turnout											
						Highest office						Maximum vote				
		Total	Percent of VAP	Rank by percent of VAP	Actual	Total	Office	Percent total REG	Rank by percent of REG	Percent of VAP	Rank by percent of VAP	Total	Percent total REG	Rank by percent of REG	Percent total VAP	Rank by percent of VAP
1992	22,668,000	15,101,473	66.6	39	11,374,565	11,131,721	P	73.7	35	49.1	47	11,374,565	75.3	33	50.2	46
1990	22,124,000	13,478,030	60.9	40	7,899,131	7,699,420	G	57.1	26	34.8	37	7,899,131	58.6	27	35.7	35
1988	21,006,000	14,004,873	66.7	35	10,194,539	9,887,065	P	70.6	29	47.1	39	10,194,539	72.8	27	48.5	36
1986	20,043,000	12,883,920	64.3	37	7,617,142	7,443,551	G	57.8	22	37.1	32	7,617,142	59.1	20	38.0	31
1984	19,152,000	13,073,630	68.3	37	9,796,375	9,505,423	P	72.7	27	49.6	41	9,796,375	74.9	26	51.2	38
1982	18,387,000	11,559,010	62.9	37	8,064,314	7,876,698	G	68.1	11	42.8	26	8,064,314	69.8	12	43.9	27
1980	17,548,000	11,361,020	64.7	40	8,775,459	8,587,063	P	75.6	21	48.9	38	8,775,459	77.2	19	50.0	37
1978	16,546,000	10,129,986	61.2	39	7,132,210	6,922,378	G	68.3	5	41.8	22	7,132,210	70.4	5	43.1	21
1976	15,598,000	9,980,488	64.0	40	8,137,202	7,867,117	P	78.8	15	50.4	34	8,137,202	81.5	10	52.2	32
1974	14,751,000	9,928,364	67.3	32	6,364,597	6,248,070	G	62.9	17	42.4	23	6,364,597	64.1	16	43.1	25
1972	14,062,000	10,466,215	74.4	24	8,595,590	8,367,862	P	80.0	9	59.5	23	8,595,590	82.1	10	61.1	20
1970	12,376,000	8,706,347	70.3	30	6,633,400	6,510,072	G	74.8	9	52.6	16	6,633,400	76.2	8	53.6	18
1968	11,771,000	8,587,673	73.0	27	7,363,711	7,251,587	P	84.4	12	61.6	29	7,363,711	85.7	9	62.6	29
1966	11,220,000	8,340,868	74.3	24	6,605,866	6,503,445	G	78.0	4	58.0	9	6,605,866	79.2	4	58.9	10
1964	10,789,000	8,184,143	75.9	24	7,233,067	7,057,586	P	86.2	10	65.4	28	7,233,067	88.4	9	67.0	28
1962	10,622,000	7,531,211	70.9	23	5,929,602	5,853,270	G	77.7	6	55.1	18	5,929,602	78.7	5	55.8	18
1960	9,895,000	7,464,626	75.4	19	6,592,591	6,506,578	P	87.2	13	65.8	31	6,592,591	88.3	12	66.6	31
1958	8,716,000	6,752,421	77.5	14	5,366,053	5,255,777	G	77.8	6	60.3	9	5,366,053	79.5	5	61.6	9
1956	8,412,000	6,408,821	76.2	17	5,547,621	5,466,355	P	85.3	10	65.0	28	5,547,621	86.6	9	65.9	28
1954	8,018,000	5,885,327	73.4	17	4,101,692	4,030,368	G	68.5	11	50.3	24	4,101,692	69.7	11	51.2	24
1952	7,096,000	5,998,300	84.5	11	5,209,692	5,141,849	P	85.7	11	72.5	17	5,209,692	86.9	9	73.4	16
1950	7,092,000	5,244,837	74.0	10	3,845,837	3,796,090	G	72.4	9	53.5	18	3,845,837	73.3	9	54.2	18
1948	6,802,000	5,061,997	74.4	11	4,086,981	4,021,538	P	79.4	9	59.1	24	4,086,981	80.7	8	60.1	24

CALIFORNIA

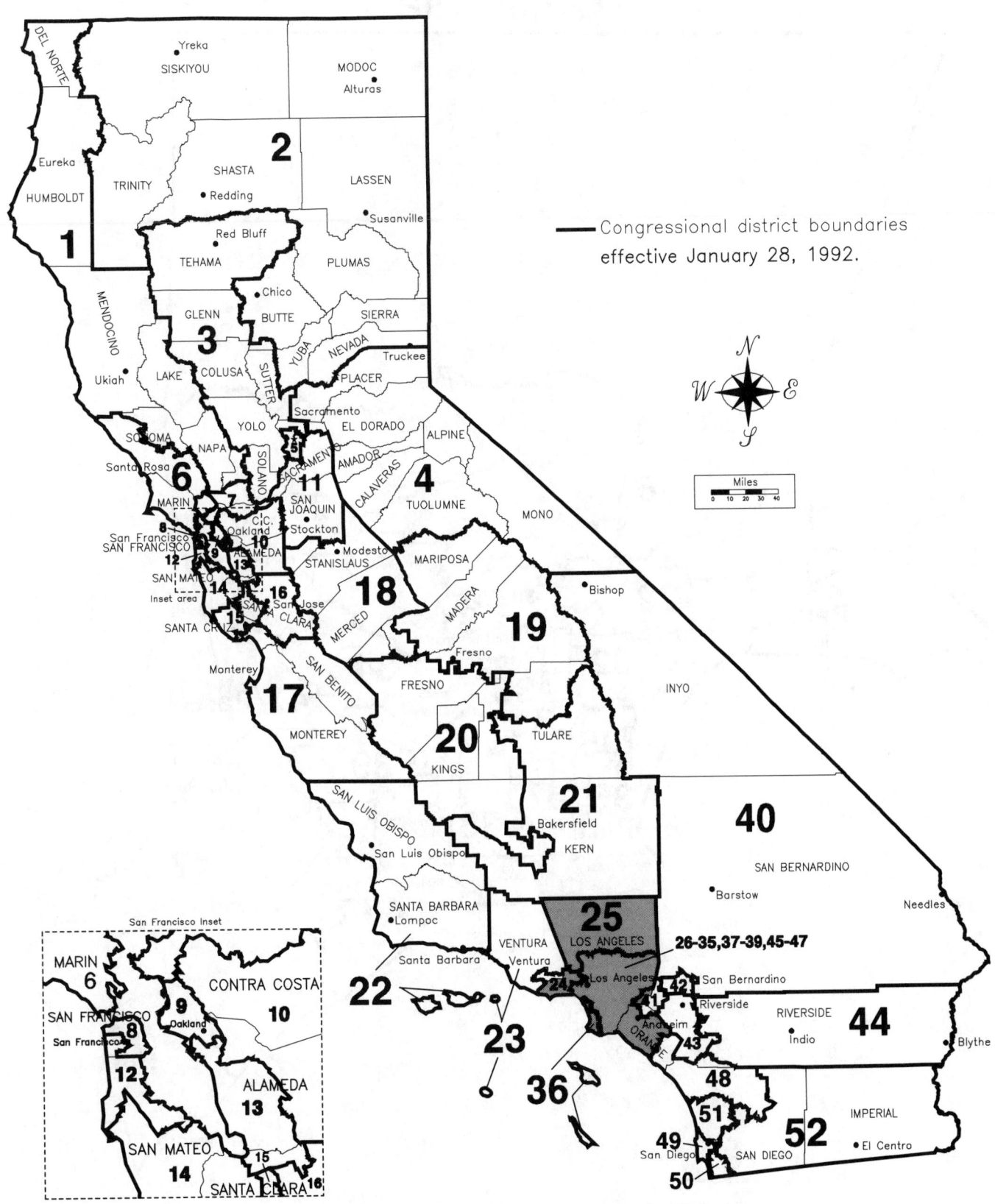

Congressional district boundaries effective January 28, 1992.

Los Angeles County & Metropolitan Area, California

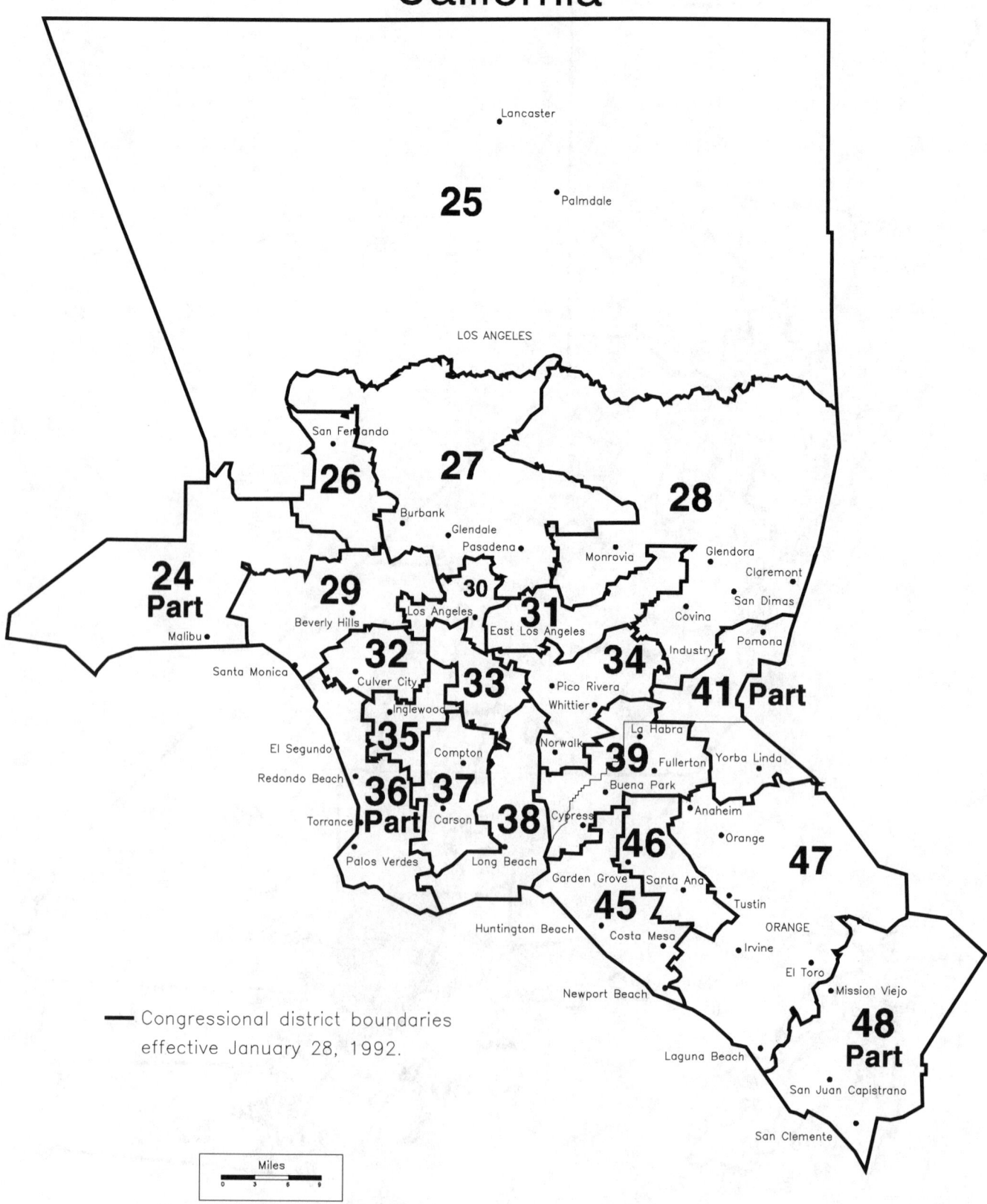

Lancaster

25

Palmdale

LOS ANGELES

San Fernando

26

27

28

Burbank

Glendale

Pasadena

Monrovia

Glendora

Claremont

24
Part

29

30

Los Angeles

31

East Los Angeles

San Dimas

Covina

Pomona

Beverly Hills

Industry

Malibu

32

Santa Monica

Culver City

33

Pico Rivera

Whittier

34

41 Part

Inglewood

35

El Segundo

Compton

Norwalk

La Habra

39

Fullerton

Yorba Linda

Redondo Beach

36
Part

37

38

Buena Park

Torrance

Carson

Cypress

Anaheim

46

Orange

47

Palos Verdes

Long Beach

Garden Grove

Santa Ana

45

Tustin

ORANGE

Huntington Beach

Costa Mesa

Irvine

El Toro

Mission Viejo

Newport Beach

48
Part

— Congressional district boundaries
effective January 28, 1992.

Laguna Beach

San Juan Capistrano

San Clemente

Miles
0   3   6   9

Table A. — 1990 Population by Race and Ethnic Origin

State/county code	County	Total persons	Percent of total persons White	Black	Asian and Pacific Islander	Native American	Other	Hispanic	Rank Total	Percent of total persons Non-Hispanic White	Black	Hispanic	Percent contribution to state population Total	Non-Hispanic White	Black	Hispanic
06 001	Alameda	1,279,182	53.2	17.4	14.4	0.5	0.2	14.2	6	52	1	27	4.3	4.0	10.7	2.4
06 003	Alpine	1,113	69.4	0.4	0.4	23.1	0.0	6.6	58	33	53	49	<.1	<.1	<.1	<.1
06 005	Amador	30,039	83.7	5.6	0.7	1.5	0.2	8.4	46	21	12	41	0.1	0.1	<.1	<.1
06 007	Butte	182,120	86.9	1.2	2.7	1.6	<.1	7.5	25	14	37	45	0.6	0.9	0.1	0.2
06 009	Calaveras	31,998	91.5	0.6	0.6	1.9	<.1	5.4	45	3	47	52	0.1	0.2	<.1	<.1
06 011	Colusa	16,275	62.1	0.5	2.0	1.9	0.3	33.3	52	42	49	9	<.1	<.1	<.1	<.1
06 013	Contra Costa	803,732	69.7	9.1	9.2	0.6	0.2	11.4	9	32	5	33	2.7	3.3	3.5	1.2
06 015	Del Norte	23,460	78.0	3.6	1.8	6.0	0.2	10.3	49	26	20	38	<.1	0.1	<.1	<.1
06 017	El Dorado	125,995	89.7	0.5	1.8	1.0	<.1	7.0	30	7	51	48	0.4	0.7	<.1	0.1
06 019	Fresno	667,490	50.7	4.7	8.1	0.8	0.3	35.5	12	55	17	5	2.2	2.0	1.5	3.1
06 021	Glenn	24,798	74.4	0.5	3.1	1.8	0.1	20.0	48	28	48	22	<.1	0.1	<.1	<.1
06 023	Humboldt	119,118	87.9	0.8	1.9	5.2	<.1	4.2	31	11	42	55	0.4	0.6	<.1	<.1
06 025	Imperial	109,303	29.0	2.1	1.5	1.4	0.1	65.8	33	58	28	1	0.4	0.2	0.1	0.9
06 027	Inyo	18,281	81.1	0.4	0.9	9.1	<.1	8.4	51	23	56	40	<.1	<.1	<.1	<.1
06 029	Kern	543,477	62.7	5.3	2.7	1.0	0.2	28.0	14	41	13	11	1.8	2.0	1.4	2.0
06 031	Kings	101,469	53.6	7.6	3.4	0.9	0.4	34.1	34	51	8	7	0.3	0.3	0.4	0.4
06 033	Lake	50,631	88.1	1.8	0.9	2.0	<.1	7.2	40	10	30	47	0.2	0.3	<.1	0.1
06 035	Lassen	27,598	79.4	6.2	1.1	2.9	<.1	10.4	47	25	9	36	<.1	0.1	<.1	<.1
06 037	Los Angeles	8,863,164	40.8	10.5	10.2	0.3	0.2	37.8	1	57	3	4	29.8	21.3	44.7	43.6
06 039	Madera	88,090	60.1	2.6	1.2	1.3	0.2	34.5	35	46	24	6	0.3	0.3	0.1	0.4
06 041	Marin	230,096	84.6	3.3	3.9	0.3	0.1	7.8	22	17	22	43	0.8	1.1	0.4	0.2
06 043	Mariposa	14,302	89.3	0.8	0.8	4.1	<.1	4.9	53	8	40	53	<.1	<.1	<.1	<.1
06 045	Mendocino	80,345	84.4	0.6	1.1	3.6	<.1	10.3	36	18	45	39	0.3	0.4	<.1	0.1
06 047	Merced	178,403	54.2	4.4	7.9	0.6	0.3	32.6	26	50	18	10	0.6	0.6	0.4	0.8
06 049	Modoc	9,678	87.6	0.8	0.4	3.9	<.1	7.2	56	13	41	46	<.1	<.1	<.1	<.1
06 051	Mono	9,956	83.7	0.4	1.1	3.4	<.1	11.3	55	20	54	34	<.1	<.1	<.1	<.1
06 053	Monterey	355,660	52.3	6.0	7.1	0.6	0.3	33.6	19	53	10	8	1.2	1.1	1.0	1.6
06 055	Napa	110,765	80.8	1.1	3.1	0.6	0.1	14.4	32	24	38	26	0.4	0.5	<.1	0.2
06 057	Nevada	78,510	93.9	0.2	0.8	0.9	<.1	4.2	37	1	57	56	0.3	0.4	<.1	<.1
06 059	Orange	2,410,556	64.5	1.6	10.0	0.4	0.1	23.4	3	39	32	17	8.1	9.1	1.9	7.3
06 061	Placer	172,796	88.3	0.6	2.1	0.9	<.1	8.0	27	9	46	42	0.6	0.9	<.1	0.2
06 063	Plumas	19,739	91.2	0.8	0.6	2.8	<.1	4.6	50	4	43	54	<.1	0.1	<.1	<.1
06 065	Riverside	1,170,413	64.4	5.1	3.3	0.7	0.2	26.3	7	40	16	15	3.9	4.4	2.9	4.0
06 067	Sacramento	1,041,219	69.3	9.0	8.8	0.9	0.2	11.7	8	34	6	31	3.5	4.2	4.5	1.6
06 069	San Benito	36,697	51.2	0.5	1.8	0.6	0.2	45.8	44	54	52	2	0.1	0.1	<.1	0.2
06 071	San Bernardino	1,418,380	60.8	7.7	3.9	0.7	0.2	26.7	5	44	7	12	4.8	5.1	5.2	4.9
06 073	San Diego	2,498,016	65.4	6.0	7.4	0.6	0.2	20.4	2	38	11	20	8.4	9.6	7.2	6.6
06 075	San Francisco	723,959	46.6	10.5	28.4	0.4	0.2	13.9	10	56	4	28	2.4	2.0	3.6	1.3
06 077	San Joaquin	480,628	58.8	5.2	11.6	0.8	0.2	23.4	15	47	15	16	1.6	1.7	1.2	1.5
06 079	San Luis Obispo	217,162	81.2	2.0	2.7	0.8	0.1	13.3	24	22	29	30	0.7	1.0	0.2	0.4
06 081	San Mateo	649,623	60.4	5.2	16.2	0.4	0.1	17.6	13	45	14	24	2.2	2.3	1.6	1.5
06 083	Santa Barbara	369,608	66.1	2.5	4.1	0.6	0.1	26.6	18	36	25	13	1.2	1.4	0.4	1.3
06 085	Santa Clara	1,497,577	58.1	3.5	16.8	0.4	0.2	21.0	4	48	21	19	5.0	5.1	2.5	4.1
06 087	Santa Cruz	229,734	74.5	1.0	3.3	0.6	0.2	20.4	23	27	39	21	0.8	1.0	0.1	0.6
06 089	Shasta	147,036	91.1	0.7	1.8	2.5	<.1	3.8	28	5	44	57	0.5	0.8	<.1	<.1
06 091	Sierra	3,318	92.2	0.2	0.2	1.8	<.1	5.5	57	2	58	51	<.1	<.1	<.1	<.1
06 093	Siskiyou	43,531	87.9	1.6	0.8	3.9	<.1	5.9	43	12	33	50	0.1	0.2	<.1	<.1
06 095	Solano	340,421	60.9	12.9	11.9	0.7	0.2	13.4	20	43	2	29	1.1	1.2	2.1	0.6
06 097	Sonoma	388,222	84.3	1.4	2.6	0.9	0.1	10.6	16	19	36	35	1.3	1.9	0.3	0.5
06 099	Stanislaus	370,522	70.5	1.6	4.9	0.9	0.2	21.8	17	31	31	18	1.2	1.5	0.3	1.1
06 101	Sutter	64,415	71.6	1.5	8.9	1.3	0.2	16.4	38	30	34	25	0.2	0.3	<.1	0.1
06 103	Tehama	49,625	86.7	0.5	0.7	1.7	<.1	10.3	41	15	50	37	0.2	0.3	<.1	<.1
06 105	Trinity	13,063	91.0	0.4	0.8	4.5	<.1	3.3	54	6	55	58	<.1	<.1	<.1	<.1
06 107	Tulare	311,921	54.6	1.4	4.0	1.0	0.2	38.8	21	49	35	3	1.0	1.0	0.2	1.6
06 109	Tuolumne	48,456	86.4	3.2	0.7	1.8	0.2	7.7	42	16	23	44	0.2	0.2	<.1	<.1
06 111	Ventura	669,016	65.9	2.2	4.9	0.5	0.1	26.4	11	37	26	14	2.2	2.6	0.7	2.3
06 113	Yolo	141,092	68.6	2.1	8.1	1.0	0.2	20.0	29	35	27	23	0.5	0.6	0.1	0.4
06 115	Yuba	58,228	73.7	4.0	7.9	2.6	0.1	11.6	39	29	19	32	0.2	0.3	0.1	<.1
06	CALIFORNIA	29,760,021	57.2	7.0	9.1	0.6	0.2	25.8					100.0	100.0	100.0	100.0
	CONGRESSIONAL															
	District 1	573,082	79.2	3.7	3.4	2.4	0.1	11.2	13	5	30	47	1.9	2.7	1.0	0.8
	District 2	573,322	87.9	1.5	2.3	2.2	<.1	6.0	8	1	50	52	1.9	3.0	0.4	0.4
	District 3	571,374	76.1	3.1	5.2	1.2	0.2	14.2	43	8	32	38	1.9	2.6	0.8	1.1
	District 4	571,033	87.6	1.7	2.0	1.1	<.1	7.4	48	2	47	51	1.9	2.9	0.5	0.6
	District 5	573,684	59.1	12.4	12.6	0.9	0.2	14.7	1	30	7	36	1.9	2.0	3.4	1.1
	District 6	571,227	84.8	2.2	3.3	0.7	0.1	8.9	46	3	42	49	1.9	2.8	0.6	0.7
	District 7	572,773	56.0	16.2	13.6	0.6	0.2	13.3	20	35	5	42	1.9	1.9	4.4	1.0
	District 8	573,247	44.3	12.4	27.0	0.4	0.2	15.7	10	39	8	33	1.9	1.5	3.4	1.2

Table A. — 1990 Population by Race and Ethnic Origin (cont)

State/county code	County	Total persons	Percent of total persons Non-Hispanic White	Black	Asian and Pacific Islander	Native American	Other	Hispanic	Rank Total	Percent of total persons Non-Hispanic White	Black	Hispanic	Percent contribution to state population Total	Non-Hispanic White	Black	Hispanic
	District 9	573,458	41.1	31.0	15.1	0.5	0.3	12.0	6	40	4	46	1.9	1.4	8.5	0.9
	District 10	572,008	82.3	2.2	6.1	0.5	0.1	8.7	31	4	41	50	1.9	2.8	0.6	0.7
	District 11	571,772	61.8	5.4	10.8	0.8	0.2	21.1	33	27	18	26	1.9	2.1	1.5	1.6
	District 12	571,535	56.3	4.0	25.0	0.3	0.2	14.3	37	34	26	37	1.9	1.9	1.1	1.1
	District 13	572,441	55.2	7.1	18.5	0.6	0.2	18.4	29	36	12	29	1.9	1.9	1.9	1.4
	District 14	571,131	69.4	4.7	11.9	0.3	0.1	13.5	47	20	23	40	1.9	2.3	1.3	1.0
	District 15	572,485	75.5	2.1	10.9	0.5	0.1	10.8	28	10	44	48	1.9	2.5	0.6	0.8
	District 16	571,551	37.5	4.8	20.1	0.5	0.2	36.8	36	41	22	11	1.9	1.3	1.3	2.7
	District 17	570,981	57.7	4.1	5.7	0.6	0.2	31.6	49	31	25	13	1.9	1.9	1.1	2.3
	District 18	571,393	64.7	2.7	5.7	0.8	0.2	26.0	41	23	37	18	1.9	2.2	0.7	1.9
	District 19	573,043	65.0	3.1	7.0	1.0	0.2	23.6	15	22	33	22	1.9	2.2	0.8	1.8
	District 20	573,282	32.6	6.0	5.0	0.6	0.4	55.4	9	44	14	5	1.9	1.1	1.7	4.1
	District 21	571,300	71.4	3.9	3.0	1.2	0.2	20.3	44	18	27	28	1.9	2.4	1.1	1.5
	District 22	572,891	72.0	2.4	3.6	0.6	0.1	21.3	19	17	39	25	1.9	2.4	0.7	1.6
	District 23	571,483	62.0	2.3	4.9	0.6	0.1	30.0	40	26	40	16	1.9	2.1	0.6	2.2
	District 24	572,563	77.9	2.0	6.3	0.3	0.1	13.5	26	6	45	41	1.9	2.6	0.5	1.0
	District 25	573,105	72.4	4.2	6.3	0.6	0.2	16.4	12	16	24	31	1.9	2.4	1.1	1.2
	District 26	571,523	34.2	5.7	6.8	0.3	0.3	52.7	38	43	15	6	1.9	1.1	1.6	3.9
	District 27	572,594	60.8	7.9	10.2	0.3	0.2	20.6	25	29	10	27	1.9	2.0	2.1	1.5
	District 28	572,927	57.4	5.4	12.6	0.3	0.2	24.1	18	33	17	21	1.9	1.9	1.5	1.8
	District 29	571,566	75.7	3.3	7.4	0.2	0.1	13.2	35	9	31	43	1.9	2.5	0.9	1.0
	District 30	572,538	15.2	3.0	19.8	0.3	0.3	61.5	27	49	35	3	1.9	0.5	0.8	4.6
	District 31	572,643	17.5	1.5	22.1	0.2	0.2	58.5	23	48	51	4	1.9	0.6	0.4	4.4
	District 32	572,595	23.6	38.2	7.4	0.3	0.4	30.2	24	47	2	15	1.9	0.8	10.5	2.3
	District 33	570,943	8.1	3.8	3.8	0.3	0.4	83.7	50	52	29	1	1.9	0.3	1.0	6.2
	District 34	573,047	26.7	1.7	8.7	0.3	0.2	62.3	14	46	48	2	1.9	0.9	0.5	4.6
	District 35	570,882	10.4	40.4	5.5	0.2	0.4	43.1	51	51	1	9	1.9	0.3	11.0	3.2
	District 36	573,663	69.4	3.0	12.2	0.4	0.1	14.9	2	21	34	34	1.9	2.3	0.8	1.1
	District 37	572,049	12.0	32.2	10.1	0.3	0.3	45.1	30	50	3	8	1.9	0.4	8.8	3.4
	District 38	572,657	57.5	7.4	8.6	0.5	0.2	25.7	22	32	11	19	1.9	1.9	2.0	1.9
	District 39	573,574	60.8	2.5	13.3	0.4	0.1	22.8	4	28	38	23	1.9	2.0	0.7	1.7
	District 40	573,625	74.1	5.2	3.3	1.2	0.1	16.1	3	13	19	32	1.9	2.5	1.4	1.2
	District 41	572,663	51.9	6.3	9.7	0.3	0.2	31.5	21	37	13	14	1.9	1.7	1.7	2.3
	District 42	571,844	50.5	10.6	3.7	0.6	0.3	34.3	32	38	9	12	1.9	1.7	2.9	2.6
	District 43	571,231	64.6	5.6	4.0	0.6	0.2	25.0	45	24	16	20	1.9	2.2	1.5	1.9
	District 44	571,583	63.5	4.8	2.6	0.8	0.2	28.1	34	25	21	17	1.9	2.1	1.3	2.1
	District 45	570,874	72.8	1.2	10.7	0.4	<.1	14.8	52	15	52	35	1.9	2.4	0.3	1.1
	District 46	571,380	35.6	2.2	11.7	0.3	0.2	50.0	42	42	43	7	1.9	1.2	0.6	3.7
	District 47	571,518	75.4	1.7	9.4	0.3	<.1	13.1	39	11	46	44	1.9	2.5	0.5	1.0
	District 48	572,928	73.8	3.8	4.2	0.8	0.1	17.2	17	14	28	30	1.9	2.5	1.0	1.3
	District 49	573,362	75.3	5.0	6.2	0.6	0.1	12.8	7	12	20	45	1.9	2.5	1.4	1.0
	District 50	573,463	31.5	13.6	13.7	0.4	0.3	40.6	5	45	6	10	1.9	1.1	3.7	3.0
	District 51	572,982	76.4	1.7	7.8	0.4	<.1	13.6	16	7	49	39	1.9	2.6	0.5	1.0
	District 52	573,203	70.7	2.9	2.7	0.9	0.1	22.6	11	19	36	24	1.9	2.4	0.8	1.7

Table B. — 1990 Voting Age Population (VAP) by Race and Ethnic Origin

County	Total Voting Age Population	Percent of total VAP — Non-Hispanic White	Black	Asian and Pacific Islander	Native American	Other	Hispanic	Rank Total	Rank Non-Hisp White	Rank Non-Hisp Black	Rank Hispanic	Pct contrib Total	Pct contrib White	Pct contrib Black	Pct contrib Hispanic	VAP % total pop Total	White	Black	Asian and Pacific Islander	Native American	Other	Hispanic
Alameda	975,777	56.4	16.3	13.9	0.5	0.2	12.7	6	54	1	26	4.4	4.1	10.8	2.5	76.3	80.9	71.4	73.2	76.4	60.9	68.3
Alpine	831	75.1	0.6	0.5	18.8	0.0	5.1	58	30	45	49	<.1	<.1	<.1	<.1	74.7	80.8	100.0	80.0	60.7	0.0	56.8
Amador	24,383	82.6	6.6	0.6	1.3	0.2	8.6	45	23	10	38	0.1	0.1	0.1	<.1	81.2	80.2	96.5	77.5	70.5	91.5	83.1
Butte	139,236	89.1	1.1	2.1	1.5	<.1	6.1	25	15	37	45	0.6	0.9	0.1	0.2	76.5	78.4	68.7	59.8	68.5	59.1	62.6
Calaveras	24,061	92.6	0.5	0.5	1.8	<.1	4.6	46	5	46	52	0.1	0.2	<.1	<.1	75.2	76.0	72.8	69.5	69.8	26.1	64.1
Colusa	11,272	67.1	0.5	2.0	1.8	0.2	28.4	52	41	49	10	<.1	<.1	<.1	<.1	69.3	74.8	69.1	71.3	65.9	64.3	59.0
Contra Costa	601,644	72.5	8.3	8.6	0.6	0.1	9.9	10	34	6	34	2.7	3.2	3.4	1.2	74.9	77.9	68.3	69.9	75.6	55.0	65.5
Del Norte	17,133	79.0	4.8	1.3	4.8	0.2	9.9	49	26	17	36	<.1	0.1	<.1	<.1	73.0	74.0	96.1	51.5	58.2	83.7	70.2
El Dorado	92,750	90.7	0.4	1.8	0.9	<.1	6.1	30	7	54	46	0.4	0.6	<.1	0.1	73.6	74.4	67.7	72.1	68.9	68.8	64.7
Fresno	458,454	56.8	4.3	6.4	0.8	0.2	31.5	13	52	19	5	2.1	1.9	1.3	2.9	68.7	76.9	63.1	54.3	68.5	61.1	61.1
Glenn	17,238	79.1	0.5	1.8	1.6	<.1	16.9	48	25	48	23	<.1	0.1	<.1	<.1	69.5	73.8	68.7	40.8	62.4	50.0	58.6
Humboldt	88,511	89.8	0.7	1.5	4.3	<.1	3.6	31	11	42	55	0.4	0.6	<.1	<.1	74.3	76.0	68.4	57.9	61.8	65.4	63.6
Imperial	71,844	34.3	2.3	1.7	1.4	0.1	60.3	33	58	26	1	0.3	0.2	0.1	0.9	65.7	77.6	71.2	73.7	63.1	61.6	60.2
Inyo	13,844	84.0	0.4	0.8	7.6	0.1	7.0	51	21	55	44	<.1	<.1	<.1	<.1	75.7	78.5	80.3	68.0	62.9	100.0	63.2
Kern	372,490	66.9	5.0	2.8	1.1	0.2	24.1	14	42	13	11	1.7	1.9	1.3	1.8	68.5	73.1	64.2	69.2	71.9	58.4	59.0
Kings	70,681	56.6	8.5	3.1	0.8	0.4	30.6	34	53	5	6	0.3	0.3	0.4	0.4	69.7	73.5	77.5	63.8	61.3	73.1	62.7
Lake	38,538	90.1	1.7	0.8	1.7	<.1	5.8	40	9	30	47	0.2	0.3	<.1	<.1	76.1	77.7	72.0	68.9	64.9	59.5	61.4
Lassen	20,775	77.9	7.7	1.1	2.4	<.1	10.9	47	29	8	31	<.1	0.1	0.1	<.1	75.3	73.9	93.8	75.1	63.4	61.5	78.6
Los Angeles	6,537,054	45.6	10.2	10.3	0.3	0.2	33.3	1	57	3	4	29.7	22.1	45.5	43.9	73.8	82.4	71.5	74.4	76.7	59.8	65.0
Madera	60,707	65.1	2.6	1.2	1.3	0.2	29.6	35	43	24	7	0.3	0.3	0.1	0.4	68.9	74.6	68.0	68.2	70.1	56.1	59.2
Marin	186,160	85.4	3.2	3.7	0.3	<.1	7.3	22	19	23	42	0.8	1.2	0.4	0.3	80.9	81.7	79.8	75.2	79.1	54.7	76.1
Mariposa	11,036	90.6	1.0	0.7	3.5	<.1	4.2	53	8	38	53	<.1	<.1	<.1	<.1	77.2	78.3	93.3	66.4	64.4	50.0	67.0
Mendocino	58,393	86.9	0.5	1.1	3.1	<.1	8.3	37	16	50	39	0.3	0.4	<.1	<.1	72.7	74.9	59.8	72.4	63.2	64.9	58.9
Merced	117,737	60.0	4.4	5.9	0.7	0.2	28.9	27	50	18	8	0.5	0.5	0.4	0.7	66.0	73.0	65.4	49.1	72.3	57.4	58.5
Modoc	7,055	89.6	0.9	0.4	3.4	<.1	5.7	56	12	41	48	<.1	<.1	<.1	<.1	72.9	74.6	79.5	71.4	63.0	100.0	56.9
Mono	7,522	85.4	0.4	1.1	2.7	<.1	10.4	55	20	53	32	<.1	<.1	<.1	<.1	75.6	77.1	78.0	71.9	59.5	20.0	69.5
Monterey	257,709	57.1	6.1	7.2	0.6	0.2	28.7	18	51	11	9	1.2	1.1	1.1	1.5	72.5	79.1	73.2	72.8	75.5	65.6	61.9
Napa	85,045	83.1	1.0	3.0	0.6	0.1	12.2	32	22	39	29	0.4	0.5	<.1	0.2	76.8	79.0	69.5	75.1	74.4	74.6	65.1
Nevada	59,518	94.7	0.2	0.7	0.9	<.1	3.5	36	1	57	56	0.3	0.4	<.1	<.1	75.8	76.5	68.0	69.4	69.0	68.4	63.0
Orange	1,821,253	68.0	1.5	9.4	0.4	<.1	20.6	3	40	31	17	8.3	9.2	1.9	7.6	75.6	79.7	70.4	71.1	77.3	61.4	66.4
Placer	127,570	89.5	0.5	2.0	0.9	<.1	7.1	26	13	47	43	0.6	0.8	<.1	0.2	73.8	74.8	68.3	71.3	70.6	59.6	64.9
Plumas	14,700	92.8	0.6	0.5	2.4	<.1	3.7	50	3	43	54	<.1	0.1	<.1	<.1	74.5	75.8	61.6	63.4	62.4	41.7	59.4
Riverside	837,152	68.7	4.8	3.1	0.7	0.1	22.5	7	39	16	15	3.8	4.3	2.7	3.8	71.5	76.3	67.0	68.7	69.5	59.1	61.3
Sacramento	766,240	72.6	8.1	8.0	0.9	0.1	10.2	8	33	7	33	3.5	4.1	4.2	1.6	73.6	77.1	65.9	66.8	71.5	55.0	64.3
San Benito	25,296	55.5	0.4	1.9	0.6	0.2	41.4	44	55	56	2	0.1	0.1	<.1	0.2	68.9	74.7	60.5	74.9	78.1	56.8	62.3
San Bernardino	979,157	64.7	7.1	3.8	0.7	0.2	23.5	5	44	9	12	4.4	4.7	4.7	4.6	69.0	73.4	63.8	68.0	69.5	57.2	60.7
San Diego	1,887,070	69.2	5.5	6.9	0.6	0.1	17.6	2	38	12	20	8.6	9.7	7.1	6.7	75.5	80.0	69.5	70.5	73.2	56.3	65.1
San Francisco	607,076	50.7	9.5	26.7	0.4	0.1	12.6	9	56	4	27	2.8	2.3	3.9	1.5	83.9	91.2	75.5	78.9	84.4	66.2	75.9
San Joaquin	338,378	63.3	4.8	9.6	0.8	0.1	21.3	15	47	15	16	1.5	1.6	1.1	1.5	70.4	75.8	65.7	58.3	70.7	54.3	64.0
San Luis Obispo	169,631	82.6	2.0	2.8	0.8	0.1	11.8	24	24	29	30	0.8	1.0	0.2	0.4	78.1	79.5	77.3	81.3	77.4	74.4	69.3
San Mateo	507,137	63.9	4.9	15.3	0.4	0.1	15.5	11	45	14	24	2.3	2.4	1.7	1.6	78.1	82.6	72.8	73.5	77.2	61.3	68.5
Santa Barbara	283,721	70.2	2.4	4.1	0.6	0.1	22.6	17	36	25	14	1.3	1.5	0.5	1.3	76.8	81.6	71.5	76.8	76.1	64.8	65.4
Santa Clara	1,138,370	61.7	3.3	16.0	0.4	0.1	18.5	4	48	22	19	5.2	5.2	2.6	4.2	76.0	80.7	71.6	72.4	76.1	61.3	66.9
Santa Cruz	175,030	78.0	0.9	3.4	0.6	0.1	17.0	23	28	40	21	0.8	1.0	0.1	0.6	76.2	79.7	69.3	77.7	76.7	60.9	63.5
Shasta	106,625	92.7	0.6	1.2	2.3	<.1	3.1	29	4	44	57	0.5	0.7	<.1	<.1	72.5	73.8	61.9	50.4	67.1	52.4	58.2
Sierra	2,449	93.5	0.1	0.3	1.5	<.1	4.6	57	2	58	51	<.1	<.1	<.1	<.1	73.8	74.8	50.0	87.5	61.0	100.0	60.9
Siskiyou	31,890	89.9	1.5	0.6	3.4	<.1	4.7	43	10	34	50	0.1	0.2	<.1	<.1	73.3	74.9	67.9	58.7	63.4	66.7	58.3
Solano	242,581	63.4	12.3	11.2	0.7	0.1	12.2	20	46	2	28	1.1	1.1	2.0	0.6	71.3	74.2	67.8	67.3	71.3	52.7	65.1
Sonoma	292,446	86.3	1.2	2.4	0.9	<.1	9.2	16	17	36	37	1.3	1.9	0.2	0.5	75.3	77.1	64.8	69.3	69.6	50.4	65.0
Stanislaus	257,151	74.9	1.5	3.9	1.0	0.1	18.5	19	31	32	18	1.2	1.4	0.3	1.0	69.4	73.7	62.7	55.9	73.8	61.8	58.8
Sutter	46,012	74.8	1.5	8.5	1.3	0.2	13.8	38	32	33	25	0.2	0.3	<.1	0.1	71.4	74.6	68.0	67.6	73.0	60.7	59.9
Tehama	36,110	89.2	0.5	0.6	1.6	<.1	8.0	42	14	51	40	0.2	0.2	<.1	<.1	72.8	74.9	68.7	64.0	68.7	59.4	56.7
Trinity	9,615	92.0	0.5	0.5	4.1	<.1	2.9	54	6	52	58	<.1	<.1	<.1	<.1	73.6	74.4	84.9	48.5	66.5	60.0	65.2
Tulare	208,784	60.6	1.3	3.5	1.0	0.2	33.4	21	49	35	3	0.9	0.9	0.2	1.4	66.9	74.3	63.2	57.8	66.1	55.0	57.7
Tuolumne	37,561	86.0	4.0	0.6	1.6	0.2	7.5	41	18	20	41	0.2	0.2	0.1	<.1	77.5	77.1	97.6	67.4	70.3	85.5	76.1
Ventura	486,030	69.3	2.1	4.7	0.5	0.1	23.2	12	37	27	13	2.2	2.5	0.7	2.3	72.6	76.5	69.4	70.5	74.1	60.2	63.8
Yolo	107,088	71.4	2.1	8.5	0.9	0.2	16.9	28	35	28	22	0.5	0.6	0.2	0.4	75.9	79.0	74.8	79.4	73.3	55.5	64.3
Yuba	39,775	78.3	3.8	5.6	2.4	<.1	9.9	39	27	21	35	0.2	0.2	0.1	<.1	68.3	72.5	64.9	47.9	61.3	46.3	58.5
CALIFORNIA	**22,009,296**	**61.2**	**6.7**	**8.9**	**0.6**	**0.2**	**22.5**					**100.0**	**100.0**	**100.0**	**100.0**	**74.0**	**79.1**	**70.3**	**71.9**	**72.0**	**59.6**	**64.5**
CONGRESSIONAL																						
District 1	423,418	81.4	3.5	3.1	2.1	<.1	9.8	25	5	29	47	1.9	2.6	1.0	0.8	73.9	75.9	70.8	68.2	63.5	62.5	64.6
District 2	424,975	89.8	1.4	1.7	2.0	<.1	5.0	23	1	51	52	1.9	2.8	0.4	0.4	74.1	75.7	71.9	54.4	65.8	55.6	62.3
District 3	417,336	78.7	2.8	5.2	1.1	0.1	12.0	30	7	33	39	1.9	2.4	0.8	1.0	73.0	75.5	66.9	72.0	70.1	53.6	61.9
District 4	426,723	88.1	2.0	1.9	1.1	<.1	6.8	20	2	44	51	1.9	2.8	0.6	0.6	74.7	75.2	85.8	70.6	69.4	72.1	68.7
District 5	421,787	63.9	10.9	11.4	0.9	0.2	12.7	26	30	8	37	1.9	2.0	3.1	1.1	73.5	79.5	64.6	66.0	71.6	55.0	63.6
District 6	443,956	86.2	2.1	3.0	0.6	<.1	7.9	12	3	43	49	2.0	2.8	0.6	0.7	77.7	79.0	73.8	72.2	71.6	50.5	69.1
District 7	421,122	59.8	14.9	12.7	0.6	0.1	11.7	27	34	5	41	1.9	1.9	4.3	1.0	73.5	78.5	67.7	68.7	74.1	52.8	65.0
District 8	481,160	48.7	11.1	25.5	0.4	0.2	14.1	2	39	7	32	2.2	1.7	3.6	1.4	83.9	92.2	75.3	79.3	85.1	66.7	75.5

Table B. — 1990 Voting Age Population (VAP) by Race and Ethnic Origin (cont)

County	Total Voting Age Population	Percent of total VAP — Non-Hispanic White	Black	Asian and Pacific Islander	Native American	Other	Hispanic	Rank — Percent of total VAP Total	Non-Hispanic White	Black	Hispanic	Percent contribution to state VAP Total	Non-Hispanic White	Black	Hispanic	VAP percent of total population Total	Non-Hispanic White	Black	Asian and Pacific Islander	Native American	Other	Hispanic
District 9	446,911	45.6	28.5	14.6	0.5	0.2	10.7	9	40	4	46	2.0	1.5	8.7	1.0	77.9	86.3	71.8	75.0	77.0	60.0	69.2
District 10	431,405	83.7	2.1	5.7	0.5	0.1	7.8	18	4	42	50	2.0	2.7	0.6	0.7	75.4	76.7	72.4	70.5	76.2	62.5	67.3
District 11	404,673	66.1	4.9	9.1	0.8	0.1	19.0	39	26	17	25	1.8	2.0	1.4	1.6	70.8	75.7	64.9	59.6	71.5	51.4	63.7
District 12	455,454	59.5	3.8	23.5	0.3	0.1	12.8	6	35	27	36	2.1	2.0	1.2	1.2	79.7	84.2	75.6	74.9	78.8	60.5	71.6
District 13	426,316	58.3	6.6	17.8	0.6	0.2	16.6	21	36	12	29	1.9	1.8	1.9	1.4	74.5	78.7	68.9	71.5	75.8	60.6	67.2
District 14	456,226	72.3	4.3	11.2	0.3	<.1	11.7	5	21	23	42	2.1	2.4	1.3	1.1	79.9	83.2	72.8	75.6	80.6	60.6	69.3
District 15	444,446	77.5	1.9	10.3	0.4	<.1	9.7	11	11	45	48	2.0	2.6	0.6	0.9	77.6	79.6	70.8	73.1	76.5	62.3	69.9
District 16	409,054	41.3	4.7	19.8	0.5	0.2	33.4	36	41	21	11	1.9	1.3	1.3	2.8	71.6	78.8	70.6	70.5	72.8	62.4	64.9
District 17	419,952	62.5	4.1	5.8	0.6	0.2	26.8	28	32	25	14	1.9	1.9	1.2	2.3	73.5	79.7	72.9	74.1	76.4	63.7	62.3
District 18	391,176	69.6	2.6	4.4	0.9	0.2	22.4	47	23	37	18	1.8	2.0	0.7	1.8	68.5	73.7	66.7	53.0	73.3	61.1	58.9
District 19	404,642	70.2	2.7	5.4	1.0	0.2	20.5	40	22	35	22	1.8	2.1	0.7	1.7	70.6	76.3	62.3	54.5	68.8	61.4	61.1
District 20	373,560	37.4	6.2	4.7	0.6	0.3	50.7	52	44	13	5	1.7	1.0	1.6	3.8	65.2	74.8	67.4	60.5	67.9	60.8	59.7
District 21	398,248	75.3	2.6	2.6	1.2	0.2	17.1	46	16	28	28	1.8	2.2	1.0	1.4	69.7	73.5	64.2	61.5	69.2	58.0	58.8
District 22	442,869	75.1	2.3	3.6	0.6	0.1	18.2	13	17	38	27	2.0	2.5	0.7	1.6	77.3	80.7	73.4	78.0	76.8·	67.7	66.2
District 23	412,637	65.8	2.2	4.8	0.6	0.1	26.5	34	27	40	15	1.9	2.0	0.6	2.2	72.2	76.6	69.2	70.7	73.4	61.5	63.6
District 24	450,849	79.9	1.8	5.9	0.3	<.1	12.0	7	6	46	40	2.0	2.7	0.6	1.1	78.7	80.8	73.3	73.5	80.7	58.3	70.2
District 25	414,953	74.4	4.0	6.1	0.5	0.1	14.9	33	18	26	31	1.9	2.3	1.1	1.2	72.4	74.4	68.9	70.8	71.1	52.3	65.5
District 26	410,112	39.9	5.5	7.1	0.4	0.2	46.9	35	43	16	6	1.9	1.2	1.5	3.9	71.8	83.7	69.6	74.9	76.4	61.6	63.9
District 27	445,260	64.3	7.2	9.7	0.4	0.1	18.4	10	29	10	26	2.0	2.1	2.2	1.7	77.8	82.2	71.4	74.0	80.3	61.1	69.2
District 28	423,910	61.4	4.9	11.9	0.4	0.1	21.3	24	33	18	21	1.9	1.9	1.4	1.8	74.0	79.2	66.8	70.3	75.6	60.9	65.2
District 29	496,536	77.4	3.2	7.2	0.3	0.1	11.7	1	12	32	44	2.3	2.9	1.1	1.2	86.9	88.8	85.6	84.9	89.0	67.3	77.2
District 30	415,463	18.2	3.2	20.9	0.3	0.2	57.1	32	49	31	3	1.9	0.6	0.9	4.8	72.6	86.9	79.9	76.6	74.8	54.3	67.5
District 31	403,689	20.7	1.5	23.6	0.3	0.2	53.8	41	48	50	4	1.8	0.6	0.4	4.4	70.5	83.4	73.2	75.2	76.7	61.3	64.8
District 32	435,038	27.0	38.0	8.0	0.3	0.3	26.4	16	47	2	16	2.0	0.9	11.2	2.3	76.0	87.2	75.5	82.9	80.2	60.2	66.3
District 33	384,158	10.5	4.7	4.6	0.3	0.3	79.5	49	52	20	1	1.7	0.3	1.2	6.2	67.3	87.9	84.0	82.7	73.6	56.2	63.9
District 34	402,266	30.7	1.6	9.0	0.3	0.2	58.1	42	46	47	2	1.8	0.9	0.4	4.7	70.2	80.6	65.7	73.1	73.6	64.3	65.5
District 35	389,470	12.8	41.9	6.3	0.2	0.3	38.5	48	51	1	9	1.8	0.4	11.1	3.0	68.2	83.8	70.8	77.8	76.4	60.2	70.7
District 36	462,022	72.4	2.8	11.3	0.4	0.1	13.1	4	20	34	35	2.1	2.5	0.9	1.2	80.5	84.0	74.0	74.6	80.0	63.2	70.7
District 37	375,216	15.2	32.9	10.5	0.3	0.3	40.8	51	50	3	8	1.7	0.4	8.4	3.1	65.6	82.7	67.1	68.4	74.6	57.1	59.3
District 38	435,049	63.1	6.6	7.8	0.5	0.2	21.9	15	31	11	20	2.0	2.0	1.9	1.9	76.0	83.3	67.2	68.3	75.6	60.8	64.8
District 39	430,089	64.4	2.3	12.6	0.4	0.1	20.3	19	28	39	23	2.0	2.1	0.7	1.8	75.0	79.3	67.7	70.9	77.7	61.7	66.6
District 40	407,236	77.1	4.8	3.2	1.2	0.1	13.6	37	13	19	33	1.9	2.3	1.3	1.1	71.0	73.9	64.7	69.3	67.6	54.5	64.3
District 41	400,070	55.2	6.1	9.5	0.4	0.2	28.5	44	37	14	13	1.8	1.6	1.7	2.3	69.9	74.3	67.6	68.5	73.7	65.3	63.3
District 42	381,173	55.1	9.8	3.7	0.6	0.2	30.6	50	38	9	12	1.7	1.6	2.5	2.4	66.7	72.7	61.6	66.6	68.8	54.9	59.4
District 43	401,020	67.6	5.6	4.0	0.6	0.2	22.0	43	25	15	19	1.8	2.0	1.5	1.8	70.2	73.5	69.4	70.2	71.8	59.8	61.9
District 44	417,411	69.2	4.2	2.3	0.8	0.1	23.3	29	24	24	17	1.9	2.1	1.2	2.0	73.0	79.6	64.2	66.4	68.0	59.1	60.6
District 45	450,058	75.7	1.1	9.7	0.4	<.1	13.1	8	15	52	34	2.0	2.5	0.3	1.2	78.8	81.9	71.2	71.9	76.8	63.4	69.5
District 46	405,602	40.5	2.2	11.5	0.3	0.2	45.3	38	42	41	7	1.8	1.2	0.6	3.7	71.0	80.8	70.5	75.4	75.4	63.3	64.4
District 47	441,680	77.5	1.6	8.8	0.3	<.1	11.7	14	10	48	43	2.0	2.5	0.5	1.0	77.3	79.4	71.5	72.3	79.4	57.0	69.3
District 48	426,279	76.5	3.5	4.1	0.8	<.1	15.0	22	14	30	30	1.9	2.4	1.0	1.3	74.4	77.1	69.1	71.4	71.1	52.6	64.9
District 49	480,143	77.9	4.7	5.6	0.5	0.1	11.2	3	9	22	45	2.2	2.8	1.5	1.1	83.7	86.6	78.1	75.2	80.5	63.5	73.4
District 50	398,704	36.5	13.1	13.3	0.4	0.2	36.4	45	45	6	10	1.8	1.1	3.6	2.9	69.5	80.5	67.1	68.0	72.1	55.6	62.4
District 51	431,928	78.5	1.5	7.4	0.4	<.1	12.1	17	8	49	38	2.0	2.5	0.5	1.1	75.4	77.5	70.4	70.7	74.0	56.1	67.0
District 52	415,866	74.3	2.6	2.7	0.9	<.1	19.4	31	19	36	24	1.9	2.3	0.7	1.6	72.6	76.2	66.4	72.3	68.4	54.2	62.1

Table C. — Voter Participation: November 3, 1992, General Election

County	Estimated Voting Age Population (VAP) 1992	Voter registration (REG) Total	% contribution to state REG	% of 1992 VAP	Rank by % of 1992 VAP	Voter turnout — Highest office Actual	Total	Office[1]	% of 1992 VAP	Maximum vote Total	% contribution to state turnout	% of REG	Rank by % of REG	% of 1992 VAP	Rank by % 1992 VAP	Percent drop-off, by office President	Senator (1)[2]	Senator (2)[3]	Representative
Alameda	976,370	758,435	5.0	77.7	23	541,928	530,145	P	54.3	541,928	4.8	71.5	54	55.5	33	2.2	5.5	4.7	7.4
Alpine	810	733	<.1	90.5	2	638	631	P	77.9	638	<.1	87.0	2	78.8	2	1.1	5.6	6.1	4.9
Amador	25,651	17,915	0.1	69.8	36	15,692	15,434	P	60.2	15,692	0.1	87.6	1	61.2	23	1.6	4.0	3.4	2.9
Butte	141,537	112,424	0.7	79.4	18	88,446	85,014	P	60.1	88,446	0.8	78.7	31	62.5	21	3.9	4.8	5.4	6.3
Calaveras	25,958	20,823	0.1	80.2	16	17,516	16,991	P	65.5	17,516	0.2	84.1	6	67.5	10	3.0	4.7	4.0	4.1
Colusa	11,788	7,173	<.1	60.9	51	5,860	5,635	P	47.8	5,860	<.1	81.7	20	49.7	42	3.8	5.5	5.4	5.4
Contra Costa	613,606	507,451	3.4	82.7	11	389,391	382,823	P	62.4	389,391	3.4	76.7	37	63.5	18	1.7	5.2	6.2	8.6
Del Norte	17,669	12,272	<.1	69.5	37	9,687	9,353	P	52.9	9,687	<.1	78.9	29	54.8	36	3.4	5.2	4.8	4.3
El Dorado	100,004	81,200	0.5	81.2	14	66,949	64,887	P	64.9	66,949	0.6	82.4	14	66.9	12	3.1	4.9	4.6	4.1
Fresno	477,250	311,952	2.1	65.4	43	224,241	219,161	P	45.9	224,241	2.0	71.9	50	47.0	48	2.3	5.4	6.0	6.7
Glenn	17,542	11,145	<.1	63.5	46	9,143	8,816	P	50.3	9,143	<.1	82.0	17	52.1	39	3.6	5.5	5.4	5.4
Humboldt	87,164	76,796	0.5	88.1	4	61,030	60,021	P	68.9	61,030	0.5	79.5	26	70.0	7	1.7	5.9	3.6	3.5
Imperial	74,155	39,797	0.3	53.7	57	27,597	26,008	S	35.1	27,597	0.2	69.3	57	37.2	57	8.3	5.8	6.7	7.3
Inyo	13,493	10,518	<.1	78.0	22	8,588	8,464	P	62.7	8,588	<.1	81.7	21	63.6	17	1.4	3.7	4.5	6.2
Kern	392,366	252,324	1.7	64.3	45	185,781	179,263	P	45.7	185,781	1.6	73.6	43	47.3	47	3.5	5.6	5.6	8.8
Kings	74,737	36,690	0.2	49.1	58	26,326	25,651	P	34.3	26,326	0.2	71.8	52	35.2	58	2.6	6.4	8.5	7.9
Lake	40,981	29,470	0.2	71.9	32	24,035	23,213	P	56.6	24,035	0.2	81.6	22	58.6	28	3.4	4.0	3.9	4.6
Lassen	21,311	12,509	<.1	58.7	53	10,510	10,362	P	48.6	10,510	<.1	84.0	7	49.3	43	1.4	6.1	5.7	6.9
Los Angeles	6,616,370	3,744,096	24.8	56.6	55	2,831,077	2,753,403	P	41.6	2,831,077	24.9	75.6	39	42.8	54	2.7	5.2	6.6	8.3
Madera	65,253	43,869	0.3	67.2	39	31,222	30,245	P	46.4	31,222	0.3	71.2	55	47.8	46	3.1	5.6	6.0	5.3
Marin	181,832	153,338	1.0	84.3	7	132,422	130,707	P	71.9	132,422	1.2	86.4	3	72.8	4	1.3	3.7	2.3	5.3
Mariposa	11,423	10,139	<.1	88.8	3	8,469	8,287	P	72.5	8,469	<.1	83.5	9	74.1	3	2.1	4.2	4.2	4.8
Mendocino	59,572	47,038	0.3	79.0	19	37,658	36,538	P	61.3	37,658	0.3	80.1	25	63.2	19	3.0	6.0	3.6	3.8
Merced	123,536	69,659	0.5	56.4	56	49,958	49,284	P	39.9	49,958	0.4	71.7	53	40.4	56	1.3	8.9	7.5	18.5
Modoc	7,136	5,936	<.1	83.2	10	4,702	4,625	P	64.8	4,702	<.1	79.2	27	65.9	14	1.6	6.9	6.5	6.7
Mono	7,483	5,687	<.1	76.0	26	4,499	4,355	P	58.2	4,499	<.1	79.1	28	60.1	25	3.2	4.2	4.8	5.7
Monterey	261,282	160,821	1.1	61.6	50	118,303	116,689	P	44.7	118,303	1.0	73.6	44	45.3	51	1.4	5.5	4.7	3.6
Napa	84,176	65,171	0.4	77.4	24	55,090	53,455	P	63.5	55,090	0.5	84.5	4	65.4	16	3.0	5.8	4.9	6.4
Nevada	65,065	54,739	0.4	84.1	8	45,414	44,201	P	67.9	45,414	0.4	83.0	11	69.8	8	2.7	4.6	4.1	7.6
Orange	1,869,133	1,240,778	8.2	66.4	41	979,024	972,549	P	52.0	979,024	8.6	78.9	30	52.4	38	0.7	2.9	3.4	9.7
Placer	138,128	113,122	0.7	81.9	12	93,438	91,366	P	66.1	93,438	0.8	82.6	12	67.6	9	2.2	5.0	5.2	5.0
Plumas	14,702	12,460	<.1	84.8	6	10,521	10,007	S2	68.1	10,521	<.1	84.4	5	71.6	5	5.4	5.3	4.9	7.5
Riverside	947,935	597,020	4.0	63.0	48	434,316	430,275	P	45.4	434,316	3.8	72.7	48	45.8	50	0.9	2.8	3.1	6.6
Sacramento	799,059	629,200	4.2	78.7	21	461,887	453,512	P	56.8	461,887	4.1	73.4	45	57.8	29	1.8	4.8	4.3	5.1
San Benito	27,414	17,299	0.1	63.1	47	13,207	12,739	P	46.5	13,207	0.1	76.3	38	48.2	44	3.5	6.1	5.4	4.7
San Bernardino	1,092,014	682,980	4.5	62.5	49	482,162	474,070	P	43.4	482,162	4.2	70.6	56	44.2	53	1.7	7.5	6.0	8.7
San Diego	1,961,574	1,382,383	9.2	70.5	35	1,002,914	986,646	P	50.3	1,002,914	8.8	72.5	49	51.1	41	1.6	5.6	6.0	7.0
San Francisco	597,642	477,740	3.2	79.9	17	329,695	322,207	P	53.9	329,695	2.9	69.0	58	55.2	34	2.3	7.7	5.6	10.2
San Joaquin	357,510	230,858	1.5	64.6	44	165,909	157,728	S	44.1	165,909	1.5	71.9	51	46.4	49	7.1	4.9	4.9	5.5
San Luis Obispo	176,388	128,898	0.9	73.1	29	107,144	104,619	P	59.3	107,144	0.9	83.1	10	60.7	24	2.4	5.3	4.9	5.3
San Mateo	503,031	347,694	2.3	69.1	38	281,791	276,508	P	55.0	281,791	2.5	81.0	24	56.0	32	1.9	5.3	4.0	5.5
Santa Barbara	285,188	209,998	1.4	73.6	28	164,705	162,756	P	57.1	164,705	1.4	78.4	33	57.8	30	1.2	4.4	4.7	6.5
Santa Clara	1,145,351	820,028	5.4	71.6	34	610,002	602,055	P	52.6	610,002	5.4	74.4	42	53.3	37	1.3	4.6	3.6	6.5
Santa Cruz	177,283	148,281	1.0	83.6	9	116,527	113,992	P	64.3	116,527	1.0	78.6	32	65.7	15	2.2	4.8	3.5	3.8
Shasta	110,214	84,450	0.6	76.6	25	69,223	68,359	P	62.0	69,223	0.6	82.0	18	62.8	20	1.2	4.0	4.1	5.2
Sierra	2,412	2,331	<.1	96.6	1	1,918	1,875	P	77.7	1,918	<.1	82.3	15	79.5	1	2.2	5.0	5.5	6.2
Siskiyou	31,835	25,645	0.2	80.6	15	21,428	20,679	P	65.0	21,428	0.2	83.6	8	67.3	11	3.5	6.7	5.7	6.2
Solano	260,331	173,167	1.1	66.5	40	134,444	132,111	P	50.7	134,444	1.2	77.6	34	51.6	40	1.7	3.9	3.4	5.3
Sonoma	302,307	245,538	1.6	81.2	13	201,499	197,691	P	65.4	201,499	1.8	82.1	16	66.7	13	1.9	4.7	4.1	5.9
Stanislaus	273,578	179,471	1.2	65.6	42	131,398	128,005	P	46.8	131,398	1.2	73.2	47	48.0	45	2.6	5.9	5.7	9.2
Sutter	47,173	34,418	0.2	73.0	30	26,456	25,860	P	54.8	26,456	0.2	76.9	36	56.1	31	2.3	5.4	5.2	5.3
Tehama	37,500	27,129	0.2	72.3	31	22,071	21,005	S	56.0	22,071	0.2	81.4	23	58.9	27	4.9	4.8	4.9	5.5
Trinity	9,599	8,248	<.1	85.9	5	6,806	6,469	C	67.4	6,806	<.1	82.5	13	70.9	6	11.4	5.5	5.0	5.0
Tulare	217,426	125,167	0.8	57.6	54	91,659	88,553	P	40.7	91,659	0.8	73.2	46	42.2	55	3.4	5.5	6.3	6.8
Tuolumne	39,974	29,932	0.2	74.9	27	24,526	24,178	P	60.5	24,526	0.2	81.9	19	61.4	22	1.4	6.6	4.1	4.0
Ventura	501,210	359,236	2.4	71.7	33	276,404	267,647	P	53.4	276,404	2.4	76.9	35	55.1	35	3.2	4.7	4.7	5.2
Yolo	106,603	84,116	0.6	78.9	20	63,394	62,436	P	58.6	63,394	0.6	75.4	41	59.5	26	1.5	5.2	4.5	4.8
Yuba	39,966	23,766	0.2	59.5	52	17,925	16,904	S2	42.3	17,925	0.2	75.4	40	44.9	52	5.7	7.6	5.7	6.3
CALIFORNIA	22,668,000	15,101,473	100.0	66.6		11,374,565	11,136,462		49.1	11,374,565	100.0	75.3		50.2		2.1	5.1	5.2	7.4

[1]S = six-year U.S. Senate term; S2 = two-year U.S. Senate term. [2]Six-year U.S. Senate term. [3]Two-year U.S. Senate term. There was no governor's contest in California in 1992.

Table D. — Voter Registration by Political Party Affiliation: November 3, 1992, General Election

County	Total voter registration	Political party affiliation					Percent of total registration						Percent contribution to state registration			
		Democrat (DEM)	Republican (REP)	Independent (IND)	Plurality Total	Plurality Party	DEM	REP	IND	Rank DEM	Rank REP	Rank IND	Total	DEM	REP	IND
Alameda	758,435	467,462	172,045	83,822	295,417	D	64.6	23.8	11.6	2	57	16	5.0	6.3	3.1	5.4
Alpine	733	281	310	112	29	R	40.0	44.1	15.9	54	19	1	<.1	<.1	<.1	<.1
Amador	17,915	8,401	7,395	1,492	1,006	D	48.6	42.8	8.6	32	22	49	0.1	0.1	0.1	<.1
Butte	112,424	49,845	46,133	11,873	3,712	D	46.2	42.8	11.0	41	23	22	0.7	0.7	0.8	0.8
Calaveras	20,823	9,280	8,979	1,781	301	D	46.3	44.8	8.9	40	17	46	0.1	0.1	0.2	0.1
Colusa	7,173	3,312	3,110	504	202	D	47.8	44.9	7.3	36	16	57	<.1	<.1	<.1	<.1
Contra Costa	507,451	257,830	179,763	43,466	78,067	D	53.6	37.4	9.0	20	42	45	3.4	3.5	3.2	2.8
Del Norte	12,272	5,703	4,396	1,659	1,307	D	48.5	37.4	14.1	35	40	4	<.1	<.1	<.1	0.1
El Dorado	81,200	33,822	36,696	7,796	2,874	R	43.2	46.9	10.0	48	7	32	0.5	0.5	0.7	0.5
Fresno	311,952	163,988	115,774	22,166	48,214	D	54.3	38.3	7.3	16	33	56	2.1	2.2	2.1	1.4
Glenn	11,145	5,002	4,793	1,037	209	D	46.2	44.2	9.6	39	18	37	<.1	<.1	<.1	<.1
Humboldt	76,796	40,863	23,371	7,431	17,492	D	57.0	32.6	10.4	11	53	29	0.5	0.6	0.4	0.5
Imperial	39,797	21,289	13,762	3,709	7,527	D	54.9	35.5	9.6	9	46	36	0.3	0.3	0.2	0.2
Inyo	10,518	4,182	5,102	861	920	R	41.2	50.3	8.5	51	3	51	<.1	<.1	<.1	<.1
Kern	252,324	111,753	111,635	20,936	118	D	45.7	45.7	8.6	43	11	50	1.7	1.5	2.0	1.3
Kings	36,690	18,739	13,494	3,443	5,245	D	52.5	37.8	9.7	19	35	34	0.2	0.3	0.2	0.2
Lake	29,470	15,548	10,216	2,752	5,332	D	54.5	35.8	9.7	15	45	35	0.2	0.2	0.2	0.2
Lassen	12,509	6,004	4,664	1,322	1,340	D	50.1	38.9	11.0	29	32	21	<.1	<.1	<.1	<.1
Los Angeles	3,744,096	2,061,025	1,211,010	361,136	850,015	D	56.7	33.3	9.9	7	48	31	24.8	27.8	21.7	23.2
Madera	43,869	22,179	17,301	3,174	4,878	D	52.0	40.6	7.4	22	27	55	0.3	0.3	0.3	0.2
Marin	153,338	80,087	47,082	19,708	33,005	D	54.5	32.1	13.4	18	51	6	1.0	1.1	0.8	1.3
Mariposa	10,139	4,338	4,216	1,086	122	D	45.0	43.7	11.3	46	20	20	<.1	<.1	<.1	<.1
Mendocino	47,038	25,578	13,763	5,231	11,815	D	57.4	30.9	11.7	8	55	15	0.3	0.3	0.2	0.3
Merced	69,659	36,972	24,187	6,456	12,785	D	54.7	35.8	9.5	12	44	38	0.5	0.5	0.4	0.4
Modoc	5,936	2,631	2,574	532	57	D	45.9	44.9	9.3	42	15	41	<.1	<.1	<.1	<.1
Mono	5,687	2,014	2,556	861	542	R	37.1	47.1	15.9	57	9	2	<.1	<.1	<.1	<.1
Monterey	160,821	79,064	55,384	20,063	23,680	D	51.2	35.8	13.0	25	47	9	1.1	1.1	1.0	1.3
Napa	65,171	33,072	23,943	5,857	9,129	D	52.6	38.1	9.3	21	37	40	0.4	0.4	0.4	0.4
Nevada	54,739	20,509	25,476	5,891	4,967	R	39.5	49.1	11.4	55	4	19	0.4	0.3	0.5	0.4
Orange	1,240,778	428,035	648,996	127,563	220,961	R	35.5	53.9	10.6	58	1	25	8.2	5.8	11.6	8.2
Placer	113,122	46,176	52,430	10,936	6,254	R	42.2	47.9	10.0	50	5	30	0.7	0.6	0.9	0.7
Plumas	12,460	5,954	4,786	1,314	1,168	D	49.4	39.7	10.9	30	29	23	<.1	<.1	<.1	<.1
Riverside	597,020	256,694	269,489	48,809	12,795	R	44.6	46.9	8.5	45	8	53	4.0	3.5	4.8	3.1
Sacramento	629,200	332,183	224,324	54,023	107,859	D	54.4	36.7	8.8	14	41	44	4.2	4.5	4.0	3.5
San Benito	17,299	8,511	6,324	1,942	2,187	D	50.7	37.7	11.6	24	38	14	0.1	0.1	0.1	0.1
San Bernardino	682,980	306,962	297,777	57,511	9,185	D	46.4	45.0	8.7	38	14	47	4.5	4.1	5.3	3.7
San Diego	1,382,383	517,551	627,617	183,768	110,066	R	38.9	47.2	13.8	56	6	5	9.2	7.0	11.2	11.8
San Francisco	477,740	301,053	81,605	69,078	219,448	D	66.6	18.1	15.3	1	58	9	3.2	4.1	1.5	4.4
San Joaquin	230,858	121,917	86,200	14,719	35,717	D	54.7	38.7	6.6	13	31	58	1.5	1.6	1.5	0.9
San Luis Obispo	128,898	50,220	57,358	15,143	7,138	R	40.9	46.7	12.3	52	10	11	0.9	0.7	1.0	1.0
San Mateo	347,694	182,432	111,328	42,953	71,104	D	54.2	33.1	12.8	17	49	10	2.3	2.5	2.0	2.8
Santa Barbara	209,998	89,323	84,497	26,454	4,826	D	44.6	42.2	13.2	47	24	8	1.4	1.2	1.5	1.7
Santa Clara	820,028	402,642	285,125	103,840	117,517	D	50.9	36.0	13.1	26	43	7	5.4	5.4	5.1	6.7
Santa Cruz	148,281	81,707	39,006	17,071	42,701	D	59.3	28.3	12.4	6	56	12	1.0	1.1	0.7	1.1
Shasta	84,450	36,380	37,001	8,329	621	R	44.5	45.3	10.2	44	13	28	0.6	0.5	0.7	0.5
Sierra	2,331	1,072	894	266	178	D	48.0	40.1	11.9	37	30	13	<.1	<.1	<.1	<.1
Siskiyou	25,645	12,653	9,428	2,644	3,225	D	51.2	38.1	10.7	23	36	24	0.2	0.2	0.2	0.2
Solano	173,167	96,391	53,162	19,059	43,229	D	57.2	31.5	11.3	5	52	17	1.1	1.3	1.0	1.2
Sonoma	245,538	137,500	75,817	23,372	61,683	D	58.1	32.0	9.9	3	50	33	1.6	1.9	1.4	1.5
Stanislaus	179,471	95,732	64,865	13,074	30,867	D	55.1	37.3	7.5	10	39	54	1.2	1.3	1.2	0.8
Sutter	34,418	13,359	16,943	2,816	3,584	R	40.3	51.2	8.5	53	2	52	0.2	0.2	0.3	0.2
Tehama	27,129	13,038	10,424	2,378	2,614	D	50.5	40.3	9.2	28	28	42	0.2	0.2	0.2	0.2
Trinity	8,248	3,889	3,052	763	837	D	50.5	39.6	9.9	31	34	39	<.1	<.1	<.1	<.1
Tulare	125,167	58,549	51,831	10,754	6,718	D	48.3	42.8	8.9	33	21	43	0.8	0.8	0.9	0.7
Tuolumne	29,932	14,557	11,937	2,515	2,620	D	50.2	41.1	8.7	27	25	48	0.2	0.2	0.2	0.2
Ventura	359,236	147,680	157,631	38,986	9,951	R	42.9	45.8	11.3	49	12	18	2.4	2.0	2.8	2.5
Yolo	84,116	46,894	24,957	8,646	21,937	D	58.3	31.0	10.7	4	54	26	0.6	0.6	0.4	0.6
Yuba	23,766	11,087	9,421	2,372	1,666	D	48.5	41.2	10.4	34	26	27	0.2	0.1	0.2	0.2
CALIFORNIA[1]	**15,101,473**	**7,410,914**	**5,593,355**	**1,557,255**	**1,817,559**	**D**	**50.9**	**38.4**	**10.7**				**100.0**	**100.0**	**100.0**	**100.0**

[1]Total voter registration also includes 247,415 for American Independent party, 98,724 for Green party, 71,148 for Libertarian party, 70,176 for Peace and Freedom party, and 52,486 for miscellaneous.

Table E. — Vote for President: November 3, 1992, General Election

County	All candidates					Plurality		Percent of total vote				Rank			Percent contribution to state vote				Major party Percent of vote	
	Total	Clinton (DEM)	Bush (REP)	Perot (IND)	Other	Total	Party	DEM	REP	IND	Other	DEM	REP	IND	Total	DEM	REP	IND	DEM	REP
Alameda	530,145	334,224	109,292	81,643	4,986	224,932	D	63.0	20.6	15.4	0.9	2	57	57	4.8	6.5	3.0	3.6	75.4	24.6
Alpine	631	215	222	186	8	7	R	34.1	35.2	29.5	1.3	46	37	3	<.1	<.1	<.1	<.1	49.2	50.8
Amador	15,434	5,286	5,477	4,553	118	191	R	34.2	35.5	29.5	0.8	43	30	2	0.1	0.1	0.2	0.2	49.1	50.9
Butte	85,014	32,489	31,608	20,231	686	881	D	38.2	37.2	23.8	0.8	31	20	27	0.8	0.6	0.9	0.9	50.7	49.3
Calaveras	16,991	5,989	6,006	4,848	148	17	R	35.2	35.3	28.5	0.9	39	34	6	0.2	0.1	0.2	0.2	49.9	50.1
Colusa	5,635	1,798	2,589	1,206	42	791	R	31.9	45.9	21.4	0.7	53	2	38	<.1	<.1	<.1	<.1	41.0	59.0
Contra Costa	382,823	194,960	112,965	72,518	2,380	81,995	D	50.9	29.5	18.9	0.6	9	45	48	3.4	3.8	3.1	3.2	63.3	36.7
Del Norte	9,353	3,639	3,083	2,575	56	556	D	38.9	33.0	27.5	0.6	27	39	9	<.1	<.1	<.1	0.1	54.1	45.9
El Dorado	64,887	21,012	25,906	17,503	466	4,894	R	32.4	39.9	27.0	0.7	51	14	11	0.6	0.4	0.7	0.8	44.8	55.2
Fresno	219,161	92,418	89,137	36,299	1,307	3,281	D	42.2	40.7	16.6	0.6	20	13	56	2.0	1.8	2.5	1.6	50.9	49.1
Glenn	8,816	2,666	3,812	2,278	60	1,146	R	30.2	43.2	25.8	0.7	58	8	20	<.1	<.1	0.1	<.1	41.2	58.8
Humboldt	60,021	28,854	18,299	12,340	528	10,555	D	48.1	30.5	20.6	0.9	13	44	42	0.5	0.6	0.5	0.5	61.2	38.8
Imperial	25,318	11,109	9,759	4,247	203	1,350	D	43.9	38.5	16.8	0.8	17	17	55	0.2	0.2	0.3	0.2	53.2	46.8
Inyo	8,464	2,695	3,689	1,999	81	994	R	31.8	43.6	23.6	1.0	54	6	30	<.1	<.1	0.1	<.1	42.2	57.8
Kern	179,263	60,510	80,762	36,891	1,100	20,252	R	33.8	45.1	20.6	0.6	47	4	41	1.6	1.2	2.2	1.6	42.8	57.2
Kings	25,651	9,982	10,673	4,899	97	691	R	38.9	41.6	19.1	0.4	26	11	46	0.2	0.2	0.3	0.2	48.3	51.7
Lake	23,213	10,548	6,678	5,797	190	3,870	D	45.4	28.8	25.0	0.8	15	49	24	0.2	0.2	0.2	0.3	61.2	38.8
Lassen	10,362	3,388	3,836	3,004	134	448	R	32.7	37.0	29.0	1.3	49	22	4	<.1	<.1	0.1	0.1	46.9	53.1
Los Angeles	2,753,403	1,446,529	799,607	488,624	18,643	646,922	D	52.5	29.0	17.7	0.7	8	48	52	24.7	28.2	22.0	21.3	64.4	35.6
Madera	30,245	10,863	13,066	6,156	160	2,203	R	35.9	43.2	20.4	0.5	37	9	43	0.3	0.2	0.4	0.3	45.4	54.6
Marin	130,707	76,158	30,479	22,986	1,084	45,679	D	58.3	23.3	17.6	0.8	3	54	54	1.2	1.5	0.8	1.0	71.4	28.6
Mariposa	8,287	3,023	2,982	2,211	71	41	D	36.5	36.0	26.7	0.9	36	28	15	<.1	<.1	<.1	<.1	50.3	49.7
Mendocino	36,538	18,344	7,958	9,753	483	8,591	D	50.2	21.8	26.7	1.3	10	56	14	0.3	0.4	0.2	0.4	69.7	30.3
Merced	49,284	20,133	17,981	10,914	256	2,152	D	40.9	36.5	22.1	0.5	24	25	33	0.4	0.4	0.5	0.5	52.8	47.2
Modoc	4,625	1,489	1,803	1,269	64	314	R	32.2	39.0	27.4	1.4	52	16	10	<.1	<.1	<.1	<.1	45.2	54.8
Mono	4,355	1,489	1,570	1,248	48	81	R	34.2	36.1	28.7	1.1	45	27	5	<.1	<.1	<.1	<.1	48.7	51.3
Monterey	116,689	54,861	36,461	24,472	895	18,400	D	47.0	31.2	21.0	0.8	14	43	40	1.0	1.1	1.0	1.1	60.1	39.9
Napa	53,455	24,215	15,662	13,150	428	8,553	D	45.3	29.3	24.6	0.8	16	47	25	0.5	0.5	0.4	0.6	60.7	39.3
Nevada	44,201	15,433	17,343	11,072	353	1,910	R	34.9	39.2	25.0	0.8	41	15	22	0.4	0.3	0.5	0.5	47.1	52.9
Orange	972,549	306,930	426,613	232,394	6,612	119,683	R	31.6	43.9	23.9	0.7	56	5	26	8.7	6.0	11.8	10.1	41.8	58.2
Placer	91,366	30,783	38,298	21,741	544	7,515	R	33.7	41.9	23.8	0.6	48	10	28	0.8	0.6	1.1	0.9	44.6	55.4
Plumas	9,949	3,742	3,599	2,551	57	143	D	37.6	36.2	25.6	0.6	33	26	21	<.1	<.1	<.1	0.1	51.0	49.0
Riverside	430,275	166,241	159,457	102,233	2,344	6,784	D	38.6	37.1	23.8	0.5	29	21	29	3.9	3.2	4.4	4.5	51.0	49.0
Sacramento	453,512	197,540	160,366	91,412	4,194	37,174	D	43.6	35.4	20.2	0.9	18	33	45	4.1	3.9	4.4	4.0	55.2	44.8
San Benito	12,739	5,354	4,112	3,182	91	1,242	D	42.0	32.3	25.0	0.7	21	40	23	0.1	0.1	0.1	0.1	56.6	43.4
San Bernardino	474,070	183,634	176,563	109,183	4,690	7,071	D	38.7	37.2	23.0	1.0	28	19	31	4.3	3.6	4.9	4.8	51.0	49.0
San Diego	986,646	367,397	352,125	259,249	7,875	15,272	D	37.2	35.7	26.3	0.8	34	29	17	8.9	7.2	9.7	11.3	51.1	48.9
San Francisco	322,207	233,263	57,352	29,018	2,574	175,911	D	72.4	17.8	9.0	0.8	1	58	58	2.9	4.6	1.6	1.3	80.3	19.7
San Joaquin	154,210	63,655	58,355	31,205	995	5,300	D	41.3	37.8	20.2	0.6	22	18	44	1.4	1.2	1.6	1.4	52.2	47.8
San Luis Obispo	104,619	40,136	36,384	27,314	785	3,752	D	38.4	34.8	26.1	0.8	30	38	18	0.9	0.8	1.0	1.2	52.5	47.5
San Mateo	276,508	149,232	75,080	50,465	1,731	74,152	D	54.0	27.2	18.3	0.6	5	52	51	2.5	2.9	2.1	2.2	66.5	33.5
Santa Barbara	162,756	69,215	57,375	35,105	1,061	11,840	D	42.5	35.3	21.6	0.7	19	36	35	1.5	1.4	1.6	1.5	54.7	45.3
Santa Clara	602,055	296,265	170,870	128,895	6,025	125,395	D	49.2	28.4	21.4	1.0	11	50	37	5.4	5.8	4.7	5.6	63.4	36.6
Santa Cruz	113,992	66,183	24,916	21,615	1,278	41,267	D	58.1	21.9	19.0	1.1	4	55	47	1.0	1.3	0.7	0.9	72.6	27.4
Shasta	68,359	21,605	28,190	17,990	574	6,585	R	31.6	41.2	26.3	0.8	55	12	16	0.6	0.4	0.8	0.8	43.4	56.6
Sierra	1,875	653	691	519	12	38	R	34.8	36.9	27.7	0.6	42	24	8	<.1	<.1	<.1	<.1	48.6	51.4
Siskiyou	20,679	8,254	6,660	5,567	198	1,594	D	39.9	32.2	26.9	1.0	25	41	12	0.2	0.2	0.2	0.2	55.3	44.7
Solano	132,111	64,320	38,883	27,851	1,057	25,437	D	48.7	29.4	21.1	0.8	12	46	39	1.2	1.3	1.1	1.2	62.3	37.7
Sonoma	197,691	104,334	47,619	43,859	1,879	56,715	D	52.8	24.1	22.2	1.0	7	53	32	1.8	2.0	1.3	1.9	68.7	31.3
Stanislaus	128,005	52,415	47,275	27,651	664	5,140	D	40.9	36.9	21.6	0.5	23	23	34	1.1	1.0	1.3	1.2	52.6	47.4
Sutter	25,860	7,883	12,956	4,881	140	5,073	R	30.5	50.1	18.9	0.5	57	1	49	0.2	0.2	0.4	0.2	37.8	62.2
Tehama	20,979	7,508	7,419	5,884	168	89	D	35.8	35.4	28.0	0.8	38	32	7	0.2	0.1	0.2	0.3	50.3	49.7
Trinity	6,029	1,967	1,886	2,092	84	125	I	32.6	31.3	34.7	1.4	50	42	1	<.1	<.1	<.1	<.1	51.1	48.9
Tulare	88,553	31,188	40,482	16,430	453	9,294	R	35.2	45.7	18.6	0.5	40	3	51	0.8	0.6	1.1	0.7	43.5	56.5
Tuolumne	24,178	9,216	8,525	6,294	143	691	D	38.1	35.3	26.0	0.6	32	35	19	0.2	0.2	0.2	0.3	51.9	48.1
Ventura	267,647	99,011	94,911	71,844	1,881	4,100	D	37.0	35.5	26.8	0.7	35	31	13	2.4	1.9	2.6	3.1	51.1	48.9
Yolo	62,436	33,297	17,574	11,073	492	15,723	D	53.3	28.1	17.7	0.8	6	51	53	0.6	0.7	0.5	0.5	65.5	34.5
Yuba	16,895	5,785	7,333	3,637	140	1,548	R	34.2	43.4	21.5	0.8	44	7	36	0.2	0.1	0.2	0.2	44.1	55.9
CALIFORNIA	11,131,721	5,121,325	3,630,574	2,296,006	83,816	1,490,751	D	46.0	32.6	20.6	0.8				100.0	100.0	100.0	100.0	58.5	41.5

Table F. — Vote for U.S. Senator: November 3, 1992, General Election (six-year term)

County	Total	Boxer (DEM)	Herschen-sohn (REP)	Other	Plurality Total	Party	DEM	REP	Other	Rank DEM	Rank REP	Rank Other	Total	DEM	REP	Other
Alameda	512,393	343,020	128,489	40,884	214,531	D	66.9	25.1	8.0	2	57	53	4.7	6.6	2.8	4.2
Alpine	602	272	260	70	12	D	45.2	43.2	11.6	18	41	13	<.1	<.1	<.1	<.1
Amador	15,061	6,082	7,366	1,613	1,284	R	40.4	48.9	10.7	31	27	24	0.1	0.1	0.2	0.2
Butte	84,207	31,505	43,338	9,364	11,833	R	37.4	51.5	11.1	41	18	20	0.8	0.6	0.9	1.0
Calaveras	16,693	6,402	8,269	2,022	1,867	R	38.4	49.5	12.1	38	23	9	0.2	0.1	0.2	0.2
Colusa	5,538	1,859	3,112	567	1,253	R	33.6	56.2	10.2	47	11	35	<.1	<.1	<.1	<.1
Contra Costa	368,952	203,563	131,923	33,466	71,640	D	55.2	35.8	9.1	9	49	45	3.4	3.9	2.8	3.4
Del Norte	9,186	3,891	4,289	1,006	398	R	42.4	46.7	11.0	24	35	21	<.1	<.1	<.1	0.1
El Dorado	63,636	24,601	32,368	6,667	7,767	R	38.7	50.9	10.5	37	19	29	0.6	0.5	0.7	0.7
Fresno	212,059	78,321	117,891	15,847	39,570	R	36.9	55.6	7.5	42	12	56	2.0	1.5	2.5	1.6
Glenn	8,644	2,271	5,373	1,000	3,102	R	26.3	62.2	11.6	58	2	15	<.1	<.1	0.1	0.1
Humboldt	57,402	27,916	24,757	4,729	3,159	D	48.6	43.1	8.2	16	42	52	0.5	0.5	0.5	0.5
Imperial	26,008	11,614	11,389	3,005	225	D	44.7	43.8	11.6	21	40	16	0.2	0.2	0.2	0.3
Inyo	8,273	2,563	4,847	863	2,284	R	31.0	58.6	10.4	52	7	31	<.1	<.1	0.1	<.1
Kern	175,366	53,141	106,916	15,309	53,775	R	30.3	61.0	8.7	55	3	46	1.6	1.0	2.3	1.6
Kings	24,636	8,151	14,079	2,406	5,928	R	33.1	57.1	9.8	49	9	41	0.2	0.2	0.3	0.2
Lake	23,080	10,805	9,357	2,918	1,448	D	46.8	40.5	12.6	17	45	7	0.2	0.2	0.2	0.3
Lassen	9,873	3,761	4,823	1,289	1,062	R	38.1	48.9	13.1	39	28	5	<.1	<.1	0.1	0.1
Los Angeles	2,684,066	1,410,423	1,062,974	210,669	347,449	D	52.5	39.6	7.8	11	47	55	24.9	27.3	22.9	21.5
Madera	29,475	9,401	17,609	2,465	8,208	R	31.9	59.7	8.4	51	4	51	0.3	0.2	0.4	0.3
Marin	127,472	80,902	37,150	9,420	43,752	D	63.5	29.1	7.4	3	56	57	1.2	1.6	0.8	1.0
Mariposa	8,110	2,989	4,211	910	1,222	R	36.9	51.9	11.2	44	15	19	<.1	<.1	<.1	<.1
Mendocino	35,397	19,818	11,718	3,861	8,100	D	56.0	33.1	10.9	8	51	23	0.3	0.4	0.3	0.4
Merced	45,519	17,848	22,360	5,311	4,512	R	39.2	49.1	11.7	35	26	12	0.4	0.3	0.5	0.5
Modoc	4,378	1,429	2,367	582	938	R	32.6	54.1	13.3	50	13	3	<.1	<.1	<.1	<.1
Mono	4,310	1,820	2,034	456	214	R	42.2	47.2	10.6	25	34	27	<.1	<.1	<.1	<.1
Monterey	111,810	54,400	45,903	11,507	8,497	D	48.7	41.1	10.3	15	43	33	1.0	1.1	1.0	1.2
Napa	51,878	25,746	20,655	5,477	5,091	D	49.6	39.8	10.6	13	46	28	0.5	0.5	0.4	0.6
Nevada	43,328	17,091	21,609	4,628	4,518	R	39.4	49.9	10.7	33	22	25	0.4	0.3	0.5	0.5
Orange	950,977	317,740	550,502	82,735	232,762	R	33.4	57.9	8.7	48	8	47	8.8	6.1	11.9	8.4
Placer	88,740	34,905	44,813	9,022	9,908	R	39.3	50.5	10.2	34	21	36	0.8	0.7	1.0	0.9
Plumas	9,960	4,032	4,728	1,200	696	R	40.5	47.5	12.0	30	32	10	<.1	<.1	0.1	0.1
Riverside	422,134	160,630	218,778	42,726	58,148	R	38.1	51.8	10.1	40	16	38	3.9	3.1	4.7	4.4
Sacramento	439,717	215,853	179,844	44,020	36,009	D	49.1	40.9	10.0	14	44	39	4.1	4.2	3.9	4.5
San Benito	12,396	5,415	5,527	1,454	112	R	43.7	44.6	11.7	22	39	11	0.1	0.1	0.1	0.1
San Bernardino	446,114	164,620	231,143	50,351	66,523	R	36.9	51.8	11.3	43	17	18	4.1	3.2	5.0	5.1
San Diego	946,429	399,087	448,181	99,161	49,094	R	42.2	47.4	10.5	26	33	30	8.8	7.7	9.7	10.1
San Francisco	304,372	233,068	56,972	14,332	176,096	D	76.6	18.7	4.7	1	58	58	2.8	4.5	1.2	1.5
San Joaquin	157,728	66,484	75,032	16,212	8,548	R	42.2	47.6	10.3	27	31	34	1.5	1.3	1.6	1.7
San Luis Obispo	101,437	41,824	49,945	9,668	8,121	R	41.2	49.2	9.5	28	25	43	0.9	0.8	1.1	1.0
San Mateo	266,885	158,490	87,209	21,186	71,281	D	59.4	32.7	7.9	5	53	54	2.5	3.1	1.9	2.2
Santa Barbara	157,394	70,998	72,793	13,603	1,795	R	45.1	46.2	8.6	19	36	49	1.5	1.4	1.6	1.4
Santa Clara	581,983	314,884	206,913	60,186	107,971	D	54.1	35.6	10.3	10	50	32	5.4	6.1	4.5	6.1
Santa Cruz	110,971	67,927	32,482	10,562	35,445	D	61.2	29.3	9.5	4	55	44	1.0	1.3	0.7	1.1
Shasta	66,467	18,868	39,507	8,092	20,639	R	28.4	59.4	12.2	57	5	8	0.6	0.4	0.9	0.8
Sierra	1,822	705	878	239	173	R	38.7	48.2	13.1	36	29	4	<.1	<.1	<.1	<.1
Siskiyou	19,989	8,115	9,568	2,306	1,453	R	40.6	47.9	11.5	29	30	17	0.2	0.2	0.2	0.2
Solano	129,175	67,007	47,148	15,020	19,859	D	51.9	36.5	11.6	12	48	14	1.2	1.3	1.0	1.5
Sonoma	192,026	108,991	62,696	20,339	46,295	D	56.8	32.6	10.6	7	54	26	1.8	2.1	1.4	2.1
Stanislaus	123,681	55,688	55,875	12,118	187	R	45.0	45.2	9.8	20	38	40	1.1	1.1	1.2	1.2
Sutter	25,040	7,719	14,783	2,538	7,064	R	30.8	59.0	10.1	53	6	37	0.2	0.1	0.3	0.3
Tehama	21,005	6,450	11,893	2,662	5,443	R	30.7	56.6	12.7	54	10	6	0.2	0.1	0.3	0.3
Trinity	6,431	2,261	3,184	986	923	R	35.2	49.5	15.3	45	24	1	<.1	<.1	<.1	0.1
Tulare	86,573	25,311	53,856	7,406	28,545	R	29.2	62.2	8.6	56	1	50	0.8	0.5	1.2	0.8
Tuolumne	22,915	9,811	10,596	2,508	785	R	42.8	46.2	10.9	23	37	22	0.2	0.2	0.2	0.3
Ventura	263,309	104,335	133,274	25,700	28,939	R	39.6	50.6	9.8	32	20	42	2.4	2.0	2.9	2.6
Yolo	60,113	35,006	19,900	5,207	15,106	D	58.2	33.1	8.7	6	52	48	0.6	0.7	0.4	0.5
Yuba	16,568	5,638	8,726	2,204	3,088	R	34.0	52.7	13.3	46	14	2	0.2	0.1	0.2	0.2
CALIFORNIA	10,799,703	5,173,467	4,644,182	982,054	529,285	D	47.9	43.0	9.1				100.0	100.0	100.0	100.0

Table F2. — Vote for U.S. Senator: November 3, 1992, General Election (two-year term)[1]

County	Total	Feinstein (DEM)	Seymour (REP)	Other	Plurality Total	Party	DEM	REP	Other	Rank DEM	Rank REP	Rank Other	Total	DEM	REP	Other
Alameda	516,367	374,675	113,223	28,469	261,452	D	72.6	21.9	5.5	2	57	54	4.8	6.4	2.8	3.4
Alpine	599	287	252	60	35	D	47.9	42.1	10.0	26	36	14	<.1	<.1	<.1	<.1
Amador	15,157	7,319	6,463	1,375	856	D	48.3	42.6	9.1	25	35	28	0.1	0.1	0.2	0.2
Butte	83,630	37,396	38,111	8,123	715	R	44.7	45.6	9.7	40	19	20	0.8	0.6	0.9	1.0
Calaveras	16,807	7,839	7,059	1,909	780	R	46.6	42.0	11.4	30	37	5	0.2	0.1	0.2	0.2
Colusa	5,543	2,083	3,014	446	931	R	37.6	54.4	8.0	52	4	38	<.1	<.1	<.1	<.1
Contra Costa	365,298	229,988	115,507	19,803	114,481	D	63.0	31.6	5.4	6	50	55	3.4	3.9	2.8	2.4
Del Norte	9,223	4,696	3,658	869	1,038	D	50.9	39.7	9.4	19	40	21	<.1	<.1	<.1	0.1
El Dorado	63,870	28,957	29,101	5,812	144	R	45.3	45.6	9.1	35	20	27	0.6	0.5	0.7	0.7
Fresno	210,751	94,988	102,172	13,591	7,184	R	45.1	48.5	6.4	39	12	52	2.0	1.6	2.5	1.6
Glenn	8,652	2,864	4,908	880	2,044	R	33.1	56.7	10.2	58	1	12	<.1	<.1	0.1	0.1
Humboldt	58,817	35,178	19,513	4,126	15,665	D	59.8	33.2	7.0	12	47	48	0.5	0.6	0.5	0.5
Imperial	25,494	12,433	11,070	1,991	1,363	D	48.8	43.4	7.8	24	32	42	0.2	0.2	0.3	0.2
Inyo	8,199	3,067	4,318	814	1,251	R	37.4	52.7	9.9	53	7	17	<.1	<.1	0.1	<.1
Kern	175,334	63,661	95,483	16,190	31,822	R	36.3	54.5	9.2	55	3	23	1.6	1.1	2.3	1.9
Kings	24,091	9,805	12,115	2,171	2,310	R	40.7	50.3	9.0	46	11	29	0.2	0.2	0.3	0.3
Lake	23,106	12,732	8,096	2,278	4,636	D	55.1	35.0	9.9	17	44	19	0.2	0.2	0.2	0.3
Lassen	9,916	4,005	4,724	1,187	719	R	40.4	47.6	12.0	47	14	4	<.1	<.1	0.1	0.1
Los Angeles	2,643,495	1,552,223	899,656	191,616	652,567	D	58.7	34.0	7.2	14	46	47	24.5	26.5	22.0	22.9
Madera	29,360	11,682	15,309	2,369	3,627	R	39.8	52.1	8.1	49	8	37	0.3	0.2	0.4	0.3
Marin	129,401	92,205	31,846	5,350	60,359	D	71.3	24.6	4.1	3	56	57	1.2	1.6	0.8	0.6
Mariposa	8,112	3,681	3,568	863	113	D	45.4	44.0	10.6	34	26	8	<.1	<.1	<.1	0.1
Mendocino	36,310	22,000	10,993	3,317	11,007	D	60.6	30.3	9.1	10	52	26	0.3	0.4	0.3	0.4
Merced	46,233	22,010	20,246	3,977	1,764	D	47.6	43.8	8.6	27	28	31	0.4	0.4	0.5	0.5
Modoc	4,395	1,572	2,327	496	755	R	35.8	52.9	11.3	56	6	6	<.1	<.1	<.1	<.1
Mono	4,281	1,931	1,911	439	20	D	45.1	44.6	10.3	38	24	10	<.1	<.1	<.1	<.1
Monterey	112,774	66,417	39,182	7,175	27,235	D	58.9	34.7	6.4	13	45	53	1.0	1.1	1.0	0.9
Napa	52,398	29,875	18,539	3,984	11,336	D	57.0	35.4	7.6	15	43	45	0.5	0.5	0.5	0.5
Nevada	43,538	20,044	19,476	4,018	568	D	46.0	44.7	9.2	32	23	24	0.4	0.3	0.5	0.5
Orange	946,081	377,170	481,810	87,101	104,640	R	39.9	50.9	9.2	48	10	25	8.8	6.4	11.8	10.4
Placer	88,555	40,511	40,497	7,547	14	D	45.7	45.7	8.5	33	17	33	0.8	0.7	1.0	0.9
Plumas	10,007	4,647	4,367	993	280	D	46.4	43.6	9.9	31	30	18	<.1	<.1	0.1	0.1
Riverside	420,935	187,548	191,258	42,129	3,710	R	44.6	45.4	10.0	41	21	15	3.9	3.2	4.7	5.0
Sacramento	442,098	237,722	168,318	36,058	69,404	D	53.8	38.1	8.2	18	41	36	4.1	4.1	4.1	4.3
San Benito	12,498	6,938	4,637	923	2,301	D	55.5	37.1	7.4	16	42	46	0.1	0.1	0.1	0.1
San Bernardino	453,136	200,979	206,969	45,188	5,990	R	44.4	45.7	10.0	42	18	16	4.2	3.4	5.1	5.4
San Diego	942,868	442,855	411,362	88,651	31,493	D	47.0	43.6	9.4	29	31	22	8.7	7.6	10.0	10.6
San Francisco	311,361	250,972	49,165	11,224	201,807	D	80.6	15.8	3.6	1	58	58	2.9	4.3	1.2	1.3
San Joaquin	156,665	76,607	67,531	12,527	9,076	D	48.9	43.1	8.0	23	33	39	1.5	1.3	1.6	1.5
San Luis Obispo	101,902	48,376	44,775	8,751	3,601	D	47.5	43.9	8.6	28	27	32	0.9	0.8	1.1	1.0
San Mateo	270,605	181,990	75,470	13,145	106,520	D	67.3	27.9	4.9	5	54	56	2.5	3.1	1.8	1.6
Santa Barbara	156,965	77,900	67,043	12,022	10,857	D	49.6	42.7	7.7	22	34	44	1.5	1.3	1.6	1.4
Santa Clara	586,933	364,997	181,858	40,078	183,139	D	62.2	31.0	6.8	8	51	49	5.4	6.2	4.4	4.8
Santa Cruz	112,449	76,327	28,562	7,560	47,765	D	67.9	25.4	6.7	4	55	50	1.0	1.3	0.7	0.9
Shasta	66,417	25,111	34,192	7,114	9,081	R	37.8	51.5	10.7	51	9	7	0.6	0.4	0.8	0.9
Sierra	1,813	818	808	187	10	D	45.1	44.6	10.3	37	25	9	<.1	<.1	<.1	<.1
Siskiyou	20,210	8,963	9,180	2,067	217	R	44.3	45.4	10.2	43	22	11	0.2	0.2	0.2	0.2
Solano	129,936	77,739	41,970	10,227	35,769	D	59.8	32.3	7.9	11	48	40	1.2	1.3	1.0	1.2
Sonoma	193,314	121,471	56,793	15,050	64,678	D	62.8	29.4	7.8	7	53	43	1.8	2.1	1.4	1.8
Stanislaus	123,953	62,110	51,549	10,294	10,561	D	50.1	41.6	8.3	21	38	35	1.1	1.1	1.3	1.2
Sutter	25,079	9,135	13,427	2,517	4,292	R	36.4	53.5	10.0	54	5	13	0.2	0.2	0.3	0.3
Tehama	20,992	8,253	10,116	2,623	1,863	R	39.3	48.2	12.5	50	13	3	0.2	0.1	0.2	0.3
Trinity	6,468	2,743	2,824	901	81	R	42.4	43.7	13.9	44	29	1	<.1	<.1	<.1	0.1
Tulare	85,884	30,665	48,493	6,726	17,828	R	35.7	56.5	7.8	57	2	41	0.8	0.5	1.2	0.8
Tuolumne	23,527	11,895	9,550	2,082	2,345	D	50.6	40.6	8.8	20	39	30	0.2	0.2	0.2	0.2
Ventura	263,499	119,366	122,064	22,069	2,698	R	45.3	46.3	8.4	36	16	34	2.4	2.0	3.0	2.6
Yolo	60,538	37,340	19,191	4,007	18,149	D	61.7	31.7	6.6	9	49	51	0.6	0.6	0.5	0.5
Yuba	16,904	6,890	7,882	2,132	992	R	40.8	46.6	12.6	45	15	2	0.2	0.1	0.2	0.3
CALIFORNIA	10,782,743	5,853,651	4,093,501	835,591	1,760,150	D	54.3	38.0	7.7				100.0	100.0	100.0	100.0

[1]For remaining two years of term vacated by Pete Wilson (R), who was elected governor of California in 1990. Incumbent John Seymour (R) appointed as interim senator in January 1991.

California 119

Table H. — Vote for U.S. Representative in Congress: November 3, 1992, General Election

Congressional district and county	Total	Democrat (DEM)	Republican (REP)	Other	Plurality Total	Party	Percent of total vote DEM	REP	Other	Rank within district DEM	REP	Other	Percent contribution to district vote Total	DEM	REP	Other
District 1	**251,206**	**119,676**	**113,266**	**18,264**	**6,410**	**D**	**47.6**	**45.1**	**7.3**				**100.0**	**100.0**	**100.0**	**100.0**
Del Norte	9,269	3,964	4,799	506	835	R	42.8	51.8	5.5	7	1	6	3.7	3.3	4.2	2.8
Humboldt	58,909	29,703	26,336	2,870	3,367	D	50.4	44.7	4.9	1	5	7	23.5	24.8	23.3	15.7
Lake	22,937	10,280	11,007	1,650	727	R	44.8	48.0	7.2	6	2	3	9.1	8.6	9.7	9.0
Mendocino	36,238	17,301	14,883	4,054	2,418	D	47.7	41.1	11.2	3	7	1	14.4	14.5	13.1	22.2
Napa	51,544	23,859	24,368	3,317	509	R	46.3	47.3	6.4	5	3	5	20.5	19.9	21.5	18.2
Solano (pt)	49,129	23,802	21,033	4,294	2,769	D	48.4	42.8	8.7	2	6	2	19.6	19.9	18.6	23.5
Sonoma (pt)	23,180	10,767	10,840	1,573	73	R	46.4	46.8	6.8	4	4	4	9.2	9.0	9.6	8.6
District 2	**256,556**	**71,780**	**167,247**	**17,529**	**95,467**	**R**	**28.0**	**65.2**	**6.8**				**100.0**	**100.0**	**100.0**	**100.0**
Butte (pt)	79,918	23,385	50,106	6,427	26,721	R	29.3	62.7	8.0	6	6	2	31.2	32.6	30.0	36.7
Lassen	9,783	3,144	5,932	707	2,788	R	32.1	60.6	7.2	3	8	3	3.8	4.4	3.5	4.0
Modoc	4,388	1,269	2,889	230	1,620	R	28.9	65.8	5.2	7	4	9	1.7	1.8	1.7	1.3
Nevada	41,961	13,534	24,881	3,546	11,347	R	32.3	59.3	8.5	2	9	1	16.4	18.9	14.9	20.2
Plumas	9,731	3,425	5,603	703	2,178	R	35.2	57.6	7.2	1	10	4	3.8	4.8	3.4	4.0
Shasta	65,602	14,014	48,139	3,449	34,125	R	21.4	73.4	5.3	10	1	8	25.6	19.5	28.8	19.7
Sierra	1,799	572	1,116	111	544	R	31.8	62.0	6.2	4	7	6	0.7	0.8	0.7	0.6
Siskiyou	20,109	6,242	12,900	967	6,658	R	31.0	64.2	4.8	5	5	10	7.8	8.7	7.7	5.5
Trinity	6,469	1,703	4,320	446	2,617	R	26.3	66.8	6.9	9	3	5	2.5	2.4	2.6	2.5
Yuba	16,796	4,492	11,361	943	6,869	R	26.7	67.6	5.6	8	2	7	6.5	6.3	6.8	5.4
District 3	**238,685**	**122,149**	**96,092**	**20,444**	**26,057**	**D**	**51.2**	**40.3**	**8.6**				**100.0**	**100.0**	**100.0**	**100.0**
Butte (pt)	2,962	1,249	1,451	262	202	R	42.2	49.0	8.8	7	2	4	1.2	1.0	1.5	1.3
Colusa	5,546	2,916	2,288	342	628	D	52.6	41.3	6.2	2	6	7	2.3	2.4	2.4	1.7
Glenn	8,645	4,245	3,754	646	491	D	49.1	43.4	7.5	4	4	6	3.6	3.5	3.9	3.2
Sacramento (pt)	92,348	45,403	38,084	8,861	7,319	D	49.2	41.2	9.6	3	7	2	38.7	37.2	39.6	43.3
Solano (pt)	22,956	10,858	10,063	2,035	795	D	47.3	43.8	8.9	5	3	3	9.6	8.9	10.5	10.0
Sutter	25,056	9,643	13,491	1,922	3,848	R	38.5	53.8	7.7	8	1	5	10.5	7.9	14.0	9.4
Tehama	20,847	9,449	8,713	2,685	736	D	45.3	41.8	12.9	6	5	1	8.7	7.7	9.1	13.1
Yolo	60,325	38,386	18,248	3,691	20,138	D	63.6	30.2	6.1	1	8	8	25.3	31.4	19.0	18.1
District 4	**283,365**	**129,489**	**141,155**	**12,721**	**11,666**	**R**	**45.7**	**49.8**	**4.5**				**100.0**	**100.0**	**100.0**	**100.0**
Alpine	607	306	273	28	33	D	50.4	45.0	4.6	1	8	3	0.2	0.2	0.2	0.2
Amador	15,244	7,102	7,518	624	416	R	46.6	49.3	4.1	4	5	8	5.4	5.5	5.3	4.9
Calaveras	16,795	7,887	8,061	847	174	R	47.0	48.0	5.0	3	6	2	5.9	6.1	5.7	6.7
El Dorado	64,180	28,663	32,607	2,910	3,944	R	44.7	50.8	4.5	6	2	4	22.6	22.1	23.1	22.9
Mono	4,243	1,860	2,102	281	242	R	43.8	49.5	6.6	8	4	1	1.5	1.4	1.5	2.2
Placer	88,787	40,649	44,223	3,915	3,574	R	45.8	49.8	4.4	5	3	6	31.3	31.4	31.3	30.8
Sacramento (pt)	69,954	31,207	35,636	3,111	4,429	R	44.6	50.9	4.4	7	1	5	24.7	24.1	25.2	24.5
Tuolumne	23,555	11,815	10,735	1,005	1,080	D	50.2	45.6	4.3	2	7	7	8.3	9.1	7.6	7.9
District 5	**230,560**	**158,250**	**58,698**	**13,612**	**99,552**	**D**	**68.6**	**25.5**	**5.9**				**100.0**	**100.0**	**100.0**	**100.0**
Sacramento (pt)	230,560	158,250	58,698	13,612	99,552	D	68.6	25.5	5.9	1	1	1	100.0	100.0	100.0	100.0
District 6	**291,786**	**190,322**	**98,171**	**3,293**	**92,151**	**D**	**65.2**	**33.6**	**1.1**				**100.0**	**100.0**	**100.0**	**100.0**
Marin	125,432	79,931	44,847	654	35,084	D	63.7	35.8	0.5	2	1	2	43.0	42.0	45.7	19.9
Sonoma (pt)	166,354	110,391	53,324	2,639	57,067	D	66.4	32.1	1.6	1	2	1	57.0	58.0	54.3	80.1
District 7	**217,982**	**153,320**	**54,822**	**9,840**	**98,498**	**D**	**70.3**	**25.1**	**4.5**				**100.0**	**100.0**	**100.0**	**100.0**
Contra Costa (pt)	162,748	117,751	37,982	7,015	79,769	D	72.4	23.3	4.3	1	2	2	74.7	76.8	69.3	71.3
Solano (pt)	55,234	35,569	16,840	2,825	18,729	D	64.4	30.5	5.1	2	1	1	25.3	23.2	30.7	28.7
District 8	**232,691**	**191,906**	**25,693**	**15,092**	**166,213**	**D**	**82.5**	**11.0**	**6.5**				**100.0**	**100.0**	**100.0**	**100.0**
San Francisco (pt)	232,691	191,906	25,693	15,092	166,213	D	82.5	11.0	6.5	1	1	1	100.0	100.0	100.0	100.0
District 9	**228,467**	**164,265**	**53,707**	**10,495**	**110,558**	**D**	**71.9**	**23.5**	**4.6**				**100.0**	**100.0**	**100.0**	**100.0**
Alameda (pt)	228,467	164,265	53,707	10,495	110,558	D	71.9	23.5	4.6	1	1	1	100.0	100.0	100.0	100.0
District 10	**280,429**	**134,635**	**145,702**	**92**	**11,067**	**R**	**48.0**	**52.0**	**<.1**				**100.0**	**100.0**	**100.0**	**100.0**
Alameda (pt)	87,247	43,919	43,285	43	634	D	50.3	49.6	<.1	1	2	1	31.1	32.6	29.7	46.7
Contra Costa (pt)	193,182	90,716	102,417	49	11,701	R	47.0	53.0	<.1	2	1	2	68.9	67.4	70.3	53.3
District 11	**198,490**	**90,539**	**94,453**	**13,498**	**3,914**	**R**	**45.6**	**47.6**	**6.8**				**100.0**	**100.0**	**100.0**	**100.0**
Sacramento (pt)	45,349	19,859	22,241	3,249	2,382	R	43.8	49.0	7.2	2	1	1	22.8	21.9	23.5	24.1
San Joaquin (pt)	153,141	70,680	72,212	10,249	1,532	R	46.2	47.2	6.7	1	2	2	77.2	78.1	76.5	75.9
District 12	**228,407**	**157,205**	**53,278**	**17,924**	**103,927**	**D**	**68.8**	**23.3**	**7.8**				**100.0**	**100.0**	**100.0**	**100.0**
San Francisco (pt)	63,219	43,972	11,956	7,291	32,016	D	69.6	18.9	11.5	1	2	1	27.7	28.0	22.4	40.7
San Mateo (pt)	165,188	113,233	41,322	10,633	71,911	D	68.5	25.0	6.4	2	1	2	72.3	72.0	77.6	59.3
District 13	**205,516**	**123,795**	**64,953**	**16,768**	**58,842**	**D**	**60.2**	**31.6**	**8.2**				**100.0**	**100.0**	**100.0**	**100.0**
Alameda (pt)	186,072	113,577	57,754	14,741	55,823	D	61.0	31.0	7.9	1	2	2	90.5	91.7	88.9	87.9
Santa Clara (pt)	19,444	10,218	7,199	2,027	3,019	D	52.6	37.0	10.4	2	1	1	9.5	8.3	11.1	12.1
District 14	**259,222**	**146,873**	**101,202**	**11,147**	**45,671**	**D**	**56.7**	**39.0**	**4.3**				**100.0**	**100.0**	**100.0**	**100.0**
San Mateo (pt)	101,178	58,457	38,693	4,028	19,764	D	57.8	38.2	4.0	1	2	2	39.0	39.8	38.2	36.1

Congressional district and county	Total	Democrat (DEM)	Republican (REP)	Other	Plurality Total	Party	Percent of total vote DEM	REP	Other	Rank within district DEM	REP	Other	Percent contribution to district vote Total	DEM	REP	Other
District 14 (cont)																
Santa Clara (pt)	158,044	88,416	62,509	7,119	25,907	D	55.9	39.6	4.5	2	1	1	61.0	60.2	61.8	63.9
District 15	265,370	168,617	82,875	13,878	85,742	D	63.5	31.2	5.2				100.0	100.0	100.0	100.0
Santa Clara (pt)	236,961	150,859	74,345	11,757	76,514	D	63.7	31.4	5.0	1	1	2	89.3	89.5	89.7	84.7
Santa Cruz (pt)	28,409	17,758	8,530	2,121	9,228	D	62.5	30.0	7.5	2	2	1	10.7	10.5	10.3	15.3
District 16	155,883	96,661	49,843	9,379	46,818	D	62.0	32.0	6.0				100.0	100.0	100.0	100.0
Santa Clara (pt)	155,883	96,661	49,843	9,379	46,818	D	62.0	32.0	6.0	1	1	1	100.0	100.0	100.0	100.0
District 17	210,367	151,565	49,947	8,855	101,618	D	72.0	23.7	4.2				100.0	100.0	100.0	100.0
Monterey	114,083	78,569	31,267	4,247	47,302	D	68.9	27.4	3.7	2	2	3	54.2	51.8	62.6	48.0
San Benito	12,589	8,400	3,678	511	4,722	D	66.7	29.2	4.1	3	1	2	6.0	5.5	7.4	5.8
Santa Cruz (pt)	83,695	64,596	15,002	4,097	49,594	D	77.2	17.9	4.9	1	3	1	39.8	42.6	30.0	46.3
District 18	165,011	139,704	-	25,307	114,397	D	84.7	-	15.3				100.0	100.0	-	100.0
Fresno (pt)	1,106	944	-	162	782	D	85.4	-	14.6	1	-	5	0.7	0.7	-	0.6
Madera (pt)	277	211	-	66	145	D	76.2	-	23.8	4	-	2	0.2	0.2	-	0.3
Merced	40,708	34,302	-	6,406	27,896	D	84.3	-	15.7	3	-	3	24.7	24.6	-	25.3
San Joaquin (pt)	3,587	2,504	-	1,083	1,421	D	69.8	-	30.2	5	-	1	2.2	1.8	-	4.3
Stanislaus	119,333	101,743	-	17,590	84,153	D	85.3	-	14.7	2	-	4	72.3	72.8	-	69.5
District 19	216,642	101,620	100,590	14,432	1,030	D	46.9	46.4	6.7				100.0	100.0	100.0	100.0
Fresno (pt)	160,902	77,059	73,180	10,663	3,879	D	47.9	45.5	6.6	1	4	2	74.3	75.8	72.8	73.9
Madera (pt)	29,276	13,591	13,805	1,880	214	R	46.4	47.2	6.4	2	3	3	13.5	13.4	13.7	13.0
Mariposa	8,063	3,437	3,913	713	476	R	42.6	48.5	8.8	3	2	1	3.7	3.4	3.9	4.9
Tulare (pt)	18,401	7,533	9,692	1,176	2,159	R	40.9	52.7	6.4	4	1	4	8.5	7.4	9.6	8.1
District 20	112,067	72,679	39,388	-	33,291	D	64.9	35.1	-				100.0	100.0	100.0	-
Fresno (pt)	47,320	30,507	16,813	-	13,694	D	64.5	35.5	-	2	3	-	42.2	42.0	42.7	-
Kern (pt)	25,754	17,725	8,029	-	9,696	D	68.8	31.2	-	1	4	-	23.0	24.4	20.4	-
Kings	24,236	15,236	9,000	-	6,236	D	62.9	37.1	-	3	2	-	21.6	21.0	22.8	-
Tulare (pt)	14,757	9,211	5,546	-	3,665	D	62.4	37.6	-	4	1	-	13.2	12.7	14.1	-
District 21	195,965	68,058	127,758	149	59,700	R	34.7	65.2	<.1				100.0	100.0	100.0	100.0
Kern (pt)	143,739	47,923	95,672	144	47,749	R	33.3	66.6	0.1	2	1	1	73.3	70.4	74.9	96.6
Tulare (pt)	52,226	20,135	32,086	5	11,951	R	38.6	61.4	<.1	1	2	2	26.7	29.6	25.1	3.4
District 22	249,924	87,328	131,242	31,354	43,914	R	34.9	52.5	12.5				100.0	100.0	100.0	100.0
San Luis Obispo	101,475	35,471	55,093	10,911	19,622	R	35.0	54.3	10.8	1	1	2	40.6	40.6	42.0	34.8
Santa Barbara (pt)	148,449	51,857	76,149	20,443	24,292	R	34.9	51.3	13.8	2	2	1	59.4	59.4	58.0	65.2
District 23	212,881	88,225	115,504	9,152	27,279	R	41.4	54.3	4.3				100.0	100.0	100.0	100.0
Santa Barbara (pt)	5,498	3,139	2,171	188	968	D	57.1	39.5	3.4	1	2	2	2.6	3.6	1.9	2.1
Ventura (pt)	207,383	85,086	113,333	8,964	28,247	R	41.0	54.6	4.3	2	1	1	97.4	96.4	98.1	97.9
District 24	255,267	141,742	99,835	13,690	41,907	D	55.5	39.1	5.4				100.0	100.0	100.0	100.0
Los Angeles (pt)	200,730	120,480	69,223	11,027	51,257	D	60.0	34.5	5.5	1	2	1	78.6	85.0	69.3	80.5
Ventura (pt)	54,537	21,262	30,612	2,663	9,350	R	39.0	56.1	4.9	2	1	2	21.4	15.0	30.7	19.5
District 25	218,715	72,233	113,611	32,871	41,378	R	33.0	51.9	15.0				100.0	100.0	100.0	100.0
Los Angeles (pt)	218,715	72,233	113,611	32,871	41,378	R	33.0	51.9	15.0	1	1	1	100.0	100.0	100.0	100.0
District 26	120,908	73,807	36,453	10,648	37,354	D	61.0	30.1	8.8				100.0	100.0	100.0	100.0
Los Angeles (pt)	120,908	73,807	36,453	10,648	37,354	D	61.0	30.1	8.8	1	1	1	100.0	100.0	100.0	100.0
District 27	212,450	83,805	105,521	23,124	21,716	R	39.4	49.7	10.9				100.0	100.0	100.0	100.0
Los Angeles (pt)	212,450	83,805	105,521	23,124	21,716	R	39.4	49.7	10.9	1	1	1	100.0	100.0	100.0	100.0
District 28	209,382	76,525	122,353	10,504	45,828	R	36.5	58.4	5.0				100.0	100.0	100.0	100.0
Los Angeles (pt)	209,382	76,525	122,353	10,504	45,828	R	36.5	58.4	5.0	1	1	1	100.0	100.0	100.0	100.0
District 29	261,486	160,312	67,141	34,033	93,171	D	61.3	25.7	13.0				100.0	100.0	100.0	100.0
Los Angeles (pt)	261,486	160,312	67,141	34,033	93,171	D	61.3	25.7	13.0	1	1	1	100.0	100.0	100.0	100.0
District 30	83,543	48,800	20,034	14,709	28,766	D	58.4	24.0	17.6				100.0	100.0	100.0	100.0
Los Angeles (pt)	83,543	48,800	20,034	14,709	28,766	D	58.4	24.0	17.6	1	1	1	100.0	100.0	100.0	100.0
District 31	109,197	68,324	40,873	0	27,451	D	62.6	37.4	0.0				100.0	100.0	100.0	0.0
Los Angeles (pt)	109,197	68,324	40,873	0	27,451	D	62.6	37.4	0.0	1	1	1	100.0	100.0	100.0	0.0
District 32	172,812	150,644	-	22,168	128,476	D	87.2	-	12.8				100.0	100.0	-	100.0
Los Angeles (pt)	172,812	150,644	-	22,168	128,476	D	87.2	-	12.8	1	-	1	100.0	100.0	-	100.0
District 33	50,779	32,010	15,428	3,341	16,582	D	63.0	30.4	6.6				100.0	100.0	100.0	100.0
Los Angeles (pt)	50,779	32,010	15,428	3,341	16,582	D	63.0	30.4	6.6	1	1	1	100.0	100.0	100.0	100.0

Congressional district and county	Total	Democrat (DEM)	Republican (REP)	Other	Plurality Total	Plurality Party	DEM	REP	Other	Rank DEM	Rank REP	Rank Other	Total	DEM	REP	Other
District 34	**149,718**	**91,738**	**50,907**	**7,073**	**40,831**	D	61.3	34.0	4.7				100.0	100.0	100.0	100.0
Los Angeles (pt)	149,718	91,738	50,907	7,073	40,831	D	61.3	34.0	4.7	1	1	1	100.0	100.0	100.0	100.0
District 35	**124,776**	**102,941**	**17,417**	**4,418**	**85,524**	D	82.5	14.0	3.5				100.0	100.0	100.0	100.0
Los Angeles (pt)	124,776	102,941	17,417	4,418	85,524	D	82.5	14.0	3.5	1	1	1	100.0	100.0	100.0	100.0
District 36	**259,757**	**125,751**	**109,684**	**24,322**	**16,067**	D	48.4	42.2	9.4				100.0	100.0	100.0	100.0
Los Angeles (pt)	259,757	125,751	109,684	24,322	16,067	D	48.4	42.2	9.4	1	1	1	100.0	100.0	100.0	100.0
District 37	**113,337**	**97,159**	**-**	**16,178**	**80,981**	D	85.7	-	14.3				100.0	100.0	-	100.0
Los Angeles (pt)	113,337	97,159	-	16,178	80,981	D	85.7	-	14.3	1	-	1	100.0	100.0	-	100.0
District 38	**189,321**	**82,108**	**92,038**	**15,175**	**9,930**	R	43.4	48.6	8.0				100.0	100.0	100.0	100.0
Los Angeles (pt)	189,321	82,108	92,038	15,175	9,930	R	43.4	48.6	8.0	1	1	1	100.0	100.0	100.0	100.0
District 39	**213,684**	**81,728**	**122,472**	**9,484**	**40,744**	R	38.2	57.3	4.4				100.0	100.0	100.0	100.0
Los Angeles (pt)	70,555	27,763	39,482	3,310	11,719	R	39.3	56.0	4.7	1	2	1	33.0	34.0	32.2	34.9
Orange (pt)	143,129	53,965	82,990	6,174	29,025	R	37.7	58.0	4.3	2	1	2	67.0	66.0	67.8	65.1
District 40	**205,283**	**63,881**	**129,563**	**11,839**	**65,682**	R	31.1	63.1	5.8				100.0	100.0	100.0	100.0
Inyo	8,057	2,380	5,179	498	2,799	R	29.5	64.3	6.2	2	1	1	3.9	3.7	4.0	4.2
San Bernardino (pt)	197,226	61,501	124,384	11,341	62,883	R	31.2	63.1	5.8	1	2	2	96.1	96.3	96.0	95.8
District 41	**170,666**	**58,777**	**101,753**	**10,136**	**42,976**	R	34.4	59.6	5.9				100.0	100.0	100.0	100.0
Los Angeles (pt)	50,039	19,781	27,328	2,930	7,547	R	39.5	54.6	5.9	1	3	2	29.3	33.7	26.9	28.9
Orange (pt)	35,153	8,925	24,433	1,795	15,508	R	25.4	69.5	5.1	3	1	3	20.6	15.2	24.0	17.7
San Bernardino (pt)	85,474	30,071	49,992	5,411	19,921	R	35.2	58.5	6.3	2	2	1	50.1	51.2	49.1	53.4
District 42	**157,455**	**79,780**	**69,251**	**8,424**	**10,529**	D	50.7	44.0	5.4				100.0	100.0	100.0	100.0
San Bernardino (pt)	157,455	79,780	69,251	8,424	10,529	D	50.7	44.0	5.4	1	1	1	100.0	100.0	100.0	100.0
District 43	**190,639**	**88,468**	**88,987**	**13,184**	**519**	R	46.4	46.7	6.9				100.0	100.0	100.0	100.0
Riverside (pt)	190,639	88,468	88,987	13,184	519	R	46.4	46.7	6.9	1	1	1	100.0	100.0	100.0	100.0
District 44	**203,541**	**81,693**	**110,333**	**11,515**	**28,640**	R	40.1	54.2	5.7				100.0	100.0	100.0	100.0
Riverside (pt)	203,541	81,693	110,333	11,515	28,640	R	40.1	54.2	5.7	1	1	1	100.0	100.0	100.0	100.0
District 45	**227,016**	**88,508**	**123,731**	**14,777**	**35,223**	R	39.0	54.5	6.5				100.0	100.0	100.0	100.0
Orange (pt)	227,016	88,508	123,731	14,777	35,223	R	39.0	54.5	6.5	1	1	1	100.0	100.0	100.0	100.0
District 46	**110,806**	**45,435**	**55,659**	**9,712**	**10,224**	R	41.0	50.2	8.8				100.0	100.0	100.0	100.0
Orange (pt)	110,806	45,435	55,659	9,712	10,224	R	41.0	50.2	8.8	1	1	1	100.0	100.0	100.0	100.0
District 47	**254,257**	**76,924**	**165,004**	**12,329**	**88,080**	R	30.3	64.9	4.8				100.0	100.0	100.0	100.0
Orange (pt)	254,257	76,924	165,004	12,329	88,080	R	30.3	64.9	4.8	1	1	1	100.0	100.0	100.0	100.0
District 48	**230,495**	**67,415**	**140,935**	**22,145**	**73,520**	R	29.2	61.1	9.6				100.0	100.0	100.0	100.0
Orange (pt)	113,588	31,715	71,882	9,991	40,167	R	27.9	63.3	8.8	3	2	2	49.3	47.0	51.0	45.1
Riverside (pt)	11,354	3,203	7,289	862	4,086	R	28.2	64.2	7.6	2	1	3	4.9	4.8	5.2	3.9
San Diego (pt)	105,553	32,497	61,764	11,292	29,267	R	30.8	58.5	10.7	1	3	1	45.8	48.2	43.8	51.0
District 49	**248,898**	**127,280**	**106,170**	**15,448**	**21,110**	D	51.1	42.7	6.2				100.0	100.0	100.0	100.0
San Diego (pt)	248,898	127,280	106,170	15,448	21,110	D	51.1	42.7	6.2	1	1	1	100.0	100.0	100.0	100.0
District 50	**136,626**	**77,293**	**39,531**	**19,802**	**37,762**	D	56.6	28.9	14.5				100.0	100.0	100.0	100.0
San Diego (pt)	136,626	77,293	39,531	19,802	37,762	D	56.6	28.9	14.5	1	1	1	100.0	100.0	100.0	100.0
District 51	**252,995**	**85,148**	**141,890**	**25,957**	**56,742**	R	33.7	56.1	10.3				100.0	100.0	100.0	100.0
San Diego (pt)	252,995	85,148	141,890	25,957	56,742	R	33.7	56.1	10.3	1	1	1	100.0	100.0	100.0	100.0
District 52	**213,784**	**88,076**	**112,995**	**12,713**	**24,919**	R	41.2	52.9	5.9				100.0	100.0	100.0	100.0
Imperial	25,576	10,604	14,080	892	3,476	R	41.5	55.1	3.5	1	1	2	12.0	12.0	12.5	7.0
San Diego (pt)	188,208	77,472	98,915	11,821	21,443	R	41.2	52.6	6.3	2	2	1	88.0	88.0	87.5	93.0
CALIFORNIA	**10,535,065**	**5,446,966**	**4,365,155**	**722,944**	**1,081,811**	D	51.7	41.4	6.9							

County	Total	Clinton	Brown	Tsongas	McCarthy	Kerrey	Agran	LaRouche		Clinton	Brown	Tsongas	Clinton	Brown	Tsongas	Total	Clinton	Brown	Tsongas
				Top candidates							Percent of total vote			Rank			Percent contribution to state vote		
Alameda	178,779	80,718	78,573	11,725	3,042	2,224	1,379	1,118	-	45.1	43.9	6.6	37	12	51	6.2	5.9	6.8	5.5
Alpine	149	48	84	9	4	1	1	2	-	32.2	56.4	6.0	58	1	57	<.1	<.1	<.1	<.1
Amador	4,267	2,107	1,582	349	120	61	17	31	-	49.4	37.1	8.2	24	33	33	0.1	0.2	0.1	0.2
Butte	19,041	9,143	7,019	1,730	611	226	149	163	-	48.0	36.9	9.1	27	35	19	0.7	0.7	0.6	0.8
Calaveras	4,248	1,848	1,759	340	170	63	19	49	-	43.5	41.4	8.0	41	20	38	0.1	0.1	0.2	0.2
Colusa	1,623	849	503	137	67	26	22	19	-	52.3	31.0	8.4	14	49	27	<.1	<.1	<.1	<.1
Contra Costa	102,217	49,470	41,133	8,037	1,755	862	481	479	-	48.4	40.2	7.9	25	25	40	3.6	3.6	3.6	3.8
Del Norte	2,743	1,471	909	240	42	31	20	30	-	53.6	33.1	8.7	12	44	23	<.1	0.1	<.1	0.1
El Dorado	14,260	5,691	6,192	1,504	467	214	81	111	-	39.9	43.4	10.5	50	14	1	0.5	0.4	0.5	0.7
Fresno	49,905	27,642	15,247	4,159	1,420	713	378	346	-	55.4	30.6	8.3	6	50	30	1.7	2.0	1.3	2.0
Glenn	2,254	1,247	594	232	87	37	27	30	-	55.3	26.4	10.3	7	57	2	<.1	<.1	<.1	0.1
Humboldt	18,461	7,334	8,156	1,835	469	234	201	232	-	39.7	44.2	9.9	51	11	5	0.6	0.5	0.7	0.9
Imperial	6,265	3,161	2,145	381	346	97	64	71	-	50.5	34.2	6.1	19	42	55	0.2	0.2	0.2	0.2
Inyo	2,029	936	719	192	78	47	18	39	-	46.1	35.4	9.5	34	39	15	<.1	<.1	<.1	<.1
Kern	36,937	20,657	11,116	2,805	1,101	597	253	408	-	55.9	30.1	7.6	4	51	42	1.3	1.5	1.0	1.3
Kings	5,782	3,317	1,737	397	181	68	36	46	-	57.4	30.0	6.9	1	52	49	0.2	0.2	0.2	0.2
Lake	6,486	3,374	2,419	415	133	72	33	40	-	52.0	37.3	6.4	16	32	53	0.2	0.2	0.2	0.2
Lassen	3,019	1,510	967	289	112	51	22	68	-	50.0	32.0	9.6	20	48	13	0.1	0.1	<.1	0.1
Los Angeles	834,756	426,646	317,751	50,636	16,657	8,652	7,574	6,840	-	51.1	38.1	6.1	17	31	56	29.2	31.4	27.6	23.8
Madera	6,101	3,369	1,739	489	192	226	37	49	-	55.2	28.5	8.0	8	56	37	0.2	0.2	0.2	0.2
Marin	43,744	15,993	22,989	3,321	744	319	199	179	-	36.6	52.6	7.6	54	4	43	1.5	1.2	2.0	1.6
Mariposa	2,022	974	718	202	71	24	17	16	-	48.2	35.5	10.0	26	38	4	<.1	<.1	<.1	<.1
Mendocino	13,319	4,795	6,976	919	263	118	120	128	-	36.0	52.4	6.9	55	5	47	0.5	0.4	0.6	0.4
Merced	12,399	6,686	3,981	1,089	275	197	79	92	-	53.9	32.1	8.8	10	47	22	0.4	0.5	0.3	0.5
Modoc	1,440	791	378	130	71	28	12	30	-	54.9	26.3	9.0	9	58	20	<.1	<.1	<.1	<.1
Mono	847	278	452	80	21	10	3	3	-	32.8	53.4	9.4	57	3	17	<.1	<.1	<.1	<.1
Monterey	26,018	11,605	10,871	2,264	580	291	205	202	-	44.6	41.8	8.7	38	18	24	0.9	0.9	0.9	1.1
Napa	15,771	7,318	6,427	1,286	350	142	96	152	-	46.4	40.8	8.2	32	22	34	0.6	0.5	0.6	0.6
Nevada	9,331	3,777	4,202	839	305	94	47	67	-	40.5	45.0	9.0	49	10	21	0.3	0.3	0.4	0.4
Orange	151,999	69,620	59,439	12,538	3,240	2,115	3,688	1,359	-	45.8	39.1	8.2	35	27	32	5.3	5.1	5.2	5.9
Placer	19,633	8,451	8,165	1,945	538	301	97	136	-	43.0	41.6	9.9	42	19	6	0.7	0.6	0.7	0.9
Plumas	3,144	1,481	1,141	301	124	54	16	27	-	47.1	36.3	9.6	30	37	11	0.1	0.1	<.1	0.1
Riverside	80,087	44,848	26,393	4,979	1,811	848	675	533	-	56.0	33.0	6.2	3	45	54	2.8	3.3	2.3	2.3
Sacramento	130,221	58,069	52,067	12,110	3,605	2,299	998	1,073	-	44.6	40.0	9.3	39	26	18	4.5	4.3	4.5	5.7
San Benito	3,196	1,484	1,234	308	77	24	30	39	-	46.4	38.6	9.6	31	29	10	0.1	0.1	0.1	0.1
San Bernardino	93,260	46,298	34,510	6,545	1,903	1,625	1,054	1,325	-	49.6	37.0	7.0	22	34	45	3.3	3.4	3.0	3.1
San Diego	193,451	91,587	75,130	16,377	4,162	3,099	1,537	1,559	-	47.3	38.8	8.5	29	28	26	6.8	6.7	6.5	7.7
San Francisco	117,778	48,731	58,703	6,855	1,762	746	452	529	-	41.4	49.8	5.8	47	7	58	4.1	3.6	5.1	3.2
San Joaquin	38,119	18,920	14,656	2,455	1,304	364	194	226	-	49.6	38.4	6.4	23	30	52	1.3	1.4	1.3	1.2
San Luis Obispo	23,042	8,714	11,056	2,206	425	365	122	154	-	37.8	48.0	9.6	53	8	12	0.8	0.6	1.0	1.0
San Mateo	81,904	33,926	38,068	6,844	1,425	760	395	486	-	41.4	46.5	8.4	46	9	29	2.9	2.5	3.3	3.2
Santa Barbara	36,469	15,341	15,868	3,449	742	564	284	221	-	42.1	43.5	9.5	45	13	16	1.3	1.1	1.4	1.6
Santa Clara	169,535	74,717	71,806	16,354	2,822	1,633	1,114	1,089	-	44.1	42.4	9.6	40	17	9	5.9	5.5	6.2	7.7
Santa Cruz	35,521	12,208	19,211	2,443	528	300	628	203	-	34.4	54.1	6.9	56	2	48	1.2	0.9	1.7	1.1
Shasta	16,132	8,623	4,771	1,656	400	266	229	187	-	53.5	29.6	10.3	13	54	3	0.6	0.6	0.4	0.8
Sierra	533	219	215	52	25	10	5	7	-	41.1	40.3	9.8	48	24	7	<.1	<.1	<.1	<.1
Siskiyou	6,130	3,099	2,162	533	135	78	44	79	-	50.6	35.3	8.7	18	40	25	0.2	0.2	0.2	0.3
Solano	34,897	15,765	14,394	2,837	820	397	337	347	-	45.2	41.2	8.1	36	21	36	1.2	1.2	1.3	1.3
Sonoma	59,951	23,428	30,451	3,949	1,028	534	283	278	-	39.1	50.8	6.6	52	6	50	2.1	1.7	2.6	1.9
Stanislaus	29,217	15,676	9,895	2,042	828	432	131	213	-	53.7	33.9	7.0	11	43	46	1.0	1.2	0.9	1.0
Sutter	5,464	2,845	1,761	519	161	74	60	44	-	52.1	32.2	9.5	15	46	14	0.2	0.2	0.2	0.2
Tehama	5,746	3,251	1,682	468	149	83	41	72	-	56.6	29.3	8.1	2	55	35	0.2	0.2	0.1	0.2
Trinity	1,894	901	695	159	54	33	23	29	-	47.6	36.7	8.4	28	36	28	<.1	<.1	<.1	<.1
Tulare	18,564	10,378	5,573	1,452	654	260	116	131	-	55.9	30.0	7.8	5	53	41	0.6	0.8	0.5	0.7
Tuolumne	6,558	2,800	2,839	518	141	159	39	62	-	42.7	43.3	7.9	44	15	39	0.2	0.2	0.2	0.2
Ventura	53,194	24,602	21,469	4,405	1,315	563	443	397	-	46.2	40.4	8.3	33	23	31	1.9	1.8	1.9	2.1
Yolo	19,470	8,331	8,359	1,881	505	175	129	90	-	42.8	42.9	9.7	43	16	8	0.7	0.6	0.7	0.9
Yuba	4,097	2,044	1,409	311	218	49	30	36	-	49.9	34.4	7.6	21	41	44	0.1	0.2	0.1	0.1
CALIFORNIA	2,863,419	1,359,112	1,150,460	212,522	60,635	33,935	24,784	21,971	-	47.5	40.2	7.4				100.0	100.0	100.0	100.0

Table J. — Vote for Presidential Preference: June 2, 1992, Republican Primary Election

| County | Top candidates | | | | | Top four candidates (state vote) | | | | | | | | | | | | |
| | | | | | | Percent of total vote | | | | Rank | | | | Percent contribution to state vote | | | | |
	Total	Bush	Bu-chanan			Bush	Bu-chanan			Bush	Bu-chanan			Total	Bush	Bu-chanan		
Alameda	61,319	47,077	14,242	-	-	76.8	23.2	-	-	23	36	-	-	2.8	3.0	2.5	-	-
Alpine	200	158	42	-	-	79.0	21.0	-	-	11	48	-	-	<.1	<.1	<.1	-	-
Amador	3,926	3,023	903	-	-	77.0	23.0	-	-	21	38	-	-	0.2	0.2	0.2	-	-
Butte	19,958	14,984	4,974	-	-	75.1	24.9	-	-	37	22	-	-	0.9	0.9	0.9	-	-
Calaveras	4,105	3,057	1,048	-	-	74.5	25.5	-	-	45	14	-	-	0.2	0.2	0.2	-	-
Colusa	1,812	1,442	370	-	-	79.6	20.4	-	-	8	51	-	-	<.1	<.1	<.1	-	-
Contra Costa	66,093	52,997	13,096	-	-	80.2	19.8	-	-	4	55	-	-	3.1	3.3	2.3	-	-
Del Norte	2,175	1,608	567	-	-	73.9	26.1	-	-	47	12	-	-	0.1	0.1	<.1	-	-
El Dorado	15,914	11,912	4,002	-	-	74.9	25.1	-	-	41	18	-	-	0.7	0.8	0.7	-	-
Fresno	43,561	33,950	9,611	-	-	77.9	22.1	-	-	16	43	-	-	2.0	2.1	1.7	-	-
Glenn	2,388	1,757	631	-	-	73.6	26.4	-	-	48	11	-	-	0.1	0.1	0.1	-	-
Humboldt	11,642	8,375	3,267	-	-	71.9	28.1	-	-	54	5	-	-	0.5	0.5	0.6	-	-
Imperial	6,060	4,886	1,174	-	-	80.6	19.4	-	-	3	56	-	-	0.3	0.3	0.2	-	-
Inyo	2,785	2,120	665	-	-	76.1	23.9	-	-	29	30	-	-	0.1	0.1	0.1	-	-
Kern	45,201	33,931	11,270	-	-	75.1	24.9	-	-	38	21	-	-	2.1	2.1	2.0	-	-
Kings	4,919	4,022	897	-	-	81.8	18.2	-	-	1	58	-	-	0.2	0.3	0.2	-	-
Lake	4,314	3,263	1,051	-	-	75.6	24.4	-	-	33	26	-	-	0.2	0.2	0.2	-	-
Lassen	2,412	1,809	603	-	-	75.0	25.0	-	-	39	20	-	-	0.1	0.1	0.1	-	-
Los Angeles	472,335	330,500	141,835	-	-	70.0	30.0	-	-	57	2	-	-	21.9	20.8	24.9	-	-
Madera	6,238	4,792	1,446	-	-	76.8	23.2	-	-	22	37	-	-	0.3	0.3	0.3	-	-
Marin	21,926	17,131	4,795	-	-	78.1	21.9	-	-	15	44	-	-	1.0	1.1	0.8	-	-
Mariposa	2,044	1,559	485	-	-	76.3	23.7	-	-	28	31	-	-	<.1	<.1	<.1	-	-
Mendocino	7,003	5,062	1,941	-	-	72.3	27.7	-	-	52	7	-	-	0.3	0.3	0.3	-	-
Merced	8,388	6,438	1,950	-	-	76.8	23.2	-	-	24	35	-	-	0.4	0.4	0.3	-	-
Modoc	1,413	1,065	348	-	-	75.4	24.6	-	-	34	25	-	-	<.1	<.1	<.1	-	-
Mono	1,046	838	208	-	-	80.1	19.9	-	-	5	54	-	-	<.1	<.1	<.1	-	-
Monterey	19,440	15,359	4,081	-	-	79.0	21.0	-	-	10	49	-	-	0.9	1.0	0.7	-	-
Napa	11,202	8,720	2,482	-	-	77.8	22.2	-	-	17	42	-	-	0.5	0.5	0.4	-	-
Nevada	12,006	8,963	3,043	-	-	74.7	25.3	-	-	44	15	-	-	0.6	0.6	0.5	-	-
Orange	236,699	171,450	65,249	-	-	72.4	27.6	-	-	50	9	-	-	11.0	10.8	11.5	-	-
Placer	22,207	16,627	5,580	-	-	74.9	25.1	-	-	40	19	-	-	1.0	1.0	1.0	-	-
Plumas	2,625	2,023	602	-	-	77.1	22.9	-	-	20	39	-	-	0.1	0.1	0.1	-	-
Riverside	94,579	70,302	24,277	-	-	74.3	25.7	-	-	46	13	-	-	4.4	4.4	4.3	-	-
Sacramento	95,270	69,800	25,470	-	-	73.3	26.7	-	-	49	10	-	-	4.4	4.4	4.5	-	-
San Benito	2,590	2,044	546	-	-	78.9	21.1	-	-	12	47	-	-	0.1	0.1	<.1	-	-
San Bernardino	100,162	70,144	30,018	-	-	70.0	30.0	-	-	56	3	-	-	4.6	4.4	5.3	-	-
San Diego	228,414	162,083	66,331	-	-	71.0	29.0	-	-	55	4	-	-	10.6	10.2	11.7	-	-
San Francisco	26,363	21,017	5,346	-	-	79.7	20.3	-	-	7	52	-	-	1.2	1.3	0.9	-	-
San Joaquin	31,770	25,451	6,319	-	-	80.1	19.9	-	-	6	53	-	-	1.5	1.6	1.1	-	-
San Luis Obispo	26,766	20,265	6,501	-	-	75.7	24.3	-	-	32	27	-	-	1.2	1.3	1.1	-	-
San Mateo	45,138	34,950	10,188	-	-	77.4	22.6	-	-	19	40	-	-	2.1	2.2	1.8	-	-
Santa Barbara	40,089	31,137	8,952	-	-	77.7	22.3	-	-	18	41	-	-	1.9	2.0	1.6	-	-
Santa Clara	111,878	85,683	26,195	-	-	76.6	23.4	-	-	25	34	-	-	5.2	5.4	4.6	-	-
Santa Cruz	16,078	12,280	3,798	-	-	76.4	23.6	-	-	27	32	-	-	0.7	0.8	0.7	-	-
Shasta	17,146	12,417	4,729	-	-	72.4	27.6	-	-	51	8	-	-	0.8	0.8	0.8	-	-
Sierra	483	384	99	-	-	79.5	20.5	-	-	9	50	-	-	<.1	<.1	<.1	-	-
Siskiyou	4,703	3,537	1,166	-	-	75.2	24.8	-	-	35	24	-	-	0.2	0.2	0.2	-	-
Solano	19,757	14,846	4,911	-	-	75.1	24.9	-	-	36	23	-	-	0.9	0.9	0.9	-	-
Sonoma	31,691	24,268	7,423	-	-	76.6	23.4	-	-	26	33	-	-	1.5	1.5	1.3	-	-
Stanislaus	23,718	18,691	5,027	-	-	78.8	21.2	-	-	13	46	-	-	1.1	1.2	0.9	-	-
Sutter	8,254	6,487	1,767	-	-	78.6	21.4	-	-	14	45	-	-	0.4	0.4	0.3	-	-
Tehama	4,884	3,654	1,230	-	-	74.8	25.2	-	-	42	17	-	-	0.2	0.2	0.2	-	-
Trinity	1,559	1,071	488	-	-	68.7	31.3	-	-	58	1	-	-	<.1	<.1	<.1	-	-
Tulare	21,727	17,607	4,120	-	-	81.0	19.0	-	-	2	57	-	-	1.0	1.1	0.7	-	-
Tuolumne	5,863	4,381	1,482	-	-	74.7	25.3	-	-	43	16	-	-	0.3	0.3	0.3	-	-
Ventura	59,483	42,922	16,561	-	-	72.2	27.8	-	-	53	6	-	-	2.8	2.7	2.9	-	-
Yolo	10,585	8,044	2,541	-	-	76.0	24.0	-	-	31	28	-	-	0.5	0.5	0.4	-	-
Yuba	3,955	3,006	949	-	-	76.0	24.0	-	-	30	29	-	-	0.2	0.2	0.2	-	-
CALIFORNIA	**2,156,261**	**1,587,369**	**568,892**	-	-	**73.6**	**26.4**	-	-					**100.0**	**100.0**	**100.0**	-	-

1992 Vote for President
Percent for Clinton (D), by County

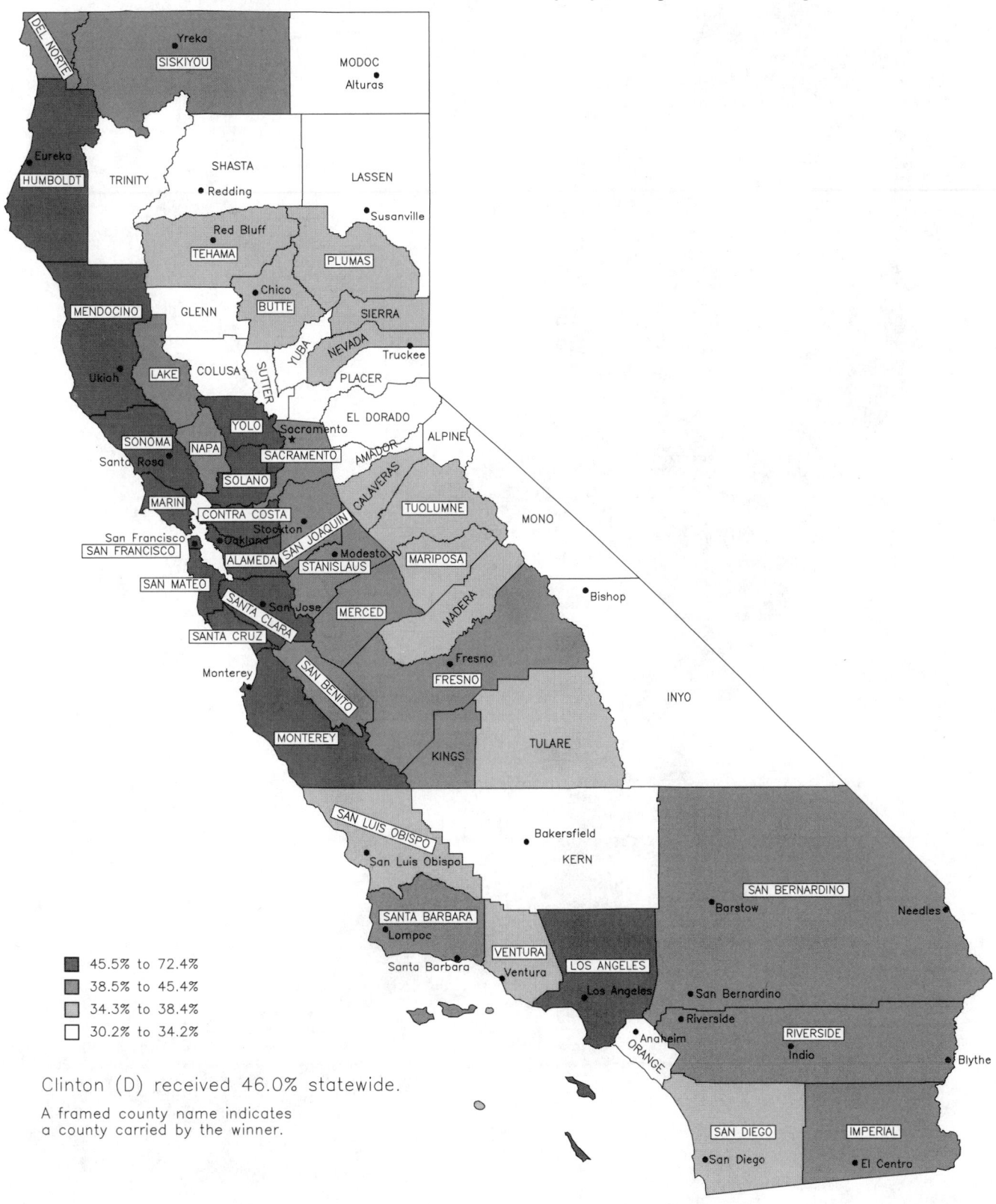

Del Norte
Yreka •
SISKIYOU
MODOC
Alturas •

Eureka •
HUMBOLDT
TRINITY
SHASTA
• Redding
LASSEN
Susanville •

Red Bluff •
TEHAMA
PLUMAS

MENDOCINO
GLENN
• Chico
BUTTE
SIERRA

Ukiah •
LAKE
COLUSA
SUTTER
YUBA
NEVADA
• Truckee

PLACER

YOLO
Sacramento ★
EL DORADO
ALPINE

SONOMA
NAPA
SACRAMENTO
AMADOR

Santa Rosa •
SOLANO
CALAVERAS
TUOLUMNE
MONO

MARIN
CONTRA COSTA
Stockton •
SAN JOAQUIN

San Francisco •
SAN FRANCISCO
• Oakland
ALAMEDA
STANISLAUS
• Modesto
MARIPOSA

SAN MATEO
SANTA CLARA
• San Jose
MERCED
MADERA
• Bishop

SANTA CRUZ
SAN BENITO

Monterey •
Fresno •
FRESNO
INYO

MONTEREY
KINGS
TULARE

SAN LUIS OBISPO
• Bakersfield
San Luis Obispo •
KERN
SAN BERNARDINO
• Barstow
Needles •

SANTA BARBARA
Lompoc •
VENTURA
LOS ANGELES
Santa Barbara •
Ventura •
Los Angeles •
• San Bernardino
• Riverside
RIVERSIDE
Anaheim •
ORANGE
Indio •
• Blythe

SAN DIEGO
IMPERIAL
• San Diego
• El Centro

Legend:
- ■ 45.5% to 72.4%
- ▨ 38.5% to 45.4%
- ▥ 34.3% to 38.4%
- □ 30.2% to 34.2%

Clinton (D) received 46.0% statewide.

A framed county name indicates
a county carried by the winner.

California 125

1992 Vote for U.S. Senator
Percent for Boxer (D), by County

- 48.9% to 76.6%
- 40.6% to 48.8%
- 37.0% to 40.5%
- 26.3% to 36.9%

Boxer (D) received 47.9% statewide.

A framed county name indicates
a county carried by the winner.

1992 Vote for U.S. Senator*
Percent for Feinstein (D), by County

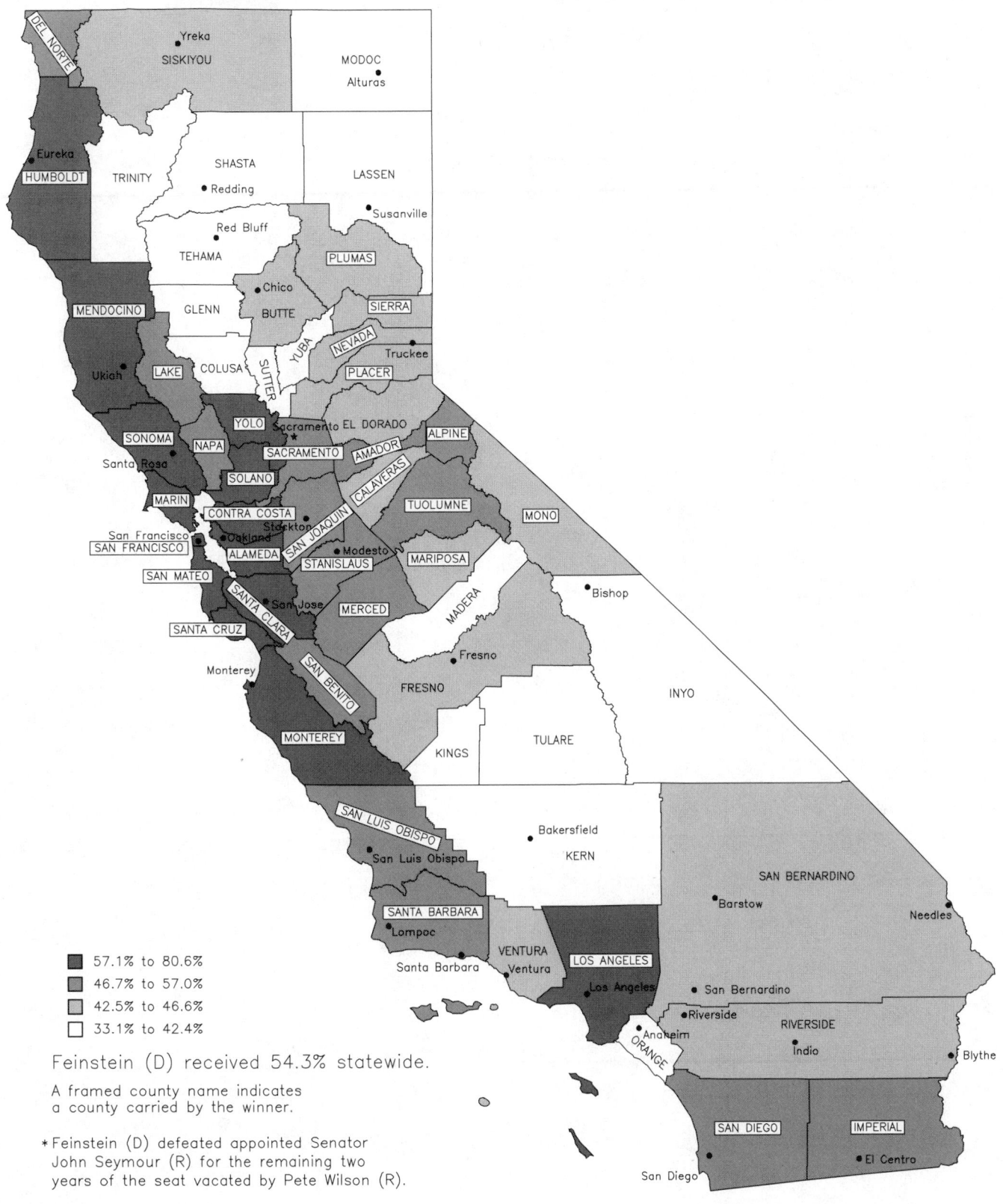

Feinstein (D) received 54.3% statewide.

57.1% to 80.6%
46.7% to 57.0%
42.5% to 46.6%
33.1% to 42.4%

A framed county name indicates
a county carried by the winner.

*Feinstein (D) defeated appointed Senator
John Seymour (R) for the remaining two
years of the seat vacated by Pete Wilson (R).

COLORADO

Congressional Districts 6
  Average Population 549,066
State Senate Districts 35
  Average Population 94,126
State House Districts 65
  Average Population 50,683

Electoral College Votes...8
Counties 63
Voting Precincts 2,805

Alternative Registration Methods:
  ....Motor-voter

Registration Deadline (Days before Election) 25

Voting Equipment Use (Counties)

Datavote Punch Card	3	Paper Ballot	19
Electronic	1	Other Punch Card	17
Lever Machine	11	Mixed Systems	0
Optical Scanner	12		

Party Control	DEM	REP	IND	VAC
1993 State Senate	16	19	0	0
1992 State Senate	12	23	0	0
1993 State House	31	34	0	0
1992 State House	27	38	0	0

Population Statistics 1990

Race/ Ethnicity	Total Population		Voting Age Population		Voting Age Population % of total population
	Number	%	Number	%	
Non-Hispanic					
White	2,658,945	80.7	2,016,316	82.9	75.8
Black	128,057	3.9	87,858	3.6	68.6
Asian/Pacific Islander	56,773	1.7	39,812	1.6	70.1
Native American	22,068	0.7	15,136	0.6	68.6
Other	4,249	<.1	2,375	<.1	55.9
All Hispanic	424,302	12.9	271,631	11.2	64.0
TOTAL	3,294,394	100.0	2,433,128	100.0	73.9

Estimated Voting Age Population 1992 (VAP) 2,501,000
Number of Registered Voters................................. 2,003,375
  % of estimated VAP.. 80.1
Voter Turnout (Actual) 1,597,166
  % of VAP 63.9
  % of Registration 79.7
Persons Not Voting—of Voting Age 903,834
  % of VAP 36.1
Persons Not Voting—of Registered 406,209
  % of Registration 20.3
Straight Ticket Voting .... No

State Officials and Members of Congress

Governor:
Roy Romer (D) 1986, elected to a four-year term in 1990.

U.S. Senators:
Hank Brown (R) 1990, elected to a six-year term in 1990.
Ben Nighthorse Campbell (D) 1992, elected to a six-year term in 1992.

U.S. Representative in Congress:
(District, Name, Party, Date first elected)

1. Schroeder (D) 1972
2. Skaggs (D) 1986
3. McInnis (R) 1992
4. Allard (R) 1990
5. Hefley (R) 1986
6. Schaefer (R) 1983

Candidates: General Election, November 3, 1992

Candidate(s)	Total vote	Percent	Party	Status	First elected
President/Vice President					
Clinton/Gore	629,681	40.13%	Democrat	Challenger	1992
Bush/Quayle	562,850	35.87%	Republican	Incumbent	1988
Perot/Stockdale	366,010	23.32%	Independent	Challenger	
Marrou/Lord	8,669	0.55%	Libertarian	Challenger	
Fulani/Munoz	1,608	0.10%	New Alliance	Challenger	
Gritz/Minett	274	0.02%	Write in	Challenger	
Hagelin/Tompkins	47	<.01%	Write in	Challenger	
Dodge/Ormbsy	21	<.01%	Write in	Challenger	
LaRouche/Bevel	20	<.01%	Write in	Challenger	
U.S. Senator					
Ben Nighthorse Campbell	803,725	51.78%	Democrat	Challenger	1992
Terry Considine	662,893	42.70%	Republican	Challenger	
Richard Grimes	42,455	2.73%	Perot Independent	Challenger	
Matt Noah	22,846	1.47%	Pro-Life	Challenger	
Dan Winters	20,347	1.31%	Independent	Challenger	
Hue Futch	23	<.01%	Libertarian	Challenger	
Governor (No Contest)					
U.S. Representative in Congress					
District 1					
Patricia Schroeder	156,629	68.84%	Democrat	Incumbent	1972
Raymond Aragon	70,902	31.16%	Republican	Challenger	
District 2					
David Skaggs	164,790	60.73%	Democrat	Incumbent	1986
Bryan Day	88,470	32.60%	Republican	Challenger	
Vern Tharp	18,101	6.67%	Grassroots	Challenger	
District 3					
Scott McInnis	143,293	54.70%	Republican	Challenger	1992
Mike Callihan	114,480	43.70%	Democrat	Challenger	
Ki R. Nelson	4,189	1.60%	Populist	Challenger	
Jim Hayes	2	<.01%	Unknown	Challenger	
District 4					
Wayne Allard	139,884	57.84%	Republican	Incumbent	1990
Tom Redder	101,957	42.16%	Democrat	Challenger	
District 5					
Joel Hefley	173,096	71.11%	Republican	Incumbent	1986
Charles Oriez	62,550	25.70%	Democrat	Challenger	
Keith Hamburger	7,769	3.19%	Libertarian	Challenger	
District 6					
Dan Schaefer	142,021	60.93%	Republican	Incumbent	1983
Tom Kolbe	91,073	39.07%	Democrat	Challenger	
Earl Higgerson	3	<.01%	Unknown	Challenger	

Candidates: March 3, 1992, Primary Election

Candidate	Total vote	Percent	Candidate	Total vote	Percent
Presidential Preference, Democratic			**Presidential Preference, Republican**		
Jerry Brown	69,073	28.82%	George Bush	132,100	67.50%
Bill Clinton	64,470	26.90%	Patrick Buchanan	58,753	30.02%
Paul Tsongas	61,360	25.60%	George Zimmermann	1,592	0.81%
Bob Kerrey	29,572	12.34%	Paul Jensen	1,332	0.68%
Tom Harkin	5,866	2.45%	Terrance Scott	719	0.37%
Noncommitted	5,356	2.23%	Stephen Koczak	659	0.34%
Charles Woods	1,051	0.44%	Tennie Rogers	535	0.27%
Larry Agran	672	0.28%			
Stephen Burke	532	0.22%			
Eugene McCarthy	488	0.20%			
Lyndon LaRouche, Jr.	328	0.14%			
Jim Hayes	279	0.12%			
Leonard Talbow	202	0.08%			
Tom Hawks	165	0.07%			
Tom Shiekman	76	0.03%			
Jeffrey Marsh	59	0.02%			
J. Louis McAlpine	48	0.02%			
Ray Rollinson	46	0.02%			

Voter Registration and Turnout, 1948-1992 Elections

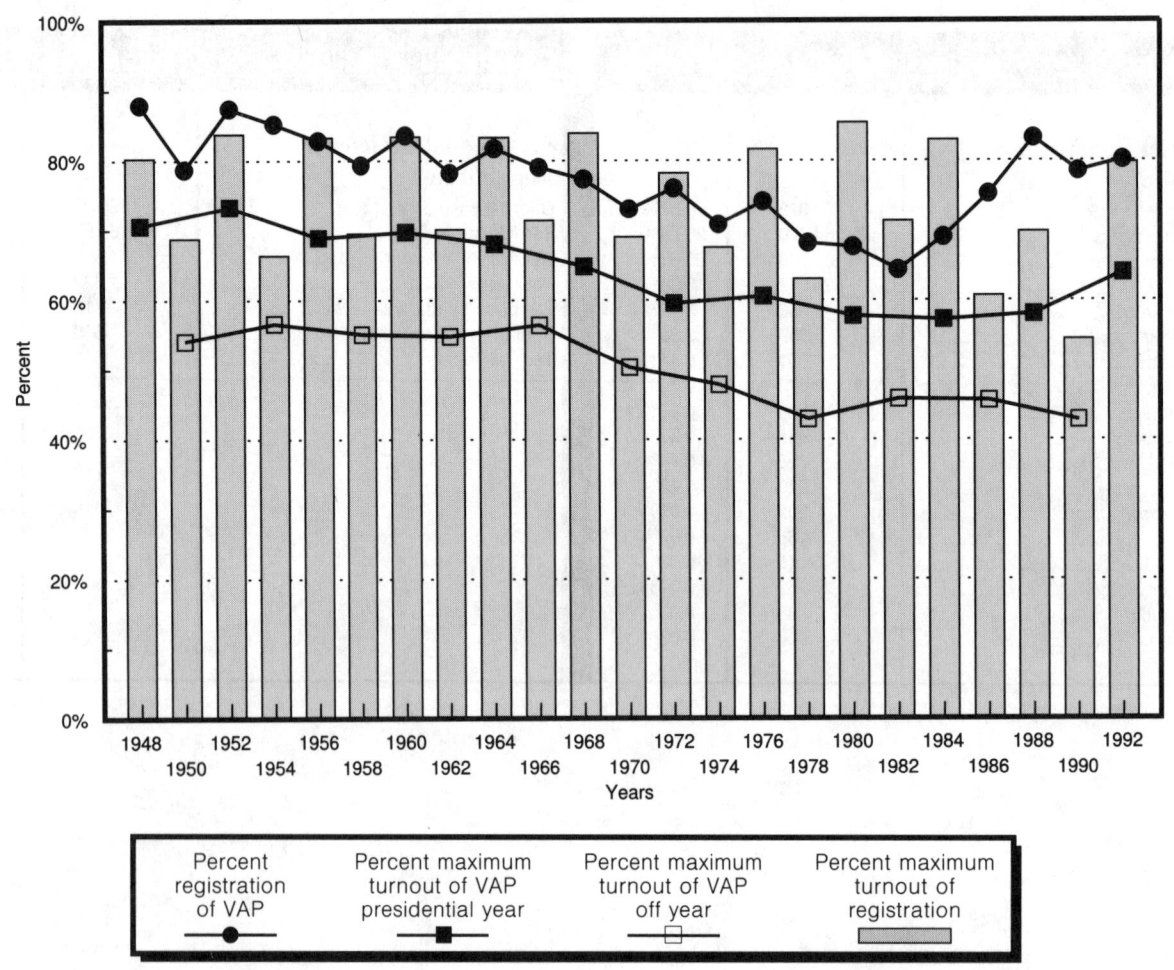

Year	Estimated Voting Age Population (VAP)	Voter registration (REG)			Voter turnout											
						Highest office						Maximum vote				
		Total	Percent of VAP	Rank by percent of VAP	Actual	Total	Office	Percent total REG	Rank by percent of REG	Percent of VAP	Rank by percent of VAP	Total	Percent total REG	Rank by percent of REG	Percent total VAP	Rank by percent of VAP
1992	2,501,000	2,003,375	80.1	14	1,597,166	1,569,180	P	78.3	20	62.7	17	1,597,166	79.7	22	63.9	15
1990	2,447,000	1,921,653	78.5	11	1,046,139	1,022,027	S	53.2	34	41.8	19	1,046,139	54.4	34	42.8	19
1988	2,440,000	2,029,518	83.2	8	1,416,265	1,372,394	P	67.6	37	56.2	14	1,416,265	69.8	34	58.0	14
1986	2,407,000	1,810,998	75.2	13	1,096,867	1,060,765	S	58.6	18	44.1	13	1,096,867	60.6	19	45.6	14
1984	2,350,000	1,621,306	69.0	34	1,343,437	1,295,380	P	79.9	6	55.1	26	1,343,437	82.9	2	57.2	20
1982	2,264,000	1,455,734	64.3	34	1,037,774	956,021	G	65.7	17	42.2	30	1,037,774	71.3	8	45.8	21
1980	2,123,000	1,434,257	67.6	33	1,225,549	1,184,415	P	82.6	2	55.8	24	1,225,549	85.4	2	57.7	22
1978	1,974,000	1,345,004	68.1	26	847,765	823,807	G	61.2	14	41.7	23	847,765	63.0	13	42.9	23
1976	1,838,000	1,361,570	74.1	22	1,111,599	1,081,554	P	79.4	13	58.8	17	1,111,599	81.6	9	60.5	16
1974	1,734,000	1,227,492	70.8	23	-	828,968	G	67.5	10	47.8	12	828,968	67.5	11	47.8	13
1972	1,604,000	1,219,591	76.0	20	-	953,884	P	78.2	14	59.5	24	953,884	78.2	19	59.5	24
1970	1,328,000	968,982	73.0	24	-	668,496	G	69.0	15	50.3	26	668,496	69.0	18	50.3	28
1968	1,251,000	966,700	77.3	21	-	811,199	P	83.9	14	64.8	24	811,199	83.9	16	64.8	25
1966	1,171,000	924,968	79.0	17	-	660,063	G	71.4	15	56.4	17	660,063	71.4	16	56.4	19
1964	1,142,000	933,312	81.7	16	-	776,986	P	83.3	16	68.0	22	776,986	83.3	18	68.0	22
1962	1,124,000	879,475	78.2	20	-	616,481	G	70.1	18	54.8	19	616,481	70.1	18	54.8	19
1960	1,056,000	882,422	83.6	11	-	736,236	P	83.4	21	69.7	28	736,236	83.4	22	69.7	28
1958	997,000	790,706	79.3	12	-	549,808	G	69.5	16	55.1	21	549,808	69.5	18	55.1	23
1956	953,000	789,204	82.8	12	-	657,074	P	83.3	14	68.9	17	657,074	83.3	15	68.9	19
1954	865,000	737,027	85.2	5	-	489,540	G	66.4	13	56.6	14	489,540	66.4	14	56.6	16
1952	860,000	752,030	87.4	6	-	630,103	P	83.8	13	73.3	15	630,103	83.8	13	73.3	17
1950	833,000	655,626	78.7	7	-	450,994	G	68.8	12	54.1	17	450,994	68.8	12	54.1	19
1948	730,000	641,747	87.9	2	-	515,237	P	80.3	8	70.6	3	515,237	80.3	9	70.6	3

COLORADO

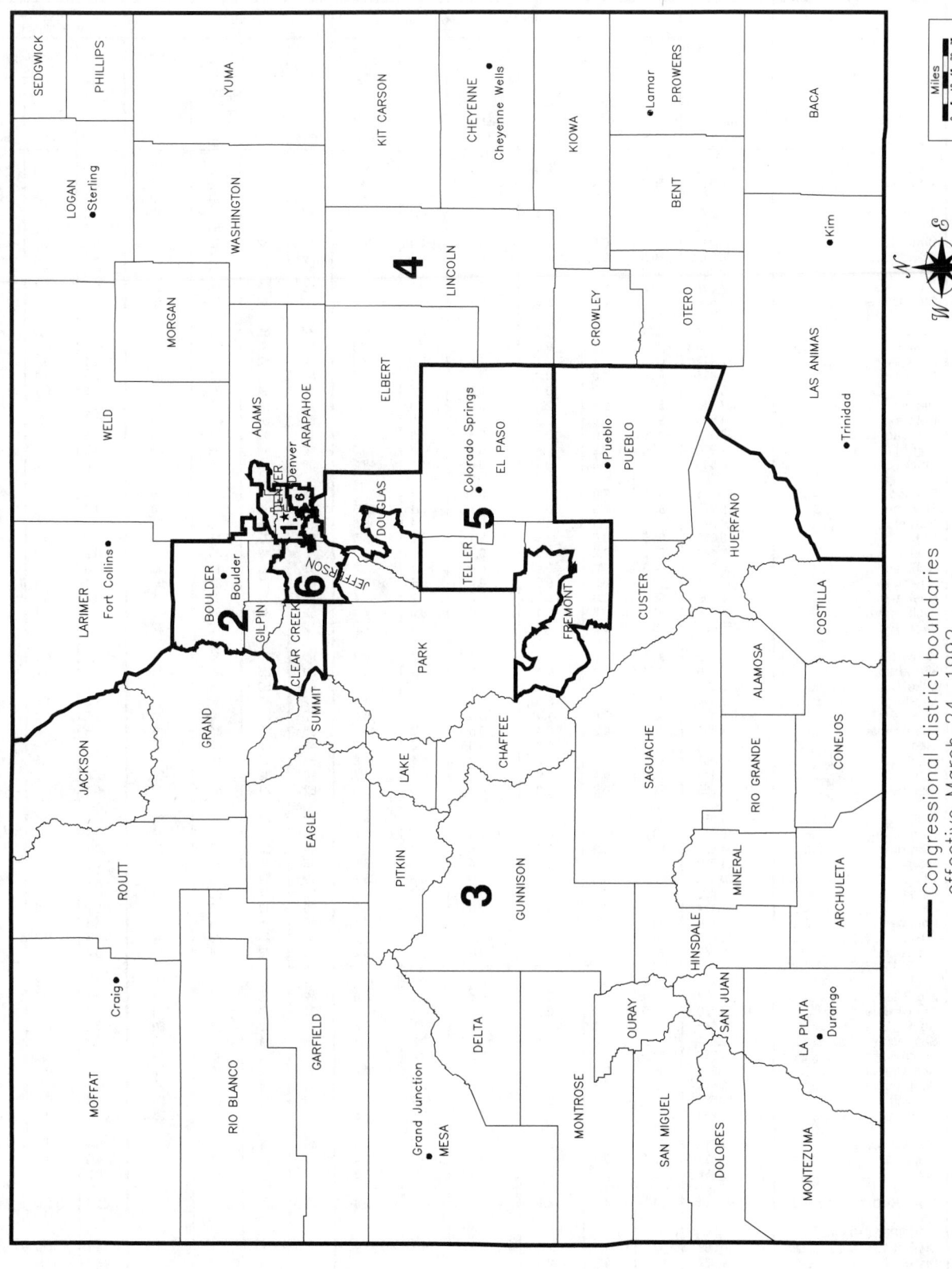

Congressional district boundaries effective March 24, 1992.

Copyright © 1993 by Election Data Services, Inc.

Colorado 133

Table A. — 1990 Population by Race and Ethnic Origin

State/ county code	County	Total persons	Percent of total persons — Non-Hispanic: White	Black	Asian and Pacific Islander	Native American	Other	Hispanic	Rank: Total	Rank Non-Hispanic: White	Black	Hispanic	Percent contribution: Total	Non-Hispanic: White	Black	Hispanic
08 001	Adams	265,038	75.0	3.2	2.4	0.7	0.2	18.6	5	49	5	17	8.0	7.5	6.6	11.6
08 003	Alamosa	13,617	59.2	0.4	0.7	0.6	0.4	38.6	24	57	19	7	0.4	0.3	<.1	1.2
08 005	Arapahoe	391,511	85.4	5.8	2.8	0.5	<.1	5.6	4	41	4	39	11.9	12.6	17.7	5.1
08 007	Archuleta	5,345	74.4	<.1	0.5	1.7	<.1	23.3	43	51	47	12	0.2	0.1	<.1	0.3
08 009	Baca	4,556	92.8	<.1	0.2	1.4	<.1	5.6	47	27	53	37	0.1	0.2	<.1	<.1
08 011	Bent	5,048	71.1	0.6	0.5	0.6	<.1	27.2	44	52	12	10	0.2	0.1	<.1	0.3
08 013	Boulder	225,339	89.5	0.8	2.4	0.5	<.1	6.7	6	36	9	33	6.8	7.6	1.5	3.6
08 015	Chaffee	12,684	87.9	1.6	0.3	0.7	<.1	9.5	27	37	8	23	0.4	0.4	0.2	0.3
08 017	Cheyenne	2,397	96.2	0.0	0.1	0.2	0.0	3.5	55	8	56	47	<.1	<.1	0.0	<.1
08 019	Clear Creek	7,619	95.6	0.2	0.5	0.3	<.1	3.3	36	16	31	48	0.2	0.3	<.1	<.1
08 021	Conejos	7,453	39.4	0.1	0.2	0.3	0.2	59.9	37	62	44	2	0.2	0.1	<.1	1.1
08 023	Costilla	3,190	21.6	0.2	0.9	0.3	0.2	76.9	52	63	32	1	<.1	<.1	<.1	0.6
08 025	Crowley	3,946	68.3	6.4	0.7	1.4	0.0	23.1	50	53	3	14	0.1	0.1	0.2	0.2
08 027	Custer	1,926	95.6	0.0	0.2	1.3	<.1	2.9	57	14	57	56	<.1	<.1	0.0	<.1
08 029	Delta	20,980	89.8	0.3	0.2	0.5	<.1	9.1	18	34	25	24	0.6	0.7	<.1	0.5
08 031	Denver	467,610	61.4	12.4	2.2	0.8	0.3	23.0	1	55	1	15	14.2	10.8	45.1	25.3
08 033	Dolores	1,504	94.1	0.0	0.0	2.7	0.0	3.2	60	24	58	50	<.1	<.1	0.0	<.1
08 035	Douglas	60,391	95.0	0.6	0.8	0.4	<.1	3.2	11	19	11	52	1.8	2.2	0.3	0.5
08 037	Eagle	21,928	85.6	0.2	0.5	0.5	<.1	13.3	17	40	39	20	0.7	0.7	<.1	0.7
08 039	Elbert	9,646	96.3	0.5	0.4	0.6	<.1	2.2	33	6	17	61	0.3	0.3	<.1	<.1
08 041	El Paso	397,014	81.2	7.0	2.3	0.7	0.1	8.7	3	44	2	25	12.1	12.1	21.6	8.1
08 043	Fremont	32,273	87.7	2.6	0.3	0.8	<.1	8.5	13	39	6	28	1.0	1.1	0.7	0.7
08 045	Garfield	29,974	93.1	0.3	0.4	0.6	<.1	5.6	14	25	26	38	0.9	1.0	<.1	0.4
08 047	Gilpin	3,070	94.5	0.5	0.4	1.1	0.0	3.6	53	22	18	46	<.1	0.1	<.1	<.1
08 049	Grand	7,966	95.9	0.2	0.5	0.4	<.1	3.1	35	12	35	53	0.2	0.3	<.1	<.1
08 051	Gunnison	10,273	94.9	0.6	0.4	0.5	<.1	3.6	32	20	13	45	0.3	0.4	<.1	<.1
08 053	Hinsdale	467	98.5	0.2	0.0	0.4	0.0	0.9	63	1	33	63	<.1	<.1	<.1	<.1
08 055	Huerfano	6,009	58.2	0.3	0.2	0.6	0.2	40.4	40	59	22	5	0.2	0.1	<.1	0.6
08 057	Jackson	1,605	91.0	0.0	<.1	1.6	0.0	7.4	59	30	59	31	<.1	<.1	0.0	<.1
08 059	Jefferson	438,430	90.1	0.7	1.7	0.5	<.1	7.0	2	33	10	32	13.3	14.9	2.4	7.3
08 061	Kiowa	1,688	96.0	0.0	0.0	0.7	<.1	3.3	58	10	60	49	<.1	<.1	0.0	<.1
08 063	Kit Carson	7,140	92.9	0.1	0.1	0.2	<.1	6.6	39	26	45	35	0.2	0.2	<.1	0.1
08 065	Lake	6,007	74.9	0.2	0.3	0.5	0.3	23.9	41	50	38	11	0.2	0.2	<.1	0.3
08 067	La Plata	32,284	83.9	0.2	0.5	4.2	<.1	11.1	12	42	40	22	1.0	1.0	<.1	0.8
08 069	Larimer	186,136	90.9	0.6	1.4	0.5	<.1	6.6	7	31	14	34	5.7	6.4	0.8	2.9
08 071	Las Animas	13,765	54.5	0.2	0.4	0.5	0.2	44.2	23	60	30	4	0.4	0.3	<.1	1.4
08 073	Lincoln	4,529	97.4	<.1	0.2	0.6	0.0	1.7	48	2	48	62	0.1	0.2	<.1	<.1
08 075	Logan	17,567	91.5	0.1	0.2	0.2	<.1	7.9	21	29	46	30	0.5	0.6	<.1	0.3
08 077	Mesa	93,145	90.2	0.4	0.6	0.6	<.1	8.1	10	32	20	29	2.8	3.2	0.3	1.8
08 079	Mineral	558	94.6	0.0	0.0	0.5	0.0	4.8	62	21	61	40	<.1	<.1	0.0	<.1
08 081	Moffat	11,357	92.7	<.1	0.3	0.7	<.1	6.1	30	28	49	36	0.3	0.4	<.1	0.2
08 083	Montezuma	18,672	80.0	<.1	0.2	11.0	<.1	8.6	20	46	50	26	0.6	0.6	<.1	0.4
08 085	Montrose	24,423	87.8	0.2	0.2	0.5	<.1	11.2	15	38	27	21	0.7	0.8	<.1	0.6
08 087	Morgan	21,939	80.5	0.2	0.3	0.4	0.1	18.4	16	45	34	18	0.7	0.7	<.1	1.0
08 089	Otero	20,185	62.9	0.5	0.5	0.6	0.3	35.2	19	54	16	9	0.6	0.5	<.1	1.7
08 091	Ouray	2,295	95.3	0.0	<.1	0.1	0.0	4.5	56	17	62	41	<.1	<.1	0.0	<.1
08 093	Park	7,174	95.7	0.5	0.2	0.6	<.1	2.9	38	13	15	55	0.2	0.3	<.1	<.1
08 095	Phillips	4,189	95.6	0.0	0.2	<.1	<.1	4.1	49	15	63	42	0.1	0.2	0.0	<.1
08 097	Pitkin	12,661	94.4	0.3	1.1	0.4	<.1	3.8	28	23	23	44	0.4	0.4	<.1	0.1
08 099	Prowers	13,347	75.5	0.3	0.3	0.6	0.1	23.2	25	48	24	13	0.4	0.4	<.1	0.7
08 101	Pueblo	123,051	61.3	1.6	0.5	0.5	0.3	35.8	9	56	7	8	3.7	2.8	1.6	10.4
08 103	Rio Blanco	5,972	95.0	0.2	0.3	0.6	0.0	4.0	42	18	41	43	0.2	0.2	<.1	<.1
08 105	Rio Grande	10,770	59.0	<.1	0.1	0.5	<.1	40.3	31	58	52	6	0.3	0.2	<.1	1.0
08 107	Routt	14,088	96.7	<.1	0.3	0.4	<.1	2.5	22	3	51	60	0.4	0.5	<.1	<.1
08 109	Saguache	4,619	51.3	0.2	<.1	2.6	0.2	45.6	46	61	29	3	0.1	<.1	<.1	0.5
08 111	San Juan	745	83.2	0.1	0.3	0.5	0.0	15.8	61	43	43	19	<.1	<.1	<.1	<.1
08 113	San Miguel	3,653	96.4	0.1	0.2	0.3	<.1	2.8	51	5	42	57	0.1	0.1	<.1	<.1
08 115	Sedgwick	2,690	89.6	0.2	1.2	0.4	0.0	8.6	54	35	36	27	<.1	<.1	<.1	<.1
08 117	Summit	12,881	95.9	0.2	0.7	0.5	<.1	2.5	26	11	28	59	0.4	0.5	<.1	<.1
08 119	Teller	12,468	96.1	0.2	0.4	0.7	<.1	2.6	29	9	37	58	0.4	0.5	<.1	<.1
08 121	Washington	4,812	96.7	<.1	0.2	0.2	0.0	2.9	45	4	55	54	0.1	0.2	<.1	<.1
08 123	Weld	131,821	77.4	0.4	0.8	0.4	0.1	20.9	8	47	21	16	4.0	3.8	0.4	6.5
08 125	Yuma	8,954	96.3	<.1	0.1	0.4	<.1	3.2	34	7	54	51	0.3	0.3	<.1	<.1
08	**COLORADO**	3,294,394	80.7	3.9	1.7	0.7	<.1	12.9					100.0	100.0	100.0	100.0
	CONGRESSIONAL															
	District 1	549,068	62.3	12.4	2.3	0.8	0.3	21.9	3	6	1	1	16.7	12.9	53.4	28.4
	District 2	549,072	86.8	0.8	2.4	0.5	<.1	9.5	1	2	4	4	16.7	17.9	3.4	12.2
	District 3	549,062	80.3	0.6	0.5	1.1	0.1	17.4	5	5	6	2	16.7	16.6	2.6	22.5
	District 4	549,070	83.0	0.6	1.0	0.5	0.1	14.7	2	4	5	3	16.7	17.1	2.8	19.1
	District 5	549,066	84.5	5.4	2.1	0.6	0.1	7.4	4	3	2	5	16.7	17.4	23.1	9.5
	District 6	549,056	87.4	3.4	2.2	0.5	<.1	6.4	6	1	3	6	16.7	18.1	14.7	8.3

Table B. — 1990 Voting Age Population (VAP) by Race and Ethnic Origin

County	Total Voting Age Population	Percent of total VAP: White	Black	Asian and Pacific Islander	Native American	Other	Hispanic	Rank Total	Rank White	Rank Black	Rank Hispanic	Pct contribution Total	White	Black	Hispanic	VAP % of total pop Total	White	Black	Asian and Pacific Islander	Native American	Other	Hispanic
Adams	188,107	77.6	2.8	2.3	0.7	0.1	16.5	5	49	6	18	7.7	7.2	5.9	11.4	71.0	73.5	61.8	66.2	68.0	56.3	63.2
Alamosa	9,647	62.4	0.5	0.8	0.7	0.3	35.3	27	58	16	7	0.4	0.3	<.1	1.3	70.8	74.6	82.0	79.6	79.1	60.0	64.8
Arapahoe	285,281	86.7	5.3	2.6	0.4	<.1	4.9	4	41	4	38	11.7	12.3	17.2	5.2	72.9	74.0	66.6	68.9	70.6	40.8	64.9
Archuleta	3,764	76.9	<.1	0.5	1.4	<.1	21.1	43	51	44	12	0.2	0.1	<.1	0.3	70.4	72.8	60.0	80.0	56.7	60.0	63.8
Baca	3,405	94.0	0.0	0.2	1.1	<.1	4.7	46	26	53	39	0.1	0.2	0.0	<.1	74.7	75.6	0.0	100.0	60.3	100.0	62.7
Bent	3,722	74.4	0.6	0.5	0.6	<.1	23.9	44	52	11	10	0.2	0.1	<.1	0.3	73.7	77.2	68.8	78.3	65.6	50.0	64.9
Boulder	173,460	90.8	0.8	2.3	0.4	<.1	5.6	6	35	9	33	7.1	7.8	1.6	3.6	77.0	78.1	74.1	74.1	67.6	51.8	64.0
Chaffee	9,793	87.6	2.0	0.3	0.7	0.1	9.3	26	38	7	23	0.4	0.4	0.2	0.3	77.2	77.0	98.5	75.0	79.1	90.9	75.7
Cheyenne	1,641	97.0	0.0	0.0	0.1	0.0	2.9	56	6	54	47	<.1	<.1	0.0	<.1	68.5	69.0	0.0	0.0	50.0	0.0	57.8
Clear Creek	5,640	96.4	0.2	0.4	0.4	0.0	2.6	36	14	29	49	0.2	0.3	<.1	<.1	74.0	74.7	76.5	56.4	76.9	0.0	58.7
Conejos	4,870	38.7	<.1	0.2	0.3	0.2	60.6	39	62	51	2	0.2	<.1	<.1	1.1	65.3	64.2	22.2	62.5	70.0	75.0	66.1
Costilla	2,278	24.5	0.2	1.1	0.3	0.2	73.7	53	63	31	1	<.1	<.1	<.1	0.6	71.4	81.1	71.4	89.3	77.8	83.3	68.4
Crowley	3,117	68.8	8.1	0.7	1.4	0.0	21.0	49	53	2	13	0.1	0.1	0.3	0.2	79.0	79.7	99.2	75.9	75.4	0.0	71.7
Custer	1,416	95.8	0.0	0.2	1.6	<.1	2.3	57	18	55	53	<.1	<.1	0.0	<.1	73.5	73.7	0.0	100.0	88.0	100.0	60.0
Delta	15,833	91.3	0.3	0.2	0.5	<.1	7.6	17	33	24	27	0.7	0.7	<.1	0.4	75.5	76.7	79.7	69.4	77.6	64.3	63.2
Denver	364,731	66.9	11.2	2.0	0.7	0.2	19.0	1	55	1	15	15.0	12.1	46.4	25.5	78.0	85.0	70.6	72.2	67.9	57.6	64.5
Dolores	1,089	94.9	0.0	0.0	2.7	0.0	2.4	60	23	56	52	<.1	<.1	0.0	<.1	72.4	73.0	0.0	0.0	72.5	0.0	54.2
Douglas	41,671	95.5	0.6	0.7	0.4	<.1	2.8	11	20	12	48	1.7	2.0	0.3	0.4	69.0	69.4	62.4	61.7	69.6	23.1	60.8
Eagle	16,323	87.6	0.2	0.4	0.5	<.1	11.3	16	39	34	20	0.7	0.7	<.1	0.7	74.4	76.2	80.0	68.7	78.0	70.0	63.1
Elbert	6,679	96.3	0.5	0.4	0.7	0.0	2.1	33	15	15	58	0.3	0.3	<.1	<.1	69.2	69.3	76.1	64.3	77.2	0.0	65.9
El Paso	287,588	82.9	6.3	2.3	0.6	<.1	7.7	3	44	3	26	11.8	11.8	20.7	8.1	72.4	74.0	66.0	71.6	69.4	48.1	64.2
Fremont	24,975	87.4	3.2	0.3	0.9	<.1	8.2	12	40	5	24	1.0	1.1	0.9	0.8	77.4	77.1	96.8	69.2	82.7	83.3	74.0
Garfield	21,704	93.8	0.3	0.3	0.6	<.1	5.0	14	27	23	37	0.9	1.0	<.1	0.4	72.4	72.9	87.0	58.7	73.5	40.0	64.3
Gilpin	2,335	95.2	0.4	0.2	1.0	0.0	3.2	52	22	20	45	<.1	0.1	<.1	<.1	76.1	76.6	64.3	38.5	70.6	0.0	68.8
Grand	5,951	96.6	0.2	0.4	0.3	0.0	2.5	35	12	33	50	0.2	0.3	<.1	<.1	74.7	75.2	75.0	64.9	64.3	0.0	61.7
Gunnison	8,141	95.2	0.6	0.4	0.5	<.1	3.3	30	21	13	44	0.3	0.4	<.1	<.1	79.2	79.5	79.7	77.8	76.4	100.0	73.0
Hinsdale	381	98.7	0.0	0.0	0.5	0.0	0.8	63	1	57	63	<.1	<.1	0.0	<.1	81.6	81.7	0.0	0.0	100.0	0.0	75.0
Huerfano	4,457	60.7	0.2	0.1	0.6	0.2	38.2	40	59	30	5	0.2	0.1	<.1	0.6	74.2	77.3	50.0	46.2	65.8	75.0	70.1
Jackson	1,194	93.1	0.0	<.1	1.1	0.0	5.7	59	29	58	32	<.1	<.1	0.0	<.1	74.4	76.2	0.0	100.0	50.0	0.0	57.6
Jefferson	322,262	91.2	0.6	1.5	0.5	<.1	6.2	2	34	10	31	13.2	14.6	2.3	7.3	73.5	74.4	67.9	66.3	72.9	51.9	64.6
Kiowa	1,203	96.8	0.0	0.0	0.6	<.1	2.5	58	8	59	51	<.1	<.1	0.0	<.1	71.3	71.9	0.0	0.0	63.6	100.0	54.5
Kit Carson	5,057	94.4	<.1	0.1	0.3	<.1	5.1	38	25	48	36	0.2	0.2	<.1	<.1	70.8	72.0	37.5	77.8	76.5	100.0	54.9
Lake	4,333	77.3	0.2	0.3	0.4	0.2	21.6	41	50	40	11	0.2	0.2	<.1	0.3	72.1	74.4	63.6	83.3	63.3	58.8	65.1
La Plata	24,040	85.5	0.2	0.6	3.8	<.1	9.8	13	42	36	21	1.0	1.0	<.1	0.9	74.5	75.9	67.2	82.3	67.9	76.7	65.9
Larimer	139,075	92.2	0.5	1.4	0.4	<.1	5.4	7	31	14	35	5.7	6.4	0.9	2.8	74.2	75.8	72.0	73.7	72.4	53.8	61.2
Las Animas	10,261	57.5	0.3	0.5	0.5	0.1	41.2	24	60	26	3	0.4	0.3	<.1	1.6	74.5	78.5	87.1	84.5	73.8	62.5	69.5
Lincoln	3,336	92.0	<.1	<.1	0.7	0.0	1.2	47	2	47	62	0.1	0.2	<.1	<.1	73.7	74.1	50.0	37.5	79.3	0.0	53.3
Logan	12,885	93.0	<.1	0.2	0.2	<.1	6.4	20	30	43	30	0.5	0.6	<.1	0.3	73.3	74.6	57.9	66.7	82.4	44.4	59.4
Mesa	68,145	91.6	0.3	0.6	0.6	<.1	6.9	10	32	22	29	2.8	3.1	0.3	1.7	73.2	74.3	61.7	70.4	70.9	60.6	61.9
Mineral	433	95.8	0.0	0.0	0.5	0.0	3.7	62	17	60	40	<.1	<.1	0.0	<.1	77.6	78.6	0.0	0.0	66.7	0.0	59.3
Moffat	7,679	93.3	<.1	0.3	0.7	<.1	5.6	31	28	45	34	0.3	0.4	<.1	0.2	67.6	68.0	60.0	53.8	69.5	100.0	61.6
Montezuma	12,840	82.9	<.1	0.2	9.2	<.1	7.6	21	45	50	28	0.5	0.5	<.1	0.4	68.8	71.2	50.0	64.4	57.2	66.7	60.9
Montrose	17,725	89.4	0.2	0.2	0.5	<.1	9.7	15	37	32	22	0.7	0.8	<.1	0.6	72.6	73.9	62.3	59.3	72.2	80.0	62.5
Morgan	15,432	84.1	0.2	0.3	0.3	0.1	15.0	18	43	36	19	0.6	0.6	<.1	0.9	70.3	73.4	62.2	70.3	58.6	56.3	57.3
Otero	14,346	67.2	0.5	0.6	0.6	0.2	30.9	19	54	17	9	0.6	0.5	<.1	1.6	71.1	75.9	64.2	85.1	71.4	59.3	62.4
Ouray	1,725	96.3	0.0	<.1	0.1	0.0	3.5	55	16	61	42	<.1	<.1	0.0	<.1	72.7	75.9	0.0	0.0	66.7	0.0	59.2
Park	5,218	96.5	0.4	0.2	0.6	<.1	2.2	37	13	18	57	0.2	0.2	<.1	<.1	72.7	73.4	56.4	53.3	73.3	66.7	55.3
Phillips	3,089	96.6	0.0	0.2	<.1	<.1	3.0	50	10	50	46	0.1	0.1	0.0	<.1	73.7	74.5	0.0	66.7	100.0	100.0	55.3
Pitkin	10,529	94.8	0.3	1.0	0.4	<.1	3.5	23	24	25	43	0.4	0.5	<.1	0.1	83.2	83.5	81.6	74.6	85.4	100.0	76.6
Prowers	9,182	79.3	0.3	0.2	0.6	0.2	19.5	28	48	21	14	0.4	0.4	<.1	0.7	68.8	72.3	81.6	52.8	65.0	70.0	57.6
Pueblo	90,572	65.1	1.7	0.5	0.5	0.2	32.0	9	56	8	8	3.7	2.9	1.7	10.7	73.6	78.2	74.8	76.2	72.3	66.8	65.8
Rio Blanco	4,178	95.5	0.2	0.3	0.5	0.0	3.5	42	19	38	41	0.2	0.2	<.1	<.1	70.0	70.4	77.8	55.0	57.1	0.0	62.7
Rio Grande	7,519	63.1	<.1	0.1	0.4	<.1	36.3	32	57	49	6	0.3	0.2	<.1	1.0	69.8	74.6	80.0	84.6	56.9	71.4	62.9
Routt	10,541	97.1	<.1	0.2	0.3	<.1	2.2	22	5	46	55	0.4	0.5	<.1	<.1	74.8	75.1	87.5	64.1	63.6	100.0	66.3
Saguache	3,153	56.4	0.2	0.1	2.1	0.1	41.2	48	61	41	4	0.1	<.1	<.1	0.5	68.3	74.9	45.5	100.0	54.6	50.0	61.6
San Juan	523	82.4	0.2	0.4	0.4	0.0	16.6	61	46	35	17	<.1	<.1	<.1	<.1	70.2	69.5	100.0	100.0	50.0	0.0	73.7
San Miguel	2,828	96.9	0.2	0.3	0.4	<.1	2.2	51	7	37	56	0.1	0.1	<.1	<.1	77.8	77.8	100.0	100.0	91.7	50.0	60.8
Sedgwick	2,037	90.3	0.2	1.2	0.5	0.0	7.7	54	36	27	25	<.1	<.1	<.1	<.1	75.7	76.3	100.0	78.1	91.7	0.0	68.3
Summit	10,233	96.7	0.2	0.6	0.5	<.1	2.0	25	9	28	61	0.4	0.5	<.1	<.1	79.4	80.0	77.4	67.0	75.4	40.0	62.2
Teller	8,872	96.6	0.1	0.4	0.8	<.1	2.1	29	11	42	60	0.4	0.4	<.1	<.1	71.7	71.6	52.2	66.0	77.5	50.0	57.1
Washington	3,512	97.6	0.0	<.1	0.3	0.0	2.1	45	3	63	59	0.1	0.2	0.0	<.1	73.0	73.7	0.0	12.5	75.0	0.0	52.5
Weld	94,808	80.8	0.4	0.8	0.4	0.1	17.5	8	47	19	16	3.9	3.8	0.4	6.1	71.9	75.1	75.4	71.5	66.3	63.3	60.2
Yuma	6,364	97.2	<.1	0.1	0.3	<.1	2.3	34	4	52	54	0.3	0.3	<.1	<.1	71.1	71.8	50.0	58.3	64.7	50.0	51.8
COLORADO	**2,433,128**	**82.9**	**3.6**	**1.6**	**0.6**	**<.1**	**11.2**					**100.0**	**100.0**	**100.0**	**100.0**	**73.9**	**75.8**	**68.6**	**70.1**	**68.6**	**55.9**	**64.0**
CONGRESSIONAL																						
District 1	424,133	67.5	11.2	2.1	0.7	0.2	18.3	1	6	1	1	17.4	14.2	53.9	28.6	77.2	83.7	69.3	72.2	67.7	57.4	64.5
District 2	407,402	88.5	0.7	2.2	0.5	<.1	8.1	2	2	4	4	16.7	17.9	3.4	12.2	74.2	75.6	67.9	68.1	68.4	49.9	63.6
District 3	403,933	82.5	0.6	0.4	1.0	0.1	15.4	3	4	5	2	16.6	16.5	2.8	22.8	73.6	75.5	74.2	72.0	69.5	66.6	65.1
District 4	396,906	85.3	0.6	1.0	0.5	<.1	12.5	5	4	5	3	16.3	16.8	2.9	18.3	72.3	74.3	71.4	71.9	69.4	59.6	61.4
District 5	394,039	85.6	5.0	2.0	0.6	<.1	6.6	6	3	2	5	16.2	16.7	22.6	9.6	71.8	72.8	67.1	69.8	71.0	48.4	64.7
District 6	406,715	88.7	3.1	2.1	0.5	<.1	5.6	3	1	3	6	16.7	17.9	14.4	8.5	74.1	75.1	67.3	69.2	73.4	46.0	65.5

Table C. — Voter Participation: November 3, 1992, General Election

County	Estimated Voting Age Population (VAP) 1992	Voter registration (REG) Total	% contribution to state REG	% of 1992 VAP	Rank by % of 1992 VAP	Voter turnout — Highest office: Actual	Total	Office	% of 1992 VAP	Maximum vote Total	% contribution to state turnout	% of REG	Rank by % of REG	% of 1992 VAP	Rank by % of 1992 VAP	President	Senator	Governor	Representative
Adams	189,814	135,594	6.8	71.4	59	105,060	103,077	P	54.3	105,060	6.6	77.5	55	55.3	62	1.9	3.0	-	10.4
Alamosa	9,642	6,624	0.3	68.7	62	5,550	4,617	P	47.9	5,550	0.3	83.8	16	57.6	60	16.8	16.9	-	18.8
Arapahoe	306,130	245,088	12.2	80.1	45	185,793	183,935	P	60.1	185,793	11.6	75.8	61	60.7	53	1.0	2.5	-	6.7
Archuleta	4,163	3,651	0.2	87.7	32	2,859	2,816	P	67.6	2,859	0.2	78.3	52	68.7	38	1.5	1.7	-	5.3
Baca	3,286	3,046	0.2	92.7	20	2,652	2,622	P	79.8	2,652	0.2	87.1	2	80.7	10	1.1	1.9	-	4.0
Bent	3,543	2,800	0.1	79.0	48	2,317	2,257	P	63.7	2,317	0.1	82.8	23	65.4	46	2.6	2.6	-	4.1
Boulder	176,260	157,074	7.8	89.1	29	130,858	128,359	S	72.8	130,858	8.2	83.3	18	74.2	24	3.1	1.9	-	3.1
Chaffee	9,546	7,636	0.4	80.0	46	6,377	6,282	P	65.8	6,377	0.4	83.5	17	66.8	44	1.5	2.3	-	4.1
Cheyenne	1,683	1,433	<.1	85.1	34	1,228	1,212	P	72.0	1,228	<.1	85.7	4	73.0	26	1.3	1.7	-	3.5
Clear Creek	5,704	5,475	0.3	96.0	14	4,503	4,460	P	78.2	4,503	0.3	82.2	28	78.9	13	1.0	2.1	-	3.4
Conejos	4,907	4,411	0.2	89.9	24	3,662	3,465	P	70.6	3,662	0.2	83.0	20	74.6	23	5.4	5.5	-	7.0
Costilla	2,272	2,323	0.1	102.2	9	1,809	1,753	P	77.2	1,809	0.1	77.9	53	79.6	12	3.1	7.4	-	11.0
Crowley	3,305	1,813	<.1	54.9	63	1,480	1,469	S	44.4	1,480	<.1	81.6	33	44.8	63	1.5	0.7	-	2.4
Custer	1,522	1,755	<.1	115.3	3	1,415	1,392	S	91.5	1,415	<.1	80.6	40	93.0	3	2.8	1.6	-	4.9
Delta	15,686	12,641	0.6	80.6	43	10,770	10,494	P	66.9	10,770	0.7	85.2	8	68.7	39	2.6	3.2	-	4.3
Denver	356,877	288,879	14.4	80.9	41	220,653	217,919	P	61.1	220,653	13.8	76.4	60	61.8	49	1.2	5.0	-	8.7
Dolores	1,079	1,035	<.1	95.9	15	860	846	P	78.4	860	<.1	83.1	19	79.7	11	1.6	3.7	-	9.2
Douglas	52,717	51,547	2.6	97.8	12	40,474	40,060	P	76.0	40,474	2.5	78.5	51	76.8	18	1.0	1.4	-	6.2
Eagle	18,571	13,777	0.7	74.2	55	11,010	10,870	P	58.5	11,010	0.7	79.9	46	59.3	56	1.3	2.7	-	6.0
Elbert	7,455	6,682	0.3	89.6	26	5,368	5,281	S	70.8	5,368	0.3	80.3	43	72.0	28	6.0	1.6	-	4.5
El Paso	302,845	208,331	10.4	68.8	61	169,709	167,169	P	55.2	169,709	10.6	81.5	34	56.0	61	1.5	2.0	-	5.9
Fremont	25,599	19,765	1.0	77.2	51	15,292	15,131	P	59.1	15,292	1.0	77.4	56	59.7	55	1.1	1.3	-	4.1
Garfield	23,061	16,809	0.8	72.9	56	14,107	13,976	P	60.6	14,107	0.9	83.9	14	61.2	51	0.9	1.2	-	2.2
Gilpin	2,487	2,300	0.1	92.5	21	1,772	1,759	P	70.7	1,772	0.1	77.0	58	71.3	29	0.7	1.5	-	3.4
Grand	6,022	6,507	0.3	108.1	6	4,980	4,918	P	81.7	4,980	0.3	76.5	59	82.7	9	1.2	1.5	-	5.8
Gunnison	7,550	7,079	0.4	93.8	18	5,817	5,759	P	76.3	5,817	0.4	82.2	29	77.0	16	1.0	1.5	-	4.6
Hinsdale	384	588	<.1	153.1	1	483	478	S	124.5	483	<.1	82.1	30	125.8	1	1.4	1.0	-	7.0
Huerfano	4,442	3,870	0.2	87.1	33	3,105	3,016	S	67.9	3,105	0.2	80.2	44	69.9	32	25.5	2.9	-	6.5
Jackson	1,147	1,149	<.1	100.2	10	973	966	P	84.2	973	<.1	84.7	12	84.8	8	0.7	1.8	-	7.0
Jefferson	335,114	281,880	14.1	84.1	37	225,930	223,203	P	66.6	225,930	14.1	80.2	45	67.4	43	1.2	2.2	-	15.3
Kiowa	1,197	1,244	<.1	103.9	7	1,044	1,030	P	86.0	1,044	<.1	83.9	15	87.2	7	1.3	1.5	-	2.4
Kit Carson	4,992	4,461	0.2	89.4	27	3,698	3,658	P	73.3	3,698	0.2	82.9	22	74.1	25	1.1	1.6	-	3.1
Lake	3,948	3,613	0.2	91.5	22	2,965	2,923	P	74.0	2,965	0.2	82.1	31	75.1	22	1.4	2.6	-	6.7
La Plata	24,337	19,081	1.0	78.4	50	16,022	15,613	P	64.2	16,022	1.0	84.0	13	65.8	45	2.6	3.6	-	6.0
Larimer	143,580	122,170	6.1	85.1	35	100,718	99,660	P	69.4	100,718	6.3	82.4	26	70.1	31	1.1	2.3	-	3.3
Las Animas	9,952	8,335	0.4	83.8	38	6,774	6,569	P	66.0	6,774	0.4	81.3	35	68.1	40	3.0	3.3	-	7.8
Lincoln	3,312	2,738	0.1	82.7	40	2,326	2,306	P	69.6	2,326	0.1	85.0	10	70.2	30	0.9	1.3	-	3.5
Logan	12,401	9,949	0.5	80.2	44	8,550	8,345	P	67.3	8,550	0.5	85.9	3	68.9	37	2.4	3.0	-	3.0
Mesa	69,553	56,063	2.8	80.6	42	45,074	44,067	P	63.4	45,074	2.8	80.4	42	64.8	48	2.2	2.6	-	3.2
Mineral	394	573	<.1	145.4	2	455	450	S	114.2	455	<.1	79.4	48	115.5	2	1.3	1.1	-	4.4
Moffat	7,447	7,012	0.4	94.2	17	5,185	5,095	P	68.4	5,185	0.3	73.9	62	69.6	33	1.7	1.9	-	4.7
Montezuma	13,277	9,466	0.5	71.3	60	7,799	7,638	P	57.5	7,799	0.5	82.4	27	58.7	58	2.1	2.9	-	4.6
Montrose	17,717	14,041	0.7	79.3	47	11,957	11,723	P	66.2	11,957	0.7	85.2	9	67.5	42	2.0	2.5	-	3.4
Morgan	15,267	10,934	0.5	71.6	58	9,018	8,930	P	58.5	9,018	0.6	82.5	25	59.1	57	1.0	5.2	-	8.8
Otero	13,978	10,527	0.5	75.3	52	8,526	8,313	P	59.5	8,526	0.5	81.0	37	61.0	52	2.5	5.0	-	11.0
Ouray	1,808	1,876	<.1	103.8	8	1,602	1,586	S	87.7	1,602	0.1	85.4	5	88.6	6	1.2	1.0	-	2.9
Park	5,647	5,453	0.3	96.6	13	4,342	4,276	P	75.7	4,342	0.3	79.6	47	76.9	17	1.5	3.5	-	10.7
Phillips	3,062	2,734	0.1	89.3	28	2,334	2,303	P	75.2	2,334	0.1	85.4	6	76.2	19	1.3	1.9	-	3.9
Pitkin	10,882	9,687	0.5	89.0	30	7,543	7,469	P	68.6	7,543	0.5	77.9	54	69.3	35	1.0	3.5	-	6.3
Prowers	9,236	6,853	0.3	74.2	54	5,565	5,377	P	58.2	5,565	0.3	81.2	36	60.3	54	3.4	7.0	-	12.7
Pueblo	89,542	70,402	3.5	78.6	49	58,409	56,594	S	63.2	58,409	3.7	83.0	21	65.2	47	3.4	3.1	-	4.0
Rio Blanco	4,153	3,881	0.2	93.5	19	2,867	2,850	P	68.6	2,867	0.2	73.9	63	69.0	36	0.6	5.0	-	9.2
Rio Grande	7,604	5,652	0.3	74.3	53	4,665	4,547	P	59.8	4,665	0.3	82.5	24	61.3	50	2.8	2.5	-	4.5
Routt	10,525	10,413	0.5	98.9	11	8,238	8,161	P	77.5	8,238	0.5	79.1	50	78.3	14	0.9	1.7	-	5.5
Saguache	3,303	2,747	0.1	83.2	39	2,248	2,177	S	65.9	2,248	0.1	81.8	32	68.1	41	3.3	3.2	-	4.9
San Juan	517	572	<.1	110.6	5	460	453	P	87.6	460	<.1	80.4	41	89.0	5	1.5	2.0	-	7.4
San Miguel	2,898	3,319	0.2	114.5	4	2,681	2,663	P	91.9	2,681	0.2	80.8	39	92.5	4	0.7	2.0	-	7.4
Sedgwick	1,960	1,735	<.1	88.5	31	1,533	1,146	P	58.5	1,533	<.1	88.4	1	78.2	15	25.2	26.9	-	27.5
Summit	11,109	10,633	0.5	95.7	16	8,419	8,370	P	75.3	8,419	0.5	79.2	49	75.8	21	0.6	1.6	-	6.3
Teller	10,124	9,111	0.5	90.0	23	7,033	6,914	P	68.3	7,033	0.4	77.2	57	69.5	34	1.7	2.8	-	5.2
Washington	3,479	3,121	0.2	89.7	25	2,651	2,613	P	75.1	2,651	0.2	84.9	11	76.2	20	1.4	2.0	-	4.2
Weld	94,661	68,075	3.4	71.9	57	55,041	54,042	S	57.1	55,041	3.4	80.9	38	58.1	59	1.8	1.8	-	3.2
Yuma	6,325	5,342	0.3	84.5	36	4,558	4,505	P	71.2	4,558	0.3	85.3	7	72.1	27	1.2	2.1	-	3.0
COLORADO	2,501,000	2,003,375	100.0	80.1		1,597,166	1,571,927		62.9	1,597,166	100.0	79.7		63.9		1.8	2.8	-	7.4

136 Colorado

Table D. — Voter Registration by Political Party Affiliation: November 3, 1992, General Election

County	Total voter registration	Political party affiliation Democrat (DEM)	Republican (REP)	Independent (IND)	Plurality Total	Party	Percent of total registration DEM	REP	IND	Rank DEM	REP	IND	Percent contribution to state registration Total	DEM	REP	IND
Adams	135,594	55,247	33,667	46,596	8,651	D	40.8	24.8	34.4	16	54	16	6.8	8.1	5.0	7.2
Alamosa	6,624	2,840	2,121	1,661	719	D	42.9	32.0	25.1	14	41	38	0.3	0.4	0.3	0.3
Arapahoe	245,088	67,342	94,800	82,719	12,081	R	27.5	38.7	33.8	45	23	18	12.2	9.9	14.2	12.8
Archuleta	3,651	1,136	1,936	579	800	R	31.1	53.0	15.9	33	7	56	0.2	0.2	0.3	<.1
Baca	3,046	1,607	1,040	399	567	D	52.8	34.1	13.1	9	38	58	0.2	0.2	0.2	<.1
Bent	2,800	1,412	722	666	690	D	50.4	25.8	23.8	10	53	42	0.1	0.2	0.1	0.1
Boulder.......................	157,074	57,227	41,668	57,944	717	I	36.5	26.6	36.9	20	52	8	7.8	8.4	6.2	8.9
Chaffee	7,636	2,714	2,684	2,236	30	D	35.6	35.2	29.3	22	36	29	0.4	0.4	0.4	0.3
Cheyenne	1,433	381	810	240	429	R	26.6	56.6	16.8	48	4	53	<.1	<.1	0.1	<.1
Clear Creek	5,475	1,598	1,730	2,137	407	I	29.2	31.7	39.1	39	42	5	0.3	0.2	0.3	0.3
Conejos	4,411	2,513	1,576	309	937	D	57.1	35.8	7.0	7	32	62	0.2	0.4	0.2	<.1
Costilla	2,323	1,975	211	137	1,764	D	85.0	9.1	5.9	1	63	63	0.1	0.3	<.1	<.1
Crowley	1,813	760	752	300	8	D	41.9	41.5	16.6	15	19	55	<.1	0.1	0.1	<.1
Custer	1,755	394	947	412	535	R	22.5	54.0	23.5	57	5	43	<.1	<.1	0.1	<.1
Delta..........................	12,641	4,069	5,397	3,157	1,328	R	32.2	42.8	25.0	30	17	39	0.6	0.6	0.8	0.5
Denver........................	288,879	139,863	67,382	76,499	63,364	D	49.3	23.7	27.0	12	55	36	14.4	20.5	10.1	11.8
Dolores.......................	1,035	556	275	203	281	D	53.8	26.6	19.6	8	51	50	<.1	<.1	<.1	<.1
Douglas	51,547	9,623	25,019	16,839	8,180	R	18.7	48.6	32.7	63	13	20	2.6	1.4	3.7	2.6
Eagle..........................	13,777	3,496	4,210	6,059	1,849	I	25.4	30.6	44.0	50	47	3	0.7	0.5	0.6	0.9
Elbert	6,682	1,609	2,525	2,542	17	I	24.1	37.8	38.1	53	26	6	0.3	0.2	0.4	0.4
El Paso	208,331	48,493	88,041	71,666	16,375	R	23.3	42.3	34.4	54	18	15	10.4	7.1	13.2	11.1
Fremont	19,765	6,820	7,453	5,473	633	R	34.5	37.7	27.7	23	28	32	1.0	1.0	1.1	0.8
Garfield.......................	16,809	5,333	5,289	6,173	840	I	31.8	31.5	36.8	31	44	9	0.8	0.8	0.8	1.0
Gilpin	2,300	777	773	742	4	D	33.9	33.7	32.4	25	39	23	0.1	0.1	0.1	0.1
Grand	6,507	1,254	3,491	1,755	1,736	R	19.3	53.7	27.0	62	6	34	0.3	0.2	0.5	0.3
Gunnison	7,079	2,347	2,219	2,506	159	I	33.2	31.4	35.4	27	45	14	0.4	0.3	0.3	0.4
Hinsdale	588	136	397	55	261	R	23.1	67.5	9.4	56	1	61	<.1	<.1	<.1	<.1
Huerfano	3,870	3,000	444	422	2,556	D	77.6	11.5	10.9	2	62	60	0.2	0.4	<.1	<.1
Jackson	1,149	235	607	307	300	R	20.5	52.8	26.7	60	8	35	<.1	<.1	<.1	<.1
Jefferson	281,880	80,690	100,141	100,820	679	I	28.6	35.6	35.8	42	33	12	14.1	11.9	15.0	15.6
Kiowa	1,244	475	533	236	58	R	38.2	42.8	19.0	19	16	52	<.1	<.1	<.1	<.1
Kit Carson	4,461	1,165	2,322	974	1,157	R	26.1	52.1	21.8	49	9	48	0.2	0.2	0.3	0.2
Lake	3,613	2,076	622	902	1,174	D	57.7	17.3	25.1	6	59	40	0.2	0.3	<.1	0.1
La Plata	19,081	6,515	6,219	6,323	192	D	34.2	32.6	33.2	24	40	19	1.0	1.0	0.9	1.0
Larimer.......................	122,170	33,652	46,633	41,764	4,869	R	27.6	38.2	34.2	44	24	17	6.1	4.9	7.0	6.4
Las Animas	8,335	6,179	1,112	1,038	5,067	D	74.2	13.4	12.5	3	61	59	0.4	0.9	0.2	0.2
Lincoln	2,738	844	1,343	548	499	R	30.9	49.1	20.0	35	12	49	0.1	0.1	0.2	<.1
Logan	9,949	3,306	3,509	3,131	203	R	33.2	35.3	31.5	26	34	24	0.5	0.5	0.5	0.5
Mesa	56,063	17,515	21,205	17,291	3,690	R	31.3	37.9	30.9	32	25	27	2.8	2.6	3.2	2.7
Mineral	573	385	92	95	290	D	67.3	16.1	16.6	4	60	54	<.1	<.1	<.1	<.1
Moffat	7,012	1,925	3,256	1,830	1,331	R	27.5	46.4	26.1	46	15	37	0.4	0.3	0.5	0.3
Montezuma..................	9,466	3,371	3,476	2,600	105	R	35.7	36.8	27.5	21	30	33	0.5	0.5	0.5	0.4
Montrose	14,041	4,326	5,162	4,537	625	R	30.8	36.8	32.3	39	29	21	0.7	0.6	0.8	0.7
Morgan	10,934	3,181	4,359	3,387	972	R	29.1	39.9	31.0	40	22	26	0.5	0.5	0.7	0.5
Otero..........................	10,527	4,265	3,268	2,989	997	D	40.5	31.1	28.4	17	46	31	0.5	0.6	0.5	0.5
Ouray	1,876	370	1,225	278	855	R	19.8	65.4	14.8	61	2	57	<.1	<.1	0.2	<.1
Park	5,453	1,507	1,918	2,017	99	I	27.7	35.2	37.1	43	35	7	0.3	0.2	0.3	0.3
Phillips	2,734	731	1,326	675	595	R	26.8	48.5	24.7	47	14	41	0.1	0.1	0.2	0.1
Pitkin	9,687	2,865	2,209	4,603	1,738	I	29.6	22.8	47.6	37	56	1	0.5	0.4	0.3	0.7
Prowers	6,853	2,131	2,510	2,211	299	R	31.1	36.6	32.3	34	31	22	0.3	0.3	0.4	0.3
Pueblo........................	70,402	41,591	13,169	15,631	25,960	D	59.1	18.7	22.2	5	58	47	3.5	6.1	2.0	2.4
Rio Blanco	3,881	831	1,925	1,125	800	R	21.4	49.6	29.0	58	11	30	0.2	0.1	0.3	0.2
Rio Grande..................	5,652	2,194	2,135	1,323	59	D	38.8	37.8	23.4	18	27	44	0.3	0.3	0.3	0.2
Routt	10,413	3,400	3,288	3,708	308	I	32.7	31.6	35.7	28	43	13	0.5	0.5	0.5	0.6
Saguache	2,747	1,359	761	627	598	D	49.5	27.7	22.8	11	49	46	0.1	0.2	0.1	<.1
San Juan	572	185	158	229	44	I	32.3	27.6	40.0	29	50	4	<.1	<.1	<.1	<.1
San Miguel	3,319	1,550	722	1,043	507	D	46.8	21.8	31.5	13	57	25	0.2	0.2	0.1	0.2
Sedgwick	1,735	436	893	406	457	R	25.1	51.5	23.4	51	10	45	<.1	<.1	0.1	<.1
Summit	10,633	2,671	3,119	4,826	1,707	I	25.2	29.4	45.5	52	48	2	0.5	0.4	0.5	0.7
Teller	9,111	2,116	3,657	3,320	337	R	23.3	40.2	36.5	55	21	10	0.5	0.3	0.5	0.5
Washington..................	3,121	667	1,853	597	1,186	R	21.4	59.4	19.2	59	3	51	0.2	<.1	0.3	<.1
Weld	68,075	19,994	23,554	24,494	940	I	29.4	34.6	36.0	38	37	11	3.4	2.9	3.5	3.8
Yuma	5,342	1,548	2,191	1,595	596	R	29.0	41.1	29.9	41	20	28	0.3	0.2	0.3	0.2
COLORADO[1]................	**2,003,375**	**680,773**	**668,051**	**647,906**	**12,722**	**D**	**34.1**	**33.5**	**32.4**				**100.0**	**100.0**	**100.0**	**100.0**

[1]Total voter registration also includes 1,660 for Libertarian party, 36 for Prohibition party, 12 for Concerns of the People party, 57 for Populist party, 18 for Colorado Taxpayers Party, and 4,862 for other.

Colorado 137

Table E. — Vote for President: November 3, 1992, General Election

County	Total	Clinton (DEM)	Bush (REP)	Perot (IND)	Other	Plurality Total	Party	DEM	REP	IND	Other	Rank DEM	Rank REP	Rank IND	Contrib Total	Contrib DEM	Contrib REP	Contrib IND	Major DEM	Major REP
Adams	103,077	45,357	30,856	26,379	485	14,501	D	44.0	29.9	25.6	0.5	12	48	33	6.6	7.2	5.5	7.2	59.5	40.5
Alamosa	4,617	1,928	1,572	1,089	28	356	D	41.8	34.0	23.6	0.6	15	42	48	0.3	0.3	0.3	0.3	55.1	44.9
Arapahoe	183,935	66,607	72,221	44,363	744	5,614	R	36.2	39.3	24.1	0.4	28	29	44	11.7	10.6	12.8	12.1	48.0	52.0
Archuleta	2,816	819	1,242	741	14	423	R	29.1	44.1	26.3	0.5	47	13	25	0.2	0.1	0.2	0.2	39.7	60.3
Baca	2,622	726	1,240	647	9	514	R	27.7	47.3	24.7	0.3	52	6	40	0.2	0.1	0.2	0.2	36.9	63.1
Bent	2,257	985	759	506	7	226	D	43.6	33.6	22.4	0.3	13	43	51	0.1	0.2	0.1	0.1	56.5	43.5
Boulder	126,771	64,567	33,553	27,762	889	31,014	D	50.9	26.5	21.9	0.7	8	56	53	8.1	10.3	6.0	7.6	65.8	34.2
Chaffee	6,282	2,284	2,419	1,549	30	135	R	36.4	38.5	24.7	0.5	26	32	41	0.4	0.4	0.4	0.4	48.6	51.4
Cheyenne	1,212	301	615	292	4	314	R	24.8	50.7	24.1	0.3	61	2	45	<.1	<.1	0.1	<.1	32.9	67.1
Clear Creek	4,460	1,744	1,356	1,308	52	388	D	39.1	30.4	29.3	1.2	19	47	15	0.3	0.3	0.2	0.4	56.3	43.7
Conejos	3,465	1,705	1,160	578	22	545	D	49.2	33.5	16.7	0.6	9	44	60	0.2	0.3	0.2	0.2	59.5	40.5
Costilla	1,753	1,180	366	199	8	814	D	67.3	20.9	11.4	0.5	1	62	63	0.1	0.2	<.1	<.1	76.3	23.7
Crowley	1,458	570	602	276	10	32	R	39.1	41.3	18.9	0.7	20	22	57	<.1	<.1	0.1	<.1	48.6	51.4
Custer	1,375	343	651	368	13	283	R	24.9	47.3	26.8	0.9	59	5	22	<.1	<.1	0.1	0.1	34.5	65.5
Delta	10,494	3,424	4,359	2,627	84	935	R	32.6	41.5	25.0	0.8	38	20	38	0.7	0.5	0.8	0.7	44.0	56.0
Denver	217,919	121,961	55,418	37,298	3,242	66,543	D	56.0	25.4	17.1	1.5	3	59	59	13.9	19.4	9.8	10.2	68.8	31.2
Dolores	846	242	315	285	4	30	R	28.6	37.2	33.7	0.5	48	34	5	<.1	<.1	<.1	<.1	43.4	56.6
Douglas	40,060	9,991	18,592	11,329	148	7,263	R	24.9	46.4	28.3	0.4	60	9	19	2.6	1.6	3.3	3.1	35.0	65.0
Eagle	10,870	3,870	3,100	3,821	79	49	D	35.6	28.5	35.2	0.7	30	53	3	0.7	0.6	0.6	1.0	55.5	44.5
Elbert	5,045	1,237	2,205	1,567	36	638	R	24.5	43.7	31.1	0.7	62	15	10	0.3	0.2	0.4	0.4	35.9	64.1
El Paso	167,169	45,827	86,044	34,346	952	40,217	R	27.4	51.5	20.5	0.6	53	1	55	10.7	7.3	15.3	9.4	34.8	65.2
Fremont	15,131	5,356	5,961	3,709	105	605	R	35.4	39.4	24.5	0.7	31	28	42	1.0	0.9	1.1	1.0	47.3	52.7
Garfield	13,976	5,082	4,404	4,408	82	674	D	36.4	31.5	31.5	0.6	25	45	8	0.9	0.8	0.8	1.2	53.6	46.4
Gilpin	1,759	726	462	545	26	181	D	41.3	26.3	31.0	1.5	17	57	11	0.1	0.1	<.1	0.1	61.1	38.9
Grand	4,918	1,678	1,763	1,454	23	85	R	34.1	35.8	29.6	0.5	34	37	12	0.3	0.3	0.3	0.4	48.8	51.2
Gunnison	5,759	2,389	1,662	1,671	37	718	D	41.5	28.9	29.0	0.6	16	51	16	0.4	0.4	0.3	0.5	59.0	41.0
Hinsdale	476	151	188	136	1	37	R	31.7	39.5	28.6	0.2	41	27	18	<.1	<.1	<.1	<.1	44.5	55.5
Huerfano	2,313	1,224	685	385	19	539	D	52.9	29.6	16.6	0.8	5	49	61	0.1	0.2	0.1	0.1	64.1	35.9
Jackson	966	216	422	326	2	96	R	22.4	43.7	33.7	0.2	63	16	4	<.1	<.1	<.1	<.1	33.9	66.1
Jefferson	223,203	80,834	82,705	58,404	1,260	1,871	R	36.2	37.1	26.2	0.6	27	35	27	14.2	12.8	14.7	16.0	49.4	50.6
Kiowa	1,030	290	472	267	1	182	R	28.2	45.8	25.9	<.1	50	10	30	<.1	<.1	<.1	<.1	38.1	61.9
Kit Carson	3,658	925	1,801	919	13	876	R	25.3	49.2	25.1	0.4	57	3	36	0.2	0.1	0.3	0.3	33.9	66.1
Lake	2,923	1,426	605	863	29	563	D	48.8	20.7	29.5	1.0	10	63	13	0.2	0.2	0.1	0.2	70.2	29.8
La Plata	15,613	5,913	5,522	4,083	95	391	D	37.9	35.4	26.2	0.6	24	41	28	1.0	0.9	1.0	1.1	51.7	48.3
Larimer	99,660	38,232	35,995	24,879	554	2,237	D	38.4	36.1	25.0	0.6	22	36	39	6.4	6.1	6.4	6.8	51.5	48.5
Las Animas	6,569	3,847	1,739	953	30	2,108	D	58.6	26.5	14.5	0.5	2	55	62	0.4	0.6	0.3	0.3	68.9	31.1
Lincoln	2,306	640	1,079	581	6	439	R	27.8	46.8	25.2	0.3	51	7	35	0.1	0.1	0.2	0.2	37.2	62.8
Logan	8,345	2,718	3,420	2,184	23	702	R	32.6	41.0	26.2	0.3	39	25	26	0.5	0.4	0.6	0.6	44.3	55.7
Mesa	44,067	15,162	18,169	10,474	262	3,007	R	34.4	41.2	23.8	0.6	33	24	47	2.8	2.4	3.2	2.9	45.5	54.5
Mineral	449	171	159	117	2	12	D	38.1	35.4	26.1	0.4	23	40	29	<.1	<.1	<.1	<.1	51.8	48.2
Moffat	5,095	1,386	1,809	1,875	25	66	I	27.2	35.5	36.8	0.5	55	39	2	0.3	0.2	0.3	0.5	43.4	56.6
Montezuma	7,638	2,270	3,124	2,205	39	854	R	29.7	40.9	28.9	0.5	45	26	17	0.5	0.4	0.6	0.6	42.1	57.9
Montrose	11,723	3,713	4,847	3,093	70	1,134	R	31.7	41.3	26.4	0.6	42	21	24	0.7	0.6	0.9	0.8	43.4	56.6
Morgan	8,930	2,985	3,724	2,175	46	739	R	33.4	41.7	24.4	0.5	36	19	43	0.6	0.5	0.7	0.6	44.5	55.5
Otero	8,313	3,485	3,120	1,590	118	365	D	41.9	37.5	19.1	1.4	14	33	56	0.5	0.6	0.6	0.4	52.8	47.2
Ouray	1,583	461	653	466	3	187	R	29.1	41.3	29.4	0.2	46	23	14	0.1	<.1	0.1	0.1	41.4	58.6
Park	4,276	1,307	1,530	1,396	43	134	R	30.6	35.8	32.6	1.0	43	38	6	0.3	0.2	0.3	0.4	46.1	53.9
Phillips	2,303	692	1,075	525	11	383	R	30.0	46.7	22.8	0.5	44	8	52	0.1	0.1	0.2	0.1	39.2	60.8
Pitkin	7,469	3,820	1,686	1,907	56	1,913	D	51.1	22.6	25.5	0.7	7	61	34	0.5	0.6	0.3	0.5	69.4	30.6
Prowers	5,377	1,770	2,371	1,184	52	601	R	32.9	44.1	22.0	1.0	37	14	52	0.3	0.3	0.4	0.3	42.7	57.3
Pueblo	56,438	30,261	16,120	9,841	216	14,141	D	53.6	28.6	17.4	0.4	4	52	58	3.6	4.8	2.9	2.7	65.2	34.8
Rio Blanco	2,850	778	1,231	794	47	437	R	27.3	43.2	27.9	1.6	54	17	21	0.2	0.1	0.2	0.2	38.7	61.3
Rio Grande	4,533	1,541	1,927	1,043	22	386	R	34.0	42.5	23.0	0.5	35	18	49	0.3	0.2	0.3	0.3	44.4	55.6
Routt	8,161	3,188	2,358	2,564	51	624	D	39.1	28.9	31.4	0.6	21	50	9	0.5	0.5	0.4	0.7	57.5	42.5
Saguache	2,174	1,011	675	471	17	336	D	46.5	31.0	21.7	0.8	11	46	54	0.1	0.2	0.1	0.1	60.0	40.0
San Juan	453	147	118	183	5	36	I	32.5	26.0	40.4	1.1	40	58	1	<.1	<.1	<.1	<.1	55.5	44.5
San Miguel	2,663	1,380	628	634	21	746	D	51.8	23.6	23.8	0.8	6	60	46	0.2	0.2	0.1	0.2	68.7	31.3
Sedgwick	1,146	397	447	295	7	50	R	34.6	39.0	25.7	0.6	32	30	31	<.1	<.1	<.1	<.1	47.0	53.0
Summit	8,370	3,344	2,256	2,715	55	629	D	40.0	27.0	32.4	0.7	18	54	7	0.5	0.5	0.4	0.7	59.7	40.3
Teller	6,914	1,873	3,050	1,927	64	1,123	R	27.1	44.1	27.9	0.9	56	12	20	0.4	0.3	0.5	0.5	38.0	62.0
Washington	2,613	660	1,266	671	16	595	R	25.3	48.5	25.7	0.6	58	4	32	0.2	0.1	0.2	0.2	34.3	65.7
Weld	54,029	19,295	20,958	13,571	205	1,663	R	35.7	38.8	25.1	0.4	29	31	37	3.4	3.1	3.7	3.7	47.9	52.1
Yuma	4,505	1,269	2,019	1,197	20	750	R	28.2	44.8	26.6	0.4	49	11	23	0.3	0.2	0.4	0.3	38.6	61.4
COLORADO	1,569,180	629,681	562,850	366,010	10,639	66,831	D	40.1	35.9	23.3	0.7				100.0	100.0	100.0	100.0	52.8	47.2

Table F. — Vote for U.S. Senator: November 3, 1992, General Election

County	Total	Campbell (DEM)	Considine (REP)	Other	Plurality Total	Party	Percent of total vote DEM	REP	Other	Rank DEM	REP	Other	Percent contribution to state vote Total	DEM	REP	Other
Adams	101,960	57,395	37,843	6,722	19,552	D	56.3	37.1	6.6	27	38	11	6.6	7.1	5.7	7.8
Alamosa	4,611	2,963	1,462	186	1,501	D	64.3	31.7	4.0	14	47	53	0.3	0.4	0.2	0.2
Arapahoe	181,133	86,474	85,953	8,706	521	D	47.7	47.5	4.8	45	18	44	11.7	10.8	13.0	10.2
Archuleta	2,810	1,452	1,181	177	271	D	51.7	42.0	6.3	34	31	15	0.2	0.2	0.2	0.2
Baca	2,602	1,024	1,469	109	445	R	39.4	56.5	4.2	59	3	50	0.2	0.1	0.2	0.1
Bent	2,257	1,135	1,043	79	92	D	50.3	46.2	3.5	39	23	58	0.1	0.1	0.2	< .1
Boulder	128,359	79,437	41,118	7,804	38,319	D	61.9	32.0	6.1	18	46	18	8.3	9.9	6.2	9.1
Chaffee	6,232	3,231	2,651	350	580	D	51.8	42.5	5.6	33	30	28	0.4	0.4	0.4	0.4
Cheyenne	1,207	474	692	41	218	R	39.3	57.3	3.4	60	2	59	< .1	< .1	0.1	< .1
Clear Creek	4,410	2,543	1,553	314	990	D	57.7	35.2	7.1	24	42	7	0.3	0.3	0.2	0.4
Conejos	3,460	2,357	970	133	1,387	D	68.1	28.0	3.8	7	56	54	0.2	0.3	0.1	0.2
Costilla	1,676	1,291	322	63	969	D	77.0	19.2	3.8	1	63	55	0.1	0.2	< .1	< .1
Crowley	1,469	673	750	46	77	R	45.8	51.1	3.1	48	13	60	< .1	< .1	0.1	< .1
Custer	1,392	571	723	98	152	R	41.0	51.9	7.0	57	10	8	< .1	< .1	0.1	0.1
Delta	10,427	5,412	4,464	551	948	D	51.9	42.8	5.3	32	29	36	0.7	0.7	0.7	0.6
Denver	209,639	135,430	63,524	10,685	71,906	D	64.6	30.3	5.1	13	49	39	13.5	16.9	9.6	12.5
Dolores	828	454	314	60	140	D	54.8	37.9	7.2	30	37	6	< .1	< .1	< .1	< .1
Douglas	39,919	15,552	22,087	2,280	6,535	R	39.0	55.3	5.7	61	4	25	2.6	1.9	3.3	2.7
Eagle	10,716	6,928	3,163	625	3,765	D	64.7	29.5	5.8	12	51	22	0.7	0.9	0.5	0.7
Elbert	5,281	2,271	2,652	358	381	R	43.0	50.2	6.8	54	14	10	0.3	0.3	0.4	0.4
El Paso	166,250	51,130	106,106	9,014	54,976	R	30.8	63.8	5.4	63	1	33	10.7	6.4	16.0	10.5
Fremont	15,090	6,511	7,728	851	1,217	R	43.1	51.2	5.6	53	12	27	1.0	0.8	1.2	1.0
Garfield	13,939	8,259	4,793	887	3,466	D	59.3	34.4	6.4	22	44	14	0.9	1.0	0.7	1.0
Gilpin	1,745	1,086	511	148	575	D	62.2	29.3	8.5	17	52	3	0.1	0.1	< .1	0.2
Grand	4,904	2,745	1,874	285	871	D	56.0	38.2	5.8	28	36	23	0.3	0.3	0.3	0.3
Gunnison	5,731	3,763	1,694	274	2,069	D	65.7	29.6	4.8	10	50	45	0.4	0.5	0.3	0.3
Hinsdale	478	275	177	26	98	D	57.5	37.0	5.4	25	39	32	< .1	< .1	< .1	< .1
Huerfano	3,016	2,047	877	92	1,170	D	67.9	29.1	3.1	8	54	62	0.2	0.3	0.1	0.1
Jackson	955	571	330	54	241	D	59.8	34.6	5.7	21	43	26	< .1	< .1	< .1	< .1
Jefferson	220,895	108,708	98,091	14,096	10,617	D	49.2	44.4	6.4	40	25	13	14.2	13.5	14.8	16.5
Kiowa	1,028	457	534	37	77	R	44.5	51.9	3.6	51	9	57	< .1	< .1	< .1	< .1
Kit Carson	3,640	1,672	1,768	200	96	R	45.9	48.6	5.5	47	17	31	0.2	0.2	0.3	0.2
Lake	2,887	2,016	670	201	1,346	D	69.8	23.2	7.0	4	61	9	0.2	0.3	0.1	0.2
La Plata	15,448	9,833	4,844	771	4,989	D	63.7	31.4	5.0	15	48	42	1.0	1.2	0.7	0.9
Larimer	98,374	50,373	42,897	5,104	7,476	D	51.2	43.6	5.2	36	28	38	6.3	6.3	6.5	6.0
Las Animas	6,549	3,749	2,530	270	1,219	D	57.2	38.6	4.1	26	35	51	0.4	0.5	0.4	0.3
Lincoln	2,295	974	1,199	122	225	R	42.4	52.2	5.3	55	8	35	0.1	0.1	0.2	0.1
Logan	8,291	4,001	3,831	459	170	D	48.3	46.2	5.5	44	24	30	0.5	0.5	0.6	0.5
Mesa	43,899	21,375	20,290	2,234	1,085	D	48.7	46.2	5.1	42	22	40	2.8	2.7	3.1	2.6
Mineral	450	312	126	12	186	D	69.3	28.0	2.7	5	57	63	< .1	< .1	< .1	< .1
Moffat	5,086	3,010	1,695	381	1,315	D	59.2	33.3	7.5	23	45	4	0.3	0.4	0.3	0.4
Montezuma	7,572	4,022	3,051	499	971	D	53.1	40.3	6.6	31	33	12	0.5	0.5	0.5	0.6
Montrose	11,662	5,977	5,101	584	876	D	51.3	43.7	5.0	35	27	41	0.8	0.7	0.8	0.7
Morgan	8,550	3,808	4,211	531	403	R	44.5	49.3	6.2	50	16	16	0.6	0.5	0.6	0.6
Otero	8,099	3,628	4,033	438	405	R	44.8	49.8	5.4	49	15	34	0.5	0.5	0.6	0.5
Ouray	1,586	798	700	88	98	D	50.3	44.1	5.5	38	26	29	0.1	< .1	0.1	0.1
Park	4,190	2,119	1,710	361	409	D	50.6	40.8	8.6	37	32	2	0.3	0.3	0.3	0.4
Phillips	2,289	993	1,203	93	210	R	43.4	52.6	4.1	52	7	52	0.1	0.1	0.2	0.1
Pitkin	7,280	5,313	1,589	378	3,724	D	73.0	21.8	5.2	2	62	37	0.5	0.7	0.2	0.4
Prowers	5,173	2,068	2,801	304	733	R	40.0	54.1	5.9	58	6	21	0.3	0.3	0.4	0.4
Pueblo	56,594	34,253	20,571	1,770	13,682	D	60.5	36.3	3.1	19	40	61	3.6	4.3	3.1	2.1
Rio Blanco	2,723	1,511	1,056	156	455	D	55.5	38.8	5.7	29	34	24	0.2	0.2	0.2	0.2
Rio Grande	4,547	2,733	1,617	197	1,116	D	60.1	35.6	4.3	20	41	49	0.3	0.3	0.2	0.2
Routt	8,096	5,525	2,185	386	3,340	D	68.2	27.0	4.8	6	59	46	0.5	0.7	0.3	0.5
Saguache	2,177	1,457	623	97	834	D	66.9	28.6	4.5	9	55	48	0.1	0.2	< .1	0.1
San Juan	451	285	123	43	162	D	63.2	27.3	9.5	16	58	1	< .1	< .1	< .1	< .1
San Miguel	2,628	1,880	625	123	1,255	D	71.5	23.8	4.7	3	60	47	0.2	0.2	< .1	0.1
Sedgwick	1,121	551	528	42	23	D	49.2	47.1	3.7	41	19	56	< .1	< .1	< .1	< .1
Summit	8,282	5,376	2,415	491	2,961	D	64.9	29.2	5.9	11	53	20	0.5	0.7	0.4	0.6
Teller	6,839	2,595	3,743	501	1,148	R	37.9	54.7	7.3	62	5	5	0.4	0.3	0.6	0.6
Washington	2,588	1,097	1,336	155	239	R	42.4	51.6	6.0	56	11	19	0.2	0.1	0.2	0.2
Weld	54,042	25,641	25,093	3,308	548	D	47.4	46.4	6.1	46	21	17	3.5	3.2	3.8	3.9
Yuma	4,462	2,161	2,080	221	81	D	48.4	46.6	5.0	43	20	43	0.3	0.3	0.3	0.3
COLORADO	**1,552,289**	**803,725**	**662,893**	**85,671**	**140,832**	**D**	**51.8**	**42.7**	**5.5**				**100.0**	**100.0**	**100.0**	**100.0**

Table H. — Vote for U.S. Representative in Congress: November 3, 1992, General Election

Congressional district and county	Total	Democrat (DEM)	Republican (REP)	Other	Plurality Total	Party	Percent of total vote DEM	REP	Other	Rank within district DEM	REP	Other	Percent contribution to district vote Total	DEM	REP	Other
District 1	**227,531**	**156,629**	**70,902**	-	**85,727**	**D**	**68.8**	**31.2**	-				**100.0**	**100.0**	**100.0**	-
Adams (pt)	14,634	9,517	5,117	-	4,400	D	65.0	35.0	-	2	2	-	6.4	6.1	7.2	-
Arapahoe (pt)	11,550	7,105	4,445	-	2,660	D	61.5	38.5	-	3	1	-	5.1	4.5	6.3	-
Denver	201,347	140,007	61,340	-	78,667	D	69.5	30.5	-	1	3	-	88.5	89.4	86.5	-
District 2	**271,361**	**164,790**	**88,470**	**18,101**	**76,320**	**D**	**60.7**	**32.6**	**6.7**				**100.0**	**100.0**	**100.0**	**100.0**
Adams (pt)	62,908	36,466	22,425	4,017	14,041	D	58.0	35.6	6.4	4	2	5	23.2	22.1	25.3	22.2
Boulder	126,751	83,762	34,360	8,629	49,402	D	66.1	27.1	6.8	1	5	3	46.7	50.8	38.8	47.7
Clear Creek	4,348	2,582	1,372	394	1,210	D	59.4	31.6	9.1	3	3	2	1.6	1.6	1.6	2.2
Gilpin	1,711	1,025	487	199	538	D	59.9	28.5	11.6	2	4	1	0.6	0.6	0.6	1.1
Jefferson (pt)	75,643	40,955	29,826	4,862	11,129	D	54.1	39.4	6.4	5	1	4	27.9	24.9	33.7	26.9
District 3	**261,964**	**114,480**	**143,293**	**4,191**	**28,813**	**R**	**43.7**	**54.7**	**1.6**				**100.0**	**100.0**	**100.0**	**100.0**
Alamosa	4,508	2,399	2,035	74	364	D	53.2	45.1	1.6	8	29	25	1.7	2.1	1.4	1.8
Archuleta	2,707	911	1,725	71	814	R	33.7	63.7	2.6	31	7	6	1.0	0.8	1.2	1.7
Chaffee	6,116	2,465	3,561	90	1,096	R	40.3	58.2	1.5	19	17	28	2.3	2.2	2.5	2.1
Conejos	3,407	2,149	1,200	58	949	D	63.1	35.2	1.7	2	35	24	1.3	1.9	0.8	1.4
Costilla	1,610	1,230	347	33	883	D	76.4	21.6	2.0	1	36	13	0.6	1.1	0.2	0.8
Custer	1,346	424	896	26	472	R	31.5	66.6	1.9	32	5	17	0.5	0.4	0.6	0.6
Delta	10,305	3,880	6,205	220	2,325	R	37.7	60.2	2.1	24	13	11	3.9	3.4	4.3	5.2
Dolores	781	367	389	25	22	R	47.0	49.8	3.2	11	26	2	0.3	0.3	0.3	0.6
Douglas (pt)	1,699	518	1,147	34	629	R	30.5	67.5	2.0	33	4	15	0.6	0.5	0.8	0.8
Eagle	10,346	3,765	6,381	200	2,616	R	36.4	61.7	1.9	26	11	16	3.9	3.3	4.5	4.8
Fremont (pt)	7,122	2,962	4,076	84	1,114	R	41.6	57.2	1.2	15	20	34	2.7	2.6	2.8	2.0
Garfield	13,798	4,105	9,510	183	5,405	R	29.8	68.9	1.3	34	3	33	5.3	3.6	6.6	4.4
Grand	4,689	1,619	2,968	102	1,349	R	34.5	63.3	2.2	29	9	10	1.8	1.4	2.1	2.4
Gunnison	5,552	2,828	2,629	95	199	D	50.9	47.4	1.7	10	27	23	2.1	2.5	1.8	2.3
Hinsdale	449	179	262	8	83	R	39.9	58.4	1.8	20	16	21	0.2	0.2	0.2	0.2
Huerfano	2,903	1,700	1,164	39	536	D	58.6	40.1	1.3	5	32	32	1.1	1.5	0.8	0.9
Jackson	905	241	656	8	415	R	26.6	72.5	0.9	35	2	36	0.3	0.2	0.5	0.2
Jefferson (pt)	1,513	593	864	56	271	R	39.2	57.1	3.7	22	21	1	0.6	0.5	0.6	1.3
Lake	2,767	1,614	1,077	76	537	D	58.3	38.9	2.7	6	33	5	1.1	1.4	0.8	1.8
La Plata	15,060	6,226	8,575	259	2,349	R	41.3	56.9	1.7	16	22	22	5.7	5.4	6.0	6.2
Mesa	43,647	15,239	27,813	595	12,574	R	34.9	63.7	1.4	28	8	30	16.7	13.3	19.4	14.2
Mineral	435	224	202	9	22	D	51.5	46.4	2.1	9	28	12	0.2	0.2	0.1	0.2
Moffat	4,940	1,692	3,154	94	1,462	R	34.3	63.8	1.9	30	6	18	1.9	1.5	2.2	2.2
Montezuma	7,437	2,874	4,397	166	1,523	R	38.6	59.1	2.2	23	14	9	2.8	2.5	3.1	4.0
Montrose	11,545	4,543	6,769	233	2,226	R	39.4	58.6	2.0	21	15	14	4.4	4.0	4.7	5.6
Ouray	1,556	549	984	23	435	R	35.3	63.2	1.5	27	10	27	0.6	0.5	0.7	0.5
Park	3,876	1,413	2,343	120	930	R	36.5	60.4	3.1	25	12	3	1.5	1.2	1.6	2.9
Pitkin	7,071	2,854	4,106	111	1,252	R	40.4	58.1	1.6	18	18	26	2.7	2.5	2.9	2.6
Pueblo	56,091	32,918	22,634	539	10,284	D	58.7	40.4	1.0	4	31	35	21.4	28.8	15.8	12.9
Rio Blanco	2,603	536	2,032	35	1,496	R	20.6	78.1	1.3	36	1	31	1.0	0.5	1.4	0.8
Rio Grande	4,455	1,948	2,423	84	475	R	43.7	54.4	1.9	13	23	19	1.7	1.7	1.7	2.0
Routt	7,787	3,189	4,459	139	1,270	R	41.0	57.3	1.8	17	19	20	3.0	2.8	3.1	3.3
Saguache	2,138	1,215	892	31	323	D	56.8	41.7	1.5	7	30	29	0.8	1.1	0.6	0.7
San Juan	426	199	214	13	15	R	46.7	50.2	3.1	12	25	4	0.2	0.2	0.1	0.3
San Miguel	2,483	1,489	934	60	555	D	60.0	37.6	2.4	3	34	8	0.9	1.3	0.7	1.4
Summit	7,891	3,423	4,270	198	847	R	43.4	54.1	2.5	14	24	7	3.0	3.0	3.0	4.7
District 4	**241,841**	**101,957**	**139,884**	-	**37,927**	**R**	**42.2**	**57.8**	-				**100.0**	**100.0**	**100.0**	-
Adams (pt)	16,563	8,727	7,836	-	891	D	52.7	47.3	-	2	20	-	6.8	8.6	5.6	-
Arapahoe (pt)	9,645	3,510	6,135	-	2,625	R	36.4	63.6	-	8	14	-	4.0	3.4	4.4	-
Baca	2,546	725	1,821	-	1,096	R	28.5	71.5	-	18	4	-	1.1	0.7	1.3	-
Bent	2,221	893	1,328	-	435	R	40.2	59.8	-	6	16	-	0.9	0.9	0.9	-
Cheyenne	1,185	307	878	-	571	R	25.9	74.1	-	20	2	-	0.5	0.3	0.6	-
Crowley	1,444	559	885	-	326	R	38.7	61.3	-	7	15	-	0.6	0.5	0.6	-
Elbert	5,125	1,813	3,312	-	1,499	R	35.4	64.6	-	9	13	-	2.1	1.8	2.4	-
Kiowa	1,019	306	713	-	407	R	30.0	70.0	-	17	5	-	0.4	0.3	0.5	-
Kit Carson	3,585	950	2,635	-	1,685	R	26.5	73.5	-	19	3	-	1.5	0.9	1.9	-
Larimer	97,437	44,349	53,088	-	8,739	R	45.5	54.5	-	3	19	-	40.3	43.5	38.0	-
Las Animas	6,244	3,551	2,693	-	858	D	56.9	43.1	-	1	21	-	2.6	3.5	1.9	-
Lincoln	2,244	701	1,543	-	842	R	31.2	68.8	-	16	6	-	0.9	0.7	1.1	-
Logan	8,295	2,790	5,505	-	2,715	R	33.6	66.4	-	13	9	-	3.4	2.7	3.9	-
Morgan	8,224	2,907	5,317	-	2,410	R	35.3	64.7	-	10	12	-	3.4	2.9	3.8	-
Otero	7,588	3,064	4,524	-	1,460	R	40.4	59.6	-	5	17	-	3.1	3.0	3.2	-
Phillips	2,244	745	1,499	-	754	R	33.2	66.8	-	14	8	-	0.9	0.7	1.1	-
Prowers	4,859	1,638	3,221	-	1,583	R	33.7	66.3	-	12	10	-	2.0	1.6	2.3	-
Sedgwick	1,111	387	724	-	337	R	34.8	65.2	-	11	11	-	0.5	0.4	0.5	-
Washington	2,539	654	1,885	-	1,231	R	25.8	74.2	-	21	1	-	1.0	0.6	1.3	-
Weld	53,304	21,977	31,327	-	9,350	R	41.2	58.8	-	4	18	-	22.0	21.6	22.4	-
Yuma	4,419	1,404	3,015	-	1,611	R	31.8	68.2	-	15	7	-	1.8	1.4	2.2	-
District 5	**243,415**	**62,550**	**173,096**	**7,769**	**110,546**	**R**	**25.7**	**71.1**	**3.2**				**100.0**	**100.0**	**100.0**	**100.0**
Arapahoe (pt)	33,288	10,208	22,186	894	11,978	R	30.7	66.6	2.7	2	4	5	13.7	16.3	12.8	11.5
Douglas (pt)	36,259	10,337	24,824	1,098	14,487	R	28.5	68.5	3.0	3	3	4	14.9	16.5	14.3	14.1

140 Colorado

Congressional district and county	Total	Democrat (DEM)	Republican (REP)	Other	Plurality		Percent of total vote								Percent contribution to district vote			
										Rank within district								
					Total	Party	DEM	REP	Other	DEM	REP	Other		Total	DEM	REP	Other
District 5 (cont)																	
El Paso	159,654	37,820	116,752	5,082	78,932	R	23.7	73.1	3.2	5	1	3		65.6	60.5	67.4	65.4
Fremont (pt)	7,544	2,578	4,605	361	2,027	R	34.2	61.0	4.8	1	5	2		3.1	4.1	2.7	4.6
Teller	6,670	1,607	4,729	334	3,122	R	24.1	70.9	5.0	4	2	1		2.7	2.6	2.7	4.3
District 6	**233,097**	**91,073**	**142,021**	**3**	**50,948**	**R**	**39.1**	**60.9**	**<.1**					**100.0**	**100.0**	**100.0**	**100.0**
Arapahoe (pt)	118,872	45,766	73,103	3	27,337	R	38.5	61.5	<.1	2	1	1		51.0	50.3	51.5	100.0
Jefferson (pt)	114,225	45,307	68,918	0	23,611	R	39.7	60.3	0.0	1	2	2		49.0	49.7	48.5	0.0
COLORADO	**1,479,209**	**691,479**	**757,666**	**30,064**	**66,187**	**R**	**46.7**	**51.2**	**2.0**								

Table I. — Vote for Presidential Preference: March 3, 1992, Democratic Primary Election

County	Top candidates									Top three candidates (state vote)								
										Percent of total vote			Rank			Percent contribution to state vote		
	Total	Brown	Clinton	Tsongas	Kerrey	Harkin	Uncommitted	Woods	Other	Brown	Clinton	Tsongas	Brown	Clinton	Tsongas	Total	Brown	Clinton	Tsongas
Adams	15,229	3,862	5,094	3,169	2,123	392	398	33	158	25.4	33.4	20.8	26	24	37	6.4	5.6	7.9	5.2
Alamosa	752	139	257	198	101	24	19	1	13	18.5	34.2	26.3	39	20	18	0.3	0.2	0.4	0.3
Arapahoe	24,982	6,977	6,059	7,483	3,293	514	497	33	126	27.9	24.3	30.0	24	45	4	10.4	10.1	9.4	12.2
Archuleta	241	59	69	62	33	1	8	1	8	24.5	28.6	25.7	31	34	21	0.1	<.1	0.1	0.1
Baca	563	96	221	102	61	16	36	13	18	17.1	39.3	18.1	47	13	50	0.2	0.1	0.3	0.2
Bent	442	80	173	54	52	13	26	3	41	18.1	39.1	12.2	41	14	61	0.2	0.1	0.3	<.1
Boulder	24,170	10,334	3,631	6,578	2,446	540	444	19	178	42.8	15.0	27.2	2	59	14	10.1	15.0	5.6	10.7
Chaffee	802	184	241	172	132	28	21	6	18	22.9	30.0	21.4	34	31	34	0.3	0.3	0.4	0.3
Cheyenne	169	37	52	23	32	16	5	2	2	21.9	30.8	13.6	37	28	59	<.1	<.1	<.1	<.1
Clear Creek	656	245	110	167	92	14	17	0	11	37.3	16.8	25.5	7	57	22	0.3	0.4	0.2	0.3
Conejos	502	67	293	68	44	6	9	3	12	13.3	58.4	13.5	58	2	60	0.2	<.1	0.5	0.1
Costilla	561	56	403	47	28	6	10	2	9	10.0	71.8	8.4	63	1	63	0.2	<.1	0.6	<.1
Crowley	285	44	144	46	31	4	6	2	8	15.4	50.5	16.1	53	5	54	0.1	<.1	0.2	<.1
Custer	149	31	50	32	21	4	8	0	3	20.8	33.6	21.5	38	23	33	<.1	<.1	<.1	<.1
Delta	1,564	387	498	290	244	40	51	9	45	24.7	31.8	18.5	28	26	44	0.7	0.6	0.8	0.5
Denver	48,530	15,466	12,845	13,207	4,673	906	854	59	520	31.9	26.5	27.2	16	40	15	20.3	22.4	19.9	21.5
Dolores	174	26	78	31	30	0	0	3	6	14.9	44.8	17.8	55	6	52	<.1	<.1	0.1	<.1
Douglas	2,819	854	561	861	412	57	51	6	17	30.3	19.9	30.5	20	51	3	1.2	1.2	0.9	1.4
Eagle	1,040	375	190	263	155	23	22	1	11	36.1	18.3	25.3	8	54	23	0.4	0.5	0.3	0.4
Elbert	502	145	129	126	69	12	14	7	0	28.9	25.7	25.1	22	42	24	0.2	0.2	0.2	0.2
El Paso	15,239	3,575	4,347	4,519	1,673	288	491	181	165	23.5	28.5	29.7	33	35	5	6.4	5.2	6.7	7.4
Fremont	2,076	362	887	418	283	36	30	37	23	17.4	42.7	20.1	45	9	40	0.9	0.5	1.4	0.7
Garfield	2,115	659	518	437	361	62	42	3	33	31.2	24.5	20.7	18	44	38	0.9	1.0	0.8	0.7
Gilpin	261	109	39	74	26	5	6	0	2	41.8	14.9	28.4	3	60	8	0.1	0.2	<.1	0.1
Grand	448	123	105	122	71	8	12	1	6	27.5	23.4	27.2	25	46	13	0.2	0.2	0.2	0.2
Gunnison	905	423	145	166	121	16	20	5	9	46.7	16.0	18.3	1	58	47	0.4	0.6	0.2	0.3
Hinsdale	55	19	6	20	9	0	1	0	0	34.5	10.9	36.4	11	63	1	<.1	<.1	<.1	<.1
Huerfano	951	215	423	136	114	10	25	13	15	22.6	44.5	14.3	36	7	57	0.4	0.3	0.7	0.2
Jackson	85	14	29	17	12	5	6	0	2	16.5	34.1	20.0	49	21	41	<.1	<.1	<.1	<.1
Jefferson	33,416	10,119	7,514	9,606	4,233	707	816	66	355	30.3	22.5	28.7	21	47	7	13.9	14.6	11.7	15.7
Kiowa	187	19	105	26	27	4	5	0	1	10.2	56.1	13.9	62	3	58	<.1	<.1	0.2	<.1
Kit Carson	422	77	161	81	71	14	11	2	5	18.2	38.2	19.2	40	15	43	0.2	0.1	0.2	0.1
Lake	680	191	193	150	94	17	17	3	15	28.1	28.4	22.1	23	36	29	0.3	0.3	0.3	0.2
La Plata	1,911	623	364	537	238	52	65	1	31	32.6	19.0	28.1	15	52	11	0.8	0.9	0.6	0.9
Larimer	12,019	3,662	2,442	3,379	1,773	335	268	10	150	30.5	20.3	28.1	19	50	10	5.0	5.3	3.8	5.5
Las Animas	2,402	246	646	278	127	702	37	167	199	10.2	26.9	11.6	61	39	62	1.0	0.4	1.0	0.5
Lincoln	366	51	156	62	57	12	19	4	5	13.9	42.6	16.9	57	10	53	0.2	<.1	0.2	0.1
Logan	1,076	193	326	226	264	23	28	1	15	17.9	30.3	21.0	42	29	36	0.4	0.3	0.5	0.4
Mesa	7,239	1,825	1,970	1,531	1,347	182	167	104	113	25.2	27.2	21.1	27	38	35	3.0	2.6	3.1	2.5
Mineral	129	22	46	32	14	3	9	1	2	17.1	35.7	24.8	46	17	26	<.1	<.1	<.1	<.1
Moffat	535	128	141	141	55	41	19	1	9	23.9	26.4	26.4	32	41	17	0.2	0.2	0.2	0.2
Montezuma	974	222	284	214	137	38	45	10	24	22.8	29.2	22.0	35	32	31	0.4	0.3	0.4	0.3
Montrose	1,664	408	458	306	332	39	61	14	46	24.5	27.5	18.4	30	37	45	0.7	0.6	0.7	0.5
Morgan	851	151	342	166	134	29	18	0	11	17.7	40.2	19.5	43	12	42	0.4	0.2	0.5	0.3
Otero	1,076	158	477	195	143	15	29	16	43	14.7	44.3	18.1	56	8	48	0.4	0.2	0.7	0.3
Ouray	150	50	28	36	23	5	3	1	4	33.3	18.7	24.0	13	53	27	<.1	<.1	<.1	<.1
Park	523	178	112	130	61	13	22	1	6	34.0	21.4	24.9	12	48	25	0.2	0.3	0.2	0.2
Phillips	275	46	79	56	79	8	6	0	1	16.7	28.7	20.4	48	33	39	0.1	<.1	0.1	<.1
Pitkin	1,045	405	121	307	122	24	25	2	39	38.8	11.6	29.4	4	62	6	0.4	0.6	0.2	0.5
Prowers	582	94	236	107	98	13	22	5	7	16.2	40.5	18.4	50	11	46	0.2	0.1	0.4	0.2
Pueblo	14,623	2,291	7,418	2,279	1,824	221	239	175	176	15.7	50.7	15.6	52	4	56	6.1	3.3	11.5	3.7
Rio Blanco	309	47	97	56	60	13	8	0	28	15.2	31.4	18.1	54	27	49	0.1	<.1	0.2	<.1
Rio Grande	570	101	202	152	54	19	24	5	13	17.7	35.4	26.7	44	18	16	0.2	0.1	0.3	0.2
Routt	1,141	403	241	296	139	22	26	1	13	35.3	21.1	25.9	9	49	20	0.5	0.6	0.4	0.5
Saguache	344	113	104	62	33	4	10	1	17	32.8	30.2	18.0	14	30	51	0.1	0.2	0.2	0.1
San Juan	69	26	12	19	12	0	0	0	0	37.7	17.4	27.5	6	55	12	<.1	<.1	<.1	<.1
San Miguel	408	157	70	115	41	6	9	2	8	38.5	17.2	28.2	5	56	9	0.2	0.2	0.1	0.2
Sedgwick	146	19	50	23	38	4	7	0	5	13.0	34.2	15.8	60	19	55	<.1	<.1	<.1	<.1
Summit	789	275	103	245	117	21	20	1	7	34.9	13.1	31.1	10	61	2	0.3	0.4	0.2	0.4
Teller	695	217	173	163	88	24	19	1	10	31.2	24.9	23.5	17	43	28	0.3	0.3	0.3	0.3
Washington	260	34	94	68	38	11	6	1	8	13.1	36.2	26.2	59	16	19	0.1	<.1	0.1	0.1
Weld	5,960	1,473	1,925	1,309	857	181	135	12	68	24.7	32.3	22.0	29	25	32	2.5	2.1	3.0	2.1
Yuma	540	86	183	119	100	18	32	0	2	15.9	33.9	22.0	51	22	30	0.2	0.1	0.3	0.2
COLORADO	239,643	69,073	64,470	61,360	29,572	5,866	5,356	1,051	2,895	28.8	26.9	25.6				100.0	100.0	100.0	100.0

Table J. — Vote for Presidential Preference: March 3, 1992, Republican Primary Election

County	Total	Bush	Bu-chanan	Zimmer-mann	Other	Bush	Bu-chanan	Zimmer-mann	Other	Bush	Bu-chanan	Zimmer-mann	Other	Total	Bush	Bu-chanan	Zimmer-mann	Other
						Percent of total vote				*Rank*				*Percent contribution to state vote*				
Adams	7,917	5,222	2,467	80	148	66.0	31.2	1.0	1.9	41	24	14	20	4.0	4.0	4.2	5.0	4.6
Alamosa	579	444	124	4	7	76.7	21.4	0.7	1.2	3	60	29	42	0.3	0.3	0.2	0.3	0.2
Arapahoe	27,979	19,129	8,224	230	396	68.4	29.4	0.8	1.4	26	36	23	35	14.3	14.5	14.0	14.4	12.2
Archuleta	417	285	128	2	2	68.3	30.7	0.5	0.5	27	28	40	61	0.2	0.2	0.2	0.1	<.1
Baca	409	308	97	1	3	75.3	23.7	0.2	0.7	7	56	51	56	0.2	0.2	0.2	<.1	<.1
Bent	222	151	68	1	2	68.0	30.6	0.5	0.9	31	29	44	51	0.1	0.1	0.1	<.1	<.1
Boulder	11,775	7,917	3,554	71	233	67.2	30.2	0.6	2.0	36	32	35	17	6.0	6.0	6.0	4.5	7.2
Chaffee	811	524	246	9	32	64.6	30.3	1.1	3.9	46	30	11	4	0.4	0.4	0.4	0.6	1.0
Cheyenne	283	176	102	0	5	62.2	36.0	0.0	1.8	53	7	55	25	0.1	0.1	0.2	0.0	0.2
Clear Creek	509	311	182	4	12	61.1	35.8	0.8	2.4	56	8	26	13	0.3	0.2	0.3	0.3	0.4
Conejos	419	286	121	7	5	68.3	28.9	1.7	1.2	29	41	1	43	0.2	0.2	0.2	0.4	0.2
Costilla	55	34	18	0	3	61.8	32.7	0.0	5.5	55	16	56	2	<.1	<.1	<.1	0.0	<.1
Crowley	295	235	50	3	7	79.7	16.9	1.0	2.4	2	63	13	11	0.2	0.2	<.1	0.2	0.2
Custer	339	246	80	4	9	72.6	23.6	1.2	2.7	11	57	7	9	0.2	0.2	0.1	0.3	0.3
Delta	2,142	1,389	705	9	39	64.8	32.9	0.4	1.8	45	14	46	24	1.1	1.1	1.2	0.6	1.2
Denver	20,050	13,750	5,608	294	398	68.6	28.0	1.5	2.0	25	45	2	16	10.2	10.4	9.5	18.5	12.3
Dolores	86	50	33	1	2	58.1	38.4	1.2	2.3	60	4	8	14	<.1	<.1	<.1	<.1	<.1
Douglas	4,688	3,122	1,498	21	47	66.6	32.0	0.4	1.0	37	19	45	50	2.4	2.4	2.5	1.3	1.4
Eagle	900	585	288	12	15	65.0	32.0	1.3	1.7	44	18	3	31	0.5	0.4	0.5	0.8	0.5
Elbert	688	472	206	4	6	68.6	29.9	0.6	0.9	24	34	36	53	0.4	0.4	0.4	0.3	0.2
El Paso	25,122	16,706	8,010	136	270	66.5	31.9	0.5	1.1	38	20	37	49	12.8	12.6	13.6	8.5	8.3
Fremont	2,200	1,539	609	15	37	70.0	27.7	0.7	1.7	18	46	30	30	1.1	1.2	1.0	0.9	1.1
Garfield	1,724	1,185	500	9	30	68.7	29.0	0.5	1.7	23	39	38	27	0.9	0.9	0.9	0.6	0.9
Gilpin	166	91	67	2	6	54.8	40.4	1.2	3.6	62	1	6	5	<.1	<.1	0.1	0.1	0.2
Grand	1,140	721	386	12	21	63.2	33.9	1.1	1.8	51	12	12	23	0.6	0.5	0.7	0.8	0.6
Gunnison	626	379	230	6	11	60.5	36.7	1.0	1.8	58	6	17	26	0.3	0.3	0.4	0.4	0.3
Hinsdale	148	86	57	0	5	58.1	38.5	0.0	3.4	61	3	57	6	<.1	<.1	<.1	0.0	0.2
Huerfano	141	114	27	0	0	80.9	19.1	0.0	0.0	1	61	58	62	<.1	<.1	<.1	0.0	0.0
Jackson	208	158	48	1	1	76.0	23.1	0.5	0.5	4	58	39	60	0.1	0.1	<.1	<.1	<.1
Jefferson	32,398	21,418	10,166	255	559	66.1	31.4	0.8	1.7	40	22	25	28	16.6	16.2	17.3	16.0	17.2
Kiowa	176	133	42	0	1	75.6	23.9	0.0	0.6	5	55	59	59	<.1	0.1	<.1	0.0	<.1
Kit Carson	851	600	243	2	6	70.5	28.6	0.2	0.7	16	42	52	57	0.4	0.5	0.4	0.1	0.2
Lake	209	133	69	1	6	63.6	33.0	0.5	2.9	50	13	41	8	0.1	0.1	0.1	<.1	0.2
La Plata	1,869	1,228	585	21	35	65.7	31.3	1.1	1.9	43	23	10	19	1.0	0.9	1.0	1.3	1.1
Larimer	13,053	8,852	3,809	151	241	67.8	29.2	1.2	1.8	32	38	9	22	6.7	6.7	6.5	9.5	7.4
Las Animas	351	176	63	3	109	50.1	17.9	0.9	31.1	63	62	22	1	0.2	0.1	0.1	0.2	3.4
Lincoln	583	398	171	5	9	68.3	29.3	0.9	1.5	28	37	21	32	0.3	0.3	0.3	0.3	0.3
Logan	1,216	858	332	9	17	70.6	27.3	0.7	1.4	15	47	27	36	0.6	0.6	0.6	0.6	0.5
Mesa	7,915	5,356	2,348	64	147	67.7	29.7	0.8	1.9	35	35	24	21	4.0	4.1	4.0	4.0	4.5
Mineral	45	29	14	0	2	64.4	31.1	0.0	4.4	47	25	60	3	<.1	<.1	<.1	0.0	<.1
Moffat	883	547	306	8	22	61.9	34.7	0.9	2.5	54	10	19	10	0.5	0.4	0.5	0.5	0.7
Montezuma	1,027	657	337	13	20	64.0	32.8	1.3	1.9	48	15	5	18	0.5	0.5	0.6	0.8	0.6
Montrose	1,930	1,269	624	13	24	65.8	32.3	0.7	1.2	42	17	31	41	1.0	1.0	1.1	0.8	0.7
Morgan	1,266	925	324	2	15	73.1	25.6	0.2	1.2	10	52	54	44	0.6	0.7	0.6	0.1	0.5
Otero	942	657	242	12	31	69.7	25.7	1.3	3.3	19	51	4	7	0.5	0.5	0.4	0.8	1.0
Ouray	408	290	108	4	6	71.1	26.5	1.0	1.5	14	49	15	33	0.2	0.2	0.2	0.3	0.2
Park	549	333	202	1	13	60.7	36.8	0.2	2.4	57	5	53	12	0.3	0.3	0.3	<.1	0.4
Phillips	458	322	129	3	4	70.3	28.2	0.7	0.9	17	44	33	52	0.2	0.2	0.2	0.2	0.1
Pitkin	579	398	164	5	12	68.7	28.3	0.9	2.1	22	43	20	15	0.3	0.3	0.3	0.3	0.4
Prowers	595	449	135	4	7	75.5	22.7	0.7	1.2	6	59	32	45	0.3	0.3	0.2	0.3	0.2
Pueblo	4,238	3,103	1,032	31	72	73.2	24.4	0.7	1.7	9	54	28	29	2.2	2.3	1.8	1.9	2.2
Rio Blanco	622	413	196	4	9	66.4	31.5	0.6	1.4	39	21	34	34	0.3	0.3	0.3	0.3	0.3
Rio Grande	646	465	166	6	9	72.0	25.7	0.9	1.4	12	50	18	37	0.3	0.4	0.3	0.4	0.3
Routt	729	466	248	7	8	63.9	34.0	1.0	1.1	49	11	16	48	0.4	0.4	0.4	0.4	0.2
Saguache	254	182	69	1	2	71.7	27.2	0.4	0.8	13	48	47	54	0.1	0.1	0.1	<.1	<.1
San Juan	48	29	19	0	0	60.4	39.6	0.0	0.0	59	2	61	63	<.1	<.1	<.1	0.0	0.0
San Miguel	223	151	69	0	3	67.7	30.9	0.0	1.3	33	26	62	40	0.1	0.1	0.1	0.0	<.1
Sedgwick	288	195	89	0	4	67.7	30.9	0.0	1.4	34	27	63	38	0.1	0.1	0.2	0.0	0.1
Summit	664	457	199	3	5	68.8	30.0	0.5	0.8	21	33	43	55	0.3	0.3	0.3	0.2	0.2
Teller	952	648	288	3	13	68.1	30.3	0.3	1.4	30	31	48	39	0.5	0.5	0.5	0.2	0.4
Washington	630	396	224	3	7	62.9	35.6	0.5	1.1	52	9	42	46	0.3	0.3	0.4	0.2	0.2
Weld	6,323	4,406	1,829	18	70	69.7	28.9	0.3	1.1	20	40	49	47	3.2	3.3	3.1	1.1	2.2
Yuma	732	546	179	2	5	74.6	24.5	0.3	0.7	8	53	50	58	0.4	0.4	0.3	0.1	0.2
COLORADO	195,690	132,100	58,753	1,592	3,245	67.5	30.0	0.8	1.7					100.0	100.0	100.0	100.0	100.0

1992 Vote for President
Percent for Clinton (D), by County

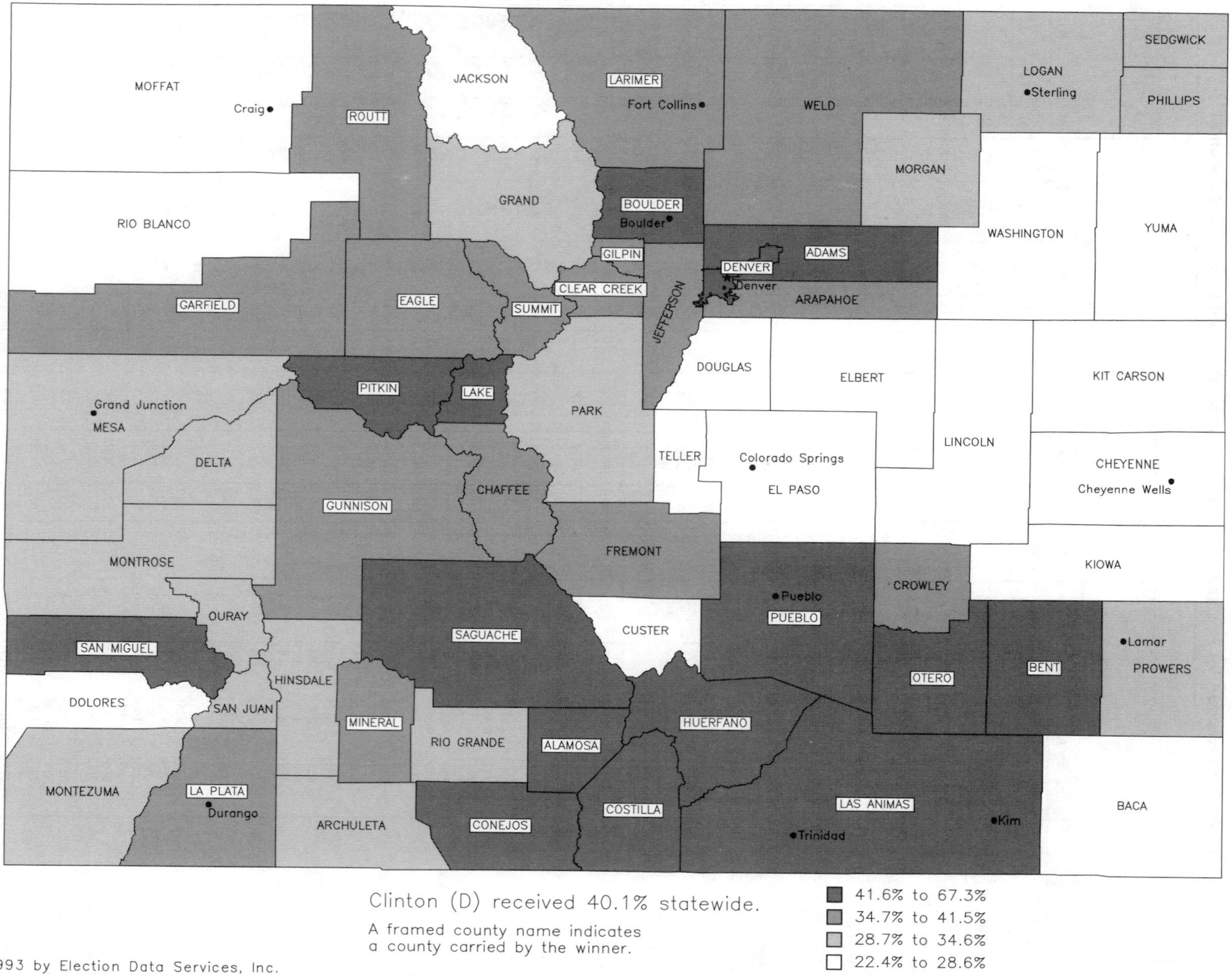

SEDGWICK

PHILLIPS

YUMA

KIT CARSON

CHEYENNE
•Cheyenne Wells

KIOWA

PROWERS
•Lamar

BACA

LOGAN
•Sterling

WASHINGTON

LINCOLN

BENT

•Kim

MORGAN

ELBERT

CROWLEY

OTERO

LAS ANIMAS
•Trinidad

WELD

ADAMS

ARAPAHOE

Colorado Springs
EL PASO

PUEBLO
•Pueblo

HUERFANO

DENVER
•Denver

DOUGLAS

LARIMER
Fort Collins•

BOULDER
Boulder•

GILPIN

CLEAR CREEK

JEFFERSON

TELLER

FREMONT

CUSTER

COSTILLA

ALAMOSA

CONEJOS

JACKSON

GRAND

SUMMIT

PARK

CHAFFEE

SAGUACHE

RIO GRANDE

MINERAL

ARCHULETA

ROUTT

EAGLE

LAKE

PITKIN

GUNNISON

HINSDALE

SAN JUAN

LA PLATA
Durango•

Craig•

MOFFAT

RIO BLANCO

GARFIELD

Grand Junction•
MESA•

DELTA

MONTROSE

OURAY

SAN MIGUEL

DOLORES

MONTEZUMA

41.6% to 67.3%
34.7% to 41.5%
28.7% to 34.6%
22.4% to 28.6%

Clinton (D) received 40.1% statewide.

A framed county name indicates
a county carried by the winner.

144 Colorado

1992 Vote for U.S. Senator
Percent for Campbell (D), by County

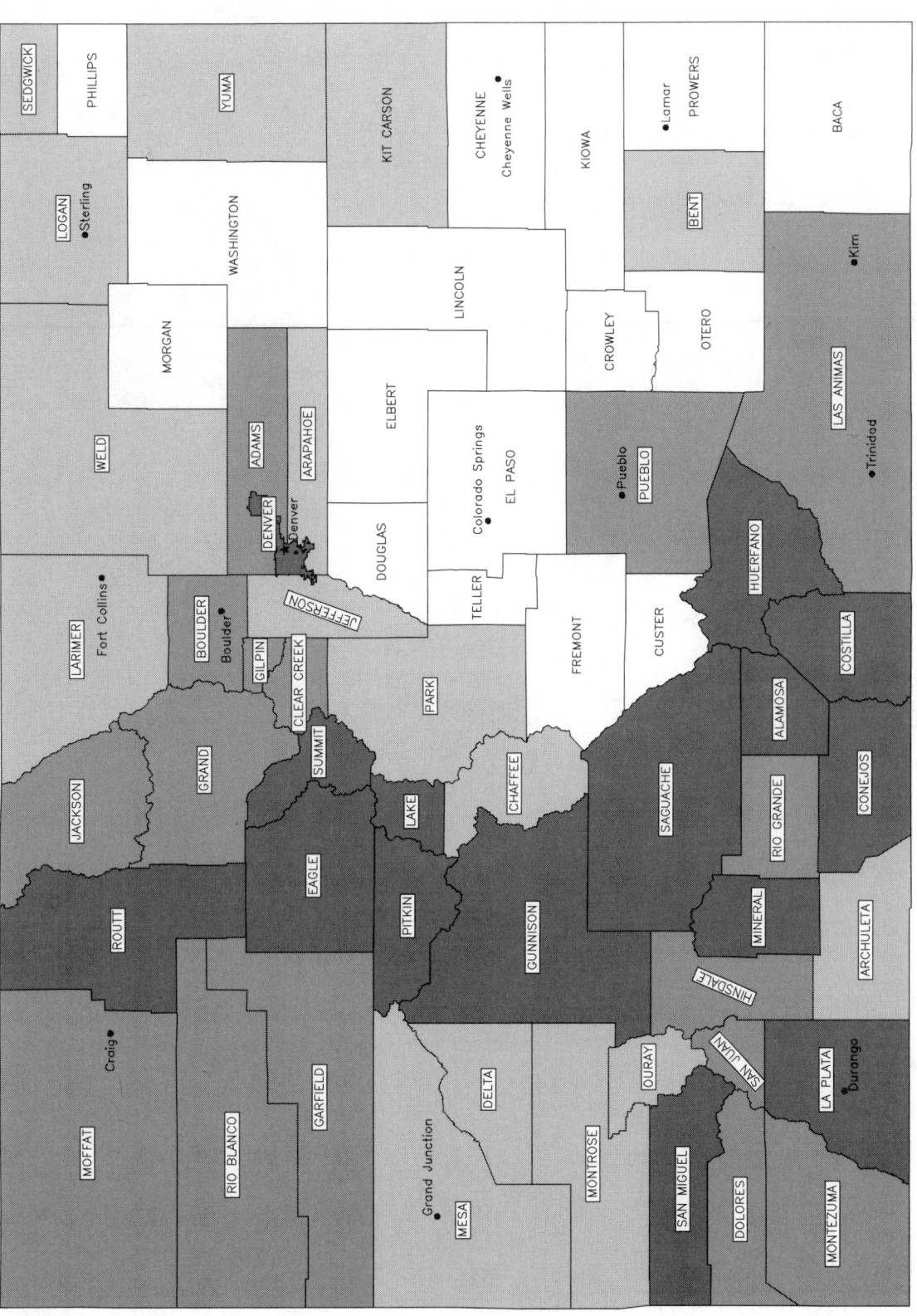

Campbell (D) received 51.8% statewide.

A framed county name indicates
a county carried by the winner.

■	63.3% to 77.0%
▨	52.0% to 63.2%
▨	45.9% to 51.9%
☐	30.8% to 45.8%

Copyright © 1993 by Election Data Services, Inc.

Colorado 145

CONNECTICUT

Congressional Districts 6
    Average Population 547,853
State Senate Districts 36
    Average Population 91,309
State House Districts 151
    Average Population 21,769

Electoral College Votes..8
Counties[1] 8
Voting Precincts 770

Alternative Registration Methods:
    ....Agency-based, Deputized Registrars, Mail-in

Registration Deadline[2] (Days before Election)....................14

Voting Equipment Use (Towns)[3]

Datavote Punch Card	0	Paper Ballot	0
Electronic	0	Other Punch Card	0
Lever Machine	169	Mixed Systems	0
Optical Scanner	0		

Party Control	DEM	REP	IND	VAC
1993 State Senate	19	17	0	0
1992 State Senate	20	16	0	0
1993 State House	87	64	0	0
1992 State House	87	64	0	0

Population Statistics 1990

Race/ Ethnicity	Total Population		Voting Age Population		Voting Age Population % of total population
	Number	%	Number	%	
Non-Hispanic					
White	2,754,184	83.8	2,179,747	85.9	79.1
Black	260,840	7.9	180,656	7.1	69.3
Asian/Pacific Islander	49,114	1.5	34,757	1.4	70.8
Native American	5,950	0.2	4,474	0.2	75.2
Other	3,912	<.1	2,126	<.1	54.3
All Hispanic	213,116	6.5	135,775	5.4	63.7
TOTAL	3,287,116	100.0	2,537,535	100.0	77.2

Estimated Voting Age Population 1992 (VAP) 2,535,000
Number of Registered Voters................................. 1,961,503
    % of estimated VAP... 77.4
Voter Turnout (Actual) 1,645,609
    % of VAP 64.9
    % of Registration 83.9
Persons Not Voting—of Voting Age 889,391
    % of VAP 35.1
Persons Not Voting—of Registered 315,894
    % of Registration 16.1
Straight Ticket Voting .... No

State Officials and Members of Congress

Governor:
Lowell P. Weicker (I) 1990, elected to a four-year term in 1990.

U.S. Senators:
Christopher Dodd (D) 1980, elected to a six-year term in 1992.
Joseph I. Lieberman (D) 1988, elected to a six-year term in 1988.

U.S. Representative in Congress:
(District, Name, Party, Date first elected)

1. Kennelly (D) 1982
2. Gejdenson (D) 1980

3. DeLauro (D) 1990
4. Shays (R) 1987

5. Franks (R) 1990

6. Johnson (R) 1982

---

[1]Elections administered by 169 towns rather than counties. Data presented for counties and 95 towns with more than one voting precinct. [2]Deadline for primary election is one day before election. [3]Reported for all 169 towns, including those with a single voting precinct.

Candidates: General Election, November 3, 1992

Candidate(s)	Total vote	Percent	Party	Status	First elected
President/Vice President					
Clinton/Gore	682,318	42.21%	Democrat	Challenger	1992
Bush/Quayle	578,313	35.78%	Republican	Incumbent	1988
Perot/Stockdale	348,771	21.58%	Americans for Perot	Challenger	
Marrou/Lord	5,391	0.33%	Libertarian	Challenger	
Fulani/Munoz	1,363	0.08%	New Alliance	Challenger	
Hagelin/Tompkins	75	<0.01	Write in	Challenger	
Gritz/Minett	72	<0.01	Write in	Challenger	
Phillips/Knight	20	<0.01	Write in	Challenger	
Warren/DeBates	5	<0.01	Write in	Challenger	
LaRouche/Bevel	4	<0.01	Write in	Challenger	
U.S. Senator					
Christopher Dodd	882,569	58.81%	Total	Incumbent	1980
	(577,662)	(65.45)	Democrat		
	(304,907)	(34.56)	A Connecticut Party		
Brook Johnson	572,036	38.12%	Republican	Challenger	
Richard Gregory	35,315	2.35%	Concerned Citizens	Challenger	
Howard Grayson, Jr.	10,741	0.72%	Libertarian	Challenger	
Clarisse DiCandia	41	<0.01	Write in	Challenger	
Will Wilkin	6	<0.01	Write in	Challenger	
Peter Rumbin	1	<0.01	Write in	Challenger	
Governor (No Contest)					
U.S. Representative in Congress					
District 1					
Barbara Kennelly	164,735	67.12%	Total	Incumbent	1982
	(112,838)	(68.50)	Democrat		
	(51,897)	(31.50)	A Connecticut Party		
Philip Steele	75,113	30.60%	Republican	Challenger	
Gary Garneau	5,577	2.27%	Concerned Citizens	Challenger	
Tom Hall	5	<0.01	Write in	Challenger	
District 2					
Sam Gejdenson	123,291	50.80%	Total	Incumbent	1980
	(83,197)	(67.48)	Democrat		
	(40,094)	(32.52)	A Connecticut Party		
Edward Munster	119,416	49.20%	Republican	Challenger	
District 3					
Rosa DeLauro	162,568	65.68%	Total	Incumbent	1990
	(112,022)	(68.91)	Democrat		
	(50,546)	(31.09)	A Connecticut Party		
Tom Scott	84,952	34.32%	Republican	Challenger	
William Russell	9	<0.01	Write in	Challenger	
Peter Krala	2	<0.01	Write in	Challenger	
District 4					
Christopher Shays	147,816	67.31%	Republican	Incumbent	1987
Dave Schropfer	58,666	26.71%	Democrat	Challenger	
Al Smith	11,679	5.32%	A Connecticut Party	Challenger	
Ronald Fried	1,445	0.66%	Natural Law	Challenger	
Edward Tonkin	9	<.01%	Write in	Challenger	
District 5					
Gary Franks	104,891	43.65%	Republican	Incumbent	1990
James Lawlor	74,791	31.13%	Democrat	Challenger	
Lynn Taborsak	54,022	22.48%	A Connecticut Party	Challenger	
Rosita Rodriguez	5,090	2.12%	Concerned Citizens	Challenger	
Bernard Nevas	864	0.36%	Natural Law	Challenger	
David LaPointe	625	0.26%	Independent	Challenger	

Candidate(s)	Total vote	Percent	Party	Status	First elected
U.S. Representative in Congress (cont)					
District 6					
Nancy Johnson	166,967	69.69%	Republican	Incumbent	1982
Eugene Slason	60,373	25.20%	Democrat	Challenger	
Daniel Plawecki	9,544	3.98%	Concerned Citizens	Challenger	
Charles Pearl	1,677	0.70%	Independent	Challenger	
Ralph Economu	1,036	0.43%	Independent	Challenger	

Candidates: March 24, 1992, Primary Election

Candidate	Total vote	Percent	Candidate	Total vote	Percent
Presidential Preference, Democratic			**Presidential Preference, Republican**		
Jerry Brown	64,472	37.24%	George Bush	66,356	66.71%
Bill Clinton	61,698	35.64%	Patrick Buchanan	21,815	21.93%
Paul Tsongas	33,811	19.53%	Uncommitted	9,008	9.06%
Uncommitted	5,430	3.14%	David Duke	2,294	2.31%
Larry Agran	2,688	1.55%			
Tom Harkin	1,919	1.11%			
Bob Kerrey	1,169	0.68%			
Eugene McCarthy	1,036	0.60%			
Lyndon LaRouche, Jr.	896	0.52%			

Voter Registration and Turnout, 1948-1992 Elections

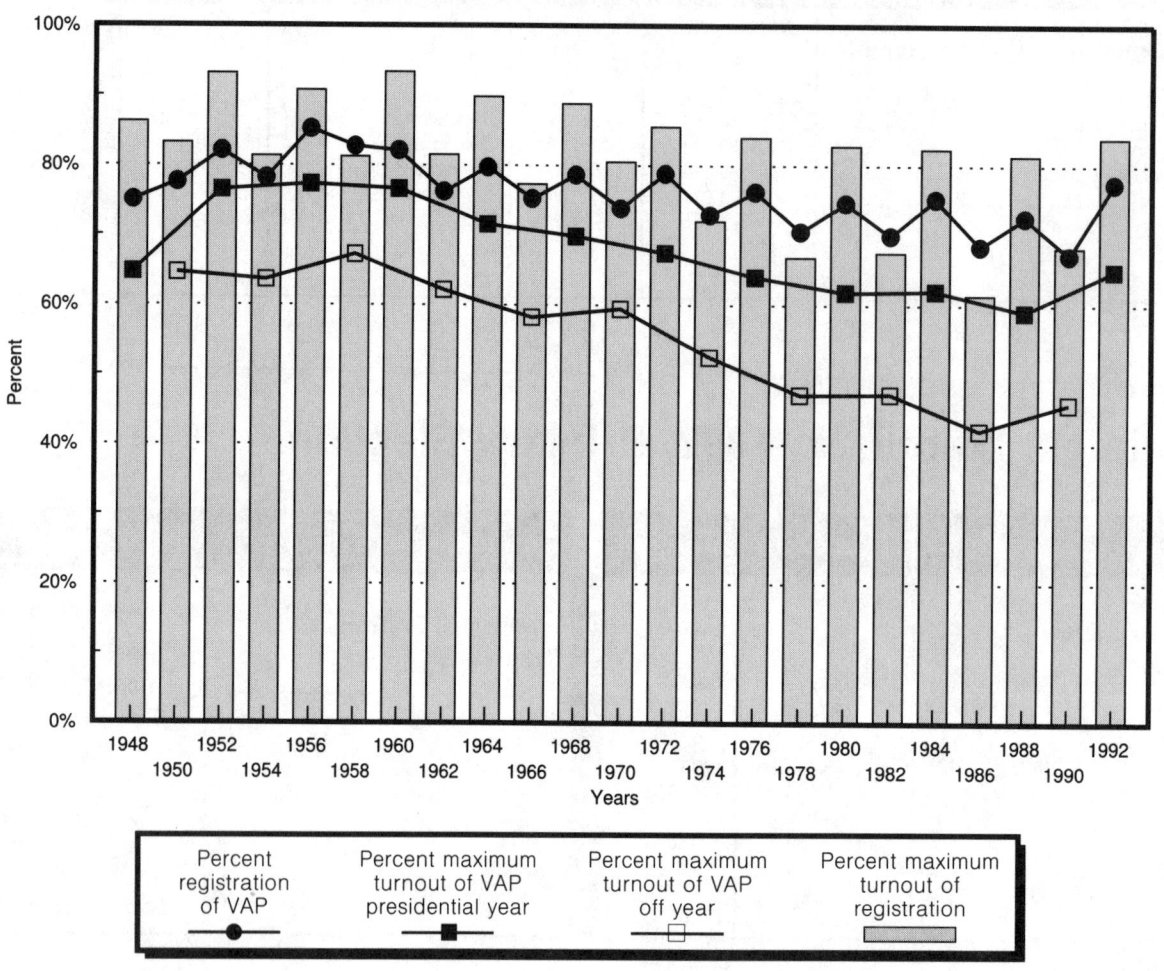

Legend:
- Percent registration of VAP (●)
- Percent maximum turnout of VAP presidential year (■)
- Percent maximum turnout of VAP off year (□)
- Percent maximum turnout of registration (bar)

Year	Estimated Voting Age Population (VAP)	Voter registration (REG)			Voter turnout											
						Highest office						Maximum vote				
		Total	Percent of VAP	Rank by percent of VAP	Actual	Total	Office	Percent total REG	Rank by percent of REG	Percent of VAP	Rank by percent of VAP	Total	Percent total REG	Rank by percent of REG	Percent total VAP	Rank by percent of VAP
1992	2,535,000	1,961,503	77.4	20	1,645,609	1,616,332	P	82.4	7	63.8	13	1,645,609	83.9	6	64.9	13
1990	2,534,000	1,700,871	67.1	29	1,159,361	1,141,101	G	67.1	7	45.0	16	1,159,361	68.2	7	45.8	16
1988	2,476,000	1,795,419	72.5	22	1,461,962	1,443,394	P	80.4	1	58.3	8	1,461,962	81.4	5	59.0	10
1986	2,442,000	1,670,798	68.4	27	1,025,605	993,692	G	59.5	17	40.7	21	1,025,605	61.4	15	42.0	21
1984	2,405,000	1,809,017	75.2	21	1,490,946	1,466,900	P	81.1	1	61.0	10	1,490,946	82.4	4	62.0	10
1982	2,356,000	1,647,514	69.9	22	1,112,428	1,084,156	G	65.8	15	46.0	18	1,112,428	67.5	17	47.2	17
1980	2,304,000	1,719,108	74.6	21	1,423,403	1,406,285	P	81.8	3	61.0	11	1,423,403	82.8	3	61.8	11
1978	2,254,000	1,588,077	70.5	21	1,061,022	1,036,608	G	65.3	7	46.0	11	1,061,022	66.8	7	47.1	11
1976	2,201,000	1,677,449	76.2	19	1,408,480	1,381,526	P	82.4	2	62.8	9	1,408,480	84.0	3	64.0	7
1974	2,143,000	1,562,228	72.9	19	1,124,858	1,102,773	G	70.6	3	51.5	6	1,124,858	72.0	3	52.5	6
1972	2,091,000	1,648,017	78.8	16	1,409,221	1,384,277	P	84.0	4	66.2	6	1,409,221	85.5	4	67.4	6
1970	1,886,000	1,392,659	73.8	22	1,121,090	1,089,353	S	78.2	4	57.8	10	1,121,090	80.5	4	59.4	7
1968	1,826,000	1,435,298	78.6	20	1,274,526	1,256,232	P	87.5	3	68.8	11	1,274,526	88.8	3	69.8	11
1966	1,773,000	1,333,974	75.2	23	1,031,631	1,008,557	G	75.6	7	56.9	14	1,031,631	77.3	6	58.2	12
1964	1,724,000	1,373,443	79.7	22	1,233,043	1,218,578	P	88.7	5	70.7	14	1,233,043	89.8	4	71.5	15
1962	1,679,000	1,279,754	76.2	21	1,043,299	1,031,902	G	80.6	3	61.5	9	1,043,299	81.5	3	62.1	11
1960	1,608,000	1,320,954	82.1	14	1,231,885	1,222,868	P	92.6	5	76.0	10	1,231,885	93.3	5	76.6	10
1958	1,464,000	1,211,204	82.7	7	983,232	974,509	G	80.5	4	66.6	1	983,232	81.2	4	67.2	1
1956	1,458,000	1,242,267	85.2	9	1,126,452	1,116,916	P	89.9	5	76.6	2	1,126,452	90.7	5	77.3	2
1954	1,485,000	1,161,686	78.2	13	944,582	936,753	G	80.6	3	63.1	3	944,582	81.3	3	63.6	2
1952	1,443,000	1,185,234	82.1	13	1,103,598	1,096,906	P	92.5	3	76.0	9	1,103,598	93.1	2	76.5	11
1950	1,378,000	1,069,321	77.6	8	889,973	878,735	G	82.2	2	63.8	2	889,973	83.2	3	64.6	2
1948	1,378,000	1,033,901	75.0	10	890,909	883,518	P	85.5	4	64.1	14	890,909	86.2	4	64.7	13

CONNECTICUT

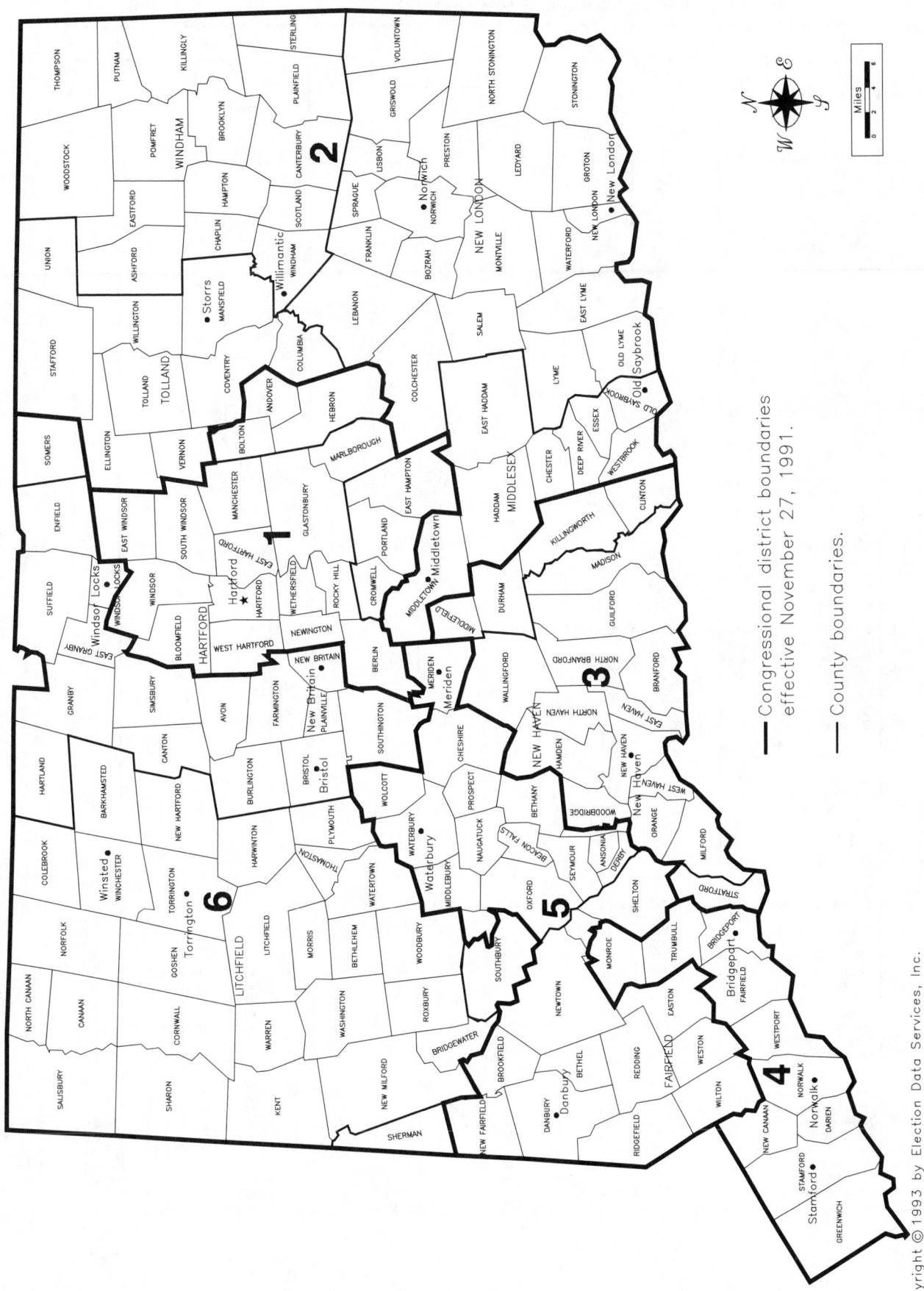

Congressional district boundaries effective November 27, 1991.

County boundaries.

Table A. — 1990 Population by Race and Ethnic Origin

State/ county code	County	Total persons	White	Black	Asian and Pacific Islander	Native American	Other	Hispanic	Total	White	Black	Hispanic	Total	White	Black	Hispanic
			Percent of total persons						**Rank**				**Percent contribution to state population**			
			Non-Hispanic						Percent of total persons				Non-Hispanic			
										Non-Hispanic						
09 001	Fairfield	827,645	79.8	9.4	2.0	0.1	0.1	8.6	2	8	3	1	25.2	24.0	29.7	33.2
09 003	Hartford	851,783	80.2	9.6	1.5	0.1	0.1	8.4	1	7	2	2	25.9	24.8	31.4	33.6
09 005	Litchfield	174,092	97.0	0.9	0.8	0.2	<.1	1.1	5	1	8	8	5.3	6.1	0.6	0.9
09 007	Middlesex	143,196	92.6	4.1	1.1	0.2	<.1	2.0	6	4	5	6	4.4	4.8	2.2	1.4
09 009	New Haven	804,219	82.3	9.8	1.3	0.2	0.1	6.3	3	6	1	3	24.5	24.0	30.3	23.9
09 011	New London	254,957	90.3	4.5	1.2	0.5	0.1	3.3	4	5	4	5	7.8	8.4	4.4	4.0
09 013	Tolland	128,699	94.2	2.0	1.9	0.2	<.1	1.7	7	2	6	7	3.9	4.4	1.0	1.0
09 015	Windham	102,525	93.7	1.0	0.7	0.3	<.1	4.2	8	3	7	4	3.1	3.5	0.4	2.0
09	**CONNECTICUT**	**3,287,116**	**83.8**	**7.9**	**1.5**	**0.2**	**<.1**	**6.5**					**100.0**	**100.0**	**100.0**	**100.0**
	SELECTED TOWNS															
09 009	Ansonia town	18,403	88.4	8.1	0.6	0.2	0.1	2.6	52	75	13	31	0.6	0.6	0.6	0.2
09 003	Berlin town	16,787	97.1	0.5	1.0	<.1	0.0	1.3	59	16	85	65	0.5	0.6	<.1	0.1
09 001	Bethel town	17,541	94.4	1.2	2.1	<.1	<.1	2.1	55	58	55	39	0.5	0.6	<.1	0.2
09 003	Bloomfield town	19,483	54.3	40.9	1.4	0.2	0.2	3.0	51	92	1	24	0.6	0.4	3.1	0.3
09 009	Branford town	27,603	95.8	1.1	1.3	<.1	<.1	1.6	35	38	57	58	0.8	1.0	0.1	0.2
09 001	Bridgeport town	141,686	45.6	25.1	2.2	0.2	0.3	26.5	1	94	4	2	4.3	2.3	13.7	17.6
09 003	Bristol town	60,640	94.4	1.9	0.8	0.2	<.1	2.7	9	57	41	28	1.8	2.1	0.4	0.8
09 001	Brookfield town	14,113	96.0	0.7	1.7	<.1	<.1	1.6	70	34	78	59	0.4	0.5	<.1	0.1
09 015	Brooklyn town	6,681	94.7	1.3	1.2	0.2	<.1	2.5	91	53	53	32	0.2	0.2	<.1	<.1
09 009	Cheshire town	25,684	91.5	3.7	1.9	<.1	<.1	2.8	37	71	23	27	0.8	0.9	0.4	0.3
09 007	Clinton town	12,767	94.8	1.0	1.0	0.2	<.1	2.9	75	52	60	26	0.4	0.4	<.1	0.2
09 013	Coventry town	10,063	97.6	0.7	0.2	0.2	<.1	1.2	82	9	75	76	0.3	0.4	<.1	<.1
09 001	Danbury town	65,585	81.8	6.1	3.8	0.2	0.4	7.7	8	83	19	11	2.0	1.9	1.5	2.4
09 001	Darien town	18,196	95.7	0.4	2.0	<.1	<.1	1.9	53	39	88	49	0.6	0.6	<.1	0.2
09 009	Derby town	12,199	92.2	2.3	0.8	0.2	0.1	4.4	77	68	32	14	0.4	0.4	0.1	0.3
09 003	East Granby town	4,302	96.9	1.5	0.4	<.1	0.0	1.2	95	23	47	75	0.1	0.2	<.1	<.1
09 003	East Hartford town	50,452	83.4	8.1	2.2	0.2	0.2	6.0	17	81	14	12	1.5	1.5	1.6	1.4
09 009	East Haven town	26,144	96.7	0.9	0.4	<.1	<.1	1.9	36	27	69	47	0.8	0.9	<.1	0.2
09 011	East Lyme town	15,340	92.4	3.5	1.4	0.3	<.1	2.4	66	66	24	35	0.5	0.5	0.2	0.2
09 003	East Windsor town	10,081	93.3	3.4	1.3	0.4	<.1	1.6	81	65	25	57	0.3	0.3	0.1	<.1
09 003	Enfield town	45,532	94.0	2.5	1.0	0.1	<.1	2.3	20	60	28	37	1.4	1.6	0.4	0.5
09 007	Essex town	5,904	97.6	1.0	0.4	<.1	<.1	1.0	93	10	63	85	0.2	0.2	<.1	<.1
09 001	Fairfield town	53,418	96.0	0.8	1.2	<.1	<.1	1.9	14	35	72	50	1.6	1.9	0.2	0.5
09 003	Farmington town	20,608	95.3	1.3	2.0	<.1	<.1	1.2	48	42	52	77	0.6	0.7	0.1	0.1
09 003	Glastonbury town	27,901	94.6	0.9	2.4	<.1	<.1	2.0	33	55	68	44	0.8	1.0	<.1	0.3
09 003	Granby town	9,369	97.7	0.5	0.7	0.2	<.1	0.9	84	5	86	88	0.3	0.3	<.1	<.1
09 001	Greenwich town	58,441	90.0	2.0	3.4	<.1	0.1	4.4	12	72	40	13	1.8	1.9	0.4	1.2
09 011	Griswold town	10,384	97.5	0.7	0.4	0.4	<.1	1.0	80	11	77	86	0.3	0.4	<.1	<.1
09 011	Groton town	45,144	87.3	6.4	1.9	0.6	0.1	3.7	21	79	18	15	1.4	1.4	1.1	0.8
09 009	Guilford town	19,848	96.9	0.5	0.8	<.1	<.1	1.6	50	20	83	60	0.6	0.7	<.1	0.1
09 007	Haddam town	6,769	97.7	0.5	0.6	0.2	<.1	1.0	90	6	84	84	0.2	0.2	<.1	<.1
09 009	Hamden town	52,434	87.5	8.5	1.7	<.1	<.1	2.0	15	78	12	43	1.6	1.7	1.7	0.5
09 003	Hartford town	139,739	30.5	35.9	1.3	0.2	0.4	31.6	2	95	2	1	4.3	1.5	19.3	20.7
09 015	Killingly town	15,889	96.8	0.7	1.2	0.4	<.1	0.8	63	24	79	94	0.5	0.6	<.1	<.1
09 011	Ledyard town	14,913	94.3	2.0	1.6	0.6	<.1	1.5	67	59	37	62	0.5	0.5	0.1	0.1
09 005	Litchfield town	8,365	97.4	0.9	0.5	0.2	<.1	0.8	88	12	66	91	0.3	0.3	<.1	<.1
09 009	Madison town	15,485	97.6	0.4	0.8	<.1	0.0	1.2	65	8	90	74	0.5	0.5	<.1	<.1
09 003	Manchester town	51,618	92.0	3.7	1.6	0.2	<.1	2.4	16	69	22	34	1.6	1.7	0.7	0.6
09 013	Mansfield town	21,103	87.9	3.1	6.0	0.1	<.1	2.7	45	76	26	29	0.6	0.7	0.3	0.3
09 009	Meriden town	59,479	81.5	3.9	0.7	0.2	<.1	13.7	11	84	21	5	1.8	1.8	0.9	3.8
09 009	Middlebury town	6,145	97.9	0.3	1.0	<.1	0.0	0.8	92	4	93	95	0.2	0.2	<.1	<.1
09 007	Middletown town	42,762	83.7	10.8	1.9	0.2	0.1	3.3	22	80	11	19	1.3	1.3	1.8	0.7
09 009	Milford town	49,938	95.0	1.5	1.0	0.1	<.1	2.3	18	47	48	36	1.5	1.7	0.3	0.5
09 001	Monroe town	16,896	94.9	1.6	1.3	0.1	<.1	2.1	58	50	43	41	0.5	0.6	0.1	0.2
09 011	Montville town	16,673	92.3	2.8	1.4	0.8	0.1	2.6	60	67	27	30	0.5	0.6	0.2	0.2
09 009	Naugatuck town	30,625	93.8	1.6	0.9	0.2	0.2	3.1	29	61	42	23	0.9	1.0	0.2	0.4
09 003	New Britain town	75,491	74.7	7.0	1.7	0.2	0.2	16.3	7	87	17	3	2.3	2.0	2.0	5.8
09 001	New Fairfield town	12,911	96.8	0.2	1.2	0.1	<.1	1.6	73	25	94	55	0.4	0.5	<.1	<.1
09 005	New Hartford town	5,769	98.0	0.3	0.7	<.1	0.0	0.8	94	3	91	93	0.2	0.2	<.1	<.1
09 009	New Haven town	130,474	49.0	35.0	2.3	0.3	0.2	13.2	3	93	3	7	4.0	2.3	17.5	8.1
09 011	New London town	28,540	69.3	15.8	2.0	0.6	0.2	12.1	32	91	7	8	0.9	0.7	1.7	1.6
09 005	New Milford town	23,629	95.2	1.4	1.2	0.2	<.1	1.9	40	44	50	48	0.7	0.8	0.1	0.3
09 003	Newington town	29,208	95.0	1.4	1.4	0.1	<.1	2.1	31	48	51	42	0.9	1.0	0.2	0.3
09 001	Newtown town	20,779	95.9	1.0	1.2	0.2	<.1	1.7	47	36	65	53	0.6	0.7	<.1	0.2
09 009	North Branford town	12,996	97.2	1.2	0.5	0.1	<.1	0.9	72	15	56	90	0.4	0.5	<.1	<.1
09 009	North Haven town	22,247	94.9	2.1	1.8	<.1	<.1	1.2	41	49	36	78	0.7	0.8	0.2	0.1
09 001	Norwalk town	78,331	73.8	14.9	1.6	0.1	0.2	9.4	6	88	8	10	2.4	2.1	4.5	3.4
09 011	Norwich town	37,391	89.8	5.1	1.0	0.6	0.3	3.1	25	73	20	22	1.1	1.2	0.7	0.5

Table A. — 1990 Population by Race and Ethnic Origin (cont)

State/ county code	County	Total persons	Percent of total persons						Rank				Percent contribution to state population			
			Non-Hispanic							Percent of total persons				Non-Hispanic		
			White	Black	Asian and Pacific Islander	Native American	Other	Hispanic	Total	Non-Hispanic		Hispanic	Total	White	Black	Hispanic
										White	Black					
09 007	Old Saybrook town	9,552	96.3	1.5	1.0	<.1	<.1	1.1	83	31	46	81	0.3	0.3	<.1	<.1
09 009	Orange town	12,830	95.6	0.8	2.4	<.1	<.1	1.2	74	40	71	79	0.4	0.4	<.1	<.1
09 015	Plainfield town..............	14,363	97.3	0.5	0.5	0.2	<.1	1.5	68	14	87	63	0.4	0.5	<.1	0.2
09 003	Plainville town..............	17,392	94.4	2.3	0.9	<.1	0.1	2.1	56	56	31	40	0.5	0.6	0.2	0.2
09 005	Plymouth town	11,822	98.1	0.4	0.4	0.1	<.1	0.9	78	2	89	89	0.4	0.4	<.1	<.1
09 009	Prospect town	7,775	96.2	2.0	0.5	0.1	<.1	1.2	89	32	38	72	0.2	0.3	<.1	<.1
09 015	Putnam town	9,031	96.8	1.1	0.4	0.4	0.1	1.2	86	26	58	73	0.3	0.3	<.1	<.1
09 001	Ridgefield town	20,919	96.4	0.5	1.3	0.1	<.1	1.5	46	28	82	61	0.6	0.7	<.1	0.2
09 003	Rocky Hill town	16,554	93.8	2.5	1.6	0.1	<.1	2.0	61	62	29	46	0.5	0.6	0.2	0.2
09 009	Seymour town	14,288	97.0	0.8	0.8	<.1	<.1	1.3	69	18	73	69	0.4	0.5	<.1	0.2
09 001	Shelton town	35,418	95.1	0.9	1.3	0.2	<.1	2.5	26	45	67	33	1.1	1.2	0.1	0.4
09 003	Simsbury town...............	22,023	96.3	0.8	1.7	<.1	<.1	1.2	44	30	74	80	0.7	0.8	<.1	0.1
09 013	Somers town	9,108	88.4	7.7	0.7	0.1	0.0	3.0	85	74	16	25	0.3	0.3	0.3	0.1
09 003	South Windsor town	22,090	93.4	2.3	2.4	0.2	<.1	1.7	42	64	33	54	0.7	0.7	0.2	0.2
09 009	Southbury town	15,818	97.7	0.6	0.7	<.1	<.1	1.0	64	7	80	87	0.5	0.6	<.1	<.1
09 003	Southington town............	38,518	97.0	0.9	0.7	<.1	<.1	1.3	24	19	70	67	1.2	1.4	0.1	0.2
09 013	Stafford town	11,091	96.9	0.3	1.2	0.2	<.1	1.4	79	22	92	64	0.3	0.4	<.1	<.1
09 001	Stamford town	108,056	70.6	16.9	2.5	<.1	0.1	9.8	5	90	5	9	3.3	2.8	7.0	5.0
09 011	Stonington town.............	16,919	97.4	0.6	0.5	0.2	<.1	1.3	57	13	81	70	0.5	0.6	<.1	0.1
09 001	Stratford town	49,389	87.6	7.7	0.8	0.1	0.1	3.6	19	77	15	16	1.5	1.6	1.5	0.8
09 015	Thompson town.............	8,668	98.4	0.2	0.3	0.3	<.1	0.8	87	1	95	92	0.3	0.3	<.1	<.1
09 005	Torrington town	33,687	95.9	1.6	1.2	0.2	<.1	1.1	27	37	44	82	1.0	1.2	0.2	0.2
09 001	Trumbull town	32,016	95.2	1.3	1.6	<.1	<.1	1.8	28	43	54	51	1.0	1.1	0.2	0.3
09 013	Vernon town	29,841	93.6	2.2	2.0	0.2	<.1	2.0	30	63	34	45	0.9	1.0	0.2	0.3
09 009	Wallingford town	40,822	94.8	1.0	0.9	0.1	<.1	3.2	23	51	64	20	1.2	1.4	0.2	0.6
09 009	Waterbury town	108,961	73.3	12.1	0.7	0.3	0.2	13.4	4	89	10	6	3.3	2.9	5.1	6.8
09 011	Waterford town	17,930	94.6	2.0	1.3	0.3	<.1	1.7	54	54	39	52	0.5	0.6	0.1	0.1
09 005	Watertown town	20,456	97.1	0.7	0.8	0.2	<.1	1.2	49	17	76	71	0.6	0.7	<.1	0.1
09 003	West Hartford town	60,110	91.8	2.1	2.8	<.1	0.1	3.1	10	70	35	21	1.8	2.0	0.5	0.9
09 009	West Haven town	54,021	81.9	12.2	2.0	0.2	0.1	3.6	13	82	9	17	1.6	1.6	2.5	0.9
09 001	Westport town	24,410	95.0	1.0	1.6	0.1	<.1	2.2	39	46	61	38	0.7	0.8	<.1	0.3
09 003	Wethersfield town	25,651	96.4	1.1	0.8	0.1	<.1	1.6	38	29	59	56	0.8	0.9	0.1	0.2
09 001	Wilton town	15,989	96.1	1.0	1.5	<.1	<.1	1.3	62	33	62	66	0.5	0.6	<.1	<.1
09 015	Windham town...............	22,039	81.0	2.4	1.0	0.4	0.2	15.1	43	85	30	4	0.7	0.6	0.2	1.6
09 003	Windsor Locks town	12,358	95.4	1.4	1.7	0.1	<.1	1.3	76	41	49	68	0.4	0.4	<.1	<.1
09 003	Windsor town................	27,817	77.2	16.8	2.4	0.1	0.1	3.4	34	86	6	18	0.8	0.8	1.8	0.4
09 009	Wolcott town	13,700	96.9	1.5	0.4	0.1	0.0	1.0	71	21	45	83	0.4	0.5	<.1	<.1
	CONGRESSIONAL															
	District 1......................	548,016	74.6	13.3	1.6	0.2	0.2	10.1	2	5	1	2	16.7	14.8	28.0	25.9
	District 2......................	548,041	91.7	3.5	1.3	0.3	<.1	3.0	1	2	5	6	16.7	18.2	7.4	7.7
	District 3......................	547,765	81.7	11.6	1.5	0.2	0.1	4.9	3	4	3	4	16.7	16.3	24.3	12.7
	District 4......................	547,765	74.0	12.5	2.1	0.1	0.2	11.1	4	6	2	1	16.7	14.7	26.2	28.6
	District 5......................	547,764	87.6	4.5	1.3	0.2	0.1	6.2	6	3	4	3	16.7	17.4	9.5	16.0
	District 6......................	547,765	93.1	2.2	1.0	0.1	<.1	3.5	5	1	6	5	16.7	18.5	4.5	9.1

Table B. — 1990 Voting Age Population (VAP) by Race and Ethnic Origin

County	Total Voting Age Population	Percent of total VAP — Non-Hispanic White	Black	Asian and Pacific Islander	Native American	Other	Hispanic	Rank Total	Rank White	Rank Black	Rank Hispanic	% contribution to state VAP Total	White	Black	Hispanic	VAP % of total pop Total	White	Black	Asian and Pacific Islander	Native American	Other	Hispanic
Fairfield	640,520	82.2	8.4	1.8	0.1	0.1	7.4	2	8	3	1	25.2	24.2	29.6	34.8	77.4	79.8	69.1	69.0	77.8	56.1	66.8
Hartford	659,440	83.0	8.7	1.4	0.1	0.1	6.6	1	7	1	2	26.0	25.1	31.8	32.2	77.4	80.2	70.2	69.9	78.1	60.4	61.1
Litchfield	133,373	97.3	0.8	0.7	0.2	<.1	1.0	5	1	8	8	5.3	6.0	0.6	1.0	76.6	76.9	71.6	62.7	74.7	46.8	68.2
Middlesex	111,795	93.7	3.5	1.0	0.2	<.1	1.6	6	4	5	6	4.4	4.8	2.2	1.3	78.1	79.0	67.2	73.3	81.0	29.6	62.6
New Haven	621,601	84.7	8.6	1.2	0.2	<.1	5.2	3	6	2	3	24.5	24.2	29.7	23.7	77.3	79.6	68.0	74.4	72.9	52.4	63.1
New London	194,951	91.4	4.2	1.1	0.5	<.1	2.8	4	5	4	5	7.7	8.2	4.5	4.0	76.5	77.4	70.0	71.0	74.3	45.5	64.1
Tolland	99,693	94.3	2.1	1.9	0.2	<.1	1.6	7	3	6	7	3.9	4.3	1.2	1.2	77.5	77.5	82.1	76.2	73.3	50.0	72.4
Windham	76,162	94.9	0.9	0.6	0.3	<.1	3.2	8	2	7	4	3.0	3.3	0.4	1.8	74.3	75.2	70.5	66.5	67.4	24.3	57.9
CONNECTICUT	**2,537,535**	85.9	7.1	1.4	0.2	<.1	5.4					100.0	100.0	100.0	100.0	77.2	79.1	69.3	70.8	75.2	54.3	63.7
SELECTED TOWNS																						
Ansonia town	14,102	90.1	6.8	0.6	0.2	<.1	2.3	53	74	15	32	0.6	0.6	0.5	0.2	76.6	78.1	63.9	67.8	81.6	15.8	69.6
Berlin town	12,963	97.4	0.5	0.8	<.1	0.0	1.3	58	16	86	62	0.5	0.6	<.1	0.1	77.2	77.5	73.8	59.9	75.0	0.0	74.6
Bethel town	12,815	94.7	1.3	1.8	<.1	<.1	2.1	59	59	51	36	0.5	0.6	<.1	0.2	73.1	73.3	78.4	61.8	71.4	37.5	71.2
Bloomfield town	15,775	59.1	36.8	1.4	0.2	<.1	2.5	48	92	1	28	0.6	0.4	3.2	0.3	81.0	88.1	72.8	80.1	74.3	33.3	67.1
Branford town	22,325	96.2	1.0	1.1	<.1	<.1	1.4	33	37	58	58	0.9	1.0	0.1	0.2	80.9	81.2	73.5	72.9	91.7	52.2	74.1
Bridgeport town	104,694	52.3	22.8	2.1	0.2	0.3	22.4	1	94	4	2	4.1	2.5	13.2	17.2	73.9	84.6	66.9	71.6	78.3	58.6	62.4
Bristol town	47,239	95.3	1.7	0.7	0.1	<.1	2.2	10	54	42	35	1.9	2.1	0.4	0.8	77.9	78.7	66.5	70.7	70.3	28.2	63.1
Brookfield town	10,556	96.3	0.7	1.4	<.1	<.1	1.5	69	36	73	52	0.4	0.5	<.1	0.1	74.8	75.0	79.0	63.7	100.0	100.0	72.3
Brooklyn town	5,007	94.7	1.3	0.9	0.2	<.1	2.9	91	58	52	22	0.2	0.2	<.1	0.1	74.9	75.0	77.6	54.9	56.3	100.0	84.1
Cheshire town	19,347	91.0	4.2	1.6	0.1	<.1	3.0	39	72	20	19	0.8	0.8	0.5	0.4	75.3	74.9	86.0	63.3	96.0	76.5	82.8
Clinton town	9,442	95.5	0.8	0.9	0.3	<.1	2.5	76	47	66	29	0.4	0.4	<.1	0.2	74.0	74.5	61.2	66.2	80.6	16.7	62.8
Coventry town	7,469	98.0	0.8	0.2	0.2	<.1	0.9	83	5	70	85	0.3	0.3	<.1	<.1	74.2	74.5	77.3	56.0	54.2	66.7	54.2
Danbury town	51,284	83.5	5.7	3.3	0.2	0.3	7.1	8	85	19	11	2.0	2.0	1.6	2.7	78.2	79.8	72.7	67.0	81.2	63.2	72.1
Darien town	13,743	96.0	0.4	1.7	<.1	<.1	1.9	55	40	88	42	0.5	0.6	<.1	0.2	75.5	75.8	75.7	62.9	100.0	60.0	75.0
Derby town	9,873	93.3	2.0	0.7	0.1	<.1	3.8	74	67	36	14	0.4	0.4	0.1	0.3	80.9	81.9	69.3	70.2	63.6	38.5	70.3
East Granby town	3,297	97.0	1.5	0.3	0.1	0.0	1.0	95	26	44	77	0.1	0.1	<.1	<.1	76.6	76.7	79.4	68.8	100.0	0.0	66.7
East Hartford town	40,578	85.9	6.8	2.0	0.2	0.1	5.0	16	81	14	12	1.6	1.6	1.5	1.5	80.4	82.8	67.8	74.1	79.3	61.4	72.6
East Haven town	20,867	96.9	0.9	0.4	<.1	<.1	1.8	37	28	64	45	0.8	0.9	0.1	0.3	79.8	80.0	80.3	80.4	76.9	70.0	72.6
East Lyme town	11,991	91.7	4.2	1.2	0.3	<.1	2.5	63	70	21	27	0.5	0.5	0.3	0.2	78.2	77.6	94.8	66.7	78.3	66.7	82.7
East Windsor town	7,930	94.2	3.1	1.1	0.3	<.1	1.2	80	62	25	63	0.3	0.3	0.1	<.1	78.7	79.5	72.5	66.4	53.8	50.0	59.8
Enfield town	35,200	93.8	2.9	0.8	0.1	<.1	2.4	20	65	27	31	1.4	1.5	0.6	0.6	77.3	77.1	87.1	63.3	87.5	18.2	80.2
Essex town	4,760	97.9	0.8	0.3	0.1	0.0	0.9	93	10	65	82	0.2	0.2	<.1	<.1	80.6	80.9	70.2	61.9	100.0	0.0	71.7
Fairfield town	43,038	96.4	0.7	1.1	<.1	<.1	1.7	13	33	74	48	1.7	1.9	0.2	0.5	80.6	80.9	75.3	68.7	84.2	42.9	73.0
Farmington town	16,238	95.1	1.2	1.8	<.1	<.1	1.0	46	42	55	76	0.6	0.7	0.1	0.1	78.8	79.2	71.4	68.9	75.0	35.7	70.0
Glastonbury town	21,417	95.5	0.8	2.0	0.1	<.1	1.6	34	49	72	50	0.8	0.9	<.1	0.3	78.8	77.5	66.9	65.4	88.0	33.3	62.3
Granby town	6,993	98.0	0.5	0.6	0.1	<.1	0.8	85	4	84	89	0.3	0.3	<.1	<.1	74.6	74.8	79.5	60.9	62.5	100.0	62.5
Greenwich town	46,670	90.9	1.9	2.9	<.1	<.1	4.2	11	73	37	13	1.8	1.9	0.5	1.4	79.9	80.6	76.0	67.1	81.8	71.2	75.8
Griswold town	7,583	97.7	0.6	0.4	0.4	<.1	0.9	82	13	79	83	0.3	0.3	<.1	<.1	73.0	73.2	64.9	65.9	76.3	16.7	66.7
Groton town	34,107	88.4	6.0	1.7	0.6	<.1	3.1	22	77	18	17	1.3	1.4	1.1	0.8	75.6	76.5	71.3	69.2	75.3	41.0	65.0
Guilford town	14,885	97.2	0.6	0.6	0.1	<.1	1.5	51	23	82	56	0.6	0.7	<.1	0.2	75.0	75.2	77.6	60.5	78.9	50.0	71.4
Haddam town	5,189	97.9	0.6	0.4	0.2	<.1	0.8	90	9	81	87	0.2	0.2	<.1	<.1	76.7	76.8	93.9	54.8	83.3	100.0	62.9
Hamden town	42,347	88.7	7.9	1.5	<.1	<.1	1.7	15	76	13	47	1.7	1.7	1.9	0.5	80.8	81.8	74.7	72.0	79.6	50.0	68.7
Hartford town	101,349	37.5	34.5	1.4	0.3	0.4	25.9	2	95	2	1	4.0	1.7	19.4	19.3	72.5	89.2	69.7	77.5	81.6	74.7	59.4
Killingly town	11,707	97.3	0.6	1.1	0.4	<.1	0.6	65	22	80	93	0.5	0.5	<.1	<.1	73.7	74.0	64.3	63.5	66.7	22.2	60.2
Ledyard town	10,695	94.8	2.0	1.4	0.5	<.1	1.2	68	57	34	64	0.4	0.5	0.1	<.1	71.7	72.1	71.4	66.0	61.9	25.0	56.1
Litchfield town	6,430	97.9	0.8	0.4	0.3	0.0	0.6	88	6	69	95	0.3	0.3	<.1	<.1	76.9	77.3	64.1	58.7	85.0	0.0	53.5
Madison town	11,612	97.9	0.2	0.6	<.1	0.0	1.2	66	11	94	69	0.5	0.5	<.1	<.1	75.0	75.2	52.7	61.7	78.6	0.0	72.4
Manchester town	40,500	93.3	3.1	1.4	0.1	<.1	2.0	17	66	26	38	1.6	1.7	0.7	0.6	78.5	79.6	64.8	68.6	67.0	44.7	65.4
Mansfield town	18,701	88.1	3.1	5.9	0.1	<.1	2.7	40	78	24	24	0.7	0.8	0.3	0.4	88.6	88.8	88.9	86.0	72.4	93.3	88.0
Meriden town	45,368	84.8	3.4	0.6	0.1	<.1	11.0	12	83	23	5	1.8	1.8	0.8	3.7	76.3	79.4	66.1	67.9	68.1	18.2	61.6
Middlebury town	4,801	97.9	0.3	1.0	<.1	0.0	0.7	92	7	89	92	0.2	0.2	<.1	<.1	78.1	78.2	84.2	73.0	66.7	0.0	74.5
Middletown town	34,524	86.3	9.1	1.9	0.2	<.1	2.5	21	79	12	26	1.4	1.4	1.7	0.6	80.7	83.3	67.7	78.7	87.1	30.2	61.9
Milford town	39,139	95.5	1.4	0.9	0.1	<.1	2.0	19	50	48	37	1.5	1.7	0.3	0.6	78.4	78.8	73.7	72.0	79.5	75.9	68.5
Monroe town	12,283	95.3	1.6	1.1	0.1	<.1	1.8	62	52	43	43	0.5	0.5	0.1	0.2	72.7	73.1	71.0	62.1	80.0	100.0	63.3
Montville town	12,621	92.7	2.7	1.3	0.8	<.1	2.4	61	69	28	30	0.5	0.5	0.2	0.2	75.7	76.0	74.2	74.1	68.1	47.1	70.1
Naugatuck town	22,632	94.5	1.7	0.8	0.2	0.1	2.8	32	61	41	23	0.9	1.0	0.2	0.5	73.9	74.4	57.7	60.0	64.6		66.4
New Britain town	59,553	79.9	6.1	1.6	0.2	0.1	12.1	7	86	17	3	2.3	2.2	2.0	5.3	78.9	84.4	69.5	71.8	78.0	48.9	58.8
New Fairfield town	9,379	97.1	0.3	1.0	0.1	<.1	1.5	77	25	93	53	0.4	0.4	<.1	0.1	72.6	72.9	83.3	59.0	86.7	100.0	66.2
New Hartford town	4,322	98.3	0.3	0.5	<.1	0.0	0.7	94	2	91	91	0.2	0.2	<.1	<.1	74.9	75.1	68.4	54.8	100.0	0.0	66.7
New Haven town	99,538	55.9	30.4	2.7	0.3	0.1	10.6	3	93	3	6	3.9	2.6	16.8	7.8	76.3	87.0	66.4	86.2	79.1	50.9	61.2
New London town	22,772	74.4	13.5	1.9	0.6	<.1	9.5	31	90	7	8	0.9	0.8	1.7	1.6	79.8	85.7	68.0	78.9	83.4	31.0	62.4
New Milford town	17,311	95.6	1.3	1.1	0.2	<.1	1.7	42	45	50	46	0.7	0.8	0.1	0.2	73.3	73.6	69.7	65.1	71.4	47.6	66.6
Newington town	23,571	95.6	1.2	1.2	0.1	<.1	1.9	29	46	54	41	0.9	1.0	0.2	0.3	80.7	81.2	71.7	67.2	82.9	46.7	72.5
Newtown town	15,425	96.1	1.1	1.1	0.1	<.1	1.5	50	38	57	51	0.6	0.7	<.1	0.2	74.2	74.4	82.5	66.3	71.9	100.0	66.4
North Branford town	9,781	97.4	1.2	0.4	0.1	<.1	0.8	75	17	53	90	0.4	0.4	<.1	<.1	75.3	75.4	75.2	65.2	57.9	33.3	66.4
North Haven town	17,670	95.4	2.0	1.5	<.1	<.1	1.0	41	51	33	78	0.7	0.8	0.2	0.1	79.4	79.8	77.1	69.2	100.0	44.4	68.1
Norwalk town	62,574	76.7	13.4	1.5	0.1	0.1	8.2	6	89	8	8	2.5	2.2	4.7	3.8	79.9	83.0	72.0	74.1	82.4	45.3	69.8
Norwich town	28,406	91.7	4.2	1.0	0.6	0.3	2.3	25	71	22	33	1.1	1.2	0.7	0.5	76.0	77.5	62.4	71.2	73.8	55.8	56.8
Old Saybrook town	7,655	96.8	1.4	0.9	<.1	0.0	0.8	81	29	46	86	0.3	0.3	<.1	<.1	80.1	80.6	75.4	72.0	100.0	0.0	60.2

¹Separate rankings for eight counties and 95 towns.

Table B. — 1990 Voting Age Population (VAP) by Race and Ethnic Origin (cont)

County	Total Voting Age Population	Percent of total VAP — Non-Hispanic White	Non-Hispanic Black	Non-Hispanic Asian and Pacific Islander	Non-Hispanic Native American	Non-Hispanic Other	Hispanic	Rank¹ Total	Rank¹ Percent of total VAP Non-Hispanic White	Non-Hispanic Black	Hispanic	Percent contribution to state VAP Total	Non-Hispanic White	Non-Hispanic Black	Hispanic	VAP percent of total population Total	Non-Hispanic White	Non-Hispanic Black	Non-Hispanic Asian and Pacific Islander	Non-Hispanic Native American	Non-Hispanic Other	Hispanic
Orange town	9,990	96.1	0.7	2.0	<.1	<.1	1.1	72	39	75	72	0.4	0.4	<.1	<.1	77.9	78.3	70.2	66.4	75.0	42.9	73.0
Plainfield town	10,288	97.8	0.4	0.4	0.2	0.0	1.2	71	12	87	67	0.4	0.5	<.1	<.1	71.6	72.0	68.2	58.7	58.1	0.0	56.3
Plainville town	13,779	94.9	2.1	0.8	<.1	<.1	2.0	54	56	32	40	0.5	0.6	0.2	0.2	79.2	79.6	71.7	73.0	81.3	38.9	73.3
Plymouth town	8,909	98.3	0.3	0.4	0.1	<.1	0.9	78	3	90	84	0.4	0.4	<.1	<.1	75.4	75.5	67.4	69.6	68.8	100.0	70.3
Prospect town	5,973	96.6	2.0	0.3	0.1	<.1	1.0	89	32	35	79	0.2	0.3	<.1	<.1	76.8	77.1	77.4	48.6	72.7	100.0	62.4
Putnam town	6,766	97.3	0.9	0.4	0.4	<.1	1.0	86	21	62	80	0.3	0.3	<.1	<.1	74.9	75.4	60.4	70.3	77.8	9.1	60.2
Ridgefield town	15,776	96.7	0.5	1.1	0.1	<.1	1.5	47	30	83	57	0.6	0.7	<.1	0.2	75.4	75.6	73.7	64.0	74.2	100.0	71.0
Rocky Hill town	13,636	94.2	2.5	1.4	0.1	<.1	1.8	56	63	29	44	0.5	0.6	0.2	0.2	82.4	82.7	82.3	73.1	78.9	55.6	74.5
Seymour town	11,205	97.6	0.7	0.6	<.1	<.1	1.1	67	15	77	73	0.4	0.5	<.1	<.1	78.4	78.8	67.0	61.6	90.0	100.0	64.2
Shelton town	27,247	95.7	0.8	1.1	0.2	<.1	2.3	26	44	67	34	1.1	1.2	0.1	0.5	76.9	77.4	68.3	66.4	64.1	50.0	70.0
Simsbury town	16,386	96.7	0.8	1.4	<.1	0.0	1.0	45	31	71	75	0.6	0.7	<.1	0.1	74.4	74.7	74.3	63.9	87.5	0.0	66.9
Somers town	7,136	86.1	9.7	0.6	0.1	0.0	3.6	84	80	11	15	0.3	0.3	0.4	0.2	78.3	76.3	98.1	60.6	90.0	0.0	92.7
South Windsor town	16,650	94.0	2.3	2.0	0.2	<.1	1.5	44	64	30	54	0.7	0.7	0.2	0.2	75.4	75.8	77.1	62.7	82.5	67.3	67.3
Southbury town	12,783	97.9	0.6	0.5	<.1	<.1	0.8	60	8	78	88	0.6	0.6	<.1	<.1	80.8	81.0	88.2	63.0	78.6	100.0	68.4
Southington town	29,392	97.4	0.8	0.5	<.1	<.1	1.2	24	19	68	66	1.2	1.3	0.1	0.3	76.3	76.6	73.0	59.1	87.1	35.0	68.3
Stafford town	8,160	97.3	0.3	1.1	0.2	<.1	1.1	79	20	92	71	0.3	0.4	<.1	<.1	73.6	73.9	66.7	68.2	72.7	100.0	57.4
Stamford town	86,283	73.8	14.7	2.3	<.1	<.1	9.0	4	91	6	9	3.4	2.9	7.0	5.7	79.9	83.5	69.3	74.8	76.8	43.9	73.7
Stonington town	13,489	97.6	0.5	0.2	0.0	0.0	1.2	57	14	85	68	0.5	0.6	<.1	0.1	79.7	79.9	70.5	77.3	84.2	0.0	71.4
Stratford town	39,402	89.4	6.6	0.6	0.1	<.1	3.1	18	75	16	18	1.6	1.6	1.4	0.9	79.8	81.4	68.5	63.6	68.1	50.0	68.6
Thompson town	6,523	98.8	0.1	0.2	0.2	0.0	0.6	87	1	95	94	0.3	0.3	<.1	<.1	75.3	75.6	52.9	62.5	42.9	0.0	56.2
Torrington town	26,652	96.4	1.5	1.0	0.1	<.1	0.9	27	34	45	81	1.1	1.2	0.2	0.2	79.1	79.5	72.8	65.2	76.5	50.0	70.3
Trumbull town	24,849	95.9	1.2	1.4	<.1	<.1	1.5	28	41	56	55	1.0	1.1	0.2	0.3	77.6	78.2	72.0	64.3	54.2	16.7	65.2
Vernon town	23,028	94.6	1.8	1.7	0.2	<.1	1.6	30	60	38	49	0.9	1.0	0.2	0.3	77.2	78.0	65.7	66.6	74.0	24.0	63.2
Wallingford town	31,416	95.3	0.9	0.7	0.1	<.1	3.0	23	55	63	20	1.2	1.4	0.2	0.7	77.0	77.3	71.1	61.5	76.2	62.5	71.7
Waterbury town	83,400	77.7	10.8	0.6	0.2	0.2	10.5	5	88	10	7	3.3	3.0	5.0	6.5	76.5	81.1	67.8	69.0	65.1	64.0	60.3
Waterford town	14,448	95.3	1.8	1.2	0.3	<.1	1.4	52	53	40	59	0.6	0.6	0.1	0.2	80.6	81.2	72.0	71.7	72.7	62.5	66.8
Watertown town	15,622	97.4	0.7	0.6	0.2	<.1	1.1	49	18	76	70	0.6	0.7	<.1	0.1	76.4	76.6	75.8	58.1	68.4	66.7	70.6
West Hartford town	48,391	93.0	1.8	2.4	<.1	<.1	2.6	9	68	39	25	1.9	2.1	0.5	0.9	80.5	81.6	69.4	70.1	77.5	52.5	67.5
West Haven town	42,529	83.7	10.9	2.0	0.2	<.1	3.2	14	84	9	16	1.7	1.6	2.6	1.0	78.7	80.5	70.3	78.6	64.8	32.9	70.5
Westport town	19,492	95.5	1.0	1.4	0.1	0.0	2.0	38	48	59	39	0.8	0.9	0.1	0.3	79.9	80.2	80.4	69.5	96.0	0.0	70.6
Wethersfield town	21,043	97.0	0.9	0.6	0.1	<.1	1.4	36	27	61	60	0.8	0.9	0.1	0.2	82.0	82.5	71.7	63.5	80.0	54.5	68.2
Wilton town	11,948	96.4	0.9	1.3	<.1	<.1	1.3	64	35	60	61	0.5	0.5	<.1	0.1	74.7	74.9	72.4	64.0	75.0	50.0	73.6
Windham town	16,936	85.2	2.3	1.0	0.3	<.1	11.1	43	82	31	4	0.7	0.7	0.2	1.4	76.8	80.8	73.7	73.8	74.7	31.4	56.6
Windsor Locks town	9,922	95.8	1.4	1.5	0.1	<.1	1.2	73	43	49	65	0.4	0.4	<.1	<.1	80.3	80.7	76.4	68.1	75.0	50.0	73.0
Windsor town	21,378	79.4	15.4	2.1	0.1	<.1	2.9	35	87	5	21	0.8	0.8	1.8	0.5	76.9	79.1	70.5	68.3	77.1	37.9	65.2
Wolcott town	10,527	97.1	1.4	0.3	0.1	0.0	1.0	70	24	47	74	0.4	0.5	<.1	<.1	76.8	77.0	70.5	63.2	80.0	0.0	76.9
CONGRESSIONAL																						
District 1	423,317	78.2	12.1	1.5	0.2	0.1	7.9	4	5	1	2	16.7	15.2	28.3	24.7	77.2	80.9	70.0	70.9	77.8	65.1	60.9
District 2	421,044	92.7	3.2	1.3	0.3	<.1	2.5	5	2	5	6	16.6	17.9	7.5	7.6	76.8	77.6	70.0	73.1	73.5	41.9	63.0
District 3	426,557	84.2	10.1	1.5	0.2	<.1	4.1	1	4	3	4	16.8	16.5	23.8	12.8	77.9	80.2	67.8	76.4	76.3	50.0	64.3
District 4	426,140	77.3	11.0	1.9	0.1	0.1	9.5	2	6	2	1	16.8	15.1	26.0	29.7	77.8	81.3	68.8	70.6	79.4	54.2	66.2
District 5	416,643	89.2	4.1	1.2	0.2	<.1	5.3	6	3	4	3	16.4	17.0	9.5	16.2	76.1	77.4	69.4	65.6	70.7	58.2	64.3
District 6	423,834	94.0	2.0	0.9	0.1	<.1	2.9	3	1	6	5	16.7	18.3	4.8	9.0	77.4	78.2	73.6	66.5	77.2	42.9	62.9

¹Separate rankings for eight counties and 95 towns.

Table C. – Voter Participation: November 3, 1992, General Election

County	Estimated Voting Age Population (VAP) 1992	Voter registration (REG) Total	% contribution to state REG	% of 1992 VAP	Rank by % of 1992 VAP	Voter turnout Highest office Actual	Total	Office	% of 1992 VAP	Maximum vote Total	% contribution to state turnout	% of REG	Rank by % of REG¹	% of 1992 VAP	Rank by % of 1992 VAP	Percent drop-off President	Senator	Governor	Representative
Fairfield	637,509	488,559	24.9	76.6	5	416,238	409,410	P	64.2	416,238	25.3	85.2	4	65.3	4	1.6	9.8	-	15.1
Hartford	658,792	509,750	26.0	77.4	4	421,126	414,804	P	63.0	421,126	25.6	82.6	7	63.9	6	1.5	7.3	-	12.7
Litchfield	135,391	108,010	5.5	79.8	2	94,494	93,213	P	68.8	94,494	5.7	87.5	2	69.8	2	1.4	7.7	-	14.7
Middlesex	112,818	94,049	4.8	83.4	1	82,034	81,027	P	71.8	82,034	5.0	87.2	3	72.7	1	1.2	7.1	-	10.2
New Haven	619,311	485,083	24.7	78.3	3	395,583	385,132	P	62.2	395,583	24.0	81.5	8	63.9	7	2.6	10.3	-	12.0
New London	194,537	143,102	7.3	73.6	8	119,596	117,767	P	60.5	119,596	7.3	83.6	6	61.5	8	1.5	8.1	-	9.5
Tolland	99,427	74,603	3.8	75.0	7	66,988	66,215	P	66.6	66,988	4.1	89.8	1	67.4	3	1.2	7.2	-	11.1
Windham	77,215	58,347	3.0	75.6	6	49,550	48,588	P	62.9	49,550	3.0	84.9	5	64.2	5	1.9	10.0	-	11.5
CONNECTICUT	2,535,000	1,961,503	100.0	77.4		1,645,609	1,616,156		63.8	1,645,609	100.0	83.9		64.9		1.8	8.8	-	12.8
SELECTED TOWNS																			
Ansonia town	-	11,255	0.6	-	-	8,813	8,481	P	-	8,813	0.5	78.3	91	-	-	3.8	8.2	-	15.3
Berlin town	-	11,379	0.6	-	-	10,376	10,219	P	-	10,376	0.6	91.2	5	-	-	1.5	8.3	-	13.2
Bethel town	-	10,501	0.5	-	-	9,435	9,337	P	-	9,435	0.6	89.8	17	-	-	1.0	10.8	-	11.5
Bloomfield town	-	13,081	0.7	-	-	10,844	10,572	P	-	10,844	0.7	82.9	78	-	-	2.5	7.6	-	9.8
Branford town	-	18,104	0.9	-	-	15,625	15,263	P	-	15,625	0.9	86.3	52	-	-	2.3	9.4	-	9.9
Bridgeport town	-	61,934	3.2	-	-	44,218	41,956	P	-	44,218	2.7	71.4	93	-	-	5.1	17.1	-	26.2
Bristol town	-	34,840	1.8	-	-	28,608	28,274	P	-	28,608	1.7	82.1	82	-	-	1.2	8.4	-	19.2
Brookfield town	-	9,689	0.5	-	-	8,486	8,446	P	-	8,486	0.5	87.6	38	-	-	0.5	7.4	-	8.6
Brooklyn town	-	3,771	0.2	-	-	3,312	3,252	P	-	3,312	0.2	87.8	36	-	-	1.8	7.5	-	9.2
Cheshire town	-	16,238	0.8	-	-	14,715	14,556	P	-	14,715	0.9	90.6	11	-	-	1.1	6.6	-	10.5
Clinton town	-	7,957	0.4	-	-	7,031	6,968	P	-	7,031	0.4	88.4	29	-	-	0.9	8.2	-	8.9
Coventry town	-	6,358	0.3	-	-	5,669	5,601	P	-	5,669	0.3	89.2	24	-	-	1.2	7.1	-	10.9
Danbury town	-	32,029	1.6	-	-	26,324	25,840	P	-	26,324	1.6	82.2	80	-	-	1.8	12.1	-	12.5
Darien town	-	12,286	0.6	-	-	11,133	10,987	P	-	11,133	0.7	90.6	12	-	-	1.3	7.1	-	10.4
Derby town	-	6,816	0.3	-	-	5,845	5,725	P	-	5,845	0.4	85.8	59	-	-	2.1	10.8	-	16.7
East Granby town	-	2,936	0.1	-	-	2,610	2,582	P	-	2,610	0.2	88.9	26	-	-	1.1	6.1	-	13.0
East Hartford town	-	27,746	1.4	-	-	23,826	23,512	P	-	23,826	1.4	85.9	57	-	-	1.3	8.0	-	11.7
East Haven town	-	16,098	0.8	-	-	13,864	13,640	P	-	13,864	0.8	86.1	53	-	-	1.6	13.6	-	10.8
East Lyme town	-	9,884	0.5	-	-	8,491	8,356	P	-	8,491	0.5	85.9	56	-	-	1.6	7.5	-	9.7
East Windsor town	-	5,936	0.3	-	-	4,858	4,818	P	-	4,858	0.3	81.8	84	-	-	0.8	8.7	-	12.5
Enfield town	-	27,333	1.4	-	-	22,377	22,036	P	-	22,377	1.4	81.9	83	-	-	1.5	8.3	-	18.6
Essex town	-	4,365	0.2	-	-	3,804	3,764	P	-	3,804	0.2	87.1	42	-	-	1.1	5.6	-	9.3
Fairfield town	-	36,370	1.9	-	-	32,486	32,120	P	-	32,486	2.0	89.3	22	-	-	1.1	7.2	-	15.8
Farmington town	-	14,102	0.7	-	-	12,459	12,374	P	-	12,459	0.8	88.3	30	-	-	0.7	6.5	-	14.0
Glastonbury town	-	19,251	1.0	-	-	17,766	17,586	P	-	17,766	1.1	92.3	2	-	-	1.0	5.3	-	7.4
Granby town	-	6,519	0.3	-	-	5,633	5,590	P	-	5,633	0.3	86.4	50	-	-	0.8	5.6	-	12.1
Greenwich town	-	37,437	1.9	-	-	32,769	32,476	P	-	32,769	2.0	87.5	39	-	-	0.9	8.2	-	15.4
Griswold town	-	5,340	0.3	-	-	4,458	4,325	P	-	4,458	0.3	83.5	74	-	-	3.0	11.1	-	13.1
Groton town	-	19,302	1.0	-	-	15,374	15,202	P	-	15,374	0.9	79.6	88	-	-	1.1	9.0	-	10.5
Guilford town	-	13,618	0.7	-	-	11,836	11,714	P	-	11,836	0.7	86.9	44	-	-	1.0	7.2	-	8.0
Haddam town	-	4,927	0.3	-	-	4,356	4,317	P	-	4,356	0.3	88.4	28	-	-	0.9	7.2	-	6.7
Hamden town	-	35,697	1.8	-	-	29,086	28,487	P	-	29,086	1.8	81.5	85	-	-	2.1	9.1	-	9.3
Hartford town	-	66,675	3.4	-	-	38,136	36,797	P	-	38,136	2.3	57.2	95	-	-	3.5	9.5	-	13.5
Killingly town	-	7,967	0.4	-	-	6,739	6,479	P	-	6,739	0.4	84.6	69	-	-	3.9	11.8	-	11.9
Ledyard town	-	8,639	0.4	-	-	7,245	7,140	P	-	7,245	0.4	83.9	72	-	-	1.4	10.0	-	7.7
Litchfield town	-	5,599	0.3	-	-	4,767	4,615	P	-	4,767	0.3	85.1	65	-	-	3.2	6.7	-	13.5
Madison town	-	11,501	0.6	-	-	10,103	9,999	P	-	10,103	0.6	87.8	35	-	-	1.0	7.5	-	8.8
Manchester town	-	33,148	1.7	-	-	28,547	28,271	P	-	28,547	1.7	86.1	54	-	-	1.0	6.3	-	9.9
Mansfield town	-	8,778	0.4	-	-	7,992	7,900	P	-	7,992	0.5	91.0	6	-	-	1.2	6.6	-	9.7
Meriden town	-	31,528	1.6	-	-	26,732	25,979	P	-	26,732	1.6	84.8	68	-	-	2.8	11.4	-	18.3
Middlebury town	-	4,227	0.2	-	-	3,845	3,798	P	-	3,845	0.2	91.0	8	-	-	1.2	9.1	-	8.7
Middletown town	-	25,172	1.3	-	-	21,581	21,114	P	-	21,581	1.3	85.7	60	-	-	2.2	9.1	-	13.0
Milford town	-	33,079	1.7	-	-	27,173	26,708	P	-	27,173	1.7	82.1	81	-	-	1.7	11.1	-	9.2
Monroe town	-	10,719	0.5	-	-	9,732	9,643	P	-	9,732	0.6	90.8	9	-	-	0.9	7.7	-	17.5
Montville town	-	9,220	0.5	-	-	8,287	8,198	P	-	8,287	0.5	89.9	15	-	-	1.1	7.2	-	9.4
Naugatuck town	-	16,327	0.8	-	-	14,124	13,883	P	-	14,124	0.9	86.5	48	-	-	1.7	9.7	-	11.7
New Britain town	-	32,048	1.6	-	-	27,094	26,317	P	-	27,094	1.6	84.5	70	-	-	2.9	11.7	-	20.2
New Fairfield town	-	8,074	0.4	-	-	7,254	7,209	P	-	7,254	0.4	89.8	18	-	-	0.6	10.3	-	10.7
New Hartford town	-	3,892	0.2	-	-	3,481	3,450	P	-	3,481	0.2	89.4	21	-	-	0.9	6.3	-	12.6
New Haven town	-	71,716	3.7	-	-	46,020	43,261	P	-	46,020	2.8	64.2	94	-	-	6.0	12.7	-	16.9
New London town	-	13,683	0.7	-	-	9,989	9,738	P	-	9,989	0.6	73.0	92	-	-	2.5	13.3	-	13.1
New Milford town	-	13,419	0.7	-	-	11,836	11,760	P	-	11,836	0.7	88.2	32	-	-	0.6	8.6	-	16.7
Newington town	-	19,698	1.0	-	-	17,072	16,823	P	-	17,072	1.0	86.7	45	-	-	1.5	6.8	-	10.1
Newtown town	-	12,633	0.6	-	-	11,499	11,410	P	-	11,499	0.7	91.0	7	-	-	0.8	9.2	-	11.7
North Branford town	-	9,082	0.5	-	-	7,220	7,115	P	-	7,220	0.4	79.5	89	-	-	1.5	10.5	-	11.3
North Haven town	-	15,590	0.8	-	-	13,707	13,518	P	-	13,707	0.8	87.9	34	-	-	1.4	10.0	-	9.9
Norwalk town	-	45,217	2.3	-	-	37,518	37,455	P	-	37,518	2.3	83.0	77	-	-	0.2	8.1	-	15.6
Norwich town	-	18,983	1.0	-	-	16,202	15,850	P	-	16,202	1.0	85.4	64	-	-	2.2	8.7	-	10.4
Old Saybrook town	-	7,057	0.4	-	-	6,018	6,053	P	-	6,053	0.4	85.8	58	-	-	0.0	6.6	-	9.5

¹Separate rankings for eight counties and 95 cities and towns.

Table C. — **Voter Participation: November 3, 1992, General Election (cont)**

| County | Estimated Voting Age Population (VAP) 1992 | Voter registration (REG) | | | | Voter turnout | | | | | | | | | | | | | |
| | | | | | | | Highest office | | | Maximum vote | | | | | | Percent drop-off, by office | | | |
		Total	% contribution to state REG	% of 1992 VAP	Rank by % of 1992 VAP	Actual	Total	Office	% of 1992 VAP	Total	% contribution to state turnout	% of REG	Rank by % of REG¹	% of 1992 VAP	Rank by % 1992 VAP	President	Senator	Governor	Representative
Orange town..................	-	9,553	0.5	-	-	8,341	8,290	P	-	8,341	0.5	87.3	41	-	-	0.6	7.4	-	7.5
Plainfield town	-	7,400	0.4	-	-	6,147	6,010	P	-	6,147	0.4	83.1	75	-	-	2.2	9.8	-	11.1
Plainville town	-	9,909	0.5	-	-	8,830	8,684	P	-	8,830	0.5	89.1	25	-	-	1.7	8.7	-	16.6
Plymouth town	-	6,562	0.3	-	-	5,508	5,445	P	-	5,508	0.3	83.9	71	-	-	1.1	5.7	-	14.1
Prospect town	-	5,215	0.3	-	-	4,702	4,657	P	-	4,702	0.3	90.2	14	-	-	1.0	8.2	-	10.2
Putnam town	-	5,298	0.3	-	-	4,265	4,168	P	-	4,265	0.3	80.5	87	-	-	2.3	10.5	-	12.8
Ridgefield town	-	14,976	0.8	-	-	13,408	13,291	P	-	13,408	0.8	89.5	20	-	-	0.9	7.0	-	8.4
Rocky Hill town	-	11,180	0.6	-	-	9,557	9,447	P	-	9,557	0.6	85.5	62	-	-	1.2	7.4	-	10.9
Seymour town	-	8,960	0.5	-	-	7,746	7,737	P	-	7,746	0.5	86.5	49	-	-	0.1	7.2	-	13.1
Shelton town	-	22,170	1.1	-	-	19,605	18,899	P	-	19,605	1.2	88.4	27	-	-	3.6	8.3	-	11.9
Simsbury town	-	15,598	0.8	-	-	13,921	13,776	P	-	13,921	0.8	89.2	23	-	-	1.0	4.6	-	10.8
Somers town	-	4,932	0.3	-	-	4,556	4,478	P	-	4,556	0.3	92.4	1	-	-	1.7	7.6	-	13.3
South Windsor town........	-	14,478	0.7	-	-	13,313	13,084	P	-	13,313	0.8	92.0	3	-	-	1.7	6.3	-	10.5
Southbury town	-	11,312	0.6	-	-	9,786	9,705	P	-	9,786	0.6	86.5	47	-	-	0.8	6.0	-	11.7
Southington town	-	23,785	1.2	-	-	20,444	20,210	P	-	20,444	1.2	86.0	55	-	-	1.1	6.9	-	14.4
Stafford town	-	6,935	0.4	-	-	6,076	5,969	P	-	6,076	0.4	87.6	37	-	-	1.8	9.5	-	13.1
Stamford town	-	59,453	3.0	-	-	50,775	49,926	P	-	50,775	3.1	85.4	63	-	-	1.7	11.2	-	17.5
Stonington town	-	11,648	0.6	-	-	9,669	9,534	P	-	9,669	0.6	83.0	76	-	-	1.4	9.6	-	12.1
Stratford town	-	31,923	1.6	-	-	27,131	26,769	P	-	27,131	1.6	85.0	66	-	-	1.3	10.5	-	12.0
Thompson town	-	5,166	0.3	-	-	4,564	4,515	P	-	4,564	0.3	88.3	31	-	-	1.1	12.7	-	13.8
Torrington town	-	19,609	1.0	-	-	17,273	16,995	P	-	17,273	1.0	88.1	33	-	-	1.6	8.0	-	15.6
Trumbull town	-	23,487	1.2	-	-	20,288	19,974	P	-	20,288	1.2	86.4	51	-	-	1.5	8.8	-	16.8
Vernon town	-	16,830	0.9	-	-	15,097	14,893	P	-	15,097	0.9	89.7	19	-	-	1.4	7.6	-	11.9
Wallingford town	-	25,400	1.3	-	-	22,205	22,011	P	-	22,205	1.3	87.4	40	-	-	0.9	9.1	-	9.4
Waterbury town	-	56,498	2.9	-	-	44,578	41,896	P	-	44,578	2.7	78.9	90	-	-	6.0	12.4	-	12.4
Waterford town	-	12,536	0.6	-	-	10,120	9,966	S	-	10,120	0.6	80.7	86	-	-	1.7	1.5	-	3.3
Watertown town	-	12,998	0.7	-	-	11,250	11,088	P	-	11,250	0.7	86.6	46	-	-	1.4	9.6	-	14.7
West Hartford town	-	43,957	2.2	-	-	37,311	37,046	P	-	37,311	2.3	84.9	67	-	-	0.7	4.9	-	6.6
West Haven town	-	31,242	1.6	-	-	26,122	25,599	P	-	26,122	1.6	83.6	73	-	-	2.0	13.0	-	12.6
Westport town	-	18,224	0.9	-	-	16,376	16,216	P	-	16,376	1.0	89.9	16	-	-	1.0	7.9	-	13.5
Wethersfield town	-	18,244	0.9	-	-	16,486	16,305	P	-	16,486	1.0	90.4	13	-	-	1.1	6.8	-	9.4
Wilton town....................	-	11,090	0.6	-	-	10,117	10,022	P	-	10,117	0.6	91.2	4	-	-	0.9	5.8	-	10.1
Windham town	-	11,741	0.6	-	-	9,713	9,512	P	-	9,713	0.6	82.7	79	-	-	2.1	10.7	-	14.0
Windsor Locks town	-	7,861	0.4	-	-	6,834	6,695	P	-	6,834	0.4	86.9	43	-	-	2.0	8.5	-	17.4
Windsor town	-	17,702	0.9	-	-	15,153	15,046	P	-	15,153	0.9	85.6	61	-	-	0.7	6.5	-	10.0
Wolcott town..................	-	8,817	0.4	-	-	8,004	7,872	P	-	8,004	0.5	90.8	10	-	-	1.6	9.3	-	12.2

¹Separate rankings for eight counties and 95 cities and towns.

Table D. — Voter Registration by Political Party Affiliation: November 3, 1992, General Election

County	Total voter registration	Political party affiliation Democrat (DEM)[1]	Republican (REP)[1]	Independent (IND)[1]	Plurality Total	Plurality Party	Percent of total registration DEM	REP	IND	Rank[2] DEM	REP	IND	Percent contribution to state registration Total	DEM	REP	IND
Fairfield	488,559	156,037	159,875	168,675	8,800	I	32.2	33.0	34.8	7	1	7	24.9	21.2	31.6	23.8
Hartford	509,750	234,285	118,358	153,842	80,443	D	46.3	23.4	30.4	1	7	8	26.0	31.8	23.4	21.7
Litchfield	108,010	30,981	33,951	42,685	8,734	I	28.8	31.5	39.7	8	2	3	5.5	4.2	6.7	6.0
Middlesex..............	94,049	32,414	24,944	36,488	4,074	I	34.5	26.6	38.9	4	3	5	4.8	4.4	4.9	5.1
New Haven.............	485,083	190,041	103,063	191,061	1,020	I	39.3	21.3	39.5	2	8	4	24.7	25.8	20.4	27.0
New London	143,102	47,627	33,976	61,030	13,403	I	33.4	23.8	42.8	5	5	2	7.3	6.5	6.7	8.6
Tolland	74,603	24,685	17,346	32,642	7,957	I	33.1	23.2	43.7	6	6	1	3.8	3.3	3.4	4.6
Windham.................	58,347	20,844	14,602	22,161	1,317	I	36.2	25.3	38.5	3	4	6	3.0	2.8	2.9	3.1
CONNECTICUT[3]	**1,961,503**	**736,914**	**506,115**	**708,584**	**28,330**	**D**	**37.8**	**25.9**	**36.3**				**100.0**	**100.0**	**100.0**	**100.0**
SELECTED TOWNS																
Ansonia town	11,255	5,078	1,825	4,217	861	D	45.7	16.4	37.9	19	89	50	0.6	0.7	0.4	0.6
Berlin town.................	11,379	5,299	3,212	2,857	2,087	D	46.6	28.3	25.1	13	36	89	0.6	0.7	0.6	0.4
Bethel town	10,501	2,526	3,033	4,842	1,809	I	24.3	29.2	46.6	75	33	18	0.5	0.3	0.6	0.7
Bloomfield town	13,081	6,834	2,548	3,591	3,243	D	52.7	19.6	27.7	6	74	86	0.7	0.9	0.5	0.5
Branford town	18,104	5,307	3,326	9,408	4,101	I	29.4	18.4	52.1	54	82	3	0.9	0.7	0.7	1.3
Bridgeport town	61,934	36,194	9,956	15,310	20,884	D	58.9	16.2	24.9	4	90	90	3.2	4.9	2.0	2.2
Bristol town	34,840	15,541	6,792	11,942	3,599	D	45.3	19.8	34.8	20	72	65	1.8	2.1	1.3	1.7
Brookfield town	9,689	2,160	4,034	3,489	545	R	22.3	41.7	36.0	82	10	58	0.5	0.3	0.8	0.5
Brooklyn town	3,771	1,221	803	1,730	509	I	32.5	21.4	46.1	44	64	20	0.2	0.2	0.2	0.2
Cheshire town	16,238	3,511	4,774	7,913	3,139	I	21.7	29.5	48.9	86	31	11	0.8	0.5	0.9	1.1
Clinton town	7,957	2,303	2,646	2,994	348	I	29.0	33.3	37.7	56	22	49	0.4	0.3	0.5	0.4
Coventry town	6,358	2,071	1,505	2,757	686	I	32.7	23.8	43.5	43	54	31	0.3	0.3	0.3	0.4
Danbury town	32,029	10,507	7,601	13,591	3,084	I	33.1	24.0	42.9	41	53	36	1.6	1.4	1.5	1.9
Darien town................	12,286	2,032	7,840	2,369	5,471	R	16.6	64.0	19.4	95	1	93	0.6	0.3	1.5	0.3
Derby town.................	6,816	3,469	1,077	2,178	1,291	D	51.6	16.0	32.4	7	92	64	0.3	0.5	0.2	0.3
East Granby town	2,936	774	1,060	1,091	31	I	26.5	36.2	37.3	68	17	51	0.1	0.1	0.2	0.2
East Hartford town	27,746	15,452	4,438	7,632	7,820	D	56.1	16.1	27.7	5	91	85	1.4	2.1	0.9	1.1
East Haven town	16,098	7,337	3,001	7,534	197	I	41.1	16.8	42.2	16	78	15	0.8	1.0	0.6	1.1
East Lyme town	9,884	2,699	2,726	4,392	1,666	I	27.5	27.8	44.7	62	37	27	0.5	0.4	0.5	0.6
East Windsor town........	5,936	2,008	1,337	2,417	409	I	34.8	23.2	41.9	39	59	40	0.3	0.3	0.3	0.3
Enfield town	27,333	11,778	5,528	9,911	1,867	D	43.3	20.3	36.4	25	69	57	1.4	1.6	1.1	1.4
Essex town	4,365	980	1,652	1,722	70	I	22.5	37.9	39.5	79	15	44	0.2	0.1	0.3	0.2
Fairfield town	36,370	9,662	11,971	14,508	2,537	I	26.7	33.1	40.1	67	24	43	1.9	1.3	2.4	2.0
Farmington town	14,102	4,324	4,596	5,121	525	I	30.8	32.7	36.5	49	25	56	0.7	0.6	0.9	0.7
Glastonbury town	19,251	6,089	6,607	6,445	162	R	31.8	34.5	33.7	45	21	72	1.0	0.8	1.3	0.9
Granby town................	6,519	1,620	2,435	2,464	29	I	24.9	37.4	37.8	71	16	48	0.3	0.2	0.5	0.3
Greenwich town	37,437	7,480	17,193	12,735	4,458	R	20.0	46.0	34.0	89	4	67	1.9	1.0	3.4	1.8
Griswold town	5,340	2,556	982	1,777	779	D	48.1	18.5	33.4	9	81	73	0.3	0.3	0.2	0.3
Groton town	19,302	5,517	4,786	8,770	3,253	I	28.9	25.1	46.0	57	50	22	1.0	0.7	0.9	1.2
Guilford town	13,618	3,694	4,296	5,540	1,244	I	27.3	31.8	40.9	64	28	41	0.7	0.5	0.8	0.8
Haddam town	4,927	1,527	1,271	2,111	584	I	31.1	25.9	43.0	47	44	33	0.3	0.2	0.3	0.3
Hamden town	35,697	11,775	7,920	15,281	3,506	I	33.7	22.6	43.7	40	62	34	1.8	1.6	1.6	2.2
Hartford town	66,675	49,998	6,139	10,211	39,787	D	75.4	9.3	15.4	1	94	95	3.4	6.8	1.2	1.4
Killingly town	7,967	1,490	2,752	3,659	907	I	18.9	34.8	46.3	93	20	19	0.4	0.2	0.5	0.5
Ledyard town	8,639	2,111	2,658	3,953	1,295	I	24.2	30.5	45.3	73	29	21	0.4	0.3	0.5	0.6
Litchfield town	5,599	1,455	2,182	1,932	250	R	26.1	39.2	34.7	69	13	63	0.3	0.2	0.4	0.3
Madison town..............	11,501	2,279	4,518	4,685	167	I	19.8	39.3	40.8	90	11	39	0.6	0.3	0.9	0.7
Manchester town..........	33,148	13,206	8,989	10,866	2,340	D	39.9	27.2	32.9	33	40	77	1.7	1.8	1.8	1.5
Mansfield town.............	8,778	3,791	1,694	3,231	560	D	43.5	19.4	37.1	23	75	54	0.4	0.5	0.3	0.5
Meriden town	31,528	10,831	5,608	14,988	4,157	I	34.5	17.8	47.7	37	84	12	1.6	1.5	1.1	2.1
Middlebury town	4,227	943	1,836	1,428	408	R	22.4	43.6	33.9	81	6	70	0.2	0.1	0.4	0.2
Middletown town	25,172	11,958	4,690	8,595	3,363	D	47.4	18.6	34.0	10	79	66	1.3	1.6	0.9	1.2
Milford town	33,079	9,227	8,005	15,552	6,325	I	28.1	24.4	47.4	59	52	14	1.7	1.3	1.6	2.2
Monroe town	10,719	2,060	3,089	5,606	2,517	I	19.2	28.7	52.1	92	34	2	0.5	0.3	0.6	0.8
Montville town	9,220	2,755	1,757	4,767	2,012	I	29.7	18.9	51.4	53	76	5	0.5	0.4	0.3	0.7
Naugatuck town	16,327	6,220	2,788	7,194	974	I	38.4	17.2	44.4	35	87	28	0.8	0.8	0.6	1.0
New Britain town	32,048	20,296	6,349	5,110	13,947	D	63.9	20.0	16.1	3	71	94	1.6	2.8	1.3	0.7
New Fairfield town.........	8,074	1,647	3,369	2,999	370	R	20.5	42.0	37.4	87	9	52	0.4	0.2	0.7	0.4
New Haven town	71,716	50,273	5,606	15,245	35,028	D	70.7	7.9	21.4	2	95	91	3.7	6.8	1.1	2.2
New London town	13,683	6,479	2,293	4,881	1,598	D	47.5	16.8	35.8	11	88	59	0.7	0.9	0.5	0.7
New Milford town..........	13,419	3,149	4,665	5,502	837	I	23.6	35.0	41.3	76	19	38	0.7	0.4	0.9	0.8
Newington town	19,698	8,615	4,599	6,495	2,120	D	43.7	23.3	33.0	22	55	75	1.0	1.2	0.9	0.9
Newtown town	12,633	3,193	4,962	4,405	557	R	25.4	39.5	35.1	70	12	61	0.6	0.4	1.0	0.6
North Branford town	9,082	1,994	1,966	5,066	3,072	I	22.1	21.8	56.1	83	63	1	0.5	0.3	0.4	0.7
North Haven town	15,590	3,141	5,173	7,192	2,019	I	20.3	33.4	46.4	88	23	17	0.8	0.4	1.0	1.0
Norwalk town	45,217	14,796	11,347	16,676	1,880	I	34.6	26.5	38.9	42	49	53	2.3	2.0	2.2	2.4
Norwich town..............	18,983	8,009	3,518	7,419	590	D	42.3	18.6	39.2	27	80	45	1.0	1.1	0.7	1.0
Old Saybrook town	7,057	1,700	3,041	2,278	763	R	24.2	43.3	32.5	74	7	79	0.4	0.2	0.6	0.3

[1]Data from report dated October 20, 1992; sum of registrants by party differs slightly from total voter registration reported with November 1992 general election returns.
[2]Separate rankings for eight counties and 95 towns. [3]Total voter registration also includes 1,770 for A Connecticut Party (ACP), 58 for Concerned Citizens party, 42 for Green party, 637 for Independent party, 1,006 for Independent Party of Norwalk, 21 for Libertarian party, 33 for North Haven party, 31 for Taxpayers' party, and 57 for other (as reported October 20, 1992).

County	Total voter registration	Political party affiliation			Plurality		Percent of total registration			Rank[2]			Percent contribution to state registration			
		Democrat (DEM)[1]	Republican (REP)[1]	Independent (IND)[1]	Total	Party	DEM	REP	IND	DEM	REP	IND	Total	DEM	REP	IND
Orange town.................	9,553	1,873	3,055	4,849	1,794	I	19.2	31.2	49.6	91	27	7	0.5	0.3	0.6	0.7
Plainfield town	7,400	2,936	1,270	3,093	157	I	40.2	17.4	42.4	34	86	37	0.4	0.4	0.3	0.4
Plainville town	9,909	4,277	2,275	3,358	919	D	43.2	23.0	33.9	24	57	69	0.5	0.6	0.4	0.5
Plymouth town	6,562	1,869	1,394	3,280	1,411	I	28.6	21.3	50.1	58	65	8	0.3	0.3	0.3	0.5
Prospect town	5,215	1,192	1,689	2,231	542	I	23.3	33.0	43.6	78	26	35	0.3	0.2	0.3	0.3
Putnam town	5,298	2,343	1,109	1,820	523	D	44.4	21.0	34.5	21	67	64	0.3	0.3	0.2	0.3
Ridgefield town	14,976	3,686	7,273	4,033	3,240	R	24.6	48.5	26.9	72	3	88	0.8	0.5	1.4	0.6
Rocky Hill town	11,180	4,811	2,588	3,774	1,037	D	43.1	23.2	33.8	26	56	71	0.6	0.7	0.5	0.5
Seymour town	8,960	2,003	2,291	4,640	2,349	I	22.4	25.6	51.9	80	46	4	0.5	0.3	0.5	0.7
Shelton town	22,170	4,829	6,315	10,862	4,547	I	21.9	28.7	49.4	84	35	10	1.1	0.7	1.2	1.5
Simsbury town	15,598	4,226	6,935	4,385	2,550	R	27.2	44.6	28.2	65	5	84	0.8	0.6	1.4	0.6
Somers town	4,932	1,362	1,338	2,224	862	I	27.7	27.2	45.2	60	39	24	0.3	0.2	0.3	0.3
South Windsor town.......	14,478	5,485	3,637	5,328	157	D	38.0	25.2	36.9	36	47	55	0.7	0.7	0.7	0.8
Southbury town	11,312	2,078	4,842	4,336	506	R	18.5	43.0	38.5	94	8	47	0.6	0.3	1.0	0.6
Southington town	23,785	8,063	5,328	10,348	2,285	I	34.0	22.4	43.6	38	60	29	1.2	1.1	1.1	1.5
Stafford town	6,935	3,213	983	2,704	509	D	46.6	14.2	39.2	15	93	46	0.4	0.4	0.2	0.4
Stamford town	59,453	27,079	20,923	11,840	6,156	D	45.3	35.0	19.8	17	18	92	3.0	3.7	4.1	1.7
Stonington town	11,648	3,410	2,926	5,250	1,840	I	29.4	25.3	45.3	55	48	25	0.6	0.5	0.6	0.7
Stratford town	31,923	8,744	6,692	16,475	7,731	I	27.4	21.0	51.6	61	66	6	1.6	1.2	1.3	2.3
Thompson town	5,166	2,405	1,060	1,674	731	D	46.8	20.6	32.6	14	68	78	0.3	0.3	0.2	0.2
Torrington town	19,609	7,816	5,301	6,455	1,361	D	39.9	27.1	33.0	32	41	76	1.0	1.1	1.0	0.9
Trumbull town	23,487	5,476	6,959	11,057	4,098	I	23.3	29.6	47.1	77	30	13	1.2	0.7	1.4	1.6
Vernon town..................	16,830	5,249	3,745	7,769	2,520	I	31.3	22.3	46.3	46	61	16	0.9	0.7	0.7	1.1
Wallingford town	25,400	7,802	4,949	12,492	4,690	I	30.9	19.6	49.5	48	73	9	1.3	1.1	1.0	1.8
Waterbury town	56,498	28,338	11,402	16,731	11,607	D	50.2	20.2	29.6	8	70	83	2.9	3.8	2.3	2.4
Waterford town	12,536	3,819	3,046	5,643	1,824	I	30.5	24.4	45.1	51	51	26	0.6	0.5	0.6	0.8
Watertown town	12,998	3,531	3,557	5,874	2,317	I	27.2	27.4	45.3	63	38	23	0.7	0.5	0.7	0.8
West Hartford town	43,957	18,362	11,430	13,666	4,696	D	42.3	26.3	31.4	29	43	82	2.2	2.5	2.3	1.9
West Haven town	31,242	14,692	5,426	11,116	3,576	D	47.0	17.4	35.6	12	85	60	1.6	2.0	1.1	1.6
Westport town	18,224	5,446	6,984	5,722	1,262	R	30.0	38.5	31.5	52	14	81	0.9	0.7	1.4	0.8
Wethersfield town	18,244	7,475	4,701	6,046	1,429	D	41.0	25.8	33.2	30	45	74	0.9	1.0	0.9	0.9
Wilton town...................	11,090	2,404	5,524	3,007	2,517	R	22.0	50.5	27.5	85	2	87	0.6	0.3	1.1	0.4
Windham town	11,741	5,346	2,103	4,059	1,287	D	46.5	18.3	35.3	18	83	62	0.6	0.7	0.4	0.6
Windsor Locks town	7,861	3,191	1,475	3,173	18	D	40.7	18.8	40.5	31	77	42	0.4	0.4	0.3	0.4
Windsor town	17,702	7,428	4,049	6,015	1,413	D	42.5	23.1	34.4	28	58	68	0.9	1.0	0.8	0.8
Wolcott town.................	8,817	2,695	2,315	3,787	1,092	I	30.6	26.3	43.0	50	42	32	0.4	0.4	0.5	0.5

[1]Data from report dated October 20, 1992; sum of registrants by party differs slightly from total voter registration reported with November 1992 general election returns.
[2]Separate rankings for eight counties and 95 towns.

Table E. – Vote for President: November 3, 1992, General Election

County	Total	Clinton (DEM)	Bush (REP)	Perot (IND)	Other	Plurality Total	Party	DEM	REP	IND	Other	Rank[1] DEM	REP	IND	Total	DEM	REP	IND	DEM	REP
Fairfield	409,410	160,202	175,158	72,532	1,518	14,956	R	39.1	42.8	17.7	0.4	7	1	8	25.3	23.5	30.3	20.8	47.8	52.2
Hartford	414,804	195,495	132,591	85,005	1,713	62,904	D	47.1	32.0	20.5	0.4	1	4	7	25.7	28.7	22.9	24.4	59.6	40.4
Litchfield	93,213	33,686	34,492	24,639	396	806	R	36.1	37.0	26.4	0.4	8	2	4	5.8	4.9	6.0	7.1	49.4	50.6
Middlesex	81,027	34,707	24,646	21,306	368	10,061	D	42.8	30.4	26.3	0.5	2	7	5	5.0	5.1	4.3	6.1	58.5	41.5
New Haven	385,132	161,374	141,264	80,817	1,677	20,110	D	41.9	36.7	21.0	0.4	4	3	6	23.8	23.7	24.4	23.2	53.3	46.7
New London	117,767	49,808	34,567	32,736	656	15,241	D	42.3	29.4	27.8	0.6	3	8	2	7.3	7.3	6.0	9.4	59.0	41.0
Tolland	66,215	27,425	20,632	17,930	228	6,793	D	41.4	31.2	27.1	0.3	5	5	3	4.1	4.0	3.6	5.1	57.1	42.9
Windham	48,588	19,621	14,963	13,806	198	4,658	D	40.4	30.8	28.4	0.4	6	6	1	3.0	2.9	2.6	4.0	56.7	43.3
CONNECTICUT[2]	**1,616,332**	**682,318**	**578,313**	**348,771**	**6,930**	**104,005**	**D**	**42.2**	**35.8**	**21.6**	**0.4**				**100.0**	**100.0**	**100.0**	**100.0**	**54.1**	**45.9**
SELECTED TOWNS																				
Ansonia town	8,481	3,273	3,277	1,883	48	4	R	38.6	38.6	22.2	0.6	52	40	58	0.5	0.5	0.6	0.5	50.0	50.0
Berlin town	10,219	4,177	3,625	2,379	38	552	D	40.9	35.5	23.3	0.4	38	53	51	0.6	0.6	0.6	0.7	53.5	46.5
Bethel town	9,337	3,178	3,974	2,160	25	796	R	34.0	42.6	23.1	0.3	78	20	53	0.6	0.5	0.7	0.6	44.4	55.6
Bloomfield town	10,572	6,914	2,341	1,266	51	4,573	D	65.4	22.1	12.0	0.5	3	93	93	0.7	1.0	0.4	0.4	74.7	25.3
Branford town	15,263	6,575	5,622	3,018	48	953	D	43.1	36.8	19.8	0.3	26	46	73	0.9	1.0	1.0	0.9	53.9	46.1
Bridgeport town	41,956	22,321	13,149	6,263	223	9,172	D	53.2	31.3	14.9	0.5	8	72	86	2.6	3.3	2.3	1.8	62.9	37.1
Bristol town	28,274	11,872	8,407	7,890	105	3,465	D	42.0	29.7	27.9	0.4	31	78	13	1.7	1.7	1.5	2.3	58.5	41.5
Brookfield town	8,446	2,657	3,750	2,012	27	1,093	R	31.5	44.4	23.8	0.3	85	16	43	0.5	0.4	0.6	0.6	41.5	58.5
Brooklyn town	3,252	1,220	1,072	941	19	148	D	37.5	33.0	28.9	0.6	61	63	12	0.2	0.2	0.2	0.3	53.2	46.8
Cheshire town	14,556	5,096	6,484	2,935	41	1,388	R	35.0	44.5	20.2	0.3	73	14	72	0.9	0.7	1.1	0.8	44.0	56.0
Clinton town	6,968	2,563	2,531	1,850	24	32	D	36.8	36.3	26.5	0.3	65	48	22	0.4	0.4	0.4	0.5	50.3	49.7
Coventry town	5,601	2,393	1,465	1,721	22	672	D	42.7	26.2	30.7	0.4	27	87	7	0.3	0.4	0.3	0.5	62.0	38.0
Danbury town	25,840	9,909	10,310	5,517	104	401	R	38.3	39.9	21.4	0.4	55	29	63	1.6	1.5	1.8	1.6	49.0	51.0
Darien town	10,987	3,089	6,396	1,463	39	3,307	R	28.1	58.2	13.3	0.4	92	1	92	0.7	0.5	1.1	0.4	32.6	67.4
Derby town	5,725	2,150	2,246	1,305	24	96	R	37.6	39.2	22.8	0.4	60	34	55	0.4	0.3	0.4	0.4	48.9	51.1
East Granby town	2,582	952	1,005	608	17	53	R	36.9	38.9	23.5	0.7	64	36	46	0.2	0.1	0.2	0.2	48.6	51.4
East Hartford town	23,512	11,450	6,472	5,478	112	4,978	D	48.7	27.5	23.3	0.5	12	83	50	1.5	1.7	1.1	1.6	63.9	36.1
East Haven town	13,640	5,645	4,747	3,196	52	898	D	41.4	34.8	23.4	0.4	36	55	48	0.8	0.8	0.8	0.9	54.3	45.7
East Lyme town	8,356	3,425	2,717	2,173	41	708	D	41.0	32.5	26.0	0.5	37	65	27	0.5	0.5	0.5	0.6	55.8	44.2
East Windsor town	4,818	1,891	1,598	1,313	16	293	D	39.2	33.2	27.3	0.3	48	61	15	0.3	0.3	0.3	0.4	54.2	45.8
Enfield town	22,036	9,248	7,043	5,646	99	2,205	D	42.0	32.0	25.6	0.4	32	69	30	1.4	1.4	1.2	1.6	56.8	43.2
Essex town	3,764	1,503	1,391	855	15	112	D	39.9	37.0	22.7	0.4	44	45	56	0.2	0.2	0.2	0.2	51.9	48.1
Fairfield town	32,120	12,099	13,968	5,941	112	1,869	R	37.7	43.5	18.5	0.3	59	17	78	2.0	1.8	2.4	1.7	46.4	53.6
Farmington town	12,374	4,917	4,893	2,520	44	24	D	39.7	39.5	20.4	0.4	45	31	70	0.8	0.7	0.8	0.7	50.1	49.9
Glastonbury town	17,586	6,976	6,840	3,707	63	136	D	39.7	38.9	21.1	0.4	46	37	65	1.1	1.0	1.2	1.1	50.5	49.5
Granby town	5,590	1,998	2,182	1,392	18	184	R	35.7	39.0	24.9	0.3	69	35	36	0.3	0.3	0.4	0.4	47.8	52.2
Greenwich town	32,476	11,893	15,885	4,584	114	3,992	R	36.6	48.9	14.1	0.4	66	4	88	2.0	1.7	2.7	1.3	42.8	57.2
Griswold town	4,325	1,815	1,024	1,469	17	346	D	42.0	23.7	34.0	0.4	33	91	1	0.3	0.3	0.2	0.4	63.9	36.1
Groton town	15,202	6,350	4,795	3,965	92	1,555	D	41.8	31.5	26.1	0.6	35	71	26	0.9	0.9	0.8	1.1	57.0	43.0
Guilford town	11,714	4,933	4,164	2,584	33	769	D	42.1	35.5	22.1	0.3	30	52	59	0.7	0.7	0.7	0.7	54.2	45.8
Haddam town	4,317	1,666	1,263	1,372	16	294	D	38.6	29.3	31.8	0.4	53	79	5	0.3	0.2	0.2	0.4	56.9	43.1
Hamden town	28,487	13,484	10,273	4,645	85	3,211	D	47.3	36.1	16.3	0.3	14	50	84	1.8	2.0	1.8	1.3	56.8	43.2
Hartford town	36,797	26,971	6,180	3,390	256	20,791	D	73.3	16.8	9.2	0.7	1	95	95	2.3	4.0	1.1	1.0	81.4	18.6
Killingly town	6,479	2,467	2,106	1,880	26	361	D	38.1	32.5	29.0	0.4	58	66	10	0.4	0.4	0.4	0.5	53.9	46.1
Ledyard town	7,140	2,534	2,656	1,907	43	122	R	35.5	37.2	26.7	0.6	71	44	20	0.4	0.4	0.5	0.5	48.8	51.2
Litchfield town	4,615	1,621	1,872	1,090	32	251	R	35.1	40.6	23.6	0.7	72	26	45	0.3	0.2	0.3	0.3	46.4	53.6
Madison town	9,999	3,437	4,476	2,062	24	1,039	R	34.4	44.8	20.6	0.2	77	13	68	0.6	0.5	0.8	0.6	43.4	56.6
Manchester town	28,271	12,266	9,132	6,759	114	3,134	D	43.4	32.3	23.9	0.4	22	68	41	1.7	1.8	1.6	1.9	57.3	42.7
Mansfield town	7,900	4,677	1,754	1,440	29	2,923	D	59.2	22.2	18.2	0.4	4	92	82	0.5	0.7	0.3	0.4	72.7	27.3
Meriden town	25,979	11,318	8,198	6,318	145	3,120	D	43.6	31.6	24.3	0.6	21	70	39	1.6	1.7	1.4	1.8	58.0	42.0
Middlebury town	3,798	1,050	1,937	801	10	887	R	27.6	51.0	21.1	0.3	94	3	64	0.2	0.2	0.3	0.2	35.2	64.8
Middletown town	21,114	11,338	5,092	4,598	86	6,246	D	53.7	24.1	21.8	0.4	7	90	62	1.3	1.7	0.9	1.3	69.0	31.0
Milford town	26,708	9,278	10,686	6,681	63	1,408	R	34.7	40.0	25.0	0.2	75	28	34	1.7	1.4	1.8	1.9	46.5	53.5
Monroe town	9,643	2,745	4,607	2,266	25	1,862	R	28.5	47.8	23.5	0.3	88	6	47	0.6	0.4	0.8	0.6	37.3	62.7
Montville town	8,198	3,275	2,259	2,601	63	674	D	39.9	27.6	31.7	0.8	43	82	6	0.5	0.5	0.4	0.7	59.2	40.8
Naugatuck town	13,883	4,410	5,371	4,021	81	961	R	31.8	38.7	29.0	0.6	84	39	11	0.9	0.6	0.9	1.2	45.1	54.9
New Britain town	26,317	14,159	7,040	4,983	135	7,119	D	53.8	26.8	18.9	0.5	6	84	76	1.6	2.1	1.2	1.4	66.8	33.2
New Fairfield town	7,209	2,047	3,426	1,723	13	1,379	R	28.4	47.5	23.9	0.2	89	7	42	0.4	0.3	0.6	0.5	37.4	62.6
New Hartford town	3,450	1,340	1,189	907	14	151	D	38.8	34.5	26.3	0.4	50	57	25	0.2	0.2	0.2	0.3	53.0	47.0
New Haven town	43,261	29,774	8,931	4,130	426	20,843	D	68.8	20.6	9.5	1.0	2	94	94	2.7	4.4	1.5	1.2	76.9	23.1
New London town	9,738	5,520	2,368	1,796	54	3,152	D	56.7	24.3	18.4	0.6	5	89	79	0.6	0.8	0.4	0.5	70.0	30.0
New Milford town	11,760	3,807	4,650	3,270	33	843	R	32.4	39.5	27.8	0.3	81	32	14	0.7	0.6	0.8	0.9	45.0	55.0
Newington town	16,823	7,687	5,598	3,482	56	2,089	D	45.7	33.3	20.7	0.3	17	60	67	1.0	1.1	1.0	1.0	57.9	42.1
Newtown town	11,410	3,783	4,940	2,646	41	1,157	R	33.2	43.3	23.2	0.4	80	18	52	0.7	0.6	0.9	0.8	43.4	56.6
North Branford town	7,115	2,455	2,856	1,787	17	401	R	34.5	40.1	25.1	0.2	76	27	33	0.4	0.4	0.5	0.5	46.2	53.8
North Haven town	13,518	5,027	5,649	2,801	41	622	R	37.2	41.8	20.7	0.3	62	24	66	0.8	0.7	1.0	0.8	47.1	52.9
Norwalk town	37,455	16,488	14,743	6,046	178	1,745	D	44.0	39.4	16.1	0.5	20	33	85	2.3	2.4	2.5	1.7	52.8	47.2
Norwich town	15,850	7,412	4,081	4,287	70	3,125	D	46.8	25.7	27.0	0.4	15	88	17	1.0	1.1	0.7	1.2	64.5	35.5
Old Saybrook town	6,053	2,233	2,353	1,440	27	120	R	36.9	38.9	23.8	0.4	63	38	44	0.4	0.3	0.4	0.4	48.7	51.3

[1]Separate rankings for eight counties and 95 towns. [2]Includes the following write-in votes reported only at the state level: 72 for Gritz, 75 for Hagelin, 4 for LaRouche, 20 for Phillips, and 5 for Warren; total of 176.

Table E. — Vote for President: November 3, 1992, General Election (cont)

County	Total	Clinton (DEM)	Bush (REP)	Perot (IND)	Other	Plurality Total	Party	DEM	REP	IND	Other	Rank DEM	Rank REP	Rank IND	Total	DEM	REP	IND	DEM	REP
Orange town..............	8,290	2,902	3,842	1,526	20	940	R	35.0	46.3	18.4	0.2	74	11	80	0.5	0.4	0.7	0.4	43.0	57.0
Plainfield town	6,010	2,412	1,607	1,967	24	445	D	40.1	26.7	32.7	0.4	42	85	4	0.4	0.4	0.3	0.6	60.0	40.0
Plainville town	8,684	3,763	2,669	2,209	43	1,094	D	43.3	30.7	25.4	0.5	23	75	31	0.5	0.6	0.5	0.6	58.5	41.5
Plymouth town	5,445	1,963	1,659	1,808	15	155	D	36.1	30.5	33.2	0.3	68	76	2	0.3	0.3	0.3	0.5	54.2	45.8
Prospect town	4,657	1,146	2,118	1,376	17	742	R	24.6	45.5	29.5	0.4	95	12	9	0.3	0.2	0.4	0.4	35.1	64.9
Putnam town	4,168	1,685	1,412	1,050	21	273	D	40.4	33.9	25.2	0.5	41	59	32	0.3	0.2	0.2	0.3	54.4	45.6
Ridgefield town	13,291	4,729	6,166	2,328	68	1,437	R	35.6	46.4	17.5	0.5	70	10	83	0.8	0.7	1.1	0.7	43.4	56.6
Rocky Hill town	9,447	4,091	3,269	2,070	17	822	D	43.3	34.6	21.9	0.2	24	56	61	0.6	0.6	0.6	0.6	55.6	44.4
Seymour town	7,737	2,382	3,247	2,070	38	865	R	30.8	42.0	26.8	0.5	87	22	19	0.5	0.3	0.6	0.6	42.3	57.7
Shelton town	18,899	5,354	8,963	4,546	36	3,609	R	28.3	47.4	24.1	0.2	90	9	40	1.2	0.8	1.5	1.3	37.4	62.6
Simsbury town	13,776	5,440	5,788	2,520	28	348	R	39.5	42.0	18.3	0.2	47	21	81	0.9	0.8	1.0	0.7	48.5	51.5
Somers town	4,478	1,397	1,915	1,151	15	518	R	31.2	42.8	25.7	0.3	86	19	29	0.3	0.2	0.3	0.3	42.2	57.8
South Windsor town.......	13,084	5,333	4,702	3,012	37	631	D	40.8	35.9	23.0	0.3	39	51	54	0.8	0.8	0.8	0.9	53.1	46.9
Southbury town	9,705	3,103	4,683	1,899	20	1,580	R	32.0	48.3	19.6	0.2	82	5	74	0.6	0.5	0.8	0.5	39.9	60.1
Southington town	20,210	7,740	7,346	5,038	86	394	D	38.3	36.3	24.9	0.4	56	47	35	1.3	1.1	1.3	1.4	51.3	48.7
Stafford town	5,969	2,294	1,660	1,979	36	315	D	38.4	27.8	33.2	0.6	54	81	3	0.4	0.3	0.3	0.6	58.0	42.0
Stamford town	49,926	23,185	19,809	6,763	169	3,376	D	46.4	39.7	13.5	0.3	16	30	89	3.1	3.4	3.4	1.9	53.9	46.1
Stonington town	9,534	4,045	2,858	2,580	51	1,187	D	42.4	30.0	27.1	0.5	29	77	16	0.6	0.6	0.5	0.7	58.6	41.4
Stratford town	26,769	9,796	10,914	5,986	73	1,118	R	36.6	40.8	22.4	0.3	67	25	57	1.7	1.4	1.9	1.7	47.3	52.7
Thompson town	4,515	1,725	1,582	1,197	11	143	D	38.2	35.0	26.5	0.2	57	54	23	0.3	0.3	0.3	0.3	52.2	47.8
Torrington town	16,995	6,882	5,508	4,528	77	1,374	D	40.5	32.4	26.6	0.5	40	67	21	1.1	1.0	1.0	1.3	55.5	44.5
Trumbull town	19,974	6,353	9,486	4,067	68	3,133	R	31.8	47.5	20.4	0.3	83	8	71	1.2	0.9	1.6	1.2	40.1	59.9
Vernon town..............	14,893	6,241	4,905	3,699	48	1,336	D	41.9	32.9	24.8	0.3	34	64	37	0.9	0.9	0.8	1.1	56.0	44.0
Wallingford town	22,011	8,539	7,942	5,445	85	597	D	38.8	36.1	24.7	0.4	51	49	38	1.4	1.3	1.4	1.6	51.8	48.2
Waterbury town	41,896	16,366	16,155	9,188	187	211	D	39.1	38.6	21.9	0.4	49	41	60	2.6	2.4	2.8	2.6	50.3	49.7
Waterford town	9,944	4,484	2,784	2,630	46	1,700	D	45.1	28.0	26.4	0.5	18	80	24	0.6	0.7	0.5	0.8	61.7	38.3
Watertown town	11,088	3,130	4,937	2,977	44	1,807	R	28.2	44.5	26.8	0.4	91	15	18	0.7	0.5	0.9	0.9	38.8	61.2
West Hartford town	37,046	19,623	12,266	5,017	140	7,357	D	53.0	33.1	13.5	0.4	9	62	90	2.3	2.9	2.1	1.4	61.5	38.5
West Haven town..........	25,599	11,523	8,742	5,249	85	2,781	D	45.0	34.1	20.5	0.3	19	58	69	1.6	1.7	1.5	1.5	56.9	43.1
Westport town	16,216	7,799	6,166	2,196	55	1,633	D	48.1	38.0	13.5	0.3	13	42	91	1.0	1.1	1.1	0.6	55.8	44.2
Wethersfield town	16,305	7,035	6,187	3,035	48	848	D	43.1	37.9	18.6	0.3	25	43	77	1.0	1.0	1.1	0.9	53.2	46.8
Wilton town..................	10,022	3,402	5,143	1,452	25	1,741	R	33.9	51.3	14.5	0.2	79	2	87	0.6	0.5	0.9	0.4	39.8	60.2
Windham town	9,512	4,744	2,506	2,222	40	2,238	D	49.9	26.3	23.4	0.4	10	86	49	0.6	0.7	0.4	0.6	65.4	34.6
Windsor Locks town	6,695	2,857	2,071	1,737	30	786	D	42.7	30.9	25.9	0.4	28	73	28	0.4	0.4	0.4	0.5	58.0	42.0
Windsor town..................	15,046	7,456	4,633	2,898	59	2,823	D	49.6	30.8	19.3	0.4	11	74	75	0.9	1.1	0.8	0.8	61.7	38.3
Wolcott town..................	7,872	2,204	3,293	2,340	35	953	R	28.0	41.8	29.7	0.4	93	23	8	0.5	0.3	0.6	0.7	40.1	59.9

[1]Separate rankings for eight counties and 95 towns.

Table F. — Vote for U.S. Senator: November 3, 1992, General Election

County	Total	Dodd[1] (DEM)	Johnson (REP)	Other	Plurality[1] Total	Party	DEM	REP	Other	Rank[2] DEM	REP	Other	Total	DEM	REP	Other
Fairfield	375,509	203,801	162,912	8,796	40,889	D	54.3	43.4	2.3	8	1	8	25.0	23.1	28.5	19.1
Hartford	390,190	243,148	134,365	12,677	108,783	D	62.3	34.4	3.2	1	8	4	26.0	27.6	23.5	27.5
Litchfield	87,184	47,431	36,335	3,418	11,096	D	54.4	41.7	3.9	7	2	1	5.8	5.4	6.4	7.4
Middlesex	76,199	46,634	27,362	2,203	19,272	D	61.2	35.9	2.9	2	7	7	5.1	5.3	4.8	4.8
New Haven	354,850	214,520	127,992	12,338	86,528	D	60.5	36.1	3.5	3	6	2	23.6	24.3	22.4	26.8
New London	109,959	65,524	41,246	3,189	24,278	D	59.6	37.5	2.9	4	5	6	7.3	7.4	7.2	6.9
Tolland	62,151	36,707	23,497	1,947	13,210	D	59.1	37.8	3.1	5	4	5	4.1	4.2	4.1	4.2
Windham	44,619	24,804	18,327	1,488	6,477	D	55.6	41.1	3.3	6	3	3	3.0	2.8	3.2	3.2
CONNECTICUT[3]	**1,500,709**	**882,569**	**572,036**	**46,104**	**310,533**	**D**	**58.8**	**38.1**	**3.1**				**100.0**	**100.0**	**100.0**	**100.0**
SELECTED TOWNS																
Ansonia town	8,092	5,040	2,731	321	2,309	D	62.3	33.7	4.0	19	78	15	0.5	0.6	0.5	0.7
Berlin town	9,518	5,495	3,727	296	1,768	D	57.7	39.2	3.1	49	51	44	0.6	0.6	0.7	0.6
Bethel town	8,420	4,666	3,472	282	1,194	D	55.4	41.2	3.3	60	35	35	0.6	0.5	0.6	0.6
Bloomfield town	10,018	7,259	2,468	291	4,791	D	72.5	24.6	2.9	3	93	51	0.7	0.8	0.4	0.6
Branford town	14,152	8,693	5,212	247	3,481	D	61.4	36.8	1.7	20	62	89	0.9	1.0	0.9	0.5
Bridgeport town	36,663	24,578	10,930	1,155	13,648	D	67.0	29.8	3.2	7	89	42	2.4	2.8	1.9	2.5
Bristol town	26,201	16,385	8,842	974	7,543	D	62.5	33.7	3.7	18	79	24	1.7	1.9	1.5	2.1
Brookfield town	7,856	3,780	3,878	198	98	R	48.1	49.4	2.5	88	7	67	0.5	0.4	0.7	0.4
Brooklyn town	3,062	1,577	1,388	97	189	D	51.5	45.3	3.2	80	17	41	0.2	0.2	0.2	0.2
Cheshire town	13,748	7,539	5,816	393	1,723	D	54.8	42.3	2.9	65	30	55	0.9	0.9	1.0	0.9
Clinton town	6,455	3,647	2,646	162	1,001	D	56.5	41.0	2.5	55	36	69	0.4	0.4	0.5	0.4
Coventry town	5,268	3,174	1,914	180	1,260	D	60.3	36.3	3.4	32	65	33	0.4	0.4	0.3	0.4
Danbury town	23,150	13,273	9,124	753	4,149	D	57.3	39.4	3.3	52	48	37	1.5	1.5	1.6	1.6
Darien town	10,348	4,007	6,208	133	2,201	R	38.7	60.0	1.3	95	1	95	0.7	0.5	1.1	0.3
Derby town	5,216	3,194	1,811	211	1,383	D	61.2	34.7	4.0	23	73	12	0.3	0.4	0.3	0.5
East Granby town	2,451	1,329	1,025	97	304	D	54.2	41.8	4.0	69	34	17	0.2	0.2	0.2	0.2
East Hartford town	21,913	14,434	6,679	800	7,755	D	65.9	30.5	3.7	9	87	26	1.5	1.6	1.2	1.7
East Haven town	11,973	7,500	4,183	290	3,317	D	62.6	34.9	2.4	17	72	71	0.8	0.8	0.7	0.6
East Lyme town	7,857	4,551	3,135	171	1,416	D	57.9	39.9	2.2	48	46	80	0.5	0.5	0.5	0.4
East Windsor town	4,437	2,628	1,645	164	983	D	59.2	37.1	3.7	37	60	25	0.3	0.3	0.3	0.4
Enfield town	20,509	12,525	7,095	889	5,430	D	61.1	34.6	4.3	26	75	9	1.4	1.4	1.2	1.9
Essex town	3,591	1,912	1,597	82	315	D	53.2	44.5	2.3	74	21	77	0.2	0.2	0.3	0.2
Fairfield town	30,160	16,347	13,214	599	3,133	D	54.2	43.8	2.0	71	22	85	2.0	1.9	2.3	1.3
Farmington town	11,655	6,444	4,898	313	1,546	D	55.3	42.0	2.7	62	32	61	0.8	0.7	0.9	0.7
Glastonbury town	16,819	8,914	7,504	401	1,410	D	53.0	44.6	2.4	75	19	72	1.1	1.0	1.3	0.9
Granby town	5,316	2,765	2,368	183	397	D	52.0	44.5	3.4	78	20	31	0.4	0.3	0.4	0.4
Greenwich town	30,097	14,494	15,175	428	681	R	48.2	50.4	1.4	87	5	94	2.0	1.6	2.7	0.9
Griswold town	3,965	2,422	1,391	152	1,031	D	61.1	35.1	3.8	25	71	21	0.3	0.3	0.2	0.3
Groton town	13,996	8,253	5,339	404	2,914	D	59.0	38.1	2.9	42	54	52	0.9	0.9	0.9	0.9
Guilford town	10,984	6,313	4,455	216	1,858	D	57.5	40.6	2.0	51	41	86	0.7	0.7	0.8	0.5
Haddam town	4,044	2,480	1,434	130	1,046	D	61.3	35.5	3.2	21	70	39	0.3	0.3	0.3	0.3
Hamden town	26,442	17,179	8,711	552	8,468	D	65.0	32.9	2.1	12	82	82	1.8	1.9	1.5	1.2
Hartford town	34,502	27,679	5,565	1,258	22,114	D	80.2	16.1	3.6	1	95	27	2.3	3.1	1.0	2.7
Killingly town	5,941	3,282	2,424	235	858	D	55.2	40.8	4.0	63	38	18	0.4	0.4	0.4	0.5
Ledyard town	6,517	3,548	2,803	166	745	D	54.4	43.0	2.5	67	26	66	0.4	0.4	0.5	0.4
Litchfield town	4,446	2,308	2,001	137	307	D	51.9	45.0	3.1	79	18	45	0.3	0.3	0.3	0.3
Madison town	9,343	4,686	4,501	156	185	D	50.2	48.2	1.7	83	12	90	0.6	0.5	0.8	0.3
Manchester town	26,742	16,387	9,484	871	6,903	D	61.3	35.5	3.3	22	69	36	1.8	1.9	1.7	1.9
Mansfield town	7,464	5,314	1,956	194	3,358	D	71.2	26.2	2.6	4	92	63	0.5	0.6	0.3	0.4
Meriden town	23,675	15,039	7,681	955	7,358	D	63.5	32.4	4.0	16	84	13	1.6	1.7	1.3	2.1
Middlebury town	3,496	1,509	1,893	94	384	R	43.2	54.1	2.7	94	3	60	0.2	0.2	0.3	0.2
Middletown town	19,626	13,447	5,591	588	7,856	D	68.5	28.5	3.0	6	90	48	1.3	1.5	1.0	1.3
Milford town	24,164	13,706	9,831	627	3,875	D	56.7	40.7	2.6	54	40	64	1.6	1.6	1.7	1.4
Monroe town	8,982	4,301	4,449	232	148	R	47.9	49.5	2.6	89	6	65	0.6	0.5	0.8	0.5
Montville town	7,690	4,568	2,872	250	1,696	D	59.4	37.3	3.3	35	58	38	0.5	0.5	0.5	0.5
Naugatuck town	12,751	7,184	5,010	557	2,174	D	56.3	39.3	4.4	57	50	8	0.8	0.8	0.9	1.2
New Britain town	23,912	15,826	7,183	903	8,643	D	66.2	30.0	3.8	8	88	23	1.6	1.8	1.3	2.0
New Fairfield town	6,504	3,058	3,199	247	141	R	47.0	49.2	3.8	90	10	22	0.4	0.3	0.6	0.5
New Hartford town	3,261	1,740	1,369	152	371	D	53.4	42.0	4.7	72	33	5	0.2	0.2	0.2	0.3
New Haven town	40,193	30,353	7,140	2,700	23,213	D	75.5	17.8	6.7	2	94	1	2.7	3.4	1.2	5.9
New London town	8,665	6,017	2,385	263	3,632	D	69.4	27.5	3.0	5	91	46	0.6	0.7	0.4	0.6
New Milford town	10,818	5,768	4,669	381	1,099	D	53.3	43.2	3.5	73	24	29	0.7	0.7	0.8	0.8
Newington town	15,911	9,692	5,672	547	4,020	D	60.9	35.6	3.4	27	68	32	1.1	1.1	1.0	1.2
Newtown town	10,440	5,701	4,458	281	1,243	D	54.6	42.7	2.7	66	27	59	0.7	0.6	0.8	0.6
North Branford town	6,460	3,720	2,583	157	1,137	D	57.6	40.0	2.4	50	44	70	0.4	0.4	0.5	0.3
North Haven town	12,335	7,011	5,053	271	1,958	D	56.8	41.0	2.2	53	37	79	0.8	0.8	0.9	0.6
Norwalk town	34,220	19,883	13,369	968	6,514	D	58.1	39.1	2.8	45	52	56	2.3	2.3	2.3	2.1
Norwich town	14,790	9,677	4,677	436	5,000	D	65.4	31.6	2.9	11	85	50	1.0	1.1	0.8	0.9
Old Saybrook town	5,656	3,128	2,398	130	730	D	55.3	42.4	2.3	61	29	76	0.4	0.4	0.4	0.3

[1]Includes votes cast for Christopher Dodd as both the nominee of the Democratic party and A Connecticut Party (ACP). [2]Separate rankings for eight counties and 95 towns. [3]Includes the following write-in votes reported only at the state level: 1 for Rumbin, 41 for DiCandia, and 6 for Wilkin; total of 48.

County	Total	Dodd[1] (DEM)	Johnson (REP)	Other	Plurality[1] Total	Party	Percent of total vote DEM	REP	Other	Rank DEM	REP	Other	Percent contribution to state vote Total	DEM	REP	Other
Orange town..................	7,727	4,072	3,545	110	527	D	52.7	45.9	1.4	76	15	93	0.5	0.5	0.6	0.2
Plainfield town	5,547	3,126	2,228	193	898	D	56.4	40.2	3.5	56	42	30	0.4	0.4	0.4	0.4
Plainville town	8,060	4,931	2,791	338	2,140	D	61.2	34.6	4.2	24	74	10	0.5	0.6	0.5	0.7
Plymouth town	5,196	3,095	1,767	334	1,328	D	59.6	34.0	6.4	34	77	2	0.3	0.4	0.3	0.7
Prospect town	4,316	2,021	2,123	172	102	R	46.8	49.2	4.0	91	9	14	0.3	0.2	0.4	0.4
Putnam town	3,816	2,076	1,621	119	455	D	54.4	42.5	3.1	68	28	43	0.3	0.2	0.3	0.3
Ridgefield town	12,476	6,101	6,147	228	46	R	48.9	49.3	1.8	86	8	88	0.8	0.7	1.1	0.5
Rocky Hill town	8,850	5,342	3,264	244	2,078	D	60.4	36.9	2.8	30	61	57	0.6	0.6	0.6	0.5
Seymour town	7,187	4,034	2,868	285	1,166	D	56.1	39.9	4.0	58	45	16	0.5	0.5	0.5	0.6
Shelton town	17,976	9,176	8,223	577	953	D	51.0	45.7	3.2	81	16	40	1.2	1.0	1.4	1.3
Simsbury town	13,285	7,203	5,772	310	1,431	D	54.2	43.4	2.3	70	23	75	0.9	0.8	1.0	0.7
Somers town	4,208	2,113	1,953	142	160	D	50.2	46.4	3.4	82	14	34	0.3	0.2	0.3	0.3
South Windsor town.......	12,474	7,240	4,940	294	2,300	D	58.0	39.6	2.4	46	47	73	0.8	0.8	0.9	0.6
Southbury town	9,197	4,199	4,795	203	596	R	45.7	52.1	2.2	92	4	78	0.6	0.5	0.8	0.4
Southington town	19,034	11,485	6,805	744	4,680	D	60.3	35.8	3.9	31	67	19	1.3	1.3	1.2	1.6
Stafford town	5,497	3,244	2,041	212	1,203	D	59.0	37.1	3.9	40	59	20	0.4	0.4	0.4	0.5
Stamford town	45,090	26,962	17,188	940	9,774	D	59.8	38.1	2.1	33	55	83	3.0	3.1	3.0	2.0
Stonington town	8,744	5,184	3,321	239	1,863	D	59.3	38.0	2.7	36	57	58	0.6	0.6	0.6	0.5
Stratford town	24,278	13,492	10,214	572	3,278	D	55.6	42.1	2.4	59	31	74	1.6	1.5	1.8	1.2
Thompson town	3,983	2,197	1,623	163	574	D	55.2	40.7	4.1	64	39	11	0.3	0.2	0.3	0.4
Torrington town	15,896	9,386	5,729	781	3,657	D	59.0	36.0	4.9	39	66	3	1.1	1.1	1.0	1.7
Trumbull town	18,497	9,191	8,928	378	263	D	49.7	48.3	2.0	84	11	84	1.2	1.0	1.6	0.8
Vernon town..................	13,947	8,236	5,299	412	2,937	D	59.1	38.0	3.0	38	56	49	0.9	0.9	0.9	0.9
Wallingford town	20,175	12,219	7,377	579	4,842	D	60.6	36.6	2.9	29	64	54	1.3	1.4	1.3	1.3
Waterbury town	39,072	22,938	14,307	1,827	8,631	D	58.7	36.6	4.7	43	63	4	2.6	2.6	2.5	4.0
Waterford town...............	9,966	5,881	3,872	213	2,009	D	59.0	38.9	2.1	41	53	81	0.7	0.7	0.7	0.5
Watertown town	10,171	5,027	4,775	369	252	D	49.4	46.9	3.6	85	13	28	0.7	0.6	0.8	0.8
West Hartford town	35,490	22,850	11,966	674	10,884	D	64.4	33.7	1.9	14	80	87	2.4	2.6	2.1	1.5
West Haven town	22,715	14,909	7,152	654	7,757	D	65.6	31.5	2.9	10	86	53	1.5	1.7	1.3	1.4
Westport town	15,088	8,818	6,050	220	2,768	D	58.4	40.1	1.5	44	43	92	1.0	1.0	1.1	0.5
Wethersfield town	15,362	8,910	6,044	408	2,866	D	58.0	39.3	2.7	47	49	62	1.0	1.0	1.1	0.9
Wilton town...................	9,534	4,128	5,253	153	1,125	R	43.3	55.1	1.6	93	2	91	0.6	0.5	0.9	0.3
Windham town	8,672	5,599	2,855	218	2,744	D	64.6	32.9	2.5	13	83	68	0.6	0.6	0.5	0.5
Windsor Locks town	6,255	3,805	2,160	290	1,645	D	60.8	34.5	4.6	28	76	6	0.4	0.4	0.4	0.6
Windsor town................	14,173	9,032	4,716	425	4,316	D	63.7	33.3	3.0	15	81	47	0.9	1.0	0.8	0.9
Wolcott town.................	7,262	3,797	3,129	336	668	D	52.3	43.1	4.6	77	25	7	0.5	0.4	0.5	0.7

[1]Includes votes cast for Christopher Dodd as both the nominee of the Democratic party and A Connecticut Party (ACP).

Connecticut 163

Table H. — Vote for U.S. Representative in Congress: November 3, 1992, General Election

Congressional district and county	Total	Democrat (DEM)[1]	Republican (REP)	Other	Plurality[1] Total	Party	DEM	REP	Other	Rank within district DEM	REP	Other	Pct. contrib. Total	DEM	REP	Other
District 1[2]	**245,430**	**164,735**	**75,113**	**5,582**	**89,622**	**D**	**67.1**	**30.6**	**2.3**				**100.0**	**100.0**	**100.0**	**100.0**
Hartford (pt)	221,393	149,841	66,564	4,988	83,277	D	67.7	30.1	2.3	1	3	3	90.2	91.0	88.6	89.4
Middlesex (pt)	16,498	10,368	5,723	407	4,645	D	62.8	34.7	2.5	2	2	1	6.7	6.3	7.6	7.3
Tolland (pt)	7,534	4,526	2,826	182	1,700	D	60.1	37.5	2.4	3	1	2	3.1	2.7	3.8	3.3
District 2	**242,707**	**123,291**	**119,416**	**-**	**3,875**	**D**	**50.8**	**49.2**	**-**				**100.0**	**100.0**	**100.0**	**-**
Middlesex (pt)	42,498	22,610	19,888	-	2,722	D	53.2	46.8	-	2	3	-	17.5	18.3	16.7	-
New London	108,284	52,655	55,629	-	2,974	R	48.6	51.4	-	3	2	-	44.6	42.7	46.6	-
Tolland (pt)	48,070	27,282	20,788	-	6,494	D	56.8	43.2	-	1	4	-	19.8	22.1	17.4	-
Windham	43,855	20,744	23,111	-	2,367	R	47.3	52.7	-	4	1	-	18.1	16.8	19.4	-
District 3[3]	**247,531**	**162,568**	**84,952**	**11**	**77,616**	**D**	**65.7**	**34.3**	**-**				**100.0**	**100.0**	**100.0**	**-**
Fairfield (pt)	23,869	13,948	9,921	-	4,027	D	58.4	41.6	-	3	1	-	9.6	8.6	11.7	-
Middlesex (pt)	14,633	9,176	5,457	-	3,719	D	62.7	37.3	-	2	2	-	5.9	5.6	6.4	-
New Haven (pt)	209,018	139,444	69,574	-	69,870	D	66.7	33.3	-	1	3	-	84.4	85.8	81.9	-
District 4	**219,615**	**58,666**	**147,816**	**13,133**	**89,150**	**R**	**26.7**	**67.3**	**6.0**				**100.0**	**100.0**	**100.0**	**100.0**
Fairfield (pt)	219,615	58,666	147,816	13,133	89,150	R	26.7	67.3	6.0	1	1	1	100.0	100.0	100.0	99.9
District 5	**240,283**	**74,791**	**104,891**	**60,601**	**30,100**	**R**	**31.1**	**43.7**	**25.2**				**100.0**	**100.0**	**100.0**	**100.0**
Fairfield (pt)	108,379	24,082	51,763	32,534	19,229	R	22.2	47.8	30.0	2	1	1	45.1	32.2	49.3	53.7
New Haven (pt)	131,904	50,709	53,128	28,067	2,419	R	38.4	40.3	21.3	1	2	2	54.9	67.8	50.7	46.3
District 6	**239,597**	**60,373**	**166,967**	**12,257**	**106,594**	**R**	**25.2**	**69.7**	**5.1**				**100.0**	**100.0**	**100.0**	**100.0**
Fairfield (pt)	1,563	341	1,154	68	813	R	21.8	73.8	4.4	4	2	3	0.7	0.6	0.7	0.6
Hartford (pt)	146,368	37,719	101,045	7,604	63,326	R	25.8	69.0	5.2	1	5	2	61.1	62.5	60.5	62.0
Litchfield	80,605	19,778	56,581	4,246	36,803	R	24.5	70.2	5.3	2	4	1	33.6	32.8	33.9	34.6
New Haven (pt)	7,113	1,723	5,218	172	3,495	R	24.2	73.4	2.4	3	3	5	3.0	2.9	3.1	1.4
Tolland (pt)	3,948	812	2,969	167	2,157	R	20.6	75.2	4.2	5	1	4	1.6	1.3	1.8	1.4
CONNECTICUT	**1,435,163**	**644,424**	**699,155**	**91,584**	**54,731**	**R**	**44.9**	**48.7**	**6.4**							

[1] Includes votes cast for candidates as both the nominees of the Democratic party and A Connecticut Party (ACP) in districts 1, 3 and 4.   [2] Includes five (5) write-in votes reported only at the district level for Hall.   [3] Includes the following write-in votes reported only at the district level: 9 for Russell and 2 for Krala; total of 11.

Table I. — Vote for Presidential Preference: March 24, 1992, Democratic Primary Election

County	Total	Brown	Clinton	Tsongas	Uncom-mitted	Agran	Harkin	Kerrey	Other	Brown	Clinton	Tsongas	Rank Brown	Rank Clinton	Rank Tsongas	Total	Brown	Clinton	Tsongas
Fairfield	35,328	14,411	12,256	5,905	1,084	583	516	235	338	40.8	34.7	16.7	2	5	7	20.4	22.4	19.9	17.5
Hartford	56,811	18,618	20,631	13,335	1,960	643	620	364	640	32.8	36.3	23.5	8	3	2	32.8	28.9	33.4	39.4
Litchfield	8,387	3,468	2,629	1,627	343	100	82	35	103	41.3	31.3	19.4	1	7	5	4.8	5.4	4.3	4.8
Middlesex	8,290	3,180	2,901	1,721	244	74	56	47	67	38.4	35.0	20.8	6	4	3	4.8	4.9	4.7	5.1
New Haven	40,373	15,906	14,780	6,264	1,027	1,045	451	338	562	39.4	36.6	15.5	5	2	8	23.3	24.7	24.0	18.5
New London	11,687	3,986	4,810	2,161	328	143	84	75	100	34.1	41.2	18.5	7	1	6	6.8	6.2	7.8	6.4
Tolland	7,243	2,905	2,068	1,771	260	62	55	46	76	40.1	28.6	24.5	3	8	1	4.2	4.5	3.4	5.2
Windham	5,000	1,998	1,623	1,027	184	38	55	29	46	40.0	32.5	20.5	4	6	4	2.9	3.1	2.6	3.0
CONNECTICUT	**173,119**	**64,472**	**61,698**	**33,811**	**5,430**	**2,688**	**1,919**	**1,169**	**1,932**	**37.2**	**35.6**	**19.5**				**100.0**	**100.0**	**100.0**	**100.0**
SELECTED TOWNS																			
Ansonia town	986	411	384	134	16	6	17	8	10	41.7	38.9	13.6	30	19	84	0.6	0.6	0.6	0.4
Berlin town	1,357	496	433	299	74	12	15	6	22	36.6	31.9	22.0	57	61	33	0.8	0.8	0.7	0.9
Bethel town	624	306	176	99	24	4	7	1	7	49.0	28.2	15.9	4	76	72	0.4	0.5	0.3	0.3
Bloomfield town	1,857	415	949	342	59	41	14	11	26	22.3	51.1	18.4	95	1	59	1.1	0.6	1.5	1.0
Branford town	1,311	593	398	231	38	17	6	17	11	45.2	30.4	17.6	16	69	66	0.8	0.9	0.6	0.7
Bridgeport town	4,816	1,920	2,122	322	84	184	91	50	43	39.9	44.1	6.7	36	7	95	2.8	3.0	3.4	1.0
Bristol town	3,826	1,473	1,399	713	91	51	44	25	30	38.5	36.6	18.6	47	30	56	2.2	2.3	2.3	2.1
Brookfield town	520	223	150	115	20	4	2	4	2	42.9	28.8	22.1	22	74	32	0.3	0.3	0.2	0.3
Brooklyn town	260	73	72	80	24	1	3	6	1	28.1	27.7	30.8	93	80	5	0.2	0.1	0.1	0.2
Cheshire town	1,045	447	284	269	23	6	4	2	10	42.8	27.2	25.7	23	86	13	0.6	0.7	0.5	0.8
Clinton town	642	251	243	119	23	1	0	2	3	39.1	37.9	18.5	41	26	57	0.4	0.4	0.4	0.4
Coventry town	622	293	177	118	21	7	1	2	3	47.1	28.5	19.0	8	75	51	0.4	0.5	0.3	0.3
Danbury town	1,831	717	662	325	55	15	24	13	20	39.2	36.2	17.7	40	33	64	1.1	1.1	1.1	1.0
Darien town	644	243	191	159	27	8	6	2	8	37.7	29.7	24.7	50	71	21	0.4	0.4	0.3	0.5
Derby town	770	308	302	101	15	11	20	8	5	40.0	39.2	13.1	35	17	88	0.4	0.5	0.5	0.3
East Granby town	195	73	55	50	8	2	2	3	2	37.4	28.2	25.6	51	77	14	0.1	0.1	< .1	0.1
East Hartford town	3,563	1,124	1,359	778	133	57	39	22	51	31.5	38.1	21.8	86	24	34	2.1	1.7	2.2	2.3
East Haven town	1,061	356	528	98	13	24	24	8	10	33.6	49.8	9.2	75	2	93	0.6	0.6	0.9	0.3
East Lyme town	706	295	251	123	16	8	4	3	6	41.8	35.6	17.4	29	42	67	0.4	0.5	0.4	0.4
East Windsor town	510	186	187	107	13	3	6	1	7	36.5	36.7	21.0	58	29	40	0.3	0.3	0.3	0.3
Enfield town	2,795	1,038	929	650	109	15	22	7	25	37.1	33.2	23.3	53	52	25	1.6	1.6	1.5	1.9
Essex town	337	124	109	91	6	1	1	3	2	36.8	32.3	27.0	56	58	10	0.2	0.2	0.2	0.3
Fairfield town	2,665	1,237	770	487	72	37	29	13	20	46.4	28.9	18.3	10	73	60	1.5	1.9	1.2	1.4
Farmington town	1,205	450	321	351	40	10	6	6	21	37.3	26.6	29.1	52	88	7	0.7	0.7	0.5	1.0
Glastonbury town	2,051	742	492	685	80	9	15	5	23	36.2	24.0	33.4	63	94	3	1.2	1.2	0.8	2.0
Granby town	489	168	121	167	16	6	1	4	6	34.4	24.7	34.2	72	92	2	0.3	0.3	0.2	0.5
Greenwich town	1,889	736	623	374	56	52	14	8	26	39.0	33.0	19.8	42	56	46	1.1	1.1	1.0	1.1
Griswold town	479	157	196	100	12	4	2	3	5	32.8	40.9	20.9	79	14	41	0.3	0.2	0.3	0.3
Groton town	1,305	423	566	234	38	15	10	8	11	32.4	43.4	17.9	81	8	62	0.8	0.7	0.9	0.7
Guilford town	1,127	480	311	260	52	10	5	2	7	42.6	27.6	23.1	24	81	27	0.7	0.7	0.5	0.8
Haddam town	472	196	157	95	11	2	3	4	4	41.5	33.3	20.1	31	51	43	0.3	0.3	0.3	0.3
Hamden town	2,735	1,061	973	516	76	53	23	12	21	38.8	35.6	18.9	45	41	54	1.6	1.6	1.6	1.5
Hartford town	6,689	1,913	3,186	1,035	164	110	125	98	58	28.6	47.6	15.5	92	3	75	3.9	3.0	5.2	3.1
Killingly town	496	160	180	124	15	4	4	5	4	32.3	36.3	25.0	82	31	20	0.3	0.2	0.3	0.4
Ledyard town	566	220	182	122	21	4	4	5	8	38.9	32.2	21.6	44	59	36	0.3	0.3	0.3	0.4
Litchfield town	411	191	101	87	13	8	3	2	6	46.5	24.6	21.2	9	93	39	0.2	0.3	0.2	0.3
Madison town	670	289	187	155	20	2	4	6	7	43.1	27.9	23.1	20	78	26	0.4	0.4	0.3	0.5
Manchester town	3,194	1,158	1,025	817	100	22	28	16	28	36.3	32.1	25.6	62	60	15	1.8	1.8	1.7	2.4
Mansfield town	1,381	621	346	336	38	13	9	7	11	45.0	25.1	24.3	18	90	22	0.8	1.0	0.6	1.0
Meriden town	3,080	1,209	1,159	451	104	44	54	33	26	39.3	37.6	14.6	39	27	81	1.8	1.9	1.9	1.3
Middlebury town	298	121	82	75	13	2	1	2	2	40.6	27.5	25.2	33	83	18	0.2	0.2	0.1	0.2
Middletown town	2,681	941	1,064	506	71	31	32	10	26	35.1	39.7	18.9	66	16	53	1.5	1.5	1.7	1.5
Milford town	1,958	895	700	258	40	19	21	13	12	45.7	35.8	13.2	15	38	86	1.1	1.4	1.1	0.8
Monroe town	540	289	157	71	10	3	5	2	3	53.5	29.1	13.1	1	72	87	0.3	0.4	0.3	0.2
Montville town	665	218	286	105	24	8	9	4	11	32.8	43.0	15.8	78	9	73	0.4	0.3	0.5	0.3
Naugatuck town	1,387	597	519	171	37	20	15	14	14	43.0	37.4	12.3	21	28	90	0.8	0.9	0.8	0.5
New Britain town	5,886	1,871	2,523	909	252	93	111	58	69	31.8	42.9	15.4	84	11	76	3.4	2.9	4.1	2.7
New Fairfield town	318	147	87	64	11	4	4	1	0	46.2	27.4	20.1	14	85	44	0.2	0.2	0.1	0.2
New Hartford town	300	118	99	68	5	3	1	2	4	39.3	33.0	22.7	38	55	30	0.2	0.2	0.2	0.2
New Haven town	9,159	3,059	3,762	1,188	206	521	78	85	260	33.4	41.1	13.0	76	13	89	5.3	4.7	6.1	3.5
New London town	1,208	438	561	147	19	21	8	6	8	36.3	46.4	12.2	61	5	91	0.7	0.7	0.9	0.4
New Milford town	954	442	263	190	38	5	8	3	5	46.3	27.6	19.9	12	82	45	0.6	0.7	0.4	0.6
Newington town	2,254	738	807	568	84	16	13	9	19	32.7	35.8	25.2	80	37	17	1.3	1.1	1.3	1.7
Newtown town	838	388	230	163	32	2	8	7	8	46.3	27.4	19.5	13	84	50	0.5	0.6	0.4	0.5
North Branford town	375	130	146	83	9	3	1	1	2	34.7	38.9	22.1	69	20	31	0.2	0.2	0.2	0.2
North Haven town	841	338	267	173	19	13	12	10	9	40.2	31.7	20.6	34	62	42	0.5	0.5	0.4	0.5
Norwalk town	2,930	1,156	1,003	571	71	46	40	14	29	39.5	34.2	19.5	37	45	49	1.7	1.8	1.6	1.7
Norwich town	2,039	591	875	443	50	37	16	13	14	29.0	42.9	21.7	91	10	35	1.2	0.9	1.4	1.3
Old Saybrook town	456	188	139	98	17	5	1	2	6	41.2	30.5	21.5	32	68	37	0.3	0.3	0.2	0.3

[1]Separate rankings for eight counties and 95 towns.

Connecticut 165

Table I. – Vote for Presidential Preference: March 24, 1992, Democratic Primary Election (cont)

County	Total	Brown	Clinton	Tsongas	Uncom-mitted	Agran	Harkin	Kerrey	Other	Brown	Clinton	Tsongas	Brown	Clinton	Tsongas	Total	Brown	Clinton	Tsongas
			Top candidates							Percent of total vote			Rank[1]			Percent contribution to state vote			
Orange town	538	185	187	135	13	6	4	4	4	34.4	34.8	25.1	71	44	19	0.3	0.3	0.3	0.4
Plainfield town	563	178	262	83	20	6	9	5	0	31.6	46.5	14.7	85	4	80	0.3	0.3	0.4	0.2
Plainville town	1,129	380	435	203	60	9	21	9	12	33.7	38.5	18.0	74	21	61	0.7	0.6	0.7	0.6
Plymouth town	381	141	153	63	7	5	5	1	6	37.0	40.2	16.5	55	15	71	0.2	0.2	0.2	0.2
Prospect town	237	126	59	40	6	2	2	1	1	53.2	24.9	16.9	2	91	69	0.1	0.2	<.1	0.1
Putnam town	327	96	103	96	14	7	2	3	6	29.4	31.5	29.4	90	63	6	0.2	0.1	0.2	0.3
Ridgefield town	942	395	261	224	36	8	3	3	12	41.9	27.7	23.8	27	79	24	0.5	0.6	0.4	0.7
Rocky Hill town	1,115	368	395	257	54	8	9	11	13	33.0	35.4	23.0	77	43	28	0.6	0.6	0.6	0.8
Seymour town	438	184	157	67	10	8	3	6	3	42.0	35.8	15.3	26	35	77	0.3	0.3	0.3	0.2
Shelton town	1,253	594	379	190	40	10	19	7	14	47.4	30.2	15.2	7	70	79	0.7	0.9	0.6	0.6
Simsbury town	1,308	391	328	522	31	8	5	6	17	29.9	25.1	39.9	89	89	1	0.8	0.6	0.5	1.5
Somers town	396	147	106	109	19	3	6	2	4	37.1	26.8	27.5	54	87	9	0.2	0.2	0.2	0.3
South Windsor town	1,389	505	430	353	48	13	12	7	21	36.4	31.0	25.4	59	67	16	0.8	0.8	0.7	1.0
Southbury town	741	255	284	140	33	12	3	2	12	34.4	38.3	18.9	70	23	52	0.4	0.4	0.5	0.4
Southington town	1,959	752	702	384	59	14	16	10	22	38.4	35.8	19.6	48	36	48	1.1	1.2	1.1	1.1
Stafford town	876	318	313	165	49	4	10	9	8	36.3	35.7	18.8	60	39	55	0.5	0.5	0.5	0.5
Stamford town	7,610	2,644	2,922	1,272	303	106	200	67	96	34.7	38.4	16.7	67	22	70	4.4	4.1	4.7	3.8
Stonington town	873	313	342	161	26	12	5	7	7	35.9	39.2	18.4	64	18	58	0.5	0.5	0.6	0.5
Stratford town	1,963	959	712	171	58	18	26	12	7	48.9	36.3	8.7	5	32	94	1.1	1.5	1.2	0.5
Thompson town	511	181	182	101	26	4	7	3	7	35.4	35.6	19.8	65	40	47	0.3	0.3	0.3	0.3
Torrington town	2,003	774	762	304	84	25	23	6	25	38.6	38.0	15.2	46	25	78	1.2	1.2	1.2	0.9
Trumbull town	1,193	575	397	170	22	6	11	9	3	48.2	33.3	14.2	6	50	83	0.7	0.9	0.6	0.5
Vernon town	1,354	463	442	357	50	11	9	3	19	34.2	32.6	26.4	73	57	12	0.8	0.7	0.7	1.1
Wallingford town	1,993	898	665	309	44	24	17	25	11	45.1	33.4	15.5	17	49	74	1.2	1.4	1.1	0.9
Waterbury town	5,318	2,249	1,757	773	132	183	92	51	81	42.3	33.0	14.5	25	54	82	3.1	3.5	2.8	2.3
Waterford town	913	286	409	161	25	10	5	7	10	31.3	44.8	17.6	87	6	65	0.5	0.4	0.7	0.5
Watertown town	639	278	201	114	23	7	10	1	5	43.5	31.5	17.8	19	64	63	0.4	0.4	0.3	0.3
West Hartford town	6,418	1,789	2,129	2,105	168	75	51	23	78	27.9	33.2	32.8	94	53	4	3.7	2.8	3.5	6.2
West Haven town	2,571	1,000	1,089	285	68	37	41	22	29	38.9	42.4	11.1	43	12	92	1.5	1.6	1.8	0.8
Westport town	2,042	772	687	434	72	51	10	3	13	37.8	33.6	21.3	49	48	38	1.2	1.2	1.1	1.3
Wethersfield town	2,396	750	812	644	110	26	20	12	22	31.3	33.9	26.9	88	47	11	1.4	1.2	1.3	1.9
Wilton town	711	298	167	204	21	4	6	3	8	41.9	23.5	28.7	28	95	8	0.4	0.5	0.3	0.6
Windham town	1,267	624	398	171	39	6	15	3	11	49.3	31.4	13.5	3	65	85	0.7	1.0	0.6	0.5
Windsor Locks town	695	241	236	158	23	11	12	3	11	34.7	34.0	22.7	68	46	29	0.4	0.4	0.4	0.5
Windsor town	1,742	557	627	420	72	20	18	6	22	32.0	36.0	24.1	83	34	23	1.0	0.9	1.0	1.2
Wolcott town	513	238	159	87	20	4	0	2	3	46.4	31.0	17.0	11	66	68	0.3	0.4	0.3	0.3

[1]Separate rankings for eight counties and 95 towns.

Table J. — Vote for Presidential Preference: March 24, 1992, Republican Primary Election

County	Top candidates					Top four candidates (state vote)												
						Percent of total vote								Percent contribution to state vote				
										Rank[1]								
	Total	Bush	Bu-chanan	Uncom-mitted	Duke	Bush	Bu-chanan	Uncom-mitted	Other	Bush	Bu-chanan	Uncom-mitted	Other	Total	Bush	Bu-chanan	Uncom-mitted	Other
Fairfield	30,111	21,152	6,043	2,302	614	70.2	20.1	7.6	2.0	1	8	7	8	30.3	31.9	27.7	25.6	26.8
Hartford	25,984	17,029	5,605	2,790	560	65.5	21.6	10.7	2.2	4	7	2	6	26.1	25.7	25.7	31.0	24.4
Litchfield	7,004	4,607	1,523	726	148	65.8	21.7	10.4	2.1	3	6	5	7	7.0	6.9	7.0	8.1	6.5
Middlesex	5,192	3,344	1,172	552	124	64.4	22.6	10.6	2.4	6	5	3	5	5.2	5.0	5.4	6.1	5.4
New Haven	18,269	12,298	4,226	1,257	488	67.3	23.1	6.9	2.7	2	4	8	3	18.4	18.5	19.4	14.0	21.3
New London	6,838	4,106	1,823	713	196	60.0	26.7	10.4	2.9	8	1	4	1	6.9	6.2	8.4	7.9	8.5
Tolland	3,602	2,215	850	441	96	61.5	23.6	12.2	2.7	7	2	1	4	3.6	3.3	3.9	4.9	4.2
Windham	2,473	1,605	573	227	68	64.9	23.2	9.2	2.7	5	3	6	2	2.5	2.4	2.6	2.5	3.0
CONNECTICUT	99,473	66,356	21,815	9,008	2,294	66.7	21.9	9.1	2.3					100.0	100.0	100.0	100.0	100.0
SELECTED TOWNS																		
Ansonia town	331	227	67	16	21	68.6	20.2	4.8	6.3	32	72	88	2	0.3	0.3	0.3	0.2	0.9
Berlin town	670	418	170	66	16	62.4	25.4	9.9	2.4	73	24	40	46	0.7	0.6	0.8	0.7	0.7
Bethel town	507	368	112	18	9	72.6	22.1	3.6	1.8	7	49	95	68	0.5	0.6	0.5	0.2	0.4
Bloomfield town	639	431	112	88	8	67.4	17.5	13.8	1.3	40	88	4	86	0.6	0.6	0.5	1.0	0.3
Branford town	543	382	95	55	11	70.3	17.5	10.1	2.0	14	89	35	56	0.5	0.6	0.4	0.6	0.5
Bridgeport town	1,293	897	285	60	51	69.4	22.0	4.6	3.9	22	50	90	11	1.3	1.4	1.3	0.7	2.2
Bristol town	1,363	828	395	105	35	60.7	29.0	7.7	2.6	80	9	60	39	1.4	1.2	1.8	1.2	1.5
Brookfield town	703	484	160	47	12	68.8	22.8	6.7	1.7	29	42	72	71	0.7	0.7	0.7	0.5	0.5
Brooklyn town	180	130	23	21	6	72.2	12.8	11.7	3.3	9	95	14	20	0.2	0.2	0.1	0.2	0.3
Cheshire town	1,017	696	236	75	10	68.4	23.2	7.4	1.0	33	38	64	93	1.0	1.0	1.1	0.8	0.4
Clinton town	523	379	101	35	8	72.5	19.3	6.7	1.5	8	78	71	76	0.5	0.6	0.5	0.4	0.3
Coventry town	298	164	82	45	7	55.0	27.5	15.1	2.3	93	15	2	48	0.3	0.2	0.4	0.5	0.3
Danbury town	920	633	223	36	28	68.8	24.2	3.9	3.0	30	29	93	26	0.9	1.0	1.0	0.4	1.2
Darien town	1,759	1,267	327	131	34	72.0	18.6	7.4	1.9	12	83	62	60	1.8	1.9	1.5	1.5	1.5
Derby town	147	86	36	15	10	58.5	24.5	10.2	6.8	87	27	34	1	0.1	0.1	0.2	0.2	0.4
East Granby town	246	160	57	24	5	65.0	23.2	9.8	2.0	64	39	41	55	0.2	0.2	0.3	0.3	0.2
East Hartford town	885	579	187	96	23	65.4	21.1	10.8	2.6	59	57	22	36	0.9	0.9	0.9	1.1	1.0
East Haven town	315	219	68	20	8	69.5	21.6	6.3	2.5	21	52	76	41	0.3	0.3	0.3	0.2	0.3
East Lyme town	564	324	169	61	10	57.4	30.0	10.8	1.8	88	6	23	69	0.6	0.5	0.8	0.7	0.4
East Windsor town	215	141	42	24	8	65.6	19.5	11.2	3.7	57	76	19	13	0.2	0.2	0.2	0.3	0.3
Enfield town	1,196	755	288	121	32	63.1	24.1	10.1	2.7	70	31	36	34	1.2	1.1	1.3	1.3	1.4
Essex town	423	305	73	40	5	72.1	17.3	9.5	1.2	10	90	44	87	0.4	0.5	0.3	0.4	0.2
Fairfield town	2,427	1,678	503	199	47	69.1	20.7	8.2	1.9	24	63	53	59	2.4	2.5	2.3	2.2	2.0
Farmington town	915	598	186	110	21	65.4	20.3	12.0	2.3	61	70	9	50	0.9	0.9	0.9	1.2	0.9
Glastonbury town	1,570	1,073	291	182	24	68.3	18.5	11.6	1.5	34	84	17	77	1.6	1.6	1.3	2.0	1.0
Granby town	544	324	128	85	7	59.6	23.5	15.6	1.3	85	36	1	85	0.5	0.5	0.6	0.9	0.3
Greenwich town	3,225	2,347	584	252	42	72.8	18.1	7.8	1.3	5	86	59	84	3.2	3.5	2.7	2.8	1.8
Griswold town	140	90	39	10	1	64.3	27.9	7.1	0.7	67	12	67	95	0.1	0.1	0.2	0.1	<.1
Groton town	931	547	258	108	18	58.8	27.7	11.6	1.9	86	13	16	61	0.9	0.8	1.2	1.2	0.8
Guilford town	818	549	153	103	13	67.1	18.7	12.6	1.6	41	81	5	75	0.8	0.8	0.7	1.1	0.6
Haddam town	295	189	67	27	12	64.1	22.7	9.2	4.1	68	43	46	9	0.3	0.3	0.3	0.3	0.5
Hamden town	1,161	801	263	66	31	69.0	22.7	5.7	2.7	27	44	81	35	1.2	1.2	1.2	0.7	1.4
Hartford town	751	461	179	81	30	61.4	23.8	10.8	4.0	76	33	24	10	0.8	0.7	0.8	0.9	1.3
Killingly town	268	183	60	22	3	68.3	22.4	8.2	1.1	35	47	52	89	0.3	0.3	0.3	0.2	0.1
Ledyard town	546	307	171	58	10	56.2	31.3	10.6	1.8	90	4	26	66	0.5	0.5	0.8	0.6	0.4
Litchfield town	464	304	95	51	14	65.5	20.5	11.0	3.0	58	66	20	29	0.5	0.5	0.4	0.6	0.6
Madison town	1,024	710	213	90	11	69.3	20.8	8.8	1.1	23	61	50	91	1.0	1.1	1.0	1.0	0.5
Manchester town	1,811	1,194	390	183	44	65.9	21.5	10.1	2.4	53	54	37	44	1.8	1.8	1.8	2.0	1.9
Mansfield town	348	230	68	43	7	66.1	19.5	12.4	2.0	50	75	8	58	0.3	0.3	0.3	0.5	0.3
Meriden town	1,513	989	358	116	50	65.4	23.7	7.7	3.3	60	35	61	21	1.5	1.5	1.6	1.3	2.2
Middlebury town	400	246	121	27	6	61.5	30.3	6.8	1.5	74	5	70	78	0.4	0.4	0.6	0.3	0.3
Middletown town	798	481	214	83	20	60.3	26.8	10.4	2.5	83	16	30	43	0.8	0.7	1.0	0.9	0.9
Milford town	1,286	844	326	77	39	65.6	25.3	6.0	3.0	56	25	78	28	1.3	1.3	1.5	0.9	1.7
Monroe town	519	374	111	28	6	72.1	21.4	5.4	1.2	11	56	83	88	0.5	0.6	0.5	0.3	0.3
Montville town	329	178	105	34	12	54.1	31.9	10.3	3.6	95	2	31	14	0.3	0.3	0.5	0.4	0.5
Naugatuck town	545	361	142	25	17	66.2	26.1	4.6	3.1	48	19	91	25	0.5	0.5	0.7	0.3	0.7
New Britain town	1,484	895	354	170	65	60.3	23.9	11.5	4.4	81	32	18	7	1.5	1.3	1.6	1.9	2.8
New Fairfield town	467	309	105	44	9	66.2	22.5	9.4	1.9	49	46	45	62	0.5	0.5	0.5	0.5	0.4
New Hartford town	202	132	42	25	3	65.3	20.8	12.4	1.5	62	62	7	79	0.2	0.2	0.2	0.3	0.1
New Haven town	732	487	149	71	25	66.5	20.4	9.7	3.4	45	68	42	18	0.7	0.7	0.7	0.8	1.1
New London town	370	222	98	38	12	60.0	26.5	10.3	3.2	84	18	33	23	0.4	0.3	0.4	0.4	0.5
New Milford town	978	682	186	89	21	69.7	19.0	9.1	2.1	20	79	48	51	1.0	1.0	0.9	1.0	0.9
Newington town	1,041	680	218	123	20	65.3	20.9	11.8	1.9	63	60	12	63	1.0	1.0	1.0	1.4	0.9
Newtown town	789	554	161	63	11	70.2	20.4	8.0	1.4	15	67	54	83	0.8	0.8	0.7	0.7	0.5
North Branford town	277	206	52	12	7	74.4	18.8	4.3	2.5	3	80	92	42	0.3	0.3	0.2	0.1	0.3
North Haven town	926	639	212	51	24	69.0	22.9	5.5	2.6	26	40	82	38	0.9	1.0	1.0	0.6	1.0
Norwalk town	1,731	1,196	391	112	32	69.1	22.6	6.5	1.8	25	45	74	65	1.7	1.8	1.8	1.2	1.4
Norwich town	670	373	194	72	31	55.7	29.0	10.7	4.6	91	10	25	4	0.7	0.6	0.9	0.8	1.4
Old Saybrook town	772	512	160	82	18	66.3	20.7	10.6	2.3	47	64	27	49	0.8	0.8	0.7	0.9	0.8

[1]Separate rankings for eight counties and 95 towns.

| County | Top candidates | | | | | Top four candidates (state vote) | | | | | | | | | | | | |
| | | | | | | Percent of total vote | | | | Rank[1] | | | | Percent contribution to state vote | | | | |
	Total	Bush	Bu-chanan	Uncom-mitted	Duke	Bush	Bu-chanan	Uncom-mitted	Other	Bush	Bu-chanan	Uncom-mitted	Other	Total	Bush	Bu-chanan	Uncom-mitted	Other
Orange town................	571	406	114	34	17	71.1	20.0	6.0	3.0	13	73	79	31	0.6	0.6	0.5	0.4	0.7
Plainfield town	231	154	60	11	6	66.7	26.0	4.8	2.6	44	21	89	37	0.2	0.2	0.3	0.1	0.3
Plainville town	536	353	110	49	24	65.9	20.5	9.1	4.5	54	65	47	5	0.5	0.5	0.5	0.5	1.0
Plymouth town	242	139	76	23	4	57.4	31.4	9.5	1.7	89	3	43	72	0.2	0.2	0.3	0.3	0.2
Prospect town	262	158	78	16	10	60.3	29.8	6.1	3.8	82	7	77	12	0.3	0.2	0.4	0.2	0.4
Putnam town	117	76	23	14	4	65.0	19.7	12.0	3.4	65	74	10	17	0.1	0.1	0.1	0.2	0.2
Ridgefield town	1,136	754	269	90	23	66.4	23.7	7.9	2.0	46	34	57	57	1.1	1.1	1.2	1.0	1.0
Rocky Hill town	510	345	99	54	12	67.6	19.4	10.6	2.4	39	77	28	47	0.5	0.5	0.5	0.6	0.5
Seymour town	432	285	106	22	19	66.0	24.5	5.1	4.4	52	26	85	6	0.4	0.4	0.5	0.2	0.8
Shelton town	1,341	908	306	79	48	67.7	22.8	5.9	3.6	38	41	80	16	1.3	1.4	1.4	0.9	2.1
Simsbury town	1,573	1,070	294	187	22	68.0	18.7	11.9	1.4	36	82	11	82	1.6	1.6	1.3	2.1	1.0
Somers town	292	178	76	30	8	61.0	26.0	10.3	2.7	78	20	32	33	0.3	0.3	0.3	0.3	0.3
South Windsor town........	797	533	171	80	13	66.9	21.5	10.0	1.6	43	55	38	74	0.8	0.8	0.8	0.9	0.6
Southbury town	1,330	985	224	97	24	74.1	16.8	7.3	1.8	4	91	66	67	1.3	1.5	1.0	1.1	1.0
Southington town	1,133	748	276	80	29	66.0	24.4	7.1	2.6	51	28	68	40	1.1	1.1	1.3	0.9	1.3
Stafford town	193	118	49	16	10	61.1	25.4	8.3	5.2	77	23	51	3	0.2	0.2	0.2	0.2	0.4
Stamford town	4,779	3,341	969	379	90	69.9	20.3	7.9	1.9	18	71	56	64	4.8	5.0	4.4	4.2	3.9
Stonington town	632	398	174	47	13	63.0	27.5	7.4	2.1	72	14	63	54	0.6	0.6	0.8	0.5	0.6
Stratford town	1,395	959	293	93	50	68.7	21.0	6.7	3.6	31	59	73	15	1.4	1.4	1.3	1.0	2.2
Thompson town	203	158	33	10	2	77.8	16.3	4.9	1.0	1	92	86	92	0.2	0.2	0.2	0.1	<.1
Torrington town	1,031	628	276	102	25	60.9	26.8	9.9	2.4	79	17	39	45	1.0	0.9	1.3	1.1	1.1
Trumbull town	1,131	790	247	60	34	69.8	21.8	5.3	3.0	19	51	84	30	1.1	1.2	1.1	0.7	1.5
Vernon town.................	796	533	162	87	14	67.0	20.4	10.9	1.8	42	69	21	70	0.8	0.8	0.7	1.0	0.6
Wallingford town	918	667	204	34	13	72.7	22.2	3.7	1.4	6	48	94	81	0.9	1.0	0.9	0.4	0.6
Waterbury town	1,507	826	556	74	51	54.8	36.9	4.9	3.4	94	1	87	19	1.5	1.2	2.5	0.8	2.2
Waterford town.............	566	372	137	45	12	65.7	24.2	8.0	2.1	55	30	55	52	0.6	0.6	0.6	0.5	0.5
Watertown town	606	393	156	39	18	64.9	25.7	6.4	3.0	66	22	75	32	0.6	0.6	0.7	0.4	0.8
West Hartford town	2,961	2,072	535	311	43	70.0	18.1	10.5	1.5	17	87	29	80	3.0	3.1	2.5	3.5	1.9
West Haven town..........	775	543	142	57	33	70.1	18.3	7.4	4.3	16	85	65	8	0.8	0.8	0.7	0.6	1.4
Westport town	1,876	1,292	287	266	31	68.9	15.3	14.2	1.7	28	93	3	73	1.9	1.9	1.3	3.0	1.4
Wethersfield town	1,333	903	281	121	28	67.7	21.1	9.1	2.1	37	58	49	53	1.3	1.4	1.3	1.3	1.2
Wilton town	1,076	825	154	85	12	76.7	14.3	7.9	1.1	2	94	58	90	1.1	1.2	0.7	0.9	0.5
Windham town	366	203	108	43	12	55.5	29.5	11.7	3.3	92	8	13	22	0.4	0.3	0.5	0.5	0.5
Windsor Locks town	362	231	78	42	11	63.8	21.5	11.6	3.0	69	53	15	27	0.4	0.3	0.4	0.5	0.5
Windsor town................	961	606	226	121	8	63.1	23.5	12.6	0.8	71	37	6	94	1.0	0.9	1.0	1.3	0.3
Wolcott town.................	384	236	109	27	12	61.5	28.4	7.0	3.1	75	11	69	24	0.4	0.4	0.5	0.3	0.5

[1]Separate rankings for eight counties and 95 towns.

1992 Vote for President
Percent for Clinton (D), by Minor Civil Division

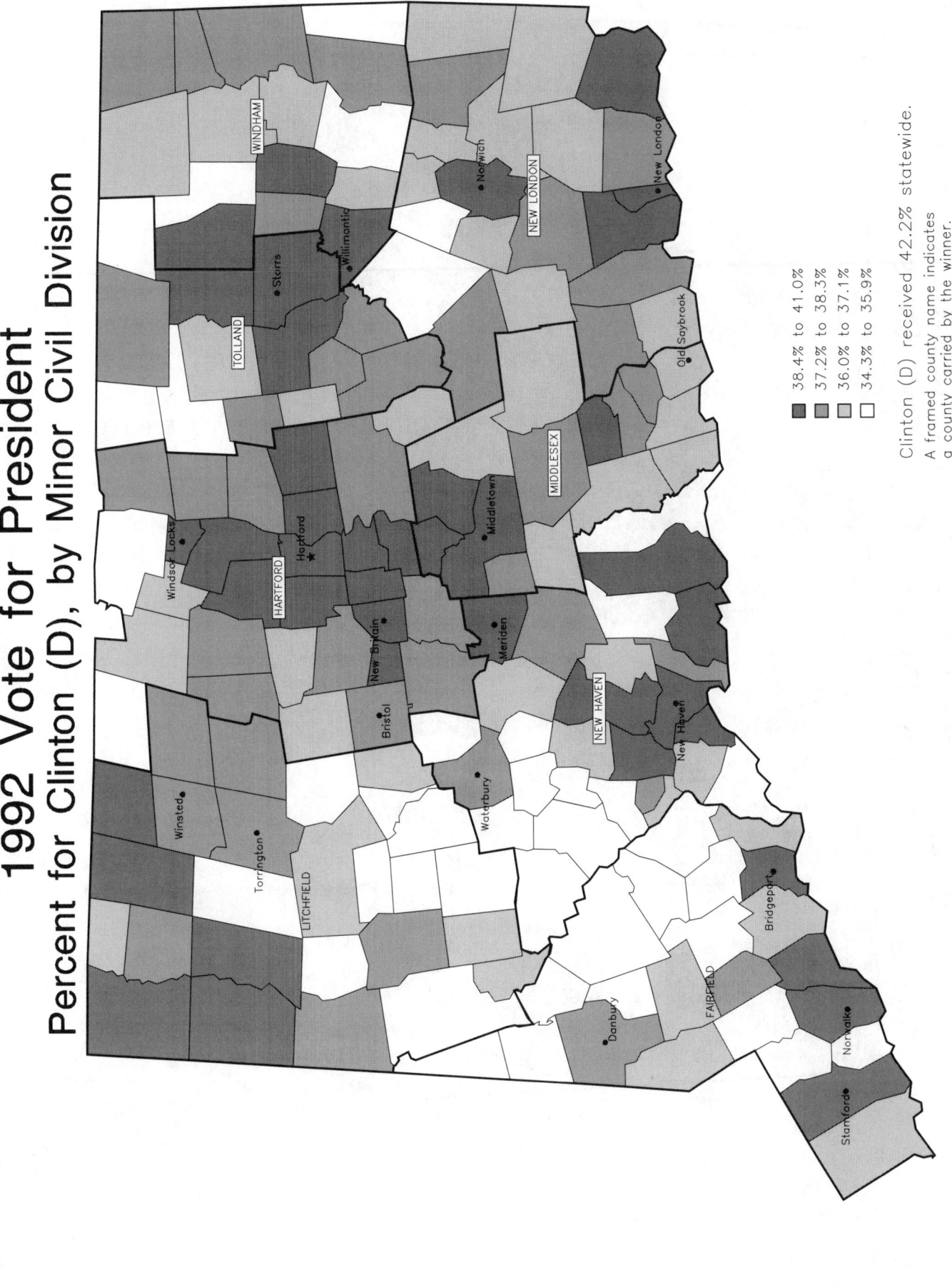

Clinton (D) received 42.2% statewide.

A framed county name indicates
a county carried by the winner.

- 38.4% to 41.0%
- 37.2% to 38.3%
- 36.0% to 37.1%
- 34.3% to 35.9%

Copyright ©1993 by Election Data Services, Inc.

Connecticut 169

1992 Vote for U.S. Senator
Percent for Dodd (D), by Minor Civil Division

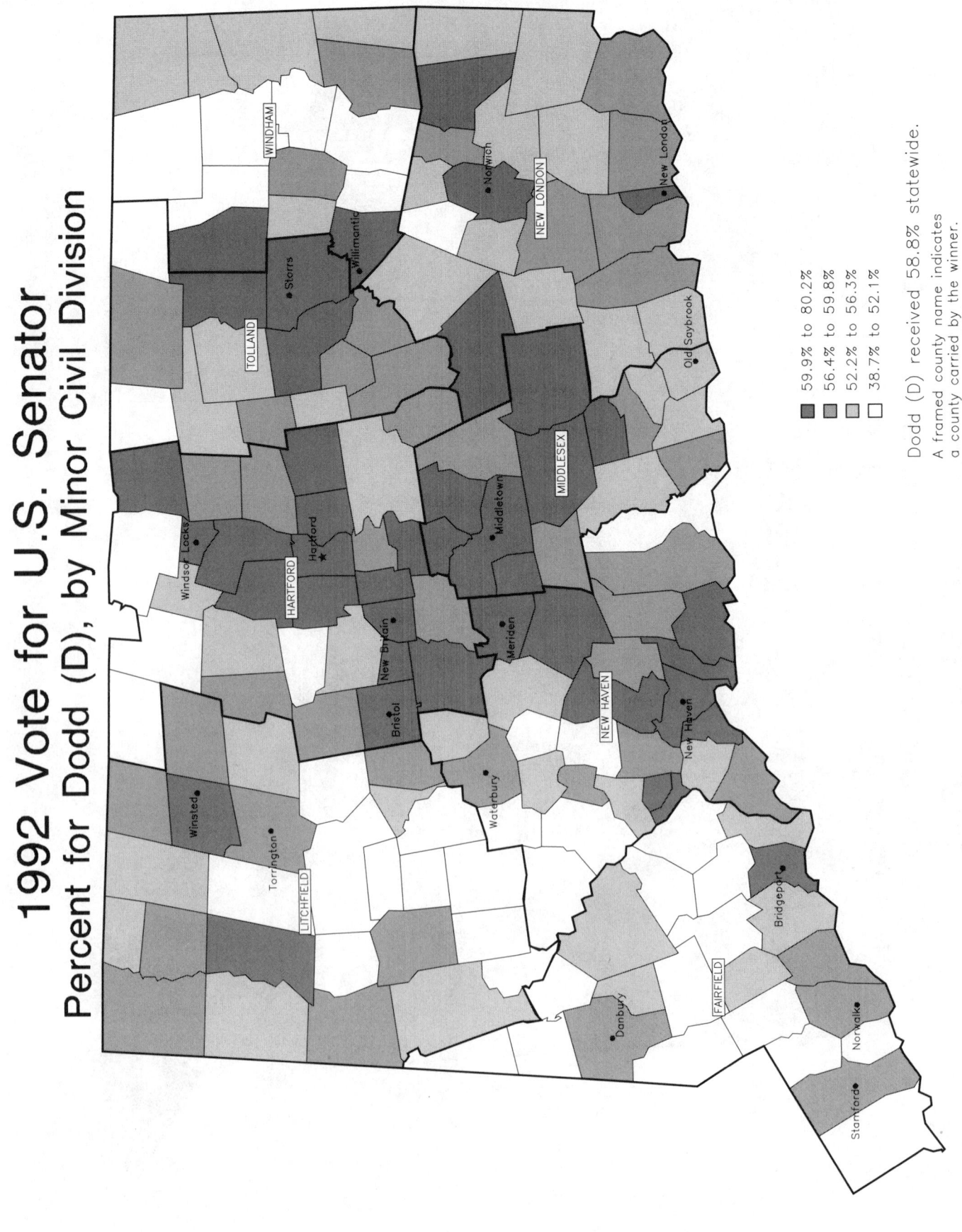

Dodd (D) received 58.8% statewide.

A framed county name indicates a county carried by the winner.

- 59.9% to 80.2%
- 56.4% to 59.8%
- 52.2% to 56.3%
- 38.7% to 52.1%

Copyright © 1993 by Election Data Services, Inc.

DELAWARE

Congressional Districts 1
   Average Population 666,168
State Senate Districts 21
   Average Population 31,722
State House Districts 41
   Average Population 16,248

Electoral College Votes...3
Counties 3
Voting Precincts 364

Alternative Registration Methods:
   ....Deputized Registrars, Mail-in

Registration Deadline[1] .... 3rd Sat. in October

Voting Equipment Use (Counties)

Datavote Punch Card	0	Paper Ballot	0
Electronic	0	Other Punch Card	0
Lever Machine	3	Mixed Systems	0
Optical Scanner	0		

Party Control	DEM	REP	IND	VAC
1993 State Senate	15	6	0	0
1992 State Senate	15	6	0	0
1993 State House	18	23	0	0
1992 State House	17	24	0	0

Population Statistics 1990

Race/Ethnicity	Total Population		Voting Age Population		Voting Age Population % of total population
	Number	%	Number	%	
Non-Hispanic					
White	528,092	79.3	408,510	81.2	77.4
Black	111,011	16.7	76,059	15.1	68.5
Asian/Pacific Islander	8,854	1.3	6,307	1.3	71.2
Native American	1,938	0.3	1,468	0.3	75.7
Other	453	<.1	252	<.1	55.6
All Hispanic	15,820	2.4	10,231	2.0	64.7
TOTAL	666,168	100.0	502,827	100.0	75.5

Estimated Voting Age Population 1992 (VAP) 525,000
Number of Registered Voters................................... 342,088
   % of estimated VAP... 65.2
Voter Turnout (Actual) 290,836
   % of VAP 55.4
   % of Registration 85.0
Persons Not Voting—of Voting Age 234,164
   % of VAP 44.6
Persons Not Voting—of Registered 51,252
   % of Registration 15.0
Straight Ticket Voting .... No

State Officials and Members of Congress

Governor:
Thomas R. Carper (D) 1992, elected to a four-year term in 1992.

U.S. Senators:
William V. Roth (R) 1970, elected to a six-year term in 1988.
Joseph R. Biden, Jr. (D) 1972, elected to a six-year term in 1990.

U.S. Representative in Congress:
(District, Name, Party, Date first elected)

At-Large. Castle (R) 1992

---

[1] Deadline for primary election is 21 days before election.

Candidates: General Election, November 3, 1992

Candidate(s)	Total vote	Percent	Party	Status	First elected
President/Vice President					
Clinton/Gore	126,054	43.51%	Democrat	Challenger	1992
Bush/Quayle	102,313	35.31%	Republican	Incumbent	1988
Perot/Stockdale	59,213	20.44%	Independent	Challenger	
Fulani/Munoz	1,105	0.38%	New Alliance	Challenger	
Marrou/Lord	935	0.32%	Libertarian	Challenger	
Write ins	115	0.04%	Write in	Challenger	
U.S. Senator (No Contest)					
Governor					
Thomas Carper	179,365	64.74%	Democrat	Challenger	1992
Gary Scott	90,725	32.75%	Republican	Challenger	
Floyd McDowell, Sr.	3,779	1.36%	A Delaware Party	Challenger	
Richard Cohen	3,165	1.14%	Libertarian	Challenger	
U.S. Representative in Congress					
District At-Large					
Michael Castle	153,037	55.42%	Republican	Challenger	1992
S.B. Woo	117,426	42.53%	Democrat	Challenger	
Peggy Schmitt	5,661	2.05%	Libertarian	Challenger	

Voter Registration and Turnout, 1948-1992 Elections

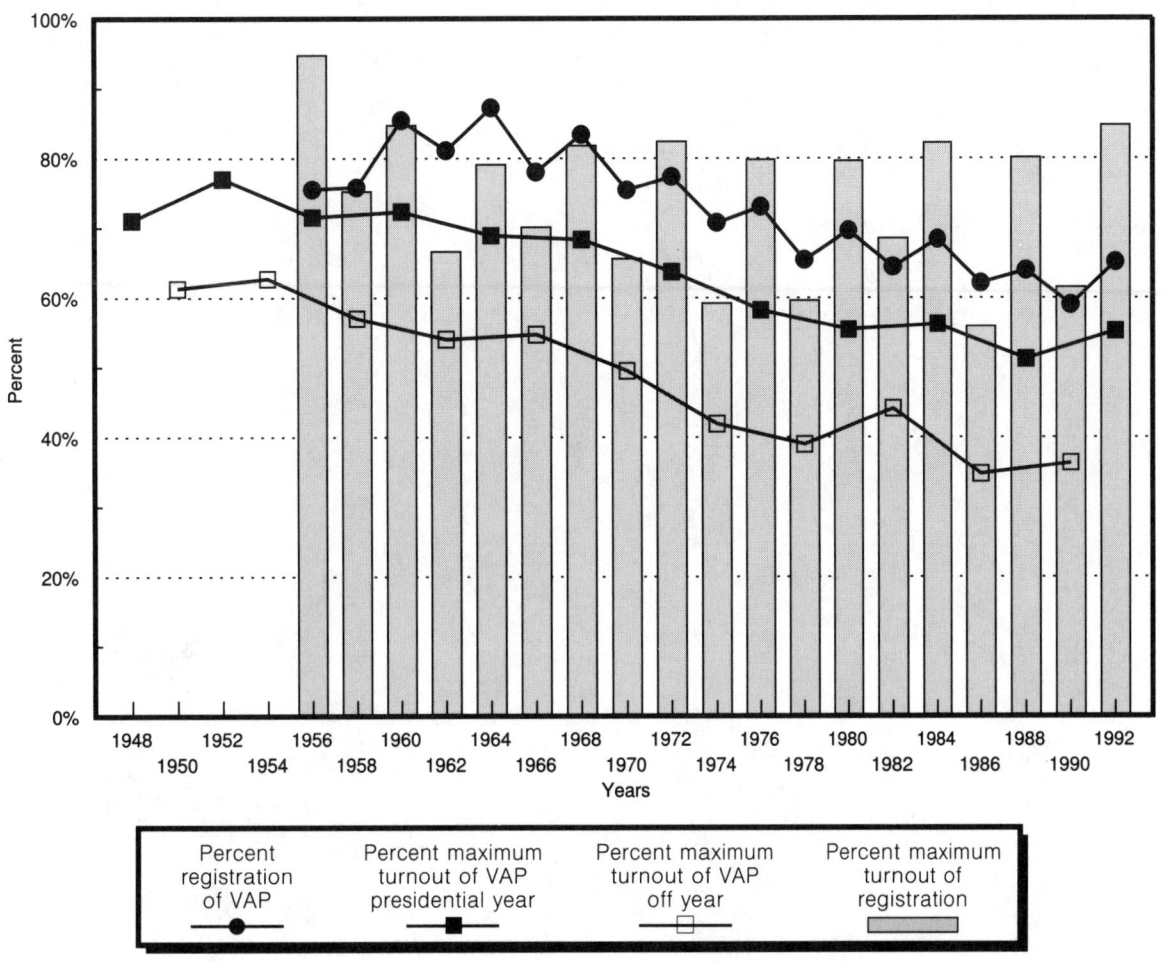

Legend			
Percent registration of VAP (●)	Percent maximum turnout of VAP presidential year (■)	Percent maximum turnout of VAP off year (□)	Percent maximum turnout of registration (bar)

Year	Estimated Voting Age Population (VAP)	Voter registration (REG)			Voter turnout										
						Highest office						Maximum vote			
		Total	Percent of VAP	Rank by percent of VAP	Actual	Total	Office	Percent total REG	Rank by percent of REG	Percent of VAP	Rank by percent of VAP	Total	Percent total REG	Rank by percent of REG	Percent total VAP	Rank by percent of VAP
1992	525,000	342,088	65.2	42	290,836	289,735	P	84.7	3	55.2	30	290,836	85.0	2	55.4	30
1990	507,000	299,081	59.0	43	183,977	180,152	S	60.2	19	35.5	33	183,977	61.5	20	36.3	34
1988	498,000	318,362	63.9	40	254,973	249,891	P	78.5	7	50.2	30	254,973	80.1	7	51.2	29
1986	477,000	296,436	62.1	39	165,563	160,757	C	54.2	27	33.7	38	165,563	55.9	28	34.7	37
1984	459,000	314,034	68.4	36	258,182	254,572	P	81.1	2	55.5	24	258,182	82.2	5	56.2	26
1982	444,000	285,736	64.4	33	195,726	190,960	S	66.8	14	43.0	24	195,726	68.5	16	44.1	26
1980	432,000	300,600	69.6	30	239,136	235,900	P	78.5	9	54.6	27	239,136	79.6	11	55.4	26
1978	426,000	278,507	65.4	36	166,045	162,072	S	58.2	20	38.0	27	166,045	59.6	19	39.0	28
1976	412,000	300,919	73.0	24	239,984	235,834	P	78.4	16	57.2	24	239,984	79.8	16	58.2	22
1974	395,000	279,364	70.7	24	165,345	160,328	C	57.4	25	40.6	31	165,345	59.2	25	41.9	30
1972	379,000	293,078	77.3	19	241,512	235,516	P	80.4	8	62.1	15	241,512	82.4	9	63.7	14
1970	326,000	245,945	75.4	18	-	161,439	S	65.6	26	49.5	29	161,439	65.6	27	49.5	30
1968	314,000	262,032	83.4	11	-	214,367	P	81.8	18	68.3	12	214,367	81.8	21	68.3	13
1966	301,000	234,731	78.0	18	-	164,549	S	70.1	16	54.7	21	164,549	70.1	18	54.7	21
1964	292,000	254,494	87.2	13	-	201,320	P	79.1	26	68.9	19	201,320	79.1	28	68.9	21
1962	284,000	230,315	81.1	11	-	153,356	C	66.6	19	54.0	20	153,356	66.6	22	54.0	21
1960	272,000	232,333	85.4	10	-	196,683	P	84.7	18	72.3	17	196,683	84.7	19	72.3	18
1958	271,000	205,445	75.8	18	-	154,432	S	75.2	10	57.0	15	154,432	75.2	10	57.0	17
1956	249,000	188,026	75.5	18	-	177,988	P	94.7	3	71.5	13	177,988	94.7	3	71.5	15
1954	231,000	-	-	-	-	144,900	S	-	-	62.7	4	144,900	-	-	62.7	4
1952	226,000	-	-	-	-	174,025	P	-	-	77.0	6	174,025	-	-	77.0	7
1950	211,000	-	-	-	-	129,404	C	-	-	61.3	5	129,404	-	-	61.3	6
1948	196,000	-	-	-	-	139,073	P	-	-	71.0	2	139,073	-	-	71.0	2

DELAWARE

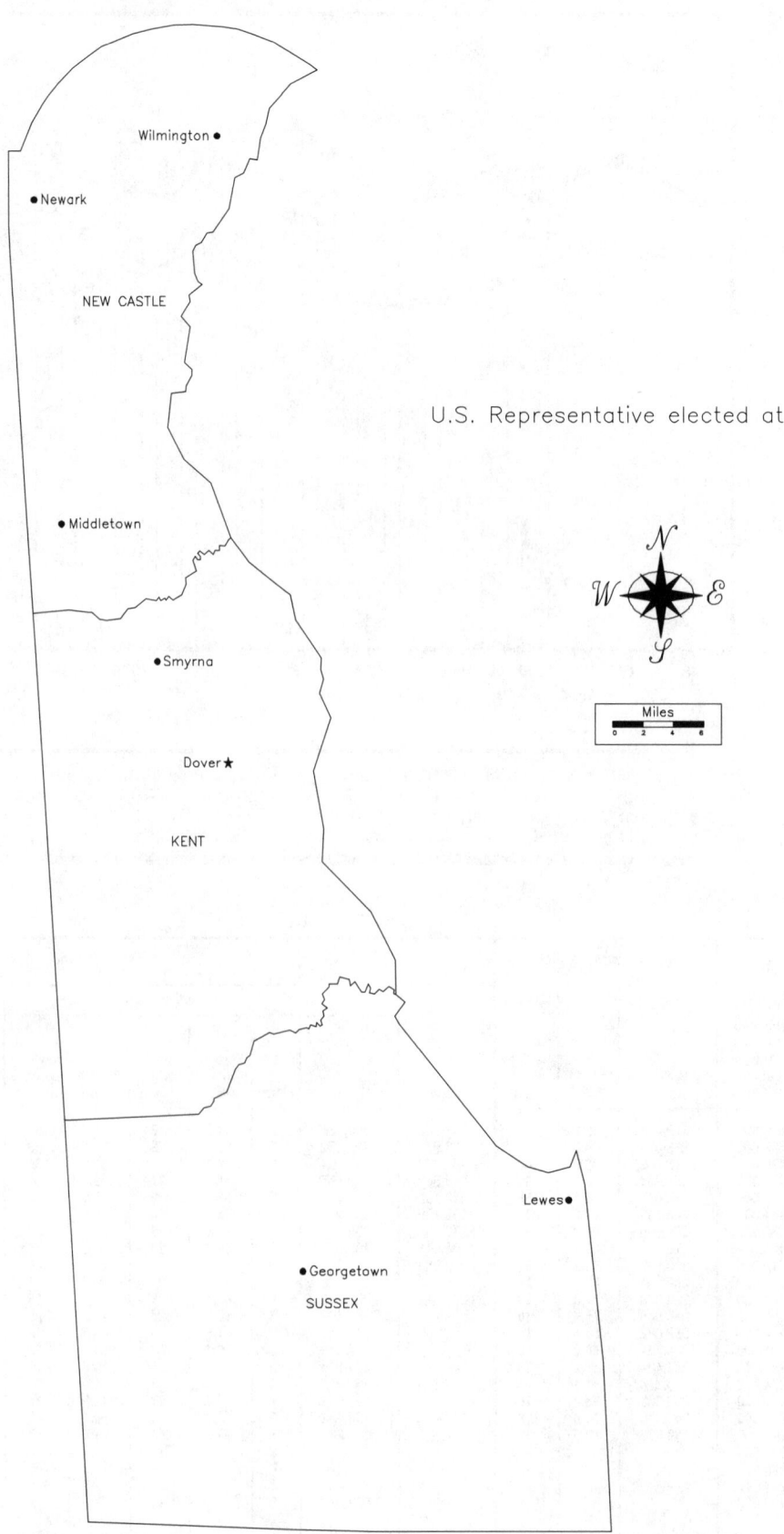

Wilmington •

• Newark

NEW CASTLE

U.S. Representative elected at large.

• Middletown

• Smyrna

Dover ★

KENT

Lewes •

• Georgetown
SUSSEX

Table A. – 1990 Population by Race and Ethnic Origin

State/county code	County	Total persons	Percent of total persons — Non-Hispanic — White	Black	Asian and Pacific Islander	Native American	Other	Hispanic	Rank — Percent of total persons — Total	Non-Hispanic — White	Black	Hispanic	Percent contribution to state population — Total	Non-Hispanic — White	Black	Hispanic
10 001	Kent	110,993	77.5	18.3	1.2	0.5	0.1	2.3	3	3	1	2	16.7	16.3	18.3	16.1
10 003	New Castle	441,946	79.3	16.3	1.6	0.2	<.1	2.7	1	2	3	1	66.3	66.3	64.8	74.6
10 005	Sussex	113,229	81.0	16.6	0.5	0.6	<.1	1.3	2	1	2	3	17.0	17.4	16.9	9.3
10	**DELAWARE**	**666,168**	**79.3**	**16.7**	**1.3**	**0.3**	**<.1**	**2.4**					**100.0**	**100.0**	**100.0**	**100.0**
	CONGRESSIONAL District At-Large	666,168	79.3	16.7	1.3	0.3	<.1	2.4								

Table B. – 1990 Voting Age Population (VAP) by Race and Ethnic Origin

County	Total Voting Age Population	Percent of total VAP — Non-Hispanic — White	Black	Asian and Pacific Islander	Native American	Other	Hispanic	Rank — Percent of total VAP — Total	Non-Hispanic — White	Black	Hispanic	Percent contribution to state VAP — Total	Non-Hispanic — White	Black	Hispanic	VAP percent of total population — Total	Non-Hispanic — White	Black	Asian and Pacific Islander	Native American	Other	Hispanic
Kent	80,819	79.2	17.0	1.2	0.5	<.1	2.0	3	3	1	2	16.1	15.7	18.0	15.6	72.8	74.3	67.6	73.3	73.5	69.0	62.8
New Castle	335,867	81.2	14.8	1.5	0.2	<.1	2.3	1	2	2	1	66.8	66.8	65.5	75.1	76.0	77.9	69.3	70.9	76.6	51.7	65.1
Sussex	86,141	83.3	14.5	0.5	0.6	<.1	1.1	2	1	3	3	17.1	17.6	16.4	9.3	76.1	78.3	66.4	70.4	76.9	45.7	64.6
DELAWARE	**502,827**	**81.2**	**15.1**	**1.3**	**0.3**	**<.1**	**2.0**					**100.0**	**100.0**	**100.0**	**100.0**	**75.5**	**77.4**	**68.5**	**71.2**	**75.7**	**55.6**	**64.7**
CONGRESSIONAL District At-Large	502,827	81.2	15.1	1.3	0.3	<.1	2.0									75.5	77.4	68.5	71.2	75.7	55.6	64.7

Table C. – Voter Participation: November 3, 1992, General Election

County	Estimated Voting Age Population (VAP) 1992	Voter registration (REG) — Total	% contribution to state REG	% of 1992 VAP	Rank by % of 1992 VAP	Voter turnout — Highest office — Actual	Total	Office	% of 1992 VAP	Maximum vote — Total	% contribution to state turnout	% of REG	Rank by % of REG	% of 1992 VAP	Rank by % of 1992 VAP	Percent drop-off, by office — President	Senator	Governor	Representative
Kent	84,721	46,814	13.7	55.3	3	40,508	40,255	P	47.5	40,508	13.9	86.5	1	47.8	3	0.6	-	3.3	4.3
New Castle	349,122	234,121	68.4	67.1	2	197,416	196,904	P	56.4	197,416	67.9	84.3	3	56.5	2	0.3	-	4.6	4.8
Sussex	91,157	61,153	17.9	67.1	1	52,912	52,576	P	57.7	52,912	18.2	86.5	2	58.0	1	0.6	-	6.2	6.6
DELAWARE	**525,000**	**342,088**	**100.0**	**65.2**		**290,836**	**289,735**		**55.2**	**290,836**	**100.0**	**85.0**		**55.4**		**0.4**	**-**	**4.7**	**5.1**

Table D. — Voter Registration by Political Party Affiliation: November 3, 1992, General Election

County	Total voter registration	Political party affiliation Democrat (DEM)	Republican (REP)	Independent (IND)	Plurality Total	Plurality Party	Percent of total registration DEM	REP	IND	Rank DEM	REP	IND	Percent contribution to state registration Total	DEM	REP	IND
Kent	46,814	20,186	17,212	9,416	2,974	D	43.1	36.8	20.1	3	2	2	13.7	13.6	13.7	13.9
New Castle	234,121	101,581	83,836	48,704	17,745	D	43.4	35.8	20.8	2	3	1	68.4	68.4	66.6	71.9
Sussex	61,153	26,775	24,781	9,597	1,994	D	43.8	40.5	15.7	1	1	3	17.9	18.0	19.7	14.2
DELAWARE	**342,088**	**148,542**	**125,829**	**67,717**	**22,713**	**D**	**43.4**	**36.8**	**19.8**				**100.0**	**100.0**	**100.0**	**100.0**

Table E. — Vote for President: November 3, 1992, General Election

County	Total	Clinton (DEM)	Bush (REP)	Perot (IND)	Other	Plurality Total	Plurality Party	Percent of total vote DEM	REP	IND	Other	Rank DEM	REP	IND	Percent contribution to state vote Total	DEM	REP	IND	Major party Percent of vote DEM	REP
Kent	40,255	15,364	15,562	8,916	413	198	R	38.2	38.7	22.1	1.0	2	2	2	13.9	12.2	15.2	15.1	49.7	50.3
New Castle	196,904	91,516	66,311	37,581	1,496	25,205	D	46.5	33.7	19.1	0.8	1	3	3	68.0	72.6	64.8	63.5	58.0	42.0
Sussex	52,576	19,174	20,440	12,716	246	1,266	R	36.5	38.9	24.2	0.5	3	1	1	18.1	15.2	20.0	21.5	48.4	51.6
DELAWARE	**289,735**	**126,054**	**102,313**	**59,213**	**2,155**	**23,741**	**D**	**43.5**	**35.3**	**20.4**	**0.7**				**100.0**	**100.0**	**100.0**	**100.0**	**55.2**	**44.8**

Table G. — Vote for Governor: November 3, 1992, General Election

County	Total	Carper (DEM)	Scott (REP)	Other	Plurality Total	Plurality Party	Percent of total vote DEM	REP	Other	Rank DEM	REP	Other	Percent contribution to state vote Total	DEM	REP	Other
Kent	39,154	24,734	13,406	1,014	11,328	D	63.2	34.2	2.6	2	2	2	14.1	13.8	14.8	14.6
New Castle	188,240	124,601	58,609	5,030	65,992	D	66.2	31.1	2.7	1	3	1	67.9	69.5	64.6	72.4
Sussex	49,640	30,030	18,710	900	11,320	D	60.5	37.7	1.8	3	1	3	17.9	16.7	20.6	13.0
DELAWARE	**277,034**	**179,365**	**90,725**	**6,944**	**88,640**	**D**	**64.7**	**32.7**	**2.5**				**100.0**	**100.0**	**100.0**	**100.0**

Table H. — **Vote for U.S. Representative in Congress: November 3, 1992, General Election**

Congressional district and county	Total	Democrat (DEM)	Republican (REP)	Other	Plurality Total	Plurality Party	Percent of total vote DEM	REP	Other	Rank within district DEM	REP	Other	Percent contribution to district vote Total	DEM	REP	Other
District At-Large	**276,124**	**117,426**	**153,037**	**5,661**	**35,611**	**R**	**42.5**	**55.4**	**2.1**				**100.0**	**100.0**	**100.0**	**100.0**
Kent	38,764	17,399	20,460	905	3,061	R	44.9	52.8	2.3	1	3	1	14.0	14.8	13.4	16.0
New Castle	187,940	81,716	102,399	3,825	20,683	R	43.5	54.5	2.0	2	2	2	68.1	69.6	66.9	67.6
Sussex	49,420	18,311	30,178	931	11,867	R	37.1	61.1	1.9	3	1	3	17.9	15.6	19.7	16.4
DELAWARE	**276,124**	**117,426**	**153,037**	**5,661**	**35,611**	**R**	**42.5**	**55.4**	**2.1**							

1992 Vote for President
Percent for Clinton (D), by County

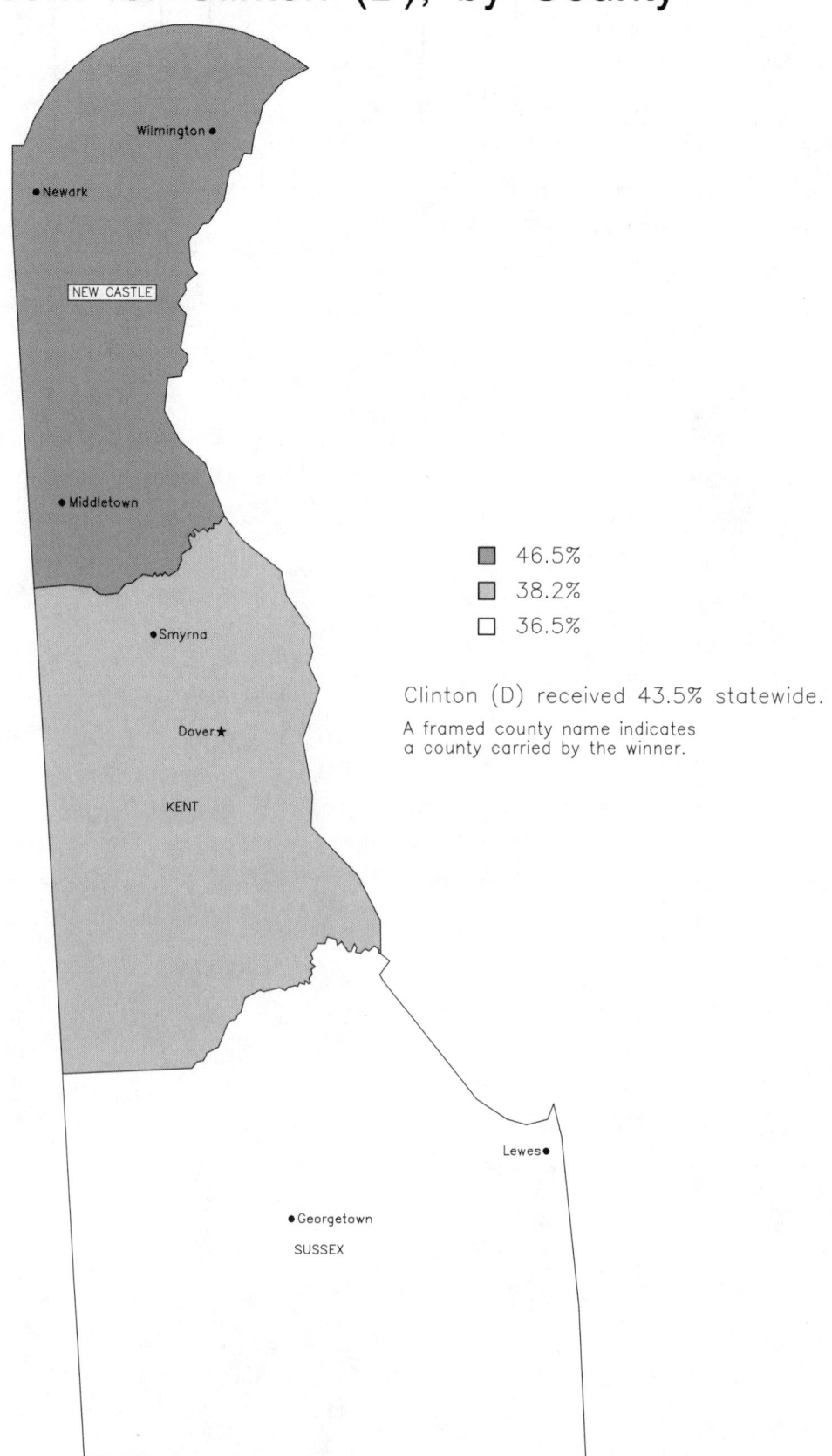

Wilmington ●

● Newark

NEW CASTLE

● Middletown

■ 46.5%
▨ 38.2%
□ 36.5%

● Smyrna

Clinton (D) received 43.5% statewide.

A framed county name indicates
a county carried by the winner.

Dover ★

KENT

Lewes ●

● Georgetown

SUSSEX

1992 Vote for Governor
Percent for Carper (D), by County

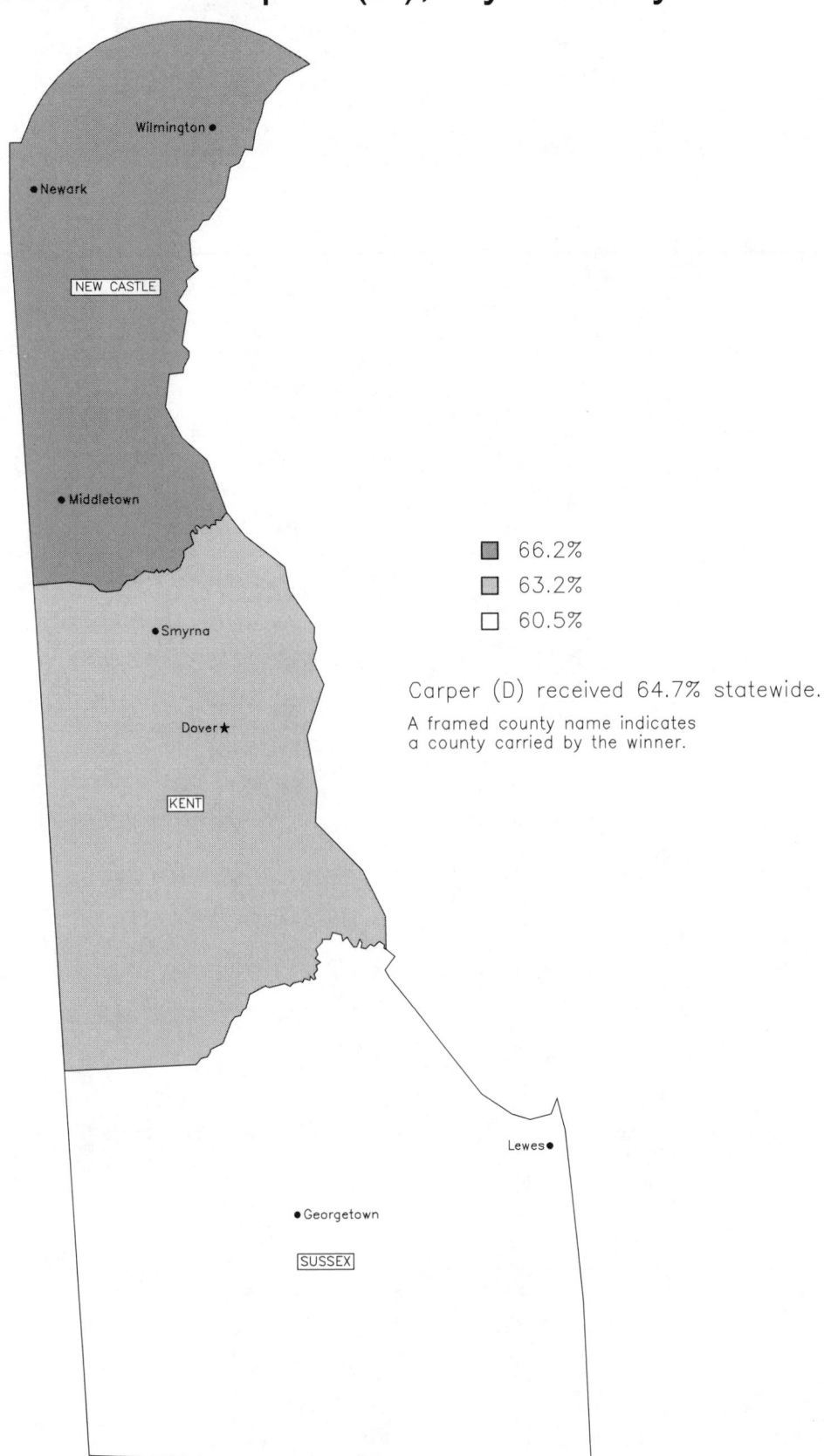

Wilmington ●

● Newark

NEW CASTLE

● Middletown

■ 66.2%
■ 63.2%
□ 60.5%

● Smyrna

Dover ★

KENT

Carper (D) received 64.7% statewide.

A framed county name indicates
a county carried by the winner.

Lewes ●

● Georgetown

SUSSEX

FLORIDA

Congressional Districts 23
    Average Population 562,519
State Senate Districts 40
    Average Population 323,448
State House Districts 120
    Average Population 107,816

Electoral College Votes..25
Counties 67
Voting Precincts 5,152

Alternative Registration Methods:
....Deputized Registrars

Registration Deadline (Days before Election) 30

Population Statistics 1990

Race/ Ethnicity	Total Population		Voting Age Population		Voting Age Population % of total population
	Number	%	Number	%	
Non-Hispanic					
White	9,475,326	73.2	7,646,760	75.9	80.7
Black	1,701,103	13.1	1,109,710	11.0	65.2
Asian/Pacific Islander	146,159	1.1	105,233	1.0	72.0
Native American	32,910	0.3	24,550	0.2	74.6
Other	8,285	<.1	3,982	<.1	48.1
All Hispanic	1,574,143	12.2	1,181,454	11.7	75.1
TOTAL	12,937,926	100.0	10,071,689	100.0	77.8

Voting Equipment Use (Counties)

Datavote Punch Card	23	Paper Ballot	2
Electronic	2	Other Punch Card	16
Lever Machine	13	Mixed Systems	0
Optical Scanner	11		

Party Control	DEM	REP	IND	VAC
1993 State Senate	20	20	0	0
1992 State Senate	21	19	0	0
1993 State House	71	49	0	0
1992 State House	74	46	0	0

Estimated Voting Age Population 1992 (VAP) 10,586,000
Number of Registered Voters................................. 6,541,825
    % of estimated VAP... 61.8
Voter Turnout (Maximum Vote)[1]........................... 5,438,617
    % of VAP 51.4
    % of Registration 83.1
Persons Not Voting—of Voting Age 5,147,383
    % of VAP 48.6
Persons Not Voting—of Registered 1,103,208
    % of Registration 16.9
Straight Ticket Voting .... No

State Officials and Members of Congress

Governor:
Lawton Chiles (D) 1990, elected to a four-year term in 1990.

U.S. Senators:
Bob Graham (D) 1986, elected to a six-year term in 1992.
Connie Mack (R) 1988, elected to a six-year term in 1988.

U.S. Representative in Congress:
(District, Name, Party, Date first elected)

1. Hutto (D) 1978
2. Peterson (D) 1990
3. Brown (D) 1992
4. Fowler (R) 1992
5. Thurman (D) 1992
6. Stearns (R) 1988
7. Mica (R) 1992
8. McCollum (R) 1980
9. Bilirakis (R) 1982
10. Young (R) 1970
11. Gibbons (D) 1962
12. Canady (R) 1992
13. Miller (R) 1992
14. Goss (R) 1988
15. Bacchus (D) 1990
16. Lewis (R) 1982
17. Meek (D) 1992
18. Ros-Lehtinen (R) 1989
19. Johnston (D) 1988
20. Deutsch (D) 1992
21. Diaz-Balart (R) 1992
22. Shaw (R) 1980
23. Hastings (D) 1992

---

[1]Maximum vote turnout from Table C exceeds reported statewide actual voter turnout because in one or more counties the vote for highest office is greater than reported actual turnout.

Candidates: General Election, November 3, 1992

Candidate(s)	Total vote	Percent	Party	Status	First elected
President/Vice President					
Bush/Quayle	2,173,310	40.89%	Republican	Incumbent	1988
Clinton/Gore	2,072,698	39.00%	Democrat	Challenger	1992
Perot/Stockdale	1,053,067	19.82%	Ross Perot	Challenger	
Marrou/Lord	15,079	0.28%	Libertarian	Challenger	
Hagelin/Tompkins	214	<.01%	Natural Law	Challenger	
Write ins[1]	24	<.01%	Write in	Unknown/NA	
U.S. Senator					
Bob Graham	3,245,565	65.40%	Democrat	Incumbent	1986
Bill Grant	1,716,505	34.59%	Republican	Challenger	
Charles Evans	86	<.01%	Write in	Challenger	
Wayne Wiechart	71	<.01%	Write in	Challenger	
Dan Fein	63	<.01%	Write in	Challenger	

Governor (No Contest)

U.S. Representative in Congress

Candidate(s)	Total vote	Percent	Party	Status	First elected
District 1					
Earl Hutto	118,941	52.02%	Democrat	Incumbent	1978
Terry Ketchel	100,349	43.89%	Republican	Challenger	
Barbara Rodgers-Hendricks	9,342	4.09%	Green	Challenger	
District 2					
Pete Peterson	167,215	73.43%	Democrat	Incumbent	1990
Ray Wagner	60,425	26.53%	Republican	Challenger	
Dennis Prescott	86	0.04%	Write in	Challenger	
District 3					
Corrine Brown	91,915	59.29%	Democrat	Challenger	1992
Don Weidner	63,114	40.71%	Republican	Challenger	
District 4					
Tillie Fowler	135,883	56.74%	Republican	Challenger	1992
Mattox Hair	103,531	43.23%	Democrat	Challenger	
Cliff Taylor	57	0.02%	Write in	Challenger	
District 5					
Karen Thurman	129,698	49.21%	Democrat	Challenger	1992
Tom Hogan	114,356	43.39%	Republican	Challenger	
Cindy Munkittrick	19,462	7.38%	Independent	Challenger	
Belinda Noah	33	0.01%	Write in	Challenger	
District 6					
Clifford Stearns	144,195	65.36%	Republican	Incumbent	1988
Phil Denton	76,419	34.64%	Democrat	Challenger	
District 7					
John Mica	125,823	56.42%	Republican	Challenger	1992
Dan Webster	96,945	43.47%	Democrat	Challenger	
Ken McCarthy	213	0.10%	Write in	Challenger	
Roy Davis	42	0.02%	Write in	Challenger	
District 8					
Bill McCollum	141,977	68.55%	Republican	Incumbent	1980
Chuck Kovaleski	65,145	31.45%	Democrat	Challenger	
District 9					
Michael Bilirakis	158,028	58.93%	Republican	Incumbent	1982
Cheryl Knapp	110,135	41.07%	Democrat	Challenger	
District 10					
C. W. Bill Young	149,606	56.58%	Republican	Incumbent	1970
Karen Moffitt	114,809	43.42%	Democrat	Challenger	

[1] Votes for Write in candidates include 16 for Brisben/Edwards, 4 for Anthony Bellizi, 2 for Jean Joie Nate, and 1 each for Barbara Eastman and J.P. Miller.

Candidate(s)	Total vote	Percent	Party	Status	First elected
U.S. Representative in Congress (cont)					
District 11					
Sam Gibbons	100,984	52.77%	Democrat	Incumbent	1962
Mark Sharpe	77,640	40.57%	Republican	Challenger	
Joe De Minico	12,730	6.65%	Independent	Challenger	
District 12					
Charles Canady	100,484	52.11%	Republican	Challenger	1992
Tom Mims	92,346	47.89%	Democrat	Challenger	
District 13					
Dan Miller	158,881	57.85%	Republican	Challenger	1992
Rand Snell	115,767	42.15%	Democrat	Challenger	
District 14					
Porter Goss	220,351	82.06%	Republican	Incumbent	1988
James King	48,160	17.94%	Independent	Challenger	
District 15					
Jim Bacchus	132,412	50.68%	Democrat	Incumbent	1990
Bill Tolley	128,873	49.32%	Republican	Challenger	
District 16					
Tom Lewis	157,322	60.85%	Republican	Incumbent	1982
John Comerford	101,237	39.15%	Democrat	Challenger	
District 17					
Carrie Meek	102,784	99.99%	Democrat	Challenger	1992
Jill Fein	15	0.01%	Write in	Challenger	
District 18					
Ileana Ros-Lehtinen	104,755	66.77%	Republican	Incumbent	1989
Magda Montiel Davis	52,142	33.23%	Democrat	Challenger	
District 19					
Harry Johnston	177,423	63.07%	Democrat	Incumbent	1988
Larry Metz	103,867	36.92%	Republican	Challenger	
Kenneth Hemmerle, Sr.	4	<.01%	Write in	Challenger	
District 20					
Peter Deutsch	130,959	55.05%	Democrat	Challenger	1992
Beverly Kennedy	91,589	38.50%	Republican	Challenger	
James Blackburn	15,341	6.45%	Independent	Challenger	
District 22					
E. Clay Shaw	128,400	51.97%	Republican	Incumbent	1980
Gwen Margolis	91,625	37.08%	Democrat	Challenger	
Richard Stephens	15,469	6.26%	Independent	Challenger	
Michael Petrie	6,312	2.55%	Independent	Challenger	
Bernard Anscher	5,274	2.13%	Independent	Challenger	
Bill Lambert	8	<.01%	Write in	Challenger	
District 23					
Alcee Hastings	84,249	58.53%	Democrat	Challenger	1992
Ed Fielding	44,807	31.13%	Republican	Challenger	
Al Woods	14,879	10.34%	Independent	Challenger	
U.S. Representative in Congress					
District 21 (Primary Election, September, 1, 1992)[1]					
Lincoln Diaz-Balart	15,192	68.64%	Republican	Challenger	1992
Javier Souto	6,941	31.36%	Republican	Challenger	

Because there was no Democratic primary and no qualified write-in candidate, Republican primary winner was declared elected and did not appear on the general election ballot.

Candidates: March 10, 1992, Primary Election

Candidate	Total vote	Percent	Candidate	Total vote	Percent
Presidential Preference, Democratic			**Presidential Preference, Republican**		
Bill Clinton	570,566	50.77%	George Bush	608,077	68.06%
Paul Tsongas	388,124	34.54%	Patrick Buchanan	285,386	31.94%
Jerry Brown	139,569	12.42%			
Tom Harkin	13,587	1.21%			
Bob Kerrey	12,011	1.07%			

Voter Registration and Turnout, 1948-1992 Elections

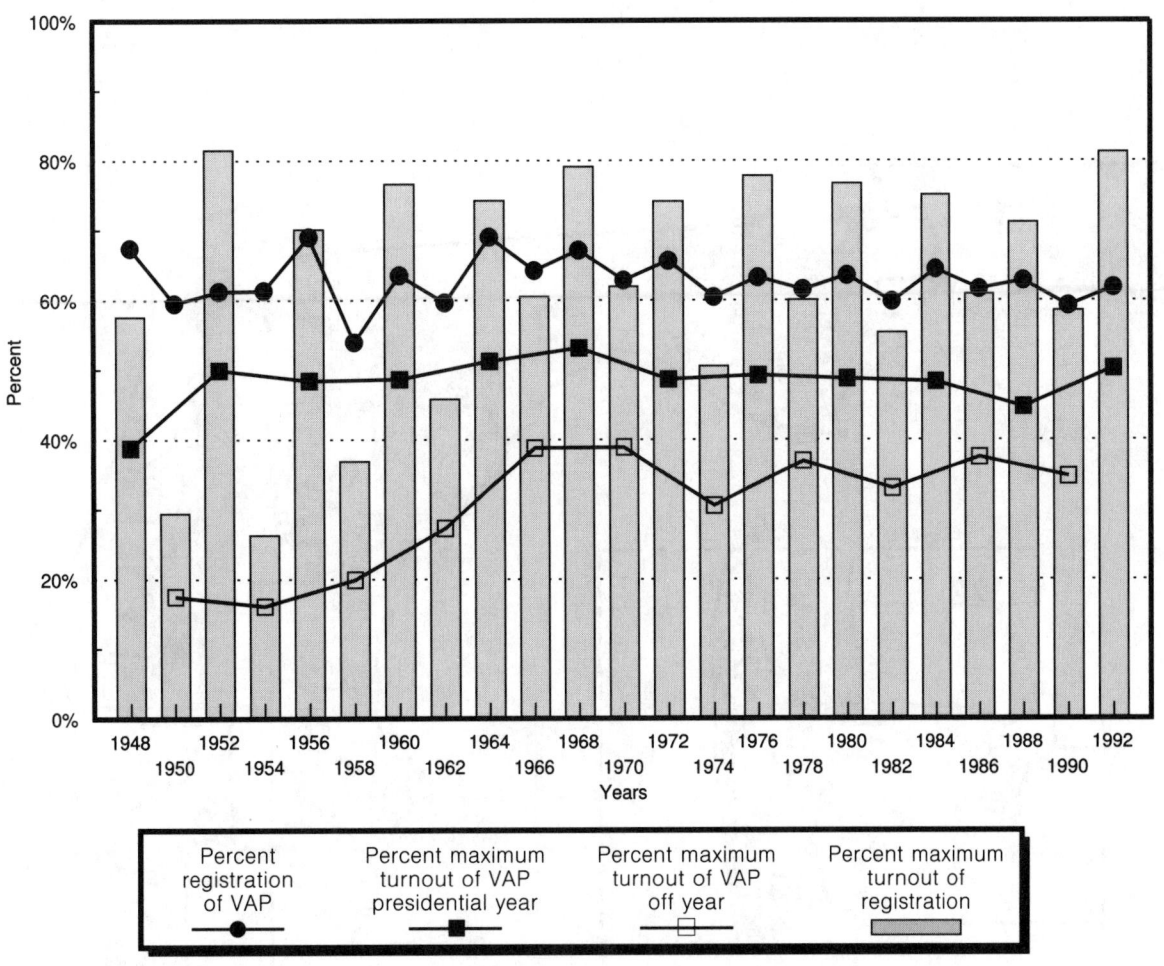

Percent registration of VAP	Percent maximum turnout of VAP presidential year	Percent maximum turnout of VAP off year	Percent maximum turnout of registration
—●—	—■—	—□—	▨

Year	Estimated Voting Age Population (VAP)	Voter registration (REG)				Voter turnout										
						Highest office						Maximum vote				
		Total	Percent of VAP	Rank by percent of VAP	Actual	Total	Office	Percent total REG	Rank by percent of REG	Percent of VAP	Rank by percent of VAP	Total	Percent total REG	Rank by percent of REG	Percent total VAP	Rank by percent of VAP
1992	10,586,000	6,541,825	61.8	47	5,438,612	5,314,392	P	81.2	14	50.2	43	5,438,612	83.1	9	51.4	42
1990	10,180,000	6,031,161	59.2	42	3,623,327	3,530,871	G	58.5	25	34.7	38	3,530,871	58.5	28	34.7	39
1988	9,632,000	6,047,347	62.8	46	-	4,302,313	P	71.1	26	44.7	44	4,302,313	71.1	31	44.7	45
1986	9,146,000	5,631,188	61.6	41	-	3,429,996	S	60.9	14	37.5	29	3,429,996	60.9	17	37.5	32
1984	8,651,000	5,574,472	64.4	44	-	4,180,051	P	75.0	21	48.3	43	4,180,051	75.0	24	48.3	43
1982	8,138,000	4,865,636	59.8	41	-	2,688,566	G	55.3	36	33.0	44	2,688,566	55.3	39	33.0	44
1980	7,578,000	4,809,717	63.5	42	-	3,686,930	P	76.7	16	48.7	40	3,686,930	76.7	23	48.7	42
1978	6,862,000	4,217,187	61.5	38	-	2,530,468	G	60.0	16	36.9	33	2,530,468	60.0	17	36.9	34
1976	6,408,000	4,047,596	63.2	42	-	3,150,631	P	77.8	18	49.2	36	3,150,631	77.8	18	49.2	38
1974	5,999,000	3,621,256	60.4	42	-	1,828,392	G	50.5	38	30.5	42	1,828,392	50.5	39	30.5	42
1972	5,313,000	3,487,458	65.6	39	-	2,583,283	P	74.1	26	48.6	37	2,583,283	74.1	27	48.6	39
1970	4,451,000	2,797,000	62.8	38	-	1,730,813	G	61.9	31	38.9	42	1,730,813	61.9	31	38.9	42
1968	4,124,000	2,765,316	67.1	35	-	2,187,805	P	79.1	27	53.1	42	2,187,805	79.1	28	53.1	42
1966	3,839,000	2,463,832	64.2	36	-	1,489,661	G	60.5	29	38.8	40	1,489,661	60.5	29	38.8	40
1964	3,623,000	2,500,466	69.0	28	-	1,854,481	P	74.2	32	51.2	41	1,854,481	74.2	32	51.2	41
1962	3,442,000	2,052,134	59.6	28	-	939,207	S	45.8	33	27.3	43	939,207	45.8	33	27.3	43
1960	3,176,000	2,016,586	63.5	27	-	1,544,176	P	76.6	30	48.6	41	1,544,176	76.6	30	48.6	41
1958	2,725,000	1,468,609	53.9	28	-	542,069	S	36.9	27	19.9	42	542,069	36.9	27	19.9	42
1956	2,327,000	1,606,532	69.0	21	-	1,125,762	P	70.1	25	48.4	38	1,125,762	70.1	26	48.4	38
1954	2,217,000	1,359,780	61.3	19	-	357,783	G	26.3	24	16.1	43	357,783	26.3	24	16.1	43
1952	1,982,000	1,213,472	61.2	20	-	989,337	P	81.5	15	49.9	39	989,337	81.5	16	49.9	39
1950	1,794,000	1,067,155	59.5	18	-	313,487	S	29.4	21	17.5	40	313,487	29.4	20	17.5	40
1948	1,488,000	1,003,503	67.4	14	-	577,643	P	57.6	20	38.8	38	577,643	57.6	20	38.8	38

Florida 185

FLORIDA

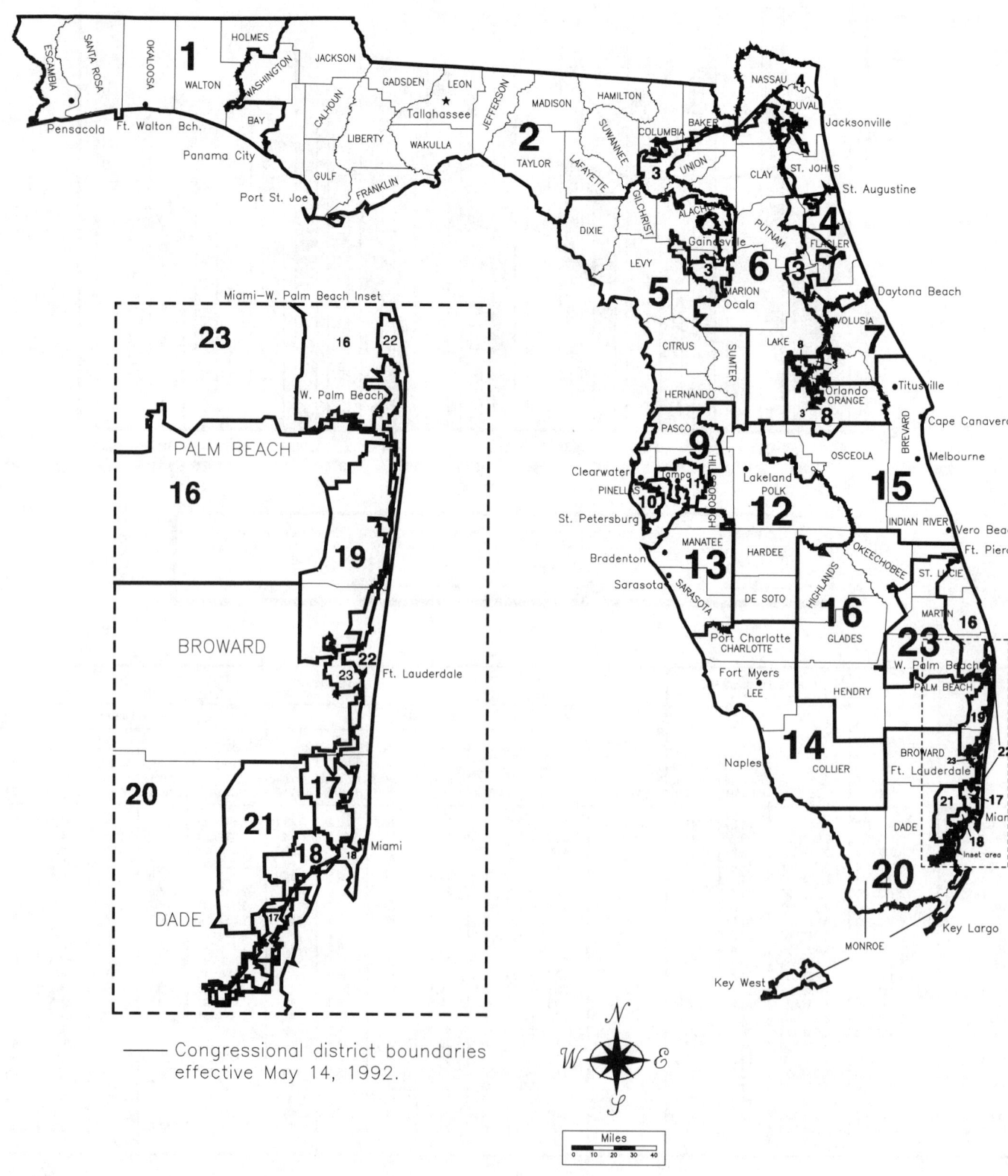

— Congressional district boundaries
effective May 14, 1992.

Miles
0 10 20 30 40

Table A. — 1990 Population by Race and Ethnic Origin

State/county code	County	Total persons	Percent of total persons: Non-Hispanic White	Black	Asian and Pacific Islander	Native American	Other	Hispanic	Rank: Percent of total persons Total	Non-Hispanic White	Black	Hispanic	Percent contribution to state population Total	Non-Hispanic White	Black	Hispanic
12 001	Alachua	181,596	74.7	18.8	2.5	0.2	0.1	3.7	19	52	12	24	1.4	1.4	2.0	0.4
12 003	Baker	18,486	83.5	14.8	0.2	0.3	<.1	1.1	51	30	24	59	0.1	0.2	0.2	<.1
12 005	Bay	126,994	85.0	10.7	1.7	0.7	<.1	1.8	24	25	37	50	1.0	1.1	0.8	0.1
12 007	Bradford	22,515	77.3	20.0	0.4	0.3	<.1	1.9	49	49	9	47	0.2	0.2	0.3	<.1
12 009	Brevard	398,978	87.5	7.7	1.3	0.3	<.1	3.1	9	18	49	28	3.1	3.7	1.8	0.8
12 011	Broward	1,255,488	74.9	14.9	1.3	0.2	<.1	8.6	2	51	23	11	9.7	9.9	11.0	6.9
12 013	Calhoun	11,011	82.6	15.0	0.1	1.2	<.1	1.1	59	33	22	60	<.1	<.1	<.1	<.1
12 015	Charlotte	110,975	93.2	3.5	0.6	0.2	<.1	2.5	25	3	65	37	0.9	1.1	0.2	0.2
12 017	Citrus	93,515	95.1	2.3	0.4	0.3	<.1	1.8	30	1	66	49	0.7	0.9	0.1	0.1
12 019	Clay	105,986	90.4	5.1	1.5	0.3	<.1	2.6	27	9	57	34	0.8	1.0	0.3	0.2
12 021	Collier	152,099	82.0	3.8	0.3	0.2	<.1	13.6	21	35	63	4	1.2	1.3	0.3	1.3
12 023	Columbia	42,613	79.7	17.9	0.6	0.2	<.1	1.5	38	45	15	54	0.3	0.4	0.4	<.1
12 025	Dade	1,937,094	30.2	19.1	1.2	0.1	0.1	49.2	1	67	11	1	15.0	6.2	21.7	60.6
12 027	DeSoto	23,865	74.3	15.4	0.4	0.3	<.1	9.6	48	53	21	10	0.2	0.2	0.2	0.1
12 029	Dixie	10,585	90.0	8.7	0.1	0.3	<.1	0.9	61	10	43	63	<.1	0.1	<.1	<.1
12 031	Duval	672,971	71.2	24.1	1.8	0.3	<.1	2.6	7	59	6	36	5.2	5.1	9.5	1.1
12 033	Escambia	262,798	75.4	19.9	1.8	1.0	<.1	1.9	15	50	10	46	2.0	2.1	3.1	0.3
12 035	Flagler	28,701	86.6	7.9	0.9	0.2	<.1	4.4	43	21	48	19	0.2	0.3	0.1	<.1
12 037	Franklin	8,967	86.2	12.3	0.2	0.5	<.1	0.7	64	22	34	66	<.1	<.1	<.1	<.1
12 039	Gadsden	41,105	39.8	57.5	0.2	0.2	<.1	2.3	40	66	1	42	0.3	0.2	1.4	<.1
12 041	Gilchrist	9,667	89.5	8.4	0.2	0.3	<.1	1.6	63	11	45	52	<.1	<.1	<.1	<.1
12 043	Glades	7,591	74.2	12.1	0.1	5.6	<.1	8.0	65	54	35	12	<.1	<.1	<.1	<.1
12 045	Gulf	11,504	79.9	18.7	0.2	0.5	0.0	0.7	57	44	13	65	<.1	<.1	0.1	<.1
12 047	Hamilton	10,930	58.2	38.6	0.2	0.4	<.1	2.7	60	63	4	33	<.1	<.1	0.2	<.1
12 049	Hardee	19,499	70.8	5.2	0.2	0.3	0.1	23.4	50	61	56	2	0.2	0.1	<.1	0.3
12 051	Hendry	25,773	58.9	16.2	0.4	2.0	0.1	22.3	47	62	18	3	0.2	0.2	0.2	0.4
12 053	Hernando	101,115	92.7	3.8	0.4	0.2	<.1	2.9	28	5	64	31	0.8	1.0	0.2	0.2
12 055	Highlands	68,432	84.2	9.8	0.5	0.3	<.1	5.1	35	28	39	15	0.5	0.6	0.4	0.2
12 057	Hillsborough	834,054	72.7	12.8	1.3	0.3	<.1	12.8	5	57	31	5	6.4	6.4	6.3	6.8
12 059	Holmes	15,778	92.7	4.9	0.3	1.0	<.1	1.1	55	6	60	57	0.1	0.2	<.1	<.1
12 061	Indian River	90,208	88.0	8.4	0.5	0.1	<.1	3.0	31	17	46	30	0.7	0.8	0.4	0.2
12 063	Jackson	41,375	71.0	25.9	0.2	0.5	<.1	2.4	39	60	5	41	0.3	0.3	0.6	<.1
12 065	Jefferson	11,296	55.2	43.2	0.2	0.2	<.1	1.2	58	65	2	56	<.1	<.1	0.3	<.1
12 067	Lafayette	5,578	81.6	13.8	0.2	0.3	0.0	4.1	66	37	28	21	<.1	<.1	<.1	<.1
12 069	Lake	152,104	87.5	9.1	0.4	0.2	<.1	2.8	20	19	40	32	1.2	1.4	0.8	0.3
12 071	Lee	335,113	88.3	6.4	0.5	0.2	<.1	4.5	11	14	53	17	2.6	3.1	1.3	1.0
12 073	Leon	192,493	71.9	24.0	1.4	0.2	<.1	2.4	18	58	7	38	1.5	1.5	2.7	0.3
12 075	Levy	25,923	84.9	12.4	0.4	0.4	<.1	1.9	46	27	33	48	0.2	0.2	0.2	<.1
12 077	Liberty	5,569	80.2	17.3	<.1	0.5	<.1	1.9	67	42	17	45	<.1	<.1	<.1	<.1
12 079	Madison	16,569	56.8	41.4	<.1	0.3	<.1	1.4	54	64	3	55	0.1	<.1	0.4	<.1
12 081	Manatee	211,707	87.2	7.5	0.6	0.2	<.1	4.5	16	20	51	18	1.6	1.9	0.9	0.6
12 083	Marion	194,833	83.6	12.6	0.5	0.3	<.1	3.0	17	29	32	29	1.5	1.7	1.4	0.4
12 085	Martin	100,900	88.8	5.8	0.5	0.1	<.1	4.7	29	12	55	16	0.8	0.9	0.3	0.3
12 087	Monroe	78,024	81.6	5.0	0.8	0.3	<.1	12.3	34	38	59	6	0.6	0.7	0.2	0.6
12 089	Nassau	43,941	88.1	10.3	0.3	0.3	<.1	1.1	37	16	38	58	0.3	0.4	0.3	<.1
12 091	Okaloosa	143,776	85.0	8.9	2.4	0.5	<.1	3.1	23	26	41	27	1.1	1.3	0.8	0.3
12 093	Okeechobee	29,627	80.8	6.3	0.5	0.4	0.1	11.8	42	41	54	8	0.2	0.3	0.1	0.2
12 095	Orange	677,491	73.3	14.8	2.0	0.3	<.1	9.6	6	55	25	9	5.2	5.2	5.9	4.1
12 097	Osceola	107,728	81.2	5.1	1.4	0.3	<.1	11.9	26	39	58	7	0.8	0.9	0.3	0.8
12 099	Palm Beach	863,518	79.1	12.0	1.0	0.1	<.1	7.7	3	46	36	13	6.7	7.2	6.1	4.2
12 101	Pasco	281,131	94.0	1.9	0.5	0.3	<.1	3.3	13	2	67	25	2.2	2.8	0.6	0.6
12 103	Pinellas	851,659	88.6	7.6	1.1	0.2	<.1	2.4	4	13	50	40	6.6	8.0	3.8	1.3
12 105	Polk	405,382	81.8	13.2	0.6	0.3	<.1	4.1	8	36	29	20	3.1	3.5	3.1	1.1
12 107	Putnam	65,070	78.6	18.2	0.3	0.2	<.1	2.6	36	48	14	35	0.5	0.5	0.7	0.1
12 109	St. Johns	83,829	88.3	8.7	0.6	0.2	<.1	2.3	32	15	44	43	0.6	0.8	0.4	0.1
12 111	St. Lucie	150,171	79.0	16.1	0.7	0.2	<.1	4.0	22	47	19	23	1.2	1.3	1.4	0.4
12 113	Santa Rosa	81,608	92.5	4.0	1.1	0.9	<.1	1.5	33	7	62	53	0.6	0.8	0.2	<.1
12 115	Sarasota	277,776	92.9	4.3	0.5	0.2	<.1	2.1	14	4	61	44	2.1	2.7	0.7	0.4
12 117	Seminole	287,529	83.3	8.3	1.6	0.3	<.1	6.5	12	31	47	14	2.2	2.5	1.4	1.2
12 119	Sumter	31,577	80.8	16.0	0.2	0.5	<.1	2.4	41	40	20	39	0.2	0.3	0.3	<.1
12 121	Suwannee	26,780	83.2	14.6	0.2	0.4	<.1	1.6	45	32	26	51	0.2	0.2	0.2	<.1
12 123	Taylor	17,111	80.0	17.9	0.2	0.9	0.0	1.0	52	43	16	62	0.1	0.1	0.2	<.1
12 125	Union	10,252	73.1	22.6	0.4	0.6	<.1	3.3	62	56	8	26	<.1	<.1	0.1	<.1
12 127	Volusia	370,712	86.1	8.9	0.7	0.2	<.1	4.0	10	23	42	22	2.9	3.4	1.9	0.9
12 129	Wakulla	14,202	85.6	12.9	0.2	0.7	<.1	0.6	56	24	30	67	0.1	0.1	0.1	<.1
12 131	Walton	27,760	90.5	6.7	0.4	1.5	<.1	0.9	44	8	52	64	0.2	0.3	0.1	<.1
12 133	Washington	16,919	82.4	14.5	0.5	1.6	<.1	1.1	53	34	27	61	0.1	0.1	0.1	<.1
12	FLORIDA	12,937,926	73.2	13.1	1.1	0.3	<.1	12.2					100.0	100.0	100.0	100.0

Table A. — 1990 Population by Race and Ethnic Origin (cont)

State/ county code	County	Total persons	Percent of total persons — Non-Hispanic White	Black	Asian and Pacific Islander	Native American	Other	Hispanic	Rank — Percent of total persons Total	Non-Hispanic White	Black	Hispanic	Percent contribution to state population Total	Non-Hispanic White	Black	Hispanic
	CONGRESSIONAL															
	District 1	562,518	82.6	12.7	1.7	0.9	<.1	2.1	13	13	6	22	4.3	4.9	4.2	0.7
	District 2	562,519	73.6	23.0	0.9	0.4	<.1	2.0	8	17	4	23	4.3	4.4	7.6	0.7
	District 3	562,519	41.7	54.5	0.7	0.2	<.1	2.8	12	19	2	20	4.3	2.5	18.0	1.0
	District 4	562,518	89.4	5.7	1.5	0.2	<.1	3.1	18	5	11	17	4.3	5.3	1.9	1.1
	District 5	562,518	90.3	5.5	1.1	0.2	<.1	2.8	19	2	12	19	4.3	5.4	1.8	1.0
	District 6	562,518	88.5	7.2	1.1	0.3	<.1	2.9	20	8	10	18	4.3	5.3	2.4	1.1
	District 7	562,518	89.1	3.8	1.2	0.3	<.1	5.5	21	6	18	13	4.3	5.3	1.3	2.0
	District 8	562,518	81.1	4.9	2.2	0.3	<.1	11.4	22	15	15	7	4.3	4.8	1.6	4.1
	District 9	562,518	91.3	3.4	1.0	0.2	<.1	4.1	23	1	19	15	4.3	5.4	1.1	1.5
	District 10	562,518	86.8	9.3	1.3	0.2	<.1	2.3	14	11	8	21	4.3	5.2	3.1	0.8
	District 11	562,519	67.7	16.7	1.4	0.3	<.1	13.9	1	18	5	4	4.3	4.0	5.5	5.0
	District 12	562,519	80.5	12.4	0.6	0.3	<.1	6.1	2	16	7	12	4.3	4.8	4.1	2.2
	District 13	562,518	89.6	5.3	0.5	0.2	<.1	4.3	15	4	14	14	4.3	5.3	1.7	1.5
	District 14	562,518	87.4	5.3	0.5	0.2	<.1	6.6	16	10	13	9	4.3	5.2	1.8	2.4
	District 15	562,519	87.7	7.4	1.1	0.3	<.1	3.4	3	9	9	16	4.3	5.2	2.5	1.2
	District 16	562,519	88.6	3.9	0.8	0.3	<.1	6.3	4	7	17	10	4.3	5.3	1.3	2.3
	District 17	562,519	19.8	55.7	1.2	0.1	0.1	23.0	5	23	1	3	4.3	1.2	18.4	8.2
	District 18	562,519	29.2	2.9	1.1	<.1	0.1	66.7	6	21	21	2	4.3	1.7	1.0	23.8
	District 19	562,519	89.7	2.6	1.4	0.1	<.1	6.2	7	3	23	11	4.3	5.3	0.8	2.2
	District 20	562,518	81.6	4.1	1.5	0.3	<.1	12.3	17	14	16	6	4.3	4.8	1.4	4.4
	District 21	562,518	25.5	3.3	1.4	<.1	0.1	69.6	9	22	20	1	4.3	1.5	1.1	24.9
	District 22	562,519	83.4	2.6	1.0	0.1	<.1	12.8	10	12	22	5	4.3	4.9	0.9	4.6
	District 23	562,519	39.3	50.2	0.9	0.2	0.1	9.4	11	20	3	8	4.3	2.3	16.6	3.3

Table B. — 1990 Voting Age Population (VAP) by Race and Ethnic Origin

County	Total Voting Age Population	Percent of total VAP — Non-Hispanic White	Black	Asian and Pacific Islander	Native American	Other	Hispanic	Rank — Total	White	Black	Hispanic	Pct contribution to state VAP — Total	White	Black	Hispanic	VAP percent of total population — Total	White	Black	Asian and Pacific Islander	Native American	Other	Hispanic
Alachua	142,081	77.5	15.9	2.6	0.2	<.1	3.8	19	52	15	20	1.4	1.4	2.0	0.5	78.2	81.2	66.0	81.9	76.9	51.6	79.8
Baker	12,855	83.2	14.8	0.3	0.4	<.1	1.3	51	39	18	56	0.1	0.1	0.2	<.1	69.5	69.3	69.7	77.3	84.5	100.0	82.5
Bay	94,745	86.9	9.3	1.5	0.7	<.1	1.6	24	26	38	51	0.9	1.1	0.8	0.1	74.6	76.3	64.4	67.1	68.7	40.7	66.8
Bradford	17,109	77.2	20.0	0.4	0.3	<.1	2.1	49	54	9	44	0.2	0.2	0.3	<.1	76.0	75.9	75.8	72.4	79.7	50.0	83.8
Brevard	311,524	89.2	6.4	1.2	0.3	<.1	2.8	8	19	49	27	3.1	3.6	1.8	0.7	78.1	79.6	64.8	73.0	77.5	38.7	71.6
Broward	998,870	78.5	12.1	1.2	0.2	<.1	8.0	2	49	28	11	9.9	10.3	10.9	6.8	79.6	83.4	64.7	71.5	73.7	53.7	73.6
Calhoun	8,140	83.2	14.5	<.1	1.1	<.1	1.0	58	40	19	58	<.1	<.1	0.1	<.1	73.9	74.5	71.5	61.5	69.5	100.0	72.0
Charlotte	93,687	94.0	3.0	0.6	0.2	<.1	2.2	25	4	63	40	0.9	1.2	0.3	0.2	84.4	85.2	74.0	74.0	81.3	42.1	74.1
Citrus	77,049	95.9	1.9	0.3	0.3	<.1	1.7	29	1	66	50	0.8	1.0	0.1	0.1	82.4	83.0	66.3	68.7	71.9	25.0	75.9
Clay	75,452	91.3	4.5	1.4	0.3	<.1	2.4	30	9	58	36	0.7	0.9	0.3	0.2	71.2	71.9	63.3	66.5	72.3	43.2	64.7
Collier	121,759	85.3	3.0	0.3	0.2	<.1	11.2	21	30	64	6	1.2	1.4	0.3	1.2	80.1	83.3	63.9	72.8	71.7	63.0	65.6
Columbia	30,712	81.7	16.1	0.6	0.3	<.1	1.4	39	46	14	54	0.3	0.3	0.4	<.1	72.1	73.8	64.6	72.7	85.0	25.0	68.0
Dade	1,469,084	31.8	16.3	1.2	<.1	<.1	50.5	1	67	13	1	14.6	6.1	21.6	62.8	75.8	79.7	64.9	75.3	72.7	48.6	77.8
DeSoto	18,199	77.3	13.5	0.4	0.3	<.1	8.5	47	53	23	10	0.2	0.2	0.2	0.1	76.3	79.4	66.9	75.3	66.2	71.4	67.7
Dixie	7,997	90.1	8.6	0.1	0.4	0.0	0.9	60	14	39	63	<.1	<.1	<.1	<.1	75.6	75.6	74.5	91.7	82.4	0.0	72.9
Duval	498,625	73.8	21.7	1.7	0.3	<.1	2.4	7	59	8	35	5.0	4.8	9.8	1.0	74.1	76.8	66.8	69.7	75.7	39.7	70.4
Escambia	196,418	78.4	17.2	1.6	1.0	<.1	1.8	15	50	11	47	2.0	2.0	3.1	0.3	74.7	77.7	64.7	65.5	73.4	43.1	71.9
Flagler	23,222	88.4	6.7	0.9	0.2	<.1	3.9	42	21	48	17	0.2	0.3	0.1	0.1	80.9	82.6	68.3	74.3	86.0	27.3	72.1
Franklin	6,814	88.1	10.4	0.2	0.6	<.1	0.6	64	22	34	66	<.1	<.1	<.1	<.1	76.0	77.7	64.3	76.5	83.7	50.0	67.7
Gadsden	28,941	45.2	52.3	0.2	0.2	<.1	2.1	40	66	1	41	0.3	0.2	1.4	<.1	70.4	79.9	64.0	80.0	75.0	46.7	64.3
Gilchrist	7,245	89.3	8.5	0.1	0.3	<.1	1.7	63	18	40	49	<.1	<.1	<.1	<.1	74.9	74.8	76.2	44.4	80.0	50.0	81.3
Glades	5,735	79.2	9.5	0.1	4.4	<.1	6.7	65	48	36	13	<.1	<.1	<.1	<.1	75.6	80.7	59.7	70.0	59.8	100.0	63.1
Gulf	8,681	81.7	16.9	0.2	0.5	0.0	0.7	57	45	12	65	<.1	<.1	0.1	<.1	75.5	77.2	68.5	69.6	77.4	0.0	68.6
Hamilton	7,774	61.2	35.7	0.2	0.3	0.0	2.6	61	63	4	31	<.1	<.1	0.3	<.1	71.1	74.8	65.8	70.6	57.1	0.0	69.8
Hardee	13,811	76.1	4.6	0.2	0.3	0.1	18.7	50	56	57	3	0.1	0.1	<.1	0.2	70.8	76.1	63.3	64.7	61.8	73.9	56.6
Hendry	17,695	63.1	13.9	0.4	1.9	<.1	20.5	48	62	21	2	0.2	0.1	0.2	0.3	68.7	73.6	58.9	70.7	65.3	46.4	63.1
Hernando	82,467	94.0	3.0	0.3	0.2	<.1	2.5	27	5	65	34	0.8	1.0	0.2	0.2	81.6	82.7	64.1	68.3	77.2	52.4	69.8
Highlands	55,614	87.7	7.4	0.5	0.3	<.1	4.2	35	24	44	16	0.6	0.6	0.4	0.2	81.3	84.7	61.2	69.3	67.8	47.1	66.3
Hillsborough	631,780	75.2	10.9	1.3	0.3	<.1	12.4	5	57	31	4	6.3	6.2	6.2	6.6	75.7	78.3	64.5	72.7	77.6	45.4	73.1
Holmes	11,857	92.3	5.4	0.3	1.0	<.1	1.0	55	7	53	59	0.1	0.1	<.1	<.1	75.1	74.9	82.9	64.0	72.4	100.0	68.8
Indian River	72,722	90.1	6.7	0.4	0.1	<.1	2.6	31	13	47	33	0.7	0.9	0.4	0.2	80.6	82.6	65.0	66.2	73.4	41.7	68.8
Jackson	31,096	72.5	24.1	0.2	0.5	<.1	2.7	38	60	5	28	0.3	0.3	0.7	<.1	75.2	76.7	69.9	72.0	72.1	57.1	86.2
Jefferson	8,028	59.1	39.3	0.2	0.2	0.0	1.2	59	65	2	57	<.1	<.1	0.3	<.1	71.1	76.1	64.6	66.7	88.2	0.0	74.6
Lafayette	4,198	80.4	14.4	0.2	0.4	0.0	4.7	67	47	20	15	<.1	<.1	<.1	<.1	75.3	74.1	78.4	88.9	88.2	0.0	86.7
Lake	121,841	89.8	7.3	0.3	0.2	<.1	2.3	20	16	45	38	1.2	1.4	0.8	0.2	80.1	82.2	64.8	70.1	74.9	42.5	65.1
Lee	269,543	91.0	4.7	0.5	0.2	<.1	3.6	11	10	56	21	2.7	3.2	1.2	0.8	80.4	82.8	59.5	69.7	76.3	45.8	65.2
Leon	149,368	73.8	22.0	1.4	0.2	<.1	2.6	18	58	7	32	1.5	1.4	3.0	0.3	77.6	79.7	71.1	76.8	77.5	47.4	81.5
Levy	19,644	86.9	10.7	0.4	0.4	0.0	1.7	46	27	32	48	0.2	0.2	0.2	<.1	75.8	77.5	65.5	68.0	75.2	0.0	68.0
Liberty	4,221	77.8	19.3	<.1	0.5	<.1	2.3	66	51	10	37	<.1	<.1	<.1	<.1	75.8	73.5	84.6	100.0	73.1	100.0	90.7
Madison	12,009	60.0	38.1	<.1	0.3	0.0	1.6	54	64	3	52	0.1	<.1	0.4	<.1	72.5	76.5	66.6	87.5	75.0	0.0	81.8
Manatee	171,091	89.9	5.9	0.5	0.2	<.1	3.5	16	15	51	23	1.7	2.0	0.9	0.5	80.8	83.4	63.4	69.6	72.4	38.1	62.8
Marion	151,741	86.0	10.6	0.4	0.3	<.1	2.7	17	29	33	29	1.5	1.7	1.4	0.3	77.9	80.1	65.3	70.9	76.9	55.2	69.9
Martin	83,162	90.7	4.9	0.4	0.1	<.1	3.9	26	11	55	18	0.8	1.0	0.4	0.3	82.4	84.2	69.2	69.0	76.1	45.8	67.9
Monroe	64,469	83.4	4.3	0.7	0.3	<.1	11.3	33	38	59	5	0.6	0.7	0.2	0.6	82.6	84.4	70.7	74.3	83.7	57.6	76.0
Nassau	32,037	89.0	9.4	0.3	0.3	<.1	1.0	37	20	37	60	0.3	0.4	0.3	<.1	72.9	73.7	67.1	77.5	75.0	33.3	63.8
Okaloosa	106,461	86.5	7.8	2.3	0.5	<.1	2.9	23	28	41	26	1.1	1.2	0.8	0.3	74.0	75.3	65.0	70.3	72.6	30.1	68.8
Okeechobee	21,577	84.6	4.9	0.4	0.4	0.1	9.5	43	34	54	8	0.2	0.2	<.1	0.2	72.8	76.2	56.6	61.5	70.9	56.8	58.9
Orange	516,005	76.4	12.6	1.9	0.3	<.1	8.8	6	55	26	9	5.1	5.2	5.9	3.8	76.2	79.4	64.9	71.7	77.7	48.1	69.9
Osceola	80,579	83.5	4.2	1.4	0.3	<.1	10.6	28	37	60	7	0.8	0.9	0.3	0.7	74.8	77.0	61.5	71.1	76.7	42.5	66.4
Palm Beach	693,965	82.5	9.6	0.9	0.1	<.1	6.9	4	43	35	12	6.9	7.5	6.0	4.0	80.4	83.7	64.4	72.9	78.2	51.5	71.7
Pasco	230,908	95.2	1.4	0.4	0.2	<.1	2.7	13	2	67	30	2.3	2.9	0.3	0.5	82.1	83.2	62.9	68.7	74.6	43.3	66.9
Pinellas	700,203	90.6	6.1	0.9	0.2	<.1	2.1	3	12	50	42	7.0	8.3	3.9	1.3	82.2	84.0	65.7	68.9	77.0	44.5	74.6
Polk	307,640	84.8	11.0	0.5	0.3	<.1	3.4	9	33	30	25	3.1	3.4	3.1	0.9	75.9	78.6	63.3	68.4	73.4	51.1	63.1
Putnam	48,528	82.2	15.0	0.3	0.3	<.1	2.2	36	44	17	39	0.5	0.5	0.7	<.1	74.6	78.0	61.5	67.7	78.2	36.8	63.0
St. Johns	65,196	89.7	7.5	0.5	0.2	<.1	2.1	32	17	43	43	0.6	0.8	0.4	0.1	77.8	79.0	66.9	72.7	71.9	25.0	72.7
St. Lucie	115,549	82.5	13.1	0.6	0.2	<.1	3.6	22	41	24	22	1.1	1.2	1.4	0.3	76.9	80.4	62.4	68.7	72.2	46.3	69.4
Santa Rosa	59,434	93.2	3.5	1.1	0.8	<.1	1.3	34	6	61	55	0.6	0.7	0.2	<.1	72.8	73.4	64.5	72.3	71.2	45.8	63.8
Sarasota	234,065	94.3	3.3	0.4	0.2	<.1	1.8	12	3	62	46	2.3	2.9	0.7	0.4	84.3	85.5	64.8	71.6	81.1	43.0	73.3
Seminole	214,622	84.9	7.2	1.5	0.3	<.1	6.0	14	32	46	14	2.1	2.4	1.4	1.1	74.6	76.1	65.3	70.4	72.3	44.0	69.5
Sumter	24,572	83.8	13.6	0.2	0.5	<.1	2.0	41	36	22	45	0.2	0.3	0.3	<.1	77.8	80.7	66.0	72.5	68.5	50.0	63.9
Suwannee	19,682	85.1	12.8	0.2	0.4	<.1	1.5	45	31	25	53	0.2	0.2	0.2	<.1	73.5	75.1	64.2	63.1	78.2	80.0	72.7
Taylor	12,288	82.5	15.6	0.2	0.8	0.0	0.9	53	42	16	61	0.1	0.1	0.2	<.1	71.8	74.1	62.3	67.6	66.7	0.0	65.5
Union	7,617	71.2	23.9	0.4	0.7	<.1	3.8	62	61	6	19	<.1	<.1	0.2	<.1	74.3	72.3	78.4	76.3	94.7	100.0	86.9
Volusia	297,689	88.1	7.6	0.7	0.2	<.1	3.4	10	23	42	24	3.0	3.4	2.0	0.9	80.3	82.1	68.6	75.5	78.2	54.1	68.8
Wakulla	10,182	87.1	11.5	0.2	0.6	<.1	0.6	56	25	29	67	0.1	0.1	0.1	<.1	71.7	72.9	63.7	66.7	66.0	33.3	75.9
Walton	21,166	91.7	5.8	0.4	1.4	<.1	0.9	44	8	52	64	0.2	0.3	0.1	<.1	76.2	77.2	65.3	70.1	76.6	33.3	70.1
Washington	12,649	84.5	12.6	0.5	1.6	<.1	0.9	52	35	27	62	0.1	0.1	0.1	<.1	74.8	76.7	65.0	71.6	71.9	50.0	63.3
FLORIDA	**10,071,689**	**75.9**	**11.0**	**1.0**	**0.2**	**<.1**	**11.7**					**100.0**	**100.0**	**100.0**	**100.0**	**77.8**	**80.7**	**65.2**	**72.0**	**74.6**	**48.1**	**75.1**

Table B. – 1990 Voting Age Population (VAP) by Race and Ethnic Origin (cont)

| County | Total Voting Age Population | Percent of total VAP | | | | | | Rank | | | | Percent contribution to state VAP | | | | VAP percent of total population | | | | | | |
| | | Non-Hispanic | | | | | Hispanic | Percent of total VAP | Non-Hispanic | | Hispanic | Total | Non-Hispanic | | Hispanic | Total | Non-Hispanic | | | | | Hispanic |
		White	Black	Asian and Pacific Islander	Native American	Other		Total	White	Black			White	Black			White	Black	Asian and Pacific Islander	Native American	Other	
CONGRESSIONAL																						
District 1	419,490	84.6	11.1	1.6	0.8	<.1	1.9	20	13	6	23	4.2	4.6	4.2	0.7	74.6	76.4	64.9	68.4	72.3	37.6	69.7
District 2	419,703	75.8	20.9	0.9	0.4	<.1	2.0	19	17	4	22	4.2	4.2	7.9	0.7	74.6	76.8	67.7	72.1	73.0	45.7	76.0
District 3	400,759	46.2	50.1	0.7	0.3	<.1	2.7	22	19	2	18	4.0	2.4	18.1	0.9	71.2	78.9	65.5	71.3	78.5	34.9	68.9
District 4	436,058	90.6	5.0	1.4	0.2	<.1	2.8	13	5	11	17	4.3	5.2	2.0	1.0	77.5	78.5	68.1	70.2	75.3	44.3	70.0
District 5	460,123	91.5	4.6	1.0	0.2	<.1	2.6	5	3	12	20	4.6	5.5	1.9	1.0	81.8	82.9	68.1	78.5	74.9	50.4	75.4
District 6	427,389	89.9	6.2	1.0	0.3	<.1	2.6	16	9	9	19	4.2	5.0	2.4	0.9	76.0	77.2	65.9	68.8	76.7	43.9	67.2
District 7	435,985	90.2	3.3	1.2	0.2	<.1	5.0	14	7	17	13	4.3	5.1	1.3	1.8	77.5	78.5	67.2	71.9	73.1	49.5	70.0
District 8	436,210	83.1	4.3	2.0	0.3	<.1	10.2	12	16	13	7	4.3	4.7	1.7	3.8	77.5	79.4	68.6	71.8	77.8	50.3	69.6
District 9	447,843	92.5	2.8	0.8	0.2	<.1	3.7	8	1	20	14	4.4	5.4	1.1	1.4	79.6	80.6	65.4	66.9	76.4	40.5	71.7
District 10	462,536	89.1	7.5	1.1	0.2	<.1	2.1	3	11	8	21	4.6	5.4	3.1	0.8	82.2	84.4	66.2	69.8	76.7	48.4	74.3
District 11	430,766	70.6	14.1	1.3	0.3	<.1	13.7	15	18	5	4	4.3	4.0	5.5	5.0	76.6	79.9	64.4	74.8	77.5	45.3	75.5
District 12	419,836	83.6	10.5	0.5	0.3	<.1	5.1	18	14	7	12	4.2	4.6	4.0	1.8	74.6	77.5	62.8	68.3	73.1	50.6	61.7
District 13	465,139	91.8	4.1	0.5	0.2	<.1	3.5	2	2	14	15	4.6	5.6	1.7	1.4	82.7	84.7	64.2	71.0	77.6	43.7	66.2
District 14	455,977	89.9	4.0	0.4	0.2	<.1	5.4	6	8	15	11	4.5	5.4	1.7	2.1	81.1	83.5	61.7	71.2	75.3	49.7	65.9
District 15	440,627	89.4	6.2	1.0	0.3	<.1	3.0	10	10	10	16	4.4	5.2	2.5	1.1	78.3	79.9	65.2	72.4	77.1	40.2	69.8
District 16	447,765	90.5	3.1	0.7	0.3	<.1	5.4	9	6	19	10	4.4	5.3	1.2	2.1	79.6	81.2	63.1	69.6	68.5	47.3	68.7
District 17	391,015	23.1	51.3	1.2	0.1	0.1	24.1	23	23	1	3	3.9	1.2	18.1	8.0	69.5	81.0	64.1	74.1	70.2	48.7	72.7
District 18	450,048	28.9	2.4	1.1	<.1	<.1	67.5	7	21	21	2	4.5	1.7	1.0	25.7	80.0	79.3	67.3	78.8	79.0	44.3	80.9
District 19	461,448	91.1	2.1	1.2	<.1	<.1	5.5	4	4	23	9	4.6	5.5	0.9	2.1	82.0	83.3	66.8	71.3	76.9	53.2	72.1
District 20	440,467	83.3	3.6	1.4	0.3	<.1	11.5	11	15	16	6	4.4	4.8	1.4	4.3	78.3	79.9	68.3	70.8	69.3	52.3	72.7
District 21	424,355	24.7	3.2	1.4	<.1	<.1	70.6	17	22	18	1	4.2	1.4	1.2	25.3	75.4	73.0	74.0	73.8	80.0	45.3	76.5
District 22	490,832	85.1	2.1	0.9	0.1	<.1	11.7	1	12	22	5	4.9	5.5	0.9	4.9	87.3	89.1	70.4	76.3	82.5	64.2	79.6
District 23	407,318	45.4	44.4	0.9	0.2	<.1	9.1	21	20	3	8	4.0	2.4	16.3	3.1	72.4	83.7	64.0	73.2	75.2	52.1	70.0

190 Florida

Table C. — Voter Participation: November 3, 1992, General Election

County	Estimated Voting Age Population (VAP) 1992	Voter registration (REG) Total	% contribution to state REG	% of 1992 VAP	Rank by % of 1992 VAP	Highest office Actual	Total	Office	% of 1992 VAP	Maximum vote Total	% contribution to state turnout	% of REG	Rank by % of REG	% of 1992 VAP	Rank by % 1992 VAP	Pres-ident	Sen-ator	Gov-ernor	Repre-sent-ative
Alachua	140,126	89,559	1.4	63.9	45	77,488	76,372	P	54.5	77,488	1.4	86.5	10	55.3	34	1.4	3.2	-	7.1
Baker	13,440	9,870	0.2	73.4	19	7,638	7,336	S	54.6	7,638	0.1	77.4	53	56.8	25	11.5	4.0	-	12.3
Bay	99,479	59,696	0.9	60.0	55	46,662	45,689	P	45.9	46,662	0.9	78.2	49	46.9	61	2.1	13.5	-	11.9
Bradford	17,256	10,049	0.2	58.2	60	8,519	8,341	P	48.3	8,519	0.2	84.8	19	49.4	53	2.1	3.8	-	11.6
Brevard	334,787	228,514	3.5	68.3	34	199,467	195,860	P	58.5	199,467	3.7	87.3	6	59.6	14	1.8	3.4	-	4.8
Broward	1,031,106	657,548	10.1	63.8	46	542,547	533,050	P	51.7	542,547	10.0	82.5	28	52.6	44	1.8	17.6	-	5.4
Calhoun	8,324	6,126	<.1	73.6	18	4,649	4,579	P	55.0	4,649	<.1	75.9	55	55.9	30	1.5	10.7	-	13.1
Charlotte	106,686	80,696	1.2	75.6	10	63,656	62,064	P	58.2	63,656	1.2	78.9	44	59.7	12	2.5	4.1	-	8.1
Citrus	85,057	57,216	0.9	67.3	35	47,231	45,386	S	53.4	47,231	0.9	82.5	27	55.5	33	5.3	3.9	-	4.4
Clay	85,262	53,042	0.8	62.2	50	46,347	45,485	P	53.3	46,347	0.9	87.4	5	54.4	39	1.9	3.1	-	7.3
Collier	135,154	76,187	1.2	56.4	63	73,117	71,944	P	53.2	73,117	1.3	96.0	1	54.1	42	1.6	4.0	-	7.8
Columbia	31,641	19,379	0.3	61.2	52	16,047	15,043	S	47.5	16,047	0.3	82.8	25	50.7	48	6.8	6.3	-	7.8
Dade	1,510,041	675,286	10.3	44.7	67	557,909	544,841	P	36.1	557,909	10.3	82.6	26	36.9	67	2.3	6.4	-	37.8
DeSoto	18,780	10,610	0.2	56.5	61	8,008	7,676	S	40.9	8,008	0.1	75.5	57	42.6	65	7.2	4.1	-	8.8
Dixie	8,433	7,526	0.1	89.2	3	4,891	4,731	S	56.1	4,891	<.1	65.0	67	58.0	19	10.6	3.3	-	6.4
Duval	506,780	349,984	5.3	69.1	32	255,683	249,926	P	49.3	255,683	4.7	73.1	59	50.5	59	2.3	15.3	-	6.3
Escambia	196,352	125,098	1.9	63.7	47	106,714	105,221	P	53.6	106,714	2.0	85.3	16	54.3	40	1.4	5.5	-	4.5
Flagler	29,495	19,264	0.3	65.3	37	16,760	16,355	P	55.5	16,760	0.3	87.0	8	56.8	26	2.4	5.3	-	8.3
Franklin	6,890	6,371	<.1	92.5	1	4,591	4,380	P	63.6	4,591	<.1	72.1	61	66.6	2	4.6	15.9	-	27.8
Gadsden	28,695	18,571	0.3	64.7	40	14,571	14,394	P	50.2	14,571	0.3	78.5	48	50.8	47	1.2	12.1	-	17.0
Gilchrist	7,856	5,455	<.1	69.4	31	4,440	4,305	S	54.8	4,440	<.1	81.4	33	56.5	27	9.5	3.0	-	5.1
Glades	6,001	4,974	<.1	82.9	5	3,537	3,407	S	56.8	3,537	<.1	71.1	62	58.9	16	4.6	3.7	-	7.2
Gulf	8,681	7,959	0.1	91.7	2	6,008	5,854	P	67.4	6,008	0.1	75.5	56	69.2	1	2.6	4.8	-	6.5
Hamilton	8,138	5,800	<.1	71.3	22	3,880	3,725	P	45.8	3,880	<.1	66.9	65	47.7	57	4.0	4.4	-	8.1
Hardee	13,602	8,235	0.1	60.5	54	6,609	6,433	P	47.3	6,609	0.1	80.3	37	48.6	55	2.7	4.1	-	8.6
Hendry	18,929	10,252	0.2	54.2	65	8,167	8,016	P	42.3	8,167	0.2	79.7	40	43.1	63	1.8	3.7	-	5.2
Hernando	99,295	74,036	1.1	74.6	14	58,293	54,948	S	55.3	58,293	1.1	78.7	47	58.7	17	15.8	5.7	-	6.7
Highlands	59,561	38,246	0.6	64.2	43	33,157	32,391	P	54.4	33,157	0.6	86.7	9	55.7	31	2.3	3.8	-	12.6
Hillsborough	659,808	372,439	5.7	56.4	62	316,006	310,502	P	47.1	316,006	5.8	84.8	18	47.9	56	1.7	3.5	-	8.4
Holmes	11,893	8,405	0.1	70.7	24	6,539	6,528	P	54.9	6,539	0.1	77.8	51	55.0	36	0.2	4.7	-	4.7
Indian River	76,949	53,800	0.8	69.9	28	45,591	43,962	P	57.1	45,591	0.8	84.7	20	59.2	15	3.6	4.7	-	9.5
Jackson	31,017	19,119	0.3	61.6	51	15,426	14,723	S	47.5	15,426	0.3	80.7	35	49.7	52	4.9	4.6	-	6.8
Jefferson	8,006	6,002	<.1	75.0	11	4,939	4,714	S	58.9	4,939	<.1	82.3	29	61.7	7	5.3	4.6	-	7.4
Lafayette	4,506	3,360	<.1	74.6	13	2,610	2,549	S	56.6	2,610	<.1	77.7	52	57.9	20	3.3	2.3	-	5.7
Lake	131,779	79,947	1.2	60.7	53	70,288	69,787	P	53.0	70,288	1.3	87.9	4	53.3	43	0.7	2.1	-	7.7
Lee	292,651	190,625	2.9	65.1	38	168,453	166,001	P	56.7	168,453	3.1	88.4	3	57.6	23	1.5	10.5	-	5.1
Leon	152,008	116,033	1.8	76.3	9	97,726	97,294	P	64.0	97,726	1.8	84.2	22	64.3	3	0.4	1.8	-	4.3
Levy	20,578	14,356	0.2	69.8	29	11,320	10,936	P	53.1	11,320	0.2	78.9	46	55.0	35	3.4	3.7	-	5.9
Liberty	4,435	3,292	<.1	74.2	16	2,648	2,576	P	58.1	2,648	<.1	80.4	36	59.7	11	2.7	9.4	-	6.3
Madison	12,069	7,762	0.1	64.3	41	6,220	6,018	S	49.9	6,220	0.1	80.1	38	51.5	46	6.1	3.2	-	5.6
Manatee	183,702	128,875	2.0	70.2	26	102,046	100,220	P	54.6	102,046	1.9	79.2	41	55.5	32	1.8	3.5	-	6.5
Marion	164,094	106,681	1.6	65.0	39	88,801	86,989	P	53.0	88,801	1.6	83.2	24	54.1	41	2.0	4.0	-	10.1
Martin	89,144	64,048	1.0	71.8	21	55,340	53,184	P	59.7	55,340	1.0	86.4	11	62.1	6	3.9	8.9	-	14.0
Monroe	66,143	41,373	0.6	62.6	49	29,989	28,789	P	43.5	29,989	0.6	72.5	60	45.3	62	4.0	5.9	-	9.4
Nassau	34,129	21,923	0.3	64.2	42	18,719	18,174	P	53.3	18,719	0.3	85.4	15	54.8	38	2.9	4.1	-	5.2
Okaloosa	111,614	76,622	1.2	68.6	33	62,521	61,769	P	55.3	62,521	1.1	81.6	32	56.0	29	1.2	4.2	-	3.2
Okeechobee	23,419	13,991	0.2	59.7	57	9,559	9,370	P	40.0	9,559	0.2	68.3	63	40.8	66	2.0	2.7	-	5.9
Orange	553,274	267,878	4.1	48.4	66	238,650	237,011	P	42.8	238,650	4.4	89.1	2	43.1	64	0.7	2.4	-	4.0
Osceola	97,296	58,382	0.9	60.0	56	46,042	45,267	P	46.5	46,042	0.8	78.9	45	47.3	59	1.7	8.1	-	7.9
Palm Beach	739,125	484,440	7.4	65.5	36	414,050	405,251	P	54.8	414,050	7.6	85.5	14	56.0	28	2.1	14.2	-	7.3
Pasco	243,538	169,753	2.6	69.7	30	141,856	135,962	P	55.8	141,856	2.6	83.6	23	58.2	18	4.2	13.4	-	7.1
Pinellas	712,416	504,465	7.7	70.8	23	429,674	422,851	P	59.4	429,674	7.9	85.2	17	60.3	10	1.6	12.3	-	3.3
Polk	317,838	172,251	2.6	54.2	64	150,237	145,900	P	45.9	150,237	2.8	87.2	7	47.3	60	2.9	2.9	-	4.3
Putnam	50,802	40,299	0.6	79.3	8	26,543	25,661	P	50.5	26,543	0.5	65.9	66	52.2	45	3.3	4.9	-	10.9
St. Johns	70,875	51,628	0.8	72.8	20	40,798	39,986	P	56.4	40,798	0.8	79.0	42	57.6	22	2.0	4.0	-	5.6
St. Lucie	127,402	89,539	1.4	70.3	25	69,908	68,233	P	53.6	69,908	1.3	78.1	50	54.9	37	2.4	10.4	-	6.7
Santa Rosa	64,629	54,695	0.8	84.6	4	36,936	36,029	C	55.7	36,936	0.7	67.5	64	57.2	24	11.3	3.8	-	2.5
Sarasota	247,921	184,437	2.8	74.4	15	158,622	156,352	P	63.1	158,622	2.9	86.0	12	64.0	4	1.4	22.0	-	6.6
Seminole	235,892	139,451	2.1	59.1	58	119,500	117,560	P	49.8	119,500	2.2	85.7	13	50.7	49	1.6	4.4	-	7.4
Sumter	25,545	14,907	0.2	58.4	59	12,598	12,329	P	48.3	12,598	0.2	84.5	21	49.3	54	2.1	18.1	-	9.9
Suwannee	20,419	14,300	0.2	70.0	27	11,760	11,374	P	55.7	11,760	0.2	82.2	30	57.6	21	3.3	3.4	-	6.3
Taylor	12,235	9,036	0.1	73.9	17	7,298	7,213	P	59.0	7,298	0.1	80.8	34	59.6	13	1.2	3.3	-	6.8
Union	7,597	4,871	<.1	64.1	44	3,602	3,606	S	47.5	3,606	<.1	74.0	58	47.5	58	1.0	0.0	-	9.8
Volusia	319,108	201,509	3.1	63.1	48	160,769	155,500	P	48.7	160,769	3.0	79.8	39	50.4	51	3.3	5.9	-	9.6
Wakulla	10,884	8,708	0.1	80.0	6	6,879	6,714	P	61.7	6,879	0.1	79.0	43	63.2	5	2.4	2.5	-	4.4
Walton	22,416	16,730	0.3	74.6	12	13,693	13,554	P	60.5	13,693	0.3	81.8	31	61.1	8	1.0	5.5	-	3.9
Washington	12,997	10,344	0.2	79.6	7	7,870	7,871	P	60.6	7,871	0.1	76.1	54	60.6	9	0.0	3.4	-	7.9
FLORIDA[1]	**10,586,000**	**6,541,825**	**100.0**	**61.8**		**5,438,612**	**5,326,061**		**50.3**	**5,438,617**	**100.0**	**83.1**		**51.4**		**2.3**	**8.8**	**-**	**9.6**

[1]Florida reports voter registration by political party affiliation (see Table D) and by race. State voter registration by race is 5,844,956 (89.3%) for white, 619,905 (9.5%) for black, and 76,964 (1.2%) for other.

Table D. — Voter Registration by Political Party Affiliation: November 3, 1992, General Election

County	Total voter registration	Democrat (DEM)	Republican (REP)	Independent (IND)	Plurality Total	Plurality Party	Percent of total registration DEM	REP	IND	Rank DEM	REP	IND	Percent contribution to state registration Total	DEM	REP	IND
Alachua	89,559	55,181	26,274	7,888	28,907	D	61.8	29.4	8.8	35	35	15	1.4	1.7	1.0	1.4
Baker	9,870	9,263	546	61	8,717	D	93.9	5.5	0.6	7	61	62	0.2	0.3	<.1	<.1
Bay	59,696	38,186	17,867	3,620	20,319	D	64.0	29.9	6.1	33	34	32	0.9	1.2	0.7	0.7
Bradford	10,049	8,704	1,079	264	7,625	D	86.6	10.7	2.6	19	52	44	0.2	0.3	<.1	<.1
Brevard	228,514	100,352	110,634	17,310	10,282	R	44.0	48.5	7.6	54	12	24	3.5	3.0	4.1	3.2
Broward	657,548	364,950	233,066	59,309	131,884	D	55.5	35.5	9.0	39	31	13	10.1	11.0	8.7	10.9
Calhoun	6,126	5,853	246	27	5,607	D	95.5	4.0	0.4	5	63	64	<.1	0.2	<.1	<.1
Charlotte	80,696	31,192	43,794	5,674	12,602	R	38.7	54.3	7.0	61	5	28	1.2	0.9	1.6	1.0
Citrus	57,216	29,618	22,366	5,218	7,252	D	51.8	39.1	9.1	42	26	10	0.9	0.9	0.8	1.0
Clay	53,042	20,865	26,802	5,350	5,937	R	39.4	50.6	10.1	60	10	5	0.8	0.6	1.0	1.0
Collier	76,187	20,259	49,851	6,035	29,592	R	26.6	65.5	7.9	67	1	21	1.2	0.6	1.9	1.1
Columbia	19,379	15,039	3,782	557	11,257	D	77.6	19.5	2.9	24	44	42	0.3	0.5	0.1	0.1
Dade	675,286	358,648	254,688	61,414	103,960	D	53.2	37.7	9.1	41	28	11	10.3	10.8	9.5	11.2
DeSoto	10,610	8,028	2,309	273	5,719	D	75.7	21.8	2.6	26	42	45	0.2	0.2	<.1	<.1
Dixie	7,526	6,865	551	106	6,314	D	91.3	7.3	1.4	11	58	52	0.1	0.2	<.1	<.1
Duval	349,984	216,766	110,849	22,189	105,917	D	62.0	31.7	6.3	34	33	29	5.3	6.5	4.1	4.1
Escambia	125,098	76,649	42,564	5,813	34,085	D	61.3	34.0	4.6	36	32	36	1.9	2.3	1.6	1.1
Flagler	19,264	8,754	8,731	1,772	23	D	45.5	45.3	9.2	53	16	9	0.3	0.3	0.3	0.3
Franklin	6,371	5,876	433	61	5,443	D	92.2	6.8	1.0	9	59	56	<.1	0.2	<.1	<.1
Gadsden	18,571	17,203	1,118	250	16,085	D	92.6	6.0	1.3	8	60	53	0.3	0.5	<.1	<.1
Gilchrist	5,455	4,772	586	96	4,186	D	87.5	10.7	1.8	17	51	49	<.1	0.1	<.1	<.1
Glades	4,974	3,995	850	41	3,145	D	81.8	17.4	0.8	22	45	57	<.1	0.1	<.1	<.1
Gulf	7,959	7,241	660	55	6,581	D	91.0	8.3	0.7	12	56	59	0.1	0.2	<.1	<.1
Hamilton	5,800	5,551	224	2	5,327	D	96.1	3.9	<.1	4	64	67	<.1	0.2	<.1	<.1
Hardee	8,235	6,966	1,139	129	5,827	D	84.6	13.8	1.6	20	48	50	0.1	0.2	<.1	<.1
Hendry	10,252	7,889	2,067	295	5,822	D	77.0	20.2	2.9	25	43	41	0.2	0.2	<.1	<.1
Hernando	74,036	33,998	33,864	6,150	134	D	45.9	45.8	8.3	52	15	17	1.1	1.0	1.3	1.1
Highlands	38,246	19,659	16,788	1,790	2,871	D	51.4	43.9	4.7	43	18	35	0.6	0.6	0.6	0.3
Hillsborough	372,439	198,798	135,417	37,893	63,381	D	53.4	36.4	10.2	40	29	4	5.7	6.0	5.1	6.9
Holmes	8,405	7,939	414	52	7,525	D	94.5	4.9	0.6	6	62	61	0.1	0.2	<.1	<.1
Indian River	53,800	18,255	31,604	3,928	13,349	R	33.9	58.8	7.3	64	4	25	0.8	0.6	1.2	0.7
Jackson	19,119	16,762	2,136	219	14,626	D	87.7	11.2	1.1	16	49	54	0.3	0.5	<.1	<.1
Jefferson	6,002	5,302	578	44	4,724	D	89.5	9.8	0.7	14	54	58	<.1	0.2	<.1	<.1
Lafayette	3,360	3,219	125	16	3,094	D	95.8	3.7	0.5	3	65	63	<.1	<.1	<.1	<.1
Lake	79,947	32,566	42,343	5,016	9,777	R	40.7	53.0	6.3	58	8	30	1.2	1.0	1.6	0.9
Lee	190,625	71,892	101,605	17,031	29,713	R	37.7	53.3	8.9	62	7	14	2.9	2.2	3.8	3.1
Leon	116,033	76,157	28,765	10,945	47,392	D	65.7	24.8	9.4	32	37	7	1.8	2.3	1.1	2.0
Levy	14,356	11,530	2,446	380	9,084	D	80.3	17.0	2.6	23	46	43	0.2	0.3	<.1	<.1
Liberty	3,292	3,203	83	5	3,120	D	97.3	2.5	0.2	1	67	65	<.1	<.1	<.1	<.1
Madison	7,762	7,002	674	86	6,328	D	90.2	8.7	1.1	13	55	55	0.1	0.2	<.1	<.1
Manatee	128,875	51,801	66,378	10,628	14,577	R	40.2	51.5	8.3	59	9	18	2.0	1.6	2.5	1.9
Marion	106,681	53,731	44,608	8,286	9,123	D	50.4	41.8	7.8	45	22	23	1.6	1.6	1.7	1.5
Martin	64,048	19,011	40,002	5,007	20,991	R	29.7	62.5	7.8	66	2	22	1.0	0.6	1.5	0.9
Monroe	41,373	20,765	16,659	3,891	4,106	D	50.3	40.3	9.4	46	25	8	0.6	0.6	0.6	0.7
Nassau	21,923	15,614	5,420	881	10,194	D	71.2	24.7	4.0	30	38	38	0.3	0.5	0.2	0.2
Okaloosa	76,622	32,762	38,393	5,424	5,631	R	42.8	50.1	7.1	56	11	27	1.2	1.0	1.4	1.0
Okeechobee	13,991	10,486	3,173	332	7,313	D	74.9	22.7	2.4	27	39	46	0.2	0.3	0.1	<.1
Orange	267,878	117,091	127,288	23,196	10,197	R	43.8	47.6	8.7	55	13	16	4.1	3.5	4.8	4.2
Osceola	58,382	27,414	25,158	5,777	2,256	D	47.0	43.1	9.9	50	20	6	0.9	0.8	0.9	1.1
Palm Beach	484,440	232,349	195,175	56,730	37,174	D	48.0	40.3	11.7	48	24	1	7.4	7.0	7.3	10.4
Pasco	169,753	80,499	73,749	15,423	6,750	D	47.4	43.5	9.1	49	19	12	2.6	2.4	2.8	2.8
Pinellas	504,465	209,365	239,000	55,769	29,635	R	41.5	47.4	11.1	57	14	3	7.7	6.3	8.9	10.2
Polk	172,251	98,809	66,307	7,079	32,502	D	57.4	38.5	4.1	38	27	37	2.6	3.0	2.5	1.3
Putnam	40,299	29,154	9,090	2,014	20,064	D	72.4	22.6	5.0	29	40	33	0.6	0.9	0.3	0.4
St. Johns	51,628	25,683	22,753	3,143	2,930	D	49.8	44.1	6.1	47	17	31	0.8	0.8	0.9	0.6
St. Lucie	89,539	41,119	38,471	9,905	2,648	D	45.9	43.0	11.1	51	21	2	1.4	1.2	1.4	1.8
Santa Rosa	54,695	32,167	19,875	2,636	12,292	D	58.8	36.3	4.8	37	30	34	0.8	1.0	0.7	0.5
Sarasota	184,437	60,244	109,326	14,804	49,082	R	32.7	59.3	8.0	65	3	20	2.8	1.8	4.1	2.7
Seminole	139,451	52,503	75,379	11,426	22,876	R	37.7	54.1	8.2	63	6	19	2.1	1.6	2.8	2.1
Sumter	14,907	10,370	3,982	552	6,388	D	69.6	26.7	3.7	31	36	39	0.2	0.3	0.1	0.1
Suwannee	14,300	11,849	2,176	269	9,673	D	82.9	15.2	1.9	21	47	48	0.2	0.4	<.1	<.1
Taylor	9,036	8,251	729	56	7,522	D	91.3	8.1	0.6	10	57	60	0.1	0.2	<.1	<.1
Union	4,871	4,673	167	6	4,506	D	96.4	3.4	0.1	2	66	66	<.1	0.1	<.1	<.1
Volusia	201,509	102,716	84,082	14,596	18,634	D	51.0	41.8	7.2	44	23	26	3.1	3.1	3.1	2.7
Wakulla	8,708	7,555	969	173	6,586	D	86.9	11.1	2.0	18	50	47	0.1	0.2	<.1	<.1
Walton	16,730	12,503	3,681	543	8,822	D	74.7	22.0	3.2	28	41	40	0.3	0.4	0.1	<.1
Washington	10,344	9,134	1,060	148	8,074	D	88.3	10.2	1.4	15	53	51	0.2	0.3	<.1	<.1
FLORIDA[1]	**6,541,825**	**3,318,565**	**2,672,968**	**546,058**	**645,597**	**D**	**50.8**	**40.9**	**8.4**				**100.0**	**100.0**	**100.0**	**100.0**

[1]Total voter registration also includes 280 for American party, 2,909 for Libertarian party, 600 for Populist party, 367 for Green party, 58 for Socialist Workers party, 15 for U.S. Taxpayer party, and 5 for Natural Law party.

Table E. — Vote for President: November 3, 1992, General Election

County	Total	Clinton (DEM)	Bush (REP)	Perot (IND)	Other	Plurality Total	Party	DEM	REP	IND	Other	Rank DEM	Rank REP	Rank IND	Total	DEM	REP	IND	DEM	REP
Alachua	76,372	37,888	22,813	15,296	375	15,075	D	49.6	29.9	20.0	0.5	3	66	48	1.4	1.8	1.0	1.5	62.4	37.6
Baker	6,756	1,976	3,418	1,315	47	1,442	R	29.2	50.6	19.5	0.7	58	6	50	0.1	<.1	0.2	0.1	36.6	63.4
Bay	45,689	12,846	22,842	9,712	289	9,996	R	28.1	50.0	21.3	0.6	61	9	40	0.9	0.6	1.1	0.9	36.0	64.0
Bradford	8,341	3,041	3,672	1,574	54	631	R	36.5	44.0	18.9	0.6	27	23	56	0.2	0.1	0.2	0.1	45.3	54.7
Brevard	195,860	61,091	84,585	49,509	675	23,494	R	31.2	43.2	25.3	0.3	53	29	18	3.7	2.9	3.9	4.7	41.9	58.1
Broward	533,050	276,361	164,832	90,937	920	111,529	D	51.8	30.9	17.1	0.2	2	65	63	10.0	13.3	7.6	8.6	62.6	37.4
Calhoun	4,579	1,665	1,721	1,176	17	56	R	36.4	37.6	25.7	0.4	28	47	14	<.1	<.1	<.1	0.1	49.2	50.8
Charlotte	62,064	22,907	24,311	14,720	126	1,404	R	36.9	39.2	23.7	0.2	24	40	27	1.2	1.1	1.1	1.4	48.5	51.5
Citrus	44,746	15,937	16,412	12,314	83	475	R	35.6	36.7	27.5	0.2	30	49	6	0.8	0.8	0.8	1.2	49.3	50.7
Clay	45,485	10,610	26,360	8,423	92	15,750	R	23.3	58.0	18.5	0.2	65	1	59	0.9	0.5	1.2	0.8	28.7	71.3
Collier	71,944	18,796	38,448	14,518	182	19,652	R	26.1	53.4	20.2	0.3	64	2	46	1.4	0.9	1.8	1.4	32.8	67.2
Columbia	14,954	5,528	6,492	2,906	28	964	R	37.0	43.4	19.4	0.2	23	26	51	0.3	0.3	0.3	0.3	46.0	54.0
Dade	544,841	254,607	235,313	54,003	918	19,294	D	46.7	43.2	9.9	0.2	6	28	67	10.3	12.3	10.8	5.1	52.0	48.0
DeSoto	7,429	2,646	3,070	1,687	26	424	R	35.6	41.3	22.7	0.4	31	35	34	0.1	0.1	0.1	0.2	46.3	53.7
Dixie	4,373	1,855	1,401	1,094	23	454	D	42.4	32.0	25.0	0.5	10	64	20	<.1	<.1	<.1	0.1	57.0	43.0
Duval	249,926	92,098	123,631	33,388	809	31,533	R	36.9	49.5	13.4	0.3	25	10	65	4.7	4.4	5.7	3.2	42.7	57.3
Escambia	105,221	32,045	52,868	19,923	385	20,823	R	30.5	50.2	18.9	0.4	55	8	54	2.0	1.5	2.4	1.9	37.7	62.3
Flagler	16,355	6,693	6,246	3,390	26	447	R	40.9	38.2	20.7	0.2	13	42	42	0.3	0.3	0.3	0.3	51.7	48.3
Franklin	4,380	1,535	1,664	1,144	37	129	R	35.0	38.0	26.1	0.8	36	44	12	<.1	<.1	<.1	0.1	48.0	52.0
Gadsden	14,394	8,486	3,975	1,871	62	4,511	D	59.0	27.6	13.0	0.4	1	67	66	0.3	0.4	0.2	0.2	68.1	31.9
Gilchrist	4,017	1,511	1,395	1,090	21	116	D	37.6	34.7	27.1	0.5	20	56	7	<.1	<.1	<.1	0.1	52.0	48.0
Glades	3,374	1,305	1,185	878	6	120	D	38.7	35.1	26.0	0.2	18	54	13	<.1	<.1	<.1	<.1	52.4	47.6
Gulf	5,854	1,938	2,651	1,245	20	713	R	33.1	45.3	21.3	0.3	48	17	39	0.1	<.1	0.1	0.1	42.2	57.8
Hamilton	3,725	1,622	1,402	695	6	220	D	43.5	37.6	18.7	0.2	9	45	58	<.1	<.1	<.1	<.1	53.6	46.4
Hardee	6,433	2,018	2,900	1,499	16	882	R	31.4	45.1	23.3	0.2	52	19	30	0.1	<.1	0.1	0.1	41.0	59.0
Hendry	8,016	2,691	3,279	2,032	14	588	R	33.6	40.9	25.3	0.2	45	37	17	0.2	0.1	0.2	0.2	45.1	54.9
Hernando	49,086	19,174	17,902	11,848	162	1,272	D	39.1	36.5	24.1	0.3	17	50	24	0.9	0.9	0.8	1.1	51.7	48.3
Highlands	32,391	11,237	14,499	6,593	62	3,262	R	34.7	44.8	20.4	0.2	41	20	43	0.6	0.5	0.7	0.6	43.7	56.3
Hillsborough	310,502	115,282	130,643	63,054	1,523	15,361	R	37.1	42.1	20.3	0.5	22	34	44	5.8	5.6	6.0	6.0	46.9	53.1
Holmes	6,528	1,877	3,196	1,427	28	1,319	R	28.8	49.0	21.9	0.4	59	11	37	0.1	<.1	0.1	0.1	37.0	63.0
Indian River	43,962	12,360	19,140	12,375	87	6,765	R	28.1	43.5	28.1	0.2	62	25	5	0.8	0.6	0.9	1.2	39.2	60.8
Jackson	14,676	5,482	6,725	2,450	19	1,243	R	37.4	45.8	16.7	0.1	21	16	64	0.3	0.3	0.3	0.2	44.9	55.1
Jefferson	4,678	2,271	1,506	895	6	765	D	48.5	32.2	19.1	0.1	5	63	53	<.1	0.1	<.1	<.1	60.1	39.9
Lafayette	2,525	867	1,039	612	7	172	R	34.3	41.1	24.2	0.3	43	36	23	<.1	<.1	<.1	<.1	45.5	54.5
Lake	69,787	23,200	30,825	15,614	148	7,625	R	33.2	44.2	22.4	0.2	46	22	35	1.3	1.1	1.4	1.5	42.9	57.1
Lee	166,001	53,660	73,436	38,452	453	19,776	R	32.3	44.2	23.2	0.3	49	21	33	3.1	2.6	3.4	3.7	42.2	57.8
Leon	97,294	47,791	31,983	17,212	308	15,808	D	49.1	32.9	17.7	0.3	4	62	62	1.8	2.3	1.5	1.6	59.9	40.1
Levy	10,936	4,330	3,796	2,784	26	534	D	39.6	34.7	25.5	0.2	15	58	16	0.2	0.2	0.2	0.3	53.3	46.7
Liberty	2,576	820	1,126	617	13	306	R	31.8	43.7	24.0	0.5	51	24	25	<.1	<.1	<.1	<.1	42.1	57.9
Madison	5,840	2,650	2,007	1,174	9	643	D	45.4	34.4	20.1	0.2	8	61	47	0.1	0.1	<.1	0.1	56.9	43.1
Manatee	100,220	33,841	42,725	23,290	364	8,884	R	33.8	42.6	23.2	0.4	44	31	32	1.9	1.6	2.0	2.2	44.2	55.8
Marion	86,989	30,829	35,442	20,529	189	4,613	R	35.4	40.7	23.6	0.2	33	38	28	1.6	1.5	1.6	1.9	46.5	53.5
Martin	53,184	14,802	24,800	13,442	140	9,998	R	27.8	46.6	25.3	0.3	63	14	19	1.0	0.7	1.1	1.3	37.4	62.6
Monroe	28,789	10,450	9,898	8,314	127	552	D	36.3	34.4	28.9	0.4	29	60	2	0.5	0.5	0.5	0.8	51.4	48.6
Nassau	18,174	5,503	9,367	3,255	49	3,864	R	30.3	51.5	17.9	0.3	57	5	61	0.3	0.3	0.4	0.3	37.0	63.0
Okaloosa	61,769	12,038	32,818	16,671	242	16,147	R	19.5	53.1	27.0	0.4	67	3	8	1.2	0.6	1.5	1.6	26.8	73.2
Okeechobee	9,370	3,418	3,298	2,647	7	120	D	36.5	35.2	28.2	<.1	26	53	4	0.2	0.2	0.2	0.3	50.9	49.1
Orange	237,011	82,683	108,788	44,844	696	26,105	R	34.9	45.9	18.9	0.3	40	15	55	4.5	4.0	5.0	4.3	43.2	56.8
Osceola	45,267	15,010	19,143	11,021	93	4,133	R	33.2	42.3	24.3	0.2	47	32	22	0.9	0.7	0.9	1.0	43.9	56.1
Palm Beach	405,251	187,869	140,350	76,243	789	47,519	D	46.4	34.6	18.8	0.2	7	59	57	7.6	9.1	6.5	7.2	57.2	42.8
Pasco	135,962	53,130	47,735	34,654	443	5,395	D	39.1	35.1	25.5	0.3	16	55	15	2.6	2.6	2.2	3.3	52.7	47.3
Pinellas	422,851	160,528	159,121	101,257	1,945	1,407	D	38.0	37.6	23.9	0.5	19	46	26	8.0	7.7	7.3	9.6	50.2	49.8
Polk	145,900	51,450	65,963	28,204	283	14,513	R	35.3	45.2	19.3	0.2	34	18	52	2.7	2.5	3.0	2.7	43.8	56.2
Putnam	25,661	10,709	8,910	5,979	63	1,799	D	41.7	34.7	23.3	0.2	12	57	31	0.5	0.5	0.4	0.6	54.6	45.4
St. Johns	39,986	12,291	20,188	7,400	107	7,897	R	30.7	50.5	18.5	0.3	54	7	60	0.8	0.6	0.9	0.7	37.8	62.2
St. Lucie	68,233	23,876	24,400	19,817	140	524	R	35.0	35.8	29.0	0.2	37	51	1	1.3	1.2	1.1	1.9	49.5	50.5
Santa Rosa	32,717	6,556	17,339	8,788	94	8,551	R	20.0	52.9	26.8	0.3	66	4	9	0.6	0.3	0.8	0.8	27.4	72.6
Sarasota	156,352	54,552	66,855	34,289	656	12,303	R	34.9	42.8	21.9	0.4	39	30	36	2.9	2.6	3.1	3.3	44.9	55.1
Seminole	117,560	35,660	57,101	24,487	312	21,441	R	30.3	48.6	20.8	0.3	56	12	41	2.2	1.7	2.6	2.3	38.4	61.6
Sumter	12,329	5,027	4,366	2,901	35	661	D	40.8	35.4	23.5	0.3	14	52	29	0.2	0.2	0.2	0.3	53.5	46.5
Suwannee	11,374	3,988	4,576	2,791	19	588	R	35.1	40.2	24.5	0.2	35	39	21	0.2	0.2	0.2	0.3	46.6	53.4
Taylor	7,213	2,568	2,693	1,929	23	125	R	35.6	37.3	26.7	0.3	32	48	10	0.1	0.1	0.1	0.2	48.8	51.2
Union	3,571	1,248	1,546	770	7	298	R	34.9	43.3	21.6	0.2	38	27	38	<.1	<.1	<.1	<.1	44.7	55.3
Volusia	155,500	65,223	59,172	30,823	282	6,051	D	41.9	38.1	19.8	0.2	11	43	49	2.9	3.1	2.7	2.9	52.4	47.6
Wakulla	6,714	2,320	2,586	1,790	18	266	R	34.6	38.5	26.7	0.3	42	41	11	0.1	0.1	0.1	0.2	47.3	52.7
Walton	13,554	3,888	5,726	3,890	50	1,836	R	28.7	42.2	28.7	0.4	60	33	3	0.3	0.2	0.3	0.4	40.4	59.6
Washington	7,871	2,544	3,695	1,596	36	1,151	R	32.3	46.9	20.3	0.5	50	13	45	0.1	0.1	0.2	0.2	40.8	59.2
FLORIDA	5,314,392	2,072,698	2,173,310	1,053,067	15,317	100,612	R	39.0	40.9	19.8	0.3				100.0	100.0	100.0	100.0	48.8	51.2

County	Total	Graham (DEM)	Grant (REP)	Other	Plurality Total	Plurality Party	Percent of total vote DEM	Percent of total vote REP	Percent of total vote Other	Rank DEM	Rank REP	Rank Other	Percent contribution to state vote Total	Percent contribution to state vote DEM	Percent contribution to state vote REP	Percent contribution to state vote Other
Alachua	74,985	54,963	20,018	4	34,945	D	73.3	26.7	<.1	7	61	8	1.5	1.7	1.2	1.8
Baker	7,336	4,689	2,647	0	2,042	D	63.9	36.1	0.0	35	33	19	0.1	0.1	0.2	0.0
Bay	40,341	21,930	18,410	1	3,520	D	54.4	45.6	<.1	63	5	14	0.8	0.7	1.1	0.5
Bradford	8,192	5,791	2,401	0	3,390	D	70.7	29.3	0.0	15	53	20	0.2	0.2	0.1	0.0
Brevard	192,658	110,490	82,168	0	28,322	D	57.4	42.6	0.0	57	11	21	3.9	3.4	4.8	0.0
Broward	446,872	339,439	107,432	1	232,007	D	76.0	24.0	<.1	5	63	22	9.0	10.5	6.3	0.5
Calhoun	4,153	2,890	1,263	0	1,627	D	69.6	30.4	0.0	18	50	23	<.1	<.1	<.1	0.0
Charlotte	61,056	36,382	24,674	0	11,708	D	59.6	40.4	0.0	52	16	24	1.2	1.1	1.4	0.0
Citrus	45,386	27,680	17,705	1	9,975	D	61.0	39.0	<.1	48	20	15	0.9	0.9	1.0	0.5
Clay	44,928	23,724	21,204	0	2,520	D	52.8	47.2	0.0	65	3	25	0.9	0.7	1.2	0.0
Collier	70,215	36,389	33,826	0	2,563	D	51.8	48.2	0.0	66	2	26	1.4	1.1	2.0	0.0
Columbia	15,043	9,478	5,565	0	3,913	D	63.0	37.0	0.0	39	29	27	0.3	0.3	0.3	0.0
Dade	522,231	410,754	111,475	2	299,279	D	78.7	21.3	<.1	2	66	28	10.5	12.7	6.5	0.9
DeSoto	7,676	5,021	2,655	0	2,366	D	65.4	34.6	0.0	26	42	29	0.2	0.2	0.2	0.0
Dixie	4,731	3,346	1,385	0	1,961	D	70.7	29.3	0.0	14	54	30	<.1	0.1	<.1	0.0
Duval	216,559	136,552	79,999	8	56,553	D	63.1	36.9	<.1	38	30	10	4.4	4.2	4.7	3.6
Escambia	100,842	57,085	43,757	0	13,328	D	56.6	43.4	0.0	59	9	31	2.0	1.8	2.5	0.0
Flagler	15,872	10,083	5,789	0	4,294	D	63.5	36.5	0.0	36	32	32	0.3	0.3	0.3	0.0
Franklin	3,860	2,450	1,409	1	1,041	D	63.5	36.5	<.1	37	31	3	<.1	<.1	<.1	0.5
Gadsden	12,815	10,487	2,328	0	8,159	D	81.8	18.2	0.0	1	67	33	0.3	0.3	0.1	0.0
Gilchrist	4,305	2,990	1,315	0	1,675	D	69.5	30.5	0.0	19	49	34	<.1	<.1	<.1	0.0
Glades	3,407	2,350	1,057	0	1,293	D	69.0	31.0	0.0	21	47	35	<.1	<.1	<.1	0.0
Gulf	5,722	3,491	2,231	0	1,260	D	61.0	39.0	0.0	47	21	36	0.1	0.1	0.1	0.0
Hamilton	3,709	2,669	1,040	0	1,629	D	72.0	28.0	0.0	11	57	37	<.1	<.1	<.1	0.0
Hardee	6,339	4,131	2,208	0	1,923	D	65.2	34.8	0.0	28	40	38	0.1	0.1	0.1	0.0
Hendry	7,868	5,498	2,370	0	3,128	D	69.9	30.1	0.0	17	51	39	0.2	0.2	0.1	0.0
Hernando	54,948	35,314	19,634	0	15,680	D	64.3	35.7	0.0	32	36	40	1.1	1.1	1.1	0.0
Highlands	31,888	18,811	13,077	0	5,734	D	59.0	41.0	0.0	54	14	41	0.6	0.6	0.8	0.0
Hillsborough	304,925	187,287	117,636	2	69,651	D	61.4	38.6	<.1	45	23	17	6.1	5.8	6.9	0.9
Holmes	6,234	3,740	2,494	0	1,246	D	60.0	40.0	0.0	50	18	42	0.1	0.1	0.1	0.0
Indian River	43,431	23,310	20,121	0	3,189	D	53.7	46.3	0.0	64	4	43	0.9	0.7	1.2	0.0
Jackson	14,723	9,586	5,137	0	4,449	D	65.1	34.9	0.0	29	39	44	0.3	0.3	0.3	0.0
Jefferson	4,714	3,632	1,082	0	2,550	D	77.0	23.0	0.0	3	65	45	<.1	0.1	<.1	0.0
Lafayette	2,549	1,749	800	0	949	D	68.6	31.4	0.0	22	46	46	<.1	<.1	<.1	0.0
Lake	68,784	42,945	25,839	0	17,106	D	62.4	37.6	0.0	40	27	47	1.4	1.3	1.5	0.0
Lee	150,709	88,282	62,424	3	25,858	D	58.6	41.4	<.1	55	13	16	3.0	2.7	3.6	1.4
Leon	95,974	73,423	22,525	26	50,898	D	76.5	23.5	<.1	4	64	2	1.9	2.3	1.3	11.8
Levy	10,902	7,259	3,643	0	3,616	D	66.6	33.4	0.0	24	44	48	0.2	0.2	0.2	0.0
Liberty	2,398	1,703	695	0	1,008	D	71.0	29.0	0.0	13	55	49	<.1	<.1	<.1	0.0
Madison	6,018	4,390	1,627	1	2,763	D	72.9	27.0	<.1	8	60	5	0.1	0.1	<.1	0.5
Manatee	98,499	58,583	39,913	3	18,670	D	59.5	40.5	<.1	53	15	13	2.0	1.8	2.3	1.4
Marion	85,268	52,873	32,395	0	20,478	D	62.0	38.0	0.0	43	25	50	1.7	1.6	1.9	0.0
Martin	50,441	28,366	22,075	0	6,291	D	56.2	43.8	0.0	61	7	51	1.0	0.9	1.3	0.0
Monroe	28,214	18,199	10,015	0	8,184	D	64.5	35.5	0.0	31	37	52	0.6	0.6	0.6	0.0
Nassau	17,956	10,934	7,022	0	3,912	D	60.9	39.1	0.0	49	19	53	0.4	0.3	0.4	0.0
Okaloosa	59,903	29,801	30,102	0	301	R	49.7	50.3	0.0	67	1	54	1.2	0.9	1.8	0.0
Okeechobee	9,301	6,158	3,143	0	3,015	D	66.2	33.8	0.0	25	43	55	0.2	0.2	0.2	0.0
Orange	233,025	143,057	89,965	3	53,092	D	61.4	38.6	<.1	46	22	18	4.7	4.4	5.2	1.4
Osceola	42,322	26,394	15,928	0	10,466	D	62.4	37.6	0.0	42	26	56	0.9	0.8	0.9	0.0
Palm Beach	355,188	249,219	105,968	1	143,251	D	70.2	29.8	<.1	16	52	57	7.2	7.7	6.2	0.5
Pasco	122,821	78,514	44,307	0	34,207	D	63.9	36.1	0.0	34	34	58	2.5	2.4	2.6	0.0
Pinellas	376,855	243,410	133,415	30	109,995	D	64.6	35.4	<.1	30	38	7	7.6	7.5	7.8	13.6
Polk	145,824	90,346	55,478	0	34,868	D	62.0	38.0	0.0	44	24	59	2.9	2.8	3.2	0.0
Putnam	25,234	18,224	7,009	1	11,215	D	72.2	27.8	<.1	10	58	11	0.5	0.6	0.4	0.5
St. Johns	39,151	22,076	17,075	0	5,001	D	56.4	43.6	0.0	60	8	61	0.8	0.7	1.0	0.0
St. Lucie	62,663	40,091	22,569	3	17,522	D	64.0	36.0	<.1	33	35	9	1.3	1.2	1.3	1.4
Santa Rosa	35,524	19,448	16,076	0	3,372	D	54.7	45.3	0.0	62	6	60	0.7	0.6	0.9	0.0
Sarasota	123,705	70,709	52,968	28	17,741	D	57.2	42.8	<.1	58	10	4	2.5	2.2	3.1	12.7
Seminole	114,185	65,932	48,249	4	17,683	D	57.7	42.3	<.1	56	12	12	2.3	2.0	2.8	1.8
Sumter	10,324	7,337	2,987	0	4,350	D	71.1	28.9	0.0	12	56	62	0.2	0.2	0.2	0.0
Suwannee	11,355	7,421	3,934	0	3,487	D	65.4	34.6	0.0	27	41	63	0.2	0.2	0.2	0.0
Taylor	7,058	4,896	2,162	0	2,734	D	69.4	30.6	0.0	20	48	64	0.1	0.2	0.1	0.0
Union	3,606	2,624	982	0	1,642	D	72.8	27.2	0.0	9	59	65	<.1	<.1	<.1	0.0
Volusia	151,324	101,365	49,863	96	51,502	D	67.0	33.0	<.1	23	45	1	3.0	3.1	2.9	43.6
Wakulla	6,705	4,934	1,771	0	3,163	D	73.6	26.4	0.0	6	62	66	0.1	0.2	0.1	0.0
Walton	12,935	7,723	5,212	0	2,511	D	59.7	40.3	0.0	51	17	67	0.3	0.2	0.3	0.0
Washington	7,606	4,748	2,857	1	1,891	D	62.4	37.6	<.1	41	28	6	0.2	0.1	0.2	0.5
FLORIDA	**4,962,290**	**3,245,565**	**1,716,505**	**220**	**1,529,060**	**D**	**65.4**	**34.6**	**<.1**				**100.0**	**100.0**	**100.0**	**100.0**

Table H. — Vote for U.S. Representative in Congress: November 3, 1992, General Election

Congressional district and county	Total	Democrat (DEM)	Republican (REP)	Other	Plurality Total	Party	Percent of total vote DEM	REP	Other	Rank within district DEM	REP	Other	Percent contribution to district vote Total	DEM	REP	Other
District 1	**228,632**	**118,941**	**100,349**	**9,342**	**18,592**	**D**	**52.0**	**43.9**	**4.1**				**100.0**	**100.0**	**100.0**	**100.0**
Bay (pt)	10,743	4,809	5,595	339	786	R	44.8	52.1	3.2	6	1	6	4.7	4.0	5.6	3.6
Escambia	101,926	56,158	41,519	4,249	14,639	D	55.1	40.7	4.2	2	5	2	44.6	47.2	41.4	45.5
Holmes	6,229	3,809	2,193	227	1,616	D	61.1	35.2	3.6	1	6	5	2.7	3.2	2.2	2.4
Okaloosa	60,548	28,260	29,789	2,499	1,529	R	46.7	49.2	4.1	5	2	3	26.5	23.8	29.7	26.8
Santa Rosa	36,029	18,890	15,698	1,441	3,192	D	52.4	43.6	4.0	4	3	4	15.8	15.9	15.6	15.4
Walton	13,157	7,015	5,555	587	1,460	D	53.3	42.2	4.5	3	4	1	5.8	5.9	5.5	6.3
District 2	**227,726**	**167,215**	**60,425**	**86**	**106,790**	**D**	**73.4**	**26.5**	**<.1**				**100.0**	**100.0**	**100.0**	**100.0**
Baker (pt)	3,956	2,537	1,419	0	1,118	D	64.1	35.9	0.0	17	2	6	1.7	1.5	2.3	0.0
Bay (pt)	30,350	18,288	12,059	3	6,229	D	60.3	39.7	<.1	18	1	5	13.3	10.9	20.0	3.5
Calhoun	4,042	3,129	913	0	2,216	D	77.4	22.6	0.0	7	12	7	1.8	1.9	1.5	0.0
Columbia (pt)	9,806	6,388	3,418	0	2,970	D	65.1	34.9	0.0	16	3	8	4.3	3.8	5.7	0.0
Franklin	3,313	2,409	903	1	1,506	D	72.7	27.3	<.1	11	8	2	1.5	1.4	1.5	1.2
Gadsden	12,099	10,268	1,831	0	8,437	D	84.9	15.1	0.0	1	18	9	5.3	6.1	3.0	0.0
Gulf	5,616	3,960	1,656	0	2,304	D	70.5	29.5	0.0	13	6	10	2.5	2.4	2.7	0.0
Hamilton	3,564	2,819	745	0	2,074	D	79.1	20.9	0.0	5	14	11	1.6	1.7	1.2	0.0
Jackson	14,376	10,035	4,338	3	5,697	D	69.8	30.2	<.1	14	5	4	6.3	6.0	7.2	3.5
Jefferson	4,575	3,687	887	1	2,800	D	80.6	19.4	<.1	2	17	3	2.0	2.2	1.5	1.2
Lafayette	2,460	1,946	514	0	1,432	D	79.1	20.9	0.0	4	15	12	1.1	1.2	0.9	0.0
Leon	93,564	72,067	21,419	78	50,648	D	77.0	22.9	<.1	8	11	1	41.1	43.1	35.4	90.7
Liberty	2,481	1,993	488	0	1,505	D	80.3	19.7	0.0	3	16	13	1.1	1.2	0.8	0.0
Madison	5,872	4,589	1,283	0	3,306	D	78.2	21.8	0.0	6	13	14	2.6	2.7	2.1	0.0
Suwannee	11,021	7,859	3,162	0	4,697	D	71.3	28.7	0.0	12	7	15	4.8	4.7	5.2	0.0
Taylor	6,805	5,183	1,622	0	3,561	D	76.2	23.8	0.0	10	9	16	3.0	3.1	2.7	0.0
Wakulla	6,579	5,016	1,563	0	3,453	D	76.2	23.8	0.0	9	10	17	2.9	3.0	2.6	0.0
Washington	7,247	5,042	2,205	0	2,837	D	69.6	30.4	0.0	15	4	18	3.2	3.0	3.6	0.0
District 3	**155,029**	**91,915**	**63,114**	**-**	**28,801**	**D**	**59.3**	**40.7**	**-**				**100.0**	**100.0**	**100.0**	**-**
Alachua (pt)	10,748	7,067	3,681	-	3,386	D	65.8	34.2	-	6	9	-	6.9	7.7	5.8	-
Baker (pt)	953	622	331	-	291	D	65.3	34.7	-	7	8	-	0.6	0.7	0.5	-
Clay (pt)	4,037	958	3,079	-	2,121	R	23.7	76.3	-	14	1	-	2.6	1.0	4.9	-
Columbia (pt)	4,987	2,442	2,545	-	103	R	49.0	51.0	-	12	3	-	3.2	2.7	4.0	-
Duval (pt)	76,721	43,057	33,664	-	9,393	D	56.1	43.9	-	11	4	-	49.5	46.8	53.3	-
Flagler (pt)	515	318	197	-	121	D	61.7	38.3	-	10	5	-	0.3	0.3	0.3	-
Lake (pt)	428	312	116	-	196	D	72.9	27.1	-	4	11	-	0.3	0.3	0.2	-
Levy (pt)	569	424	145	-	279	D	74.5	25.5	-	3	12	-	0.4	0.5	0.2	-
Marion (pt)	5,736	3,640	2,096	-	1,544	D	63.5	36.5	-	8	7	-	3.7	4.0	3.3	-
Orange (pt)	24,508	17,365	7,143	-	10,222	D	70.9	29.1	-	5	10	-	15.8	18.9	11.3	-
Putnam (pt)	9,162	3,688	5,474	-	1,786	R	40.3	59.7	-	13	2	-	5.9	4.0	8.7	-
St. Johns (pt)	1,985	1,601	384	-	1,217	D	80.7	19.3	-	1	14	-	1.3	1.7	0.6	-
Seminole (pt)	5,999	3,718	2,281	-	1,437	D	62.0	38.0	-	9	6	-	3.9	4.0	3.6	-
Volusia (pt)	8,681	6,703	1,978	-	4,725	D	77.2	22.8	-	2	13	-	5.6	7.3	3.1	-
District 4	**239,471**	**103,531**	**135,883**	**57**	**32,352**	**R**	**43.2**	**56.7**	**<.1**				**100.0**	**100.0**	**100.0**	**100.0**
Duval (pt)	135,014	56,171	78,828	15	22,657	R	41.6	58.4	<.1	5	1	3	56.4	54.3	58.0	26.3
Flagler (pt)	14,849	6,889	7,951	9	1,062	R	46.4	53.5	<.1	2	4	2	6.2	6.7	5.9	15.8
Nassau	17,747	8,677	9,070	0	393	R	48.9	51.1	0.0	1	5	4	7.4	8.4	6.7	0.0
St. Johns (pt)	36,541	15,879	20,662	0	4,783	R	43.5	56.5	0.0	4	2	5	15.3	15.3	15.2	0.0
Volusia (pt)	35,320	15,915	19,372	33	3,457	R	45.1	54.8	<.1	3	3	1	14.7	15.4	14.3	57.9
District 5	**263,549**	**129,698**	**114,356**	**19,495**	**15,342**	**D**	**49.2**	**43.4**	**7.4**				**100.0**	**100.0**	**100.0**	**100.0**
Alachua (pt)	61,202	30,852	26,188	4,162	4,664	D	50.4	42.8	6.8	3	5	6	23.2	23.8	22.9	21.3
Citrus	45,165	22,341	19,536	3,288	2,805	D	49.5	43.3	7.3	4	3	5	17.1	17.2	17.1	16.9
Dixie	4,580	2,524	1,672	384	852	D	55.1	36.5	8.4	2	9	4	1.7	1.9	1.5	2.0
Gilchrist	4,213	1,996	1,760	457	236	D	47.4	41.8	10.8	7	7	1	1.6	1.5	1.5	2.3
Hernando	54,399	25,536	25,273	3,590	263	D	46.9	46.5	6.6	8	2	7	20.6	19.7	22.1	18.4
Levy (pt)	10,088	4,728	4,319	1,041	409	D	46.9	42.8	10.3	9	4	2	3.8	3.6	3.8	5.3
Marion (pt)	11,760	5,666	5,546	548	120	D	48.2	47.2	4.7	6	1	9	4.5	4.4	4.8	2.8
Pasco (pt)	60,786	29,646	25,801	5,339	3,845	D	48.8	42.4	8.8	5	6	3	23.1	22.9	22.6	27.4
Sumter	11,356	6,409	4,261	686	2,148	D	56.4	37.5	6.0	1	8	8	4.3	4.9	3.7	3.5
District 6	**220,614**	**76,419**	**144,195**	**-**	**67,776**	**R**	**34.6**	**65.4**	**-**				**100.0**	**100.0**	**100.0**	**-**
Baker (pt)	1,788	794	994	-	200	R	44.4	55.6	-	4	5	-	0.8	1.0	0.7	-
Bradford	7,535	3,658	3,877	-	219	R	48.5	51.5	-	3	6	-	3.4	4.8	2.7	-
Clay (pt)	38,934	11,288	27,646	-	16,358	R	29.0	71.0	-	8	1	-	17.6	14.8	19.2	-
Duval (pt)	27,885	8,773	19,112	-	10,339	R	31.5	68.5	-	7	2	-	12.6	11.5	13.3	-
Lake (pt)	64,429	22,701	41,728	-	19,027	R	35.2	64.8	-	5	4	-	29.2	29.7	28.9	-
Marion (pt)	62,299	20,358	41,941	-	21,583	R	32.7	67.3	-	6	3	-	28.2	26.6	29.1	-
Putnam (pt)	14,493	7,198	7,295	-	97	R	49.7	50.3	-	2	7	-	6.6	9.4	5.1	-
Union	3,251	1,649	1,602	-	47	D	50.7	49.3	-	1	8	-	1.5	2.2	1.1	-
District 7	**223,023**	**96,945**	**125,823**	**255**	**28,878**	**R**	**43.5**	**56.4**	**0.1**				**100.0**	**100.0**	**100.0**	**100.0**
Orange (pt)	16,968	6,907	10,061	0	3,154	R	40.7	59.3	0.0	2	2	2	7.6	7.1	8.0	0.0
Seminole (pt)	104,683	38,646	66,037	0	27,391	R	36.9	63.1	0.0	3	1	3	46.9	39.9	52.5	0.0
Volusia (pt)	101,372	51,392	49,725	255	1,667	D	50.7	49.1	0.3	1	3	1	45.5	53.0	39.5	100.0

Congressional district and county	Total	Democrat (DEM)	Republican (REP)	Other	Plurality Total	Plurality Party	Percent of total vote DEM	Percent of total vote REP	Percent of total vote Other	Rank within district DEM	Rank within district REP	Rank within district Other	Percent contribution to district vote Total	Percent contribution to district vote DEM	Percent contribution to district vote REP	Percent contribution to district vote Other
District 8	**207,122**	**65,145**	**141,977**	**-**	**76,832**	**R**	**31.5**	**68.5**	**-**				**100.0**	**100.0**	**100.0**	**-**
Orange (pt)	187,623	58,390	129,233	-	70,843	R	31.1	68.9	-	2	1	-	90.6	89.6	91.0	-
Osceola (pt)	19,499	6,755	12,744	-	5,989	R	34.6	65.4	-	1	2	-	9.4	10.4	9.0	-
District 9	**268,163**	**110,135**	**158,028**	**-**	**47,893**	**R**	**41.1**	**58.9**	**-**				**100.0**	**100.0**	**100.0**	**-**
Hillsborough (pt)	53,309	20,931	32,378	-	11,447	R	39.3	60.7	-	3	1	-	19.9	19.0	20.5	-
Pasco (pt)	63,697	26,046	37,651	-	11,605	R	40.9	59.1	-	2	2	-	23.8	23.6	23.8	-
Pinellas (pt)	151,157	63,158	87,999	-	24,841	R	41.8	58.2	-	1	3	-	56.4	57.3	55.7	-
District 10	**264,415**	**114,809**	**149,606**	**-**	**34,797**	**R**	**43.4**	**56.6**	**-**				**100.0**	**100.0**	**100.0**	**-**
Pinellas (pt)	264,415	114,809	149,606	-	34,797	R	43.4	56.6	-	1	1	-	100.0	100.0	100.0	-
District 11	**191,354**	**100,984**	**77,640**	**12,730**	**23,344**	**D**	**52.8**	**40.6**	**6.7**				**100.0**	**100.0**	**100.0**	**100.0**
Hillsborough (pt)	191,354	100,984	77,640	12,730	23,344	D	52.8	40.6	6.7	1	1	1	100.0	100.0	100.0	100.0
District 12	**192,830**	**92,346**	**100,484**	**-**	**8,138**	**R**	**47.9**	**52.1**	**-**				**100.0**	**100.0**	**100.0**	**-**
DeSoto	7,306	3,960	3,346	-	614	D	54.2	45.8	-	2	5	-	3.8	4.3	3.3	-
Hardee	6,041	3,029	3,012	-	17	D	50.1	49.9	-	3	4	-	3.1	3.3	3.0	-
Highlands (pt)	4,714	2,038	2,676	-	638	R	43.2	56.8	-	5	2	-	2.4	2.2	2.7	-
Hillsborough (pt)	30,891	13,267	17,624	-	4,357	R	42.9	57.1	-	6	1	-	16.0	14.4	17.5	-
Pasco (pt)	7,290	3,960	3,330	-	630	D	54.3	45.7	-	1	6	-	3.8	4.3	3.3	-
Polk (pt)	136,588	66,092	70,496	-	4,404	R	48.4	51.6	-	4	3	-	70.8	71.6	70.2	-
District 13	**274,648**	**115,767**	**158,881**	**-**	**43,114**	**R**	**42.2**	**57.8**	**-**				**100.0**	**100.0**	**100.0**	**-**
Charlotte (pt)	17,259	8,582	8,677	-	95	R	49.7	50.3	-	1	4	-	6.3	7.4	5.5	-
Hillsborough (pt)	13,882	5,359	8,523	-	3,164	R	38.6	61.4	-	4	1	-	5.1	4.6	5.4	-
Manatee	95,367	39,447	55,920	-	16,473	R	41.4	58.6	-	3	2	-	34.7	34.1	35.2	-
Sarasota	148,140	62,379	85,761	-	23,382	R	42.1	57.9	-	2	3	-	53.9	53.9	54.0	-
District 14	**268,511**	**-**	**220,351**	**48,160**	**172,191**	**R**	**-**	**82.1**	**17.9**				**100.0**	**-**	**100.0**	**100.0**
Charlotte (pt)	41,233	-	33,436	7,797	25,639	R	-	81.1	18.9	-	2	2	15.4	-	15.2	16.2
Collier	67,413	-	53,288	14,125	39,163	R	-	79.0	21.0	-	3	1	25.1	-	24.2	29.3
Lee	159,865	-	133,627	26,238	107,389	R	-	83.6	16.4	-	1	3	59.5	-	60.6	54.5
District 15	**261,285**	**132,412**	**128,873**	**-**	**3,539**	**D**	**50.7**	**49.3**	**-**				**100.0**	**100.0**	**100.0**	**-**
Brevard	189,906	99,990	89,916	-	10,074	D	52.7	47.3	-	1	4	-	72.7	75.5	69.8	-
Indian River	41,282	17,223	24,059	-	6,836	R	41.7	58.3	-	4	1	-	15.8	13.0	18.7	-
Osceola (pt)	22,888	11,719	11,169	-	550	D	51.2	48.8	-	2	3	-	8.8	8.9	8.7	-
Polk (pt)	7,209	3,480	3,729	-	249	R	48.3	51.7	-	3	2	-	2.8	2.6	2.9	-
District 16	**258,559**	**101,237**	**157,322**	**-**	**56,085**	**R**	**39.2**	**60.8**	**-**				**100.0**	**100.0**	**100.0**	**-**
Glades	3,281	1,291	1,990	-	699	R	39.3	60.7	-	4	4	-	1.3	1.3	1.3	-
Hendry (pt)	6,893	1,998	4,895	-	2,897	R	29.0	71.0	-	7	1	-	2.7	2.0	3.1	-
Highlands (pt)	24,269	10,065	14,204	-	4,139	R	41.5	58.5	-	2	6	-	9.4	9.9	9.0	-
Martin (pt)	46,384	14,729	31,655	-	16,926	R	31.8	68.2	-	5	3	-	17.9	14.5	20.1	-
Okeechobee (pt)	5,891	1,833	4,058	-	2,225	R	31.1	68.9	-	6	2	-	2.3	1.8	2.6	-
Palm Beach (pt)	113,675	47,264	66,411	-	19,147	R	41.6	58.4	-	1	7	-	44.0	46.7	42.2	-
St. Lucie (pt)	58,166	24,057	34,109	-	10,052	R	41.4	58.6	-	3	5	-	22.5	23.8	21.7	-
District 17	**102,799**	**102,784**	**-**	**15**	**102,769**	**D**	**100.0**	**-**	**<.1**				**100.0**	**100.0**	**-**	**100.0**
Dade (pt)	102,799	102,784	-	15	102,769	D	100.0	-	<.1	1	-	1	100.0	100.0	-	100.0
District 18	**156,897**	**52,142**	**104,755**	**-**	**52,613**	**R**	**33.2**	**66.8**	**-**				**100.0**	**100.0**	**100.0**	**-**
Dade (pt)	156,897	52,142	104,755	-	52,613	R	33.2	66.8	-	1	1	-	100.0	100.0	100.0	-
District 19	**281,294**	**177,423**	**103,867**	**4**	**73,556**	**D**	**63.1**	**36.9**	**<.1**				**100.0**	**100.0**	**100.0**	**100.0**
Broward (pt)	129,620	82,715	46,902	3	35,813	D	63.8	36.2	<.1	1	2	1	46.1	46.6	45.2	75.0
Palm Beach (pt)	151,674	94,708	56,965	1	37,743	D	62.4	37.6	<.1	2	1	2	53.9	53.4	54.8	25.0
District 20	**237,889**	**130,959**	**91,589**	**15,341**	**39,370**	**D**	**55.1**	**38.5**	**6.4**				**100.0**	**100.0**	**100.0**	**100.0**
Broward (pt)	189,847	107,845	69,933	12,069	37,912	D	56.8	36.8	6.4	1	3	3	79.8	82.4	76.4	78.7
Dade (pt)	20,874	9,547	9,803	1,524	256	R	45.7	47.0	7.3	3	1	1	8.8	7.3	10.7	9.9
Monroe	27,168	13,567	11,853	1,748	1,714	D	49.9	43.6	6.4	2	2	2	11.4	10.4	12.9	11.4
District 22	**247,088**	**91,625**	**128,400**	**27,063**	**36,775**	**R**	**37.1**	**52.0**	**11.0**				**100.0**	**100.0**	**100.0**	**100.0**
Broward (pt)	118,156	36,234	68,795	13,127	32,561	R	30.7	58.2	11.1	2	2	1	47.8	39.5	53.6	48.5
Dade (pt)	62,451	36,213	19,663	6,575	16,550	D	58.0	31.5	10.5	1	3	3	25.3	39.5	15.3	24.3
Palm Beach (pt)	66,481	19,178	39,942	7,361	20,764	R	28.8	60.1	11.1	3	1	2	26.9	20.9	31.1	27.2
District 23	**143,935**	**84,249**	**44,807**	**14,879**	**39,442**	**D**	**58.5**	**31.1**	**10.3**				**100.0**	**100.0**	**100.0**	**100.0**
Broward (pt)	75,508	47,208	20,324	7,976	26,884	D	62.5	26.9	10.6	4	4	4	52.5	56.0	45.4	53.6
Dade (pt)	4,213	3,043	874	296	2,169	D	72.2	20.7	7.0	2	6	5	2.9	3.6	2.0	2.0
Hendry (pt)	852	731	87	34	644	D	85.8	10.2	4.0	1	7	7	0.6	0.9	0.2	0.2
Martin (pt)	1,199	392	657	150	265	R	32.7	54.8	12.5	7	1	2	0.8	0.5	1.5	1.0
Okeechobee (pt)	3,100	1,295	1,393	412	98	R	41.8	44.9	13.3	6	2	1	2.2	1.5	3.1	2.8
Palm Beach (pt)	52,025	26,734	19,743	5,548	6,991	D	51.4	37.9	10.7	5	3	3	36.1	31.7	44.1	37.3

Table H. — Vote for U.S. Representative in Congress: November 3, 1992, General Election (cont)

Congressional district and county	Total	Democrat (DEM)	Republican (REP)	Other	Plurality Total	Party	DEM	REP	Other	Rank within district DEM	REP	Other	Total	DEM	REP	Other
District 23 (cont)																
St. Lucie (pt)	7,038	4,846	1,729	463	3,117	D	68.9	24.6	6.6	3	5	6	4.9	5.8	3.9	3.1
FLORIDA	**4,914,833**	**2,256,681**	**2,510,725**	**147,427**	**254,044**	**R**	**45.9**	**51.1**	**3.0**							
District 21 (9/1/92																
Primary)[1]	**22,133**	**15,192**	**6,941**	-	**8,251**		**68.6**	**31.4**	-				**100.0**	**100.0**	**100.0**	-
Dade (pt)[1]	22,133	15,192	6,941	-	8,251		68.6	31.4	-	1	1	-	100.0	100.0	100.0	-

[1]Representative elected from Republican primary; vote shown in Democrat (DEM) columns is for winning Republican candidate.

Table I. — Vote for Presidential Preference: March 10, 1992, Democratic Primary Election

County	Total	Clinton	Tsongas	Brown	Harkin	Kerrey				Percent of total vote Clinton	Tsongas	Brown	Rank Clinton	Tsongas	Brown	Percent contribution to state vote Total	Clinton	Tsongas	Brown
Alachua	23,428	9,363	9,380	3,898	478	309	-	-	-	40.0	40.0	16.6	64	6	8	2.1	1.6	2.4	2.8
Baker	1,477	953	307	165	26	26	-	-	-	64.5	20.8	11.2	11	55	45	0.1	0.2	<.1	0.1
Bay	8,272	4,223	2,632	1,069	189	159	-	-	-	51.1	31.8	12.9	49	24	25	0.7	0.7	0.7	0.8
Bradford	2,156	1,296	565	215	44	36	-	-	-	60.1	26.2	10.0	21	40	58	0.2	0.2	0.1	0.2
Brevard	36,627	16,646	13,675	5,467	429	410	-	-	-	45.4	37.3	14.9	58	10	13	3.3	2.9	3.5	3.9
Broward	140,205	75,205	48,451	14,435	1,247	867	-	-	-	53.6	34.6	10.3	40	15	55	12.5	13.2	12.5	10.3
Calhoun	1,022	645	202	135	26	14	-	-	-	63.1	19.8	13.2	13	56	21	<.1	0.1	<.1	<.1
Charlotte	9,965	5,456	3,003	1,262	143	101	-	-	-	54.8	30.1	12.7	36	31	26	0.9	1.0	0.8	0.9
Citrus	12,384	6,605	4,185	1,294	159	141	-	-	-	53.3	33.8	10.4	42	19	53	1.1	1.2	1.1	0.9
Clay	7,355	3,826	2,343	904	139	143	-	-	-	52.0	31.9	12.3	44	23	33	0.7	0.7	0.6	0.6
Collier	8,838	3,954	3,262	1,316	187	119	-	-	-	44.7	36.9	14.9	59	11	14	0.8	0.7	0.8	0.9
Columbia	4,665	2,853	1,130	519	63	100	-	-	-	61.2	24.2	11.1	18	50	47	0.4	0.5	0.3	0.4
Dade	120,031	64,777	41,055	11,705	1,421	1,073	-	-	-	54.0	34.2	9.8	37	17	60	10.7	11.4	10.6	8.4
DeSoto	1,852	1,121	477	195	37	22	-	-	-	60.5	25.8	10.5	19	42	52	0.2	0.2	0.1	0.1
Dixie	1,572	1,050	306	164	27	25	-	-	-	66.8	19.5	10.4	5	57	54	0.1	0.2	<.1	0.1
Duval	56,483	29,188	17,913	7,692	833	857	-	-	-	51.7	31.7	13.6	47	25	18	5.0	5.1	4.6	5.5
Escambia	32,150	17,201	9,311	3,960	798	880	-	-	-	53.5	29.0	12.3	41	35	32	2.9	3.0	2.4	2.8
Flagler	2,961	1,504	988	410	26	33	-	-	-	50.8	33.4	13.8	50	20	17	0.3	0.3	0.3	0.3
Franklin	917	508	226	147	15	21	-	-	-	55.4	24.6	16.0	34	47	11	<.1	<.1	<.1	0.1
Gadsden	3,797	2,346	568	759	55	69	-	-	-	61.8	15.0	20.0	17	66	4	0.3	0.4	0.1	0.5
Gilchrist	1,415	810	351	207	22	25	-	-	-	57.2	24.8	14.6	28	46	16	<.1	0.1	<.1	0.1
Glades	935	586	213	99	25	12	-	-	-	62.7	22.8	10.6	14	52	51	<.1	0.1	<.1	<.1
Gulf	1,348	782	332	159	38	37	-	-	-	58.0	24.6	11.8	26	48	41	0.1	0.1	<.1	0.1
Hamilton	777	581	120	58	9	9	-	-	-	74.8	15.4	7.5	1	64	67	<.1	0.1	<.1	<.1
Hardee	1,626	1,043	404	136	27	16	-	-	-	64.1	24.8	8.4	12	45	65	0.1	0.2	0.1	<.1
Hendry	1,825	1,076	447	216	59	27	-	-	-	59.0	24.5	11.8	25	49	39	0.2	0.2	0.1	0.2
Hernando	14,077	8,049	4,426	1,358	147	97	-	-	-	57.2	31.4	9.6	29	26	61	1.3	1.4	1.1	1.0
Highlands	8,198	4,699	2,335	968	103	93	-	-	-	57.3	28.5	11.8	27	37	40	0.7	0.8	0.6	0.7
Hillsborough	61,960	30,378	22,621	7,701	684	576	-	-	-	49.0	36.5	12.4	53	13	29	5.5	5.3	5.8	5.5
Holmes	1,674	1,107	313	187	41	26	-	-	-	66.1	18.7	11.2	7	59	46	0.1	0.2	<.1	0.1
Indian River	6,498	2,835	2,727	784	82	70	-	-	-	43.6	42.0	12.1	61	3	35	0.6	0.5	0.7	0.6
Jackson	3,981	2,596	683	521	92	89	-	-	-	65.2	17.2	13.1	10	63	22	0.4	0.5	0.2	0.4
Jefferson	1,795	1,207	320	217	20	31	-	-	-	67.2	17.8	12.1	4	61	34	0.2	0.2	<.1	0.2
Lafayette	703	512	108	55	11	17	-	-	-	72.8	15.4	7.8	2	65	66	<.1	<.1	<.1	<.1
Lake	14,520	7,500	4,450	2,312	136	122	-	-	-	51.7	30.6	15.9	48	29	12	1.3	1.3	1.1	1.7
Lee	24,351	13,348	6,739	3,593	334	337	-	-	-	54.8	27.7	14.8	35	39	15	2.2	2.3	1.7	2.6
Leon	27,479	13,236	7,882	5,750	251	360	-	-	-	48.2	28.7	20.9	55	36	3	2.4	2.3	2.0	4.1
Levy	3,022	1,715	849	375	46	37	-	-	-	56.8	28.1	12.4	31	38	30	0.3	0.3	0.2	0.3
Liberty	565	383	82	76	7	17	-	-	-	67.8	14.5	13.5	3	67	20	<.1	<.1	<.1	<.1
Madison	1,622	1,082	304	202	12	22	-	-	-	66.7	18.7	12.5	6	58	28	0.1	0.2	<.1	0.1
Manatee	17,697	9,174	6,011	2,102	214	196	-	-	-	51.8	34.0	11.9	46	18	38	1.6	1.6	1.5	1.5
Marion	17,827	9,573	5,784	2,015	242	213	-	-	-	53.7	32.4	11.3	39	22	44	1.6	1.7	1.5	1.4
Martin	6,242	2,229	3,180	679	81	73	-	-	-	35.7	50.9	10.9	67	1	50	0.6	0.4	0.8	0.5
Monroe	6,787	2,683	2,604	1,284	127	89	-	-	-	39.5	38.4	18.9	65	8	5	0.6	0.5	0.7	0.9
Nassau	4,080	2,293	1,182	474	71	60	-	-	-	56.2	29.0	11.6	33	34	42	0.4	0.4	0.3	0.3
Okaloosa	10,201	5,119	3,347	1,230	251	254	-	-	-	50.2	32.8	12.1	52	21	36	0.9	0.9	0.9	0.9
Okeechobee	2,034	1,158	638	175	27	36	-	-	-	56.9	31.4	8.6	30	27	64	0.2	0.2	0.2	0.1
Orange	38,550	15,809	13,677	8,444	328	292	-	-	-	41.0	35.5	21.9	63	14	1	3.4	2.8	3.5	6.1
Osceola	7,525	3,913	2,221	1,213	101	77	-	-	-	52.0	29.5	16.1	45	32	10	0.7	0.7	0.6	0.9
Palm Beach	92,388	40,635	41,605	8,667	791	690	-	-	-	44.0	45.0	9.4	60	2	62	8.2	7.1	10.7	6.2
Pasco	31,778	17,991	9,939	3,240	326	282	-	-	-	56.6	31.3	10.2	32	28	57	2.8	3.2	2.6	2.3
Pinellas	78,681	38,270	30,037	8,927	779	668	-	-	-	48.6	38.2	11.3	54	9	43	7.0	6.7	7.7	6.4
Polk	30,606	18,254	8,968	2,732	318	334	-	-	-	59.6	29.3	8.9	23	33	63	2.7	3.2	2.3	2.0
Putnam	7,601	4,561	1,991	843	98	108	-	-	-	60.0	26.2	11.1	22	41	48	0.7	0.8	0.5	0.6
St. Johns	7,758	3,310	2,859	1,378	85	126	-	-	-	42.7	36.9	17.8	62	12	6	0.7	0.6	0.7	1.0
St. Lucie	11,828	5,440	4,900	1,213	155	120	-	-	-	46.0	41.4	10.3	56	4	56	1.1	1.0	1.3	0.9
Santa Rosa	7,349	3,871	2,227	920	157	174	-	-	-	52.7	30.3	12.5	43	30	27	0.7	0.7	0.6	0.7
Sarasota	22,786	10,473	9,129	2,809	198	177	-	-	-	46.0	40.1	12.3	57	5	31	2.0	1.8	2.4	2.0
Seminole	16,813	6,405	6,488	3,662	131	127	-	-	-	38.1	38.6	21.8	66	7	2	1.5	1.1	1.7	2.6
Sumter	3,306	2,064	799	366	44	33	-	-	-	62.4	24.2	11.1	16	51	49	0.3	0.4	0.2	0.3
Suwannee	2,950	1,780	734	352	38	46	-	-	-	60.3	24.9	11.9	20	44	37	0.3	0.3	0.2	0.3
Taylor	2,066	1,356	369	270	38	33	-	-	-	65.6	17.9	13.1	9	60	24	0.2	0.2	<.1	0.2
Union	761	501	167	75	9	9	-	-	-	65.8	21.9	9.9	8	54	59	<.1	<.1	<.1	<.1
Volusia	34,964	17,566	12,060	4,758	328	252	-	-	-	50.2	34.5	13.6	51	16	19	3.1	3.1	3.1	3.4
Wakulla	1,790	1,120	318	299	28	25	-	-	-	62.6	17.8	16.7	15	62	7	0.2	0.2	<.1	0.2
Walton	3,125	1,683	789	517	85	51	-	-	-	53.9	25.2	16.5	38	43	9	0.3	0.3	0.2	0.4
Washington	1,836	1,090	416	240	49	41	-	-	-	59.4	22.7	13.1	24	53	23	0.2	0.2	0.1	0.2
FLORIDA	1,123,857	570,566	388,124	139,569	13,587	12,011	-	-	-	50.8	34.5	12.4				100.0	100.0	100.0	100.0

Table J. — Vote for Presidential Preference: March 10, 1992, Republican Primary Election

County	Total	Bush	Bu-chanan			Bush	Bu-chanan			Bush	Bu-chanan			Total	Bush	Bu-chanan		
										Rank								
Alachua	9,362	5,853	3,509	-	-	62.5	37.5	-	-	60	8	-	-	1.0	1.0	1.2	-	-
Baker	114	71	43	-	-	62.3	37.7	-	-	61	7	-	-	<.1	<.1	<.1	-	-
Bay	4,102	2,635	1,467	-	-	64.2	35.8	-	-	50	18	-	-	0.5	0.4	0.5	-	-
Bradford	385	251	134	-	-	65.2	34.8	-	-	43	25	-	-	<.1	<.1	<.1	-	-
Brevard	39,653	26,546	13,107	-	-	66.9	33.1	-	-	31	37	-	-	4.4	4.4	4.6	-	-
Broward	71,143	48,857	22,286	-	-	68.7	31.3	-	-	16	52	-	-	8.0	8.0	7.8	-	-
Calhoun	88	57	31	-	-	64.8	35.2	-	-	48	20	-	-	<.1	<.1	<.1	-	-
Charlotte	14,703	9,572	5,131	-	-	65.1	34.9	-	-	45	23	-	-	1.6	1.6	1.8	-	-
Citrus	8,791	5,750	3,041	-	-	65.4	34.6	-	-	41	27	-	-	1.0	0.9	1.1	-	-
Clay	7,495	5,297	2,198	-	-	70.7	29.3	-	-	9	59	-	-	0.8	0.9	0.8	-	-
Collier	25,815	17,672	8,143	-	-	68.5	31.5	-	-	17	51	-	-	2.9	2.9	2.9	-	-
Columbia	1,218	776	442	-	-	63.7	36.3	-	-	53	15	-	-	0.1	0.1	0.2	-	-
Dade	77,622	63,489	14,133	-	-	81.8	18.2	-	-	1	67	-	-	8.7	10.4	5.0	-	-
DeSoto	613	419	194	-	-	68.4	31.6	-	-	18	50	-	-	<.1	<.1	<.1	-	-
Dixie	137	92	45	-	-	67.2	32.8	-	-	29	39	-	-	<.1	<.1	<.1	-	-
Duval	26,472	18,524	7,948	-	-	70.0	30.0	-	-	11	57	-	-	3.0	3.0	2.8	-	-
Escambia	16,396	11,786	4,610	-	-	71.9	28.1	-	-	6	62	-	-	1.8	1.9	1.6	-	-
Flagler	2,675	1,684	991	-	-	63.0	37.0	-	-	56	12	-	-	0.3	0.3	0.3	-	-
Franklin	128	87	41	-	-	68.0	32.0	-	-	19	49	-	-	<.1	<.1	<.1	-	-
Gadsden	281	169	112	-	-	60.1	39.9	-	-	64	4	-	-	<.1	<.1	<.1	-	-
Gilchrist	169	120	49	-	-	71.0	29.0	-	-	7	61	-	-	<.1	<.1	<.1	-	-
Glades	227	157	70	-	-	69.2	30.8	-	-	13	55	-	-	<.1	<.1	<.1	-	-
Gulf	179	135	44	-	-	75.4	24.6	-	-	3	65	-	-	<.1	<.1	<.1	-	-
Hamilton	51	34	17	-	-	66.7	33.3	-	-	32	36	-	-	<.1	<.1	<.1	-	-
Hardee	311	91	220	-	-	29.3	70.7	-	-	67	1	-	-	<.1	<.1	<.1	-	-
Hendry	637	423	214	-	-	66.4	33.6	-	-	37	31	-	-	<.1	<.1	<.1	-	-
Hernando	13,653	8,559	5,094	-	-	62.7	37.3	-	-	59	9	-	-	1.5	1.4	1.8	-	-
Highlands	7,616	5,383	2,233	-	-	70.7	29.3	-	-	8	60	-	-	0.9	0.9	0.8	-	-
Hillsborough	38,582	26,207	12,375	-	-	67.9	32.1	-	-	21	47	-	-	4.3	4.3	4.3	-	-
Holmes	114	77	37	-	-	67.5	32.5	-	-	26	42	-	-	<.1	<.1	<.1	-	-
Indian River	12,725	8,586	4,139	-	-	67.5	32.5	-	-	27	41	-	-	1.4	1.4	1.5	-	-
Jackson	541	360	181	-	-	66.5	33.5	-	-	34	34	-	-	<.1	<.1	<.1	-	-
Jefferson	217	129	88	-	-	59.4	40.6	-	-	65	3	-	-	<.1	<.1	<.1	-	-
Lafayette	36	26	10	-	-	72.2	27.8	-	-	5	63	-	-	<.1	<.1	<.1	-	-
Lake	19,215	12,741	6,474	-	-	66.3	33.7	-	-	38	30	-	-	2.2	2.1	2.3	-	-
Lee	38,070	24,834	13,236	-	-	65.2	34.8	-	-	42	26	-	-	4.3	4.1	4.6	-	-
Leon	8,850	5,829	3,021	-	-	65.9	34.1	-	-	39	29	-	-	1.0	1.0	1.1	-	-
Levy	762	491	271	-	-	64.4	35.6	-	-	49	19	-	-	<.1	<.1	<.1	-	-
Liberty	32	26	6	-	-	81.3	18.8	-	-	2	66	-	-	<.1	<.1	<.1	-	-
Madison	175	114	61	-	-	65.1	34.9	-	-	44	24	-	-	<.1	<.1	<.1	-	-
Manatee	23,710	15,973	7,737	-	-	67.4	32.6	-	-	28	40	-	-	2.7	2.6	2.7	-	-
Marion	14,079	9,253	4,826	-	-	65.7	34.3	-	-	40	28	-	-	1.6	1.5	1.7	-	-
Martin	12,845	8,863	3,982	-	-	69.0	31.0	-	-	14	54	-	-	1.4	1.5	1.4	-	-
Monroe	5,225	3,476	1,749	-	-	66.5	33.5	-	-	35	33	-	-	0.6	0.6	0.6	-	-
Nassau	1,545	1,026	519	-	-	66.4	33.6	-	-	36	32	-	-	0.2	0.2	0.2	-	-
Okaloosa	11,825	8,035	3,790	-	-	67.9	32.1	-	-	20	48	-	-	1.3	1.3	1.3	-	-
Okeechobee	632	427	205	-	-	67.6	32.4	-	-	25	43	-	-	<.1	<.1	<.1	-	-
Orange	40,432	27,323	13,109	-	-	67.6	32.4	-	-	23	45	-	-	4.5	4.5	4.6	-	-
Osceola	6,535	4,383	2,152	-	-	67.1	32.9	-	-	30	38	-	-	0.7	0.7	0.8	-	-
Palm Beach	69,238	48,890	20,348	-	-	70.6	29.4	-	-	10	58	-	-	7.7	8.0	7.1	-	-
Pasco	27,913	17,071	10,842	-	-	61.2	38.8	-	-	63	5	-	-	3.1	2.8	3.8	-	-
Pinellas	87,386	54,987	32,399	-	-	62.9	37.1	-	-	57	11	-	-	9.8	9.0	11.4	-	-
Polk	21,414	14,541	6,873	-	-	67.9	32.1	-	-	22	46	-	-	2.4	2.4	2.4	-	-
Putnam	2,257	1,424	833	-	-	63.1	36.9	-	-	55	13	-	-	0.3	0.2	0.3	-	-
St. Johns	6,598	4,192	2,406	-	-	63.5	36.5	-	-	54	14	-	-	0.7	0.7	0.8	-	-
St. Lucie	11,721	7,593	4,128	-	-	64.8	35.2	-	-	47	21	-	-	1.3	1.2	1.4	-	-
Santa Rosa	4,327	2,883	1,444	-	-	66.6	33.4	-	-	33	35	-	-	0.5	0.5	0.5	-	-
Sarasota	43,127	29,649	13,478	-	-	68.7	31.3	-	-	15	53	-	-	4.8	4.9	4.7	-	-
Seminole	22,232	14,216	8,016	-	-	63.9	36.1	-	-	52	16	-	-	2.5	2.3	2.8	-	-
Sumter	1,496	1,037	459	-	-	69.3	30.7	-	-	12	56	-	-	0.2	0.2	0.2	-	-
Suwannee	632	393	239	-	-	62.2	37.8	-	-	62	6	-	-	<.1	<.1	<.1	-	-
Taylor	209	152	57	-	-	72.7	27.3	-	-	4	64	-	-	<.1	<.1	<.1	-	-
Union	44	25	19	-	-	56.8	43.2	-	-	66	2	-	-	<.1	<.1	<.1	-	-
Volusia	26,982	17,269	9,713	-	-	64.0	36.0	-	-	51	17	-	-	3.0	2.8	3.4	-	-
Wakulla	276	179	97	-	-	64.9	35.1	-	-	46	22	-	-	<.1	<.1	<.1	-	-
Walton	1,169	733	436	-	-	62.7	37.3	-	-	58	10	-	-	0.1	0.1	0.2	-	-
Washington	259	175	84	-	-	67.6	32.4	-	-	24	44	-	-	<.1	<.1	<.1	-	-
FLORIDA	**893,463**	**608,077**	**285,386**	-	-	**68.1**	**31.9**	-	-					**100.0**	**100.0**	**100.0**		

1992 Vote for President
Percent for Bush (R), by County

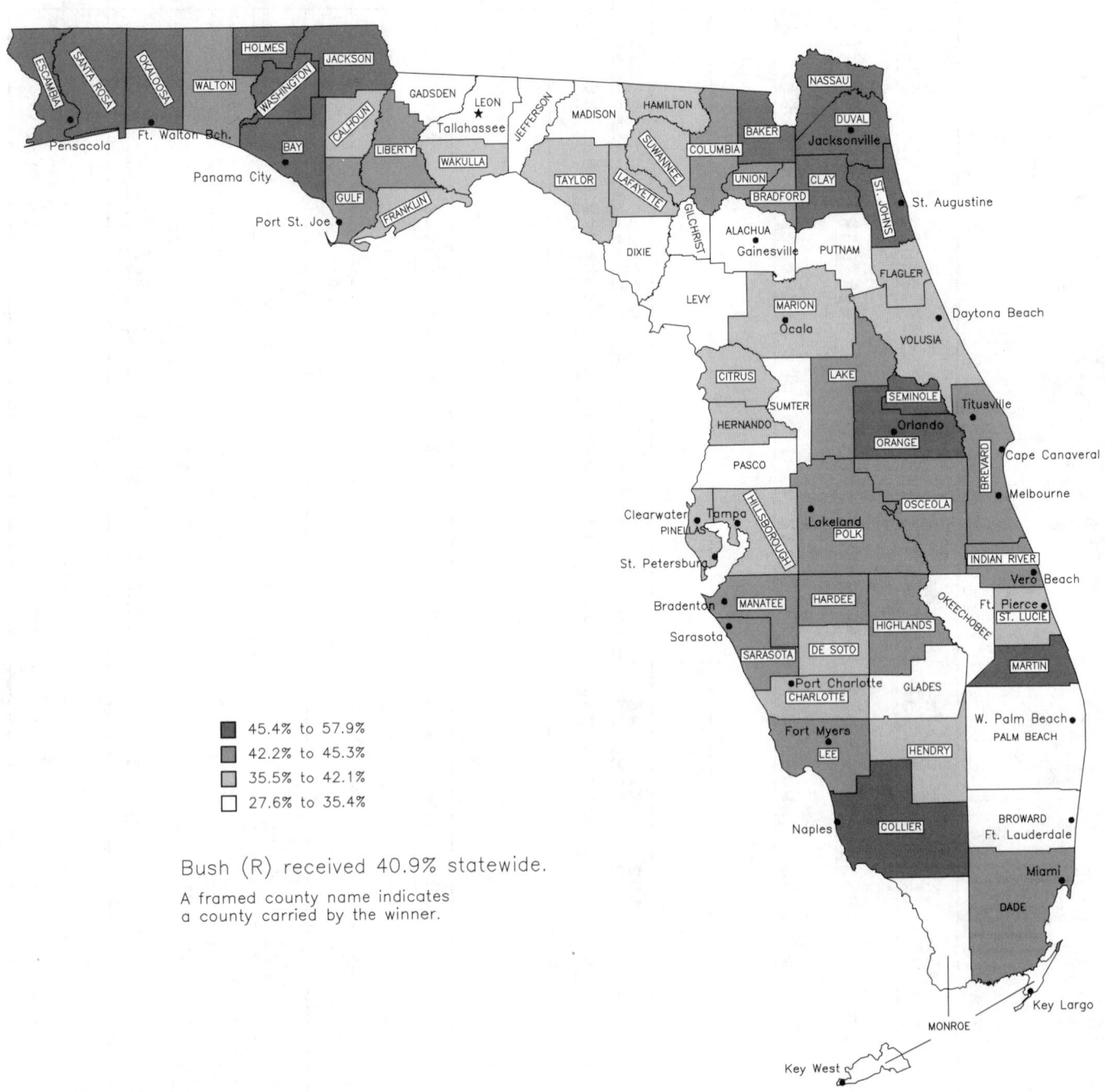

Legend:
- 45.4% to 57.9%
- 42.2% to 45.3%
- 35.5% to 42.1%
- 27.6% to 35.4%

Bush (R) received 40.9% statewide.

A framed county name indicates
a county carried by the winner.

200 Florida

1992 Vote for U.S. Senator
Percent for Graham (D), by County

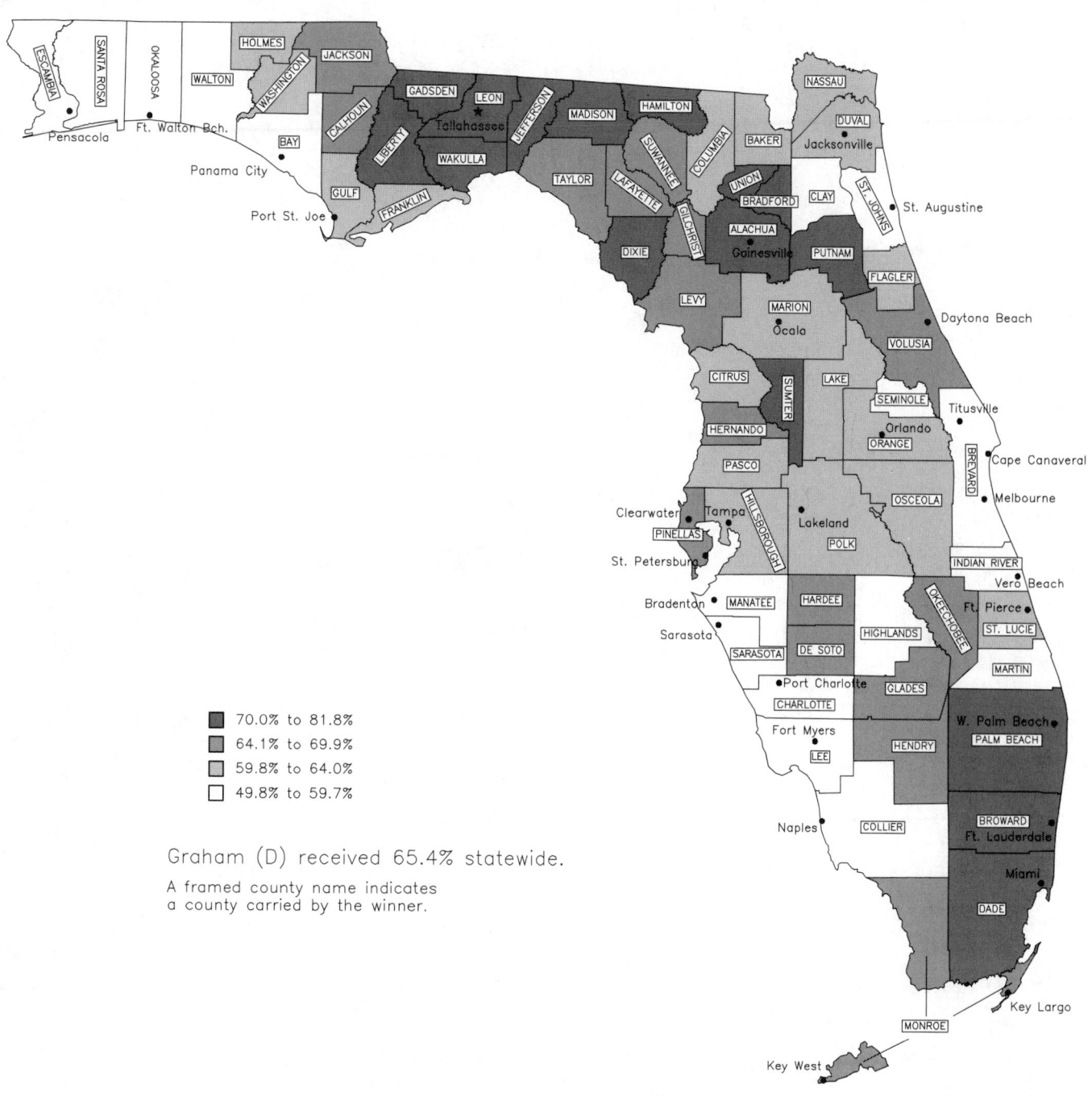

70.0% to 81.8%
64.1% to 69.9%
59.8% to 64.0%
49.8% to 59.7%

Graham (D) received 65.4% statewide.

A framed county name indicates
a county carried by the winner.

Florida 201

GEORGIA

Congressional Districts 11
  Average Population 588,929
State Senate Districts 56
  Average Population 115,682
State House Districts 180
  Average Population 35,990

Electoral College Votes..13
Counties 159
Voting Precincts 2,350

Alternative Registration Methods:
  ....Deputized Registrars

Registration Deadline (Days before Election) 30

Voting Equipment Use (Counties)

Datavote Punch Card	8	Paper Ballot	16
Electronic	2	Other Punch Card	28
Lever Machine	81	Mixed Systems	2
Optical Scanner	22		

Party Control	DEM	REP	IND	VAC
1993 State Senate	41	15	0	0
1992 State Senate	45	11	0	0
1993 State House	128	52	0	0
1992 State House	145	35	0	0

Population Statistics 1990

Race/ Ethnicity	Total Population		Voting Age Population		Voting Age Population % of total population
	Number	%	Number	%	
Non-Hispanic					
White	4,543,425	70.1	3,450,274	72.6	75.9
Black	1,737,165	26.8	1,162,105	24.5	66.9
Asian/Pacific Islander	73,725	1.1	51,858	1.1	70.3
Native American	12,621	0.2	9,433	0.2	74.7
Other	2,358	<.1	1,025	<.1	43.5
All Hispanic	108,922	1.7	76,218	1.6	70.0
TOTAL	6,478,216	100.0	4,750,913	100.0	73.3

Estimated Voting Age Population 1992 (VAP) 4,950,000
Number of Registered Voters................................... 3,177,061
  % of estimated VAP.. 64.2
Voter Turnout (Highest Office) 2,325,470
  % of VAP 47.0
  % of Registration 73.2
Persons Not Voting—of Voting Age 2,624,530
  % of VAP 53.0
Persons Not Voting—of Registered 851,591
  % of Registration 26.8
Straight Ticket Voting .... Yes, Exception

State Officials and Members of Congress

Governor:
Zell Miller (D) 1990, elected to a four-year term in 1990.

U.S. Senators:
Sam Nunn (D) 1972, elected to a six-year term in 1990.
Paul Coverdell (R) 1992, elected to a six-year term in 1992.

U.S. Representative in Congress:
(District, Name, Party, Date first elected)

1. Kingston (R) 1992
2. Bishop (D) 1992
3. Collins (R) 1992

4. Linder (R) 1992
5. Lewis (D) 1986
6. Gingrich (R) 1978

7. Darden (D) 1983
8. Rowland (D) 1982
9. Deal (D) 1992

10. Johnson (D) 1992
11. McKinney (D) 1992

Candidates: General Election, November 3, 1992

Candidate(s)	Total vote	Percent	Party	Status	First elected
President/Vice President					
Clinton/Gore	1,008,966	43.47%	Democrat	Challenger	1992
Bush/Quayle	995,252	42.88%	Republican	Incumbent	1988
Perot/Stockdale	309,657	13.34%	Ross Perot	Challenger	
Marrou/Lord	7,110	0.31%	Libertarian	Challenger	
Bo Gritz	78	<.01%	Populist	Challenger	
Lenora Fulani	44	<.01%	New Alliance	Challenger	
James Warren	9	<.01%	Socialist Worker	Challenger	
Howard Phillips	7	<.01%	Taxpayers	Challenger	
Kim Peterson	2	<.01%	Write in	Challenger	
U.S. Senator [1]					
Wyche Fowler	1,108,416	49.23%	Democrat	Incumbent	1986
Paul Coverdell	1,073,282	47.67%	Republican	Challenger	
Jim Hudson	69,878	3.10%	Libertarian	Challenger	
Miguel Zarate	8	<.01%	Write in	Challenger	
Mitchell Williams	3	<.01%	Write in	Challenger	
U.S. Senator (Runoff Election, November 24, 1992)[1]					
Paul Coverdell	635,114	50.65%	Republican	Challenger	
Wyche Fowler	618,877	49.35%	Democrat	Incumbent	1986
Governor (No Contest)					
U.S. Representative in Congress					
District 1					
Jack Kingston	103,932	57.82%	Republican	Challenger	1992
Barbara Christmas	75,808	42.18%	Democrat	Challenger	
District 2					
Sanford Bishop	95,789	63.70%	Democrat	Challenger	1992
Jim Dudley	54,593	36.30%	Republican	Challenger	
District 3					
Mac Collins	114,107	54.76%	Republican	Challenger	1992
Richard Ray	94,271	45.24%	Democrat	Incumbent	1982
District 4					
John Linder	126,495	50.53%	Republican	Challenger	1992
Cathey Steinberg	123,819	49.47%	Democrat	Challenger	
District 5					
John Lewis	147,445	72.13%	Democrat	Incumbent	1986
Paul Stabler	56,960	27.87%	Republican	Challenger	
Virginia O'Riley	2	<.01%	Write in	Challenger	
District 6					
Newt Gingrich	158,761	57.74%	Republican	Incumbent	1978
Tony Center	116,196	42.26%	Democrat	Challenger	
District 7					
Buddy Darden	111,374	57.32%	Democrat	Incumbent	1983
Al Beverly	82,915	42.68%	Republican	Challenger	
District 8					
J. Roy Rowland	108,472	55.71%	Democrat	Incumbent	1982
Bob Cunningham	86,220	44.29%	Republican	Challenger	
District 9					
Nathan Neal	113,024	59.19%	Democrat	Challenger	1992
Daniel Becker	77,919	40.81%	Republican	Challenger	

[1]Runoff election required because no candidate received a majority of vote.

Candidate(s)	Total vote	Percent	Party	Status	First elected
U.S. Representative in Congress (cont)					
District 10					
Don Johnson	108,426	53.81%	Democrat	Challenger	1992
Ralph Hudgens	93,059	46.19%	Republican	Challenger	
District 11					
Cynthia McKinney	120,168	73.09%	Democrat	Challenger	1992
Woodrow Lovett	44,221	26.90%	Republican	Challenger	
Joe Turner	11	<.01%	Write in	Challenger	

Candidates: March 10, 1992, Primary Election

Candidate	Total vote	Percent	Candidate	Total vote	Percent
Presidential Preference, Democratic			**Presidential Preference, Republican**		
Bill Clinton	259,907	57.17%	George Bush	291,905	64.30%
Paul Tsongas	109,148	24.01%	Patrick Buchanan	162,085	35.70%
Jerry Brown	36,808	8.10%			
Bob Kerrey	22,033	4.85%			
Uncommitted	17,256	3.80%			
Tom Harkin	9,479	2.08%			

Voter Registration and Turnout, 1948-1992 Elections

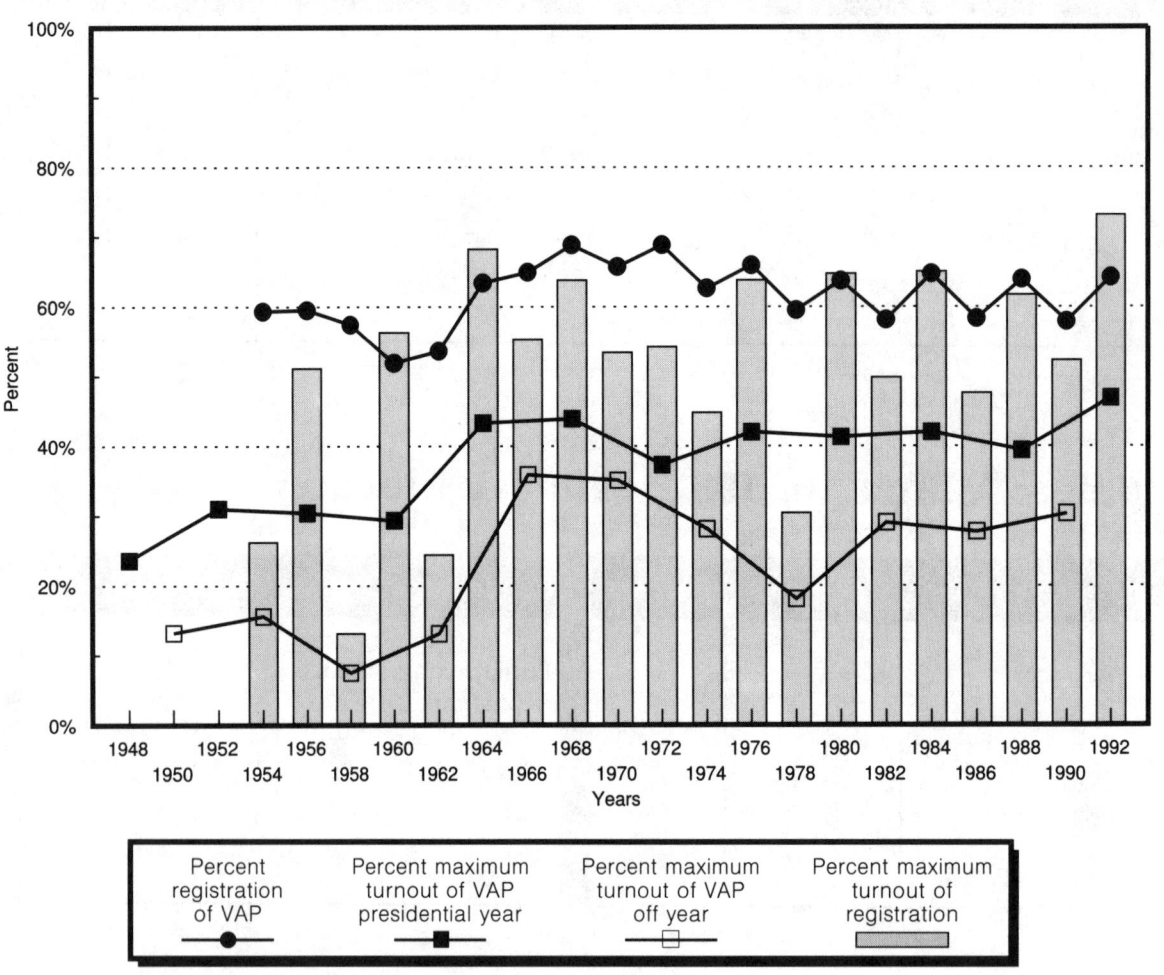

Percent registration of VAP	Percent maximum turnout of VAP presidential year	Percent maximum turnout of VAP off year	Percent maximum turnout of registration

Year	Estimated Voting Age Population (VAP)	Voter registration (REG)			Voter turnout											
						Highest office						Maximum vote				
		Total	Percent of VAP	Rank by percent of VAP	Actual	Total	Office	Percent total REG	Rank by percent of REG	Percent of VAP	Rank by percent of VAP	Total	Percent total REG	Rank by percent of REG	Percent total VAP	Rank by percent of VAP
1992	4,950,000	3,177,061	64.2	43	-	2,321,125	P	73.1	36	46.9	49	2,321,125	73.1	37	46.9	49
1990	4,791,000	2,773,025	57.9	46	-	1,449,652	G	52.3	35	30.3	45	1,449,652	52.3	37	30.3	47
1988	4,593,000	2,934,487	63.9	41	-	1,809,672	P	61.7	45	39.4	50	1,809,672	61.7	46	39.4	51
1986	4,421,000	2,575,815	58.3	45	-	1,224,948	S	47.6	38	27.7	47	1,224,948	47.6	39	27.7	48
1984	4,224,000	2,734,202	64.7	43	-	1,776,120	P	65.0	45	42.0	49	1,776,120	65.0	47	42.0	51
1982	4,038,000	2,346,544	58.1	44	-	1,169,041	G	49.8	43	29.0	48	1,169,041	49.8	43	29.0	48
1980	3,870,000	2,466,786	63.7	41	-	1,596,695	P	64.7	45	41.3	48	1,596,695	64.7	45	41.3	50
1978	3,667,000	2,182,938	59.5	43	-	662,862	G	30.4	47	18.1	50	662,862	30.4	47	18.1	50
1976	3,494,000	2,301,575	65.9	38	-	1,467,458	P	63.8	47	42.0	49	1,467,458	63.8	47	42.0	49
1974	3,338,000	2,090,267	62.6	38	-	936,438	G	44.8	41	28.1	43	936,438	44.8	41	28.1	44
1972	3,153,000	2,167,888	68.8	34	-	1,174,772	P	54.2	46	37.3	50	1,174,772	54.2	46	37.3	50
1970	2,985,000	1,961,013	65.7	35	-	1,046,663	G	53.4	39	35.1	43	1,046,663	53.4	39	35.1	43
1968	2,851,000	1,960,436	68.8	34	-	1,250,266	P	63.8	45	43.9	50	1,250,266	63.8	45	43.9	50
1966	2,717,000	1,763,486	64.9	33	-	975,019	G	55.3	33	35.9	44	975,019	55.3	33	35.9	44
1964	2,634,000	1,669,778	63.4	33	-	1,139,335	P	68.2	38	43.3	46	1,139,335	68.2	38	43.3	46
1962	2,546,000	1,364,988	53.6	33	-	333,374	G	24.4	36	13.1	50	333,374	24.4	36	13.1	50
1960	2,507,000	1,302,139	51.9	32	-	733,349	P	56.3	35	29.3	49	733,349	56.3	35	29.3	49
1958	2,242,000	1,286,021	57.4	25	-	168,497	G	13.1	31	7.5	46	168,497	13.1	31	7.5	46
1956	2,202,000	1,310,586	59.5	26	-	669,665	P	51.1	28	30.4	45	669,665	51.1	28	30.4	45
1954	2,147,000	1,273,793	59.3	21	-	333,936	S	26.2	25	15.6	44	333,936	26.2	25	15.6	44
1952	2,116,000	-	-	-	-	655,785	P	-	-	31.0	45	655,785	-	-	31.0	45
1950	1,980,000	-	-	-	-	261,293	S	-	-	13.2	42	261,293	-	-	13.2	42
1948	1,776,000	-	-	-	-	418,844	P	-	-	23.6	42	418,844	-	-	23.6	42

GEORGIA

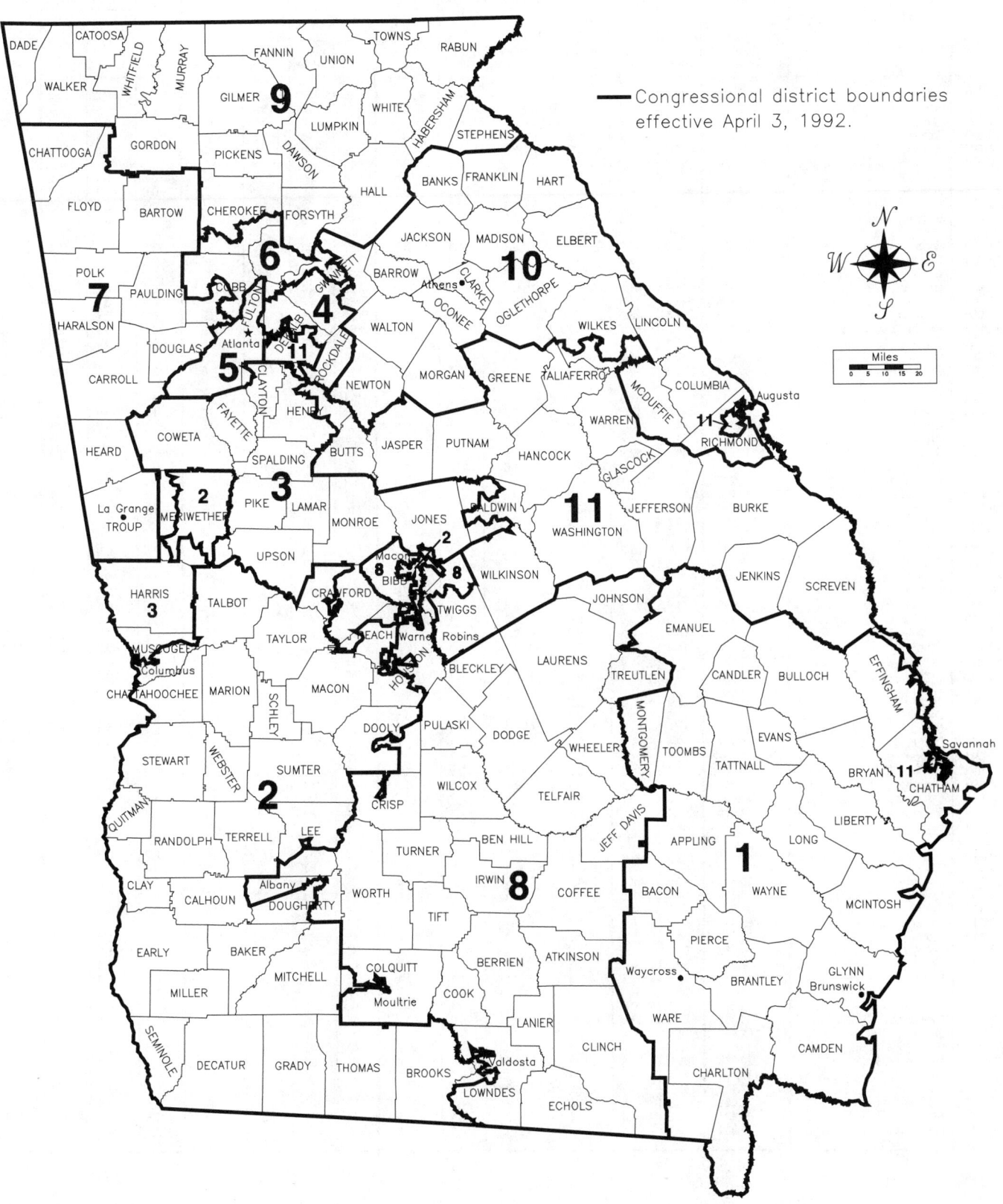

Congressional district boundaries effective April 3, 1992.

Table A. — 1990 Population by Race and Ethnic Origin

State/county code	County	Total persons	White	Black	Asian and Pacific Islander	Native American	Other	Hispanic	Total	White	Black	Hispanic	Total	White	Black	Hispanic
			Percent of total persons — Non-Hispanic					Hispanic	Rank — Percent of total persons	Non-Hispanic		Hispanic	Percent contribution to state population	Non-Hispanic		Hispanic
13 001	Appling	15,744	78.0	20.7	0.2	0.1	<.1	0.9	85	56	103	62	0.2	0.3	0.2	0.1
13 003	Atkinson	6,213	70.8	26.6	<.1	<.1	0.0	2.5	142	79	84	13	<.1	<.1	<.1	0.1
13 005	Bacon	9,566	83.5	15.4	0.1	<.1	<.1	0.9	118	48	111	64	0.1	0.2	<.1	0.1
13 007	Baker	3,615	48.3	51.1	<.1	<.1	0.0	0.6	152	145	14	98	<.1	<.1	0.1	<.1
13 009	Baldwin	39,530	56.2	42.2	0.7	0.1	<.1	0.9	37	126	31	60	0.6	0.5	1.0	0.3
13 011	Banks	10,308	95.5	3.5	0.3	0.2	0.0	0.5	112	14	145	111	0.2	0.2	<.1	<.1
13 013	Barrow	29,721	86.9	11.3	0.7	0.2	<.1	0.9	48	36	122	66	0.5	0.6	0.2	0.2
13 015	Bartow	55,911	89.6	9.0	0.2	0.2	<.1	0.9	25	29	129	58	0.9	1.1	0.3	0.5
13 017	Ben Hill	16,245	68.0	31.2	0.2	<.1	<.1	0.5	83	88	66	115	0.3	0.2	0.3	<.1
13 019	Berrien	14,153	86.0	11.6	0.2	0.2	0.0	2.0	91	39	121	21	0.2	0.3	<.1	0.3
13 021	Bibb	149,967	57.2	41.6	0.5	0.1	<.1	0.6	9	123	35	97	2.3	1.9	3.6	0.8
13 023	Bleckley	10,430	76.5	22.3	0.7	<.1	0.0	0.4	111	57	99	126	0.2	0.2	0.1	<.1
13 025	Brantley	11,077	94.0	5.4	<.1	0.3	0.0	0.3	107	19	138	146	0.2	0.2	<.1	<.1
13 027	Brooks	15,398	56.7	41.3	0.2	0.2	<.1	1.6	87	124	37	30	0.2	0.2	0.4	0.2
13 029	Bryan	15,438	83.8	14.8	0.4	0.1	<.1	0.9	86	47	113	61	0.2	0.3	0.1	0.1
13 031	Bulloch	43,125	72.5	26.0	0.5	0.1	<.1	0.8	32	68	88	69	0.7	0.7	0.6	0.3
13 033	Burke	20,579	47.2	52.2	0.1	<.1	<.1	0.3	64	147	12	145	0.3	0.2	0.6	<.1
13 035	Butts	15,326	63.4	35.4	0.3	0.2	0.0	0.7	88	110	48	83	0.2	0.2	0.3	0.1
13 037	Calhoun	5,013	40.8	58.7	<.1	0.2	0.0	0.2	150	151	8	155	<.1	<.1	0.2	<.1
13 039	Camden	30,167	76.1	20.1	1.3	0.5	<.1	2.1	46	60	105	16	0.5	0.5	0.3	0.6
13 043	Candler	7,744	67.0	31.0	0.1	<.1	0.0	1.8	134	95	67	27	0.1	0.1	0.1	0.1
13 045	Carroll	71,422	83.0	15.7	0.3	0.2	<.1	0.8	18	50	110	70	1.1	1.3	0.6	0.5
13 047	Catoosa	42,464	98.1	0.8	0.4	0.2	<.1	0.5	33	10	150	114	0.7	0.9	<.1	0.2
13 049	Charlton	8,496	71.4	27.7	<.1	0.4	0.0	0.4	128	75	79	127	0.1	0.1	0.1	<.1
13 051	Chatham	216,935	59.5	37.9	1.0	0.2	<.1	1.3	5	115	43	41	3.3	2.8	4.7	2.6
13 053	Chattahoochee	16,934	55.6	30.4	2.6	0.6	0.3	10.6	80	128	70	1	0.3	0.2	0.3	1.6
13 055	Chattooga	22,242	90.7	8.7	<.1	0.2	0.0	0.3	59	25	131	144	0.3	0.4	0.1	<.1
13 057	Cherokee	90,204	96.3	1.9	0.3	0.3	<.1	1.2	12	12	147	47	1.4	1.9	<.1	1.0
13 059	Clarke	87,594	69.6	26.1	2.4	0.1	<.1	1.7	14	81	87	28	1.4	1.3	1.3	1.4
13 061	Clay	3,364	38.8	60.4	<.1	0.1	0.0	0.6	154	155	4	102	<.1	<.1	0.1	<.1
13 063	Clayton	182,052	71.3	23.6	2.7	0.2	<.1	2.1	7	78	96	19	2.8	2.9	2.5	3.4
13 065	Clinch	6,160	71.6	27.2	<.1	0.1	0.0	1.0	144	73	83	55	<.1	<.1	<.1	<.1
13 067	Cobb	447,745	86.2	9.8	1.7	0.2	<.1	2.1	3	38	127	15	6.9	8.5	2.5	8.6
13 069	Coffee	29,592	72.3	25.3	0.4	0.1	<.1	1.9	49	70	93	24	0.5	0.5	0.4	0.5
13 071	Colquitt	36,645	71.4	24.0	0.1	0.2	<.1	4.3	40	76	95	5	0.6	0.6	0.5	1.5
13 073	Columbia	66,031	85.0	11.0	2.3	0.2	<.1	1.5	20	43	124	36	1.0	1.2	0.4	0.9
13 075	Cook	13,456	68.0	29.9	0.2	0.3	<.1	1.6	94	87	74	32	0.2	0.2	0.2	0.2
13 077	Coweta	53,853	76.2	22.6	0.3	0.2	<.1	0.7	29	59	98	85	0.8	0.9	0.7	0.4
13 079	Crawford	8,991	67.2	30.6	0.1	0.4	0.0	1.7	121	94	68	29	0.1	0.1	0.2	0.1
13 081	Crisp	20,011	58.7	40.7	0.1	0.2	<.1	0.3	69	118	39	149	0.3	0.3	0.5	<.1
13 083	Dade	13,147	98.2	0.8	0.2	0.3	0.0	0.5	97	8	151	112	0.2	0.3	<.1	<.1
13 085	Dawson	9,429	98.6	<.1	<.1	0.8	0.0	0.4	119	6	156	125	0.1	0.2	<.1	<.1
13 087	Decatur	25,511	58.8	38.9	0.2	0.2	<.1	1.9	54	116	41	25	0.4	0.3	0.6	0.4
13 089	DeKalb	545,837	52.0	41.9	2.9	0.2	<.1	2.9	2	137	33	12	8.4	6.3	13.2	14.3
13 091	Dodge	17,607	71.4	27.5	0.2	<.1	<.1	0.8	77	77	81	68	0.3	0.3	0.3	0.1
13 093	Dooly	9,901	50.1	48.8	0.3	<.1	0.0	0.8	115	140	20	77	0.2	0.1	0.3	<.1
13 095	Dougherty	96,311	48.4	50.1	0.4	0.2	<.1	0.8	10	144	16	67	1.5	1.0	2.8	0.7
13 097	Douglas	71,120	90.3	7.8	0.5	0.2	<.1	1.1	19	26	134	51	1.1	1.4	0.3	0.7
13 099	Early	11,854	55.4	43.8	0.1	0.3	<.1	0.4	104	129	28	136	0.2	0.1	0.3	<.1
13 101	Echols	2,334	85.3	11.0	<.1	1.7	0.0	1.9	156	42	123	23	<.1	<.1	<.1	<.1
13 103	Effingham	25,687	84.8	14.0	0.2	0.2	<.1	0.7	53	44	115	92	0.4	0.5	0.2	0.2
13 105	Elbert	18,949	68.9	30.1	0.2	<.1	<.1	0.7	73	86	72	86	0.3	0.3	0.3	0.1
13 107	Emanuel	20,546	66.9	32.4	0.2	<.1	0.0	0.4	65	96	60	131	0.3	0.3	0.4	<.1
13 109	Evans	8,724	64.7	33.8	0.2	<.1	<.1	1.2	123	106	55	43	0.1	0.1	0.2	0.1
13 111	Fannin	15,992	99.2	<.1	<.1	0.2	0.0	0.4	84	2	157	132	0.2	0.3	<.1	<.1
13 113	Fayette	62,415	91.3	5.3	1.7	0.1	<.1	1.6	22	22	139	33	1.0	1.3	0.2	0.9
13 115	Floyd	81,251	84.7	13.6	0.5	0.2	<.1	1.0	15	45	116	53	1.3	1.5	0.6	0.8
13 117	Forsyth	44,083	98.1	<.1	0.2	0.2	<.1	1.4	31	9	158	37	0.7	1.0	<.1	0.6
13 119	Franklin	16,650	89.2	10.1	0.2	0.2	0.0	0.5	81	32	126	117	0.3	0.3	<.1	<.1
13 121	Fulton	648,951	46.8	49.7	1.3	0.1	<.1	2.1	1	148	19	17	10.0	6.7	18.6	12.3
13 123	Gilmer	13,368	98.7	0.3	0.1	0.1	<.1	0.8	95	5	153	78	0.2	0.3	<.1	<.1
13 125	Glascock	2,357	87.1	12.6	0.0	<.1	0.0	0.3	155	35	118	153	<.1	<.1	<.1	<.1
13 127	Glynn	62,496	73.0	25.4	0.5	0.2	<.1	0.9	21	67	92	56	1.0	1.0	0.9	0.5
13 129	Gordon	35,072	95.1	3.7	0.3	0.2	<.1	0.6	42	16	144	101	0.5	0.7	<.1	0.2
13 131	Grady	20,279	66.8	31.3	<.1	0.4	<.1	1.4	66	97	65	39	0.3	0.3	0.4	0.3
13 133	Greene	11,793	49.3	49.7	<.1	0.1	0.0	0.8	105	143	18	71	0.2	0.1	0.3	<.1
13 135	Gwinnett	352,910	89.4	5.1	2.9	0.2	<.1	2.4	4	31	140	14	5.4	6.9	1.0	7.8
13 137	Habersham	27,621	91.1	5.5	1.8	0.2	<.1	1.2	50	23	137	44	0.4	0.6	<.1	0.3
13 139	Hall	95,428	85.8	8.6	0.6	0.2	<.1	4.8	11	40	132	4	1.5	1.8	0.5	4.2
13 141	Hancock	8,908	20.1	79.0	0.0	<.1	0.1	0.7	122	159	1	87	0.1	<.1	0.4	<.1

Table A. — 1990 Population by Race and Ethnic Origin (cont)

State/county code	County	Total persons	Percent of total persons - Non-Hispanic White	Black	Asian and Pacific Islander	Native American	Other	Hispanic	Rank - Percent of total persons Total	Non-Hispanic White	Black	Hispanic	Percent contribution to state population Total	Non-Hispanic White	Black	Hispanic
13 143	Haralson	21,966	92.8	6.5	0.2	0.1	0.0	0.4	60	20	136	134	0.3	0.4	<.1	<.1
13 145	Harris	17,788	73.3	25.6	0.2	0.3	0.0	0.5	74	65	90	104	0.3	0.3	0.3	<.1
13 147	Hart	19,712	79.2	20.2	0.2	<.1	0.0	0.4	71	55	104	133	0.3	0.3	0.2	<.1
13 149	Heard	8,628	85.5	13.3	0.2	0.1	0.0	0.8	127	41	117	73	0.1	0.2	<.1	<.1
13 151	Henry	58,741	88.2	10.3	0.5	0.2	0.0	0.8	23	33	125	74	0.9	1.1	0.3	0.4
13 153	Houston	89,208	75.3	21.6	1.1	0.3	<.1	1.6	13	61	101	31	1.4	1.5	1.1	1.3
13 155	Irwin	8,649	69.1	30.1	0.2	<.1	0.0	0.6	125	84	71	96	0.1	0.1	0.1	<.1
13 157	Jackson	30,005	89.4	9.7	0.2	0.2	<.1	0.5	47	30	128	107	0.5	0.6	0.2	0.1
13 159	Jasper	8,453	64.3	34.7	0.1	0.2	<.1	0.7	129	109	49	91	0.1	0.1	0.2	<.1
13 161	Jeff Davis	12,032	83.3	15.2	0.2	<.1	<.1	1.2	102	49	112	46	0.2	0.2	0.1	0.1
13 163	Jefferson	17,408	43.9	55.7	<.1	<.1	<.1	0.2	78	149	11	154	0.3	0.2	0.6	<.1
13 165	Jenkins	8,247	58.2	41.4	0.2	<.1	0.0	0.2	131	119	36	156	0.1	0.1	0.2	<.1
13 167	Johnson	8,329	65.5	33.9	<.1	<.1	<.1	0.4	130	102	54	122	0.1	0.1	0.2	<.1
13 169	Jones	20,739	73.6	25.6	0.2	0.1	<.1	0.4	63	64	91	135	0.3	0.3	0.3	<.1
13 171	Lamar	13,038	65.3	34.1	<.1	0.1	0.0	0.4	99	105	52	137	0.2	0.2	0.3	<.1
13 173	Lanier	5,531	71.5	26.3	0.3	0.7	0.0	1.2	149	74	86	45	<.1	<.1	<.1	<.1
13 175	Laurens	39,988	66.0	33.1	0.3	<.1	<.1	0.5	36	100	57	119	0.6	0.6	0.8	0.2
13 177	Lee	16,250	79.7	19.2	0.3	0.2	<.1	0.7	82	52	108	88	0.3	0.3	0.2	0.1
13 179	Liberty	52,745	52.7	38.5	2.1	0.5	0.2	6.1	30	135	42	2	0.8	0.6	1.2	3.0
13 181	Lincoln	7,442	61.4	37.6	0.1	<.1	0.0	0.8	136	112	46	81	0.1	0.1	0.2	<.1
13 183	Long	6,202	74.3	21.6	0.6	0.4	<.1	3.0	143	63	102	10	<.1	0.1	<.1	0.2
13 185	Lowndes	75,981	65.8	31.8	0.8	0.3	<.1	1.3	16	101	62	40	1.2	1.1	1.4	0.9
13 187	Lumpkin	14,573	95.0	1.6	0.3	1.6	<.1	1.5	89	17	149	35	0.2	0.3	<.1	0.2
13 189	McDuffie	20,119	62.9	36.3	0.1	0.2	0.0	0.4	68	111	47	123	0.3	0.3	0.4	<.1
13 191	McIntosh	8,634	56.2	42.9	<.1	0.1	0.0	0.7	126	125	30	84	0.1	0.1	0.2	<.1
13 193	Macon	13,114	40.7	58.5	0.2	0.1	<.1	0.4	98	152	9	120	0.2	0.1	0.4	<.1
13 195	Madison	21,050	90.0	8.8	0.2	0.1	0.0	0.9	62	27	130	65	0.3	0.4	0.1	0.2
13 197	Marion	5,590	57.9	41.1	0.2	0.3	0.0	0.4	148	120	38	128	<.1	<.1	0.1	<.1
13 199	Meriwether	22,411	54.9	44.4	<.1	0.1	<.1	0.5	57	130	27	105	0.3	0.3	0.6	0.1
13 201	Miller	6,280	72.0	27.5	<.1	<.1	<.1	0.3	141	71	82	148	<.1	<.1	<.1	<.1
13 205	Mitchell	20,275	51.0	47.4	<.1	0.3	0.0	1.3	67	138	21	42	0.3	0.2	0.6	0.2
13 207	Monroe	17,113	67.5	31.5	0.2	0.2	<.1	0.6	79	92	64	103	0.3	0.3	0.3	<.1
13 209	Montgomery	7,163	69.5	28.2	0.2	<.1	<.1	2.0	137	82	78	20	0.1	0.1	0.1	0.1
13 211	Morgan	12,883	64.4	34.4	0.2	<.1	0.0	0.9	101	107	50	59	0.2	0.2	0.3	0.1
13 213	Murray	26,147	98.9	0.2	0.2	0.2	<.1	0.5	52	4	155	109	0.4	0.6	<.1	0.1
13 215	Muscogee	179,278	57.7	37.7	1.3	0.3	<.1	3.0	8	121	45	11	2.8	2.3	3.9	4.9
13 217	Newton	41,808	76.4	22.2	0.2	0.2	<.1	0.9	34	58	100	57	0.6	0.7	0.5	0.4
13 219	Oconee	17,618	90.9	7.4	0.5	0.2	<.1	1.0	76	24	135	54	0.3	0.4	<.1	0.2
13 221	Oglethorpe	9,763	74.4	24.6	<.1	0.2	<.1	0.7	117	62	94	90	0.2	0.2	0.1	<.1
13 223	Paulding	41,611	95.0	3.9	0.2	0.3	<.1	0.6	35	18	142	93	0.6	0.9	<.1	0.2
13 225	Peach	21,189	50.2	47.3	0.3	0.3	<.1	1.8	61	139	22	26	0.3	0.2	0.6	0.3
13 227	Pickens	14,432	97.6	1.7	0.1	0.2	0.0	0.3	90	11	148	147	0.2	0.3	<.1	<.1
13 229	Pierce	13,328	87.2	11.7	<.1	0.2	0.0	0.8	96	34	120	76	0.2	0.3	<.1	<.1
13 231	Pike	10,224	79.2	20.0	0.2	0.1	<.1	0.5	114	54	106	108	0.2	0.2	0.1	<.1
13 233	Polk	33,815	84.0	14.1	0.3	0.2	<.1	1.4	44	46	114	38	0.5	0.6	0.3	0.4
13 235	Pulaski	8,108	66.4	32.4	0.2	<.1	0.0	1.0	132	99	61	52	0.1	0.1	0.2	<.1
13 237	Putnam	14,137	65.5	33.4	0.3	0.1	<.1	0.7	92	103	56	89	0.2	0.2	0.3	<.1
13 239	Quitman	2,209	49.4	50.1	0.1	0.3	0.0	<.1	158	142	15	157	<.1	<.1	<.1	<.1
13 241	Rabun	11,648	98.6	0.4	0.1	0.3	<.1	0.6	106	7	152	100	0.2	0.3	<.1	<.1
13 243	Randolph	8,023	41.2	57.7	0.6	<.1	<.1	0.5	133	150	10	113	0.1	<.1	0.3	<.1
13 245	Richmond	189,719	54.3	41.8	1.7	0.3	<.1	2.0	6	132	34	22	2.9	2.3	4.6	3.4
13 247	Rockdale	54,091	89.7	8.0	0.9	0.2	<.1	1.1	28	28	133	49	0.8	1.1	0.2	0.5
13 249	Schley	3,588	64.3	34.0	0.0	<.1	<.1	1.5	153	108	53	34	<.1	<.1	<.1	<.1
13 251	Screven	13,842	54.7	44.8	<.1	<.1	<.1	0.4	93	131	26	141	0.2	0.2	0.4	<.1
13 253	Seminole	9,010	61.2	32.6	0.1	0.2	0.0	5.9	120	113	59	3	0.1	0.1	0.2	0.5
13 255	Spalding	54,457	69.9	28.9	0.4	0.2	<.1	0.6	27	80	77	99	0.8	0.8	0.9	0.3
13 257	Stephens	23,257	86.9	11.9	0.4	0.1	<.1	0.6	56	37	119	95	0.4	0.4	0.2	0.1
13 259	Stewart	5,654	36.0	63.1	0.2	0.2	0.0	0.5	147	158	2	118	<.1	<.1	0.2	<.1
13 261	Sumter	30,228	52.3	46.3	0.4	0.3	<.1	0.6	45	136	23	94	0.5	0.3	0.8	0.2
13 263	Talbot	6,524	37.0	62.0	<.1	0.2	0.0	0.8	140	157	3	75	0.1	<.1	0.2	<.1
13 265	Taliaferro	1,915	38.4	60.2	0.2	<.1	<.1	1.1	159	156	5	50	<.1	<.1	<.1	<.1
13 267	Tattnall	17,722	67.4	29.1	0.3	0.1	<.1	3.1	75	93	76	9	0.3	0.3	0.3	0.5
13 269	Taylor	7,642	56.1	43.0	<.1	<.1	0.0	0.8	135	127	29	79	0.1	<.1	0.2	<.1
13 271	Telfair	11,000	65.4	34.1	<.1	<.1	0.0	0.4	108	104	51	139	0.2	0.2	0.2	<.1
13 273	Terrell	10,653	39.8	59.7	<.1	<.1	0.0	0.4	109	153	7	138	0.2	<.1	0.4	<.1
13 275	Thomas	38,986	61.1	37.8	0.2	0.2	<.1	0.7	38	114	44	82	0.6	0.5	0.8	0.3
13 277	Tift	34,998	69.3	26.5	0.5	0.1	<.1	3.5	43	83	85	6	0.5	0.5	0.5	1.1
13 279	Toombs	24,072	72.5	23.4	0.6	0.1	<.1	3.4	55	69	97	7	0.4	0.4	0.3	0.8
13 281	Towns	6,754	99.5	0.0	<.1	0.2	0.0	0.3	139	1	159	151	0.1	0.1	0.0	<.1
13 283	Treutlen	5,994	66.6	33.1	0.0	<.1	<.1	0.3	146	98	58	152	<.1	<.1	0.1	<.1

Table A. — 1990 Population by Race and Ethnic Origin (cont)

State/county code	County	Total persons	Percent of total persons Non-Hispanic White	Black	Asian and Pacific Islander	Native American	Other	Hispanic	Rank Percent of total persons Total	Non-Hispanic White	Black	Hispanic	Percent contribution to state population Total	Non-Hispanic White	Black	Hispanic
13 285	Troup	55,536	68.9	29.9	0.5	<.1	<.1	0.5	26	85	75	110	0.9	0.8	1.0	0.3
13 287	Turner	8,703	58.8	40.5	0.2	<.1	0.0	0.4	124	117	40	130	0.1	0.1	0.2	<.1
13 289	Twiggs	9,806	53.7	45.7	<.1	<.1	0.0	0.5	116	133	25	116	0.2	0.1	0.3	<.1
13 291	Union	11,993	99.1	0.2	0.1	0.2	0.0	0.4	103	3	154	129	0.2	0.3	<.1	<.1
13 293	Upson	26,300	71.6	27.6	0.2	0.1	<.1	0.4	51	72	80	140	0.4	0.4	0.4	<.1
13 295	Walker	58,340	95.3	3.8	0.2	0.2	<.1	0.4	24	15	143	142	0.9	1.2	0.1	0.2
13 297	Walton	38,586	80.2	18.3	0.3	0.2	<.1	0.9	39	51	109	63	0.6	0.7	0.4	0.3
13 299	Ware	35,471	73.1	25.9	0.3	0.2	<.1	0.5	41	66	89	106	0.5	0.6	0.5	0.2
13 301	Warren	6,078	39.7	60.2	0.1	<.1	0.0	<.1	145	154	6	159	<.1	<.1	0.2	<.1
13 303	Washington	19,112	48.0	51.4	0.1	<.1	<.1	0.3	72	146	13	143	0.3	0.2	0.6	<.1
13 305	Wayne	22,356	79.5	19.4	0.2	0.2	<.1	0.8	58	53	107	72	0.3	0.4	0.2	0.2
13 307	Webster	2,263	49.8	50.0	0.0	0.2	0.0	<.1	157	141	17	158	<.1	<.1	<.1	<.1
13 309	Wheeler	4,903	67.7	30.0	0.1	<.1	<.1	2.1	151	91	73	18	<.1	<.1	<.1	<.1
13 311	White	13,006	95.7	2.8	0.4	0.3	<.1	0.8	100	13	146	80	0.2	0.3	<.1	<.1
13 313	Whitfield	72,462	92.2	4.0	0.4	0.2	<.1	3.2	17	21	141	8	1.1	1.5	0.2	2.1
13 315	Wilcox	7,008	67.7	31.7	<.1	0.1	0.0	0.4	138	90	63	121	0.1	0.1	0.1	<.1
13 317	Wilkes	10,597	53.2	46.2	<.1	0.1	0.0	0.4	110	134	24	124	0.2	0.1	0.3	<.1
13 319	Wilkinson	10,228	57.5	42.0	<.1	<.1	<.1	0.3	113	122	32	150	0.2	0.1	0.2	<.1
13 321	Worth	19,745	67.9	30.5	0.2	0.3	0.0	1.1	70	89	69	48	0.3	0.3	0.3	0.2
13	**GEORGIA**	**6,478,216**	**70.1**	**26.8**	**1.1**	**0.2**	**<.1**	**1.7**					**100.0**	**100.0**	**100.0**	**100.0**
	CONGRESSIONAL															
	District 1	589,546	74.7	22.5	0.8	0.2	<.1	1.8	5	8	4	4	9.1	9.7	7.6	9.5
	District 2	591,699	41.3	56.3	0.5	0.2	<.1	1.7	1	9	3	6	9.1	5.4	19.2	9.1
	District 3	591,328	79.5	17.7	1.2	0.2	<.1	1.4	4	6	7	8	9.1	10.3	6.0	7.4
	District 4	588,293	81.3	11.4	3.6	0.2	<.1	3.4	6	4	9	1	9.1	10.5	3.9	18.5
	District 5	586,485	34.9	62.0	1.1	0.1	<.1	1.8	9	10	2	3	9.1	4.5	20.9	9.6
	District 6	587,118	89.8	5.9	2.0	0.2	<.1	2.1	8	2	10	2	9.1	11.6	2.0	11.1
	District 7	588,071	85.3	12.8	0.5	0.2	<.1	1.1	7	3	8	10	9.1	11.0	4.3	6.0
	District 8	591,615	77.0	20.9	0.5	0.2	<.1	1.4	3	7	5	7	9.1	10.0	7.1	7.6
	District 9	586,222	94.0	3.6	0.4	0.3	<.1	1.7	10	1	11	5	9.0	12.1	1.2	9.0
	District 10	591,644	79.6	18.0	1.0	0.2	<.1	1.2	2	5	6	9	9.1	10.4	6.1	6.4
	District 11	586,195	34.1	63.8	0.9	0.1	<.1	1.1	11	11	1	11	9.0	4.4	21.5	5.7

Table B. — 1990 Voting Age Population (VAP) by Race and Ethnic Origin

County	Total Voting Age Population	Percent of total VAP — Non-Hispanic White	Black	Asian and Pacific Islander	Native American	Other	Hispanic	Rank — Non-Hispanic Total	White	Black	Hispanic	Percent contribution to state VAP — Total	Non-Hispanic White	Black	Hispanic	VAP percent of total population — Total	Non-Hispanic White	Black	Asian and Pacific Islander	Native American	Other	Hispanic
Appling	11,160	81.3	17.6	0.2	<.1	<.1	0.8	85	54	106	65	0.2	0.3	0.2	0.1	70.9	73.9	60.0	66.7	64.7	50.0	63.8
Atkinson	4,351	73.6	24.0	<.1	<.1	0.0	2.3	143	79	84	14	<.1	<.1	<.1	0.1	70.0	72.8	63.2	100.0	100.0	0.0	64.3
Bacon	6,708	86.6	12.3	0.2	<.1	<.1	0.8	119	44	116	61	0.1	0.2	<.1	0.1	70.1	72.7	56.4	84.6	66.7	33.3	67.5
Baker	2,535	52.2	47.0	<.1	<.1	<.1	0.7	153	143	15	72	<.1	<.1	0.1	<.1	70.1	75.9	64.5	50.0	100.0	0.0	85.7
Baldwin	30,372	58.8	39.5	0.6	0.1	<.1	1.0	34	130	29	50	0.6	0.5	1.0	0.4	76.8	80.4	71.9	73.2	88.6	100.0	87.1
Banks	7,571	95.8	3.4	0.2	0.2	0.0	0.4	111	14	145	121	0.2	0.2	<.1	0.1	73.4	73.7	70.9	58.1	76.5	0.0	59.6
Barrow	21,407	87.9	10.5	0.6	0.2	<.1	0.8	46	36	122	63	0.5	0.5	0.2	0.2	72.0	72.8	66.8	62.4	73.4	25.0	67.2
Bartow	40,535	90.0	8.6	0.3	0.2	<.1	0.9	25	30	129	58	0.9	1.1	0.3	0.5	72.5	72.8	69.6	75.9	80.0	33.3	67.0
Ben Hill	11,263	72.0	27.3	0.2	<.1	<.1	0.4	84	84	71	119	0.2	0.2	0.3	<.1	69.3	73.4	60.6	67.6	62.5	50.0	60.3
Berrien	10,244	87.9	9.8	0.3	0.2	0.0	1.9	92	37	124	22	0.2	0.3	<.1	0.2	72.4	73.9	61.4	89.7	70.4	0.0	68.6
Bibb	110,104	61.0	37.8	0.5	0.1	<.1	0.6	9	123	35	91	2.3	1.9	3.6	0.9	73.4	78.3	66.8	68.7	78.3	54.8	72.3
Bleckley	7,681	79.5	19.4	0.6	<.1	0.0	0.4	110	56	102	123	0.2	0.2	0.1	<.1	73.6	76.6	64.1	61.5	66.7	0.0	72.1
Brantley	7,712	94.5	4.9	<.1	0.2	0.0	0.3	109	19	140	139	0.2	0.2	<.1	<.1	69.6	70.0	63.6	40.0	53.1	0.0	69.4
Brooks	10,806	61.8	36.1	0.1	0.2	0.0	1.8	89	120	38	28	0.2	0.2	0.3	0.3	70.2	76.5	61.3	59.3	81.5	0.0	75.9
Bryan	10,434	84.7	13.8	0.4	0.1	<.1	0.9	91	48	112	53	0.2	0.3	0.1	0.1	67.6	68.4	63.0	67.2	59.1	100.0	72.1
Bulloch	33,288	75.9	22.5	0.5	0.1	<.1	0.8	31	66	90	60	0.7	0.7	0.6	0.4	66.8	73.2	60.9	73.1	92.3	75.0	76.1
Burke	13,750	51.8	47.6	0.1	<.1	<.1	0.4	72	146	14	128	0.3	0.2	0.6	0.1	66.8	75.9	71.5	53.5	81.6	0.0	67.3
Butts	11,379	64.8	34.1	0.2	0.3	0.0	0.7	83	113	46	81	0.2	0.2	0.3	<.1	74.2	75.9	71.5	53.5	81.6	0.0	67.3
Calhoun	3,557	45.2	54.4	<.1	0.2	0.0	0.1	150	153	7	156	<.1	<.1	0.2	<.1	71.0	78.6	65.7	100.0	58.3	0.0	50.0
Camden	21,017	77.1	19.3	1.1	0.5	<.1	1.9	49	61	104	20	0.4	0.5	0.3	0.5	69.7	70.6	66.9	62.3	73.9	62.5	65.6
Candler	5,640	70.6	27.7	0.2	0.1	0.0	1.4	134	93	68	34	0.1	0.1	0.1	0.1	72.8	76.8	65.0	100.0	100.0	0.0	58.7
Carroll	52,281	84.3	14.5	0.3	0.2	<.1	0.7	18	50	110	74	1.1	1.3	0.7	0.5	73.2	74.3	67.8	71.4	76.7	50.0	61.8
Catoosa	31,441	98.2	0.8	0.3	0.2	<.1	0.3	33	9	150	118	0.7	0.9	<.1	0.2	74.0	74.1	72.6	70.9	75.3	100.0	64.9
Charlton	5,855	73.9	25.3	0.1	0.4	0.0	0.3	131	76	81	144	0.1	0.1	0.1	<.1	73.6	78.1	66.9	69.9	76.4	50.0	66.6
Chatham	159,649	63.2	34.4	1.0	0.2	<.1	1.2	5	117	43	44	3.4	2.9	4.7	2.4	73.6	78.1	66.9	69.9	76.4	50.0	66.6
Chattahoochee	12,204	58.4	28.7	2.4	0.7	0.2	9.6	81	131	62	1	0.3	0.2	0.3	1.5	72.1	75.7	68.2	68.3	85.6	48.9	65.0
Chattooga	16,548	91.4	8.0	<.1	0.2	0.0	0.3	57	24	131	137	0.3	0.4	0.1	<.1	71.9	72.0	71.1	70.2	69.9	47.4	66.6
Cherokee	64,861	96.5	1.9	0.3	0.3	<.1	1.1	12	13	147	47	1.4	1.8	0.1	0.9	71.9	72.0	71.1	70.2	69.9	47.4	66.6
Clarke	70,042	74.0	21.8	2.4	0.1	<.1	1.6	11	75	95	30	1.5	1.5	1.3	1.5	80.0	85.0	66.7	80.9	78.0	43.8	77.3
Clay	2,381	43.6	55.4	0.1	0.2	0.0	0.7	154	155	5	79	<.1	<.1	0.1	<.1	70.8	79.5	65.0	100.0	80.0	0.0	84.2
Clayton	131,197	73.6	21.8	2.4	0.2	<.1	1.9	7	78	94	21	2.8	2.8	2.5	3.3	72.1	74.4	66.4	65.4	72.1	56.6	67.1
Clinch	4,316	74.7	24.0	<.1	<.1	0.0	1.1	145	71	86	45	<.1	<.1	<.1	<.1	74.7	75.5	69.7	68.6	76.3	42.4	69.8
Cobb	334,501	87.1	9.1	1.6	0.2	<.1	1.9	3	40	126	19	7.0	8.4	2.6	8.6	70.1	72.8	62.3	66.1	67.7	100.0	68.8
Coffee	20,738	75.2	22.5	0.3	0.1	<.1	1.8	50	69	92	23	0.4	0.5	0.4	0.5	71.7	75.1	60.8	59.0	71.9	87.5	76.8
Colquitt	26,268	74.7	20.3	<.1	0.2	<.1	4.6	40	70	99	4	0.6	0.6	0.5	1.6	69.5	69.6	70.7	64.1	76.0	33.3	64.9
Columbia	45,887	85.1	11.2	2.1	0.2	<.1	1.4	21	47	119	35	1.0	1.1	0.4	0.8	71.3	75.2	62.5	63.6	64.7	0.0	73.7
Cook	9,595	71.7	26.2	0.1	0.2	0.0	1.7	97	88	76	29	0.2	0.2	0.2	0.2	71.3	75.2	62.5	63.6	64.7	0.0	73.7
Coweta	38,502	78.2	20.6	0.3	0.2	<.1	0.7	29	58	96	75	0.8	0.9	0.7	0.4	71.7	72.7	69.1	84.6	72.7	33.3	69.9
Crawford	6,450	68.2	29.5	0.2	0.4	0.0	1.8	121	105	59	26	0.1	0.1	0.2	0.2	71.7	72.7	69.1	84.6	72.7	0.0	77.9
Crisp	14,016	64.3	35.0	0.1	0.2	<.1	0.3	68	116	40	149	0.3	0.3	0.4	<.1	70.0	76.8	60.3	74.1	80.6	28.6	59.7
Dade	9,725	98.2	0.8	0.2	0.3	0.0	0.5	96	8	151	110	0.2	0.3	<.1	<.1	74.0	74.0	77.2	84.0	71.4	0.0	70.3
Dawson	6,814	98.8	<.1	<.1	0.7	0.0	0.4	117	5	157	117	0.1	0.2	<.1	<.1	72.3	72.4	50.0	28.6	64.1	0.0	74.4
Decatur	17,911	62.7	34.8	0.2	0.3	<.1	2.0	53	118	41	17	0.4	0.3	0.5	0.5	70.2	74.8	62.9	72.5	78.7	11.1	76.9
DeKalb	416,284	56.7	37.6	2.7	0.2	<.1	2.8	2	135	36	9	8.8	6.8	13.5	15.1	76.3	83.1	68.3	71.4	74.5	37.6	73.9
Dodge	13,047	73.4	25.4	0.2	0.1	<.1	0.9	76	80	80	57	0.3	0.3	0.3	0.2	74.1	76.2	68.6	62.9	93.8	100.0	77.7
Dooly	6,911	55.5	43.5	0.3	<.1	0.0	0.6	116	139	21	86	0.1	0.1	0.3	<.1	69.8	77.4	62.2	70.0	66.7	0.0	57.1
Dougherty	66,994	53.4	45.1	0.4	0.3	<.1	0.8	12	142	18	67	1.4	1.0	2.6	0.7	69.6	76.7	62.7	69.2	74.9	55.6	64.6
Douglas	50,971	91.1	7.1	0.5	0.2	<.1	1.0	19	25	134	52	1.1	1.3	0.3	0.6	71.7	72.3	65.6	69.0	71.3	21.1	64.9
Early	8,290	60.7	38.5	0.1	0.3	<.1	0.4	105	124	31	130	0.2	0.1	0.3	<.1	69.9	76.6	61.5	76.9	67.7	100.0	66.7
Echols	1,637	87.4	8.9	0.1	1.5	0.0	2.0	158	38	127	18	<.1	<.1	<.1	<.1	70.1	71.9	56.8	100.0	62.5	0.0	73.3
Effingham	17,712	86.1	13.0	0.2	0.2	<.1	0.5	54	45	113	105	0.4	0.4	0.2	0.1	69.0	70.0	63.7	73.2	53.7	53.8	53.3
Elbert	13,861	71.8	27.3	0.2	<.1	0.0	0.6	69	85	70	92	0.3	0.3	0.3	0.1	73.1	76.3	66.4	73.3	75.0	0.0	60.4
Emanuel	14,301	71.6	27.8	0.2	<.1	0.0	0.4	66	90	66	127	0.3	0.3	0.3	<.1	69.6	74.5	59.6	58.5	65.0	0.0	67.1
Evans	6,166	68.7	30.0	0.2	<.1	0.0	1.1	125	101	55	46	0.1	0.1	0.2	<.1	70.0	75.1	62.6	78.6	100.0	0.0	62.4
Fannin	12,285	99.3	<.1	<.1	0.3	0.0	0.3	80	2	156	143	0.3	0.4	<.1	<.1	76.8	76.9	80.0	60.0	81.6	0.0	61.3
Fayette	44,188	91.9	5.0	1.5	0.1	<.1	1.5	22	22	139	32	0.9	1.2	0.2	0.9	70.8	71.3	66.3	64.1	68.8	61.5	66.6
Floyd	61,782	86.6	11.9	0.4	0.2	<.1	0.9	15	43	138	56	1.3	1.6	0.6	0.7	74.0	77.7	66.7	66.5	78.9	42.9	67.7
Forsyth	32,710	98.2	<.1	0.1	0.2	<.1	1.4	32	10	158	33	0.7	0.9	<.1	0.6	74.2	74.2	100.0	59.3	67.4	88.9	74.6
Franklin	12,697	90.5	8.8	0.1	0.2	<.1	0.4	77	29	128	124	0.3	0.3	<.1	<.1	76.3	77.4	66.5	69.2	71.4	0.0	66.2
Fulton	491,766	50.9	45.6	1.2	0.2	<.1	2.1	1	148	17	15	10.4	7.3	19.3	13.3	75.8	82.5	69.5	73.2	83.4	44.5	76.1
Gilmer	10,004	98.7	0.3	0.1	0.1	<.1	0.7	94	6	153	82	0.2	0.3	<.1	<.1	74.8	74.8	91.9	75.0	93.3	100.0	64.7
Glascock	1,802	87.2	12.5	0.0	0.1	0.0	0.2	155	39	115	155	<.1	<.1	<.1	<.1	76.5	76.6	75.8	0.0	100.0	0.0	50.0
Glynn	46,253	76.2	22.3	0.4	0.2	<.1	0.9	20	64	93	59	1.0	1.0	0.9	0.5	74.0	77.3	65.0	71.2	78.1	16.7	67.9
Gordon	25,574	95.4	3.5	0.3	0.2	<.1	0.6	42	17	144	98	0.5	0.7	<.1	0.2	72.9	73.2	67.3	67.8	75.6	20.0	73.0
Grady	14,553	70.0	28.3	<.1	0.4	<.1	1.3	65	96	64	38	0.3	0.3	0.4	0.3	71.8	75.2	66.8	68.4	69.3	100.0	66.8
Greene	8,183	54.6	44.6	<.1	0.1	0.0	0.7	106	141	20	83	0.2	0.1	0.3	<.1	69.4	76.8	62.2	100.0	92.3	0.0	56.3
Gwinnett	254,196	89.7	5.0	2.7	0.2	<.1	2.3	4	32	138	13	5.4	6.6	1.1	7.6	72.0	72.3	71.1	68.6	74.4	50.4	68.8
Habersham	21,087	90.6	6.4	1.5	0.2	<.1	1.2	48	27	136	43	0.4	0.6	0.1	0.3	76.3	75.9	88.0	65.2	75.4	100.0	71.3
Hall	70,969	86.8	7.7	0.6	0.2	<.1	4.6	10	42	132	5	1.5	1.8	0.5	4.3	74.4	75.3	66.9	73.4	77.4	60.8	71.3
Hancock	6,115	24.7	74.4	0.0	<.1	0.1	0.7	126	159	1	76	0.1	<.1	0.4	<.1	68.6	84.5	64.7	0.0	66.7	58.3	66.7

Table B. — 1990 Voting Age Population (VAP) by Race and Ethnic Origin (cont)

County	Total Voting Age Population	Percent of total VAP Non-Hispanic White	Black	Asian and Pacific Islander	Native American	Other	Hispanic	Rank Total	Rank NH White	Rank NH Black	Rank Hispanic	Pct contribution Total	Pct contribution NH White	Pct contribution NH Black	Pct contribution Hispanic	VAP pct of total pop Total	NH White	Black	Asian and Pacific Islander	Native American	Other	Hispanic
Haralson	16,144	93.4	5.9	0.2	0.1	0.0	0.3	58	20	137	147	0.3	0.4	<.1	<.1	73.5	74.0	67.2	66.7	77.8	0.0	58.3
Harris	13,288	74.4	24.5	0.2	0.3	0.0	0.6	75	73	83	95	0.3	0.3	0.3	0.1	74.7	75.8	71.4	71.8	76.9	0.0	79.4
Hart	14,821	82.0	17.4	0.2	<.1	0.0	0.3	64	51	107	140	0.3	0.4	0.2	<.1	75.2	77.9	64.8	69.7	80.0	0.0	63.2
Heard	6,179	86.9	12.2	0.2	0.1	0.0	0.6	123	41	117	93	0.1	0.2	<.1	<.1	71.6	72.8	65.6	55.0	66.7	0.0	52.9
Henry	42,525	88.5	10.1	0.5	0.2	0.0	0.7	24	33	123	73	0.9	1.1	0.4	0.4	72.4	72.7	70.9	68.1	73.8	0.0	64.4
Houston	64,026	77.9	19.2	1.1	0.3	<.1	1.5	14	60	105	31	1.3	1.4	1.1	1.3	71.8	74.3	63.6	70.5	71.2	31.4	66.6
Irwin	6,167	73.2	26.1	0.1	<.1	0.0	0.5	124	81	77	102	0.1	0.1	0.1	<.1	71.3	75.5	61.8	69.2	66.7	0.0	62.3
Jackson	22,054	89.8	9.3	0.2	0.2	<.1	0.5	45	31	125	103	0.5	0.6	0.2	0.1	73.5	73.8	70.6	68.0	80.0	80.0	70.6
Jasper	6,068	66.9	32.3	0.1	0.1	0.0	0.6	127	108	50	88	0.1	0.1	0.2	<.1	71.8	74.7	66.7	70.0	46.7	0.0	66.7
Jeff Davis	8,655	84.4	14.0	0.2	<.1	<.1	1.4	104	49	111	36	0.2	0.2	0.1	0.2	71.9	72.9	66.2	58.3	88.9	25.0	81.3
Jefferson	12,160	48.2	51.4	<.1	<.1	0.0	0.2	82	149	11	154	0.3	0.2	0.5	<.1	69.9	76.6	64.6	62.5	85.7	0.0	56.1
Jenkins	5,812	62.5	37.0	0.2	<.1	0.0	0.2	132	119	37	153	0.1	0.1	0.2	<.1	70.5	75.7	63.1	56.3	80.0	0.0	92.3
Johnson	5,890	70.3	29.1	<.1	<.1	<.1	0.4	130	94	60	125	0.1	0.1	0.1	<.1	70.7	75.9	60.7	71.4	66.7	50.0	65.7
Jones	14,951	74.5	24.8	0.2	0.2	<.1	0.3	63	72	82	134	0.3	0.3	0.3	<.1	72.1	72.9	69.7	72.3	77.4	100.0	65.8
Lamar	9,594	67.9	31.6	<.1	0.1	0.0	0.3	98	106	51	142	0.2	0.2	0.3	<.1	73.6	76.5	68.2	72.7	68.4	0.0	63.3
Lanier	3,915	74.3	23.9	0.2	0.4	0.0	1.2	149	74	87	42	<.1	<.1	<.1	<.1	70.8	73.5	64.4	60.0	41.7	0.0	69.1
Laurens	28,730	69.5	29.6	0.3	<.1	<.1	0.5	37	38	58	112	0.6	0.6	0.7	0.2	71.8	75.6	64.3	73.3	80.0	25.0	72.8
Lee	11,034	79.3	19.5	0.3	0.2	0.0	0.7	86	57	101	77	0.2	0.3	0.2	<.1	67.9	67.6	69.3	63.6	83.3	0.0	67.0
Liberty	36,702	55.6	36.0	2.2	0.5	0.1	5.6	30	138	39	3	0.8	0.6	1.1	2.7	69.6	73.4	65.2	74.0	74.0	36.5	63.8
Lincoln	5,454	64.4	34.8	0.1	<.1	0.0	0.6	137	115	42	89	0.1	0.1	0.2	<.1	73.3	76.9	67.7	77.8	33.3	0.0	60.7
Long	4,322	76.7	19.9	0.6	0.3	0.0	2.6	144	62	100	12	<.1	<.1	<.1	0.1	69.7	71.9	64.2	62.5	60.9	0.0	59.3
Lowndes	54,740	69.1	28.6	0.8	0.3	<.1	1.2	16	100	63	40	1.2	1.1	1.3	0.9	72.0	75.6	64.7	71.0	78.4	50.0	68.1
Lumpkin	11,025	95.5	1.6	0.2	1.3	0.0	1.3	87	15	149	37	0.2	0.3	<.1	0.2	75.7	76.1	74.3	59.5	63.0	0.0	69.0
McDuffie	14,208	66.2	33.0	0.2	0.2	0.0	0.4	67	109	49	131	0.3	0.3	0.4	<.1	70.6	74.3	64.3	85.7	76.3	0.0	60.7
McIntosh	6,211	58.9	40.4	<.1	0.1	0.0	0.5	122	128	27	108	0.1	0.1	0.2	<.1	71.9	75.5	67.7	100.0	88.9	0.0	47.6
Macon	8,972	44.2	55.1	0.1	0.1	<.1	0.4	103	154	6	116	0.2	0.1	0.4	<.1	68.4	74.3	64.5	44.0	66.7	16.7	70.2
Madison	15,434	90.6	8.3	0.3	0.1	0.0	0.7	61	28	130	71	0.3	0.4	0.1	0.1	73.3	73.8	69.3	75.0	80.8	0.0	62.6
Marion	3,992	60.7	38.5	0.1	0.3	0.0	0.5	148	125	32	114	<.1	<.1	0.1	<.1	71.4	74.8	66.8	36.4	61.1	0.0	78.3
Meriwether	15,871	58.9	40.4	<.1	0.1	0.0	0.5	59	129	26	111	0.3	0.3	0.6	<.1	70.8	76.0	64.6	90.9	72.0	0.0	60.3
Miller	4,550	75.5	24.0	<.1	0.1	0.0	0.3	141	68	85	138	<.1	<.1	<.1	<.1	72.5	75.9	63.3	50.0	100.0	0.0	75.0
Mitchell	13,847	56.0	42.5	<.1	0.3	0.0	1.2	70	137	24	41	0.3	0.2	0.5	0.2	68.3	75.0	61.2	73.3	70.6	0.0	65.4
Monroe	12,487	68.3	30.7	0.2	0.2	0.0	0.6	79	104	54	96	0.3	0.2	0.3	<.1	73.0	73.8	71.2	69.4	72.2	0.0	75.0
Montgomery	5,301	70.9	27.0	0.2	<.1	0.0	1.8	138	92	73	24	0.1	0.1	0.1	0.1	74.0	75.4	70.8	91.7	75.0	0.0	67.6
Morgan	9,321	65.8	33.1	0.2	0.1	0.0	0.7	100	110	48	70	0.2	0.2	0.3	<.1	72.4	74.0	69.5	76.9	100.0	0.0	59.0
Murray	18,729	99.2	0.1	0.2	0.2	0.0	0.4	52	3	155	129	0.4	0.5	<.1	<.1	71.6	71.8	58.5	57.4	74.4	0.0	50.0
Muscogee	130,837	61.4	34.2	1.3	0.3	<.1	2.7	8	122	45	10	2.8	2.3	3.9	4.6	73.0	77.7	66.3	73.3	77.9	39.6	66.5
Newton	30,132	78.2	20.5	0.2	0.2	<.1	0.8	35	59	97	62	0.6	0.7	0.5	0.3	72.1	73.8	66.6	70.4	71.9	33.3	63.3
Oconee	12,560	91.7	6.8	0.4	0.2	<.1	0.9	78	23	135	55	0.3	0.3	<.1	0.2	71.3	71.9	65.6	62.5	69.7	33.3	64.6
Oglethorpe	7,210	76.5	22.5	<.1	0.3	<.1	0.6	115	63	91	90	0.2	0.2	0.1	<.1	73.9	75.9	67.6	85.7	82.6	100.0	66.7
Paulding	29,500	95.3	3.7	0.2	0.3	0.0	0.6	36	18	143	97	0.6	0.8	<.1	0.2	70.9	71.1	66.7	69.9	77.1	0.0	62.8
Peach	15,424	51.9	45.6	0.3	0.4	<.1	1.8	62	144	16	25	0.3	0.2	0.6	0.4	72.8	75.2	70.2	72.2	75.0	62.5	73.5
Pickens	10,816	97.7	1.7	<.1	0.3	0.0	0.3	88	11	148	141	0.2	0.3	<.1	<.1	74.9	75.0	73.1	52.6	93.5	0.0	76.1
Pierce	9,575	88.5	10.7	<.1	0.2	0.0	0.6	99	34	121	99	0.2	0.2	<.1	<.1	71.8	72.8	65.6	90.0	75.0	0.0	51.9
Pike	7,430	79.8	19.4	0.2	0.1	<.1	0.5	113	55	103	104	0.2	0.2	0.1	<.1	72.7	73.2	70.6	66.7	72.7	100.0	70.4
Polk	24,875	85.5	12.8	0.3	0.1	<.1	1.2	44	46	114	39	0.5	0.6	0.3	0.4	73.6	74.9	67.0	72.4	58.6	100.0	63.6
Pulaski	5,924	69.9	28.9	0.2	<.1	0.0	1.0	129	97	61	51	0.1	0.1	0.1	<.1	73.1	76.9	65.3	64.3	57.1	0.0	69.9
Putnam	10,499	69.1	29.9	0.2	0.1	0.0	0.7	91	99	56	84	0.2	0.2	0.3	<.1	74.2	76.4	66.5	54.8	52.4	0.0	71.1
Quitman	1,639	54.9	44.7	0.1	0.2	0.0	<.1	156	140	19	157	<.1	<.1	<.1	<.1	74.2	82.4	66.1	66.7	66.7	0.0	100.0
Rabun	9,090	98.5	0.4	0.1	0.3	<.1	0.6	102	7	152	85	0.2	0.3	<.1	<.1	78.0	78.0	92.7	64.7	75.8	100.0	86.6
Randolph	5,666	46.5	52.1	0.8	<.1	<.1	0.6	133	150	10	94	0.1	<.1	0.3	<.1	70.6	79.7	63.7	93.5	100.0	100.0	84.6
Richmond	138,246	58.2	37.9	1.7	0.3	<.1	1.8	6	132	34	27	2.9	2.3	4.5	3.3	72.9	78.1	66.2	75.6	79.6	46.7	67.0
Rockdale	38,764	90.6	7.3	0.8	0.2	<.1	1.0	28	26	133	48	0.8	1.0	0.2	0.5	71.7	72.4	65.7	62.4	67.6	25.0	68.2
Schley	2,572	67.5	31.5	0.0	<.1	0.0	0.9	152	107	52	54	<.1	<.1	<.1	<.1	71.7	75.2	66.4	0.0	50.0	50.0	43.6
Screven	9,789	59.1	40.3	<.1	0.1	<.1	0.4	95	127	28	122	0.2	0.2	0.3	<.1	70.7	76.5	63.6	81.8	84.6	100.0	78.4
Seminole	6,645	64.9	27.6	<.1	0.2	0.0	7.2	120	112	69	2	0.1	0.1	0.2	0.6	73.8	74.2	62.5	60.0	68.4	0.0	90.4
Spalding	39,147	73.1	25.8	0.4	0.2	<.1	0.5	27	82	78	101	0.8	0.8	0.9	0.3	71.9	75.2	64.1	64.4	72.7	15.4	66.5
Stephens	17,649	88.1	10.8	0.4	0.1	0.0	0.5	55	35	120	100	0.4	0.5	0.2	0.1	75.9	77.0	68.8	69.7	78.1	0.0	66.0
Stewart	4,109	39.1	60.2	0.2	0.2	0.0	0.3	147	158	2	135	<.1	<.1	0.2	<.1	72.7	78.8	69.4	58.3	61.5	0.0	53.8
Sumter	21,393	57.4	41.4	0.4	0.3	<.1	0.5	47	133	25	107	0.5	0.4	0.8	0.1	70.8	77.7	63.2	82.6	62.0	25.0	56.1
Talbot	4,757	40.2	58.8	<.1	0.3	0.0	0.7	140	157	3	78	0.1	<.1	0.2	<.1	72.9	79.4	69.1	100.0	100.0	0.0	62.7
Taliaferro	1,385	41.8	57.2	0.1	<.1	0.0	0.8	159	156	4	64	<.1	<.1	<.1	<.1	72.3	78.7	68.8	50.0	100.0	0.0	52.4
Tattnall	13,439	68.6	28.1	0.3	0.1	<.1	2.9	74	103	65	7	0.3	0.3	0.3	0.5	75.8	77.2	73.2	77.8	78.3	50.0	72.0
Taylor	5,506	59.8	39.4	<.1	<.1	0.0	0.8	136	126	30	69	0.1	<.1	0.2	<.1	72.0	76.8	65.9	75.0	50.0	0.0	60.3
Telfair	7,955	68.6	31.0	<.1	<.1	0.0	0.3	107	102	53	150	0.2	0.2	0.2	<.1	73.2	75.9	65.7	100.0	44.4	0.0	46.3
Terrell	7,489	45.7	53.7	<.1	0.1	0.0	0.4	112	151	9	126	0.2	<.1	0.3	<.1	70.3	80.8	63.3	62.5	100.0	0.0	72.5
Thomas	27,827	64.7	34.3	0.2	0.2	<.1	0.6	39	114	44	87	0.6	0.5	0.8	0.2	71.4	76.5	64.8	77.4	63.4	57.1	61.2
Tift	24,940	72.8	22.9	0.5	0.1	<.1	3.6	43	83	89	6	0.5	0.5	0.5	1.2	71.3	74.9	61.5	75.7	70.0	44.4	73.6
Toombs	16,976	76.1	20.5	0.5	0.1	<.1	2.7	56	65	98	11	0.4	0.4	0.3	0.6	70.5	74.1	61.9	66.2	73.5	50.0	55.2
Towns	5,578	99.4	0.0	<.1	0.2	0.0	0.3	135	1	159	146	0.1	0.2	0.0	<.1	82.6	82.5	0.0	100.0	92.3	0.0	94.4
Treutlen	4,291	70.0	29.8	0.0	<.1	0.0	0.2	146	95	57	151	<.1	<.1	0.1	<.1	71.6	75.2	64.4	0.0	50.0	0.0	62.5

Table B. — 1990 Voting Age Population (VAP) by Race and Ethnic Origin (cont)

County	Total Voting Age Population	Percent of total VAP						Rank				Percent contribution to state VAP				VAP percent of total population						
			Non-Hispanic						Non-Hispanic				Non-Hispanic					Non-Hispanic				
		White	Black	Asian and Pacific Islander	Native American	Other	Hispanic	Total	White	Black	Hispanic	Total	White	Black	Hispanic	Total	White	Black	Asian and Pacific Islander	Native American	Other	Hispanic
Troup	40,030	71.8	27.2	0.5	0.1	<.1	0.5	26	86	72	113	0.8	0.8	0.9	0.2	72.1	75.0	65.5	67.1	79.2	40.0	63.0
Turner	5,983	65.7	33.5	0.2	<.1	0.0	0.5	128	111	47	109	0.1	0.1	0.2	<.1	68.7	76.8	56.8	70.0	100.0	0.0	80.0
Twiggs	6,809	56.7	42.7	<.1	<.1	0.0	0.4	118	134	23	120	0.1	0.1	0.3	<.1	69.4	73.4	64.9	83.3	37.5	0.0	60.9
Union	9,320	99.1	0.2	0.1	0.2	0.0	0.4	101	4	154	133	0.2	0.3	<.1	<.1	77.7	77.8	78.9	68.8	84.0	0.0	67.3
Upson	19,621	73.7	25.6	0.2	0.1	<.1	0.3	51	77	79	145	0.4	0.4	0.4	<.1	74.6	76.8	69.1	71.4	82.4	33.3	61.2
Walker	43,317	95.4	3.8	0.2	0.2	<.1	0.3	23	16	141	136	0.9	1.2	0.1	0.2	74.2	74.3	73.9	66.1	75.8	20.0	68.2
Walton	27,854	81.8	16.9	0.3	0.2	<.1	0.8	38	53	109	68	0.6	0.7	0.4	0.3	72.2	73.6	66.6	61.9	71.8	14.3	64.8
Ware	25,971	75.6	23.4	0.3	0.2	<.1	0.5	41	67	88	106	0.5	0.6	0.5	0.2	73.2	75.8	66.1	69.2	74.5	100.0	68.4
Warren	4,361	45.4	54.4	0.1	<.1	0.0	<.1	142	152	8	158	<.1	<.1	0.2	<.1	71.8	82.1	64.9	85.7	50.0	0.0	100.0
Washington	13,479	51.4	48.1	0.1	<.1	<.1	0.3	73	148	12	148	0.3	0.2	0.6	<.1	70.5	75.4	66.0	76.0	70.0	50.0	63.1
Wayne	15,861	81.9	17.0	0.2	0.2	<.1	0.8	60	52	108	66	0.3	0.4	0.2	0.2	70.9	73.1	62.2	64.1	60.0	50.0	70.6
Webster	1,638	51.8	48.0	0.0	0.1	0.0	0.0	157	145	13	159	<.1	<.1	<.1	0.0	72.4	75.4	69.5	0.0	50.0	0.0	0.0
Wheeler	3,495	71.3	26.4	<.1	<.1	<.1	2.1	151	91	75	16	<.1	<.1	<.1	<.1	71.3	75.1	62.7	60.0	50.0	100.0	71.3
White	10,015	96.1	2.6	0.4	0.2	<.1	0.7	93	13	146	80	0.2	0.3	<.1	<.1	77.0	77.3	71.3	67.2	64.9	100.0	68.4
Whitfield	53,527	92.9	3.7	0.4	0.2	<.1	2.8	17	21	142	8	1.1	1.4	0.2	2.0	73.9	74.4	69.7	65.7	62.1	46.7	65.5
Wilcox	5,022	71.7	27.8	<.1	0.1	0.0	0.4	139	87	67	132	0.1	0.1	0.1	<.1	71.7	75.9	62.7	50.0	77.8	0.0	60.0
Wilkes	7,789	56.0	43.3	<.1	0.1	0.0	0.4	108	136	22	115	0.2	0.1	0.3	<.1	73.5	77.4	68.9	60.0	73.3	0.0	79.5
Wilkinson	7,219	61.5	38.1	<.1	<.1	0.0	0.2	114	121	33	152	0.2	0.1	0.2	<.1	70.6	75.5	64.0	100.0	100.0	0.0	53.3
Worth	13,755	71.6	26.9	0.2	0.3	0.0	1.0	71	89	74	49	0.3	0.3	0.3	0.2	69.7	73.5	61.4	81.1	69.8	0.0	62.2
GEORGIA	**4,750,913**	**72.6**	**24.5**	**1.1**	**0.2**	**<.1**	**1.6**					**100.0**	**100.0**	**100.0**	**100.0**	**73.3**	**75.9**	**66.9**	**70.3**	**74.7**	**43.5**	**70.0**
CONGRESSIONAL																						
District 1	429,078	77.2	20.2	0.8	0.2	<.1	1.6	8	8	4	6	9.0	9.6	7.5	8.8	72.8	75.3	65.3	70.8	73.2	41.8	64.9
District 2	415,781	45.6	52.1	0.5	0.2	<.1	1.6	10	9	3	4	8.8	5.5	18.6	8.8	70.3	77.6	64.9	73.0	75.4	39.3	68.0
District 3	429,343	81.2	16.2	1.1	0.2	<.1	1.3	7	5	7	8	9.0	10.1	6.0	7.1	72.6	74.2	66.3	66.6	72.8	47.0	67.4
District 4	448,179	82.5	10.6	3.4	0.2	<.1	3.3	1	4	9	1	9.4	10.7	4.1	19.3	76.2	77.3	71.0	70.8	73.0	42.2	72.9
District 5	440,910	39.7	57.2	1.1	0.2	<.1	1.8	2	10	2	3	9.3	5.1	21.7	10.5	75.2	85.5	69.4	73.2	83.3	46.3	75.9
District 6	438,847	90.3	5.8	1.8	0.2	<.1	1.9	4	2	10	2	9.2	11.5	2.2	11.2	74.7	75.1	72.4	68.6	76.9	47.6	70.7
District 7	431,939	86.6	11.6	0.5	0.2	<.1	1.0	6	3	8	11	9.1	10.8	4.3	5.7	73.5	74.6	66.7	68.3	75.1	34.1	66.0
District 8	427,443	79.6	18.3	0.5	0.2	<.1	1.4	9	7	5	7	9.0	9.9	6.7	7.7	72.3	74.8	63.2	69.6	71.9	49.2	70.7
District 9	436,725	94.4	3.5	0.4	0.2	<.1	1.6	5	1	11	5	9.2	11.9	1.3	9.0	74.5	74.8	70.5	68.3	71.3	54.4	69.7
District 10	439,254	81.2	16.5	1.0	0.2	<.1	1.1	3	6	6	9	9.2	10.3	6.2	6.4	74.2	75.7	67.9	74.0	77.2	46.5	70.3
District 11	413,414	37.8	60.1	0.9	0.2	<.1	1.0	11	11	1	10	8.7	4.5	21.4	5.5	70.5	78.3	66.5	70.2	76.7	37.0	67.3

Table C. — Voter Participation: November 3, 1992, General Election

County	Estimated Voting Age Population (VAP) 1992	Voter registration (REG)					Voter turnout												
							Highest office			Maximum vote						Percent drop-off, by office[1]			
		Total	% contribution to state REG	% of 1992 VAP	Rank by % of 1992 VAP	Actual	Total	Office	% of 1992 VAP	Total	% contribution to state turnout	% of REG	Rank by % of REG	% of 1992 VAP	Rank by % 1992 VAP	President	Senator	Governor	Representative
Appling	11,286	9,193	0.3	81.5	22	-	6,027	P	53.4	6,027	0.3	65.6	125	53.4	27	0.0	13.9	-	8.9
Atkinson	4,379	3,862	0.1	88.2	11	-	2,185	P	49.9	2,185	<.1	56.6	156	49.9	57	0.0	23.8	-	25.2
Bacon	6,810	5,033	0.2	73.9	46	-	3,335	P	49.0	3,335	0.1	66.3	119	49.0	63	0.0	18.9	-	10.7
Baker	2,537	2,409	<.1	95.0	4	-	1,468	P	57.9	1,468	<.1	60.9	145	57.9	9	0.0	16.3	-	18.6
Baldwin	30,854	15,534	0.5	50.3	156	-	11,788	P	38.2	11,788	0.5	75.9	25	38.2	155	0.0	12.5	-	19.9
Banks	7,954	5,019	0.2	63.1	106	-	3,712	S	46.7	3,712	0.2	74.0	41	46.7	89	1.1	0.0	-	0.5
Barrow	23,124	13,497	0.4	58.4	127	-	10,007	S	43.3	10,007	0.4	74.1	39	43.3	117	0.2	0.0	-	2.8
Bartow	43,757	22,923	0.7	52.4	154	-	16,990	P	38.8	16,990	0.7	74.1	40	38.8	153	0.0	10.6	-	15.4
Ben Hill	11,436	7,573	0.2	66.2	93	-	4,464	P	39.0	4,464	0.2	58.9	152	39.0	149	0.0	3.0	-	8.2
Berrien	10,259	6,958	0.2	67.8	81	-	4,755	S	46.3	4,755	0.2	68.3	102	46.3	93	4.5	0.0	-	1.0
Bibb	108,903	72,042	2.3	66.2	95	-	54,049	P	49.6	54,049	2.3	75.0	32	49.6	59	0.0	0.7	-	1.7
Bleckley	7,487	5,743	0.2	76.7	39	-	3,956	P	52.8	3,956	0.2	68.9	94	52.8	30	0.0	14.2	-	15.6
Brantley	8,264	6,593	0.2	79.8	27	-	4,274	P	51.7	4,274	0.2	64.8	130	51.7	36	0.0	16.6	-	12.0
Brooks	10,773	6,232	0.2	57.8	132	-	4,315	P	40.1	4,315	0.2	69.2	87	40.1	142	0.0	14.7	-	22.1
Bryan	11,835	8,644	0.3	73.0	50	-	5,928	P	50.1	5,928	0.3	68.6	97	50.1	51	0.0	11.2	-	4.8
Bulloch	32,457	18,691	0.6	57.6	135	-	12,715	C	39.2	12,715	0.5	68.0	104	39.2	148	0.3	1.4	-	0.0
Burke	14,116	10,259	0.3	72.7	52	-	6,859	P	48.6	6,859	0.3	66.9	113	48.6	71	0.0	13.9	-	10.9
Butts	11,607	7,024	0.2	60.5	122	-	4,851	P	41.8	4,851	0.2	69.1	89	41.8	131	0.0	0.8	-	1.2
Calhoun	3,475	2,935	<.1	84.5	16	-	2,085	S	60.0	2,085	<.1	71.0	70	60.0	5	3.2	0.0	-	0.5
Camden	25,619	10,906	0.3	42.6	157	-	7,572	P	29.6	7,572	0.3	69.4	85	29.6	157	0.0	18.8	-	6.7
Candler	5,697	4,137	0.1	72.6	53	-	2,755	P	48.4	2,755	0.1	66.6	116	48.4	74	0.0	14.8	-	4.4
Carroll	54,780	29,871	0.9	54.5	149	-	22,586	P	41.2	22,586	1.0	75.6	26	41.2	133	0.0	0.3	-	2.0
Catoosa	32,375	19,607	0.6	60.6	121	-	14,731	P	45.5	14,731	0.6	75.1	30	45.5	98	0.0	0.9	-	0.3
Charlton	6,034	4,373	0.1	72.5	54	-	2,892	P	47.9	2,892	0.1	66.1	120	47.9	81	0.0	32.5	-	19.4
Chatham	160,088	97,549	3.1	60.9	115	-	72,069	P	45.0	72,069	3.1	73.9	43	45.0	102	0.0	6.6	-	8.1
Chattahoochee	10,910	2,002	<.1	18.4	159	-	1,198	P	11.0	1,198	<.1	59.8	148	11.0	159	0.0	19.4	-	21.1
Chattooga	16,536	10,060	0.3	60.8	120	-	6,434	S	38.9	6,434	0.3	64.0	134	38.9	152	0.5	0.0	-	0.8
Cherokee	73,183	42,301	1.3	57.8	134	-	29,214	P	39.9	29,214	1.3	69.1	90	39.9	144	0.0	1.7	-	7.4
Clarke	68,520	39,609	1.2	57.8	133	-	28,998	P	42.3	28,998	1.2	73.2	50	42.3	128	0.0	4.8	-	10.9
Clay	2,347	1,826	<.1	77.8	34	-	1,197	P	51.0	1,197	<.1	65.6	126	51.0	42	0.0	8.7	-	7.7
Clayton	136,924	75,280	2.4	55.0	148	-	57,989	P	42.4	57,989	2.5	77.0	20	42.4	126	0.0	0.6	-	6.3
Clinch	4,278	3,801	0.1	88.8	8	-	1,837	P	42.9	1,837	<.1	48.3	158	42.9	119	0.0	24.7	-	26.2
Cobb	369,739	250,422	7.9	67.7	85	-	197,129	P	53.3	197,129	8.5	78.7	12	53.3	29	0.0	0.9	-	1.7
Coffee	21,187	13,277	0.4	62.7	107	-	8,339	P	39.4	8,339	0.4	62.8	138	39.4	146	0.0	16.7	-	18.4
Colquitt	26,397	14,556	0.5	55.1	147	-	10,276	P	38.9	10,276	0.4	70.6	74	38.9	151	0.0	7.2	-	12.1
Columbia	52,827	35,488	1.1	67.2	88	-	28,200	P	53.4	28,200	1.2	79.5	10	53.4	28	0.0	0.1	-	3.5
Cook	9,594	6,000	0.2	62.5	108	-	3,788	S	39.5	3,788	0.2	63.1	137	39.5	145	4.8	0.0	-	0.9
Coweta	41,757	25,844	0.8	61.9	110	-	20,552	P	49.2	20,552	0.9	79.5	8	49.2	62	0.0	0.1	-	2.4
Crawford	6,690	4,263	0.1	63.7	105	-	3,183	P	47.6	3,183	0.1	74.7	36	47.6	84	0.0	12.7	-	20.1
Crisp	14,161	8,530	0.3	60.2	123	-	5,709	P	40.3	5,709	0.2	66.9	112	40.3	139	0.0	10.3	-	17.8
Dade	9,748	6,695	0.2	68.7	72	-	4,804	P	49.3	4,804	0.2	71.8	63	49.3	61	0.0	21.0	-	21.9
Dawson	8,093	4,851	0.2	59.9	124	-	3,892	P	48.1	3,892	0.2	80.2	4	48.1	78	0.0	2.4	-	4.7
Decatur	18,043	10,981	0.3	60.9	117	-	7,419	P	41.1	7,419	0.3	67.6	107	41.1	135	0.0	13.2	-	16.8
DeKalb	423,900	289,933	9.1	68.4	76	-	215,433	P	50.8	215,433	9.3	74.3	38	50.8	44	0.0	0.4	-	2.4
Dodge	13,049	10,251	0.3	78.6	31	-	6,278	P	48.1	6,278	0.3	61.2	143	48.1	77	0.0	17.1	-	15.1
Dooly	6,783	4,838	0.2	71.3	55	-	3,387	P	49.9	3,387	0.1	70.0	82	49.9	54	0.0	17.4	-	29.0
Dougherty	65,793	42,569	1.3	64.7	100	-	31,215	S	47.4	31,215	1.3	73.3	47	47.4	86	0.9	0.0	-	1.9
Douglas	54,508	33,275	1.0	61.0	114	-	26,657	P	48.9	26,657	1.1	80.1	5	48.9	64	0.0	0.4	-	2.4
Early	8,113	5,519	0.2	68.0	79	-	4,143	P	51.1	4,143	0.2	75.1	31	51.1	41	0.0	5.3	-	6.1
Echols	1,658	1,439	<.1	86.8	13	-	911	P	54.9	911	<.1	63.3	136	54.9	22	0.0	24.3	-	33.0
Effingham	19,592	11,193	0.4	57.1	138	-	7,963	P	40.6	7,963	0.3	71.1	68	40.6	138	0.0	6.2	-	5.6
Elbert	13,762	8,895	0.3	64.6	101	-	6,167	P	44.8	6,167	0.3	69.3	86	44.8	104	0.0	5.1	-	3.7
Emanuel	14,348	9,962	0.3	69.4	66	-	6,425	P	44.8	6,425	0.3	64.5	132	44.8	105	0.0	17.9	-	15.9
Evans	6,197	4,564	0.1	73.6	48	-	2,960	P	47.8	2,960	0.1	64.9	129	47.8	83	0.0	10.3	-	4.2
Fannin	12,456	9,961	0.3	80.0	25	-	7,200	S	57.8	7,200	0.3	72.3	58	57.8	11	0.0	0.0	-	1.9
Fayette	54,065	38,466	1.2	71.1	56	-	31,687	P	58.6	31,687	1.4	82.4	1	58.6	7	0.0	0.4	-	3.3
Floyd	60,912	35,475	1.1	58.2	131	-	27,860	P	45.7	27,860	1.2	78.5	13	45.7	97	0.0	0.1	-	0.4
Forsyth	36,881	21,517	0.7	58.3	128	-	17,099	S	46.4	17,099	0.7	79.5	9	46.4	92	0.1	0.1	-	2.2
Franklin	12,769	8,837	0.3	69.2	70	-	6,075	C	47.6	6,075	0.3	68.7	95	47.6	85	2.5	1.3	-	0.0
Fulton	495,770	367,710	11.6	74.2	45	-	257,825	S	52.0	257,825	11.1	70.1	80	52.0	34	0.2	0.0	-	2.0
Gilmer	10,460	8,043	0.3	76.9	37	-	5,888	P	56.3	5,888	0.3	73.2	51	56.3	15	0.0	12.9	-	23.9
Glascock	1,784	1,517	<.1	85.0	15	-	1,013	P	56.8	1,013	<.1	66.8	114	56.8	12	0.0	19.1	-	36.6
Glynn	47,043	33,156	1.0	70.5	61	-	22,932	P	48.7	22,932	1.0	69.2	88	48.7	67	0.0	0.1	-	0.3
Gordon	26,620	18,688	0.6	70.2	62	-	11,213	P	42.1	11,213	0.5	60.0	147	42.1	129	0.0	11.5	-	21.8
Grady	14,648	8,598	0.3	58.7	125	-	6,033	P	41.2	6,033	0.3	70.2	78	41.2	134	0.0	15.9	-	19.7
Greene	8,334	5,718	0.2	68.6	74	-	4,066	C	48.8	4,066	0.2	71.1	69	48.8	66	0.2	0.4	-	0.0
Gwinnett	309,883	188,754	5.9	60.9	116	-	150,576	P	48.6	150,576	6.5	79.8	6	48.6	70	0.0	0.8	-	0.7
Habersham	20,997	11,811	0.4	56.3	144	-	9,134	P	43.5	9,134	0.4	77.3	19	43.5	115	0.0	4.3	-	8.2
Hall	74,322	41,087	1.3	55.3	146	-	32,746	S	44.1	32,746	1.4	79.7	7	44.1	108	1.0	0.0	-	0.3
Hancock	6,067	5,329	0.2	87.8	12	-	3,157	P	52.0	3,157	0.1	59.2	150	52.0	33	0.0	24.1	-	20.2

[1]Percent drop-off is zero for any office used as highest office turnout.

Table C. — **Voter Participation: November 3, 1992, General Election (cont)**

County	Estimated Voting Age Population (VAP) 1992	Voter registration (REG)					Voter turnout										Percent drop-off, by office[1]			
							Highest office				Maximum vote										
		Total	% contribution to state REG	% of 1992 VAP	Rank by % of 1992 VAP	Actual	Total	Office	% of 1992 VAP	Total	% contribution to state turnout	% of REG	Rank by % of REG	% of 1992 VAP	Rank by % 1992 VAP	President	Senator	Governor	Representative
Haralson	16,704	11,350	0.4	67.9	80	-	7,675	S	45.9	7,675	0.3	67.6	106	45.9	95	0.7	0.0	-	1.3
Harris	13,723	9,702	0.3	70.7	60	-	6,960	P	50.7	6,960	0.3	71.7	64	50.7	45	0.0	9.8	-	12.8
Hart	14,889	10,442	0.3	70.1	63	-	7,609	P	51.1	7,609	0.3	72.9	53	51.1	40	0.0	18.6	-	11.1
Heard	6,704	4,749	0.1	70.8	57	-	3,273	P	48.8	3,273	0.1	68.9	92	48.8	65	0.0	0.9	-	4.0
Henry	47,346	30,658	1.0	64.8	99	-	24,610	S	52.0	24,610	1.1	80.3	3	52.0	35	1.3	0.0	-	1.3
Houston	66,011	42,601	1.3	64.5	102	-	32,748	P	49.6	32,748	1.4	76.9	21	49.6	60	0.0	0.7	-	2.1
Irwin	6,045	4,044	0.1	66.9	90	-	2,820	P	46.7	2,820	0.1	69.7	84	46.7	90	0.0	7.6	-	12.4
Jackson	22,892	13,340	0.4	58.3	130	-	9,165	P	40.0	9,165	0.4	68.7	96	40.0	143	0.0	0.5	-	1.1
Jasper	6,227	4,318	0.1	69.3	68	-	3,023	P	48.5	3,023	0.1	70.0	81	48.5	72	0.0	7.5	-	16.6
Jeff Davis	8,745	6,760	0.2	77.3	36	-	4,952	P	56.6	4,952	0.2	73.3	48	56.6	13	0.0	18.0	-	17.6
Jefferson	11,993	8,754	0.3	73.0	51	-	5,989	P	49.9	5,989	0.3	68.4	101	49.9	53	0.0	16.3	-	18.6
Jenkins	5,690	4,436	0.1	78.0	33	-	2,728	P	47.9	2,728	0.1	61.5	142	47.9	80	0.0	11.3	-	17.9
Johnson	5,888	4,907	0.2	83.3	18	-	3,295	P	56.0	3,295	0.1	67.1	110	56.0	18	0.0	15.6	-	7.7
Jones	15,792	10,862	0.3	68.8	71	-	7,279	P	46.1	7,279	0.3	67.0	111	46.1	94	0.0	7.0	-	13.4
Lamar	9,635	6,434	0.2	66.8	91	-	4,410	P	45.8	4,410	0.2	68.5	98	45.8	96	0.0	5.7	-	9.8
Lanier	3,895	2,875	<.1	73.8	47	-	1,713	P	44.0	1,713	<.1	59.6	149	44.0	109	0.0	20.9	-	29.5
Laurens	29,291	18,796	0.6	64.2	103	-	14,059	P	48.0	14,059	0.6	74.8	35	48.0	79	0.0	17.3	-	14.5
Lee	12,209	8,080	0.3	66.2	94	-	5,908	P	48.4	5,908	0.3	73.1	52	48.4	73	0.0	1.8	-	0.1
Liberty	38,909	11,041	0.3	28.4	158	-	7,895	P	20.3	7,895	0.3	71.5	66	20.3	158	0.0	14.1	-	8.6
Lincoln	5,573	4,555	0.1	81.7	21	-	3,019	S	54.2	3,019	0.1	66.3	118	54.2	24	2.0	0.0	-	3.5
Long	4,619	2,875	<.1	62.2	109	-	1,957	P	42.4	1,957	<.1	68.1	103	42.4	125	0.0	15.2	-	7.1
Lowndes	55,240	30,564	1.0	55.3	145	-	22,192	P	40.2	22,192	1.0	72.6	57	40.2	140	0.0	0.7	-	2.0
Lumpkin	11,483	6,988	0.2	60.9	118	-	5,044	S	43.9	5,044	0.2	72.2	61	43.9	110	0.2	0.0	-	1.2
McDuffie	14,522	9,848	0.3	67.8	82	-	6,468	P	44.5	6,468	0.3	65.7	123	44.5	107	0.0	8.4	-	17.5
McIntosh	6,324	5,103	0.2	80.7	24	-	3,517	P	55.6	3,517	0.2	68.9	93	55.6	19	0.0	13.0	-	7.8
Macon	8,899	6,692	0.2	75.2	43	-	3,806	P	42.8	3,806	0.2	56.9	155	42.8	122	0.0	10.2	-	8.0
Madison	16,046	9,056	0.3	56.4	143	-	6,893	P	43.0	6,893	0.3	76.1	23	43.0	118	0.0	9.2	-	10.2
Marion	4,037	3,051	<.1	75.6	42	-	2,056	P	50.9	2,056	<.1	67.4	108	50.9	43	0.0	6.2	-	6.4
Meriwether	16,097	10,910	0.3	67.8	83	-	7,476	S	46.4	7,476	0.3	68.5	99	46.4	91	2.1	0.0	-	3.8
Miller	4,421	3,296	0.1	74.6	44	-	2,217	P	50.1	2,217	<.1	67.3	109	50.1	49	0.0	16.6	-	18.1
Mitchell	13,839	8,873	0.3	64.1	104	-	6,033	C	43.6	6,033	0.3	68.0	105	43.6	113	3.9	0.3	-	0.0
Monroe	12,908	8,476	0.3	65.7	96	-	6,236	S	48.3	6,236	0.3	73.6	44	48.3	75	1.1	0.0	-	2.5
Montgomery	5,230	4,176	0.1	79.8	26	-	2,617	P	50.0	2,617	0.1	62.7	139	50.0	52	0.0	11.0	-	4.4
Morgan	9,538	7,228	0.2	75.8	41	-	4,495	S	47.1	4,495	0.2	62.2	141	47.1	88	0.9	0.0	-	3.2
Murray	20,138	10,977	0.3	54.5	150	-	7,214	P	35.8	7,214	0.3	65.7	122	35.8	156	0.0	1.3	-	1.5
Muscogee	130,684	71,038	2.2	54.4	151	-	51,280	P	39.2	51,280	2.2	72.2	60	39.2	147	0.0	0.5	-	1.3
Newton	31,236	17,635	0.6	56.5	142	-	13,659	P	43.7	13,659	0.6	77.5	16	43.7	112	0.0	1.3	-	3.5
Oconee	13,714	10,020	0.3	73.1	49	-	8,076	P	58.9	8,076	0.3	80.6	2	58.9	6	0.0	1.2	-	4.9
Oglethorpe	7,318	4,921	0.2	67.2	87	-	3,703	P	50.6	3,703	0.2	75.2	29	50.6	46	0.0	2.1	-	2.1
Paulding	33,371	19,160	0.6	57.4	137	-	15,088	P	45.2	15,088	0.6	78.7	11	45.2	99	0.0	0.6	-	2.1
Peach	15,452	9,508	0.3	61.5	111	-	6,973	P	45.1	6,973	0.3	73.3	46	45.1	100	0.0	7.1	-	10.2
Pickens	11,365	7,428	0.2	65.4	97	-	5,748	P	50.6	5,748	0.2	77.4	17	50.6	47	0.0	9.6	-	19.5
Pierce	9,930	6,726	0.2	67.7	84	-	4,472	P	45.0	4,472	0.2	66.5	117	45.0	101	0.0	10.5	-	6.4
Pike	7,647	5,304	0.2	69.4	67	-	4,104	P	53.7	4,104	0.2	77.4	18	53.7	25	0.0	1.7	-	3.2
Polk	25,059	14,221	0.4	56.8	141	-	10,668	P	42.6	10,668	0.5	75.0	33	42.6	123	0.0	8.5	-	16.1
Pulaski	5,749	4,920	0.2	85.6	14	-	3,451	P	60.0	3,451	0.1	70.1	79	60.0	4	0.0	13.3	-	15.4
Putnam	11,349	6,657	0.2	58.7	126	-	4,694	P	41.4	4,694	0.2	70.5	75	41.4	132	0.0	7.4	-	14.1
Quitman	1,590	1,406	<.1	88.4	9	-	922	P	58.0	922	<.1	65.6	124	58.0	8	0.0	29.2	-	28.4
Rabun	9,219	6,401	0.2	69.4	65	-	4,622	P	50.1	4,622	0.2	72.2	59	50.1	50	0.0	7.5	-	9.7
Randolph	5,364	4,492	0.1	83.7	17	-	2,959	P	55.2	2,959	0.1	65.9	121	55.2	21	0.0	6.5	-	5.5
Richmond	137,030	84,215	2.7	61.5	112	-	59,718	S	43.6	59,718	2.6	70.9	71	43.6	114	0.3	0.0	-	0.9
Rockdale	43,038	28,980	0.9	67.3	86	-	22,690	P	52.7	22,690	1.0	78.3	14	52.7	31	0.0	0.0	-	0.4
Schley	2,599	1,839	<.1	70.8	59	-	1,296	P	49.9	1,296	<.1	70.5	77	49.9	58	0.0	11.0	-	9.6
Screven	9,750	7,633	0.2	78.3	32	-	4,366	P	44.8	4,366	0.2	57.2	154	44.8	106	0.0	20.9	-	24.2
Seminole	6,587	5,121	0.2	77.7	35	-	2,791	S	42.4	2,791	0.1	54.5	157	42.4	124	9.7	0.0	-	2.1
Spalding	40,369	22,989	0.7	56.9	140	-	15,734	P	39.0	15,734	0.7	68.4	100	39.0	150	0.0	6.1	-	16.1
Stephens	17,646	11,846	0.4	67.1	89	-	8,493	P	48.1	8,493	0.4	71.7	65	48.1	76	0.0	11.0	-	13.0
Stewart	4,066	3,727	0.1	91.7	6	-	2,909	P	71.5	2,909	0.1	78.1	15	71.5	2	0.0	37.8	-	34.6
Sumter	21,410	14,655	0.5	68.4	75	-	9,168	P	42.8	9,168	0.4	62.6	140	42.8	120	0.0	11.3	-	6.0
Talbot	4,779	4,677	0.1	97.9	3	-	2,682	P	56.1	2,682	0.1	57.3	153	56.1	17	0.0	27.7	-	26.1
Taliaferro	1,388	1,553	<.1	111.9	1	-	1,106	P	79.7	1,106	<.1	71.2	67	79.7	1	0.0	3.8	-	11.3
Tattnall	13,228	9,156	0.3	69.2	69	-	5,942	P	44.9	5,942	0.3	64.9	128	44.9	103	0.0	13.5	-	3.4
Taylor	5,478	4,501	0.1	82.2	20	-	2,872	P	52.4	2,872	0.1	63.8	135	52.4	32	0.0	0.4	-	2.9
Telfair	7,847	6,493	0.2	82.7	19	-	4,192	P	53.4	4,192	0.2	64.6	131	53.4	26	0.0	20.9	-	22.4
Terrell	7,251	5,866	0.2	80.9	23	-	3,474	P	47.9	3,474	0.1	59.2	151	47.9	82	0.0	13.3	-	10.2
Thomas	27,984	17,122	0.5	61.2	113	-	11,980	S	42.8	11,980	0.5	70.0	83	42.8	121	0.3	0.0	-	1.3
Tift	25,015	12,683	0.4	50.7	155	-	9,569	P	38.3	9,569	0.4	75.4	28	38.3	154	0.0	4.1	-	9.5
Toombs	17,229	11,239	0.4	65.2	98	-	7,490	P	43.5	7,490	0.3	66.6	115	43.5	116	0.0	13.5	-	6.3
Towns	5,529	4,878	0.2	88.2	10	-	3,704	P	67.0	3,704	0.2	75.9	24	67.0	3	0.0	6.6	-	9.2
Treutlen	4,307	3,837	0.1	89.1	7	-	2,344	P	54.4	2,344	0.1	61.1	144	54.4	23	0.0	20.3	-	49.9

[1]Percent drop-off is zero for any office used as highest office turnout.

Table C. – **Voter Participation: November 3, 1992, General Election (cont)**

County	Estimated Voting Age Population (VAP) 1992	Voter registration (REG)				Voter turnout											Percent drop-off, by office[1]			
							Highest office			Maximum vote										
		Total	% contribution to state REG	% of 1992 VAP	Rank by % of 1992 VAP	Actual	Total	Office	% of 1992 VAP	Total	% contribution to state turnout	% of REG	Rank by % of REG	% of 1992 VAP	Rank by % 1992 VAP	President	Senator	Governor	Representative
Troup	40,920	23,372	0.7	57.1	139	-	17,171	S	42.0	17,171	0.7	73.5	45	42.0	130	0.8	0.0	-	2.0
Turner	5,868	4,000	0.1	68.2	78	-	3,024	P	51.5	3,024	0.1	75.6	27	51.5	37	0.0	5.0	-	6.0
Twiggs	6,882	5,290	0.2	76.9	38	-	3,452	S	50.2	3,452	0.1	65.3	127	50.2	48	1.7	0.0	-	3.4
Union	9,779	7,769	0.2	79.4	28	-	5,656	P	57.8	5,656	0.2	72.8	54	57.8	10	0.0	3.3	-	4.4
Upson	19,557	13,372	0.4	68.4	77	-	9,234	S	47.2	9,234	0.4	69.1	91	47.2	87	2.5	0.0	-	1.0
Walker	43,572	23,368	0.7	53.6	152	-	17,488	P	40.1	17,488	0.8	74.8	34	40.1	141	0.0	3.4	-	1.8
Walton	29,263	17,053	0.5	58.3	129	-	12,391	P	42.3	12,391	0.5	72.7	56	42.3	127	0.0	5.4	-	11.3
Ware	25,620	14,733	0.5	57.5	136	-	10,424	P	40.7	10,424	0.4	70.8	73	40.7	137	0.0	11.8	-	9.1
Warren	4,253	3,375	0.1	79.4	30	-	2,175	P	51.1	2,175	<.1	64.4	133	51.1	39	0.0	19.3	-	29.1
Washington	13,477	9,538	0.3	70.8	58	-	6,725	P	49.9	6,725	0.3	70.5	76	49.9	56	0.0	13.3	-	22.4
Wayne	16,146	10,736	0.3	66.5	92	-	7,860	C	48.7	7,860	0.3	73.2	49	48.7	69	3.9	2.5	-	0.0
Webster	1,620	1,287	<.1	79.4	29	-	911	P	56.2	911	<.1	70.8	72	56.2	16	0.0	23.5	-	15.0
Wheeler	3,488	3,701	0.1	106.1	2	-	1,699	P	48.7	1,699	<.1	45.9	159	48.7	68	0.0	15.1	-	5.9
White	10,476	7,193	0.2	68.7	73	-	5,229	P	49.9	5,229	0.2	72.7	55	49.9	55	0.0	0.8	-	2.1
Whitfield	54,534	29,186	0.9	53.5	153	-	22,239	P	40.8	22,239	1.0	76.2	22	40.8	136	0.0	0.5	-	1.5
Wilcox	4,910	4,519	0.1	92.0	5	-	2,723	P	55.5	2,723	0.1	60.3	146	55.5	20	0.0	11.4	-	11.5
Wilkes	7,696	5,359	0.2	69.6	64	-	3,962	P	51.5	3,962	0.2	73.9	42	51.5	38	0.0	14.6	-	20.1
Wilkinson	7,206	5,468	0.2	75.9	40	-	4,072	P	56.5	4,072	0.2	74.5	37	56.5	14	0.0	17.8	-	32.3
Worth	14,100	8,580	0.3	60.9	119	-	6,176	S	43.8	6,176	0.3	72.0	62	43.8	111	5.5	0.0	-	1.7
GEORGIA[2]	4,950,000	3,177,061	100.0	64.2		-	2,325,470		47.0	2,325,470	100.0	73.2		47.0		0.2	3.2	-	4.8

[1]Percent drop-off is zero for any office used as highest office turnout. [2]Georgia does not report voter registration by political party, but does report registration by race. State voter registration by race is 2,451,242 (77.2%) for white, 698,305 (22.0%) for black, 22,449 (0.7%) for other, and 5,065 (0.2%) for unknown.

County	Total	Clinton (DEM)	Bush (REP)	Perot (IND)	Other	Plurality Total	Plurality Party	Pct DEM	Pct REP	Pct IND	Pct Other	Rank DEM	Rank REP	Rank IND	Contrib Total	Contrib DEM	Contrib REP	Contrib IND	Major DEM	Major REP
Appling	6,027	2,455	2,514	1,047	11	59	R	40.7	41.7	17.4	0.2	104	68	28	0.3	0.2	0.3	0.3	49.4	50.6
Atkinson	2,185	1,056	779	342	8	277	D	48.3	35.7	15.7	0.4	51	119	61	<.1	0.1	<.1	0.1	57.5	42.5
Bacon	3,335	1,423	1,301	604	7	122	D	42.7	39.0	18.1	0.2	87	93	17	0.1	0.1	0.1	0.2	52.2	47.8
Baker	1,468	864	391	210	3	473	D	58.9	26.6	14.3	0.2	10	151	97	<.1	<.1	<.1	<.1	68.8	31.2
Baldwin	11,788	5,813	4,262	1,679	34	1,551	D	49.3	36.2	14.2	0.3	43	114	99	0.5	0.6	0.4	0.5	57.7	42.3
Banks	3,671	1,530	1,551	583	7	21	R	41.7	42.3	15.9	0.2	93	66	56	0.2	0.2	0.2	0.2	49.7	50.3
Barrow	9,982	3,991	4,328	1,633	30	337	R	40.0	43.4	16.4	0.3	114	58	44	0.4	0.4	0.4	0.5	48.0	52.0
Bartow	16,990	6,675	7,742	2,500	73	1,067	R	39.3	45.6	14.7	0.4	117	39	85	0.7	0.7	0.8	0.8	46.3	53.7
Ben Hill	4,464	2,348	1,476	619	21	872	D	52.6	33.1	13.9	0.5	30	137	104	0.2	0.2	0.1	0.2	61.4	38.6
Berrien	4,543	2,103	1,637	796	7	466	D	46.3	36.0	17.5	0.2	62	117	25	0.2	0.2	0.2	0.3	56.2	43.8
Bibb	54,049	28,070	19,847	6,021	111	8,223	D	51.9	36.7	11.1	0.2	33	109	142	2.3	2.8	2.0	1.9	58.6	41.4
Bleckley	3,956	1,710	1,570	662	14	140	D	43.2	39.7	16.7	0.4	84	83	37	0.2	0.2	0.2	0.2	52.1	47.9
Brantley	4,274	1,883	1,541	840	10	342	D	44.1	36.1	19.7	0.2	78	116	6	0.2	0.2	0.2	0.3	55.0	45.0
Brooks	4,315	1,895	1,779	630	11	116	D	43.9	41.2	14.6	0.3	80	72	91	0.2	0.2	0.2	0.2	51.6	48.4
Bryan	5,928	2,031	2,789	1,095	13	758	R	34.3	47.0	18.5	0.2	141	29	14	0.3	0.2	0.3	0.4	42.1	57.9
Bulloch	12,644	4,903	5,690	2,020	31	787	R	38.8	45.0	16.0	0.2	123	48	51	0.5	0.5	0.6	0.7	46.3	53.7
Burke	6,859	3,647	2,390	807	15	1,257	D	53.2	34.8	11.8	0.2	25	124	134	0.3	0.4	0.2	0.3	60.4	39.6
Butts	4,851	2,448	1,768	619	16	680	D	50.5	36.4	12.8	0.3	38	111	122	0.2	0.2	0.2	0.2	58.1	41.9
Calhoun	2,018	1,301	464	248	5	837	D	64.5	23.0	12.3	0.2	7	156	126	<.1	0.1	<.1	<.1	73.7	26.3
Camden	7,572	2,952	3,517	1,077	26	565	R	39.0	46.4	14.2	0.3	120	32	100	0.3	0.3	0.4	0.3	45.6	54.4
Candler	2,755	1,192	1,014	541	8	178	D	43.3	36.8	19.6	0.3	83	107	7	0.1	0.1	0.1	0.2	54.0	46.0
Carroll	22,586	8,404	10,750	3,358	74	2,346	R	37.2	47.6	14.9	0.3	130	26	42	1.0	0.8	1.1	1.1	43.9	56.1
Catoosa	14,731	4,817	7,599	2,290	25	2,782	R	32.7	51.6	15.5	0.2	149	10	66	0.6	0.5	0.8	0.7	38.8	61.2
Charlton	2,892	1,127	1,333	427	5	206	R	39.0	46.1	14.8	0.2	121	35	84	0.1	0.1	0.1	0.1	45.8	54.2
Chatham	72,069	31,533	31,925	8,269	342	392	R	43.8	44.3	11.5	0.5	82	53	137	3.1	3.1	3.2	2.7	49.7	50.3
Chattahoochee	1,198	604	413	177	4	191	D	50.4	34.5	14.8	0.3	39	129	83	<.1	<.1	<.1	<.1	59.4	40.6
Chattooga	6,404	2,976	2,439	965	24	537	D	46.5	38.1	15.1	0.4	60	102	75	0.3	0.3	0.2	0.3	55.0	45.0
Cherokee	29,214	8,113	16,054	4,950	97	7,941	R	27.8	55.0	16.9	0.3	157	3	34	1.3	0.8	1.6	1.6	33.6	66.4
Clarke	28,998	15,403	10,459	2,987	149	4,944	D	53.1	36.1	10.3	0.5	26	115	147	1.2	1.5	1.1	1.0	59.6	40.4
Clay	1,197	778	264	155	0	514	D	65.0	22.1	12.9	0.0	6	158	117	<.1	<.1	<.1	<.1	74.7	25.3
Clayton	57,989	25,890	23,965	7,942	192	1,925	D	44.6	41.3	13.7	0.3	74	71	106	2.5	2.6	2.4	2.6	51.9	48.1
Clinch	1,837	759	790	286	2	31	R	41.3	43.0	15.6	0.1	98	61	64	<.1	<.1	<.1	<.1	49.0	51.0
Cobb	197,129	63,960	103,734	28,747	688	39,774	R	32.4	52.6	14.6	0.3	150	7	92	8.5	6.3	10.4	9.3	38.1	61.9
Coffee	8,339	3,275	3,778	1,256	30	503	R	39.3	45.3	15.1	0.4	118	42	77	0.4	0.3	0.4	0.4	46.4	53.6
Colquitt	10,276	3,891	4,680	1,682	23	789	R	37.9	45.5	16.4	0.2	126	40	42	0.4	0.4	0.5	0.5	45.4	54.6
Columbia	28,200	7,115	16,657	4,379	49	9,542	R	25.2	59.1	15.5	0.2	159	1	67	1.2	0.7	1.7	1.4	29.9	70.1
Cook	3,605	1,731	1,318	537	19	413	D	48.0	36.6	14.9	0.5	52	110	80	0.2	0.2	0.1	0.2	56.8	43.2
Coweta	20,552	7,093	9,814	3,587	58	2,721	R	34.5	47.8	17.5	0.3	140	22	26	0.9	0.7	1.0	1.2	42.0	58.0
Crawford	3,183	1,648	974	549	12	674	D	51.8	30.6	17.2	0.4	35	146	30	0.1	0.2	<.1	0.2	62.9	37.1
Crisp	5,709	2,610	2,253	823	23	357	D	45.7	39.5	14.4	0.4	67	85	95	0.2	0.3	0.2	0.3	53.7	46.3
Dade	4,804	1,782	2,191	823	8	409	R	37.1	45.6	17.1	0.2	131	38	31	0.2	0.2	0.2	0.3	44.9	55.1
Dawson	3,892	1,399	1,696	790	7	297	R	35.9	43.6	20.3	0.2	133	56	4	0.2	0.1	0.2	0.3	45.2	54.8
Decatur	7,419	3,198	3,142	1,068	11	56	D	43.1	42.4	14.4	0.1	85	65	96	0.3	0.3	0.3	0.3	50.4	49.6
DeKalb	215,433	124,559	70,282	19,741	851	54,277	D	57.8	32.6	9.2	0.4	12	139	152	9.3	12.3	7.1	6.4	63.9	36.1
Dodge	6,278	3,002	2,287	978	11	715	D	47.8	36.4	15.6	0.2	53	112	63	0.3	0.3	0.2	0.3	56.8	43.2
Dooly	3,387	1,993	1,034	350	10	959	D	58.8	30.5	10.3	0.3	11	147	146	0.1	0.2	0.1	0.1	65.8	34.2
Dougherty	30,931	15,236	12,455	3,178	62	2,781	D	49.3	40.3	10.3	0.2	44	80	148	1.3	1.5	1.3	1.0	55.0	45.0
Douglas	26,657	8,869	13,349	4,362	77	4,480	R	33.3	50.1	16.4	0.3	147	14	43	1.1	0.9	1.3	1.4	39.9	60.1
Early	4,143	1,970	1,457	652	64	513	D	47.6	35.2	15.7	1.5	55	122	59	0.2	0.2	0.1	0.2	57.5	42.5
Echols	911	312	361	238	0	49	R	34.2	39.6	26.1	0.0	142	84	1	<.1	<.1	<.1	<.1	46.4	53.6
Effingham	7,963	2,690	3,814	1,443	16	1,124	R	33.8	47.9	18.1	0.2	145	21	16	0.3	0.3	0.4	0.5	41.4	58.6
Elbert	6,167	3,025	2,372	757	13	653	D	49.1	38.5	12.3	0.2	46	99	127	0.3	0.3	0.2	0.2	56.0	44.0
Emanuel	6,425	2,951	2,662	755	57	289	D	45.9	41.4	11.8	0.9	64	70	135	0.3	0.3	0.3	0.2	52.6	47.4
Evans	2,960	1,230	1,244	480	6	14	R	41.6	42.0	16.2	0.2	94	67	46	0.1	0.1	0.1	0.2	49.7	50.3
Fannin	7,195	2,902	3,255	1,028	10	353	R	40.3	45.2	14.3	0.1	110	43	98	0.3	0.3	0.3	0.3	47.1	52.9
Fayette	31,687	8,430	17,576	5,598	83	9,146	R	26.6	55.5	17.7	0.3	158	2	23	1.4	0.8	1.8	1.8	32.4	67.6
Floyd	27,860	11,614	12,378	3,779	89	764	R	41.7	44.4	13.6	0.3	92	51	110	1.2	1.2	1.2	1.2	48.4	51.6
Forsyth	17,086	4,936	8,652	3,453	45	3,716	R	28.9	50.6	20.2	0.3	156	13	5	0.7	0.5	0.9	1.1	36.3	63.7
Franklin	5,923	2,505	2,391	1,014	13	114	D	42.3	40.4	17.1	0.2	89	78	32	0.3	0.2	0.2	0.3	51.2	48.8
Fulton	257,406	147,459	85,451	23,578	918	62,008	D	57.3	33.2	9.2	0.4	13	135	153	11.1	14.6	8.6	7.6	63.3	36.7
Gilmer	5,888	2,311	2,661	879	37	350	R	39.2	45.2	14.9	0.6	119	44	79	0.3	0.2	0.3	0.3	46.5	53.5
Glascock	1,013	316	516	180	1	200	R	31.2	50.9	17.8	<.1	152	12	22	<.1	<.1	<.1	<.1	38.0	62.0
Glynn	22,932	8,581	11,242	3,053	56	2,661	R	37.4	49.0	13.3	0.2	129	17	113	1.0	0.9	1.1	1.0	43.3	56.7
Gordon	11,213	4,103	5,265	1,818	27	1,162	R	36.6	47.0	16.2	0.2	132	30	47	0.5	0.4	0.5	0.6	43.8	56.2
Grady	6,033	2,520	2,370	1,126	17	150	D	41.8	39.3	18.7	0.3	91	89	12	0.3	0.2	0.2	0.4	51.5	48.5
Greene	4,058	2,259	1,307	483	9	952	D	55.7	32.2	11.9	0.2	19	141	133	0.2	0.2	0.1	0.2	63.3	36.7
Gwinnett	150,576	44,253	81,822	23,926	575	37,569	R	29.4	54.3	15.9	0.4	155	4	55	6.5	4.4	8.2	7.7	35.1	64.9
Habersham	9,134	3,098	4,569	1,444	23	1,471	R	33.9	50.0	15.8	0.3	144	15	58	0.4	0.3	0.5	0.5	40.4	59.6
Hall	32,433	11,214	16,108	5,043	68	4,894	R	34.6	49.7	15.5	0.2	138	16	65	1.4	1.1	1.6	1.6	41.0	59.0
Hancock	3,157	2,461	506	189	1	1,955	D	78.0	16.0	6.0	<.1	1	159	159	0.1	0.2	<.1	<.1	82.9	17.1

Table E. – Vote for President: November 3, 1992, General Election (cont)

County	Total	Clinton (DEM)	Bush (REP)	Perot (IND)	Other	Plurality Total	Party	DEM	REP	IND	Other	Rank DEM	Rank REP	Rank IND	Total	DEM	REP	IND	DEM	REP
Haralson	7,621	3,281	3,142	1,167	31	139	D	43.1	41.2	15.3	0.4	86	73	72	0.3	0.3	0.3	0.4	51.1	48.9
Harris	6,960	2,679	3,316	954	11	637	R	38.5	47.6	13.7	0.2	124	24	105	0.3	0.3	0.3	0.3	44.7	55.3
Hart	7,609	3,614	2,607	1,376	12	1,007	D	47.5	34.3	18.1	0.2	56	130	18	0.3	0.4	0.3	0.4	58.1	41.9
Heard	3,273	1,456	1,190	617	10	266	D	44.5	36.4	18.9	0.3	75	113	10	0.1	0.1	0.1	0.2	55.0	45.0
Henry	24,284	7,817	12,634	3,769	64	4,817	R	32.2	52.0	15.5	0.3	151	8	68	1.0	0.8	1.3	1.2	38.2	61.8
Houston	32,748	12,270	14,119	6,263	96	1,849	R	37.5	43.1	19.1	0.3	128	60	9	1.4	1.2	1.4	2.0	46.5	53.5
Irwin	2,820	1,366	973	465	16	393	D	48.4	34.5	16.5	0.6	50	128	39	0.1	0.1	<.1	0.2	58.4	41.6
Jackson	9,165	3,792	3,976	1,381	16	184	R	41.4	43.4	15.1	0.2	97	57	76	0.4	0.4	0.4	0.4	48.8	51.2
Jasper	3,023	1,485	1,153	373	12	332	D	49.1	38.1	12.3	0.4	45	101	125	0.1	0.1	0.1	0.1	56.3	43.7
Jeff Davis	4,952	2,031	1,947	958	16	84	D	41.0	39.3	19.3	0.3	101	88	8	0.2	0.2	0.2	0.3	51.1	48.9
Jefferson	5,989	3,220	2,077	685	7	1,143	D	53.8	34.7	11.4	0.1	23	125	138	0.3	0.3	0.2	0.2	60.8	39.2
Jenkins	2,728	1,401	929	394	4	472	D	51.4	34.1	14.4	0.1	36	131	94	0.1	0.1	<.1	0.1	60.1	39.9
Johnson	3,295	1,473	1,314	502	6	159	D	44.7	39.9	15.2	0.2	72	82	73	0.1	0.1	0.1	0.1	52.9	47.1
Jones	7,279	3,338	2,770	1,159	12	568	D	45.9	38.1	15.9	0.2	65	103	52	0.3	0.3	0.3	0.4	54.6	45.4
Lamar	4,410	2,065	1,707	600	38	358	D	46.8	38.7	13.6	0.9	59	97	107	0.2	0.2	0.2	0.2	54.7	45.3
Lanier	1,713	811	600	298	4	211	D	47.3	35.0	17.4	0.2	58	123	27	<.1	<.1	<.1	<.1	57.5	42.5
Laurens	14,059	6,184	6,146	1,602	127	38	D	44.0	43.7	11.4	0.9	79	55	140	0.6	0.6	0.6	0.5	50.2	49.8
Lee	5,908	1,811	3,061	1,024	12	1,250	R	30.7	51.8	17.3	0.2	154	9	29	0.3	0.2	0.3	0.3	37.2	62.8
Liberty	7,895	3,853	2,832	1,176	34	1,021	D	48.8	35.9	14.9	0.4	48	118	81	0.3	0.4	0.3	0.4	57.6	42.4
Lincoln	2,958	1,327	1,149	479	3	178	D	44.9	38.8	16.2	0.1	71	95	48	0.1	0.1	0.1	0.2	53.6	46.4
Long	1,957	874	719	355	9	155	D	44.7	36.7	18.1	0.5	73	108	15	<.1	<.1	<.1	0.1	54.9	45.1
Lowndes	22,192	9,019	10,276	2,864	33	1,257	R	40.6	46.3	12.9	0.1	105	33	118	1.0	0.9	1.0	0.9	46.7	53.3
Lumpkin	5,036	2,010	1,972	1,035	19	38	D	39.9	39.2	20.6	0.4	115	91	2	0.2	0.2	0.2	0.3	50.5	49.5
McDuffie	6,468	2,640	2,955	860	13	315	R	40.8	45.7	13.3	0.2	102	37	114	0.3	0.3	0.3	0.3	47.2	52.8
McIntosh	3,517	1,925	1,027	550	15	898	D	54.7	29.2	15.6	0.4	21	150	62	0.2	0.2	0.1	0.2	65.2	34.8
Macon	3,806	2,491	944	363	8	1,547	D	65.4	24.8	9.5	0.2	5	154	151	0.2	0.2	<.1	0.1	72.5	27.5
Madison	6,893	2,393	3,351	1,129	20	958	R	34.7	48.6	16.4	0.3	137	18	41	0.3	0.2	0.3	0.4	41.7	58.3
Marion	2,056	1,145	711	198	2	434	D	55.7	34.6	9.6	<.1	18	126	150	<.1	0.1	<.1	<.1	61.7	38.3
Meriwether	7,320	4,002	2,364	942	12	1,638	D	54.7	32.3	12.9	0.2	22	140	120	0.3	0.4	0.2	0.2	62.9	37.1
Miller	2,217	934	826	455	2	108	D	42.1	37.3	20.5	<.1	90	106	3	<.1	<.1	<.1	0.1	53.1	46.9
Mitchell	5,795	3,052	1,917	818	8	1,135	D	52.7	33.1	14.1	0.1	29	136	102	0.2	0.3	0.2	0.3	61.4	38.6
Monroe	6,168	2,774	2,423	949	22	351	D	45.0	39.3	15.4	0.4	70	90	71	0.3	0.3	0.2	0.3	53.4	46.6
Montgomery	2,617	1,185	1,009	416	7	176	D	45.3	38.6	15.9	0.3	69	98	54	0.1	0.1	0.1	0.1	54.0	46.0
Morgan	4,455	2,057	1,797	596	5	260	D	46.2	40.3	13.4	0.1	63	79	111	0.2	0.2	0.2	0.2	53.4	46.6
Murray	7,214	2,764	3,256	1,186	8	492	R	38.3	45.1	16.4	0.1	125	46	40	0.3	0.3	0.3	0.4	45.9	54.1
Muscogee	51,280	25,476	21,386	4,327	91	4,090	D	49.7	41.7	8.4	0.2	41	69	155	2.2	2.5	2.1	1.4	54.4	45.6
Newton	13,659	5,811	5,804	1,998	46	7	D	42.5	42.5	14.6	0.3	88	63	88	0.6	0.6	0.6	0.6	50.0	50.0
Oconee	8,076	2,745	4,125	1,182	24	1,380	R	34.0	51.1	14.6	0.3	143	11	87	0.3	0.3	0.4	0.4	40.0	60.0
Oglethorpe	3,703	1,491	1,590	620	2	99	R	40.3	42.9	16.7	<.1	111	62	36	0.2	0.1	0.2	0.2	48.4	51.6
Paulding	15,088	5,212	7,180	2,654	42	1,968	R	34.5	47.6	17.6	0.3	139	27	24	0.7	0.5	0.7	0.9	42.1	57.9
Peach	6,973	3,677	2,327	947	22	1,350	D	52.7	33.4	13.6	0.3	28	134	108	0.3	0.4	0.2	0.3	61.2	38.8
Pickens	5,748	2,359	2,332	1,037	20	27	D	41.0	40.6	18.0	0.3	100	77	19	0.2	0.2	0.2	0.3	50.3	49.7
Pierce	4,472	1,852	1,899	708	13	47	R	41.4	42.5	15.8	0.3	96	64	57	0.2	0.2	0.2	0.2	49.4	50.6
Pike	4,104	1,651	1,822	623	8	171	R	40.2	44.4	15.2	0.2	112	52	74	0.2	0.2	0.2	0.2	47.5	52.5
Polk	10,668	4,872	4,158	1,598	40	714	D	45.7	39.0	15.0	0.4	68	94	78	0.5	0.5	0.4	0.5	54.0	46.0
Pulaski	3,451	1,756	1,075	614	6	681	D	50.9	31.2	17.8	0.2	37	143	21	0.1	0.2	0.1	0.2	62.0	38.0
Putnam	4,694	2,149	1,756	775	14	393	D	45.8	37.4	16.5	0.3	66	105	38	0.2	0.2	0.2	0.2	55.0	45.0
Quitman	922	523	284	113	2	239	D	56.7	30.8	12.3	0.2	15	145	128	<.1	<.1	<.1	<.1	64.8	35.2
Rabun	4,622	1,878	1,902	825	17	24	R	40.6	41.2	17.8	0.4	106	74	20	0.2	0.2	0.2	0.3	49.7	50.3
Randolph	2,959	1,756	887	315	1	869	D	59.3	30.0	10.6	<.1	9	149	144	0.1	0.2	<.1	0.1	66.4	33.6
Richmond	59,523	28,910	24,227	6,290	96	4,683	D	48.6	40.7	10.6	0.2	49	76	145	2.6	2.9	2.4	2.0	54.4	45.6
Rockdale	22,690	7,003	11,945	3,664	78	4,942	R	30.9	52.6	16.1	0.3	153	6	50	1.0	0.7	1.2	1.2	37.0	63.0
Schley	1,296	601	511	180	4	90	D	46.4	39.4	13.9	0.3	61	87	103	<.1	<.1	<.1	<.1	54.0	46.0
Screven	4,366	1,940	1,705	709	12	235	D	44.4	39.1	16.2	0.3	76	92	45	0.2	0.2	0.2	0.2	53.2	46.8
Seminole	2,519	1,193	850	468	8	343	D	47.4	33.7	18.6	0.3	57	132	13	0.1	0.1	<.1	0.2	58.4	41.6
Spalding	15,734	6,392	7,262	2,044	36	870	R	40.6	46.2	13.0	0.2	107	34	116	0.7	0.6	0.7	0.7	46.8	53.2
Stephens	8,493	2,976	4,047	1,448	22	1,071	R	35.0	47.7	17.0	0.3	136	23	33	0.4	0.3	0.4	0.5	42.4	57.6
Stewart	2,909	1,540	1,186	175	8	354	D	52.9	40.8	6.0	0.3	27	75	158	0.1	0.2	0.1	<.1	56.5	43.5
Sumter	9,168	4,489	3,616	1,046	17	873	D	49.0	39.4	11.4	0.2	47	86	139	0.4	0.4	0.4	0.3	55.4	44.6
Talbot	2,682	1,768	671	238	5	1,097	D	65.9	25.0	8.9	0.2	3	153	154	0.1	0.2	<.1	<.1	72.5	27.5
Taliaferro	1,106	755	269	80	2	486	D	68.3	24.3	7.2	0.2	2	155	157	<.1	<.1	<.1	<.1	73.7	26.3
Tattnall	5,942	2,360	2,566	996	20	206	R	39.7	43.2	16.8	0.3	116	59	35	0.3	0.2	0.3	0.3	47.9	52.1
Taylor	2,872	1,508	1,078	281	5	430	D	52.5	37.5	9.8	0.2	31	104	149	0.1	0.1	0.1	<.1	58.3	41.7
Telfair	4,192	2,238	1,324	613	17	914	D	53.4	31.6	14.6	0.4	24	142	89	0.2	0.2	0.1	0.2	62.8	37.2
Terrell	3,474	1,942	1,143	384	5	799	D	55.9	32.9	11.1	0.1	17	138	143	0.1	0.2	0.1	0.1	62.9	37.1
Thomas	11,948	4,841	5,500	1,591	16	659	R	40.5	46.0	13.3	0.1	108	30	113	0.5	0.5	0.6	0.5	46.8	53.2
Tift	9,569	3,930	4,485	1,139	15	555	R	41.1	46.9	11.9	0.2	99	31	132	0.4	0.4	0.5	0.4	46.7	53.3
Toombs	7,490	2,648	3,609	1,210	23	961	R	35.4	48.2	16.2	0.3	135	20	49	0.3	0.3	0.4	0.4	42.3	57.7
Towns	3,704	1,487	1,674	537	6	187	R	40.1	45.2	14.5	0.2	113	45	93	0.2	0.1	0.2	0.2	47.0	53.0
Treutlen	2,344	1,116	898	318	12	218	D	47.6	38.3	13.6	0.5	54	100	109	0.1	0.1	<.1	0.1	55.4	44.6

Table E. – **Vote for President: November 3, 1992, General Election (cont)**

County	Total	Clinton (DEM)	Bush (REP)	Perot (IND)	Other	Plurality Total	Party	DEM	REP	IND	Other	Rank DEM	Rank REP	Rank IND	Total	DEM	REP	IND	DEM	REP
Troup	17,039	6,412	8,118	2,488	21	1,706	R	37.6	47.6	14.6	0.1	127	25	90	0.7	0.6	0.8	0.8	44.1	55.9
Turner	3,024	1,669	936	370	49	733	D	55.2	31.0	12.2	1.6	20	144	129	0.1	0.2	<.1	0.1	64.1	35.9
Twiggs	3,392	2,097	853	432	10	1,244	D	61.8	25.1	12.7	0.3	8	152	123	0.1	0.2	<.1	0.1	71.1	28.9
Union	5,656	2,304	2,533	804	15	229	R	40.7	44.8	14.2	0.3	103	49	101	0.2	0.2	0.3	0.3	47.6	52.4
Upson	9,001	3,740	4,053	1,186	22	313	R	41.6	45.0	13.2	0.2	95	47	115	0.4	0.4	0.4	0.4	48.0	52.0
Walker	17,488	6,217	8,489	2,748	34	2,272	R	35.6	48.5	15.7	0.2	134	19	60	0.8	0.6	0.9	0.9	42.3	57.7
Walton	12,391	4,821	5,619	1,923	28	798	R	38.9	45.3	15.5	0.2	122	41	69	0.5	0.5	0.6	0.6	46.2	53.8
Ware	10,424	4,573	4,573	1,263	15	0	D	43.9	43.9	12.1	0.1	81	54	131	0.4	0.5	0.5	0.4	50.0	50.0
Warren	2,175	1,239	751	180	5	488	D	57.0	34.5	8.3	0.2	14	127	156	<.1	0.1	<.1	<.1	62.3	37.7
Washington	6,725	3,508	2,384	820	13	1,124	D	52.2	35.4	12.2	0.2	32	120	130	0.3	0.3	0.2	0.3	59.5	40.5
Wayne	7,552	3,052	3,381	1,107	12	329	R	40.4	44.8	14.7	0.2	109	50	86	0.3	0.3	0.3	0.4	47.4	52.6
Webster	911	600	208	103	0	392	D	65.9	22.8	11.3	0.0	4	157	141	<.1	<.1	<.1	<.1	74.3	25.7
Wheeler	1,699	880	601	214	4	279	D	51.8	35.4	12.6	0.2	34	121	124	<.1	<.1	<.1	<.1	59.4	40.6
White	5,229	1,756	2,477	981	15	721	R	33.6	47.4	18.8	0.3	146	28	11	0.2	0.2	0.2	0.3	41.5	58.5
Whitfield	22,239	7,335	12,003	2,866	35	4,668	R	33.0	54.0	12.9	0.2	148	5	119	1.0	0.7	1.2	0.9	37.9	62.1
Wilcox	2,723	1,365	916	433	9	449	D	50.1	33.6	15.9	0.3	40	133	53	0.1	0.1	<.1	0.1	59.8	40.2
Wilkes	3,962	1,955	1,535	464	8	420	D	49.3	38.7	11.7	0.2	42	96	136	0.2	0.2	0.2	0.1	56.0	44.0
Wilkinson	4,072	2,286	1,232	520	34	1,054	D	56.1	30.3	12.8	0.8	16	148	121	0.2	0.2	0.1	0.2	65.0	35.0
Worth	5,837	2,578	2,344	905	10	234	D	44.2	40.2	15.5	0.2	77	81	70	0.3	0.3	0.2	0.3	52.4	47.6
GEORGIA	**2,321,125**	**1,008,966**	**995,252**	**309,657**	**7,250**	**13,714**	**D**	**43.5**	**42.9**	**13.3**	**0.3**				**100.0**	**100.0**	**100.0**	**100.0**	**50.3**	**49.7**

Table F. — Vote for U.S. Senator: November 3, 1992, General Election[1]

County	Total	Fowler (DEM)	Coverdell (REP)	Other	Plurality Total	Party	Percent of total vote DEM	REP	Other	Rank DEM	REP	Other	Percent contribution to state vote Total	DEM	REP	Other
Appling	5,192	2,413	2,616	163	203	R	46.5	50.4	3.1	113	48	81	0.2	0.2	0.2	0.2
Atkinson	1,665	1,059	533	73	526	D	63.6	32.0	4.4	30	138	13	<.1	<.1	<.1	0.1
Bacon	2,706	1,441	1,129	136	312	D	53.3	41.7	5.0	76	93	8	0.1	0.1	0.1	0.2
Baker	1,229	881	308	40	573	D	71.7	25.1	3.3	5	155	76	<.1	<.1	<.1	<.1
Baldwin	10,319	5,956	4,006	357	1,950	D	57.7	38.8	3.5	55	107	57	0.5	0.5	0.4	0.5
Banks	3,712	1,814	1,729	169	85	D	48.9	46.6	4.6	96	69	12	0.2	0.2	0.2	0.2
Barrow	10,007	4,473	5,027	507	554	R	44.7	50.2	5.1	121	49	7	0.4	0.4	0.5	0.7
Bartow	15,195	6,657	7,986	552	1,329	R	43.8	52.6	3.6	128	33	46	0.7	0.6	0.7	0.8
Ben Hill	4,332	2,796	1,404	132	1,392	D	64.5	32.4	3.0	23	137	89	0.2	0.3	0.1	0.2
Berrien	4,755	2,797	1,771	187	1,026	D	58.8	37.2	3.9	49	114	27	0.2	0.3	0.2	0.3
Bibb	53,688	32,778	19,779	1,131	12,999	D	61.1	36.8	2.1	38	117	145	2.4	3.0	1.8	1.6
Bleckley	3,393	1,995	1,272	126	723	D	58.8	37.5	3.7	50	113	44	0.2	0.2	0.1	0.2
Brantley	3,564	2,000	1,437	127	563	D	56.1	40.3	3.6	61	102	50	0.2	0.2	0.1	0.2
Brooks	3,680	2,163	1,418	99	745	D	58.8	38.5	2.7	51	109	119	0.2	0.2	0.1	0.1
Bryan	5,267	2,207	2,933	127	726	R	41.9	55.7	2.4	136	21	135	0.2	0.2	0.3	0.2
Bulloch	12,536	5,839	6,349	348	510	R	46.6	50.6	2.8	111	45	113	0.6	0.5	0.6	0.5
Burke	5,903	2,866	2,853	184	13	D	48.6	48.3	3.1	99	59	83	0.3	0.3	0.3	0.3
Butts	4,814	2,781	1,894	139	887	D	57.8	39.3	2.9	54	105	102	0.2	0.3	0.2	0.2
Calhoun	2,085	1,617	434	34	1,183	D	77.6	20.8	1.6	2	158	151	<.1	0.1	<.1	<.1
Camden	6,147	2,970	3,041	136	71	R	48.3	49.5	2.2	102	52	140	0.3	0.3	0.3	0.2
Candler	2,348	1,224	1,052	72	172	D	52.1	44.8	3.1	81	78	88	0.1	0.1	<.1	0.1
Carroll	22,526	10,009	11,742	775	1,733	R	44.4	52.1	3.4	124	37	60	1.0	0.9	1.1	1.1
Catoosa	14,603	4,867	9,322	414	4,455	R	33.3	63.8	2.8	156	4	108	0.6	0.4	0.9	0.6
Charlton	1,953	1,043	790	120	253	D	53.4	40.5	6.1	75	100	2	<.1	<.1	<.1	0.2
Chatham	67,303	33,189	32,633	1,481	556	D	49.3	48.5	2.2	95	57	142	3.0	3.0	3.0	2.1
Chattahoochee	965	525	403	37	122	D	54.4	41.8	3.8	69	92	31	<.1	<.1	<.1	<.1
Chattooga	6,434	3,114	3,064	256	50	D	48.4	47.6	4.0	101	63	26	0.3	0.3	0.3	0.4
Cherokee	28,714	9,639	18,203	872	8,564	R	33.6	63.4	3.0	155	5	92	1.3	0.9	1.7	1.2
Clarke	27,597	15,444	10,881	1,272	4,563	D	56.0	39.4	4.6	63	103	11	1.2	1.4	1.0	1.8
Clay	1,093	769	295	29	474	D	70.4	27.0	2.7	8	153	121	<.1	<.1	<.1	<.1
Clayton	57,639	28,682	26,766	2,191	1,916	D	49.8	46.4	3.8	93	71	37	2.6	2.6	2.5	3.1
Clinch	1,383	892	440	51	452	D	64.5	31.8	3.7	24	140	45	<.1	<.1	<.1	<.1
Cobb	195,375	73,213	115,558	6,604	42,345	R	37.5	59.1	3.4	149	11	68	8.7	6.6	10.8	9.4
Coffee	6,947	3,582	2,996	369	586	D	51.6	43.1	5.3	84	83	5	0.3	0.3	0.3	0.5
Colquitt	9,535	4,779	4,463	293	316	D	50.1	46.8	3.1	91	67	87	0.4	0.4	0.4	0.4
Columbia	28,159	7,639	19,686	834	12,047	R	27.1	69.9	3.0	159	1	94	1.3	0.7	1.8	1.2
Cook	3,788	2,327	1,364	97	963	D	61.4	36.0	2.6	37	123	125	0.2	0.2	0.1	0.1
Coweta	20,525	8,404	11,405	716	3,001	R	40.9	55.6	3.5	138	23	54	0.9	0.8	1.1	1.0
Crawford	2,779	1,745	939	95	806	D	62.8	33.8	3.4	33	129	62	0.1	0.2	<.1	0.1
Crisp	5,123	3,050	1,899	174	1,151	D	59.5	37.1	3.4	47	115	66	0.2	0.3	0.2	0.2
Dade	3,796	1,208	2,459	129	1,251	R	31.8	64.8	3.4	158	2	65	0.2	0.1	0.2	0.2
Dawson	3,799	1,704	2,013	82	309	R	44.9	53.0	2.2	119	30	144	0.2	0.2	0.2	0.1
Decatur	6,436	3,566	2,650	220	916	D	55.4	41.2	3.4	65	95	63	0.3	0.3	0.2	0.3
DeKalb	214,586	130,372	77,573	6,641	52,799	D	60.8	36.2	3.1	40	122	85	9.5	11.8	7.2	9.5
Dodge	5,204	3,313	1,705	186	1,608	D	63.7	32.8	3.6	28	134	49	0.2	0.3	0.2	0.3
Dooly	2,799	2,004	702	93	1,302	D	71.6	25.1	3.3	6	154	71	0.1	0.2	<.1	0.1
Dougherty	31,215	17,355	13,225	635	4,130	D	55.6	42.4	2.0	64	88	147	1.4	1.6	1.2	0.9
Douglas	26,563	10,626	14,931	1,006	4,305	R	40.0	56.2	3.8	141	19	38	1.2	1.0	1.4	1.4
Early	3,925	2,718	1,111	96	1,607	D	69.2	28.3	2.4	10	150	132	0.2	0.2	0.1	0.1
Echols	690	439	227	24	212	D	63.6	32.9	3.5	29	133	55	<.1	<.1	<.1	<.1
Effingham	7,468	3,070	4,197	201	1,127	R	41.1	56.2	2.7	137	20	118	0.3	0.3	0.4	0.3
Elbert	5,853	3,549	2,227	77	1,322	D	60.6	38.0	1.3	42	110	154	0.3	0.3	0.2	0.1
Emanuel	5,272	2,480	2,676	116	196	R	47.0	50.8	2.2	109	44	143	0.2	0.2	0.2	0.2
Evans	2,655	1,281	1,296	78	15	R	48.2	48.8	2.9	104	56	96	0.1	0.1	0.1	0.1
Fannin	7,200	2,764	4,248	188	1,484	R	38.4	59.0	2.6	146	12	123	0.3	0.2	0.4	0.3
Fayette	31,548	10,149	20,375	1,024	10,226	R	32.2	64.6	3.2	157	3	77	1.4	0.9	1.9	1.5
Floyd	27,846	13,595	13,484	767	111	D	48.8	48.4	2.8	97	58	114	1.2	1.2	1.3	1.1
Forsyth	17,099	6,314	10,133	652	3,819	R	36.9	59.3	3.8	150	10	35	0.8	0.6	0.9	0.9
Franklin	5,998	3,222	2,544	232	678	D	53.7	42.4	3.9	73	87	29	0.3	0.3	0.2	0.3
Fulton	257,825	155,975	95,001	6,849	60,974	D	60.5	36.8	2.7	44	116	120	11.5	14.1	8.9	9.8
Gilmer	5,127	1,998	2,911	218	913	R	39.0	56.8	4.3	145	17	17	0.2	0.2	0.3	0.3
Glascock	820	310	476	34	166	R	37.8	58.0	4.1	148	14	21	<.1	<.1	<.1	<.1
Glynn	22,904	10,100	12,299	505	2,199	R	44.1	53.7	2.2	127	28	141	1.0	0.9	1.1	0.7
Gordon	9,925	4,323	5,291	311	968	R	43.6	53.3	3.1	130	29	82	0.4	0.4	0.5	0.4
Grady	5,072	2,851	2,050	171	801	D	56.2	40.4	3.4	59	101	69	0.2	0.3	0.2	0.2
Greene	4,050	2,464	1,454	132	1,010	D	60.8	35.9	3.3	39	124	75	0.2	0.2	0.1	0.2
Gwinnett	149,400	51,543	92,467	5,390	40,924	R	34.5	61.9	3.6	154	8	47	6.6	4.7	8.6	7.7
Habersham	8,740	3,819	4,709	212	890	R	43.7	53.9	2.4	129	27	133	0.4	0.3	0.4	0.3
Hall	32,746	14,476	17,298	972	2,822	R	44.2	52.8	3.0	126	31	93	1.5	1.3	1.6	1.4
Hancock	2,396	1,875	398	123	1,477	D	78.3	16.6	5.1	1	159	6	0.1	0.2	<.1	0.2

[1]Runoff election required because no candidate received a majority of vote.

County	Total	Fowler (DEM)	Coverdell (REP)	Other	Plurality Total	Party	DEM	REP	Other	Rank DEM	Rank REP	Rank Other	Total	DEM	REP	Other
Haralson	7,675	3,859	3,493	323	366	D	50.3	45.5	4.2	90	73	19	0.3	0.3	0.3	0.5
Harris	6,278	2,805	3,294	179	489	R	44.7	52.5	2.9	122	35	105	0.3	0.3	0.3	0.3
Hart	6,193	3,503	2,329	361	1,174	D	56.6	37.6	5.8	58	112	3	0.3	0.3	0.2	0.5
Heard	3,242	1,721	1,369	152	352	D	53.1	42.2	4.7	77	90	9	0.1	0.2	0.1	0.2
Henry	24,610	9,424	14,381	805	4,957	R	38.3	58.4	3.3	147	13	74	1.1	0.9	1.3	1.2
Houston	32,503	16,426	15,035	1,042	1,391	D	50.5	46.3	3.2	88	72	78	1.4	1.5	1.4	1.5
Irwin	2,606	1,688	853	65	835	D	64.8	32.7	2.5	21	135	129	0.1	0.2	<.1	<.1
Jackson	9,120	4,405	4,328	387	77	D	48.3	47.5	4.2	103	65	18	0.4	0.4	0.4	0.6
Jasper	2,797	1,509	1,191	97	318	D	54.0	42.6	3.5	72	85	56	0.1	0.1	0.1	0.1
Jeff Davis	4,060	1,862	2,056	142	194	R	45.9	50.6	3.5	115	46	52	0.2	0.2	0.2	0.2
Jefferson	5,014	2,603	2,256	155	347	D	51.9	45.0	3.1	82	75	86	0.2	0.2	0.2	0.2
Jenkins	2,419	1,133	1,195	91	62	R	46.8	49.4	3.8	110	53	42	0.1	0.1	0.1	0.1
Johnson	2,782	1,821	928	33	893	D	65.5	33.4	1.2	17	130	156	0.1	0.2	<.1	<.1
Jones	6,771	3,964	2,617	190	1,347	D	58.5	38.7	2.8	52	108	109	0.3	0.4	0.2	0.3
Lamar	4,160	2,293	1,774	93	519	D	55.1	42.6	2.2	67	84	139	0.2	0.2	0.2	0.1
Lanier	1,355	870	429	56	441	D	64.2	31.7	4.1	25	141	22	<.1	<.1	<.1	<.1
Laurens	11,627	6,858	4,375	394	2,483	D	59.0	37.6	3.4	48	111	67	0.5	0.6	0.4	0.6
Lee	5,803	2,466	3,167	170	701	R	42.5	54.6	2.9	135	25	97	0.3	0.2	0.3	0.2
Liberty	6,778	3,565	2,935	278	630	D	52.6	43.3	4.1	80	82	25	0.3	0.3	0.3	0.4
Lincoln	3,019	1,378	1,527	114	149	R	45.6	50.6	3.8	116	47	39	0.1	0.1	0.1	0.2
Long	1,660	838	745	77	93	D	50.5	44.9	4.6	89	76	10	<.1	<.1	<.1	0.1
Lowndes	22,031	11,300	10,289	442	1,011	D	51.3	46.7	2.0	86	68	148	1.0	1.0	1.0	0.6
Lumpkin	5,044	2,395	2,430	219	35	R	47.5	48.2	4.3	108	60	14	0.2	0.2	0.2	0.3
McDuffie	5,925	2,579	3,119	227	540	R	43.5	52.6	3.8	131	32	32	0.3	0.2	0.3	0.3
McIntosh	3,061	1,858	1,120	83	738	D	60.7	36.6	2.7	41	118	117	0.1	0.2	0.1	0.1
Macon	3,418	2,322	967	129	1,355	D	67.9	28.3	3.8	13	151	40	0.2	0.2	<.1	0.2
Madison	6,256	2,696	3,138	422	442	R	43.1	50.2	6.7	133	50	1	0.3	0.2	0.3	0.6
Marion	1,928	1,165	698	65	467	D	60.4	36.2	3.4	45	121	70	<.1	0.1	<.1	<.1
Meriwether	7,476	4,532	2,731	213	1,801	D	60.6	36.5	2.8	43	119	106	0.3	0.4	0.3	0.3
Miller	1,850	1,206	590	54	616	D	65.2	31.9	2.9	19	139	99	<.1	0.1	<.1	<.1
Mitchell	6,016	4,095	1,778	143	2,317	D	68.1	29.6	2.4	12	147	138	0.3	0.4	0.2	0.2
Monroe	6,236	3,420	2,554	262	866	D	54.8	41.0	4.2	68	97	20	0.3	0.3	0.2	0.4
Montgomery	2,330	1,265	1,033	32	232	D	54.3	44.3	1.4	70	80	153	0.1	0.1	<.1	<.1
Morgan	4,495	2,369	1,969	157	400	D	52.7	43.8	3.5	78	81	53	0.2	0.2	0.2	0.2
Murray	7,119	2,789	4,075	255	1,286	R	39.2	57.2	3.6	144	16	48	0.3	0.3	0.4	0.4
Muscogee	51,011	28,164	21,568	1,279	6,596	D	55.2	42.3	2.5	66	89	128	2.3	2.5	2.0	1.8
Newton	13,479	6,498	6,468	513	30	D	48.2	48.0	3.8	105	61	36	0.6	0.6	0.6	0.7
Oconee	7,976	3,222	4,410	344	1,188	R	40.4	55.3	4.3	139	24	15	0.4	0.3	0.4	0.5
Oglethorpe	3,627	1,573	1,848	206	275	R	43.4	51.0	5.7	132	40	4	0.2	0.1	0.2	0.3
Paulding	14,995	6,027	8,350	618	2,323	R	40.2	55.7	4.1	140	22	23	0.7	0.5	0.8	0.9
Peach	6,479	4,061	2,204	214	1,857	D	62.7	34.0	3.3	34	128	72	0.3	0.4	0.2	0.3
Pickens	5,194	2,521	2,459	214	62	D	48.5	47.3	4.1	100	66	24	0.2	0.2	0.2	0.3
Pierce	4,002	2,241	1,659	102	582	D	56.0	41.5	2.5	62	94	126	0.2	0.2	0.2	0.1
Pike	4,036	1,822	2,071	143	249	R	45.1	51.3	3.5	118	38	51	0.2	0.2	0.2	0.2
Polk	9,763	5,141	4,350	272	791	D	52.7	44.6	2.8	79	79	111	0.4	0.5	0.4	0.4
Pulaski	2,991	2,005	893	93	1,112	D	67.0	29.9	3.1	15	146	84	0.1	0.2	<.1	0.1
Putnam	4,347	2,354	1,830	163	524	D	54.2	42.1	3.7	71	91	43	0.2	0.2	0.2	0.2
Quitman	653	417	217	19	200	D	63.9	33.2	2.9	27	131	100	<.1	<.1	<.1	<.1
Rabun	4,274	2,059	2,092	123	33	R	48.2	48.9	2.9	106	55	103	0.2	0.2	0.2	0.2
Randolph	2,768	1,979	762	27	1,217	D	71.5	27.5	1.0	7	152	157	0.1	0.2	<.1	<.1
Richmond	59,718	29,608	28,439	1,671	1,169	D	49.6	47.6	2.8	94	64	110	2.7	2.7	2.6	2.4
Rockdale	22,680	8,362	13,544	774	5,182	R	36.9	59.7	3.4	151	9	64	1.0	0.8	1.3	1.1
Schley	1,154	618	491	45	127	D	53.6	42.5	3.9	74	86	28	<.1	<.1	<.1	<.1
Screven	3,453	1,569	1,765	119	196	R	45.4	51.1	3.4	117	39	59	0.2	0.1	0.2	0.2
Seminole	2,791	1,783	923	85	860	D	63.9	33.1	3.0	26	132	90	0.1	0.2	<.1	0.1
Spalding	14,779	6,292	8,019	468	1,727	R	42.6	54.3	3.2	134	26	79	0.7	0.6	0.7	0.7
Stephens	7,562	3,371	3,971	220	600	R	44.6	52.5	2.9	123	34	101	0.3	0.3	0.4	0.3
Stewart	1,808	1,183	556	69	627	D	65.4	30.8	3.8	18	143	34	<.1	0.1	<.1	<.1
Sumter	8,133	4,717	3,202	214	1,515	D	58.0	39.4	2.6	53	104	122	0.4	0.4	0.3	0.3
Talbot	1,939	1,274	590	75	684	D	65.7	30.4	3.9	16	144	30	<.1	0.1	<.1	0.1
Taliaferro	1,064	676	374	14	302	D	63.5	35.2	1.3	31	125	155	<.1	<.1	<.1	<.1
Tattnall	5,138	2,649	2,338	151	311	D	51.6	45.5	2.9	85	74	95	0.2	0.2	0.2	0.2
Taylor	2,861	1,789	1,000	72	789	D	62.5	35.0	2.5	35	126	127	0.1	0.2	<.1	0.1
Telfair	3,316	2,160	1,031	125	1,129	D	65.1	31.1	3.8	20	142	41	0.1	0.2	<.1	0.2
Terrell	3,013	2,024	907	82	1,117	D	67.2	30.1	2.7	14	145	116	0.1	0.2	<.1	0.1
Thomas	11,980	5,840	5,913	227	73	R	48.7	49.4	1.9	98	54	150	0.5	0.5	0.6	0.3
Tift	9,181	4,575	4,387	219	188	D	49.8	47.8	2.4	92	62	137	0.4	0.4	0.4	0.3
Toombs	6,482	2,584	3,737	161	1,153	R	39.9	57.7	2.5	142	15	131	0.3	0.2	0.3	0.2
Towns	3,458	1,660	1,732	66	72	R	48.0	50.1	1.9	107	51	149	0.2	0.1	0.2	<.1
Treutlen	1,868	1,123	728	17	395	D	60.1	39.0	0.9	46	106	158	<.1	0.1	<.1	<.1

[1] Runoff election required because no candidate received a majority of vote.

County	Total	Fowler (DEM)	Coverdell (REP)	Other	Plurality Total	Party	DEM	REP	Other	Rank DEM	Rank REP	Rank Other	Total	DEM	REP	Other
Troup	17,171	7,981	8,744	446	763	R	46.5	50.9	2.6	112	42	124	0.8	0.7	0.8	0.6
Turner	2,873	1,978	836	59	1,142	D	68.8	29.1	2.1	11	148	146	0.1	0.2	<.1	<.1
Twiggs	3,452	2,517	830	105	1,687	D	72.9	24.0	3.0	3	157	91	0.2	0.2	<.1	0.2
Union	5,467	2,526	2,781	160	255	R	46.2	50.9	2.9	114	43	98	0.2	0.2	0.3	0.2
Upson	9,234	4,682	4,290	262	392	D	50.7	46.5	2.8	87	70	107	0.4	0.4	0.4	0.4
Walker	16,886	5,856	10,546	484	4,690	R	34.7	62.5	2.9	153	6	104	0.8	0.5	1.0	0.7
Walton	11,726	5,250	5,973	503	723	R	44.8	50.9	4.3	120	41	16	0.5	0.5	0.6	0.7
Ware	9,194	5,224	3,741	229	1,483	D	56.8	40.7	2.5	57	98	130	0.4	0.5	0.3	0.3
Warren	1,756	986	722	48	264	D	56.2	41.1	2.7	60	96	115	<.1	<.1	<.1	<.1
Washington	5,829	3,609	2,020	200	1,589	D	61.9	34.7	3.4	36	127	61	0.3	0.3	0.2	0.3
Wayne	7,660	3,399	4,019	242	620	R	44.4	52.5	3.2	125	36	80	0.3	0.3	0.4	0.3
Webster	697	502	172	23	330	D	72.0	24.7	3.3	4	156	73	<.1	<.1	<.1	<.1
Wheeler	1,442	912	524	6	388	D	63.2	36.3	0.4	32	120	159	<.1	<.1	<.1	<.1
White	5,187	2,067	2,922	198	855	R	39.8	56.3	3.8	143	18	33	0.2	0.2	0.3	0.3
Whitfield	22,129	7,782	13,815	532	6,033	R	35.2	62.4	2.4	152	7	136	1.0	0.7	1.3	0.8
Wilcox	2,413	1,678	696	39	982	D	69.5	28.8	1.6	9	149	152	0.1	0.2	<.1	<.1
Wilkes	3,384	1,749	1,518	117	231	D	51.7	44.9	3.5	83	77	58	0.2	0.2	0.1	0.2
Wilkinson	3,346	2,166	1,087	93	1,079	D	64.7	32.5	2.8	22	136	112	0.1	0.2	0.1	0.1
Worth	6,176	3,527	2,500	149	1,027	D	57.1	40.5	2.4	56	99	134	0.3	0.3	0.2	0.2
GEORGIA	2,251,587	1,108,416	1,073,282	69,889	35,134	D	49.2	47.7	3.1				100.0	100.0	100.0	100.0

[1]Runoff election required because no candidate received a majority of vote.

Table F2. — Vote for U.S. Senator: November 24, 1992, Runoff Election[1]

County	Total	Fowler (DEM)	Coverdell (REP)		Plurality Total	Party	Percent of total vote DEM	REP		Rank DEM	REP		Percent contribution to state vote Total	DEM	REP	
Appling	2,748	1,255	1,493	-	238	R	45.7	54.3	-	109	51	-	0.2	0.2	0.2	-
Atkinson	1,024	611	413	-	198	D	59.7	40.3	-	36	124	-	<.1	<.1	<.1	-
Bacon	1,301	636	665	-	29	R	48.9	51.1	-	91	69	-	0.1	0.1	0.1	-
Baker	874	669	205	-	464	D	76.5	23.5	-	4	156	-	<.1	0.1	<.1	-
Baldwin	6,474	3,492	2,982	-	510	D	53.9	46.1	-	61	99	-	0.5	0.6	0.5	-
Banks	1,758	856	902	-	46	R	48.7	51.3	-	93	67	-	0.1	0.1	0.1	-
Barrow	4,812	2,321	2,491	-	170	R	48.2	51.8	-	97	63	-	0.4	0.4	0.4	-
Bartow	8,039	3,847	4,192	-	345	R	47.9	52.1	-	99	61	-	0.6	0.6	0.7	-
Ben Hill	2,067	1,334	733	-	601	D	64.5	35.5	-	21	139	-	0.2	0.2	0.1	-
Berrien	2,242	1,391	851	-	540	D	62.0	38.0	-	28	132	-	0.2	0.2	0.1	-
Bibb	33,786	19,688	14,098	-	5,590	D	58.3	41.7	-	44	116	-	2.7	3.2	2.2	-
Bleckley	1,987	1,040	947	-	93	D	52.3	47.7	-	70	90	-	0.2	0.2	0.1	-
Brantley	1,914	982	932	-	50	D	51.3	48.7	-	77	83	-	0.2	0.2	0.1	-
Brooks	2,342	1,297	1,045	-	252	D	55.4	44.6	-	51	109	-	0.2	0.2	0.2	-
Bryan	2,890	1,176	1,714	-	538	R	40.7	59.3	-	133	27	-	0.2	0.2	0.3	-
Bulloch	6,951	3,161	3,790	-	629	R	45.5	54.5	-	111	49	-	0.6	0.5	0.6	-
Burke	4,101	2,052	2,049	-	3	D	50.0	50.0	-	84	76	-	0.3	0.3	0.3	-
Butts	2,637	1,544	1,093	-	451	D	58.6	41.4	-	40	120	-	0.2	0.2	0.2	-
Calhoun	1,270	1,049	221	-	828	D	82.6	17.4	-	1	159	-	0.1	0.2	<.1	-
Camden	3,064	1,247	1,817	-	570	R	40.7	59.3	-	132	28	-	0.2	0.2	0.3	-
Candler	1,463	711	752	-	41	R	48.6	51.4	-	94	66	-	0.1	0.1	0.1	-
Carroll	12,076	5,506	6,570	-	1,064	R	45.6	54.4	-	110	50	-	1.0	0.9	1.0	-
Catoosa	7,802	2,239	5,563	-	3,324	R	28.7	71.3	-	156	4	-	0.6	0.4	0.9	-
Charlton	1,076	395	681	-	286	R	36.7	63.3	-	148	12	-	<.1	<.1	0.1	-
Chatham	42,567	21,424	21,143	-	281	D	50.3	49.7	-	82	78	-	3.4	3.5	3.3	-
Chattahoochee	446	250	196	-	54	D	56.1	43.9	-	50	110	-	<.1	<.1	<.1	-
Chattooga	3,266	1,562	1,704	-	142	R	47.8	52.2	-	100	60	-	0.3	0.3	0.3	-
Cherokee	15,649	5,502	10,147	-	4,645	R	35.2	64.8	-	150	10	-	1.2	0.9	1.6	-
Clarke	16,991	9,873	7,118	-	2,755	D	58.1	41.9	-	45	115	-	1.4	1.6	1.1	-
Clay	630	493	137	-	356	D	78.3	21.7	-	3	157	-	<.1	<.1	<.1	-
Clayton	29,230	15,119	14,111	-	1,008	D	51.7	48.3	-	74	86	-	2.3	2.4	2.2	-
Clinch	751	394	357	-	37	D	52.5	47.5	-	68	92	-	<.1	<.1	<.1	-
Cobb	99,540	37,469	62,071	-	24,602	R	37.6	62.4	-	146	14	-	7.9	6.1	9.8	-
Coffee	3,845	1,975	1,870	-	105	D	51.4	48.6	-	75	85	-	0.3	0.3	0.3	-
Colquitt	5,748	3,047	2,701	-	346	D	53.0	47.0	-	65	95	-	0.5	0.5	0.4	-
Columbia	16,549	3,508	13,041	-	9,533	R	21.2	78.8	-	159	1	-	1.3	0.6	2.1	-
Cook	1,991	1,301	690	-	611	D	65.3	34.7	-	20	140	-	0.2	0.2	0.1	-
Coweta	10,541	4,238	6,303	-	2,065	R	40.2	59.8	-	135	25	-	0.8	0.7	1.0	-
Crawford	1,762	1,029	733	-	296	D	58.4	41.6	-	43	117	-	0.1	0.2	0.1	-
Crisp	2,818	1,646	1,172	-	474	D	58.4	41.6	-	42	118	-	0.2	0.3	0.2	-
Dade	2,135	578	1,557	-	979	R	27.1	72.9	-	158	2	-	0.2	<.1	0.2	-
Dawson	1,748	771	977	-	206	R	44.1	55.9	-	118	42	-	0.1	0.1	0.2	-
Decatur	3,824	1,921	1,903	-	18	D	50.2	49.8	-	83	77	-	0.3	0.3	0.3	-
DeKalb	124,015	76,313	47,702	-	28,611	D	61.5	38.5	-	30	130	-	9.9	12.3	7.5	-
Dodge	3,078	1,768	1,310	-	458	D	57.4	42.6	-	47	113	-	0.2	0.3	0.2	-
Dooly	2,261	1,712	549	-	1,163	D	75.7	24.3	-	5	155	-	0.2	0.3	<.1	-
Dougherty	19,347	10,687	8,660	-	2,027	D	55.2	44.8	-	53	107	-	1.5	1.7	1.4	-
Douglas	12,334	5,205	7,129	-	1,924	R	42.2	57.8	-	125	35	-	1.0	0.8	1.1	-
Early	1,900	1,314	586	-	728	D	69.2	30.8	-	14	146	-	0.2	0.2	<.1	-
Echols	312	154	158	-	4	R	49.4	50.6	-	88	72	-	<.1	<.1	<.1	-
Effingham	4,146	1,673	2,473	-	800	R	40.4	59.6	-	134	26	-	0.3	0.3	0.4	-
Elbert	2,925	1,339	1,586	-	247	R	45.8	54.2	-	108	52	-	0.2	0.2	0.2	-
Emanuel	3,096	1,324	1,772	-	448	R	42.8	57.2	-	123	37	-	0.2	0.2	0.3	-
Evans	1,517	721	796	-	75	R	47.5	52.5	-	101	59	-	0.1	0.1	0.1	-
Fannin	3,552	1,401	2,151	-	750	R	39.4	60.6	-	139	21	-	0.3	0.2	0.3	-
Fayette	18,307	5,765	12,542	-	6,777	R	31.5	68.5	-	154	6	-	1.5	0.9	2.0	-
Floyd	18,316	9,399	8,917	-	482	D	51.3	48.7	-	76	84	-	1.5	1.5	1.4	-
Forsyth	8,411	3,306	5,105	-	1,799	R	39.3	60.7	-	141	19	-	0.7	0.5	0.8	-
Franklin	2,561	1,133	1,428	-	295	R	44.2	55.8	-	117	43	-	0.2	0.2	0.2	-
Fulton	143,987	90,022	53,965	-	36,057	D	62.5	37.5	-	26	134	-	11.5	14.5	8.5	-
Gilmer	3,722	1,734	1,988	-	254	R	46.6	53.4	-	105	55	-	0.3	0.3	0.3	-
Glascock	528	149	379	-	230	R	28.2	71.8	-	157	3	-	<.1	<.1	<.1	-
Glynn	13,049	5,161	7,888	-	2,727	R	39.6	60.4	-	138	22	-	1.0	0.8	1.2	-
Gordon	5,240	2,341	2,899	-	558	R	44.7	55.3	-	115	45	-	0.4	0.4	0.5	-
Grady	3,046	1,684	1,362	-	322	D	55.3	44.7	-	52	108	-	0.2	0.3	0.2	-
Greene	2,113	1,299	814	-	485	D	61.5	38.5	-	31	129	-	0.2	0.2	0.1	-
Gwinnett	73,728	26,205	47,523	-	21,318	R	35.5	64.5	-	149	11	-	5.9	4.2	7.5	-
Habersham	5,015	2,185	2,830	-	645	R	43.6	56.4	-	120	40	-	0.4	0.4	0.4	-
Hall	16,488	7,178	9,310	-	2,132	R	43.5	56.5	-	121	39	-	1.3	1.2	1.5	-
Hancock	1,475	1,200	275	-	925	D	81.4	18.6	-	2	158	-	0.1	0.2	<.1	-

[1]Runoff election required because no candidate received a majority of vote in November 3, 1992, general election.

County	Total	Fowler (DEM)	Coverdell (REP)		Plurality Total	Party	DEM	REP		Rank DEM	Rank REP		Total	DEM	REP	
Haralson	3,824	1,988	1,836	-	152	D	52.0	48.0	-	71	89	-	0.3	0.3	0.3	-
Harris	3,840	1,502	2,338	-	836	R	39.1	60.9	-	142	18	-	0.3	0.2	0.4	-
Hart	3,070	1,359	1,711	-	352	R	44.3	55.7	-	116	44	-	0.2	0.2	0.3	-
Heard	1,471	854	617	-	237	D	58.1	41.9	-	46	114	-	0.1	0.1	<.1	-
Henry	13,001	5,065	7,936	-	2,871	R	39.0	61.0	-	143	17	-	1.0	0.8	1.2	-
Houston	18,186	7,875	10,311	-	2,436	R	43.3	56.7	-	122	38	-	1.5	1.3	1.6	-
Irwin	1,571	1,101	470	-	631	D	70.1	29.9	-	12	148	-	0.1	0.2	<.1	-
Jackson	5,017	2,494	2,523	-	29	R	49.7	50.3	-	85	75	-	0.4	0.4	0.4	-
Jasper	1,898	1,026	872	-	154	D	54.1	45.9	-	59	101	-	0.2	0.2	0.1	-
Jeff Davis	1,848	774	1,074	-	300	R	41.9	58.1	-	126	34	-	0.1	0.1	0.2	-
Jefferson	3,569	1,801	1,768	-	33	D	50.5	49.5	-	81	79	-	0.3	0.3	0.3	-
Jenkins	1,307	611	696	-	85	R	46.7	53.3	-	103	57	-	0.1	<.1	0.1	-
Johnson	2,055	1,010	1,045	-	35	R	49.1	50.9	-	90	70	-	0.2	0.2	0.2	-
Jones	4,365	2,269	2,096	-	173	D	52.0	48.0	-	72	88	-	0.3	0.4	0.3	-
Lamar	2,595	1,397	1,198	-	199	D	53.8	46.2	-	62	98	-	0.2	0.2	0.2	-
Lanier	737	450	287	-	163	D	61.1	38.9	-	32	128	-	<.1	<.1	<.1	-
Laurens	7,505	3,838	3,667	-	171	D	51.1	48.9	-	78	82	-	0.6	0.6	0.6	-
Lee	3,301	1,372	1,929	-	557	R	41.6	58.4	-	128	32	-	0.3	0.2	0.3	-
Liberty	3,719	2,117	1,602	-	515	D	56.9	43.1	-	49	111	-	0.3	0.3	0.3	-
Lincoln	1,467	577	890	-	313	R	39.3	60.7	-	140	20	-	0.1	<.1	0.1	-
Long	861	491	370	-	121	D	57.0	43.0	-	48	112	-	<.1	<.1	<.1	-
Lowndes	12,280	5,908	6,372	-	464	R	48.1	51.9	-	98	62	-	1.0	1.0	1.0	-
Lumpkin	2,437	1,205	1,232	-	27	R	49.4	50.6	-	87	73	-	0.2	0.2	0.2	-
McDuffie	3,873	1,352	2,521	-	1,169	R	34.9	65.1	-	151	9	-	0.3	0.2	0.4	-
McIntosh	1,834	1,095	739	-	356	D	59.7	40.3	-	35	125	-	0.1	0.2	0.1	-
Macon	2,427	1,722	705	-	1,017	D	71.0	29.0	-	11	149	-	0.2	0.3	0.1	-
Madison	3,699	1,359	2,340	-	981	R	36.7	63.3	-	147	13	-	0.3	0.2	0.4	-
Marion	1,162	727	435	-	292	D	62.6	37.4	-	25	135	-	<.1	0.1	<.1	-
Meriwether	3,926	2,440	1,486	-	954	D	62.1	37.9	-	27	133	-	0.3	0.4	0.2	-
Miller	915	564	351	-	213	D	61.6	38.4	-	29	131	-	<.1	<.1	<.1	-
Mitchell	3,643	2,688	955	-	1,733	D	73.8	26.2	-	7	153	-	0.3	0.4	0.2	-
Monroe	3,714	1,924	1,790	-	134	D	51.8	48.2	-	73	87	-	0.3	0.3	0.3	-
Montgomery	1,323	592	731	-	139	R	44.7	55.3	-	114	46	-	0.1	<.1	0.1	-
Morgan	2,602	1,412	1,190	-	222	D	54.3	45.7	-	58	102	-	0.2	0.2	0.2	-
Murray	2,757	1,048	1,709	-	661	R	38.0	62.0	-	145	15	-	0.2	0.2	0.3	-
Muscogee	29,633	15,773	13,860	-	1,913	D	53.2	46.8	-	63	97	-	2.4	2.5	2.2	-
Newton	7,553	3,979	3,574	-	405	D	52.7	47.3	-	66	94	-	0.6	0.6	0.6	-
Oconee	4,866	2,038	2,828	-	790	R	41.9	58.1	-	127	33	-	0.4	0.3	0.4	-
Oglethorpe	2,092	862	1,230	-	368	R	41.2	58.8	-	130	30	-	0.2	0.1	0.2	-
Paulding	6,607	2,791	3,816	-	1,025	R	42.2	57.8	-	124	36	-	0.5	0.5	0.6	-
Peach	4,477	2,635	1,842	-	793	D	58.9	41.1	-	38	122	-	0.4	0.4	0.3	-
Pickens	4,345	2,346	1,999	-	347	D	54.0	46.0	-	60	100	-	0.3	0.4	0.3	-
Pierce	2,172	1,100	1,072	-	28	D	50.6	49.4	-	80	80	-	0.2	0.2	0.2	-
Pike	2,277	1,001	1,276	-	275	R	44.0	56.0	-	119	41	-	0.2	0.2	0.2	-
Polk	5,524	3,041	2,483	-	558	D	55.1	44.9	-	54	106	-	0.4	0.5	0.4	-
Pulaski	1,898	1,245	653	-	592	D	65.6	34.4	-	19	141	-	0.2	0.2	0.1	-
Putnam	2,579	1,412	1,167	-	245	D	54.7	45.3	-	56	104	-	0.2	0.2	0.2	-
Quitman	367	217	150	-	67	D	59.1	40.9	-	37	123	-	<.1	<.1	<.1	-
Rabun	2,369	1,061	1,308	-	247	R	44.8	55.2	-	113	47	-	0.2	0.2	0.2	-
Randolph	1,628	1,226	402	-	824	D	75.3	24.7	-	6	154	-	0.1	0.2	<.1	-
Richmond	35,826	16,199	19,627	-	3,428	R	45.2	54.8	-	112	48	-	2.9	2.6	3.1	-
Rockdale	12,512	4,862	7,650	-	2,788	R	38.9	61.1	-	144	16	-	1.0	0.8	1.2	-
Schley	648	341	307	-	34	D	52.6	47.4	-	67	93	-	<.1	<.1	<.1	-
Screven	2,172	998	1,174	-	176	R	45.9	54.1	-	107	53	-	0.2	0.2	0.2	-
Seminole	1,168	741	427	-	314	D	63.4	36.6	-	24	136	-	<.1	0.1	<.1	-
Spalding	8,449	3,380	5,069	-	1,689	R	40.0	60.0	-	136	24	-	0.7	0.5	0.8	-
Stephens	4,081	1,618	2,463	-	845	R	39.6	60.4	-	137	23	-	0.3	0.3	0.4	-
Stewart	1,298	928	370	-	558	D	71.5	28.5	-	10	150	-	0.1	0.1	<.1	-
Sumter	4,580	2,739	1,841	-	898	D	59.8	40.2	-	34	126	-	0.4	0.4	0.3	-
Talbot	1,305	874	431	-	443	D	67.0	33.0	-	17	143	-	0.1	0.1	<.1	-
Taliaferro	527	355	172	-	183	D	67.4	32.6	-	16	144	-	<.1	<.1	<.1	-
Tattnall	2,821	1,437	1,384	-	53	D	50.9	49.1	-	79	81	-	0.2	0.2	0.2	-
Taylor	1,606	878	728	-	150	D	54.7	45.3	-	57	103	-	0.1	0.1	0.1	-
Telfair	1,814	1,161	653	-	508	D	64.0	36.0	-	22	138	-	0.1	0.2	0.1	-
Terrell	2,018	1,398	620	-	778	D	69.3	30.7	-	13	147	-	0.2	0.2	<.1	-
Thomas	6,812	3,174	3,638	-	464	R	46.6	53.4	-	104	56	-	0.5	0.5	0.6	-
Tift	5,352	2,847	2,505	-	342	D	53.2	46.8	-	64	96	-	0.4	0.5	0.4	-
Toombs	4,156	1,421	2,735	-	1,314	R	34.2	65.8	-	152	8	-	0.3	0.2	0.4	-
Towns	1,669	786	883	-	97	R	47.1	52.9	-	102	58	-	0.1	0.1	0.1	-
Treutlen	1,192	700	492	-	208	D	58.7	41.3	-	39	121	-	<.1	0.1	<.1	-

[1]Runoff election required because no candidate received a majority of vote in November 3, 1992, general election.

County	Total	Fowler (DEM)	Coverdell (REP)		Plurality Total	Party	Percent of total vote DEM	REP		Rank DEM	REP		Percent contribution to state vote Total	DEM	REP	
Troup	8,716	3,620	5,096	-	1,476	R	41.5	58.5	-	129	31	-	0.7	0.6	0.8	-
Turner	1,427	1,039	388	-	651	D	72.8	27.2	-	9	151	-	0.1	0.2	<.1	-
Twiggs	2,020	1,392	628	-	764	D	68.9	31.1	-	15	145	-	0.2	0.2	<.1	-
Union	2,742	1,270	1,472	-	202	R	46.3	53.7	-	106	54	-	0.2	0.2	0.2	-
Upson	4,309	2,119	2,190	-	71	R	49.2	50.8	-	89	71	-	0.3	0.3	0.3	-
Walker	9,395	2,806	6,589	-	3,783	R	29.9	70.1	-	155	5	-	0.7	0.5	1.0	-
Walton..........................	6,785	3,287	3,498	-	211	R	48.4	51.6	-	96	64	-	0.5	0.5	0.6	-
Ware	5,827	2,841	2,986	-	145	R	48.8	51.2	-	92	68	-	0.5	0.5	0.5	-
Warren	1,281	672	609	-	63	D	52.5	47.5	-	69	91	-	0.1	0.1	<.1	-
Washington....................	3,827	2,239	1,588	-	651	D	58.5	41.5	-	41	119	-	0.3	0.4	0.3	-
Wayne..........................	4,042	1,960	2,082	-	122	R	48.5	51.5	-	95	65	-	0.3	0.3	0.3	-
Webster	471	346	125	-	221	D	73.5	26.5	-	8	152	-	<.1	<.1	<.1	-
Wheeler	725	399	326	-	73	D	55.0	45.0	-	55	105	-	<.1	<.1	<.1	-
White..........................	2,726	1,114	1,612	-	498	R	40.9	59.1	-	131	29	-	0.2	0.2	0.3	-
Whitfield	10,491	3,398	7,093	-	3,695	R	32.4	67.6	-	153	7	-	0.8	0.5	1.1	-
Wilcox	1,326	875	451	-	424	D	66.0	34.0	-	18	142	-	0.1	0.1	<.1	-
Wilkes	2,345	1,164	1,181	-	17	R	49.6	50.4	-	86	74	-	0.2	0.2	0.2	-
Wilkinson	2,500	1,594	906	-	688	D	63.8	36.2	-	23	137	-	0.2	0.3	0.1	-
Worth	3,646	2,200	1,446	-	754	D	60.3	39.7	-	33	127	-	0.3	0.4	0.2	-
GEORGIA	**1,253,991**	**618,877**	**635,114**	**-**	**16,237**	**R**	**49.4**	**50.6**	**-**				**100.0**	**100.0**	**100.0**	**-**

[1]Runoff election required because no candidate received a majority of vote in November 3, 1992, general election.

Table H. — Vote for U.S. Representative in Congress: November 3, 1992, General Election

Congressional district and county	Total	Democrat (DEM)	Republican (REP)	Other	Plurality Total	Plurality Party	Percent of total vote DEM	REP	Other	Rank within district DEM	REP	Other	Percent contribution to district vote Total	DEM	REP	Other
District 1	**179,740**	**75,808**	**103,932**	-	**28,124**	**R**	**42.2**	**57.8**	-			-	**100.0**	**100.0**	**100.0**	-
Appling	5,491	2,246	3,245	-	999	R	40.9	59.1	-	19	4	-	3.1	3.0	3.1	-
Bacon	2,977	1,335	1,642	-	307	R	44.8	55.2	-	13	10	-	1.7	1.8	1.6	-
Brantley	3,763	1,671	2,092	-	421	R	44.4	55.6	-	14	9	-	2.1	2.2	2.0	-
Bryan	5,643	2,341	3,302	-	961	R	41.5	58.5	-	17	6	-	3.1	3.1	3.2	-
Bulloch	12,715	5,864	6,851	-	987	R	46.1	53.9	-	8	15	-	7.1	7.7	6.6	-
Camden	7,067	3,906	3,161	-	745	D	55.3	44.7	-	4	19	-	3.9	5.2	3.0	-
Candler	2,634	1,203	1,431	-	228	R	45.7	54.3	-	10	13	-	1.5	1.6	1.4	-
Charlton	2,331	943	1,388	-	445	R	40.5	59.5	-	20	3	-	1.3	1.2	1.3	-
Chatham (pt)	49,685	16,239	33,446	-	17,207	R	32.7	67.3	-	22	1	-	27.6	21.4	32.2	-
Effingham (pt)	7,267	2,596	4,671	-	2,075	R	35.7	64.3	-	21	2	-	4.0	3.4	4.5	-
Emanuel	5,405	2,450	2,955	-	505	R	45.3	54.7	-	11	12	-	3.0	3.2	2.8	-
Evans	2,835	1,394	1,441	-	47	R	49.2	50.8	-	7	16	-	1.6	1.8	1.4	-
Glynn	22,870	9,632	13,238	-	3,606	R	42.1	57.9	-	16	7	-	12.7	12.7	12.7	-
Liberty	7,218	3,685	3,533	-	152	D	51.1	48.9	-	6	17	-	4.0	4.9	3.4	-
Long	1,819	930	889	-	41	D	51.1	48.9	-	5	18	-	1.0	1.2	0.9	-
McIntosh	3,242	1,855	1,387	-	468	D	57.2	42.8	-	3	20	-	1.8	2.4	1.3	-
Montgomery	2,502	1,473	1,029	-	444	D	58.9	41.1	-	2	21	-	1.4	1.9	1.0	-
Pierce	4,185	1,844	2,341	-	497	R	44.1	55.9	-	15	8	-	2.3	2.4	2.3	-
Tattnall	5,738	3,454	2,284	-	1,170	D	60.2	39.8	-	1	22	-	3.2	4.6	2.2	-
Toombs	7,016	3,173	3,843	-	670	R	45.2	54.8	-	12	11	-	3.9	4.2	3.7	-
Ware	9,477	4,338	5,139	-	801	R	45.8	54.2	-	9	14	-	5.3	5.7	4.9	-
Wayne	7,860	3,236	4,624	-	1,388	R	41.2	58.8	-	18	5	-	4.4	4.3	4.4	-
District 2	**150,382**	**95,789**	**54,593**	-	**41,196**	**D**	**63.7**	**36.3**	-			-	**100.0**	**100.0**	**100.0**	-
Baker	1,195	648	547	-	101	D	54.2	45.8	-	23	13	-	0.8	0.7	1.0	-
Bibb (pt)	20,643	16,978	3,665	-	13,313	D	82.2	17.8	-	3	33	-	13.7	17.7	6.7	-
Brooks	3,362	1,731	1,631	-	100	D	51.5	48.5	-	26	10	-	2.2	1.8	3.0	-
Calhoun	2,074	1,286	788	-	498	D	62.0	38.0	-	15	21	-	1.4	1.3	1.4	-
Chattahoochee	945	545	400	-	145	D	57.7	42.3	-	20	16	-	0.6	0.6	0.7	-
Clay	1,105	688	417	-	271	D	62.3	37.7	-	13	23	-	0.7	0.7	0.8	-
Colquitt	1,334	929	405	-	524	D	69.6	30.4	-	9	27	-	0.9	1.0	0.7	-
Crawford (pt)	473	368	105	-	263	D	77.8	22.2	-	6	30	-	0.3	0.4	0.2	-
Crisp (pt)	657	619	38	-	581	D	94.2	5.8	-	1	35	-	0.4	0.6	0.1	-
Decatur	6,173	2,949	3,224	-	275	R	47.8	52.2	-	30	6	-	4.1	3.1	5.9	-
Dooly (pt)	2,119	1,237	882	-	355	D	58.4	41.6	-	19	17	-	1.4	1.3	1.6	-
Dougherty (pt)	12,648	10,205	2,443	-	7,762	D	80.7	19.3	-	4	32	-	8.4	10.7	4.5	-
Early	3,890	1,928	1,962	-	34	R	49.6	50.4	-	27	9	-	2.6	2.0	3.6	-
Grady	4,842	1,949	2,893	-	944	R	40.3	59.7	-	33	3	-	3.2	2.0	5.3	-
Houston (pt)	6,529	4,360	2,169	-	2,191	D	66.8	33.2	-	10	26	-	4.3	4.6	4.0	-
Lee (pt)	1,130	666	464	-	202	D	58.9	41.1	-	18	18	-	0.8	0.7	0.8	-
Lowndes (pt)	5,317	3,815	1,502	-	2,313	D	71.8	28.2	-	8	28	-	3.5	4.0	2.8	-
Macon	3,502	2,172	1,330	-	842	D	62.0	38.0	-	14	22	-	2.3	2.3	2.4	-
Marion	1,925	994	931	-	63	D	51.6	48.4	-	25	11	-	1.3	1.0	1.7	-
Meriwether (pt)	4,221	2,794	1,427	-	1,367	D	66.2	33.8	-	11	25	-	2.8	2.9	2.6	-
Miller	1,816	641	1,175	-	534	R	35.3	64.7	-	35	1	-	1.2	0.7	2.2	-
Mitchell	6,033	2,934	3,099	-	165	R	48.6	51.4	-	28	8	-	4.0	3.1	5.7	-
Muscogee (pt)	17,416	14,780	2,636	-	12,144	D	84.9	15.1	-	2	34	-	11.6	15.4	4.8	-
Peach (pt)	2,661	2,146	515	-	1,631	D	80.6	19.4	-	5	31	-	1.8	2.2	0.9	-
Quitman	660	415	245	-	170	D	62.9	37.1	-	12	24	-	0.4	0.4	0.4	-
Randolph	2,796	1,674	1,122	-	552	D	59.9	40.1	-	16	20	-	1.9	1.7	2.1	-
Schley	1,171	476	695	-	219	R	40.6	59.4	-	32	4	-	0.8	0.5	1.3	-
Seminole	2,731	1,326	1,405	-	79	R	48.6	51.4	-	29	7	-	1.8	1.4	2.6	-
Stewart	1,902	1,125	777	-	348	D	59.1	40.9	-	17	19	-	1.3	1.2	1.4	-
Sumter	8,621	3,328	5,293	-	1,965	R	38.6	61.4	-	34	2	-	5.7	3.5	9.7	-
Talbot	1,983	1,442	541	-	901	D	72.7	27.3	-	7	29	-	1.3	1.5	1.0	-
Taylor	2,788	1,569	1,219	-	350	D	56.3	43.7	-	21	15	-	1.9	1.6	2.2	-
Terrell	3,121	1,678	1,443	-	235	D	53.8	46.2	-	24	12	-	2.1	1.8	2.6	-
Thomas	11,825	4,973	6,852	-	1,879	R	42.1	57.9	-	31	5	-	7.9	5.2	12.6	-
Webster	774	421	353	-	68	D	54.4	45.6	-	22	14	-	0.5	0.4	0.6	-
District 3	**208,378**	**94,271**	**114,107**	-	**19,836**	**R**	**45.2**	**54.8**	-			-	**100.0**	**100.0**	**100.0**	-
Baldwin (pt)	2,837	1,522	1,315	-	207	D	53.6	46.4	-	9	8	-	1.4	1.6	1.2	-
Clayton (pt)	45,765	19,896	25,869	-	5,973	R	43.5	56.5	-	13	4	-	22.0	21.1	22.7	-
Coweta	20,066	8,590	11,476	-	2,886	R	42.8	57.2	-	14	3	-	9.6	9.1	10.1	-
Crawford (pt)	2,069	1,411	658	-	753	D	68.2	31.8	-	1	16	-	1.0	1.5	0.6	-
Fayette	30,638	9,610	21,028	-	11,418	R	31.4	68.6	-	16	1	-	14.7	10.2	18.4	-
Harris	6,071	3,361	2,710	-	651	D	55.4	44.6	-	8	9	-	2.9	3.6	2.4	-
Henry (pt)	19,779	6,695	13,084	-	6,389	R	33.8	66.2	-	15	2	-	9.5	7.1	11.5	-
Jones (pt)	5,012	3,079	1,933	-	1,146	D	61.4	38.6	-	4	13	-	2.4	3.3	1.7	-
Lamar	3,978	2,350	1,628	-	722	D	59.1	40.9	-	5	12	-	1.9	2.5	1.4	-
Meriwether (pt)	2,973	1,974	999	-	975	D	66.4	33.6	-	2	15	-	1.4	2.1	0.9	-
Monroe	6,078	3,525	2,553	-	972	D	58.0	42.0	-	7	10	-	2.9	3.7	2.2	-
Muscogee (pt)	33,194	16,662	16,532	-	130	D	50.2	49.8	-	11	6	-	15.9	17.7	14.5	-
Peach (pt)	3,601	2,347	1,254	-	1,093	D	65.2	34.8	-	3	14	-	1.7	2.5	1.1	-
Pike	3,974	2,060	1,914	-	146	D	51.8	48.2	-	10	7	-	1.9	2.2	1.7	-

226 Georgia

Congressional district and county	Total	Democrat (DEM)	Republican (REP)	Other	Plurality Total	Party	Percent of total vote DEM	REP	Other	Rank within district DEM	REP	Other	Percent contribution to district vote Total	DEM	REP	Other
District 3 (cont)																
Spalding	13,199	5,798	7,401	-	1,603	R	43.9	56.1	-	12	5	-	6.3	6.2	6.5	-
Upson	9,144	5,391	3,753	-	1,638	D	59.0	41.0	-	6	11	-	4.4	5.7	3.3	-
District 4	250,314	123,819	126,495	-	2,676	R	49.5	50.5	-				100.0	100.0	100.0	-
DeKalb (pt)	117,580	69,970	47,610	-	22,360	D	59.5	40.5	-	2	3	-	47.0	56.5	37.6	-
Fulton (pt)	6,605	4,634	1,971	-	2,663	D	70.2	29.8	-	1	4	-	2.6	3.7	1.6	-
Gwinnett (pt)	103,538	40,456	63,082	-	22,626	R	39.1	60.9	-	3	2	-	41.4	32.7	49.9	-
Rockdale	22,591	8,759	13,832	-	5,073	R	38.8	61.2	-	4	1	-	9.0	7.1	10.9	-
District 5	204,407	147,445	56,960	2	90,485	D	72.1	27.9	<.1				100.0	100.0	100.0	100.0
Clayton (pt)	8,553	6,064	2,489	0	3,575	D	70.9	29.1	0.0	3	2	2	4.2	4.1	4.4	0.0
Cobb (pt)	2,474	1,557	917	0	640	D	62.9	37.1	0.0	4	1	3	1.2	1.1	1.6	0.0
DeKalb (pt)	5,744	5,479	265	0	5,214	D	95.4	4.6	0.0	1	4	4	2.8	3.7	0.5	0.0
Fulton (pt)	187,636	134,345	53,289	2	81,056	D	71.6	28.4	<.1	2	3	1	91.8	91.1	93.6	100.0
District 6	274,957	116,196	158,761	-	42,565	R	42.3	57.7	-				100.0	100.0	100.0	-
Cherokee (pt)	17,588	7,093	10,495	-	3,402	R	40.3	59.7	-	3	3	-	6.4	6.1	6.6	-
Cobb (pt)	144,956	64,381	80,575	-	16,194	R	44.4	55.6	-	1	5	-	52.7	55.4	50.8	-
DeKalb (pt)	24,237	10,542	13,695	-	3,153	R	43.5	56.5	-	2	4	-	8.8	9.1	8.6	-
Fulton (pt)	58,315	22,276	36,039	-	13,763	R	38.2	61.8	-	5	1	-	21.2	19.2	22.7	-
Gwinnett (pt)	29,861	11,904	17,957	-	6,053	R	39.9	60.1	-	4	2	-	10.9	10.2	11.3	-
District 7	194,289	111,374	82,915	-	28,459	D	57.3	42.7	-				100.0	100.0	100.0	-
Bartow	14,368	8,493	5,875	-	2,618	D	59.1	40.9	-	7	5	-	7.4	7.6	7.1	-
Carroll	22,140	11,888	10,252	-	1,636	D	53.7	46.3	-	10	2	-	11.4	10.7	12.4	-
Chattooga	6,381	3,788	2,593	-	1,195	D	59.4	40.6	-	5	7	-	3.3	3.4	3.1	-
Cobb (pt)	46,370	25,952	20,418	-	5,534	D	56.0	44.0	-	8	4	-	23.9	23.3	24.6	-
Douglas	26,023	12,543	13,480	-	937	R	48.2	51.8	-	11	1	-	13.4	11.3	16.3	-
Floyd	27,735	17,721	10,014	-	7,707	D	63.9	36.1	-	3	9	-	14.3	15.9	12.1	-
Haralson	7,578	4,768	2,810	-	1,958	D	62.9	37.1	-	4	8	-	3.9	4.3	3.4	-
Heard	3,142	2,086	1,056	-	1,030	D	66.4	33.6	-	2	10	-	1.6	1.9	1.3	-
Paulding	14,777	8,002	6,775	-	1,227	D	54.2	45.8	-	9	3	-	7.6	7.2	8.2	-
Polk	8,953	6,150	2,803	-	3,347	D	68.7	31.3	-	1	11	-	4.6	5.5	3.4	-
Troup	16,822	9,983	6,839	-	3,144	D	59.3	40.7	-	6	6	-	8.7	9.0	8.2	-
District 8	194,692	108,472	86,220	-	22,252	D	55.7	44.3	-				100.0	100.0	100.0	-
Atkinson	1,634	1,132	502	-	630	D	69.3	30.7	-	11	22	-	0.8	1.0	0.6	-
Ben Hill	4,100	2,652	1,448	-	1,204	D	64.7	35.3	-	18	15	-	2.1	2.4	1.7	-
Berrien	4,707	2,999	1,708	-	1,291	D	63.7	36.3	-	19	14	-	2.4	2.8	2.0	-
Bibb (pt)	32,501	17,285	15,216	-	2,069	D	53.2	46.8	-	25	8	-	16.7	15.9	17.6	-
Bleckley	3,340	2,237	1,103	-	1,134	D	67.0	33.0	-	16	17	-	1.7	2.1	1.3	-
Clinch	1,355	948	407	-	541	D	70.0	30.0	-	9	24	-	0.7	0.9	0.5	-
Coffee	6,801	4,091	2,710	-	1,381	D	60.2	39.8	-	23	10	-	3.5	3.8	3.1	-
Colquitt (pt)	7,698	3,680	4,018	-	338	R	47.8	52.2	-	29	4	-	4.0	3.4	4.7	-
Cook	3,754	2,301	1,453	-	848	D	61.3	38.7	-	22	11	-	1.9	2.1	1.7	-
Crisp (pt)	4,038	2,476	1,562	-	914	D	61.3	38.7	-	21	12	-	2.1	2.3	1.8	-
Dodge	5,327	3,774	1,553	-	2,221	D	70.8	29.2	-	7	26	-	2.7	3.5	1.8	-
Dooly (pt)	286	204	82	-	122	D	71.3	28.7	-	6	27	-	0.1	0.2	0.1	-
Dougherty (pt)	17,971	7,409	10,562	-	3,153	R	41.2	58.8	-	31	2	-	9.2	6.8	12.3	-
Echols	610	388	222	-	166	D	63.6	36.4	-	20	13	-	0.3	0.4	0.3	-
Houston (pt)	25,515	12,464	13,051	-	587	R	48.8	51.2	-	27	6	-	13.1	11.5	15.1	-
Irwin	2,469	1,668	801	-	867	D	67.6	32.4	-	15	18	-	1.3	1.5	0.9	-
Jeff Davis	4,082	2,148	1,934	-	214	D	52.6	47.4	-	26	7	-	2.1	2.0	2.2	-
Johnson	3,042	2,389	653	-	1,736	D	78.5	21.5	-	1	32	-	1.6	2.2	0.8	-
Jones (pt)	1,294	853	441	-	412	D	65.9	34.1	-	17	16	-	0.7	0.8	0.5	-
Lanier	1,208	830	378	-	452	D	68.7	31.3	-	13	20	-	0.6	0.8	0.4	-
Laurens	12,017	8,606	3,411	-	5,195	D	71.6	28.4	-	5	28	-	6.2	7.9	4.0	-
Lee (pt)	4,774	1,816	2,958	-	1,142	R	38.0	62.0	-	32	1	-	2.5	1.7	3.4	-
Lowndes (pt)	16,427	7,703	8,724	-	1,021	R	46.9	53.1	-	30	3	-	8.4	7.1	10.1	-
Pulaski	2,919	2,018	901	-	1,117	D	69.1	30.9	-	12	21	-	1.5	1.9	1.0	-
Telfair	3,255	2,266	989	-	1,277	D	69.6	30.4	-	10	23	-	1.7	2.1	1.1	-
Tift	8,664	4,190	4,474	-	284	R	48.4	51.6	-	28	5	-	4.5	3.9	5.2	-
Treutlen	1,174	886	288	-	598	D	75.5	24.5	-	2	31	-	0.6	0.8	0.3	-
Turner	2,842	1,944	898	-	1,046	D	68.4	31.6	-	14	19	-	1.5	1.8	1.0	-
Twiggs (pt)	805	568	237	-	331	D	70.6	29.4	-	8	25	-	0.4	0.5	0.3	-
Wheeler	1,599	1,174	425	-	749	D	73.4	26.6	-	4	29	-	0.8	1.1	0.5	-
Wilcox	2,410	1,778	632	-	1,146	D	73.8	26.2	-	3	30	-	1.2	1.6	0.7	-
Worth	6,074	3,595	2,479	-	1,116	D	59.2	40.8	-	24	9	-	3.1	3.3	2.9	-
District 9	190,943	113,024	77,919	-	35,105	D	59.2	40.8	-				100.0	100.0	100.0	-
Catoosa	14,688	8,211	6,477	-	1,734	D	55.9	44.1	-	13	8	-	7.7	7.3	8.3	-
Cherokee (pt)	9,458	4,786	4,672	-	114	D	50.6	49.4	-	19	2	-	5.0	4.2	6.0	-
Dade	3,750	1,984	1,766	-	218	D	52.9	47.1	-	18	3	-	2.0	1.8	2.3	-
Dawson	3,709	2,423	1,286	-	1,137	D	65.3	34.7	-	3	18	-	1.9	2.1	1.7	-
Fannin	7,060	3,768	3,292	-	476	D	53.4	46.6	-	17	4	-	3.7	3.3	4.2	-
Forsyth	16,729	9,331	7,398	-	1,933	D	55.8	44.2	-	14	7	-	8.8	8.3	9.5	-

Georgia 227

Congressional district and county	Total	Democrat (DEM)	Republican (REP)	Other	Plurality Total	Party	Percent of total vote DEM	REP	Other	Rank within district DEM	REP	Other	Percent contribution to district vote Total	DEM	REP	Other
District 9 (cont)																
Gilmer	4,478	2,440	2,038	-	402	D	54.5	45.5	-	16	5	-	2.3	2.2	2.6	-
Gordon	8,774	5,458	3,316	-	2,142	D	62.2	37.8	-	6	15	-	4.6	4.8	4.3	-
Habersham	8,383	4,892	3,491	-	1,401	D	58.4	41.6	-	10	11	-	4.4	4.3	4.5	-
Hall	32,657	22,615	10,042	-	12,573	D	69.3	30.7	-	1	20	-	17.1	20.0	12.9	-
Lumpkin	4,981	3,387	1,594	-	1,793	D	68.0	32.0	-	2	19	-	2.6	3.0	2.0	-
Murray	7,106	4,305	2,801	-	1,504	D	60.6	39.4	-	9	12	-	3.7	3.8	3.6	-
Pickens	4,625	2,942	1,683	-	1,259	D	63.6	36.4	-	4	17	-	2.4	2.6	2.2	-
Rabun	4,175	2,427	1,748	-	679	D	58.1	41.9	-	11	10	-	2.2	2.1	2.2	-
Stephens	7,391	3,685	3,706	-	21	R	49.9	50.1	-	20	1	-	3.9	3.3	4.8	-
Towns	3,364	2,062	1,302	-	760	D	61.3	38.7	-	7	14	-	1.8	1.8	1.7	-
Union	5,409	3,279	2,130	-	1,149	D	60.6	39.4	-	8	13	-	2.8	2.9	2.7	-
Walker	17,179	9,506	7,673	-	1,833	D	55.3	44.7	-	15	6	-	9.0	8.4	9.8	-
White	5,119	3,191	1,928	-	1,263	D	62.3	37.7	-	5	16	-	2.7	2.8	2.5	-
Whitfield	21,908	12,332	9,576	-	2,756	D	56.3	43.7	-	12	9	-	11.5	10.9	12.3	-
District 10	201,485	108,426	93,059	-	15,367	D	53.8	46.2	-				100.0	100.0	100.0	-
Banks	3,695	2,490	1,205	-	1,285	D	67.4	32.6	-	3	17	-	1.8	2.3	1.3	-
Barrow	9,726	5,783	3,943	-	1,840	D	59.5	40.5	-	11	9	-	4.8	5.3	4.2	-
Clarke	25,827	16,745	9,082	-	7,663	D	64.8	35.2	-	4	16	-	12.8	15.4	9.8	-
Columbia	27,199	9,923	17,276	-	7,353	R	36.5	63.5	-	19	1	-	13.5	9.2	18.6	-
Elbert	5,939	3,840	2,099	-	1,741	D	64.7	35.3	-	5	15	-	2.9	3.5	2.3	-
Franklin	6,075	4,117	1,958	-	2,159	D	67.8	32.2	-	2	18	-	3.0	3.8	2.1	-
Gwinnett (pt)	16,167	6,992	9,175	-	2,183	R	43.2	56.8	-	18	2	-	8.0	6.4	9.9	-
Hart	6,764	4,885	1,879	-	3,006	D	72.2	27.8	-	1	19	-	3.4	4.5	2.0	-
Jackson	9,062	5,777	3,285	-	2,492	D	63.7	36.3	-	7	13	-	4.5	5.3	3.5	-
Lincoln	2,913	1,743	1,170	-	573	D	59.8	40.2	-	10	10	-	1.4	1.6	1.3	-
McDuffie	5,334	2,970	2,364	-	606	D	55.7	44.3	-	13	7	-	2.6	2.7	2.5	-
Madison	6,192	3,349	2,843	-	506	D	54.1	45.9	-	14	6	-	3.1	3.1	3.1	-
Morgan	4,349	2,736	1,613	-	1,123	D	62.9	37.1	-	8	12	-	2.2	2.5	1.7	-
Newton	13,185	7,421	5,764	-	1,657	D	56.3	43.7	-	12	8	-	6.5	6.8	6.2	-
Oconee	7,681	3,858	3,823	-	35	D	50.2	49.8	-	16	4	-	3.8	3.6	4.1	-
Oglethorpe	3,626	1,889	1,737	-	152	D	52.1	47.9	-	15	5	-	1.8	1.7	1.9	-
Richmond (pt)	34,653	15,945	18,708	-	2,763	R	46.0	54.0	-	17	3	-	17.2	14.7	20.1	-
Walton	10,991	6,604	4,387	-	2,217	D	60.1	39.9	-	9	11	-	5.5	6.1	4.7	-
Wilkes (pt)	2,107	1,359	748	-	611	D	64.5	35.5	-	6	14	-	1.0	1.3	0.8	-
District 11	164,400	120,168	44,221	11	75,947	D	73.1	26.9	<.1				100.0	100.0	100.0	100.0
Baldwin (pt)	6,607	3,743	2,863	1	880	D	56.7	43.3	<.1	14	9	2	4.0	3.1	6.5	9.1
Burke	6,113	3,181	2,932	0	249	D	52.0	48.0	0.0	17	6	4	3.7	2.6	6.6	0.0
Butts	4,792	2,618	2,174	0	444	D	54.6	45.4	0.0	16	7	5	2.9	2.2	4.9	0.0
Chatham (pt)	16,512	14,026	2,486	0	11,540	D	84.9	15.1	0.0	1	22	6	10.0	11.7	5.6	0.0
DeKalb (pt)	62,767	53,000	9,759	8	43,241	D	84.4	15.5	<.1	2	21	3	38.2	44.1	22.1	72.7
Effingham (pt)	254	156	98	0	58	D	61.4	38.6	0.0	10	13	7	0.2	0.1	0.2	0.0
Glascock	642	249	393	0	144	R	38.8	61.2	0.0	21	2	8	0.4	0.2	0.9	0.0
Greene	4,066	2,540	1,526	0	1,014	D	62.5	37.5	0.0	9	14	9	2.5	2.1	3.5	0.0
Hancock	2,520	2,081	439	0	1,642	D	82.6	17.4	0.0	3	20	10	1.5	1.7	1.0	0.0
Henry (pt)	4,519	1,562	2,957	0	1,395	R	34.6	65.4	0.0	22	1	11	2.7	1.3	6.7	0.0
Jasper	2,522	1,462	1,058	2	404	D	58.0	42.0	<.1	12	11	1	1.5	1.2	2.4	18.2
Jefferson	4,877	2,699	2,178	0	521	D	55.3	44.7	0.0	15	8	12	3.0	2.2	4.9	0.0
Jenkins	2,239	1,112	1,127	0	15	R	49.7	50.3	0.0	19	4	13	1.4	0.9	2.5	0.0
Putnam	4,030	2,065	1,965	0	100	D	51.2	48.8	0.0	18	5	14	2.5	1.7	4.4	0.0
Richmond (pt)	24,544	19,269	5,275	0	13,994	D	78.5	21.5	0.0	4	19	15	14.9	16.0	11.9	0.0
Screven	3,308	1,535	1,773	0	238	R	46.4	53.6	0.0	20	3	16	2.0	1.3	4.0	0.0
Taliaferro	981	732	249	0	483	D	74.6	25.4	0.0	5	18	17	0.6	0.6	0.6	0.0
Twiggs (pt)	2,531	1,801	730	0	1,071	D	71.2	28.8	0.0	6	17	18	1.5	1.5	1.7	0.0
Warren	1,543	974	569	0	405	D	63.1	36.9	0.0	8	15	19	0.9	0.8	1.3	0.0
Washington	5,218	2,971	2,247	0	724	D	56.9	43.1	0.0	13	10	20	3.2	2.5	5.1	0.0
Wilkes (pt)	1,059	726	333	0	393	D	68.6	31.4	0.0	7	16	21	0.6	0.6	0.8	0.0
Wilkinson	2,756	1,666	1,090	0	576	D	60.4	39.6	0.0	11	12	22	1.7	1.4	2.5	0.0
GEORGIA	2,213,987	1,214,792	999,182	13	215,610	D	54.9	45.1	<.1							

Table I. — Vote for Presidential Preference: March 10, 1992, Democratic Primary Election

County	Total	Clinton	Tsongas	Brown	Kerrey	Uncom-mitted	Harkin			Clinton	Tsongas	Brown	Clinton	Tsongas	Brown	Total	Clinton	Tsongas	Brown
										Percent of total vote			Rank			Percent contribution to state vote			
Appling	895	617	106	72	39	40	21	-	-	68.9	11.8	8.0	51	126	55	0.2	0.2	<.1	0.2
Atkinson	504	391	44	29	19	4	17	-	-	77.6	8.7	5.8	4	153	123	0.1	0.2	<.1	<.1
Bacon	460	326	73	18	20	16	7	-	-	70.9	15.9	3.9	32	79	153	0.1	0.1	<.1	<.1
Baker	253	169	45	19	7	4	9	-	-	66.8	17.8	7.5	71	58	63	<.1	<.1	<.1	<.1
Baldwin	2,575	1,574	466	219	155	92	69	-	-	61.1	18.1	8.5	118	54	42	0.6	0.6	0.4	0.6
Banks	845	587	108	53	56	27	14	-	-	69.5	12.8	6.3	43	118	107	0.2	0.2	<.1	0.1
Barrow	1,933	1,231	348	140	109	62	43	-	-	63.7	18.0	7.2	98	56	72	0.4	0.5	0.3	0.4
Bartow	4,017	2,557	715	273	196	190	86	-	-	63.7	17.8	6.8	99	57	88	0.9	1.0	0.7	0.7
Ben Hill	1,126	734	179	77	46	59	31	-	-	65.2	15.9	6.8	82	78	84	0.2	0.3	0.2	0.2
Berrien	818	583	115	31	31	31	27	-	-	71.3	14.1	3.8	26	104	155	0.2	0.2	0.1	<.1
Bibb	12,480	8,974	1,817	528	487	390	284	-	-	71.9	14.6	4.2	18	98	150	2.7	3.5	1.7	1.4
Bleckley	1,404	998	145	94	71	74	22	-	-	71.1	10.3	6.7	29	139	92	0.3	0.4	0.1	0.3
Brantley	728	495	81	44	50	38	20	-	-	68.0	11.1	6.0	57	131	112	0.2	0.2	<.1	0.1
Brooks	678	421	108	64	37	30	18	-	-	62.1	15.9	9.4	110	77	32	0.1	0.2	<.1	0.2
Bryan	782	489	147	47	33	55	11	-	-	62.5	18.8	6.0	107	45	113	0.2	0.2	0.1	0.1
Bulloch	1,786	1,070	385	123	87	74	47	-	-	59.9	21.6	6.9	128	28	81	0.4	0.4	0.4	0.3
Burke	1,137	789	115	132	29	37	35	-	-	69.4	10.1	11.6	44	142	9	0.3	0.3	0.1	0.4
Butts	1,675	1,095	261	113	79	88	39	-	-	65.4	15.6	6.7	80	83	90	0.4	0.4	0.2	0.3
Calhoun	501	363	65	18	14	21	20	-	-	72.5	13.0	3.6	16	113	157	0.1	0.1	<.1	<.1
Camden	1,082	601	233	108	65	31	44	-	-	55.5	21.5	10.0	144	30	22	0.2	0.2	0.2	0.3
Candler	450	306	66	29	21	20	8	-	-	68.0	14.7	6.4	55	94	101	<.1	0.1	<.1	<.1
Carroll	4,334	2,494	1,062	345	242	124	67	-	-	57.5	24.5	8.0	140	12	56	1.0	1.0	1.0	0.9
Catoosa	2,195	1,428	402	94	82	100	89	-	-	65.1	18.3	4.3	85	52	149	0.5	0.5	0.4	0.3
Charlton	864	520	122	57	54	55	56	-	-	60.2	14.1	6.6	124	102	95	0.2	0.2	0.1	0.2
Chatham	12,366	7,289	2,754	970	607	474	272	-	-	58.9	22.3	7.8	132	21	59	2.7	2.8	2.5	2.6
Chattahoochee	235	153	25	25	11	12	9	-	-	65.1	10.6	10.6	83	136	12	<.1	<.1	<.1	<.1
Chattooga	2,703	1,781	394	134	116	204	74	-	-	65.9	14.6	5.0	75	97	138	0.6	0.7	0.4	0.4
Cherokee	5,194	2,801	1,317	497	301	186	92	-	-	53.9	25.4	9.6	148	10	31	1.1	1.1	1.2	1.4
Clarke	7,537	2,537	2,807	1,299	506	144	244	-	-	33.7	37.2	17.2	159	1	2	1.7	1.0	2.6	3.5
Clay	324	237	29	19	11	16	12	-	-	73.1	9.0	5.9	12	152	118	<.1	<.1	<.1	<.1
Clayton	11,398	6,659	2,570	844	693	424	208	-	-	58.4	22.5	7.4	136	19	67	2.5	2.6	2.4	2.3
Clinch	280	176	45	29	10	11	9	-	-	62.9	16.1	10.4	104	75	14	<.1	<.1	<.1	<.1
Cobb	28,350	12,460	9,901	2,760	1,916	819	494	-	-	44.0	34.9	9.7	156	4	26	6.2	4.8	9.1	7.5
Coffee	1,468	947	273	92	68	60	28	-	-	64.5	18.6	6.3	91	46	108	0.3	0.4	0.3	0.2
Colquitt	1,717	1,108	363	104	59	48	35	-	-	64.5	21.1	6.1	90	33	111	0.4	0.4	0.3	0.3
Columbia	2,622	1,538	565	162	126	154	77	-	-	58.7	21.5	6.2	134	29	109	0.6	0.6	0.5	0.4
Cook	893	623	120	50	42	33	25	-	-	69.8	13.4	5.6	40	111	125	0.2	0.2	0.1	0.1
Coweta	3,308	1,937	734	226	227	107	77	-	-	58.6	22.2	6.8	135	25	85	0.7	0.7	0.7	0.6
Crawford	818	583	76	61	41	33	24	-	-	71.3	9.3	7.5	27	146	64	0.2	0.2	<.1	0.2
Crisp	916	596	149	75	43	34	19	-	-	65.1	16.3	8.2	84	74	49	0.2	0.2	0.1	0.2
Dade	1,372	859	211	91	65	111	35	-	-	62.6	15.4	6.6	106	87	93	0.3	0.3	0.2	0.2
Dawson	700	431	148	52	28	27	14	-	-	61.6	21.1	7.4	114	32	66	0.2	0.2	0.1	0.1
Decatur	1,166	692	186	135	70	40	43	-	-	59.3	16.0	11.6	131	76	10	0.3	0.3	0.2	0.4
DeKalb	51,426	23,108	18,160	5,458	2,298	1,560	842	-	-	44.9	35.3	10.6	154	2	13	11.3	8.9	16.6	14.8
Dodge	1,247	969	88	82	38	44	26	-	-	77.7	7.1	6.6	3	158	98	0.3	0.4	<.1	0.2
Dooly	891	636	98	72	40	24	21	-	-	71.4	11.0	8.1	25	132	54	0.2	0.2	<.1	0.2
Dougherty	6,259	3,847	1,485	284	237	247	159	-	-	61.5	23.7	4.5	115	14	145	1.4	1.5	1.4	0.8
Douglas	4,691	2,696	1,040	384	315	174	82	-	-	57.5	22.2	8.2	141	26	50	1.0	1.0	1.0	1.0
Early	853	570	150	47	34	27	25	-	-	66.8	17.6	5.5	70	62	127	0.2	0.2	0.1	0.1
Echols	120	83	12	11	8	4	2	-	-	69.2	10.0	9.2	46	143	36	<.1	<.1	<.1	<.1
Effingham	1,206	792	184	89	56	52	33	-	-	65.7	15.3	7.4	76	88	69	0.3	0.3	0.2	0.2
Elbert	1,956	1,317	250	94	82	166	47	-	-	67.3	12.8	4.8	62	119	142	0.4	0.5	0.2	0.3
Emanuel	957	659	145	51	51	24	27	-	-	68.9	15.2	5.3	52	89	132	0.2	0.3	0.1	0.1
Evans	489	345	52	35	23	27	7	-	-	70.6	10.6	7.2	34	137	73	0.1	0.1	<.1	<.1
Fannin	974	674	145	67	51	16	21	-	-	69.2	14.9	6.9	45	92	82	0.2	0.3	0.1	0.2
Fayette	4,295	1,888	1,493	435	304	112	63	-	-	44.0	34.8	10.1	155	5	19	0.9	0.7	1.4	1.2
Floyd	5,843	3,513	1,180	338	350	255	207	-	-	60.1	20.2	5.8	125	35	122	1.3	1.4	1.1	0.9
Forsyth	3,819	2,118	850	312	231	207	101	-	-	55.5	22.3	8.2	145	22	51	0.8	0.8	0.8	0.8
Franklin	2,147	1,445	255	102	84	197	64	-	-	67.3	11.9	4.8	63	123	144	0.5	0.6	0.2	0.3
Fulton	59,496	30,599	18,630	5,396	2,251	1,804	816	-	-	51.4	31.3	9.1	152	6	37	13.1	11.8	17.1	14.7
Gilmer	898	592	159	59	51	22	15	-	-	65.9	17.7	6.6	74	59	99	0.2	0.2	0.1	0.2
Glascock	97	65	10	9	2	9	2	-	-	67.0	10.3	9.3	68	140	34	<.1	<.1	<.1	<.1
Glynn	3,551	1,889	941	224	221	160	116	-	-	53.2	26.5	6.3	150	9	106	0.8	0.7	0.9	0.6
Gordon	2,214	1,384	392	153	162	78	45	-	-	62.5	17.7	6.9	108	60	80	0.5	0.5	0.4	0.4
Grady	1,219	790	188	119	41	49	32	-	-	64.8	15.4	9.8	87	86	25	0.3	0.3	0.2	0.3
Greene	1,063	757	160	59	30	33	24	-	-	71.2	15.1	5.6	28	90	126	0.2	0.3	0.1	0.2
Gwinnett	19,712	8,590	6,903	2,009	1,307	504	399	-	-	43.6	35.0	10.2	158	3	15	4.3	3.3	6.3	5.5
Habersham	1,997	1,197	387	176	114	89	34	-	-	59.9	19.4	8.8	127	43	39	0.4	0.5	0.4	0.5
Hall	6,456	3,440	1,446	437	416	590	127	-	-	53.3	22.4	6.8	149	20	89	1.4	1.3	1.3	1.2
Hancock	906	625	123	92	16	30	20	-	-	69.0	13.6	10.2	49	109	17	0.2	0.2	0.1	0.2

Table I. – Vote for Presidential Preference: March 10, 1992, Democratic Primary Election (cont)

County	Top candidates									Top three candidates (state vote)									
										Percent of total vote			Rank			Percent contribution to state vote			
	Total	Clinton	Tsongas	Brown	Kerrey	Uncom- mitted	Harkin			Clinton	Tsongas	Brown	Clinton	Tsongas	Brown	Total	Clinton	Tsongas	Brown
Haralson	1,773	1,275	260	87	89	38	24	-	-	71.9	14.7	4.9	17	95	141	0.4	0.5	0.2	0.2
Harris	1,348	859	237	137	42	44	29	-	-	63.7	17.6	10.2	97	63	16	0.3	0.3	0.2	0.4
Hart	1,296	814	221	94	72	44	51	-	-	62.8	17.1	7.3	105	65	71	0.3	0.3	0.2	0.3
Heard	966	647	125	61	51	64	18	-	-	67.0	12.9	6.3	69	115	105	0.2	0.2	0.1	0.2
Henry	3,847	2,239	855	316	223	141	73	-	-	58.2	22.2	8.2	137	23	48	0.8	0.9	0.8	0.9
Houston	7,232	4,736	1,181	368	425	357	165	-	-	65.5	16.3	5.1	78	72	136	1.6	1.8	1.1	1.0
Irwin	479	309	93	23	23	15	16	-	-	64.5	19.4	4.8	92	41	143	0.1	0.1	<.1	<.1
Jackson	2,240	1,513	372	115	98	107	35	-	-	67.5	16.6	5.1	61	66	135	0.5	0.6	0.3	0.3
Jasper	823	496	136	79	45	49	18	-	-	60.3	16.5	9.6	123	68	30	0.2	0.2	0.1	0.2
Jeff Davis	786	549	90	62	15	51	19	-	-	69.8	11.5	7.9	39	129	58	0.2	0.2	<.1	0.2
Jefferson	943	643	117	123	30	2	28	-	-	68.2	12.4	13.0	53	121	5	0.2	0.2	0.1	0.3
Jenkins	395	246	36	56	11	34	12	-	-	62.3	9.1	14.2	109	150	4	<.1	<.1	<.1	0.2
Johnson	651	510	48	26	18	37	12	-	-	78.3	7.4	4.0	1	157	152	0.1	0.2	<.1	<.1
Jones	1,699	1,217	216	121	60	48	37	-	-	71.6	12.7	7.1	24	120	74	0.4	0.5	0.2	0.3
Lamar	1,094	693	197	75	46	38	45	-	-	63.3	18.0	6.9	101	55	83	0.2	0.3	0.2	0.3
Lanier	280	181	44	15	13	16	11	-	-	64.6	15.7	5.4	88	81	131	<.1	<.1	<.1	<.1
Laurens	2,693	1,963	321	148	104	93	64	-	-	72.9	11.9	5.5	14	122	128	0.6	0.8	0.3	0.4
Lee	1,102	668	225	48	63	65	33	-	-	60.6	20.4	4.4	121	34	147	0.2	0.3	0.2	0.1
Liberty	1,357	867	225	119	45	61	40	-	-	63.9	16.6	8.8	94	67	40	0.3	0.3	0.2	0.3
Lincoln	544	386	50	41	25	29	13	-	-	71.0	9.2	7.5	31	148	62	0.1	0.1	<.1	0.2
Long	413	287	49	24	21	20	12	-	-	69.5	11.9	5.8	42	124	119	<.1	0.1	<.1	<.1
Lowndes	2,759	1,595	613	182	161	109	99	-	-	57.8	22.2	6.6	139	24	96	0.6	0.6	0.6	0.5
Lumpkin	1,586	862	361	118	90	125	30	-	-	54.4	22.8	7.4	147	17	65	0.3	0.3	0.3	0.3
McDuffie	2,428	1,539	288	200	98	214	89	-	-	63.4	11.9	8.2	100	125	47	0.5	0.6	0.3	0.5
McIntosh	779	447	144	77	31	59	21	-	-	57.4	18.5	9.9	142	48	24	0.2	0.2	0.1	0.2
Macon	1,041	699	135	128	32	19	28	-	-	67.1	13.0	12.3	65	114	7	0.2	0.3	0.1	0.3
Madison	1,322	789	241	124	68	62	38	-	-	59.7	18.2	9.4	129	53	33	0.3	0.3	0.2	0.3
Marion	525	362	72	46	15	23	7	-	-	69.0	13.7	8.8	50	106	41	0.1	0.1	<.1	0.1
Meriwether	1,829	1,300	251	97	83	65	33	-	-	71.1	13.7	5.3	30	105	133	0.4	0.5	0.2	0.3
Miller	354	254	32	19	31	11	7	-	-	71.8	9.0	5.4	21	151	130	<.1	<.1	<.1	<.1
Mitchell	1,352	933	223	67	42	40	47	-	-	69.0	16.5	5.0	48	70	139	0.3	0.4	0.2	0.2
Monroe	1,321	900	207	79	55	42	38	-	-	68.1	15.7	6.0	54	82	114	0.3	0.3	0.2	0.2
Montgomery	507	344	48	22	30	49	14	-	-	67.9	9.5	4.3	58	145	148	0.1	0.1	<.1	<.1
Morgan	1,503	897	288	95	88	112	23	-	-	59.7	19.2	6.3	130	44	104	0.3	0.3	0.3	0.3
Murray	1,368	874	239	77	57	92	29	-	-	63.9	17.5	5.6	95	64	124	0.3	0.3	0.2	0.2
Muscogee	11,549	8,498	1,662	485	369	312	223	-	-	73.6	14.4	4.2	11	99	151	2.5	3.3	1.5	1.3
Newton	3,883	2,373	777	232	199	228	74	-	-	61.1	20.0	6.0	119	36	115	0.9	0.9	0.7	0.6
Oconee	1,596	700	488	196	129	59	24	-	-	43.9	30.6	12.3	157	7	8	0.4	0.3	0.4	0.5
Oglethorpe	835	476	195	81	38	26	19	-	-	57.0	23.4	9.7	143	15	27	0.2	0.2	0.2	0.2
Paulding	2,720	1,736	537	149	170	70	58	-	-	63.8	19.7	5.5	96	37	129	0.6	0.7	0.5	0.4
Peach	2,226	1,595	249	181	78	71	52	-	-	71.7	11.2	8.1	23	130	53	0.5	0.6	0.2	0.5
Pickens	1,537	969	284	125	75	61	23	-	-	63.0	18.5	8.1	102	49	52	0.3	0.4	0.3	0.3
Pierce	818	554	105	57	35	42	25	-	-	67.7	12.8	7.0	60	116	78	0.2	0.2	<.1	0.2
Pike	846	568	124	65	28	43	18	-	-	67.1	14.7	7.7	66	96	61	0.2	0.2	0.1	0.2
Polk	2,653	1,874	392	161	119	67	40	-	-	70.6	14.8	6.1	33	93	110	0.6	0.7	0.4	0.4
Pulaski	793	595	93	47	34	16	8	-	-	75.0	11.7	5.9	8	127	116	0.2	0.2	<.1	0.1
Putnam	1,057	710	150	84	57	33	23	-	-	67.2	14.2	7.9	64	101	57	0.2	0.3	0.1	0.2
Quitman	158	110	15	16	6	7	4	-	-	69.6	9.5	10.1	41	144	20	<.1	<.1	<.1	<.1
Rabun	1,444	908	284	102	56	73	21	-	-	62.9	19.7	7.1	103	39	75	0.3	0.3	0.3	0.3
Randolph	725	509	102	51	22	21	20	-	-	70.2	14.1	7.0	35	103	76	0.2	0.2	<.1	0.1
Richmond	7,856	5,272	1,297	534	264	311	178	-	-	67.1	16.5	6.8	67	69	87	1.7	2.0	1.2	1.5
Rockdale	4,104	2,013	1,162	339	267	239	84	-	-	49.0	28.3	8.3	153	8	46	0.9	0.8	1.1	0.9
Schley	306	202	54	27	11	8	4	-	-	66.0	17.6	8.8	73	61	38	<.1	<.1	<.1	<.1
Screven	801	533	109	77	33	26	23	-	-	66.5	13.6	9.6	72	108	29	0.2	0.2	<.1	0.2
Seminole	570	409	78	33	19	15	16	-	-	71.8	13.7	5.8	20	107	121	0.1	0.2	<.1	<.1
Spalding	3,500	2,141	753	242	161	128	75	-	-	61.2	21.5	6.9	117	31	79	0.8	0.8	0.7	0.7
Stephens	2,336	1,411	383	171	104	196	71	-	-	60.4	16.4	7.3	122	71	70	0.5	0.5	0.4	0.5
Stewart	848	440	59	309	17	7	16	-	-	51.9	7.0	36.4	151	159	1	0.2	0.2	<.1	0.8
Sumter	1,749	1,015	429	146	48	89	22	-	-	58.0	24.5	8.3	138	11	45	0.4	0.4	0.4	0.4
Talbot	660	473	71	67	24	14	11	-	-	71.7	10.8	10.2	22	134	18	0.1	0.2	<.1	0.2
Taliaferro	166	126	17	11	6	0	6	-	-	75.9	10.2	6.6	5	141	94	<.1	<.1	<.1	<.1
Tattnall	1,000	680	128	85	40	43	24	-	-	68.0	12.8	8.5	56	117	43	0.2	0.3	0.1	0.2
Taylor	661	483	69	51	18	32	8	-	-	73.1	10.4	7.7	13	138	60	0.1	0.2	<.1	0.1
Telfair	825	577	109	70	29	20	20	-	-	69.9	13.2	8.5	38	112	44	0.2	0.2	<.1	0.2
Terrell	657	401	144	74	19	7	12	-	-	61.0	21.9	11.3	120	27	11	0.2	0.2	0.1	0.2
Thomas	1,582	930	358	101	71	76	46	-	-	58.8	22.6	6.4	133	18	103	0.3	0.4	0.3	0.3
Tift	1,858	1,206	341	125	83	66	37	-	-	64.9	18.4	6.7	86	50	91	0.4	0.5	0.3	0.3
Toombs	1,055	690	164	74	49	55	23	-	-	65.4	15.5	7.0	79	84	77	0.2	0.3	0.2	0.2
Towns	640	396	126	41	49	21	7	-	-	61.9	19.7	6.4	111	38	102	0.1	0.2	0.1	0.1
Treutlen	400	301	43	13	12	24	7	-	-	75.3	10.8	3.3	6	135	158	<.1	0.1	<.1	<.1

Table I. — Vote for Presidential Preference: March 10, 1992, Democratic Primary Election (cont)

| County | Top candidates | | | | | | | | | Top three candidates(state vote) | | | | | | | | |
| | | | | | | | | | | Percent of total vote | | | | Rank | | Percent contribution to state vote | | |
	Total	Clinton	Tsongas	Brown	Kerrey	Uncom-mitted	Harkin			Clinton	Tsongas	Brown	Clinton	Tsongas	Brown	Total	Clinton	Tsongas	Brown
Troup	2,626	1,624	602	129	112	125	34	-	-	61.8	22.9	4.9	112	16	140	0.6	0.6	0.6	0.4
Turner	546	402	78	24	12	19	11	-	-	73.6	14.3	4.4	10	100	146	0.1	0.2	<.1	<.1
Twiggs	896	666	82	59	30	39	20	-	-	74.3	9.2	6.6	9	149	97	0.2	0.3	<.1	0.2
Union	1,202	738	223	89	76	55	21	-	-	61.4	18.6	7.4	116	47	68	0.3	0.3	0.2	0.2
Upson	1,661	1,194	271	63	54	59	20	-	-	71.9	16.3	3.8	19	73	154	0.4	0.5	0.2	0.2
Walker	2,815	1,840	516	148	131	104	76	-	-	65.4	18.3	5.3	81	51	134	0.6	0.7	0.5	0.4
Walton	3,450	2,133	669	224	149	199	76	-	-	61.8	19.4	6.5	113	42	100	0.8	0.8	0.6	0.6
Ware	2,277	1,494	341	155	76	125	86	-	-	65.6	15.0	6.8	77	91	86	0.5	0.6	0.3	0.4
Warren	506	324	55	66	14	32	15	-	-	64.0	10.9	13.0	93	133	6	0.1	0.1	<.1	0.2
Washington	1,691	1,187	197	170	46	60	31	-	-	70.2	11.6	10.1	36	128	21	0.4	0.5	0.2	0.5
Wayne	1,469	996	198	54	67	73	81	-	-	67.8	13.5	3.7	59	110	156	0.3	0.4	0.2	0.1
Webster	227	159	21	21	10	10	6	-	-	70.0	9.3	9.3	37	147	35	<.1	<.1	<.1	<.1
Wheeler	265	183	22	40	5	14	1	-	-	69.1	8.3	15.1	47	155	3	<.1	<.1	<.1	0.1
White	1,446	786	282	140	100	112	26	-	-	54.4	19.5	9.7	146	40	28	0.3	0.3	0.3	0.4
Whitfield	3,029	1,821	738	176	110	108	76	-	-	60.1	24.4	5.8	126	13	120	0.7	0.7	0.7	0.5
Wilcox	643	483	53	32	27	28	20	-	-	75.1	8.2	5.0	7	156	137	0.1	0.2	<.1	<.1
Wilkes	724	468	112	72	23	31	18	-	-	64.6	15.5	9.9	89	85	23	0.2	0.2	0.1	0.2
Wilkinson	1,253	975	109	74	30	39	26	-	-	77.8	8.7	5.9	2	154	117	0.3	0.4	<.1	0.2
Worth	1,185	860	187	35	40	40	23	-	-	72.6	15.8	3.0	15	80	159	0.3	0.3	0.2	<.1
GEORGIA	**454,631**	**259,907**	**109,148**	**36,808**	**22,033**	**17,256**	**9,479**	**-**	**-**	**57.2**	**24.0**	**8.1**				**100.0**	**100.0**	**100.0**	**100.0**

Georgia 231

Table J. — Vote for Presidential Preference: March 10, 1992, Republican Primary Election

| County | Top candidates | | | | | Top four candidates (state vote) | | | | | | | | Percent contribution to state vote | | | | |
| | | | | | | Percent of total vote | | | | Rank | | | | | | | | |
	Total	Bush	Bu-chanan			Bush	Bu-chanan			Bush	Bu-chanan			Total	Bush	Bu-chanan		
Appling	820	465	355	-	-	56.7	43.3	-	-	115	45	-	-	0.2	0.2	0.2	-	-
Atkinson	262	157	105	-	-	59.9	40.1	-	-	90	70	-	-	<.1	<.1	<.1	-	-
Bacon	405	223	182	-	-	55.1	44.9	-	-	124	36	-	-	<.1	<.1	0.1	-	-
Baker	153	85	68	-	-	55.6	44.4	-	-	120	39	-	-	<.1	<.1	<.1	-	-
Baldwin	2,305	1,354	951	-	-	58.7	41.3	-	-	100	60	-	-	0.5	0.5	0.6	-	-
Banks	561	358	203	-	-	63.8	36.2	-	-	54	106	-	-	0.1	0.1	0.1	-	-
Barrow	1,973	1,192	781	-	-	60.4	39.6	-	-	87	73	-	-	0.4	0.4	0.5	-	-
Bartow	3,280	2,209	1,071	-	-	67.3	32.7	-	-	21	139	-	-	0.7	0.8	0.7	-	-
Ben Hill	849	414	435	-	-	48.8	51.2	-	-	149	11	-	-	0.2	0.1	0.3	-	-
Berrien	522	294	228	-	-	56.3	43.7	-	-	117	43	-	-	0.1	0.1	0.1	-	-
Bibb	10,139	5,621	4,518	-	-	55.4	44.6	-	-	122	38	-	-	2.2	1.9	2.8	-	-
Bleckley	1,160	586	574	-	-	50.5	49.5	-	-	142	18	-	-	0.3	0.2	0.4	-	-
Brantley	433	235	198	-	-	54.3	45.7	-	-	130	30	-	-	<.1	<.1	0.1	-	-
Brooks	563	341	222	-	-	60.6	39.4	-	-	85	75	-	-	0.1	0.1	0.1	-	-
Bryan	1,067	702	365	-	-	65.8	34.2	-	-	34	126	-	-	0.2	0.2	0.2	-	-
Bulloch	2,338	1,456	882	-	-	62.3	37.7	-	-	72	88	-	-	0.5	0.5	0.5	-	-
Burke	1,092	600	492	-	-	54.9	45.1	-	-	126	34	-	-	0.2	0.2	0.3	-	-
Butts	1,112	774	338	-	-	69.6	30.4	-	-	8	152	-	-	0.2	0.3	0.2	-	-
Calhoun	193	96	97	-	-	49.7	50.3	-	-	147	13	-	-	<.1	<.1	<.1	-	-
Camden	1,062	628	434	-	-	59.1	40.9	-	-	97	63	-	-	0.2	0.2	0.3	-	-
Candler	459	269	190	-	-	58.6	41.4	-	-	102	58	-	-	0.1	<.1	0.1	-	-
Carroll	4,672	3,055	1,617	-	-	65.4	34.6	-	-	39	121	-	-	1.0	1.0	1.0	-	-
Catoosa	2,761	1,695	1,066	-	-	61.4	38.6	-	-	77	83	-	-	0.6	0.6	0.7	-	-
Charlton	522	332	190	-	-	63.6	36.4	-	-	57	103	-	-	0.1	0.1	0.1	-	-
Chatham	18,124	12,797	5,327	-	-	70.6	29.4	-	-	5	155	-	-	4.0	4.4	3.3	-	-
Chattahoochee	134	64	70	-	-	47.8	52.2	-	-	153	7	-	-	<.1	<.1	<.1	-	-
Chattooga	1,688	1,127	561	-	-	66.8	33.2	-	-	26	134	-	-	0.4	0.4	0.3	-	-
Cherokee	8,512	5,617	2,895	-	-	66.0	34.0	-	-	32	128	-	-	1.9	1.9	1.8	-	-
Clarke	4,579	2,997	1,582	-	-	65.5	34.5	-	-	38	122	-	-	1.0	1.0	1.0	-	-
Clay	108	54	54	-	-	50.0	50.0	-	-	144	16	-	-	<.1	<.1	<.1	-	-
Clayton	12,078	7,575	4,503	-	-	62.7	37.3	-	-	65	95	-	-	2.7	2.6	2.8	-	-
Clinch	147	90	57	-	-	61.2	38.8	-	-	79	81	-	-	<.1	<.1	<.1	-	-
Cobb	45,385	30,400	14,985	-	-	67.0	33.0	-	-	23	137	-	-	10.0	10.4	9.2	-	-
Coffee	1,169	671	498	-	-	57.4	42.6	-	-	112	48	-	-	0.3	0.2	0.3	-	-
Colquitt	1,522	964	558	-	-	63.3	36.7	-	-	60	100	-	-	0.3	0.3	0.3	-	-
Columbia	6,648	3,546	3,102	-	-	53.3	46.7	-	-	133	27	-	-	1.5	1.2	1.9	-	-
Cook	496	321	175	-	-	64.7	35.3	-	-	42	118	-	-	0.1	0.1	0.1	-	-
Coweta	4,723	2,886	1,837	-	-	61.1	38.9	-	-	81	79	-	-	1.0	1.0	1.1	-	-
Crawford	507	216	291	-	-	42.6	57.4	-	-	158	2	-	-	0.1	<.1	0.2	-	-
Crisp	798	461	337	-	-	57.8	42.2	-	-	108	52	-	-	0.2	0.2	0.2	-	-
Dade	1,387	935	452	-	-	67.4	32.6	-	-	19	141	-	-	0.3	0.3	0.3	-	-
Dawson	721	443	278	-	-	61.4	38.6	-	-	76	84	-	-	0.2	0.2	0.2	-	-
Decatur	1,069	700	369	-	-	65.5	34.5	-	-	36	124	-	-	0.2	0.2	0.2	-	-
DeKalb	37,850	26,305	11,545	-	-	69.5	30.5	-	-	9	151	-	-	8.3	9.0	7.1	-	-
Dodge	913	385	528	-	-	42.2	57.8	-	-	159	1	-	-	0.2	0.1	0.3	-	-
Dooly	445	231	214	-	-	51.9	48.1	-	-	138	22	-	-	<.1	<.1	0.1	-	-
Dougherty	5,859	3,995	1,864	-	-	68.2	31.8	-	-	17	143	-	-	1.3	1.4	1.2	-	-
Douglas	6,090	3,825	2,265	-	-	62.8	37.2	-	-	62	98	-	-	1.3	1.3	1.4	-	-
Early	626	361	265	-	-	57.7	42.3	-	-	109	51	-	-	0.1	0.1	0.2	-	-
Echols	56	40	16	-	-	71.4	28.6	-	-	3	157	-	-	<.1	<.1	<.1	-	-
Effingham	1,510	1,011	499	-	-	67.0	33.0	-	-	24	136	-	-	0.3	0.3	0.3	-	-
Elbert	1,159	781	378	-	-	67.4	32.6	-	-	20	140	-	-	0.3	0.3	0.2	-	-
Emanuel	931	513	418	-	-	55.1	44.9	-	-	123	37	-	-	0.2	0.2	0.3	-	-
Evans	525	327	198	-	-	62.3	37.7	-	-	71	89	-	-	0.1	0.1	0.1	-	-
Fannin	1,456	1,027	429	-	-	70.5	29.5	-	-	6	154	-	-	0.3	0.4	0.3	-	-
Fayette	9,022	5,968	3,054	-	-	66.1	33.9	-	-	30	130	-	-	2.0	2.0	1.9	-	-
Floyd	5,515	3,661	1,854	-	-	66.4	33.6	-	-	29	131	-	-	1.2	1.3	1.1	-	-
Forsyth	4,707	3,179	1,528	-	-	67.5	32.5	-	-	18	142	-	-	1.0	1.1	0.9	-	-
Franklin	1,320	882	438	-	-	66.8	33.2	-	-	25	135	-	-	0.3	0.3	0.3	-	-
Fulton	38,799	28,003	10,796	-	-	72.2	27.8	-	-	2	158	-	-	8.5	9.6	6.7	-	-
Gilmer	1,393	694	699	-	-	49.8	50.2	-	-	146	14	-	-	0.3	0.2	0.4	-	-
Glascock	184	103	81	-	-	56.0	44.0	-	-	119	41	-	-	<.1	<.1	<.1	-	-
Glynn	5,178	3,229	1,949	-	-	62.4	37.6	-	-	70	90	-	-	1.1	1.1	1.2	-	-
Gordon	2,064	1,328	736	-	-	64.3	35.7	-	-	46	114	-	-	0.5	0.5	0.5	-	-
Grady	833	506	327	-	-	60.7	39.3	-	-	83	77	-	-	0.2	0.2	0.2	-	-
Greene	547	373	174	-	-	68.2	31.8	-	-	16	144	-	-	0.1	0.1	0.1	-	-
Gwinnett	34,772	23,148	11,624	-	-	66.6	33.4	-	-	28	132	-	-	7.7	7.9	7.2	-	-
Habersham	1,697	1,078	619	-	-	63.5	36.5	-	-	59	101	-	-	0.4	0.4	0.4	-	-
Hall	6,519	4,478	2,041	-	-	68.7	31.3	-	-	15	145	-	-	1.4	1.5	1.3	-	-
Hancock	201	119	82	-	-	59.2	40.8	-	-	96	64	-	-	<.1	<.1	<.1	-	-

County	Top candidates					Top four candidates (state vote)											
						Percent of total vote								Percent contribution to state vote			
									Rank								
	Total	Bush	Bu-chanan			Bush	Bu-chanan			Bush	Bu-chanan			Total	Bush	Bu-chanan	
Haralson	1,388	815	573	-	-	58.7	41.3	-	-	101	59	-	-	0.3	0.3	0.4	-	-
Harris	1,488	960	528	-	-	64.5	35.5	-	-	44	116	-	-	0.3	0.3	0.3	-	-
Hart	881	561	320	-	-	63.7	36.3	-	-	56	104	-	-	0.2	0.2	0.2	-	-
Heard	642	378	264	-	-	58.9	41.1	-	-	99	61	-	-	0.1	0.1	0.2	-	-
Henry	5,659	3,438	2,221	-	-	60.8	39.2	-	-	82	78	-	-	1.2	1.2	1.4	-	-
Houston	7,629	3,686	3,943	-	-	48.3	51.7	-	-	150	10	-	-	1.7	1.3	2.4	-	-
Irwin	373	186	187	-	-	49.9	50.1	-	-	145	15	-	-	<.1	<.1	0.1	-	-
Jackson	1,768	1,132	636	-	-	64.0	36.0	-	-	50	110	-	-	0.4	0.4	0.4	-	-
Jasper	661	415	246	-	-	62.8	37.2	-	-	63	97	-	-	0.1	0.1	0.2	-	-
Jeff Davis	507	256	251	-	-	50.5	49.5	-	-	143	17	-	-	0.1	<.1	0.2	-	-
Jefferson	870	488	382	-	-	56.1	43.9	-	-	118	42	-	-	0.2	0.2	0.2	-	-
Jenkins	350	151	199	-	-	43.1	56.9	-	-	157	3	-	-	<.1	<.1	0.1	-	-
Johnson	550	291	259	-	-	52.9	47.1	-	-	134	26	-	-	0.1	<.1	0.2	-	-
Jones	1,389	712	677	-	-	51.3	48.7	-	-	141	19	-	-	0.3	0.2	0.4	-	-
Lamar	972	563	409	-	-	57.9	42.1	-	-	106	54	-	-	0.2	0.2	0.3	-	-
Lanier	160	110	50	-	-	68.8	31.3	-	-	14	146	-	-	<.1	<.1	<.1	-	-
Laurens	2,247	1,290	957	-	-	57.4	42.6	-	-	111	49	-	-	0.5	0.4	0.6	-	-
Lee	1,284	824	460	-	-	64.2	35.8	-	-	49	111	-	-	0.3	0.3	0.3	-	-
Liberty	1,233	829	404	-	-	67.2	32.8	-	-	22	138	-	-	0.3	0.3	0.2	-	-
Lincoln	553	327	226	-	-	59.1	40.9	-	-	98	62	-	-	0.1	0.1	0.1	-	-
Long	238	146	92	-	-	61.3	38.7	-	-	78	82	-	-	<.1	<.1	<.1	-	-
Lowndes	3,328	2,002	1,326	-	-	60.2	39.8	-	-	89	71	-	-	0.7	0.7	0.8	-	-
Lumpkin	1,092	722	370	-	-	66.1	33.9	-	-	31	129	-	-	0.2	0.2	0.2	-	-
McDuffie	2,385	1,525	860	-	-	63.9	36.1	-	-	52	108	-	-	0.5	0.5	0.5	-	-
McIntosh	415	242	173	-	-	58.3	41.7	-	-	103	57	-	-	<.1	<.1	0.1	-	-
Macon	504	304	200	-	-	60.3	39.7	-	-	88	72	-	-	0.1	0.1	0.1	-	-
Madison	1,303	834	469	-	-	64.0	36.0	-	-	51	109	-	-	0.3	0.3	0.3	-	-
Marion	299	181	118	-	-	60.5	39.5	-	-	86	74	-	-	<.1	<.1	<.1	-	-
Meriwether	1,221	787	434	-	-	64.5	35.5	-	-	45	115	-	-	0.3	0.3	0.3	-	-
Miller	250	149	101	-	-	59.6	40.4	-	-	93	67	-	-	<.1	<.1	<.1	-	-
Mitchell	678	411	267	-	-	60.6	39.4	-	-	84	76	-	-	0.1	0.1	0.2	-	-
Monroe	1,215	675	540	-	-	55.6	44.4	-	-	121	40	-	-	0.3	0.2	0.3	-	-
Montgomery	381	207	174	-	-	54.3	45.7	-	-	129	31	-	-	<.1	<.1	0.1	-	-
Morgan	1,096	760	336	-	-	69.3	30.7	-	-	11	149	-	-	0.2	0.3	0.2	-	-
Murray	1,098	675	423	-	-	61.5	38.5	-	-	75	85	-	-	0.2	0.2	0.3	-	-
Muscogee	10,877	7,521	3,356	-	-	69.1	30.9	-	-	13	147	-	-	2.4	2.6	2.1	-	-
Newton	3,653	2,531	1,122	-	-	69.3	30.7	-	-	12	148	-	-	0.8	0.9	0.7	-	-
Oconee	1,872	1,230	642	-	-	65.7	34.3	-	-	35	125	-	-	0.4	0.4	0.4	-	-
Oglethorpe	781	542	239	-	-	69.4	30.6	-	-	10	150	-	-	0.2	0.2	0.1	-	-
Paulding	2,743	1,718	1,025	-	-	62.6	37.4	-	-	67	93	-	-	0.6	0.6	0.6	-	-
Peach	1,435	645	790	-	-	44.9	55.1	-	-	154	6	-	-	0.3	0.2	0.5	-	-
Pickens	1,775	1,128	647	-	-	63.5	36.5	-	-	58	102	-	-	0.4	0.4	0.4	-	-
Pierce	500	275	225	-	-	55.0	45.0	-	-	125	35	-	-	0.1	<.1	0.1	-	-
Pike	944	559	385	-	-	59.2	40.8	-	-	95	65	-	-	0.2	0.2	0.2	-	-
Polk	1,895	1,210	685	-	-	63.9	36.1	-	-	53	107	-	-	0.4	0.4	0.4	-	-
Pulaski	516	227	289	-	-	44.0	56.0	-	-	156	4	-	-	0.1	<.1	0.2	-	-
Putnam	818	445	373	-	-	54.4	45.6	-	-	128	32	-	-	0.2	0.2	0.2	-	-
Quitman	94	70	24	-	-	74.5	25.5	-	-	1	159	-	-	<.1	<.1	<.1	-	-
Rabun	993	655	338	-	-	66.0	34.0	-	-	33	127	-	-	0.2	0.2	0.2	-	-
Randolph	348	187	161	-	-	53.7	46.3	-	-	131	29	-	-	<.1	<.1	<.1	-	-
Richmond	11,187	5,805	5,382	-	-	51.9	48.1	-	-	139	21	-	-	2.5	2.0	3.3	-	-
Rockdale	6,348	4,233	2,115	-	-	66.7	33.3	-	-	27	133	-	-	1.4	1.5	1.3	-	-
Schley	263	152	111	-	-	57.8	42.2	-	-	107	53	-	-	<.1	<.1	<.1	-	-
Screven	809	503	306	-	-	62.2	37.8	-	-	73	87	-	-	0.2	0.2	0.2	-	-
Seminole	314	202	112	-	-	64.3	35.7	-	-	47	113	-	-	<.1	<.1	<.1	-	-
Spalding	3,693	2,315	1,378	-	-	62.7	37.3	-	-	66	94	-	-	0.8	0.8	0.9	-	-
Stephens	1,624	1,036	588	-	-	63.8	36.2	-	-	55	105	-	-	0.4	0.4	0.4	-	-
Stewart	267	167	100	-	-	62.5	37.5	-	-	68	92	-	-	<.1	<.1	<.1	-	-
Sumter	1,478	779	699	-	-	52.7	47.3	-	-	135	25	-	-	0.3	0.3	0.4	-	-
Talbot	299	192	107	-	-	64.2	35.8	-	-	48	112	-	-	<.1	<.1	<.1	-	-
Taliaferro	82	53	29	-	-	64.6	35.4	-	-	43	117	-	-	<.1	<.1	<.1	-	-
Tattnall	838	528	310	-	-	63.0	37.0	-	-	61	99	-	-	0.2	0.2	0.2	-	-
Taylor	431	236	195	-	-	54.8	45.2	-	-	127	33	-	-	<.1	<.1	0.1	-	-
Telfair	518	250	268	-	-	48.3	51.7	-	-	151	9	-	-	0.1	<.1	0.2	-	-
Terrell	510	296	214	-	-	58.0	42.0	-	-	105	55	-	-	0.1	0.1	0.1	-	-
Thomas	1,744	1,132	612	-	-	64.9	35.1	-	-	40	120	-	-	0.4	0.4	0.4	-	-
Tift	1,860	1,162	698	-	-	62.5	37.5	-	-	69	91	-	-	0.4	0.4	0.4	-	-
Toombs	1,357	777	580	-	-	57.3	42.7	-	-	113	47	-	-	0.3	0.3	0.4	-	-
Towns	506	361	145	-	-	71.3	28.7	-	-	4	156	-	-	0.1	0.1	<.1	-	-
Treutlen	325	184	141	-	-	56.6	43.4	-	-	116	44	-	-	<.1	<.1	<.1	-	-

County	Top candidates					Top four candidates (state vote)												
						Percent of total vote				Rank				Percent contribution to state vote				
	Total	Bush	Bu-chanan			Bush	Bu-chanan			Bush	Bu-chanan			Total	Bush	Bu-chanan		
Troup	3,495	1,674	1,821	-	-	47.9	52.1	-	-	152	8	-	-	0.8	0.6	1.1	-	-
Turner	281	139	142	-	-	49.5	50.5	-	-	148	12	-	-	<.1	<.1	<.1	-	-
Twiggs	417	223	194	-	-	53.5	46.5	-	-	132	28	-	-	<.1	<.1	0.1	-	-
Union	796	521	275	-	-	65.5	34.5	-	-	37	123	-	-	0.2	0.2	0.2	-	-
Upson	1,729	997	732	-	-	57.7	42.3	-	-	110	50	-	-	0.4	0.3	0.5	-	-
Walker	3,088	1,829	1,259	-	-	59.2	40.8	-	-	94	66	-	-	0.7	0.6	0.8	-	-
Walton	3,153	2,046	1,107	-	-	64.9	35.1	-	-	41	119	-	-	0.7	0.7	0.7	-	-
Ware	1,781	1,104	677	-	-	62.0	38.0	-	-	74	86	-	-	0.4	0.4	0.4	-	-
Warren	364	212	152	-	-	58.2	41.8	-	-	104	56	-	-	<.1	<.1	<.1	-	-
Washington	1,101	658	443	-	-	59.8	40.2	-	-	91	69	-	-	0.2	0.2	0.3	-	-
Wayne	1,117	666	451	-	-	59.6	40.4	-	-	92	68	-	-	0.2	0.2	0.3	-	-
Webster	124	64	60	-	-	51.6	48.4	-	-	140	20	-	-	<.1	<.1	<.1	-	-
Wheeler	177	92	85	-	-	52.0	48.0	-	-	137	23	-	-	<.1	<.1	<.1	-	-
White	1,261	880	381	-	-	69.8	30.2	-	-	7	153	-	-	0.3	0.3	0.2	-	-
Whitfield	3,987	2,438	1,549	-	-	61.1	38.9	-	-	80	80	-	-	0.9	0.8	1.0	-	-
Wilcox	362	162	200	-	-	44.8	55.2	-	-	155	5	-	-	<.1	<.1	0.1	-	-
Wilkes	561	352	209	-	-	62.7	37.3	-	-	64	96	-	-	0.1	0.1	0.1	-	-
Wilkinson	634	333	301	-	-	52.5	47.5	-	-	136	24	-	-	0.1	0.1	0.2	-	-
Worth	1,089	622	467	-	-	57.1	42.9	-	-	114	46	-	-	0.2	0.2	0.3	-	-
GEORGIA	453,990	291,905	162,085	-	-	64.3	35.7	-	-					100.0	100.0	100.0	-	-

1992 Vote for President
Percent for Clinton (D), by County

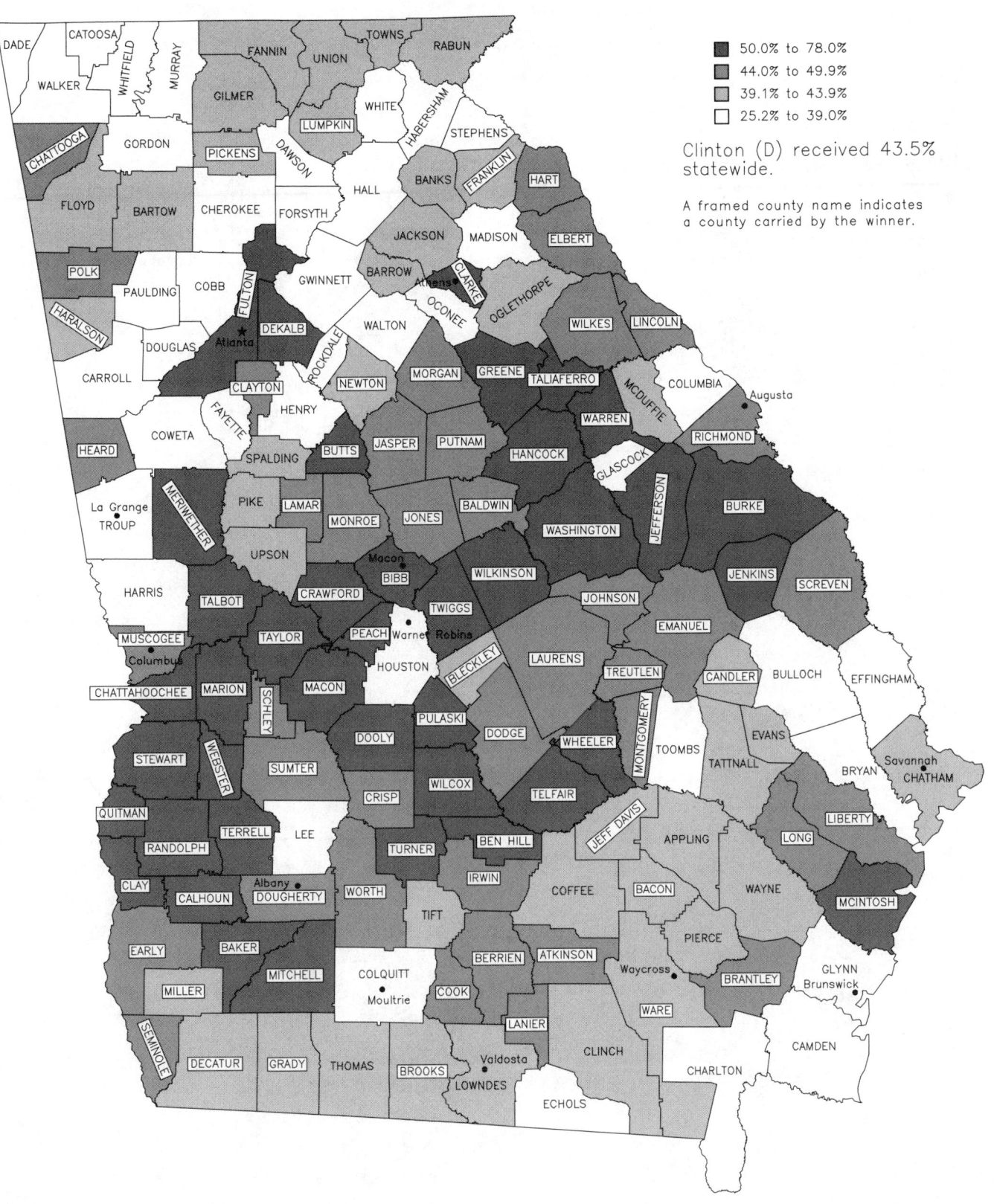

■	50.0% to 78.0%
▨	44.0% to 49.9%
▨	39.1% to 43.9%
☐	25.2% to 39.0%

Clinton (D) received 43.5% statewide.

A framed county name indicates a county carried by the winner.

Georgia 235

1992 Vote for U.S. Senator
Percent for Fowler*(D), by County

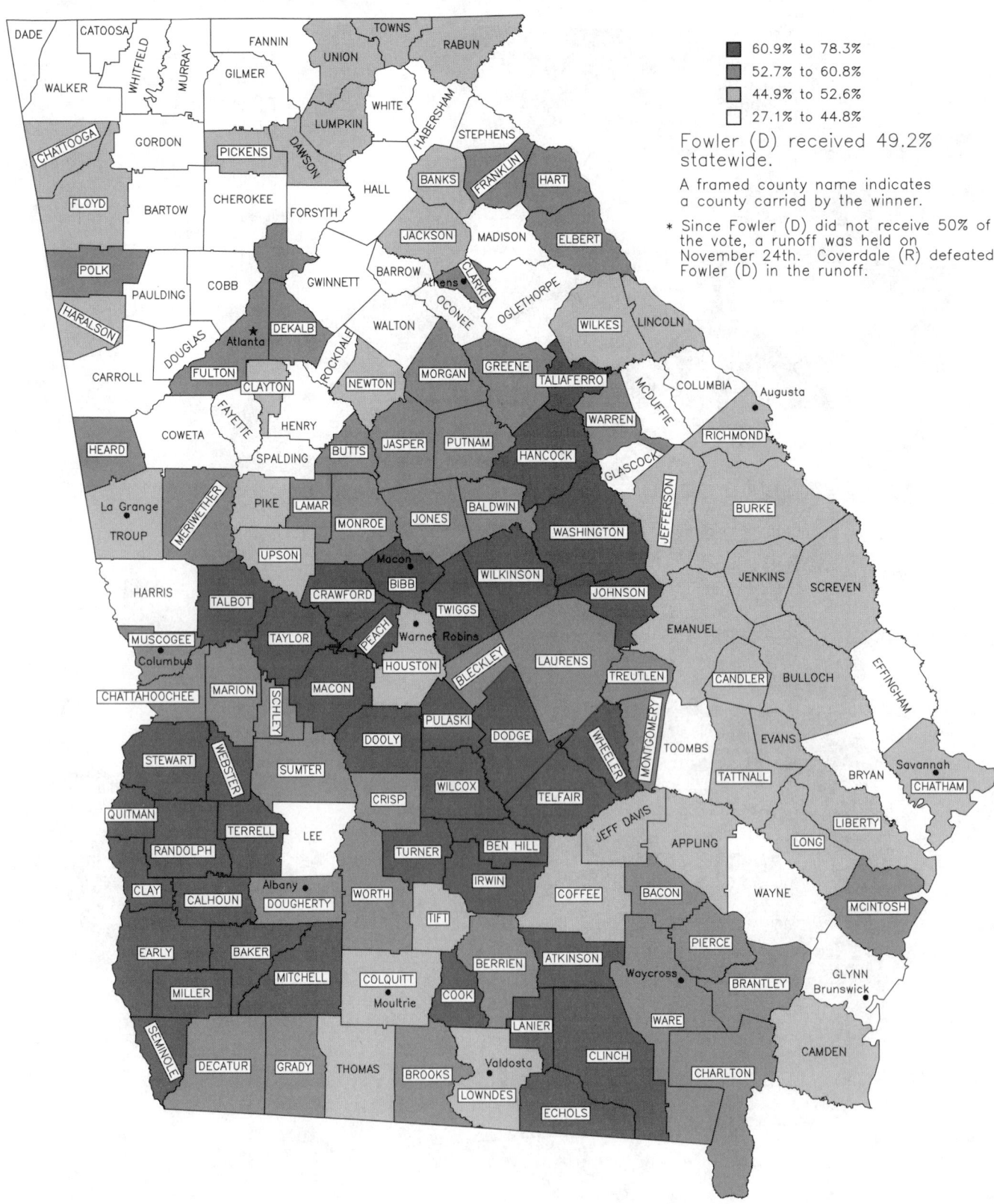

Legend:
- 60.9% to 78.3%
- 52.7% to 60.8%
- 44.9% to 52.6%
- 27.1% to 44.8%

Fowler (D) received 49.2% statewide.

A framed county name indicates a county carried by the winner.

* Since Fowler (D) did not receive 50% of the vote, a runoff was held on November 24th. Coverdale (R) defeated Fowler (D) in the runoff.

1992 Vote for U.S. Senator*
Percent for Coverdale (R), by County

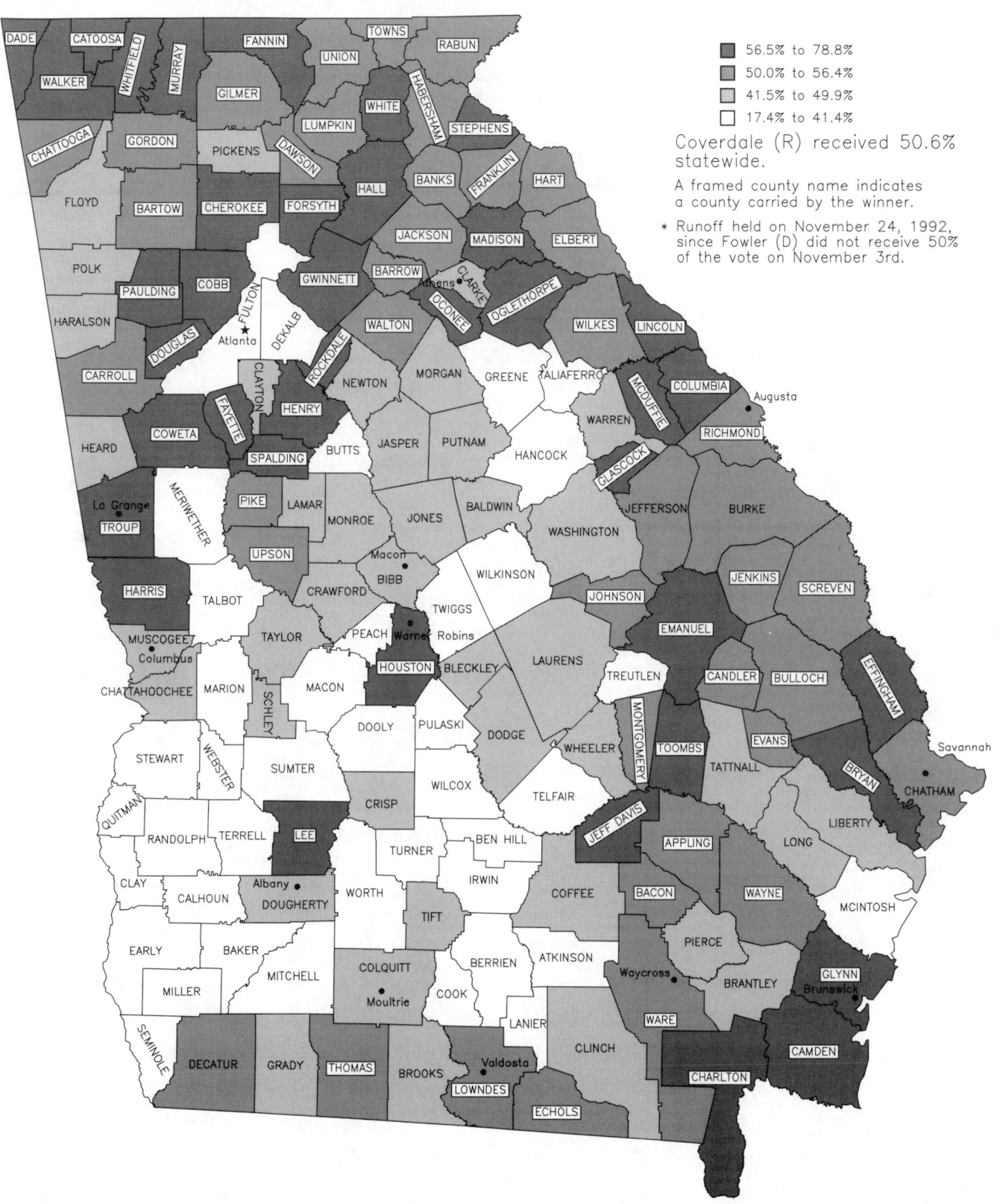

Legend:
- 56.5% to 78.8%
- 50.0% to 56.4%
- 41.5% to 49.9%
- 17.4% to 41.4%

Coverdale (R) received 50.6% statewide.

A framed county name indicates a county carried by the winner.

* Runoff held on November 24, 1992, since Fowler (D) did not receive 50% of the vote on November 3rd.

HAWAII

Alternative Registration Methods:
    Agency-based, Deputized Registrars, Mail-in, Motor-voter

Registration Deadline (Days before Election) 30

Voting Equipment Use (Counties)[1]

Datavote Punch Card	4	Paper Ballot	0
Electronic	0	Other Punch Card	0
Lever Machine	0	Mixed Systems	0
Optical Scanner	0		

Party Control	DEM	REP	IND	VAC
1993 State Senate	22	3	0	0
1992 State Senate	22	3	0	0
1993 State House	47	4	0	0
1992 State House	45	6	0	0

Population Statistics 1990

Race/ Ethnicity	Total Population		Voting Age Population		Voting Age Population % of total population
	Number	%	Number	%	
Non-Hispanic					
White	347,644	31.4	270,580	32.7	77.8
Black	25,916	2.3	18,191	2.2	70.2
Asian/Pacific Islander	646,404	58.3	484,758	58.5	75.0
Native American	4,001	0.4	2,871	0.3	71.8
Other	2,874	0.3	1,503	0.2	52.3
All Hispanic	81,390	7.3	50,200	6.1	61.7
TOTAL	1,108,229	100.0	828,103	100.0	74.7

Estimated Voting Age Population 1992 (VAP) 889,000
Number of Registered Voters.................................... 464,495
    % of estimated VAP.. 52.2
Voter Turnout (Actual) 382,882
    % of VAP 43.1
    % of Registration 82.4
Persons Not Voting—of Voting Age 506,118
    % of VAP 56.9
Persons Not Voting—of Registered 81,613
    % of Registration 17.6
Straight Ticket Voting .... No

State Officials and Members of Congress

Governor:
John D. Waihee III (D) 1986, elected to a four-year term in 1990.

U.S. Senators:
Daniel Inouye (D) 1962, elected to a six-year term in 1992.
Daniel Akaka (D) 1990, elected to a six-year term in 1990.

U.S. Representative in Congress:
(District, Name, Party, Date first elected)

1. Abercrombie (D) 1990   2. Mink (D) 1990

---

[1]Less than total number of counties because Kalawao and Maui counties are combined for elections administration purposes.

Candidates: General Election, November 3, 1992

Candidate(s)	Total vote	Percent	Party	Status	First elected
President/Vice President					
Clinton/Gore	179,310	48.09%	Democrat	Challenger	1992
Bush/Quayle	136,822	36.70%	Republican	Incumbent	1988
Perot/Stockdale	53,003	14.22%	Independent	Challenger	
Gritz/Minett	1,452	0.39%	Independent	Challenger	
Marrou/Lord	1,119	0.30%	Libertarian	Challenger	
Fulani/Munoz	720	0.19%	New Alliance	Challenger	
Hagelin/Tompkins	416	0.11%	Natural Law	Challenger	
U.S. Senator					
Daniel K. Inouye	208,266	57.27%	Democrat	Incumbent	1962
Rick Reed	97,928	26.93%	Republican	Challenger	
Linda Martin	49,921	13.73%	Green	Challenger	
Richard Rowland	7,547	2.08%	Libertarian	Challenger	

Governor (No Contest)

U.S. Representative in Congress

District 1

Candidate(s)	Total vote	Percent	Party	Status	First elected
Neil Abercrombie	129,332	72.87%	Democrat	Incumbent	1990
Warner Sutton	41,575	23.43%	Republican	Challenger	
Rockne Johnson	6,569	3.70%	Libertarian	Challenger	

District 2

Candidate(s)	Total vote	Percent	Party	Status	First elected
Patsy Mink	131,454	72.64%	Democrat	Incumbent	1990
Kamuela Price	40,070	22.14%	Republican	Challenger	
Lloyd Mallan	9,431	5.21%	Libertarian	Challenger	

Voter Registration and Turnout, 1948-1992 Elections

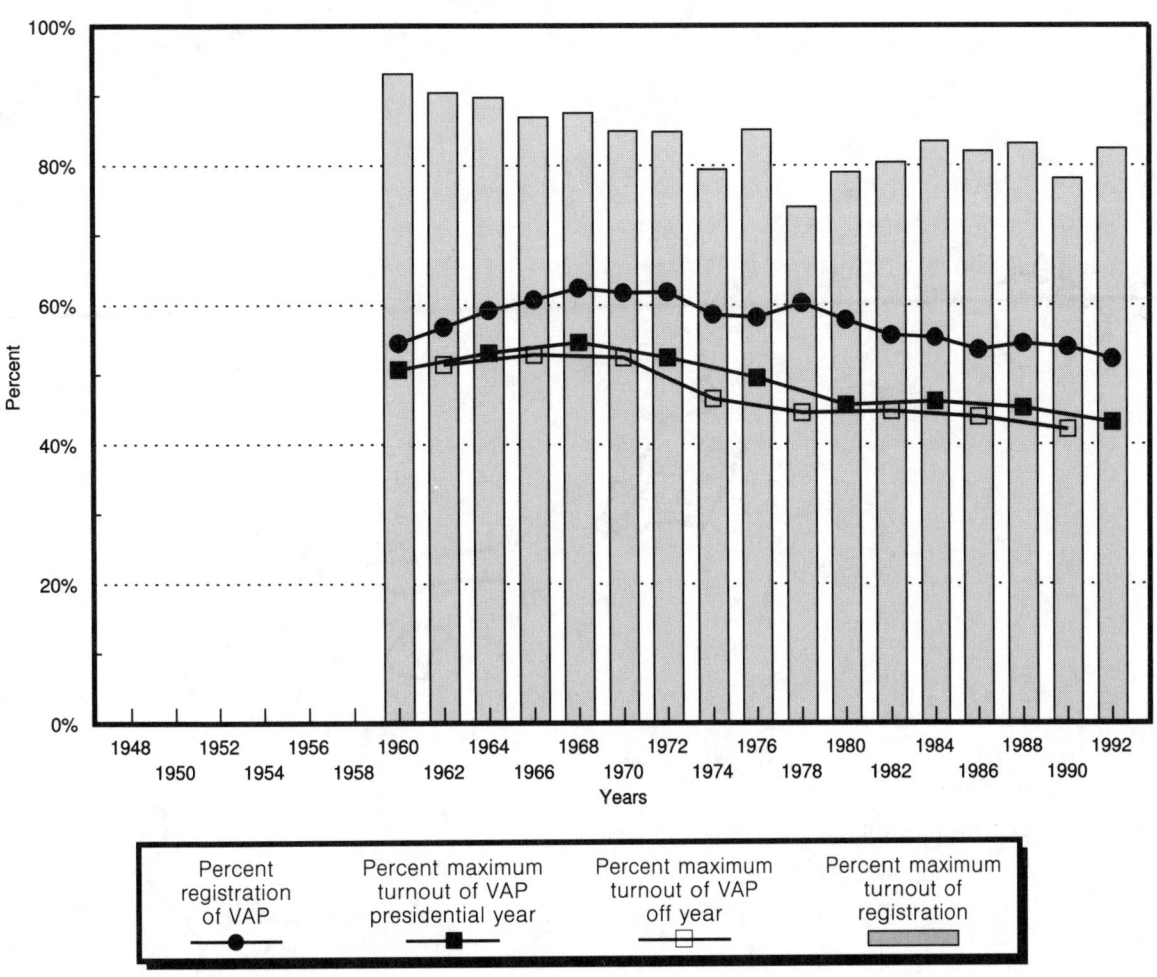

Percent registration of VAP	Percent maximum turnout of VAP presidential year	Percent maximum turnout of VAP off year	Percent maximum turnout of registration

Year	Estimated Voting Age Population (VAP)	Voter registration (REG)				Voter turnout											
							Highest office						Maximum vote				
		Total	Percent of VAP	Rank by percent of VAP	Actual	Total	Office	Percent total REG	Rank by percent of REG	Percent of VAP	Rank by percent of VAP	Total	Percent total REG	Rank by percent of REG	Percent total VAP	Rank by percent of VAP
1992	889,000	464,495	52.2	49	382,882	372,842	P	80.3	17	41.9	51	382,882	82.4	15	43.1	51
1990	841,000	453,389	53.9	48	354,144	349,666	S	77.1	1	41.6	20	354,144	78.1	1	42.1	20
1988	815,000	443,742	54.4	49	368,567	354,461	P	79.9	4	43.5	47	368,567	83.1	1	45.2	44
1986	784,000	419,794	53.5	47	344,416	334,115	G	79.6	1	42.6	18	344,416	82.0	1	43.9	15
1984	757,000	418,898	55.3	48	349,253	335,846	P	80.2	4	44.4	47	349,253	83.4	1	46.1	47
1982	728,000	405,005	55.6	45	325,459	311,853	G	77.0	1	42.8	27	325,459	80.4	1	44.7	24
1980	697,000	402,795	57.8	46	318,026	303,287	P	75.3	23	43.5	46	318,026	79.0	14	45.6	46
1978	657,000	395,292	60.2	41	292,690	281,587	G	71.2	2	42.9	20	292,690	74.0	1	44.5	16
1976	624,000	363,045	58.2	45	309,025	291,301	P	80.2	8	46.7	43	309,025	85.1	2	49.5	36
1974	586,000	343,404	58.6	45	272,545	259,427	C	75.5	1	44.3	19	272,545	79.4	1	46.5	18
1972	547,000	337,837	61.8	45	286,593	270,274	P	80.0	10	49.4	36	286,593	84.8	5	52.4	34
1970	473,000	291,681	61.7	42	247,740	240,760	S	82.5	2	50.9	24	247,740	84.9	2	52.4	20
1968	439,000	274,104	62.4	42	239,765	236,218	P	86.2	5	53.8	39	239,765	87.5	4	54.6	36
1966	417,000	253,242	60.7	38	220,137	213,164	G	84.2	1	51.1	27	220,137	86.9	1	52.8	25
1964	404,000	239,361	59.2	36	214,694	207,271	P	86.6	9	51.3	40	214,694	89.7	5	53.1	37
1962	390,000	221,650	56.8	31	200,441	196,361	S	88.6	1	50.3	27	200,441	90.4	1	51.4	27
1960	371,000	202,059	54.5	31	188,206	184,705	P	91.4	6	49.8	39	188,206	93.1	6	50.7	39
1958	-	-	-	-	-	-	-	-	-	-	-	-	-	-	-	-
1956	-	-	-	-	-	-	-	-	-	-	-	-	-	-	-	-
1954	-	-	-	-	-	-	-	-	-	-	-	-	-	-	-	-
1952	-	-	-	-	-	-	-	-	-	-	-	-	-	-	-	-
1950	-	-	-	-	-	-	-	-	-	-	-	-	-	-	-	-
1948	-	-	-	-	-	-	-	-	-	-	-	-	-	-	-	-

HAWAII

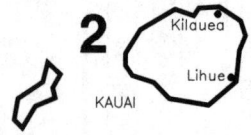

Kilauea

Lihue•

KAUAI

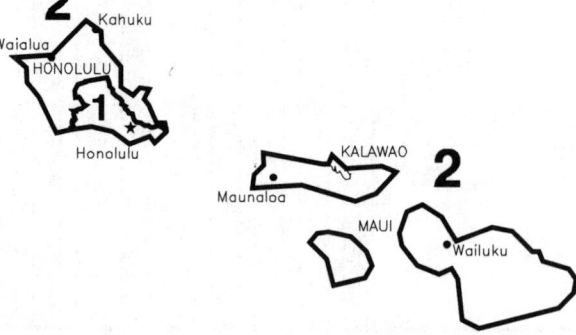

2

Kahuku

Waialua

HONOLULU

1

Honolulu

KALAWAO

Maunaloa

2

MAUI

•Wailuku

—Congressional district boundaries
effective July 27, 1991.

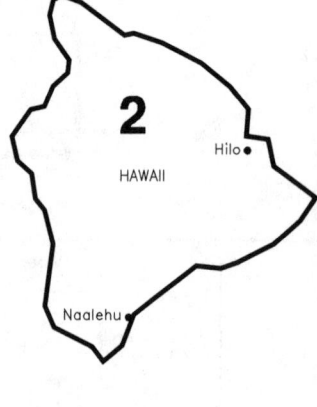

2

Hilo•

HAWAII

Naalehu•

N
W ✦ *E*
S

Miles
0 10 20 30

Table A. — 1990 Population by Race and Ethnic Origin

State/county code	County	Total persons	Percent of total persons — Non-Hispanic White	Black	Asian and Pacific Islander	Native American	Other	Hispanic	Rank Total	Rank Non-Hispanic White	Black	Asian and Pacific Islander[1]	Percent contribution to state population Total	Non-Hispanic White	Black	Asian and Pacific Islander[1]
15 001	Hawaii	120,317	36.9	0.5	52.5	0.5	0.3	9.3	2	2	2	5	10.9	12.8	2.2	9.8
15 003	Honolulu	836,231	29.9	3.0	59.8	0.3	0.3	6.8	1	4	1	2	75.5	71.8	95.4	72.4
15 005	Kalawao	130	18.5	0.0	73.1	0.0	0.0	8.5	5	5	5	1	<.1	<.1	0.0	<.1
15 007	Kauai	51,177	31.7	0.4	56.5	0.3	0.2	10.9	4	3	4	3	4.6	4.7	0.7	4.5
15 009	Maui	100,374	37.2	0.4	54.0	0.4	0.2	7.8	3	1	3	4	9.1	10.7	1.7	8.4
15	HAWAII	1,108,229	31.4	2.3	58.3	0.4	0.3	7.3					100.0	100.0	100.0	100.0
	CONGRESSIONAL															
	District 1	554,119	27.6	2.4	64.0	0.3	0.2	5.5	1	2	1	1	50.0	44.0	50.9	54.9
	District 2	554,110	35.1	2.3	52.7	0.4	0.3	9.2	2	1	2	2	50.0	56.0	49.1	45.1

[1]Non-Hispanic Asian and Pacific Islander.

Table B. — 1990 Voting Age Population (VAP) by Race and Ethnic Origin

County	Total Voting Age Population	Percent of total VAP — Non-Hispanic White	Black	Asian and Pacific Islander	Native American	Other	Hispanic	Rank Total	Rank Non-Hispanic White	Black	Asian and Pacific Islander[1]	Percent contribution to state VAP Total	Non-Hispanic White	Black	Asian and Pacific Islander[1]	VAP percent of total population Total	Non-Hispanic White	Black	Asian and Pacific Islander	Native American	Other	Hispanic
Hawaii	85,802	39.4	0.4	52.2	0.5	0.2	7.3	2	2	2	5	10.4	12.5	2.1	9.2	71.3	76.1	66.6	70.8	68.4	52.9	55.9
Honolulu	631,618	30.9	2.7	60.2	0.3	0.2	5.7	1	4	1	2	76.3	72.1	95.4	78.4	75.5	78.2	70.2	76.0	72.6	52.6	62.9
Kalawao	130	18.5	0.0	73.1	0.0	0.0	8.5	5	5	5	1	<.1	<.1	0.0	<.1	100.0	100.0	0.0	100.0	0.0	0.0	100.0
Kauai	37,062	33.5	0.4	56.5	0.3	0.1	9.2	4	3	4	3	4.5	4.6	0.8	4.3	72.4	76.5	72.5	72.5	71.8	50.0	60.8
Maui	73,491	39.8	0.4	52.8	0.4	0.2	6.5	3	1	3	4	8.9	10.8	1.7	8.0	73.2	78.2	70.9	71.6	71.1	49.8	61.3
HAWAII	828,103	32.7	2.2	58.5	0.3	0.2	6.1					100.0	100.0	100.0	100.0	74.7	77.8	70.2	75.0	71.8	52.3	61.7
CONGRESSIONAL																						
District 1	431,485	28.4	2.2	64.3	0.3	0.2	4.7	1	2	2	1	52.1	45.3	51.6	57.2	77.9	80.1	71.2	78.3	76.5	53.9	66.1
District 2	396,618	37.3	2.2	52.3	0.4	0.2	7.6	2	1	1	2	47.9	54.7	48.4	42.8	71.6	76.0	69.2	71.0	68.8	51.1	59.0

[1]Non-Hispanic Asian and Pacific Islander.

Table C. — Voter Participation: November 3, 1992, General Election

County	Estimated Voting Age Population (VAP) 1992	Voter registration (REG) Total	% contribution to state REG	% of 1992 VAP	Rank by % of 1992 VAP	Voter turnout — Highest office Actual	Total	Office	% of 1992 VAP	Maximum vote Total	% contribution to state turnout	% of REG	Rank by % of REG	% of 1992 VAP	Rank by % 1992 VAP	Percent drop-off, by office President	Senator	Governor	Representative
Hawaii	95,877	62,023	13.4	64.7	2	52,529	50,916	P	53.1	52,529	13.7	84.7	1	54.8	1	3.1	4.4	-	6.2
Honolulu	667,642	328,463	70.7	49.2	4	272,081	265,841	P	39.8	272,081	71.1	82.8	2	40.8	4	2.3	5.0	-	6.0
Kauai	41,292	26,771	5.8	64.8	1	19,864	18,960	P	45.9	19,864	5.2	74.2	4	48.1	2	4.6	6.4	-	9.2
Maui[1]	84,189	47,238	10.2	56.1	3	38,408	37,125	P	44.1	38,408	10.0	81.3	3	45.6	3	3.3	5.2	-	8.2
HAWAII	889,000	464,495	100.0	52.2		382,882	372,842		41.9	382,882	100.0	82.4		43.1		2.6	5.0	-	6.4

[1]Includes Kalawao county.

Table E. – Vote for President: November 3, 1992, General Election

County	Total	Clinton (DEM)	Bush (REP)	Perot (IND)	Other	Plurality Total	Party	DEM	REP	IND	Other	Rank DEM	Rank REP	Rank IND	Total	DEM	REP	IND	DEM	REP
Hawaii	50,916	25,725	15,460	8,889	842	10,265	D	50.5	30.4	17.5	1.7	3	3	2	13.7	14.3	11.3	16.8	62.5	37.5
Honolulu	265,841	123,908	103,937	35,728	2,268	19,971	D	46.6	39.1	13.4	0.9	4	1	3	71.3	69.1	76.0	67.4	54.4	45.6
Kauai	18,960	10,715	6,274	1,756	215	4,441	D	56.5	33.1	9.3	1.1	1	2	4	5.1	6.0	4.6	3.3	63.1	36.9
Maui[1]	37,125	18,962	11,151	6,630	382	7,811	D	51.1	30.0	17.9	1.0	2	4	1	10.0	10.6	8.2	12.5	63.0	37.0
HAWAII	372,842	179,310	136,822	53,003	3,707	42,488	D	48.1	36.7	14.2	1.0				100.0	100.0	100.0	100.0	56.7	43.3

[1]Includes Kalawao county.

Table F. – Vote for U.S. Senator: November 3, 1992, General Election

County	Total	Inouye (DEM)	Reed (REP)	Other	Plurality Total	Party	DEM	REP	Other	Rank DEM	Rank REP	Rank Other	Total	DEM	REP	Other
Hawaii	50,231	27,461	15,130	7,640	12,331	D	54.7	30.1	15.2	3	2	2	13.8	13.2	15.5	13.3
Honolulu	258,407	148,831	66,094	43,482	82,737	D	57.6	25.6	16.8	2	3	1	71.1	71.5	67.5	75.7
Kauai	18,602	13,213	4,058	1,331	9,155	D	71.0	21.8	7.2	1	4	4	5.1	6.3	4.1	2.3
Maui[1]	36,422	18,761	12,646	5,015	6,115	D	51.5	34.7	13.8	4	1	3	10.0	9.0	12.9	8.7
HAWAII	363,662	208,266	97,928	57,468	110,338	D	57.3	26.9	15.8				100.0	100.0	100.0	100.0

[1]Includes Kalawao county.

Table H. – Vote for U.S. Representative in Congress: November 3, 1992, General Election

Congressional district and county	Total	Democrat (DEM)	Republican (REP)	Other	Plurality Total	Party	DEM	REP	Other	Rank within district DEM	Rank within district REP	Rank within district Other	Total	DEM	REP	Other
District 1	177,476	129,332	41,575	6,569	87,757	D	72.9	23.4	3.7				100.0	100.0	100.0	100.0
Honolulu (pt)	177,476	129,332	41,575	6,569	87,757	D	72.9	23.4	3.7	1	1	1	100.0	100.0	100.0	100.0
District 2	180,955	131,454	40,070	9,431	91,384	D	72.6	22.1	5.2				100.0	100.0	100.0	100.0
Hawaii	49,279	35,697	10,783	2,799	24,914	D	72.4	21.9	5.7	3	2	1	27.2	27.2	26.9	29.7
Honolulu (pt)	78,374	54,943	19,264	4,167	35,679	D	70.1	24.6	5.3	4	1	2	43.3	41.8	48.1	44.2
Kauai	18,040	14,803	2,600	637	12,203	D	82.1	14.4	3.5	1	4	4	10.0	11.3	6.5	6.8
Maui[1]	35,262	26,011	7,423	1,828	18,588	D	73.8	21.1	5.2	2	3	3	19.5	19.8	18.5	19.4
HAWAII	358,431	260,786	81,645	16,000	179,141	D	72.8	22.8	4.5							

[1]Includes Kalawao county.

1992 Vote for President
Percent for Clinton (D), by County

Kilauea

Lihue

KAUAI

Kahuku

Waialua

HONOLULU

Honolulu

KALAWAO*

Maunaloa

MAUI

Wailuku

Hilo

HAWAII

Naalehu

■ 56.5%
■ 51.1%
■ 50.5%
□ 46.6%

Clinton (D) received 48.1% statewide.

A framed county name indicates
a county carried by the winner.

*Kalawao county returns are reported
with the returns of Maui county.

1992 Vote for U.S. Senator
Percent for Inouye (D), by County

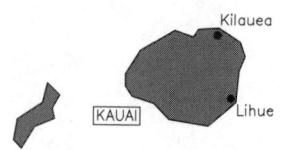

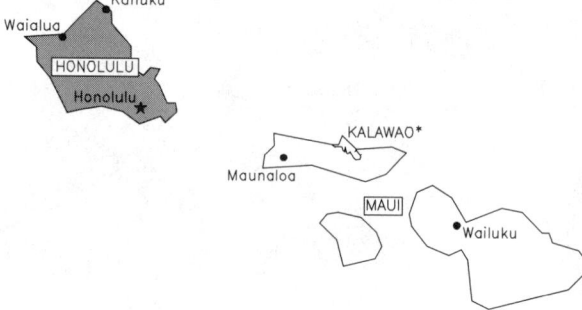

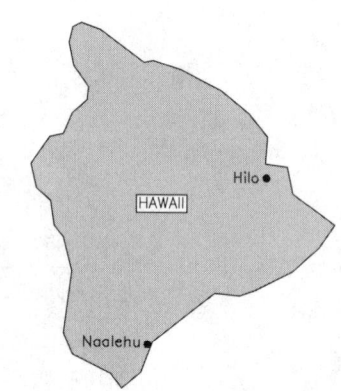

■ 71.0%
■ 57.6%
■ 54.7%
□ 51.5%

Inouye (D) received 57.3% statewide.

A framed county name indicates
a county carried by the winner.

*Kalawao county returns are reported
with the returns of Maui county.

IDAHO

Voting Equipment Use (Counties)

Datavote Punch Card	0	Paper Ballot	22
Electronic	0	Other Punch Card	17
Lever Machine	0	Mixed Systems	0
Optical Scanner	5		

Party Control	DEM	REP	IND	VAC
1993 State Senate	12	23	0	0
1992 State Senate	21	21	0	0
1993 State House	20	50	0	0
1992 State House	28	56	0	0

Population Statistics 1990

Race/ Ethnicity	Total Population		Voting Age Population		Voting Age Population % of total population
	Number	%	Number	%	
Non-Hispanic					
White	928,661	92.2	651,417	93.3	70.1
Black	3,211	0.3	2,056	0.3	64.0
Asian/Pacific Islander	9,053	0.9	6,199	0.9	68.5
Native American	12,418	1.2	7,984	1.1	64.3
Other	479	<.1	234	<.1	48.9
All Hispanic	52,927	5.3	30,454	4.4	57.5
TOTAL	1,006,749	100.0	698,344	100.0	69.4

Estimated Voting Age Population 1992 (VAP) 740,000
Number of Registered Voters.................................... 611,121
    % of estimated VAP... 82.6
Voter Turnout (Actual) 491,725
    % of VAP 66.4
    % of Registration 80.5
Persons Not Voting—of Voting Age 248,275
    % of VAP 33.6
Persons Not Voting—of Registered 119,396
    % of Registration 19.5
Straight Ticket Voting .... No

State Officials and Members of Congress

Governor:
Cecil Andrus (D) 1970, elected to a four-year term in 1990.

U.S. Senators:
Larry Craig (R) 1990, elected to a six-year term in 1990.
Dirk Kempthorne (R) 1992, elected to a six-year term in 1992.

U.S. Representative in Congress:
(District, Name, Party, Date first elected)

1. LaRocco (D) 1990   2. Crapo (R) 1992

Candidates: General Election, November 3, 1992

Candidate(s)	Total vote	Percent	Party	Status	First elected
President/Vice President					
Bush/Quayle	202,645	42.03%	Republican	Incumbent	1988
Clinton/Gore	137,013	28.42%	Democrat	Challenger	1992
Perot/Stockdale	130,395	27.04%	Independent	Challenger	
Gritz/Minett	10,281	2.13%	Independent	Challenger	
Marrou/Lord	1,167	0.24%	Libertarian	Challenger	
Fulani/Munoz	613	0.13%	Independent	Challenger	
Write ins[1]	28	<0.1%	Unknown	Challenger	
U.S. Senator					
Dirk Kempthorne	270,468	56.52%	Republican	Challenger	1992
Richard Stallings	208,036	43.48%	Democrat	Challenger	
David Shepherd	18	<.01%	Independent	Challenger	
Governor (No Contest)					
U.S. Representative in Congress					
District 1					
Larry LaRocco	140,985	58.07%	Democrat	Incumbent	1990
Rachel Gilbert	90,983	37.47%	Republican	Challenger	
John Abel	6,255	2.58%	Independent	Challenger	
Henry Kinsey	4,567	1.88%	Independent	Challenger	
District 2					
Michael Crapo	139,783	60.79%	Republican	Challenger	1992
J. D. Williams	81,450	35.42%	Democrat	Challenger	
Steven Kauer	4,917	2.14%	Independent	Challenger	
David Mansfield	3,807	1.66%	Independent	Challenger	

[1]Votes for Write in candidates include 24 for John Hagelin, 3 for J. Quinn Brisben, and 1 for Lyndon LaRouche, Jr.

Candidates: March 3, 1992, Primary Election

Candidate	Total vote	Percent	Candidate	Total vote	Percent
Presidential Preference, Democratic			**Presidential Preference, Republican**		
Bill Clinton	27,004	48.99%	George Bush	73,297	63.46%
None of the Above	16,029	29.08%	None of the Above	27,038	23.41%
Jerry Brown	9,212	16.71%	Patrick Buchanan	15,167	13.13%
Lyndon LaRouche, Jr.	2,011	3.65%			
Larry Agran	868	1.57%			

Voter Registration and Turnout, 1948-1992 Elections

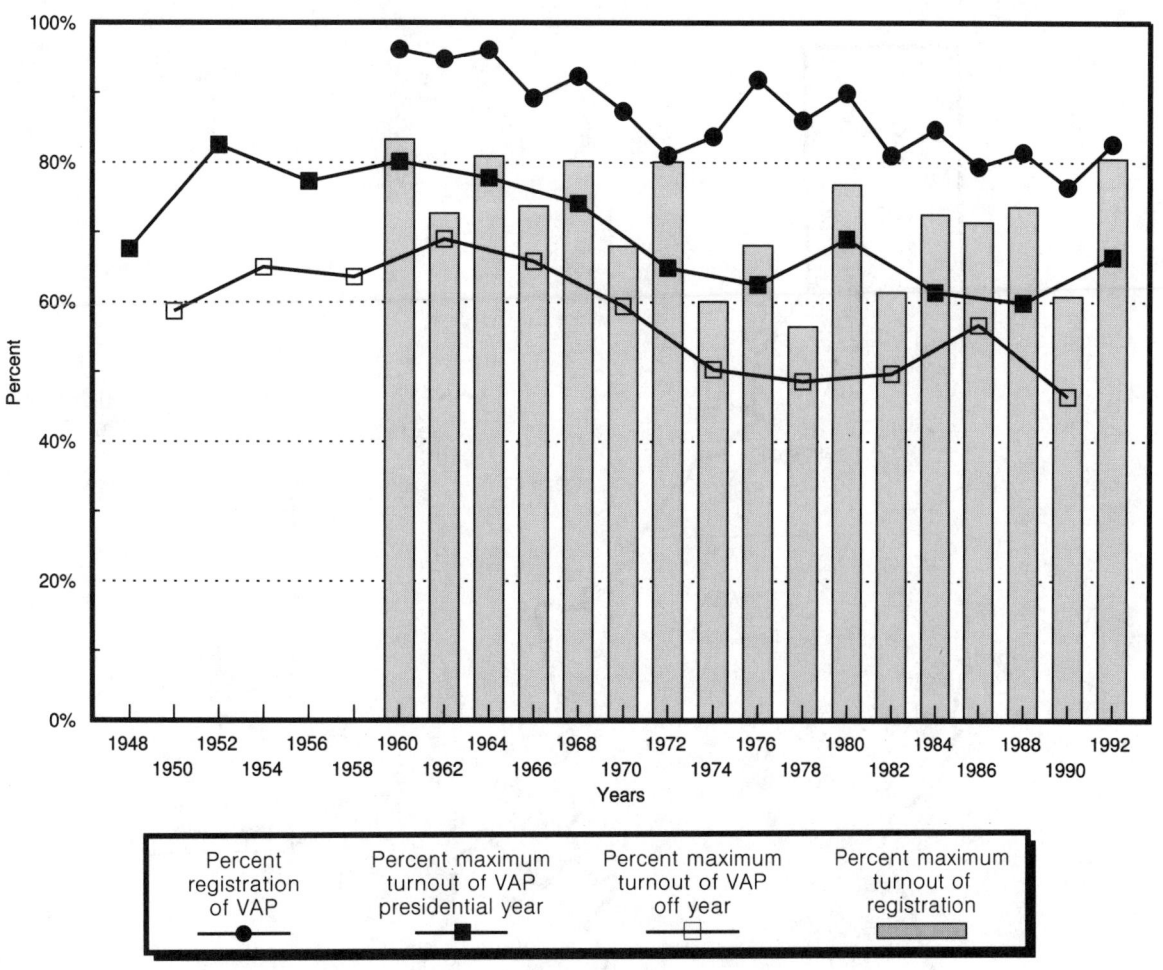

	Percent registration of VAP	Percent maximum turnout of VAP presidential year	Percent maximum turnout of VAP off year	Percent maximum turnout of registration

Year	Estimated Voting Age Population (VAP)	Voter registration (REG)			Voter turnout											
						Highest office							Maximum vote			
		Total	Percent of VAP	Rank by percent of VAP	Actual	Total	Office	Percent total REG	Rank by percent of REG	Percent of VAP	Rank by percent of VAP	Total	Percent total REG	Rank by percent of REG	Percent total VAP	Rank by percent of VAP
1992.......	740,000	611,121	82.6	10	482,142	482,114	P	78.9	19	65.2	11	491,725	80.5	20	66.4	10
1990.......	707,000	540,247	76.4	14	328,340	320,610	G	59.3	23	45.3	15	328,340	60.8	22	46.4	15
1988.......	703,000	572,430	81.4	12	421,213	408,968	P	71.4	25	58.2	9	421,213	73.6	23	59.9	9
1986.......	693,000	549,934	79.4	10	392,909	387,426	G	70.4	6	55.9	3	392,909	71.4	6	56.7	3
1984.......	687,000	582,196	84.7	9	421,935	411,144	P	70.6	35	59.8	11	421,935	72.5	33	61.4	11
1982.......	668,000	541,164	81.0	8	332,237	326,522	G	60.3	29	48.9	10	332,237	61.4	31	49.7	10
1980.......	646,000	581,006	89.9	5	446,045	437,431	P	75.3	24	67.7	2	446,045	76.8	21	69.0	2
1978.......	612,000	526,253	86.0	5	297,363	288,566	G	54.8	29	47.2	8	297,363	56.5	31	48.6	6
1976.......	567,000	520,384	91.8	2	354,566	344,071	P	66.1	42	60.7	12	354,566	68.1	40	62.5	11
1974.......	526,000	440,114	83.7	4	264,330	259,632	G	59.0	23	49.4	9	264,330	60.1	22	50.3	8
1972.......	490,000	397,019	81.0	13	318,179	310,379	P	78.2	15	63.3	10	318,179	80.1	13	64.9	10
1970.......	418,000	364,992	87.3	5	248,147	245,112	G	67.2	22	58.6	7	248,147	68.0	22	59.4	8
1968.......	397,000	366,532	92.3	5	294,085	291,183	P	79.4	24	73.3	3	294,085	80.2	26	74.1	3
1966[1].....	384,000	342,581	89.2	5	233,883	252,593	G	73.7	10	65.8	2	252,593	73.7	10	65.8	3
1964.......	379,000	364,231	96.1	3	294,717	292,477	P	80.3	20	77.2	2	294,717	80.9	20	77.8	2
1962.......	385,000	364,925	94.8	3	265,477	258,786	S	70.9	15	67.2	1	265,477	72.7	15	69.0	1
1960.......	377,000	362,704	96.2	2	302,155	300,450	P	82.8	23	79.7	1	302,155	83.3	23	80.1	2
1958.......	376,000	-	-	-	-	239,046	G	-	-	63.6	4	239,046	-	-	63.6	5
1956.......	353,000	-	-	-	-	272,989	P	-	-	77.3	1	272,989	-	-	77.3	3
1954.......	352,000	-	-	-	-	228,685	G	-	-	65.0	1	228,685	-	-	65.0	1
1952.......	335,000	-	-	-	-	276,254	P	-	-	82.5	1	276,254	-	-	82.5	1
1950.......	349,000	-	-	-	-	204,792	G	-	-	58.7	9	204,792	-	-	58.7	9
1948.......	318,000	-	-	-	-	214,816	P	-	-	67.6	7	214,816	-	-	67.6	9

[1]Vote for Governor (highest office turnout) exceeds actual voter turnout because actual turnout data are missing from three counties that did not report.

IDAHO

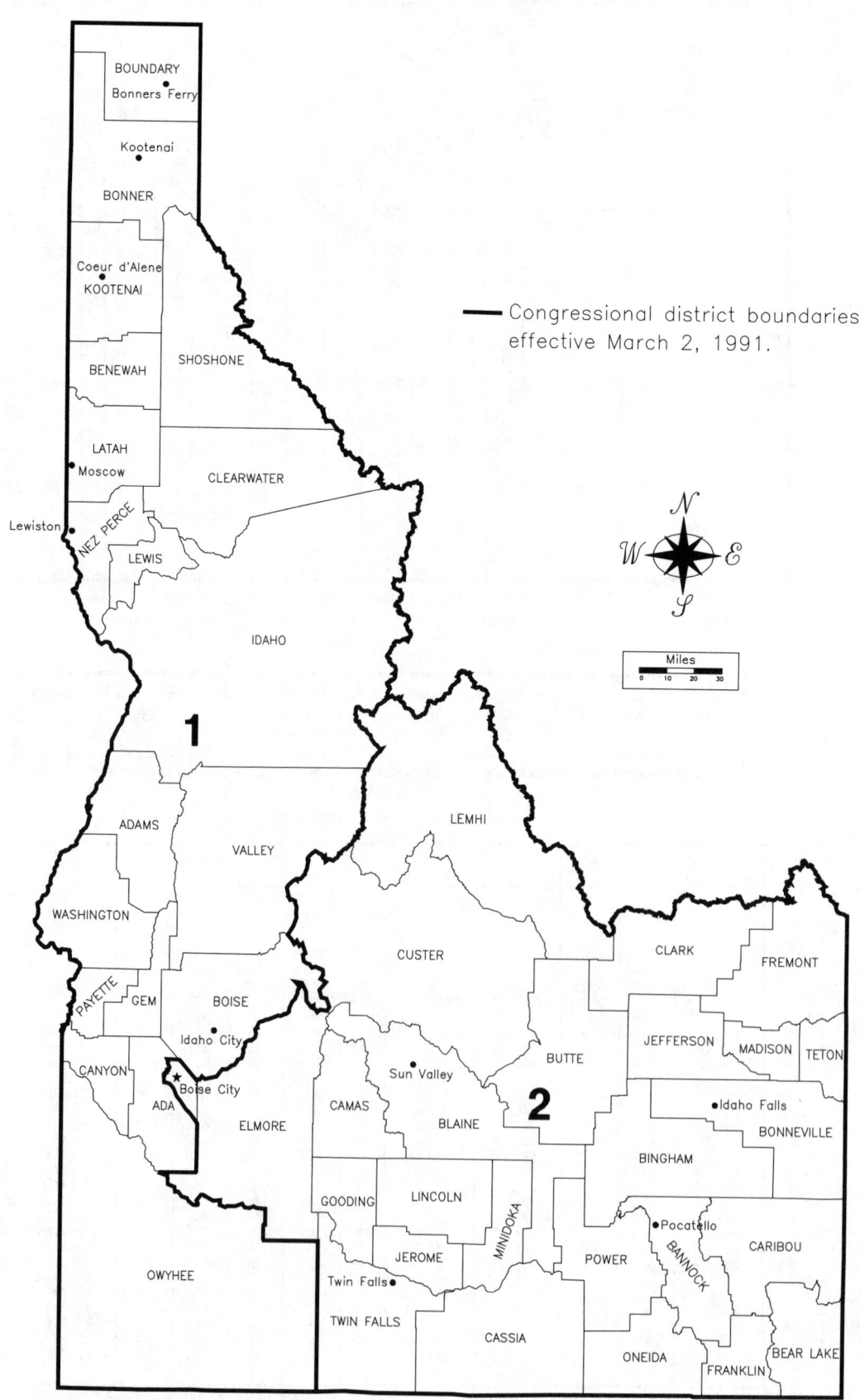

Congressional district boundaries effective March 2, 1991.

Copyright © 1993 by Election Data Services, Inc.

Table A. — 1990 Population by Race and Ethnic Origin

State/ county code	County	Total persons	Percent of total persons Non-Hispanic White	Black	Asian and Pacific Islander	Native American	Other	Hispanic	Rank Percent of total persons Total	Non-Hispanic White	Black	Hispanic	Percent contribution to state population Total	Non-Hispanic White	Black	Hispanic
16 001	Ada	205,775	94.8	0.4	1.4	0.6	<.1	2.7	1	20	4	26	20.4	21.0	28.8	10.5
16 003	Adams	3,254	97.5	<.1	<.1	1.3	0.0	1.2	41	4	28	42	0.3	0.3	<.1	<.1
16 005	Bannock	66,026	91.8	0.6	1.1	2.3	<.1	4.1	5	32	2	20	6.6	6.5	12.9	5.2
16 007	Bear Lake	6,084	97.4	0.0	<.1	0.2	0.0	2.2	34	5	41	29	0.6	0.6	0.0	0.3
16 009	Benewah	7,937	90.6	<.1	0.4	7.3	<.1	1.6	29	33	35	35	0.8	0.8	<.1	0.2
16 011	Bingham	37,583	83.6	<.1	0.7	5.9	<.1	9.6	7	41	23	8	3.7	3.4	1.0	6.8
16 013	Blaine	13,552	95.9	<.1	0.7	0.3	<.1	2.9	20	16	24	24	1.3	1.4	0.3	0.8
16 015	Boise	3,509	96.1	<.1	0.4	1.0	<.1	2.4	37	15	32	28	0.3	0.4	<.1	0.2
16 017	Bonner	26,622	97.5	0.1	0.2	0.8	<.1	1.3	10	3	13	38	2.6	2.8	1.1	0.7
16 019	Bonneville	72,207	94.0	0.4	0.9	0.5	<.1	4.2	3	22	5	19	7.2	7.3	8.9	5.7
16 021	Boundary	8,332	94.2	<.1	0.3	1.8	<.1	3.7	28	21	36	21	0.8	0.8	<.1	0.6
16 023	Butte	2,918	95.6	0.0	0.2	0.7	0.0	3.5	42	17	42	22	0.3	0.3	0.0	0.2
16 025	Camas	727	97.7	0.3	0.4	1.1	0.0	0.6	44	1	6	44	<.1	<.1	<.1	<.1
16 027	Canyon	90,076	84.9	0.2	1.0	0.7	<.1	13.1	2	40	8	5	8.9	8.2	5.1	22.4
16 029	Caribou	6,963	96.7	<.1	0.2	0.3	<.1	2.8	31	10	37	25	0.7	0.7	<.1	0.4
16 031	Cassia	19,532	85.3	<.1	0.5	0.7	<.1	13.4	13	39	40	3	1.9	1.8	<.1	5.0
16 033	Clark	762	89.0	0.0	0.0	0.7	0.0	10.4	43	36	43	7	<.1	<.1	0.0	0.1
16 035	Clearwater	8,505	96.3	<.1	0.2	2.1	0.0	1.3	26	14	19	39	0.8	0.9	0.2	0.2
16 037	Custer	4,133	96.6	<.1	0.4	0.8	0.0	2.2	35	12	34	30	0.4	0.4	<.1	0.2
16 039	Elmore	21,205	86.1	3.6	2.0	0.7	0.1	7.5	12	38	1	10	2.1	2.0	23.8	3.0
16 041	Franklin	9,232	96.9	<.1	0.1	0.3	<.1	2.6	24	8	33	27	0.9	1.0	0.2	0.4
16 043	Fremont	10,937	92.0	<.1	0.3	0.6	<.1	7.0	23	30	25	13	1.1	1.1	0.2	1.4
16 045	Gem	11,844	93.3	<.1	0.4	0.9	<.1	5.2	21	24	20	18	1.2	1.2	0.3	1.2
16 047	Gooding	11,633	90.6	<.1	0.2	0.3	<.1	8.8	22	35	29	9	1.2	1.1	0.2	1.9
16 049	Idaho	13,783	96.4	<.1	0.2	2.4	<.1	0.9	19	13	38	43	1.4	1.4	<.1	0.2
16 051	Jefferson	16,543	92.0	<.1	0.2	0.7	0.1	7.0	15	31	39	12	1.6	1.6	<.1	2.2
16 053	Jerome	15,138	92.2	<.1	0.3	0.6	<.1	6.7	17	29	30	15	1.5	1.5	0.3	1.9
16 055	Kootenai	69,795	97.0	0.1	0.4	0.9	<.1	1.5	4	6	12	36	6.9	7.3	2.8	2.0
16 057	Latah	30,617	95.0	0.6	2.3	0.6	<.1	1.5	9	19	3	37	3.0	3.1	5.3	0.8
16 059	Lemhi	6,899	97.0	0.0	0.3	0.6	0.0	2.0	32	7	44	31	0.7	0.7	0.0	0.3
16 061	Lewis	3,516	93.5	0.1	0.4	4.8	0.0	1.2	36	23	17	41	0.3	0.4	0.1	<.1
16 063	Lincoln	3,308	93.0	<.1	0.4	0.7	<.1	5.9	40	26	21	16	0.3	0.3	<.1	0.4
16 065	Madison	23,674	95.0	0.1	1.2	0.4	<.1	3.2	11	18	10	23	2.4	2.4	1.1	1.4
16 067	Minidoka	19,361	79.1	0.1	0.5	0.9	<.1	19.3	14	44	9	1	1.9	1.6	0.9	7.1
16 069	Nez Perce	33,754	93.2	0.1	0.6	4.8	<.1	1.2	8	25	11	40	3.4	3.4	1.4	0.8
16 071	Oneida	3,492	97.6	0.1	0.2	0.5	0.0	1.6	38	2	15	34	0.3	0.4	0.1	0.1
16 073	Owyhee	8,392	79.2	0.3	0.9	2.9	<.1	16.8	27	43	7	2	0.8	0.7	0.7	2.7
16 075	Payette	16,434	90.6	<.1	1.0	1.1	<.1	7.3	16	34	27	11	1.6	1.6	0.3	2.3
16 077	Power	7,086	83.4	<.1	0.5	2.8	<.1	13.2	30	42	22	4	0.7	0.6	0.2	1.8
16 079	Shoshone	13,931	96.6	0.1	0.3	1.2	<.1	1.8	18	11	18	32	1.4	1.4	0.4	0.5
16 081	Teton	3,439	92.6	<.1	<.1	0.4	<.1	6.9	39	27	31	14	0.3	0.3	<.1	0.4
16 083	Twin Falls	53,580	92.6	0.1	1.0	0.5	<.1	5.8	6	28	14	17	5.3	5.3	1.9	5.9
16 085	Valley	6,109	96.8	0.1	0.4	1.0	0.0	1.8	33	9	16	33	0.6	0.6	0.2	0.2
16 087	Washington	8,550	87.2	<.1	1.4	0.5	<.1	10.7	25	37	26	6	0.8	0.8	0.2	1.7
16	**IDAHO**	1,006,749	92.2	0.3	0.9	1.2	<.1	5.3					100.0	100.0	100.0	100.0
	CONGRESSIONAL															
	District 1	503,357	93.0	0.2	0.9	1.3	<.1	4.6	2	1	2	2	50.0	50.4	32.8	43.6
	District 2	503,392	91.5	0.4	0.9	1.2	<.1	5.9	1	2	1	1	50.0	49.6	67.2	56.4

Idaho 251

Table B. — 1990 Voting Age Population (VAP) by Race and Ethnic Origin

County	Total Voting Age Population	Percent of total VAP — Non-Hispanic White	Black	Asian and Pacific Islander	Native American	Other	Hispanic	Rank Total	Rank Non-Hispanic White	Black	Hispanic	Percent contribution to state VAP Total	Non-Hispanic White	Black	Hispanic	VAP percent of total population Total	Non-Hispanic White	Black	Asian and Pacific Islander	Native American	Other	Hispanic
Ada	147,532	95.3	0.4	1.3	0.6	<.1	2.4	1	18	4	25	21.1	21.6	28.8	11.7	71.7	72.0	64.2	66.8	69.8	42.4	64.1
Adams	2,329	97.7	<.1	<.1	0.9	0.0	1.3	38	3	29	36	0.3	0.3	<.1	<.1	71.6	71.8	50.0	100.0	51.2	0.0	78.9
Bannock	44,544	92.6	0.7	1.1	2.1	<.1	3.5	5	31	2	21	6.4	6.3	14.6	5.1	67.5	68.0	72.3	72.3	61.4	48.7	56.5
Bear Lake	3,807	98.0	0.0	0.1	0.2	0.0	1.7	34	2	39	29	0.5	0.6	0.0	0.2	62.6	62.9	0.0	80.0	53.3	0.0	48.5
Benewah	5,590	92.3	0.0	0.4	6.1	<.1	1.1	28	33	40	39	0.8	0.8	0.0	0.2	70.4	71.7	0.0	75.0	58.7	60.0	50.8
Bingham	23,061	84.8	<.1	0.8	5.8	<.1	8.5	9	42	24	7	3.3	3.0	0.7	6.4	61.4	62.2	48.4	65.5	60.5	51.5	54.2
Blaine	9,947	96.4	<.1	0.6	0.4	<.1	2.5	18	16	25	24	1.4	1.5	0.3	0.8	73.4	73.8	60.0	61.9	78.3	66.7	63.5
Boise	2,516	96.8	<.1	0.3	1.1	<.1	1.6	37	14	19	30	0.4	0.4	<.1	0.1	71.7	72.2	100.0	57.1	77.1	100.0	48.8
Bonner	19,029	98.0	<.1	0.2	0.7	<.1	1.0	10	1	22	40	2.7	2.9	0.6	0.6	71.5	71.8	38.2	65.2	67.6	50.0	51.4
Bonneville	46,822	94.6	0.4	0.9	0.5	<.1	3.6	4	22	5	20	6.7	6.8	8.8	5.5	64.8	65.3	62.9	66.8	61.8	23.1	55.6
Boundary	5,632	94.5	<.1	0.2	1.5	0.0	3.7	26	23	34	19	0.8	0.8	<.1	0.7	67.6	67.9	33.3	60.9	57.8	0.0	66.8
Butte	1,894	96.0	0.0	0.1	0.6	0.0	3.3	42	17	41	22	0.3	0.3	0.0	0.2	64.9	65.1	0.0	40.0	57.1	0.0	61.4
Camas	511	97.7	0.0	0.6	1.0	0.0	0.8	44	5	42	43	<.1	<.1	0.0	<.1	70.3	70.3	0.0	100.0	62.5	0.0	100.0
Canyon	62,364	87.5	0.2	1.0	0.7	<.1	10.6	2	37	8	6	8.9	8.4	5.2	21.6	69.2	71.4	64.2	69.4	70.4	55.1	55.6
Caribou	4,318	97.2	<.1	0.1	0.3	<.1	2.3	33	10	27	26	0.6	0.6	<.1	0.3	62.0	62.3	100.0	46.2	63.6	100.0	51.6
Cassia	12,388	87.0	<.1	0.5	0.7	<.1	11.8	14	40	35	3	1.8	1.7	<.1	4.8	63.4	64.7	66.7	62.8	61.0	41.2	55.7
Clark	530	87.4	0.0	0.0	0.9	0.0	11.7	43	38	43	4	<.1	<.1	0.0	0.2	69.6	68.3	0.0	0.0	100.0	0.0	78.5
Clearwater	6,358	96.5	<.1	0.3	1.9	0.0	1.3	24	15	20	37	0.9	0.9	0.2	0.3	74.8	74.9	62.5	84.2	68.0	0.0	72.3
Custer	2,872	96.9	<.1	0.3	0.8	0.0	1.8	35	13	21	28	0.4	0.4	<.1	0.2	69.5	69.7	100.0	62.5	75.0	0.0	57.8
Elmore	14,526	87.1	3.3	2.0	0.7	<.1	6.8	12	39	1	10	2.1	1.9	23.1	3.3	68.5	69.3	62.3	68.9	75.0	38.5	62.3
Franklin	5,563	97.5	<.1	<.1	0.2	0.0	2.1	29	7	15	27	0.8	0.8	0.2	0.4	60.3	60.6	100.0	50.0	40.6	0.0	48.9
Fremont	6,797	92.7	<.1	0.3	0.6	<.1	6.4	23	29	28	13	1.0	1.0	0.1	1.4	62.1	62.6	37.5	54.8	60.0	42.9	57.0
Gem	8,507	94.4	<.1	0.4	0.7	<.1	4.4	21	24	26	18	1.2	1.2	0.2	1.2	71.8	72.6	45.5	62.3	60.0	25.0	60.7
Gooding	8,114	91.4	<.1	0.2	0.4	<.1	8.0	22	35	37	9	1.2	1.1	<.1	2.1	69.7	70.4	14.3	65.5	75.0	100.0	63.7
Idaho	9,938	97.0	<.1	0.2	2.0	<.1	0.8	19	12	32	42	1.4	1.5	<.1	0.3	72.1	72.5	66.7	48.5	59.8	100.0	66.9
Jefferson	9,860	92.4	<.1	0.2	0.7	<.1	6.6	20	32	38	12	1.4	1.4	<.1	2.1	59.6	59.9	33.3	50.0	64.2	52.9	55.9
Jerome	10,281	93.3	<.1	0.4	0.7	<.1	5.6	17	27	33	16	1.5	1.5	<.1	1.9	67.9	68.8	22.2	70.6	71.1	66.7	56.1
Kootenai	50,854	97.4	0.1	0.4	0.9	<.1	1.2	3	8	13	38	7.3	7.6	2.5	2.0	72.9	73.1	56.0	66.7	71.5	63.6	59.0
Latah	23,616	95.2	0.6	2.3	0.6	<.1	1.3	8	19	3	35	3.4	3.5	6.4	1.0	77.1	77.3	77.5	78.3	69.3	54.5	69.5
Lemhi	5,001	97.7	0.0	0.2	0.6	0.0	1.5	30	4	44	31	0.7	0.8	0.0	0.2	72.5	73.0	0.0	47.8	65.9	0.0	52.9
Lewis	2,526	94.7	0.2	0.3	4.1	0.0	0.8	36	21	9	44	0.4	0.4	0.2	<.1	71.8	72.8	100.0	50.0	61.5	0.0	45.2
Lincoln	2,269	92.7	<.1	0.5	0.9	0.0	5.8	40	30	16	14	0.3	0.3	<.1	0.4	68.6	68.4	66.7	100.0	90.9	0.0	67.7
Madison	16,044	95.0	0.2	1.4	0.4	<.1	3.0	11	20	7	23	2.3	2.3	1.6	1.6	67.8	67.7	94.3	77.8	74.7	85.7	63.3
Minidoka	12,571	81.9	0.1	0.5	0.8	<.1	16.5	13	43	12	1	1.8	1.6	0.6	6.8	64.9	67.3	44.8	72.6	60.2	47.4	55.7
Nez Perce	25,349	94.3	0.1	0.6	4.0	<.1	0.9	7	25	11	41	3.6	3.7	1.4	0.8	75.1	76.0	62.2	72.5	62.8	100.0	57.3
Oneida	2,194	97.6	0.1	0.2	0.6	0.0	1.5	41	6	31	33	0.3	0.3	0.1	0.1	62.8	62.8	75.0	62.5	76.5	0.0	57.1
Owyhee	5,617	81.3	0.3	0.9	2.8	<.1	14.6	27	44	6	2	0.8	0.7	0.7	2.7	66.9	68.7	68.2	73.6	65.8	33.3	58.4
Payette	11,439	92.3	<.1	1.0	1.0	<.1	5.7	15	34	30	15	1.6	1.6	0.1	2.1	69.6	70.9	27.3	74.5	64.0	42.9	54.2
Power	4,604	86.1	<.1	0.3	2.5	<.1	10.9	31	41	18	5	0.7	0.6	0.2	1.6	65.0	67.1	66.7	48.5	59.1	75.0	53.4
Shoshone	10,333	97.3	<.1	0.2	1.1	<.1	1.3	16	9	23	34	1.5	1.5	0.3	0.4	74.2	74.7	50.0	58.3	68.4	50.0	55.5
Teton	2,284	92.9	<.1	<.1	0.4	0.0	6.6	39	28	17	11	0.3	0.3	<.1	0.5	66.4	66.6	100.0	100.0	61.5	0.0	63.7
Twin Falls	37,534	93.8	<.1	0.8	0.5	<.1	4.8	6	26	14	17	5.4	5.4	1.8	5.9	70.1	71.0	58.1	60.2	70.3	52.2	57.4
Valley	4,405	97.1	<.1	0.4	1.0	0.0	1.5	32	11	31	32	0.6	0.7	<.1	0.2	72.1	72.4	14.3	72.0	72.9	0.0	60.7
Washington	6,074	89.5	<.1	1.5	0.5	<.1	8.4	25	36	36	8	0.9	0.8	<.1	1.7	71.0	72.9	16.7	72.4	73.3	71.4	55.8
IDAHO	698,344	93.3	0.3	0.9	1.1	<.1	4.4					100.0	100.0	100.0	100.0	69.4	70.1	64.0	68.5	64.3	48.9	57.5
CONGRESSIONAL																						
District 1	358,537	94.1	0.2	0.9	1.2	<.1	3.7	1	1	2	2	51.3	51.8	31.2	43.5	71.2	72.0	61.0	68.2	65.4	51.6	57.4
District 2	339,807	92.5	0.4	0.9	1.1	<.1	5.1	2	2	1	1	48.7	48.2	68.8	56.5	67.5	68.2	65.5	68.7	63.1	47.0	57.6

Table C. — Voter Participation: November 3, 1992, General Election

County	Estimated Voting Age Population (VAP) 1992	Voter registration (REG) Total	% contribution to state REG	% of 1992 VAP	Rank by % of 1992 VAP	Voter turnout — Highest office Actual	Total	Office	% of 1992 VAP	Maximum vote Total	% contribution to state turnout	% of REG	Rank by % of REG	% of 1992 VAP	Rank by % 1992 VAP	Percent drop-off, by office President	Senator	Governor	Representative
Ada	160,011	136,808	22.4	85.5	20	111,798	110,392	S	69.0	111,798	22.7	81.7	19	69.9	18	1.5	1.3	-	3.3
Adams	2,423	2,396	0.4	98.9	5	1,948	1,937	P	79.9	1,948	0.4	81.3	21	80.4	6	0.6	2.1	-	3.7
Bannock	46,553	40,942	6.7	87.9	15	32,806	32,418	S	69.6	32,806	6.7	80.1	30	70.5	16	1.8	1.2	-	3.6
Bear Lake	3,887	3,593	0.6	92.4	10	3,025	2,857	S	73.5	3,025	0.6	84.2	6	77.8	8	5.7	5.6	-	7.2
Benewah	5,835	4,788	0.8	82.1	29	3,788	3,705	P	63.5	3,788	0.8	79.1	35	64.9	32	2.2	6.3	-	5.9
Bingham	24,875	20,304	3.3	81.6	31	16,339	16,060	S	64.6	16,339	3.3	80.5	28	65.7	31	2.1	1.7	-	2.8
Blaine	11,182	10,261	1.7	91.8	11	8,124	8,022	P	71.7	8,124	1.7	79.2	34	72.7	12	1.3	1.8	-	5.9
Boise	2,723	2,759	0.5	101.3	3	2,329	2,320	P	85.2	2,329	0.5	84.4	5	85.5	3	0.4	2.2	-	3.4
Bonner	20,244	17,419	2.9	86.0	18	14,055	13,823	P	68.3	14,055	2.9	80.7	26	69.4	20	1.7	5.5	-	5.2
Bonneville	50,387	43,408	7.1	86.1	17	35,837	35,400	S	70.3	35,837	7.3	82.6	13	71.1	14	1.3	1.2	-	2.9
Boundary	6,189	4,946	0.8	79.9	32	3,850	3,774	P	61.0	3,850	0.8	77.8	39	62.2	34	2.0	6.4	-	6.5
Butte	2,002	1,829	0.3	91.4	12	1,529	1,503	P	75.1	1,529	0.3	83.6	9	76.4	9	1.7	1.8	-	3.6
Camas	536	584	<.1	109.0	2	495	489	P	91.2	495	0.1	84.8	4	92.4	1	1.2	2.6	-	5.1
Canyon	66,269	48,013	7.9	72.5	38	38,588	37,987	S	57.3	38,588	7.8	80.4	29	58.2	39	1.9	1.6	-	3.5
Caribou	4,434	3,900	0.6	88.0	14	3,367	3,287	P	73.0	3,367	0.7	86.3	2	75.9	11	3.9	3.9	-	5.9
Cassia	13,122	9,485	1.6	72.3	39	7,791	7,696	S	58.6	7,791	1.6	82.1	15	59.4	38	2.2	1.2	-	3.4
Clark	550	555	<.1	100.9	4	450	423	P	76.9	450	<.1	81.1	24	81.8	4	6.0	6.9	-	8.0
Clearwater	6,418	5,093	0.8	79.4	35	3,852	3,732	P	58.1	3,852	0.8	75.6	43	60.0	37	3.1	4.2	-	4.6
Custer	3,203	2,679	0.4	83.6	21	2,201	2,164	P	67.6	2,201	0.4	82.2	14	68.7	22	1.7	3.6	-	5.5
Elmore	15,093	9,128	1.5	60.5	44	7,025	6,890	P	45.7	7,025	1.4	77.0	41	46.5	44	1.9	8.1	-	5.5
Franklin	6,043	5,022	0.8	83.1	24	4,151	4,067	S	67.3	4,151	0.8	82.7	12	68.7	23	2.4	2.0	-	4.1
Fremont	7,301	6,045	1.0	82.8	25	5,039	4,954	P	67.9	5,039	1.0	83.4	11	69.0	21	1.7	2.4	-	3.0
Gem	8,830	7,287	1.2	82.5	27	5,945	5,827	S	66.0	5,945	1.2	81.6	20	67.3	25	3.7	2.0	-	3.3
Gooding	8,481	6,961	1.1	82.1	28	5,709	5,564	P	65.6	5,709	1.2	82.0	16	67.3	26	2.5	7.1	-	4.4
Idaho	10,255	8,392	1.4	81.8	30	6,869	6,735	P	65.7	6,869	1.4	81.9	18	67.0	29	2.0	5.3	-	5.6
Jefferson	10,847	8,654	1.4	79.8	33	7,268	7,159	S	66.0	7,268	1.5	84.0	8	67.0	28	2.1	1.5	-	2.9
Jerome	10,819	8,501	1.4	78.6	36	6,898	6,720	P	62.1	6,898	1.4	81.1	23	63.8	33	2.6	5.8	-	3.7
Kootenai	54,885	46,971	7.7	85.6	19	36,999	36,328	P	66.2	36,999	7.5	78.8	36	67.4	24	1.8	3.8	-	4.4
Latah	23,837	22,516	3.7	94.5	8	16,707	16,331	P	68.5	16,707	3.4	74.2	44	70.1	17	2.3	2.9	-	5.1
Lemhi	5,091	4,847	0.8	95.2	6	3,877	3,821	P	75.1	3,877	0.8	80.0	31	76.2	10	1.4	7.1	-	4.4
Lewis	2,570	2,250	0.4	87.5	16	1,814	1,778	P	69.2	1,814	0.4	80.6	27	70.6	15	2.0	5.1	-	4.7
Lincoln	2,404	1,986	0.3	82.6	26	1,724	1,700	P	70.7	1,724	0.4	86.8	1	71.7	13	1.4	2.8	-	3.7
Madison	15,139	9,631	1.6	63.6	43	7,891	7,763	P	51.3	7,891	1.6	81.9	17	52.1	43	1.6	3.3	-	1.9
Minidoka	13,312	9,401	1.5	70.6	41	7,620	7,512	S	56.4	7,620	1.5	81.1	25	57.2	41	2.7	1.4	-	3.7
Nez Perce	26,213	21,906	3.6	83.6	23	17,389	16,974	P	64.8	17,389	3.5	79.4	33	66.3	30	2.4	2.8	-	3.9
Oneida	2,344	2,220	0.4	94.7	7	1,907	1,866	P	79.6	1,907	0.4	85.9	3	81.4	5	2.2	7.9	-	3.0
Owyhee	5,893	3,866	0.6	65.6	42	3,138	3,072	S	52.1	3,138	0.6	81.2	22	53.2	42	2.1	3.7	-	5.3
Payette	12,088	8,682	1.4	71.8	40	6,938	6,751	S	55.8	6,938	1.4	79.9	32	57.4	40	2.7	2.7	-	4.2
Power	4,966	3,870	0.6	77.9	37	3,035	2,977	P	59.9	3,035	0.6	78.4	37	61.1	36	1.9	3.2	-	2.9
Shoshone	10,076	8,948	1.5	88.8	13	6,770	6,549	P	65.0	6,770	1.4	75.7	42	67.2	27	3.3	4.5	-	4.6
Teton	2,482	2,326	0.4	93.7	9	1,957	1,918	P	77.3	1,957	0.4	84.1	7	78.8	7	2.0	3.4	-	5.6
Twin Falls	39,205	31,257	5.1	79.7	34	24,262	23,506	P	60.0	24,262	4.9	77.6	40	61.9	35	3.1	5.4	-	3.8
Valley	4,658	5,402	0.9	116.0	1	4,210	4,153	P	89.2	4,210	0.9	77.9	38	90.4	2	1.4	3.3	-	4.7
Washington	6,325	5,290	0.9	83.6	22	4,411	4,281	P	67.7	4,411	0.9	83.4	10	69.7	19	2.9	4.9	-	6.3
IDAHO	740,000	611,121	100.0	82.6		491,725	483,135		65.3	491,725	100.0	80.5		66.4		1.9	2.7	-	3.9

Idaho 253

County	Total	Clinton (DEM)	Bush (REP)	Perot (IND)	Other	Plurality Total	Party	DEM	REP	IND	Other	Rank DEM	Rank REP	Rank IND	Total	DEM	REP	IND	DEM	REP
Ada	110,174	31,941	49,000	28,192	1,041	17,059	R	29.0	44.5	25.6	0.9	15	15	35	22.9	23.3	24.2	21.6	39.5	60.5
Adams	1,937	457	754	695	31	59	R	23.6	38.9	35.9	1.6	32	30	1	0.4	0.3	0.4	0.5	37.7	62.3
Bannock	32,211	11,091	12,016	8,116	988	925	R	34.4	37.3	25.2	3.1	8	34	37	6.7	8.1	5.9	6.2	48.0	52.0
Bear Lake	2,854	562	1,419	684	189	735	R	19.7	49.7	24.0	6.6	37	5	39	0.6	0.4	0.7	0.5	28.4	71.6
Benewah	3,705	1,270	1,223	1,165	47	47	D	34.3	33.0	31.4	1.3	9	38	10	0.8	0.9	0.6	0.9	50.9	49.1
Bingham	15,991	3,565	7,333	4,144	949	3,189	R	22.3	45.9	25.9	5.9	35	11	32	3.3	2.6	3.6	3.2	32.7	67.3
Blaine	8,022	2,865	2,243	2,831	83	34	D	35.7	28.0	35.3	1.0	7	43	2	1.7	2.1	1.1	2.2	56.1	43.9
Boise	2,320	623	912	754	31	158	R	26.9	39.3	32.5	1.3	23	27	6	0.5	0.5	0.5	0.6	40.6	59.4
Bonner	13,823	4,995	3,937	4,645	246	350	D	36.1	28.5	33.6	1.8	6	42	5	2.9	3.6	1.9	3.6	55.9	44.1
Bonneville	35,377	7,014	16,557	10,241	1,565	6,316	R	19.8	46.8	28.9	4.4	36	9	18	7.3	5.1	8.2	7.9	29.8	70.2
Boundary	3,774	1,095	1,479	1,136	64	343	R	29.0	39.2	30.1	1.7	14	28	15	0.8	0.8	0.7	0.9	42.5	57.5
Butte	1,503	433	602	392	76	169	R	28.8	40.1	26.1	5.1	16	25	30	0.3	0.3	0.3	0.3	41.8	58.2
Camas	489	134	202	145	8	57	R	27.4	41.3	29.7	1.6	21	22	16	0.1	< .1	< .1	0.1	39.9	60.1
Canyon	37,850	9,095	19,220	8,974	561	10,125	R	24.0	50.8	23.7	1.5	31	4	40	7.9	6.6	9.5	6.9	32.1	67.9
Caribou	3,237	562	1,350	1,088	237	262	R	17.4	41.7	33.6	7.3	41	21	4	0.7	0.4	0.7	0.8	29.4	70.6
Cassia	7,622	1,351	4,052	1,785	434	2,267	R	17.7	53.2	23.4	5.7	40	2	41	1.6	1.0	2.0	1.4	25.0	75.0
Clark	423	95	195	119	14	76	R	22.5	46.1	28.1	3.3	33	10	22	< .1	< .1	< .1	< .1	32.8	67.2
Clearwater	3,732	1,433	1,152	1,098	49	281	D	38.4	30.9	29.4	1.3	4	41	17	0.8	1.0	0.6	0.8	55.4	44.6
Custer	2,164	564	829	729	42	100	R	26.1	38.3	33.7	1.9	26	32	3	0.4	0.4	0.4	0.6	40.5	59.5
Elmore	6,890	1,858	3,087	1,867	78	1,220	R	27.0	44.8	27.1	1.1	22	13	28	1.4	1.4	1.5	1.4	37.6	62.4
Franklin	4,050	524	2,115	890	521	1,225	R	12.9	52.2	22.0	12.9	43	3	44	0.8	0.4	1.0	0.7	19.9	80.1
Fremont	4,954	903	2,333	1,349	369	984	R	18.2	47.1	27.2	7.4	39	8	26	1.0	0.7	1.2	1.0	27.9	72.1
Gem	5,723	1,609	2,455	1,555	104	846	R	28.1	42.9	27.2	1.8	18	19	27	1.2	1.2	1.2	1.2	39.6	60.4
Gooding	5,564	1,530	2,178	1,591	265	587	R	27.5	39.1	28.6	4.8	20	29	20	1.2	1.1	1.1	1.2	41.3	58.7
Idaho	6,735	1,974	2,709	1,900	152	735	R	29.3	40.2	28.2	2.3	13	24	21	1.4	1.4	1.3	1.5	42.2	57.8
Jefferson	7,116	978	3,471	2,164	503	1,307	R	13.7	48.8	30.4	7.1	42	6	14	1.5	0.7	1.7	1.7	22.0	78.0
Jerome	6,720	1,739	2,972	1,768	241	1,204	R	25.9	44.2	26.3	3.6	27	16	29	1.4	1.3	1.5	1.4	36.9	63.1
Kootenai	36,328	11,553	13,065	11,261	449	1,512	R	31.8	36.0	31.0	1.2	10	36	11	7.5	8.4	6.4	8.6	46.9	53.1
Latah	16,331	7,233	5,353	3,602	143	1,880	D	44.3	32.8	22.1	0.9	2	39	43	3.4	5.3	2.6	2.8	57.5	42.5
Lemhi	3,821	996	1,540	1,175	110	365	R	26.1	40.3	30.8	2.9	25	23	12	0.8	0.7	0.8	0.9	39.3	60.7
Lewis	1,778	674	593	491	20	81	D	37.9	33.4	27.6	1.1	5	37	25	0.4	0.5	0.3	0.4	53.2	46.8
Lincoln	1,700	514	656	441	89	142	R	30.2	38.6	25.9	5.2	12	31	31	0.4	0.4	0.3	0.3	43.9	56.1
Madison	7,763	741	4,591	1,920	511	2,671	R	9.5	59.1	24.7	6.6	44	1	38	1.6	0.5	2.3	1.5	13.9	86.1
Minidoka	7,417	1,815	3,304	1,875	423	1,429	R	24.5	44.5	25.3	5.7	30	14	36	1.5	1.3	1.6	1.4	35.5	64.5
Nez Perce	16,974	7,069	5,431	4,363	111	1,638	D	41.6	32.0	25.7	0.7	3	40	34	3.5	5.2	2.7	3.3	56.6	43.4
Oneida	1,866	351	713	590	212	123	R	18.8	38.2	31.6	11.4	38	33	8	0.4	0.3	0.4	0.5	33.0	67.0
Owyhee	3,072	686	1,469	862	55	607	R	22.3	47.8	28.1	1.8	34	7	24	0.6	0.5	0.7	0.7	31.8	68.2
Payette	6,748	1,656	2,895	2,055	142	840	R	24.5	42.9	30.5	2.1	29	18	13	1.4	1.2	1.4	1.6	36.4	63.6
Power	2,977	837	1,352	697	91	515	R	28.1	45.4	23.4	3.1	17	12	42	0.6	0.6	0.7	0.5	38.2	61.8
Shoshone	6,549	3,182	1,441	1,878	48	1,304	D	48.6	22.0	28.7	0.7	1	44	19	1.4	2.3	0.7	1.4	68.8	31.2
Teton	1,918	472	762	608	76	154	R	24.6	39.7	31.7	4.0	28	26	7	0.4	0.3	0.4	0.5	38.2	61.8
Twin Falls	23,506	6,593	10,335	6,043	535	3,742	R	28.0	44.0	25.7	2.3	19	17	33	4.9	4.8	5.1	4.6	38.9	61.1
Valley	4,153	1,259	1,548	1,313	33	235	R	30.3	37.3	31.6	0.8	11	35	9	0.9	0.9	0.8	1.0	44.9	55.1
Washington	4,281	1,122	1,802	1,204	153	598	R	26.2	42.1	28.1	3.6	24	20	23	0.9	0.8	0.9	0.9	38.4	61.6
IDAHO	**482,142**	**137,013**	**202,645**	**130,395**	**12,089**	**65,632**	**R**	**28.4**	**42.0**	**27.0**	**2.5**				**100.0**	**100.0**	**100.0**	**100.0**	**40.3**	**59.7**

Table F. — Vote for U.S. Senator: November 3, 1992, General Election

County	Total[1]	Stallings (DEM)	Kemp-thorne (REP)		Plurality Total	Party	Percent of total vote DEM	REP		Rank DEM	Rank REP		Percent contribution to state vote Total	DEM	REP	
Ada	110,392	42,875	67,517	-	24,642	R	38.8	61.2	-	30	15	-	23.1	20.6	25.0	-
Adams	1,908	636	1,272	-	636	R	33.3	66.7	-	40	5	-	0.4	0.3	0.5	-
Bannock	32,418	17,953	14,465	-	3,488	D	55.4	44.6	-	3	42	-	6.8	8.6	5.3	-
Bear Lake	2,857	862	1,995	-	1,133	R	30.2	69.8	-	44	1	-	0.6	0.4	0.7	-
Benewah	3,551	1,762	1,789	-	27	R	49.6	50.4	-	15	30	-	0.7	0.8	0.7	-
Bingham	16,060	7,652	8,408	-	756	R	47.6	52.4	-	21	24	-	3.4	3.7	3.1	-
Blaine	7,976	4,309	3,667	-	642	D	54.0	46.0	-	6	39	-	1.7	2.1	1.4	-
Boise	2,278	820	1,458	-	638	R	36.0	64.0	-	37	8	-	0.5	0.4	0.5	-
Bonner	13,282	6,741	6,541	-	200	D	50.8	49.2	-	13	32	-	2.8	3.2	2.4	-
Bonneville	35,400	14,633	20,767	-	6,134	R	41.3	58.7	-	26	19	-	7.4	7.0	7.7	-
Boundary	3,605	1,600	2,005	-	405	R	44.4	55.6	-	22	23	-	0.8	0.8	0.7	-
Butte	1,501	793	708	-	85	D	52.8	47.2	-	9	36	-	0.3	0.4	0.3	-
Camas	482	232	250	-	18	R	48.1	51.9	-	20	25	-	0.1	0.1	<.1	-
Canyon	37,987	11,819	26,168	-	14,349	R	31.1	68.9	-	43	2	-	7.9	5.7	9.7	-
Caribou	3,235	1,265	1,970	-	705	R	39.1	60.9	-	28	17	-	0.7	0.6	0.7	-
Cassia	7,696	3,715	3,981	-	266	R	48.3	51.7	-	19	26	-	1.6	1.8	1.5	-
Clark	419	162	257	-	95	R	38.7	61.3	-	31	14	-	<.1	<.1	<.1	-
Clearwater	3,690	1,973	1,717	-	256	D	53.5	46.5	-	8	37	-	0.8	0.9	0.6	-
Custer	2,122	843	1,279	-	436	R	39.7	60.3	-	27	18	-	0.4	0.4	0.5	-
Elmore	6,456	2,474	3,982	-	1,508	R	38.3	61.7	-	32	13	-	1.3	1.2	1.5	-
Franklin	4,067	1,433	2,634	-	1,201	R	35.2	64.8	-	39	6	-	0.8	0.7	1.0	-
Fremont	4,916	2,041	2,875	-	834	R	41.5	58.5	-	25	20	-	1.0	1.0	1.1	-
Gem	5,827	2,216	3,611	-	1,395	R	38.0	62.0	-	33	12	-	1.2	1.1	1.3	-
Gooding	5,306	2,628	2,678	-	50	R	49.5	50.5	-	16	29	-	1.1	1.3	1.0	-
Idaho	6,504	2,529	3,975	-	1,446	R	38.9	61.1	-	29	16	-	1.4	1.2	1.5	-
Jefferson	7,159	2,672	4,487	-	1,815	R	37.3	62.7	-	34	11	-	1.5	1.3	1.7	-
Jerome	6,496	3,199	3,297	-	98	R	49.2	50.8	-	17	28	-	1.4	1.5	1.2	-
Kootenai	35,605	15,202	20,403	-	5,201	R	42.7	57.3	-	24	21	-	7.4	7.3	7.5	-
Latah	16,222	8,317	7,905	-	412	D	51.3	48.7	-	11	34	-	3.4	4.0	2.9	-
Lemhi	3,600	1,272	2,328	-	1,056	R	35.3	64.7	-	38	7	-	0.8	0.6	0.9	-
Lewis	1,722	860	862	-	2	R	49.9	50.1	-	14	31	-	0.4	0.4	0.3	-
Lincoln	1,675	984	691	-	293	D	58.7	41.3	-	2	43	-	0.4	0.5	0.3	-
Madison	7,633	3,281	4,352	-	1,071	R	43.0	57.0	-	23	22	-	1.6	1.6	1.6	-
Minidoka	7,512	4,125	3,387	-	738	D	54.9	45.1	-	4	41	-	1.6	2.0	1.3	-
Nez Perce	16,900	9,049	7,851	-	1,198	D	53.5	46.5	-	7	38	-	3.5	4.3	2.9	-
Oneida	1,756	899	857	-	42	D	51.2	48.8	-	12	33	-	0.4	0.4	0.3	-
Owyhee	3,023	977	2,046	-	1,069	R	32.3	67.7	-	42	3	-	0.6	0.5	0.8	-
Payette	6,751	2,245	4,506	-	2,261	R	33.3	66.7	-	41	4	-	1.4	1.1	1.7	-
Power	2,937	1,600	1,337	-	263	D	54.5	45.5	-	5	40	-	0.6	0.8	0.5	-
Shoshone	6,464	4,135	2,329	-	1,806	D	64.0	36.0	-	1	44	-	1.4	2.0	0.9	-
Teton	1,891	989	902	-	87	D	52.3	47.7	-	10	35	-	0.4	0.5	0.3	-
Twin Falls	22,959	11,251	11,708	-	457	R	49.0	51.0	-	18	27	-	4.8	5.4	4.3	-
Valley	4,069	1,501	2,568	-	1,067	R	36.9	63.1	-	35	10	-	0.9	0.7	0.9	-
Washington	4,195	1,512	2,683	-	1,171	R	36.0	64.0	-	36	9	-	0.9	0.7	1.0	-
IDAHO	**478,504**	**208,036**	**270,468**	**-**	**62,432**	**R**	**43.5**	**56.5**	**-**				**100.0**	**100.0**	**100.0**	**-**

Does not include Write in votes for independent candidate Shepherd (statewide total 18).

Table H. — Vote for U.S. Representative in Congress: November 3, 1992, General Election

Congressional district and county	Total	Democrat (DEM)	Republican (REP)	Other	Plurality Total	Plurality Party	Percent of total vote DEM	Percent of total vote REP	Percent of total vote Other	Rank within district DEM	Rank within district REP	Rank within district Other	Percent contribution to district vote Total	Percent contribution to district vote DEM	Percent contribution to district vote REP	Percent contribution to district vote Other
District 1	**242,790**	**140,985**	**90,983**	**10,822**	**50,002**	**D**	**58.1**	**37.5**	**4.5**				**100.0**	**100.0**	**100.0**	**100.0**
Ada (pt)	71,153	41,827	26,203	3,123	15,624	D	58.8	36.8	4.4	9	11	11	29.3	29.7	28.8	28.9
Adams	1,876	979	820	77	159	D	52.2	43.7	4.1	16	4	13	0.8	0.7	0.9	0.7
Benewah	3,563	2,246	1,180	137	1,066	D	63.0	33.1	3.8	4	16	15	1.5	1.6	1.3	1.3
Boise	2,250	1,293	839	118	454	D	57.5	37.3	5.2	10	10	4	0.9	0.9	0.9	1.1
Bonner	13,324	8,019	4,493	812	3,526	D	60.2	33.7	6.1	8	14	1	5.5	5.7	4.9	7.5
Boundary	3,599	2,007	1,456	136	551	D	55.8	40.5	3.8	13	6	16	1.5	1.4	1.6	1.3
Canyon	37,226	18,855	16,642	1,729	2,213	D	50.7	44.7	4.6	17	3	8	15.3	13.4	18.3	16.0
Clearwater	3,673	2,266	1,234	173	1,032	D	61.7	33.6	4.7	6	15	7	1.5	1.6	1.4	1.6
Gem	5,746	3,222	2,219	305	1,003	D	56.1	38.6	5.3	12	9	2	2.4	2.3	2.4	2.8
Idaho	6,481	3,235	2,951	295	284	D	49.9	45.5	4.6	18	2	9	2.7	2.3	3.2	2.7
Kootenai	35,376	19,890	13,921	1,565	5,969	D	56.2	39.4	4.4	11	8	10	14.6	14.1	15.3	14.5
Latah	15,855	10,487	4,743	625	5,744	D	66.1	29.9	3.9	3	17	14	6.5	7.4	5.2	5.8
Lewis	1,729	1,069	587	73	482	D	61.8	34.0	4.2	5	13	12	0.7	0.8	0.6	0.7
Nez Perce	16,714	11,196	4,972	546	6,224	D	67.0	29.7	3.3	2	18	19	6.9	7.9	5.5	5.0
Owyhee	2,972	1,436	1,426	110	10	D	48.3	48.0	3.7	19	1	17	1.2	1.0	1.6	1.0
Payette	6,648	3,487	2,809	352	678	D	52.5	42.3	5.3	15	5	3	2.7	2.5	3.1	3.3
Shoshone	6,460	4,740	1,411	309	3,329	D	73.4	21.8	4.8	1	19	6	2.7	3.4	1.6	2.9
Valley	4,012	2,469	1,408	135	1,061	D	61.5	35.1	3.4	7	12	18	1.7	1.8	1.5	1.2
Washington	4,133	2,262	1,669	202	593	D	54.7	40.4	4.9	14	7	5	1.7	1.6	1.8	1.9
District 2	**229,957**	**81,450**	**139,783**	**8,724**	**58,333**	**R**	**35.4**	**60.8**	**3.8**				**100.0**	**100.0**	**100.0**	**100.0**
Ada (pt)	36,942	14,346	21,417	1,179	7,071	R	38.8	58.0	3.2	8	19	18	16.1	17.6	15.3	13.5
Bannock	31,637	14,775	15,805	1,057	1,030	R	46.7	50.0	3.3	3	24	17	13.8	18.1	11.3	12.1
Bear Lake	2,807	965	1,756	86	791	R	34.4	62.6	3.1	14	9	21	1.2	1.2	1.3	1.0
Bingham	15,884	5,559	9,470	855	3,911	R	35.0	59.6	5.4	13	16	2	6.9	6.8	6.8	9.8
Blaine	7,644	3,504	3,836	304	332	R	45.8	50.2	4.0	4	23	13	3.3	4.3	2.7	3.5
Bonneville	34,802	9,202	24,170	1,430	14,968	R	26.4	69.5	4.1	24	3	11	15.1	11.3	17.3	16.4
Butte	1,474	613	797	64	184	R	41.6	54.1	4.3	7	20	10	0.6	0.8	0.6	0.7
Camas	470	160	295	15	135	R	34.0	62.8	3.2	17	8	19	0.2	0.2	0.2	0.2
Caribou	3,167	1,040	1,973	154	933	R	32.8	62.3	4.9	19	10	4	1.4	1.3	1.4	1.8
Cassia	7,529	2,149	5,159	221	3,010	R	28.5	68.5	2.9	22	4	23	3.3	2.6	3.7	2.5
Clark	414	141	255	18	114	R	34.1	61.6	4.3	16	11	9	0.2	0.2	0.2	0.2
Custer	2,080	714	1,267	99	553	R	34.3	60.9	4.8	15	13	7	0.9	0.9	0.9	1.1
Elmore	6,640	2,500	3,875	265	1,375	R	37.7	58.4	4.0	9	18	12	2.9	3.1	2.8	3.0
Franklin	3,981	1,683	2,145	153	462	R	42.3	53.9	3.8	6	21	14	1.7	2.1	1.5	1.8
Fremont	4,887	1,324	3,329	234	2,005	R	27.1	68.1	4.8	23	5	6	2.1	1.6	2.4	2.7
Gooding	5,458	1,962	3,306	190	1,344	R	35.9	60.6	3.5	11	14	16	2.4	2.4	2.4	2.2
Jefferson	7,060	1,735	4,950	375	3,215	R	24.6	70.1	5.3	25	2	3	3.1	2.1	3.5	4.3
Jerome	6,640	2,095	4,349	196	2,254	R	31.6	65.5	3.0	21	6	22	2.9	2.6	3.1	2.2
Lemhi	3,708	1,192	2,246	270	1,054	R	32.1	60.6	7.3	20	15	1	1.6	1.5	1.6	3.1
Lincoln	1,661	727	882	52	155	R	43.8	53.1	3.1	5	22	20	0.7	0.9	0.6	0.6
Madison	7,741	1,496	5,873	372	4,377	R	19.3	75.9	4.8	26	1	5	3.4	1.8	4.2	4.3
Minidoka	7,339	2,577	4,490	272	1,913	R	35.1	61.2	3.7	12	12	15	3.2	3.2	3.2	3.1
Oneida	1,849	1,126	669	54	457	D	60.9	36.2	2.9	1	26	24	0.8	1.4	0.5	0.6
Power	2,948	1,510	1,358	80	152	D	51.2	46.1	2.7	2	25	26	1.3	1.9	1.0	0.9
Teton	1,848	677	1,086	85	409	R	36.6	58.8	4.6	10	17	8	0.8	0.8	0.8	1.0
Twin Falls	23,347	7,678	15,025	644	7,347	R	32.9	64.4	2.8	18	7	25	10.2	9.4	10.7	7.4
IDAHO	**472,747**	**222,435**	**230,766**	**19,546**	**8,331**	**R**	**47.1**	**48.8**	**4.1**							

Table I. — Vote for Presidential Preference: March 3, 1992, Democratic Primary Election

County	Top candidates									Top three candidates(state vote)									
										Percent of total vote			Rank			Percent contribution to state vote			
	Total	Clinton	None of Above	Brown	LaRouche	Agran				Clinton	None of Above	Brown	Clinton	None of Above	Brown	Total	Clinton	None of Above	Brown
Ada	9,193	4,307	2,902	1,670	240	74	-	-	-	46.9	31.6	18.2	33	14	14	16.7	15.9	18.1	18.1
Adams	193	105	35	34	11	8	-	-	-	54.4	18.1	17.6	16	35	17	0.4	0.4	0.2	0.4
Bannock	3,794	2,116	595	826	164	93	-	-	-	55.8	15.7	21.8	13	41	5	6.9	7.8	3.7	9.0
Bear Lake	225	150	18	41	12	4	-	-	-	66.7	8.0	18.2	1	44	13	0.4	0.6	0.1	0.4
Benewah	671	396	109	125	31	10	-	-	-	59.0	16.2	18.6	7	40	10	1.2	1.5	0.7	1.4
Bingham	1,472	660	494	213	79	26	-	-	-	44.8	33.6	14.5	38	6	29	2.7	2.4	3.1	2.3
Blaine	1,048	290	478	263	12	5	-	-	-	27.7	45.6	25.1	44	1	1	1.9	1.1	3.0	2.9
Boise	259	140	54	50	11	4	-	-	-	54.1	20.8	19.3	18	31	8	0.5	0.5	0.3	0.5
Bonner	3,118	1,586	634	734	124	40	-	-	-	50.9	20.3	23.5	27	33	2	5.7	5.9	4.0	8.0
Bonneville	2,100	995	627	352	94	32	-	-	-	47.4	29.9	16.8	32	16	20	3.8	3.7	3.9	3.8
Boundary	448	260	94	69	20	5	-	-	-	58.0	21.0	15.4	9	30	25	0.8	1.0	0.6	0.7
Butte	284	142	90	32	14	6	-	-	-	50.0	31.7	11.3	28	12	41	0.5	0.5	0.6	0.3
Camas	68	34	17	12	4	1	-	-	-	50.0	25.0	17.6	29	21	16	0.1	0.1	0.1	0.1
Canyon	2,549	1,406	550	425	126	42	-	-	-	55.2	21.6	16.7	14	28	21	4.6	5.2	3.4	4.6
Caribou	344	183	50	75	29	7	-	-	-	53.2	14.5	21.8	20	42	4	0.6	0.7	0.3	0.8
Cassia	572	293	143	90	38	8	-	-	-	51.2	25.0	15.7	25	22	24	1.0	1.1	0.9	1.0
Clark	20	11	4	4	1	0	-	-	-	55.0	20.0	20.0	15	34	7	<.1	<.1	<.1	<.1
Clearwater	1,057	514	343	147	40	13	-	-	-	48.6	32.5	13.9	31	8	30	1.9	1.9	2.1	1.6
Custer	238	125	53	45	13	2	-	-	-	52.5	22.3	18.9	22	25	9	0.4	0.5	0.3	0.5
Elmore	1,366	699	442	172	43	10	-	-	-	51.2	32.4	12.6	26	9	35	2.5	2.6	2.8	1.9
Franklin	313	138	98	55	11	11	-	-	-	44.1	31.3	17.6	41	15	18	0.6	0.5	0.6	0.6
Fremont	477	206	154	66	34	17	-	-	-	43.2	32.3	13.8	43	10	32	0.9	0.8	1.0	0.7
Gem	644	349	204	58	25	8	-	-	-	54.2	31.7	9.0	17	13	44	1.2	1.3	1.3	0.6
Gooding	382	248	64	52	12	6	-	-	-	64.9	16.8	13.6	2	38	33	0.7	0.9	0.4	0.6
Idaho	1,357	711	376	188	58	24	-	-	-	52.4	27.7	13.9	23	19	31	2.5	2.6	2.3	2.0
Jefferson	447	203	149	56	28	11	-	-	-	45.4	33.3	12.5	36	7	36	0.8	0.8	0.9	0.6
Jerome	407	236	67	66	33	5	-	-	-	58.0	16.5	16.2	10	39	23	0.7	0.9	0.4	0.7
Kootenai	4,782	2,113	1,633	883	116	37	-	-	-	44.2	34.1	18.5	40	5	12	8.7	7.8	10.2	9.6
Latah	2,463	1,107	644	456	63	193	-	-	-	44.9	26.1	18.5	37	20	11	4.5	4.1	4.0	5.0
Lemhi	428	250	105	54	14	5	-	-	-	58.4	24.5	12.6	8	23	34	0.8	0.9	0.7	0.6
Lewis	809	378	309	84	28	10	-	-	-	46.7	38.2	10.4	34	3	43	1.5	1.4	1.9	0.9
Lincoln	137	85	15	29	4	4	-	-	-	62.0	10.9	21.2	3	43	6	0.2	0.3	<.1	0.3
Madison	346	185	84	42	26	9	-	-	-	53.5	24.3	12.1	19	24	38	0.6	0.7	0.5	0.5
Minidoka	633	282	177	110	45	19	-	-	-	44.5	28.0	17.4	39	18	19	1.1	1.0	1.1	1.2
Nez Perce	4,018	1,863	1,515	487	122	31	-	-	-	46.4	37.7	12.1	35	4	39	7.3	6.9	9.5	5.3
Oneida	270	133	86	33	12	6	-	-	-	49.3	31.9	12.2	30	11	37	0.5	0.5	0.5	0.4
Owyhee	298	177	53	45	18	5	-	-	-	59.4	17.8	15.1	6	36	26	0.5	0.7	0.3	0.5
Payette	647	340	184	95	22	6	-	-	-	52.6	28.4	14.7	21	17	28	1.2	1.3	1.1	1.0
Power	366	211	81	54	15	5	-	-	-	57.7	22.1	14.8	11	27	27	0.7	0.8	0.5	0.6
Shoshone	4,562	2,009	1,856	530	133	34	-	-	-	44.0	40.7	11.6	42	2	40	8.3	7.4	11.6	5.8
Teton	193	109	41	32	7	4	-	-	-	56.5	21.2	16.6	12	29	22	0.4	0.4	0.3	0.3
Twin Falls	1,388	831	242	247	47	21	-	-	-	59.9	17.4	17.8	5	37	15	2.5	3.1	1.5	2.7
Valley	275	143	57	62	10	3	-	-	-	52.0	20.7	22.5	24	32	3	0.5	0.5	0.4	0.7
Washington	463	285	103	49	22	4	-	-	-	61.6	22.2	10.6	4	26	42	0.8	1.1	0.6	0.5
IDAHO	55,124	27,004	16,029	9,212	2,011	868	-	-	-	49.0	29.1	16.7				100.0	100.0	100.0	100.0

Table J. — Vote for Presidential Preference: March 3, 1992, Republican Primary Election

County	Top candidates					Top four candidates (state vote)									Percent contribution to state vote				
						Percent of total vote													
										Rank									
	Total	Bush	None of Above	Bu-chanan	-	Bush	None of Above	Bu-chanan	-	Bush	None of Above	Bu-chanan	-	Total	Bush	None of Above	Bu-chanan	-
Ada	28,357	17,932	7,633	2,792	-	63.2	26.9	9.8	-	27	7	41	-	24.6	24.5	28.2	18.4	-
Adams	713	437	155	121	-	61.3	21.7	17.0	-	32	22	5	-	0.6	0.6	0.6	0.8	-
Bannock	3,313	2,514	276	523	-	75.9	8.3	15.8	-	2	43	12	-	2.9	3.4	1.0	3.4	-
Bear Lake	1,225	919	136	170	-	75.0	11.1	13.9	-	3	41	26	-	1.1	1.3	0.5	1.1	-
Benewah	562	421	63	78	-	74.9	11.2	13.9	-	5	40	25	-	0.5	0.6	0.2	0.5	-
Bingham	5,437	3,228	1,454	755	-	59.4	26.7	13.9	-	35	8	24	-	4.7	4.4	5.4	5.0	-
Blaine	808	472	267	69	-	58.4	33.0	8.5	-	37	2	43	-	0.7	0.6	1.0	0.5	-
Boise	641	454	96	91	-	70.8	15.0	14.2	-	11	37	21	-	0.6	0.6	0.4	0.6	-
Bonner	1,804	1,428	193	183	-	79.2	10.7	10.1	-	1	42	40	-	1.6	1.9	0.7	1.2	-
Bonneville	12,021	7,183	2,959	1,879	-	59.8	24.6	15.6	-	34	14	17	-	10.4	9.8	10.9	12.4	-
Boundary	571	386	95	90	-	67.6	16.6	15.8	-	16	33	13	-	0.5	0.5	0.4	0.6	-
Butte	349	230	77	42	-	65.9	22.1	12.0	-	21	19	35	-	0.3	0.3	0.3	0.3	-
Camas	172	129	31	12	-	75.0	18.0	7.0	-	4	27	44	-	0.1	0.2	0.1	<.1	-
Canyon	11,572	7,517	2,602	1,453	-	65.0	22.5	12.6	-	24	18	33	-	10.0	10.3	9.6	9.6	-
Caribou	910	678	62	170	-	74.5	6.8	18.7	-	6	44	2	-	0.8	0.9	0.2	1.1	-
Cassia	2,047	1,357	464	226	-	66.3	22.7	11.0	-	20	17	37	-	1.8	1.9	1.7	1.5	-
Clark	251	139	64	48	-	55.4	25.5	19.1	-	42	13	1	-	0.2	0.2	0.2	0.3	-
Clearwater	300	206	47	47	-	68.7	15.7	15.7	-	13	36	15	-	0.3	0.3	0.2	0.3	-
Custer	852	484	248	120	-	56.8	29.1	14.1	-	39	6	23	-	0.7	0.7	0.9	0.8	-
Elmore	1,435	1,035	249	151	-	72.1	17.4	10.5	-	9	29	39	-	1.2	1.4	0.9	1.0	-
Franklin	858	622	153	83	-	72.5	17.8	9.7	-	8	28	42	-	0.7	0.8	0.6	0.5	-
Fremont	1,552	1,067	222	263	-	68.8	14.3	16.9	-	12	38	7	-	1.3	1.5	0.8	1.7	-
Gem	1,295	787	344	164	-	60.8	26.6	12.7	-	33	9	31	-	1.1	1.1	1.3	1.1	-
Gooding	2,068	1,167	547	354	-	56.4	26.5	17.1	-	40	10	4	-	1.8	1.6	2.0	2.3	-
Idaho	1,598	1,078	270	250	-	67.5	16.9	15.6	-	17	31	16	-	1.4	1.5	1.0	1.6	-
Jefferson	2,966	1,631	870	465	-	55.0	29.3	15.7	-	43	5	14	-	2.6	2.2	3.2	3.1	-
Jerome	2,262	1,425	462	375	-	63.0	20.4	16.6	-	28	24	9	-	2.0	1.9	1.7	2.5	-
Kootenai	3,275	2,132	717	426	-	65.1	21.9	13.0	-	23	21	28	-	2.8	2.9	2.7	2.8	-
Latah	1,306	867	218	221	-	66.4	16.7	16.9	-	19	32	8	-	1.1	1.2	0.8	1.5	-
Lemhi	1,514	849	471	194	-	56.1	31.1	12.8	-	41	3	29	-	1.3	1.2	1.7	1.3	-
Lewis	152	104	25	23	-	68.4	16.4	15.1	-	15	34	19	-	0.1	0.1	<.1	0.2	-
Lincoln	617	364	159	94	-	59.0	25.8	15.2	-	36	12	18	-	0.5	0.5	0.6	0.6	-
Madison	3,405	2,330	578	497	-	68.4	17.0	14.6	-	14	30	20	-	2.9	3.2	2.1	3.3	-
Minidoka	3,387	1,637	1,160	590	-	48.3	34.2	17.4	-	44	1	3	-	2.9	2.2	4.3	3.9	-
Nez Perce	1,345	954	245	146	-	70.9	18.2	10.9	-	10	26	38	-	1.2	1.3	0.9	1.0	-
Oneida	790	503	157	130	-	63.7	19.9	16.5	-	25	25	10	-	0.7	0.7	0.6	0.9	-
Owyhee	879	591	139	149	-	67.2	15.8	17.0	-	18	35	6	-	0.8	0.8	0.5	1.0	-
Payette	1,773	1,098	459	216	-	61.9	25.9	12.2	-	31	11	34	-	1.5	1.5	1.7	1.4	-
Power	510	370	71	69	-	72.5	13.9	13.5	-	7	39	27	-	0.4	0.5	0.3	0.5	-
Shoshone	236	154	52	30	-	65.3	22.0	12.7	-	22	20	30	-	0.2	0.2	0.2	0.2	-
Teton	587	369	122	96	-	62.9	20.8	16.4	-	29	23	11	-	0.5	0.5	0.5	0.6	-
Twin Falls	6,718	4,194	1,573	951	-	62.4	23.4	14.2	-	30	16	22	-	5.8	5.7	5.8	6.3	-
Valley	1,740	1,013	533	194	-	58.2	30.6	11.1	-	38	4	36	-	1.5	1.4	2.0	1.3	-
Washington	1,329	842	320	167	-	63.4	24.1	12.6	-	26	15	32	-	1.2	1.1	1.2	1.1	-
IDAHO	115,502	73,297	27,038	15,167	-	63.5	23.4	13.1	-					100.0	100.0	100.0	100.0	-

1992 Vote for President
Percent for Bush (R), by County

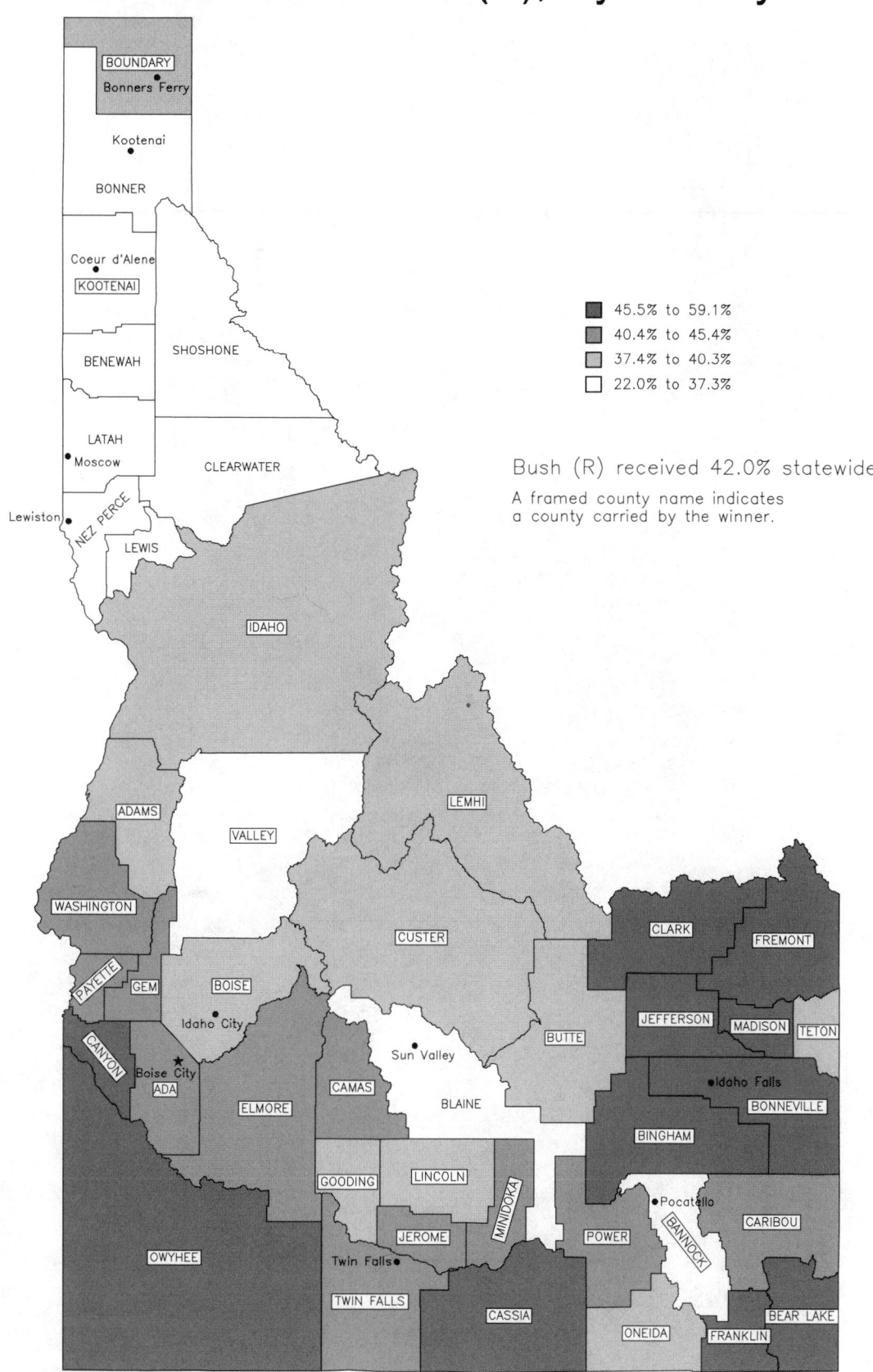

45.5% to 59.1%
40.4% to 45.4%
37.4% to 40.3%
22.0% to 37.3%

Bush (R) received 42.0% statewide.

A framed county name indicates
a county carried by the winner.

BOUNDARY
Bonners Ferry
Kootenai
BONNER
Coeur d'Alene
KOOTENAI
SHOSHONE
BENEWAH
LATAH
Moscow
CLEARWATER
Lewiston
NEZ PERCE
LEWIS
IDAHO
ADAMS
VALLEY
LEMHI
WASHINGTON
CUSTER
CLARK
FREMONT
PAYETTE
GEM
BOISE
Idaho City
JEFFERSON
MADISON
TETON
CANYON
Boise City
ADA
Sun Valley
BUTTE
Idaho Falls
BONNEVILLE
ELMORE
CAMAS
BLAINE
BINGHAM
GOODING
LINCOLN
MINIDOKA
Pocatello
CARIBOU
OWYHEE
JEROME
POWER
BANNOCK
Twin Falls
TWIN FALLS
CASSIA
ONEIDA
FRANKLIN
BEAR LAKE

Idaho 259

1992 Vote for U.S. Senator
Percent for Kempthorne (R), by County

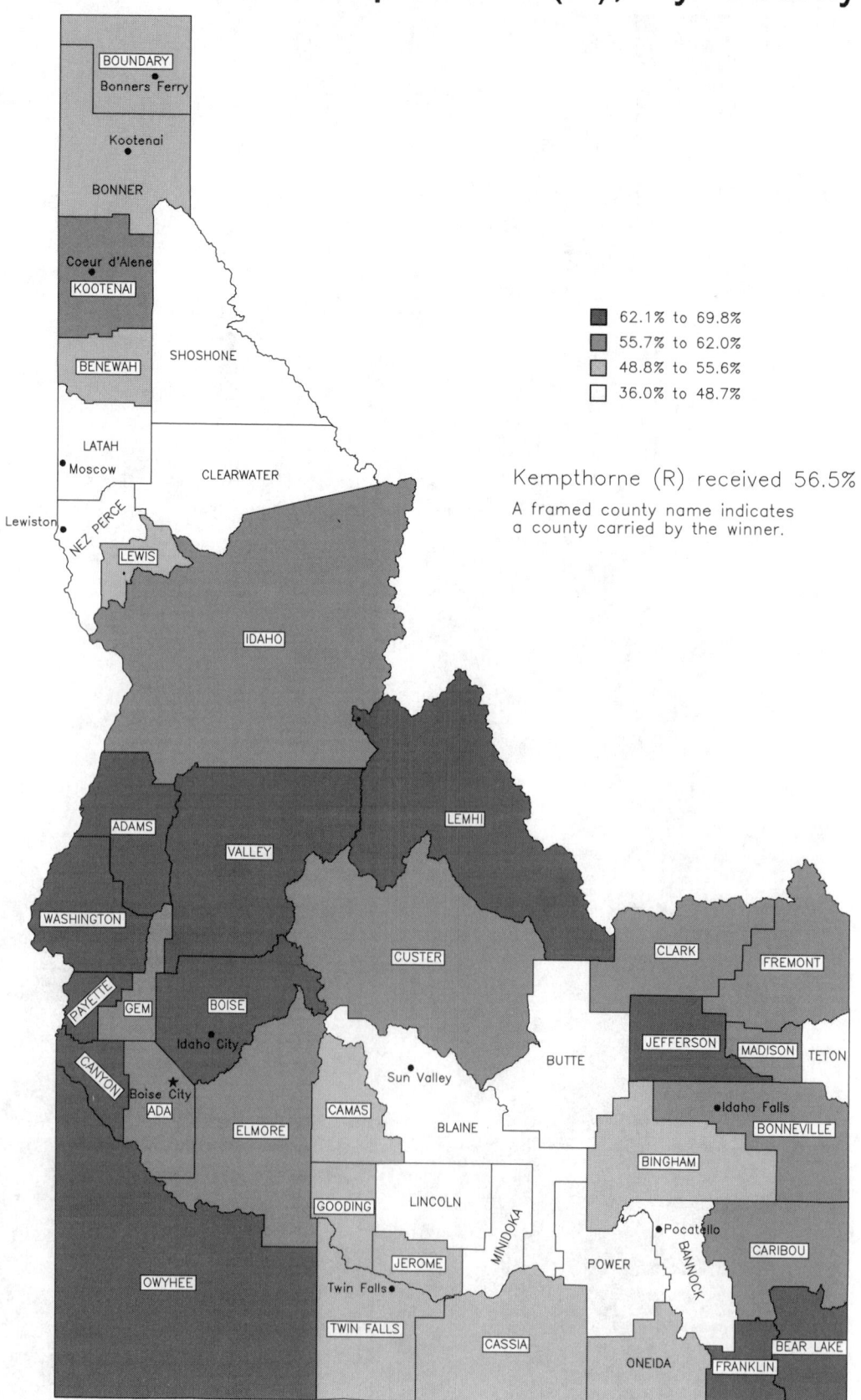

■ 62.1% to 69.8%
■ 55.7% to 62.0%
■ 48.8% to 55.6%
□ 36.0% to 48.7%

Kempthorne (R) received 56.5% statewide.

A framed county name indicates
a county carried by the winner.

ILLINOIS

Congressional Districts 20
  Average Population 571,530
State Senate Districts 59
  Average Population 193,739
State House Districts 118
  Average Population 96,870

Electoral College Votes..22
Counties[1] 102
Voting Precincts 11,284

Alternative Registration Methods:
  ....Agency-based, Deputized Registrars

Registration Deadline (Days before Election) 28

Voting Equipment Use (Counties)[1]

Datavote Punch Card	0	Paper Ballot	1
Electronic	0	Other Punch Card	108
Lever Machine	1	Mixed Systems	1
Optical Scanner	0		

Party Control	DEM	REP	IND	VAC
1993 State Senate	27	32	0	0
1992 State Senate	31	28	0	0
1993 State House	67	51	0	0
1992 State House	72	46	0	0

Population Statistics 1990

Race/ Ethnicity	Total Population		Voting Age Population		Voting Age Population % of total population
	Number	%	Number	%	
Non-Hispanic					
White	8,550,208	74.8	6,567,688	77.4	76.8
Black	1,673,703	14.6	1,128,332	13.3	67.4
Asian/Pacific Islander	275,568	2.4	197,458	2.3	71.7
Native American	18,213	0.2	13,410	0.2	73.6
Other	8,464	<.1	3,954	<.1	46.7
All Hispanic	904,446	7.9	573,394	6.8	63.4
TOTAL	11,430,602	100.0	8,484,236	100.0	74.2

Estimated Voting Age Population 1992 (VAP) 8,568,000
Number of Registered Voters................................. 6,600,358
  % of estimated VAP... 77.0
Voter Turnout (Actual) 5,164,357
  % of VAP 60.3
  % of Registration 78.2
Persons Not Voting—of Voting Age 3,403,643
  % of VAP 39.7
Persons Not Voting—of Registered 1,436,001
  % of Registration 21.8
Straight Ticket Voting .... Yes, Exception

State Officials and Members of Congress

Governor:
Jim Edgar (R) 1990, elected to a four-year term in 1990.

U.S. Senators:
Paul Simon (D) 1984, elected to a six-year term in 1990.
Carol Moseley Braun (D) 1992, elected to a six-year term in 1992.

U.S. Representative in Congress:
(District, Name, Party, Date first elected)

1. Rush (D) 1992
2. Reynolds (D) 1992
3. Lipinski (D) 1982
4. Gutierrez (D) 1992
5. Rostenkowski (D) 1958

6. Hyde (R) 1974
7. Collins (D) 1973
8. Crane (R) 1969
9. Yates (D) 1964
10. Porter (R) 1980

11. Sangmeister (D) 1988
12. Costello (D) 1988
13. Fawell (R) 1984
14. Hastert (R) 1986
15. Ewing (R) 1991

16. Manzullo (R) 1992
17. Evans (D) 1982
18. Michel (R) 1956
19. Poshard (D) 1988
20. Durbin (D) 1982

[1]Because several cities administer elections independently, exceeds total number of counties.

Candidates: General Election, November 3, 1992

Candidate(s)	Total vote	Percent	Party	Status	First elected
President/Vice President					
Clinton/Gore	2,453,350	48.58%	Democrat	Challenger	1992
Bush/Quayle	1,734,096	34.34%	Republican	Incumbent	1988
Perot/Stockdale	840,515	16.64%	Ross Perot	Challenger	
Marrou/Lord	9,218	0.18%	Libertarian	Challenger	
Fulani/Munoz	5,267	0.10%	New Alliance	Challenger	
Gritz/Minett	3,577	0.07%	Populist	Challenger	
Hagelin/Tompkins	2,751	0.05%	Natural Law	Challenger	
Warren/Reid	1,361	0.03%	Socialist Worker	Challenger	
Write ins[1]	22	<0.1%	Write in	Challenger	
U.S. Senator					
Carol Moseley Braun	2,631,229	53.27%	Democrat	Challenger	1992
Richard Williamson	2,126,833	43.06%	Republican	Challenger	
Chad Koppie	100,422	2.03%	Conservative	Challenger	
Andrew Spiegel	34,527	0.70%	Libertarian	Challenger	
Charles Winter	15,118	0.31%	Natural Law	Challenger	
Alan Port	12,689	0.26%	New Alliance	Challenger	
Kathleen Kaku	10,056	0.20%	Socialist Worker	Challenger	
John Justice	8,656	0.18%	Populist	Challenger	
Don Torgersen	26	<0.1%	Write in	Challenger	
Walter Feiss	1	<0.1%	Write in	Challenger	
Roe Conn	1	<0.1%	Write in	Challenger	

Governor (No Contest)

U.S. Representative in Congress

Candidate(s)	Total vote	Percent	Party	Status	First elected
District 1					
Bobby Rush	209,258	82.81%	Democrat	Challenger	1992
Jay Walker	43,453	17.19%	Republican	Challenger	
District 2					
Mel Reynolds	182,614	78.09%	Democrat	Challenger	1992
Ron Blackstone	31,957	13.66%	Republican	Challenger	
Louanner Peters	19,293	8.25%	Unknown	Challenger	
District 3					
William Lipinski	162,165	63.52%	Democrat	Incumbent	1982
Harry Lepinske	93,128	36.48%	Republican	Challenger	
District 4					
Luis Gutierrez	90,452	77.57%	Democrat	Challenger	1992
Hildegarde Rodriguez-Schieman	26,154	22.43%	Republican	Challenger	
District 5					
Dan Rostenkowski	132,889	57.26%	Democrat	Incumbent	1958
Elias Zenkich	90,738	39.10%	Republican	Challenger	
Blaise Grenke	8,456	3.64%	Libertarian	Challenger	
District 6					
Henry Hyde	165,009	65.50%	Republican	Incumbent	1974
Barry Watkins	86,891	34.49%	Democrat	Challenger	
Keith Petropoulos	4	<0.1%	Write in	Challenger	
District 7					
Cardiss Collins	182,811	81.15%	Democrat	Incumbent	1973
Norman Boccio	35,346	15.69%	Republican	Challenger	
Rose-Marie Love	4,711	2.09%	Economic Recovery	Challenger	
Geri McLauchlan	2,413	1.07%	Natural Law	Challenger	

[1]Votes for Write in candidates include 12 for Paul Tsongas, 4 for J. Quinn Brisben, and 1 each for Willie Carter, Eugene Hern, Lyndon LaRouche, Jr., Julie Moyer, Moyer/Anderson, and Roy Tyree.

Candidate(s)	Total vote	Percent	Party	Status	First elected
U.S. Representative in Congress (cont)					
District 8					
Philip Crane	132,887	55.69%	Republican	Incumbent	1969
Sheila Smith	96,419	40.40%	Democrat	Challenger	
Joe M. Dillier	9,327	3.91%	Independent	Challenger	
District 9					
Sidney Yates	162,942	67.98%	Democrat	Incumbent	1964
Herb Sohn	64,760	27.02%	Republican	Challenger	
Sheila Jones	12,001	5.01%	Unknown	Challenger	
District 10					
John Porter	155,230	64.51%	Republican	Incumbent	1980
Michael J. Kennedy	85,400	35.49%	Democrat	Challenger	
District 11					
George Sangmeister	135,387	55.66%	Democrat	Incumbent	1988
Robert Herbolsheimer	107,860	44.34%	Republican	Challenger	
District 12					
Jerry F. Costello	168,762	71.24%	Democrat	Incumbent	1988
Mike Starr	68,115	28.76%	Republican	Challenger	
District 13					
Harris Fawell	179,257	68.35%	Republican	Incumbent	1984
Dennis Temple	82,985	31.64%	Democrat	Challenger	
Ralph Miron	13	<.01%	Write in	Challenger	
District 14					
J. Dennis Hastert	155,271	67.33%	Republican	Incumbent	1986
Jonathan Reich	75,294	32.65%	Democrat	Challenger	
Yvonne Dinwiddie	59	0.03%	Write in	Challenger	
District 15					
Thomas Ewing	142,167	59.34%	Republican	Incumbent	1991
Charles Mattis	97,190	40.57%	Democrat	Challenger	
Gerard Archibald	229	0.10%	Write in	Challenger	
District 16					
Donald Manzullo	142,388	55.63%	Republican	Challenger	
John Cox	113,555	44.37%	Democrat	Incumbent	1992
District 17					
Lane Evans	156,233	60.10%	Democrat	Incumbent	1982
Ken Schloemer	103,719	39.90%	Republican	Challenger	
District 18					
Robert Michel	156,533	57.77%	Republican	Incumbent	1956
Ronald Hawkins	114,413	42.22%	Democrat	Challenger	
Carl Gifford	30	0.01%	Write in	Challenger	
District 19					
Glenn Poshard	187,156	69.14%	Democrat	Incumbent	1988
Douglas Lee	83,526	30.86%	Republican	Challenger	
Pat Riker	3	<.01%	Write in	Challenger	
District 20					
Richard Durbin	154,869	56.50%	Democrat	Incumbent	1982
John Shimkus	119,219	43.50%	Republican	Challenger	

Candidates: March 17, 1992, Primary Election

Candidate	Total vote	Percent	Candidate	Total vote	Percent
Presidential Preference, Democratic			**Presidential Preference, Republican**		
Bill Clinton	776,829	51.65%	George Bush	634,588	76.35%
Paul Tsongas	387,891	25.79%	Patrick Buchanan	186,915	22.49%
Jerry Brown	220,346	14.65%	Maurice Horton	9,637	1.16%
Uncommitted	67,612	4.50%			
Tom Harkin	30,710	2.04%			
Bob Kerrey	10,916	0.73%			
Lyndon LaRouche, Jr.	6,599	0.44%			
Lawrence Agran	3,227	0.21%			

Voter Registration and Turnout, 1948-1992 Elections

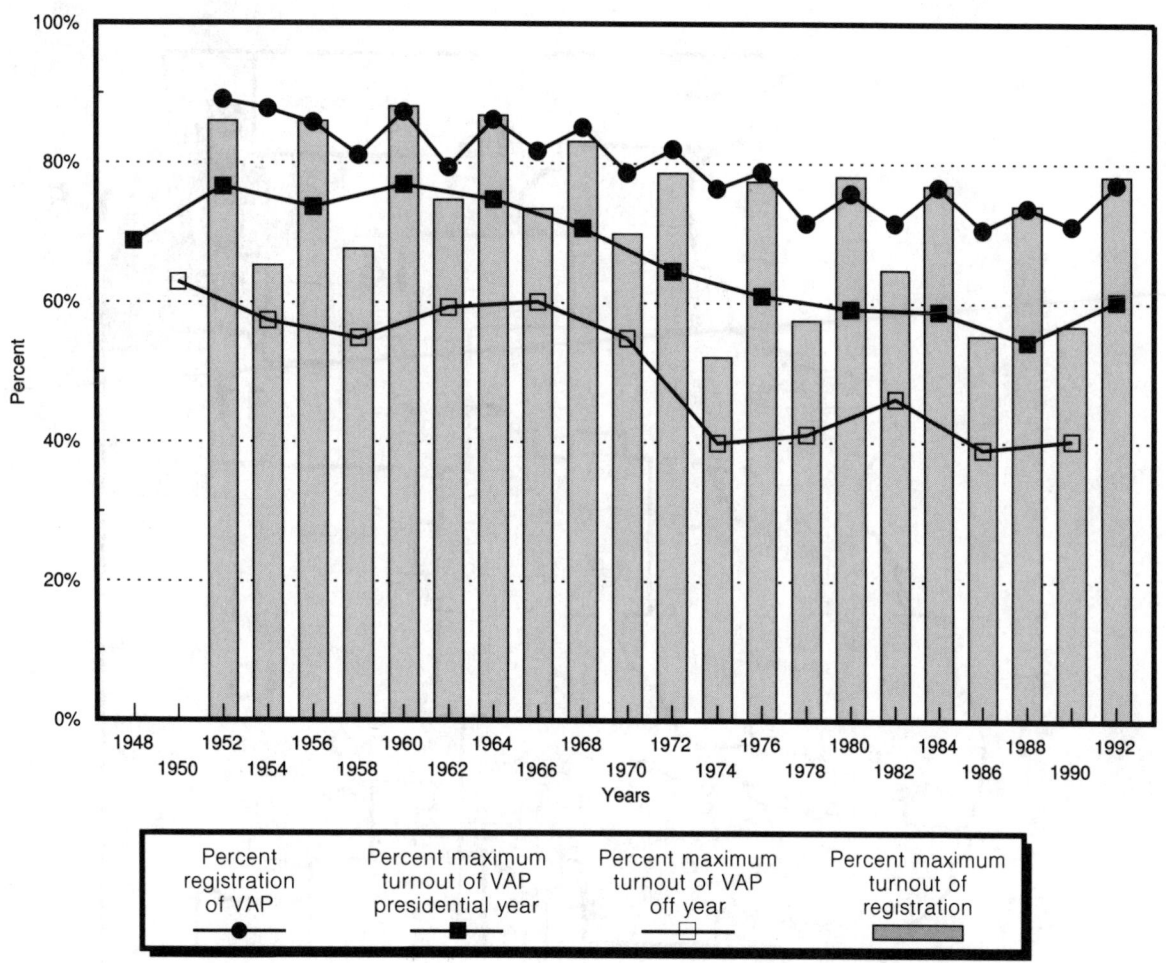

Legend			
Percent registration of VAP ●	Percent maximum turnout of VAP presidential year ■	Percent maximum turnout of VAP off year ☐	Percent maximum turnout of registration ▨

Year	Estimated Voting Age Population (VAP)	Voter registration (REG)			Voter turnout											
						Highest office						Maximum vote				
		Total	Percent of VAP	Rank by percent of VAP	Actual	Total	Office	Percent total REG	Rank by percent of REG	Percent of VAP	Rank by percent of VAP	Total	Percent total REG	Rank by percent of REG	Percent total VAP	Rank by percent of VAP
1992	8,568,000	6,600,358	77.0	21	5,164,357	5,050,157	P	76.5	28	58.9	26	5,164,357	78.2	27	60.3	25
1990	8,495,000	6,031,858	71.0	19	3,420,720	3,257,410	G	54.0	32	38.3	27	3,420,720	56.7	30	40.3	25
1988	8,636,000	6,356,940	73.6	19	4,697,192	4,559,120	P	71.7	24	52.8	24	4,697,192	73.9	22	54.4	23
1986	8,517,000	6,003,811	70.5	23	3,322,657	3,144,185	G	52.4	34	36.9	33	3,322,657	55.3	32	39.0	29
1984	8,448,000	6,470,438	76.6	18	4,969,352	4,819,088	P	74.5	23	57.0	19	4,969,352	76.8	19	58.8	17
1982	8,354,000	5,965,514	71.4	20	3,856,875	3,673,681	G	61.6	26	44.0	21	3,856,875	64.7	23	46.2	19
1980	8,235,000	6,230,332	75.7	18	4,868,890	4,749,721	P	76.2	17	57.7	16	4,868,890	78.1	15	59.1	16
1978	8,132,000	5,809,045	71.4	19	3,342,985	3,184,764	S	54.8	30	39.2	26	3,342,985	57.5	26	41.1	25
1976	7,939,000	6,253,654	78.8	17	4,838,961	4,718,914	P	75.5	23	59.4	16	4,838,961	77.4	20	61.0	14
1974	7,727,000	5,905,633	76.4	11	3,084,675	2,914,666	S	49.4	39	37.7	35	3,084,675	52.2	37	39.9	33
1972	7,576,000	6,215,331	82.0	11	4,882,865	4,723,236	P	76.0	22	62.3	14	4,882,865	78.6	16	64.5	11
1970	6,795,000	5,337,692	78.6	13	3,731,006	3,599,272	S	67.4	20	53.0	15	3,731,006	69.9	15	54.9	13
1968	6,667,000	5,676,131	85.1	10	4,714,943	4,619,749	P	81.4	21	69.3	10	4,714,943	83.1	17	70.7	9
1966	6,542,000	5,341,722	81.7	13	3,928,478	3,822,725	S	71.6	14	58.4	8	3,928,478	73.5	11	60.1	7
1964	6,422,000	5,534,676	86.2	15	4,805,928	4,702,841	P	85.0	12	73.2	8	4,805,928	86.8	11	74.8	5
1962	6,430,000	5,105,120	79.4	15	3,812,120	3,709,216	S	72.7	11	57.7	16	3,812,120	74.7	10	59.3	14
1960	6,298,000	5,499,469	87.3	8	4,845,319	4,757,409	P	86.5	14	75.5	12	4,845,319	88.1	13	76.9	9
1958	6,238,000	5,060,686	81.1	10	3,427,278	3,229,864	C	63.8	20	51.8	25	3,427,278	67.7	19	54.9	24
1956	6,082,000	5,217,858	85.8	7	4,484,956	4,407,407	P	84.5	11	72.5	8	4,484,956	86.0	10	73.7	9
1954	6,023,000	5,287,979	87.8	4	3,455,173	3,368,025	S	63.7	15	55.9	14	3,455,173	65.3	15	57.4	14
1952	5,955,000	5,303,521	89.1	5	4,563,305	4,481,058	P	84.5	12	75.2	11	4,563,305	86.0	11	76.6	10
1950	5,931,000	-	-	-	3,731,618	3,622,673	S	-	-	61.1	6	3,731,618	-	-	62.9	4
1948	5,927,000	-	-	-	4,078,146	3,984,046	P	-	-	67.2	8	4,078,146	-	-	68.8	5

ILLINOIS

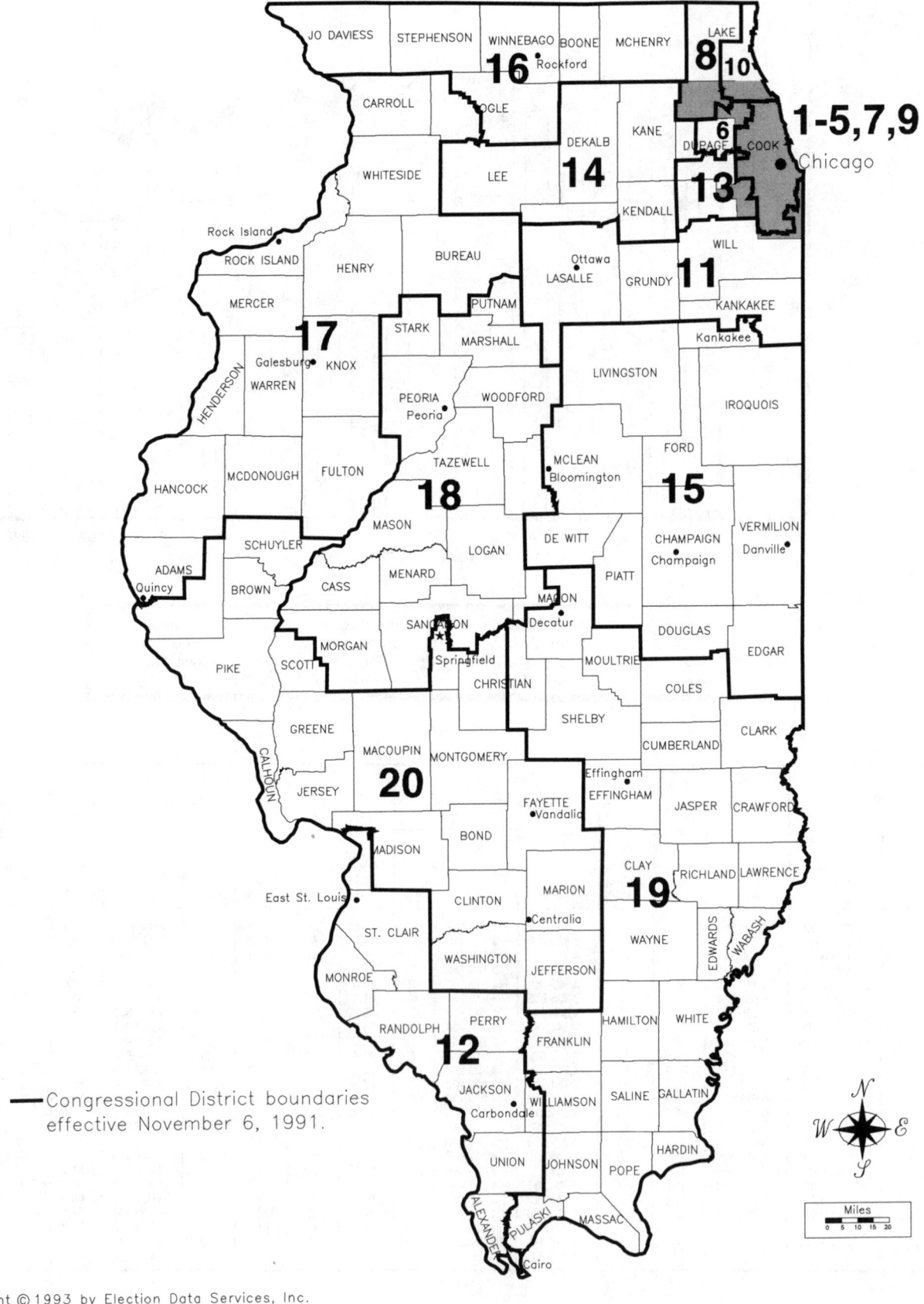

—— Congressional District boundaries
effective November 6, 1991.

Cook County, Illinois

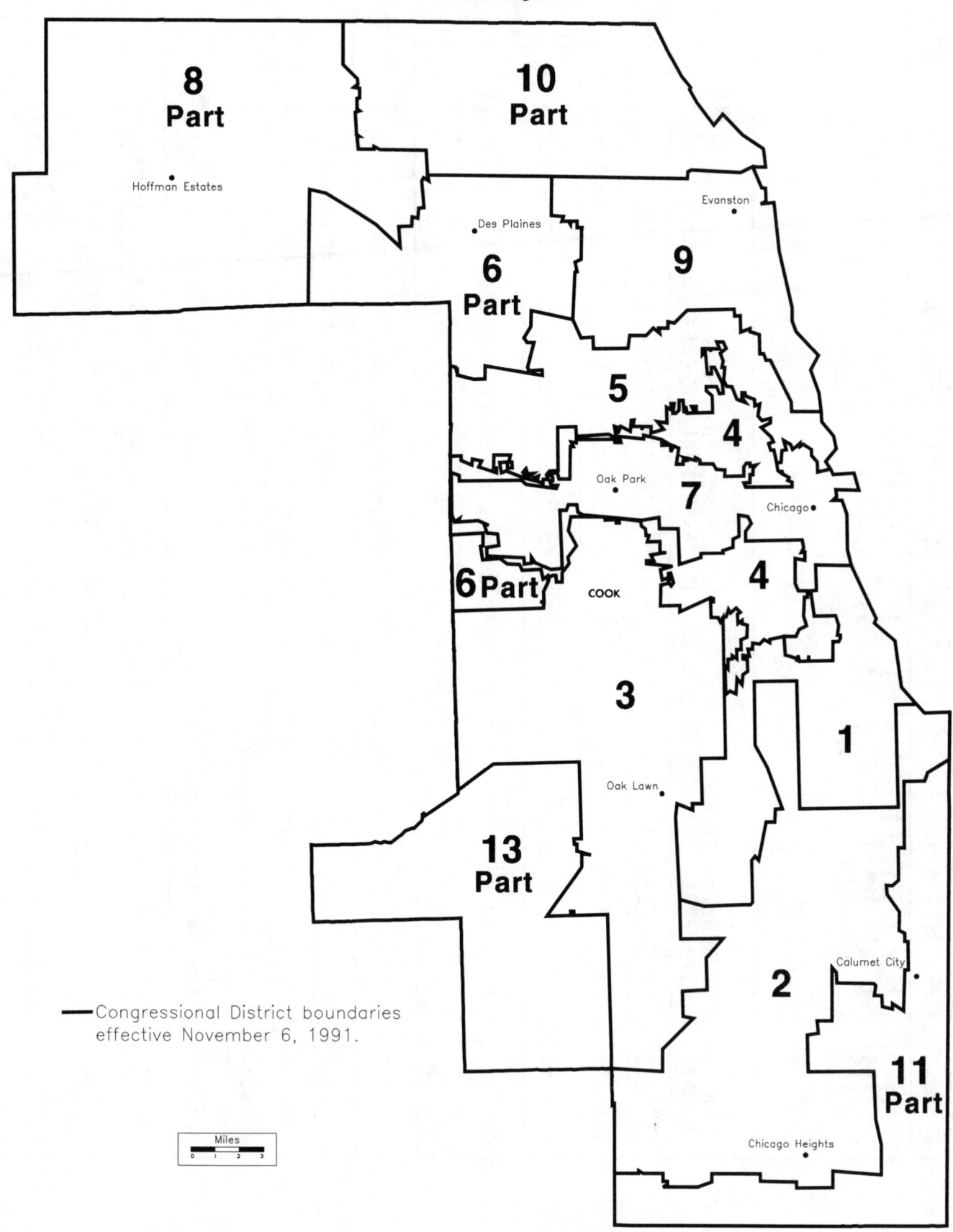

—Congressional District boundaries
effective November 6, 1991.

Copyright © 1993 by Election Data Services, Inc.

Table A. – 1990 Population by Race and Ethnic Origin

State/county code	County	Total persons	Percent of total persons — Non-Hispanic: White	Black	Asian and Pacific Islander	Native American	Other	Hispanic	Rank — Percent of total persons: Total	Non-Hispanic: White	Black	Hispanic	Percent contribution to state population: Total	Non-Hispanic: White	Black	Hispanic
17 001	Adams	66,090	96.4	2.5	0.4	0.1	0.1	0.4	21	57	38	75	0.6	0.7	0.1	<.1
17 003	Alexander	10,626	66.1	32.7	0.5	0.2	<.1	0.5	88	101	1	62	<.1	<.1	0.2	<.1
17 005	Bond	14,991	96.3	2.8	<.1	0.2	<.1	0.5	76	60	35	61	0.1	0.2	<.1	<.1
17 007	Boone	30,806	92.3	0.4	0.5	0.1	<.1	6.7	47	76	58	5	0.3	0.3	<.1	0.2
17 009	Brown	5,836	88.7	9.3	<.1	0.2	<.1	1.8	97	87	11	24	<.1	<.1	<.1	<.1
17 011	Bureau	35,688	96.4	0.1	0.5	0.2	<.1	2.8	38	58	73	15	0.3	0.4	<.1	0.1
17 013	Calhoun	5,322	99.3	<.1	0.3	0.2	0.0	0.2	100	8	100	99	<.1	<.1	<.1	<.1
17 015	Carroll	16,805	97.0	0.7	0.4	0.2	<.1	1.8	67	51	52	26	0.1	0.2	<.1	<.1
17 017	Cass	13,437	99.2	0.1	0.2	<.1	0.0	0.4	82	16	76	72	0.1	0.2	<.1	<.1
17 019	Champaign	173,025	83.7	9.5	4.6	0.2	<.1	2.0	12	93	10	23	1.5	1.7	1.0	0.4
17 021	Christian	34,418	99.1	0.2	0.3	0.1	<.1	0.3	41	25	65	89	0.3	0.4	<.1	<.1
17 023	Clark	15,921	99.3	<.1	0.2	0.2	0.0	0.3	73	12	85	97	0.1	0.2	<.1	<.1
17 025	Clay	14,460	99.3	<.1	0.2	0.1	<.1	0.4	79	13	98	76	0.1	0.2	<.1	<.1
17 027	Clinton	33,944	95.6	3.0	0.3	0.1	<.1	1.0	43	63	34	41	0.3	0.4	<.1	<.1
17 029	Coles	51,644	96.6	1.8	0.6	0.1	<.1	0.8	26	55	44	43	0.5	0.6	<.1	<.1
17 031	Cook	5,105,067	57.1	25.5	3.6	0.2	<.1	13.6	1	102	4	2	44.7	34.1	77.7	76.8
17 033	Crawford	19,464	98.8	0.3	0.2	0.2	<.1	0.4	60	31	60	73	0.2	0.2	<.1	<.1
17 035	Cumberland	10,670	99.3	<.1	0.2	<.1	0.0	0.4	87	9	91	81	<.1	0.1	<.1	<.1
17 037	DeKalb	77,932	92.0	2.6	2.2	0.1	<.1	3.0	20	79	37	14	0.7	0.8	0.1	0.3
17 039	De Witt	16,516	98.9	0.2	0.3	0.2	0.0	0.5	70	29	70	65	0.1	0.2	<.1	<.1
17 041	Douglas	19,464	98.1	<.1	0.2	0.2	0.0	1.5	61	43	83	30	0.2	0.2	<.1	<.1
17 043	DuPage	781,666	88.5	1.9	5.0	0.1	<.1	4.4	2	88	40	9	6.8	8.1	0.9	3.8
17 045	Edgar	19,595	99.1	0.3	0.1	0.1	0.0	0.3	59	22	59	96	0.2	0.2	<.1	<.1
17 047	Edwards	7,440	99.2	<.1	0.2	0.1	<.1	0.4	94	17	81	74	<.1	<.1	<.1	<.1
17 049	Effingham	31,704	99.2	<.1	0.3	0.1	<.1	0.4	46	20	96	80	0.3	0.4	<.1	<.1
17 051	Fayette	20,893	96.2	2.8	0.1	0.2	<.1	0.7	57	61	36	47	0.2	0.2	<.1	<.1
17 053	Ford	14,275	98.7	0.3	0.3	<.1	<.1	0.6	80	35	62	57	0.1	0.2	<.1	<.1
17 055	Franklin	40,319	99.2	<.1	0.2	0.3	<.1	0.3	32	21	80	92	0.4	0.5	<.1	<.1
17 057	Fulton	38,080	97.1	1.7	0.3	0.2	<.1	0.6	35	49	45	52	0.3	0.4	<.1	<.1
17 059	Gallatin	6,909	98.9	0.6	0.2	0.1	0.0	0.2	95	30	54	98	<.1	<.1	<.1	<.1
17 061	Greene	15,317	99.2	<.1	<.1	0.3	0.0	0.3	75	14	79	91	0.1	0.2	<.1	<.1
17 063	Grundy	32,337	97.2	<.1	0.3	0.1	<.1	2.3	45	46	92	18	0.3	0.4	<.1	<.1
17 065	Hamilton	8,499	99.3	<.1	0.2	0.1	0.0	0.3	90	11	97	85	<.1	<.1	<.1	<.1
17 067	Hancock	21,373	99.3	0.1	0.2	<.1	<.1	0.3	56	7	75	94	0.2	0.2	<.1	<.1
17 069	Hardin	5,189	97.2	1.6	0.3	0.3	<.1	0.6	101	45	46	56	<.1	<.1	<.1	<.1
17 071	Henderson	8,096	98.8	<.1	0.1	0.3	0.0	0.7	91	34	78	49	<.1	<.1	<.1	<.1
17 073	Henry	51,159	96.8	1.3	0.2	0.1	<.1	1.6	27	53	47	29	0.4	0.6	<.1	<.1
17 075	Iroquois	30,787	97.0	0.5	0.2	<.1	0.0	2.1	49	52	55	19	0.3	0.3	<.1	<.1
17 077	Jackson	61,067	84.2	10.2	3.5	0.2	<.1	1.8	22	92	9	25	0.5	0.6	0.4	0.1
17 079	Jasper	10,609	99.4	<.1	0.2	0.1	<.1	0.3	89	5	102	88	<.1	0.1	<.1	<.1
17 081	Jefferson	37,020	93.9	5.2	0.3	0.1	<.1	0.4	36	70	25	70	0.3	0.4	0.1	<.1
17 083	Jersey	20,539	98.7	0.5	0.2	0.2	<.1	0.5	58	38	57	64	0.2	0.2	<.1	<.1
17 085	Jo Daviess	21,821	99.3	<.1	0.1	<.1	0.0	0.4	54	10	87	69	0.2	0.3	<.1	<.1
17 087	Johnson	11,347	88.8	9.2	0.1	0.2	<.1	1.7	85	85	12	27	<.1	0.1	<.1	<.1
17 089	Kane	317,471	78.9	5.8	1.3	0.2	<.1	13.7	5	98	23	1	2.8	2.9	1.1	4.8
17 091	Kankakee	96,255	82.3	14.8	0.6	0.1	<.1	2.0	18	97	5	22	0.8	0.9	0.9	0.2
17 093	Kendall	39,413	94.2	0.5	0.5	0.1	<.1	4.6	33	68	56	8	0.3	0.4	<.1	0.2
17 095	Knox	56,393	91.8	5.0	0.6	0.1	<.1	2.5	25	80	26	16	0.5	0.6	0.2	0.2
17 097	Lake	516,418	83.4	6.5	2.3	0.2	<.1	7.5	3	95	18	3	4.5	5.0	2.0	4.3
17 099	La Salle	106,913	95.2	1.1	0.5	0.2	<.1	3.0	17	65	48	12	0.9	1.2	<.1	0.4
17 101	Lawrence	15,972	98.4	0.9	0.1	0.2	<.1	0.4	72	42	49	83	0.1	0.2	<.1	<.1
17 103	Lee	34,392	93.6	3.5	0.5	0.2	<.1	2.1	42	71	31	20	0.3	0.4	<.1	<.1
17 105	Livingston	39,301	92.0	5.3	0.3	0.1	<.1	2.1	34	78	24	21	0.3	0.4	0.1	<.1
17 107	Logan	30,798	94.1	4.2	0.4	0.1	<.1	1.1	48	69	28	35	0.3	0.3	<.1	<.1
17 109	McDonough	35,244	93.1	3.5	2.2	0.2	<.1	1.0	39	73	33	39	0.3	0.4	<.1	<.1
17 111	McHenry	183,241	95.7	0.2	0.7	0.2	<.1	3.3	9	62	68	10	1.6	2.1	<.1	0.7
17 113	McLean	129,180	93.0	4.2	1.2	0.1	<.1	1.3	14	74	27	34	1.1	1.4	0.3	0.2
17 115	Macon	117,206	86.9	12.0	0.4	0.1	<.1	0.5	16	89	7	66	1.0	1.2	0.8	<.1
17 117	Macoupin	47,679	98.4	0.8	0.2	0.2	<.1	0.4	29	41	50	78	0.4	0.5	<.1	<.1
17 119	Madison	249,238	91.6	6.4	0.5	0.3	<.1	1.1	8	81	19	36	2.2	2.7	1.0	0.3
17 121	Marion	41,561	95.0	3.6	0.5	0.3	<.1	0.6	31	66	30	59	0.4	0.5	<.1	<.1
17 123	Marshall	12,846	98.8	0.1	0.2	0.2	<.1	0.6	84	32	74	54	0.1	0.1	<.1	<.1
17 125	Mason	16,269	99.2	<.1	0.2	0.2	<.1	0.4	71	19	90	82	0.1	0.2	<.1	<.1
17 127	Massac	14,752	93.3	5.9	0.2	0.3	<.1	0.3	78	72	22	90	0.1	0.2	<.1	<.1
17 129	Menard	11,164	99.2	<.1	0.1	0.3	0.0	0.3	86	18	82	86	<.1	0.1	<.1	<.1
17 131	Mercer	17,290	98.8	0.2	0.2	0.2	<.1	0.6	65	33	67	53	0.2	0.2	<.1	<.1
17 133	Monroe	22,422	98.7	<.1	0.3	0.2	<.1	0.7	52	36	95	46	0.2	0.3	<.1	<.1
17 135	Montgomery	30,728	97.1	1.8	0.2	0.1	<.1	0.8	50	50	43	45	0.3	0.3	<.1	<.1
17 137	Morgan	36,397	94.5	4.1	0.3	0.1	0.2	0.8	37	67	29	42	0.3	0.4	<.1	<.1
17 139	Moultrie	13,930	99.4	<.1	<.1	0.2	0.0	0.3	81	6	88	93	0.1	0.2	<.1	<.1

268 Illinois

Table A. — 1990 Population by Race and Ethnic Origin (cont)

State/ county code	County	Total persons	Percent of total persons Non-Hispanic White	Black	Asian and Pacific Islander	Native American	Other	Hispanic	Rank Percent of total persons Total	Non-Hispanic White	Black	Hispanic	Percent contribution to state population Total	Non-Hispanic White	Black	Hispanic
17 141	Ogle	45,957	96.3	0.1	0.3	0.2	<.1	3.0	30	59	72	13	0.4	0.5	<.1	0.2
17 143	Peoria	182,827	83.6	13.5	1.2	0.2	0.1	1.4	10	94	6	32	1.6	1.8	1.5	0.3
17 145	Perry	21,412	97.2	1.8	0.3	0.1	<.1	0.6	55	47	42	58	0.2	0.2	<.1	<.1
17 147	Piatt	15,548	99.5	<.1	<.1	0.1	0.0	0.2	74	3	89	100	0.1	0.2	<.1	<.1
17 149	Pike	17,577	99.2	<.1	0.2	0.1	0.0	0.4	64	15	93	77	0.2	0.2	<.1	<.1
17 151	Pope	4,373	92.3	5.9	0.1	0.3	0.0	1.3	102	75	21	33	<.1	<.1	<.1	<.1
17 153	Pulaski	7,523	66.7	32.7	<.1	0.1	<.1	0.4	92	100	2	79	<.1	<.1	0.1	<.1
17 155	Putnam	5,730	97.2	0.2	0.1	0.1	<.1	2.4	98	48	69	17	<.1	<.1	<.1	<.1
17 157	Randolph	34,583	90.3	8.2	0.2	0.2	<.1	1.0	40	83	15	40	0.3	0.4	0.2	<.1
17 159	Richland	16,545	99.1	0.1	0.2	0.1	<.1	0.4	68	24	77	68	0.1	0.2	<.1	<.1
17 161	Rock Island	148,723	86.7	6.9	0.7	0.2	<.1	5.4	13	90	17	7	1.3	1.5	0.6	0.9
17 163	St. Clair	262,852	70.5	27.0	0.7	0.2	<.1	1.5	6	99	3	31	2.3	2.2	4.2	0.4
17 165	Saline	26,551	95.5	3.5	0.1	0.2	0.1	0.5	51	64	32	63	0.2	0.3	<.1	<.1
17 167	Sangamon	178,386	90.3	8.0	0.8	0.2	<.1	0.7	11	84	16	48	1.6	1.9	0.9	0.1
17 169	Schuyler	7,498	99.7	<.1	<.1	0.1	0.0	<.1	93	1	99	102	<.1	<.1	<.1	<.1
17 171	Scott	5,644	99.6	<.1	<.1	0.1	0.0	0.3	99	2	101	95	<.1	<.1	<.1	<.1
17 173	Shelby	22,261	99.5	<.1	<.1	0.1	0.0	0.5	53	4	86	101	0.2	0.3	<.1	<.1
17 175	Stark	6,534	99.0	<.1	0.3	0.1	0.0	0.5	96	26	84	67	<.1	<.1	<.1	<.1
17 177	Stephenson	48,052	92.2	6.4	0.6	0.1	<.1	0.6	28	77	20	55	0.4	0.5	0.2	<.1
17 179	Tazewell	123,692	98.7	0.1	0.3	0.2	<.1	0.7	15	39	71	51	1.1	1.4	<.1	<.1
17 181	Union	17,619	97.9	0.7	0.3	0.1	0.0	1.0	63	44	51	38	0.2	0.2	<.1	<.1
17 183	Vermilion	88,257	88.8	8.8	0.5	0.2	<.1	1.6	19	86	14	28	0.8	0.9	0.5	0.2
17 185	Wabash	13,111	98.5	0.3	0.6	<.1	<.1	0.6	83	40	63	60	0.1	0.2	<.1	<.1
17 187	Warren	19,181	96.5	1.9	0.4	0.1	<.1	1.1	62	56	41	37	0.2	0.2	<.1	<.1
17 189	Washington	14,965	99.0	0.3	0.2	0.2	<.1	0.3	77	27	61	87	0.1	0.2	<.1	<.1
17 191	Wayne	17,241	99.1	<.1	0.3	0.2	<.1	0.4	66	23	94	71	0.2	0.2	<.1	<.1
17 193	White	16,522	99.0	0.2	0.2	0.2	<.1	0.4	69	28	64	84	0.1	0.2	<.1	<.1
17 195	Whiteside	60,186	91.5	0.6	0.3	0.1	<.1	7.4	23	82	53	4	0.5	0.6	<.1	0.5
17 197	Will	357,313	82.3	10.6	1.3	0.2	<.1	5.6	4	96	8	6	3.1	3.4	2.3	2.2
17 199	Williamson	57,733	96.7	2.0	0.4	0.2	<.1	0.8	24	54	39	44	0.5	0.7	<.1	<.1
17 201	Winnebago	252,913	86.4	9.1	1.1	0.2	<.1	3.1	7	91	13	11	2.2	2.6	1.4	0.9
17 203	Woodford	32,653	98.7	0.2	0.3	0.1	<.1	0.7	44	37	66	50	0.3	0.4	<.1	<.1
17	**ILLINOIS**	**11,430,602**	**74.8**	**14.6**	**2.4**	**0.2**	**<.1**	**7.9**					**100.0**	**100.0**	**100.0**	**100.0**
	CONGRESSIONAL															
	District 1	571,530	25.9	69.3	1.0	0.1	<.1	3.6	5	19	1	12	5.0	1.7	23.7	2.3
	District 2	571,530	24.6	68.0	0.5	0.1	<.1	6.6	12	20	2	7	5.0	1.6	23.2	4.2
	District 3	571,531	89.2	1.9	1.4	0.1	<.1	7.4	4	7	17	5	5.0	6.0	0.6	4.7
	District 4	571,530	26.8	5.5	2.2	0.2	0.3	65.0	13	18	9	1	5.0	1.8	1.9	41.1
	District 5	571,530	79.4	1.4	5.6	0.2	<.1	13.3	14	15	20	2	5.0	5.3	0.5	8.4
	District 6	571,530	88.3	1.4	4.8	0.1	<.1	5.3	15	10	19	10	5.0	5.9	0.5	3.3
	District 7	571,530	27.2	65.2	3.1	0.1	<.1	4.3	16	17	3	11	5.0	1.8	22.2	2.7
	District 8	571,530	88.7	1.6	4.0	0.1	<.1	5.5	17	9	18	9	5.0	5.9	0.5	3.5
	District 9	571,530	68.4	11.6	9.8	0.3	0.2	9.7	18	16	5	4	5.0	4.6	4.0	6.2
	District 10	571,530	82.8	6.0	4.0	0.1	<.1	7.1	6	13	8	6	5.0	5.5	2.0	4.5
	District 11	571,528	84.2	8.4	0.6	0.2	<.1	6.5	19	11	6	8	5.0	5.6	2.9	4.1
	District 12	571,530	80.6	16.9	0.9	0.2	<.1	1.3	7	14	4	17	5.0	5.4	5.8	0.8
	District 13	571,531	89.7	3.1	4.1	0.1	<.1	3.0	3	6	16	15	5.0	6.0	1.1	1.9
	District 14	571,530	84.2	4.0	1.7	0.2	<.1	9.8	8	12	13	3	5.0	5.6	1.4	6.2
	District 15	571,532	88.9	7.4	1.8	0.1	<.1	1.6	2	8	7	16	5.0	5.9	2.5	1.0
	District 16	571,530	91.2	4.7	0.8	0.2	<.1	3.1	9	5	11	13	5.0	6.1	1.6	1.9
	District 17	571,530	93.0	3.2	0.5	0.2	<.1	3.0	10	4	15	14	5.0	6.2	1.1	1.9
	District 18	571,580	93.1	5.1	0.7	0.2	<.1	0.9	1	3	10	18	5.0	6.2	1.7	0.6
	District 19	571,530	95.2	3.8	0.3	0.2	<.1	0.5	11	1	14	20	5.0	6.4	1.3	0.3
	District 20	571,480	94.5	4.2	0.4	0.2	<.1	0.7	20	2	12	19	5.0	6.3	1.4	0.4

Table B. — 1990 Voting Age Population (VAP) by Race and Ethnic Origin

County	Total Voting Age Population	Percent of total VAP — Non-Hispanic White	Black	Asian and Pacific Islander	Native American	Other	Hispanic	Rank Total	Rank Non-Hispanic White	Rank Non-Hispanic Black	Rank Hispanic	Pct contribution to state VAP Total	Non-Hispanic White	Non-Hispanic Black	Hispanic	VAP percent of total pop Total	Non-Hispanic White	Black	Asian and Pacific Islander	Native American	Other	Hispanic
Adams	49,047	97.0	2.2	0.3	0.2	<.1	0.3	22	52	39	73	0.6	0.7	<.1	<.1	74.2	74.7	63.3	62.3	77.3	7.4	61.1
Alexander	7,561	72.0	26.9	0.5	0.1	0.0	0.4	89	100	2	63	<.1	<.1	0.2	<.1	71.2	77.5	58.5	72.9	82.4	0.0	55.6
Bond	11,310	96.7	2.5	<.1	0.2	<.1	0.5	75	58	37	56	0.1	0.2	<.1	<.1	75.4	75.8	66.6	78.6	70.6	16.7	66.3
Boone	22,199	93.7	0.3	0.4	0.1	<.1	5.4	49	72	58	5	0.3	0.3	<.1	0.2	72.1	73.2	57.9	60.5	71.1	57.1	58.0
Brown	4,555	85.6	11.8	<.1	0.2	<.1	2.3	97	92	6	16	<.1	<.1	<.1	<.1	78.1	75.3	99.8	80.0	91.7	100.0	99.0
Bureau	26,263	96.9	0.1	0.4	0.2	0.0	2.4	39	55	73	13	0.3	0.4	<.1	0.1	73.6	74.0	54.0	58.8	67.2	0.0	62.7
Calhoun	4,031	99.3	<.1	0.2	0.2	0.0	0.3	100	18	96	83	<.1	<.1	<.1	<.1	75.7	75.7	100.0	46.7	100.0	0.0	91.7
Carroll	12,582	97.6	0.6	0.3	0.1	<.1	1.4	68	48	52	27	0.1	0.2	<.1	<.1	74.9	75.3	70.0	59.0	53.6	28.6	58.4
Cass	9,955	99.4	0.1	0.1	<.1	0.0	0.3	82	14	72	71	0.1	0.2	<.1	<.1	74.1	74.2	68.8	56.5	75.0	0.0	58.9
Champaign	135,259	84.9	8.0	4.8	0.2	<.1	2.1	10	96	13	18	1.6	1.7	1.0	0.5	78.2	79.3	66.1	82.6	77.6	35.9	80.9
Christian	25,707	99.1	0.2	0.2	0.2	0.0	0.2	41	29	63	94	0.3	0.4	<.1	<.1	74.7	74.8	75.3	70.1	80.4	0.0	55.3
Clark	12,005	99.4	<.1	0.2	0.2	0.0	0.2	73	10	97	99	0.1	0.2	<.1	<.1	75.4	75.5	30.0	63.9	84.0	0.0	57.1
Clay	10,782	99.3	<.1	0.2	0.1	<.1	0.3	79	17	95	70	0.1	0.2	<.1	<.1	74.6	74.6	75.0	60.7	82.4	100.0	63.2
Clinton	24,779	94.9	3.6	0.3	0.1	<.1	1.0	43	68	33	37	0.3	0.4	<.1	<.1	73.0	72.5	88.9	63.3	81.4	14.3	75.6
Coles	40,938	96.8	1.8	0.6	0.1	<.1	0.7	26	57	43	45	0.5	0.5	<.1	<.1	79.3	79.4	79.0	70.1	74.7	15.8	73.1
Cook	3,825,022	61.6	23.2	3.5	0.1	<.1	11.5	1	102	4	2	45.1	35.9	78.7	77.0	74.9	80.8	68.2	73.2	73.7	55.2	63.6
Crawford	14,641	99.2	0.2	0.2	0.2	<.1	0.3	59	28	65	78	0.2	0.2	<.1	<.1	75.2	75.5	43.5	63.8	64.7	50.0	52.5
Cumberland	7,680	99.5	<.1	0.2	<.1	0.0	0.2	87	6	89	92	<.1	0.1	<.1	<.1	72.0	72.1	60.0	60.9	66.7	0.0	46.2
DeKalb	61,250	92.2	2.6	2.3	0.1	<.1	2.7	20	79	36	11	0.7	0.9	0.1	0.3	78.6	78.7	77.6	82.8	80.0	51.0	70.6
De Witt	12,263	99.1	0.1	0.3	0.2	0.0	0.4	69	31	68	67	0.1	0.2	<.1	<.1	74.2	74.4	68.0	72.1	61.1	0.0	55.0
Douglas	13,976	98.4	<.1	0.1	0.1	0.0	1.3	62	43	79	29	0.2	0.2	<.1	<.1	71.8	72.0	66.7	51.4	100.0	0.0	59.9
DuPage	575,250	89.7	1.7	4.5	0.1	<.1	4.0	2	85	44	8	6.8	7.9	0.9	4.0	73.6	74.5	66.1	66.6	74.1	42.7	66.0
Edgar	14,588	99.3	0.3	0.1	<.1	0.0	0.2	60	21	59	101	0.2	0.2	<.1	<.1	74.4	74.6	67.6	75.0	58.3	0.0	46.2
Edwards	5,610	99.5	<.1	<.1	0.1	0.0	0.2	93	5	80	93	<.1	<.1	<.1	<.1	75.4	75.6	66.7	35.7	75.0	0.0	43.3
Effingham	22,145	99.3	<.1	0.2	0.1	0.0	0.3	50	15	99	87	0.3	0.3	<.1	<.1	69.8	70.0	33.3	60.0	62.8	0.0	48.8
Fayette	15,680	95.2	3.7	0.1	0.2	<.1	0.8	57	66	32	41	0.2	0.2	<.1	<.1	75.0	74.3	99.3	61.3	78.4	100.0	86.4
Ford	10,585	98.9	0.3	0.2	<.1	<.1	0.5	80	34	61	55	0.1	0.2	<.1	<.1	74.2	74.3	64.3	57.5	75.0	25.0	64.2
Franklin	30,636	99.3	<.1	0.2	0.3	<.1	0.2	31	23	78	95	0.4	0.5	<.1	<.1	76.0	76.1	66.7	60.5	74.5	71.4	61.8
Fulton	28,776	96.7	2.2	0.2	0.2	<.1	0.7	34	59	40	47	0.3	0.4	<.1	<.1	75.6	75.2	94.1	67.7	75.9	28.6	80.3
Gallatin	5,271	98.9	0.6	0.2	<.1	0.0	0.2	95	35	53	97	<.1	<.1	<.1	<.1	76.3	76.4	76.2	72.7	50.0	0.0	68.8
Greene	11,258	99.4	<.1	<.1	0.2	0.0	0.3	76	13	87	79	0.1	0.2	<.1	<.1	73.5	73.6	35.7	46.2	62.2	0.0	72.7
Grundy	23,401	97.6	<.1	0.3	0.1	<.1	2.0	45	49	90	20	0.3	0.3	<.1	<.1	72.4	72.6	60.0	69.5	68.6	100.0	62.0
Hamilton	6,456	99.3	<.1	0.2	0.2	0.0	0.3	90	20	101	75	<.1	<.1	<.1	<.1	76.0	76.0	33.3	75.0	100.0	0.0	72.4
Hancock	15,887	99.4	<.1	0.2	<.1	<.1	0.3	55	11	77	89	0.2	0.2	<.1	<.1	74.3	74.4	53.8	69.4	70.0	33.3	69.0
Hardin	3,958	96.9	2.1	0.2	0.3	0.0	0.5	101	54	41	54	<.1	<.1	<.1	<.1	76.3	76.1	98.8	53.8	68.8	0.0	66.7
Henderson	6,026	99.0	<.1	0.1	0.2	0.0	0.6	91	32	93	50	<.1	<.1	<.1	<.1	74.4	74.6	25.0	90.0	54.2	0.0	64.3
Henry	37,404	97.4	1.0	0.2	0.1	<.1	1.2	27	54	48	31	0.4	0.6	<.1	<.1	73.1	73.6	60.6	60.3	87.0	5.0	56.2
Iroquois	22,816	97.6	0.5	0.2	<.1	<.1	1.6	48	47	55	25	0.3	0.3	<.1	<.1	74.1	74.6	67.5	72.1	66.7	0.0	55.8
Jackson	49,467	85.3	9.1	3.7	0.2	<.1	1.6	21	93	12	24	0.6	0.6	0.4	0.1	81.0	82.1	71.6	85.6	87.1	61.5	73.9
Jasper	7,611	99.4	0.0	0.1	0.1	0.0	0.3	88	7	102	77	<.1	0.1	0.0	<.1	71.7	71.8	0.0	62.5	72.7	0.0	75.0
Jefferson	27,073	95.3	3.9	0.3	0.2	<.1	0.4	38	65	29	66	0.3	0.4	<.1	<.1	73.1	74.2	54.9	65.9	84.6	8.3	63.1
Jersey	15,031	98.9	0.3	0.2	0.2	<.1	0.4	58	36	60	62	0.2	0.2	<.1	<.1	73.2	73.4	44.7	71.9	80.0	33.3	60.2
Jo Daviess	16,105	99.4	<.1	0.1	0.1	0.0	0.3	54	9	94	76	0.2	0.2	<.1	<.1	73.8	73.9	38.5	76.0	94.7	0.0	54.3
Johnson	9,099	86.5	11.3	<.1	0.2	<.1	1.8	85	91	7	22	0.1	0.1	<.1	<.1	80.2	78.1	98.9	53.8	84.6	100.0	88.4
Kane	222,946	82.0	5.0	1.2	0.2	<.1	11.6	5	98	25	1	2.6	2.8	1.0	4.5	70.2	73.0	60.3	64.0	71.0	31.5	59.5
Kankakee	69,165	85.2	12.4	0.6	0.2	<.1	1.6	18	94	5	26	0.8	0.9	0.8	0.2	71.9	74.4	60.1	62.6	77.9	30.0	57.0
Kendall	27,620	95.1	0.4	0.5	0.1	<.1	3.9	36	67	56	9	0.3	0.4	<.1	0.2	70.1	70.7	60.0	61.9	80.4	38.5	59.2
Knox	42,913	92.2	4.9	0.5	0.1	<.1	2.1	25	80	26	17	0.5	0.6	0.2	0.2	76.1	76.5	75.3	73.0	69.5	64.3	64.8
Lake	373,946	84.9	6.1	2.2	0.2	<.1	6.6	3	95	19	3	4.4	4.8	2.0	4.3	72.4	73.8	67.1	67.4	76.8	42.8	63.7
La Salle	79,719	96.0	1.1	0.4	0.2	<.1	2.4	17	63	47	14	0.9	1.2	<.1	0.3	74.6	75.1	76.9	61.3	67.3	59.1	58.1
Lawrence	12,177	98.5	0.9	0.1	0.2	<.1	0.3	71	41	49	69	0.1	0.2	<.1	<.1	76.2	76.3	69.5	70.0	83.9	20.0	73.2
Lee	25,477	93.3	4.2	0.4	0.2	<.1	1.8	42	74	27	23	0.3	0.4	<.1	<.1	74.1	73.9	88.4	62.9	76.1	61.9	62.2
Livingston	29,490	90.6	6.9	0.3	0.1	<.1	2.0	33	83	16	19	0.3	0.4	0.2	0.1	75.0	73.9	97.3	63.0	75.4	86.2	71.9
Logan	23,466	93.2	5.1	0.4	0.1	<.1	1.2	44	75	24	32	0.3	0.3	0.1	<.1	76.2	75.5	93.2	69.1	72.2	7.7	80.5
McDonough	28,757	92.8	3.7	2.3	0.1	<.1	1.0	35	77	31	38	0.3	0.4	<.1	<.1	81.6	81.3	87.4	84.3	77.4	83.3	81.6
McHenry	129,969	96.1	0.1	0.6	0.2	<.1	3.0	12	62	69	10	1.5	1.9	<.1	0.7	70.9	71.2	58.2	64.3	71.5	48.4	64.6
McLean	99,358	93.7	3.8	1.2	0.1	<.1	1.1	14	71	30	35	1.2	1.4	0.3	0.2	76.9	77.5	68.4	74.8	71.1	31.6	66.8
Macon	86,799	89.3	9.8	0.4	0.1	<.1	0.4	16	86	9	65	1.0	1.2	0.8	<.1	74.1	76.1	60.6	65.3	74.7	16.0	62.6
Macoupin	35,348	98.6	0.7	0.2	0.2	0.0	0.3	29	40	51	72	0.4	0.5	<.1	<.1	74.1	74.3	64.0	69.3	77.8	0.0	63.6
Madison	185,490	92.7	5.5	0.5	0.3	<.1	1.0	8	78	21	39	2.2	2.6	0.9	0.3	74.4	75.3	63.9	69.6	71.8	32.8	65.3
Marion	30,482	95.7	3.2	0.4	0.3	0.0	0.4	32	64	34	64	0.4	0.4	<.1	<.1	73.3	73.9	64.2	56.8	77.4	0.0	52.2
Marshall	9,612	98.9	0.1	0.2	0.2	<.1	0.5	84	33	67	57	0.1	0.1	<.1	<.1	74.8	74.9	82.4	73.1	75.9	50.0	57.0
Mason	12,034	99.3	<.1	0.2	0.2	<.1	0.3	72	19	88	80	0.1	0.2	<.1	<.1	74.0	74.1	62.5	60.5	73.1	50.0	58.6
Massac	11,249	93.9	5.4	0.2	0.2	0.0	0.3	77	70	22	82	0.1	0.2	<.1	<.1	76.3	76.8	69.6	74.2	64.9	0.0	68.2
Menard	8,097	99.3	<.1	0.1	0.3	0.0	0.2	86	16	91	90	<.1	0.1	<.1	<.1	72.5	72.6	33.3	64.3	72.4	0.0	54.1
Mercer	12,687	99.2	<.1	0.1	0.1	<.1	0.5	66	27	75	58	0.1	0.2	<.1	<.1	73.4	73.7	40.0	42.9	57.6	100.0	54.1
Monroe	16,432	98.9	<.1	0.2	0.2	<.1	0.7	53	39	83	46	0.2	0.2	<.1	<.1	73.3	73.4	100.0	47.4	66.7	14.3	68.7
Montgomery	22,907	96.6	2.3	0.2	0.1	<.1	0.8	47	60	38	44	0.3	0.3	<.1	<.1	74.5	74.2	95.5	58.7	74.4	87.5	73.6
Morgan	27,528	94.9	3.9	0.3	0.1	<.1	0.8	37	69	28	43	0.3	0.4	<.1	<.1	75.6	76.0	72.1	64.5	76.1	15.0	73.1
Moultrie	10,268	99.4	<.1	<.1	0.1	0.0	0.3	81	8	82	84	0.1	0.2	<.1	<.1	73.7	73.7	75.0	76.9	68.2	0.0	73.7

Table B. — 1990 Voting Age Population (VAP) by Race and Ethnic Origin (cont)

County	Total Voting Age Population	Percent of total VAP — White	Black	Asian and Pacific Islander	Native American	Other	Hispanic	Rank Total	Rank White	Rank Black	Rank Hispanic	Pct contribution Total	White	Black	Hispanic	VAP% Total	White	Black	Asian and Pacific Islander	Native American	Other	Hispanic
Ogle	33,358	97.2	0.1	0.2	0.2	<.1	2.3	30	51	70	15	0.4	0.5	<.1	0.1	72.6	73.2	63.6	62.9	70.9	33.3	54.8
Peoria	135,322	86.9	10.7	1.1	0.2	<.1	1.2	9	90	8	34	1.6	1.8	1.3	0.3	74.0	76.9	58.3	69.1	71.9	20.2	61.1
Perry	15,764	97.7	1.6	0.2	0.1	0.0	0.4	56	46	46	60	0.2	0.2	<.1	<.1	73.6	74.0	64.9	42.9	69.6	0.0	57.5
Piatt	11,559	99.6	<.1	<.1	0.1	0.0	0.2	74	3	92	98	0.1	0.2	<.1	<.1	74.3	74.4	50.0	63.6	75.0	0.0	68.6
Pike	13,212	99.4	<.1	0.2	0.1	0.0	0.3	64	12	86	81	0.2	0.2	<.1	<.1	75.2	75.3	75.0	65.6	66.7	0.0	53.6
Pope	3,365	91.9	6.4	0.1	0.4	0.0	1.2	102	81	18	33	<.1	<.1	<.1	<.1	76.9	76.7	82.3	83.3	85.7	0.0	70.2
Pulaski	5,351	70.8	28.6	0.1	0.1	0.0	0.3	94	101	1	88	<.1	<.1	0.1	<.1	71.1	75.5	62.3	100.0	100.0	0.0	48.3
Putnam	4,232	97.9	<.1	<.1	0.1	<.1	1.8	98	45	81	21	<.1	<.1	<.1	<.1	73.9	74.4	33.3	42.9	83.3	100.0	56.5
Randolph	26,189	89.0	9.5	0.2	0.2	<.1	1.1	40	88	11	36	0.3	0.4	0.2	<.1	75.7	74.6	87.5	65.1	83.0	13.3	84.3
Richland	12,243	99.3	<.1	0.2	0.2	0.0	0.3	70	22	76	82	0.1	0.2	<.1	<.1	74.0	74.2	64.7	60.5	82.6	0.0	45.9
Rock Island	110,814	89.1	5.8	0.6	0.2	<.1	4.4	13	87	20	7	1.3	1.5	0.6	0.8	74.5	76.5	62.5	65.1	66.8	32.9	59.8
St. Clair	188,043	73.9	23.9	0.7	0.2	<.1	1.3	6	99	3	28	2.2	2.1	4.0	0.4	71.5	74.9	63.3	69.2	71.2	33.1	63.4
Saline	20,143	96.4	2.8	0.1	0.2	<.1	0.4	51	61	35	61	0.2	0.3	<.1	<.1	75.9	76.6	59.9	49.2	69.7	25.8	62.2
Sangamon	132,835	91.8	6.7	0.7	0.2	<.1	0.6	11	82	17	49	1.6	1.9	0.8	0.1	74.5	75.7	62.2	70.3	76.2	19.5	64.4
Schuyler	5,639	99.6	<.1	<.1	0.2	0.0	0.1	92	1	100	102	<.1	<.1	<.1	<.1	75.2	75.2	50.0	50.0	100.0	0.0	100.0
Scott	4,165	99.6	<.1	0.0	0.1	0.0	0.2	99	4	98	91	<.1	<.1	<.1	<.1	73.8	73.8	100.0	0.0	100.0	0.0	66.7
Shelby	16,510	99.6	<.1	<.1	0.1	0.0	0.3	52	2	84	100	0.2	0.3	<.1	<.1	74.2	74.2	64.3	50.0	69.2	0.0	64.4
Stark	4,854	99.2	0.1	0.3	0.1	0.0	0.3	96	25	74	74	<.1	<.1	<.1	<.1	74.3	74.4	100.0	61.9	75.0	0.0	53.3
Stephenson	35,661	93.6	5.4	0.5	0.1	<.1	0.5	28	73	23	59	0.4	0.5	0.2	<.1	74.2	75.3	62.3	58.1	75.0	24.0	58.7
Tazewell	90,993	98.9	0.1	0.3	0.2	<.1	0.5	15	37	71	53	1.1	1.4	<.1	<.1	73.6	73.7	61.2	61.5	74.2	18.2	57.2
Union	13,532	97.9	0.8	0.3	0.1	0.0	0.9	63	44	50	40	0.2	0.2	<.1	<.1	76.8	76.9	87.7	70.0	86.4	0.0	64.3
Vermilion	65,389	90.3	7.9	0.4	0.2	<.1	1.2	19	84	14	30	0.8	0.9	0.5	0.1	74.1	75.3	66.1	59.7	67.1	34.7	56.2
Wabash	9,701	98.4	0.3	0.6	<.1	0.0	0.6	83	42	57	51	0.1	0.1	<.1	<.1	74.0	74.0	94.3	67.5	81.8	0.0	78.1
Warren	14,207	96.9	1.7	0.4	<.1	<.1	0.8	61	56	45	42	0.2	0.2	<.1	<.1	74.3	74.3	69.3	88.4	60.0	8.3	57.5
Washington	11,034	99.1	0.2	0.2	0.2	0.0	0.4	78	30	62	85	0.1	0.2	<.1	<.1	73.7	73.8	58.7	78.3	74.2	0.0	62.5
Wayne	13,015	99.2	<.1	0.2	0.2	<.1	0.4	65	24	85	68	0.2	0.2	<.1	<.1	75.5	75.6	75.0	63.6	79.3	100.0	63.9
White	12,614	99.2	0.2	0.1	0.2	<.1	0.4	67	26	64	66	0.1	0.2	<.1	<.1	76.3	76.5	70.7	51.4	84.8	100.0	46.6
Whiteside	44,028	93.0	0.5	0.2	0.1	<.1	6.1	23	76	54	4	0.5	0.6	<.1	0.5	73.2	74.3	59.1	62.9	60.8	47.8	60.4
Will	250,866	84.0	9.7	1.2	0.2	<.1	4.9	4	97	10	6	3.0	3.2	2.1	2.2	70.2	71.7	64.2	64.4	71.8	35.8	61.9
Williamson	43,898	96.9	1.8	0.4	0.2	<.1	0.6	24	53	42	48	0.5	0.6	<.1	<.1	76.0	76.3	71.5	70.6	75.2	38.5	62.9
Winnebago	186,609	88.7	7.6	1.0	0.2	<.1	2.5	7	89	15	12	2.2	2.5	1.3	0.8	73.8	75.8	61.3	64.0	73.5	31.1	59.5
Woodford	23,217	98.9	0.2	0.2	0.1	0.0	0.6	46	38	66	52	0.3	0.3	<.1	<.1	71.1	71.2	67.2	57.9	72.3	0.0	58.4
ILLINOIS	8,484,236	77.4	13.3	2.3	0.2	<.1	6.8					100.0	100.0	100.0	100.0	74.2	76.8	67.4	71.7	73.6	46.7	63.4
CONGRESSIONAL																						
District 1	418,800	28.0	67.5	1.1	0.1	<.1	3.1	13	19	1	12	4.9	1.8	25.1	2.3	73.3	79.5	71.3	83.3	76.4	54.9	63.7
District 2	402,216	27.8	65.6	0.5	0.1	<.1	5.9	19	20	2	7	4.7	1.7	23.4	4.1	70.4	79.6	67.9	68.6	74.7	54.0	62.3
District 3	442,224	90.9	1.7	1.2	0.1	<.1	6.1	3	6	17	6	5.2	6.1	0.7	4.7	77.4	78.8	68.6	70.7	68.9	55.1	63.8
District 4	383,497	32.7	5.3	2.4	0.2	0.2	59.2	20	18	9	1	4.5	1.9	1.8	39.6	67.1	81.9	63.9	73.7	70.1	60.9	61.1
District 5	467,584	82.3	1.3	5.1	0.2	<.1	11.0	1	15	20	2	5.5	5.9	0.5	9.0	81.8	84.8	74.7	74.3	55.5		68.0
District 6	437,195	89.7	1.3	4.3	0.1	<.1	4.6	4	10	19	10	5.2	6.0	0.5	3.5	76.5	77.7	67.7	68.2	74.7	47.0	66.5
District 7	406,971	32.9	59.3	3.4	0.1	<.1	4.1	18	17	3	11	4.8	2.0	21.4	2.9	71.2	86.0	64.8	79.5	76.6	48.8	68.1
District 8	420,358	89.9	1.4	3.6	0.1	<.1	4.9	12	9	18	9	5.0	5.8	0.5	3.6	73.5	74.5	67.4	67.4	72.9	44.2	65.1
District 9	467,139	72.0	10.3	8.9	0.3	<.1	8.4	2	16	5	3	5.5	5.1	4.3	6.8	81.7	86.0	72.4	74.7	75.6	53.0	70.3
District 10	425,243	84.6	5.4	3.5	0.2	<.1	6.3	8	13	8	5	5.0	5.5	2.0	4.6	74.4	76.1	67.4	66.2	76.4	44.1	65.5
District 11	417,919	86.5	7.4	0.6	0.2	<.1	5.4	14	11	6	8	4.9	5.5	2.7	4.0	73.1	75.0	63.9	64.7	72.5	43.1	61.2
District 12	421,442	82.9	14.8	0.9	0.2	<.1	1.2	11	14	4	17	5.0	5.3	5.5	0.9	73.7	75.9	64.3	75.9	73.5	35.7	65.6
District 13	412,733	90.4	2.9	3.8	0.1	<.1	2.7	16	7	15	13	4.9	5.7	1.1	2.0	72.2	72.8	68.4	65.8	74.1	38.5	66.6
District 14	407,741	86.3	3.6	1.6	0.2	<.1	8.3	17	12	13	4	4.8	5.4	1.3	5.9	71.3	73.1	63.5	68.1	72.9	36.6	60.5
District 15	433,422	90.0	6.4	1.9	0.1	<.1	1.5	5	8	7	16	5.1	5.9	2.5	1.1	75.8	76.7	66.0	79.4	72.7	37.0	68.9
District 16	415,480	92.6	3.9	0.7	0.2	<.1	2.6	15	5	11	14	4.9	5.9	1.4	1.9	72.7	73.8	61.4	60.7	73.2	35.1	60.7
District 17	427,877	94.0	2.9	0.5	0.2	<.1	2.5	7	4	16	15	5.0	6.1	1.1	1.9	74.9	75.6	67.3	70.4	69.1	29.8	61.0
District 18	421,986	94.2	4.2	0.6	0.2	<.1	0.8	10	3	10	18	5.0	6.1	1.6	0.6	73.8	74.7	61.1	67.3	72.6	18.3	62.0
District 19	429,589	95.8	3.3	0.3	0.2	<.1	0.4	6	1	14	20	5.1	6.3	1.3	0.3	75.2	75.7	64.7	66.0	75.1	24.0	65.1
District 20	424,820	95.1	3.7	0.4	0.2	<.1	0.6	9	2	12	19	5.0	6.2	1.4	0.4	74.3	74.8	66.2	67.8	76.6	24.8	68.8

Table C. — Voter Participation: November 3, 1992, General Election

| County | Estimated Voting Age Population (VAP) 1992 | Voter registration (REG) | | | | Voter turnout | | | | | | | | | | | | | |
| | | Total | % contribution to state REG | % of 1992 VAP | Rank by % of 1992 VAP | Highest office | | | | Maximum vote | | | | | | Percent drop-off, by office | | | |
						Actual	Total	Office	% of 1992 VAP	Total	% contribution to state turnout	% of REG	Rank by % of REG	% of 1992 VAP	Rank by % 1992 VAP	President	Senator	Governor	Representative
Adams	48,470	39,956	0.6	82.4	57	32,274	31,579	P	65.2	32,274	0.6	80.8	50	66.6	46	2.2	4.9	-	6.0
Alexander	7,429	8,046	0.1	108.3	1	4,513	4,362	P	58.7	4,513	<.1	56.1	102	60.7	84	3.3	7.3	-	10.2
Bond	11,152	10,575	0.2	94.8	12	7,848	7,548	P	67.7	7,848	0.2	74.2	87	70.4	19	3.8	8.6	-	8.5
Boone	22,972	15,540	0.2	67.6	101	13,836	13,627	P	59.3	13,836	0.3	89.0	2	60.2	88	1.5	3.2	-	2.6
Brown	4,654	3,604	<.1	77.4	72	2,761	2,689	P	57.8	2,761	<.1	76.6	71	59.3	92	2.6	6.2	-	5.3
Bureau	26,146	22,306	0.3	85.3	43	18,311	17,907	P	68.5	18,311	0.4	82.1	40	70.0	25	2.2	4.8	-	4.4
Calhoun	4,009	3,726	<.1	92.9	15	2,897	2,803	P	69.9	2,897	<.1	77.8	66	72.3	12	3.2	8.1	-	5.0
Carroll	12,408	9,696	0.1	78.1	69	7,968	7,679	P	61.9	7,968	0.2	82.2	37	64.2	65	3.6	5.6	-	6.7
Cass	9,877	9,601	0.1	97.2	8	6,616	6,447	P	65.3	6,616	0.1	68.9	100	67.0	45	2.6	5.5	-	5.4
Champaign	131,514	91,710	1.4	69.7	95	77,254	76,092	P	57.9	77,254	1.5	84.2	16	58.7	95	1.5	4.4	-	10.3
Christian	25,614	23,579	0.4	92.1	16	17,956	17,590	P	68.7	17,956	0.3	76.2	75	70.1	24	2.0	3.9	-	3.8
Clark	12,063	10,634	0.2	88.2	32	8,195	7,979	P	66.1	8,195	0.2	77.1	68	67.9	36	2.6	5.7	-	6.1
Clay	10,862	9,379	0.1	86.3	38	6,852	6,652	P	61.2	6,852	0.1	73.1	92	63.1	72	2.9	6.0	-	5.9
Clinton	25,298	19,309	0.3	76.3	77	16,293	15,822	P	62.5	16,293	0.3	84.4	14	64.4	62	2.9	6.9	-	6.7
Coles	39,486	30,165	0.5	76.4	76	22,839	22,300	P	56.5	22,839	0.4	75.7	77	57.8	97	2.4	4.2	-	6.8
Cook	3,840,168	2,924,493	44.3	76.2	79	2,199,608	2,146,655	P	55.9	2,199,608	42.6	75.2	83	57.3	99	2.4	4.3	-	7.1
Crawford	14,620	12,205	0.2	83.5	54	9,903	9,671	P	66.1	9,903	0.2	81.1	48	67.7	40	2.3	5.7	-	6.1
Cumberland	7,733	8,226	0.1	106.4	2	5,387	5,202	P	67.3	5,387	0.1	65.5	101	69.7	27	3.4	6.0	-	6.9
DeKalb	59,332	40,618	0.6	68.5	99	34,863	34,232	P	57.7	34,863	0.7	85.8	9	58.8	94	1.8	3.6	-	7.2
De Witt	12,160	9,969	0.2	82.0	58	7,906	7,759	P	63.8	7,906	0.2	79.3	59	65.0	57	1.9	4.7	-	5.7
Douglas	14,191	10,798	0.2	76.1	80	8,585	8,276	P	58.3	8,585	0.2	79.5	56	60.5	86	3.6	5.8	-	9.5
DuPage	604,559	431,876	6.5	71.4	93	376,837	370,987	P	61.4	376,837	7.3	87.3	3	62.3	75	1.6	3.3	-	5.7
Edgar	14,567	12,222	0.2	83.9	50	10,052	9,776	P	67.1	10,052	0.2	82.2	36	69.0	30	2.7	6.2	-	10.4
Edwards	5,579	4,766	<.1	85.4	42	3,663	3,552	P	63.7	3,663	<.1	76.9	69	65.7	53	3.0	9.4	-	7.6
Effingham	22,497	16,853	0.3	74.9	84	15,299	14,981	P	66.6	15,299	0.3	90.8	1	68.0	34	2.1	5.1	-	6.0
Fayette	15,653	12,048	0.2	77.0	75	10,383	10,118	P	64.6	10,383	0.2	86.2	8	66.3	47	2.6	5.3	-	5.2
Ford	10,534	7,788	0.1	73.9	88	6,679	6,481	P	61.5	6,679	0.1	85.8	10	63.4	71	3.0	5.4	-	6.6
Franklin	30,616	29,785	0.5	97.3	6	21,956	21,481	P	70.2	21,956	0.4	73.7	90	71.7	13	2.2	6.0	-	3.6
Fulton	28,269	24,018	0.4	85.0	45	18,142	17,701	P	62.6	18,142	0.4	75.5	78	64.2	66	2.4	4.1	-	3.7
Gallatin	5,211	4,944	<.1	94.9	11	4,052	3,944	P	75.7	4,052	<.1	82.0	44	77.8	5	2.7	9.3	-	4.4
Greene	11,196	9,130	0.1	81.5	60	7,239	7,032	P	62.8	7,239	0.1	79.3	60	64.7	60	2.9	7.4	-	4.3
Grundy	24,230	19,487	0.3	80.4	63	16,503	16,265	P	67.1	16,503	0.3	84.7	12	68.1	33	1.4	3.7	-	5.2
Hamilton	6,452	6,160	<.1	95.5	10	5,149	4,974	P	77.1	5,149	<.1	83.6	25	79.8	3	3.4	13.9	-	8.3
Hancock	15,759	13,502	0.2	85.7	39	10,283	10,069	P	63.9	10,283	0.2	76.2	74	65.3	54	2.1	5.5	-	7.0
Hardin	3,968	3,866	<.1	97.4	5	3,334	3,173	P	80.0	3,334	<.1	86.2	5	84.0	1	4.8	12.0	-	7.3
Henderson	5,944	5,089	<.1	85.6	40	4,119	4,048	P	68.1	4,119	<.1	80.9	49	69.3	29	1.7	4.6	-	2.8
Henry	36,986	33,254	0.5	89.9	27	25,050	24,371	P	65.9	25,050	0.5	75.3	82	67.7	41	2.7	5.2	-	4.8
Iroquois	22,799	17,696	0.3	77.6	71	14,816	14,530	P	63.7	14,816	0.3	83.7	21	65.0	58	1.9	4.3	-	6.5
Jackson	47,132	35,604	0.5	75.5	81	24,935	24,434	P	51.8	24,935	0.5	70.0	98	52.9	102	2.0	3.7	-	6.3
Jasper	7,627	7,013	0.1	91.9	18	5,625	5,480	P	71.9	5,625	0.1	80.2	54	73.8	8	2.6	6.7	-	6.1
Jefferson	27,521	21,800	0.3	79.2	67	17,957	17,597	P	63.9	17,957	0.3	82.4	35	65.2	55	2.0	5.5	-	6.5
Jersey	15,155	12,757	0.2	84.2	48	10,270	10,093	P	66.6	10,270	0.2	80.5	52	67.8	38	1.7	5.2	-	4.3
Jo Daviess	16,106	12,882	0.2	80.0	65	10,660	10,454	P	64.9	10,660	0.2	82.8	30	66.2	49	1.9	5.7	-	3.2
Johnson	9,530	6,601	0.1	69.3	97	5,546	5,391	P	56.6	5,546	0.1	84.0	17	58.2	96	2.8	6.6	-	3.8
Kane	233,374	158,611	2.4	68.0	100	130,088	127,938	P	54.8	130,088	2.5	82.0	41	55.7	100	1.7	3.4	-	6.4
Kankakee	68,925	48,955	0.7	71.0	94	40,972	40,071	P	58.1	40,972	0.8	83.7	23	59.4	91	2.2	3.7	-	6.9
Kendall	28,700	22,972	0.3	80.0	64	18,950	18,406	P	64.1	18,950	0.4	82.5	32	66.0	51	2.9	3.7	-	4.8
Knox	42,367	31,559	0.5	74.5	85	25,909	25,296	P	59.7	25,909	0.5	82.1	38	61.2	82	2.4	4.7	-	3.5
Lake	389,271	271,375	4.1	69.7	96	229,473	223,987	P	57.5	229,473	4.4	84.6	13	58.9	93	2.4	5.8	-	12.8
La Salle	79,367	61,394	0.9	77.4	73	50,996	49,931	P	62.9	50,996	1.0	83.1	28	64.3	64	2.1	4.5	-	5.2
Lawrence	11,975	9,675	0.1	80.8	62	7,661	7,488	P	62.5	7,661	0.1	79.2	61	64.0	69	2.3	6.8	-	6.9
Lee	25,474	18,808	0.3	73.8	89	15,788	15,417	P	60.5	15,788	0.3	83.9	19	62.0	76	2.3	4.4	-	8.7
Livingston	29,546	20,254	0.3	68.6	98	17,571	17,098	P	57.9	17,571	0.3	86.8	4	59.5	90	2.7	4.5	-	4.6
Logan	23,260	20,770	0.3	89.3	30	14,505	14,195	P	62.4	14,505	0.3	69.8	99	62.4	74	2.1	4.8	-	6.2
McDonough	26,600	17,124	0.3	64.4	102	14,164	13,922	P	52.3	14,164	0.3	82.7	31	53.2	101	1.7	4.7	-	4.8
McHenry	139,033	113,358	1.7	81.5	61	89,334	88,294	P	63.5	89,334	1.7	78.8	64	64.3	63	1.2	3.1	-	4.8
McLean	98,439	73,273	1.1	74.4	86	60,430	59,285	P	60.2	60,430	1.2	82.5	33	61.4	81	1.9	3.2	-	6.3
Macon	85,714	71,855	1.1	83.8	51	56,623	55,580	P	64.8	56,623	1.1	78.8	65	66.1	50	1.8	3.2	-	4.6
Macoupin	35,547	31,811	0.5	89.5	28	24,003	23,661	P	66.6	24,003	0.5	75.5	80	67.5	42	1.4	4.1	-	3.8
Madison	187,552	141,321	2.1	75.4	82	115,893	114,095	P	60.8	115,893	2.2	82.0	42	61.8	78	1.6	4.3	-	3.8
Marion	30,574	25,810	0.4	84.4	47	19,399	18,883	P	61.8	19,399	0.4	75.2	84	63.4	70	2.7	5.7	-	5.8
Marshall	9,482	8,070	0.1	85.1	44	6,650	6,496	P	68.5	6,650	0.1	82.4	34	70.1	23	2.3	4.2	-	5.8
Mason	11,741	9,680	0.1	82.4	56	7,881	7,702	P	65.6	7,881	0.2	81.4	47	67.1	44	2.3	4.5	-	4.6
Massac	11,411	10,370	0.2	90.9	23	7,306	7,056	P	61.8	7,306	0.1	70.5	97	64.0	68	3.4	7.0	-	5.4
Menard	8,208	7,462	0.1	90.9	22	6,431	6,299	P	76.7	6,431	0.1	86.2	7	78.4	4	2.1	4.4	-	5.4
Mercer	12,590	11,074	0.2	88.0	33	8,738	8,540	P	67.8	8,738	0.2	78.9	63	69.4	28	2.3	4.6	-	2.9
Monroe	17,027	15,329	0.2	90.0	26	12,861	12,542	P	73.7	12,861	0.2	83.9	20	75.5	6	2.5	6.1	-	6.2
Montgomery	22,996	18,208	0.3	79.2	68	15,114	14,837	P	64.5	15,114	0.3	83.0	29	65.7	52	1.8	4.7	-	3.4
Morgan	27,299	20,121	0.3	73.7	90	16,819	16,297	P	59.7	16,819	0.3	83.6	24	61.6	80	3.1	4.6	-	5.7
Moultrie	10,318	7,958	0.1	77.1	74	6,661	6,465	P	62.7	6,661	0.1	83.7	22	64.6	61	2.9	5.2	-	6.4

Table C. — **Voter Participation: November 3, 1992, General Election (cont)**

County	Estimated Voting Age Population (VAP) 1992	Voter registration (REG)				Voter turnout													
						Highest office				Maximum vote							Percent drop-off, by office		
		Total	% contribution to state REG	% of 1992 VAP	Rank by % of 1992 VAP	Actual	Total	Office	% of 1992 VAP	Total	% contribution to state turnout	% of REG	Rank by % of REG	% of 1992 VAP	Rank by % 1992 VAP	President	Senator	Governor	Representative
Ogle	33,740	26,870	0.4	79.6	66	20,529	20,109	P	59.6	20,529	0.4	76.4	73	60.8	83	2.0	4.4	-	5.7
Peoria	133,703	98,304	1.5	73.5	91	82,842	81,328	P	60.8	82,842	1.6	84.3	15	62.0	77	1.8	4.0	-	4.3
Perry	16,012	14,939	0.2	93.3	13	11,446	11,086	P	69.2	11,446	0.2	76.6	70	71.5	15	3.1	6.5	-	8.0
Piatt	11,580	10,047	0.2	86.8	36	8,571	8,447	P	72.9	8,571	0.2	85.3	11	74.0	7	1.4	3.8	-	6.1
Pike	13,147	12,061	0.2	91.7	20	9,226	9,037	P	68.7	9,226	0.2	76.5	72	70.2	22	2.0	5.5	-	3.2
Pope	3,389	3,117	<.1	92.0	17	2,465	2,411	P	71.1	2,465	<.1	79.1	62	72.7	10	2.2	6.5	-	4.2
Pulaski	5,266	5,119	<.1	97.2	7	3,752	3,549	P	67.4	3,752	<.1	73.3	91	71.2	16	5.4	8.7	-	7.8
Putnam	4,238	4,232	<.1	99.9	3	3,386	3,308	P	78.1	3,386	<.1	80.0	55	79.9	2	2.3	5.4	-	7.4
Randolph	26,384	21,559	0.3	81.7	59	17,125	16,565	P	62.8	17,125	0.3	79.4	57	64.9	59	3.3	5.5	-	6.1
Richland	12,118	10,963	0.2	90.5	24	8,272	8,061	P	66.5	8,272	0.2	75.5	81	68.3	32	2.6	6.0	-	5.9
Rock Island	108,720	91,938	1.4	84.6	46	73,751	72,039	P	66.3	73,751	1.4	80.2	53	67.8	37	2.3	4.4	-	4.8
St. Clair	190,474	148,101	2.2	77.8	70	109,638	107,541	P	56.5	109,638	2.1	74.0	89	57.6	98	1.9	4.8	-	5.3
Saline	20,113	16,705	0.3	83.1	55	13,626	13,254	P	65.9	13,626	0.3	81.6	45	67.7	39	2.7	7.2	-	3.5
Sangamon	134,893	121,873	1.8	90.3	25	98,301	96,860	P	71.8	98,301	1.9	80.7	51	72.9	9	1.5	3.0	-	3.8
Schuyler	5,605	5,479	<.1	97.8	4	4,066	3,995	P	71.3	4,066	<.1	74.2	88	72.5	11	1.7	4.5	-	4.8
Scott	4,189	3,746	<.1	89.4	29	2,848	2,783	P	66.4	2,848	<.1	76.0	76	68.0	35	2.3	4.8	-	4.1
Shelby	16,424	13,761	0.2	83.8	52	11,491	11,175	P	68.0	11,491	0.2	83.5	26	70.0	26	2.8	5.2	-	7.2
Stark	4,782	4,155	<.1	86.9	35	3,407	3,351	P	70.1	3,407	<.1	82.0	43	71.2	17	1.6	5.0	-	4.8
Stephenson	35,702	26,826	0.4	75.1	83	22,023	21,656	P	60.7	22,023	0.4	82.1	39	61.7	79	1.7	4.6	-	3.2
Tazewell	90,987	79,136	1.2	87.0	34	61,311	59,994	P	65.9	61,311	1.2	77.5	67	67.4	43	2.1	4.1	-	4.5
Union	13,652	12,483	0.2	91.4	21	9,355	9,083	P	66.5	9,355	0.2	74.9	85	68.5	31	2.9	6.1	-	8.1
Vermilion	65,288	47,246	0.7	72.4	92	39,333	38,461	P	58.9	39,333	0.8	83.3	27	60.2	87	2.2	4.5	-	7.4
Wabash	9,748	8,704	0.1	89.3	31	6,345	6,240	P	64.0	6,345	0.1	72.9	94	65.1	56	1.7	6.1	-	5.4
Warren	13,916	11,908	0.2	85.6	41	8,681	8,446	P	60.7	8,681	0.2	72.9	93	62.4	73	2.7	4.7	-	3.7
Washington	11,143	9,642	0.1	86.5	37	7,857	7,555	P	67.8	7,857	0.2	81.5	46	70.5	18	3.8	8.2	-	8.1
Wayne	13,052	12,143	0.2	93.0	14	9,165	8,872	P	68.0	9,165	0.2	75.5	79	70.2	21	3.2	8.4	-	7.0
White	12,578	12,102	0.2	96.2	9	9,009	8,811	P	70.1	9,009	0.2	74.4	86	71.6	14	2.2	7.2	-	4.6
Whiteside	43,766	32,555	0.5	74.4	87	28,073	27,153	P	62.0	28,073	0.5	86.2	6	64.1	67	3.3	5.2	-	5.9
Will	261,641	219,528	3.3	83.9	49	156,597	152,123	P	58.1	156,597	3.0	71.3	96	59.9	89	2.9	4.0	-	5.5
Williamson	44,558	40,968	0.6	91.9	19	29,552	28,760	P	64.5	29,552	0.6	72.1	95	66.3	48	2.7	5.1	-	4.4
Winnebago	188,879	144,016	2.2	76.2	78	114,374	112,215	P	59.4	114,374	2.2	79.4	58	60.6	85	1.9	3.7	-	2.9
Woodford	23,475	19,659	0.3	83.7	53	16,506	16,305	P	69.5	16,506	0.3	84.0	18	70.3	20	1.2	3.8	-	4.3
ILLINOIS	**8,568,000**	**6,600,358**	**100.0**	**77.0**		**5,164,357**	**5,050,157**		**58.9**	**5,164,357**	**100.0**	**78.2**		**60.3**		**2.2**	**4.4**	**-**	**6.5**

Table E. — Vote for President: November 3, 1992, General Election

County	Total	Clinton (DEM)	Bush (REP)	Perot (IND)	Other	Plurality Total	Party	DEM	REP	IND	Other	Rank DEM	Rank REP	Rank IND	Total	DEM	REP	IND	DEM	REP
Adams	31,579	11,748	13,529	6,157	145	1,781	R	37.2	42.8	19.5	0.5	85	18	44	0.6	0.5	0.8	0.7	46.5	53.5
Alexander	4,362	2,566	1,301	474	21	1,265	D	58.8	29.8	10.9	0.5	3	86	101	<.1	0.1	<.1	<.1	66.4	33.6
Bond	7,548	3,428	2,715	1,373	32	713	D	45.4	36.0	18.2	0.4	42	61	58	0.1	0.1	0.2	0.2	55.8	44.2
Boone	13,627	5,114	5,589	2,880	44	475	R	37.5	41.0	21.1	0.3	84	22	21	0.3	0.2	0.3	0.3	47.8	52.2
Brown	2,689	1,146	1,029	504	10	117	D	42.6	38.3	18.7	0.4	55	43	54	<.1	<.1	<.1	<.1	52.7	47.3
Bureau	17,907	7,551	6,836	3,465	55	715	D	42.2	38.2	19.4	0.3	57	44	45	0.4	0.3	0.4	0.4	52.5	47.5
Calhoun	2,803	1,519	745	532	7	774	D	54.2	26.6	19.0	0.2	10	100	50	<.1	<.1	<.1	<.1	67.1	32.9
Carroll	7,679	2,854	3,297	1,502	26	443	R	37.2	42.9	19.6	0.3	86	16	43	0.2	0.1	0.2	0.2	46.4	53.6
Cass	6,447	3,200	2,162	1,072	13	1,038	D	49.6	33.5	16.6	0.2	25	70	83	0.1	0.1	0.1	0.1	59.7	40.3
Champaign	76,092	35,003	27,096	13,571	422	7,907	D	46.0	35.6	17.8	0.6	39	64	67	1.5	1.4	1.6	1.6	56.4	43.6
Christian	17,590	9,042	5,087	3,401	60	3,955	D	51.4	28.9	19.3	0.3	18	92	47	0.3	0.4	0.3	0.4	64.0	36.0
Clark	7,979	3,338	3,175	1,450	16	163	D	41.8	39.8	18.2	0.2	60	30	60	0.2	0.1	0.2	0.2	51.3	48.7
Clay	6,652	2,962	2,471	1,193	26	491	D	44.5	37.1	17.9	0.4	45	52	65	0.1	0.1	0.1	0.1	54.5	45.5
Clinton	15,822	6,686	5,771	3,315	50	915	D	42.3	36.5	21.0	0.3	56	57	25	0.3	0.3	0.3	0.4	53.7	46.3
Coles	22,300	9,402	8,098	4,707	93	1,304	D	42.2	36.3	21.1	0.4	58	60	23	0.4	0.4	0.5	0.6	53.7	46.3
Cook	2,146,655	1,249,533	605,300	281,999	9,823	644,233	D	58.2	28.2	13.1	0.5	4	95	99	42.5	50.9	34.9	33.6	67.4	32.6
Crawford	9,671	3,964	3,606	2,062	39	358	D	41.0	37.3	21.3	0.4	67	51	15	0.2	0.2	0.2	0.2	52.4	47.6
Cumberland	5,202	2,111	1,860	1,209	22	251	D	40.6	35.8	23.2	0.4	69	63	4	0.1	<.1	0.1	0.1	53.2	46.8
DeKalb	34,232	13,744	12,655	7,680	153	1,089	D	40.1	37.0	22.4	0.4	71	54	7	0.7	0.6	0.7	0.9	52.1	47.9
De Witt	7,759	3,009	3,164	1,543	43	155	R	38.8	40.8	19.9	0.6	79	24	41	0.2	0.1	0.2	0.2	48.7	51.3
Douglas	8,276	3,341	3,309	1,600	26	32	D	40.4	40.0	19.3	0.3	70	28	48	0.2	0.1	0.2	0.2	50.2	49.8
DuPage	370,987	114,564	178,271	76,839	1,313	63,707	R	30.9	48.1	20.7	0.4	99	2	30	7.3	4.7	10.3	9.1	39.1	60.9
Edgar	9,776	4,014	3,790	1,930	42	224	D	41.1	38.8	19.7	0.4	66	38	42	0.2	0.2	0.2	0.2	51.4	48.6
Edwards	3,552	1,299	1,601	634	18	302	R	36.6	45.1	17.8	0.5	87	9	66	<.1	<.1	<.1	<.1	44.8	55.2
Effingham	14,981	5,221	6,329	3,354	77	1,108	R	34.9	42.2	22.4	0.5	94	19	9	0.3	0.2	0.4	0.4	45.2	54.8
Fayette	10,118	4,833	3,508	1,730	47	1,325	D	47.8	34.7	17.1	0.5	31	67	78	0.2	0.2	0.2	0.2	57.9	42.1
Ford	6,481	2,175	3,046	1,222	38	871	R	33.6	47.0	18.9	0.6	97	4	53	0.1	<.1	0.2	0.1	41.7	58.3
Franklin	21,481	12,744	5,504	3,180	53	7,240	D	59.3	25.6	14.8	0.2	2	101	96	0.4	0.5	0.3	0.4	69.8	30.2
Fulton	17,701	9,725	5,062	2,874	40	4,663	D	54.9	28.6	16.2	0.2	6	93	89	0.4	0.4	0.3	0.3	65.8	34.2
Gallatin	3,944	2,371	990	568	15	1,381	D	60.1	25.1	14.4	0.4	1	102	98	<.1	<.1	<.1	<.1	70.5	29.5
Greene	7,032	3,164	2,391	1,461	16	773	D	45.0	34.0	20.8	0.2	44	68	28	0.1	0.1	0.1	0.2	57.0	43.0
Grundy	16,265	6,122	6,346	3,724	73	224	R	37.6	39.0	22.9	0.4	82	37	5	0.3	0.2	0.4	0.4	49.1	50.9
Hamilton	4,974	2,582	1,521	862	9	1,061	D	51.9	30.6	17.3	0.2	14	83	76	<.1	0.1	<.1	0.1	62.9	37.1
Hancock	10,069	4,213	3,714	2,091	51	499	D	41.8	36.9	20.8	0.5	59	55	29	0.2	0.2	0.2	0.2	53.1	46.9
Hardin	3,173	1,665	985	515	8	680	D	52.5	31.0	16.2	0.3	12	82	90	<.1	<.1	<.1	<.1	62.8	37.2
Henderson	4,048	2,013	1,310	715	10	703	D	49.7	32.4	17.7	0.2	24	76	69	<.1	<.1	<.1	<.1	60.6	39.4
Henry	24,371	11,077	8,989	4,231	74	2,088	D	45.5	36.9	17.4	0.3	41	56	74	0.5	0.5	0.5	0.5	55.2	44.8
Iroquois	14,530	4,440	6,948	3,073	69	2,508	R	30.6	47.8	21.1	0.5	100	3	20	0.3	0.2	0.4	0.4	39.0	61.0
Jackson	24,434	13,373	6,899	3,995	167	6,474	D	54.7	28.2	16.4	0.7	8	94	88	0.5	0.5	0.4	0.5	66.0	34.0
Jasper	5,480	2,284	1,996	1,160	40	288	D	41.7	36.4	21.2	0.7	62	58	19	0.1	<.1	0.1	0.1	53.4	46.6
Jefferson	17,597	8,665	5,497	3,403	32	3,168	D	49.2	31.2	19.3	0.2	28	81	46	0.3	0.4	0.3	0.4	61.2	38.8
Jersey	10,093	4,749	2,933	2,363	48	1,816	D	47.1	29.1	23.4	0.5	35	91	3	0.2	0.2	0.2	0.3	61.8	38.2
Jo Daviess	10,454	4,044	4,249	2,102	59	205	R	38.7	40.6	20.1	0.6	80	26	37	0.2	0.2	0.2	0.3	48.8	51.2
Johnson	5,391	2,299	2,124	944	24	175	D	42.6	39.4	17.5	0.4	54	33	71	0.1	<.1	0.1	0.1	52.0	48.0
Kane	127,938	44,568	55,684	27,179	507	11,116	R	34.8	43.5	21.2	0.4	95	13	16	2.5	1.8	3.2	3.2	44.5	55.5
Kankakee	40,071	17,229	15,411	7,264	167	1,818	D	43.0	38.5	18.1	0.4	53	39	61	0.8	0.7	0.9	0.9	52.8	47.2
Kendall	18,406	5,423	8,521	4,394	68	3,098	R	29.5	46.3	23.9	0.4	101	7	2	0.4	0.2	0.5	0.5	38.9	61.1
Knox	25,296	12,524	8,331	4,357	84	4,193	D	49.5	32.9	17.2	0.3	26	73	77	0.5	0.5	0.5	0.5	60.1	39.9
Lake	223,987	81,693	99,000	42,384	910	17,307	R	36.5	44.2	18.9	0.4	89	12	51	4.4	3.3	5.7	5.0	45.2	54.8
La Salle	49,931	23,276	16,078	10,434	143	7,198	D	46.6	32.2	20.9	0.3	38	78	26	1.0	0.9	0.9	1.2	59.1	40.9
Lawrence	7,488	3,270	2,681	1,498	39	589	D	43.7	35.8	20.0	0.5	49	62	38	0.1	0.1	0.2	0.2	54.9	45.1
Lee	15,417	5,530	6,652	3,191	44	1,122	R	35.9	43.1	20.7	0.3	92	15	31	0.3	0.2	0.4	0.4	45.4	54.6
Livingston	17,098	6,007	8,004	3,029	58	1,997	R	35.1	46.8	17.7	0.3	93	6	68	0.3	0.2	0.5	0.4	42.9	57.1
Logan	14,195	5,169	6,567	2,420	39	1,398	R	36.4	46.3	17.0	0.3	90	8	79	0.3	0.2	0.4	0.3	44.0	56.0
McDonough	13,922	5,814	5,297	2,770	41	517	D	41.8	38.0	19.9	0.3	61	45	40	0.3	0.2	0.3	0.3	52.3	47.7
McHenry	88,294	24,783	41,356	21,817	338	16,573	R	28.1	46.8	24.7	0.4	102	5	1	1.7	1.0	2.4	2.6	37.5	62.5
McLean	59,285	23,090	25,726	10,282	187	2,636	R	38.9	43.4	17.3	0.3	78	14	75	1.2	0.9	1.5	1.2	47.3	52.7
Macon	55,580	27,449	18,684	9,236	211	8,765	D	49.4	33.6	16.6	0.4	27	69	84	1.1	1.1	1.1	1.1	59.5	40.5
Macoupin	23,661	12,050	6,518	5,018	75	5,532	D	50.9	27.5	21.2	0.3	21	99	18	0.5	0.5	0.4	0.6	64.9	35.1
Madison	114,095	58,484	32,167	23,110	334	26,317	D	51.3	28.2	20.3	0.3	19	96	36	2.3	2.4	1.9	2.7	64.5	35.5
Marion	18,883	9,669	5,764	3,407	43	3,905	D	51.2	30.5	18.0	0.2	20	84	62	0.4	0.4	0.3	0.4	62.7	37.3
Marshall	6,496	2,819	2,491	1,169	17	328	D	43.4	38.3	18.0	0.2	50	41	63	0.1	0.1	0.1	0.1	53.1	46.9
Mason	7,702	3,969	2,473	1,245	15	1,496	D	51.5	32.1	16.2	0.2	16	79	93	0.2	0.2	0.1	0.1	61.6	38.4
Massac	7,056	3,347	2,754	892	63	593	D	47.4	39.0	12.6	0.9	33	36	100	0.1	0.1	0.2	0.1	54.9	45.1
Menard	6,299	2,264	2,834	1,179	22	570	R	35.9	45.0	18.7	0.3	91	10	55	0.1	<.1	0.2	0.1	44.4	55.6
Mercer	8,540	3,990	2,983	1,535	32	1,007	D	46.7	34.9	18.0	0.4	37	65	64	0.2	0.2	0.2	0.2	57.2	42.8
Monroe	12,542	4,894	4,807	2,813	28	87	D	39.0	38.3	22.4	0.2	76	42	8	0.2	0.2	0.3	0.3	50.4	49.6
Montgomery	14,837	7,424	4,407	2,956	50	3,017	D	50.0	29.7	19.9	0.3	22	88	39	0.3	0.3	0.3	0.4	62.8	37.2
Morgan	16,297	6,351	6,566	3,317	63	215	R	39.0	40.3	20.4	0.4	77	27	35	0.3	0.3	0.4	0.4	49.2	50.8
Moultrie	6,465	3,056	2,065	1,322	22	991	D	47.3	31.9	20.4	0.3	34	80	32	0.1	0.1	0.1	0.2	59.7	40.3

Table E. — Vote for President: November 3, 1992, General Election (cont)

County	Total	Clinton (DEM)	Bush (REP)	Perot (IND)	Other	Plurality Total	Party	DEM	REP	IND	Other	Rank DEM	Rank REP	Rank IND	Total	DEM	REP	IND	DEM	REP
Ogle	20,109	6,512	9,008	4,455	134	2,496	R	32.4	44.8	22.2	0.7	98	11	10	0.4	0.3	0.5	0.5	42.0	58.0
Peoria	81,328	38,099	30,718	12,195	316	7,381	D	46.8	37.8	15.0	0.4	36	48	95	1.6	1.6	1.8	1.5	55.4	44.6
Perry	11,086	6,009	3,105	1,955	17	2,904	D	54.2	28.0	17.6	0.2	9	97	70	0.2	0.2	0.2	0.2	65.9	34.1
Piatt	8,447	3,520	3,076	1,822	29	444	D	41.7	36.4	21.6	0.3	63	59	12	0.2	0.1	0.2	0.2	53.4	46.6
Pike	9,037	4,016	3,342	1,643	36	674	D	44.4	37.0	18.2	0.4	46	53	59	0.2	0.2	0.2	0.2	54.6	45.4
Pope	2,411	1,063	951	391	6	112	D	44.1	39.4	16.2	0.2	47	32	91	<.1	<.1	<.1	<.1	52.8	47.2
Pulaski	3,549	1,987	1,169	379	14	818	D	56.0	32.9	10.7	0.4	5	72	102	<.1	<.1	<.1	<.1	63.0	37.0
Putnam	3,308	1,574	969	752	13	605	D	47.6	29.3	22.7	0.4	32	90	6	<.1	<.1	<.1	<.1	61.9	38.1
Randolph	16,565	8,529	4,899	3,092	45	3,630	D	51.5	29.6	18.7	0.3	17	89	56	0.3	0.3	0.3	0.4	63.5	36.5
Richland	8,061	3,286	3,053	1,689	33	233	D	40.8	37.9	21.0	0.4	68	46	24	0.2	0.1	0.2	0.2	51.8	48.2
Rock Island	72,039	37,412	23,212	10,416	999	14,200	D	51.9	32.2	14.5	1.4	13	77	97	1.4	1.5	1.3	1.2	61.7	38.3
St. Clair	107,541	57,625	31,951	17,592	373	25,674	D	53.6	29.7	16.4	0.3	11	87	87	2.1	2.3	1.8	2.1	64.3	35.7
Saline	13,254	7,258	3,667	2,302	27	3,591	D	54.8	27.7	17.4	0.2	7	98	73	0.3	0.3	0.2	0.3	66.4	33.6
Sangamon	96,860	40,052	39,641	16,861	306	411	D	41.4	40.9	17.4	0.3	64	23	72	1.9	1.6	2.3	2.0	50.3	49.7
Schuyler	3,995	1,650	1,512	815	18	138	D	41.3	37.8	20.4	0.5	65	47	34	<.1	<.1	<.1	<.1	52.2	47.8
Scott	2,783	1,057	1,132	588	6	75	R	38.0	40.7	21.1	0.2	81	25	22	<.1	<.1	<.1	<.1	48.3	51.7
Shelby	11,175	5,101	3,631	2,401	42	1,470	D	45.6	32.5	21.5	0.4	40	75	14	0.2	0.2	0.2	0.3	58.4	41.6
Stark	3,351	1,336	1,384	625	6	48	R	39.9	41.3	18.7	0.2	72	21	57	<.1	<.1	<.1	<.1	49.1	50.9
Stephenson	21,656	7,899	9,005	4,677	75	1,106	R	36.5	41.6	21.6	0.3	88	20	11	0.4	0.3	0.5	0.6	46.7	53.3
Tazewell	59,994	26,428	23,469	9,927	170	2,959	D	44.1	39.1	16.5	0.3	48	35	86	1.2	1.1	1.4	1.2	53.0	47.0
Union	9,083	4,681	3,003	1,373	26	1,678	D	51.5	33.1	15.1	0.3	15	71	94	0.2	0.2	0.2	0.2	60.9	39.1
Vermilion	38,461	18,383	11,703	8,162	213	6,680	D	47.8	30.4	21.2	0.6	30	85	17	0.8	0.7	0.7	1.0	61.1	38.9
Wabash	6,240	2,436	2,485	1,302	17	49	R	39.0	39.8	20.9	0.3	75	29	27	0.1	<.1	0.1	0.2	49.5	50.5
Warren	8,446	3,661	3,325	1,436	24	336	D	43.3	39.4	17.0	0.3	51	34	80	0.2	0.1	0.2	0.2	52.4	47.6
Washington	7,555	2,986	3,003	1,542	24	17	R	39.5	39.7	20.4	0.3	73	31	33	0.1	0.1	0.2	0.2	49.9	50.1
Wayne	8,872	3,332	3,809	1,702	29	477	R	37.6	42.9	19.2	0.3	83	17	49	0.2	0.1	0.2	0.2	46.7	53.3
White	8,811	4,308	3,057	1,428	18	1,251	D	48.9	34.7	16.2	0.2	29	66	92	0.2	0.2	0.2	0.2	58.5	41.5
Whiteside	27,153	12,329	10,146	4,589	89	2,183	D	45.4	37.4	16.9	0.3	43	50	81	0.5	0.5	0.6	0.5	54.9	45.1
Will	152,123	59,633	58,337	32,788	1,365	1,296	D	39.2	38.3	21.6	0.9	74	40	13	3.0	2.4	3.4	3.9	50.5	49.5
Williamson	28,760	14,361	9,462	4,779	158	4,899	D	49.9	32.9	16.6	0.5	23	74	85	0.6	0.6	0.5	0.6	60.3	39.7
Winnebago	112,215	48,298	42,221	21,227	469	6,077	D	43.0	37.6	18.9	0.4	52	49	52	2.2	2.0	2.4	2.5	53.4	46.6
Woodford	16,305	5,490	8,032	2,733	50	2,542	R	33.7	49.3	16.8	0.3	96	1	82	0.3	0.2	0.5	0.3	40.6	59.4
ILLINOIS	5,050,157	2,453,350	1,734,096	840,515	22,196	719,254	D	48.6	34.3	16.6	0.4				100.0	100.0	100.0	100.0	58.6	41.4

County	Total	Braun (DEM)	Williamson (REP)	Other	Plurality Total	Party	DEM	REP	Other	Rank DEM	Rank REP	Rank Other	Total	DEM	REP	Other
Adams	30,697	13,473	15,759	1,465	2,286	R	43.9	51.3	4.8	80	30	24	0.6	0.5	0.7	0.8
Alexander	4,182	2,517	1,576	89	941	D	60.2	37.7	2.1	4	94	100	<.1	<.1	<.1	<.1
Bond	7,171	3,723	3,137	311	586	D	51.9	43.7	4.3	31	71	41	0.1	0.1	0.1	0.2
Boone	13,392	5,648	6,830	914	1,182	R	42.2	51.0	6.8	87	32	4	0.3	0.2	0.3	0.5
Brown	2,591	1,160	1,331	100	171	R	44.8	51.4	3.9	73	28	68	<.1	<.1	<.1	<.1
Bureau	17,434	8,438	8,326	670	112	D	48.4	47.8	3.8	52	46	69	0.4	0.3	0.4	0.4
Calhoun	2,663	1,654	953	56	701	D	62.1	35.8	2.1	2	101	101	<.1	<.1	<.1	<.1
Carroll	7,521	3,064	4,140	317	1,076	R	40.7	55.0	4.2	91	7	44	0.2	0.1	0.2	0.2
Cass	6,253	3,361	2,654	238	707	D	53.8	42.4	3.8	25	78	70	0.1	0.1	0.1	0.1
Champaign	73,854	38,103	32,236	3,515	5,867	D	51.6	43.6	4.8	33	72	25	1.5	1.4	1.5	1.9
Christian	17,263	9,561	6,951	751	2,610	D	55.4	40.3	4.4	21	87	40	0.3	0.4	0.3	0.4
Clark	7,724	3,636	3,815	273	179	R	47.1	49.4	3.5	62	37	76	0.2	0.1	0.2	0.2
Clay	6,440	3,157	3,014	269	143	D	49.0	46.8	4.2	50	53	48	0.1	0.1	0.1	0.1
Clinton	15,163	7,467	7,068	628	399	D	49.2	46.6	4.1	47	54	50	0.3	0.3	0.3	0.3
Coles	21,878	10,704	10,300	874	404	D	48.9	47.1	4.0	51	52	58	0.4	0.4	0.5	0.5
Cook	2,105,233	1,294,440	754,945	55,848	539,495	D	61.5	35.9	2.7	3	100	97	42.6	49.2	35.5	30.8
Crawford	9,336	4,106	4,965	265	859	R	44.0	53.2	2.8	79	16	95	0.2	0.2	0.2	0.1
Cumberland	5,064	2,359	2,444	261	85	R	46.6	48.3	5.2	64	42	19	0.1	<.1	0.1	0.1
DeKalb	33,602	16,133	15,596	1,873	537	D	48.0	46.4	5.6	54	56	12	0.7	0.6	0.7	1.0
De Witt	7,538	3,299	3,872	367	573	R	43.8	51.4	4.9	81	29	23	0.2	0.1	0.2	0.2
Douglas	8,083	3,708	4,095	280	387	R	45.9	50.7	3.5	68	33	80	0.2	0.1	0.2	0.2
DuPage	364,557	139,402	210,818	14,337	71,416	R	38.2	57.8	3.9	99	3	62	7.4	5.3	9.9	7.9
Edgar	9,427	4,187	5,000	240	813	R	44.4	53.0	2.5	76	17	98	0.2	0.2	0.2	0.1
Edwards	3,319	1,478	1,711	130	233	R	44.5	51.6	3.9	75	27	64	<.1	<.1	<.1	<.1
Effingham	14,525	5,896	7,639	990	1,743	R	40.6	52.6	6.8	92	19	5	0.3	0.2	0.4	0.5
Fayette	9,836	4,977	4,452	407	525	D	50.6	45.3	4.1	38	60	51	0.2	0.2	0.2	0.2
Ford	6,315	2,431	3,530	354	1,099	R	38.5	55.9	5.6	98	5	11	0.1	<.1	0.2	0.2
Franklin	20,640	12,391	7,438	811	4,953	D	60.0	36.0	3.9	6	99	63	0.4	0.5	0.3	0.4
Fulton	17,399	10,393	6,325	681	4,068	D	59.7	36.4	3.9	7	96	65	0.4	0.4	0.3	0.4
Gallatin	3,674	2,442	1,118	114	1,324	D	66.5	30.4	3.1	1	102	90	<.1	<.1	<.1	<.1
Greene	6,704	3,444	2,994	266	450	D	51.4	44.7	4.0	35	67	60	0.1	0.1	0.1	0.1
Grundy	15,898	6,759	8,406	733	1,647	R	42.5	52.9	4.6	84	18	29	0.3	0.3	0.4	0.4
Hamilton	4,433	2,285	2,066	82	219	D	51.5	46.6	1.8	34	55	102	<.1	<.1	<.1	<.1
Hancock	9,720	4,651	4,610	459	41	D	47.8	47.4	4.7	56	48	26	0.2	0.2	0.2	0.3
Hardin	2,933	1,616	1,232	85	384	D	55.1	42.0	2.9	22	79	93	<.1	<.1	<.1	<.1
Henderson	3,928	2,178	1,627	123	551	D	55.4	41.4	3.1	20	82	88	<.1	<.1	<.1	<.1
Henry	23,757	11,690	11,197	870	493	D	49.2	47.1	3.7	48	50	72	0.5	0.4	0.5	0.5
Iroquois	14,180	5,066	8,368	746	3,302	R	35.7	59.0	5.3	102	1	15	0.3	0.2	0.4	0.4
Jackson	24,009	13,665	9,342	1,002	4,323	D	56.9	38.9	4.2	12	92	49	0.5	0.5	0.4	0.6
Jasper	5,249	2,430	2,353	466	77	D	46.3	44.8	8.9	67	66	1	0.1	<.1	0.1	0.3
Jefferson	16,964	8,435	7,783	746	652	D	49.7	45.9	4.4	45	58	38	0.3	0.3	0.4	0.4
Jersey	9,741	5,572	3,729	440	1,843	D	57.2	38.3	4.5	10	93	33	0.2	0.2	0.2	0.2
Jo Daviess	10,051	4,493	5,136	422	643	R	44.7	51.1	4.2	74	31	46	0.2	0.2	0.2	0.2
Johnson	5,180	2,234	2,780	166	546	R	43.1	53.7	3.2	83	13	86	0.1	<.1	0.1	<.1
Kane	125,631	53,407	65,092	7,132	11,685	R	42.5	51.8	5.7	85	23	9	2.5	2.0	3.1	3.9
Kankakee	39,450	18,795	18,924	1,731	129	R	47.6	48.0	4.4	58	45	39	0.8	0.7	0.9	1.0
Kendall	18,245	6,740	10,582	923	3,842	R	36.9	58.0	5.1	101	2	20	0.4	0.3	0.5	0.5
Knox	24,702	13,001	10,877	824	2,124	D	52.6	44.0	3.3	30	70	84	0.5	0.5	0.5	0.5
Lake	216,211	93,996	113,541	8,674	19,545	R	43.5	52.5	4.0	82	20	56	4.4	3.6	5.3	4.8
La Salle	48,702	24,556	21,993	2,153	2,563	D	50.4	45.2	4.4	41	62	37	1.0	0.9	1.0	1.2
Lawrence	7,142	3,612	3,286	244	326	D	50.6	46.0	3.4	39	57	82	0.1	0.1	0.2	0.1
Lee	15,090	6,240	8,179	671	1,939	R	41.4	54.2	4.4	90	10	36	0.3	0.2	0.4	0.4
Livingston	16,788	6,776	9,321	691	2,545	R	40.4	55.5	4.1	93	6	52	0.3	0.3	0.4	0.4
Logan	13,802	5,558	7,469	775	1,911	R	40.3	54.1	5.6	95	12	10	0.3	0.2	0.4	0.4
McDonough	13,504	6,430	6,490	584	60	R	47.6	48.1	4.3	59	44	43	0.3	0.2	0.3	0.3
McHenry	86,560	32,339	49,057	5,164	16,718	R	37.4	56.7	6.0	100	4	8	1.8	1.2	2.3	2.8
McLean	58,487	26,585	29,619	2,283	3,034	R	45.5	50.6	3.9	69	34	66	1.2	1.0	1.4	1.3
Macon	54,833	28,897	23,421	2,515	5,476	D	52.7	42.7	4.6	29	75	32	1.1	1.1	1.1	1.4
Macoupin	23,016	13,842	8,361	813	5,481	D	60.1	36.3	3.5	5	97	77	0.5	0.5	0.4	0.4
Madison	110,950	66,228	40,243	4,479	25,985	D	59.7	36.3	4.0	8	98	55	2.2	2.5	1.9	2.5
Marion	18,302	10,372	7,216	714	3,156	D	56.7	39.4	3.9	14	90	67	0.4	0.4	0.3	0.4
Marshall	6,370	3,211	2,883	276	328	D	50.4	45.3	4.3	42	61	42	0.1	0.1	0.1	0.2
Mason	7,524	4,205	3,018	301	1,187	D	55.9	40.1	4.0	17	88	57	0.2	0.2	0.1	0.2
Massac	6,792	3,348	3,198	246	150	D	49.3	47.1	3.6	46	51	74	0.1	0.1	0.2	0.1
Menard	6,147	2,565	3,274	308	709	R	41.7	53.3	5.0	89	15	22	0.1	<.1	0.2	0.2
Mercer	8,337	4,033	4,045	259	12	R	48.4	48.5	3.1	53	40	89	0.2	0.2	0.2	0.1
Monroe	12,076	5,461	6,109	506	648	R	45.2	50.6	4.2	71	35	47	0.2	0.2	0.3	0.3
Montgomery	14,410	8,104	5,659	647	2,445	D	56.2	39.3	4.5	15	91	34	0.3	0.3	0.3	0.4
Morgan	16,046	7,104	8,351	591	1,247	R	44.3	52.0	3.7	78	21	71	0.3	0.3	0.4	0.3
Moultrie	6,317	3,369	2,697	251	672	D	53.3	42.7	4.0	26	76	59	0.1	0.1	0.1	0.1

County	Total	Braun (DEM)	Williamson (REP)	Other	Plurality Total	Party	DEM	REP	Other	Rank DEM	Rank REP	Rank Other	Total	DEM	REP	Other
Ogle	19,622	7,565	10,664	1,393	3,099	R	38.6	54.3	7.1	97	9	2	0.4	0.3	0.5	0.8
Peoria	79,495	41,204	34,541	3,750	6,663	D	51.8	43.5	4.7	32	73	27	1.6	1.6	1.6	2.1
Perry	10,699	5,820	4,327	552	1,493	D	54.4	40.4	5.2	24	85	18	0.2	0.2	0.2	0.3
Piatt	8,247	3,953	3,908	386	45	D	47.9	47.4	4.7	55	49	28	0.2	0.2	0.2	0.2
Pike	8,719	4,277	4,145	297	132	D	49.1	47.5	3.4	49	47	83	0.2	0.2	0.2	0.2
Pope	2,306	1,043	1,194	69	151	R	45.2	51.8	3.0	70	24	91	<.1	<.1	<.1	<.1
Pulaski	3,427	1,924	1,429	74	495	D	56.1	41.7	2.2	16	80	99	<.1	<.1	<.1	<.1
Putnam	3,203	1,823	1,290	90	533	D	56.9	40.3	2.8	13	86	96	<.1	<.1	<.1	<.1
Randolph	16,188	9,033	6,569	586	2,464	D	55.8	40.6	3.6	18	84	75	0.3	0.3	0.3	0.3
Richland	7,776	3,601	3,764	411	163	R	46.3	48.4	5.3	66	41	14	0.2	0.1	0.2	0.2
Rock Island	70,504	37,465	30,072	2,967	7,393	D	53.1	42.7	4.2	28	77	45	1.4	1.4	1.4	1.6
St. Clair	104,370	61,508	39,200	3,662	22,308	D	58.9	37.6	3.5	9	95	78	2.1	2.3	1.8	2.0
Saline	12,650	7,230	5,044	376	2,186	D	57.2	39.9	3.0	11	89	92	0.3	0.3	0.2	0.2
Sangamon	95,308	44,248	47,743	3,317	3,495	R	46.4	50.1	3.5	65	36	79	1.9	1.7	2.2	1.8
Schuyler	3,883	1,837	1,867	179	30	R	47.3	48.1	4.6	60	43	30	<.1	<.1	<.1	<.1
Scott	2,710	1,150	1,450	110	300	R	42.4	53.5	4.1	86	14	54	<.1	<.1	<.1	<.1
Shelby	10,896	5,510	4,801	585	709	D	50.6	44.1	5.4	40	69	13	0.2	0.2	0.2	0.3
Stark	3,237	1,508	1,584	145	76	R	46.6	48.9	4.5	63	39	35	<.1	<.1	<.1	<.1
Stephenson	21,016	8,820	10,936	1,260	2,116	R	42.0	52.0	6.0	88	22	7	0.4	0.3	0.5	0.7
Tazewell	58,822	29,362	26,387	3,073	2,975	D	49.9	44.9	5.2	44	65	16	1.2	1.1	1.2	1.7
Union	8,787	4,837	3,658	292	1,179	D	55.0	41.6	3.3	23	81	85	0.2	0.2	0.2	0.2
Vermilion	37,558	19,990	16,079	1,489	3,911	D	53.2	42.8	4.0	27	74	61	0.8	0.8	0.8	0.8
Wabash	5,957	3,048	2,635	274	413	D	51.2	44.2	4.6	37	68	31	0.1	0.1	0.1	0.2
Warren	8,277	3,958	4,080	239	122	R	47.8	49.3	2.9	57	38	94	0.2	0.2	0.2	0.1
Washington	7,214	3,247	3,719	248	472	R	45.0	51.6	3.4	72	26	81	0.1	0.1	0.2	0.1
Wayne	8,397	3,306	4,545	546	1,239	R	39.4	54.1	6.5	96	11	6	0.2	0.1	0.2	0.3
White	8,360	4,656	3,437	267	1,219	D	55.7	41.1	3.2	19	83	87	0.2	0.2	0.2	0.1
Whiteside	26,619	13,650	12,003	966	1,647	D	51.3	45.1	3.6	36	63	73	0.5	0.5	0.6	0.5
Will	150,328	66,660	77,550	6,118	10,890	R	44.3	51.6	4.1	77	25	53	3.0	2.5	3.6	3.4
Williamson	28,042	14,037	12,587	1,418	1,450	D	50.1	44.9	5.1	43	64	21	0.6	0.5	0.6	0.8
Winnebago	110,105	51,962	50,404	7,739	1,558	D	47.2	45.8	7.0	61	59	3	2.2	2.0	2.4	4.3
Woodford	15,881	6,397	8,655	829	2,258	R	40.3	54.5	5.2	94	8	17	0.3	0.2	0.4	0.5
ILLINOIS	**4,939,558**	**2,631,229**	**2,126,833**	**181,496**	**504,396**	**D**	**53.3**	**43.1**	**3.7**				**100.0**	**100.0**	**100.0**	**100.0**

Congressional district and county	Total	Democrat (DEM)	Republican (REP)	Other	Plurality Total	Party	DEM	REP	Other	DEM	REP	Other	Total	DEM	REP	Other
District 1	252,711	209,258	43,453	-	165,805	D	82.8	17.2	-	1	1	-	100.0	100.0	100.0	-
Cook (pt)	252,711	209,258	43,453	-	165,805	D	82.8	17.2	-	1	1	-	100.0	100.0	100.0	-
District 2	233,864	182,614	31,957	19,293	150,657	D	78.1	13.7	8.2	1	1	1	100.0	100.0	100.0	100.0
Cook (pt)	233,864	182,614	31,957	19,293	150,657	D	78.1	13.7	8.2	1	1	1	100.0	100.0	100.0	100.0
District 3	255,293	162,165	93,128	-	69,037	D	63.5	36.5	-	1	1	-	100.0	100.0	100.0	-
Cook (pt)	255,293	162,165	93,128	-	69,037	D	63.5	36.5	-	1	1	-	100.0	100.0	100.0	-
District 4	116,606	90,452	26,154	-	64,298	D	77.6	22.4	-	1	1	-	100.0	100.0	100.0	-
Cook (pt)	116,606	90,452	26,154	-	64,298	D	77.6	22.4	-	1	1	-	100.0	100.0	100.0	-
District 5	232,083	132,889	90,738	8,456	42,151	D	57.3	39.1	3.6	1	1	1	100.0	100.0	100.0	100.0
Cook (pt)	232,083	132,889	90,738	8,456	42,151	D	57.3	39.1	3.6	1	1	1	100.0	100.0	100.0	100.0
District 6	251,904	86,891	165,009	4	78,118	R	34.5	65.5	<.1				100.0	100.0	100.0	100.0
Cook (pt)	88,464	32,342	56,122	0	23,780	R	36.6	63.4	0.0	1	2	2	35.1	37.2	34.0	0.0
DuPage (pt)	163,440	54,549	108,887	4	54,338	R	33.4	66.6	<.1	2	1	1	64.9	62.8	66.0	100.0
District 7	225,281	182,811	35,346	7,124	147,465	D	81.1	15.7	3.2	1	1	1	100.0	100.0	100.0	100.0
Cook (pt)	225,281	182,811	35,346	7,124	147,465	D	81.1	15.7	3.2	1	1	1	100.0	100.0	100.0	100.0
District 8	238,633	96,419	132,887	9,327	36,468	R	40.4	55.7	3.9				100.0	100.0	100.0	100.0
Cook (pt)	151,345	63,821	81,660	5,864	17,839	R	42.2	54.0	3.9	1	2	2	63.4	66.2	61.5	62.9
Lake (pt)	87,288	32,598	51,227	3,463	18,629	R	37.3	58.7	4.0	2	1	1	36.6	33.8	38.5	37.1
District 9	239,703	162,942	64,760	12,001	98,182	D	68.0	27.0	5.0	1	1	1	100.0	100.0	100.0	100.0
Cook (pt)	239,703	162,942	64,760	12,001	98,182	D	68.0	27.0	5.0	1	1	1	100.0	100.0	100.0	100.0
District 10	240,630	85,400	155,230	-	69,830	R	35.5	64.5	-				100.0	100.0	100.0	-
Cook (pt)	127,927	41,916	86,011	-	44,095	R	32.8	67.2	-	2	1	-	53.2	49.1	55.4	-
Lake (pt)	112,703	43,484	69,219	-	25,735	R	38.6	61.4	-	1	2	-	46.8	50.9	44.6	-
District 11	243,247	135,387	107,860	-	27,527	D	55.7	44.3	-				100.0	100.0	100.0	-
Cook (pt)	69,604	40,835	28,769	-	12,066	D	58.7	41.3	-	2	4	-	28.6	30.2	26.7	-
Grundy	15,642	7,639	8,003	-	364	R	48.8	51.2	-	4	2	-	6.4	5.6	7.4	-
Kankakee (pt)	25,461	12,430	13,031	-	601	R	48.8	51.2	-	5	1	-	10.5	9.2	12.1	-
La Salle (pt)	41,724	20,619	21,105	-	486	R	49.4	50.6	-	3	3	-	17.2	15.2	19.6	-
Will (pt)	90,816	53,864	36,952	-	16,912	D	59.3	40.7	-	1	5	-	37.3	39.8	34.3	-
District 12	236,877	168,762	68,115	-	100,647	D	71.2	28.8	-				100.0	100.0	100.0	-
Alexander	4,052	2,862	1,190	-	1,672	D	70.6	29.4	-	3	7	-	1.7	1.7	1.7	-
Jackson	23,352	15,157	8,195	-	6,962	D	64.9	35.1	-	7	3	-	9.9	9.0	12.0	-
Madison (pt)	53,517	41,009	12,508	-	28,501	D	76.6	23.4	-	1	9	-	22.6	24.3	18.4	-
Monroe	12,059	7,056	5,003	-	2,053	D	58.5	41.5	-	9	1	-	5.1	4.2	7.3	-
Perry	10,535	7,102	3,433	-	3,669	D	67.4	32.6	-	5	5	-	4.4	4.2	5.0	-
Randolph	16,074	10,989	5,085	-	5,904	D	68.4	31.6	-	4	6	-	6.8	6.5	7.5	-
St. Clair	103,825	75,911	27,914	-	47,997	D	73.1	26.9	-	2	8	-	43.8	45.0	41.0	-
Union	8,601	5,520	3,081	-	2,439	D	64.2	35.8	-	8	2	-	3.6	3.3	4.5	-
Williamson (pt)	4,862	3,156	1,706	-	1,450	D	64.9	35.1	-	6	4	-	2.1	1.9	2.5	-
District 13	262,255	82,985	179,257	13	96,272	R	31.6	68.4	<.1				100.0	100.0	100.0	100.0
Cook (pt)	50,717	17,788	32,929	0	15,141	R	35.1	64.9	0.0	2	2	2	19.3	21.4	18.4	0.0
DuPage (pt)	154,308	42,933	111,362	13	68,429	R	27.8	72.2	<.1	3	1	1	58.8	51.7	62.1	100.0
Will (pt)	57,230	22,264	34,966	0	12,702	R	38.9	61.1	0.0	1	3	3	21.8	26.8	19.5	0.0
District 14	230,624	75,294	155,271	59	79,977	R	32.6	67.3	<.1				100.0	100.0	100.0	100.0
DeKalb	32,342	11,456	20,886	0	9,430	R	35.4	64.6	0.0	2	5	4	14.0	15.2	13.5	0.0
DuPage (pt)	37,428	10,533	26,891	4	16,358	R	28.1	71.8	<.1	5	2	2	16.2	14.0	17.3	6.8
Kane	121,753	40,936	80,763	54	39,827	R	33.6	66.3	<.1	3	4	1	52.8	54.4	52.0	91.5
Kendall	18,045	5,043	13,002	0	7,959	R	27.9	72.1	0.0	6	1	5	7.8	6.7	8.4	0.0
La Salle (pt)	6,637	2,158	4,479	0	2,321	R	32.5	67.5	0.0	4	3	6	2.9	2.9	2.9	0.0
Lee	14,419	5,168	9,250	1	4,082	R	35.8	64.2	<.1	1	6	3	6.3	6.9	6.0	1.7
District 15	239,586	97,190	142,167	229	44,977	R	40.6	59.3	<.1				100.0	100.0	100.0	100.0
Champaign	69,304	30,668	38,407	229	7,739	R	44.3	55.4	0.3	3	9	1	28.9	31.6	27.0	100.0
De Witt	7,452	2,664	4,788	0	2,124	R	35.7	64.3	0.0	7	5	2	3.1	2.7	3.4	0.0
Douglas	7,773	3,010	4,763	0	1,753	R	38.7	61.3	0.0	5	7	3	3.2	3.1	3.4	0.0
Edgar	9,010	3,847	5,163	0	1,316	R	42.7	57.3	0.0	4	8	4	3.8	4.0	3.6	0.0
Ford	6,239	1,758	4,481	0	2,723	R	28.2	71.8	0.0	10	2	5	2.6	1.8	3.2	0.0
Iroquois	13,852	3,938	9,914	0	5,976	R	28.4	71.6	0.0	9	3	6	5.8	4.1	7.0	0.0
Kankakee (pt)	12,690	6,012	6,678	0	666	R	47.4	52.6	0.0	2	10	7	5.3	6.2	4.7	0.0
Livingston	16,762	4,589	12,173	0	7,584	R	27.4	72.6	0.0	11	1	8	7.0	4.7	8.6	0.0
McLean (pt)	52,027	17,530	34,497	0	16,967	R	33.7	66.3	0.0	8	4	9	21.7	18.0	24.3	0.0
Piatt	8,047	3,018	5,029	0	2,011	R	37.5	62.5	0.0	6	6	10	3.4	3.1	3.5	0.0
Vermilion	36,430	20,156	16,274	0	3,882	D	55.3	44.7	0.0	1	11	11	15.2	20.7	11.4	0.0

Congressional district and county	Total	Democrat (DEM)	Republican (REP)	Other	Plurality Total	Party	DEM	REP	Other	Rank within district DEM	REP	Other	Total	DEM	REP	Other
District 16	**255,943**	**113,555**	**142,388**	-	**28,833**	**R**	**44.4**	**55.6**	**-**				**100.0**	**100.0**	**100.0**	**-**
Boone	13,473	6,046	7,427	-	1,381	R	44.9	55.1	-	3	4	-	5.3	5.3	5.2	-
Jo Daviess	10,317	5,706	4,611	-	1,095	D	55.3	44.7	-	1	6	-	4.0	5.0	3.2	-
McHenry	85,015	29,356	55,659	-	26,303	R	34.5	65.5	-	6	1	-	33.2	25.9	39.1	-
Ogle (pt)	14,801	6,245	8,556	-	2,311	R	42.2	57.8	-	5	2	-	5.8	5.5	6.0	-
Stephenson	21,316	9,331	11,985	-	2,654	R	43.8	56.2	-	4	3	-	8.3	8.2	8.4	-
Winnebago	111,021	56,871	54,150	-	2,721	D	51.2	48.8	-	2	5	-	43.4	50.1	38.0	-
District 17	**259,952**	**156,233**	**103,719**	**-**	**52,514**	**D**	**60.1**	**39.9**	**-**				**100.0**	**100.0**	**100.0**	**-**
Adams (pt)	23,613	12,658	10,955	-	1,703	D	53.6	46.4	-	12	3	-	9.1	8.1	10.6	-
Bureau	17,506	10,942	6,564	-	4,378	D	62.5	37.5	-	5	10	-	6.7	7.0	6.3	-
Carroll	7,431	3,521	3,910	-	389	R	47.4	52.6	-	13	2	-	2.9	2.3	3.8	-
Fulton	17,462	12,230	5,232	-	6,998	D	70.0	30.0	-	1	14	-	6.7	7.8	5.0	-
Hancock	9,559	5,228	4,331	-	897	D	54.7	45.3	-	11	4	-	3.7	3.3	4.2	-
Henderson	4,002	2,512	1,490	-	1,022	D	62.8	37.2	-	4	11	-	1.5	1.6	1.4	-
Henry	23,847	14,059	9,788	-	4,271	D	59.0	41.0	-	6	9	-	9.2	9.0	9.4	-
Knox	25,004	16,470	8,534	-	7,936	D	65.9	34.1	-	2	13	-	9.6	10.5	8.2	-
McDonough	13,490	7,705	5,785	-	1,920	D	57.1	42.9	-	9	6	-	5.2	4.9	5.6	-
Mercer	8,482	4,834	3,648	-	1,186	D	57.0	43.0	-	10	5	-	3.3	3.1	3.5	-
Ogle (pt)	4,568	1,623	2,945	-	1,322	R	35.5	64.5	-	14	1	-	1.8	1.0	2.8	-
Rock Island	70,217	44,094	26,123	-	17,971	D	62.8	37.2	-	3	12	-	27.0	28.2	25.2	-
Warren	8,357	4,833	3,524	-	1,309	D	57.8	42.2	-	8	7	-	3.2	3.1	3.4	-
Whiteside	26,414	15,524	10,890	-	4,634	D	58.8	41.2	-	7	8	-	10.2	9.9	10.5	-
District 18	**270,976**	**114,413**	**156,533**	**30**	**42,120**	**R**	**42.2**	**57.8**	**<.1**				**100.0**	**100.0**	**100.0**	**100.0**
Cass	6,256	2,842	3,414	0	572	R	45.4	54.6	0.0	6	9	3	2.3	2.5	2.2	0.0
Logan	13,605	4,522	9,083	0	4,561	R	33.2	66.8	0.0	14	1	4	5.0	4.0	5.8	0.0
McLean (pt)	4,584	1,527	3,057	0	1,530	R	33.3	66.7	0.0	13	2	5	1.7	1.3	2.0	0.0
Macon (pt)	4,814	1,690	3,124	0	1,434	R	35.1	64.9	0.0	11	4	6	1.8	1.5	2.0	0.0
Marshall	6,264	2,875	3,389	0	514	R	45.9	54.1	0.0	4	11	7	2.3	2.5	2.2	0.0
Mason	7,515	3,847	3,668	0	179	D	51.2	48.8	0.0	2	13	8	2.8	3.4	2.3	0.0
Menard	6,081	2,107	3,974	0	1,867	R	34.6	65.4	0.0	12	3	9	2.2	1.8	2.5	0.0
Morgan	15,858	5,797	10,061	0	4,264	R	36.6	63.4	0.0	8	7	10	5.9	5.1	6.4	0.0
Peoria	79,277	36,064	43,197	16	7,133	R	45.5	54.5	<.1	5	10	2	29.3	31.5	27.6	53.3
Putnam	3,135	1,614	1,521	0	93	D	51.5	48.5	0.0	1	14	11	1.2	1.4	1.0	0.0
Sangamon (pt)	46,016	16,678	29,338	0	12,660	R	36.2	63.8	0.0	10	5	12	17.0	14.6	18.7	0.0
Stark	3,243	1,425	1,818	0	393	R	43.9	56.1	0.0	7	8	13	1.2	1.2	1.2	0.0
Tazewell	58,524	27,675	30,835	14	3,160	R	47.3	52.7	<.1	3	12	1	21.6	24.2	19.7	46.7
Woodford	15,804	5,750	10,054	0	4,304	R	36.4	63.6	0.0	9	6	14	5.8	5.0	6.4	0.0
District 19	**270,685**	**187,156**	**83,526**	**3**	**103,630**	**D**	**69.1**	**30.9**	**<.1**				**100.0**	**100.0**	**100.0**	**100.0**
Christian (pt)	6,301	4,347	1,954	0	2,393	D	69.0	31.0	0.0	11	17	2	2.3	2.3	2.3	0.0
Clark	7,694	4,241	3,453	0	788	D	55.1	44.9	0.0	27	1	3	2.8	2.3	4.1	0.0
Clay	6,447	4,173	2,274	0	1,899	D	64.7	35.3	0.0	15	13	4	2.4	2.2	2.7	0.0
Coles	21,290	12,174	9,113	3	3,061	D	57.2	42.8	<.1	26	2	1	7.9	6.5	10.9	100.0
Crawford	9,295	5,626	3,669	0	1,957	D	60.5	39.5	0.0	23	5	5	3.4	3.0	4.4	0.0
Cumberland	5,016	3,031	1,985	0	1,046	D	60.4	39.6	0.0	24	4	6	1.9	1.6	2.4	0.0
Edwards	3,384	2,117	1,267	0	850	D	62.6	37.4	0.0	21	7	7	1.3	1.1	1.5	0.0
Effingham	14,384	9,033	5,351	0	3,682	D	62.8	37.2	0.0	20	8	8	5.3	4.8	6.4	0.0
Franklin	21,157	18,083	3,074	0	15,009	D	85.5	14.5	0.0	2	26	9	7.8	9.7	3.7	0.0
Gallatin	3,872	3,352	520	0	2,832	D	86.6	13.4	0.0	1	27	10	1.4	1.8	0.6	0.0
Hamilton	4,720	3,708	1,012	0	2,696	D	78.6	21.4	0.0	6	22	11	1.7	2.0	1.2	0.0
Hardin	3,090	2,467	623	0	1,844	D	79.8	20.2	0.0	5	23	12	1.1	1.3	0.7	0.0
Jasper	5,282	3,614	1,668	0	1,946	D	68.4	31.6	0.0	13	15	13	2.0	1.9	2.0	0.0
Johnson	5,338	4,053	1,285	0	2,768	D	75.9	24.1	0.0	8	20	14	2.0	2.2	1.5	0.0
Lawrence	7,131	4,501	2,630	0	1,871	D	63.1	36.9	0.0	19	9	15	2.6	2.4	3.1	0.0
Macon (pt)	49,215	31,406	17,809	0	13,597	D	63.8	36.2	0.0	17	11	16	18.2	16.8	21.3	0.0
Massac	6,912	5,184	1,728	0	3,456	D	75.0	25.0	0.0	10	18	17	2.6	2.8	2.1	0.0
Moultrie	6,232	3,985	2,247	0	1,738	D	63.9	36.1	0.0	16	12	18	2.3	2.1	2.7	0.0
Pope	2,362	1,622	740	0	882	D	68.7	31.3	0.0	12	16	19	0.9	0.9	0.9	0.0
Pulaski	3,461	2,663	798	0	1,865	D	76.9	23.1	0.0	7	21	20	1.3	1.4	1.0	0.0
Richland	7,786	4,640	3,146	0	1,494	D	59.6	40.4	0.0	25	3	21	2.9	2.5	3.8	0.0
Saline	13,143	10,835	2,308	0	8,527	D	82.4	17.6	0.0	4	24	22	4.9	5.8	2.8	0.0
Shelby	10,660	7,052	3,608	0	3,444	D	66.2	33.8	0.0	14	14	23	3.9	3.8	4.3	0.0
Wabash	6,000	3,816	2,184	0	1,632	D	63.6	36.4	0.0	18	10	24	2.2	2.0	2.6	0.0
Wayne	8,520	5,299	3,221	0	2,078	D	62.2	37.8	0.0	22	6	25	3.1	2.8	3.9	0.0
White	8,591	6,457	2,134	0	4,323	D	75.2	24.8	0.0	9	19	26	3.2	3.5	2.6	0.0
Williamson (pt)	23,402	19,677	3,725	0	15,952	D	84.1	15.9	0.0	3	25	27	8.6	10.5	4.5	0.0
District 20	**274,088**	**154,869**	**119,219**	**-**	**35,650**	**D**	**56.5**	**43.5**	**-**				**100.0**	**100.0**	**100.0**	**-**
Adams (pt)	6,724	4,016	2,708	-	1,308	D	59.7	40.3	-	5	15	-	2.5	2.6	2.3	-
Bond	7,178	4,137	3,041	-	1,096	D	57.6	42.4	-	9	11	-	2.6	2.7	2.6	-
Brown	2,614	1,424	1,190	-	234	D	54.5	45.5	-	15	5	-	1.0	0.9	1.0	-
Calhoun	2,751	1,822	929	-	893	D	66.2	33.8	-	1	19	-	1.0	1.2	0.8	-
Christian (pt)	10,975	6,565	4,410	-	2,155	D	59.8	40.2	-	4	16	-	4.0	4.2	3.7	-
Clinton	15,202	8,478	6,724	-	1,754	D	55.8	44.2	-	12	8	-	5.5	5.5	5.6	-

Congressional district and county	Total	Democrat (DEM)	Republican (REP)	Other	Plurality		Percent of total vote			Rank within district			Percent contribution to district vote			
					Total	Party	DEM	REP	Other	DEM	REP	Other	Total	DEM	REP	Other
District 20 (cont)																
Fayette	9,846	5,519	4,327	-	1,192	D	56.1	43.9	-	11	9	-	3.6	3.6	3.6	-
Greene	6,928	3,999	2,929	-	1,070	D	57.7	42.3	-	8	12	-	2.5	2.6	2.5	-
Jefferson	16,791	9,209	7,582	-	1,627	D	54.8	45.2	-	14	6	-	6.1	5.9	6.4	-
Jersey	9,827	5,983	3,844	-	2,139	D	60.9	39.1	-	3	17	-	3.6	3.9	3.2	-
Macoupin	23,102	14,813	8,289	-	6,524	D	64.1	35.9	-	2	18	-	8.4	9.6	7.0	-
Madison (pt)	57,935	30,280	27,655	-	2,625	D	52.3	47.7	-	16	4	-	21.1	19.6	23.2	-
Marion	18,274	10,697	7,577	-	3,120	D	58.5	41.5	-	6	14	-	6.7	6.9	6.4	-
Montgomery	14,607	8,454	6,153	-	2,301	D	57.9	42.1	-	7	13	-	5.3	5.5	5.2	-
Pike	8,928	4,966	3,962	-	1,004	D	55.6	44.4	-	13	7	-	3.3	3.2	3.3	-
Sangamon (pt)	48,589	27,784	20,805	-	6,979	D	57.2	42.8	-	10	10	-	17.7	17.9	17.5	-
Schuyler	3,869	1,852	2,017	-	165	R	47.9	52.1	-	19	1	-	1.4	1.2	1.7	-
Scott	2,731	1,376	1,355	-	21	D	50.4	49.6	-	17	3	-	1.0	0.9	1.1	-
Washington	7,217	3,495	3,722	-	227	R	48.4	51.6	-	18	2	-	2.6	2.3	3.1	-
ILLINOIS	4,830,941	2,677,685	2,096,717	56,539	580,968	D	55.4	43.4	1.2							

Table I. — Vote for Presidential Preference: March 17, 1992, Democratic Primary Election

County	Total	Clinton	Tsongas	Brown	Uncommitted	Harkin	Kerrey	LaRouche	Agran	Clinton	Tsongas	Brown	Clinton	Tsongas	Brown	Total	Clinton	Tsongas	Brown
	Top candidates									**Top three candidates (state vote)** — Percent of total vote			Rank			Percent contribution to state vote			
Adams	6,180	3,672	1,212	777	236	188	65	25	5	59.4	19.6	12.6	57	41	50	0.4	0.5	0.3	0.4
Alexander	1,565	1,208	101	103	87	42	11	10	3	77.2	6.5	6.6	2	101	99	0.1	0.2	<.1	<.1
Bond	1,676	1,184	181	188	52	54	14	1	2	70.6	10.8	11.2	12	92	59	0.1	0.2	<.1	<.1
Boone	2,326	1,343	466	391	52	47	16	6	5	57.7	20.0	16.8	62	38	13	0.2	0.2	0.1	0.2
Brown	563	385	81	53	18	21	3	2	0	68.4	14.4	9.4	20	72	82	<.1	<.1	<.1	<.1
Bureau	4,901	2,620	860	689	413	255	35	21	8	53.5	17.5	14.1	81	51	36	0.3	0.3	0.2	0.3
Calhoun	807	590	76	71	30	24	13	3	0	73.1	9.4	8.8	5	96	89	<.1	<.1	<.1	<.1
Carroll	954	485	229	153	33	42	9	2	1	50.8	24.0	16.0	88	18	23	<.1	<.1	<.1	<.1
Cass	1,479	912	307	141	61	39	10	7	2	61.7	20.8	9.5	47	32	80	<.1	0.1	<.1	<.1
Champaign	16,562	6,012	6,343	3,063	655	276	85	24	104	36.3	38.3	18.5	101	3	8	1.1	0.8	1.6	1.4
Christian	6,509	4,131	1,165	628	339	149	56	27	14	63.5	17.9	9.6	39	46	77	0.4	0.5	0.3	0.3
Clark	1,676	1,098	212	215	85	41	18	5	2	65.5	12.6	12.8	31	85	46	0.1	0.1	<.1	<.1
Clay	1,570	1,020	234	155	64	62	23	10	2	65.0	14.9	9.9	35	66	73	0.1	0.1	<.1	<.1
Clinton	2,523	1,735	329	289	97	42	22	8	1	68.8	13.0	11.5	17	81	57	0.2	0.2	<.1	0.1
Coles	4,860	2,620	1,199	612	215	135	44	21	14	53.9	24.7	12.6	78	16	49	0.3	0.3	0.3	0.3
Cook	867,003	435,599	236,101	126,551	40,754	15,863	5,915	4,093	2,127	50.2	27.2	14.6	90	11	31	57.6	56.1	60.9	57.4
Crawford	2,055	1,238	276	297	125	87	23	5	4	60.2	13.4	14.5	54	78	32	0.1	0.2	<.1	0.1
Cumberland	1,291	794	218	134	85	41	13	5	1	61.5	16.9	10.4	51	55	69	<.1	0.1	<.1	<.1
DeKalb	5,730	2,444	1,770	1,209	158	61	34	23	31	42.7	30.9	21.1	98	6	2	0.4	0.3	0.5	0.5
De Witt	1,277	850	215	139	46	17	6	2	2	66.6	16.8	10.9	26	57	64	<.1	0.1	<.1	<.1
Douglas	1,617	1,022	326	166	51	37	7	4	4	63.2	20.2	10.3	40	37	70	0.1	0.1	<.1	<.1
DuPage	61,563	20,515	26,130	12,272	1,623	602	242	121	58	33.3	42.4	19.9	102	1	3	4.1	2.6	6.7	5.6
Edgar	1,649	1,097	245	183	50	47	21	6	0	66.5	14.9	11.1	27	67	61	0.1	0.1	<.1	<.1
Edwards	768	485	113	83	59	18	4	5	1	63.2	14.7	10.8	41	68	68	<.1	<.1	<.1	<.1
Effingham	3,737	1,940	904	540	159	131	42	15	6	51.9	24.2	14.5	86	17	34	0.2	0.2	0.2	0.2
Fayette	1,920	1,288	280	190	66	65	15	14	2	67.1	14.6	9.9	25	71	72	0.1	0.2	<.1	<.1
Ford	838	490	189	98	24	17	10	5	5	58.5	22.6	11.7	60	25	54	<.1	<.1	<.1	<.1
Franklin	11,114	8,024	1,121	875	706	246	93	43	6	72.2	10.1	7.9	9	95	96	0.7	1.0	0.3	0.4
Fulton	6,573	4,189	926	741	404	220	65	23	5	63.7	14.1	11.3	38	75	58	0.4	0.5	0.2	0.3
Gallatin	2,293	1,737	202	127	125	68	21	9	4	75.8	8.8	5.5	4	98	101	0.2	0.2	<.1	<.1
Greene	1,945	1,344	250	167	109	48	16	9	2	69.1	12.9	8.6	16	84	91	0.1	0.2	<.1	<.1
Grundy	2,763	1,464	657	484	74	54	19	8	3	53.0	23.8	17.5	84	20	11	0.2	0.2	0.2	0.2
Hamilton	2,486	1,805	261	174	152	55	30	7	2	72.6	10.5	7.0	6	93	98	0.2	0.2	<.1	<.1
Hancock	1,601	918	323	214	49	77	13	6	1	57.3	20.2	13.4	65	36	41	0.1	0.1	<.1	<.1
Hardin	1,151	835	101	73	84	31	12	9	6	72.5	8.8	6.3	8	99	100	<.1	0.1	<.1	<.1
Henderson	853	454	152	113	44	77	9	3	1	53.2	17.8	13.2	82	48	43	<.1	<.1	<.1	<.1
Henry	4,103	2,034	984	593	192	246	35	12	7	49.6	24.0	14.5	91	19	33	0.3	0.3	0.3	0.3
Iroquois	1,721	948	398	283	28	36	14	13	1	55.1	23.1	16.4	74	22	16	0.1	0.1	0.1	0.1
Jackson	6,936	4,271	1,319	900	254	117	50	13	12	61.6	19.0	13.0	49	43	45	0.5	0.5	0.3	0.4
Jasper	1,941	1,195	316	170	132	69	29	22	8	61.6	16.3	8.8	50	60	90	0.1	0.2	<.1	<.1
Jefferson	6,689	4,363	983	594	478	183	47	32	9	65.2	14.7	8.9	32	69	87	0.4	0.6	0.3	0.3
Jersey	3,011	2,103	354	327	132	55	24	13	3	69.8	11.8	10.9	14	87	65	0.2	0.3	<.1	0.1
Jo Daviess	2,324	1,077	546	388	137	138	28	7	3	46.3	23.5	16.7	94	21	14	0.2	0.1	0.1	0.2
Johnson	1,395	983	200	112	46	26	16	9	3	70.5	14.3	8.0	13	73	95	<.1	0.1	<.1	<.1
Kane	20,402	8,927	6,431	4,010	529	300	115	51	39	43.8	31.5	19.7	96	5	5	1.4	1.1	1.7	1.8
Kankakee	5,309	2,849	1,180	1,035	86	112	29	13	5	53.7	22.2	19.5	79	26	6	0.4	0.4	0.3	0.5
Kendall	2,415	1,138	697	475	39	46	11	6	3	47.1	28.9	19.7	93	7	4	0.2	0.1	0.2	0.2
Knox	4,578	2,392	913	713	270	219	52	8	11	52.2	19.9	15.6	85	39	27	0.3	0.3	0.2	0.3
Lake	43,965	16,393	17,940	7,266	1,502	462	214	100	88	37.3	40.8	16.5	100	2	15	2.9	2.1	4.6	3.3
La Salle	12,436	6,840	2,543	2,021	543	332	114	31	12	55.0	20.4	16.3	75	34	20	0.8	0.9	0.7	0.9
Lawrence	2,086	1,290	273	239	125	113	32	12	2	61.8	13.1	11.5	46	80	56	0.1	0.2	<.1	0.1
Lee	2,316	1,341	413	373	61	102	15	4	7	57.9	17.8	16.1	61	47	22	0.2	0.2	0.1	0.2
Livingston	1,817	1,047	348	284	60	54	14	6	4	57.6	19.2	15.6	64	42	26	0.1	0.1	<.1	0.1
Logan	1,574	983	291	185	65	29	10	6	5	62.5	18.5	11.8	45	45	53	0.1	0.1	<.1	0.1
McDonough	2,051	1,098	529	272	54	73	19	2	4	53.5	25.8	13.3	80	13	42	0.1	0.1	0.1	0.1
McHenry	11,907	4,700	3,936	2,671	339	151	69	32	9	39.5	33.1	22.4	99	4	1	0.8	0.6	1.0	1.2
McLean	9,395	4,346	2,684	1,709	355	209	65	17	10	46.3	28.6	18.2	95	8	9	0.6	0.6	0.7	0.8
Macon	15,585	9,263	3,457	1,802	573	297	119	49	25	59.4	22.2	11.6	56	27	55	1.0	1.2	0.9	0.8
Macoupin	7,971	5,100	1,141	984	420	196	87	30	13	64.0	14.3	12.3	37	74	51	0.5	0.7	0.3	0.4
Madison	37,007	23,295	5,631	5,052	1,607	926	314	149	33	62.9	15.2	13.7	43	65	38	2.5	3.0	1.5	2.3
Marion	6,362	4,334	840	595	368	119	67	30	9	68.1	13.2	9.4	21	79	85	0.4	0.6	0.2	0.3
Marshall	1,257	788	198	171	50	36	7	5	2	62.7	15.8	13.6	44	62	39	<.1	0.1	<.1	<.1
Mason	2,029	1,366	280	192	99	67	15	7	3	67.3	13.8	9.5	23	77	81	0.1	0.2	<.1	<.1
Massac	2,364	1,559	329	208	138	58	52	12	8	65.9	13.9	8.8	30	76	88	0.2	0.2	<.1	<.1
Menard	765	463	163	84	23	15	13	1	3	60.5	21.3	11.0	53	30	62	<.1	<.1	<.1	<.1
Mercer	1,980	1,050	402	278	89	130	17	7	7	53.0	20.3	14.0	83	35	37	0.1	0.1	0.1	0.1
Monroe	2,026	1,202	346	307	97	46	14	12	2	59.3	17.1	15.2	58	54	29	0.1	0.2	<.1	0.1
Montgomery	3,921	2,548	600	424	187	94	36	28	4	65.0	15.3	10.8	34	64	67	0.3	0.3	0.2	0.2
Morgan	2,366	1,335	610	259	81	40	28	9	4	56.4	25.8	10.9	69	14	63	0.2	0.2	0.2	0.1
Moultrie	1,867	1,176	370	175	87	34	15	6	4	63.0	19.8	9.4	42	40	83	0.1	0.2	<.1	<.1

Table I. — Vote for Presidential Preference: March 17, 1992, Democratic Primary Election (cont)

| County | Top candidates | | | | | | | | | Top three candidates (state vote) | | | | | | | | | |
| | | | | | | | | | | Percent of total vote | | | Rank | | | Percent contribution to state vote | | | |
	Total	Clinton	Tsongas	Brown	Uncom-mitted	Harkin	Kerrey	LaRouche	Agran	Clinton	Tsongas	Brown	Clinton	Tsongas	Brown	Total	Clinton	Tsongas	Brown
Ogle	2,504	1,432	475	432	67	53	26	12	7	57.2	19.0	17.3	67	44	12	0.2	0.2	0.1	0.2
Peoria	15,963	8,982	3,274	2,520	506	423	179	54	25	56.3	20.5	15.8	71	33	24	1.1	1.2	0.8	1.1
Perry	2,837	2,168	231	236	68	88	31	10	5	76.4	8.1	8.3	3	100	93	0.2	0.3	<.1	0.1
Piatt	1,640	938	379	221	53	27	12	4	6	57.2	23.1	13.5	66	23	40	0.1	0.1	<.1	0.1
Pike	2,409	1,621	280	200	142	116	32	16	2	67.3	11.6	8.3	24	90	94	0.2	0.2	<.1	<.1
Pope	616	423	72	63	33	18	4	3	0	68.7	11.7	10.2	18	89	71	<.1	<.1	<.1	<.1
Pulaski	929	774	54	37	26	26	9	0	3	83.3	5.8	4.0	1	102	102	<.1	<.1	<.1	<.1
Putnam	1,400	769	220	179	139	72	12	9	0	54.9	15.7	12.8	76	63	47	0.1	0.1	0.1	0.1
Randolph	5,780	3,934	605	541	399	228	41	27	5	68.1	10.5	9.4	22	94	84	0.4	0.5	0.2	0.2
Richland	2,101	1,183	363	299	128	77	36	11	4	56.3	17.3	14.2	70	53	35	0.1	0.2	<.1	0.1
Rock Island	20,781	8,903	5,684	3,209	1,327	1,307	184	107	60	42.8	27.4	15.4	97	9	28	1.4	1.1	1.5	1.5
St. Clair	37,402	23,033	5,480	4,446	2,581	879	418	484	81	61.6	14.7	11.9	48	70	52	2.5	3.0	1.4	2.0
Saline	6,227	4,401	711	525	355	132	59	25	19	70.7	11.4	8.4	11	91	92	0.4	0.6	0.2	0.2
Sangamon	17,077	9,235	4,665	1,908	785	272	129	50	33	54.1	27.3	11.2	77	10	60	1.1	1.2	1.2	0.9
Schuyler	687	456	113	64	33	11	7	1	2	66.4	16.4	9.3	28	58	86	<.1	<.1	<.1	<.1
Scott	440	286	72	42	24	14	1	1	0	65.0	16.4	9.5	33	59	79	<.1	<.1	<.1	<.1
Shelby	3,590	2,313	632	348	175	69	31	17	5	64.4	17.6	9.7	36	50	75	0.2	0.3	0.2	0.2
Stark	646	391	112	82	27	25	7	1	1	60.5	17.3	12.7	52	52	48	<.1	<.1	<.1	<.1
Stephenson	2,907	1,616	616	475	80	77	28	9	6	55.6	21.2	16.3	72	31	19	0.2	0.2	0.2	0.2
Tazewell	11,238	6,686	1,895	1,663	585	266	106	27	10	59.5	16.9	14.8	55	56	30	0.7	0.9	0.5	0.8
Union	3,938	2,859	363	381	188	90	31	16	10	72.6	9.2	9.7	7	97	76	0.3	0.4	<.1	0.2
Vermilion	8,395	4,959	1,483	1,374	219	217	92	32	19	59.1	17.7	16.4	59	49	17	0.6	0.6	0.4	0.6
Wabash	1,688	973	271	264	118	40	17	3	2	57.6	16.1	15.6	63	61	25	0.1	0.1	<.1	<.1
Warren	1,178	606	296	153	48	56	10	6	3	51.4	25.1	13.0	87	15	44	<.1	<.1	<.1	<.1
Washington	1,271	901	149	138	34	32	13	3	1	70.9	11.7	10.9	10	88	66	<.1	0.1	<.1	<.1
Wayne	1,843	1,287	230	145	86	68	18	7	2	69.8	12.5	7.9	15	86	97	0.1	0.2	<.1	0.1
White	3,856	2,546	501	369	275	95	39	20	11	66.0	13.0	9.6	29	83	78	0.3	0.3	0.1	0.2
Whiteside	4,269	2,146	977	753	120	198	45	22	8	50.3	22.9	17.6	89	24	10	0.3	0.3	0.3	0.3
Will	34,080	16,601	8,948	6,309	1,229	606	184	151	52	48.7	26.3	18.5	92	12	7	2.3	2.1	2.3	2.9
Williamson	11,422	7,840	1,485	1,118	591	225	103	45	15	68.6	13.0	9.8	19	82	74	0.8	1.0	0.4	0.5
Winnebago	24,842	14,160	5,442	4,028	482	444	176	79	31	57.0	21.9	16.2	68	28	21	1.7	1.8	1.4	1.8
Woodford	1,925	1,063	413	315	59	50	16	6	3	55.2	21.5	16.4	73	29	18	0.1	0.1	0.1	0.1
ILLINOIS	1,504,130	776,829	387,891	220,346	67,612	30,710	10,916	6,599	3,227	51.6	25.8	14.6				100.0	100.0	100.0	100.0

Table J. — Vote for Presidential Preference: March 17, 1992, Republican Primary Election

County	Top candidates					Top four candidates (state vote)												
						Percent of total vote				Rank				Percent contribution to state vote				
	Total	Bush	Bu-chanan	Horton		Bush	Bu-chanan	Horton		Bush	Bu-chanan	Horton		Total	Bush	Bu-chanan	Horton	
Adams	5,632	4,506	1,054	72	-	80.0	18.7	1.3	-	8	96	48	-	0.7	0.7	0.6	0.7	-
Alexander	350	264	82	4	-	75.4	23.4	1.1	-	55	43	63	-	<.1	<.1	<.1	<.1	-
Bond	1,281	1,041	228	12	-	81.3	17.8	0.9	-	4	99	87	-	0.2	0.2	0.1	0.1	-
Boone	4,370	3,193	1,114	63	-	73.1	25.5	1.4	-	88	16	29	-	0.5	0.5	0.6	0.7	-
Brown	577	447	123	7	-	77.5	21.3	1.2	-	29	73	57	-	<.1	<.1	<.1	<.1	-
Bureau	3,383	2,580	760	43	-	76.3	22.5	1.3	-	46	58	49	-	0.4	0.4	0.4	0.4	-
Calhoun	385	300	80	5	-	77.9	20.8	1.3	-	24	79	44	-	<.1	<.1	<.1	<.1	-
Carroll	2,071	1,564	490	17	-	75.5	23.7	0.8	-	54	38	95	-	0.2	0.2	0.3	0.2	-
Cass	1,186	945	227	14	-	79.7	19.1	1.2	-	14	91	60	-	0.1	0.1	0.1	0.1	-
Champaign	12,515	9,314	3,087	114	-	74.4	24.7	0.9	-	73	22	91	-	1.5	1.5	1.7	1.2	-
Christian	2,851	2,170	648	33	-	76.1	22.7	1.2	-	49	54	61	-	0.3	0.3	0.3	0.3	-
Clark	1,553	1,135	402	16	-	73.1	25.9	1.0	-	87	12	77	-	0.2	0.2	0.2	0.2	-
Clay	1,131	840	275	16	-	74.3	24.3	1.4	-	77	26	32	-	0.1	0.1	0.1	0.2	-
Clinton	1,853	1,413	410	30	-	76.3	22.1	1.6	-	47	65	14	-	0.2	0.2	0.2	0.3	-
Coles	5,497	3,988	1,421	88	-	72.5	25.9	1.6	-	91	13	15	-	0.7	0.6	0.8	0.9	-
Cook	198,916	153,799	42,900	2,217	-	77.3	21.6	1.1	-	33	69	67	-	23.9	24.2	23.0	23.0	-
Crawford	2,146	1,587	528	31	-	74.0	24.6	1.4	-	79	23	27	-	0.3	0.3	0.3	0.3	-
Cumberland	924	665	248	11	-	72.0	26.8	1.2	-	96	7	59	-	0.1	0.1	0.1	0.1	-
DeKalb	6,654	5,016	1,543	95	-	75.4	23.2	1.4	-	58	46	31	-	0.8	0.8	0.8	1.0	-
De Witt	2,531	1,808	698	25	-	71.4	27.6	1.0	-	97	4	83	-	0.3	0.3	0.4	0.3	-
Douglas	2,344	1,700	612	32	-	72.5	26.1	1.4	-	93	10	37	-	0.3	0.3	0.3	0.3	-
DuPage	105,667	81,741	22,863	1,063	-	77.4	21.6	1.0	-	32	67	81	-	12.7	12.9	12.2	11.0	-
Edgar	2,589	1,906	655	28	-	73.6	25.3	1.1	-	83	19	71	-	0.3	0.3	0.4	0.3	-
Edwards	945	712	227	6	-	75.3	24.0	0.6	-	59	35	101	-	0.1	0.1	0.1	<.1	-
Effingham	2,430	1,787	617	26	-	73.5	25.4	1.1	-	84	17	73	-	0.3	0.3	0.3	0.3	-
Fayette	1,871	1,495	349	27	-	79.9	18.7	1.4	-	9	97	28	-	0.2	0.2	0.2	0.3	-
Ford	2,581	1,946	600	35	-	75.4	23.2	1.4	-	57	45	40	-	0.3	0.3	0.3	0.4	-
Franklin	1,806	1,373	416	17	-	76.0	23.0	0.9	-	50	49	86	-	0.2	0.2	0.2	0.2	-
Fulton	2,417	1,927	460	30	-	79.7	19.0	1.2	-	12	93	53	-	0.3	0.3	0.2	0.3	-
Gallatin	352	283	66	3	-	80.4	18.8	0.9	-	5	94	94	-	<.1	<.1	<.1	<.1	-
Greene	1,409	1,097	301	11	-	77.9	21.4	0.8	-	25	71	98	-	0.2	0.2	0.2	0.1	-
Grundy	3,442	2,685	715	42	-	78.0	20.8	1.2	-	21	80	56	-	0.4	0.4	0.4	0.4	-
Hamilton	884	648	222	14	-	73.3	25.1	1.6	-	86	20	18	-	0.1	0.1	0.1	0.1	-
Hancock	1,827	1,351	444	32	-	73.9	24.3	1.8	-	80	29	12	-	0.2	0.2	0.2	0.3	-
Hardin	464	372	86	6	-	80.2	18.5	1.3	-	6	98	45	-	<.1	<.1	<.1	<.1	-
Henderson	971	757	200	14	-	78.0	20.6	1.4	-	23	81	30	-	0.1	0.1	0.1	0.1	-
Henry	4,253	3,349	860	44	-	78.7	20.2	1.0	-	19	85	76	-	0.5	0.5	0.5	0.5	-
Iroquois	3,781	2,789	919	73	-	73.8	24.3	1.9	-	82	28	6	-	0.5	0.4	0.5	0.8	-
Jackson	2,765	1,952	776	37	-	70.6	28.1	1.3	-	100	3	41	-	0.3	0.3	0.4	0.4	-
Jasper	698	537	147	14	-	76.9	21.1	2.0	-	35	77	3	-	<.1	<.1	<.1	0.1	-
Jefferson	2,030	1,622	380	28	-	79.9	18.7	1.4	-	10	95	35	-	0.2	0.3	0.2	0.3	-
Jersey	1,629	1,253	358	18	-	76.9	22.0	1.1	-	36	66	69	-	0.2	0.2	0.2	0.2	-
Jo Daviess	3,392	2,544	797	51	-	75.0	23.5	1.5	-	66	42	24	-	0.4	0.4	0.4	0.5	-
Johnson	1,652	1,267	352	33	-	76.7	21.3	2.0	-	39	74	4	-	0.2	0.2	0.2	0.3	-
Kane	39,551	29,729	9,311	511	-	75.2	23.5	1.3	-	61	40	46	-	4.8	4.7	5.0	5.3	-
Kankakee	5,285	3,986	1,217	82	-	75.4	23.0	1.6	-	56	50	20	-	0.6	0.6	0.7	0.9	-
Kendall	6,003	4,460	1,469	74	-	74.3	24.5	1.2	-	76	25	54	-	0.7	0.7	0.8	0.8	-
Knox	5,517	4,101	1,341	75	-	74.3	24.3	1.4	-	75	27	38	-	0.7	0.6	0.7	0.8	-
Lake	58,072	44,950	12,393	729	-	77.4	21.3	1.3	-	31	72	52	-	7.0	7.1	6.6	7.6	-
La Salle	8,750	6,684	1,945	121	-	76.4	22.2	1.4	-	43	62	33	-	1.1	1.1	1.0	1.3	-
Lawrence	2,417	1,787	581	49	-	73.9	24.0	2.0	-	81	34	2	-	0.3	0.3	0.3	0.5	-
Lee	4,146	3,112	987	47	-	75.1	23.8	1.1	-	63	36	64	-	0.5	0.5	0.5	0.5	-
Livingston	7,399	5,645	1,669	85	-	76.3	22.6	1.1	-	44	56	62	-	0.9	0.9	0.9	0.9	-
Logan	5,593	4,212	1,318	63	-	75.3	23.6	1.1	-	60	39	66	-	0.7	0.7	0.7	0.7	-
McDonough	4,435	3,320	1,044	71	-	74.9	23.5	1.6	-	70	41	16	-	0.5	0.5	0.6	0.7	-
McHenry	29,370	21,877	7,103	390	-	74.5	24.2	1.3	-	72	32	43	-	3.5	3.4	3.8	4.0	-
McLean	19,705	15,113	4,409	183	-	76.7	22.4	0.9	-	38	59	89	-	2.4	2.4	2.4	1.9	-
Macon	8,762	6,843	1,858	61	-	78.1	21.2	0.7	-	20	76	100	-	1.1	1.1	1.0	0.6	-
Macoupin	2,300	1,833	438	29	-	79.7	19.0	1.3	-	13	92	50	-	0.3	0.3	0.2	0.3	-
Madison	8,598	6,451	2,036	111	-	75.0	23.7	1.3	-	65	37	47	-	1.0	1.0	1.1	1.2	-
Marion	2,192	1,737	425	30	-	79.2	19.4	1.4	-	16	89	36	-	0.3	0.3	0.2	0.3	-
Marshall	1,500	1,143	344	13	-	76.2	22.9	0.9	-	48	52	93	-	0.2	0.2	0.2	0.1	-
Mason	1,536	1,229	298	9	-	80.0	19.4	0.6	-	7	88	102	-	0.2	0.2	0.2	<.1	-
Massac	1,074	858	206	10	-	79.9	19.2	0.9	-	11	90	88	-	0.1	0.1	0.1	0.1	-
Menard	2,689	2,064	596	29	-	76.8	22.2	1.1	-	37	63	72	-	0.3	0.3	0.3	0.3	-
Mercer	1,501	1,185	299	17	-	78.9	19.9	1.1	-	17	86	65	-	0.2	0.2	0.2	0.2	-
Monroe	2,377	1,781	551	45	-	74.9	23.2	1.9	-	68	47	7	-	0.3	0.3	0.3	0.5	-
Montgomery	2,421	1,850	544	27	-	76.4	22.5	1.1	-	42	57	68	-	0.3	0.3	0.3	0.3	-
Morgan	3,389	2,576	767	46	-	76.0	22.6	1.4	-	51	55	39	-	0.4	0.4	0.4	0.5	-
Moultrie	1,324	958	342	24	-	72.4	25.8	1.8	-	94	15	9	-	0.2	0.2	0.2	0.2	-

Table J. — Vote for Presidential Preference: March 17, 1992, Republican Primary Election (cont)

| County | Top candidates | | | | | Top four candidates (state vote) | | | | | | | | | | | | |
| | | | | | | Percent of total vote | | | | Rank | | | | Percent contribution to state vote | | | | |
	Total	Bush	Bu-chanan	Horton		Bush	Bu-chanan	Horton		Bush	Bu-chanan	Horton		Total	Bush	Bu-chanan	Horton	
Ogle	7,599	5,524	1,964	111	-	72.7	25.8	1.5	-	89	14	26	-	0.9	0.9	1.1	1.2	-
Peoria	14,266	11,242	2,911	113	-	78.8	20.4	0.8	-	18	83	97	-	1.7	1.8	1.6	1.2	-
Perry	1,382	955	397	30	-	69.1	28.7	2.2	-	102	2	1	-	0.2	0.2	0.2	0.3	-
Piatt	1,750	1,299	430	21	-	74.2	24.6	1.2	-	78	24	58	-	0.2	0.2	0.2	0.2	-
Pike	1,391	1,134	240	17	-	81.5	17.3	1.2	-	3	100	55	-	0.2	0.2	0.1	0.2	-
Pope	781	602	167	12	-	77.1	21.4	1.5	-	34	70	22	-	<.1	<.1	<.1	0.1	-
Pulaski	1,096	795	284	17	-	72.5	25.9	1.6	-	92	11	21	-	0.1	0.1	0.2	0.2	-
Putnam	362	307	51	4	-	84.8	14.1	1.1	-	1	102	70	-	<.1	<.1	<.1	<.1	-
Randolph	1,628	1,233	371	24	-	75.7	22.8	1.5	-	53	53	25	-	0.2	0.2	0.2	0.2	-
Richland	1,665	1,199	443	23	-	72.0	26.6	1.4	-	95	8	34	-	0.2	0.2	0.2	0.2	-
Rock Island	8,072	6,402	1,589	81	-	79.3	19.7	1.0	-	15	87	82	-	1.0	1.0	0.9	0.8	-
St. Clair	9,316	6,974	2,175	167	-	74.9	23.3	1.8	-	69	44	11	-	1.1	1.1	1.2	1.7	-
Saline	1,687	1,313	347	27	-	77.8	20.6	1.6	-	26	82	17	-	0.2	0.2	0.2	0.3	-
Sangamon	27,272	21,111	5,885	276	-	77.4	21.6	1.0	-	30	68	79	-	3.3	3.3	3.1	2.9	-
Schuyler	1,050	817	214	19	-	77.8	20.4	1.8	-	27	84	10	-	0.1	0.1	0.1	0.2	-
Scott	842	612	222	8	-	72.7	26.4	1.0	-	90	9	84	-	0.1	<.1	0.1	<.1	-
Shelby	1,656	1,214	420	22	-	73.3	25.4	1.3	-	85	18	42	-	0.2	0.2	0.2	0.2	-
Stark	1,180	894	263	23	-	75.8	22.3	1.9	-	52	61	5	-	0.1	0.1	0.1	0.2	-
Stephenson	7,632	5,448	2,067	117	-	71.4	27.1	1.5	-	98	5	23	-	0.9	0.9	1.1	1.2	-
Tazewell	10,117	7,716	2,323	78	-	76.3	23.0	0.8	-	45	51	99	-	1.2	1.2	1.2	0.8	-
Union	1,503	1,172	315	16	-	78.0	21.0	1.1	-	22	78	74	-	0.2	0.2	0.2	0.2	-
Vermilion	6,097	4,352	1,646	99	-	71.4	27.0	1.6	-	99	6	13	-	0.7	0.7	0.9	1.0	-
Wabash	1,731	1,298	419	14	-	75.0	24.2	0.8	-	67	31	96	-	0.3	0.3	0.3	0.1	-
Warren	2,628	2,013	582	33	-	76.6	22.1	1.3	-	41	64	51	-	0.3	0.3	0.3	0.3	-
Washington	1,683	1,264	388	31	-	75.1	23.1	1.8	-	62	48	8	-	0.2	0.2	0.2	0.3	-
Wayne	3,553	2,467	1,030	56	-	69.4	29.0	1.6	-	101	1	19	-	0.4	0.4	0.6	0.6	-
White	1,082	894	177	11	-	82.6	16.4	1.0	-	2	101	78	-	0.1	0.1	<.1	0.1	-
Whiteside	4,249	3,258	948	43	-	76.7	22.3	1.0	-	40	60	80	-	0.5	0.5	0.5	0.4	-
Will	31,551	23,566	7,656	329	-	74.7	24.3	1.0	-	71	30	75	-	3.8	3.7	4.1	3.4	-
Williamson	2,638	2,052	561	25	-	77.8	21.3	0.9	-	28	75	85	-	0.3	0.3	0.3	0.3	-
Winnebago	24,250	18,202	5,837	211	-	75.1	24.1	0.9	-	64	33	92	-	2.9	2.9	3.1	2.2	-
Woodford	5,520	4,107	1,362	51	-	74.4	24.7	0.9	-	74	21	90	-	0.7	0.6	0.7	0.5	-
ILLINOIS	831,140	634,588	186,915	9,637	-	76.4	22.5	1.2	-					100.0	100.0	100.0	100.0	-

1992 Vote for President
Percent for Clinton (D), by County

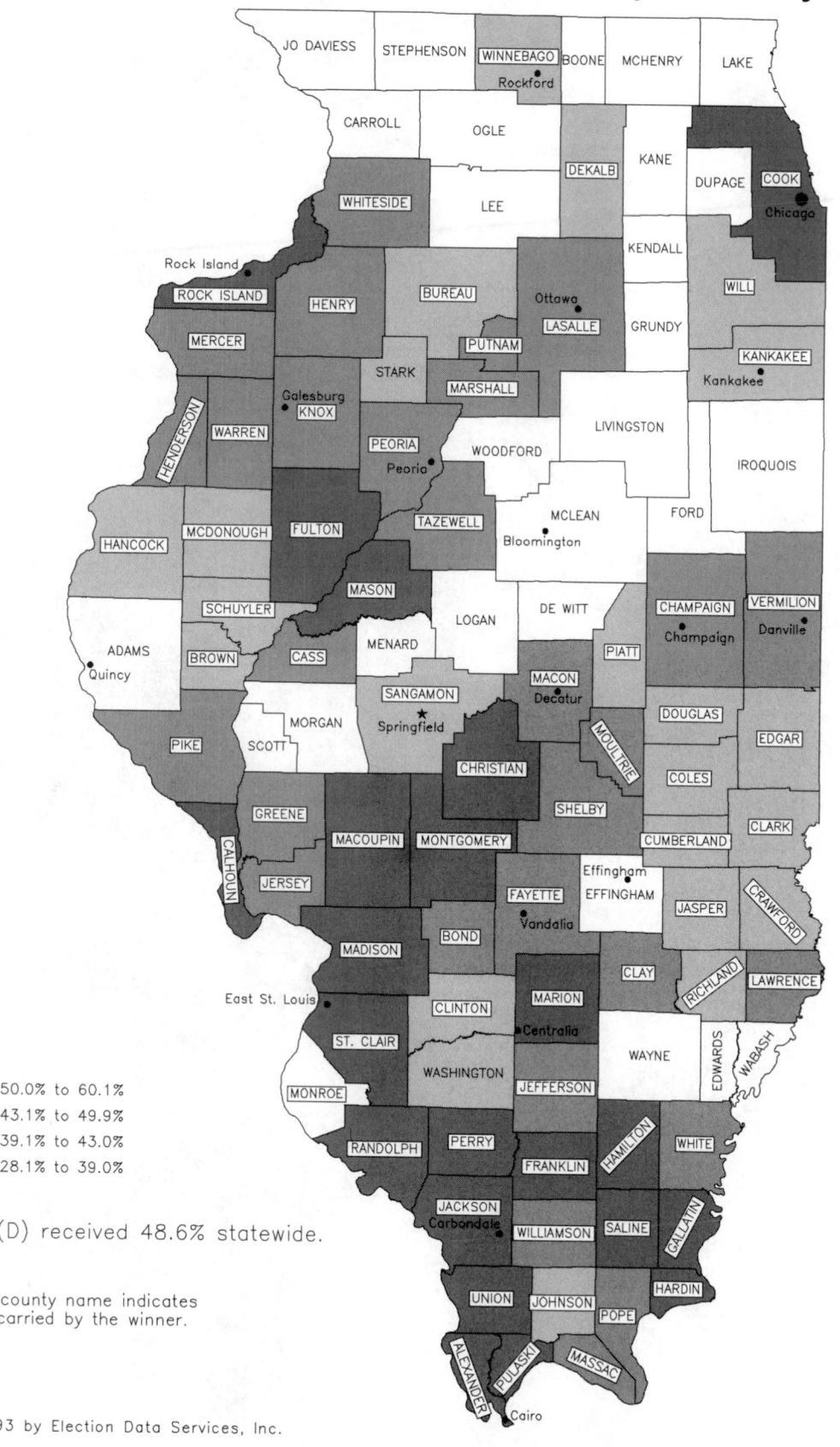

Clinton (D) received 48.6% statewide.

A framed county name indicates
a county carried by the winner.

Legend:
- 50.0% to 60.1%
- 43.1% to 49.9%
- 39.1% to 43.0%
- 28.1% to 39.0%

Copyright © 1993 by Election Data Services, Inc.

1992 Vote for U.S. Senator
Percent for Moseley-Braun (D), by County

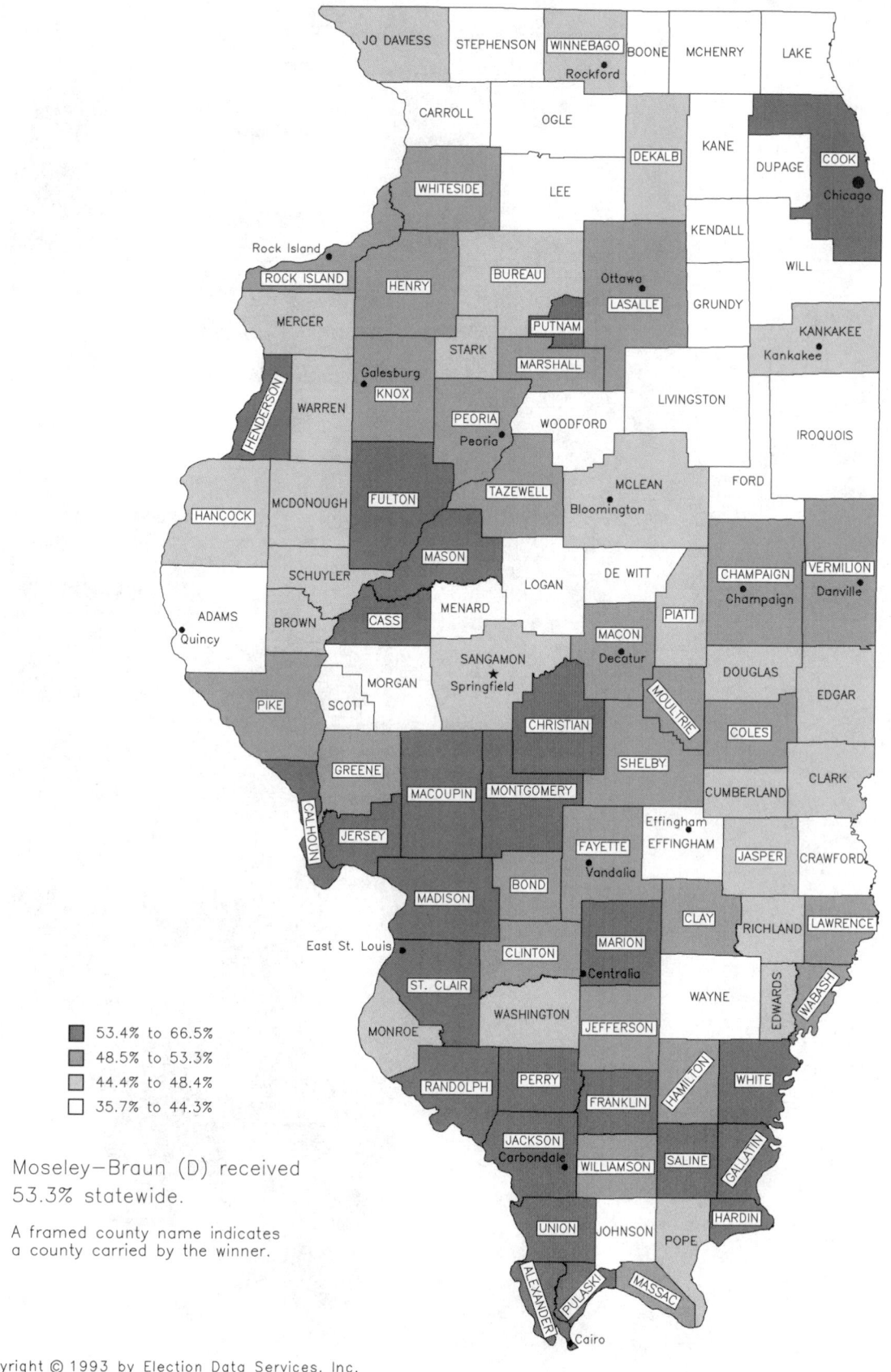

53.4% to 66.5%
48.5% to 53.3%
44.4% to 48.4%
35.7% to 44.3%

Moseley—Braun (D) received
53.3% statewide.

A framed county name indicates
a county carried by the winner.

INDIANA

Congressional Districts 10
  Average Population 554,416
State Senate Districts 50
  Average Population 110,883
State House Districts 100
  Average Population 55,442

Electoral College Votes.......................................12
Counties 92
Voting Precincts 4,837

Alternative Registration Methods:
....Deputized Registrars

Registration Deadline (Days before Election) 29

Voting Equipment Use (Counties)

Datavote Punch Card	2	Paper Ballot	5
Electronic	14	Other Punch Card	35
Lever Machine	31	Mixed Systems	0
Optical Scanner	5		

Party Control	DEM	REP	IND	VAC
1993 State Senate	22	28	0	0
1992 State Senate	24	26	0	0
1993 State House	55	45	0	0
1992 State House	52	48	0	0

Population Statistics 1990

Race/ Ethnicity	Total Population		Voting Age Population		Voting Age Population % of total population
	Number	%	Number	%	
Non-Hispanic					
White	4,965,242	89.6	3,703,471	90.6	74.6
Black	428,612	7.7	286,298	7.0	66.8
Asian/Pacific Islander	36,618	0.7	26,725	0.7	73.0
Native American	11,999	0.2	8,626	0.2	71.9
Other	2,900	<.1	905	<.1	31.2
All Hispanic	98,788	1.8	62,170	1.5	62.9
TOTAL	5,544,159	100.0	4,088,195	100.0	73.7

Estimated Voting Age Population 1992 (VAP) 4,176,000
Number of Registered Voters..................................3,180,157
  % of estimated VAP.......................................76.2
Voter Turnout (Maximum Vote)[1]...........................2,348,650
  % of VAP...56.2
  % of Registration 73.9
Persons Not Voting—of Voting Age 1,827,350
  % of VAP...43.8
Persons Not Voting—of Registered 831,507
  % of Registration 26.1
Straight Ticket Voting .... Yes, Exception

State Officials and Members of Congress

Governor:
Evan Bayh (D) 1988, elected to a four-year term in 1992.

U.S. Senators:
Richard Lugar (R) 1976, elected to a six-year term in 1988.
Daniel Coats (R) 1989, elected to a six-year term in 1990.

U.S. Representative in Congress:
(District, Name, Party, Date first elected)

1. Visclosky (D) 1984
2. Sharp (D) 1974
3. Roemer (D) 1990
4. Long (D) 1989
5. Buyer (R) 1992
6. Burton (R) 1982
7. Myers (R) 1966
8. McCloskey (D) 1982
9. Hamilton (D) 1964
10. Jacobs (D) 1974

---

[1]Maximum vote turnout from Table C exceeds reported statewide actual voter turnout because in one or more counties the vote for highest office is greater than reported actual turnout.

Candidates: General Election, November 3, 1992

Candidate(s)	Total vote	Percent	Party	Status	First elected
President/Vice President					
Bush/Quayle	989,375	42.91%	Republican	Incumbent	1988
Clinton/Gore	848,420	36.79%	Democrat	Challenger	1992
Perot/Stockdale	455,934	19.77%	Ross Perot	Challenger	
Marrou/Lord	7,936	0.34%	Libertarian	Challenger	
Fulani/Munoz	2,583	0.11%	New Alliance	Challenger	
Gritz/Minett	1,467	0.06%	Write in	Challenger	
Hagelin/Tompkins	126	<.01%	Write in	Challenger	
Write ins[1]	30	<.01%	Write in	Challenger	
U.S. Senator					
Daniel Coats	1,267,972	57.34%	Republican	Incumbent	1989
Joseph Hogsett	900,148	40.70%	Democrat	Challenger	
Steve Dillon	35,733	1.62%	Libertarian	Challenger	
Raymond Tirado	7,474	0.34%	New Alliance	Challenger	
John Plemons	78	<.01%	Write in	Challenger	
Georgia D. Irey	18	<.01%	Write in	Challenger	
Governor					
Bayh/O'Bannon	1,382,151	62.00%	Democrat	Incumbent	1988
Pearson/Green	822,533	36.90%	Republican	Challenger	
Barton/Wellington	24,378	1.09%	New Alliance	Challenger	
Gary Montgomery	36	<.01%	Write in	Challenger	
Paul Galanti	18	<.01%	Write in	Challenger	
U.S. Representative in Congress					
District 1					
Peter J. Visclosky	147,054	69.42%	Democrat	Incumbent	1984
David J. Vucich	64,770	30.58%	Republican	Challenger	
District 2					
Philip Sharp	130,881	57.08%	Democrat	Incumbent	1974
William Frazier	90,593	39.51%	Republican	Challenger	
Theodore Shaver	7,821	3.41%	Independent	Challenger	
District 3					
Tim Roemer	121,269	57.45%	Democrat	Incumbent	1990
Carl Baxmeyer	89,834	42.55%	Republican	Challenger	
District 4					
Jill Long	134,907	62.06%	Democrat	Incumbent	1989
Charles Pierson	82,468	37.94%	Republican	Challenger	
District 5					
Steve Buyer	111,116	51.37%	Republican	Challenger	1992
James Jontz	105,209	48.63%	Democrat	Incumbent	1986
District 6					
Dan Burton	186,499	72.16%	Republican	Incumbent	1982
Natalie Bruner	71,952	27.84%	Democrat	Challenger	
John Peterson	4	<.01%	Write in	Challenger	
District 7					
John Myers	129,189	59.48%	Republican	Incumbent	1966
Ellen Wedum	88,005	40.52%	Democrat	Challenger	
District 8					
Frank McCloskey	125,244	52.54%	Democrat	Incumbent	1982
Richard Mourdock	108,054	45.33%	Republican	Challenger	
John Taylor	3,098	1.30%	Independent	Challenger	
Jimmy Funkhouser	2,001	0.84%	Libertarian	Challenger	

[1]Votes for Write in candidates include 16 for Brisben/Garson and 14 for Lyndon LaRouche, Jr.

Candidate(s)	Total vote	Percent	Party	Status	First elected
U.S. Representative in Congress (cont)					
District 9					
Lee Hamilton	160,980	69.68%	Democrat	Incumbent	1964
Michael Bailey	70,057	30.32%	Republican	Challenger	
District 10					
Andrew Jacobs, Jr.	117,604	63.97%	Democrat	Incumbent	1974
Janos Horvath	64,378	35.02%	Republican	Challenger	
Carolyn Sackett	1,849	1.01%	New Alliance	Challenger	

Candidates: May 5, 1992, Primary Election

Candidate	Total vote	Percent	Candidate	Total vote	Percent
Presidential Preference, Democratic			**Presidential Preference, Republican**		
Bill Clinton	301,905	63.31%	George Bush	374,666	80.12%
Jerry Brown	102,377	21.47%	Patrick Buchanan	92,949	19.88%
Paul Tsongas	58,215	12.21%			
Bob Kerrey	14,353	3.01%			

Voter Registration and Turnout, 1948-1992 Elections

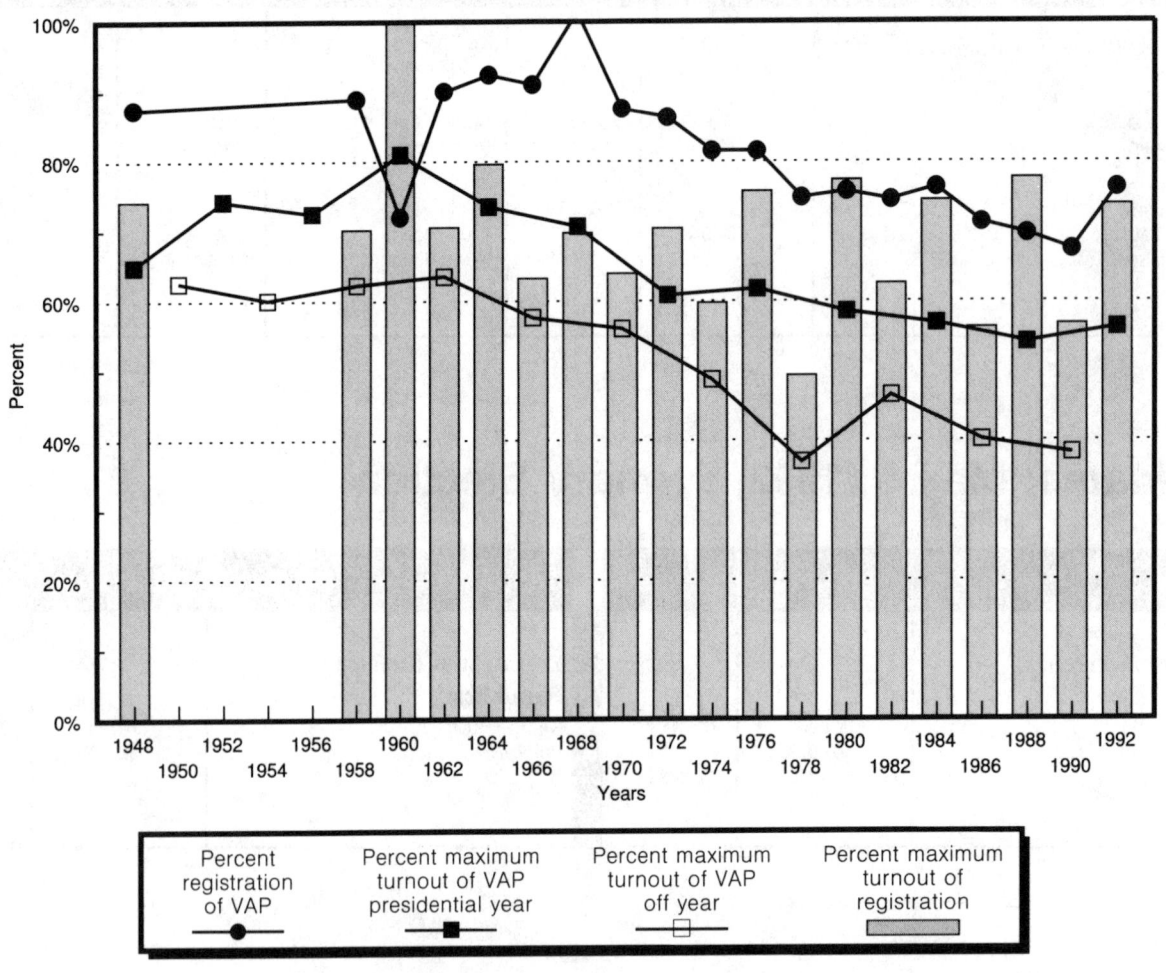

Legend:
- Percent registration of VAP ●
- Percent maximum turnout of VAP presidential year ■
- Percent maximum turnout of VAP off year ☐
- Percent maximum turnout of registration ▨

Year	Estimated Voting Age Population (VAP)	Voter registration (REG)			Voter turnout												
						Highest office						Maximum vote					
		Total	Percent of VAP	Rank by percent of VAP	Actual	Total	Office	Percent total REG	Rank by percent of REG	Percent of VAP	Rank by percent of VAP	Total	Percent total REG	Rank by percent of REG	Percent total VAP	Rank by percent of VAP
1992.......	4,176,000	3,180,157	76.2	23	2,347,912	2,305,871	P	72.5	39	55.2	31	2,347,912	73.8	36	56.2	29
1990.......	4,105,000	2,764,768	67.4	27	1,566,371	1,513,093	C	54.7	31	36.9	31	1,566,371	56.7	31	38.2	30
1988.......	4,111,000	2,865,852	69.7	29	2,222,811	2,168,621	P	75.7	14	52.8	25	2,222,811	77.6	11	54.1	25
1986.......	4,040,000	2,878,498	71.3	20	1,619,005	1,555,507	C	54.0	29	38.5	26	1,619,005	56.2	27	40.1	25
1984.......	3,995,000	3,049,590	76.3	19	2,268,493	2,233,069	P	73.2	25	55.9	22	2,268,493	74.4	28	56.8	23
1982.......	3,942,000	2,936,978	74.5	15	1,834,225	1,817,287	S	61.9	25	46.1	17	1,834,225	62.5	27	46.5	18
1980.......	3,892,000	2,944,311	75.7	19	2,275,433	2,242,033	P	76.1	18	57.6	17	2,275,433	77.3	17	58.5	19
1978.......	3,812,000	2,850,684	74.8	15	1,405,399	1,448,863	C	50.8	37	38.0	28	1,405,399	49.3	40	36.9	35
1976.......	3,692,000	3,010,439	81.5	12	2,278,621	2,220,362	P	73.8	28	60.1	13	2,278,621	75.7	25	61.7	13
1974.......	3,603,000	2,937,114	81.5	7	-	1,752,978	S	59.7	21	48.7	10	1,752,978	59.7	23	48.7	12
1972.......	3,498,000	3,018,578	86.3	7	-	2,125,529	P	70.4	32	60.8	19	2,125,529	70.4	33	60.8	22
1970.......	3,104,000	2,717,331	87.5	4	-	1,737,697	S	63.9	29	56.0	11	1,737,697	63.9	29	56.0	12
1968[1].....	3,003,000	3,044,186	101.4	2	-	2,123,597	P	69.8	43	70.7	6	2,123,597	69.8	43	70.7	10
1966.......	2,915,000	2,653,219	91.0	4	-	1,678,037	C	63.2	27	57.6	12	1,678,037	63.2	27	57.6	15
1964.......	2,845,000	2,628,627	92.4	5	-	2,091,606	P	79.6	22	73.5	7	2,091,606	79.6	24	73.5	9
1962.......	2,836,000	2,551,303	90.0	4	-	1,800,038	S	70.6	17	63.5	3	1,800,038	70.6	17	63.5	4
1960[2].....	2,799,000	2,013,887	72.0	23	2,268,420	2,135,360	P	106.0	2	76.3	9	2,268,420	112.6	2	81.0	1
1958[3].....	2,766,000	2,458,140	88.9	3	1,724,311	1,724,598	S	70.2	14	62.3	7	1,724,598	70.2	16	62.3	8
1956.......	2,729,000	-	-	-	1,978,218	1,974,607	P	-	-	72.4	9	1,978,218	-	-	72.5	10
1954[4].....	2,648,000	-	-	-	-	1,590,901	C	-	-	60.1	9	1,590,901	-	-	60.1	10
1952.......	2,631,000	-	-	-	-	1,955,049	P	-	-	74.3	14	1,955,049	-	-	74.3	15
1950.......	2,555,000	-	-	-	-	1,598,742	S	-	-	62.6	4	1,598,742	-	-	62.6	5
1948.......	2,558,000	2,236,591	87.4	3	1,660,904	1,656,212	P	74.1	11	64.7	11	1,660,904	74.3	13	64.9	12

[1]Total voter registration reported by Indiana Secretary of State exceeds estimated voting age population (VAP). [2]Actual voter turnout exceeds total voter registration reported by Indiana Secretary of State. [3]Votes for U.S. Senator (highest office turnout) exceed actual voter turnout reported by Indiana Secretary of State. [4]No statewide office on 1954 ballot. Voter turnout is higher than indicated by highest office turnout, which is based on combined total votes for U.S. Representative in Congress.

INDIANA

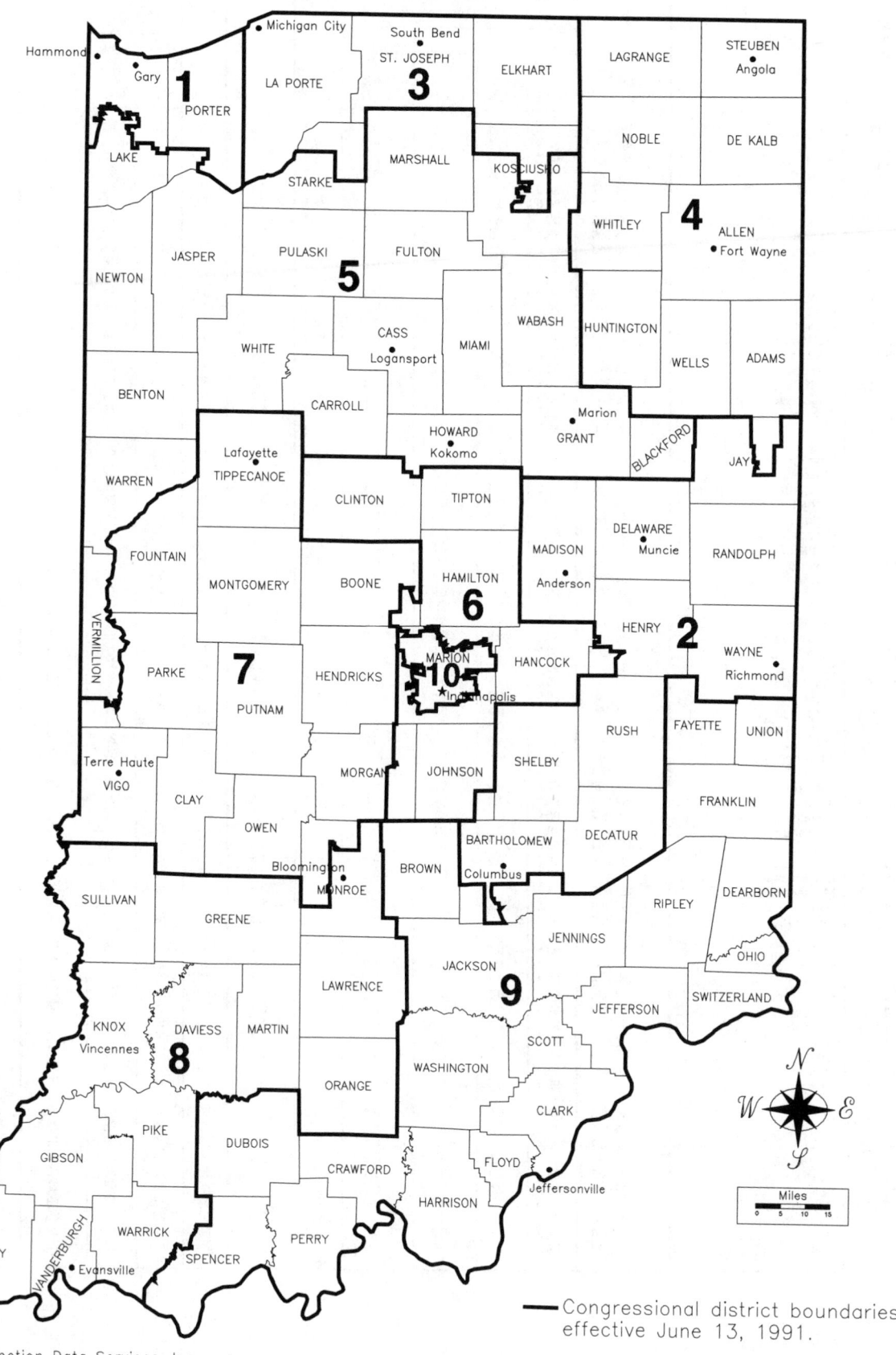

Copyright © 1993 by Election Data Services, Inc.

——Congressional district boundaries
effective June 13, 1991.

Indiana 291

Table A. — 1990 Population by Race and Ethnic Origin

State/county code	County	Total persons	Percent of total persons — Non-Hispanic White	Black	Asian and Pacific Islander	Native American	Other	Hispanic	Rank Total	Rank Non-Hispanic White	Black	Hispanic	Contribution Total	Contribution Non-Hispanic White	Black	Hispanic
18 001	Adams	31,095	97.0	0.1	0.2	0.1	<.1	2.6	44	70	66	3	0.6	0.6	<.1	0.8
18 003	Allen	300,836	86.8	10.0	0.8	0.3	0.1	1.9	3	89	3	7	5.4	5.3	7.0	5.9
18 005	Bartholomew	63,657	96.6	1.6	0.9	0.1	<.1	0.7	23	72	22	39	1.1	1.2	0.2	0.4
18 007	Benton	9,441	98.6	<.1	<.1	0.2	0.0	1.1	88	39	82	21	0.2	0.2	<.1	0.1
18 009	Blackford	14,067	98.9	<.1	0.1	0.3	<.1	0.6	82	21	85	46	0.3	0.3	<.1	<.1
18 011	Boone	38,147	98.6	0.2	0.2	0.2	<.1	0.7	34	35	56	44	0.7	0.8	<.1	0.3
18 013	Brown	14,080	98.7	<.1	0.1	0.3	<.1	0.7	81	30	73	41	0.3	0.3	<.1	<.1
18 015	Carroll	18,809	99.1	0.1	<.1	0.1	<.1	0.6	73	15	70	45	0.3	0.4	<.1	0.1
18 017	Cass	38,413	97.9	0.8	0.3	0.4	<.1	0.6	33	59	31	50	0.7	0.8	<.1	0.2
18 019	Clark	87,777	93.4	5.3	0.4	0.2	<.1	0.6	16	79	12	47	1.6	1.7	1.1	0.6
18 021	Clay	24,705	99.0	0.5	<.1	0.2	<.1	0.3	59	17	44	87	0.4	0.5	<.1	<.1
18 023	Clinton	30,974	98.1	0.1	0.2	0.2	<.1	1.5	45	55	67	15	0.6	0.6	<.1	0.5
18 025	Crawford	9,914	99.4	<.1	0.1	0.3	0.0	0.2	87	4	74	90	0.2	0.2	<.1	<.1
18 027	Daviess	27,533	99.2	0.4	<.1	<.1	<.1	0.3	52	13	49	82	0.5	0.5	<.1	<.1
18 029	Dearborn	38,835	98.7	0.6	0.2	0.1	<.1	0.3	32	29	39	77	0.7	0.8	<.1	0.1
18 031	Decatur	23,645	98.8	0.2	0.5	<.1	<.1	0.4	63	25	61	68	0.4	0.5	<.1	<.1
18 033	De Kalb	35,324	98.5	0.1	0.2	0.3	<.1	0.9	40	40	69	26	0.6	0.7	<.1	0.3
18 035	Delaware	119,659	92.5	5.9	0.5	0.2	<.1	0.7	10	81	9	33	2.2	2.2	1.7	0.9
18 037	Dubois	36,616	99.0	<.1	0.1	<.1	<.1	0.7	38	20	75	42	0.7	0.7	<.1	0.2
18 039	Elkhart	156,198	92.6	4.5	0.6	0.3	<.1	1.9	6	80	14	9	2.8	2.9	1.6	3.0
18 041	Fayette	26,015	97.6	1.7	0.3	0.1	<.1	0.3	55	64	21	80	0.5	0.5	0.1	<.1
18 043	Floyd	64,404	95.1	4.1	0.3	0.1	<.1	0.4	22	75	15	67	1.2	1.2	0.6	0.3
18 045	Fountain	17,808	99.2	<.1	0.1	0.1	0.0	0.5	76	9	88	54	0.3	0.4	<.1	<.1
18 047	Franklin	19,580	99.4	<.1	0.1	0.2	0.0	0.3	68	3	84	88	0.4	0.4	<.1	<.1
18 049	Fulton	18,840	98.0	0.8	0.2	0.2	<.1	0.7	72	57	34	32	0.3	0.4	<.1	0.1
18 051	Gibson	31,913	97.3	1.8	0.3	0.1	<.1	0.4	43	69	20	63	0.6	0.6	0.1	0.1
18 053	Grant	74,169	90.3	6.7	0.5	0.4	<.1	2.0	19	87	8	5	1.3	1.3	1.2	1.5
18 055	Greene	30,410	99.1	<.1	0.2	0.2	<.1	0.5	46	14	87	55	0.5	0.6	<.1	0.1
18 057	Hamilton	108,936	97.5	0.6	1.1	0.1	<.1	0.7	12	67	40	43	2.0	2.1	0.2	0.7
18 059	Hancock	45,527	98.7	<.1	0.4	0.1	<.1	0.7	26	32	76	31	0.8	0.9	<.1	0.3
18 061	Harrison	29,890	98.9	0.4	0.1	0.2	<.1	0.4	48	23	47	62	0.5	0.6	<.1	0.1
18 063	Hendricks	75,717	98.1	0.9	0.4	0.2	<.1	0.5	18	56	29	56	1.4	1.5	0.2	0.4
18 065	Henry	48,139	98.2	1.0	0.2	0.2	<.1	0.4	25	51	27	61	0.9	1.0	0.1	0.2
18 067	Howard	80,827	92.4	5.4	0.5	0.3	<.1	1.3	17	83	11	16	1.5	1.5	1.0	1.1
18 069	Huntington	35,427	98.3	0.1	0.4	0.4	<.1	0.8	39	48	63	28	0.6	0.7	<.1	0.3
18 071	Jackson	37,730	98.6	0.3	0.5	0.2	<.1	0.3	36	36	50	76	0.7	0.7	<.1	0.1
18 073	Jasper	24,960	97.9	0.4	0.2	0.2	<.1	1.3	58	58	46	18	0.5	0.5	<.1	0.3
18 075	Jay	21,512	98.7	0.1	0.3	0.1	<.1	0.7	66	33	64	38	0.4	0.4	<.1	0.2
18 077	Jefferson	29,797	97.7	1.2	0.4	0.2	0.1	0.4	49	62	23	64	0.5	0.6	<.1	0.1
18 079	Jennings	23,661	98.4	0.9	0.2	0.1	<.1	0.4	62	43	30	69	0.4	0.5	<.1	<.1
18 081	Johnson	88,109	97.6	0.9	0.6	0.2	<.1	0.7	15	66	28	34	1.6	1.7	0.2	0.6
18 083	Knox	39,884	97.7	1.2	0.4	0.2	<.1	0.5	31	63	24	53	0.7	0.8	0.1	0.2
18 085	Kosciusko	65,294	96.9	0.5	0.5	0.2	<.1	1.9	21	71	45	8	1.2	1.3	<.1	1.3
18 087	Lagrange	29,477	98.1	0.1	0.3	0.2	<.1	1.2	50	54	65	20	0.5	0.6	<.1	0.4
18 089	Lake	475,594	65.6	24.3	0.6	0.1	<.1	9.4	2	92	1	1	8.6	6.3	26.9	45.1
18 091	La Porte	107,066	88.9	8.9	0.4	0.2	<.1	1.5	13	88	5	14	1.9	1.9	2.2	1.6
18 093	Lawrence	42,836	99.0	0.3	0.2	0.2	<.1	0.3	28	19	55	74	0.8	0.9	<.1	0.1
18 095	Madison	130,669	91.2	7.5	0.3	0.2	<.1	0.7	7	85	6	40	2.4	2.4	2.3	0.9
18 097	Marion	797,159	76.5	21.2	0.9	0.2	<.1	1.1	1	91	2	22	14.4	12.3	39.4	8.6
18 099	Marshall	42,182	97.3	0.2	0.4	0.2	<.1	2.0	29	68	60	6	0.8	0.8	<.1	0.8
18 101	Martin	10,369	99.5	0.1	0.1	0.1	0.0	0.1	86	1	68	91	0.2	0.2	<.1	<.1
18 103	Miami	36,897	93.4	3.0	0.6	1.5	<.1	1.5	37	78	16	13	0.7	0.7	0.3	0.6
18 105	Monroe	108,978	93.4	2.6	2.5	0.2	0.1	1.3	11	77	18	19	2.0	2.1	0.7	1.4
18 107	Montgomery	34,436	98.4	0.6	0.4	0.2	<.1	0.5	42	45	41	57	0.6	0.7	<.1	0.2
18 109	Morgan	55,920	99.2	<.1	0.2	0.2	<.1	0.4	24	12	89	65	1.0	1.1	<.1	0.2
18 111	Newton	13,551	98.2	<.1	0.2	0.3	0.0	1.3	83	53	80	17	0.2	0.3	<.1	0.2
18 113	Noble	37,877	97.7	0.2	0.3	0.2	<.1	1.7	35	60	62	10	0.7	0.7	<.1	0.6
18 115	Ohio	5,315	98.8	0.8	0.2	0.2	0.0	0.1	92	27	35	92	<.1	0.1	<.1	<.1
18 117	Orange	18,409	98.7	0.7	0.1	0.2	<.1	0.3	74	34	38	78	0.3	0.4	<.1	<.1
18 119	Owen	17,281	99.1	0.3	<.1	0.3	0.0	0.3	77	16	54	81	0.3	0.3	<.1	<.1
18 121	Parke	15,410	98.3	0.8	0.1	0.3	<.1	0.6	80	49	36	48	0.3	0.3	<.1	<.1
18 123	Perry	19,107	98.3	1.1	0.2	0.2	<.1	0.3	70	50	26	73	0.3	0.4	<.1	<.1
18 125	Pike	12,509	99.4	<.1	0.1	0.1	<.1	0.3	85	2	90	79	0.2	0.3	<.1	<.1
18 127	Porter	128,932	95.7	0.3	0.7	0.2	<.1	3.0	9	74	51	2	2.3	2.5	0.1	3.9
18 129	Posey	25,968	98.2	1.1	0.1	0.1	<.1	0.4	56	52	25	66	0.5	0.5	<.1	0.1
18 131	Pulaski	12,643	98.3	0.5	0.2	0.2	0.0	0.8	84	46	43	27	0.2	0.3	<.1	0.1
18 133	Putnam	30,315	96.0	2.7	0.5	0.2	<.1	0.6	47	73	17	49	0.5	0.6	0.2	0.2
18 135	Randolph	27,148	98.8	0.2	0.1	0.2	<.1	0.7	54	28	57	35	0.5	0.5	<.1	0.2
18 137	Ripley	24,616	99.3	<.1	0.2	0.2	<.1	0.3	60	5	81	89	0.4	0.5	<.1	<.1
18 139	Rush	18,129	98.5	0.8	0.3	<.1	<.1	0.3	75	41	37	75	0.3	0.4	<.1	<.1

Table A. — 1990 Population by Race and Ethnic Origin (cont)

State/county code	County	Total persons	Percent of total persons						Rank				Percent contribution to state population			
			Non-Hispanic							Percent of total persons				Non-Hispanic		
			White	Black	Asian and Pacific Islander	Native American	Other	Hispanic	Total	Non-Hispanic		Hispanic	Total	White	Black	Hispanic
										White	Black					
18 141	St. Joseph	247,052	86.8	9.7	1.0	0.3	<.1	2.1	4	90	4	4	4.5	4.3	5.6	5.3
18 143	Scott	20,991	98.9	<.1	0.2	0.1	<.1	0.7	67	22	79	36	0.4	0.4	<.1	0.1
18 145	Shelby	40,307	98.4	0.8	0.4	0.2	<.1	0.3	30	44	33	84	0.7	0.8	<.1	0.1
18 147	Spencer	19,490	98.6	0.6	0.2	0.2	<.1	0.5	69	38	42	58	0.4	0.4	<.1	<.1
18 149	Starke	22,747	97.6	0.3	0.1	0.4	<.1	1.6	65	65	52	11	0.4	0.4	<.1	0.4
18 151	Steuben	27,446	98.4	0.2	0.5	0.2	<.1	0.7	53	42	59	37	0.5	0.5	<.1	0.2
18 153	Sullivan	18,993	99.3	<.1	<.1	0.2	<.1	0.3	71	7	78	83	0.3	0.4	<.1	<.1
18 155	Switzerland	7,738	99.2	0.2	0.1	0.2	0.0	0.3	90	11	58	85	0.1	0.2	<.1	<.1
18 157	Tippecanoe	130,598	92.4	2.0	3.7	0.2	<.1	1.6	8	82	19	12	2.4	2.4	0.6	2.1
18 159	Tipton	16,119	98.7	<.1	0.3	0.1	<.1	0.8	79	31	83	30	0.3	0.3	<.1	0.1
18 161	Union	6,976	98.8	0.3	0.3	0.2	0.0	0.4	91	26	53	72	0.1	0.1	<.1	<.1
18 163	Vanderburgh	165,058	91.2	7.5	0.5	0.2	<.1	0.5	5	86	7	51	3.0	3.0	2.9	0.9
18 165	Vermillion	16,773	99.2	<.1	0.2	0.2	<.1	0.4	78	10	77	71	0.3	0.3	<.1	<.1
18 167	Vigo	106,107	92.2	5.5	1.1	0.3	<.1	0.9	14	84	10	24	1.9	2.0	1.4	1.0
18 169	Wabash	35,069	97.7	0.4	0.3	0.7	<.1	0.9	41	61	48	25	0.6	0.7	<.1	0.3
18 171	Warren	8,176	99.3	<.1	0.2	0.2	0.0	0.3	89	6	91	86	0.1	0.2	<.1	<.1
18 173	Warrick	44,920	98.3	0.8	0.3	0.2	<.1	0.4	27	47	32	70	0.8	0.9	<.1	0.2
18 175	Washington	23,717	99.3	<.1	<.1	<.1	<.1	0.5	61	8	72	60	0.4	0.5	<.1	0.1
18 177	Wayne	71,951	93.6	5.2	0.4	0.2	<.1	0.5	20	76	13	52	1.3	1.4	0.9	0.4
18 179	Wells	25,948	98.6	<.1	0.2	0.2	<.1	1.0	57	37	86	23	0.5	0.5	<.1	0.3
18 181	White	23,265	98.9	<.1	0.2	0.2	<.1	0.8	64	24	92	29	0.4	0.5	<.1	0.2
18 183	Whitley	27,651	99.0	0.1	0.1	0.3	<.1	0.5	51	18	71	59	0.5	0.6	<.1	0.1
18	**INDIANA**	**5,544,159**	**89.6**	**7.7**	**0.7**	**0.2**	**<.1**	**1.8**					**100.0**	**100.0**	**100.0**	**100.0**
	CONGRESSIONAL															
	District 1	554,416	69.8	20.8	0.6	0.1	<.1	8.5	1	9	2	1	10.0	7.8	27.0	47.9
	District 2	554,416	94.6	4.1	0.4	0.2	<.1	0.6	3	6	5	8	10.0	10.6	5.3	3.4
	District 3	554,416	89.6	7.3	0.7	0.3	<.1	1.9	4	8	3	2	10.0	10.0	9.5	10.8
	District 4	554,416	92.0	5.5	0.6	0.3	<.1	1.6	5	7	4	3	10.0	10.3	7.1	8.9
	District 5	554,415	95.8	2.1	0.3	0.4	<.1	1.3	10	3	7	4	10.0	10.7	2.7	7.6
	District 6	554,416	97.2	1.1	0.8	0.1	<.1	0.8	6	2	10	7	10.0	10.8	1.4	4.4
	District 7	554,416	95.8	1.9	1.2	0.2	<.1	0.8	7	4	8	6	10.0	10.7	2.5	4.7
	District 8	554,416	95.4	3.1	0.8	0.2	<.1	0.6	8	5	6	9	10.0	10.7	4.0	3.3
	District 9	554,416	97.4	1.7	0.2	0.2	<.1	0.4	9	1	9	10	10.0	10.9	2.2	2.5
	District 10	554,416	68.0	29.7	0.9	0.2	0.1	1.2	2	10	1	5	10.0	7.6	38.4	6.5

Table B. — 1990 Voting Age Population (VAP) by Race and Ethnic Origin

County	Total Voting Age Population	Percent of total VAP — Non-Hispanic White	Black	Asian and Pacific Islander	Native American	Other	Hispanic	Rank Total	NH White	Black	Hispanic	% contribution Total	NH White	Black	Hispanic	VAP % of total population Total	White	Black	Asian and Pacific Islander	Native American	Other	Hispanic
Adams	21,235	97.2	0.1	0.2	0.1	<.1	2.3	49	71	66	3	0.5	0.6	<.1	0.8	68.3	68.5	62.9	69.1	73.0	100.0	60.6
Allen	217,332	88.8	8.5	0.8	0.3	<.1	1.6	3	89	3	6	5.3	5.2	6.4	5.7	72.2	73.9	61.3	67.9	65.9	23.2	60.7
Bartholomew	47,182	97.0	1.4	0.9	0.1	<.1	0.5	22	72	22	45	1.2	1.2	0.2	0.4	74.1	74.4	67.2	69.4	78.7	15.0	58.4
Benton	6,783	98.9	<.1	<.1	0.2	0.0	0.9	88	28	74	23	0.2	0.2	<.1	<.1	71.8	72.0	83.3	100.0	81.3	0.0	54.6
Blackford	10,495	99.1	<.1	<.1	0.3	0.0	0.5	82	19	87	50	0.3	0.3	<.1	<.1	74.6	74.8	33.3	56.3	76.7	0.0	54.4
Boone	27,710	98.7	0.2	0.2	0.2	<.1	0.6	34	37	58	34	0.7	0.7	<.1	0.3	72.6	72.7	68.7	59.6	72.1	33.3	69.2
Brown	10,612	98.9	<.1	0.1	0.3	<.1	0.6	81	29	79	33	0.3	0.3	<.1	0.1	75.4	75.5	53.8	72.2	65.2	55.6	71.3
Carroll	13,833	99.3	<.1	<.1	0.1	0.0	0.5	71	10	70	47	0.3	0.4	<.1	0.1	73.5	73.7	57.9	100.0	77.3	0.0	57.9
Cass	28,256	98.0	0.9	0.3	0.3	0.0	0.5	32	61	32	46	0.7	0.7	<.1	0.2	73.6	73.6	78.4	71.8	70.8	0.0	63.0
Clark	65,228	94.0	4.8	0.4	0.2	<.1	0.6	15	78	12	42	1.6	1.7	1.1	0.6	74.3	74.8	67.6	67.3	75.1	17.3	64.3
Clay	18,253	99.0	0.5	<.1	0.1	<.1	0.2	58	21	43	85	0.4	0.5	<.1	<.1	73.9	73.9	81.4	86.7	65.0	66.7	65.2
Clinton	22,422	98.6	<.1	0.2	0.1	<.1	1.0	46	43	73	19	0.5	0.6	<.1	0.4	72.4	72.8	51.5	62.7	64.0	100.0	51.9
Crawford	7,186	99.4	0.1	0.1	0.2	0.0	0.1	87	6	64	92	0.2	0.2	<.1	<.1	72.5	72.5	100.0	81.8	61.5	0.0	62.5
Daviess	19,578	99.1	0.4	<.1	0.1	0.0	0.3	53	18	46	78	0.5	0.5	<.1	<.1	71.1	71.1	77.6	90.0	80.8	0.0	64.0
Dearborn	27,729	98.8	0.6	0.2	0.1	<.1	0.3	33	31	41	75	0.7	0.7	<.1	0.1	71.4	71.5	63.6	72.5	65.3	33.3	63.2
Decatur	16,823	99.1	<.1	0.5	<.1	<.1	0.3	64	20	82	71	0.4	0.5	<.1	<.1	71.1	71.3	17.9	63.7	72.2	100.0	60.9
De Kalb	25,099	98.8	<.1	0.2	0.2	0.0	0.7	42	32	71	28	0.6	0.7	<.1	0.3	71.1	71.3	54.1	65.3	66.7	0.0	52.6
Delaware	93,244	93.3	5.3	0.5	0.2	<.1	0.6	10	81	9	32	2.3	2.3	1.7	1.0	71.9	78.6	69.2	78.3	75.1	30.0	69.9
Dubois	26,322	99.3	<.1	0.1	<.1	0.0	0.5	38	11	77	48	0.6	0.7	<.1	0.2	71.9	72.1	57.6	56.0	65.5	0.0	52.5
Elkhart	111,721	93.7	3.9	0.6	0.3	<.1	1.6	6	79	14	7	2.7	2.8	1.5	2.9	71.5	72.3	61.1	63.4	73.6	27.2	60.5
Fayette	19,112	97.8	1.6	0.2	0.2	<.1	0.2	55	64	21	84	0.5	0.5	0.1	<.1	73.5	73.6	70.7	63.2	82.9	66.7	55.4
Floyd	47,362	95.7	3.5	0.2	0.1	<.1	0.4	21	74	15	68	1.2	1.2	0.6	0.3	73.5	74.1	63.7	62.8	72.2	12.9	65.4
Fountain	13,196	99.3	<.1	0.1	0.2	0.0	0.4	75	7	90	66	0.3	0.4	<.1	<.1	74.1	74.2	33.3	72.0	80.0	0.0	53.4
Franklin	13,794	99.5	<.1	0.1	0.1	<.1	0.2	73	2	83	83	0.3	0.4	<.1	<.1	70.4	70.5	50.0	59.3	58.1	0.0	65.4
Fulton	13,824	98.3	0.7	0.2	0.3	0.0	0.5	72	55	37	43	0.3	0.4	<.1	0.1	73.4	73.6	62.3	66.7	80.9	0.0	56.3
Gibson	23,714	97.5	1.8	0.3	0.1	<.1	0.3	43	69	20	70	0.6	0.6	0.1	0.1	74.3	74.4	71.4	71.3	81.1	7.1	61.7
Grant	55,799	91.6	5.9	0.4	0.4	<.1	1.7	18	87	8	5	1.4	1.4	1.1	1.5	75.2	76.3	65.5	63.5	71.9	34.4	62.9
Greene	22,681	99.2	<.1	0.2	0.2	<.1	0.4	45	15	86	57	0.6	0.6	<.1	0.1	74.6	74.6	50.0	80.7	74.5	66.7	62.3
Hamilton	77,313	97.7	0.6	1.0	0.2	<.1	0.6	14	66	40	39	1.9	2.0	0.2	0.7	71.0	71.1	70.6	63.6	77.8	13.3	62.9
Hancock	32,982	98.8	<.1	0.4	0.1	0.0	0.7	26	33	75	30	0.8	0.9	<.1	0.3	72.4	72.5	58.5	73.8	84.0	0.0	64.6
Harrison	21,440	98.9	0.4	<.1	0.2	<.1	0.4	48	27	47	58	0.5	0.6	<.1	<.1	71.7	71.8	67.5	58.8	82.8	50.0	67.5
Hendricks	54,605	98.1	0.9	0.3	0.2	<.1	0.4	19	57	31	56	1.3	1.4	0.2	0.4	72.1	72.2	72.6	67.5	80.1	66.7	63.5
Henry	36,302	98.4	0.9	0.1	0.2	<.1	0.4	25	54	29	60	0.9	1.0	0.1	0.2	75.4	75.5	70.1	70.1	80.3	30.0	65.4
Howard	59,285	93.1	5.0	0.5	0.3	<.1	1.1	17	82	11	18	1.5	1.5	1.0	1.0	73.3	73.9	67.5	71.6	71.8	31.0	59.8
Huntington	25,623	98.6	0.1	0.3	0.4	<.1	0.6	41	42	62	37	0.6	0.7	<.1	0.2	72.3	72.6	70.0	60.5	60.9	25.0	54.1
Jackson	27,550	98.8	0.3	0.4	0.2	<.1	0.3	35	34	49	79	0.7	0.7	<.1	0.1	73.0	73.1	72.0	65.0	73.8	25.0	59.8
Jasper	17,787	98.0	0.5	0.1	0.2	<.1	1.1	59	60	44	16	0.4	0.5	<.1	0.3	71.3	71.3	78.0	52.5	86.0	50.0	63.4
Jay	15,812	98.7	0.2	0.3	0.2	<.1	0.6	66	36	61	35	0.4	0.4	<.1	0.1	73.5	73.5	85.7	75.8	83.9	37.5	63.6
Jefferson	22,342	97.9	1.2	0.4	0.2	<.1	0.4	47	63	25	63	0.5	0.6	<.1	0.1	75.0	75.1	75.7	68.6	61.8	27.8	66.7
Jennings	17,275	98.4	0.9	0.2	0.1	0.0	0.4	61	49	30	65	0.4	0.5	<.1	<.1	73.0	73.0	75.8	60.8	70.0	0.0	68.9
Johnson	64,292	97.7	1.0	0.6	0.2	<.1	0.7	16	67	27	29	1.6	1.7	0.2	0.7	73.0	73.0	73.4	66.5	83.7	33.3	67.5
Knox	30,649	97.6	1.3	0.5	0.2	<.1	0.5	29	68	24	51	0.7	0.8	0.1	0.2	76.8	76.8	85.6	81.9	70.6	50.0	68.8
Kosciusko	46,520	97.5	0.4	0.4	0.2	<.1	1.6	23	70	48	8	1.1	1.2	<.1	1.2	71.2	71.6	57.0	62.7	69.6	25.0	57.9
Lagrange	19,135	98.4	<.1	0.3	0.2	<.1	1.1	54	51	85	17	0.5	0.5	<.1	0.3	64.9	65.1	16.2	56.3	64.3	75.0	57.5
Lake	342,427	68.8	22.3	0.5	0.1	<.1	8.2	2	92	1	1	8.4	6.4	26.6	45.0	72.0	75.5	66.1	69.3	70.6	51.6	62.9
La Porte	79,953	89.6	8.4	0.4	0.3	<.1	1.3	13	88	4	12	2.0	1.9	2.4	1.6	74.7	75.3	70.9	69.9	82.6	30.0	64.1
Lawrence	31,902	99.1	0.2	0.2	0.2	<.1	0.3	28	17	55	81	0.8	0.9	<.1	0.1	74.5	74.6	64.8	71.6	78.2	50.0	56.6
Madison	98,294	92.1	6.8	0.3	0.2	<.1	0.6	8	86	6	38	2.4	2.4	2.3	0.9	75.2	75.9	68.1	69.8	76.6	34.4	65.8
Marion	593,974	78.7	19.2	0.9	0.2	<.1	0.9	1	91	2	21	14.5	12.6	39.8	8.9	74.5	76.6	67.6	72.9	75.5	23.8	65.8
Marshall	30,154	97.8	0.2	0.3	0.2	<.1	1.5	30	65	60	9	0.7	0.8	<.1	0.7	71.5	71.8	75.7	66.9	76.1	50.0	55.8
Martin	7,567	99.5	<.1	0.1	0.2	0.0	0.1	86	3	67	91	0.2	0.2	<.1	<.1	73.0	73.0	63.6	78.6	85.7	0.0	78.6
Miami	26,413	94.2	2.7	0.6	1.3	<.1	1.2	37	76	17	15	0.6	0.7	0.2	0.5	71.6	72.2	64.4	72.3	63.2	22.7	56.4
Monroe	88,911	93.5	2.5	2.6	0.2	<.1	1.2	11	80	18	14	2.2	2.2	0.8	1.7	81.6	81.6	79.8	84.9	84.2	59.0	78.8
Montgomery	25,756	98.5	0.5	0.4	0.2	<.1	0.4	40	44	42	59	0.6	0.7	<.1	0.2	74.8	74.9	66.0	77.5	64.2	12.5	62.9
Morgan	40,351	99.2	<.1	0.2	0.2	<.1	0.3	24	13	89	69	1.0	1.1	<.1	0.2	72.2	72.2	44.4	80.2	63.2	25.0	61.4
Newton	9,627	98.6	<.1	0.1	0.3	0.0	0.9	83	41	76	22	0.2	0.3	<.1	0.1	71.0	71.4	77.8	59.1	65.8	0.0	49.2
Noble	26,764	98.1	0.1	0.2	0.2	<.1	1.3	36	58	63	11	0.7	0.7	<.1	0.6	70.7	71.0	60.3	57.1	67.5	50.0	57.0
Ohio	3,923	98.6	0.9	0.2	0.1	0.0	0.2	92	40	28	89	<.1	0.1	<.1	<.1	73.8	73.7	87.8	66.7	62.5	0.0	85.7
Orange	13,487	98.8	0.6	0.1	0.2	0.0	0.3	74	35	38	77	0.3	0.4	<.1	<.1	73.3	73.3	66.1	70.0	78.9	0.0	64.4
Owen	12,656	99.0	0.3	0.1	0.3	0.0	0.3	77	23	54	76	0.3	0.3	<.1	<.1	73.2	73.2	77.3	76.5	91.1	0.0	65.5
Parke	11,541	98.4	0.9	<.1	0.2	0.0	0.4	80	50	33	54	0.3	0.3	<.1	<.1	74.9	75.0	85.5	43.8	62.5	0.0	52.6
Perry	14,157	97.9	1.4	0.1	0.2	<.1	0.4	69	62	23	61	0.3	0.4	<.1	<.1	74.1	73.8	98.0	56.3	75.0	100.0	80.3
Pike	9,445	99.4	0.0	0.1	0.1	0.0	0.3	84	5	91	72	0.2	0.3	0.0	<.1	75.5	75.5	0.0	61.1	86.7	0.0	77.5
Porter	93,409	96.5	0.3	0.6	0.2	<.1	2.4	9	73	51	2	2.3	2.4	0.1	3.6	72.4	73.0	65.0	65.8	74.7	38.1	57.7
Posey	18,684	98.4	1.0	0.1	0.2	0.0	0.4	56	53	26	64	0.5	0.5	<.1	0.1	72.0	72.1	63.3	76.5	78.4	0.0	65.4
Pulaski	9,024	98.5	0.4	<.1	0.2	0.0	0.8	85	48	45	25	0.2	0.2	<.1	0.1	71.4	71.5	60.0	45.0	90.5	0.0	65.1
Putnam	23,309	95.5	3.2	0.5	0.2	<.1	0.6	44	75	16	36	0.6	0.6	0.3	0.2	76.9	76.5	90.5	74.3	80.3	50.0	77.5
Randolph	20,122	98.9	0.2	0.1	0.1	0.0	0.6	51	26	56	41	0.5	0.5	<.1	0.2	74.1	74.2	78.6	75.7	59.6	0.0	60.9
Ripley	17,597	99.3	<.1	0.2	0.2	0.0	0.2	60	8	78	87	0.4	0.5	<.1	<.1	71.5	71.5	75.0	89.2	70.5	0.0	64.5
Rush	13,069	98.7	0.7	0.2	<.1	<.1	0.3	76	39	36	80	0.3	0.3	<.1	<.1	72.1	72.2	68.6	53.4	64.3	50.0	55.7

Table B. — 1990 Voting Age Population (VAP) by Race and Ethnic Origin (cont)

County	Total Voting Age Population	Percent of total VAP — Non-Hispanic White	Black	Asian and Pacific Islander	Native American	Other	Hispanic	Rank — Percent of total VAP Total	Non-Hispanic White	Black	Hispanic	Percent contribution to state VAP Total	Non-Hispanic White	Black	Hispanic	VAP percent of total population Total	Non-Hispanic White	Black	Asian and Pacific Islander	Native American	Other	Hispanic
St. Joseph	184,589	88.7	8.3	1.0	0.3	<.1	1.7	4	90	5	4	4.5	4.4	5.3	5.1	74.7	76.4	63.8	71.9	63.6	35.3	60.8
Scott	15,159	99.0	<.1	0.2	<.1	<.1	0.6	67	22	68	40	0.4	0.4	<.1	0.1	72.2	72.3	87.5	60.4	54.2	100.0	60.1
Shelby	29,302	98.5	0.8	0.3	0.2	0.0	0.3	31	46	35	82	0.7	0.8	<.1	0.1	72.7	72.8	67.8	60.6	77.4	0.0	62.7
Spencer	14,170	98.5	0.6	0.2	0.2	<.1	0.4	68	45	39	52	0.3	0.4	<.1	0.1	72.7	72.6	79.3	75.8	85.7	100.0	70.8
Starke	16,367	98.0	0.3	0.2	0.3	<.1	1.2	65	59	53	13	0.4	0.4	<.1	0.3	72.0	72.3	62.5	87.1	58.0	100.0	55.0
Steuben	20,270	98.5	0.2	0.5	0.2	<.1	0.5	50	47	57	44	0.5	0.5	<.1	0.2	73.9	73.9	86.3	82.4	66.1	100.0	57.5
Sullivan	14,157	99.5	<.1	<.1	0.1	0.0	0.2	70	1	69	88	0.3	0.4	<.1	<.1	74.5	74.7	80.0	60.0	58.3	0.0	52.5
Switzerland	5,646	99.3	0.2	0.1	0.2	0.0	0.2	90	12	59	86	0.1	0.2	<.1	<.1	73.0	73.0	73.3	60.0	75.0	0.0	59.1
Tippecanoe	103,214	92.4	2.0	3.9	0.2	<.1	1.5	7	83	19	10	2.5	2.6	0.7	2.4	79.0	79.0	77.8	84.4	72.2	58.1	72.4
Tipton	11,904	98.7	<.1	0.3	0.1	<.1	0.7	79	38	80	26	0.3	0.3	<.1	0.1	73.9	73.9	70.0	71.4	75.0	71.4	73.6
Union	5,026	98.8	0.3	0.3	0.2	0.0	0.3	91	30	50	74	0.1	0.1	<.1	<.1	72.0	72.1	80.0	71.4	80.0	0.0	60.0
Vanderburgh	125,648	92.3	6.5	0.5	0.2	<.1	0.5	5	85	7	49	3.1	3.1	2.9	1.0	76.1	77.0	66.5	68.9	75.9	19.2	67.3
Vermillion	12,603	99.2	<.1	0.2	0.2	<.1	0.3	78	14	72	73	0.3	0.3	<.1	<.1	75.1	75.2	66.7	76.9	89.3	25.0	65.6
Vigo	81,728	92.4	5.2	1.1	0.3	<.1	1.0	12	84	10	20	2.0	2.0	1.5	1.3	77.0	77.2	74.1	79.9	75.1	30.9	80.2
Wabash	25,852	98.1	0.3	0.3	0.6	<.1	0.7	39	56	52	27	0.6	0.7	<.1	0.3	73.7	74.0	56.2	68.0	62.9	50.0	57.0
Warren	6,035	99.4	<.1	0.2	0.2	0.0	0.1	89	4	88	90	0.1	0.2	<.1	<.1	73.8	73.9	100.0	73.3	81.3	0.0	39.1
Warrick	32,197	98.4	0.8	0.3	0.2	0.0	0.4	27	52	34	67	0.8	0.9	<.1	0.2	71.7	71.8	70.1	58.9	65.9	0.0	67.3
Washington	17,224	99.3	0.1	<.1	0.1	<.1	0.4	62	9	65	62	0.4	0.5	<.1	0.1	72.6	72.7	95.5	71.4	78.3	100.0	59.3
Wayne	53,808	94.2	4.8	0.4	0.2	<.1	0.4	20	77	13	53	1.3	1.4	0.9	0.4	74.8	75.3	68.5	68.5	74.1	20.4	63.4
Wells	18,570	98.9	<.1	0.1	0.1	<.1	0.8	57	25	84	24	0.5	0.5	<.1	0.2	71.6	71.8	60.0	52.5	65.0	40.0	55.3
White	16,977	99.0	0.0	0.2	0.2	0.0	0.6	63	24	92	31	0.4	0.5	0.0	0.2	73.0	73.1	0.0	73.7	67.3	0.0	62.3
Whitley	19,796	99.2	<.1	<.1	0.2	<.1	0.4	52	16	81	55	0.5	0.5	<.1	0.1	71.6	71.7	39.3	51.4	68.6	42.9	65.1
INDIANA	**4,088,195**	**90.6**	**7.0**	**0.7**	**0.2**	**<.1**	**1.5**					**100.0**	**100.0**	**100.0**	**100.0**	**73.7**	**74.6**	**66.8**	**73.0**	**71.9**	**31.2**	**62.9**
CONGRESSIONAL																						
District 1	400,197	72.8	19.1	0.6	0.1	<.1	7.4	9	9	2	1	9.8	7.9	26.7	47.6	72.2	75.2	66.0	68.3	70.8	49.5	62.5
District 2	416,400	95.1	3.7	0.4	0.2	<.1	0.5	3	6	5	9	10.2	10.7	5.4	3.5	75.1	75.5	68.5	70.5	75.5	26.2	65.1
District 3	407,768	90.9	6.5	0.7	0.3	<.1	1.6	6	8	3	2	10.0	10.0	9.2	10.5	73.5	74.6	64.9	69.2	69.0	31.6	60.8
District 4	396,224	93.2	4.7	0.5	0.2	<.1	1.3	10	7	4	3	9.7	10.0	6.5	8.5	71.5	72.4	61.2	67.3	65.8	25.8	59.7
District 5	403,843	96.3	2.0	0.3	0.3	<.1	1.1	8	3	7	4	9.9	10.5	2.8	7.1	72.8	73.2	67.0	68.3	69.7	27.3	59.2
District 6	408,057	97.4	1.0	0.8	0.1	<.1	0.7	5	2	10	7	10.0	10.7	1.4	4.5	73.6	73.8	69.5	68.6	74.6	22.7	63.8
District 7	418,523	95.7	1.9	1.3	0.2	<.1	0.8	2	4	8	6	10.2	10.8	2.8	5.3	75.5	75.5	75.8	81.9	73.9	41.3	71.6
District 8	421,765	95.7	2.8	0.8	0.2	<.1	0.6	1	5	6	8	10.3	10.9	4.1	3.7	76.1	76.3	69.5	79.7	76.7	43.9	71.2
District 9	404,813	97.6	1.6	0.2	0.2	<.1	0.4	7	1	9	10	9.9	10.7	2.2	2.5	73.0	73.2	68.1	66.0	72.0	24.9	63.3
District 10	410,605	70.8	27.1	0.9	0.2	<.1	1.0	4	10	1	5	10.0	7.8	38.8	6.8	74.1	77.1	67.5	74.1	76.4	24.3	65.9

County	Estimated Voting Age Population (VAP) 1992	Voter registration (REG)				Voter turnout										Percent drop-off, by office			
						Highest office				Maximum vote									
		Total	% contribution to state REG	% of 1992 VAP	Rank by % of 1992 VAP	Actual	Total	Office	% of 1992 VAP	Total	% contribution to state turnout	% of REG	Rank by % of REG	% of 1992 VAP	Rank by % 1992 VAP	President	Senator	Governor	Representative
Adams	22,000	15,851	0.5	72.1	73	12,893	12,708	P	57.8	12,893	0.5	81.3	5	58.6	43	1.4	1.7	2.3	2.6
Allen	223,056	170,307	5.4	76.4	50	124,153	121,577	P	54.5	124,153	5.3	72.9	75	55.7	65	2.1	3.6	4.5	4.9
Bartholomew	47,987	36,368	1.1	75.8	56	28,033	27,440	P	57.2	28,033	1.2	77.1	28	58.4	47	2.1	4.2	4.3	5.6
Benton	6,855	5,477	0.2	79.9	27	4,385	4,323	P	63.1	4,385	0.2	80.1	8	64.0	15	1.4	5.8	2.4	1.8
Blackford	10,517	7,782	0.2	74.0	69	5,886	5,778	P	54.9	5,886	0.3	75.6	42	56.0	60	1.8	3.4	4.0	7.8
Boone	28,673	22,578	0.7	78.7	32	17,159	17,358	P	60.5	17,358	0.7	76.9	30	60.5	28	0.0	4.2	2.1	5.1
Brown	11,231	8,732	0.3	77.7	39	6,496	6,325	P	56.3	6,496	0.3	74.4	60	57.8	50	2.6	10.1	6.1	6.8
Carroll	14,081	10,961	0.3	77.8	38	8,562	8,562	P	60.8	8,562	0.4	78.1	17	60.8	24	0.0	2.5	1.5	3.2
Cass	28,607	22,567	0.7	78.9	30	16,788	16,237	P	56.8	16,788	0.7	74.4	61	58.7	42	3.3	7.8	6.5	5.0
Clark	66,823	50,144	1.6	75.0	61	36,691	36,694	P	54.9	36,694	1.6	73.2	73	54.9	68	0.0	12.0	9.2	5.3
Clay	18,584	13,857	0.4	74.6	66	10,313	10,164	P	54.7	10,313	0.4	74.4	59	55.5	67	1.4	2.3	2.3	3.2
Clinton	22,976	17,669	0.6	76.9	45	12,509	12,224	P	53.2	12,509	0.5	70.8	86	54.4	71	2.3	4.5	3.8	6.6
Crawford	7,419	7,139	0.2	96.2	1	5,354	4,994	P	67.3	5,354	0.2	75.0	50	72.2	3	6.7	13.4	10.7	14.6
Daviess	20,019	14,387	0.5	71.9	74	10,823	10,520	P	52.6	10,823	0.5	75.2	49	54.1	73	2.8	4.7	5.2	4.2
Dearborn	29,442	20,029	0.6	68.0	86	15,964	15,567	P	52.9	15,964	0.7	79.7	10	54.2	72	2.5	13.7	11.9	7.3
Decatur	17,354	13,846	0.4	79.8	28	10,537	10,291	P	59.3	10,537	0.4	76.1	38	60.7	27	2.3	3.2	3.2	4.2
De Kalb	26,149	19,657	0.6	75.2	59	15,202	15,022	P	57.4	15,202	0.6	77.3	24	58.1	49	1.2	5.1	8.0	4.6
Delaware	90,419	72,681	2.3	80.4	26	51,624	50,721	P	56.1	51,624	2.2	71.0	85	57.1	54	1.7	4.9	3.8	3.6
Dubois	27,269	21,050	0.7	77.2	44	16,162	15,989	P	58.6	16,162	0.7	76.8	31	59.3	34	1.1	8.2	6.8	8.6
Elkhart	117,205	71,380	2.2	60.9	91	52,754	52,184	P	44.5	52,754	2.2	73.9	68	45.0	91	1.1	4.5	2.2	2.1
Fayette	19,461	15,773	0.5	81.0	22	10,826	10,710	P	55.0	10,826	0.5	68.6	89	55.6	66	1.1	8.0	6.9	6.3
Floyd	49,254	39,683	1.2	80.6	23	29,651	29,651	P	60.2	29,651	1.3	74.7	54	60.2	30	0.0	7.9	5.9	3.5
Fountain	13,277	11,041	0.3	83.2	16	8,524	8,410	P	63.3	8,524	0.4	77.2	26	64.2	14	1.3	2.3	2.1	2.8
Franklin	14,232	10,885	0.3	76.5	49	8,325	8,167	P	57.4	8,325	0.4	76.5	34	58.5	44	1.9	6.1	7.6	3.8
Fulton	14,058	10,784	0.3	76.7	47	8,627	8,527	P	60.7	8,627	0.4	80.0	9	61.4	22	1.2	4.8	2.2	2.1
Gibson	24,066	20,523	0.6	85.3	13	16,817	14,800	P	61.5	16,817	0.7	81.9	4	69.9	4	12.0	13.6	15.9	12.9
Grant	55,408	41,445	1.3	74.8	64	29,756	28,738	P	51.9	29,756	1.3	71.8	81	53.7	74	3.4	5.7	6.2	6.6
Greene	23,276	18,095	0.6	77.7	40	13,702	13,608	P	58.5	13,702	0.6	75.7	41	58.9	41	0.7	6.3	4.5	3.4
Hamilton	85,203	73,004	2.3	85.7	12	56,406	55,434	P	65.1	56,406	2.4	77.3	25	66.2	7	1.7	3.4	4.0	6.8
Hancock	34,376	27,063	0.9	78.7	34	20,874	20,639	P	60.0	20,874	0.9	77.1	27	60.7	26	1.1	2.2	2.3	4.1
Harrison	22,613	17,814	0.6	78.8	31	13,915	13,671	P	60.5	13,915	0.6	78.1	18	61.5	21	1.8	3.3	2.8	3.2
Hendricks	57,496	43,609	1.4	75.8	55	33,887	33,136	P	57.6	33,887	1.4	77.7	21	58.9	40	2.2	4.2	4.7	7.3
Henry	36,489	27,677	0.9	75.9	54	20,460	19,989	P	54.8	20,460	0.9	73.9	67	56.1	59	2.3	3.5	3.2	4.0
Howard	59,799	46,293	1.5	77.4	41	34,975	34,340	P	57.4	34,975	1.5	75.6	43	58.5	45	1.8	3.7	5.6	3.3
Huntington	26,115	21,016	0.7	80.5	24	16,072	16,013	P	61.3	16,072	0.7	76.5	35	61.5	20	0.4	4.0	4.5	4.1
Jackson	28,504	21,814	0.7	76.5	48	16,323	16,170	P	56.7	16,323	0.7	74.8	52	57.3	53	0.9	8.3	6.1	4.9
Jasper	17,964	13,512	0.4	75.2	58	10,235	9,890	P	55.1	10,235	0.4	75.7	40	57.0	55	3.4	6.1	6.4	6.4
Jay	15,960	10,302	0.3	64.5	89	8,970	8,836	P	55.4	8,970	0.4	87.1	1	56.2	58	1.5	5.5	3.0	2.9
Jefferson	22,566	17,751	0.6	78.7	35	13,364	13,191	P	58.5	13,364	0.6	75.3	48	59.2	35	1.3	9.1	6.0	6.1
Jennings	17,930	13,690	0.4	76.4	51	10,482	10,295	P	57.4	10,482	0.4	76.6	33	58.5	46	1.8	10.5	6.9	7.1
Johnson	67,749	50,912	1.6	75.1	60	37,852	37,438	P	55.3	37,852	1.6	74.3	62	55.9	64	1.1	7.3	3.2	3.9
Knox	29,791	23,028	0.7	77.3	43	17,574	17,284	P	58.0	17,574	0.7	76.3	37	59.0	39	1.7	6.8	5.7	5.2
Kosciusko	48,372	32,725	1.0	67.7	87	24,977	24,683	P	51.0	24,977	1.1	76.3	36	51.6	83	1.2	1.8	2.1	3.1
Lagrange	20,419	9,903	0.3	48.5	92	7,617	7,444	P	36.5	7,617	0.3	76.9	29	37.3	92	2.3	6.0	5.1	4.2
Lake	347,031	271,911	8.6	78.4	36	194,053	186,298	P	53.7	194,053	8.3	71.4	82	55.9	63	4.0	8.3	7.8	9.8
La Porte	81,490	57,770	1.8	70.9	77	43,155	42,463	P	52.1	43,155	1.8	74.7	56	53.0	77	1.6	4.0	4.5	3.4
Lawrence	32,796	24,328	0.8	74.2	68	17,332	16,781	P	51.2	17,332	0.7	71.2	83	52.8	79	3.2	6.0	6.4	8.1
Madison	98,832	82,053	2.6	83.0	17	59,788	59,058	P	59.8	59,788	2.5	72.9	76	60.5	29	1.2	2.3	2.2	3.2
Marion	609,995	468,408	14.7	76.8	46	327,043	323,790	P	53.1	327,043	13.9	69.8	87	53.6	75	1.0	7.0	5.7	7.0
Marshall	31,438	22,052	0.7	70.1	80	16,635	16,567	P	52.7	16,635	0.7	75.4	44	52.9	78	0.4	5.1	4.3	5.0
Martin	7,664	7,374	0.2	96.2	2	5,606	5,438	P	71.0	5,606	0.2	76.0	39	73.1	2	3.0	7.4	5.6	6.4
Miami	26,725	18,916	0.6	70.8	78	14,107	13,918	P	52.1	14,107	0.6	74.6	57	52.8	80	1.3	7.3	5.8	5.3
Monroe	86,908	63,695	2.0	73.3	70	44,390	43,587	P	50.2	44,390	1.9	69.7	88	51.1	85	1.8	6.0	5.6	8.2
Montgomery	25,918	19,726	0.6	76.1	53	14,704	14,564	P	56.2	14,704	0.6	74.5	58	56.7	56	1.0	5.1	2.3	2.7
Morgan	42,369	29,531	0.9	69.7	82	21,599	21,107	P	49.8	21,599	0.9	73.1	74	51.0	86	2.3	4.7	4.9	8.7
Newton	9,719	6,937	0.2	71.4	76	5,439	5,344	P	55.0	5,439	0.2	78.4	16	56.0	61	1.7	6.7	3.0	2.9
Noble	27,870	17,982	0.6	64.5	90	14,019	13,713	P	49.2	14,019	0.6	78.0	50	50.3	90	2.2	3.3	4.7	4.6
Ohio	4,047	3,468	0.1	85.7	11	2,570	2,514	P	62.1	2,570	0.1	74.1	64	63.5	16	2.2	4.5	4.5	3.7
Orange	13,833	12,006	0.4	86.8	8	8,203	8,015	P	57.9	8,203	0.3	68.3	90	59.3	33	2.3	4.1	3.5	4.6
Owen	13,301	9,213	0.3	69.3	84	6,760	6,555	P	49.3	6,760	0.3	73.4	71	50.8	87	3.0	5.4	5.6	7.8
Parke	11,666	9,553	0.3	81.9	19	7,206	7,099	P	60.9	7,206	0.3	75.4	45	61.8	19	1.5	1.9	2.1	2.4
Perry	14,467	12,757	0.4	88.2	6	9,165	9,382	P	64.9	9,382	0.4	73.5	70	64.9	12	0.0	3.9	2.1	4.9
Pike	9,522	8,802	0.3	92.4	3	6,507	6,371	P	66.9	6,507	0.3	73.9	66	68.3	5	2.1	3.4	3.0	3.2
Porter	97,293	67,601	2.1	77.4	83	57,510	57,067	P	58.7	57,510	2.4	85.1	3	59.1	36	0.8	2.3	2.1	4.0
Posey	19,092	14,778	0.5	77.4	42	11,597	11,453	P	60.0	11,597	0.5	78.5	15	60.7	25	1.2	2.0	2.2	4.4
Pulaski	9,188	7,545	0.2	82.1	18	5,969	5,916	P	64.4	5,969	0.3	79.1	11	65.0	10	0.9	6.5	4.4	3.7
Putnam	23,396	16,464	0.5	70.4	79	12,306	12,048	P	51.5	12,306	0.5	74.7	53	52.6	81	2.1	4.0	5.7	4.5
Randolph	20,269	15,192	0.5	75.0	62	11,958	11,784	P	58.1	11,958	0.5	78.7	14	59.0	37	1.5	2.3	2.3	2.3
Ripley	18,185	14,500	0.5	79.7	29	10,914	10,937	P	60.1	10,937	0.5	75.4	46	60.1	31	0.0	9.9	6.0	3.7
Rush	13,292	11,258	0.4	84.7	14	8,124	8,008	P	60.2	8,124	0.3	72.2	79	61.1	23	1.4	2.0	2.3	3.6

Table C. – **Voter Participation: November 3, 1992, General Election (cont)**

County	Estimated Voting Age Population (VAP) 1992	Voter registration (REG)				Voter turnout													
							Highest office			Maximum vote									
																Percent drop-off, by office			
		Total	% contribution to state REG	% of 1992 VAP	Rank by % of 1992 VAP	Actual	Total	Office	% of 1992 VAP	Total	% contribution to state turnout	% of REG	Rank by % of REG	% of 1992 VAP	Rank by % 1992 VAP	President	Senator	Governor	Representative
St. Joseph	186,767	139,554	4.4	74.7	65	104,178	104,465	P	55.9	104,465	4.4	74.9	51	55.9	62	0.0	6.2	5.0	3.4
Scott	15,755	11,695	0.4	74.2	67	7,970	7,859	P	49.9	7,970	0.3	68.1	91	50.6	88	1.4	13.2	15.8	5.6
Shelby	30,222	21,966	0.7	72.7	72	16,547	16,211	P	53.6	16,547	0.7	75.3	47	54.8	69	2.0	4.7	4.6	6.1
Spencer	14,606	13,259	0.4	90.8	4	11,507	9,579	P	65.6	11,507	0.5	86.8	2	78.8	1	16.8	19.9	19.5	19.7
Starke	16,914	12,151	0.4	71.8	75	8,848	8,758	P	51.8	8,848	0.4	72.8	77	52.3	82	1.0	9.9	7.0	7.4
Steuben	21,088	14,207	0.4	67.4	88	11,505	11,469	P	54.4	11,505	0.5	81.0	6	54.6	70	0.3	10.2	4.7	3.9
Sullivan	14,219	12,477	0.4	87.7	7	9,242	9,168	P	64.5	9,242	0.4	74.1	65	65.0	9	0.8	12.7	6.0	9.9
Switzerland	5,935	4,776	0.2	80.5	25	3,400	3,388	P	57.1	3,400	0.1	71.2	84	57.3	52	0.4	17.4	10.6	6.4
Tippecanoe	101,092	68,985	2.2	68.2	85	50,879	50,334	P	49.8	50,879	2.2	73.8	69	50.3	89	1.1	4.6	2.7	4.2
Tipton	12,140	10,964	0.3	90.3	5	7,874	7,883	P	64.9	7,883	0.3	71.9	80	64.9	11	0.0	1.4	2.5	6.7
Union	5,241	3,815	0.1	72.8	71	3,016	2,968	P	56.6	3,016	0.1	79.1	12	57.5	51	1.6	5.2	6.1	4.4
Vanderburgh	126,322	108,858	3.4	86.2	10	78,648	76,840	P	60.8	78,648	3.3	72.2	78	62.3	18	2.3	4.9	4.6	3.0
Vermillion	12,710	10,742	0.3	84.5	15	7,974	7,832	P	61.6	7,974	0.3	74.2	63	62.7	17	1.8	2.7	2.2	57.5
Vigo	80,595	63,456	2.0	78.7	33	42,875	42,161	P	52.3	42,875	1.8	67.6	92	53.2	76	1.7	6.6	3.0	3.3
Wabash	26,039	19,494	0.6	74.9	63	15,210	15,101	P	58.0	15,210	0.6	78.0	19	58.4	48	0.7	6.1	6.3	5.1
Warren	6,068	5,256	0.2	86.6	9	4,073	4,003	P	66.0	4,073	0.2	77.5	22	67.1	6	1.7	3.6	4.6	2.8
Warrick	33,842	27,539	0.9	81.4	21	22,214	20,614	P	60.9	22,214	0.9	80.7	7	65.6	8	7.2	8.1	7.9	10.0
Washington	18,075	13,631	0.4	75.4	57	10,183	10,057	P	55.6	10,183	0.4	74.7	55	56.3	57	1.2	9.5	8.1	4.2
Wayne	53,992	37,871	1.2	70.1	81	27,777	27,346	P	50.6	27,777	1.2	73.3	72	51.4	84	1.6	3.9	3.8	3.7
Wells	19,057	15,576	0.5	81.7	20	12,273	12,039	P	63.2	12,273	0.5	78.8	13	64.4	13	1.9	2.7	2.5	4.0
White	17,314	13,524	0.4	78.1	37	10,380	10,221	P	59.0	10,380	0.4	76.8	32	60.0	32	1.5	3.3	5.4	2.4
Whitley	20,648	15,737	0.5	76.2	52	12,181	12,056	P	58.4	12,181	0.5	77.4	23	59.0	38	1.0	4.6	2.2	1.8
INDIANA	**4,176,000**	**3,180,157**	**100.0**	**76.2**		**2,347,912**	**2,305,871**		**55.2**	**2,348,650**	**100.0**	**73.9**		**56.2**		**1.8**	**5.8**	**5.1**	**5.7**

Table E. — Vote for President: November 3, 1992, General Election

County	Total	Clinton (DEM)	Bush (REP)	Perot (IND)	Other	Plurality Total	Party	DEM	REP	IND	Other	Rank DEM	Rank REP	Rank IND	Pct contrib Total	Pct DEM	Pct REP	Pct IND	Major DEM	Major REP
Adams	12,708	3,708	6,078	2,865	57	2,370	R	29.2	47.8	22.5	0.4	72	23	36	0.6	0.4	0.6	0.6	37.9	62.1
Allen	121,577	39,629	55,003	25,809	1,136	15,374	R	32.6	45.2	21.2	0.9	51	38	51	5.3	4.7	5.6	5.7	41.9	58.1
Bartholomew	27,440	8,284	13,146	5,882	128	4,862	R	30.2	47.9	21.4	0.5	62	22	49	1.2	1.0	1.3	1.3	38.7	61.3
Benton	4,323	1,221	2,030	1,056	16	809	R	28.2	47.0	24.4	0.4	76	25	13	0.2	0.1	0.2	0.2	37.6	62.4
Blackford	5,778	2,088	2,347	1,319	24	259	R	36.1	40.6	22.8	0.4	37	61	30	0.3	0.2	0.2	0.3	47.1	52.9
Boone	17,358	3,982	9,485	3,826	65	5,503	R	22.9	54.6	22.0	0.4	88	5	41	0.8	0.5	1.0	0.8	29.6	70.4
Brown	6,325	2,029	2,633	1,635	28	604	R	32.1	41.6	25.8	0.4	54	57	3	0.3	0.2	0.3	0.4	43.5	56.5
Carroll	8,562	2,561	3,800	2,173	28	1,239	R	29.9	44.4	25.4	0.3	67	45	7	0.4	0.3	0.4	0.5	40.3	59.7
Cass	16,237	4,757	7,421	3,944	115	2,664	R	29.3	45.7	24.3	0.7	70	37	15	0.7	0.6	0.8	0.9	39.1	60.9
Clark	36,694	17,460	13,333	5,653	248	4,127	D	47.6	36.3	15.4	0.7	4	82	88	1.6	2.1	1.3	1.2	56.7	43.3
Clay	10,164	3,306	4,696	2,134	28	1,390	R	32.5	46.2	21.0	0.3	52	31	52	0.4	0.4	0.5	0.5	41.3	58.7
Clinton	12,224	3,490	6,141	2,535	58	2,651	R	28.6	50.2	20.7	0.5	74	13	54	0.5	0.4	0.6	0.6	36.2	63.8
Crawford	4,994	2,260	1,903	819	12	357	D	45.3	38.1	16.4	0.2	10	78	82	0.2	0.3	0.2	0.2	54.3	45.7
Daviess	10,520	3,201	5,591	1,695	33	2,390	R	30.4	53.1	16.1	0.3	60	9	86	0.5	0.4	0.6	0.4	36.4	63.6
Dearborn	15,567	5,116	6,974	3,384	93	1,858	R	32.9	44.8	21.7	0.6	49	41	44	0.7	0.6	0.7	0.7	42.3	57.7
Decatur	10,291	2,774	5,195	2,299	23	2,421	R	27.0	50.5	22.3	0.2	83	12	38	0.4	0.3	0.5	0.5	34.8	65.2
De Kalb	15,022	4,652	6,682	3,554	134	2,030	R	31.0	44.5	23.7	0.9	58	44	22	0.7	0.5	0.7	0.8	41.0	59.0
Delaware	50,721	19,556	20,473	10,453	239	917	R	38.6	40.4	20.6	0.5	27	62	56	2.2	2.3	2.1	2.3	48.9	51.1
Dubois	15,989	5,878	6,785	3,195	131	907	R	36.8	42.4	20.0	0.8	34	54	62	0.7	0.7	0.7	0.7	46.4	53.6
Elkhart	52,184	14,660	27,920	9,450	154	13,260	R	28.1	53.5	18.1	0.3	79	8	76	2.3	1.7	2.8	2.1	34.4	65.6
Fayette	10,710	3,969	4,376	2,299	66	407	R	37.1	40.9	21.5	0.6	31	59	48	0.5	0.5	0.4	0.5	47.6	52.4
Floyd	29,651	13,166	11,932	4,421	132	1,234	D	44.4	40.2	14.9	0.4	13	64	91	1.3	1.6	1.2	1.0	52.5	47.5
Fountain	8,410	2,829	3,391	2,162	28	562	R	33.6	40.3	25.7	0.3	45	63	4	0.4	0.3	0.3	0.5	45.5	54.5
Franklin	8,167	2,456	3,831	1,858	22	1,375	R	30.1	46.9	22.8	0.3	63	26	31	0.4	0.3	0.4	0.4	39.1	60.9
Fulton	8,527	2,552	3,982	1,963	30	1,430	R	29.9	46.7	23.0	0.4	65	28	26	0.4	0.3	0.4	0.4	39.1	60.9
Gibson	14,800	6,909	5,172	2,680	39	1,737	D	46.7	34.9	18.1	0.3	5	86	77	0.6	0.8	0.5	0.6	57.2	42.8
Grant	28,738	9,211	13,806	5,597	124	4,595	R	32.1	48.0	19.5	0.4	55	21	63	1.2	1.1	1.4	1.2	40.0	60.0
Greene	13,608	5,431	5,410	2,610	157	21	D	39.9	39.8	19.2	1.2	24	68	69	0.6	0.6	0.5	0.6	50.1	49.9
Hamilton	55,434	10,215	34,622	10,365	232	24,257	R	18.4	62.5	18.7	0.4	92	1	72	2.4	1.2	3.5	2.3	22.8	77.2
Hancock	20,639	4,752	11,072	4,752	63	6,320	R	23.0	53.6	23.0	0.3	87	7	25	0.9	0.6	1.1	1.0	30.0	70.0
Harrison	13,671	5,768	5,403	2,469	31	365	D	42.2	39.5	18.1	0.2	17	72	78	0.6	0.7	0.5	0.5	51.6	48.4
Hendricks	33,136	7,071	18,373	7,519	173	10,854	R	21.3	55.4	22.7	0.5	91	4	33	1.4	0.8	1.9	1.6	27.8	72.2
Henry	19,989	6,794	8,720	4,416	59	1,926	R	34.0	43.6	22.1	0.3	42	48	40	0.9	0.8	0.9	1.0	43.8	56.2
Howard	34,340	10,288	15,306	8,575	171	5,018	R	30.0	44.6	25.0	0.5	64	43	10	1.5	1.2	1.5	1.9	40.2	59.8
Huntington	16,013	3,855	9,093	2,967	98	5,238	R	24.1	56.8	18.5	0.6	84	3	74	0.7	0.5	0.9	0.7	29.8	70.2
Jackson	16,170	5,663	7,246	3,148	113	1,583	R	35.0	44.8	19.5	0.7	38	40	64	0.7	0.7	0.7	0.7	43.9	56.1
Jasper	9,890	3,033	4,809	2,019	29	1,776	R	30.7	48.6	20.4	0.3	59	16	60	0.4	0.4	0.5	0.4	38.7	61.3
Jay	8,836	3,208	3,609	1,994	25	401	R	36.3	40.8	22.6	0.3	36	60	35	0.4	0.4	0.4	0.4	47.1	52.9
Jefferson	13,191	5,510	4,937	2,565	179	573	D	41.8	37.4	19.4	1.4	20	80	65	0.6	0.6	0.5	0.6	52.7	47.3
Jennings	10,295	3,471	4,392	2,370	62	921	R	33.7	42.7	23.0	0.6	43	52	27	0.4	0.4	0.4	0.5	44.1	55.9
Johnson	37,438	8,712	20,353	8,246	127	11,641	R	23.3	54.4	22.0	0.3	85	6	42	1.6	1.0	2.1	1.8	30.0	70.0
Knox	17,284	6,718	6,683	3,719	164	35	D	38.9	38.7	21.5	0.9	25	76	47	0.8	0.8	0.7	0.8	50.1	49.9
Kosciusko	24,683	5,307	14,179	5,115	82	8,872	R	21.5	57.4	20.7	0.3	90	2	55	1.1	0.6	1.4	1.1	27.2	72.8
Lagrange	7,444	2,093	3,584	1,736	31	1,491	R	28.1	48.1	23.3	0.4	78	20	23	0.3	0.2	0.4	0.4	36.9	63.1
Lake	186,298	102,778	53,867	28,635	1,018	48,911	D	55.2	28.9	15.4	0.5	1	92	89	8.1	12.1	5.4	6.3	65.6	34.4
La Porte	42,463	17,717	14,962	9,641	143	2,755	D	41.7	35.2	22.7	0.3	21	85	31	1.8	2.1	1.5	2.1	54.2	45.8
Lawrence	16,781	5,557	7,712	3,452	60	2,155	R	33.1	46.0	20.6	0.4	46	34	58	0.7	0.7	0.8	0.8	41.9	58.1
Madison	59,058	22,276	23,479	13,100	203	1,203	R	37.7	39.8	22.2	0.3	29	69	39	2.6	2.6	2.4	2.9	48.7	51.3
Marion	323,790	122,234	141,369	57,878	2,309	19,135	R	37.8	43.7	17.9	0.7	28	47	80	14.0	14.4	14.3	12.7	46.4	53.6
Marshall	16,567	4,912	8,048	3,522	85	3,136	R	29.6	48.6	21.3	0.5	68	17	50	0.7	0.6	0.8	0.8	37.9	62.1
Martin	5,438	2,018	2,523	883	14	505	R	37.1	46.4	16.2	0.3	30	30	84	0.2	0.2	0.3	0.2	44.4	55.6
Miami	13,918	3,967	6,416	3,428	107	2,449	R	28.5	46.1	24.6	0.8	75	32	12	0.6	0.5	0.6	0.8	38.2	61.8
Monroe	43,587	19,712	16,661	6,943	271	3,051	D	45.2	38.2	15.9	0.6	11	77	87	1.9	2.3	1.7	1.5	54.2	45.8
Montgomery	14,564	3,371	7,602	3,511	80	4,091	R	23.1	52.2	24.1	0.5	86	10	17	0.6	0.4	0.8	0.8	30.7	69.3
Morgan	21,107	4,690	10,939	5,375	103	5,564	R	22.2	51.8	25.5	0.5	89	11	6	0.9	0.6	1.1	1.2	30.0	70.0
Newton	5,344	1,757	2,295	1,274	18	538	R	32.9	42.9	23.8	0.3	48	50	21	0.2	0.2	0.2	0.3	43.4	56.6
Noble	13,713	4,411	5,883	3,328	91	1,472	R	32.2	42.9	24.3	0.7	53	51	16	0.6	0.5	0.6	0.7	42.9	57.1
Ohio	2,514	970	1,009	527	8	39	R	38.6	40.1	21.0	0.3	26	66	53	0.1	0.1	0.1	0.1	49.0	51.0
Orange	8,015	2,948	3,738	1,296	33	790	R	36.8	46.6	16.2	0.4	33	29	85	0.3	0.3	0.4	0.3	44.1	55.9
Owen	6,555	2,207	2,753	1,563	32	546	R	33.7	42.0	23.8	0.5	44	55	20	0.3	0.3	0.3	0.3	44.5	55.5
Parke	7,099	2,429	2,953	1,696	21	524	R	34.2	41.6	23.9	0.3	40	58	19	0.3	0.3	0.3	0.4	45.1	54.9
Perry	9,382	4,829	2,973	1,560	20	1,856	D	51.5	31.7	16.6	0.2	3	90	81	0.4	0.6	0.3	0.3	61.9	38.1
Pike	6,371	2,960	2,156	1,238	17	804	D	46.5	33.8	19.4	0.3	7	87	66	0.3	0.3	0.2	0.3	57.9	42.1
Porter	57,067	21,022	22,644	13,096	305	1,622	R	36.8	39.7	22.9	0.5	32	70	28	2.5	2.5	2.3	2.9	48.1	51.9
Posey	11,453	4,632	4,435	2,357	29	197	D	40.4	38.7	20.6	0.3	23	75	57	0.5	0.5	0.4	0.5	51.1	48.9
Pulaski	5,916	1,950	2,712	1,214	40	762	R	33.0	45.8	20.5	0.7	47	35	59	0.3	0.2	0.3	0.3	41.8	58.2
Putnam	12,048	3,487	5,341	3,174	46	1,854	R	28.9	44.3	26.3	0.4	73	46	2	0.5	0.4	0.5	0.7	39.5	60.5
Randolph	11,784	3,870	4,937	2,939	38	1,067	R	32.8	41.9	24.9	0.3	50	56	11	0.5	0.5	0.5	0.6	43.9	56.1
Ripley	10,937	3,480	5,033	2,406	18	1,553	R	31.8	46.0	22.0	0.2	56	33	43	0.5	0.4	0.5	0.5	40.9	59.1
Rush	8,008	2,168	3,873	1,948	19	1,705	R	27.1	48.4	24.3	0.2	81	18	14	0.3	0.3	0.4	0.4	35.9	64.1

Table E. – Vote for President: November 3, 1992, General Election (cont)

County	Total	Clinton (DEM)	Bush (REP)	Perot (IND)	Other	Plurality Total	Party	Percent of total vote DEM	REP	IND	Other	Rank DEM	REP	IND	Percent contribution to state vote Total	DEM	REP	IND	Major party Percent of vote DEM	REP
St. Joseph	104,465	46,203	38,934	18,828	500	7,269	D	44.2	37.3	18.0	0.5	14	81	79	4.5	5.4	3.9	4.1	54.3	45.7
Scott	7,859	4,085	2,649	1,092	33	1,436	D	52.0	33.7	13.9	0.4	2	88	92	0.3	0.5	0.3	0.2	60.7	39.3
Shelby	16,211	4,560	8,075	3,521	55	3,515	R	28.1	49.8	21.7	0.3	77	14	45	0.7	0.5	0.8	0.8	36.1	63.9
Spencer	9,579	4,301	3,789	1,464	25	512	D	44.9	39.6	15.3	0.3	12	71	90	0.4	0.5	0.4	0.3	53.2	46.8
Starke	8,758	3,695	3,100	1,885	78	595	D	42.2	35.4	21.5	0.9	18	84	46	0.4	0.4	0.3	0.4	54.4	45.6
Steuben	11,469	3,630	4,868	2,896	75	1,238	R	31.7	42.4	25.3	0.7	57	53	9	0.5	0.4	0.5	0.6	42.7	57.3
Sullivan	9,168	4,211	3,052	1,857	48	1,159	D	45.9	33.3	20.3	0.5	8	89	61	0.4	0.5	0.3	0.4	58.0	42.0
Switzerland	3,388	1,535	1,211	636	6	324	D	45.3	35.7	18.8	0.2	9	83	70	0.1	0.2	0.1	0.1	55.9	44.1
Tippecanoe	50,334	17,343	23,050	9,684	257	5,707	R	34.5	45.8	19.2	0.5	39	36	68	2.2	2.0	2.3	2.1	42.9	57.1
Tipton	7,883	2,125	3,906	1,816	36	1,781	R	27.0	49.5	23.0	0.5	82	15	24	0.3	0.3	0.4	0.4	35.2	64.8
Union	2,968	898	1,394	664	12	496	R	30.3	47.0	22.4	0.4	61	24	37	0.1	0.1	0.1	0.1	39.2	60.8
Vanderburgh	76,840	33,799	30,271	12,513	257	3,528	D	44.0	39.4	16.3	0.3	15	73	83	3.3	4.0	3.1	2.7	52.8	47.2
Vermillion	7,832	3,652	2,360	1,794	26	1,292	D	46.6	30.1	22.9	0.3	6	91	29	0.3	0.4	0.2	0.4	60.7	39.3
Vigo	42,161	18,050	15,834	8,141	136	2,216	D	42.8	37.6	19.3	0.3	16	79	67	1.8	2.1	1.6	1.8	53.3	46.7
Wabash	15,101	4,518	7,062	3,424	97	2,544	R	29.9	46.8	22.7	0.6	66	27	34	0.7	0.5	0.7	0.8	39.0	61.0
Warren	4,003	1,367	1,601	1,020	15	234	R	34.1	40.0	25.5	0.4	41	67	5	0.2	0.2	0.2	0.2	46.1	53.9
Warrick	20,614	8,612	8,087	3,862	53	525	D	41.8	39.2	18.7	0.3	19	74	71	0.9	1.0	0.8	0.8	51.6	48.4
Washington	10,057	4,092	4,043	1,846	76	49	D	40.7	40.2	18.4	0.8	22	65	75	0.4	0.5	0.4	0.4	50.3	49.7
Wayne	27,346	9,960	12,221	5,095	70	2,261	R	36.4	44.7	18.6	0.3	35	42	73	1.2	1.2	1.2	1.1	44.9	55.1
Wells	12,039	3,282	5,799	2,890	68	2,517	R	27.3	48.2	24.0	0.6	80	19	18	0.5	0.4	0.6	0.6	36.1	63.9
White	10,221	2,988	4,622	2,582	29	1,634	R	29.2	45.2	25.3	0.3	71	39	8	0.4	0.4	0.5	0.6	39.3	60.7
Whitley	12,056	3,569	5,217	3,195	75	1,648	R	29.6	43.3	26.5	0.6	69	49	1	0.5	0.4	0.5	0.7	40.6	59.4
INDIANA	2,305,871	848,420	989,375	455,934	12,142	140,955	R	36.8	42.9	19.8	0.5				100.0	100.0	100.0	100.0	46.2	53.8

Table F. — Vote for U.S. Senator: November 3, 1992, General Election

County	Total	Hogsett (DEM)	Coats (REP)	Other	Plurality Total	Party	DEM	REP	Other	Rank DEM	Rank REP	Rank Other	Total	DEM	REP	Other
Adams	12,668	4,149	8,345	174	4,196	R	32.8	65.9	1.4	80	12	75	0.6	0.5	0.7	0.4
Allen	119,697	41,499	75,991	2,207	34,492	R	34.7	63.5	1.8	71	21	46	5.4	4.6	6.0	5.1
Bartholomew	26,843	9,178	17,034	631	7,856	R	34.2	63.5	2.4	75	22	21	1.2	1.0	1.3	1.5
Benton	4,130	1,590	2,442	98	852	R	38.5	59.1	2.4	55	38	17	0.2	0.2	0.2	0.2
Blackford	5,685	2,342	3,253	90	911	R	41.2	57.2	1.6	40	49	61	0.3	0.3	0.3	0.2
Boone	16,633	4,360	12,043	230	7,683	R	26.2	72.4	1.4	89	3	74	0.8	0.5	0.9	0.5
Brown	5,843	2,103	3,591	149	1,488	R	36.0	61.5	2.6	65	29	11	0.3	0.2	0.3	0.3
Carroll	8,346	3,477	4,752	117	1,275	R	41.7	56.9	1.4	38	53	72	0.4	0.4	0.4	0.3
Cass	15,486	6,470	8,759	257	2,289	R	41.8	56.6	1.7	37	56	54	0.7	0.7	0.7	0.6
Clark	32,291	17,716	14,200	375	3,516	D	54.9	44.0	1.2	5	88	81	1.5	2.0	1.1	0.9
Clay	10,077	4,026	5,890	161	1,864	R	40.0	58.4	1.6	47	42	57	0.5	0.4	0.5	0.4
Clinton	11,944	4,186	7,514	244	3,328	R	35.0	62.9	2.0	70	26	32	0.5	0.5	0.6	0.6
Crawford	4,638	2,489	2,109	40	380	D	53.7	45.5	0.9	6	86	91	0.2	0.3	0.2	<.1
Daviess	10,313	3,809	6,395	109	2,586	R	36.9	62.0	1.1	63	28	83	0.5	0.4	0.5	0.3
Dearborn	13,777	5,573	7,882	322	2,309	R	40.5	57.2	2.3	44	50	22	0.6	0.6	0.6	0.7
Decatur	10,200	3,500	6,481	219	2,981	R	34.3	63.5	2.1	74	20	26	0.5	0.4	0.5	0.5
De Kalb	14,427	5,099	9,117	211	4,018	R	35.3	63.2	1.5	69	23	70	0.7	0.6	0.7	0.5
Delaware	49,072	18,982	28,811	1,279	9,829	R	38.7	58.7	2.6	53	41	9	2.2	2.1	2.3	3.0
Dubois	14,834	6,254	8,359	221	2,105	R	42.2	56.4	1.5	33	57	67	0.7	0.7	0.7	0.5
Elkhart	50,358	14,949	34,644	765	19,695	R	29.7	68.8	1.5	84	9	66	2.3	1.7	2.7	1.8
Fayette	9,963	4,481	5,334	148	853	R	45.0	53.5	1.5	24	68	68	0.5	0.5	0.4	0.3
Floyd	27,301	14,181	12,847	273	1,334	D	51.9	47.1	1.0	9	83	89	1.2	1.6	1.0	0.6
Fountain	8,328	3,578	4,565	185	987	R	43.0	54.8	2.2	31	64	24	0.4	0.4	0.4	0.4
Franklin	7,819	3,061	4,546	212	1,485	R	39.1	58.1	2.7	50	44	6	0.4	0.3	0.4	0.5
Fulton	8,210	3,175	4,874	161	1,699	R	38.7	59.4	2.0	54	37	39	0.4	0.4	0.4	0.4
Gibson	14,535	7,424	6,936	175	488	D	51.1	47.7	1.2	11	82	79	0.7	0.8	0.5	0.4
Grant	28,071	9,930	17,696	445	7,766	R	35.4	63.0	1.6	67	24	59	1.3	1.1	1.4	1.0
Greene	12,841	5,954	6,637	250	683	R	46.4	51.7	1.9	22	72	41	0.6	0.7	0.5	0.6
Hamilton	54,513	10,145	43,173	1,195	33,028	R	18.6	79.2	2.2	92	1	25	2.5	1.1	3.4	2.8
Hancock	20,421	5,648	14,267	506	8,619	R	27.7	69.9	2.5	87	6	14	0.9	0.6	1.1	1.2
Harrison	13,451	6,982	6,256	213	726	D	51.9	46.5	1.6	10	84	60	0.6	0.8	0.5	0.5
Hendricks	32,469	7,863	23,938	668	16,075	R	24.2	73.7	2.1	91	2	30	1.5	0.9	1.9	1.5
Henry	19,742	7,873	11,465	404	3,592	R	39.9	58.1	2.0	48	46	31	0.9	0.9	0.9	0.9
Howard	33,694	13,412	19,306	976	5,894	R	39.8	57.3	2.9	49	48	4	1.5	1.5	1.5	2.3
Huntington	15,430	4,750	10,511	169	5,761	R	30.8	68.1	1.1	83	10	82	0.7	0.5	0.8	0.4
Jackson	14,972	6,151	8,590	231	2,439	R	41.1	57.4	1.5	42	47	64	0.7	0.7	0.7	0.5
Jasper	9,613	3,602	5,877	134	2,275	R	37.5	61.1	1.4	60	31	73	0.4	0.4	0.5	0.3
Jay	8,477	3,141	5,195	141	2,054	R	37.1	61.3	1.7	62	30	53	0.4	0.3	0.4	0.3
Jefferson	12,149	6,067	5,835	247	232	D	49.9	48.0	2.0	12	81	34	0.5	0.7	0.5	0.6
Jennings	9,382	3,936	5,224	222	1,288	R	42.0	55.7	2.4	35	60	19	0.4	0.4	0.4	0.5
Johnson	35,075	9,131	25,069	875	15,938	R	26.0	71.5	2.5	90	5	12	1.6	1.0	2.0	2.0
Knox	16,386	7,239	8,683	464	1,444	R	44.2	53.0	2.8	26	69	5	0.7	0.8	0.7	1.1
Kosciusko	24,532	6,533	17,624	375	11,091	R	26.6	71.8	1.5	88	4	65	1.1	0.7	1.4	0.9
Lagrange	7,160	2,240	4,792	128	2,552	R	31.3	66.9	1.8	82	11	48	0.3	0.2	0.4	0.3
Lake	177,933	108,174	66,132	3,627	42,042	D	60.8	37.2	2.0	1	92	33	8.0	12.0	5.2	8.4
La Porte	41,438	20,082	20,525	831	443	R	48.5	49.5	2.0	16	78	35	1.9	2.2	1.6	1.9
Lawrence	16,296	6,706	9,315	275	2,609	R	41.2	57.2	1.7	41	51	51	0.7	0.7	0.7	0.6
Madison	58,418	25,279	31,709	1,430	6,430	R	43.3	54.3	2.4	29	67	15	2.6	2.8	2.5	3.3
Marion	303,993	118,781	179,213	5,999	60,432	R	39.1	59.0	2.0	51	39	37	13.7	13.2	14.1	13.9
Marshall	15,790	5,357	10,268	165	4,911	R	33.9	65.0	1.0	76	15	84	0.7	0.6	0.8	0.4
Martin	5,189	2,450	2,685	54	235	R	47.2	51.7	1.0	20	71	85	0.2	0.3	0.2	0.1
Miami	13,078	5,248	7,638	192	2,390	R	40.1	58.4	1.5	45	43	69	0.6	0.6	0.6	0.4
Monroe	41,745	16,685	23,409	1,651	6,724	R	40.0	56.1	4.0	46	58	1	1.9	1.9	1.8	3.8
Montgomery	13,950	3,860	9,718	372	5,858	R	27.7	69.7	2.7	86	7	7	0.6	0.4	0.8	0.9
Morgan	20,594	5,807	14,260	527	8,453	R	28.2	69.2	2.6	85	8	10	0.9	0.6	1.1	1.2
Newton	5,072	1,931	3,021	120	1,090	R	38.1	59.6	2.4	59	36	20	0.2	0.2	0.2	0.3
Noble	13,563	4,692	8,646	225	3,954	R	34.6	63.7	1.7	72	19	55	0.6	0.5	0.7	0.5
Ohio	2,454	1,164	1,244	46	80	R	47.4	50.7	1.9	19	74	45	0.1	0.1	<.1	0.1
Orange	7,870	3,459	4,280	131	821	R	44.0	54.4	1.7	27	65	52	0.4	0.4	0.3	0.3
Owen	6,393	2,450	3,716	227	1,266	R	38.3	58.1	3.6	57	45	2	0.3	0.3	0.3	0.5
Parke	7,069	2,958	3,962	149	1,004	R	41.8	56.0	2.1	36	59	29	0.3	0.3	0.3	0.3
Perry	9,017	5,167	3,759	91	1,408	D	57.3	41.7	1.0	3	90	88	0.4	0.6	0.3	0.2
Pike	6,288	3,084	3,104	100	20	R	49.0	49.4	1.6	15	79	58	0.3	0.3	0.2	0.2
Porter	56,159	24,109	30,862	1,188	6,753	R	42.9	55.0	2.1	32	61	28	2.5	2.7	2.4	2.7
Posey	11,367	4,720	6,433	214	1,713	R	41.5	56.6	1.9	39	55	44	0.5	0.5	0.5	0.5
Pulaski	5,584	2,353	3,176	55	823	R	42.1	56.9	1.0	34	54	90	0.3	0.3	0.3	0.1
Putnam	11,813	3,864	7,639	310	3,775	R	32.7	64.7	2.6	81	17	8	0.5	0.4	0.6	0.7
Randolph	11,685	4,372	7,086	227	2,714	R	37.4	60.6	1.9	61	33	42	0.5	0.5	0.6	0.5
Ripley	9,856	3,754	5,977	125	2,223	R	38.1	60.6	1.3	58	32	78	0.4	0.4	0.5	0.3
Rush	7,965	3,719	4,090	156	371	R	46.7	51.3	2.0	21	73	40	0.4	0.4	0.3	0.4

300 Indiana

Table F. — Vote for U.S. Senator: November 3, 1992, General Election (cont)

County	Total	Hogsett (DEM)	Coats (REP)	Other	Plurality Total	Party	DEM	REP	Other	Rank DEM	Rank REP	Rank Other	Total	DEM	REP	Other
St. Joseph	98,040	43,785	53,260	995	9,475	R	44.7	54.3	1.0	25	66	87	4.4	4.9	4.2	2.3
Scott	6,920	4,061	2,778	81	1,283	D	58.7	40.1	1.2	2	91	80	0.3	0.5	0.2	0.2
Shelby	15,770	5,299	10,227	244	4,928	R	33.6	64.9	1.5	77	16	63	0.7	0.6	0.8	0.6
Spencer	9,220	4,549	4,630	41	81	R	49.3	50.2	0.4	13	77	92	0.4	0.5	0.4	<.1
Starke	7,968	3,816	4,014	138	198	R	47.9	50.4	1.7	18	76	49	0.4	0.4	0.3	0.3
Steuben	10,331	3,573	6,611	147	3,038	R	34.6	64.0	1.4	73	18	71	0.5	0.4	0.5	0.3
Sullivan	8,069	4,282	3,649	138	633	D	53.1	45.2	1.7	8	87	50	0.4	0.5	0.3	0.3
Switzerland	2,808	1,500	1,279	29	221	D	53.4	45.5	1.0	7	85	86	0.1	0.2	0.1	<.1
Tippecanoe	48,557	17,867	29,129	1,561	11,262	R	36.8	60.0	3.2	64	34	3	2.2	2.0	2.3	3.6
Tipton	7,776	2,584	5,063	129	2,479	R	33.2	65.1	1.7	78	14	56	0.4	0.3	0.4	0.3
Union	2,859	1,097	1,705	57	608	R	38.4	59.6	2.0	56	35	36	0.1	0.1	0.1	0.1
Vanderburgh	74,802	32,300	41,079	1,423	8,779	R	43.2	54.9	1.9	30	62	43	3.4	3.6	3.2	3.3
Vermillion	7,757	4,286	3,293	178	993	D	55.3	42.5	2.3	4	89	23	0.4	0.5	0.3	0.4
Vigo	40,043	19,659	19,436	948	223	D	49.1	48.5	2.4	14	80	18	1.8	2.2	1.5	2.2
Wabash	14,280	5,099	8,992	189	3,893	R	35.7	63.0	1.3	66	25	77	0.6	0.6	0.7	0.4
Warren	3,928	1,793	2,051	84	258	R	45.6	52.2	2.1	23	70	27	0.2	0.2	0.2	0.2
Warrick	20,415	8,850	11,194	371	2,344	R	43.4	54.8	1.8	28	63	47	0.9	1.0	0.9	0.9
Washington	9,219	4,433	4,661	125	228	R	48.1	50.6	1.4	17	75	76	0.4	0.5	0.4	0.3
Wayne	26,684	10,914	15,246	524	4,332	R	40.9	57.1	2.0	43	52	38	1.2	1.2	1.2	1.2
Wells	11,946	3,926	7,834	186	3,908	R	32.9	65.6	1.6	79	13	62	0.5	0.4	0.6	0.4
White	10,037	3,895	5,893	249	1,998	R	38.8	58.7	2.5	52	40	13	0.5	0.4	0.5	0.6
Whitley	11,619	4,107	7,229	283	3,122	R	35.3	62.2	2.4	68	27	16	0.5	0.5	0.6	0.7
INDIANA	**2,211,423**	**900,148**	**1,267,972**	**43,303**	**367,824**	**R**	**40.7**	**57.3**	**2.0**				**100.0**	**100.0**	**100.0**	**100.0**

County	Total	Bayh (DEM)	Pearson (REP)	Other	Plurality Total	Party	DEM	REP	Other	Rank DEM	Rank REP	Rank Other	Total	DEM	REP	Other
Adams	12,602	7,906	4,533	163	3,373	D	62.7	36.0	1.3	30	65	42	0.6	0.6	0.6	0.7
Allen	118,506	71,007	46,056	1,443	24,951	D	59.9	38.9	1.2	46	44	47	5.3	5.1	5.6	5.9
Bartholomew	26,832	16,355	10,183	294	6,172	D	61.0	38.0	1.1	40	54	51	1.2	1.2	1.2	1.2
Benton	4,281	2,457	1,743	81	714	D	57.4	40.7	1.9	64	33	8	0.2	0.2	0.2	0.3
Blackford	5,651	3,770	1,807	74	1,963	D	66.7	32.0	1.3	18	76	39	0.3	0.3	0.2	0.3
Boone	16,991	8,568	8,365	58	203	D	50.4	49.2	0.3	88	3	81	0.8	0.6	1.0	0.2
Brown	6,097	3,941	2,094	62	1,847	D	64.6	34.3	1.0	25	69	55	0.3	0.3	0.3	0.3
Carroll	8,435	4,919	3,474	42	1,445	D	58.3	41.2	0.5	58	29	70	0.4	0.4	0.4	0.2
Cass	15,702	8,932	6,720	50	2,212	D	56.9	42.8	0.3	68	22	84	0.7	0.6	0.8	0.2
Clark	33,330	23,825	9,384	121	14,441	D	71.5	28.2	0.4	4	87	78	1.5	1.7	1.1	0.5
Clay	10,080	6,744	3,230	106	3,514	D	66.9	32.0	1.1	17	75	53	0.5	0.5	0.4	0.4
Clinton	12,029	5,309	6,640	80	1,331	R	44.1	55.2	0.7	92	1	62	0.5	0.4	0.8	0.3
Crawford	4,782	3,005	1,765	12	1,240	D	62.8	36.9	0.3	29	58	88	0.2	0.2	0.2	<.1
Daviess	10,260	5,755	4,439	66	1,316	D	56.1	43.3	0.6	72	17	64	0.5	0.4	0.5	0.3
Dearborn	14,069	7,699	6,265	105	1,434	D	54.7	44.5	0.7	79	12	60	0.6	0.6	0.8	0.4
Decatur	10,200	6,328	3,713	159	2,615	D	62.0	36.4	1.6	35	60	24	0.5	0.5	0.5	0.7
De Kalb	13,981	7,565	6,357	59	1,208	D	54.1	45.5	0.4	83	10	75	0.6	0.5	0.8	0.2
Delaware	49,656	32,802	15,932	922	16,870	D	66.1	32.1	1.9	19	74	9	2.2	2.4	1.9	3.8
Dubois	15,070	9,884	5,151	35	4,733	D	65.6	34.2	0.2	21	70	89	0.7	0.7	0.6	0.1
Elkhart	51,569	28,271	22,616	682	5,655	D	54.8	43.9	1.3	78	16	37	2.3	2.0	2.7	2.8
Fayette	10,080	6,257	3,778	45	2,479	D	62.1	37.5	0.4	34	57	73	0.5	0.5	0.5	0.2
Floyd	27,892	18,956	8,875	61	10,081	D	68.0	31.8	0.2	14	77	90	1.3	1.4	1.1	0.2
Fountain	8,347	4,989	3,215	143	1,774	D	59.8	38.5	1.7	47	50	14	0.4	0.4	0.4	0.6
Franklin	7,693	4,564	2,974	155	1,590	D	59.3	38.7	2.0	51	46	4	0.3	0.3	0.4	0.6
Fulton	8,434	4,877	3,428	129	1,449	D	57.8	40.6	1.5	61	34	25	0.4	0.4	0.4	0.5
Gibson	14,147	9,832	4,153	162	5,679	D	69.5	29.4	1.1	9	85	50	0.6	0.7	0.5	0.7
Grant	27,902	16,566	11,043	293	5,523	D	59.4	39.6	1.1	50	39	54	1.3	1.2	1.3	1.2
Greene	13,081	8,594	4,440	47	4,154	D	65.7	33.9	0.4	20	71	79	0.6	0.6	0.5	0.2
Hamilton	54,125	27,499	26,040	586	1,459	D	50.8	48.1	1.1	87	6	52	2.4	2.0	3.2	2.4
Hancock	20,386	11,434	8,604	348	2,830	D	56.1	42.2	1.7	73	27	15	0.9	0.8	1.0	1.4
Harrison	13,524	9,581	3,726	217	5,855	D	70.8	27.6	1.6	6	89	20	0.6	0.7	0.5	0.9
Hendricks	32,301	16,453	15,412	436	1,041	D	50.9	47.7	1.3	86	7	33	1.4	1.2	1.9	1.8
Henry	19,806	12,323	7,174	309	5,149	D	62.2	36.2	1.6	33	63	23	0.9	0.9	0.9	1.3
Howard	33,011	19,824	12,730	457	7,094	D	60.1	38.6	1.4	45	48	31	1.5	1.4	1.5	1.9
Huntington	15,354	8,455	6,756	143	1,699	D	55.1	44.0	0.9	77	14	57	0.7	0.6	0.8	0.6
Jackson	15,323	9,352	5,919	52	3,433	D	61.0	38.6	0.3	39	47	82	0.7	0.7	0.7	0.2
Jasper	9,580	4,671	4,781	128	110	R	48.8	49.9	1.3	91	2	34	0.4	0.3	0.6	0.5
Jay	8,697	5,413	3,147	137	2,266	D	62.2	36.2	1.6	31	64	22	0.4	0.4	0.4	0.6
Jefferson	12,559	7,637	4,841	81	2,796	D	60.8	38.5	0.6	41	49	63	0.6	0.6	0.6	0.3
Jennings	9,762	5,399	4,292	71	1,107	D	55.3	44.0	0.7	76	15	61	0.4	0.4	0.5	0.3
Johnson	36,657	20,391	15,587	679	4,804	D	55.6	42.5	1.9	75	26	10	1.6	1.5	1.9	2.8
Knox	16,564	10,264	6,109	191	4,155	D	62.0	36.9	1.2	36	59	49	0.7	0.7	0.7	0.8
Kosciusko	24,462	12,258	11,897	307	361	D	50.1	48.6	1.3	90	4	46	1.1	0.9	1.4	1.3
Lagrange	7,230	3,936	3,291	3	645	D	54.4	45.5	<.1	81	9	92	0.3	0.3	0.4	<.1
Lake	178,945	122,861	53,720	2,364	69,141	D	68.7	30.0	1.3	12	82	38	8.0	8.9	6.5	9.7
La Porte	41,192	26,963	13,547	682	13,416	D	65.5	32.9	1.7	22	73	17	1.8	2.0	1.6	2.8
Lawrence	16,215	9,418	6,650	147	2,768	D	58.1	41.0	0.9	59	31	58	0.7	0.7	0.8	0.6
Madison	58,462	38,130	19,294	1,038	18,836	D	65.2	33.0	1.8	23	72	13	2.6	2.8	2.3	4.2
Marion	308,491	189,575	117,400	1,516	72,175	D	61.5	38.1	0.5	38	53	71	13.8	13.7	14.3	6.2
Marshall	15,914	9,007	6,844	63	2,163	D	56.6	43.0	0.4	70	19	77	0.7	0.7	0.8	0.3
Martin	5,291	3,354	1,918	19	1,436	D	63.4	36.3	0.4	27	62	80	0.2	0.2	0.2	<.1
Miami	13,292	7,586	5,652	54	1,934	D	57.1	42.5	0.4	66	25	76	0.6	0.5	0.7	0.2
Monroe	41,893	28,193	12,834	866	15,359	D	67.3	30.6	2.1	16	80	2	1.9	2.0	1.6	3.5
Montgomery	14,368	7,859	6,216	293	1,643	D	54.7	43.3	2.0	80	18	3	0.6	0.6	0.8	1.2
Morgan	20,540	10,325	9,911	304	414	D	50.3	48.3	1.5	89	5	26	0.9	0.7	1.2	1.2
Newton	5,275	2,776	2,394	105	382	D	52.6	45.4	2.0	84	11	6	0.2	0.2	0.3	0.4
Noble	13,354	7,717	5,451	186	2,266	D	57.8	40.8	1.4	62	32	30	0.6	0.6	0.7	0.8
Ohio	2,454	1,449	957	48	492	D	59.0	39.0	2.0	55	43	7	0.1	0.1	0.1	0.2
Orange	7,915	4,294	3,513	108	781	D	54.3	44.4	1.4	82	13	32	0.4	0.3	0.4	0.4
Owen	6,382	3,972	2,319	91	1,653	D	62.2	36.3	1.4	32	61	28	0.3	0.3	0.3	0.4
Parke	7,056	4,445	2,497	114	1,948	D	63.0	35.4	1.6	28	66	19	0.3	0.3	0.3	0.5
Perry	9,189	6,338	2,827	24	3,511	D	69.0	30.8	0.3	11	79	87	0.4	0.5	0.3	<.1
Pike	6,314	4,264	1,969	81	2,295	D	67.5	31.2	1.3	15	78	44	0.3	0.3	0.2	0.3
Porter	56,322	33,533	21,658	1,131	11,875	D	59.5	38.5	2.0	49	51	5	2.5	2.4	2.6	4.6
Posey	11,343	7,827	3,324	192	4,503	D	69.0	29.3	1.7	10	86	16	0.5	0.6	0.4	0.8
Pulaski	5,705	3,383	2,306	16	1,077	D	59.3	40.4	0.3	52	35	86	0.3	0.3	0.3	<.1
Putnam	11,605	6,797	4,653	155	2,144	D	58.6	40.1	1.3	57	37	35	0.5	0.5	0.6	0.6
Randolph	11,681	6,861	4,612	208	2,249	D	58.7	39.5	1.8	56	40	12	0.5	0.5	0.6	0.9
Ripley	10,281	5,828	4,401	52	1,427	D	56.7	42.8	0.5	69	21	69	0.5	0.4	0.5	0.2
Rush	7,940	4,745	3,100	95	1,645	D	59.8	39.0	1.2	48	42	48	0.4	0.3	0.4	0.4

County	Total	Bayh (DEM)	Pearson (REP)	Other	Plurality Total	Party	DEM	REP	Other	Rank DEM	Rank REP	Rank Other	Total	DEM	REP	Other
St. Joseph	99,212	69,742	29,164	306	40,578	D	70.3	29.4	0.3	7	84	85	4.5	5.0	3.5	1.3
Scott	6,713	4,694	1,990	29	2,704	D	69.9	29.6	0.4	8	83	74	0.3	0.3	0.2	0.1
Shelby	15,785	9,322	6,324	139	2,998	D	59.1	40.1	0.9	54	38	59	0.7	0.7	0.8	0.6
Spencer	9,266	5,695	3,561	10	2,134	D	61.5	38.4	0.1	37	52	91	0.4	0.4	0.4	< .1
Starke	8,226	5,322	2,855	49	2,467	D	64.7	34.7	0.6	24	68	65	0.4	0.4	0.3	0.2
Steuben	10,965	6,201	4,706	58	1,495	D	56.6	42.9	0.5	71	20	67	0.5	0.4	0.6	0.2
Sullivan	8,692	6,488	2,159	45	4,329	D	74.6	24.8	0.5	2	90	68	0.4	0.5	0.3	0.2
Switzerland	3,039	1,950	1,075	14	875	D	64.2	35.4	0.5	26	67	72	0.1	0.1	0.1	< .1
Tippecanoe	49,482	29,840	18,742	900	11,098	D	60.3	37.9	1.8	44	55	11	2.2	2.2	2.3	3.7
Tipton	7,683	4,450	3,157	76	1,293	D	57.9	41.1	1.0	60	30	56	0.3	0.3	0.4	0.3
Union	2,832	1,457	1,339	36	118	D	51.4	47.3	1.3	85	8	45	0.1	0.1	0.2	0.1
Vanderburgh	75,004	53,240	20,782	982	32,458	D	71.0	27.7	1.3	5	88	40	3.4	3.9	2.5	4.0
Vermillion	7,797	5,924	1,746	127	4,178	D	76.0	22.4	1.6	1	92	18	0.3	0.4	0.2	0.5
Vigo	41,600	31,036	10,030	534	21,006	D	74.6	24.1	1.3	3	91	43	1.9	2.2	1.2	2.2
Wabash	14,250	8,124	6,080	46	2,044	D	57.0	42.7	0.3	67	24	83	0.6	0.6	0.7	0.2
Warren	3,885	2,359	1,471	55	888	D	60.7	37.9	1.4	43	56	29	0.2	0.2	0.2	0.2
Warrick	20,453	13,951	6,202	300	7,749	D	68.2	30.3	1.5	13	81	27	0.9	1.0	0.8	1.2
Washington	9,359	5,685	3,619	55	2,066	D	60.7	38.7	0.6	42	45	66	0.4	0.4	0.4	0.2
Wayne	26,714	15,261	11,106	347	4,155	D	57.1	41.6	1.3	65	28	41	1.2	1.1	1.4	1.4
Wells	11,964	6,694	5,111	159	1,583	D	56.0	42.7	1.3	74	23	36	0.5	0.5	0.6	0.7
White	9,819	5,800	3,862	157	1,938	D	59.1	39.3	1.6	53	41	21	0.4	0.4	0.5	0.6
Whitley	11,917	6,849	4,806	262	2,043	D	57.5	40.3	2.2	63	36	1	0.5	0.5	0.6	1.1
INDIANA	**2,229,116**	**1,382,151**	**822,533**	**24,432**	**559,618**	**D**	**62.0**	**36.9**	**1.1**				**100.0**	**100.0**	**100.0**	**100.0**

Table H. — Vote for U.S. Representative in Congress: November 3, 1992, General Election

Congressional district and county	Total	Democrat (DEM)	Republican (REP)	Other	Plurality Total	Party	Percent of total vote DEM	REP	Other	Rank within district DEM	REP	Other	Percent contribution to district vote Total	DEM	REP	Other
District 1	**211,824**	**147,054**	**64,770**	-	**82,284**	**D**	**69.4**	**30.6**	**-**				**100.0**	**100.0**	**100.0**	**-**
Lake (pt)	158,696	117,247	41,449	-	75,798	D	73.9	26.1	-	1	2	-	74.9	79.7	64.0	-
Porter (pt)	53,128	29,807	23,321	-	6,486	D	56.1	43.9	-	2	1	-	25.1	20.3	36.0	-
District 2	**229,295**	**130,881**	**90,593**	**7,821**	**40,288**	**D**	**57.1**	**39.5**	**3.4**				**100.0**	**100.0**	**100.0**	**100.0**
Bartholomew (pt)	22,953	12,018	10,223	712	1,795	D	52.4	44.5	3.1	11	2	7	10.0	9.2	11.3	9.1
Decatur	10,092	5,665	4,141	286	1,524	D	56.1	41.0	2.8	6	5	9	4.4	4.3	4.6	3.7
Delaware	49,758	31,593	16,558	1,607	15,035	D	63.5	33.3	3.2	1	11	6	21.7	24.1	18.3	20.5
Henry (pt)	18,051	10,634	6,804	613	3,830	D	58.9	37.7	3.4	5	8	5	7.9	8.1	7.5	7.8
Jay (pt)	7,364	4,594	2,549	221	2,045	D	62.4	34.6	3.0	2	10	8	3.2	3.5	2.8	2.8
Johnson (pt)	1,407	832	521	54	311	D	59.1	37.0	3.8	4	9	3	0.6	0.6	0.6	0.7
Madison	57,869	32,068	23,305	2,496	8,763	D	55.4	40.3	4.3	7	6	1	25.2	24.5	25.7	31.9
Randolph	11,681	6,932	4,418	331	2,514	D	59.3	37.8	2.8	3	7	10	5.1	5.3	4.9	4.2
Rush	7,833	4,150	3,413	270	737	D	53.0	43.6	3.4	9	3	4	3.4	3.2	3.8	3.5
Shelby	15,531	8,195	6,680	656	1,515	D	52.8	43.0	4.2	10	4	2	6.8	6.3	7.4	8.4
Wayne	26,756	14,200	11,981	575	2,219	D	53.1	44.8	2.1	8	1	11	11.7	10.8	13.2	7.4
District 3	**211,103**	**121,269**	**89,834**	**-**	**31,435**	**D**	**57.4**	**42.6**	**-**				**100.0**	**100.0**	**100.0**	**-**
Elkhart	51,624	23,218	28,406	-	5,188	R	45.0	55.0	-	4	2	-	24.5	19.1	31.6	-
Kosciusko (pt)	14,350	5,456	8,894	-	3,438	R	38.0	62.0	-	5	1	-	6.8	4.5	9.9	-
La Porte	41,669	26,634	15,035	-	11,599	D	63.9	36.1	-	2	4	-	19.7	22.0	16.7	-
St. Joseph	100,921	64,312	36,609	-	27,703	D	63.7	36.3	-	3	3	-	47.8	53.0	40.8	-
Starke (pt)	2,539	1,649	890	-	759	D	64.9	35.1	-	1	5	-	1.2	1.4	1.0	-
District 4	**217,375**	**134,907**	**82,468**	**-**	**52,439**	**D**	**62.1**	**37.9**	**-**				**100.0**	**100.0**	**100.0**	**-**
Adams	12,562	7,859	4,703	-	3,156	D	62.6	37.4	-	5	6	-	5.8	5.8	5.7	-
Allen	118,068	73,481	44,587	-	28,894	D	62.2	37.8	-	6	5	-	54.3	54.5	54.1	-
De Kalb	14,509	8,928	5,581	-	3,347	D	61.5	38.5	-	7	4	-	6.7	6.6	6.8	-
Huntington	15,409	8,342	7,067	-	1,275	D	54.1	45.9	-	10	1	-	7.1	6.2	8.6	-
Jay (pt)	1,347	859	488	-	371	D	63.8	36.2	-	4	7	-	0.6	0.6	0.6	-
Lagrange	7,300	4,468	2,832	-	1,636	D	61.2	38.8	-	8	3	-	3.4	3.3	3.4	-
Noble	13,369	8,733	4,636	-	4,097	D	65.3	34.7	-	2	9	-	6.2	6.5	5.6	-
Steuben	11,059	7,088	3,971	-	3,117	D	64.1	35.9	-	3	8	-	5.1	5.3	4.8	-
Wells	11,786	7,111	4,675	-	2,436	D	60.3	39.7	-	9	2	-	5.4	5.3	5.7	-
Whitley	11,966	8,038	3,928	-	4,110	D	67.2	32.8	-	1	10	-	5.5	6.0	4.8	-
District 5	**216,325**	**105,209**	**111,116**	**-**	**5,907**	**R**	**48.6**	**51.4**	**-**				**100.0**	**100.0**	**100.0**	**-**
Benton	4,307	2,132	2,175	-	43	R	49.5	50.5	-	9	11	-	2.0	2.0	2.0	-
Blackford	5,429	3,182	2,247	-	935	D	58.6	41.4	-	2	18	-	2.5	3.0	2.0	-
Carroll	8,289	3,881	4,408	-	527	R	46.8	53.2	-	13	7	-	3.8	3.7	4.0	-
Cass	15,946	7,845	8,101	-	256	R	49.2	50.8	-	11	9	-	7.4	7.5	7.3	-
Fulton	8,449	4,101	4,348	-	247	R	48.5	51.5	-	12	8	-	3.9	3.9	3.9	-
Grant	27,786	13,727	14,059	-	332	R	49.4	50.6	-	10	10	-	12.8	13.0	12.7	-
Howard	33,828	15,693	18,135	-	2,442	R	46.4	53.6	-	14	6	-	15.6	14.9	16.3	-
Jasper	9,576	4,357	5,219	-	862	R	45.5	54.5	-	15	5	-	4.4	4.1	4.7	-
Kosciusko (pt)	9,854	4,352	5,502	-	1,150	R	44.2	55.8	-	18	2	-	4.6	4.1	5.0	-
Lake (pt)	16,405	9,120	7,285	-	1,835	D	55.6	44.4	-	4	16	-	7.6	8.7	6.6	-
Marshall	15,802	7,001	8,801	-	1,800	R	44.3	55.7	-	17	3	-	7.3	6.7	7.9	-
Miami	13,362	6,073	7,289	-	1,216	R	45.4	54.6	-	16	4	-	6.2	5.8	6.6	-
Newton	5,281	2,822	2,459	-	363	D	53.4	46.6	-	6	14	-	2.4	2.7	2.2	-
Porter (pt)	2,093	1,254	839	-	415	D	59.9	40.1	-	1	19	-	1.0	1.2	0.8	-
Pulaski	5,751	2,999	2,752	-	247	D	52.1	47.9	-	7	13	-	2.7	2.9	2.5	-
Starke (pt)	5,651	3,276	2,375	-	901	D	58.0	42.0	-	3	17	-	2.6	3.1	2.1	-
Wabash	14,428	6,211	8,217	-	2,006	R	43.0	57.0	-	19	1	-	6.7	5.9	7.4	-
Warren	3,957	2,151	1,806	-	345	D	54.4	45.6	-	5	15	-	1.8	2.0	1.6	-
White	10,131	5,032	5,099	-	67	R	49.7	50.3	-	8	12	-	4.7	4.8	4.6	-
District 6	**258,455**	**71,952**	**186,499**	**4**	**114,547**	**R**	**27.8**	**72.2**	**<.1**				**100.0**	**100.0**	**100.0**	**100.0**
Boone (pt)	5,707	1,396	4,311	0	2,915	R	24.5	75.5	0.0	8	2	3	2.2	1.9	2.3	0.0
Clinton	11,680	4,107	7,573	0	3,466	R	35.2	64.8	0.0	1	9	4	4.5	5.7	4.1	0.0
Hamilton	52,550	11,241	41,309	0	30,068	R	21.4	78.6	0.0	9	1	5	20.3	15.6	22.1	0.0
Hancock	20,020	5,508	14,512	0	9,004	R	27.5	72.5	0.0	7	3	6	7.7	7.7	7.8	0.0
Henry (pt)	1,599	459	1,140	0	681	R	28.7	71.3	0.0	5	5	7	0.6	0.6	0.6	0.0
Johnson (pt)	34,979	9,960	25,019	0	15,059	R	28.5	71.5	0.0	6	4	8	13.5	13.8	13.4	0.0
Marion (pt)	120,184	35,699	84,482	3	48,783	R	29.7	70.3	<.1	4	6	2	46.5	49.6	45.3	75.0
Morgan (pt)	4,379	1,345	3,033	1	1,688	R	30.7	69.3	<.1	2	8	1	1.7	1.9	1.6	25.0
Tipton	7,357	2,237	5,120	0	2,883	R	30.4	69.6	0.0	3	7	9	2.8	3.1	2.7	0.0
District 7	**217,194**	**88,005**	**129,189**	**-**	**41,184**	**R**	**40.5**	**59.5**	**-**				**100.0**	**100.0**	**100.0**	**-**
Boone (pt)	10,764	3,721	7,043	-	3,322	R	34.6	65.4	-	11	3	-	5.0	4.2	5.5	-
Clay	9,982	4,526	5,456	-	930	R	45.3	54.7	-	5	9	-	4.6	5.1	4.2	-
Fountain	8,287	3,989	4,298	-	309	R	48.1	51.9	-	3	11	-	3.8	4.5	3.3	-
Hendricks	31,401	8,926	22,475	-	13,549	R	28.4	71.6	-	13	1	-	14.5	10.1	17.4	-
Monroe (pt)	8,480	2,973	5,507	-	2,534	R	35.1	64.9	-	10	4	-	3.9	3.4	4.3	-
Montgomery	14,304	5,240	9,064	-	3,824	R	36.6	63.4	-	9	5	-	6.6	6.0	7.0	-
Morgan (pt)	15,337	4,467	10,870	-	6,403	R	29.1	70.9	-	12	2	-	7.1	5.1	8.4	-

Congressional district and county	Total	Democrat (DEM)	Republican (REP)	Other	Plurality Total	Plurality Party	Percent of total vote DEM	Percent of total vote REP	Percent of total vote Other	Rank within district DEM	Rank within district REP	Rank within district Other	Percent contribution to district vote Total	Percent contribution to district vote DEM	Percent contribution to district vote REP	Percent contribution to district vote Other
District 7 (cont)																
Owen	6,234	2,499	3,735	-	1,236	R	40.1	59.9	-	7	7	-	2.9	2.8	2.9	-
Parke	7,036	3,350	3,686	-	336	R	47.6	52.4	-	4	10	-	3.2	3.8	2.9	-
Putnam	11,757	4,668	7,089	-	2,421	R	39.7	60.3	-	8	6	-	5.4	5.3	5.5	-
Tippecanoe	48,758	20,756	28,002	-	7,246	R	42.6	57.4	-	6	8	-	22.4	23.6	21.7	-
Vermillion	3,389	1,800	1,589	-	211	D	53.1	46.9	-	1	13	-	1.6	2.0	1.2	-
Vigo	41,465	21,090	20,375	-	715	D	50.9	49.1	-	2	12	-	19.1	24.0	15.8	-
District 8	238,397	125,244	108,054	5,099	17,190	D	52.5	45.3	2.1				100.0	100.0	100.0	100.0
Daviess	10,366	5,008	5,142	216	134	R	48.3	49.6	2.1	10	4	6	4.3	4.0	4.8	4.2
Gibson	14,647	8,270	6,119	258	2,151	D	56.5	41.8	1.8	4	10	10	6.1	6.6	5.7	5.1
Greene	13,236	7,286	5,595	355	1,691	D	55.0	42.3	2.7	5	9	2	5.6	5.8	5.2	7.0
Knox	16,654	7,616	8,707	331	1,091	R	45.7	52.3	2.0	11	3	9	7.0	6.1	8.1	6.5
Lawrence	15,935	7,185	8,407	343	1,222	R	45.1	52.8	2.2	12	1	4	6.7	5.7	7.8	6.7
Martin	5,246	3,094	2,119	33	975	D	59.0	40.4	0.6	3	11	11	2.2	2.5	2.0	0.6
Monroe (pt)	32,267	16,745	14,153	1,369	2,592	D	51.9	43.9	4.2	9	8	1	13.5	13.4	13.1	26.8
Orange	7,828	3,524	4,104	200	580	R	45.0	52.4	2.6	13	2	3	3.3	2.8	3.8	3.9
Pike	6,298	3,878	2,294	126	1,584	D	61.6	36.4	2.0	1	13	8	2.6	3.1	2.1	2.5
Posey	11,316	5,915	5,389	12	526	D	52.3	47.6	0.1	8	5	13	4.7	4.7	5.0	0.2
Sullivan	8,327	5,115	3,034	178	2,081	D	61.4	36.4	2.1	2	12	5	3.5	4.1	2.8	3.5
Vanderburgh	76,289	40,620	34,089	1,580	6,531	D	53.2	44.7	2.1	7	6	7	32.0	32.4	31.5	31.0
Warrick	19,988	10,988	8,902	98	2,086	D	55.0	44.5	0.5	6	7	12	8.4	8.8	8.2	1.9
District 9	231,037	160,980	70,057	-	90,923	D	69.7	30.3	-				100.0	100.0	100.0	-
Bartholomew (pt)	3,516	2,346	1,170	-	1,176	D	66.7	33.3	-	13	9	-	1.5	1.5	1.7	-
Brown	6,057	3,984	2,073	-	1,911	D	65.8	34.2	-	15	7	-	2.6	2.5	3.0	-
Clark	34,737	26,371	8,366	-	18,005	D	75.9	24.1	-	2	20	-	15.0	16.4	11.9	-
Crawford	4,572	3,178	1,394	-	1,784	D	69.5	30.5	-	7	15	-	2.0	2.0	2.0	-
Dearborn	14,805	9,228	5,577	-	3,651	D	62.3	37.7	-	19	3	-	6.4	5.7	8.0	-
Dubois	14,780	10,129	4,651	-	5,478	D	68.5	31.5	-	11	11	-	6.4	6.3	6.6	-
Fayette	10,147	6,983	3,164	-	3,819	D	68.8	31.2	-	10	12	-	4.4	4.3	4.5	-
Floyd	28,620	21,529	7,091	-	14,438	D	75.2	24.8	-	4	18	-	12.4	13.4	10.1	-
Franklin	8,009	4,595	3,414	-	1,181	D	57.4	42.6	-	21	1	-	3.5	2.9	4.9	-
Harrison	13,471	9,599	3,872	-	5,727	D	71.3	28.7	-	6	16	-	5.8	6.0	5.5	-
Jackson	15,531	10,632	4,899	-	5,733	D	68.5	31.5	-	12	10	-	6.7	6.6	7.0	-
Jefferson	12,546	9,087	3,459	-	5,628	D	72.4	27.6	-	5	17	-	5.4	5.6	4.9	-
Jennings	9,740	6,225	3,515	-	2,710	D	63.9	36.1	-	17	5	-	4.2	3.9	5.0	-
Ohio	2,474	1,705	769	-	936	D	68.9	31.1	-	9	13	-	1.1	1.1	1.1	-
Perry	8,919	6,743	2,176	-	4,567	D	75.6	24.4	-	3	19	-	3.9	4.2	3.1	-
Ripley	10,537	6,540	3,997	-	2,543	D	62.1	37.9	-	20	2	-	4.6	4.1	5.7	-
Scott	7,523	5,759	1,764	-	3,995	D	76.6	23.4	-	1	21	-	3.3	3.6	2.5	-
Spencer	9,239	5,802	3,437	-	2,365	D	62.8	37.2	-	18	4	-	4.0	3.6	4.9	-
Switzerland	3,181	2,194	987	-	1,207	D	69.0	31.0	-	8	14	-	1.4	1.4	1.4	-
Union	2,882	1,865	1,017	-	848	D	64.7	35.3	-	16	6	-	1.2	1.2	1.5	-
Washington	9,751	6,486	3,265	-	3,221	D	66.5	33.5	-	14	8	-	4.2	4.0	4.7	-
District 10	183,831	117,604	64,378	1,849	53,226	D	64.0	35.0	1.0				100.0	100.0	100.0	100.0
Marion (pt)	183,831	117,604	64,378	1,849	53,226	D	64.0	35.0	1.0	1	1	1	100.0	100.0	100.0	100.0
INDIANA	2,214,836	1,203,105	996,958	14,773	206,147	D	54.3	45.0	0.7							

Table I. — Vote for Presidential Preference: May 5, 1992, Democratic Primary Election

County	Total	Clinton	Brown	Tsongas	Kerrey					Clinton	Brown	Tsongas	Rank Clinton	Rank Brown	Rank Tsongas	Total	Clinton	Brown	Tsongas
Adams	3,249	1,963	727	428	131	-	-	-	-	60.4	22.4	13.2	81	17	32	0.7	0.7	0.7	0.7
Allen	17,220	9,397	5,436	1,956	431	-	-	-	-	54.6	31.6	11.4	91	3	67	3.6	3.1	5.3	3.4
Bartholomew	4,153	2,684	779	560	130	-	-	-	-	64.6	18.8	13.5	57	39	22	0.9	0.9	0.8	1.0
Benton	544	355	92	75	22	-	-	-	-	65.3	16.9	13.8	50	59	18	0.1	0.1	< .1	0.1
Blackford	1,662	1,061	328	234	39	-	-	-	-	63.8	19.7	14.1	62	31	13	0.3	0.4	0.3	0.4
Boone	1,553	936	322	241	54	-	-	-	-	60.3	20.7	15.5	82	25	5	0.3	0.3	0.3	0.4
Brown	1,586	900	401	241	44	-	-	-	-	56.7	25.3	15.2	89	5	7	0.3	0.3	0.4	0.4
Carroll	1,416	994	210	154	58	-	-	-	-	70.2	14.8	10.9	12	83	78	0.3	0.3	0.2	0.3
Cass	3,114	1,912	728	344	130	-	-	-	-	61.4	23.4	11.0	78	10	73	0.7	0.6	0.7	0.6
Clark	13,798	9,970	2,182	1,386	260	-	-	-	-	72.3	15.8	10.0	8	72	85	2.9	3.3	2.1	2.4
Clay	2,664	1,777	451	336	100	-	-	-	-	66.7	16.9	12.6	38	57	43	0.6	0.6	0.4	0.6
Clinton	1,800	1,229	288	221	62	-	-	-	-	68.3	16.0	12.3	25	70	50	0.4	0.4	0.3	0.4
Crawford	1,953	1,456	241	178	78	-	-	-	-	74.6	12.3	9.1	2	90	91	0.4	0.5	0.2	0.3
Daviess	1,917	1,242	395	232	48	-	-	-	-	64.8	20.6	12.1	54	26	53	0.4	0.4	0.4	0.4
Dearborn	2,643	1,761	440	348	94	-	-	-	-	66.6	16.6	13.2	40	61	33	0.6	0.6	0.4	0.6
Decatur	1,269	795	240	182	52	-	-	-	-	62.6	18.9	14.3	73	37	10	0.3	0.3	0.2	0.3
De Kalb	2,519	1,591	588	267	73	-	-	-	-	63.2	23.3	10.6	68	11	81	0.5	0.5	0.6	0.5
Delaware	13,828	9,077	2,644	1,603	504	-	-	-	-	65.6	19.1	11.6	46	36	64	2.9	3.0	2.6	2.8
Dubois	5,348	3,298	1,146	745	159	-	-	-	-	61.7	21.4	13.9	77	23	17	1.1	1.1	1.1	1.3
Elkhart	5,799	3,525	1,325	796	153	-	-	-	-	60.8	22.8	13.7	80	14	20	1.2	1.2	1.3	1.4
Fayette	2,439	1,640	454	289	56	-	-	-	-	67.2	18.6	11.8	31	43	57	0.5	0.5	0.4	0.5
Floyd	7,100	4,871	1,237	834	158	-	-	-	-	68.6	17.4	11.7	21	54	60	1.5	1.6	1.2	1.4
Fountain	1,375	960	198	178	39	-	-	-	-	69.8	14.4	12.9	16	85	35	0.3	0.3	0.2	0.3
Franklin	1,977	1,338	269	282	88	-	-	-	-	67.7	13.6	14.3	27	88	11	0.4	0.4	0.3	0.5
Fulton	1,326	875	219	185	47	-	-	-	-	66.0	16.5	14.0	45	64	15	0.3	0.3	0.2	0.3
Gibson	4,329	2,885	701	556	187	-	-	-	-	66.6	16.2	12.8	39	68	36	0.9	1.0	0.7	1.0
Grant	4,485	2,940	901	512	132	-	-	-	-	65.6	20.1	11.4	49	30	66	0.9	1.0	0.9	0.9
Greene	3,864	2,695	600	422	147	-	-	-	-	69.7	15.5	10.9	17	75	77	0.8	0.9	0.6	0.7
Hamilton	3,460	1,982	784	608	86	-	-	-	-	57.3	22.7	17.6	87	16	1	0.7	0.7	0.8	1.0
Hancock	2,247	1,395	393	298	161	-	-	-	-	62.1	17.5	13.3	76	53	29	0.5	0.5	0.4	0.5
Harrison	4,900	3,310	778	635	177	-	-	-	-	67.6	15.9	13.0	28	71	34	1.0	1.1	0.8	1.1
Hendricks	2,847	1,699	625	433	90	-	-	-	-	59.7	22.0	15.2	83	21	6	0.6	0.6	0.6	0.7
Henry	4,273	2,858	763	527	125	-	-	-	-	66.9	17.9	12.3	35	51	49	0.9	0.9	0.7	0.9
Howard	6,444	4,157	1,265	788	234	-	-	-	-	64.5	19.6	12.2	58	32	51	1.4	1.4	1.2	1.4
Huntington	2,080	1,355	465	194	66	-	-	-	-	65.1	22.4	9.3	51	18	89	0.4	0.4	0.5	0.3
Jackson	3,810	2,552	686	475	97	-	-	-	-	67.0	18.0	12.5	33	50	45	0.8	0.8	0.7	0.8
Jasper	1,433	1,021	230	144	38	-	-	-	-	71.2	16.1	10.0	10	69	84	0.3	0.3	0.2	0.2
Jay	2,001	1,405	308	225	63	-	-	-	-	70.2	15.4	11.2	11	76	70	0.4	0.5	0.3	0.4
Jefferson	3,734	2,594	608	451	81	-	-	-	-	69.5	16.3	12.1	18	66	54	0.8	0.9	0.6	0.8
Jennings	2,605	1,725	456	331	93	-	-	-	-	66.2	17.5	12.7	43	52	40	0.5	0.6	0.4	0.6
Johnson	3,877	2,311	918	512	136	-	-	-	-	59.6	23.7	13.2	84	7	30	0.8	0.8	0.9	0.9
Knox	5,727	3,644	1,046	802	235	-	-	-	-	63.6	18.3	14.0	64	48	14	1.2	1.2	1.0	1.4
Kosciusko	2,197	1,372	450	294	81	-	-	-	-	62.4	20.5	13.4	75	27	25	0.5	0.5	0.4	0.5
Lagrange	1,061	684	200	134	43	-	-	-	-	64.5	18.9	12.6	59	38	42	0.2	0.2	0.2	0.2
Lake	72,374	47,819	14,797	7,797	1,961	-	-	-	-	66.1	20.4	10.8	44	28	80	15.2	15.8	14.5	13.4
La Porte	12,023	7,674	2,420	1,600	329	-	-	-	-	63.8	20.1	13.3	63	29	27	2.5	2.5	2.4	2.7
Lawrence	2,460	1,683	451	266	60	-	-	-	-	68.4	18.3	10.8	23	47	79	0.5	0.6	0.4	0.5
Madison	14,168	9,488	2,578	1,680	422	-	-	-	-	67.0	18.2	11.9	34	49	56	3.0	3.1	2.5	2.9
Marion	52,049	28,998	16,521	5,506	1,024	-	-	-	-	55.7	31.7	10.6	90	2	82	10.9	9.6	16.1	9.5
Marshall	2,057	1,306	440	243	68	-	-	-	-	63.5	21.4	11.8	66	24	58	0.4	0.4	0.4	0.4
Martin	2,387	1,611	377	298	101	-	-	-	-	67.5	15.8	12.5	30	73	44	0.5	0.5	0.4	0.5
Miami	2,179	1,392	484	240	63	-	-	-	-	63.9	22.2	11.0	61	19	75	0.5	0.5	0.5	0.4
Monroe	8,063	3,395	3,197	1,317	154	-	-	-	-	42.1	39.7	16.3	92	1	3	1.7	1.1	3.1	2.3
Montgomery	1,548	993	289	213	53	-	-	-	-	64.1	18.7	13.8	60	41	19	0.3	0.3	0.3	0.4
Morgan	2,088	1,307	453	245	83	-	-	-	-	62.6	21.7	11.7	74	22	61	0.4	0.4	0.4	0.4
Newton	906	635	137	105	29	-	-	-	-	70.1	15.1	11.6	14	78	65	0.2	0.2	0.1	0.2
Noble	2,368	1,485	554	261	68	-	-	-	-	62.7	23.4	11.0	71	9	74	0.5	0.5	0.5	0.4
Ohio	454	343	51	45	15	-	-	-	-	75.6	11.2	9.9	1	92	87	< .1	0.1	< .1	< .1
Orange	1,450	1,048	206	149	47	-	-	-	-	72.3	14.2	10.3	7	87	83	0.3	0.3	0.2	0.3
Owen	1,810	1,171	334	242	63	-	-	-	-	64.7	18.5	13.4	55	44	26	0.4	0.4	0.3	0.4
Parke	1,706	1,169	254	219	64	-	-	-	-	68.5	14.9	12.8	22	82	37	0.4	0.4	0.2	0.4
Perry	4,887	3,310	796	608	173	-	-	-	-	67.7	16.3	12.4	26	65	47	1.0	1.1	0.8	1.0
Pike	2,261	1,505	367	303	86	-	-	-	-	66.6	16.2	13.4	41	67	24	0.5	0.5	0.4	0.5
Porter	11,056	6,493	2,594	1,615	354	-	-	-	-	58.7	23.5	14.6	86	8	9	2.3	2.2	2.5	2.8
Posey	2,515	1,636	378	393	108	-	-	-	-	65.0	15.0	15.6	53	79	4	0.5	0.5	0.4	0.7
Pulaski	1,132	778	212	113	29	-	-	-	-	68.7	18.7	10.0	20	40	86	0.2	0.3	0.2	0.2
Putnam	2,041	1,363	339	261	78	-	-	-	-	66.8	16.6	12.8	36	63	38	0.4	0.5	0.3	0.4
Randolph	1,632	1,190	243	155	44	-	-	-	-	72.9	14.9	9.5	5	81	88	0.3	0.4	0.2	0.3
Ripley	1,578	1,035	267	213	63	-	-	-	-	65.6	16.9	13.5	48	58	21	0.3	0.3	0.3	0.4
Rush	1,004	686	167	125	26	-	-	-	-	68.3	16.6	12.5	24	62	46	0.2	0.2	0.2	0.2

County	Top candidates										Top three candidates(state vote)									
											Percent of total vote						Percent contribution to state vote			
															Rank						
	Total	Clinton	Brown	Tsongas	Kerrey						Clinton	Brown	Tsongas	Clinton	Brown	Tsongas	Total	Clinton	Brown	Tsongas
St. Joseph	25,021	14,773	5,782	3,538	928	-	-	-	-		59.0	23.1	14.1	85	12	12	5.2	4.9	5.6	6.1
Scott	3,379	2,466	507	313	93	-	-	-	-		73.0	15.0	9.3	4	80	90	0.7	0.8	0.5	0.5
Shelby	2,588	1,722	482	302	82	-	-	-	-		66.5	18.6	11.7	42	42	62	0.5	0.6	0.5	0.5
Spencer	2,507	1,739	360	306	102	-	-	-	-		69.4	14.4	12.2	19	86	52	0.5	0.6	0.4	0.5
Starke	3,011	2,160	555	209	87	-	-	-	-		71.7	18.4	6.9	9	45	92	0.6	0.7	0.5	0.4
Steuben	1,406	860	359	154	33	-	-	-	-		61.2	25.5	11.0	79	4	76	0.3	0.3	0.4	0.3
Sullivan	3,729	2,518	585	495	131	-	-	-	-		67.5	15.7	13.3	29	74	28	0.8	0.8	0.6	0.9
Switzerland	1,404	1,022	177	165	40	-	-	-	-		72.8	12.6	11.8	6	89	59	0.3	0.3	0.2	0.3
Tippecanoe	6,832	3,889	1,573	1,173	197	-	-	-	-		56.9	23.0	17.2	88	13	2	1.4	1.3	1.5	2.0
Tipton	1,329	893	225	165	46	-	-	-	-		67.2	16.9	12.4	32	56	48	0.3	0.3	0.2	0.3
Union	365	255	53	49	8	-	-	-	-		69.9	14.5	13.4	15	84	23	<.1	<.1	<.1	<.1
Vanderburgh	10,436	6,751	2,046	1,320	319	-	-	-	-		64.7	19.6	12.6	56	33	41	2.2	2.2	2.0	2.3
Vermillion	3,732	2,490	627	477	138	-	-	-	-		66.7	16.8	12.8	37	60	39	0.8	0.8	0.6	0.8
Vigo	14,829	9,428	2,559	2,198	644	-	-	-	-		63.6	17.3	14.8	65	55	8	3.1	3.1	2.5	3.8
Wabash	3,095	1,960	747	343	45	-	-	-	-		63.3	24.1	11.1	67	6	72	0.6	0.6	0.7	0.6
Warren	637	468	77	72	20	-	-	-	-		73.5	12.1	11.3	3	91	68	0.1	0.2	<.1	0.1
Warrick	5,293	3,319	1,014	738	222	-	-	-	-		62.7	19.2	13.9	72	35	16	1.1	1.1	1.0	1.3
Washington	2,422	1,700	372	272	78	-	-	-	-		70.2	15.4	11.2	13	77	71	0.5	0.6	0.4	0.5
Wayne	3,236	2,123	622	388	103	-	-	-	-		65.6	19.2	12.0	47	34	55	0.7	0.7	0.6	0.7
Wells	2,000	1,256	454	226	64	-	-	-	-		62.8	22.7	11.3	70	15	69	0.4	0.4	0.4	0.4
White	1,591	1,036	293	210	52	-	-	-	-		65.1	18.4	13.2	52	46	31	0.3	0.3	0.3	0.4
Whitley	2,186	1,373	485	254	74	-	-	-	-		62.8	22.2	11.6	69	20	63	0.5	0.5	0.5	0.4
INDIANA	**476,850**	**301,905**	**102,377**	**58,215**	**14,353**	-	-	-	-		**63.3**	**21.5**	**12.2**				**100.0**	**100.0**	**100.0**	**100.0**

Table J. — Vote for Presidential Preference: May 5, 1992, Republican Primary Election

County	Top candidates					Top four candidates (state vote)												
						Percent of total vote								Percent contribution to state vote				
										Rank								
	Total	Bush	Bu-chanan			Bush	Bu-chanan			Bush	Bu-chanan			Total	Bush	Bu-chanan		
Adams	1,832	1,415	417	-	-	77.2	22.8	-	-	85	8	-	-	0.4	0.4	0.4	-	-
Allen	21,528	15,395	6,133	-	-	71.5	28.5	-	-	92	1	-	-	4.6	4.1	6.6	-	-
Bartholomew	6,373	5,252	1,121	-	-	82.4	17.6	-	-	31	62	-	-	1.4	1.4	1.2	-	-
Benton	1,413	1,097	316	-	-	77.6	22.4	-	-	82	11	-	-	0.3	0.3	0.3	-	-
Blackford	851	811	40	-	-	95.3	4.7	-	-	1	92	-	-	0.2	0.2	<.1	-	-
Boone	5,569	4,551	1,018	-	-	81.7	18.3	-	-	40	53	-	-	1.2	1.2	1.1	-	-
Brown	1,177	960	217	-	-	81.6	18.4	-	-	42	51	-	-	0.3	0.3	0.2	-	-
Carroll	2,315	1,865	450	-	-	80.6	19.4	-	-	58	35	-	-	0.5	0.5	0.5	-	-
Cass	4,265	3,391	874	-	-	79.5	20.5	-	-	66	27	-	-	0.9	0.9	0.9	-	-
Clark	3,486	2,931	555	-	-	84.1	15.9	-	-	16	77	-	-	0.7	0.8	0.6	-	-
Clay	2,017	1,669	348	-	-	82.7	17.3	-	-	28	65	-	-	0.4	0.4	0.4	-	-
Clinton	4,157	3,500	657	-	-	84.2	15.8	-	-	15	78	-	-	0.9	0.9	0.7	-	-
Crawford	743	638	105	-	-	85.9	14.1	-	-	6	87	-	-	0.2	0.2	0.1	-	-
Daviess	3,815	3,198	617	-	-	83.8	16.2	-	-	19	74	-	-	0.8	0.9	0.7	-	-
Dearborn	2,086	1,759	327	-	-	84.3	15.7	-	-	13	80	-	-	0.4	0.5	0.4	-	-
Decatur	2,180	1,842	338	-	-	84.5	15.5	-	-	11	82	-	-	0.5	0.5	0.4	-	-
De Kalb	4,623	3,506	1,117	-	-	75.8	24.2	-	-	88	5	-	-	1.0	0.9	1.2	-	-
Delaware	9,872	8,369	1,503	-	-	84.8	15.2	-	-	9	84	-	-	2.1	2.2	1.6	-	-
Dubois	1,555	1,312	243	-	-	84.4	15.6	-	-	12	81	-	-	0.3	0.4	0.3	-	-
Elkhart	12,314	9,906	2,408	-	-	80.4	19.6	-	-	60	33	-	-	2.6	2.6	2.6	-	-
Fayette	1,840	1,586	254	-	-	86.2	13.8	-	-	4	89	-	-	0.4	0.4	0.3	-	-
Floyd	3,064	2,570	494	-	-	83.9	16.1	-	-	18	75	-	-	0.7	0.7	0.5	-	-
Fountain	1,817	1,427	390	-	-	78.5	21.5	-	-	76	17	-	-	0.4	0.4	0.4	-	-
Franklin	1,500	1,253	247	-	-	83.5	16.5	-	-	22	71	-	-	0.3	0.3	0.3	-	-
Fulton	2,314	1,872	442	-	-	80.9	19.1	-	-	51	42	-	-	0.5	0.5	0.5	-	-
Gibson	1,277	1,030	247	-	-	80.7	19.3	-	-	56	37	-	-	0.3	0.3	0.3	-	-
Grant	6,490	5,399	1,091	-	-	83.2	16.8	-	-	23	70	-	-	1.4	1.4	1.2	-	-
Greene	2,741	2,243	498	-	-	81.8	18.2	-	-	39	54	-	-	0.6	0.6	0.5	-	-
Hamilton	21,148	17,233	3,915	-	-	81.5	18.5	-	-	43	50	-	-	4.5	4.6	4.2	-	-
Hancock	5,713	4,515	1,198	-	-	79.0	21.0	-	-	72	21	-	-	1.2	1.2	1.3	-	-
Harrison	2,110	1,751	359	-	-	83.0	17.0	-	-	25	68	-	-	0.5	0.5	0.4	-	-
Hendricks	10,768	8,535	2,233	-	-	79.3	20.7	-	-	69	24	-	-	2.3	2.3	2.4	-	-
Henry	5,014	4,223	791	-	-	84.2	15.8	-	-	14	79	-	-	1.1	1.1	0.9	-	-
Howard	7,409	6,002	1,407	-	-	81.0	19.0	-	-	49	44	-	-	1.6	1.6	1.5	-	-
Huntington	3,885	3,226	659	-	-	83.0	17.0	-	-	24	69	-	-	0.8	0.9	0.7	-	-
Jackson	2,626	2,176	450	-	-	82.9	17.1	-	-	26	67	-	-	0.6	0.6	0.5	-	-
Jasper	3,913	3,065	848	-	-	78.3	21.7	-	-	77	16	-	-	0.8	0.8	0.9	-	-
Jay	2,339	1,889	450	-	-	80.8	19.2	-	-	53	44	-	-	0.5	0.5	0.5	-	-
Jefferson	2,234	1,903	331	-	-	85.2	14.8	-	-	8	85	-	-	0.5	0.5	0.4	-	-
Jennings	2,553	2,102	451	-	-	82.3	17.7	-	-	33	60	-	-	0.5	0.6	0.5	-	-
Johnson	11,297	8,945	2,352	-	-	79.2	20.8	-	-	71	22	-	-	2.4	2.4	2.5	-	-
Knox	2,961	2,477	484	-	-	83.7	16.3	-	-	21	72	-	-	0.6	0.7	0.5	-	-
Kosciusko	7,032	5,596	1,436	-	-	79.6	20.4	-	-	64	29	-	-	1.5	1.5	1.5	-	-
Lagrange	2,456	1,984	472	-	-	80.8	19.2	-	-	52	41	-	-	0.5	0.5	0.5	-	-
Lake	15,138	12,219	2,919	-	-	80.7	19.3	-	-	54	39	-	-	3.2	3.3	3.1	-	-
La Porte	7,525	5,993	1,532	-	-	79.6	20.4	-	-	63	30	-	-	1.6	1.6	1.6	-	-
Lawrence	5,238	4,097	1,141	-	-	78.2	21.8	-	-	79	14	-	-	1.1	1.1	1.2	-	-
Madison	11,749	9,694	2,055	-	-	82.5	17.5	-	-	30	63	-	-	2.5	2.6	2.2	-	-
Marion	70,143	55,619	14,524	-	-	79.3	20.7	-	-	68	25	-	-	15.0	14.8	15.6	-	-
Marshall	3,899	3,191	708	-	-	81.8	18.2	-	-	38	55	-	-	0.8	0.9	0.8	-	-
Martin	1,083	916	167	-	-	84.6	15.4	-	-	10	83	-	-	0.2	0.2	0.2	-	-
Miami	3,566	2,818	748	-	-	79.0	21.0	-	-	73	20	-	-	0.8	0.8	0.8	-	-
Monroe	6,635	5,438	1,197	-	-	82.0	18.0	-	-	37	56	-	-	1.4	1.5	1.3	-	-
Montgomery	5,672	4,504	1,168	-	-	79.4	20.6	-	-	67	26	-	-	1.2	1.2	1.3	-	-
Morgan	7,197	5,595	1,602	-	-	77.7	22.3	-	-	81	12	-	-	1.5	1.5	1.7	-	-
Newton	2,301	1,723	578	-	-	74.9	25.1	-	-	89	4	-	-	0.5	0.5	0.6	-	-
Noble	3,135	2,386	749	-	-	76.1	23.9	-	-	87	6	-	-	0.7	0.6	0.8	-	-
Ohio	270	245	25	-	-	90.7	9.3	-	-	2	91	-	-	<.1	<.1	<.1	-	-
Orange	2,943	2,386	557	-	-	81.1	18.9	-	-	48	45	-	-	0.6	0.6	0.6	-	-
Owen	1,581	1,276	305	-	-	80.7	19.3	-	-	55	38	-	-	0.3	0.3	0.3	-	-
Parke	1,998	1,639	359	-	-	82.0	18.0	-	-	36	57	-	-	0.4	0.4	0.4	-	-
Perry	604	516	88	-	-	85.4	14.6	-	-	7	86	-	-	0.1	0.1	<.1	-	-
Pike	925	746	179	-	-	80.6	19.4	-	-	57	36	-	-	0.2	0.2	0.2	-	-
Porter	12,742	9,526	3,216	-	-	74.8	25.2	-	-	91	2	-	-	2.7	2.5	3.5	-	-
Posey	984	803	181	-	-	81.6	18.4	-	-	41	52	-	-	0.2	0.2	0.2	-	-
Pulaski	1,798	1,455	343	-	-	80.9	19.1	-	-	50	43	-	-	0.4	0.4	0.4	-	-
Putnam	3,219	2,550	669	-	-	79.2	20.8	-	-	70	23	-	-	0.7	0.7	0.7	-	-
Randolph	3,574	2,819	755	-	-	78.9	21.1	-	-	75	18	-	-	0.8	0.8	0.8	-	-
Ripley	1,765	1,477	288	-	-	83.7	16.3	-	-	20	73	-	-	0.4	0.4	0.3	-	-
Rush	2,907	2,386	521	-	-	82.1	17.9	-	-	35	58	-	-	0.6	0.6	0.6	-	-

Table J.   —   Vote for Presidential Preference: May 5, 1992, Republican Primary Election (cont)

County	Top candidates					Top four candidates (state vote)												
	Total	Bush	Bu-chanan			Percent of total vote								Percent contribution to state vote				
						Bush	Bu-chanan			Rank				Total	Bush	Bu-chanan		
										Bush	Bu-chanan							
St. Joseph	13,582	10,914	2,668	-	-	80.4	19.6	-	-	61	32	-	-	2.9	2.9	2.9	-	-
Scott	724	587	137	-	-	81.1	18.9	-	-	47	46	-	-	0.2	0.2	0.1	-	-
Shelby	3,286	2,706	580	-	-	82.3	17.7	-	-	32	61	-	-	0.7	0.7	0.6	-	-
Spencer	2,037	1,750	287	-	-	85.9	14.1	-	-	5	88	-	-	0.4	0.5	0.3	-	-
Starke	1,268	1,021	247	-	-	80.5	19.5	-	-	59	34	-	-	0.3	0.3	0.3	-	-
Steuben	3,595	2,812	783	-	-	78.2	21.8	-	-	78	15	-	-	0.8	0.8	0.8	-	-
Sullivan	1,011	804	207	-	-	79.5	20.5	-	-	65	28	-	-	0.2	0.2	0.2	-	-
Switzerland	408	354	54	-	-	86.8	13.2	-	-	3	90	-	-	<.1	<.1	<.1	-	-
Tippecanoe	12,798	10,110	2,688	-	-	79.0	21.0	-	-	74	19	-	-	2.7	2.7	2.9	-	-
Tipton	2,388	2,007	381	-	-	84.0	16.0	-	-	17	76	-	-	0.5	0.5	0.4	-	-
Union	1,241	994	247	-	-	80.1	19.9	-	-	62	31	-	-	0.3	0.3	0.3	-	-
Vanderburgh	7,097	5,875	1,222	-	-	82.8	17.2	-	-	27	66	-	-	1.5	1.6	1.3	-	-
Vermillion	532	413	119	-	-	77.6	22.4	-	-	83	10	-	-	0.1	0.1	0.1	-	-
Vigo	4,886	3,787	1,099	-	-	77.5	22.5	-	-	84	9	-	-	1.0	1.0	1.2	-	-
Wabash	6,359	5,181	1,178	-	-	81.5	18.5	-	-	44	49	-	-	1.4	1.4	1.3	-	-
Warren	915	699	216	-	-	76.4	23.6	-	-	86	7	-	-	0.2	0.2	0.2	-	-
Warrick	2,356	1,917	439	-	-	81.4	18.6	-	-	45	48	-	-	0.5	0.5	0.5	-	-
Washington	2,471	2,042	429	-	-	82.6	17.4	-	-	29	64	-	-	0.5	0.5	0.5	-	-
Wayne	7,355	6,049	1,306	-	-	82.2	17.8	-	-	34	59	-	-	1.6	1.6	1.4	-	-
Wells	2,373	1,851	522	-	-	78.0	22.0	-	-	80	13	-	-	0.5	0.5	0.6	-	-
White	2,608	2,116	492	-	-	81.1	18.9	-	-	46	47	-	-	0.6	0.6	0.5	-	-
Whitley	3,062	2,291	771	-	-	74.8	25.2	-	-	90	3	-	-	0.7	0.6	0.8	-	-
INDIANA	**467,615**	**374,666**	**92,949**	-	-	**80.1**	**19.9**	-	-					**100.0**	**100.0**	**100.0**	-	-

1992 Vote for President
Percent for Bush (R), by County

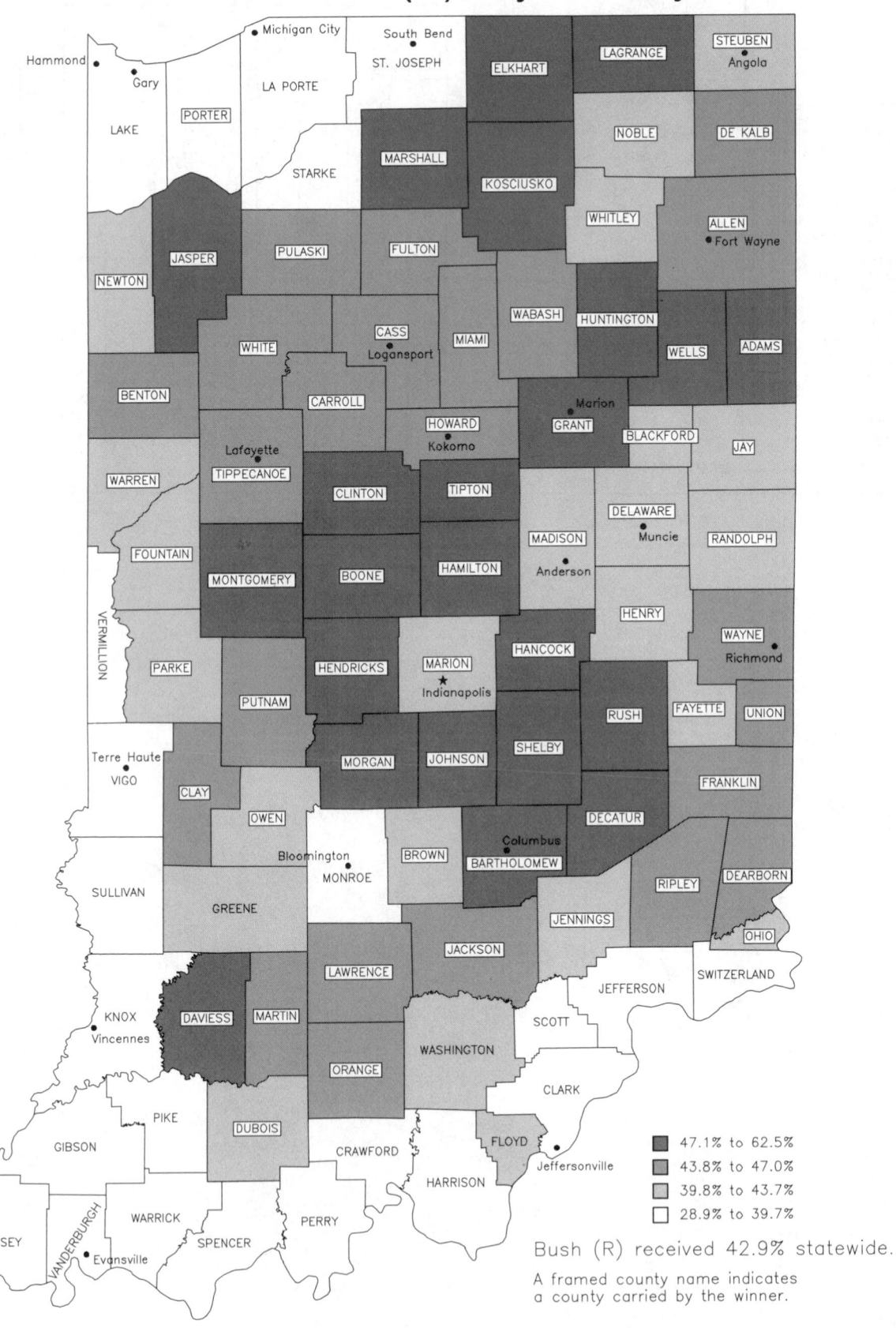

Bush (R) received 42.9% statewide.

A framed county name indicates
a county carried by the winner.

- 47.1% to 62.5%
- 43.8% to 47.0%
- 39.8% to 43.7%
- 28.9% to 39.7%

1992 Vote for U.S. Senator
Percent for Coats (R), by County

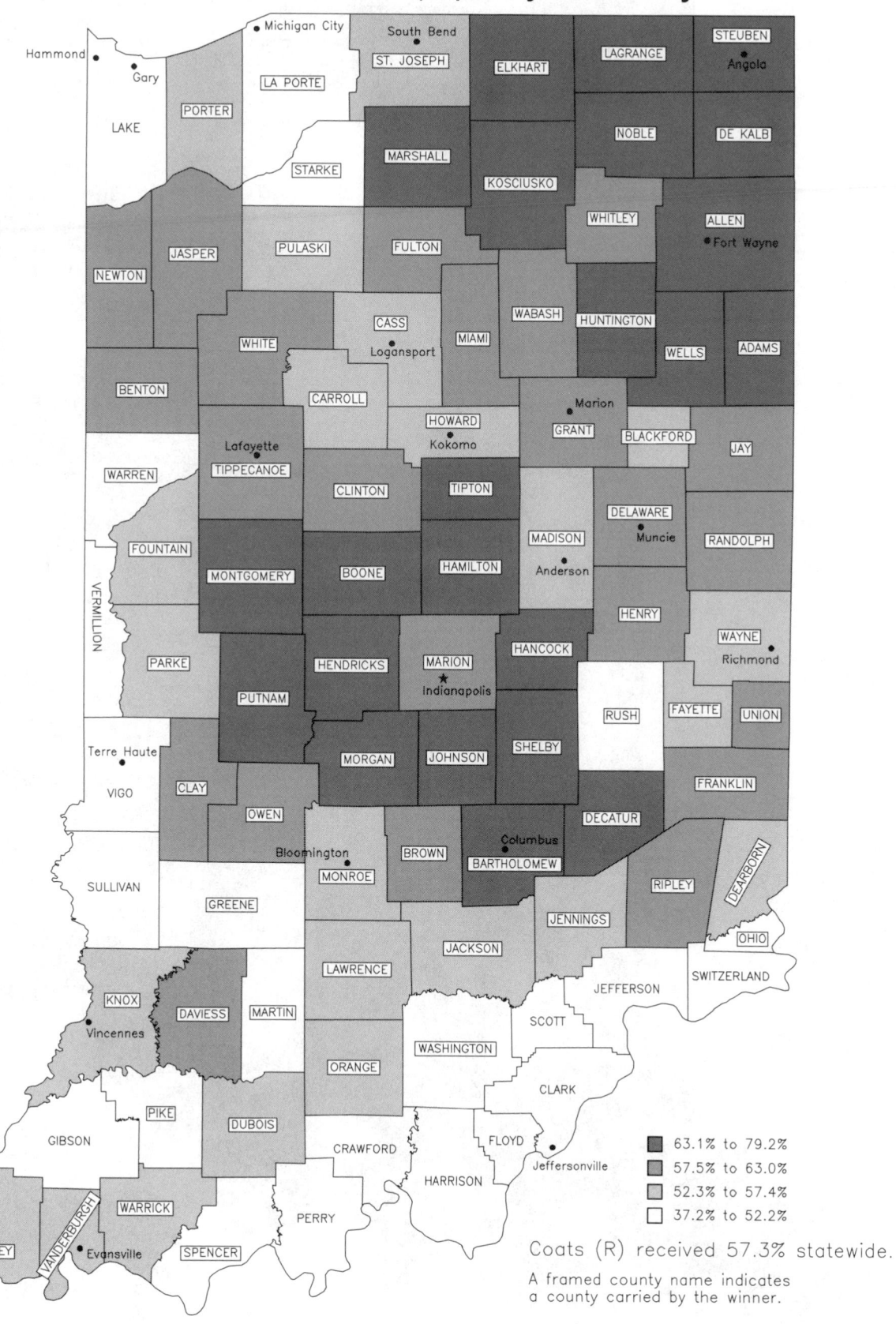

Hammond
• Michigan City
South Bend
• Gary
STEUBEN
LAGRANGE
• Angola
LA PORTE
ST. JOSEPH
ELKHART
PORTER
LAKE
STARKE
MARSHALL
NOBLE
DE KALB
KOSCIUSKO
JASPER
PULASKI
FULTON
WHITLEY
ALLEN
• Fort Wayne
NEWTON
WABASH
HUNTINGTON
CASS
MIAMI
WELLS
ADAMS
WHITE
Logansport
BENTON
CARROLL
Marion
•
GRANT
BLACKFORD
JAY
HOWARD
Lafayette
•
Kokomo
TIPPECANOE
DELAWARE
CLINTON
TIPTON
• Muncie
MADISON
RANDOLPH
FOUNTAIN
Anderson
•
WARREN
MONTGOMERY
BOONE
HAMILTON
VERMILLION
HENRY
WAYNE
PARKE
HENDRICKS
MARION
HANCOCK
• Richmond
★
PUTNAM
Indianapolis
RUSH
FAYETTE
UNION
Terre Haute
•
SHELBY
VIGO
CLAY
MORGAN
JOHNSON
FRANKLIN
OWEN
DECATUR
Bloomington
BROWN
•
Columbus
DEARBORN
MONROE
BARTHOLOMEW
RIPLEY
SULLIVAN
GREENE
JENNINGS
OHIO
JACKSON
LAWRENCE
SWITZERLAND
JEFFERSON
KNOX
DAVIESS
MARTIN
SCOTT
Vincennes
•
WASHINGTON
ORANGE
CLARK
PIKE
FLOYD
• Jeffersonville
GIBSON
DUBOIS
CRAWFORD
HARRISON
POSEY
WARRICK
PERRY
VANDERBURGH
• Evansville
SPENCER

■ 63.1% to 79.2%
■ 57.5% to 63.0%
□ 52.3% to 57.4%
□ 37.2% to 52.2%

Coats (R) received 57.3% statewide.

A framed county name indicates
a county carried by the winner.

Copyright © 1993 by Election Data Services, Inc.

Indiana 311

1992 Vote for Governor
Percent for Bayh (D), by County

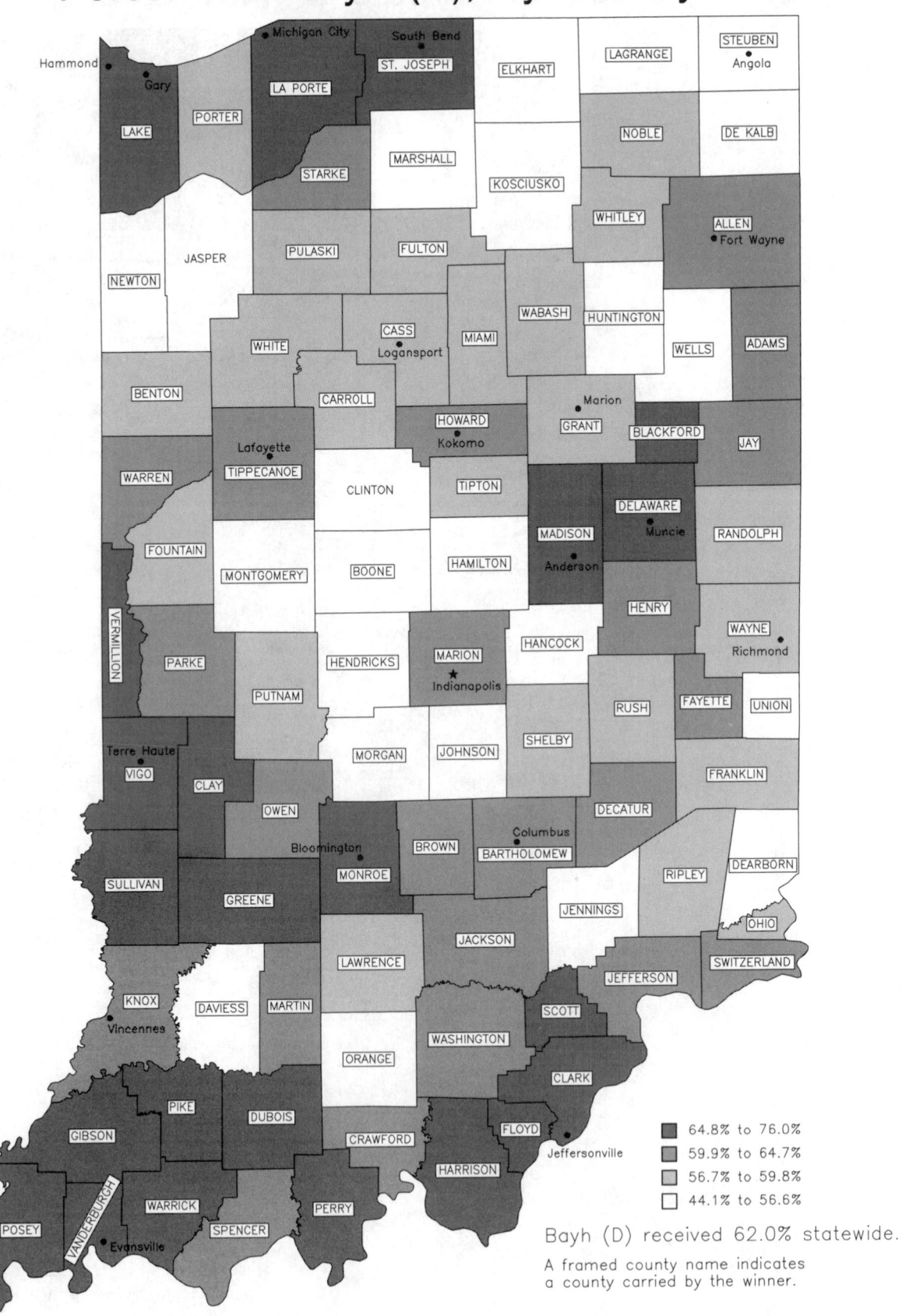

Legend:
- 64.8% to 76.0%
- 59.9% to 64.7%
- 56.7% to 59.8%
- 44.1% to 56.6%

Bayh (D) received 62.0% statewide.

A framed county name indicates
a county carried by the winner.

312 Indiana

IOWA

Congressional Districts 5
   Average Population 555,351
State Senate Districts 50
   Average Population 55,535
State House Districts 100
   Average Population 27,768

Electoral College Votes 7
Counties 99
Voting Precincts 2,469

Alternative Registration Methods:
   Agency-based, Deputized Registrars, Mail-in, Motor-voter

Registration Deadline (Days before Election) 10

Voting Equipment Use (Counties)

Datavote Punch Card	0	Paper Ballot	10
Electronic	3	Other Punch Card	0
Lever Machine	44	Mixed Systems	0
Optical Scanner	42		

Party Control	DEM	REP	IND	VAC
1993 State Senate	27	23	0	0
1992 State Senate	28	22	' 0	0
1993 State House	49	51	0	0
1992 State House	55	45	0	0

Population Statistics 1990

Race/ Ethnicity	Total Population		Voting Age Population		Voting Age Population % of total population
	Number	%	Number	%	
Non-Hispanic					
White	2,663,840	95.9	1,986,950	96.6	74.6
Black	47,493	1.7	30,128	1.5	63.4
Asian/Pacific Islander	24,926	0.9	16,430	0.8	65.9
Native American	6,765	0.2	4,272	0.2	63.1
Other	1,084	<.1	307	<.1	28.3
All Hispanic	32,647	1.2	19,788	1.0	60.6
TOTAL	2,776,755	100.0	2,057,875	100.0	74.1

Estimated Voting Age Population 1992 (VAP) 2,075,000
Number of Registered Voters 1,703,532
   % of estimated VAP 82.1
Voter Turnout (Maximum Vote)[1] 1,375,751
   % of VAP 66.3
   % of Registration 80.8
Persons Not Voting—of Voting Age 699,249
   % of VAP 33.7
Persons Not Voting—of Registered 327,781
   % of Registration 19.2
Straight Ticket Voting .... Yes, Exception

State Officials and Members of Congress

Governor:
Terry E. Branstad (R) 1982, elected to a four-year term in 1990.

U.S. Senators:
Charles E. Grassley (R) 1980, elected to a six-year term in 1992.
Tom Harkin (D) 1984, elected to a six-year term in 1990.

U.S. Representative in Congress:
(District, Name, Party, Date first elected)

1. Leach (R) 1976
2. Nussle (R) 1990

3. Lightfoot (R) 1984

4. Smith (D) 1958

5. Grandy (R) 1986

---

[1]Maximum vote turnout from Table C exceeds reported statewide actual voter turnout because in one or more counties the vote for highest office is greater than reported actual turnout. Actual voter turnout not officially certified by Iowa Secretary of State at time of publication.

Candidates: General Election, November 3, 1992

Candidate(s)	Total vote	Percent	Party	Status	First elected
President/Vice President					
Clinton/Gore	586,353	43.29%	Democrat	Challenger	1992
Bush/Quayle	504,891	37.27%	Republican	Incumbent	1988
Perot/Stockdale	253,468	18.71%	Independent	Challenger	
Hagelin/Tompkins	3,079	0.23%	Natural Law	Challenger	
Gritz/Minett	1,177	0.09%	America First	Challenger	
Ehlers/Wendt	1,149	0.08%	Independent	Challenger	
Marrou/Lord	1,076	0.08%	Libertarian	Challenger	
Scattering (other)	741	0.05%	Composited Others	Challenger	
Herer/Grimmer	669	0.05%	Grass Roots	Challenger	
Yiamouyiannis/McCone	604	0.04%	Independent	Challenger	
Phillips/Knight	480	0.04%	Taxpayers	Challenger	
Warren/Reid	273	0.02%	Socialist Workers	Challenger	
LaRouche/Bevel	238	0.02%	Ind. Econ. Recovery	Challenger	
Daniels/Tupahache	212	0.02%	Campaign New Tomorrow	Challenger	
Fulani/Munoz	197	0.01%	New Alliance	Challenger	
U.S. Senator					
Charles Grassley	899,761	69.61%	Republican	Incumbent	1980
Jean Lloyd-Jones	351,561	27.20%	Democrat	Challenger	
Stuart Zimmerman	16,403	1.27%	Natural Law	Challenger	
Sue Atkinson	6,277	0.49%	Independent	Challenger	
Mel Boring	5,508	0.43%	Independent	Challenger	
Rosanne Freeburg	4,999	0.39%	Independent	Challenger	
Carl Olsen	3,404	0.26%	Grass Roots	Challenger	
Richard Hughes	2,918	0.23%	Independent	Challenger	
Cleve Pulley	1,370	0.11%	Socialist Workers	Challenger	
Scattering (other)	293	0.02%	Composited Others	Challenger	

Governor (No Contest)

U.S. Representative in Congress

Candidate(s)	Total vote	Percent	Party	Status	First elected
District 1					
Jim Leach	178,042	68.13%	Republican	Incumbent	1976
Jan Zonneveld	81,600	31.23%	Democrat	Challenger	
Scattering (other)	1,667	0.64%	Composited Others	Challenger	
District 2					
Jim Nussle	134,536	50.22%	Republican	Incumbent	1992
David Nagle	131,570	49.11%	Democrat	Incumbent	1990
Albert Schoeman	1,757	0.66%	Grass Roots	Challenger	
Scattering (other)	29	0.01%	Composited Others	Challenger	
District 3					
Jim Ross Lightfoot	125,931	48.95%	Republican	Challenger	1984
Elaine Baxter	121,063	47.06%	Democrat	Challenger	
Larry Chroman	10,181	3.96%	Natural Law	Challenger	
Scattering (other)	101	0.04%	Composited Others	Challenger	
District 4					
Neal Smith	158,610	61.57%	Democrat	Incumbent	1958
Paul Lunde	94,045	36.51%	Republican	Challenger	
Jerry Yellin	2,427	0.94%	Natural Law	Challenger	
William Oviatt	2,359	0.92%	Grass Roots	Challenger	
Scattering (other)	152	0.06%	Composited Others	Challenger	
District 5					
Fred Grandy	196,942	99.28%	Republican	Incumbent	1986
Scattering (other)	1,424	0.72%	Composited Others	Challenger	

Voter Registration and Turnout, 1948-1992 Elections

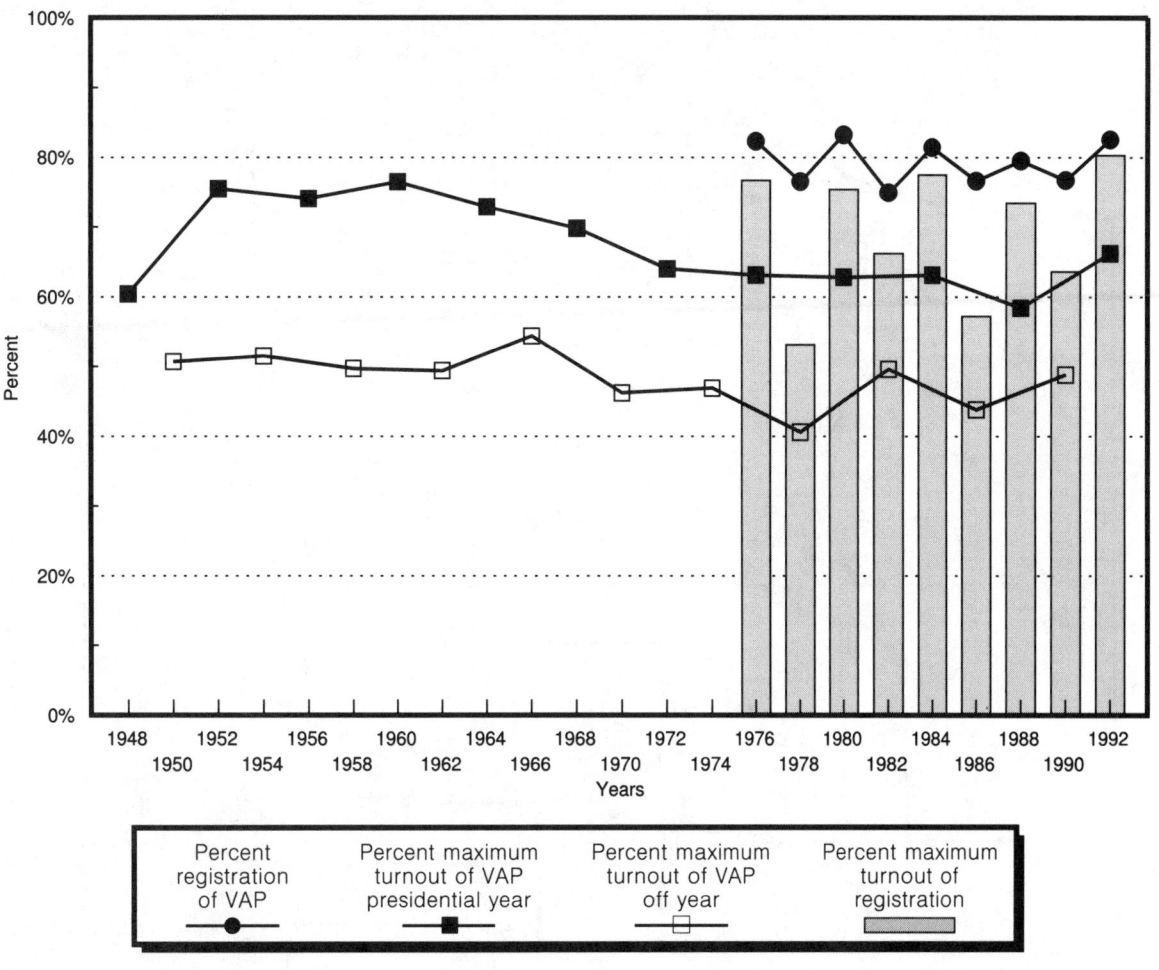

| | | Percent registration of VAP | | Percent maximum turnout of VAP presidential year | | Percent maximum turnout of VAP off year | | Percent maximum turnout of registration | |

Year	Estimated Voting Age Population (VAP)	Voter registration (REG)			Voter turnout										
						Highest office						Maximum vote			
		Total	Percent of VAP	Rank by percent of VAP	Actual	Total	Office	Percent total REG	Rank by percent of REG	Percent of VAP	Rank by percent of VAP	Total	Percent total REG	Rank by percent of REG	Percent total VAP	Rank by percent of VAP
1992¹	2,075,000	1,703,532	82.1	11	1,374,111	1,354,607	P	79.5	18	65.3	10	1,374,111	80.7	19	66.2	11
1990	2,061,000	1,580,160	76.7	13	1,004,908	983,933	S	62.3	14	47.7	12	1,004,908	63.6	14	48.8	12
1988	2,125,000	1,690,093	79.5	14	1,240,854	1,225,614	P	72.5	21	57.7	11	1,240,854	73.4	24	58.4	13
1986	2,105,000	1,611,438	76.6	11	922,094	910,623	G	56.5	24	43.3	16	922,094	57.2	26	43.8	16
1984	2,125,000	1,728,808	81.4	11	1,339,886	1,319,805	P	76.3	16	62.1	7	1,339,886	77.5	17	63.1	7
1982	2,117,000	1,586,345	74.9	14	1,050,495	1,038,229	P	65.4	18	49.0	9	1,050,495	66.2	20	49.6	11
1980	2,099,000	1,746,725	83.2	11	1,314,258	1,317,661	P	75.4	22	62.8	9	1,317,661	75.4	26	62.8	9
1978	2,075,000	1,587,723	76.5	11	-	843,190	G	53.1	36	40.6	25	843,190	53.1	36	40.6	26
1976	2,026,000	1,666,909	82.3	11	-	1,279,306	P	76.7	20	63.1	8	1,279,306	76.7	22	63.1	9
1974	1,961,000	-	-	-	-	920,458	G	-	-	46.9	15	920,458	-	-	46.9	16
1972	1,917,000	-	-	-	-	1,225,944	P	-	-	64.0	8	1,225,944	-	-	64.0	12
1970	1,712,000	-	-	-	-	791,241	G	-	-	46.2	33	791,241	-	-	46.2	34
1968	1,673,000	-	-	-	-	1,167,931	P	-	-	69.8	8	1,167,931	-	-	69.8	12
1966	1,641,000	-	-	-	-	893,175	G	-	-	54.4	22	893,175	-	-	54.4	22
1964	1,625,000	-	-	-	-	1,184,539	P	-	-	72.9	9	1,184,539	-	-	72.9	11
1962	1,661,000	-	-	-	-	819,854	G	-	-	49.4	28	819,854	-	-	49.4	28
1960	1,666,000	-	-	-	-	1,273,810	P	-	-	76.5	7	1,273,810	-	-	76.5	11
1958	1,730,000	-	-	-	-	859,095	G	-	-	49.7	29	859,095	-	-	49.7	30
1956	1,666,000	-	-	-	-	1,234,564	P	-	-	74.1	7	1,234,564	-	-	74.1	8
1954	1,648,000	-	-	-	-	848,592	G	-	-	51.5	22	848,592	-	-	51.5	23
1952	1,680,000	-	-	-	-	1,268,773	P	-	-	75.5	10	1,268,773	-	-	75.5	13
1950	1,694,000	-	-	-	-	858,523	S	-	-	50.7	23	858,523	-	-	50.7	25
1948	1,718,000	-	-	-	-	1,038,264	P	-	-	60.4	20	1,038,264	-	-	60.4	20

¹Actual voter turnout not officially certified by Iowa Secretary of State at time of publication.

IOWA

ALLAMAKEE
WINNESHIEK
HOWARD
MITCHELL
WORTH
WINNEBAGO
KOSSUTH
EMMET
DICKINSON
OSCEOLA
O'BRIEN
CLAY
PALO ALTO
LYON
SIOUX
PLYMOUTH
CHEROKEE
BUENA VISTA
POCAHONTAS
HUMBOLDT
WRIGHT
FRANKLIN
BUTLER
CHICKASAW
CERRO GORDO
FLOYD
Mason City
CLAYTON
FAYETTE
BREMER
Waterloo
BLACK HAWK
BUCHANAN
DELAWARE
DUBUQUE
Dubuque
JACKSON
CLINTON
Clinton
SCOTT
Davenport
MUSCATINE
JONES
CEDAR
LINN
Cedar Rapids
JOHNSON
Iowa City
BENTON
IOWA
TAMA
POWESHIEK
WASHINGTON
LOUISA
DES MOINES
Burlington
LEE
Keokuk
HENRY
VAN BUREN
JEFFERSON
KEOKUK
MAHASKA
WAPELLO
Ottumwa
DAVIS
MARSHALL
Marshalltown
JASPER
MARION
MONROE
APPANOOSE
STORY
Ames
POLK
Des Moines
WARREN
LUCAS
WAYNE
BOONE
DALLAS
MADISON
CLARKE
DECATUR
UNION
RINGGOLD
GREENE
GUTHRIE
ADAIR
ADAMS
TAYLOR
CARROLL
AUDUBON
CASS
MONTGOMERY
PAGE
CRAWFORD
SHELBY
POTTAWATTAMIE
Council Bluffs
MILLS
FREMONT
HARRISON
MONONA
WOODBURY
Sioux City
IDA
SAC
CALHOUN
HAMILTON
HARDIN
GRUNDY
HANCOCK
Fort Dodge
WEBSTER
MITCHELL

1
2
3
4
5

Miles
0 5 10 15 20

— Congressional district boundaries
effective May 30, 1991.

316 Iowa

Copyright © 1993 by Election Data Services, Inc.

Table A. — 1990 Population by Race and Ethnic Origin

State/county code	County	Total persons	Percent of total persons — Non-Hispanic — White	Black	Asian and Pacific Islander	Native American	Other	Hispanic	Rank — Percent of total persons — Total	Non-Hispanic — White	Black	Hispanic	Percent contribution to state population — Total	Non-Hispanic — White	Black	Hispanic
19 001	Adair	8,409	99.4	<.1	0.1	<.1	0.0	0.4	85	14	96	55	0.3	0.3	<.1	0.1
19 003	Adams	4,866	99.4	<.1	<.1	0.1	<.1	0.4	99	11	61	62	0.2	0.2	<.1	<.1
19 005	Allamakee	13,855	99.4	<.1	0.2	0.1	<.1	0.3	58	18	90	77	0.5	0.5	<.1	0.1
19 007	Appanoose	13,743	98.4	0.6	0.3	0.2	<.1	0.5	59	70	19	47	0.5	0.5	0.2	0.2
19 009	Audubon	7,334	99.6	0.0	<.1	<.1	0.0	0.3	94	1	99	79	0.3	0.3	0.0	<.1
19 011	Benton	22,429	99.2	<.1	0.2	0.1	0.0	0.4	26	30	54	56	0.8	0.8	<.1	0.3
19 013	Black Hawk	123,798	91.4	6.9	0.8	0.2	<.1	0.7	4	97	1	25	4.5	4.2	17.9	2.8
19 015	Boone	25,186	99.0	0.2	0.3	<.1	<.1	0.4	23	47	35	59	0.9	0.9	0.1	0.3
19 017	Bremer	22,813	98.8	0.3	0.6	<.1	<.1	0.3	25	58	30	75	0.8	0.8	0.1	0.2
19 019	Buchanan	20,844	98.9	0.2	0.2	0.1	<.1	0.5	31	48	44	45	0.8	0.8	<.1	0.3
19 021	Buena Vista	19,965	97.0	0.3	1.9	<.1	<.1	0.8	32	84	31	21	0.7	0.7	0.1	0.5
19 023	Butler	15,731	99.5	<.1	0.2	<.1	<.1	0.2	50	2	88	92	0.6	0.6	<.1	0.1
19 025	Calhoun	11,508	99.1	0.3	0.2	<.1	<.1	0.3	74	40	32	67	0.4	0.4	<.1	0.1
19 027	Carroll	21,423	99.4	<.1	0.3	<.1	0.0	0.3	29	13	83	87	0.8	0.8	<.1	0.2
19 029	Cass	15,128	99.4	<.1	<.1	0.1	0.0	0.3	52	6	63	76	0.5	0.6	<.1	0.1
19 031	Cedar	17,381	98.9	<.1	0.3	<.1	0.0	0.6	44	52	51	33	0.6	0.6	<.1	0.3
19 033	Cerro Gordo	46,733	96.6	0.6	0.5	<.1	<.1	2.1	11	86	17	5	1.7	1.7	0.6	3.0
19 035	Cherokee	14,098	99.1	0.1	0.2	0.2	<.1	0.4	57	43	49	63	0.5	0.5	<.1	0.2
19 037	Chickasaw	13,295	99.5	<.1	0.1	<.1	<.1	0.3	60	3	87	78	0.5	0.5	<.1	0.1
19 039	Clarke	8,287	99.4	<.1	0.3	<.1	0.0	0.2	89	10	82	93	0.3	0.3	<.1	<.1
19 041	Clay	17,585	99.1	<.1	0.5	0.2	0.0	0.3	42	42	74	89	0.6	0.7	<.1	0.1
19 043	Clayton	19,054	99.4	<.1	0.1	<.1	<.1	0.3	38	7	86	73	0.7	0.7	<.1	0.2
19 045	Clinton	51,040	97.4	1.4	0.4	0.2	<.1	0.6	10	82	12	37	1.8	1.9	1.5	0.9
19 047	Crawford	16,775	98.4	0.4	0.5	0.2	<.1	0.6	47	71	28	35	0.6	0.6	0.1	0.3
19 049	Dallas	29,755	98.8	0.2	0.2	0.1	<.1	0.6	22	57	38	34	1.1	1.1	0.1	0.5
19 051	Davis	8,312	98.9	<.1	0.3	0.3	0.0	0.5	88	49	89	50	0.3	0.3	<.1	0.1
19 053	Decatur	8,338	98.0	0.4	0.9	0.2	<.1	0.5	87	76	26	42	0.3	0.3	<.1	0.1
19 055	Delaware	18,035	99.3	<.1	0.2	<.1	<.1	0.4	41	25	62	61	0.6	0.7	<.1	0.2
19 057	Des Moines	42,614	95.1	3.1	0.5	0.2	<.1	1.2	12	90	4	13	1.5	1.5	2.8	1.5
19 059	Dickinson	14,909	99.2	<.1	0.2	0.1	<.1	0.3	53	31	50	66	0.5	0.6	<.1	0.2
19 061	Dubuque	86,403	98.5	0.4	0.5	<.1	<.1	0.5	7	66	27	48	3.1	3.2	0.7	1.3
19 063	Emmet	11,569	98.9	0.1	0.3	<.1	<.1	0.5	73	53	47	40	0.4	0.4	<.1	0.2
19 065	Fayette	21,843	98.6	0.2	0.2	<.1	<.1	0.9	27	60	37	19	0.8	0.8	<.1	0.6
19 067	Floyd	17,058	99.1	<.1	0.2	<.1	0.0	0.5	45	39	73	44	0.6	0.6	<.1	0.3
19 069	Franklin	11,364	98.4	<.1	0.1	<.1	<.1	1.3	75	69	66	10	0.4	0.4	<.1	0.5
19 071	Fremont	8,226	99.0	<.1	0.2	0.1	0.0	0.6	90	45	71	31	0.3	0.3	<.1	0.2
19 073	Greene	10,045	99.3	<.1	0.3	<.1	<.1	0.3	80	26	69	80	0.4	0.4	<.1	<.1
19 075	Grundy	12,029	99.4	<.1	0.2	<.1	0.0	0.3	69	5	64	84	0.4	0.4	<.1	0.1
19 077	Guthrie	10,935	99.3	<.1	0.1	0.2	<.1	0.3	76	20	60	74	0.4	0.4	<.1	0.1
19 079	Hamilton	16,071	98.6	<.1	0.5	0.1	0.0	0.7	49	62	65	27	0.6	0.6	<.1	0.4
19 081	Hancock	12,638	98.7	<.1	0.2	<.1	<.1	1.0	64	59	98	16	0.5	0.5	<.1	0.4
19 083	Hardin	19,094	98.4	0.6	0.3	0.1	0.0	0.6	37	68	18	39	0.7	0.7	0.2	0.3
19 085	Harrison	14,730	99.1	<.1	0.3	0.1	<.1	0.3	54	38	59	69	0.5	0.5	<.1	0.2
19 087	Henry	19,226	96.9	1.1	1.1	0.2	<.1	0.7	36	85	13	28	0.7	0.7	0.4	0.4
19 089	Howard	9,809	99.4	<.1	0.2	<.1	<.1	0.2	82	9	76	91	0.4	0.4	<.1	<.1
19 091	Humboldt	10,756	99.2	<.1	0.2	0.1	0.0	0.3	78	32	52	68	0.4	0.4	<.1	0.1
19 093	Ida	8,365	99.4	<.1	0.2	<.1	<.1	0.3	86	8	97	85	0.3	0.3	<.1	<.1
19 095	Iowa	14,630	99.4	<.1	0.2	<.1	<.1	0.3	55	12	72	86	0.5	0.5	<.1	0.1
19 097	Jackson	19,950	99.2	<.1	0.1	0.1	<.1	0.5	33	33	55	52	0.7	0.7	<.1	0.3
19 099	Jasper	34,795	98.6	0.2	0.5	0.2	<.1	0.6	19	61	43	38	1.3	1.3	0.1	0.6
19 101	Jefferson	16,310	97.6	0.6	0.8	0.1	<.1	0.9	48	79	20	20	0.6	0.6	0.2	0.4
19 103	Johnson	96,119	92.3	2.0	4.0	0.2	<.1	1.5	6	95	7	9	3.5	3.3	4.1	4.4
19 105	Jones	19,444	97.7	1.5	0.1	0.2	<.1	0.5	35	78	11	51	0.7	0.7	0.6	0.3
19 107	Keokuk	11,624	99.4	<.1	0.2	0.2	<.1	0.2	71	16	67	98	0.4	0.4	<.1	<.1
19 109	Kossuth	18,591	99.1	<.1	0.3	<.1	<.1	0.5	40	37	80	49	0.7	0.7	<.1	0.3
19 111	Lee	38,687	94.8	2.8	0.3	0.2	<.1	1.9	15	91	5	6	1.4	1.4	2.3	2.2
19 113	Linn	168,767	96.0	1.9	0.8	0.2	<.1	0.9	2	87	8	18	6.1	6.1	6.9	4.9
19 115	Louisa	11,592	95.2	0.7	0.2	0.2	0.0	3.7	72	89	15	2	0.4	0.4	0.2	1.3
19 117	Lucas	9,070	98.9	<.1	0.2	0.2	<.1	0.6	84	55	84	36	0.3	0.3	<.1	0.2
19 119	Lyon	11,952	99.5	<.1	0.3	0.1	0.0	<.1	70	4	93	99	0.4	0.4	<.1	<.1
19 121	Madison	12,483	99.1	<.1	0.1	0.2	<.1	0.5	65	41	79	46	0.4	0.5	<.1	0.2
19 123	Mahaska	21,522	98.5	0.2	0.8	<.1	<.1	0.4	28	67	41	54	0.8	0.8	<.1	0.3
19 125	Marion	30,001	98.0	0.3	0.9	0.1	<.1	0.5	20	75	29	43	1.1	1.1	0.2	0.5
19 127	Marshall	38,276	97.5	0.7	0.8	0.2	<.1	0.8	16	81	16	24	1.4	1.4	0.6	0.9
19 129	Mills	13,202	98.9	0.2	0.1	0.2	<.1	0.5	62	50	46	41	0.5	0.5	<.1	0.2
19 131	Mitchell	10,928	99.4	<.1	0.2	<.1	<.1	0.4	77	15	91	57	0.4	0.4	<.1	0.1
19 133	Monona	10,034	99.3	<.1	0.1	0.2	<.1	0.3	81	27	70	81	0.4	0.4	<.1	<.1
19 135	Monroe	8,114	98.9	0.2	0.4	0.2	0.0	0.2	91	51	36	95	0.3	0.3	<.1	<.1
19 137	Montgomery	12,076	99.3	<.1	<.1	<.1	<.1	0.4	68	21	77	53	0.4	0.5	<.1	0.2
19 139	Muscatine	39,907	91.3	0.5	0.7	0.2	<.1	7.3	14	98	23	1	1.4	1.4	0.4	8.9

Table A. — 1990 Population by Race and Ethnic Origin (cont)

State/county code	County	Total persons	Percent of total persons Non-Hispanic White	Black	Asian and Pacific Islander	Native American	Other	Hispanic	Rank Percent of total persons Total	Non-Hispanic White	Black	Hispanic	Percent contribution to state population Total	Non-Hispanic White	Black	Hispanic
19 141	O'Brien	15,444	99.2	<.1	0.3	0.2	<.1	0.3	51	35	68	88	0.6	0.6	<.1	0.1
19 143	Osceola	7,267	99.4	<.1	0.2	0.1	<.1	0.2	95	17	78	97	0.3	0.3	<.1	<.1
19 145	Page	16,870	97.6	0.5	0.5	0.3	<.1	1.2	46	80	22	12	0.6	0.6	0.2	0.6
19 147	Palo Alto	10,669	99.3	<.1	0.2	0.2	0.0	0.2	79	23	57	94	0.4	0.4	<.1	<.1
19 149	Plymouth	23,388	99.3	0.2	0.2	<.1	<.1	0.2	24	28	39	90	0.8	0.9	<.1	0.2
19 151	Pocahontas	9,525	99.3	<.1	0.2	0.1	<.1	0.3	83	22	75	70	0.3	0.4	<.1	<.1
19 153	Polk	327,140	91.5	4.5	1.8	0.3	<.1	1.9	1	96	3	7	11.8	11.2	30.8	18.9
19 155	Pottawattamie	82,628	97.0	0.5	0.3	0.3	<.1	1.8	8	83	21	8	3.0	3.0	1.0	4.6
19 157	Poweshiek	19,033	98.1	0.5	0.9	0.1	<.1	0.4	39	74	25	64	0.7	0.7	0.2	0.2
19 159	Ringgold	5,420	99.2	<.1	0.3	0.2	<.1	0.3	98	36	92	82	0.2	0.2	<.1	<.1
19 161	Sac	12,324	99.3	<.1	0.2	0.1	0.0	0.4	66	19	85	65	0.4	0.5	<.1	0.1
19 163	Scott	150,979	90.7	5.2	0.9	0.3	0.1	2.8	3	99	2	3	5.4	5.1	16.6	13.0
19 165	Shelby	13,230	99.3	<.1	0.2	0.2	<.1	0.3	61	24	81	71	0.5	0.5	<.1	0.1
19 167	Sioux	29,903	98.9	<.1	0.7	0.1	<.1	0.2	21	56	53	96	1.1	1.1	<.1	0.2
19 169	Story	74,252	92.5	1.6	4.6	0.1	<.1	1.1	9	94	10	15	2.7	2.6	2.5	2.6
19 171	Tama	17,419	94.1	0.2	0.4	4.6	<.1	0.7	43	92	45	26	0.6	0.6	<.1	0.4
19 173	Taylor	7,114	99.0	<.1	0.3	<.1	0.0	0.6	96	46	94	29	0.3	0.3	<.1	0.1
19 175	Union	12,750	99.0	<.1	0.4	0.2	<.1	0.3	63	44	56	72	0.5	0.5	<.1	0.1
19 177	Van Buren	7,676	99.2	0.1	0.2	<.1	0.0	0.4	93	29	48	60	0.3	0.3	<.1	<.1
19 179	Wapello	35,687	97.9	0.8	0.4	0.2	<.1	0.6	18	77	14	32	1.3	1.3	0.6	0.7
19 181	Warren	36,033	98.5	0.2	0.4	0.1	<.1	0.8	17	64	34	23	1.3	1.3	0.2	0.8
19 183	Washington	19,612	98.2	0.5	0.3	<.1	<.1	1.0	34	73	24	17	0.7	0.7	0.2	0.6
19 185	Wayne	7,067	99.2	<.1	0.2	0.1	<.1	0.4	97	34	95	58	0.3	0.3	<.1	<.1
19 187	Webster	40,342	95.9	2.2	0.4	0.3	<.1	1.2	13	88	6	11	1.5	1.5	1.9	1.5
19 189	Winnebago	12,122	98.3	0.3	0.6	0.1	<.1	0.8	67	72	33	22	0.4	0.4	<.1	0.3
19 191	Winneshiek	20,847	98.6	0.2	0.9	<.1	<.1	0.3	30	63	40	83	0.8	0.8	<.1	0.2
19 193	Woodbury	98,276	92.5	1.9	1.3	1.5	<.1	2.8	5	93	9	4	3.5	3.4	3.9	8.3
19 195	Worth	7,991	98.5	0.2	0.2	<.1	0.0	1.1	92	65	42	14	0.3	0.3	<.1	0.3
19 197	Wright	14,269	98.9	<.1	0.3	0.1	0.0	0.6	56	54	58	30	0.5	0.5	<.1	0.3
19	IOWA	2,776,755	95.9	1.7	0.9	0.2	<.1	1.2					100.0	100.0	100.0	100.0
	CONGRESSIONAL															
	District 1	555,229	93.8	2.6	1.3	0.2	<.1	2.0	5	5	2	1	20.0	19.6	30.3	34.0
	District 2	555,494	96.9	1.7	0.4	0.2	<.1	0.7	1	3	3	5	20.0	20.2	19.9	11.3
	District 3	555,299	97.0	0.9	1.1	0.2	<.1	0.8	3	2	4	4	20.0	20.2	10.8	13.7
	District 4	555,276	94.3	2.7	1.2	0.2	<.1	1.5	4	4	1	2	20.0	19.7	32.0	25.5
	District 5	555,457	97.6	0.6	0.5	0.4	<.1	0.9	2	1	5	3	20.0	20.3	6.9	15.5

Table B. — 1990 Voting Age Population (VAP) by Race and Ethnic Origin

County	Total Voting Age Population	Percent of total VAP — Non-Hispanic White	Black	Asian and Pacific Islander	Native American	Other	Hispanic	Rank Percent of total VAP — Total	Non-Hispanic White	Black	Hispanic	Percent contribution to state VAP — Total	Non-Hispanic White	Black	Hispanic	VAP percent of total population — Total	Non-Hispanic White	Black	Asian and Pacific Islander	Native American	Other	Hispanic
Adair	6,298	99.5	<.1	<.1	<.1	0.0	0.3	86	15	92	59	0.3	0.3	<.1	0.1	74.9	75.0	100.0	33.3	80.0	0.0	57.1
Adams	3,677	99.3	<.1	<.1	0.2	<.1	0.4	99	41	80	39	0.2	0.2	<.1	<.1	75.6	75.5	33.3	100.0	100.0	100.0	88.9
Allamakee	10,081	99.5	<.1	0.1	<.1	0.0	0.3	59	20	88	57	0.5	0.5	<.1	0.2	72.8	72.9	66.7	42.3	38.9	0.0	78.6
Appanoose	10,285	98.7	0.5	0.2	0.2	<.1	0.4	57	70	18	38	0.5	0.5	0.2	0.2	74.8	75.0	68.4	50.0	65.4	40.0	62.5
Audubon	5,461	99.7	0.0	<.1	<.1	0.0	0.2	94	2	96	78	0.3	0.3	0.0	<.1	74.5	74.5	0.0	50.0	66.7	0.0	54.5
Benton	16,210	99.4	<.1	0.1	0.1	0.0	0.3	26	32	53	69	0.8	0.8	<.1	0.3	72.3	72.4	61.1	47.2	73.3	0.0	48.4
Black Hawk	92,396	93.2	5.4	0.6	0.1	<.1	0.6	4	94	1	24	4.5	4.3	16.6	2.8	74.6	76.1	58.9	60.1	59.9	17.2	60.6
Boone	19,017	99.2	0.2	0.2	<.1	0.0	0.3	23	49	36	65	0.9	0.9	0.1	0.3	75.5	75.7	69.4	51.9	84.2	0.0	56.6
Bremer	17,051	98.9	0.3	0.5	<.1	0.1	0.3	24	62	32	66	0.8	0.8	0.2	0.2	74.7	74.8	65.7	69.5	71.4	75.0	66.7
Buchanan	14,425	99.2	0.1	0.2	<.1	0.0	0.4	33	45	46	47	0.7	0.7	<.1	0.3	69.2	69.4	44.7	57.1	58.3	0.0	50.0
Buena Vista	14,790	97.4	0.3	1.6	0.1	<.1	0.6	31	83	33	21	0.7	0.7	0.1	0.5	74.1	74.4	69.8	62.1	93.8	100.0	60.0
Butler	11,582	99.6	<.1	<.1	<.1	0.0	0.2	50	6	82	76	0.6	0.6	<.1	0.1	73.6	73.7	75.0	36.0	58.3	0.0	70.3
Calhoun	8,619	99.1	0.3	0.2	0.1	0.0	0.3	70	54	29	71	0.4	0.4	<.1	0.1	74.9	74.9	93.3	63.6	81.8	0.0	57.5
Carroll	15,064	99.5	<.1	0.2	<.1	0.0	0.2	30	17	65	87	0.7	0.8	<.1	0.2	70.3	70.4	85.7	48.2	50.0	0.0	54.4
Cass	11,248	99.6	<.1	<.1	<.1	0.0	0.2	53	10	81	74	0.6	0.6	<.1	0.1	74.4	74.5	33.3	53.3	52.9	0.0	56.5
Cedar	12,748	99.2	<.1	0.1	<.1	0.0	0.5	43	46	54	28	0.6	0.6	<.1	0.2	73.3	73.6	50.0	39.1	62.5	0.0	58.7
Cerro Gordo	35,163	97.2	0.5	0.4	<.1	<.1	1.8	11	84	20	5	1.7	1.7	0.6	3.2	75.2	75.7	61.6	54.5	65.9	33.3	63.4
Cherokee	10,271	99.4	<.1	0.1	0.2	0.0	0.2	58	34	49	83	0.5	0.5	<.1	0.1	72.9	73.1	44.4	46.4	54.5	0.0	43.1
Chickasaw	9,558	99.6	<.1	0.1	<.1	0.0	0.2	62	9	75	79	0.5	0.5	<.1	0.1	71.9	72.0	75.0	55.6	100.0	0.0	52.5
Clarke	6,119	99.4	<.1	0.2	0.1	0.0	0.2	87	28	71	85	0.3	0.3	<.1	<.1	73.8	73.9	66.7	57.1	87.5	0.0	68.4
Clay	12,781	99.3	<.1	0.4	0.2	0.0	0.2	42	43	76	92	0.6	0.6	<.1	0.1	72.7	72.8	50.0	59.3	64.5	0.0	52.3
Clayton	13,732	99.6	<.1	<.1	<.1	0.0	0.2	39	5	69	82	0.7	0.7	<.1	0.1	72.1	72.2	83.3	33.3	53.3	0.0	49.2
Clinton	37,421	97.8	1.2	0.3	0.2	<.1	0.4	10	79	13	42	1.8	1.8	1.5	0.8	73.3	73.7	62.2	61.7	65.5	20.8	53.1
Crawford	12,158	98.7	0.3	0.4	0.2	<.1	0.4	48	68	28	44	0.6	0.6	0.1	0.2	72.5	72.8	69.5	50.6	59.4	50.0	50.0
Dallas	21,469	99.1	0.2	0.2	0.1	<.1	0.4	21	56	43	40	1.0	1.1	0.1	0.5	72.2	72.3	59.7	61.8	66.7	100.0	52.3
Davis	6,050	99.2	<.1	0.2	0.3	0.0	0.3	90	53	72	56	0.3	0.3	<.1	0.2	76.7	76.7	85.7	80.3	73.3	100.0	71.1
Decatur	6,397	97.9	0.5	0.9	0.2	<.1	0.5	85	29	24	29	0.3	0.3	<.1	0.2	76.1	76.3	83.8	41.9	73.3	0.0	58.8
Delaware	12,495	99.4	<.1	0.1	<.1	0.0	0.3	46	29	56	58	0.6	0.6	<.1	0.2	69.3	69.4	63.6	41.9	73.3	0.0	58.8
Des Moines	31,662	96.2	2.3	0.4	0.1	<.1	0.9	12	89	5	13	1.5	1.5	2.4	1.5	74.3	75.2	56.3	58.4	63.2	35.3	60.4
Dickinson	11,403	99.5	<.1	0.1	0.1	<.1	0.2	51	24	60	81	0.6	0.6	<.1	0.1	76.5	76.7	35.7	48.0	71.4	66.7	48.1
Dubuque	63,002	98.5	0.4	0.5	<.1	<.1	0.5	7	73	25	35	3.1	3.1	0.9	1.4	72.9	73.0	73.8	73.4	70.6	20.6	65.4
Emmet	8,496	99.1	0.2	0.2	<.1	0.0	0.4	72	55	45	43	0.4	0.4	<.1	0.2	73.4	73.6	76.5	64.5	54.5	0.0	55.6
Fayette	16,063	98.8	0.2	0.2	<.1	<.1	0.7	27	65	35	20	0.8	0.8	<.1	0.6	73.5	73.7	84.8	54.2	80.0	100.0	60.5
Floyd	12,633	99.4	<.1	<.1	<.1	0.0	0.4	45	27	74	48	0.6	0.6	<.1	0.2	74.1	74.3	50.0	25.0	58.3	0.0	53.3
Franklin	8,438	98.8	<.1	<.1	<.1	<.1	1.0	73	67	51	11	0.4	0.4	<.1	0.4	74.3	74.5	100.0	46.2	50.0	100.0	57.2
Fremont	6,080	99.2	<.1	0.2	<.1	0.0	0.4	88	47	57	36	0.3	0.3	<.1	0.1	73.9	74.1	75.0	81.3	66.7	0.0	50.9
Greene	7,559	99.5	<.1	0.2	<.1	0.0	0.2	81	22	83	75	0.4	0.4	<.1	<.1	75.3	75.4	40.0	50.0	70.0	0.0	56.7
Grundy	8,952	99.7	<.1	<.1	<.1	0.0	0.2	69	1	94	88	0.4	0.4	<.1	<.1	74.4	74.6	14.3	21.1	44.4	0.0	52.9
Guthrie	8,212	99.5	<.1	<.1	0.1	0.0	0.3	76	3	58	72	0.4	0.4	<.1	0.1	75.1	75.2	57.1	46.2	70.6	0.0	60.0
Hamilton	11,990	99.0	<.1	0.4	0.1	0.0	0.5	49	58	84	30	0.6	0.6	<.1	0.3	74.6	74.9	33.3	58.5	61.9	0.0	50.9
Hancock	9,077	98.9	<.1	0.2	<.1	<.1	0.8	65	61	95	16	0.4	0.5	<.1	0.4	71.8	72.0	100.0	53.8	60.0	44.4	59.7
Hardin	14,319	98.9	0.5	0.2	<.1	0.0	0.4	38	63	23	52	0.7	0.7	0.2	0.3	75.0	75.3	58.1	62.3	47.8	0.0	49.1
Harrison	10,771	99.4	<.1	0.2	<.1	<.1	0.3	56	35	68	62	0.5	0.5	<.1	0.2	73.1	73.3	40.0	41.2	46.7	100.0	64.0
Henry	14,379	96.9	1.3	1.0	0.2	<.1	0.5	35	86	12	26	0.7	0.7	0.6	0.4	74.8	74.8	88.1	67.5	83.3	40.0	59.1
Howard	7,180	99.6	<.1	<.1	<.1	<.1	0.2	82	11	64	90	0.3	0.4	<.1	<.1	73.2	73.3	75.0	16.7	66.7	100.0	58.3
Humboldt	8,014	99.4	<.1	0.1	<.1	0.0	0.3	78	30	55	70	0.4	0.4	<.1	0.1	74.5	74.7	55.6	44.0	53.3	0.0	59.5
Ida	6,031	99.7	0.0	<.1	<.1	0.0	0.2	91	3	97	91	0.3	0.3	0.0	<.1	72.1	72.3	0.0	26.3	100.0	0.0	47.8
Iowa	10,885	99.5	<.1	0.2	<.1	0.0	0.2	54	14	89	80	0.5	0.5	<.1	0.1	74.4	74.5	28.6	50.0	60.0	0.0	61.5
Jackson	14,385	99.3	<.1	0.1	0.1	0.0	0.4	34	39	59	45	0.7	0.7	<.1	0.3	72.1	72.2	43.8	62.5	69.6	0.0	59.4
Jasper	25,883	98.9	0.2	0.3	0.2	0.0	0.4	18	59	44	41	1.3	1.3	0.1	0.4	74.4	74.7	62.5	43.9	75.4	0.0	57.2
Jefferson	12,323	97.5	0.6	0.9	0.1	<.1	0.9	47	81	17	15	0.6	0.6	0.2	0.6	75.6	75.5	77.4	81.8	77.3	100.0	78.7
Johnson	76,772	92.6	1.9	4.0	0.2	<.1	1.4	5	99	7	9	3.7	3.6	4.8	5.3	79.9	80.1	75.1	80.1	77.0	49.3	72.6
Jones	14,454	97.2	2.0	<.1	0.2	<.1	0.5	32	85	6	27	0.7	0.7	0.9	0.4	74.3	74.0	97.3	61.9	82.4	66.7	77.9
Keokuk	8,603	99.5	<.1	0.2	0.1	0.0	0.1	71	18	70	97	0.4	0.4	<.1	<.1	74.0	74.1	50.0	51.9	63.2	25.0	57.9
Kossuth	13,376	99.4	<.1	0.2	<.1	0.0	0.4	40	36	87	50	0.7	0.7	<.1	0.3	71.9	72.1	42.9	46.0	71.4	0.0	53.2
Lee	28,716	95.1	2.7	0.3	0.1	<.1	1.7	15	92	4	6	1.4	1.4	2.6	2.5	74.2	74.5	72.2	59.4	70.5	26.7	66.3
Linn	126,337	96.8	1.6	0.7	0.2	<.1	0.8	2	87	9	19	6.1	6.2	6.6	4.8	72.7	73.1	73.3	64.1	63.4	21.1	59.8
Louisa	8,430	95.7	0.7	<.1	0.3	0.0	3.2	74	91	14	2	0.4	0.4	0.2	1.4	72.7	73.1	73.3	38.9	78.6	0.0	64.0
Lucas	6,836	99.2	<.1	0.1	0.2	<.1	0.5	84	50	78	32	0.3	0.3	<.1	0.2	75.4	75.6	66.7	41.2	66.7	22.2	62.3
Lyon	8,338	99.6	0.0	0.2	0.1	0.0	<.1	75	7	98	99	0.4	0.4	0.0	<.1	69.8	69.8	0.0	47.1	66.7	0.0	63.6
Madison	9,039	99.3	<.1	<.1	0.2	0.0	0.4	67	40	73	54	0.4	0.5	<.1	0.2	72.4	72.6	60.0	56.3	69.2	0.0	47.8
Mahaska	15,898	98.7	0.2	0.6	<.1	<.1	0.4	28	69	37	46	0.8	0.8	0.1	0.3	73.9	74.0	87.8	53.4	73.3	57.1	68.5
Marion	22,317	98.4	0.4	0.6	0.1	0.0	0.4	20	74	26	37	1.1	1.1	0.3	0.4	74.4	74.6	86.3	50.9	77.5	0.0	61.1
Marshall	28,678	97.9	0.7	0.6	0.2	<.1	0.6	16	77	16	25	1.4	1.4	0.6	0.8	74.9	75.3	68.7	57.8	70.2	70.0	55.5
Mills	9,577	99.0	0.2	0.1	0.3	0.0	0.4	61	57	41	49	0.5	0.5	<.1	0.1	72.5	72.6	86.4	70.6	85.7	0.0	51.4
Mitchell	8,080	99.6	<.1	<.1	<.1	0.0	0.3	77	12	85	63	0.4	0.4	<.1	0.1	73.9	74.1	100.0	35.0	100.0	0.0	53.3
Monona	7,578	99.5	<.1	<.1	0.2	0.0	0.2	80	21	66	89	0.4	0.4	<.1	<.1	75.5	75.7	60.0	46.2	66.7	0.0	50.0
Monroe	6,055	99.4	0.2	0.1	0.1	0.0	0.2	89	37	39	95	0.3	0.3	<.1	<.1	74.6	75.0	68.4	18.2	50.0	0.0	55.6
Montgomery	9,102	99.4	<.1	<.1	<.1	<.1	0.4	64	31	61	53	0.4	0.5	<.1	0.1	75.4	75.4	80.0	66.7	66.7	50.0	63.5
Muscatine	28,767	93.1	0.4	0.6	0.2	<.1	5.7	14	95	27	1	1.4	1.3	0.4	8.3	72.1	73.5	60.2	60.5	72.6	41.7	56.3

County	Total Voting Age Population	Percent of total VAP — Non-Hispanic White	Black	Asian and Pacific Islander	Native American	Other	Hispanic	Rank Percent of total VAP Non-Hispanic Total	White	Black	Hispanic	Percent contribution to state VAP Total	Non-Hispanic White	Black	Hispanic	VAP percent of total population Total	Non-Hispanic White	Black	Asian and Pacific Islander	Native American	Other	Hispanic
O'Brien	11,320	99.5	<.1	0.2	0.1	0.0	0.2	52	25	90	86	0.6	0.6	<.1	0.1	73.3	73.5	25.0	40.8	50.0	0.0	61.5
Osceola	5,288	99.6	<.1	0.1	0.1	0.0	0.1	97	8	67	98	0.3	0.3	<.1	<.1	72.8	73.0	66.7	37.5	77.8	0.0	37.5
Page	12,656	97.8	0.5	0.4	0.3	<.1	0.9	44	80	19	14	0.6	0.6	0.2	0.6	75.0	75.2	79.3	65.0	76.5	66.7	59.4
Palo Alto	7,821	99.6	<.1	0.1	0.1	0.0	0.2	79	13	93	94	0.4	0.4	<.1	<.1	73.3	73.5	12.5	50.0	43.5	0.0	54.2
Plymouth	16,596	99.5	0.2	0.1	<.1	<.1	0.2	25	26	42	93	0.8	0.8	<.1	0.1	71.0	71.1	61.7	42.9	64.3	60.0	50.0
Pocahontas	7,047	99.6	<.1	<.1	<.1	<.1	0.2	83	4	63	84	0.3	0.4	<.1	<.1	74.0	74.2	75.0	11.8	30.0	100.0	46.9
Polk	245,169	92.7	4.0	1.5	0.2	<.1	1.6	1	97	3	7	11.9	11.4	32.3	19.5	74.9	75.9	66.5	62.5	72.1	26.2	62.7
Pottawattamie	60,101	97.4	0.5	0.3	0.2	<.1	1.5	8	82	21	8	2.9	2.9	1.0	4.5	72.7	73.1	68.0	64.0	67.1	35.3	59.2
Poweshiek	14,370	98.2	0.5	0.8	0.1	<.1	0.3	36	75	22	61	0.7	0.7	0.2	0.2	75.5	75.6	84.9	64.4	68.2	100.0	66.2
Ringgold	4,122	99.3	<.1	0.2	0.2	0.0	0.3	98	42	86	60	0.2	0.2	<.1	<.1	76.1	76.1	100.0	50.0	70.0	0.0	81.3
Sac	9,046	99.5	<.1	0.1	<.1	0.0	0.2	66	16	62	73	0.4	0.5	<.1	0.1	73.4	73.5	100.0	50.0	46.2	0.0	50.0
Scott	108,792	92.6	4.1	0.8	0.3	<.1	2.3	3	98	2	4	5.3	5.1	14.7	12.5	72.1	73.6	56.2	62.0	63.6	16.9	58.1
Shelby	9,644	99.5	<.1	<.1	0.1	<.1	0.3	60	23	77	67	0.5	0.5	<.1	0.1	72.9	73.0	60.0	45.0	50.0	50.0	61.4
Sioux	20,962	99.2	0.1	0.5	<.1	0.0	0.2	22	52	48	96	1.0	1.0	<.1	0.2	70.1	70.3	84.0	54.4	34.4	0.0	48.5
Story	59,572	92.7	1.6	4.5	0.1	<.1	1.0	9	96	10	10	2.9	2.8	3.1	3.2	80.2	80.4	79.6	78.9	68.3	35.7	74.3
Tama	12,871	95.8	0.1	0.2	3.5	<.1	0.4	41	90	47	51	0.6	0.6	<.1	0.2	73.9	75.3	43.3	40.0	56.0	50.0	36.7
Taylor	5,292	99.2	0.0	0.1	0.1	0.0	0.6	96	51	99	23	0.3	0.3	0.0	0.2	74.4	74.5	0.0	33.3	85.7	0.0	69.6
Union	9,458	99.2	<.1	0.3	0.2	<.1	0.2	63	48	50	77	0.5	0.5	<.1	0.1	74.2	74.3	70.0	64.6	77.3	25.0	50.0
Van Buren	5,661	99.4	<.1	0.2	<.1	0.0	0.4	93	38	52	55	0.3	0.3	<.1	0.1	73.7	73.9	40.0	50.0	100.0	0.0	69.0
Wapello	27,119	98.2	0.7	0.3	0.2	<.1	0.5	17	76	15	33	1.3	1.3	0.7	0.6	76.0	76.3	73.0	57.1	68.6	39.1	57.1
Warren	25,847	98.8	0.2	0.3	0.1	<.1	0.6	19	64	38	22	1.3	1.3	0.2	0.8	71.7	72.0	62.9	50.0	73.2	40.0	57.4
Washington	14,358	98.6	0.3	0.2	<.1	0.0	0.8	37	72	30	17	0.7	0.7	0.2	0.6	73.2	73.5	51.1	59.6	81.3	0.0	59.7
Wayne	5,410	99.4	<.1	0.1	0.1	0.0	0.3	95	33	91	64	0.3	0.3	<.1	<.1	76.6	76.7	100.0	46.7	100.0	0.0	55.2
Webster	29,859	96.7	1.7	0.3	0.2	<.1	1.0	13	88	8	12	1.5	1.5	1.7	1.5	74.0	74.6	57.7	59.9	63.3	26.3	61.8
Winnebago	9,032	98.8	0.3	0.4	<.1	<.1	0.5	68	66	31	34	0.4	0.4	<.1	0.2	74.5	74.9	80.6	49.3	57.1	100.0	43.3
Winneshiek	15,716	98.6	0.2	0.8	<.1	<.1	0.3	29	71	34	68	0.8	0.8	0.1	0.2	75.4	75.4	92.9	69.6	80.0	100.0	72.1
Woodbury	70,697	94.0	1.5	1.1	1.1	<.1	2.3	6	93	11	3	3.4	3.3	3.6	8.2	71.9	73.1	58.3	61.3	53.7	23.9	59.6
Worth	6,009	98.9	0.2	<.1	<.1	0.0	0.8	92	60	40	18	0.3	0.3	<.1	0.2	75.2	75.5	80.0	21.4	100.0	0.0	52.7
Wright	10,784	99.2	<.1	0.1	0.1	0.0	0.5	55	44	79	31	0.5	0.5	<.1	0.3	75.6	75.8	30.0	37.5	73.3	0.0	57.6
IOWA	2,057,875	96.6	1.5	0.8	0.2	<.1	1.0					100.0	100.0	100.0	100.0	74.1	74.6	63.4	65.9	63.1	28.3	60.6
CONGRESSIONAL																						
District 1	413,721	94.8	2.1	1.2	0.2	<.1	1.6	2	5	2	1	20.1	19.7	29.2	33.7	74.5	75.3	61.1	71.9	66.9	26.1	60.0
District 2	408,469	97.5	1.4	0.4	0.2	<.1	0.5	4	2	3	5	19.8	20.0	18.8	11.2	73.5	74.0	59.7	59.5	59.0	22.5	60.2
District 3	417,743	97.3	0.9	1.0	0.2	<.1	0.7	1	3	4	4	20.3	20.4	12.0	14.5	75.2	75.4	70.4	69.9	72.0	40.5	64.2
District 4	412,171	95.1	2.5	1.0	0.2	<.1	1.2	3	4	1	2	20.0	19.7	33.6	25.9	74.2	74.8	66.5	62.3	70.2	28.0	61.5
District 5	405,771	98.1	0.5	0.4	0.3	<.1	0.7	5	1	5	3	19.7	20.0	6.5	14.7	73.1	73.4	59.2	56.9	55.6	27.3	57.5

Table C. – Voter Participation: November 3, 1992, General Election

County	Estimated Voting Age Population (VAP) 1992	REG Total	REG % contribution to state REG	REG % of 1992 VAP	REG Rank by % of 1992 VAP	Actual[1]	Highest office Total	Office	% of 1992 VAP	Max Total	% contribution to state turnout	% of REG	Rank by % of REG	% of 1992 VAP	Rank by % 1992 VAP	President	Senator	Governor	Representative
Adair	6,296	5,170	0.3	82.1	59	4,362	4,194	P	66.6	4,362	0.3	84.4	8	69.3	20	3.9	15.0	-	21.7
Adams	3,636	3,122	0.2	85.9	19	2,620	2,596	P	71.4	2,620	0.2	83.9	10	72.1	5	0.9	7.7	-	6.6
Allamakee	10,127	8,398	0.5	82.9	50	6,742	6,679	P	66.0	6,742	0.5	80.3	51	66.6	59	0.9	13.7	-	5.1
Appanoose	10,212	8,163	0.5	79.9	79	6,414	6,373	P	62.4	6,414	0.5	78.6	80	62.8	80	0.6	13.6	-	12.4
Audubon	5,410	4,390	0.3	81.1	70	3,894	3,873	P	71.6	3,894	0.3	88.7	1	72.0	6	0.5	15.3	-	23.3
Benton	16,432	13,502	0.8	82.2	57	11,065	10,841	C	66.0	11,065	0.8	82.0	26	67.3	45	5.7	2.5	-	2.0
Black Hawk	91,047	77,931	4.6	85.6	21	61,662	61,550	P	67.6	61,662	4.5	79.1	72	67.7	38	0.2	8.0	-	2.2
Boone	19,155	15,739	0.9	82.2	58	12,458	12,219	P	63.8	12,458	0.9	79.2	70	65.0	67	1.9	4.1	-	41.0
Bremer	16,977	14,742	0.9	86.8	12	11,645	11,714	P	69.0	11,714	0.9	79.5	68	69.0	22	0.0	3.7	-	3.3
Buchanan	14,617	12,024	0.7	82.3	55	9,780	9,715	C	66.5	9,780	0.7	81.3	32	66.9	51	1.3	1.3	-	0.7
Buena Vista	14,832	11,757	0.7	79.3	82	9,223	9,257	P	62.4	9,257	0.7	78.7	77	62.4	87	0.0	10.8	-	22.0
Butler	11,637	8,919	0.5	76.6	89	7,177	7,137	P	61.3	7,177	0.5	80.5	48	61.7	91	0.6	3.2	-	2.6
Calhoun	8,489	6,921	0.4	81.5	66	5,584	5,388	S	63.5	5,584	0.4	80.7	41	65.8	64	5.6	3.5	-	19.3
Carroll	15,196	12,390	0.7	81.5	65	9,989	9,565	S	62.9	9,989	0.7	80.6	42	65.7	65	5.1	4.2	-	26.5
Cass	11,253	9,531	0.6	84.7	34	7,642	7,298	S	64.9	7,642	0.6	80.2	55	67.9	36	7.6	4.5	-	8.3
Cedar	12,896	10,277	0.6	79.7	80	8,216	8,240	P	63.9	8,240	0.6	80.2	56	63.9	75	0.0	1.4	-	3.3
Cerro Gordo	35,385	31,045	1.8	87.7	10	24,209	24,293	P	68.7	24,293	1.8	78.3	83	68.7	27	0.0	10.5	-	4.3
Cherokee	10,288	8,696	0.5	84.5	36	7,340	7,172	S	69.7	7,340	0.5	84.4	7	71.3	7	6.1	2.3	-	15.6
Chickasaw	9,494	8,184	0.5	86.2	17	6,544	6,640	P	69.9	6,640	0.5	81.1	34	69.9	14	0.0	1.2	-	0.7
Clarke	6,199	5,530	0.3	89.2	5	4,328	4,260	P	68.7	4,328	0.3	78.3	82	69.8	17	1.6	2.4	-	2.7
Clay	12,736	10,466	0.6	82.2	56	8,392	8,380	P	65.8	8,392	0.6	80.2	54	65.9	62	0.1	15.4	-	26.0
Clayton	13,852	11,495	0.7	83.0	49	9,252	9,190	P	66.3	9,252	0.7	80.5	45	66.8	54	0.7	14.6	-	4.5
Clinton	37,467	32,325	1.9	86.3	14	24,948	24,960	P	66.6	24,960	1.8	77.2	89	66.6	58	0.0	13.2	-	12.9
Crawford	12,130	9,822	0.6	81.0	72	7,737	7,672	P	63.2	7,737	0.6	78.8	76	63.8	76	0.8	17.6	-	39.9
Dallas	22,111	18,774	1.1	84.9	33	15,042	14,861	P	67.2	15,042	1.1	80.1	58	68.0	33	1.2	1.8	-	3.5
Davis	6,098	4,997	0.3	81.9	61	4,100	4,041	P	66.3	4,100	0.3	82.0	24	67.2	47	1.4	5.8	-	7.3
Decatur	6,112	5,215	0.3	85.3	26	4,125	3,986	P	65.2	4,125	0.3	79.1	73	67.5	42	3.4	5.6	-	5.5
Delaware	12,704	10,560	0.6	83.1	46	8,450	8,492	P	66.8	8,492	0.6	80.4	50	66.8	52	0.0	11.6	-	1.8
Des Moines	31,932	26,692	1.6	83.6	45	21,382	21,190	P	66.4	21,382	1.6	80.1	60	67.0	49	0.9	15.0	-	8.3
Dickinson	11,574	10,330	0.6	89.3	4	8,402	8,304	P	71.7	8,402	0.6	81.3	33	72.6	3	1.2	12.6	-	26.8
Dubuque	63,131	50,866	3.0	80.6	73	42,925	42,968	P	68.1	42,968	3.1	84.5	6	68.1	32	0.0	2.4	-	1.5
Emmet	8,396	6,402	0.4	76.3	92	5,255	5,098	S	60.7	5,255	0.4	82.1	23	62.6	85	4.3	3.0	-	18.4
Fayette	15,880	13,496	0.8	85.0	31	10,793	10,861	P	68.4	10,861	0.8	80.5	47	68.4	30	0.0	9.6	-	3.0
Floyd	12,562	10,283	0.6	81.9	62	7,879	7,750	P	61.7	7,879	0.6	76.6	92	62.7	82	1.6	2.9	-	2.9
Franklin	8,403	6,396	0.4	76.1	94	5,236	5,266	P	62.7	5,266	0.4	82.3	18	62.7	84	0.0	7.1	-	25.3
Fremont	6,051	5,125	0.3	84.7	35	4,040	3,911	P	64.6	4,040	0.3	78.8	74	66.8	56	3.2	4.3	-	9.1
Greene	7,419	6,636	0.4	89.4	3	5,417	5,353	P	72.2	5,417	0.4	81.6	31	73.0	2	1.2	4.5	-	23.6
Grundy	8,871	7,476	0.4	84.3	37	6,172	6,156	P	69.4	6,172	0.4	82.6	15	69.6	18	0.3	7.1	-	3.5
Guthrie	8,266	6,964	0.4	84.2	38	5,511	5,453	P	66.0	5,511	0.4	79.1	71	66.7	57	1.1	7.0	-	19.6
Hamilton	12,013	9,661	0.6	80.4	76	8,162	7,951	S	66.2	8,162	0.6	84.5	5	67.9	35	5.9	2.6	-	24.7
Hancock	9,117	7,341	0.4	80.5	75	5,871	5,806	P	63.7	5,871	0.4	80.0	64	64.4	73	1.1	1.6	-	14.6
Hardin	14,099	12,429	0.7	88.2	8	9,511	9,246	S	65.6	9,511	0.7	76.5	93	67.5	44	5.6	2.8	-	21.0
Harrison	10,776	8,679	0.5	80.5	74	6,985	6,868	P	63.7	6,985	0.5	80.5	46	64.8	70	1.7	10.7	-	15.8
Henry	14,676	11,386	0.7	77.6	86	8,869	8,743	S	59.6	8,869	0.6	77.9	86	60.4	94	2.7	1.4	-	2.6
Howard	7,158	5,995	0.4	83.8	41	4,999	4,897	C	68.4	4,999	0.4	83.4	11	69.8	16	2.7	3.9	-	2.0
Humboldt	7,923	6,635	0.4	83.7	42	5,466	5,305	S	67.0	5,466	0.4	82.4	17	69.0	23	5.1	2.9	-	16.2
Ida	6,106	5,224	0.3	85.6	23	4,268	4,239	P	69.4	4,268	0.3	81.7	29	69.9	15	0.7	16.7	-	24.9
Iowa	10,945	8,934	0.5	81.6	64	7,309	7,285	C	66.6	7,309	0.5	81.8	28	66.8	55	4.7	1.1	-	0.3
Jackson	14,424	11,721	0.7	81.3	67	9,503	9,305	P	64.5	9,503	0.7	81.1	35	65.9	63	2.1	11.7	-	11.3
Jasper	26,412	22,429	1.3	84.9	32	18,148	18,012	P	68.2	18,148	1.3	80.9	37	68.7	26	0.7	1.0	-	1.4
Jefferson	12,604	10,723	0.6	85.1	30	8,520	8,416	S	66.8	8,520	0.6	79.5	69	67.6	39	2.1	1.2	-	1.8
Johnson	78,336	71,612	4.2	91.4	1	52,355	51,774	P	66.1	52,355	3.8	73.1	98	66.8	53	1.1	2.5	-	6.0
Jones	14,665	11,128	0.7	75.9	95	9,147	8,903	S	60.7	9,147	0.7	82.2	20	62.4	88	2.7	2.7	-	7.5
Keokuk	8,634	7,002	0.4	81.1	71	5,643	5,577	P	64.6	5,643	0.4	80.6	43	65.4	66	1.2	13.9	-	12.9
Kossuth	13,253	11,410	0.7	86.1	18	9,181	9,059	P	68.4	9,181	0.7	80.5	49	69.3	21	1.3	3.3	-	17.5
Lee	28,765	23,577	1.4	82.0	60	17,985	17,660	C	61.4	17,985	1.3	76.3	94	62.5	86	4.6	2.1	-	1.8
Linn	128,216	102,628	6.0	80.0	78	90,408	88,885	P	69.3	90,408	6.6	88.1	2	70.5	11	1.7	2.2	-	5.4
Louisa	8,601	6,361	0.4	74.0	99	4,896	4,844	P	56.3	4,896	0.4	77.0	91	56.9	99	1.1	1.7	-	2.1
Lucas	6,818	5,826	0.3	85.5	24	4,702	4,674	P	68.6	4,702	0.3	80.7	40	69.0	24	0.6	4.4	-	7.9
Lyon	8,487	7,340	0.4	86.5	13	5,772	5,726	P	67.5	5,772	0.4	78.6	79	68.0	34	0.8	13.4	-	21.7
Madison	9,315	8,030	0.5	86.2	16	6,468	6,379	S	68.5	6,468	0.5	80.5	44	69.4	19	4.9	1.4	-	3.1
Mahaska	16,014	12,493	0.7	78.0	85	10,226	10,247	P	64.0	10,247	0.7	82.0	25	64.0	74	0.0	9.9	-	7.9
Marion	22,729	18,458	1.1	81.2	69	13,697	13,533	P	59.5	13,697	1.0	74.2	97	60.3	95	1.2	4.3	-	5.0
Marshall	28,761	23,720	1.4	82.5	54	18,985	18,818	P	65.4	18,985	1.4	80.0	62	66.0	61	3.7	0.9	-	2.1
Mills	9,959	7,917	0.5	79.5	81	6,173	6,166	P	61.9	6,173	0.4	78.0	85	62.0	90	0.1	15.2	-	22.7
Mitchell	8,069	6,882	0.4	85.3	27	5,697	5,576	S	69.1	5,697	0.4	82.8	13	70.6	10	6.1	2.1	-	2.8
Monona	7,482	6,187	0.4	82.7	51	4,854	4,849	P	64.8	4,854	0.4	78.5	81	64.9	69	0.1	8.6	-	30.1
Monroe	6,032	4,976	0.3	82.5	53	4,072	3,926	S	65.1	4,072	0.3	81.8	27	67.5	40	7.1	3.6	-	4.9
Montgomery	9,069	7,102	0.4	78.3	84	5,692	5,537	S	61.1	5,692	0.4	80.1	57	62.8	81	5.7	2.7	-	6.1
Muscatine	29,467	22,234	1.3	75.5	97	16,699	16,858	P	57.2	16,858	1.2	75.8	96	57.2	98	0.0	12.3	-	10.8

[1] Actual voter turnout for all counties not officially certified by Iowa Secretary of State at time of publication.

Table C. — Voter Participation: November 3, 1992, General Election (cont)

County	Estimated Voting Age Population (VAP) 1992	Voter registration (REG)				Voter turnout													
						Highest office				Maximum vote						Percent drop-off, by office			
		Total	% contribution to state REG	% of 1992 VAP	Rank by % of 1992 VAP	Actual¹	Total	Office	% of 1992 VAP	Total	% contribution to state turnout	% of REG	Rank by % of REG	% of 1992 VAP	Rank by % 1992 VAP	President	Senator	Governor	Representative
O'Brien	11,381	9,246	0.5	81.2	68	7,629	7,584	P	66.6	7,629	0.6	82.5	16	67.0	48	0.6	3.1	-	14.5
Osceola	5,261	4,405	0.3	83.7	43	3,616	3,598	P	68.4	3,616	0.3	82.1	22	68.7	25	0.5	12.9	-	24.8
Page	12,694	9,456	0.6	74.5	98	7,576	7,516	C	59.2	7,576	0.6	80.1	59	59.7	96	3.5	2.8	-	0.8
Palo Alto	7,631	6,761	0.4	88.6	7	5,426	5,379	P	70.5	5,426	0.4	80.3	52	71.1	8	0.9	17.5	-	38.6
Plymouth	16,808	12,838	0.8	76.4	91	10,539	10,484	P	62.4	10,539	0.8	82.1	21	62.7	83	0.5	15.9	-	24.2
Pocahontas	6,942	6,099	0.4	87.9	9	4,871	4,760	S	68.6	4,871	0.4	79.9	65	70.2	13	4.1	2.3	-	15.6
Polk	253,691	195,906	11.5	77.2	87	170,754	167,258	P	65.9	170,754	12.4	87.2	4	67.3	46	2.0	2.4	-	4.2
Pottawattamie	60,983	46,496	2.7	76.2	93	36,859	37,115	P	60.9	37,115	2.7	79.8	66	60.9	92	0.0	11.7	-	17.8
Poweshiek	14,367	12,021	0.7	83.7	44	9,155	9,047	P	63.0	9,155	0.7	76.2	95	63.7	77	1.2	10.0	-	10.4
Ringgold	4,097	3,634	0.2	88.7	6	2,910	2,869	P	70.0	2,910	0.2	80.1	61	71.0	9	1.4	1.7	-	2.2
Sac	9,018	7,100	0.4	78.7	83	5,466	5,428	S	60.2	5,466	0.4	77.0	90	60.6	93	4.6	0.7	-	13.9
Scott	109,971	93,736	5.5	85.2	28	74,255	74,662	P	67.9	74,662	5.4	79.7	67	67.9	37	0.0	11.3	-	8.1
Shelby	9,611	8,180	0.5	85.1	29	6,539	6,544	P	68.1	6,544	0.5	80.0	63	68.1	31	0.0	18.1	-	21.1
Sioux	20,986	17,911	1.1	85.3	25	14,628	14,730	P	70.2	14,730	1.1	82.2	19	70.2	12	0.0	8.5	-	15.8
Story	58,044	52,133	3.1	89.8	2	36,633	36,290	P	62.5	36,633	2.7	70.3	99	63.1	79	0.9	4.5	-	6.5
Tama	12,840	10,494	0.6	81.7	63	8,667	8,566	C	66.7	8,667	0.6	82.6	14	67.5	41	3.6	1.6	-	1.2
Taylor	5,246	4,572	0.3	87.2	11	3,596	3,551	P	67.7	3,596	0.3	78.7	78	68.5	28	1.3	8.7	-	6.2
Union	9,518	7,908	0.5	83.1	48	6,179	6,102	P	64.1	6,179	0.4	78.1	84	64.9	68	1.2	11.1	-	6.7
Van Buren	5,616	4,644	0.3	82.7	52	3,759	3,710	P	66.1	3,759	0.3	80.9	36	66.9	50	1.3	11.8	-	10.5
Wapello	26,969	22,409	1.3	83.1	47	17,428	16,919	S	62.7	17,428	1.3	77.8	87	64.6	72	7.7	2.9	-	3.3
Warren	26,692	23,022	1.4	86.3	15	19,325	19,158	P	71.8	19,325	1.4	83.9	9	72.4	4	0.9	10.2	-	8.3
Washington	14,603	11,248	0.7	77.0	88	9,097	9,018	P	61.8	9,097	0.7	80.9	38	62.3	89	0.9	6.0	-	14.2
Wayne	5,333	4,487	0.3	84.1	39	3,598	3,584	P	67.2	3,598	0.3	80.2	53	67.5	43	0.4	5.1	-	8.4
Webster	29,509	23,645	1.4	80.1	77	19,114	18,921	P	64.1	19,114	1.4	80.8	39	64.8	71	1.0	10.9	-	42.9
Winnebago	8,932	7,483	0.4	83.8	40	6,112	6,078	P	68.0	6,112	0.4	81.7	30	68.4	29	0.6	17.2	-	37.2
Winneshiek	15,424	13,203	0.8	85.6	20	10,200	10,048	C	65.1	10,200	0.7	77.3	88	66.1	60	5.6	3.0	-	1.5
Woodbury	71,944	54,399	3.2	75.6	96	42,676	42,864	P	59.6	42,864	3.1	78.8	75	59.6	97	0.0	2.0	-	22.8
Worth	5,996	5,132	0.3	85.6	22	4,475	4,448	P	74.2	4,475	0.3	87.2	3	74.6	1	0.6	2.7	-	9.6
Wright	10,695	8,173	0.5	76.4	90	6,814	6,665	P	62.3	6,814	0.5	83.4	12	63.7	78	2.2	7.0	-	29.6
IOWA	**2,075,000**	**1,703,532**	**100.0**	**82.1**		**1,374,111**	**1,360,856**		**65.6**	**1,375,751**	**100.0**	**80.8**		**66.3**		**1.5**	**6.1**	**-**	**9.7**

¹Actual voter turnout for all counties not officially certified by Iowa Secretary of State at time of publication.

Table D. — Voter Registration by Political Party Affiliation: November 3, 1992, General Election

County	Total voter registration	Political party affiliation Democrat (DEM)	Republican (REP)	Independent (IND)	Plurality Total	Party	Percent of total registration DEM	REP	IND	Rank DEM	REP	IND	Percent contribution to state registration Total	DEM	REP	IND
Adair	5,170	1,550	2,258	1,362	708	R	30.0	43.7	26.3	64	17	80	0.3	0.2	0.4	0.3
Adams	3,122	1,092	1,191	839	99	R	35.0	38.1	26.9	47	28	76	0.2	0.2	0.2	0.2
Allamakee	8,398	1,881	4,045	2,472	1,573	R	22.4	48.2	29.4	90	11	58	0.5	0.3	0.8	0.5
Appanoose	8,163	3,588	2,662	1,913	926	D	44.0	32.6	23.4	17	52	90	0.5	0.6	0.5	0.4
Audubon	4,390	2,016	1,332	1,042	684	D	45.9	30.3	23.7	9	69	88	0.3	0.3	0.3	0.2
Benton	13,502	4,566	3,364	5,572	1,006	I	33.8	24.9	41.3	53	88	4	0.8	0.7	0.6	1.0
Black Hawk	77,931	30,164	22,263	25,504	4,660	D	38.7	28.6	32.7	28	76	35	4.6	4.7	4.2	4.8
Boone	15,739	6,928	3,746	5,065	1,863	D	44.0	23.8	32.2	14	90	39	0.9	1.1	0.7	0.9
Bremer	14,742	3,699	4,729	6,314	1,585	I	25.1	32.1	42.8	85	56	1	0.9	0.6	0.9	1.2
Buchanan	12,024	4,614	3,141	4,269	345	D	38.4	26.1	35.5	30	85	19	0.7	0.7	0.6	0.8
Buena Vista	11,757	3,356	4,239	4,162	77	R	28.5	36.1	35.4	69	38	20	0.7	0.5	0.8	0.8
Butler	8,919	1,913	4,549	2,457	2,092	R	21.4	51.0	27.5	93	9	71	0.5	0.3	0.9	0.5
Calhoun	6,921	2,032	2,178	2,711	533	I	29.4	31.5	39.2	68	60	5	0.4	0.3	0.4	0.5
Carroll	12,390	6,391	2,398	3,601	2,790	D	51.6	19.4	29.1	4	97	60	0.7	1.0	0.5	0.7
Cass	9,531	2,072	5,253	2,206	3,047	R	21.7	55.1	23.1	91	5	91	0.6	0.3	1.0	0.4
Cedar	10,277	3,056	3,293	3,928	635	I	29.7	32.0	38.2	66	57	9	0.6	0.5	0.6	0.7
Cerro Gordo	31,045	10,871	9,481	10,693	178	D	35.0	30.5	34.4	46	65	26	1.8	1.7	1.8	2.0
Cherokee	8,696	2,901	3,170	2,625	269	R	33.4	36.5	30.2	58	34	54	0.5	0.5	0.6	0.5
Chickasaw	8,184	3,410	2,069	2,705	705	D	41.7	25.3	33.1	20	87	34	0.5	0.5	0.4	0.5
Clarke	5,530	2,211	1,721	1,598	490	D	40.0	31.1	28.9	26	62	61	0.3	0.3	0.3	0.3
Clay	10,466	2,851	3,982	3,633	349	R	27.2	38.0	34.7	77	29	23	0.6	0.4	0.7	0.7
Clayton	11,495	3,859	3,461	4,175	316	I	33.6	30.1	36.3	55	70	17	0.7	0.6	0.7	0.8
Clinton	32,325	10,367	9,407	12,551	2,184	I	32.1	29.1	38.8	60	75	7	1.9	1.6	1.8	2.3
Crawford	9,822	3,767	2,670	3,385	382	D	38.4	27.2	34.5	31	83	25	0.6	0.6	0.5	0.6
Dallas	18,774	7,949	4,996	5,829	2,120	D	42.3	26.6	31.0	19	84	46	1.1	1.2	0.9	1.1
Davis	4,997	2,593	1,384	1,020	1,209	D	51.9	27.7	20.4	3	81	97	0.3	0.4	0.3	0.2
Decatur	5,215	2,341	1,623	1,251	718	D	44.9	31.1	24.0	10	61	87	0.3	0.4	0.3	0.2
Delaware	10,560	2,978	3,636	3,946	310	I	28.2	34.4	37.4	70	43	12	0.6	0.5	0.7	0.7
Des Moines	26,692	11,803	6,228	8,661	3,142	D	44.2	23.3	32.4	13	91	37	1.6	1.9	1.2	1.6
Dickinson	10,330	2,787	3,515	4,028	513	I	27.0	34.0	39.0	78	45	6	0.6	0.4	0.7	0.8
Dubuque	50,866	25,640	9,711	15,515	10,125	D	50.4	19.1	30.5	5	98	51	3.0	4.0	1.8	2.9
Emmet	6,402	2,642	2,073	1,687	569	D	41.3	32.4	26.4	22	54	79	0.4	0.4	0.4	0.3
Fayette	13,496	4,538	4,466	4,492	46	D	33.6	33.1	33.3	54	51	32	0.8	0.7	0.8	0.8
Floyd	10,283	3,449	3,326	3,508	59	I	33.5	32.3	34.1	56	55	29	0.6	0.5	0.6	0.7
Franklin	6,396	1,789	2,928	1,679	1,139	R	28.0	45.8	26.3	72	14	82	0.4	0.3	0.6	0.3
Fremont	5,125	1,659	2,038	1,428	379	R	32.4	39.8	27.9	59	24	69	0.3	0.3	0.4	0.3
Greene	6,636	2,532	2,107	1,997	425	D	38.2	31.8	30.1	33	58	55	0.4	0.4	0.4	0.4
Grundy	7,476	1,455	4,047	1,974	2,073	R	19.5	54.1	26.4	95	7	78	0.4	0.2	0.8	0.4
Guthrie	6,964	2,466	2,637	1,861	171	R	35.4	37.9	26.7	45	31	77	0.4	0.4	0.5	0.3
Hamilton	9,661	3,361	3,202	3,098	159	D	34.8	33.1	32.1	48	50	40	0.6	0.5	0.6	0.6
Hancock	7,341	1,950	3,149	2,242	907	R	26.6	42.9	30.5	79	18	50	0.4	0.3	0.6	0.4
Hardin	12,429	3,971	4,490	3,968	519	R	31.9	36.1	31.9	62	37	41	0.7	0.6	0.8	0.7
Harrison	8,679	3,286	2,954	2,439	332	D	37.9	34.0	28.1	35	44	66	0.5	0.5	0.6	0.5
Henry	11,386	2,831	4,787	3,768	1,019	R	24.9	42.0	33.1	86	21	33	0.7	0.4	0.9	0.7
Howard	5,995	2,260	1,823	1,912	348	D	37.7	30.4	31.9	36	68	42	0.4	0.4	0.3	0.4
Humboldt	6,635	1,970	2,386	2,279	107	R	29.7	36.0	34.3	67	39	27	0.4	0.3	0.4	0.4
Ida	5,224	1,446	2,300	1,478	822	R	27.7	44.0	28.3	73	16	65	0.3	0.2	0.4	0.3
Iowa	8,934	2,434	3,255	3,245	10	R	27.2	36.4	36.3	76	35	16	0.5	0.4	0.6	0.6
Jackson	11,721	5,748	2,370	3,603	2,145	D	49.0	20.2	30.7	7	94	48	0.7	0.9	0.4	0.7
Jasper	22,429	9,805	6,145	6,479	3,326	D	43.7	27.4	28.9	18	82	62	1.3	1.5	1.2	1.2
Jefferson	10,723	2,784	3,473	4,466	993	I	26.0	32.4	41.6	82	53	2	0.6	0.4	0.7	0.8
Johnson	71,612	31,789	15,000	24,823	6,966	D	44.4	20.9	34.7	12	93	24	4.2	5.0	2.8	4.6
Jones	11,128	4,226	3,386	3,516	710	D	38.0	30.4	31.6	34	66	44	0.7	0.7	0.6	0.7
Keokuk	7,002	2,682	2,356	1,964	326	D	38.3	33.6	28.0	32	47	68	0.4	0.4	0.4	0.4
Kossuth	11,410	4,671	3,207	3,532	1,139	D	40.9	28.1	31.0	24	78	47	0.7	0.7	0.6	0.7
Lee	23,577	10,371	4,745	8,461	1,910	D	44.0	20.1	35.9	15	96	18	1.4	1.6	0.9	1.6
Linn	102,628	37,960	25,174	39,494	1,534	I	37.0	24.5	38.5	40	89	8	6.0	6.0	4.7	7.4
Louisa	6,361	1,741	2,906	1,714	1,165	R	27.4	45.7	26.9	75	15	74	0.4	0.3	0.5	0.3
Lucas	5,826	2,181	2,114	1,531	67	D	37.4	36.3	26.3	37	36	81	0.3	0.3	0.4	0.3
Lyon	7,340	1,282	4,673	1,385	3,288	R	17.5	63.7	18.9	98	2	99	0.4	0.2	0.9	0.3
Madison	8,030	3,312	2,546	2,172	766	D	41.2	31.7	27.0	23	59	73	0.5	0.5	0.5	0.4
Mahaska	12,493	3,994	5,134	3,365	1,140	R	32.0	41.1	26.9	61	22	75	0.7	0.6	1.0	0.6
Marion	18,458	7,650	5,509	5,299	2,141	D	41.4	29.8	28.7	21	72	63	1.1	1.2	1.0	1.0
Marshall	23,720	8,494	8,267	6,959	227	D	35.8	34.9	29.3	44	42	59	1.4	1.3	1.6	1.3
Mills	7,917	1,713	4,345	1,859	2,486	R	21.6	54.9	23.5	92	6	89	0.5	0.3	0.8	0.3
Mitchell	6,882	1,939	2,600	2,343	257	R	28.2	37.8	34.0	71	32	30	0.4	0.3	0.5	0.4
Monona	6,187	2,309	1,582	2,296	13	D	37.3	25.6	37.1	38	86	13	0.4	0.4	0.3	0.4
Monroe	4,976	2,475	1,382	1,119	1,093	D	49.7	27.8	22.5	6	79	93	0.3	0.4	0.3	0.2
Montgomery	7,102	1,341	3,917	1,844	2,073	R	18.9	55.2	26.0	96	4	83	0.4	0.2	0.7	0.3
Muscatine	22,234	5,707	8,154	8,373	219	I	25.7	36.7	37.7	83	33	10	1.3	0.9	1.5	1.6

County	Total voter registration	Democrat (DEM)	Republican (REP)	Independent (IND)	Plurality Total	Plurality Party	DEM	REP	IND	Rank DEM	Rank REP	Rank IND	Total	DEM	REP	IND
O'Brien	9,246	1,861	4,489	2,896	1,593	R	20.1	48.6	31.3	94	10	45	0.5	0.3	0.8	0.5
Osceola	4,405	1,031	2,541	833	1,510	R	23.4	57.7	18.9	89	3	98	0.3	0.2	0.5	0.2
Page	9,456	1,784	4,864	2,808	2,056	R	18.9	51.4	29.7	97	8	57	0.6	0.3	0.9	0.5
Palo Alto	6,761	3,659	1,361	1,741	1,918	D	54.1	20.1	25.8	2	95	84	0.4	0.6	0.3	0.3
Plymouth	12,838	3,406	4,954	4,478	476	R	26.5	38.6	34.9	80	27	22	0.8	0.5	0.9	0.8
Pocahontas	6,099	2,039	1,775	2,285	246	I	33.4	29.1	37.5	57	74	11	0.4	0.3	0.3	0.4
Polk	195,906	94,047	58,593	43,266	35,454	D	48.0	29.9	22.1	8	71	94	11.5	14.8	11.0	8.1
Pottawattamie	46,496	15,799	17,649	13,048	1,850	R	34.0	38.0	28.1	52	30	67	2.7	2.5	3.3	2.4
Poweshiek	12,021	4,652	3,704	3,665	948	D	38.7	30.8	30.5	29	64	52	0.7	0.7	0.7	0.7
Ringgold	3,634	1,346	1,539	749	193	R	37.0	42.4	20.6	39	20	96	0.2	0.2	0.3	0.1
Sac	7,100	1,794	2,802	2,504	298	R	25.3	39.5	35.3	84	26	21	0.4	0.3	0.5	0.5
Scott	93,736	31,871	27,732	34,133	2,262	I	34.0	29.6	36.4	51	73	15	5.5	5.0	5.2	6.4
Shelby	8,180	2,791	2,730	2,659	61	D	34.1	33.4	32.5	50	49	36	0.5	0.4	0.5	0.5
Sioux	17,911	1,985	12,025	3,901	8,124	R	11.1	67.1	21.8	99	1	95	1.1	0.3	2.3	0.7
Story	52,133	18,122	14,728	19,283	1,161	I	34.8	28.3	37.0	49	77	14	3.1	2.8	2.8	3.6
Tama	10,494	4,095	3,254	3,145	841	D	39.0	31.0	30.0	27	63	56	0.6	0.6	0.6	0.6
Taylor	4,572	1,383	1,943	1,246	560	R	30.2	42.5	27.3	63	19	72	0.3	0.2	0.4	0.2
Union	7,908	2,837	2,650	2,421	187	D	35.9	33.5	30.6	43	48	49	0.5	0.4	0.5	0.5
Van Buren	4,644	1,383	2,209	1,052	826	R	29.8	47.6	22.7	65	12	92	0.3	0.2	0.4	0.2
Wapello	22,409	12,874	3,929	5,606	7,268	D	57.5	17.5	25.0	1	99	85	1.3	2.0	0.7	1.0
Warren	23,022	10,122	6,383	6,517	3,605	D	44.0	27.7	28.3	16	80	64	1.4	1.6	1.2	1.2
Washington	11,248	2,667	5,182	3,399	1,783	R	23.7	46.1	30.2	88	13	53	0.7	0.4	1.0	0.6
Wayne	4,487	1,799	1,582	1,106	217	D	40.1	35.3	24.6	25	41	86	0.3	0.3	0.3	0.2
Webster	23,645	10,601	5,508	7,536	3,065	D	44.8	23.3	31.9	11	92	43	1.4	1.7	1.0	1.4
Winnebago	7,483	1,841	2,537	3,105	568	I	24.6	33.9	41.5	87	46	3	0.4	0.3	0.5	0.6
Winneshiek	13,203	3,445	5,245	4,513	732	R	26.1	39.7	34.2	81	25	28	0.8	0.5	1.0	0.8
Woodbury	54,399	19,686	16,549	18,164	1,522	D	36.2	30.4	33.4	42	67	31	3.2	3.1	3.1	3.4
Worth	5,132	1,887	1,818	1,427	69	D	36.8	35.4	27.8	41	40	70	0.3	0.3	0.3	0.3
Wright	8,173	2,262	3,279	2,632	647	R	27.7	40.1	32.2	74	23	38	0.5	0.4	0.6	0.5
IOWA	**1,703,532**	**636,528**	**532,202**	**534,802**	**101,726**	**D**	**37.4**	**31.2**	**31.4**				**100.0**	**100.0**	**100.0**	**100.0**

County	All candidates					Plurality		Percent of total vote				Rank			Percent contribution to state vote				Major party Percent of vote	
	Total	Clinton (DEM)	Bush (REP)	Perot (IND)	Other	Total	Party	DEM	REP	IND	Other	DEM	REP	IND	Total	DEM	REP	IND	DEM	REP
Adair	4,194	1,655	1,713	814	12	58	R	39.5	40.8	19.4	0.3	65	22	60	0.3	0.3	0.3	0.3	49.1	50.9
Adams	2,596	1,034	863	679	20	171	D	39.8	33.2	26.2	0.8	64	85	2	0.2	0.2	0.2	0.3	54.5	45.5
Allamakee	6,679	2,362	2,627	1,543	147	265	R	35.4	39.3	23.1	2.2	84	34	24	0.5	0.4	0.5	0.6	47.3	52.7
Appanoose	6,373	2,810	2,346	1,161	56	464	D	44.1	36.8	18.2	0.9	32	51	68	0.5	0.5	0.5	0.5	54.5	45.5
Audubon	3,873	1,589	1,373	887	24	216	D	41.0	35.5	22.9	0.6	49	64	26	0.3	0.3	0.3	0.3	53.6	46.4
Benton	10,439	4,467	3,469	2,454	49	998	D	42.8	33.2	23.5	0.5	38	86	20	0.8	0.8	0.7	1.0	56.3	43.7
Black Hawk	61,550	29,584	21,398	10,182	386	8,186	D	48.1	34.8	16.5	0.6	8	71	89	4.5	5.0	4.2	4.0	58.0	42.0
Boone	12,219	5,913	4,148	2,070	88	1,765	D	48.4	33.9	16.9	0.7	6	79	85	0.9	1.0	0.8	0.8	58.8	41.2
Bremer	11,714	4,774	4,482	2,338	120	292	D	40.8	38.3	20.0	1.0	52	37	56	0.9	0.8	0.9	0.9	51.6	48.4
Buchanan	9,654	4,166	3,313	2,126	49	853	D	43.2	34.3	22.0	0.5	37	75	38	0.7	0.7	0.7	0.8	55.7	44.3
Buena Vista	9,257	3,374	3,863	1,955	65	489	R	36.4	41.7	21.1	0.7	77	19	45	0.7	0.6	0.8	0.8	46.6	53.4
Butler	7,137	2,548	3,209	1,333	47	661	R	35.7	45.0	18.7	0.7	82	10	64	0.5	0.4	0.6	0.5	44.3	55.7
Calhoun	5,274	2,140	2,169	946	19	29	R	40.6	41.1	17.9	0.4	57	20	70	0.4	0.4	0.4	0.4	49.7	50.3
Carroll	9,475	3,800	3,439	2,192	44	361	D	40.1	36.3	23.1	0.5	60	54	23	0.7	0.6	0.7	0.9	52.5	47.5
Cass	7,058	2,231	3,176	1,608	43	945	R	31.6	45.0	22.8	0.6	89	9	28	0.5	0.4	0.6	0.6	41.3	58.7
Cedar	8,240	3,296	2,965	1,945	34	331	D	40.0	36.0	23.6	0.4	61	58	18	0.6	0.6	0.6	0.8	52.6	47.4
Cerro Gordo	24,293	11,415	8,250	4,498	130	3,165	D	47.0	34.0	18.5	0.5	13	78	67	1.8	1.9	1.6	1.8	58.0	42.0
Cherokee	6,893	2,590	2,768	1,503	32	178	R	37.6	40.2	21.8	0.5	72	27	41	0.5	0.4	0.5	0.6	48.3	51.7
Chickasaw	6,640	2,913	2,129	1,566	32	784	D	43.9	32.1	23.6	0.5	33	90	19	0.5	0.5	0.4	0.6	57.8	42.2
Clarke	4,260	1,921	1,417	899	23	504	D	45.1	33.3	21.1	0.5	24	82	46	0.3	0.3	0.3	0.4	57.5	42.5
Clay	8,380	3,346	3,011	1,964	59	335	D	39.9	35.9	23.4	0.7	63	60	22	0.6	0.6	0.6	0.6	52.6	47.4
Clayton	9,190	3,742	3,044	2,309	95	698	D	40.7	33.1	25.1	1.0	53	87	8	0.7	0.6	0.6	0.9	55.1	44.9
Clinton	24,960	11,683	8,746	4,414	117	2,937	D	46.8	35.0	17.7	0.5	16	67	75	1.8	2.0	1.7	1.7	57.2	42.8
Crawford	7,672	3,004	2,693	1,905	70	311	D	39.2	35.1	24.8	0.9	69	66	12	0.6	0.5	0.5	0.8	52.7	47.3
Dallas	14,861	6,554	5,587	2,665	55	967	D	44.1	37.6	17.9	0.4	31	45	71	1.1	1.1	1.1	1.1	54.0	46.0
Davis	4,041	1,962	1,344	718	17	618	D	48.6	33.3	17.8	0.4	5	83	74	0.3	0.3	0.3	0.3	59.3	40.7
Decatur	3,986	1,866	1,316	786	18	550	D	46.8	33.0	19.7	0.5	10	84	58	0.3	0.3	0.3	0.3	58.6	41.4
Delaware	8,492	3,093	3,195	2,144	60	102	R	36.4	37.6	25.2	0.7	78	44	7	0.6	0.5	0.6	0.8	49.2	50.8
Des Moines	21,190	11,309	6,378	3,386	117	4,931	D	53.4	30.1	16.0	0.6	4	96	92	1.6	1.9	1.3	1.3	63.9	36.1
Dickinson	8,304	3,106	3,196	1,974	28	90	R	37.4	38.5	23.8	0.3	75	36	17	0.6	0.5	0.6	0.8	49.3	50.7
Dubuque	42,968	20,539	14,007	8,208	214	6,532	D	47.8	32.6	19.1	0.5	9	89	62	3.2	3.5	2.8	3.2	59.5	40.5
Emmet	5,031	2,239	1,749	1,010	33	490	D	44.5	34.8	20.1	0.7	28	72	55	0.4	0.4	0.3	0.4	56.1	43.9
Fayette	10,861	4,412	3,879	2,493	77	533	D	40.6	35.7	23.0	0.7	55	62	25	0.8	0.8	0.8	1.0	53.2	46.8
Floyd	7,750	3,688	2,404	1,611	47	1,284	D	47.6	31.0	20.8	0.6	10	93	51	0.6	0.6	0.5	0.6	60.5	39.5
Franklin	5,266	2,049	2,137	1,045	35	88	R	38.9	40.6	19.8	0.7	70	24	57	0.4	0.3	0.4	0.4	48.9	51.1
Fremont	3,911	1,422	1,459	1,003	27	37	R	36.4	37.3	25.6	0.7	79	47	4	0.3	0.2	0.3	0.4	49.4	50.6
Greene	5,353	2,422	1,952	956	23	470	D	45.2	36.5	17.9	0.4	21	52	73	0.4	0.4	0.4	0.4	55.4	44.6
Grundy	6,156	1,895	3,160	1,069	32	1,265	R	30.8	51.3	17.4	0.5	90	3	78	0.5	0.3	0.6	0.4	37.5	62.5
Guthrie	5,453	2,234	1,962	1,216	41	272	D	41.0	36.0	22.3	0.8	50	59	32	0.4	0.4	0.4	0.5	53.2	46.8
Hamilton	7,681	3,262	3,031	1,348	40	231	D	42.5	39.5	17.5	0.5	40	32	77	0.6	0.6	0.6	0.5	51.8	48.2
Hancock	5,806	2,175	2,428	1,170	33	253	R	37.5	41.8	20.2	0.6	74	18	54	0.4	0.4	0.5	0.5	47.3	52.7
Hardin	8,979	3,792	3,590	1,547	50	202	D	42.2	40.0	17.2	0.6	41	28	82	0.7	0.6	0.7	0.6	51.4	48.6
Harrison	6,868	2,349	2,763	1,691	65	414	R	34.2	40.2	24.6	0.9	85	26	14	0.5	0.4	0.5	0.7	46.0	54.0
Henry	8,628	3,544	3,435	1,522	127	109	D	41.1	39.8	17.6	1.5	47	29	76	0.6	0.6	0.7	0.6	50.8	49.2
Howard	4,862	2,099	1,516	1,193	54	583	D	43.2	31.2	24.5	1.1	35	91	15	0.4	0.4	0.3	0.5	58.1	41.9
Humboldt	5,185	1,765	2,299	1,093	28	534	R	34.0	44.3	21.1	0.5	87	13	47	0.4	0.3	0.5	0.4	43.4	56.6
Ida	4,239	1,449	1,714	1,061	15	265	R	34.2	40.4	25.0	0.4	86	25	10	0.3	0.2	0.3	0.4	45.8	54.2
Iowa	6,965	2,560	2,656	1,709	40	96	R	36.8	38.1	24.5	0.6	76	40	16	0.5	0.4	0.5	0.7	49.1	50.9
Jackson	9,305	4,421	2,673	2,096	115	1,748	D	47.5	28.7	22.5	1.2	11	97	30	0.7	0.8	0.5	0.8	62.3	37.7
Jasper	18,012	8,120	6,866	2,972	54	1,254	D	45.1	38.1	16.5	0.3	25	41	90	1.3	1.4	1.4	1.2	54.2	45.8
Jefferson	8,341	2,562	2,541	1,241	1,997	21	D	30.7	30.5	14.9	23.9	91	94	95	0.6	0.4	0.5	0.5	50.2	49.8
Johnson	51,774	28,656	14,041	8,625	452	14,615	D	55.3	27.1	16.7	0.9	1	99	88	3.8	4.9	2.8	3.4	67.1	32.9
Jones	8,900	3,508	3,071	2,306	15	437	D	39.4	34.5	25.9	0.2	67	74	3	0.7	0.6	0.6	0.9	53.3	46.7
Keokuk	5,577	2,329	1,981	1,238	29	348	D	41.8	35.5	22.2	0.5	44	63	33	0.4	0.4	0.4	0.5	54.0	46.0
Kossuth	9,059	3,660	3,464	1,906	29	196	D	40.4	38.2	21.0	0.3	58	38	48	0.7	0.6	0.7	0.8	51.4	48.6
Lee	17,152	9,366	4,777	2,920	89	4,589	D	54.6	27.9	17.0	0.5	2	98	83	1.3	1.6	0.9	1.2	66.2	33.8
Linn	88,885	38,567	30,215	19,643	460	8,352	D	43.4	34.0	22.1	0.5	34	77	36	6.6	6.6	6.0	7.7	56.1	43.9
Louisa	4,844	2,091	1,691	1,044	18	400	D	43.2	34.9	21.6	0.4	36	70	45	0.4	0.4	0.4	0.4	55.3	44.7
Lucas	4,674	2,072	1,734	848	20	338	D	44.3	37.1	18.1	0.4	29	48	69	0.3	0.4	0.3	0.3	54.4	45.6
Lyon	5,726	1,331	3,272	1,068	55	1,941	R	23.2	57.1	18.7	1.0	98	2	65	0.4	0.2	0.6	0.4	28.9	71.1
Madison	6,149	2,525	2,421	1,168	35	104	D	41.1	39.4	19.0	0.6	48	33	63	0.5	0.4	0.5	0.5	51.1	48.9
Mahaska	10,247	3,714	4,953	1,508	72	1,239	R	36.2	48.3	14.7	0.7	81	8	96	0.8	0.6	1.0	0.5	42.9	57.1
Marion	13,533	5,531	6,062	1,896	44	531	R	40.9	44.8	14.0	0.3	51	11	98	1.0	0.9	1.2	0.7	47.7	52.3
Marshall	18,289	8,303	6,784	3,100	102	1,519	D	45.4	37.1	17.0	0.6	19	49	84	1.4	1.4	1.3	1.2	55.0	45.0
Mills	6,166	1,798	2,699	1,638	31	901	R	29.2	43.8	26.6	0.5	94	14	1	0.5	0.3	0.5	0.6	40.0	60.0
Mitchell	5,347	2,177	1,933	1,199	38	244	D	40.7	36.2	22.4	0.7	54	56	31	0.4	0.4	0.4	0.5	53.0	47.0
Monona	4,849	1,939	1,660	1,231	19	279	D	40.0	34.2	25.4	0.4	62	76	6	0.4	0.3	0.3	0.5	53.9	46.1
Monroe	3,782	1,829	1,323	612	18	506	D	48.4	35.0	16.2	0.5	7	69	91	0.3	0.3	0.3	0.3	58.0	42.0
Montgomery	5,369	1,599	2,404	1,341	25	805	R	29.8	44.8	25.0	0.5	93	12	11	0.4	0.3	0.5	0.5	39.9	60.1
Muscatine	16,858	7,089	6,087	3,583	99	1,002	D	42.1	36.1	21.3	0.6	42	57	44	1.2	1.2	1.2	1.4	53.8	46.2

Iowa 325

Table E. – Vote for President: November 3, 1992, General Election (cont)

County	Total	Clinton (DEM)	Bush (REP)	Perot (IND)	Other	Plurality Total	Party	DEM	REP	IND	Other	Rank DEM	Rank REP	Rank IND	Total	DEM	REP	IND	DEM	REP
O'Brien	7,584	2,122	3,869	1,557	36	1,747	R	28.0	51.0	20.5	0.5	95	4	52	0.6	0.4	0.8	0.6	35.4	64.6
Osceola	3,598	990	1,756	813	39	766	R	27.5	48.8	22.6	1.1	96	7	29	0.3	0.2	0.3	0.3	36.1	63.9
Page	7,312	1,951	3,670	1,669	22	1,719	R	26.7	50.2	22.8	0.3	97	5	27	0.5	0.3	0.7	0.7	34.7	65.3
Palo Alto	5,379	2,374	1,789	1,186	30	585	D	44.1	33.3	22.0	0.6	30	84	37	0.4	0.4	0.4	0.5	57.0	43.0
Plymouth	10,484	3,171	5,196	2,039	78	2,025	R	30.2	49.6	19.4	0.7	92	6	59	0.8	0.5	1.0	0.8	37.9	62.1
Pocahontas	4,669	1,919	1,743	942	65	176	D	41.1	37.3	20.2	1.4	46	46	53	0.3	0.3	0.3	0.4	52.4	47.6
Polk	167,258	78,585	63,708	24,155	810	14,877	D	47.0	38.1	14.4	0.5	14	42	97	12.3	13.4	12.6	9.5	55.2	44.8
Pottawattamie	37,115	13,228	15,671	8,035	181	2,443	R	35.6	42.2	21.6	0.5	83	17	42	2.7	2.3	3.1	3.2	45.8	54.2
Poweshiek	9,047	4,056	3,245	1,680	66	811	D	44.8	35.9	18.6	0.7	27	61	66	0.7	0.7	0.6	0.7	55.6	44.4
Ringgold	2,869	1,341	967	551	10	374	D	46.7	33.7	19.2	0.3	17	81	61	0.2	0.2	0.2	0.2	58.1	41.9
Sac	5,215	1,896	2,138	1,157	24	242	R	36.4	41.0	22.2	0.5	80	21	34	0.4	0.3	0.4	0.5	47.0	53.0
Scott	74,662	33,765	28,844	11,423	630	4,921	D	45.2	38.6	15.3	0.8	22	35	94	5.5	5.8	5.7	4.5	53.9	46.1
Shelby	6,544	2,094	2,809	1,614	27	715	R	32.0	42.9	24.7	0.4	88	15	13	0.5	0.4	0.6	0.6	42.7	57.3
Sioux	14,730	2,226	10,637	1,771	96	8,411	R	15.1	72.2	12.0	0.7	99	1	99	1.1	0.4	2.1	0.7	17.3	82.7
Story	36,290	17,118	12,702	6,275	195	4,416	D	47.2	35.0	17.3	0.5	12	68	80	2.7	2.9	2.5	2.5	57.4	42.6
Tama	8,351	3,573	2,948	1,748	82	625	D	42.8	35.3	20.9	1.0	39	65	50	0.6	0.6	0.6	0.7	54.8	45.2
Taylor	3,551	1,430	1,200	910	11	230	D	40.3	33.8	25.6	0.3	59	80	5	0.3	0.2	0.2	0.4	54.4	45.6
Union	6,102	2,565	2,224	1,280	33	341	D	42.0	36.4	21.0	0.5	43	53	49	0.5	0.4	0.4	0.5	53.6	46.4
Van Buren	3,710	1,464	1,418	811	17	46	D	39.5	38.2	21.9	0.5	66	39	40	0.3	0.2	0.3	0.3	50.8	49.2
Wapello	16,083	8,670	4,852	2,513	48	3,818	D	53.9	30.2	15.6	0.3	3	95	93	1.2	1.5	1.0	1.0	64.1	35.9
Warren	19,158	8,612	7,242	3,217	87	1,370	D	45.0	37.8	16.8	0.5	26	43	86	1.4	1.5	1.4	1.3	54.3	45.7
Washington	9,018	3,384	3,576	1,994	64	192	R	37.5	39.7	22.1	0.7	73	30	35	0.7	0.6	0.7	0.8	48.6	51.4
Wayne	3,584	1,632	1,299	642	11	333	D	45.5	36.2	17.9	0.3	18	55	72	0.3	0.3	0.3	0.3	55.7	44.3
Webster	18,921	8,562	6,992	3,272	95	1,570	D	45.3	37.0	17.3	0.5	20	50	79	1.4	1.5	1.4	1.3	55.0	45.0
Winnebago	6,078	2,322	2,407	1,329	20	85	R	38.2	39.6	21.9	0.3	71	31	39	0.4	0.4	0.5	0.5	49.1	50.9
Winneshiek	9,624	3,791	3,331	2,416	86	460	D	39.4	34.6	25.1	0.9	68	73	9	0.7	0.6	0.7	1.0	53.2	46.8
Woodbury	42,864	17,398	18,148	7,182	136	750	R	40.6	42.3	16.8	0.3	56	16	87	3.2	3.0	3.6	2.8	48.9	51.1
Worth	4,448	2,009	1,382	1,044	13	627	D	45.2	31.1	23.5	0.3	23	92	21	0.3	0.3	0.3	0.4	59.2	40.8
Wright	6,665	2,776	2,708	1,151	30	68	D	41.7	40.6	17.3	0.5	45	23	81	0.5	0.5	0.5	0.5	50.6	49.4
IOWA	1,354,607	586,353	504,891	253,468	9,895	81,462	D	43.3	37.3	18.7	0.7				100.0	100.0	100.0	100.0	53.7	46.3

Table F. — Vote for U.S. Senator: November 3, 1992, General Election

County	Total	Lloyd-Jones (DEM)	Grassley (REP)	Other	Plurality Total	Party	DEM	REP	Other	Rank DEM	Rank REP	Rank Other	Total	DEM	REP	Other
Adair	3,706	875	2,741	90	1,866	R	23.6	74.0	2.4	47	47	70	0.3	0.2	0.3	0.2
Adams	2,419	569	1,798	52	1,229	R	23.5	74.3	2.1	49	44	83	0.2	0.2	0.2	0.1
Allamakee	5,815	1,273	4,370	172	3,097	R	21.9	75.2	3.0	61	37	45	0.4	0.4	0.5	0.4
Appanoose	5,543	1,790	3,573	180	1,783	R	32.3	64.5	3.2	5	94	31	0.4	0.5	0.4	0.4
Audubon	3,300	824	2,364	112	1,540	R	25.0	71.6	3.4	39	62	23	0.3	0.2	0.3	0.3
Benton	10,785	2,416	8,073	296	5,657	R	22.4	74.9	2.7	55	39	54	0.8	0.7	0.9	0.7
Black Hawk	56,717	16,958	38,192	1,567	21,234	R	29.9	67.3	2.8	14	85	53	4.4	4.8	4.2	3.8
Boone	11,941	3,338	8,268	335	4,930	R	28.0	69.2	2.8	20	75	50	0.9	0.9	0.9	0.8
Bremer	11,286	2,263	8,819	204	6,556	R	20.1	78.1	1.8	78	20	90	0.9	0.6	1.0	0.5
Buchanan	9,652	2,075	7,329	248	5,254	R	21.5	75.9	2.6	66	31	64	0.7	0.6	0.8	0.6
Buena Vista	8,254	1,628	6,366	260	4,738	R	19.7	77.1	3.2	79	24	37	0.6	0.5	0.7	0.6
Butler	6,945	1,322	5,486	137	4,164	R	19.0	79.0	2.0	82	14	86	0.5	0.4	0.6	0.3
Calhoun	5,388	1,175	4,051	162	2,876	R	21.8	75.2	3.0	62	36	40	0.4	0.3	0.5	0.4
Carroll	9,565	2,228	7,049	288	4,821	R	23.3	73.7	3.0	50	49	39	0.7	0.6	0.8	0.7
Cass	7,298	1,471	5,588	239	4,117	R	20.2	76.6	3.3	77	26	30	0.6	0.4	0.6	0.6
Cedar	8,127	1,831	6,079	217	4,248	R	22.5	74.8	2.7	54	40	60	0.6	0.5	0.7	0.5
Cerro Gordo	21,753	5,818	15,405	530	9,587	R	26.7	70.8	2.4	31	65	69	1.7	1.7	1.7	1.3
Cherokee	7,172	1,289	5,692	191	4,403	R	18.0	79.4	2.7	87	12	61	0.6	0.4	0.6	0.5
Chickasaw	6,563	1,323	5,094	146	3,771	R	20.2	77.6	2.2	76	21	79	0.5	0.4	0.6	0.4
Clarke	4,222	1,179	2,875	168	1,696	R	27.9	68.1	4.0	22	81	10	0.3	0.3	0.3	0.4
Clay	7,101	1,772	5,034	295	3,262	R	25.0	70.9	4.2	40	64	6	0.5	0.5	0.6	0.7
Clayton	7,899	1,659	5,944	296	4,285	R	21.0	75.3	3.7	70	35	13	0.6	0.5	0.7	0.7
Clinton	21,658	6,760	14,203	695	7,443	R	31.2	65.6	3.2	8	92	33	1.7	1.9	1.6	1.7
Crawford	6,378	1,240	4,800	338	3,560	R	19.4	75.3	5.3	81	33	5	0.5	0.4	0.5	0.8
Dallas	14,766	4,006	10,209	551	6,203	R	27.1	69.1	3.7	29	77	14	1.1	1.1	1.1	1.3
Davis	3,861	1,225	2,586	50	1,361	R	31.7	67.0	1.3	6	93	98	0.3	0.3	0.3	0.1
Decatur	3,894	1,051	2,694	149	1,643	R	27.0	69.2	3.8	30	76	12	0.3	0.3	0.3	0.4
Delaware	7,509	1,420	5,888	201	4,468	R	18.9	78.4	2.7	83	18	59	0.6	0.4	0.7	0.5
Des Moines	18,177	7,387	10,261	529	2,874	R	40.6	56.5	2.9	2	97	47	1.4	2.1	1.1	1.3
Dickinson	7,341	1,593	5,477	271	3,884	R	21.7	74.6	3.7	64	41	15	0.6	0.5	0.6	0.7
Dubuque	41,952	12,713	28,334	905	15,621	R	30.3	67.5	2.2	11	82	82	3.2	3.6	3.1	2.2
Emmet	5,098	1,399	3,567	132	2,168	R	27.4	70.0	2.6	24	69	63	0.4	0.4	0.4	0.3
Fayette	9,813	2,455	7,063	295	4,608	R	25.0	72.0	3.0	38	59	41	0.8	0.7	0.8	0.7
Floyd	7,652	1,684	5,542	426	3,858	R	22.0	72.4	5.6	59	55	3	0.6	0.5	0.6	1.0
Franklin	4,893	896	3,886	111	2,990	R	18.3	79.4	2.3	86	11	74	0.4	0.3	0.4	0.3
Fremont	3,865	954	2,777	134	1,823	R	24.7	71.8	3.5	42	61	21	0.3	0.3	0.3	0.3
Greene	5,175	1,266	3,830	79	2,564	R	24.5	74.0	1.5	43	46	96	0.4	0.4	0.4	0.2
Grundy	5,733	895	4,708	130	3,813	R	15.6	82.1	2.3	95	6	75	0.4	0.3	0.5	0.3
Guthrie	5,126	1,316	3,656	154	2,340	R	25.7	71.3	3.0	35	63	42	0.4	0.4	0.4	0.4
Hamilton	7,951	1,912	5,805	234	3,893	R	24.0	73.0	2.9	45	52	46	0.6	0.5	0.6	0.6
Hancock	5,778	921	4,762	95	3,841	R	15.9	82.4	1.6	94	4	93	0.4	0.3	0.5	0.2
Hardin	9,246	2,182	6,856	208	4,674	R	23.6	74.2	2.2	48	45	77	0.7	0.6	0.8	0.5
Harrison	6,236	1,703	4,371	162	2,668	R	27.3	70.1	2.6	26	68	62	0.5	0.5	0.5	0.4
Henry	8,743	2,111	6,390	242	4,279	R	24.1	73.1	2.8	44	51	52	0.7	0.6	0.7	0.6
Howard	4,806	985	3,727	94	2,742	R	20.5	77.5	2.0	72	23	88	0.4	0.3	0.4	0.2
Humboldt	5,305	986	4,191	128	3,205	R	18.6	79.0	2.4	84	13	71	0.4	0.3	0.5	0.3
Ida	3,557	593	2,840	124	2,247	R	16.7	79.8	3.5	92	9	20	0.3	0.2	0.3	0.3
Iowa	7,227	1,298	5,769	160	4,471	R	18.0	79.8	2.2	88	10	81	0.6	0.4	0.6	0.4
Jackson	8,395	2,152	6,041	202	3,889	R	25.6	72.0	2.4	36	60	72	0.6	0.6	0.7	0.5
Jasper	17,966	5,345	12,115	506	6,770	R	29.8	67.4	2.8	16	83	49	1.4	1.5	1.3	1.2
Jefferson	8,416	1,464	4,404	2,548	1,856	R	17.4	52.3	30.3	90	98	1	0.7	0.4	0.5	6.2
Johnson	51,029	19,494	29,663	1,872	10,169	R	38.2	58.1	3.7	4	95	16	3.9	5.5	3.3	4.5
Jones	8,903	1,855	6,806	242	4,951	R	20.8	76.4	2.7	71	27	57	0.7	0.5	0.8	0.6
Keokuk	4,857	1,130	3,541	186	2,411	R	23.3	72.9	3.8	51	53	11	0.4	0.3	0.4	0.5
Kossuth	8,880	1,806	6,889	185	5,083	R	20.3	77.6	2.1	74	22	85	0.7	0.5	0.8	0.4
Lee	17,602	7,812	9,204	586	1,392	R	44.4	52.3	3.3	1	99	26	1.4	2.2	1.0	1.4
Linn	88,394	24,077	61,450	2,867	37,373	R	27.2	69.5	3.2	27	74	32	6.8	6.8	6.8	7.0
Louisa	4,813	1,199	3,483	131	2,284	R	24.9	72.4	2.7	41	57	56	0.4	0.3	0.4	0.3
Lucas	4,497	1,156	3,253	88	2,097	R	25.7	72.3	2.0	34	58	87	0.3	0.3	0.4	0.2
Lyon	4,999	710	4,195	94	3,485	R	14.2	83.9	1.9	97	2	89	0.4	0.2	0.5	0.2
Madison	6,379	1,675	4,450	254	2,775	R	26.3	69.8	4.0	32	71	9	0.5	0.5	0.5	0.6
Mahaska	9,230	2,059	6,946	225	4,887	R	22.3	75.3	2.4	56	34	68	0.7	0.6	0.8	0.5
Marion	13,103	3,567	9,241	295	5,674	R	27.2	70.5	2.3	28	67	76	1.0	1.0	1.0	0.7
Marshall	18,818	5,295	13,087	436	7,792	R	28.1	69.5	2.3	19	73	73	1.5	1.5	1.5	1.1
Mills	5,232	1,140	3,811	281	2,671	R	21.8	72.8	5.4	63	54	4	0.4	0.3	0.4	0.7
Mitchell	5,576	1,094	4,384	98	3,290	R	19.6	78.6	1.8	80	15	91	0.4	0.3	0.5	0.2
Monona	4,437	976	3,329	132	2,353	R	22.0	75.0	3.0	60	38	44	0.3	0.3	0.4	0.3
Monroe	3,926	1,075	2,707	144	1,632	R	27.4	69.0	3.7	25	79	17	0.3	0.3	0.3	0.3
Montgomery	5,537	1,124	4,230	183	3,106	R	20.3	76.4	3.3	75	28	28	0.4	0.3	0.5	0.4
Muscatine	14,792	4,066	10,128	598	6,062	R	27.5	68.5	4.0	23	80	8	1.1	1.2	1.1	1.5

County	Total	Lloyd-Jones (DEM)	Grassley (REP)	Other	Plurality Total	Party	DEM	REP	Other	Rank DEM	Rank REP	Rank Other	Total	DEM	REP	Other
O'Brien	7,393	1,018	6,177	198	5,159	R	13.8	83.6	2.7	98	3	58	0.6	0.3	0.7	0.5
Osceola	3,151	469	2,596	86	2,127	R	14.9	82.4	2.7	96	5	55	0.2	0.1	0.3	0.2
Page	7,361	1,227	5,978	156	4,751	R	16.7	81.2	2.1	93	7	84	0.6	0.3	0.7	0.4
Palo Alto	4,475	1,058	3,283	134	2,225	R	23.6	73.4	3.0	46	50	43	0.3	0.3	0.4	0.3
Plymouth	8,864	1,570	6,969	325	5,399	R	17.7	78.6	3.7	89	16	18	0.7	0.4	0.8	0.8
Pocahontas	4,760	878	3,733	149	2,855	R	18.4	78.4	3.1	85	17	38	0.4	0.2	0.4	0.4
Polk	166,631	50,318	110,972	5,341	60,654	R	30.2	66.6	3.2	12	88	34	12.9	14.3	12.3	13.0
Pottawattamie	32,766	10,278	21,343	1,145	11,065	R	31.4	65.1	3.5	7	93	19	2.5	2.9	2.4	2.8
Poweshiek	8,235	2,453	5,552	230	3,099	R	29.8	67.4	2.8	15	84	51	0.6	0.7	0.6	0.6
Ringgold	2,861	609	2,180	72	1,571	R	21.3	76.2	2.5	68	29	65	0.2	0.2	0.2	0.2
Sac	5,428	936	4,338	154	3,402	R	17.2	79.9	2.8	91	8	48	0.4	0.3	0.5	0.4
Scott	66,226	20,354	43,640	2,232	23,286	R	30.7	65.9	3.4	10	90	24	5.1	5.8	4.9	5.4
Shelby	5,357	1,183	3,953	221	2,770	R	22.1	73.8	4.1	58	48	7	0.4	0.3	0.4	0.5
Sioux	13,483	1,051	12,253	179	11,202	R	7.8	90.9	1.3	99	1	97	1.0	0.3	1.4	0.4
Story	34,973	10,869	22,953	1,151	12,084	R	31.1	65.6	3.3	9	91	29	2.7	3.1	2.6	2.8
Tama	8,526	1,841	6,496	189	4,655	R	21.6	76.2	2.2	65	30	80	0.7	0.5	0.7	0.5
Taylor	3,283	704	2,526	53	1,822	R	21.4	76.9	1.6	67	25	94	0.3	0.2	0.3	0.1
Union	5,491	1,436	3,882	173	2,446	R	26.2	70.7	3.2	33	66	36	0.4	0.4	0.4	0.4
Van Buren	3,317	927	2,316	74	1,389	R	27.9	69.8	2.2	21	70	78	0.3	0.3	0.3	0.2
Wapello	16,919	6,674	9,679	566	3,005	R	39.4	57.2	3.3	3	96	25	1.3	1.9	1.1	1.4
Warren	17,357	5,228	11,537	592	6,309	R	30.1	66.5	3.4	13	89	22	1.3	1.5	1.3	1.4
Washington	8,551	1,969	6,368	214	4,399	R	23.0	74.5	2.5	52	43	66	0.7	0.6	0.7	0.5
Wayne	3,413	1,001	2,359	53	1,358	R	29.3	69.1	1.6	18	78	95	0.3	0.3	0.3	0.1
Webster	17,032	5,045	11,443	544	6,398	R	29.6	67.2	3.2	17	86	35	1.3	1.4	1.3	1.3
Winnebago	5,059	1,063	3,519	477	2,456	R	21.0	69.6	9.4	69	72	2	0.4	0.3	0.4	1.2
Winneshiek	9,896	2,187	7,381	328	5,194	R	22.1	74.6	3.3	57	42	27	0.8	0.6	0.8	0.8
Woodbury	42,026	10,575	30,415	1,036	19,840	R	25.2	72.4	2.5	37	56	67	3.3	3.0	3.4	2.5
Worth	4,354	890	3,408	56	2,518	R	20.4	78.3	1.3	73	19	99	0.3	0.3	0.4	0.1
Wright	6,334	1,452	4,773	109	3,321	R	22.9	75.4	1.7	53	32	92	0.5	0.4	0.5	0.3
IOWA	**1,292,494**	**351,561**	**899,761**	**41,172**	**548,200**	**R**	**27.2**	**69.6**	**3.2**				**100.0**	**100.0**	**100.0**	**100.0**

Congressional district and county	Total	Democrat (DEM)	Republican (REP)	Other	Plurality Total	Party	DEM	REP	Other	Rank within district DEM	REP	Other	Percent contribution to district vote Total	DEM	REP	Other
District 1	**261,309**	**81,600**	**178,042**	**1,667**	**96,442**	**R**	**31.2**	**68.1**	**0.6**				**100.0**	**100.0**	**100.0**	**100.0**
Cedar	7,966	1,964	5,964	38	4,000	R	24.7	74.9	0.5	8	1	4	3.0	2.4	3.3	2.3
Clinton	21,744	7,576	14,166	2	6,590	R	34.8	65.1	<.1	1	7	8	8.3	9.3	8.0	0.1
Johnson	49,190	16,479	32,332	379	15,853	R	33.5	65.7	0.8	3	6	2	18.8	20.2	18.2	22.7
Jones	8,459	2,464	5,947	48	3,483	R	29.1	70.3	0.6	4	5	3	3.2	3.0	3.3	2.9
Linn	85,501	29,122	55,215	1,164	26,093	R	34.1	64.6	1.4	2	8	1	32.7	35.7	31.0	69.8
Louisa	4,795	1,250	3,535	10	2,285	R	26.1	73.7	0.2	6	3	5	1.8	1.5	2.0	0.6
Muscatine	15,041	3,843	11,188	10	7,345	R	25.6	74.4	<.1	7	2	6	5.8	4.7	6.3	0.6
Scott	68,613	18,902	49,695	16	30,793	R	27.5	72.4	<.1	5	4	7	26.3	23.2	27.9	1.0
District 2	**267,892**	**131,570**	**134,536**	**1,786**	**2,966**	**R**	**49.1**	**50.2**	**0.7**				**100.0**	**100.0**	**100.0**	**100.0**
Allamakee	6,400	2,238	4,128	34	1,890	R	35.0	64.5	0.5	20	2	15	2.4	1.7	3.1	1.9
Benton	10,841	5,220	5,531	90	311	R	48.2	51.0	0.8	10	12	9	4.0	4.0	4.1	5.0
Black Hawk	60,303	33,313	26,690	300	6,623	D	55.2	44.3	0.5	4	18	16	22.5	25.3	19.8	16.8
Bremer	11,326	5,364	5,888	74	524	R	47.4	52.0	0.7	12	10	12	4.2	4.1	4.4	4.1
Buchanan	9,715	4,273	5,358	84	1,085	R	44.0	55.2	0.9	14	8	8	3.6	3.2	4.0	4.7
Butler	6,991	2,910	4,037	44	1,127	R	41.6	57.7	0.6	17	5	14	2.6	2.2	3.0	2.5
Cerro Gordo	23,250	12,070	11,018	162	1,052	D	51.9	47.4	0.7	6	15	11	8.7	9.2	8.2	9.1
Chickasaw	6,594	3,847	2,743	4	1,104	D	58.3	41.6	<.1	1	21	21	2.5	2.9	2.0	0.2
Clayton	8,839	3,615	5,183	41	1,568	R	40.9	58.6	0.5	18	4	17	3.3	2.7	3.9	2.3
Delaware	8,343	2,832	5,488	23	2,656	R	33.9	65.8	0.3	21	1	20	3.1	2.2	4.1	1.3
Dubuque	42,343	20,993	20,971	379	22	D	49.6	49.5	0.9	9	13	6	15.8	16.0	15.6	21.2
Fayette	10,536	4,515	5,983	38	1,468	R	42.9	56.8	0.4	15	6	18	3.9	3.4	4.4	2.1
Floyd	7,649	4,275	3,303	71	972	D	55.9	43.2	0.9	2	20	3	2.9	3.2	2.5	4.0
Grundy	5,953	2,209	3,723	21	1,514	R	37.1	62.5	0.4	19	3	19	2.2	1.7	2.8	1.2
Howard	4,897	2,538	2,320	39	218	D	51.8	47.4	0.8	7	16	10	1.8	1.9	1.7	2.2
Iowa	7,285	3,120	4,095	70	975	R	42.8	56.2	1.0	16	7	2	2.7	2.4	3.0	3.9
Jackson	8,427	4,204	4,169	54	35	D	49.9	49.5	0.6	8	14	13	3.1	3.2	3.1	3.0
Mitchell	5,539	2,661	2,827	51	166	R	48.0	51.0	0.9	11	11	4	2.1	2.0	2.1	2.9
Tama	8,566	4,603	3,887	76	716	D	53.7	45.4	0.9	5	17	7	3.2	3.5	2.9	4.3
Winneshiek	10,048	4,529	5,429	90	900	R	45.1	54.0	0.9	13	9	5	3.8	3.4	4.0	5.0
Worth	4,047	2,241	1,765	41	476	D	55.4	43.6	1.0	3	19	1	1.5	1.7	1.3	2.3
District 3	**257,276**	**121,063**	**125,931**	**10,282**	**4,868**	**R**	**47.1**	**48.9**	**4.0**				**100.0**	**100.0**	**100.0**	**100.0**
Adams	2,446	921	1,511	14	590	R	37.7	61.8	0.6	22	3	26	1.0	0.8	1.2	0.1
Appanoose	5,618	2,775	2,774	69	1	D	49.4	49.4	1.2	6	18	18	2.2	2.3	2.2	0.7
Clarke	4,211	1,778	2,172	261	394	R	42.2	51.6	6.2	18	14	3	1.6	1.5	1.7	2.5
Davis	3,802	1,943	1,835	24	108	D	51.1	48.3	0.6	4	19	24	1.5	1.6	1.5	0.2
Decatur	3,899	1,633	2,026	240	393	R	41.9	52.0	6.2	19	12	4	1.5	1.3	1.6	2.3
Des Moines	19,600	11,248	8,165	187	3,083	D	57.4	41.7	1.0	2	25	21	7.6	9.3	6.5	1.8
Henry	8,642	4,002	4,325	315	323	R	46.3	50.0	3.6	14	17	10	3.4	3.3	3.4	3.1
Jasper	17,899	8,331	8,576	992	245	R	46.5	47.9	5.5	13	20	5	7.0	6.9	6.8	9.6
Jefferson	8,365	2,616	3,236	2,513	620	R	31.3	38.7	30.0	26	26	1	3.3	2.2	2.6	24.4
Keokuk	4,913	2,312	2,540	61	228	R	47.1	51.7	1.2	10	13	17	1.9	1.9	2.0	0.6
Lee	17,660	10,311	6,600	749	3,711	D	58.4	37.4	4.2	1	27	8	6.9	8.5	5.2	7.3
Lucas	4,329	2,056	2,207	66	151	R	47.5	51.0	1.5	9	16	15	1.7	1.7	1.8	0.6
Mahaska	9,435	3,533	5,778	124	2,245	R	37.4	61.2	1.3	23	4	16	3.7	2.9	4.6	1.2
Marion	13,007	5,420	7,232	355	1,812	R	41.7	55.6	2.7	20	7	12	5.1	4.5	5.7	3.5
Marshall	18,591	9,084	8,576	931	508	D	48.9	46.1	5.0	7	22	7	7.2	7.5	6.8	9.1
Monroe	3,874	1,736	1,848	290	112	R	44.8	47.7	7.5	16	21	2	1.5	1.4	1.5	2.8
Page	7,516	1,841	5,518	157	3,677	R	24.5	73.4	2.1	27	1	13	2.9	1.5	4.4	1.5
Poweshiek	8,201	3,846	4,265	90	419	R	46.9	52.0	1.1	11	11	20	3.2	3.2	3.4	0.9
Ringgold	2,845	1,027	1,717	101	690	R	36.1	60.4	3.6	24	5	11	1.1	0.8	1.4	1.0
Story	34,257	17,362	15,460	1,435	1,902	D	50.7	45.1	4.2	5	23	9	13.3	14.3	12.3	14.0
Taylor	3,373	1,155	2,199	19	1,044	R	34.2	65.2	0.6	25	2	27	1.3	1.0	1.7	0.2
Union	5,763	2,356	3,303	104	947	R	40.9	57.3	1.8	21	6	14	2.2	1.9	2.6	1.0
Van Buren	3,365	1,537	1,803	25	266	R	45.7	53.6	0.7	15	9	23	1.3	1.3	1.4	0.2
Wapello	16,855	8,819	7,157	879	1,662	D	52.3	42.5	5.2	3	24	6	6.6	7.3	5.7	8.5
Warren	17,712	8,470	9,045	197	575	R	47.8	51.1	1.1	8	15	19	6.9	7.0	7.2	1.9
Washington	7,803	3,416	4,322	65	906	R	43.8	55.4	0.8	17	8	22	3.0	2.8	3.4	0.6
Wayne	3,295	1,535	1,741	19	206	R	46.6	52.8	0.6	12	10	25	1.3	1.3	1.4	0.2
District 4	**257,593**	**158,610**	**94,045**	**4,938**	**64,565**	**D**	**61.6**	**36.5**	**1.9**				**100.0**	**100.0**	**100.0**	**100.0**
Adair	3,415	2,026	1,366	23	660	D	59.3	40.0	0.7	5	8	12	1.3	1.3	1.5	0.5
Audubon	2,985	1,868	1,102	15	766	D	62.6	36.9	0.5	3	10	13	1.2	1.2	1.2	0.3
Cass	7,011	3,396	3,456	159	60	R	48.4	49.3	2.3	12	2	3	2.7	2.1	3.7	3.2
Dallas	14,511	9,298	4,861	352	4,437	D	64.1	33.5	2.4	2	12	1	5.6	5.9	5.2	7.1
Fremont	3,672	2,153	1,447	72	706	D	58.6	39.4	2.0	6	9	6	1.4	1.4	1.5	1.5
Guthrie	4,433	2,554	1,846	33	708	D	57.6	41.6	0.7	7	7	11	1.7	1.6	2.0	0.7
Harrison	5,883	3,339	2,490	54	849	D	56.8	42.3	0.9	8	6	9	2.3	2.1	2.6	1.1
Madison	6,267	3,868	2,247	152	1,621	D	61.7	35.9	2.4	4	11	2	2.4	2.4	2.4	3.1
Mills	4,769	2,594	2,096	79	498	D	54.4	44.0	1.7	10	4	7	1.9	1.6	2.2	1.6
Montgomery	5,345	2,526	2,700	119	174	R	47.3	50.5	2.2	13	1	4	2.1	1.6	2.9	2.4
Polk	163,637	106,735	53,478	3,424	53,257	D	65.2	32.7	2.1	1	13	5	63.5	67.3	56.9	69.3
Pottawattamie	30,500	15,355	14,736	409	619	D	50.3	48.3	1.3	11	3	8	11.8	9.7	15.7	8.3
Shelby	5,165	2,898	2,220	47	678	D	56.1	43.0	0.9	9	5	10	2.0	1.8	2.4	1.0

Congressional district and county	Total	Democrat (DEM)	Republican (REP)	Other	Plurality Total	Party	Percent of total vote DEM	REP	Other	Rank within district DEM	REP	Other	Percent contribution to district vote Total	DEM	REP	Other
District 5	**198,366**	-	**196,942**	**1,424**	**195,518**	**R**	-	**99.3**	**0.7**	-	**11**	**20**	**100.0**	-	**100.0**	**100.0**
Boone	7,355	-	7,349	6	7,343	R	-	99.9	<.1	-	11	20	3.7	-	3.7	0.4
Buena Vista	7,219	-	7,214	5	7,209	R	-	99.9	<.1	-	10	21	3.6	-	3.7	0.4
Calhoun	4,508	-	4,493	15	4,478	R	-	99.7	0.3	-	18	13	2.3	-	2.3	1.1
Carroll	7,345	-	7,311	34	7,277	R	-	99.5	0.5	-	20	11	3.7	-	3.7	2.4
Cherokee	6,198	-	6,154	44	6,110	R	-	99.3	0.7	-	24	7	3.1	-	3.1	3.1
Clay	6,212	-	6,194	18	6,176	R	-	99.7	0.3	-	17	14	3.1	-	3.1	1.3
Crawford	4,650	-	4,650	0	4,650	R	-	100.0	0.0	-	1	25	2.3	-	2.4	0.0
Dickinson	6,152	-	6,151	1	6,150	R	-	100.0	<.1	-	7	24	3.1	-	3.1	0.1
Emmet	4,286	-	4,255	31	4,224	R	-	99.3	0.7	-	26	5	2.2	-	2.2	2.2
Franklin	3,932	-	3,924	8	3,916	R	-	99.8	0.2	-	14	17	2.0	-	2.0	0.6
Greene	4,138	-	4,117	21	4,096	R	-	99.5	0.5	-	21	10	2.1	-	2.1	1.5
Hamilton	6,150	-	6,106	44	6,062	R	-	99.3	0.7	-	25	6	3.1	-	3.1	3.1
Hancock	5,013	-	4,985	28	4,957	R	-	99.4	0.6	-	22	9	2.5	-	2.5	2.0
Hardin	7,518	-	7,452	66	7,386	R	-	99.1	0.9	-	27	4	3.8	-	3.8	4.6
Humboldt	4,581	-	4,568	13	4,555	R	-	99.7	0.3	-	16	15	2.3	-	2.3	0.9
Ida	3,206	-	3,203	3	3,200	R	-	99.9	<.1	-	12	19	1.6	-	1.6	0.2
Kossuth	7,576	-	7,523	53	7,470	R	-	99.3	0.7	-	23	8	3.8	-	3.8	3.7
Lyon	4,521	-	4,520	1	4,519	R	-	100.0	<.1	-	8	23	2.3	-	2.3	0.1
Monona	3,394	-	3,394	0	3,394	R	-	100.0	0.0	-	2	26	1.7	-	1.7	0.0
O'Brien	6,525	-	6,362	163	6,199	R	-	97.5	2.5	-	30	1	3.3	-	3.2	11.4
Osceola	2,719	-	2,679	40	2,639	R	-	98.5	1.5	-	28	3	1.4	-	1.4	2.8
Palo Alto	3,332	-	3,332	0	3,332	R	-	100.0	0.0	-	3	27	1.7	-	1.7	0.0
Plymouth	7,989	-	7,989	0	7,989	R	-	100.0	0.0	-	4	28	4.0	-	4.1	0.0
Pocahontas	4,109	-	4,090	19	4,071	R	-	99.5	0.5	-	19	12	2.1	-	2.1	1.3
Sac	4,706	-	4,706	0	4,706	R	-	100.0	0.0	-	5	29	2.4	-	2.4	0.0
Sioux	12,404	-	12,370	34	12,336	R	-	99.7	0.3	-	15	16	6.3	-	6.3	2.4
Webster	10,916	-	10,916	0	10,916	R	-	100.0	0.0	-	6	30	5.5	-	5.5	0.0
Winnebago	3,836	-	3,829	7	3,822	R	-	99.8	0.2	-	13	18	1.9	-	1.9	0.5
Woodbury	33,080	-	32,313	767	31,546	R	-	97.7	2.3	-	29	2	16.7	-	16.4	53.9
Wright	4,796	-	4,793	3	4,790	R	-	99.9	<.1	-	9	22	2.4	-	2.4	0.2
IOWA	**1,242,436**	**492,843**	**729,496**	**20,097**	**236,653**	**R**	**39.7**	**58.7**	**1.6**							

1992 Vote for President
Percent for Clinton (D), by County

45.1% to 55.3%
41.0% to 45.0%
37.5% to 40.9%
15.1% to 37.4%

Clinton (D) received 43.3% statewide.

A framed county name indicates
a county carried by the winner.

Copyright © 1993 by Election Data Services, Inc.

Iowa 331

1992 Vote for U.S. Senator
Percent for Grassley (R), by County

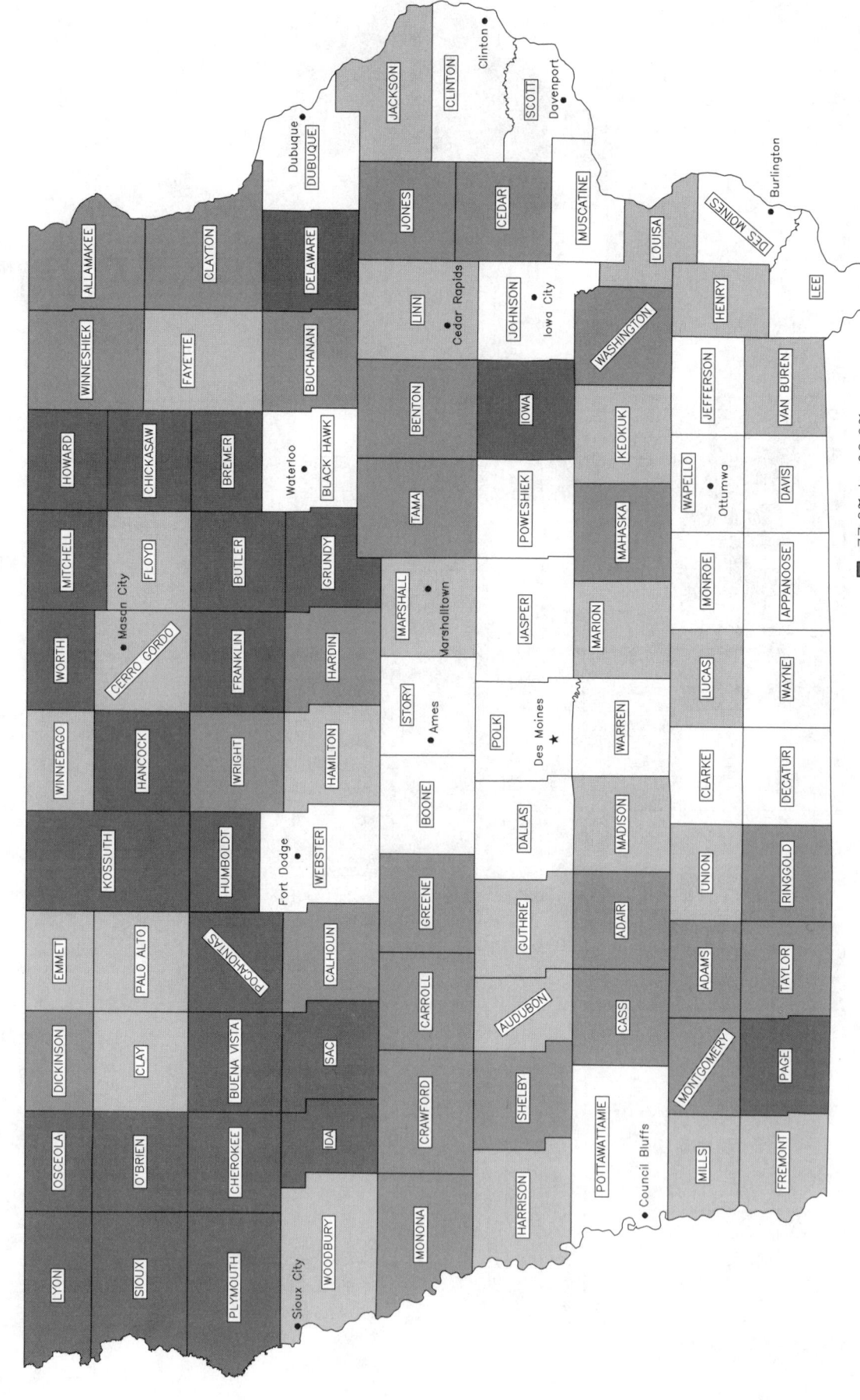

Grassley (R) received 69.6% statewide.

A framed county name indicates
a county carried by the winner.

- 77.0% to 90.9%
- 73.5% to 76.9%
- 69.3% to 73.4%
- 52.3% to 69.2%

332 Iowa

KANSAS

Congressional Districts 4
    Average Population 619,394
State Senate Districts 40
    Average Population 61,939
State House Districts 125
    Average Population 19,821

Electoral College Votes..6
Counties 105
Voting Precincts 3,007

Alternative Registration Methods:
    ....Deputized Registrars, Mail-in

Registration Deadline (Days before Election) 15

Voting Equipment Use (Counties)

Datavote Punch Card	0	Paper Ballot	63
Electronic	0	Other Punch Card	0
Lever Machine	4	Mixed Systems	0
Optical Scanner	38		

Party Control	DEM	REP	IND	VAC
1993 State Senate	14	26	0	0
1992 State Senate	18	22	0	0
1993 State House	59	66	0	0
1992 State House	63	62	0	0

Population Statistics 1990

Race/ Ethnicity	Total Population		Voting Age Population		Voting Age Population % of total population
	Number	%	Number	%	
Non-Hispanic					
White	2,190,524	88.4	1,630,411	89.8	74.4
Black	140,761	5.7	93,177	5.1	66.2
Asian/Pacific Islander	30,814	1.2	20,998	1.2	68.1
Native American	20,363	0.8	13,815	0.8	67.8
Other	1,442	<.1	620	<.1	43.0
All Hispanic	93,670	3.8	56,939	3.1	60.8
TOTAL	2,477,574	100.0	1,815,960	100.0	73.3

Estimated Voting Age Population 1992 (VAP) 1,836,000
Number of Registered Voters................................... 1,365,849
    % of estimated VAP.. 74.4
Voter Turnout (Maximum Vote)[1]........................... 1,167,216
    % of VAP 63.6
    % of Registration 85.5
Persons Not Voting—of Voting Age 668,784
    % of VAP 36.4
Persons Not Voting—of Registered 198,633
    % of Registration 14.5
Straight Ticket Voting .... No

State Officials and Members of Congress

Governor:
Joan Finney (D) 1990, elected to a four-year term in 1990.

U.S. Senators:
Bob Dole (R) 1968, elected to a six-year term in 1992.
Nancy Kassebaum (R) 1978, elected to a six-year term in 1990.

U.S. Representative in Congress:
(District, Name, Party, Date first elected)

1. Roberts (R) 1980   2. Slattery (D) 1982   3. Meyers (R) 1984   4. Glickman (D) 1976

[1]Maximum vote turnout from Table C exceeds reported statewide actual voter turnout because in one or more counties the vote for highest office is greater than reported actual turnout.

Candidates: General Election, November 3, 1992

Candidate(s)	Total vote	Percent	Party	Status	First elected
President/Vice President					
Bush/Quayle	449,951	38.88%	Republican	Incumbent	1988
Clinton/Gore	390,434	33.74%	Democrat	Challenger	1992
Perot/Stockdale	312,358	26.99%	Independent	Challenger	
Marrou/Lord	4,314	0.37%	Libertarian	Challenger	
Gritz/Minett	81	<0.01%	Write in	Challenger	
Hagelin/Tompkins	76	<0.01%	Write in	Challenger	
Write ins	74	<0.01%	Write in	Challenger	
Phillips/Knight	28	<0.01%	Write in	Challenger	
Fulani/Munoz	19	<0.01%	Write in	Challenger	
U.S. Senator					
Bob Dole	706,246	62.70%	Republican	Incumbent	1968
Gloria O'Dell	349,525	31.03%	Democrat	Challenger	
Christina Campbell-Cline	45,423	4.03%	Independent	Challenger	
Mark Kirk	25,253	2.24%	Libertarian	Challenger	
Governor (No Contest)					
U.S. Representative in Congress					
District 1					
Pat Roberts	194,912	68.32%	Republican	Incumbent	1980
Duane West	83,620	29.31%	Democrat	Challenger	
Steven Rosile	6,765	2.37%	Libertarian	Challenger	
District 2					
Jim Slattery	151,019	56.18%	Democrat	Incumbent	1982
Jim Van Slyke	109,801	40.85%	Republican	Challenger	
Arthur Clack	7,986	2.97%	Libertarian	Challenger	
District 3					
Jan Meyers	169,929	58.04%	Republican	Incumbent	1984
Tom Love	110,076	37.59%	Democrat	Challenger	
Frank Kaul	12,791	4.37%	Libertarian	Challenger	
District 4					
Dan Glickman	143,671	51.68%	Democrat	Incumbent	1976
Eric Yost	117,070	42.11%	Republican	Challenger	
Seth Warren	17,275	6.21%	Libertarian	Challenger	

Candidates: April 7, 1992, Primary Election

Candidate	Total vote	Percent	Candidate	Total vote	Percent
Presidential Preference, Democratic			**Presidential Preference, Republican**		
Bill Clinton	82,145	51.26%	George Bush	132,131	61.98%
Paul Tsongas	24,413	15.23%	None of the Above	35,450	16.63%
None of the Above	22,159	13.83%	Patrick Buchanan	31,494	14.77%
Jerry Brown	20,811	12.99%	Pat Paulsen	5,105	2.39%
Bob Kerrey	2,215	1.38%	David Duke	3,837	1.80%
Gary Hauptli	1,303	0.81%	Isabell Masters	1,303	0.61%
Charles Woods	1,119	0.70%	Philip Skow	1,105	0.52%
Don Beamgard	1,009	0.63%	George Zimmermann	766	0.36%
Tom Harkin	940	0.59%	Jack Beemont	735	0.34%
John Barnes	892	0.56%	Charles Doty	417	0.20%
Tod Hawks	765	0.48%	Stephen Koczak	262	0.12%
Lyndon LaRouche, Jr.	631	0.39%	Paul Daugherty	236	0.11%
Ralph Spelbring	537	0.34%	Jack Fellure	164	0.08%
Raymond Vanskiver	510	0.32%	Tennie Rogers	85	0.04%
William Pawley	364	0.23%	Hubert Patty	62	0.03%
Jeffrey Marsh	160	0.10%	Thomas Fabish	44	0.02%
Larry Agran	147	0.09%			
M. Louis McAlpine	131	0.08%			

Voter Registration and Turnout, 1948-1992 Elections

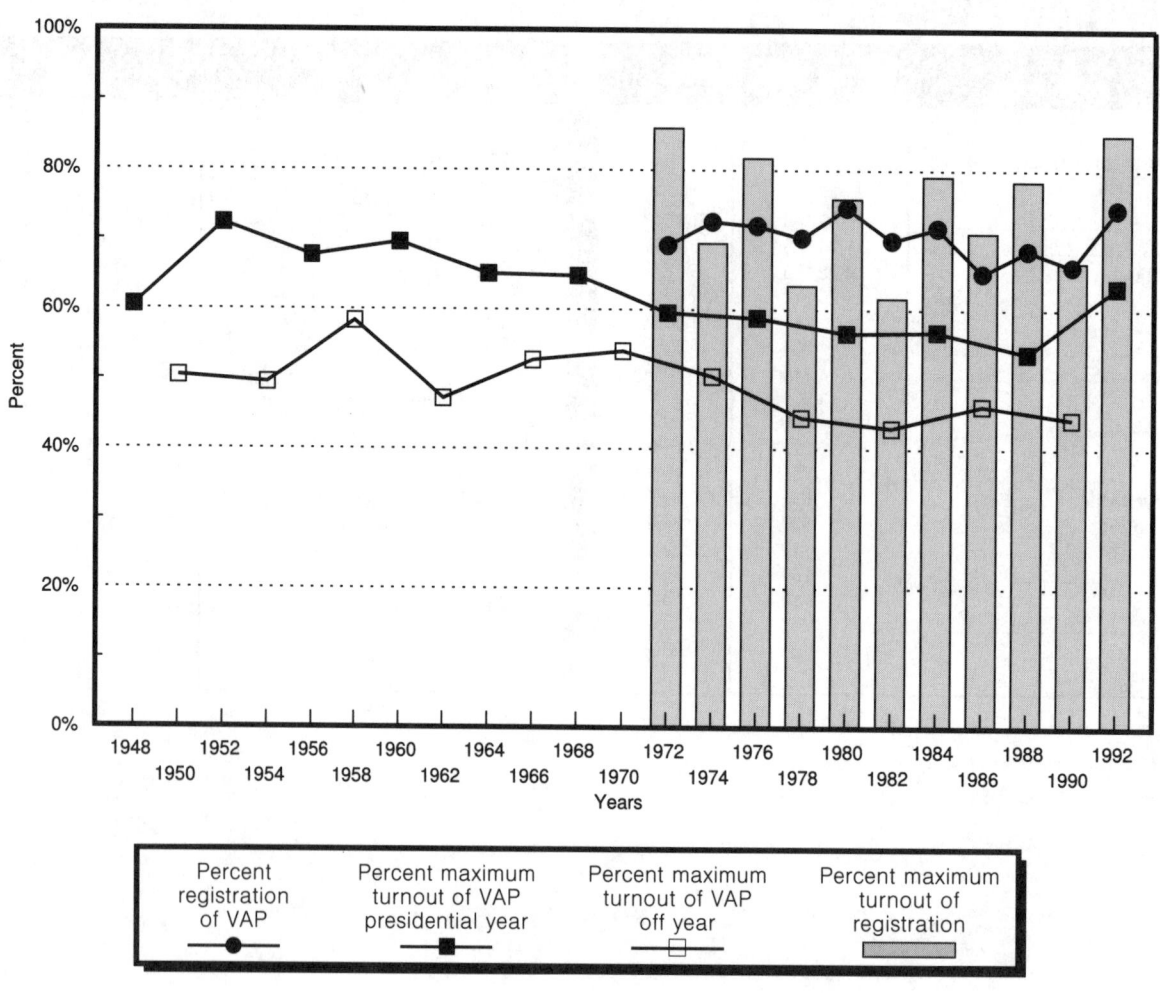

Year	Estimated Voting Age Population (VAP)	Voter registration (REG)				Voter turnout									
						Highest office						Maximum vote			
		Total	Percent of VAP	Rank by percent of VAP	Actual	Total	Office	Percent total REG	Rank by percent of REG	Percent of VAP	Rank by percent of VAP	Total	Percent total REG	Rank by percent of REG	Percent total VAP	Rank by percent of VAP
1992	1,836,000	1,365,849	74.4	26	1,161,044	1,157,335	P	84.7	2	63.0	16	1,161,044	85.0	3	63.2	17
1990	1,819,000	1,204,574	66.2	30	805,251	786,096	S	65.3	9	43.2	17	805,251	66.8	9	44.3	18
1988	1,848,000	1,265,958	68.5	33	-	993,044	P	78.4	8	53.7	21	993,044	78.4	10	53.7	26
1986	1,818,000	1,184,486	65.2	33	-	840,605	G	71.0	4	46.2	11	840,605	71.0	7	46.2	12
1984	1,800,000	1,291,416	71.7	29	-	1,021,991	P	79.1	7	56.8	20	1,021,991	79.1	11	56.8	24
1982	1,773,000	1,238,505	69.9	23	-	763,263	G	61.6	27	43.0	25	763,263	61.6	30	43.0	29
1980	1,730,000	1,290,539	74.6	22	-	979,795	P	75.9	20	56.6	22	979,795	75.9	25	56.6	24
1978	1,681,000	1,182,032	70.3	22	-	748,839	S	63.4	9	44.5	15	748,839	63.4	11	44.5	17
1976	1,628,000	1,172,151	72.0	27	-	957,845	P	81.7	3	58.8	18	957,845	81.7	8	58.8	21
1974	1,575,000	1,143,027	72.6	20	-	794,437	S	69.5	4	50.4	7	794,437	69.5	7	50.4	7
1972	1,539,000	1,065,730	69.2	33	-	916,095	P	86.0	3	59.5	25	916,095	86.0	3	59.5	25
1970	1,380,000	-	-	-	-	745,196	G	-	-	54.0	14	745,196	-	-	54.0	15
1968	1,346,000	-	-	-	-	872,783	P	-	-	64.8	25	872,783	-	-	64.8	26
1966	1,316,000	-	-	-	-	692,955	G	-	-	52.7	24	692,955	-	-	52.7	26
1964	1,318,000	-	-	-	-	857,901	P	-	-	65.1	29	857,901	-	-	65.1	29
1962	1,352,000	-	-	-	-	638,798	S	-	-	47.2	33	638,798	-	-	47.2	33
1960	1,334,000	-	-	-	-	928,825	P	-	-	69.6	29	928,825	-	-	69.6	29
1958	1,263,000	-	-	-	-	735,939	G	-	-	58.3	10	735,939	-	-	58.3	14
1956	1,280,000	-	-	-	-	866,243	P	-	-	67.7	21	866,243	-	-	67.7	22
1954	1,259,000	-	-	-	-	622,633	G	-	-	49.5	26	622,633	-	-	49.5	29
1952	1,240,000	-	-	-	-	896,166	P	-	-	72.3	19	896,166	-	-	72.3	21
1950	1,230,000	-	-	-	-	619,310	G	-	-	50.4	26	619,310	-	-	50.4	27
1948	1,303,000	-	-	-	-	788,819	P	-	-	60.5	19	788,819	-	-	60.5	19

KANSAS

Leavenworth
Kansas City
WYANDOTTE

3

DONIPHAN

Atchison
ATCHISON

LEAVENWORTH

Lawrence

JEFFERSON

DOUGLAS

JOHNSON

MIAMI

LINN

BOURBON

CRAWFORD

CHEROKEE
Columbus

BROWN

JACKSON

SHAWNEE

★
Topeka

OSAGE

FRANKLIN

2

ANDERSON

ALLEN

NEOSHO

LABETTE

NEMAHA

COFFEY

WOODSON

WILSON

MONTGOMERY

MARSHALL

POTTAWATOMIE

WABAUNSEE

LYON
• Emporia

GREENWOOD

ELK

CHAUTAUQUA

RILEY

Manhattan •

GEARY

MORRIS

CHASE

BUTLER

4

COWLEY

WASHINGTON

CLAY

• Abilene
DICKINSON

MARION

HARVEY

Wichita •
SEDGWICK

SUMNER

REPUBLIC
• Republic

CLOUD

OTTAWA

Salina •
SALINE

MCPHERSON

Hutchinson •
RENO

KINGMAN

HARPER

JEWELL

MITCHELL

LINCOLN

ELLSWORTH

RICE

SMITH

OSBORNE

RUSSELL

BARTON

STAFFORD

PRATT

BARBER

PHILLIPS

ROOKS

ELLIS
• Hays

RUSH

PAWNEE

EDWARDS

KIOWA

COMANCHE

NORTON

GRAHAM

TREGO

NESS

1

HODGEMAN

Dodge City
• FORD

CLARK

DECATUR

SHERIDAN

GOVE

LANE

GRAY

MEADE

RAWLINS

THOMAS

Oakley •
LOGAN

SCOTT

FINNEY
Garden City •

HASKELL

SEWARD
Liberal •

CHEYENNE

SHERMAN

WALLACE

GREELEY

WICHITA

KEARNY

HAMILTON

GRANT

STANTON

STEVENS

MORTON

Miles
0 5 10 15 20 25

N
W   E
S

—— Congressional district boundaries
effective June 3, 1992.

Copyright © 1993 by Election Data Services, Inc.

Kansas 337

Table A. — 1990 Population by Race and Ethnic Origin

State/ county code	County	Total persons	\<Pct of total persons\> White	Black	Asian and Pacific Islander	Native American	Other	Hispanic	\<Rank\> Total	White	Black	Hispanic	\<Pct contribution to state pop\> Total	White	Black	Hispanic
20 001	Allen	14,638	95.4	1.8	0.3	0.7	<.1	1.8	35	63	24	47	0.6	0.6	0.2	0.3
20 003	Anderson	7,803	98.0	0.5	<.1	0.8	0.0	0.7	53	33	49	80	0.3	0.3	<.1	<.1
20 005	Atchison	16,932	91.1	5.5	0.8	0.4	<.1	2.2	30	85	9	36	0.7	0.7	0.7	0.4
20 007	Barber	5,874	98.0	0.2	<.1	0.5	<.1	1.2	67	34	64	58	0.2	0.3	<.1	<.1
20 009	Barton	29,382	95.2	1.2	0.3	0.4	<.1	2.8	18	65	32	31	1.2	1.3	0.2	0.9
20 011	Bourbon	14,966	96.2	2.8	0.1	0.4	<.1	0.5	34	54	16	89	0.6	0.7	0.3	<.1
20 013	Brown	11,128	90.8	1.2	0.1	6.0	0.1	1.7	39	86	30	50	0.4	0.5	<.1	0.2
20 015	Butler	50,580	96.6	0.7	0.3	0.9	<.1	1.5	9	52	37	54	2.0	2.2	0.3	0.8
20 017	Chase	3,021	98.1	0.2	<.1	0.4	0.0	1.3	96	31	73	57	0.1	0.1	<.1	<.1
20 019	Chautauqua	4,407	94.9	0.5	0.1	3.4	0.0	1.0	75	69	47	66	0.2	0.2	<.1	<.1
20 021	Cherokee	21,374	95.0	0.5	0.1	3.5	<.1	0.8	26	67	45	74	0.9	0.9	<.1	0.2
20 023	Cheyenne	3,243	98.9	0.2	0.3	<.1	0.0	0.6	92	13	74	82	0.1	0.1	<.1	<.1
20 025	Clark	2,418	96.9	0.0	0.3	1.0	0.0	1.7	98	48	100	49	<.1	0.1	0.0	<.1
20 027	Clay	9,158	98.9	0.2	0.3	0.2	<.1	0.4	45	16	66	92	0.4	0.4	<.1	<.1
20 029	Cloud	11,023	98.8	0.3	<.1	0.1	<.1	0.7	40	18	59	79	0.4	0.5	<.1	<.1
20 031	Coffey	8,404	98.4	0.1	0.2	0.6	0.0	0.7	46	27	80	78	0.3	0.4	<.1	<.1
20 033	Comanche	2,313	98.7	0.3	0.0	0.5	0.0	0.6	102	22	61	88	<.1	0.1	<.1	<.1
20 035	Cowley	36,915	91.5	2.8	0.9	1.8	<.1	3.0	12	83	15	29	1.5	1.5	0.7	1.2
20 037	Crawford	35,568	95.7	1.3	1.2	0.8	<.1	0.9	13	61	27	69	1.4	1.6	0.3	0.3
20 039	Decatur	4,021	99.4	<.1	<.1	0.2	0.0	0.3	81	5	93	98	0.2	0.2	<.1	<.1
20 041	Dickinson	18,958	96.9	0.6	0.3	0.3	<.1	1.8	27	50	38	45	0.8	0.8	<.1	0.4
20 043	Doniphan	8,134	96.1	1.9	0.2	1.2	<.1	0.6	50	55	23	85	0.3	0.4	0.1	<.1
20 045	Douglas	81,798	87.7	4.0	3.1	2.5	<.1	2.6	5	90	11	33	3.3	3.3	2.3	2.3
20 047	Edwards	3,787	94.2	0.1	0.2	0.3	0.0	5.2	84	73	81	18	0.2	0.2	<.1	0.2
20 049	Elk	3,327	96.3	0.2	<.1	1.5	0.1	1.8	91	53	75	46	0.1	0.1	<.1	<.1
20 051	Ellis	26,004	98.0	0.4	0.6	0.2	<.1	0.8	21	32	52	76	1.0	1.2	<.1	0.2
20 053	Ellsworth	6,586	94.6	2.0	0.2	0.3	<.1	2.8	62	71	20	30	0.3	0.3	<.1	0.2
20 055	Finney	33,070	69.3	1.2	3.5	0.6	0.2	25.3	15	103	29	1	1.3	1.0	0.3	8.9
20 057	Ford	27,463	80.5	1.6	2.4	0.5	0.1	14.9	19	100	26	6	1.1	1.0	0.3	4.4
20 059	Franklin	21,994	95.4	1.3	0.4	0.8	<.1	2.1	25	64	28	38	0.9	1.0	0.2	0.5
20 061	Geary	30,453	66.4	22.9	3.8	0.6	0.2	6.1	17	104	2	14	1.2	0.9	5.0	2.0
20 063	Gove	3,231	99.4	0.1	<.1	0.2	0.0	0.3	93	4	77	100	0.1	0.1	<.1	<.1
20 065	Graham	3,543	95.8	2.9	0.3	0.4	0.0	0.6	88	58	14	81	0.1	0.2	<.1	<.1
20 067	Grant	7,159	76.8	<.1	0.5	1.0	0.1	21.6	56	101	98	2	0.3	0.3	<.1	1.6
20 069	Gray	5,396	95.1	0.1	<.1	0.4	<.1	4.2	69	66	76	23	0.2	0.2	<.1	0.2
20 071	Greeley	1,774	93.5	0.2	<.1	<.1	0.2	6.0	105	75	72	15	<.1	<.1	<.1	0.1
20 073	Greenwood	7,847	97.8	0.1	0.0	0.9	0.0	1.2	51	39	78	63	0.3	0.4	<.1	<.1
20 075	Hamilton	2,388	92.6	0.2	1.0	0.3	<.1	5.8	99	77	65	16	<.1	0.1	<.1	0.1
20 077	Harper	7,124	97.6	0.2	<.1	0.6	0.0	1.5	57	41	71	52	0.3	0.3	<.1	0.1
20 079	Harvey	31,028	91.9	1.7	0.7	0.5	<.1	5.2	16	82	25	17	1.3	1.3	0.4	1.7
20 081	Haskell	3,886	85.0	<.1	0.1	0.4	<.1	14.3	82	94	92	7	0.2	0.2	<.1	0.6
20 083	Hodgeman	2,177	97.4	1.0	<.1	<.1	0.0	1.5	103	44	35	53	<.1	<.1	<.1	<.1
20 085	Jackson	11,525	92.6	0.3	<.1	5.9	<.1	1.1	38	79	57	64	0.5	0.5	<.1	0.1
20 087	Jefferson	15,905	97.5	0.5	0.4	0.8	<.1	0.8	32	43	50	73	0.6	0.7	<.1	0.1
20 089	Jewell	4,251	99.4	0.0	<.1	0.3	0.0	0.2	76	3	101	103	0.2	0.2	0.0	<.1
20 091	Johnson	355,054	94.1	1.9	1.6	0.3	<.1	2.0	2	74	22	41	14.3	15.3	4.8	7.5
20 093	Kearny	4,027	82.5	<.1	0.1	0.6	<.1	16.7	80	97	88	5	0.2	0.2	<.1	0.7
20 095	Kingman	8,292	98.6	0.1	0.1	0.3	0.0	0.9	47	24	79	67	0.3	0.4	<.1	<.1
20 097	Kiowa	3,660	97.9	0.2	0.3	0.4	<.1	1.1	86	35	68	65	0.1	0.2	<.1	<.1
20 099	Labette	23,693	91.4	4.3	0.4	1.7	<.1	2.2	23	84	10	37	1.0	1.0	0.7	0.6
20 101	Lane	2,375	97.9	<.1	0.0	0.2	0.0	1.9	100	37	95	44	<.1	0.1	<.1	<.1
20 103	Leavenworth	64,371	83.8	10.7	1.4	0.6	<.1	3.4	7	95	3	27	2.6	2.5	4.9	2.3
20 105	Lincoln	3,653	99.2	<.1	<.1	0.3	<.1	0.4	87	9	99	95	0.1	0.2	<.1	<.1
20 107	Linn	8,254	98.5	0.4	<.1	0.5	0.0	0.4	49	26	51	94	0.3	0.4	<.1	<.1
20 109	Logan	3,081	98.5	0.4	0.0	0.3	0.0	0.4	94	25	54	72	0.1	0.1	<.1	<.1
20 111	Lyon	34,732	89.4	2.0	1.8	0.5	<.1	6.1	14	87	21	13	1.4	1.4	0.5	2.3
20 113	McPherson	27,268	97.2	0.7	0.4	0.4	<.1	1.2	20	45	36	61	1.1	1.2	0.1	0.3
20 115	Marion	12,888	97.9	0.6	0.2	0.3	<.1	0.9	36	36	39	68	0.5	0.6	<.1	0.1
20 117	Marshall	11,705	99.1	<.1	<.1	0.3	<.1	0.4	37	10	87	91	0.5	0.5	<.1	<.1
20 119	Meade	4,247	94.7	0.0	0.3	0.3	0.1	4.7	77	70	102	20	0.2	0.2	0.0	0.2
20 121	Miami	23,466	95.7	2.4	0.1	0.5	<.1	1.2	24	59	18	62	0.9	1.0	0.4	0.3
20 123	Mitchell	7,203	98.6	0.6	0.1	0.2	0.0	0.4	55	23	41	96	0.3	0.3	<.1	<.1
20 125	Montgomery	38,816	89.2	6.2	0.4	2.3	<.1	1.9	11	88	7	42	1.6	1.6	1.7	0.8
20 127	Morris	6,198	97.6	0.3	0.2	0.5	0.0	1.5	64	42	60	55	0.3	0.3	<.1	<.1
20 129	Morton	3,480	88.0	<.1	1.1	0.7	<.1	10.1	89	89	97	10	0.1	0.1	<.1	0.4
20 131	Nemaha	10,446	99.2	0.4	0.2	0.1	<.1	0.1	42	7	55	105	0.4	0.5	<.1	<.1
20 133	Neosho	17,035	95.8	1.1	0.2	0.8	0.0	2.1	29	56	34	39	0.7	0.7	0.1	0.4
20 135	Ness	4,033	99.2	0.0	0.1	<.1	0.0	0.6	79	8	103	87	0.2	0.2	0.0	<.1
20 137	Norton	5,947	95.7	2.3	0.3	0.2	<.1	1.4	66	60	19	56	0.2	0.3	<.1	<.1
20 139	Osage	15,248	97.8	0.2	0.1	0.7	0.0	1.2	33	38	69	59	0.6	0.7	<.1	0.2

Table A. — 1990 Population by Race and Ethnic Origin (cont)

State/county code	County	Total persons	Percent of total persons						Rank				Percent contribution to state population			
			Non-Hispanic							Percent of total persons				Non-Hispanic		
			White	Black	Asian and Pacific Islander	Native American	Other	Hispanic	Total	Non-Hispanic		Hispanic	Total	White	Black	Hispanic
										White	Black					
20 141	Osborne	4,867	99.1	<.1	0.1	0.4	0.0	0.3	74	12	85	97	0.2	0.2	<.1	<.1
20 143	Ottawa	5,634	98.9	<.1	0.1	0.3	0.0	0.6	68	14	89	84	0.2	0.3	<.1	<.1
20 145	Pawnee	7,555	92.3	3.1	0.7	0.3	0.1	3.4	54	81	12	28	0.3	0.3	0.2	0.3
20 147	Phillips	6,590	98.7	0.2	0.4	0.1	0.0	0.5	61	21	63	90	0.3	0.3	<.1	<.1
20 149	Pottawatomie	16,128	96.9	0.6	0.4	0.6	<.1	1.5	31	49	42	51	0.7	0.7	<.1	0.3
20 151	Pratt	9,702	95.8	1.2	0.3	0.6	0.2	1.9	44	57	31	43	0.4	0.4	<.1	0.2
20 153	Rawlins	3,404	98.7	<.1	0.2	0.1	0.0	0.8	90	20	83	75	0.1	0.2	<.1	<.1
20 155	Reno	62,389	92.4	2.7	0.3	0.5	<.1	4.0	8	80	17	25	2.5	2.6	1.2	2.6
20 157	Republic	6,482	99.4	<.1	0.2	0.2	0.0	0.2	63	6	94	102	0.3	0.3	<.1	<.1
20 159	Rice	10,610	95.6	1.1	0.2	0.5	<.1	2.6	41	62	33	32	0.4	0.5	<.1	0.3
20 161	Riley	67,139	81.6	10.0	3.5	0.7	0.1	4.2	6	99	4	24	2.7	2.5	4.7	3.0
20 163	Rooks	6,039	98.7	0.6	<.1	0.2	0.0	0.4	65	19	43	93	0.2	0.3	<.1	<.1
20 165	Rush	3,842	98.8	0.0	0.1	0.1	<.1	0.9	83	17	104	70	0.2	0.2	0.0	<.1
20 167	Russell	7,835	98.4	0.5	<.1	0.4	0.0	0.6	52	28	44	86	0.3	0.4	<.1	<.1
20 169	Saline	49,301	93.0	3.0	1.1	0.4	<.1	2.5	10	76	13	35	2.0	2.1	1.1	1.3
20 171	Scott	5,289	96.8	<.1	0.3	0.2	0.0	2.6	71	51	82	34	0.2	0.2	<.1	0.1
20 173	Sedgwick	403,662	83.7	8.8	2.1	1.0	<.1	4.3	1	96	5	22	16.3	15.4	25.2	18.6
20 175	Seward	18,743	71.6	5.8	2.4	0.6	0.1	19.5	28	102	8	3	0.8	0.6	0.8	3.9
20 177	Shawnee	160,976	85.3	8.1	0.7	1.0	<.1	4.8	4	93	6	19	6.5	6.3	9.3	8.3
20 179	Sheridan	3,043	98.9	0.0	0.2	<.1	0.0	0.9	95	15	105	71	0.1	0.1	0.0	<.1
20 181	Sherman	6,926	92.6	0.2	0.2	<.1	0.0	6.8	59	78	62	11	0.3	0.3	<.1	0.5
20 183	Smith	5,078	99.6	<.1	<.1	0.1	<.1	0.1	72	1	86	104	0.2	0.2	<.1	<.1
20 185	Stafford	5,365	97.1	0.2	0.2	0.4	0.0	2.1	70	47	70	40	0.2	0.2	<.1	0.1
20 187	Stanton	2,333	82.1	<.1	0.2	0.7	<.1	16.8	101	98	84	4	<.1	<.1	<.1	0.4
20 189	Stevens	5,048	87.6	0.5	0.2	0.8	0.0	10.9	73	91	48	9	0.2	0.2	<.1	0.6
20 191	Sumner	25,841	94.6	0.5	0.3	1.1	<.1	3.4	22	72	46	26	1.0	1.1	<.1	0.9
20 193	Thomas	8,258	97.8	0.4	0.4	0.2	<.1	1.2	48	40	56	60	0.3	0.4	<.1	0.1
20 195	Trego	3,694	99.1	<.1	0.5	0.2	0.0	0.2	85	11	91	101	0.1	0.2	<.1	<.1
20 197	Wabaunsee	6,603	97.2	0.6	0.1	0.4	0.0	1.8	60	46	40	48	0.3	0.3	<.1	0.1
20 199	Wallace	1,821	94.9	0.3	0.2	0.2	0.0	4.3	104	68	58	21	<.1	<.1	<.1	<.1
20 201	Washington	7,073	99.5	<.1	0.0	<.1	0.0	0.3	58	2	90	99	0.3	0.3	<.1	<.1
20 203	Wichita	2,758	87.5	<.1	0.3	0.3	<.1	11.8	97	92	96	8	0.1	0.1	<.1	0.3
20 205	Wilson	10,289	98.3	0.2	<.1	0.6	<.1	0.7	43	29	67	77	0.4	0.5	<.1	<.1
20 207	Woodson	4,116	98.2	0.4	0.1	0.7	0.0	0.6	78	30	53	83	0.2	0.2	<.1	<.1
20 209	Wyandotte	161,993	64.2	27.2	1.1	0.6	<.1	6.8	3	105	1	12	6.5	4.7	31.4	11.7
20	KANSAS	2,477,574	88.4	5.7	1.2	0.8	<.1	3.8					100.0	100.0	100.0	100.0
	CONGRESSIONAL															
	District 1	619,370	92.4	1.3	0.8	0.4	<.1	5.2	4	1	4	1	25.0	26.1	5.6	34.1
	District 2	619,391	88.7	6.1	1.1	1.1	<.1	3.0	2	2	3	4	25.0	25.1	27.0	19.6
	District 3	619,439	85.5	8.8	1.6	0.7	<.1	3.3	1	4	1	3	25.0	24.2	38.9	21.8
	District 4	619,374	87.1	6.5	1.5	1.1	<.1	3.7	3	3	2	2	25.0	24.6	28.5	24.5

Table B. — 1990 Voting Age Population (VAP) by Race and Ethnic Origin

County	Total Voting Age Population	Percent of total VAP — Non-Hispanic White	Black	Asian and Pacific Islander	Native American	Other	Hispanic	Rank Percent of total VAP Total	Non-Hispanic White	Black	Hispanic	Percent contribution to state VAP Total	Non-Hispanic White	Black	Hispanic	VAP percent of total population Total	Non-Hispanic White	Black	Asian and Pacific Islander	Native American	Other	Hispanic
Allen	10,654	96.0	1.6	0.3	0.6	0.0	1.5	35	61	24	43	0.6	0.6	0.2	0.3	72.8	73.2	66.0	67.4	65.7	0.0	61.2
Anderson	5,741	98.5	0.3	<.1	0.6	0.0	0.6	53	30	59	76	0.3	0.3	<.1	<.1	73.6	73.9	43.2	66.7	56.3	0.0	62.7
Atchison	12,255	92.4	5.0	0.6	0.4	<.1	1.6	30	85	8	41	0.7	0.7	0.7	0.3	72.4	73.4	66.0	60.2	68.1	20.0	53.0
Barber	4,305	98.3	0.3	<.1	0.4	<.1	1.0	67	34	61	59	0.2	0.3	<.1	<.1	73.3	73.6	84.6	33.3	60.7	50.0	57.5
Barton	21,457	96.0	1.2	0.3	0.4	<.1	2.1	17	62	31	33	1.2	1.3	0.3	0.8	73.0	73.6	75.4	69.3	66.7	42.1	54.0
Bourbon	11,089	96.1	2.9	0.1	0.4	<.1	0.4	34	58	14	83	0.6	0.7	0.3	<.1	74.1	74.1	78.4	71.4	77.2	16.7	60.8
Brown	8,069	92.4	1.1	0.1	4.9	<.1	1.4	40	84	33	45	0.4	0.5	<.1	0.2	72.5	73.8	67.2	80.0	59.4	14.3	58.3
Butler	35,973	96.9	0.7	0.3	0.9	<.1	1.2	10	53	36	53	2.0	2.1	0.3	0.7	71.1	71.4	74.2	64.6	68.6	66.7	56.9
Chase	2,267	98.4	0.2	<.1	0.4	0.0	1.0	94	32	64	60	0.1	0.1	<.1	<.1	75.0	75.2	100.0	100.0	81.8	0.0	55.0
Chautauqua	3,374	95.6	0.4	0.1	3.1	0.0	0.7	75	68	50	71	0.2	0.2	<.1	<.1	76.6	77.1	65.2	83.3	68.9	0.0	52.3
Cherokee	15,733	95.7	0.5	<.1	3.1	<.1	0.6	26	67	44	74	0.9	0.9	<.1	0.2	73.6	74.1	69.6	50.0	64.4	100.0	56.6
Cheyenne	2,461	99.2	0.1	0.2	<.1	0.0	0.4	91	16	76	81	0.1	0.1	<.1	<.1	75.9	76.1	60.0	44.4	100.0	0.0	55.0
Clark	1,812	97.4	0.0	0.2	1.1	0.0	1.3	98	50	99	48	<.1	0.1	0.0	<.1	74.9	75.3	0.0	42.9	80.0	0.0	57.1
Clay	6,818	99.0	0.1	0.2	0.2	0.0	0.4	45	19	74	90	0.4	0.4	<.1	<.1	74.4	74.6	50.0	63.0	81.3	0.0	68.4
Cloud	8,500	98.8	0.4	<.1	0.2	<.1	0.6	38	23	56	73	0.5	0.5	<.1	<.1	77.1	77.1	83.3	100.0	86.7	100.0	71.1
Coffey	6,116	98.8	0.1	0.2	0.4	0.0	0.5	47	24	75	79	0.3	0.4	<.1	<.1	72.8	73.0	88.9	76.9	55.1	0.0	50.8
Comanche	1,749	98.9	0.1	0.0	0.5	0.0	0.5	100	21	78	77	0.1	0.1	<.1	<.1	75.6	75.8	33.3	0.0	72.7	0.0	69.2
Cowley	27,129	92.5	2.8	0.7	1.6	<.1	2.4	13	83	16	31	1.5	1.5	0.8	1.2	73.5	74.3	72.6	62.9	64.6	27.8	59.7
Crawford	27,284	95.9	1.3	1.4	0.7	<.1	0.8	12	64	27	66	1.5	1.6	0.4	0.4	76.7	76.9	72.6	89.7	63.6	33.3	64.0
Decatur	2,983	99.5	0.0	<.1	0.2	0.0	0.2	79	5	100	97	0.2	0.2	0.0	<.1	74.2	74.3	0.0	100.0	77.8	0.0	53.8
Dickinson	14,013	97.5	0.6	0.2	0.3	<.1	1.4	27	49	42	44	0.8	0.8	<.1	0.4	73.9	74.3	63.9	59.3	63.5	25.0	59.2
Doniphan	6,015	96.4	2.0	0.2	1.0	0.0	0.5	49	55	22	80	0.3	0.4	0.1	<.1	73.9	74.2	78.7	55.6	60.4	0.0	60.4
Douglas	65,070	88.3	3.5	3.3	2.3	<.1	2.5	5	92	11	30	3.6	3.5	2.5	2.8	79.5	80.1	70.5	85.0	75.4	33.3	74.8
Edwards	2,840	95.3	0.1	0.1	0.4	0.0	4.0	82	72	72	19	0.2	0.2	<.1	0.2	75.0	75.9	100.0	37.5	100.0	0.0	57.9
Elk	2,610	97.3	0.2	0.1	1.1	<.1	1.2	89	51	69	52	0.1	0.2	<.1	<.1	78.4	79.3	100.0	100.0	56.9	50.0	52.5
Ellis	19,273	98.1	0.4	0.6	0.2	<.1	0.7	21	39	52	72	1.1	1.2	<.1	0.2	74.1	74.2	72.0	78.7	76.9	50.0	62.9
Ellsworth	5,027	94.3	2.6	0.2	0.3	<.1	2.7	59	77	19	29	0.3	0.3	0.1	0.2	76.3	76.0	96.3	100.0	61.9	100.0	72.6
Finney	21,768	73.2	1.2	3.0	0.6	0.1	21.9	16	103	29	1	1.2	1.0	0.3	8.4	65.8	69.5	66.3	57.4	62.0	62.7	57.0
Ford	19,508	83.0	1.5	1.9	0.4	0.1	13.0	20	100	26	6	1.1	1.0	0.3	4.5	71.0	73.2	65.6	58.2	68.0	64.7	62.1
Franklin	15,835	95.8	1.2	0.5	0.7	<.1	1.8	25	66	28	38	0.9	0.9	0.2	0.5	72.0	72.3	70.5	83.2	68.1	60.0	59.7
Geary	21,457	68.9	21.2	4.0	0.6	<.1	5.3	18	104	2	12	1.2	0.9	4.9	2.0	70.5	73.2	65.1	72.6	66.8	29.4	61.5
Gove	2,362	99.7	<.1	<.1	0.1	0.0	0.1	93	3	92	102	0.1	0.1	<.1	<.1	73.1	73.3	25.0	50.0	60.0	0.0	33.3
Graham	2,616	95.9	3.1	0.3	0.3	0.0	0.4	88	65	13	89	0.1	0.2	<.1	<.1	73.8	73.9	80.4	58.3	69.2	0.0	43.5
Grant	4,691	80.5	<.1	0.4	1.0	<.1	18.0	63	101	91	2	0.3	0.2	<.1	1.5	65.5	68.6	100.0	55.9	64.3	40.0	54.8
Gray	3,668	96.2	0.1	<.1	0.3	<.1	3.3	73	56	80	24	0.2	0.2	<.1	0.2	68.0	68.8	57.1	100.0	54.5	25.0	52.4
Greeley	1,227	94.9	0.2	<.1	<.1	0.2	4.6	105	73	62	16	<.1	<.1	<.1	<.1	69.2	70.2	100.0	100.0	100.0	66.7	52.3
Greenwood	5,981	98.1	0.1	0.0	0.9	0.0	1.0	51	41	73	61	0.3	0.4	<.1	0.1	76.2	76.4	88.9	0.0	68.9	0.0	62.6
Hamilton	1,772	94.3	0.2	0.7	0.2	0.0	4.6	99	76	71	15	<.1	0.1	<.1	0.1	74.2	75.5	60.0	52.2	50.0	0.0	59.0
Harper	5,318	98.2	0.2	<.1	0.4	0.0	1.2	56	37	70	51	0.3	0.3	<.1	0.1	74.6	75.1	76.9	60.0	45.7	0.0	61.0
Harvey	22,858	93.2	1.5	0.6	0.4	<.1	4.2	15	80	25	17	1.3	1.3	0.4	1.7	73.7	74.7	67.6	67.6	65.2	16.7	59.6
Haskell	2,621	87.1	<.1	0.1	0.5	0.0	12.2	87	93	86	7	0.1	0.1	<.1	0.6	67.4	69.1	100.0	75.0	76.5	0.0	57.3
Hodgeman	1,566	97.8	1.0	<.1	0.1	0.0	1.0	103	44	35	56	<.1	<.1	<.1	<.1	71.9	72.3	68.2	100.0	100.0	0.0	50.0
Jackson	8,223	93.6	0.3	<.1	5.2	<.1	0.8	39	79	57	64	0.5	0.5	<.1	0.1	71.3	72.2	71.8	55.6	62.6	50.0	51.6
Jefferson	11,543	97.7	0.5	0.4	0.7	<.1	0.8	31	46	43	69	0.6	0.7	<.1	0.1	72.6	72.7	86.3	75.8	62.1	25.0	62.1
Jewell	3,235	99.7	0.0	0.0	0.2	0.0	<.1	76	2	101	104	0.2	0.2	0.0	<.1	76.1	76.3	0.0	0.0	50.0	0.0	37.5
Johnson	259,938	94.7	1.7	1.5	0.3	<.1	1.8	2	74	23	39	14.3	15.1	4.8	8.0	73.2	73.7	65.5	66.8	72.4	31.6	65.3
Kearny	2,685	85.2	0.1	0.2	0.5	<.1	14.0	86	96	79	5	0.1	0.1	<.1	0.7	66.7	68.9	100.0	100.0	56.5	50.0	55.9
Kingman	5,996	98.7	0.1	0.1	0.3	0.0	0.8	50	25	77	65	0.3	0.4	<.1	<.1	72.3	72.4	77.8	70.0	70.8	0.0	59.7
Kiowa	2,711	98.4	0.3	0.2	0.4	<.1	0.7	85	31	60	67	0.1	0.2	<.1	<.1	74.1	74.4	100.0	45.5	68.8	33.3	51.3
Labette	17,401	92.3	4.0	0.3	1.5	0.0	1.8	23	86	10	37	1.0	1.0	0.8	0.6	73.4	74.2	68.3	64.1	64.7	0.0	60.9
Lane	1,720	98.1	<.1	0.0	0.2	0.0	1.6	101	38	88	42	<.1	0.1	<.1	<.1	72.4	72.6	100.0	0.0	80.0	0.0	61.4
Leavenworth	47,207	83.5	11.2	1.3	0.6	<.1	3.3	7	98	3	23	2.6	2.4	5.7	2.8	73.3	73.1	76.4	68.6	78.1	54.8	71.7
Lincoln	2,780	99.1	<.1	<.1	0.4	0.0	0.4	83	17	97	84	0.2	0.2	<.1	<.1	76.1	76.0	100.0	100.0	100.0	0.0	80.0
Linn	6,147	98.8	0.4	<.1	0.5	0.0	0.2	46	22	53	98	0.3	0.4	<.1	<.1	74.5	74.7	64.9	50.0	72.7	0.0	41.2
Logan	2,265	98.7	0.5	0.0	0.1	0.0	0.7	95	26	47	70	0.1	0.1	<.1	<.1	73.5	73.6	100.0	0.0	37.5	0.0	61.5
Lyon	25,442	90.8	2.1	1.7	0.5	<.1	4.9	14	87	21	14	1.4	1.4	0.6	2.2	73.3	74.3	74.6	69.3	66.9	54.5	58.8
McPherson	20,163	97.5	0.7	0.4	0.3	<.1	1.0	19	48	37	57	1.1	1.2	0.2	0.4	73.9	74.2	71.4	60.7	67.3	46.2	63.4
Marion	9,875	98.2	0.7	0.2	0.2	<.1	0.7	36	36	38	68	0.5	0.6	<.1	0.1	76.6	76.8	82.9	53.1	67.6	100.0	60.2
Marshall	8,607	99.3	<.1	<.1	0.2	0.0	0.3	37	12	83	91	0.5	0.5	<.1	<.1	73.5	73.7	77.8	63.6	47.1	0.0	59.2
Meade	3,090	95.5	0.0	0.2	0.3	0.1	3.8	78	69	102	21	0.2	0.2	0.0	0.2	72.8	73.4	0.0	58.3	90.9	80.0	59.1
Miami	16,948	95.9	2.4	0.1	0.5	<.1	1.0	24	63	20	58	0.9	1.0	0.4	0.3	72.2	72.4	72.6	74.2	70.3	20.0	62.0
Mitchell	5,279	99.4	0.2	<.1	0.2	0.0	0.2	57	9	66	99	0.3	0.3	<.1	<.1	73.3	73.8	25.6	20.0	56.3	0.0	41.4
Montgomery	28,793	90.4	5.6	0.3	2.0	<.1	1.6	11	89	7	40	1.6	1.6	1.7	0.8	74.2	75.2	67.3	64.4	65.8	41.2	62.7
Morris	4,640	98.1	0.3	0.2	0.3	0.0	1.1	64	40	58	55	0.3	0.3	<.1	<.1	74.9	75.2	77.8	81.8	51.7	0.0	56.7
Morton	2,422	90.5	<.1	1.0	0.8	<.1	7.6	92	88	93	10	0.1	0.1	<.1	0.3	69.6	71.6	100.0	63.2	73.1	100.0	52.6
Nemaha	7,445	99.3	0.4	<.1	0.1	0.0	0.1	43	13	54	103	0.4	0.5	<.1	<.1	71.3	71.5	75.7	43.8	69.2	0.0	57.1
Neosho	12,637	96.0	1.1	0.2	0.6	0.0	2.0	29	60	32	34	0.7	0.7	0.1	0.5	74.2	74.3	76.4	65.8	61.2	0.0	71.2
Ness	2,973	99.4	0.0	0.1	0.1	0.0	0.3	80	7	103	93	0.2	0.2	0.0	<.1	73.7	73.9	0.0	80.0	100.0	0.0	39.1
Norton	4,624	95.4	2.9	0.3	0.2	<.1	1.2	65	71	15	54	0.3	0.3	0.1	<.1	77.8	77.5	99.3	70.0	64.3	75.0	65.9
Osage	11,128	98.3	<.1	<.1	0.5	0.0	0.9	33	33	82	62	0.6	0.7	<.1	0.2	73.0	73.4	34.5	64.7	57.7	0.0	55.6

Table B. — **1990 Voting Age Population (VAP) by Race and Ethnic Origin (cont)**

County	Total Voting Age Population	Percent of total VAP — Non-Hispanic White	Non-Hispanic Black	Non-Hispanic Asian and Pacific Islander	Non-Hispanic Native American	Non-Hispanic Other	Hispanic	Rank — Total	Rank — NH White	Rank — NH Black	Rank — Hispanic	Pct contribution to state VAP — Total	NH White	NH Black	Hispanic	VAP pct of total pop — Total	NH White	NH Black	NH Asian and Pacific Islander	NH Native American	NH Other	Hispanic
Osborne	3,690	99.3	<.1	0.1	0.2	0.0	0.3	72	11	84	95	0.2	0.2	<.1	<.1	75.8	76.0	75.0	66.7	44.4	0.0	58.8
Ottawa	4,197	99.3	<.1	<.1	0.3	0.0	0.3	68	15	81	94	0.2	0.3	<.1	<.1	74.5	74.8	100.0	57.1	68.8	0.0	35.3
Pawnee	5,598	92.7	3.2	0.7	0.4	<.1	2.9	54	82	12	27	0.3	0.3	0.2	0.3	74.1	74.4	76.4	71.4	76.9	62.5	63.7
Phillips	4,938	98.9	0.2	0.4	0.2	0.0	0.3	61	20	67	92	0.3	0.3	<.1	<.1	74.9	75.1	62.5	70.4	100.0	0.0	46.9
Pottawatomie	11,384	97.3	0.5	0.3	0.6	0.0	1.3	32	52	45	49	0.6	0.7	<.1	0.3	70.6	70.8	60.2	59.0	69.3	0.0	61.5
Pratt	7,204	96.5	1.2	0.3	0.5	0.1	1.3	44	54	30	47	0.4	0.4	<.1	0.2	74.3	74.8	77.2	65.5	62.3	42.1	52.5
Rawlins	2,503	99.1	<.1	0.2	0.2	0.0	0.4	90	18	85	82	0.1	0.2	<.1	<.1	73.5	73.8	66.7	62.5	100.0	0.0	40.7
Reno	46,498	93.2	2.7	0.3	0.5	<.1	3.2	8	81	18	25	2.6	2.7	1.4	2.6	77.3	77.3	66.7	75.0	58.3	0.0	60.0
Republic	5,008	99.5	<.1	0.2	0.1	0.0	0.2	60	6	94	101	0.3	0.3	<.1	<.1	73.7	74.1	72.4	72.2	70.6	80.0	59.5
Rice	7,821	96.1	1.1	0.2	0.5	<.1	2.1	41	57	34	32	0.4	0.5	<.1	0.3	73.7	74.1	72.4	72.2	70.6	80.0	59.5
Riley	52,682	83.0	9.0	3.4	0.6	<.1	3.8	6	99	4	20	2.9	2.7	5.1	3.5	78.5	79.8	71.3	77.4	72.3	46.4	71.8
Rooks	4,427	98.6	0.6	0.1	0.2	0.0	0.4	66	27	39	88	0.2	0.3	<.1	<.1	73.3	73.2	82.4	100.0	83.3	0.0	68.0
Rush	2,966	99.4	0.0	0.1	0.1	<.1	0.4	81	8	104	86	0.2	0.2	0.0	<.1	76.9	77.1	62.8	50.0	60.0	100.0	34.3
Russell	6,024	98.6	0.4	<.1	0.5	0.0	0.4	48	28	49	87	0.3	0.4	<.1	<.1	73.7	74.5	66.4	63.7	70.3	20.8	59.4
Saline	36,327	93.9	2.7	0.9	0.4	<.1	2.0	9	78	17	35	2.0	2.1	1.1	1.3	73.7	74.5	66.4	63.7	77.8	50.0	50.0
Scott	3,758	97.7	<.1	0.3	0.2	0.0	1.8	71	47	89	36	0.2	0.2	<.1	0.1	72.3	74.2	63.3	65.3	65.5	43.2	58.5
Sedgwick	291,703	85.9	7.7	1.9	0.9	<.1	3.5	1	95	5	22	16.1	15.4	24.1	17.9	68.6	72.9	57.3	56.0	75.6	58.3	57.6
Seward	12,865	76.1	4.8	1.9	0.7	0.1	16.4	28	102	9	3	0.7	0.6	0.7	3.7	74.1	75.6	65.9	70.5	68.9	49.2	63.4
Shawnee	119,283	87.0	7.2	0.7	1.0	<.1	4.1	3	94	6	18	6.6	6.4	9.2	8.7	71.3	71.6	65.9	66.7	68.9	49.2	63.4
Sheridan	2,170	99.4	0.0	0.2	<.1	0.0	0.4	96	10	105	85	0.1	0.1	0.0	<.1	71.3	71.6	0.0	66.7	100.0	0.0	34.6
Sherman	5,087	94.5	0.2	0.2	<.1	0.0	4.9	58	75	63	13	0.3	0.3	<.1	0.4	73.4	75.0	70.6	75.0	100.0	0.0	52.7
Smith	3,940	99.8	<.1	0.0	0.1	0.0	<.1	70	1	98	105	0.2	0.2	<.1	<.1	77.6	77.8	25.0	0.0	83.3	0.0	28.6
Stafford	3,988	97.9	0.2	0.2	0.4	0.0	1.4	69	43	68	46	0.2	0.2	<.1	<.1	74.3	75.0	80.0	66.7	58.3	0.0	48.2
Stanton	1,582	84.3	<.1	0.3	0.9	0.1	14.3	102	97	87	4	<.1	<.1	<.1	0.4	69.4	71.5	76.9	77.8	76.3	0.0	51.4
Stevens	3,503	90.3	0.6	0.2	0.8	0.0	8.1	74	90	41	9	0.2	0.2	<.1	0.5	69.4	71.5	76.9	77.8	76.3	0.0	51.4
Sumner	18,347	95.5	0.5	0.2	1.0	<.1	2.8	22	70	46	28	1.0	1.1	<.1	0.9	71.0	71.6	65.2	60.9	64.3	54.5	57.4
Thomas	5,922	98.0	0.4	0.4	0.2	<.1	0.9	52	42	55	63	0.3	0.4	<.1	<.1	71.7	71.9	75.9	74.3	76.5	66.7	53.5
Trego	2,728	99.3	<.1	0.3	0.1	0.0	0.3	84	14	95	96	0.2	0.2	<.1	<.1	73.8	74.0	50.0	52.9	50.0	0.0	77.8
Wabaunsee	4,817	97.7	0.6	0.1	0.3	0.0	1.3	62	45	40	50	0.3	0.3	<.1	0.1	73.0	73.4	68.3	71.4	58.3	0.0	53.4
Wallace	1,292	96.1	0.5	0.2	0.2	0.0	3.1	104	59	48	26	<.1	<.1	<.1	<.1	71.0	71.8	100.0	50.0	100.0	0.0	50.6
Washington	5,336	99.6	<.1	0.0	0.1	0.0	0.2	55	4	96	100	0.3	0.3	<.1	<.1	75.4	75.5	50.0	0.0	100.0	0.0	54.5
Wichita	1,884	90.0	<.1	0.2	0.4	<.1	9.3	97	91	90	8	0.1	0.1	<.1	0.3	68.3	70.3	100.0	50.0	87.5	100.0	53.7
Wilson	7,650	98.6	0.2	0.1	0.5	<.1	0.6	42	29	65	75	0.4	0.5	<.1	<.1	74.4	74.5	80.0	88.9	60.9	100.0	60.5
Woodson	3,128	98.2	0.4	0.1	0.7	0.0	0.5	77	35	51	78	0.2	0.2	<.1	<.1	76.0	76.0	86.7	80.0	76.7	0.0	64.0
Wyandotte	115,928	68.0	24.6	0.9	0.6	<.1	5.8	4	105	1	11	6.4	4.8	30.7	11.8	71.6	75.8	64.7	58.4	70.4	43.9	61.3
KANSAS	1,815,960	89.8	5.1	1.2	0.8	<.1	3.1					100.0	100.0	100.0	100.0	73.3	74.4	66.2	68.1	67.8	43.0	60.8
CONGRESSIONAL																						
District 1	452,729	93.6	1.2	0.6	0.4	<.1	4.1	3	1	4	1	24.9	26.0	6.0	32.5	73.1	74.1	70.2	61.9	69.3	52.1	57.9
District 2	458,157	89.6	5.7	1.1	1.0	<.1	2.6	1	2	2	4	25.2	25.2	28.1	20.9	74.0	74.7	69.0	73.9	73.4	36.5	64.8
District 3	455,833	87.0	7.8	1.5	0.7	<.1	2.9	2	4	1	3	25.1	24.3	38.4	23.0	73.6	74.9	65.3	69.9	73.4	36.5	64.1
District 4	449,241	88.9	5.7	1.4	1.0	<.1	3.0	4	3	3	2	24.7	24.5	27.5	23.6	72.5	74.0	64.0	65.3	65.5	41.0	58.7

Table C. – Voter Participation: November 3, 1992, General Election

County	Estimated Voting Age Population (VAP) 1992	Voter registration (REG) Total	% contribution to state REG	% of 1992 VAP	Rank by % of 1992 VAP	Highest office Actual	Highest office Total	Office	% of 1992 VAP	Maximum vote Total	% contribution to state turnout	% of REG	Rank by % of REG	% of 1992 VAP	Rank by % 1992 VAP	Drop-off President	Drop-off Senator	Drop-off Governor	Drop-off Representative
Allen	10,485	7,538	0.6	71.9	93	6,466	6,430	P	61.3	6,466	0.6	85.8	38	61.7	92	0.6	1.6	-	2.9
Anderson	5,644	4,415	0.3	78.2	66	3,619	3,687	P	65.3	3,687	0.3	83.5	69	65.3	74	0.0	1.3	-	3.3
Atchison	11,937	8,276	0.6	69.3	96	7,709	7,533	P	63.1	7,709	0.7	93.1	1	64.6	78	2.3	2.9	-	3.4
Barber	4,264	3,625	0.3	85.0	29	2,896	2,881	P	67.6	2,896	0.2	79.9	99	67.9	52	0.5	2.3	-	3.4
Barton	20,909	15,369	1.1	73.5	88	13,779	13,582	P	65.0	13,779	1.2	89.7	8	65.9	69	1.4	2.7	-	2.5
Bourbon	10,898	8,626	0.6	79.2	61	7,229	7,162	P	65.7	7,229	0.6	83.8	64	66.3	63	0.9	2.2	-	3.6
Brown	8,070	6,385	0.5	79.1	62	5,331	5,294	P	65.6	5,331	0.5	83.5	70	66.1	67	0.7	1.6	-	2.0
Butler	37,317	28,809	2.1	77.2	69	23,087	23,629	P	63.3	23,629	2.0	82.0	83	63.3	83	0.0	0.7	-	1.1
Chase	2,235	1,915	0.1	85.7	27	1,732	1,685	P	75.4	1,732	0.1	90.4	6	77.5	10	2.7	3.5	-	6.2
Chautauqua	3,265	2,601	0.2	79.7	58	2,039	2,073	P	63.5	2,073	0.2	79.7	101	63.5	81	0.0	2.5	-	3.0
Cherokee	15,777	11,843	0.9	75.1	86	9,881	9,757	P	61.8	9,881	0.8	83.4	71	62.6	86	1.3	2.0	-	3.5
Cheyenne	2,431	2,097	0.2	86.3	24	1,778	1,755	P	72.2	1,778	0.2	84.8	54	73.1	25	1.3	1.7	-	2.4
Clark	1,809	1,514	0.1	83.7	38	1,350	1,315	P	72.7	1,350	0.1	89.2	12	74.6	18	2.6	3.3	-	3.1
Clay	6,766	5,556	0.4	82.1	45	4,649	4,590	P	67.8	4,649	0.4	83.7	66	68.7	47	1.3	3.6	-	5.7
Cloud	8,071	6,554	0.5	81.2	49	5,530	5,448	P	67.5	5,530	0.5	84.4	60	68.5	50	1.5	2.4	-	4.4
Coffey	6,019	5,347	0.4	88.8	13	4,336	4,300	P	71.4	4,336	0.4	81.1	90	72.0	28	0.8	1.4	-	2.4
Comanche	1,723	1,490	0.1	86.5	20	1,300	1,286	S	74.6	1,300	0.1	87.2	25	75.4	16	1.2	1.1	-	2.4
Cowley	27,164	18,668	1.4	68.7	98	15,662	15,784	P	58.1	15,784	1.4	84.6	57	58.1	97	0.0	0.6	-	0.8
Crawford	26,654	20,715	1.5	77.7	68	15,515	16,591	P	62.2	16,591	1.4	80.1	96	62.2	88	0.0	1.3	-	2.6
Decatur	2,924	2,551	0.2	87.2	18	2,142	2,089	P	71.4	2,142	0.2	84.0	63	73.3	24	2.5	3.5	-	4.8
Dickinson	13,939	10,716	0.8	76.9	74	8,645	9,222	P	66.2	9,222	0.8	86.1	34	66.2	66	0.0	1.1	-	2.4
Doniphan	5,757	4,975	0.4	86.4	21	3,836	3,976	P	69.1	3,976	0.3	79.9	98	69.1	44	0.0	1.9	-	2.6
Douglas	64,531	49,628	3.6	76.9	73	41,917	42,265	P	65.5	42,265	3.6	85.2	48	65.5	70	0.0	1.5	-	5.3
Edwards	2,814	2,342	0.2	83.2	42	1,954	1,925	P	68.4	1,954	0.2	83.4	72	69.4	42	1.5	1.9	-	2.5
Elk	2,511	2,061	0.2	82.1	46	1,763	1,742	P	69.4	1,763	0.2	85.5	42	70.2	37	1.2	2.6	-	3.1
Ellis	18,881	15,366	1.1	81.4	48	12,629	12,453	P	66.0	12,629	1.1	82.2	81	66.9	59	1.4	2.1	-	3.5
Ellsworth	5,068	4,094	0.3	80.8	51	3,275	3,239	P	63.9	3,275	0.3	80.0	97	64.6	77	1.1	2.8	-	4.2
Finney	23,720	12,955	0.9	54.6	102	10,788	10,933	P	46.1	10,933	0.9	84.4	58	46.1	103	0.0	0.8	-	0.9
Ford	19,811	12,816	0.9	64.7	99	10,386	10,358	P	52.3	10,386	0.9	81.0	91	52.4	100	0.3	0.9	-	0.9
Franklin	15,918	11,266	0.8	70.8	94	9,907	9,883	P	62.1	9,907	0.8	87.9	18	62.2	89	0.2	1.4	-	3.0
Geary	21,279	9,906	0.7	46.6	105	7,644	7,556	P	35.5	7,644	0.7	77.2	104	35.9	105	1.2	2.0	-	2.3
Gove	2,312	1,996	0.1	86.3	23	1,752	1,706	P	73.8	1,752	0.2	87.8	20	75.8	15	2.6	3.4	-	4.5
Graham	2,580	2,328	0.2	90.2	7	1,735	1,912	P	74.1	1,912	0.2	82.1	82	74.1	20	0.0	0.6	-	2.2
Grant	4,816	3,825	0.3	79.4	60	3,113	3,024	S	62.8	3,113	0.3	81.4	87	64.6	76	3.0	2.9	-	3.9
Gray	3,763	2,587	0.2	68.7	97	2,208	2,173	P	57.7	2,208	0.2	85.3	46	58.7	96	1.6	2.5	-	2.8
Greeley	1,237	1,037	<.1	83.8	37	891	874	S	70.7	891	<.1	85.9	35	72.0	29	2.0	1.9	-	2.1
Greenwood	5,897	4,827	0.4	81.9	47	3,919	3,853	P	65.3	3,919	0.3	81.2	89	66.5	62	1.7	2.0	-	3.1
Hamilton	1,762	1,649	0.1	93.6	4	1,412	1,378	P	78.2	1,412	0.1	85.6	40	80.1	3	2.4	3.8	-	3.5
Harper	5,272	4,023	0.3	76.3	77	3,439	3,378	P	64.1	3,439	0.3	85.5	43	65.2	75	1.8	2.3	-	2.5
Harvey	22,769	18,269	1.3	80.2	52	15,174	15,012	P	65.9	15,174	1.3	83.1	76	66.6	61	1.1	1.5	-	1.8
Haskell	2,682	2,015	0.1	75.1	83	1,633	1,826	P	68.1	1,826	0.2	90.6	3	68.1	51	0.0	1.1	-	1.0
Hodgeman	1,589	1,416	0.1	89.1	12	1,252	1,229	P	77.3	1,252	0.1	88.4	16	78.8	8	1.8	2.4	-	3.0
Jackson	8,285	6,924	0.5	83.6	40	5,286	5,563	C	67.1	5,563	0.5	80.3	93	67.1	57	0.2	0.9	-	0.0
Jefferson	11,758	9,259	0.7	78.7	64	7,755	7,781	P	66.2	7,781	0.7	84.0	62	66.2	65	0.0	1.3	-	4.1
Jewell	3,142	2,825	0.2	89.9	8	2,339	2,300	P	73.2	2,339	0.2	82.8	78	74.4	19	1.3	3.4	-	5.7
Johnson	278,583	222,815	16.3	80.0	55	197,262	194,924	P	70.0	197,262	16.9	88.5	15	70.8	35	1.2	4.5	-	5.4
Kearny	2,800	2,108	0.2	75.3	81	1,723	1,709	P	61.0	1,723	0.1	81.7	85	61.5	93	0.8	1.9	-	1.7
Kingman	5,987	5,123	0.4	85.6	28	4,740	4,163	P	69.5	4,740	0.4	92.5	2	79.2	5	12.2	13.3	-	13.0
Kiowa	2,675	2,386	0.2	89.2	11	1,912	1,891	P	70.7	1,912	0.2	80.1	94	71.5	33	1.1	2.4	-	2.5
Labette	17,044	12,991	1.0	76.2	78	10,258	10,177	P	59.7	10,258	0.9	79.0	103	60.2	94	0.8	2.0	-	3.8
Lane	1,719	1,451	0.1	84.4	33	1,308	1,299	P	75.6	1,308	0.1	90.1	7	76.1	13	0.7	2.2	-	2.1
Leavenworth	49,559	26,157	1.9	52.8	103	23,304	23,177	P	46.8	23,304	2.0	89.1	14	47.0	102	0.5	1.6	-	3.0
Lincoln	2,759	2,589	0.2	93.8	3	2,202	2,172	P	78.7	2,202	0.2	85.1	50	79.8	4	1.4	3.5	-	4.5
Linn	6,192	5,182	0.4	83.7	39	4,124	4,134	P	66.8	4,134	0.4	79.8	100	66.8	60	0.0	1.0	-	3.7
Logan	2,194	1,999	0.1	91.1	6	1,731	1,709	P	77.9	1,731	0.1	86.6	29	78.9	7	1.3	2.6	-	3.5
Lyon	24,756	18,294	1.3	73.9	87	14,594	14,656	P	59.2	14,656	1.3	80.1	95	59.2	95	0.0	0.5	-	2.7
McPherson	20,012	15,035	1.1	75.1	84	13,082	12,991	P	64.9	13,082	1.1	87.0	28	65.4	73	0.7	1.2	-	2.8
Marion	9,781	7,790	0.6	79.6	59	6,457	6,351	P	64.9	6,457	0.6	82.9	77	66.0	68	1.6	2.6	-	4.4
Marshall	8,362	6,900	0.5	82.5	44	5,954	5,858	P	70.1	5,954	0.5	86.3	31	71.2	34	1.6	3.1	-	1.8
Meade	3,056	2,576	0.2	84.3	35	2,195	2,164	P	70.8	2,195	0.2	85.2	47	71.8	30	1.4	3.5	-	2.3
Miami	17,452	13,109	1.0	75.1	85	11,203	11,096	P	63.6	11,203	1.0	85.5	44	64.2	79	1.0	1.8	-	2.8
Mitchell	5,186	4,377	0.3	84.4	34	3,721	3,650	P	70.4	3,721	0.3	85.0	51	71.8	31	1.9	3.5	-	3.9
Montgomery	27,981	19,719	1.4	70.5	95	16,058	15,912	P	56.9	16,058	1.4	81.4	86	57.4	98	0.9	2.0	-	2.6
Morris	4,649	3,585	0.3	77.1	71	3,156	3,111	P	66.9	3,156	0.3	88.0	17	67.9	53	1.4	2.8	-	6.1
Morton	2,459	1,973	0.1	80.2	53	1,764	1,670	P	67.9	1,764	0.2	89.4	10	71.7	32	5.3	6.8	-	6.9
Nemaha	7,370	6,581	0.5	89.3	10	5,195	5,619	P	76.2	5,619	0.5	85.4	45	76.2	12	0.0	3.8	-	0.7
Neosho	12,228	9,341	0.7	76.4	76	7,998	7,893	P	64.5	7,998	0.7	85.6	41	65.4	71	1.3	6.7	-	3.7
Ness	2,962	2,516	0.2	84.9	30	2,249	2,218	P	74.9	2,249	0.2	89.4	11	75.9	14	1.4	2.8	-	2.5
Norton	4,499	3,519	0.3	78.2	67	3,093	3,068	P	68.2	3,093	0.3	87.9	19	68.7	45	0.8	1.7	-	1.4
Osage	11,264	8,692	0.6	77.2	70	7,460	7,421	P	65.9	7,460	0.6	85.8	36	66.2	64	0.5	1.3	-	1.4

Table C. — Voter Participation: November 3, 1992, General Election (cont)

County	Estimated Voting Age Population (VAP) 1992	Voter registration (REG)				Voter turnout												
						Highest office				Maximum vote						Percent drop-off, by office			
		Total	% contribution to state REG	% of 1992 VAP	Rank by % of 1992 VAP	Actual	Total	Office	% of 1992 VAP	Total	% contribution to state turnout	% of REG	Rank by % of REG	% of 1992 VAP	Rank by % 1992 VAP	President	Senator	Governor	Representative
Osborne	3,556	3,149	0.2	88.6	15	2,633	2,607	P	73.3	2,633	0.2	83.6	67	74.0	21	1.0	2.8	-	2.8
Ottawa	4,171	3,536	0.3	84.8	31	2,861	2,820	P	67.6	2,861	0.2	80.9	92	68.6	49	1.4	2.0	-	3.0
Pawnee	5,642	4,887	0.4	86.6	19	3,500	3,585	P	63.5	3,585	0.3	73.4	105	63.5	80	0.0	1.8	-	1.4
Phillips	4,847	4,081	0.3	84.2	36	3,417	3,388	P	69.9	3,417	0.3	83.7	65	70.5	36	0.8	2.5	-	3.0
Pottawatomie	11,673	9,728	0.7	83.3	41	8,083	8,016	P	68.7	8,083	0.7	83.1	74	69.2	43	0.8	1.8	-	1.8
Pratt	7,114	5,700	0.4	80.1	54	4,828	4,786	P	67.3	4,828	0.4	84.7	56	67.9	54	0.9	2.2	-	3.1
Rawlins	2,421	2,354	0.2	97.2	1	1,984	1,935	P	79.9	1,984	0.2	84.3	61	81.9	2	2.5	9.4	-	4.2
Reno	45,701	35,223	2.6	77.1	72	28,619	28,379	P	62.1	28,619	2.5	81.3	88	62.6	87	0.8	2.2	-	3.0
Republic	4,867	4,251	0.3	87.3	17	3,851	3,806	P	78.2	3,851	0.3	90.6	4	79.1	6	1.2	2.4	-	3.4
Rice	7,558	6,127	0.4	81.1	50	5,274	5,271	P	69.7	5,274	0.5	86.1	33	69.8	39	0.1	0.4	-	1.4
Riley	50,172	25,579	1.9	51.0	104	21,942	21,797	P	43.4	21,942	1.9	85.8	37	43.7	104	0.7	2.0	-	3.5
Rooks	4,318	3,824	0.3	88.6	14	3,145	3,090	P	71.6	3,145	0.3	82.2	80	72.8	27	1.7	3.1	-	3.6
Rush	2,896	2,590	0.2	89.4	9	2,163	2,118	P	73.1	2,163	0.2	83.5	68	74.7	17	2.1	2.4	-	2.9
Russell	5,851	4,580	0.3	78.3	65	3,993	4,015	P	68.6	4,015	0.3	87.7	22	68.6	48	0.0	0.5	-	1.0
Saline	36,278	27,450	2.0	75.7	80	23,727	23,623	P	65.1	23,727	2.0	86.4	30	65.4	72	0.4	1.0	-	2.2
Scott	3,713	2,958	0.2	79.7	57	2,586	2,535	P	68.3	2,586	0.2	87.4	24	69.6	41	2.0	2.7	-	4.0
Sedgwick	297,844	216,089	15.8	72.6	90	188,195	186,574	P	62.6	188,195	16.1	87.1	26	63.2	84	0.9	7.0	-	3.7
Seward	13,115	8,192	0.6	62.5	101	6,722	6,806	P	51.9	6,806	0.6	83.1	75	51.9	101	0.0	3.2	-	2.3
Shawnee	120,444	96,014	7.0	79.7	56	82,778	82,294	P	68.3	82,778	7.1	86.2	32	68.7	46	0.0	2.0	-	1.8
Sheridan	2,161	1,858	0.1	86.0	25	1,682	1,636	P	75.7	1,682	0.1	90.5	5	77.8	9	2.7	3.7	-	3.9
Sherman	4,904	3,729	0.3	76.0	79	3,323	3,278	P	66.8	3,323	0.3	89.1	13	67.8	55	1.4	4.0	-	3.0
Smith	3,845	3,548	0.3	92.3	5	2,932	2,852	P	74.2	2,932	0.3	82.6	79	76.3	11	2.7	3.6	-	5.0
Stafford	3,956	3,271	0.2	82.7	43	2,752	2,760	P	69.8	2,760	0.2	84.4	59	69.8	40	0.0	1.2	-	1.6
Stanton	1,598	1,155	<.1	72.3	91	1,013	998	P	62.5	1,013	<.1	87.7	21	63.4	82	1.5	2.7	-	2.4
Stevens	3,601	3,165	0.2	87.9	16	2,520	2,477	P	68.8	2,520	0.2	79.6	102	70.0	38	1.7	4.7	-	4.7
Sumner	18,781	13,672	1.0	72.8	89	11,124	11,589	P	61.7	11,589	1.0	84.8	55	61.7	90	0.0	0.3	-	0.6
Thomas	5,849	4,607	0.3	78.8	63	2,987	3,923	P	67.1	3,923	0.3	85.2	49	67.1	58	0.0	0.5	-	1.0
Trego	2,672	2,307	0.2	86.3	22	1,960	1,912	P	71.6	1,960	0.2	85.0	52	73.4	23	2.4	2.8	-	4.1
Wabaunsee	4,848	4,105	0.3	84.7	32	3,575	3,386	P	69.8	3,575	0.3	87.1	27	73.7	22	5.3	6.3	-	9.8
Wallace	1,282	1,243	<.1	97.0	2	1,088	1,066	P	83.2	1,088	<.1	87.5	23	84.9	1	2.0	3.4	-	4.1
Washington	5,154	4,428	0.3	85.9	26	3,760	3,702	P	71.8	3,760	0.3	84.9	53	73.0	26	1.5	3.4	-	5.2
Wichita	1,856	1,396	0.1	75.2	82	1,249	1,230	P	66.3	1,249	0.1	89.5	9	67.3	56	1.5	2.2	-	1.8
Wilson	7,414	5,693	0.4	76.8	75	4,667	4,635	P	62.5	4,667	0.4	82.0	84	62.9	85	0.7	2.1	-	4.1
Woodson	3,087	2,220	0.2	71.9	92	1,904	1,866	P	60.4	1,904	0.2	85.8	39	61.7	91	2.0	3.1	-	4.9
Wyandotte	114,827	73,333	5.4	63.9	100	60,782	61,133	P	53.2	61,133	5.2	83.4	73	53.2	99	0.0	7.0	-	7.1
KANSAS	**1,836,000**	**1,365,849**	**100.0**	**74.4**		**1,161,044**	**1,157,353**		**63.0**	**1,167,216**	**100.0**	**85.5**		**63.6**		**0.8**	**3.5**	**-**	**3.6**

Table D. — Voter Registration by Political Party Affiliation: November 3, 1992, General Election

County	Total voter registration	Democrat (DEM)[1]	Republican (REP)[1]	Independent (IND)[1]	Plurality Total	Plurality Party	DEM	REP	IND	Rank DEM	Rank REP	Rank IND	Total	DEM	REP	IND
Allen	7,538	2,282	3,787	1,399	1,505	R	30.6	50.7	18.7	35	54	64	0.6	0.5	0.6	0.4
Anderson	4,415	1,494	1,848	1,068	354	R	33.9	41.9	24.2	20	82	34	0.3	0.4	0.3	0.3
Atchison	8,276	3,262	2,734	2,267	528	D	39.5	33.1	27.4	7	101	19	0.6	0.8	0.5	0.6
Barber	3,625	874	1,738	1,009	729	R	24.1	48.0	27.9	73	65	17	0.3	0.2	0.3	0.3
Barton	15,369	4,474	7,338	3,547	2,864	R	29.1	47.8	23.1	46	66	43	1.1	1.1	1.2	1.0
Bourbon	8,626	3,542	3,627	1,404	85	R	41.3	42.3	16.4	5	80	81	0.6	0.8	0.6	0.4
Brown	6,385	1,292	4,042	1,051	2,750	R	20.2	63.3	16.5	95	9	80	0.5	0.3	0.7	0.3
Butler	28,809	9,487	12,085	7,144	2,598	R	33.0	42.1	24.9	24	81	29	2.1	2.2	2.1	2.0
Chase	1,915	415	1,155	339	740	R	21.7	60.5	17.8	89	17	71	0.1	<.1	0.2	<.1
Chautauqua	2,601	593	1,593	412	1,000	R	22.8	61.3	15.9	79	12	85	0.2	0.1	0.3	0.1
Cherokee	11,843	5,480	3,639	2,724	1,841	D	46.3	30.7	23.0	2	103	45	0.9	1.3	0.6	0.8
Cheyenne	2,097	516	1,282	295	766	R	24.7	61.3	14.1	68	13	92	0.2	0.1	0.2	<.1
Clark	1,514	449	829	220	380	R	30.0	55.3	14.7	38	40	90	0.1	0.1	0.1	<.1
Clay	5,556	869	4,037	650	3,168	R	15.6	72.7	11.7	104	2	100	0.4	0.2	0.7	0.2
Cloud	6,554	1,690	3,259	1,605	1,569	R	25.8	49.7	24.5	62	55	32	0.5	0.4	0.6	0.5
Coffey	5,347	1,306	3,033	983	1,727	R	24.5	57.0	18.5	70	32	65	0.4	0.3	0.5	0.3
Comanche	1,490	401	949	136	548	R	27.0	63.9	9.2	59	8	103	0.1	<.1	0.2	<.1
Cowley	18,668	6,569	7,710	4,372	1,141	R	35.2	41.3	23.4	14	85	40	1.4	1.5	1.3	1.2
Crawford	20,715	8,923	6,668	4,943	2,255	D	43.5	32.5	24.1	4	102	37	1.5	2.1	1.1	1.4
Decatur	2,551	774	1,292	485	518	R	30.3	50.6	19.0	34	53	59	0.2	0.2	0.2	0.1
Dickinson	10,716	2,172	5,722	2,822	2,900	R	20.3	53.4	26.3	94	45	23	0.8	0.5	1.0	0.8
Doniphan	4,975	995	2,960	997	1,963	R	20.1	59.8	20.1	96	22	52	0.4	0.2	0.5	0.3
Douglas	49,628	14,604	17,307	17,336	29	I	29.7	35.1	35.2	42	99	3	3.6	3.4	2.9	5.0
Edwards	2,342	692	1,157	493	465	R	29.5	49.4	21.1	39	57	48	0.2	0.2	0.2	0.1
Elk	2,061	627	1,260	174	633	R	30.4	61.1	8.4	32	14	104	0.2	0.1	0.2	<.1
Ellis	15,366	6,667	4,541	4,109	2,126	D	43.5	29.6	26.8	3	104	22	1.1	1.6	0.8	1.2
Ellsworth	4,094	1,565	2,015	498	450	R	38.4	49.4	12.2	8	61	98	0.3	0.4	0.3	0.1
Finney	12,955	2,876	5,026	5,047	21	I	22.2	38.8	39.0	85	93	1	0.9	0.7	0.9	1.4
Ford	12,816	3,779	5,176	3,850	1,326	R	29.5	40.4	30.1	41	90	9	0.9	0.9	0.9	1.1
Franklin	11,266	3,636	5,370	2,176	1,734	R	32.5	48.0	19.5	29	67	57	0.8	0.9	0.9	0.6
Geary	9,906	3,384	3,832	2,682	448	R	34.2	38.7	27.1	18	94	20	0.7	0.8	0.7	0.8
Gove	1,996	579	831	586	245	R	29.0	41.6	29.4	47	84	12	0.1	0.1	0.1	0.2
Graham	2,328	454	1,537	337	1,083	R	19.5	66.0	14.5	99	5	91	0.2	0.1	0.3	<.1
Grant	3,825	930	2,137	725	1,207	R	24.5	56.4	19.1	71	36	61	0.3	0.2	0.4	0.2
Gray	2,587	887	970	716	83	R	34.5	37.7	27.8	17	95	18	0.2	0.2	0.2	0.2
Greeley	1,037	185	686	166	501	R	17.8	66.2	16.0	100	4	83	<.1	<.1	0.1	<.1
Greenwood	4,827	1,592	2,568	667	976	R	33.0	53.2	13.8	23	46	94	0.4	0.4	0.4	0.2
Hamilton	1,649	537	906	206	369	R	32.6	54.9	12.5	27	39	95	0.1	0.1	0.2	<.1
Harper	4,023	1,213	1,936	874	723	R	30.2	48.1	21.7	36	64	47	0.3	0.3	0.3	0.2
Harvey	18,269	4,813	8,364	5,087	3,277	R	26.4	45.8	27.9	61	70	16	1.3	1.1	1.4	1.5
Haskell	2,015	413	1,200	402	787	R	20.5	59.6	20.0	93	21	54	0.1	<.1	0.2	0.1
Hodgeman	1,416	362	808	244	446	R	25.6	57.1	17.3	63	30	78	0.1	<.1	0.1	<.1
Jackson	6,924	2,018	3,219	1,661	1,201	R	29.3	46.7	24.1	45	69	35	0.5	0.5	0.5	0.5
Jefferson	9,259	2,442	3,815	2,982	833	R	26.4	41.3	32.3	60	86	6	0.7	0.6	0.6	0.9
Jewell	2,825	464	1,685	674	1,011	R	16.4	59.7	23.9	103	20	38	0.2	0.1	0.3	0.2
Johnson	222,815	46,271	104,078	71,904	32,174	R	20.8	46.8	32.4	92	68	5	16.3	10.9	17.7	20.6
Kearny	2,108	469	1,220	417	751	R	22.3	57.9	19.8	84	27	55	0.2	0.1	0.2	0.1
Kingman	5,123	1,289	2,488	1,344	1,144	R	25.2	48.6	26.2	66	63	25	0.4	0.3	0.4	0.4
Kiowa	2,386	474	1,474	436	1,000	R	19.9	61.8	18.3	98	11	67	0.2	0.1	0.3	0.1
Labette	12,991	4,641	4,760	3,512	119	R	35.9	36.9	27.2	12	98	21	1.0	1.1	0.8	1.0
Lane	1,451	318	880	251	562	R	21.9	60.7	17.3	88	15	77	0.1	<.1	0.1	<.1
Leavenworth	26,157	9,746	8,737	7,645	1,009	D	37.3	33.4	29.3	9	100	13	1.9	2.3	1.5	2.2
Lincoln	2,589	589	1,473	527	884	R	22.8	56.9	20.4	80	31	51	0.2	0.1	0.3	0.2
Linn	5,182	1,625	2,693	803	1,068	R	31.7	52.6	15.7	31	48	87	0.4	0.4	0.5	0.2
Logan	1,999	482	1,152	365	670	R	24.1	57.6	18.3	72	28	68	0.1	0.1	0.2	0.1
Lyon	18,294	5,078	7,471	5,573	1,898	R	28.0	41.2	30.8	56	88	8	1.3	1.2	1.3	1.6
McPherson	15,035	3,402	8,129	3,475	4,654	R	22.7	54.2	23.2	81	43	41	1.1	0.8	1.4	1.0
Marion	7,790	1,780	4,383	1,616	2,603	R	22.9	56.3	20.8	77	34	49	0.6	0.4	0.7	0.5
Marshall	6,900	2,287	3,407	1,198	1,120	R	33.2	49.4	17.4	22	59	75	0.5	0.5	0.6	0.3
Meade	2,576	574	1,272	727	545	R	22.3	49.4	28.3	83	58	15	0.2	0.1	0.2	0.2
Miami	13,109	4,787	4,868	3,383	81	R	36.7	37.3	25.9	11	96	28	1.0	1.1	0.8	1.0
Mitchell	4,377	1,213	2,345	816	1,132	R	27.7	53.6	18.7	57	44	62	0.3	0.3	0.4	0.2
Montgomery	19,719	6,736	9,754	3,127	3,018	R	34.3	49.7	15.9	19	56	84	1.4	1.6	1.7	0.9
Morris	3,585	1,080	1,822	666	742	R	30.3	51.1	18.7	37	51	63	0.3	0.3	0.3	0.2
Morton	1,973	725	1,002	246	277	R	36.7	50.8	12.5	10	52	96	0.1	0.2	0.2	<.1
Nemaha	6,581	2,602	2,951	1,028	349	R	39.5	44.8	15.6	6	73	86	0.5	0.6	0.5	0.3
Neosho	9,341	3,010	4,178	2,062	1,168	R	32.5	45.2	22.3	30	74	46	0.7	0.7	0.7	0.6
Ness	2,516	713	1,290	513	577	R	28.3	51.3	20.4	51	50	50	0.2	0.2	0.2	0.1
Norton	3,519	780	2,126	611	1,346	R	22.2	60.4	17.4	86	16	74	0.3	0.2	0.4	0.2
Osage	8,692	2,836	3,823	2,004	987	R	32.7	44.1	23.1	25	76	44	0.6	0.7	0.7	0.6

[1]Data from report dated October 20, 1992; sum of registrants by party differs slightly from total voter registration reported with November 1992 general election returns.

344 Kansas

Table D. – Voter Registration by Political Party Affiliation: November 3, 1992, General Election (cont)

County	Total voter registration	Democrat (DEM)[1]	Republican (REP)[1]	Independent (IND)[1]	Plurality Total	Plurality Party	DEM	REP	IND	Rank DEM	Rank REP	Rank IND	Total	DEM	REP	IND
Osborne	3,149	930	1,867	352	937	R	29.5	59.3	11.2	40	23	101	0.2	0.2	0.3	0.1
Ottawa	3,536	755	1,725	1,053	672	R	21.4	48.8	29.8	91	62	10	0.3	0.2	0.3	0.3
Pawnee	4,887	1,374	2,044	1,453	591	R	28.2	42.0	29.8	52	83	11	0.4	0.3	0.3	0.4
Phillips	4,081	685	2,646	750	1,896	R	16.8	64.8	18.4	102	7	66	0.3	0.2	0.5	0.2
Pottawatomie	9,728	2,378	5,400	1,844	3,022	R	24.7	56.1	19.2	69	37	60	0.7	0.6	0.9	0.5
Pratt	5,700	1,602	2,607	1,491	1,005	R	28.1	45.7	26.2	53	71	26	0.4	0.4	0.4	0.4
Rawlins	2,354	560	1,551	243	991	R	23.8	65.9	10.3	75	6	102	0.2	0.1	0.3	<.1
Reno	35,223	11,855	14,880	8,420	3,025	R	33.7	42.3	24.0	21	78	36	2.6	2.8	2.5	2.4
Republic	4,251	959	2,536	748	1,577	R	22.6	59.8	17.6	82	19	72	0.3	0.2	0.4	0.2
Rice	6,127	1,753	2,789	1,583	1,036	R	28.6	45.5	25.8	49	72	27	0.4	0.4	0.5	0.5
Riley	25,579	6,511	10,797	7,989	2,808	R	25.7	42.7	31.6	65	79	7	1.9	1.5	1.8	2.3
Rooks	3,824	918	2,216	669	1,298	R	24.1	58.3	17.6	74	26	73	0.3	0.2	0.4	0.2
Rush	2,590	787	1,336	467	549	R	30.4	51.6	18.0	33	49	69	0.2	0.2	0.2	0.1
Russell	4,580	1,277	2,753	550	1,476	R	27.9	60.1	12.0	55	18	99	0.3	0.3	0.5	0.2
Saline	27,450	7,541	11,989	7,920	4,069	R	27.5	43.7	28.9	58	77	14	2.0	1.8	2.0	2.3
Scott	2,958	588	1,857	513	1,269	R	19.9	62.8	17.3	97	10	76	0.2	0.1	0.3	0.1
Sedgwick	216,089	74,327	88,939	52,294	14,612	R	34.5	41.3	24.3	16	87	33	15.8	17.5	15.1	14.9
Seward	8,192	2,092	4,045	2,023	1,953	R	25.6	49.6	24.8	64	60	30	0.6	0.5	0.7	0.6
Shawnee	96,014	33,125	37,328	25,215	4,203	R	34.6	39.0	26.4	15	92	24	7.0	7.8	6.4	7.2
Sheridan	1,858	605	824	429	219	R	32.6	44.3	23.1	28	75	42	0.1	0.1	0.1	0.1
Sherman	3,729	1,091	2,022	606	931	R	29.3	54.4	16.3	44	42	82	0.3	0.3	0.3	0.2
Smith	3,548	809	2,029	710	1,220	R	22.8	57.2	20.0	78	29	53	0.3	0.2	0.3	0.2
Stafford	3,271	1,066	1,728	453	662	R	32.8	53.2	14.0	26	47	93	0.2	0.3	0.3	0.1
Stanton	1,155	323	635	195	312	R	28.0	55.1	16.9	54	38	79	<.1	<.1	0.1	<.1
Stevens	3,165	789	1,771	605	982	R	24.9	56.0	19.1	67	35	58	0.2	0.2	0.3	0.2
Sumner	13,672	4,819	5,455	3,350	636	R	35.4	40.0	24.6	13	91	31	1.0	1.1	0.9	1.0
Thomas	4,607	1,348	2,515	710	1,167	R	29.5	55.0	15.5	43	41	88	0.3	0.3	0.4	0.2
Trego	2,307	659	855	792	63	R	28.6	37.1	34.3	50	97	4	0.2	0.2	0.1	0.2
Wabaunsee	4,105	904	2,389	806	1,485	R	22.1	58.3	19.7	87	24	56	0.3	0.2	0.4	0.2
Wallace	1,243	188	967	87	779	R	15.1	77.9	7.0	105	1	105	<.1	<.1	0.2	<.1
Washington	4,428	747	3,127	544	2,380	R	16.9	70.8	12.3	101	3	97	0.3	0.2	0.5	0.2
Wichita	1,396	302	570	524	46	R	21.6	40.8	37.5	90	89	2	0.1	<.1	<.1	0.1
Wilson	5,693	1,351	3,305	1,014	1,954	R	23.8	58.3	17.9	76	25	70	0.4	0.3	0.6	0.3
Woodson	2,220	639	1,251	330	612	R	28.8	56.4	14.9	48	33	89	0.2	0.2	0.2	<.1
Wyandotte	73,333	42,736	13,106	17,319	25,417	D	58.4	17.9	23.7	1	105	39	5.4	10.1	2.2	5.0
KANSAS[2]	**1,365,849**	**424,478**	**587,303**	**349,864**	**162,825**	**R**	**31.2**	**43.1**	**25.7**				**100.0**	**100.0**	**100.0**	**100.0**

[1]Data from report dated October 20, 1992; sum of registrants by party differs slightly from total voter registration reported with November 1992 general election returns.
[2]Total voter registration also includes 4,204 for Libertarian party (as reported October 20, 1992).

Table E. — Vote for President: November 3, 1992, General Election

County	Total	Clinton (DEM)	Bush (REP)	Perot (IND)	Other	Plurality Total	Party	DEM	REP	IND	Other	Rank DEM	Rank REP	Rank IND	Total	DEM	REP	IND	DEM	REP
Allen	6,430	2,312	2,351	1,746	21	39	R	36.0	36.6	27.2	0.3	10	81	70	0.6	0.6	0.5	0.6	49.6	50.4
Anderson	3,687	1,178	1,218	1,282	9	64	I	32.0	33.0	34.8	0.2	28	99	3	0.3	0.3	0.3	0.4	49.2	50.8
Atchison	7,533	2,959	2,521	2,020	33	438	D	39.3	33.5	26.8	0.4	6	96	75	0.7	0.8	0.6	0.6	54.0	46.0
Barber	2,881	759	1,225	893	4	332	R	26.3	42.5	31.0	0.1	64	44	37	0.2	0.2	0.3	0.3	38.3	61.7
Barton	13,582	3,846	5,113	4,574	49	539	R	28.3	37.6	33.7	0.4	50	73	12	1.2	1.0	1.1	1.5	42.9	57.1
Bourbon	7,162	2,509	2,876	1,763	14	367	R	35.0	40.2	24.6	0.2	12	58	91	0.6	0.6	0.6	0.6	46.6	53.4
Brown	5,294	1,476	2,203	1,603	12	600	R	27.9	41.6	30.3	0.2	57	49	45	0.5	0.4	0.5	0.5	40.1	59.9
Butler	23,629	7,029	9,166	7,355	79	1,811	R	29.7	38.8	31.1	0.3	41	65	35	2.0	1.8	2.0	2.4	43.4	56.6
Chase	1,685	470	610	600	5	10	R	27.9	36.2	35.6	0.3	56	83	2	0.1	0.1	0.1	0.2	43.5	56.5
Chautauqua	2,073	598	853	607	15	246	R	28.8	41.1	29.3	0.7	48	51	52	0.2	0.2	0.2	0.2	41.2	58.8
Cherokee	9,757	4,083	3,589	2,067	18	494	D	41.8	36.8	21.2	0.2	4	79	101	0.8	1.0	0.8	0.7	53.2	46.8
Cheyenne	1,755	407	863	477	8	386	R	23.2	49.2	27.2	0.5	84	23	69	0.2	0.1	0.2	0.2	32.0	68.0
Clark	1,315	293	676	341	5	335	R	22.3	51.4	25.9	0.4	87	17	80	0.1	<.1	0.2	0.1	30.2	69.8
Clay	4,590	947	2,198	1,434	11	764	R	20.6	47.9	31.2	0.2	94	25	32	0.4	0.2	0.5	0.5	30.1	69.9
Cloud	5,448	1,720	2,131	1,578	19	411	R	31.6	39.1	29.0	0.3	31	64	54	0.5	0.4	0.5	0.5	44.7	55.3
Coffey	4,300	1,021	1,824	1,443	12	381	R	23.7	42.4	33.6	0.2	82	45	13	0.4	0.3	0.4	0.5	35.9	64.1
Comanche	1,285	325	636	324	0	311	R	25.3	49.5	25.2	0.0	71	21	85	0.1	<.1	0.1	0.1	33.8	66.2
Cowley	15,784	5,405	5,422	4,911	46	17	R	34.2	34.4	31.1	0.3	17	94	36	1.4	1.4	1.2	1.2	49.9	50.1
Crawford	16,591	7,366	5,468	3,706	51	1,898	D	44.4	33.0	22.3	0.3	3	101	97	1.4	1.9	1.2	1.2	57.4	42.6
Decatur	2,089	576	940	565	8	364	R	27.6	45.0	27.0	0.4	60	36	72	0.2	0.1	0.2	0.2	38.0	62.0
Dickinson	9,222	2,518	3,851	2,833	20	1,018	R	27.3	41.8	30.7	0.2	61	47	38	0.8	0.6	0.9	0.9	39.5	60.5
Doniphan	3,976	1,177	1,579	1,200	20	379	R	29.6	39.7	30.2	0.5	42	61	47	0.3	0.3	0.4	0.4	42.7	57.3
Douglas	42,265	19,439	12,949	9,630	247	6,490	D	46.0	30.6	22.8	0.6	2	104	95	3.7	5.0	2.9	3.1	60.0	40.0
Edwards	1,925	567	769	584	5	185	R	29.5	39.9	30.3	0.3	45	60	43	0.2	0.1	0.2	0.2	42.4	57.6
Elk	1,742	485	748	503	6	245	R	27.8	42.9	28.9	0.3	58	43	55	0.2	0.1	0.2	0.2	39.3	60.7
Ellis	12,453	4,544	3,985	3,887	37	559	D	36.5	32.0	31.2	0.3	8	102	33	1.1	1.2	0.9	1.2	53.3	46.7
Ellsworth	3,239	1,010	1,197	1,020	12	177	R	31.2	37.0	31.5	0.4	33	78	29	0.3	0.3	0.3	0.3	45.8	54.2
Finney	10,933	2,612	5,278	3,011	32	2,267	R	23.9	48.3	27.5	0.3	79	24	63	0.9	0.7	1.2	1.0	33.1	66.9
Ford	10,358	2,635	4,342	3,341	40	1,001	R	25.4	41.9	32.3	0.4	69	46	21	0.9	0.7	1.0	1.1	37.8	62.2
Franklin	9,883	2,968	3,699	3,184	32	515	R	30.0	37.4	32.2	0.3	39	74	22	0.9	0.8	0.8	1.0	44.5	55.5
Geary	7,556	2,559	2,928	2,057	12	369	R	33.9	38.8	27.2	0.2	18	66	67	0.7	0.7	0.7	0.7	46.6	53.4
Gove	1,706	379	792	532	3	260	R	22.2	46.4	31.2	0.2	88	32	34	0.1	<.1	0.2	0.2	32.4	67.6
Graham	1,912	554	752	603	3	149	R	29.0	39.3	31.5	0.2	47	63	27	0.2	0.1	0.2	0.2	42.4	57.6
Grant	3,019	619	1,561	835	4	726	R	20.5	51.7	27.7	0.1	95	16	62	0.3	0.2	0.3	0.3	28.4	71.6
Gray	2,173	443	1,039	686	5	353	R	20.4	47.8	31.6	0.2	97	27	26	0.2	0.1	0.2	0.2	29.9	70.1
Greeley	873	191	504	175	3	313	R	21.9	57.7	20.0	0.3	89	2	104	<.1	<.1	0.1	<.1	27.5	72.5
Greenwood	3,853	1,262	1,411	1,167	13	149	R	32.8	36.6	30.3	0.3	23	80	44	0.3	0.3	0.3	0.4	47.2	52.8
Hamilton	1,378	386	716	271	5	330	R	28.0	52.0	19.7	0.4	55	14	105	0.1	<.1	0.2	<.1	35.0	65.0
Harper	3,378	845	1,371	1,151	11	220	R	25.0	40.6	34.1	0.3	73	54	10	0.3	0.2	0.3	0.4	38.1	61.9
Harvey	15,012	5,047	6,259	3,653	53	1,212	R	33.6	41.7	24.3	0.4	19	48	94	1.3	1.3	1.4	1.2	44.6	55.4
Haskell	1,826	336	1,023	462	5	561	R	18.4	56.0	25.3	0.3	103	5	83	0.2	<.1	0.2	0.1	24.7	75.3
Hodgeman	1,229	258	625	343	3	282	R	21.0	50.9	27.9	0.2	92	19	61	0.1	<.1	0.1	0.1	29.2	70.8
Jackson	5,552	1,639	1,970	1,927	16	43	R	29.5	35.5	34.7	0.3	43	87	5	0.5	0.4	0.4	0.6	45.4	54.6
Jefferson	7,781	2,538	2,569	2,642	32	73	I	32.6	33.0	34.0	0.4	26	100	11	0.7	0.7	0.6	0.8	49.7	50.3
Jewell	2,300	546	1,050	698	6	352	R	23.7	45.7	30.3	0.3	83	33	42	0.2	0.1	0.2	0.2	34.2	65.8
Johnson	194,924	59,573	85,418	49,136	797	25,845	R	30.6	43.8	25.2	0.4	38	39	86	16.8	15.3	19.0	15.7	41.1	58.9
Kearny	1,709	384	943	376	6	559	R	22.5	55.2	22.0	0.4	85	9	99	0.1	<.1	0.2	0.1	28.9	71.1
Kingman	4,163	1,100	1,680	1,370	13	310	R	26.4	40.4	32.9	0.3	63	57	18	0.4	0.3	0.4	0.4	39.6	60.4
Kiowa	1,891	355	1,057	475	4	582	R	18.8	55.9	25.1	0.2	102	6	87	0.2	<.1	0.2	0.2	25.1	74.9
Labette	10,177	4,196	3,368	2,577	36	828	D	41.2	33.1	25.3	0.4	5	98	81	0.9	1.1	0.7	0.8	55.5	44.5
Lane	1,299	265	674	356	4	318	R	20.4	51.9	27.4	0.3	96	15	65	0.1	<.1	0.1	0.1	28.2	71.8
Leavenworth	23,177	8,077	7,738	7,306	56	339	D	34.8	33.4	31.5	0.2	13	97	28	2.0	2.1	1.7	2.3	51.1	48.9
Lincoln	2,172	612	893	657	10	236	R	28.2	41.1	30.2	0.5	51	52	46	0.2	0.2	0.2	0.2	40.7	59.3
Linn	4,134	1,353	1,413	1,358	10	55	R	32.7	34.2	32.8	0.2	24	95	19	0.4	0.3	0.3	0.4	48.9	51.1
Logan	1,709	355	905	446	3	459	R	20.8	53.0	26.1	0.2	93	11	79	0.1	<.1	0.2	0.1	28.2	71.8
Lyon	14,656	4,811	5,090	4,717	38	279	R	32.8	34.7	32.2	0.3	22	90	23	1.3	1.2	1.1	1.5	48.6	51.4
McPherson	12,991	3,645	5,745	3,561	40	2,100	R	28.1	44.2	27.4	0.3	54	37	64	1.1	0.9	1.3	1.1	38.8	61.2
Marion	6,351	1,627	3,142	1,557	25	1,515	R	25.6	49.5	24.5	0.4	67	22	92	0.5	0.4	0.7	0.5	34.1	65.9
Marshall	5,858	2,022	2,030	1,786	20	8	R	34.5	34.7	30.5	0.3	15	91	41	0.5	0.5	0.5	0.6	49.9	50.1
Meade	2,164	430	1,135	592	7	543	R	19.9	52.4	27.4	0.3	99	13	66	0.2	0.1	0.3	0.2	27.5	72.5
Miami	11,096	3,835	3,528	3,701	32	134	D	34.6	31.8	33.4	0.3	14	103	16	1.0	1.0	0.8	1.2	52.1	47.9
Mitchell	3,650	938	1,601	1,098	13	503	R	25.7	43.9	30.1	0.4	66	38	49	0.3	0.2	0.4	0.4	36.9	63.1
Montgomery	15,912	5,453	6,848	3,570	41	1,395	R	34.3	43.0	22.4	0.3	16	42	96	1.4	1.4	1.5	1.1	44.3	55.7
Morris	3,111	957	1,071	1,071	12	0	-	30.8	34.4	34.4	0.4	35	93	15	0.3	0.2	0.2	0.3	47.2	52.8
Morton	1,670	398	915	350	7	517	R	23.8	54.8	21.0	0.4	80	10	102	0.1	0.1	0.2	0.1	30.3	69.7
Nemaha	5,619	1,580	2,220	1,804	15	416	R	28.1	39.5	32.1	0.3	53	62	24	0.5	0.4	0.5	0.6	41.6	58.4
Neosho	7,893	2,799	2,926	2,136	32	127	R	35.5	37.1	27.1	0.4	11	76	71	0.7	0.7	0.7	0.7	48.9	51.1
Ness	2,218	565	967	678	8	289	R	25.5	43.6	30.6	0.4	68	40	40	0.2	0.1	0.2	0.2	36.9	63.1
Norton	3,068	779	1,469	815	5	654	R	25.4	47.9	26.6	0.2	70	26	78	0.3	0.2	0.3	0.3	34.7	65.3
Osage	7,421	2,297	2,561	2,532	31	29	R	31.0	34.5	34.1	0.4	34	92	9	0.6	0.6	0.6	0.8	47.3	52.7

346 Kansas

County	Total	Clinton (DEM)	Bush (REP)	Perot (IND)	Other	Plurality Total	Plurality Party	DEM	REP	IND	Other	Rank DEM	Rank REP	Rank IND	Total	DEM	REP	IND	DEM	REP
Osborne	2,607	779	1,003	819	6	184	R	29.9	38.5	31.4	0.2	40	70	30	0.2	0.2	0.2	0.3	43.7	56.3
Ottawa	2,820	764	1,284	762	10	520	R	27.1	45.5	27.0	0.4	62	34	73	0.2	0.2	0.3	0.2	37.3	62.7
Pawnee	3,585	1,118	1,357	1,097	13	239	R	31.2	37.9	30.6	0.4	32	72	39	0.3	0.3	0.3	0.4	45.2	54.8
Phillips	3,388	843	1,579	955	11	624	R	24.9	46.6	28.2	0.3	75	30	60	0.3	0.2	0.4	0.3	34.8	65.2
Pottawatomie	8,016	2,099	3,106	2,759	52	347	R	26.2	38.7	34.4	0.6	65	67	7	0.7	0.5	0.7	0.9	40.3	59.7
Pratt	4,786	1,466	1,779	1,528	13	251	R	30.6	37.2	31.9	0.3	37	75	25	0.4	0.4	0.4	0.5	45.2	54.8
Rawlins	1,935	393	1,023	517	2	506	R	20.3	52.9	26.7	0.1	98	12	76	0.2	0.1	0.2	0.2	27.8	72.2
Reno	28,379	9,257	11,377	7,636	109	2,120	R	32.6	40.1	26.9	0.4	25	59	74	2.5	2.4	2.5	2.4	44.9	55.1
Republic	3,806	939	1,767	1,084	16	683	R	24.7	46.4	28.5	0.4	77	31	58	0.3	0.2	0.4	0.3	34.7	65.3
Rice	5,271	1,555	2,158	1,543	15	603	R	29.5	40.9	29.3	0.3	44	53	53	0.5	0.4	0.5	0.5	41.9	58.1
Riley	21,797	7,933	8,394	5,387	83	461	R	36.4	38.5	24.7	0.4	9	69	89	1.9	2.0	1.9	1.7	48.6	51.4
Rooks	3,090	771	1,249	1,063	7	186	R	25.0	40.4	34.4	0.2	74	56	8	0.3	0.2	0.3	0.3	38.2	61.8
Rush	2,118	689	756	665	8	67	R	32.5	35.7	31.4	0.4	27	85	31	0.2	0.2	0.2	0.2	47.7	52.3
Russell	4,015	1,178	1,434	1,395	8	39	R	29.3	35.7	34.7	0.2	46	84	4	0.3	0.3	0.3	0.4	45.1	54.9
Saline	23,623	7,890	8,565	7,108	60	675	R	33.4	36.3	30.1	0.3	21	82	48	2.0	2.0	1.9	2.3	47.9	52.1
Scott	2,535	480	1,426	621	8	805	R	18.9	56.3	24.5	0.3	101	4	93	0.2	0.1	0.3	0.2	25.2	74.8
Sedgwick	186,574	62,670	75,577	47,238	1,089	12,907	R	33.6	40.5	25.3	0.6	20	55	82	16.1	16.1	16.8	15.1	45.3	54.7
Seward	6,806	1,488	3,477	1,818	23	1,659	R	21.9	51.1	26.7	0.3	90	18	77	0.6	0.4	0.8	0.6	30.0	70.0
Shawnee	82,294	31,972	29,344	20,653	325	2,628	D	38.9	35.7	25.1	0.4	7	86	88	7.1	8.2	6.5	6.6	52.1	47.9
Sheridan	1,636	347	739	546	4	193	R	21.2	45.2	33.4	0.2	91	35	15	0.1	<.1	0.2	0.2	32.0	68.0
Sherman	3,278	810	1,630	828	10	802	R	24.7	49.7	25.3	0.3	76	20	84	0.3	0.2	0.4	0.3	33.2	66.8
Smith	2,852	789	1,236	816	11	420	R	27.7	43.3	28.6	0.4	59	41	57	0.2	0.2	0.3	0.3	39.0	61.0
Stafford	2,760	777	1,064	910	9	154	R	28.2	38.6	33.0	0.3	52	68	17	0.2	0.2	0.2	0.3	42.2	57.8
Stanton	998	224	556	214	4	332	R	22.4	55.7	21.4	0.4	86	7	100	<.1	<.1	0.1	<.1	28.7	71.3
Stevens	2,477	390	1,408	674	5	734	R	15.7	56.8	27.2	0.2	104	3	68	0.2	<.1	0.3	0.2	21.7	78.3
Sumner	11,589	3,564	4,087	3,887	51	200	R	30.8	35.3	33.5	0.4	36	89	14	1.0	0.9	0.9	1.2	46.6	53.4
Thomas	3,923	932	1,849	1,129	13	720	R	23.8	47.1	28.8	0.3	81	28	56	0.3	0.2	0.4	0.4	33.5	66.5
Trego	1,912	608	727	574	3	119	R	31.8	38.0	30.0	0.2	29	71	50	0.2	0.2	0.2	0.2	45.5	54.5
Wabaunsee	3,386	851	1,254	1,258	23	4	I	25.1	37.0	37.2	0.7	72	77	1	0.3	0.2	0.3	0.4	40.4	59.6
Wallace	1,066	164	679	219	4	460	R	15.4	63.7	20.5	0.4	105	1	103	<.1	<.1	0.2	<.1	19.5	80.5
Washington	3,702	893	1,740	1,054	15	686	R	24.1	47.0	28.5	0.4	78	29	59	0.3	0.2	0.4	0.3	33.9	66.1
Wichita	1,230	241	681	303	5	378	R	19.6	55.4	24.6	0.4	100	8	90	0.1	<.1	0.2	<.1	26.1	73.9
Wilson	4,635	1,331	1,925	1,365	14	560	R	28.7	41.5	29.4	0.3	49	50	51	0.4	0.3	0.4	0.4	40.9	59.1
Woodson	1,866	590	662	604	10	58	R	31.6	35.5	32.4	0.5	30	88	20	0.2	0.2	0.1	0.2	47.1	52.9
Wyandotte	61,133	34,397	12,872	13,620	244	20,777	D	56.3	21.1	22.3	0.4	1	105	98	5.3	8.8	2.9	4.4	72.8	27.2
KANSAS	1,157,335	390,434	449,951	312,358	4,592	59,517	R	33.7	38.9	27.0	0.4				100.0	100.0	100.0	100.0	46.5	53.5

County	Total	O'Dell (DEM)	Dole (REP)	Other	Plurality Total	Party	DEM	REP	Other	Rank DEM	Rank REP	Rank Other	Total	DEM	REP	Other
Allen	6,363	2,196	3,615	552	1,419	R	34.5	56.8	8.7	28	91	4	0.6	0.6	0.5	0.8
Anderson	3,638	1,568	1,729	341	161	R	43.1	47.5	9.4	2	105	2	0.3	0.4	0.2	0.5
Atchison	7,483	2,600	4,472	411	1,872	R	34.7	59.8	5.5	25	74	54	0.7	0.7	0.6	0.6
Barber	2,830	850	1,781	199	931	R	30.0	62.9	7.0	56	57	17	0.3	0.2	0.3	0.3
Barton	13,404	4,122	8,360	922	4,238	R	30.8	62.4	6.9	50	60	20	1.2	1.2	1.2	1.3
Bourbon	7,071	2,610	4,067	394	1,457	R	36.9	57.5	5.6	16	85	53	0.6	0.7	0.6	0.6
Brown	5,245	1,720	3,206	319	1,486	R	32.8	61.1	6.1	43	68	39	0.5	0.5	0.5	0.5
Butler	23,462	6,713	15,220	1,529	8,507	R	28.6	64.9	6.5	70	46	28	2.1	1.9	2.2	2.2
Chase	1,671	600	934	137	334	R	35.9	55.9	8.2	20	93	6	0.1	0.2	0.1	0.2
Chautauqua	2,022	569	1,289	164	720	R	28.1	63.7	8.1	75	53	8	0.2	0.2	0.2	0.2
Cherokee	9,681	3,748	5,333	600	1,585	R	38.7	55.1	6.2	9	96	36	0.9	1.1	0.8	0.8
Cheyenne	1,747	395	1,228	124	833	R	22.6	70.3	7.1	98	12	16	0.2	0.1	0.2	0.2
Clark	1,305	397	829	79	432	R	30.4	63.5	6.1	54	54	41	0.1	0.1	0.1	0.1
Clay	4,482	1,186	3,069	227	1,883	R	26.5	68.5	5.1	83	20	73	0.4	0.3	0.4	0.3
Cloud	5,397	1,750	3,233	414	1,483	R	32.4	59.9	7.7	46	73	9	0.5	0.5	0.5	0.6
Coffey	4,276	1,301	2,679	296	1,378	R	30.4	62.7	6.9	53	58	18	0.4	0.4	0.4	0.4
Comanche	1,286	367	840	79	473	R	28.5	65.3	6.1	72	41	37	0.1	0.1	0.1	0.1
Cowley	15,688	5,267	9,414	1,007	4,147	R	33.6	60.0	6.4	38	72	31	1.4	1.5	1.3	1.4
Crawford	16,381	6,634	8,830	917	2,196	R	40.5	53.9	5.6	5	99	52	1.5	1.9	1.3	1.3
Decatur	2,066	555	1,399	112	844	R	26.9	67.7	5.4	82	24	58	0.2	0.2	0.2	0.2
Dickinson	9,120	3,024	5,603	493	2,579	R	33.2	61.4	5.4	42	66	60	0.8	0.9	0.8	0.7
Doniphan	3,900	1,058	2,545	297	1,487	R	27.1	65.3	7.6	79	42	10	0.3	0.3	0.4	0.4
Douglas	41,625	14,380	24,740	2,505	10,360	R	34.5	59.4	6.0	26	78	42	3.7	4.1	3.5	3.5
Edwards	1,916	650	1,143	123	493	R	33.9	59.7	6.4	31	76	30	0.2	0.2	0.2	0.2
Elk	1,717	502	1,101	114	599	R	29.2	64.1	6.6	62	51	24	0.2	0.1	0.2	0.2
Ellis	12,362	4,627	7,181	554	2,554	R	37.4	58.1	4.5	15	83	90	1.1	1.3	1.0	0.8
Ellsworth	3,184	1,057	2,017	110	960	R	33.2	63.3	3.5	41	55	105	0.3	0.3	0.3	0.2
Finney	10,849	3,054	7,265	530	4,211	R	28.2	67.0	4.9	74	29	78	1.0	0.9	1.0	0.7
Ford	10,291	2,855	6,911	525	4,056	R	27.7	67.2	5.1	77	27	69	0.9	0.8	1.0	0.7
Franklin	9,766	3,586	5,480	700	1,894	R	36.7	56.1	7.2	18	92	15	0.9	1.0	0.8	1.0
Geary	7,490	2,299	4,858	333	2,559	R	30.7	64.9	4.4	51	47	91	0.7	0.7	0.7	0.5
Gove	1,693	550	1,057	86	507	R	32.5	62.4	5.1	45	59	72	0.2	0.2	0.1	0.1
Graham	1,901	732	1,086	83	354	R	38.5	57.1	4.4	11	86	93	0.2	0.2	0.2	0.1
Grant	3,024	655	2,229	140	1,574	R	21.7	73.7	4.6	102	4	87	0.3	0.2	0.3	0.2
Gray	2,152	515	1,527	110	1,012	R	23.9	71.0	5.1	95	9	68	0.2	0.1	0.2	0.2
Greeley	874	237	582	55	345	R	27.1	66.6	6.3	80	32	35	<.1	<.1	<.1	<.1
Greenwood	3,839	1,301	2,291	247	990	R	33.9	59.7	6.4	32	75	29	0.3	0.4	0.3	0.3
Hamilton	1,359	389	911	59	522	R	28.6	67.0	4.3	69	28	95	0.1	0.1	0.1	<.1
Harper	3,361	880	2,283	198	1,403	R	26.2	67.9	5.9	85	23	44	0.3	0.3	0.3	0.3
Harvey	14,943	4,309	9,781	853	5,472	R	28.8	65.5	5.7	66	39	47	1.3	1.2	1.4	1.2
Haskell	1,806	397	1,338	71	941	R	22.0	74.1	3.9	100	2	102	0.2	0.1	0.2	0.1
Hodgeman	1,222	300	875	47	575	R	24.5	71.6	3.8	92	7	103	0.1	<.1	0.1	<.1
Jackson	5,515	2,213	3,047	255	834	R	40.1	55.2	4.6	6	95	88	0.5	0.6	0.4	0.4
Jefferson	7,680	3,078	4,099	503	1,021	R	40.1	53.4	6.5	8	100	27	0.7	0.9	0.6	0.7
Jewell	2,259	660	1,486	113	826	R	29.2	65.8	5.0	63	37	75	0.2	0.2	0.2	0.2
Johnson	188,396	45,537	132,067	10,792	86,530	R	24.2	70.1	5.7	94	14	46	16.7	13.0	18.7	15.3
Kearny	1,691	401	1,208	82	807	R	23.7	71.4	4.8	96	8	80	0.2	0.1	0.2	0.1
Kingman	4,108	1,156	2,690	262	1,534	R	28.1	65.5	6.4	76	38	33	0.4	0.3	0.4	0.4
Kiowa	1,867	405	1,357	105	952	R	21.7	72.7	5.6	101	6	51	0.2	0.1	0.2	0.1
Labette	10,049	3,345	6,116	588	2,771	R	33.3	60.9	5.9	40	69	45	0.9	1.0	0.9	0.8
Lane	1,279	277	942	60	665	R	21.7	73.7	4.7	103	5	86	0.1	<.1	0.1	<.1
Leavenworth	22,928	7,979	13,206	1,743	5,227	R	34.8	57.6	7.6	24	84	11	2.0	2.3	1.9	2.5
Lincoln	2,126	617	1,420	89	803	R	29.0	66.8	4.2	64	30	97	0.2	0.2	0.2	0.1
Linn	4,091	1,375	2,458	258	1,083	R	33.6	60.1	6.3	37	71	34	0.4	0.4	0.3	0.4
Logan	1,686	435	1,156	95	721	R	25.8	68.6	5.6	88	19	50	0.1	0.1	0.2	0.1
Lyon	14,579	5,632	8,013	934	2,381	R	38.6	55.0	6.4	10	97	32	1.3	1.6	1.1	1.3
McPherson	12,926	3,748	8,550	628	4,802	R	29.0	66.1	4.9	65	35	79	1.1	1.1	1.2	0.9
Marion	6,292	1,791	4,238	263	2,447	R	28.5	67.4	4.2	73	26	98	0.6	0.5	0.6	0.4
Marshall	5,771	2,514	2,948	309	434	R	43.6	51.1	5.4	1	103	61	0.5	0.7	0.4	0.4
Meade	2,119	560	1,434	125	874	R	26.4	67.7	5.9	84	25	43	0.2	0.2	0.2	0.2
Miami	11,005	3,838	6,410	757	2,572	R	34.9	58.2	6.9	23	80	21	1.0	1.1	0.9	1.1
Mitchell	3,590	1,027	2,345	218	1,318	R	28.6	65.3	6.1	71	40	40	0.3	0.3	0.3	0.3
Montgomery	15,738	5,622	8,983	1,133	3,361	R	35.7	57.1	7.2	21	87	14	1.4	1.6	1.3	1.6
Morris	3,068	1,230	1,672	166	442	R	40.1	54.5	5.4	7	98	59	0.3	0.4	0.2	0.2
Morton	1,644	430	1,136	78	706	R	26.2	69.1	4.7	86	17	84	0.1	0.1	0.2	0.1
Nemaha	5,403	2,066	3,079	258	1,013	R	38.2	57.0	4.8	12	88	82	0.5	0.6	0.4	0.4
Neosho	7,465	2,748	4,152	565	1,404	R	36.8	55.6	7.6	17	94	12	0.7	0.8	0.6	0.8
Ness	2,187	652	1,420	115	768	R	29.8	64.9	5.3	58	44	64	0.2	0.2	0.2	0.2
Norton	3,039	889	1,878	272	989	R	29.3	61.8	9.0	61	62	3	0.3	0.3	0.3	0.4
Osage	7,361	3,066	3,876	419	810	R	41.7	52.7	5.7	4	101	48	0.7	0.9	0.5	0.6

Table F. — Vote for U.S. Senator: November 3, 1992, General Election (cont)

County	Total	O'Dell (DEM)	Dole (REP)	Other	Plurality Total	Party	Percent of total vote DEM	REP	Other	Rank DEM	REP	Other	Percent contribution to state vote Total	DEM	REP	Other
Osborne	2,560	874	1,581	105	707	R	34.1	61.8	4.1	30	64	100	0.2	0.3	0.2	0.1
Ottawa	2,803	894	1,765	144	871	R	31.9	63.0	5.1	47	56	67	0.2	0.3	0.2	0.2
Pawnee	3,520	1,113	2,245	162	1,132	R	31.6	63.8	4.6	48	52	89	0.3	0.3	0.3	0.2
Phillips	3,333	901	2,213	219	1,312	R	27.0	66.4	6.6	81	33	25	0.3	0.3	0.3	0.3
Pottawatomie	7,936	2,677	4,864	395	2,187	R	33.7	61.3	5.0	34	67	76	0.7	0.8	0.7	0.6
Pratt	4,723	1,418	3,055	250	1,637	R	30.0	64.7	5.3	57	48	63	0.4	0.4	0.4	0.4
Rawlins	1,797	374	1,325	98	951	R	20.8	73.7	5.5	104	3	56	0.2	0.1	0.2	0.1
Reno	27,986	9,600	16,669	1,717	7,069	R	34.3	59.6	6.1	29	77	38	2.5	2.7	2.4	2.4
Republic	3,757	1,076	2,424	257	1,348	R	28.6	64.5	6.8	68	49	23	0.3	0.3	0.3	0.4
Rice	5,253	1,621	3,411	221	1,790	R	30.9	64.9	4.2	49	43	96	0.5	0.5	0.5	0.3
Riley	21,508	6,294	14,325	889	8,031	R	29.3	66.6	4.1	60	31	99	1.9	1.8	2.0	1.3
Rooks	3,049	1,018	1,884	147	866	R	33.4	61.8	4.8	39	63	81	0.3	0.3	0.3	0.2
Rush	2,111	742	1,254	115	512	R	35.1	59.4	5.4	22	79	57	0.2	0.2	0.2	0.2
Russell	3,993	1,092	2,761	140	1,669	R	27.3	69.1	3.5	78	16	104	0.4	0.3	0.4	0.2
Saline	23,481	7,940	14,435	1,106	6,495	R	33.8	61.5	4.7	33	65	85	2.1	2.3	2.0	1.6
Scott	2,517	620	1,786	111	1,166	R	24.6	71.0	4.4	91	10	92	0.2	0.2	0.3	0.2
Sedgwick	175,030	42,842	119,486	12,702	76,644	R	24.5	68.3	7.3	93	22	13	15.5	12.3	16.9	18.0
Seward	6,591	1,462	4,676	453	3,214	R	22.2	70.9	6.9	99	11	22	0.6	0.4	0.7	0.6
Shawnee	81,095	34,905	42,020	4,170	7,115	R	43.0	51.8	5.1	3	102	66	7.2	10.0	5.9	5.9
Sheridan	1,619	494	1,043	82	549	R	30.5	64.4	5.1	52	50	74	0.1	0.1	0.1	0.1
Sherman	3,189	833	2,181	175	1,348	R	26.1	68.4	5.5	87	21	55	0.3	0.2	0.3	0.2
Smith	2,827	953	1,761	113	808	R	33.7	62.3	4.0	35	61	101	0.3	0.3	0.2	0.2
Stafford	2,726	822	1,769	135	947	R	30.2	64.9	5.0	55	45	77	0.2	0.2	0.3	0.2
Stanton	986	252	678	56	426	R	25.6	68.8	5.7	89	18	49	<.1	<.1	<.1	<.1
Stevens	2,402	548	1,688	166	1,140	R	22.8	70.3	6.9	97	13	19	0.2	0.2	0.2	0.2
Sumner	11,551	3,772	7,020	759	3,248	R	32.7	60.8	6.6	44	70	26	1.0	1.1	1.0	1.1
Thomas	3,902	1,163	2,569	170	1,406	R	29.8	65.8	4.4	59	36	94	0.3	0.3	0.4	0.2
Trego	1,906	699	1,110	97	411	R	36.7	58.2	5.1	19	81	71	0.2	0.2	0.2	0.1
Wabaunsee	3,351	1,270	1,908	173	638	R	37.9	56.9	5.2	14	89	65	0.3	0.4	0.3	0.2
Wallace	1,051	208	787	56	579	R	19.8	74.9	5.3	105	1	62	<.1	<.1	0.1	<.1
Washington	3,634	1,043	2,406	185	1,363	R	28.7	66.2	5.1	67	34	70	0.3	0.3	0.3	0.3
Wichita	1,221	311	852	58	541	R	25.5	69.8	4.8	90	15	83	0.1	<.1	0.1	<.1
Wilson	4,571	1,539	2,661	371	1,122	R	33.7	58.2	8.1	36	82	7	0.4	0.4	0.4	0.5
Woodson	1,845	637	1,049	159	412	R	34.5	56.9	8.6	27	90	5	0.2	0.2	0.1	0.2
Wyandotte	56,869	21,722	28,868	6,279	7,146	R	38.2	50.8	11.0	13	104	1	5.0	6.2	4.1	8.9
KANSAS	1,126,447	349,525	706,246	70,676	356,721	R	31.0	62.7	6.3				100.0	100.0	100.0	100.0

Congressional district and county	Total	Democrat (DEM)	Republican (REP)	Other	Plurality Total	Party	DEM	REP	Other	Rank within district DEM	REP	Other	Total	DEM	REP	Other
District 1	**285,297**	**83,620**	**194,912**	**6,765**	**111,292**	**R**	**29.3**	**68.3**	**2.4**				**100.0**	**100.0**	**100.0**	**100.0**
Barber	2,797	621	2,103	73	1,482	R	22.2	75.2	2.6	57	12	11	1.0	0.7	1.1	1.1
Barton	13,439	4,022	9,132	285	5,110	R	29.9	68.0	2.1	19	47	24	4.7	4.8	4.7	4.2
Chase	1,624	425	1,131	68	706	R	26.2	69.6	4.2	43	38	2	0.6	0.5	0.6	1.0
Cheyenne	1,736	344	1,360	32	1,016	R	19.8	78.3	1.8	61	5	34	0.6	0.4	0.7	0.5
Clark	1,308	338	949	21	611	R	25.8	72.6	1.6	45	21	49	0.5	0.4	0.5	0.3
Clay	4,386	840	3,428	118	2,588	R	19.2	78.2	2.7	64	6	10	1.5	1.0	1.8	1.7
Cloud	5,287	1,641	3,489	157	1,848	R	31.0	66.0	3.0	14	56	6	1.9	2.0	1.8	2.3
Comanche	1,269	304	942	23	638	R	24.0	74.2	1.8	50	16	38	0.4	0.4	0.5	0.3
Decatur	2,039	534	1,483	22	949	R	26.2	72.7	1.1	42	20	64	0.7	0.6	0.8	0.3
Dickinson	9,002	2,340	6,434	228	4,094	R	26.0	71.5	2.5	44	27	12	3.2	2.8	3.3	3.4
Edwards	1,906	507	1,358	41	851	R	26.6	71.2	2.2	39	28	23	0.7	0.6	0.7	0.6
Ellis	12,193	5,151	6,735	307	1,584	R	42.2	55.2	2.5	2	65	14	4.3	6.2	3.5	4.5
Ellsworth	3,138	830	2,251	57	1,421	R	26.5	71.7	1.8	40	25	37	1.1	1.0	1.2	0.8
Finney	10,834	5,120	5,459	255	339	R	47.3	50.4	2.4	1	66	18	3.8	6.1	2.8	3.8
Ford	10,288	2,716	7,424	148	4,708	R	26.4	72.2	1.4	41	23	54	3.6	3.2	3.8	2.2
Gove	1,673	521	1,122	30	601	R	31.1	67.1	1.8	13	54	41	0.6	0.6	0.6	0.4
Graham	1,869	609	1,227	33	618	R	32.6	65.7	1.8	8	59	44	0.7	0.7	0.6	0.5
Grant	2,991	904	2,039	48	1,135	R	30.2	68.2	1.6	18	46	50	1.0	1.1	1.0	0.7
Gray	2,147	605	1,508	34	903	R	28.2	70.2	1.6	29	33	52	0.8	0.7	0.8	0.5
Greeley	872	240	617	15	377	R	27.5	70.8	1.7	35	30	47	0.3	0.3	0.3	0.2
Hamilton	1,362	479	864	19	385	R	35.2	63.4	1.4	5	61	56	0.5	0.6	0.4	0.3
Haskell	1,807	536	1,243	28	707	R	29.7	68.8	1.5	22	42	53	0.6	0.6	0.6	0.4
Hodgeman	1,215	285	915	15	630	R	23.5	75.3	1.2	53	9	61	0.4	0.3	0.5	0.2
Jewell	2,205	506	1,658	41	1,152	R	22.9	75.2	1.9	55	11	32	0.8	0.6	0.9	0.6
Kearny	1,694	628	1,035	31	407	R	37.1	61.1	1.8	4	63	35	0.6	0.8	0.5	0.5
Kiowa	1,865	338	1,506	21	1,168	R	18.1	80.8	1.1	66	1	63	0.7	0.4	0.8	0.3
Lane	1,281	363	894	24	531	R	28.3	69.8	1.9	28	37	30	0.4	0.4	0.5	0.4
Lincoln	2,104	476	1,584	44	1,108	R	22.6	75.3	2.1	56	10	25	0.7	0.6	0.8	0.7
Logan	1,671	449	1,199	23	750	R	26.9	71.8	1.4	38	24	57	0.6	0.5	0.6	0.3
Lyon	14,263	5,837	7,887	539	2,050	R	40.9	55.3	3.8	3	64	3	5.0	7.0	4.0	8.0
McPherson	12,713	2,817	9,545	351	6,728	R	22.2	75.1	2.8	58	13	9	4.5	3.4	4.9	5.2
Marion (pt)	5,471	1,073	4,297	101	3,224	R	19.6	78.5	1.8	62	4	33	1.9	1.3	2.2	1.5
Marshall	5,849	1,995	3,708	146	1,713	R	34.1	63.4	2.5	6	62	15	2.1	2.4	1.9	2.2
Meade	2,145	578	1,538	29	960	R	26.9	71.7	1.4	37	26	58	0.8	0.7	0.8	0.4
Mitchell	3,577	822	2,683	72	1,861	R	23.0	75.0	2.0	54	14	28	1.3	1.0	1.4	1.1
Morris	2,965	829	2,034	102	1,205	R	28.0	68.6	3.4	31	44	4	1.0	1.0	1.0	1.5
Morton	1,643	490	1,123	30	633	R	29.8	68.4	1.8	20	45	36	0.6	0.6	0.6	0.4
Ness	2,192	677	1,487	28	810	R	30.9	67.8	1.3	15	50	59	0.8	0.8	0.8	0.4
Norton	3,050	898	2,109	43	1,211	R	29.4	69.1	1.4	25	40	55	1.1	1.1	1.1	0.6
Osborne	2,560	736	1,792	32	1,056	R	28.8	70.0	1.3	26	36	60	0.9	0.9	0.9	0.5
Ottawa	2,776	655	2,060	61	1,405	R	23.6	74.2	2.2	51	17	20	1.0	0.8	1.1	0.9
Pawnee	3,535	976	2,491	68	1,515	R	27.6	70.5	1.9	34	31	29	1.2	1.2	1.3	1.0
Phillips	3,313	723	2,522	68	1,799	R	21.8	76.1	2.1	60	7	26	1.2	0.9	1.3	1.0
Pratt	4,677	1,275	3,284	118	2,009	R	27.3	70.2	2.5	36	34	13	1.6	1.5	1.7	1.7
Rawlins	1,901	368	1,499	34	1,131	R	19.4	78.9	1.8	63	3	42	0.7	0.4	0.8	0.5
Reno	27,751	8,235	18,661	855	10,426	R	29.7	67.2	3.1	21	53	5	9.7	9.8	9.6	12.6
Republic	3,721	875	2,765	81	1,890	R	23.5	74.3	2.2	52	15	21	1.3	1.0	1.4	1.2
Rice	5,199	1,265	3,821	113	2,556	R	24.3	73.5	2.2	49	19	22	1.8	1.5	2.0	1.7
Rooks	3,032	968	1,991	73	1,023	R	31.9	65.7	2.4	11	58	17	1.1	1.2	1.0	1.1
Rush	2,100	678	1,385	37	707	R	32.3	66.0	1.8	10	57	45	0.7	0.8	0.7	0.5
Russell	3,973	1,204	2,698	71	1,494	R	30.3	67.9	1.8	17	49	43	1.4	1.4	1.4	1.0
Saline	23,204	6,623	15,936	645	9,313	R	28.5	68.7	2.8	27	43	8	8.1	7.9	8.2	9.5
Scott	2,483	736	1,687	60	951	R	29.6	67.9	2.4	23	48	16	0.9	0.9	0.9	0.9
Seward	6,650	1,838	4,620	192	2,782	R	27.6	69.5	2.9	33	39	7	2.3	2.2	2.4	2.8
Sheridan	1,616	507	1,094	15	587	R	31.4	67.7	0.9	12	51	66	0.6	0.6	0.6	0.2
Sherman	3,223	904	2,261	58	1,357	R	28.0	70.2	1.8	30	35	39	1.1	1.1	1.2	0.9
Smith	2,784	777	1,957	50	1,180	R	27.9	70.3	1.8	32	32	40	1.0	0.9	1.0	0.7
Stafford	2,715	664	2,006	45	1,342	R	24.5	73.9	1.7	48	18	48	1.0	0.8	1.0	0.7
Stanton	989	253	716	20	463	R	25.6	72.4	2.0	46	22	27	0.3	0.3	0.4	0.3
Stevens	2,402	737	1,620	45	883	R	30.7	67.4	1.9	16	52	31	0.8	0.9	0.8	0.7
Thomas	3,883	1,149	2,672	62	1,523	R	29.6	68.8	1.6	24	41	51	1.4	1.4	1.4	0.9
Trego	1,880	622	1,225	33	603	R	33.1	65.2	1.8	7	60	46	0.7	0.7	0.6	0.5
Wabaunsee	3,226	797	2,289	140	1,492	R	24.7	71.0	4.3	47	29	1	1.1	1.0	1.2	2.1
Wallace	1,043	192	839	12	647	R	18.4	80.4	1.2	65	2	62	0.4	0.2	0.4	0.2
Washington	3,564	778	2,703	83	1,925	R	21.8	75.8	2.3	59	8	19	1.2	0.9	1.4	1.2
Wichita	1,227	397	818	12	421	R	32.4	66.7	1.0	9	55	65	0.4	0.5	0.4	0.2
District 2	**268,806**	**151,019**	**109,801**	**7,986**	**41,218**	**D**	**56.2**	**40.8**	**3.0**				**100.0**	**100.0**	**100.0**	**100.0**
Allen	6,277	3,057	2,979	241	78	D	48.7	47.5	3.8	23	5	6	2.3	2.0	2.7	3.0
Anderson	3,567	1,816	1,614	137	202	D	50.9	45.2	3.8	18	8	5	1.3	1.2	1.5	1.7
Atchison	7,449	4,837	2,406	206	2,431	D	64.9	32.3	2.8	1	25	17	2.8	3.2	2.2	2.6
Bourbon	6,966	3,413	3,372	181	41	D	49.0	48.4	2.6	20	3	19	2.6	2.3	3.1	2.3
Brown	5,224	2,902	2,204	118	698	D	55.6	42.2	2.3	14	11	21	1.9	1.9	2.0	1.5
Cherokee	9,537	5,703	3,625	209	2,078	D	59.8	38.0	2.2	5	20	23	3.5	3.8	3.3	2.6
Coffey	4,230	1,809	2,292	129	483	R	42.8	54.2	3.0	25	1	13	1.6	1.2	2.1	1.6

Congressional district and county	Total	Democrat (DEM)	Republican (REP)	Other	Plurality Total	Plurality Party	Percent of total vote DEM	Percent of total vote REP	Percent of total vote Other	Rank within district DEM	Rank within district REP	Rank within district Other	Percent contribution to district vote Total	Percent contribution to district vote DEM	Percent contribution to district vote REP	Percent contribution to district vote Other
District 2 (cont)																
Crawford	16,162	9,728	6,001	433	3,727	D	60.2	37.1	2.7	4	23	18	6.0	6.4	5.5	5.4
Doniphan	3,871	2,269	1,488	114	781	D	58.6	38.4	2.9	6	19	16	1.4	1.5	1.4	1.4
Douglas (pt)	1,605	919	637	49	282	D	57.3	39.7	3.1	11	15	12	0.6	0.6	0.6	0.6
Franklin	9,607	4,740	4,505	362	235	D	49.3	46.9	3.8	19	7	7	3.6	3.1	4.1	4.5
Geary	7,469	4,282	2,961	226	1,321	D	57.3	39.6	3.0	9	16	14	2.8	2.8	2.7	2.8
Jackson	5,563	3,363	2,110	90	1,253	D	60.5	37.9	1.6	3	21	25	2.1	2.2	1.9	1.1
Jefferson	7,465	4,157	3,036	272	1,121	D	55.7	40.7	3.6	13	13	8	2.8	2.8	2.8	3.4
Labette	9,868	5,774	3,801	293	1,973	D	58.5	38.5	3.0	7	18	15	3.7	3.8	3.5	3.7
Leavenworth	22,604	12,800	8,891	913	3,909	D	56.6	39.3	4.0	12	17	4	8.4	8.5	8.1	11.4
Linn	3,982	1,860	1,941	181	81	R	46.7	48.7	4.5	24	2	2	1.5	1.2	1.8	2.3
Nemaha	5,582	3,423	2,044	115	1,379	D	61.3	36.6	2.1	2	24	24	2.1	2.3	1.9	1.4
Neosho	7,704	3,980	3,455	269	525	D	51.7	44.8	3.5	17	9	9	2.9	2.6	3.1	3.4
Osage	7,354	3,907	3,271	176	636	D	53.1	44.5	2.4	16	10	20	2.7	2.6	3.0	2.2
Pottawatomie	7,934	4,370	3,287	277	1,083	D	55.1	41.4	3.5	15	12	10	3.0	2.9	3.0	3.5
Riley	21,177	12,246	7,951	980	4,295	D	57.8	37.5	4.6	8	22	1	7.9	8.1	7.2	12.3
Shawnee	81,322	46,587	32,937	1,798	13,650	D	57.3	40.5	2.2	10	14	22	30.3	30.8	30.0	22.5
Wilson	4,476	2,191	2,142	143	49	D	49.0	47.9	3.2	21	4	11	1.7	1.5	2.0	1.8
Woodson	1,811	886	851	74	35	D	48.9	47.0	4.1	22	6	3	0.7	0.6	0.8	0.9
District 3	292,796	110,076	169,929	12,791	59,853	R	37.6	58.0	4.4				100.0	100.0	100.0	100.0
Douglas (pt)	38,413	14,736	19,783	3,894	5,047	R	38.4	51.5	10.1	3	3	1	13.1	13.4	11.6	30.4
Johnson	186,676	57,286	123,365	6,025	66,079	R	30.7	66.1	3.2	4	1	4	63.8	52.0	72.6	47.1
Miami	10,891	4,668	5,751	472	1,083	R	42.9	52.8	4.3	2	2	2	3.7	4.2	3.4	3.7
Wyandotte	56,816	33,386	21,030	2,400	12,356	D	58.8	37.0	4.2	1	4	3	19.4	30.3	12.4	18.8
District 4	278,016	143,671	117,070	17,275	26,601	D	51.7	42.1	6.2				100.0	100.0	100.0	100.0
Butler	23,366	11,927	9,739	1,700	2,188	D	51.0	41.7	7.3	6	8	3	8.4	8.3	8.3	9.8
Chautauqua	2,011	722	1,186	103	464	R	35.9	59.0	5.1	11	2	10	0.7	0.5	1.0	0.6
Cowley	15,659	8,663	5,924	1,072	2,739	D	55.3	37.8	6.8	1	12	4	5.6	6.0	5.1	6.2
Elk	1,708	712	894	102	182	R	41.7	52.3	6.0	10	3	7	0.6	0.5	0.8	0.6
Greenwood	3,799	1,730	1,834	235	104	R	45.5	48.3	6.2	9	4	6	1.4	1.2	1.6	1.4
Harper	3,353	1,747	1,415	191	332	D	52.1	42.2	5.7	4	7	8	1.2	1.2	1.2	1.1
Harvey	14,899	7,714	6,449	736	1,265	D	51.8	43.3	4.9	5	6	11	5.4	5.4	5.5	4.3
Kingman	4,125	2,019	1,876	230	143	D	48.9	45.5	5.6	8	5	9	1.5	1.4	1.6	1.3
Marion (pt)	703	357	284	62	73	D	50.8	40.4	8.8	7	10	1	0.3	0.2	0.2	0.4
Montgomery	15,644	5,559	9,581	504	4,022	R	35.5	61.2	3.2	12	1	12	5.6	3.9	8.2	2.9
Sedgwick	181,224	96,260	73,494	11,470	22,766	D	53.1	40.6	6.3	3	9	5	65.2	67.0	62.8	66.4
Sumner	11,525	6,261	4,394	870	1,867	D	54.3	38.1	7.5	2	11	2	4.1	4.4	3.8	5.0
KANSAS	1,124,915	488,386	591,712	44,817	103,326	R	43.4	52.6	4.0							

Table I. — Vote for Presidential Preference: April 7, 1992, Democratic Primary Election

County	Total	Clinton	Tsongas	None of Above	Brown	Kerrey	Hauptli	Woods	Other	Clinton	Tsongas	None of Above	Rank Clinton	Rank Tsongas	Rank None of Above	Total	Clinton	Tsongas	None of Above
Allen	1,132	657	125	172	95	10	6	15	52	58.0	11.0	15.2	15	65	64	0.7	0.8	0.5	0.8
Anderson	446	271	55	52	39	4	4	1	20	60.8	12.3	11.7	12	53	92	0.3	0.3	0.2	0.2
Atchison	840	401	154	115	103	14	8	2	43	47.7	18.3	13.7	69	5	75	0.5	0.5	0.6	0.5
Barber	498	261	64	102	40	6	4	2	19	52.4	12.9	20.5	39	46	25	0.3	0.3	0.3	0.5
Barton	1,578	767	218	284	203	24	18	12	52	48.6	13.8	18.0	63	36	37	1.0	0.9	0.9	1.3
Bourbon	893	488	120	139	83	9	9	12	33	54.6	13.4	15.6	25	39	61	0.6	0.6	0.5	0.6
Brown	510	271	66	83	46	17	2	2	23	53.1	12.9	16.3	33	44	54	0.3	0.3	0.3	0.4
Butler	3,578	1,919	505	596	365	30	13	39	111	53.6	14.1	16.7	30	33	50	2.2	2.3	2.1	2.7
Chase	167	91	16	32	15	2	1	1	9	54.5	9.6	19.2	26	90	32	0.1	0.1	<.1	0.1
Chautauqua	227	146	31	24	15	0	2	1	8	64.3	13.7	10.6	5	37	98	0.1	0.2	0.1	0.1
Cherokee	2,005	1,418	156	236	114	13	5	19	44	70.7	7.8	11.8	1	100	91	1.3	1.7	0.6	1.1
Cheyenne	193	89	30	19	8	7	0	0	40	46.1	15.5	9.8	79	21	99	0.1	0.1	0.1	<.1
Clark	155	78	20	36	10	2	1	0	8	50.3	12.9	23.2	50	45	15	<.1	<.1	<.1	0.2
Clay	267	131	34	46	27	11	6	3	9	49.1	12.7	17.2	58	49	42	0.2	0.2	0.1	0.2
Cloud	960	481	103	121	115	47	31	13	49	50.1	10.7	12.6	54	70	85	0.6	0.6	0.4	0.5
Coffey	365	198	39	62	33	4	2	11	16	54.2	10.7	17.0	29	71	43	0.2	0.2	0.2	0.3
Comanche	162	86	27	28	11	1	2	0	7	53.1	16.7	17.3	34	12	41	0.1	0.1	0.1	0.1
Cowley	2,289	1,315	310	321	226	12	6	25	74	57.4	13.5	14.0	16	38	70	1.4	1.6	1.3	1.4
Crawford	2,776	1,782	245	360	254	16	5	14	100	64.2	8.8	13.0	6	98	83	1.7	2.2	1.0	1.6
Decatur	311	169	24	46	10	13	3	0	46	54.3	7.7	14.8	27	101	67	0.2	0.2	<.1	0.2
Dickinson	867	497	96	118	79	11	24	11	31	57.3	11.1	13.6	17	64	77	0.5	0.6	0.4	0.5
Doniphan	214	132	23	28	12	10	2	0	7	61.7	10.7	13.1	10	69	82	0.1	0.2	0.1	0.1
Douglas	4,839	1,809	1,145	545	1,133	64	7	27	109	37.4	23.7	11.3	104	1	95	3.0	2.2	4.7	2.5
Edwards	340	154	48	96	21	2	4	2	13	45.3	14.1	28.2	86	32	5	0.2	0.2	0.2	0.4
Elk	253	140	33	36	18	4	4	4	14	55.3	13.0	14.2	24	42	69	0.2	0.2	0.1	0.2
Ellis	3,403	1,705	409	475	503	58	49	14	190	50.1	12.0	14.0	55	57	72	2.1	2.1	1.7	2.1
Ellsworth	941	455	96	194	107	18	31	9	31	48.4	10.2	20.6	65	79	24	0.6	0.6	0.4	0.9
Finney	1,133	483	201	219	160	17	8	7	38	42.6	17.7	19.3	97	8	30	0.7	0.6	0.8	1.0
Ford	2,064	967	249	531	175	32	12	4	94	46.9	12.1	25.7	74	56	9	1.3	1.2	1.0	2.4
Franklin	1,091	580	176	149	107	17	2	12	48	53.2	16.1	13.7	32	15	76	0.7	0.7	0.7	0.7
Geary	894	471	145	108	126	11	4	12	17	52.7	16.2	12.1	36	14	90	0.6	0.6	0.6	0.5
Gove	203	83	20	34	23	9	3	0	31	40.9	9.9	16.7	100	86	48	0.1	0.1	<.1	0.2
Graham	173	78	20	16	31	3	4	0	21	45.1	11.6	9.2	87	60	100	0.1	<.1	<.1	<.1
Grant	327	166	52	70	16	7	1	2	13	50.8	15.9	21.4	49	17	21	0.2	0.2	0.2	0.3
Gray	298	130	40	69	37	6	5	2	9	43.6	13.4	23.2	92	40	16	0.2	0.2	0.2	0.3
Greeley	67	31	5	21	2	4	0	0	4	46.3	7.5	31.3	78	102	1	<.1	<.1	<.1	<.1
Greenwood	785	482	80	149	41	7	1	5	20	61.4	10.2	19.0	11	80	33	0.5	0.6	0.3	0.7
Hamilton	162	78	21	34	11	3	2	3	10	48.1	13.0	21.0	67	43	23	0.1	<.1	<.1	0.2
Harper	470	269	60	78	37	5	1	5	15	57.2	12.8	16.6	18	48	52	0.3	0.3	0.2	0.4
Harvey	2,537	1,202	454	425	326	30	16	16	68	47.4	17.9	16.8	70	7	47	1.6	1.5	1.9	1.9
Haskell	189	105	18	40	10	1	1	1	13	55.6	9.5	21.2	23	91	22	0.1	0.1	<.1	0.2
Hodgeman	120	51	11	33	8	4	1	0	12	42.5	9.2	27.5	98	95	6	<.1	<.1	<.1	0.1
Jackson	726	373	104	121	75	13	0	13	27	51.4	14.3	16.7	45	29	49	0.5	0.5	0.4	0.5
Jefferson	858	403	134	144	116	8	3	15	35	47.0	15.6	16.8	73	20	46	0.5	0.5	0.5	0.6
Jewell	142	68	18	25	13	16	0	1	1	47.9	12.7	17.6	68	50	39	<.1	<.1	<.1	0.1
Johnson	16,698	7,367	3,675	2,292	2,501	314	26	40	483	44.1	22.0	13.7	90	3	74	10.4	9.0	15.1	10.3
Kearny	213	96	32	49	21	1	2	1	11	45.1	15.0	23.0	88	23	17	0.1	0.1	0.1	0.2
Kingman	573	279	81	124	43	7	5	5	29	48.7	14.1	21.6	60	31	20	0.4	0.3	0.3	0.6
Kiowa	242	119	27	65	18	3	0	0	10	49.2	11.2	26.9	57	63	7	0.2	0.1	0.1	0.3
Labette	1,564	1,047	157	133	148	8	5	10	56	66.9	10.0	8.5	2	84	104	1.0	1.3	0.6	0.6
Lane	112	43	19	30	9	1	0	0	10	38.4	17.0	26.8	102	11	8	<.1	<.1	<.1	0.1
Leavenworth	2,485	1,246	435	337	337	39	10	8	73	50.1	17.5	13.6	53	10	78	1.6	1.5	1.8	1.5
Lincoln	202	113	21	25	19	6	11	0	7	55.9	10.4	12.4	19	76	87	0.1	0.1	<.1	0.1
Linn	434	285	47	38	34	7	4	4	15	65.7	10.8	8.8	3	67	103	0.3	0.3	0.2	0.2
Logan	177	104	15	22	10	6	0	0	20	58.8	8.5	12.4	14	99	86	0.1	0.1	<.1	<.1
Lyon	1,706	799	281	266	233	32	12	24	59	46.8	16.5	15.6	75	13	60	1.1	1.0	1.2	1.2
McPherson	1,428	652	227	288	169	24	28	11	29	45.7	15.9	20.2	82	18	28	0.9	0.8	0.9	1.3
Marion	694	372	97	107	62	10	7	2	37	53.6	14.0	15.4	31	34	62	0.4	0.5	0.4	0.5
Marshall	783	408	74	126	86	45	5	13	26	52.1	9.5	16.1	41	92	55	0.5	0.5	0.3	0.6
Meade	271	116	31	82	18	5	1	1	17	42.8	11.4	30.3	96	61	2	0.2	0.1	0.1	0.4
Miami	2,182	1,185	303	379	184	27	9	8	87	54.3	13.9	17.4	28	35	40	1.4	1.4	1.2	1.7
Mitchell	458	198	30	59	31	19	111	0	10	43.2	6.6	12.9	95	104	84	0.3	0.2	0.1	0.3
Montgomery	2,235	1,430	225	312	112	17	7	25	107	64.0	10.1	14.0	7	83	71	1.4	1.7	0.9	1.4
Morris	409	213	41	83	46	5	2	6	13	52.1	10.0	20.3	42	85	27	0.3	0.3	0.2	0.4
Morton	346	158	55	79	33	3	4	1	13	45.7	15.9	22.8	81	19	18	0.2	0.2	0.2	0.4
Nemaha	642	300	65	116	88	31	4	10	28	46.7	10.1	18.1	76	81	36	0.4	0.4	0.3	0.5
Neosho	1,018	640	124	118	66	9	5	11	45	62.9	12.2	11.6	8	55	93	0.6	0.8	0.5	0.5
Ness	260	145	25	49	21	4	2	1	13	55.8	9.6	18.8	20	88	34	0.2	0.2	0.1	0.2
Norton	327	168	40	43	23	22	4	0	27	51.4	12.2	13.1	46	54	81	0.2	0.2	0.2	0.2
Osage	956	533	100	159	113	8	4	16	23	55.8	10.5	16.6	21	75	51	0.6	0.6	0.4	0.7

Table I. — Vote for Presidential Preference: April 7, 1992, Democratic Primary Election (cont)

County	Total	Clinton	Tsongas	None of Above	Brown	Kerrey	Hauptli	Woods	Other	Clinton	Tsongas	None of Above	Clinton	Tsongas	None of Above	Total	Clinton	Tsongas	None of Above
											Percent of total vote			**Rank**			**Percent contribution to state vote**		
Osborne	294	143	42	47	21	13	16	0	12	48.6	14.3	16.0	62	30	57	0.2	0.2	0.2	0.2
Ottawa	314	158	29	45	30	8	31	4	9	50.3	9.2	14.3	51	93	68	0.2	0.2	0.1	0.2
Pawnee	454	198	83	107	37	9	1	0	19	43.6	18.3	23.6	93	6	13	0.3	0.2	0.3	0.5
Phillips	268	125	27	41	30	15	11	0	19	46.6	10.1	15.3	77	82	63	0.2	0.2	0.1	0.2
Pottawatomie	1,091	480	136	246	150	20	5	16	38	44.0	12.5	22.5	91	52	19	0.7	0.6	0.6	1.1
Pratt	790	415	99	161	72	7	2	5	29	52.5	12.5	20.4	38	51	26	0.5	0.5	0.4	0.7
Rawlins	339	89	19	19	22	7	2	0	181	26.3	5.6	5.6	105	105	105	0.2	0.1	<.1	<.1
Reno	4,052	1,971	477	969	421	37	27	44	106	48.6	11.8	23.9	61	59	12	2.5	2.4	2.0	4.4
Republic	372	152	39	63	34	44	17	2	21	40.9	10.5	16.9	101	74	44	0.2	0.2	0.2	0.3
Rice	747	340	108	175	75	11	8	4	26	45.5	14.5	23.4	85	27	14	0.5	0.4	0.4	0.8
Riley	2,453	1,028	568	301	419	43	15	19	60	41.9	23.2	12.3	99	2	89	1.5	1.3	2.3	1.4
Rooks	403	199	36	71	41	16	5	4	31	49.4	8.9	17.6	56	97	38	0.3	0.2	0.1	0.3
Rush	343	172	51	55	31	6	7	1	20	50.1	14.9	16.0	52	25	56	0.2	0.2	0.2	0.2
Russell	604	318	59	102	76	4	12	3	30	52.6	9.8	16.9	37	87	45	0.4	0.4	0.2	0.5
Saline	2,832	1,385	339	381	310	32	311	20	54	48.9	12.0	13.5	59	58	79	1.8	1.7	1.4	1.7
Scott	219	95	44	41	19	4	1	3	12	43.4	20.1	18.7	94	4	35	0.1	0.1	0.2	0.2
Sedgwick	35,186	18,623	6,179	3,113	5,542	294	102	204	1,129	52.9	17.6	8.8	35	9	102	22.0	22.7	25.3	14.0
Seward	927	476	133	178	78	13	10	3	36	51.3	14.3	19.2	47	28	31	0.6	0.6	0.5	0.8
Shawnee	11,850	5,722	1,725	1,637	2,012	141	47	146	420	48.3	14.6	13.8	66	26	73	7.4	7.0	7.1	7.4
Sheridan	202	77	31	32	22	8	3	1	28	38.1	15.3	15.8	103	22	59	0.1	<.1	0.1	0.1
Sherman	772	353	81	123	79	19	9	2	106	45.7	10.5	15.9	80	73	58	0.5	0.4	0.3	0.6
Smith	219	112	25	33	14	19	8	0	8	51.1	11.4	15.1	48	62	65	0.1	0.1	0.1	0.1
Stafford	388	177	40	110	28	3	2	4	24	45.6	10.3	28.4	84	77	4	0.2	0.2	0.2	0.5
Stanton	144	64	23	35	11	0	2	0	9	44.4	16.0	24.3	89	16	10	<.1	<.1	<.1	0.2
Stevens	454	220	58	109	32	3	1	0	31	48.5	12.8	24.0	64	47	11	0.3	0.3	0.2	0.5
Sumner	2,396	1,332	314	390	219	24	9	27	81	55.6	13.1	16.3	22	41	53	1.5	1.6	1.3	1.8
Thomas	640	292	69	85	51	23	13	2	105	45.6	10.8	13.3	83	68	80	0.4	0.4	0.3	0.4
Trego	266	139	24	40	21	10	3	6	23	52.3	9.0	15.0	40	96	66	0.2	0.2	<.1	0.2
Wabaunsee	438	206	45	86	54	14	1	10	22	47.0	10.3	19.6	72	78	29	0.3	0.3	0.2	0.4
Wallace	73	38	7	9	6	2	1	1	9	52.1	9.6	12.3	43	89	88	<.1	<.1	<.1	<.1
Washington	266	138	28	24	32	18	7	2	17	51.9	10.5	9.0	44	72	101	0.2	0.2	0.1	0.1
Wichita	121	57	18	36	3	1	1	1	4	47.1	14.9	29.8	71	24	3	<.1	<.1	<.1	0.2
Wilson	501	328	46	57	37	3	0	10	20	65.5	9.2	11.4	4	94	94	0.3	0.4	0.2	0.3
Woodson	257	161	18	28	27	2	3	1	17	62.6	7.0	10.9	9	103	97	0.2	0.2	<.1	0.1
Wyandotte	10,713	6,415	1,166	1,197	1,331	87	29	40	448	59.9	10.9	11.2	13	66	96	6.7	7.8	4.8	5.4
KANSAS	160,251	82,145	24,413	22,159	20,811	2,215	1,303	1,119	6,086	51.3	15.2	13.8				100.0	100.0	100.0	100.0

Table J. — Vote for Presidential Preference: April 7, 1992, Republican Primary Election

| County | Top candidates | | | | | Top four candidates (state vote) | | | | | | | | | | | | |
| | | | | | | Percent of total vote | | | | Rank | | | | Percent contribution to state vote | | | | |
	Total	Bush	None of Above	Bu-chanan	Other	Bush	None of Above	Bu-chanan	Other	Bush	None of Above	Bu-chanan	Other	Total	Bush	None of Above	Bu-chanan	Other
Allen	1,803	1,116	324	231	132	61.9	18.0	12.8	7.3	39	52	70	55	0.8	0.8	0.9	0.7	0.9
Anderson	493	298	80	69	46	60.4	16.2	14.0	9.3	53	75	50	14	0.2	0.2	0.2	0.2	0.3
Atchison	677	432	85	100	60	63.8	12.6	14.8	8.9	26	101	39	21	0.3	0.3	0.2	0.3	0.4
Barber	918	501	180	156	81	54.6	19.6	17.0	8.8	90	37	8	22	0.4	0.4	0.5	0.5	0.6
Barton	2,274	1,313	484	323	154	57.7	21.3	14.2	6.8	75	21	47	71	1.1	1.0	1.4	1.0	1.1
Bourbon	829	549	141	98	41	66.2	17.0	11.8	4.9	12	62	86	100	0.4	0.4	0.4	0.3	0.3
Brown	1,542	929	309	182	122	60.2	20.0	11.8	7.9	55	34	87	38	0.7	0.7	0.9	0.6	0.9
Butler	3,992	2,486	598	645	263	62.3	15.0	16.2	6.6	35	87	17	74	1.9	1.9	1.7	2.0	1.9
Chase	359	191	77	55	36	53.2	21.4	15.3	10.0	95	20	29	8	0.2	0.1	0.2	0.2	0.3
Chautauqua	563	335	99	82	47	59.5	17.6	14.6	8.3	58	56	41	33	0.3	0.3	0.3	0.3	0.3
Cherokee	1,265	902	154	154	55	71.3	12.2	12.2	4.3	1	103	82	104	0.6	0.7	0.4	0.5	0.4
Cheyenne	352	239	43	46	24	67.9	12.2	13.1	6.8	8	102	67	69	0.2	0.2	0.1	0.1	0.2
Clark	309	190	68	30	21	61.5	22.0	9.7	6.8	42	17	102	70	0.1	0.1	0.2	<.1	0.1
Clay	1,137	689	248	116	84	60.6	21.8	10.2	7.4	50	18	100	51	0.5	0.5	0.7	0.4	0.6
Cloud	1,598	946	292	244	116	59.2	18.3	15.3	7.3	61	48	30	57	0.7	0.7	0.8	0.8	0.8
Coffey	759	442	150	105	62	58.2	19.8	13.8	8.2	71	36	52	34	0.4	0.3	0.4	0.3	0.4
Comanche	351	214	70	46	21	61.0	19.9	13.1	6.0	47	35	65	84	0.2	0.2	0.2	0.1	0.1
Cowley	2,699	1,673	450	410	166	62.0	16.7	15.2	6.2	38	69	32	79	1.3	1.3	1.3	1.3	1.2
Crawford	1,671	1,074	271	209	117	64.3	16.2	12.5	7.0	22	76	77	63	0.8	0.8	0.8	0.7	0.8
Decatur	425	267	58	66	34	62.8	13.6	15.5	8.0	31	95	24	37	0.2	0.2	0.2	0.2	0.2
Dickinson	1,842	1,045	340	301	156	56.7	18.5	16.3	8.5	83	45	14	31	0.9	0.8	1.0	1.0	1.1
Doniphan	562	309	91	108	54	55.0	16.2	19.2	9.6	89	77	1	11	0.3	0.2	0.3	0.3	0.4
Douglas	4,282	2,498	896	617	271	58.3	20.9	14.4	6.3	70	25	43	76	2.0	1.9	2.5	2.0	1.9
Edwards	544	272	160	64	48	50.0	29.4	11.8	8.8	104	2	88	23	0.3	0.2	0.5	0.2	0.3
Elk	437	296	50	59	32	67.7	11.4	13.5	7.3	9	104	58	54	0.2	0.2	0.1	0.2	0.2
Ellis	2,121	1,356	321	314	130	63.9	15.1	14.8	6.1	25	86	38	80	1.0	1.0	0.9	1.0	0.9
Ellsworth	1,177	726	205	154	92	61.7	17.4	13.1	7.8	41	58	66	39	0.6	0.5	0.6	0.5	0.7
Finney	1,730	1,157	256	217	100	66.9	14.8	12.5	5.8	10	89	75	89	0.8	0.9	0.7	0.7	0.7
Ford	2,687	1,720	557	266	144	64.0	20.7	9.9	5.4	24	28	101	94	1.3	1.3	1.6	0.8	1.0
Franklin	1,469	797	288	248	136	54.3	19.6	16.9	9.3	91	38	9	16	0.7	0.6	0.8	0.8	1.0
Geary	957	626	161	116	54	65.4	16.8	12.1	5.6	16	64	83	92	0.4	0.5	0.5	0.4	0.4
Gove	319	184	67	40	28	57.7	21.0	12.5	8.8	77	24	76	25	0.1	0.1	0.2	0.1	0.2
Graham	572	324	101	87	60	56.6	17.7	15.2	10.5	84	55	31	4	0.3	0.2	0.3	0.3	0.4
Grant	741	480	141	85	35	64.8	19.0	11.5	4.7	20	41	90	103	0.3	0.4	0.4	0.3	0.2
Gray	318	186	58	51	23	58.5	18.2	16.0	7.2	69	49	19	59	0.1	0.1	0.2	0.2	0.2
Greeley	227	122	70	21	14	53.7	30.8	9.3	6.2	93	1	104	78	0.1	<.1	0.2	<.1	<.1
Greenwood	1,155	704	186	184	81	61.0	16.1	15.9	7.0	48	79	21	61	0.5	0.5	0.5	0.6	0.6
Hamilton	233	161	33	25	14	69.1	14.2	10.7	6.0	2	91	97	83	0.1	0.1	<.1	<.1	<.1
Harper	747	472	131	90	54	63.2	17.5	12.0	7.2	30	57	84	60	0.4	0.4	0.4	0.3	0.4
Harvey	4,098	2,547	687	633	231	62.2	16.8	15.4	5.6	37	66	25	93	1.9	1.9	1.9	2.0	1.6
Haskell	518	343	86	62	27	66.2	16.6	12.0	5.2	13	70	85	97	0.2	0.3	0.2	0.2	0.2
Hodgeman	275	157	52	35	31	57.1	18.9	12.7	11.3	81	42	73	2	0.1	0.1	0.1	0.1	0.2
Jackson	1,130	644	264	144	78	57.0	23.4	12.7	6.9	82	12	72	67	0.5	0.5	0.7	0.5	0.6
Jefferson	1,137	603	242	180	112	53.0	21.3	15.8	9.9	96	22	22	9	0.5	0.5	0.7	0.6	0.8
Jewell	480	297	79	79	25	61.9	16.5	16.5	5.2	40	72	13	98	0.2	0.2	0.2	0.3	0.2
Johnson	33,041	20,699	5,526	4,935	1,881	62.6	16.7	14.9	5.7	32	67	36	91	15.5	15.7	15.6	15.7	13.3
Kearny	524	357	88	54	25	68.1	16.8	10.3	4.8	7	65	99	102	0.2	0.3	0.2	0.2	0.2
Kingman	975	498	244	162	71	51.1	25.0	16.6	7.3	102	7	10	56	0.5	0.4	0.7	0.5	0.5
Kiowa	698	426	147	85	40	61.0	21.1	12.2	5.7	45	23	80	90	0.3	0.3	0.4	0.3	0.3
Labette	1,384	881	223	188	92	63.7	16.1	13.6	6.6	27	78	56	73	0.6	0.7	0.6	0.6	0.7
Lane	292	200	52	25	15	68.5	17.8	8.6	5.1	4	53	105	99	0.1	0.2	0.1	<.1	0.1
Leavenworth	2,195	1,321	367	376	131	60.2	16.7	17.1	6.0	56	68	7	85	1.0	1.0	1.0	1.2	0.9
Lincoln	389	220	93	53	23	56.6	23.9	13.6	5.9	86	10	55	86	0.2	0.2	0.3	0.2	0.2
Linn	606	362	96	99	49	59.7	15.8	16.3	8.1	57	81	15	35	0.3	0.3	0.3	0.3	0.3
Logan	291	172	45	48	26	59.1	15.5	16.5	8.9	62	84	11	20	0.1	0.1	0.1	0.2	0.2
Lyon	2,260	1,212	466	365	217	53.6	20.6	16.2	9.6	94	30	18	12	1.1	0.9	1.3	1.2	1.5
McPherson	2,801	1,645	602	370	184	58.7	21.5	13.2	6.6	66	19	64	75	1.3	1.2	1.7	1.2	1.3
Marion	1,716	1,124	280	221	91	65.5	16.3	12.9	5.3	14	74	69	96	0.8	0.9	-0.8	0.7	0.6
Marshall	1,049	555	231	173	90	52.9	22.0	16.5	8.6	97	16	12	28	0.5	0.4	0.7	0.5	0.6
Meade	626	379	127	93	27	60.5	20.3	14.9	4.3	52	32	37	105	0.3	0.3	0.4	0.3	0.2
Miami	1,994	1,170	400	286	138	58.7	20.1	14.3	6.9	67	33	46	66	0.9	0.9	1.1	0.9	1.0
Mitchell	858	505	156	114	83	58.9	18.2	13.3	9.7	64	50	61	10	0.4	0.4	0.4	0.4	0.6
Montgomery	3,251	2,126	445	431	249	65.4	13.7	13.3	7.7	17	94	63	43	1.5	1.6	1.3	1.4	1.8
Morris	592	304	132	85	71	51.4	22.3	14.4	12.0	101	15	45	1	0.3	0.2	0.4	0.3	0.5
Morton	444	264	59	81	40	59.5	13.3	18.2	9.0	59	98	2	17	0.2	0.2	0.2	0.3	0.3
Nemaha	773	491	122	108	52	63.5	15.8	14.0	6.7	28	82	51	72	0.4	0.4	0.3	0.3	0.4
Neosho	1,304	812	198	205	89	62.3	15.2	15.7	6.8	36	85	23	68	0.6	0.6	0.6	0.7	0.6
Ness	385	218	96	41	30	56.6	24.9	10.6	7.8	85	8	98	40	0.2	0.2	0.3	0.1	0.2
Norton	838	513	141	113	71	61.2	16.8	13.5	8.5	44	63	59	30	0.4	0.4	0.4	0.4	0.5
Osage	1,074	547	242	184	101	50.9	22.5	17.1	9.4	103	14	6	13	0.5	0.4	0.7	0.6	0.7

Table J. — Vote for Presidential Preference: April 7, 1992, Republican Primary Election (cont)

| County | Top candidates | | | | | Top four candidates (state vote) | | | | | | | | | | | | |
| | | | | | | Percent of total vote | | | | Rank | | | | Percent contribution to state vote | | | | |
	Total	Bush	None of Above	Bu-chanan	Other	Bush	None of Above	Bu-chanan	Other	Bush	None of Above	Bu-chanan	Other	Total	Bush	None of Above	Bu-chanan	Other
Osborne	528	322	90	76	40	61.0	17.0	14.4	7.6	46	60	44	46	0.2	0.2	0.3	0.2	0.3
Ottawa	684	403	126	103	52	58.9	18.4	15.1	7.6	63	47	33	45	0.3	0.3	0.4	0.3	0.4
Pawnee	646	375	171	62	38	58.0	26.5	9.6	5.9	73	6	103	87	0.3	0.3	0.5	0.2	0.3
Phillips	805	502	126	107	70	62.4	15.7	13.3	8.7	34	83	60	27	0.4	0.4	0.4	0.3	0.5
Pottawatomie	2,544	1,370	518	462	194	53.9	20.4	18.2	7.6	92	31	3	44	1.2	1.0	1.5	1.5	1.4
Pratt	1,261	749	247	177	88	59.4	19.6	14.0	7.0	60	39	48	64	0.6	0.6	0.7	0.6	0.6
Rawlins	854	584	111	96	63	68.4	13.0	11.2	7.4	5	99	94	53	0.4	0.4	0.3	0.3	0.4
Reno	4,478	2,365	1,247	583	283	52.8	27.8	13.0	6.3	98	4	68	77	2.1	1.8	3.5	1.9	2.0
Republic	878	575	130	107	66	65.5	14.8	12.2	7.5	15	88	79	48	0.4	0.4	0.4	0.3	0.5
Rice	1,044	597	254	132	61	57.2	24.3	12.6	5.8	80	9	74	88	0.5	0.5	0.7	0.4	0.4
Riley	3,869	2,423	688	524	234	62.6	17.8	13.5	6.0	33	54	57	82	1.8	1.8	1.9	1.7	1.7
Rooks	883	508	160	122	93	57.5	18.1	13.8	10.5	78	51	53	3	0.4	0.4	0.5	0.4	0.7
Rush	563	310	134	70	49	55.1	23.8	12.4	8.7	88	11	78	26	0.3	0.2	0.4	0.2	0.3
Russell	1,190	624	276	190	100	52.4	23.2	16.0	8.4	99	13	20	32	0.6	0.5	0.8	0.6	0.7
Saline	3,944	2,276	814	580	274	57.7	20.6	14.7	6.9	76	29	40	65	1.8	1.7	2.3	1.8	1.9
Scott	665	456	84	75	50	68.6	12.6	11.3	7.5	3	100	92	47	0.3	0.3	0.2	0.2	0.4
Sedgwick	42,896	29,235	4,389	6,995	2,277	68.2	10.2	16.3	5.3	6	105	16	95	20.1	22.1	12.4	22.2	16.1
Seward	1,997	1,327	328	220	122	66.4	16.4	11.0	6.1	11	73	95	81	0.9	1.0	0.9	0.7	0.9
Shawnee	14,327	8,416	2,640	2,202	1,069	58.7	18.4	15.4	7.5	65	46	27	49	6.7	6.4	7.4	7.0	7.6
Sheridan	278	163	58	32	25	58.6	20.9	11.5	9.0	68	26	89	18	0.1	0.1	0.2	0.1	0.2
Sherman	1,379	885	187	183	124	64.2	13.6	13.3	9.0	23	97	62	19	0.6	0.7	0.5	0.6	0.9
Smith	470	303	80	53	34	64.5	17.0	11.3	7.2	21	61	93	58	0.2	0.2	0.2	0.2	0.2
Stafford	518	270	151	57	40	52.1	29.2	11.0	7.7	100	3	96	42	0.2	0.2	0.4	0.2	0.3
Stanton	271	176	43	33	19	64.9	15.9	12.2	7.0	19	80	81	62	0.1	0.1	0.1	0.1	0.1
Stevens	1,024	628	190	116	90	61.3	18.6	11.3	8.8	43	44	91	24	0.5	0.5	0.5	0.4	0.6
Sumner	2,547	1,474	437	439	197	57.9	17.2	17.2	7.7	74	59	5	41	1.2	1.1	1.2	1.4	1.4
Thomas	1,044	662	147	151	84	63.4	14.1	14.5	8.0	29	92	42	36	0.5	0.5	0.4	0.5	0.6
Trego	293	168	55	45	25	57.3	18.8	15.4	8.5	79	43	28	29	0.1	0.1	0.2	0.1	0.2
Wabaunsee	967	476	269	132	90	49.2	27.8	13.7	9.3	105	5	54	15	0.5	0.4	0.8	0.4	0.6
Wallace	260	158	36	39	27	60.8	13.8	15.0	10.4	49	93	34	5	0.1	0.1	0.1	0.1	0.2
Washington	853	475	166	149	63	55.7	19.5	17.5	7.4	87	40	4	52	0.4	0.4	0.5	0.5	0.4
Wichita	207	125	43	29	10	60.4	20.8	14.0	4.8	54	27	49	101	<.1	<.1	0.1	<.1	<.1
Wilson	1,106	720	163	141	82	65.1	14.7	12.7	7.4	18	90	71	50	0.5	0.5	0.5	0.4	0.6
Woodson	492	298	67	76	51	60.6	13.6	15.4	10.4	51	96	26	6	0.2	0.2	0.2	0.2	0.4
Wyandotte	3,297	1,920	544	494	339	58.2	16.5	15.0	10.3	72	71	35	7	1.5	1.5	1.5	1.6	2.4
KANSAS	213,196	132,131	35,450	31,494	14,121	62.0	16.6	14.8	6.6					100.0	100.0	100.0	100.0	100.0

1992 Vote for President
Percent for Bush (R), by County

47.9% to 63.7%
40.7% to 47.8%
36.7% to 40.6%
21.1% to 36.6%

Bush (R) received 38.9% statewide.

A framed county name indicates
a county carried by the winner.

Copyright © 1993 by Election Data Services, Inc.

356 Kansas

1992 Vote for U.S. Senator
Percent for Dole (R), by County

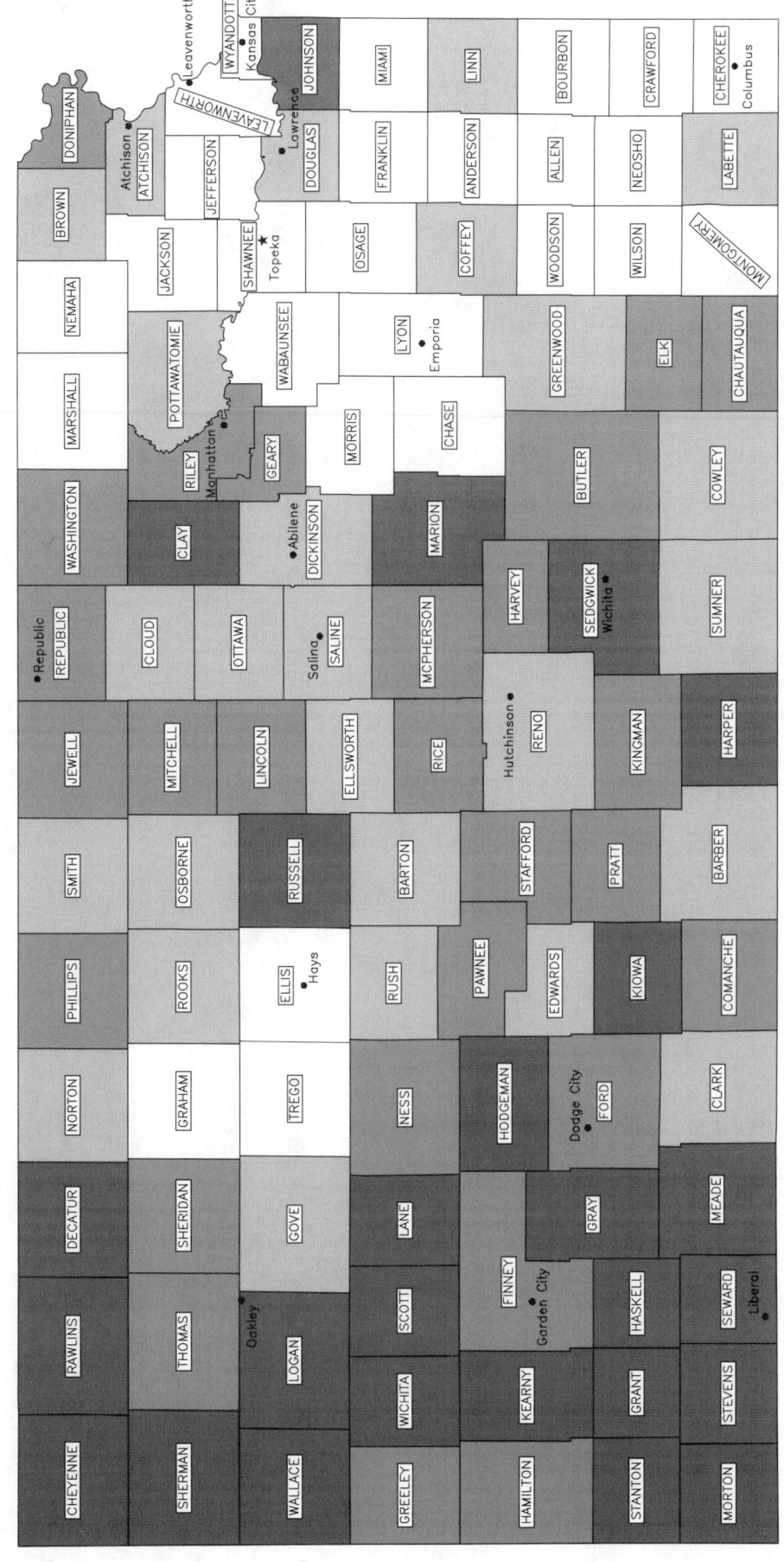

67.3% to 74.9%
63.6% to 67.2%
58.3% to 63.5%
47.5% to 58.2%

Dole (R) received 62.7% statewide.

A framed county name indicates
a county carried by the winner.

Kansas 357

KENTUCKY

Population Statistics 1990

Race/ Ethnicity	Total Population		Voting Age Population		Voting Age Population % of total population
	Number	%	Number	%	
Non-Hispanic					
White	3,378,022	91.7	2,520,863	92.3	74.6
Black	261,360	7.1	178,976	6.6	68.5
Asian/Pacific Islander	17,201	0.5	12,035	0.4	70.0
Native American	5,518	0.1	4,172	0.2	75.6
Other	1,211	<0.1	275	<0.1	22.7
All Hispanic	21,984	0.6	14,881	0.5	67.7
TOTAL	3,685,296	100.0	2,731,202	100.0	74.1

Voting Equipment Use (Counties)

Datavote Punch Card	1	Paper Ballot	0
Electronic	37	Other Punch Card	3
Lever Machine	79	Mixed Systems	0
Optical Scanner	0		

Party Control	DEM	REP	IND	VAC
1993 State Senate	25	13	0	0
1992 State Senate	27	11	0	0
1993 State House	72	28	0	0
1992 State House	68	32	0	0

Estimated Voting Age Population 1992 (VAP) 2,779,000
Number of Registered Voters 2,076,263
  % of estimated VAP 74.7
Voter Turnout (Highest Office) 1,492,900
  % of VAP 53.7
  % of Registration 71.9
Persons Not Voting—of Voting Age 1,286,100
  % of VAP 46.3
Persons Not Voting—of Registered 583,363
  % of Registration 28.1
Straight Ticket Voting .... Yes, Exception

State Officials and Members of Congress

Governor:
Brereton Jones (D) 1991, elected to a four-year term in 1991.

U.S. Senators:
Wendell H. Ford (D) 1974, elected to a six-year term in 1992.
Mitch McConnell (R) 1984, elected to a six-year term in 1990.

U.S. Representative in Congress:
(District, Name, Party, Date first elected)

1. Barlow (D) 1992
2. Natcher (D) 1953
3. Mazzoli (D) 1970
4. Bunning (R) 1986
5. Rogers (R) 1980
6. Baesler (D) 1992

Candidates: General Election, November 3, 1992

Candidate(s)	Total vote	Percent	Party	Status	First elected
President/Vice President					
Clinton/Gore	665,104	44.55%	Democrat	Challenger	1992
Bush/Quayle	617,178	41.34%	Republican	Incumbent	1988
Perot/Stockdale	203,944	13.66%	Independent	Challenger	
Marrou/Lord	4,513	0.30%	Libertarian	Challenger	
Phillips/Knight	989	0.07%	Taxpayers	Challenger	
Hagelin/Tompkins	695	0.05%	Natural Law	Challenger	
Fulani/Munoz	430	0.03%	New Alliance	Challenger	
Gritz/Minett	47	<0.01%	Write in	Challenger	
U.S. Senator					
Wendell Ford	836,888	62.88%	Democrat	Incumbent	1974
David Williams	476,604	35.81%	Republican	Challenger	
James A. Ridenour	17,366	1.30%	Libertarian	Challenger	
Governor (General Election November 5, 1991)					
Brereton Jones	540,468	64.73%	Democrat	Challenger	1991
Larry Hopkins	294,452	35.27%	Republican	Challenger	
U.S. Representative in Congress					
District 1					
Tom Barlow	128,524	60.46%	Democrat	Challenger	1992
Steve Hamrick	83,088	39.09%	Republican	Challenger	
Marvin Seat	962	0.45%	Reform	Challenger	
District 2					
William Natcher	126,894	61.43%	Democrat	Incumbent	1953
Bruce Bartley	79,684	38.57%	Republican	Challenger	
District 3					
Romano Mazzoli	148,066	52.74%	Democrat	Incumbent	1970
Susan Stokes	132,689	47.26%	Republican	Challenger	
Patricia Metten	15	<0.01%	Write in	Challenger	
District 4					
Jim Bunning	139,634	61.64%	Republican	Incumbent	1986
Floyd Poore	86,890	38.36%	Democrat	Challenger	
District 5					
Harold Rogers	115,255	54.62%	Republican	Incumbent	1980
John Doug Hays	95,760	45.38%	Democrat	Challenger	
District 6					
Scotty Baesler	135,613	60.69%	Democrat	Challenger	1992
Charles Ellinger	87,816	39.30%	Republican	Challenger	
Mark Gailey	21	<0.01%	Write in	Challenger	

Candidates: May 26, 1992, Primary Election

Candidate	Total vote	Percent	Candidate	Total vote	Percent
Presidential Preference, Democratic			**Presidential Preference, Republican**		
Bill Clinton	207,804	56.08%	George Bush	75,371	74.54%
Uncommitted	103,590	27.95%	Uncommitted	25,748	25.46%
Jerry Brown	30,709	8.29%			
Paul Tsongas	18,097	4.88%			
Tom Harkin	7,136	1.93%			
Bob Kerrey	3,242	0.87%			

Voter Registration and Turnout, 1948-1992 Elections

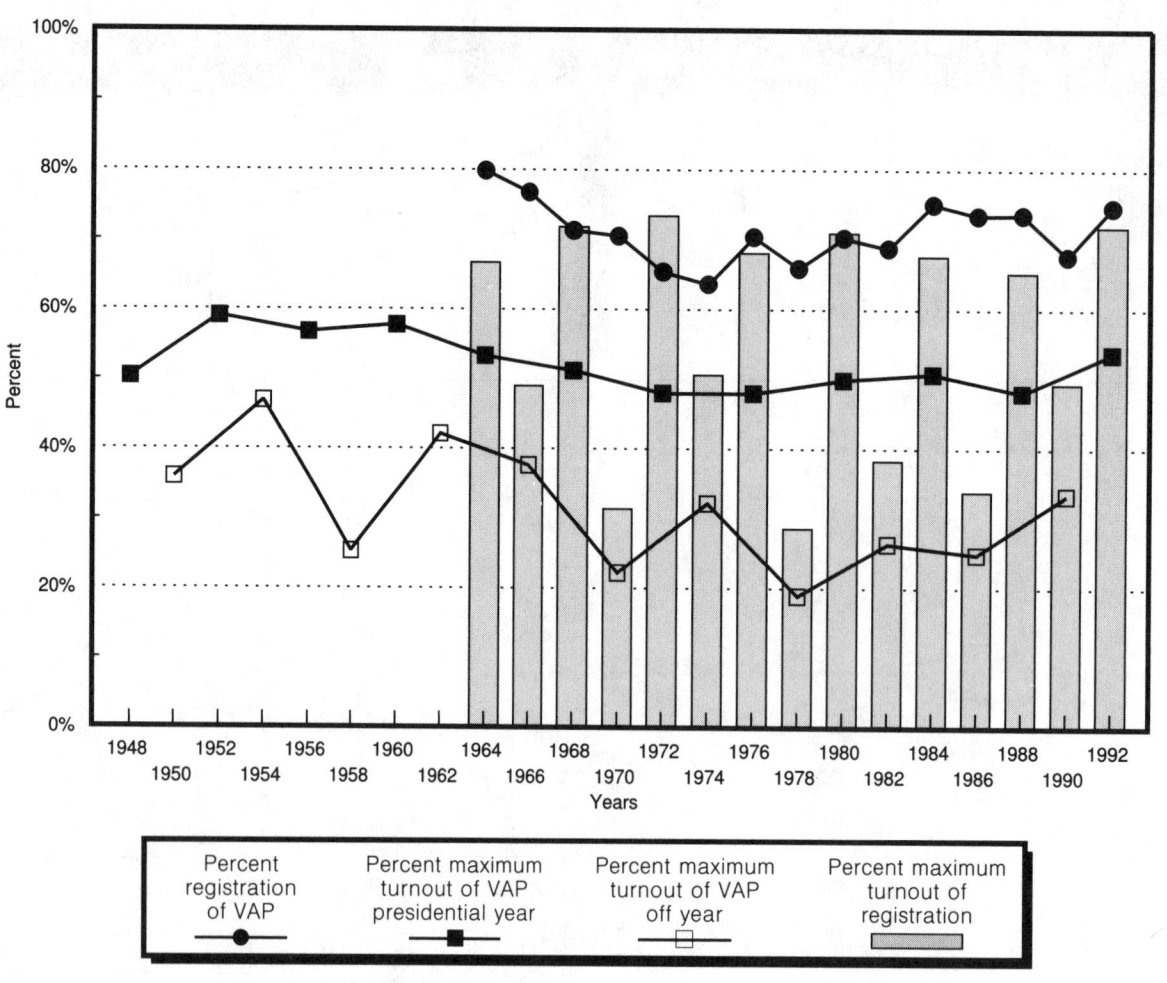

Legend:
- Percent registration of VAP (●)
- Percent maximum turnout of VAP presidential year (■)
- Percent maximum turnout of VAP off year (□)
- Percent maximum turnout of registration (bar)

Year	Estimated Voting Age Population (VAP)	Voter registration (REG)				Voter turnout									
						Highest office						Maximum vote			
		Total	Percent of VAP	Rank by percent of VAP	Actual	Total	Office	Percent total REG	Rank by percent of REG	Percent of VAP	Rank by percent of VAP	Total	Percent total REG	Rank by percent of REG	Percent total VAP	Rank by percent of VAP
1992	2,779,000	2,076,263	74.7	24	–	1,492,900	P	71.9	41	53.7	35	1,492,900	71.9	41	53.7	37
1990	2,740,000	1,854,315	67.7	26	–	916,010	S	49.4	41	33.4	41	916,010	49.4	41	33.4	42
1988	2,752,000	2,026,307	73.6	20	–	1,322,517	P	65.3	40	48.1	35	1,322,517	65.3	42	48.1	37
1986	2,720,000	1,998,899	73.5	16	–	677,280	S	33.9	48	24.9	51	677,280	33.9	48	24.9	51
1984	2,695,000	2,022,995	75.1	22	–	1,369,345	P	67.7	42	50.8	38	1,369,345	67.7	42	50.8	39
1982	2,656,000	1,826,590	68.8	25	–	700,603	C	38.4	47	26.4	49	700,603	38.4	47	26.4	49
1980	2,596,000	1,824,469	70.3	29	–	1,294,627	P	71.0	35	49.9	37	1,294,627	71.0	37	49.9	38
1978	2,528,000	1,666,133	65.9	34	–	477,461	C	28.7	48	18.9	49	477,461	28.7	48	18.9	49
1976	2,434,000	1,713,297	70.4	32	–	1,167,142	P	68.1	40	48.0	40	1,167,142	68.1	41	48.0	41
1974	2,315,000	1,473,228	63.6	37	–	745,994	S	50.6	37	32.2	41	745,994	50.6	38	32.2	41
1972	2,223,000	1,454,575	65.4	41	–	1,067,499	P	73.4	27	48.0	39	1,067,499	73.4	28	48.0	41
1970	2,136,000	1,506,347	70.5	28	–	473,663	C	31.4	45	22.2	50	473,663	31.4	45	22.2	50
1968	2,063,000	1,471,343	71.3	30	–	1,055,893	P	71.8	41	51.2	44	1,055,893	71.8	42	51.2	45
1966	1,996,000	1,531,441	76.7	21	–	749,884	S	49.0	38	37.6	43	749,884	49.0	38	37.6	43
1964	1,964,000	1,567,629	79.8	21	–	1,046,105	P	66.7	40	53.3	36	1,046,105	66.7	40	53.3	36
1962	1,950,000	-	-	-	–	820,088	S	-	-	42.1	37	820,088	-	-	42.1	37
1960	1,950,000	-	-	-	–	1,124,462	P	-	-	57.7	35	1,124,462	-	-	57.7	35
1958	1,883,000	-	-	-	–	475,818	C	-	-	25.3	38	475,818	-	-	25.3	38
1956	1,858,000	-	-	-	–	1,053,805	P	-	-	56.7	35	1,053,805	-	-	56.7	35
1954	1,698,000	-	-	-	–	797,057	S	-	-	46.9	32	797,057	-	-	46.9	32
1952	1,683,000	-	-	-	–	993,148	P	-	-	59.0	35	993,148	-	-	59.0	35
1950	1,721,000	-	-	-	–	617,121	S	-	-	35.9	37	617,121	-	-	35.9	37
1948	1,635,000	-	-	-	–	822,658	P	-	-	50.3	32	822,658	-	-	50.3	32

KENTUCKY

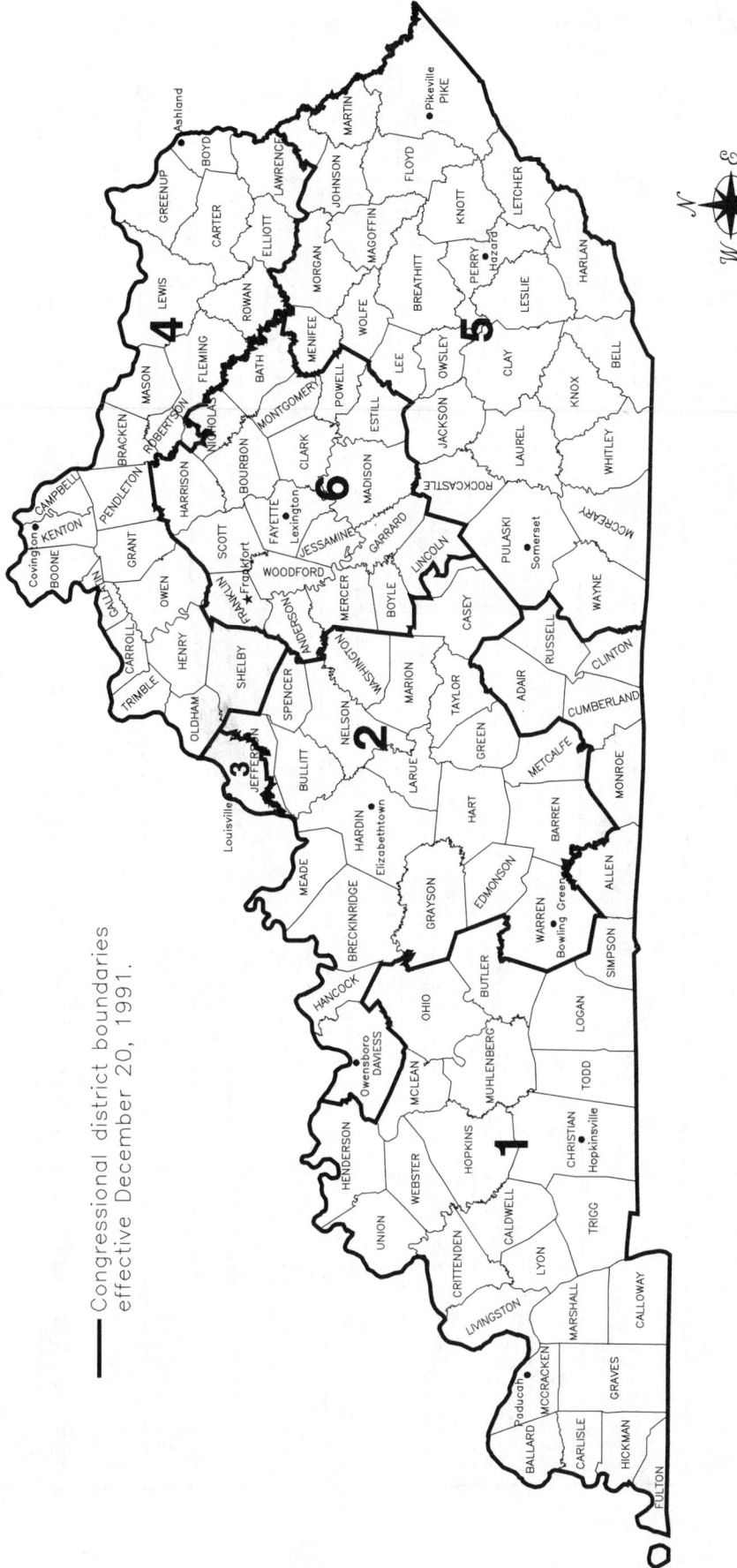

— Congressional district boundaries
effective December 20, 1991.

Copyright © 1993 by Election Data Services, Inc.

Kentucky 363

Table A. – 1990 Population by Race and Ethnic Origin

State/county code	County	Total persons	Percent of total persons — Non-Hispanic White	Black	Asian and Pacific Islander	Native American	Other	Hispanic	Rank Total	Rank Non-Hispanic White	Black	Hispanic	Pct contribution Total	Non-Hispanic White	Black	Hispanic
21 001	Adair	15,360	96.2	3.0	0.2	<.1	<.1	0.6	64	70	53	10	0.4	0.4	0.2	0.4
21 003	Allen	14,628	98.5	1.1	<.1	0.1	<.1	0.2	69	41	75	110	0.4	0.4	<.1	0.1
21 005	Anderson	14,571	96.4	3.0	0.1	<.1	0.0	0.5	71	66	54	25	0.4	0.4	0.2	0.3
21 007	Ballard	7,902	96.2	3.0	<.1	0.2	0.0	0.5	104	69	51	18	0.2	0.2	<.1	0.2
21 009	Barren	34,001	94.5	4.9	0.2	<.1	<.1	0.3	23	87	34	73	0.9	1.0	0.6	0.4
21 011	Bath	9,692	96.7	2.8	<.1	<.1	<.1	0.3	95	64	57	62	0.3	0.3	0.1	0.1
21 013	Bell	31,506	96.8	2.6	0.3	0.1	0.0	0.2	27	62	58	88	0.9	0.9	0.3	0.4
21 015	Boone	57,589	98.0	0.6	0.6	0.1	<.1	0.6	11	47	89	14	1.6	1.7	0.1	1.4
21 017	Bourbon	19,236	90.7	8.6	0.1	<.1	<.1	0.4	52	103	17	34	0.5	0.5	0.6	0.4
21 019	Boyd	51,150	96.8	1.9	0.3	0.1	<.1	0.9	13	63	61	5	1.4	1.5	0.4	2.0
21 021	Boyle	25,641	89.7	9.5	0.3	<.1	<.1	0.4	37	108	13	35	0.7	0.7	0.9	0.5
21 023	Bracken	7,766	99.1	0.6	<.1	0.1	0.0	0.2	106	24	90	113	0.2	0.2	<.1	<.1
21 025	Breathitt	15,703	99.4	0.2	0.1	<.1	0.0	0.2	62	12	102	109	0.4	0.5	<.1	0.1
21 027	Breckinridge	16,312	95.9	3.6	<.1	0.2	<.1	0.3	59	73	45	75	0.4	0.5	0.2	0.2
21 029	Bullitt	47,567	98.9	0.4	0.2	0.2	<.1	0.3	15	32	94	53	1.3	1.4	<.1	0.7
21 031	Butler	11,245	98.9	0.5	0.1	0.2	0.0	0.3	89	31	92	56	0.3	0.3	<.1	0.2
21 033	Caldwell	13,232	93.7	5.8	<.1	0.3	<.1	0.2	76	92	29	96	0.4	0.4	0.3	0.1
21 035	Calloway	30,735	95.8	3.1	0.4	<.1	<.1	0.5	29	75	49	17	0.8	0.9	0.4	0.7
21 037	Campbell	83,866	98.2	1.0	0.3	0.1	<.1	0.4	6	45	77	45	2.3	2.4	0.3	1.5
21 039	Carlisle	5,238	98.3	1.1	<.1	0.2	0.0	0.4	117	44	76	41	0.1	0.2	<.1	<.1
21 041	Carroll	9,292	97.3	2.1	<.1	0.2	<.1	0.2	97	60	60	92	0.3	0.3	<.1	0.1
21 043	Carter	24,340	99.5	<.1	<.1	<.1	<.1	0.2	40	8	111	87	0.7	0.7	<.1	0.3
21 045	Casey	14,211	99.0	0.3	0.1	0.2	0.2	0.3	72	29	101	59	0.4	0.4	<.1	0.2
21 047	Christian	68,941	70.7	24.2	1.2	0.4	<.1	3.4	9	120	1	1	1.9	1.4	6.4	10.6
21 049	Clark	29,496	93.8	5.5	0.1	0.3	<.1	0.3	34	90	31	57	0.8	0.8	0.6	0.4
21 051	Clay	21,746	97.9	1.5	0.1	0.2	<.1	0.2	44	52	70	100	0.6	0.6	0.1	0.2
21 053	Clinton	9,135	99.4	<.1	<.1	<.1	0.0	0.4	99	15	112	40	0.2	0.3	<.1	0.2
21 055	Crittenden	9,196	98.7	0.8	<.1	0.1	0.0	0.3	98	37	80	81	0.2	0.3	<.1	0.1
21 057	Cumberland	6,784	94.9	4.5	<.1	0.2	0.0	0.3	109	85	35	55	0.2	0.2	0.1	0.1
21 059	Daviess	87,189	95.1	4.1	0.3	0.1	<.1	0.4	5	82	41	50	2.4	2.5	1.4	1.4
21 061	Edmonson	10,357	98.0	1.6	<.1	0.1	0.0	0.2	94	51	69	89	0.3	0.3	<.1	0.1
21 063	Elliott	6,455	99.7	<.1	0.0	<.1	0.0	0.2	113	1	120	94	0.2	0.2	<.1	<.1
21 065	Estill	14,614	99.6	<.1	<.1	<.1	<.1	0.3	70	7	114	64	0.4	0.4	<.1	0.2
21 067	Fayette	225,366	83.8	13.3	1.6	0.1	<.1	1.1	2	116	5	4	6.1	5.6	11.4	11.6
21 069	Fleming	12,292	97.7	1.8	<.1	<.1	<.1	0.5	81	56	63	26	0.3	0.4	<.1	0.3
21 071	Floyd	43,586	98.8	0.7	0.2	<.1	0.0	0.3	18	35	85	69	1.2	1.3	0.1	0.6
21 073	Franklin	43,781	91.4	7.5	0.5	0.1	<.1	0.4	17	101	21	39	1.2	1.2	1.3	0.8
21 075	Fulton	8,271	80.8	18.5	0.2	0.1	<.1	0.3	103	119	2	66	0.2	0.2	0.6	0.1
21 077	Gallatin	5,393	97.8	1.7	0.1	<.1	<.1	0.1	116	54	65	116	0.1	0.2	<.1	<.1
21 079	Garrard	11,579	95.6	3.9	<.1	0.1	<.1	0.3	87	76	43	78	0.3	0.3	0.2	0.1
21 081	Grant	15,737	99.4	0.2	0.1	<.1	<.1	0.2	61	14	105	95	0.4	0.5	<.1	0.2
21 083	Graves	33,550	95.0	4.5	0.1	0.1	<.1	0.3	24	84	36	72	0.9	0.9	0.6	0.4
21 085	Grayson	21,050	98.9	0.3	0.1	0.2	<.1	0.4	47	30	99	32	0.6	0.6	<.1	0.4
21 087	Green	10,371	95.8	3.4	0.1	0.1	0.0	0.6	92	74	46	11	0.3	0.3	0.1	0.3
21 089	Greenup	36,742	99.0	0.4	0.3	0.1	<.1	0.2	21	28	95	101	1.0	1.1	<.1	0.3
21 091	Hancock	7,864	98.0	1.2	0.2	0.2	0.0	0.4	105	49	74	44	0.2	0.2	<.1	0.1
21 093	Hardin	89,240	83.9	10.9	1.9	0.4	<.1	2.8	4	115	8	2	2.4	2.2	3.7	11.4
21 095	Harlan	36,574	96.2	3.3	0.1	<.1	<.1	0.3	22	71	47	68	1.0	1.0	0.5	0.5
21 097	Harrison	16,248	96.5	2.9	<.1	0.1	<.1	0.3	60	65	55	83	0.4	0.5	0.2	0.2
21 099	Hart	14,890	92.2	7.1	<.1	0.1	<.1	0.4	66	98	22	30	0.4	0.4	0.4	0.3
21 101	Henderson	43,044	92.1	7.1	0.3	0.2	<.1	0.4	20	99	23	42	1.2	1.2	1.2	0.8
21 103	Henry	12,823	95.4	4.2	<.1	0.1	<.1	0.2	79	78	39	97	0.3	0.4	0.2	0.1
21 105	Hickman	5,566	90.5	9.0	<.1	<.1	0.0	0.3	115	105	14	54	0.2	0.1	0.2	<.1
21 107	Hopkins	46,126	92.6	6.6	0.3	0.1	<.1	0.4	16	96	24	38	1.3	1.3	1.2	0.9
21 109	Jackson	11,955	99.6	<.1	<.1	0.1	0.0	0.3	83	6	119	82	0.3	0.4	<.1	0.1
21 111	Jefferson	664,937	81.5	17.0	0.7	0.2	<.1	0.7	1	118	3	7	18.0	16.0	43.2	19.9
21 113	Jessamine	30,508	95.5	3.2	0.4	0.2	<.1	0.6	30	77	48	9	0.8	0.9	0.4	0.8
21 115	Johnson	23,248	99.3	0.1	0.3	<.1	<.1	0.2	43	18	108	111	0.6	0.7	<.1	0.2
21 117	Kenton	142,031	96.0	2.9	0.4	0.1	<.1	0.5	3	72	56	21	3.9	4.0	1.6	3.2
21 119	Knott	17,906	99.0	0.6	0.1	<.1	<.1	0.2	54	26	87	104	0.5	0.5	<.1	0.2
21 121	Knox	29,676	98.4	1.0	<.1	0.2	<.1	0.3	33	43	78	79	0.8	0.9	0.1	0.4
21 123	Larue	11,679	95.1	4.2	<.1	0.2	<.1	0.5	85	83	38	24	0.3	0.3	0.2	0.3
21 125	Laurel	43,438	98.6	0.6	0.2	0.3	<.1	0.4	19	40	91	43	1.2	1.3	<.1	0.8
21 127	Lawrence	13,998	99.3	0.2	0.2	0.2	0.0	0.2	73	17	106	107	0.4	0.4	<.1	0.1
21 129	Lee	7,422	99.4	0.0	0.0	<.1	0.0	0.1	107	11	98	117	0.2	0.2	<.1	<.1
21 131	Leslie	13,642	99.5	<.1	<.1	<.1	0.0	0.3	75	9	110	70	0.4	0.4	<.1	0.2
21 133	Letcher	27,000	98.8	0.7	0.1	0.1	<.1	0.2	36	33	83	93	0.7	0.8	<.1	0.3
21 135	Lewis	13,029	99.4	0.2	<.1	0.2	0.0	0.2	78	13	103	103	0.4	0.4	<.1	0.1
21 137	Lincoln	20,045	96.4	3.1	<.1	0.2	<.1	0.3	49	67	50	98	0.5	0.6	0.2	0.2
21 139	Livingston	9,062	99.2	0.2	<.1	0.2	0.0	0.3	100	20	107	60	0.2	0.3	<.1	0.1

State/county code	County	Total persons	Percent of total persons						Rank				Percent contribution to state population			
			Non-Hispanic						Percent of total persons				Non-Hispanic			
										Non-Hispanic						
			White	Black	Asian and Pacific Islander	Native American	Other	Hispanic	Total	White	Black	Hispanic	Total	White	Black	Hispanic
21 141	Logan	24,416	90.8	8.5	<.1	0.2	<.1	0.3	39	102	18	61	0.7	0.7	0.8	0.4
21 143	Lyon	6,624	92.6	6.5	0.2	0.3	0.0	0.4	111	97	25	33	0.2	0.2	0.2	0.1
21 145	McCracken	62,879	89.0	10.0	0.3	0.1	<.1	0.5	10	110	10	19	1.7	1.7	2.4	1.5
21 147	McCreary	15,603	98.7	0.8	<.1	0.4	0.0	0.2	63	38	82	115	0.4	0.5	<.1	0.1
21 149	McLean	9,628	99.3	0.5	<.1	<.1	0.0	0.2	96	19	93	112	0.3	0.3	<.1	<.1
21 151	Madison	57,508	93.9	5.1	0.6	0.1	<.1	0.3	12	89	33	58	1.6	1.6	1.1	0.9
21 153	Magoffin	13,077	99.7	<.1	<.1	0.1	0.0	0.1	77	2	117	118	0.4	0.4	<.1	<.1
21 155	Marion	16,499	90.6	8.9	0.1	<.1	<.1	0.3	58	104	15	85	0.4	0.4	0.6	0.2
21 157	Marshall	27,205	99.2	<.1	0.1	0.2	<.1	0.4	35	21	115	31	0.7	0.8	<.1	0.5
21 159	Martin	12,526	99.6	<.1	<.1	<.1	0.0	0.2	80	4	113	108	0.3	0.4	<.1	<.1
21 161	Mason	16,666	91.7	7.6	0.1	<.1	<.1	0.5	56	100	20	27	0.5	0.5	0.5	0.3
21 163	Meade	24,170	86.5	9.7	1.0	0.3	<.1	2.4	41	114	12	3	0.7	0.6	0.9	2.6
21 165	Menifee	5,092	97.6	1.7	<.1	<.1	0.0	0.5	118	58	67	16	0.1	0.1	<.1	0.1
21 167	Mercer	19,148	94.8	4.2	0.4	0.1	<.1	0.5	53	86	37	28	0.5	0.5	0.3	0.4
21 169	Metcalfe	8,963	96.9	2.5	0.1	0.2	0.0	0.3	102	61	59	67	0.2	0.3	<.1	0.1
21 171	Monroe	11,401	96.2	3.0	<.1	<.1	<.1	0.6	88	68	52	12	0.3	0.3	0.1	0.3
21 173	Montgomery	19,561	95.4	4.1	<.1	<.1	<.1	0.3	51	80	40	71	0.5	0.6	0.3	0.3
21 175	Morgan	11,648	98.7	0.9	<.1	<.1	0.0	0.4	86	39	79	49	0.3	0.3	<.1	0.2
21 177	Muhlenberg	31,318	95.4	4.1	0.1	0.1	<.1	0.3	28	79	42	80	0.8	0.9	0.5	0.4
21 179	Nelson	29,710	93.2	6.0	0.2	<.1	<.1	0.4	32	93	28	29	0.8	0.8	0.7	0.6
21 181	Nicholas	6,725	98.1	1.3	0.2	<.1	<.1	0.2	110	46	72	91	0.2	0.2	<.1	<.1
21 183	Ohio	21,105	98.4	0.8	0.1	0.2	0.0	0.4	46	42	81	46	0.6	0.6	<.1	0.4
21 185	Oldham	33,263	95.2	3.6	0.3	0.2	<.1	0.6	26	81	44	8	0.9	0.9	0.5	0.9
21 187	Owen	9,035	97.9	1.7	<.1	0.1	0.0	0.2	101	53	64	114	0.2	0.3	<.1	<.1
21 189	Owsley	5,036	99.4	0.3	<.1	<.1	0.0	0.3	119	16	100	84	0.1	0.1	<.1	<.1
21 191	Pendleton	12,036	99.1	0.4	<.1	0.2	<.1	0.2	82	22	97	90	0.3	0.4	<.1	0.1
21 193	Perry	30,283	97.8	1.7	0.2	<.1	<.1	0.2	31	55	66	106	0.8	0.9	0.2	0.2
21 195	Pike	72,583	99.1	0.4	0.2	<.1	<.1	0.3	8	25	96	86	2.0	2.1	0.1	0.8
21 197	Powell	11,686	98.8	0.7	<.1	<.1	0.0	0.4	84	34	84	51	0.3	0.3	<.1	0.2
21 199	Pulaski	49,489	98.0	1.2	0.2	0.2	<.1	0.4	14	50	73	37	1.3	1.4	0.2	0.9
21 201	Robertson	2,124	99.6	0.2	0.0	0.0	0.0	0.2	120	5	104	105	<.1	<.1	<.1	<.1
21 203	Rockcastle	14,803	99.4	<.1	<.1	0.1	<.1	0.4	67	10	118	52	0.4	0.4	<.1	0.2
21 205	Rowan	20,353	97.5	1.5	0.5	0.2	<.1	0.4	48	59	71	47	0.6	0.6	0.1	0.3
21 207	Russell	14,716	99.0	0.6	<.1	<.1	0.0	0.3	68	27	88	74	0.4	0.4	<.1	0.2
21 209	Scott	23,867	92.7	6.3	0.4	<.1	<.1	0.4	42	95	27	36	0.6	0.7	0.6	0.5
21 211	Shelby	24,824	89.3	9.9	0.4	<.1	<.1	0.4	38	109	11	48	0.7	0.7	0.9	0.4
21 213	Simpson	15,145	88.3	11.0	0.2	0.2	<.1	0.3	65	112	7	63	0.4	0.4	0.6	0.2
21 215	Spencer	6,801	98.0	1.7	0.2	<.1	0.0	<.1	108	48	68	119	0.2	0.2	<.1	<.1
21 217	Taylor	21,146	94.5	5.1	0.1	<.1	0.0	0.2	45	88	32	99	0.6	0.6	0.4	0.2
21 219	Todd	10,940	88.3	10.9	<.1	0.1	<.1	0.5	90	111	9	20	0.3	0.3	0.5	0.3
21 221	Trigg	10,361	87.6	11.8	0.1	0.1	<.1	0.3	93	113	6	76	0.3	0.3	0.5	0.1
21 223	Trimble	6,090	99.1	<.1	<.1	0.3	<.1	0.5	114	23	116	23	0.2	0.2	<.1	0.1
21 225	Union	16,557	83.6	15.2	0.2	0.2	<.1	0.7	57	117	4	6	0.4	0.4	1.0	0.6
21 227	Warren	76,673	90.4	8.1	0.8	0.1	<.1	0.6	7	107	19	13	2.1	2.1	2.4	2.0
21 229	Washington	10,441	90.4	8.7	0.2	<.1	<.1	0.5	91	106	16	15	0.3	0.3	0.3	0.3
21 231	Wayne	17,468	97.6	1.8	<.1	0.2	<.1	0.3	55	57	62	65	0.5	0.5	0.1	0.2
21 233	Webster	13,955	93.8	5.6	0.2	0.2	<.1	0.2	74	91	30	102	0.4	0.4	0.3	0.1
21 235	Whitley	33,326	98.8	0.6	0.2	0.2	0.0	0.3	25	36	86	77	0.9	1.0	<.1	0.4
21 237	Wolfe	6,503	99.7	0.1	<.1	<.1	0.0	<.1	112	3	109	120	0.2	0.2	<.1	<.1
21 239	Woodford	19,955	92.7	6.5	0.1	0.1	<.1	0.5	50	94	26	22	0.5	0.5	0.5	0.4
21	**KENTUCKY**	**3,685,296**	**91.7**	**7.1**	**0.5**	**0.1**	**<.1**	**0.6**					**100.0**	**100.0**	**100.0**	**100.0**
	CONGRESSIONAL															
	District 1	614,226	91.0	7.7	0.3	0.2	<.1	0.7	4	4	3	2	16.7	16.6	18.2	20.3
	District 2	614,833	93.0	5.4	0.6	0.2	<.1	0.8	1	3	4	1	16.7	16.9	12.8	23.2
	District 3	613,603	80.2	18.2	0.7	0.2	<.1	0.7	6	6	1	3	16.7	14.6	42.8	18.5
	District 4	614,245	97.0	2.1	0.3	0.1	<.1	0.4	3	2	5	5	16.7	17.6	5.0	12.1
	District 5	614,119	98.5	1.0	0.1	0.1	<.1	0.3	5	1	6	6	16.7	17.9	2.2	7.4
	District 6	614,270	90.3	8.1	0.8	0.1	<.1	0.7	2	5	2	4	16.7	16.4	19.0	18.4

Table B. – 1990 Voting Age Population (VAP) by Race and Ethnic Origin

County	Total Voting Age Population	Percent of total VAP — Non-Hispanic — White	Black	Asian and Pacific Islander	Native American	Other	Hispanic	Rank — Percent of total VAP — Non-Hispanic — Total	White	Black	Hispanic	Percent contribution to state VAP — Total	Non-Hispanic — White	Black	Hispanic	VAP percent of total population — Total	Non-Hispanic — White	Black	Asian and Pacific Islander	Native American	Other	Hispanic
Adair	11,582	96.1	3.1	0.2	<.1	<.1	0.5	61	74	51	13	0.4	0.4	0.2	0.4	75.4	75.4	77.6	79.2	100.0	100.0	64.0
Allen	10,761	98.6	1.1	<.1	0.1	0.0	0.1	69	41	75	117	0.4	0.4	<.1	<.1	73.6	73.6	74.5	66.7	64.7	0.0	50.0
Anderson	10,720	96.6	3.0	<.1	<.1	0.0	0.4	70	67	52	43	0.4	0.4	0.2	0.3	73.6	73.7	73.4	50.0	50.0	0.0	55.9
Ballard	6,054	96.6	2.7	<.1	0.2	0.0	0.4	104	66	55	21	0.2	0.2	<.1	0.2	76.6	76.9	68.8	83.3	84.6	0.0	63.4
Barren	25,539	94.9	4.6	0.1	<.1	<.1	0.3	23	86	34	68	0.9	1.0	0.7	0.5	75.1	75.4	70.1	56.9	80.6	25.0	71.3
Bath	7,253	96.7	2.9	<.1	<.1	<.1	0.3	95	63	54	65	0.3	0.3	0.1	0.1	74.8	74.9	75.5	85.7	85.7	25.0	64.5
Bell	22,969	96.9	2.5	0.2	0.1	0.0	0.2	29	61	59	87	0.8	0.9	0.3	0.3	72.9	72.9	72.4	61.4	83.8	0.0	67.5
Boone	40,676	98.1	0.6	0.6	0.2	<.1	0.5	12	47	88	12	1.5	1.6	0.1	1.4	70.6	70.7	72.5	67.6	75.3	18.8	63.2
Bourbon	14,185	90.9	8.5	0.1	0.1	<.1	0.4	53	106	14	28	0.5	0.5	0.7	0.4	73.7	73.9	72.4	65.2	89.5	20.0	67.9
Boyd	39,167	96.6	2.0	0.3	0.1	<.1	1.0	13	68	61	5	1.4	1.5	0.4	2.7	76.6	76.4	81.5	72.7	82.1	23.1	90.3
Boyle	19,446	90.3	9.0	0.2	<.1	<.1	0.4	36	109	12	35	0.7	0.7	1.0	0.4	75.8	76.4	72.1	55.7	71.4	28.6	66.7
Bracken	5,747	99.1	0.6	<.1	0.1	0.0	0.1	105	27	87	111	0.2	0.2	<.1	<.1	74.0	74.0	78.7	100.0	87.5	0.0	66.7
Breathitt	11,203	99.4	0.2	0.2	<.1	0.0	0.1	63	13	101	113	0.4	0.4	<.1	0.1	71.3	71.3	75.8	90.0	58.3	0.0	57.7
Breckinridge	11,977	96.3	3.2	<.1	0.2	0.0	0.3	58	70	48	74	0.4	0.5	0.2	0.2	73.4	73.7	65.9	73.3	70.4	0.0	68.2
Bullitt	33,644	98.9	0.4	0.2	0.2	<.1	0.3	16	33	93	56	1.2	1.3	<.1	0.7	70.7	70.8	73.3	59.8	73.8	60.0	61.6
Butler	8,253	99.0	0.4	0.1	0.2	0.0	0.3	88	31	94	60	0.3	0.3	<.1	0.2	73.4	73.4	65.5	78.6	83.3	0.0	63.2
Caldwell	10,081	94.1	5.3	<.1	0.3	<.1	0.2	74	90	31	91	0.4	0.4	0.3	0.1	76.2	76.6	70.1	77.8	79.4	50.0	73.3
Calloway	24,744	95.8	3.1	0.4	0.1	<.1	0.5	25	75	50	15	0.9	0.9	0.4	0.8	80.5	80.5	80.9	78.9	90.0	22.2	73.8
Campbell	61,367	98.3	0.9	0.3	0.1	<.1	0.4	6	45	80	44	2.2	2.4	0.3	1.5	73.2	73.3	66.4	67.6	73.5	5.9	68.0
Carlisle	3,973	98.4	1.0	<.1	0.2	0.0	0.4	116	44	77	22	0.1	0.2	<.1	0.1	75.8	76.0	70.9	33.3	50.0	0.0	81.0
Carroll	6,771	97.4	2.1	<.1	0.2	<.1	0.2	100	59	60	106	0.2	0.3	<.1	<.1	72.9	72.9	71.9	62.5	88.2	50.0	50.0
Carter	17,836	99.6	<.1	<.1	<.1	<.1	0.2	40	8	111	99	0.7	0.7	<.1	0.2	73.3	73.3	78.9	93.8	58.3	66.7	55.0
Casey	10,433	99.2	0.2	0.1	0.2	<.1	0.3	72	24	102	47	0.4	0.4	<.1	0.2	73.4	73.6	56.8	81.3	72.0	4.5	74.5
Christian	50,986	73.5	22.1	1.1	0.4	<.1	2.9	9	120	1	1	1.9	1.5	6.3	10.0	74.0	76.8	67.4	69.7	71.3	46.9	63.7
Clark	21,867	93.9	5.4	0.1	0.2	<.1	0.3	31	91	30	55	0.8	0.8	0.7	0.4	74.1	74.2	73.8	63.6	68.9	25.0	67.3
Clay	15,160	97.9	1.6	0.1	0.1	<.1	0.2	48	51	70	98	0.6	0.6	0.1	0.2	69.7	69.7	72.2	53.1	66.7	75.0	67.4
Clinton	6,866	99.4	<.1	<.1	0.1	0.0	0.4	99	14	110	29	0.3	0.3	<.1	0.2	75.2	75.2	100.0	75.0	100.0	0.0	70.3
Crittenden	6,906	98.6	0.9	0.1	0.0	0.0	0.2	98	39	81	77	0.3	0.3	<.1	0.1	75.1	75.1	79.5	75.0	76.9	0.0	70.8
Cumberland	5,172	95.0	4.5	<.1	0.2	0.0	0.4	109	85	35	37	0.2	0.2	0.1	0.1	76.2	76.3	75.2	100.0	66.7	0.0	82.6
Daviess	63,506	95.8	3.6	0.2	0.1	<.1	0.3	5	76	44	58	2.3	2.4	1.3	1.2	72.8	73.4	63.7	60.6	70.1	7.7	59.6
Edmonson	7,634	98.0	1.6	<.1	0.1	0.0	0.2	93	50	71	95	0.3	0.3	<.1	0.1	73.7	73.8	72.0	66.7	83.3	0.0	64.0
Elliott	4,576	99.8	<.1	0.0	<.1	0.0	0.1	113	1	116	114	0.2	0.2	<.1	<.1	70.9	70.9	100.0	0.0	100.0	0.0	40.0
Estill	10,713	99.6	<.1	<.1	<.1	0.0	0.2	71	5	112	72	0.4	0.4	<.1	0.2	73.3	73.4	62.5	33.3	100.0	0.0	58.7
Fayette	174,950	85.4	11.7	1.6	0.1	<.1	1.1	2	115	5	4	6.4	5.9	11.5	13.2	77.6	79.2	68.7	75.0	79.3	19.7	76.6
Fleming	9,171	97.8	1.7	<.1	<.1	<.1	0.4	79	54	67	19	0.3	0.4	<.1	0.3	74.6	74.7	71.8	50.0	75.0	25.0	71.4
Floyd	31,024	98.9	0.6	0.2	<.1	0.0	0.2	20	32	89	79	1.1	1.2	0.1	0.5	71.2	71.3	62.2	67.1	77.4	0.0	58.1
Franklin	33,215	91.8	7.2	0.4	0.2	<.1	0.3	17	101	20	41	1.2	1.2	1.3	0.8	75.9	76.2	73.4	65.2	78.1	23.1	66.9
Fulton	6,203	83.8	15.5	0.2	0.1	0.0	0.3	103	118	2	46	0.2	0.2	0.5	0.1	75.0	77.8	62.7	75.0	80.0	0.0	84.0
Gallatin	3,857	97.8	1.8	0.1	0.1	<.1	0.2	117	56	64	110	0.1	0.1	<.1	<.1	71.5	71.5	76.3	57.1	80.0	25.0	75.0
Garrard	8,792	95.6	3.9	<.1	0.1	0.0	0.3	81	78	42	66	0.3	0.3	0.2	0.2	75.9	75.9	76.5	50.0	80.0	0.0	77.4
Grant	11,193	99.5	0.1	<.1	<.1	<.1	0.2	64	10	108	96	0.4	0.4	<.1	0.2	71.1	71.2	44.4	64.7	80.0	100.0	63.9
Graves	25,411	95.4	4.1	0.1	0.1	0.0	0.2	24	80	38	80	0.9	1.0	0.6	0.4	75.7	76.1	68.7	59.1	85.7	0.0	65.6
Grayson	15,556	99.0	0.3	0.1	0.2	0.0	0.4	46	30	98	27	0.6	0.6	<.1	0.4	73.9	74.0	68.6	73.1	68.6	0.0	70.8
Green	7,964	96.2	3.2	<.1	<.1	<.1	0.5	92	73	49	16	0.3	0.3	0.1	0.3	76.8	77.1	72.5	54.5	63.6	0.0	63.3
Greenup	27,320	99.1	0.4	0.2	<.1	0.0	0.3	21	26	95	107	1.0	1.1	<.1	0.3	74.4	74.5	73.5	58.2	65.0	0.0	57.9
Hancock	5,570	98.3	1.2	0.1	0.1	0.0	0.3	106	46	73	63	0.2	0.2	<.1	0.1	70.8	71.0	69.1	47.1	57.1	0.0	53.3
Hardin	63,976	84.9	10.1	1.9	0.4	<.1	2.6	4	116	9	2	2.3	2.2	3.6	11.2	71.7	72.6	66.5	71.5	77.6	35.4	66.4
Harlan	26,057	96.2	3.3	0.1	<.1	0.0	0.3	22	72	47	61	1.0	1.0	0.5	0.5	71.2	71.3	70.1	68.0	75.0	0.0	68.8
Harrison	11,908	96.6	2.9	<.1	0.1	<.1	0.2	59	64	53	92	0.4	0.5	0.2	0.2	73.3	73.4	71.8	78.6	73.9	33.3	61.9
Hart	11,009	92.4	7.0	<.1	0.2	<.1	0.4	66	98	23	34	0.4	0.4	0.4	0.3	73.9	74.1	72.8	75.0	81.8	50.0	63.1
Henderson	31,596	92.6	6.6	0.3	0.2	0.0	0.4	18	97	24	42	1.2	1.2	1.2	0.8	73.4	73.8	69.1	61.7	73.5	0.0	68.1
Henry	9,568	95.4	4.1	<.1	0.1	<.1	0.3	76	81	37	70	0.4	0.4	0.2	0.2	74.6	74.6	74.3	50.0	80.0	66.7	86.2
Hickman	4,279	91.3	8.3	<.1	<.1	0.0	0.3	115	103	16	71	0.2	0.2	0.2	<.1	76.9	77.6	70.4	100.0	80.0	0.0	57.9
Hopkins	34,081	93.3	6.0	0.2	0.1	<.1	0.4	15	94	27	33	1.2	1.3	1.1	0.9	73.9	74.5	67.1	48.0	80.8	37.5	67.6
Jackson	8,535	99.6	<.1	0.0	0.2	0.0	0.2	86	6	118	94	0.3	0.3	<.1	0.1	71.4	71.4	50.0	0.0	100.0	0.0	58.1
Jefferson	502,361	83.4	15.2	0.6	0.2	<.1	0.6	1	119	3	7	18.4	16.6	42.6	20.2	75.6	77.4	67.5	69.7	77.5	20.0	69.0
Jessamine	22,160	95.5	3.3	0.4	0.2	<.1	0.5	30	79	45	10	0.8	0.8	0.4	0.8	72.6	72.6	74.3	76.0	72.1	20.0	64.7
Johnson	16,912	99.4	0.1	0.3	0.1	0.0	0.1	42	16	107	116	0.6	0.7	<.1	0.1	72.7	72.8	72.7	60.8	85.0	0.0	52.6
Kenton	102,810	96.4	2.6	0.4	0.1	<.1	0.4	3	69	58	18	3.8	3.9	1.5	3.0	72.4	72.7	63.8	69.1	79.1	16.2	63.8
Knott	12,658	99.1	0.6	0.1	<.1	0.0	0.2	55	28	90	97	0.5	0.5	<.1	0.2	70.7	70.7	64.6	77.8	100.0	0.0	76.5
Knox	21,249	98.4	1.0	<.1	0.2	<.1	0.2	33	43	76	85	0.8	0.8	0.1	0.3	71.6	71.6	75.9	72.0	65.7	33.3	62.8
Larue	8,754	95.3	4.0	<.1	0.2	<.1	0.4	82	82	41	23	0.3	0.3	0.2	0.2	75.0	75.1	71.6	70.0	95.2	100.0	67.3
Laurel	31,447	98.7	0.5	0.1	0.3	0.0	0.3	19	37	91	49	1.2	1.2	<.1	0.7	72.4	72.5	67.5	54.8	73.8	0.0	61.4
Lawrence	10,038	99.3	0.2	0.1	0.2	0.0	0.2	75	20	104	108	0.4	0.4	<.1	0.1	71.7	71.7	86.4	60.9	81.8	0.0	66.7
Lee	5,363	99.4	0.4	0.0	<.1	0.0	0.2	108	17	96	102	0.2	0.2	<.1	<.1	72.3	72.2	80.8	0.0	57.1	0.0	90.0
Leslie	9,506	99.5	<.1	<.1	<.1	0.0	0.2	77	9	109	86	0.3	0.4	<.1	0.1	69.7	69.7	75.0	62.5	88.9	0.0	55.0
Letcher	19,245	98.9	0.7	<.1	0.1	0.0	0.2	37	34	85	88	0.7	0.8	<.1	0.3	71.3	71.3	68.4	63.3	73.0	0.0	67.2
Lewis	9,419	99.5	<.1	<.1	0.2	0.0	0.2	78	12	103	109	0.3	0.4	<.1	0.1	72.3	72.3	72.0	25.0	72.7	0.0	60.0
Lincoln	14,702	96.3	3.3	<.1	0.2	0.0	0.2	49	71	46	101	0.5	0.6	0.3	0.2	73.3	73.3	77.5	83.3	60.0	0.0	58.1
Livingston	6,998	99.3	0.1	<.1	0.2	0.0	0.3	97	22	106	64	0.3	0.3	<.1	0.1	77.2	77.2	71.4	85.7	94.1	0.0	66.7

Table B. – 1990 Voting Age Population (VAP) by Race and Ethnic Origin (cont)

Percent of total VAP columns (White, Black, Asian and Pacific Islander, Native American, Other) are Non-Hispanic. Rank, Percent contribution to state VAP, and VAP percent of total population groups likewise list Non-Hispanic White/Black.

County	Total Voting Age Population	Percent of total VAP — White	Black	Asian and Pacific Islander	Native American	Other	Hispanic	Rank — Total	Rank White	Rank Black	Rank Hispanic	Pct contribution to state VAP — Total	White	Black	Hispanic	VAP pct of total population — Total	White	Black	Asian and Pacific Islander	Native American	Other	Hispanic
Logan	18,004	91.7	7.7	<.1	0.2	<.1	0.2	39	102	18	75	0.7	0.7	0.8	0.3	73.7	74.5	67.0	73.9	66.7	50.0	57.0
Lyon	5,534	91.9	7.2	0.2	0.3	0.0	0.4	107	100	21	30	0.2	0.2	0.2	0.1	83.5	82.9	92.6	83.3	85.7	0.0	75.0
McCracken	47,559	90.6	8.6	0.3	0.2	<.1	0.4	10	107	13	17	1.7	1.7	2.3	1.4	75.6	76.9	64.8	67.8	83.7	5.3	65.1
McCreary	10,854	98.8	0.7	<.1	0.4	0.0	0.1	67	36	84	112	0.4	0.4	<.1	0.1	69.6	69.7	60.5	100.0	65.5	0.0	62.5
McLean	7,224	99.3	0.5	<.1	<.1	0.0	0.1	96	18	92	115	0.3	0.3	<.1	<.1	75.0	75.1	71.7	66.7	37.5	0.0	60.0
Madison	44,652	93.8	5.2	0.6	0.1	<.1	0.3	11	92	32	48	1.6	1.7	1.3	1.0	77.6	77.6	79.3	81.1	84.6	20.7	78.0
Magoffin	9,025	99.7	<.1	<.1	0.2	0.0	0.1	80	4	117	118	0.3	0.4	<.1	<.1	69.0	69.0	50.0	60.0	83.3	0.0	66.7
Marion	11,981	90.4	9.2	<.1	<.1	<.1	0.3	57	108	11	59	0.4	0.4	0.6	0.2	72.6	72.4	74.9	52.4	68.8	33.3	83.3
Marshall	20,898	99.3	<.1	<.1	0.2	<.1	0.4	35	19	115	36	0.8	0.8	<.1	0.5	76.8	76.9	80.0	60.0	72.9	100.0	65.3
Martin	8,553	99.7	<.1	<.1	<.1	0.0	0.2	84	3	119	100	0.3	0.3	<.1	<.1	68.3	68.3	12.5	71.4	55.6	0.0	71.4
Mason	12,388	92.4	7.1	<.1	<.1	0.0	0.4	56	99	22	24	0.5	0.5	0.5	0.3	74.3	74.9	69.4	43.5	45.5	0.0	68.4
Meade	16,184	88.4	8.4	1.0	0.3	<.1	1.9	43	114	15	3	0.6	0.6	0.8	2.1	67.0	68.4	57.6	63.6	58.0	50.0	54.3
Menifee	3,693	97.6	1.8	<.1	0.1	0.0	0.4	119	58	66	20	0.1	0.1	<.1	0.1	72.5	72.5	75.9	66.3	76.2	0.0	59.3
Mercer	14,454	95.1	4.0	0.4	0.1	0.0	0.4	51	84	40	25	0.5	0.5	0.3	0.4	75.5	75.7	71.9	66.3	87.5	0.0	63.0
Metcalfe	6,749	96.8	2.6	0.1	0.2	0.0	0.3	101	62	57	73	0.2	0.3	<.1	0.3	75.3	75.2	79.4	80.0	100.0	50.0	65.6
Monroe	8,577	96.6	2.7	<.1	<.1	<.1	0.5	83	65	56	14	0.3	0.3	0.1	0.3	73.6	73.5	77.6	72.2	82.4	16.7	67.9
Montgomery	14,402	95.2	4.4	<.1	<.1	<.1	0.3	52	83	36	67	0.5	0.5	0.3	0.3	72.4	72.4	78.0	66.7	66.7	0.0	64.3
Morgan	8,437	98.6	0.9	<.1	<.1	0.0	0.3	87	38	78	51	0.3	0.3	<.1	0.2	74.3	74.5	69.8	51.5	82.5	20.0	74.4
Muhlenberg	23,260	95.7	3.9	<.1	0.1	<.1	0.3	28	77	43	69	0.9	0.9	0.5	0.4	70.9	71.3	66.1	71.7	85.3	0.0	58.8
Nelson	21,069	93.7	5.6	0.2	<.1	0.0	0.4	34	93	28	39	0.8	0.8	0.7	0.5	74.5	74.6	76.1	73.3	83.7	0.0	68.8
Nicholas	5,013	98.1	1.3	0.2	<.1	0.0	0.2	110	48	72	90	0.2	0.2	<.1	<.1	72.9	72.9	78.8	63.3	67.5	0.0	68.8
Ohio	15,379	98.4	0.9	0.1	0.2	0.0	0.4	47	42	79	45	0.6	0.6	<.1	0.4	71.4	71.1	81.0	61.8	69.9	15.4	62.6
Oldham	23,734	94.9	4.1	0.3	0.2	<.1	0.5	27	87	39	9	0.9	0.9	0.5	0.9	73.3	73.7	77.8	80.0	61.5	0.0	78.6
Owen	6,625	97.8	1.9	<.1	0.1	0.0	0.2	102	53	63	103	0.2	0.3	<.1	<.1	73.5	73.5	64.3	100.0	66.7	0.0	84.6
Owsley	3,700	99.4	0.2	<.1	<.1	0.0	0.3	118	15	100	57	0.1	0.1	<.1	<.1	70.9	71.0	60.5	33.3	73.9	0.0	69.0
Pendleton	8,539	99.2	0.3	<.1	0.2	0.0	0.2	85	23	99	84	0.3	0.3	<.1	0.2	71.5	71.6	67.0	63.5	82.8	100.0	67.9
Perry	21,663	97.9	1.6	0.2	0.1	<.1	0.2	32	52	69	104	0.8	0.8	0.2	0.2	72.2	72.2	68.1	69.2	73.8	0.0	63.0
Pike	52,402	99.1	0.4	0.2	<.1	0.0	0.2	8	25	97	89	1.9	2.1	0.1	0.1	72.2	72.2	68.1	69.2	73.8	0.0	48.8
Powell	8,210	98.8	0.8	<.1	<.1	0.0	0.2	89	35	83	78	0.3	0.3	<.1	0.1	70.3	70.3	78.0	75.0	88.9	0.0	78.0
Pulaski	37,272	98.1	1.2	0.2	0.2	<.1	0.4	14	49	74	32	1.4	1.5	0.2	0.9	75.3	75.4	72.2	65.9	68.6	33.3	68.8
Robertson	1,615	99.6	0.2	0.0	0.0	0.0	0.2	120	7	105	76	<.1	<.1	<.1	<.1	76.0	76.0	75.0	0.0	0.0	0.0	100.0
Rockcastle	10,854	99.5	<.1	<.1	0.1	<.1	0.3	68	11	120	50	0.4	0.4	<.1	0.2	73.3	73.4	33.3	44.4	76.5	66.7	67.3
Rowan	16,155	97.4	1.6	0.5	0.2	<.1	0.3	44	60	68	54	0.6	0.6	0.3	0.3	79.4	79.3	86.2	84.9	75.0	66.7	66.2
Russell	11,240	99.0	0.6	<.1	<.1	0.0	0.2	62	29	86	93	0.4	0.4	<.1	0.2	76.4	76.4	79.3	66.7	83.3	0.0	60.0
Scott	17,473	93.0	6.1	0.4	0.1	<.1	0.4	41	95	26	38	0.6	0.6	0.6	0.4	74.7	75.1	72.2	63.3	75.0	33.3	63.3
Shelby	18,554	89.7	9.5	0.3	<.1	<.1	0.3	38	110	10	52	0.7	0.7	1.0	0.4	73.4	74.1	68.4	66.7	69.6	0.0	66.7
Simpson	11,111	89.2	10.3	0.1	0.1	0.0	0.3	65	112	7	62	0.4	0.4	0.6	0.4	73.4	72.9	87.6	54.5	100.0	0.0	33.3
Spencer	4,970	97.8	2.0	0.1	<.1	0.0	<.1	111	55	62	120	0.2	0.2	<.1	<.1	75.2	75.3	72.4	65.5	76.5	0.0	84.4
Taylor	15,898	94.7	4.9	0.1	<.1	0.0	0.2	45	88	33	81	0.6	0.6	0.4	0.3	73.7	74.5	68.6	77.8	62.5	100.0	52.7
Todd	8,063	89.3	10.2	<.1	0.1	<.1	0.4	90	111	8	40	0.3	0.3	0.5	0.2	73.7	74.5	68.6	77.8	62.5	100.0	52.7
Trigg	8,004	89.1	10.4	<.1	0.1	0.0	0.2	91	113	6	83	0.3	0.3	0.5	0.1	77.3	78.6	68.0	50.0	80.0	0.0	67.9
Trimble	4,480	99.3	<.1	0.0	0.3	0.0	0.4	114	21	113	31	0.2	0.2	<.1	0.1	73.6	73.7	100.0	0.0	60.0	0.0	58.6
Union	11,844	84.4	14.6	0.2	0.2	<.1	0.6	60	117	4	6	0.4	0.4	1.0	0.5	75.7	76.4	68.6	67.7	73.3	20.0	73.7
Warren	58,032	91.2	7.4	0.7	0.1	<.1	0.5	7	104	19	8	2.1	2.1	2.4	2.1	75.7	76.4	68.6	89.5	50.0	33.3	67.9
Washington	7,624	91.1	8.1	0.2	<.1	<.1	0.5	94	105	17	11	0.3	0.3	0.3	0.3	73.0	73.5	67.9	57.1	80.0	100.0	73.6
Wayne	12,751	97.6	1.8	<.1	0.2	<.1	0.3	54	57	65	53	0.5	0.5	0.1	0.3	73.7	74.0	71.5	38.5	60.9	0.0	60.7
Webster	10,289	94.1	5.5	<.1	0.1	0.0	0.2	73	89	29	105	0.4	0.4	0.3	0.1	72.8	72.7	90.6	67.3	85.0	0.0	64.4
Whitley	24,276	98.6	0.8	0.1	0.2	0.0	0.2	26	40	82	82	0.9	0.9	0.1	0.4	71.1	71.2	25.0	66.7	100.0	0.0	60.1
Wolfe	4,626	99.7	<.1	<.1	0.1	0.0	0.1	112	2	114	119	0.2	0.2	<.1	<.1	71.1	71.2	25.0	66.7	100.0	0.0	100.0
Woodford	14,685	93.0	6.4	0.1	0.1	0.0	0.4	50	96	25	26	0.5	0.5	0.5	0.5	73.6	73.8	72.7	70.4	75.6	0.0	61.2
KENTUCKY	**2,731,202**	**92.3**	**6.6**	**0.4**	**0.2**	**<.1**	**0.5**					**100.0**	**100.0**	**100.0**	**100.0**	**74.1**	**74.6**	**68.5**	**70.0**	**75.6**	**22.7**	**67.7**
CONGRESSIONAL																						
District 1	460,899	91.9	7.0	0.3	0.2	<.1	0.6	3	4	3	3	16.9	16.8	18.1	19.5	75.0	75.7	68.1	67.2	75.5	31.9	65.0
District 2	448,145	93.5	5.0	0.5	0.2	<.1	0.7	5	3	4	1	16.4	16.6	12.6	22.2	72.9	73.3	67.3	68.2	73.9	23.1	64.9
District 3	465,460	82.3	16.2	0.7	0.2	<.1	0.6	1	6	1	4	17.0	15.2	42.2	19.0	75.9	77.9	67.5	70.2	78.0	20.9	69.5
District 4	449,632	97.1	2.1	0.3	0.1	<.1	0.4	4	2	5	5	16.5	17.3	5.2	12.3	73.2	73.3	70.0	67.7	74.6	21.8	68.7
District 5	441,914	98.5	0.9	0.1	0.1	<.1	0.2	6	1	6	6	16.2	17.3	2.3	7.1	72.0	72.0	70.8	65.1	74.5	36.4	65.0
District 6	465,152	90.9	7.6	0.8	0.1	<.1	0.6	2	5	2	2	17.0	16.8	19.6	19.8	75.7	76.2	70.9	73.9	77.5	19.2	72.8

Table C. — Voter Participation: November 3, 1992, General Election

County	Estimated Voting Age Population (VAP) 1992	Voter registration (REG)				Highest office				Maximum vote							Percent drop-off, by office[1]			
		Total	% contribution to state REG	% of 1992 VAP	Rank by % of 1992 VAP	Actual	Total	Office	% of 1992 VAP	Total	% contribution to state turnout	% of REG	Rank by % of REG	% of 1992 VAP	Rank by % of 1992 VAP	President	Senator	Governor	Representative
Adair	11,779	9,857	0.5	83.7	34	-	6,424	P	54.5	6,424	0.4	65.2	80	54.5	51	0.0	11.2	-	23.6
Allen	11,041	8,413	0.4	76.2	70	-	5,415	P	49.0	5,415	0.4	64.4	84	49.0	96	0.0	14.0	-	17.4
Anderson	11,351	8,770	0.4	77.3	67	-	6,472	P	57.0	6,472	0.4	73.8	23	57.0	32	0.0	10.9	-	9.7
Ballard	6,053	5,196	0.3	85.8	30	-	3,880	P	64.1	3,880	0.3	74.7	18	64.1	3	0.0	3.6	-	3.1
Barren	25,920	19,549	0.9	75.4	76	-	12,973	P	50.1	12,973	0.9	66.4	74	50.1	88	0.0	11.7	-	13.9
Bath	7,324	7,113	0.3	97.1	7	-	4,204	P	57.4	4,204	0.3	59.1	103	57.4	29	0.0	19.7	-	15.1
Bell	23,151	19,874	1.0	85.8	29	-	11,575	P	50.0	11,575	0.8	58.2	107	50.0	90	0.0	27.3	-	9.6
Boone	43,829	30,111	1.5	68.7	109	-	23,575	P	53.8	23,575	1.6	78.3	7	53.8	56	0.0	9.8	-	4.1
Bourbon	14,438	10,102	0.5	70.0	104	-	6,920	P	47.9	6,920	0.5	68.5	62	47.9	103	0.0	12.5	-	9.4
Boyd	39,005	28,524	1.4	73.1	93	-	21,147	P	54.2	21,147	1.4	74.1	21	54.2	54	0.0	7.7	-	5.5
Boyle	19,649	13,110	0.6	66.7	113	-	9,278	P	47.2	9,278	0.6	70.8	43	47.2	106	0.0	10.5	-	8.6
Bracken	5,860	4,109	0.2	70.1	103	-	2,932	P	50.0	2,932	0.2	71.4	38	50.0	89	0.0	18.6	-	10.7
Breathitt	11,311	11,021	0.5	97.4	6	-	5,336	P	47.2	5,336	0.4	48.4	120	47.2	107	0.0	8.7	-	5.8
Breckinridge	12,141	9,731	0.5	80.1	54	-	7,013	P	57.8	7,013	0.5	72.1	33	57.8	26	0.0	7.8	-	10.7
Bullitt	35,495	25,962	1.3	73.1	92	-	18,969	P	53.4	18,969	1.3	73.1	28	53.4	60	0.0	8.4	-	12.8
Butler	8,481	6,936	0.3	81.8	48	-	4,806	P	56.7	4,806	0.3	69.3	51	56.7	35	0.0	14.7	-	20.8
Caldwell	10,212	7,646	0.4	74.9	82	-	5,651	P	55.3	5,651	0.4	73.9	22	55.3	45	0.0	6.1	-	6.6
Calloway	24,079	18,158	0.9	75.4	77	-	12,740	P	52.9	12,740	0.9	70.2	47	52.9	64	0.0	8.7	-	7.1
Campbell	62,229	41,771	2.0	67.1	112	-	32,840	P	52.8	32,840	2.2	78.6	4	52.8	66	0.0	16.3	-	6.4
Carlisle	3,986	3,506	0.2	88.0	21	-	2,545	P	63.8	2,545	0.2	72.6	29	63.8	4	0.0	11.5	-	10.2
Carroll	6,917	5,742	0.3	83.0	40	-	3,746	P	54.2	3,746	0.3	65.2	78	54.2	55	0.0	15.4	-	9.4
Carter	18,183	13,761	0.7	75.7	73	-	8,560	P	47.1	8,560	0.6	62.2	93	47.1	108	0.0	10.5	-	6.6
Casey	10,663	8,728	0.4	81.9	47	-	5,302	P	49.7	5,302	0.4	60.7	100	49.7	91	0.0	15.8	-	31.5
Christian	51,305	23,768	1.1	46.3	120	-	16,288	P	31.7	16,288	1.1	68.5	59	31.7	120	0.0	12.0	-	8.9
Clark	22,433	15,533	0.7	69.2	107	-	11,517	P	51.3	11,517	0.8	74.1	20	51.3	80	0.0	16.2	-	13.1
Clay	15,536	13,510	0.7	87.0	25	-	7,427	P	47.8	7,427	0.5	55.0	116	47.8	104	0.0	25.8	-	10.8
Clinton	7,010	6,980	0.3	99.6	5	-	4,436	P	63.3	4,436	0.3	63.6	90	63.3	6	0.0	19.7	-	35.4
Crittenden	7,018	5,086	0.2	72.5	98	-	3,820	P	54.4	3,820	0.3	75.1	17	54.4	53	0.0	12.3	-	14.3
Cumberland	5,141	4,726	0.2	91.9	16	-	3,061	P	59.5	3,061	0.2	64.8	82	59.5	18	0.0	6.7	-	35.9
Daviess	64,663	47,366	2.3	73.3	90	-	36,929	P	57.1	36,929	2.5	78.0	9	57.1	30	0.0	10.5	-	16.8
Edmonson	7,900	6,830	0.3	86.5	26	-	4,585	P	58.0	4,585	0.3	67.1	66	58.0	24	0.0	15.2	-	11.4
Elliott	4,626	4,492	0.2	97.1	8	-	2,525	P	54.6	2,525	0.2	56.2	114	54.6	50	0.0	11.4	-	8.4
Estill	11,009	8,723	0.4	79.2	59	-	5,039	P	45.8	5,039	0.3	57.8	108	45.8	111	0.0	7.0	-	7.9
Fayette	178,184	115,672	5.6	64.9	115	-	95,534	P	53.6	95,534	6.4	82.6	1	53.6	57	0.0	14.6	-	9.0
Fleming	9,353	7,643	0.4	81.7	49	-	5,135	P	54.9	5,135	0.3	67.2	65	54.9	47	0.0	16.6	-	11.6
Floyd	31,229	29,025	1.4	92.9	12	-	18,674	P	59.8	18,674	1.3	64.3	86	59.8	16	0.0	16.9	-	7.5
Franklin	34,107	27,068	1.3	79.4	58	-	21,031	P	61.7	21,031	1.4	77.7	10	61.7	10	0.0	14.1	-	16.4
Fulton	6,182	4,821	0.2	78.0	64	-	3,204	P	51.8	3,204	0.2	66.5	72	51.8	75	0.0	17.5	-	17.6
Gallatin	4,050	3,231	0.2	79.8	55	-	2,329	P	57.5	2,329	0.2	72.1	32	57.5	28	0.0	18.9	-	9.7
Garrard	9,108	7,160	0.3	78.6	60	-	4,797	P	52.7	4,797	0.3	67.0	68	52.7	67	0.0	10.6	-	8.6
Grant	12,019	7,377	0.4	61.4	118	-	5,395	P	44.9	5,395	0.4	73.1	26	44.9	114	0.0	12.5	-	4.3
Graves	25,780	19,540	0.9	75.8	71	-	15,341	P	59.5	15,341	1.0	78.5	6	59.5	19	0.0	16.3	-	15.4
Grayson	15,902	12,428	0.6	78.2	63	-	8,507	P	53.5	8,507	0.6	68.5	63	53.5	59	0.0	11.4	-	17.7
Green	8,023	7,432	0.4	92.6	14	-	4,986	P	62.1	4,986	0.3	67.1	67	62.1	9	0.0	9.4	-	22.0
Greenup	27,651	20,366	1.0	73.7	87	-	14,414	P	52.1	14,414	1.0	70.8	42	52.1	71	0.0	10.5	-	7.5
Hancock	5,771	4,778	0.2	82.8	41	-	3,605	P	62.5	3,605	0.2	75.5	15	62.5	8	0.0	14.5	-	18.8
Hardin	64,226	36,387	1.8	56.7	119	-	25,958	P	40.4	25,958	1.7	71.3	39	40.4	118	0.0	7.9	-	10.8
Harlan	26,050	21,519	1.0	82.6	44	-	12,203	P	46.8	12,203	0.8	56.7	111	46.8	110	0.0	18.3	-	6.7
Harrison	12,451	8,791	0.4	70.6	100	-	6,189	P	49.7	6,189	0.4	70.4	45	49.7	92	0.0	7.7	-	6.3
Hart	11,237	9,464	0.5	84.2	33	-	5,858	P	52.1	5,858	0.4	61.9	95	52.1	70	0.0	12.5	-	15.1
Henderson	32,565	21,974	1.1	67.5	110	-	16,126	P	49.5	16,126	1.1	73.4	25	49.5	94	0.0	7.2	-	9.4
Henry	9,742	7,218	0.3	74.1	85	-	5,219	P	53.6	5,219	0.3	72.3	31	53.6	58	0.0	11.6	-	10.4
Hickman	4,230	3,264	0.2	77.2	68	-	2,457	P	58.1	2,457	0.2	75.3	16	58.1	23	0.0	4.8	-	5.3
Hopkins	34,826	25,592	1.2	73.5	88	-	17,531	P	50.3	17,531	1.2	68.5	61	50.3	86	0.0	8.9	-	10.6
Jackson	8,792	8,138	0.4	92.6	15	-	4,533	P	51.6	4,533	0.3	55.7	115	51.6	78	0.0	20.8	-	11.1
Jefferson	505,110	379,521	18.3	75.1	80	-	309,793	P	61.3	309,793	20.8	81.6	2	61.3	12	0.0	3.0	-	2.4
Jessamine	23,284	18,113	0.9	77.8	65	-	12,339	P	53.0	12,339	0.8	68.1	64	53.0	63	0.0	10.9	-	7.5
Johnson	17,287	14,918	0.7	86.3	28	-	8,436	P	48.8	8,436	0.6	56.5	112	48.8	98	0.0	12.2	-	10.1
Kenton	105,193	68,007	3.3	64.6	116	-	53,135	P	50.5	53,135	3.6	78.1	8	50.5	85	0.0	11.3	-	4.3
Knott	13,015	12,065	0.6	92.7	13	-	7,328	P	56.3	7,328	0.5	60.7	101	56.3	37	0.0	15.8	-	6.5
Knox	21,649	18,020	0.9	83.2	37	-	9,825	P	45.4	9,825	0.7	54.5	117	45.4	113	0.0	17.4	-	5.5
Larue	8,890	7,396	0.4	83.2	38	-	4,930	P	55.5	4,930	0.3	66.7	71	55.5	43	0.0	9.5	-	12.8
Laurel	33,150	24,239	1.2	73.1	94	-	15,050	P	45.4	15,050	1.0	62.1	94	45.4	112	0.0	10.6	-	3.6
Lawrence	10,388	8,650	0.4	83.3	36	-	5,057	P	48.7	5,057	0.3	58.5	106	48.7	99	0.0	11.9	-	8.9
Lee	5,444	5,138	0.2	94.4	9	-	3,158	P	58.0	3,158	0.2	61.5	98	58.0	25	0.0	16.7	-	8.5
Leslie	9,643	8,775	0.4	91.0	17	-	4,936	P	51.2	4,936	0.3	56.3	113	51.2	82	0.0	19.8	-	5.7
Letcher	19,366	16,028	0.8	82.8	42	-	10,090	P	52.1	10,090	0.7	63.0	91	52.1	72	0.0	26.8	-	11.6
Lewis	9,486	7,687	0.4	81.0	51	-	4,904	P	51.7	4,904	0.3	63.8	88	51.7	76	0.0	14.8	-	8.2
Lincoln	15,224	10,135	0.5	66.6	114	-	5,946	P	39.1	5,946	0.4	58.7	104	39.1	119	0.0	5.9	-	9.6
Livingston	7,112	5,582	0.3	78.5	61	-	4,312	P	60.6	4,312	0.3	77.2	11	60.6	14	0.0	11.6	-	13.4

[1]Percent drop-off is zero for any office used as highest office turnout.

368 Kentucky

Table C. — Voter Participation: November 3, 1992, General Election (cont)

County	Estimated Voting Age Population (VAP) 1992	Voter registration (REG) Total	% contribution to state REG	% of 1992 VAP	Rank by % of 1992 VAP	Voter turnout Highest office Actual	Total	Office	% of 1992 VAP	Maximum vote Total	% contribution to state turnout	% of REG	Rank by % of REG	% of 1992 VAP	Rank by % 1992 VAP	Percent drop-off, by office President	Senator	Governor	Representative
Logan	18,392	13,914	0.7	75.7	74	-	8,849	P	48.1	8,849	0.6	63.6	89	48.1	102	0.0	10.3	-	10.6
Lyon	5,607	3,921	0.2	69.9	105	-	2,703	P	48.2	2,703	0.2	68.9	55	48.2	101	0.0	3.0	-	3.6
McCracken	48,586	35,367	1.7	72.8	97	-	27,153	P	55.9	27,153	1.8	76.8	12	55.9	40	0.0	6.9	-	6.5
McCreary	11,212	10,061	0.5	89.7	19	-	6,210	P	55.4	6,210	0.4	61.7	97	55.4	44	0.0	37.2	-	15.7
McLean	7,286	5,706	0.3	78.3	62	-	4,129	P	56.7	4,129	0.3	72.4	30	56.7	34	0.0	8.6	-	13.7
Madison	44,467	29,879	1.4	67.2	111	-	19,841	P	44.6	19,841	1.3	66.4	73	44.6	115	0.0	8.8	-	7.7
Magoffin	9,291	9,748	0.5	104.9	1	-	5,711	P	61.5	5,711	0.4	58.6	105	61.5	11	0.0	18.8	-	14.3
Marion	11,974	9,635	0.5	80.5	52	-	6,324	P	52.8	6,324	0.4	65.6	77	52.8	65	0.0	15.6	-	18.8
Marshall	21,410	16,220	0.8	75.8	72	-	12,749	P	59.5	12,749	0.9	78.6	5	59.5	17	0.0	6.4	-	5.8
Martin	8,663	8,173	0.4	94.3	10	-	4,095	P	47.3	4,095	0.3	50.1	119	47.3	105	0.0	11.8	-	12.3
Mason	12,435	8,731	0.4	70.2	102	-	6,029	P	48.5	6,029	0.4	69.1	53	48.5	100	0.0	11.3	-	7.9
Meade	16,830	10,666	0.5	63.4	117	-	7,365	P	43.8	7,365	0.5	69.1	54	43.8	116	0.0	8.1	-	10.6
Menifee	3,763	3,303	0.2	87.8	23	-	2,145	P	57.0	2,145	0.1	64.9	81	57.0	33	0.0	14.6	-	15.7
Mercer	14,735	10,901	0.5	74.0	86	-	7,653	P	51.9	7,653	0.5	70.2	46	51.9	74	0.0	19.6	-	15.6
Metcalfe	6,819	5,967	0.3	87.5	24	-	3,813	P	55.9	3,813	0.3	63.9	87	55.9	38	0.0	13.2	-	22.5
Monroe	8,590	8,756	0.4	101.9	4	-	5,803	P	67.6	5,803	0.4	66.3	75	67.6	1	0.0	28.8	-	36.3
Montgomery	14,750	11,105	0.5	75.3	78	-	7,611	P	51.6	7,611	0.5	68.5	58	51.6	77	0.0	14.9	-	12.0
Morgan	8,652	7,291	0.4	84.3	32	-	4,411	P	51.0	4,411	0.3	60.5	102	51.0	83	0.0	18.7	-	15.7
Muhlenberg	23,621	18,827	0.9	79.7	56	-	13,114	P	55.5	13,114	0.9	69.7	49	55.5	42	0.0	11.1	-	16.4
Nelson	21,893	15,235	0.7	69.6	106	-	11,672	P	53.3	11,672	0.8	76.6	13	53.3	61	0.0	17.7	-	23.3
Nicholas	5,093	4,210	0.2	82.7	43	-	2,789	P	54.8	2,789	0.2	66.2	76	54.8	49	0.0	23.2	-	19.2
Ohio	15,656	12,702	0.6	81.1	50	-	8,865	P	56.6	8,865	0.6	69.8	48	56.6	36	0.0	8.0	-	12.7
Oldham	25,472	20,422	1.0	80.2	53	-	16,639	P	65.3	16,639	1.1	81.5	3	65.3	2	0.0	8.8	-	7.3
Owen	6,814	4,980	0.2	73.1	96	-	3,569	P	52.4	3,569	0.2	71.7	34	52.4	69	0.0	9.8	-	6.9
Owsley	3,674	3,822	0.2	104.0	2	-	2,342	P	63.7	2,342	0.2	61.3	99	63.7	5	0.0	32.1	-	17.1
Pendleton	8,907	6,539	0.3	73.4	89	-	4,669	P	52.4	4,669	0.3	71.4	37	52.4	68	0.0	22.6	-	10.2
Perry	21,872	19,586	0.9	89.5	20	-	12,103	P	55.3	12,103	0.8	61.8	96	55.3	46	0.0	21.5	-	9.5
Pike	52,836	43,642	2.1	82.6	45	-	28,082	P	53.1	28,082	1.9	64.3	85	53.1	62	0.0	12.6	-	5.2
Powell	8,537	7,733	0.4	90.6	18	-	5,041	P	59.0	5,041	0.3	65.2	79	59.0	20	0.0	24.0	-	18.5
Pulaski	38,641	28,249	1.4	73.1	95	-	19,414	P	50.2	19,414	1.3	68.7	57	50.2	87	0.0	19.0	-	6.6
Robertson	1,615	1,323	<.1	81.9	46	-	945	P	58.5	945	<.1	71.4	36	58.5	21	0.0	14.4	-	13.8
Rockcastle	11,263	8,517	0.4	75.6	75	-	4,897	P	43.5	4,897	0.3	57.5	109	43.5	117	0.0	10.2	-	5.9
Rowan	15,502	11,643	0.6	75.1	81	-	7,274	P	46.9	7,274	0.5	62.5	92	46.9	109	0.0	11.2	-	10.6
Russell	11,567	10,893	0.5	94.2	11	-	7,285	P	63.0	7,285	0.5	66.9	70	63.0	7	0.0	9.9	-	23.7
Scott	18,007	12,684	0.6	70.4	101	-	9,273	P	51.5	9,273	0.6	73.1	27	51.5	79	0.0	10.3	-	8.5
Shelby	19,174	14,026	0.7	73.2	91	-	10,445	P	54.5	10,445	0.7	74.5	19	54.5	52	0.0	9.8	-	9.3
Simpson	11,382	8,522	0.4	74.9	83	-	5,840	P	51.3	5,840	0.4	68.5	60	51.3	81	0.0	17.5	-	20.8
Spencer	5,261	4,465	0.2	84.9	31	-	3,167	P	60.2	3,167	0.2	70.9	41	60.2	15	0.0	15.3	-	19.5
Taylor	16,044	13,322	0.6	83.0	39	-	8,920	P	55.6	8,920	0.6	67.0	69	55.6	41	0.0	7.6	-	17.6
Todd	8,083	6,080	0.3	75.2	79	-	4,202	P	52.0	4,202	0.3	69.1	52	52.0	73	0.0	28.2	-	28.6
Trigg	8,313	6,599	0.3	79.4	57	-	4,855	P	58.4	4,855	0.3	73.6	24	58.4	22	0.0	14.5	-	14.9
Trimble	4,574	3,820	0.2	83.5	35	-	2,631	P	57.5	2,631	0.2	68.9	56	57.5	27	0.0	4.4	-	4.3
Union	11,749	8,086	0.4	68.8	108	-	5,739	P	48.8	5,739	0.4	71.0	40	48.8	97	0.0	7.5	-	10.5
Warren	58,664	41,847	2.0	71.3	99	-	29,896	P	51.0	29,896	2.0	71.4	35	51.0	84	0.0	6.3	-	6.3
Washington	7,692	6,757	0.3	87.8	22	-	4,695	P	61.0	4,695	0.3	69.5	50	61.0	13	0.0	17.2	-	23.3
Wayne	13,139	11,344	0.5	86.3	27	-	6,507	P	49.5	6,507	0.4	57.4	110	49.5	93	0.0	18.3	-	5.3
Webster	10,328	8,027	0.4	77.7	66	-	5,665	P	54.9	5,665	0.4	70.6	44	54.9	48	0.0	8.3	-	11.2
Whitley	24,623	18,786	0.9	76.3	69	-	12,167	P	49.4	12,167	0.8	64.8	83	49.4	95	0.0	24.8	-	12.1
Wolfe	4,800	4,947	0.2	103.1	3	-	2,684	P	55.9	2,684	0.2	54.3	118	55.9	39	0.0	18.0	-	14.0
Woodford	15,285	11,418	0.5	74.7	84	-	8,725	P	57.1	8,725	0.6	76.4	14	57.1	31	0.0	8.4	-	6.9
KENTUCKY[2]	**2,779,000**	**2,076,263**	**100.0**	**74.7**		**-**	**1,492,900**		**53.7**	**1,492,900**	**100.0**	**71.9**		**53.7**		**0.0**	**10.9**	**-**	**8.8**

[1]Percent drop-off is zero for any office used as highest office turnout. [2]Kentucky reports voter registration by political party affiliation (see Table D) and by race. State voter registration by race is 1,963,544 (94.6%) for white and 112,719 (5.4%) for black.

Table D. — Voter Registration by Political Party Affiliation: November 3, 1992, General Election

County	Total voter registration	Democrat (DEM)	Republican (REP)	Independent (IND)	Plurality Total	Plurality Party	Pct DEM	Pct REP	Pct IND	Rank DEM	Rank REP	Rank IND	Contrib Total	Contrib DEM	Contrib REP	Contrib IND
Adair	9,857	3,576	6,178	32	2,602	R	36.5	63.1	0.3	102	19	80	0.5	0.3	1.0	<.1
Allen	8,413	3,415	4,919	42	1,504	R	40.8	58.7	0.5	99	22	63	0.4	0.2	0.8	<.1
Anderson	8,770	7,357	1,281	104	6,076	D	84.2	14.7	1.2	43	76	31	0.4	0.5	0.2	0.2
Ballard	5,196	4,943	232	4	4,711	D	95.4	4.5	<.1	9	112	111	0.3	0.4	<.1	<.1
Barren	19,549	14,181	4,995	155	9,186	D	73.4	25.8	0.8	69	51	44	0.9	1.0	0.8	0.3
Bath	7,113	6,544	539	18	6,005	D	92.2	7.6	0.2	21	98	92	0.3	0.5	<.1	<.1
Bell	19,874	10,776	8,852	87	1,924	D	54.7	44.9	0.4	90	30	69	1.0	0.8	1.4	0.1
Boone	30,111	16,417	10,414	2,017	6,003	D	56.9	36.1	7.0	89	39	3	1.5	1.2	1.7	3.3
Bourbon	10,102	8,766	1,109	148	7,657	D	87.5	11.1	1.5	38	84	21	0.5	0.6	0.2	0.2
Boyd	28,524	18,216	9,465	610	8,751	D	64.4	33.5	2.2	78	40	12	1.4	1.3	1.5	1.0
Boyle	13,110	10,093	2,530	101	7,563	D	79.3	19.9	0.8	61	64	45	0.6	0.7	0.4	0.2
Bracken	4,109	3,705	355	14	3,350	D	90.9	8.7	0.3	25	93	76	0.2	0.3	<.1	<.1
Breathitt	11,021	10,571	400	17	10,171	D	96.2	3.6	0.2	5	116	105	0.5	0.8	<.1	<.1
Breckinridge	9,731	5,831	3,699	84	2,132	D	60.7	38.5	0.9	81	36	42	0.5	0.4	0.6	0.1
Bullitt	25,962	19,744	4,976	682	14,768	D	77.7	19.6	2.7	65	65	8	1.3	1.4	0.8	1.1
Butler	6,936	1,848	5,019	32	3,171	R	26.8	72.7	0.5	108	13	66	0.3	0.1	0.8	<.1
Caldwell	7,646	6,417	1,164	26	5,253	D	84.4	15.3	0.3	42	72	77	0.4	0.5	0.2	<.1
Calloway	18,158	15,135	2,191	236	12,944	D	86.2	12.5	1.3	45	81	24	0.9	1.1	0.4	0.4
Campbell	41,771	23,566	14,490	2,020	9,076	D	58.8	36.2	5.0	85	38	7	2.0	1.7	2.4	3.3
Carlisle	3,506	3,404	92	1	3,312	D	97.3	2.6	<.1	3	118	117	0.2	0.2	<.1	<.1
Carroll	5,742	5,347	327	8	5,020	D	94.1	5.8	0.1	18	106	106	0.3	0.4	<.1	<.1
Carter	13,761	8,244	5,178	153	3,066	D	60.7	38.1	1.1	82	37	35	0.7	0.6	0.8	0.2
Casey	8,728	2,360	6,301	28	3,941	R	27.2	72.5	0.3	107	14	83	0.4	0.2	1.0	<.1
Christian	23,768	19,564	3,583	428	15,981	D	83.0	15.2	1.8	48	73	16	1.1	1.4	0.6	0.7
Clark	15,533	12,568	2,640	99	9,928	D	82.1	17.2	0.6	52	68	54	0.7	0.9	0.4	0.2
Clay	13,510	2,464	10,988	58	8,524	R	18.2	81.3	0.4	117	4	70	0.7	0.2	1.8	<.1
Clinton	6,980	1,570	5,371	18	3,801	R	22.6	77.2	0.3	113	8	91	0.3	0.1	0.9	<.1
Crittenden	5,086	2,820	2,175	44	645	D	56.0	43.2	0.9	88	32	41	0.2	0.2	0.4	<.1
Cumberland	4,726	1,111	3,597	9	2,486	R	23.6	76.3	0.2	112	9	100	0.2	<.1	0.6	<.1
Daviess	47,366	36,047	9,899	604	26,148	D	77.4	21.3	1.3	64	59	28	2.3	2.6	1.6	1.0
Edmonson	6,830	2,172	4,617	23	2,445	R	31.9	67.8	0.3	105	16	78	0.3	0.2	0.7	<.1
Elliott	4,492	4,413	74	3	4,339	D	98.3	1.6	<.1	1	120	113	0.2	0.3	<.1	<.1
Estill	8,723	3,832	4,804	0	972	R	44.4	55.6	0.0	95	26	120	0.4	0.3	0.8	0.0
Fayette	115,672	69,120	37,535	8,926	31,585	D	59.8	32.5	7.7	83	42	2	5.6	5.0	6.1	14.4
Fleming	7,643	5,933	1,640	36	4,293	D	78.0	21.6	0.5	59	58	65	0.4	0.4	0.3	<.1
Floyd	29,025	26,706	2,091	50	24,615	D	92.6	7.2	0.2	20	100	103	1.4	1.9	0.3	<.1
Franklin	27,068	24,017	2,406	350	21,611	D	89.7	9.0	1.3	31	92	26	1.3	1.7	0.4	0.6
Fulton	4,821	4,596	197	11	4,399	D	95.7	4.1	0.2	8	113	96	0.2	0.3	<.1	<.1
Gallatin	3,231	2,911	269	16	2,642	D	91.1	8.4	0.5	26	96	64	0.2	0.2	<.1	<.1
Garrard	7,160	2,961	4,012	130	1,051	R	41.7	56.5	1.8	97	25	15	0.3	0.2	0.7	0.2
Grant	7,377	5,999	1,088	149	4,911	D	82.9	15.0	2.1	51	75	13	0.4	0.4	0.2	0.2
Graves	19,540	18,274	1,135	63	17,139	D	93.8	5.8	0.3	14	105	82	0.9	1.3	0.2	0.1
Grayson	12,428	4,796	7,407	95	2,611	R	39.0	60.2	0.8	100	21	46	0.6	0.3	1.2	0.2
Green	7,432	3,526	3,855	24	329	R	47.6	52.1	0.3	93	28	81	0.4	0.3	0.6	<.1
Greenup	20,366	13,400	6,332	341	7,068	D	66.8	31.5	1.7	77	45	19	1.0	1.0	1.0	0.6
Hancock	4,778	3,318	1,388	28	1,930	D	70.1	29.3	0.6	72	46	55	0.2	0.2	0.2	<.1
Hardin	36,387	25,540	8,740	923	16,800	D	72.6	24.8	2.6	71	52	9	1.8	1.9	1.4	1.5
Harlan	21,519	16,406	4,883	123	11,523	D	76.6	22.8	0.6	63	55	59	1.0	1.2	0.8	0.2
Harrison	8,791	7,887	744	21	7,143	D	91.2	8.6	0.2	27	94	94	0.4	0.6	0.1	<.1
Hart	9,464	7,192	2,201	34	4,991	D	76.3	23.3	0.4	66	54	75	0.5	0.5	0.4	<.1
Henderson	21,974	19,284	2,317	177	16,967	D	88.5	10.6	0.8	34	85	43	1.1	1.4	0.4	0.3
Henry	7,218	6,582	492	88	6,090	D	91.9	6.9	1.2	23	101	30	0.3	0.5	<.1	0.1
Hickman	3,264	3,121	119	19	3,002	D	95.8	3.7	0.6	7	115	57	0.2	0.2	<.1	<.1
Hopkins	25,592	20,962	3,847	562	17,115	D	82.6	15.2	2.2	50	74	11	1.2	1.5	0.6	0.9
Jackson	8,138	1,059	7,035	11	5,976	R	13.1	86.8	0.1	119	2	108	0.4	<.1	1.1	<.1
Jefferson	379,521	237,632	109,926	29,314	127,706	D	63.1	29.2	7.8	79	47	1	18.3	17.3	17.9	47.3
Jessamine	18,113	12,416	4,932	362	7,484	D	70.1	27.8	2.0	73	49	14	0.9	0.9	0.8	0.6
Johnson	14,918	6,134	8,684	28	2,550	R	41.3	58.5	0.2	98	23	101	0.7	0.4	1.4	<.1
Kenton	68,007	39,002	22,050	3,770	16,952	D	60.2	34.0	5.8	84	43	4	3.3	2.8	3.6	6.1
Knott	12,065	11,738	250	9	11,488	D	97.8	2.1	<.1	2	119	112	0.6	0.9	<.1	<.1
Knox	18,020	6,843	11,045	25	4,202	R	38.2	61.7	0.1	101	20	107	0.9	0.5	1.8	<.1
Larue	7,396	6,461	849	22	5,612	D	88.1	11.6	0.3	36	83	87	0.4	0.5	0.1	<.1
Laurel	24,239	6,023	17,798	286	11,775	R	25.0	73.8	1.2	111	11	32	1.2	0.4	2.9	0.5
Lawrence	8,650	5,208	3,334	45	1,874	D	60.6	38.8	0.5	80	35	62	0.4	0.4	0.5	<.1
Lee	5,138	2,333	2,774	9	441	R	45.6	54.2	0.2	94	27	102	0.2	0.2	0.5	<.1
Leslie	8,775	1,095	7,613	22	6,518	R	12.5	87.2	0.3	120	1	93	0.4	<.1	1.2	<.1
Letcher	16,028	12,507	3,339	73	9,168	D	78.6	21.0	0.5	58	60	67	0.8	0.9	0.5	0.1
Lewis	7,687	1,960	5,627	51	3,667	R	25.7	73.7	0.7	109	12	52	0.4	0.1	0.9	<.1
Lincoln	10,135	5,699	4,333	30	1,366	D	56.6	43.1	0.3	86	33	88	0.5	0.4	0.7	<.1
Livingston	5,582	5,156	376	17	4,780	D	92.9	6.8	0.3	19	102	85	0.3	0.4	<.1	<.1

County	Total voter registration	Political party affiliation			Plurality		Percent of total registration			Rank			Percent contribution to state registration			
		Democrat (DEM)	Republican (REP)	Independent (IND)	Total	Party	DEM	REP	IND	DEM	REP	IND	Total	DEM	REP	IND
Logan	13,914	12,084	1,647	105	10,437	D	87.3	11.9	0.8	37	82	48	0.7	0.9	0.3	0.2
Lyon	3,921	3,569	297	22	3,272	D	91.8	7.6	0.6	24	99	60	0.2	0.3	<.1	<.1
McCracken	35,367	29,911	4,527	534	25,384	D	85.5	12.9	1.5	40	80	20	1.7	2.2	0.7	0.9
McCreary	10,061	2,801	7,113	4	4,312	R	28.2	71.7	<.1	106	15	116	0.5	0.2	1.2	<.1
McLean	5,706	4,718	907	30	3,811	D	83.4	16.0	0.5	46	69	61	0.3	0.3	0.1	<.1
Madison	29,879	19,995	8,264	674	11,731	D	69.1	28.6	2.3	76	48	10	1.4	1.5	1.3	1.1
Magoffin	9,748	6,541	3,186	10	3,355	D	67.2	32.7	0.1	75	41	109	0.5	0.5	0.5	<.1
Marion	9,635	9,229	372	16	8,857	D	96.0	3.9	0.2	6	114	104	0.5	0.7	<.1	<.1
Marshall	16,220	14,534	1,371	162	13,163	D	90.5	8.5	1.0	29	95	40	0.8	1.1	0.2	0.3
Martin	8,173	1,567	6,565	23	4,998	R	19.2	80.5	0.3	116	5	90	0.4	0.1	1.1	<.1
Mason..........................	8,731	6,902	1,596	121	5,306	D	80.1	18.5	1.4	56	67	23	0.4	0.5	0.3	0.2
Meade..........................	10,666	8,784	1,537	190	7,247	D	83.6	14.6	1.8	47	77	17	0.5	0.6	0.2	0.3
Menifee........................	3,303	3,018	252	10	2,766	D	92.0	7.7	0.3	22	97	86	0.2	0.2	<.1	<.1
Mercer.........................	10,901	8,969	1,707	114	7,262	D	83.1	15.8	1.1	49	71	37	0.5	0.7	0.3	0.2
Metcalfe.......................	5,967	4,008	1,875	62	2,133	D	67.4	31.5	1.0	74	44	38	0.3	0.3	0.3	0.1
Monroe.........................	8,756	1,425	7,235	19	5,810	R	16.4	83.4	0.2	118	3	98	0.4	0.1	1.2	<.1
Montgomery	11,105	9,766	1,135	81	8,631	D	88.9	10.3	0.7	33	87	49	0.5	0.7	0.2	0.1
Morgan.........................	7,291	7,024	248	3	6,776	D	96.5	3.4	<.1	4	117	115	0.4	0.5	<.1	<.1
Muhlenberg	18,827	15,007	3,503	233	11,504	D	80.1	18.7	1.2	55	66	29	0.9	1.1	0.6	0.4
Nelson	15,235	13,114	1,594	260	11,520	D	87.6	10.6	1.7	39	86	18	0.7	1.0	0.3	0.4
Nicholas	4,210	3,959	219	13	3,740	D	94.5	5.2	0.3	12	108	84	0.2	0.3	<.1	<.1
Ohio	12,702	6,226	6,200	183	26	D	49.4	49.2	1.5	92	29	22	0.6	0.5	1.0	0.3
Oldham	20,422	10,921	7,885	1,085	3,036	D	54.9	39.6	5.5	91	34	5	1.0	0.8	1.3	1.8
Owen	4,980	4,638	306	3	4,332	D	93.8	6.2	<.1	17	104	114	0.2	0.3	<.1	<.1
Owsley	3,822	773	3,043	1	2,270	R	20.3	79.7	<.1	115	6	118	0.2	<.1	0.5	<.1
Pendleton	6,539	5,529	896	43	4,633	D	85.5	13.9	0.7	41	79	53	0.3	0.4	0.1	<.1
Perry	19,586	14,820	4,635	87	10,185	D	75.8	23.7	0.4	67	53	68	0.9	1.1	0.8	0.1
Pike	43,642	33,673	9,409	290	24,264	D	77.6	21.7	0.7	60	57	51	2.1	2.4	1.5	0.5
Powell	7,733	6,165	1,493	18	4,672	D	80.3	19.5	0.2	54	63	95	0.4	0.4	0.2	<.1
Pulaski	28,249	9,296	18,323	322	9,027	R	33.3	65.6	1.2	103	18	34	1.4	0.7	3.0	0.5
Robertson.....................	1,323	1,170	133	10	1,037	D	89.1	10.1	0.8	32	88	47	<.1	<.1	<.1	<.1
Rockcastle	8,517	1,778	6,686	19	4,908	R	21.0	78.8	0.2	114	7	97	0.4	0.1	1.1	<.1
Rowan	11,643	8,273	2,975	151	5,298	D	72.6	26.1	1.3	70	50	25	0.6	0.6	0.5	0.2
Russell	10,893	3,519	7,246	32	3,727	R	32.6	67.1	0.3	104	17	89	0.5	0.3	1.2	<.1
Scott	12,684	10,191	2,011	129	8,180	D	82.6	16.3	1.0	53	70	39	0.6	0.7	0.3	0.2
Shelby..........................	14,026	11,693	2,008	147	9,685	D	84.4	14.5	1.1	44	78	36	0.7	0.9	0.3	0.2
Simpson	8,522	7,451	803	57	6,648	D	89.7	9.7	0.7	35	89	50	0.4	0.5	0.1	<.1
Spencer	4,465	3,993	408	51	3,585	D	89.7	9.2	1.1	30	90	33	0.2	0.3	<.1	<.1
Taylor	13,322	7,415	5,723	78	1,692	D	56.1	43.3	0.6	87	31	56	0.6	0.5	0.9	0.1
Todd	6,080	5,753	284	5	5,469	D	95.2	4.7	<.1	11	110	110	0.3	0.4	<.1	<.1
Trigg	6,599	5,914	599	38	5,315	D	90.3	9.1	0.6	28	91	58	0.3	0.4	<.1	<.1
Trimble	3,820	3,568	215	16	3,353	D	93.9	5.7	0.4	16	107	71	0.2	0.3	<.1	<.1
Union	8,086	7,669	367	27	7,302	D	95.1	4.6	0.3	10	111	79	0.4	0.6	<.1	<.1
Warren	41,847	30,637	9,152	2,038	21,485	D	73.2	21.9	4.9	68	56	6	2.0	2.2	1.5	3.3
Washington...................	6,757	5,291	1,382	28	3,909	D	79.0	20.6	0.4	57	61	72	0.3	0.4	0.2	<.1
Wayne..........................	11,344	4,792	6,425	46	1,633	R	42.5	57.0	0.4	96	24	73	0.5	0.3	1.0	<.1
Webster	8,027	7,531	414	16	7,117	D	94.6	5.2	0.2	13	109	99	0.4	0.5	<.1	<.1
Whitley.........................	18,786	4,692	13,827	74	9,135	R	25.2	74.4	0.4	110	10	74	0.9	0.3	2.2	0.1
Wolfe...........................	4,947	4,626	312	1	4,314	D	93.7	6.3	<.1	15	103	119	0.2	0.3	<.1	<.1
Woodford	11,418	8,723	2,305	146	6,418	D	78.1	20.6	1.3	62	62	27	0.5	0.6	0.4	0.2
KENTUCKY[1]	**2,076,263**	**1,374,459**	**615,732**	**61,972**	**758,727**	**D**	**67.0**	**30.0**	**3.0**				**100.0**	**100.0**	**100.0**	**100.0**

[1]Total voter registration also includes 24,100 for other.

Table E. — Vote for President: November 3, 1992, General Election

County	All candidates																			Major party	
						Plurality		Percent of total vote				Rank			Percent contribution to state vote				Percent of vote	
	Total	Clinton (DEM)	Bush (REP)	Perot (IND)	Other	Total	Party	DEM	REP	IND	Other	DEM	REP	IND	Total	DEM	REP	IND	DEM	REP
Adair	6,424	2,044	3,740	617	23	1,696	R	31.8	58.2	9.6	0.4	104	12	103	0.4	0.3	0.6	0.3	35.3	64.7
Allen	5,415	2,040	2,747	606	22	707	R	37.7	50.7	11.2	0.4	90	26	88	0.4	0.3	0.4	0.3	42.6	57.4
Anderson	6,472	2,491	2,731	1,219	31	240	R	38.5	42.2	18.8	0.5	88	47	7	0.4	0.4	0.4	0.6	47.7	52.3
Ballard	3,880	2,268	1,108	500	4	1,160	D	58.5	28.6	12.9	0.1	12	109	59	0.3	0.3	0.2	0.2	67.2	32.8
Barren	12,973	5,688	5,467	1,778	40	221	D	43.8	42.1	13.7	0.3	66	48	54	0.9	0.9	0.9	0.9	51.0	49.0
Bath	4,204	2,229	1,259	694	22	970	D	53.0	29.9	16.5	0.5	27	106	26	0.3	0.3	0.2	0.3	63.9	36.1
Bell	11,575	5,745	4,501	1,193	136	1,244	D	49.6	38.9	10.3	1.2	38	68	96	0.8	0.9	0.7	0.6	56.1	43.9
Boone	23,575	6,514	12,306	4,676	79	5,792	R	27.6	52.2	19.8	0.3	114	21	3	1.6	1.0	2.0	2.3	34.6	65.4
Bourbon	6,920	2,895	2,707	1,290	28	188	D	41.8	39.1	18.6	0.4	76	66	8	0.5	0.4	0.4	0.6	51.7	48.3
Boyd	21,147	10,496	7,387	3,195	69	3,109	D	49.6	34.9	15.1	0.3	37	81	36	1.4	1.6	1.2	1.6	58.7	41.3
Boyle	9,278	3,894	4,019	1,335	30	125	R	42.0	43.3	14.4	0.3	74	45	46	0.6	0.6	0.7	0.7	49.2	50.8
Bracken	2,932	1,259	1,162	500	11	97	D	42.9	39.6	17.1	0.4	69	63	20	0.2	0.2	0.2	0.2	52.0	48.0
Breathitt	5,336	3,496	1,303	515	22	2,193	D	65.5	24.4	9.7	0.4	4	117	102	0.4	0.5	0.2	0.3	72.8	27.2
Breckinridge	7,013	3,113	2,941	945	14	172	D	44.4	41.9	13.5	0.2	62	50	55	0.5	0.5	0.5	0.5	51.4	48.6
Bullitt	18,969	7,830	7,745	3,333	61	85	D	41.3	40.8	17.6	0.3	77	57	13	1.3	1.2	1.3	1.6	50.3	49.7
Butler	4,806	1,468	2,729	596	13	1,261	R	30.5	56.8	12.4	0.3	107	15	67	0.3	0.2	0.4	0.3	35.0	65.0
Caldwell	5,651	3,000	1,966	670	15	1,034	D	53.1	34.8	11.9	0.3	26	84	74	0.4	0.5	0.3	0.3	60.4	39.6
Calloway	12,740	6,181	4,654	1,853	52	1,527	D	48.5	36.5	14.5	0.4	45	75	44	0.9	0.9	0.8	0.9	57.0	43.0
Campbell	32,840	10,673	16,382	5,659	126	5,709	R	32.5	49.9	17.2	0.4	102	27	16	2.2	1.6	2.7	2.8	39.4	60.6
Carlisle	2,545	1,383	844	309	9	539	D	54.3	33.2	12.1	0.4	22	94	70	0.2	0.2	0.1	0.2	62.1	37.9
Carroll	3,746	2,119	1,046	566	15	1,073	D	56.6	27.9	15.1	0.4	17	112	37	0.3	0.3	0.2	0.3	67.0	33.0
Carter	8,560	4,224	3,305	989	42	919	D	49.3	38.6	11.6	0.5	39	70	82	0.6	0.6	0.5	0.5	56.1	43.9
Casey	5,302	1,409	3,317	542	34	1,908	R	26.6	62.6	10.2	0.6	117	7	97	0.4	0.2	0.5	0.3	29.8	70.2
Christian	16,288	6,709	7,737	1,789	53	1,028	R	41.2	47.5	11.0	0.3	78	35	91	1.1	1.0	1.3	0.9	46.4	53.6
Clark	11,517	4,892	4,625	1,955	45	267	D	42.5	40.2	17.0	0.4	72	61	21	0.8	0.7	0.7	1.0	51.4	48.6
Clay	7,427	2,012	4,747	648	20	2,735	R	27.1	63.9	8.7	0.3	115	4	113	0.5	0.3	0.8	0.3	29.8	70.2
Clinton	4,436	1,241	2,830	348	17	1,589	R	28.0	63.8	7.8	0.4	113	5	117	0.3	0.2	0.5	0.2	30.5	69.5
Crittenden	3,820	1,740	1,576	495	9	164	D	45.5	41.3	13.0	0.2	56	52	58	0.3	0.3	0.3	0.2	52.5	47.5
Cumberland	3,061	917	1,866	268	10	949	R	30.0	61.0	8.8	0.3	110	9	112	0.2	0.1	0.3	0.1	33.0	67.0
Daviess	36,929	16,592	14,936	5,112	289	1,656	D	44.9	40.4	13.8	0.8	59	58	50	2.5	2.5	2.4	2.5	52.6	47.4
Edmonson	4,585	1,653	2,486	438	8	833	R	36.1	54.2	9.6	0.2	97	17	105	0.3	0.2	0.4	0.2	39.9	60.1
Elliott	2,525	1,796	444	273	12	1,352	D	71.1	17.6	10.8	0.5	3	119	93	0.2	0.3	<.1	0.1	80.2	19.8
Estill	5,039	1,837	2,453	736	13	616	R	36.5	48.7	14.6	0.3	93	32	42	0.3	0.3	0.4	0.4	42.8	57.2
Fayette	95,534	38,306	41,908	14,215	1,105	3,602	R	40.1	43.9	14.9	1.2	80	42	39	6.4	5.8	6.8	7.0	47.8	52.2
Fleming	5,135	2,257	2,045	815	18	212	D	44.0	39.8	15.9	0.4	65	62	29	0.3	0.3	0.3	0.4	52.5	47.5
Floyd	18,674	13,351	3,540	1,723	60	9,811	D	71.5	19.0	9.2	0.3	2	118	108	1.3	2.0	0.6	0.8	79.0	21.0
Franklin	21,031	9,896	7,591	3,340	204	2,305	D	47.1	36.1	15.9	1.0	50	76	28	1.4	1.5	1.2	1.6	56.6	43.4
Fulton	3,204	1,813	1,073	306	12	740	D	56.6	33.5	9.6	0.4	16	93	106	0.2	0.3	0.2	0.2	62.8	37.2
Gallatin	2,329	1,171	699	445	14	472	D	50.3	30.0	19.1	0.6	34	104	6	0.2	0.2	0.1	0.2	62.6	37.4
Garrard	4,797	1,730	2,359	697	11	629	R	36.1	49.2	14.5	0.2	96	31	45	0.3	0.3	0.4	0.3	42.3	57.7
Grant	5,395	2,097	2,128	1,149	21	31	R	38.9	39.4	21.3	0.4	84	64	2	0.4	0.3	0.3	0.6	49.6	50.4
Graves	15,341	8,001	5,311	1,943	86	2,690	D	52.2	34.6	12.7	0.6	29	86	64	1.0	1.2	0.9	1.0	60.1	39.9
Grayson	8,507	2,909	4,533	993	72	1,624	R	34.2	53.3	11.7	0.8	100	18	81	0.6	0.4	0.7	0.5	39.1	60.9
Green	4,986	1,760	2,709	500	17	949	R	35.3	54.3	10.0	0.3	98	16	99	0.3	0.3	0.4	0.2	39.4	60.6
Greenup	14,414	7,214	4,975	2,188	37	2,239	D	50.0	34.5	15.2	0.3	36	87	35	1.0	1.1	0.8	1.1	59.2	40.8
Hancock	3,605	1,714	1,261	551	79	453	D	47.5	35.0	15.3	2.2	48	80	33	0.2	0.3	0.2	0.3	57.6	42.4
Hardin	25,958	9,417	12,299	4,026	216	2,882	R	36.3	47.4	15.5	0.8	94	36	31	1.7	1.4	2.0	2.0	43.4	56.6
Harlan	12,203	6,796	3,970	1,391	46	2,826	D	55.7	32.5	11.4	0.4	18	97	84	0.8	1.0	0.6	0.7	63.1	36.9
Harrison	6,189	2,795	2,148	1,225	21	647	D	45.2	34.7	19.8	0.3	58	85	4	0.4	0.4	0.3	0.6	56.5	43.5
Hart	5,858	2,852	2,401	579	26	451	D	48.7	41.0	9.9	0.4	43	56	101	0.4	0.4	0.4	0.3	54.3	45.7
Henderson	16,126	8,270	5,125	2,678	53	3,145	D	51.3	31.8	16.6	0.3	31	99	25	1.1	1.2	0.8	1.3	61.7	38.3
Henry	5,219	2,838	1,640	720	21	1,198	D	54.4	31.4	13.8	0.4	21	100	52	0.3	0.4	0.3	0.4	63.4	36.6
Hickman	2,457	1,296	861	294	6	435	D	52.7	35.0	12.0	0.2	28	79	72	0.2	0.2	0.1	0.1	60.1	39.9
Hopkins	17,531	8,881	6,032	2,565	53	2,849	D	50.7	34.4	14.6	0.3	33	88	41	1.2	1.3	1.0	1.3	59.6	40.4
Jackson	4,533	776	3,398	341	18	2,622	R	17.1	75.0	7.5	0.4	120	1	120	0.3	0.1	0.6	0.2	18.6	81.4
Jefferson	309,793	152,728	116,566	39,822	677	36,162	D	49.3	37.6	12.9	0.2	40	73	60	20.8	23.0	18.9	19.5	56.7	43.3
Jessamine	12,339	3,764	6,474	2,059	42	2,710	R	30.5	52.5	16.7	0.3	108	19	23	0.8	0.6	1.0	1.0	36.8	63.2
Johnson	8,436	3,669	3,614	1,118	35	55	D	43.5	42.8	13.3	0.4	68	46	57	0.6	0.6	0.6	0.5	50.4	49.6
Kenton	53,135	16,344	27,261	9,336	194	10,917	R	30.8	51.3	17.6	0.4	106	22	14	3.6	2.5	4.4	4.6	37.5	62.5
Knott	7,328	5,500	1,243	560	25	4,257	D	75.1	17.0	7.6	0.3	1	120	119	0.5	0.8	0.2	0.3	81.6	18.4
Knox	9,825	3,787	5,011	972	55	1,224	R	38.5	51.0	9.9	0.6	87	24	100	0.7	0.6	0.8	0.5	43.0	57.0
Larue	4,930	2,190	2,154	582	4	36	D	44.4	43.7	11.8	<.1	61	43	77	0.3	0.3	0.3	0.3	50.4	49.6
Laurel	15,050	4,560	8,583	1,859	48	4,023	R	30.3	57.0	12.4	0.3	109	14	69	1.0	0.7	1.4	0.9	34.7	65.3
Lawrence	5,057	2,400	2,084	557	16	316	D	47.5	41.2	11.0	0.3	49	53	90	0.3	0.4	0.3	0.3	53.5	46.5
Lee	3,158	1,170	1,617	356	15	447	R	37.0	51.2	11.3	0.5	92	34	87	0.2	0.2	0.3	0.2	42.0	58.0
Leslie	4,936	1,591	2,879	450	16	1,288	R	32.2	58.3	9.1	0.3	103	11	109	0.3	0.2	0.5	0.2	35.6	64.4
Letcher	10,090	5,817	3,011	1,206	56	2,806	D	57.7	29.8	12.0	0.6	14	107	73	0.7	0.9	0.5	0.6	65.9	34.1
Lewis	4,904	1,713	2,493	673	25	780	R	34.9	50.8	13.7	0.5	99	25	53	0.3	0.3	0.4	0.4	40.7	59.3
Lincoln	5,946	2,532	2,624	762	28	92	R	42.6	44.1	12.8	0.5	71	40	61	0.4	0.4	0.4	0.4	49.1	50.9
Livingston	4,312	2,386	1,339	578	9	1,047	D	55.3	31.1	13.4	0.2	19	101	56	0.3	0.4	0.2	0.3	64.1	35.9

County	Total	Clinton (DEM)	Bush (REP)	Perot (IND)	Other	Plurality Total	Party	DEM	REP	IND	Other	Rank DEM	Rank REP	Rank IND	Total	DEM	REP	IND	DEM	REP
Logan	8,849	4,064	3,710	1,043	32	354	D	45.9	41.9	11.8	0.4	55	51	79	0.6	0.6	0.6	0.5	52.3	47.7
Lyon	2,703	1,583	820	293	7	763	D	58.6	30.3	10.8	0.3	11	103	92	0.2	0.2	0.1	0.1	65.9	34.1
McCracken	27,153	13,341	10,657	3,077	78	2,684	D	49.1	39.2	11.3	0.3	41	65	85	1.8	2.0	1.7	1.5	55.6	44.4
McCreary	6,210	1,934	3,588	624	64	1,654	R	31.1	57.8	10.0	1.0	105	13	98	0.4	0.3	0.6	0.3	35.0	65.0
McLean	4,129	2,223	1,355	529	22	868	D	53.8	32.8	12.8	0.5	23	96	62	0.3	0.3	0.2	0.3	62.1	37.9
Madison	19,841	8,005	8,719	3,038	79	714	R	40.3	43.9	15.3	0.4	79	41	32	1.3	1.2	1.4	1.5	47.9	52.1
Magoffin	5,711	3,261	1,992	440	18	1,269	D	57.1	34.9	7.7	0.3	15	82	118	0.4	0.5	0.3	0.2	62.1	37.9
Marion	6,324	3,403	2,091	805	25	1,312	D	53.8	33.1	12.7	0.4	24	95	63	0.4	0.5	0.3	0.4	61.9	38.1
Marshall	12,749	6,576	4,368	1,773	32	2,208	D	51.6	34.3	13.9	0.3	30	89	48	0.9	1.0	0.7	0.9	60.1	39.9
Martin	4,095	1,715	1,961	393	26	246	R	41.9	47.9	9.6	0.6	75	34	104	0.3	0.3	0.3	0.2	46.7	53.3
Mason	6,029	2,657	2,432	916	24	225	D	44.1	40.3	15.2	0.4	64	59	34	0.4	0.4	0.4	0.4	52.2	47.8
Meade	7,365	3,387	2,641	1,298	39	746	D	46.0	35.9	17.6	0.5	54	78	11	0.5	0.5	0.4	0.6	56.2	43.8
Menifee	2,145	1,311	557	254	23	754	D	61.1	26.0	11.8	1.1	7	115	75	0.1	0.2	<.1	0.1	70.2	29.8
Mercer	7,653	3,010	3,211	1,298	134	201	R	39.3	42.0	17.0	1.8	82	49	22	0.5	0.5	0.5	0.6	48.4	51.6
Metcalfe	3,813	1,703	1,683	409	18	20	D	44.7	44.1	10.7	0.5	60	39	95	0.3	0.3	0.3	0.2	50.3	49.7
Monroe	5,803	1,515	3,776	480	32	2,261	R	26.1	65.1	8.3	0.6	118	3	116	0.4	0.2	0.6	0.2	28.6	71.4
Montgomery	7,611	3,686	2,590	1,308	27	1,096	D	48.4	34.0	17.2	0.4	46	91	17	0.5	0.6	0.4	0.6	58.7	41.3
Morgan	4,411	2,655	1,239	498	19	1,416	D	60.2	28.1	11.3	0.4	9	110	86	0.3	0.4	0.2	0.2	68.2	31.8
Muhlenberg	13,114	7,901	3,551	1,624	38	4,350	D	60.2	27.1	12.4	0.3	8	113	68	0.9	1.2	0.6	0.8	69.0	31.0
Nelson	11,672	5,437	4,495	1,638	102	942	D	46.6	38.5	14.0	0.9	51	71	47	0.8	0.8	0.7	0.8	54.7	45.3
Nicholas	2,789	1,341	894	513	41	447	D	48.1	32.1	18.4	1.5	47	98	9	0.2	0.2	0.1	0.3	60.0	40.0
Ohio	8,865	4,022	3,385	1,423	35	637	D	45.4	38.2	16.1	0.4	57	72	27	0.6	0.6	0.5	0.7	54.3	45.7
Oldham	16,639	5,457	8,263	2,855	64	2,806	R	32.8	49.7	17.2	0.4	101	28	19	1.1	0.8	1.3	1.4	39.8	60.2
Owen	3,569	1,830	1,108	613	18	722	D	51.3	31.0	17.2	0.5	32	102	18	0.2	0.3	0.2	0.3	62.3	37.7
Owsley	2,342	678	1,437	209	18	759	R	28.9	61.4	8.9	0.8	111	8	111	0.2	0.1	0.2	0.1	32.1	67.9
Pendleton	4,669	1,740	1,810	1,086	33	70	R	37.3	38.8	23.3	0.7	91	69	1	0.3	0.3	0.3	0.5	49.0	51.0
Perry	12,103	6,619	4,128	1,308	48	2,491	D	54.7	34.1	10.8	0.4	20	90	94	0.8	1.0	0.7	0.6	61.6	38.4
Pike	28,082	17,358	8,212	2,444	68	9,146	D	61.8	29.2	8.7	0.2	6	108	114	1.9	2.6	1.3	1.2	67.9	32.1
Powell	5,041	2,323	1,809	874	35	514	D	46.1	35.9	17.3	0.7	53	77	15	0.3	0.3	0.3	0.4	56.2	43.8
Pulaski	19,414	5,465	11,423	2,449	77	5,958	R	28.1	58.8	12.6	0.4	112	10	65	1.3	0.8	1.9	1.2	32.4	67.6
Robertson	945	439	329	170	7	110	D	46.5	34.8	18.0	0.7	52	83	10	<.1	<.1	<.1	<.1	57.2	42.8
Rockcastle	4,897	1,144	3,287	446	20	2,143	R	23.4	67.1	9.1	0.4	119	2	110	0.3	0.2	0.5	0.2	25.8	74.2
Rowan	7,274	3,558	2,469	1,212	35	1,089	D	48.9	33.9	16.7	0.5	42	92	24	0.5	0.5	0.4	0.6	59.0	41.0
Russell	7,285	1,950	4,641	673	21	2,691	R	26.8	63.7	9.2	0.3	116	6	107	0.5	0.3	0.8	0.3	29.6	70.4
Scott	9,273	3,639	3,810	1,800	24	171	R	39.2	41.1	19.4	0.3	83	55	5	0.6	0.5	0.6	0.9	48.9	51.1
Shelby	10,445	4,398	4,550	1,451	46	152	R	42.1	43.6	13.9	0.4	73	44	49	0.7	0.7	0.7	0.7	49.2	50.8
Simpson	5,840	2,834	2,280	708	18	554	D	48.5	39.0	12.1	0.3	44	67	71	0.4	0.4	0.4	0.3	55.4	44.6
Spencer	3,167	1,383	1,305	466	13	78	D	43.7	41.2	14.7	0.4	67	54	40	0.2	0.2	0.2	0.2	51.5	48.5
Taylor	8,920	3,518	4,319	1,044	39	801	R	39.4	48.4	11.7	0.4	81	33	80	0.6	0.5	0.7	0.5	44.9	55.1
Todd	4,202	1,858	1,691	612	41	167	D	44.2	40.2	14.6	1.0	63	60	43	0.3	0.3	0.3	0.3	52.4	47.6
Trigg	4,855	2,438	1,820	573	24	618	D	50.2	37.5	11.8	0.5	35	74	78	0.3	0.4	0.3	0.3	57.3	42.7
Trimble	2,631	1,413	789	413	16	624	D	53.7	30.0	15.7	0.6	25	105	30	0.2	0.2	0.1	0.2	64.2	35.8
Union	5,739	3,325	1,605	794	15	1,720	D	57.9	28.0	13.8	0.3	13	111	51	0.4	0.5	0.3	0.4	67.4	32.6
Warren	29,896	11,529	14,748	3,533	86	3,219	R	38.6	49.3	11.8	0.3	86	29	76	2.0	1.7	2.4	1.7	43.9	56.1
Washington	4,695	2,008	2,098	542	47	90	R	42.8	44.7	11.5	1.0	70	38	83	0.3	0.3	0.3	0.3	48.9	51.1
Wayne	6,507	2,516	3,412	560	19	896	R	38.7	52.4	8.6	0.3	85	20	115	0.4	0.4	0.6	0.3	42.4	57.6
Webster	5,665	3,380	1,408	854	23	1,972	D	59.7	24.9	15.1	0.4	10	116	38	0.4	0.5	0.2	0.4	70.6	29.4
Whitley	12,167	4,600	5,998	1,533	36	1,398	R	37.8	49.3	12.6	0.3	89	30	66	0.8	0.7	1.0	0.8	43.4	56.6
Wolfe	2,684	1,674	697	297	16	977	D	62.4	26.0	11.1	0.6	5	114	89	0.2	0.3	0.1	0.1	70.6	29.4
Woodford	8,725	3,161	3,992	1,535	37	831	R	36.2	45.8	17.6	0.4	95	37	12	0.6	0.5	0.6	0.8	44.2	55.8
KENTUCKY	**1,492,900**	**665,104**	**617,178**	**203,944**	**6,674**	**47,926**	**D**	**44.6**	**41.3**	**13.7**	**0.4**				**100.0**	**100.0**	**100.0**	**100.0**	**51.9**	**48.1**

Table F. — Vote for U.S. Senator: November 3, 1992, General Election

County	Total	Ford (DEM)	Williams (REP)	Ridenour (LIB)[1]	Plurality Total	Party	Percent of total vote DEM	REP	LIB	Rank DEM	REP	LIB	Percent contribution to state vote Total	DEM	REP	LIB
Adair	5,703	2,378	3,280	45	902	R	41.7	57.5	0.8	113	9	97	0.4	0.3	0.7	0.3
Allen	4,658	2,203	2,417	38	214	R	47.3	51.9	0.8	106	15	96	0.4	0.3	0.5	0.2
Anderson	5,768	3,543	2,145	80	1,398	D	61.4	37.2	1.4	78	44	28	0.4	0.4	0.5	0.5
Ballard	3,741	3,128	579	34	2,549	D	83.6	15.5	0.9	4	117	86	0.3	0.4	0.1	0.2
Barren	11,450	6,990	4,375	85	2,615	D	61.0	38.2	0.7	80	41	101	0.9	0.8	0.9	0.5
Bath	3,375	2,616	724	35	1,892	D	77.5	21.5	1.0	13	106	67	0.3	0.3	0.2	0.2
Bell	8,412	5,364	2,901	147	2,463	D	63.8	34.5	1.7	65	58	16	0.6	0.6	0.6	0.8
Boone	21,261	11,372	9,525	364	1,847	D	53.5	44.8	1.7	94	28	18	1.6	1.4	2.0	2.1
Bourbon	6,055	4,188	1,777	90	2,411	D	69.2	29.3	1.5	46	75	23	0.5	0.5	0.4	0.5
Boyd	19,516	13,256	6,076	184	7,180	D	67.9	31.1	0.9	51	68	83	1.5	1.6	1.3	1.1
Boyle	8,308	5,025	3,210	73	1,815	D	60.5	38.6	0.9	82	39	90	0.6	0.6	0.7	0.4
Bracken	2,387	1,740	609	38	1,131	D	72.9	25.5	1.6	31	93	20	0.2	0.2	0.1	0.2
Breathitt	4,873	3,910	931	32	2,979	D	80.2	19.1	0.7	8	113	108	0.4	0.5	0.2	0.2
Breckinridge	6,468	4,314	2,112	42	2,202	D	66.7	32.7	0.6	57	63	109	0.5	0.5	0.4	0.2
Bullitt	17,375	10,954	6,205	216	4,749	D	63.0	35.7	1.2	70	52	38	1.3	1.3	1.3	1.2
Butler	4,098	1,817	2,255	26	438	R	44.3	55.0	0.6	111	10	111	0.3	0.2	0.5	0.1
Caldwell	5,305	3,644	1,626	35	2,018	D	68.7	30.7	0.7	48	71	107	0.4	0.4	0.3	0.2
Calloway	11,632	7,452	4,058	122	3,394	D	64.1	34.9	1.0	63	56	65	0.9	0.9	0.9	0.7
Campbell	27,477	15,765	11,181	531	4,584	D	57.4	40.7	1.9	85	37	11	2.1	1.9	2.3	3.1
Carlisle	2,253	1,760	480	13	1,280	D	78.1	21.3	0.6	10	108	114	0.2	0.2	0.1	< .1
Carroll	3,169	2,449	664	56	1,785	D	77.3	21.0	1.8	15	111	15	0.2	0.3	0.1	0.3
Carter	7,657	4,973	2,628	56	2,345	D	64.9	34.3	0.7	61	59	103	0.6	0.6	0.6	0.3
Casey	4,466	1,832	2,581	53	749	R	41.0	57.8	1.2	114	7	46	0.3	0.2	0.5	0.3
Christian	14,328	7,982	6,210	136	1,772	D	55.7	43.3	0.9	90	31	82	1.1	1.0	1.3	0.8
Clark	9,655	6,106	3,442	107	2,664	D	63.2	35.6	1.1	67	54	55	0.7	0.7	0.7	0.6
Clay	5,513	2,250	3,210	53	960	R	40.8	58.2	1.0	115	6	80	0.4	0.3	0.7	0.3
Clinton	3,561	1,297	2,222	42	925	R	36.4	62.4	1.2	118	4	48	0.3	0.2	0.5	0.2
Crittenden	3,351	2,120	1,210	21	910	D	63.3	36.1	0.6	66	49	112	0.3	0.3	0.3	0.1
Cumberland	2,855	1,041	1,804	10	763	R	36.5	63.2	0.4	117	3	120	0.2	0.1	0.4	< .1
Daviess	33,046	22,194	10,374	478	11,820	D	67.2	31.4	1.4	56	67	27	2.5	2.7	2.2	2.8
Edmonson	3,886	1,782	2,082	22	300	R	45.9	53.6	0.6	109	12	115	0.3	0.2	0.4	0.1
Elliott	2,237	1,944	268	25	1,676	D	86.9	12.0	1.1	1	120	53	0.2	0.2	< .1	0.1
Estill	4,687	2,623	2,013	51	610	D	56.0	42.9	1.1	89	32	60	0.4	0.3	0.4	0.3
Fayette	81,609	45,941	34,047	1,621	11,894	D	56.3	41.7	2.0	88	34	9	6.1	5.5	7.1	9.3
Fleming	4,281	2,909	1,321	51	1,588	D	68.0	30.9	1.2	50	70	44	0.3	0.3	0.3	0.3
Floyd	15,516	13,138	2,223	155	10,915	D	84.7	14.3	1.0	3	118	76	1.2	1.6	0.5	0.9
Franklin	18,065	12,717	4,986	362	7,731	D	70.4	27.6	2.0	40	84	8	1.4	1.5	1.0	2.1
Fulton	2,644	1,999	616	29	1,383	D	75.6	23.3	1.1	19	99	58	0.2	0.2	0.1	0.2
Gallatin	1,888	1,419	432	37	987	D	75.2	22.9	2.0	21	104	10	0.1	0.2	< .1	0.2
Garrard	4,289	2,359	1,901	29	458	D	55.0	44.3	0.7	91	30	106	0.3	0.3	0.4	0.2
Grant	4,719	3,297	1,338	84	1,959	D	69.9	28.4	1.8	43	80	14	0.4	0.4	0.3	0.5
Graves	12,848	9,596	3,115	137	6,481	D	74.7	24.2	1.1	23	96	63	1.0	1.1	0.7	0.8
Grayson	7,535	3,753	3,694	88	59	D	49.8	49.0	1.2	102	19	49	0.6	0.4	0.8	0.5
Green	4,518	2,100	2,394	24	294	R	46.5	53.0	0.5	107	14	118	0.3	0.3	0.5	0.1
Greenup	12,903	8,691	4,096	116	4,595	D	67.4	31.7	0.9	55	65	88	1.0	1.0	0.9	0.7
Hancock	3,082	2,141	855	86	1,286	D	69.5	27.7	2.8	44	83	1	0.2	0.3	0.2	0.5
Hardin	23,907	14,858	8,728	321	6,130	D	62.1	36.5	1.3	75	48	32	1.8	1.8	1.8	1.8
Harlan	9,965	7,370	2,500	95	4,870	D	74.0	25.1	1.0	27	94	81	0.7	0.9	0.5	0.5
Harrison	5,710	4,084	1,567	59	2,517	D	71.5	27.4	1.0	36	85	70	0.4	0.5	0.3	0.3
Hart	5,128	3,351	1,744	33	1,607	D	65.3	34.0	0.6	59	60	110	0.4	0.4	0.4	0.2
Henderson	14,957	10,891	3,912	154	6,979	D	72.8	26.2	1.0	33	88	72	1.1	1.3	0.8	0.9
Henry	4,611	3,483	1,065	63	2,418	D	75.5	23.1	1.4	20	101	29	0.3	0.4	0.2	0.4
Hickman	2,338	1,808	493	37	1,315	D	77.3	21.1	1.6	14	109	21	0.2	0.2	0.1	0.2
Hopkins	15,973	11,672	4,127	174	7,545	D	73.1	25.8	1.1	30	90	59	1.2	1.4	0.9	1.0
Jackson	3,590	1,011	2,543	36	1,532	R	28.2	70.8	1.0	120	1	75	0.3	0.1	0.5	0.2
Jefferson	300,588	195,253	100,956	4,379	94,297	D	65.0	33.6	1.5	60	62	25	22.6	23.3	21.2	25.2
Jessamine	10,996	5,778	5,101	117	677	D	52.5	46.4	1.1	97	24	64	0.8	0.7	1.1	0.7
Johnson	7,410	4,672	2,650	88	2,022	D	63.0	35.8	1.2	69	51	45	0.6	0.6	0.6	0.5
Kenton	47,116	24,978	21,040	1,098	3,938	D	53.0	44.7	2.3	96	29	6	3.5	3.0	4.4	6.3
Knott	6,171	5,299	799	73	4,500	D	85.9	12.9	1.2	2	119	47	0.5	0.6	0.2	0.4
Knox	8,119	4,594	3,443	82	1,151	D	56.6	42.4	1.0	87	33	73	0.6	0.5	0.7	0.5
Larue	4,462	3,006	1,412	44	1,594	D	67.4	31.6	1.0	54	66	78	0.3	0.4	0.3	0.3
Laurel	13,448	6,202	7,127	119	925	R	46.1	53.0	0.9	108	13	89	1.0	0.7	1.5	0.7
Lawrence	4,453	2,813	1,601	39	1,212	D	63.2	36.0	0.9	68	50	91	0.3	0.3	0.3	0.2
Lee	2,631	1,395	1,207	29	188	D	53.0	45.9	1.1	95	26	57	0.2	0.2	0.3	0.2
Leslie	3,958	1,766	2,171	21	405	R	44.6	54.9	0.5	110	11	119	0.3	0.2	0.5	0.1
Letcher	7,390	5,488	1,775	127	3,713	D	74.3	24.0	1.7	26	97	17	0.6	0.7	0.4	0.7
Lewis	4,180	2,001	2,122	57	121	R	47.9	50.8	1.4	104	16	30	0.3	0.2	0.4	0.3
Lincoln	5,598	3,501	2,049	48	1,452	D	62.5	36.6	0.9	73	47	92	0.4	0.4	0.4	0.3
Livingston	3,812	2,886	876	50	2,010	D	75.7	23.0	1.3	18	102	34	0.3	0.3	0.2	0.3

[1]Libertarian candidate Ridenour was the only minor candidate (only three candidates on ballot).

Table F. — Vote for U.S. Senator: November 3, 1992, General Election (cont)

County	Total	Ford (DEM)	Williams (REP)	Ridenour (LIB)[1]	Plurality Total	Party	Percent of total vote DEM	REP	LIB	Rank DEM	REP	LIB	Percent contribution to state vote Total	DEM	REP	LIB
Logan	7,938	4,903	2,953	82	1,950	D	61.8	37.2	1.0	77	43	71	0.6	0.6	0.6	0.5
Lyon	2,623	1,998	596	29	1,402	D	76.2	22.7	1.1	16	105	56	0.2	0.2	0.1	0.2
McCracken	25,278	17,841	7,262	175	10,579	D	70.6	28.7	0.7	39	78	105	1.9	2.1	1.5	1.0
McCreary	3,897	1,853	1,948	96	95	R	47.5	50.0	2.5	105	18	4	0.3	0.2	0.4	0.6
McLean	3,773	2,759	967	47	1,792	D	73.1	25.6	1.2	29	92	37	0.3	0.3	0.2	0.3
Madison	18,086	10,976	6,914	196	4,062	D	60.7	38.2	1.1	81	40	61	1.4	1.3	1.5	1.1
Magoffin	4,640	3,256	1,327	57	1,929	D	70.2	28.6	1.2	41	79	41	0.3	0.4	0.3	0.3
Marion	5,339	4,149	1,125	65	3,024	D	77.7	21.1	1.2	12	110	42	0.4	0.5	0.2	0.4
Marshall	11,934	8,648	3,199	87	5,449	D	72.5	26.8	0.7	34	87	104	0.9	1.0	0.7	0.5
Martin	3,610	2,097	1,466	47	631	D	58.1	40.6	1.3	83	38	35	0.3	0.3	0.3	0.3
Mason	5,345	3,552	1,737	56	1,815	D	66.5	32.5	1.0	58	64	66	0.4	0.4	0.4	0.3
Meade	6,765	4,776	1,891	98	2,885	D	70.6	28.0	1.4	38	82	26	0.5	0.6	0.4	0.6
Menifee	1,831	1,423	391	17	1,032	D	77.7	21.4	0.9	11	107	84	0.1	0.2	<.1	<.1
Mercer	6,153	3,829	2,195	129	1,634	D	62.2	35.7	2.1	74	53	7	0.5	0.5	0.5	0.7
Metcalfe	3,309	1,895	1,377	37	518	D	57.3	41.6	1.1	86	35	54	0.2	0.2	0.3	0.2
Monroe	4,129	1,464	2,618	47	1,154	R	35.5	63.4	1.1	119	2	52	0.3	0.2	0.5	0.3
Montgomery	6,475	4,719	1,669	87	3,050	D	72.9	25.8	1.3	32	91	31	0.5	0.6	0.4	0.5
Morgan	3,584	2,928	620	36	2,308	D	81.7	17.3	1.0	5	115	74	0.3	0.3	0.1	0.2
Muhlenberg	11,654	8,685	2,870	99	5,815	D	74.5	24.6	0.8	25	95	93	0.9	1.0	0.6	0.6
Nelson	9,607	6,617	2,827	163	3,790	D	68.9	29.4	1.7	47	74	19	0.7	0.8	0.6	0.9
Nicholas	2,142	1,597	492	53	1,105	D	74.6	23.0	2.5	24	103	3	0.2	0.2	0.1	0.3
Ohio	8,155	5,106	2,985	64	2,121	D	62.6	36.6	0.8	72	46	99	0.6	0.6	0.6	0.4
Oldham	15,175	7,612	7,425	138	187	D	50.2	48.9	0.9	101	20	87	1.1	0.9	1.6	0.8
Owen	3,220	2,418	765	37	1,653	D	75.1	23.8	1.1	22	98	51	0.2	0.3	0.2	0.2
Owsley	1,591	854	717	20	137	D	53.7	45.1	1.3	92	27	36	0.1	0.1	0.2	0.1
Pendleton	3,613	2,480	1,047	86	1,433	D	68.6	29.0	2.4	49	77	5	0.3	0.3	0.2	0.5
Perry	9,503	6,656	2,768	79	3,888	D	70.0	29.1	0.8	42	76	95	0.7	0.8	0.6	0.5
Pike	24,557	18,032	6,372	153	11,660	D	73.4	25.9	0.6	28	89	113	1.8	2.2	1.3	0.9
Powell	3,831	2,586	1,174	71	1,412	D	67.5	30.6	1.9	53	72	12	0.3	0.3	0.2	0.4
Pulaski	15,719	7,623	7,964	132	341	R	48.5	50.7	0.8	103	17	94	1.2	0.9	1.7	0.8
Robertson	809	582	217	10	365	D	71.9	26.8	1.2	35	86	40	<.1	<.1	<.1	<.1
Rockcastle	4,396	1,839	2,533	24	694	R	41.8	57.6	0.5	112	8	117	0.3	0.2	0.5	0.1
Rowan	6,458	4,572	1,819	67	2,753	D	70.8	28.2	1.0	37	81	68	0.5	0.5	0.4	0.4
Russell	6,561	2,560	3,953	48	1,393	R	39.0	60.3	0.7	116	5	102	0.5	0.3	0.8	0.3
Scott	8,315	5,305	2,913	97	2,392	D	63.8	35.0	1.2	64	55	50	0.6	0.6	0.6	0.6
Shelby	9,425	5,754	3,577	94	2,177	D	61.1	38.0	1.0	79	42	77	0.7	0.7	0.8	0.5
Simpson	4,818	2,991	1,789	38	1,202	D	62.1	37.1	0.8	76	45	98	0.4	0.4	0.4	0.2
Spencer	2,684	1,862	793	29	1,069	D	69.4	29.5	1.1	45	73	62	0.2	0.2	0.2	0.2
Taylor	8,239	4,413	3,780	46	633	D	53.6	45.9	0.6	93	25	116	0.6	0.5	0.8	0.3
Todd	3,019	1,893	1,050	76	843	D	62.7	34.8	2.5	71	57	2	0.2	0.2	0.2	0.4
Trigg	4,151	2,804	1,283	64	1,521	D	67.6	30.9	1.5	52	69	22	0.3	0.3	0.3	0.4
Trimble	2,514	1,905	583	26	1,322	D	75.8	23.2	1.0	17	100	69	0.2	0.2	0.1	0.1
Union	5,308	4,286	981	41	3,305	D	80.7	18.5	0.8	7	114	100	0.4	0.5	0.2	0.2
Warren	28,008	14,177	13,558	273	619	D	50.6	48.4	1.0	98	22	79	2.1	1.7	2.8	1.6
Washington	3,889	2,502	1,315	72	1,187	D	64.3	33.8	1.9	62	61	13	0.3	0.3	0.3	0.4
Wayne	5,314	2,675	2,590	49	85	D	50.3	48.7	0.9	100	21	85	0.4	0.3	0.5	0.3
Webster	5,197	4,240	894	63	3,346	D	81.6	17.2	1.2	6	116	43	0.4	0.5	0.2	0.4
Whitley	9,150	4,610	4,404	136	206	D	50.4	48.1	1.5	99	23	24	0.7	0.6	0.9	0.8
Wolfe	2,200	1,730	441	29	1,289	D	78.6	20.0	1.3	9	112	33	0.2	0.2	<.1	0.2
Woodford	7,993	4,624	3,270	99	1,354	D	57.9	40.9	1.2	84	36	39	0.6	0.6	0.7	0.6
KENTUCKY	1,330,858	836,888	476,604	17,366	360,284	D	62.9	35.8	1.3				100.0	100.0	100.0	100.0

[1] Libertarian candidate Ridenour was the only minor candidate (only three candidates on ballot).

Table G. — Vote for Governor: November 5, 1991, General Election

County	Total	Jones (DEM)	Hopkins (REP)		Plurality Total	Party	DEM	REP		Rank DEM	Rank REP		Total	DEM	REP	
Adair	3,921	1,827	2,094	-	267	R	46.6	53.4	-	111	10	-	0.5	0.3	0.7	-
Allen	2,559	1,317	1,242	-	75	D	51.5	48.5	-	103	18	-	0.3	0.2	0.4	-
Anderson	4,636	2,972	1,664	-	1,308	D	64.1	35.9	-	66	55	-	0.6	0.5	0.6	-
Ballard	2,197	1,658	539	-	1,119	D	75.5	24.5	-	20	101	-	0.3	0.3	0.2	-
Barren	6,490	4,127	2,363	-	1,764	D	63.6	36.4	-	69	52	-	0.8	0.8	0.8	-
Bath	3,853	2,843	1,010	-	1,833	D	73.8	26.2	-	25	96	-	0.5	0.5	0.3	-
Bell	5,496	3,448	2,048	-	1,400	D	62.7	37.3	-	73	48	-	0.7	0.6	0.7	-
Boone	9,840	5,759	4,081	-	1,678	D	58.5	41.5	-	86	35	-	1.2	1.1	1.4	-
Bourbon	4,419	2,608	1,811	-	797	D	59.0	41.0	-	84	37	-	0.5	0.5	0.6	-
Boyd	12,485	8,442	4,043	-	4,399	D	67.6	32.4	-	47	74	-	1.5	1.6	1.4	-
Boyle	5,994	3,489	2,505	-	984	D	58.2	41.8	-	87	34	-	0.7	0.6	0.9	-
Bracken	1,891	1,055	836	-	219	D	55.8	44.2	-	96	25	-	0.2	0.2	0.3	-
Breathitt	3,134	2,594	540	-	2,054	D	82.8	17.2	-	4	117	-	0.4	0.5	0.2	-
Breckinridge	4,365	2,754	1,611	-	1,143	D	63.1	36.9	-	71	50	-	0.5	0.5	0.5	-
Bullitt	9,366	6,428	2,938	-	3,490	D	68.6	31.4	-	42	79	-	1.1	1.2	1.0	-
Butler	2,404	1,164	1,240	-	76	R	48.4	51.6	-	109	12	-	0.3	0.2	0.4	-
Caldwell	3,902	2,810	1,092	-	1,718	D	72.0	28.0	-	32	89	-	0.5	0.5	0.4	-
Calloway	5,525	3,735	1,790	-	1,945	D	67.6	32.4	-	48	73	-	0.7	0.7	0.6	-
Campbell	16,832	10,236	6,596	-	3,640	D	60.8	39.2	-	77	44	-	2.0	1.9	2.2	-
Carlisle	1,583	1,087	496	-	591	D	68.7	31.3	-	41	80	-	0.2	0.2	0.2	-
Carroll	2,022	1,561	461	-	1,100	D	77.2	22.8	-	11	110	-	0.2	0.3	0.2	-
Carter	4,098	2,681	1,417	-	1,264	D	65.4	34.6	-	59	62	-	0.5	0.5	0.5	-
Casey	3,414	1,382	2,032	-	650	R	40.5	59.5	-	116	5	-	0.4	0.3	0.7	-
Christian	7,396	4,800	2,596	-	2,204	D	64.9	35.1	-	62	59	-	0.9	0.9	0.9	-
Clark	7,159	4,393	2,766	-	1,627	D	61.4	38.6	-	76	45	-	0.9	0.8	0.9	-
Clay	4,010	2,231	1,779	-	452	D	55.6	44.4	-	97	24	-	0.5	0.4	0.6	-
Clinton	3,219	1,117	2,102	-	985	R	34.7	65.3	-	120	1	-	0.4	0.2	0.7	-
Crittenden	2,093	1,215	878	-	337	D	58.1	41.9	-	89	32	-	0.3	0.2	0.3	-
Cumberland	1,565	677	888	-	211	R	43.3	56.7	-	114	7	-	0.2	0.1	0.3	-
Daviess	20,568	12,712	7,856	-	4,856	D	61.8	38.2	-	75	46	-	2.5	2.4	2.7	-
Edmonson	2,636	1,200	1,436	-	236	R	45.5	54.5	-	112	9	-	0.3	0.2	0.5	-
Elliott	1,173	1,003	170	-	833	D	85.5	14.5	-	2	119	-	0.1	0.2	<.1	-
Estill	3,545	2,133	1,412	-	721	D	60.2	39.8	-	79	42	-	0.4	0.4	0.5	-
Fayette	52,732	30,063	22,669	-	7,394	D	57.0	43.0	-	92	29	-	6.3	5.6	7.7	-
Fleming	3,286	2,148	1,138	-	1,010	D	65.4	34.6	-	60	61	-	0.4	0.4	0.4	-
Floyd	11,736	10,294	1,442	-	8,852	D	87.7	12.3	-	1	120	-	1.4	1.9	0.5	-
Franklin	17,118	12,797	4,321	-	8,476	D	74.8	25.2	-	23	98	-	2.1	2.4	1.5	-
Fulton	1,842	1,330	512	-	818	D	72.2	27.8	-	31	90	-	0.2	0.2	0.2	-
Gallatin	984	733	251	-	482	D	74.5	25.5	-	24	97	-	0.1	0.1	<.1	-
Garrard	2,761	1,402	1,359	-	43	D	50.8	49.2	-	107	14	-	0.3	0.3	0.5	-
Grant	2,874	1,951	923	-	1,028	D	67.9	32.1	-	45	76	-	0.3	0.4	0.3	-
Graves	7,857	5,197	2,660	-	2,537	D	66.1	33.9	-	53	68	-	0.9	1.0	0.9	-
Grayson	4,779	2,448	2,331	-	117	D	51.2	48.8	-	105	16	-	0.6	0.5	0.8	-
Green	2,793	1,423	1,370	-	53	D	50.9	49.1	-	106	15	-	0.3	0.3	0.5	-
Greenup	8,277	5,378	2,899	-	2,479	D	65.0	35.0	-	61	60	-	1.0	1.0	1.0	-
Hancock	1,922	1,289	633	-	656	D	67.1	32.9	-	49	72	-	0.2	0.2	0.2	-
Hardin	13,901	8,983	4,918	-	4,065	D	64.6	35.4	-	63	58	-	1.7	1.7	1.7	-
Harlan	6,008	4,132	1,876	-	2,256	D	68.8	31.2	-	40	81	-	0.7	0.8	0.6	-
Harrison	3,859	2,485	1,374	-	1,111	D	64.4	35.6	-	64	57	-	0.5	0.5	0.5	-
Hart	3,040	1,939	1,101	-	838	D	63.8	36.2	-	68	53	-	0.4	0.4	0.4	-
Henderson	9,712	7,502	2,210	-	5,292	D	77.2	22.8	-	10	111	-	1.2	1.4	0.8	-
Henry	3,226	2,449	777	-	1,672	D	75.9	24.1	-	18	103	-	0.4	0.5	0.3	-
Hickman	1,675	952	723	-	229	D	56.8	43.2	-	93	28	-	0.2	0.2	0.2	-
Hopkins	9,795	7,335	2,460	-	4,875	D	74.9	25.1	-	22	99	-	1.2	1.4	0.8	-
Jackson	2,303	814	1,489	-	675	R	35.3	64.7	-	119	2	-	0.3	0.2	0.5	-
Jefferson	172,582	115,520	57,062	-	58,458	D	66.9	33.1	-	50	71	-	20.7	21.4	19.4	-
Jessamine	6,812	3,869	2,943	-	926	D	56.8	43.2	-	94	27	-	0.8	0.7	1.0	-
Johnson	4,232	2,678	1,554	-	1,124	D	63.3	36.7	-	70	51	-	0.5	0.5	0.5	-
Kenton	27,699	16,060	11,639	-	4,421	D	58.0	42.0	-	90	31	-	3.3	3.0	4.0	-
Knott	5,098	4,293	805	-	3,488	D	84.2	15.8	-	3	118	-	0.6	0.8	0.3	-
Knox	5,415	3,144	2,271	-	873	D	58.1	41.9	-	88	33	-	0.6	0.6	0.8	-
Larue	2,566	1,772	794	-	978	D	69.1	30.9	-	38	83	-	0.3	0.3	0.3	-
Laurel	9,388	4,551	4,837	-	286	R	48.5	51.5	-	108	13	-	1.1	0.8	1.6	-
Lawrence	2,600	1,715	885	-	830	D	66.0	34.0	-	54	67	-	0.3	0.3	0.3	-
Lee	2,750	1,544	1,206	-	338	D	56.1	43.9	-	95	26	-	0.3	0.3	0.4	-
Leslie	2,422	1,247	1,175	-	72	D	51.5	48.5	-	102	19	-	0.3	0.2	0.4	-
Letcher	6,955	5,353	1,602	-	3,751	D	77.0	23.0	-	13	108	-	0.8	1.0	0.5	-
Lewis	3,070	1,241	1,829	-	588	R	40.4	59.6	-	117	4	-	0.4	0.2	0.6	-
Lincoln	3,603	2,164	1,439	-	725	D	60.1	39.9	-	81	40	-	0.4	0.4	0.5	-
Livingston	2,663	1,885	778	-	1,107	D	70.8	29.2	-	35	86	-	0.3	0.3	0.3	-

Table G. — Vote for Governor: November 5, 1991, General Election (cont)

County	Total	Jones (DEM)	Hopkins (REP)		Plurality Total	Party	Percent of total vote DEM	REP		Rank DEM	REP		Percent contribution to state vote Total	DEM	REP	
Logan	3,957	3,017	940	-	2,077	D	76.2	23.8	-	16	105	-	0.5	0.6	0.3	-
Lyon	1,951	1,430	521	-	909	D	73.3	26.7	-	27	94	-	0.2	0.3	0.2	-
McCracken	14,882	10,072	4,810	-	5,262	D	67.7	32.3	-	46	75	-	1.8	1.9	1.6	-
McCreary	2,018	1,034	984	-	50	D	51.2	48.8	-	104	17	-	0.2	0.2	0.3	-
McLean	2,300	1,677	623	-	1,054	D	72.9	27.1	-	28	93	-	0.3	0.3	0.2	-
Madison	11,250	6,647	4,603	-	2,044	D	59.1	40.9	-	83	38	-	1.3	1.2	1.6	-
Magoffin	4,365	3,333	1,032	-	2,301	D	76.4	23.6	-	15	106	-	0.5	0.6	0.4	-
Marion	3,544	2,600	944	-	1,656	D	73.4	26.6	-	26	95	-	0.4	0.5	0.3	-
Marshall	6,612	4,818	1,794	-	3,024	D	72.9	27.1	-	29	92	-	0.8	0.9	0.6	-
Martin	1,525	884	641	-	243	D	58.0	42.0	-	91	30	-	0.2	0.2	0.2	-
Mason	3,770	2,472	1,298	-	1,174	D	65.6	34.4	-	58	63	-	0.5	0.5	0.4	-
Meade	3,847	2,659	1,188	-	1,471	D	69.1	30.9	-	37	84	-	0.5	0.5	0.4	-
Menifee	1,323	1,013	310	-	703	D	76.6	23.4	-	14	107	-	0.2	0.2	0.1	-
Mercer	5,111	2,996	2,115	-	881	D	58.6	41.4	-	85	36	-	0.6	0.6	0.7	-
Metcalfe	2,114	1,176	938	-	238	D	55.6	44.4	-	98	23	-	0.3	0.2	0.3	-
Monroe	2,591	946	1,645	-	699	R	36.5	63.5	-	118	3	-	0.3	0.2	0.6	-
Montgomery	5,810	3,881	1,929	-	1,952	D	66.8	33.2	-	51	70	-	0.7	0.7	0.7	-
Morgan	2,157	1,781	376	-	1,405	D	82.6	17.4	-	5	116	-	0.3	0.3	0.1	-
Muhlenberg	6,179	4,765	1,414	-	3,351	D	77.1	22.9	-	12	109	-	0.7	0.9	0.5	-
Nelson	6,007	4,296	1,711	-	2,585	D	71.5	28.5	-	33	88	-	0.7	0.8	0.6	-
Nicholas	1,814	1,135	679	-	456	D	62.6	37.4	-	74	47	-	0.2	0.2	0.2	-
Ohio	4,439	2,670	1,769	-	901	D	60.1	39.9	-	80	41	-	0.5	0.5	0.6	-
Oldham	8,049	4,765	3,284	-	1,481	D	59.2	40.8	-	82	39	-	1.0	0.9	1.1	-
Owen	2,437	1,905	532	-	1,373	D	78.2	21.8	-	9	112	-	0.3	0.4	0.2	-
Owsley	1,294	573	721	-	148	R	44.3	55.7	-	113	8	-	0.2	0.1	0.2	-
Pendleton	2,618	1,738	880	-	858	D	66.4	33.6	-	52	69	-	0.3	0.3	0.3	-
Perry	9,088	6,858	2,230	-	4,628	D	75.5	24.5	-	21	100	-	1.1	1.3	0.8	-
Pike	12,705	10,151	2,554	-	7,597	D	79.9	20.1	-	7	114	-	1.5	1.9	0.9	-
Powell	2,747	1,959	788	-	1,171	D	71.3	28.7	-	34	87	-	0.3	0.4	0.3	-
Pulaski	9,521	5,243	4,278	-	965	D	55.1	44.9	-	99	22	-	1.1	1.0	1.5	-
Robertson	698	440	258	-	182	D	63.0	37.0	-	72	49	-	<.1	<.1	<.1	-
Rockcastle	2,617	1,242	1,375	-	133	R	47.5	52.5	-	110	11	-	0.3	0.2	0.5	-
Rowan	4,751	3,331	1,420	-	1,911	D	70.1	29.9	-	36	85	-	0.6	0.6	0.5	-
Russell	4,776	2,050	2,726	-	676	R	42.9	57.1	-	115	6	-	0.6	0.4	0.9	-
Scott	5,799	3,705	2,094	-	1,611	D	63.9	36.1	-	67	54	-	0.7	0.7	0.7	-
Shelby	6,312	4,143	2,169	-	1,974	D	65.6	34.4	-	57	64	-	0.8	0.8	0.7	-
Simpson	2,833	1,942	891	-	1,051	D	68.5	31.5	-	43	78	-	0.3	0.4	0.3	-
Spencer	1,664	1,138	526	-	612	D	68.4	31.6	-	44	77	-	0.2	0.2	0.2	-
Taylor	4,481	2,709	1,772	-	937	D	60.5	39.5	-	78	43	-	0.5	0.5	0.6	-
Todd	1,695	1,291	404	-	887	D	76.2	23.8	-	17	104	-	0.2	0.2	0.1	-
Trigg	2,846	2,069	777	-	1,292	D	72.7	27.3	-	30	91	-	0.3	0.4	0.3	-
Trimble	1,384	912	472	-	440	D	65.9	34.1	-	55	66	-	0.2	0.2	0.2	-
Union	3,494	2,763	731	-	2,032	D	79.1	20.9	-	8	113	-	0.4	0.5	0.2	-
Warren	16,663	10,707	5,956	-	4,751	D	64.3	35.7	-	65	56	-	2.0	2.0	2.0	-
Washington	2,784	1,834	950	-	884	D	65.9	34.1	-	56	65	-	0.3	0.3	0.3	-
Wayne	4,199	2,300	1,899	-	401	D	54.8	45.2	-	100	21	-	0.5	0.4	0.6	-
Webster	3,568	2,935	633	-	2,302	D	82.3	17.7	-	6	115	-	0.4	0.5	0.2	-
Whitley	6,606	3,581	3,025	-	556	D	54.2	45.8	-	101	20	-	0.8	0.7	1.0	-
Wolfe	1,555	1,180	375	-	805	D	75.9	24.1	-	19	102	-	0.2	0.2	0.1	-
Woodford	6,045	4,164	1,881	-	2,283	D	68.9	31.1	-	39	82	-	0.7	0.8	0.6	-
KENTUCKY	**834,920**	**540,468**	**294,452**	-	**246,016**	**D**	**64.7**	**35.3**	-			-	**100.0**	**100.0**	**100.0**	-

Table H. — Vote for U.S. Representative in Congress: November 3, 1992, General Election

Congressional district and county	Total	Democrat (DEM)	Republican (REP)	Other	Plurality Total	Plurality Party	Percent of total vote DEM	Percent of total vote REP	Percent of total vote Other	Rank within district DEM	Rank within district REP	Rank within district Other	Percent contribution to district vote Total	Percent contribution to district vote DEM	Percent contribution to district vote REP	Percent contribution to district vote Other
District 1	**212,574**	**128,524**	**83,088**	962	**45,436**	D	**60.5**	**39.1**	**0.5**				**100.0**	**100.0**	**100.0**	**100.0**
Adair (pt)	4,897	1,995	2,887	15	892	R	40.7	59.0	0.3	26	6	17	2.3	1.6	3.5	1.6
Allen	4,471	2,063	2,386	22	323	R	46.1	53.4	0.5	24	8	9	2.1	1.6	2.9	2.3
Ballard	3,760	2,968	768	24	2,200	D	78.9	20.4	0.6	3	29	8	1.8	2.3	0.9	2.5
Butler	3,805	1,532	2,261	12	729	R	40.3	59.4	0.3	27	5	16	1.8	1.2	2.7	1.2
Caldwell	5,276	3,534	1,727	15	1,807	D	67.0	32.7	0.3	12	20	20	2.5	2.7	2.1	1.6
Calloway	11,831	6,175	5,608	48	567	D	52.2	47.4	0.4	23	9	11	5.6	4.8	6.7	5.0
Carlisle	2,285	1,518	761	6	757	D	66.4	33.3	0.3	13	19	22	1.1	1.2	0.9	0.6
Christian	14,846	6,835	7,979	32	1,144	R	46.0	53.7	0.2	25	7	25	7.0	5.3	9.6	3.3
Clinton	2,864	924	1,921	19	997	R	32.3	67.1	0.7	30	2	7	1.3	0.7	2.3	2.0
Crittenden	3,275	1,945	1,321	9	624	D	59.4	40.3	0.3	20	12	21	1.5	1.5	1.6	0.9
Cumberland	1,961	704	1,254	3	550	R	35.9	63.9	0.2	29	3	30	0.9	0.5	1.5	0.3
Fulton	2,640	1,828	719	93	1,109	D	69.2	27.2	3.5	9	26	1	1.2	1.4	0.9	9.7
Graves	12,971	7,974	4,855	142	3,119	D	61.5	37.4	1.1	16	17	5	6.1	6.2	5.8	14.8
Henderson	14,613	10,491	4,061	61	6,430	D	71.8	27.8	0.4	6	25	10	6.9	8.2	4.9	6.3
Hickman	2,326	1,590	658	78	932	D	68.4	28.3	3.4	10	24	2	1.1	1.2	0.8	8.1
Hopkins	15,679	10,930	4,702	47	6,228	D	69.7	30.0	0.3	8	22	18	7.4	8.5	5.7	4.9
Livingston	3,735	2,631	1,076	28	1,555	D	70.4	28.8	0.7	7	23	6	1.8	2.0	1.3	2.9
Logan	7,911	4,349	3,546	16	803	D	55.0	44.8	0.2	22	10	27	3.7	3.4	4.3	1.7
Lyon	2,607	1,773	798	36	975	D	68.0	30.6	1.4	11	21	3	1.2	1.4	1.0	3.7
McCracken	25,375	15,366	9,948	61	5,418	D	60.6	39.2	0.2	19	13	24	11.9	12.0	12.0	6.3
McLean	3,564	2,596	956	12	1,640	D	72.8	26.8	0.3	5	27	15	1.7	2.0	1.2	1.2
Marshall	12,007	7,566	4,400	41	3,166	D	63.0	36.6	0.3	14	18	14	5.6	5.9	5.3	4.3
Monroe	3,696	1,041	2,640	15	1,599	R	28.2	71.4	0.4	31	1	12	1.7	0.8	3.2	1.6
Muhlenberg	10,961	8,078	2,867	16	5,211	D	73.7	26.2	0.1	4	28	31	5.2	6.3	3.5	1.7
Ohio	7,735	4,717	3,006	12	1,711	D	61.0	38.9	0.2	17	15	29	3.6	3.7	3.6	1.2
Russell	5,555	2,112	3,431	12	1,319	R	38.0	61.8	0.2	28	4	26	2.6	1.6	4.1	1.2
Simpson	4,628	2,851	1,765	12	1,086	D	61.6	38.1	0.3	15	16	23	2.2	2.2	2.1	1.2
Todd	3,000	1,744	1,221	35	523	D	58.1	40.7	1.2	21	11	4	1.4	1.4	1.5	3.6
Trigg	4,134	2,509	1,610	15	899	D	60.7	38.9	0.4	18	14	13	1.9	2.0	1.9	1.6
Union	5,136	4,136	990	10	3,146	D	80.5	19.3	0.2	1	30	28	2.4	3.2	1.2	1.0
Webster	5,030	4,049	966	15	3,083	D	80.5	19.2	0.3	2	31	19	2.4	3.2	1.2	1.6
District 2	**206,578**	**126,894**	**79,684**	-	**47,210**	D	**61.4**	**38.6**	-				**100.0**	**100.0**	**100.0**	
Adair (pt)	12	7	5	-	2	D	58.3	41.7	-	15	9	-	0.0	0.0	0.0	-
Barren	11,166	7,198	3,968	-	3,230	D	64.5	35.5	-	11	13	-	5.4	5.7	5.0	-
Breckinridge	6,266	4,183	2,083	-	2,100	D	66.8	33.2	-	9	15	-	3.0	3.3	2.6	-
Bullitt	16,533	10,224	6,309	-	3,915	D	61.8	38.2	-	12	12	-	8.0	8.1	7.9	-
Casey	3,630	1,346	2,284	-	938	R	37.1	62.9	-	23	1	-	1.8	1.1	2.9	-
Daviess	30,707	20,754	9,953	-	10,801	D	67.6	32.4	-	7	17	-	14.9	16.4	12.5	-
Edmonson	4,064	2,315	1,749	-	566	D	57.0	43.0	-	17	7	-	2.0	1.8	2.2	-
Grayson	6,999	3,752	3,247	-	505	D	53.6	46.4	-	18	6	-	3.4	3.0	4.1	-
Green	3,887	1,850	2,037	-	187	R	47.6	52.4	-	22	2	-	1.9	1.5	2.6	-
Hancock	2,929	2,150	779	-	1,371	D	73.4	26.6	-	2	22	-	1.4	1.7	1.0	-
Hardin	23,147	13,890	9,257	-	4,633	D	60.0	40.0	-	13	11	-	11.2	10.9	11.6	-
Hart	4,971	3,371	1,600	-	1,771	D	67.8	32.2	-	6	18	-	2.4	2.7	2.0	-
Jefferson (pt)	21,708	10,985	10,723	-	262	D	50.6	49.4	-	21	3	-	10.5	8.7	13.5	-
Larue	4,299	2,884	1,415	-	1,469	D	67.1	32.9	-	8	16	-	2.1	2.3	1.8	-
Lincoln (pt)	1,110	573	537	-	36	D	51.6	48.4	-	19	5	-	0.5	0.5	0.7	-
Marion	5,138	4,160	978	-	3,182	D	81.0	19.0	-	1	23	-	2.5	3.3	1.2	-
Meade	6,583	4,611	1,972	-	2,639	D	70.0	30.0	-	5	19	-	3.2	3.6	2.5	-
Metcalfe	2,954	1,706	1,248	-	458	D	57.8	42.2	-	16	8	-	1.4	1.3	1.6	-
Nelson	8,953	6,358	2,595	-	3,763	D	71.0	29.0	-	4	20	-	4.3	5.0	3.3	-
Spencer	2,548	1,818	730	-	1,088	D	71.4	28.6	-	3	21	-	1.2	1.4	0.9	-
Taylor	7,351	3,792	3,559	-	233	D	51.6	48.4	-	20	4	-	3.6	3.0	4.5	-
Warren	28,024	16,610	11,414	-	5,196	D	59.3	40.7	-	14	10	-	13.6	13.1	14.3	-
Washington	3,599	2,357	1,242	-	1,115	D	65.5	34.5	-	10	14	-	1.7	1.9	1.6	-
District 3	**280,770**	**148,066**	**132,689**	15	**15,377**	D	**52.7**	**47.3**	**<.1**				**100.0**	**100.0**	**100.0**	**100.0**
Jefferson (pt)	280,770	148,066	132,689	15	15,377	D	52.7	47.3	<.1	1	1	1	100.0	100.0	100.0	100.0
District 4	**226,524**	**86,890**	**139,634**	-	**52,744**	R	**38.4**	**61.6**	-				**100.0**	**100.0**	**100.0**	-
Boone	22,609	6,778	15,831	-	9,053	R	30.0	70.0	-	21	4	-	10.0	7.8	11.3	-
Boyd	19,994	10,422	9,572	-	850	D	52.1	47.9	-	7	18	-	8.8	12.0	6.9	-
Bracken	2,617	1,000	1,617	-	617	R	38.2	61.8	-	18	7	-	1.2	1.2	1.2	-
Campbell	30,723	8,717	22,006	-	13,289	R	28.4	71.6	-	24	1	-	13.6	10.0	15.8	-
Carroll	3,395	1,637	1,758	-	121	R	48.2	51.8	-	13	12	-	1.5	1.9	1.3	-
Carter	7,992	3,822	4,170	-	348	R	47.8	52.2	-	14	11	-	3.5	4.4	3.0	-
Elliott	2,313	1,751	562	-	1,189	D	75.7	24.3	-	1	24	-	1.0	2.0	0.4	-
Fleming	4,539	2,325	2,214	-	111	D	51.2	48.8	-	9	16	-	2.0	2.7	1.6	-
Gallatin	2,104	1,120	984	-	136	D	53.2	46.8	-	5	20	-	0.9	1.3	0.7	-
Grant	5,165	2,318	2,847	-	529	R	44.9	55.1	-	16	9	-	2.3	2.7	2.0	-
Greenup	13,339	7,192	6,147	-	1,045	D	53.9	46.1	-	4	21	-	5.9	8.3	4.4	-
Henry	4,675	2,439	2,236	-	203	D	52.2	47.8	-	6	19	-	2.1	2.8	1.6	-
Kenton	50,829	14,756	36,073	-	21,317	R	29.0	71.0	-	22	3	-	22.4	17.0	25.8	-
Lawrence (pt)	3,725	1,912	1,813	-	99	D	51.3	48.7	-	8	17	-	1.6	2.2	1.3	-

Congressional district and county	Total	Democrat (DEM)	Republican (REP)	Other	Plurality Total	Party	Percent of total vote DEM	REP	Other	Rank within district DEM	REP	Other	Percent contribution to district vote Total	DEM	REP	Other
District 4 (cont)																
Lewis	4,501	1,548	2,953	-	1,405	R	34.4	65.6	-	20	5	-	2.0	1.8	2.1	-
Mason	5,552	2,596	2,956	-	360	R	46.8	53.2	-	15	10	-	2.5	3.0	2.1	-
Nicholas (pt)	208	119	89	-	30	D	57.2	42.8	-	2	23	-	0.1	0.1	0.1	-
Oldham	15,430	4,463	10,967	-	6,504	R	28.9	71.1	-	23	2	-	6.8	5.1	7.9	-
Owen	3,321	1,661	1,660	-	1	D	50.0	50.0	-	10	14	-	1.5	1.9	1.2	-
Pendleton	4,191	1,555	2,636	-	1,081	R	37.1	62.9	-	19	6	-	1.9	1.8	1.9	-
Robertson	815	444	371	-	73	D	54.5	45.5	-	3	22	-	0.4	0.5	0.3	-
Rowan	6,500	3,251	3,249	-	2	D	50.0	50.0	-	11	15	-	2.9	3.7	2.3	-
Shelby	9,469	3,826	5,643	-	1,817	R	40.4	59.6	-	17	8	-	4.2	4.4	4.0	-
Trimble	2,518	1,238	1,280	-	42	R	49.2	50.8	-	12	13	-	1.1	1.4	0.9	-
District 5	211,015	95,760	115,255	-	19,495	R	45.4	54.6	-				100.0	100.0	100.0	-
Bell	10,463	3,834	6,629	-	2,795	R	36.6	63.4	-	15	13	-	5.0	4.0	5.8	-
Breathitt	5,025	3,402	1,623	-	1,779	D	67.7	32.3	-	4	24	-	2.4	3.6	1.4	-
Clay	6,624	1,535	5,089	-	3,554	R	23.2	76.8	-	22	6	-	3.1	1.6	4.4	-
Floyd	17,267	12,986	4,281	-	8,705	D	75.2	24.8	-	2	26	-	8.2	13.6	3.7	-
Harlan	11,380	5,822	5,558	-	264	D	51.2	48.8	-	11	17	-	5.4	6.1	4.8	-
Jackson	4,031	675	3,356	-	2,681	R	16.7	83.3	-	27	1	-	1.9	0.7	2.9	-
Johnson	7,580	3,304	4,276	-	972	R	43.6	56.4	-	14	14	-	3.6	3.5	3.7	-
Knott	6,854	5,376	1,478	-	3,898	D	78.4	21.6	-	1	27	-	3.2	5.6	1.3	-
Knox	9,289	2,561	6,728	-	4,167	R	27.6	72.4	-	20	8	-	4.4	2.7	5.8	-
Laurel	14,504	3,657	10,847	-	7,190	R	25.2	74.8	-	21	7	-	6.9	3.8	9.4	-
Lawrence (pt)	884	405	479	-	74	R	45.8	54.2	-	12	16	-	0.4	0.4	0.4	-
Lee	2,888	987	1,901	-	914	R	34.2	65.8	-	16	12	-	1.4	1.0	1.6	-
Leslie	4,657	1,428	3,229	-	1,801	R	30.7	69.3	-	17	11	-	2.2	1.5	2.8	-
Letcher	8,924	5,321	3,603	-	1,718	D	59.6	40.4	-	7	21	-	4.2	5.6	3.1	-
McCreary	5,236	1,015	4,221	-	3,206	R	19.4	80.6	-	26	2	-	2.5	1.1	3.7	-
Magoffin	4,894	2,877	2,017	-	860	D	58.8	41.2	-	8	20	-	2.3	3.0	1.8	-
Martin	3,593	1,572	2,021	-	449	R	43.8	56.2	-	13	15	-	1.7	1.6	1.8	-
Menifee	1,808	1,200	608	-	592	D	66.4	33.6	-	5	23	-	0.9	1.3	0.5	-
Morgan	3,718	2,162	1,556	-	606	D	58.1	41.9	-	9	19	-	1.8	2.3	1.4	-
Owsley	1,941	433	1,508	-	1,075	R	22.3	77.7	-	24	4	-	0.9	0.5	1.3	-
Perry	10,948	6,357	4,591	-	1,766	D	58.1	41.9	-	10	18	-	5.2	6.6	4.0	-
Pike	26,611	17,283	9,328	-	7,955	D	64.9	35.1	-	6	22	-	12.6	18.0	8.1	-
Pulaski	18,126	4,074	14,052	-	9,978	R	22.5	77.5	-	23	5	-	8.6	4.3	12.2	-
Rockcastle	4,609	973	3,636	-	2,663	R	21.1	78.9	-	25	3	-	2.2	1.0	3.2	-
Wayne	6,163	1,815	4,348	-	2,533	R	29.4	70.6	-	18	10	-	2.9	1.9	3.8	-
Whitley	10,691	3,116	7,575	-	4,459	R	29.1	70.9	-	19	9	-	5.1	3.3	6.6	-
Wolfe	2,307	1,590	717	-	873	D	68.9	31.1	-	3	25	-	1.1	1.7	0.6	-
District 6	223,450	135,613	87,816	21	47,797	D	60.7	39.3	<.1				100.0	100.0	100.0	100.0
Anderson	5,844	3,505	2,339	0	1,166	D	60.0	40.0	0.0	14	6	5	2.6	2.6	2.7	0.0
Bath	3,570	2,628	942	0	1,686	D	73.6	26.4	0.0	1	19	6	1.6	1.9	1.1	0.0
Bourbon	6,270	4,236	2,034	0	2,202	D	67.6	32.4	0.0	6	14	7	2.8	3.1	2.3	0.0
Boyle	8,479	5,247	3,232	0	2,015	D	61.9	38.1	0.0	12	8	8	3.8	3.9	3.7	0.0
Clark	10,005	6,390	3,615	0	2,775	D	63.9	36.1	0.0	9	11	9	4.5	4.7	4.1	0.0
Estill	4,641	2,553	2,088	0	465	D	55.0	45.0	0.0	17	3	10	2.1	1.9	2.4	0.0
Fayette	86,978	48,736	38,238	4	10,498	D	56.0	44.0	<.1	16	4	4	38.9	35.9	43.5	19.0
Franklin	17,577	12,604	4,972	1	7,632	D	71.7	28.3	<.1	4	16	3	7.9	9.3	5.7	4.8
Garrard	4,385	2,412	1,973	0	439	D	55.0	45.0	0.0	18	2	11	2.0	1.8	2.2	0.0
Harrison	5,798	4,110	1,688	0	2,422	D	70.9	29.1	0.0	5	15	12	2.6	3.0	1.9	0.0
Jessamine	11,415	5,754	5,661	0	93	D	50.4	49.6	0.0	19	1	13	5.1	4.2	6.4	0.0
Lincoln (pt)	4,267	2,687	1,580	0	1,107	D	63.0	37.0	0.0	10	10	14	1.9	2.0	1.8	0.0
Madison	18,309	11,808	6,486	15	5,322	D	64.5	35.4	<.1	8	12	1	8.2	8.7	7.4	71.4
Mercer	6,459	3,960	2,499	0	1,461	D	61.3	38.7	0.0	13	7	15	2.9	2.9	2.8	0.0
Montgomery	6,694	4,838	1,856	0	2,982	D	72.3	27.7	0.0	2	18	16	3.0	3.6	2.1	0.0
Nicholas (pt)	2,045	1,476	568	1	908	D	72.2	27.8	<.1	3	17	2	0.9	1.1	0.6	4.8
Powell	4,107	2,680	1,427	0	1,253	D	65.3	34.7	0.0	7	13	17	1.8	2.0	1.6	0.0
Scott	8,481	5,306	3,175	0	2,131	D	62.6	37.4	0.0	11	9	18	3.8	3.9	3.6	0.0
Woodford	8,126	4,683	3,443	0	1,240	D	57.6	42.4	0.0	15	5	19	3.6	3.5	3.9	0.0
KENTUCKY	1,360,911	721,747	638,166	998	83,581	D	53.0	46.9	<.1							

Table I. — Vote for Presidential Preference: May 26, 1992, Democratic Primary Election

County	Total	Clinton	Uncom-mitted	Brown	Tsongas	Harkin	Kerrey			Clinton	Uncom-mitted	Brown	Clinton	Uncom-mitted	Brown	Total	Clinton	Uncom-mitted	Brown
											Percent of total vote			Rank			Percent contribution to state vote		
Adair	655	471	107	25	24	22	6	-	-	71.9	16.3	3.8	21	98	110	0.2	0.2	0.1	<.1
Allen	492	368	76	20	16	11	1	-	-	74.8	15.4	4.1	8	104	109	0.1	0.2	<.1	<.1
Anderson	1,829	866	677	158	81	38	9	-	-	47.3	37.0	8.6	111	9	21	0.5	0.4	0.7	0.5
Ballard	1,967	1,217	582	61	68	23	16	-	-	61.9	29.6	3.1	58	40	118	0.5	0.6	0.6	0.2
Barren	3,334	2,100	815	150	151	88	30	-	-	63.0	24.4	4.5	55	64	98	0.9	1.0	0.8	0.5
Bath	935	609	227	43	27	14	15	-	-	65.1	24.3	4.6	46	65	96	0.3	0.3	0.2	0.1
Bell	1,405	984	225	60	56	70	10	-	-	70.0	16.0	4.3	29	100	107	0.4	0.5	0.2	0.2
Boone	4,980	1,922	2,264	372	309	76	37	-	-	38.6	45.5	7.5	119	2	32	1.3	0.9	2.2	1.2
Bourbon	1,448	737	462	148	63	22	16	-	-	50.9	31.9	10.2	101	26	9	0.4	0.4	0.4	0.5
Boyd	4,789	2,851	1,227	373	185	108	45	-	-	59.5	25.6	7.8	63	59	28	1.3	1.4	1.2	1.2
Boyle	3,411	1,675	1,264	258	155	39	20	-	-	49.1	37.1	7.6	108	8	31	0.9	0.8	1.2	0.8
Bracken	495	268	154	28	20	20	5	-	-	54.1	31.1	5.7	88	32	72	0.1	0.1	0.1	<.1
Breathitt	3,216	2,283	591	190	79	36	37	-	-	71.0	18.4	5.9	24	88	64	0.9	1.1	0.6	0.6
Breckinridge	2,087	1,344	467	142	79	34	21	-	-	64.4	22.4	6.8	50	74	45	0.6	0.6	0.5	0.5
Bullitt	4,510	2,462	1,126	469	225	188	40	-	-	54.6	25.0	10.4	84	62	8	1.2	1.2	1.1	1.5
Butler	496	382	72	15	12	9	6	-	-	77.0	14.5	3.0	3	109	119	0.1	0.2	<.1	<.1
Caldwell	2,048	1,178	631	90	84	40	25	-	-	57.5	30.8	4.4	73	35	102	0.6	0.6	0.6	0.3
Calloway	3,866	2,043	1,361	185	183	65	29	-	-	52.8	35.2	4.8	94	14	90	1.0	1.0	1.3	0.6
Campbell	4,307	1,902	1,471	440	309	133	52	-	-	44.2	34.2	10.2	115	19	10	1.2	0.9	1.4	1.4
Carlisle	1,192	723	343	51	51	20	4	-	-	60.7	28.8	4.3	60	43	106	0.3	0.3	0.3	0.2
Carroll	757	449	214	43	21	24	6	-	-	59.3	28.3	5.7	65	48	71	0.2	0.2	0.2	0.1
Carter	1,727	1,206	277	129	65	40	10	-	-	69.8	16.0	7.5	31	99	33	0.5	0.6	0.3	0.4
Casey	533	343	123	26	22	17	2	-	-	64.4	23.1	4.9	51	69	89	0.1	0.2	0.1	<.1
Christian	6,049	2,902	2,211	348	350	160	78	-	-	48.0	36.6	5.8	110	12	69	1.6	1.4	2.1	1.1
Clark	4,328	2,143	1,626	285	167	70	37	-	-	49.5	37.6	6.6	105	7	50	1.2	1.0	1.6	0.9
Clay	651	440	117	31	26	29	8	-	-	67.6	18.0	4.8	36	91	91	0.2	0.2	0.1	0.1
Clinton	243	197	19	8	8	10	1	-	-	81.1	7.8	3.3	1	120	115	<.1	<.1	<.1	<.1
Crittenden	1,028	729	213	35	29	21	1	-	-	70.9	20.7	3.4	26	78	113	0.3	0.4	0.2	0.1
Cumberland	211	154	32	10	8	5	2	-	-	73.0	15.2	4.7	16	105	92	<.1	<.1	<.1	<.1
Daviess	7,275	3,584	2,462	526	387	223	93	-	-	49.3	33.8	7.2	106	20	39	2.0	1.7	2.4	1.7
Edmonson	378	281	57	17	15	5	3	-	-	74.3	15.1	4.5	11	106	99	0.1	0.1	<.1	<.1
Elliott	592	444	80	26	20	14	8	-	-	75.0	13.5	4.4	6	112	103	0.2	0.2	<.1	<.1
Estill	653	457	116	48	14	14	4	-	-	70.0	17.8	7.4	30	92	36	0.2	0.2	0.1	0.2
Fayette	19,189	8,192	7,038	2,169	1,334	297	159	-	-	42.7	36.7	11.3	116	11	4	5.2	3.9	6.8	7.1
Fleming	893	597	164	63	33	28	8	-	-	66.9	18.4	7.1	40	89	42	0.2	0.3	0.2	0.2
Floyd	10,322	7,543	1,692	483	287	197	120	-	-	73.1	16.4	4.7	15	97	94	2.8	3.6	1.6	1.6
Franklin	10,050	3,794	4,748	709	480	230	89	-	-	37.8	47.2	7.1	120	1	43	2.7	1.8	4.6	2.3
Fulton	1,789	1,075	553	57	65	29	10	-	-	60.1	30.9	3.2	61	34	117	0.5	0.5	0.5	0.2
Gallatin	1,017	527	357	59	39	22	13	-	-	51.8	35.1	5.8	98	15	66	0.3	0.3	0.3	0.2
Garrard	627	396	166	37	17	8	3	-	-	63.2	26.5	5.9	54	57	65	0.2	0.2	0.2	0.1
Grant	929	466	326	61	36	32	8	-	-	50.2	35.1	6.6	103	16	53	0.3	0.2	0.3	0.2
Graves	7,179	4,141	2,297	234	316	140	51	-	-	57.7	32.0	3.3	72	25	116	1.9	2.0	2.2	0.8
Grayson	1,497	979	336	101	41	32	8	-	-	65.4	22.4	6.7	44	73	49	0.4	0.5	0.3	0.3
Green	468	336	68	26	17	16	5	-	-	71.8	14.5	5.6	22	108	75	0.1	0.2	<.1	<.1
Greenup	3,304	2,245	661	224	98	58	18	-	-	67.9	20.0	6.8	35	80	48	0.9	1.1	0.6	0.7
Hancock	645	400	159	35	27	18	6	-	-	62.0	24.7	5.4	57	63	77	0.2	0.2	0.2	0.1
Hardin	9,369	4,497	3,267	838	527	154	86	-	-	48.0	34.9	8.9	109	17	18	2.5	2.2	3.2	2.7
Harlan	5,912	3,788	1,349	362	198	150	65	-	-	64.1	22.8	6.1	52	71	59	1.6	1.8	1.3	1.2
Harrison	1,551	839	491	114	86	11	10	-	-	54.1	31.7	7.4	90	30	37	0.4	0.4	0.5	0.4
Hart	1,560	1,079	266	80	69	42	24	-	-	69.2	17.1	5.1	32	93	82	0.4	0.5	0.3	0.3
Henderson	7,601	3,360	3,325	440	313	107	56	-	-	44.2	43.7	5.8	114	4	68	2.1	1.6	3.2	1.4
Henry	1,538	866	416	125	65	54	12	-	-	56.3	27.0	8.1	76	54	24	0.4	0.4	0.4	0.4
Hickman	1,218	719	396	28	47	20	8	-	-	59.0	32.5	2.3	66	24	120	0.3	0.3	0.4	<.1
Hopkins	4,609	2,580	1,427	287	207	76	32	-	-	56.0	31.0	6.2	79	33	57	1.2	1.2	1.4	0.9
Jackson	146	90	33	12	5	5	1	-	-	61.6	22.6	8.2	59	72	22	<.1	<.1	<.1	<.1
Jefferson	73,874	40,301	17,293	10,280	4,624	836	540	-	-	54.6	23.4	13.9	85	66	2	19.9	19.4	16.7	33.5
Jessamine	2,624	1,204	971	249	129	41	30	-	-	45.9	37.0	9.5	112	10	15	0.7	0.6	0.9	0.8
Johnson	1,454	993	288	71	59	33	10	-	-	68.3	19.8	4.9	34	82	88	0.4	0.5	0.3	0.2
Kenton	6,340	2,556	2,419	697	467	141	60	-	-	40.3	38.2	11.0	117	6	5	1.7	1.2	2.3	2.3
Knott	3,777	2,739	586	210	116	87	39	-	-	72.5	15.5	5.6	19	102	74	1.0	1.3	0.6	0.7
Knox	1,215	857	207	67	37	33	14	-	-	70.5	17.0	5.5	27	94	76	0.3	0.4	0.2	0.2
Larue	1,636	908	437	157	72	46	16	-	-	55.5	26.7	9.6	81	56	12	0.4	0.4	0.4	0.5
Laurel	1,529	1,031	304	91	58	31	14	-	-	67.4	19.9	6.0	37	81	63	0.4	0.5	0.3	0.3
Lawrence	1,080	797	155	70	28	24	6	-	-	73.8	14.4	6.5	12	110	54	0.3	0.4	0.1	0.2
Lee	599	391	114	47	12	25	10	-	-	65.3	19.0	7.8	45	85	27	0.2	0.2	0.1	0.2
Leslie	363	278	41	28	8	2	6	-	-	76.6	11.3	7.7	4	115	30	<.1	0.1	<.1	<.1
Letcher	3,949	2,769	711	240	112	92	25	-	-	70.1	18.0	6.1	28	90	62	1.1	1.3	0.7	0.8
Lewis	339	245	54	23	10	6	1	-	-	72.3	15.9	6.8	20	101	47	<.1	0.1	<.1	<.1
Lincoln	1,207	786	282	76	26	14	23	-	-	65.1	23.4	6.3	47	67	56	0.3	0.4	0.3	0.2
Livingston	1,645	1,068	416	61	59	27	14	-	-	64.9	25.3	3.7	48	61	111	0.4	0.5	0.4	0.2

Table I. – Vote for Presidential Preference: May 26, 1992, Democratic Primary Election (cont)

County	Total	Clinton	Uncom-mitted	Brown	Tsongas	Harkin	Kerrey			Clinton	Uncom-mitted	Brown	Clinton (Rank)	Uncom-mitted (Rank)	Brown (Rank)	Total	Clinton	Uncom-mitted	Brown
Logan	2,802	1,630	799	152	141	60	20	-	-	58.2	28.5	5.4	68	44	79	0.8	0.8	0.8	0.5
Lyon	1,198	661	398	53	57	18	11	-	-	55.2	33.2	4.4	82	23	101	0.3	0.3	0.4	0.2
McCracken	11,162	5,930	3,945	524	553	133	77	-	-	53.1	35.3	4.7	93	13	93	3.0	2.9	3.8	1.7
McCreary	585	373	110	37	25	31	9	-	-	63.8	18.8	6.3	53	87	55	0.2	0.2	0.1	0.1
McLean	1,088	623	346	47	40	25	7	-	-	57.3	31.8	4.3	74	28	105	0.3	0.3	0.3	0.2
Madison	3,592	1,928	1,093	319	179	40	33	-	-	53.7	30.4	8.9	92	36	19	1.0	0.9	1.1	1.0
Magoffin	1,319	1,048	144	61	21	33	12	-	-	79.5	10.9	4.6	2	116	95	0.4	0.5	0.1	0.2
Marion	1,273	757	333	90	61	23	9	-	-	59.5	26.2	7.1	64	58	41	0.3	0.4	0.3	0.3
Marshall	4,935	2,649	1,687	251	224	84	40	-	-	53.7	34.2	5.1	91	18	85	1.3	1.3	1.6	0.8
Martin	431	323	53	24	10	14	7	-	-	74.9	12.3	5.6	7	114	73	0.1	0.2	<.1	<.1
Mason	902	502	243	86	51	12	8	-	-	55.7	26.9	9.5	80	55	14	0.2	0.2	0.2	0.3
Meade	3,145	1,705	894	330	146	42	28	-	-	54.2	28.4	10.5	87	46	7	0.8	0.8	0.9	1.1
Menifee	690	506	107	42	16	11	8	-	-	73.3	15.5	6.1	14	103	61	0.2	0.2	0.1	0.1
Mercer	2,923	1,526	926	215	150	73	33	-	-	52.2	31.7	7.4	96	29	35	0.8	0.7	0.9	0.7
Metcalfe	664	482	89	34	17	36	6	-	-	72.6	13.4	5.1	18	113	83	0.2	0.2	<.1	0.1
Monroe	230	172	25	12	11	8	2	-	-	74.8	10.9	5.2	9	117	81	<.1	<.1	<.1	<.1
Montgomery	1,792	1,039	503	118	71	41	20	-	-	58.0	28.1	6.6	70	50	51	0.5	0.5	0.5	0.4
Morgan	1,935	1,330	383	105	62	36	19	-	-	68.7	19.8	5.4	33	83	78	0.5	0.6	0.4	0.3
Muhlenberg	3,854	2,580	837	168	131	103	35	-	-	66.9	21.7	4.4	39	75	104	1.0	1.2	0.8	0.5
Nelson	2,363	1,203	658	251	133	88	30	-	-	50.9	27.8	10.6	100	51	6	0.6	0.6	0.6	0.8
Nicholas	589	380	111	48	15	25	10	-	-	64.5	18.8	8.1	49	86	23	0.2	0.2	0.1	0.2
Ohio	1,526	1,002	313	78	59	61	13	-	-	65.7	20.5	5.1	42	79	84	0.4	0.5	0.3	0.3
Oldham	2,312	1,031	696	338	159	72	16	-	-	44.6	30.1	14.6	113	38	1	0.6	0.5	0.7	1.1
Owen	1,050	601	287	78	41	36	7	-	-	57.2	27.3	7.4	75	53	34	0.3	0.3	0.3	0.3
Owsley	368	271	37	25	21	7	7	-	-	73.6	10.1	6.8	13	118	46	<.1	0.1	<.1	<.1
Pendleton	769	390	257	47	34	33	8	-	-	50.7	33.4	6.1	102	22	60	0.2	0.2	0.2	0.2
Perry	4,482	2,941	857	327	168	136	53	-	-	65.6	19.1	7.3	43	84	38	1.2	1.4	0.8	1.1
Pike	13,269	9,903	1,929	698	419	206	114	-	-	74.6	14.5	5.3	10	107	80	3.6	4.8	1.9	2.3
Powell	1,358	855	312	98	54	28	11	-	-	63.0	23.0	7.2	56	70	40	0.4	0.4	0.3	0.3
Pulaski	2,069	1,194	588	119	75	74	19	-	-	57.7	28.4	5.8	71	47	70	0.6	0.6	0.6	0.4
Robertson	207	109	62	12	7	16	1	-	-	52.7	30.0	5.8	95	39	67	<.1	<.1	<.1	<.1
Rockcastle	321	245	32	28	11	3	2	-	-	76.3	10.0	8.7	5	119	20	<.1	0.1	<.1	<.1
Rowan	2,460	1,334	717	191	134	54	30	-	-	54.2	29.1	7.8	86	41	29	0.7	0.6	0.7	0.6
Russell	937	628	202	42	34	22	9	-	-	67.0	21.6	4.5	38	76	100	0.3	0.3	0.2	0.1
Scott	2,034	1,008	683	205	100	21	17	-	-	49.6	33.6	10.1	104	21	11	0.5	0.5	0.7	0.7
Shelby	2,604	1,327	713	321	163	62	18	-	-	51.0	27.4	12.3	99	52	3	0.7	0.6	0.7	1.0
Simpson	787	441	224	49	45	21	7	-	-	56.0	28.5	6.2	77	45	58	0.2	0.2	0.2	0.2
Spencer	719	389	182	69	44	29	6	-	-	54.1	25.3	9.6	89	60	13	0.2	0.2	0.2	0.2
Taylor	972	690	165	64	32	14	7	-	-	71.0	17.0	6.6	25	95	52	0.3	0.3	0.2	0.2
Todd	1,760	971	533	59	116	55	26	-	-	55.2	30.3	3.4	83	37	114	0.5	0.5	0.5	0.2
Trigg	1,635	948	476	83	74	40	14	-	-	58.0	29.1	5.1	69	42	86	0.4	0.5	0.5	0.3
Trimble	553	324	156	44	19	6	4	-	-	58.6	28.2	8.0	67	49	26	0.1	0.2	0.2	0.1
Union	2,584	1,272	1,007	127	105	56	17	-	-	49.2	39.0	4.9	107	5	87	0.7	0.6	1.0	0.4
Warren	4,179	2,180	1,320	292	264	86	37	-	-	52.2	31.6	7.0	97	31	44	1.1	1.0	1.3	1.0
Washington	827	495	193	75	32	19	13	-	-	59.9	23.3	9.1	62	68	17	0.2	0.2	0.2	0.2
Wayne	683	497	114	29	18	22	3	-	-	72.8	16.7	4.2	17	96	108	0.2	0.2	0.1	<.1
Webster	2,185	1,224	695	80	114	45	27	-	-	56.0	31.8	3.7	78	27	112	0.6	0.6	0.7	0.3
Whitley	1,038	687	220	47	33	37	14	-	-	66.2	21.2	4.5	41	77	97	0.3	0.3	0.2	0.2
Wolfe	1,840	1,308	259	148	51	50	24	-	-	71.1	14.1	8.0	23	111	25	0.5	0.6	0.3	0.5
Woodford	2,647	1,046	1,175	248	124	37	17	-	-	39.5	44.4	9.4	118	3	16	0.7	0.5	1.1	0.8
KENTUCKY	**370,578**	**207,804**	**103,590**	**30,709**	**18,097**	**7,136**	**3,242**	**-**	**-**	**56.1**	**28.0**	**8.3**				**100.0**	**100.0**	**100.0**	**100.0**

Table J. — Vote for Presidential Preference: May 26, 1992, Republican Primary Election

County	Total	Bush	Uncommitted			Bush	Uncommitted			Rank Bush	Rank Uncommitted			Total	Bush	Uncommitted		
Adair	689	577	112	-	-	83.7	16.3	-	-	15	106	-	-	0.7	0.8	0.4	-	-
Allen	440	366	74	-	-	83.2	16.8	-	-	18	103	-	-	0.4	0.5	0.3	-	-
Anderson	187	148	39	-	-	79.1	20.9	-	-	40	81	-	-	0.2	0.2	0.2	-	-
Ballard	40	28	12	-	-	70.0	30.0	-	-	100	21	-	-	<.1	<.1	<.1	-	-
Barren	541	426	115	-	-	78.7	21.3	-	-	42	79	-	-	0.5	0.6	0.4	-	-
Bath	53	38	15	-	-	71.7	28.3	-	-	89	32	-	-	<.1	<.1	<.1	-	-
Bell	903	700	203	-	-	77.5	22.5	-	-	50	71	-	-	0.9	0.9	0.8	-	-
Boone	1,358	976	382	-	-	71.9	28.1	-	-	87	34	-	-	1.3	1.3	1.5	-	-
Bourbon	149	99	50	-	-	66.4	33.6	-	-	111	10	-	-	0.1	0.1	0.2	-	-
Boyd	1,716	1,239	477	-	-	72.2	27.8	-	-	85	36	-	-	1.7	1.6	1.9	-	-
Boyle	392	298	94	-	-	76.0	24.0	-	-	61	60	-	-	0.4	0.4	0.4	-	-
Bracken	71	57	14	-	-	80.3	19.7	-	-	36	85	-	-	<.1	<.1	<.1	-	-
Breathitt	92	75	17	-	-	81.5	18.5	-	-	32	89	-	-	<.1	<.1	<.1	-	-
Breckinridge	549	430	119	-	-	78.3	21.7	-	-	46	75	-	-	0.5	0.6	0.5	-	-
Bullitt	743	549	194	-	-	73.9	26.1	-	-	78	43	-	-	0.7	0.7	0.8	-	-
Butler	1,086	835	251	-	-	76.9	23.1	-	-	55	66	-	-	1.1	1.1	1.0	-	-
Caldwell	215	162	53	-	-	75.3	24.7	-	-	67	54	-	-	0.2	0.2	0.2	-	-
Calloway	227	131	96	-	-	57.7	42.3	-	-	119	2	-	-	0.2	0.2	0.4	-	-
Campbell	1,726	1,249	477	-	-	72.4	27.6	-	-	84	37	-	-	1.7	1.7	1.9	-	-
Carlisle	33	25	8	-	-	75.8	24.2	-	-	62	59	-	-	<.1	<.1	<.1	-	-
Carroll	41	29	12	-	-	70.7	29.3	-	-	96	25	-	-	<.1	<.1	<.1	-	-
Carter	678	539	139	-	-	79.5	20.5	-	-	39	82	-	-	0.7	0.7	0.5	-	-
Casey	984	821	163	-	-	83.4	16.6	-	-	17	104	-	-	1.0	1.1	0.6	-	-
Christian	433	309	124	-	-	71.4	28.6	-	-	95	26	-	-	0.4	0.4	0.5	-	-
Clark	495	314	181	-	-	63.4	36.6	-	-	115	6	-	-	0.5	0.4	0.7	-	-
Clay	2,599	2,048	551	-	-	78.8	21.2	-	-	41	80	-	-	2.6	2.7	2.1	-	-
Clinton	521	429	92	-	-	82.3	17.7	-	-	24	97	-	-	0.5	0.6	0.4	-	-
Crittenden	313	229	84	-	-	73.2	26.8	-	-	82	39	-	-	0.3	0.3	0.3	-	-
Cumberland	659	565	94	-	-	85.7	14.3	-	-	10	111	-	-	0.7	0.7	0.4	-	-
Daviess	1,042	734	308	-	-	70.4	29.6	-	-	98	23	-	-	1.0	1.0	1.2	-	-
Edmonson	425	334	91	-	-	78.6	21.4	-	-	44	77	-	-	0.4	0.4	0.4	-	-
Elliott	18	16	2	-	-	88.9	11.1	-	-	5	116	-	-	<.1	<.1	<.1	-	-
Estill	799	636	163	-	-	79.6	20.4	-	-	38	83	-	-	0.8	0.8	0.6	-	-
Fayette	6,851	4,653	2,198	-	-	67.9	32.1	-	-	105	16	-	-	6.8	6.2	8.5	-	-
Fleming	162	143	19	-	-	88.3	11.7	-	-	8	113	-	-	0.2	0.2	<.1	-	-
Floyd	495	368	127	-	-	74.3	25.7	-	-	73	48	-	-	0.5	0.5	0.5	-	-
Franklin	613	397	216	-	-	64.8	35.2	-	-	113	8	-	-	0.6	0.5	0.8	-	-
Fulton	117	96	21	-	-	82.1	17.9	-	-	25	96	-	-	0.1	0.1	<.1	-	-
Gallatin	46	38	8	-	-	82.6	17.4	-	-	21	100	-	-	<.1	<.1	<.1	-	-
Garrard	453	355	98	-	-	78.4	21.6	-	-	45	76	-	-	0.4	0.5	0.4	-	-
Grant	113	81	32	-	-	71.7	28.3	-	-	90	31	-	-	0.1	0.1	0.1	-	-
Graves	184	139	45	-	-	75.5	24.5	-	-	63	58	-	-	0.2	0.2	0.2	-	-
Grayson	972	794	178	-	-	81.7	18.3	-	-	30	91	-	-	1.0	1.1	0.7	-	-
Green	424	387	37	-	-	91.3	8.7	-	-	1	120	-	-	0.4	0.5	0.1	-	-
Greenup	871	657	214	-	-	75.4	24.6	-	-	65	56	-	-	0.9	0.9	0.8	-	-
Hancock	186	145	41	-	-	78.0	22.0	-	-	49	72	-	-	0.2	0.2	0.2	-	-
Hardin	1,653	1,216	437	-	-	73.6	26.4	-	-	79	42	-	-	1.6	1.6	1.7	-	-
Harlan	1,028	762	266	-	-	74.1	25.9	-	-	77	44	-	-	1.0	1.0	1.0	-	-
Harrison	127	93	34	-	-	73.2	26.8	-	-	81	40	-	-	0.1	0.1	0.1	-	-
Hart	241	215	26	-	-	89.2	10.8	-	-	4	117	-	-	0.2	0.3	0.1	-	-
Henderson	502	324	178	-	-	64.5	35.5	-	-	114	7	-	-	0.5	0.4	0.7	-	-
Henry	63	51	12	-	-	81.0	19.0	-	-	33	88	-	-	<.1	<.1	<.1	-	-
Hickman	25	21	4	-	-	84.0	16.0	-	-	14	107	-	-	<.1	<.1	<.1	-	-
Hopkins	336	235	101	-	-	69.9	30.1	-	-	101	20	-	-	0.3	0.3	0.4	-	-
Jackson	921	785	136	-	-	85.2	14.8	-	-	12	109	-	-	0.9	1.0	0.5	-	-
Jefferson	24,122	17,634	6,488	-	- .	73.1	26.9	-	-	83	38	-	-	23.9	23.4	25.2	-	-
Jessamine	563	429	134	-	-	76.2	23.8	-	-	60	61	-	-	0.6	0.6	0.5	-	-
Johnson	1,588	1,165	423	-	-	73.4	26.6	-	-	80	41	-	-	1.6	1.5	1.6	-	-
Kenton	2,179	1,573	606	-	-	72.2	27.8	-	-	86	35	-	-	2.2	2.1	2.4	-	-
Knott	44	36	8	-	-	81.8	18.2	-	-	28	92	-	-	<.1	<.1	<.1	-	-
Knox	1,835	1,402	433	-	-	76.4	23.6	-	-	59	62	-	-	1.8	1.9	1.7	-	-
Larue	125	93	32	-	-	74.4	25.6	-	-	72	49	-	-	0.1	0.1	0.1	-	-
Laurel	3,396	2,428	968	-	-	71.5	28.5	-	-	93	28	-	-	3.4	3.2	3.8	-	-
Lawrence	583	493	90	-	-	84.6	15.4	-	-	13	108	-	-	0.6	0.7	0.3	-	-
Lee	634	519	115	-	-	81.9	18.1	-	-	27	94	-	-	0.6	0.7	0.4	-	-
Leslie	1,004	784	220	-	-	78.1	21.9	-	-	48	73	-	-	1.0	1.0	0.9	-	-
Letcher	869	671	198	-	-	77.2	22.8	-	-	53	68	-	-	0.9	0.9	0.8	-	-
Lewis	550	449	101	-	-	81.6	18.4	-	-	31	90	-	-	0.5	0.6	0.4	-	-
Lincoln	412	330	82	-	-	80.1	19.9	-	-	37	84	-	-	0.4	0.4	0.3	-	-
Livingston	72	54	18	-	-	75.0	25.0	-	-	68	53	-	-	<.1	<.1	<.1	-	-

Table J. — Vote for Presidential Preference: May 26, 1992, Republican Primary Election (cont)

County	Top candidates					Top four candidates (state vote)									Percent contribution to state vote				
						Percent of total vote				Rank									
	Total	Bush	Uncom-mitted			Bush	Uncom-mitted			Bush	Uncom-mitted			Total	Bush	Uncom-mitted		
Logan	195	147	48	-	-	75.4	24.6	-	-	66	55	-	-	0.2	0.2	0.2	-	-
Lyon	57	38	19	-	-	66.7	33.3	-	-	109	11	-	-	<.1	<.1	<.1	-	-
McCracken	737	500	237	-	-	67.8	32.2	-	-	106	15	-	-	0.7	0.7	0.9	-	-
McCreary	1,936	1,514	422	-	-	78.2	21.8	-	-	47	74	-	-	1.9	2.0	1.6	-	-
McLean	101	71	30	-	-	70.3	29.7	-	-	99	22	-	-	<.1	<.1	0.1	-	-
Madison	847	631	216	-	-	74.5	25.5	-	-	71	50	-	-	0.8	0.8	0.8	-	-
Magoffin	377	334	43	-	-	88.6	11.4	-	-	6	115	-	-	0.4	0.4	0.2	-	-
Marion	51	34	17	-	-	66.7	33.3	-	-	110	12	-	-	<.1	<.1	<.1	-	-
Marshall	247	168	79	-	-	68.0	32.0	-	-	104	17	-	-	0.2	0.2	0.3	-	-
Martin	918	657	261	-	-	71.6	28.4	-	-	91	30	-	-	0.9	0.9	1.0	-	-
Mason	175	134	41	-	-	76.6	23.4	-	-	56	65	-	-	0.2	0.2	0.2	-	-
Meade	251	192	59	-	-	76.5	23.5	-	-	57	64	-	-	0.2	0.3	0.2	-	-
Menifee	41	28	13	-	-	68.3	31.7	-	-	102	19	-	-	<.1	<.1	<.1	-	-
Mercer	284	217	67	-	-	76.4	23.6	-	-	58	63	-	-	0.3	0.3	0.3	-	-
Metcalfe	219	197	22	-	-	90.0	10.0	-	-	3	118	-	-	0.2	0.3	<.1	-	-
Monroe	486	382	104	-	-	78.6	21.4	-	-	43	78	-	-	0.5	0.5	0.4	-	-
Montgomery	151	108	43	-	-	71.5	28.5	-	-	92	29	-	-	0.1	0.1	0.2	-	-
Morgan	74	61	13	-	-	82.4	17.6	-	-	22	99	-	-	<.1	<.1	<.1	-	-
Muhlenberg	399	296	103	-	-	74.2	25.8	-	-	76	45	-	-	0.4	0.4	0.4	-	-
Nelson	201	142	59	-	-	70.6	29.4	-	-	97	24	-	-	0.2	0.2	0.2	-	-
Nicholas	35	27	8	-	-	77.1	22.9	-	-	54	67	-	-	<.1	<.1	<.1	-	-
Ohio	1,067	727	340	-	-	68.1	31.9	-	-	103	18	-	-	1.1	1.0	1.3	-	-
Oldham	1,003	717	286	-	-	71.5	28.5	-	-	94	27	-	-	1.0	1.0	1.1	-	-
Owen	68	41	27	-	-	60.3	39.7	-	-	118	3	-	-	<.1	<.1	0.1	-	-
Owsley	672	540	132	-	-	80.4	19.6	-	-	34	87	-	-	0.7	0.7	0.5	-	-
Pendleton	99	74	25	-	-	74.7	25.3	-	-	70	51	-	-	<.1	<.1	<.1	-	-
Perry	934	724	210	-	-	77.5	22.5	-	-	51	70	-	-	0.9	1.0	0.8	-	-
Pike	1,538	1,271	267	-	-	82.6	17.4	-	-	20	101	-	-	1.5	1.7	1.0	-	-
Powell	242	198	44	-	-	81.8	18.2	-	-	29	93	-	-	0.2	0.3	0.2	-	-
Pulaski	3,476	2,580	896	-	-	74.2	25.8	-	-	75	46	-	-	3.4	3.4	3.5	-	-
Robertson	26	23	3	-	-	88.5	11.5	-	-	7	114	-	-	<.1	<.1	<.1	-	-
Rockcastle	607	502	105	-	-	82.7	17.3	-	-	19	102	-	-	0.6	0.7	0.4	-	-
Rowan	581	435	146	-	-	74.9	25.1	-	-	69	52	-	-	0.6	0.6	0.6	-	-
Russell	1,195	1,000	195	-	-	83.7	16.3	-	-	16	105	-	-	1.2	1.3	0.8	-	-
Scott	225	149	76	-	-	66.2	33.8	-	-	112	9	-	-	0.2	0.2	0.3	-	-
Shelby	253	191	62	-	-	75.5	24.5	-	-	64	57	-	-	0.3	0.3	0.2	-	-
Simpson	66	53	13	-	-	80.3	19.7	-	-	35	86	-	-	<.1	<.1	<.1	-	-
Spencer	62	48	14	-	-	77.4	22.6	-	-	52	69	-	-	<.1	<.1	<.1	-	-
Taylor	652	534	118	-	-	81.9	18.1	-	-	26	95	-	-	0.6	0.7	0.5	-	-
Todd	41	25	16	-	-	61.0	39.0	-	-	117	4	-	-	<.1	<.1	<.1	-	-
Trigg	77	47	30	-	-	61.0	39.0	-	-	116	5	-	-	<.1	<.1	0.1	-	-
Trimble	28	24	4	-	-	85.7	14.3	-	-	11	110	-	-	<.1	<.1	<.1	-	-
Union	58	29	29	-	-	50.0	50.0	-	-	120	1	-	-	<.1	<.1	0.1	-	-
Warren	918	682	236	-	-	74.3	25.7	-	-	74	47	-	-	0.9	0.9	0.9	-	-
Washington	136	112	24	-	-	82.4	17.6	-	-	23	98	-	-	0.1	0.1	<.1	-	-
Wayne	697	607	90	-	-	87.1	12.9	-	-	9	112	-	-	0.7	0.8	0.3	-	-
Webster	78	56	22	-	-	71.8	28.2	-	-	88	33	-	-	<.1	<.1	<.1	-	-
Whitley	3,516	2,358	1,158	-	-	67.1	32.9	-	-	108	13	-	-	3.5	3.1	4.5	-	-
Wolfe	77	70	7	-	-	90.9	9.1	-	-	2	119	-	-	<.1	<.1	<.1	-	-
Woodford	369	250	119	-	-	67.8	32.2	-	-	107	14	-	-	0.4	0.3	0.5	-	-
KENTUCKY	101,119	75,371	25,748	-	-	74.5	25.5	-	-					100.0	100.0	100.0	-	-

1992 Vote for President
Percent for Clinton (D), by County

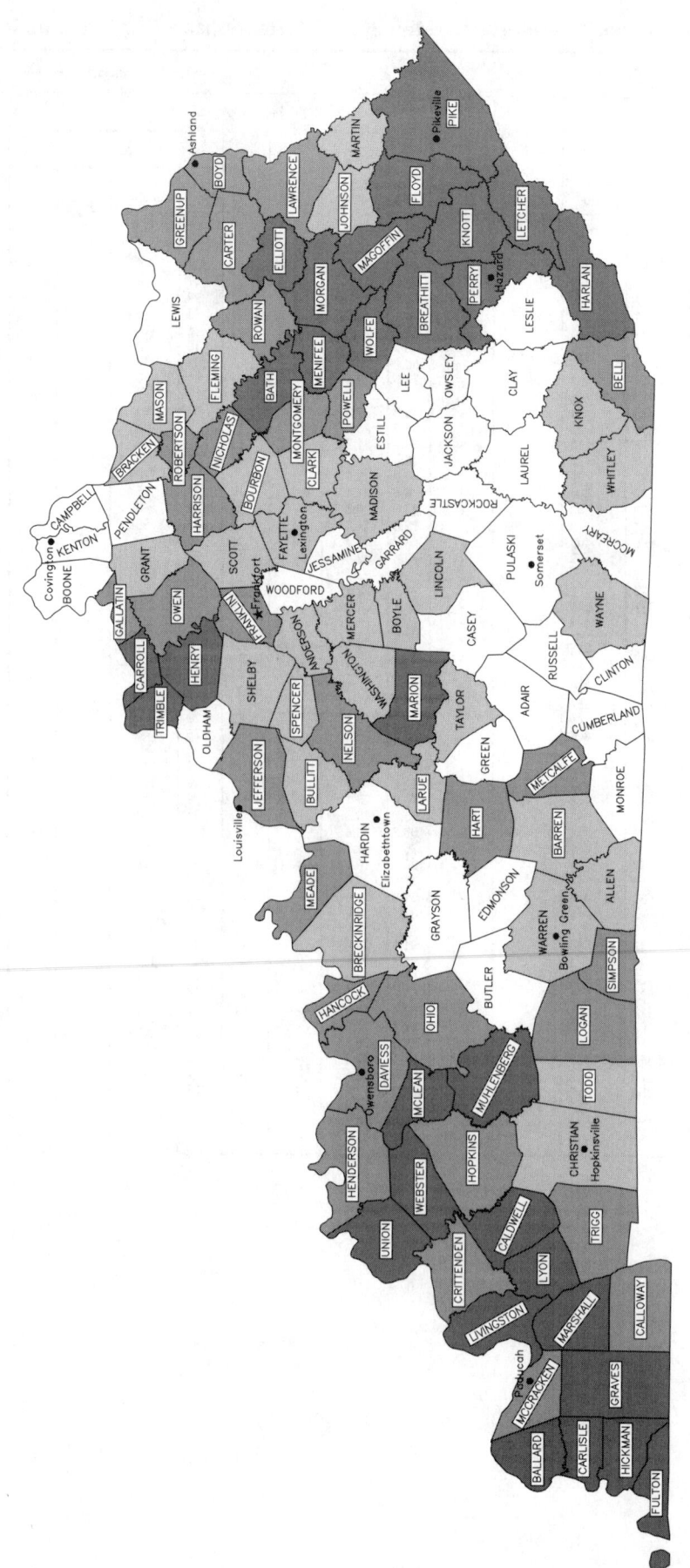

Clinton (D) received 44.6% statewide.

A framed county name indicates
a county carried by the winner.

51.4% to 75.1%
44.5% to 51.3%
37.4% to 44.4%
17.1% to 37.3%

384 Kentucky

1992 Vote for U.S. Senator
Percent for Ford (D), by County

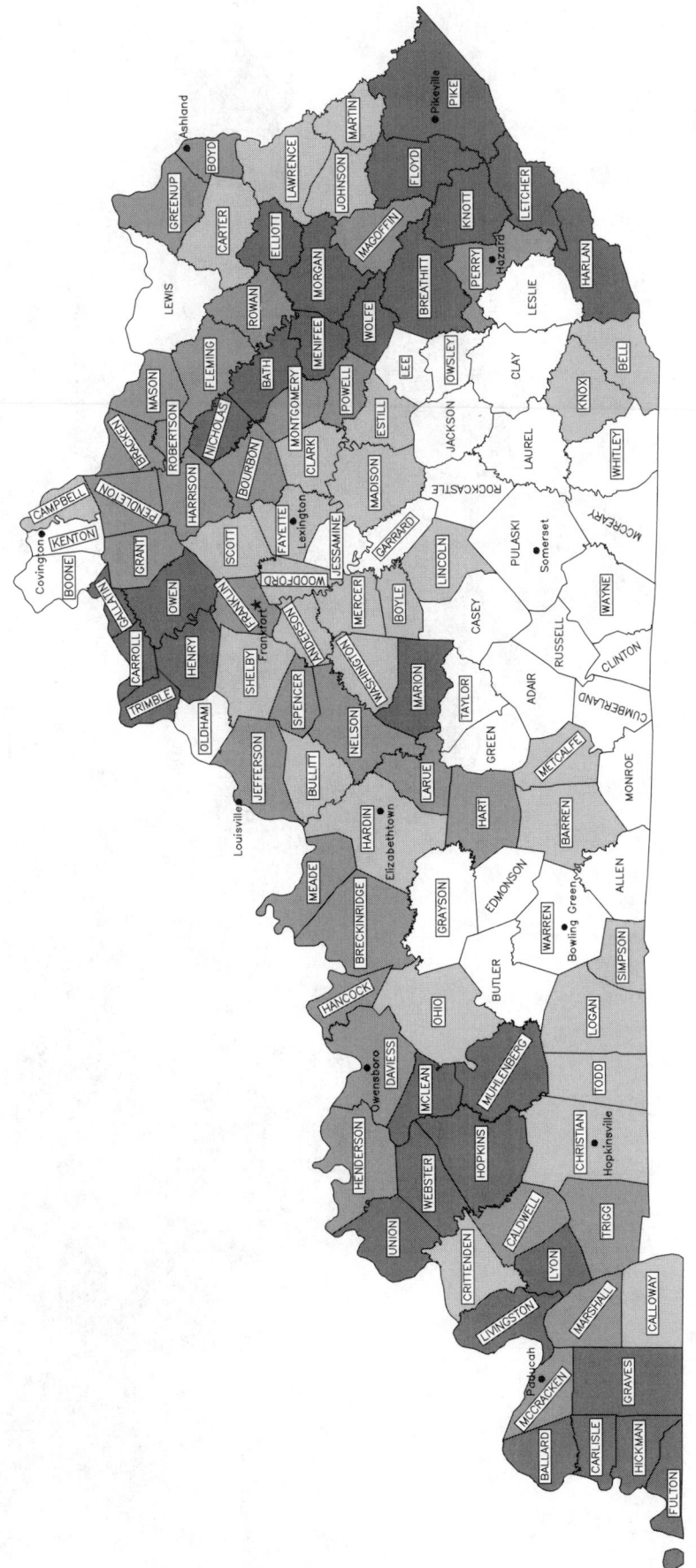

Ford (D) received 62.9% statewide.

A framed county name indicates
a county carried by the winner.

- 73.0% to 86.9%
- 65.0% to 72.9%
- 55.1% to 64.9%
- 28.2% to 55.0%

Copyright © 1993 by Election Data Services, Inc.

Kentucky 385

1991 Vote for Governor
Percent for Jones (D), by County

Jones (D) received 64.7% statewide.

A framed county name indicates a county carried by the winner.

Legend:
- 72.3% to 87.7%
- 65.1% to 72.2%
- 58.1% to 65.0%
- 34.7% to 58.0%

PIKE · Pikeville
MARTIN
BOYD · Ashland
GREENUP
CARTER
LAWRENCE
JOHNSON
FLOYD
KNOTT
LETCHER
ELLIOTT
MORGAN
MAGOFFIN
BREATHITT
PERRY · Hazard
HARLAN
LEWIS
ROWAN
MENIFEE
WOLFE
LESLIE
FLEMING
BATH
POWELL
LEE
OWSLEY
CLAY
BELL
MASON
MONTGOMERY
ESTILL
KNOX
BRACKEN
NICHOLAS
CLARK
MADISON
JACKSON
LAUREL
WHITLEY
ROBERTSON
BOURBON
ROCKCASTLE
HARRISON
FAYETTE · Lexington
JESSAMINE
GARRARD
PULASKI · Somerset
MCCREARY
CAMPBELL
PENDLETON
SCOTT
Frankfort
LINCOLN
WAYNE
KENTON
Covington
GRANT
WOODFORD
BOYLE
CASEY
BOONE
FRANKLIN
MERCER
RUSSELL
CLINTON
CALLATIN
OWEN
ANDERSON
WASHINGTON
ADAIR
CARROLL
HENRY
SHELBY
SPENCER
MARION
TAYLOR
GREEN
CUMBERLAND
TRIMBLE
NELSON
LARUE
METCALFE
MONROE
OLDHAM
BULLITT
JEFFERSON
Louisville
HART
BARREN
MEADE
HARDIN · Elizabethtown
ALLEN
BRECKINRIDGE
GRAYSON
EDMONSON
WARREN · Bowling Green
SIMPSON
BUTLER
HANCOCK
OHIO
LOGAN
DAVIESS · Owensboro
MCLEAN
MUHLENBERG
TODD
CHRISTIAN · Hopkinsville
HENDERSON
HOPKINS
WEBSTER
UNION
CALDWELL
TRIGG
CRITTENDEN
LYON
LIVINGSTON
MARSHALL
CALLOWAY
BALLARD
MCCRACKEN · Paducah
GRAVES
CARLISLE
HICKMAN
FULTON

LOUISIANA

Population Statistics 1990

Race/ Ethnicity	Total Population		Voting Age Population		Voting Age Population % of total population
	Number	%	Number	%	
Non-Hispanic					
White	2,776,022	65.8	2,058,777	68.8	74.2
Black	1,291,470	30.6	828,866	27.7	64.2
Asian/Pacific Islander	39,302	0.9	25,731	0.9	65.5
Native American	17,539	0.4	11,376	0.4	64.9
Other	2,596	<0.1	1,712	<0.1	65.9
All Hispanic	93,044	2.2	66,242	2.2	71.2
TOTAL	4,219,973	100.0	2,992,704	100.0	70.9

Voting Equipment Use (Parishes)

Datavote Punch Card	0	Paper Ballot	0
Electronic	2	Other Punch Card	0
Lever Machine	62	Mixed Systems	0
Optical Scanner	0		

Party Control	DEM	REP	IND	VAC
1993 State Senate	33	6	0	0
1992 State Senate	34	5	0	0
1993 State House	88	16	1	0
1992 State House	88	16	1	0

Estimated Voting Age Population 1992 (VAP) 2,992,000
Number of Registered Voters.................................. 2,292,129
    % of estimated VAP... 76.6
Voter Turnout (Maximum Vote)[1]........................... 1,800,641
    % of VAP 60.2
    % of Registration 78.6
Persons Not Voting—of Voting Age 1,191,359
    % of VAP 39.8
Persons Not Voting—of Registered 491,488
    % of Registration 21.4
Straight Ticket Voting .... No

State Officials and Members of Congress

Governor:
Edwin Edwards (D) 1971, elected to a four-year term in 1991.

U.S. Senators:
J. Bennett Johnston (D) 1972, elected to a six-year term in 1990.
John B. Breaux (D) 1986, elected to a six-year term in 1992.

U.S. Representative in Congress:
(District, Name, Party, Date first elected)

1. Livingston (R) 1977
2. Jefferson (D) 1990
3. Tauzin (D) 1980
4. Fields (D) 1992
5. McCrery (R) 1988
6. Baker (R) 1986
7. Hayes (D) 1986

[1]Maximum vote turnout from Table C exceeds reported statewide actual voter turnout because in one or more counties the vote for highest office is greater than reported actual turnout.

Candidates: General Election, November 3, 1992

Candidate(s)	Total vote	Percent	Party	Status	First elected
President/Vice President					
Clinton/Gore	815,971	45.58%	Democrat	Challenger	1992
Bush/Quayle	733,386	40.97%	Republican	Incumbent	1988
Perot/Stockdale	211,478	11.81%	Prudence Action Res.	Challenger	
Gritz/Minett	18,545	1.04%	America First	Challenger	
Marrou/Lord	3,155	0.18%	Libertarian	Challenger	
Daniels/Tupahache	1,663	0.09%	Equal Justice & Opp.	Challenger	
Phillips/Graves	1,552	0.09%	Taxpayers	Challenger	
Fulani/Munoz	1,434	0.08%	More Perfect Dem.	Challenger	
LaRouche/Bevel	1,136	0.06%	Just. Industry Agric.	Challenger	
Hagelin/Tompkins	889	0.05%	Natural Law	Challenger	
Yiamouyiannis/McCone	808	0.05%	Independent	Challenger	
U.S. Senator (Primary Election, October 3, 1992)[1]					
John B. Breaux	616,021	73.07%	Democrat	Incumbent	1986
Jon Khachaturian	74,785	8.87%	Independent	Challenger	
Lyle Stockstill	69,986	8.30%	Republican	Challenger	
Nick Joseph Accardo	45,839	5.44%	Democrat	Challenger	
Fred Strong	36,406	4.32%	Republican	Challenger	
Governor (General Election, November 16, 1991)					
Edwin Edwards	1,057,031	61.17%	Democrat	Challenger	1991
David Duke	671,009	38.83%	Republican	Challenger	
U.S. Representative in Congress					
District 1: (Primary Election, October 3, 1992)[1]					
Robert Livingston	83,685	72.74%	Republican	Incumbent	1977
Anne Thompson	11,620	10.10%	Republican	Challenger	
Vincent Bruno	7,874	6.84%	Republican	Challenger	
Richie Martin	4,789	4.16%	Republican	Challenger	
Jules Hillery	4,442	3.86%	Independent	Challenger	
Greg Reinhard	2,641	2.30%	Independent	Challenger	
District 2: (Primary Election, October 3, 1992)[1]					
William Jefferson	67,030	73.46%	Democrat	Incumbent	1990
Wilma Irvin	14,121	15.48%	Democrat	Challenger	
Roger Johnson	10,090	11.06%	Independent	Challenger	
District 3: (Primary Election, October 3, 1992)[1]					
Billy Tauzin	82,047	81.68%	Democrat	Incumbent	1980
Paul Boynton	18,402	18.32%	Republican	Challenger	
District 4					
Cleo Fields	143,980	73.90%	Democrat	Challenger	1992
Charles Jones	50,851	26.10%	Democrat	Challenger	
District 5					
Jim McCrery	153,501	63.02%	Republican	Incumbent	1988
Jerry Huckaby	90,079	36.98%	Democrat	Incumbent	1976
District 6					
Richard Baker	123,953	50.56%	Republican	Incumbent	1986
Clyde Holloway	121,225	49.44%	Republican	Incumbent	1986
District 7: (Primary Election, October 3, 1992)[1]					
James Hayes	84,149	73.04%	Democrat	Incumbent	1986
Fredric Hayes	23,870	20.72%	Republican	Challenger	
Robert Nain	7,184	6.24%	Republican	Challenger	

[1] Winning candidate elected from primary election received more than 50 percent of vote.

Candidates: March 10, 1992, Primary Election

Candidate	Total vote	Percent	Candidate	Total vote	Percent
Presidential Preference, Democratic			**Presidential Preference, Republican**		
Bill Clinton	267,002	69.46%	George Bush	83,744	61.98%
Paul Tsongas	42,508	11.06%	Patrick Buchanan	36,525	27.03%
Jerry Brown	25,480	6.63%	David Duke	11,955	8.85%
Eugene McCarthy	15,129	3.94%	Pat Paulsen	1,186	0.88%
Charles Woods	8,989	2.34%	Tennie Rogers	1,111	0.82%
Stephen Burke	4,294	1.12%	George Zimmermann	474	0.35%
Tom Harkin	4,033	1.05%	Thomas Fabish	114	0.08%
Larry Agran	3,511	0.91%			
Lyndon LaRouche, Jr.	3,082	0.80%			
Bob Kerrey	2,984	0.78%			
Jeffrey Marsh	2,120	0.55%			
Tom Laughlin	1,857	0.48%			
Tom Hawks	1,469	0.38%			
Ray Rollinson	1,069	0.28%			
J. Louis McAlpine	870	0.23%			

Voter Registration and Turnout, 1948-1992 Elections

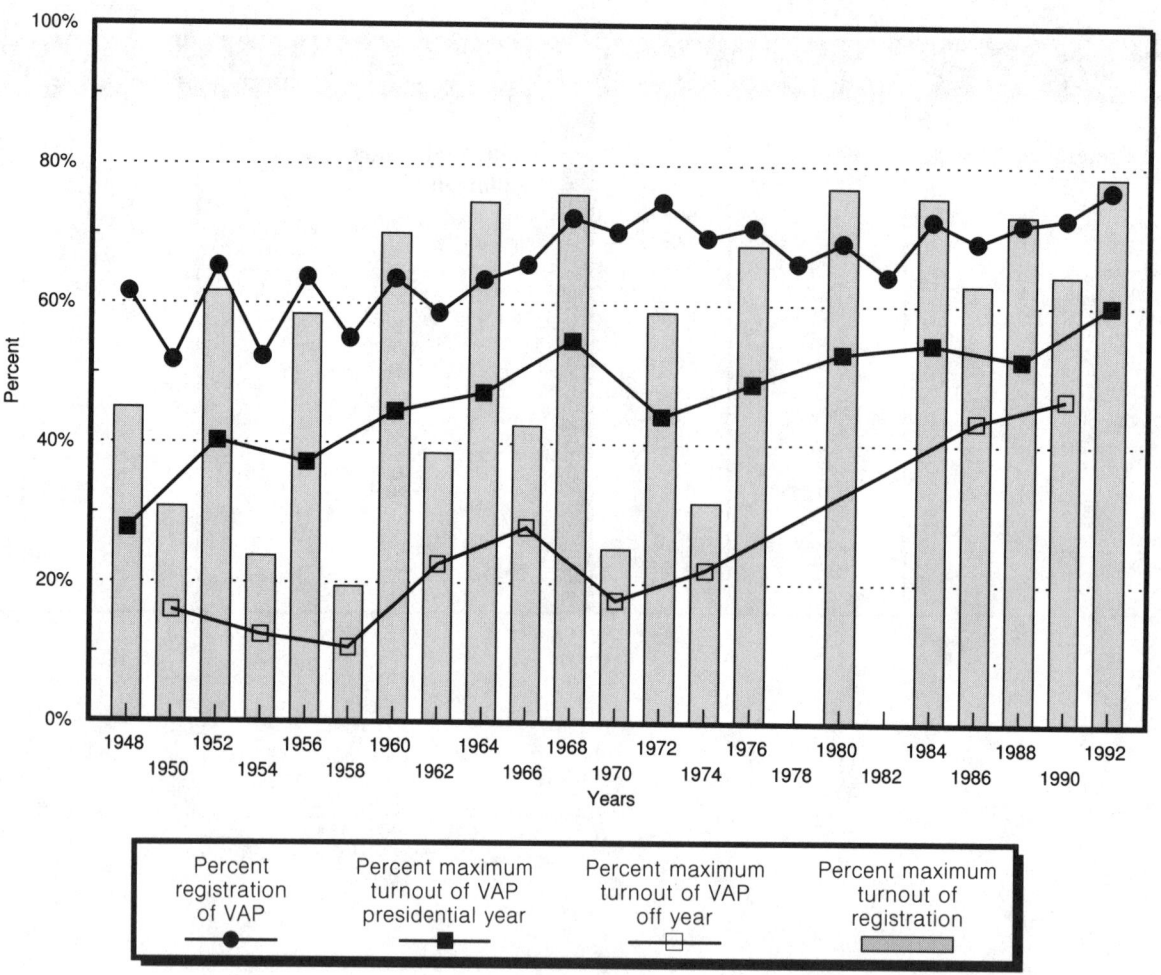

Legend:
- Percent registration of VAP (line with filled circles)
- Percent maximum turnout of VAP presidential year (line with filled squares)
- Percent maximum turnout of VAP off year (line with open squares)
- Percent maximum turnout of registration (bars)

Year	Estimated Voting Age Population (VAP)	Voter registration (REG)			Actual	Voter turnout										
						Highest office						Maximum vote				
		Total	Percent of VAP	Rank by percent of VAP		Total	Office	Percent total REG	Rank by percent of REG	Percent of VAP	Rank by percent of VAP	Total	Percent total REG	Rank by percent of REG	Percent total VAP	Rank by percent of VAP
1992.......	2,992,000	2,292,129	76.6	22	1,799,596	1,790,017	P	78.1	22	59.8	24	1,799,596	78.5	25	60.1	26
1990[1]	2,988,000	2,169,222	72.6	16	-	1,396,113	S	64.4	10	46.7	14	1,396,113	64.4	13	46.7	14
1988.......	3,112,000	2,231,857	71.7	23	-	1,628,202	P	73.0	20	52.3	27	1,628,202	73.0	25	52.3	28
1986.......	3,153,000	2,179,317	69.1	25	-	1,369,897	S	62.9	10	43.4	14	1,369,897	62.9	12	43.4	17
1984.......	3,131,000	2,262,101	72.2	27	-	1,706,822	P	75.5	19	54.5	27	1,706,822	75.5	22	54.5	29
1982.......	3,063,000	1,965,422	64.2	35	-	-	-	-	-	-	-	-	-	-	-	-
1980.......	2,919,000	2,015,402	69.0	32	-	1,548,591	P	76.8	15	53.1	29	1,548,591	76.8	22	53.1	29
1978.......	2,760,000	1,821,026	66.0	33	-	-	-	-	-	-	-	-	-	-	-	-
1976.......	2,623,000	1,866,117	71.1	30	-	1,278,439	P	68.5	39	48.7	37	1,278,439	68.5	39	48.7	39
1974.......	2,480,000	1,726,693	69.6	28	-	546,042	C	31.6	46	22.0	48	546,042	31.6	46	22.0	48
1972.......	2,389,000	1,784,890	74.7	23	-	1,051,491	P	58.9	44	44.0	45	1,051,491	58.9	44	44.0	45
1970.......	2,058,000	1,449,332	70.4	29	-	507,507	C	35.0	43	24.7	49	363,048	25.0	45	17.6	50
1968.......	2,002,000	1,449,231	72.4	28	-	1,097,450	P	75.7	34	54.8	34	1,097,450	75.7	34	54.8	35
1966.......	1,950,000	1,281,181	65.7	32	-	546,258	C	42.6	41	28.0	49	546,258	42.6	41	28.0	49
1964.......	1,894,000	1,201,785	63.5	32	-	896,293	P	74.6	31	47.3	43	896,293	74.6	31	47.3	43
1962.......	1,859,000	1,091,808	58.7	30	-	421,904	S	38.6	35	22.7	46	421,904	38.6	35	22.7	46
1960.......	1,813,000	1,152,398	63.6	26	-	807,891	P	70.1	32	44.6	42	807,891	70.1	32	44.6	43
1958.......	1,707,000	938,942	55.0	27	-	182,124	C	19.4	29	10.7	45	182,124	19.4	29	10.7	45
1956.......	1,659,000	1,057,687	63.8	23	-	617,544	P	58.4	27	37.2	43	617,544	58.4	27	37.2	43
1954.......	1,663,000	871,635	52.4	24	-	207,115	S	23.8	26	12.5	47	207,115	23.8	26	12.5	47
1952.......	1,619,000	1,056,720	65.3	19	-	651,952	P	61.7	23	40.3	42	651,952	61.7	23	40.3	42
1950.......	1,578,000	818,031	51.8	19	-	251,838	S	30.8	20	16.0	41	251,838	30.8	20	16.0	41
1948.......	1,502,000	924,705	61.6	18	-	416,336	P	45.0	21	27.7	41	416,336	45.0	21	27.7	41

[1]Highest office voter turnout is U.S. Senate contest from October 6, 1990, primary election; winning candidate elected from primary election received more than 50 percent of vote.

LOUISIANA

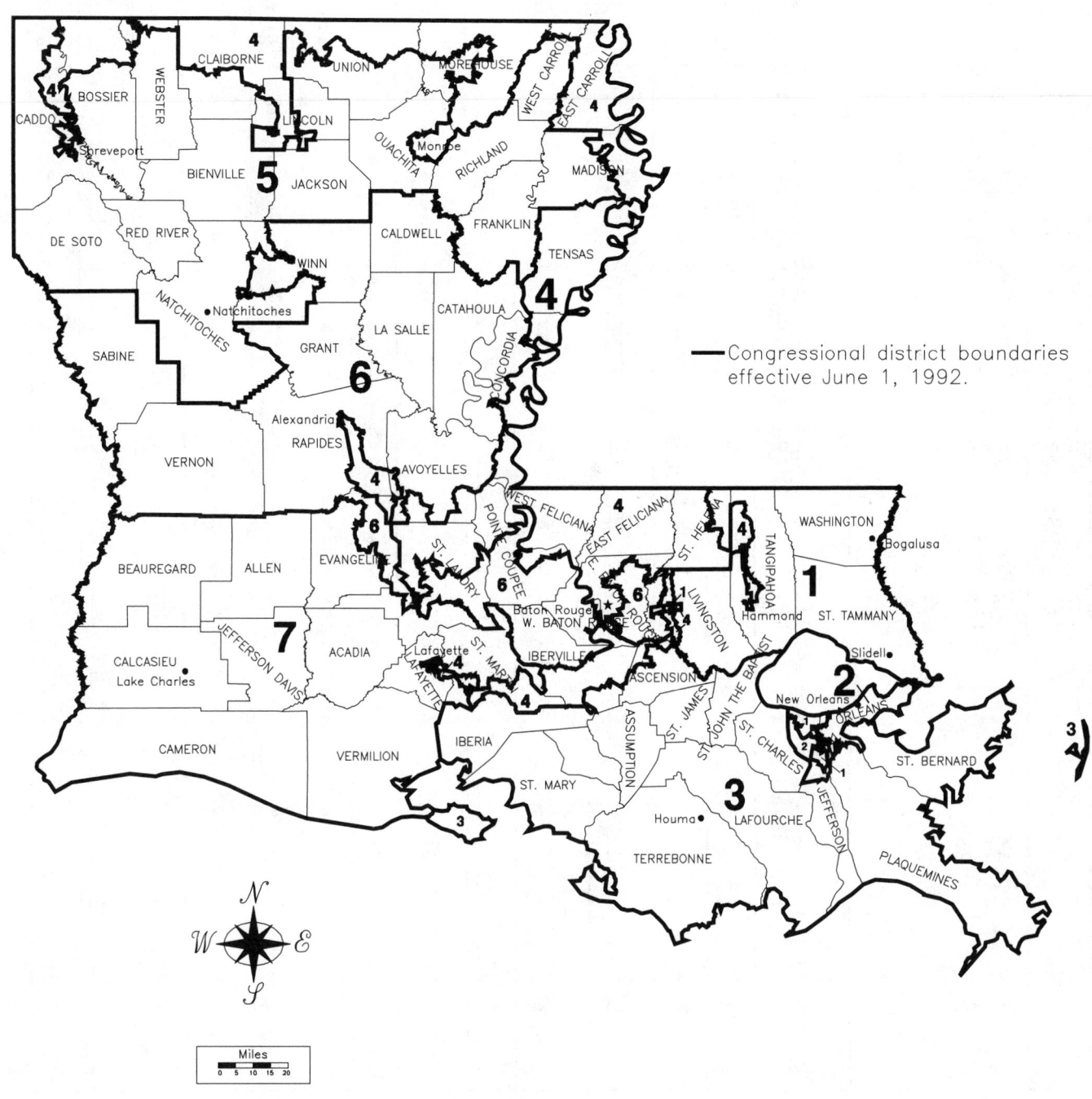

Congressional district boundaries effective June 1, 1992.

Table A. — 1990 Population by Race and Ethnic Origin

State/ county code	Parish	Total persons	Percent of total persons						Rank				Percent contribution to state population			
			White	Black	Asian and Pacific Islander	Native American	Other	Hispanic	Total	White	Black	Hispanic	Total	White	Black	Hispanic
			Non-Hispanic							Non-Hispanic				Non-Hispanic		
										Percent of total persons						
22 001	Acadia	55,882	81.0	18.1	0.1	<.1	<.1	0.7	21	11	50	48	1.3	1.6	0.8	0.4
22 003	Allen	21,226	74.6	20.7	0.2	1.3	<.1	3.2	42	20	46	6	0.5	0.6	0.3	0.7
22 005	Ascension	58,214	75.3	22.7	0.3	0.1	<.1	1.6	19	18	44	16	1.4	1.6	1.0	1.0
22 007	Assumption	22,753	66.1	32.1	0.3	0.2	<.1	1.3	38	38	26	27	0.5	0.5	0.6	0.3
22 009	Avoyelles	39,159	71.2	26.8	0.1	0.3	<.1	1.6	29	26	38	17	0.9	1.0	0.8	0.7
22 011	Beauregard	30,083	83.0	14.8	0.4	0.4	<.1	1.4	35	9	56	25	0.7	0.9	0.3	0.4
22 013	Bienville	15,979	55.9	43.4	<.1	0.1	<.1	0.5	52	53	12	59	0.4	0.3	0.5	<.1
22 015	Bossier	86,088	76.4	20.1	1.0	0.3	<.1	2.1	11	15	48	11	2.0	2.4	1.3	1.9
22 017	Caddo	248,253	58.4	39.9	0.4	0.2	<.1	1.0	4	50	16	35	5.9	5.2	7.7	2.8
22 019	Calcasieu	168,134	75.5	22.8	0.3	0.2	0.1	1.1	5	17	43	33	4.0	4.6	3.0	2.0
22 021	Caldwell	9,810	80.2	17.9	0.1	<.1	<.1	1.6	60	12	51	15	0.2	0.3	0.1	0.2
22 023	Cameron	9,260	92.7	5.4	0.2	0.2	<.1	1.5	63	2	63	20	0.2	0.3	<.1	0.2
22 025	Catahoula	11,065	73.2	25.9	<.1	0.1	0.0	0.6	58	22	40	52	0.3	0.3	0.2	<.1
22 027	Claiborne	17,405	53.4	46.1	<.1	0.2	<.1	0.2	50	55	9	64	0.4	0.3	0.6	<.1
22 029	Concordia	20,828	62.8	36.3	0.1	0.1	<.1	0.6	44	41	21	53	0.5	0.5	0.6	0.1
22 031	De Soto	25,346	54.4	43.8	<.1	0.2	<.1	1.5	37	54	11	22	0.6	0.5	0.9	0.4
22 033	East Baton Rouge	380,105	62.2	34.7	1.4	0.2	<.1	1.5	3	44	24	21	9.0	8.5	10.2	6.2
22 035	East Carroll	9,709	33.9	64.6	0.2	<.1	0.0	1.2	61	63	1	28	0.2	0.1	0.5	0.1
22 037	East Feliciana	19,211	51.8	47.0	0.1	0.1	0.0	1.0	48	56	8	37	0.5	0.4	0.7	0.2
22 039	Evangeline	33,274	72.8	26.0	0.1	<.1	0.2	0.8	31	24	39	45	0.8	0.9	0.7	0.3
22 041	Franklin	22,387	67.9	31.3	0.1	0.1	0.0	0.5	41	34	29	57	0.5	0.5	0.5	0.1
22 043	Grant	17,526	84.1	14.4	0.2	0.4	<.1	0.9	49	6	57	42	0.4	0.5	0.2	0.2
22 045	Iberia	68,297	67.5	29.2	1.1	0.2	0.1	1.9	16	37	33	13	1.6	1.7	1.5	1.4
22 047	Iberville	31,049	51.6	46.1	0.1	0.2	<.1	1.9	33	57	10	14	0.7	0.6	1.1	0.6
22 049	Jackson	15,705	70.2	29.2	0.1	0.1	<.1	0.3	53	29	34	63	0.4	0.4	0.4	<.1
22 051	Jefferson	448,306	74.0	17.5	2.2	0.4	<.1	5.9	2	21	53	2	10.6	12.0	6.1	28.6
22 053	Jefferson Davis	30,722	80.0	18.9	0.1	0.2	<.1	0.7	34	13	49	49	0.7	0.9	0.4	0.2
22 055	Lafayette	164,762	74.9	22.2	0.9	0.2	<.1	1.6	6	19	45	18	3.9	4.4	2.8	2.8
22 057	Lafourche	85,860	83.2	12.4	0.7	2.2	<.1	1.5	12	8	59	23	2.0	2.6	0.8	1.3
22 059	La Salle	13,662	89.6	9.2	0.3	0.6	0.0	0.3	54	3	61	62	0.3	0.4	<.1	<.1
22 061	Lincoln	41,745	58.5	39.6	0.8	<.1	<.1	0.9	27	49	17	40	1.0	0.9	1.3	0.4
22 063	Livingston	70,526	93.1	5.5	0.2	0.2	<.1	0.9	15	1	62	41	1.7	2.4	0.3	0.7
22 065	Madison	12,463	39.5	59.3	<.1	0.1	<.1	1.0	56	62	3	36	0.3	0.2	0.6	0.1
22 067	Morehouse	31,938	58.0	41.4	0.1	<.1	0.0	0.4	32	51	13	61	0.8	0.7	1.0	0.1
22 069	Natchitoches	36,689	60.1	37.4	0.4	0.4	0.4	1.3	30	47	19	26	0.9	0.8	1.1	0.5
22 071	Orleans	496,938	33.1	61.4	1.8	0.1	0.1	3.5	1	64	2	5	11.8	5.9	23.6	18.5
22 073	Ouachita	142,191	67.5	30.9	0.5	0.2	<.1	0.8	8	36	30	44	3.4	3.5	3.4	1.3
22 075	Plaquemines	25,575	70.7	23.1	1.9	1.8	0.2	2.3	36	28	42	9	0.6	0.7	0.5	0.6
22 077	Pointe Coupee	22,540	58.0	41.0	<.1	0.1	<.1	0.7	40	52	14	47	0.5	0.5	0.7	0.2
22 079	Rapides	131,556	69.9	27.9	0.7	0.4	<.1	1.2	9	31	36	30	3.1	3.3	2.8	1.6
22 081	Red River	9,387	60.9	38.2	<.1	0.2	0.0	0.6	62	46	18	50	0.2	0.2	0.3	<.1
22 083	Richland	20,629	62.6	36.3	<.1	<.1	<.1	1.0	46	43	20	38	0.5	0.5	0.6	0.2
22 085	Sabine	22,646	75.7	17.5	0.1	2.1	<.1	4.6	39	16	52	4	0.5	0.6	0.3	1.1
22 087	St. Bernard	66,631	87.7	4.6	0.9	0.5	<.1	6.3	17	4	64	1	1.6	2.1	0.2	4.5
22 089	St. Charles	42,437	72.8	24.0	0.4	0.3	<.1	2.5	25	23	41	7	1.0	1.1	0.8	1.2
22 091	St. Helena	9,874	47.6	51.7	<.1	0.1	<.1	0.5	59	59	6	60	0.2	0.2	0.4	<.1
22 093	St. James	20,879	49.9	49.5	<.1	<.1	<.1	0.5	43	58	7	58	0.5	0.4	0.8	0.1
22 095	St. John the Baptist	39,996	61.0	35.9	0.4	0.2	<.1	2.4	28	45	22	8	0.9	0.9	1.1	1.0
22 097	St. Landry	80,331	58.7	40.1	0.2	<.1	0.1	0.8	14	48	15	46	1.9	1.7	2.5	0.7
22 099	St. Martin	43,978	64.7	32.8	0.7	0.2	0.4	1.1	23	39	25	31	1.0	1.0	1.1	0.5
22 101	St. Mary	58,086	63.5	31.4	1.7	1.4	<.1	1.9	20	40	28	12	1.4	1.3	1.4	1.2
22 103	St. Tammany	144,508	85.9	10.9	0.5	0.3	<.1	2.2	7	5	60	10	3.4	4.5	1.2	3.4
22 105	Tangipahoa	85,709	69.9	28.5	0.3	0.2	<.1	1.1	13	30	35	32	2.0	2.2	1.9	1.0
22 107	Tensas	7,103	46.2	53.0	<.1	0.2	<.1	0.6	64	60	5	54	0.2	0.1	0.3	<.1
22 109	Terrebonne	96,982	76.5	16.4	0.7	5.0	<.1	1.4	10	14	55	24	2.3	2.7	1.2	1.5
22 111	Union	20,690	71.4	27.8	0.1	<.1	0.0	0.6	45	25	37	51	0.5	0.5	0.4	0.1
22 113	Vermilion	50,055	83.4	13.8	1.3	0.2	<.1	1.2	22	7	58	29	1.2	1.5	0.5	0.6
22 115	Vernon	61,961	71.0	20.4	2.3	0.7	0.1	5.5	18	27	47	3	1.5	1.6	1.0	3.7
22 117	Washington	43,185	68.4	30.8	0.1	0.1	0.0	0.6	24	33	31	55	1.0	1.1	1.0	0.3
22 119	Webster	41,989	67.6	31.5	0.1	0.2	<.1	0.5	26	35	27	56	1.0	1.0	1.0	0.2
22 121	West Baton Rouge	19,419	62.7	35.9	0.1	0.1	<.1	1.1	47	42	23	34	0.5	0.4	0.5	0.2
22 123	West Carroll	12,093	82.1	16.6	<.1	0.3	0.0	1.0	57	10	54	39	0.3	0.4	0.2	0.1
22 125	West Feliciana	12,915	43.1	54.9	<.1	0.3	<.1	1.6	55	61	4	19	0.3	0.2	0.5	0.2
22 127	Winn	16,269	69.3	29.4	0.1	0.4	<.1	0.9	51	32	32	43	0.4	0.4	0.4	0.1
22	LOUISIANA	4,219,973	65.8	30.6	0.9	0.4	<.1	2.2					100.0	100.0	100.0	100.0
	CONGRESSIONAL															
	District 1	602,859	84.5	10.0	1.1	0.3	<.1	4.1	4	1	7	1	14.3	18.4	4.7	26.4
	District 2	602,689	33.5	60.4	2.1	0.2	<.1	3.7	7	6	2	2	14.3	7.3	28.2	23.8

State/county code	Parish	Total persons	Percent of total persons						Rank				Percent contribution to state population			
			Non-Hispanic							Percent of total persons				Non-Hispanic		
										Non-Hispanic						
			White	Black	Asian and Pacific Islander	Native American	Other	Hispanic	Total	White	Black	Hispanic	Total	White	Black	Hispanic
	District 3........................	602,950	73.5	21.7	0.9	1.5	<.1	2.4	1	5	4	3	14.3	16.0	10.1	15.8
	District 4........................	602,884	32.4	66.2	0.3	0.1	<.1	0.9	3	7	1	7	14.3	7.0	30.9	5.8
	District 5........................	602,816	76.1	22.0	0.5	0.2	<.1	1.1	6	4	3	6	14.3	16.5	10.3	7.3
	District 6........................	602,854	82.1	14.4	1.1	0.4	<.1	2.0	5	2	6	4	14.3	17.8	6.7	12.8
	District 7........................	602,921	78.5	19.4	0.6	0.2	<.1	1.3	2	3	5	5	14.3	17.0	9.1	8.1

Parish	Total Voting Age Population	Pct VAP Non-Hisp White	Black	Asian and Pacific Islander	Native American	Other	Hispanic	Rank Total	Rank Non-Hisp White	Rank Black	Rank Hispanic	% contrib Total	% contrib White	% contrib Black	% contrib Hispanic	VAP% Total	VAP% White	VAP% Black	VAP% Asian and Pacific Islander	VAP% Native American	VAP% Other	VAP% Hispanic
Acadia	38,002	82.8	16.3	0.1	<.1	<.1	0.7	21	11	51	49	1.3	1.5	0.7	0.4	68.0	69.6	61.0	69.9	59.6	60.0	68.3
Allen	15,118	74.9	19.4	0.2	1.3	<.1	4.1	42	24	46	5	0.5	0.6	0.4	0.9	71.2	71.6	66.6	78.9	69.7	71.4	93.3
Ascension	39,563	77.6	20.4	0.3	0.2	<.1	1.6	19	17	44	18	1.3	1.5	1.0	1.0	68.0	70.0	61.0	67.8	72.6	72.7	68.4
Assumption	15,539	68.7	29.5	0.2	0.2	<.1	1.4	40	38	26	21	0.5	0.5	0.6	0.3	68.3	71.0	62.8	41.7	70.5	50.0	73.3
Avoyelles	27,655	74.0	23.9	0.1	0.2	<.1	1.7	28	26	38	16	0.9	1.0	0.8	0.7	70.6	73.4	63.0	72.7	65.0	69.2	75.4
Beauregard	21,294	83.7	14.2	0.4	0.4	<.1	1.3	34	10	56	28	0.7	0.9	0.4	0.4	70.8	71.4	67.8	71.8	69.3	71.4	65.5
Bienville	11,466	58.5	40.8	<.1	0.2	<.1	0.5	52	53	12	57	0.4	0.3	0.6	<.1	71.8	75.0	67.5	91.7	85.7	100.0	70.4
Bossier	60,904	79.0	17.6	1.0	0.4	<.1	1.9	11	15	48	12	2.0	2.3	1.3	1.8	70.7	73.1	62.0	72.3	80.7	62.9	65.5
Caddo	177,354	62.9	35.4	0.4	0.2	<.1	1.0	4	48	17	36	5.9	5.4	7.6	2.7	71.4	77.0	63.3	72.1	76.9	73.8	67.9
Calcasieu	118,999	77.6	20.8	0.3	0.2	<.1	1.0	5	18	43	35	4.0	4.5	3.0	1.9	70.8	72.7	64.5	70.6	72.4	67.6	67.1
Caldwell	6,979	81.7	16.7	0.1	0.1	<.1	1.3	59	13	50	25	0.2	0.3	0.1	0.1	71.1	72.5	66.1	83.3	77.8	100.0	58.1
Cameron	6,421	93.1	5.1	0.3	0.2	<.1	1.3	62	2	62	24	0.2	0.3	<.1	0.1	69.3	69.6	65.9	85.0	73.3	100.0	60.1
Catahoula	7,679	76.0	23.4	<.1	0.2	0.0	0.4	58	21	39	59	0.3	0.3	0.2	<.1	69.4	72.0	62.6	100.0	81.3	0.0	45.1
Claiborne	12,959	55.5	44.1	<.1	0.2	<.1	0.2	49	55	9	64	0.4	0.3	0.7	<.1	74.5	77.3	71.2	69.2	71.4	50.0	70.0
Concordia	14,453	65.9	33.2	<.1	0.2	<.1	0.6	44	42	22	50	0.5	0.5	0.6	0.1	69.4	72.8	63.4	58.3	88.9	100.0	70.8
De Soto	17,796	57.4	40.9	<.1	0.2	<.1	1.4	36	54	11	22	0.6	0.5	0.9	0.4	70.2	74.0	65.6	77.8	81.5	66.7	65.0
East Baton Rouge	275,524	65.5	31.4	1.4	0.2	<.1	1.6	3	43	24	19	9.2	8.8	10.4	6.5	72.5	76.3	65.6	72.1	76.0	65.9	74.8
East Carroll	6,209	40.1	58.4	0.1	<.1	0.0	1.3	63	63	1	26	0.2	0.1	0.4	0.1	64.0	75.5	57.8	45.0	100.0	0.0	68.3
East Feliciana	13,484	53.8	44.7	0.1	0.1	0.0	1.2	48	57	8	30	0.5	0.4	0.7	0.2	70.2	72.9	66.8	68.2	81.0	0.0	86.0
Evangeline	22,784	75.9	23.0	<.1	<.1	0.1	0.8	31	22	40	45	0.8	0.8	0.6	0.3	68.5	71.3	60.7	57.9	56.7	60.7	65.9
Franklin	15,507	72.1	27.1	<.1	0.1	<.1	0.6	41	32	30	53	0.5	0.5	0.5	0.1	69.3	73.6	62.5	54.8	0.0		73.3
Grant	12,302	85.3	13.3	0.2	0.3	<.1	0.8	50	8	57	39	0.4	0.5	0.2	0.2	70.2	71.2	65.0	75.9	50.0	83.3	67.3
Iberia	46,357	70.5	26.5	0.9	0.2	0.1	1.9	17	36	34	14	1.5	1.6	1.5	1.3	67.9	70.9	61.5	54.0	68.0	74.3	65.9
Iberville	21,809	54.4	43.0	0.2	0.2	<.1	2.2	33	56	10	10	0.7	0.6	1.1	0.7	70.2	74.0	65.6	84.8	71.4	80.0	79.6
Jackson	11,236	72.3	27.1	0.1	0.1	<.1	0.3	53	31	31	62	0.4	0.4	0.4	<.1	71.5	73.7	66.5	77.8	56.5	60.0	70.0
Jefferson	327,867	77.1	14.7	1.9	0.3	<.1	5.8	2	19	53	2	11.0	12.3	5.8	28.9	73.1	76.2	61.7	64.5	66.6	60.8	71.9
Jefferson Davis	21,161	82.0	17.1	0.1	0.1	<.1	0.6	35	12	49	51	0.7	0.8	0.4	0.2	68.9	70.5	62.3	68.2	52.6	45.0	65.2
Lafayette	116,867	77.0	20.1	1.0	0.2	0.1	1.6	6	20	45	17	3.9	4.4	2.8	2.8	70.9	72.9	64.0	76.5	67.4	75.9	71.5
Lafourche	60,046	85.8	10.6	0.5	1.7	<.1	1.4	12	6	59	20	2.0	2.5	0.8	1.3	69.9	72.1	59.5	49.2	54.5	70.6	66.7
La Salle	9,912	91.0	8.1	0.2	0.4	0.0	0.3	55	3	61	63	0.3	0.4	<.1	<.1	72.6	73.7	64.2	52.8	53.2	0.0	56.5
Lincoln	32,151	59.2	38.9	0.9	0.1	<.1	0.9	23	52	13	37	1.1	0.9	1.5	0.5	77.0	77.9	75.5	83.3	84.6	79.2	78.7
Livingston	48,350	93.7	5.1	0.2	0.2	<.1	0.8	16	1	63	40	1.6	2.2	0.3	0.6	68.6	68.9	62.7	72.3	75.0	88.9	62.3
Madison	8,131	45.3	53.6	<.1	0.1	<.1	0.8	57	61	4	40	0.3	0.2	0.5	0.1	65.2	74.9	59.0	75.0	80.0	57.1	54.0
Morehouse	22,131	62.6	36.8	0.2	<.1	0.0	0.4	32	49	16	61	0.7	0.7	1.0	0.1	69.3	74.8	61.7	82.9	66.7	0.0	59.6
Natchitoches	25,713	64.4	33.2	0.3	0.5	0.4	1.4	30	46	21	23	0.9	0.8	1.0	0.5	70.1	75.1	62.2	49.0	72.1	72.2	71.7
Orleans	360,476	38.8	55.8	1.6	0.1	<.1	3.6	1	64	3	6	12.0	6.8	24.3	19.8	72.5	84.9	65.9	62.9	79.7	63.3	76.2
Ouachita	100,445	71.9	26.6	0.6	0.2	<.1	0.8	8	33	33	42	3.4	3.5	3.2	1.2	70.6	75.2	60.6	76.2	80.2	76.9	67.4
Plaquemines	17,559	73.0	21.4	1.6	1.7	0.2	2.2	37	28	42	9	0.6	0.6	0.5	0.6	68.7	70.8	63.7	56.1	64.1	65.9	65.6
Pointe Coupee	15,709	60.9	38.1	<.1	0.1	<.1	0.8	39	51	14	44	0.5	0.5	0.7	0.2	69.7	73.1	64.8	50.0	75.9	76.9	74.1
Rapides	93,358	72.7	25.1	0.7	0.4	<.1	1.1	9	30	35	34	3.1	3.3	2.8	1.5	71.0	73.8	63.9	69.1	73.7	58.3	67.0
Red River	6,462	65.4	33.5	<.1	0.2	0.0	0.8	61	44	20	48	0.2	0.2	0.3	<.1	68.8	73.9	60.5	83.3	82.4	0.0	80.3
Richland	14,295	67.3	31.8	<.1	<.1	<.1	0.8	45	41	23	46	0.5	0.5	0.5	0.2	69.3	74.5	60.6	69.2	100.0	100.0	55.8
Sabine	16,192	78.9	14.5	0.1	2.0	<.1	4.4	38	16	54	4	0.5	0.6	0.3	1.1	71.5	74.5	59.3	91.3	66.7	66.7	69.8
St. Bernard	48,492	88.4	4.2	0.8	0.4	<.1	6.1	15	4	64	1	1.6	2.1	0.2	4.5	72.8	73.4	65.2	70.6	64.0	55.2	71.0
St. Charles	29,058	75.0	22.0	0.3	0.2	<.1	2.4	27	23	41	7	1.0	1.1	0.8	1.1	68.5	70.5	62.9	62.4	64.9	59.1	65.0
St. Helena	6,764	50.7	48.7	0.0	0.1	<.1	0.4	60	60	5	60	0.2	0.2	0.3	<.1	68.5	73.0	64.5	0.0	66.7	71.4	56.5
St. James	14,244	52.9	46.5	<.1	<.1	<.1	0.6	46	58	7	55	0.5	0.4	0.8	0.1	68.2	72.3	64.1	56.3	80.0	50.0	73.8
St. John the Baptist	26,348	63.4	33.6	0.4	0.3	<.1	2.4	29	47	19	8	0.9	0.8	1.1	0.9	65.9	68.4	61.5	61.6	69.1	53.8	65.9
St. Landry	54,804	61.8	37.1	0.2	<.1	0.1	0.8	14	50	15	47	1.8	1.6	2.5	0.6	68.2	71.7	63.2	61.5	55.7	73.0	65.4
St. Martin	29,743	67.4	30.3	0.6	0.2	0.4	1.2	26	39	25	29	1.0	1.0	1.1	0.6	67.6	70.5	62.3	54.2	57.7	61.1	71.7
St. Mary	39,388	67.4	28.2	1.1	1.2	<.1	1.9	20	40	28	13	1.3	1.3	1.3	1.1	67.8	72.0	60.9	46.4	59.5	91.7	66.6
St. Tammany	100,460	87.1	9.9	0.5	0.4	<.1	2.1	7	5	60	11	3.4	4.2	1.2	3.2	69.5	70.4	62.9	64.8	72.8	67.9	66.7
Tangipahoa	59,786	73.7	24.6	0.3	0.2	<.1	1.2	13	27	37	31	2.0	2.1	1.8	1.0	69.8	73.6	60.2	69.8	69.7	60.0	73.1
Tensas	4,799	51.0	48.3	<.1	0.1	<.1	0.5	64	59	6	58	0.2	0.1	0.3	<.1	67.6	74.6	61.7	100.0	58.3	50.0	51.2
Terrebonne	65,598	79.2	14.8	0.5	4.2	<.1	1.3	10	14	52	27	2.2	2.5	1.2	1.3	67.6	70.0	60.9	50.2	57.2	44.4	62.5
Union	14,888	74.2	25.0	0.1	<.1	0.0	0.6	43	25	36	54	0.5	0.5	0.4	0.1	72.0	74.7	64.9	86.4	77.8	0.0	63.2
Vermilion	34,678	85.5	12.2	1.0	0.1	<.1	1.1	22	7	58	32	1.2	1.4	0.5	0.6	69.3	71.0	61.0	49.6	66.2	65.0	66.7
Vernon	43,838	72.7	19.2	2.3	0.7	<.1	5.0	18	29	47	3	1.5	1.5	1.0	3.3	70.8	72.4	66.7	71.8	70.7	49.4	64.0
Washington	30,766	71.1	28.1	0.1	0.1	0.0	0.6	24	35	29	52	1.0	1.1	1.0	0.3	71.2	74.1	64.9	68.8	69.0	0.0	74.9
Webster	30,516	70.2	28.9	0.1	0.2	<.1	0.5	25	37	27	56	1.0	1.0	1.1	0.2	72.7	75.5	66.6	80.4	86.8	100.0	66.4
West Baton Rouge	13,640	64.5	34.0	0.1	0.2	<.1	1.1	47	45	18	33	0.5	0.4	0.6	0.2	70.2	72.3	66.5	64.0	75.9	76.5	74.3
West Carroll	8,567	84.3	14.5	<.1	0.3	0.0	0.8	56	9	55	38	0.3	0.4	0.1	0.1	70.8	72.7	61.7	66.7	82.9	0.0	62.6
West Feliciana	10,366	40.9	56.8	<.1	0.3	<.1	1.8	54	62	2	15	0.3	0.2	0.7	0.3	80.3	76.3	83.0	75.0	83.3	100.0	93.6
Winn	11,743	71.7	27.0	0.1	0.4	<.1	0.8	51	34	32	43	0.4	0.4	0.4	0.1	72.2	74.7	66.4	59.1	75.4	100.0	66.9
LOUISIANA	2,992,704	68.8	27.7	0.9	0.4	<.1	2.2					100.0	100.0	100.0	100.0	70.9	74.2	64.2	65.5	64.9	65.9	71.2
CONGRESSIONAL																						
District 1	444,144	86.0	8.6	1.0	0.3	<.1	4.0	1	1	7	1	14.8	18.6	4.6	27.1	73.7	75.0	63.3	68.2	71.9	65.6	73.0
District 2	426,275	38.4	55.7	1.8	0.2	<.1	3.8	4	6	2	2	14.2	7.9	28.6	24.5	70.7	81.1	65.2	61.4	70.5	62.5	73.3

Parish	Total Voting Age Population	Percent of total VAP						Rank				Percent contribution to state VAP				VAP percent of total population						
		Non-Hispanic							Non-Hispanic				Non-Hispanic				Non-Hispanic					
								Percent of total VAP															
									Non-Hispanic														
		White	Black	Asian and Pacific Islander	Native American	Other	Hispanic	Total	White	Black	Hispanic	Total	White	Black	Hispanic	Total	White	Black	Asian and Pacific Islander	Native American	Other	Hispanic
District 3	414,995	76.2	19.4	0.7	1.2	<.1	2.4	6	5	3	3	13.9	15.4	9.7	15.1	68.8	71.4	61.6	55.7	58.1	65.8	68.0
District 4	413,500	36.2	62.3	0.3	0.1	<.1	0.9	7	7	1	7	13.8	7.3	31.1	5.9	68.6	76.5	64.6	69.3	76.2	64.8	73.1
District 5	437,021	78.7	19.4	0.5	0.2	<.1	1.1	2	4	4	6	14.6	16.7	10.2	6.9	72.5	75.0	63.9	73.7	77.4	71.1	67.6
District 6	434,678	83.7	12.8	1.1	0.4	<.1	1.9	3	2	6	4	14.5	17.7	6.7	12.5	72.1	73.6	64.1	71.9	70.4	65.4	69.2
District 7	422,091	80.3	17.5	0.6	0.2	<.1	1.3	5	3	5	5	14.1	16.5	8.9	8.0	70.0	71.7	63.3	67.9	67.1	68.5	70.4

Table C. — **Voter Participation: November 3, 1992, General Election**

Parish	Estimated Voting Age Population (VAP) 1992	Voter registration (REG)				Voter turnout													
						Highest office				Maximum vote						Percent drop-off, by office[1]			
		Total	% contribution to state REG	% of 1992 VAP	Rank by % of 1992 VAP	Actual	Total	Office	% of 1992 VAP	Total	% contribution to state turnout	% of REG	Rank by % of REG	% of 1992 VAP	Rank by % 1992 VAP	President	Senator	Governor	Representative
Acadia	38,084	33,230	1.4	87.3	21	24,929	24,568	P	64.5	24,929	1.4	75.0	41	65.5	26	1.4	-	-	-
Allen	15,110	13,189	0.6	87.3	20	10,010	10,017	P	66.3	10,017	0.6	75.9	36	66.3	23	0.0	-	-	-
Ascension	41,317	34,571	1.5	83.7	34	28,135	27,748	P	67.2	28,135	1.6	81.4	9	68.1	16	1.4	-	-	85.7
Assumption	15,712	13,938	0.6	88.7	18	10,477	10,453	P	66.5	10,477	0.6	75.2	40	66.7	22	0.2	-	-	-
Avoyelles	27,249	23,175	1.0	85.0	31	16,761	16,549	P	60.7	16,761	0.9	72.3	56	61.5	38	1.3	-	-	12.0
Beauregard	21,403	16,506	0.7	77.1	46	12,596	12,551	P	58.6	12,596	0.7	76.3	32	58.9	50	0.4	-	-	-
Bienville	11,293	10,202	0.4	90.3	14	7,551	7,432	P	65.8	7,551	0.4	74.0	49	66.9	21	1.6	-	-	10.4
Bossier	61,613	40,353	1.8	65.5	62	33,134	32,801	P	53.2	33,134	1.8	82.1	6	53.8	61	1.0	-	-	12.4
Caddo	176,229	127,562	5.6	72.4	57	103,040	102,678	P	58.3	103,040	5.7	80.8	11	58.5	52	0.4	-	-	8.9
Calcasieu	118,602	86,206	3.8	72.7	56	69,743	69,862	P	58.9	69,862	3.9	81.0	10	58.9	49	0.0	-	-	-
Caldwell	6,926	6,814	0.3	98.4	6	4,708	4,684	P	67.6	4,708	0.3	69.1	62	68.0	17	0.5	-	-	21.0
Cameron	6,416	6,149	0.3	95.8	10	4,370	4,338	P	67.6	4,370	0.2	71.1	60	68.1	15	0.7	-	-	-
Catahoula	7,543	7,722	0.3	102.4	2	5,541	5,471	P	72.5	5,541	0.3	71.8	58	73.5	6	1.3	-	-	16.5
Claiborne	12,797	9,489	0.4	74.2	53	7,052	6,996	P	54.7	7,052	0.4	74.3	46	55.1	60	0.8	-	-	27.2
Concordia	14,180	12,296	0.5	86.7	24	9,254	9,148	P	64.5	9,254	0.5	75.3	39	65.3	29	1.1	-	-	22.0
De Soto	17,738	14,652	0.6	82.6	36	11,146	11,021	P	62.1	11,146	0.6	76.1	35	62.8	35	1.1	-	-	11.0
East Baton Rouge	275,771	202,253	8.8	73.3	55	167,135	166,691	P	60.4	167,135	9.3	82.6	2	60.6	45	0.3	-	-	5.2
East Carroll	6,013	5,678	0.2	94.4	11	3,423	3,375	P	56.1	3,423	0.2	60.3	64	56.9	55	1.4	-	-	19.8
East Feliciana	13,630	10,957	0.5	80.4	43	7,988	7,895	P	57.9	7,988	0.4	72.9	54	58.6	51	1.2	-	-	13.0
Evangeline	22,791	21,862	1.0	95.9	9	16,683	16,376	P	71.9	16,683	0.9	76.3	33	73.2	8	1.8	-	-	85.1
Franklin	15,438	13,409	0.6	86.9	23	9,808	9,653	P	62.5	9,808	0.5	73.1	52	63.5	34	1.6	-	-	7.9
Grant	12,437	10,755	0.5	86.5	25	7,985	7,878	P	63.3	7,985	0.4	74.2	47	64.2	31	1.3	-	-	8.9
Iberia	47,063	38,862	1.7	82.6	37	30,848	30,530	P	64.9	30,848	1.7	79.4	17	65.5	25	1.0	-	-	-
Iberville	21,613	20,362	0.9	94.2	12	15,873	15,594	P	72.2	15,873	0.9	78.0	24	73.4	7	1.8	-	-	17.8
Jackson	11,058	9,527	0.4	86.2	27	7,685	7,566	P	68.4	7,685	0.4	80.7	13	69.5	12	1.5	-	-	7.9
Jefferson	326,807	227,468	9.9	69.6	60	186,567	187,038	P	57.2	187,038	10.4	82.2	4	57.2	53	0.0	-	-	-
Jefferson Davis	21,034	17,931	0.8	85.2	28	13,822	13,838	P	65.8	13,838	0.8	77.2	28	65.8	24	0.0	-	-	-
Lafayette	117,949	90,052	3.9	76.3	48	72,206	71,762	P	60.8	72,206	4.0	80.2	15	61.2	40	0.6	-	-	89.3
Lafourche	60,269	44,346	1.9	73.6	54	35,807	35,645	P	59.1	35,807	2.0	80.7	12	59.4	48	0.5	-	-	-
La Salle	9,491	9,214	0.4	97.1	8	6,804	6,723	P	70.8	6,804	0.4	73.8	50	71.7	9	1.2	-	-	10.9
Lincoln	30,131	21,655	0.9	71.9	59	16,728	16,561	P	55.0	16,728	0.9	77.2	27	55.5	59	1.0	-	-	13.7
Livingston	50,983	40,236	1.8	78.9	45	31,417	31,421	P	61.6	31,421	1.7	78.1	23	61.6	37	0.0	-	-	49.2
Madison	7,953	7,769	0.3	97.7	7	5,202	5,106	P	64.2	5,202	0.3	67.0	63	65.4	27	1.8	-	-	15.7
Morehouse	21,918	17,395	0.8	79.4	44	13,475	13,463	P	61.4	13,475	0.7	77.5	26	61.5	39	0.1	-	-	12.9
Natchitoches	24,726	20,615	0.9	83.4	35	15,000	14,779	P	59.8	15,000	0.8	72.8	55	60.7	43	1.5	-	-	11.1
Orleans	351,270	262,258	11.4	74.7	51	198,902	197,349	P	56.2	198,902	11.0	75.8	37	56.6	57	0.8	-	-	-
Ouachita	100,315	72,307	3.2	72.1	58	56,883	56,502	P	56.3	56,883	3.2	78.7	21	56.7	56	0.7	-	-	8.4
Plaquemines	17,541	14,935	0.7	85.1	29	11,291	11,257	P	64.2	11,291	0.6	75.6	38	64.4	30	0.3	-	-	-
Pointe Coupee	15,496	14,557	0.6	93.9	13	11,529	11,322	P	73.1	11,529	0.6	79.2	18	74.4	5	1.8	-	-	8.9
Rapides	92,716	70,133	3.1	75.6	50	52,432	51,882	P	56.0	52,432	2.9	74.8	44	56.6	58	1.0	-	-	9.3
Red River	6,281	6,190	0.3	98.6	3	4,764	4,680	P	74.5	4,764	0.3	77.0	30	75.8	3	1.8	-	-	8.8
Richland	14,141	11,876	0.5	84.0	33	9,079	8,903	P	63.0	9,079	0.5	76.4	31	64.2	32	1.9	-	-	7.7
Sabine	15,800	13,658	0.6	86.4	26	9,496	9,348	P	59.2	9,496	0.5	69.5	61	60.1	47	1.6	-	-	20.7
St. Bernard	48,653	40,051	1.7	82.3	39	33,051	32,938	P	67.7	33,051	1.8	82.5	3	67.9	18	0.3	-	-	-
St. Charles	29,923	25,412	1.1	84.9	32	20,610	20,877	P	69.8	20,877	1.2	82.2	5	69.8	11	0.0	-	-	-
St. Helena	6,777	7,908	0.3	116.7	1	5,655	5,618	P	82.9	5,655	0.3	71.5	59	83.4	1	0.7	-	-	41.0
St. James	14,133	13,910	0.6	98.4	5	11,118	11,186	P	79.1	11,186	0.6	80.4	14	79.1	2	0.0	-	-	-
St. John the Baptist	28,014	22,679	1.0	81.0	41	17,759	17,851	P	63.7	17,851	1.0	78.7	20	63.7	33	0.0	-	-	-
St. Landry	54,213	48,945	2.1	90.3	15	37,240	36,815	P	67.9	37,240	2.1	76.1	34	68.7	13	1.1	-	-	52.0
St. Martin	30,446	25,897	1.1	85.1	30	20,496	20,426	P	67.1	20,496	1.1	79.1	19	67.3	19	0.3	-	-	88.6
St. Mary	38,505	31,730	1.4	82.4	38	23,494	23,440	P	60.9	23,494	1.3	74.0	48	61.0	42	0.2	-	-	-
St. Tammany	108,079	81,885	3.6	75.8	49	67,153	66,921	P	61.9	67,153	3.7	82.0	7	62.1	36	0.3	-	-	-
Tangipahoa	60,212	46,308	2.0	76.9	47	34,428	34,245	P	56.9	34,428	1.9	74.3	45	57.2	54	0.5	-	-	83.6
Tensas	4,669	4,597	0.2	98.5	4	3,305	3,266	P	70.0	3,305	0.2	71.9	57	70.8	10	1.2	-	-	18.8
Terrebonne	66,126	43,858	1.9	66.3	61	35,000	34,664	P	52.4	35,000	1.9	79.8	16	52.9	62	1.0	-	-	-
Union	14,847	13,044	0.6	87.9	19	10,114	10,069	P	67.8	10,114	0.6	77.5	25	68.1	14	0.4	-	-	15.0
Vermilion	34,983	30,466	1.3	87.1	22	23,470	23,444	P	67.0	23,470	1.3	77.0	29	67.1	20	0.1	-	-	-
Vernon	44,492	20,507	0.9	46.1	64	14,956	14,767	P	33.2	14,956	0.8	72.9	53	33.6	64	1.3	-	-	15.1
Washington	30,770	25,111	1.1	81.6	40	18,822	18,753	P	60.9	18,822	1.0	75.0	42	61.2	41	0.4	-	-	-
Webster	30,151	22,368	1.0	74.2	52	18,274	18,264	P	60.6	18,274	1.0	81.7	8	60.6	44	0.1	-	-	12.8
West Baton Rouge	13,657	12,269	0.5	89.8	16	10,214	9,976	P	73.0	10,214	0.6	83.3	1	74.8	4	2.3	-	-	7.0
West Carroll	8,506	6,883	0.3	80.9	42	5,152	5,120	P	60.2	5,152	0.3	74.9	43	60.6	46	0.6	-	-	12.5
West Feliciana	10,452	5,691	0.2	54.4	63	4,458	4,374	P	41.8	4,458	0.2	78.3	22	42.7	63	1.9	-	-	13.7
Winn	11,545	10,296	0.4	89.2	17	7,548	7,549	P	65.4	7,549	0.4	73.3	51	65.4	28	0.1	-	-	14.5
LOUISIANA[2]	2,992,000	2,292,129	100.0	76.6		1,799,596	1,790,017		59.8	1,800,641	100.0	78.6		60.2		0.6	-	-	62.0

[1]Percent drop-off is zero for any office used as highest office turnout. [2]Louisiana reports voter registration and turnout by political party affiliation and by race. See Table D-registration by party. State voter turnout by party is 1,289,778 (71.7%) for Democratic party, 353,342 (19.6%) for Republican party, and 156,476 (8.7%) for other. State voter registration by race is 1,639,233 (71.5%) for white, 633,049 (27.6%) for black, and 19,847 (0.9%) for other. State voter turnout by race is 1,336,057 (74.2%) for white, 449,177 (25.0%) for black, and 14,362 (0.8%) for other.

Table D. — Voter Registration by Political Party Affiliation: November 3, 1992, General Election

Parish	Total voter registration	Political party affiliation Democrat (DEM)	Republican (REP)	Independent (IND)	Plurality Total	Party	Percent of total registration DEM	REP	IND	Rank DEM	REP	IND	Percent contribution to state registration Total	DEM	REP	IND
Acadia	33,230	28,572	3,353	1,305	25,219	D	86.0	10.1	3.9	8	51	58	1.4	1.7	0.8	0.6
Allen	13,189	11,318	1,215	656	10,103	D	85.8	9.2	5.0	9	54	52	0.6	0.7	0.3	0.3
Ascension	34,571	26,644	4,619	3,308	22,025	D	77.1	13.4	9.6	38	35	22	1.5	1.6	1.1	1.5
Assumption	13,938	12,325	959	654	11,366	D	88.4	6.9	4.7	4	62	53	0.6	0.8	0.2	0.3
Avoyelles	23,175	19,654	1,999	1,522	17,655	D	84.8	8.6	6.6	11	56	39	1.0	1.2	0.5	0.7
Beauregard	16,506	12,044	2,638	1,824	9,406	D	73.0	16.0	11.1	51	19	9	0.7	0.7	0.6	0.8
Bienville	10,202	8,843	968	391	7,875	D	86.7	9.5	3.8	7	53	59	0.4	0.5	0.2	0.2
Bossier	40,353	23,385	11,894	5,074	11,491	D	58.0	29.5	12.6	63	2	3	1.8	1.4	2.7	2.3
Caddo	127,562	80,782	32,240	14,540	48,542	D	63.3	25.3	11.4	58	6	7	5.6	4.9	7.4	6.6
Calcasieu	86,206	64,603	13,702	7,901	50,901	D	74.9	15.9	9.2	44	21	25	3.8	4.0	3.1	3.6
Caldwell	6,814	5,393	998	423	4,395	D	79.1	14.6	6.2	31	32	44	0.3	0.3	0.2	0.2
Cameron	6,149	5,197	479	473	4,718	D	84.5	7.8	7.7	13	59	32	0.3	0.3	0.1	0.2
Catahoula	7,722	6,545	855	322	5,690	D	84.8	11.1	4.2	12	45	57	0.3	0.4	0.2	0.1
Claiborne	9,489	7,429	1,428	632	6,001	D	78.3	15.0	6.7	34	28	37	0.4	0.5	0.3	0.3
Concordia	12,296	10,002	1,600	694	8,402	D	81.3	13.0	5.6	23	39	49	0.5	0.6	0.4	0.3
De Soto	14,652	11,888	1,620	1,144	10,268	D	81.1	11.1	7.8	24	46	31	0.6	0.7	0.4	0.5
East Baton Rouge	202,253	127,810	52,821	21,622	74,989	D	63.2	26.1	10.7	59	5	10	8.8	7.8	12.1	9.8
East Carroll	5,678	4,656	657	365	3,999	D	82.0	11.6	6.4	20	43	40	0.2	0.3	0.2	0.2
East Feliciana	10,957	8,861	1,415	681	7,446	D	80.9	12.9	6.2	26	41	43	0.5	0.5	0.3	0.3
Evangeline	21,862	19,767	1,633	462	18,134	D	90.4	7.5	2.1	2	60	64	1.0	1.2	0.4	0.2
Franklin	13,409	11,182	1,752	475	9,430	D	83.4	13.1	3.5	17	37	62	0.6	0.7	0.4	0.2
Grant	10,755	8,450	1,623	682	6,827	D	78.6	15.1	6.3	33	27	42	0.5	0.5	0.4	0.3
Iberia	38,862	29,569	6,162	3,131	23,407	D	76.1	15.9	8.1	39	22	28	1.7	1.8	1.4	1.4
Iberville	20,362	18,168	1,291	903	16,877	D	89.2	6.3	4.4	3	63	55	0.9	1.1	0.3	0.4
Jackson	9,527	7,663	1,424	440	6,239	D	80.4	14.9	4.6	27	30	54	0.4	0.5	0.3	0.2
Jefferson	227,468	132,707	66,579	28,182	66,128	D	58.3	29.3	12.4	62	3	5	9.9	8.1	15.2	12.8
Jefferson Davis	17,931	14,299	1,898	1,734	12,401	D	79.7	10.6	9.7	29	50	20	0.8	0.9	0.4	0.8
Lafayette	90,052	56,625	22,183	11,244	34,442	D	62.9	24.6	12.5	60	7	4	3.9	3.5	5.1	5.1
Lafourche	44,346	35,611	5,228	3,507	30,383	D	80.3	11.8	7.9	28	42	29	1.9	2.2	1.2	1.6
La Salle	9,214	7,499	1,191	524	6,308	D	81.4	12.9	5.7	21	40	48	0.4	0.5	0.3	0.2
Lincoln	21,655	14,326	5,050	2,279	9,276	D	66.2	23.3	10.5	57	8	12	0.9	0.9	1.2	1.0
Livingston	40,236	29,429	6,769	4,038	22,660	D	73.1	16.8	10.0	50	17	17	1.8	1.8	1.5	1.8
Madison	7,769	5,686	1,397	686	4,289	D	73.2	18.0	8.8	49	13	27	0.3	0.3	0.3	0.3
Morehouse	17,395	12,643	3,075	1,677	9,568	D	72.7	17.7	9.6	52	14	21	0.8	0.8	0.7	0.8
Natchitoches	20,615	15,572	3,162	1,881	12,410	D	75.5	15.3	9.1	42	24	26	0.9	1.0	0.7	0.9
Orleans	262,258	199,457	37,836	24,965	161,621	D	76.1	14.4	9.5	40	33	23	11.4	12.2	8.6	11.4
Ouachita	72,307	44,508	19,294	8,505	25,214	D	61.6	26.7	11.8	61	4	6	3.2	2.7	4.4	3.9
Plaquemines	14,935	11,767	2,145	1,023	9,622	D	78.8	14.4	6.8	32	34	34	0.7	0.7	0.5	0.5
Pointe Coupee	14,557	12,841	1,071	645	11,770	D	88.2	7.4	4.4	5	61	56	0.6	0.8	0.2	0.3
Rapides	70,133	48,862	14,197	7,074	34,665	D	69.7	20.2	10.1	54	9	16	3.1	3.0	3.2	3.2
Red River	6,190	5,103	664	423	4,439	D	82.4	10.7	6.8	19	47	35	0.3	0.3	0.2	0.2
Richland	11,876	8,961	2,071	844	6,890	D	75.5	17.4	7.1	43	15	33	0.5	0.5	0.5	0.4
Sabine	13,658	11,066	1,784	808	9,282	D	81.0	13.1	5.9	25	38	46	0.6	0.7	0.4	0.4
St. Bernard	40,051	31,334	6,025	2,692	25,309	D	78.2	15.0	6.7	35	29	36	1.7	1.9	1.4	1.2
St. Charles	25,412	17,694	4,871	2,847	12,823	D	69.6	19.2	11.2	55	11	8	1.1	1.1	1.1	1.3
St. Helena	7,908	6,714	692	502	6,022	D	84.9	8.8	6.3	10	55	41	0.3	0.4	0.2	0.2
St. James	13,910	12,580	799	531	11,781	D	90.4	5.7	3.8	1	64	60	0.6	0.8	0.2	0.2
St. John the Baptist	22,679	16,981	3,471	2,227	13,510	D	74.9	15.3	9.8	45	25	18	1.0	1.0	0.8	1.0
St. Landry	48,945	40,931	5,184	2,830	35,747	D	83.6	10.6	5.8	16	49	47	2.1	2.5	1.2	1.3
St. Martin	25,897	22,785	2,187	925	20,598	D	88.0	8.4	3.6	6	57	61	1.1	1.4	0.5	0.4
St. Mary	31,730	23,294	5,167	3,269	18,127	D	73.4	16.3	10.3	48	18	15	1.4	1.4	1.2	1.5
St. Tammany	81,885	40,686	29,116	12,083	11,570	D	49.7	35.6	14.8	64	1	1	3.6	2.5	6.7	5.5
Tangipahoa	46,308	34,184	7,342	4,782	26,842	D	73.8	15.9	10.3	47	23	14	2.0	2.1	1.7	2.2
Tensas	4,597	3,741	732	124	3,009	D	81.4	15.9	2.7	22	20	63	0.2	0.2	0.2	<.1
Terrebonne	43,858	30,466	8,746	4,646	21,720	D	69.5	19.9	10.6	56	10	11	1.9	1.9	2.0	2.1
Union	13,044	10,167	2,212	665	7,955	D	77.9	17.0	5.1	36	16	50	0.6	0.6	0.5	0.3
Vermilion	30,466	25,567	2,513	2,386	23,054	D	83.9	8.2	7.8	14	58	30	1.3	1.6	0.6	1.1
Vernon	20,507	14,558	3,010	2,939	11,548	D	71.0	14.7	14.3	53	31	2	0.9	0.9	0.7	1.3
Washington	25,111	20,725	2,874	1,512	17,851	D	82.5	11.4	6.0	18	44	45	1.1	1.3	0.7	0.7
Webster	22,368	16,634	3,421	2,313	13,213	D	74.4	15.3	10.3	46	26	13	1.0	1.0	0.8	1.1
West Baton Rouge	12,269	10,264	1,194	811	9,070	D	83.7	9.7	6.6	15	52	38	0.5	0.6	0.3	0.4
West Carroll	6,883	5,225	1,311	347	3,914	D	75.9	19.0	5.0	41	12	51	0.3	0.3	0.3	0.2
West Feliciana	5,691	4,404	750	537	3,654	D	77.4	13.2	9.4	37	36	24	0.2	0.3	0.2	0.2
Winn	10,296	8,186	1,104	1,006	7,082	D	79.5	10.7	9.8	30	48	19	0.4	0.5	0.3	0.5
LOUISIANA[1]	**2,292,129**	**1,634,832**	**437,660**	**219,637**	**1,197,172**	**D**	**71.3**	**19.1**	**9.6**				**100.0**	**100.0**	**100.0**	**100.0**

[1]State voter turnout by party as a percentage of voter registration by party is 1,289,778 (78.9%) for Democrat, 353,342 (80.7%) for Republican, and 156,476 (71.2%) for independent (other parties).

Table E. — Vote for President: November 3, 1992, General Election

Parish	Total	Clinton (DEM)	Bush (REP)	Perot (IND)	Other	Plurality Total	Party	DEM	REP	IND	Other	Rank DEM	Rank REP	Rank IND	Total	DEM	REP	IND	DEM	REP
Acadia	24,568	12,276	9,017	3,145	130	3,259	D	50.0	36.7	12.8	0.5	24	36	32	1.4	1.5	1.2	1.5	57.7	42.3
Allen	10,017	5,626	3,069	1,245	77	2,557	D	56.2	30.6	12.4	0.8	5	56	37	0.6	0.7	0.4	0.6	64.7	35.3
Ascension	27,748	13,036	10,275	4,295	142	2,761	D	47.0	37.0	15.5	0.5	28	35	8	1.6	1.6	1.4	2.0	55.9	44.1
Assumption	10,453	5,639	2,928	1,358	528	2,711	D	53.9	28.0	13.0	5.1	10	62	28	0.6	0.7	0.4	0.6	65.8	34.2
Avoyelles	16,549	8,696	4,851	2,139	863	3,845	D	52.5	29.3	12.9	5.2	14	60	30	0.9	1.1	0.7	1.0	64.2	35.8
Beauregard	12,551	5,037	5,119	2,103	292	82	R	40.1	40.8	16.8	2.3	52	20	2	0.7	0.6	0.7	1.0	49.6	50.4
Bienville	7,432	3,899	2,412	832	289	1,487	D	52.5	32.5	11.2	3.9	15	52	51	0.4	0.5	0.3	0.4	61.8	38.2
Bossier	32,801	11,313	15,628	4,863	997	4,315	R	34.5	47.6	14.8	3.0	62	6	12	1.8	1.4	2.1	2.3	42.0	58.0
Caddo	102,678	47,733	42,665	11,830	450	5,068	D	46.5	41.6	11.5	0.4	33	17	49	5.7	5.8	5.8	5.6	52.8	47.2
Calcasieu	69,862	33,570	24,847	10,980	465	8,723	D	48.1	35.6	15.7	0.7	26	41	6	3.9	4.1	3.4	5.2	57.5	42.5
Caldwell	4,684	2,061	1,752	653	218	309	D	44.0	37.4	13.9	4.7	42	33	19	0.3	0.3	0.2	0.3	54.1	45.9
Cameron	4,338	1,985	1,329	995	29	656	D	45.8	30.6	22.9	0.7	35	57	1	0.2	0.2	0.2	0.5	59.9	40.1
Catahoula	5,471	2,570	1,976	773	152	594	D	47.0	36.1	14.1	2.8	29	38	18	0.3	0.3	0.3	0.4	56.5	43.5
Claiborne	6,996	3,263	2,599	926	208	664	D	46.6	37.1	13.2	3.0	32	34	25	0.4	0.4	0.4	0.4	55.7	44.3
Concordia	9,148	4,283	3,223	1,317	325	1,060	D	46.8	35.2	14.4	3.6	31	45	14	0.5	0.5	0.4	0.6	57.1	42.9
De Soto	11,021	5,671	3,643	1,358	349	2,028	D	51.5	33.1	12.3	3.2	18	50	39	0.6	0.7	0.5	0.6	60.9	39.1
East Baton Rouge	166,691	68,622	81,072	16,102	895	12,450	R	41.2	48.6	9.7	0.5	48	5	60	9.3	8.4	11.1	7.6	45.8	54.2
East Carroll	3,375	1,835	1,142	283	115	693	D	54.4	33.8	8.4	3.4	8	47	63	0.2	0.2	0.2	0.1	61.6	38.4
East Feliciana	7,895	4,093	2,813	932	57	1,280	D	51.8	35.6	11.8	0.7	17	40	44	0.4	0.5	0.4	0.4	59.3	40.7
Evangeline	16,376	8,564	5,147	2,124	541	3,417	D	52.3	31.4	13.0	3.3	16	55	29	0.9	1.0	0.7	1.0	62.5	37.5
Franklin	9,653	4,127	3,889	1,311	326	238	D	42.8	40.3	13.6	3.4	44	23	21	0.5	0.5	0.5	0.6	51.5	48.5
Grant	7,878	3,122	3,214	1,174	368	92	R	39.6	40.8	14.9	4.7	56	19	11	0.4	0.4	0.4	0.6	49.3	50.7
Iberia	30,530	13,040	11,905	4,337	1,248	1,135	D	42.7	39.0	14.2	4.1	45	26	17	1.7	1.6	1.6	2.1	52.3	47.7
Iberville	15,594	8,218	5,211	1,543	622	3,007	D	52.7	33.4	9.9	4.0	12	48	59	0.9	1.0	0.7	0.7	61.2	38.8
Jackson	7,566	3,370	3,072	882	242	298	D	44.5	40.6	11.7	3.2	40	22	47	0.4	0.4	0.4	0.4	52.3	47.7
Jefferson	187,038	64,302	100,493	21,278	965	36,191	R	34.4	53.7	11.4	0.5	63	2	50	10.4	7.9	13.7	10.1	39.0	61.0
Jefferson Davis	13,838	7,022	4,513	2,221	82	2,509	D	50.7	32.6	16.1	0.6	21	51	3	0.8	0.9	0.6	1.1	60.9	39.1
Lafayette	71,762	28,583	32,406	9,124	1,649	3,823	R	39.8	45.2	12.7	2.3	53	9	34	4.0	3.5	4.4	4.3	46.9	53.1
Lafourche	35,645	16,182	12,744	5,077	1,642	3,438	D	45.4	35.8	14.2	4.6	37	39	16	2.0	2.0	1.7	2.4	55.9	44.1
La Salle	6,723	2,389	3,068	993	273	679	R	35.5	45.6	14.8	4.1	61	8	13	0.4	0.3	0.4	0.5	43.8	56.2
Lincoln	16,561	7,205	7,220	1,751	385	15	R	43.5	43.6	10.6	2.3	43	14	56	0.9	0.9	1.0	0.8	49.9	50.1
Livingston	31,421	11,499	14,808	4,971	143	3,309	R	36.6	47.1	15.8	0.5	60	7	5	1.8	1.4	2.0	2.4	43.7	56.3
Madison	5,106	2,773	1,702	469	162	1,071	D	54.3	33.3	9.2	3.2	9	49	61	0.3	0.3	0.2	0.2	62.0	38.0
Morehouse	13,463	6,013	5,364	1,727	359	649	D	44.7	39.8	12.8	2.7	38	25	31	0.8	0.7	0.7	0.8	52.9	47.1
Natchitoches	14,779	6,974	5,694	1,606	505	1,280	D	47.2	38.5	10.9	3.4	27	29	53	0.8	0.9	0.8	0.8	55.1	44.9
Orleans	197,349	133,261	52,019	10,889	1,180	81,242	D	67.5	26.4	5.5	0.6	1	64	64	11.0	16.3	7.1	5.1	71.9	28.1
Ouachita	56,502	20,835	27,600	6,612	1,455	6,765	R	36.9	48.8	11.7	2.6	59	4	46	3.2	2.6	3.8	3.1	43.0	57.0
Plaquemines	11,257	4,467	5,018	1,729	43	551	R	39.7	44.6	15.4	0.4	55	10	9	0.6	0.5	0.7	0.8	47.1	52.9
Pointe Coupee	11,322	6,512	3,563	1,157	90	2,949	D	57.5	31.5	10.2	0.8	4	54	58	0.6	0.8	0.5	0.5	64.6	35.4
Rapides	51,882	20,873	22,783	6,599	1,627	1,910	R	40.2	43.9	12.7	3.1	51	12	33	2.9	2.6	3.1	3.1	47.8	52.2
Red River	4,680	2,360	1,649	566	105	711	D	50.4	35.2	12.1	2.2	22	44	41	0.3	0.3	0.2	0.3	58.9	41.1
Richland	8,903	3,706	3,808	1,054	335	102	R	41.6	42.8	11.8	3.8	47	15	43	0.5	0.5	0.5	0.5	49.3	50.7
Sabine	9,348	4,173	3,586	1,219	370	587	D	44.6	38.4	13.0	4.0	39	30	27	0.5	0.5	0.5	0.6	53.8	46.2
St. Bernard	32,938	12,305	16,131	4,308	194	3,826	R	37.4	49.0	13.1	0.6	58	3	26	1.8	1.5	2.2	2.0	43.3	56.7
St. Charles	20,877	8,810	9,158	2,593	316	348	R	42.2	43.9	12.4	1.5	46	13	38	1.2	1.1	1.2	1.2	49.0	51.0
St. Helena	5,618	3,416	1,515	589	98	1,901	D	60.8	27.0	10.5	1.7	2	63	57	0.3	0.4	0.2	0.3	69.3	30.7
St. James	11,186	6,609	3,339	993	245	3,270	D	59.1	29.8	8.9	2.2	3	59	62	0.6	0.8	0.5	0.5	66.4	33.6
St. John the Baptist	17,851	8,977	6,730	1,922	222	2,247	D	50.3	37.7	10.8	1.2	23	31	55	1.0	1.1	0.9	0.9	57.2	42.8
St. Landry	36,815	20,383	11,882	4,266	284	8,501	D	55.4	32.3	11.6	0.8	6	53	48	2.1	2.5	1.6	2.0	63.2	36.8
St. Martin	20,426	11,252	5,909	2,573	692	5,343	D	55.1	28.9	12.6	3.4	7	61	35	1.1	1.4	0.8	1.2	65.6	34.4
St. Mary	23,440	10,648	8,792	3,257	743	1,856	D	45.4	37.5	13.9	3.2	36	32	20	1.3	1.3	1.2	1.5	54.8	45.2
St. Tammany	66,921	19,735	37,839	9,005	342	18,104	R	29.5	56.5	13.5	0.5	64	1	23	3.7	2.4	5.2	4.3	34.3	65.7
Tangipahoa	34,245	15,194	14,128	4,612	311	1,066	D	44.4	41.3	13.5	0.9	41	18	22	1.9	1.9	1.9	2.2	51.8	48.2
Tensas	3,266	1,666	1,153	353	94	513	D	51.0	35.3	10.8	2.9	20	43	54	0.2	0.2	0.2	0.2	59.1	40.9
Terrebonne	34,664	13,325	14,662	5,505	1,172	1,337	R	38.4	42.3	15.9	3.4	57	16	4	1.9	1.6	2.0	2.6	47.6	52.4
Union	10,069	4,005	4,434	1,209	421	429	R	39.8	44.0	12.0	4.2	54	11	42	0.6	0.5	0.6	0.6	47.5	52.5
Vermilion	23,444	12,324	7,062	3,127	931	5,262	D	52.6	30.1	13.3	4.0	13	58	24	1.3	1.5	1.0	1.5	63.6	36.4
Vernon	14,767	6,005	5,912	2,313	537	93	D	40.7	40.0	15.7	3.6	49	24	7	0.8	0.7	0.8	1.1	50.4	49.6
Washington	18,753	9,095	7,227	2,303	128	1,868	D	48.5	38.5	12.3	0.7	25	28	40	1.0	1.1	1.0	1.1	55.7	44.3
Webster	18,264	8,380	6,640	2,629	615	1,740	D	45.9	36.4	14.4	3.4	34	37	15	1.0	1.0	0.9	1.2	55.8	44.2
West Baton Rouge	9,976	5,131	3,522	1,249	74	1,609	D	51.4	35.3	12.5	0.7	19	42	36	0.6	0.6	0.5	0.6	59.3	40.7
West Carroll	5,120	2,068	2,082	771	199	14	R	40.4	40.7	15.1	3.9	50	21	10	0.3	0.3	0.3	0.4	49.8	50.2
West Feliciana	4,374	2,328	1,501	516	29	827	D	53.2	34.3	11.8	0.7	11	46	45	0.2	0.3	0.2	0.2	60.8	39.2
Winn	7,549	3,537	2,932	843	237	605	D	46.9	38.8	11.2	3.1	30	27	52	0.4	0.4	0.4	0.4	54.7	45.3
LOUISIANA	**1,790,017**	**815,971**	**733,386**	**211,478**	**29,182**	**82,585**	**D**	**45.6**	**41.0**	**11.8**	**1.6**				**100.0**	**100.0**	**100.0**	**100.0**	**52.7**	**47.3**

Table FS. — Vote for U.S. Senator: October 3, Primary Election[1]

Parish	Top candidates — Total	Breaux	Khacha-turian	Stock-still	Other	Pct of total vote — Breaux	Khacha-turian	Stock-still	Other	Rank — Breaux	Khacha-turian	Stock-still	Other	Pct contribution to state vote — Total	Breaux	Khacha-turian	Stock-still	Other
Acadia	10,581	7,882	457	1,290	952	74.5	4.3	12.2	9.0	41	52	4	54	1.3	1.3	0.6	1.8	1.2
Allen	5,876	4,880	208	311	477	83.0	3.5	5.3	8.1	2	58	41	58	0.7	0.8	0.3	0.4	0.6
Ascension	11,299	8,401	568	1,147	1,183	74.4	5.0	10.2	10.5	42	40	10	35	1.3	1.4	0.8	1.6	1.4
Assumption	3,348	2,684	182	122	360	80.2	5.4	3.6	10.8	10	34	62	30	0.4	0.4	0.2	0.2	0.4
Avoyelles	8,483	6,770	431	300	982	79.8	5.1	3.5	11.6	12	39	63	22	1.0	1.1	0.6	0.4	1.2
Beauregard	4,479	3,430	210	304	535	76.6	4.7	6.8	11.9	34	47	26	16	0.5	0.6	0.3	0.4	0.7
Bienville	4,371	3,405	215	193	558	77.9	4.9	4.4	12.8	22	41	54	7	0.5	0.6	0.3	0.3	0.7
Bossier	16,338	11,670	1,337	1,586	1,745	71.4	8.2-	9.7	10.7	54	17	13	32	1.9	1.9	1.8	2.3	2.1
Caddo	55,372	42,176	4,375	4,927	3,894	76.2	7.9	8.9	7.0	36	19	19	62	6.6	6.8	5.9	7.0	4.7
Calcasieu	31,769	24,585	1,462	2,903	2,819	77.4	4.6	9.1	8.9	26	48	17	55	3.8	4.0	2.0	4.1	3.4
Caldwell	2,379	1,848	165	114	252	77.7	6.9	4.8	10.6	24	23	47	33	0.3	0.3	0.2	0.2	0.3
Cameron	1,721	1,426	38	97	160	82.9	2.2	5.6	9.3	3	64	36	50	0.2	0.2	<.1	0.1	0.2
Catahoula	2,691	2,108	111	137	335	78.3	4.1	5.1	12.4	19	54	43	9	0.3	0.3	0.1	0.2	0.4
Claiborne	3,071	2,375	161	175	360	77.3	5.2	5.7	11.7	27	37	35	19	0.4	0.4	0.2	0.3	0.4
Concordia	4,090	3,129	210	308	443	76.5	5.1	7.5	10.8	35	38	23	29	0.5	0.5	0.3	0.4	0.5
De Soto	6,635	5,319	377	298	641	80.2	5.7	4.5	9.7	11	32	51	45	0.8	0.9	0.5	0.4	0.8
East Baton Rouge	93,035	67,013	5,793	13,083	7,146	72.0	6.2	14.1	7.7	51	26	3	59	11.0	10.9	7.7	18.7	8.7
East Carroll	2,039	1,649	86	58	246	80.9	4.2	2.8	12.1	7	53	64	12	0.2	0.3	0.1	<.1	0.3
East Feliciana	3,461	2,605	151	398	307	75.3	4.4	11.5	8.9	38	51	7	56	0.4	0.4	0.2	0.6	0.4
Evangeline	10,846	8,367	622	500	1,357	77.1	5.7	4.6	12.5	28	29	49	8	1.3	1.4	0.8	0.7	1.6
Franklin	6,089	4,829	294	242	724	79.3	4.8	4.0	11.9	17	44	58	17	0.7	0.8	0.4	0.3	0.9
Grant	5,466	4,019	504	290	653	73.5	9.2	5.3	11.9	45	11	40	15	0.6	0.7	0.7	0.4	0.8
Iberia	15,952	11,568	1,205	1,577	1,602	72.5	7.6	9.9	10.0	49	21	11	41	1.9	1.9	1.6	2.3	1.9
Iberville	12,668	10,093	459	625	1,491	79.7	3.6	4.9	11.8	13	56	45	18	1.5	1.6	0.6	0.9	1.8
Jackson	5,594	4,556	220	212	606	81.4	3.9	3.8	10.8	5	55	61	28	0.7	0.7	0.3	0.3	0.7
Jefferson	85,709	53,341	15,405	8,035	8,928	62.2	18.0	9.4	10.4	62	3	16	36	10.2	8.7	20.6	11.5	10.9
Jefferson Davis	7,096	5,746	197	538	615	81.0	2.8	7.6	8.7	6	63	21	57	0.8	0.9	0.3	0.8	0.7
Lafayette	30,616	21,257	2,818	3,637	2,904	69.4	9.2	11.9	9.5	57	12	6	47	3.6	3.5	3.8	5.2	3.5
Lafourche	12,306	9,052	1,369	689	1,196	73.6	11.1	5.6	9.7	44	7	37	43	1.5	1.5	1.8	1.0	1.5
La Salle	3,008	2,161	217	157	473	71.8	7.2	5.2	15.7	53	22	42	5	0.4	0.4	0.3	0.2	0.6
Lincoln	9,249	7,360	501	545	843	79.6	5.4	5.9	9.1	15	36	33	51	1.1	1.2	0.7	0.8	1.0
Livingston	13,939	9,933	834	1,682	1,490	71.3	6.0	12.1	10.7	55	28	5	31	1.7	1.6	1.1	2.4	1.8
Madison	3,372	2,726	99	141	406	80.8	2.9	4.2	12.0	8	62	55	13	0.4	0.4	0.1	0.2	0.5
Morehouse	6,699	5,075	413	387	824	75.8	6.2	5.8	12.3	37	27	34	11	0.8	0.8	0.6	0.6	1.0
Natchitoches	7,507	5,757	367	449	934	76.7	4.9	6.0	12.4	32	43	32	10	0.9	0.9	0.5	0.6	1.1
Orleans	82,063	63,305	9,772	3,140	5,846	77.1	11.9	3.8	7.1	29	5	60	61	9.7	10.3	13.1	4.5	7.1
Ouachita	32,695	24,464	2,643	2,476	3,112	74.8	8.1	7.6	9.5	39	18	22	46	3.9	4.0	3.5	3.5	3.8
Plaquemines	5,089	3,362	500	912	315	66.1	9.8	17.9	6.2	60	9	1	64	0.6	0.5	0.7	1.3	0.4
Pointe Coupee	5,492	4,574	187	358	373	83.3	3.4	6.5	6.8	1	59	27	63	0.7	0.7	0.3	0.5	0.5
Rapides	25,168	18,108	2,935	1,359	2,766	71.9	11.7	5.4	11.0	52	6	39	26	3.0	2.9	3.9	1.9	3.4
Red River	2,789	2,219	158	140	272	79.6	5.7	5.0	9.8	16	33	44	42	0.3	0.4	0.2	0.2	0.3
Richland	5,980	4,697	394	231	658	78.5	6.6	3.9	11.0	18	24	59	25	0.7	0.8	0.5	0.3	0.8
Sabine	4,312	3,351	192	276	493	77.7	4.5	6.4	11.4	23	50	28	23	0.5	0.5	0.3	0.4	0.6
St. Bernard	8,529	5,585	1,616	526	802	65.5	18.9	6.2	9.4	61	2	30	48	1.0	0.9	2.2	0.8	1.0
St. Charles	4,610	3,131	558	433	488	67.9	12.1	9.4	10.6	59	4	15	34	0.5	0.5	0.7	0.6	0.6
St. Helena	2,243	1,676	110	229	228	74.7	4.9	10.2	10.2	40	42	8	40	0.3	0.3	0.1	0.3	0.3
St. James	3,517	2,542	169	162	644	72.3	4.8	4.6	18.3	50	45	50	2	0.4	0.4	0.2	0.2	0.8
St. John the Baptist	6,804	3,913	600	545	1,746	57.5	8.8	8.0	25.7	63	14	20	1	0.8	0.6	0.8	0.8	2.1
St. Landry	18,524	14,337	831	1,681	1,675	77.4	4.5	9.1	9.0	25	49	18	52	2.2	2.3	1.1	2.4	2.0
St. Martin	7,436	5,713	403	556	764	76.8	5.4	7.5	10.3	33	35	24	38	0.9	0.9	0.5	0.8	0.9
St. Mary	10,584	7,398	803	468	1,915	69.9	7.6	4.4	18.1	56	20	53	3	1.3	1.2	1.1	0.7	2.3
St. Tammany	17,672	9,206	3,583	2,964	1,919	52.1	20.3	16.8	10.9	64	1	2	27	2.1	1.5	4.8	4.2	2.3
Tangipahoa	13,655	9,359	1,268	1,387	1,641	68.5	9.3	10.2	12.0	58	10	9	14	1.6	1.5	1.7	2.0	2.0
Tensas	2,353	1,895	72	113	273	80.5	3.1	4.8	11.6	9	60	46	21	0.3	0.3	<.1	0.2	0.3
Terrebonne	17,916	13,289	1,971	977	1,679	74.2	11.0	5.5	9.4	43	8	38	49	2.1	2.2	2.6	1.4	2.0
Union	5,471	4,270	311	329	561	78.0	5.7	6.0	10.3	21	31	31	39	0.6	0.7	0.4	0.5	0.7
Vermilion	8,376	6,138	732	532	974	73.3	8.7	6.4	11.6	46	15	29	20	1.0	1.0	1.0	0.8	1.2
Vernon	6,894	5,487	328	308	771	79.6	4.8	4.5	11.2	14	46	52	24	0.8	0.9	0.4	0.4	0.9
Washington	10,327	7,505	847	977	998	72.7	8.2	9.5	9.7	47	16	14	44	1.2	1.2	1.1	1.4	1.2
Webster	11,403	8,749	1,007	473	1,174	76.7	8.8	4.1	10.3	31	13	56	37	1.4	1.4	1.3	0.7	1.4
West Baton Rouge	6,542	5,385	235	446	476	82.3	3.6	6.8	7.3	4	57	25	60	0.8	0.9	0.3	0.6	0.6
West Carroll	2,330	1,690	150	93	397	72.5	6.4	4.0	17.0	48	25	57	4	0.3	0.3	0.2	0.1	0.5
West Feliciana	2,104	1,644	63	207	190	78.1	3.0	9.8	9.0	20	61	12	53	0.2	0.3	<.1	0.3	0.2
Winn	5,005	3,834	286	231	654	76.6	5.7	4.6	13.1	33	30	48	6	0.6	0.6	0.4	0.3	0.8
LOUISIANA	843,037	616,021	74,785	69,986	82,245	73.1	8.9	8.3	9.8					100.0	100.0	100.0	100.0	100.0

[1]Winning candidate elected from primary election received more than 50% of vote.

Table G. — Vote for Governor: November 16, 1991, General Election

Parish	Total	Edwards (DEM)	Duke (REP)		Plurality Total	Party	DEM	REP		Rank DEM	Rank REP		Total	DEM	REP	
Acadia	24,700	14,928	9,772	-	5,156	D	60.4	39.6	-	22	43	-	1.4	1.4	1.5	-
Allen	10,207	6,171	4,036	-	2,135	D	60.5	39.5	-	21	44	-	0.6	0.6	0.6	-
Ascension	27,659	14,792	12,867	-	1,925	D	53.5	46.5	-	41	24	-	1.6	1.4	1.9	-
Assumption	10,873	6,488	4,385	-	2,103	D	59.7	40.3	-	24	41	-	0.6	0.6	0.7	-
Avoyelles	16,836	9,044	7,792	-	1,252	D	53.7	46.3	-	40	25	-	1.0	0.9	1.2	-
Beauregard	11,936	5,585	6,351	-	766	R	46.8	53.2	-	51	14	-	0.7	0.5	0.9	-
Bienville	7,901	4,685	3,216	-	1,469	D	59.3	40.7	-	28	37	-	0.5	0.4	0.5	-
Bossier	28,993	14,536	14,457	-	79	D	50.1	49.9	-	45	20	-	1.7	1.4	2.2	-
Caddo	93,524	59,933	33,591	-	26,342	D	64.1	35.9	-	13	52	-	5.4	5.7	5.0	-
Calcasieu	61,810	40,617	21,193	-	19,424	D	65.7	34.3	-	5	60	-	3.6	3.8	3.2	-
Caldwell	5,702	2,112	3,590	-	1,478	R	37.0	63.0	-	62	3	-	0.3	0.2	0.5	-
Cameron	4,122	2,669	1,453	-	1,216	D	64.8	35.2	-	6	59	-	0.2	0.3	0.2	-
Catahoula	6,285	2,815	3,470	-	655	R	44.8	55.2	-	54	11	-	0.4	0.3	0.5	-
Claiborne	7,503	4,329	3,174	-	1,155	D	57.7	42.3	-	34	31	-	0.4	0.4	0.5	-
Concordia	9,584	4,544	5,040	-	496	R	47.4	52.6	-	48	17	-	0.6	0.4	0.8	-
De Soto	11,178	6,607	4,571	-	2,036	D	59.1	40.9	-	31	34	-	0.6	0.6	0.7	-
East Baton Rouge	150,794	100,138	50,656	-	49,482	D	66.4	33.6	-	3	62	-	8.7	9.5	7.5	-
East Carroll	4,374	3,017	1,357	-	1,660	D	69.0	31.0	-	2	63	-	0.3	0.3	0.2	-
East Feliciana	8,311	4,949	3,362	-	1,587	D	59.5	40.5	-	25	40	-	0.5	0.5	0.5	-
Evangeline	16,417	8,947	7,470	-	1,477	D	54.5	45.5	-	39	26	-	1.0	0.8	1.1	-
Franklin	10,589	4,410	6,179	-	1,769	R	41.6	58.4	-	59	6	-	0.6	0.4	0.9	-
Grant	8,016	3,516	4,500	-	984	R	43.9	56.1	-	57	8	-	0.5	0.3	0.7	-
Iberia	29,408	16,594	12,814	-	3,780	D	56.4	43.6	-	35	30	-	1.7	1.6	1.9	-
Iberville	16,563	10,693	5,870	-	4,823	D	64.6	35.4	-	9	56	-	1.0	1.0	0.9	-
Jackson	7,518	3,345	4,173	-	828	R	44.5	55.5	-	55	10	-	0.4	0.3	0.6	-
Jefferson	172,444	102,261	70,183	-	32,078	D	59.3	40.7	-	27	38	-	10.0	9.7	10.5	-
Jefferson Davis	13,451	8,581	4,870	-	3,711	D	63.8	36.2	-	14	51	-	0.8	0.8	0.7	-
Lafayette	63,152	40,816	22,336	-	18,480	D	64.6	35.4	-	8	57	-	3.7	3.9	3.3	-
Lafourche	36,001	21,346	14,655	-	6,691	D	59.3	40.7	-	29	36	-	2.1	2.0	2.2	-
La Salle	7,342	2,432	4,910	-	2,478	R	33.1	66.9	-	63	2	-	0.4	0.2	0.7	-
Lincoln	15,325	9,382	5,943	-	3,439	D	61.2	38.8	-	19	46	-	0.9	0.9	0.9	-
Livingston	30,706	12,152	18,554	-	6,402	R	39.6	60.4	-	61	4	-	1.8	1.1	2.8	-
Madison	5,828	3,562	2,266	-	1,296	D	61.1	38.9	-	20	45	-	0.3	0.3	0.3	-
Morehouse	13,778	6,517	7,261	-	744	R	47.3	52.7	-	49	16	-	0.8	0.6	1.1	-
Natchitoches	15,230	8,870	6,360	-	2,510	D	58.2	41.8	-	33	32	-	0.9	0.8	0.9	-
Orleans	199,665	173,744	25,921	-	147,823	D	87.0	13.0	-	1	64	-	11.6	16.4	3.9	-
Ouachita	52,859	26,137	26,722	-	585	R	49.4	50.6	-	46	19	-	3.1	2.5	4.0	-
Plaquemines	11,990	6,689	5,301	-	1,388	D	55.8	44.2	-	38	27	-	0.7	0.6	0.8	-
Pointe Coupee	12,117	7,430	4,687	-	2,743	D	61.3	38.7	-	18	47	-	0.7	0.7	0.7	-
Rapides	49,400	27,638	21,762	-	5,876	D	55.9	44.1	-	36	29	-	2.9	2.6	3.2	-
Red River	5,013	2,674	2,339	-	335	D	53.3	46.7	-	42	23	-	0.3	0.3	0.3	-
Richland	9,149	3,970	5,179	-	1,209	R	43.4	56.6	-	58	7	-	0.5	0.4	0.8	-
Sabine	9,886	4,635	5,251	-	616	R	46.9	53.1	-	50	15	-	0.6	0.4	0.8	-
St. Bernard	32,547	14,394	18,153	-	3,759	R	44.2	55.8	-	56	9	-	1.9	1.4	2.7	-
St. Charles	20,565	12,680	7,885	-	4,795	D	61.7	38.3	-	15	50	-	1.2	1.2	1.2	-
St. Helena	6,148	3,700	2,448	-	1,252	D	60.2	39.8	-	23	42	-	0.4	0.4	0.4	-
St. James	12,102	8,028	4,074	-	3,954	D	66.3	33.7	-	4	61	-	0.7	0.8	0.6	-
St. John the Baptist	18,678	11,993	6,685	-	5,308	D	64.2	35.8	-	11	54	-	1.1	1.1	1.0	-
St. Landry	38,087	23,362	14,725	-	8,637	D	61.3	38.7	-	17	48	-	2.2	2.2	2.2	-
St. Martin	19,821	12,726	7,095	-	5,631	D	64.2	35.8	-	12	53	-	1.1	1.2	1.1	-
St. Mary	24,486	15,039	9,447	-	5,592	D	61.4	38.6	-	16	49	-	1.4	1.4	1.4	-
St. Tammany	58,478	32,678	25,800	-	6,878	D	55.9	44.1	-	37	28	-	3.4	3.1	3.8	-
Tangipahoa	35,268	18,779	16,489	-	2,290	D	53.2	46.8	-	43	22	-	2.0	1.8	2.5	-
Tensas	3,387	1,993	1,394	-	599	D	58.8	41.2	-	32	33	-	0.2	0.2	0.2	-
Terrebonne	33,461	19,799	13,662	-	6,137	D	59.2	40.8	-	30	35	-	1.9	1.9	2.0	-
Union	10,049	4,029	6,020	-	1,991	R	40.1	59.9	-	60	5	-	0.6	0.4	0.9	-
Vermilion	22,359	14,477	7,882	-	6,595	D	64.7	35.3	-	7	58	-	1.3	1.4	1.2	-
Vernon	13,532	6,676	6,856	-	180	R	49.3	50.7	-	47	18	-	0.8	0.6	1.0	-
Washington	19,734	9,157	10,577	-	1,420	R	46.4	53.6	-	52	13	-	1.1	0.9	1.6	-
Webster	17,430	9,024	8,406	-	618	D	51.8	48.2	-	44	21	-	1.0	0.9	1.3	-
West Baton Rouge	10,108	6,016	4,092	-	1,924	D	59.5	40.5	-	26	39	-	0.6	0.6	0.6	-
West Carroll	5,221	1,625	3,596	-	1,971	R	31.1	68.9	-	64	1	-	0.3	0.2	0.5	-
West Feliciana	4,492	2,896	1,596	-	1,300	D	64.5	35.5	-	10	55	-	0.3	0.3	0.2	-
Winn	7,948	3,660	4,288	-	628	R	46.0	54.0	-	53	12	-	0.5	0.3	0.6	-
LOUISIANA	1,728,040	1,057,031	671,009	-	386,022	D	61.2	38.8	-				100.0	100.0	100.0	-

Table H. — Vote for U.S. Representative in Congress: November 3, 1992, General Election

Congressional district and parish	Total	Candidate #1[1]	Candidate #2[1]		Plurality[2] Total	Party	Percent of total vote #1	#2		Rank within district #1	#2		Percent contribution to district vote Total	#1	#2	
District 4[3]	194,831	143,980	50,851	-	93,129	C1	73.9	26.1	-			-	100.0	100.0	100.0	-
Ascension	4,013	2,463	1,550	-	913	C1	61.4	38.6	-	20	9	-	2.1	1.7	3.0	-
Avoyelles (pt)	1,514	1,279	235	-	1,044	C1	84.5	15.5	-	4	25	-	0.8	0.9	0.5	-
Bossier (pt)	1,840	1,359	481	-	878	C1	73.9	26.1	-	13	16	-	0.9	0.9	0.9	-
Caddo (pt)	22,941	19,262	3,679	-	15,583	C1	84.0	16.0	-	6	23	-	11.8	13.4	7.2	-
Claiborne (pt)	3,163	1,844	1,319	-	525	C1	58.3	41.7	-	22	7	-	1.6	1.3	2.6	-
Concordia (pt)	4,375	2,056	2,319	-	263	C2	47.0	53.0	-	24	5	-	2.2	1.4	4.6	-
East Baton Rouge (pt)	58,090	48,838	9,252	-	39,586	C1	84.1	15.9	-	5	24	-	29.8	33.9	18.2	-
East Carroll	2,744	1,065	1,679	-	614	C2	38.8	61.2	-	26	3	-	1.4	0.7	3.3	-
East Feliciana	6,952	5,028	1,924	-	3,104	C1	72.3	27.7	-	15	14	-	3.6	3.5	3.8	-
Iberville (pt)	7,153	5,934	1,219	-	4,715	C1	83.0	17.0	-	7	22	-	3.7	4.1	2.4	-
Lafayette	7,727	6,700	1,027	-	5,673	C1	86.7	13.3	-	3	26	-	4.0	4.7	2.0	-
Lincoln (pt)	5,905	3,550	2,355	-	1,195	C1	60.1	39.9	-	21	8	-	3.0	2.5	4.6	-
Livingston (pt)	4,528	2,799	1,729	-	1,070	C1	61.8	38.2	-	18	11	-	2.3	1.9	3.4	-
Madison (pt)	2,188	909	1,279	-	370	C2	41.5	58.5	-	25	4	-	1.1	0.6	2.5	-
Morehouse (pt)	4,349	1,678	2,671	-	993	C2	38.6	61.4	-	27	2	-	2.2	1.2	5.3	-
Ouachita (pt)	12,163	4,334	7,829	-	3,495	C2	35.6	64.4	-	28	1	-	6.2	3.0	15.4	-
Pointe Coupee (pt)	3,352	2,939	413	-	2,526	C1	87.7	12.3	-	2	27	-	1.7	2.0	0.8	-
Rapides (pt)	7,284	5,953	1,331	-	4,622	C1	81.7	18.3	-	8	21	-	3.7	4.1	2.6	-
St. Helena	3,336	2,709	627	-	2,082	C1	81.2	18.8	-	9	20	-	1.7	1.9	1.2	-
St. Landry (pt)	9,551	7,574	1,977	-	5,597	C1	79.3	20.7	-	11	18	-	4.9	5.3	3.9	-
St. Martin	2,342	1,883	459	-	1,424	C1	80.4	19.6	-	10	19	-	1.2	1.3	0.9	-
Tangipahoa	5,650	4,154	1,496	-	2,658	C1	73.5	26.5	-	14	15	-	2.9	2.9	2.9	-
Tensas	2,683	1,652	1,031	-	621	C1	61.6	38.4	-	19	10	-	1.4	1.1	2.0	-
Union (pt)	2,039	1,098	941	-	157	C1	53.8	46.2	-	23	6	-	1.0	0.8	1.9	-
Webster (pt)	2,404	1,682	722	-	960	C1	70.0	30.0	-	16	13	-	1.2	1.2	1.4	-
West Baton Rouge (pt)	2,222	2,050	172	-	1,878	C1	92.3	7.7	-	1	28	-	1.1	1.4	0.3	-
West Carroll (pt)	477	299	178	-	121	C1	62.7	37.3	-	17	12	-	0.2	0.2	0.4	-
West Feliciana	3,846	2,889	957	-	1,932	C1	75.1	24.9	-	12	17	-	2.0	2.0	1.9	-
District 5[4]	243,580	90,079	153,501	-	63,422	C2	37.0	63.0	-			-	100.0	100.0	100.0	-
Bienville	6,769	4,227	2,542	-	1,685	C1	62.4	37.6	-	2	17	-	2.8	4.7	1.7	-
Bossier (pt)	27,197	6,836	20,361	-	13,525	C2	25.1	74.9	-	17	2	-	11.2	7.6	13.3	-
Caddo (pt)	70,906	17,055	53,851	-	36,796	C2	24.1	75.9	-	18	1	-	29.1	18.9	35.1	-
Claiborne (pt)	1,970	680	1,290	-	610	C2	34.5	65.5	-	15	4	-	0.8	0.8	0.8	-
De Soto	9,919	4,225	5,694	-	1,469	C2	42.6	57.4	-	12	7	-	4.1	4.7	3.7	-
Franklin	9,035	4,794	4,241	-	553	C1	53.1	46.9	-	6	13	-	3.7	5.3	2.8	-
Jackson	7,079	3,882	3,197	-	685	C1	54.8	45.2	-	4	15	-	2.9	4.3	2.1	-
Lincoln (pt)	8,537	2,835	5,702	-	2,867	C2	33.2	66.8	-	16	3	-	3.5	3.1	3.7	-
Madison (pt)	2,195	1,101	1,094	-	7	C1	50.2	49.8	-	8	11	-	0.9	1.2	0.7	-
Morehouse (pt)	7,388	3,536	3,852	-	316	C2	47.9	52.1	-	10	9	-	3.0	3.9	2.5	-
Natchitoches	13,332	7,487	5,845	-	1,642	C1	56.2	43.8	-	3	16	-	5.5	8.3	3.8	-
Ouachita (pt)	39,945	14,339	25,606	-	11,267	C2	35.9	64.1	-	14	5	-	16.4	15.9	16.7	-
Red River	4,346	2,018	2,328	-	310	C2	46.4	53.6	-	11	8	-	1.8	2.2	1.5	-
Richland	8,378	4,452	3,926	-	526	C1	53.1	46.9	-	5	14	-	3.4	4.9	2.6	-
Union (pt)	6,555	3,243	3,312	-	69	C2	49.5	50.5	-	9	10	-	2.7	3.6	2.2	-
Webster (pt)	13,527	5,529	7,998	-	2,469	C2	40.9	59.1	-	13	6	-	5.6	6.1	5.2	-
West Carroll (pt)	4,031	2,105	1,926	-	179	C1	52.2	47.8	-	7	12	-	1.7	2.3	1.3	-
Winn (pt)	2,471	1,735	736	-	999	C1	70.2	29.8	-	1	18	-	1.0	1.9	0.5	-
District 6[5]	245,178	123,953	121,225	-	2,728	C1	50.6	49.4	-			-	100.0	100.0	100.0	-
Avoyelles (pt)	13,240	4,183	9,057	-	4,874	C2	31.6	68.4	-	14	4	-	5.4	3.4	7.5	-
Caldwell	3,718	1,428	2,290	-	862	C2	38.4	61.6	-	7	11	-	1.5	1.2	1.9	-
Catahoula	4,625	1,728	2,897	-	1,169	C2	37.4	62.6	-	8	10	-	1.9	1.4	2.4	-
Concordia (pt)	2,843	1,223	1,620	-	397	C2	43.0	57.0	-	5	13	-	1.2	1.0	1.3	-
East Baton Rouge (pt)	100,371	72,154	28,217	-	43,937	C1	71.9	28.1	-	1	17	-	40.9	58.2	23.3	-
Evangeline	2,486	429	2,057	-	1,628	C2	17.3	82.7	-	17	1	-	1.0	0.3	1.7	-
Grant	7,274	2,501	4,773	-	2,272	C2	34.4	65.6	-	10	8	-	3.0	2.0	3.9	-
Iberville (pt)	5,897	2,421	3,476	-	1,055	C2	41.1	58.9	-	6	12	-	2.4	2.0	2.9	-
La Salle	6,060	2,018	4,042	-	2,024	C2	33.3	66.7	-	13	5	-	2.5	1.6	3.3	-
Livingston (pt)	11,429	7,760	3,669	-	4,091	C1	67.9	32.1	-	2	16	-	4.7	6.3	3.0	-
Pointe Coupee (pt)	7,150	2,430	4,720	-	2,290	C2	34.0	66.0	-	12	6	-	2.9	2.0	3.9	-
Rapides (pt)	40,277	11,545	28,732	-	17,187	C2	28.7	71.3	-	15	3	-	16.4	9.3	23.7	-
Sabine	7,529	2,582	4,947	-	2,365	C2	34.3	65.7	-	11	7	-	3.1	2.1	4.1	-
St. Landry (pt)	8,322	1,980	6,342	-	4,362	C2	23.8	76.2	-	16	2	-	3.4	1.6	5.2	-
Vernon	12,701	4,564	8,137	-	3,573	C2	35.9	64.1	-	9	9	-	5.2	3.7	6.7	-
West Baton Rouge (pt)	7,276	3,292	3,984	-	692	C2	45.2	54.8	-	3	15	-	3.0	2.7	3.3	-
Winn (pt)	3,980	1,715	2,265	-	550	C2	43.1	56.9	-	4	14	-	1.6	1.4	1.9	-
LOUISIANA[6]	683,589	284,910	398,679	-	113,769	R	41.7	58.3	-			-				

[1]Candidates in the general election may be from the same party because of Louisiana's open primary law, which states that the top two candidates from the primary election run in the general election (regardless of party affiliation) if no one received a majority of the vote in the primary. [2]C1 = Candidate #1; C2 = Candidate #2. [3]Both candidates are Democrats (#1 = Fields, #2 = Jones). [4]Candidate #1 is a Democrat (Huckaby); candidate #2, Republican (McCrery). [5]Both candidates are Republicans (#1 = Baker, #2 = Holloway). [6]The vote for all Democratic candidates is shown under Candidate #1; the vote for all Republican candidates, under Candidate #2.

Table H2. — Vote for U.S. Representative in Congress: October 3, 1992, Primary Election

Congressional district and parish	Total	Candidate #1[1]	Candidate #2[1]	Other	Plurality[2] Total	Plurality[2] Party	Percent of total vote #1	#2	Other	Rank within district #1	#2	Other	Percent contribution to district vote Total	#1	#2	Other
District 1 (10/3/92 Pri.)[3] ..	**115,051**	**83,685**	**11,620**	**19,746**	**63,939**	**C1**	**72.7**	**10.1**	**17.2**				**100.0**	**100.0**	**100.0**	**100.0**
Jefferson (pt)	60,080	44,626	6,104	9,350	35,276	C1	74.3	10.2	15.6	2	4	6	52.2	53.3	52.5	47.4
Livingston (pt)	5,837	4,069	518	1,250	2,819	C1	69.7	8.9	21.4	5	6	2	5.1	4.9	4.5	6.3
Orleans (pt)	11,122	8,739	929	1,454	7,285	C1	78.6	8.4	13.1	1	7	7	9.7	10.4	8.0	7.4
St. Helena (pt)	635	448	70	117	331	C1	70.6	11.0	18.4	4	1	4	0.6	0.5	0.6	0.6
St. Tammany	17,552	12,638	1,912	3,002	9,636	C1	72.0	10.9	17.1	3	3	5	15.3	15.1	16.5	15.2
Tangipahoa (pt)	10,326	6,641	1,048	2,637	4,004	C1	64.3	10.1	25.5	7	5	1	9.0	7.9	9.0	13.4
Washington	9,499	6,524	1,039	1,936	4,588	C1	68.7	10.9	20.4	6	2	3	8.3	7.8	8.9	9.8
District 2 (10/3/92 Pri.)[4] ..	**91,241**	**67,030**	**14,121**	**10,090**	**52,909**	**C1**	**73.5**	**15.5**	**11.1**				**100.0**	**100.0**	**100.0**	**100.0**
Jefferson (pt)	21,244	12,767	4,988	3,489	7,779	C1	60.1	23.5	16.4	2	1	1	23.3	19.0	35.3	34.6
Orleans (pt)	69,997	54,263	9,133	6,601	45,130	C1	77.5	13.0	9.4	1	2	2	76.7	81.0	64.7	65.4
District 3 (10/3/92 Pri.)[5] ..	**100,449**	**82,047**	**18,402**	**-**	**63,645**	**C1**	**81.7**	**18.3**	**-**				**100.0**	**100.0**	**100.0**	**-**
Ascension (pt)	9,260	7,600	1,660	-	5,940	C1	82.1	17.9	-	8	7	-	9.2	9.3	9.0	-
Assumption	3,295	2,880	415	-	2,465	C1	87.4	12.6	-	3	12	-	3.3	3.5	2.3	-
Iberia	15,672	13,125	2,547	-	10,578	C1	83.7	16.3	-	6	9	-	15.6	16.0	13.8	-
Iberville (pt)	397	354	43	-	311	C1	89.2	10.8	-	2	13	-	0.4	0.4	0.2	-
Jefferson (pt)	4,468	3,164	1,304	-	1,860	C1	70.8	29.2	-	14	1	-	4.4	3.9	7.1	-
Lafourche	12,242	9,859	2,383	-	7,476	C1	80.5	19.5	-	10	5	-	12.2	12.0	12.9	-
Plaquemines	4,617	3,736	881	-	2,855	C1	80.9	19.1	-	9	6	-	4.6	4.6	4.8	-
St. Bernard	8,076	6,194	1,882	-	4,312	C1	76.7	23.3	-	13	2	-	8.0	7.5	10.2	-
St. Charles	4,427	3,413	1,014	-	2,399	C1	77.1	22.9	-	12	3	-	4.4	4.2	5.5	-
St. James	3,368	2,920	448	-	2,472	C1	86.7	13.3	-	4	11	-	3.4	3.6	2.4	-
St. John the Baptist....	6,235	4,868	1,367	-	3,501	C1	78.1	21.9	-	11	4	-	6.2	5.9	7.4	-
St. Martin (pt)............	167	149	18	-	131	C1	89.2	10.8	-	1	14	-	0.2	0.2	0.1	-
St. Mary	10,416	8,957	1,459	-	7,498	C1	86.0	14.0	-	5	10	-	10.4	10.9	7.9	-
Terrebonne	17,809	14,828	2,981	-	11,847	C1	83.3	16.7	-	7	8	-	17.7	18.1	16.2	-
District 7 (10/3/92 Pri.)[6] ..	**115,203**	**84,149**	**23,870**	**7,184**	**60,279**	**C1**	**73.0**	**20.7**	**6.2**				**100.0**	**100.0**	**100.0**	**100.0**
Acadia	10,453	8,188	1,738	527	6,450	C1	78.3	16.6	5.0	2	8	8	9.1	9.7	7.3	7.3
Allen.......................	5,639	4,402	891	346	3,511	C1	78.1	15.8	6.1	3	9	3	4.9	5.2	3.7	4.8
Beauregard	4,383	3,165	969	249	2,196	C1	72.2	22.1	5.7	9	3	6	3.8	3.8	4.1	3.5
Calcasieu	31,217	22,417	7,069	1,731	15,348	C1	71.8	22.6	5.5	10	2	7	27.1	26.6	29.6	24.1
Cameron	1,697	1,291	340	66	951	C1	76.1	20.0	3.9	8	4	11	1.5	1.5	1.4	0.9
Evangeline (pt)	8,013	6,403	1,141	469	5,262	C1	79.9	14.2	5.9	1	11	5	7.0	7.6	4.8	6.5
Jefferson Davis	6,905	5,305	1,319	281	3,986	C1	76.8	19.1	4.1	6	5	10	6.0	6.3	5.5	3.9
Lafayette (pt)	25,427	16,422	6,744	2,261	9,678	C1	64.6	26.5	8.9	11	1	1	22.1	19.5	28.3	31.5
St. Landry (pt)	7,606	5,926	1,178	502	4,748	C1	77.9	15.5	6.6	4	10	2	6.6	7.0	4.9	7.0
St. Martin (pt)	5,663	4,375	944	344	3,431	C1	77.3	16.7	6.1	5	7	4	4.9	5.2	4.0	4.8
Vermilion	8,200	6,255	1,537	408	4,718	C1	76.3	18.7	5.0	7	6	9	7.1	7.4	6.4	5.7

[1]Under Louisiana's open primary law, where all candidates appear on the same ballot (regardless of party affiliation), a candidate may be elected to office if he or she receives a majority of the vote in the primary. Candidate #1 received the highest number of votes; candidate #2, the second highest. [2]C1 = Candidate #1; C2 = Candidate #2. [3]Candidate #1 (Livingston) and candidate #2 (Thompson) are both Republicans. Other includes two independents and two other Republicans. [4]Both candidates are Democrats (#1 = Jefferson, #2 = Irvin). Other is an independent. [5]Candidate #1 is a Democrat (Tauzin); candidate #2, Republican (Boynton). [6]Candidate #1 is a Democrat (J. Hayes); candidate #2, Republican (F. Hayes). Other is also a Republican.

Table I. — Vote for Presidential Preference: March 10, 1992, Democratic Primary Election

| Parish | Top candidates | | | | | | | | | Top three candidates (state vote) | | | | | | | | |
| | | | | | | | | | | Percent of total vote | | | Rank | | | Percent contribution to state vote | | | |
	Total	Clinton	Tsongas	Brown	McCarthy	Woods	Burke	Harkin	Other	Clinton	Tsongas	Brown	Clinton	Tsongas	Brown	Total	Clinton	Tsongas	Brown
Acadia	3,509	2,505	323	222	32	163	37	43	184	71.4	9.2	6.3	37	19	23	0.9	0.9	0.8	0.9
Allen	3,582	2,574	280	252	42	217	41	33	143	71.9	7.8	7.0	32	31	15	0.9	1.0	0.7	1.0
Ascension	4,261	3,143	370	266	32	159	64	41	186	73.8	8.7	6.2	17	21	25	1.1	1.2	0.9	1.0
Assumption	6,141	3,744	361	330	721	216	86	90	593	61.0	5.9	5.4	61	44	33	1.6	1.4	0.8	1.3
Avoyelles	9,817	6,031	731	613	976	292	167	144	863	61.4	7.4	6.2	60	34	24	2.6	2.3	1.7	2.4
Beauregard	1,847	1,259	196	117	65	117	11	12	70	68.2	10.6	6.3	48	15	22	0.5	0.5	0.5	0.5
Bienville	1,876	1,360	72	63	204	63	10	12	92	72.5	3.8	3.4	27	62	55	0.5	0.5	0.2	0.2
Bossier	4,558	3,438	349	203	262	150	9	30	117	75.4	7.7	4.5	11	32	45	1.2	1.3	0.8	0.8
Caddo	14,978	12,028	1,387	755	39	360	55	99	255	80.3	9.3	5.0	1	18	36	3.9	4.5	3.3	3.0
Calcasieu	13,931	9,530	1,600	1,225	67	813	112	135	449	68.4	11.5	8.8	46	11	2	3.6	3.6	3.8	4.8
Caldwell	1,489	1,083	79	46	155	48	8	9	61	72.7	5.3	3.1	23	49	59	0.4	0.4	0.2	0.2
Cameron	686	489	45	49	5	64	6	5	23	71.3	6.6	7.1	39	41	14	0.2	0.2	0.1	0.2
Catahoula	3,601	2,388	162	170	397	117	48	50	269	66.3	4.5	4.7	53	55	42	0.9	0.9	0.4	0.7
Claiborne	1,648	1,206	121	57	147	42	8	13	54	73.2	7.3	3.5	20	36	51	0.4	0.5	0.3	0.2
Concordia	3,668	2,502	203	178	369	90	53	34	239	68.2	5.5	4.9	47	47	39	1.0	0.9	0.5	0.7
De Soto	2,603	1,967	114	86	180	81	27	36	112	75.6	4.4	3.3	9	58	56	0.7	0.7	0.3	0.3
East Baton Rouge	25,000	17,957	3,387	1,727	126	658	178	207	760	71.8	13.5	6.9	33	7	17	6.5	6.7	8.0	6.8
East Carroll	878	633	39	28	111	8	5	5	49	72.1	4.4	3.2	29	56	57	0.2	0.2	<.1	0.1
East Feliciana	3,614	2,850	192	181	26	167	49	35	114	78.9	5.3	5.0	2	48	37	0.9	1.1	0.5	0.7
Evangeline	2,874	2,094	130	137	166	88	40	43	176	72.9	4.5	4.8	21	54	40	0.7	0.8	0.3	0.5
Franklin	3,641	2,766	148	125	278	112	34	35	143	76.0	4.1	3.4	7	60	52	0.9	1.0	0.3	0.5
Grant	2,197	1,569	172	92	189	25	15	15	120	71.4	7.8	4.2	36	30	48	0.6	0.6	0.4	0.4
Iberia	4,178	2,394	528	278	485	118	39	37	299	57.3	12.6	6.7	64	8	19	1.1	0.9	1.2	1.1
Iberville	3,274	2,425	257	210	38	79	42	42	181	74.1	7.8	6.4	16	29	20	0.9	0.9	0.6	0.8
Jackson	1,692	1,264	84	44	172	46	5	12	65	74.7	5.0	2.6	13	52	61	0.4	0.5	0.2	0.2
Jefferson	30,254	19,387	5,817	2,535	198	235	514	361	1,207	64.1	19.2	8.4	57	1	5	7.9	7.3	13.7	9.9
Jefferson Davis	2,303	1,718	176	156	19	137	24	9	64	74.6	7.6	6.8	14	33	18	0.6	0.6	0.4	0.6
Lafayette	20,655	12,482	3,028	1,820	956	718	240	256	1,155	60.4	14.7	8.8	62	4	1	5.4	4.7	7.1	7.1
Lafourche	6,148	4,038	665	333	613	62	55	50	332	65.7	10.8	5.4	55	14	32	1.6	1.5	1.6	1.3
La Salle	1,321	960	75	42	137	33	8	10	56	72.7	5.7	3.2	24	45	58	0.3	0.4	0.2	0.2
Lincoln	2,517	1,752	218	111	255	63	14	16	88	69.6	8.7	4.4	43	22	46	0.7	0.7	0.5	0.4
Livingston	8,520	6,072	742	478	82	536	106	123	381	71.3	8.7	5.6	40	20	30	2.2	2.3	1.7	1.9
Madison	1,017	732	40	65	93	10	3	6	68	72.0	3.9	6.4	31	61	21	0.3	0.3	<.1	0.3
Morehouse	3,399	2,493	209	105	320	49	25	31	167	73.3	6.1	3.1	19	43	60	0.9	0.9	0.5	0.4
Natchitoches	3,951	2,531	323	200	505	85	36	38	233	64.1	8.2	5.1	58	24	35	1.0	0.9	0.8	0.8
Orleans	59,717	43,316	8,266	4,703	406	256	636	480	1,654	72.5	13.8	7.9	26	6	9	15.5	16.2	19.4	18.5
Ouachita	13,984	10,017	969	590	1,344	263	79	109	613	71.6	6.9	4.2	34	39	47	3.6	3.8	2.3	2.3
Plaquemines	1,848	1,336	220	134	11	13	31	23	80	72.3	11.9	7.3	28	10	12	0.5	0.5	0.5	0.5
Pointe Coupee	1,888	1,419	135	88	28	68	36	23	91	75.2	7.2	4.7	12	38	43	0.5	0.5	0.3	0.3
Rapides	8,008	5,225	910	470	764	79	43	93	424	65.2	11.4	5.9	56	12	28	2.1	2.0	2.1	1.8
Red River	1,065	837	33	36	70	40	2	7	40	78.6	3.1	3.4	3	63	54	0.3	0.3	<.1	0.1
Richland	1,424	1,018	63	32	185	35	13	10	68	71.5	4.4	2.2	35	57	63	0.4	0.4	0.1	0.1
Sabine	1,877	1,297	106	99	217	50	5	8	95	69.1	5.6	5.3	45	46	34	0.5	0.5	0.2	0.4
St. Bernard	6,621	4,436	990	525	60	60	125	91	334	67.0	15.0	7.9	51	3	8	1.7	1.7	2.3	2.1
St. Charles	3,155	2,210	437	270	22	33	36	33	114	70.0	13.9	8.6	42	5	3	0.8	0.8	1.0	1.1
St. Helena	1,341	1,013	40	75	14	56	27	26	90	75.5	3.0	5.6	10	64	31	0.3	0.4	<.1	0.3
St. James	1,739	1,354	117	122	10	14	20	24	78	77.9	6.7	7.0	4	40	16	0.5	0.5	0.3	0.5
St. John the Baptist	2,521	1,854	273	202	21	18	28	29	96	73.5	10.8	8.0	18	13	7	0.7	0.7	0.6	0.8
St. Landry	5,009	3,639	406	389	40	175	80	71	209	72.6	8.1	7.8	25	25	10	1.3	1.4	1.0	1.5
St. Martin	8,951	5,145	720	649	719	396	240	221	861	57.5	8.0	7.3	63	26	13	2.3	1.9	1.7	2.5
St. Mary	3,719	2,522	367	185	323	95	27	26	174	67.8	9.9	5.0	49	16	38	1.0	0.9	0.9	0.7
St. Tammany	15,192	10,103	2,577	1,277	105	150	167	192	621	66.5	17.0	8.4	52	2	4	4.0	3.8	6.1	5.0
Tangipahoa	6,960	4,936	674	566	69	161	124	113	317	70.9	9.7	8.1	41	17	6	1.8	1.8	1.6	2.2
Tensas	1,272	908	55	47	151	14	13	12	72	71.4	4.3	3.7	38	59	50	0.3	0.3	0.1	0.2
Terrebonne	5,522	3,823	665	318	330	59	33	47	247	69.2	12.0	5.8	44	9	29	1.4	1.4	1.6	1.2
Union	3,499	2,521	179	86	408	69	62	31	143	72.0	5.1	2.5	30	51	62	0.9	0.9	0.4	0.3
Vermilion	4,194	2,685	336	193	487	192	36	28	237	64.0	8.0	4.6	59	27	44	1.1	1.0	0.8	0.8
Vernon	2,553	1,713	220	151	207	86	20	19	137	67.1	8.6	5.9	50	23	27	0.7	0.6	0.5	0.6
Washington	8,479	6,171	617	653	116	145	166	124	487	72.8	7.3	7.7	22	37	11	2.2	2.3	1.5	2.6
Webster	3,151	2,432	162	108	203	115	11	22	98	77.2	5.1	3.4	5	50	53	0.8	0.9	0.4	0.4
West Baton Rouge	1,745	1,325	138	83	20	54	20	26	79	75.9	7.9	4.8	8	28	41	0.5	0.5	0.3	0.3
West Carroll	964	719	47	15	108	13	9	10	43	74.6	4.9	1.6	15	53	64	0.3	0.3	0.1	<.1
West Feliciana	943	723	70	56	7	30	17	8	32	76.7	7.4	5.9	6	35	26	0.2	0.3	0.2	0.2
Winn	1,428	941	93	59	222	29	14	10	60	65.9	6.5	4.1	54	42	49	0.4	0.4	0.2	0.2
LOUISIANA	384,397	267,002	42,508	25,480	15,129	8,989	4,294	4,033	16,962	69.5	11.1	6.6				100.0	100.0	100.0	100.0

Table J. — Vote for Presidential Preference: March 10, 1992, Republican Primary Election

Parish	Top candidates					Top four candidates (state vote)												
						Percent of total vote				Rank				Percent contribution to state vote				
	Total	Bush	Bu-chanan	Duke	Other	Bush	Bu-chanan	Duke	Other	Bush	Bu-chanan	Duke	Other	Total	Bush	Bu-chanan	Duke	Other
Acadia	695	393	241	59	2	56.5	34.7	8.5	0.3	34	8	48	62	0.5	0.5	0.7	0.5	<.1
Allen	386	268	66	48	4	69.4	17.1	12.4	1.0	2	60	33	42	0.3	0.3	0.2	0.4	0.1
Ascension	988	549	344	87	8	55.6	34.8	8.8	0.8	40	7	46	49	0.7	0.7	0.9	0.7	0.3
Assumption	498	269	110	58	61	54.0	22.1	11.6	12.2	45	38	38	1	0.4	0.3	0.3	0.5	2.1
Avoyelles	1,058	533	246	198	81	50.4	23.3	18.7	7.7	55	32	9	11	0.8	0.6	0.7	1.7	2.8
Beauregard	575	372	111	83	9	64.7	19.3	14.4	1.6	13	54	21	39	0.4	0.4	0.3	0.7	0.3
Bienville	271	170	56	29	16	62.7	20.7	10.7	5.9	14	46	42	19	0.2	0.2	0.2	0.2	0.6
Bossier	2,834	1,860	574	238	162	65.6	20.3	8.4	5.7	9	49	51	21	2.1	2.2	1.6	2.0	5.6
Caddo	8,701	6,331	1,694	614	62	72.8	19.5	7.1	0.7	1	53	59	54	6.4	7.6	4.6	5.1	2.1
Calcasieu	3,870	2,673	877	283	37	69.1	22.7	7.3	1.0	3	35	57	45	2.9	3.2	2.4	2.4	1.3
Caldwell	318	153	72	66	27	48.1	22.6	20.8	8.5	60	36	6	6	0.2	0.2	0.2	0.6	0.9
Cameron	71	38	27	6	0	53.5	38.0	8.5	0.0	48	3	49	63	<.1	<.1	<.1	<.1	0.0
Catahoula	485	245	89	112	39	50.5	18.4	23.1	8.0	54	56	3	9	0.4	0.3	0.2	0.9	1.4
Claiborne	413	280	61	48	24	67.8	14.8	11.6	5.8	5	64	39	20	0.3	0.3	0.2	0.4	0.8
Concordia	717	403	164	120	30	56.2	22.9	16.7	4.2	36	33	12	26	0.5	0.5	0.4	1.0	1.0
De Soto	430	261	82	67	20	60.7	19.1	15.6	4.7	20	55	15	25	0.3	0.3	0.2	0.6	0.7
East Baton Rouge	15,538	10,353	4,287	773	125	66.6	27.6	5.0	0.8	6	25	63	50	11.5	12.4	11.7	6.5	4.3
East Carroll	210	125	33	34	18	59.5	15.7	16.2	8.6	25	63	13	5	0.2	0.1	<.1	0.3	0.6
East Feliciana	587	315	178	88	6	53.7	30.3	15.0	1.0	46	18	19	43	0.4	0.4	0.5	0.7	0.2
Evangeline	360	157	116	78	9	43.6	32.2	21.7	2.5	64	13	5	33	0.3	0.2	0.3	0.7	0.3
Franklin	782	359	165	229	29	45.9	21.1	29.3	3.7	62	42	2	29	0.6	0.4	0.5	1.9	1.0
Grant	474	287	81	72	34	60.5	17.1	15.2	7.2	21	61	17	15	0.4	0.3	0.2	0.6	1.2
Iberia	1,445	774	435	122	114	53.6	30.1	8.4	7.9	47	20	50	10	1.1	0.9	1.2	1.0	4.0
Iberville	385	252	88	41	4	65.5	22.9	10.6	1.0	11	34	43	41	0.3	0.3	0.2	0.3	0.1
Jackson	332	185	79	56	12	55.7	23.8	16.9	3.6	37	30	11	31	0.2	0.2	0.2	0.5	0.4
Jefferson	20,954	12,143	6,546	2,112	153	58.0	31.2	10.1	0.7	31	17	45	53	15.5	14.5	17.9	17.7	5.3
Jefferson Davis	394	262	83	46	3	66.5	21.1	11.7	0.8	7	43	37	52	0.3	0.3	0.2	0.4	0.1
Lafayette	9,248	5,742	2,896	460	150	62.1	31.3	5.0	1.6	18	16	64	37	6.8	6.9	7.9	3.8	5.2
Lafourche	1,343	745	399	100	99	55.5	29.7	7.4	7.4	41	22	56	13	1.0	0.9	1.1	0.8	3.4
La Salle	273	166	50	38	19	60.8	18.3	13.9	7.0	19	57	24	16	0.2	0.2	0.1	0.3	0.7
Lincoln	1,339	877	271	93	98	65.5	20.2	6.9	7.3	10	50	60	14	1.0	1.0	0.7	0.8	3.4
Livingston	1,940	1,111	557	259	13	57.3	28.7	13.4	0.7	32	24	28	57	1.4	1.3	1.5	2.2	0.5
Madison	424	236	89	79	20	55.7	21.0	18.6	4.7	39	45	10	24	0.3	0.3	0.2	0.7	0.7
Morehouse	936	560	204	151	21	59.8	21.8	16.1	2.2	24	39	14	34	0.7	0.7	0.6	1.3	0.7
Natchitoches	853	498	172	114	69	58.4	20.2	13.4	8.1	30	51	27	8	0.6	0.6	0.5	1.0	2.4
Orleans	14,165	9,303	3,718	940	204	65.7	26.2	6.6	1.4	8	28	62	40	10.5	11.1	10.2	7.9	7.1
Ouachita	6,881	4,691	1,414	492	284	68.2	20.5	7.2	4.1	4	47	58	27	5.1	5.6	3.9	4.1	9.8
Plaquemines	465	246	165	50	4	52.9	35.5	10.8	0.9	50	6	41	48	0.3	0.3	0.5	0.4	0.1
Pointe Coupee	298	166	94	36	2	55.7	31.5	12.1	0.7	38	14	36	56	0.2	0.2	0.3	0.3	<.1
Rapides	3,167	2,053	746	244	124	64.8	23.6	7.7	3.9	12	31	53	28	2.3	2.5	2.0	2.0	4.3
Red River	137	80	25	27	5	58.4	18.2	19.7	3.6	29	58	7	30	0.1	<.1	<.1	0.2	0.2
Richland	483	266	109	75	33	55.1	22.6	15.5	6.8	42	37	16	18	0.4	0.3	0.3	0.6	1.1
Sabine	419	239	90	61	29	57.0	21.5	14.6	6.9	33	40	20	17	0.3	0.3	0.2	0.5	1.0
St. Bernard	1,584	806	540	227	11	50.9	34.1	14.3	0.7	53	10	22	55	1.2	1.0	1.5	1.9	0.4
St. Charles	1,391	872	404	107	8	62.7	29.0	7.7	0.6	15	23	54	60	1.0	1.0	1.1	0.9	0.3
St. Helena	252	118	53	77	4	46.8	21.0	30.6	1.6	61	44	1	38	0.2	0.1	0.1	0.6	0.1
St. James	162	78	63	20	1	48.1	38.9	12.3	0.6	59	1	34	59	0.1	<.1	0.2	0.2	<.1
St. John the Baptist	876	495	300	76	5	56.5	34.2	8.7	0.6	35	9	47	61	0.6	0.6	0.8	0.6	0.2
St. Landry	1,018	502	394	114	8	49.3	38.7	11.2	0.8	58	2	40	51	0.8	0.6	1.1	1.0	0.3
St. Martin	885	443	267	125	50	50.1	30.2	14.1	5.6	56	19	23	22	0.7	0.5	0.7	1.0	1.7
St. Mary	1,259	762	343	127	27	60.5	27.2	10.1	2.1	22	26	44	35	0.9	0.9	0.9	1.1	0.9
St. Tammany	11,455	7,124	3,430	788	113	62.2	29.9	6.9	1.0	17	21	61	44	8.5	8.5	9.4	6.6	3.9
Tangipahoa	2,034	1,120	640	256	18	55.1	31.5	12.6	0.9	43	15	32	46	1.5	1.3	1.8	2.1	0.6
Tensas	326	203	69	43	11	62.3	21.2	13.2	3.4	16	41	30	32	0.2	0.2	0.2	0.4	0.4
Terrebonne	2,384	1,300	859	182	43	54.5	36.0	7.6	1.8	44	5	55	36	1.8	1.6	2.4	1.5	1.5
Union	884	529	145	123	87	59.8	16.4	13.9	9.8	23	62	25	3	0.7	0.6	0.4	1.0	3.0
Vermilion	602	310	198	49	45	51.5	32.9	8.1	7.5	51	11	52	12	0.4	0.4	0.5	0.4	1.6
Vernon	535	318	106	81	30	59.4	19.8	15.1	5.6	26	52	18	23	0.4	0.4	0.3	0.7	1.0
Washington	1,259	648	316	284	11	51.5	25.1	22.6	0.9	52	29	4	47	0.9	0.8	0.9	2.4	0.4
Webster	919	538	166	121	94	58.5	18.1	13.2	10.2	28	59	31	2	0.7	0.6	0.5	1.0	3.3
West Baton Rouge	312	166	102	42	2	53.2	32.7	13.5	0.6	49	12	26	58	0.2	0.2	0.3	0.4	<.1
West Carroll	339	153	90	65	31	45.1	26.5	19.2	9.1	63	27	8	4	0.3	0.2	0.2	0.5	1.1
West Feliciana	212	105	79	28	0	49.5	37.3	13.2	0.0	57	4	29	64	0.2	0.1	0.2	0.2	0.0
Winn	279	165	57	34	23	59.1	20.4	12.2	8.2	27	48	35	7	0.2	0.2	0.2	0.3	0.8
LOUISIANA	135,109	83,744	36,525	11,955	2,885	62.0	27.0	8.8	2.1					100.0	100.0	100.0	100.0	100.0

1992 Vote for President
Percent for Clinton (D), by County

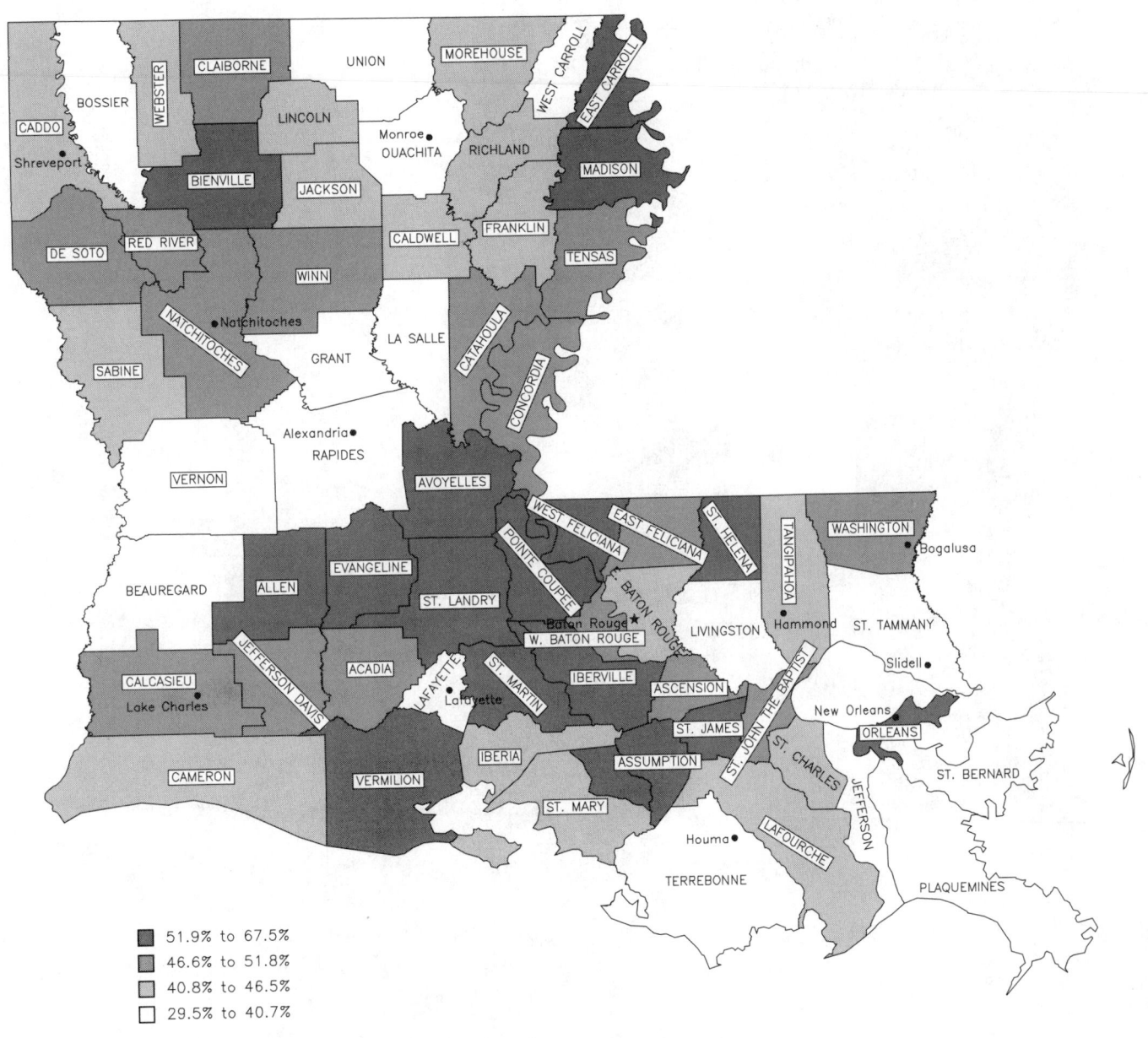

Legend:
- 51.9% to 67.5%
- 46.6% to 51.8%
- 40.8% to 46.5%
- 29.5% to 40.7%

Clinton (D) received 45.6% statewide.

A framed parish name indicates
a parish carried by the winner.

1992 Vote for U.S. Senator
Percent for Breaux (D), by County

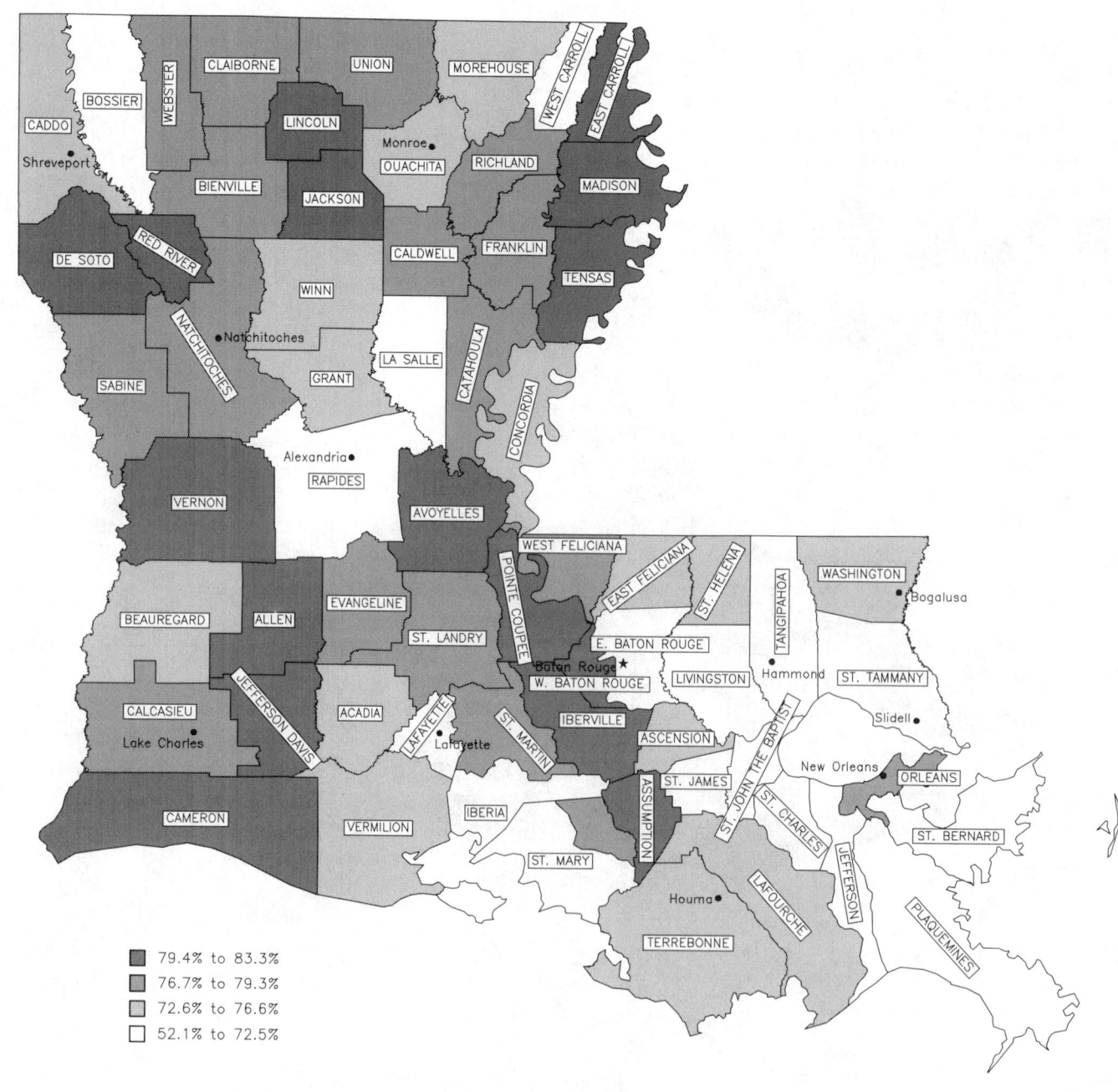

79.4% to 83.3%
76.7% to 79.3%
72.6% to 76.6%
52.1% to 72.5%

Breaux (D) received 73.1% statewide.

A framed parish name indicates
a parish carried by the winner.

1991 Vote for Governor
Percent for Edwards (D), by County

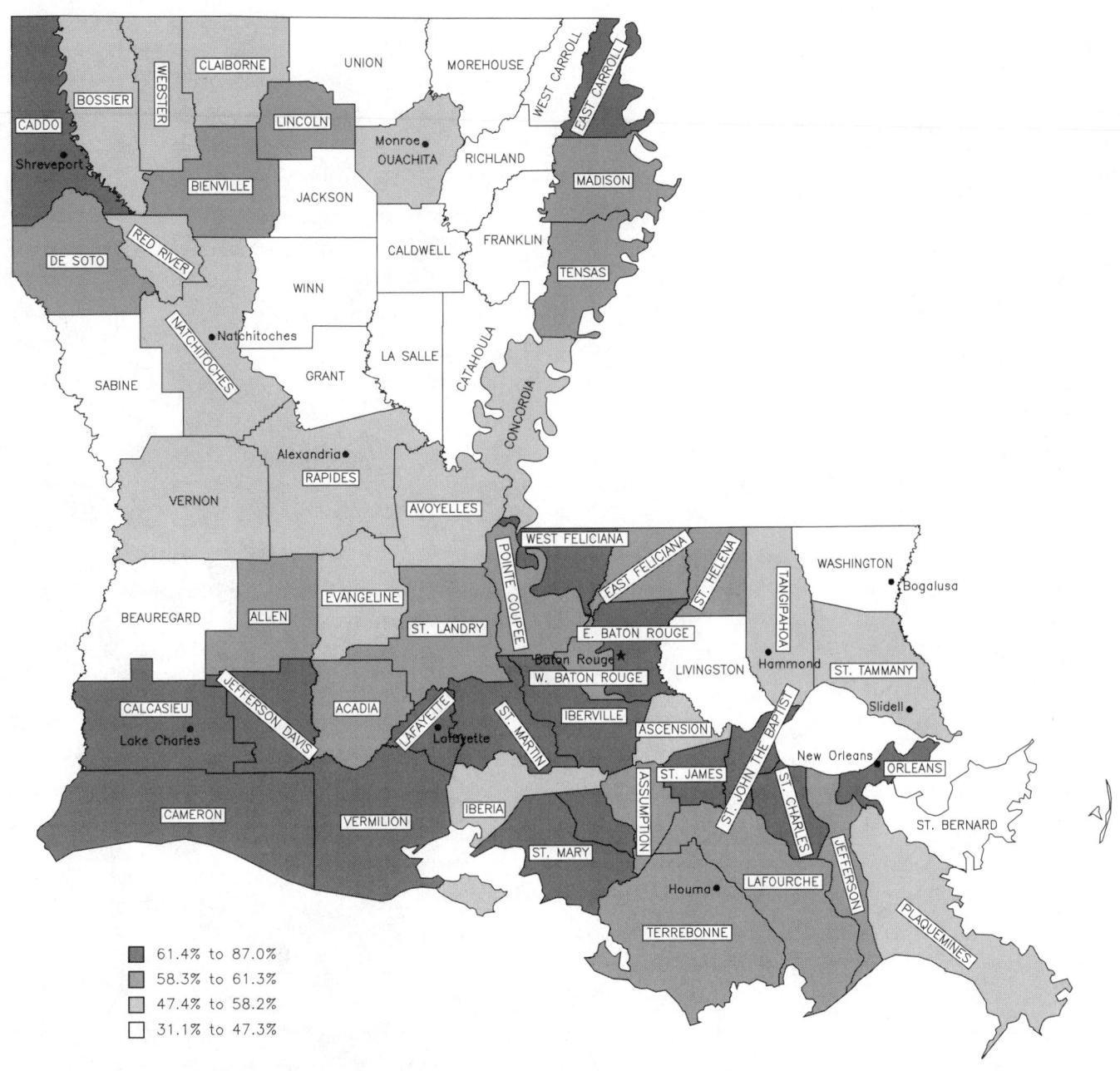

Legend:
- 61.4% to 87.0%
- 58.3% to 61.3%
- 47.4% to 58.2%
- 31.1% to 47.3%

Edwards (D) received 61.2% statewide.

A framed parish name indicates
a parish carried by the winner.

MAINE

Congressional Districts 2
  Average Population 613,964
State Senate Districts 35
  Average Population 35,084
State House Districts 151
  Average Population 8,132

Electoral College Votes...4
Counties[1] 16
Voting Precincts 657

Alternative Registration Methods:
    Deputized Registrars, Election day, Mail-in, Motor-voter

Registration Deadline (Days before Election) 0

Voting Equipment Use (Cities and Towns)[2]

Datavote Punch Card	0	Paper Ballot	449
Electronic	1	Other Punch Card	0
Lever Machine	4	Mixed Systems	0
Optical Scanner	37		

Party Control	DEM	REP	IND	VAC
1993 State Senate	20	15	0	0
1992 State Senate	22	13	0	0
1993 State House	90	61	0	0
1992 State House	97	54	0	0

Population Statistics 1990

Race/ Ethnicity	Total Population		Voting Age Population		Voting Age Population % of total population
	Number	%	Number	%	
Non-Hispanic					
White	1,203,357	98.0	903,031	98.3	75.0
Black	4,937	0.4	3,315	0.4	67.1
Asian/Pacific Islander	6,505	0.5	4,330	0.5	66.6
Native American	5,898	0.5	3,811	0.4	64.6
Other	402	<.1	132	<.1	32.8
All Hispanic	6,829	0.6	4,307	0.5	63.1
TOTAL	1,227,928	100.0	918,926	100.0	74.8

Estimated Voting Age Population 1992 (VAP) 944,000
Number of Registered Voters[3] 974,605
  % of estimated VAP.. 103.2
Voter Turnout (Highest Office) 679,499
  % of VAP 72.0
  % of Registration 69.7
Persons Not Voting—of Voting Age 264,501
  % of VAP 28.0
Persons Not Voting—of Registered 295,106
  % of Registration 30.3
Straight Ticket Voting .... No

State Officials and Members of Congress

Governor:
John R. McKernan, Jr. (R) 1986, elected to a four-year term in
1990.

U.S. Senators:
William S. Cohen (R) 1978, elected to a six-year term in 1990.
George J. Mitchell (D) 1980, elected to a six-year term in 1988.

U.S. Representative in Congress:
(District, Name, Party, Date first elected)

1. Andrews (D) 1990   2. Snowe (R) 1978

---

[1]Elections administered by 491 cities and towns rather than counties. Data presented for counties and 33 cities and towns with more than one voting precinct. [2]Reported for all 491 cities and towns, including those with a single voting precinct. [3]Total voter registration reported by Maine Secretary of State exceeds estimated voting age population (VAP).

Candidates: General Election, November 3, 1992

Candidate(s)	Total vote	Percent	Party	Status	First elected
President/Vice President					
Clinton/Gore	263,420	38.77%	Democrat	Challenger	1992
Perot/Stockdale	206,820	30.44%	Independent	Challenger	
Bush/Quayle	206,504	30.39%	Republican	Incumbent	1988
Marrou/Lord	1,681	0.25%	Libertarian	Challenger	
Fulani/Munoz	519	0.08%	New Alliance	Challenger	
Phillips/Knight	464	0.07%	Taxpayers	Challenger	
Others	91	0.01%	Composited Others	Challenger	
U.S. Senator (No Contest)					
Governor (No Contest)					
U.S. Representative in Congress					
District 1					
Thomas Andrews	232,696	64.97%	Democrat	Incumbent	1990
Linda Bean	125,236	34.97%	Republican	Challenger	
Others	216	0.06%	Composited Others	Challenger	
District 2					
Olympia Snowe	153,022	49.13%	Republican	Incumbent	1978
Patrick McGowan	130,824	42.01%	Democrat	Challenger	
Jonathan Carter	27,526	8.84%	Green	Challenger	
Others	61	0.02%	Composited Others	Challenger	

Voter Registration and Turnout, 1948-1992 Elections

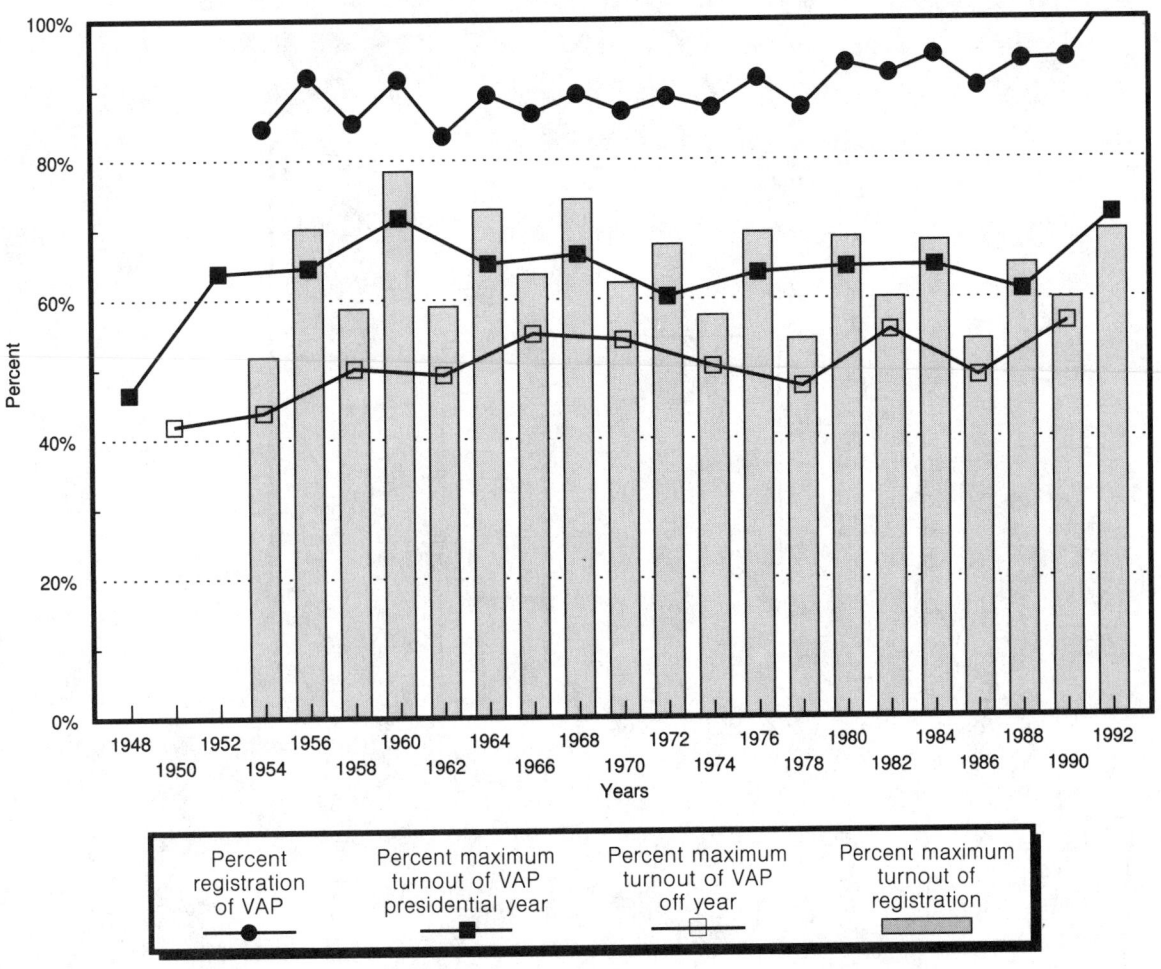

Year	Estimated Voting Age Population (VAP)	Voter registration (REG)			Actual	Voter turnout									
						Highest office						Maximum vote			
		Total	Percent of VAP	Rank by percent of VAP		Total	Office	Percent total REG	Rank by percent of REG	Percent of VAP	Rank by percent of VAP	Total	Percent total REG	Rank by percent of REG	Percent total VAP	Rank by percent of VAP
1992¹	944,000	974,605	103.2	1	-	679,499	P	69.7	44	72.0	1	679,499	69.7	45	72.0	1
1990........	924,000	871,697	94.3	1	-	522,181	G	59.9	20	56.5	1	522,181	59.9	23	56.5	2
1988........	908,000	854,764	94.1	1	-	555,035	P	64.9	42	61.1	4	555,035	64.9	43	61.1	6
1986........	875,000	790,247	90.3	1	-	426,861	G	54.0	30	48.8	7	426,861	54.0	34	48.8	9
1984........	855,000	810,661	94.8	1	-	553,144	P	68.2	40	64.7	3	553,144	68.2	41	64.7	4
1982........	831,000	766,285	92.2	1	-	460,295	G	60.1	30	55.4	5	460,295	60.1	25	55.4	6
1980........	811,000	759,978	93.7	2	-	523,011	P	68.8	39	64.5	8	523,011	68.8	41	64.5	8
1978........	791,000	691,617	87.4	4	-	375,172	S	54.2	33	47.4	6	375,172	54.2	34	47.4	10
1976........	759,000	695,595	91.6	3	-	483,216	P	69.5	36	63.7	6	483,216	69.5	36	63.7	8
1974²	723,000	631,873	87.4	2	-	363,945	G	57.6	24	50.3	8	363,945	57.6	27	50.3	9
1972........	692,000	615,546	89.0	3	-	417,042	P	67.8	37	60.3	21	417,042	67.8	37	60.3	23
1970........	601,000	522,044	86.9	6	-	325,386	G	62.3	30	54.1	13	325,386	62.3	30	54.1	14
1968........	592,000	529,137	89.4	7	-	392,936	P	74.3	37	66.4	19	392,936	74.3	38	66.4	19
1966........	589,000	509,888	86.6	8	-	323,838	G	63.5	26	55.0	20	323,838	63.5	26	55.0	20
1964........	585,000	522,236	89.3	9	-	380,965	P	72.9	33	65.1	30	380,965	72.9	33	65.1	30
1962........	595,000	496,029	83.4	8	-	292,725	G	59.0	29	49.2	29	292,725	59.0	29	49.2	30
1960........	588,000	537,922	91.5	4	-	421,767	P	78.4	28	71.7	21	421,767	78.4	28	71.7	21
1958........	567,000	483,875	85.3	5	-	284,226	S	58.7	25	50.1	28	284,226	58.7	25	50.1	29
1956........	545,000	500,922	91.9	4	-	351,706	P	70.2	24	64.5	31	351,706	70.2	25	64.5	32
1954........	569,000	480,658	84.5	6	-	248,971	G	51.8	20	43.8	36	248,971	51.8	20	43.8	37
1952........	551,000	-	-	-	-	351,786	P	-	-	63.8	33	351,786	-	-	63.8	34
1950........	576,000	-	-	-	-	241,177	G	-	-	41.9	35	241,177	-	-	41.9	35
1948........	570,000	-	-	-	-	264,787	P	-	-	46.5	36	264,787	-	-	46.5	36

¹Total voter registration reported by Maine Secretary of State exceeds estimated voting age population (VAP). ²Law establishing election day voter registration enacted 1973.

MAINE

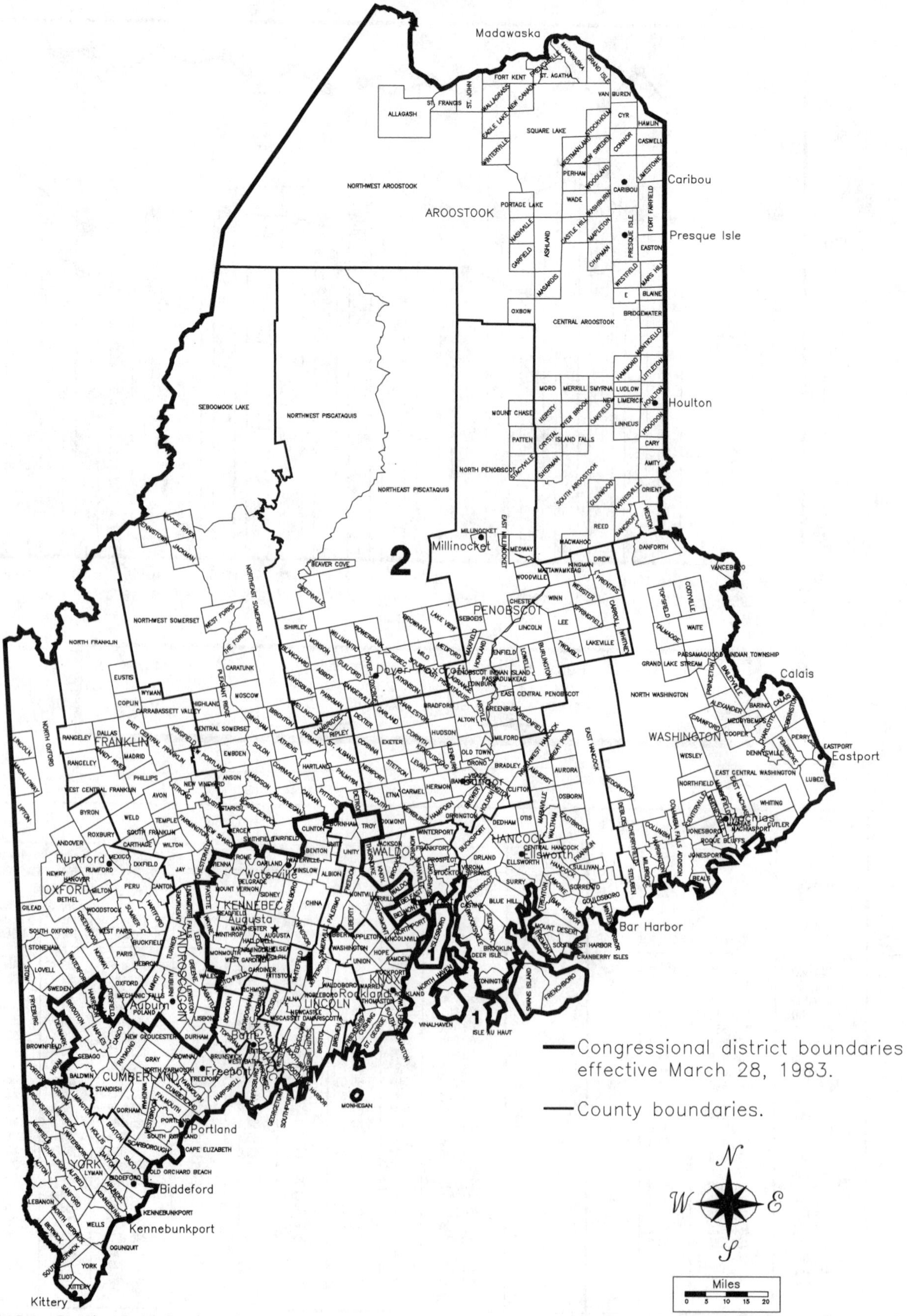

Madawaska

St. John

ALLAGASH · ST FRANCIS

AROOSTOOK

Caribou

Presque Isle

SEBOOMOOK LAKE

NORTHWEST PISCATAQUIS

Houlton

NORTHEAST PISCATAQUIS

2

Millinocket

PENOBSCOT

NORTHWEST SOMERSET

WEST FORKS

FRANKLIN

Dover-Foxcroft

WASHINGTON

Calais

Eastport

Machias

RUMFORD

OXFORD

KENNEBEC

Waterville

Augusta

HANCOCK

Ellsworth

Bar Harbor

ANDROSCOGGIN

Auburn

KNOX

Rockland

LINCOLN

1

1

CUMBERLAND

Bath

Freeport

MONHEGAN

Portland

Cape Elizabeth

YORK

Biddeford

Kennebunkport

Kittery

—— Congressional district boundaries
effective March 28, 1983.

—— County boundaries.

N
W · E
S

Miles
0 5 10 15 20

Table A. — 1990 Population by Race and Ethnic Origin

State/ county code	County	Total persons	Percent of total persons — Non-Hispanic White	Black	Asian and Pacific Islander	Native American	Other	Hispanic	Rank¹ Total	White	Black	Hispanic	Pct contribution Total	White	Black	Hispanic
23 001	Androscoggin	105,259	98.0	0.4	0.5	0.2	<.1	0.7	5	11	4	2	8.6	8.6	9.4	11.4
23 003	Aroostook	86,936	96.9	1.0	0.5	0.9	<.1	0.6	6	15	1	4	7.1	7.0	18.4	8.1
23 005	Cumberland	243,135	97.6	0.6	0.9	0.2	<.1	0.6	1	13	3	3	19.8	19.7	30.2	22.8
23 007	Franklin	29,008	98.9	0.1	0.3	0.3	<.1	0.4	15	4	14	13	2.4	2.4	0.6	1.6
23 009	Hancock	46,948	98.6	0.2	0.3	0.4	<.1	0.6	9	8	8	6	3.8	3.8	1.9	3.9
23 011	Kennebec	115,904	98.6	0.2	0.4	0.3	<.1	0.4	4	9	7	9	9.4	9.5	5.2	7.6
23 013	Knox	36,310	98.9	0.1	0.2	0.3	<.1	0.4	10	6	10	12	3.0	3.0	1.1	2.1
23 015	Lincoln	30,357	99.1	<.1	0.1	0.3	<.1	0.4	14	1	16	10	2.5	2.5	0.5	1.8
23 017	Oxford	52,602	99.0	0.1	0.3	0.2	<.1	0.4	7	2	11	11	4.3	4.3	1.3	3.0
23 019	Penobscot	146,601	97.7	0.4	0.6	0.9	<.1	0.5	3	12	5	8	11.9	11.9	10.6	10.3
23 021	Piscataquis	18,653	98.8	<.1	0.3	0.4	<.1	0.4	16	7	15	14	1.5	1.5	0.4	1.0
23 023	Sagadahoc	33,535	97.1	1.0	0.7	0.2	<.1	1.0	12	14	2	1	2.7	2.7	6.5	4.9
23 025	Somerset	49,767	99.0	0.1	0.2	0.3	<.1	0.3	8	3	12	16	4.1	4.1	1.2	2.5
23 027	Waldo	33,018	98.9	0.1	0.2	0.2	<.1	0.5	13	5	13	7	2.7	2.7	0.8	2.5
23 029	Washington	35,308	95.2	0.2	0.2	4.0	0.0	0.4	11	16	9	15	2.9	2.8	1.3	1.9
23 031	York	164,587	98.2	0.3	0.7	0.2	<.1	0.6	2	10	6	5	13.4	13.4	10.7	14.5
23	**MAINE**	**1,227,928**	**98.0**	**0.4**	**0.5**	**0.5**	**<.1**	**0.6**					**100.0**	**100.0**	**100.0**	**100.0**
	CITIES AND TOWNS															
23 001	Auburn city	24,309	98.1	0.5	0.7	0.2	<.1	0.5	4	19	10	18	2.0	2.0	2.3	1.9
23 011	Augusta city	21,325	97.9	0.3	0.8	0.4	<.1	0.5	6	22	16	17	1.7	1.7	1.4	1.7
23 019	Bangor city	33,181	96.7	0.9	1.0	0.7	<.1	0.6	3	28	4	12	2.7	2.7	6.1	3.1
23 023	Bath city	9,799	95.9	1.9	0.6	0.2	<.1	1.3	17	30	1	2	0.8	0.8	3.8	1.8
23 027	Belfast city	6,355	99.0	<.1	0.2	0.3	0.0	0.4	24	3	30	26	0.5	0.5	0.1	0.4
23 031	Biddeford city	20,710	98.1	0.3	0.8	0.3	<.1	0.5	8	18	20	22	1.7	1.7	1.1	1.4
23 019	Brewer city	9,021	98.6	0.2	0.2	0.4	<.1	0.5	19	10	22	19	0.7	0.7	0.4	0.7
23 005	Brunswick town	20,906	95.2	1.8	1.3	0.2	<.1	1.4	7	33	2	1	1.7	1.7	7.8	4.2
23 029	Calais city	3,963	98.4	0.1	0.2	0.9	0.0	0.4	28	17	28	25	0.3	0.3	0.1	0.2
23 009	Cranberry Isles town	189	98.4	0.5	0.0	0.0	1.1	0.0	33	16	9	33	<.1	<.1	<.1	0.0
23 005	Cumberland town	5,836	98.8	0.1	0.4	0.2	<.1	0.5	26	7	29	23	0.5	0.5	0.1	0.4
23 009	Ellsworth city	5,975	98.7	0.2	0.4	0.3	0.0	0.4	25	8	25	31	0.5	0.5	0.2	0.3
23 005	Falmouth town	7,610	98.8	0.1	0.6	<.1	0.0	0.4	22	6	27	30	0.6	0.6	0.2	0.4
23 011	Gardiner city	6,746	98.5	0.3	0.3	0.3	<.1	0.5	23	13	12	20	0.5	0.6	0.5	0.5
23 005	Gorham town	11,856	98.5	0.3	0.4	0.2	<.1	0.4	14	12	14	24	1.0	1.0	0.8	0.8
23 011	Hallowell city	2,534	98.4	0.2	0.5	0.3	<.1	0.6	30	15	21	15	0.2	0.2	0.1	0.2
23 005	Harpswell town	5,012	98.5	<.1	0.4	0.2	0.0	0.8	27	11	31	6	0.4	0.4	<.1	0.6
23 017	Hiram town	1,260	99.0	0.0	0.3	0.2	0.2	0.4	32	4	32	29	0.1	0.1	0.0	<.1
23 001	Lewiston city	39,757	97.7	0.6	0.7	0.2	<.1	0.7	2	24	5	8	3.2	3.2	5.2	4.2
23 001	Lisbon town	9,457	97.8	0.3	0.5	0.3	<.1	1.0	18	23	15	4	0.8	0.8	0.6	1.3
23 011	Monmouth town	3,353	99.0	0.3	0.1	0.2	<.1	0.3	29	2	18	32	0.3	0.3	0.2	0.2
23 009	Mount Desert town	1,899	99.0	0.0	0.3	0.3	0.0	0.4	31	1	33	27	0.2	0.2	0.0	0.1
23 019	Old Town city	8,317	95.2	0.3	1.9	1.8	<.1	0.7	20	32	13	10	0.7	0.7	0.6	0.8
23 019	Orono town	10,573	95.8	0.6	1.7	0.8	<.1	1.0	15	31	6	3	0.9	0.8	1.3	1.6
23 005	Portland city	64,358	96.0	1.1	1.6	0.4	<.1	0.8	1	29	3	7	5.2	5.1	14.0	7.5
23 003	Presque Isle city	10,550	97.5	0.5	0.5	0.8	<.1	0.6	16	26	8	14	0.9	0.9	1.2	1.0
23 031	Saco city	15,181	98.5	0.3	0.6	0.1	<.1	0.5	12	14	19	16	1.2	1.2	0.8	1.2
23 031	Sanford town	20,463	96.9	0.2	1.7	0.3	<.1	0.9	9	27	26	5	1.7	1.6	0.7	2.6
23 005	South Portland city	23,163	97.6	0.3	1.1	0.3	<.1	0.7	5	25	17	9	1.9	1.9	1.3	2.4
23 011	Waterville city	17,173	98.0	0.5	0.6	0.3	<.1	0.6	10	21	11	11	1.4	1.4	1.6	1.6
23 005	Westbrook city	16,121	98.1	0.6	0.6	0.2	<.1	0.5	11	20	7	21	1.3	1.3	2.0	1.1
23 005	Windham town	13,020	98.8	0.2	0.2	0.2	0.1	0.4	13	5	24	28	1.1	1.1	0.6	0.8
23 005	Yarmouth town	7,862	98.6	0.2	0.4	<.1	<.1	0.6	21	9	23	13	0.6	0.6	0.3	0.7
	CONGRESSIONAL															
	District 1	636,486	98.1	0.4	0.6	0.2	<.1	0.6	1	1	1	1	51.8	51.9	54.5	54.8
	District 2	591,442	97.9	0.4	0.4	0.7	<.1	0.5	2	2	2	2	48.2	48.1	45.5	45.2

¹Separate rankings for 16 counties and for 33 cities and towns.

Table B. — 1990 Voting Age Population (VAP) by Race and Ethnic Origin

County	Total Voting Age Population	Percent of total VAP — Non-Hispanic White	Black	Asian and Pacific Islander	Native American	Other	Hispanic	Rank Total	Rank White	Rank Black	Rank Hispanic	% contrib to state VAP Total	White	Black	Hispanic	VAP % of total pop Total	White	Black	Asian and Pacific Islander	Native American	Other	Hispanic
Androscoggin	78,104	98.3	0.3	0.5	0.2	<.1	0.6	5	11	5	2	8.5	8.5	7.8	11.5	74.2	74.4	56.2	70.1	73.8	14.3	63.7
Aroostook	64,584	97.3	1.0	0.4	0.7	<.1	0.5	6	14	1	4	7.0	7.0	19.5	8.1	74.3	74.6	71.1	70.1	58.9	31.6	63.4
Cumberland	186,207	97.9	0.6	0.7	0.2	<.1	0.6	1	12	3	3	20.3	20.2	32.0	24.1	76.6	76.8	71.2	64.8	71.0	40.3	66.5
Franklin	21,409	99.0	<.1	0.3	0.3	0.0	0.3	15	7	12	11	2.3	2.3	0.6	1.6	73.8	73.9	66.7	69.1	78.3	0.0	61.8
Hancock	35,613	98.8	0.2	0.2	0.3	<.1	0.5	9	8	8	6	3.9	3.9	2.1	3.8	75.9	76.0	71.6	66.4	67.1	36.4	61.3
Kennebec	86,652	98.8	0.2	0.4	0.3	<.1	0.4	4	9	7	9	9.4	9.5	5.0	7.4	74.8	74.9	65.2	62.7	71.2	27.0	62.0
Knox	27,446	99.1	0.1	0.2	0.3	<.1	0.3	10	4	9	13	3.0	3.0	1.2	1.9	75.6	75.7	72.2	64.9	69.1	22.2	56.3
Lincoln	22,736	99.3	<.1	<.1	0.2	0.0	0.3	14	1	15	10	2.5	2.5	0.4	1.7	74.9	75.1	52.2	58.3	52.9	0.0	59.5
Oxford	38,726	99.2	<.1	0.2	0.2	<.1	0.3	7	2	13	12	4.2	4.3	1.0	2.6	73.6	73.8	51.6	64.2	68.8	60.0	54.9
Penobscot	110,990	97.9	0.3	0.6	0.7	<.1	0.4	3	13	4	7	12.1	12.0	11.3	11.1	75.7	75.9	71.5	72.9	65.7	35.7	67.9
Piscataquis	13,773	99.0	<.1	0.2	0.4	<.1	0.3	16	6	16	14	1.5	1.5	0.1	0.9	73.8	74.0	22.2	51.9	78.7	100.0	58.0
Sagadahoc	24,598	97.3	0.9	0.7	0.2	<.1	0.9	12	15	2	1	2.7	2.7	6.6	5.2	73.4	73.5	67.7	70.2	83.6	13.3	65.9
Somerset	36,121	99.2	<.1	0.2	0.3	<.1	0.3	8	3	14	15	3.9	4.0	0.9	2.2	72.6	72.7	50.8	62.6	64.3	40.0	55.2
Waldo	24,087	99.1	0.1	0.2	0.2	<.1	0.4	13	5	11	8	2.6	2.6	0.8	2.2	73.0	73.1	68.4	68.7	66.2	25.0	54.7
Washington	26,268	96.4	0.1	0.2	3.0	0.0	0.2	11	16	10	16	2.9	2.8	1.1	1.5	74.4	75.3	57.8	76.5	56.1	0.0	50.4
York	121,612	98.5	0.3	0.6	0.2	<.1	0.5	2	10	6	5	13.2	13.3	9.7	14.2	73.9	74.1	60.7	63.2	73.5	42.1	61.7
MAINE	**918,926**	**98.3**	**0.4**	**0.5**	**0.4**	**<.1**	**0.5**					**100.0**	**100.0**	**100.0**	**100.0**	**74.8**	**75.0**	**67.1**	**66.6**	**64.6**	**32.8**	**63.1**
CITIES AND TOWNS																						
Auburn city	18,155	98.3	0.3	0.6	0.2	<.1	0.5	4	20	12	15	2.0	2.0	1.7	2.0	74.7	74.9	51.8	66.3	84.0	30.8	66.7
Augusta city	16,644	98.2	0.3	0.7	0.4	<.1	0.5	6	22	18	14	1.8	1.8	1.3	1.9	78.0	78.3	63.2	62.2	75.6	44.4	70.7
Bangor city	25,887	97.0	0.8	0.9	0.7	<.1	0.6	3	28	4	11	2.8	2.8	6.6	3.4	78.0	78.3	72.7	71.9	70.5	42.9	69.2
Bath city	7,399	96.2	1.8	0.6	0.3	0.0	1.1	17	30	2	2	0.8	0.8	4.0	2.0	75.5	75.7	70.0	68.3	95.7	0.0	68.3
Belfast city	4,809	99.1	<.1	0.1	0.3	0.0	0.4	24	1	31	16	0.5	0.5	<.1	0.5	75.7	75.7	50.0	60.0	68.2	0.0	77.8
Biddeford city	15,909	98.4	0.2	0.7	0.3	<.1	0.4	8	19	22	17	1.7	1.7	0.8	1.6	76.8	77.0	52.8	65.9	73.3	62.5	69.7
Brewer city	6,927	98.9	0.2	0.2	0.3	0.0	0.4	18	9	21	22	0.8	0.8	0.5	0.7	76.8	77.0	81.0	70.0	54.5	0.0	57.1
Brunswick town	16,061	95.5	1.9	1.2	0.2	<.1	1.2	7	33	1	1	1.7	1.7	9.1	4.6	76.8	77.1	78.7	68.6	70.2	64.3	67.8
Calais city	3,033	98.6	0.1	0.2	0.7	0.0	0.3	28	17	26	31	0.3	0.3	0.1	0.2	76.5	76.7	80.0	100.0	61.8	0.0	52.9
Cranberry Isles town	140	99.3	0.7	0.0	0.0	0.0	0.0	33	1	5	33	<.1	<.1	<.1	0.0	74.1	74.7	100.0	0.0	0.0	0.0	0.0
Cumberland town	4,243	99.1	<.1	0.2	0.2	<.1	0.4	26	4	29	18	0.5	0.5	0.1	0.4	72.7	72.9	57.1	47.6	63.6	33.3	66.7
Ellsworth city	4,570	98.8	0.2	0.4	0.2	0.0	0.4	25	11	25	27	0.5	0.5	0.2	0.4	76.5	76.6	58.3	83.3	52.6	0.0	72.7
Falmouth town	5,965	99.1	<.1	0.5	<.1	0.0	0.3	22	2	30	32	0.6	0.7	0.2	0.4	78.4	78.6	50.0	65.1	83.3	0.0	53.3
Gardiner city	4,956	98.7	0.3	0.2	0.3	0.0	0.4	23	15	14	19	0.5	0.5	0.4	0.5	73.5	73.6	60.9	57.1	80.0	0.0	63.6
Gorham town	8,856	98.8	0.3	0.3	0.2	0.0	0.4	15	12	16	24	1.0	1.0	0.7	0.8	74.7	74.9	61.5	55.3	71.4	0.0	64.2
Hallowell city	1,995	98.7	0.3	0.3	0.3	0.0	0.4	30	14	13	23	0.2	0.2	0.2	0.2	78.7	79.0	100.0	50.0	71.4	0.0	57.1
Harpswell town	3,964	98.7	0.1	0.3	0.2	0.0	0.8	27	16	28	5	0.4	0.4	0.1	0.7	79.1	79.2	100.0	60.0	75.0	0.0	75.6
Hiram town	881	98.9	0.0	0.3	0.2	0.2	0.3	32	10	32	29	<.1	<.1	0.0	<.1	69.9	69.8	0.0	75.0	100.0	100.0	60.0
Lewiston city	30,704	98.0	0.5	0.7	0.2	<.1	0.6	2	25	7	9	3.3	3.3	4.6	4.3	77.2	77.5	59.3	76.6	75.8	6.3	65.5
Lisbon town	6,784	98.0	0.3	0.4	0.4	<.1	0.8	19	23	11	4	0.7	0.7	0.7	1.3	71.7	71.9	74.2	62.5	75.8	11.1	59.3
Monmouth town	2,381	99.0	0.3	<.1	0.2	<.1	0.4	29	5	19	25	0.3	0.3	0.2	0.2	71.0	71.0	66.7	40.0	62.5	100.0	81.8
Mount Desert town	1,535	99.0	0.0	0.4	0.3	0.0	0.3	31	6	33	30	0.2	0.2	0.0	0.1	80.8	80.8	0.0	100.0	100.0	0.0	62.5
Old Town city	6,415	95.9	0.3	1.9	1.3	<.1	0.7	20	32	15	8	0.7	0.7	0.5	1.0	77.1	77.6	64.3	76.1	54.7	33.3	76.8
Orono town	9,427	96.1	0.6	1.6	0.7	<.1	0.9	14	31	6	3	1.0	1.0	1.8	2.0	89.2	89.4	92.2	83.8	86.3	66.7	79.8
Portland city	51,597	96.5	1.0	1.4	0.4	<.1	0.7	1	29	3	6	5.6	5.5	15.1	8.6	80.2	80.6	72.3	66.6	77.1	39.1	72.3
Presque Isle city	7,966	98.0	0.5	0.5	0.6	<.1	0.4	16	26	8	20	0.9	0.9	1.1	0.8	75.5	75.9	63.2	65.5	63.8	16.7	50.0
Saco city	11,512	98.8	0.1	0.6	<.1	<.1	0.4	12	13	27	21	1.3	1.3	0.4	1.1	75.8	76.1	35.0	75.3	62.5	100.0	56.6
Sanford town	14,573	97.4	0.2	1.4	0.3	<.1	0.7	9	27	24	7	1.6	1.6	0.7	2.3	71.2	71.6	65.7	58.6	70.5	12.5	56.1
South Portland city	17,880	98.0	0.3	0.9	0.2	<.1	0.6	5	24	17	10	1.9	1.9	1.4	2.4	77.2	77.5	73.8	62.2	67.7	9.1	63.6
Waterville city	13,719	98.2	0.4	0.6	0.3	<.1	0.5	10	21	9	12	1.5	1.5	1.8	1.7	79.9	80.0	75.9	81.4	72.9	20.0	66.7
Westbrook city	12,197	98.5	0.4	0.5	0.2	<.1	0.3	11	18	10	28	1.3	1.3	1.5	1.0	75.7	76.0	52.6	72.2	65.0	50.0	53.8
Windham town	9,767	98.9	0.2	0.2	0.2	0.1	0.4	13	8	20	26	1.1	1.1	0.7	0.8	75.0	75.1	85.7	72.7	71.0	66.7	66.7
Yarmouth town	5,970	98.9	0.2	0.3	0.1	<.1	0.5	21	7	23	13	0.6	0.7	0.3	0.7	75.9	76.1	58.8	56.3	85.7	100.0	60.0
CONGRESSIONAL																						
District 1	478,547	98.3	0.4	0.5	0.2	<.1	0.5	1	1	1	1	52.1	52.1	55.1	55.4	75.2	75.4	67.9	64.5	71.0	35.6	63.8
District 2	440,379	98.2	0.3	0.4	0.6	<.1	0.4	2	2	2	2	47.9	47.9	44.9	44.6	74.5	74.7	66.2	69.9	62.3	28.8	62.2

[1]Separate rankings for 16 counties and for 33 cities and towns.

Table C. — Voter Participation: November 3, 1992, General Election

County	Estimated Voting Age Population (VAP) 1992	Voter registration (REG)				Voter turnout										Percent drop-off, by office[2]			
						Highest office				Maximum vote									
		Total	% contribution to state REG	% of 1992 VAP	Rank by % of 1992 VAP	Actual	Total	Office	% of 1992 VAP	Total	% contribution to state turnout	% of REG	Rank by % of REG[1]	% of 1992 VAP	Rank by % of 1992 VAP	President	Senator	Governor	Representative
Androscoggin	79,389	79,816	8.2	100.5	11	-	55,144	P	69.5	55,144	8.1	69.1	9	69.5	14	0.0	-	-	0.3
Aroostook	64,514	59,169	6.1	91.7	16	-	38,585	P	59.8	38,585	5.7	65.2	16	59.8	16	0.0	-	-	0.9
Cumberland	191,636	205,903	21.1	107.4	5	-	141,522	P	73.8	141,522	20.8	68.7	10	73.8	5	0.0	-	-	2.0
Franklin	21,702	24,503	2.5	112.9	1	-	16,523	P	76.1	16,523	2.4	67.4	14	76.1	3	0.0	-	-	0.5
Hancock	36,701	40,498	4.2	110.3	2	-	28,805	P	78.5	28,805	4.2	71.1	5	78.5	2	0.0	-	-	1.4
Kennebec	88,174	90,687	9.3	102.9	9	-	63,921	P	72.5	63,921	9.4	70.5	7	72.5	8	0.0	-	-	1.5
Knox	28,231	30,564	3.1	108.3	4	-	20,338	P	72.0	20,338	3.0	66.5	15	72.0	9	0.0	-	-	2.4
Lincoln	23,885	26,144	2.7	109.5	3	-	19,036	P	79.7	19,036	2.8	72.8	2	79.7	1	0.0	-	-	2.4
Oxford	39,761	41,741	4.3	105.0	7	-	29,356	P	73.8	29,356	4.3	70.3	8	73.8	6	0.0	-	-	1.6
Penobscot........................	112,391	111,175	11.4	98.9	12	-	80,444	P	71.6	80,444	11.8	72.4	3	71.6	11	0.0	-	-	1.1
Piscataquis.......................	14,150	13,962	1.4	98.7	13	-	10,031	P	70.9	10,031	1.5	71.8	4	70.9	12	0.0	-	-	0.9
Sagadahoc	25,698	25,159	2.6	97.9	15	-	18,513	P	72.0	18,513	2.7	73.6	1	72.0	10	0.0	-	-	2.2
Somerset	37,831	38,797	4.0	102.6	10	-	26,424	P	69.8	26,424	3.9	68.1	12	69.8	13	0.0	-	-	0.4
Waldo.............................	25,230	27,066	2.8	107.3	6	-	18,529	P	73.4	18,529	2.7	68.5	11	73.4	7	0.0	-	-	2.0
Washington.......................	26,669	26,190	2.7	98.2	14	-	17,765	P	66.6	17,765	2.6	67.8	13	66.6	15	0.0	-	-	0.7
York	128,038	133,231	13.7	104.1	8	-	94,563	P	73.9	94,563	13.9	71.0	6	73.9	4	0.0	-	-	1.8
MAINE[3]	**944,000**	**974,605**	**100.0**	**103.2**		**-**	**679,499**		**72.0**	**679,499**	**100.0**	**69.7**		**72.0**		**0.0**	**-**	**-**	**1.5**
CITIES AND TOWNS																			
Auburn city	-	16,610	1.7	-	-	-	12,693	P	-	12,693	1.9	76.4	7	-	-	0.0	-	-	0.2
Augusta city	-	15,190	1.6	-	-	-	10,702	P	-	10,702	1.6	70.5	22	-	-	0.0	-	-	0.9
Bangor city	-	22,066	2.3	-	-	-	16,771	P	-	16,771	2.5	76.0	8	-	-	0.0	-	-	1.1
Bath city	-	7,095	0.7	-	-	-	5,093	P	-	5,093	0.7	71.8	17	-	-	0.0	-	-	2.9
Belfast city	-	5,113	0.5	-	-	-	3,214	P	-	3,214	0.5	62.9	30	-	-	0.0	-	-	2.3
Biddeford city	-	16,092	1.7	-	-	-	10,239	C	-	10,239	1.5	63.6	28	-	-	0.1	-	-	0.0
Brewer city	-	6,905	0.7	-	-	-	5,349	P	-	5,349	0.8	77.5	5	-	-	0.0	-	-	1.1
Brunswick town	-	14,272	1.5	-	-	-	10,060	P	-	10,060	1.5	70.5	21	-	-	0.0	-	-	1.2
Calais city........................	-	2,678	0.3	-	-	-	1,773	P	-	1,773	0.3	66.2	26	-	-	0.0	-	-	1.0
Cranberry Isles town......	-	194	<.1	-	-	-	160	P	-	160	<.1	82.5	1	-	-	0.0	-	-	0.0
Cumberland town...........	-	5,229	0.5	-	-	-	4,140	P	-	4,140	0.6	79.2	3	-	-	0.0	-	-	3.6
Ellsworth city	-	5,217	0.5	-	-	-	3,526	P	-	3,526	0.5	67.6	25	-	-	0.0	-	-	0.1
Falmouth town	-	7,055	0.7	-	-	-	5,321	P	-	5,321	0.8	75.4	10	-	-	0.0	-	-	3.3
Gardiner city	-	5,050	0.5	-	-	-	3,572	P	-	3,572	0.5	70.7	20	-	-	0.0	-	-	1.7
Gorham town	-	9,325	1.0	-	-	-	6,972	P	-	6,972	1.0	74.8	11	-	-	0.0	-	-	1.9
Hallowell city	-	2,618	0.3	-	-	-	1,617	P	-	1,617	0.2	61.8	31	-	-	0.0	-	-	1.8
Harpswell town	-	4,224	0.4	-	-	-	3,360	P	-	3,360	0.5	79.5	2	-	-	0.0	-	-	2.7
Hiram town	-	963	<.1	-	-	-	695	P	-	695	0.1	72.2	15	-	-	0.0	-	-	11.2
Lewiston city	-	31,747	3.3	-	-	-	19,998	C	-	19,998	2.9	63.0	29	-	-	0.6	-	-	0.0
Lisbon town	-	7,196	0.7	-	-	-	4,880	P	-	4,880	0.7	67.8	24	-	-	0.0	-	-	2.7
Monmouth town	-	2,671	0.3	-	-	-	2,017	P	-	2,017	0.3	75.5	9	-	-	0.0	-	-	2.1
Mount Desert town	-	1,946	0.2	-	-	-	1,397	P	-	1,397	0.2	71.8	16	-	-	0.0	-	-	2.4
Old Town city	-	6,519	0.7	-	-	-	4,766	P	-	4,766	0.7	73.1	13	-	-	0.0	-	-	1.3
Orono town......................	-	8,842	0.9	-	-	-	5,671	P	-	5,671	0.8	64.1	27	-	-	0.0	-	-	2.0
Portland city	-	59,111	6.1	-	-	-	35,274	P	-	35,274	5.2	59.7	32	-	-	0.0	-	-	1.0
Presque Isle city	-	8,732	0.9	-	-	-	4,783	P	-	4,783	0.7	54.8	33	-	-	0.0	-	-	0.0
Saco city.........................	-	12,479	1.3	-	-	-	9,095	P	-	9,095	1.3	72.9	14	-	-	0.0	-	-	2.4
Sanford town	-	12,848	1.3	-	-	-	10,149	P	-	10,149	1.5	79.0	4	-	-	0.0	-	-	3.5
South Portland city	-	17,791	1.8	-	-	-	12,712	P	-	12,712	1.9	71.5	18	-	-	0.0	-	-	0.9
Waterville city	-	10,355	1.1	-	-	-	7,977	P	-	7,977	1.2	77.0	6	-	-	0.0	-	-	1.2
Westbrook city	-	12,764	1.3	-	-	-	9,109	P	-	9,109	1.3	71.4	19	-	-	0.0	-	-	6.4
Windham town	-	9,884	1.0	-	-	-	7,315	P	-	7,315	1.1	74.0	12	-	-	0.0	-	-	1.2
Yarmouth town..................	-	7,661	0.8	-	-	-	5,321	P	-	5,321	0.8	69.5	23	-	-	0.0	-	-	2.5

[1]Separate rankings for 16 counties and for 33 cities and towns. [2]Percent drop-off is zero for any office used as highest office turnout. [3]Total voter registration reported by Maine Secretary of State exceeds estimated voting age population (VAP).

Table E. – Vote for President: November 3, 1992, General Election

County	Total	Clinton (DEM)	Bush (REP)	Perot (IND)	Other	Plurality Total	Party	DEM	REP	IND	Other	Rank[1] DEM	Rank[1] REP	Rank[1] IND	Total	DEM	REP	IND	DEM	REP
Androscoggin	55,144	22,247	14,174	18,518	205	3,729	D	40.3	25.7	33.6	0.4	4	15	5	8.1	8.4	6.9	9.0	61.1	38.9
Aroostook	38,585	15,682	12,409	10,376	118	3,273	D	40.6	32.2	26.9	0.3	3	4	15	5.7	6.0	6.0	5.0	55.8	44.2
Cumberland	141,522	60,781	45,752	34,443	546	15,029	D	42.9	32.3	24.3	0.4	1	3	16	20.8	23.1	22.2	16.7	57.1	42.9
Franklin	16,523	6,739	4,608	5,115	61	1,624	D	40.8	27.9	31.0	0.4	2	13	11	2.4	2.6	2.2	2.5	59.4	40.6
Hancock	28,805	10,126	8,657	9,865	157	261	D	35.2	30.1	34.2	0.5	13	9	4	4.2	3.8	4.2	4.8	53.9	46.1
Kennebec	63,921	25,125	17,135	21,436	225	3,689	D	39.3	26.8	33.5	0.4	5	14	6	9.4	9.5	8.3	10.4	59.5	40.5
Knox	20,338	7,631	6,310	6,303	94	1,321	D	37.5	31.0	31.0	0.5	8	6	10	3.0	2.9	3.1	3.0	54.7	45.3
Lincoln	19,036	6,714	6,405	5,808	109	309	D	35.3	33.6	30.5	0.6	12	2	13	2.8	2.5	3.1	2.8	51.2	48.8
Oxford	29,356	11,202	8,194	9,815	145	1,387	D	38.2	27.9	33.4	0.5	6	12	7	4.3	4.3	4.0	4.7	57.8	42.2
Penobscot	80,444	29,485	24,218	26,437	304	3,048	D	36.7	30.1	32.9	0.4	10	8	9	11.8	11.2	11.7	12.8	54.9	45.1
Piscataquis	10,031	3,323	2,970	3,688	50	365	I	33.1	29.6	36.8	0.5	16	10	2	1.5	1.3	1.4	1.8	52.8	47.2
Sagadahoc	18,513	6,828	5,917	5,705	63	911	D	36.9	32.0	30.8	0.3	9	5	12	2.7	2.6	2.9	2.8	53.6	46.4
Somerset	26,424	9,274	6,780	10,293	77	1,019	I	35.1	25.7	39.0	0.3	14	16	1	3.9	3.5	3.3	5.0	57.8	42.2
Waldo	18,529	6,472	5,241	6,702	114	230	I	34.9	28.3	36.2	0.6	15	11	3	2.7	2.5	2.5	3.2	55.3	44.7
Washington	17,765	6,284	5,493	5,894	94	390	D	35.4	30.9	33.2	0.5	11	7	8	2.6	2.4	2.7	2.8	53.4	46.6
York	94,563	35,507	32,241	26,422	393	3,266	D	37.5	34.1	27.9	0.4	7	1	14	13.9	13.5	15.6	12.8	52.4	47.6
MAINE	**679,499**	**263,420**	**206,504**	**206,820**	**2,755**	**56,600**	**D**	**38.8**	**30.4**	**30.4**	**0.4**				**100.0**	**100.0**	**100.0**	**100.0**	**56.1**	**43.9**
CITIES AND TOWNS																				
Auburn city	12,693	5,025	3,653	3,964	51	1,061	D	39.6	28.8	31.2	0.4	16	23	7	1.9	1.9	1.8	1.9	57.9	42.1
Augusta city	10,702	4,657	3,003	3,002	40	1,654	D	43.5	28.1	28.1	0.4	12	26	17	1.6	1.8	1.5	1.5	60.8	39.2
Bangor city	16,771	6,826	5,185	4,689	71	1,641	D	40.7	30.9	28.0	0.4	13	16	18	2.5	2.6	2.5	2.3	56.8	43.2
Bath city	5,093	1,988	1,630	1,458	17	358	D	39.0	32.0	28.6	0.3	18	12	14	0.7	0.8	0.8	0.7	54.9	45.1
Belfast city	3,214	1,180	993	1,024	17	156	D	36.7	30.9	31.9	0.5	23	17	4	0.5	0.4	0.5	0.5	54.3	45.7
Biddeford city	10,225	4,945	2,533	2,717	30	2,228	D	48.4	24.8	26.6	0.3	5	28	23	1.5	1.9	1.2	1.3	66.1	33.9
Brewer city	5,349	1,788	1,907	1,625	29	119	R	33.4	35.7	30.4	0.5	29	6	11	0.8	0.7	0.9	0.8	48.4	51.6
Brunswick town	10,060	4,686	3,058	2,282	34	1,628	D	46.6	30.4	22.7	0.3	10	19	27	1.5	1.8	1.5	1.1	60.5	39.5
Calais city	1,773	639	608	523	3	31	D	36.0	34.3	29.5	0.2	26	9	12	0.3	0.2	0.3	0.3	51.2	48.8
Cranberry Isles town	160	77	46	36	1	31	D	48.1	28.8	22.5	0.6	6	24	28	<.1	<.1	<.1	<.1	62.6	37.4
Cumberland town	4,140	1,473	1,763	884	20	290	R	35.6	42.6	21.4	0.5	27	1	31	0.6	0.6	0.9	0.4	45.5	54.5
Ellsworth city	3,526	1,050	1,303	1,159	14	144	R	29.8	37.0	32.9	0.4	33	4	3	0.5	0.4	0.6	0.6	44.6	55.4
Falmouth town	5,321	2,002	2,240	1,066	13	238	R	37.6	42.1	20.0	0.2	22	2	32	0.8	0.8	1.1	0.5	47.2	52.8
Gardiner city	3,572	1,391	1,054	1,115	12	276	D	38.9	29.5	31.2	0.3	19	21	8	0.5	0.5	0.5	0.5	56.9	43.1
Gorham town	6,972	2,516	2,422	2,015	19	94	D	36.1	34.7	28.9	0.3	25	8	13	1.0	1.0	1.2	1.0	51.0	49.0
Hallowell city	1,617	813	413	378	13	400	D	50.3	25.5	23.4	0.8	2	27	26	0.2	0.3	0.2	0.2	66.3	33.7
Harpswell town	3,360	1,296	1,098	953	13	198	D	38.6	32.7	28.4	0.4	20	11	15	0.5	0.5	0.5	0.5	54.1	45.9
Hiram town	695	236	230	221	8	6	D	34.0	33.1	31.8	1.2	28	10	5	0.1	<.1	0.1	0.1	50.6	49.4
Lewiston city	19,886	9,265	4,372	6,180	69	3,085	D	46.6	22.0	31.1	0.3	9	33	9	2.9	3.5	2.1	3.0	67.9	32.1
Lisbon town	4,880	1,629	1,381	1,853	17	224	I	33.4	28.3	38.0	0.3	31	25	1	0.7	0.6	0.7	0.9	54.1	45.9
Monmouth town	2,017	668	586	757	6	89	I	33.1	29.1	37.5	0.3	32	22	2	0.3	0.3	0.3	0.4	53.3	46.7
Mount Desert town	1,397	557	444	389	7	113	D	39.9	31.8	27.8	0.5	15	14	19	0.2	0.2	0.2	0.2	55.6	44.4
Old Town city	4,766	2,272	1,173	1,302	19	970	D	47.7	24.6	27.3	0.4	7	29	22	0.7	0.9	0.6	0.6	66.0	34.0
Orono town	5,671	2,813	1,336	1,502	20	1,311	D	49.6	23.6	26.5	0.4	3	31	24	0.8	1.1	0.6	0.7	67.8	32.2
Portland city	35,274	19,510	8,660	6,910	194	10,850	D	55.3	24.6	19.6	0.6	1	30	33	5.2	7.4	4.2	3.3	69.3	30.7
Presque Isle city	4,783	1,750	1,709	1,318	6	41	D	36.6	35.7	27.6	0.1	24	5	21	0.7	0.7	0.8	0.6	50.6	49.4
Saco city	9,095	4,000	2,769	2,303	23	1,231	D	44.0	30.4	25.3	0.3	11	18	25	1.3	1.5	1.3	1.1	59.1	40.9
Sanford town	10,149	3,854	3,030	3,215	50	639	D	38.0	29.9	31.7	0.5	21	20	6	1.5	1.5	1.5	1.6	56.0	44.0
South Portland city	12,712	5,933	3,999	2,734	46	1,934	D	46.7	31.5	21.5	0.4	8	15	30	1.9	2.3	1.9	1.3	59.7	40.3
Waterville city	7,977	3,868	1,832	2,257	20	1,611	D	48.5	23.0	28.3	0.3	4	32	16	1.2	1.5	0.9	1.1	67.9	32.1
Westbrook city	9,109	3,665	2,904	2,512	28	761	D	40.2	31.9	27.6	0.3	14	13	20	1.3	1.4	1.4	1.2	55.8	44.2
Windham town	7,315	2,444	2,603	2,250	18	159	R	33.4	35.6	30.8	0.2	30	7	10	1.1	0.9	1.3	1.1	48.4	51.6
Yarmouth town	5,321	2,078	2,027	1,191	25	51	D	39.1	38.1	22.4	0.5	17	3	29	0.8	0.8	1.0	0.6	50.6	49.4

[1]Separate rankings for 16 counties and for 33 cities and towns.

Table H. — Vote for U.S. Representative in Congress: November 3, 1992, General Election

Congressional district and county	Total	Democrat (DEM)	Republican (REP)	Other	Plurality Total	Plurality Party	Percent of total vote DEM	Percent of total vote REP	Percent of total vote Other	Rank within district DEM	Rank within district REP	Rank within district Other	Percent contribution to district vote Total	Percent contribution to district vote DEM	Percent contribution to district vote REP	Percent contribution to district vote Other
District 1	**358,148**	**232,696**	**125,236**	**216**	**107,460**	**D**	**65.0**	**35.0**	**< .1**				**100.0**	**100.0**	**100.0**	**100.0**
Cumberland	138,692	97,608	40,949	135	56,659	D	70.4	29.5	< .1	1	7	1	38.7	41.9	32.7	62.5
Kennebec	62,950	40,541	22,385	24	18,156	D	64.4	35.6	< .1	3	5	5	17.6	17.4	17.9	11.1
Knox	19,846	11,603	8,224	19	3,379	D	58.5	41.4	< .1	6	2	2	5.5	5.0	6.6	8.8
Lincoln	18,585	10,947	7,629	9	3,318	D	58.9	41.0	< .1	5	3	4	5.2	4.7	6.1	4.2
Sagadahoc	18,106	11,774	6,323	9	5,451	D	65.0	34.9	< .1	2	6	3	5.1	5.1	5.0	4.2
Waldo (pt)	7,091	3,863	3,228	0	635	D	54.5	45.5	0.0	7	1	7	2.0	1.7	2.6	0.0
York	92,878	56,360	36,498	20	19,862	D	60.7	39.3	< .1	4	4	6	25.9	24.2	29.1	9.3
District 2	**311,433**	**130,824**	**153,022**	**27,587**	**22,198**	**R**	**42.0**	**49.1**	**8.9**				**100.0**	**100.0**	**100.0**	**100.0**
Androscoggin	54,992	27,831	23,983	3,178	3,848	D	50.6	43.6	5.8	2	9	10	17.7	21.3	15.7	11.5
Aroostook	38,222	15,443	20,241	2,538	4,798	R	40.4	53.0	6.6	5	3	8	12.3	11.8	13.2	9.2
Franklin	16,434	6,863	7,911	1,660	1,048	R	41.8	48.1	10.1	4	8	3	5.3	5.2	5.2	6.0
Hancock	28,407	8,168	15,932	4,307	7,764	R	28.8	56.1	15.2	10	1	1	9.1	6.2	10.4	15.6
Oxford	28,886	13,045	14,007	1,834	962	R	45.2	48.5	6.3	3	7	9	9.3	10.0	9.2	6.6
Penobscot	79,527	31,313	40,350	7,864	9,037	R	39.4	50.7	9.9	6	6	5	25.5	23.9	26.4	28.5
Piscataquis	9,945	3,745	5,365	835	1,620	R	37.7	53.9	8.4	8	2	6	3.2	2.9	3.5	3.0
Somerset	26,317	13,806	10,436	2,075	3,370	D	52.5	39.7	7.9	1	10	7	8.5	10.6	6.8	7.5
Waldo (pt)	11,061	3,759	5,751	1,551	1,992	R	34.0	52.0	14.0	9	4	2	3.6	2.9	3.8	5.6
Washington	17,642	6,851	9,046	1,745	2,195	R	38.8	51.3	9.9	7	5	4	5.7	5.2	5.9	6.3
MAINE	**669,581**	**363,520**	**278,258**	**27,803**	**85,262**	**D**	**54.3**	**41.6**	**4.2**							

1992 Vote for President
Percent for Clinton (D), by Minor Civil Division

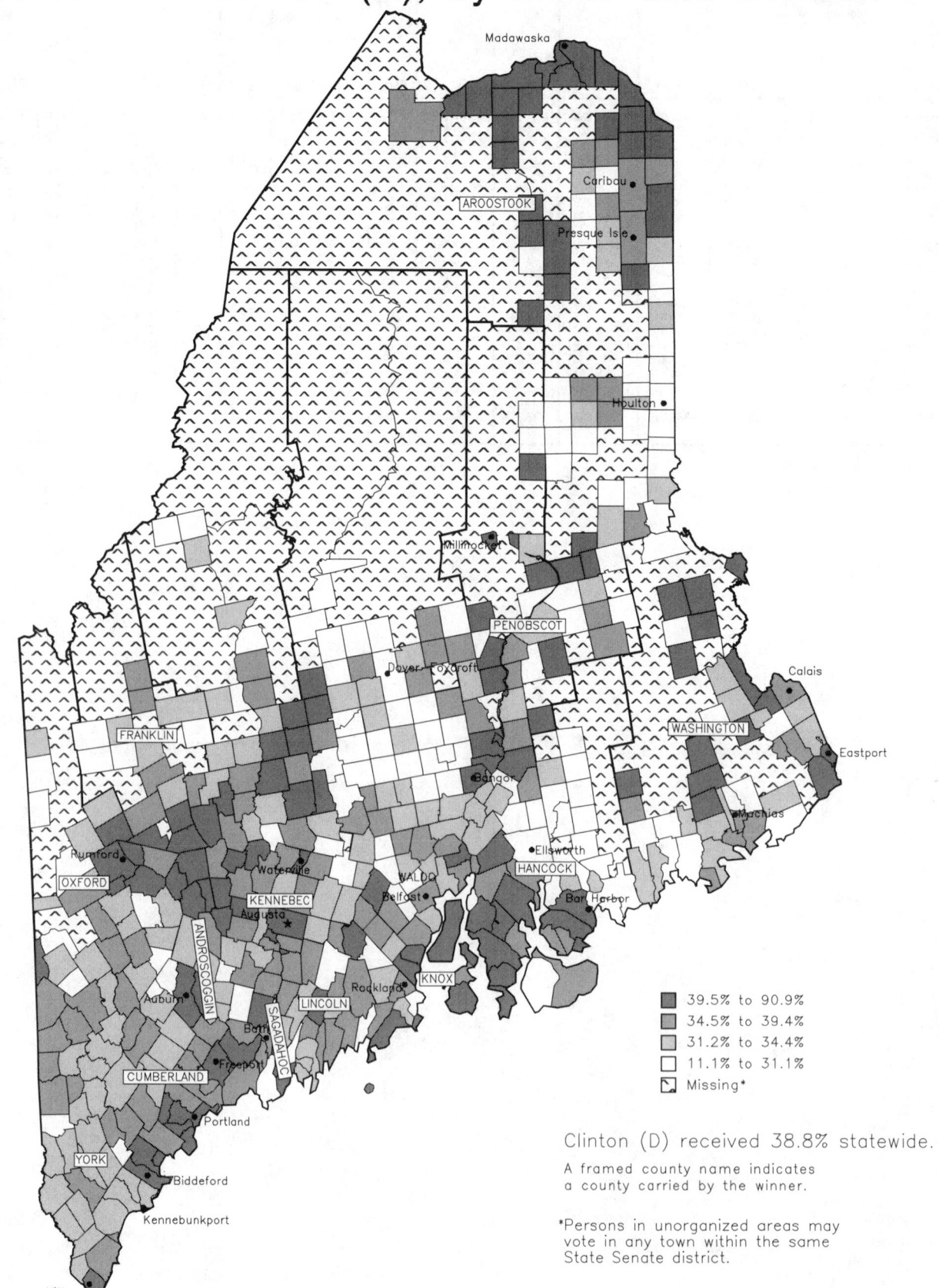

39.5% to 90.9%
34.5% to 39.4%
31.2% to 34.4%
11.1% to 31.1%
Missing*

Clinton (D) received 38.8% statewide.

A framed county name indicates
a county carried by the winner.

*Persons in unorganized areas may
vote in any town within the same
State Senate district.

418 Maine

MARYLAND

Alternative Registration Methods:
.... Agency-based, Mail-in, Motor-voter

Registration Deadline (Days before Election) 29

Voting Equipment Use (Counties)[1]

Datavote Punch Card	1	Paper Ballot	0
Electronic	0	Other Punch Card	2
Lever Machine	17	Mixed Systems	0
Optical Scanner	4		

Party Control	DEM	REP	IND	VAC
1993 State Senate	38	9	0	0
1992 State Senate	38	9	0	0
1993 State House	116	25	0	0
1992 State House	116	25	0	0

Population Statistics 1990

Race/Ethnicity	Total Population		Voting Age Population		Voting Age Population % of total population
	Number	%	Number	%	
Non-Hispanic					
White	3,326,109	69.6	2,580,083	71.3	77.6
Black	1,177,823	24.6	840,675	23.2	71.4
Asian/Pacific Islander	136,619	2.9	99,026	2.7	72.5
Native American	12,143	0.3	9,027	0.2	74.3
Other	3,672	<.1	1,625	<.1	44.3
All Hispanic	125,102	2.6	88,791	2.5	71.0
TOTAL	4,781,468	100.0	3,619,227	100.0	75.7

Estimated Voting Age Population 1992 (VAP) 3,719,000
Number of Registered Voters.................................. 2,463,010
    % of estimated VAP.. 66.2
Voter Turnout (Maximum Vote)[2].......................... 1,999,503
    % of VAP... 53.8
    % of Registration 81.2
Persons Not Voting—of Voting Age 1,719,497
    % of VAP... 46.2
Persons Not Voting—of Registered 463,507
    % of Registration 18.8
Straight Ticket Voting .... No

State Officials and Members of Congress

Governor:
William Donald Schaefer (D) 1986, elected to a four-year term in 1990.

U.S. Senators:
Paul Sarbanes (D) 1976, elected to a six-year term in 1988.
Barbara A. Mikulski (D) 1986, elected to a six-year term in 1992.

U.S. Representative in Congress:
(District, Name, Party, Date first elected)

1. Gilchrest (R) 1990
2. Bentley (R) 1984

3. Cardin (D) 1986
4. Wynn (D) 1992

5. Hoyer (D) 1981
6. Bartlett (R) 1992

7. Mfume (D) 1986
8. Morella (R) 1986

---

[1]Includes city of Baltimore. [2]Maximum vote turnout from Table C exceeds reported statewide actual voter turnout because in one or more counties the vote for highest office is greater than reported actual turnout.

Candidates: General Election, November 3, 1992

Candidate(s)	Total vote	Percent	Party	Status	First elected
President/Vice President					
Clinton/Gore	988,571	49.80%	Democrat	Challenger	1992
Bush/Quayle	707,094	35.62%	Republican	Incumbent	1988
Perot/Stockdale	281,414	14.18%	Ross Perot	Challenger	
Marrou/Lord	4,715	0.24%	Libertarian	Challenger	
Fulani/Munoz	2,786	0.14%	New Alliance	Challenger	
Hagelin/Tompkins	191	<.01%	Write in	Challenger	
Ron Daniels	167	<.01%	Write in	Challenger	
Gritz/Minett	41	<.01%	Write in	Challenger	
Warren/Debates	25	<.01%	Write in	Challenger	
Phillips/Knight	22	<.01%	Write in	Challenger	
LaRouche/Bevel	18	<.01%	Write in	Challenger	
Don Allensworth	1	<.01%	Write in	Challenger	
George Muzyk	1	<.01%	Write in	Challenger	
U.S. Senator					
Barbara Mikulski	1,307,610	71.00%	Democrat	Incumbent	1986
Alan Keyes	533,688	28.98%	Republican	Challenger	
Tomas Estrada-Palma	196	0.01%	Write in	Challenger	
John Gaige	84	<.01%	Write in	Challenger	
Gene Zarwell	72	<.01%	Write in	Challenger	
John Clapp	63	<.01%	Write in	Challenger	
Joan Bowman	20	<.01%	Write in	Challenger	
Jon Thompson	2	<.01%	Write in	Challenger	

Governor (No Contest)

U.S. Representative in Congress

Candidate(s)	Total vote	Percent	Party	Status	First elected
District 1					
Wayne Gilchrest	120,084	51.27%	Republican	Incumbent	1990
Thomas McMillen	112,771	48.15%	Democrat	Incumbent	1986
Ralph Gies	1,320	0.56%	Write in	Challenger	
Louise Meyers Beauregard	24	0.01%	Write in	Challenger	
William Stephens	4	<.01%	Write in	Challenger	
District 2					
Helen Bentley	165,443	65.11%	Republican	Incumbent	1984
Michael Hickey	88,658	34.89%	Democrat	Challenger	
James Godfrey	5	<.01%	Write in	Challenger	
District 3					
Benjamin Cardin	163,354	73.50%	Democrat	Incumbent	1986
William Bricker	58,869	26.49%	Republican	Challenger	
James Fitzgerald	29	0.01%	Write in	Challenger	
Eric Ashelman	3	<.01%	Write in	Challenger	
District 4					
Albert Wynn	136,902	75.14%	Democrat	Challenger	1992
Michele Dyson	45,166	24.79%	Republican	Challenger	
Maria Turner	68	0.04%	Write in	Challenger	
R. Chinelo Haney	47	0.03%	Write in	Challenger	
Steve Kramer	2	<.01%	Write in	Challenger	
District 5					
Steny Hoyer	118,312	52.98%	Democrat	Incumbent	1981
Lawrence Hogan, Jr.	97,982	43.87%	Republican	Challenger	
William Johnston	6,990	3.13%	Independent	Challenger	
James McLaughlin	40	0.02%	Write in	Challenger	
Lisa Ashelman	2	<.01%	Write in	Challenger	

Candidate(s)	Total vote	Percent	Party	Status	First elected
U.S. Representative in Congress (cont)					
District 6					
Roscoe Bartlett	125,564	54.13%	Republican	Challenger	1992
Thomas Hattery	106,224	45.79%	Democrat	Challenger	
Edward Miller	102	0.04%	Write in	Challenger	
Wayne Dougherty	60	0.03%	Write in	Challenger	
Kevin Condon	9	<.01%	Write in	Challenger	
District 7					
Kweisi Mfume	152,689	85.30%	Democrat	Incumbent	1986
Kenneth Kondner	26,304	14.70%	Republican	Challenger	
Glova Scott	4	<.01%	Write in	Challenger	
Margaret Ashelman	1	<.01%	Write in	Challenger	
District 8					
Constance Morella	203,377	72.51%	Republican	Incumbent	1986
Edward Heffernan	77,042	27.47%	Democrat	Challenger	
David Lonsdorf	56	0.02%	Write in	Challenger	

Candidates: March 3, 1992, Primary Election

Candidate	Total vote	Percent	Candidate	Total vote	Percent
Presidential Preference, Democratic			**Presidential Preference, Republican**		
Paul Tsongas	230,490	40.63%	George Bush	168,374	70.15%
Bill Clinton	189,906	33.48%	Patrick Buchanan	71,647	29.85%
Jerry Brown	46,480	8.19%			
Uncommitted	36,155	6.37%			
Tom Harkin	32,899	5.80%			
Bob Kerrey	27,035	4.77%			
Lyndon LaRouche, Jr.	4,259	0.75%			

Voter Registration and Turnout, 1948-1992 Elections

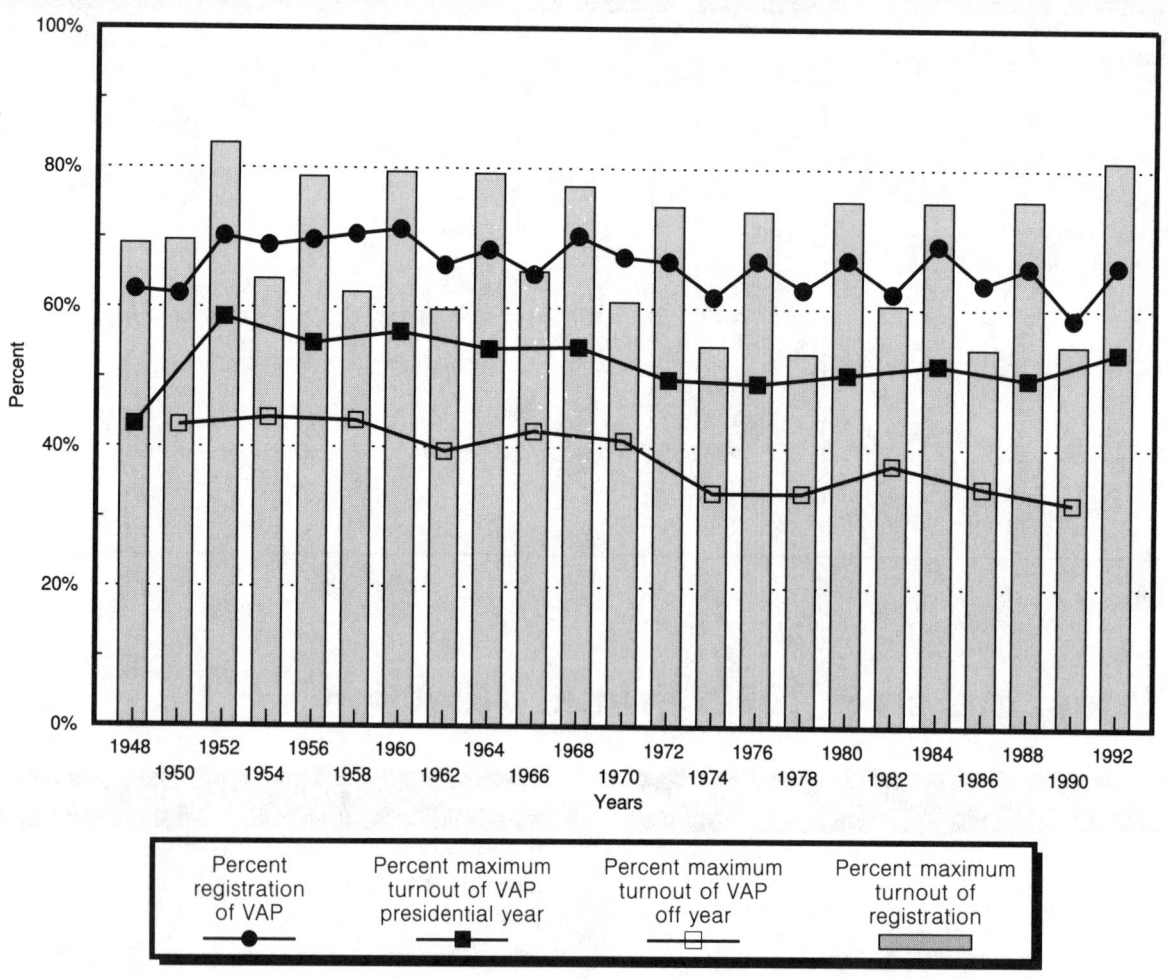

	Percent registration of VAP ●—	Percent maximum turnout of VAP presidential year ■—	Percent maximum turnout of VAP off year □—	Percent maximum turnout of registration

Year	Estimated Voting Age Population (VAP)	Voter registration (REG)			Voter turnout											
						Highest office						Maximum vote				
		Total	Percent of VAP	Rank by percent of VAP	Actual	Total	Office	Percent total REG	Rank by percent of REG	Percent of VAP	Rank by percent of VAP	Total	Percent total REG	Rank by percent of REG	Percent total VAP	Rank by percent of VAP
1992	3,719,000	2,463,010	66.2	40	1,999,486	1,985,046	P	80.6	15	53.4	36	1,999,486	81.2	18	53.8	36
1990	3,640,000	2,134,732	58.6	44	1,170,867	1,111,088	G	52.0	37	30.5	44	1,170,867	54.8	33	32.2	43
1988	3,498,000	2,310,080	66.0	37	1,747,350	1,714,358	P	74.2	17	49.0	33	1,747,350	75.6	19	50.0	33
1986	3,372,000	2,139,690	63.5	38	1,161,136	1,112,637	S	52.0	36	33.0	40	1,161,136	54.3	33	34.4	38
1984	3,259,000	2,253,150	69.1	33	1,695,924	1,675,873	P	74.4	24	51.4	35	1,695,924	75.3	23	52.0	35
1982	3,165,000	1,968,498	62.2	38	1,190,011	1,139,149	G	57.9	34	36.0	41	1,190,011	60.5	32	37.6	38
1980	3,080,000	2,064,883	67.0	34	1,557,709	1,540,496	P	74.6	27	50.0	36	1,557,709	75.4	27	50.6	36
1978	3,014,000	1,888,313	62.7	37	-	1,011,963	G	53.6	34	33.6	41	1,011,963	53.6	35	33.6	41
1976	2,920,000	1,949,753	66.8	37	-	1,439,897	P	73.9	27	49.3	35	1,439,897	73.9	31	49.3	37
1974	2,822,000	1,737,870	61.6	39	-	949,097	G	54.6	31	33.6	39	949,097	54.6	33	33.6	39
1972	2,721,000	1,815,784	66.7	37	-	1,353,812	P	74.6	23	49.8	34	1,353,812	74.6	26	49.8	36
1970	2,372,000	1,596,916	67.3	34	-	973,099	G	60.9	32	41.0	40	973,099	60.9	33	41.0	40
1968	2,271,000	1,595,779	70.3	32	-	1,235,039	P	77.4	32	54.4	35	1,235,039	77.4	32	54.4	37
1966	2,174,000	1,409,756	64.8	34	-	918,761	G	65.2	23	42.3	37	918,761	65.2	24	42.3	39
1964	2,065,000	1,410,281	68.3	29	-	1,116,457	P	79.2	25	54.1	35	1,116,457	79.2	27	54.1	35
1962	1,966,000	1,298,951	66.1	25	-	775,101	G	59.7	27	39.4	38	775,101	59.7	27	39.4	39
1960	1,867,000	1,329,279	71.2	24	-	1,055,349	P	79.4	26	56.5	36	1,055,349	79.4	26	56.5	36
1958	1,741,000	1,227,434	70.5	21	-	763,234	G	62.2	23	43.8	35	763,234	62.2	23	43.8	35
1956	1,700,000	1,185,231	69.7	20	-	932,827	P	78.7	21	54.9	36	932,827	78.7	22	54.9	36
1954	1,585,000	1,092,730	68.9	18	-	700,484	G	64.1	14	44.2	34	700,484	64.1	16	44.2	35
1952	1,540,000	1,081,135	70.2	17	-	902,704	P	83.5	14	58.6	36	902,704	83.5	14	58.6	36
1950	1,498,000	927,988	61.9	16	-	645,631	G	69.6	11	43.1	34	645,631	69.6	11	43.1	34
1948	1,382,000	863,951	62.5	17	-	596,748	P	69.1	17	43.2	37	596,748	69.1	17	43.2	37

MARYLAND

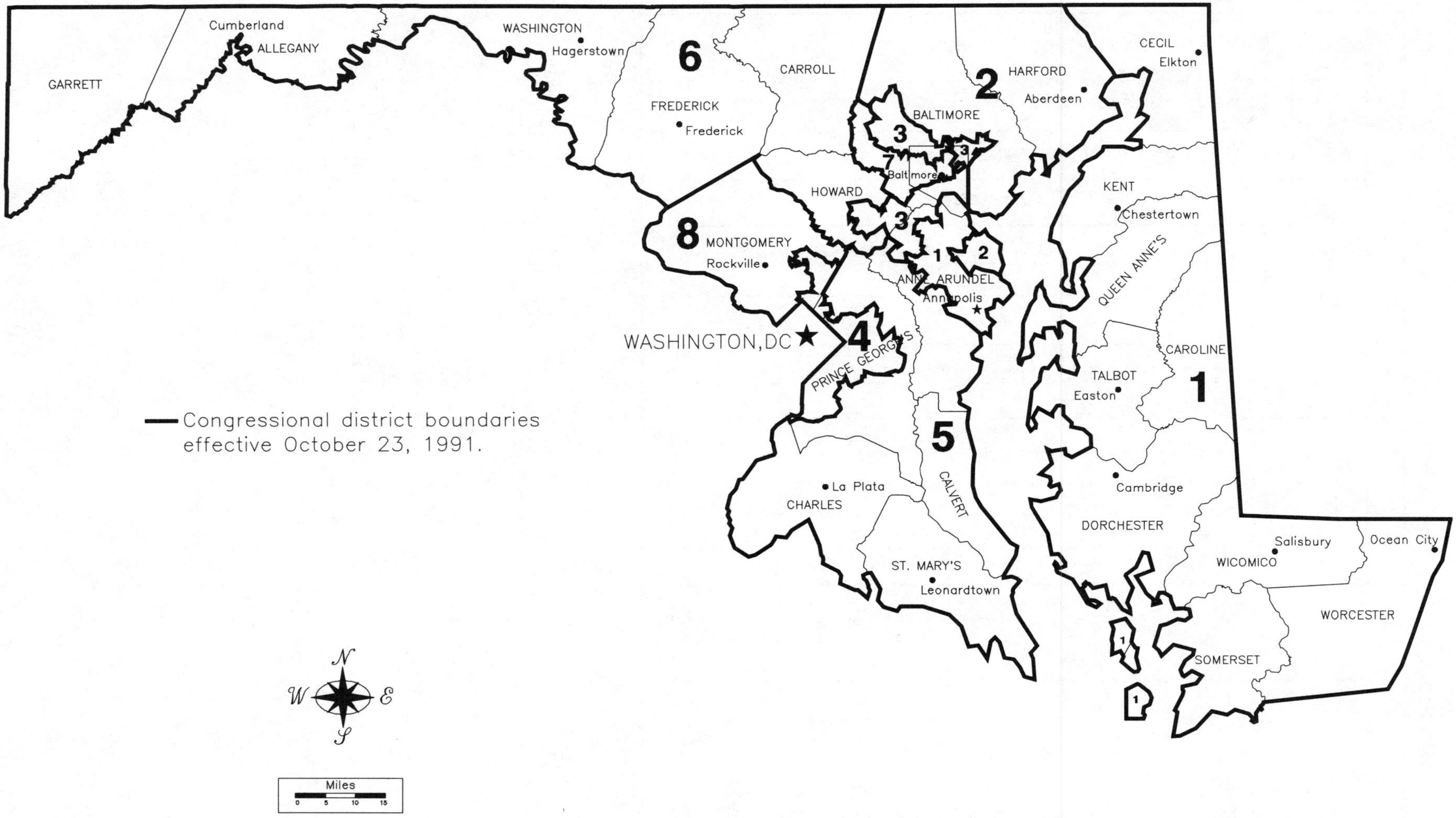

Elkton •
CECIL

CHESTERTOWN •
KENT

QUEEN ANNE'S

1
CAROLINE

Ocean City •
WORCESTER

Salisbury •
WICOMICO

SOMERSET

1

1

Aberdeen •
HARFORD
2

Cambridge •
TALBOT
Easton •
DORCHESTER

BALTIMORE
2

3

Baltimore •
3

ANNE ARUNDEL
1
2
Annapolis ★

5
CALVERT

Leonardtown •
ST. MARY'S

7

HOWARD
3

CARROLL

FREDERICK
Frederick •
6

PRINCE GEORGES
4

La Plata •
CHARLES

WASHINGTON
Hagerstown •

MONTGOMERY
Rockville •
8

WASHINGTON, DC ★

ALLEGANY
Cumberland •

GARRETT

— Congressional district boundaries
effective October 23, 1991.

Miles
0   5   10   15

Maryland 423

Table A. — 1990 Population by Race and Ethnic Origin

| State/county code | County | Total persons | Percent of total persons | | | | | | Rank | | | | Percent contribution to state population | | | |
| | | | Non-Hispanic | | | | | Hispanic | Total | Non-Hispanic | | Hispanic | Non-Hispanic | | | Hispanic |
			White	Black	Asian and Pacific Islander	Native American	Other			White	Black		Total	White	Black	
24 001	Allegany	74,946	97.0	2.0	0.4	<.1	<.1	0.4	13	2	23	23	1.6	2.2	0.1	0.3
24 003	Anne Arundel	427,239	84.6	11.7	1.7	0.3	<.1	1.6	5	9	15	7	8.9	10.9	4.2	5.4
24 005	Baltimore	692,134	84.1	12.2	2.2	0.2	<.1	1.2	4	10	13	9	14.5	17.5	7.2	6.5
24 009	Calvert	51,372	82.6	15.6	0.5	0.2	<.1	1.0	16	12	11	12	1.1	1.3	0.7	0.4
24 011	Caroline	27,035	82.2	16.4	0.3	0.2	<.1	0.9	22	13	10	15	0.6	0.7	0.4	0.2
24 013	Carroll	123,372	96.2	2.3	0.6	0.1	<.1	0.7	9	3	22	19	2.6	3.6	0.2	0.7
24 015	Cecil	71,347	94.0	4.5	0.4	0.2	<.1	0.9	15	4	21	14	1.5	2.0	0.3	0.5
24 017	Charles	101,154	78.2	18.1	1.3	0.7	<.1	1.7	11	16	8	5	2.1	2.4	1.6	1.4
24 019	Dorchester	30,236	71.0	27.7	0.4	0.2	<.1	0.6	20	21	4	20	0.6	0.6	0.7	0.1
24 021	Frederick	150,208	92.4	5.3	1.0	0.2	<.1	1.1	8	6	20	10	3.1	4.2	0.7	1.4
24 023	Garrett	28,138	99.0	0.4	0.1	<.1	<.1	0.4	21	1	24	24	0.6	0.8	<.1	<.1
24 025	Harford	182,132	88.4	8.4	1.3	0.2	<.1	1.5	7	7	18	8	3.8	4.8	1.3	2.3
24 027	Howard	187,328	81.9	11.6	4.3	0.2	<.1	2.0	6	14	16	4	3.9	4.6	1.8	3.0
24 029	Kent	17,842	77.2	19.7	0.3	0.1	<.1	2.6	24	18	7	3	0.4	0.4	0.3	0.4
24 031	Montgomery	757,027	72.4	11.8	8.1	0.2	0.1	7.4	1	20	14	1	15.8	16.5	7.6	44.5
24 033	Prince George's	729,268	41.6	50.1	3.7	0.3	0.1	4.1	3	23	2	2	15.3	9.1	31.0	24.0
24 035	Queen Anne's	33,953	87.7	11.2	0.4	0.1	<.1	0.6	18	8	17	21	0.7	0.9	0.3	0.2
24 037	St. Mary's	75,974	83.4	13.4	1.1	0.3	<.1	1.6	12	11	12	6	1.6	1.9	0.9	1.0
24 039	Somerset	23,440	60.5	37.9	0.4	0.2	<.1	1.0	23	22	3	13	0.5	0.4	0.8	0.2
24 041	Talbot	30,549	81.0	17.9	0.3	0.1	<.1	0.5	19	15	9	22	0.6	0.7	0.5	0.1
24 043	Washington	121,393	92.5	5.9	0.6	0.2	<.1	0.7	10	5	19	18	2.5	3.4	0.6	0.7
24 045	Wicomico	74,339	75.9	22.2	0.9	0.2	<.1	0.8	14	19	5	16	1.6	1.7	1.4	0.5
24 047	Worcester	35,028	77.3	21.3	0.5	0.2	<.1	0.8	17	17	6	17	0.7	0.8	0.6	0.2
24 510	Baltimore City	736,014	38.6	58.9	1.0	0.3	<.1	1.0	2	24	1	11	15.4	8.5	36.8	6.1
24	**MARYLAND**	**4,781,468**	**69.6**	**24.6**	**2.9**	**0.3**	**<.1**	**2.6**					**100.0**	**100.0**	**100.0**	**100.0**
	CONGRESSIONAL															
	District 1	597,684	82.7	14.9	1.0	0.2	<.1	1.1	3	3	5	6	12.5	14.9	7.6	5.3
	District 2	597,683	90.9	5.8	1.8	0.2	<.1	1.2	4	2	7	5	12.5	16.3	3.0	5.8
	District 3	597,680	78.5	17.3	2.2	0.3	<.1	1.7	7	4	4	4	12.5	14.1	8.8	8.2
	District 4	597,690	31.1	57.7	4.4	0.3	0.2	6.4	1	7	2	1	12.5	5.6	29.3	30.3
	District 5	597,681	75.8	18.3	3.0	0.4	<.1	2.4	6	6	3	3	12.5	13.6	9.3	11.6
	District 6	597,688	93.2	4.4	1.3	0.2	<.1	0.9	2	1	8	7	12.5	16.7	2.2	4.4
	District 7	597,680	26.9	70.6	1.3	0.3	<.1	0.9	8	8	1	8	12.5	4.8	35.8	4.2
	District 8	597,682	77.5	8.0	7.9	0.2	0.1	6.3	5	5	6	2	12.5	13.9	4.0	30.2

Table B. — 1990 Voting Age Population (VAP) by Race and Ethnic Origin

County	Total Voting Age Population	Percent of total VAP — Non-Hispanic White	Black	Asian and Pacific Islander	Native American	Other	Hispanic	Rank — Total	Non-Hispanic White	Black	Hispanic	Pct contribution to state VAP — Total	Non-Hispanic White	Black	Hispanic	VAP percent of total population — Total	Non-Hispanic White	Black	Asian and Pacific Islander	Native American	Other	Hispanic
Allegany	58,581	97.4	1.8	0.3	<.1	<.1	0.4	12	2	23	23	1.6	2.2	0.1	0.2	78.2	78.5	69.8	63.5	82.5	38.5	68.0
Anne Arundel	322,051	85.5	11.1	1.7	0.3	<.1	1.5	5	10	16	6	8.9	10.7	4.3	5.3	75.4	76.1	71.7	71.8	76.5	33.3	68.6
Baltimore	540,972	85.6	11.1	2.0	0.2	<.1	1.1	4	9	15	9	14.9	17.9	7.2	6.6	78.2	79.5	71.2	71.4	74.2	44.2	71.8
Calvert	36,772	82.9	15.4	0.5	0.3	<.1	0.9	16	13	11	13	1.0	1.2	0.7	0.4	71.6	71.8	70.8	67.6	81.1	44.4	62.7
Caroline	19,935	83.2	15.6	0.2	0.2	<.1	0.7	22	12	10	16	0.6	0.6	0.4	0.2	73.7	74.7	70.0	60.8	69.0	28.6	63.2
Carroll	90,602	96.3	2.4	0.5	0.1	<.1	0.6	10	3	22	18	2.5	3.4	0.3	0.6	73.4	73.5	76.1	65.9	75.6	25.0	63.5
Cecil	51,839	94.3	4.3	0.4	0.2	<.1	0.8	15	4	21	14	1.4	1.9	0.3	0.5	72.7	72.9	70.1	65.5	73.8	50.0	63.9
Charles	71,398	79.0	17.6	1.2	0.7	<.1	1.5	11	17	8	5	2.0	2.2	1.5	1.2	70.6	71.3	68.7	64.6	70.4	40.7	62.8
Dorchester	23,319	73.5	25.4	0.4	0.2	<.1	0.5	20	21	4	20	0.6	0.7	0.7	0.1	77.1	79.8	70.6	73.3	70.6	61.5	67.2
Frederick	110,477	92.8	5.1	0.9	0.2	<.1	1.0	8	5	20	10	3.1	4.0	0.7	1.3	73.5	73.9	71.0	68.8	68.5	17.9	67.0
Garrett	20,518	99.3	0.2	0.1	<.1	<.1	0.3	21	1	24	24	0.6	0.8	<.1	<.1	72.9	73.1	36.3	65.0	54.5	50.0	55.5
Harford	133,350	89.2	7.9	1.3	0.2	<.1	1.4	7	7	18	8	3.7	4.6	1.2	2.1	73.2	73.9	68.5	68.7	73.8	48.9	64.9
Howard	138,846	82.6	11.4	3.9	0.2	<.1	1.8	6	14	13	4	3.8	4.4	1.9	2.8	74.1	74.8	73.2	68.2	79.2	31.0	67.5
Kent	14,037	78.6	18.6	0.3	0.1	<.1	2.4	24	18	7	3	0.4	0.4	0.3	0.4	78.7	80.1	74.2	64.5	94.7	25.0	72.4
Montgomery	578,783	74.1	11.1	7.6	0.2	<.1	6.9	1	20	14	1	16.0	16.6	7.7	45.1	76.5	78.2	72.3	72.0	76.9	47.6	71.9
Prince George's	551,323	44.7	47.2	3.7	0.3	<.1	3.9	3	23	2	2	15.2	9.6	31.0	24.3	75.6	81.4	71.2	75.4	75.9	46.3	71.9
Queen Anne's	25,612	88.1	11.0	0.3	0.1	0.0	0.5	18	8	17	21	0.7	0.9	0.3	0.1	75.4	75.7	73.6	68.3	82.2	0.0	68.8
St. Mary's	54,421	84.1	13.1	1.1	0.3	<.1	1.4	14	11	12	7	1.5	1.8	0.8	0.9	71.6	72.2	69.7	68.2	71.8	34.4	64.1
Somerset	18,713	60.7	37.7	0.4	0.2	<.1	0.9	23	22	3	12	0.5	0.4	0.8	0.2	79.8	80.1	79.4	86.0	80.0	68.8	74.7
Talbot	24,116	82.0	17.1	0.2	0.1	<.1	0.5	19	15	9	22	0.7	0.8	0.5	0.1	78.9	79.9	75.6	56.0	85.7	29.6	65.9
Washington	93,857	92.4	6.3	0.5	0.2	<.1	0.6	9	6	19	19	2.6	3.4	0.7	0.6	77.3	77.2	82.5	64.8	85.2	33.3	63.5
Wicomico	56,229	78.0	20.2	0.8	0.2	<.1	0.8	13	19	5	15	1.6	1.7	1.4	0.5	75.6	77.8	68.9	72.0	74.4	19.1	70.7
Worcester	27,331	79.6	19.2	0.4	0.2	<.1	0.7	17	16	6	17	0.8	0.8	0.6	0.2	78.0	80.3	70.3	61.4	82.4	18.8	70.9
Baltimore City	556,145	42.0	55.5	1.1	0.3	<.1	1.0	2	24	1	11	15.4	9.1	36.7	6.3	75.6	82.2	71.2	80.2	69.7	53.1	73.5
MARYLAND	**3,619,227**	**71.3**	**23.2**	**2.7**	**0.2**	**<.1**	**2.5**					**100.0**	**100.0**	**100.0**	**100.0**	**75.7**	**77.6**	**71.4**	**72.5**	**74.3**	**44.3**	**71.0**
CONGRESSIONAL																						
District 1	454,929	83.7	14.1	0.9	0.2	<.1	1.0	3	3	5	6	12.6	14.8	7.6	5.2	76.1	77.1	71.7	71.3	77.6	33.9	70.5
District 2	457,326	91.8	5.3	1.6	0.2	<.1	1.1	2	2	7	5	12.6	16.3	2.9	5.6	76.5	77.3	68.9	70.0	74.1	44.2	68.7
District 3	458,953	80.6	15.5	2.0	0.3	<.1	1.6	1	4	4	4	12.7	14.3	8.5	8.0	76.8	78.9	68.9	71.9	70.8	40.3	69.6
District 4	447,101	34.1	55.1	4.3	0.3	0.1	6.1	8	7	2	1	12.4	5.9	29.3	30.6	74.8	82.0	71.5	72.9	76.6	48.4	71.6
District 5	450,198	76.7	17.6	3.0	0.4	<.1	2.3	5	6	3	3	12.4	13.4	9.4	11.5	75.3	76.3	72.3	75.2	74.1	44.3	70.4
District 6	447,788	93.4	4.5	1.1	0.2	<.1	0.8	7	1	8	8	12.4	16.2	2.4	4.1	74.9	75.1	75.4	66.8	76.8	29.0	65.8
District 7	448,189	29.9	67.6	1.4	0.2	<.1	0.9	6	8	1	7	12.4	5.2	36.0	4.4	75.0	83.5	71.7	78.9	71.1	54.4	73.5
District 8	454,743	79.0	7.3	7.5	0.2	<.1	6.0	4	5	6	2	12.6	13.9	3.9	30.6	76.1	77.6	69.6	71.9	75.8	44.5	71.9

Table C. — Voter Participation: November 3, 1992, General Election

County	Estimated Voting Age Population (VAP) 1992	Voter registration (REG) Total	% contribution to state REG	% of 1992 VAP	Rank by % of 1992 VAP	Voter turnout Highest office Actual	Total	Office	% of 1992 VAP	Maximum vote Total	% contribution to state turnout	% of REG	Rank by % of REG	% of 1992 VAP	Rank by % 1992 VAP	Percent drop-off, by office President	Senator	Governor	Representative
Allegany	56,602	38,870	1.6	68.7	7	30,847	30,595	P	54.1	30,847	1.5	79.4	19	54.5	12	0.8	15.5	-	22.6
Anne Arundel	330,748	214,050	8.7	64.7	14	186,427	185,634	P	56.1	186,427	9.3	87.1	2	56.4	8	0.4	2.9	-	4.0
Baltimore	540,797	401,278	16.3	74.2	2	324,870	323,220	P	59.8	324,870	16.2	81.0	15	60.1	3	0.5	9.6	-	11.7
Calvert	41,111	28,562	1.2	69.5	4	23,354	23,249	P	56.6	23,354	1.2	81.8	12	56.8	7	0.4	15.4	-	9.1
Caroline	20,621	10,642	0.4	51.6	24	8,504	8,459	P	41.0	8,504	0.4	79.9	17	41.2	24	0.5	15.9	-	11.1
Carroll	95,879	65,337	2.7	68.1	8	55,912	54,930	P	57.3	55,912	2.8	85.6	3	58.3	6	1.8	3.8	-	9.6
Cecil	54,018	33,819	1.4	62.6	17	27,420	27,319	P	50.6	27,420	1.4	81.1	14	50.8	16	0.4	15.7	-	12.0
Charles	78,223	49,058	2.0	62.7	16	38,437	38,454	P	49.2	38,454	1.9	78.4	22	49.2	17	0.0	15.5	-	11.2
Dorchester	23,011	14,032	0.6	61.0	19	11,130	10,957	P	47.6	11,130	0.6	79.3	20	48.4	19	1.6	18.1	-	11.0
Frederick	117,848	77,498	3.1	65.8	12	65,649	64,691	P	54.9	65,649	3.3	84.7	7	55.7	9	1.5	4.3	-	5.8
Garrett	20,893	12,918	0.5	61.8	18	10,634	10,580	P	50.6	10,634	0.5	82.3	10	50.9	15	0.5	20.1	-	19.4
Harford	140,230	96,392	3.9	68.7	6	81,883	80,687	P	57.5	81,883	4.1	84.9	5	58.4	5	1.5	3.4	-	4.8
Howard	157,422	113,764	4.6	72.3	3	100,471	99,798	P	63.4	100,471	5.0	88.3	1	63.8	1	0.7	3.1	-	8.7
Kent	13,887	9,357	0.4	67.4	9	7,701	7,628	P	54.9	7,701	0.4	82.3	11	55.5	11	0.9	18.4	-	9.8
Montgomery	618,021	428,740	17.4	69.4	5	365,128	362,613	P	58.7	365,128	18.3	85.2	4	59.1	4	0.7	3.1	-	6.0
Prince George's	558,117	318,524	12.9	57.1	21	258,699	256,859	P	46.0	258,699	12.9	81.2	13	46.4	20	0.7	11.8	-	10.3
Queen Anne's	27,342	17,180	0.7	62.8	15	14,561	14,514	P	53.1	14,561	0.7	84.8	6	53.3	13	0.3	14.2	-	8.9
St. Mary's	57,112	31,782	1.3	55.6	22	25,127	25,085	P	43.9	25,127	1.3	79.1	21	44.0	22	0.2	14.5	-	9.0
Somerset	19,242	10,034	0.4	52.1	23	8,017	7,936	P	41.2	8,017	0.4	79.9	18	41.7	23	1.0	18.5	-	12.0
Talbot	24,841	16,723	0.7	67.3	10	13,785	13,708	P	55.2	13,785	0.7	82.4	9	55.5	10	0.6	17.3	-	11.0
Washington	94,527	54,947	2.2	58.1	20	46,382	46,208	P	48.9	46,382	2.3	84.4	8	49.1	18	0.4	14.3	-	18.3
Wicomico	57,493	37,617	1.5	65.4	13	30,418	30,272	P	52.7	30,418	1.5	80.9	16	52.9	14	0.5	13.3	-	10.5
Worcester	27,813	21,481	0.9	77.2	1	16,820	16,559	P	59.5	16,820	0.8	78.3	23	60.5	2	1.6	6.2	-	4.2
Baltimore City	543,202	360,405	14.6	66.3	11	247,310	245,091	P	45.1	247,310	12.4	68.6	24	45.5	21	0.9	8.6	-	14.6
MARYLAND[1]	3,719,000	2,463,010	100.0	66.2		1,999,486	1,985,046		53.4	1,999,503	100.0	81.2		53.8		0.7	7.9	-	9.6

[1]Maryland reports voter registration and turnout by political party affiliation. See Table D-registration by party. State voter turnout by party is 1,227,778 (61.4%) for Democratic party, 591,654 (29.6%) for Republican party, 1,916 (0.1%) for Libertarian party, 32 (<.1%) for Alliance party, and 178,106 (8.9%) for registrants who declined to affiliate and other parties.

Table D. — Voter Registration by Political Party Affiliation: November 3, 1992, General Election

County	Total voter registration	Political party affiliation Democrat (DEM)	Republican (REP)	Independent (IND)	Plurality Total	Plurality Party	Percent of total registration DEM	REP	IND	Rank DEM	Rank REP	Rank IND	Percent contribution to state registration Total	DEM	REP	IND
Allegany	38,870	17,991	18,825	2,030	834	R	46.3	48.5	5.2	21	2	21	1.6	1.2	2.6	0.9
Anne Arundel	214,050	111,763	80,257	21,726	31,506	R	52.3	37.5	10.2	15	10	6	8.7	7.4	11.2	9.2
Baltimore	401,278	265,812	108,308	26,737	157,504	D	66.3	27.0	6.7	3	22	19	16.3	17.6	15.1	11.3
Calvert	28,562	14,503	11,317	2,709	3,186	D	50.8	39.7	9.5	16	8	8	1.2	1.0	1.6	1.1
Caroline	10,642	5,899	3,885	858	2,014	D	55.4	36.5	8.1	10	12	13	0.4	0.4	0.5	0.4
Carroll	65,337	28,626	31,193	5,462	2,567	R	43.9	47.8	8.4	23	3	10	2.7	1.9	4.3	2.3
Cecil	33,819	18,381	11,571	3,786	6,810	D	54.5	34.3	11.2	12	17	4	1.4	1.2	1.6	1.6
Charles	49,058	24,127	20,048	4,794	4,079	D	49.3	40.9	9.8	18	7	7	2.0	1.6	2.8	2.0
Dorchester	14,032	9,027	4,355	641	4,672	D	64.4	31.1	4.6	4	21	23	0.6	0.6	0.6	0.3
Frederick	77,498	34,102	34,027	9,221	75	D	44.1	44.0	11.9	22	4	3	3.1	2.3	4.7	3.9
Garrett	12,918	4,443	8,030	432	3,587	R	34.4	62.2	3.3	24	1	24	0.5	0.3	1.1	0.2
Harford	96,392	52,726	35,628	7,971	17,098	D	54.7	37.0	8.3	11	11	11	3.9	3.5	5.0	3.4
Howard	113,764	56,106	41,285	16,296	14,821	D	49.4	36.3	14.3	17	13	2	4.6	3.7	5.8	6.9
Kent	9,357	5,472	3,242	639	2,230	D	58.5	34.7	6.8	7	16	18	0.4	0.4	0.5	0.3
Montgomery	428,740	228,489	136,048	63,702	92,441	D	53.4	31.8	14.9	14	19	1	17.4	15.2	18.9	27.0
Prince George's	318,524	220,420	62,817	34,886	157,603	D	69.3	19.7	11.0	2	23	5	12.9	14.6	8.7	14.8
Queen Anne's	17,180	9,272	6,527	1,378	2,745	D	54.0	38.0	8.0	13	9	14	0.7	0.6	0.9	0.6
St. Mary's	31,782	18,624	10,338	2,801	8,286	D	58.6	32.5	8.8	6	18	9	1.3	1.2	1.4	1.2
Somerset	10,034	6,398	3,137	491	3,261	D	63.8	31.3	4.9	5	20	22	0.4	0.4	0.4	0.2
Talbot	16,723	8,092	7,252	1,359	840	D	48.4	43.4	8.1	20	5	12	0.7	0.5	1.0	0.6
Washington	54,947	26,816	23,754	4,293	3,062	D	48.9	43.3	7.8	19	6	17	2.2	1.8	3.3	1.8
Wicomico	37,617	21,120	13,471	2,963	7,649	D	56.2	35.9	7.9	9	14	16	1.5	1.4	1.9	1.3
Worcester	21,481	12,183	7,575	1,714	4,608	D	56.7	35.3	8.0	8	15	15	0.9	0.8	1.1	0.7
Baltimore City	360,405	305,792	35,073	19,224	270,719	D	84.9	9.7	5.3	1	24	20	14.6	20.3	4.9	8.1
MARYLAND[1]	2,463,010	1,506,184	717,963	236,113	788,221	D	61.2	29.2	9.6				100.0	100.0	100.0	100.0

[1]Total voter registration also includes 2,692 for Libertarian party and 58 for Alliance party. State voter turnout as a percentage of voter registration by party is 1,227,778 (81.5%) for Democrat, 591,654 (82.4%) for Republican, and 178,106 (75.4%) for independent.

Table E. — Vote for President: November 3, 1992, General Election

County	Total	Clinton (DEM)	Bush (REP)	Perot (IND)	Other	Plurality Total	Party	Pct DEM	Pct REP	Pct IND	Pct Other	Rank DEM	Rank REP	Rank IND	Contrib Total	Contrib DEM	Contrib REP	Contrib IND	Major DEM	Major REP
Allegany	30,595	11,501	13,862	5,081	151	2,361	R	37.6	45.3	16.6	0.5	10	9	16	1.5	1.2	2.0	1.8	45.3	54.7
Anne Arundel	185,634	68,629	81,467	35,191	347	12,838	R	37.0	43.9	19.0	0.2	13	14	8	9.4	6.9	11.5	12.5	45.7	54.3
Baltimore	323,220	143,498	126,728	51,757	1,237	16,770	D	44.4	39.2	16.0	0.4	5	20	20	16.3	14.5	17.9	18.4	53.1	46.9
Calvert	23,249	8,619	10,026	4,499	105	1,407	R	37.1	43.1	19.4	0.5	12	17	7	1.2	0.9	1.4	1.6	46.2	53.8
Caroline	8,459	2,822	3,856	1,729	52	1,034	R	33.4	45.6	20.4	0.6	21	8	3	0.4	0.3	0.5	0.6	42.3	57.7
Carroll	54,930	15,447	28,405	10,965	113	12,958	R	28.1	51.7	20.0	0.2	23	2	5	2.8	1.6	4.0	3.9	35.2	64.8
Cecil	27,319	10,232	10,784	6,115	188	552	R	37.5	39.5	22.4	0.7	11	19	1	1.4	1.0	1.5	2.2	48.7	51.3
Charles	38,454	14,498	17,293	6,501	162	2,795	R	37.7	45.0	16.9	0.4	9	12	15	1.9	1.5	2.4	2.3	45.6	54.4
Dorchester	10,957	3,933	4,934	2,010	80	1,001	R	35.9	45.0	18.3	0.7	15	11	11	0.6	0.4	0.7	0.7	44.4	55.6
Frederick	64,691	21,848	31,290	11,373	180	9,442	R	33.8	48.4	17.6	0.3	19	4	13	3.3	2.2	4.4	4.0	41.1	58.9
Garrett	10,580	2,856	5,714	1,987	23	2,858	R	27.0	54.0	18.8	0.2	24	1	9	0.5	0.3	0.8	0.7	33.3	66.7
Harford	80,687	27,164	36,350	17,002	171	9,186	R	33.7	45.1	21.1	0.2	20	10	2	4.1	2.7	5.1	6.0	42.8	57.2
Howard	99,798	44,763	38,594	16,182	259	6,169	D	44.9	38.7	16.2	0.3	4	21	19	5.0	4.5	5.5	5.8	53.7	46.3
Kent	7,628	3,093	3,094	1,411	30	1	R	40.5	40.6	18.5	0.4	6	18	10	0.4	0.3	0.4	0.5	50.0	50.0
Montgomery	362,613	199,757	119,705	41,971	1,180	80,052	D	55.1	33.0	11.6	0.3	3	22	22	18.3	20.2	16.9	14.9	62.5	37.5
Prince George's	256,859	168,691	62,955	23,355	1,858	105,736	D	65.7	24.5	9.1	0.7	2	23	23	12.9	17.1	8.9	8.3	72.8	27.2
Queen Anne's	14,514	4,668	6,829	2,958	59	2,161	R	32.2	47.1	20.4	0.4	22	6	4	0.7	0.5	1.0	1.1	40.6	59.4
St. Mary's	25,085	8,931	11,485	4,550	119	2,554	R	35.6	45.8	18.1	0.5	17	7	12	1.3	0.9	1.6	1.6	43.7	56.3
Somerset	7,936	3,210	3,450	1,230	46	240	R	40.4	43.5	15.5	0.6	7	16	21	0.4	0.3	0.5	0.4	48.2	51.8
Talbot	13,708	4,642	6,774	2,233	59	2,132	R	33.9	49.4	16.3	0.4	18	3	18	0.7	0.5	1.0	0.8	40.7	59.3
Washington	46,208	16,495	21,977	7,537	199	5,482	R	35.7	47.6	16.3	0.4	16	5	17	2.3	1.7	3.1	2.7	42.9	57.1
Wicomico	30,272	11,481	13,560	5,140	91	2,079	R	37.9	44.8	17.0	0.3	8	13	14	1.5	1.2	1.9	1.8	45.8	54.2
Worcester	16,559	6,040	7,237	3,256	26	1,197	R	36.5	43.7	19.7	0.2	14	15	6	0.8	0.6	1.0	1.2	45.5	54.5
Baltimore City	245,091	185,753	40,725	17,381	1,232	145,028	D	75.8	16.6	7.1	0.5	1	24	24	12.3	18.8	5.8	6.2	82.0	18.0
MARYLAND	1,985,046	988,571	707,094	281,414	7,967	281,477	D	49.8	35.6	14.2	0.4				100.0	100.0	100.0	100.0	58.3	41.7

Table F. — Vote for U.S. Senator: November 3, 1992, General Election

County	Total	Mikulski (DEM)	Keyes (REP)	Other	Plurality Total	Party	Pct DEM	Pct REP	Pct Other	Rank DEM	Rank REP	Rank Other	Contrib Total	Contrib DEM	Contrib REP	Contrib Other
Allegany	26,072	16,872	9,199	1	7,673	D	64.7	35.3	<.1	14	11	15	1.4	1.3	1.7	0.2
Anne Arundel	180,997	121,290	59,512	195	61,778	D	67.0	32.9	0.1	11	14	1	9.8	9.3	11.2	44.6
Baltimore	293,539	208,164	85,374	1	122,790	D	70.9	29.1	<.1	5	20	16	15.9	15.9	16.0	0.2
Calvert	19,761	11,980	7,781	0	4,199	D	60.6	39.4	0.0	21	4	17	1.1	0.9	1.5	0.0
Caroline	7,154	4,622	2,531	1	2,091	D	64.6	35.4	<.1	17	8	8	0.4	0.4	0.5	0.2
Carroll	53,799	30,495	23,293	11	7,202	D	56.7	43.3	<.1	23	2	6	2.9	2.3	4.4	2.5
Cecil	23,120	14,744	8,374	2	6,370	D	63.8	36.2	<.1	18	7	11	1.3	1.1	1.6	0.5
Charles	32,494	20,053	12,439	2	7,614	D	61.7	38.3	<.1	19	6	13	1.8	1.5	2.3	0.5
Dorchester	9,111	6,346	2,765	0	3,581	D	69.7	30.3	0.0	8	17	18	0.5	0.5	0.5	0.0
Frederick	62,854	36,788	26,055	11	10,733	D	58.5	41.5	<.1	22	3	7	3.4	2.8	4.9	2.5
Garrett	8,501	3,473	5,028	0	1,555	R	40.9	59.1	0.0	24	1	19	0.5	0.3	0.9	0.0
Harford	79,066	51,096	27,966	4	23,130	D	64.6	35.4	<.1	16	9	14	4.3	3.9	5.2	0.9
Howard	97,354	65,681	31,664	9	34,017	D	67.5	32.5	<.1	9	16	12	5.3	5.0	5.9	2.1
Kent	6,282	4,550	1,732	0	2,818	D	72.4	27.6	0.0	4	21	20	0.3	0.3	0.3	0.0
Montgomery	353,628	247,505	105,997	126	141,508	D	70.0	30.0	<.1	6	19	3	19.2	18.9	19.9	28.8
Prince George's	228,249	180,129	48,093	27	132,036	D	78.9	21.1	<.1	2	23	9	12.4	13.8	9.0	6.2
Queen Anne's	12,493	8,079	4,414	0	3,665	D	64.7	35.3	0.0	15	10	21	0.7	0.6	0.8	0.0
St. Mary's	21,493	13,943	7,541	9	6,402	D	64.9	35.1	<.1	13	12	2	1.2	1.1	1.4	2.1
Somerset	6,535	4,565	1,970	0	2,595	D	69.9	30.1	0.0	7	18	22	0.4	0.3	0.4	0.0
Talbot	11,407	7,437	3,966	4	3,471	D	65.2	34.8	<.1	12	13	4	0.6	0.6	0.7	0.9
Washington	39,750	24,499	15,240	11	9,259	D	61.6	38.3	<.1	20	5	5	2.2	1.9	2.9	2.5
Wicomico	26,364	17,713	8,651	0	9,062	D	67.2	32.8	0.0	10	15	23	1.4	1.4	1.6	0.0
Worcester	15,769	11,500	4,269	0	7,231	D	72.9	27.1	0.0	3	22	24	0.9	0.9	0.8	0.0
Baltimore City	225,943	196,086	29,834	23	166,252	D	86.8	13.2	<.1	1	24	10	12.3	15.0	5.6	5.3
MARYLAND	1,841,735	1,307,610	533,688	437	773,922	D	71.0	29.0	<.1				100.0	100.0	100.0	100.0

Maryland 427

Table H. — Vote for U.S. Representative in Congress: November 3, 1992, General Election

Congressional district and county	Total	Democrat (DEM)	Republican (REP)	Other	Plurality Total	Plurality Party	Percent of total vote DEM	REP	Other	Rank within district DEM	REP	Other	Percent contribution to district vote Total	DEM	REP	Other
District 1	**234,203**	**112,771**	**120,084**	**1,348**	**7,313**	**R**	**48.2**	**51.3**	**0.6**				**100.0**	**100.0**	**100.0**	**100.0**
Anne Arundel (pt)	107,195	61,411	44,516	1,268	16,895	D	57.3	41.5	1.2	2	10	1	45.8	54.5	37.1	94.1
Caroline	7,564	2,560	4,988	16	2,428	R	33.8	65.9	0.2	8	4	3	3.2	2.3	4.2	1.2
Cecil	24,119	11,705	12,412	2	707	R	48.5	51.5	<.1	3	9	7	10.3	10.4	10.3	0.1
Dorchester	9,909	4,135	5,735	39	1,600	R	41.7	57.9	0.4	6	6	2	4.2	3.7	4.8	2.9
Kent	6,945	1,959	4,975	11	3,016	R	28.2	71.6	0.2	10	2	4	3.0	1.7	4.1	0.8
Queen Anne's	13,260	4,212	9,048	0	4,836	R	31.8	68.2	0.0	9	3	8	5.7	3.7	7.5	0.0
Somerset	7,053	3,259	3,794	0	535	R	46.2	53.8	0.0	4	8	9	3.0	2.9	3.2	0.0
Talbot	12,269	3,152	9,108	9	5,956	R	25.7	74.2	<.1	11	1	6	5.2	2.8	7.6	0.7
Wicomico	27,215	11,094	16,121	0	5,027	R	40.8	59.2	0.0	7	5	10	11.6	9.8	13.4	0.0
Worcester	16,119	7,408	8,711	0	1,303	R	46.0	54.0	0.0	5	7	11	6.9	6.6	7.3	0.0
Baltimore City (pt)	2,555	1,876	676	3	1,200	D	73.4	26.5	0.1	1	11	5	1.1	1.7	0.6	0.2
District 2	**254,106**	**88,658**	**165,443**	**5**	**76,785**	**R**	**34.9**	**65.1**	**<.1**				**100.0**	**100.0**	**100.0**	**100.0**
Anne Arundel (pt)	20,929	7,031	13,894	4	6,863	R	33.6	66.4	<.1	2	2	1	8.2	7.9	8.4	80.0
Baltimore (pt)	155,222	51,074	104,148	0	53,074	R	32.9	67.1	0.0	3	1	3	61.1	57.6	63.0	0.0
Harford	77,955	30,553	47,401	1	16,848	R	39.2	60.8	<.1	1	3	2	30.7	34.5	28.7	20.0
District 3	**222,255**	**163,354**	**58,869**	**32**	**104,485**	**D**	**73.5**	**26.5**	**<.1**				**100.0**	**100.0**	**100.0**	**100.0**
Anne Arundel (pt)	18,414	11,273	7,120	21	4,153	D	61.2	38.7	0.1	4	1	1	8.3	6.9	12.1	65.6
Baltimore (pt)	83,227	59,147	24,080	0	35,067	D	71.1	28.9	0.0	2	3	3	37.4	36.2	40.9	0.0
Howard (pt)	42,542	28,507	14,024	11	14,483	D	67.0	33.0	<.1	3	2	2	19.1	17.5	23.8	34.4
Baltimore City (pt)	78,072	64,427	13,645	0	50,782	D	82.5	17.5	0.0	1	4	4	35.1	39.4	23.2	0.0
District 4	**182,185**	**136,902**	**45,166**	**117**	**91,736**	**D**	**75.1**	**24.8**	**<.1**				**100.0**	**100.0**	**100.0**	**100.0**
Montgomery (pt)	62,915	37,024	25,836	55	11,188	D	58.8	41.1	<.1	2	1	1	34.5	27.0	57.2	47.0
Prince George's (pt)	119,270	99,878	19,330	62	80,548	D	83.7	16.2	<.1	1	2	2	65.5	73.0	42.8	53.0
District 5	**223,326**	**118,312**	**97,982**	**7,032**	**20,330**	**D**	**53.0**	**43.9**	**3.1**				**100.0**	**100.0**	**100.0**	**100.0**
Anne Arundel (pt)	32,413	14,754	15,605	2,054	851	R	45.5	48.1	6.3	3	4	2	14.5	12.5	15.9	29.2
Calvert	21,230	9,011	10,798	1,421	1,787	R	42.4	50.9	6.7	5	2	1	9.5	7.6	11.0	20.2
Charles	34,132	16,035	17,116	981	1,081	R	47.0	50.1	2.9	2	3	3	15.3	13.6	17.5	14.0
Prince George's (pt)	112,685	68,147	42,558	1,980	25,589	D	60.5	37.8	1.8	1	5	5	50.5	57.6	43.4	28.2
St. Mary's	22,866	10,365	11,905	596	1,540	R	45.3	52.1	2.6	4	1	4	10.2	8.8	12.2	8.5
District 6	**231,959**	**106,224**	**125,564**	**171**	**19,340**	**R**	**45.8**	**54.1**	**<.1**				**100.0**	**100.0**	**100.0**	**100.0**
Allegany	23,863	11,970	11,888	5	82	D	50.2	49.8	<.1	2	5	6	10.3	11.3	9.5	2.9
Carroll	50,544	22,979	27,544	21	4,565	R	45.5	54.5	<.1	3	4	4	21.8	21.6	21.9	12.3
Frederick	61,849	25,578	36,206	65	10,628	R	41.4	58.5	0.1	5	2	2	26.7	24.1	28.8	38.0
Garrett	8,567	3,132	5,431	4	2,299	R	36.6	63.4	<.1	6	1	3	3.7	2.9	4.3	2.3
Howard (pt)	49,220	26,409	22,800	11	3,609	D	53.7	46.3	<.1	1	6	5	21.2	24.9	18.2	6.4
Washington	37,916	16,156	21,695	65	5,539	R	42.6	57.2	0.2	4	3	1	16.3	15.2	17.3	38.0
District 7	**178,998**	**152,689**	**26,304**	**5**	**126,385**	**D**	**85.3**	**14.7**	**<.1**				**100.0**	**100.0**	**100.0**	**100.0**
Baltimore (pt)	48,384	30,946	17,438	0	13,508	D	64.0	36.0	0.0	2	1	2	27.0	20.3	66.3	0.0
Baltimore City (pt)	130,614	121,743	8,866	5	112,877	D	93.2	6.8	<.1	1	2	1	73.0	79.7	33.7	100.0
District 8	**280,475**	**77,042**	**203,377**	**56**	**126,335**	**R**	**27.5**	**72.5**	**<.1**				**100.0**	**100.0**	**100.0**	**100.0**
Montgomery (pt)	280,475	77,042	203,377	56	126,335	R	27.5	72.5	<.1	1	1	1	100.0	100.0	100.0	100.0
MARYLAND	**1,807,507**	**955,952**	**842,789**	**8,766**	**113,163**	**D**	**52.9**	**46.6**	**0.5**							

Table I. — Vote for Presidential Preference: March 3, 1992, Democratic Primary Election

| County | Top candidates | | | | | | | | | Top three candidates (state vote) | | | | | | | | | |
| | | | | | | | | | | Percent of total vote | | | Rank | | | Percent contribution to state vote | | | |
	Total	Tsongas	Clinton	Brown	Uncommitted	Harkin	Kerrey	LaRouche		Tsongas	Clinton	Brown	Tsongas	Clinton	Brown	Total	Tsongas	Clinton	Brown
Allegany	7,374	2,482	2,581	674	473	605	431	128	-	33.7	35.0	9.1	16	16	6	1.3	1.1	1.4	1.5
Anne Arundel	47,891	19,745	14,205	3,976	4,715	2,502	2,460	288	-	41.2	29.7	8.3	5	21	17	8.4	8.6	7.5	8.6
Baltimore	101,473	44,355	30,203	9,389	5,928	5,667	5,066	865	-	43.7	29.8	9.3	4	20	4	17.9	19.2	15.9	20.2
Calvert	5,256	1,862	2,060	447	243	249	341	54	-	35.4	39.2	8.5	12	7	14	0.9	0.8	1.1	1.0
Caroline	2,072	618	916	183	134	91	101	29	-	29.8	44.2	8.8	22	3	12	0.4	0.3	0.5	0.4
Carroll	11,639	5,236	3,197	1,065	859	612	596	74	-	45.0	27.5	9.2	3	22	5	2.1	2.3	1.7	2.3
Cecil	6,087	1,896	2,618	576	378	301	239	79	-	35.4	43.0	9.5	19	4	3	1.1	0.8	1.4	1.2
Charles	7,342	2,601	2,796	598	524	324	405	94	-	35.4	38.1	8.1	13	9	18	1.3	1.1	1.5	1.3
Dorchester	3,014	838	1,289	205	262	199	168	53	-	27.8	42.8	6.8	23	5	24	0.5	0.4	0.7	0.4
Frederick	13,950	5,397	4,317	1,247	1,046	958	900	85	-	38.7	30.9	8.9	8	19	10	2.5	2.3	2.3	2.7
Garrett	1,721	529	642	156	171	121	81	21	-	30.7	37.3	9.1	21	11	7	0.3	0.2	0.3	0.3
Harford	20,083	8,233	6,237	2,023	1,552	946	960	132	-	41.0	31.1	10.1	7	18	1	3.5	3.6	3.3	4.4
Howard	24,127	12,540	5,674	2,028	1,457	1,137	1,217	74	-	52.0	23.5	8.4	1	24	15	4.3	5.4	3.0	4.4
Kent	2,256	828	845	217	179	89	87	11	-	36.7	37.5	9.6	10	10	2	0.4	0.4	0.4	0.5
Montgomery	103,109	51,880	24,277	7,217	7,052	6,748	5,637	298	-	50.3	23.5	7.0	2	23	23	18.2	22.5	12.8	15.5
Prince George's	76,022	26,179	31,276	5,323	4,503	4,827	3,352	562	-	34.4	41.1	7.0	14	6	22	13.4	11.4	16.5	11.5
Queen Anne's	3,666	1,336	1,405	330	248	148	168	31	-	36.4	38.3	9.0	11	8	9	0.6	0.6	0.7	0.7
St. Mary's	6,720	2,500	2,504	544	440	275	399	58	-	37.2	37.3	8.1	9	12	19	1.2	1.1	1.3	1.2
Somerset	2,141	559	980	168	217	86	95	36	-	26.1	45.8	7.8	24	1	21	0.4	0.2	0.5	0.4
Talbot	2,864	1,176	992	245	194	87	147	23	-	41.1	34.6	8.6	6	17	13	0.5	0.5	0.5	0.5
Washington	10,911	3,630	3,914	862	932	766	691	116	-	33.3	35.9	7.9	17	15	20	1.9	1.6	2.1	1.9
Wicomico	7,353	2,315	2,677	665	900	430	288	78	-	31.5	36.4	9.0	18	13	8	1.3	1.0	1.4	1.4
Worcester	4,142	1,289	1,498	368	569	189	200	29	-	31.1	36.2	8.9	20	14	11	0.7	0.6	0.8	0.8
Baltimore City	96,011	32,466	42,803	7,974	3,179	5,542	3,006	1,041	-	33.8	44.6	8.3	15	2	16	16.9	14.1	22.5	17.2
MARYLAND	**567,224**	**230,490**	**189,906**	**46,480**	**36,155**	**32,899**	**27,035**	**4,259**	-	**40.6**	**33.5**	**8.2**				**100.0**	**100.0**	**100.0**	**100.0**

Table J. — Vote for Presidential Preference: March 3, 1992, Republican Primary Election

| County | Top candidates | | | | | Top four candidates (state vote) | | | | | | | | | Percent contribution to state vote | | | | |
| | | | | | | Percent of total vote | | | | Rank | | | | | | | | | |
	Total	Bush	Buchanan			Bush	Buchanan			Bush	Buchanan			Total	Bush	Buchanan		
Allegany	7,281	5,017	2,264	-	-	68.9	31.1	-	-	19	6	-	-	3.0	3.0	3.2	-	-
Anne Arundel	29,512	20,792	8,720	-	-	70.5	29.5	-	-	11	14	-	-	12.3	12.3	12.2	-	-
Baltimore	33,825	24,472	9,353	-	-	72.3	27.7	-	-	4	21	-	-	14.1	14.5	13.1	-	-
Calvert	3,554	2,392	1,162	-	-	67.3	32.7	-	-	22	3	-	-	1.5	1.4	1.6	-	-
Caroline	1,268	893	375	-	-	70.4	29.6	-	-	12	13	-	-	0.5	0.5	0.5	-	-
Carroll	10,750	7,554	3,196	-	-	70.3	29.7	-	-	14	11	-	-	4.5	4.5	4.5	-	-
Cecil	3,368	2,415	953	-	-	71.7	28.3	-	-	7	18	-	-	1.4	1.4	1.3	-	-
Charles	4,992	3,328	1,664	-	-	66.7	33.3	-	-	24	1	-	-	2.1	2.0	2.3	-	-
Dorchester	1,512	1,116	396	-	-	73.8	26.2	-	-	3	22	-	-	0.6	0.7	0.6	-	-
Frederick	11,912	8,414	3,498	-	-	70.6	29.4	-	-	9	16	-	-	5.0	5.0	4.9	-	-
Garrett	3,065	2,201	864	-	-	71.8	28.2	-	-	6	19	-	-	1.3	1.3	1.2	-	-
Harford	11,836	8,511	3,325	-	-	71.9	28.1	-	-	5	20	-	-	4.9	5.1	4.6	-	-
Howard	12,988	9,083	3,905	-	-	69.9	30.1	-	-	16	9	-	-	5.4	5.4	5.5	-	-
Kent	1,349	1,010	339	-	-	74.9	25.1	-	-	1	24	-	-	0.6	0.6	0.5	-	-
Montgomery	49,262	34,288	14,974	-	-	69.6	30.4	-	-	17	8	-	-	20.5	20.4	20.9	-	-
Prince George's	20,271	13,713	6,558	-	-	67.6	32.4	-	-	21	4	-	-	8.4	8.1	9.2	-	-
Queen Anne's	2,326	1,653	673	-	-	71.1	28.9	-	-	8	17	-	-	1.0	1.0	0.9	-	-
St. Mary's	2,951	2,009	942	-	-	68.1	31.9	-	-	20	5	-	-	1.2	1.2	1.3	-	-
Somerset	1,185	829	356	-	-	70.0	30.0	-	-	15	10	-	-	0.5	0.5	0.5	-	-
Talbot	2,838	2,108	730	-	-	74.3	25.7	-	-	2	23	-	-	1.2	1.3	1.0	-	-
Washington	8,149	5,751	2,398	-	-	70.6	29.4	-	-	10	15	-	-	3.4	3.4	3.3	-	-
Wicomico	4,948	3,479	1,469	-	-	70.3	29.7	-	-	13	12	-	-	2.1	2.1	2.1	-	-
Worcester	2,376	1,638	738	-	-	68.9	31.1	-	-	18	7	-	-	1.0	1.0	1.0	-	-
Baltimore City	8,503	5,708	2,795	-	-	67.1	32.9	-	-	23	2	-	-	3.5	3.4	3.9	-	-
MARYLAND	**240,021**	**168,374**	**71,647**	-	-	**70.1**	**29.9**	-	-					**100.0**	**100.0**	**100.0**		

1992 Vote for President
Percent for Clinton (D), by County

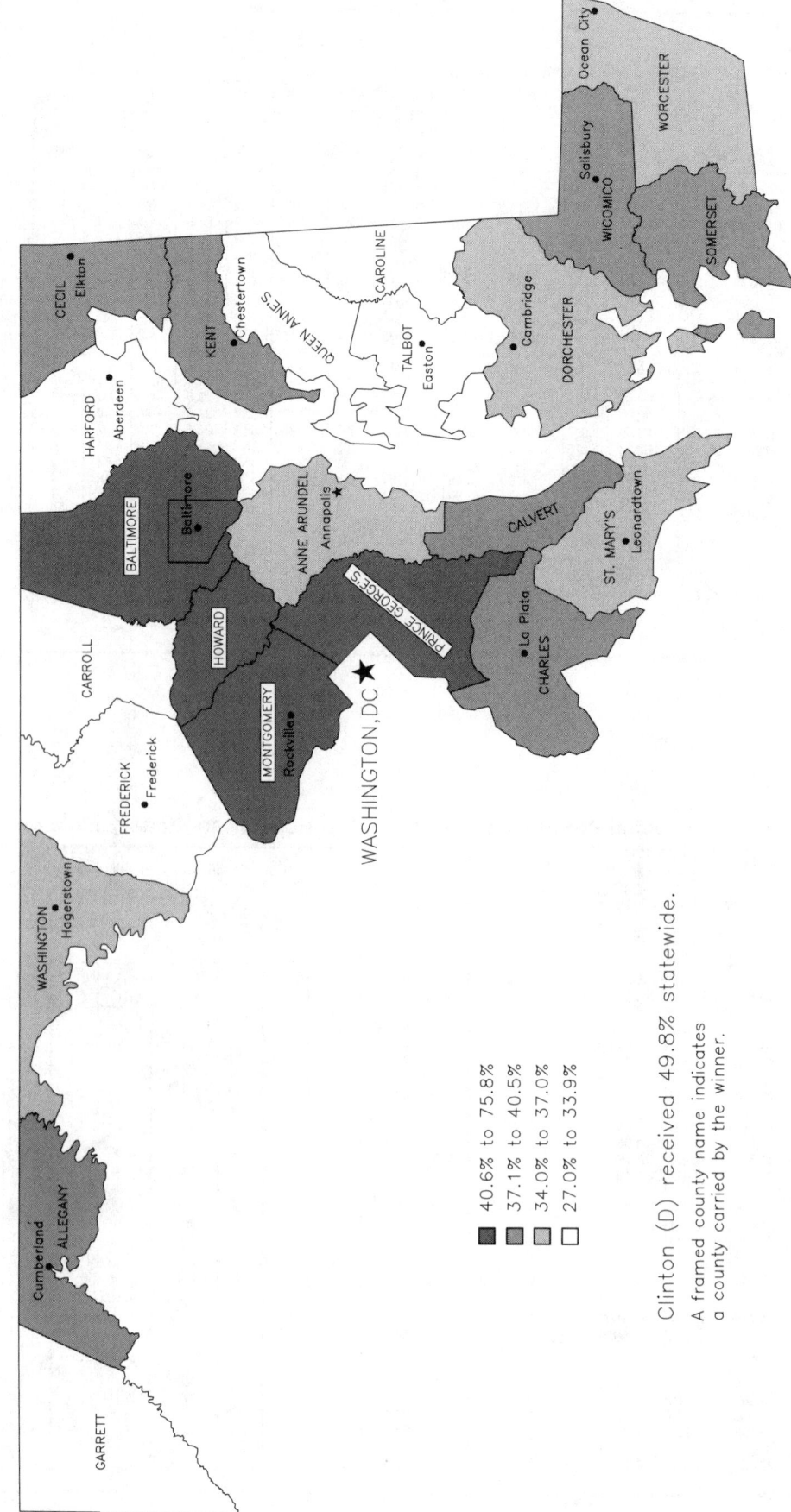

40.6% to 75.8%
37.1% to 40.5%
34.0% to 37.0%
27.0% to 33.9%

Clinton (D) received 49.8% statewide.

A framed county name indicates
a county carried by the winner.

GARRETT

ALLEGANY
Cumberland

WASHINGTON
Hagerstown

FREDERICK
Frederick

CARROLL

MONTGOMERY
Rockville

HOWARD

BALTIMORE
Baltimore

HARFORD
Aberdeen

CECIL
Elkton

KENT
Chestertown

QUEEN ANNE'S

CAROLINE

TALBOT
Easton

ANNE ARUNDEL
Annapolis

PRINCE GEORGE'S

WASHINGTON,DC

CHARLES
La Plata

CALVERT

ST. MARY'S
Leonardtown

DORCHESTER
Cambridge

WICOMICO
Salisbury

WORCESTER
Ocean City

SOMERSET

1992 Vote for U.S. Senator
Percent for Mikulski (D), by County

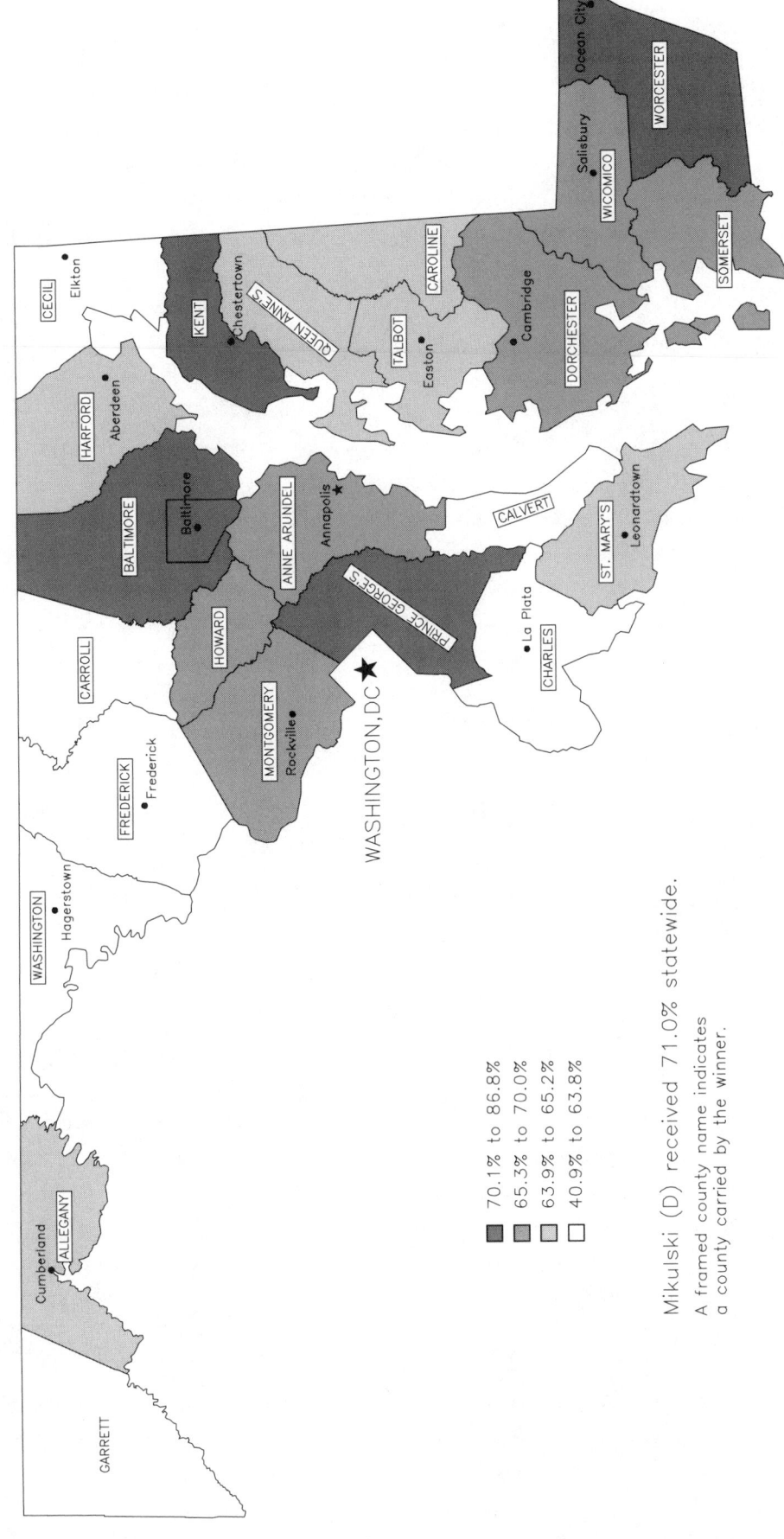

70.1% to 86.8%
65.3% to 70.0%
63.9% to 65.2%
40.9% to 63.8%

Mikulski (D) received 71.0% statewide.

A framed county name indicates
a county carried by the winner.

Copyright © 1993 by Election Data Services, Inc.

Maryland 431

MASSACHUSETTS

Congressional Districts 10
   Average Population 601,643
State Senate Districts 40
   Average Population 150,411
State House Districts 160
   Average Population 37,603

Electoral College Votes... 12
Counties[1] 14
Voting Precincts 2,138

Alternative Registration Methods:
....Deputized Registrars

Registration Deadline (Days before Election) 28

Voting Equipment Use (Cities and Towns)[2]

Datavote Punch Card	16	Paper Ballot	176
Electronic	19	Other Punch Card	57
Lever Machine	42	Mixed Systems	1
Optical Scanner	40		

Party Control	DEM	REP	IND	VAC
1993 State Senate	31	9	0	0
1992 State Senate	24	15	0	1
1993 State House	124	35	1	0
1992 State House	120	37	1	2

Population Statistics 1990

Race/ Ethnicity	Total Population		Voting Age Population		Voting Age Population % of total population
	Number	%	Number	%	
Non-Hispanic					
White	5,280,292	87.8	4,169,437	89.4	79.0
Black	274,464	4.6	190,895	4.1	69.6
Asian/Pacific Islander	140,338	2.3	100,122	2.1	71.3
Native American	10,545	0.2	7,653	0.2	72.6
Other	23,237	0.4	14,869	0.3	64.0
All Hispanic	287,549	4.8	180,374	3.9	62.7
TOTAL	6,016,425	100.0	4,663,350	100.0	77.5

Estimated Voting Age Population 1992 (VAP) 4,607,000
Number of Registered Voters..................................... 3,351,918
   % of estimated VAP.. 72.8
Voter Turnout (Actual) 2,822,962
   % of VAP 61.3
   % of Registration 84.2
Persons Not Voting—of Voting Age 1,784,038
   % of VAP 38.7
Persons Not Voting—of Registered 528,956
   % of Registration 15.8
Straight Ticket Voting .... No

State Officials and Members of Congress

Governor:
William Weld (R) 1990, elected to a four-year term in 1990.

U.S. Senators:
Edward M. Kennedy (D) 1962, elected to a six-year term in 1988.
John Kerry (D) 1984, elected to a six-year term in 1990.

U.S. Representative in Congress:
(District, Name, Party, Date first elected)

1. Olver (D) 1991
2. Neal (D) 1988
3. Blute (R) 1992

4. Frank (D) 1980
5. Meehan (D) 1992
6. Torkildsen (R) 1992

7. Markey (D) 1976
8. Kennedy (D) 1986

9. Moakley (D) 1972
10. Studds (D) 1972

---

[1]Elections administered by 351 cities and towns rather than counties. Data presented for counties and 213 cities and towns with more than one voting precinct. [2]Reports for all 351 cities and towns, including those with a single voting precinct.

Candidates: General Election, November 3, 1992

Candidate(s)	Total vote	Percent	Party	Status	First elected
President/Vice President					
Clinton/Gore	1,318,662	47.54%	Democrat	Challenger	1992
Bush/Quayle	805,049	29.02%	Republican	Incumbent	1988
Perot/Stockdale	630,731	22.74%	Independent	Challenger	
Marrou/Lord	9,024	0.33%	Libertarian	Challenger	
Fulani/Munoz	3,172	0.11%	New Alliance	Challenger	
Phillips/Knight	2,218	0.08%	Independent Voters	Challenger	
Others	1,990	0.07%	Unknown	Challenger	
Hagelin/Tompkins	1,812	0.07%	Natural Law	Challenger	
LaRouche/Bevel	1,027	0.04%	LaRouche for Pres.	Challenger	
Brisben/Garson	13	<.01%	Write in	Challenger	
Dodge/Ormsby	2	<.01%	Write in	Challenger	
U.S. Senator (No Contest)					
Governor (No Contest)					
U.S. Representative in Congress					
District 1					
John Olver	135,049	51.52%	Democrat	Incumbent	1991
Patrick Larkin	113,828	43.43%	Republican	Challenger	
Louis Godena	7,162	2.73%	Peace Jobs Justice	Challenger	
Dennis Kelly	4,355	1.66%	Pro-Democracy Reform	Challenger	
Jeffrey Rebello	1,598	0.61%	Freedom for LaRouche	Challenger	
Others	128	0.05%	Composited Others	Challenger	
District 2					
Richard Neal	131,215	53.09%	Democrat	Incumbent	1988
Anthony Ravosa, Jr.	76,795	31.07%	Republican	Challenger	
Thomas Sheehan	38,963	15.76%	For the People	Challenger	
Others[1]	190	0.08%	Composited Others	Challenger	
District 3					
Peter Blute	131,476	50.39%	Republican	Challenger	
Joseph Early	115,592	44.30%	Democrat	Incumbent	1992
Leonard Umina	9,692	3.71%	Independent Voters	Challenger	
Michael Moore	4,130	1.58%	Natural Law	Challenger	
Others	51	0.02%	Composited Others	Challenger	
District 4					
Barney Frank	182,633	67.69%	Democrat	Incumbent	1980
Edward McCormick III	70,666	26.19%	Republican	Challenger	
Luke Lumina	13,671	5.07%	Independent	Challenger	
Dennis Ingalls	2,797	1.04%	Freedom for LaRouche	Challenger	
Others	47	0.02%	Composited Others	Challenger	
District 5					
Martin Meehan	133,844	52.17%	Democrat	Challenger	1992
Paul Cronin	96,206	37.50%	Republican	Challenger	
Mary Farinelli	19,077	7.44%	Independent	Challenger	
David Coleman	7,214	2.81%	Independent	Challenger	
Others	223	0.09%	Composited Others	Challenger	
District 6					
Peter Torkildsen	159,165	54.83%	Republican	Challenger	1992
Nicholas Mavroules	130,248	44.86%	Democrat	Incumbent	1978
Others	899	0.31%	Composited Others	Challenger	
District 7					
Edward Markey	174,837	62.10%	Democrat	Incumbent	1976
Stephen Sohn	78,262	27.80%	Republican	Challenger	
Robert Antonelli	28,421	10.09%	Independent	Challenger	
Others	38	0.01%	Composited Others	Challenger	

[1]Total vote for other candidates corrected to 178 in published election results (The Elections Division, Office of Massachusetts Secretary of State, *Massachusetts Election Statistics 1992,* Public Document 43).

434 Massachusetts

Candidate(s)	Total vote	Percent	Party	Status	First elected
U.S. Representative in Congress (cont)					
District 8					
Joseph Kennedy II	149,907	83.05%	Democrat	Incumbent	1986
Alice Nakash	30,406	16.85%	Independent	Challenger	
Others	179	0.10%	Composited Others	Challenger	
District 9					
John Joseph Moakley	175,550	69.21%	Democrat	Incumbent	1972
Martin Conboy	54,291	21.41%	Republican	Challenger	
Lawrence Mackin	15,637	6.17%	Independent	Challenger	
Robert Horan	8,084	3.19%	Independent	Challenger	
Others	72	0.03%	Composited Others	Challenger	
District 10					
Gerry Studds	189,343	60.75%	Democrat	Incumbent	1972
Daniel Daly	75,887	24.35%	Republican	Challenger	
Jon Bryan	39,265	12.60%	Independent	Challenger	
Michael Umina	6,020	1.93%	Independent Voters	Challenger	
Robert Knapp	1,106	0.35%	Freedom for LaRouche	Challenger	
Others	30	<.01%	Composited Others	Challenger	

Candidates: March 10, 1992, Primary Election

Candidate	Total vote	Percent	Candidate	Total vote	Percent
Presidential Preference, Democratic			**Presidential Preference, Republican**		
Paul Tsongas	526,297	66.38%	George Bush	176,868	65.58%
Jerry Brown	115,746	14.60%	Patrick Buchanan	74,797	27.73%
Bill Clinton	86,817	10.95%	No Preference	10,132	3.76%
Ralph Nader	32,881	4.15%	David Duke	5,557	2.06%
No Preference[1]	12,198	1.54%	Others[1]	2,347	0.87%
Bob Kerrey	5,409	0.68%			
Tom Harkin	3,764	0.47%			
Eugene McCarthy	3,127	0.39%			
Others[1]	2,255	0.28%			
Larry Agran	2,224	0.28%			
Lyndon LaRouche, Jr.	2,167	0.27%			

[1]Total vote in Democratic primary for no preference corrected to 12,218 and vote for other candidates corrected to 3,465; and total vote in Republican primary for other candidates corrected to 2,348 in published election results (Elections Division, *Massachusetts Election Statistics 1992*, Public Document 43).

Voter Registration and Turnout, 1948-1992 Elections

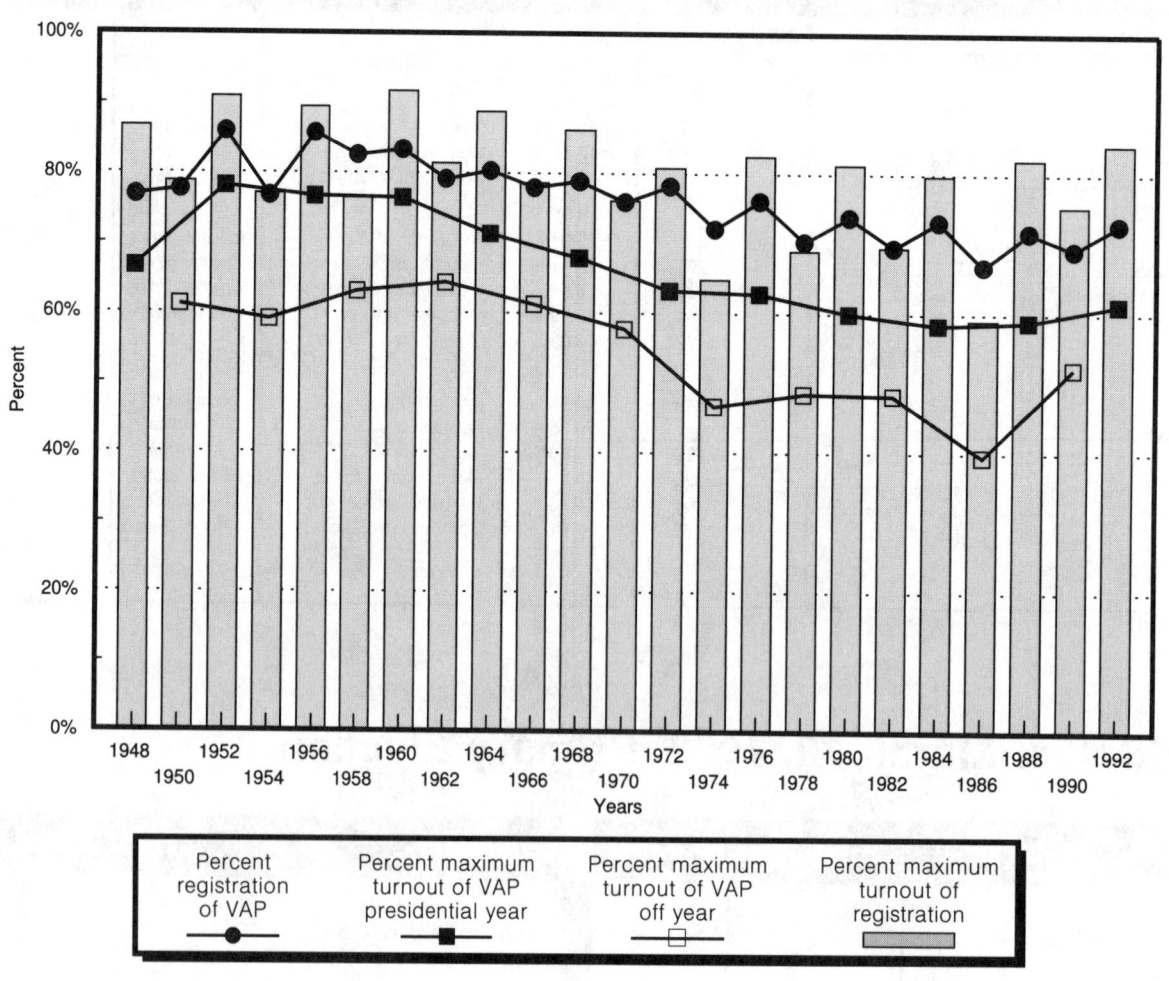

Percent registration of VAP	Percent maximum turnout of VAP presidential year	Percent maximum turnout of VAP off year	Percent maximum turnout of registration

Year	Estimated Voting Age Population (VAP)	Voter registration (REG)			Voter turnout										
						Highest office						Maximum vote			
		Total	Percent of VAP	Rank by percent of VAP	Actual	Total	Office	Percent total REG	Rank by percent of REG	Percent of VAP	Rank by percent of VAP	Total	Percent total REG	Rank by percent of REG	Percent total VAP	Rank by percent of VAP
1992	4,607,000	3,351,918	72.8	30	2,822,962	2,773,700	P	82.7	6	60.2	22	2,822,962	84.2	5	61.3	23
1990	4,646,000	3,213,763	69.2	22	2,424,579	2,341,990	G	72.9	4	50.4	9	2,424,579	75.4	3	52.2	6
1988	4,565,000	3,274,777	71.7	24	2,689,857	2,632,801	P	80.4	2	57.7	12	2,689,857	82.1	3	58.9	11
1986	4,502,000	3,005,729	66.8	31	1,777,276	1,684,079	G	56.0	25	37.4	30	1,777,276	59.1	21	39.5	26
1984	4,447,000	3,253,785	73.2	26	2,595,054	2,559,453	P	78.7	10	57.6	17	2,595,054	79.8	9	58.4	18
1982	4,354,000	3,026,868	69.5	24	2,103,780	2,050,769	S	67.8	12	47.1	15	2,103,780	69.5	13	48.3	14
1980	4,278,000	3,156,672	73.8	24	2,566,807	2,524,298	P	80.0	6	59.0	13	2,566,807	81.3	5	60.0	13
1978	4,213,000	2,962,904	70.3	23	2,044,076	1,985,700	S	67.0	6	47.1	9	2,044,076	69.0	6	48.5	7
1976	4,132,000	3,145,551	76.1	20	2,594,262	2,547,558	P	81.0	4	61.7	10	2,594,262	82.5	4	62.8	10
1974	4,060,000	2,927,990	72.1	22	1,896,421	1,854,798	G	63.3	15	45.7	16	1,896,421	64.8	15	46.7	17
1972	3,963,000	3,099,877	78.2	17	2,503,494	2,458,756	P	79.3	11	62.0	17	2,503,494	80.8	11	63.2	15
1970	3,538,000	2,684,636	75.9	17	2,043,087	1,935,607	S	72.1	11	54.7	12	2,043,087	76.1	9	57.7	11
1968	3,459,000	2,725,058	78.8	19	2,348,005	2,331,752	P	85.6	6	67.4	14	2,348,005	86.2	7	67.9	14
1966	3,391,000	2,641,538	77.9	19	2,076,826	2,041,177	G	77.3	5	60.2	5	2,076,826	78.6	5	61.2	6
1964	3,349,000	2,688,699	80.3	20	2,388,230	2,344,798	P	87.2	8	70.0	16	2,388,230	88.8	7	71.3	16
1962	3,333,000	2,635,085	79.1	17	2,144,051	2,109,089	G	80.0	4	63.3	4	2,144,051	81.4	4	64.3	3
1960	3,266,000	2,720,359	83.3	13	2,495,504	2,469,480	P	90.8	7	75.6	11	2,495,504	91.7	7	76.4	12
1958	3,099,000	2,556,300	82.5	8	1,952,855	1,899,117	G	74.3	11	61.3	8	1,952,855	76.4	9	63.0	6
1956	3,118,000	2,671,369	85.7	8	2,388,129	2,348,506	P	87.9	7	75.3	4	2,388,129	89.4	6	76.6	4
1954	3,289,000	2,523,414	76.7	14	1,942,071	1,903,774	G	75.4	6	57.9	12	1,942,071	77.0	5	59.0	13
1952	3,104,000	2,666,025	85.9	10	2,424,548	2,383,398	P	89.4	5	76.8	7	2,424,548	90.9	5	78.1	5
1950	3,188,000	2,475,396	77.6	9	1,947,071	1,910,180	G	77.2	6	59.9	7	1,947,071	78.7	5	61.1	7
1948	3,236,000	2,484,938	76.8	8	2,155,347	2,107,146	P	84.8	5	65.1	10	2,155,347	86.7	3	66.6	10

MASSACHUSETTS

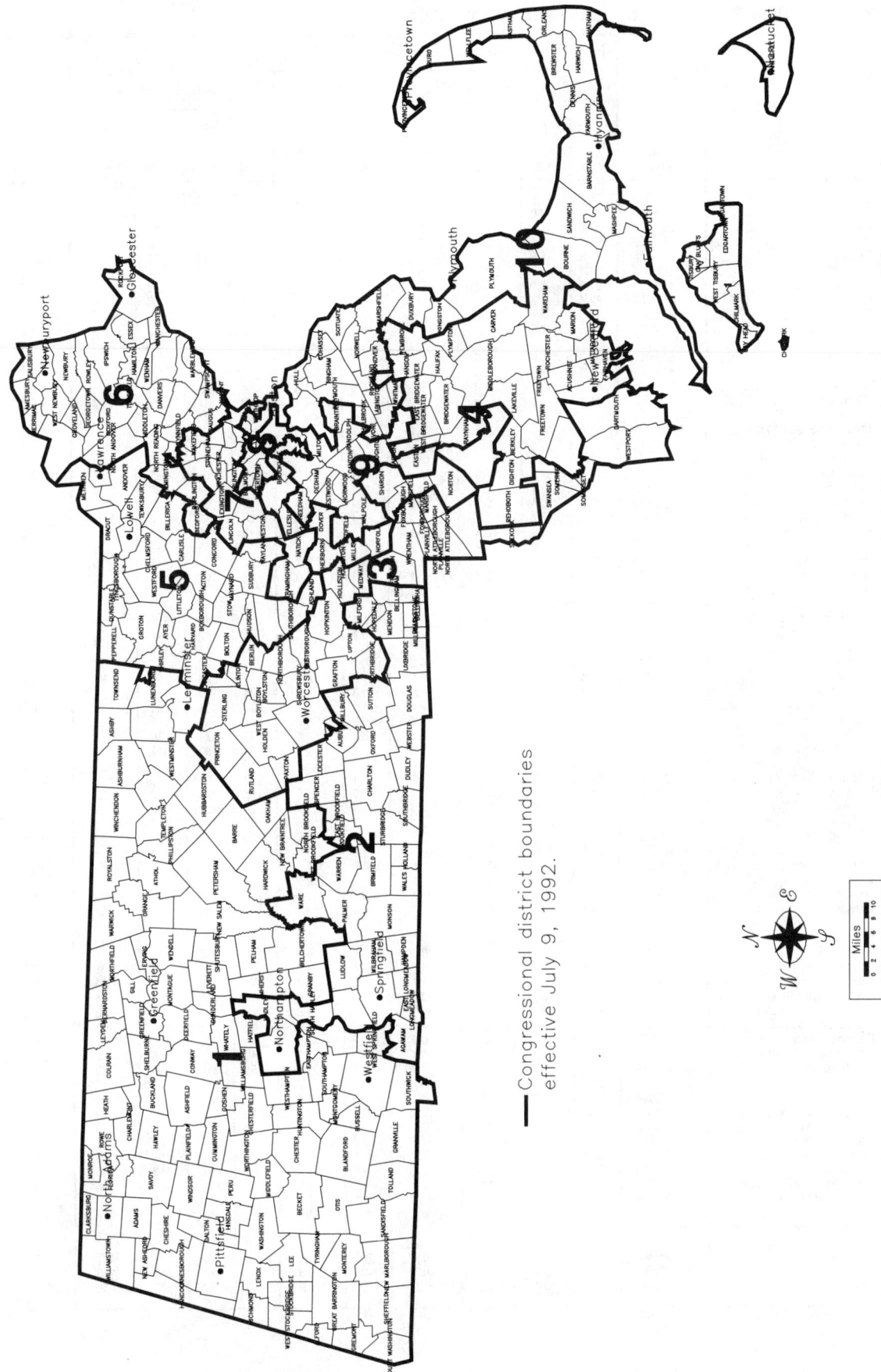

Congressional district boundaries effective July 9, 1992.

Miles
0 2 4 6 8 10

Table A. — 1990 Population by Race and Ethnic Origin

State/ county code	County	Total persons	White	Black	Asian and Pacific Islander	Native American	Other	Hispanic	Total	White	Black	Hispanic	Total	White	Black	Hispanic
					Percent of total persons — Non-Hispanic					**Rank¹** — Percent of total persons — Non-Hispanic				**Percent contribution to state population** — Non-Hispanic		
25 001	Barnstable	186,605	95.4	1.5	0.5	0.6	0.8	1.2	9	4	12	10	3.1	3.4	1.0	0.8
25 003	Berkshire	139,352	96.3	1.8	0.7	0.2	<.1	1.0	11	2	9	13	2.3	2.5	0.9	0.5
25 005	Bristol	506,325	93.6	1.4	0.9	0.2	1.2	2.7	6	6	13	6	8.4	9.0	2.6	4.7
25 007	Dukes	11,639	93.6	2.8	0.3	2.0	0.2	1.0	13	7	4	12	0.2	0.2	0.1	<.1
25 009	Essex	670,080	89.6	1.5	1.4	0.1	0.1	7.2	3	12	11	3	11.1	11.4	3.7	16.8
25 011	Franklin	70,092	97.1	0.7	0.7	0.3	<.1	1.2	12	1	14	11	1.2	1.3	0.2	0.3
25 013	Hampden	456,310	81.8	7.0	0.8	0.1	0.1	10.0	7	13	2	2	7.6	7.1	11.7	15.9
25 015	Hampshire	146,568	92.4	1.7	3.0	0.2	0.1	2.7	10	8	10	7	2.4	2.6	0.9	1.4
25 017	Middlesex	1,398,468	90.0	2.7	3.7	0.1	0.1	3.4	1	11	5	5	23.2	23.8	13.7	16.5
25 019	Nantucket	6,012	95.8	2.3	0.3	<.1	0.7	0.8	14	3	6	14	<.1	0.1	<.1	<.1
25 021	Norfolk	616,087	93.7	1.9	2.9	0.1	0.1	1.4	5	5	8	9	10.2	10.9	4.2	2.9
25 023	Plymouth	435,276	92.3	3.4	0.8	0.2	1.1	2.2	8	9	3	8	7.2	7.6	5.5	3.3
25 025	Suffolk	663,906	62.1	20.9	4.9	0.3	0.9	11.0	4	14	1	1	11.0	7.8	50.5	25.3
25 027	Worcester	709,705	91.6	1.9	1.6	0.2	<.1	4.6	2	10	7	4	11.8	12.3	4.9	11.5
25	**MASSACHUSETTS**	**6,016,425**	**87.8**	**4.6**	**2.3**	**0.2**	**0.4**	**4.8**					**100.0**	**100.0**	**100.0**	**100.0**
	CITIES AND TOWNS															
25 023	Abington town	13,817	98.5	0.3	0.3	0.2	<.1	0.7	124	23	181	169	0.2	0.3	<.1	<.1
25 017	Acton town	17,872	93.9	0.8	3.6	0.1	<.1	1.5	91	154	97	72	0.3	0.3	<.1	<.1
25 005	Acushnet town	9,554	98.2	0.4	0.2	0.2	0.4	0.5	162	32	176	199	0.2	0.2	<.1	<.1
25 003	Adams town	9,445	99.1	0.2	0.2	<.1	<.1	0.4	164	3	206	208	0.2	0.2	<.1	<.1
25 013	Agawam town	27,323	97.4	0.9	0.5	0.1	<.1	1.1	57	82	93	100	0.5	0.5	<.1	0.1
25 009	Amesbury town	14,997	98.0	0.6	0.4	0.2	0.1	0.6	113	43	138	179	0.2	0.3	<.1	<.1
25 015	Amherst town	35,228	82.6	4.4	7.8	0.2	0.2	4.7	40	203	12	25	0.6	0.6	0.6	0.6
25 009	Andover town	29,151	93.8	0.8	3.7	<.1	<.1	1.5	48	157	98	67	0.5	0.5	<.1	0.2
25 017	Arlington town	44,630	93.9	1.3	3.0	<.1	<.1	1.7	26	156	66	63	0.7	0.8	0.2	0.3
25 027	Ashburnham town	5,433	98.5	0.1	0.4	0.1	<.1	0.8	206	19	209	151	<.1	0.1	<.1	<.1
25 017	Ashland town	12,066	94.0	1.9	2.0	<.1	0.1	2.0	138	152	42	52	0.2	0.2	<.1	<.1
25 027	Athol town	11,451	97.6	0.4	0.6	0.5	<.1	0.9	146	71	165	130	0.2	0.2	<.1	<.1
25 005	Attleboro city	38,383	93.4	1.0	2.4	0.2	0.1	2.9	32	163	87	37	0.6	0.7	0.1	0.4
25 027	Auburn town	15,005	98.3	0.3	0.7	0.1	<.1	0.6	112	28	191	190	0.2	0.3	<.1	<.1
25 017	Ayer town	6,871	81.8	9.5	3.0	0.5	0.3	4.9	195	204	5	22	0.1	0.1	0.2	0.1
25 001	Barnstable town	40,949	93.3	2.6	0.7	0.7	1.0	1.7	30	164	31	61	0.7	0.7	0.4	0.2
25 027	Barre town	4,546	98.1	0.6	0.6	<.1	0.0	0.6	209	35	133	187	<.1	<.1	<.1	<.1
25 017	Bedford town	12,996	92.5	2.7	3.1	0.2	0.1	1.5	132	171	30	71	0.2	0.2	0.1	<.1
25 015	Belchertown town	10,579	97.4	0.5	1.0	<.1	0.1	0.9	151	80	147	128	0.2	0.2	<.1	<.1
25 021	Bellingham town	14,877	97.1	1.0	0.8	0.2	<.1	0.9	114	91	83	124	0.2	0.3	<.1	<.1
25 017	Belmont town	24,720	94.5	0.8	3.3	<.1	<.1	1.3	68	146	102	83	0.4	0.4	<.1	0.1
25 009	Beverly city	38,195	96.8	0.8	1.0	0.1	<.1	1.1	34	108	104	99	0.6	0.7	0.1	0.2
25 017	Billerica town	37,609	96.0	1.1	1.5	0.1	<.1	1.3	37	126	77	84	0.6	0.7	0.1	0.2
25 027	Blackstone town	8,023	97.8	0.3	0.8	0.1	<.1	0.8	180	52	184	142	0.1	0.1	<.1	<.1
25 025	Boston city	574,283	59.0	23.8	5.2	0.3	1.0	10.8	1	211	1	6	9.5	6.4	49.9	21.5
25 001	Bourne town	16,064	95.7	1.3	0.6	0.5	0.6	1.2	107	133	62	87	0.3	0.3	<.1	<.1
25 009	Boxford town	6,266	97.6	0.7	1.1	<.1	<.1	0.5	203	72	125	198	0.1	0.1	<.1	<.1
25 021	Braintree town	33,836	96.8	0.6	1.5	<.1	0.1	0.9	41	109	139	134	0.6	0.6	<.1	0.1
25 001	Brewster town	8,440	98.3	0.4	0.4	0.1	<.1	0.8	177	29	169	152	0.1	0.2	<.1	<.1
25 023	Bridgewater town	21,249	91.5	4.1	0.8	0.2	0.2	3.2	78	179	13	33	0.4	0.4	0.3	0.2
25 023	Brockton city	92,788	77.5	11.7	1.7	0.3	2.6	6.3	7	206	4	17	1.5	1.4	3.9	2.0
25 021	Brookline town	54,718	85.4	3.0	8.3	0.1	0.2	2.9	18	195	24	38	0.9	0.9	0.6	0.6
25 017	Burlington town	23,302	93.1	1.1	4.5	<.1	<.1	1.2	72	167	75	94	0.4	0.4	<.1	0.1
25 017	Cambridge city	95,802	71.6	12.7	8.3	0.2	0.4	6.8	6	208	3	14	1.6	1.3	4.4	2.3
25 021	Canton town	18,530	96.6	1.2	1.2	<.1	0.1	0.8	89	113	73	143	0.3	0.3	<.1	<.1
25 023	Carver town	10,590	95.8	1.9	0.4	0.2	1.0	0.7	150	131	41	166	0.2	0.2	<.1	<.1
25 001	Chatham town	6,579	98.6	0.4	0.2	0.2	<.1	0.6	200	13	167	193	0.1	0.1	<.1	<.1
25 017	Chelmsford town	32,383	95.4	0.5	3.0	<.1	<.1	1.0	43	135	156	112	0.5	0.6	<.1	0.1
25 025	Chelsea city	28,710	59.0	4.0	4.8	0.2	0.7	31.4	51	212	16	2	0.5	0.3	0.4	3.1
25 013	Chicopee city	56,632	93.9	1.7	0.6	0.1	<.1	3.6	17	155	46	32	0.9	1.0	0.4	0.7
25 003	Clarksburg town	1,745	99.4	0.3	0.0	0.0	0.0	0.2	212	1	180	212	<.1	<.1	<.1	<.1
25 027	Clinton town	13,222	89.7	1.5	0.9	<.1	<.1	7.8	129	187	59	13	0.2	0.2	<.1	0.4
25 021	Cohasset town	7,075	98.6	0.3	0.4	<.1	0.0	0.6	192	12	190	188	0.1	0.1	<.1	<.1
25 017	Concord town	17,076	92.5	2.3	2.0	0.1	<.1	3.0	97	172	34	35	0.3	0.3	0.1	0.2
25 003	Dalton town	7,155	98.5	0.4	0.5	<.1	0.0	0.6	191	18	163	195	0.1	0.1	<.1	<.1
25 009	Danvers town	24,174	97.5	0.5	1.0	<.1	<.1	1.1	69	78	159	105	0.4	0.4	<.1	<.1
25 005	Dartmouth town	27,244	96.3	0.7	0.8	<.1	1.1	1.0	59	119	122	107	0.5	0.5	<.1	<.1
25 021	Dedham town	23,782	97.0	0.8	1.1	0.1	<.1	1.0	71	96	107	108	0.4	0.4	<.1	<.1
25 011	Deerfield town	5,018	98.3	0.2	0.7	<.1	<.1	0.8	208	30	195	157	<.1	<.1	<.1	<.1
25 001	Dennis town	13,864	96.9	1.0	0.3	0.4	0.5	0.9	122	102	84	137	0.2	0.3	<.1	<.1
25 017	Dracut town	25,594	97.2	0.5	1.2	0.1	<.1	0.9	63	87	142	123	0.4	0.5	<.1	<.1
25 027	Dudley town	9,540	97.0	0.4	0.9	<.1	<.1	1.6	163	101	172	65	0.2	0.2	<.1	<.1

¹Separate rankings for 14 counties and 213 cities and towns.

438 Massachusetts

Table A. — 1990 Population by Race and Ethnic Origin (cont)

State/ county code	County	Total persons	Percent of total persons — Non-Hispanic White	Black	Asian and Pacific Islander	Native American	Other	Hispanic	Rank Total	Rank % Non-Hispanic White	Black	Hispanic	Pct contrib Total	Non-Hispanic White	Black	Hispanic
25 023	Duxbury town	13,895	97.7	0.9	0.5	<.1	0.2	0.7	121	61	94	170	0.2	0.3	<.1	<.1
25 023	East Bridgewater town	11,104	97.7	0.7	0.3	0.2	0.2	0.9	148	67	110	125	0.2	0.2	<.1	<.1
25 013	East Longmeadow town	13,367	98.5	0.5	0.4	<.1	<.1	0.5	127	17	145	204	0.2	0.2	<.1	<.1
25 015	Easthampton town	15,537	97.1	0.3	0.7	<.1	<.1	1.8	108	93	182	58	0.3	0.3	<.1	<.1
25 005	Easton town	19,807	96.5	1.7	1.0	<.1	0.2	0.6	85	116	47	183	0.3	0.4	0.1	<.1
25 011	Erving town	1,372	98.5	0.5	0.4	0.4	0.0	0.2	213	20	148	213	<.1	<.1	<.1	<.1
25 017	Everett city	35,701	91.2	2.9	1.7	0.2	0.1	3.8	39	181	27	30	0.6	0.6	0.4	0.5
25 005	Fairhaven town	16,132	97.0	0.5	0.5	0.1	1.0	0.8	105	94	149	139	0.3	0.3	<.1	<.1
25 005	Fall River city	92,703	95.8	1.0	1.3	<.1	0.2	1.7	8	130	85	62	1.5	1.7	0.3	0.5
25 001	Falmouth town	27,960	93.7	1.7	0.7	0.6	1.9	1.5	54	160	49	70	0.5	0.5	0.2	0.1
25 027	Fitchburg city	41,194	84.7	2.9	2.5	0.2	<.1	9.6	29	198	26	8	0.7	0.7	0.4	1.4
25 021	Foxborough town	14,637	97.6	0.5	1.0	0.1	<.1	0.7	115	68	151	164	0.2	0.3	<.1	<.1
25 017	Framingham town	64,989	85.2	3.3	2.9	0.1	0.3	8.1	14	197	21	12	1.1	1.0	0.8	1.8
25 021	Franklin town	22,095	97.5	0.7	1.0	0.1	<.1	0.6	76	74	126	177	0.4	0.4	<.1	<.1
25 005	Freetown town	8,522	97.1	0.5	0.4	0.2	1.1	0.8	175	90	157	154	0.1	0.2	<.1	<.1
25 027	Gardner city	20,125	94.3	2.0	0.8	0.1	<.1	2.8	82	150	40	41	0.3	0.4	0.1	0.2
25 009	Gloucester city	28,716	98.5	0.2	0.3	<.1	<.1	0.9	50	24	198	121	0.5	0.5	<.1	<.1
25 027	Grafton town	13,035	96.1	1.3	1.2	0.1	<.1	1.3	131	124	69	79	0.2	0.2	<.1	<.1
25 003	Great Barrington town	7,725	94.7	2.6	0.8	0.1	<.1	1.7	183	143	33	59	0.1	0.1	<.1	<.1
25 011	Greenfield town	18,666	96.8	0.8	0.9	0.2	<.1	1.2	88	103	99	97	0.3	0.3	<.1	<.1
25 017	Groton town	7,511	97.6	0.6	0.8	0.1	<.1	0.8	187	70	129	141	0.1	0.1	<.1	<.1
25 009	Groveland town	5,214	98.9	0.1	0.3	0.2	<.1	0.5	207	5	211	200	<.1	<.1	<.1	<.1
25 009	Hamilton town	7,280	96.8	0.5	1.3	0.1	0.0	1.2	190	105	155	93	0.1	0.1	<.1	<.1
25 023	Hanover town	11,912	97.8	0.6	0.8	<.1	<.1	0.6	142	56	130	178	0.2	0.2	<.1	<.1
25 023	Hanson town	9,028	97.0	1.4	0.5	<.1	0.5	0.6	170	100	61	192	0.2	0.2	<.1	<.1
25 027	Hardwick town	2,385	98.7	0.3	<.1	0.3	<.1	0.7	211	7	194	171	<.1	<.1	<.1	<.1
25 009	Haverhill city	51,418	92.2	1.5	0.8	0.2	<.1	5.3	21	175	57	20	0.9	0.9	0.3	0.9
25 023	Hingham town	19,821	97.8	0.4	0.8	0.1	<.1	0.8	84	58	168	140	0.3	0.4	<.1	<.1
25 021	Holbrook town	11,041	94.4	2.9	0.9	0.2	0.2	1.4	149	147	28	73	0.2	0.2	0.1	<.1
25 027	Holden town	14,628	98.0	0.2	1.0	0.1	<.1	0.7	116	46	199	173	0.2	0.3	<.1	<.1
25 017	Holliston town	12,926	96.8	0.9	1.0	<.1	<.1	1.2	133	106	88	98	0.2	0.2	<.1	<.1
25 013	Holyoke city	43,704	65.3	2.6	0.7	0.2	0.2	31.1	27	209	32	3	0.7	0.5	0.4	4.7
25 017	Hopkinton town	9,191	97.1	0.3	1.1	<.1	<.1	1.3	167	89	186	81	0.2	0.2	<.1	<.1
25 017	Hudson town	17,233	95.0	0.8	1.2	0.1	0.1	2.7	96	139	95	42	0.3	0.3	<.1	0.2
25 023	Hull town	10,466	97.2	0.8	0.6	0.2	<.1	1.1	153	85	96	104	0.2	0.2	<.1	<.1
25 009	Ipswich town	11,873	98.5	0.3	0.4	<.1	<.1	0.6	144	22	183	175	0.2	0.2	<.1	<.1
25 023	Kingston town	9,045	98.1	0.8	0.2	0.1	0.4	0.4	169	36	108	207	0.2	0.2	<.1	<.1
25 009	Lawrence city	70,207	54.7	1.7	1.5	0.1	0.3	41.6	13	213	45	1	1.2	0.7	0.4	10.2
25 027	Leicester town	10,191	97.2	0.8	0.6	0.1	<.1	1.2	157	88	105	86	0.2	0.2	<.1	<.1
25 027	Leominster city	38,145	87.8	2.0	1.6	0.1	0.1	8.3	35	194	36	11	0.6	0.6	0.3	1.1
25 017	Lexington town	28,974	91.1	1.1	6.5	<.1	<.1	1.2	49	182	76	89	0.5	0.5	0.1	0.1
25 017	Lincoln town	7,666	88.9	5.0	3.7	<.1	0.2	2.1	185	189	9	48	0.1	0.1	0.1	<.1
25 017	Littleton town	7,051	97.7	0.7	0.8	<.1	<.1	0.6	193	66	113	186	0.1	0.1	<.1	<.1
25 013	Longmeadow town	15,467	95.9	0.8	2.5	<.1	<.1	0.7	111	127	106	165	0.3	0.3	<.1	<.1
25 017	Lowell city	103,439	76.5	2.0	10.9	0.1	0.3	10.1	4	207	37	7	1.7	1.5	0.8	3.7
25 013	Ludlow town	18,820	97.1	0.2	0.6	<.1	<.1	2.0	87	92	203	49	0.3	0.3	<.1	0.1
25 027	Lunenburg town	9,117	97.6	0.7	0.7	<.1	0.0	1.0	168	69	127	117	0.2	0.2	<.1	<.1
25 009	Lynn city	81,245	80.2	6.7	3.5	0.2	0.2	9.1	11	205	7	10	1.4	1.2	2.0	2.6
25 009	Lynnfield town	11,274	97.6	<.1	1.6	<.1	<.1	0.6	147	73	212	176	0.2	0.2	<.1	<.1
25 017	Malden city	53,884	87.9	4.0	5.2	0.1	0.1	2.6	20	192	14	43	0.9	0.9	0.8	0.5
25 005	Mansfield town	16,568	96.1	1.6	0.9	0.1	<.1	1.2	101	123	51	95	0.3	0.3	<.1	<.1
25 009	Marblehead town	19,971	97.8	0.4	0.9	<.1	<.1	0.8	83	55	173	147	0.3	0.4	<.1	<.1
25 017	Marlborough city	31,813	91.6	1.7	1.9	0.2	0.5	4.2	44	178	50	26	0.5	0.6	0.2	0.5
25 023	Marshfield town	21,531	97.8	0.7	0.5	0.1	0.2	0.7	77	60	120	172	0.4	0.4	<.1	<.1
25 001	Mashpee town	7,884	88.2	3.9	0.4	4.8	1.2	1.5	181	191	18	69	0.1	0.1	0.1	<.1
25 017	Maynard town	10,325	94.9	0.8	1.8	0.1	0.1	2.3	155	141	109	44	0.2	0.2	<.1	<.1
25 021	Medfield town	10,531	97.8	0.7	0.9	<.1	<.1	0.6	152	54	124	194	0.2	0.2	<.1	<.1
25 017	Medford city	57,407	92.2	3.9	2.0	0.1	<.1	1.7	16	176	17	60	1.0	1.0	0.8	0.3
25 021	Medway town	9,931	97.5	0.7	1.0	<.1	<.1	0.7	159	77	121	159	0.2	0.2	<.1	<.1
25 017	Melrose city	28,150	97.4	0.5	1.1	<.1	<.1	0.8	53	79	141	146	0.5	0.5	<.1	<.1
25 009	Methuen town	39,990	92.7	0.7	1.3	0.1	<.1	5.2	31	170	117	21	0.7	0.7	0.1	0.7
25 023	Middleborough town	17,867	96.5	1.4	0.3	0.4	0.5	1.0	92	117	60	120	0.3	0.3	<.1	<.1
25 027	Milford town	25,355	93.5	1.2	1.0	0.1	0.2	4.0	65	162	72	29	0.4	0.4	0.1	0.4
25 027	Millbury town	12,228	98.1	0.3	1.0	<.1	<.1	0.6	137	40	192	189	0.2	0.2	<.1	<.1
25 021	Millis town	7,613	98.0	0.4	0.7	<.1	<.1	0.8	186	48	164	149	0.1	0.1	<.1	<.1
25 021	Milton town	25,725	93.1	4.6	1.2	<.1	<.1	1.0	62	166	11	109	0.4	0.5	0.4	<.1
25 013	Monson town	7,776	98.4	0.5	0.2	0.1	0.1	0.7	182	25	146	174	0.1	0.1	<.1	<.1
25 011	Montague town	8,316	97.0	0.5	0.5	0.5	<.1	1.3	178	99	144	80	0.1	0.2	<.1	<.1
25 017	Natick town	30,510	93.7	2.0	2.3	<.1	<.1	1.8	45	159	39	57	0.5	0.5	0.2	0.2
25 021	Needham town	27,557	96.2	0.6	2.2	<.1	<.1	1.0	55	122	134	119	0.5	0.5	<.1	<.1

[1]Separate rankings for 14 counties and 213 cities and towns.

State/county code	County	Total persons	Percent of total persons Non-Hispanic White	Black	Asian and Pacific Islander	Native American	Other	Hispanic	Rank¹ Percent of total persons Total	Non-Hispanic White	Black	Hispanic	Percent contribution to state population Total	Non-Hispanic White	Black	Hispanic
25 005	New Bedford city	99,922	84.4	3.5	0.4	0.4	4.7	6.7	5	201	20	16	1.7	1.6	1.3	2.3
25 009	Newbury town	5,623	98.7	0.2	0.2	<.1	<.1	0.8	205	8	204	153	<.1	0.1	<.1	<.1
25 009	Newburyport city	16,317	98.6	0.5	0.3	<.1	<.1	0.6	103	14	160	196	0.3	0.3	<.1	<.1
25 017	Newton city	82,585	91.3	2.0	4.5	<.1	<.1	2.0	10	180	38	50	1.4	1.4	0.6	0.6
25 021	Norfolk town	9,270	89.3	4.7	0.9	0.3	<.1	4.8	166	188	10	23	0.2	0.2	0.2	0.2
25 003	North Adams city	16,797	96.7	1.3	0.5	0.3	<.1	1.2	98	110	67	96	0.3	0.3	<.1	<.1
25 009	North Andover town	22,792	95.9	0.7	2.0	<.1	<.1	1.3	73	128	118	77	0.4	0.4	<.1	0.1
25 005	North Attleborough town	25,038	97.4	0.5	1.2	<.1	<.1	0.8	66	81	143	145	0.4	0.5	<.1	<.1
25 017	North Reading town	12,002	98.1	0.3	0.8	<.1	0.0	0.7	140	34	187	163	0.2	0.2	<.1	<.1
25 015	Northampton city	29,289	91.1	1.7	2.8	0.2	<.1	4.1	47	183	48	27	0.5	0.5	0.2	0.4
25 027	Northborough town	11,929	94.3	0.6	3.9	0.1	<.1	1.1	141	151	135	103	0.2	0.2	<.1	<.1
25 027	Northbridge town	13,371	98.3	0.4	0.3	0.1	0.0	0.8	126	26	171	144	0.2	0.2	<.1	<.1
25 005	Norton town	14,265	96.3	1.3	0.9	0.2	<.1	1.2	119	120	63	91	0.2	0.3	<.1	<.1
25 023	Norwell town	9,279	98.3	0.3	0.9	<.1	<.1	0.3	165	27	185	209	0.2	0.2	<.1	<.1
25 021	Norwood town	28,700	95.7	1.5	1.5	0.1	<.1	1.1	52	132	55	101	0.5	0.5	0.2	0.1
25 011	Orange town	7,312	97.7	0.5	0.4	0.1	<.1	1.2	189	62	158	92	0.1	0.1	<.1	<.1
25 001	Orleans town	5,838	98.9	0.2	0.5	<.1	0.0	0.3	204	4	205	211	<.1	0.1	<.1	<.1
25 027	Oxford town	12,588	97.7	0.6	0.7	0.1	<.1	0.9	135	63	140	131	0.2	0.2	<.1	<.1
25 013	Palmer town	12,054	98.1	0.7	0.4	0.2	<.1	0.6	139	41	111	185	0.2	0.2	<.1	<.1
25 009	Peabody city	47,039	95.1	0.9	1.1	<.1	<.1	2.9	24	137	92	39	0.8	0.8	0.1	0.5
25 023	Pembroke town	14,544	98.6	0.5	0.4	<.1	<.1	0.4	117	15	150	205	0.2	0.3	<.1	<.1
25 017	Pepperell town	10,098	97.5	0.7	0.7	<.1	<.1	1.0	158	76	112	114	0.2	0.2	<.1	<.1
25 003	Pittsfield city	48,622	94.8	3.0	0.7	0.2	0.2	1.1	23	142	23	102	0.8	0.9	0.5	0.2
25 021	Plainville town	6,871	97.7	0.6	0.7	<.1	<.1	0.9	196	64	137	132	0.1	0.1	<.1	<.1
25 023	Plymouth town	45,608	95.9	1.7	0.6	0.2	0.4	1.2	25	129	44	90	0.8	0.8	0.3	0.2
25 021	Quincy city	84,985	90.8	1.1	6.5	0.2	<.1	1.4	9	185	79	74	1.4	1.5	0.3	0.4
25 021	Randolph town	30,093	84.4	7.8	5.5	0.2	0.3	1.8	46	199	6	55	0.5	0.5	0.9	0.2
25 005	Raynham town	9,867	97.3	0.8	0.8	0.1	0.2	0.9	160	84	103	133	0.2	0.2	<.1	<.1
25 017	Reading town	22,539	97.9	0.2	1.0	0.1	<.1	0.7	74	49	196	168	0.4	0.4	<.1	<.1
25 005	Rehoboth town	8,656	98.2	0.5	0.5	<.1	0.2	0.6	173	33	161	182	0.1	0.2	<.1	<.1
25 025	Revere city	42,786	91.0	1.3	3.5	0.2	0.2	3.8	28	184	68	31	0.7	0.7	0.2	0.6
25 023	Rockland town	16,123	96.5	1.5	0.7	0.1	<.1	1.0	106	114	53	115	0.3	0.3	<.1	<.1
25 009	Rockport town	7,482	98.8	0.2	0.4	0.1	<.1	0.5	188	6	197	202	0.1	0.1	<.1	<.1
25 009	Salem city	38,091	90.2	1.5	1.3	0.2	0.2	6.7	36	186	56	15	0.6	0.7	0.2	0.9
25 009	Salisbury town	6,882	98.6	0.1	0.2	0.3	<.1	0.7	194	9	210	160	0.1	0.1	<.1	<.1
25 001	Sandwich town	15,489	97.8	0.4	0.5	0.3	0.2	0.8	110	59	178	138	0.3	0.3	<.1	<.1
25 009	Saugus town	25,549	97.8	0.5	0.7	<.1	<.1	0.9	64	57	154	126	0.4	0.5	<.1	<.1
25 023	Scituate town	16,786	97.0	0.4	0.4	<.1	1.3	0.8	99	98	177	158	0.3	0.3	<.1	<.1
25 005	Seekonk town	13,046	97.0	0.7	1.2	0.2	0.3	0.6	130	95	123	197	0.2	0.2	<.1	<.1
25 021	Sharon town	15,517	93.8	3.0	2.2	<.1	<.1	0.9	109	158	22	129	0.3	0.3	0.2	<.1
25 027	Shrewsbury town	24,146	93.7	1.0	3.7	<.1	0.1	1.4	70	161	80	76	0.4	0.4	<.1	0.1
25 005	Somerset town	17,655	98.3	0.1	0.7	<.1	<.1	0.8	94	31	208	150	0.3	0.3	<.1	<.1
25 017	Somerville city	76,210	84.4	5.2	3.7	0.1	0.3	6.3	12	200	8	18	1.3	1.2	1.5	1.7
25 015	South Hadley town	16,685	95.2	1.0	2.3	<.1	<.1	1.3	100	136	82	85	0.3	0.3	<.1	<.1
25 027	Southborough town	6,628	96.5	0.6	2.1	<.1	<.1	0.7	198	115	136	162	0.1	0.1	<.1	<.1
25 027	Southbridge town	17,816	85.2	0.3	1.5	0.1	<.1	12.8	93	196	189	5	0.3	0.3	<.1	0.8
25 013	Southwick town	7,667	98.0	0.5	0.2	0.2	<.1	1.0	184	42	152	118	0.1	0.1	<.1	<.1
25 027	Spencer town	11,645	98.5	0.2	0.2	0.2	<.1	0.9	145	21	202	135	0.2	0.2	<.1	<.1
25 013	Springfield city	156,983	63.6	18.1	1.0	0.2	0.2	16.9	3	210	2	4	2.6	1.9	10.4	9.2
25 017	Stoneham town	22,203	96.4	0.6	1.5	<.1	<.1	1.3	75	118	131	78	0.4	0.4	<.1	0.1
25 021	Stoughton town	26,777	92.9	3.8	1.1	0.1	0.3	1.8	60	169	19	56	0.4	0.5	0.4	0.2
25 017	Sudbury town	14,358	94.7	1.3	2.9	0.1	<.1	0.9	118	144	65	122	0.2	0.3	<.1	<.1
25 027	Sutton town	6,824	99.2	<.1	0.3	0.1	<.1	0.3	197	2	213	210	0.1	0.1	<.1	<.1
25 009	Swampscott town	13,650	97.9	0.4	0.6	<.1	<.1	1.0	125	51	170	111	0.2	0.3	<.1	<.1
25 005	Taunton city	49,832	91.9	1.7	0.4	0.1	1.1	4.7	22	177	43	24	0.8	0.9	0.3	0.8
25 027	Templeton town	6,438	98.6	0.4	0.2	<.1	0.0	0.8	201	11	175	155	0.1	0.1	<.1	<.1
25 017	Tewksbury town	27,266	96.8	0.8	1.3	0.2	<.1	0.9	58	107	101	127	0.5	0.5	<.1	<.1
25 017	Townsend town	8,496	98.1	0.9	0.2	<.1	<.1	0.7	176	37	91	161	0.1	0.2	<.1	<.1
25 017	Tyngsborough town	8,642	98.0	0.5	0.9	<.1	0.0	0.6	174	47	162	184	0.1	0.2	<.1	<.1
25 027	Uxbridge town	10,415	98.6	0.3	0.3	<.1	<.1	0.6	154	10	179	191	0.2	0.2	<.1	<.1
25 017	Wakefield town	24,825	98.0	0.4	0.8	<.1	<.1	0.8	67	45	174	156	0.4	0.5	<.1	<.1
25 021	Walpole town	20,212	96.2	1.5	0.6	0.1	<.1	1.5	81	121	58	66	0.3	0.4	0.1	0.1
25 017	Waltham city	57,878	87.9	2.8	3.5	0.1	0.1	5.6	15	193	29	19	1.0	1.0	0.6	1.1
25 015	Ware town	9,808	97.4	0.3	0.5	0.3	<.1	1.5	161	83	193	68	0.2	0.2	<.1	<.1
25 023	Wareham town	19,232	88.9	2.2	0.5	0.5	4.9	3.0	86	190	35	34	0.3	0.3	0.2	0.2
25 027	Warren town	4,437	97.8	0.5	0.2	0.3	<.1	1.0	210	53	153	110	<.1	<.1	<.1	<.1
25 017	Watertown town	33,284	94.4	1.2	2.2	0.1	<.1	2.0	42	149	70	53	0.6	0.6	0.2	0.2
25 017	Wayland town	11,874	94.4	1.0	3.3	<.1	0.0	1.2	143	148	81	88	0.2	0.2	<.1	<.1
25 027	Webster town	16,196	96.0	0.7	0.6	0.4	<.1	2.2	104	125	116	46	0.3	0.3	<.1	0.1
25 021	Wellesley town	26,615	92.3	1.5	3.9	<.1	<.1	2.2	61	174	54	47	0.4	0.5	0.1	0.2

¹Separate rankings for 14 counties and 213 cities and towns.

Table A. — 1990 Population by Race and Ethnic Origin (cont)

State/county code	County	Total persons	Percent of total persons						Rank[1]				Percent contribution to state population			
			Non-Hispanic					Hispanic	Percent of total persons				Non-Hispanic			Hispanic
			White	Black	Asian and Pacific Islander	Native American	Other		Total	Non-Hispanic		Hispanic	Total	White	Black	
										White	Black					
25 027	West Boylston town	6,611	95.1	1.3	0.7	<.1	0.1	2.8	199	138	64	40	0.1	0.1	<.1	<.1
25 023	West Bridgewater town ..	6,389	97.7	0.6	0.7	<.1	0.4	0.5	202	65	128	201	0.1	0.1	<.1	<.1
25 013	West Springfield town	27,537	94.5	1.2	1.1	0.2	<.1	3.0	56	145	71	36	0.5	0.5	0.1	0.3
25 027	Westborough town	14,133	93.3	1.6	3.0	<.1	0.1	2.0	120	165	52	51	0.2	0.2	<.1	<.1
25 013	Westfield city	38,372	93.9	0.8	0.7	<.1	0.3	4.1	33	153	100	28	0.6	0.7	0.1	0.5
25 017	Westford town................	16,392	97.0	0.2	1.6	0.1	<.1	1.0	102	97	200	113	0.3	0.3	<.1	<.1
25 017	Weston town	10,200	93.0	0.7	4.7	0.0	<.1	1.6	156	168	114	64	0.2	0.2	<.1	<.1
25 005	Westport town................	13,852	98.5	0.1	0.5	<.1	0.2	0.6	123	16	207	181	0.2	0.3	<.1	<.1
25 021	Westwood town	12,557	97.5	0.3	1.5	<.1	<.1	0.6	136	75	188	180	0.2	0.2	<.1	<.1
25 021	Weymouth town	54,063	96.8	1.0	0.9	0.1	0.1	1.0	19	104	86	106	0.9	1.0	0.2	0.2
25 023	Whitman town................	13,240	98.1	0.6	0.2	0.2	0.2	0.7	128	38	132	167	0.2	0.2	<.1	<.1
25 013	Wilbraham town	12,635	96.6	1.2	1.3	<.1	<.1	0.8	134	112	74	148	0.2	0.2	<.1	<.1
25 003	Williamstown town	8,220	92.4	3.0	2.6	0.2	<.1	1.8	179	173	25	54	0.1	0.1	<.1	<.1
25 017	Wilmington town	17,651	98.0	0.4	1.0	<.1	<.1	0.5	95	44	166	203	0.3	0.3	<.1	<.1
25 027	Winchendon town	8,805	97.9	0.2	0.7	0.2	<.1	1.0	172	50	201	116	0.1	0.2	<.1	<.1
25 017	Winchester town	20,267	95.4	0.9	2.6	<.1	<.1	0.9	80	134	90	136	0.3	0.4	<.1	<.1
25 025	Winthrop town	18,127	97.2	0.7	0.7	<.1	<.1	1.3	90	86	115	82	0.3	0.3	<.1	<.1
25 017	Woburn city...................	35,943	95.0	0.9	1.5	0.2	<.1	2.3	38	140	89	45	0.6	0.6	0.1	0.3
25 027	Worcester city................	169,759	83.3	4.0	2.7	0.3	0.2	9.6	2	202	15	9	2.8	2.7	2.5	5.7
25 021	Wrentham town	9,006	98.1	0.7	0.7	<.1	<.1	0.4	171	39	119	206	0.1	0.2	<.1	<.1
25 001	Yarmouth town	21,174	96.6	1.1	0.4	0.2	0.3	1.4	79	111	78	75	0.4	0.4	<.1	0.1
	CONGRESSIONAL															
	District 1	601,643	92.1	1.5	1.3	0.2	0.1	4.8	1	4	10	4	10.0	10.5	3.3	10.1
	District 2	601,642	87.5	5.3	0.9	0.2	<.1	6.0	7	7	3	3	10.0	10.0	11.7	12.6
	District 3	601,642	92.6	1.6	1.7	0.1	0.2	3.7	8	3	7	6	10.0	10.6	3.6	7.8
	District 4	601,642	92.1	2.0	2.1	0.2	1.2	2.5	9	5	5	9	10.0	10.5	4.4	5.2
	District 5	601,643	86.5	1.6	3.5	0.1	0.1	8.1	2	8	8	2	10.0	9.9	3.5	17.0
	District 6	601,643	94.0	1.5	1.4	0.1	<.1	2.9	3	2	9	8	10.0	10.7	3.4	6.0
	District 7	601,642	91.9	2.1	2.8	0.1	0.1	3.0	10	6	4	7	10.0	10.5	4.7	6.3
	District 8	601,643	61.2	21.8	5.4	0.2	0.6	10.6	4	10	1	1	10.0	7.0	47.9	22.3
	District 9	601,643	85.6	6.1	2.7	0.2	0.8	4.6	5	9	2	5	10.0	9.7	13.3	9.7
	District 10	601,642	94.3	1.9	1.5	0.3	0.6	1.4	6	1	6	10	10.0	10.7	4.2	3.0

[1]Separate rankings for 14 counties and 213 cities and towns.

Table B. — 1990 Voting Age Population (VAP) by Race and Ethnic Origin

County	Total Voting Age Population	Percent of total VAP — Non-Hisp. White	Black	Asian and Pacific Islander	Native American	Other	Hispanic	Rank Pct of total VAP — Total	White	Black	Hispanic	Pct contribution to state VAP — Total	Non-Hisp. White	Black	Hispanic	VAP pct of total population — Total	Non-Hisp. White	Black	Asian and Pacific Islander	Native American	Other	Hispanic
Barnstable	147,375	96.1	1.2	0.4	0.5	0.7	1.0	9	3	13	10	3.2	3.4	1.0	0.8	79.0	79.6	66.8	63.1	66.9	66.0	65.5
Berkshire	107,663	96.8	1.6	0.6	0.1	<.1	0.9	11	2	10	12	2.3	2.5	0.9	0.5	77.3	77.6	68.1	71.3	73.8	23.9	66.8
Bristol	382,444	94.5	1.2	0.7	0.2	1.1	2.2	6	5	12	7	8.2	8.7	2.5	4.7	75.5	76.3	66.1	62.6	69.6	69.9	61.9
Dukes	8,935	93.9	2.9	0.3	1.9	0.2	0.9	13	7	4	13	0.2	0.2	0.1	<.1	76.8	77.0	80.8	64.1	71.8	68.2	62.8
Essex	511,503	91.9	1.3	1.2	0.1	<.1	5.5	4	11	11	3	11.0	11.3	3.5	15.5	76.3	78.3	65.2	62.5	70.6	34.1	57.9
Franklin	52,788	97.6	0.6	0.6	0.2	<.1	0.9	12	1	14	11	1.1	1.2	0.2	0.3	75.3	75.7	67.4	69.1	66.2	27.1	58.6
Hampden	342,448	85.5	6.2	0.7	0.1	<.1	7.3	7	13	2	2	7.3	7.0	11.1	13.9	75.0	78.4	66.3	68.0	72.0	51.4	54.6
Hampshire	118,334	92.9	1.6	3.0	0.2	<.1	2.3	10	10	9	6	2.5	2.6	1.0	1.5	80.7	81.2	76.6	81.0	77.2	57.1	69.1
Middlesex	1,107,476	91.0	2.5	3.3	0.1	0.1	2.9	1	12	5	5	23.7	24.2	14.5	18.1	79.2	80.1	73.6	71.3	78.7	64.3	68.8
Nantucket	4,758	96.1	2.1	0.3	<.1	0.6	0.8	14	4	6	14	0.1	0.1	<.1	<.1	79.1	79.4	72.9	83.3	60.0	72.5	72.0
Norfolk	486,400	94.2	1.7	2.7	0.1	<.1	1.3	5	6	7	9	10.4	11.0	4.4	3.4	78.9	79.4	72.9	73.0	74.8	62.3	72.5
Plymouth	320,999	93.2	3.1	0.7	0.2	1.0	1.9	8	8	3	8	6.9	7.2	5.1	3.4	73.7	74.5	65.4	63.6	74.7	66.2	63.4
Suffolk	535,721	67.1	18.1	4.7	0.2	0.7	9.2	3	14	1	1	11.5	8.6	50.9	27.2	80.7	87.2	70.0	76.6	72.7	63.9	67.4
Worcester	536,506	93.1	1.7	1.3	0.2	<.1	3.6	2	9	8	4	11.5	12.0	4.7	10.7	75.6	76.8	67.1	64.9	70.2	42.0	58.8
MASSACHUSETTS	**4,663,350**	**89.4**	**4.1**	**2.1**	**0.2**	**0.3**	**3.9**					**100.0**	**100.0**	**100.0**	**100.0**	**77.5**	**79.0**	**69.6**	**71.3**	**72.6**	**64.0**	**62.7**
CITIES AND TOWNS																						
Abington town	10,349	98.6	0.4	0.2	0.2	<.1	0.6	125	26	168	168	0.2	0.2	<.1	<.1	74.9	75.0	78.7	62.2	81.5	62.5	61.7
Acton town	13,386	94.6	0.8	3.2	<.1	<.1	1.2	94	154	87	76	0.3	0.3	<.1	<.1	74.9	75.4	75.8	67.2	68.4	40.0	61.2
Acushnet town	7,309	98.4	0.3	0.1	0.2	0.4	0.5	161	36	170	189	0.2	0.2	<.1	<.1	76.5	76.6	67.6	45.5	84.2	80.0	66.0
Adams town	7,449	99.4	0.1	<.1	<.1	0.0	0.3	157	2	206	210	0.2	0.2	<.1	<.1	78.9	79.1	62.5	36.8	75.0	0.0	53.8
Agawam town	21,299	97.7	0.8	0.4	0.1	<.1	0.9	56	78	93	98	0.5	0.5	<.1	0.1	78.0	78.2	71.3	63.6	71.9	50.0	65.3
Amesbury town	11,039	98.5	0.5	0.4	0.2	<.1	0.5	115	33	144	185	0.2	0.3	<.1	<.1	73.6	73.9	59.1	60.9	69.7	25.0	55.2
Amherst town	31,032	84.3	3.8	7.3	0.2	0.2	4.2	31	203	13	21	0.7	0.6	0.6	0.7	88.1	89.9	75.9	82.4	79.8	69.7	77.7
Andover town	21,548	94.7	0.8	3.2	<.1	<.1	1.2	54	152	92	77	0.5	0.5	<.1	0.1	73.9	74.6	72.2	63.2	67.9	35.7	59.1
Arlington town	37,188	94.5	1.1	2.8	<.1	<.1	1.5	24	155	71	62	0.8	0.8	0.2	0.3	83.3	83.9	71.8	76.7	97.0	36.8	75.2
Ashburnham town	3,804	98.9	<.1	0.4	0.1	0.0	0.5	208	10	213	174	<.1	<.1	<.1	<.1	70.0	70.3	28.6	62.5	57.1	0.0	47.6
Ashland town	9,409	94.3	1.8	1.8	<.1	0.1	1.8	136	162	40	52	0.2	0.2	<.1	<.1	78.0	78.3	76.2	73.4	100.0	68.8	69.7
Athol town	8,311	98.3	0.3	0.5	0.3	<.1	0.6	148	43	183	155	0.2	0.2	<.1	<.1	72.6	73.1	45.1	59.4	45.5	33.3	51.0
Attleboro city	28,705	94.4	0.8	1.9	0.2	0.1	2.6	37	160	90	40	0.6	0.6	0.1	0.4	74.8	75.6	64.9	61.1	65.2	63.5	65.1
Auburn town	11,736	98.6	0.2	0.6	0.1	<.1	0.5	110	28	190	183	0.3	0.3	<.1	<.1	78.2	78.4	64.3	66.0	71.4	60.0	67.1
Ayer town	5,201	83.5	8.8	2.9	0.4	0.2	4.1	197	205	5	22	0.1	0.1	0.2	0.1	75.7	77.3	70.1	75.4	64.5	55.0	62.9
Barnstable town	32,223	94.1	2.4	0.5	0.6	0.8	1.5	28	164	31	61	0.7	0.7	0.4	0.3	78.7	79.4	70.9	63.4	71.6	66.3	70.6
Barre town	3,296	98.8	0.4	0.4	<.1	0.0	0.4	209	16	160	194	<.1	<.1	<.1	<.1	72.5	73.0	46.4	41.4	100.0	0.0	51.9
Bedford town	10,414	93.0	2.8	2.7	0.2	<.1	1.3	123	173	24	69	0.2	0.2	0.2	<.1	80.1	80.5	83.5	70.5	79.2	50.0	72.1
Belchertown town	7,856	97.5	0.6	1.0	<.1	<.1	0.8	153	94	129	117	0.2	0.2	<.1	<.1	74.3	74.3	81.5	77.5	100.0	23.1	69.5
Bellingham town	10,988	97.4	0.9	0.7	0.2	<.1	0.8	116	99	79	115	0.2	0.3	<.1	<.1	73.9	74.1	70.3	64.6	58.6	40.0	66.9
Belmont town	20,129	95.2	0.7	2.9	<.1	<.1	1.1	63	147	108	82	0.4	0.5	<.1	0.1	81.4	82.0	70.2	71.6	72.7	55.6	69.8
Beverly city	29,979	97.4	0.7	0.8	0.1	<.1	0.9	34	96	110	104	0.6	0.7	0.1	0.2	78.5	79.0	68.1	63.4	75.5	38.2	63.3
Billerica town	27,975	96.0	1.1	1.4	0.2	<.1	1.3	41	133	67	72	0.6	0.6	0.2	0.2	74.4	74.4	80.5	70.5	80.8	50.0	74.4
Blackstone town	5,806	98.4	0.3	0.5	0.1	<.1	0.7	183	34	178	152	0.1	0.1	<.1	<.1	72.4	72.8	65.4	40.9	80.0	20.0	57.6
Boston city	464,450	64.3	20.7	5.0	0.2	0.8	9.1	1	212	1	6	10.0	7.2	50.3	23.4	80.9	88.1	70.1	78.4	73.0	64.5	68.0
Bourne town	12,090	96.3	1.1	0.5	0.5	0.5	1.1	104	128	69	86	0.3	0.3	<.1	<.1	75.3	75.7	62.5	71.1	75.6	65.0	63.5
Boxford town	4,532	98.2	0.7	0.8	<.1	<.1	0.3	204	57	112	206	<.1	0.1	<.1	<.1	72.3	72.8	73.8	49.3	40.0	100.0	44.1
Braintree town	27,089	97.3	0.5	1.3	<.1	0.1	0.7	42	103	135	132	0.6	0.6	<.1	0.1	80.1	80.5	72.5	67.8	59.4	61.7	66.9
Brewster town	6,537	98.9	0.2	0.2	<.1	<.1	0.5	173	9	195	172	0.1	0.2	<.1	<.1	77.5	78.0	35.1	42.4	66.7	100.0	53.8
Bridgewater town	16,648	90.4	4.7	0.8	0.2	0.2	3.7	77	187	9	26	0.4	0.4	0.4	0.3	78.3	77.4	91.1	72.4	92.5	80.4	90.4
Brockton city	68,183	81.2	9.8	1.5	0.3	2.2	5.0	9	207	4	19	1.5	1.3	3.5	1.9	73.5	77.0	61.9	66.4	72.8	61.0	58.5
Brookline town	46,068	86.7	2.6	7.8	0.1	0.2	2.6	17	199	29	38	1.0	1.0	0.6	0.7	84.2	85.5	74.4	78.6	72.2	58.7	75.2
Burlington town	18,161	93.7	1.1	4.1	<.1	<.1	1.1	72	169	73	83	0.4	0.4	0.1	0.1	77.9	78.4	74.2	70.8	73.9	44.4	71.2
Cambridge city	82,190	74.4	10.8	8.4	0.3	0.3	5.8	4	209	3	15	1.8	1.5	4.7	2.6	85.8	89.2	73.2	86.7	86.9	64.0	73.1
Canton town	14,484	97.0	1.1	1.0	<.1	<.1	0.7	88	115	68	139	0.3	0.3	<.1	<.1	78.5	78.5	73.5	66.2	76.5	50.0	67.3
Carver town	7,382	95.7	1.9	0.4	0.2	1.2	0.7	158	138	39	134	0.2	0.2	<.1	<.1	69.7	69.6	68.7	63.4	73.9	79.8	72.6
Chatham town	5,594	98.8	0.3	0.2	0.2	<.1	0.5	186	15	179	177	0.1	0.1	<.1	<.1	85.0	85.2	55.2	75.0	78.6	100.0	78.4
Chelmsford town	24,748	96.1	0.4	2.6	<.1	<.1	0.8	44	131	158	120	0.5	0.6	<.1	0.1	76.4	77.0	65.8	65.1	64.5	61.1	62.5
Chelsea city	21,423	65.7	3.5	4.0	0.2	0.4	26.2	55	211	17	2	0.5	0.3	0.4	3.1	74.6	83.1	66.3	61.7	74.5	45.8	62.3
Chicopee city	44,124	95.2	1.5	0.5	0.1	<.1	2.7	18	148	52	36	0.9	1.0	0.3	0.7	77.9	79.0	67.4	72.7	77.6	37.5	57.6
Clarksburg town	1,347	99.7	0.1	0.0	0.0	0.0	0.1	212	1	204	213	<.1	<.1	<.1	<.1	77.2	77.4	33.3	0.0	0.0	0.0	50.0
Clinton town	10,263	91.0	1.3	0.8	<.1	<.1	6.6	126	186	60	13	0.2	0.2	<.1	0.4	77.6	78.8	70.8	70.5	100.0	66.7	66.1
Cohasset town	5,438	98.9	0.3	0.4	<.1	0.0	0.4	190	13	186	196	0.1	0.1	<.1	<.1	76.9	77.1	70.0	64.5	83.3	0.0	54.8
Concord town	13,609	92.1	2.7	1.7	0.1	<.1	3.4	92	181	26	29	0.3	0.3	0.2	0.3	79.7	79.4	92.5	65.5	94.4	70.0	89.3
Dalton town	5,293	98.6	0.5	0.4	<.1	0.0	0.4	195	23	148	191	0.1	0.1	<.1	<.1	74.0	74.1	75.0	69.7	100.0	0.0	57.5
Danvers town	19,030	97.9	0.4	0.8	<.1	0.0	0.9	68	75	157	102	0.4	0.4	<.1	<.1	78.7	79.1	68.8	61.7	100.0	0.0	68.7
Dartmouth town	21,283	96.5	0.7	0.8	<.1	1.0	1.0	58	124	116	88	0.5	0.5	<.1	0.1	78.1	78.2	76.1	74.8	75.0	71.6	78.5
Dedham town	18,970	97.4	0.7	1.0	0.1	<.1	0.9	69	100	117	108	0.4	0.4	<.1	<.1	79.8	80.0	67.4	72.6	80.0	40.0	71.1
Deerfield town	3,937	98.2	0.3	0.8	<.1	<.1	0.7	206	50	187	143	<.1	<.1	<.1	<.1	78.5	78.4	83.3	88.2	100.0	100.0	71.1
Dennis town	11,266	97.7	0.8	0.2	0.3	0.4	0.6	112	80	97	161	0.2	0.3	<.1	<.1	81.3	82.0	63.7	47.9	64.3	55.3	57.1
Dracut town	19,223	97.4	0.5	1.1	0.1	<.1	0.9	66	98	132	112	0.4	0.4	<.1	<.1	75.1	75.3	77.8	66.2	88.5	33.3	70.1
Dudley town	7,318	97.6	0.3	0.8	<.1	<.1	1.2	160	87	171	74	0.2	0.2	<.1	<.1	76.7	77.2	62.5	64.0	83.3	20.0	60.1

¹Separate rankings for 14 counties and 213 cities and towns.

County	Total Voting Age Population	Percent of total VAP — Non-Hispanic White	Black	Asian and Pacific Islander	Native American	Other	Hispanic	Rank¹ Percent of total VAP — Total	Non-Hispanic White	Black	Hispanic	Percent contribution to state VAP — Total	Non-Hispanic White	Black	Hispanic	VAP percent of total population — Total	Non-Hispanic White	Black	Asian and Pacific Islander	Native American	Other	Hispanic
Duxbury town	9,960	98.0	0.9	0.3	<.1	0.2	0.5	128	68	81	176	0.2	0.2	<.1	<.1	71.7	71.9	76.7	43.1	80.0	81.8	55.3
East Bridgewater town	8,049	97.7	0.7	0.3	0.1	0.2	0.9	151	79	99	103	0.2	0.2	<.1	<.1	72.5	72.5	73.2	69.7	57.9	56.5	72.8
East Longmeadow town	10,257	98.6	0.4	0.4	<.1	<.1	0.6	127	22	150	199	0.2	0.2	<.1	<.1	76.7	76.8	65.2	74.5	83.3	100.0	68.9
Easthampton town	11,979	97.5	0.3	0.7	0.1	<.1	1.4	106	91	176	66	0.3	0.3	<.1	<.1	77.1	77.5	72.5	67.2	80.0	50.0	61.5
Easton town	15,014	97.0	1.5	0.8	<.1	0.1	0.5	86	116	49	171	0.3	0.3	0.1	<.1	75.8	76.2	67.5	60.3	64.7	62.9	66.4
Erving town	1,029	98.5	0.4	0.3	0.5	0.0	0.3	213	29	162	209	<.1	<.1	<.1	<.1	75.0	75.1	57.1	60.0	83.3	0.0	100.0
Everett city	28,686	92.1	2.7	1.5	0.2	0.1	3.4	38	180	27	30	0.6	0.6	0.4	0.5	80.4	81.2	75.1	71.3	73.6	60.0	70.5
Fairhaven town	12,598	97.3	0.5	0.4	0.1	1.0	0.7	102	102	146	145	0.3	0.3	<.1	<.1	78.1	78.3	72.8	68.0	66.7	80.6	63.2
Fall River city	70,157	96.6	0.8	0.9	<.1	0.1	1.5	8	123	96	64	1.5	1.6	0.3	0.6	75.7	76.3	59.6	54.9	63.6	67.9	65.7
Falmouth town	21,758	94.5	1.4	0.6	0.4	1.7	1.4	52	156	56	68	0.5	0.5	0.2	0.2	77.8	78.5	65.9	69.6	58.4	69.3	70.8
Fitchburg city	31,184	88.8	2.3	1.8	0.2	<.1	6.8	29	194	32	11	0.7	0.7	0.4	1.2	75.7	79.3	61.0	55.7	64.8	38.2	54.0
Foxborough town	11,189	97.8	0.6	0.9	0.1	<.1	0.6	114	76	130	164	0.2	0.3	<.1	<.1	76.4	76.6	84.9	66.9	88.9	100.0	63.1
Framingham town	52,337	86.8	3.1	2.6	0.1	0.3	7.0	13	198	22	9	1.1	1.1	0.8	2.0	80.5	82.1	74.7	73.3	80.6	69.4	69.7
Franklin town	16,446	97.6	0.7	0.9	0.1	<.1	0.6	78	85	113	162	0.4	0.4	<.1	<.1	74.4	74.5	76.0	68.5	80.0	54.5	68.5
Freetown town	6,134	97.2	0.3	0.4	0.2	1.2	0.7	177	110	172	135	0.1	0.1	<.1	<.1	72.0	72.0	52.5	69.7	86.7	75.8	67.7
Gardner city	15,568	94.6	1.8	0.7	0.1	<.1	2.7	82	153	42	37	0.3	0.4	0.1	0.2	77.4	77.6	72.1	71.0	91.3	53.8	74.2
Gloucester city	22,577	98.6	0.2	0.2	<.1	<.1	0.9	50	27	199	106	0.5	0.5	<.1	0.1	78.6	78.7	58.5	72.6	76.0	37.5	75.7
Grafton town	9,887	96.6	1.3	0.9	0.1	0.0	1.1	130	122	64	84	0.2	0.2	<.1	<.1	75.8	76.3	76.4	61.3	64.7	0.0	60.9
Great Barrington town	5,832	95.6	2.1	0.5	<.1	<.1	1.5	182	139	34	59	0.1	0.1	<.1	<.1	75.5	76.2	62.6	51.6	62.5	57.1	67.2
Greenfield town	14,255	97.5	0.7	0.7	0.2	<.1	0.9	90	92	107	107	0.3	0.3	<.1	<.1	76.4	76.9	64.9	59.8	77.5	11.1	58.8
Groton town	5,440	98.0	0.5	0.6	0.2	0.0	0.7	189	72	134	146	0.1	0.1	<.1	<.1	72.4	72.7	60.4	58.6	90.9	0.0	59.7
Groveland town	3,849	98.9	0.1	0.3	0.2	<.1	0.5	207	8	207	182	<.1	<.1	<.1	<.1	73.8	73.9	62.5	62.5	75.0	100.0	70.4
Hamilton town	5,456	97.5	0.4	1.1	<.1	0.0	0.9	188	93	155	110	0.1	0.1	<.1	<.1	74.9	75.4	65.7	62.2	50.0	0.0	56.3
Hanover town	8,652	98.2	0.6	0.5	<.1	<.1	0.5	145	48	125	187	0.2	0.2	<.1	<.1	72.6	73.0	69.3	46.9	100.0	100.0	53.2
Hanson town	6,557	97.1	1.4	0.4	<.1	0.5	0.5	172	144	97	170	0.1	0.2	<.1	<.1	72.6	72.7	74.6	57.4	100.0	75.0	70.6
Hardwick town	1,764	99.0	0.3	<.1	0.2	0.0	0.4	211	7	180	200	<.1	<.1	<.1	<.1	74.0	74.2	83.3	100.0	66.7	0.0	43.8
Haverhill city	39,062	93.8	1.3	0.8	0.1	<.1	4.0	21	168	63	23	0.8	0.9	0.3	0.9	76.0	77.3	68.0	71.3	73.1	26.0	57.1
Hingham town	15,018	98.1	0.4	0.7	0.1	0.0	0.7	85	63	151	144	0.3	0.4	<.1	<.1	75.8	76.0	75.9	62.7	71.4	0.0	66.2
Holbrook town	8,544	94.7	2.8	0.9	0.2	0.2	1.2	147	151	25	73	0.2	0.2	0.1	<.1	77.4	77.6	74.7	78.0	76.5	73.1	66.2
Holden town	10,911	98.4	0.2	0.8	<.1	0.0	0.5	118	37	198	179	0.2	0.3	<.1	<.1	74.6	74.9	57.6	61.5	53.3	0.0	58.3
Holliston town	9,394	97.3	0.9	0.8	<.1	0.0	1.0	137	104	84	93	0.2	0.2	<.1	<.1	72.7	73.0	68.9	60.2	54.5	0.0	61.2
Holyoke city	31,035	74.9	2.3	0.7	0.2	<.1	21.9	30	208	33	3	0.7	0.6	0.4	3.8	71.0	81.5	61.4	68.2	67.5	36.8	50.0
Hopkinton town	6,611	97.2	0.4	0.9	0.1	<.1	1.4	171	105	165	65	0.1	0.2	<.1	<.1	71.9	72.0	86.2	55.2	100.0	33.3	77.0
Hudson town	13,265	95.5	0.7	1.1	0.1	<.1	2.5	96	142	98	41	0.3	0.3	<.1	0.2	77.0	77.3	67.8	72.3	85.0	35.3	71.0
Hull town	8,052	97.6	0.7	0.5	0.2	<.1	1.0	150	88	100	97	0.2	0.2	<.1	<.1	76.9	77.2	68.2	66.2	73.7	40.0	68.1
Ipswich town	9,308	98.8	0.3	0.3	<.1	<.1	0.5	138	17	182	178	0.2	0.2	<.1	<.1	78.4	78.6	66.7	62.0	75.0	44.4	62.3
Kingston town	6,754	98.0	0.8	0.2	0.2	0.4	0.4	169	65	95	193	0.1	0.2	<.1	<.1	74.7	74.6	76.8	80.0	100.0	73.0	74.4
Lawrence city	48,064	62.6	1.6	1.5	0.1	0.1	34.1	15	213	47	1	1.0	0.7	0.4	9.1	68.5	78.4	62.7	65.0	61.0	29.9	56.0
Leicester town	7,625	97.4	0.8	0.6	0.1	0.0	1.0	156	97	88	92	0.2	0.2	<.1	<.1	74.8	75.0	79.0	75.8	73.3	0.0	60.6
Leominster city	29,266	89.9	1.9	1.3	0.2	<.1	6.7	36	190	38	12	0.6	0.6	0.3	1.1	76.7	78.5	70.7	64.7	82.5	37.5	62.3
Lexington town	22,763	92.5	1.1	5.3	<.1	<.1	1.0	49	176	74	94	0.5	0.5	0.1	0.1	78.6	79.8	80.3	64.6	80.0	30.0	63.0
Lincoln town	5,368	90.1	4.2	3.6	0.1	0.1	1.8	192	188	11	51	0.1	0.1	0.1	<.1	70.0	71.0	58.8	69.3	100.0	35.3	59.9
Littleton town	5,428	98.1	0.6	0.7	0.1	<.1	0.4	191	61	121	195	0.1	0.1	<.1	<.1	77.0	77.3	68.0	64.4	85.7	25.0	54.8
Longmeadow town	11,742	96.4	0.7	2.1	<.1	<.1	0.7	109	127	103	137	0.3	0.3	<.1	<.1	75.9	76.3	69.4	64.6	77.8	50.0	77.6
Lowell city	76,438	81.5	1.8	8.4	0.1	0.2	7.9	5	206	41	7	1.6	1.5	0.7	3.3	73.9	78.7	66.9	57.2	77.1	62.7	57.3
Ludlow town	14,589	97.2	0.2	0.5	<.1	<.1	2.0	87	107	194	45	0.3	0.3	<.1	0.2	77.5	77.6	83.8	62.2	68.8	62.5	77.1
Lunenburg town	6,809	97.9	0.7	0.6	0.1	0.0	0.7	168	73	115	138	0.1	0.2	<.1	<.1	74.7	74.9	75.0	66.7	88.9	0.0	54.5
Lynn city	61,188	84.2	5.6	2.6	0.2	0.1	7.3	12	204	8	8	1.3	1.2	1.8	2.5	75.3	79.1	63.3	55.3	69.4	32.8	59.9
Lynnfield town	8,786	98.1	<.1	1.3	<.1	0.0	0.5	143	62	211	188	0.2	0.2	<.1	<.1	77.9	78.4	72.7	62.7	100.0	0.0	56.2
Malden city	43,314	88.8	3.6	4.8	0.1	<.1	2.6	19	193	15	39	0.9	0.9	0.8	0.6	80.4	81.2	72.4	74.0	76.1	60.3	78.6
Mansfield town	12,031	96.7	1.4	0.9	0.1	<.1	1.0	105	121	59	96	0.3	0.3	<.1	<.1	72.6	73.1	61.4	68.7	54.2	16.7	58.9
Marblehead town	16,026	98.2	0.3	0.7	<.1	<.1	0.7	79	51	169	151	0.3	0.4	<.1	<.1	80.2	80.6	70.0	62.8	90.0	46.7	66.3
Marlborough city	24,912	92.5	1.4	1.8	0.1	0.5	3.7	43	177	55	27	0.5	0.6	0.2	0.8	78.3	79.1	66.6	72.7	67.3	79.7	68.8
Marshfield town	15,772	98.0	0.6	0.4	0.1	0.2	0.6	81	66	122	157	0.3	0.4	<.1	<.1	73.3	73.5	66.2	52.1	65.4	75.5	69.0
Mashpee town	5,953	89.9	3.6	0.3	4.3	0.9	1.4	180	189	14	85	0.1	0.1	0.1	<.1	75.5	76.9	70.1	65.5	66.7	52.6	54.3
Maynard town	8,024	95.8	0.6	1.5	0.1	1.8	1.8	152	136	118	49	0.2	0.2	<.1	<.1	77.7	78.5	66.7	64.9	92.3	53.8	61.3
Medfield town	7,698	98.0	0.7	0.8	<.1	<.1	0.5	155	69	114	184	0.2	0.2	<.1	<.1	73.1	73.2	71.8	63.0	100.0	66.7	62.7
Medford city	47,349	92.7	3.6	1.9	<.1	<.1	1.6	16	175	16	56	1.0	1.1	0.9	0.4	82.5	83.0	75.0	78.8	69.8	76.4	77.4
Medway town	7,171	97.9	0.6	0.7	0.1	<.1	0.7	163	74	119	154	0.2	0.2	<.1	<.1	72.2	72.5	66.2	51.0	100.0	100.0	61.6
Melrose city	22,325	97.8	0.5	1.0	<.1	<.1	0.7	51	77	143	150	0.5	0.5	<.1	<.1	79.3	79.6	69.5	73.0	66.7	37.5	65.5
Methuen town	30,505	94.4	0.6	1.2	<.1	<.1	3.7	33	159	128	25	0.7	0.7	<.1	0.6	76.3	77.7	65.6	67.8	62.8	33.3	55.0
Middleborough town	12,784	96.7	1.3	0.3	0.4	0.5	0.8	101	120	62	125	0.3	0.3	<.1	<.1	71.6	71.7	65.8	70.0	71.9	77.8	59.4
Milford town	19,172	94.5	1.0	0.9	0.2	0.1	3.3	67	157	78	32	0.4	0.4	<.1	0.4	75.6	76.5	59.9	71.0	82.9	56.4	62.6
Millbury town	9,551	98.4	0.3	0.9	<.1	<.1	0.6	134	38	188	205	0.2	0.2	<.1	<.1	78.1	78.4	70.6	76.1	100.0	0.0	49.3
Millis town	5,661	98.1	0.4	0.7	0.1	<.1	0.6	185	58	149	159	0.1	0.1	<.1	<.1	74.4	74.5	73.5	76.0	85.7	50.0	58.3
Milton town	19,976	93.9	4.0	1.0	<.1	<.1	0.9	64	166	12	109	0.4	0.5	0.4	0.1	77.7	78.4	68.5	65.5	66.7	55.6	69.3
Monson town	5,853	98.7	0.5	0.1	0.1	0.1	0.5	181	20	139	181	0.1	0.1	<.1	<.1	75.3	75.5	72.5	43.8	70.0	75.0	56.9
Montague town	6,340	97.7	0.4	0.4	0.4	<.1	1.0	174	82	156	90	0.1	0.1	<.1	<.1	76.2	76.8	60.5	60.5	54.5	42.9	58.6
Natick town	24,441	94.3	1.9	2.1	<.1	<.1	1.6	45	163	37	58	0.5	0.6	0.2	0.2	80.1	80.6	77.1	72.9	88.0	50.0	70.2
Needham town	21,295	96.8	0.5	1.8	<.1	<.1	0.8	57	117	140	129	0.5	0.5	<.1	<.1	77.3	77.8	62.1	65.1	93.3	42.9	62.1

¹Separate rankings for 14 counties and 213 cities and towns.

Table B. — 1990 Voting Age Population (VAP) by Race and Ethnic Origin (cont)

County	Total Voting Age Population	Percent of total VAP — Non-Hispanic White	Black	Asian and Pacific Islander	Native American	Other	Hispanic	Rank Total	Rank Non-Hispanic White	Black	Hispanic	Contribution to state VAP Total	Non-Hispanic White	Black	Hispanic	VAP % of total pop Total	Non-Hispanic White	Black	Asian and Pacific Islander	Native American	Other	Hispanic
New Bedford city	74,969	86.6	3.1	0.4	0.4	4.4	5.2	6	200	21	18	1.6	1.6	1.2	2.1	75.0	77.0	66.8	70.7	72.5	70.1	58.1
Newbury town	4,180	99.1	<.1	0.2	0.1	0.0	0.5	205	4	210	175	<.1	<.1	<.1	<.1	74.3	74.6	40.0	50.0	100.0	0.0	51.2
Newburyport city	12,966	98.7	0.5	0.2	0.1	<.1	0.5	99	18	147	186	0.3	0.3	<.1	<.1	79.5	79.6	78.7	59.1	87.5	25.0	68.1
Newton city	67,275	91.9	2.0	4.1	0.1	<.1	1.9	10	184	36	48	1.4	1.5	0.7	0.7	81.5	82.0	82.8	73.0	92.4	53.9	77.2
Norfolk town	6,850	86.9	6.2	0.7	0.4	<.1	5.9	167	197	7	14	0.1	0.1	0.2	0.2	73.9	71.8	97.2	54.9	100.0	100.0	91.2
North Adams city	13,149	97.2	1.1	0.4	0.2	<.1	1.0	98	106	76	89	0.3	0.3	<.1	<.1	78.3	78.7	66.7	64.4	69.0	50.0	67.8
North Andover town	17,364	96.4	0.6	1.7	<.1	<.1	1.2	76	126	123	79	0.4	0.4	<.1	0.1	76.2	76.6	68.2	66.2	63.6	100.0	65.1
North Attleborough town	18,631	97.7	0.5	1.0	<.1	<.1	0.6	71	81	137	153	0.4	0.4	<.1	<.1	74.4	74.7	71.5	64.4	81.3	100.0	59.4
North Reading town	9,086	98.5	0.2	0.6	<.1	0.0	0.6	141	30	189	165	0.2	0.2	<.1	<.1	75.7	76.0	58.3	59.8	80.0	0.0	61.2
Northampton city	24,210	92.3	1.6	2.7	0.2	<.1	3.2	46	178	45	34	0.5	0.5	0.2	0.4	82.7	83.7	80.4	79.3	81.6	48.3	63.5
Northborough town	8,715	95.3	0.6	3.2	0.1	<.1	0.8	144	144	127	123	0.2	0.2	<.1	<.1	73.1	73.9	71.2	59.5	66.7	25.0	53.5
Northbridge town	9,758	98.5	0.4	0.3	0.2	0.0	0.7	132	31	164	148	0.2	0.2	<.1	<.1	73.0	73.1	64.9	73.7	94.4	0.0	61.1
Norton town	10,664	96.1	1.5	1.0	0.1	<.1	1.2	121	129	54	78	0.2	0.2	<.1	<.1	74.8	74.6	83.3	81.3	54.2	71.4	72.4
Norwell town	6,914	98.6	0.3	0.8	<.1	<.1	0.2	166	25	173	212	0.1	0.2	<.1	<.1	74.5	74.7	76.7	63.9	75.0	28.6	48.4
Norwood town	23,245	96.4	1.3	1.2	0.1	<.1	0.9	48	125	65	100	0.5	0.5	0.2	0.1	81.0	81.6	67.4	68.5	71.4	46.7	69.0
Orange town	5,272	98.4	0.3	0.3	0.2	<.1	0.8	196	39	174	118	0.1	0.1	<.1	<.1	72.1	72.6	50.0	57.1	88.9	16.7	48.9
Orleans town	4,964	99.1	0.1	0.4	<.1	0.0	0.3	199	5	208	207	0.1	0.1	<.1	<.1	85.0	85.2	60.0	64.5	80.0	0.0	94.1
Oxford town	9,161	98.0	0.5	0.6	0.2	<.1	0.7	140	67	145	133	0.2	0.2	<.1	<.1	72.8	73.0	61.4	69.0	77.8	0.0	60.0
Palmer town	9,274	98.4	0.5	0.4	0.3	<.1	0.4	139	40	133	192	0.2	0.2	<.1	<.1	76.9	77.2	56.8	76.7	86.7	50.0	55.6
Peabody city	37,059	95.9	0.7	0.8	<.1	<.1	2.5	25	135	101	42	0.8	0.9	0.1	0.5	78.8	79.4	67.2	62.5	95.0	52.4	67.6
Pembroke town	10,399	98.7	0.5	0.3	<.1	<.1	0.4	124	19	136	203	0.2	0.2	<.1	<.1	71.5	71.6	72.6	55.9	100.0	37.5	61.5
Pepperell town	6,993	97.7	0.7	0.6	0.1	<.1	0.8	164	83	111	119	0.2	0.2	<.1	<.1	69.3	69.4	66.7	65.2	87.5	50.0	57.6
Pittsfield city	37,588	95.6	2.6	0.7	0.2	<.1	0.9	23	140	28	111	0.8	0.9	0.5	0.2	77.3	78.0	66.9	71.2	74.4	20.5	62.2
Plainville town	5,295	98.2	0.4	0.7	<.1	<.1	0.7	194	56	167	147	0.1	0.1	<.1	<.1	77.1	77.4	46.3	72.0	100.0	80.0	60.0
Plymouth town	33,129	96.0	1.7	0.5	0.2	0.3	1.2	27	132	43	75	0.7	0.8	0.3	0.2	72.6	72.8	71.9	60.9	67.7	66.1	72.4
Quincy city	70,450	91.8	0.9	5.8	0.2	<.1	1.3	7	185	82	71	1.5	1.6	0.3	0.5	82.9	83.9	71.5	73.7	71.9	66.7	74.5
Randolph town	23,801	86.3	6.9	4.8	0.2	0.2	1.6	47	201	6	57	0.5	0.5	0.9	0.2	79.1	80.9	70.2	69.4	69.2	60.2	68.6
Raynham town	7,240	97.7	0.6	0.6	0.1	0.2	0.8	162	84	124	122	0.2	0.2	<.1	<.1	73.4	73.7	55.7	57.9	72.7	87.5	61.6
Reading town	17,367	98.4	0.2	0.8	<.1	<.1	0.4	75	41	193	190	0.4	0.4	<.1	<.1	77.1	77.4	69.8	61.9	73.9	57.1	50.6
Rehoboth town	6,326	98.5	0.4	0.3	<.1	<.1	0.6	175	32	154	166	0.1	0.1	<.1	<.1	73.1	73.3	69.2	43.2	100.0	57.1	66.7
Revere city	34,697	92.9	1.1	2.4	0.2	0.1	3.4	26	174	75	31	0.7	0.8	0.2	0.6	81.1	82.8	69.4	54.5	67.4	64.9	71.3
Rockland town	11,964	96.7	1.5	0.7	0.1	<.1	0.9	107	119	53	105	0.3	0.3	<.1	<.1	74.2	74.4	71.3	67.5	77.3	40.0	69.6
Rockport town	6,036	99.0	0.2	0.3	0.1	0.0	0.3	179	6	200	208	0.1	0.1	<.1	<.1	80.7	80.9	58.8	77.8	100.0	0.0	54.3
Salem city	30,870	92.0	1.4	1.2	0.1	<.1	5.2	32	182	58	17	0.7	0.7	0.2	0.9	81.0	82.7	74.6	73.6	63.5	45.0	63.1
Salisbury town	5,198	98.8	0.1	0.2	0.3	<.1	0.6	198	14	209	163	0.1	0.1	<.1	<.1	75.5	75.7	75.0	75.0	70.0	33.3	62.0
Sandwich town	11,269	98.4	0.3	0.3	0.2	0.2	0.6	111	35	177	158	0.2	0.3	<.1	<.1	72.8	73.2	60.7	39.5	52.2	58.1	53.4
Saugus town	20,306	98.0	0.4	0.7	<.1	<.1	0.8	62	64	152	121	0.4	0.5	<.1	<.1	79.5	79.7	71.0	73.4	71.4	30.0	70.3
Scituate town	12,862	97.6	0.2	0.8	<.1	1.2	0.6	100	86	192	169	0.3	0.3	<.1	<.1	76.6	77.1	44.6	55.6	78.6	71.3	57.1
Seekonk town	9,807	97.3	0.7	0.9	0.1	0.3	0.5	131	101	105	173	0.2	0.2	<.1	<.1	75.2	75.4	79.5	57.4	60.9	76.2	72.2
Sharon town	11,223	94.1	3.1	2.0	<.1	<.1	0.8	113	165	23	128	0.2	0.3	0.2	<.1	72.3	72.6	72.5	65.9	80.0	66.7	62.6
Shrewsbury town	18,814	94.4	0.9	3.2	<.1	0.1	1.3	70	161	80	70	0.4	0.4	<.1	0.1	77.9	78.5	70.5	67.4	75.0	67.7	72.5
Somerset town	14,037	98.2	0.1	0.6	<.1	<.1	0.9	91	53	205	114	0.3	0.3	<.1	<.1	79.5	79.5	87.0	76.9	70.6	64.3	87.6
Somerville city	64,343	85.7	4.5	3.6	0.1	0.3	5.7	11	202	10	16	1.4	1.3	1.5	2.0	84.4	85.8	73.5	82.8	76.0	80.5	76.7
South Hadley town	13,585	95.3	1.0	2.4	<.1	<.1	1.1	93	145	77	80	0.3	0.3	<.1	<.1	81.4	81.5	80.7	84.7	73.3	53.8	74.3
Southborough town	4,948	97.1	0.6	1.6	0.1	<.1	0.6	200	112	120	167	0.1	0.1	<.1	<.1	74.7	75.1	77.5	58.8	100.0	25.0	59.6
Southbridge town	13,347	88.7	0.3	1.2	0.1	<.1	9.6	95	195	184	5	0.3	0.3	<.1	0.7	74.9	78.0	72.5	61.5	66.7	50.0	56.5
Southwick town	5,581	98.2	0.4	0.3	0.2	<.1	0.8	187	54	153	116	0.1	0.1	<.1	<.1	72.8	72.9	63.2	84.2	84.6	33.3	63.5
Spencer town	8,552	98.7	0.2	0.3	0.2	<.1	0.7	146	21	201	131	0.2	0.2	<.1	<.1	73.4	73.6	56.0	82.1	60.0	100.0	62.0
Springfield city	114,885	69.6	16.4	0.9	0.2	0.1	12.8	3	210	2	4	2.5	1.9	9.9	8.2	73.2	80.0	66.3	69.5	70.6	41.2	55.5
Stoneham town	17,696	96.8	0.5	1.3	<.1	<.1	1.4	73	118	142	67	0.4	0.4	<.1	0.1	79.7	80.0	61.9	69.3	68.8	64.3	79.9
Stoughton town	20,823	93.6	3.4	1.0	<.1	0.2	1.7	60	170	18	55	0.5	0.5	0.4	0.2	77.8	78.4	69.3	69.0	63.0	73.9	72.1
Sudbury town	10,498	95.2	1.3	2.5	<.1	<.1	0.8	122	146	61	124	0.2	0.2	<.1	<.1	73.1	73.5	76.0	63.9	62.5	15.4	61.0
Sutton town	4,893	99.3	<.1	0.3	0.1	0.0	0.3	202	3	212	211	0.1	0.1	<.1	<.1	71.7	71.7	100.0	70.0	85.7	0.0	59.1
Swampscott town	10,891	98.0	0.4	0.5	0.1	<.1	1.0	119	70	166	91	0.2	0.3	<.1	<.1	79.8	79.9	67.8	67.5	92.3	42.9	82.2
Taunton city	37,887	93.2	1.5	0.4	0.1	0.9	3.9	22	172	51	24	0.8	0.8	0.3	0.8	76.0	77.2	64.5	64.3	65.8	65.0	62.4
Templeton town	4,773	98.9	0.2	0.1	<.1	0.0	0.7	203	12	191	142	0.1	0.1	<.1	<.1	74.1	74.3	44.0	53.8	100.0	0.0	67.3
Tewksbury town	20,577	97.1	0.8	1.2	0.1	<.1	0.8	61	111	94	127	0.4	0.5	<.1	<.1	75.7	75.7	74.0	70.4	63.4	60.0	65.3
Townsend town	5,728	98.3	0.8	0.2	<.1	0.0	0.6	184	47	91	160	0.1	0.1	<.1	<.1	67.4	67.5	61.0	72.2	100.0	0.0	57.4
Tyngsborough town	6,100	98.3	0.4	0.9	<.1	0.0	0.4	178	45	161	198	0.1	0.1	<.1	<.1	70.6	70.8	61.5	64.2	100.0	0.0	48.1
Uxbridge town	7,719	98.9	0.3	0.3	0.1	<.1	0.4	154	11	185	197	0.2	0.2	<.1	<.1	74.1	74.3	58.3	65.6	88.9	33.3	54.2
Wakefield town	19,478	98.3	0.3	0.7	<.1	<.1	0.7	65	44	175	149	0.4	0.5	<.1	<.1	78.5	78.7	63.3	63.2	85.7	100.0	69.3
Walpole town	15,462	96.1	1.7	0.6	0.1	<.1	1.5	83	130	44	60	0.3	0.4	0.1	0.1	76.5	76.4	87.8	66.7	69.6	50.0	77.0
Waltham city	48,967	89.3	2.5	3.2	0.1	0.1	4.7	14	192	30	20	1.1	1.0	0.6	1.3	84.6	86.0	76.6	78.1	93.2	71.8	70.9
Ware town	7,358	98.1	0.1	0.5	0.2	<.1	0.9	159	59	202	101	0.2	0.2	<.1	<.1	75.0	75.6	42.3	78.4	51.5	25.0	47.6
Wareham town	14,409	89.4	2.1	0.4	0.5	4.7	2.8	89	191	35	35	0.3	0.3	0.2	0.2	74.7	75.4	70.9	68.2	81.5	71.8	69.8
Warren town	3,240	98.4	0.4	0.2	0.3	<.1	0.7	210	42	159	136	<.1	<.1	<.1	<.1	73.0	73.4	59.1	50.0	73.3	25.0	51.1
Watertown town	28,578	95.0	1.1	2.1	0.1	<.1	1.7	39	149	72	53	0.6	0.7	0.2	0.3	85.9	86.4	75.0	80.5	94.3	59.1	75.6
Wayland town	9,011	95.3	0.9	2.7	<.1	0.0	1.0	142	143	83	87	0.2	0.2	<.1	<.1	73.2	73.6	66.4	61.8	100.0	0.0	63.9
Webster town	12,507	97.2	0.5	0.5	0.3	<.1	1.5	103	108	138	63	0.3	0.3	<.1	0.1	77.2	78.1	55.4	61.9	66.1	50.0	50.8
Wellesley town	21,216	92.2	1.6	3.9	<.1	<.1	2.2	59	179	46	44	0.5	0.5	0.2	0.3	79.7	79.6	83.9	80.5	80.0	73.3	78.4

¹Separate rankings for 14 counties and 213 cities and towns.

Table B. – 1990 Voting Age Population (VAP) by Race and Ethnic Origin (cont)

County	Total Voting Age Population	Percent of total VAP						Rank[1]				Percent contribution to state VAP				VAP percent of total population						
		Non-Hispanic						Percent of total VAP				Non-Hispanic				Non-Hispanic						
									Non-Hispanic													
		White	Black	Asian and Pacific Islander	Native American	Other	Hispanic	Total	White	Black	Hispanic	Total	White	Black	Hispanic	Total	White	Black	Asian and Pacific Islander	Native American	Other	Hispanic
West Boylston town	5,342	94.4	1.6	0.5	<.1	<.1	3.4	193	158	48	28	0.1	0.1	<.1	0.1	80.8	80.3	97.6	60.0	75.0	50.0	97.8
West Bridgewater town	4,898	98.1	0.6	0.6	<.1	0.3	0.4	201	60	131	201	0.1	0.1	<.1	<.1	76.7	77.0	65.9	69.0	100.0	53.6	57.6
West Springfield town	21,642	95.5	1.1	0.9	0.1	<.1	2.3	53	141	70	43	0.5	0.5	0.1	0.3	78.6	79.4	69.1	66.0	65.3	66.7	62.3
Westborough town	10,981	93.9	1.5	2.5	<.1	0.1	1.8	117	167	50	50	0.2	0.2	<.1	0.1	77.7	78.3	72.3	67.0	70.0	76.2	72.0
Westfield city	29,437	94.9	0.7	0.7	0.1	0.4	3.2	35	150	106	33	0.6	0.7	0.1	0.5	76.7	77.5	66.8	68.9	78.9	88.0	61.0
Westford town	11,773	97.4	0.2	1.5	<.1	<.1	0.9	108	95	196	113	0.3	0.3	<.1	<.1	71.8	72.1	62.2	64.0	47.1	40.0	62.3
Weston town	8,099	93.6	0.7	4.0	0.0	<.1	1.7	149	171	109	54	0.2	0.2	<.1	<.1	79.4	79.9	77.8	68.8	0.0	33.3	82.0
Westport town	10,722	98.6	0.1	0.4	<.1	0.1	0.6	120	24	203	156	0.2	0.3	<.1	<.1	77.4	77.5	84.2	65.1	100.0	66.7	76.1
Westwood town	9,888	98.0	0.3	1.2	<.1	0.0	0.5	129	71	181	180	0.2	0.2	<.1	<.1	78.7	79.1	75.7	62.4	100.0	0.0	61.3
Weymouth town	43,125	97.2	0.9	0.7	0.1	0.1	0.9	20	109	48	99	0.9	1.0	0.2	0.2	79.8	80.0	73.6	67.5	84.5	60.8	72.2
Whitman town	9,543	98.2	0.5	0.2	0.2	0.2	0.7	135	49	141	141	0.2	0.2	<.1	<.1	72.1	72.2	57.3	61.3	78.3	69.2	72.5
Wilbraham town	9,625	97.1	1.2	1.0	<.1	<.1	0.7	133	113	66	140	0.2	0.2	<.1	<.1	76.2	76.6	73.4	57.6	100.0	55.6	66.3
Williamstown town	6,927	91.9	3.2	2.8	0.2	<.1	1.9	165	183	20	47	0.1	0.2	0.1	<.1	84.3	83.8	89.8	92.9	100.0	14.3	86.8
Wilmington town	13,186	98.3	0.4	0.8	0.1	<.1	0.4	97	46	163	202	0.3	0.3	<.1	<.1	74.7	74.9	65.4	62.2	82.4	50.0	63.0
Winchendon town	6,165	98.2	0.2	0.6	0.2	<.1	0.8	176	55	197	126	0.1	0.1	<.1	<.1	70.0	70.2	63.2	62.5	62.5	100.0	55.8
Winchester town	15,829	95.9	0.9	2.4	<.1	<.1	0.8	80	134	86	130	0.3	0.4	<.1	<.1	78.1	78.5	74.3	69.4	91.7	35.7	68.4
Winthrop town	15,151	97.5	0.6	0.6	<.1	<.1	1.1	84	90	126	81	0.3	0.4	<.1	<.1	83.6	83.9	72.2	75.6	72.7	71.4	71.7
Woburn city	28,471	95.7	0.8	1.4	0.1	<.1	1.9	40	137	89	46	0.6	0.7	0.1	0.3	79.2	79.8	70.8	73.9	53.6	61.3	65.2
Worcester city	131,916	87.0	3.3	2.3	0.2	<.1	7.0	2	196	19	10	2.8	2.8	2.3	5.1	77.7	81.2	64.9	66.7	67.6	40.4	56.7
Wrentham town	6,714	98.2	0.7	0.6	<.1	<.1	0.4	170	52	104	204	0.1	0.2	<.1	<.1	74.6	74.7	77.4	65.1	83.3	33.3	64.1
Yarmouth town	17,446	97.5	0.7	0.3	0.2	0.2	1.0	74	89	102	95	0.4	0.4	<.1	<.1	82.4	83.2	55.8	72.8	73.5	52.9	57.6
CONGRESSIONAL																						
District 1	457,863	93.7	1.4	1.2	0.2	<.1	3.6	8	4	9	5	9.8	10.3	3.3	9.0	76.1	77.4	67.8	71.6	71.3	48.4	56.4
District 2	454,404	89.7	4.7	0.9	0.1	<.1	4.5	9	7	3	3	9.7	9.8	11.2	11.4	75.5	77.5	66.6	70.3	72.3	42.4	56.7
District 3	458,187	93.9	1.4	1.5	0.1	0.1	2.9	7	3	8	6	9.8	10.3	3.4	7.4	76.2	77.2	66.3	65.2	70.1	58.4	59.7
District 4	461,073	92.7	1.9	2.0	0.2	1.1	2.2	6	6	5	9	9.9	10.2	4.6	5.6	76.6	77.1	73.8	73.2	75.3	70.6	67.0
District 5	446,756	89.0	1.5	2.9	0.1	<.1	6.4	10	8	7	2	9.6	9.5	3.6	15.8	74.3	76.4	71.3	61.5	71.7	53.3	58.1
District 6	465,983	95.1	1.3	1.2	0.1	<.1	2.3	5	1	10	8	10.0	10.6	3.2	5.9	77.5	78.4	66.3	63.2	73.2	36.4	61.8
District 7	485,704	92.8	1.9	2.5	0.1	<.1	2.6	2	5	4	7	10.4	10.8	4.9	7.1	80.7	81.5	73.6	71.3	76.1	62.3	71.2
District 8	494,335	66.1	18.8	5.4	0.2	0.5	9.0	1	10	1	1	10.6	7.8	48.8	24.6	82.2	88.7	70.9	81.0	75.9	66.4	69.3
District 9	472,887	87.6	5.2	2.5	0.1	0.6	3.8	3	9	2	4	10.1	9.9	12.9	10.0	78.6	80.5	67.4	72.3	72.4	62.0	64.6
District 10	466,158	95.0	1.7	1.3	0.3	0.5	1.2	4	2	6	10	10.0	10.6	4.0	3.1	77.5	78.1	66.2	70.0	69.7	65.1	65.3

[1]Separate rankings for 14 counties and 213 cities and towns.

Table C. – Voter Participation: November 3, 1992, General Election

County	Estimated Voting Age Population (VAP), 1992	Voter registration (REG) Total	% contribution to state REG	% of 1992 VAP	Rank by % of 1992 VAP	Voter turnout Highest office Actual	Total	Office	% of 1992 VAP	Maximum vote Total	% contribution to state turnout	% of REG	Rank by % of REG[1]	% of 1992 VAP	Rank by % 1992 VAP	Percent drop-off, by office President	Senator	Governor	Representative
Barnstable	152,484	129,036	3.8	84.6	3	111,880	108,997	P	71.5	111,880	4.0	86.7	4	73.4	3	2.6	-	-	4.1
Berkshire	104,145	80,700	2.4	77.5	7	68,456	67,746	P	65.0	68,456	2.4	84.8	8	65.7	7	1.0	-	-	3.7
Bristol	382,364	255,380	7.6	66.8	12	215,519	211,754	P	55.4	215,519	7.6	84.4	11	56.4	13	1.7	-	-	8.1
Dukes	9,409	9,048	0.3	96.2	2	7,931	7,888	P	83.8	7,931	0.3	87.7	1	84.3	2	0.5	-	-	1.9
Essex	508,203	384,383	11.5	75.6	8	328,180	322,328	P	63.4	328,180	11.6	85.4	7	64.6	8	1.8	-	-	7.4
Franklin	53,064	42,570	1.3	80.2	5	36,021	35,827	P	67.5	36,021	1.3	84.6	10	67.9	5	0.5	-	-	2.6
Hampden	337,818	225,086	6.7	66.6	13	190,853	188,265	P	55.7	190,853	6.8	84.8	9	56.5	12	1.4	-	-	6.1
Hampshire	112,233	80,899	2.4	72.1	10	70,869	70,072	P	62.4	70,869	2.5	87.6	2	63.1	10	1.1	-	-	5.9
Middlesex	1,085,272	815,979	24.3	75.2	9	699,754	689,452	P	63.5	699,754	24.8	85.8	5	64.5	9	1.5	-	-	8.2
Nantucket	4,857	5,164	0.2	106.3	1	4,240	4,216	P	86.8	4,240	0.2	82.1	12	87.3	1	0.6	-	-	2.4
Norfolk	477,450	382,485	11.4	80.1	6	332,589	324,390	P	67.9	332,589	11.8	87.0	3	69.7	4	2.5	-	-	7.6
Plymouth	322,070	262,907	7.8	81.6	4	212,511	207,710	P	64.5	212,511	7.5	80.8	13	66.0	6	2.3	-	-	5.7
Suffolk	521,766	303,727	9.1	58.2	14	224,223	219,273	P	42.0	224,223	7.9	73.8	14	43.0	14	2.2	-	-	12.1
Worcester	535,865	374,554	11.2	69.9	11	319,936	315,782	P	58.9	319,936	11.3	85.4	6	59.7	11	1.3	-	-	6.6
MASSACHUSETTS	4,607,000	3,351,918	100.0	72.8		2,822,962	2,773,700		60.2	2,822,962	100.0	84.2		61.3		1.7	-	-	7.4
CITIES AND TOWNS																			
Abington town	-	8,372	0.2	-	-	7,174	6,924	P	-	7,174	0.3	85.7	136	-	-	3.5	-	-	8.3
Acton town	-	11,402	0.3	-	-	10,393	10,338	P	-	10,393	0.4	91.2	16	-	-	0.5	-	-	6.2
Acushnet town	-	5,646	0.2	-	-	4,909	4,863	P	-	4,909	0.2	86.9	97	-	-	0.9	-	-	5.1
Adams town	-	5,720	0.2	-	-	4,777	4,726	P	-	4,777	0.2	83.5	173	-	-	1.1	-	-	2.6
Agawam town	-	15,692	0.5	-	-	13,548	13,498	P	-	13,548	0.5	86.3	117	-	-	0.4	-	-	4.7
Amesbury town	-	8,177	0.2	-	-	7,013	6,966	P	-	7,013	0.2	85.8	134	-	-	0.7	-	-	5.4
Amherst town	-	13,225	0.4	-	-	11,830	11,775	P	-	11,830	0.4	89.5	40	-	-	0.5	-	-	7.7
Andover town	-	19,133	0.6	-	-	16,927	16,836	P	-	16,927	0.6	88.5	64	-	-	0.5	-	-	4.5
Arlington town	-	29,647	0.9	-	-	26,724	25,685	P	-	26,724	0.9	90.1	28	-	-	3.9	-	-	11.9
Ashburnham town	-	2,921	<.1	-	-	2,603	2,578	P	-	2,603	<.1	89.1	50	-	-	1.0	-	-	5.0
Ashland town	-	7,663	0.2	-	-	6,655	6,495	P	-	6,655	0.2	86.8	103	-	-	2.4	-	-	11.4
Athol town	-	5,715	0.2	-	-	4,787	4,751	P	-	4,787	0.2	83.8	168	-	-	0.8	-	-	4.8
Attleboro city	-	18,379	0.5	-	-	15,492	15,114	P	-	15,492	0.5	84.3	158	-	-	2.4	-	-	7.9
Auburn town	-	9,733	0.3	-	-	8,457	8,215	P	-	8,457	0.3	86.9	98	-	-	2.9	-	-	11.5
Ayer town	-	2,841	<.1	-	-	2,487	2,472	P	-	2,487	<.1	87.5	85	-	-	0.6	-	-	5.1
Barnstable town	-	25,908	0.8	-	-	22,747	21,584	P	-	22,747	0.8	87.8	80	-	-	5.1	-	-	6.1
Barre town	-	2,827	<.1	-	-	2,434	2,424	P	-	2,434	<.1	86.1	126	-	-	0.4	-	-	8.2
Bedford town	-	7,834	0.2	-	-	6,777	6,747	P	-	6,777	0.2	86.5	113	-	-	0.4	-	-	8.0
Belchertown town	-	6,155	0.2	-	-	5,479	5,306	P	-	5,479	0.2	89.0	51	-	-	3.2	-	-	6.8
Bellingham town	-	8,333	0.2	-	-	7,260	7,140	P	-	7,260	0.3	87.1	92	-	-	1.7	-	-	13.7
Belmont town	-	17,058	0.5	-	-	15,093	14,656	P	-	15,093	0.5	88.5	63	-	-	2.9	-	-	18.2
Beverly city	-	23,321	0.7	-	-	20,423	19,791	P	-	20,423	0.7	87.6	84	-	-	3.1	-	-	15.4
Billerica town	-	20,444	0.6	-	-	17,658	17,042	P	-	17,658	0.6	86.4	115	-	-	3.5	-	-	7.7
Blackstone town	-	4,364	0.1	-	-	3,733	3,630	P	-	3,733	0.1	85.5	139	-	-	2.8	-	-	13.7
Boston city	-	256,487	7.7	-	-	186,900	183,131	P	-	186,900	6.6	72.9	208	-	-	2.0	-	-	12.5
Bourne town	-	8,858	0.3	-	-	7,885	7,760	P	-	7,885	0.3	89.0	52	-	-	1.6	-	-	2.4
Boxford town	-	4,261	0.1	-	-	3,927	3,912	P	-	3,927	0.1	92.2	8	-	-	0.4	-	-	2.8
Braintree town	-	21,174	0.6	-	-	18,913	18,730	P	-	18,913	0.7	89.3	48	-	-	1.0	-	-	6.4
Brewster town	-	6,086	0.2	-	-	5,480	5,438	P	-	5,480	0.2	90.0	32	-	-	0.8	-	-	1.6
Bridgewater town	-	10,701	0.3	-	-	8,831	8,221	P	-	8,831	0.3	82.5	184	-	-	6.9	-	-	11.3
Brockton city	-	42,538	1.3	-	-	31,647	29,799	P	-	31,647	1.1	74.4	205	-	-	5.8	-	-	10.1
Brookline town	-	35,241	1.1	-	-	27,727	27,547	P	-	27,727	1.0	78.7	200	-	-	0.6	-	-	6.3
Burlington town	-	14,597	0.4	-	-	12,791	12,697	P	-	12,791	0.5	87.6	82	-	-	0.7	-	-	6.1
Cambridge city	-	50,347	1.5	-	-	42,237	41,158	P	-	42,237	1.5	83.9	165	-	-	2.6	-	-	19.8
Canton town	-	12,235	0.4	-	-	11,135	10,834	P	-	11,135	0.4	91.0	17	-	-	2.7	-	-	10.1
Carver town	-	6,005	0.2	-	-	5,186	5,176	P	-	5,186	0.2	86.4	116	-	-	0.2	-	-	4.6
Chatham town	-	5,211	0.2	-	-	4,558	4,523	P	-	4,558	0.2	87.5	86	-	-	0.8	-	-	1.3
Chelmsford town	-	20,396	0.6	-	-	18,418	18,302	P	-	18,418	0.7	90.3	27	-	-	0.6	-	-	5.9
Chelsea city	-	10,920	0.3	-	-	8,084	7,847	P	-	8,084	0.3	74.0	206	-	-	2.9	-	-	9.6
Chicopee city	-	28,469	0.8	-	-	24,282	24,129	P	-	24,282	0.9	85.3	146	-	-	0.6	-	-	2.6
Clarksburg town	-	1,077	<.1	-	-	935	929	P	-	935	<.1	86.8	105	-	-	0.6	-	-	3.0
Clinton town	-	7,659	0.2	-	-	6,301	6,263	P	-	6,301	0.2	82.3	185	-	-	0.6	-	-	2.2
Cohasset town	-	5,270	0.2	-	-	4,577	4,333	C	-	4,577	0.2	86.9	102	-	-	6.8	-	-	5.3
Concord town	-	11,037	0.3	-	-	10,001	9,967	P	-	10,001	0.4	90.6	22	-	-	0.3	-	-	6.8
Dalton town	-	4,219	0.1	-	-	3,675	3,624	P	-	3,675	0.1	87.1	93	-	-	1.4	-	-	2.9
Danvers town	-	15,457	0.5	-	-	13,358	13,088	P	-	13,358	0.5	86.3	114	-	-	2.0	-	-	11.3
Dartmouth town	-	14,664	0.4	-	-	12,997	12,934	P	-	12,997	0.5	88.6	61	-	-	0.5	-	-	11.0
Dedham town	-	14,551	0.4	-	-	13,466	13,056	P	-	13,466	0.5	92.5	5	-	-	3.0	-	-	9.6
Deerfield town	-	3,932	0.1	-	-	3,004	2,995	P	-	3,004	0.1	76.4	204	-	-	0.3	-	-	2.0
Dennis town	-	9,818	0.3	-	-	8,732	8,438	P	-	8,732	0.3	88.9	54	-	-	3.4	-	-	5.7
Dracut town	-	15,885	0.5	-	-	13,575	12,588	P	-	13,575	0.5	85.5	141	-	-	7.3	-	-	9.6
Dudley town	-	5,033	0.2	-	-	4,319	4,196	P	-	4,319	0.2	85.8	132	-	-	2.8	-	-	12.8

[1]Separate rankings for 14 counties and 213 cities and towns.

Table C. – **Voter Participation: November 3, 1992, General Election (cont)**

County	Estimated Voting Age Population (VAP), 1992	Voter registration (REG)				Voter turnout										Percent drop-off, by office			
							Highest office			Maximum vote									
		Total	% contribution to state REG	% of 1992 VAP	Rank by % of 1992 VAP	Actual	Total	Office	% of 1992 VAP	Total	% contribution to state turnout	% of REG	Rank by % of REG[1]	% of 1992 VAP	Rank by % 1992 VAP	President	Senator	Governor	Representative
Duxbury town	-	9,506	0.3	-	-	8,393	8,337	P	-	8,393	0.3	88.3	67	-	-	0.7	-	-	2.0
East Bridgewater town....	-	6,546	0.2	-	-	5,644	5,624	P	-	5,644	0.2	86.2	122	-	-	0.4	-	-	7.9
East Longmeadow town..	-	8,448	0.3	-	-	7,566	7,513	P	-	7,566	0.3	89.6	38	-	-	0.7	-	-	3.9
Easthampton town	-	8,980	0.3	-	-	7,963	7,937	P	-	7,963	0.3	88.7	60	-	-	0.3	-	-	2.2
Easton town	-	11,785	0.4	-	-	10,375	10,337	P	-	10,375	0.4	88.0	75	-	-	0.4	-	-	5.5
Erving town.....................	-	905	<.1	-	-	771	766	P	-	771	<.1	85.2	147	-	-	0.6	-	-	2.2
Everett city	-	18,371	0.5	-	-	15,441	15,250	P	-	15,441	0.5	84.1	163	-	-	1.2	-	-	7.7
Fairhaven town	-	9,511	0.3	-	-	7,934	7,903	P	-	7,934	0.3	83.4	174	-	-	0.4	-	-	6.3
Fall River city	-	39,923	1.2	-	-	31,921	31,210	P	-	31,921	1.1	80.0	195	-	-	2.2	-	-	11.1
Falmouth town	-	20,152	0.6	-	-	16,377	15,996	P	-	16,377	0.6	81.3	192	-	-	2.3	-	-	5.2
Fitchburg city	-	18,102	0.5	-	-	14,404	13,731	P	-	14,404	0.5	79.6	196	-	-	4.7	-	-	10.5
Foxborough town	-	9,245	0.3	-	-	8,139	8,092	P	-	8,139	0.3	88.0	74	-	-	0.6	-	-	5.6
Framingham town	-	35,167	1.0	-	-	30,143	29,542	P	-	30,143	1.1	85.7	135	-	-	2.0	-	-	10.7
Franklin town	-	13,414	0.4	-	-	11,678	11,487	P	-	11,678	0.4	87.1	94	-	-	1.6	-	-	7.7
Freetown town	-	4,807	0.1	-	-	4,143	4,126	P	-	4,143	0.1	86.2	124	-	-	0.4	-	-	3.5
Gardner city	-	9,763	0.3	-	-	8,289	8,157	P	-	8,289	0.3	84.9	152	-	-	1.6	-	-	7.0
Gloucester city	-	17,741	0.5	-	-	14,336	14,099	P	-	14,336	0.5	80.8	193	-	-	1.7	-	-	5.4
Grafton town	-	8,209	0.2	-	-	6,835	6,779	P	-	6,835	0.2	83.3	177	-	-	0.8	-	-	3.6
Great Barrington town....	-	4,075	0.1	-	-	3,496	3,452	P	-	3,496	0.1	85.8	133	-	-	1.3	-	-	4.5
Greenfield town	-	9,728	0.3	-	-	8,628	8,591	P	-	8,628	0.3	88.7	59	-	-	0.4	-	-	3.1
Groton town	-	4,777	0.1	-	-	4,345	4,333	P	-	4,345	0.2	91.0	18	-	-	0.3	-	-	5.6
Groveland town	-	3,535	0.1	-	-	3,041	3,028	P	-	3,041	0.1	86.0	127	-	-	0.4	-	-	3.2
Hamilton town................	-	4,686	0.1	-	-	4,277	4,254	P	-	4,277	0.2	91.3	15	-	-	0.5	-	-	4.0
Hanover town	-	7,486	0.2	-	-	6,899	6,841	P	-	6,899	0.2	92.2	9	-	-	0.8	-	-	2.4
Hanson town	-	5,449	0.2	-	-	4,656	4,100	P	-	4,656	0.2	85.4	143	-	-	11.9	-	-	13.8
Hardwick town	-	1,254	<.1	-	-	1,236	1,229	P	-	1,236	<.1	98.6	1	-	-	0.6	-	-	4.4
Haverhill city..................	-	27,020	0.8	-	-	22,890	22,678	P	-	22,890	0.8	84.7	156	-	-	0.9	-	-	4.6
Hingham town	-	13,923	0.4	-	-	12,478	12,378	P	-	12,478	0.4	89.6	37	-	-	0.8	-	-	2.3
Holbrook town	-	6,573	0.2	-	-	5,738	5,670	P	-	5,738	0.2	87.3	88	-	-	1.2	-	-	4.5
Holden town	-	9,742	0.3	-	-	8,593	8,559	P	-	8,593	0.3	88.2	70	-	-	0.4	-	-	3.2
Holliston town	-	9,442	0.3	-	-	7,691	7,534	P	-	7,691	0.3	81.5	191	-	-	2.0	-	-	6.8
Holyoke city	-	21,822	0.7	-	-	15,896	15,582	P	-	15,896	0.6	72.8	209	-	-	2.0	-	-	8.1
Hopkinton town	-	6,100	0.2	-	-	5,517	5,491	P	-	5,517	0.2	90.4	25	-	-	0.5	-	-	3.9
Hudson town	-	10,054	0.3	-	-	8,432	8,389	P	-	8,432	0.3	83.9	166	-	-	0.5	-	-	5.9
Hull town........................	-	7,624	0.2	-	-	5,466	5,318	P	-	5,466	0.2	71.7	211	-	-	2.7	-	-	5.9
Ipswich town	-	8,116	0.2	-	-	7,177	7,137	P	-	7,177	0.3	88.4	66	-	-	0.6	-	-	3.9
Kingston town	-	5,682	0.2	-	-	5,033	4,981	P	-	5,033	0.2	88.6	62	-	-	1.0	-	-	3.2
Lawrence city	-	22,240	0.7	-	-	16,352	16,139	P	-	16,352	0.6	73.5	207	-	-	1.3	-	-	5.0
Leicester town	-	5,696	0.2	-	-	5,069	5,043	P	-	5,069	0.2	89.0	53	-	-	0.5	-	-	10.5
Leominster city	-	20,086	0.6	-	-	17,027	16,832	P	-	17,027	0.6	84.8	154	-	-	1.1	-	-	7.7
Lexington town	-	21,179	0.6	-	-	18,071	17,960	P	-	18,071	0.6	85.3	145	-	-	0.6	-	-	6.5
Lincoln town	-	3,564	0.1	-	-	3,296	3,131	P	-	3,296	0.1	92.5	7	-	-	5.0	-	-	9.7
Littleton town	-	4,709	0.1	-	-	4,137	4,114	P	-	4,137	0.1	87.9	79	-	-	0.6	-	-	5.0
Longmeadow town	-	10,492	0.3	-	-	9,374	8,937	P	-	9,374	0.3	89.3	47	-	-	4.7	-	-	10.1
Lowell city	-	42,136	1.3	-	-	32,989	32,123	P	-	32,989	1.2	78.3	201	-	-	2.6	-	-	7.8
Ludlow town	-	10,174	0.3	-	-	8,838	8,615	P	-	8,838	0.3	86.9	100	-	-	2.5	-	-	9.0
Lunenburg town	-	5,647	0.2	-	-	4,703	4,634	P	-	4,703	0.2	83.3	176	-	-	1.5	-	-	8.6
Lynn city	-	38,582	1.2	-	-	32,053	30,477	P	-	32,053	1.1	83.1	180	-	-	4.9	-	-	13.4
Lynnfield town	-	7,838	0.2	-	-	6,966	6,901	P	-	6,966	0.2	88.9	55	-	-	0.9	-	-	3.7
Malden city	-	27,934	0.8	-	-	23,374	23,192	P	-	23,374	0.8	83.7	170	-	-	0.8	-	-	7.3
Mansfield town	-	9,941	0.3	-	-	8,831	8,783	P	-	8,831	0.3	88.8	56	-	-	0.5	-	-	5.4
Marblehead town	-	14,138	0.4	-	-	12,738	12,605	P	-	12,738	0.5	90.1	30	-	-	1.0	-	-	4.1
Marlborough city	-	17,946	0.5	-	-	14,989	14,796	P	-	14,989	0.5	83.5	172	-	-	1.3	-	-	6.2
Marshfield town	-	14,622	0.4	-	-	12,321	12,239	P	-	12,321	0.4	84.3	159	-	-	0.7	-	-	2.5
Mashpee town	-	5,422	0.2	-	-	4,619	4,597	P	-	4,619	0.2	85.2	148	-	-	0.5	-	-	1.7
Maynard town	-	6,619	0.2	-	-	5,554	5,534	P	-	5,554	0.2	83.9	164	-	-	0.4	-	-	6.5
Medfield town	-	6,944	0.2	-	-	6,352	6,321	P	-	6,352	0.2	91.5	12	-	-	0.5	-	-	7.8
Medford city	-	32,716	1.0	-	-	28,339	27,987	P	-	28,339	1.0	86.6	108	-	-	1.2	-	-	5.5
Medway town	-	6,278	0.2	-	-	5,491	5,343	P	-	5,491	0.2	87.5	87	-	-	2.7	-	-	9.8
Melrose city	-	18,589	0.6	-	-	16,394	16,232	P	-	16,394	0.6	88.2	71	-	-	1.0	-	-	5.5
Methuen town	-	23,586	0.7	-	-	19,921	19,677	P	-	19,921	0.7	84.5	157	-	-	1.2	-	-	5.1
Middleborough town	-	9,423	0.3	-	-	8,005	7,966	P	-	8,005	0.3	85.0	151	-	-	0.5	-	-	5.5
Milford town	-	13,318	0.4	-	-	11,717	11,561	P	-	11,717	0.4	88.0	76	-	-	1.3	-	-	9.2
Millbury town	-	7,186	0.2	-	-	6,269	6,204	P	-	6,269	0.2	87.2	90	-	-	1.0	-	-	10.0
Millis town	-	4,673	0.1	-	-	4,212	4,202	P	-	4,212	0.1	90.1	29	-	-	0.2	-	-	4.8
Milton town	-	17,589	0.5	-	-	15,175	14,999	P	-	15,175	0.5	86.3	119	-	-	1.2	-	-	8.1
Monson town	-	4,255	0.1	-	-	3,764	3,705	P	-	3,764	0.1	88.5	65	-	-	1.6	-	-	9.0
Montague town	-	5,181	0.2	-	-	4,108	4,071	P	-	4,108	0.1	79.3	197	-	-	0.9	-	-	1.9
Natick town	-	21,370	0.6	-	-	17,481	17,296	P	-	17,481	0.6	81.8	189	-	-	1.1	-	-	8.1
Needham town	-	19,520	0.6	-	-	17,530	17,101	P	-	17,530	0.6	89.8	35	-	-	2.4	-	-	9.7

[1]Separate rankings for 14 counties and 213 cities and towns.

Table C. – Voter Participation: November 3, 1992, General Election (cont)

County	Estimated Voting Age Population (VAP), 1992	Voter registration (REG)				Voter turnout										Percent drop-off, by office			
							Highest office			Maximum vote									
		Total	% contribution to state REG	% of 1992 VAP	Rank by % of 1992 VAP	Actual	Total	Office	% of 1992 VAP	Total	% contribution to state turnout	% of REG	Rank by % of REG[1]	% of 1992 VAP	Rank by % 1992 VAP	President	Senator	Governor	Representative
New Bedford city	-	39,947	1.2	-	-	33,608	33,322	P	-	33,608	1.2	84.1	161	-	-	0.9	-	-	5.8
Newbury town	-	4,233	0.1	-	-	3,675	3,662	P	-	3,675	0.1	86.8	104	-	-	0.4	-	-	3.5
Newburyport city	-	11,323	0.3	-	-	9,524	9,438	P	-	9,524	0.3	84.1	162	-	-	0.9	-	-	4.7
Newton city	-	50,969	1.5	-	-	44,916	44,705	P	-	44,916	1.6	88.1	73	-	-	0.5	-	-	5.1
Norfolk town	-	4,895	0.1	-	-	4,439	4,416	P	-	4,439	0.2	90.7	21	-	-	0.5	-	-	2.8
North Adams city	-	7,711	0.2	-	-	6,457	6,389	P	-	6,457	0.2	83.7	169	-	-	1.1	-	-	3.3
North Andover town	-	14,660	0.4	-	-	12,636	12,569	P	-	12,636	0.4	86.2	123	-	-	0.5	-	-	5.2
North Attleborough town	-	13,102	0.4	-	-	11,402	10,654	P	-	11,402	0.4	87.0	96	-	-	6.6	-	-	9.1
North Reading town	-	7,857	0.2	-	-	7,073	7,036	P	-	7,073	0.3	90.0	33	-	-	0.5	-	-	4.6
Northampton city	-	17,398	0.5	-	-	15,252	15,174	P	-	15,252	0.5	87.7	81	-	-	0.5	-	-	7.1
Northborough town	-	7,231	0.2	-	-	6,632	6,567	P	-	6,632	0.2	91.7	11	-	-	1.0	-	-	3.0
Northbridge town	-	7,461	0.2	-	-	6,373	6,347	P	-	6,373	0.2	85.4	144	-	-	0.4	-	-	3.6
Norton town	-	7,844	0.2	-	-	6,765	6,729	P	-	6,765	0.2	86.2	121	-	-	0.5	-	-	4.3
Norwell town	-	6,275	0.2	-	-	5,652	5,639	P	-	5,652	0.2	90.1	31	-	-	0.2	-	-	2.6
Norwood town	-	17,577	0.5	-	-	15,460	15,001	P	-	15,460	0.5	88.0	77	-	-	3.0	-	-	10.2
Orange town	-	3,829	0.1	-	-	3,313	3,302	P	-	3,313	0.1	86.5	112	-	-	0.3	-	-	3.7
Orleans town	-	4,753	0.1	-	-	4,251	4,142	P	-	4,251	0.2	89.4	43	-	-	2.6	-	-	4.5
Oxford town	-	6,651	0.2	-	-	5,692	5,658	P	-	5,692	0.2	85.6	138	-	-	0.6	-	-	10.6
Palmer town	-	7,204	0.2	-	-	6,035	5,748	P	-	6,035	0.2	83.8	167	-	-	4.8	-	-	12.5
Peabody city	-	28,625	0.9	-	-	24,981	24,704	P	-	24,981	0.9	87.3	89	-	-	1.1	-	-	2.8
Pembroke town	-	8,894	0.3	-	-	7,893	7,842	P	-	7,893	0.3	88.7	58	-	-	0.6	-	-	5.1
Pepperell town	-	5,626	0.2	-	-	4,873	4,863	P	-	4,873	0.2	86.6	109	-	-	0.2	-	-	5.2
Pittsfield city	-	27,510	0.8	-	-	23,180	22,882	P	-	23,180	0.8	84.3	160	-	-	1.3	-	-	3.8
Plainville town	-	3,882	0.1	-	-	3,361	3,300	P	-	3,361	0.1	86.6	110	-	-	1.8	-	-	8.4
Plymouth town	-	33,737	1.0	-	-	21,722	21,614	P	-	21,722	0.8	64.4	213	-	-	0.5	-	-	4.3
Quincy city	-	48,207	1.4	-	-	41,202	40,495	P	-	41,202	1.5	85.5	140	-	-	1.7	-	-	7.1
Randolph town	-	16,595	0.5	-	-	14,383	14,245	P	-	14,383	0.5	86.7	107	-	-	1.0	-	-	7.4
Raynham town	-	6,070	0.2	-	-	5,350	5,195	P	-	5,350	0.2	88.1	72	-	-	2.9	-	-	8.9
Reading town	-	14,922	0.4	-	-	13,621	13,446	P	-	13,621	0.5	91.3	14	-	-	1.3	-	-	8.7
Rehoboth town	-	5,172	0.2	-	-	4,566	4,539	P	-	4,566	0.2	88.3	68	-	-	0.6	-	-	3.9
Revere city	-	24,042	0.7	-	-	19,686	18,826	P	-	19,686	0.7	81.9	188	-	-	4.4	-	-	12.8
Rockland town	-	9,395	0.3	-	-	8,064	7,610	P	-	8,064	0.3	85.8	131	-	-	5.6	-	-	7.6
Rockport town	-	5,208	0.2	-	-	4,520	4,497	P	-	4,520	0.2	86.8	106	-	-	0.5	-	-	4.5
Salem city	-	21,310	0.6	-	-	18,353	17,985	P	-	18,353	0.6	86.1	125	-	-	2.0	-	-	13.2
Salisbury town	-	4,464	0.1	-	-	3,531	3,138	P	-	3,531	0.1	79.1	199	-	-	11.1	-	-	16.7
Sandwich town	-	10,209	0.3	-	-	9,151	9,116	P	-	9,151	0.3	89.6	36	-	-	0.4	-	-	1.7
Saugus town	-	15,999	0.5	-	-	13,897	13,405	P	-	13,897	0.5	86.9	101	-	-	3.5	-	-	15.1
Scituate town	-	12,329	0.4	-	-	10,592	10,494	P	-	10,592	0.4	85.9	130	-	-	0.9	-	-	2.4
Seekonk town	-	7,598	0.2	-	-	6,790	6,491	P	-	6,790	0.2	89.4	46	-	-	4.4	-	-	10.8
Sharon town	-	10,367	0.3	-	-	9,266	9,211	P	-	9,266	0.3	89.4	45	-	-	0.6	-	-	2.6
Shrewsbury town	-	15,430	0.5	-	-	13,802	13,494	P	-	13,802	0.5	89.4	41	-	-	2.2	-	-	5.1
Somerset town	-	11,515	0.3	-	-	9,941	9,893	P	-	9,941	0.4	86.3	118	-	-	0.5	-	-	6.4
Somerville city	-	42,829	1.3	-	-	30,768	30,399	P	-	30,768	1.1	71.8	210	-	-	1.2	-	-	5.9
South Hadley town	-	10,431	0.3	-	-	8,647	8,272	P	-	8,647	0.3	82.9	181	-	-	4.3	-	-	10.8
Southborough town	-	4,577	0.1	-	-	4,095	4,084	P	-	4,095	0.1	89.5	39	-	-	0.3	-	-	6.4
Southbridge town	-	8,767	0.3	-	-	7,182	7,158	P	-	7,182	0.3	81.9	187	-	-	0.3	-	-	12.9
Southwick town	-	4,116	0.1	-	-	3,703	3,641	P	-	3,703	0.1	90.0	34	-	-	1.7	-	-	4.9
Spencer town	-	6,456	0.2	-	-	5,371	5,288	P	-	5,371	0.2	83.2	179	-	-	1.5	-	-	10.4
Springfield city	-	59,850	1.8	-	-	50,859	50,111	P	-	50,859	1.8	85.0	150	-	-	1.5	-	-	7.5
Stoneham town	-	13,329	0.4	-	-	11,723	11,629	P	-	11,723	0.4	88.0	78	-	-	0.8	-	-	3.9
Stoughton town	-	15,531	0.5	-	-	13,171	13,065	P	-	13,171	0.5	84.8	153	-	-	0.8	-	-	7.2
Sudbury town	-	10,057	0.3	-	-	8,990	8,967	P	-	8,990	0.3	89.4	44	-	-	0.3	-	-	9.2
Sutton town	-	4,228	0.1	-	-	3,753	3,710	P	-	3,753	0.1	88.8	57	-	-	1.1	-	-	10.5
Swampscott town	-	10,067	0.3	-	-	8,328	8,227	P	-	8,328	0.3	82.7	183	-	-	1.2	-	-	5.0
Taunton city	-	25,681	0.8	-	-	20,048	19,483	P	-	20,048	0.7	78.1	202	-	-	2.8	-	-	12.6
Templeton town	-	3,545	0.1	-	-	3,005	2,991	P	-	3,005	0.1	84.8	155	-	-	0.5	-	-	5.0
Tewksbury town	-	15,277	0.5	-	-	14,076	14,038	P	-	14,076	0.5	92.1	10	-	-	0.3	-	-	4.8
Townsend town	-	4,622	0.1	-	-	4,001	3,953	P	-	4,001	0.1	86.6	111	-	-	1.2	-	-	8.8
Tyngsborough town	-	4,654	0.1	-	-	4,251	4,238	P	-	4,251	0.2	91.3	13	-	-	0.3	-	-	4.9
Uxbridge town	-	5,554	0.2	-	-	5,281	5,256	P	-	5,281	0.2	95.1	2	-	-	0.5	-	-	9.7
Wakefield town	-	14,871	0.4	-	-	13,973	13,776	P	-	13,973	0.5	94.0	3	-	-	1.4	-	-	7.1
Walpole town	-	13,059	0.4	-	-	11,525	11,257	P	-	11,525	0.4	88.3	69	-	-	2.3	-	-	9.8
Waltham city	-	29,726	0.9	-	-	24,243	23,975	P	-	24,243	0.9	81.6	190	-	-	1.1	-	-	11.2
Ware town	-	5,369	0.2	-	-	4,682	4,657	P	-	4,682	0.2	87.2	91	-	-	0.5	-	-	4.8
Wareham town	-	12,558	0.4	-	-	8,935	8,887	P	-	8,935	0.3	71.1	212	-	-	0.5	-	-	4.2
Warren town	-	2,446	<.1	-	-	2,035	2,023	P	-	2,035	<.1	83.2	178	-	-	0.6	-	-	3.6
Watertown town	-	19,882	0.6	-	-	17,413	17,239	P	-	17,413	0.6	87.6	83	-	-	1.0	-	-	6.0
Wayland town	-	8,302	0.2	-	-	7,681	7,629	P	-	7,681	0.3	92.5	6	-	-	0.7	-	-	8.9
Webster town	-	8,224	0.2	-	-	6,758	6,576	P	-	6,758	0.2	82.2	186	-	-	2.7	-	-	11.3
Wellesley town	-	16,208	0.5	-	-	15,159	14,691	P	-	15,159	0.5	93.5	4	-	-	3.1	-	-	7.9

[1]Separate rankings for 14 counties and 213 cities and towns.

Table C. – **Voter Participation: November 3, 1992, General Election (cont)**

County	Estimated Voting Age Population (VAP), 1992	Voter registration (REG)				Voter turnout										Percent drop-off, by office			
							Highest office			Maximum vote									
		Total	% contribution to state REG	% of 1992 VAP	Rank by % of 1992 VAP	Actual	Total	Office	% of 1992 VAP	Total	% contribution to state turnout	% of REG	Rank by % of REG[1]	% of 1992 VAP	Rank by % 1992 VAP	President	Senator	Governor	Representative
West Boylston town	-	3,925	0.1	-	-	3,562	3,548	P	-	3,562	0.1	90.8	20	-	-	0.4	-	-	1.8
West Bridgewater town ..	-	4,373	0.1	-	-	3,799	3,774	P	-	3,799	0.1	86.9	99	-	-	0.7	-	-	5.9
West Springfield town	-	14,590	0.4	-	-	12,700	12,649	P	-	12,700	0.4	87.0	95	-	-	0.4	-	-	4.7
Westborough town	-	8,917	0.3	-	-	7,976	7,955	P	-	7,976	0.3	89.4	42	-	-	0.3	-	-	3.8
Westfield city	-	20,718	0.6	-	-	17,259	17,170	P	-	17,259	0.6	83.3	175	-	-	0.5	-	-	3.1
Westford town................	-	10,553	0.3	-	-	9,588	9,516	P	-	9,588	0.3	90.9	19	-	-	0.8	-	-	5.3
Weston town	-	7,106	0.2	-	-	6,429	6,131	P	-	6,429	0.2	90.5	24	-	-	4.6	-	-	9.0
Westport town................	-	8,476	0.3	-	-	7,243	7,088	P	-	7,243	0.3	85.5	142	-	-	2.1	-	-	10.0
Westwood town	-	9,294	0.3	-	-	8,395	8,290	P	-	8,395	0.3	90.3	26	-	-	1.3	-	-	7.0
Weymouth town	-	34,017	1.0	-	-	28,454	26,215	C	-	28,454	1.0	83.6	171	-	-	11.1	-	-	7.9
Whitman town................	-	7,584	0.2	-	-	6,519	6,432	P	-	6,519	0.2	86.0	128	-	-	1.3	-	-	5.8
Wilbraham town	-	8,341	0.2	-	-	7,554	7,527	P	-	7,554	0.3	90.6	23	-	-	0.4	-	-	5.7
Williamstown town	-	4,906	0.1	-	-	4,217	4,152	P	-	4,217	0.1	86.0	129	-	-	1.5	-	-	4.8
Wilmington town.............	-	11,691	0.3	-	-	9,956	9,919	P	-	9,956	0.4	85.2	149	-	-	0.4	-	-	7.9
Winchendon town	-	4,319	0.1	-	-	3,422	3,307	P	-	3,422	0.1	79.2	198	-	-	3.4	-	-	11.1
Winchester town.............	-	14,300	0.4	-	-	12,744	12,668	P	-	12,744	0.5	89.1	49	-	-	0.6	-	-	5.9
Winthrop town................	-	12,278	0.4	-	-	9,553	9,469	P	-	9,553	0.3	77.8	203	-	-	0.9	-	-	5.2
Woburn city...................	-	22,387	0.7	-	-	18,551	18,466	P	-	18,551	0.7	82.9	182	-	-	0.5	-	-	5.7
Worcester city................	-	75,988	2.3	-	-	61,147	60,307	P	-	61,147	2.2	80.5	194	-	-	1.4	-	-	3.6
Wrentham town	-	5,251	0.2	-	-	4,486	4,496	P	-	4,496	0.2	85.6	137	-	-	0.0	-	-	9.2
Yarmouth town	-	14,912	0.4	-	-	12,862	12,421	P	-	12,862	0.5	86.3	120	-	-	3.4	-	-	5.5

[1]Separate rankings for 14 counties and 213 cities and towns.

Table D. — Voter Registration by Political Party Affiliation: November 3, 1992, General Election

County	Total voter registration	Political party affiliation Democrat (DEM)	Republican (REP)	Independent (IND)	Plurality Total	Party	Percent of total registration DEM	REP	IND	Rank[1] DEM	REP	IND	Percent contribution to state registration Total	DEM	REP	IND
Barnstable	129,036	33,584	27,263	67,862	34,278	I	26.1	21.2	52.7	12	1	5	3.8	2.5	6.1	4.4
Berkshire	80,700	30,407	11,092	39,112	8,705	I	37.7	13.8	48.5	7	10	9	2.4	2.3	2.5	2.5
Bristol	255,380	111,490	29,416	113,710	2,220	I	43.8	11.6	44.7	3	12	12	7.6	8.3	6.6	7.3
Dukes	9,048	2,283	1,472	5,278	2,995	I	25.3	16.3	58.4	13	3	2	0.3	0.2	0.3	0.3
Essex	384,383	136,571	56,264	190,983	54,412	I	35.6	14.7	49.8	9	5	6	11.5	10.1	12.6	12.3
Franklin	42,570	11,386	6,112	24,954	13,568	I	26.8	14.4	58.8	11	6	1	1.3	0.8	1.4	1.6
Hampden	225,086	103,582	31,534	89,598	13,984	D	46.1	14.0	39.9	2	8	13	6.7	7.7	7.1	5.8
Hampshire	80,899	32,289	8,696	39,371	7,082	I	40.2	10.8	49.0	5	13	8	2.4	2.4	1.9	2.5
Middlesex	815,979	337,608	102,260	373,982	36,374	I	41.5	12.6	46.0	4	11	11	24.3	25.1	22.9	24.1
Nantucket	5,164	1,265	927	2,960	1,695	I	24.6	18.0	57.5	14	2	3	0.2	<.1	0.2	0.2
Norfolk	382,485	148,923	53,968	178,739	29,816	I	39.0	14.1	46.8	6	7	10	11.4	11.1	12.1	11.5
Plymouth	262,907	81,195	41,527	139,814	58,619	I	30.9	15.8	53.3	10	4	4	7.8	6.0	9.3	9.0
Suffolk	303,727	178,413	24,289	98,183	80,230	D	59.3	8.1	32.6	1	14	14	9.1	13.3	5.4	6.3
Worcester	374,554	137,101	52,361	184,072	46,971	I	36.7	14.0	49.3	8	9	7	11.2	10.2	11.7	11.9
MASSACHUSETTS	**3,351,918**	**1,346,097**	**447,181**	**1,548,618**	**202,521**	**I**	**40.3**	**13.4**	**46.3**				**100.0**	**100.0**	**100.0**	**100.0**
CITIES AND TOWNS																
Abington town	8,372	2,920	1,039	4,396	1,476	I	34.9	12.4	52.6	89	129	104	0.2	0.2	0.2	0.3
Acton town	11,402	1,986	1,562	7,812	5,826	I	17.5	13.8	68.8	206	104	4	0.3	0.1	0.3	0.5
Acushnet town	5,646	2,819	318	2,435	384	D	50.6	5.7	43.7	26	212	174	0.2	0.2	<.1	0.2
Adams town	5,720	2,473	572	2,658	185	I	43.4	10.0	46.6	48	172	155	0.2	0.2	0.1	0.2
Agawam town	15,692	5,764	2,243	7,657	1,893	I	36.8	14.3	48.9	78	98	140	0.5	0.4	0.5	0.5
Amesbury town	8,177	2,585	1,219	4,362	1,777	I	31.7	14.9	53.4	109	91	90	0.2	0.2	0.3	0.3
Amherst town	13,225	6,906	1,334	4,848	2,058	D	52.8	10.2	36.7	18	171	190	0.4	0.5	0.3	0.3
Andover town	19,133	5,864	4,210	8,990	3,126	I	30.8	22.1	47.2	117	20	152	0.6	0.4	0.9	0.6
Arlington town	29,647	16,366	3,546	9,617	6,749	D	55.4	12.0	32.6	15	141	200	0.9	1.2	0.8	0.6
Ashburnham town	2,921	806	431	1,677	871	I	27.7	14.8	57.5	141	92	51	<.1	<.1	<.1	0.1
Ashland town	7,663	1,993	994	4,664	2,671	I	26.0	13.0	61.0	156	119	29	0.2	0.1	0.2	0.3
Athol town	5,715	1,567	886	3,245	1,678	I	27.5	15.5	56.9	144	83	60	0.2	0.1	0.2	0.2
Attleboro city	18,379	4,283	2,248	11,786	7,503	I	23.4	12.3	64.3	177	132	9	0.5	0.3	0.5	0.8
Auburn town	9,733	3,296	1,210	5,176	1,880	I	34.0	12.5	53.5	94	128	94	0.3	0.2	0.3	0.3
Ayer town	2,841	836	366	1,639	803	I	29.4	12.9	57.7	128	121	49	<.1	<.1	<.1	0.1
Barnstable town	25,908	6,983	5,733	13,162	6,179	I	27.0	22.2	50.9	149	18	122	0.8	0.5	1.3	0.8
Barre town	2,827	978	357	1,492	514	I	34.6	12.6	52.8	90	125	100	<.1	<.1	<.1	<.1
Bedford town	7,834	1,827	1,119	4,879	3,052	I	23.3	14.3	62.4	176	99	19	0.2	0.1	0.3	0.3
Belchertown town	6,155	1,797	835	3,466	1,669	I	29.5	13.7	56.8	131	109	65	0.2	0.1	0.2	0.2
Bellingham town	8,333	3,214	1,003	4,087	873	I	38.7	12.1	49.2	68	137	137	0.2	0.2	0.2	0.3
Belmont town	17,058	5,277	1,940	9,831	4,554	I	31.0	11.4	57.7	113	154	50	0.5	0.4	0.4	0.6
Beverly city	23,321	6,345	3,639	13,310	6,965	I	27.2	15.6	57.1	147	80	55	0.7	0.5	0.8	0.9
Billerica town	20,444	7,757	2,492	10,168	2,411	I	38.0	12.2	49.8	71	133	131	0.6	0.6	0.6	0.7
Blackstone town	4,364	1,846	324	2,174	328	I	42.5	7.5	50.0	53	206	130	0.1	0.1	<.1	0.1
Boston city	256,487	150,375	20,655	82,693	67,682	D	59.3	8.1	32.6	9	199	202	7.7	11.2	4.6	5.3
Bourne town	8,858	1,991	1,344	5,504	3,513	I	22.5	15.2	62.3	187	88	22	0.3	0.1	0.3	0.4
Boxford town	4,261	468	1,097	2,696	1,599	I	11.0	25.7	63.3	213	5	14	0.1	<.1	0.2	0.2
Braintree town	21,174	10,307	3,275	7,568	2,739	D	48.7	15.5	35.8	30	84	193	0.6	0.8	0.7	0.5
Brewster town	6,086	1,323	1,445	3,312	1,867	I	21.8	23.8	54.5	190	9	85	0.2	<.1	0.3	0.2
Bridgewater town	10,701	2,929	1,569	6,179	3,250	I	27.4	14.7	57.9	145	95	47	0.3	0.2	0.4	0.4
Brockton city	42,538	21,279	5,278	15,940	5,339	D	50.1	12.4	37.5	25	130	186	1.3	1.6	1.2	1.0
Brookline town	35,241	15,227	3,840	16,124	897	I	43.3	10.9	45.8	49	162	164	1.1	1.1	0.9	1.0
Burlington town	14,597	6,044	1,849	6,661	617	I	41.5	12.7	45.8	56	123	165	0.4	0.4	0.4	0.4
Cambridge city	50,347	31,772	3,538	14,769	17,003	D	63.4	7.1	29.5	4	208	206	1.5	2.4	0.8	1.0
Canton town	12,235	5,010	1,592	5,624	614	I	41.0	13.0	46.0	58	117	162	0.4	0.4	0.4	0.4
Carver town	6,005	1,953	1,062	2,974	1,021	I	32.6	17.7	49.7	101	60	133	0.2	0.1	0.2	0.2
Chatham town	5,211	850	1,678	2,683	1,005	I	16.3	32.2	51.5	208	2	113	0.2	<.1	0.4	0.2
Chelmsford town	20,396	5,341	3,363	11,623	6,282	I	26.3	16.5	57.2	155	71	56	0.6	0.4	0.8	0.8
Chelsea city	10,920	7,118	705	3,079	4,039	D	65.3	6.5	28.2	2	211	209	0.3	0.5	0.2	0.2
Chicopee city	28,469	16,144	2,566	9,680	6,464	D	56.9	9.0	34.1	13	190	197	0.8	1.2	0.6	0.6
Clarksburg town	1,077	199	123	754	555	I	18.5	11.4	70.1	203	152	3	<.1	<.1	<.1	<.1
Clinton town	7,659	3,583	1,052	3,004	579	D	46.9	13.8	39.3	38	103	183	0.2	0.3	0.2	0.2
Cohasset town	5,270	1,151	1,124	2,991	1,840	I	21.9	21.3	56.8	189	21	61	0.2	<.1	0.3	0.2
Concord town	11,037	3,118	2,218	5,654	2,536	I	28.4	20.2	51.4	136	32	117	0.3	0.2	0.5	0.4
Dalton town	4,219	1,228	667	2,323	1,095	I	29.1	15.8	55.1	132	78	79	0.1	<.1	0.1	0.2
Danvers town	15,457	3,780	2,540	9,131	5,351	I	24.5	16.4	59.1	164	72	36	0.5	0.3	0.6	0.6
Dartmouth town	14,664	7,004	1,745	5,911	1,093	D	47.8	11.9	40.3	33	143	182	0.4	0.5	0.4	0.4
Dedham town	14,551	5,964	1,581	7,000	1,036	I	41.0	10.9	48.1	57	163	144	0.4	0.4	0.4	0.5
Deerfield town	3,932	1,114	476	2,342	1,228	I	28.3	12.1	59.6	135	135	32	0.1	<.1	0.1	0.2
Dennis town	9,818	2,220	2,183	5,408	3,188	I	22.6	22.3	55.1	185	17	78	0.3	0.2	0.5	0.3
Dracut town	15,885	7,174	2,010	6,684	490	D	45.2	12.7	42.1	40	124	177	0.5	0.5	0.4	0.4
Dudley town	5,033	2,185	438	2,408	223	I	43.4	8.7	47.9	46	192	146	0.2	0.2	<.1	0.2

[1]Separate rankings for 14 counties and 213 cities and towns.

County	Total voter registration	Democrat (DEM)	Republican (REP)	Independent (IND)	Plurality Total	Plurality Party	% DEM	% REP	% IND	Rank[1] DEM	Rank[1] REP	Rank[1] IND	Total	DEM	REP	IND
Duxbury town	9,506	1,914	2,334	5,251	2,917	I	20.1	24.6	55.3	197	7	75	0.3	0.1	0.5	0.3
East Bridgewater town	6,546	1,749	1,163	3,625	1,876	I	26.8	17.8	55.5	153	56	73	0.2	0.1	0.3	0.2
East Longmeadow town	8,448	2,696	1,766	3,977	1,281	I	31.9	20.9	47.1	105	23	151	0.3	0.2	0.4	0.3
Easthampton town	8,980	3,053	847	5,054	2,001	I	34.1	9.5	56.4	93	181	66	0.3	0.2	0.2	0.3
Easton town	11,785	2,938	2,455	6,220	3,282	I	25.3	21.1	53.6	162	24	99	0.4	0.2	0.5	0.4
Erving town	905	176	117	612	436	I	19.4	12.9	67.6	199	120	5	<.1	<.1	<.1	<.1
Everett city	18,371	10,438	1,433	6,473	3,965	D	56.9	7.8	35.3	12	201	195	0.5	0.8	0.3	0.4
Fairhaven town	9,511	3,962	802	4,747	785	I	41.7	8.4	49.9	55	194	129	0.3	0.3	0.2	0.3
Fall River city	39,923	28,772	2,982	8,006	20,766	D	72.4	7.5	20.1	1	204	212	1.2	2.1	0.7	0.5
Falmouth town	20,152	6,383	3,522	10,219	3,836	I	31.7	17.5	50.8	108	63	123	0.6	0.5	0.8	0.7
Fitchburg city	18,102	7,725	1,890	8,380	655	I	42.9	10.5	46.6	52	167	157	0.5	0.6	0.4	0.5
Foxborough town	9,245	2,478	1,640	5,113	2,635	I	26.8	17.8	55.4	151	57	74	0.3	0.2	0.4	0.3
Framingham town	35,167	12,291	4,074	18,725	6,434	I	35.0	11.6	53.4	88	147	92	1.0	0.9	0.9	1.2
Franklin town	13,414	3,286	1,642	8,453	5,167	I	24.6	12.3	63.2	163	131	16	0.4	0.2	0.4	0.5
Freetown town	4,807	1,505	546	2,750	1,245	I	31.3	11.4	57.3	112	155	54	0.1	0.1	0.1	0.2
Gardner town	9,763	4,775	1,328	3,593	1,182	D	49.2	13.7	37.1	29	107	189	0.3	0.4	0.3	0.2
Gloucester city	17,741	4,910	2,126	10,700	5,790	I	27.7	12.0	60.3	140	140	30	0.5	0.4	0.5	0.7
Grafton town	8,209	2,135	947	5,107	2,972	I	26.1	11.6	62.4	157	149	20	0.2	0.2	0.2	0.3
Great Barrington town	4,075	1,292	634	2,148	856	I	31.7	15.6	52.7	107	82	101	0.1	<.1	0.1	0.1
Greenfield town	9,728	2,857	1,607	5,248	2,391	I	29.4	16.5	54.0	129	68	87	0.3	0.2	0.4	0.3
Groton town	4,777	1,060	895	2,813	1,753	I	22.2	18.8	59.0	188	45	37	0.1	<.1	0.2	0.2
Groveland town	3,535	1,009	701	1,825	816	I	28.5	19.8	51.6	133	35	112	0.1	<.1	0.2	0.1
Hamilton town	4,686	674	1,128	2,884	1,756	I	14.4	24.1	61.5	212	8	25	0.1	<.1	0.3	0.2
Hanover town	7,486	2,250	1,354	3,876	1,626	I	30.1	18.1	51.8	123	52	110	0.2	0.2	0.3	0.3
Hanson town	5,449	1,397	867	3,178	1,781	I	25.7	15.9	58.4	160	75	44	0.2	0.1	0.2	0.2
Hardwick town	1,254	526	121	607	81	I	41.9	9.6	48.4	54	179	142	<.1	<.1	<.1	<.1
Haverhill city	27,020	10,105	3,633	13,267	3,162	I	37.4	13.5	49.1	75	111	136	0.8	0.8	0.8	0.9
Hingham town	13,923	3,323	2,668	7,927	4,604	I	23.9	19.2	57.0	170	41	57	0.4	0.2	0.6	0.5
Holbrook town	6,573	2,298	823	3,445	1,147	I	35.0	12.5	52.5	87	126	105	0.2	0.2	0.2	0.2
Holden town	9,742	1,946	2,298	5,461	3,163	I	20.1	23.7	56.3	198	11	69	0.3	0.1	0.5	0.4
Holliston town	9,442	2,203	1,817	5,412	3,209	I	23.4	19.3	57.4	175	40	53	0.3	0.2	0.4	0.3
Holyoke city	21,822	10,684	1,871	9,236	1,448	D	49.0	8.6	42.4	28	193	175	0.7	0.8	0.4	0.6
Hopkinton town	6,100	1,628	1,127	3,341	1,713	I	26.7	18.5	54.8	154	46	81	0.2	0.1	0.3	0.2
Hudson town	10,054	2,385	1,154	6,498	4,113	I	23.8	11.5	64.7	174	150	8	0.3	0.2	0.3	0.4
Hull town	7,624	2,615	628	4,373	1,758	I	34.3	8.2	57.4	92	197	52	0.2	0.2	0.1	0.3
Ipswich town	8,116	1,759	1,538	4,819	3,060	I	21.7	19.0	59.4	192	43	34	0.2	0.1	0.3	0.3
Kingston town	5,682	1,562	1,094	3,019	1,457	I	27.5	19.3	53.2	142	39	95	0.2	0.1	0.2	0.2
Lawrence city	22,240	13,775	3,022	5,285	8,490	D	62.4	13.7	23.9	6	108	211	0.7	1.0	0.7	0.3
Leicester town	5,696	2,526	558	2,607	81	I	44.4	9.8	45.8	42	177	163	0.2	0.2	0.1	0.2
Leominster city	20,086	6,713	2,065	11,202	4,489	I	33.6	10.3	56.1	98	168	71	0.6	0.5	0.5	0.7
Lexington town	21,179	9,071	3,748	8,259	812	D	43.0	17.8	39.2	51	59	184	0.6	0.7	0.8	0.5
Lincoln town	3,564	1,074	647	1,841	767	I	30.2	18.2	51.7	121	51	111	0.1	<.1	0.1	0.1
Littleton town	4,709	1,118	688	2,898	1,780	I	23.8	14.6	61.6	173	96	26	0.1	<.1	0.2	0.2
Longmeadow town	10,492	3,285	3,247	3,882	597	I	31.5	31.2	37.3	111	4	187	0.3	0.2	0.7	0.3
Lowell city	42,136	20,167	4,759	17,182	2,985	D	47.9	11.3	40.8	32	157	180	1.3	1.5	1.1	1.1
Ludlow town	10,174	6,340	931	2,889	3,451	D	62.4	9.2	28.4	5	188	207	0.3	0.5	0.2	0.2
Lunenburg town	5,647	1,306	1,041	3,285	1,979	I	23.2	18.5	58.3	180	47	45	0.2	<.1	0.2	0.2
Lynn city	38,582	20,430	3,229	14,895	5,535	D	53.0	8.4	38.6	17	196	185	1.2	1.5	0.7	1.0
Lynnfield town	7,838	1,818	1,728	4,292	2,474	I	23.2	22.0	54.8	178	19	82	0.2	0.1	0.4	0.3
Malden city	27,934	14,409	2,093	11,389	3,020	D	51.7	7.5	40.8	19	203	181	0.8	1.1	0.5	0.7
Mansfield town	9,941	2,362	1,692	5,824	3,462	I	23.9	17.1	59.0	172	66	40	0.3	0.2	0.4	0.4
Marblehead town	14,138	3,652	3,209	7,277	3,625	I	25.8	22.7	51.5	159	16	114	0.4	0.3	0.7	0.5
Marlborough city	17,946	6,386	2,286	9,164	2,778	I	35.8	12.8	51.4	84	122	119	0.5	0.5	0.5	0.6
Marshfield town	14,622	4,503	2,180	7,931	3,428	I	30.8	14.9	54.3	114	90	86	0.4	0.3	0.5	0.5
Mashpee town	5,422	1,600	825	2,978	1,378	I	29.6	15.3	55.1	126	87	80	0.2	0.1	0.2	0.2
Maynard town	6,619	2,196	780	3,615	1,419	I	33.3	11.8	54.8	99	145	83	0.2	0.2	0.2	0.2
Medfield town	6,944	1,226	1,269	4,449	3,180	I	17.7	18.3	64.1	205	48	10	0.2	<.1	0.3	0.3
Medford city	32,716	16,418	2,481	13,777	2,641	D	50.2	7.6	42.2	24	202	176	1.0	1.2	0.6	0.9
Medway town	6,278	1,510	843	3,923	2,413	I	24.1	13.4	62.5	167	112	18	0.2	0.1	0.2	0.3
Melrose city	18,589	6,733	3,178	8,648	1,915	I	36.3	17.1	46.6	80	65	154	0.6	0.5	0.7	0.6
Methuen town	23,586	12,074	3,591	7,902	4,172	D	51.2	15.2	33.5	21	86	199	0.7	0.9	0.8	0.5
Middleborough town	9,423	1,983	1,490	5,923	3,940	I	21.1	15.9	63.0	195	77	17	0.3	0.1	0.3	0.4
Milford town	13,318	5,894	1,586	5,838	56	D	44.3	11.9	43.8	43	142	168	0.4	0.4	0.4	0.4
Millbury town	7,186	3,171	687	3,308	137	I	44.3	9.6	46.2	44	180	161	0.2	0.2	0.2	0.2
Millis town	4,673	1,117	665	2,889	1,772	I	23.9	14.2	61.8	169	100	24	0.1	<.1	0.1	0.2
Milton town	17,589	8,849	2,326	6,414	2,435	D	50.3	13.2	36.5	23	115	191	0.5	0.7	0.5	0.4
Monson town	4,255	1,615	531	2,107	492	I	38.0	12.5	49.5	70	127	134	0.1	0.1	0.1	0.1
Montague town	5,181	1,813	610	2,752	939	I	35.0	11.8	53.2	86	146	97	0.2	0.1	0.1	0.2
Natick town	21,370	7,177	2,968	11,139	3,962	I	33.7	13.9	52.3	96	102	108	0.6	0.5	0.7	0.7
Needham town	19,520	6,297	3,915	9,209	2,912	I	32.4	20.2	47.4	102	33	150	0.6	0.5	0.9	0.6

[1]Separate rankings for 14 counties and 213 cities and towns.

Massachusetts 451

Table D. — Voter Registration by Political Party Affiliation: November 3, 1992, General Election (cont)

County	Total voter registration	Political party affiliation Democrat (DEM)	Republican (REP)	Independent (IND)	Plurality Total	Party	Percent of total registration DEM	REP	IND	Rank[1] DEM	REP	IND	Percent contribution to state registration Total	DEM	REP	IND
New Bedford city	39,947	24,639	3,291	11,947	12,692	D	61.8	8.3	30.0	8	196	205	1.2	1.8	0.7	0.8
Newbury town	4,233	622	765	2,846	2,081	I	14.7	18.1	67.2	211	53	6	0.1	<.1	0.2	0.2
Newburyport city	11,323	3,743	1,870	5,702	1,959	I	33.1	16.5	50.4	100	69	125	0.3	0.3	0.4	0.4
Newton city	50,969	23,140	5,803	22,020	1,120	D	45.4	11.4	43.2	39	153	173	1.5	1.7	1.3	1.4
Norfolk town	4,895	884	988	3,003	2,015	I	18.1	20.3	61.6	204	30	27	0.1	<.1	0.2	0.2
North Adams city	7,711	2,914	926	3,859	945	I	37.8	12.0	50.1	72	138	128	0.2	0.2	0.2	0.2
North Andover town	14,660	3,979	2,068	8,611	4,632	I	27.1	14.1	58.7	148	101	39	0.4	0.3	0.5	0.6
North Attleborough town	13,102	2,799	2,713	7,559	4,760	I	21.4	20.8	57.8	193	25	48	0.4	0.2	0.6	0.5
North Reading town	7,857	2,411	1,304	4,127	1,716	I	30.7	16.6	52.6	116	67	103	0.2	0.2	0.3	0.3
Northampton city	17,398	8,284	1,230	7,626	658	D	48.3	7.2	44.5	34	207	169	0.5	0.6	0.3	0.5
Northborough town	7,231	1,641	1,471	4,112	2,471	I	22.7	20.4	56.9	183	29	59	0.2	0.1	0.3	0.3
Northbridge town	7,461	2,049	1,179	4,209	2,160	I	27.6	15.9	56.6	143	79	64	0.2	0.2	0.3	0.3
Norton town	7,844	1,806	1,204	4,795	2,989	I	23.1	15.4	61.4	181	85	28	0.2	0.1	0.3	0.3
Norwell town	6,275	1,751	1,426	3,063	1,312	I	28.1	22.9	49.1	138	15	139	0.2	0.1	0.3	0.2
Norwood town	17,577	7,556	1,894	8,103	547	I	43.0	10.8	46.2	50	164	159	0.5	0.6	0.4	0.5
Orange town	3,829	866	672	2,278	1,412	I	22.7	17.6	59.7	184	62	33	0.1	<.1	0.1	0.1
Orleans town	4,753	757	1,476	2,520	1,044	I	15.9	31.1	53.0	209	3	98	0.1	<.1	0.3	0.2
Oxford town	6,651	2,494	698	3,452	958	I	37.5	10.5	52.0	74	166	109	0.2	0.2	0.2	0.2
Palmer town	7,204	2,843	704	3,650	807	I	39.5	9.8	50.7	61	178	124	0.2	0.2	0.2	0.2
Peabody city	28,625	11,282	1,933	15,402	4,120	I	39.4	6.8	53.8	63	209	88	0.9	0.8	0.4	1.0
Pembroke town	8,894	2,795	1,410	4,682	1,887	I	31.5	15.9	52.7	110	76	102	0.3	0.2	0.3	0.3
Pepperell town	5,626	1,410	997	3,181	1,771	I	25.2	17.8	56.9	161	58	62	0.2	0.1	0.2	0.2
Pittsfield city	27,510	14,052	3,694	9,764	4,288	D	51.1	13.4	35.5	22	113	194	0.8	1.0	0.8	0.6
Plainville town	3,882	750	709	2,413	1,663	I	19.4	18.3	62.3	200	49	21	0.1	<.1	0.2	0.2
Plymouth town	33,737	7,816	4,388	21,454	13,638	I	23.2	13.0	63.7	179	118	12	1.0	0.6	1.0	1.4
Quincy city	48,207	27,808	6,894	13,346	14,462	D	57.9	14.3	27.8	10	97	210	1.4	2.1	1.5	0.9
Randolph town	16,595	7,850	1,330	7,198	652	D	47.9	8.1	43.9	36	200	172	0.5	0.6	0.3	0.5
Raynham town	6,070	1,628	1,002	3,431	1,803	I	26.9	16.5	56.6	150	70	63	0.2	0.1	0.2	0.2
Reading town	14,922	4,737	2,892	7,258	2,521	I	31.8	19.4	48.8	106	37	141	0.4	0.4	0.6	0.5
Rehoboth town	5,172	818	1,090	3,262	2,172	I	15.8	21.1	63.1	210	22	15	0.2	<.1	0.2	0.2
Revere city	24,042	14,830	1,785	7,381	7,449	D	61.8	7.4	30.8	7	205	204	0.7	1.1	0.4	0.5
Rockland town	9,395	3,155	1,042	5,189	2,034	I	33.6	11.1	55.3	97	158	77	0.3	0.2	0.2	0.3
Rockport town	5,208	1,129	1,022	3,049	1,920	I	21.7	19.7	58.6	191	36	41	0.2	<.1	0.2	0.2
Salem city	21,310	9,215	1,997	9,974	759	I	43.5	9.4	47.1	47	184	153	0.6	0.7	0.4	0.6
Salisbury town	4,464	1,316	544	2,604	1,288	I	29.5	12.2	58.3	127	134	43	0.1	<.1	0.1	0.2
Sandwich town	10,209	2,441	1,948	5,742	3,301	I	24.1	19.2	56.7	168	42	67	0.3	0.2	0.4	0.4
Saugus town	15,999	6,391	1,919	7,647	1,256	I	40.1	12.0	47.9	59	139	147	0.5	0.5	0.4	0.5
Scituate town	12,329	3,936	2,548	5,840	1,904	I	31.9	20.7	47.4	104	26	149	0.4	0.3	0.6	0.4
Seekonk town	7,598	1,412	750	5,424	4,012	I	18.6	9.9	71.5	202	175	2	0.2	0.1	0.2	0.4
Sharon town	10,367	3,651	977	5,726	2,075	I	35.3	9.4	55.3	85	182	76	0.3	0.3	0.2	0.4
Shrewsbury town	15,430	5,525	2,751	7,141	1,616	I	35.8	17.8	46.3	83	54	158	0.5	0.4	0.6	0.5
Somerset town	11,515	5,406	1,082	5,026	380	D	47.0	9.4	43.7	37	183	170	0.3	0.4	0.2	0.3
Somerville city	42,829	27,660	2,853	12,146	15,514	D	64.8	6.7	28.5	3	210	167	1.3	2.1	0.6	0.8
South Hadley town	10,431	3,836	437	1,575	2,261	D	65.6	7.5	26.9	77	213	213	0.3	0.3	<.1	0.1
Southborough town	4,577	1,226	945	2,397	1,171	I	26.8	20.7	52.5	152	27	106	0.1	<.1	0.2	0.2
Southbridge town	8,767	4,717	867	3,175	1,542	D	53.9	9.9	36.2	16	174	192	0.3	0.4	0.2	0.2
Southwick town	4,116	1,250	797	2,069	819	I	30.4	19.4	50.3	118	38	126	0.1	<.1	0.2	0.1
Spencer town	6,456	2,356	881	3,210	854	I	36.5	13.7	49.8	79	106	132	0.2	0.2	0.2	0.2
Springfield city	59,850	34,524	5,934	19,346	15,178	D	57.7	9.9	32.3	11	173	201	1.8	2.6	1.3	1.2
Stoneham town	13,329	5,204	1,821	6,186	982	I	39.4	13.8	46.8	66	105	156	0.4	0.4	0.4	0.4
Stoughton town	15,531	5,571	1,693	8,250	2,679	I	35.9	10.9	53.2	81	161	96	0.5	0.4	0.4	0.5
Sudbury town	10,057	2,614	2,029	5,398	2,784	I	26.0	20.2	53.8	158	31	89	0.3	0.2	0.5	0.3
Sutton town	4,228	720	387	3,109	2,389	I	17.1	9.2	73.7	207	187	1	0.1	<.1	<.1	0.2
Swampscott town	10,067	2,803	1,034	6,228	3,425	I	27.8	10.3	61.9	139	169	23	0.3	0.2	0.2	0.4
Taunton city	25,681	10,072	2,525	13,069	2,997	I	39.2	9.8	50.9	65	176	120	0.8	0.7	0.6	0.8
Templeton town	3,545	1,073	389	2,075	1,002	I	30.3	11.0	58.7	120	160	42	0.1	<.1	<.1	0.1
Tewksbury town	15,277	5,886	1,847	7,480	1,594	I	38.7	12.1	49.2	69	136	138	0.5	0.4	0.4	0.5
Townsend town	4,622	871	720	3,025	2,154	I	18.9	15.6	65.5	201	81	7	0.1	<.1	0.2	0.2
Tyngsborough town	4,654	1,395	631	2,603	1,208	I	30.1	13.6	56.2	124	110	70	0.1	0.1	0.1	0.2
Uxbridge town	5,554	1,564	636	3,320	1,756	I	28.3	11.5	60.1	137	151	31	0.2	0.1	0.1	0.2
Wakefield town	14,871	5,862	2,382	6,619	757	I	39.4	16.0	44.5	62	74	167	0.4	0.4	0.5	0.4
Walpole town	13,059	3,961	1,953	7,109	3,148	I	30.4	15.0	54.6	119	89	84	0.4	0.3	0.4	0.5
Waltham city	29,726	11,867	3,440	14,328	2,461	I	40.0	11.6	48.3	60	148	143	0.9	0.9	0.8	0.9
Ware town	5,369	2,551	481	2,335	216	D	47.5	9.0	43.5	35	191	171	0.2	0.2	0.1	0.2
Wareham town	12,558	3,715	2,155	6,688	2,973	I	29.6	17.2	53.3	125	64	91	0.4	0.3	0.5	0.4
Warren town	2,446	963	225	1,257	294	I	39.4	9.2	51.4	64	186	115	<.1	<.1	<.1	<.1
Watertown town	19,882	11,110	2,012	6,677	4,433	D	56.1	10.2	33.7	14	170	198	0.6	0.8	0.4	0.4
Wayland town	8,302	2,008	1,460	4,828	2,820	I	24.2	17.6	58.2	166	61	46	0.2	0.1	0.3	0.3
Webster town	8,224	3,598	673	3,953	355	I	43.8	8.2	48.1	45	198	145	0.2	0.3	0.2	0.3
Wellesley town	16,208	4,626	3,841	7,727	3,101	I	28.6	23.7	47.7	134	10	148	0.5	0.3	0.9	0.5

[1]Separate rankings for 14 counties and 213 cities and towns.

County	Total voter registration	Political party affiliation					Percent of total registration						Percent contribution to state registration			
		Democrat (DEM)	Republican (REP)	Independent (IND)	Plurality		DEM	REP	IND	Rank[1]			Total	DEM	REP	IND
					Total	Party				DEM	REP	IND				
West Boylston town	3,925	801	632	2,491	1,690	I	20.4	16.1	63.5	196	73	13	0.1	<.1	0.1	0.2
West Bridgewater town ..	4,373	930	872	2,571	1,641	I	21.3	19.9	58.8	194	34	38	0.1	<.1	0.2	0.2
West Springfield town	14,590	5,667	4,784	8,190	2,523	I	30.4	25.7	43.9	67	1	68	0.4	0.4	1.1	0.5
Westborough town	8,917	2,432	2,078	4,400	1,968	I	27.3	23.3	49.4	146	14	135	0.3	0.2	0.5	0.3
Westfield city	20,718	7,733	2,348	6,548	1,185	D	46.5	14.1	39.4	76	156	203	0.6	0.6	0.5	0.4
Westford town..................	10,553	3,240	1,926	5,367	2,127	I	30.8	18.3	51.0	115	50	121	0.3	0.2	0.4	0.3
Weston town	7,106	1,630	1,825	3,650	1,825	I	22.9	25.7	51.4	182	6	116	0.2	0.1	0.4	0.2
Westport town.................	8,476	4,077	1,249	3,132	945	D	48.2	14.8	37.0	31	93	188	0.3	0.3	0.3	0.2
Westwood town	9,294	2,719	1,915	4,660	1,941	I	29.3	20.6	50.1	130	28	127	0.3	0.2	0.4	0.3
Weymouth town	34,017	12,811	3,763	17,419	4,608	I	37.7	11.1	51.2	73	159	118	1.0	1.0	0.8	1.1
Whitman town..................	7,584	2,427	1,116	4,035	1,608	I	32.0	14.7	53.2	103	94	93	0.2	0.2	0.2	0.3
Wilbraham town	8,341	2,885	1,951	3,504	619	I	34.6	23.4	42.0	91	13	178	0.2	0.2	0.4	0.2
Williamstown town	4,906	1,475	639	2,792	1,317	I	30.1	13.0	56.9	122	116	58	0.1	0.1	0.1	0.2
Wilmington town.............	11,691	3,939	1,241	6,480	2,541	I	33.8	10.6	55.6	95	165	72	0.3	0.3	0.3	0.4
Winchendon town...........	4,319	1,055	511	2,749	1,694	I	24.4	11.8	63.7	165	144	11	0.1	<.1	0.1	0.2
Winchester town.............	14,300	5,122	2,702	6,461	1,339	I	35.9	18.9	45.2	82	44	166	0.4	0.4	0.6	0.4
Winthrop town.................	12,278	6,090	1,144	5,030	1,060	D	49.7	9.3	41.0	27	185	179	0.4	0.5	0.3	0.3
Woburn city....................	22,387	10,000	2,037	10,312	312	I	44.7	9.1	46.1	41	189	160	0.7	0.7	0.5	0.7
Worcester city................	75,988	39,134	10,160	26,432	12,702	D	51.7	13.4	34.9	20	114	196	2.3	2.9	2.3	1.7
Wrentham town	5,251	1,183	933	3,108	1,925	I	22.6	17.9	59.5	186	55	35	0.2	<.1	0.2	0.2
Yarmouth town	14,912	3,553	3,514	7,777	4,224	I	23.9	23.7	52.4	171	12	107	0.4	0.3	0.8	0.5

[1]Separate rankings for 14 counties and 213 cities and towns.

Table E. — Vote for President: November 3, 1992, General Election

County	Total	Clinton (DEM)	Bush (REP)	Perot (IND)	Other	Plurality Total	Plurality Party	Percent of total vote DEM	REP	IND	Other	Rank[1] DEM	REP	IND	Percent contribution to state vote Total	DEM	REP	IND	Major party Percent of vote DEM	REP
Barnstable	108,997	46,641	33,916	27,727	713	12,725	D	42.8	31.1	25.4	0.7	13	5	4	3.9	3.5	4.2	4.4	57.9	42.1
Berkshire	67,746	36,857	14,726	15,799	364	21,058	D	54.4	21.7	23.3	0.5	3	14	9	2.4	2.8	1.8	2.5	71.5	28.5
Bristol	211,754	102,406	52,370	55,845	1,133	46,561	D	48.4	24.7	26.4	0.5	6	9	3	7.6	7.8	6.5	8.9	66.2	33.8
Dukes	7,888	4,292	1,827	1,714	55	2,465	D	54.4	23.2	21.7	0.7	2	12	11	0.3	0.3	0.2	0.3	70.1	29.9
Essex	322,328	140,593	102,212	77,459	2,064	38,381	D	43.6	31.7	24.0	0.6	12	4	6	11.6	10.7	12.7	12.3	57.9	42.1
Franklin	35,827	17,246	8,691	9,596	294	7,650	D	48.1	24.3	26.8	0.8	8	10	2	1.3	1.3	1.1	1.5	66.5	33.5
Hampden	188,265	86,026	54,621	46,678	940	31,405	D	45.7	29.0	24.8	0.5	10	6	5	6.8	6.5	6.8	7.4	61.2	38.8
Hampshire	70,072	37,879	15,694	15,705	794	22,174	D	54.1	22.4	22.4	1.1	4	13	10	2.5	2.9	1.9	2.5	70.7	29.3
Middlesex	689,452	343,994	193,703	146,831	4,924	150,291	D	49.9	28.1	21.3	0.7	5	7	12	24.9	26.1	24.1	23.3	64.0	36.0
Nantucket	4,216	2,037	1,158	989	32	879	D	48.3	27.5	23.5	0.8	7	8	7	0.2	0.2	0.1	0.2	63.8	36.2
Norfolk	324,390	150,488	103,255	67,537	3,110	47,233	D	46.4	31.8	20.8	1.0	9	3	13	11.7	11.4	12.8	10.7	59.3	40.7
Plymouth	207,710	79,160	69,514	57,886	1,150	9,646	D	38.1	33.5	27.9	0.6	14	1	1	7.5	6.0	8.6	9.2	53.2	46.8
Suffolk	219,273	132,921	51,378	32,914	2,060	81,543	D	60.6	23.4	15.0	0.9	1	11	14	7.9	10.1	6.4	5.2	72.1	27.9
Worcester	315,782	138,122	101,984	74,051	1,625	36,138	D	43.7	32.3	23.5	0.5	11	2	8	11.4	10.5	12.7	11.7	57.5	42.5
MASSACHUSETTS	**2,773,700**	**1,318,662**	**805,049**	**630,731**	**19,258**	**513,613**	**D**	**47.5**	**29.0**	**22.7**	**0.7**				**100.0**	**100.0**	**100.0**	**100.0**	**62.1**	**37.9**
CITIES AND TOWNS																				
Abington town	6,924	2,570	2,452	1,870	32	118	D	37.1	35.4	27.0	0.5	175	35	74	0.2	0.2	0.3	0.3	51.2	48.8
Acton town	10,338	4,980	3,136	2,142	80	1,844	D	48.2	30.3	20.7	0.8	52	124	171	0.4	0.4	0.4	0.3	61.4	38.6
Acushnet town	4,863	2,568	826	1,448	21	1,120	D	52.8	17.0	29.8	0.4	25	210	28	0.2	0.2	0.1	0.2	75.7	24.3
Adams town	4,726	2,618	848	1,238	22	1,380	D	55.4	17.9	26.2	0.5	19	207	89	0.2	0.2	0.1	0.2	75.5	24.5
Agawam town	13,498	5,479	4,239	3,742	38	1,240	D	40.6	31.4	27.7	0.3	132	105	58	0.5	0.4	0.5	0.6	56.4	43.6
Amesbury town	6,966	2,857	1,978	2,103	28	754	D	41.0	28.4	30.2	0.4	126	152	24	0.3	0.2	0.2	0.3	59.1	40.9
Amherst town	11,775	8,563	1,646	1,436	130	6,917	D	72.7	14.0	12.2	1.1	2	213	210	0.4	0.6	0.2	0.2	83.9	16.1
Andover town	16,836	6,649	6,487	3,590	110	162	D	39.5	38.5	21.3	0.7	143	18	166	0.6	0.5	0.8	0.6	50.6	49.4
Arlington town	25,685	14,453	6,646	4,384	202	7,807	D	56.3	25.9	17.1	0.8	15	174	196	0.9	1.1	0.8	0.7	68.5	31.5
Ashburnham town	2,578	1,045	811	693	29	234	D	40.5	31.5	26.9	1.1	133	103	78	<.1	<.1	0.1	0.1	56.3	43.7
Ashland town	6,495	2,962	1,931	1,566	36	1,031	D	45.6	29.7	24.1	0.6	73	131	125	0.2	0.2	0.2	0.2	60.5	39.5
Athol town	4,751	1,811	1,437	1,453	50	358	D	38.1	30.2	30.6	1.1	163	126	19	0.2	0.1	0.2	0.2	55.8	44.2
Attleboro city	15,114	5,831	4,779	4,413	91	1,052	D	38.6	31.6	29.2	0.6	153	96	38	0.5	0.4	0.6	0.7	55.0	45.0
Auburn town	8,215	3,488	2,879	1,814	34	609	D	42.5	35.0	22.1	0.4	105	42	159	0.3	0.3	0.4	0.3	54.8	45.2
Ayer town	2,472	1,063	730	654	25	333	D	43.0	29.5	26.5	1.0	96	132	84	<.1	<.1	<.1	0.1	59.3	40.7
Barnstable town	21,584	8,972	6,558	5,920	134	2,414	D	41.6	30.4	27.4	0.6	118	122	64	0.8	0.7	0.8	0.9	57.8	42.2
Barre town	2,424	1,057	740	603	24	317	D	43.6	30.5	24.9	1.0	89	120	115	<.1	<.1	<.1	<.1	58.8	41.2
Bedford town	6,747	3,027	2,230	1,441	49	797	D	44.9	33.1	21.4	0.7	80	73	164	0.2	0.2	0.3	0.2	57.6	42.4
Belchertown town	5,306	2,372	1,287	1,622	25	750	D	44.7	24.3	30.6	0.5	82	186	20	0.2	0.2	0.2	0.3	64.8	35.2
Bellingham town	7,140	2,922	2,062	2,127	29	795	D	40.9	28.9	29.8	0.4	128	143	27	0.3	0.2	0.3	0.3	58.6	41.4
Belmont town	14,656	7,588	4,684	2,294	90	2,904	D	51.8	32.0	15.7	0.6	32	91	203	0.5	0.6	0.6	0.4	61.8	38.2
Beverly city	19,791	8,507	6,174	4,979	131	2,333	D	43.0	31.2	25.2	0.7	99	109	103	0.7	0.6	0.8	0.8	57.9	42.1
Billerica town	17,042	6,501	4,958	5,429	154	1,072	D	38.1	29.1	31.9	0.9	162	140	12	0.6	0.5	0.6	0.9	56.7	43.3
Blackstone town	3,630	1,411	1,027	1,169	23	242	D	38.9	28.3	32.2	0.6	149	154	10	0.1	0.1	0.1	0.2	57.9	42.1
Boston city	183,131	114,260	41,868	25,189	1,814	72,392	D	62.4	22.9	13.8	1.0	9	194	207	6.6	8.7	5.2	4.0	73.2	26.8
Bourne town	7,760	2,984	2,595	2,137	44	389	D	38.5	33.4	27.5	0.6	155	66	63	0.3	0.2	0.3	0.3	53.5	46.5
Boxford town	3,912	1,153	1,738	984	37	585	R	29.5	44.4	25.2	0.9	213	1	104	0.1	<.1	0.2	0.2	39.9	60.1
Braintree town	18,730	7,702	6,598	4,350	80	1,104	D	41.1	35.2	23.2	0.4	125	37	137	0.7	0.6	0.8	0.7	53.9	46.1
Brewster town	5,438	2,285	1,587	1,510	56	698	D	42.0	29.2	27.8	1.0	110	138	56	0.2	0.2	0.2	0.2	59.0	41.0
Bridgewater town	8,221	2,950	2,757	2,427	87	193	D	35.9	33.5	29.5	1.1	189	64	32	0.3	0.2	0.3	0.4	51.7	48.3
Brockton city	29,799	13,209	8,863	7,579	148	4,346	D	44.3	29.7	25.4	0.5	86	130	100	1.1	1.0	1.1	1.2	59.8	40.2
Brookline town	27,547	19,848	4,892	2,629	178	14,956	D	72.1	17.8	9.5	0.6	3	208	212	1.0	1.5	0.6	0.4	80.2	19.8
Burlington town	12,697	5,145	4,192	3,278	82	953	D	40.5	33.0	25.8	0.6	134	75	94	0.5	0.4	0.5	0.5	55.1	44.9
Cambridge city	41,158	30,737	5,847	4,106	468	24,890	D	74.7	14.2	10.0	1.1	1	212	211	1.5	2.3	0.7	0.7	84.0	16.0
Canton town	10,834	4,464	3,808	2,516	46	656	D	41.2	35.1	23.2	0.4	122	39	138	0.4	0.3	0.5	0.4	54.0	46.0
Carver town	5,176	1,875	1,629	1,643	29	232	D	36.2	31.5	31.7	0.6	186	100	13	0.2	0.1	0.2	0.3	53.5	46.5
Chatham town	4,523	1,665	1,770	1,059	29	105	R	36.8	39.1	23.4	0.6	180	17	135	0.2	0.1	0.2	0.2	48.5	51.5
Chelmsford town	18,302	6,832	6,151	5,175	144	681	D	37.3	33.6	28.3	0.8	174	62	47	0.7	0.5	0.8	0.8	52.6	47.4
Chelsea city	7,847	4,408	1,957	1,441	41	2,451	D	56.2	24.9	18.4	0.5	16	178	191	0.3	0.3	0.2	0.2	69.3	30.7
Chicopee city	24,129	11,433	6,138	6,452	106	4,981	D	47.4	25.4	26.7	0.4	60	176	80	0.9	0.9	0.8	1.0	65.1	34.9
Clarksburg town	929	458	184	285	2	173	D	49.3	19.8	30.7	0.2	42	203	18	<.1	<.1	<.1	<.1	71.3	28.7
Clinton town	6,263	2,905	1,934	1,398	26	971	D	46.4	30.9	22.3	0.4	67	114	152	0.2	0.2	0.2	0.2	60.0	40.0
Cohasset town	4,268	1,576	1,757	911	24	181	R	36.9	41.2	21.3	0.6	179	8	165	0.2	0.1	0.2	0.1	47.3	52.7
Concord town	9,967	5,153	3,145	1,595	74	2,008	D	51.7	31.6	16.0	0.7	33	98	201	0.4	0.4	0.4	0.3	62.1	37.9
Dalton town	3,624	1,807	867	942	8	865	D	49.9	23.9	26.0	0.2	40	192	91	0.1	0.1	0.1	0.1	67.6	32.4
Danvers town	13,088	4,947	4,640	3,440	61	307	D	37.8	35.5	26.3	0.5	171	33	88	0.5	0.4	0.6	0.5	51.6	48.4
Dartmouth town	12,934	6,571	2,846	3,437	80	3,134	D	50.8	22.0	26.6	0.6	37	196	83	0.5	0.5	0.4	0.5	69.8	30.2
Dedham town	13,056	5,675	4,409	2,907	65	1,266	D	43.5	33.8	22.3	0.5	92	57	154	0.5	0.5	0.5	0.5	56.3	43.7
Deerfield town	2,995	1,474	645	867	9	607	D	49.2	21.5	28.9	0.3	44	198	41	0.1	0.1	<.1	0.1	69.6	30.4
Dennis town	8,438	3,476	2,815	2,087	60	661	D	41.2	33.4	24.7	0.7	124	68	117	0.3	0.3	0.3	0.3	55.3	44.7
Dracut town	12,588	4,509	3,667	4,360	52	149	D	35.8	29.1	34.6	0.4	190	139	4	0.5	0.3	0.5	0.7	55.1	44.9
Dudley town	4,196	1,782	1,273	1,117	24	509	D	42.5	30.3	26.6	0.6	104	123	82	0.2	0.1	0.2	0.2	58.3	41.7

[1] Separate rankings for 14 counties and 213 cities and towns.

454 Massachusetts

Table E. — Vote for President: November 3, 1992, General Election (cont)

County	Total	Clinton (DEM)	Bush (REP)	Perot (IND)	Other	Plurality Total	Party	DEM	REP	IND	Other	Rank¹ DEM	Rank¹ REP	Rank¹ IND	Total	DEM	REP	IND	DEM	REP
Duxbury town	8,337	2,909	3,473	1,909	46	564	R	34.9	41.7	22.9	0.6	196	7	143	0.3	0.2	0.4	0.3	45.6	54.4
East Bridgewater town	5,624	1,796	2,123	1,667	38	327	R	31.9	37.7	29.6	0.7	210	22	29	0.2	0.1	0.3	0.3	45.8	54.2
East Longmeadow town	7,513	2,844	2,818	1,833	18	26	D	37.9	37.5	24.4	0.2	169	23	123	0.3	0.2	0.4	0.3	50.2	49.8
Easthampton town	7,937	3,655	1,950	2,293	39	1,362	D	46.1	24.6	28.9	0.5	69	183	42	0.3	0.3	0.2	0.4	65.2	34.8
Easton town	10,337	3,736	3,906	2,637	58	170	R	36.1	37.8	25.5	0.6	187	21	97	0.4	0.3	0.5	0.4	48.9	51.1
Erving town	766	264	219	277	6	13	I	34.5	28.6	36.2	0.8	205	148	1	<.1	<.1	<.1	<.1	54.7	45.3
Everett city	15,250	8,037	4,063	3,051	99	3,974	D	52.7	26.6	20.0	0.6	26	167	183	0.5	0.6	0.5	0.5	66.4	33.6
Fairhaven town	7,903	4,061	1,584	2,222	36	1,839	D	51.4	20.0	28.1	0.5	34	201	51	0.3	0.3	0.2	0.4	71.9	28.1
Fall River city	31,210	18,652	5,456	6,922	180	11,730	D	59.8	17.5	22.2	0.6	11	209	156	1.1	1.4	0.7	1.1	77.4	22.6
Falmouth town	15,996	7,622	4,514	3,771	89	3,108	D	47.6	28.2	23.6	0.6	57	156	131	0.6	0.6	0.6	0.6	62.8	37.2
Fitchburg city	13,731	6,713	3,812	3,108	98	2,901	D	48.9	27.8	22.6	0.7	46	160	147	0.5	0.5	0.5	0.5	63.8	36.2
Foxborough town	8,092	3,153	2,844	2,051	44	309	D	39.0	35.1	25.3	0.5	148	40	102	0.3	0.2	0.4	0.3	52.6	47.4
Framingham town	29,542	15,165	8,114	6,089	174	7,051	D	51.3	27.5	20.6	0.6	35	163	174	1.1	1.2	1.0	1.0	65.1	34.9
Franklin town	11,487	4,844	3,698	2,864	81	1,146	D	42.2	32.2	24.9	0.7	107	86	111	0.4	0.4	0.5	0.5	56.7	43.3
Freetown town	4,126	1,584	1,062	1,458	22	126	D	38.4	25.7	35.3	0.5	156	175	2	0.1	0.1	0.1	0.2	59.9	40.1
Gardner town	8,157	3,973	2,231	1,920	33	1,742	D	48.7	27.4	23.5	0.4	48	164	133	0.3	0.3	0.3	0.3	64.0	36.0
Gloucester city	14,099	6,808	3,982	3,232	77	2,826	D	48.3	28.2	22.9	0.5	51	155	142	0.5	0.5	0.5	0.5	63.1	36.9
Grafton town	6,779	2,828	2,331	1,597	23	497	D	41.7	34.4	23.6	0.3	115	50	132	0.2	0.2	0.3	0.3	54.8	45.2
Great Barrington town	3,452	1,907	826	697	22	1,081	D	55.2	23.9	20.2	0.6	20	191	177	0.1	0.1	0.1	0.1	69.8	30.2
Greenfield town	8,591	4,130	2,073	2,326	62	1,804	D	48.1	24.1	27.1	0.7	54	189	72	0.3	0.3	0.3	0.4	66.6	33.4
Groton town	4,333	1,765	1,378	1,166	24	387	D	40.7	31.8	26.9	0.6	131	94	76	0.2	0.2	0.2	0.2	56.2	43.8
Groveland town	3,028	1,119	1,013	814	82	106	D	37.0	33.5	26.9	2.7	177	65	77	0.1	<.1	0.1	0.1	52.5	47.5
Hamilton town	4,254	1,428	1,860	941	25	432	R	33.6	43.7	22.1	0.6	207	2	158	0.2	0.1	0.2	0.1	43.4	56.6
Hanover town	6,841	2,382	2,561	1,866	32	179	R	34.8	37.4	27.3	0.5	198	25	69	0.2	0.2	0.3	0.3	48.2	51.8
Hanson town	4,100	1,365	1,383	1,327	25	18	R	33.3	33.7	32.4	0.6	208	59	9	0.1	0.1	0.2	0.2	49.7	50.3
Hardwick town	1,229	555	310	362	2	193	D	45.2	25.2	29.5	0.2	76	177	33	<.1	<.1	<.1	<.1	64.2	35.8
Haverhill city	22,678	10,216	6,854	5,450	158	3,362	D	45.0	30.2	24.0	0.7	79	127	127	0.8	0.8	0.9	0.9	59.8	40.2
Hingham town	12,378	4,702	4,899	2,705	72	197	R	38.0	39.6	21.9	0.6	166	14	161	0.4	0.4	0.6	0.4	49.0	51.0
Holbrook town	5,670	2,388	1,873	1,386	23	515	D	42.1	33.0	24.4	0.4	109	74	122	0.2	0.2	0.2	0.2	56.0	44.0
Holden town	8,559	3,127	3,736	1,676	20	609	R	36.5	43.7	19.6	0.2	182	3	185	0.3	0.2	0.5	0.3	45.6	54.4
Holliston town	7,534	3,224	2,380	1,886	44	844	D	42.8	31.6	25.0	0.6	101	97	109	0.3	0.2	0.3	0.3	57.5	42.5
Holyoke city	15,582	7,812	4,476	3,207	87	3,336	D	50.1	28.7	20.6	0.6	38	144	175	0.6	0.6	0.6	0.5	63.6	36.4
Hopkinton town	5,491	2,199	1,902	1,348	42	297	D	40.0	34.6	24.5	0.8	140	45	120	0.2	0.2	0.2	0.2	53.6	46.4
Hudson town	8,389	3,461	2,581	2,292	55	880	D	41.3	30.8	27.3	0.7	121	116	67	0.3	0.3	0.3	0.4	57.3	42.7
Hull town	5,318	2,620	1,259	1,403	36	1,217	D	49.3	23.7	26.4	0.7	43	193	87	0.2	0.2	0.2	0.2	67.5	32.5
Ipswich town	7,137	2,862	2,514	1,716	45	348	D	40.1	35.2	24.0	0.6	137	38	126	0.3	0.2	0.3	0.3	53.2	46.8
Kingston town	4,981	1,822	1,764	1,377	18	58	D	36.6	35.4	27.6	0.4	181	34	60	0.2	0.1	0.2	0.2	50.8	49.2
Lawrence city	16,139	7,698	5,079	3,245	117	2,619	D	47.7	31.5	20.1	0.7	56	101	180	0.6	0.6	0.6	0.5	60.2	39.8
Leicester town	5,043	2,064	1,630	1,334	15	434	D	40.9	32.3	26.5	0.3	127	83	85	0.2	0.2	0.2	0.2	55.9	44.1
Leominster city	16,832	7,302	5,293	4,157	80	2,009	D	43.4	31.4	24.7	0.5	93	104	119	0.6	0.6	0.7	0.7	58.0	42.0
Lexington town	17,960	10,015	5,001	2,796	148	5,014	D	55.8	27.8	15.6	0.8	18	159	204	0.6	0.8	0.6	0.4	66.7	33.3
Lincoln town	3,131	1,748	868	491	24	880	D	55.8	27.7	15.7	0.8	17	161	202	0.1	0.1	0.1	<.1	66.8	33.2
Littleton town	4,114	1,641	1,330	1,110	33	311	D	39.9	32.3	27.0	0.8	141	82	75	0.1	0.1	0.2	0.2	55.2	44.8
Longmeadow town	8,937	4,105	3,216	1,568	48	889	D	45.9	36.0	17.5	0.5	71	31	193	0.3	0.3	0.4	0.3	56.1	43.9
Lowell city	32,123	14,492	8,467	8,893	271	5,599	D	45.1	26.4	27.7	0.8	78	169	59	1.2	1.1	1.1	1.4	63.1	36.9
Ludlow town	8,615	3,898	2,244	2,396	77	1,502	D	45.2	26.0	27.8	0.9	75	171	55	0.3	0.3	0.3	0.4	63.5	36.5
Lunenburg town	4,634	1,808	1,546	1,252	28	262	D	39.0	33.4	27.0	0.6	147	67	73	0.2	0.1	0.2	0.2	53.9	46.1
Lynn city	30,477	15,275	7,350	7,665	187	7,610	D	50.1	24.1	25.2	0.6	39	190	106	1.1	1.2	0.9	1.2	67.5	32.5
Lynnfield town	6,901	2,259	2,905	1,706	31	646	R	32.7	42.1	24.7	0.4	209	5	118	0.2	0.2	0.4	0.3	43.7	56.3
Malden city	23,192	12,653	5,725	4,673	141	6,928	D	54.6	24.7	20.1	0.6	22	182	179	0.8	1.0	0.7	0.7	68.8	31.2
Mansfield town	8,783	3,356	2,908	2,476	43	448	D	38.2	33.1	28.2	0.5	161	72	49	0.3	0.3	0.4	0.4	53.6	46.4
Marblehead town	12,605	5,844	4,237	2,443	81	1,607	D	46.4	33.6	19.4	0.6	68	60	187	0.5	0.4	0.5	0.4	58.0	42.0
Marlborough city	14,796	6,213	4,525	3,962	96	1,688	D	42.0	30.6	26.8	0.6	112	119	79	0.5	0.5	0.6	0.6	57.9	42.1
Marshfield town	12,239	4,682	4,153	3,342	62	529	D	38.3	33.9	27.3	0.5	160	56	68	0.4	0.4	0.5	0.5	53.0	47.0
Mashpee town	4,597	1,941	1,329	1,311	16	612	D	42.2	28.9	28.5	0.3	106	142	46	0.2	0.1	0.2	0.2	59.4	40.6
Maynard town	5,534	2,526	1,588	1,387	33	938	D	45.6	28.7	25.1	0.6	72	145	107	0.2	0.2	0.2	0.2	61.4	38.6
Medfield town	6,321	2,456	2,503	1,340	22	47	R	38.9	39.6	21.2	0.3	150	13	169	0.2	0.2	0.3	0.2	49.5	50.5
Medford city	27,987	14,690	7,690	5,480	127	7,000	D	52.5	27.5	19.6	0.5	27	162	186	1.0	1.1	1.0	0.9	65.6	34.4
Medway town	5,343	2,124	1,729	1,464	26	395	D	39.8	32.4	27.4	0.5	142	80	66	0.2	0.2	0.2	0.2	55.1	44.9
Melrose city	16,232	7,464	5,108	3,582	78	2,356	D	46.0	31.5	22.1	0.5	70	102	160	0.6	0.6	0.6	0.6	59.4	40.6
Methuen town	19,677	7,727	6,954	4,905	91	773	D	39.3	35.3	24.9	0.5	145	36	112	0.7	0.6	0.9	0.8	52.6	47.4
Middleborough town	7,966	2,687	2,509	2,727	43	40	I	33.7	31.5	34.2	0.5	206	99	5	0.3	0.2	0.3	0.4	51.7	48.3
Milford town	11,561	5,583	3,306	2,632	40	2,277	D	48.3	28.6	22.8	0.3	50	147	145	0.4	0.4	0.4	0.4	62.8	37.2
Millbury town	6,204	2,655	2,007	1,520	22	648	D	42.8	32.4	24.5	0.4	100	81	121	0.2	0.2	0.2	0.2	56.9	43.1
Millis town	4,202	1,714	1,419	1,052	17	295	D	40.8	33.8	25.0	0.4	130	58	108	0.2	0.1	0.2	0.2	54.7	45.3
Milton town	14,999	6,634	5,409	2,900	56	1,225	D	44.2	36.1	19.3	0.4	87	30	188	0.5	0.5	0.7	0.5	55.1	44.9
Monson town	3,705	1,411	1,055	1,220	19	191	D	38.1	28.5	32.9	0.5	164	150	6	0.1	0.1	0.1	0.2	57.2	42.8
Montague town	4,071	2,123	883	1,048	17	1,075	D	52.1	21.7	25.7	0.4	30	197	95	0.1	0.2	0.1	0.2	70.6	29.4
Natick town	17,296	8,529	5,220	3,446	101	3,309	D	49.3	30.2	19.9	0.6	41	128	184	0.6	0.6	0.6	0.5	62.0	38.0
Needham town	17,101	8,287	5,880	2,816	118	2,407	D	48.5	34.4	16.5	0.7	49	51	199	0.6	0.6	0.7	0.4	58.5	41.5

¹Separate rankings for 14 counties and 213 cities and towns.

Massachusetts 455

Table E. — Vote for President: November 3, 1992, General Election (cont)

County	All candidates Total	Clinton (DEM)	Bush (REP)	Perot (IND)	Other	Plurality Total	Party	DEM	REP	IND	Other	Rank[1] DEM	Rank[1] REP	Rank[1] IND	% contrib Total	% contrib DEM	% contrib REP	% contrib IND	Major party DEM	Major party REP
New Bedford city	33,322	20,880	5,255	6,965	222	13,915	D	62.7	15.8	20.9	0.7	8	211	170	1.2	1.6	0.7	1.1	79.9	20.1
Newbury town	3,662	1,405	1,214	1,020	23	191	D	38.4	33.2	27.9	0.6	158	70	54	0.1	0.1	0.2	0.2	53.6	46.4
Newburyport city	9,438	4,543	2,735	2,097	63	1,808	D	48.1	29.0	22.2	0.7	53	141	155	0.3	0.3	0.3	0.3	62.4	37.6
Newton city	44,705	29,136	9,623	5,685	261	19,513	D	65.2	21.5	12.7	0.6	4	199	209	1.6	2.2	1.2	0.9	75.2	24.8
Norfolk town	4,416	1,402	1,781	1,220	13	379	R	31.7	40.3	27.6	0.3	211	10	61	0.2	0.1	0.2	0.2	44.0	56.0
North Adams city	6,389	3,733	1,256	1,379	21	2,354	D	58.4	19.7	21.6	0.3	12	204	162	0.2	0.3	0.2	0.2	74.8	25.2
North Andover town	12,569	4,652	4,937	2,891	89	285	R	37.0	39.3	23.0	0.7	176	16	140	0.5	0.4	0.6	0.5	48.5	51.5
North Attleborough town	10,654	3,699	3,683	3,227	45	16	D	34.7	34.6	30.3	0.4	201	46	22	0.4	0.3	0.5	0.5	50.1	49.9
North Reading town	7,036	2,663	2,469	1,858	46	194	D	37.8	35.1	26.4	0.7	170	41	86	0.3	0.2	0.3	0.3	51.9	48.1
Northampton city	15,174	9,750	2,741	2,513	170	7,009	D	64.3	18.1	16.6	1.1	6	206	198	0.5	0.7	0.3	0.4	78.1	21.9
Northborough town	6,567	2,537	2,416	1,561	53	121	D	38.6	36.8	23.8	0.8	152	28	128	0.2	0.2	0.3	0.2	51.2	48.8
Northbridge town	6,347	2,615	2,158	1,543	31	457	D	41.2	34.0	24.3	0.5	123	55	124	0.2	0.2	0.3	0.2	54.8	45.2
Norton town	6,729	2,562	2,150	1,979	38	412	D	38.1	32.0	29.4	0.6	165	92	34	0.2	0.2	0.3	0.3	54.4	45.6
Norwell town	5,639	1,956	2,224	1,431	28	268	R	34.7	39.4	25.4	0.5	202	15	101	0.2	0.1	0.3	0.2	46.8	53.2
Norwood town	15,001	6,803	4,882	3,224	92	1,921	D	45.4	32.5	21.5	0.6	74	79	163	0.5	0.5	0.6	0.5	58.2	41.8
Orange town	3,302	1,190	1,077	1,021	14	113	D	36.0	32.6	30.9	0.4	188	77	17	0.1	<.1	0.1	0.2	52.5	47.5
Orleans town	4,142	1,590	1,533	978	41	57	D	38.4	37.0	23.6	1.0	157	27	129	0.1	0.1	0.2	0.2	50.9	49.1
Oxford town	5,658	2,282	1,773	1,581	22	509	D	40.3	31.3	27.9	0.4	136	107	53	0.2	0.2	0.2	0.3	56.3	43.7
Palmer town	5,748	2,485	1,530	1,698	35	787	D	43.2	26.6	29.5	0.6	94	168	31	0.2	0.2	0.2	0.3	61.9	38.1
Peabody city	24,704	11,694	6,709	6,155	146	4,985	D	47.3	27.2	24.9	0.6	61	165	114	0.9	0.9	0.8	1.0	63.5	36.5
Pembroke town	7,842	2,728	2,636	2,457	21	92	D	34.8	33.6	31.3	0.3	200	61	15	0.3	0.2	0.3	0.4	50.9	49.1
Pepperell town	4,863	1,693	1,550	1,577	43	116	D	34.8	31.9	32.4	0.9	199	93	8	0.2	0.1	0.2	0.3	52.2	47.8
Pittsfield city	22,882	13,012	4,541	5,189	140	7,823	D	56.9	19.8	22.7	0.6	14	202	146	0.8	1.0	0.6	0.8	74.1	25.9
Plainville town	3,300	1,219	1,135	929	17	84	D	36.9	34.4	28.2	0.5	178	48	50	0.1	<.1	0.1	0.1	51.8	48.2
Plymouth town	21,614	8,360	6,620	6,521	113	1,740	D	38.7	30.6	30.2	0.5	151	118	25	0.8	0.6	0.8	1.0	55.8	44.2
Quincy city	40,495	18,891	12,306	9,068	230	6,585	D	46.7	30.4	22.4	0.6	64	121	150	1.5	1.4	1.5	1.4	60.6	39.4
Randolph town	14,245	7,817	3,443	2,915	70	4,374	D	54.9	24.2	20.5	0.5	21	188	176	0.5	0.6	0.4	0.5	69.4	30.6
Raynham town	5,195	1,839	1,771	1,561	24	68	D	35.4	34.1	30.0	0.5	192	53	26	0.2	0.1	0.2	0.2	50.9	49.1
Reading town	13,446	5,753	4,516	3,083	94	1,237	D	42.8	33.6	22.9	0.7	102	63	141	0.5	0.4	0.6	0.5	56.0	44.0
Rehoboth town	4,539	1,652	1,452	1,405	30	200	D	36.4	32.0	31.0	0.7	183	90	16	0.2	0.1	0.2	0.2	53.2	46.8
Revere city	18,826	9,628	4,896	4,175	127	4,732	D	51.1	26.0	22.2	0.7	36	172	157	0.7	0.7	0.6	0.7	66.3	33.7
Rockland town	7,610	2,970	2,457	2,138	45	513	D	39.0	32.3	28.1	0.6	146	84	52	0.3	0.2	0.3	0.3	54.7	45.3
Rockport town	4,497	2,091	1,411	958	37	680	D	46.5	31.4	21.3	0.8	65	106	167	0.2	0.2	0.2	0.2	59.7	40.3
Salem city	17,985	9,385	4,471	4,025	104	4,914	D	52.2	24.9	22.4	0.6	29	180	151	0.6	0.7	0.6	0.6	67.7	32.3
Salisbury town	3,138	1,300	924	897	17	376	D	41.4	29.4	28.6	0.5	120	134	44	0.1	<.1	0.1	0.1	58.5	41.5
Sandwich town	9,116	3,460	2,936	2,677	43	524	D	38.0	32.2	29.4	0.5	167	85	35	0.3	0.3	0.4	0.4	54.1	45.9
Saugus town	13,405	5,764	3,938	3,637	66	1,826	D	43.0	29.4	27.1	0.5	97	135	70	0.5	0.4	0.5	0.6	59.4	40.6
Scituate town	10,494	4,129	3,609	2,678	78	520	D	39.3	34.4	25.5	0.7	144	49	96	0.4	0.3	0.4	0.4	53.4	46.6
Seekonk town	6,491	2,735	2,001	1,694	61	734	D	42.1	30.8	26.1	0.9	108	115	90	0.2	0.2	0.2	0.3	57.7	42.3
Sharon town	9,211	5,656	1,964	1,538	53	3,692	D	61.4	21.3	16.7	0.6	10	200	197	0.3	0.4	0.2	0.2	74.2	25.8
Shrewsbury town	13,494	5,670	5,044	2,708	72	626	D	42.0	37.4	20.1	0.5	111	26	181	0.5	0.4	0.6	0.4	52.9	47.1
Somerset town	9,893	5,155	2,392	2,318	28	2,763	D	52.1	24.2	23.4	0.3	31	187	134	0.4	0.4	0.3	0.4	68.3	31.7
Somerville city	30,399	19,792	5,883	4,416	308	13,909	D	65.1	19.4	14.5	1.0	5	205	205	1.1	1.5	0.7	0.7	77.1	22.9
South Hadley town	8,272	3,694	2,461	2,070	47	1,233	D	44.7	29.8	25.0	0.6	83	129	110	0.3	0.3	0.3	0.3	60.0	40.0
Southborough town	4,084	1,637	1,403	1,018	26	234	D	40.1	34.4	24.9	0.6	138	52	113	0.1	0.1	0.2	0.2	53.8	46.2
Southbridge town	7,158	3,385	1,914	1,824	35	1,471	D	47.3	26.7	25.5	0.5	62	166	99	0.3	0.3	0.2	0.3	63.9	36.1
Southwick town	3,641	1,268	1,187	1,168	18	81	D	34.8	32.6	32.1	0.5	197	78	11	0.1	<.1	0.1	0.2	51.6	48.4
Spencer town	5,288	1,993	1,763	1,513	19	230	D	37.7	33.3	28.6	0.4	172	69	43	0.2	0.2	0.2	0.2	53.1	46.9
Springfield city	50,111	27,302	12,200	10,361	248	15,102	D	54.5	24.3	20.7	0.5	23	185	172	1.8	2.1	1.5	1.6	69.1	30.9
Stoneham town	11,629	5,135	3,689	2,743	62	1,446	D	44.2	31.7	23.6	0.5	88	95	130	0.4	0.4	0.5	0.4	58.2	41.8
Stoughton town	13,065	6,274	3,749	2,986	56	2,525	D	48.0	28.7	22.9	0.4	55	146	144	0.5	0.5	0.5	0.5	62.6	37.4
Sudbury town	8,967	4,169	2,942	1,799	57	1,227	D	46.5	32.8	20.1	0.6	66	76	182	0.3	0.3	0.4	0.3	58.6	41.4
Sutton town	3,710	1,296	1,412	991	11	116	R	34.9	38.1	26.7	0.3	195	20	81	0.1	<.1	0.2	0.2	47.9	52.1
Swampscott town	8,227	4,315	2,301	1,551	60	2,014	D	52.4	28.0	18.9	0.7	28	158	189	0.3	0.3	0.3	0.2	65.2	34.8
Taunton city	19,483	8,683	5,049	5,673	78	3,010	D	44.6	25.9	29.1	0.4	84	173	39	0.7	0.7	0.6	0.9	63.2	36.8
Templeton town	2,991	1,247	924	811	9	323	D	41.7	30.9	27.1	0.3	116	113	71	0.1	<.1	0.1	0.1	57.4	42.6
Tewksbury town	14,038	5,328	4,340	4,276	94	988	D	38.0	30.9	30.5	0.7	168	112	21	0.5	0.4	0.5	0.7	55.1	44.9
Townsend town	3,953	1,365	1,272	1,290	26	75	D	34.5	32.2	32.6	0.7	203	87	7	0.1	0.1	0.2	0.2	51.8	48.2
Tyngsborough town	4,238	1,483	1,251	1,489	15	6	I	35.0	29.5	35.1	0.4	194	133	3	0.2	0.1	0.2	0.2	54.2	45.8
Uxbridge town	5,256	2,183	1,540	1,501	32	643	D	41.5	29.3	28.6	0.6	119	137	45	0.2	0.2	0.2	0.2	58.6	41.4
Wakefield town	13,776	5,922	4,300	3,465	89	1,622	D	43.0	31.2	25.2	0.6	98	108	105	0.5	0.4	0.5	0.5	57.9	42.1
Walpole town	11,257	4,317	4,288	2,592	60	29	D	38.3	38.1	23.0	0.5	159	19	139	0.4	0.3	0.5	0.4	50.2	49.8
Waltham city	23,975	11,333	7,365	5,092	185	3,968	D	47.3	30.7	21.2	0.8	63	117	168	0.9	0.9	0.9	0.8	60.6	39.4
Ware town	4,657	2,216	1,136	1,292	13	924	D	47.6	24.4	27.7	0.3	58	184	57	0.2	0.2	0.1	0.2	66.1	33.9
Wareham town	8,887	3,870	2,516	2,454	47	1,354	D	43.5	28.3	27.6	0.5	90	153	62	0.3	0.3	0.3	0.4	60.6	39.4
Warren town	2,023	846	532	635	10	211	D	41.8	26.3	31.4	0.5	113	170	14	<.1	<.1	0.1	0.1	61.4	38.6
Watertown town	17,239	9,977	4,293	2,824	145	5,684	D	57.9	24.9	16.4	0.8	13	179	200	0.6	0.8	0.5	0.4	69.9	30.1
Wayland town	7,629	3,733	2,450	1,379	67	1,283	D	48.9	32.1	18.1	0.9	45	88	192	0.3	0.3	0.3	0.2	60.4	39.6
Webster town	6,576	2,943	1,927	1,676	30	1,016	D	44.8	29.3	25.5	0.5	81	136	98	0.2	0.2	0.2	0.3	60.4	39.6
Wellesley town	14,691	6,990	5,507	2,112	82	1,483	D	47.6	37.5	14.4	0.6	59	24	206	0.5	0.5	0.7	0.3	55.9	44.1

[1]Separate rankings for 14 counties and 213 cities and towns.

456 Massachusetts

County	Total	Clinton (DEM)	Bush (REP)	Perot (IND)	Other	Plurality Total	Party	DEM	REP	IND	Other	DEM (Rank¹)	REP (Rank¹)	IND (Rank¹)	Total	DEM	REP	IND	DEM	REP
West Boylston town	3,548	1,335	1,481	716	16	146	R	37.6	41.7	20.2	0.5	173	6	178	0.1	0.1	0.2	0.1	47.4	52.6
West Bridgewater town ..	3,774	1,142	1,498	1,118	16	356	R	30.3	39.7	29.6	0.4	212	12	30	0.1	<.1	0.2	0.2	43.3	56.7
West Springfield town	12,649	5,122	4,190	3,274	63	932	D	40.5	33.1	25.9	0.5	135	71	93	0.5	0.4	0.5	0.5	55.0	45.0
Westborough town	7,955	3,187	2,916	1,800	52	271	D	40.1	36.7	22.6	0.7	139	29	148	0.3	0.2	0.4	0.3	52.2	47.8
Westfield city	17,170	7,023	5,206	4,854	87	1,817	D	40.9	30.3	28.3	0.5	129	125	48	0.6	0.5	0.6	0.8	57.4	42.6
Westford town..............	9,516	3,341	3,303	2,794	78	38	D	35.1	34.7	29.4	0.8	193	43	36	0.3	0.3	0.4	0.4	50.3	49.7
Weston town	6,131	2,561	2,454	1,073	43	107	D	41.8	40.0	17.5	0.7	114	11	194	0.2	0.2	0.3	0.2	51.1	48.9
Westport town	7,088	3,150	1,757	2,145	36	1,005	D	44.4	24.8	30.3	0.5	85	181	23	0.3	0.2	0.2	0.3	64.2	35.8
Westwood town	8,290	3,007	3,529	1,710	44	522	R	36.3	42.6	20.6	0.5	184	4	173	0.3	0.2	0.4	0.3	46.0	54.0
Weymouth town	25,295	10,762	7,849	6,552	132	2,913	D	42.5	31.0	25.9	0.5	103	111	92	0.9	0.8	1.0	1.0	57.8	42.2
Whitman town................	6,432	2,283	2,232	1,879	38	51	D	35.5	34.7	29.2	0.6	191	44	37	0.2	0.2	0.3	0.3	50.6	49.4
Wilbraham town	7,527	2,730	3,062	1,691	44	332	R	36.3	40.7	22.5	0.6	185	9	149	0.3	0.2	0.4	0.3	47.1	52.9
Williamstown town	4,152	2,618	945	563	26	1,673	D	63.1	22.8	13.6	0.6	7	195	208	0.1	0.2	0.1	<.1	73.5	26.5
Wilmington town............	9,919	3,817	3,174	2,886	42	643	D	38.5	32.0	29.1	0.4	154	89	40	0.4	0.3	0.4	0.5	54.6	45.4
Winchendon town..........	3,307	1,439	940	907	21	499	D	43.5	28.4	27.4	0.6	91	151	65	0.1	0.1	0.1	0.1	60.5	39.5
Winchester town............	12,668	5,717	4,506	2,378	67	1,211	D	45.1	35.6	18.8	0.5	77	32	190	0.5	0.4	0.6	0.4	55.9	44.1
Winthrop town................	9,469	4,625	2,657	2,109	78	1,968	D	48.8	28.1	22.3	0.8	47	157	153	0.3	0.4	0.3	0.3	63.5	36.5
Woburn city..................	18,466	7,983	5,743	4,581	159	2,240	D	43.2	31.1	24.8	0.9	95	110	116	0.7	0.6	0.7	0.7	58.2	41.8
Worcester city..............	60,307	32,326	17,228	10,488	265	15,098	D	53.6	28.6	17.4	0.4	24	149	195	2.2	2.5	2.1	1.7	65.2	34.8
Wrentham town	4,496	1,550	1,531	4	1,411	19	D	34.5	34.1	<.1	31.4	204	54	213	0.2	0.1	0.2	<.1	50.3	49.7
Yarmouth town	12,421	5,168	4,283	2,890	80	885	D	41.6	34.5	23.3	0.6	117	47	136	0.4	0.4	0.5	0.5	54.7	45.3

¹Separate rankings for 14 counties and 213 cities and towns.

Table H. – Vote for U.S. Representative in Congress: November 3, 1992, General Election

Congressional district and county	Total	Democrat (DEM)	Republican (REP)	Other	Plurality Total	Plurality Party	Percent of total vote DEM	Percent of total vote REP	Percent of total vote Other	Rank within district DEM	Rank within district REP	Rank within district Other	Percent contribution to district vote Total	Percent contribution to district vote DEM	Percent contribution to district vote REP	Percent contribution to district vote Other
District 1	262,120	135,049	113,828	13,243	21,221	D	51.5	43.4	5.1				100.0	100.0	100.0	100.0
Berkshire	65,936	33,556	30,892	1,488	2,664	D	50.9	46.9	2.3	4	2	6	25.2	24.8	27.1	11.2
Franklin	35,098	19,168	15,040	890	4,128	D	54.6	42.9	2.5	2	4	5	13.4	14.2	13.2	6.7
Hampden (pt)	50,219	26,194	22,504	1,521	3,690	D	52.2	44.8	3.0	3	3	4	19.2	19.4	19.8	11.5
Hampshire (pt)	37,665	22,554	13,941	1,170	8,613	D	59.9	37.0	3.1	1	6	3	14.4	16.7	12.2	8.8
Middlesex (pt)	4,981	1,794	2,559	628	765	R	36.0	51.4	12.6	6	1	1	1.9	1.3	2.2	4.7
Worcester (pt)	68,221	31,783	28,892	7,546	2,891	D	46.6	42.4	11.1	5	5	2	26.0	23.5	25.4	57.0
District 2'	247,163	131,215	76,795	39,153	54,420	D	53.1	31.1	15.8				100.0	100.0	100.0	100.0
Hampden (pt)'	129,013	71,155	37,896	19,962	33,259	D	55.2	29.4	15.5	1	4	3	52.2	54.2	49.3	51.0
Hampshire (pt)'	29,000	15,623	9,039	4,338	6,584	D	53.9	31.2	15.0	2	3	4	11.7	11.9	11.8	11.1
Norfolk (pt)'	6,262	2,711	2,211	1,340	500	D	43.3	35.3	21.4	4	1	1	2.5	2.1	2.9	3.4
Worcester (pt)'	82,888	41,726	27,649	13,513	14,077	D	50.3	33.4	16.3	3	2	2	33.5	31.8	36.0	34.5
District 3	260,941	115,592	131,476	13,873	15,884	R	44.3	50.4	5.3				100.0	100.0	100.0	100.0
Bristol (pt)	83,724	40,239	37,979	5,506	2,260	D	48.1	45.4	6.6	1	4	3	32.1	34.8	28.9	39.7
Middlesex (pt)	12,470	4,076	7,385	1,009	3,309	R	32.7	59.2	8.1	4	1	1	4.8	3.5	5.6	7.3
Norfolk (pt)	26,663	9,718	15,025	1,920	5,307	R	36.4	56.4	7.2	3	2	2	10.2	8.4	11.4	13.8
Worcester (pt)	138,084	61,559	71,087	5,438	9,528	R	44.6	51.5	3.9	2	3	4	52.9	53.3	54.1	39.2
District 4	269,814	182,633	70,666	16,515	111,967	D	67.7	26.2	6.1				100.0	100.0	100.0	100.0
Bristol (pt)	91,611	65,406	20,258	5,947	45,148	D	71.4	22.1	6.5	2	3	2	34.0	35.8	28.7	36.0
Middlesex (pt)	45,194	35,289	7,908	1,997	27,381	D	78.1	17.5	4.4	1	4	3	16.8	19.3	11.2	12.1
Norfolk (pt)	64,264	44,945	17,386	1,933	27,559	D	69.9	27.1	3.0	3	2	4	23.8	24.6	24.6	11.7
Plymouth (pt)	68,745	36,993	25,114	6,638	11,879	D	53.8	36.5	9.7	4	1	1	25.5	20.3	35.5	40.2
District 5	256,564	133,844	96,206	26,514	37,638	D	52.2	37.5	10.3				100.0	100.0	100.0	100.0
Essex (pt)	50,593	22,354	21,207	7,032	1,147	D	44.2	41.9	13.9	2	2	1	19.7	16.7	22.0	26.5
Middlesex (pt)	196,303	107,291	70,480	18,532	36,811	D	54.7	35.9	9.4	1	3	3	76.5	80.2	73.3	69.9
Worcester (pt)	9,668	4,199	4,519	950	320	R	43.4	46.7	9.8	3	1	2	3.8	3.1	4.7	3.6
District 6	290,312	130,248	159,165	899	28,917	R	44.9	54.8	0.3				100.0	100.0	100.0	100.0
Essex (pt)	253,453	118,891	133,742	820	14,851	R	46.9	52.8	0.3	1	2	1	87.3	91.3	84.0	91.2
Middlesex (pt)	36,859	11,357	25,423	79	14,066	R	30.8	69.0	0.2	2	1	2	12.7	8.7	16.0	8.8
District 7	281,558	174,837	78,262	28,459	96,575	D	62.1	27.8	10.1				100.0	100.0	100.0	100.0
Middlesex (pt)	255,330	156,323	73,336	25,671	82,987	D	61.2	28.7	10.1	2	1	2	90.7	89.4	93.7	90.2
Suffolk (pt)	26,228	18,514	4,926	2,788	13,588	D	70.6	18.8	10.6	1	2	1	9.3	10.6	6.3	9.8
District 8	180,492	149,907	-	30,585	119,322	D	83.1	-	16.9				100.0	100.0	-	100.0
Middlesex (pt)	91,570	74,506	-	17,064	57,442	D	81.4	-	18.6	2	-	1	50.7	49.7	-	55.8
Suffolk (pt)	88,922	75,401	-	13,521	61,880	D	84.8	-	15.2	1	-	2	49.3	50.3	-	44.2
District 9	253,634	175,550	54,291	23,793	121,259	D	69.2	21.4	9.4				100.0	100.0	100.0	100.0
Bristol (pt)	22,620	14,107	6,897	1,616	7,210	D	62.4	30.5	7.1	3	2	4	8.9	8.0	12.7	6.8
Norfolk (pt)	133,120	85,591	33,236	14,293	52,355	D	64.3	25.0	10.7	2	3	1	52.5	48.8	61.2	60.1
Plymouth (pt)	16,043	9,662	4,996	1,385	4,666	D	60.2	31.1	8.6	4	1	2	6.3	5.5	9.2	5.8
Suffolk (pt)	81,851	66,190	9,162	6,499	57,028	D	80.9	11.2	7.9	1	4	3	32.3	37.7	16.9	27.3
District 10	311,651	189,343	75,887	46,421	113,456	D	60.8	24.4	14.9				100.0	100.0	100.0	100.0
Barnstable	107,269	68,335	19,751	19,183	48,584	D	63.7	18.4	17.9	3	3	1	34.4	36.1	26.0	41.3
Dukes	7,777	6,394	833	550	5,561	D	82.2	10.7	7.1	1	5	4	2.5	3.4	1.1	1.2
Nantucket	4,140	3,195	659	286	2,536	D	77.2	15.9	6.9	2	4	5	1.3	1.7	0.9	0.6
Norfolk (pt)	76,839	44,631	21,524	10,684	23,107	D	58.1	28.0	13.9	4	2	2	24.7	23.6	28.4	23.0
Plymouth (pt)	115,626	66,788	33,120	15,718	33,668	D	57.8	28.6	13.6	5	1	3	37.1	35.3	43.6	33.9
MASSACHUSETTS	2,614,249	1,518,218	856,576	239,455	661,642	D	58.1	32.8	9.2							

'Does not include corrected vote for other candidates from Secretary of State's publication, *Massachusetts Election Statistics 1992*, Public Document 43 (district total vote for other candidates of 190 corrected to 178).

Table I. — Vote for Presidential Preference: March 10, 1992, Democratic Primary Election

County	Top candidates									Top three candidates (state vote)								
										Percent of total vote			Rank[2]			Percent contribution to state vote		
	Total[1]	Tsongas	Brown	Clinton	Nader	No Pre-ference[1]	Kerrey	Harkin	Other[1]	Tsongas	Brown	Clinton	Tsongas	Brown	Clinton	Total	Tsongas	Brown	Clinton
Barnstable	25,238	16,604	4,323	2,623	890	237	160	107	294	65.8	17.1	10.4	6	7	9	3.2	3.2	3.7	3.0
Berkshire	13,438	8,185	1,905	1,675	1,031	248	84	75	235	60.9	14.2	12.5	10	11	4	1.7	1.6	1.6	1.9
Bristol	51,328	31,382	6,496	8,922	1,942	914	544	322	806	61.1	12.7	17.4	9	12	1	6.5	6.0	5.6	10.3
Dukes	2,746	1,570	594	334	101	60	25	19	43	57.2	21.6	12.2	13	2	5	0.3	0.3	0.5	0.4
Essex	95,445	64,653	13,864	9,184	4,323	1,381	641	411	988	67.7	14.5	9.6	4	9	10	12.0	12.3	12.0	10.6
Franklin	8,228	4,694	1,969	747	534	82	48	46	108	57.0	23.9	9.1	14	1	13	1.0	0.9	1.7	0.9
Hampden	39,720	27,437	3,679	4,311	2,573	779	225	130	586	69.1	9.3	10.9	2	14	7	5.0	5.2	3.2	5.0
Hampshire	17,925	10,397	3,860	1,710	1,289	274	78	100	217	58.0	21.5	9.5	12	3	12	2.3	2.0	3.3	2.0
Middlesex	231,139	161,879	32,771	20,479	8,124	2,777	1,242	1,017	2,850	70.0	14.2	8.9	1	10	14	29.2	30.8	28.3	23.6
Nantucket	929	570	192	111	22	9	8	2	15	61.4	20.7	11.9	8	4	6	0.1	0.1	0.2	0.1
Norfolk	99,681	67,616	14,663	9,551	3,911	1,782	641	455	1,062	67.8	14.7	9.6	3	8	11	12.6	12.8	12.7	11.0
Plymouth	49,513	31,765	8,501	5,252	2,088	772	370	251	514	64.2	17.2	10.6	7	6	8	6.2	6.0	7.3	6.0
Suffolk	77,564	46,322	13,519	10,858	3,019	1,523	665	436	1,222	59.7	17.4	14.0	11	5	2	9.8	8.8	11.7	12.5
Worcester	79,991	53,223	9,410	11,060	3,034	1,360	678	393	833	66.5	11.8	13.8	5	13	3	10.1	10.1	8.1	12.7
MASSACHUSETTS	**792,885**	**526,297**	**115,746**	**86,817**	**32,881**	**12,198**	**5,409**	**3,764**	**9,773**	**66.4**	**14.6**	**10.9**				**100.0**	**100.0**	**100.0**	**100.0**
CITIES AND TOWNS																			
Abington town	1,734	1,118	285	169	75	45	15	9	18	64.5	16.4	9.7	144	49	116	0.2	0.2	0.2	0.2
Acton town	3,038	2,355	413	154	63	12	8	10	23	77.5	13.6	5.1	6	118	210	0.4	0.4	0.4	0.2
Acushnet town	1,453	824	195	318	46	28	21	7	14	56.7	13.4	21.9	207	125	2	0.2	0.2	0.2	0.4
Adams town	974	646	122	129	43	13	9	3	9	66.3	12.5	13.2	120	156	49	0.1	0.1	0.1	0.1
Agawam town	2,317	1,584	248	244	166	36	10	5	24	68.4	10.7	10.5	86	187	99	0.3	0.3	0.2	0.2
Amesbury town	1,786	1,028	356	178	77	15	29	33	70	57.6	19.9	10.0	205	11	115	0.2	0.2	0.3	0.2
Amherst town	3,787	1,911	1,044	404	287	62	15	34	30	50.5	27.6	10.7	212	1	93	0.5	0.4	0.9	0.5
Andover town	4,733	3,471	703	267	211	40	18	10	13	73.3	14.9	5.6	27	87	205	0.6	0.7	0.6	0.3
Arlington town	11,296	7,747	1,712	865	507	186	82	57	140	68.6	15.2	7.7	82	78	171	1.4	1.5	1.5	1.0
Ashburnham town	591	371	109	77	18	4	3	2	7	62.8	18.4	13.0	174	21	52	<.1	<.1	<.1	<.1
Ashland town	1,579	1,077	252	135	61	21	9	10	14	68.2	16.0	8.5	91	55	145	0.2	0.2	0.2	0.2
Athol town	826	517	99	133	28	17	8	8	16	62.6	12.0	16.1	176	162	25	0.1	<.1	<.1	0.2
Attleboro city	2,683	1,703	416	336	135	34	15	17	27	63.5	15.5	12.5	162	63	60	0.3	0.3	0.4	0.4
Auburn town	1,971	1,346	227	264	61	34	12	9	18	68.3	11.5	13.4	89	172	47	0.2	0.3	0.2	0.3
Ayer town	651	452	86	88	8	3	7	2	5	69.4	13.2	13.5	67	132	44	<.1	<.1	<.1	0.1
Barnstable town	4,941	3,261	806	546	185	49	34	18	42	66.0	16.3	11.1	128	52	84	0.6	0.6	0.7	0.6
Barre town	604	374	92	97	21	6	5	2	7	61.9	15.2	16.1	181	71	26	<.1	<.1	<.1	0.1
Bedford town	2,173	1,691	277	118	46	16	6	6	13	77.8	12.7	5.4	4	148	208	0.3	0.3	0.2	0.1
Belchertown town	983	621	190	84	59	12	2	4	11	63.2	19.3	8.5	166	13	146	0.1	0.1	0.2	<.1
Bellingham town	1,643	1,059	217	222	51	37	17	10	30	64.5	13.2	13.5	148	133	45	0.2	0.2	0.2	0.3
Belmont town	5,018	3,566	735	370	164	67	32	20	64	71.1	14.6	7.4	48	90	180	0.6	0.7	0.6	0.4
Beverly city	5,185	3,491	920	407	173	89	33	22	50	67.3	17.7	7.8	107	29	164	0.7	0.7	0.8	0.5
Billerica town	5,094	3,679	662	371	216	84	27	21	34	72.2	13.0	7.3	37	139	183	0.6	0.7	0.6	0.4
Blackstone town	936	591	86	162	37	23	10	11	16	63.1	9.2	17.3	167	200	15	0.1	0.1	<.1	0.2
Boston city	64,666	38,095	11,805	9,170	2,439	1,186	554	380	1,037	58.9	18.3	14.2	201	23	39	8.2	7.2	10.2	10.6
Bourne town	1,796	1,142	298	213	75	17	15	13	23	63.6	16.6	11.9	160	44	71	0.2	0.2	0.3	0.2
Boxford town	786	583	120	34	31	6	2	2	8	74.2	15.3	4.3	20	70	213	<.1	0.1	0.1	<.1
Braintree town	6,129	4,094	791	587	302	165	43	17	130	66.8	12.9	9.6	114	143	119	0.8	0.8	0.7	0.7
Brewster town	1,262	811	278	108	44	4	5	2	10	64.3	22.0	8.6	153	7	143	0.2	0.2	0.2	0.1
Bridgewater town	1,622	1,008	289	168	72	31	15	18	21	62.1	17.8	10.4	180	27	108	0.2	0.2	0.2	0.2
Brockton city	9,366	5,737	1,423	1,283	476	244	79	51	73	61.3	15.2	13.7	185	76	43	1.2	1.1	1.2	1.5
Brookline town	10,206	6,619	1,790	1,170	321	81	38	67	120	64.9	17.5	11.5	138	31	77	1.3	1.3	1.5	1.3
Burlington town	3,624	2,592	490	283	144	58	19	13	25	71.5	13.5	7.8	44	121	166	0.5	0.5	0.4	0.3
Cambridge city	16,790	9,480	3,821	2,015	708	221	82	123	340	56.5	22.8	12.0	208	6	69	2.1	1.8	3.3	2.3
Canton town	3,433	2,290	528	313	133	89	33	13	34	66.7	15.4	9.1	115	67	131	0.4	0.4	0.5	0.4
Carver town	1,178	742	179	173	42	15	11	3	13	63.0	15.2	14.7	171	75	35	0.1	0.1	0.2	0.2
Chatham town	918	696	123	57	21	4	8	1	8	75.8	13.4	6.2	11	129	198	0.1	0.1	0.1	<.1
Chelmsford town	5,643	4,485	585	320	151	30	23	13	36	79.5	10.4	5.7	2	191	204	0.7	0.9	0.5	0.4
Chelsea city	2,968	1,886	342	481	122	63	26	14	34	63.5	11.5	16.2	161	171	24	0.4	0.4	0.3	0.6
Chicopee city	6,270	4,354	478	702	450	99	43	11	133	69.4	7.6	11.2	66	209	82	0.8	0.8	0.4	0.8
Clarksburg town	141	104	14	12	9	2	0	0	0	73.8	9.9	8.5	22	196	149	<.1	<.1	<.1	<.1
Clinton town	1,730	1,082	217	309	46	22	14	11	29	62.5	12.5	17.9	177	155	12	0.2	0.2	0.2	0.4
Cohasset town	982	692	172	60	30	11	3	2	12	70.5	17.5	6.1	57	32	199	0.1	0.1	0.1	<.1
Concord town	3,349	2,570	463	184	72	13	11	5	31	76.7	13.8	5.5	9	110	207	0.4	0.5	0.4	0.2
Dalton town	637	379	97	66	65	4	6	9	11	59.5	15.2	10.4	196	72	107	<.1	<.1	<.1	0.1
Danvers town	3,261	2,346	460	252	106	42	22	10	23	71.9	14.1	7.7	40	103	168	0.4	0.4	0.4	0.3
Dartmouth town	3,653	2,187	463	721	125	75	27	22	33	59.9	12.7	19.7	192	149	9	0.5	0.4	0.4	0.8
Dedham town	4,380	2,979	610	409	202	102	23	28	27	68.0	13.9	9.3	95	104	123	0.6	0.6	0.5	0.5
Deerfield town	707	445	131	66	56	4	2	0	3	62.9	18.5	9.3	172	20	124	<.1	<.1	0.1	<.1
Dennis town	1,924	1,301	266	195	82	21	13	16	30	67.6	13.8	10.1	101	111	112	0.2	0.2	0.2	0.2
Dracut town	4,993	3,769	428	454	191	65	28	16	42	75.5	8.6	9.1	12	206	133	0.6	0.7	0.4	0.5
Dudley town	970	594	111	170	41	31	7	0	16	61.2	11.4	17.5	186	175	14	0.1	0.1	<.1	0.2

[1]Does not include corrected vote for no preference and other candidates from Secretary of State's publication, *Massachusetts Election Statistics 1992*, Public Document 43 (statewide total vote of 12,198 for no preference and 2,255 for other candidates corrected to 12,218 for no preference and 3,465 for other candidates). [2]Separate rankings for 14 counties and 213 cities and towns.

Table I. — Vote for Presidential Preference: March 10, 1992, Democratic Primary Election (cont)

| County | Top candidates | | | | | | | | | Top three candidates (state vote) | | | | | | | | | |
| | | | | | | | | | | Percent of total vote | | | Rank² | | | Percent contribution to state vote | | | |
	Total¹	Tsongas	Brown	Clinton	Nader	No Pre-ference¹	Kerrey	Harkin	Other¹	Tsongas	Brown	Clinton	Tsongas	Brown	Clinton	Total	Tsongas	Brown	Clinton
Duxbury town	1,595	1,094	292	108	50	13	8	5	25	68.6	18.3	6.8	81	22	187	0.2	0.2	0.3	0.1
East Bridgewater town	996	606	166	105	39	10	12	20	38	60.8	16.7	10.5	188	43	98	0.1	0.1	0.1	0.1
East Longmeadow town	1,264	960	106	95	64	20	3	1	15	75.9	8.4	7.5	10	208	174	0.2	0.2	<.1	0.1
Easthampton town	1,618	1,021	236	168	131	22	10	7	23	63.1	14.6	10.4	170	95	105	0.2	0.2	0.2	0.2
Easton town	2,366	1,615	383	201	79	41	19	8	20	68.3	16.2	8.5	90	53	150	0.3	0.3	0.3	0.2
Erving town	138	89	10	18	16	1	2	1	1	64.5	7.2	13.0	143	211	51	<.1	<.1	<.1	<.1
Everett city	4,920	3,089	671	713	218	118	41	34	36	62.8	13.6	14.5	173	115	37	0.6	0.6	0.6	0.8
Fairhaven town	2,106	1,205	293	456	79	30	16	12	15	57.2	13.9	21.7	206	106	4	0.3	0.2	0.3	0.5
Fall River city	8,774	5,464	744	1,558	299	237	166	61	245	62.3	8.5	17.8	179	207	13	1.1	1.0	0.6	1.8
Falmouth town	4,155	2,706	693	474	135	61	28	21	37	65.1	16.7	11.4	133	42	78	0.5	0.5	0.6	0.5
Fitchburg city	5,286	3,429	562	793	198	112	41	46	105	64.9	10.6	15.0	137	188	32	0.7	0.7	0.5	0.9
Foxborough town	2,103	1,444	288	221	67	43	9	7	24	68.7	13.7	10.5	78	113	101	0.3	0.3	0.2	0.3
Framingham town	9,508	6,740	1,204	908	339	114	42	43	118	70.9	12.7	9.5	51	150	120	1.2	1.3	1.0	1.0
Franklin town	2,569	1,790	332	284	79	33	16	7	28	69.7	12.9	11.1	65	142	83	0.3	0.3	0.3	0.3
Freetown town	835	490	122	150	38	9	6	3	17	58.7	14.6	18.0	202	92	11	0.1	<.1	0.1	0.2
Gardner city	2,877	1,857	253	474	117	77	40	18	41	64.5	8.8	16.5	142	204	22	0.4	0.4	0.2	0.5
Gloucester city	3,318	2,139	596	393	100	31	19	13	27	64.5	18.0	11.8	147	24	72	0.4	0.4	0.5	0.5
Grafton town	1,399	925	155	197	96	4	6	3	13	66.1	11.1	14.1	125	182	40	0.2	0.2	0.1	0.2
Great Barrington town	592	252	143	83	65	9	2	2	36	42.6	24.2	14.0	213	3	41	<.1	<.1	0.1	<.1
Greenfield town	1,762	1,136	301	161	108	15	12	7	22	64.5	17.1	9.1	146	38	129	0.2	0.2	0.3	0.2
Groton town	1,145	864	147	75	35	12	5	2	5	75.5	12.8	6.6	13	144	190	0.1	0.2	0.1	<.1
Groveland town	789	532	136	72	35	2	4	1	7	67.4	17.2	9.1	103	35	130	<.1	0.1	0.1	<.1
Hamilton town	925	632	165	58	48	4	5	4	9	68.3	17.8	6.3	88	26	196	0.1	0.1	0.1	<.1
Hanover town	1,672	1,160	244	143	81	19	11	5	9	69.4	14.6	8.6	68	94	144	0.2	0.2	0.2	0.2
Hanson town	949	607	155	102	42	13	7	4	19	64.0	16.3	10.7	157	50	90	0.1	0.1	0.1	0.1
Hardwick town	344	204	54	55	18	5	2	3	3	59.3	15.7	16.0	198	60	27	<.1	<.1	<.1	<.1
Haverhill city	7,174	4,807	980	881	272	80	44	32	78	67.0	13.7	12.3	111	114	63	0.9	0.9	0.8	1.0
Hingham town	3,167	2,185	589	204	103	36	17	21	12	69.0	18.6	6.4	73	19	192	0.4	0.4	0.5	0.2
Holbrook town	1,644	1,068	239	210	70	35	7	3	12	65.0	14.5	12.8	136	96	56	0.2	0.2	0.2	0.2
Holden town	1,922	1,435	215	175	45	24	15	6	7	74.7	11.2	9.1	19	179	132	0.2	0.3	0.2	0.2
Holliston town	2,019	1,439	296	172	64	17	11	3	17	71.3	14.7	8.5	47	89	148	0.3	0.3	0.3	0.2
Holyoke city	3,945	2,865	364	333	220	74	25	12	52	72.6	9.2	8.4	33	199	151	0.5	0.5	0.3	0.4
Hopkinton town	1,298	913	196	106	50	17	7	2	7	70.3	15.1	8.2	58	80	155	0.2	0.2	0.2	0.1
Hudson town	1,896	1,337	246	218	35	14	11	6	29	70.5	13.0	11.5	55	141	75	0.2	0.3	0.2	0.3
Hull town	1,409	816	327	143	67	16	16	14	10	57.9	23.2	10.1	204	4	111	0.2	0.2	0.3	0.2
Ipswich town	1,748	1,210	310	130	51	16	7	4	20	69.2	17.7	7.4	71	30	179	0.2	0.2	0.3	0.1
Kingston town	1,031	727	172	77	29	8	8	6	4	70.5	16.7	7.5	56	41	177	0.1	0.1	0.1	<.1
Lawrence city	6,444	4,287	643	779	410	129	58	43	95	66.5	10.0	12.1	118	195	66	0.8	0.8	0.6	0.9
Leicester town	1,361	895	160	199	43	20	17	6	21	65.8	11.8	14.6	129	167	36	0.2	0.2	0.1	0.2
Leominster city	5,995	4,061	583	902	161	168	60	25	35	67.7	9.7	15.0	98	197	31	0.8	0.8	0.5	1.0
Lexington town	6,673	5,175	800	416	167	35	21	22	37	77.6	12.0	6.2	5	161	197	0.8	1.0	0.7	0.5
Lincoln town	1,157	822	230	62	27	2	2	8	4	71.0	19.9	5.4	50	12	209	0.1	0.2	0.2	<.1
Littleton town	1,089	852	122	55	22	11	5	2	20	78.2	11.2	5.1	3	178	211	0.1	0.2	0.1	<.1
Longmeadow town	1,727	1,293	129	139	84	23	3	11	45	74.9	7.5	8.0	16	210	160	0.2	0.2	0.1	0.2
Lowell city	14,110	11,420	1,018	921	374	146	55	46	130	80.9	7.2	6.5	1	212	191	1.8	2.2	0.9	1.1
Ludlow town	2,199	1,505	154	230	157	79	12	9	53	68.4	7.0	10.5	83	213	103	0.3	0.3	0.1	0.3
Lunenburg town	1,279	887	164	138	36	24	13	8	9	69.4	12.8	10.8	69	145	89	0.2	0.2	0.1	0.2
Lynn city	10,078	6,886	1,266	1,054	470	177	75	48	102	68.3	12.6	10.5	87	152	104	1.3	1.3	1.1	1.2
Lynnfield town	1,764	1,274	245	112	77	15	11	2	28	72.2	13.9	6.3	38	107	194	0.2	0.2	0.2	0.1
Malden city	8,035	5,150	1,063	922	325	83	79	44	369	64.1	13.2	11.5	155	131	76	1.0	1.0	0.9	1.1
Mansfield town	2,113	1,437	306	224	63	39	18	11	15	68.0	14.5	10.6	96	97	96	0.3	0.3	0.3	0.3
Marblehead town	3,493	2,565	486	265	87	28	14	11	37	73.4	13.9	7.6	25	105	173	0.4	0.5	0.4	0.3
Marlborough city	3,500	2,351	484	438	100	43	18	18	48	67.2	13.8	12.5	109	109	61	0.4	0.4	0.4	0.5
Marshfield town	3,163	2,061	606	237	145	58	19	12	25	65.2	19.2	7.5	132	14	176	0.4	0.4	0.5	0.3
Mashpee town	1,086	718	182	125	36	10	7	6	2	66.1	16.8	11.5	126	40	74	0.1	0.1	0.2	0.1
Maynard town	1,649	1,115	254	175	68	9	9	6	13	67.6	15.4	10.6	102	65	94	0.2	0.2	0.2	0.2
Medfield town	1,641	1,191	241	113	42	24	4	5	21	72.6	14.7	6.9	34	88	185	0.2	0.2	0.2	0.1
Medford city	10,236	6,820	1,453	1,130	446	195	63	45	84	66.6	14.2	11.0	117	99	85	1.3	1.3	1.3	1.3
Medway town	1,270	866	196	129	39	21	7	6	6	68.2	15.4	10.2	92	64	110	0.2	0.2	0.2	0.1
Melrose city	4,786	3,401	712	382	164	57	23	24	23	71.1	14.9	8.0	49	85	162	0.6	0.6	0.6	0.4
Methuen town	8,795	5,581	960	1,116	607	333	96	42	60	63.5	10.9	12.7	163	184	57	1.1	1.1	0.8	1.3
Middleborough town	1,546	940	270	198	71	21	12	4	30	60.8	17.5	12.8	190	33	55	0.2	0.2	0.2	0.2
Milford town	3,031	2,043	340	407	105	46	22	13	55	67.4	11.2	13.4	105	177	46	0.4	0.4	0.3	0.5
Millbury town	1,252	814	147	187	45	23	19	5	12	65.0	11.7	14.9	134	168	33	0.2	0.2	0.1	0.2
Millis town	1,188	850	168	80	43	11	10	6	20	71.5	14.1	6.7	42	101	188	0.1	0.2	0.1	<.1
Milton town	5,635	3,815	946	404	207	148	45	19	51	67.7	16.8	7.2	100	39	184	0.7	0.7	0.8	0.5
Monson town	645	415	81	79	37	17	3	4	9	64.3	12.6	12.2	152	153	65	<.1	<.1	<.1	<.1
Montague town	983	585	185	111	67	15	4	4	12	59.5	18.8	11.3	195	18	81	0.1	0.1	0.2	0.1
Natick town	5,314	3,876	713	447	134	51	29	22	42	72.9	13.4	8.4	32	127	152	0.7	0.7	0.6	0.5
Needham town	5,690	4,207	745	424	144	64	18	22	66	73.9	13.1	7.5	21	135	178	0.7	0.8	0.6	0.5

¹Does not include corrected vote for no preference and other candidates from Secretary of State's publication, *Massachusetts Election Statistics 1992*, Public Document 43 (statewide total vote of 12,198 for no preference and 2,255 for other candidates corrected to 12,218 for no preference and 3,465 for other candidates).   ²Separate rankings for 14 counties and 213 cities and towns.

County	Total[1]	Tsongas	Brown	Clinton	Nader	No Preference[1]	Kerrey	Harkin	Other[1]	Percent of total vote Tsongas	Brown	Clinton	Rank[2] Tsongas	Brown	Clinton	Percent contribution to state vote Total	Tsongas	Brown	Clinton
New Bedford city	11,293	6,299	1,417	2,506	439	174	124	109	225	55.8	12.5	22.2	209	154	1	1.4	1.2	1.2	2.9
Newbury town	912	588	210	54	41	6	4	2	7	64.5	23.0	5.9	145	5	200	0.1	0.1	0.2	<.1
Newburyport city	2,566	1,667	538	188	99	26	7	13	28	65.0	21.0	7.3	135	9	182	0.3	0.3	0.5	0.2
Newton city	17,071	12,210	2,327	1,645	451	130	54	82	172	71.5	13.6	9.6	43	116	117	2.2	2.3	2.0	1.9
Norfolk town	959	684	132	72	31	13	12	3	12	71.3	13.8	7.5	46	112	175	0.1	0.1	0.1	<.1
North Adams city	1,189	820	142	165	30	11	9	2	10	69.0	11.9	13.9	75	164	42	0.2	0.2	0.1	0.2
North Andover town	3,687	2,593	482	301	172	65	31	11	32	70.3	13.1	8.2	59	136	156	0.5	0.5	0.4	0.3
North Attleborough town	1,708	1,133	260	159	108	22	8	12	6	66.3	15.2	9.3	119	73	126	0.2	0.2	0.2	0.2
North Reading town	1,986	1,404	290	136	88	30	17	3	18	70.7	14.6	6.8	52	93	186	0.3	0.3	0.3	0.2
Northampton city	5,044	2,769	1,299	407	413	53	19	26	58	54.9	25.8	8.1	211	2	159	0.6	0.5	1.1	0.5
Northborough town	1,546	1,122	208	136	41	8	7	5	19	72.6	13.5	8.8	35	123	140	0.2	0.2	0.2	0.2
Northbridge town	1,074	711	115	182	31	15	9	7	4	66.2	10.7	16.9	123	186	18	0.1	0.1	<.1	0.2
Norton town	1,183	765	193	127	58	22	7	5	6	64.7	16.3	10.7	141	51	91	0.1	0.1	0.2	0.1
Norwell town	1,275	901	211	81	43	15	8	3	13	70.7	16.5	6.4	53	46	193	0.2	0.2	0.2	<.1
Norwood town	4,649	3,217	586	427	211	92	35	23	58	69.2	12.6	9.2	72	151	127	0.6	0.6	0.5	0.5
Orange town	516	308	90	77	16	10	6	4	5	59.7	17.4	14.9	194	34	34	<.1	<.1	<.1	<.1
Orleans town	822	570	141	64	23	4	2	2	16	69.3	17.2	7.8	70	37	167	0.1	0.1	0.1	<.1
Oxford town	1,193	780	126	197	39	23	13	6	9	65.4	10.6	16.5	131	189	20	0.2	0.1	0.1	0.2
Palmer town	1,126	765	118	142	60	18	9	4	10	67.9	10.5	12.6	97	190	58	0.1	0.1	0.1	0.2
Peabody city	7,676	5,394	941	780	315	79	42	24	101	70.3	12.3	10.2	62	159	109	1.0	1.0	0.8	0.9
Pembroke town	1,758	1,164	332	135	69	30	9	8	11	66.2	18.9	7.7	122	17	170	0.2	0.2	0.3	0.2
Pepperell town	1,290	943	159	112	35	8	6	0	27	73.1	12.3	8.7	29	158	141	0.2	0.2	0.1	0.1
Pittsfield city	5,074	3,203	608	609	412	140	30	29	43	63.1	12.0	12.0	168	163	68	0.6	0.6	0.5	0.7
Plainville town	616	397	106	68	26	9	3	1	6	64.4	17.2	11.0	150	36	86	<.1	<.1	<.1	<.1
Plymouth town	4,766	3,013	910	552	170	38	39	19	25	63.2	19.1	11.6	165	15	73	0.6	0.6	0.8	0.6
Quincy city	12,900	8,206	2,004	1,339	672	354	110	82	133	63.6	15.5	10.4	159	62	106	1.6	1.6	1.7	1.5
Randolph town	4,794	3,246	623	543	216	59	33	16	58	67.7	13.0	11.3	99	140	80	0.6	0.6	0.5	0.6
Raynham town	1,119	716	181	127	43	14	21	3	14	64.0	16.2	11.3	156	54	79	0.1	0.1	0.2	0.1
Reading town	4,394	3,235	620	255	162	54	22	14	32	73.6	14.1	5.8	23	102	202	0.6	0.6	0.5	0.3
Rehoboth town	482	294	106	53	18	4	2	1	4	61.0	22.0	11.0	187	8	87	<.1	<.1	<.1	<.1
Revere city	6,613	4,195	862	857	313	186	56	32	112	63.4	13.0	13.0	164	138	53	0.8	0.8	0.7	1.0
Rockland town	2,017	1,299	301	252	82	42	19	7	15	64.4	14.9	12.5	151	83	62	0.3	0.2	0.3	0.3
Rockport town	1,196	785	247	100	39	3	7	5	10	65.6	20.7	8.4	130	10	153	0.2	0.1	0.2	0.1
Salem city	5,662	3,752	936	571	212	64	39	27	61	66.3	16.5	10.1	121	47	113	0.7	0.7	0.8	0.7
Salisbury town	889	545	130	137	46	11	6	6	8	61.3	14.6	15.4	183	91	30	0.1	0.1	0.1	0.2
Sandwich town	2,047	1,405	323	170	63	15	22	8	41	68.6	15.8	8.3	80	58	154	0.3	0.3	0.3	0.2
Saugus town	3,744	2,413	491	393	310	61	19	15	42	64.4	13.1	10.5	149	134	102	0.5	0.5	0.4	0.5
Scituate town	2,871	1,971	514	160	142	22	11	8	43	68.7	17.9	5.6	79	25	206	0.4	0.4	0.4	0.2
Seekonk town	877	560	119	110	34	19	7	6	22	63.9	13.6	12.5	158	119	59	0.1	0.1	0.1	0.1
Sharon town	3,253	2,324	436	342	82	25	17	14	13	71.4	13.4	10.5	45	128	100	0.4	0.4	0.4	0.4
Shrewsbury town	3,145	2,265	346	298	127	48	13	14	34	72.0	11.0	9.5	39	183	122	0.4	0.4	0.3	0.3
Somerset town	2,346	1,618	208	374	75	18	22	5	26	69.0	8.9	15.9	74	202	28	0.3	0.3	0.2	0.4
Somerville city	12,064	7,152	2,281	1,450	532	206	90	74	279	59.3	18.9	12.0	199	16	67	1.5	1.4	2.0	1.7
South Hadley town	1,740	1,214	194	158	107	31	7	8	21	69.8	11.1	9.1	64	181	134	0.2	0.2	0.2	0.2
Southborough town	1,018	748	130	90	25	7	6	3	9	73.5	12.8	8.8	24	147	138	0.1	0.1	0.1	0.1
Southbridge town	1,700	1,042	150	329	118	22	18	9	12	61.3	8.8	19.4	184	203	10	0.2	0.2	0.1	0.4
Southwick town	567	380	67	57	28	13	2	2	18	67.0	11.8	10.1	110	166	114	<.1	<.1	<.1	<.1
Spencer town	927	585	121	147	32	21	11	2	8	63.1	13.1	15.9	169	137	29	0.1	0.1	0.1	0.2
Springfield city	11,706	7,836	1,052	1,536	762	288	72	40	120	66.9	9.0	13.1	112	201	50	1.5	1.5	0.9	1.8
Stoneham town	2,997	2,103	403	272	126	34	19	13	27	70.2	13.4	9.1	63	124	135	0.4	0.4	0.3	0.3
Stoughton town	3,857	2,597	579	413	166	43	21	11	27	67.3	15.0	10.7	106	81	92	0.5	0.5	0.5	0.5
Sudbury town	2,541	1,961	341	150	47	16	6	8	12	77.2	13.4	5.9	7	126	201	0.3	0.4	0.3	0.2
Sutton town	624	400	74	104	25	8	7	3	3	64.1	11.9	16.7	154	165	19	<.1	<.1	<.1	0.1
Swampscott town	2,486	1,747	395	212	87	13	18	7	7	70.3	15.9	8.5	61	56	147	0.3	0.3	0.3	0.2
Taunton city	4,173	2,421	594	826	169	67	27	20	49	58.0	14.2	19.8	203	98	8	0.5	0.5	0.5	1.0
Templeton town	665	395	75	144	25	4	14	4	4	59.4	11.3	21.7	197	176	3	<.1	<.1	<.1	0.2
Tewksbury town	4,759	3,473	575	382	169	64	17	15	64	73.0	12.1	8.0	31	160	161	0.6	0.7	0.5	0.4
Townsend town	892	627	147	59	33	11	2	8	5	70.3	16.5	6.6	60	48	189	0.1	0.1	0.1	<.1
Tyngsborough town	1,453	1,094	167	111	50	12	9	3	7	75.3	11.5	7.6	14	173	172	0.2	0.2	0.1	0.1
Uxbridge town	1,228	757	123	261	32	15	17	9	14	61.6	10.0	21.3	182	194	6	0.2	0.1	0.1	0.3
Wakefield town	4,284	2,918	637	349	215	69	23	26	47	68.1	14.9	8.1	93	86	157	0.5	0.6	0.6	0.4
Walpole town	3,032	2,088	460	246	122	44	22	11	39	68.9	15.2	8.1	77	77	158	0.4	0.4	0.4	0.3
Waltham city	6,693	4,502	1,011	710	267	94	49	24	36	67.3	15.1	10.6	108	79	95	0.8	0.9	0.9	0.8
Ware town	1,024	664	88	175	40	27	11	6	13	64.8	8.6	17.1	139	205	16	0.1	0.1	<.1	0.2
Wareham town	1,656	990	255	270	56	18	21	10	36	59.8	15.4	16.3	193	66	23	0.2	0.2	0.2	0.3
Warren town	358	237	40	59	11	6	1	2	2	66.2	11.2	16.5	124	180	21	<.1	<.1	<.1	<.1
Watertown town	6,513	4,301	1,032	607	289	107	32	30	115	66.0	15.8	9.3	127	57	125	0.8	0.8	0.9	0.7
Wayland town	2,302	1,729	344	116	66	7	7	5	28	75.1	14.9	5.0	15	82	212	0.3	0.3	0.3	0.1
Webster town	1,490	881	150	319	72	32	18	5	13	59.1	10.1	21.4	200	193	5	0.2	0.2	0.1	0.4
Wellesley town	4,020	2,940	542	345	96	22	23	22	30	73.1	13.5	8.6	28	122	142	0.5	0.6	0.5	0.4

[1]Does not include corrected vote for no preference and other candidates from Secretary of State's publication, *Massachusetts Election Statistics 1992*, Public Document 43 (statewide total vote of 12,198 for no preference and 2,255 for other candidates corrected to 12,218 for no preference and 3,465 for other candidates).   [2]Separate rankings for 14 counties and 213 cities and towns.

County	Top candidates									Top three candidates (state vote)									
										Percent of total vote			Rank²			Percent contribution to state vote			
	Total¹	Tsongas	Brown	Clinton	Nader	No Pre-ference¹	Kerrey	Harkin	Other¹	Tsongas	Brown	Clinton	Tsongas	Brown	Clinton	Total	Tsongas	Brown	Clinton
West Boylston town	702	480	82	86	34	6	3	5	6	68.4	11.7	12.3	85	169	64	<.1	<.1	<.1	<.1
West Bridgewater town	712	446	118	92	35	1	6	4	10	62.6	16.6	12.9	175	45	54	<.1	<.1	0.1	0.1
West Springfield town	2,293	1,619	237	218	142	38	11	11	17	70.6	10.3	9.5	54	192	121	0.3	0.3	0.2	0.3
Westborough town	1,632	1,184	226	129	48	12	9	12	12	72.5	13.8	7.9	36	108	163	0.2	0.2	0.2	0.1
Westfield city	2,884	1,964	310	277	223	33	13	9	55	68.1	10.7	9.6	94	185	118	0.4	0.4	0.3	0.3
Westford town	2,737	2,107	317	172	82	20	12	9	18	77.0	11.6	6.3	8	170	195	0.3	0.4	0.3	0.2
Weston town	1,441	1,077	195	106	36	8	2	1	16	74.7	13.5	7.4	18	120	181	0.2	0.2	0.2	0.1
Westport town	1,662	1,002	207	283	62	35	23	12	38	60.3	12.5	17.0	191	157	17	0.2	0.2	0.2	0.3
Westwood town	2,336	1,747	311	135	78	28	10	4	23	74.8	13.3	5.8	17	130	203	0.3	0.3	0.3	0.2
Weymouth town	8,379	5,583	1,274	768	383	198	66	49	58	66.6	15.2	9.2	116	74	128	1.1	1.1	1.1	0.9
Whitman town	1,506	916	268	179	67	38	12	8	18	60.8	17.8	11.9	189	28	70	0.2	0.2	0.2	0.2
Wilbraham town	1,317	966	123	103	83	20	10	4	8	73.3	9.3	7.8	26	198	165	0.2	0.2	0.1	0.1
Williamstown town	1,032	645	161	147	45	7	4	9	14	62.5	15.6	14.2	178	61	38	0.1	0.1	0.1	0.2
Wilmington town	2,730	1,964	349	242	95	35	24	6	15	71.9	12.8	8.9	41	146	137	0.3	0.4	0.3	0.3
Winchendon town	658	362	98	135	27	11	7	8	10	55.0	14.9	20.5	210	84	7	<.1	<.1	<.1	0.2
Winchester town	3,971	2,900	540	305	128	33	33	16	16	73.0	13.6	7.7	30	117	169	0.5	0.6	0.5	0.4
Winthrop town	3,317	2,146	510	350	145	88	29	10	39	64.7	15.4	10.6	140	68	97	0.4	0.4	0.4	0.4
Woburn city	6,075	4,155	862	543	241	107	39	41	87	68.4	14.2	8.9	84	100	136	0.8	0.8	0.7	0.6
Worcester city	17,335	11,583	1,992	2,305	766	355	135	61	138	66.8	11.5	13.3	113	174	48	2.2	2.2	1.7	2.7
Wrentham town	940	648	148	83	33	13	5	4	6	68.9	15.7	8.8	76	59	139	0.1	0.1	0.1	<.1
Yarmouth town	2,648	1,785	405	291	87	16	10	12	42	67.4	15.3	11.0	104	69	88	0.3	0.3	0.3	0.3

¹Does not include corrected vote for no preference and other candidates from Secretary of State's publication, *Massachusetts Election Statistics 1992*, Public Document 43 (statewide total vote of 12,198 for no preference and 2,255 for other candidates corrected to 12,218 for no preference and 3,465 for other candidates).   ²Separate rankings for 14 counties and 213 cities and towns.

Table J. — Vote for Presidential Preference: March 10, 1992, Republican Primary Election

| County | Top candidates | | | | | Top four candidates (state vote) | | | | | | | | | | | | |
| | | | | | | Percent of total vote | | | | Rank² | | | | Percent contribution to state vote | | | | |
	Total¹	Bush	Bu-chanan	No Pre-ference	Other¹	Bush	Bu-chanan	No Pre-ference	Other	Bush	Bu-chanan	No Pre-ference	Other	Total	Bush	Bu-chanan	No Pre-ference	Other
Barnstable	15,623	10,923	3,727	591	382	69.9	23.9	3.8	2.4	1	14	7	13	5.8	6.2	5.0	5.8	4.8
Berkshire	4,755	2,906	1,376	258	215	61.1	28.9	5.4	4.5	13	3	1	2	1.8	1.6	1.8	2.5	2.7
Bristol	16,110	9,855	5,141	624	490	61.2	31.9	3.9	3.0	12	2	6	9	6.0	5.6	6.9	6.2	6.2
Dukes	1,342	902	332	67	41	67.2	24.7	5.0	3.1	5	13	2	8	0.5	0.5	0.4	0.7	0.5
Essex	36,712	24,510	9,803	1,386	1,013	66.8	26.7	3.8	2.8	6	8	8	11	13.6	13.9	13.1	13.7	12.8
Franklin	3,235	2,213	813	102	107	68.4	25.1	3.2	3.3	3	12	12	7	1.2	1.3	1.1	1.0	1.4
Hampden	14,309	9,548	3,741	474	546	66.7	26.1	3.3	3.8	7	9	10	4	5.3	5.4	5.0	4.7	6.9
Hampshire	4,687	3,082	1,287	144	174	65.8	27.5	3.1	3.7	8	7	13	5	1.7	1.7	1.7	1.4	2.2
Middlesex	66,735	43,278	18,880	2,684	1,893	64.9	28.3	4.0	2.8	11	4	4	10	24.7	24.5	25.2	26.5	23.9
Nantucket	469	316	118	11	24	67.4	25.2	2.3	5.1	4	11	14	1	0.2	0.2	0.2	0.1	0.3
Norfolk	36,533	23,952	10,208	1,437	936	65.6	27.9	3.9	2.6	9	6	5	12	13.5	13.5	13.6	14.2	11.8
Plymouth	23,968	15,610	6,764	800	794	65.1	28.2	3.3	3.3	10	5	9	6	8.9	8.8	9.0	7.9	10.0
Suffolk	11,940	6,969	3,960	490	521	58.4	33.2	4.1	4.4	14	1	3	3	4.4	3.9	5.3	4.8	6.6
Worcester	33,283	22,804	8,647	1,064	768	68.5	26.0	3.2	2.3	2	10	11	14	12.3	12.9	11.6	10.5	9.7
MASSACHUSETTS	**269,701**	**176,868**	**74,797**	**10,132**	**7,904**	**65.6**	**27.7**	**3.8**	**2.9**					**100.0**	**100.0**	**100.0**	**100.0**	**100.0**
CITIES AND TOWNS																		
Abington town	706	452	197	27	30	64.0	27.9	3.8	4.2	134	122	77	33	0.3	0.3	0.3	0.3	0.4
Acton town	1,310	914	328	41	27	69.8	25.0	3.1	2.1	37	163	147	170	0.5	0.5	0.4	0.4	0.3
Acushnet town	240	121	101	5	13	50.4	42.1	2.1	5.4	213	1	194	13	<.1	<.1	0.1	<.1	0.2
Adams town	244	138	77	8	21	56.6	31.6	3.3	8.6	206	43	130	1	0.4	0.4	0.4	0.3	0.7
Agawam town	1,025	664	277	29	55	64.8	27.0	2.8	5.4	117	132	164	14	0.4	0.4	0.4	0.3	0.7
Amesbury town	732	442	233	29	28	60.4	31.8	4.0	3.8	185	39	70	47	0.2	0.2	0.2	0.3	0.2
Amherst town	541	376	121	31	13	69.5	22.4	5.7	2.4	42	201	10	138	0.8	0.9	0.7	0.9	0.5
Andover town	2,261	1,577	550	92	42	69.7	24.3	4.1	1.9	38	173	65	186	0.9	0.9	0.9	1.3	0.8
Arlington town	2,480	1,593	687	133	67	64.2	27.7	5.4	2.7	127	124	15	118	0.1	0.1	0.1	<.1	0.2
Ashburnham town	309	199	88	6	16	64.4	28.5	1.9	5.2	123	108	200	17	0.2	0.2	0.2	0.2	0.2
Ashland town	628	412	177	20	19	65.6	28.2	3.2	3.0	94	112	141	95	0.2	0.2	0.2	0.1	0.2
Athol town	458	309	117	15	17	67.5	25.5	3.3	3.7	70	155	133	53	0.5	0.4	0.6	0.4	0.3
Attleboro city	1,251	765	420	42	24	61.2	33.6	3.4	1.9	174	14	122	181	0.3	0.3	0.3	0.2	0.2
Auburn town	771	511	216	25	19	66.3	28.0	3.2	2.5	86	119	134	135	<.1	<.1	<.1	<.1	0.1
Ayer town	244	154	73	6	11	63.1	29.9	2.5	4.5	150	69	183	23	1.2	1.2	1.1	1.1	0.9
Barnstable town	3,110	2,104	829	108	69	67.7	26.7	3.5	2.2	67	139	110	155	<.1	<.1	<.1	<.1	0.1
Barre town	221	147	59	7	8	66.5	26.7	3.2	3.6	85	138	144	56	0.3	0.3	0.3	0.3	0.2
Bedford town	843	549	251	30	13	65.1	29.8	3.6	1.5	112	71	97	195	0.1	0.1	0.1	<.1	<.1
Belchertown town	304	197	90	10	7	64.8	29.6	3.3	2.3	116	73	128	146					
Bellingham town	608	364	202	25	17	59.9	33.2	4.1	2.8	188	22	61	109	0.2	0.2	0.3	0.2	0.2
Belmont town	1,720	1,210	435	51	24	70.3	25.3	3.0	1.4	29	158	157	202	0.6	0.7	0.6	0.5	0.3
Beverly city	2,250	1,513	590	85	62	67.2	26.2	3.8	2.8	76	145	81	113	0.8	0.9	0.8	0.8	0.8
Billerica town	1,680	919	617	87	57	54.7	36.7	5.2	3.4	211	3	21	72	0.6	0.5	0.8	0.9	0.7
Blackstone town	226	145	74	3	4	64.2	32.7	1.3	1.8	128	27	209	187	<.1	<.1	<.1	<.1	<.1
Boston city	9,602	5,591	3,203	398	410	58.2	33.4	4.1	4.3	198	18	60	32	3.6	3.2	4.3	3.9	5.2
Bourne town	1,041	744	246	33	18	71.5	23.6	3.2	1.7	17	188	143	190	0.4	0.4	0.3	0.3	0.2
Boxford town	681	506	130	18	27	74.3	19.1	2.6	4.0	6	209	169	41	0.3	0.3	0.2	0.2	0.3
Braintree town	2,096	1,326	607	76	87	63.3	29.0	3.6	4.2	147	91	93	34	0.8	0.7	0.8	0.8	1.1
Brewster town	895	628	205	38	24	70.2	22.9	4.2	2.7	31	195	49	120	0.3	0.4	0.3	0.4	0.3
Bridgewater town	774	489	235	29	21	63.2	30.4	3.7	2.7	149	61	87	117	0.3	0.3	0.3	0.3	0.3
Brockton city	2,550	1,616	703	121	110	63.4	27.6	4.7	4.3	146	126	29	28	0.9	0.9	0.9	1.2	1.4
Brookline town	1,852	1,290	384	132	46	69.7	20.7	7.1	2.5	41	204	3	132	0.7	0.7	0.5	1.3	0.6
Burlington town	1,267	742	447	45	33	58.6	35.3	3.6	2.6	196	7	100	123	0.5	0.4	0.6	0.4	0.4
Cambridge city	1,534	928	432	84	90	60.5	28.2	5.5	5.9	183	115	14	10	0.6	0.5	0.6	0.8	1.1
Canton town	1,123	717	348	36	22	63.8	31.0	3.2	2.0	140	51	139	179	0.4	0.4	0.5	0.4	0.3
Carver town	580	372	169	16	23	64.1	29.1	2.8	4.0	129	84	167	40	0.2	0.2	0.2	0.2	0.3
Chatham town	892	669	175	19	29	75.0	19.6	2.1	3.3	3	208	192	79	0.3	0.4	0.2	0.2	0.4
Chelmsford town	2,493	1,525	805	83	80	61.2	32.3	3.3	3.2	173	35	125	83	0.9	0.9	1.1	0.8	1.0
Chelsea city	423	248	125	22	28	58.6	29.6	5.2	6.6	195	74	20	3	0.2	0.1	0.2	0.2	0.4
Chicopee city	1,291	802	421	22	46	62.1	32.6	1.7	3.6	162	30	207	59	0.5	0.5	0.6	0.2	0.6
Clarksburg town	46	33	8	2	3	71.7	17.4	4.3	6.5	13	212	41	4	<.1	<.1	<.1	<.1	<.1
Clinton town	522	357	131	16	18	68.4	25.1	3.1	3.4	58	161	154	67	0.2	0.2	0.2	0.2	0.2
Cohasset town	682	455	177	38	12	66.7	26.0	5.6	1.8	80	150	13	188	0.3	0.3	0.2	0.4	0.2
Concord town	1,478	1,060	338	49	31	71.7	22.9	3.3	2.1	14	197	127	162	0.5	0.6	0.5	0.5	0.4
Dalton town	314	203	90	9	12	64.6	28.7	2.9	3.8	119	101	161	48	0.1	0.1	0.1	<.1	0.2
Danvers town	1,769	1,137	529	65	38	64.3	29.9	3.7	2.1	125	70	90	159	0.7	0.6	0.7	0.6	0.5
Dartmouth town	991	597	350	20	24	60.2	35.3	2.0	2.4	186	6	196	137	0.4	0.3	0.5	0.2	0.3
Dedham town	1,618	1,037	489	55	37	64.1	30.2	3.4	2.3	130	64	117	150	0.6	0.6	0.7	0.5	0.5
Deerfield town	207	121	73	4	9	58.5	35.3	1.9	4.3	197	8	201	27	<.1	<.1	<.1	<.1	0.1
Dennis town	1,364	951	326	48	39	69.7	23.9	3.5	2.9	39	184	104	105	0.5	0.5	0.4	0.5	0.5
Dracut town	1,268	712	443	75	38	56.2	34.9	5.9	3.0	208	9	6	96	0.5	0.4	0.6	0.7	0.5
Dudley town	252	156	82	5	9	61.9	32.5	2.0	3.6	166	31	198	58	<.1	<.1	0.1	<.1	0.1

¹Does not include corrected vote for other candidates from Secretary of State's publication, *Massachusetts Election Statistics 1992*, Public Document 43 (statewide total vote of 2,347 for other candidates corrected to 2,348).   ²Separate rankings for 14 counties and 213 cities and towns.

Table J. — Vote for Presidential Preference: March 10, 1992, Republican Primary Election (cont)

County	Top candidates — Total[1]	Bush	Bu-chanan	No Pre-ference	Other[1]	Percent of total vote — Bush	Bu-chanan	No Pre-ference	Other	Rank[2] Bush	Bu-chanan	No Pre-ference	Other	Percent contribution to state vote — Total	Bush	Bu-chanan	No Pre-ference	Other
Duxbury town	1,118	738	323	42	15	66.0	28.9	3.8	1.3	90	92	84	204	0.4	0.4	0.4	0.4	0.2
East Bridgewater town	645	419	186	22	18	65.0	28.8	3.4	2.8	114	95	115	110	0.2	0.2	0.2	0.2	0.2
East Longmeadow town	905	648	207	22	28	71.6	22.9	2.4	3.1	16	196	185	90	0.3	0.4	0.3	0.2	0.4
Easthampton town	550	327	191	10	22	59.5	34.7	1.8	4.0	190	10	204	37	0.2	0.2	0.3	<.1	0.3
Easton town	1,891	1,223	540	99	29	64.7	28.6	5.2	1.5	118	105	19	196	0.7	0.7	0.7	1.0	0.4
Erving town	65	42	20	0	3	64.6	30.8	0.0	4.6	120	55	213	21	<.1	<.1	<.1	0.0	<.1
Everett city	1,075	683	315	47	30	63.5	29.3	4.4	2.8	144	77	40	111	0.4	0.4	0.4	0.5	0.4
Fairhaven town	556	337	186	14	19	60.6	33.5	2.5	3.4	178	16	179	68	0.2	0.2	0.2	0.1	0.2
Fall River city	1,098	617	390	53	38	56.2	35.5	4.8	3.5	207	5	25	66	0.4	0.3	0.5	0.5	0.5
Falmouth town	1,982	1,345	477	104	56	67.9	24.1	5.2	2.8	65	178	18	107	0.7	0.8	0.6	1.0	0.7
Fitchburg city	1,744	1,188	449	80	27	68.1	25.7	4.6	1.5	63	153	33	194	0.6	0.7	0.6	0.8	0.3
Foxborough town	1,367	892	384	57	34	65.3	28.1	4.2	2.5	104	118	56	130	0.5	0.5	0.5	0.6	0.4
Framingham town	3,027	1,998	818	128	83	66.0	27.0	4.2	2.7	91	133	52	115	1.1	1.1	1.1	1.3	1.1
Franklin town	1,102	702	318	45	37	63.7	28.9	4.1	3.4	141	93	64	76	0.4	0.4	0.4	0.4	0.5
Freetown town	351	208	115	15	13	59.3	32.8	4.3	3.7	193	26	46	54	0.1	0.1	0.2	0.1	0.2
Gardner city	954	635	268	32	19	66.6	28.1	3.4	2.0	83	117	123	175	0.4	0.4	0.4	0.3	0.2
Gloucester city	1,439	970	392	44	33	67.4	27.2	3.1	2.3	73	128	156	149	0.5	0.5	0.5	0.4	0.4
Grafton town	680	446	198	20	16	65.6	29.1	2.9	2.4	95	85	158	141	0.3	0.3	0.3	0.2	0.2
Great Barrington town	228	132	65	19	12	57.9	28.5	8.3	5.3	200	106	1	15	<.1	<.1	<.1	0.2	0.2
Greenfield town	752	520	180	36	16	69.1	23.9	4.8	2.1	47	182	26	160	0.3	0.3	0.2	0.4	0.2
Groton town	597	402	146	21	28	67.3	24.5	3.5	4.7	74	171	105	20	0.2	0.2	0.2	0.2	0.4
Groveland town	389	255	106	14	14	65.6	27.2	3.6	3.6	96	127	94	57	0.1	0.1	0.1	0.1	0.2
Hamilton town	766	532	176	32	26	69.5	23.0	4.2	3.4	43	194	55	71	0.3	0.3	0.2	0.3	0.3
Hanover town	851	555	261	15	20	65.2	30.7	1.8	2.4	106	56	206	142	0.3	0.3	0.3	0.1	0.3
Hanson town	482	325	131	16	10	67.4	27.2	3.3	2.1	71	130	126	166	0.2	0.2	0.2	0.2	0.1
Hardwick town	100	70	22	2	6	70.0	22.0	2.0	6.0	33	203	197	9	<.1	<.1	<.1	<.1	<.1
Haverhill city	2,652	1,654	802	110	86	62.4	30.2	4.1	3.2	160	63	59	80	1.0	0.9	1.1	1.1	1.1
Hingham town	1,839	1,306	427	68	38	71.0	23.2	3.7	2.1	21	191	89	169	0.7	0.7	0.6	0.7	0.5
Holbrook town	758	501	209	26	22	66.1	27.6	3.4	2.9	88	125	113	102	0.3	0.3	0.3	0.3	0.3
Holden town	1,784	1,337	359	62	26	74.9	20.1	3.5	1.5	4	205	109	198	0.7	0.8	0.5	0.6	0.3
Holliston town	992	694	243	35	20	70.0	24.5	3.5	2.0	35	169	102	173	0.4	0.4	0.3	0.3	0.3
Holyoke city	921	590	269	21	41	64.1	29.2	2.3	4.5	133	81	186	25	0.3	0.3	0.4	0.2	0.5
Hopkinton town	631	429	159	18	25	68.0	25.2	2.9	4.0	64	159	163	42	0.2	0.2	0.2	0.2	0.3
Hudson town	840	549	242	22	27	65.4	28.8	2.6	3.2	100	98	171	82	0.3	0.3	0.3	0.2	0.3
Hull town	347	177	140	16	14	51.0	40.3	4.6	4.0	212	2	32	36	0.1	0.1	0.2	0.2	0.2
Ipswich town	977	681	252	27	17	69.7	25.8	2.8	1.7	40	152	166	189	0.4	0.4	0.3	0.3	0.2
Kingston town	607	389	176	23	19	64.1	29.0	3.8	3.1	131	90	80	87	0.2	0.2	0.2	0.2	0.2
Lawrence city	1,343	858	403	52	30	63.9	30.0	3.9	2.2	138	67	74	154	0.5	0.5	0.5	0.5	0.4
Leicester town	457	300	133	14	10	65.6	29.1	3.1	2.2	93	87	155	157	0.2	0.2	0.2	0.1	0.1
Leominster city	2,382	1,649	620	82	31	69.2	26.0	3.4	1.3	45	147	111	205	0.9	0.9	0.8	0.8	0.4
Lexington town	2,023	1,398	496	87	42	69.1	24.5	4.3	2.1	48	168	44	165	0.8	0.8	0.7	0.9	0.5
Lincoln town	465	337	93	27	8	72.5	20.0	5.8	1.7	10	206	7	192	0.2	0.2	0.1	0.3	0.1
Littleton town	495	352	119	22	2	71.1	24.0	4.4	0.4	19	180	36	212	0.2	0.2	0.2	0.2	<.1
Longmeadow town	1,238	931	236	53	18	75.2	19.1	4.3	1.5	2	210	45	199	0.5	0.5	0.3	0.5	0.2
Lowell city	2,468	1,466	771	139	92	59.4	31.2	5.6	3.7	191	48	11	52	0.9	0.8	1.0	1.4	1.2
Ludlow town	421	259	123	16	23	61.5	29.2	3.8	5.5	170	80	78	11	0.2	0.1	0.2	0.2	0.3
Lunenburg town	900	621	217	40	22	69.0	24.1	4.4	2.4	50	177	37	136	0.3	0.4	0.3	0.4	0.3
Lynn city	2,053	1,323	575	73	82	64.4	28.0	3.6	4.0	121	120	98	38	0.8	0.7	0.8	0.7	1.0
Lynnfield town	1,325	941	306	50	28	71.0	23.1	3.8	2.1	20	192	82	161	0.5	0.5	0.4	0.5	0.4
Malden city	1,652	1,000	549	41	62	60.5	33.2	2.5	3.8	182	21	181	50	0.6	0.6	0.7	0.4	0.8
Mansfield town	1,403	914	378	79	32	65.1	26.9	5.6	2.3	110	137	12	151	0.5	0.5	0.5	0.8	0.4
Marblehead town	1,924	1,440	364	65	55	74.8	18.9	3.4	2.9	5	211	119	106	0.7	0.8	0.5	0.6	0.7
Marlborough city	1,210	808	338	30	34	66.8	27.9	2.5	2.8	79	121	182	108	0.4	0.5	0.5	0.3	0.4
Marshfield town	1,370	914	386	43	27	66.7	28.2	3.1	2.0	81	113	146	177	0.5	0.5	0.5	0.4	0.3
Mashpee town	518	357	125	16	20	68.9	24.1	3.1	3.9	52	176	153	44	0.2	0.2	0.2	0.2	0.3
Maynard town	561	346	177	21	17	61.7	31.6	3.7	3.0	168	45	88	94	0.2	0.2	0.2	0.2	0.2
Medfield town	965	685	248	22	10	71.0	25.7	2.3	1.0	24	154	187	210	0.4	0.4	0.3	0.2	0.1
Medford city	2,124	1,286	695	85	58	60.5	32.7	4.0	2.7	181	28	68	116	0.8	0.7	0.9	0.8	0.7
Medway town	580	380	166	22	12	65.5	28.6	3.8	2.1	97	102	79	168	0.2	0.2	0.2	0.2	0.2
Melrose city	1,948	1,296	562	51	39	66.5	28.9	2.6	2.0	84	94	172	174	0.7	0.7	0.8	0.5	0.5
Methuen town	2,926	1,966	734	184	42	67.2	25.1	6.3	1.4	78	162	5	201	1.1	1.1	1.0	1.8	0.5
Middleborough town	940	586	290	26	38	62.3	30.9	2.8	4.0	161	54	165	35	0.3	0.3	0.4	0.3	0.5
Milford town	855	536	269	33	17	62.7	31.5	3.9	2.0	154	46	75	176	0.3	0.3	0.4	0.3	0.2
Millbury town	406	275	118	6	7	67.7	29.1	1.5	1.7	66	88	208	191	0.2	0.2	0.2	<.1	<.1
Millis town	472	319	135	9	9	67.6	28.6	1.9	1.9	68	103	202	182	0.2	0.2	0.2	<.1	0.1
Milton town	1,644	1,036	502	65	41	63.0	30.5	4.0	2.5	152	57	71	128	0.6	0.6	0.7	0.6	0.5
Monson town	269	171	73	17	8	63.6	27.1	6.3	3.0	143	131	4	98	<.1	<.1	<.1	0.2	0.1
Montague town	266	169	87	5	5	63.5	32.7	1.9	1.9	145	29	203	183	<.1	<.1	0.1	<.1	<.1
Natick town	1,738	1,134	492	69	43	65.2	28.3	4.0	2.5	105	109	69	134	0.6	0.6	0.7	0.7	0.5
Needham town	2,679	1,886	602	141	50	70.4	22.5	5.3	1.9	28	199	17	185	1.0	1.1	0.8	1.4	0.6

[1]Does not include corrected vote for other candidates from Secretary of State's publication, *Massachusetts Election Statistics 1992*, Public Document 43 (statewide total vote of 2,347 for other candidates corrected to 2,348).   [2]Separate rankings for 14 counties and 213 cities and towns.

County	Total¹	Bush	Bu-chanan	No Pre-ference	Other¹	Bush	Bu-chanan	No Pre-ference	Other	Bush	Bu-chanan	No Pre-ference	Other	Total	Bush	Bu-chanan	No Pre-ference	Other
New Bedford city	1,708	943	616	56	93	55.2	36.1	3.3	5.4	209	4	131	12	0.6	0.5	0.8	0.6	1.2
Newbury town	582	393	154	18	17	67.5	26.5	3.1	2.9	69	143	152	101	0.2	0.2	0.2	0.2	0.2
Newburyport city	904	591	236	45	32	65.4	26.1	5.0	3.5	99	146	24	60	0.3	0.3	0.3	0.4	0.4
Newton city	3,519	2,400	835	203	81	68.2	23.7	5.8	2.3	61	187	8	147	1.3	1.4	1.1	2.0	1.0
Norfolk town	682	472	167	22	21	69.2	24.5	3.2	3.1	46	170	135	91	0.3	0.3	0.2	0.2	0.3
North Adams city	424	241	135	18	30	56.8	31.8	4.2	7.1	204	38	50	2	0.2	0.1	0.2	0.2	0.4
North Andover town	1,567	1,071	423	53	20	68.3	27.0	3.4	1.3	59	134	118	206	0.6	0.6	0.6	0.5	0.3
North Attleborough town	1,062	653	332	55	22	61.5	31.3	5.2	2.1	171	47	22	167	0.4	0.4	0.4	0.5	0.3
North Reading town	898	585	253	39	21	65.1	28.2	4.3	2.3	111	114	42	143	0.3	0.3	0.3	0.4	0.3
Northampton city	805	488	254	21	42	60.6	31.6	2.6	5.2	177	44	173	16	0.3	0.3	0.3	0.2	0.5
Northborough town	832	587	212	17	16	70.6	25.5	2.0	1.9	27	157	195	180	0.3	0.3	0.3	0.2	0.2
Northbridge town	494	340	131	13	10	68.8	26.5	2.6	2.0	53	141	170	172	0.2	0.2	0.2	0.1	0.1
Norton town	712	442	214	32	24	62.1	30.1	4.5	3.4	163	66	35	74	0.3	0.2	0.3	0.3	0.3
Norwell town	867	565	245	37	20	65.2	28.3	4.3	2.3	108	110	47	145	0.3	0.3	0.3	0.4	0.3
Norwood town	1,541	928	517	53	43	60.2	33.5	3.4	2.8	187	15	112	112	0.6	0.5	0.7	0.5	0.5
Orange town	397	263	96	14	24	66.2	24.2	3.5	6.0	87	175	103	8	0.1	0.1	0.1	0.1	0.3
Orleans town	882	703	148	28	3	79.7	16.8	3.2	0.3	1	213	142	213	0.3	0.4	0.2	0.3	<.1
Oxford town	458	321	119	9	9	70.1	26.0	2.0	2.0	32	148	199	178	0.2	0.2	0.2	<.1	0.1
Palmer town	361	252	92	8	9	69.8	25.5	2.2	2.5	36	156	189	129	0.1	0.1	0.1	<.1	0.1
Peabody city	1,813	1,165	531	47	70	64.3	29.3	2.6	3.9	126	78	174	45	0.7	0.7	0.7	0.5	0.9
Pembroke town	834	533	251	24	26	63.9	30.1	2.9	3.1	137	65	160	89	0.3	0.3	0.3	0.2	0.3
Pepperell town	652	394	202	31	25	60.4	31.0	4.8	3.8	184	52	28	46	0.2	0.2	0.3	0.3	0.3
Pittsfield city	1,360	748	462	106	44	55.0	34.0	7.8	3.2	210	13	2	81	0.5	0.4	0.6	1.0	0.6
Plainville town	320	219	85	13	3	68.4	26.6	4.1	0.9	56	140	66	211	0.1	0.1	0.1	0.1	<.1
Plymouth town	2,412	1,512	753	62	85	62.7	31.2	2.6	3.5	155	49	176	63	0.9	0.9	1.0	0.6	1.1
Quincy city	3,457	2,101	1,114	149	93	60.8	32.2	4.3	2.7	176	36	43	119	1.3	1.2	1.5	1.5	1.2
Randolph town	1,092	677	333	41	41	62.0	30.5	3.8	3.8	164	59	85	49	0.4	0.4	0.4	0.4	0.5
Raynham town	651	425	186	14	26	65.3	28.6	2.2	4.0	102	104	190	39	0.2	0.2	0.2	0.1	0.3
Reading town	2,149	1,449	579	90	31	67.4	26.9	4.2	1.4	72	136	53	200	0.8	0.8	0.8	0.9	0.4
Rehoboth town	433	254	139	19	21	58.7	32.1	4.4	4.8	194	37	39	19	0.2	0.1	0.2	0.2	0.3
Revere city	1,198	688	400	49	61	57.4	33.4	4.1	5.1	202	17	63	18	0.4	0.4	0.5	0.5	0.8
Rockland town	693	425	216	29	23	61.3	31.2	4.2	3.3	172	50	54	78	0.3	0.2	0.3	0.3	0.3
Rockport town	590	402	146	19	23	68.1	24.7	3.2	3.9	62	167	136	43	0.2	0.2	0.2	0.2	0.3
Salem city	1,392	869	441	50	32	62.4	31.7	3.6	2.3	159	42	95	148	0.5	0.5	0.6	0.5	0.4
Salisbury town	351	202	116	18	15	57.5	33.0	5.1	4.3	201	24	23	31	0.1	0.1	0.2	0.2	0.2
Sandwich town	1,151	741	325	45	40	64.4	28.2	3.9	3.5	124	111	72	65	0.4	0.4	0.4	0.4	0.5
Saugus town	1,252	746	397	55	54	59.6	31.7	4.4	4.3	189	41	38	30	0.5	0.4	0.5	0.5	0.7
Scituate town	1,443	945	402	51	45	65.5	27.9	3.5	3.1	98	123	101	88	0.5	0.5	0.5	0.5	0.6
Seekonk town	439	266	146	14	13	60.6	33.3	3.2	3.0	179	20	140	99	0.2	0.2	0.2	0.1	0.2
Sharon town	645	406	186	37	16	62.9	28.8	5.7	2.5	153	96	9	133	0.2	0.2	0.2	0.4	0.2
Shrewsbury town	1,617	1,148	394	55	20	71.0	24.4	3.4	1.2	23	172	116	208	0.6	0.6	0.5	0.5	0.3
Somerset town	591	343	201	21	26	58.0	34.0	3.6	4.4	199	12	99	26	0.2	0.2	0.3	0.2	0.3
Somerville city	1,337	757	442	57	81	56.6	33.1	4.3	6.1	205	23	48	7	0.5	0.4	0.6	0.6	1.0
South Hadley town	716	497	179	16	24	69.4	25.0	2.2	3.4	44	164	188	77	0.3	0.3	0.2	0.2	0.3
Southborough town	509	350	122	23	14	68.8	24.0	4.5	2.8	54	181	34	114	0.2	0.2	0.2	0.2	0.2
Southbridge town	468	315	138	10	5	67.3	29.5	2.1	1.1	75	76	191	209	0.2	0.2	0.2	<.1	<.1
Southwick town	330	208	95	7	20	63.0	28.8	2.1	6.1	151	99	193	6	0.1	0.1	0.1	<.1	0.3
Spencer town	418	273	120	15	10	65.3	28.7	3.6	2.4	101	100	96	139	0.2	0.2	0.2	0.1	0.1
Springfield city	2,573	1,691	668	103	111	65.7	26.0	4.0	4.3	92	149	67	29	1.0	1.0	0.9	1.0	1.4
Stoneham town	1,088	680	332	52	24	62.5	30.5	4.8	2.2	156	58	27	156	0.4	0.4	0.4	0.5	0.3
Stoughton town	1,303	824	385	50	44	63.2	29.5	3.8	3.4	148	75	76	73	0.5	0.5	0.5	0.5	0.6
Sudbury town	1,178	806	294	50	28	68.4	25.0	4.2	2.4	57	165	51	140	0.4	0.5	0.4	0.5	0.4
Sutton town	352	260	81	2	9	73.9	23.0	0.6	2.6	8	193	211	124	0.1	0.1	0.1	<.1	0.1
Swampscott town	833	571	215	28	19	68.5	25.8	3.4	2.3	55	151	120	152	0.3	0.3	0.3	0.3	0.2
Taunton city	1,311	835	390	48	38	63.7	29.7	3.7	2.9	142	72	91	103	0.5	0.5	0.5	0.5	0.5
Templeton town	274	175	83	9	7	63.9	30.3	3.3	2.6	139	62	129	125	0.1	<.1	0.1	<.1	<.1
Tewksbury town	1,314	749	451	34	80	57.0	34.3	2.6	6.1	203	11	175	5	0.5	0.4	0.6	0.3	1.0
Townsend town	584	380	170	22	12	65.1	29.1	3.8	2.1	113	86	83	171	0.2	0.2	0.2	0.2	0.2
Tyngsborough town	509	302	165	24	18	59.3	32.4	4.7	3.5	192	33	30	61	0.2	0.2	0.2	0.2	0.2
Uxbridge town	416	252	137	13	14	60.6	32.9	3.1	3.4	180	25	148	75	0.2	0.1	0.2	0.1	0.2
Wakefield town	1,679	1,118	457	69	35	66.6	27.2	4.1	2.1	82	129	62	163	0.6	0.6	0.6	0.7	0.4
Walpole town	1,489	954	446	52	37	64.1	30.0	3.5	2.5	132	68	107	131	0.6	0.5	0.6	0.5	0.5
Waltham city	2,043	1,350	575	67	51	66.1	28.1	3.3	2.5	89	116	132	127	0.8	0.8	0.8	0.7	0.6
Ware town	255	176	64	7	8	69.0	25.1	2.7	3.1	49	160	168	86	<.1	<.1	<.1	<.1	0.1
Wareham town	945	616	276	23	30	65.2	29.2	2.4	3.2	107	82	184	85	0.4	0.3	0.4	0.2	0.4
Warren town	120	75	40	3	2	62.5	33.3	2.5	1.7	157	19	180	193	<.1	<.1	<.1	<.1	<.1
Watertown town	1,148	748	331	29	40	65.2	28.8	2.5	3.5	109	97	178	64	0.4	0.4	0.4	0.3	0.5
Wayland town	980	686	221	28	45	70.0	22.6	2.9	4.6	34	198	162	22	0.4	0.4	0.3	0.3	0.6
Webster town	322	222	78	11	11	68.9	24.2	3.4	3.4	51	174	114	69	0.1	0.1	0.1	0.1	0.1
Wellesley town	2,552	1,843	568	82	59	72.2	22.3	3.2	2.3	11	202	137	144	0.9	1.0	0.8	0.8	0.7

¹Does not include corrected vote for other candidates from Secretary of State's publication, *Massachusetts Election Statistics 1992*, Public Document 43 (statewide total vote of 2,347 for other candidates corrected to 2,348). ²Separate rankings for 14 counties and 213 cities and towns.

Table J. — Vote for Presidential Preference: March 10, 1992, Republican Primary Election (cont)

County	Top candidates					Top four candidates (state vote)												
						Percent of total vote								Percent contribution to state vote				
										Rank[2]								
	Total[1]	Bush	Bu-chanan	No Pre-ference	Other[1]	Bush	Bu-chanan	No Pre-ference	Other	Bush	Bu-chanan	No Pre-ference	Other	Total	Bush	Bu-chanan	No Pre-ference	Other
West Boylston town	521	370	138	6	7	71.0	26.5	1.2	1.3	22	142	210	203	0.2	0.2	0.2	<.1	<.1
West Bridgewater town ..	608	444	145	3	16	73.0	23.8	0.5	2.6	9	185	212	121	0.2	0.3	0.2	<.1	0.2
West Springfield town	1,240	793	363	39	45	64.0	29.3	3.1	3.6	136	79	145	55	0.5	0.4	0.5	0.4	0.6
Westborough town	1,106	781	266	20	39	70.6	24.1	1.8	3.5	26	179	205	62	0.4	0.4	0.4	0.2	0.5
Westfield city	1,880	1,211	507	78	84	64.4	27.0	4.1	4.5	122	135	58	24	0.7	0.7	0.7	0.8	1.1
Westford town...............	1,250	816	356	42	36	65.3	28.5	3.4	2.9	103	107	121	104	0.5	0.5	0.5	0.4	0.5
Weston town	969	687	240	30	12	70.9	24.8	3.1	1.2	25	166	151	207	0.4	0.4	0.3	0.3	0.2
Westport town................	513	333	149	16	15	64.9	29.0	3.1	2.9	115	89	149	100	0.2	0.2	0.2	0.2	0.2
Westwood town	1,338	965	314	34	25	72.1	23.5	2.5	1.9	12	190	177	184	0.5	0.5	0.4	0.3	0.3
Weymouth town	2,895	1,792	941	97	65	61.9	32.5	3.4	2.2	167	32	124	153	1.1	1.0	1.3	1.0	0.8
Whitman town.................	774	495	226	24	29	64.0	29.2	3.1	3.7	135	83	150	51	0.3	0.3	0.3	0.2	0.4
Wilbraham town	876	648	175	34	19	74.0	20.0	3.9	2.2	7	207	73	158	0.3	0.4	0.2	0.3	0.2
Williamstown town	343	234	82	16	11	68.2	23.9	4.7	3.2	60	183	31	84	0.1	0.1	0.1	0.2	0.1
Wilmington town	912	565	290	38	19	62.0	31.8	4.2	2.1	165	40	57	164	0.3	0.3	0.4	0.4	0.2
Winchendon town...........	293	183	89	11	10	62.5	30.4	3.8	3.4	158	60	86	70	0.1	0.1	0.1	0.1	0.1
Winchester town.............	1,808	1,296	427	58	27	71.7	23.6	3.2	1.5	15	189	138	197	0.7	0.7	0.6	0.6	0.3
Winthrop town................	717	442	232	21	22	61.6	32.4	2.9	3.1	169	34	159	92	0.3	0.2	0.3	0.2	0.3
Woburn city...................	1,404	854	434	74	42	60.8	30.9	5.3	3.0	175	53	16	97	0.5	0.5	0.6	0.7	0.5
Worcester city...............	4,485	3,014	1,177	157	137	67.2	26.2	3.5	3.1	77	144	106	93	1.7	1.7	1.6	1.5	1.7
Wrentham town	517	363	123	18	13	70.2	23.8	3.5	2.5	30	186	108	126	0.2	0.2	0.2	0.2	0.2
Yarmouth town	1,918	1,369	429	70	50	71.4	22.4	3.6	2.6	18	200	92	122	0.7	0.8	0.6	0.7	0.6

[1]Does not include corrected vote for other candidates from Secretary of State's publication, *Massachusetts Election Statistics 1992*, Public Document 43 (statewide total vote of 2,347 for other candidates corrected to 2,348).   [2]Separate rankings for 14 counties and 213 cities and towns.

1992 Vote for President
Percent for Clinton (D), by Minor Civil Division

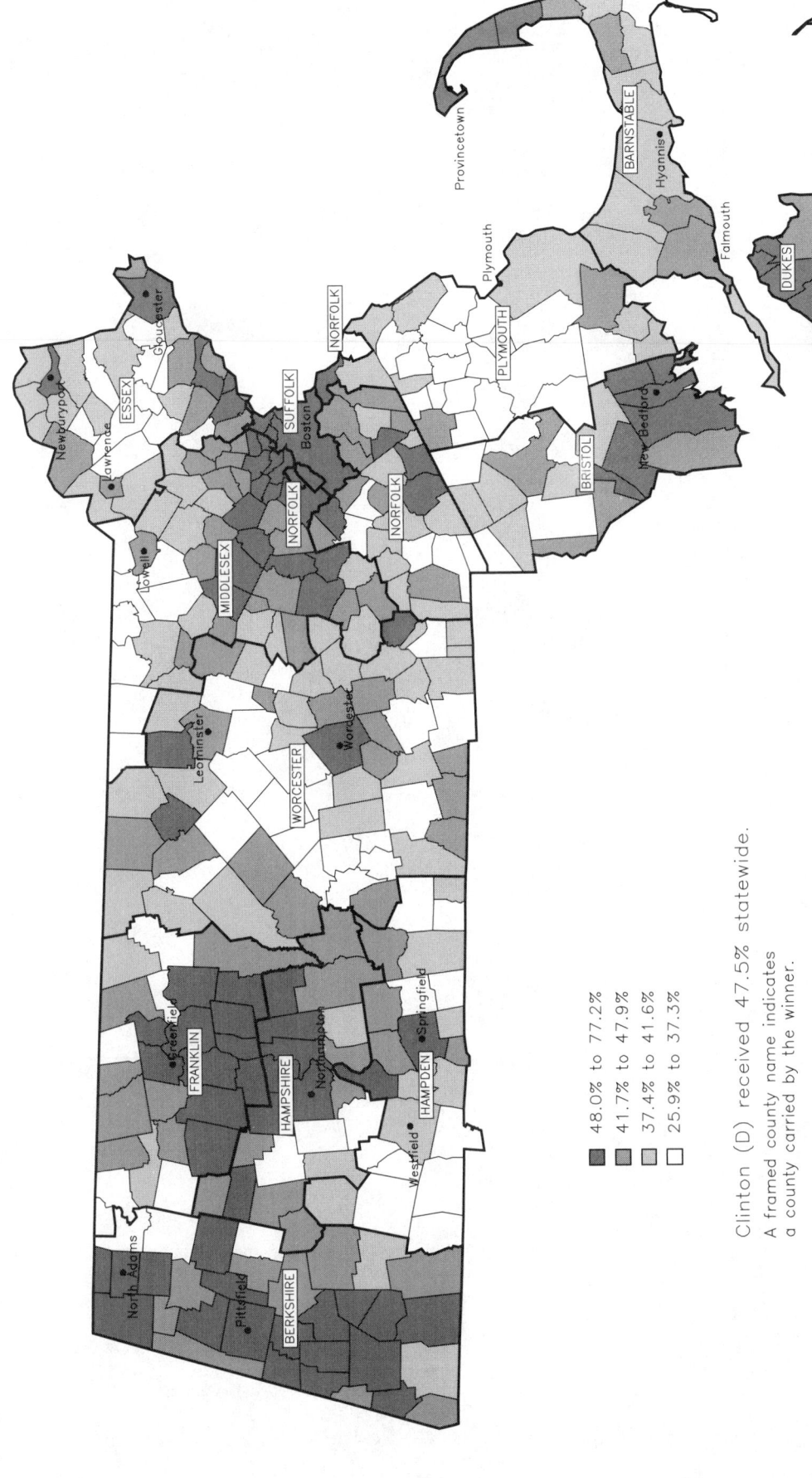

Clinton (D) received 47.5% statewide.

A framed county name indicates a county carried by the winner.

■ 48.0% to 77.2%
▨ 41.7% to 47.9%
▧ 37.4% to 41.6%
□ 25.9% to 37.3%

Copyright © 1993 by Election Data Services, Inc.

Massachusetts 467

MICHIGAN

Congressional Districts 16
   Average Population 580,956
State Senate Districts 38
   Average Population 244,613
State House Districts 110
   Average Population 84,503

Electoral College Votes... 18
Counties 83
Voting Precincts 6,395

Alternative Registration Methods:
   ....Deputized Registrars, Motor-voter

Registration Deadline (Days before Election) 30

Voting Equipment Use (Counties)

Datavote Punch Card	0	Paper Ballot	1
Electronic	0	Other Punch Card	12
Lever Machine	5	Mixed Systems	63
Optical Scanner	2		

Party Control	DEM	REP	IND	VAC
1993 State Senate	16	22	0	0
1992 State Senate	18	20	0	0
1993 State House	55	54	0	1
1992 State House	60	49	0	1

Population Statistics 1990

Race/ Ethnicity	Total Population		Voting Age Population		Voting Age Population % of total population
	Number	%	Number	%	
Non-Hispanic					
White	7,649,951	82.3	5,739,171	83.9	75.0
Black	1,282,744	13.8	867,030	12.7	67.6
Asian/Pacific Islander	102,506	1.1	68,713	1.0	67.0
Native American	52,571	0.6	34,942	0.5	66.5
Other	5,929	<.1	2,226	<.1	37.5
All Hispanic	201,596	2.2	124,450	1.8	61.7
TOTAL	9,295,297	100.0	6,836,532	100.0	73.5

Estimated Voting Age Population 1992 (VAP) 6,923,000
Number of Registered Voters................................. 6,147,083
   % of estimated VAP....................................... 88.8
Voter Turnout (Actual) 4,341,909
   % of VAP 62.7
   % of Registration 70.6
Persons Not Voting—of Voting Age 2,581,091
   % of VAP 37.3
Persons Not Voting—of Registered 1,805,174
   % of Registration 29.4
Straight Ticket Voting .... Yes, Exception

State Officials and Members of Congress

Governor:
John M. Engler (R) 1990, elected to a four-year term in 1990.

U.S. Senators:
Donald W. Riegle, Jr. (D) 1976, elected to a six-year term in 1988.
Carl Levin (D) 1978, elected to a six-year term in 1990.

U.S. Representative in Congress:
(District, Name, Party, Date first elected)

1. Stupak (D) 1992
2. Hoekstra (R) 1992
3. Henry (R) 1984
4. Camp (R) 1990

5. Barcia (D) 1992
6. Upton (R) 1986
7. Smith (R) 1992
8. Carr (D) 1982

9. Kildee (D) 1976
10. Bonior (D) 1976
11. Knollenberg (R) 1992
12. Levin (D) 1982

13. Ford (D) 1964
14. Conyers (D) 1964
15. Collins (D) 1990
16. Dingell (D) 1955

Candidates: General Election, November 3, 1992

Candidate(s)	Total vote	Percent	Party	Status	First elected
President/Vice President					
Clinton/Gore	1,871,182	43.77%	Democrat	Challenger	1992
Bush/Quayle	1,554,940	36.38%	Republican	Incumbent	1988
Perot/Stockdale	824,813	19.30%	Independent	Challenger	
Marrou/Lord	10,175	0.24%	Libertarian	Challenger	
Phillips/Tisch	8,263	0.19%	Tisch Ind. Citizens	Challenger	
Hagelin/Tompkins	2,954	0.07%	Natural Law	Challenger	
Halyard/Mazells	1,432	0.03%	Workers League	Challenger	
Write ins	711	0.02%	Write in	Challenger	
Gritz/Minett	168	<.01%	Write in	Challenger	
Fulani/Munoz	21	<.01%	Write in	Challenger	
LaRouche/Bevel	14	<.01%	Write in	Challenger	
U.S. Senator (No Contest)					
Governor (No Contest)					
U.S. Representative in Congress					
District 1					
Bart Stupak	144,857	53.93%	Democrat	Challenger	1992
Philip Ruppe	117,056	43.58%	Republican	Challenger	
Gerald Aydlott	4,094	1.52%	Libertarian	Challenger	
Lyman Clark	2,570	0.96%	Natural Law	Challenger	
Write ins	42	0.02%	Write in	Challenger	
District 2					
Peter Hoekstra	155,577	63.05%	Republican	Challenger	1992
John Miltner	86,265	34.96%	Democrat	Challenger	
Dick Jacobs	4,840	1.96%	Libertarian	Challenger	
Write ins	79	0.03%	Write in	Challenger	
District 3					
Paul Henry	162,451	61.31%	Republican	Incumbent	1984
Carol Kooistra	95,927	36.21%	Democrat	Challenger	
Richard Whitelock	3,232	1.22%	Libertarian	Challenger	
Susan Normandin	3,228	1.22%	Natural Law	Challenger	
Write ins	110	0.04%	Write in	Challenger	
District 4					
Dave Camp	157,337	62.55%	Republican	Incumbent	1990
Lisa Donaldson	87,573	34.81%	Democrat	Challenger	
Joan Dennison	3,344	1.33%	Tisch Ind. Citizens	Challenger	
Gary Bradley	2,027	0.81%	Libertarian	Challenger	
Thomas List	1,247	0.50%	Natural Law	Challenger	
Write ins	11	<.01%	Write in	Challenger	
District 5					
James Barcia	147,618	60.25%	Democrat	Challenger	1992
Keith Muxlow	93,098	38.00%	Republican	Challenger	
Lloyd Clarke	4,270	1.74%	Workers World	Challenger	
Write ins	6	<.01%	Write in	Challenger	
District 6					
Fred Upton	144,083	61.81%	Republican	Incumbent	1986
Andy Davis	89,020	38.19%	Democrat	Challenger	
Write ins	9	<.01%	Write in	Challenger	
District 7					
Nick Smith	133,972	87.64%	Republican	Challenger	1992
Kenneth Proctor	18,751	12.27%	Libertarian	Challenger	
Write ins	145	0.09%	Write in	Challenger	

Candidate(s)	Total vote	Percent	Party	Status	First elected
U.S. Representative in Congress (cont)					
District 8					
Bob Carr	135,517	47.60%	Democrat	Incumbent	1982
Dick Chrysler	131,906	46.33%	Republican	Challenger	
Frank McAlpine	12,155	4.27%	Independent	Challenger	
Michael Marotta	5,115	1.80%	Libertarian	Challenger	
Write ins	14	<.01%	Write in	Challenger	
District 9					
Dale Kildee	133,956	53.68%	Democrat	Incumbent	1976
Megan O'Neill	111,798	44.80%	Republican	Challenger	
Key Halverson	1,891	0.76%	Natural Law	Challenger	
Jerome White	1,872	0.75%	Workers League	Challenger	
Write ins	13	<.01%	Write in	Challenger	
District 10					
David Bonior	138,193	53.11%	Democrat	Incumbent	1976
Douglas Carl	114,918	44.16%	Republican	Challenger	
David Weidner	7,098	2.73%	Libertarian	Challenger	
Write ins	4	<.01%	Write in	Challenger	
District 11					
Joe Knollenberg	168,940	57.64%	Republican	Challenger	1992
Walter Briggs	117,725	40.17%	Democrat	Challenger	
Brian Wright	4,144	1.41%	Libertarian	Challenger	
Henry Clark	2,269	0.77%	Natural Law	Challenger	
Write ins	20	<.01%	Write in	Challenger	
District 12					
Sander Levin	137,514	52.62%	Democrat	Incumbent	1982
John Pappageorge	119,357	45.67%	Republican	Challenger	
Charles Hahn	2,751	1.05%	Libertarian	Challenger	
R. Montgomery	1,724	0.66%	Natural Law	Challenger	
Write ins	3	<.01%	Write in	Challenger	
District 13					
William Ford	127,642	51.91%	Democrat	Incumbent	1964
Robert Geake	105,169	42.77%	Republican	Challenger	
Randall Roe	8,626	3.51%	Natural Law	Challenger	
Paul Jensen	3,314	1.35%	Tisch Ind. Citizens	Challenger	
Larry Roberts	1,127	0.46%	Workers League	Challenger	
Write ins	10	<.01%	Write in	Challenger	
District 14					
John Conyers, Jr.	165,496	82.39%	Democrat	Incumbent	1964
John Gordon	32,036	15.95%	Republican	Challenger	
Richard Miller	2,043	1.02%	Natural Law	Challenger	
D'Artagnan Collier	1,296	0.65%	Workers League	Challenger	
Write ins	8	<.01%	Write in	Challenger	
District 15					
Barbara-Rose Collins	148,908	80.51%	Democrat	Incumbent	1990
Charles Vincent	31,849	17.22%	Republican	Challenger	
James Harris, Jr.	2,704	1.46%	Independent	Challenger	
Jane Meade	1,496	0.81%	Natural Law	Challenger	
Write ins	7	<.01%	Write in	Challenger	
District 16					
John Dingell	156,964	65.15%	Democrat	Incumbent	1955
Frank Beaumont	75,694	31.42%	Republican	Challenger	
Max Siegle	4,048	1.68%	Tisch Ind. Citizens	Challenger	
Jeff Hampton	2,387	0.99%	Libertarian	Challenger	
Martin McLaughlin	1,842	0.76%	Workers League	Challenger	
Write ins	1	<.01%	Write in	Challenger	

Candidates: March 17, 1992, Primary Election

Candidate	Total vote	Percent	Candidate	Total vote	Percent
Presidential Preference, Democratic			**Presidential Preference, Republican**		
Bill Clinton	297,280	50.73%	George Bush	301,948	67.23%
Jerry Brown	151,400	25.84%	Patrick Buchanan	112,122	24.96%
Paul Tsongas	97,017	16.56%	Uncommitted	23,809	5.30%
Uncommitted	27,836	4.75%	David Duke	10,688	2.38%
Tom Harkin	6,265	1.07%	Write ins	566	0.13%
Bob Kerrey	3,219	0.55%			
Lyndon LaRouche, Jr.	2,049	0.35%			
Write ins	906	0.15%			

Voter Registration and Turnout, 1948-1992 Elections

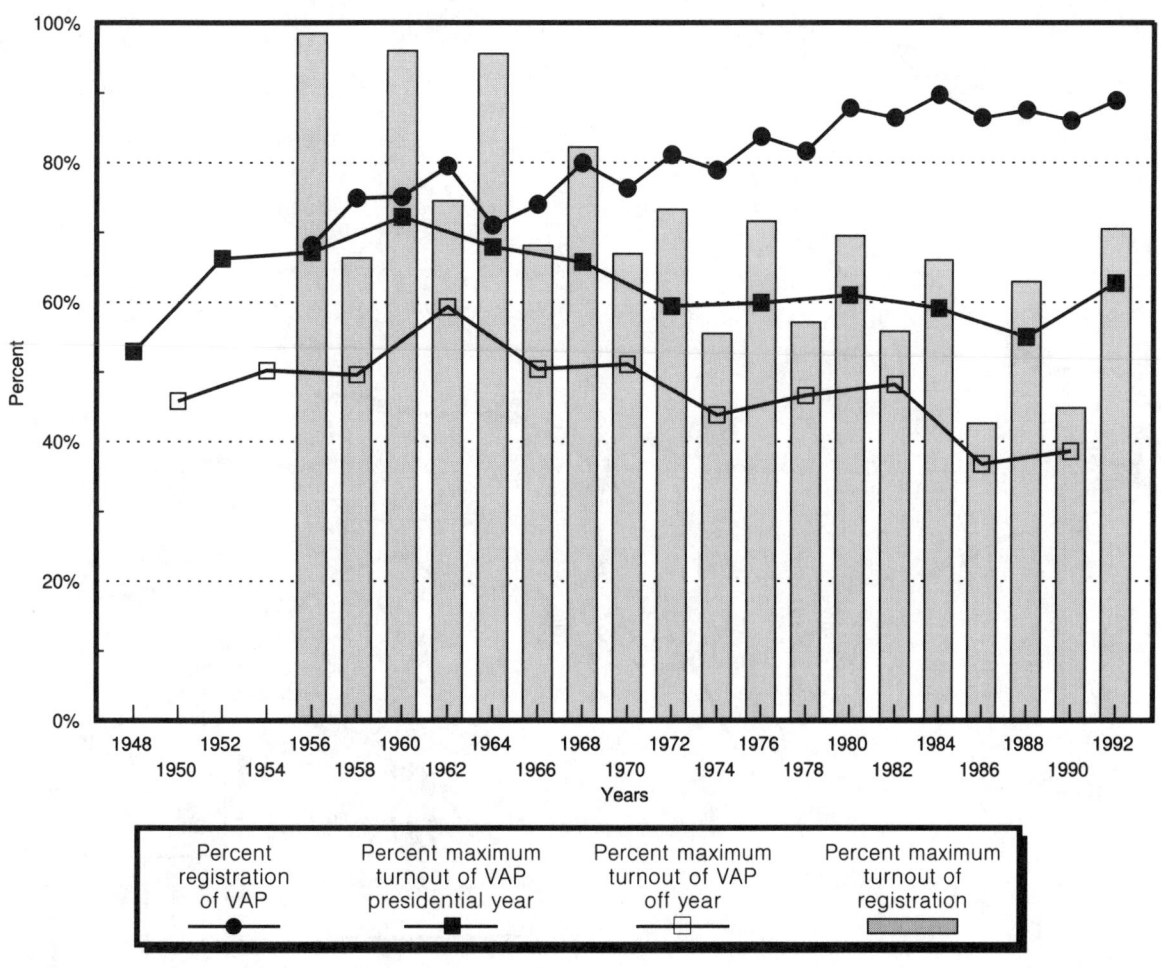

Year	Estimated Voting Age Population (VAP)	Voter registration (REG)				Voter turnout											
							Highest office						Maximum vote				
		Total	Percent of VAP	Rank by percent of VAP	Actual	Total	Office	Percent total REG	Rank by percent of REG	Percent of VAP	Rank by percent of VAP	Total	Percent total REG	Rank by percent of REG	Percent total VAP	Rank by percent of VAP
1992	6,923,000	6,147,083	88.8	7	4,341,909	4,274,673	P	69.5	45	61.7	20	4,341,909	70.6	44	62.7	19
1990	6,851,000	5,892,001	86.0	5	2,641,649	2,564,563	G	43.5	46	37.4	30	2,641,649	44.8	46	38.6	29
1988	6,805,000	5,952,513	87.5	4	3,745,751	3,669,163	P	61.6	46	53.9	20	3,745,751	62.9	44	55.0	20
1986	6,699,000	5,790,753	86.4	3	2,468,009	2,396,564	G	41.4	46	35.8	35	2,468,009	42.6	47	36.8	35
1984	6,568,000	5,888,808	89.7	4	3,884,854	3,801,658	P	64.6	46	57.9	15	3,884,854	66.0	46	59.1	16
1982	6,509,000	5,624,573	86.4	3	3,135,928	3,040,008	G	54.0	39	46.7	16	3,135,928	55.8	38	48.2	15
1980	6,520,000	5,725,713	87.8	7	3,978,647	3,909,725	P	68.3	43	60.0	12	3,978,647	69.5	39	61.0	12
1978	6,406,000	5,230,345	81.6	7	2,984,829	2,867,212	G	54.8	31	44.8	13	2,984,829	57.1	28	46.6	12
1976	6,214,000	5,202,379	83.7	9	3,722,384	3,653,749	P	70.2	35	58.8	19	3,722,384	71.6	34	59.9	19
1974	6,066,000	4,785,689	78.9	8	-	2,657,017	G	55.5	29	43.8	21	2,657,017	55.5	30	43.8	22
1972	5,876,000	4,762,764	81.1	12	-	3,489,727	P	73.3	28	59.4	26	3,489,727	73.3	29	59.4	26
1970	5,200,000	3,969,807	76.3	16	-	2,656,102	G	66.9	23	51.1	22	2,656,102	66.9	24	51.1	25
1968	5,032,000	4,022,378	79.9	16	-	3,306,250	P	82.2	17	65.7	22	3,306,250	82.2	20	65.7	22
1966	4,885,000	3,613,463	74.0	25	-	2,461,909	G	68.1	18	50.4	29	2,461,909	68.1	19	50.4	31
1964	4,719,000	3,351,730	71.0	27	-	3,203,102	P	95.6	2	67.9	23	3,203,102	95.6	2	67.9	23
1962	4,665,000	3,710,798	79.5	12	-	2,764,839	G	74.5	9	59.3	13	2,764,839	74.5	11	59.3	15
1960	4,598,000	3,454,804	75.1	20	-	3,318,097	P	96.0	4	72.2	18	3,318,097	96.0	4	72.2	19
1958	4,662,000	3,489,626	74.9	20	-	2,312,184	G	66.3	18	49.6	30	2,312,184	66.3	20	49.6	31
1956	4,593,000	3,128,573	68.1	22	-	3,080,468	P	98.5	2	67.1	23	3,080,468	98.5	2	67.1	24
1954	4,360,000	-	-	-	-	2,187,027	G	-	-	50.2	25	2,187,027	-	-	50.2	26
1952	4,227,000	-	-	-	-	2,798,592	P	-	-	66.2	31	2,798,592	-	-	66.2	31
1950	4,099,000	-	-	-	-	1,879,382	G	-	-	45.8	32	1,879,382	-	-	45.8	33
1948	3,985,000	-	-	-	-	2,109,609	P	-	-	52.9	29	2,109,609	-	-	52.9	29

MICHIGAN

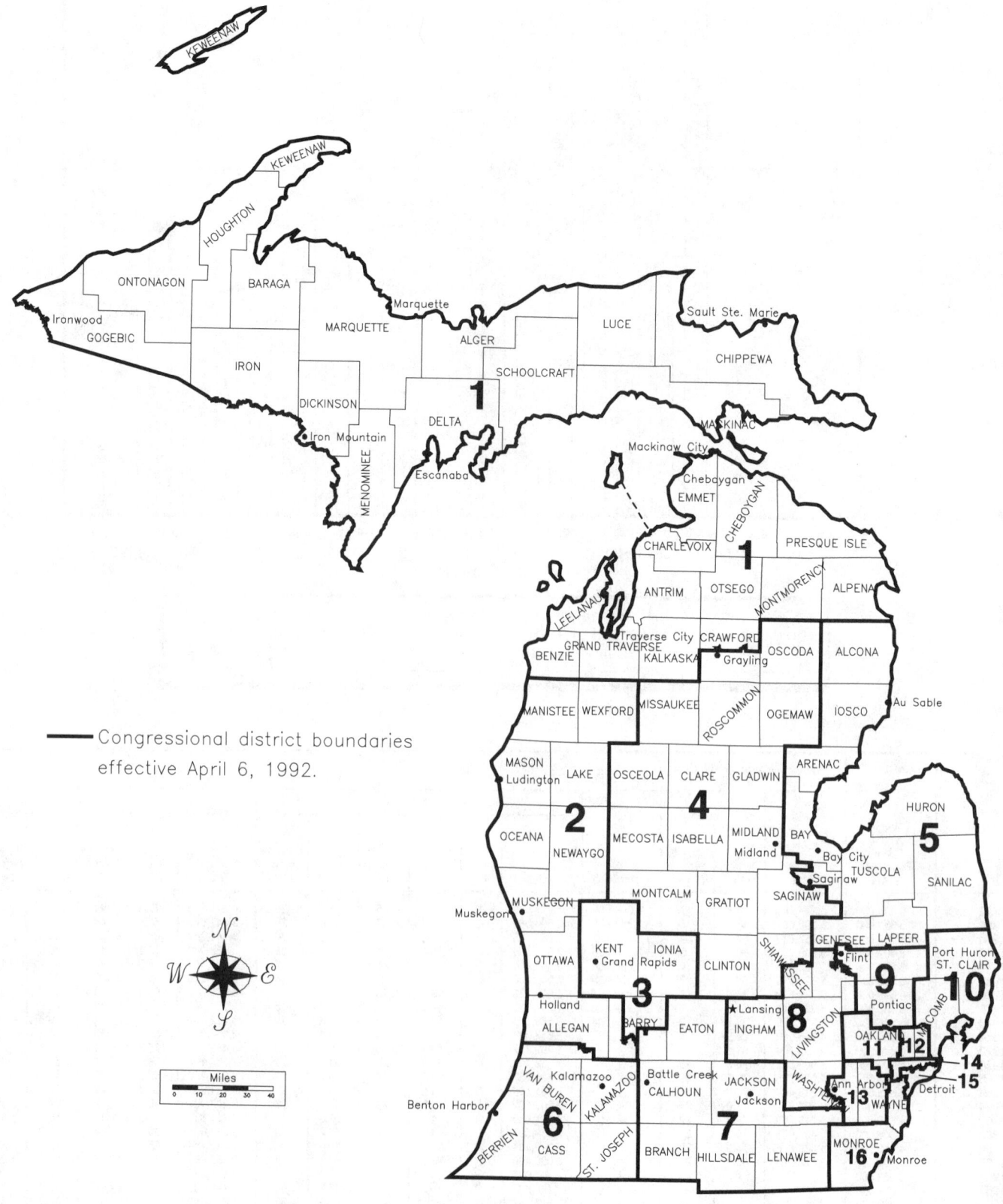

Congressional district boundaries effective April 6, 1992.

Miles
0 10 20 30 40

Table A. — 1990 Population by Race and Ethnic Origin

State/county code	County	Total persons	Percent of total persons — Non-Hispanic — White	Black	Asian and Pacific Islander	Native American	Other	Hispanic	Rank — Percent of total persons — Total	Non-Hispanic — White	Black	Hispanic	Percent contribution to state population — Total	Non-Hispanic — White	Black	Hispanic
26 001	Alcona	10,145	98.4	0.2	0.2	0.6	<.1	0.5	74	14	53	61	0.1	0.1	<.1	<.1
26 003	Alger	8,972	93.5	2.4	0.3	3.4	<.1	0.5	75	60	21	66	<.1	0.1	<.1	<.1
26 005	Allegan	90,509	94.2	1.6	0.4	0.6	<.1	3.2	21	57	29	8	1.0	1.1	0.1	1.4
26 007	Alpena	30,605	98.8	0.1	0.3	0.3	<.1	0.5	46	3	60	68	0.3	0.4	<.1	<.1
26 009	Antrim	18,185	98.0	0.1	0.1	1.2	<.1	0.5	62	22	58	63	0.2	0.2	<.1	<.1
26 011	Arenac	14,931	97.6	<.1	0.3	0.9	<.1	1.1	66	24	72	39	0.2	0.2	<.1	<.1
26 013	Baraga	7,954	87.4	0.6	0.1	11.4	<.1	0.4	80	72	40	73	<.1	<.1	<.1	<.1
26 015	Barry	50,057	98.1	0.2	0.3	0.4	<.1	1.0	34	21	54	44	0.5	0.6	<.1	0.3
26 017	Bay	111,723	94.8	1.1	0.4	0.6	<.1	3.1	18	56	35	9	1.2	1.4	<.1	1.7
26 019	Benzie	12,200	96.5	0.2	0.3	1.9	0.0	1.1	71	38	52	42	0.1	0.2	<.1	<.1
26 021	Berrien	161,378	81.7	15.3	0.9	0.4	<.1	1.7	11	79	4	27	1.7	1.7	1.9	1.3
26 023	Branch	41,502	96.3	1.7	0.4	0.5	<.1	1.1	37	39	27	38	0.4	0.5	<.1	0.2
26 025	Calhoun	135,982	86.3	10.5	0.8	0.5	0.1	1.9	15	73	8	22	1.5	1.5	1.1	1.3
26 027	Cass	49,477	89.8	7.4	0.3	0.9	0.2	1.3	35	66	13	34	0.5	0.6	0.3	0.3
26 029	Charlevoix	21,468	97.5	<.1	0.2	1.7	<.1	0.5	56	28	68	64	0.2	0.3	<.1	<.1
26 031	Cheboygan	21,398	97.1	<.1	0.3	2.2	<.1	0.4	57	31	71	76	0.2	0.3	<.1	<.1
26 033	Chippewa	34,604	81.5	6.2	0.4	11.0	<.1	0.8	45	80	16	48	0.4	0.4	0.2	0.1
26 035	Clare	24,952	98.5	0.2	0.2	0.6	<.1	0.5	52	13	56	62	0.3	0.3	<.1	<.1
26 037	Clinton	57,883	96.6	0.4	0.3	0.5	<.1	2.2	29	35	47	16	0.6	0.7	<.1	0.6
26 039	Crawford	12,260	95.7	2.1	0.3	1.2	0.0	0.6	70	46	22	55	0.1	0.2	<.1	<.1
26 041	Delta	37,780	97.2	<.1	0.3	2.1	<.1	0.4	41	29	77	79	0.4	0.5	<.1	<.1
26 043	Dickinson	26,831	98.6	<.1	0.4	0.5	<.1	0.4	48	7	65	72	0.3	0.3	<.1	<.1
26 045	Eaton	92,879	93.0	3.5	0.6	0.4	<.1	2.4	19	62	18	13	1.0	1.1	0.3	1.1
26 047	Emmet	25,040	96.0	0.5	0.3	2.7	<.1	0.5	51	42	43	69	0.3	0.3	<.1	<.1
26 049	Genesee	430,459	77.1	19.4	0.7	0.7	<.1	2.1	5	81	2	18	4.6	4.3	6.5	4.4
26 051	Gladwin	21,896	98.6	<.1	0.2	0.5	<.1	0.6	55	9	69	57	0.2	0.3	<.1	<.1
26 053	Gogebic	18,052	96.6	1.3	0.1	1.6	<.1	0.4	63	37	32	78	0.2	0.2	<.1	<.1
26 055	Grand Traverse	64,273	97.5	0.4	0.5	0.8	<.1	0.8	27	27	46	50	0.7	0.8	<.1	0.2
26 057	Gratiot	38,982	94.8	0.8	0.2	0.3	<.1	3.8	39	55	38	6	0.4	0.5	<.1	0.7
26 059	Hillsdale	43,431	98.2	0.3	0.3	0.3	<.1	0.9	36	18	49	46	0.5	0.6	<.1	0.2
26 061	Houghton	35,446	96.9	0.4	1.7	0.4	<.1	0.5	43	33	45	71	0.4	0.4	<.1	<.1
26 063	Huron	34,951	98.4	<.1	0.2	0.3	<.1	1.1	44	15	74	41	0.4	0.4	<.1	0.2
26 065	Ingham	281,912	82.1	9.7	2.6	0.6	0.2	4.8	7	78	9	4	3.0	3.0	2.1	6.7
26 067	Ionia	57,024	92.2	5.2	0.2	0.4	<.1	2.1	30	64	17	19	0.6	0.7	0.2	0.6
26 069	Iosco	30,209	95.1	2.1	0.9	0.7	<.1	1.2	47	53	23	36	0.3	0.4	<.1	0.2
26 071	Iron	13,175	98.5	<.1	0.2	0.7	<.1	0.5	69	11	79	65	0.1	0.2	<.1	<.1
26 073	Isabella	54,624	94.9	1.1	0.8	1.8	<.1	1.3	32	54	34	35	0.6	0.7	<.1	0.4
26 075	Jackson	149,756	89.7	7.9	0.4	0.4	<.1	1.5	13	67	11	30	1.6	1.8	0.9	1.1
26 077	Kalamazoo	223,411	87.5	8.8	1.4	0.4	0.1	1.8	8	71	10	24	2.4	2.6	1.5	2.0
26 079	Kalkaska	13,497	98.3	<.1	0.2	0.8	<.1	0.6	68	17	70	54	0.1	0.2	<.1	<.1
26 081	Kent	500,631	87.5	7.9	1.0	0.5	<.1	2.9	4	70	12	10	5.4	5.7	3.1	7.3
26 083	Keweenaw	1,701	98.9	<.1	0.4	0.2	<.1	0.4	83	2	73	80	<.1	<.1	<.1	<.1
26 085	Lake	8,583	85.0	13.3	0.1	0.9	<.1	0.7	78	74	6	52	<.1	<.1	<.1	<.1
26 087	Lapeer	74,768	96.6	0.6	0.4	0.4	<.1	2.0	23	36	39	21	0.8	0.9	<.1	0.7
26 089	Leelanau	16,527	95.8	<.1	0.2	2.7	<.1	1.1	65	45	62	37	0.2	0.2	<.1	<.1
26 091	Lenawee	91,476	91.6	1.5	0.5	0.3	<.1	6.0	20	65	30	3	1.0	1.1	0.1	2.7
26 093	Livingston	115,645	97.6	0.6	0.4	0.6	<.1	0.8	17	25	42	47	1.2	1.5	<.1	0.5
26 095	Luce	5,763	93.7	<.1	0.1	5.7	0.0	0.5	82	58	78	70	<.1	<.1	<.1	<.1
26 097	Mackinac	10,674	83.7	<.1	0.1	15.8	<.1	0.3	73	75	75	81	0.1	0.1	<.1	<.1
26 099	Macomb	717,400	95.8	1.4	1.2	0.4	<.1	1.1	3	44	31	40	7.7	9.0	0.8	4.0
26 101	Manistee	21,265	97.1	0.3	0.2	0.9	<.1	1.5	58	30	51	31	0.2	0.3	<.1	0.2
26 103	Marquette	70,887	95.5	1.6	0.7	1.3	<.1	0.8	24	49	28	49	0.8	0.9	<.1	0.3
26 105	Mason	25,537	96.8	0.6	0.3	0.7	<.1	1.6	50	34	41	28	0.3	0.3	<.1	0.2
26 107	Mecosta	37,308	95.1	2.6	0.5	0.7	<.1	1.0	42	52	20	43	0.4	0.5	<.1	0.2
26 109	Menominee	24,920	98.0	<.1	0.2	1.5	<.1	0.2	53	23	80	83	0.3	0.3	<.1	<.1
26 111	Midland	75,651	96.2	0.9	1.0	0.4	<.1	1.4	22	40	36	33	0.8	1.0	<.1	0.5
26 113	Missaukee	12,147	98.6	<.1	0.2	0.6	0.0	0.6	72	8	82	60	0.1	0.2	<.1	<.1
26 115	Monroe	133,600	95.9	1.7	0.4	0.3	<.1	1.6	16	43	26	29	1.4	1.7	0.2	1.0
26 117	Montcalm	53,059	95.6	1.8	0.3	0.7	<.1	1.7	33	47	25	26	0.6	0.7	<.1	0.4
26 119	Montmorency	8,936	98.6	<.1	0.1	0.5	<.1	0.7	76	6	83	53	<.1	0.1	<.1	<.1
26 121	Muskegon	158,983	83.1	13.5	0.3	0.8	<.1	2.3	12	76	5	14	1.7	1.7	1.7	1.8
26 123	Newaygo	38,202	95.4	1.2	0.2	0.6	<.1	2.5	40	51	33	11	0.4	0.5	<.1	0.5
26 125	Oakland	1,083,592	88.4	7.1	2.3	0.3	<.1	1.8	2	69	14	23	11.7	12.5	6.0	9.7
26 127	Oceana	22,454	92.3	0.3	0.2	1.0	<.1	6.2	54	63	50	2	0.2	0.3	<.1	0.7
26 129	Ogemaw	18,681	98.5	<.1	<.1	0.7	<.1	0.6	61	10	63	59	0.2	0.2	<.1	<.1
26 131	Ontonagon	8,854	98.2	<.1	0.2	1.2	0.0	0.4	77	20	76	74	<.1	0.1	<.1	<.1
26 133	Osceola	20,146	98.2	0.3	0.2	0.6	<.1	0.7	59	19	48	51	0.2	0.3	<.1	<.1
26 135	Oscoda	7,842	98.7	<.1	<.1	0.5	<.1	0.6	81	4	81	56	<.1	0.1	<.1	<.1
26 137	Otsego	17,957	98.5	0.1	0.5	0.6	<.1	0.4	64	12	61	77	0.2	0.2	<.1	<.1
26 139	Ottawa	187,768	93.7	0.5	1.3	0.3	<.1	4.2	10	59	44	5	2.0	2.3	<.1	3.9

State/county code	County	Total persons	Percent of total persons — Non-Hispanic White	Black	Asian and Pacific Islander	Native American	Other	Hispanic	Rank — Percent of total persons — Total	Non-Hispanic White	Black	Hispanic	Percent contribution to state population — Total	Non-Hispanic White	Black	Hispanic
26 141	Presque Isle	13,743	99.1	<.1	0.2	0.3	0.0	0.3	67	1	67	82	0.1	0.2	<.1	<.1
26 143	Roscommon	19,776	98.7	0.2	0.1	0.5	0.0	0.5	60	5	55	67	0.2	0.3	<.1	<.1
26 145	Saginaw	211,946	75.6	17.1	0.6	0.4	<.1	6.2	9	82	3	1	2.3	2.1	2.8	6.5
26 147	St. Clair	145,607	95.4	2.0	0.3	0.5	<.1	1.8	14	50	24	25	1.6	1.8	0.2	1.3
26 149	St. Joseph	58,913	95.6	2.7	0.4	0.4	<.1	0.9	28	48	19	45	0.6	0.7	0.1	0.3
26 151	Sanilac	39,928	97.0	<.1	0.1	0.5	<.1	2.3	38	32	64	15	0.4	0.5	<.1	0.4
26 153	Schoolcraft	8,302	93.1	<.1	0.2	6.2	0.0	0.4	79	61	66	75	<.1	0.1	<.1	<.1
26 155	Shiawassee	69,770	97.5	0.1	0.3	0.5	<.1	1.5	26	26	57	32	0.8	0.9	<.1	0.5
26 157	Tuscola	55,498	96.1	0.8	0.3	0.6	<.1	2.1	31	41	37	17	0.6	0.7	<.1	0.6
26 159	Van Buren	70,060	89.0	6.6	0.3	0.9	<.1	3.2	25	68	15	7	0.8	0.8	0.4	1.1
26 161	Washtenaw	282,937	82.3	11.1	4.1	0.3	0.1	2.0	6	77	7	20	3.0	3.0	2.4	2.8
26 163	Wayne	2,111,687	56.1	40.0	1.0	0.4	<.1	2.4	1	83	1	12	22.7	15.5	65.9	25.1
26 165	Wexford	26,360	98.3	0.1	0.3	0.7	<.1	0.6	49	16	59	58	0.3	0.3	<.1	<.1
26	**MICHIGAN**	**9,295,297**	**82.3**	**13.8**	**1.1**	**0.6**	**<.1**	**2.2**					**100.0**	**100.0**	**100.0**	**100.0**
	CONGRESSIONAL															
	District 1	580,956	95.8	0.8	0.4	2.4	<.1	0.6	2	2	16	16	6.3	7.3	0.4	1.6
	District 2	580,956	91.4	4.3	0.6	0.6	<.1	3.0	10	7	10	3	6.3	6.9	2.0	8.7
	District 3	580,956	88.4	7.3	0.9	0.5	<.1	2.8	11	10	7	6	6.3	6.7	3.3	8.0
	District 4	580,956	96.1	1.0	0.4	0.6	<.1	1.8	12	1	15	10	6.3	7.3	0.5	5.0
	District 5	580,956	87.3	8.3	0.4	0.5	<.1	3.4	13	11	6	2	6.3	6.6	3.8	9.7
	District 6	580,956	87.2	9.5	0.9	0.5	<.1	1.8	14	12	5	9	6.3	6.6	4.3	5.2
	District 7	580,957	91.0	5.6	0.5	0.4	<.1	2.4	1	8	9	7	6.3	6.9	2.5	7.0
	District 8	580,956	89.0	5.7	1.6	0.6	<.1	2.9	15	9	8	4	6.3	6.8	2.6	8.4
	District 9	580,956	78.0	17.6	1.0	0.5	<.1	2.8	16	14	3	5	6.3	5.9	8.0	8.2
	District 10	580,956	95.6	2.0	0.7	0.4	<.1	1.3	3	3	13	12	6.3	7.3	0.9	3.7
	District 11	580,956	92.0	4.1	2.3	0.2	<.1	1.3	4	6	11	13	6.3	7.0	1.8	3.7
	District 12	580,956	92.4	3.7	2.3	0.4	<.1	1.2	5	5	12	14	6.3	7.0	1.7	3.4
	District 13	580,956	84.0	10.9	2.8	0.4	<.1	1.7	6	13	4	11	6.3	6.4	5.0	5.0
	District 14	580,956	28.8	68.8	1.0	0.3	0.1	1.1	7	15	2	15	6.3	2.2	31.2	3.0
	District 15	580,956	24.9	69.7	0.7	0.4	0.1	4.3	8	16	1	1	6.3	1.9	31.6	12.3
	District 16	580,956	94.8	1.4	0.9	0.4	<.1	2.4	9	4	14	8	6.3	7.2	0.6	7.0

Table B. — 1990 Voting Age Population (VAP) by Race and Ethnic Origin

County	Total Voting Age Population	Percent of total VAP — Non-Hispanic: White	Black	Asian and Pacific Islander	Native American	Other	Hispanic	Rank: Percent of total VAP — Non-Hispanic Total	White	Black	Hispanic	Percent contribution to state VAP: Total	Non-Hispanic White	Black	Hispanic	VAP percent of total population: Total	Non-Hispanic White	Black	Asian and Pacific Islander	Native American	Other	Hispanic
Alcona	8,003	98.7	0.2	0.2	0.5	<.1	0.4	73	14	49	67	0.1	0.1	<.1	<.1	78.9	79.1	87.0	60.9	71.4	100.0	52.7
Alger	6,732	93.8	3.1	0.2	2.6	<.1	0.4	77	63	19	63	<.1	0.1	<.1	<.1	75.0	75.2	97.6	58.3	57.5	100.0	58.1
Allegan	63,644	94.9	1.7	0.3	0.5	<.1	2.7	21	58	29	7	0.9	1.1	0.1	1.4	70.3	70.8	74.5	44.4	61.7	45.5	58.7
Alpena	22,539	99.0	0.1	0.2	0.3	<.1	0.4	46	6	57	60	0.3	0.4	<.1	<.1	73.6	73.8	68.6	61.9	69.3	25.0	62.8
Antrim	13,508	98.5	<.1	<.1	0.9	<.1	0.4	63	21	59	61	0.2	0.2	<.1	<.1	74.3	74.6	52.2	50.0	61.0	66.7	56.3
Arenac	10,941	98.1	<.1	0.2	0.8	<.1	0.9	66	24	72	42	0.2	0.2	<.1	<.1	73.3	73.6	50.0	52.6	62.0	100.0	57.5
Baraga	5,848	89.4	0.8	<.1	9.4	0.0	0.3	81	72	40	74	<.1	<.1	<.1	<.1	73.5	75.2	93.8	50.0	60.7	0.0	52.9
Barry	36,068	98.4	0.2	0.2	0.4	<.1	0.8	35	23	53	43	0.5	0.6	<.1	0.2	72.1	72.3	68.9	56.6	69.4	41.7	58.7
Bay	82,344	95.8	0.9	0.3	0.5	<.1	2.4	18	49	36	8	1.2	1.4	<.1	1.6	75.8	76.3	56.7	45.7	68.6	34.9	57.6
Benzie	9,244	97.2	0.2	0.2	1.5	0.0	0.9	70	34	54	40	0.1	0.2	<.1	<.1	75.8	76.3	56.7	45.7	60.2	0.0	65.9
Berrien	117,859	84.7	12.6	0.8	0.4	<.1	1.4	11	77	5	25	1.7	1.7	1.7	1.3	73.0	75.8	60.0	69.3	70.5	46.8	62.3
Branch	29,935	96.1	2.1	0.3	0.5	<.1	1.0	37	46	24	37	0.4	0.5	<.1	0.2	72.1	71.9	92.9	63.3	68.8	25.0	63.9
Calhoun	99,789	87.9	9.3	0.7	0.5	<.1	1.5	15	73	8	23	1.5	1.5	1.1	1.2	73.4	74.8	65.3	66.6	68.4	30.9	59.6
Cass	36,112	90.7	7.0	0.3	0.8	0.1	1.1	34	66	13	36	0.5	0.6	0.3	0.3	73.0	73.7	68.1	60.8	66.1	61.2	59.0
Charlevoix	15,676	98.0	<.1	0.1	1.5	<.1	0.3	58	26	77	71	0.2	0.3	<.1	<.1	73.0	73.4	29.4	50.0	64.8	25.0	47.3
Cheboygan	15,793	97.5	<.1	0.2	2.0	0.0	0.3	57	32	65	76	0.2	0.3	<.1	<.1	73.8	74.1	60.0	54.5	66.7	0.0	52.5
Chippewa	26,524	79.9	7.9	0.5	8.3	<.1	0.8	44	80	11	45	0.4	0.4	0.2	0.2	76.7	77.6	97.3	82.9	57.8	72.7	78.1
Clare	18,417	98.7	0.1	0.2	0.6	<.1	0.4	51	12	56	64	0.3	0.3	<.1	<.1	73.8	74.0	53.8	60.4	71.8	33.3	51.5
Clinton	41,231	97.1	0.4	0.3	0.4	<.1	1.8	30	35	47	16	0.6	0.7	<.1	0.6	71.2	71.6	68.8	56.7	67.2	33.3	57.8
Crawford	9,059	95.3	2.8	0.4	1.1	0.0	0.5	71	55	20	52	0.1	0.2	<.1	<.1	73.9	73.5	96.5	81.0	67.6	0.0	62.0
Delta	27,606	97.8	<.1	0.2	1.7	<.1	0.3	41	28	80	75	0.4	0.5	<.1	<.1	73.1	73.5	33.3	52.0	59.4	33.3	54.4
Dickinson	19,859	98.9	<.1	0.2	0.4	<.1	0.4	48	8	67	68	0.3	0.3	<.1	<.1	74.0	74.2	45.5	46.9	67.7	57.1	61.2
Eaton	67,250	93.9	3.2	0.5	0.4	<.1	2.0	19	62	18	12	1.0	1.1	0.3	1.1	72.4	73.1	66.3	57.5	67.5	34.0	59.9
Emmet	18,363	96.3	0.6	0.2	2.5	<.1	0.4	52	43	41	59	0.3	0.3	<.1	<.1	73.3	73.5	80.2	58.0	68.0	42.9	63.6
Genesee	309,796	79.9	17.2	0.6	0.6	<.1	1.7	5	81	2	19	4.5	4.3	6.1	4.3	72.0	74.6	63.6	63.8	64.3	27.0	59.8
Gladwin	16,134	98.9	<.1	0.1	0.5	<.1	0.4	55	7	68	58	0.2	0.3	<.1	<.1	73.7	73.9	47.1	47.4	70.2	100.0	50.0
Gogebic	14,021	96.7	1.7	<.1	1.3	<.1	0.2	61	38	28	79	0.2	0.2	<.1	<.1	77.7	77.8	97.9	56.0	63.5	66.7	50.7
Grand Traverse	46,861	97.8	0.4	0.4	0.8	<.1	0.7	27	29	46	50	0.7	0.8	<.1	0.2	72.9	73.1	79.7	57.3	66.1	26.3	61.2
Gratiot	28,404	95.4	1.0	0.2	0.3	<.1	3.0	40	54	35	6	0.4	0.5	<.1	0.7	72.9	73.3	93.4	62.8	66.2	100.0	57.5
Hillsdale	31,175	98.6	0.2	0.2	0.3	<.1	0.7	36	19	51	47	0.5	0.5	<.1	0.2	71.8	72.0	59.3	62.7	66.1	19.0	57.7
Houghton	27,504	97.0	0.5	1.8	0.4	<.1	0.4	42	36	44	62	0.4	0.5	<.1	<.1	77.6	77.6	80.8	81.0	68.6	60.0	65.9
Huron	25,574	98.7	<.1	0.1	0.3	<.1	0.8	45	15	71	44	0.4	0.4	<.1	0.2	73.2	73.3	60.0	58.6	78.4	100.0	57.8
Ingham	213,547	84.5	8.5	2.5	0.6	<.1	3.9	7	78	9	4	3.1	3.1	2.1	6.6	72.5	78.0	66.4	71.0	69.8	30.8	61.3
Ionia	40,920	90.8	6.9	0.1	0.4	<.1	1.8	31	65	14	17	0.6	0.6	0.3	0.6	71.8	70.7	95.7	47.5	69.3	27.3	61.7
Iosco	22,245	95.6	1.8	0.7	0.7	<.1	1.1	47	51	26	33	0.3	0.4	<.1	0.2	73.6	74.0	65.1	62.8	72.3	33.3	69.5
Iron	10,245	98.9	<.1	0.1	0.6	0.0	0.4	67	10	83	69	0.1	0.2	<.1	<.1	77.8	78.1	25.0	51.7	66.3	0.0	53.7
Isabella	42,098	95.5	1.2	0.7	1.4	<.1	1.4	28	52	34	35	0.6	0.7	<.1	0.4	77.1	77.6	82.0	69.2	61.5	27.5	63.4
Jackson	111,189	89.8	8.1	0.4	0.4	<.1	1.4	13	68	10	27	1.6	1.7	1.0	1.2	74.2	74.3	76.4	62.4	69.1	25.0	65.2
Kalamazoo	168,938	89.4	7.4	1.3	0.4	<.1	1.4	8	71	12	24	2.5	2.6	1.4	1.9	75.6	77.3	63.2	72.4	71.8	33.2	60.9
Kalkaska	9,543	98.5	<.1	0.1	0.8	<.1	0.4	69	20	61	57	0.1	0.2	<.1	<.1	70.7	70.9	80.0	56.5	71.8	50.0	47.1
Kent	359,055	89.5	6.8	0.9	0.4	<.1	2.4	4	70	15	9	5.3	5.6	2.8	6.8	71.7	73.3	62.1	58.5	64.5	30.2	57.8
Keweenaw	1,362	99.4	<.1	0.1	0.3	0.0	<.1	83	1	64	83	<.1	<.1	<.1	<.1	80.1	80.5	100.0	33.3	100.0	0.0	16.7
Lake	6,428	86.0	12.7	<.1	0.8	0.0	0.5	78	75	4	53	<.1	<.1	<.1	<.1	74.9	75.8	71.3	44.4	66.2	0.0	53.3
Lapeer	52,659	96.9	0.8	0.3	0.4	<.1	1.6	26	39	39	21	0.8	0.9	<.1	0.7	70.4	70.6	90.5	50.4	68.1	50.0	57.9
Leelanau	12,217	96.7	<.1	0.1	2.3	<.1	0.9	65	40	69	41	0.2	0.2	<.1	<.1	73.9	74.6	37.5	41.0	61.8	33.3	59.0
Lenawee	65,698	92.9	1.4	0.5	0.3	<.1	4.9	20	64	31	2	1.0	1.1	0.1	2.6	71.8	72.9	68.2	64.4	71.1	43.0	58.1
Livingston	82,513	98.0	0.4	0.3	0.5	<.1	0.7	17	25	45	48	1.2	1.4	<.1	0.5	71.4	71.7	52.8	58.8	64.8	30.8	59.7
Luce	4,195	95.2	<.1	0.1	4.4	0.0	0.2	82	57	79	73	<.1	<.1	<.1	<.1	72.8	73.9	50.0	83.3	56.0	0.0	51.9
Mackinac	7,908	87.2	<.1	<.1	12.5	<.1	0.2	74	74	74	82	0.1	0.1	<.1	<.1	74.1	77.2	60.0	63.6	58.2	100.0	45.5
Macomb	545,747	96.3	1.3	1.1	0.3	<.1	1.0	3	44	32	38	8.0	9.2	0.8	4.4	76.1	76.4	68.6	66.1	70.4	30.2	67.9
Manistee	16,164	97.6	0.2	0.2	0.8	<.1	1.2	54	30	50	32	0.2	0.3	<.1	0.2	76.0	76.4	64.8	57.7	67.2	66.7	58.2
Marquette	52,488	95.7	1.8	0.7	1.1	<.1	0.7	24	50	27	49	0.8	0.9	0.1	0.3	74.0	74.2	80.9	66.9	63.2	34.5	63.3
Mason	18,826	97.4	0.6	0.2	0.6	<.1	0.9	49	33	42	31	0.3	0.3	<.1	0.2	73.7	74.1	69.7	57.3	64.4	100.0	56.4
Mecosta	29,125	95.2	2.8	0.5	0.6	<.1	0.9	38	56	21	39	0.4	0.5	<.1	0.2	78.1	78.1	82.9	72.1	69.2	58.3	69.4
Menominee	18,331	98.4	<.1	0.1	1.2	<.1	0.4	53	22	78	81	0.3	0.3	<.1	<.1	73.6	73.9	71.4	46.6	57.6	100.0	61.0
Midland	54,943	96.7	0.9	1.0	0.4	<.1	1.1	22	39	38	34	0.8	0.9	<.1	0.5	72.6	73.0	67.7	66.9	65.6	42.3	59.1
Missaukee	8,544	98.9	<.1	0.2	0.5	0.0	0.4	72	9	75	66	0.1	0.1	<.1	<.1	70.3	70.5	100.0	60.0	62.2	0.0	46.3
Monroe	95,356	96.4	1.6	0.4	0.3	<.1	1.3	16	42	30	28	1.4	1.6	0.2	1.0	71.4	71.7	65.5	60.4	66.5	29.6	61.4
Montcalm	37,858	95.5	2.4	0.2	0.6	<.1	1.3	33	53	23	29	0.6	0.6	0.1	0.4	71.4	71.3	96.3	48.6	66.2	41.7	56.2
Montmorency	6,836	99.0	<.1	<.1	0.4	<.1	0.5	75	5	81	54	0.1	0.1	<.1	<.1	76.5	76.8	100.0	50.0	63.8	33.3	51.7
Muskegon	114,319	85.2	11.9	0.3	0.7	<.1	1.8	12	76	6	15	1.7	1.7	1.6	1.7	71.9	73.8	63.6	57.1	63.8	34.3	58.2
Newaygo	26,910	96.2	1.2	0.2	0.5	<.1	1.9	43	45	33	14	0.4	0.5	<.1	0.4	70.4	71.0	71.6	50.5	62.0	50.0	52.4
Oakland	815,534	89.6	6.5	2.0	0.3	<.1	1.5	2	69	16	22	11.9	12.7	6.1	10.2	75.3	76.3	68.9	66.5	70.5	34.0	60.4
Oceana	15,812	94.3	0.3	<.1	0.9	<.1	4.4	56	61	48	3	0.2	0.3	<.1	0.6	70.4	71.9	72.4	38.5	63.5	37.5	50.3
Ogemaw	13,756	98.8	<.1	<.1	0.7	<.1	0.3	62	11	66	70	0.2	0.2	<.1	<.1	73.6	73.9	38.9	58.8	70.9	66.7	45.2
Ontonagon	6,745	98.6	<.1	<.1	1.0	0.0	0.3	76	17	73	77	<.1	0.1	<.1	<.1	76.2	76.5	75.0	40.0	64.8	0.0	46.8
Osceola	14,173	98.6	0.2	<.1	0.6	<.1	0.5	60	18	52	51	0.2	0.2	<.1	<.1	70.6	70.6	51.9	27.9	67.2	40.0	54.5
Oscoda	5,956	99.1	<.1	<.1	0.4	<.1	0.5	80	3	76	55	<.1	0.1	<.1	<.1	76.0	76.2	100.0	40.0	53.7	33.3	54.0
Otsego	12,839	98.7	0.1	0.3	0.5	<.1	0.3	64	13	58	72	0.2	0.2	<.1	<.1	71.5	71.7	72.2	52.4	63.1	40.0	64.2
Ottawa	132,690	94.7	0.5	1.0	0.3	<.1	3.6	10	60	43	5	1.9	2.2	<.1	3.8	70.7	71.4	72.3	52.8	71.8	32.3	59.4

Michigan 477

County	Total Voting Age Population	Percent of total VAP — Non-Hispanic White	Black	Asian and Pacific Islander	Native American	Other	Hispanic	Rank: Percent of total VAP — Total	Non-Hispanic White	Black	Hispanic	Percent contribution to state VAP — Total	Non-Hispanic White	Black	Hispanic	VAP percent of total population — Total	Non-Hispanic White	Black	Asian and Pacific Islander	Native American	Other	Hispanic
Presque Isle	10,240	99.2	<.1	0.2	0.3	0.0	0.2	68	2	60	80	0.1	0.2	<.1	<.1	74.5	74.6	81.8	70.0	67.4	0.0	59.5
Roscommon	15,603	99.0	<.1	<.1	0.5	0.0	0.4	59	4	82	65	0.2	0.3	<.1	<.1	78.9	79.2	5.4	65.2	74.3	0.0	60.6
Saginaw	152,369	79.3	14.7	0.5	0.4	<.1	5.1	9	82	3	1	2.2	2.1	2.6	6.3	71.9	75.4	61.6	62.0	69.0	40.0	59.1
St. Clair	105,196	96.0	1.9	0.3	0.4	<.1	1.4	14	47	25	26	1.5	1.8	0.2	1.2	72.2	72.7	67.2	59.8	65.3	19.3	57.4
St. Joseph	41,935	95.9	2.5	0.4	0.4	<.1	0.8	29	48	22	46	0.6	0.7	0.1	0.3	71.2	71.5	65.9	59.2	75.1	40.0	62.5
Sanilac	28,635	97.6	<.1	0.1	0.4	<.1	1.7	39	31	62	18	0.4	0.5	<.1	0.4	71.7	72.2	63.2	59.3	64.4	50.0	54.5
Schoolcraft	6,172	94.8	<.1	0.1	4.8	0.0	0.2	79	59	70	78	<.1	0.1	<.1	<.1	74.3	75.6	42.9	53.8	57.5	0.0	46.9
Shiawassee	49,835	97.9	0.1	0.2	0.5	<.1	1.2	25	27	55	30	0.7	0.9	<.1	0.5	71.4	71.7	67.4	55.0	71.3	31.6	57.6
Tuscola	39,672	96.6	0.9	0.3	0.5	<.1	1.7	32	41	37	20	0.6	0.7	<.1	0.5	71.5	71.8	78.9	59.9	62.1	36.8	58.1
Van Buren	49,664	90.5	6.1	0.2	0.8	<.1	2.3	26	67	17	10	0.7	0.8	0.4	0.9	70.9	72.1	65.6	56.3	62.6	48.6	51.5
Washtenaw	221,841	83.5	10.0	4.1	0.3	<.1	1.9	6	79	7	13	3.2	3.2	2.6	3.5	78.4	79.5	71.0	79.3	78.1	41.8	75.2
Wayne	1,541,050	59.1	37.5	0.9	0.3	<.1	2.1	1	83	1	11	22.5	15.9	66.6	26.1	73.0	76.8	68.3	67.0	71.6	43.1	64.3
Wexford	18,795	98.6	<.1	0.2	0.6	0.0	0.4	50	16	63	56	0.3	0.3	<.1	<.1	71.3	71.5	42.4	57.5	65.7	0.0	53.6
MICHIGAN	**6,836,532**	**83.9**	**12.7**	**1.0**	**0.5**	**<.1**	**1.8**					100.0	100.0	100.0	100.0	73.5	75.0	67.6	67.0	66.5	37.5	61.7
CONGRESSIONAL																						
District 1	431,643	96.2	1.0	0.4	1.9	<.1	0.5	6	2	16	16	6.3	7.2	0.5	1.6	74.3	74.6	89.5	65.3	60.7	40.2	60.7
District 2	414,968	92.6	3.9	0.5	0.5	<.1	2.5	15	7	10	3	6.1	6.7	1.9	8.2	71.4	72.4	65.0	52.5	65.1	39.7	58.0
District 3	416,628	90.0	6.6	0.8	0.4	<.1	2.2	14	10	7	6	6.1	6.5	3.2	7.5	71.7	73.0	64.5	58.3	65.0	30.0	58.0
District 4	425,655	96.6	1.1	0.4	0.6	<.1	1.4	9	1	15	11	6.2	7.2	0.5	4.8	73.3	73.6	74.9	62.9	66.1	46.7	58.8
District 5	418,962	89.3	7.1	0.3	0.5	<.1	2.7	12	11	6	2	6.1	6.5	3.4	9.2	72.1	73.7	62.0	58.3	66.2	33.5	58.2
District 6	426,902	89.1	8.0	0.9	0.5	<.1	1.4	8	12	5	10	6.2	6.6	4.0	5.0	73.5	75.1	62.5	69.8	68.7	42.1	58.9
District 7	424,301	91.7	5.4	0.5	0.4	<.1	2.0	10	8	8	8	6.2	6.8	2.6	7.0	73.0	73.6	70.8	63.4	69.6	32.2	61.3
District 8	431,535	90.3	5.2	1.5	0.5	<.1	2.4	7	9	9	4	6.3	6.8	2.6	8.3	74.3	75.3	67.3	68.9	68.5	31.8	61.3
District 9	420,886	80.6	15.6	0.9	0.5	<.1	2.4	11	14	3	5	6.2	5.9	7.6	8.0	72.4	74.9	64.3	65.1	68.4	31.9	60.6
District 10	434,093	96.2	1.8	0.6	0.3	<.1	1.1	5	3	13	13	6.3	7.3	0.9	3.8	74.7	75.1	67.4	64.7	68.3	22.3	63.5
District 11	444,245	92.8	3.8	2.0	0.2	<.1	1.1	1	6	11	12	6.5	7.2	2.0	4.0	76.5	77.1	72.0	66.2	70.8	39.0	67.4
District 12	442,863	93.1	3.5	2.1	0.3	<.1	1.1	2	5	12	14	6.5	7.2	1.8	3.8	76.2	76.8	71.1	67.4	70.6	34.9	69.0
District 13	442,445	85.2	9.9	2.8	0.4	<.1	1.6	3	13	4	9	6.5	6.6	5.1	5.8	76.2	77.3	69.0	76.1	75.0	37.8	70.6
District 14	408,963	32.8	65.0	0.8	0.3	<.1	1.0	16	15	2	15	6.0	2.3	30.7	3.3	70.4	80.3	66.5	61.5	70.7	34.6	66.3
District 15	418,224	27.3	67.9	0.7	0.4	<.1	3.7	13	16	1	1	6.1	2.0	32.7	12.5	72.0	79.0	70.1	75.9	71.0	52.7	62.8
District 16	434,219	95.4	1.2	0.8	0.4	<.1	2.1	4	4	14	7	6.4	7.2	0.6	7.3	74.7	75.2	67.4	65.2	70.2	46.2	64.9

Table C. – **Voter Participation: November 3, 1992, General Election**

County	Estimated Voting Age Population (VAP), 1992	Voter registration (REG)				Voter turnout												
						Highest office				Maximum vote						Percent drop-off, by office		
		Total	% contribution to state REG	% of 1992 VAP	Rank by % of 1992 VAP	Actual	Total	Office	% of 1992 VAP	Total	% contribution to state turnout	% of REG	Rank by % of REG	% of 1992 VAP	Rank by % 1992 VAP	President	Senator	Governor	Representative
Alcona	8,110	8,752	0.1	107.9	1	5,921	5,779	P	71.3	5,921	0.1	67.7	71	73.0	8	2.4	-	-	23.1
Alger	6,778	5,855	<.1	86.4	63	4,630	4,570	P	67.4	4,630	0.1	79.1	5	68.3	25	1.3	-	-	6.9
Allegan	66,288	54,161	0.9	81.7	76	41,345	40,835	P	61.6	41,345	1.0	76.3	12	62.4	62	1.2	-	-	14.1
Alpena	22,551	21,604	0.4	95.8	23	15,304	15,069	P	66.8	15,304	0.4	70.8	44	67.9	30	1.5	-	-	9.1
Antrim	14,058	14,113	0.2	100.4	11	10,172	9,991	P	71.1	10,172	0.2	72.1	36	72.4	11	1.8	-	-	12.6
Arenac	11,195	10,701	0.2	95.6	25	7,290	7,206	P	64.4	7,290	0.2	68.1	65	65.1	42	1.2	-	-	12.5
Baraga	5,824	5,788	<.1	99.4	14	3,697	3,630	P	62.3	3,697	<.1	63.9	82	63.5	54	1.8	-	-	8.0
Barry	37,440	32,824	0.5	87.7	58	24,690	24,599	P	65.7	24,690	0.6	75.2	19	65.9	36	0.4	-	-	19.9
Bay	82,215	72,285	1.2	87.9	57	54,931	54,355	P	66.1	54,931	1.3	76.0	14	66.8	32	1.0	-	-	7.5
Benzie	9,424	9,181	0.1	97.4	17	6,914	6,852	P	72.7	6,914	0.2	75.3	18	73.4	7	0.9	-	-	11.6
Berrien	117,836	102,741	1.7	87.2	60	74,260	69,615	P	59.1	74,260	1.7	72.3	32	63.0	58	6.3	-	-	11.1
Branch	30,618	24,707	0.4	80.7	79	16,836	16,593	P	54.2	16,836	0.4	68.1	64	55.0	82	1.4	-	-	44.7
Calhoun	100,005	85,426	1.4	85.4	68	59,848	58,702	P	58.7	59,848	1.4	70.1	53	59.8	68	1.9	-	-	40.5
Cass	36,791	29,929	0.5	81.3	77	20,584	20,283	P	55.1	20,584	0.5	68.8	61	55.9	79	1.5	-	-	12.9
Charlevoix	16,111	16,399	0.3	101.8	6	11,724	11,525	P	71.5	11,724	0.3	71.5	39	72.8	9	1.7	-	-	4.7
Cheboygan	16,136	15,414	0.3	95.5	26	10,970	10,864	P	67.3	10,970	0.3	71.2	42	68.0	29	1.0	-	-	10.0
Chippewa	27,580	19,942	0.3	72.3	83	13,893	13,647	P	49.5	13,893	0.3	69.7	56	50.4	83	1.8	-	-	10.9
Clare	18,756	18,916	0.3	100.9	8	12,394	12,163	P	64.8	12,394	0.3	65.5	78	66.1	34	1.9	-	-	5.7
Clinton	42,486	38,609	0.6	90.9	41	30,683	30,339	P	71.4	30,683	0.7	79.5	3	72.2	12	1.1	-	-	14.3
Crawford	9,678	8,765	0.1	90.6	44	6,023	5,925	P	61.2	6,023	0.1	68.7	62	62.2	63	1.6	-	-	6.4
Delta	27,933	23,970	0.4	85.8	65	18,183	17,962	P	64.3	18,183	0.4	75.9	15	65.1	43	1.2	-	-	5.6
Dickinson	20,468	19,634	0.3	95.9	22	13,298	13,031	P	63.7	13,298	0.3	67.7	70	65.0	46	2.0	-	-	6.4
Eaton	69,372	63,444	1.0	91.5	40	48,573	47,883	P	69.0	48,573	1.1	76.6	11	70.0	19	1.4	-	-	36.5
Emmet	18,843	17,861	0.3	94.8	30	13,374	13,232	P	70.2	13,374	0.3	74.9	20	71.0	14	1.1	-	-	4.2
Genesee	312,062	314,202	5.1	100.7	9	203,724	199,998	P	64.1	203,724	4.7	64.8	81	65.3	41	1.8	-	-	4.8
Gladwin	16,653	14,890	0.2	89.4	54	11,077	10,776	P	64.7	11,077	0.3	74.4	21	66.5	33	2.7	-	-	7.7
Gogebic	13,815	13,192	0.2	95.5	28	9,410	9,225	P	66.8	9,410	0.2	71.3	41	68.1	27	2.0	-	-	10.6
Grand Traverse	48,965	44,988	0.7	91.9	37	34,692	34,461	P	70.4	34,692	0.8	77.1	9	70.9	15	0.7	-	-	5.4
Gratiot	28,394	22,482	0.4	79.2	81	16,107	15,879	P	55.9	16,107	0.4	71.6	37	56.7	77	1.4	-	-	9.5
Hillsdale	31,733	25,651	0.4	80.8	78	18,099	17,891	P	56.4	18,099	0.4	70.6	49	57.0	75	1.1	-	-	33.7
Houghton	26,245	23,202	0.4	88.4	56	15,369	15,173	P	57.8	15,369	0.4	66.2	74	58.6	72	1.3	-	-	7.4
Huron	25,668	24,834	0.4	96.8	21	16,837	16,632	P	64.8	16,837	0.4	67.8	68	65.6	39	1.2	-	-	13.8
Ingham	210,422	196,257	3.2	93.3	34	135,138	133,792	P	63.6	135,138	3.1	68.9	59	64.2	50	1.0	-	-	2.7
Ionia	42,194	33,986	0.6	80.5	80	23,992	23,822	P	56.5	23,992	0.6	70.6	47	56.9	76	0.7	-	-	16.1
Iosco	22,695	21,223	0.3	93.5	32	13,839	13,492	P	59.4	13,839	0.3	65.2	80	61.0	67	2.5	-	-	11.1
Iron	10,292	9,430	0.2	91.6	39	7,284	7,000	P	68.0	7,284	0.2	77.2	8	70.8	16	3.9	-	-	7.0
Isabella	40,255	33,846	0.6	84.1	73	22,389	22,037	P	54.7	22,389	0.5	66.1	75	55.6	81	1.6	-	-	7.9
Jackson	111,985	94,851	1.5	84.7	71	65,974	64,644	P	57.7	65,974	1.5	69.6	57	58.9	71	2.0	-	-	38.4
Kalamazoo	169,625	142,551	2.3	84.0	74	105,480	103,858	P	61.2	105,480	2.4	74.0	23	62.2	64	1.5	-	-	8.2
Kalkaska	10,249	9,920	0.2	96.8	20	6,479	6,426	P	62.7	6,479	0.1	65.3	79	63.2	55	0.8	-	-	12.0
Kent	371,633	333,333	5.4	89.7	49	245,489	242,553	P	65.3	245,489	5.7	73.6	26	66.1	35	1.2	-	-	4.3
Keweenaw	1,355	1,458	<.1	107.6	2	1,210	1,173	P	86.6	1,210	<.1	83.0	1	89.3	1	3.1	-	-	6.0
Lake	6,592	6,632	0.1	100.6	10	4,657	4,546	P	69.0	4,657	0.1	70.2	51	70.6	17	2.4	-	-	8.4
Lapeer	54,844	47,942	0.8	87.4	59	35,551	35,084	P	64.0	35,551	0.8	74.2	22	64.8	47	1.3	-	-	8.3
Leelanau	12,760	13,518	0.2	105.9	4	10,253	10,187	P	79.8	10,253	0.2	75.8	16	80.4	2	0.6	-	-	13.5
Lenawee	67,149	57,199	0.9	85.2	69	39,879	39,365	P	58.6	39,879	0.9	69.7	55	59.4	70	1.3	-	-	55.0
Livingston	87,273	84,909	1.4	97.3	18	62,467	61,735	P	70.7	62,467	1.4	73.6	27	71.6	13	1.2	-	-	3.7
Luce	4,172	4,210	<.1	100.9	7	2,637	2,603	P	62.4	2,637	<.1	62.6	83	63.2	56	1.3	-	-	12.1
Mackinac	8,095	8,046	0.1	99.4	13	6,137	5,977	P	73.8	6,137	0.1	76.3	13	75.8	3	2.6	-	-	9.9
Macomb	552,775	481,886	7.8	87.2	61	353,851	349,238	P	63.2	353,851	8.1	73.4	30	64.0	52	1.3	-	-	9.2
Manistee	16,069	16,360	0.3	101.8	5	11,805	11,651	P	72.5	11,805	0.3	72.2	34	73.5	6	1.3	-	-	16.5
Marquette	52,033	44,635	0.7	85.8	66	32,799	31,629	P	60.8	32,799	0.8	73.5	29	63.0	57	3.6	-	-	7.3
Mason	18,886	17,995	0.3	95.3	29	13,268	13,082	P	69.3	13,268	0.3	73.7	25	70.3	18	1.4	-	-	7.2
Mecosta	27,488	22,712	0.4	82.6	75	16,030	15,835	P	57.6	16,030	0.4	70.6	48	58.3	73	1.2	-	-	13.7
Menominee	18,377	15,912	0.3	86.6	62	12,541	11,082	P	60.3	12,541	0.3	78.8	6	68.2	26	11.6	-	-	16.7
Midland	55,902	50,750	0.8	90.8	42	38,997	38,624	P	69.1	38,997	0.9	76.8	10	69.8	21	1.0	-	-	3.0
Missaukee	9,069	8,781	0.1	96.8	19	6,204	6,058	P	68.4	6,204	0.1	70.7	46	68.4	24	2.4	-	-	6.3
Monroe	97,146	83,455	1.4	85.9	64	59,727	59,031	P	60.8	59,727	1.4	71.6	38	61.5	66	1.2	-	-	13.8
Montcalm	39,621	33,600	0.5	84.8	70	22,824	22,780	P	57.5	22,824	0.5	67.9	66	57.6	74	0.2	-	-	17.1
Montmorency	7,119	6,716	0.1	94.3	31	4,843	4,791	P	67.3	4,843	0.1	72.1	35	68.0	28	1.1	-	-	12.0
Muskegon	115,854	107,255	1.7	92.6	35	72,736	71,948	P	62.1	72,736	1.7	67.8	67	62.8	60	1.1	-	-	18.4
Newaygo	28,019	25,887	0.4	92.4	36	18,210	17,916	P	63.9	18,210	0.4	70.3	50	65.0	45	1.6	-	-	16.1
Oakland	841,454	761,611	12.4	90.5	45	562,691	555,760	P	66.0	562,691	13.0	73.9	24	66.9	31	1.2	-	-	9.1
Oceana	16,230	14,540	0.2	89.6	53	10,691	10,557	P	65.0	10,691	0.2	73.5	28	65.9	38	1.3	-	-	18.8
Ogemaw	14,323	14,072	0.2	98.2	16	9,435	9,126	P	63.7	9,435	0.2	67.0	72	65.9	37	3.3	-	-	11.3
Ontonagon	6,718	6,164	0.1	91.8	38	4,938	4,745	P	70.6	4,938	0.1	80.1	2	73.5	5	3.9	-	-	8.7
Osceola	14,756	13,767	0.2	93.3	33	9,476	9,376	P	63.5	9,476	0.2	68.8	60	64.2	51	1.1	-	-	13.1
Oscoda	6,137	5,498	<.1	89.6	52	3,925	3,831	P	62.4	3,925	<.1	71.4	40	64.0	53	2.4	-	-	7.8
Otsego	13,561	13,362	0.2	98.5	15	9,369	9,207	P	67.9	9,369	0.2	70.1	52	69.1	22	1.7	-	-	9.6
Ottawa	139,033	124,983	2.0	89.9	48	97,071	96,211	P	69.2	97,071	2.2	77.7	7	69.8	20	0.9	-	-	9.2

Table C. – **Voter Participation: November 3, 1992, General Election (cont)**

County	Estimated Voting Age Population (VAP), 1992	Voter registration (REG)				Voter turnout														
							Highest office			Maximum vote						Percent drop-off, by office			
		Total	% contribution to state REG	% of 1992 VAP	Rank by % of 1992 VAP	Actual	Total	Office	% of 1992 VAP	Total	% contribution to state turnout	% of REG	Rank by % of REG	% of 1992 VAP	Rank by % 1992 VAP	President	Senator	Governor	Representative
Presque Isle	10,350	9,899	0.2	95.6	24	7,491	7,345	P	71.0	7,491	0.2	75.7	17	72.4	10	1.9	-	-	5.9
Roscommon	16,270	17,452	0.3	107.3	3	12,133	12,007	P	73.8	12,133	0.3	69.5	58	74.6	4	1.0	-	-	11.0
Saginaw	152,180	145,372	2.4	95.5	27	98,463	96,905	P	63.7	98,463	2.3	67.7	69	64.7	48	1.6	-	-	8.3
St. Clair	108,198	96,971	1.6	89.6	51	67,812	66,832	P	61.8	67,812	1.6	69.9	54	62.7	61	1.4	-	-	8.8
St. Joseph	43,164	36,974	0.6	85.7	67	24,315	23,971	P	55.5	24,315	0.6	65.8	77	56.3	78	1.4	-	-	13.1
Sanilac	29,129	26,212	0.4	90.0	47	18,944	18,758	P	64.4	18,944	0.4	72.3	33	65.0	44	1.0	-	-	11.5
Schoolcraft	6,258	6,277	0.1	100.3	12	4,311	4,129	P	66.0	4,311	<.1	68.7	63	68.9	23	4.2	-	-	10.7
Shiawassee	50,744	46,013	0.7	90.7	43	32,620	32,360	P	63.8	32,620	0.8	70.9	43	64.3	49	0.8	-	-	11.0
Tuscola	40,371	31,578	0.5	78.2	82	24,984	24,666	P	61.1	24,984	0.6	79.1	4	61.9	65	1.3	-	-	14.1
Van Buren	51,279	45,982	0.7	89.7	50	30,517	30,237	P	59.0	30,517	0.7	66.4	73	59.5	69	0.9	-	-	16.7
Washtenaw	220,597	196,243	3.2	89.0	55	139,015	137,466	P	62.3	139,015	3.2	70.8	45	63.0	59	1.1	-	-	10.6
Wayne	1,532,918	1,296,934	21.1	84.6	72	857,484	841,965	P	54.9	857,484	19.7	66.1	76	55.9	80	1.8	-	-	7.5
Wexford	19,351	17,462	0.3	90.2	46	12,682	12,575	P	65.0	12,682	0.3	72.6	31	65.5	40	0.8	-	-	13.3
MICHIGAN	**6,923,000**	**6,147,083**	**100.0**	**88.8**		**4,341,909**	**4,274,673**		**61.7**	**4,341,909**	**100.0**	**70.6**		**62.7**		**1.5**	**-**	**-**	**10.5**

Table E. — Vote for President: November 3, 1992, General Election

County	All candidates Total	Clinton (DEM)	Bush (REP)	Perot (IND)	Other	Plurality Total	Plurality Party	Percent of total vote DEM	REP	IND	Other	Rank DEM	REP	IND	Percent contribution to state vote Total	DEM	REP	IND	Major party Percent of vote DEM	REP
Alcona	5,779	2,383	2,247	1,117	32	136	D	41.2	38.9	19.3	0.6	31	26	72	0.1	0.1	0.1	0.1	51.5	48.5
Alger	4,570	2,144	1,471	941	14	673	D	46.9	32.2	20.6	0.3	12	70	65	0.1	0.1	<.1	0.1	59.3	40.7
Allegan	40,835	12,823	19,077	8,742	193	6,254	R	31.4	46.7	21.4	0.5	78	3	57	1.0	0.7	1.2	1.1	40.2	59.8
Alpena	15,069	6,894	4,878	3,236	61	2,016	D	45.7	32.4	21.5	0.4	16	66	56	0.4	0.4	0.3	0.4	58.6	41.4
Antrim	9,991	3,431	3,984	2,528	48	553	R	34.3	39.9	25.3	0.5	69	18	22	0.2	0.2	0.3	0.3	46.3	53.7
Arenac	7,206	3,244	2,330	1,608	24	914	D	45.0	32.3	22.3	0.3	20	67	51	0.2	0.2	0.1	0.2	58.2	41.8
Baraga	3,630	1,695	1,160	754	21	535	D	46.7	32.0	20.8	0.6	13	72	62	<.1	<.1	<.1	<.1	59.4	40.6
Barry	24,599	8,652	9,489	6,303	155	837	R	35.2	38.6	25.6	0.6	64	27	19	0.6	0.5	0.6	0.8	47.7	52.3
Bay	54,355	26,492	16,383	11,258	222	10,109	D	48.7	30.1	20.7	0.4	11	77	63	1.3	1.4	1.1	1.4	61.8	38.2
Benzie	6,852	2,715	2,438	1,657	42	277	D	39.6	35.6	24.2	0.6	40	47	29	0.2	0.1	0.2	0.2	52.7	47.3
Berrien	69,615	25,840	29,252	14,056	467	3,412	R	37.1	42.0	20.2	0.7	53	10	66	1.6	1.4	1.9	1.7	46.9	53.1
Branch	16,593	5,850	5,976	4,683	84	126	R	35.3	36.0	28.2	0.5	62	46	5	0.4	0.3	0.4	0.6	49.5	50.5
Calhoun	58,702	25,542	19,791	13,058	311	5,751	D	43.5	33.7	22.2	0.5	26	58	52	1.4	1.4	1.3	1.6	56.3	43.7
Cass	20,283	8,047	7,391	4,756	89	656	D	39.7	36.4	23.4	0.4	39	42	36	0.5	0.4	0.5	0.6	52.1	47.9
Charlevoix	11,525	4,063	4,017	3,360	85	46	D	35.3	34.9	29.2	0.7	63	52	3	0.3	0.2	0.3	0.4	50.3	49.7
Cheboygan	10,864	4,459	3,864	2,495	46	595	D	41.0	35.6	23.0	0.4	34	48	45	0.3	0.2	0.2	0.3	53.6	46.4
Chippewa	13,647	5,434	5,462	2,706	45	28	R	39.8	40.0	19.8	0.3	36	17	67	0.3	0.3	0.4	0.3	49.9	50.1
Clare	12,163	5,346	3,916	2,812	89	1,430	D	44.0	32.2	23.1	0.7	23	69	43	0.3	0.3	0.3	0.3	57.7	42.3
Clinton	30,339	10,116	12,216	7,877	130	2,100	R	33.3	40.3	26.0	0.4	74	15	15	0.7	0.5	0.8	1.0	45.3	54.7
Crawford	5,925	2,252	2,193	1,442	38	59	D	38.0	37.0	24.3	0.6	49	35	28	0.1	0.1	0.1	0.2	50.7	49.3
Delta	17,962	8,387	6,027	3,485	63	2,360	D	46.7	33.6	19.4	0.4	14	60	71	0.4	0.4	0.4	0.4	58.2	41.8
Dickinson	13,031	5,689	4,273	3,022	47	1,416	D	43.7	32.8	23.2	0.4	25	64	40	0.3	0.3	0.3	0.3	57.1	42.9
Eaton	47,883	16,752	18,669	12,208	254	1,917	R	35.0	39.0	25.5	0.5	67	25	20	1.1	0.9	1.2	1.5	47.3	52.7
Emmet	13,232	4,245	5,312	3,576	99	1,067	R	32.1	40.1	27.0	0.7	77	16	10	0.3	0.2	0.3	0.4	44.4	55.6
Genesee	199,998	105,156	47,834	46,259	749	57,322	D	52.6	23.9	23.1	0.4	3	83	42	4.7	5.6	3.1	5.6	68.7	31.3
Gladwin	10,776	4,457	3,616	2,649	54	841	D	41.4	33.6	24.6	0.5	30	59	25	0.3	0.2	0.2	0.3	55.2	44.8
Gogebic	9,225	4,792	2,838	1,543	52	1,954	D	51.9	30.8	16.7	0.6	5	74	81	0.2	0.3	0.2	0.2	62.8	37.2
Grand Traverse	34,461	11,148	13,629	9,495	189	2,481	R	32.3	39.5	27.6	0.5	76	19	8	0.8	0.6	0.9	1.2	45.0	55.0
Gratiot	15,879	5,678	6,280	3,866	55	602	R	35.8	39.5	24.3	0.3	60	20	27	0.4	0.3	0.4	0.5	47.5	52.5
Hillsdale	17,891	5,244	7,579	4,968	100	2,335	R	29.3	42.4	27.8	0.6	81	7	6	0.4	0.3	0.5	0.6	40.9	59.1
Houghton	15,173	6,558	5,575	2,945	95	983	D	43.2	36.7	19.4	0.6	27	39	70	0.4	0.4	0.4	0.4	54.1	45.9
Huron	16,632	6,023	6,491	4,064	54	468	R	36.2	39.0	24.4	0.3	58	23	26	0.4	0.3	0.4	0.5	48.1	51.9
Ingham	133,792	61,596	43,926	27,683	587	17,670	D	46.0	32.8	20.7	0.4	15	63	64	3.1	3.3	2.8	3.4	58.4	41.6
Ionia	23,822	8,370	9,135	6,211	106	765	R	35.1	38.3	26.1	0.4	65	29	14	0.6	0.4	0.6	0.8	47.8	52.2
Iosco	13,492	5,369	4,912	3,131	80	457	D	39.8	36.4	23.2	0.6	37	43	39	0.3	0.3	0.3	0.4	52.2	47.8
Iron	7,000	3,648	1,971	1,344	37	1,677	D	52.1	28.2	19.2	0.5	4	80	73	0.2	0.2	0.1	0.2	64.9	35.1
Isabella	22,037	8,784	7,706	5,434	113	1,078	D	39.9	35.0	24.7	0.5	35	51	24	0.5	0.5	0.5	0.7	53.3	46.7
Jackson	64,644	23,686	25,424	15,194	340	1,738	R	36.6	39.3	23.5	0.5	56	21	34	1.5	1.3	1.6	1.8	48.2	51.8
Kalamazoo	103,858	43,568	38,035	21,666	589	5,533	D	41.9	36.6	20.9	0.6	29	41	61	2.4	2.3	2.4	2.6	53.4	46.6
Kalkaska	6,426	2,297	2,173	1,915	41	124	D	35.7	33.8	29.8	0.6	61	56	2	0.2	0.1	0.1	0.2	51.4	48.6
Kent	242,553	82,305	115,285	43,707	1,256	32,980	R	33.9	47.5	18.0	0.5	72	2	76	5.7	4.4	7.4	5.3	41.7	58.3
Keweenaw	1,173	582	378	212	1	204	D	49.6	32.2	18.1	<.1	10	68	75	<.1	<.1	<.1	<.1	60.6	39.4
Lake	4,546	2,351	1,194	981	20	1,157	D	51.7	26.3	21.6	0.4	7	82	54	0.1	0.1	<.1	0.1	66.3	33.7
Lapeer	35,084	11,982	12,326	10,541	235	344	R	34.2	35.1	30.0	0.7	70	49	1	0.8	0.6	0.8	1.3	49.3	50.7
Leelanau	10,187	3,445	3,993	2,685	64	548	R	33.8	39.2	26.4	0.6	73	22	12	0.2	0.2	0.3	0.3	46.3	53.7
Lenawee	39,365	15,399	14,297	9,517	152	1,102	D	39.1	36.3	24.2	0.4	41	44	30	0.9	0.8	0.9	1.2	51.9	48.1
Livingston	61,735	17,851	27,539	15,971	374	9,688	R	28.9	44.6	25.9	0.6	82	5	17	1.4	1.0	1.8	1.9	39.3	60.7
Luce	2,603	972	958	660	13	14	D	37.3	36.8	25.4	0.5	52	38	21	<.1	<.1	<.1	<.1	50.4	49.6
Mackinac	5,977	2,293	2,278	1,379	27	15	D	38.4	38.1	23.1	0.5	47	31	44	0.1	0.1	0.1	0.2	50.2	49.8
Macomb	349,238	130,732	147,795	67,954	2,757	17,063	R	37.4	42.3	19.5	0.8	51	8	69	8.2	7.0	9.5	8.2	46.9	53.1
Manistee	11,651	5,193	3,491	2,923	44	1,702	D	44.6	30.0	25.1	0.4	21	79	23	0.3	0.3	0.2	0.4	59.8	40.2
Marquette	31,629	16,038	9,665	5,768	158	6,373	D	50.7	30.6	18.2	0.5	9	75	74	0.7	0.9	0.6	0.7	62.4	37.6
Mason	13,082	4,829	5,102	3,096	55	273	R	36.9	39.0	23.7	0.4	55	24	33	0.3	0.3	0.3	0.4	48.6	51.4
Mecosta	15,835	6,097	6,047	3,612	79	50	D	38.5	38.2	22.8	0.5	45	30	47	0.4	0.3	0.4	0.4	50.2	49.8
Menominee	11,082	4,559	3,995	2,487	41	564	D	41.1	36.0	22.4	0.4	33	45	50	0.3	0.2	0.3	0.3	53.3	46.7
Midland	38,624	13,382	16,149	8,945	148	2,767	R	34.6	41.8	23.2	0.4	68	11	41	0.9	0.7	1.0	1.1	45.3	54.7
Missaukee	6,058	1,893	2,829	1,306	30	936	R	31.2	46.7	21.6	0.5	80	4	55	0.1	0.1	0.2	0.2	40.1	59.9
Monroe	59,031	24,957	20,250	13,551	273	4,707	D	42.3	34.3	23.0	0.5	28	54	46	1.4	1.3	1.3	1.6	55.2	44.8
Montcalm	22,780	8,730	8,420	5,504	126	310	D	38.3	37.0	24.2	0.6	48	36	31	0.5	0.5	0.5	0.7	50.9	49.1
Montmorency	4,791	1,903	1,794	1,077	17	109	D	39.7	37.4	22.5	0.4	38	32	49	0.1	0.1	0.1	0.1	51.5	48.5
Muskegon	71,948	32,515	23,769	15,268	396	8,746	D	45.2	33.0	21.2	0.6	18	62	59	1.7	1.7	1.5	1.9	57.8	42.2
Newaygo	17,916	6,455	7,333	4,056	72	878	R	36.0	40.9	22.6	0.4	59	14	48	0.4	0.3	0.5	0.5	46.8	53.2
Oakland	555,760	214,733	242,160	94,911	3,956	27,427	R	38.6	43.6	17.1	0.7	44	6	79	13.0	11.5	15.6	11.5	47.0	53.0
Oceana	10,557	3,846	3,944	2,713	54	98	R	36.4	37.4	25.7	0.5	57	33	18	0.2	0.2	0.3	0.3	49.4	50.6
Ogemaw	9,126	4,016	2,936	2,122	52	1,080	D	44.0	32.2	23.3	0.6	22	71	37	0.2	0.2	0.2	0.3	57.8	42.2
Ontonagon	4,745	2,451	1,463	805	26	988	D	51.7	30.8	17.0	0.5	8	73	80	0.1	0.1	<.1	<.1	62.6	37.4
Osceola	9,376	3,529	3,606	2,199	42	77	R	37.6	38.5	23.5	0.4	50	28	35	0.2	0.2	0.2	0.3	49.5	50.5
Oscoda	3,831	1,471	1,583	755	22	112	R	38.4	41.3	19.7	0.6	46	12	68	<.1	<.1	0.1	<.1	48.2	51.8
Otsego	9,207	3,129	3,393	2,635	50	264	R	34.0	36.9	28.6	0.5	71	37	4	0.2	0.2	0.2	0.3	48.0	52.0
Ottawa	96,211	22,180	56,862	16,855	314	34,682	R	23.1	59.1	17.5	0.3	83	1	77	2.3	1.2	3.7	2.0	28.1	71.9

Michigan 481

Table E. – Vote for President: November 3, 1992, General Election (cont)

County	Total	Clinton (DEM)	Bush (REP)	Perot (IND)	Other	Plurality Total	Party	DEM	REP	IND	Other	Rank DEM	Rank REP	Rank IND	Total	DEM	REP	IND	DEM	REP
Presque Isle	7,345	3,308	2,398	1,612	27	910	D	45.0	32.6	21.9	0.4	19	65	53	0.2	0.2	0.2	0.2	58.0	42.0
Roscommon	12,007	5,243	4,170	2,551	43	1,073	D	43.7	34.7	21.2	0.4	24	53	58	0.3	0.3	0.3	0.3	55.7	44.3
Saginaw	96,905	43,819	32,103	20,523	460	11,716	D	45.2	33.1	21.2	0.5	17	61	60	2.3	2.3	2.1	2.5	57.7	42.3
St. Clair	66,832	23,385	24,508	18,523	416	1,123	R	35.0	36.7	27.7	0.6	66	40	7	1.6	1.2	1.6	2.2	48.8	51.2
St. Joseph	23,971	7,817	9,836	6,209	109	2,019	R	32.6	41.0	25.9	0.5	75	13	16	0.6	0.4	0.6	0.8	44.3	55.7
Sanilac	18,758	5,868	7,891	4,894	105	2,023	R	31.3	42.1	26.1	0.6	79	9	13	0.4	0.3	0.5	0.6	42.6	57.4
Schoolcraft	4,129	2,139	1,253	721	16	886	D	51.8	30.3	17.5	0.4	6	76	78	<.1	0.1	<.1	<.1	63.1	36.9
Shiawassee	32,360	12,629	10,930	8,632	169	1,699	D	39.0	33.8	26.7	0.5	42	57	11	0.8	0.7	0.7	1.0	53.6	46.4
Tuscola	24,666	9,138	8,636	6,765	127	502	D	37.0	35.0	27.4	0.5	54	50	9	0.6	0.5	0.6	0.8	51.4	48.6
Van Buren	30,237	12,466	10,357	7,255	159	2,109	D	41.2	34.3	24.0	0.5	32	55	32	0.7	0.7	0.7	0.9	54.6	45.4
Washtenaw	137,466	73,325	41,386	21,889	866	31,939	D	53.3	30.1	15.9	0.6	2	78	82	3.2	3.9	2.7	2.7	63.9	36.1
Wayne	841,965	508,464	227,002	102,074	4,425	281,462	D	60.4	27.0	12.1	0.5	1	81	83	19.7	27.2	14.6	12.4	69.1	30.9
Wexford	12,575	4,894	4,696	2,923	62	198	D	38.9	37.3	23.2	0.5	43	34	38	0.3	0.3	0.3	0.4	51.0	49.0
MICHIGAN	**4,274,673**	**1,871,182**	**1,554,940**	**824,813**	**23,738**	**316,242**	**D**	**43.8**	**36.4**	**19.3**	**0.6**				**100.0**	**100.0**	**100.0**	**100.0**	**54.6**	**45.4**

Table H. — Vote for U.S. Representative in Congress: November 3, 1992, General Election

Congressional district and county	Total	Democrat (DEM)	Republican (REP)	Other	Plurality Total	Party	Percent of total vote DEM	REP	Other	Rank within district DEM	REP	Other	Percent contribution to district vote Total	DEM	REP	Other
District 1	268,619	144,857	117,056	6,706	27,801	D	53.9	43.6	2.5				100.0	100.0	100.0	100.0
Alger	4,311	2,642	1,559	110	1,083	D	61.3	36.2	2.6	9	22	10	1.6	1.8	1.3	1.6
Alpena	13,916	6,925	6,778	213	147	D	49.8	48.7	1.5	21	7	19	5.2	4.8	5.8	3.2
Antrim	8,886	3,983	4,595	308	612	R	44.8	51.7	3.5	27	2	5	3.3	2.7	3.9	4.6
Baraga	3,403	2,096	1,251	56	845	D	61.6	36.8	1.6	8	21	17	1.3	1.4	1.1	0.8
Benzie	6,111	3,062	2,874	175	188	D	50.1	47.0	2.9	19	11	8	2.3	2.1	2.5	2.6
Charlevoix	11,175	5,021	5,355	799	334	R	44.9	47.9	7.1	26	9	1	4.2	3.5	4.6	11.9
Cheboygan	9,877	5,137	4,564	176	573	D	52.0	46.2	1.8	15	12	16	3.7	3.5	3.9	2.6
Chippewa	12,377	6,582	5,629	166	953	D	53.2	45.5	1.3	14	14	21	4.6	4.5	4.8	2.5
Crawford (pt)	1,340	693	608	39	85	D	51.7	45.4	2.9	16	15	7	0.5	0.5	0.5	0.6
Delta	17,168	11,217	5,776	175	5,441	D	65.3	33.6	1.0	1	27	24	6.4	7.7	4.9	2.6
Dickinson	12,453	7,378	4,969	106	2,409	D	59.2	39.9	0.9	11	18	27	4.6	5.1	4.2	1.6
Emmet	12,809	5,232	6,862	715	1,630	R	40.8	53.6	5.6	28	1	2	4.8	3.6	5.9	10.7
Gogebic	8,414	5,369	2,960	85	2,409	D	63.8	35.2	1.0	3	26	25	3.1	3.7	2.5	1.3
Grand Traverse	32,826	15,065	16,481	1,280	1,416	R	45.9	50.2	3.9	25	3	3	12.2	10.4	14.1	19.1
Houghton	14,239	7,866	6,046	327	1,820	D	55.2	42.5	2.3	12	17	11	5.3	5.4	5.2	4.9
Iron	6,771	4,410	2,266	95	2,144	D	65.1	33.5	1.4	2	28	20	2.5	3.0	1.9	1.4
Kalkaska	5,702	2,915	2,625	162	290	D	51.1	46.0	2.8	17	13	9	2.1	2.0	2.2	2.4
Keweenaw	1,137	709	410	18	299	D	62.4	36.1	1.6	5	25	18	0.4	0.5	0.4	0.3
Leelanau	8,868	4,101	4,430	337	329	R	46.2	50.0	3.8	24	4	4	3.3	2.8	3.8	5.0
Luce	2,317	1,160	1,130	27	30	D	50.1	48.8	1.2	20	6	22	0.9	0.8	1.0	0.4
Mackinac	5,531	2,787	2,641	103	146	D	50.4	47.7	1.9	18	10	13	2.1	1.9	2.3	1.5
Marquette	30,402	18,811	10,993	598	7,818	D	61.9	36.2	2.0	6	23	12	11.3	13.0	9.4	8.9
Menominee	10,445	6,593	3,768	84	2,825	D	63.1	36.1	0.8	4	24	28	3.9	4.6	3.2	1.3
Montmorency	4,260	2,074	2,107	79	33	R	48.7	49.5	1.9	22	5	14	1.6	1.4	1.8	1.2
Ontonagon	4,506	2,777	1,680	49	1,097	D	61.6	37.3	1.1	7	20	23	1.7	1.9	1.4	0.7
Otsego	8,472	4,086	4,126	260	40	R	48.2	48.7	3.1	23	8	6	3.2	2.8	3.5	3.9
Presque Isle	7,052	3,819	3,103	130	716	D	54.2	44.0	1.8	13	16	15	2.6	2.6	2.7	1.9
Schoolcraft	3,851	2,347	1,470	34	877	D	60.9	38.2	0.9	10	19	26	1.4	1.6	1.3	0.5
District 2	246,761	86,265	155,577	4,919	69,312	R	35.0	63.0	2.0				100.0	100.0	100.0	100.0
Allegan (pt)	29,764	8,801	20,225	738	11,424	R	29.6	68.0	2.5	9	2	3	12.1	10.2	13.0	15.0
Barry (pt)	8,073	3,245	4,649	179	1,404	R	40.2	57.6	2.2	5	5	5	3.3	3.8	3.0	3.6
Lake	4,264	2,343	1,777	144	566	D	54.9	41.7	3.4	1	10	2	1.7	2.7	1.1	2.9
Manistee	9,863	5,003	4,641	219	362	D	50.7	47.1	2.2	2	9	4	4.0	5.8	3.0	4.5
Mason	12,309	4,807	7,035	467	2,228	R	39.1	57.2	3.8	7	6	1	5.0	5.6	4.5	9.5
Muskegon	59,332	28,381	30,056	895	1,675	R	47.8	50.7	1.5	4	7	10	24.0	32.9	19.3	18.2
Newaygo	15,286	5,821	9,227	238	3,406	R	38.1	60.4	1.6	8	3	9	6.2	6.7	5.9	4.8
Oceana	8,685	3,409	5,135	141	1,726	R	39.3	59.1	1.6	6	4	8	3.5	4.0	3.3	2.9
Ottawa	88,184	19,186	67,310	1,688	48,124	R	21.8	76.3	1.9	10	1	6	35.7	22.2	43.3	34.3
Wexford	11,001	5,269	5,522	210	253	R	47.9	50.2	1.9	3	8	7	4.5	6.1	3.5	4.3
District 3	264,948	95,927	162,451	6,570	66,524	R	36.2	61.3	2.5				100.0	100.0	100.0	100.0
Barry (pt)	9,828	4,010	5,572	246	1,562	R	40.8	56.7	2.5	2	2	2	3.7	4.2	3.4	3.7
Ionia	20,141	8,344	11,130	667	2,786	R	41.4	55.3	3.3	1	3	1	7.6	8.7	6.9	10.2
Kent	234,979	83,573	145,749	5,657	62,176	R	35.6	62.0	2.4	3	1	3	88.7	87.1	89.7	86.1
District 4	251,539	87,573	157,337	6,629	69,764	R	34.8	62.5	2.6				100.0	100.0	100.0	100.0
Clare	11,682	3,955	7,422	305	3,467	R	33.9	63.5	2.6	10	7	7	4.6	4.5	4.7	4.6
Clinton	26,307	9,786	15,617	904	5,831	R	37.2	59.4	3.4	6	12	3	10.5	11.2	9.9	13.6
Crawford (pt)	4,295	1,380	2,754	161	1,374	R	32.1	64.1	3.7	12	5	1	1.7	1.6	1.8	2.4
Gladwin	10,225	3,653	6,330	242	2,677	R	35.7	61.9	2.4	8	9	11	4.1	4.2	4.0	3.7
Gratiot	14,576	4,204	10,038	334	5,834	R	28.8	68.9	2.3	14	3	12	5.8	4.8	6.4	5.0
Isabella	20,625	6,982	13,132	511	6,150	R	33.9	63.7	2.5	9	6	9	8.2	8.0	8.3	7.7
Mecosta	13,834	4,805	8,742	287	3,937	R	34.7	63.2	2.1	9	8	14	5.5	5.5	5.6	4.3
Midland	37,825	10,142	26,986	697	16,844	R	26.8	71.3	1.8	15	2	16	15.0	11.6	17.2	10.5
Missaukee	5,813	1,432	4,254	127	2,822	R	24.6	73.2	2.2	16	1	13	2.3	1.6	2.7	1.9
Montcalm	18,930	8,066	10,386	478	2,320	R	42.6	54.9	2.5	1	16	8	7.5	9.2	6.6	7.2
Ogemaw	8,371	3,378	4,761	232	1,383	R	40.4	56.9	2.8	2	14	6	3.3	3.9	3.0	3.5
Osceola	8,239	2,607	5,479	153	2,872	R	31.6	66.5	1.9	13	4	15	3.3	3.0	3.5	2.3
Oscoda	3,619	1,311	2,195	113	884	R	36.2	60.7	3.1	7	10	4	1.4	1.5	1.4	1.7
Roscommon	10,794	4,247	6,281	266	2,034	R	39.3	58.2	2.5	4	13	10	4.3	4.8	4.0	4.0
Saginaw (pt)	34,811	13,016	20,744	1,051	7,728	R	37.4	59.6	3.0	5	11	5	13.8	14.9	13.2	15.9
Shiawassee (pt)	21,593	8,609	12,216	768	3,607	R	39.9	56.6	3.6	3	15	2	8.6	9.8	7.8	11.6
District 5	244,992	147,618	93,098	4,276	54,520	D	60.3	38.0	1.7				100.0	100.0	100.0	100.0
Alcona	4,552	2,133	2,379	40	246	R	46.9	52.3	0.9	8	3	6	1.9	1.4	2.6	0.9
Arenac	6,381	3,944	2,388	49	1,556	D	61.8	37.4	0.8	4	7	7	2.6	2.7	2.6	1.1
Bay	50,817	38,068	12,474	275	25,594	D	74.9	24.5	0.5	1	10	10	20.7	25.8	13.4	6.4
Genesee (pt)	49,028	32,273	15,043	1,712	17,230	D	65.8	30.7	3.5	2	9	1	20.0	21.9	16.2	40.0
Huron	14,518	7,579	6,856	83	723	D	52.2	47.2	0.6	6	4	9	5.9	5.1	7.4	1.9
Iosco	12,302	6,255	5,768	279	487	D	50.8	46.9	2.3	7	5	3	5.0	4.2	6.2	6.5
Lapeer (pt)	13,651	5,977	7,241	433	1,264	R	43.8	53.0	3.2	9	2	2	5.6	4.0	7.8	10.1
Saginaw (pt)	55,522	34,715	19,761	1,046	14,954	D	62.5	35.6	1.9	3	8	4	22.7	23.5	21.2	24.5
Sanilac	16,760	4,879	11,767	114	6,888	R	29.1	70.2	0.7	10	1	8	6.8	3.3	12.6	2.7
Tuscola	21,461	11,795	9,421	245	2,374	D	55.0	43.9	1.1	5	6	5	8.8	8.0	10.1	5.7

Congressional district and county	Total	Democrat (DEM)	Republican (REP)	Other	Plurality Total	Plurality Party	Percent of total vote DEM	Percent of total vote REP	Percent of total vote Other	Rank within district DEM	Rank within district REP	Rank within district Other	Percent contribution to district vote Total	Percent contribution to district vote DEM	Percent contribution to district vote REP	Percent contribution to district vote Other
District 6	**233,112**	**89,020**	**144,083**	**9**	**55,063**	**R**	**38.2**	**61.8**	**<.1**				**100.0**	**100.0**	**100.0**	**100.0**
Allegan (pt)	5,757	2,441	3,316	0	875	R	42.4	57.6	0.0	1	6	4	2.5	2.7	2.3	0.0
Berrien	65,994	22,500	43,488	6	20,988	R	34.1	65.9	<.1	5	2	1	28.3	25.3	30.2	66.7
Cass	17,930	6,851	11,079	0	4,228	R	38.2	61.8	0.0	4	3	5	7.7	7.7	7.7	0.0
Kalamazoo	96,857	40,146	56,711	0	16,565	R	41.4	58.6	0.0	3	4	6	41.5	45.1	39.4	0.0
St. Joseph	21,139	6,406	14,731	2	8,325	R	30.3	69.7	<.1	6	1	2	9.1	7.2	10.2	22.2
Van Buren	25,435	10,676	14,758	1	4,082	R	42.0	58.0	<.1	2	5	3	10.9	12.0	10.2	11.1
District 7	**152,868**	**-**	**133,972**	**18,896**	**115,076**	**R**	**-**	**87.6**	**12.4**				**100.0**	**-**	**100.0**	**100.0**
Barry (pt)	1,878	-	1,704	174	1,530	R	-	90.7	9.3	-	4	5	1.2	-	1.3	0.9
Branch	9,307	-	8,785	522	8,263	R	-	94.4	5.6	-	2	7	6.1	-	6.6	2.8
Calhoun	35,594	-	29,739	5,855	23,884	R	-	83.6	16.4	-	7	2	23.3	-	22.2	31.0
Eaton	30,843	-	25,338	5,505	19,833	R	-	82.2	17.8	-	8	1	20.2	-	18.9	29.1
Hillsdale	11,993	-	11,120	873	10,247	R	-	92.7	7.3	-	3	6	7.8	-	8.3	4.6
Jackson	40,644	-	35,838	4,806	31,032	R	-	88.2	11.8	-	5	4	26.6	-	26.8	25.4
Lenawee	17,964	-	17,500	464	17,036	R	-	97.4	2.6	-	1	8	11.8	-	13.1	2.5
Washtenaw (pt)	4,645	-	3,948	697	3,251	R	-	85.0	15.0	-	6	3	3.0	-	2.9	3.7
District 8	**284,707**	**135,517**	**131,906**	**17,284**	**3,611**	**D**	**47.6**	**46.3**	**6.1**				**100.0**	**100.0**	**100.0**	**100.0**
Genesee (pt)	53,005	27,743	22,959	2,303	4,784	D	52.3	43.3	4.3	1	5	6	18.6	20.5	17.4	13.3
Ingham	131,509	66,339	55,540	9,630	10,799	D	50.4	42.2	7.3	2	6	1	46.2	49.0	42.1	55.7
Livingston	60,163	23,411	33,633	3,119	10,222	R	38.9	55.9	5.2	6	1	4	21.1	17.3	25.5	18.0
Oakland (pt)	5,799	2,641	2,774	384	133	R	45.5	47.8	6.6	4	3	2	2.0	1.9	2.1	2.2
Shiawassee (pt)	7,429	3,651	3,296	482	355	D	49.1	44.4	6.5	3	4	3	2.6	2.7	2.5	2.8
Washtenaw (pt)	26,802	11,732	13,704	1,366	1,972	R	43.8	51.1	5.1	5	2	5	9.4	8.7	10.4	7.9
District 9	**249,530**	**133,956**	**111,798**	**3,776**	**22,158**	**D**	**53.7**	**44.8**	**1.5**				**100.0**	**100.0**	**100.0**	**100.0**
Genesee (pt)	91,987	67,463	23,262	1,262	44,201	D	73.3	25.3	1.4	1	3	3	36.9	50.4	20.8	33.4
Lapeer (pt)	18,940	8,881	9,582	477	701	R	46.9	50.6	2.5	2	2	1	7.6	6.6	8.6	12.6
Oakland (pt)	138,603	57,612	78,954	2,037	21,342	R	41.6	57.0	1.5	3	1	2	55.5	43.0	70.6	53.9
District 10	**260,213**	**138,193**	**114,918**	**7,102**	**23,275**	**D**	**53.1**	**44.2**	**2.7**				**100.0**	**100.0**	**100.0**	**100.0**
Macomb (pt)	198,382	103,301	89,421	5,660	13,880	D	52.1	45.1	2.9	2	1	1	76.2	74.8	77.8	79.7
St. Clair	61,831	34,892	25,497	1,442	9,395	D	56.4	41.2	2.3	1	2	2	23.8	25.2	22.2	20.3
District 11	**293,098**	**117,725**	**168,940**	**6,433**	**51,215**	**R**	**40.2**	**57.6**	**2.2**				**100.0**	**100.0**	**100.0**	**100.0**
Oakland (pt)	228,569	93,425	130,811	4,333	37,386	R	40.9	57.2	1.9	1	2	2	78.0	79.4	77.4	67.4
Wayne (pt)	64,529	24,300	38,129	2,100	13,829	R	37.7	59.1	3.3	2	1	1	22.0	20.6	22.6	32.6
District 12	**261,349**	**137,514**	**119,357**	**4,478**	**18,157**	**D**	**52.6**	**45.7**	**1.7**				**100.0**	**100.0**	**100.0**	**100.0**
Macomb (pt)	122,988	62,818	57,834	2,336	4,984	D	51.1	47.0	1.9	2	1	1	47.1	45.7	48.5	52.2
Oakland (pt)	138,361	74,696	61,523	2,142	13,173	D	54.0	44.5	1.5	1	2	2	52.9	54.3	51.5	47.8
District 13	**245,888**	**127,642**	**105,169**	**13,077**	**22,473**	**D**	**51.9**	**42.8**	**5.3**				**100.0**	**100.0**	**100.0**	**100.0**
Washtenaw (pt)	92,812	56,944	32,185	3,683	24,759	D	61.4	34.7	4.0	1	2	2	37.7	44.6	30.6	28.2
Wayne (pt)	153,076	70,698	72,984	9,394	2,286	R	46.2	47.7	6.1	2	1	1	62.3	55.4	69.4	71.8
District 14	**200,879**	**165,496**	**32,036**	**3,347**	**133,460**	**D**	**82.4**	**15.9**	**1.7**				**100.0**	**100.0**	**100.0**	**100.0**
Wayne (pt)	200,879	165,496	32,036	3,347	133,460	D	82.4	15.9	1.7	1	1	1	100.0	100.0	100.0	100.0
District 15	**184,964**	**148,908**	**31,849**	**4,207**	**117,059**	**D**	**80.5**	**17.2**	**2.3**				**100.0**	**100.0**	**100.0**	**100.0**
Wayne (pt)	184,964	148,908	31,849	4,207	117,059	D	80.5	17.2	2.3	1	1	1	100.0	100.0	100.0	100.0
District 16	**240,936**	**156,964**	**75,694**	**8,278**	**81,270**	**D**	**65.1**	**31.4**	**3.4**				**100.0**	**100.0**	**100.0**	**100.0**
Monroe	51,514	33,696	16,525	1,293	17,171	D	65.4	32.1	2.5	1	1	2	21.4	21.5	21.8	15.6
Wayne (pt)	189,422	123,268	59,169	6,985	64,099	D	65.1	31.2	3.7	2	2	1	78.6	78.5	78.2	84.4
MICHIGAN	**3,884,403**	**1,913,175**	**1,855,241**	**115,987**	**57,934**	**D**	**49.3**	**47.8**	**3.0**							

| County | Top candidates | | | | | | | | | Top three candidates (state vote) | | | | | | | | |
| | | | | | | | | | | Percent of total vote | | | Rank | | | Percent contribution to state vote | | | |
	Total	Clinton	Brown	Tsongas	Uncom-mitted	Harkin	Kerrey	LaRouche	Write ins	Clinton	Brown	Tsongas	Clinton	Brown	Tsongas	Total	Clinton	Brown	Tsongas
Alcona	533	307	130	68	20	4	4	0	0	57.6	24.4	12.8	6	65	70	<.1	0.1	<.1	<.1
Alger	511	189	215	78	23	1	3	2	0	37.0	42.1	15.3	75	2	52	<.1	<.1	0.1	<.1
Allegan	2,667	1,147	853	538	95	13	8	12	1	43.0	32.0	20.2	64	20	21	0.5	0.4	0.6	0.6
Alpena	1,664	791	493	220	125	22	7	6	0	47.5	29.6	13.2	43	28	67	0.3	0.3	0.3	0.2
Antrim	753	285	262	157	32	7	5	5	0	37.8	34.8	20.8	73	10	19	0.1	<.1	0.2	0.2
Arenac	769	450	196	87	22	5	3	4	2	58.5	25.5	11.3	5	59	77	0.1	0.2	0.1	<.1
Baraga	438	223	132	54	16	6	3	4	0	50.9	30.1	12.3	30	26	74	<.1	<.1	<.1	<.1
Barry	1,785	798	518	338	91	20	4	8	8	44.7	29.0	18.9	57	32	29	0.3	0.3	0.3	0.3
Bay	7,820	3,537	2,084	1,399	492	117	109	53	29	45.2	26.6	17.9	55	49	40	1.3	1.2	1.4	1.4
Benzie	644	261	186	138	36	4	4	7	8	40.5	28.9	21.4	67	33	16	0.1	<.1	0.1	0.1
Berrien	5,838	2,993	1,312	1,197	210	42	30	27	27	51.3	22.5	20.5	29	76	20	1.0	1.0	0.9	1.2
Branch	1,273	706	240	217	70	13	15	10	2	55.5	18.9	17.0	14	83	43	0.2	0.2	0.2	0.2
Calhoun	4,843	2,601	1,095	908	175	23	13	10	18	53.7	22.6	18.7	21	74	31	0.8	0.9	0.7	0.9
Cass	1,680	862	445	274	60	18	14	7	0	51.3	26.5	16.3	28	54	47	0.3	0.3	0.3	0.3
Charlevoix	887	318	321	197	32	8	5	6	0	35.9	36.2	22.2	76	6	13	0.2	0.1	0.2	0.2
Cheboygan	929	470	221	170	42	10	8	6	2	50.6	23.8	18.3	31	71	35	0.2	0.2	0.1	0.2
Chippewa	1,711	831	443	313	88	11	9	4	12	48.6	25.9	18.3	39	54	36	0.3	0.3	0.3	0.3
Clare	1,246	737	303	138	53	8	3	3	1	59.1	24.3	11.1	4	67	79	0.2	0.2	0.2	0.1
Clinton	2,444	1,132	659	488	118	28	9	5	5	46.3	27.0	20.0	49	45	23	0.4	0.4	0.4	0.5
Crawford	413	185	128	71	25	0	3	1	0	44.8	31.0	17.2	56	23	42	<.1	<.1	<.1	<.1
Delta	1,834	812	575	330	81	16	9	5	6	44.3	31.4	18.0	58	22	39	0.3	0.3	0.4	0.3
Dickinson	1,513	690	491	243	41	17	15	11	5	45.6	32.5	16.1	53	19	48	0.3	0.3	0.3	0.3
Eaton	4,005	1,844	898	988	188	45	29	13	0	46.0	22.4	24.7	50	77	8	0.7	0.6	0.6	1.0
Emmet	891	261	366	216	33	3	4	7	1	29.3	41.1	24.2	82	3	9	0.2	<.1	0.2	0.2
Genesee	32,721	18,404	9,036	3,174	1,678	189	103	121	16	56.2	27.6	9.7	11	39	83	5.6	6.2	6.0	3.3
Gladwin	1,107	616	274	148	57	3	3	5	1	55.6	24.8	13.4	13	62	66	0.2	0.2	0.2	0.2
Gogebic	702	328	191	130	32	13	6	1	1	46.7	27.2	18.5	47	41	34	0.1	0.1	0.1	0.1
Grand Traverse	2,100	621	743	635	69	15	11	6	0	29.6	35.4	30.2	81	9	1	0.4	0.2	0.5	0.7
Gratiot	1,101	573	265	187	52	8	3	10	3	52.0	24.1	17.0	25	69	44	0.2	0.2	0.2	0.2
Hillsdale	1,208	598	293	224	74	3	5	9	2	49.5	24.3	18.5	37	68	33	0.2	0.2	0.2	0.2
Houghton	1,759	666	585	410	58	18	8	5	9	37.9	33.3	23.3	72	15	10	0.3	0.2	0.4	0.4
Huron	1,466	826	342	209	65	10	7	7	0	56.3	23.3	14.3	10	72	60	0.3	0.3	0.2	0.2
Ingham	19,494	8,215	5,145	5,121	682	141	86	37	67	42.1	26.4	26.3	66	52	6	3.3	2.8	3.4	5.3
Ionia	1,581	793	396	286	67	13	12	13	1	50.2	25.0	18.1	35	61	38	0.3	0.3	0.3	0.3
Iosco	1,382	744	340	218	62	4	4	8	2	53.8	24.6	15.8	20	63	50	0.2	0.3	0.2	0.2
Iron	1,092	483	363	183	37	13	4	1	8	44.2	33.2	16.8	60	16	45	0.2	0.2	0.2	0.2
Isabella	1,967	681	670	430	145	15	13	11	2	34.6	34.1	21.9	77	11	14	0.3	0.2	0.4	0.4
Jackson	4,933	2,480	1,213	945	209	34	25	5	22	50.3	24.6	19.2	33	64	27	0.8	0.8	0.8	1.0
Kalamazoo	10,408	3,361	3,387	3,012	533	45	50	20	0	32.3	32.5	28.9	78	18	5	1.8	1.1	2.2	3.1
Kalkaska	427	207	114	74	20	4	4	1	3	48.5	26.7	17.3	40	47	41	<.1	<.1	<.1	<.1
Kent	22,177	9,506	5,978	5,133	1,207	135	123	76	19	42.9	27.0	23.1	65	46	11	3.8	3.2	3.9	5.3
Keweenaw	195	77	64	41	8	2	0	1	2	39.5	32.8	21.0	69	17	18	<.1	<.1	<.1	<.1
Lake	650	411	129	66	25	6	3	10	0	63.2	19.8	10.2	1	82	81	0.1	0.1	<.1	<.1
Lapeer	3,369	1,472	1,229	423	158	46	25	13	3	43.7	36.5	12.6	63	4	72	0.6	0.5	0.8	0.4
Leelanau	926	267	337	271	39	4	3	4	1	28.8	36.4	29.3	83	5	4	0.2	<.1	0.2	0.3
Lenawee	3,703	1,759	1,255	541	84	27	18	18	1	47.5	33.9	14.6	44	12	55	0.6	0.6	0.8	0.6
Livingston	5,258	1,958	1,861	1,146	201	45	26	16	5	37.2	35.4	21.8	74	8	15	0.9	0.7	1.2	1.2
Luce	344	162	69	47	43	15	6	1	1	47.1	20.1	13.7	45	81	61	<.1	<.1	<.1	<.1
Mackinac	580	254	153	124	39	3	3	0	4	43.8	26.4	21.4	62	53	17	<.1	<.1	0.1	0.1
Macomb	44,203	20,658	12,952	7,019	2,541	518	270	171	74	46.7	29.3	15.9	46	29	49	7.5	6.9	8.6	7.2
Manistee	1,028	465	296	201	44	5	6	4	7	45.2	28.8	19.6	54	34	26	0.2	0.2	0.2	0.2
Marquette	3,598	1,156	1,540	654	170	27	15	11	25	32.1	42.8	18.2	79	1	37	0.6	0.4	1.0	0.7
Mason	1,329	668	342	248	41	16	2	12	0	50.3	25.7	18.7	34	57	32	0.2	0.2	0.2	0.3
Mecosta	1,146	527	321	229	45	11	7	3	3	46.0	28.0	20.0	51	37	22	0.2	0.2	0.2	0.2
Menominee	1,100	505	298	217	57	11	6	6	0	45.9	27.1	19.7	52	43	25	0.2	0.2	0.2	0.2
Midland	3,678	1,418	938	1,094	162	33	16	10	7	38.6	25.5	29.7	70	58	3	0.6	0.5	0.6	1.1
Missaukee	436	232	122	56	17	5	2	2	0	53.2	28.0	12.8	23	38	69	<.1	<.1	<.1	<.1
Monroe	7,113	3,124	2,401	1,028	390	88	44	38	0	43.9	33.8	14.5	61	14	56	1.2	1.1	1.6	1.1
Montcalm	1,600	865	432	215	63	15	6	3	1	54.1	27.0	13.4	18	44	63	0.3	0.3	0.3	0.2
Montmorency	441	241	102	66	26	5	0	1	0	54.6	23.1	15.0	15	73	53	<.1	<.1	<.1	<.1
Muskegon	8,007	4,585	1,684	1,154	368	106	55	38	17	57.3	21.0	14.4	9	80	58	1.4	1.5	1.1	1.2
Newaygo	1,506	865	360	184	72	10	8	3	4	57.4	23.9	12.2	7	70	75	0.3	0.3	0.2	0.2
Oakland	70,367	31,152	18,110	16,245	3,605	590	313	183	169	44.3	25.7	23.1	59	56	12	12.0	10.5	12.0	16.7
Oceana	873	470	233	126	26	11	3	3	1	53.8	26.7	14.4	19	48	57	0.1	0.2	0.2	0.1
Ogemaw	1,059	627	238	135	41	10	6	2	0	59.2	22.5	12.7	3	75	71	0.2	0.2	0.2	0.1
Ontonagon	630	325	163	85	27	12	6	3	9	51.6	25.9	13.5	27	55	62	0.1	0.1	0.1	<.1
Osceola	797	434	229	80	47	4	1	2	0	54.5	28.7	10.0	17	35	82	0.1	0.1	0.2	<.1
Oscoda	330	180	96	37	8	5	3	1	0	54.5	29.1	11.2	16	31	78	<.1	<.1	<.1	<.1
Otsego	664	264	225	132	31	1	4	6	1	39.8	33.9	19.9	68	13	24	0.1	<.1	0.1	0.1
Ottawa	5,066	1,930	1,483	1,328	219	34	32	37	3	38.1	29.3	26.2	71	30	7	0.9	0.6	1.0	1.4

Table I. — Vote for Presidential Preference: March 17, 1992, Democratic Primary Election (cont)

County	Top candidates									Top three candidates (state vote)									
										Percent of total vote						Percent contribution to state vote			
														Rank					
	Total	Clinton	Brown	Tsongas	Uncom-mitted	Harkin	Kerrey	LaRouche	Write ins	Clinton	Brown	Tsongas	Clinton	Brown	Tsongas	Total	Clinton	Brown	Tsongas
Presque Isle	693	398	150	99	29	9	3	5	0	57.4	21.6	14.3	8	78	59	0.1	0.1	< .1	0.1
Roscommon	1,118	589	335	131	46	4	9	1	3	52.7	30.0	11.7	24	27	76	0.2	0.2	0.2	0.1
Saginaw	10,545	5,924	2,566	1,415	451	74	46	33	36	56.2	24.3	13.4	12	66	65	1.8	2.0	1.7	1.5
St. Clair	6,579	3,069	2,089	974	310	48	55	23	11	46.6	31.8	14.8	48	21	54	1.1	1.0	1.4	1.0
St. Joseph	1,537	735	407	292	62	9	9	13	10	47.8	26.5	19.0	41	51	28	0.3	0.2	0.3	0.3
Sanilac	1,523	813	413	191	71	9	10	9	7	53.4	27.1	12.5	22	42	73	0.3	0.3	0.3	0.2
Schoolcraft	453	229	127	71	17	5	1	1	2	50.6	28.0	15.7	32	36	51	< .1	< .1	< .1	< .1
Shiawassee	3,365	1,663	1,029	452	147	18	16	38	2	49.4	30.6	13.4	38	24	64	0.6	0.6	0.7	0.5
Tuscola	2,435	1,218	738	316	127	14	4	18	0	50.0	30.3	13.0	36	25	68	0.4	0.4	0.5	0.3
Van Buren	2,638	1,260	725	495	88	32	23	12	3	47.8	27.5	18.8	42	40	30	0.5	0.4	0.5	0.5
Washtenaw	29,527	8,872	10,502	8,892	870	250	59	43	39	30.0	35.6	30.1	80	7	2	5.0	3.0	6.9	9.2
Wayne	201,738	123,350	42,478	20,966	9,771	3,014	1,302	692	165	61.1	21.1	10.4	2	79	80	34.4	41.5	28.1	21.6
Wexford	1,109	577	278	185	35	10	10	7	7	52.0	25.1	16.7	26	60	46	0.2	0.2	0.2	0.2
MICHIGAN	**585,972**	**297,280**	**151,400**	**97,017**	**27,836**	**6,265**	**3,219**	**2,049**	**906**	**50.7**	**25.8**	**16.6**				**100.0**	**100.0**	**100.0**	**100.0**

Table J. — Vote for Presidential Preference: March 17, 1992, Republican Primary Election

County	Top candidates					Top four candidates (state vote)												
						Percent of total vote				Rank				Percent contribution to state vote				
	Total	Bush	Bu-chanan	Uncom-mitted	Other	Bush	Bu-chanan	Uncom-mitted	Other	Bush	Bu-chanan	Uncom-mitted	Other	Total	Bush	Bu-chanan	Uncom-mitted	Other
Alcona	725	430	232	53	10	59.3	32.0	7.3	1.4	80	12	3	78	0.2	0.1	0.2	0.2	<.1
Alger	289	197	80	8	4	68.2	27.7	2.8	1.4	28	29	81	76	<.1	<.1	<.1	<.1	<.1
Allegan	5,734	4,006	1,360	254	114	69.9	23.7	4.4	2.0	13	59	63	62	1.3	1.3	1.2	1.1	1.0
Alpena	1,452	871	473	82	26	60.0	32.6	5.6	1.8	78	6	22	68	0.3	0.3	0.4	0.3	0.2
Antrim	1,193	790	329	54	20	66.2	27.6	4.5	1.7	43	31	58	71	0.3	0.3	0.3	0.2	0.2
Arenac	550	389	122	26	13	70.7	22.2	4.7	2.4	7	73	52	44	0.1	0.1	0.1	0.1	0.1
Baraga	226	129	78	11	8	57.1	34.5	4.9	3.5	83	1	47	8	<.1	<.1	<.1	<.1	<.1
Barry	2,558	1,750	606	152	50	68.4	23.7	5.9	2.0	27	60	14	64	0.6	0.6	0.5	0.6	0.4
Bay	4,904	2,829	1,668	298	109	57.7	34.0	6.1	2.2	82	3	11	53	1.1	0.9	1.5	1.3	1.0
Benzie	810	534	223	36	17	65.9	27.5	4.4	2.1	46	32	61	59	0.2	0.2	0.2	0.2	0.2
Berrien	9,430	6,739	2,119	408	164	71.5	22.5	4.3	1.7	4	70	66	69	2.1	2.2	1.9	1.7	1.5
Branch	1,948	1,369	428	105	46	70.3	22.0	5.4	2.4	11	75	29	45	0.4	0.5	0.4	0.4	0.4
Calhoun	5,031	3,542	1,140	224	125	70.4	22.7	4.5	2.5	10	66	60	42	1.1	1.2	1.0	0.9	1.1
Cass	2,009	1,282	560	97	70	63.8	27.9	4.8	3.5	60	28	48	10	0.4	0.4	0.5	0.4	0.6
Charlevoix	1,099	660	352	63	24	60.1	32.0	5.7	2.2	77	11	20	55	0.2	0.2	0.3	0.3	0.2
Cheboygan	1,008	611	323	47	27	60.6	32.0	4.7	2.7	73	10	56	28	0.2	0.2	0.3	0.2	0.2
Chippewa	1,975	1,276	524	116	59	64.6	26.5	5.9	3.0	53	39	16	21	0.4	0.4	0.5	0.5	0.5
Clare	1,322	875	338	58	51	66.2	25.6	4.4	3.9	44	47	64	4	0.3	0.3	0.3	0.2	0.5
Clinton	3,509	2,283	1,012	130	84	65.1	28.8	3.7	2.4	51	21	73	43	0.8	0.8	0.9	0.5	0.7
Crawford	621	386	201	22	12	62.2	32.4	3.5	1.9	67	8	77	65	0.1	0.1	0.2	<.1	0.1
Delta	1,013	658	274	67	14	65.0	27.0	6.6	1.4	52	36	6	77	0.2	0.2	0.2	0.3	0.1
Dickinson	770	495	221	32	22	64.3	28.7	4.2	2.9	54	22	68	23	0.2	0.2	0.2	0.1	0.2
Eaton	5,611	3,823	1,391	269	128	68.1	24.8	4.8	2.3	29	55	49	48	1.2	1.3	1.2	1.1	1.1
Emmet	1,211	830	306	58	17	68.5	25.3	4.8	1.4	24	51	51	75	0.3	0.3	0.3	0.2	0.2
Genesee	12,449	7,921	3,263	902	363	63.6	26.2	7.2	2.9	62	43	4	22	2.8	2.6	2.9	3.8	3.2
Gladwin	834	589	180	39	26	70.6	21.6	4.7	3.1	9	76	55	18	0.2	0.2	0.2	0.2	0.2
Gogebic	337	200	113	13	11	59.3	33.5	3.9	3.3	79	4	72	14	<.1	<.1	0.1	<.1	<.1
Grand Traverse	3,440	2,204	1,056	122	58	64.1	30.7	3.5	1.7	55	15	76	70	0.8	0.7	0.9	0.5	0.5
Gratiot	1,598	1,078	385	109	26	67.5	24.1	6.8	1.6	33	56	5	72	0.4	0.4	0.3	0.5	0.2
Hillsdale	2,227	1,579	478	112	58	70.9	21.5	5.0	2.6	6	79	42	35	0.5	0.5	0.4	0.5	0.5
Houghton	1,106	665	361	45	35	60.1	32.6	4.1	3.2	75	5	70	16	0.2	0.2	0.3	0.2	0.3
Huron	1,951	1,295	495	109	52	66.4	25.4	5.6	2.7	42	50	24	30	0.4	0.4	0.5	0.5	0.5
Ingham	14,310	9,932	3,346	727	305	69.4	23.4	5.1	2.1	18	61	39	56	3.2	3.3	3.0	3.1	2.7
Ionia	2,220	1,485	585	91	59	66.9	26.4	4.1	2.7	37	42	69	33	0.5	0.5	0.5	0.4	0.5
Iosco	1,586	1,041	419	85	41	65.6	26.4	5.4	2.6	49	40	31	37	0.4	0.3	0.4	0.4	0.4
Iron	486	302	132	32	20	62.1	27.2	6.6	4.1	68	34	7	2	0.1	0.1	0.1	0.1	0.2
Isabella	1,976	1,196	628	116	36	60.5	31.8	5.9	1.8	74	13	17	66	0.4	0.4	0.6	0.5	0.3
Jackson	6,516	4,716	1,373	293	134	72.4	21.1	4.5	2.1	3	81	59	60	1.5	1.6	1.2	1.2	1.2
Kalamazoo	10,761	7,601	2,437	564	159	70.6	22.6	5.2	1.5	8	67	34	74	2.4	2.5	2.2	2.4	1.4
Kalkaska	564	378	159	12	15	67.0	28.2	2.1	2.7	36	24	83	32	0.1	0.1	0.1	<.1	0.1
Kent	37,075	27,246	7,543	1,817	469	73.5	20.3	4.9	1.3	2	82	46	80	8.3	9.0	6.7	7.6	4.2
Keweenaw	133	91	36	3	3	68.4	27.1	2.3	2.3	26	35	82	50	<.1	<.1	<.1	<.1	<.1
Lake	490	327	114	36	13	66.7	23.3	7.3	2.7	41	63	2	34	0.1	0.1	0.1	0.2	0.1
Lapeer	3,538	2,150	1,061	226	101	60.8	30.0	6.4	2.9	72	18	8	24	0.8	0.7	0.9	0.9	0.9
Leelanau	1,269	836	356	69	8	65.9	28.1	5.4	0.6	47	25	27	83	0.3	0.3	0.3	0.3	<.1
Lenawee	3,866	2,616	931	193	126	67.7	24.1	5.0	3.3	31	57	44	11	0.9	0.9	0.8	0.8	1.1
Livingston	7,141	4,563	1,997	357	224	63.9	28.0	5.0	3.1	57	27	43	17	1.6	1.5	1.8	1.5	2.0
Luce	610	386	138	69	17	63.3	22.6	11.3	2.8	63	68	1	25	0.1	0.1	0.1	0.3	0.2
Mackinac	863	601	184	55	23	69.6	21.3	6.4	2.7	16	80	9	31	0.2	0.2	0.2	0.2	0.2
Macomb	35,975	22,300	10,538	1,866	1,271	62.0	29.3	5.2	3.5	69	20	35	9	8.0	7.4	9.4	7.8	11.3
Manistee	1,125	695	341	59	30	61.8	30.3	5.2	2.7	70	16	33	29	0.3	0.2	0.3	0.2	0.3
Marquette	1,551	979	445	84	43	63.1	28.7	5.4	2.8	64	23	28	26	0.3	0.3	0.4	0.4	0.4
Mason	1,861	1,328	414	56	63	71.4	22.2	3.0	3.4	5	71	79	12	0.4	0.4	0.4	0.2	0.6
Mecosta	1,736	1,160	444	88	44	66.8	25.6	5.1	2.5	39	46	41	38	0.4	0.4	0.4	0.4	0.4
Menominee	953	661	219	38	35	69.4	23.0	4.0	3.7	21	64	71	7	0.2	0.2	0.2	0.2	0.3
Midland	5,685	3,945	1,352	301	87	69.4	23.8	5.3	1.5	20	58	32	73	1.3	1.3	1.2	1.3	0.8
Missaukee	957	657	211	53	36	68.7	22.0	5.5	3.8	23	74	25	5	0.2	0.2	0.2	0.2	0.3
Monroe	4,638	2,963	1,298	250	127	63.9	28.0	5.4	2.7	58	26	30	27	1.0	1.0	1.2	1.1	1.1
Montcalm	2,317	1,603	500	138	76	69.2	21.6	6.0	3.3	22	77	13	13	0.5	0.5	0.4	0.6	0.7
Montmorency	553	353	153	19	28	63.8	27.7	3.4	5.1	59	30	78	1	0.1	0.1	0.1	<.1	0.2
Muskegon	6,563	4,450	1,649	299	165	67.8	25.1	4.6	2.5	30	52	57	39	1.5	1.5	1.5	1.3	1.5
Newaygo	2,142	1,504	462	131	45	70.2	21.6	6.1	2.1	12	78	10	58	0.5	0.5	0.4	0.6	0.4
Oakland	72,973	48,725	18,258	4,361	1,629	66.8	25.0	6.0	2.2	40	53	12	52	16.2	16.1	16.3	18.3	14.5
Oceana	1,328	922	300	66	40	69.4	22.6	5.0	3.0	17	69	45	20	0.3	0.3	0.3	0.3	0.4
Ogemaw	784	499	214	40	31	63.6	27.3	5.1	4.0	61	33	38	3	0.2	0.2	0.2	0.2	0.3
Ontonagon	347	216	110	18	3	62.2	31.7	5.2	0.9	66	14	36	82	<.1	<.1	<.1	<.1	<.1
Osceola	1,329	895	351	59	24	67.3	26.4	4.4	1.8	35	41	62	67	0.3	0.3	0.3	0.2	0.2
Oscoda	429	268	139	12	10	62.5	32.4	2.8	2.3	65	7	80	46	<.1	<.1	0.1	<.1	<.1
Otsego	879	512	299	48	20	58.2	34.0	5.5	2.3	81	2	26	49	0.2	0.2	0.3	0.2	0.2
Ottawa	16,380	12,676	2,927	588	189	77.4	17.9	3.6	1.2	1	83	75	81	3.6	4.2	2.6	2.5	1.7

County	Top candidates					Top four candidates (state vote)												
						Percent of total vote								Percent contribution to state vote				
										Rank								
	Total	Bush	Bu-chanan	Uncom-mitted	Other	Bush	Bu-chanan	Uncom-mitted	Other	Bush	Bu-chanan	Uncom-mitted	Other	Total	Bush	Bu-chanan	Uncom-mitted	Other
Presque Isle	666	400	214	29	23	60.1	32.1	4.4	3.5	76	9	65	11	0.1	0.1	0.2	0.1	0.2
Roscommon	1,276	817	374	60	25	64.0	29.3	4.7	2.0	56	19	53	63	0.3	0.3	0.3	0.3	0.2
Saginaw	7,544	5,044	2,008	325	167	66.9	26.6	4.3	2.2	38	38	67	54	1.7	1.7	1.8	1.4	1.5
St. Clair	7,068	4,765	1,760	359	184	67.4	24.9	5.1	2.6	34	54	40	36	1.6	1.6	1.6	1.5	1.6
St. Joseph	2,401	1,674	561	115	51	69.7	23.4	4.8	2.1	14	62	50	57	0.5	0.6	0.5	0.5	0.5
Sanilac	2,612	1,821	580	146	65	69.7	22.2	5.6	2.5	15	72	23	41	0.6	0.6	0.5	0.6	0.6
Schoolcraft	236	156	63	14	3	66.1	26.7	5.9	1.3	45	37	15	79	<.1	<.1	<.1	<.1	<.1
Shiawassee	2,876	1,892	746	149	89	65.8	25.9	5.2	3.1	48	44	37	19	0.6	0.6	0.7	0.6	0.8
Tuscola	2,281	1,404	687	133	57	61.6	30.1	5.8	2.5	71	17	19	40	0.5	0.5	0.6	0.6	0.5
Van Buren	3,162	2,136	807	148	71	67.6	25.5	4.7	2.2	32	48	54	51	0.7	0.7	0.7	0.6	0.6
Washtenaw	13,234	9,185	3,012	773	264	69.4	22.8	5.8	2.0	19	65	18	61	2.9	3.0	2.7	3.2	2.3
Wayne	71,401	46,546	18,165	4,062	2,628	65.2	25.4	5.7	3.7	50	49	21	6	15.9	15.4	16.2	17.1	23.4
Wexford	1,527	1,045	391	56	35	68.4	25.6	3.7	2.3	25	45	74	47	0.3	0.3	0.3	0.2	0.3
MICHIGAN	**449,133**	**301,948**	**112,122**	**23,809**	**11,254**	**67.2**	**25.0**	**5.3**	**2.5**					**100.0**	**100.0**	**100.0**	**100.0**	**100.0**

1992 Vote for President
Percent for Clinton (D), by County

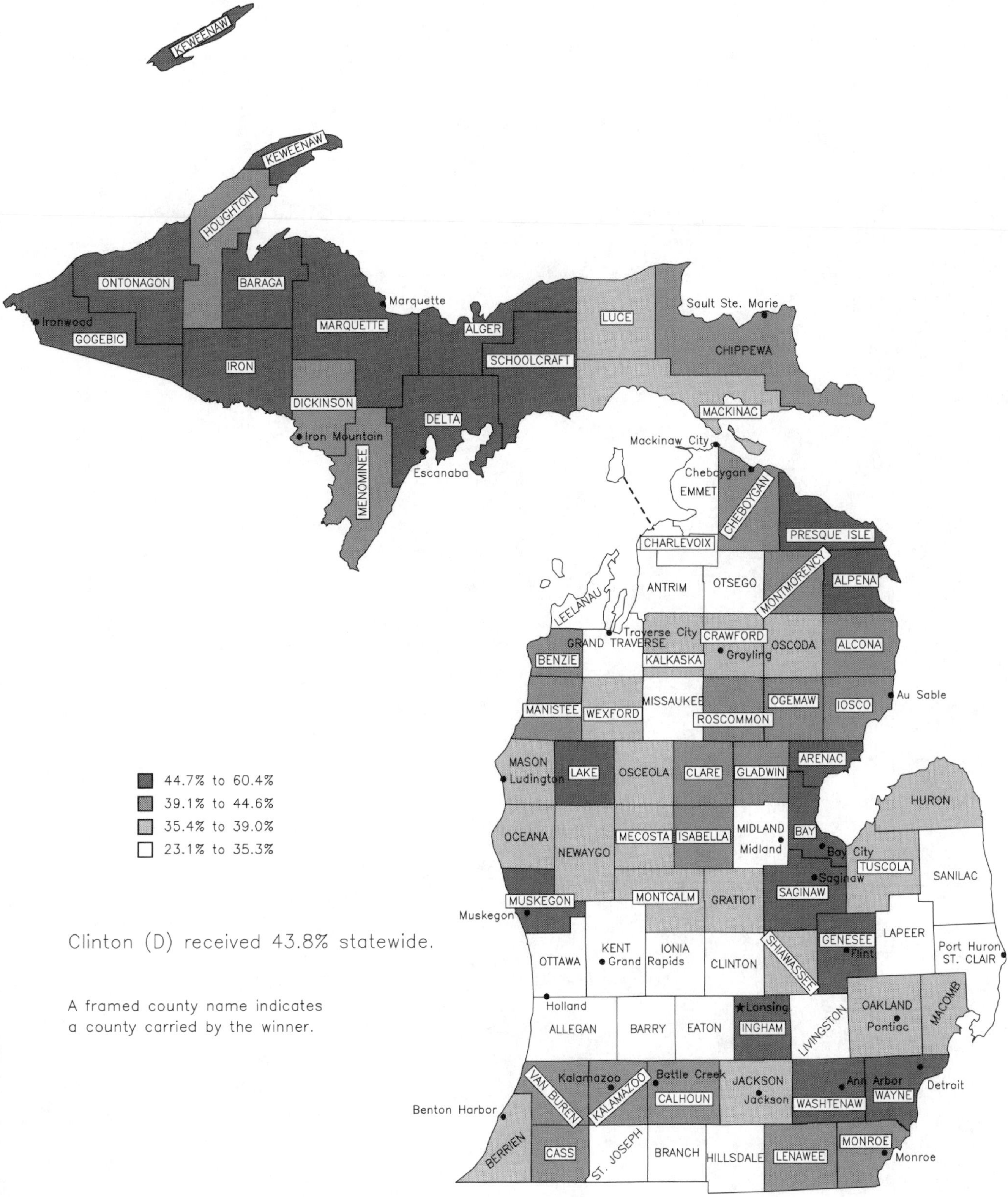

KEWEENAW

HOUGHTON

ONTONAGON

Ironwood
GOGEBIC

BARAGA

MARQUETTE

IRON

DICKINSON

DELTA

MENOMINEE

Iron Mountain

Escanaba

Marquette

ALGER

SCHOOLCRAFT

LUCE

Sault Ste. Marie

CHIPPEWA

MACKINAC

Mackinaw City

Cheboygan
EMMET

CHEBOYGAN

PRESQUE ISLE

CHARLEVOIX

ANTRIM

OTSEGO

MONTMORENCY

ALPENA

LEELANAU

Traverse City
GRAND TRAVERSE

CRAWFORD
Grayling

OSCODA

ALCONA

BENZIE

KALKASKA

MANISTEE

WEXFORD

MISSAUKEE

ROSCOMMON

OGEMAW

IOSCO

Au Sable

MASON
Ludington

LAKE

OSCEOLA

CLARE

GLADWIN

ARENAC

HURON

OCEANA

NEWAYGO

MECOSTA

ISABELLA

MIDLAND
Midland

BAY

Bay City

TUSCOLA

SANILAC

MUSKEGON

Muskegon

MONTCALM

GRATIOT

SAGINAW

Saginaw

GENESEE
Flint

LAPEER

Port Huron
ST. CLAIR

OTTAWA

KENT
Grand Rapids

IONIA

CLINTON

SHIAWASSEE

OAKLAND
Pontiac

MACOMB

Holland

ALLEGAN

BARRY

EATON

Lansing
INGHAM

LIVINGSTON

Benton Harbor

VAN BUREN

Kalamazoo
KALAMAZOO

Battle Creek

CALHOUN

JACKSON
Jackson

WASHTENAW

Ann Arbor
WAYNE

Detroit

BERRIEN

CASS

ST. JOSEPH

BRANCH

HILLSDALE

LENAWEE

MONROE
Monroe

Legend
- ■ 44.7% to 60.4%
- ▦ 39.1% to 44.6%
- ▨ 35.4% to 39.0%
- □ 23.1% to 35.3%

Clinton (D) received 43.8% statewide.

A framed county name indicates
a county carried by the winner.

Michigan 489

MINNESOTA

Congressional Districts 8
    Average Population 546,887
State Senate Districts 67
    Average Population 65,300
State House Districts 134
    Average Population 32,650

Electoral College Votes 10
Counties 87
Voting Precincts 4,061

Alternative Registration Methods:
    .... Agency-based, Election day, Mail-in, Motor-voter

Registration Deadline (Days before Election) 0

Voting Equipment Use (Counties)

Datavote Punch Card	0	Paper Ballot	36
Electronic	0	Other Punch Card	14
Lever Machine	1	Mixed Systems	8
Optical Scanner	28		

Party Control	DEM	REP	IND	VAC
1993 State Senate	45	22	0	0
1992 State Senate	46	21	0	0
1993 State House	86	48	0	0
1992 State House	78	56	0	0

Population Statistics 1990

Race/ Ethnicity	Total Population		Voting Age Population		Voting Age Population % of total population
	Number	%	Number	%	
Non-Hispanic					
White	4,101,266	93.7	3,048,950	95.0	74.3
Black	93,040	2.1	56,755	1.8	61.0
Asian/Pacific Islander	76,229	1.7	41,822	1.3	54.9
Native American	48,251	1.1	28,686	0.9	59.5
Other	2,429	<.1	717	<.1	29.5
All Hispanic	53,884	1.2	31,386	1.0	58.2
TOTAL	4,375,099	100.0	3,208,316	100.0	73.3

Estimated Voting Age Population 1992 (VAP) 3,278,000
Number of Registered Voters 3,138,901
    % of estimated VAP 95.8
Voter Turnout (Maximum Vote)[1] 2,362,280
    % of VAP 72.1
    % of Registration 75.3
Persons Not Voting—of Voting Age 915,720
    % of VAP 27.9
Persons Not Voting—of Registered 776,621
    % of Registration 24.7
Straight Ticket Voting .... No

State Officials and Members of Congress

Governor:
Arne Carlson (R) 1990, elected to a four-year term in 1990.

U.S. Senators:
Dave Durenberger (R) 1978, elected to a six-year term in 1988.
Paul Wellstone (D) 1990, elected to a six-year term in 1990.

U.S. Representative in Congress:
(District, Name, Party, Date first elected)

1. Penny (D) 1982
2. Minge (D) 1992
3. Ramstad (R) 1990
4. Vento (D) 1976
5. Sabo (D) 1978
6. Grams (R) 1992
7. Peterson (D) 1990
8. Oberstar (D) 1974

---

[1]Maximum vote turnout from Table C exceeds reported statewide actual voter turnout because in one or more counties the vote for highest office is greater than reported actual turnout.

Candidates: General Election, November 3, 1992

Candidate(s)	Total vote	Percent	Party	Status	First elected
President/Vice President					
Clinton/Gore	1,020,997	43.48%	Dem.-Farmer-Labor	Challenger	1992
Bush/Quayle	747,841	31.85%	Ind.-Republican	Incumbent	1988
Perot/Stockdale	562,506	23.96%	Independent	Challenger	
Marrou/Lord	3,374	0.14%	Libertarian	Challenger	
Gritz/Minett	3,363	0.14%	Constitution	Challenger	
Herer/Grimmer	2,659	0.11%	Grassroots	Challenger	
Write ins	2,499	0.11%	Write in	Challenger	
Hagelin/Tompkins	1,406	0.06%	Natural Law	Challenger	
Warren/Debates	990	0.04%	Socialist Workers	Challenger	
Fulani/Munoz	958	0.04%	New Alliance	Challenger	
Phillips/Knight	733	0.03%	Taxpayers	Challenger	
LaRouche/Bevel	622	0.03%	Ind. Econ. Recovery	Challenger	

U.S. Senator (No Contest)

Governor (No Contest)

U.S. Representative in Congress

Candidate(s)	Total vote	Percent	Party	Status	First elected
District 1					
Timothy Penny	206,369	73.85%	Dem.-Farmer-Labor	Incumbent	1982
Timothy Droogsma	72,367	25.90%	Ind.-Republican	Challenger	
Write ins	694	0.25%	Write in	Challenger	
District 2					
David Minge	132,156	47.81%	Dem.-Farmer-Labor	Challenger	1992
Cal Ludeman	131,587	47.61%	Ind.-Republican	Challenger	
Stan Bentz[1]	12,246	4.43%	Independent	Challenger	
Write ins	414	0.15%	Write in	Challenger	
District 3					
Jim Ramstad	200,240	63.62%	Ind.-Republican	Incumbent	1990
Paul Mandell	104,606	33.24%	Dem.-Farmer-Labor	Challenger	
Dwight Fellman	9,164	2.91%	Grassroots	Challenger	
Write ins	721	0.23%	Write in	Challenger	
District 4					
Bruce Vento	159,796	57.49%	Dem.-Farmer-Labor	Incumbent	1976
Ian Maitland	101,744	36.60%	Ind.-Republican	Challenger	
James Willess	6,732	2.42%	Independent	Challenger	
Dan Vacek	4,418	1.59%	Grassroots	Challenger	
Lynn Johnson	3,602	1.30%	Natural Law	Challenger	
Jo Rothenberg	1,236	0.44%	Socialist Workers	Challenger	
Write ins	428	0.15%	Write in	Challenger	
District 5					
Martin Olav Sabo	174,139	62.84%	Dem.-Farmer-Labor	Incumbent	1978
Stephen Moriarty	77,093	27.82%	Ind.-Republican	Challenger	
Russell Bently	6,786	2.45%	Grassroots	Challenger	
Sandra Coleman	5,927	2.14%	New Alliance	Challenger	
Mary Mellen	5,499	1.98%	Natural Law	Challenger	
Glenn Mesaros	4,809	1.74%	Independent	Challenger	
Christopher Nisan	2,062	0.74%	Socialist Workers	Challenger	
Write ins	779	0.28%	Write in	Challenger	
District 6					
Rod Grams	133,564	44.37%	Ind.-Republican	Challenger	1992
Gerry Sikorski	100,016	33.23%	Dem.-Farmer-Labor	Incumbent	1982
Dean Barkley	48,329	16.05%	Independent	Challenger	
James Peterson	16,411	5.45%	Ross Perot	Challenger	
Tom Firnstahl	2,400	0.80%	Natural Law	Challenger	
Write ins	303	0.10%	Write in	Challenger	

[1]Total vote for candidate Bentz corrected to 12,146 in published election results (Elections Division, Secretary of State, *Minnesota Election Results 1992,* Saint Paul, MN).

Candidate(s)	Total vote	Percent	Party	Status	First elected
U.S. Representative in Congress (cont)					
District 7					
Collin Peterson	133,886	50.42%	Dem.-Farmer-Labor	Incumbent	1990
Bernie Omann	130,396	49.11%	Ind.-Republican	Challenger	
Write ins	1,242	0.47%	Write in	Challenger	
District 8					
James Oberstar	167,104	59.04%	Dem.-Farmer-Labor	Incumbent	1974
Phil Herwig	83,823	29.62%	Ind.-Republican	Challenger	
Harry Welty	22,619	7.99%	Ross Perot	Challenger	
Floyd Henspeter	8,602	3.04%	Term Limits Candidate	Challenger	
Write ins	883	0.31%	Write in	Challenger	

Candidates: April 7, 1992, Primary Election

Candidate	Total vote	Percent	Candidate	Total vote	Percent
Presidential Preference, Democratic			**Presidential Preference, Republican**		
Bill Clinton	63,584	31.14%	George Bush	84,841	63.91%
Jerry Brown	62,474	30.60%	Patrick Buchanan	32,094	24.18%
Paul Tsongas	43,588	21.35%	Write ins	6,957	5.24%
Uncommitted	11,366	5.57%	Uncommitted	4,098	3.09%
Write ins	10,149	4.97%	Harold Stassen	4,074	3.07%
Tom Harkin	4,077	2.00%	Sharon Anderson	300	0.23%
Eugene McCarthy	3,704	1.81%	Beatrice Mooney	196	0.15%
Bob Kerrey	1,191	0.58%	George Zimmermann	135	0.10%
Larry Agran	1,042	0.51%	Tennie Rogers	61	0.05%
Charles Woods	990	0.48%			
Mary Rachner	620	0.30%			
Lyndon LaRouche, Jr.	532	0.26%			
Stephen Burke	348	0.17%			
J. Louis McAlpine	183	0.09%			
Tod Hawks	111	0.05%			
Jeffrey Marsh	106	0.05%			
Nathan Averick	105	0.05%			

Voter Registration and Turnout, 1948-1992 Elections

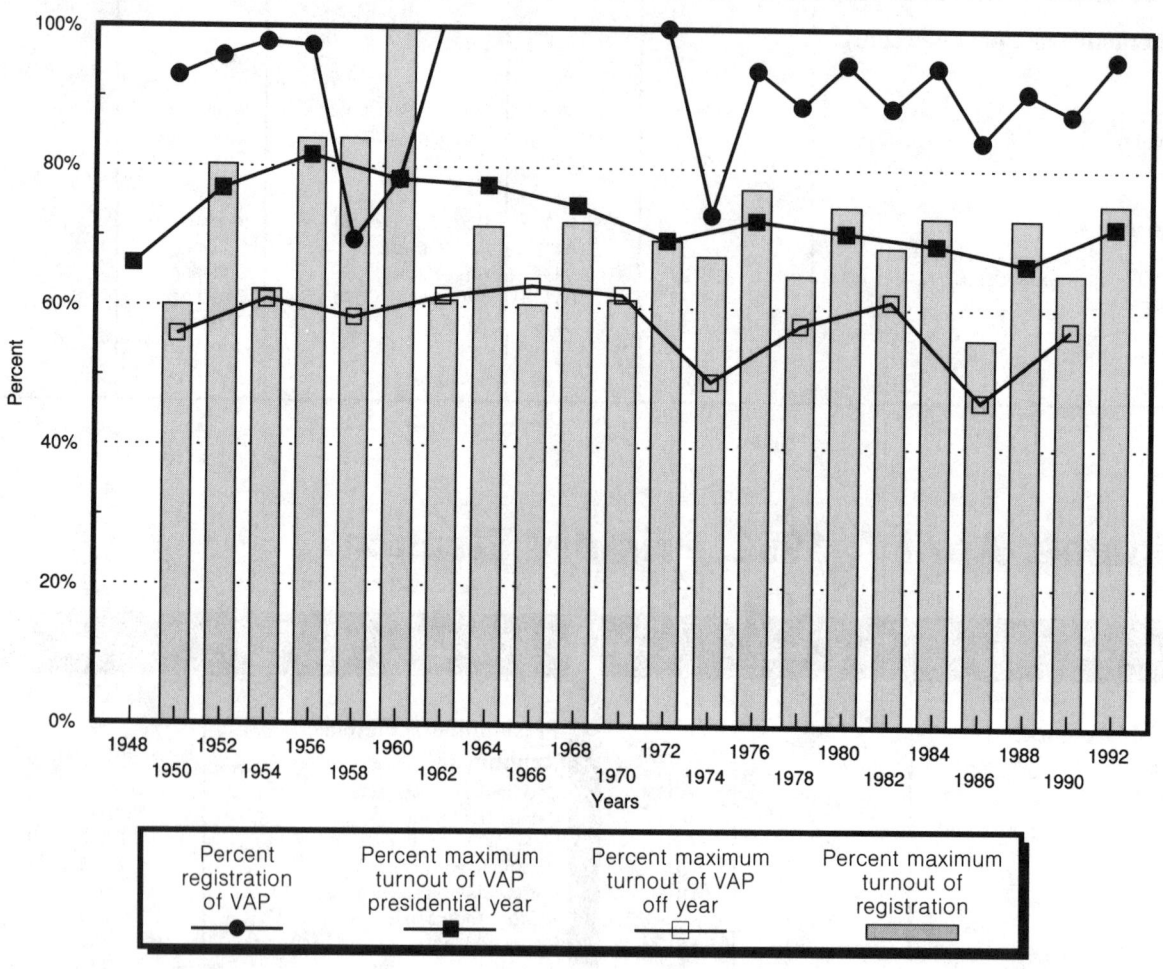

Legend:
- Percent registration of VAP
- Percent maximum turnout of VAP presidential year
- Percent maximum turnout of VAP off year
- Percent maximum turnout of registration

Year	Estimated Voting Age Population (VAP)	Voter registration (REG)			Voter turnout												
							Highest office						Maximum vote			
		Total	Percent of VAP	Rank by percent of VAP	Actual	Total	Office	Percent total REG	Rank by percent of REG	Percent of VAP	Rank by percent of VAP	Total	Percent total REG	Rank by percent of REG	Percent total VAP	Rank by percent of VAP
1992	3,278,000	3,138,901	95.8	3	2,355,796	2,347,948	P	74.8	34	71.6	2	2,355,796	75.1	34	71.9	2
1990	3,222,000	2,830,649	87.9	2	1,843,104	1,806,777	G	63.8	12	56.1	2	1,843,104	65.1	11	57.2	1
1988	3,201,000	2,916,957	91.1	3	2,125,119	2,096,790	P	71.9	23	65.5	1	2,125,119	72.9	26	66.4	1
1986	3,115,000	2,615,137	84.0	5	1,456,579	1,415,989	G	54.1	28	45.5	12	1,456,579	55.7	30	46.8	11
1984	3,057,000	2,893,049	94.6	2	2,115,317	2,084,449	P	72.1	29	68.2	1	2,115,317	73.1	31	69.2	1
1982	3,004,000	2,667,522	88.8	2	1,834,737	1,804,675	S	67.7	13	60.1	2	1,834,737	68.8	15	61.1	2
1980	2,933,000	2,787,487	95.0	1	2,079,451	2,051,980	P	73.6	29	70.0	1	2,079,451	74.6	30	70.9	1
1978	2,823,000	2,511,120	89.0	1	1,624,911	1,585,702	G	63.1	10	56.2	1	1,624,911	64.7	8	57.6	1
1976	2,726,000	2,565,686	94.1	1	1,978,590	1,949,931	P	76.0	22	71.5	1	1,978,590	77.1	21	72.6	1
1974[1]	2,620,000	1,922,462	73.4	18	1,296,209	1,252,898	G	65.2	12	47.8	13	1,296,209	67.4	12	49.5	11
1972[2]	2,546,000	2,545,344	100.0	1	1,773,838	1,741,652	P	68.4	35	68.4	3	1,773,838	69.7	34	69.7	2
1970[2]	2,248,000	2,272,712	101.1	1	1,388,525	1,365,443	G	60.1	33	60.7	5	1,388,525	61.1	32	61.8	4
1968[2]	2,154,000	2,225,080	103.3	1	1,606,307	1,588,506	P	71.4	42	73.7	2	1,606,307	72.2	41	74.6	2
1966[2]	2,082,000	2,177,448	104.6	1	1,312,288	1,295,058	G	59.5	30	62.2	4	1,312,288	60.3	30	63.0	4
1964[2]	2,050,000	2,219,816	108.3	1	1,586,173	1,554,462	P	70.0	37	75.8	3	1,586,173	71.5	35	77.4	3
1962[2]	2,062,000	2,081,220	100.9	1	1,267,502	1,246,904	G	59.9	26	60.5	11	1,267,502	60.9	25	61.5	10
1960	2,017,000	1,577,509	78.2	18	1,577,509	1,541,887	P	97.7	3	76.4	8	1,577,509	100.0	3	78.2	6
1958	2,018,000	1,402,043	69.5	22	1,178,173	1,159,915	G	82.7	3	57.5	12	1,178,173	84.0	3	58.4	12
1956	1,977,000	1,922,855	97.3	1	1,613,138	1,340,005	P	69.7	26	67.8	20	1,613,138	83.9	13	81.6	1
1954	1,917,000	1,875,510	97.8	2	1,168,101	1,151,417	G	61.4	17	60.1	10	1,168,101	62.3	17	60.9	7
1952	1,909,000	1,828,164	95.8	3	1,466,326	1,379,483	P	75.5	21	72.3	20	1,466,326	80.2	19	76.8	8
1950	1,909,000	1,775,770	93.0	1	1,067,967	1,046,632	G	58.9	17	54.8	15	1,067,967	60.1	17	55.9	16
1948	1,907,000	-	-	-	1,257,804	1,212,226	P	-	-	63.6	15	1,257,804	-	-	66.0	11

[1]Election day voter registration law enacted 1973. [2]Total voter registration reported by Minnesota Secretary of State exceeds estimated voting age population (VAP).

494 Minnesota

MINNESOTA

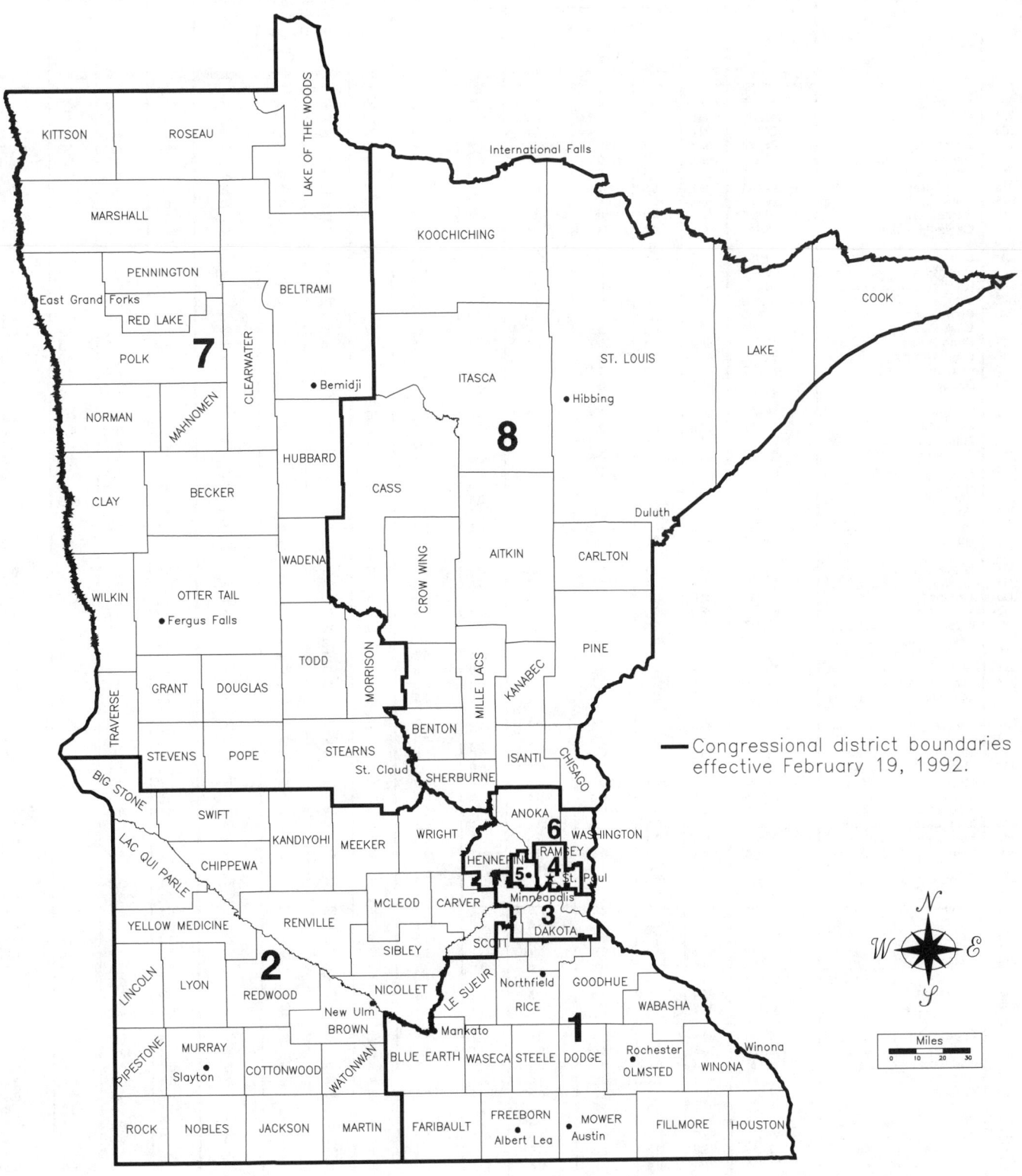

Congressional district boundaries
effective February 19, 1992.

Copyright © 1993 by Election Data Services, Inc.

Minnesota 495

Table A. — 1990 Population by Race and Ethnic Origin

State/county code	County	Total persons	Percent of total persons — Non-Hispanic White	Black	Asian and Pacific Islander	Native American	Other	Hispanic	Rank — Percent of total persons — Total	Non-Hispanic White	Black	Hispanic	Percent contribution to state population — Total	Non-Hispanic White	Black	Hispanic
27 001	Aitkin	12,425	98.0	0.1	0.2	1.4	<.1	0.3	63	50	44	76	0.3	0.3	<.1	<.1
27 003	Anoka	243,641	96.6	0.5	1.2	0.7	<.1	0.9	4	64	10	22	5.6	5.7	1.4	4.2
27 005	Becker	27,881	92.5	<.1	0.4	6.6	<.1	0.4	34	80	49	59	0.6	0.6	<.1	0.2
27 007	Beltrami	34,384	82.4	0.3	0.6	16.3	<.1	0.4	23	86	18	60	0.8	0.7	0.1	0.3
27 009	Benton	30,185	98.5	0.2	0.4	0.4	<.1	0.5	29	32	26	53	0.7	0.7	<.1	0.3
27 011	Big Stone	6,285	98.9	<.1	0.2	0.4	<.1	0.4	80	15	52	67	0.1	0.2	<.1	<.1
27 013	Blue Earth	54,044	96.9	0.5	1.5	0.2	<.1	0.9	11	62	11	25	1.2	1.3	0.3	0.9
27 015	Brown	26,984	99.0	<.1	0.4	<.1	<.1	0.6	35	12	64	43	0.6	0.7	<.1	0.3
27 017	Carlton	29,259	94.8	0.1	0.3	4.4	<.1	0.3	31	77	34	72	0.7	0.7	<.1	0.2
27 019	Carver	47,915	98.1	0.2	0.9	0.2	<.1	0.5	15	46	23	48	1.1	1.1	0.1	0.5
27 021	Cass	21,791	88.3	0.2	0.2	10.8	0.0	0.4	41	84	30	57	0.5	0.5	<.1	0.2
27 023	Chippewa	13,228	98.8	<.1	0.3	0.2	0.0	0.7	59	22	66	35	0.3	0.3	<.1	0.2
27 025	Chisago	30,521	98.6	0.2	0.3	0.4	<.1	0.4	28	27	25	55	0.7	0.7	<.1	0.3
27 027	Clay	50,422	95.4	0.3	0.8	1.1	<.1	2.3	13	73	16	6	1.2	1.2	0.2	2.2
27 029	Clearwater	8,309	92.1	<.1	0.1	7.6	0.0	0.2	76	81	79	83	0.2	0.2	<.1	<.1
27 031	Cook	3,868	92.0	0.1	0.5	7.0	0.0	0.4	87	82	38	68	<.1	<.1	<.1	<.1
27 033	Cottonwood	12,694	98.6	<.1	0.7	<.1	<.1	0.5	62	26	53	49	0.3	0.3	<.1	0.1
27 035	Crow Wing	44,249	98.4	0.2	0.3	0.7	<.1	0.4	17	34	24	65	1.0	1.1	0.1	0.3
27 037	Dakota	275,227	95.3	1.2	1.6	0.3	<.1	1.5	3	74	4	10	6.3	6.4	3.6	7.5
27 039	Dodge	15,731	98.3	<.1	0.4	0.2	<.1	1.0	54	37	50	18	0.4	0.4	<.1	0.3
27 041	Douglas	28,674	99.1	<.1	0.3	0.3	0.0	0.3	32	10	61	77	0.7	0.7	<.1	0.1
27 043	Faribault	16,937	97.6	<.1	0.3	0.1	<.1	1.9	52	53	55	7	0.4	0.4	<.1	0.6
27 045	Fillmore	20,777	99.2	<.1	0.2	0.2	0.0	0.3	44	6	69	71	0.5	0.5	<.1	0.1
27 047	Freeborn	33,060	96.1	<.1	0.4	0.2	<.1	3.3	24	67	72	4	0.8	0.8	<.1	2.0
27 049	Goodhue	40,690	98.3	0.2	0.4	0.7	<.1	0.4	20	39	27	61	0.9	1.0	<.1	0.3
27 051	Grant	6,246	99.4	<.1	0.2	0.2	0.0	0.1	81	3	62	86	0.1	0.2	<.1	<.1
27 053	Hennepin	1,032,431	88.6	5.7	2.8	1.4	0.1	1.4	1	83	1	11	23.6	22.3	63.5	25.9
27 055	Houston	18,497	98.9	0.1	0.3	0.3	0.0	0.2	48	8	37	82	0.4	0.4	<.1	<.1
27 057	Hubbard	14,939	97.8	<.1	<.1	1.8	0.0	0.2	56	52	74	79	0.3	0.4	<.1	<.1
27 059	Isanti	25,921	98.3	0.3	0.4	0.5	<.1	0.5	36	36	20	54	0.6	0.6	<.1	0.2
27 061	Itasca	40,863	96.1	<.1	0.2	3.3	<.1	0.3	19	68	46	70	0.9	1.0	<.1	0.3
27 063	Jackson	11,677	97.5	<.1	1.4	0.1	0.0	1.0	66	56	82	21	0.3	0.3	<.1	0.2
27 065	Kanabec	12,802	98.6	0.1	0.4	0.4	<.1	0.5	61	28	39	51	0.3	0.3	<.1	0.1
27 067	Kandiyohi	38,761	95.6	0.2	0.3	0.4	<.1	3.5	21	71	28	3	0.9	0.9	<.1	2.5
27 069	Kittson	5,767	98.9	0.0	0.2	<.1	0.0	0.8	82	14	84	29	0.1	0.1	0.0	<.1
27 071	Koochiching	16,299	95.5	0.3	0.3	2.7	<.1	1.1	53	72	19	15	0.4	0.4	<.1	0.3
27 073	Lac qui Parle	8,924	99.2	0.1	0.3	0.1	<.1	0.3	75	7	45	78	0.2	0.2	<.1	<.1
27 075	Lake	10,415	98.9	<.1	0.2	0.6	0.0	0.3	72	13	83	74	0.2	0.3	<.1	<.1
27 077	Lake of the Woods	4,076	98.8	<.1	0.2	0.3	0.0	0.6	86	19	78	40	<.1	<.1	<.1	<.1
27 079	Le Sueur	23,239	98.9	<.1	0.3	0.2	<.1	0.5	39	16	57	45	0.5	0.6	<.1	0.2
27 081	Lincoln	6,890	99.3	<.1	0.1	0.1	0.0	0.4	79	4	73	66	0.2	0.2	<.1	<.1
27 083	Lyon	24,789	98.1	0.2	0.5	0.3	<.1	0.9	37	44	22	28	0.6	0.6	<.1	0.4
27 085	McLeod	32,030	98.5	<.1	0.4	0.2	0.0	0.9	26	33	47	26	0.7	0.8	<.1	0.5
27 087	Mahnomen	5,044	75.9	<.1	<.1	23.5	0.0	0.5	83	87	80	44	0.1	<.1	<.1	<.1
27 089	Marshall	10,993	98.4	<.1	0.1	0.5	0.0	1.0	67	35	81	19	0.3	0.3	<.1	0.2
27 091	Martin	22,914	98.9	<.1	0.4	0.1	<.1	0.6	40	18	65	41	0.5	0.6	<.1	0.3
27 093	Meeker	20,846	98.2	0.1	0.4	0.1	<.1	1.1	43	42	42	16	0.5	0.5	<.1	0.4
27 095	Mille Lacs	18,670	95.9	0.1	0.2	3.3	<.1	0.5	47	70	36	52	0.4	0.4	<.1	0.2
27 097	Morrison	29,604	99.1	0.1	0.2	0.3	<.1	0.3	30	9	41	73	0.7	0.7	<.1	0.2
27 099	Mower	37,385	98.2	0.2	0.8	0.1	<.1	0.7	22	40	29	38	0.9	0.9	<.1	0.5
27 101	Murray	9,660	99.6	0.0	0.2	<.1	0.0	0.2	74	1	85	81	0.2	0.2	0.0	<.1
27 103	Nicollet	28,076	98.1	0.3	0.7	0.2	<.1	0.7	33	47	17	33	0.6	0.7	<.1	0.4
27 105	Nobles	20,098	96.1	0.2	2.0	0.3	<.1	1.3	45	66	21	12	0.5	0.5	<.1	0.5
27 107	Norman	7,975	98.0	<.1	0.2	0.8	0.0	0.9	77	49	60	24	0.2	0.2	<.1	0.1
27 109	Olmsted	106,470	95.1	0.7	3.0	0.3	<.1	0.9	8	75	6	23	2.4	2.5	0.8	1.8
27 111	Otter Tail	50,714	98.7	<.1	0.4	0.4	<.1	0.4	12	25	59	56	1.2	1.2	<.1	0.4
27 113	Pennington	13,306	98.0	<.1	0.4	0.8	0.0	0.8	58	48	48	30	0.3	0.3	<.1	0.2
27 115	Pine	21,264	94.7	1.5	0.4	1.7	<.1	1.6	42	78	3	9	0.5	0.5	0.3	0.6
27 117	Pipestone	10,491	97.4	<.1	0.6	1.5	<.1	0.4	71	57	56	63	0.2	0.2	<.1	<.1
27 119	Polk	32,498	94.8	0.2	0.3	1.2	<.1	3.5	25	76	32	2	0.7	0.8	<.1	2.1
27 121	Pope	10,745	99.5	<.1	0.1	0.2	<.1	<.1	68	2	63	87	0.2	0.3	<.1	<.1
27 123	Ramsey	485,765	86.7	4.5	5.0	0.9	0.1	2.9	2	85	2	5	11.1	10.3	23.7	25.8
27 125	Red Lake	4,525	98.8	0.0	<.1	0.2	0.0	1.0	84	20	86	20	0.1	0.1	0.0	<.1
27 127	Redwood	17,254	97.6	0.2	0.2	1.6	<.1	0.5	51	54	33	46	0.4	0.4	<.1	0.2
27 129	Renville	17,673	98.1	<.1	0.3	0.3	<.1	1.2	50	43	70	14	0.4	0.4	<.1	0.4
27 131	Rice	49,183	97.1	0.3	1.2	0.2	<.1	1.1	14	61	15	17	1.1	1.2	0.2	1.0
27 133	Rock	9,806	99.1	0.1	0.2	0.3	0.0	0.3	73	11	40	75	0.2	0.2	<.1	<.1
27 135	Roseau	15,026	98.2	<.1	0.6	1.0	<.1	0.2	55	41	75	85	0.3	0.4	<.1	<.1
27 137	St. Louis	198,213	96.6	0.5	0.5	1.8	<.1	0.5	5	65	8	50	4.5	4.7	1.2	1.8
27 139	Scott	57,846	97.3	0.4	0.9	0.6	<.1	0.7	10	59	12	36	1.3	1.4	0.3	0.8

State/county code	County	Total persons	Percent of total persons						Rank				Percent contribution to state population			
			Non-Hispanic					Hispanic	Total	Percent of total persons			Total	Non-Hispanic		Hispanic
			White	Black	Asian and Pacific Islander	Native American	Other			Non-Hispanic		Hispanic		White	Black	
										White	Black					
27 141	Sherburne	41,945	97.8	0.6	0.5	0.5	<.1	0.6	18	51	7	39	1.0	1.0	0.3	0.5
27 143	Sibley	14,366	98.8	<.1	0.2	0.1	0.0	0.9	57	21	68	27	0.3	0.3	<.1	0.2
27 145	Stearns	118,791	98.3	0.3	0.7	0.2	<.1	0.4	7	38	14	58	2.7	2.8	0.4	1.0
27 147	Steele	30,729	97.4	0.2	0.5	0.1	<.1	1.8	27	58	31	8	0.7	0.7	<.1	1.0
27 149	Stevens	10,634	97.3	0.5	1.1	0.5	0.1	0.5	70	60	9	47	0.2	0.3	<.1	0.1
27 151	Swift	10,724	98.5	<.1	0.3	0.3	<.1	0.7	69	30	67	31	0.2	0.3	<.1	0.1
27 153	Todd	23,363	99.3	<.1	0.2	0.2	<.1	0.2	38	5	71	80	0.5	0.6	<.1	0.1
27 155	Traverse	4,463	96.7	0.0	0.4	2.8	0.0	0.2	85	63	87	84	0.1	0.1	0.0	<.1
27 157	Wabasha	19,744	98.9	<.1	0.5	0.2	0.0	0.4	46	17	58	64	0.5	0.5	<.1	0.1
27 159	Wadena	13,154	98.7	<.1	0.3	0.6	<.1	0.4	60	23	54	69	0.3	0.3	<.1	<.1
27 161	Waseca	18,079	98.5	0.1	0.4	0.2	<.1	0.7	49	29	35	34	0.4	0.4	<.1	0.2
27 163	Washington	145,896	96.0	1.1	1.1	0.4	<.1	1.3	6	69	5	13	3.3	3.4	1.7	3.5
27 165	Watonwan	11,682	94.1	<.1	0.5	0.2	0.1	5.1	65	79	51	1	0.3	0.3	<.1	1.1
27 167	Wilkin	7,516	98.5	<.1	0.3	0.5	<.1	0.6	78	31	76	42	0.2	0.2	<.1	<.1
27 169	Winona	47,828	97.5	0.4	1.1	0.2	<.1	0.7	16	55	13	32	1.1	1.1	0.2	0.6
27 171	Wright	68,710	98.7	0.1	0.4	0.3	<.1	0.4	9	24	43	62	1.6	1.7	<.1	0.5
27 173	Yellow Medicine	11,684	98.1	<.1	0.2	1.0	<.1	0.7	64	45	77	37	0.3	0.3	<.1	0.2
27	**MINNESOTA**	4,375,099	93.7	2.1	1.7	1.1	<.1	1.2					100.0	100.0	100.0	100.0
	CONGRESSIONAL															
	District 1	546,887	97.3	0.3	1.2	0.2	<.1	1.0	4	2	6	4	12.5	13.0	1.8	9.9
	District 2	546,887	98.0	0.1	0.5	0.4	<.1	1.0	5	1	8	5	12.5	13.1	0.9	9.8
	District 3	546,888	95.3	1.3	2.0	0.3	<.1	1.1	1	6	3	3	12.5	12.7	7.7	10.9
	District 4	546,887	87.5	4.1	4.6	0.8	<.1	2.9	6	7	2	1	12.5	11.7	24.3	29.0
	District 5	546,887	82.9	9.4	3.4	2.3	0.2	1.8	7	8	1	2	12.5	11.1	55.3	18.1
	District 6	546,888	96.0	1.1	1.4	0.6	<.1	0.9	2	5	4	6	12.5	12.8	6.7	9.2
	District 7	546,888	96.4	0.2	0.5	2.2	<.1	0.8	3	4	7	7	12.5	12.9	1.0	8.0
	District 8	546,887	96.6	0.4	0.4	2.1	<.1	0.5	8	3	5	8	12.5	12.9	2.3	5.2

Table B. — 1990 Voting Age Population (VAP) by Race and Ethnic Origin

County	Total Voting Age Population	Percent of total VAP — Non-Hispanic White	Black	Asian and Pacific Islander	Native American	Other	Hispanic	Rank — Total	Rank — Non-Hispanic White	Black	Hispanic	Pct contribution — Total	Non-Hispanic White	Black	Hispanic	VAP pct of total pop — Total	Non-Hispanic White	Black	Asian and Pacific Islander	Native American	Other	Hispanic
Aitkin	9,466	98.6	<.1	<.1	1.0	<.1	0.2	60	43	35	79	0.3	0.3	<.1	<.1	76.2	76.7	61.5	30.0	58.6	50.0	45.7
Anoka	169,272	97.3	0.4	0.9	0.6	<.1	0.7	4	64	12	19	5.3	5.4	1.2	3.9	69.5	70.0	52.6	54.6	60.7	14.3	53.4
Becker	19,773	93.9	<.1	0.3	5.5	<.1	0.3	34	80	53	61	0.6	0.6	<.1	0.2	70.9	72.0	40.0	58.0	58.7	50.0	49.2
Beltrami	24,156	86.2	0.2	0.6	12.7	<.1	0.3	24	86	22	53	0.8	0.7	<.1	0.3	70.3	73.5	48.0	71.6	54.7	60.0	56.8
Benton	21,141	98.7	0.1	0.3	0.3	<.1	0.4	28	40	28	43	0.7	0.7	<.1	0.3	70.0	70.2	47.5	57.9	59.3	28.6	63.3
Big Stone	4,644	99.3	<.1	<.1	0.3	0.0	0.2	80	14	44	71	0.1	0.2	<.1	<.1	73.9	74.2	75.0	26.7	52.0	0.0	47.8
Blue Earth	41,653	97.2	0.5	1.4	0.2	<.1	0.7	10	65	9	20	1.3	1.3	0.4	0.9	77.1	77.3	81.5	72.8	67.7	35.7	61.9
Brown	19,587	99.3	<.1	0.2	<.1	<.1	0.4	35	12	59	51	0.6	0.6	<.1	0.2	72.6	72.9	54.5	40.8	91.7	100.0	46.4
Carlton	21,048	96.0	0.1	0.1	3.5	0.0	0.2	30	76	27	68	0.7	0.7	<.1	0.2	71.9	72.8	67.4	38.7	57.3	0.0	51.5
Carver	33,408	98.5	0.2	0.7	0.2	<.1	0.5	16	49	23	40	1.0	1.1	0.1	0.5	69.7	70.0	59.2	50.0	63.4	15.4	60.3
Cass	15,862	91.2	<.1	0.1	8.3	0.0	0.3	41	83	33	55	0.5	0.5	<.1	0.2	72.8	75.1	39.5	36.5	55.7	0.0	55.3
Chippewa	9,647	99.3	0.0	0.2	0.1	0.0	0.4	59	13	77	46	0.3	0.3	0.0	0.1	72.9	73.4	0.0	34.9	56.5	0.0	38.3
Chisago	21,117	99.0	0.1	0.2	0.3	<.1	0.3	29	26	26	58	0.7	0.7	<.1	0.2	69.2	69.5	49.2	42.7	58.3	15.4	47.4
Clay	37,797	96.4	0.3	0.8	0.8	<.1	1.7	12	72	18	7	1.2	1.2	0.2	2.0	75.0	75.8	62.2	74.4	55.9	45.9	53.4
Clearwater	5,890	93.7	<.1	<.1	6.2	0.0	0.1	76	81	72	84	0.2	0.2	<.1	<.1	70.9	72.1	50.0	10.0	58.0	0.0	43.8
Cook	2,932	93.0	0.1	0.1	6.5	0.0	0.2	87	82	31	70	<.1	<.1	<.1	<.1	75.8	76.6	60.0	20.0	70.8	0.0	50.0
Cottonwood	9,389	99.3	<.1	0.4	<.1	0.0	0.2	62	15	47	72	0.3	0.3	<.1	<.1	74.0	74.5	62.5	38.6	60.0	0.0	34.9
Crow Wing	32,321	98.8	0.2	0.2	0.5	<.1	0.2	17	37	24	69	1.0	1.0	<.1	0.2	73.0	73.3	59.6	58.8	58.5	33.3	44.8
Dakota	193,081	96.2	1.0	1.3	0.3	<.1	1.2	3	73	5	10	6.0	6.1	3.6	7.1	70.2	70.8	60.1	55.8	65.4	22.7	55.7
Dodge	10,782	98.8	<.1	0.1	0.2	<.1	0.8	55	39	45	17	0.3	0.3	<.1	0.3	68.5	68.9	63.6	26.3	75.0	42.9	53.7
Douglas	20,894	99.4	<.1	0.2	0.2	0.0	0.2	31	11	69	75	0.7	0.7	<.1	0.1	72.9	73.1	28.6	42.0	54.8	0.0	55.1
Faribault	12,443	98.4	<.1	0.2	<.1	<.1	1.3	64	51	67	9	0.4	0.4	<.1	0.5	73.5	74.1	30.0	42.6	63.2	25.0	50.3
Fillmore	14,996	99.5	<.1	0.1	0.1	<.1	0.2	43	6	54	73	0.5	0.5	<.1	0.1	72.2	72.4	85.7	30.6	56.3	0.0	49.3
Freeborn	24,530	97.0	<.1	0.3	0.2	<.1	2.5	23	67	62	3	0.8	0.8	<.1	1.9	74.2	74.9	63.6	50.0	77.0	60.0	56.3
Goodhue	29,240	98.8	0.1	0.2	0.5	<.1	0.3	19	35	30	56	0.9	0.9	<.1	0.3	71.9	72.3	44.4	38.1	52.2	10.0	54.3
Grant	4,629	99.7	0.0	<.1	0.2	0.0	<.1	81	3	78	86	0.1	0.2	0.0	<.1	74.1	74.3	0.0	33.3	60.0	0.0	28.6
Hennepin	793,622	91.1	4.5	2.2	1.1	<.1	1.1	1	84	1	11	24.7	23.7	63.1	28.4	76.9	79.0	60.6	59.5	59.3	26.8	63.7
Houston	13,185	99.5	<.1	<.1	0.2	0.0	0.1	48	7	57	81	0.4	0.4	<.1	<.1	71.3	71.5	20.8	25.5	60.4	0.0	51.4
Hubbard	10,850	98.2	<.1	<.1	1.5	0.0	0.2	54	54	70	76	0.3	0.3	<.1	<.1	72.6	72.9	50.0	46.2	59.8	0.0	56.8
Isanti	17,809	98.7	0.2	0.2	0.5	<.1	0.4	37	41	21	44	0.6	0.6	<.1	0.2	68.7	68.9	53.7	39.0	65.7	25.0	56.3
Itasca	29,305	96.9	<.1	0.1	2.6	<.1	0.2	18	68	49	67	0.9	0.9	<.1	0.2	71.7	72.4	38.5	42.2	58.0	100.0	50.3
Jackson	8,541	98.5	<.1	0.8	0.1	0.0	0.5	64	46	74	34	0.3	0.3	<.1	0.1	73.1	73.9	50.0	41.9	73.3	0.0	39.8
Kanabec	8,917	99.1	<.1	0.1	0.4	0.0	0.3	63	24	43	54	0.3	0.3	<.1	<.1	69.7	70.0	37.5	26.7	64.3	0.0	49.2
Kandiyohi	27,724	97.1	<.1	0.2	0.3	<.1	2.4	22	66	34	4	0.9	0.9	<.1	2.1	71.5	72.6	33.3	47.3	53.3	75.0	47.8
Kittson	4,261	99.2	0.0	<.1	0.1	0.0	0.6	82	19	79	28	0.1	0.1	0.0	<.1	73.9	74.1	0.0	30.0	100.0	0.0	54.3
Koochiching	12,150	96.1	0.3	0.2	2.3	<.1	1.1	53	74	17	12	0.4	0.4	<.1	0.4	74.5	75.0	83.7	50.0	62.4	50.0	70.3
Lac qui Parle	6,565	99.6	<.1	0.1	<.1	0.0	0.1	75	4	60	83	0.2	0.2	<.1	<.1	73.6	73.9	22.2	32.1	33.3	0.0	34.8
Lake	7,880	99.1	0.0	0.1	0.5	0.0	0.3	68	22	80	64	0.2	0.3	0.0	<.1	75.7	75.8	0.0	56.3	65.6	0.0	65.6
Lake of the Woods	2,948	99.0	<.1	0.2	0.3	0.0	0.5	86	30	58	37	<.1	<.1	<.1	<.1	72.3	72.5	100.0	50.0	76.9	0.0	56.0
Le Sueur	16,374	99.3	<.1	0.1	0.2	<.1	0.4	39	16	71	47	0.5	0.5	<.1	0.2	70.5	70.7	23.1	30.6	74.0	50.0	49.6
Lincoln	5,089	99.5	<.1	<.1	<.1	0.0	0.3	79	5	56	62	0.2	0.2	<.1	<.1	73.9	74.0	100.0	11.1	55.6	0.0	57.7
Lyon	18,050	98.6	0.2	0.4	0.2	0.0	0.6	36	44	20	29	0.6	0.6	<.1	0.3	72.8	73.1	71.2	66.9	50.8	0.0	49.1
McLeod	22,748	98.9	<.1	0.3	0.1	0.0	0.7	26	34	48	24	0.7	0.7	<.1	0.5	71.0	71.3	40.0	55.6	55.1	0.0	52.8
Mahnomen	3,470	79.9	0.0	<.1	19.5	0.0	0.5	83	87	81	39	0.1	<.1	0.0	<.1	68.8	72.5	0.0	60.0	57.3	0.0	59.3
Marshall	7,824	98.9	0.0	<.1	0.4	0.0	0.7	70	33	82	23	0.2	0.3	0.0	0.2	71.2	71.6	0.0	28.6	58.0	0.0	46.0
Martin	16,771	99.2	<.1	0.2	<.1	0.0	0.4	38	17	61	41	0.5	0.5	<.1	0.2	73.2	73.5	55.6	39.8	55.2	0.0	52.6
Meeker	14,719	98.8	<.1	0.2	0.1	<.1	0.8	42	38	46	18	0.5	0.5	<.1	0.4	70.6	71.0	39.1	38.5	51.7	80.0	51.1
Mille Lacs	13,233	96.8	<.1	0.1	2.7	0.0	0.3	47	70	40	65	0.4	0.4	<.1	0.1	70.9	71.6	38.5	45.7	57.9	0.0	40.2
Morrison	20,346	99.4	<.1	<.1	0.3	0.0	0.2	33	10	52	74	0.6	0.7	<.1	0.1	68.7	68.9	30.3	33.3	70.1	0.0	46.9
Mower	27,830	98.8	<.1	0.5	<.1	<.1	0.5	21	36	39	38	0.9	0.9	<.1	0.4	74.4	74.9	32.8	52.8	52.0	50.0	52.0
Murray	7,040	99.7	0.0	0.1	<.1	0.0	0.1	73	2	83	85	0.2	0.2	0.0	<.1	72.9	73.0	0.0	58.8	100.0	0.0	38.1
Nicollet	20,729	98.3	0.3	0.5	0.2	<.1	0.6	32	52	15	27	0.6	0.7	0.1	0.4	73.8	74.0	78.6	56.1	74.1	50.0	61.1
Nobles	14,767	96.9	0.2	1.5	0.2	<.1	1.0	44	69	19	13	0.5	0.5	<.1	0.5	73.5	74.1	73.5	56.6	54.0	42.9	58.8
Norman	5,822	98.6	0.0	<.1	0.7	0.0	0.6	77	42	84	26	0.2	0.2	0.0	0.1	73.0	73.5	0.0	31.3	59.7	0.0	48.6
Olmsted	76,942	95.9	0.7	2.3	0.2	<.1	0.8	8	77	7	16	2.4	2.4	1.0	2.0	72.3	72.9	72.8	56.4	62.9	31.7	65.8
Otter Tail	37,271	99.0	<.1	0.3	0.4	<.1	0.3	13	29	50	57	1.2	1.2	<.1	0.4	73.5	73.7	70.4	54.9	61.9	66.7	51.8
Pennington	9,744	98.6	<.1	0.2	0.6	0.0	0.6	58	45	37	31	0.3	0.3	<.1	0.2	73.2	73.6	80.0	35.4	62.0	0.0	50.9
Pine	15,221	94.5	2.0	0.2	1.4	<.1	1.9	42	79	3	6	0.5	0.5	0.5	0.9	71.6	71.4	91.7	43.2	60.4	66.7	81.6
Pipestone	7,542	99.2	<.1	0.4	1.0	<.1	0.3	72	55	55	63	0.2	0.2	<.1	<.1	71.9	72.4	50.0	47.1	51.6	100.0	52.4
Polk	23,355	96.1	0.1	0.2	1.0	<.1	2.5	25	75	29	2	0.7	0.7	<.1	1.9	71.9	72.8	60.4	48.3	62.2	60.0	51.9
Pope	7,785	99.7	<.1	<.1	0.2	0.0	<.1	71	1	73	87	0.2	0.3	<.1	<.1	72.5	72.6	20.0	25.0	60.9	0.0	42.9
Ramsey	365,661	90.0	3.7	3.3	0.7	<.1	2.3	2	85	2	5	11.4	10.8	23.7	26.2	75.3	78.2	60.8	49.8	63.9	31.3	59.3
Red Lake	3,171	99.2	0.0	0.0	0.2	0.0	0.6	85	18	85	30	<.1	0.1	0.0	<.1	70.1	70.4	0.0	85.7	0.0	0.0	39.1
Redwood	12,408	98.3	<.1	<.1	1.1	<.1	0.4	52	53	38	48	0.4	0.4	<.1	0.1	71.9	72.5	37.0	35.5	52.2	100.0	50.5
Renville	12,751	98.9	<.1	0.1	0.2	<.1	0.7	50	32	76	21	0.4	0.4	<.1	0.3	72.1	72.7	16.7	26.1	56.4	40.0	41.7
Rice	36,275	97.5	0.4	1.1	0.2	<.1	0.9	14	62	14	15	1.1	1.2	0.2	1.1	73.8	74.0	76.5	64.0	72.2	55.6	62.3
Rock	7,020	99.4	<.1	0.1	0.2	0.0	0.2	74	9	36	77	0.2	0.2	<.1	<.1	71.6	71.9	50.0	42.1	42.4	0.0	44.8
Roseau	10,343	98.5	<.1	0.5	0.9	0.0	0.1	56	48	63	82	0.3	0.3	<.1	<.1	68.8	69.1	75.0	51.1	61.0	0.0	53.8
St. Louis	149,892	97.3	0.5	0.4	1.4	<.1	0.4	5	63	10	50	4.7	4.8	1.3	1.7	75.6	76.2	67.1	55.7	58.6	30.0	57.1
Scott	39,845	97.8	0.4	0.7	0.6	0.0	0.5	11	58	11	35	1.2	1.3	0.3	0.7	68.9	69.2	64.1	51.2	65.1	0.0	51.6

Table B. — 1990 Voting Age Population (VAP) by Race and Ethnic Origin (cont)

County	Total Voting Age Population	Pct of total VAP — NH White	Black	Asian and Pacific Islander	Native American	Other	Hispanic	Rank — Total	NH White	Black	Hispanic	Pct contribution to state VAP — Total	NH White	Black	Hispanic	VAP pct of total pop — Total	NH White	Black	Asian and Pacific Islander	Native American	Other	Hispanic
Sherburne	28,627	97.8	0.8	0.3	0.6	<.1	0.5	20	60	6	33	0.9	0.9	0.4	0.5	68.2	68.2	84.7	46.1	85.0	71.4	59.1
Sibley	10,284	99.1	<.1	<.1	0.1	0.0	0.7	57	23	64	22	0.3	0.3	<.1	0.2	71.6	71.8	60.0	25.0	80.0	0.0	55.1
Stearns	85,782	98.5	0.3	0.6	0.2	<.1	0.4	7	50	16	45	2.7	2.8	0.5	1.0	72.2	72.4	65.7	62.6	66.7	50.0	62.9
Steele	21,937	98.1	0.1	0.3	0.2	0.0	1.3	27	56	32	8	0.7	0.7	<.1	0.9	76.5	76.8	75.0	66.4	66.0	30.8	60.7
Stevens	8,134	97.7	0.5	0.9	0.4	<.1	0.4	67	61	8	42	0.2	0.3	<.1	0.1	73.1	73.6	50.0	29.7	54.1	100.0	36.7
Swift	7,842	99.2	<.1	0.1	0.3	<.1	0.4	69	20	65	49	0.2	0.3	<.1	<.1	69.5	69.6	50.0	31.4	68.6	66.7	50.0
Todd	16,232	99.5	<.1	<.1	0.2	<.1	0.2	40	8	66	78	0.5	0.5	0.0	<.1	71.1	71.2	63.6	31.3	45.6	0.0	62.5
Traverse	3,292	98.0	0.0	0.2	1.7	0.0	0.2	84	57	86	80	0.1	0.1	0.0	<.1	73.8	74.8	0.0	64.0	68.1	0.0	54.4
Wabasha	14,032	99.0	<.1	0.4	0.2	0.0	0.3	46	28	51	59	0.4	0.5	<.1	0.1	71.8	72.0	87.5	37.1	58.4	0.0	51.1
Wadena	9,442	99.1	<.1	0.1	0.5	0.0	0.3	61	25	41	66	0.3	0.3	<.1	<.1	71.3	71.6	76.9	39.2	54.3	0.0	53.5
Waseca	12,895	98.9	0.2	0.2	0.1	0.0	0.5	49	31	25	32	0.4	0.4	<.1	0.2	69.6	70.1	69.0	49.8	75.0	38.5	53.8
Washington	101,581	96.7	1.1	0.8	0.5	<.1	1.0	6	71	4	14	3.2	3.2	1.9	3.2	71.9	73.0	25.0	45.6	70.0	42.9	55.1
Watonwan	8,401	95.5	<.1	0.3	0.2	<.1	3.9	66	78	68	1	0.2	0.2	0.0	<.1	71.7	72.1	0.0	47.8	51.2	100.0	44.2
Wilkin	5,390	99.0	0.0	0.2	0.4	<.1	0.4	78	27	87	52	0.2	0.2	0.2	0.7	75.5	75.7	71.0	65.5	70.3	60.0	66.6
Winona	36,098	97.8	0.4	1.0	0.2	<.1	0.6	15	59	13	25	1.1	1.2	0.2	0.4	67.4	67.7	45.9	33.1	58.9	38.9	48.9
Wright	46,325	99.1	<.1	0.2	0.3	<.1	0.3	9	21	42	60	1.4	1.5	<.1	0.4	73.0	73.3	33.3	21.1	66.7	100.0	52.4
Yellow Medicine	8,529	98.5	<.1	<.1	0.9	<.1	0.5	65	47	75	36	0.3	0.3	<.1	0.1	72.8	73.3	70.2	49.9	58.8	34.7	58.6
MINNESOTA	3,208,316	95.0	1.8	1.3	0.9	<.1	1.0					100.0	100.0	100.0	100.0	73.3	74.3	61.0	54.9	59.5	29.5	58.2
CONGRESSIONAL																						
District 1	399,063	97.8	0.3	0.9	0.2	<.1	0.8	3	2	6	4	12.4	12.8	2.1	9.9	73.0	73.3	68.7	57.4	63.7	36.4	58.3
District 2	390,480	98.6	0.1	0.3	0.3	<.1	0.7	7	1	8	6	12.2	12.6	0.8	8.5	71.4	71.8	58.2	46.3	58.2	37.8	50.7
District 3	398,813	96.2	1.1	1.6	0.3	<.1	0.8	4	6	3	3	12.4	12.6	7.8	10.7	75.1	77.7	60.8	58.4	66.4	22.7	56.9
District 4	410,455	90.6	3.3	3.1	0.7	<.1	2.2	2	7	2	1	12.8	12.2	24.2	29.3	75.1	77.7	60.8	50.0	64.1	31.7	58.9
District 5	434,263	87.0	7.2	2.6	1.7	<.1	1.5	1	8	1	2	13.5	12.4	54.8	20.4	79.4	83.4	60.4	59.7	58.4	28.7	65.7
District 6	382,305	96.7	1.0	1.1	0.5	<.1	0.7	8	5	4	5	11.9	12.1	6.7	8.6	69.9	70.4	61.2	54.7	64.7	19.7	54.9
District 7	394,926	97.2	0.1	0.4	1.7	<.1	0.6	6	4	7	7	12.3	12.6	1.0	7.4	72.2	72.8	60.0	59.3	57.0	45.2	53.6
District 8	398,011	97.3	0.4	0.3	1.7	<.1	0.4	5	3	5	8	12.4	12.7	2.6	5.2	72.8	73.3	70.2	49.9	58.8	34.7	58.6

Table C. – Voter Participation: November 3, 1992, General Election

County	Estimated Voting Age Population (VAP), 1992	Voter registration (REG)				Voter turnout										Percent drop-off, by office			
						Highest office				Maximum vote									
		Total	% contribution to state REG	% of 1992 VAP	Rank by % of 1992 VAP	Actual	Total	Office	% of 1992 VAP	Total	% contribution to state turnout	% of REG	Rank by % of REG	% of 1992 VAP	Rank by % 1992 VAP	President	Senator	Governor	Representative
Aitkin	9,396	10,590	0.3	112.7	3	7,603	7,559	P	80.4	7,603	0.3	71.8	74	80.9	4	0.6	–	–	2.4
Anoka	180,436	166,637	5.3	92.4	62	130,018	130,020	P	72.1	130,020	5.5	78.0	25	72.1	48	0.0	–	–	1.6
Becker	19,851	18,367	0.6	92.5	60	13,923	13,702	P	69.0	13,923	0.6	75.8	42	70.1	63	1.6	–	–	4.3
Beltrami	24,511	22,205	0.7	90.6	71	16,162	15,987	P	65.2	16,162	0.7	72.8	68	65.9	83	1.1	–	–	3.8
Benton	22,311	20,106	0.6	90.1	72	14,617	14,371	P	64.4	14,617	0.6	72.7	69	65.5	84	1.7	–	–	8.2
Big Stone	4,458	4,100	0.1	92.0	63	3,455	3,420	P	76.7	3,455	0.1	84.3	4	77.5	12	1.0	–	–	3.3
Blue Earth	40,634	41,470	1.3	102.1	13	28,064	27,847	P	68.5	28,064	1.2	67.7	84	69.1	70	0.8	–	–	3.2
Brown	19,257	19,087	0.6	99.1	27	13,830	13,621	P	70.7	13,830	0.6	72.5	71	71.8	49	1.5	–	–	2.8
Carlton	21,308	19,857	0.6	93.2	57	14,919	14,747	P	69.2	14,919	0.6	75.1	50	70.0	64	1.2	–	–	2.3
Carver	35,794	35,476	1.1	99.1	28	26,820	26,604	P	74.3	26,820	1.1	75.6	43	74.9	25	0.8	–	–	4.7
Cass	16,223	16,549	0.5	102.0	15	12,328	12,197	P	75.2	12,328	0.5	74.5	60	76.0	19	1.1	–	–	4.0
Chippewa	9,457	8,900	0.3	94.1	52	6,724	6,617	P	70.0	6,724	0.3	75.6	45	71.1	57	1.6	–	–	2.4
Chisago	22,307	22,756	0.7	102.0	14	17,177	17,119	P	76.7	17,177	0.7	75.5	47	77.0	15	0.3	–	–	3.3
Clay	36,709	33,938	1.1	92.5	61	23,745	23,478	P	64.0	23,745	1.0	70.0	80	64.7	85	1.1	–	–	5.8
Clearwater	5,919	5,068	0.2	85.6	86	3,806	3,758	P	63.5	3,806	0.2	75.1	51	64.3	86	1.3	–	–	2.3
Cook	2,927	3,482	0.1	119.0	1	2,628	2,618	P	89.4	2,628	0.1	75.5	48	89.8	1	0.4	–	–	2.7
Cottonwood	9,129	9,344	0.3	102.4	12	6,701	6,651	P	72.9	6,701	0.3	71.7	75	73.4	33	0.7	–	–	1.7
Crow Wing	32,945	32,581	1.0	98.9	29	24,779	24,539	P	74.5	24,779	1.0	76.1	37	75.2	23	1.0	–	–	3.7
Dakota	213,599	206,967	6.6	96.9	38	157,365	157,080	P	73.5	157,365	6.7	76.0	38	73.7	30	0.2	–	–	4.9
Dodge	11,084	10,746	0.3	97.0	35	8,027	7,972	P	71.9	8,027	0.3	74.7	59	72.4	43	0.7	–	–	2.4
Douglas	21,062	20,196	0.6	95.9	42	15,949	15,859	P	75.3	15,949	0.7	79.0	16	75.7	21	0.6	–	–	4.3
Faribault	12,101	11,432	0.4	94.5	49	9,245	9,146	P	75.6	9,245	0.4	80.9	8	76.4	17	1.1	–	–	1.8
Fillmore	14,944	13,953	0.4	93.4	56	10,732	10,658	P	71.3	10,732	0.5	76.9	32	71.8	50	0.7	–	–	1.5
Freeborn	24,103	23,012	0.7	95.5	44	17,973	17,813	P	73.9	17,973	0.8	78.1	21	74.6	28	0.9	–	–	3.9
Goodhue	29,885	26,540	0.8	88.8	80	21,593	21,250	P	71.1	21,593	0.9	81.4	6	72.3	46	1.6	–	–	3.6
Grant	4,507	5,257	0.2	116.6	2	3,688	3,666	P	81.3	3,688	0.2	70.2	79	81.8	3	0.6	–	–	2.1
Hennepin	809,508	790,678	25.2	97.7	33	588,335	586,619	P	72.5	588,335	24.9	74.4	61	72.7	39	0.3	–	–	4.2
Houston	13,349	13,125	0.4	98.3	31	10,547	10,451	P	78.3	10,547	0.4	80.4	11	79.0	7	0.9	–	–	2.5
Hubbard	11,177	11,397	0.4	102.0	17	8,660	8,589	P	76.8	8,660	0.4	76.0	40	77.5	13	0.8	–	–	2.3
Isanti	18,640	17,677	0.6	94.8	47	13,458	13,366	P	71.7	13,458	0.6	76.1	34	72.2	47	0.7	–	–	2.7
Itasca	29,643	27,100	0.9	91.4	64	21,602	20,838	P	70.3	21,602	0.9	79.7	14	72.9	37	3.5	–	–	5.5
Jackson	8,266	8,027	0.3	97.1	34	6,302	6,252	P	75.6	6,302	0.3	78.5	17	76.2	18	0.8	–	–	2.2
Kanabec	9,232	8,413	0.3	91.1	66	6,313	6,288	P	68.1	6,313	0.3	75.0	53	68.4	75	0.4	–	–	2.6
Kandiyohi	28,086	25,637	0.8	91.3	65	19,742	19,656	P	70.0	19,742	0.8	77.0	30	70.3	61	0.4	–	–	1.6
Kittson	4,146	4,407	0.1	106.3	5	3,028	2,984	P	72.0	3,028	0.1	68.7	83	73.0	35	1.5	–	–	1.8
Koochiching	12,049	9,995	0.3	83.0	87	7,500	7,465	P	62.0	7,500	0.3	75.0	54	62.2	87	0.5	–	–	2.7
Lac qui Parle	6,362	6,480	0.2	101.9	19	5,003	4,968	P	78.1	5,003	0.2	77.2	28	78.6	8	0.7	–	–	2.5
Lake	7,534	7,957	0.3	105.6	7	6,384	6,357	P	84.4	6,384	0.3	80.2	12	84.7	2	0.4	–	–	2.0
Lake of the Woods	3,015	2,623	<.1	87.0	85	2,221	2,198	P	72.9	2,221	<.1	84.7	2	73.7	31	1.0	–	–	3.1
Le Sueur	16,592	16,923	0.5	102.0	16	12,059	11,954	P	72.0	12,059	0.5	71.3	76	72.7	38	0.9	–	–	2.0
Lincoln	4,953	4,963	0.2	100.2	22	3,680	3,636	P	73.4	3,680	0.2	74.1	63	74.3	29	1.2	–	–	2.9
Lyon	17,792	17,791	0.6	100.0	25	12,432	12,324	P	69.3	12,432	0.5	69.9	81	69.9	66	0.9	–	–	1.8
McLeod	23,354	20,972	0.7	89.8	74	15,526	15,347	P	65.7	15,526	0.7	74.0	65	66.5	82	1.2	–	–	3.7
Mahnomen	3,478	3,566	0.1	102.5	11	2,403	2,389	P	68.7	2,403	0.1	67.4	85	69.1	69	0.6	–	–	1.7
Marshall	7,735	6,855	0.2	88.6	81	5,774	5,803	P	75.0	5,803	0.2	84.7	3	75.0	24	0.0	–	–	1.5
Martin	16,582	14,656	0.5	88.4	82	11,697	11,609	P	70.0	11,697	0.5	79.8	13	70.5	60	0.8	–	–	2.5
Meeker	14,978	14,771	0.5	98.6	30	10,611	10,540	P	70.4	10,611	0.4	71.8	73	70.8	59	0.7	–	–	2.3
Mille Lacs	13,452	13,038	0.4	96.9	37	9,624	9,154	P	68.0	9,624	0.4	73.8	66	71.5	53	4.9	–	–	6.4
Morrison	20,748	19,441	0.6	93.7	54	14,565	14,442	P	69.6	14,565	0.6	74.9	56	70.2	62	0.8	–	–	2.6
Mower	27,386	26,270	0.8	95.9	41	20,507	20,210	P	73.8	20,507	0.9	78.1	24	74.9	26	1.4	–	–	1.6
Murray	6,800	6,500	0.2	95.6	43	5,262	5,213	P	76.7	5,262	0.2	81.0	7	77.4	14	0.9	–	–	1.9
Nicollet	20,573	20,614	0.7	100.2	23	15,084	15,039	P	73.1	15,084	0.6	73.2	67	73.3	34	0.3	–	–	2.8
Nobles	14,492	12,973	0.4	89.5	77	10,128	9,930	P	68.5	10,128	0.4	78.1	23	69.9	65	2.0	–	–	3.7
Norman	5,736	5,476	0.2	95.5	45	4,162	4,121	P	71.8	4,162	0.2	76.0	39	72.6	40	1.0	–	–	2.3
Olmsted	79,718	76,665	2.4	96.2	39	56,863	56,662	P	71.1	56,863	2.4	74.2	62	71.3	54	0.4	–	–	2.5
Otter Tail	37,465	35,310	1.1	94.2	50	26,874	26,670	P	71.2	26,874	1.1	76.1	36	71.7	51	0.8	–	–	2.2
Pennington	9,463	8,591	0.3	90.8	69	6,450	6,359	P	67.2	6,450	0.3	75.1	52	68.2	76	1.4	–	–	2.5
Pine	15,732	15,377	0.5	97.9	32	10,878	10,813	P	68.7	10,878	0.5	70.7	78	69.1	68	0.6	–	–	2.5
Pipestone	7,387	6,466	0.2	87.5	84	5,263	5,170	P	70.0	5,263	0.2	81.4	5	71.2	56	1.8	–	–	5.2
Polk	22,957	20,207	0.6	88.0	83	15,318	14,934	P	65.1	15,318	0.6	75.8	41	66.7	81	2.5	–	–	3.1
Pope	7,735	7,931	0.3	102.5	10	6,038	5,970	P	77.2	6,038	0.3	76.1	35	78.1	9	1.1	–	–	2.5
Ramsey	368,353	333,718	10.6	90.6	70	245,462	251,915	P	68.4	251,915	10.7	75.5	46	68.4	74	0.0	–	–	3.7
Red Lake	3,112	3,212	0.1	103.2	8	2,230	2,201	P	70.7	2,230	<.1	69.4	82	71.7	52	1.3	–	–	2.1
Redwood	12,198	11,111	0.4	91.1	67	8,954	8,913	P	73.1	8,954	0.4	80.6	10	73.4	32	0.5	–	–	2.2
Renville	12,377	11,584	0.4	93.6	55	8,966	8,920	P	72.1	8,966	0.4	77.4	27	72.4	42	0.5	–	–	0.6
Rice	36,118	32,496	1.0	90.0	73	24,444	24,113	P	66.8	24,444	1.0	75.2	49	67.7	77	1.4	–	–	7.9
Rock	6,931	7,110	0.2	102.6	9	5,375	5,338	P	77.0	5,375	0.2	75.6	44	77.6	11	0.7	–	–	2.9
Roseau	10,978	9,813	0.3	89.4	78	7,341	7,269	P	66.2	7,341	0.3	74.8	57	66.9	80	1.0	–	–	2.2
St. Louis	145,726	146,833	4.7	100.8	21	109,703	108,815	P	74.7	109,703	4.6	74.7	58	75.3	22	0.8	–	–	4.3
Scott	43,331	41,569	1.3	95.9	40	32,392	32,216	P	74.3	32,392	1.4	77.9	26	74.8	27	0.5	–	–	4.3

Table C. — **Voter Participation: November 3, 1992, General Election (cont)**

| County | Estimated Voting Age Population (VAP), 1992 | Voter registration (REG) | | | | Voter turnout | | | | | | | | | | | | | |
| | | Total | % contribution to state REG | % of 1992 VAP | Rank by % of 1992 VAP | Highest office | | | | Maximum vote | | | | | | Percent drop-off, by office | | | |
						Actual	Total	Office	% of 1992 VAP	Total	% contribution to state turnout	% of REG	Rank by % of REG	% of 1992 VAP	Rank by % 1992 VAP	President	Senator	Governor	Representative
Sherburne	31,824	28,513	0.9	89.6	76	23,028	21,841	P	68.6	23,028	1.0	80.8	9	72.4	44	5.2	-	-	9.0
Sibley	10,244	9,483	0.3	92.6	59	7,267	7,185	P	70.1	7,267	0.3	76.6	33	70.9	58	1.1	-	-	2.6
Stearns	86,619	82,454	2.6	95.2	46	59,657	59,340	P	68.5	59,657	2.5	72.4	72	68.9	72	2.0	-	-	4.9
Steele	22,110	20,550	0.7	92.9	58	16,116	15,789	P	71.4	16,116	0.7	78.4	19	72.9	36	2.0	-	-	2.9
Stevens	7,666	6,820	0.2	89.0	79	5,867	5,816	P	75.9	5,867	0.2	86.0	1	76.5	16	0.9	-	-	4.2
Swift	7,564	7,637	0.2	101.0	20	6,036	5,991	P	79.2	6,036	0.3	79.0	15	79.8	5	0.7	-	-	1.8
Todd	16,311	15,411	0.5	94.5	48	11,186	11,104	P	68.1	11,186	0.5	72.6	70	68.6	73	0.8	-	-	3.7
Traverse	3,149	3,208	0.1	101.9	18	2,505	2,484	.P	78.9	2,505	0.1	78.1	22	79.5	6	1.1	-	-	2.3
Wabasha	14,243	13,420	0.4	94.2	51	10,333	10,217	P	71.7	10,333	0.4	77.0	31	72.5	41	1.1	-	-	2.3
Wadena	9,345	9,908	0.3	106.0	6	6,446	6,398	P	68.5	6,446	0.3	65.1	86	69.0	71	0.7	-	-	2.6
Waseca	12,892	12,908	0.4	100.1	24	9,192	9,006	P	69.9	9,192	0.4	71.2	77	71.3	55	2.0	-	-	2.1
Washington	109,772	109,158	3.5	99.4	26	85,684	85,499	P	77.9	85,684	3.6	78.5	18	78.1	10	0.2	-	-	2.9
Watonwan	8,343	7,584	0.2	90.9	68	5,617	5,578	P	66.9	5,617	0.2	74.1	64	67.3	78	0.7	-	-	2.6
Wilkin	5,284	4,737	0.2	89.6	75	3,550	3,510	P	66.4	3,550	0.2	74.9	55	67.2	79	1.1	-	-	6.1
Winona	35,349	38,307	1.2	108.4	4	24,666	24,518	P	69.4	24,666	1.0	64.4	87	69.8	67	0.6	-	-	2.7
Wright	48,941	45,874	1.5	93.7	53	35,364	35,160	P	71.8	35,364	1.5	77.1	29	72.3	45	0.6	-	-	3.9
Yellow Medicine	8,248	7,995	0.3	96.9	36	6,251	6,193	P	75.1	6,251	0.3	78.2	20	75.8	20	0.9	-	-	1.1
MINNESOTA	3,278,000	3,138,901	100.0	95.8		2,355,796	2,347,948		71.6	2,362,280	100.0	75.3		72.1		0.6	-	-	3.7

Table E. — Vote for President: November 3, 1992, General Election

County	Total	Clinton (DEM)	Bush (REP)	Perot (IND)	Other	Plurality Total	Party	DEM	REP	IND	Other	Rank DEM	Rank REP	Rank IND	Total	DEM	REP	IND	DEM	REP
Aitkin	7,559	3,400	2,151	1,951	57	1,249	D	45.0	28.5	25.8	0.8	16	78	44	0.3	0.3	0.3	0.3	61.3	38.7
Anoka	130,020	54,621	39,458	35,140	801	15,163	D	42.0	30.3	27.0	0.6	28	69	31	5.5	5.3	5.3	6.2	58.1	41.9
Becker	13,702	4,958	5,430	3,238	76	472	R	36.2	39.6	23.6	0.6	64	6	62	0.6	0.5	0.7	0.6	47.7	52.3
Beltrami	15,987	7,210	5,204	3,473	100	2,006	D	45.1	32.6	21.7	0.6	15	55	74	0.7	0.7	0.7	0.6	58.1	41.9
Benton	14,371	5,156	5,053	4,048	114	103	D	35.9	35.2	28.2	0.8	68	33	24	0.6	0.5	0.7	0.7	50.5	49.5
Big Stone	3,420	1,610	1,052	740	18	558	D	47.1	30.8	21.6	0.5	9	66	75	0.1	0.2	0.1	0.1	60.5	39.5
Blue Earth	27,847	11,531	8,813	7,299	204	2,718	D	41.4	31.6	26.2	0.7	32	60	45	1.2	1.1	1.2	1.3	56.7	43.3
Brown	13,621	4,278	5,390	3,845	108	1,112	R	31.4	39.6	28.2	0.8	85	7	22	0.6	0.4	0.7	0.7	44.2	55.8
Carlton	14,747	7,736	3,922	3,005	84	3,814	D	52.5	26.6	20.4	0.6	3	82	80	0.6	0.8	0.5	0.5	66.4	33.6
Carver	26,604	8,349	10,201	7,942	112	1,852	R	31.4	38.3	29.9	0.4	86	11	9	1.1	0.8	1.4	1.4	45.0	55.0
Cass	12,197	4,901	4,276	2,939	81	625	D	40.2	35.1	24.1	0.7	40	34	64	0.5	0.5	0.6	0.5	53.4	46.6
Chippewa	6,617	2,929	2,143	1,505	40	786	D	44.3	32.4	22.7	0.6	17	56	68	0.3	0.3	0.3	0.3	57.7	42.3
Chisago	17,119	7,077	4,813	5,098	131	1,979	D	41.3	28.1	29.8	0.8	33	79	10	0.7	0.7	0.6	0.9	59.5	40.5
Clay	23,478	9,845	9,666	3,835	132	179	D	41.9	41.2	16.3	0.6	29	4	87	1.0	1.0	1.3	0.7	50.5	49.5
Clearwater	3,758	1,587	1,315	841	15	272	D	42.2	35.0	22.4	0.4	27	36	73	0.2	0.2	0.2	0.1	54.7	45.3
Cook	2,618	1,005	878	704	31	127	D	38.4	33.5	26.9	1.2	49	49	32	0.1	<.1	0.1	0.1	53.4	46.6
Cottonwood	6,651	2,382	2,481	1,749	39	99	R	35.8	37.3	26.3	0.6	70	23	39	0.3	0.2	0.3	0.3	49.0	51.0
Crow Wing	24,539	8,896	9,112	6,367	164	216	R	36.3	37.1	25.9	0.7	63	25	46	1.0	0.9	1.2	1.1	49.4	50.6
Dakota	157,080	63,660	52,312	40,244	864	11,348	D	40.5	33.3	25.6	0.6	35	50	48	6.7	6.2	7.0	7.2	54.9	45.1
Dodge	7,972	2,620	3,049	2,231	72	429	R	32.9	38.2	28.0	0.9	80	14	26	0.3	0.3	0.4	0.4	46.2	53.8
Douglas	15,859	5,252	6,356	4,138	113	1,104	R	33.1	40.1	26.1	0.7	79	5	41	0.7	0.5	0.8	0.7	45.2	54.8
Faribault	9,146	3,339	3,439	2,322	46	100	R	36.5	37.6	25.4	0.5	61	20	49	0.4	0.3	0.5	0.4	49.3	50.7
Fillmore	10,658	3,977	3,583	3,011	87	394	D	37.3	33.6	28.3	0.8	55	46	21	0.5	0.4	0.5	0.5	52.6	47.4
Freeborn	17,813	7,759	5,089	4,878	87	2,670	D	43.6	28.6	27.4	0.5	20	76	28	0.8	0.8	0.7	0.9	60.4	39.6
Goodhue	21,250	7,916	7,321	5,790	223	595	D	37.3	34.5	27.2	1.0	56	41	30	0.9	0.8	1.0	1.0	52.0	48.0
Grant	3,666	1,561	1,201	885	19	360	D	42.6	32.8	24.1	0.5	24	54	59	0.2	0.2	0.2	0.2	56.5	43.5
Hennepin	586,619	278,648	179,581	123,659	4,731	99,067	D	47.5	30.6	21.1	0.8	7	68	79	25.0	27.3	24.0	22.0	60.8	39.2
Houston	10,451	3,744	3,853	2,697	157	109	R	35.8	36.9	25.8	1.5	69	26	45	0.4	0.4	0.5	0.3	49.3	50.7
Hubbard	8,589	3,362	3,227	1,949	51	135	D	39.1	37.6	22.7	0.6	46	21	69	0.4	0.3	0.4	0.3	51.0	49.0
Isanti	13,366	5,386	3,988	3,898	94	1,398	D	40.3	29.8	29.2	0.7	36	70	14	0.6	0.5	0.5	0.7	57.5	42.5
Itasca	20,838	9,621	5,952	5,147	118	3,669	D	46.2	28.6	24.7	0.6	12	77	56	0.9	0.9	0.8	0.9	61.8	38.2
Jackson	6,252	2,481	1,824	1,918	29	563	D	39.7	29.2	30.7	0.5	43	73	4	0.3	0.2	0.2	0.3	57.6	42.4
Kanabec	6,288	2,532	1,876	1,836	44	656	D	40.3	29.8	29.2	0.7	37	71	13	0.3	0.2	0.3	0.3	57.4	42.6
Kandiyohi	19,656	7,914	6,784	4,869	89	1,130	D	40.3	34.5	24.8	0.5	38	40	54	0.8	0.8	0.9	0.9	53.8	46.2
Kittson	2,984	1,307	1,098	558	21	209	D	43.8	36.8	18.7	0.7	19	28	85	0.1	0.1	0.1	<.1	54.3	45.7
Koochiching	7,465	3,474	1,954	1,993	44	1,481	D	46.5	26.2	26.7	0.6	10	84	34	0.3	0.3	0.3	0.4	64.0	36.0
Lac qui Parle	4,968	2,342	1,435	1,163	28	907	D	47.1	28.9	23.4	0.6	8	75	65	0.2	0.2	0.2	0.2	62.0	38.0
Lake	6,357	3,415	1,465	1,437	40	1,950	D	53.7	23.0	22.6	0.6	2	86	71	0.3	0.3	0.2	0.3	70.0	30.0
Lake of the Woods	2,198	794	762	629	13	32	D	36.1	34.7	28.6	0.6	66	38	19	<.1	<.1	0.1	0.1	51.0	49.0
Le Sueur	11,954	4,662	3,858	3,363	71	804	D	39.0	32.3	28.1	0.6	47	57	25	0.5	0.5	0.5	0.6	54.7	45.3
Lincoln	3,636	1,555	1,084	967	30	471	D	42.8	29.8	26.6	0.8	23	72	36	0.2	0.2	0.1	0.2	58.9	41.1
Lyon	12,324	4,481	4,591	3,180	72	110	R	36.4	37.3	25.8	0.6	62	24	46	0.5	0.4	0.6	0.6	49.4	50.6
McLeod	15,347	4,919	5,422	4,933	73	489	R	32.1	35.3	32.1	0.5	83	32	2	0.7	0.5	0.7	0.9	47.6	52.4
Mahnomen	2,389	1,035	854	483	17	181	D	43.3	35.7	20.2	0.7	21	30	81	0.1	0.1	0.1	<.1	54.8	45.2
Marshall	5,803	2,309	2,136	1,306	52	173	D	39.8	36.8	22.5	0.9	42	27	72	0.2	0.2	0.3	0.2	51.9	48.1
Martin	11,609	4,019	4,438	3,089	63	419	R	34.6	38.2	26.6	0.5	74	16	35	0.5	0.4	0.6	0.5	47.5	52.5
Meeker	10,540	3,861	3,497	3,120	62	364	D	36.6	33.2	29.6	0.6	57	52	11	0.4	0.4	0.5	0.6	52.5	47.5
Mille Lacs	9,154	3,648	2,814	2,615	77	834	D	39.9	30.7	28.6	0.8	41	67	20	0.4	0.4	0.4	0.5	56.5	43.5
Morrison	14,442	5,588	5,038	3,710	106	550	D	38.7	34.9	25.7	0.7	48	37	47	0.6	0.5	0.7	0.7	52.6	47.4
Mower	20,210	9,935	5,147	5,001	127	4,788	D	49.2	25.5	24.7	0.6	6	85	55	0.9	1.0	0.7	0.9	65.9	34.1
Murray	5,213	1,993	1,609	1,588	23	384	D	38.2	30.9	30.5	0.4	51	64	6	0.2	0.2	0.2	0.3	55.3	44.7
Nicollet	15,039	6,055	5,091	3,799	94	964	D	40.3	33.9	25.3	0.6	39	45	50	0.6	0.6	0.7	0.7	54.3	45.7
Nobles	9,930	3,756	3,548	2,586	40	208	D	37.8	35.7	26.0	0.4	52	31	42	0.4	0.4	0.5	0.5	51.4	48.6
Norman	4,121	1,784	1,541	776	20	243	D	43.3	37.4	18.8	0.5	22	22	84	0.2	0.2	0.2	0.1	53.7	46.3
Olmsted	56,662	19,039	23,404	13,806	413	4,365	R	33.6	41.3	24.4	0.7	78	3	58	2.4	1.9	3.1	2.5	44.9	55.1
Otter Tail	26,670	9,176	11,074	6,274	146	1,898	R	34.4	41.5	23.5	0.5	75	2	63	1.1	0.9	1.5	1.1	45.3	54.7
Pennington	6,359	2,578	2,155	1,598	28	423	D	40.5	33.9	25.1	0.4	34	43	51	0.3	0.3	0.3	0.3	54.5	45.5
Pine	10,813	4,929	2,841	2,952	91	1,977	D	45.6	26.3	27.3	0.8	13	83	29	0.5	0.5	0.4	0.5	63.4	36.6
Pipestone	5,170	1,773	1,953	1,429	15	180	R	34.3	37.8	27.6	0.3	76	18	27	0.2	0.2	0.3	0.3	47.6	52.4
Polk	14,934	5,850	5,817	3,176	91	33	D	39.2	39.0	21.3	0.6	45	8	78	0.6	0.6	0.8	0.6	50.1	49.9
Pope	5,970	2,619	1,886	1,390	75	733	D	43.9	31.6	23.3	1.3	18	61	67	0.3	0.3	0.3	0.2	58.1	41.9
Ramsey	251,915	130,932	68,206	50,757	2,020	62,726	D	52.0	27.1	20.1	0.8	4	80	82	10.7	12.8	9.1	9.0	65.7	34.3
Red Lake	2,201	1,020	691	472	18	329	D	46.3	31.4	21.4	0.8	11	62	76	<.1	<.1	<.1	<.1	59.6	40.4
Redwood	8,913	2,740	3,408	2,710	55	668	R	30.7	38.2	30.4	0.6	87	15	7	0.4	0.3	0.5	0.5	44.6	55.4
Renville	8,920	3,414	2,852	2,598	56	562	D	38.3	32.0	29.1	0.6	50	59	15	0.4	0.3	0.4	0.5	54.5	45.5
Rice	24,113	10,908	7,015	6,057	133	3,893	D	45.2	29.1	25.1	0.6	14	74	52	1.0	1.1	0.9	1.1	60.9	39.1
Rock	5,338	2,006	2,065	1,244	23	59	R	37.6	38.7	23.3	0.4	54	10	66	0.2	0.2	0.3	0.2	49.3	50.7
Roseau	7,269	2,346	2,785	2,099	39	439	R	32.3	38.3	28.9	0.5	82	13	17	0.3	0.2	0.4	0.4	45.7	54.3
St. Louis	108,815	61,813	24,579	21,714	709	37,234	D	56.8	22.6	20.0	0.7	1	87	83	4.6	6.1	3.3	3.9	71.5	28.5
Scott	32,216	11,225	10,936	9,881	174	289	D	34.8	33.9	30.7	0.5	73	42	5	1.4	1.1	1.5	1.8	50.7	49.3

Table E. — Vote for President: November 3, 1992, General Election (cont)

County	Total	Clinton (DEM)	Bush (REP)	Perot (IND)	Other	Plurality Total	Party	DEM	REP	IND	Other	Rank DEM	Rank REP	Rank IND	Total	DEM	REP	IND	DEM	REP
Sherburne	21,841	7,843	7,339	6,534	125	504	D	35.9	33.6	29.9	0.6	67	47	8	0.9	0.8	1.0	1.2	51.7	48.3
Sibley	7,185	2,421	2,315	2,407	42	14	D	33.7	32.2	33.5	0.6	77	58	1	0.3	0.2	0.3	0.4	51.1	48.9
Stearns	59,340	21,451	22,502	14,834	553	1,051	R	36.1	37.9	25.0	0.9	65	17	53	2.5	2.1	3.0	2.6	48.8	51.2
Steele	15,789	5,152	5,964	4,542	131	812	R	32.6	37.8	28.8	0.8	81	19	18	0.7	0.5	0.8	0.8	46.3	53.7
Stevens	5,816	2,466	2,229	1,086	35	237	D	42.4	38.3	18.7	0.6	25	12	86	0.2	0.2	0.3	0.2	52.5	47.5
Swift	5,991	2,980	1,603	1,359	49	1,377	D	49.7	26.8	22.7	0.8	5	81	70	0.3	0.3	0.2	0.2	65.0	35.0
Todd	11,104	4,059	3,990	2,976	79	69	D	36.6	35.9	26.8	0.7	60	29	33	0.5	0.4	0.5	0.5	50.4	49.6
Traverse	2,484	1,053	841	582	8	212	D	42.4	33.9	23.4	0.3	26	44	64	0.1	0.1	0.1	0.1	55.6	44.4
Wabasha	10,217	3,736	3,397	3,012	72	339	D	36.6	33.2	29.5	0.7	59	51	12	0.4	0.4	0.5	0.5	52.4	47.6
Wadena	6,398	2,340	2,492	1,535	31	152	R	36.6	38.9	24.0	0.5	58	9	61	0.3	0.2	0.3	0.3	48.4	51.6
Waseca	9,006	3,146	3,118	2,621	121	28	D	34.9	34.6	29.1	1.3	72	39	16	0.4	0.3	0.4	0.5	50.2	49.8
Washington	85,499	35,820	26,568	22,585	526	9,252	D	41.9	31.1	26.4	0.6	30	63	38	3.6	3.5	3.6	4.0	57.4	42.6
Watonwan	5,578	2,100	1,871	1,574	33	229	D	37.6	33.5	28.2	0.6	53	48	23	0.2	0.2	0.3	0.3	52.9	47.1
Wilkin	3,510	1,122	1,626	748	14	504	R	32.0	46.3	21.3	0.4	84	1	77	0.1	0.1	0.2	0.1	40.8	59.2
Winona	24,518	9,707	8,585	5,993	233	1,122	D	39.6	35.0	24.4	1.0	44	35	57	1.0	1.0	1.1	1.1	53.1	46.9
Wright	35,160	12,465	11,650	10,829	216	815	D	35.5	33.1	30.8	0.6	71	53	3	1.5	1.2	1.6	1.9	51.7	48.3
Yellow Medicine	6,193	2,593	1,909	1,645	46	684	D	41.9	30.8	26.6	0.7	31	65	37	0.3	0.3	0.3	0.3	57.6	42.4
MINNESOTA	**2,347,948**	**1,020,997**	**747,841**	**562,506**	**16,604**	**273,156**	**D**	**43.5**	**31.9**	**24.0**	**0.7**				**100.0**	**100.0**	**100.0**	**100.0**	**57.7**	**42.3**

Minnesota 503

Table H. — Vote for U.S. Representative in Congress: November 3, 1992, General Election

Congressional district and county	Total	Democrat (DEM)	Republican (REP)	Other	Plurality Total	Plurality Party	Percent of total vote DEM	REP	Other	Rank within district DEM	REP	Other	Percent contribution to district vote Total	DEM	REP	Other
District 1	**279,430**	**206,369**	**72,367**	**694**	**134,002**	**D**	**73.9**	**25.9**	**0.2**				**100.0**	**100.0**	**100.0**	**100.0**
Blue Earth	27,173	19,555	7,567	51	11,988	D	72.0	27.8	0.2	12	6	5	9.7	9.5	10.5	7.3
Dakota (pt)	3,751	2,581	1,145	25	1,436	D	68.8	30.5	0.7	16	2	3	1.3	1.3	1.6	3.6
Dodge	7,831	5,867	1,939	25	3,928	D	74.9	24.8	0.3	7	11	4	2.8	2.8	2.7	3.6
Faribault	9,079	6,677	2,402	0	4,275	D	73.5	26.5	0.0	10	8	15	3.2	3.2	3.3	0.0
Fillmore	10,574	8,256	2,310	8	5,946	D	78.1	21.8	<.1	3	15	12	3.8	4.0	3.2	1.2
Freeborn	17,269	13,524	3,623	122	9,901	D	78.3	21.0	0.7	2	16	2	6.2	6.6	5.0	17.6
Goodhue	20,822	15,304	5,513	5	9,791	D	73.5	26.5	<.1	11	7	13	7.5	7.4	7.6	0.7
Houston	10,282	7,302	2,971	9	4,331	D	71.0	28.9	<.1	14	4	11	3.7	3.5	4.1	1.3
Le Sueur	11,812	8,904	2,895	13	6,009	D	75.4	24.5	0.1	6	12	10	4.2	4.3	4.0	1.9
Mower	20,186	16,526	3,656	4	12,870	D	81.9	18.1	<.1	1	17	14	7.2	8.0	5.1	0.6
Olmsted	55,448	39,505	15,856	87	23,649	D	71.2	28.6	0.2	13	5	9	19.8	19.1	21.9	12.5
Rice	22,523	17,132	5,113	278	12,019	D	76.1	22.7	1.2	4	14	1	8.1	8.3	7.1	40.1
Scott (pt)	3,939	2,452	1,480	7	972	D	62.2	37.6	0.2	17	1	7	1.4	1.2	2.0	1.0
Steele	15,641	11,713	3,928	0	7,785	D	74.9	25.1	0.0	9	9	16	5.6	5.7	5.4	0.0
Wabasha	10,100	7,564	2,519	17	5,045	D	74.9	24.9	0.2	8	10	8	3.6	3.7	3.5	2.4
Waseca	9,002	6,831	2,171	0	4,660	D	75.9	24.1	0.0	5	13	17	3.2	3.3	3.0	0.0
Winona	23,998	16,676	7,279	43	9,397	D	69.5	30.3	0.2	15	3	6	8.6	8.1	10.1	6.2
District 2[1]	**276,403**	**132,156**	**131,587**	**12,660**	**569**	**D**	**47.8**	**47.6**	**4.6**				**100.0**	**100.0**	**100.0**	**100.0**
Big Stone	3,341	1,845	1,349	147	496	D	55.2	40.4	4.4	6	23	10	1.2	1.4	1.0	1.2
Brown	13,446	5,701	7,141	604	1,440	R	42.4	53.1	4.5	23	6	9	4.9	4.3	5.4	4.8
Carver	25,569	10,179	13,506	1,884	3,327	R	39.8	52.8	7.4	24	7	2	9.3	7.7	10.3	14.9
Chippewa	6,562	4,126	2,297	139	1,829	D	62.9	35.0	2.1	1	27	26	2.4	3.1	1.7	1.1
Cottonwood	6,586	3,014	3,332	240	318	R	45.8	50.6	3.6	18	9	13	2.4	2.3	2.5	1.9
Hennepin (pt)	2,962	1,152	1,580	230	428	R	38.9	53.3	7.8	25	5	1	1.1	0.9	1.2	1.8
Jackson	6,162	3,385	2,589	188	796	D	54.9	42.0	3.1	8	21	17	2.2	2.6	2.0	1.5
Kandiyohi	19,429	10,689	8,150	590	2,539	D	55.0	41.9	3.0	7	22	18	7.0	8.1	6.2	4.7
Lac qui Parle	4,878	2,855	1,910	113	945	D	58.5	39.2	2.3	3	25	24	1.8	2.2	1.5	0.9
Lincoln	3,572	1,559	1,925	88	366	R	43.6	53.9	2.5	21	4	23	1.3	1.2	1.5	0.7
Lyon	12,203	4,236	7,729	238	3,493	R	34.7	63.3	2.0	26	1	27	4.4	3.2	5.9	1.9
McLeod	14,954	6,545	7,560	849	1,015	R	43.8	50.6	5.7	20	10	5	5.4	5.0	5.7	6.7
Martin	11,404	5,211	5,727	466	516	R	45.7	50.2	4.1	19	11	11	4.1	3.9	4.4	3.7
Meeker	10,369	5,252	4,610	507	642	D	50.7	44.5	4.9	10	18	7	3.8	4.0	3.5	4.0
Murray	5,163	2,415	2,635	113	220	R	46.8	51.0	2.2	17	8	25	1.9	1.8	2.0	0.9
Nicollet	14,659	7,424	6,652	583	772	D	50.6	45.4	4.0	11	15	12	5.3	5.6	5.1	4.6
Nobles	9,753	5,387	4,103	263	1,284	D	55.2	42.1	2.7	5	20	21	3.5	4.1	3.1	2.1
Pipestone	4,990	2,138	2,692	160	554	R	42.8	53.9	3.2	22	3	15	1.8	1.6	2.0	1.3
Redwood	8,753	3,016	5,469	268	2,453	R	34.5	62.5	3.1	27	2	16	3.2	2.3	4.2	2.1
Renville[1]	8,910	4,434	4,040	436	394	D	49.8	45.3	4.9	12	16	6	3.2	3.4	3.1	3.4
Rock	5,218	2,475	2,605	138	130	R	47.4	49.9	2.6	16	12	22	1.9	1.9	2.0	1.1
Scott (pt)	19,239	9,153	8,807	1,279	346	D	47.6	45.8	6.6	15	14	4	7.0	6.9	6.7	10.1
Sibley	7,078	3,444	3,294	340	150	D	48.7	46.5	4.8	14	13	8	2.6	2.6	2.5	2.7
Swift	5,927	3,589	2,165	173	1,424	D	60.6	36.5	2.9	2	26	19	2.1	2.7	1.6	1.4
Watonwan	5,471	2,846	2,441	184	405	D	52.0	44.6	3.4	9	17	14	2.0	2.2	1.9	1.5
Wright (pt)	33,623	16,543	14,816	2,264	1,727	D	49.2	44.1	6.7	13	19	3	12.2	12.5	11.3	17.9
Yellow Medicine	6,182	3,543	2,463	176	1,080	D	57.3	39.8	2.8	4	24	20	2.2	2.7	1.9	1.4
District 3	**314,731**	**104,606**	**200,240**	**9,885**	**95,634**	**R**	**33.2**	**63.6**	**3.1**				**100.0**	**100.0**	**100.0**	**100.0**
Dakota (pt)	129,798	46,561	79,258	3,979	32,697	R	35.9	61.1	3.1	2	3	4	41.2	44.5	39.6	40.3
Hennepin (pt)	157,835	46,460	106,421	4,954	59,961	R	29.4	67.4	3.1	4	1	3	50.1	44.4	53.1	50.1
Scott (pt)	7,818	2,558	4,983	277	2,425	R	32.7	63.7	3.5	3	2	1	2.5	2.4	2.5	2.8
Washington (pt)	19,280	9,027	9,578	675	551	R	46.8	49.7	3.5	1	4	2	6.1	8.6	4.8	6.8
District 4	**277,956**	**159,796**	**101,744**	**16,416**	**58,052**	**D**	**57.5**	**36.6**	**5.9**				**100.0**	**100.0**	**100.0**	**100.0**
Dakota (pt)	16,077	9,450	5,716	911	3,734	D	58.8	35.6	5.7	1	3	3	5.8	5.9	5.6	5.5
Ramsey	242,484	140,510	87,699	14,275	52,811	D	57.9	36.2	5.9	2	2	2	87.2	87.9	86.2	87.0
Washington (pt)	19,395	9,836	8,329	1,230	1,507	D	50.7	42.9	6.3	3	1	1	7.0	6.2	8.2	7.5
District 5	**277,094**	**174,139**	**77,093**	**25,862**	**97,046**	**D**	**62.8**	**27.8**	**9.3**				**100.0**	**100.0**	**100.0**	**100.0**
Hennepin (pt)	277,094	174,139	77,093	25,862	97,046	D	62.8	27.8	9.3	1	1	1	100.0	100.0	100.0	100.0
District 6	**301,023**	**100,016**	**133,564**	**67,443**	**33,548**	**R**	**33.2**	**44.4**	**22.4**				**100.0**	**100.0**	**100.0**	**100.0**
Anoka	127,966	45,995	54,064	27,907	8,069	R	35.9	42.2	21.8	1	5	3	42.5	46.0	40.5	41.4
Hennepin (pt)	125,959	38,811	57,735	29,413	18,924	R	30.8	45.8	23.4	3	4	2	41.8	38.8	43.2	43.6
Sherburne (pt)	2,171	609	1,143	419	534	R	28.1	52.6	19.3	4	1	5	0.7	0.6	0.9	0.6
Washington (pt)	44,552	14,510	20,432	9,610	5,922	R	32.6	45.9	21.6	2	3	4	14.8	14.5	15.3	14.2
Wright (pt)	375	91	190	94	96	R	24.3	50.7	25.1	5	2	1	0.1	0.1	0.1	0.1
District 7	**265,524**	**133,886**	**130,396**	**1,242**	**3,490**	**D**	**50.4**	**49.1**	**0.5**				**100.0**	**100.0**	**100.0**	**100.0**
Becker	13,329	7,474	5,745	110	1,729	D	56.1	43.1	0.8	14	13	5	5.0	5.6	4.4	8.9
Beltrami	15,553	8,998	6,540	15	2,458	D	57.9	42.0	<.1	12	15	10	5.9	6.7	5.0	1.2
Benton (pt)	6,615	2,681	3,846	88	1,165	R	40.5	58.1	1.3	24	3	1	2.5	2.0	2.9	7.1
Clay	22,369	13,122	8,961	286	4,161	D	58.7	40.1	1.3	8	19	2	8.4	9.8	6.9	23.0
Clearwater	3,720	2,149	1,568	3	581	D	57.8	42.2	<.1	13	14	12	1.4	1.6	1.2	0.2
Douglas	15,258	6,813	8,357	88	1,544	R	44.7	54.8	0.6	23	4	6	5.7	5.1	6.4	7.1

[1]Does not include corrected vote of 335 in Renville County for independent candidate Bentz reported in published election results (Elections Division, Secretary of State, *Minnesota Election Results 1992*, Saint Paul, MN).

Table H. — Vote for U.S. Representative in Congress: November 3, 1992, General Election (cont)

Congressional district and county	Total	Democrat (DEM)	Republican (REP)	Other	Plurality Total	Party	Percent of total vote DEM	REP	Other	Rank within district DEM	REP	Other	Percent contribution to district vote Total	DEM	REP	Other
District 7 (cont)																
Grant	3,610	2,004	1,606	0	398	D	55.5	44.5	0.0	16	11	22	1.4	1.5	1.2	0.0
Hubbard	8,465	4,281	4,173	11	108	D	50.6	49.3	0.1	18	9	8	3.2	3.2	3.2	0.9
Kittson	2,975	1,976	999	0	977	D	66.4	33.6	0.0	3	24	23	1.1	1.5	0.8	0.0
Lake of the Woods	2,153	1,397	754	2	643	D	64.9	35.0	<.1	4	23	11	0.8	1.0	0.6	0.2
Mahnomen	2,363	1,371	991	1	380	D	58.0	41.9	<.1	11	16	17	0.9	1.0	0.8	0.1
Marshall	5,717	3,924	1,793	0	2,131	D	68.6	31.4	0.0	2	25	24	2.2	2.9	1.4	0.0
Morrison (pt)	11,342	4,185	7,152	5	2,967	R	36.9	63.1	<.1	26	1	16	4.3	3.1	5.5	0.4
Norman	4,068	2,542	1,514	12	1,028	D	62.5	37.2	0.3	6	21	7	1.5	1.9	1.2	1.0
Otter Tail	26,281	12,844	13,403	34	559	R	48.9	51.0	0.1	19	7	9	9.9	9.6	10.3	2.7
Pennington	6,287	3,998	2,289	0	1,709	D	63.6	36.4	0.0	5	22	25	2.4	3.0	1.8	0.0
Polk	14,836	8,681	6,154	1	2,527	D	58.5	41.5	<.1	9	18	21	5.6	6.5	4.7	0.1
Pope	5,889	3,167	2,721	1	446	D	53.8	46.2	<.1	17	10	20	2.2	2.4	2.1	0.1
Red Lake	2,183	1,554	628	1	926	D	71.2	28.8	<.1	1	26	15	0.8	1.2	0.5	0.1
Roseau	7,180	4,444	2,734	2	1,710	D	61.9	38.1	<.1	7	20	18	2.7	3.3	2.1	0.2
Stearns	56,725	21,967	34,223	535	12,256	R	38.7	60.3	0.9	25	2	4	21.4	16.4	26.2	43.1
Stevens	5,621	3,135	2,483	3	652	D	55.8	44.2	<.1	15	12	14	2.1	2.3	1.9	0.2
Todd	10,960	5,177	5,781	2	604	R	47.2	52.7	<.1	22	5	19	4.1	3.9	4.4	0.2
Traverse	2,413	1,403	1,010	0	393	D	58.1	41.9	0.0	10	17	26	0.9	1.0	0.8	0.0
Wadena	6,279	2,979	3,295	5	316	R	47.4	52.5	<.1	21	6	13	2.4	2.2	2.5	0.4
Wilkin	3,333	1,620	1,676	37	56	R	48.6	50.3	1.1	20	8	3	1.3	1.2	1.3	3.0
District 8	283,031	167,104	83,823	32,104	83,281	D	59.0	29.6	11.3				100.0	100.0	100.0	100.0
Aitkin	7,423	3,927	2,573	923	1,354	D	52.9	34.7	12.4	15	2	9	2.6	2.4	3.1	2.9
Benton (pt)	6,798	3,869	2,300	629	1,569	D	56.9	33.8	9.3	10	5	14	2.4	2.3	2.7	2.0
Carlton	14,574	8,723	3,839	2,012	4,884	D	59.9	26.3	13.8	5	14	3	5.1	5.2	4.6	6.3
Cass	11,829	6,384	4,027	1,418	2,357	D	54.0	34.0	12.0	12	3	12	4.2	3.8	4.8	4.4
Chisago	16,602	9,320	5,005	2,277	4,315	D	56.1	30.1	13.7	11	10	4	5.9	5.6	6.0	7.1
Cook	2,557	1,370	842	345	528	D	53.6	32.9	13.5	14	7	5	0.9	0.8	1.0	1.1
Crow Wing	23,852	12,789	8,089	2,974	4,700	D	53.6	33.9	12.5	13	4	8	8.4	7.7	9.7	9.3
Isanti	13,089	7,639	3,814	1,636	3,825	D	58.4	29.1	12.5	7	12	7	4.6	4.6	4.6	5.1
Itasca	20,420	11,638	6,444	2,338	5,194	D	57.0	31.6	11.4	9	9	13	7.2	7.0	7.7	7.3
Kanabec	6,150	3,582	1,819	749	1,763	D	58.2	29.6	12.2	8	11	10	2.2	2.1	2.2	2.3
Koochiching	7,297	4,270	2,365	662	1,905	D	58.5	32.4	9.1	6	8	16	2.6	2.6	2.8	2.1
Lake	6,256	4,094	1,614	548	2,480	D	65.4	25.8	8.8	1	15	17	2.2	2.5	1.9	1.7
Mille Lacs	9,007	4,617	3,214	1,176	1,403	D	51.3	35.7	13.1	17	1	6	3.2	2.8	3.8	3.7
Morrison (pt)	2,851	1,850	659	342	1,191	D	64.9	23.1	12.0	2	17	11	1.0	1.1	0.8	1.1
Pine	10,608	6,401	2,597	1,610	3,804	D	60.3	24.5	15.2	4	16	1	3.7	3.8	3.1	5.0
St. Louis	104,943	66,837	28,409	9,697	38,428	D	63.7	27.1	9.2	3	13	15	37.1	40.0	33.9	30.2
Sherburne (pt)	18,775	9,794	6,213	2,768	3,581	D	52.2	33.1	14.7	16	6	2	6.6	5.9	7.4	8.6
MINNESOTA	2,275,192	1,178,072	930,814	166,306	247,258	D	51.8	40.9	7.3							

Table I. — Vote for Presidential Preference: April 7, 1992, Democratic Primary Election

County	Total	Clinton	Brown	Tsongas	Uncom-mitted	Write ins	Harkin	McCarthy	Other	Clinton (% of total)	Brown (% of total)	Tsongas (% of total)	Clinton (Rank)	Brown (Rank)	Tsongas (Rank)	Total (% contrib)	Clinton (% contrib)	Brown (% contrib)	Tsongas (% contrib)
Aitkin	1,008	377	286	160	66	53	22	8	36	37.4	28.4	15.9	46	41	46	0.5	0.6	0.5	0.4
Anoka	10,208	3,035	3,241	2,130	609	587	187	143	276	29.7	31.7	20.9	77	19	14	5.0	4.8	5.2	4.9
Becker	833	342	217	122	56	40	12	14	30	41.1	26.1	14.6	34	52	60	0.4	0.5	0.3	0.3
Beltrami	1,315	470	433	189	66	68	18	22	49	35.7	32.9	14.4	53	13	61	0.6	0.7	0.7	0.4
Benton	846	239	332	120	55	30	15	27	28	28.3	39.2	14.2	81	2	66	0.4	0.4	0.5	0.3
Big Stone	369	188	91	42	30	4	6	3	5	50.9	24.7	11.4	6	56	83	0.2	0.3	0.1	<.1
Blue Earth	1,593	466	482	287	121	94	54	25	64	29.3	30.3	18.0	79	30	26	0.8	0.7	0.8	0.7
Brown	665	203	220	130	30	28	19	9	26	30.5	33.1	19.5	73	11	19	0.3	0.3	0.4	0.3
Carlton	1,879	627	701	289	91	53	36	26	56	33.4	37.3	15.4	63	4	52	0.9	1.0	1.1	0.7
Carver	1,290	341	452	297	59	80	18	17	26	26.4	35.0	23.0	86	7	9	0.6	0.5	0.7	0.7
Cass	1,238	493	361	166	84	80	15	12	27	39.8	29.2	13.4	37	39	77	0.6	0.8	0.6	0.4
Chippewa	421	178	115	62	21	11	20	8	6	42.3	27.3	14.7	26	49	59	0.2	0.3	0.2	0.1
Chisago	1,509	506	474	278	76	89	26	26	34	33.5	31.4	18.4	62	21	24	0.7	0.8	0.8	0.6
Clay	908	383	170	208	60	25	24	13	25	42.2	18.7	22.9	27	78	10	0.4	0.6	0.3	0.5
Clearwater	352	185	64	56	18	11	6	3	9	52.6	18.2	15.9	4	79	45	0.2	0.3	0.1	0.1
Cook	319	74	106	72	30	19	5	6	7	23.2	33.2	22.6	87	10	12	0.2	0.1	0.2	0.2
Cottonwood	397	158	93	57	39	14	13	1	22	39.8	23.4	14.4	38	63	62	0.2	0.2	0.1	0.1
Crow Wing	1,821	674	569	320	96	87	19	17	39	37.0	31.2	17.6	48	22	30	0.9	1.1	0.9	0.7
Dakota	10,854	3,034	3,264	2,737	628	620	204	168	199	28.0	30.1	25.2	82	32	5	5.3	4.8	5.2	6.3
Dodge	417	160	102	56	41	14	16	12	16	38.4	24.5	13.4	42	58	76	0.2	0.3	0.2	0.1
Douglas	1,023	387	291	175	66	34	20	23	27	37.8	28.4	17.1	45	40	34	0.5	0.6	0.5	0.4
Faribault	587	251	124	84	42	15	29	19	23	42.8	21.1	14.3	24	71	63	0.3	0.4	0.2	0.2
Fillmore	680	284	139	114	46	39	22	12	24	41.8	20.4	16.8	30	74	38	0.3	0.4	0.2	0.3
Freeborn	833	332	234	118	62	39	24	8	16	39.9	28.1	14.2	36	42	67	0.4	0.5	0.4	0.3
Goodhue	1,675	538	463	392	131	60	31	19	41	32.1	27.6	23.4	67	47	7	0.8	0.8	0.7	0.9
Grant	313	141	51	68	24	6	10	4	9	45.0	16.3	21.7	15	82	13	0.2	0.2	<.1	0.2
Hennepin	59,149	16,438	18,468	14,660	2,760	3,435	991	1,055	1,342	27.8	31.2	24.8	83	23	6	29.0	25.9	29.6	33.6
Houston	747	263	207	150	37	21	21	16	32	35.2	27.7	20.1	56	45	18	0.4	0.4	0.3	0.3
Hubbard	1,472	563	397	201	112	58	27	29	85	38.2	27.0	13.7	44	51	72	0.7	0.9	0.6	0.5
Isanti	1,212	419	365	207	91	59	25	16	30	34.6	30.1	17.1	59	31	35	0.6	0.7	0.6	0.5
Itasca	2,848	1,024	869	404	197	128	50	34	142	36.0	30.5	14.2	52	28	64	1.4	1.6	1.4	0.9
Jackson	335	163	78	34	21	14	10	4	11	48.7	23.3	10.1	10	64	87	0.2	0.3	0.1	<.1
Kanabec	612	226	190	91	46	24	13	10	12	36.9	31.0	14.9	50	25	57	0.3	0.4	0.3	0.2
Kandiyohi	1,175	454	303	243	61	46	18	27	23	38.6	25.8	20.7	40	54	15	0.6	0.7	0.5	0.6
Kittson	212	110	50	30	12	0	2	1	7	51.9	23.6	14.2	5	62	68	0.1	0.2	<.1	<.1
Koochiching	1,138	399	418	119	66	52	15	18	51	35.1	36.7	10.5	57	5	86	0.6	0.6	0.7	0.3
Lac qui Parle	508	232	113	75	33	18	17	6	14	45.7	22.2	14.8	14	66	58	0.2	0.4	0.2	0.2
Lake	1,032	348	345	181	71	25	19	16	27	33.7	33.4	17.5	61	9	31	0.5	0.5	0.6	0.4
Lake of the Woods	160	69	41	24	11	6	2	5	2	43.1	25.6	15.0	21	55	55	<.1	0.1	<.1	<.1
Le Sueur	775	245	244	133	71	39	16	13	14	31.6	31.5	17.2	70	20	33	0.4	0.4	0.4	0.3
Lincoln	275	130	53	32	14	13	10	3	20	47.3	19.3	11.6	12	76	82	0.1	0.2	<.1	<.1
Lyon	697	259	224	106	38	14	27	8	21	37.2	32.1	15.2	47	18	53	0.3	0.4	0.4	0.2
McLeod	569	201	171	111	27	28	10	6	15	35.3	30.1	19.5	54	33	20	0.3	0.3	0.3	0.3
Mahnomen	194	96	29	22	10	16	5	6	10	49.5	14.9	11.3	7	84	84	<.1	0.2	<.1	<.1
Marshall	405	197	73	79	15	10	13	5	13	48.6	18.0	19.5	11	80	21	0.2	0.3	0.1	0.2
Martin	390	168	86	61	23	25	5	6	16	43.1	22.1	15.6	22	67	50	0.2	0.3	0.1	0.1
Meeker	640	226	188	99	42	25	14	30	16	35.3	29.4	15.5	55	37	51	0.3	0.4	0.3	0.2
Mille Lacs	733	288	223	102	34	46	15	6	19	39.3	30.4	13.9	39	29	71	0.4	0.5	0.4	0.2
Morrison	1,081	417	323	147	86	32	17	18	41	38.6	29.9	13.6	41	35	73	0.5	0.7	0.5	0.3
Mower	1,417	593	347	201	92	66	64	23	31	41.8	24.5	14.2	28	57	65	0.7	0.9	0.6	0.5
Murray	394	173	80	67	25	13	16	2	18	43.9	20.3	17.0	19	75	36	0.2	0.3	0.1	0.2
Nicollet	876	279	262	165	63	40	24	19	24	31.8	29.9	18.8	68	34	23	0.4	0.4	0.4	0.4
Nobles	481	215	103	65	26	24	36	4	8	44.7	21.4	13.5	16	70	75	0.2	0.3	0.2	0.1
Norman	292	156	40	44	14	8	11	4	15	53.4	13.7	15.1	2	86	54	0.1	0.2	<.1	0.1
Olmsted	3,796	1,046	1,045	1,009	249	198	86	64	99	27.6	27.5	26.6	84	48	1	1.9	1.6	1.7	2.3
Otter Tail	1,583	606	430	263	103	56	32	25	68	38.3	27.2	16.6	43	50	41	0.8	1.0	0.7	0.6
Pennington	487	201	102	81	30	12	26	8	27	41.3	20.9	16.6	33	72	40	0.2	0.3	0.2	0.2
Pine	1,334	465	429	200	96	49	22	29	44	34.9	32.2	15.0	58	17	56	0.7	0.7	0.7	0.5
Pipestone	660	324	114	81	66	14	22	7	32	49.1	17.3	12.3	9	81	80	0.3	0.5	0.2	0.2
Polk	1,234	515	234	253	75	38	29	28	62	41.7	19.0	20.5	31	77	17	0.6	0.8	0.4	0.6
Pope	508	227	132	66	30	20	11	11	11	44.7	26.0	13.0	17	53	78	0.2	0.4	0.2	0.2
Ramsey	29,064	8,399	8,041	7,632	1,509	1,536	567	740	640	28.9	27.7	26.3	80	46	3	14.2	13.2	12.9	17.5
Red Lake	165	70	25	34	21	4	4	4	3	42.4	15.2	20.6	25	83	16	<.1	0.1	<.1	<.1
Redwood	519	192	126	92	43	15	19	12	20	37.0	24.3	17.7	49	59	29	0.3	0.3	0.2	0.2
Renville	539	223	123	85	29	26	23	13	17	41.4	22.8	15.8	32	65	47	0.3	0.3	0.2	0.2
Rice	1,903	603	555	440	144	61	39	28	33	31.7	29.2	23.1	69	38	8	0.9	0.9	0.9	1.0
Rock	232	124	33	27	25	4	9	3	7	53.4	14.2	11.6	1	85	81	0.1	0.2	<.1	<.1
Roseau	323	135	77	53	14	12	9	7	16	41.8	23.8	16.4	29	61	43	0.2	0.2	0.1	0.1
St. Louis	16,769	5,081	6,622	2,365	945	676	361	264	455	30.3	39.5	14.1	76	1	69	8.2	8.0	10.6	5.4
Scott	1,810	560	646	333	97	89	25	29	31	30.9	35.7	18.4	72	6	25	0.9	0.9	1.0	0.8

County	Top candidates									Top three candidates(state vote)									
										Percent of total vote						Percent contribution to state vote			
														Rank					
	Total	Clinton	Brown	Tsongas	Uncom-mitted	Write ins	Harkin	McCarthy	Other	Clinton	Brown	Tsongas	Clinton	Brown	Tsongas	Total	Clinton	Brown	Tsongas
Sherburne	1,297	394	422	251	72	83	28	22	25	30.4	32.5	19.4	75	14	22	0.6	0.6	0.7	0.6
Sibley	429	146	127	71	31	9	9	12	24	34.0	29.6	16.6	60	36	42	0.2	0.2	0.2	0.2
Stearns	3,028	897	1,166	505	155	105	51	95	54	29.6	38.5	16.7	78	3	39	1.5	1.4	1.9	1.2
Steele	779	258	239	140	45	33	31	11	22	33.1	30.7	18.0	65	27	27	0.4	0.4	0.4	0.3
Stevens	334	111	80	88	14	20	2	9	10	33.2	24.0	26.3	64	60	2	0.2	0.2	0.1	0.2
Swift	371	197	81	41	19	12	14	2	5	53.1	21.8	11.1	3	68	85	0.2	0.3	0.1	<.1
Todd	874	382	245	137	29	36	14	9	22	43.7	28.0	15.7	20	43	49	0.4	0.6	0.4	0.3
Traverse	192	95	40	26	13	4	3	3	8	49.5	20.8	13.5	8	73	74	<.1	0.1	<.1	<.1
Wabasha	597	182	200	103	32	36	14	13	17	30.5	33.5	17.3	74	8	32	0.3	0.3	0.3	0.2
Wadena	450	199	139	63	18	7	9	5	10	44.2	30.9	14.0	18	26	70	0.2	0.3	0.2	0.1
Waseca	475	174	153	77	24	13	6	9	19	36.6	32.2	16.2	51	16	44	0.2	0.3	0.2	0.2
Washington	6,431	1,706	2,007	1,669	396	280	132	118	123	26.5	31.2	26.0	85	24	4	3.1	2.7	3.2	3.8
Watonwan	374	153	104	48	20	12	12	10	15	40.9	27.8	12.8	35	44	79	<.1	<.1	<.1	<.1
Wilkin	114	49	14	26	10	3	2	2	8	43.0	12.3	22.8	23	87	11	0.8	0.8	0.8	0.6
Winona	1,588	499	512	268	100	92	41	31	45	31.4	32.2	16.9	71	15	37	1.1	1.1	1.2	0.9
Wright	2,210	710	731	396	133	94	41	41	64	32.1	33.1	17.9	66	12	28	0.3	0.4	0.2	0.2
Yellow Medicine	529	244	115	83	34	15	20	5	13	46.1	21.7	15.7	13	69	48	0.3	0.4	0.2	0.2
MINNESOTA	**204,170**	**63,584**	**62,474**	**43,588**	**11,366**	**10,149**	**4,077**	**3,704**	**5,228**	**31.1**	**30.6**	**21.3**				**100.0**	**100.0**	**100.0**	**100.0**

Table J. — Vote for Presidential Preference: April 7, 1992, Republican Primary Election

County	Top candidates — Total	Bush	Bu-chanan	Write ins	Other	Percent of total vote — Bush	Bu-chanan	Write ins	Other	Rank — Bush	Bu-chanan	Write ins	Other	Pct contribution — Total	Bush	Bu-chanan	Write ins	Other
Aitkin	512	325	118	34	35	63.5	23.0	6.6	6.8	64	36	5	28	0.4	0.4	0.4	0.5	0.4
Anoka	6,331	3,682	1,968	329	352	58.2	31.1	5.2	5.6	85	4	17	55	4.8	4.3	6.1	4.7	4.0
Becker	688	522	102	32	32	75.9	14.8	4.7	4.7	7	79	23	76	0.5	0.6	0.3	0.5	0.4
Beltrami	792	478	183	58	73	60.4	23.1	7.3	9.2	77	35	2	3	0.6	0.6	0.6	0.8	0.8
Benton	569	353	158	20	38	62.0	27.8	3.5	6.7	74	13	40	33	0.4	0.4	0.5	0.3	0.4
Big Stone	182	137	26	2	17	75.3	14.3	1.1	9.3	11	81	79	2	0.1	0.2	<.1	<.1	0.2
Blue Earth	1,265	821	276	76	92	64.9	21.8	6.0	7.3	62	45	10	21	1.0	1.0	0.9	1.1	1.0
Brown	788	523	183	28	54	66.4	23.2	3.6	6.9	57	33	39	27	0.6	0.6	0.6	0.4	0.6
Carlton	690	382	222	31	55	55.4	32.2	4.5	8.0	87	2	25	10	0.5	0.5	0.7	0.4	0.6
Carver	1,508	935	379	95	99	62.0	25.1	6.3	6.6	75	21	7	37	1.1	1.1	1.2	1.4	1.1
Cass	965	695	153	66	51	72.0	15.9	6.8	5.3	24	75	4	64	0.7	0.8	0.5	0.9	0.6
Chippewa	348	263	52	15	18	75.6	14.9	4.3	5.2	9	78	28	67	0.3	0.3	0.2	0.2	0.2
Chisago	960	563	288	39	70	58.6	30.0	4.1	7.3	84	8	32	20	0.7	0.7	0.9	0.6	0.8
Clay	719	563	99	17	40	78.3	13.8	2.4	5.6	5	83	71	54	0.5	0.7	0.3	0.2	0.5
Clearwater	194	139	32	10	13	71.6	16.5	5.2	6.7	26	74	18	32	0.1	0.2	<.1	0.1	0.1
Cook	204	141	31	23	9	69.1	15.2	11.3	4.4	39	77	1	82	0.2	0.2	<.1	0.3	0.1
Cottonwood	440	317	88	11	24	72.0	20.0	2.5	5.5	23	60	68	58	0.3	0.4	0.3	0.2	0.3
Crow Wing	1,517	1,104	257	82	74	72.8	16.9	5.4	4.9	18	71	13	72	1.1	1.3	0.8	1.2	0.8
Dakota	8,575	5,123	2,288	527	637	59.7	26.7	6.1	7.4	80	16	8	16	6.5	6.0	7.1	7.6	7.2
Dodge	516	356	110	18	32	69.0	21.3	3.5	6.2	42	50	41	43	0.4	0.4	0.3	0.3	0.4
Douglas	1,007	701	194	45	67	69.6	19.3	4.5	6.7	34	63	26	35	0.8	0.8	0.6	0.6	0.8
Faribault	514	351	110	15	38	68.3	21.4	2.9	7.4	48	49	57	17	0.4	0.4	0.3	0.2	0.4
Fillmore	703	500	119	41	43	71.1	16.9	5.8	6.1	27	72	12	44	0.5	0.6	0.4	0.6	0.5
Freeborn	679	448	173	20	38	66.0	25.5	2.9	5.6	60	20	56	53	0.5	0.5	0.5	0.3	0.4
Goodhue	1,607	1,120	291	54	142	69.7	18.1	3.4	8.8	33	66	47	4	1.2	1.3	0.9	0.8	1.6
Grant	204	165	27	1	11	80.9	13.2	0.5	5.4	4	84	85	61	0.2	0.2	<.1	<.1	0.1
Hennepin	36,756	22,925	8,593	2,554	2,684	62.4	23.4	6.9	7.3	72	31	3	19	27.7	27.0	26.8	36.7	30.3
Houston	645	442	135	30	38	68.5	20.9	4.7	5.9	45	53	24	46	0.5	0.5	0.4	0.4	0.4
Hubbard	1,367	1,008	213	72	74	73.7	15.6	5.3	5.4	14	76	16	60	1.0	1.2	0.7	1.0	0.8
Isanti	888	587	204	39	58	66.1	23.0	4.4	6.5	59	37	27	38	0.7	0.7	0.6	0.6	0.7
Itasca	1,240	798	289	63	90	64.4	23.3	5.1	7.3	63	32	19	22	0.9	0.9	0.9	0.9	1.0
Jackson	235	180	34	8	13	76.6	14.5	3.4	5.5	6	80	44	56	0.2	0.2	0.1	0.1	0.1
Kanabec	403	279	88	8	28	69.2	21.8	2.0	6.9	38	44	73	26	0.3	0.3	0.3	0.1	0.3
Kandiyohi	896	629	201	24	42	70.2	22.4	2.7	4.7	31	40	63	75	0.7	0.7	0.6	0.3	0.5
Kittson	115	83	25	1	6	72.2	21.7	0.9	5.2	20	46	81	66	<.1	<.1	<.1	<.1	<.1
Koochiching	461	344	79	7	31	74.6	17.1	1.5	6.7	12	69	76	30	0.3	0.4	0.2	0.1	0.3
Lac qui Parle	350	220	92	10	28	62.9	26.3	2.9	8.0	69	18	59	9	0.3	0.3	0.3	0.1	0.3
Lake	328	197	99	14	18	60.1	30.2	4.3	5.5	78	7	30	57	0.2	0.2	0.3	0.2	0.2
Lake of the Woods	116	85	21	4	6	73.3	18.1	3.4	5.2	16	67	43	68	<.1	0.1	<.1	<.1	<.1
Le Sueur	632	419	156	20	37	66.3	24.7	3.2	5.9	58	25	51	48	0.5	0.5	0.5	0.3	0.4
Lincoln	231	142	61	6	22	61.5	26.4	2.6	9.5	76	17	65	1	0.2	0.2	0.2	<.1	0.2
Lyon	710	492	154	21	43	69.3	21.7	3.0	6.1	37	48	55	45	0.5	0.6	0.5	0.3	0.5
McLeod	702	473	171	26	32	67.4	24.4	3.7	4.6	52	27	36	79	0.5	0.6	0.5	0.4	0.4
Mahnomen	94	63	20	5	6	67.0	21.3	5.3	6.4	55	51	14	40	<.1	<.1	<.1	<.1	<.1
Marshall	283	204	59	9	11	72.1	20.8	3.2	3.9	21	55	49	84	0.2	0.2	0.2	0.1	0.1
Martin	621	427	144	19	31	68.8	23.2	3.1	5.0	43	34	54	71	0.5	0.5	0.4	0.3	0.3
Meeker	672	470	129	22	51	69.9	19.2	3.3	7.6	32	64	48	15	0.5	0.6	0.4	0.3	0.6
Mille Lacs	472	326	96	18	32	69.1	20.3	3.8	6.8	40	58	35	29	0.4	0.4	0.3	0.3	0.4
Morrison	721	489	171	20	41	67.8	23.7	2.8	5.7	50	29	61	51	0.5	0.6	0.5	0.3	0.5
Mower	973	653	241	33	46	67.1	24.8	3.4	4.7	54	24	45	74	0.7	0.8	0.8	0.5	0.5
Murray	252	170	59	2	21	67.5	23.4	0.8	8.3	51	30	83	7	0.2	0.2	0.2	<.1	0.2
Nicollet	724	456	180	35	53	63.0	24.9	4.8	7.3	67	23	20	18	0.5	0.5	0.6	0.5	0.6
Nobles	418	303	78	10	27	72.5	18.7	2.4	6.5	19	65	70	39	0.3	0.4	0.2	0.1	0.3
Norman	240	201	30	2	7	83.8	12.5	0.8	2.9	1	85	82	87	0.2	0.2	<.1	<.1	<.1
Olmsted	4,920	3,465	1,024	212	219	70.4	20.8	4.3	4.5	30	56	29	81	3.7	4.1	3.2	3.0	2.5
Otter Tail	1,667	1,201	299	70	97	72.0	17.9	4.2	5.8	22	68	31	50	1.3	1.4	0.9	1.0	1.1
Pennington	248	182	49	3	14	73.4	19.8	1.2	5.6	15	61	78	52	0.2	0.2	0.2	<.1	0.2
Pine	730	457	208	26	39	62.6	28.5	3.6	5.3	70	11	38	62	0.5	0.5	0.6	0.4	0.4
Pipestone	584	443	100	10	31	75.9	17.1	1.7	5.3	8	70	75	63	0.4	0.5	0.3	0.1	0.3
Polk	880	665	122	35	58	75.6	13.9	4.0	6.6	10	82	33	36	0.7	0.8	0.4	0.5	0.7
Pope	391	286	66	9	30	73.1	16.9	2.3	7.7	17	73	72	13	0.3	0.3	0.2	0.1	0.3
Ramsey	14,297	8,419	3,939	849	1,090	58.9	27.6	5.9	7.6	82	14	11	14	10.8	9.9	12.3	12.2	12.3
Red Lake	90	53	31	0	6	58.9	34.4	0.0	6.7	81	1	86	34	<.1	<.1	<.1	0.0	<.1
Redwood	709	477	177	5	50	67.3	25.0	0.7	7.1	53	22	84	23	0.5	0.6	0.6	<.1	0.6
Renville	555	383	123	10	39	69.0	22.2	1.8	7.0	41	42	74	24	0.4	0.5	0.4	0.1	0.4
Rice	1,133	778	231	36	88	68.7	20.4	3.2	7.8	44	57	50	11	0.9	0.9	0.7	0.5	1.0
Rock	344	287	27	12	18	83.4	7.8	3.5	5.2	2	86	42	65	0.3	0.3	<.1	0.2	0.2
Roseau	295	220	64	0	11	74.6	21.7	0.0	3.7	13	47	87	85	0.2	0.3	0.2	0.0	0.1
St. Louis	4,886	2,874	1,533	175	304	58.8	31.4	3.6	6.2	83	3	37	42	3.7	3.4	4.8	2.5	3.4
Scott	1,382	803	425	73	81	58.1	30.8	5.3	5.9	86	6	15	47	1.0	0.9	1.3	1.0	0.9

508 Minnesota

County	Top candidates					Top four candidates (state vote)												
						Percent of total vote				Rank				Percent contribution to state vote				
	Total	Bush	Bu-chanan	Write ins	Other	Bush	Bu-chanan	Write ins	Other	Bush	Bu-chanan	Write ins	Other	Total	Bush	Bu-chanan	Write ins	Other
Sherburne	931	581	263	45	42	62.4	28.2	4.8	4.5	71	12	21	80	0.7	0.7	0.8	0.6	0.5
Sibley	455	288	134	4	29	63.3	29.5	0.9	6.4	66	9	80	41	0.3	0.3	0.4	<.1	0.3
Stearns	2,152	1,366	628	56	102	63.5	29.2	2.6	4.7	65	10	64	73	1.6	1.6	2.0	0.8	1.2
Steele	929	645	186	26	72	69.4	20.0	2.8	7.8	36	59	60	12	0.7	0.8	0.6	0.4	0.8
Stevens	265	181	60	16	8	68.3	22.6	6.0	3.0	47	39	9	86	0.2	0.2	0.2	0.2	<.1
Swift	207	129	64	5	9	62.3	30.9	2.4	4.3	73	5	69	83	0.2	0.2	0.2	<.1	0.1
Todd	627	429	153	16	29	68.4	24.4	2.6	4.6	46	26	67	78	0.5	0.5	0.5	0.2	0.3
Traverse	154	109	34	2	9	70.8	22.1	1.3	5.8	29	43	77	49	0.1	0.1	0.1	<.1	0.1
Wabasha	539	375	120	17	27	69.6	22.3	3.2	5.0	35	41	53	70	0.4	0.4	0.4	0.2	0.3
Wadena	412	292	86	13	21	70.9	20.9	3.2	5.1	28	54	52	69	0.3	0.3	0.3	0.2	0.2
Waseca	443	296	101	15	31	66.8	22.8	3.4	7.0	56	38	46	25	0.3	0.3	0.3	0.2	0.3
Washington	4,546	2,726	1,227	288	305	60.0	27.0	6.3	6.7	79	15	6	31	3.4	3.2	3.8	4.1	3.4
Watonwan	349	238	74	9	28	68.2	21.2	2.6	8.0	49	52	66	8	0.3	0.3	0.2	0.1	0.3
Wilkin	139	114	9	4	12	82.0	6.5	2.9	8.6	3	87	58	5	0.1	0.1	<.1	<.1	0.1
Winona	1,228	882	241	48	57	71.8	19.6	3.9	4.6	25	62	34	77	0.9	1.0	0.8	0.7	0.6
Wright	1,841	1,158	441	86	156	62.9	24.0	4.7	8.5	68	28	22	6	1.4	1.4	1.4	1.2	1.8
Yellow Medicine	406	267	106	11	22	65.8	26.1	2.7	5.4	61	19	62	59	0.3	0.3	0.3	0.2	0.2
MINNESOTA	**132,756**	**84,841**	**32,094**	**6,957**	**8,864**	**63.9**	**24.2**	**5.2**	**6.7**					**100.0**	**100.0**	**100.0**	**100.0**	**100.0**

1992 Vote for President
Percent for Clinton (D), by County

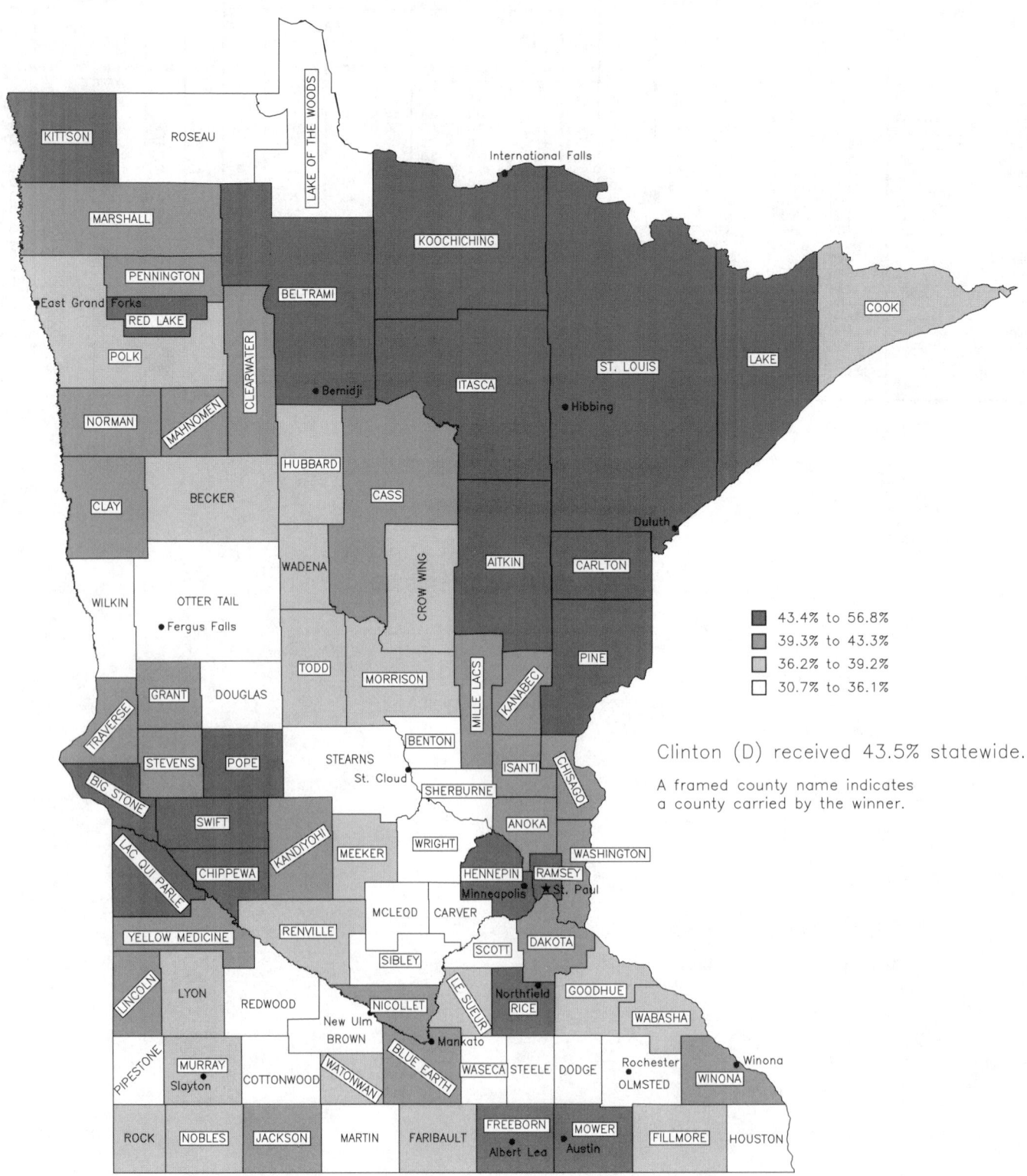

KITTSON
ROSEAU
LAKE OF THE WOODS
International Falls
MARSHALL
KOOCHICHING
PENNINGTON
East Grand Forks
RED LAKE
BELTRAMI
COOK
POLK
CLEARWATER
Bemidji
ST. LOUIS
LAKE
ITASCA
NORMAN
MAHNOMEN
Hibbing
HUBBARD
CLAY
BECKER
CASS
AITKIN
CARLTON
Duluth
WADENA
CROW WING
WILKIN
OTTER TAIL
Fergus Falls
PINE
TODD
GRANT
DOUGLAS
MORRISON
MILLE LACS
KANABEC
TRAVERSE
STEVENS
POPE
BENTON
STEARNS
St. Cloud
ISANTI
CHISAGO
BIG STONE
SHERBURNE
SWIFT
ANOKA
LAC QUI PARLE
KANDIYOHI
MEEKER
WRIGHT
WASHINGTON
CHIPPEWA
HENNEPIN
RAMSEY
Minneapolis
St. Paul
YELLOW MEDICINE
RENVILLE
MCLEOD
CARVER
DAKOTA
LINCOLN
LYON
SIBLEY
SCOTT
REDWOOD
NICOLLET
LE SUEUR
Northfield
GOODHUE
New Ulm
RICE
BROWN
WABASHA
Mankato
PIPESTONE
MURRAY
BLUE EARTH
WASECA
STEELE
DODGE
Rochester
Winona
Slayton
COTTONWOOD
WATONWAN
OLMSTED
WINONA
ROCK
NOBLES
JACKSON
MARTIN
FARIBAULT
FREEBORN
MOWER
FILLMORE
HOUSTON
Albert Lea
Austin

43.4% to 56.8%
39.3% to 43.3%
36.2% to 39.2%
30.7% to 36.1%

Clinton (D) received 43.5% statewide.

A framed county name indicates
a county carried by the winner.

510 Minnesota

MISSISSIPPI

Congressional Districts 5
   Average Population 514,643
State Senate Districts 52
   Average Population 49,485
State House Districts 122
   Average Population 21,092

Electoral College Votes...7
Counties 82
Voting Precincts 2,321

Alternative Registration Methods:
   Agency-based, Deputized Registrars, Mail-in, Motor-voter

Registration Deadline (Days before Election) 30

Voting Equipment Use (Counties)

Datavote Punch Card	0	Paper Ballot	2
Electronic	1	Other Punch Card	21
Lever Machine	14	Mixed Systems	0
Optical Scanner	44		

Party Control	DEM	REP	IND	VAC
1993 State Senate	39	13	0	0
1992 State Senate	43	9	0	0
1993 State House	93	27	2	0
1992 State House	98	23	1	0

Population Statistics 1990

Race/ Ethnicity	Total Population		Voting Age Population		Voting Age Population % of total population
	Number	%	Number	%	
Non-Hispanic					
White	1,624,198	63.1	1,226,332	67.1	75.5
Black	911,891	35.4	575,773	31.5	63.1
Asian/Pacific Islander	12,543	0.5	8,424	0.5	67.2
Native American	8,316	0.3	5,102	0.3	61.4
Other	337	<.1	169	<.1	50.1
All Hispanic	15,931	0.6	10,655	0.6	66.9
TOTAL	2,573,216	100.0	1,826,455	100.0	71.0

Estimated Voting Age Population 1992 (VAP) 1,861,000
Number of Registered Voters................................. 1,640,150
   % of estimated VAP....................................... 88.1
Voter Turnout (Maximum Vote)[1]........................... 1,026,251
   % of VAP 55.1
   % of Registration 62.6
Persons Not Voting—of Voting Age 834,749
   % of VAP 44.9
Persons Not Voting—of Registered 613,899
   % of Registration 37.4
Straight Ticket Voting .... No

State Officials and Members of Congress

Governor:
Kirk Fordice (R) 1991, elected to a four-year term in 1991.

U.S. Senators:
Thad Cochran (R) 1978, elected to a six-year term in 1990.
Trent Lott (R) 1988, elected to a six-year term in 1988.

U.S. Representative in Congress:
(District, Name, Party, Date first elected)

1. Whitten (D) 1941
2. Thompson (D) 1993[2]

3. Montgomery (D) 1966

4. Parker (D) 1988

5. Taylor (D) 1989

---

[1]Maximum vote turnout from Table C exceeds reported statewide actual voter turnout because in one or more counties the vote for highest office is greater than reported actual turnout. [2]Elected from April 13, 1993, runoff election to replace Mike Espy (D), who was appointed as U.S. Secretary of Agriculture.

Candidates: General Election, November 3, 1992

Candidate(s)	Total vote	Percent	Party	Status	First elected
President/Vice President					
Bush/Quayle	487,793	49.68%	Republican	Incumbent	1988
Clinton/Gore	400,258	40.77%	Democrat	Challenger	1992
Perot/Stockdale	85,626	8.72%	Independent	Challenger	
Fulani/Munoz	2,625	0.27%	Independent	Challenger	
Marrou/Lord	2,154	0.22%	Libertarian	Challenger	
Phillips/Knight	1,652	0.17%	Taxpayers	Challenger	
Hagelin/Tompkins	1,140	0.12%	Independent	Challenger	
Gritz/Minett	545	0.06%	Independent	Challenger	
U.S. Senator (No Contest)					
Governor (General Election November 5, 1991)					
Kirk Fordice	361,500	50.83%	Republican	Challenger	1991
Ray Mabus	338,459	47.59%	Democrat	Incumbent	1987
Shawn O'Hara	11,253	1.58%	Independent	Challenger	
U.S. Representative in Congress					
District 1					
Jamie Whitten	121,664	59.46%	Democrat	Incumbent	1941
Clyde Whitaker	82,952	40.54%	Republican	Challenger	
District 2					
Mike Espy[1]	133,361	76.38%	Democrat	Incumbent	1986
Dorothy Benford	41,248	23.62%	Republican	Challenger	
District 3					
G. V. Sonny Montgomery	162,864	81.20%	Democrat	Incumbent	1966
Michael Williams	37,710	18.80%	Republican	Challenger	
District 4					
Mike Parker	130,927	67.30%	Democrat	Incumbent	1988
Jack McMillan	43,705	22.47%	Republican	Challenger	
Liz Gilchrist	10,523	5.41%	Independent	Challenger	
James Meredith	9,389	4.83%	Independent	Challenger	
District 5					
Gene Taylor	120,766	63.21%	Democrat	Incumbent	1989
Paul Harvey	67,619	35.39%	Republican	Challenger	
Shawn O'Hara	2,673	1.40%	Independent	Challenger	

[1]Appointed as U.S. Secretary of Agriculture. Bennie Thompson (D) elected at April 13, 1993, runoff election to fill vacancy.

Candidates: March 10, 1992, Primary Election

Candidate	Total vote	Percent	Candidate	Total vote	Percent
Presidential Preference, Democratic			**Presidential Preference, Republican**		
Bill Clinton	139,893	73.11%	George Bush	111,794	72.26%
Jerry Brown	18,396	9.61%	Patrick Buchanan	25,891	16.74%
Paul Tsongas	15,538	8.12%	David Duke	16,426	10.62%
Uncommitted	11,796	6.16%	Billy Clegg	408	0.26%
Tom Harkin	2,509	1.31%	Tennie Rogers	189	0.12%
Bob Kerrey	1,660	0.87%			
Lyndon LaRouche, Jr.	1,394	0.73%			
Others	171	0.09%			

Voter Registration and Turnout, 1948-1992 Elections

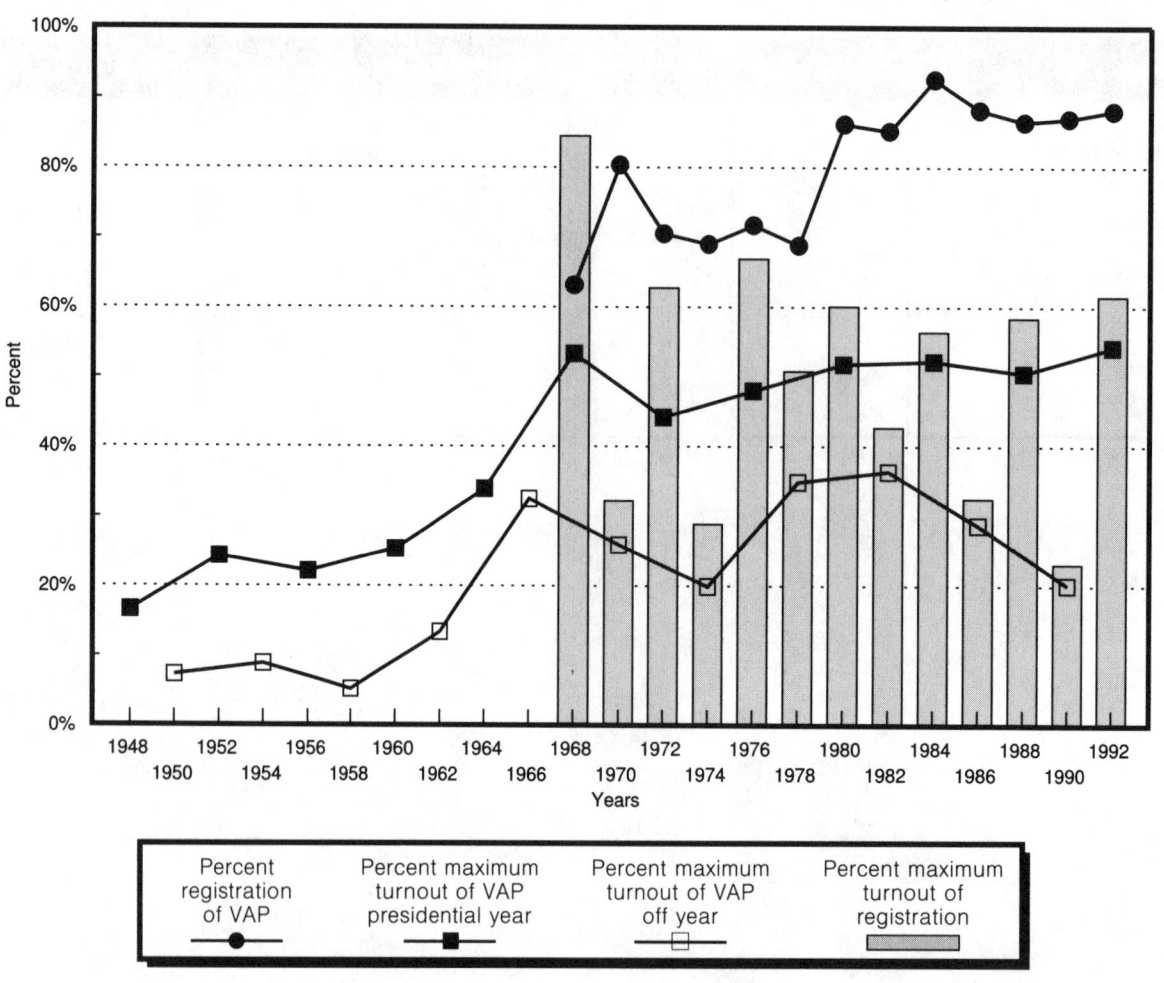

Legend:
- Percent registration of VAP (●)
- Percent maximum turnout of VAP presidential year (■)
- Percent maximum turnout of VAP off year (□)
- Percent maximum turnout of registration (bar)

Year	Estimated Voting Age Population (VAP)	Voter registration (REG)				Voter turnout										
							Highest office						Maximum vote			
		Total	Percent of VAP	Rank by percent of VAP	Actual	Total	Office	Percent total REG	Rank by percent of REG	Percent of VAP	Rank by percent of VAP	Total	Percent total REG	Rank by percent of REG	Percent total VAP	Rank by percent of VAP
1992	1,861,000	1,640,150	88.1	8	1,008,019	981,793	P	59.9	49	52.8	37	1,008,019	61.5	49	54.2	34
1990	1,832,000	1,592,992	87.0	3	-	368,502	C	23.1	49	20.1	51	368,502	23.1	49	20.1	51
1988	1,845,000	1,595,826	86.5	5	-	931,527	P	58.4	47	50.5	29	931,527	58.4	47	50.5	30
1986	1,827,000	1,610,763	88.2	2	-	523,563	C	32.5	49	28.7	46	523,563	32.5	49	28.7	46
1984	1,803,000	1,669,539	92.6	3	-	941,104	P	56.4	49	52.2	31	941,104	56.4	49	52.2	33
1982	1,771,000	1,509,669	85.2	5	-	645,026	S	42.7	46	36.4	40	645,026	42.7	46	36.4	41
1980	1,723,000	1,485,539	86.2	8	-	892,620	P	60.1	49	51.8	33	892,620	60.1	49	51.8	33
1978	1,672,000	1,150,000	68.8	25	-	583,936	S	50.8	38	34.9	39	583,936	50.8	38	34.9	39
1976	1,603,000	1,150,000	71.7	29	-	769,361	P	66.9	41	48.0	41	769,361	66.9	43	48.0	42
1974	1,537,000	1,060,000	69.0	29	-	305,909	C	28.9	48	19.9	50	305,909	28.9	48	19.9	50
1972	1,462,000	1,030,000	70.5	32	-	645,963	P	62.7	42	44.2	44	645,963	62.7	42	44.2	44
1970	1,253,000	1,006,059	80.3	10	-	324,215	S	32.2	44	25.9	48	324,215	32.2	44	25.9	48
1968	1,229,000	775,000	63.1	41	-	654,509	P	84.5	10	53.3	41	654,509	84.5	15	53.3	41
1966	1,213,000	-	-	-	-	393,900	S	-	-	32.5	45	393,900	-	-	32.5	45
1964	1,207,000	-	-	-	-	409,146	P	-	-	33.9	51	409,146	-	-	33.9	51
1962	1,205,000	-	-	-	-	161,615	C	-	-	13.4	49	161,615	-	-	13.4	49
1960	1,177,000	-	-	-	-	298,171	P	-	-	25.3	50	298,171	-	-	25.3	50
1958	1,181,000	-	-	-	-	61,464	C	-	-	5.2	48	61,464	-	-	5.2	48
1956	1,123,000	-	-	-	-	248,104	P	-	-	22.1	48	248,104	-	-	22.1	48
1954	1,181,000	-	-	-	-	105,526	S	-	-	8.9	48	105,526	-	-	8.9	48
1952	1,176,000	-	-	-	-	285,532	P	-	-	24.3	48	285,532	-	-	24.3	48
1950	1,198,000	-	-	-	-	87,756	C	-	-	7.3	47	87,756	-	-	7.3	47
1948	1,161,000	-	-	-	-	192,190	P	-	-	16.6	45	192,190	-	-	16.6	45

MISSISSIPPI

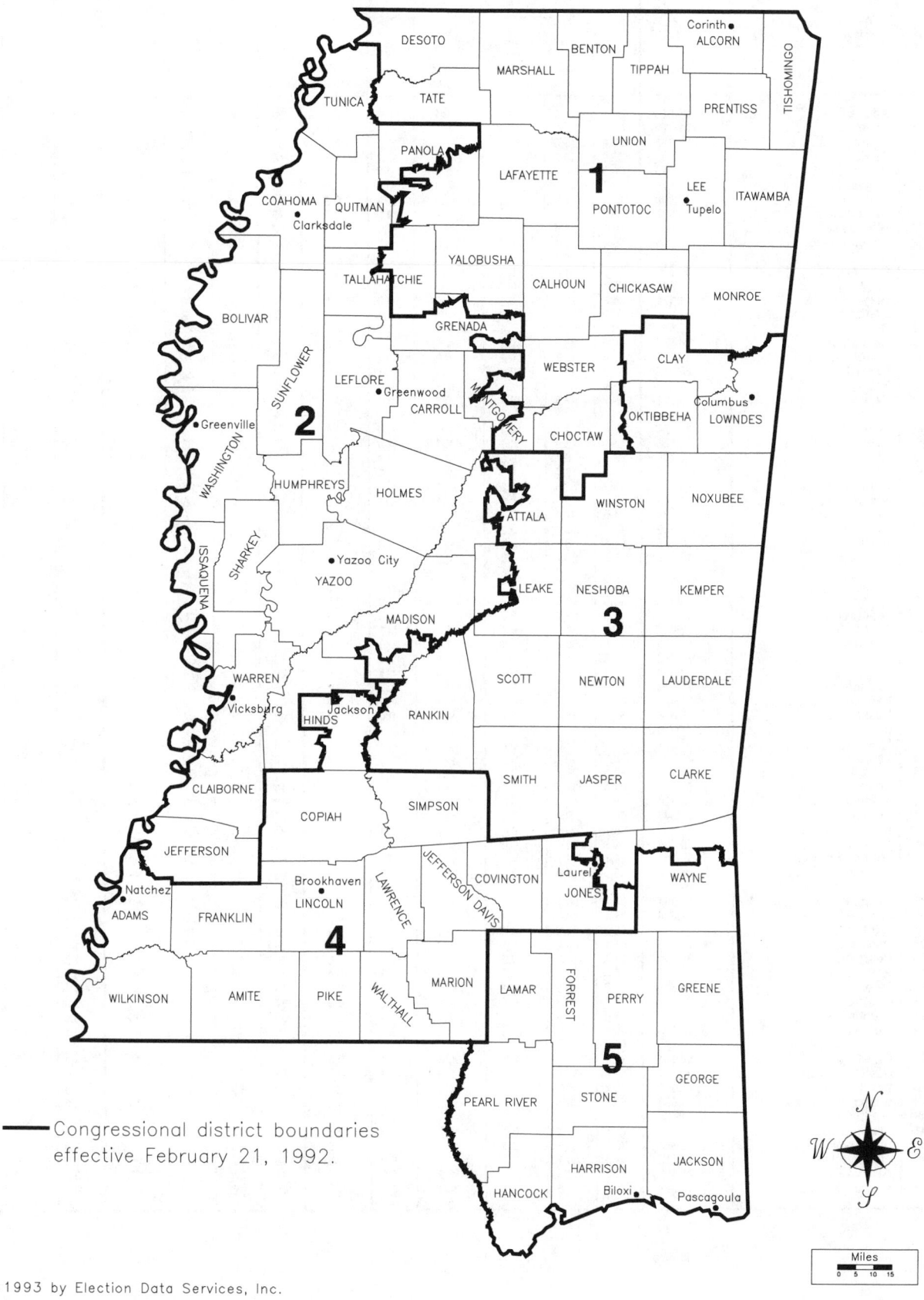

—Congressional district boundaries
effective February 21, 1992.

Copyright © 1993 by Election Data Services, Inc.

Miles
0 5 10 15

Mississippi 515

Table A. — 1990 Population by Race and Ethnic Origin

State/ county code	County	Total persons	Percent of total persons — Non-Hispanic White	Black	Asian and Pacific Islander	Native American	Other	Hispanic	Rank — Total	Rank — Non-Hispanic White	Black	Hispanic	Percent contribution to state population — Total	Non-Hispanic White	Black	Hispanic
28 001	Adams	35,356	50.7	48.5	0.2	0.1	<.1	0.4	20	58	25	47	1.4	1.1	1.9	1.0
28 003	Alcorn	31,722	88.2	11.1	0.2	<.1	<.1	0.4	24	5	78	55	1.2	1.7	0.4	0.8
28 005	Amite	13,328	54.4	45.2	<.1	<.1	0.0	0.2	61	55	28	79	0.5	0.4	0.7	0.2
28 007	Attala	18,481	60.1	39.3	0.1	0.2	<.1	0.3	48	46	35	68	0.7	0.7	0.8	0.4
28 009	Benton	8,046	60.3	39.2	<.1	<.1	0.0	0.5	80	45	36	40	0.3	0.3	0.3	0.2
28 011	Bolivar	41,875	36.1	62.6	0.3	<.1	0.0	0.9	14	72	11	5	1.6	0.9	2.9	2.4
28 013	Calhoun	14,908	72.4	27.0	<.1	<.1	<.1	0.5	57	23	58	28	0.6	0.7	0.4	0.5
28 015	Carroll	9,237	60.0	39.3	0.1	0.1	0.0	0.5	75	49	34	42	0.4	0.3	0.4	0.3
28 017	Chickasaw	18,085	60.9	38.4	<.1	0.1	<.1	0.5	50	44	38	36	0.7	0.7	0.8	0.5
28 019	Choctaw	9,071	69.4	30.1	0.1	<.1	<.1	0.3	76	26	55	64	0.4	0.4	0.3	0.2
28 021	Claiborne	11,370	17.4	81.8	0.1	0.2	0.0	0.5	67	81	2	35	0.4	0.1	1.0	0.4
28 023	Clarke	17,313	65.1	34.4	<.1	<.1	<.1	0.4	52	34	47	61	0.7	0.7	0.7	0.4
28 025	Clay	21,120	46.1	53.2	0.1	<.1	0.0	0.4	42	64	19	60	0.8	0.6	1.2	0.5
28 027	Coahoma	31,665	34.5	64.2	0.3	<.1	<.1	0.9	25	74	9	7	1.2	0.7	2.2	1.7
28 029	Copiah	27,592	49.1	50.3	<.1	<.1	0.0	0.4	30	59	24	57	1.1	0.8	1.5	0.7
28 031	Covington	16,527	64.6	35.0	0.1	<.1	0.0	0.3	55	36	45	72	0.6	0.7	0.6	0.3
28 033	DeSoto	67,910	86.4	12.7	0.2	0.2	<.1	0.5	8	8	75	43	2.6	3.6	0.9	1.9
28 035	Forrest	68,314	67.8	30.7	0.7	0.1	<.1	0.7	6	30	52	10	2.7	2.9	2.3	3.1
28 037	Franklin	8,377	63.0	36.7	<.1	<.1	0.0	0.3	78	39	42	78	0.3	0.3	0.3	0.1
28 039	George	16,673	89.9	9.5	0.1	0.2	0.0	0.3	54	3	79	74	0.6	0.9	0.2	0.3
28 041	Greene	10,220	77.8	21.4	<.1	<.1	<.1	0.6	73	15	65	14	0.4	0.5	0.2	0.4
28 043	Grenada	21,555	58.1	41.2	0.1	0.1	0.0	0.4	40	50	33	56	0.8	0.8	1.0	0.5
28 045	Hancock	31,760	88.7	8.7	0.5	0.4	<.1	1.7	23	4	80	2	1.2	1.7	0.3	3.4
28 047	Harrison	165,365	76.0	19.4	2.5	0.3	<.1	1.8	2	21	68	1	6.4	7.7	3.5	18.4
28 049	Hinds	254,441	48.2	50.8	0.5	<.1	<.1	0.5	1	62	21	44	9.9	7.5	14.2	7.2
28 051	Holmes	21,604	23.9	75.6	0.1	<.1	<.1	0.3	39	80	3	75	0.8	0.3	1.8	0.4
28 053	Humphreys	12,134	31.6	67.4	0.4	<.1	0.0	0.6	65	77	6	18	0.5	0.2	0.9	0.4
28 055	Issaquena	1,909	43.6	55.8	0.2	<.1	0.0	0.3	82	66	16	69	<.1	<.1	0.1	<.1
28 057	Itawamba	20,017	92.5	6.8	0.1	<.1	0.0	0.5	44	2	81	34	0.8	1.1	0.1	0.6
28 059	Jackson	115,243	77.5	20.4	0.9	0.2	<.1	0.9	3	16	67	4	4.5	5.5	2.6	6.7
28 061	Jasper	17,114	49.0	50.7	<.1	<.1	0.0	0.2	53	60	22	80	0.7	0.5	1.0	0.3
28 063	Jefferson	8,653	13.6	85.9	<.1	<.1	0.0	0.5	77	82	1	33	0.3	<.1	0.8	0.3
28 065	Jefferson Davis	14,051	45.0	54.4	0.2	0.1	0.0	0.3	60	65	18	70	0.5	0.4	0.8	0.3
28 067	Jones	62,031	74.3	24.9	0.1	0.3	<.1	0.3	10	22	60	65	2.4	2.8	1.7	1.3
28 069	Kemper	10,356	42.4	55.2	<.1	1.9	0.0	0.3	71	67	17	71	0.4	0.3	0.6	0.2
28 071	Lafayette	31,826	72.3	25.0	2.0	<.1	<.1	0.6	22	24	59	13	1.2	1.4	0.9	1.3
28 073	Lamar	30,424	87.0	11.9	0.4	0.1	<.1	0.6	26	7	76	22	1.2	1.6	0.4	1.1
28 075	Lauderdale	75,555	64.1	34.7	0.4	0.1	<.1	0.7	5	37	46	12	2.9	3.0	2.9	3.1
28 077	Lawrence	12,458	66.4	33.0	0.1	<.1	<.1	0.4	63	33	50	51	0.5	0.5	0.5	0.3
28 079	Leake	18,436	60.1	35.4	<.1	4.2	0.0	0.3	49	47	44	77	0.7	0.7	0.7	0.3
28 081	Lee	65,581	77.9	21.3	0.2	<.1	<.1	0.5	9	14	66	23	2.5	3.1	1.5	2.3
28 083	Leflore	37,341	38.8	60.4	0.3	<.1	<.1	0.4	17	71	12	58	1.5	0.9	2.5	0.9
28 085	Lincoln	30,278	69.8	29.8	0.1	<.1	<.1	0.2	28	25	56	82	1.2	1.3	1.0	0.4
28 087	Lowndes	59,308	61.4	37.1	0.5	0.1	<.1	0.8	11	42	41	8	2.3	2.2	2.4	3.1
28 089	Madison	53,794	55.1	44.0	0.3	<.1	<.1	0.5	12	54	29	29	2.1	1.8	2.6	1.7
28 091	Marion	25,544	69.1	30.1	0.2	<.1	<.1	0.5	31	28	54	26	1.0	1.1	0.8	0.9
28 093	Marshall	30,361	48.7	50.5	0.1	0.2	<.1	0.4	27	61	23	46	1.2	0.9	1.7	0.8
28 095	Monroe	36,582	69.2	30.1	<.1	<.1	<.1	0.5	19	27	53	31	1.4	1.6	1.2	1.2
28 097	Montgomery	12,388	55.7	43.7	0.1	<.1	0.0	0.4	64	53	30	52	0.5	0.4	0.6	0.3
28 099	Neshoba	24,800	68.1	18.6	0.1	12.8	<.1	0.4	33	29	69	49	1.0	1.0	0.5	0.7
28 101	Newton	20,291	67.2	28.7	<.1	3.6	<.1	0.4	43	31	57	50	0.8	0.8	0.6	0.5
28 103	Noxubee	12,604	31.4	68.0	<.1	0.3	0.0	0.2	62	78	5	81	0.5	0.2	0.9	0.2
28 105	Oktibbeha	38,375	62.2	34.2	2.6	<.1	<.1	0.9	16	40	49	6	1.5	1.5	1.4	2.1
28 107	Panola	29,996	51.1	48.2	0.1	0.1	<.1	0.5	29	57	26	30	1.2	0.9	1.6	1.0
28 109	Pearl River	38,714	84.4	14.3	0.2	0.4	<.1	0.8	15	11	74	9	1.5	2.0	0.6	1.9
28 111	Perry	10,865	76.4	22.5	<.1	0.6	<.1	0.4	68	20	61	48	0.4	0.5	0.3	0.3
28 113	Pike	36,882	53.8	45.4	0.1	<.1	<.1	0.5	18	56	27	37	1.4	1.2	1.8	1.1
28 115	Pontotoc	22,237	84.9	14.5	0.1	0.1	0.0	0.3	37	9	72	73	0.9	1.2	0.4	0.4
28 117	Prentiss	23,278	87.6	11.8	<.1	0.1	<.1	0.4	36	6	77	53	0.9	1.3	0.3	0.6
28 119	Quitman	10,490	40.2	59.0	0.2	0.2	0.0	0.5	70	70	13	41	0.4	0.3	0.7	0.3
28 121	Rankin	87,161	82.2	16.7	0.3	<.1	<.1	0.6	4	13	70	16	3.4	4.4	1.6	3.3
28 123	Scott	24,137	61.2	37.9	<.1	0.2	<.1	0.6	34	43	39	17	0.9	0.9	1.0	0.9
28 125	Sharkey	7,066	33.1	65.9	0.3	<.1	0.0	0.7	81	75	8	11	0.3	0.1	0.5	0.3
28 127	Simpson	23,953	67.2	32.3	<.1	0.2	0.0	0.3	35	32	51	76	0.9	1.0	0.8	0.4
28 129	Smith	14,798	77.4	21.9	<.1	0.1	<.1	0.5	58	19	63	24	0.6	0.7	0.4	0.5
28 131	Stone	10,750	77.5	21.7	0.1	0.2	<.1	0.5	69	17	64	32	0.4	0.5	0.3	0.3
28 133	Sunflower	32,867	35.2	63.9	0.3	<.1	<.1	0.6	21	73	10	20	1.3	0.7	2.3	1.2
28 135	Tallahatchie	15,210	41.0	58.1	0.3	<.1	0.0	0.5	56	69	14	25	0.6	0.4	1.0	0.5
28 137	Tate	21,432	64.8	34.3	0.1	0.2	0.0	0.6	41	35	48	19	0.8	0.9	0.8	0.8
28 139	Tippah	19,523	83.0	16.5	<.1	<.1	<.1	0.3	45	12	71	66	0.8	1.0	0.4	0.4

Table A. – 1990 Population by Race and Ethnic Origin (cont)

| State/county code | County | Total persons | Percent of total persons | | | | | | Rank | | | | Percent contribution to state population | | | |
| | | | Non-Hispanic | | | | | | | Non-Hispanic | | | | Non-Hispanic | | |
			White	Black	Asian and Pacific Islander	Native American	Other	Hispanic	Total	White	Black	Hispanic	Total	White	Black	Hispanic
28 141	Tishomingo	17,683	96.0	3.6	<.1	0.1	<.1	0.3	51	1	82	67	0.7	1.0	<.1	0.4
28 143	Tunica	8,164	24.3	74.6	<.1	<.1	<.1	1.0	79	79	4	3	0.3	0.1	0.7	0.5
28 145	Union	22,085	84.9	14.5	0.1	<.1	<.1	0.5	38	10	73	38	0.9	1.2	0.4	0.6
28 147	Walthall	14,352	57.2	42.1	0.2	0.1	0.0	0.3	59	51	31	63	0.6	0.5	0.7	0.3
28 149	Warren	47,880	60.0	38.9	0.5	<.1	<.1	0.5	13	48	37	27	1.9	1.8	2.0	1.6
28 151	Washington	67,935	41.5	57.5	0.4	<.1	<.1	0.6	7	68	15	15	2.6	1.7	4.3	2.6
28 153	Wayne	19,517	63.9	35.5	0.2	<.1	<.1	0.4	46	38	43	59	0.8	0.8	0.8	0.5
28 155	Webster	10,222	77.4	21.9	<.1	<.1	<.1	0.6	72	18	62	21	0.4	0.5	0.2	0.4
28 157	Wilkinson	9,678	32.1	67.3	<.1	0.2	<.1	0.5	74	76	7	39	0.4	0.2	0.7	0.3
28 159	Winston	19,433	57.2	41.5	<.1	0.8	0.0	0.4	47	52	32	62	0.8	0.7	0.9	0.4
28 161	Yalobusha	12,033	61.9	37.5	<.1	<.1	0.0	0.4	66	41	40	45	0.5	0.5	0.5	0.3
28 163	Yazoo	25,506	46.7	52.5	0.2	0.1	0.0	0.4	32	63	20	54	1.0	0.7	1.5	0.6
28	**MISSISSIPPI**	**2,573,216**	**63.1**	**35.4**	**0.5**	**0.3**	**<.1**	**0.6**					**100.0**	**100.0**	**100.0**	**100.0**
	CONGRESSIONAL															
	District 1	514,548	76.5	22.7	0.2	0.1	<.1	0.5	4	2	4	4	20.0	24.2	12.8	15.0
	District 2	514,845	36.4	62.7	0.2	<.1	<.1	0.5	2	5	1	3	20.0	11.5	35.4	17.1
	District 3	515,314	66.6	31.3	0.4	1.1	<.1	0.6	1	3	3	2	20.0	21.1	17.7	18.2
	District 4	513,853	58.5	40.6	0.3	<.1	<.1	0.4	5	4	2	5	20.0	18.5	22.9	13.4
	District 5	514,656	77.5	19.9	1.2	0.2	<.1	1.1	3	1	5	1	20.0	24.6	11.2	36.3

Table B. — 1990 Voting Age Population (VAP) by Race and Ethnic Origin

County	Total Voting Age Population	Percent of total VAP — Non-Hispanic White	Black	Asian and Pacific Islander	Native American	Other	Hispanic	Rank — Percent of total VAP Total	Non-Hispanic White	Black	Hispanic	Percent contribution to state VAP Total	Non-Hispanic White	Black	Hispanic	VAP percent of total population Total	Non-Hispanic White	Black	Asian and Pacific Islander	Native American	Other	Hispanic
Adams	25,114	54.2	45.1	0.2	0.1	<.1	0.4	21	58	25	35	1.4	1.1	2.0	1.0	71.0	75.9	66.0	64.5	84.2	50.0	72.4
Alcorn	23,633	89.7	9.8	0.1	<.1	<.1	0.3	22	5	78	62	1.3	1.7	0.4	0.7	74.5	75.7	65.5	60.8	63.6	20.0	61.4
Amite	9,418	58.7	40.9	<.1	0.1	0.0	0.2	61	55	28	78	0.5	0.5	0.7	0.2	70.7	76.3	63.9	83.3	90.9	0.0	57.6
Attala	13,435	64.2	35.3	0.1	<.1	0.0	0.3	48	48	34	73	0.7	0.7	0.8	0.3	72.7	77.7	65.3	65.4	37.5	0.0	60.3
Benton	5,648	66.0	33.5	<.1	<.1	0.0	0.4	78	42	39	38	0.3	0.3	0.3	0.2	70.2	76.8	60.0	100.0	80.0	0.0	64.9
Bolivar	27,708	42.7	56.0	0.4	<.1	0.0	0.8	15	72	11	6	1.5	1.0	2.7	2.2	66.2	78.3	59.2	76.5	80.0	0.0	62.3
Calhoun	10,986	75.9	23.4	<.1	<.1	<.1	0.5	56	24	58	19	0.6	0.7	0.4	0.5	73.7	77.3	64.0	66.7	83.3	66.7	74.4
Carroll	6,586	64.3	35.1	<.1	0.2	0.0	0.4	75	47	36	56	0.4	0.3	0.4	0.2	71.3	76.4	63.6	60.0	90.9	0.0	57.1
Chickasaw	12,680	65.5	33.8	<.1	0.1	0.0	0.5	51	44	38	29	0.7	0.7	0.7	0.6	70.1	75.4	61.8	41.7	90.0	0.0	71.8
Choctaw	6,331	73.4	26.1	0.1	0.1	0.0	0.3	76	25	56	65	0.3	0.4	0.3	0.2	69.8	73.8	60.7	70.0	77.8	0.0	61.3
Claiborne	8,186	19.8	79.5	0.2	0.2	0.0	0.4	66	81	2	43	0.4	0.1	1.1	0.3	72.0	82.0	69.9	93.8	65.0	0.0	58.9
Clarke	12,297	69.1	30.5	<.1	<.1	0.0	0.4	52	35	46	46	0.7	0.7	0.7	0.5	71.0	75.4	62.8	71.4	83.3	0.0	75.0
Clay	14,587	50.9	48.5	0.1	<.1	0.0	0.4	43	64	19	52	0.8	0.6	1.2	0.5	69.1	76.2	62.9	54.8	73.7	0.0	68.8
Coahoma	20,851	40.1	58.6	0.4	<.1	<.1	0.9	28	74	9	5	1.1	0.7	2.1	1.7	65.8	76.4	60.1	73.3	55.6	100.0	66.1
Copiah	19,335	53.5	45.9	<.1	<.1	0.0	0.4	30	60	23	48	1.1	0.8	1.5	0.7	70.1	76.4	63.9	68.0	76.2	0.0	68.5
Covington	11,422	69.7	29.9	<.1	<.1	0.0	0.2	55	34	48	76	0.6	0.6	0.6	0.3	69.1	74.6	59.2	52.6	88.9	0.0	57.1
DeSoto	48,298	87.7	11.6	0.2	0.2	0.0	0.4	7	8	75	44	2.6	3.5	1.0	1.8	71.1	72.1	64.6	66.4	73.7	0.0	63.1
Forrest	50,589	71.8	26.5	0.8	0.1	<.1	0.8	6	30	54	8	2.8	3.0	2.3	3.8	74.1	78.4	63.9	86.0	78.7	53.8	82.2
Franklin	5,898	67.5	32.1	<.1	<.1	0.0	0.3	77	39	42	66	0.3	0.3	0.3	0.2	70.4	75.5	61.6	75.0	100.0	0.0	81.0
George	11,624	91.1	8.4	<.1	0.2	0.0	0.2	54	3	79	75	0.6	0.9	0.2	0.3	69.7	70.6	61.4	47.1	76.3	0.0	60.4
Greene	7,148	79.8	19.3	<.1	0.1	0.0	0.6	72	19	62	13	0.4	0.5	0.2	0.4	69.9	71.8	63.3	66.7	90.0	0.0	69.2
Grenada	15,270	62.0	37.3	0.2	0.2	0.0	0.4	39	52	31	51	0.8	0.8	1.0	0.5	70.8	75.6	64.1	74.2	76.7	0.0	67.4
Hancock	23,077	90.0	7.5	0.4	0.4	<.1	1.6	23	4	80	2	1.3	1.7	0.3	3.5	72.7	73.8	63.0	62.2	72.4	50.0	67.9
Harrison	119,877	78.8	17.2	2.0	0.3	<.1	1.7	2	21	68	1	6.6	7.7	3.6	19.0	72.5	75.2	64.3	57.8	76.3	50.0	68.8
Hinds	183,463	52.6	46.4	0.5	<.1	<.1	0.4	1	61	22	34	10.0	7.9	14.8	7.6	72.1	78.7	65.9	70.5	71.2	48.6	70.3
Holmes	14,033	29.1	70.4	0.2	<.1	<.1	0.3	45	80	3	69	0.8	0.3	1.7	0.4	65.0	79.2	60.4	80.6	53.8	100.0	62.9
Humphreys	7,788	37.5	61.4	0.4	<.1	0.0	0.5	67	76	7	20	0.4	0.2	0.8	0.4	64.2	76.2	58.5	81.4	75.0	0.0	59.4
Issaquena	1,288	48.2	51.3	0.2	<.1	0.0	0.2	82	66	16	82	<.1	<.1	0.1	<.1	67.5	74.5	62.0	100.0	100.0	0.0	33.3
Itawamba	15,154	92.9	6.5	0.1	<.1	0.0	0.4	40	2	81	37	0.8	1.1	0.2	0.6	75.7	76.1	72.1	58.6	55.6	0.0	66.7
Jackson	81,028	80.5	17.6	0.8	0.2	<.1	0.9	3	17	67	3	4.4	5.3	2.5	6.8	70.3	73.0	60.6	62.1	68.7	40.0	68.6
Jasper	11,876	54.1	45.5	<.1	<.1	0.0	0.3	53	59	24	71	0.7	0.5	0.9	0.3	69.4	76.7	62.3	71.4	75.0	0.0	78.0
Jefferson	5,588	16.6	82.7	<.1	<.1	0.0	0.5	79	82	1	23	0.3	<.1	0.8	0.3	64.6	79.2	62.2	100.0	100.0	0.0	67.4
Jefferson Davis	9,691	49.9	49.5	0.2	0.1	0.0	0.3	60	65	18	68	0.5	0.4	0.8	0.3	69.0	76.5	62.8	68.2	66.7	0.0	61.4
Jones	45,069	77.8	21.5	0.1	0.3	<.1	0.3	9	22	59	64	2.5	2.9	1.7	1.3	72.7	76.1	62.6	69.0	58.8	28.6	66.8
Kemper	7,283	47.1	50.8	<.1	1.7	0.0	0.3	71	68	17	70	0.4	0.3	0.6	0.2	70.3	78.1	64.6	75.0	63.5	0.0	62.5
Lafayette	25,217	76.0	21.1	2.2	<.1	<.1	0.6	20	23	60	12	1.4	1.6	0.9	1.5	79.2	83.3	66.8	86.5	73.1	100.0	79.3
Lamar	21,318	88.5	10.5	0.3	0.1	<.1	0.5	26	7	76	17	1.2	1.5	0.4	1.1	70.1	71.2	61.8	65.5	70.3	100.0	69.0
Lauderdale	54,373	68.1	30.7	0.4	<.1	<.1	0.6	5	37	45	11	3.0	3.0	2.9	3.3	72.0	76.4	63.8	71.9	78.3	80.0	70.5
Lawrence	8,700	70.1	29.3	0.1	<.1	0.0	0.3	63	33	49	60	0.5	0.5	0.4	0.3	69.8	73.7	62.1	66.7	100.0	0.0	58.8
Leake	13,177	65.0	31.5	<.1	3.3	0.0	0.2	50	46	43	79	0.7	0.7	0.7	0.2	71.5	77.3	63.5	62.5	56.3	0.0	53.1
Lee	47,085	80.6	18.7	0.2	<.1	<.1	0.5	8	16	65	24	2.6	3.1	1.5	2.2	71.8	74.3	62.9	64.3	78.9	50.0	64.7
Leflore	25,329	43.8	55.4	0.4	<.1	<.1	0.4	19	71	12	58	1.4	0.9	2.4	0.8	67.8	76.7	62.1	71.8	69.6	100.0	61.6
Lincoln	21,686	72.8	26.8	0.1	<.1	<.1	0.2	25	29	52	80	1.2	1.3	1.0	0.4	71.6	74.7	64.5	64.4	63.2	100.0	63.3
Lowndes	41,710	65.8	32.8	0.5	0.1	<.1	0.7	11	43	41	9	2.3	2.2	2.4	2.9	70.3	75.3	62.2	71.3	80.0	38.1	62.5
Madison	37,875	59.7	39.4	0.3	<.1	<.1	0.5	12	54	29	27	2.1	1.8	2.6	1.7	70.4	76.3	63.1	69.2	77.5	100.0	66.7
Marion	17,758	72.9	26.4	0.1	0.1	<.1	0.5	31	26	55	31	1.0	1.1	0.8	0.8	69.5	73.4	61.0	45.5	78.3	33.3	59.1
Marshall	21,267	52.3	47.0	0.1	0.2	<.1	0.4	27	62	21	57	1.2	0.9	1.7	0.7	70.0	75.2	65.2	66.7	89.8	60.0	57.1
Monroe	26,092	72.9	26.6	<.1	<.1	0.0	0.4	17	27	53	55	1.4	1.6	1.2	0.9	71.3	75.1	63.0	75.0	62.5	0.0	51.6
Montgomery	8,854	60.6	38.9	0.1	0.1	0.0	0.4	62	53	30	45	0.5	0.4	0.6	0.3	71.5	77.7	63.5	68.8	81.8	0.0	70.0
Neshoba	17,395	72.8	16.8	0.1	9.9	<.1	0.4	32	28	69	59	1.0	1.0	0.5	0.6	70.1	75.0	63.5	71.4	54.1	100.0	58.7
Newton	14,709	70.9	26.0	<.1	2.6	<.1	0.4	42	32	57	49	0.8	0.9	0.7	0.5	72.5	76.4	65.7	100.0	53.5	50.0	65.9
Noxubee	8,340	36.1	63.4	<.1	0.3	0.0	0.2	65	77	6	81	0.5	0.2	0.9	0.1	66.2	76.1	61.7	83.3	63.6	0.0	48.1
Oktibbeha	29,713	67.4	29.0	2.7	<.1	<.1	0.8	14	40	50	7	1.6	1.6	1.5	2.4	77.4	83.8	65.7	78.9	82.8	58.3	76.4
Panola	20,434	57.0	42.4	<.1	<.1	0.0	0.5	29	57	26	32	1.1	1.0	1.5	0.9	68.1	76.0	59.9	54.5	54.8	0.0	60.8
Pearl River	27,510	86.2	12.5	0.2	0.3	0.0	0.7	16	11	74	10	1.5	1.9	0.6	1.8	71.1	72.6	62.5	69.6	61.0	0.0	63.3
Perry	7,460	79.3	19.8	<.1	0.5	<.1	0.3	70	20	61	61	0.4	0.5	0.3	0.2	68.7	71.3	60.4	40.0	53.0	100.0	54.3
Pike	25,784	58.3	41.1	0.1	<.1	0.0	0.4	18	56	27	40	1.4	1.2	1.8	1.0	69.9	75.8	63.1	59.1	57.7	0.0	62.4
Pontotoc	16,209	86.3	13.1	0.1	0.1	0.0	0.3	38	10	72	72	0.9	1.1	0.4	0.4	72.9	74.1	65.7	65.6	75.0	0.0	66.2
Prentiss	17,270	88.9	10.5	<.1	0.1	0.0	0.4	33	6	77	54	0.9	1.3	0.3	0.6	74.2	75.3	66.3	52.2	79.2	0.0	68.1
Quitman	7,019	46.0	53.2	0.2	0.1	0.0	0.4	73	70	13	41	0.4	0.3	0.6	0.3	66.9	76.6	60.3	88.9	56.3	0.0	60.4
Rankin	63,059	83.3	15.8	0.3	<.1	<.1	0.5	4	13	70	18	3.5	4.3	1.7	3.2	72.3	73.3	68.2	65.5	78.6	54.5	65.6
Scott	16,852	65.1	34.0	<.1	0.2	<.1	0.5	36	45	37	22	0.9	0.9	1.0	0.8	69.8	74.3	62.7	60.9	64.3	100.0	62.4
Sharkey	4,468	38.4	60.5	0.4	<.1	0.0	0.6	81	75	8	14	0.2	0.1	0.5	0.2	63.2	73.4	58.1	95.2	42.9	0.0	54.2
Simpson	16,868	71.2	28.3	<.1	0.2	0.0	0.2	35	31	51	77	0.9	1.0	0.8	0.3	70.4	74.6	61.8	72.7	69.6	0.0	55.2
Smith	10,595	80.6	18.8	<.1	0.1	0.0	0.4	57	15	64	47	0.6	0.7	0.3	0.4	71.6	74.6	61.6	71.4	68.8	0.0	50.6
Stone	7,688	80.2	18.9	0.2	0.2	<.1	0.4	68	18	63	33	0.4	0.5	0.3	0.3	71.5	74.1	62.4	100.0	70.0	100.0	63.0
Sunflower	22,422	40.6	58.4	0.3	<.1	<.1	0.5	24	73	10	21	1.2	0.7	2.3	1.1	68.2	78.7	62.4	83.3	71.4	50.0	64.1
Tallahatchie	10,167	47.1	51.9	0.3	0.1	0.0	0.5	58	67	15	30	0.6	0.4	0.9	0.5	66.8	76.9	59.8	76.7	92.9	0.0	58.5
Tate	15,150	68.7	30.4	0.1	0.2	0.0	0.6	41	36	47	16	0.8	0.8	0.8	0.8	70.7	74.9	62.7	73.1	80.6	0.0	70.2
Tippah	14,249	85.1	14.5	<.1	<.1	0.0	0.3	44	12	71	67	0.8	1.0	0.4	0.4	73.0	74.8	64.3	64.7	58.3	0.0	62.5

Table B. — 1990 Voting Age Population (VAP) by Race and Ethnic Origin (cont)

County	Total Voting Age Population	Percent of total VAP						Rank					Percent contribution to state VAP				VAP percent of total population						
			Non-Hispanic					Percent of total VAP						Non-Hispanic					Non-Hispanic				
									Non-Hispanic														
		White	Black	Asian and Pacific Islander	Native American	Other	Hispanic	Total	White	Black	Hispanic	Total	White	Black	Hispanic	Total	White	Black	Asian and Pacific Islander	Native American	Other	Hispanic
Tishomingo	13,512	96.4	3.2	<.1	<.1	<.1	0.3	47	1	82	74	0.7	1.1	<.1	0.3	76.4	76.8	68.6	38.5	66.7	100.0	62.5
Tunica	5,077	30.1	68.9	<.1	<.1	<.1	0.9	80	79	4	4	0.3	0.1	0.6	0.4	62.2	76.9	57.4	75.0	100.0	100.0	55.6
Union	16,251	86.5	12.9	<.1	<.1	<.1	0.4	37	9	73	39	0.9	1.1	0.4	0.6	73.6	75.0	65.6	60.0	88.9	50.0	67.0
Walthall	9,817	62.5	36.8	0.2	0.1	0.0	0.4	59	51	32	36	0.5	0.5	0.6	0.4	68.4	74.7	59.7	66.7	73.3	0.0	86.0
Warren	33,583	63.8	35.2	0.4	0.1	<.1	0.5	13	49	35	25	1.8	1.7	2.1	1.6	70.1	74.5	63.5	64.6	84.1	14.3	65.4
Washington	44,908	46.6	52.2	0.4	<.1	<.1	0.6	10	69	14	15	2.5	1.7	4.1	2.4	66.1	74.4	60.1	79.9	73.6	61.5	62.3
Wayne	13,420	68.0	31.4	0.2	0.1	<.1	0.4	49	38	44	53	0.7	0.7	0.7	0.5	68.8	73.2	60.8	68.8	78.9	100.0	66.7
Webster	7,474	80.9	18.4	0.1	<.1	<.1	0.5	69	14	66	28	0.4	0.5	0.2	0.3	73.1	76.4	61.6	80.0	50.0	100.0	63.2
Wilkinson	6,731	35.4	63.8	<.1	0.2	<.1	0.5	74	78	5	26	0.4	0.2	0.7	0.3	69.5	76.9	66.0	100.0	80.0	100.0	73.3
Winston	13,719	62.7	36.4	<.1	0.6	0.0	0.3	46	50	33	63	0.8	0.7	0.9	0.4	70.6	77.3	61.9	56.3	48.1	0.0	61.4
Yalobusha	8,671	66.4	33.1	<.1	<.1	0.0	0.4	64	41	40	50	0.5	0.5	0.5	0.3	72.1	77.3	63.5	60.0	80.0	0.0	62.3
Yazoo	17,231	51.9	47.4	0.2	0.1	0.0	0.4	34	63	20	42	0.9	0.7	1.4	0.7	67.6	75.0	61.0	73.5	66.7	0.0	68.0
MISSISSIPPI	**1,826,455**	**67.1**	**31.5**	**0.5**	**0.3**	**<.1**	**0.6**					**100.0**	**100.0**	**100.0**	**100.0**	**71.0**	**75.5**	**63.1**	**67.2**	**61.4**	**50.1**	**66.9**
CONGRESSIONAL																						
District 1	373,516	79.3	19.9	0.3	0.1	<.1	0.4	1	2	4	4	20.5	24.1	12.9	14.7	72.6	75.2	63.8	75.5	75.3	37.5	65.5
District 2	346,446	41.4	57.7	0.3	<.1	<.1	0.5	5	5	1	3	19.0	11.7	34.7	15.9	67.3	76.6	61.9	75.0	69.3	56.5	62.1
District 3	370,165	70.4	27.8	0.4	0.9	<.1	0.5	2	3	3	2	20.3	21.2	17.9	18.1	71.8	75.8	63.9	73.3	56.2	56.8	66.5
District 4	367,820	62.7	36.5	0.3	<.1	<.1	0.4	4	4	2	5	20.1	18.8	23.3	13.8	71.6	76.7	64.2	68.8	73.4	44.0	68.7
District 5	368,508	80.2	17.4	1.0	0.2	<.1	1.1	3	1	5	1	20.2	24.1	11.2	37.6	71.6	74.1	62.7	61.2	71.4	50.0	69.3

Table C. — Voter Participation: November 3, 1992, General Election

County	Estimated Voting Age Population (VAP), 1992	Voter registration (REG)				Voter turnout													
						Highest office				Maximum vote						Percent drop-off, by office[1]			
		Total	% contribution to state REG	% of 1992 VAP	Rank by % of 1992 VAP	Actual	Total	Office	% of 1992 VAP	Total	% contribution to state turnout	% of REG	Rank by % of REG	% of 1992 VAP	Rank by % 1992 VAP	President	Senator	Governor	Representative
Adams	24,989	25,336	1.5	101.4	36	15,374	15,877	P	63.5	15,877	1.5	62.7	41	63.5	21	0.0	-	-	3.9
Alcorn	23,783	22,004	1.3	92.5	47	14,136	14,136	P	59.4	14,136	1.4	64.2	33	59.4	42	0.0	-	-	10.6
Amite	9,621	9,442	0.6	98.1	40	6,655	6,143	C	63.8	6,655	0.6	70.5	20	69.2	8	14.6	-	-	7.7
Attala	13,431	12,364	0.8	92.1	49	7,087	7,087	P	52.8	7,087	0.7	57.3	59	52.8	67	0.0	-	-	2.3
Benton	5,748	6,305	0.4	109.7	20	4,216	3,955	P	68.8	4,216	0.4	66.9	27	73.3	5	6.2	-	-	9.1
Bolivar	27,428	23,835	1.5	86.9	57	13,863	14,226	P	51.9	14,226	1.4	59.7	52	51.9	70	0.0	-	-	12.7
Calhoun	10,965	10,271	0.6	93.7	45	6,761	6,520	C	59.5	6,761	0.7	65.8	30	61.7	30	7.2	-	-	3.6
Carroll	6,648	5,887	0.4	88.6	55	4,546	4,127	C	62.1	4,546	0.4	77.2	5	68.4	10	32.2	-	-	9.2
Chickasaw	12,898	12,041	0.7	93.4	46	7,355	7,055	C	54.7	7,355	0.7	61.1	45	57.0	54	4.7	-	-	4.1
Choctaw	6,525	7,923	0.5	121.4	4	3,768	3,768	P	57.7	3,768	0.4	47.6	79	57.7	51	0.0	-	-	1.6
Claiborne	7,603	5,861	0.4	77.1	69	4,682	4,442	C	58.4	4,682	0.5	79.9	3	61.6	31	5.8	-	-	5.1
Clarke	12,640	10,547	0.6	83.4	65	7,388	7,131	C	56.4	7,388	0.7	70.0	21	58.4	48	6.1	-	-	3.5
Clay	14,770	11,274	0.7	76.3	70	9,200	8,603	C	58.2	9,200	0.9	81.6	2	62.3	28	6.9	-	-	6.5
Coahoma	20,612	17,092	1.0	82.9	66	10,984	11,180	P	54.2	11,180	1.1	65.4	31	54.2	60	0.0	-	-	16.6
Copiah	19,574	16,649	1.0	85.1	60	10,466	9,654	C	49.3	10,466	1.0	62.9	39	53.5	65	9.7	-	-	7.8
Covington	11,797	13,678	0.8	115.9	11	7,462	7,121	C	60.4	7,462	0.7	54.6	68	63.3	24	6.2	-	-	4.6
DeSoto	51,975	40,300	2.5	77.5	68	29,716	27,917	C	53.7	29,716	2.9	73.7	13	57.2	53	7.2	-	-	6.1
Forrest	50,587	31,505	1.9	62.3	81	22,805	23,249	P	46.0	23,249	2.3	73.8	12	46.0	77	2.1	-	-	0.0
Franklin	6,042	5,781	0.4	95.7	42	4,307	4,082	C	67.6	4,307	0.4	74.5	8	71.3	7	8.6	-	-	5.2
George	12,170	13,268	0.8	109.0	24	8,081	9,509	P	78.1	9,509	0.9	71.7	14	78.1	2	0.0	-	-	22.0
Greene	7,394	9,078	0.6	122.8	2	5,047	5,014	C	67.8	5,047	0.5	55.6	62	68.3	11	8.1	-	-	0.7
Grenada	15,615	15,740	1.0	100.8	37	9,404	9,568	P	61.3	9,568	0.9	60.8	46	61.3	32	0.0	-	-	7.1
Hancock	24,971	25,509	1.6	102.2	34	13,977	13,558	C	54.3	13,977	1.4	54.8	64	56.0	57	3.8	-	-	3.0
Harrison	121,496	72,155	4.4	59.4	82	53,724	52,301	C	43.0	53,724	5.2	74.5	9	44.2	79	11.8	-	-	2.6
Hinds	184,275	149,538	9.1	81.1	67	91,594	96,024	P	52.1	96,024	9.4	64.2	34	52.1	68	0.0	-	-	11.2
Holmes	14,097	14,582	0.9	103.4	33	7,975	7,579	C	53.8	7,975	0.8	54.7	65	56.6	55	24.6	-	-	5.0
Humphreys	7,739	9,338	0.6	120.7	7	5,029	4,683	P	60.5	5,029	0.5	53.9	70	65.0	17	6.9	-	-	9.8
Issaquena	1,246	1,327	<.1	106.5	28	990	990	P	79.5	990	<.1	74.6	7	79.5	1	0.0	-	-	13.0
Itawamba	15,156	13,295	0.8	87.7	56	9,051	8,943	C	59.0	9,051	0.9	68.1	25	59.7	39	3.7	-	-	1.2
Jackson	82,328	75,300	4.6	91.5	50	45,273	44,930	P	54.6	45,273	4.4	60.1	49	55.0	59	0.8	-	-	1.7
Jasper	12,211	11,979	0.7	98.1	41	7,022	7,022	C	57.5	7,022	0.7	58.6	57	57.5	52	8.5	-	-	0.0
Jefferson	5,724	6,274	0.4	109.6	21	3,442	3,745	C	65.4	3,745	0.4	59.7	51	65.4	15	6.0	-	-	0.0
Jefferson Davis	9,985	10,181	0.6	102.0	35	6,383	5,633	P	56.4	6,383	0.6	62.7	40	63.9	20	11.8	-	-	18.8
Jones	45,513	51,115	3.1	112.3	16	24,414	24,430	P	53.7	24,430	2.4	47.8	78	53.7	63	0.0	-	-	0.5
Kemper	7,340	6,947	0.4	94.6	44	4,827	4,469	C	60.9	4,827	0.5	69.5	23	65.8	14	9.7	-	-	7.4
Lafayette	24,363	22,479	1.4	92.3	48	11,577	11,402	C	46.8	11,577	1.1	51.5	75	47.5	76	1.6	-	-	1.5
Lamar	23,127	19,385	1.2	83.8	63	13,361	13,190	C	57.0	13,361	1.3	68.9	24	57.8	50	2.5	-	-	1.3
Lauderdale	54,679	45,934	2.8	84.0	62	26,723	27,466	P	50.2	27,466	2.7	59.8	50	50.2	72	0.0	-	-	8.9
Lawrence	8,933	10,007	0.6	112.0	17	6,623	6,417	C	71.8	6,623	0.6	66.2	29	74.1	4	8.0	-	-	3.1
Leake	13,382	11,995	0.7	89.6	54	8,374	8,008	C	59.8	8,374	0.8	69.8	22	62.6	25	7.0	-	-	4.4
Lee	49,323	36,380	2.2	73.8	74	22,495	22,501	P	45.6	22,501	2.2	61.8	44	45.6	78	0.0	-	-	8.1
Leflore	25,004	30,261	1.8	121.0	5	11,844	12,498	P	50.0	12,498	1.2	41.3	81	50.0	73	0.0	-	-	13.7
Lincoln	22,315	20,057	1.2	89.9	53	14,303	13,831	C	62.0	14,303	1.4	71.3	16	64.1	19	8.5	-	-	3.3
Lowndes	42,605	31,341	1.9	73.6	75	20,815	19,179	C	45.0	20,815	2.0	66.4	28	48.9	74	9.5	-	-	7.9
Madison	41,221	34,453	2.1	83.6	64	24,524	23,721	P	57.5	24,524	2.4	71.2	17	59.5	41	3.3	-	-	4.9
Marion	18,182	21,994	1.3	121.0	6	12,013	11,613	P	63.9	12,013	1.2	54.6	66	66.1	12	3.3	-	-	4.1
Marshall	21,641	19,686	1.2	91.0	51	12,069	12,512	P	57.8	12,512	1.2	63.6	36	57.8	49	0.0	-	-	12.8
Monroe	26,605	22,418	1.4	84.3	61	14,173	13,364	C	50.2	14,173	1.4	63.2	37	53.3	66	13.8	-	-	5.7
Montgomery	8,859	9,704	0.6	109.5	22	4,794	4,776	P	53.9	4,794	0.5	49.4	77	54.1	61	0.4	-	-	0.8
Neshoba	17,989	19,268	1.2	107.1	25	10,528	10,333	C	57.4	10,528	1.0	54.6	66	58.5	47	4.6	-	-	1.9
Newton	14,886	14,238	0.9	95.6	43	8,813	8,156	C	54.8	8,813	0.9	61.9	43	59.2	43	11.4	-	-	7.5
Noxubee	8,392	8,870	0.5	105.7	29	5,018	5,037	P	60.0	5,037	0.5	56.8	60	60.0	38	0.0	-	-	11.7
Oktibbeha	28,759	18,576	1.1	64.6	80	13,791	13,156	P	45.7	13,791	1.3	74.2	11	48.0	75	4.6	-	-	5.0
Panola	21,185	22,192	1.4	104.8	30	13,090	12,036	C	56.8	13,090	1.3	59.0	55	61.8	29	12.5	-	-	8.1
Pearl River	28,821	21,887	1.3	75.9	71	14,950	15,460	C	53.6	15,460	1.5	70.6	19	53.6	64	4.3	-	-	0.0
Perry	7,851	8,398	0.5	107.0	26	4,630	4,630	C	59.0	4,630	0.5	55.1	63	59.0	44	2.8	-	-	0.0
Pike	26,428	18,955	1.2	71.7	77	14,680	14,825	C	56.1	14,825	1.4	78.2	4	56.1	56	7.7	-	-	0.0
Pontotoc	16,699	12,028	0.7	72.0	76	8,409	8,505	C	50.9	8,505	0.8	70.7	18	50.9	71	1.6	-	-	0.0
Prentiss	17,163	14,753	0.9	86.0	58	8,526	8,929	C	52.0	8,929	0.9	60.5	47	52.0	69	4.5	-	-	0.0
Quitman	6,931	7,889	0.5	113.8	14	4,093	4,399	C	63.5	4,399	0.4	55.8	61	63.5	22	7.0	-	-	0.0
Rankin	67,864	50,130	3.1	73.9	73	37,528	36,423	C	53.7	37,528	3.7	74.9	6	55.3	58	3.5	-	-	2.9
Scott	17,159	18,965	1.2	110.5	19	10,078	9,689	C	56.5	10,078	1.0	53.1	74	58.7	45	7.4	-	-	3.9
Sharkey	4,502	3,121	0.2	69.3	78	2,737	2,752	P	61.1	2,752	0.3	88.2	1	61.1	33	0.0	-	-	11.0
Simpson	17,365	13,058	0.8	75.2	72	9,326	9,326	P	53.7	9,326	0.9	71.4	15	53.7	62	0.0	-	-	0.0
Smith	10,778	9,186	0.6	85.2	59	6,828	6,788	P	63.0	6,828	0.7	74.3	10	63.4	23	0.6	-	-	14.2
Stone	7,819	8,551	0.5	109.4	23	4,097	4,660	C	59.6	4,660	0.5	54.5	69	59.6	40	9.7	-	-	0.0
Sunflower	22,393	22,165	1.4	99.0	39	9,252	9,391	P	41.9	9,391	0.9	42.4	80	41.9	82	0.0	-	-	3.6
Tallahatchie	10,136	11,747	0.7	115.9	12	6,046	7,302	C	72.0	7,302	0.7	62.2	42	72.0	6	24.4	-	-	0.0
Tate	15,422	17,586	1.1	114.0	13	9,364	8,968	C	58.2	9,364	0.9	53.2	73	60.7	37	10.6	-	-	4.2
Tippah	14,606	18,343	1.1	125.6	1	8,976	9,128	C	62.5	9,128	0.9	49.8	76	62.5	26	4.3	-	-	0.0

[1]Percent drop-off is zero for any office used as highest office turnout.

Table C. — Voter Participation: November 3, 1992, General Election (cont)

County	Estimated Voting Age Population (VAP), 1992	Voter registration (REG)				Voter turnout													
							Highest office			Maximum vote						Percent drop-off, by office[1]			
		Total	% contribution to state REG	% of 1992 VAP	Rank by % of 1992 VAP	Actual	Total	Office	% of 1992 VAP	Total	% contribution to state turnout	% of REG	Rank by % of REG	% of 1992 VAP	Rank by % 1992 VAP	President	Senator	Governor	Representative
Tishomingo	13,456	13,939	0.8	103.6	31	8,061	8,182	C	60.8	8,182	0.8	58.7	56	60.8	36	1.3	-	-	0.0
Tunica	5,111	6,228	0.4	121.9	3	2,185	2,243	P	43.9	2,243	0.2	36.0	82	43.9	80	0.0	-	-	11.6
Union	16,593	16,435	1.0	99.0	38	9,732	9,742	P	58.7	9,742	0.9	59.3	54	58.7	46	0.0	-	-	1.1
Walthall	10,197	10,890	0.7	106.8	27	6,570	5,967	P	58.5	6,570	0.6	60.3	48	64.4	18	9.2	-	-	15.7
Warren	33,756	38,231	2.3	113.3	15	17,119	20,578	P	61.0	20,578	2.0	53.8	72	61.0	34	0.0	-	-	3.5
Washington	45,395	30,960	1.9	68.2	79	19,307	19,689	P	43.4	19,689	1.9	63.6	35	43.4	81	0.0	-	-	13.0
Wayne	13,818	12,500	0.8	90.5	52	7,783	8,406	C	60.8	8,406	0.8	67.2	26	60.8	35	7.4	-	-	0.0
Webster	7,590	8,453	0.5	111.4	18	5,012	5,012	C	66.0	5,012	0.5	59.3	53	66.0	13	0.5	-	-	0.0
Wilkinson	6,748	7,883	0.5	116.8	9	5,134	4,945	P	73.3	5,134	0.5	65.1	32	76.1	3	3.7	-	-	76.9
Winston	14,099	14,604	0.9	103.6	32	8,904	9,186	C	65.2	9,186	0.9	62.9	38	65.2	16	2.4	-	-	0.0
Yalobusha	8,641	10,219	0.6	118.3	8	5,945	5,612	C	64.9	5,945	0.6	58.2	58	68.8	9	11.7	-	-	5.6
Yazoo	17,313	20,087	1.2	116.0	10	10,815	10,745	P	62.1	10,815	1.1	53.8	71	62.5	27	0.6	-	-	8.5
MISSISSIPPI	1,861,000	1,640,150	100.0	88.1		1,008,019	1,005,349		54.0	1,026,251	100.0	62.6		55.1		4.3	-	-	5.9

[1]Percent drop-off is zero for any office used as highest office turnout.

Table E. — Vote for President: November 3, 1992, General Election

County	Total	Clinton (DEM)	Bush (REP)	Perot (IND)	Other	Plurality Total	Party	Pct DEM	Pct REP	Pct IND	Pct Other	Rank DEM	Rank REP	Rank IND	Contrib Total	Contrib DEM	Contrib REP	Contrib IND	Major DEM	Major REP
Adams	15,877	8,255	5,831	1,753	38	2,424	D	52.0	36.7	11.0	0.2	21	70	10	1.6	2.1	1.2	2.0	58.6	41.4
Alcorn	14,136	6,373	6,249	1,349	165	124	D	45.1	44.2	9.5	1.2	34	53	24	1.4	1.6	1.3	1.6	50.5	49.5
Amite	5,681	2,608	2,561	498	14	47	D	45.9	45.1	8.8	0.2	29	51	37	0.6	0.7	0.5	0.6	50.5	49.5
Attala	7,087	3,015	3,520	529	23	505	R	42.5	49.7	7.5	0.3	40	36	50	0.7	0.8	0.7	0.6	46.1	53.9
Benton	3,955	2,402	1,253	293	7	1,149	D	60.7	31.7	7.4	0.2	9	75	51	0.4	0.6	0.3	0.3	65.7	34.3
Bolivar	14,226	8,801	4,752	593	80	4,049	D	61.9	33.4	4.2	0.6	8	73	78	1.4	2.2	1.0	0.7	64.9	35.1
Calhoun	6,273	2,462	3,191	607	13	729	R	39.2	50.9	9.7	0.2	54	28	23	0.6	0.6	0.7	0.7	43.6	56.4
Carroll	3,084	1,182	1,695	200	7	513	R	38.3	55.0	6.5	0.2	55	16	57	0.3	0.3	0.3	0.2	41.1	58.9
Chickasaw	7,007	3,220	3,150	629	8	70	D	46.0	45.0	9.0	0.1	28	52	34	0.7	0.8	0.6	0.7	50.5	49.5
Choctaw	3,768	1,435	2,026	298	9	591	R	38.1	53.8	7.9	0.2	57	23	42	0.4	0.4	0.4	0.3	41.5	58.5
Claiborne	4,412	3,302	935	161	14	2,367	D	74.8	21.2	3.6	0.3	2	81	81	0.4	0.8	0.2	0.2	77.9	22.1
Clarke	6,934	2,259	4,207	450	18	1,948	R	32.6	60.7	6.5	0.3	71	6	56	0.7	0.6	0.9	0.5	34.9	65.1
Clay	8,563	4,620	3,297	626	20	1,323	D	54.0	38.5	7.3	0.2	15	67	53	0.9	1.2	0.7	0.7	58.4	41.6
Coahoma	11,180	6,409	4,120	518	133	2,289	D	57.3	36.9	4.6	1.2	12	68	74	1.1	1.6	0.8	0.6	60.9	39.1
Copiah	9,449	4,397	4,600	409	43	203	R	46.5	48.7	4.3	0.5	27	41	76	1.0	1.1	0.9	0.5	48.9	51.1
Covington	6,996	2,775	3,525	654	42	750	R	39.7	50.4	9.3	0.6	51	32	26	0.7	0.7	0.7	0.8	44.0	56.0
DeSoto	27,575	8,833	16,104	2,569	69	7,271	R	32.0	58.4	9.3	0.3	73	8	27	2.8	2.2	3.3	3.0	35.4	64.6
Forrest	22,753	8,333	12,432	1,909	79	4,099	R	36.6	54.6	8.4	0.3	58	18	38	2.3	2.1	2.5	2.2	40.1	59.9
Franklin	3,938	1,587	1,942	393	16	355	R	40.3	49.3	10.0	0.4	46	39	21	0.4	0.4	0.4	0.5	45.0	55.0
George	9,509	2,650	4,141	1,335	1,383	1,491	R	27.9	43.5	14.0	14.5	79	56	5	1.0	0.7	0.8	1.6	39.0	61.0
Greene	4,636	1,664	2,406	559	7	742	R	35.9	51.9	12.1	0.2	61	27	7	0.5	0.4	0.5	0.7	40.9	59.1
Grenada	9,568	4,203	4,721	609	35	518	R	43.9	49.3	6.4	0.4	36	38	61	1.0	1.1	1.0	0.7	47.1	52.9
Hancock	13,440	4,651	6,422	2,302	65	1,771	R	34.6	47.8	17.1	0.5	65	45	1	1.4	1.2	1.3	2.7	42.0	58.0
Harrison	47,407	15,268	25,049	6,855	235	9,781	R	32.2	52.8	14.5	0.5	72	25	3	4.8	3.8	5.1	8.0	37.9	62.1
Hinds	96,024	43,434	45,031	5,341	2,218	1,597	R	45.2	46.9	5.6	2.3	33	48	68	10.9	10.9	9.2	6.2	49.1	50.9
Holmes	6,014	4,092	1,694	203	25	2,398	D	68.0	28.2	3.4	0.4	3	80	82	0.6	1.0	0.3	0.2	70.7	29.3
Humphreys	4,683	2,696	1,721	258	8	975	D	57.6	36.7	5.5	0.2	11	69	69	0.5	0.7	0.4	0.3	61.0	39.0
Issaquena	990	550	298	79	63	252	D	55.6	30.1	8.0	6.4	13	78	41	0.1	0.1	<.1	<.1	64.9	35.1
Itawamba	8,713	3,635	4,142	918	18	507	R	41.7	47.5	10.5	0.2	43	47	13	0.9	0.9	0.8	1.1	46.7	53.3
Jackson	44,930	13,017	25,321	6,484	108	12,304	R	29.0	56.4	14.4	0.2	78	13	4	4.6	3.3	5.2	7.6	34.0	66.0
Jasper	6,428	3,059	2,789	568	12	270	D	47.6	43.4	8.8	0.2	26	57	36	0.7	0.8	0.6	0.7	52.3	47.7
Jefferson	3,522	2,796	562	156	8	2,234	D	79.4	16.0	4.4	0.2	1	82	75	0.4	0.7	0.1	0.2	83.3	16.7
Jefferson Davis	5,633	2,991	2,228	382	32	763	D	53.1	39.6	6.8	0.6	18	65	55	0.6	0.7	0.5	0.4	57.3	42.7
Jones	24,430	8,035	13,824	2,523	48	5,789	R	32.9	56.6	10.3	0.2	70	10	15	2.5	2.0	2.8	2.9	36.8	63.2
Kemper	4,361	2,243	1,830	278	10	413	D	51.4	42.0	6.4	0.2	22	60	60	0.4	0.6	0.4	0.3	55.1	44.9
Lafayette	11,397	5,224	5,251	861	61	27	R	45.8	46.1	7.6	0.5	31	49	48	1.2	1.3	1.1	1.0	49.9	50.1
Lamar	13,032	3,208	8,259	1,543	22	5,051	R	24.6	63.4	11.8	0.2	81	3	9	1.3	0.8	1.7	1.8	28.0	72.0
Lauderdale	27,466	8,489	17,098	1,659	220	8,609	R	30.9	62.3	6.0	0.8	75	4	67	2.8	2.1	3.5	1.9	33.2	66.8
Lawrence	6,095	2,582	2,689	765	59	107	R	42.4	44.1	12.6	1.0	41	54	6	0.6	0.6	0.6	0.9	49.0	51.0
Leake	7,786	3,333	3,943	497	13	610	R	42.8	50.6	6.4	0.2	39	30	59	0.8	0.8	0.8	0.6	45.8	54.2
Lee	22,501	7,710	12,231	2,041	519	4,521	R	34.3	54.4	9.1	2.3	68	20	33	2.3	1.9	2.5	2.4	38.7	61.3
Leflore	12,498	6,374	5,298	611	215	1,076	D	51.0	42.4	4.9	1.7	23	58	73	1.3	1.6	1.1	0.7	54.6	45.4
Lincoln	13,091	4,744	7,040	1,281	26	2,296	R	36.2	53.8	9.8	0.2	59	22	22	1.3	1.2	1.4	1.5	40.3	59.7
Lowndes	18,835	6,552	10,509	1,716	58	3,957	R	34.8	55.8	9.1	0.3	64	15	32	1.9	1.6	2.2	2.0	38.4	61.6
Madison	23,721	9,386	12,810	1,478	47	3,424	R	39.6	54.0	6.2	0.2	52	21	64	2.4	2.3	2.6	1.7	42.3	57.7
Marion	11,613	4,654	5,776	1,162	21	1,122	R	40.1	49.7	10.0	0.2	47	35	20	1.2	1.2	1.2	1.4	44.6	55.4
Marshall	12,512	7,913	3,847	689	63	4,066	D	63.2	30.7	5.5	0.5	7	77	70	1.3	2.0	0.8	0.8	67.3	32.7
Monroe	12,224	4,933	5,994	1,255	42	1,061	R	40.4	49.0	10.3	0.3	45	40	16	1.2	1.2	1.2	1.5	45.1	54.9
Montgomery	4,776	2,076	2,324	370	6	248	R	43.5	48.7	7.7	0.1	38	42	45	0.5	0.5	0.5	0.4	47.2	52.8
Neshoba	10,042	3,090	6,135	794	23	3,045	R	30.8	61.1	7.9	0.2	76	5	43	1.0	0.8	1.3	0.9	33.5	66.5
Newton	7,806	2,146	5,128	494	38	2,982	R	27.5	65.7	6.3	0.5	80	2	63	0.8	0.5	1.1	0.6	29.5	70.5
Noxubee	5,037	3,188	1,623	203	23	1,565	D	63.3	32.2	4.0	0.5	6	74	80	0.5	0.8	0.3	0.2	66.3	33.7
Oktibbeha	13,156	5,726	6,381	984	65	655	R	43.5	48.5	7.5	0.5	37	43	49	1.3	1.4	1.3	1.1	47.3	52.7
Panola	11,460	6,066	4,644	729	21	1,422	D	52.9	40.5	6.4	0.2	19	62	62	1.2	1.5	1.0	0.9	56.6	43.4
Pearl River	14,797	4,683	7,726	2,352	36	3,043	R	31.6	52.2	15.9	0.2	74	26	2	1.5	1.2	1.6	2.7	37.7	62.3
Perry	4,501	1,490	2,538	462	11	1,048	R	33.1	56.4	10.3	0.2	69	12	17	0.5	0.4	0.5	0.5	37.0	63.0
Pike	13,679	6,279	6,005	1,380	15	274	D	45.9	43.9	10.1	0.1	30	55	18	1.4	1.6	1.2	1.6	51.1	48.9
Pontotoc	8,366	2,965	4,595	777	29	1,630	R	35.4	54.9	9.3	0.3	62	17	29	0.9	0.7	0.9	0.9	39.2	60.8
Prentiss	8,526	3,385	4,317	781	43	932	R	39.7	50.6	9.2	0.5	50	31	31	0.9	0.8	0.9	0.9	43.9	56.1
Quitman	4,093	2,422	1,451	210	10	971	D	59.2	35.5	5.1	0.2	10	72	72	0.4	0.6	0.3	0.2	62.5	37.5
Rankin	36,210	8,155	24,537	3,454	64	16,382	R	22.5	67.8	9.5	0.2	82	1	25	3.7	2.0	5.0	4.0	24.9	75.1
Scott	9,329	3,349	5,268	691	21	1,919	R	35.9	56.5	7.4	0.2	60	11	52	0.9	0.8	1.1	0.8	38.9	61.1
Sharkey	2,752	1,526	1,008	145	73	518	D	55.5	36.6	5.3	2.7	14	71	71	0.3	0.4	0.2	0.2	60.2	39.8
Simpson	9,326	3,213	5,358	726	29	2,145	R	34.5	57.5	7.8	0.3	66	9	44	0.9	0.8	1.1	0.8	37.5	62.5
Smith	6,788	1,968	4,106	680	34	2,138	R	29.0	60.5	10.0	0.5	77	7	19	0.7	0.5	0.8	0.8	32.4	67.6
Stone	4,209	1,447	2,295	447	20	848	R	34.4	54.5	10.6	0.5	67	19	11	0.4	0.4	0.5	0.5	38.7	61.3
Sunflower	9,391	5,050	3,726	600	15	1,324	D	53.8	39.7	6.4	0.2	17	64	58	1.0	1.3	0.8	0.7	57.5	42.5
Tallahatchie	5,518	2,902	2,213	380	23	689	D	52.6	40.1	6.9	0.4	20	63	54	0.6	0.7	0.5	0.4	56.7	43.3
Tate	8,371	3,519	4,196	634	22	677	R	42.0	50.1	7.6	0.3	42	33	47	0.9	0.9	0.9	0.7	45.6	54.4
Tippah	8,739	3,475	4,444	802	18	969	R	39.8	50.9	9.2	0.2	48	29	30	0.9	0.9	0.9	0.9	43.9	56.1

Table E. – Vote for President: November 3, 1992, General Election (cont)

County	All candidates																		Major party	
						Plurality		Percent of total vote							Percent contribution to state vote				Percent of vote	
												Rank								
	Total	Clinton (DEM)	Bush (REP)	Perot (IND)	Other	Total	Party	DEM	REP	IND	Other	DEM	REP	IND	Total	DEM	REP	IND	DEM	REP
Tishomingo	8,072	3,910	3,393	751	18	517	D	48.4	42.0	9.3	0.2	25	59	28	0.8	1.0	0.7	0.9	53.5	46.5
Tunica	2,243	1,451	693	96	3	758	D	64.7	30.9	4.3	0.1	5	76	77	0.2	0.4	0.1	0.1	67.7	32.3
Union	9,742	3,714	5,173	816	39	1,459	R	38.1	53.1	8.4	0.4	56	24	39	1.0	0.9	1.1	1.0	41.8	58.2
Walthall	5,967	2,476	2,728	711	52	252	R	41.5	45.7	11.9	0.9	44	50	8	0.6	0.6	0.6	0.8	47.6	52.4
Warren	20,578	8,175	10,209	2,146	48	2,034	R	39.7	49.6	10.4	0.2	49	37	14	2.1	2.0	2.1	2.5	44.5	55.5
Washington	19,689	10,588	7,598	795	708	2,990	D	53.8	38.6	4.0	3.6	16	66	79	2.0	2.6	1.6	0.9	58.2	41.8
Wayne	7,783	3,064	3,874	824	21	810	R	39.4	49.8	10.6	0.3	53	34	12	0.8	0.8	0.8	1.0	44.2	55.8
Webster	4,988	1,746	2,791	444	7	1,045	R	35.0	56.0	8.9	0.1	63	14	35	0.5	0.4	0.6	0.5	38.5	61.5
Wilkinson	4,945	3,210	1,399	307	29	1,811	D	64.9	28.3	6.2	0.6	4	79	66	0.5	0.8	0.3	0.4	69.6	30.4
Winston	8,968	3,953	4,311	688	16	358	R	44.1	48.1	7.7	0.2	35	44	46	0.9	1.0	0.9	0.8	47.8	52.2
Yalobusha	5,248	2,617	2,179	438	14	438	D	49.9	41.5	8.3	0.3	24	61	40	0.5	0.7	0.4	0.5	54.6	45.4
Yazoo	10,745	4,880	5,113	669	83	233	R	45.4	47.6	6.2	0.8	32	46	65	1.1	1.2	1.0	0.8	48.8	51.2
MISSISSIPPI	981,793	400,258	487,793	85,626	8,116	87,535	R	40.8	49.7	8.7	0.8				100.0	100.0	100.0	100.0	45.1	54.9

Table G. — Vote for Governor: November 5, 1991, General Election

County	Total	Mabus (DEM)	Fordice (REP)	O'Hara (IND)[1]	Plurality Total	Party	Percent of total vote DEM	REP	IND	Rank DEM	REP	IND	Percent contribution to state vote Total	DEM	REP	IND
Adams	11,293	6,631	4,554	108	2,077	D	58.7	40.3	1.0	16	66	66	1.6	2.0	1.3	1.0
Alcorn	6,455	3,070	3,216	169	146	R	47.6	49.8	2.6	40	47	10	0.9	0.9	0.9	1.5
Amite	4,704	2,097	2,552	55	455	R	44.6	54.3	1.2	52	30	52	0.7	0.6	0.7	0.5
Attala	5,703	2,384	3,269	50	885	R	41.8	57.3	0.9	57	22	67	0.8	0.7	0.9	0.4
Benton	2,661	1,755	861	45	894	D	66.0	32.4	1.7	7	77	28	0.4	0.5	0.2	0.4
Bolivar	8,350	5,146	3,062	142	2,084	D	61.6	36.7	1.7	13	70	26	1.2	1.5	0.8	1.3
Calhoun	5,920	2,612	3,208	100	596	R	44.1	54.2	1.7	54	33	29	0.8	0.8	0.9	0.9
Carroll	3,108	1,295	1,789	24	494	R	41.7	57.6	0.8	58	21	74	0.4	0.4	0.5	0.2
Chickasaw	5,439	2,657	2,691	91	34	R	48.9	49.5	1.7	37	49	30	0.8	0.8	0.7	0.8
Choctaw	2,999	1,611	1,354	34	257	D	53.7	45.1	1.1	25	58	55	0.4	0.5	0.4	0.3
Claiborne	4,150	3,045	1,057	48	1,988	D	73.4	25.5	1.2	3	80	53	0.6	0.9	0.3	0.4
Clarke	5,896	1,755	3,967	174	2,212	R	29.8	67.3	3.0	79	6	5	0.8	0.5	1.1	1.5
Clay	5,383	3,131	2,192	60	939	D	58.2	40.7	1.1	17	65	58	0.8	0.9	0.6	0.5
Coahoma	8,245	5,452	2,704	89	2,748	D	66.1	32.8	1.1	6	76	59	1.2	1.6	0.7	0.8
Copiah	7,993	3,703	4,212	78	509	R	46.3	52.7	1.0	47	35	63	1.1	1.1	1.2	0.7
Covington	6,347	2,270	3,948	129	1,678	R	35.8	62.2	2.0	70	15	13	0.9	0.7	1.1	1.1
DeSoto	15,727	9,993	5,486	248	4,507	D	63.5	34.9	1.6	10	73	34	2.2	3.0	1.5	2.2
Forrest	17,732	7,371	10,072	289	2,701	R	41.6	56.8	1.6	59	25	32	2.5	2.2	2.8	2.6
Franklin	3,159	1,187	1,933	39	746	R	37.6	61.2	1.2	66	17	46	0.4	0.4	0.5	0.3
George	4,548	2,119	2,352	77	233	R	46.6	51.7	1.7	44	39	27	0.6	0.6	0.7	0.7
Greene	3,314	1,372	1,884	58	512	R	41.4	56.8	1.8	60	24	21	0.5	0.4	0.5	0.5
Grenada	5,531	2,728	2,758	45	30	R	49.3	49.9	0.8	35	45	72	0.8	0.8	0.8	0.4
Hancock	9,888	6,278	3,437	173	2,841	D	63.5	34.8	1.7	11	74	22	1.4	1.9	1.0	1.5
Harrison	35,507	21,520	13,629	358	7,891	D	60.6	38.4	1.0	14	69	61	5.0	6.4	3.8	3.2
Hinds	68,939	34,574	32,399	1,966	2,175	D	50.2	47.0	2.9	32	56	7	9.7	10.2	9.0	17.5
Holmes	6,084	4,179	1,873	32	2,306	D	68.7	30.8	0.5	5	78	81	0.9	1.2	0.5	0.3
Humphreys	3,344	1,838	1,482	24	356	D	55.0	44.3	0.7	22	59	75	0.5	0.5	0.4	0.2
Issaquena	773	421	338	14	83	D	54.5	43.7	1.8	24	61	18	0.1	0.1	<.1	0.1
Itawamba	5,081	2,421	2,598	62	177	R	47.6	51.1	1.2	39	43	49	0.7	0.7	0.7	0.6
Jackson	29,357	14,955	13,986	416	969	D	50.9	47.6	1.4	31	52	41	4.1	4.4	3.9	3.7
Jasper	5,819	2,234	3,409	176	1,175	R	38.4	58.6	3.0	64	20	4	0.8	0.7	0.9	1.6
Jefferson	3,549	2,799	716	34	2,083	D	78.9	20.2	1.0	1	82	65	0.5	0.8	0.2	0.3
Jefferson Davis	4,690	2,313	2,324	53	11	R	49.3	49.6	1.1	36	48	57	0.7	0.7	0.6	0.5
Jones	18,635	5,760	12,568	307	6,808	R	30.9	67.4	1.6	77	4	31	2.6	1.7	3.5	2.7
Kemper	4,042	1,628	2,272	142	644	R	40.3	56.2	3.5	63	27	1	0.6	0.5	0.6	1.3
Lafayette	6,939	3,233	3,594	112	361	R	46.6	51.8	1.6	45	38	33	1.0	1.0	1.0	1.0
Lamar	9,774	2,892	6,706	176	3,814	R	29.6	68.6	1.8	80	2	19	1.4	0.9	1.9	1.6
Lauderdale	19,852	6,936	12,395	521	5,459	R	34.9	62.4	2.6	71	13	9	2.8	2.0	3.4	4.6
Lawrence	5,967	2,745	3,149	73	404	R	46.0	52.8	1.2	48	34	48	0.8	0.8	0.9	0.6
Leake	6,936	3,119	3,760	57	641	R	45.0	54.2	0.8	50	32	71	1.0	0.9	1.0	0.5
Lee	15,607	7,146	8,028	433	882	R	45.8	51.4	2.8	49	41	8	2.2	2.1	2.2	3.8
Leflore	9,774	5,554	3,932	288	1,622	D	56.8	40.2	2.9	19	67	6	1.4	1.6	1.1	2.6
Lincoln	9,992	3,488	6,423	81	2,935	R	34.9	64.3	0.8	72	9	73	1.4	1.0	1.8	0.7
Lowndes	13,857	7,182	6,518	157	664	D	51.8	47.0	1.1	28	55	56	1.9	2.1	1.8	1.4
Madison	15,712	7,414	8,216	82	802	R	47.2	52.3	0.5	42	36	82	2.2	2.2	2.3	0.7
Marion	8,564	3,278	5,170	116	1,892	R	38.3	60.4	1.4	65	18	43	1.2	1.0	1.4	1.0
Marshall	6,825	4,871	1,835	119	3,036	D	71.4	26.9	1.7	4	79	23	1.0	1.4	0.5	1.1
Monroe	7,722	3,962	3,665	95	297	D	51.3	47.5	1.2	29	53	47	1.1	1.2	1.0	0.8
Montgomery	3,509	1,741	1,749	19	8	R	49.6	49.8	0.5	34	46	80	0.5	0.5	0.5	0.2
Neshoba	7,559	2,324	5,105	130	2,781	R	30.7	67.5	1.7	78	3	25	1.1	0.7	1.4	1.2
Newton	7,346	2,366	4,828	152	2,462	R	32.2	65.7	2.1	76	8	12	1.0	0.7	1.3	1.4
Noxubee	4,861	3,192	1,608	61	1,584	D	65.7	33.1	1.3	8	75	45	0.7	0.9	0.4	0.5
Oktibbeha	9,576	5,103	4,333	140	770	D	53.3	45.2	1.5	26	57	37	1.3	1.5	1.2	1.2
Panola	7,213	4,173	2,955	85	1,218	D	57.9	41.0	1.2	18	64	51	1.0	1.2	0.8	0.8
Pearl River	11,510	5,386	5,895	229	509	R	46.8	51.2	2.0	43	42	15	1.6	1.6	1.6	2.0
Perry	3,710	1,086	2,502	122	1,416	R	29.3	67.4	3.3	81	5	3	0.5	0.3	0.7	1.1
Pike	9,425	4,186	5,161	78	975	R	44.4	54.8	0.8	53	28	70	1.3	1.2	1.4	0.7
Pontotoc	6,289	2,195	3,968	126	1,773	R	34.9	63.1	2.0	73	11	14	0.9	0.6	1.1	1.1
Prentiss	4,511	2,159	2,272	80	113	R	47.9	50.4	1.8	38	44	20	0.6	0.6	0.6	0.7
Quitman	3,281	2,047	1,187	47	860	D	62.4	36.2	1.4	12	71	39	0.5	0.6	0.3	0.4
Rankin	28,000	9,042	18,775	183	9,733	R	32.3	67.1	0.7	75	7	78	3.9	2.7	5.2	1.6
Scott	6,908	2,555	4,285	68	1,730	R	37.0	62.0	1.0	67	16	62	1.0	0.8	1.2	0.6
Sharkey	2,401	1,202	1,164	35	38	D	50.1	48.5	1.5	33	50	38	0.3	0.4	0.3	0.3
Simpson	8,024	2,904	5,052	68	2,148	R	36.2	63.0	0.8	69	12	68	1.1	0.9	1.4	0.6
Smith	6,052	1,652	4,321	79	2,669	R	27.3	71.4	1.3	82	1	44	0.9	0.5	1.2	0.7
Stone	4,118	1,809	2,234	75	425	R	43.9	54.2	1.8	55	31	17	0.6	0.5	0.6	0.7
Sunflower	6,997	3,871	3,068	58	803	D	55.3	43.8	0.8	21	60	69	1.0	1.1	0.8	0.5
Tallahatchie	5,167	2,861	2,230	76	631	D	55.4	43.2	1.5	20	63	36	0.7	0.8	0.6	0.7
Tate	7,335	3,752	3,495	88	257	D	51.2	47.6	1.2	30	51	50	1.0	1.1	1.0	0.8
Tippah	4,883	2,265	2,512	106	247	R	46.4	51.4	2.2	46	40	11	0.7	0.7	0.7	0.9

[1]Independent candidate O'Hara was only minor candidate (only three candidates on ballot).

Table G. — Vote for Governor: November 5, 1991, General Election (cont)

County	Total	Mabus (DEM)	Fordice (REP)	O'Hara (IND)[1]	Plurality Total	Party	Percent of total vote DEM	REP	IND	Rank DEM	REP	IND	Percent contribution to state vote Total	DEM	REP	IND
Tishomingo....................	4,066	2,228	1,775	63	453	D	54.8	43.7	1.5	23	62	35	0.6	0.7	0.5	0.6
Tunica...........................	1,912	1,427	452	33	975	D	74.6	23.6	1.7	2	81	24	0.3	0.4	0.1	0.3
Union	5,889	2,408	3,366	115	958	R	40.9	57.2	2.0	61	23	16	0.8	0.7	0.9	1.0
Walthall........................	3,664	1,556	2,066	42	510	R	42.5	56.4	1.1	56	26	54	0.5	0.5	0.6	0.4
Warren	15,120	6,090	8,925	105	2,835	R	40.3	59.0	0.7	62	19	77	2.1	1.8	2.5	0.9
Washington..................	11,327	5,889	5,357	81	532	D	52.0	47.3	0.7	27	54	76	1.6	1.7	1.5	0.7
Wayne..........................	7,108	2,366	4,505	237	2,139	R	33.3	63.4	3.3	74	10	2	1.0	0.7	1.2	2.1
Webster	4,026	1,461	2,508	57	1,047	R	36.3	62.3	1.4	68	14	42	0.6	0.4	0.7	0.5
Wilkinson	3,044	1,944	1,069	31	875	D	63.9	35.1	1.0	9	72	60	0.4	0.6	0.3	0.3
Winston........................	6,149	2,748	3,341	60	593	R	44.7	54.3	1.0	51	29	64	0.9	0.8	0.9	0.5
Yalobusha	4,200	2,489	1,651	60	838	D	59.3	39.3	1.4	15	68	40	0.6	0.7	0.5	0.5
Yazoo	8,146	3,858	4,243	45	385	R	47.4	52.1	0.6	41	37	79	1.1	1.1	1.2	0.4
MISSISSIPPI..................	**711,212**	**338,459**	**361,500**	**11,253**	**23,041**	**R**	**47.6**	**50.8**	**1.6**				**100.0**	**100.0**	**100.0**	**100.0**

[1]Independent candidate O'Hara was only minor candidate (only three candidates on ballot).

Table H. — Vote for U.S. Representative in Congress: November 3, 1992, General Election

Congressional district and county	Total	Democrat (DEM)	Republican (REP)	Other	Plurality Total	Party	Percent of total vote DEM	REP	Other	Rank within district DEM	REP	Other	Percent contribution to district vote Total	DEM	REP	Other
District 1	**204,616**	**121,664**	**82,952**	-	**38,712**	**D**	**59.5**	**40.5**	-				**100.0**	**100.0**	**100.0**	-
Alcorn	12,642	9,024	3,618	-	5,406	D	71.4	28.6	-	3	22	-	6.2	7.4	4.4	-
Benton	3,831	2,503	1,328	-	1,175	D	65.3	34.7	-	7	18	-	1.9	2.1	1.6	-
Calhoun	6,520	3,739	2,781	-	958	D	57.3	42.7	-	18	7	-	3.2	3.1	3.4	-
Chickasaw	7,055	4,291	2,764	-	1,527	D	60.8	39.2	-	12	13	-	3.4	3.5	3.3	-
Choctaw	3,707	1,906	1,801	-	105	D	51.4	48.6	-	22	3	-	1.8	1.6	2.2	-
DeSoto	27,917	10,886	17,031	-	6,145	R	39.0	61.0	-	24	1	-	13.6	8.9	20.5	-
Grenada (pt)	584	337	247	-	90	D	57.7	42.3	-	16	9	-	0.3	0.3	0.3	-
Itawamba	8,943	5,784	3,159	-	2,625	D	64.7	35.3	-	8	17	-	4.4	4.8	3.8	-
Lafayette	11,402	7,367	4,035	-	3,332	D	64.6	35.4	-	9	16	-	5.6	6.1	4.9	-
Lee	20,685	12,308	8,377	-	3,931	D	59.5	40.5	-	15	10	-	10.1	10.1	10.1	-
Marshall	10,905	7,244	3,661	-	3,583	D	66.4	33.6	-	5	20	-	5.3	6.0	4.4	-
Monroe	13,364	8,085	5,279	-	2,806	D	60.5	39.5	-	13	12	-	6.5	6.6	6.4	-
Montgomery (pt)	1,397	860	537	-	323	D	61.6	38.4	-	11	14	-	0.7	0.7	0.6	-
Oktibbeha (pt)	1,087	530	557	-	27	R	48.8	51.2	-	23	2	-	0.5	0.4	0.7	-
Panola (pt)	7,156	4,044	3,112	-	932	D	56.5	43.5	-	19	6	-	3.5	3.3	3.8	-
Pontotoc	8,505	5,119	3,386	-	1,733	D	60.2	39.8	-	14	11	-	4.2	4.2	4.1	-
Prentiss	8,929	5,865	3,064	-	2,801	D	65.7	34.3	-	6	19	-	4.4	4.8	3.7	-
Tallahatchie (pt)	3,453	2,726	727	-	1,999	D	78.9	21.1	-	1	24	-	1.7	2.2	0.9	-
Tate	8,968	5,004	3,964	-	1,040	D	55.8	44.2	-	20	5	-	4.4	4.1	4.8	-
Tippah	9,128	5,675	3,453	-	2,222	D	62.2	37.8	-	10	15	-	4.5	4.7	4.2	-
Tishomingo	8,182	6,194	1,988	-	4,206	D	75.7	24.3	-	2	23	-	4.0	5.1	2.4	-
Union	9,632	5,527	4,105	-	1,422	D	57.4	42.6	-	17	8	-	4.7	4.5	4.9	-
Webster	5,012	2,749	2,263	-	486	D	54.8	45.2	-	21	4	-	2.4	2.3	2.7	-
Yalobusha	5,612	3,897	1,715	-	2,182	D	69.4	30.6	-	4	21	-	2.7	3.2	2.1	-
District 2	**174,609**	**133,361**	**41,248**	-	**92,113**	**D**	**76.4**	**23.6**	-				**100.0**	**100.0**	**100.0**	-
Attala (pt)	2,429	1,773	656	-	1,117	D	73.0	27.0	-	19	6	-	1.4	1.3	1.6	-
Bolivar	12,423	10,320	2,103	-	8,217	D	83.1	16.9	-	9	16	-	7.1	7.7	5.1	-
Carroll	4,127	2,793	1,334	-	1,459	D	67.7	32.3	-	21	4	-	2.4	2.1	3.2	-
Claiborne	4,442	3,908	534	-	3,374	D	88.0	12.0	-	3	22	-	2.5	2.9	1.3	-
Coahoma	9,321	7,277	2,044	-	5,233	D	78.1	21.9	-	16	9	-	5.3	5.5	5.0	-
Grenada (pt)	8,304	5,685	2,619	-	3,066	D	68.5	31.5	-	20	5	-	4.8	4.3	6.3	-
Hinds (pt)	16,913	14,908	2,005	-	12,903	D	88.1	11.9	-	2	23	-	9.7	11.2	4.9	-
Holmes	7,579	6,653	926	-	5,727	D	87.8	12.2	-	4	21	-	4.3	5.0	2.2	-
Humphreys	4,537	3,936	601	-	3,335	D	86.8	13.2	-	5	20	-	2.6	3.0	1.5	-
Issaquena	861	716	145	-	571	D	83.2	16.8	-	8	17	-	0.5	0.5	0.4	-
Jefferson	3,745	3,436	309	-	3,127	D	91.7	8.3	-	1	24	-	2.1	2.6	0.7	-
Leake (pt)	1,868	1,506	362	-	1,144	D	80.6	19.4	-	12	13	-	1.1	1.1	0.9	-
Leflore	10,787	8,552	2,235	-	6,317	D	79.3	20.7	-	14	11	-	6.2	6.4	5.4	-
Madison (pt)	10,430	8,299	2,131	-	6,168	D	79.6	20.4	-	13	12	-	6.0	6.2	5.2	-
Montgomery (pt)	3,360	2,251	1,109	-	1,142	D	67.0	33.0	-	22	3	-	1.9	1.7	2.7	-
Panola (pt)	4,880	3,865	1,015	-	2,850	D	79.2	20.8	-	15	10	-	2.8	2.9	2.5	-
Quitman	4,399	3,659	740	-	2,919	D	83.2	16.8	-	7	18	-	2.5	2.7	1.8	-
Sharkey	2,449	2,024	425	-	1,599	D	82.6	17.4	-	10	15	-	1.4	1.5	1.0	-
Sunflower	9,056	7,350	1,706	-	5,644	D	81.2	18.8	-	11	14	-	5.2	5.5	4.1	-
Tallahatchie (pt)	3,849	396	3,453	-	3,057	R	10.3	89.7	-	24	1	-	2.2	0.3	8.4	-
Tunica	1,983	1,674	309	-	1,365	D	84.4	15.6	-	6	19	-	1.1	1.3	0.7	-
Warren	19,849	11,999	7,850	-	4,149	D	60.5	39.5	-	23	2	-	11.4	9.0	19.0	-
Washington	17,126	12,776	4,350	-	8,426	D	74.6	25.4	-	18	7	-	9.8	9.6	10.5	-
Yazoo	9,892	7,605	2,287	-	5,318	D	76.9	23.1	-	17	8	-	5.7	5.7	5.5	-
District 3	**200,574**	**162,864**	**37,710**	-	**125,154**	**D**	**81.2**	**18.8**	-				**100.0**	**100.0**	**100.0**	-
Attala (pt)	4,496	3,887	609	-	3,278	D	86.5	13.5	-	9	11	-	2.2	2.4	1.6	-
Clarke	7,131	6,353	778	-	5,575	D	89.1	10.9	-	3	17	-	3.6	3.9	2.1	-
Clay	8,603	7,398	1,205	-	6,193	D	86.0	14.0	-	12	8	-	4.3	4.5	3.2	-
Jasper	7,022	6,137	885	-	5,252	D	87.4	12.6	-	8	12	-	3.5	3.8	2.3	-
Jones (pt)	8,189	6,831	1,358	-	5,473	D	83.4	16.6	-	14	6	-	4.1	4.2	3.6	-
Kemper	4,469	4,019	450	-	3,569	D	89.9	10.1	-	1	19	-	2.2	2.5	1.2	-
Lauderdale	25,023	22,062	2,961	-	19,101	D	88.2	11.8	-	5	15	-	12.5	13.5	7.9	-
Leake (pt)	6,140	5,438	702	-	4,736	D	88.6	11.4	-	4	16	-	3.1	3.3	1.9	-
Lowndes	19,179	14,943	4,236	-	10,707	D	77.9	22.1	-	17	3	-	9.6	9.2	11.2	-
Madison (pt)	12,885	8,203	4,682	-	3,521	D	63.7	36.3	-	19	1	-	6.4	5.0	12.4	-
Neshoba	10,333	8,891	1,442	-	7,449	D	86.0	14.0	-	11	9	-	5.2	5.5	3.8	-
Newton	8,156	7,274	882	-	6,392	D	89.2	10.8	-	2	18	-	4.1	4.5	2.3	-
Noxubee	4,448	3,889	559	-	3,330	D	87.4	12.6	-	7	13	-	2.2	2.4	1.5	-
Oktibbeha (pt)	12,009	9,720	2,289	-	7,431	D	80.9	19.1	-	16	4	-	6.0	6.0	6.1	-
Rankin	36,423	25,585	10,838	-	14,747	D	70.2	29.8	-	18	2	-	18.2	15.7	28.7	-
Scott	9,689	8,482	1,207	-	7,275	D	87.5	12.5	-	6	14	-	4.8	5.2	3.2	-
Smith	5,861	4,869	992	-	3,877	D	83.1	16.9	-	15	5	-	2.9	3.0	2.6	-
Wayne (pt)	1,332	1,148	184	-	964	D	86.2	13.8	-	10	10	-	0.7	0.7	0.5	-
Winston	9,186	7,735	1,451	-	6,284	D	84.2	15.8	-	13	7	-	4.6	4.7	3.8	-
District 4	**194,544**	**130,927**	**43,705**	**19,912**	**87,222**	**D**	**67.3**	**22.5**	**10.2**				**100.0**	**100.0**	**100.0**	**100.0**
Adams	15,257	11,746	2,408	1,103	9,338	D	77.0	15.8	7.2	7	12	3	7.8	9.0	5.5	5.5
Amite	6,143	4,628	1,123	392	3,505	D	75.3	18.3	6.4	9	7	8	3.2	3.5	2.6	2.0

Congressional district and county	Total	Democrat (DEM)	Republican (REP)	Other	Plurality Total	Party	DEM	REP	Other	Rank within district DEM	REP	Other	Total	DEM	REP	Other
District 4 (cont)																
Copiah	9,654	7,165	1,886	603	5,279	D	74.2	19.5	6.2	11	6	10	5.0	5.5	4.3	3.0
Covington	7,121	5,326	1,426	369	3,900	D	74.8	20.0	5.2	10	5	13	3.7	4.1	3.3	1.9
Franklin	4,082	3,185	631	266	2,554	D	78.0	15.5	6.5	4	13	7	2.1	2.4	1.4	1.3
Hinds (pt)	68,328	35,752	20,528	12,048	15,224	D	52.3	30.0	17.6	14	2	2	35.1	27.3	47.0	60.5
Jefferson Davis	5,184	4,070	833	281	3,237	D	78.5	16.1	5.4	2	11	12	2.7	3.1	1.9	1.4
Jones (pt)	16,129	11,574	3,433	1,122	8,141	D	71.8	21.3	7.0	12	4	5	8.3	8.8	7.9	5.6
Lawrence	6,417	5,036	979	402	4,057	D	78.5	15.3	6.3	3	14	9	3.3	3.8	2.2	2.0
Lincoln	13,831	10,755	2,097	979	8,658	D	77.8	15.2	7.1	6	15	4	7.1	8.2	4.8	4.9
Marion	11,525	9,059	2,040	426	7,019	D	78.6	17.7	3.7	1	8	15	5.9	6.9	4.7	2.1
Pike	14,825	11,548	2,428	849	9,120	D	77.9	16.4	5.7	5	10	11	7.6	8.8	5.6	4.3
Simpson	9,323	6,498	2,419	406	4,079	D	69.7	25.9	4.4	13	3	14	4.8	5.0	5.5	2.0
Walthall	5,537	4,249	924	364	3,325	D	76.7	16.7	6.6	8	9	6	2.8	3.2	2.1	1.8
Wilkinson	1,188	336	550	302	214	R	28.3	46.3	25.4	15	1	1	0.6	0.3	1.3	1.5
District 5	191,058	120,766	67,619	2,673	53,147	D	63.2	35.4	1.4				100.0	100.0	100.0	100.0
Forrest	23,249	13,464	9,353	432	4,111	D	57.9	40.2	1.9	10	2	3	12.2	11.1	13.8	16.2
George	7,415	5,158	2,181	76	2,977	D	69.6	29.4	1.0	3	9	10	3.9	4.3	3.2	2.8
Greene	5,014	3,375	1,605	34	1,770	D	67.3	32.0	0.7	4	7	11	2.6	2.8	2.4	1.3
Hancock	13,558	8,972	4,320	266	4,652	D	66.2	31.9	2.0	5	8	2	7.1	7.4	6.4	10.0
Harrison	52,301	34,564	17,163	574	17,401	D	66.1	32.8	1.1	6	6	8	27.4	28.6	25.4	21.5
Jackson	44,507	27,605	16,411	491	11,194	D	62.0	36.9	1.1	8	4	7	23.3	22.9	24.3	18.4
Lamar	13,190	7,124	5,845	221	1,279	D	54.0	44.3	1.7	11	1	5	6.9	5.9	8.6	8.3
Pearl River	15,460	9,185	5,944	331	3,241	D	59.4	38.4	2.1	9	3	1	8.1	7.6	8.8	12.4
Perry	4,630	2,956	1,590	84	1,366	D	63.8	34.3	1.8	7	5	4	2.4	2.4	2.4	3.1
Stone	4,660	3,345	1,266	49	2,079	D	71.8	27.2	1.1	1	11	9	2.4	2.8	1.9	1.8
Wayne (pt)	7,074	5,018	1,941	115	3,077	D	70.9	27.4	1.6	2	10	6	3.7	4.2	2.9	4.3
MISSISSIPPI	965,401	669,582	273,234	22,585	396,348	D	69.4	28.3	2.3							

Table I. — Vote for Presidential Preference: March 10, 1992, Democratic Primary Election

County	Total	Clinton	Brown	Tsongas	Uncom-mitted	Harkin	Kerrey	LaRouche	Other	Clinton	Brown	Tsongas	Rank Clinton	Rank Brown	Rank Tsongas	Total	Clinton	Brown	Tsongas
Adams	3,107	2,492	264	241	0	52	34	24	0	80.2	8.5	7.8	17	40	29	1.6	1.8	1.4	1.6
Alcorn	2,481	1,969	100	259	122	13	18	0	0	79.4	4.0	10.4	22	74	12	1.3	1.4	0.5	1.7
Amite	1,133	940	56	43	61	9	14	10	0	83.0	4.9	3.8	9	68	78	0.6	0.7	0.3	0.3
Attala	1,867	1,352	215	114	143	17	18	8	0	72.4	11.5	6.1	51	18	55	1.0	1.0	1.2	0.7
Benton	1,051	937	18	49	34	2	4	4	3	89.2	1.7	4.7	1	82	72	0.5	0.7	<.1	0.3
Bolivar	2,879	2,466	181	98	38	42	28	26	0	85.7	6.3	3.4	4	58	80	1.5	1.8	1.0	0.6
Calhoun	1,562	1,219	77	97	129	14	13	13	0	78.0	4.9	6.2	24	69	52	0.8	0.9	0.4	0.6
Carroll	895	715	45	54	53	10	3	9	6	79.9	5.0	6.0	20	66	56	0.5	0.5	0.2	0.3
Chickasaw	1,631	1,144	93	138	204	16	18	18	0	70.1	5.7	8.5	64	61	21	0.9	0.8	0.5	0.9
Choctaw	875	606	73	80	81	12	8	15	0	69.3	8.3	9.1	68	41	16	0.5	0.4	0.4	0.5
Claiborne	1,188	903	157	50	32	17	17	12	0	76.0	13.2	4.2	33	10	76	0.6	0.6	0.9	0.3
Clarke	1,493	1,041	144	133	115	28	22	10	0	69.7	9.6	8.9	67	28	18	0.8	0.7	0.8	0.9
Clay	2,295	1,613	190	148	230	28	33	25	28	70.3	8.3	6.4	62	42	47	1.2	1.2	1.0	1.0
Coahoma	2,608	1,997	141	181	211	30	22	26	0	76.6	5.4	6.9	32	63	41	1.4	1.4	0.8	1.2
Copiah	2,021	1,467	300	86	108	27	25	8	0	72.6	14.8	4.3	49	7	75	1.1	1.0	1.6	0.6
Covington	1,001	755	99	85	41	13	5	3	0	75.4	9.9	8.5	37	27	20	0.5	0.5	0.5	0.5
DeSoto	4,139	3,427	152	309	199	21	15	16	0	82.8	3.7	7.5	10	77	34	2.2	2.4	0.8	2.0
Forrest	3,142	2,139	406	375	136	48	20	18	0	68.1	12.9	11.9	71	11	6	1.6	1.5	2.2	2.4
Franklin	770	613	70	37	30	1	7	7	5	79.6	9.1	4.8	21	33	71	0.4	0.4	0.4	0.2
George	1,144	809	85	106	69	49	9	17	0	70.7	7.4	9.3	60	53	15	0.6	0.6	0.5	0.7
Greene	711	570	51	48	0	25	11	6	0	80.2	7.2	6.8	18	55	44	0.4	0.4	0.3	0.3
Grenada	1,358	1,066	108	103	43	14	13	10	1	78.5	8.0	7.6	23	47	33	0.7	0.8	0.6	0.7
Hancock	2,169	1,419	203	303	182	27	17	18	0	65.4	9.4	14.0	77	30	2	1.1	1.0	1.1	2.0
Harrison	15,977	10,741	1,448	1,894	1,347	265	172	110	0	67.2	9.1	11.9	73	34	8	8.3	7.7	7.9	12.2
Hinds	19,047	13,362	3,422	1,472	459	168	102	62	0	70.2	18.0	7.7	63	4	31	10.0	9.6	18.6	9.5
Holmes	2,680	2,162	268	67	76	55	36	16	0	80.7	10.0	2.5	15	26	82	1.4	1.5	1.5	0.4
Humphreys	1,032	748	104	62	60	30	17	11	0	72.5	10.1	6.0	50	25	58	0.5	0.5	0.6	0.4
Issaquena	309	210	69	19	3	2	3	3	0	68.0	22.3	6.1	72	2	53	0.2	0.2	0.4	0.1
Itawamba	1,833	1,418	89	148	148	10	6	14	0	77.4	4.9	8.1	27	70	26	1.0	1.0	0.5	1.0
Jackson	8,192	5,113	790	976	990	208	54	61	0	62.4	9.6	11.9	80	29	7	4.3	3.7	4.3	6.3
Jasper	1,398	990	130	104	124	23	12	15	0	70.8	9.3	7.4	57	31	35	0.7	0.7	0.7	0.7
Jefferson	990	750	111	35	25	41	19	9	0	75.8	11.2	3.5	36	20	79	0.5	0.5	0.6	0.2
Jefferson Davis	1,361	978	210	55	75	22	10	11	0	71.9	15.4	4.0	53	6	77	0.7	0.7	1.1	0.4
Jones	3,179	2,328	280	286	191	33	26	35	0	73.2	8.8	9.0	46	37	17	1.7	1.7	1.5	1.8
Kemper	992	746	101	62	57	11	8	7	0	75.2	10.2	6.3	39	24	50	0.5	0.5	0.5	0.4
Lafayette	3,035	2,148	229	376	211	18	16	18	19	70.8	7.5	12.4	59	52	5	1.6	1.5	1.2	2.4
Lamar	1,235	795	143	200	61	12	16	8	0	64.4	11.6	16.2	78	16	1	0.6	0.6	0.8	1.3
Lauderdale	3,267	1,992	418	372	231	159	40	54	1	61.0	12.8	11.4	82	13	10	1.7	1.4	2.3	2.4
Lawrence	1,223	943	154	101	0	10	11	4	0	77.1	12.6	8.3	30	14	23	0.6	0.7	0.8	0.7
Leake	1,337	1,042	139	59	62	18	9	8	0	77.9	10.4	4.4	26	23	74	0.7	0.7	0.8	0.4
Lee	4,606	3,149	325	499	532	20	41	40	0	68.4	7.1	10.8	70	56	11	2.4	2.3	1.8	3.2
Leflore	2,514	2,064	149	149	0	50	54	48	0	82.1	5.9	5.9	12	60	62	1.3	1.5	0.8	1.0
Lincoln	2,104	1,584	238	125	98	30	23	6	0	75.3	11.3	5.9	38	19	61	1.1	1.1	1.3	0.8
Lowndes	2,605	1,614	205	299	404	30	30	23	0	62.0	7.9	11.5	81	50	9	1.4	1.2	1.1	1.9
Madison	5,283	3,857	760	276	208	66	61	18	37	73.0	14.4	5.2	48	8	67	2.8	2.8	4.1	1.8
Marion	1,791	1,396	148	148	68	10	11	10	0	77.9	8.3	8.3	25	43	22	0.9	1.0	0.8	1.0
Marshall	2,588	2,156	144	139	95	18	11	25	0	83.3	5.6	5.4	7	62	65	1.4	1.5	0.8	0.9
Monroe	2,734	1,890	197	217	357	26	24	23	0	69.1	7.2	7.9	69	54	27	1.4	1.4	1.1	1.4
Montgomery	1,131	836	118	66	63	25	12	11	0	73.9	10.4	5.8	42	22	64	0.6	0.6	0.6	0.4
Neshoba	1,996	1,331	176	158	266	29	20	16	0	66.7	8.8	7.9	75	36	28	1.0	1.0	1.0	1.0
Newton	1,324	926	120	93	143	15	12	8	7	69.9	9.1	7.0	65	35	38	0.7	0.7	0.7	0.6
Noxubee	754	499	58	58	103	17	9	10	0	66.2	7.7	7.7	76	51	32	0.4	0.4	0.3	0.4
Oktibbeha	2,536	1,694	201	324	254	24	13	26	0	66.8	7.9	12.8	74	48	3	1.3	1.2	1.1	2.1
Panola	3,121	2,543	117	195	204	19	16	18	9	81.5	3.7	6.2	14	76	51	1.6	1.8	0.6	1.3
Pearl River	1,766	1,342	145	219	0	31	16	13	0	76.0	8.2	12.4	34	44	4	0.9	1.0	0.8	1.4
Perry	590	440	47	40	33	14	7	6	3	74.6	8.0	6.8	41	46	43	0.3	0.3	0.3	0.3
Pike	2,403	1,855	211	178	87	23	31	18	0	77.2	8.8	7.4	29	38	36	1.3	1.3	1.1	1.1
Pontotoc	3,073	2,177	157	215	445	27	18	34	0	70.8	5.1	7.0	56	64	39	1.6	1.6	0.9	1.4
Prentiss	1,821	1,383	88	141	169	11	11	18	0	75.9	4.8	7.7	35	71	30	1.0	1.0	0.5	0.9
Quitman	1,261	1,063	26	62	68	18	9	8	7	84.3	2.1	4.9	6	81	70	0.7	0.8	0.1	0.4
Rankin	3,313	2,372	424	325	114	44	25	9	0	71.6	12.8	9.8	54	12	13	1.7	1.7	2.3	2.1
Scott	1,831	1,287	211	109	151	26	25	10	12	70.3	11.5	6.0	61	17	60	1.0	0.9	1.1	0.7
Sharkey	465	295	129	24	0	5	7	5	0	63.4	27.7	5.2	79	1	68	0.2	0.2	0.7	0.2
Simpson	1,581	1,119	247	93	92	10	11	9	0	70.8	15.6	5.9	58	5	63	0.8	0.8	1.3	0.6
Smith	954	713	83	60	82	5	8	3	0	74.7	8.7	6.3	40	39	49	0.5	0.5	0.5	0.4
Stone	807	573	66	77	55	14	14	8	0	71.0	8.2	9.5	55	45	14	0.4	0.4	0.4	0.5
Sunflower	1,508	1,253	91	81	57	16	5	5	0	83.1	6.0	5.4	8	59	66	0.8	0.9	0.5	0.5
Tallahatchie	2,367	1,743	120	168	219	46	40	31	0	73.6	5.1	7.1	45	65	37	1.2	1.2	0.7	1.1
Tate	2,063	1,756	58	126	93	16	11	3	0	85.1	2.8	6.1	5	80	54	1.1	1.3	0.3	0.8
Tippah	1,777	1,462	51	106	104	15	8	18	13	82.3	2.9	6.0	11	79	59	0.9	1.0	0.3	0.7

Table I. — Vote for Presidential Preference: March 10, 1992, Democratic Primary Election (cont)

| County | Top candidates | | | | | | | | | Top three candidates (state vote) | | | | | | | | | |
| | | | | | | | | | | Percent of total vote | | | Rank | | | Percent contribution to state vote | | | |
	Total	Clinton	Brown	Tsongas	Uncom-mitted	Harkin	Kerrey	LaRouche	Other	Clinton	Brown	Tsongas	Clinton	Brown	Tsongas	Total	Clinton	Brown	Tsongas
Tishomingo	1,696	1,305	84	139	140	10	4	14	0	76.9	5.0	8.2	31	67	24	0.9	0.9	0.5	0.9
Tunica	447	395	21	20	0	5	4	2	0	88.4	4.7	4.5	2	72	73	0.2	0.3	0.1	0.1
Union	2,310	1,860	83	160	177	6	10	14	0	80.5	3.6	6.9	16	78	42	1.2	1.3	0.5	1.0
Walthall	1,053	776	118	86	31	19	15	8	0	73.7	11.2	8.2	44	21	25	0.6	0.6	0.6	0.6
Warren	3,007	2,172	402	261	94	29	19	10	20	72.2	13.4	8.7	52	9	19	1.6	1.6	2.2	1.7
Washington	2,771	1,934	600	167	5	19	20	26	0	69.8	21.7	6.0	66	3	57	1.4	1.4	3.3	1.1
Wayne	1,242	916	113	82	72	25	13	21	0	73.8	9.1	6.6	43	32	45	0.6	0.7	0.6	0.5
Webster	1,224	894	80	85	128	16	7	14	0	73.0	6.5	6.9	47	57	40	0.6	0.6	0.4	0.5
Wilkinson	1,324	1,155	50	43	40	18	9	9	0	87.2	3.8	3.2	3	75	81	0.7	0.8	0.3	0.3
Winston	1,587	1,301	125	102	0	23	12	24	0	82.0	7.9	6.4	13	49	48	0.8	0.9	0.7	0.7
Yalobusha	1,635	1,307	67	106	118	13	12	12	0	79.9	4.1	6.5	19	73	46	0.9	0.9	0.4	0.7
Yazoo	1,787	1,381	210	92	46	26	21	11	0	77.3	11.8	5.1	28	15	69	0.9	1.0	1.1	0.6
MISSISSIPPI	**191,357**	**139,893**	**18,396**	**15,538**	**11,796**	**2,509**	**1,660**	**1,394**	**171**	**73.1**	**9.6**	**8.1**				**100.0**	**100.0**	**100.0**	**100.0**

Table J. – Vote for Presidential Preference: March 10, 1992, Republican Primary Election

| County | Top candidates | | | | | Top four candidates (state vote) | | | | | | | | | | | | |
| | | | | | | Percent of total vote | | | | Rank | | | | Percent contribution to state vote | | | | |
	Total	Bush	Bu-chanan	Duke	Other	Bush	Bu-chanan	Duke	Other	Bush	Bu-chanan	Duke	Other	Total	Bush	Bu-chanan	Duke	Other
Adams	1,323	891	303	128	1	67.3	22.9	9.7	<.1	70	7	59	65	0.9	0.8	1.2	0.8	0.2
Alcorn	619	421	149	48	1	68.0	24.1	7.8	0.2	66	6	71	49	0.4	0.4	0.6	0.3	0.2
Amite	609	350	122	137	0	57.5	20.0	22.5	0.0	81	18	1	67	0.4	0.3	0.5	0.8	0.0
Attala	1,011	741	133	132	5	73.3	13.2	13.1	0.5	38	47	30	20	0.7	0.7	0.5	0.8	0.8
Benton	218	159	47	11	1	72.9	21.6	5.0	0.5	40	11	81	22	0.1	0.1	0.2	<.1	0.2
Bolivar	1,163	901	147	114	1	77.5	12.6	9.8	<.1	15	54	57	64	0.8	0.8	0.6	0.7	0.2
Calhoun	652	468	107	76	1	71.8	16.4	11.7	0.2	49	27	45	54	0.4	0.4	0.4	0.5	0.2
Carroll	408	280	40	88	0	68.6	9.8	21.6	0.0	63	66	2	68	0.3	0.3	0.2	0.5	0.0
Chickasaw	366	252	76	35	3	68.9	20.8	9.6	0.8	62	13	62	8	0.2	0.2	0.3	0.2	0.5
Choctaw	477	311	89	74	3	65.2	18.7	15.5	0.6	74	24	15	17	0.3	0.3	0.3	0.5	0.5
Claiborne	379	287	33	58	1	75.7	8.7	15.3	0.3	24	76	17	36	0.2	0.3	0.1	0.4	0.2
Clarke	1,078	882	92	102	2	81.8	8.5	9.5	0.2	2	77	63	46	0.7	0.8	0.4	0.6	0.3
Clay	455	302	71	82	0	66.4	15.6	18.0	0.0	72	34	11	69	0.3	0.3	0.3	0.5	0.0
Coahoma	480	372	64	44	0	77.5	13.3	9.2	0.0	14	45	67	70	0.3	0.3	0.2	0.3	0.0
Copiah	1,774	1,389	173	210	2	78.3	9.8	11.8	0.1	10	67	42	60	1.1	1.2	0.7	1.3	0.3
Covington	1,008	717	128	156	7	71.1	12.7	15.5	0.7	53	53	16	11	0.7	0.6	0.5	0.9	1.2
DeSoto	3,270	2,240	831	195	4	68.5	25.4	6.0	0.1	64	4	80	57	2.1	2.0	3.2	1.2	0.7
Forrest	4,615	3,412	678	505	20	73.9	14.7	10.9	0.4	33	37	51	24	3.0	3.1	2.6	3.1	3.4
Franklin	536	409	48	78	1	76.3	9.0	14.6	0.2	22	74	23	45	0.3	0.4	0.2	0.5	0.2
George	1,080	796	145	136	3	73.7	13.4	12.6	0.3	36	44	37	34	0.7	0.7	0.6	0.8	0.5
Greene	613	478	59	74	2	78.0	9.6	12.1	0.3	12	68	39	32	0.4	0.4	0.2	0.5	0.3
Grenada	942	702	139	99	2	74.5	14.8	10.5	0.2	28	36	54	41	0.6	0.6	0.5	0.6	0.3
Hancock	2,324	1,332	638	350	4	57.3	27.5	15.1	0.2	82	3	19	48	1.5	1.2	2.5	2.1	0.7
Harrison	24,012	16,331	5,256	2,260	165	68.0	21.9	9.4	0.7	67	9	64	12	15.5	14.6	20.3	13.8	27.6
Hinds	20,695	15,649	3,292	1,712	42	75.6	15.9	8.3	0.2	25	31	69	42	13.4	14.0	12.7	10.4	7.0
Holmes	734	564	67	99	4	76.8	9.1	13.5	0.5	18	72	28	19	0.5	0.5	0.3	0.6	0.7
Humphreys	323	242	22	59	0	74.9	6.8	18.3	0.0	27	79	10	71	0.2	0.2	<.1	0.4	0.0
Issaquena	51	38	1	11	1	74.5	2.0	21.6	2.0	29	82	3	4	<.1	<.1	<.1	<.1	0.2
Itawamba	438	312	84	42	0	71.2	19.2	9.6	0.0	52	22	61	72	0.3	0.3	0.3	0.3	0.0
Jackson	10,881	7,733	2,257	854	37	71.1	20.7	7.8	0.3	55	14	70	31	7.0	6.9	8.7	5.2	6.2
Jasper	659	484	68	97	10	73.4	10.3	14.7	1.5	37	63	21	5	0.4	0.4	0.3	0.6	1.7
Jefferson	146	116	13	16	1	79.5	8.9	11.0	0.7	7	75	50	13	<.1	0.1	<.1	<.1	0.2
Jefferson Davis	751	546	75	127	3	72.7	10.0	16.9	0.4	43	65	12	26	0.5	0.5	0.3	0.8	0.5
Jones	3,521	2,703	422	394	2	76.8	12.0	11.2	<.1	19	56	49	66	2.3	2.4	1.6	2.4	0.3
Kemper	636	491	51	93	1	77.2	8.0	14.6	0.2	17	78	22	53	0.4	0.4	0.2	0.6	0.2
Lafayette	859	613	187	59	0	71.4	21.8	6.9	0.0	50	10	78	73	0.6	0.5	0.7	0.4	0.0
Lamar	2,633	1,918	374	338	3	72.8	14.2	12.8	0.1	41	40	33	59	1.7	1.7	1.4	2.1	0.5
Lauderdale	4,247	3,340	472	408	27	78.6	11.1	9.6	0.6	9	58	60	16	2.7	3.0	1.8	2.5	4.5
Lawrence	830	596	77	155	2	71.8	9.3	18.7	0.2	48	70	8	38	0.5	0.5	0.3	0.9	0.3
Leake	1,054	851	67	134	2	80.7	6.4	12.7	0.2	4	80	35	44	0.7	0.8	0.3	0.8	0.3
Lee	1,876	1,202	531	140	3	64.1	28.3	7.5	0.2	75	2	73	51	1.2	1.1	2.1	0.9	0.5
Leflore	1,262	827	249	156	30	65.5	19.7	12.4	2.4	73	20	38	2	0.8	0.7	1.0	0.9	5.0
Lincoln	2,008	1,495	208	302	3	74.5	10.4	15.0	0.1	30	62	20	56	1.3	1.3	0.8	1.8	0.5
Lowndes	1,994	1,264	492	236	2	63.4	24.7	11.8	0.1	76	5	43	63	1.3	1.1	1.9	1.4	0.3
Madison	4,967	3,796	800	360	11	76.4	16.1	7.2	0.2	21	28	75	40	3.2	3.4	3.1	2.2	1.8
Marion	1,490	1,016	192	278	4	68.2	12.9	18.7	0.3	65	50	9	35	1.0	0.9	0.7	1.7	0.7
Marshall	511	374	102	33	2	73.2	20.0	6.5	0.4	39	19	79	27	0.3	0.3	0.4	0.2	0.3
Monroe	687	483	109	93	2	70.3	15.9	13.5	0.3	57	32	27	33	0.4	0.4	0.4	0.6	0.3
Montgomery	469	352	61	56	0	75.1	13.0	11.9	0.0	26	48	40	74	0.3	0.3	0.2	0.3	0.0
Neshoba	1,241	1,046	72	121	2	84.3	5.8	9.8	0.2	1	81	58	50	0.8	0.9	0.3	0.7	0.3
Newton	1,446	1,160	130	150	6	80.2	9.0	10.4	0.4	5	73	56	25	0.9	1.0	0.5	0.9	1.0
Noxubee	347	236	70	41	0	68.0	20.2	11.8	0.0	68	17	44	75	0.2	0.2	0.3	0.2	0.0
Oktibbeha	1,605	1,145	306	148	6	71.3	19.1	9.2	0.4	51	23	65	29	1.0	1.0	1.2	0.9	1.0
Panola	760	593	98	64	5	78.0	12.9	8.4	0.7	11	49	68	14	0.5	0.5	0.4	0.4	0.8
Pearl River	2,292	1,387	521	373	11	60.5	22.7	16.3	0.5	77	8	14	21	1.5	1.2	2.0	2.3	1.8
Perry	671	488	76	102	5	72.7	11.3	15.2	0.7	42	57	18	10	0.4	0.4	0.3	0.6	0.8
Pike	1,620	1,165	259	193	3	71.9	16.0	11.9	0.2	47	30	41	47	1.0	1.0	1.0	1.2	0.5
Pontotoc	333	199	98	36	0	59.8	29.4	10.8	0.0	80	1	52	76	0.2	0.2	0.4	0.2	0.0
Prentiss	365	220	75	70	0	60.3	20.5	19.2	0.0	78	16	6	77	0.2	0.2	0.3	0.4	0.0
Quitman	293	239	32	21	1	81.6	10.9	7.2	0.3	3	60	76	30	0.2	0.2	0.1	0.1	0.2
Rankin	9,940	7,338	1,529	1,053	20	73.8	15.4	10.6	0.2	34	35	53	43	6.4	6.6	5.9	6.4	3.4
Scott	1,383	1,108	130	145	0	80.1	9.4	10.5	0.0	6	69	55	78	0.9	1.0	0.5	0.9	0.0
Sharkey	342	236	54	44	8	69.0	15.8	12.9	2.3	61	33	32	3	0.2	0.2	0.2	0.3	1.3
Simpson	1,814	1,405	167	235	7	77.5	9.2	13.0	0.4	16	71	31	28	1.2	1.3	0.6	1.4	1.2
Smith	971	679	98	182	12	69.9	10.1	18.7	1.2	59	64	7	6	0.6	0.6	0.4	1.1	2.0
Stone	863	622	120	116	5	72.1	13.9	13.4	0.6	46	43	29	18	0.6	0.6	0.5	0.7	0.8
Sunflower	961	698	123	139	1	72.6	12.8	14.5	0.1	44	52	24	62	0.6	0.6	0.5	0.8	0.2
Tallahatchie	180	134	20	26	0	74.4	11.1	14.4	0.0	31	59	25	79	0.1	0.1	<.1	0.2	0.0
Tate	648	478	134	28	8	73.8	20.7	4.3	1.2	35	15	82	7	0.4	0.4	0.5	0.2	1.3
Tippah	445	308	86	50	1	69.2	19.3	11.2	0.2	60	21	47	39	0.3	0.3	0.3	0.3	0.2

Table J. — Vote for Presidential Preference: March 10, 1992, Republican Primary Election (cont)

| County | Top candidates | | | | | Top four candidates (state vote) | | | | | | | | | | | | |
| | | | | | | Percent of total vote | | | | Rank | | | | Percent contribution to state vote | | | | |
	Total	Bush	Bu-chanan	Duke	Other	Bush	Bu-chanan	Duke	Other	Bush	Bu-chanan	Duke	Other	Total	Bush	Bu-chanan	Duke	Other
Tishomingo	311	236	50	23	2	75.9	16.1	7.4	0.6	23	29	74	15	0.2	0.2	0.2	0.1	0.3
Tunica	129	102	18	9	0	79.1	14.0	7.0	0.0	8	41	77	80	<.1	<.1	<.1	<.1	0.0
Union	660	469	139	51	1	71.1	21.1	7.7	0.2	56	12	72	55	0.4	0.4	0.5	0.3	0.2
Walthall	623	375	89	121	38	60.2	14.3	19.4	6.1	79	38	5	1	0.4	0.3	0.3	0.7	6.4
Warren	3,568	2,655	459	450	4	74.4	12.9	12.6	0.1	32	51	36	61	2.3	2.4	1.8	2.7	0.7
Washington	2,631	1,871	441	299	20	71.1	16.8	11.4	0.8	54	26	46	9	1.7	1.7	1.7	1.8	3.4
Wayne	1,094	793	156	140	5	72.5	14.3	12.8	0.5	45	39	34	23	0.7	0.7	0.6	0.9	0.8
Webster	613	415	77	121	0	67.7	12.6	19.7	0.0	69	55	4	81	0.4	0.4	0.3	0.7	0.0
Wilkinson	312	210	57	45	0	67.3	18.3	14.4	0.0	71	25	26	82	0.2	0.2	0.2	0.3	0.0
Winston	833	584	110	138	1	70.1	13.2	16.6	0.1	58	46	13	58	0.5	0.5	0.4	0.8	0.2
Yalobusha	380	291	53	35	1	76.6	13.9	9.2	0.3	20	42	66	37	0.2	0.3	0.2	0.2	0.2
Yazoo	1,900	1,481	203	213	3	77.9	10.7	11.2	0.2	13	61	48	52	1.2	1.3	0.8	1.3	0.5
MISSISSIPPI	**154,708**	**111,794**	**25,891**	**16,426**	**597**	**72.3**	**16.7**	**10.6**	**0.4**					**100.0**	**100.0**	**100.0**	**100.0**	**100.0**

1992 Vote for President
Percent for Bush (R), by County

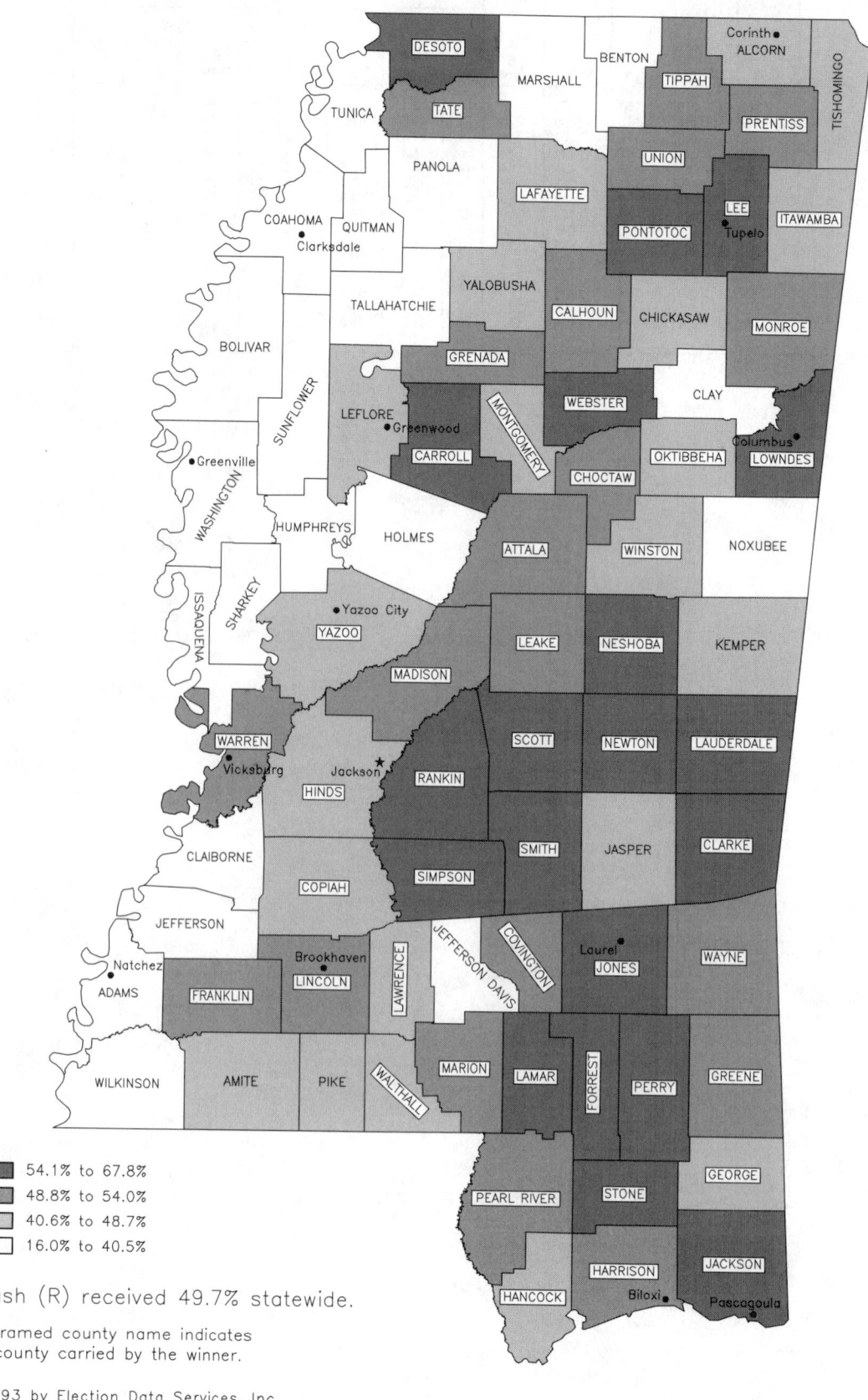

54.1% to 67.8%
48.8% to 54.0%
40.6% to 48.7%
16.0% to 40.5%

Bush (R) received 49.7% statewide.

A framed county name indicates
a county carried by the winner.

Copyright © 1993 by Election Data Services, Inc.

1991 Vote for Governor
Percent for Fordice (R), by County

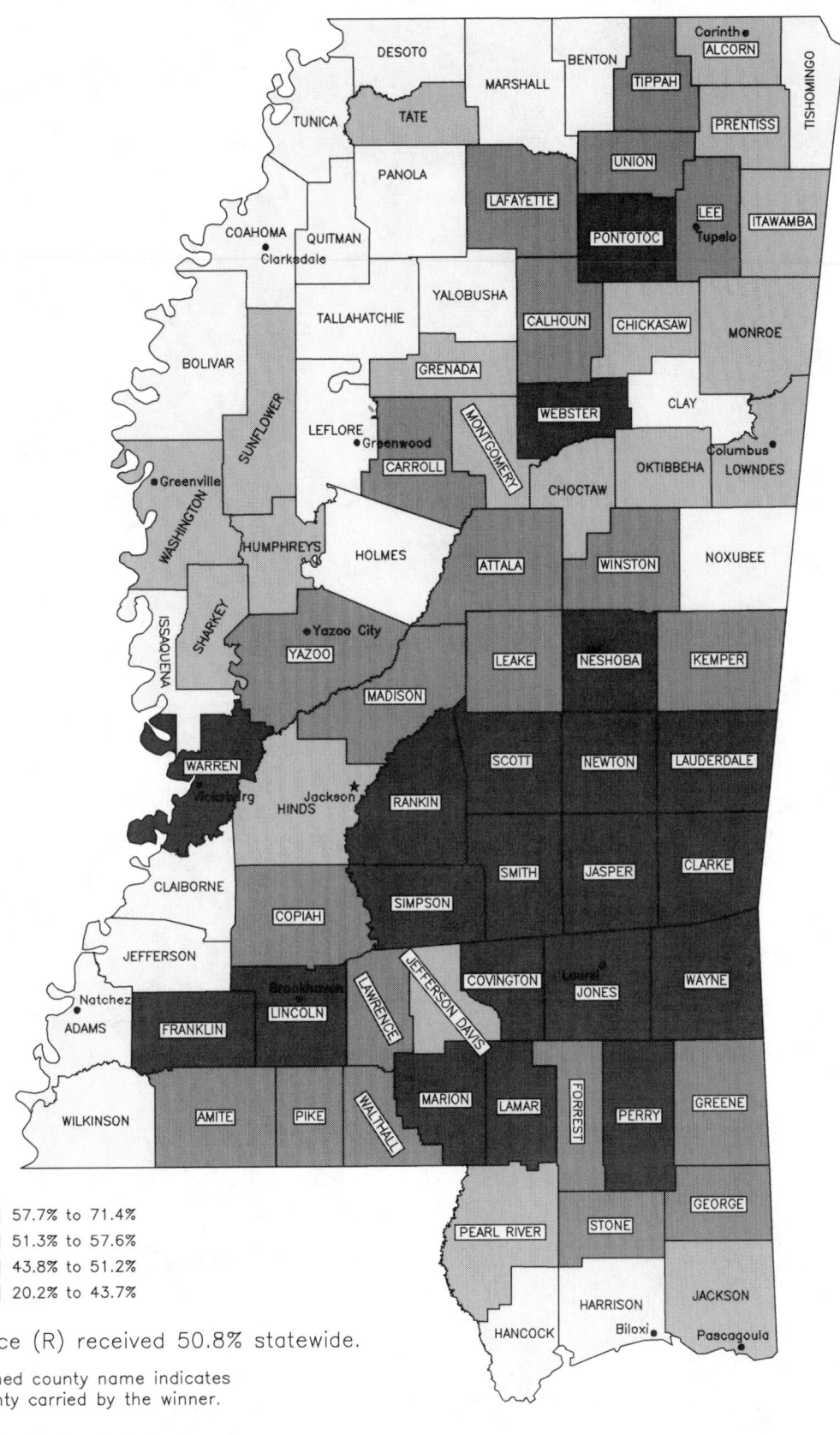

57.7% to 71.4%
51.3% to 57.6%
43.8% to 51.2%
20.2% to 43.7%

Fordice (R) received 50.8% statewide.

A framed county name indicates
a county carried by the winner.

Mississippi 533

MISSOURI

Congressional Districts 9
   Average Population 568,564
State Senate Districts 34
   Average Population 150,502
State House Districts 163
   Average Population 31,393

Electoral College Votes...11
Counties[1] 115
Voting Precincts 4,188

Alternative Registration Methods:
   ....Deputized Registrars

Registration Deadline (Days before Election) 19

Voting Equipment Use (Counties)[2]

Datavote Punch Card	0	Paper Ballot	48
Electronic	0	Other Punch Card	42
Lever Machine	2	Mixed Systems	0
Optical Scanner	24		

Party Control	DEM	REP	IND	VAC
1993 State Senate	19	15	0	0
1992 State Senate	22	12	0	0
1993 State House	100	62	0	1
1992 State House	99	64	0	0

Population Statistics 1990

Race/ Ethnicity	Total Population		Voting Age Population		Voting Age Population % of total population
	Number	%	Number	%	
Non-Hispanic					
White	4,448,465	86.9	3,351,276	88.1	75.3
Black	545,527	10.7	367,548	9.7	67.4
Asian/Pacific Islander	40,087	0.8	28,574	0.8	71.3
Native American	18,873	0.4	13,625	0.4	72.2
Other	2,419	<.1	794	<.1	32.8
All Hispanic	61,702	1.2	40,430	1.1	65.5
TOTAL	5,117,073	100.0	3,802,247	100.0	74.3

Estimated Voting Age Population 1992 (VAP) 3,858,000
Number of Registered Voters................................... 3,067,955
   % of estimated VAP... 79.5
Voter Turnout (Highest Office) 2,391,568
   % of VAP 62.0
   % of Registration 78.0
Persons Not Voting—of Voting Age 1,466,432
   % of VAP 38.0
Persons Not Voting—of Registered 676,387
   % of Registration 22.0
Straight Ticket Voting .... Yes, Exception

State Officials and Members of Congress

Governor:
Mel Carnahan (D) 1992, elected to a four-year term in 1992.

U.S. Senators:
John C. Danforth (R) 1976, elected to a six-year term in 1988.
Christopher S. Bond (R) 1986, elected to a six-year term in 1992.

U.S. Representative in Congress:
(District, Name, Party, Date first elected)

1. Clay (D) 1968
2. Talent (R) 1992
3. Gephardt (D) 1976

4. Skelton (D) 1976
5. Wheat (D) 1982

6. Danner (D) 1992
7. Hancock (R) 1988

8. Emerson (R) 1980
9. Volkmer (D) 1976

---

[1]Includes city of St. Louis.   [2]Includes cities of St. Louis and Kansas City, which administer elections independently.

Candidates: General Election, November 3, 1992

Candidate(s)	Total vote	Percent	Party	Status	First elected
President/Vice President					
Clinton/Gore	1,053,873	44.07%	Democrat	Challenger	1992
Bush/Quayle	811,159	33.92%	Republican	Incumbent	1988
Perot/Stockdale	518,741	21.69%	Independent	Challenger	
Marrou/Lord	7,497	0.31%	Libertarian	Challenger	
Write ins[1]	295	<.01%	Write in	Challenger	
U.S. Senator					
Christopher Bond	1,221,901	51.89%	Republican	Incumbent	1986
Geri Rothman-Serot	1,057,967	44.93%	Democrat	Challenger	
Jeanne Bojarski	75,048	3.19%	Libertarian	Challenger	
Write ins[2]	9	<.01%	Write in	Challenger	
Governor					
Mel Carnahan	1,375,425	58.68%	Democrat	Challenger	1992
William Webster	968,574	41.32%	Republican	Challenger	
Write ins[3]	122	<.01%	Write in	Challenger	
U.S. Representative in Congress					
District 1					
William Clay	158,693	68.06%	Democrat	Incumbent	1968
Arthur Montgomery	74,482	31.94%	Republican	Challenger	
District 2					
James Talent	157,594	50.44%	Republican	Challenger	1992
Joan Kelly Horn	148,729	47.60%	Democrat	Incumbent	1990
Jim Higgins	6,119	1.96%	Libertarian	Challenger	
David Kaplan	3	<.01%	Write in	Challenger	
District 3					
Richard Gephardt	174,000	64.01%	Democrat	Incumbent	1976
Mack Holekamp	90,006	33.11%	Republican	Challenger	
Robert Stockhausen	7,828	2.88%	Libertarian	Challenger	
District 4					
Ike Skelton	176,977	70.38%	Democrat	Incumbent	1976
John Carley	74,475	29.62%	Republican	Challenger	
District 5					
Alan Wheat	151,014	59.15%	Democrat	Incumbent	1982
Edward Moody	93,562	36.65%	Republican	Challenger	
Tom Danaher	6,107	2.39%	Green	Challenger	
Grant Stauffer	4,629	1.81%	Libertarian	Challenger	
District 6					
Patsy Ann Danner	148,887	55.45%	Democrat	Challenger	
Tom Coleman	119,637	44.55%	Republican	Incumbent	1992
District 7					
Melton Hancock	160,303	61.64%	Republican	Incumbent	1988
Thomas Deaton	99,762	38.36%	Democrat	Challenger	
District 8					
Bill Emerson	147,398	62.88%	Republican	Incumbent	1980
Thad Bullock	86,730	37.00%	Democrat	Challenger	
District 9					
Harold Volkmer	124,694	47.71%	Democrat	Incumbent	1976
Rick Hardy	118,811	45.46%	Republican	Challenger	
Jeff Barrow	10,565	4.04%	Green Party	Challenger	
Duane Burghard	7,265	2.78%	Independent	Challenger	
Write ins[4]	290	.11%	Write in	Challenger	

[1]Votes for Write in candidates include 180 for Bo Gritz, 64 for Hagelin/Tompkins, 17 for Fulani/Munoz, 13 for LaRouche/Bevel, 12 for Ron Daniels, 6 for James Warren, and 1 each for Messiah, Barbara Scott, and Robert Smith. [2]Votes for Write in candidates include 6 for Jock Peacock and 3 for David Sandor. [3]Votes for Write in candidates include 66 for Joan Dow, 42 for Jerry Branscrum, 6 for Jerry Smith, 5 for Douglas Clement, 2 for James Garrison, Jr., and 1 for Cyril Kolocotronis. [4]Votes for Write in candidates include 282 for Harry Reed and 8 for David Baugh.

Voter Registration and Turnout, 1948-1992 Elections

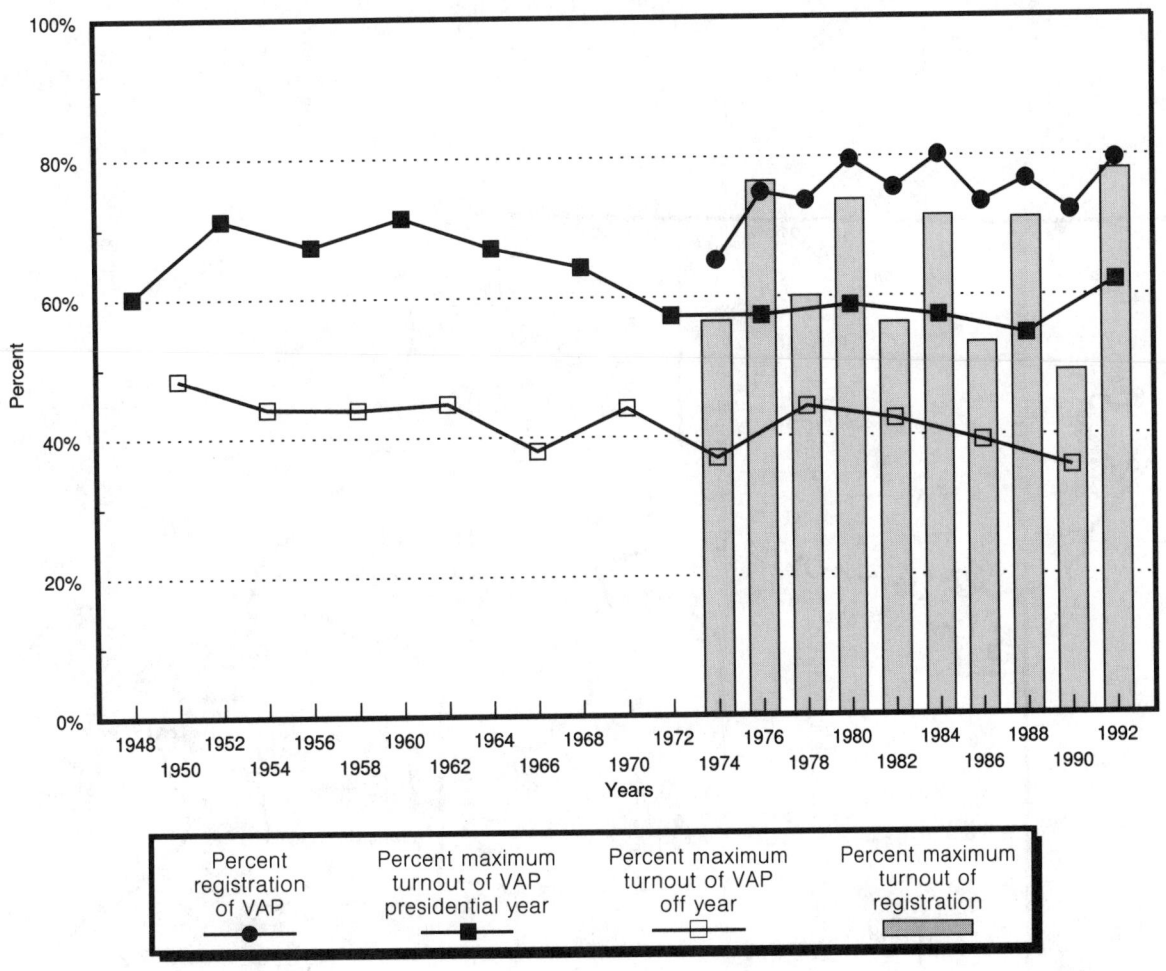

		Voter registration (REG)				Voter turnout										
							Highest office						Maximum vote			
Year	Estimated Voting Age Population (VAP)	Total	Percent of VAP	Rank by percent of VAP	Actual	Total	Office	Percent total REG	Rank by percent of REG	Percent of VAP	Rank by percent of VAP	Total	Percent total REG	Rank by percent of REG	Percent total VAP	Rank by percent of VAP
1992	3,858,000	3,067,955	79.5	17	-	2,391,565	P	78.0	23	62.0	19	2,391,565	78.0	28	62.0	21
1990	3,813,000	2,747,693	72.1	17	-	1,352,552	C	49.2	42	35.5	34	1,352,552	49.2	42	35.5	37
1988	3,840,000	2,943,024	76.6	16	-	2,093,713	P	71.1	27	54.5	18	2,093,713	71.1	32	54.5	22
1986	3,772,000	2,769,184	73.4	17	-	1,477,327	S	53.3	31	39.2	25	1,477,327	53.3	35	39.2	28
1984	3,709,000	2,969,700	80.1	16	-	2,122,783	P	71.5	32	57.2	18	2,122,783	71.5	37	57.2	21
1982	3,637,000	2,744,819	75.5	13	-	1,543,521	S	56.2	35	42.4	29	1,543,521	56.2	35	42.4	30
1980	3,578,000	2,845,023	79.5	14	-	2,099,824	P	73.8	28	58.7	14	2,099,824	73.8	32	58.7	18
1978	3,499,000	2,578,494	73.7	17	-	1,545,827	C	60.0	17	44.2	17	1,545,827	60.0	18	44.2	19
1976	3,408,000	2,552,852	74.9	21	-	1,953,600	P	76.5	21	57.3	22	1,953,600	76.5	24	57.3	26
1974	3,319,000	2,165,407	65.2	35	-	1,224,303	S	56.5	28	36.9	37	1,224,303	56.5	28	36.9	37
1972	3,240,000	-	-	-	-	1,855,803	P	-	-	57.3	28	1,855,803	-	-	57.3	32
1970	2,913,000	-	-	-	-	1,283,912	S	-	-	44.1	36	1,283,912	-	-	44.1	37
1968	2,813,000	-	-	-	-	1,809,502	P	-	-	64.3	26	1,809,502	-	-	64.3	27
1966	2,751,000	-	-	-	-	1,045,210	C	-	-	38.0	42	1,045,210	-	-	38.0	42
1964	2,709,000	-	-	-	-	1,817,879	P	-	-	67.1	25	1,817,879	-	-	67.1	27
1962	2,726,000	-	-	-	-	1,222,259	S	-	-	44.8	34	1,222,259	-	-	44.8	35
1960	2,706,000	-	-	-	-	1,934,422	P	-	-	71.5	22	1,934,422	-	-	71.5	22
1958	2,670,000	-	-	-	-	1,173,903	S	-	-	44.0	34	1,173,903	-	-	44.0	34
1956	2,717,000	-	-	-	-	1,832,562	P	-	-	67.4	22	1,832,562	-	-	67.4	22
1954	2,678,000	-	-	-	-	1,184,813	C	-	-	44.2	35	1,184,813	-	-	44.2	36
1952	2,656,000	-	-	-	-	1,892,062	P	-	-	71.2	24	1,892,062	-	-	71.2	25
1950	2,641,000	-	-	-	-	1,279,414	S	-	-	48.4	29	1,279,414	-	-	48.4	30
1948	2,624,000	-	-	-	-	1,578,628	P	-	-	60.2	21	1,578,628	-	-	60.2	23

MISSOURI

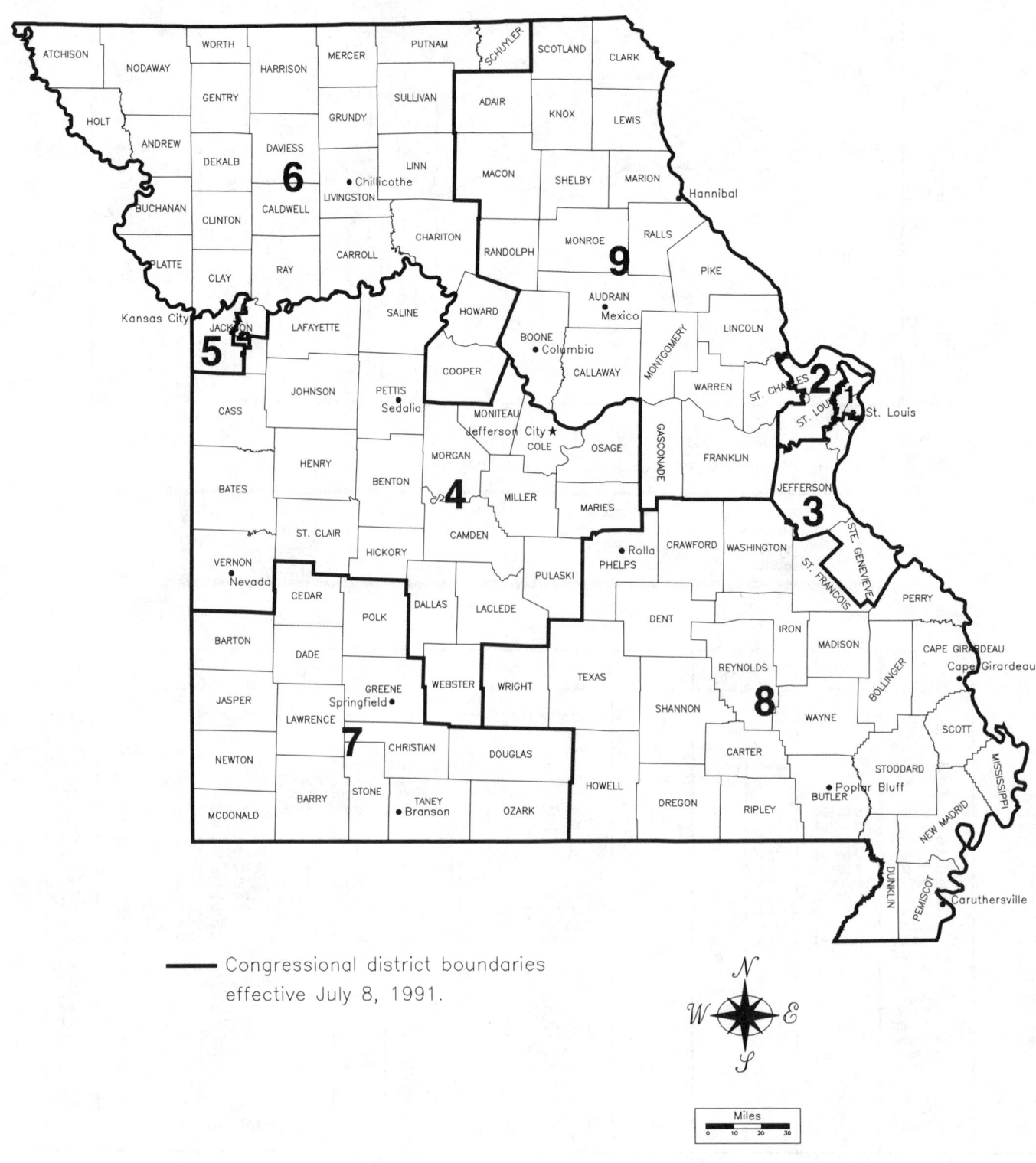

Congressional district boundaries
effective July 8, 1991.

N
W✦E
S

Miles
0 10 20 30

538 Missouri

Table A. — 1990 Population by Race and Ethnic Origin

State/ county code	County	Total persons	Percent of total persons						Rank				Percent contribution to state population			
			Non-Hispanic							Percent of total persons				Non-Hispanic		
			White	Black	Asian and Pacific Islander	Native American	Other	Hispanic	Total	Non-Hispanic		Hispanic	Total	White	Black	Hispanic
										White	Black					
29 001	Adair	24,577	97.3	0.9	0.9	0.2	<.1	0.7	37	68	53	28	0.5	0.5	<.1	0.3
29 003	Andrew	14,632	98.7	0.2	0.2	0.3	0.0	0.7	65	36	73	33	0.3	0.3	<.1	0.2
29 005	Atchison	7,457	97.1	1.1	0.2	0.2	<.1	1.4	101	71	50	8	0.1	0.2	<.1	0.2
29 007	Audrain	23,599	93.1	6.0	0.4	0.1	<.1	0.3	40	98	16	102	0.5	0.5	0.3	0.1
29 009	Barry	27,547	98.1	<.1	0.3	1.0	<.1	0.6	33	54	88	56	0.5	0.6	<.1	0.2
29 011	Barton	11,312	98.2	<.1	0.2	0.9	<.1	0.5	80	51	83	70	0.2	0.2	<.1	<.1
29 013	Bates	15,025	98.2	0.7	<.1	0.5	<.1	0.5	63	53	58	58	0.3	0.3	<.1	0.1
29 015	Benton	13,859	98.7	<.1	0.1	0.5	0.0	0.6	70	34	84	53	0.3	0.3	<.1	0.1
29 017	Bollinger	10,619	98.7	0.1	0.3	0.3	0.0	0.7	84	35	79	40	0.2	0.2	<.1	0.1
29 019	Boone	112,379	88.3	7.4	2.8	0.3	<.1	1.1	8	108	14	11	2.2	2.2	1.5	2.0
29 021	Buchanan	83,083	94.2	3.1	0.3	0.3	<.1	2.1	10	92	28	4	1.6	1.8	0.5	2.8
29 023	Butler	38,765	93.7	5.1	0.3	0.3	<.1	0.6	21	96	20	54	0.8	0.8	0.4	0.4
29 025	Caldwell	8,380	99.0	0.2	<.1	0.3	<.1	0.6	96	19	75	49	0.2	0.2	<.1	<.1
29 027	Callaway	32,809	94.0	4.8	0.4	0.3	<.1	0.5	25	94	22	64	0.6	0.6	0.3	0.3
29 029	Camden	27,495	98.6	0.2	0.2	0.4	<.1	0.6	34	37	72	46	0.5	0.6	<.1	0.2
29 031	Cape Girardeau	61,633	93.7	4.8	0.8	0.1	<.1	0.5	14	95	21	69	1.2	1.3	0.5	0.5
29 033	Carroll	10,748	97.3	2.0	0.1	0.1	<.1	0.4	82	69	36	98	0.2	0.2	<.1	<.1
29 035	Carter	5,515	98.7	<.1	<.1	0.6	0.0	0.6	109	32	112	47	0.1	0.1	<.1	<.1
29 037	Cass	63,808	96.7	1.1	0.4	0.6	<.1	1.3	12	75	51	9	1.2	1.4	0.1	1.3
29 039	Cedar	12,093	98.7	<.1	0.2	0.6	<.1	0.5	75	33	106	74	0.2	0.3	<.1	<.1
29 041	Chariton	9,202	95.8	3.7	<.1	0.2	<.1	0.2	90	83	25	112	0.2	0.2	<.1	<.1
29 043	Christian	32,644	98.4	0.1	0.2	0.6	<.1	0.7	26	45	81	39	0.6	0.7	<.1	0.4
29 045	Clark	7,547	99.5	<.1	<.1	<.1	<.1	0.3	100	3	102	101	0.1	0.2	<.1	<.1
29 047	Clay	153,411	94.7	1.7	0.7	0.5	<.1	2.3	7	90	42	3	3.0	3.3	0.5	5.7
29 049	Clinton	16,595	96.6	2.0	0.1	0.4	<.1	0.8	58	77	38	19	0.3	0.4	<.1	0.2
29 051	Cole	63,579	91.0	7.5	0.4	0.4	<.1	0.7	13	103	12	35	1.2	1.3	0.9	0.7
29 053	Cooper	14,835	90.9	7.7	0.3	0.3	<.1	0.6	64	104	10	43	0.3	0.3	0.2	0.2
29 055	Crawford	19,173	99.1	<.1	0.1	0.2	<.1	0.6	52	16	113	50	0.4	0.4	<.1	0.2
29 057	Dade	7,449	97.7	0.3	0.2	0.8	0.0	1.0	102	62	69	13	0.1	0.2	<.1	0.1
29 059	Dallas	12,646	98.5	0.1	0.1	0.7	0.0	0.5	72	40	77	66	0.2	0.3	<.1	0.1
29 061	Daviess	7,865	98.9	<.1	0.2	0.3	0.0	0.6	98	20	107	52	0.2	0.2	<.1	<.1
29 063	DeKalb	9,967	89.6	7.3	0.3	0.7	<.1	2.0	87	107	15	5	0.2	0.2	0.1	0.3
29 065	Dent	13,702	98.6	<.1	0.2	0.4	<.1	0.6	71	38	94	42	0.3	0.3	<.1	0.1
29 067	Douglas	11,876	98.3	<.1	0.1	0.7	0.0	0.8	77	46	108	24	0.2	0.3	<.1	0.1
29 069	Dunklin	33,112	91.1	7.9	0.2	0.3	<.1	0.5	24	102	9	68	0.6	0.7	0.5	0.3
29 071	Franklin	80,603	98.1	0.9	0.2	0.2	<.1	0.5	11	56	52	57	1.6	1.8	0.1	0.7
29 073	Gasconade	14,006	99.4	<.1	0.1	0.1	0.0	0.2	68	4	92	110	0.3	0.3	<.1	<.1
29 075	Gentry	6,848	99.1	<.1	<.1	0.4	<.1	0.4	105	15	87	93	0.1	0.2	<.1	<.1
29 077	Greene	207,949	96.0	1.8	0.7	0.6	<.1	0.9	5	80	41	18	4.1	4.5	0.7	2.9
29 079	Grundy	10,536	98.5	0.1	0.2	0.4	0.0	0.7	85	42	82	30	0.2	0.2	<.1	0.1
29 081	Harrison	8,469	98.9	<.1	0.2	0.4	<.1	0.4	94	23	85	82	0.2	0.2	<.1	<.1
29 083	Henry	20,044	97.5	1.1	0.2	0.4	<.1	0.7	50	65	48	31	0.4	0.4	<.1	0.2
29 085	Hickory	7,335	98.7	<.1	<.1	0.7	0.0	0.4	103	30	93	92	0.1	0.2	<.1	<.1
29 087	Holt	6,034	99.1	<.1	<.1	0.4	<.1	0.3	108	12	78	108	0.1	0.1	<.1	<.1
29 089	Howard	9,631	91.4	7.6	0.2	0.3	<.1	0.5	88	100	11	76	0.2	0.2	0.1	0.1
29 091	Howell	31,447	98.5	0.2	0.2	0.5	<.1	0.5	27	43	74	67	0.6	0.7	<.1	0.3
29 093	Iron	10,726	98.8	0.5	0.1	0.1	<.1	0.4	83	24	61	88	0.2	0.2	<.1	<.1
29 095	Jackson	633,232	74.2	21.3	1.0	0.4	<.1	3.0	2	113	3	2	12.4	10.6	24.7	30.6
29 097	Jasper	90,465	95.7	1.3	0.5	1.6	<.1	0.9	9	86	47	16	1.8	1.9	0.2	1.3
29 099	Jefferson	171,380	98.1	0.7	0.3	0.2	<.1	0.7	6	57	59	38	3.3	3.8	0.2	1.9
29 101	Johnson	42,514	90.8	5.7	1.4	0.5	<.1	1.7	18	105	18	7	0.8	0.9	0.4	1.1
29 103	Knox	4,482	99.4	0.1	<.1	0.2	0.0	0.2	112	5	76	113	<.1	0.1	<.1	<.1
29 105	Laclede	27,158	98.3	0.3	0.3	0.5	<.1	0.5	35	48	63	65	0.5	0.6	<.1	0.2
29 107	Lafayette	31,107	95.9	2.8	0.2	0.3	<.1	0.7	28	82	29	34	0.6	0.7	0.2	0.4
29 109	Lawrence	30,236	98.1	<.1	0.2	0.9	<.1	0.7	29	55	90	36	0.6	0.7	<.1	0.3
29 111	Lewis	10,233	96.0	3.3	0.2	0.2	<.1	0.3	86	81	26	109	0.2	0.2	<.1	<.1
29 113	Lincoln	28,892	96.7	2.0	0.2	0.3	<.1	0.8	31	76	37	25	0.6	0.6	0.1	0.4
29 115	Linn	13,885	98.3	0.8	<.1	0.2	<.1	0.7	69	49	56	37	0.3	0.3	<.1	0.2
29 117	Livingston	14,592	97.0	2.2	0.2	0.3	0.0	0.4	66	72	34	83	0.3	0.3	<.1	0.1
29 119	McDonald	16,938	95.8	<.1	0.2	3.2	<.1	0.7	55	84	109	32	0.3	0.4	<.1	0.2
29 121	Macon	15,345	96.8	2.4	0.1	0.3	<.1	0.4	62	73	32	95	0.3	0.3	<.1	<.1
29 123	Madison	11,127	98.8	<.1	0.3	0.3	<.1	0.6	81	28	86	55	0.2	0.2	<.1	0.1
29 125	Maries	7,976	98.8	0.3	0.1	0.2	<.1	0.5	97	26	64	71	0.2	0.2	<.1	<.1
29 127	Marion	27,682	94.4	4.5	0.4	0.2	<.1	0.4	32	91	23	85	0.5	0.6	0.2	0.2
29 129	Mercer	3,723	99.5	<.1	<.1	0.2	0.0	0.2	114	1	89	114	<.1	<.1	<.1	<.1
29 131	Miller	20,700	98.9	0.1	0.1	0.4	<.1	0.5	48	22	80	73	0.4	0.5	<.1	0.2
29 133	Mississippi	14,442	80.1	19.4	0.1	0.2	0.0	0.3	67	111	4	107	0.3	0.3	0.5	<.1
29 135	Moniteau	12,298	97.6	1.3	0.3	0.4	<.1	0.4	74	64	46	97	0.2	0.3	<.1	<.1
29 137	Monroe	9,104	95.3	3.9	0.1	0.2	0.0	0.5	91	89	24	61	0.2	0.2	<.1	<.1
29 139	Montgomery	11,355	96.8	2.5	0.2	0.1	<.1	0.4	79	74	31	91	0.2	0.2	<.1	<.1

Table A. — 1990 Population by Race and Ethnic Origin (cont)

State/ county code	County	Total persons	Percent of total persons — White	Non-Hispanic Black	Non-Hispanic Asian and Pacific Islander	Non-Hispanic Native American	Non-Hispanic Other	Hispanic	Rank — Percent of total persons Total	Non-Hispanic White	Non-Hispanic Black	Hispanic	Percent contribution to state population Total	Non-Hispanic White	Non-Hispanic Black	Hispanic
29 141	Morgan	15,574	98.3	0.6	0.2	0.4	<.1	0.4	61	47	60	80	0.3	0.3	<.1	0.1
29 143	New Madrid	20,928	83.6	15.6	0.2	0.2	<.1	0.4	47	109	5	79	0.4	0.4	0.6	0.2
29 145	Newton	44,445	96.2	0.4	0.5	2.1	<.1	0.8	17	78	62	20	0.9	1.0	<.1	0.6
29 147	Nodaway	21,709	97.7	0.8	0.8	0.2	<.1	0.6	45	63	57	45	0.4	0.5	<.1	0.2
29 149	Oregon	9,470	99.1	<.1	0.1	0.4	<.1	0.3	89	14	104	103	0.2	0.2	<.1	<.1
29 151	Osage	12,018	99.0	0.3	<.1	0.2	<.1	0.5	76	18	65	77	0.2	0.3	<.1	<.1
29 153	Ozark	8,598	98.7	<.1	0.1	0.4	<.1	0.7	92	29	110	41	0.2	0.2	<.1	<.1
29 155	Pemiscot	21,921	73.8	25.4	0.2	0.2	<.1	0.4	43	114	2	90	0.4	0.4	1.0	0.1
29 157	Perry	16,648	98.9	<.1	0.4	0.2	<.1	0.4	57	21	95	84	0.3	0.4	<.1	0.1
29 159	Pettis	35,437	95.3	3.3	0.3	0.3	<.1	0.8	22	88	27	26	0.7	0.8	0.2	0.4
29 161	Phelps	35,248	95.4	1.1	2.2	0.4	<.1	0.9	23	87	49	17	0.7	0.8	<.1	0.5
29 163	Pike	15,969	93.6	5.2	0.1	0.3	<.1	0.7	60	97	19	27	0.3	0.3	0.2	0.2
29 165	Platte	57,867	94.1	2.1	1.3	0.5	<.1	2.0	15	93	35	6	1.1	1.2	0.2	1.9
29 167	Polk	21,826	98.0	0.3	0.3	0.6	<.1	0.8	44	58	67	21	0.4	0.5	<.1	0.3
29 169	Pulaski	41,307	78.4	13.3	2.8	0.6	0.2	4.7	19	112	7	1	0.8	0.7	1.0	3.2
29 171	Putnam	5,079	99.3	<.1	<.1	0.2	0.0	0.5	110	11	111	75	<.1	0.1	<.1	<.1
29 173	Ralls	8,476	97.9	1.6	<.1	0.2	0.0	0.2	93	59	43	115	0.2	0.2	<.1	<.1
29 175	Randolph	24,370	91.1	7.5	0.3	0.3	<.1	0.7	38	101	13	29	0.5	0.5	0.3	0.3
29 177	Ray	21,971	97.4	1.3	0.2	0.5	<.1	0.5	42	67	45	59	0.4	0.5	<.1	0.2
29 179	Reynolds	6,661	99.3	<.1	<.1	0.2	<.1	0.4	106	10	100	87	0.1	0.1	<.1	<.1
29 181	Ripley	12,303	98.8	<.1	0.2	0.4	<.1	0.6	73	27	99	44	0.2	0.3	<.1	0.1
29 183	St. Charles	212,907	95.7	2.3	0.7	0.2	<.1	1.1	4	85	33	12	4.2	4.6	0.9	3.7
29 185	St. Clair	8,457	98.8	0.3	<.1	0.5	0.0	0.4	95	25	70	94	0.2	0.2	<.1	<.1
29 186	Ste. Genevieve	16,037	99.1	0.3	0.1	0.2	<.1	0.3	59	17	68	105	0.3	0.4	<.1	<.1
29 187	St. Francois	48,904	97.1	1.9	0.2	0.2	<.1	0.5	16	70	39	72	1.0	1.1	0.2	0.4
29 189	St. Louis	993,529	83.4	14.0	1.4	0.1	<.1	1.0	1	110	6	14	19.4	18.6	25.4	15.9
29 195	Saline	23,523	92.9	5.7	0.2	0.2	<.1	0.9	41	99	17	15	0.5	0.5	0.2	0.3
29 197	Schuyler	4,236	99.3	0.0	<.1	0.2	0.0	0.4	113	7	115	86	<.1	<.1	0.0	<.1
29 199	Scotland	4,822	99.5	<.1	0.0	0.2	0.0	0.2	111	2	97	111	<.1	0.1	<.1	<.1
29 201	Scott	39,376	90.3	8.9	0.2	0.2	<.1	0.5	20	106	8	63	0.8	0.8	0.6	0.3
29 203	Shannon	7,613	99.3	<.1	<.1	0.3	0.0	0.3	99	8	103	106	0.1	0.2	<.1	<.1
29 205	Shelby	6,942	98.5	0.8	<.1	0.3	<.1	0.3	104	41	55	104	0.1	0.2	<.1	<.1
29 207	Stoddard	28,895	97.8	1.4	0.1	0.2	<.1	0.5	30	61	44	78	0.6	0.6	<.1	0.2
29 209	Stone	19,078	98.5	<.1	0.2	0.7	0.0	0.6	53	44	105	48	0.4	0.4	<.1	0.2
29 211	Sullivan	6,326	99.3	<.1	<.1	0.2	0.0	0.4	107	9	114	81	0.1	0.1	<.1	<.1
29 213	Taney	25,561	98.3	<.1	0.3	0.6	<.1	0.8	36	50	96	23	0.5	0.6	<.1	0.3
29 215	Texas	21,476	98.7	<.1	0.3	0.4	<.1	0.5	46	31	91	62	0.4	0.5	<.1	0.2
29 217	Vernon	19,041	98.2	0.3	0.3	0.6	<.1	0.5	54	52	66	60	0.4	0.4	<.1	0.2
29 219	Warren	19,534	96.2	2.6	0.2	0.2	<.1	0.8	51	79	30	22	0.4	0.4	<.1	0.2
29 221	Washington	20,380	97.5	1.9	<.1	0.2	<.1	0.4	49	66	40	89	0.4	0.4	<.1	0.1
29 223	Wayne	11,543	99.1	<.1	<.1	0.4	<.1	0.4	78	13	98	96	0.2	0.3	<.1	<.1
29 225	Webster	23,753	97.8	0.8	0.2	0.6	<.1	0.6	39	60	54	51	0.5	0.5	<.1	0.2
29 227	Worth	2,440	99.3	<.1	0.2	<.1	0.0	0.4	115	6	101	99	<.1	<.1	<.1	<.1
29 229	Wright	16,758	98.6	0.2	<.1	0.7	<.1	0.4	56	39	71	100	0.3	0.4	<.1	<.1
29 510	St. Louis City	396,685	50.2	47.3	0.9	0.2	<.1	1.3	3	115	1	10	7.8	4.5	34.4	8.3
29	**MISSOURI**	**5,117,073**	**86.9**	**10.7**	**0.8**	**0.4**	**<.1**	**1.2**					**100.0**	**100.0**	**100.0**	**100.0**
	CONGRESSIONAL															
	District 1	568,285	45.8	52.2	0.9	0.2	<.1	0.9	8	9	1	6	11.1	5.8	54.3	8.2
	District 2	568,306	93.5	3.7	1.6	0.2	<.1	1.0	7	7	4	5	11.1	11.9	3.9	9.4
	District 3	568,326	95.5	2.3	0.8	0.2	<.1	1.1	6	3	7	3	11.1	12.2	2.4	10.6
	District 4	569,146	94.7	3.2	0.5	0.4	<.1	1.1	1	4	6	4	11.1	12.1	3.3	10.1
	District 5	569,130	71.8	23.5	1.0	0.5	<.1	3.2	3	8	2	1	11.1	9.2	24.5	29.2
	District 6	569,131	95.5	2.1	0.5	0.4	<.1	1.5	2	2	8	2	11.1	12.2	2.2	13.7
	District 7	568,017	96.8	0.9	0.5	1.0	<.1	0.8	9	1	9	7	11.1	12.4	1.0	7.2
	District 8	568,385	94.4	4.4	0.4	0.3	<.1	0.5	4	6	3	9	11.1	12.1	4.6	4.7
	District 9	568,347	94.5	3.7	0.8	0.3	<.1	0.7	5	5	5	8	11.1	12.1	3.8	6.8

County	Total Voting Age Population	Percent of total VAP — Non-Hispanic White	Black	Asian and Pacific Islander	Native American	Other	Hispanic	Rank — Total	Non-Hispanic White	Black	Hispanic	Percent contribution to state VAP — Total	Non-Hispanic White	Black	Hispanic	VAP percent of total population — Total	Non-Hispanic White	Black	Asian and Pacific Islander	Native American	Other	Hispanic
Adair	19,629	97.2	0.9	1.0	0.1	<.1	0.7	37	68	53	21	0.5	0.6	<.1	0.3	79.9	79.8	86.9	89.0	74.4	83.3	70.9
Andrew	10,680	98.8	0.2	0.1	0.2	0.0	0.6	67	36	72	30	0.3	0.3	<.1	0.2	73.0	73.1	73.3	65.2	66.7	0.0	63.1
Atchison	5,778	96.7	1.3	0.2	0.2	<.1	1.5	99	76	45	7	0.2	0.2	<.1	0.2	77.5	77.2	93.9	100.0	85.7	40.0	81.7
Audrain	17,376	93.9	5.4	0.3	0.1	0.0	0.3	40	96	18	100	0.5	0.5	0.3	0.1	73.6	74.3	65.9	57.8	75.8	0.0	60.5
Barry	20,570	98.4	<.1	0.2	0.9	<.1	0.4	32	51	81	60	0.5	0.6	<.1	0.2	74.7	74.9	83.3	52.1	66.2	100.0	59.2
Barton	8,326	98.5	<.1	0.2	0.8	<.1	0.4	80	46	87	78	0.2	0.2	<.1	<.1	73.6	73.8	63.6	60.7	63.7	100.0	54.4
Bates	11,097	98.4	0.8	<.1	0.5	0.0	0.3	64	52	56	92	0.3	0.3	<.1	<.1	73.9	74.0	79.4	75.0	73.9	0.0	42.7
Benton	10,882	98.7	<.1	0.1	0.6	0.0	0.5	66	43	83	42	0.3	0.3	<.1	0.1	78.5	78.5	76.9	93.8	81.3	0.0	71.8
Bollinger	7,837	98.9	0.1	0.2	0.2	0.0	0.5	86	28	76	41	0.2	0.2	<.1	0.1	73.8	74.0	83.3	57.1	60.0	0.0	60.0
Boone	87,015	89.5	6.4	2.8	0.3	<.1	1.0	8	107	14	11	2.3	2.3	1.5	2.2	77.4	78.4	67.0	78.1	71.7	25.7	71.9
Buchanan	61,630	94.9	2.8	0.2	0.3	<.1	1.8	10	92	28	5	1.6	1.7	0.5	2.7	74.2	74.8	66.6	61.1	72.1	14.6	63.1
Butler	28,802	94.7	4.2	0.3	0.3	0.0	0.5	20	93	21	55	0.8	0.8	0.3	0.3	74.3	75.1	61.1	66.4	76.2	0.0	61.3
Caldwell	6,180	99.1	0.1	<.1	0.3	<.1	0.4	96	17	75	70	0.2	0.2	<.1	<.1	73.7	73.9	57.1	100.0	90.5	50.0	50.0
Callaway	24,212	93.9	5.0	0.3	0.3	<.1	0.4	25	97	20	59	0.6	0.7	0.3	0.3	73.8	73.7	76.3	68.1	84.8	11.1	62.6
Camden	21,501	98.8	0.2	0.2	0.3	<.1	0.5	31	34	71	51	0.6	0.6	<.1	0.2	78.2	78.3	82.5	77.8	71.3	100.0	59.4
Cape Girardeau	47,004	94.5	4.1	0.8	0.2	<.1	0.5	13	95	23	53	1.2	1.3	0.5	0.5	76.3	76.9	64.1	81.4	82.6	23.8	70.0
Carroll	7,923	97.6	1.9	0.1	0.2	0.0	0.3	83	65	39	106	0.2	0.2	<.1	<.1	73.7	73.9	68.0	90.9	100.0	0.0	50.0
Carter	3,993	98.7	0.0	0.1	0.6	0.0	0.6	109	39	114	39	0.1	0.1	0.0	<.1	72.4	72.4	0.0	80.0	72.7	0.0	66.7
Cass	45,256	97.1	0.9	0.4	0.5	<.1	1.1	14	70	52	10	1.2	1.3	0.1	1.2	70.9	71.2	63.5	64.9	69.3	41.7	57.8
Cedar	9,279	98.8	<.1	0.2	0.6	0.0	0.3	72	33	105	86	0.2	0.3	<.1	<.1	76.7	76.8	100.0	80.0	80.0	76.3	53.4
Chariton	6,828	95.8	3.7	<.1	0.2	0.0	0.2	90	87	24	108	0.2	0.2	<.1	<.1	74.2	74.2	74.8	71.4	73.3	0.0	84.2
Christian	23,315	98.7	<.1	0.2	0.5	0.0	0.5	26	44	89	46	0.6	0.7	<.1	0.3	71.4	71.6	51.4	59.5	66.8	0.0	54.6
Clark	5,493	99.5	<.1	<.1	<.1	<.1	0.3	103	5	97	96	0.1	0.2	<.1	<.1	72.8	72.8	100.0	75.0	66.7	100.0	61.5
Clay	113,909	95.4	1.5	0.6	0.5	<.1	2.0	7	90	44	4	3.0	3.2	0.5	5.7	74.3	74.7	65.5	67.9	70.1	27.4	64.7
Clinton	11,977	97.0	1.8	0.1	0.4	<.1	0.6	58	73	40	23	0.3	0.3	<.1	0.1	72.2	72.5	66.9	63.6	70.4	25.0	55.4
Cole	47,660	90.0	8.6	0.4	0.4	<.1	0.7	12	106	9	22	1.3	1.3	1.1	0.8	75.0	74.2	85.3	74.5	76.1	26.3	70.0
Cooper	11,214	90.7	8.1	0.3	0.3	0.0	0.5	63	105	10	45	0.3	0.3	0.2	0.1	75.6	75.4	79.4	83.0	72.0	0.0	59.4
Crawford	14,013	99.1	<.1	0.1	0.2	0.0	0.6	54	18	113	36	0.4	0.4	<.1	0.1	73.1	73.1	33.3	66.7	72.2	0.0	70.2
Dade	5,566	98.2	0.3	0.1	0.7	0.0	0.7	102	58	69	20	0.1	0.2	<.1	<.1	74.7	75.1	80.0	66.7	61.3	0.0	50.0
Dallas	9,249	98.7	<.1	0.1	0.6	0.0	0.4	73	41	82	58	0.2	0.3	<.1	0.1	73.1	73.3	56.3	70.6	65.1	0.0	63.1
Daviess	5,747	99.1	<.1	0.1	0.2	0.0	0.5	100	15	102	47	0.2	0.2	<.1	<.1	73.1	73.2	100.0	58.3	45.8	0.0	63.0
DeKalb	7,844	87.3	9.3	0.3	0.8	0.1	2.3	85	108	8	3	0.2	0.2	0.2	0.5	78.7	76.6	99.9	71.0	90.8	100.0	91.0
Dent	10,091	98.9	<.1	0.1	0.4	0.0	0.5	71	32	91	49	0.3	0.3	<.1	0.1	73.6	73.8	77.8	53.6	75.0	0.0	53.9
Douglas	8,698	98.5	<.1	0.1	0.7	0.0	0.6	77	49	107	27	0.2	0.3	<.1	0.1	73.6	73.7	66.7	73.3	73.9	0.0	60.0
Dunklin	24,367	93.4	5.8	0.2	0.3	<.1	0.4	24	99	15	71	0.6	0.7	0.4	0.2	73.6	75.4	53.8	61.4	75.0	10.0	57.4
Franklin	57,603	98.3	0.9	0.2	0.2	<.1	0.5	11	56	54	54	1.5	1.7	0.1	0.4	71.5	71.6	69.7	56.6	70.3	13.6	60.5
Gasconade	10,518	99.4	<.1	0.1	0.1	0.0	0.3	68	9	96	104	0.3	0.3	<.1	<.1	75.1	75.1	60.0	82.4	70.0	0.0	80.0
Gentry	5,161	99.3	<.1	<.1	0.3	<.1	0.3	104	12	94	103	0.1	0.2	<.1	<.1	73.4	73.5	50.0	75.0	68.0	100.0	51.9
Greene	160,309	96.4	1.7	0.6	0.6	<.1	0.7	4	81	42	14	4.2	4.6	0.7	2.9	77.1	77.4	71.7	68.7	72.3	22.0	66.9
Grundy	8,037	98.8	<.1	0.2	0.4	0.0	0.6	82	37	80	38	0.2	0.2	<.1	0.1	76.3	76.5	72.7	54.2	74.4	0.0	58.4
Harrison	6,534	99.0	<.1	0.2	0.4	<.1	0.4	93	23	93	76	0.2	0.2	<.1	<.1	77.2	77.3	50.0	58.8	74.2	50.0	67.6
Henry	15,126	97.9	1.0	0.2	0.4	0.0	0.5	47	61	51	48	0.4	0.4	<.1	0.2	75.5	75.8	67.4	63.0	67.9	0.0	52.8
Hickory	5,923	98.9	<.1	0.1	0.7	0.0	0.3	97	29	103	94	0.2	0.2	<.1	<.1	80.7	80.9	40.0	100.0	73.6	0.0	62.1
Holt	4,491	99.2	0.1	<.1	0.3	<.1	0.2	108	13	78	109	0.1	0.1	<.1	<.1	74.4	74.5	71.4	60.0	68.2	100.0	62.5
Howard	7,246	91.6	7.5	0.2	0.3	<.1	0.4	88	102	12	80	0.2	0.2	0.1	<.1	75.2	75.4	74.3	94.1	75.0	42.9	57.8
Howell	23,185	98.7	0.1	0.2	0.5	<.1	0.4	27	40	74	67	0.6	0.7	<.1	0.2	73.7	73.9	51.6	60.0	71.3	50.0	59.6
Iron	7,862	99.1	0.3	<.1	0.2	<.1	0.3	84	21	65	88	0.2	0.2	<.1	<.1	73.3	73.5	55.1	41.7	100.0	33.3	59.1
Jackson	472,417	76.8	19.2	0.9	0.4	<.1	2.6	2	114	3	2	12.4	10.8	24.6	30.8	74.6	77.2	67.2	69.9	73.1	41.3	66.0
Jasper	67,343	96.0	1.2	0.5	1.5	<.1	0.7	9	85	48	17	1.8	1.9	0.2	1.2	74.4	74.7	66.9	60.8	70.8	32.0	61.5
Jefferson	120,382	98.2	0.7	0.3	0.3	<.1	0.6	6	57	59	37	3.2	3.5	0.2	1.7	70.2	70.4	66.9	60.8	78.9	16.2	59.2
Johnson	32,138	91.3	5.4	1.4	0.4	<.1	1.4	18	103	17	8	0.8	0.9	0.5	1.1	75.6	76.0	72.7	77.2	71.4	38.5	63.0
Knox	3,412	99.5	0.1	<.1	0.1	0.0	0.1	112	3	77	113	<.1	0.1	<.1	<.1	76.1	76.2	66.7	66.7	50.0	0.0	55.6
Laclede	19,864	98.5	0.3	0.2	0.5	0.0	0.5	36	48	64	56	0.5	0.6	<.1	0.2	73.1	73.3	72.6	63.2	64.3	0.0	64.5
Lafayette	22,871	96.3	2.6	0.2	0.3	<.1	0.6	28	82	29	33	0.6	0.7	0.2	0.3	73.5	73.8	69.1	72.7	63.1	26.7	61.2
Lawrence	22,150	98.4	<.1	0.2	0.8	<.1	0.5	29	54	84	40	0.6	0.7	<.1	0.3	73.3	73.5	83.3	60.7	66.8	42.9	56.9
Lewis	7,829	96.2	3.1	0.2	0.1	<.1	0.3	87	83	26	90	0.2	0.2	0.1	<.1	76.5	76.7	70.5	100.0	57.9	14.3	96.2
Lincoln	20,216	96.8	2.0	0.2	0.3	<.1	0.7	34	74	37	19	0.5	0.6	0.1	0.4	70.0	70.1	68.5	68.5	66.3	25.0	65.8
Linn	10,430	98.4	0.8	<.1	0.2	0.0	0.6	69	53	58	34	0.3	0.3	<.1	0.1	75.1	75.2	73.8	69.2	86.4	0.0	64.9
Livingston	10,906	96.7	2.4	0.2	0.3	0.0	0.4	65	75	32	74	0.3	0.3	<.1	0.1	74.7	74.6	83.5	85.2	73.7	0.0	66.7
McDonald	12,268	96.4	<.1	0.2	2.8	<.1	0.5	55	80	110	43	0.3	0.4	<.1	0.2	72.4	72.9	50.0	70.0	63.5	100.0	52.1
Macon	11,571	97.2	2.1	0.1	0.3	0.0	0.3	61	69	36	99	0.3	0.3	<.1	<.1	75.4	75.7	65.6	78.9	76.0	0.0	55.9
Madison	8,266	98.9	<.1	0.3	0.3	0.0	0.5	81	30	86	50	0.2	0.2	<.1	0.1	74.0	74.4	64.7	71.9	0.0	62.9
Maries	5,906	99.1	0.2	0.1	0.2	<.1	0.2	98	22	70	85	0.2	0.2	<.1	<.1	72.8	73.2	67.2	64.2	69.1	20.0	64.4
Marion	20,144	94.9	4.1	0.3	0.2	<.1	0.4	35	91	22	77	0.5	0.6	0.2	0.2	72.8	73.2	67.2	64.2	69.1	20.0	64.4
Mercer	2,884	99.5	0.1	<.1	0.1	0.0	0.2	114	2	79	110	<.1	<.1	<.1	<.1	77.5	77.5	100.0	100.0	0.0	0.0	85.7
Miller	14,916	99.0	<.1	<.1	0.4	<.1	0.4	49	25	85	65	0.4	0.4	<.1	0.2	72.1	72.1	56.5	47.6	74.7	100.0	63.4
Mississippi	10,273	83.5	15.9	<.1	0.2	0.0	0.3	70	111	4	105	0.3	0.3	0.4	<.1	71.1	74.2	58.5	66.7	80.8	0.0	67.5
Moniteau	8,908	97.4	1.6	0.3	0.4	0.0	0.5	75	67	43	44	0.2	0.3	<.1	0.1	72.4	72.2	89.8	77.8	78.4	0.0	58.7
Monroe	6,601	95.6	3.6	0.1	0.2	0.0	0.5	92	88	25	52	0.2	0.2	<.1	<.1	72.5	72.7	67.5	75.0	88.9	0.0	64.6
Montgomery	8,384	97.0	2.4	0.2	<.1	<.1	0.3	79	72	33	97	0.2	0.2	<.1	<.1	73.8	74.1	70.2	65.0	58.3	50.0	53.3

Table B. — 1990 Voting Age Population (VAP) by Race and Ethnic Origin (cont)

County	Total Voting Age Population	Percent of total VAP — Non-Hispanic: White	Black	Asian and Pacific Islander	Native American	Other	Hispanic	Rank — Percent of total VAP — Non-Hispanic: Total	White	Black	Hispanic	Percent contribution to state VAP — Non-Hispanic: Total	White	Black	Hispanic	VAP percent of total population — Non-Hispanic: Total	White	Black	Asian and Pacific Islander	Native American	Other	Hispanic
Morgan	11,970	98.4	0.6	0.1	0.4	<.1	0.4	59	50	60	75	0.3	0.4	<.1	0.1	76.9	76.9	79.8	64.0	73.5	25.0	66.7
New Madrid	14,807	86.5	12.8	0.1	0.2	<.1	0.4	50	109	5	81	0.4	0.4	0.5	0.1	70.8	73.2	58.1	52.8	79.4	100.0	57.0
Newton	32,672	96.7	0.4	0.5	1.8	<.1	0.6	17	77	61	24	0.9	0.9	<.1	0.5	73.5	73.9	69.9	68.2	64.1	50.0	59.5
Nodaway	16,831	97.5	0.9	0.8	0.2	<.1	0.6	42	66	55	26	0.4	0.5	<.1	0.3	77.5	77.4	91.5	85.4	71.1	40.0	77.8
Oregon	7,213	99.1	<.1	<.1	0.5	<.1	0.3	89	16	112	93	0.2	0.2	<.1	<.1	76.2	76.2	33.3	38.5	86.8	100.0	68.8
Osage	8,679	99.0	0.4	<.1	0.1	<.1	0.4	78	24	61	60	0.2	0.3	<.1	<.1	72.2	72.2	84.2	100.0	55.0	100.0	67.9
Ozark	6,612	98.8	<.1	0.1	0.5	<.1	0.6	91	35	111	35	0.2	0.2	<.1	<.1	76.9	76.9	50.0	66.7	88.6	33.3	67.9
Pemiscot	15,161	79.0	20.3	0.1	0.2	<.1	0.4	46	113	2	79	0.4	0.4	0.8	0.1	69.2	74.0	55.3	46.7	75.8	50.0	61.8
Perry	11,989	99.1	<.1	0.3	0.2	0.0	0.3	57	20	95	84	0.3	0.4	<.1	0.1	72.0	72.1	63.6	60.3	72.4	0.0	56.9
Pettis	26,222	95.9	3.0	0.3	0.3	<.1	0.6	23	86	27	31	0.7	0.8	0.2	0.4	74.0	74.4	67.2	58.8	74.0	14.3	59.3
Phelps	26,826	95.4	1.0	2.4	0.4	<.1	0.7	22	89	50	15	0.7	0.8	<.1	0.5	76.1	76.1	70.2	82.0	75.9	66.7	65.3
Pike	11,613	93.9	5.1	0.1	0.2	0.0	0.6	60	98	19	28	0.3	0.3	0.2	0.2	72.7	73.0	71.5	68.2	57.1	0.0	60.5
Platte	42,664	94.6	1.9	1.2	0.5	<.1	1.7	15	94	38	6	1.1	1.2	0.2	1.8	73.7	74.2	67.7	68.8	72.1	23.1	63.2
Polk	16,467	98.1	0.4	0.3	0.5	<.1	0.7	43	59	63	18	0.4	0.5	<.1	0.3	75.4	75.5	89.6	74.6	68.8	33.3	68.2
Pulaski	29,385	79.4	12.8	2.8	0.6	0.1	4.2	19	112	6	1	0.8	0.7	1.0	3.0	71.1	72.1	68.5	71.4	73.3	49.4	63.1
Putnam	3,928	99.4	<.1	<.1	0.1	0.0	0.4	110	10	106	62	0.1	0.1	<.1	<.1	77.3	77.4	100.0	50.0	62.5	0.0	70.8
Ralls	6,226	97.9	1.7	<.1	0.2	0.0	0.1	95	62	41	115	0.2	0.2	<.1	<.1	73.5	73.4	76.8	83.3	83.3	0.0	50.0
Randolph	18,282	90.8	8.0	0.3	0.3	<.1	0.6	38	104	11	25	0.5	0.5	0.4	0.2	75.0	74.8	79.9	62.0	68.8	28.6	64.2
Ray	15,707	97.7	1.3	0.1	0.4	<.1	0.4	44	63	47	57	0.4	0.5	<.1	0.2	71.5	71.7	66.9	66.7	60.6	50.0	58.8
Reynolds	4,907	99.3	<.1	<.1	0.2	<.1	0.4	107	11	101	73	0.1	0.1	<.1	<.1	73.7	73.7	66.7	100.0	57.1	100.0	67.9
Ripley	8,998	98.9	<.1	0.1	0.4	<.1	0.5	74	26	104	44	0.2	0.3	<.1	0.1	73.1	73.3	50.0	47.4	79.6	100.0	59.0
St. Charles	148,840	96.0	2.1	0.6	0.2	<.1	1.0	5	84	35	12	3.9	4.3	0.8	3.6	69.9	70.2	63.2	68.9	67.6	32.4	63.6
St. Clair	6,481	98.7	0.3	<.1	0.5	0.0	0.4	94	42	66	82	0.2	0.2	<.1	<.1	76.6	76.6	100.0	100.0	82.9	0.0	69.7
Ste. Genevieve	11,548	99.1	0.3	0.1	0.2	0.0	0.3	62	19	68	98	0.3	0.3	<.1	<.1	72.0	72.0	80.0	58.3	63.3	0.0	67.3
St. Francois	36,456	96.6	2.5	0.3	0.2	<.1	0.4	16	78	31	68	1.0	1.1	0.2	0.3	74.5	74.2	94.9	76.7	84.5	25.0	62.8
St. Louis	749,134	85.1	12.5	1.3	0.1	<.1	0.9	1	110	7	13	19.7	19.0	25.5	16.4	75.4	76.9	67.6	70.4	77.0	29.5	67.6
Saline	17,621	93.2	5.6	0.2	0.2	<.1	0.7	39	100	16	16	0.5	0.5	0.3	0.3	74.9	75.1	73.8	69.1	86.7	45.5	62.5
Schuyler	3,196	99.7	0.0	<.1	0.1	0.0	0.2	113	1	115	111	<.1	<.1	0.0	<.1	75.4	75.7	0.0	33.3	50.0	0.0	33.3
Scotland	3,597	99.4	<.1	0.0	0.2	0.0	0.3	111	8	88	87	<.1	0.1	<.1	<.1	74.6	74.5	100.0	0.0	60.0	0.0	100.0
Scott	28,185	92.4	6.8	0.2	0.2	0.0	0.4	21	101	13	63	0.7	0.8	0.5	0.3	71.6	73.3	55.3	74.2	70.7	0.0	59.2
Shannon	5,582	99.4	<.1	<.1	0.3	0.0	0.1	101	7	98	114	0.1	0.2	<.1	<.1	73.3	73.4	100.0	75.0	72.0	0.0	31.8
Shelby	5,143	98.6	0.8	<.1	0.3	<.1	0.3	105	45	57	102	0.1	0.2	<.1	<.1	74.1	74.1	70.9	100.0	77.8	100.0	60.9
Stoddard	21,676	98.0	1.3	0.1	0.2	<.1	0.3	30	60	46	83	0.6	0.6	<.1	0.2	75.0	75.2	69.4	68.3	65.5	28.6	56.8
Stone	14,978	98.8	<.1	0.2	0.6	0.0	0.4	48	38	108	69	0.4	0.4	<.1	0.2	78.5	78.7	50.0	70.3	71.0	0.0	53.5
Sullivan	4,945	99.5	<.1	<.1	0.2	0.0	0.2	106	6	109	107	0.1	0.1	<.1	<.1	78.2	78.3	100.0	100.0	78.6	0.0	42.9
Taney	20,274	98.5	<.1	0.3	0.6	<.1	0.6	33	47	92	32	0.5	0.6	<.1	0.3	79.3	79.5	81.3	70.4	77.6	50.0	61.9
Texas	15,687	98.9	<.1	0.2	0.4	0.0	0.4	45	27	90	72	0.4	0.5	<.1	0.2	73.0	73.2	68.8	54.2	81.7	0.0	54.0
Vernon	14,075	98.3	0.3	0.3	0.6	0.0	0.4	52	55	67	66	0.4	0.4	<.1	0.1	73.9	74.0	76.3	72.3	78.7	0.0	58.8
Warren	14,049	96.5	2.5	<.1	0.2	<.1	0.6	53	79	30	29	0.4	0.4	<.1	0.2	71.9	72.2	69.4	56.7	62.2	30.0	56.6
Washington	14,299	97.1	2.3	<.1	0.2	<.1	0.3	51	71	34	89	0.4	0.4	<.1	0.1	70.2	69.9	87.3	66.7	82.5	50.0	56.6
Wayne	8,810	99.1	<.1	<.1	0.4	<.1	0.3	76	14	100	91	0.2	0.3	<.1	<.1	76.3	76.4	57.1	88.9	75.6	100.0	63.6
Webster	16,948	97.7	1.1	0.2	0.6	<.1	0.4	41	64	49	64	0.4	0.5	<.1	0.2	71.4	71.3	98.4	66.7	71.7	100.0	52.1
Worth	1,854	99.5	<.1	0.2	<.1	0.0	0.2	115	4	99	112	<.1	<.1	<.1	<.1	76.0	76.1	100.0	80.0	100.0	0.0	33.3
Wright	12,050	98.9	0.2	<.1	0.6	<.1	0.3	56	31	73	101	0.3	0.4	<.1	<.1	71.9	72.1	55.6	33.3	65.0	37.5	55.7
St. Louis City	296,645	55.0	42.5	0.9	0.2	<.1	1.2	3	115	1	9	7.8	4.9	34.3	9.2	74.8	82.0	67.2	75.7	81.1	33.5	72.3
MISSOURI	3,802,247	88.1	9.7	0.8	0.4	<.1	1.1					100.0	100.0	100.0	100.0	74.3	75.3	67.4	71.3	72.2	32.8	65.5
CONGRESSIONAL																						
District 1	418,731	50.1	47.8	1.0	0.2	<.1	0.9	7	9	1	6	11.0	6.3	54.5	9.0	73.7	80.7	67.5	78.8	79.8	30.2	71.8
District 2	420,651	94.0	3.4	1.5	0.2	<.1	0.9	5	7	5	4	11.1	11.8	3.9	9.6	74.0	74.4	68.7	67.5	74.6	33.6	66.8
District 3	428,779	96.1	1.9	0.7	0.2	<.1	1.0	2	2	8	3	11.3	12.3	2.2	10.7	75.4	76.0	61.4	69.2	78.4	27.7	66.6
District 4	420,347	94.9	3.2	0.5	0.4	<.1	0.9	6	5	6	5	11.1	11.9	3.6	9.5	73.9	74.0	74.4	71.3	72.2	39.5	61.5
District 5	428,226	74.8	21.0	0.9	0.4	<.1	2.8	3	8	2	1	11.3	9.6	24.5	29.7	75.2	78.4	67.2	70.3	73.2	41.5	66.6
District 6	421,046	95.9	2.0	0.5	0.4	<.1	1.3	4	3	7	2	11.1	12.0	2.3	13.4	74.0	74.3	71.3	68.8	71.3	27.1	63.8
District 7	428,827	97.1	0.9	0.4	0.9	<.1	0.6	1	1	9	8	11.3	12.4	1.0	6.9	75.5	75.8	71.0	69.1	68.9	28.7	62.3
District 8	418,339	95.3	3.6	0.4	0.3	<.1	0.4	8	4	3	9	11.0	11.9	4.1	4.4	73.6	74.3	59.9	73.8	75.2	31.6	61.5
District 9	417,301	94.8	3.4	0.8	0.2	<.1	0.7	9	6	4	7	11.0	11.8	3.9	6.9	73.4	73.7	68.6	75.0	70.0	25.3	65.7

Table C. – **Voter Participation: November 3, 1992, General Election**

County	Estimated Voting Age Population (VAP), 1992	Voter registration (REG)				Voter turnout										Percent drop-off, by office[1]			
							Highest office			Maximum vote									
		Total	% contribution to state REG	% of 1992 VAP	Rank by % of 1992 VAP	Actual	Total	Office	% of 1992 VAP	Total	% contribution to state turnout	% of REG	Rank by % of REG	% of 1992 VAP	Rank by % 1992 VAP	President	Senator	Governor	Representative
Adair	18,318	13,000	0.4	71.0	107	–	10,640	P	58.1	10,640	0.4	81.8	14	58.1	88	0.0	2.1	2.1	2.8
Andrew	10,943	9,963	0.3	91.0	28	–	7,489	P	68.4	7,489	0.3	75.2	49	68.4	16	0.0	2.3	2.3	2.1
Atchison	5,539	4,229	0.1	76.3	89	–	3,199	P	57.8	3,199	0.1	75.6	45	57.8	92	0.0	0.5	1.1	0.2
Audrain	17,076	13,446	0.4	78.7	81	–	10,654	P	62.4	10,654	0.4	79.2	29	62.4	58	0.0	1.4	2.1	1.0
Barry	21,411	18,722	0.6	87.4	40	–	12,757	P	59.6	12,757	0.5	68.1	93	59.6	75	0.0	3.2	2.6	3.6
Barton	8,409	7,113	0.2	84.6	53	–	5,194	P	61.8	5,194	0.2	73.0	61	61.8	62	0.0	0.5	1.0	1.1
Bates	11,083	10,960	0.4	98.9	10	–	7,730	P	69.7	7,730	0.3	70.5	80	69.7	10	0.0	0.9	1.4	1.3
Benton	11,260	9,081	0.3	80.6	73	–	7,276	P	64.6	7,276	0.3	80.1	21	64.6	40	0.0	2.0	2.4	1.5
Bollinger	7,962	7,428	0.2	93.3	22	–	5,363	P	67.4	5,363	0.2	72.2	66	67.4	21	0.0	3.9	2.8	5.2
Boone	85,876	76,011	2.5	88.5	34	–	57,890	P	67.4	57,890	2.4	76.2	43	67.4	18	0.0	0.5	1.6	1.4
Buchanan	61,010	47,879	1.6	78.5	82	–	37,365	P	61.2	37,365	1.6	78.0	36	61.2	66	0.0	0.8	1.5	1.2
Butler	29,299	25,200	0.8	86.0	49	–	15,272	P	52.1	15,272	0.6	60.6	111	52.1	107	0.0	2.2	2.3	1.2
Caldwell	6,201	6,020	0.2	97.1	14	–	4,055	P	65.4	4,055	0.2	67.4	97	65.4	35	0.0	1.9	3.1	1.4
Callaway	24,255	17,780	0.6	73.3	99	–	13,981	P	57.6	13,981	0.6	78.6	31	57.6	93	0.0	0.8	1.0	1.2
Camden	23,443	18,875	0.6	80.5	74	–	14,627	P	62.4	14,627	0.6	77.5	38	62.4	57	0.0	1.6	2.0	2.5
Cape Girardeau	46,940	34,000	1.1	72.4	101	–	28,355	P	60.4	28,355	1.2	83.4	7	60.4	68	0.0	1.4	2.3	2.7
Carroll	7,821	7,500	0.2	95.9	16	–	5,378	P	68.8	5,378	0.2	71.7	72	68.8	15	0.0	2.6	2.6	2.5
Carter	4,061	3,800	0.1	93.6	21	–	2,686	P	66.1	2,686	0.1	70.7	79	66.1	31	0.0	4.4	2.7	3.5
Cass	48,411	34,000	1.1	70.2	111	–	29,905	P	61.8	29,905	1.3	88.0	2	61.8	61	0.0	1.3	2.2	2.5
Cedar	9,360	8,100	0.3	86.5	46	–	5,339	P	57.0	5,339	0.2	65.9	104	57.0	95	0.0	1.5	2.0	1.0
Chariton	6,675	6,950	0.2	104.1	7	–	4,601	P	68.9	4,601	0.2	66.2	103	68.9	13	0.0	4.8	4.6	3.8
Christian	26,320	23,000	0.7	87.4	41	–	17,145	P	65.1	17,145	0.7	74.5	54	65.1	36	0.0	0.6	1.3	1.1
Clark	5,394	5,400	0.2	100.1	9	–	3,584	P	66.4	3,584	0.1	66.4	101	66.4	28	0.0	3.7	3.5	2.1
Clay	117,472	88,585	2.9	75.4	92	–	75,778	P	64.5	75,778	3.2	85.5	4	64.5	41	0.0	5.4	4.4	4.6
Clinton	12,208	10,000	0.3	81.9	68	–	8,228	P	67.4	8,228	0.3	82.3	10	67.4	19	0.0	0.6	1.2	0.7
Cole	49,135	37,000	1.2	75.3	93	–	31,304	P	63.7	31,304	1.3	84.6	5	63.7	47	0.0	0.4	0.9	1.5
Cooper	11,066	8,978	0.3	81.1	71	–	7,339	P	66.3	7,339	0.3	81.7	15	66.3	30	0.0	0.5	1.0	1.8
Crawford	14,348	12,419	0.4	86.6	44	–	8,385	P	58.4	8,385	0.4	67.5	96	58.4	83	0.0	1.0	1.9	2.6
Dade	5,636	5,000	0.2	88.7	33	–	3,751	P	66.6	3,751	0.2	75.0	52	66.6	27	0.0	2.8	2.9	2.6
Dallas	9,471	8,300	0.3	87.6	38	–	6,051	P	63.9	6,051	0.3	72.9	62	63.9	43	0.0	4.0	3.2	7.4
Daviess	5,654	5,200	0.2	92.0	25	–	3,732	P	66.0	3,732	0.2	71.8	71	66.0	32	0.0	0.4	1.2	1.0
DeKalb	8,184	5,500	0.2	67.2	113	–	4,171	P	51.0	4,171	0.2	75.8	44	51.0	109	0.0	0.7	1.2	0.6
Dent	10,091	11,000	0.4	109.0	2	–	5,877	P	58.2	5,877	0.2	53.4	114	58.2	85	0.0	0.5	0.9	0.8
Douglas	8,838	8,700	0.3	98.4	11	–	5,792	P	65.5	5,792	0.2	66.6	100	65.5	34	0.0	4.1	3.2	2.9
Dunklin	24,097	17,300	0.6	71.8	103	–	11,479	P	47.6	11,479	0.5	66.4	102	47.6	113	0.0	6.7	4.6	5.4
Franklin	59,836	44,000	1.4	73.5	98	–	36,064	P	60.3	36,064	1.5	82.0	12	60.3	70	0.0	1.6	2.7	3.0
Gasconade	10,779	9,057	0.3	84.0	58	–	6,334	P	58.8	6,334	0.3	69.9	84	58.8	80	0.0	0.8	1.7	2.0
Gentry	4,996	4,825	0.2	96.6	15	–	3,724	P	74.5	3,724	0.2	77.2	40	74.5	2	0.0	3.0	2.6	1.8
Greene	162,486	133,033	4.3	81.9	69	–	105,713	P	65.1	105,713	4.4	79.5	26	65.1	37	0.0	1.0	1.5	1.7
Grundy	7,857	6,800	0.2	86.5	45	–	5,105	P	65.0	5,105	0.2	75.1	51	65.0	38	0.0	2.8	2.9	2.3
Harrison	6,316	5,850	0.2	92.6	24	–	4,222	P	66.8	4,222	0.2	72.2	67	66.8	22	0.0	4.1	5.0	2.2
Henry	15,300	12,600	0.4	82.4	64	–	9,740	P	63.7	9,740	0.4	77.3	39	63.7	48	0.0	2.1	2.8	2.4
Hickory	6,075	5,183	0.2	85.3	51	–	4,058	P	66.8	4,058	0.2	78.3	34	66.8	23	0.0	3.5	2.4	5.0
Holt	4,426	3,977	0.1	89.9	30	–	3,044	P	68.8	3,044	0.1	76.5	41	68.8	14	0.0	3.1	3.8	2.2
Howard	7,110	6,348	0.2	89.3	32	–	4,443	P	62.5	4,443	0.2	70.0	83	62.5	56	0.0	0.7	1.3	1.8
Howell	23,981	18,400	0.6	76.7	86	–	13,537	P	56.4	13,537	0.6	73.6	58	56.4	97	0.0	1.0	2.0	1.8
Iron	7,906	6,425	0.2	81.3	70	–	4,634	P	58.6	4,634	0.2	72.1	69	58.6	81	0.0	4.4	3.8	5.2
Jackson	474,675	374,000	12.2	78.8	80	–	291,595	P	61.4	291,595	12.2	78.0	37	61.4	64	0.0	1.5	1.8	1.5
Jasper	68,374	48,500	1.6	70.9	110	–	35,872	P	52.5	35,872	1.5	74.0	56	52.5	106	0.0	1.5	1.1	1.1
Jefferson	126,347	90,000	2.9	71.2	105	–	73,501	P	58.2	73,501	3.1	81.7	16	58.2	86	0.0	1.0	1.8	0.9
Johnson	31,311	19,193	0.6	61.3	114	–	15,203	P	48.6	15,203	0.6	79.2	30	48.6	112	0.0	0.7	1.6	1.8
Knox	3,273	3,124	0.1	95.4	19	–	2,262	P	69.1	2,262	<.1	72.4	63	69.1	12	0.0	3.4	2.7	2.7
Laclede	20,554	15,200	0.5	74.0	97	–	12,222	P	59.5	12,222	0.5	80.4	20	59.5	76	0.0	0.7	1.1	2.0
Lafayette	23,229	18,603	0.6	80.1	75	–	13,467	P	58.0	13,467	0.6	72.4	64	58.0	89	0.0	1.4	1.9	1.2
Lawrence	22,706	16,500	0.5	72.7	100	–	12,891	P	56.8	12,891	0.5	78.1	35	56.8	96	0.0	2.0	2.3	1.1
Lewis	7,511	5,809	0.2	77.3	83	–	4,562	P	60.7	4,562	0.2	78.5	32	60.7	67	0.0	4.2	4.3	3.9
Lincoln	21,962	15,424	0.5	70.2	112	–	12,765	P	58.1	12,765	0.5	82.8	8	58.1	87	0.0	0.7	1.5	1.9
Linn	10,196	9,465	0.3	92.8	23	–	6,436	P	63.1	6,436	0.3	68.0	94	63.1	50	0.0	2.1	2.6	1.6
Livingston	10,760	8,614	0.3	80.1	76	–	6,863	P	63.8	6,863	0.3	79.7	24	63.8	46	0.0	3.4	3.2	2.5
McDonald	12,735	11,434	0.4	89.8	31	–	6,875	P	54.0	6,875	0.3	60.1	113	54.0	103	0.0	2.1	2.5	1.5
Macon	11,501	9,898	0.3	86.1	48	–	7,164	P	62.3	7,164	0.3	72.4	65	62.3	60	0.0	2.4	2.8	1.6
Madison	8,456	7,354	0.2	87.0	43	–	5,082	P	60.1	5,082	0.2	69.1	89	60.1	71	0.0	0.9	1.3	0.9
Maries	6,046	5,335	0.2	88.2	36	–	4,015	P	66.4	4,015	0.2	75.3	48	66.4	29	0.0	1.2	1.2	2.1
Marion	20,104	14,429	0.5	71.8	104	–	11,783	P	58.6	11,783	0.5	81.7	17	58.6	82	0.0	1.2	1.9	0.5
Mercer	2,775	2,600	<.1	93.7	20	–	1,849	P	66.6	1,849	<.1	71.1	76	66.6	26	0.0	5.3	5.2	2.8
Miller	15,487	11,767	0.4	76.0	91	–	9,487	P	61.3	9,487	0.4	80.6	19	61.3	65	0.0	0.7	1.0	1.7
Mississippi	10,209	8,098	0.3	79.3	78	–	5,687	P	55.7	5,687	0.2	70.2	81	55.7	101	0.0	2.7	3.0	2.3
Moniteau	9,126	7,677	0.3	84.1	57	–	6,088	P	66.7	6,088	0.3	79.3	28	66.7	24	0.0	0.6	1.3	1.7
Monroe	6,556	6,005	0.2	91.6	27	–	4,187	P	63.9	4,187	0.2	69.7	85	63.9	44	0.0	0.9	1.4	0.9
Montgomery	8,453	7,038	0.2	83.3	60	–	5,319	P	62.9	5,319	0.2	75.6	46	62.9	51	0.0	2.8	2.9	3.2

[1]Percent drop-off is zero for any office used as highest office turnout.

Table C. – Voter Participation: November 3, 1992, General Election (cont)

County	Estimated Voting Age Population (VAP), 1992	Voter registration (REG)				Voter turnout													
						Highest office				Maximum vote						Percent drop-off, by office[1]			
		Total	% contribution to state REG	% of 1992 VAP	Rank by % of 1992 VAP	Actual	Total	Office	% of 1992 VAP	Total	% contribution to state turnout	% of REG	Rank by % of REG	% of 1992 VAP	Rank by % 1992 VAP	President	Senator	Governor	Representative
Morgan	12,305	9,400	0.3	76.4	87	-	7,770	P	63.1	7,770	0.3	82.7	9	63.1	49	0.0	1.0	1.6	2.1
New Madrid	14,760	12,250	0.4	83.0	63	-	8,289	P	56.2	8,289	0.3	67.7	95	56.2	99	0.0	5.0	4.5	5.1
Newton	33,548	26,688	0.9	79.6	77	-	18,479	P	55.1	18,479	0.8	69.2	87	55.1	102	0.0	7.2	6.2	6.1
Nodaway	15,915	11,800	0.4	74.1	96	-	9,388	P	59.0	9,388	0.4	79.6	25	59.0	78	0.0	1.3	1.8	0.9
Oregon	7,205	5,925	0.2	82.2	66	-	4,236	P	58.8	4,236	0.2	71.5	75	58.8	79	0.0	1.4	1.7	1.7
Osage	8,747	7,400	0.2	84.6	52	-	6,073	P	69.4	6,073	0.3	82.1	11	69.4	11	0.0	1.7	1.5	3.2
Ozark	6,793	6,646	0.2	97.8	13	-	4,271	P	62.9	4,271	0.2	64.3	107	62.9	52	0.0	2.2	2.2	2.2
Pemiscot	14,929	13,055	0.4	87.4	39	-	6,768	P	45.3	6,768	0.3	51.8	115	45.3	114	0.0	3.1	3.3	1.5
Perry	12,139	9,250	0.3	76.2	90	-	7,252	P	59.7	7,252	0.3	78.4	33	59.7	74	0.0	1.0	2.2	1.6
Pettis	26,261	23,200	0.8	88.3	35	-	16,470	P	62.7	16,470	0.7	71.0	77	62.7	53	0.0	1.2	1.9	1.3
Phelps	26,776	20,450	0.7	76.4	88	-	16,739	P	62.5	16,739	0.7	81.9	13	62.5	55	0.0	1.3	1.1	2.8
Pike	11,488	12,165	0.4	105.9	4	-	7,336	P	63.9	7,336	0.3	60.3	112	63.9	45	0.0	1.2	2.1	1.7
Platte	45,611	33,000	1.1	72.4	102	-	29,478	P	64.6	29,478	1.2	89.3	1	64.6	39	0.0	0.2	0.6	1.0
Polk	16,913	12,993	0.4	76.8	85	-	8,675	P	51.3	8,675	0.4	66.8	99	51.3	108	0.0	1.0	1.3	0.7
Pulaski	28,867	13,301	0.4	46.1	115	-	9,988	P	34.6	9,988	0.4	75.1	50	34.6	115	0.0	0.9	1.4	1.8
Putnam	3,808	3,498	0.1	91.9	26	-	2,503	P	65.7	2,503	0.1	71.6	73	65.7	33	0.0	5.2	5.3	6.0
Ralls	6,279	6,000	0.2	95.6	17	-	4,393	P	70.0	4,393	0.2	73.2	60	70.0	9	0.0	0.8	0.7	0.4
Randolph	18,187	16,000	0.5	88.0	37	-	10,210	P	56.1	10,210	0.4	63.8	108	56.1	100	0.0	1.0	1.6	1.1
Ray	16,098	13,800	0.4	85.7	50	-	9,620	P	59.8	9,620	0.4	69.7	86	59.8	72	0.0	1.4	1.1	0.3
Reynolds	4,935	5,300	0.2	107.4	3	-	3,325	P	67.4	3,325	0.1	62.7	110	67.4	20	0.0	5.2	4.0	5.8
Ripley	9,142	7,730	0.3	84.6	55	-	4,860	P	53.2	4,860	0.2	62.9	109	53.2	105	0.0	2.1	2.5	1.9
St. Charles	166,495	123,602	4.0	74.2	95	-	106,563	P	64.0	106,563	4.5	86.2	3	64.0	42	0.0	0.9	1.8	2.0
St. Clair	6,537	5,650	0.2	86.4	47	-	4,611	P	70.5	4,611	0.2	81.6	18	70.5	8	0.0	2.3	2.4	3.8
Ste. Genevieve	11,837	9,725	0.3	82.2	67	-	7,137	P	60.3	7,137	0.3	73.4	59	60.3	69	0.0	1.2	2.2	0.6
St. Francois	38,060	27,000	0.9	70.9	108	-	18,947	P	49.8	18,947	0.8	70.2	82	49.8	111	0.0	1.2	1.6	1.2
St. Louis	754,002	637,685	20.8	84.6	54	-	534,763	P	70.9	534,763	22.4	83.9	6	70.9	5	0.0	0.7	1.6	1.1
Saline	17,396	15,174	0.5	87.2	42	-	10,166	P	58.4	10,166	0.4	67.0	98	58.4	84	0.0	0.9	1.3	1.6
Schuyler	3,047	3,347	0.1	109.8	1	-	2,170	P	71.2	2,170	<.1	64.8	106	71.2	4	0.0	3.9	3.5	4.6
Scotland	3,517	3,616	0.1	102.8	8	-	2,494	P	70.9	2,494	0.1	69.0	90	70.9	6	0.0	7.4	6.0	4.7
Scott	28,498	23,850	0.8	83.7	59	-	16,507	P	57.9	16,507	0.7	69.2	88	57.9	90	0.0	4.1	3.2	3.6
Shannon	5,598	5,490	0.2	98.1	12	-	3,952	P	70.6	3,952	0.2	72.0	70	70.6	7	0.0	6.0	4.1	6.5
Shelby	5,095	4,583	0.1	90.0	29	-	3,397	C	66.7	3,397	0.1	74.1	55	66.7	25	0.1	0.4	0.4	0.0
Stoddard	21,849	15,500	0.5	70.9	109	-	12,308	P	56.3	12,308	0.5	79.4	27	56.3	98	0.0	4.7	4.5	3.8
Stone	15,910	13,400	0.4	84.2	56	-	9,196	P	57.8	9,196	0.4	68.6	92	57.8	91	0.0	1.5	2.3	1.7
Sullivan	4,728	5,000	0.2	105.8	5	-	3,436	P	72.7	3,436	0.1	68.7	91	72.7	3	0.0	3.0	3.1	2.8
Taney	21,414	16,500	0.5	77.1	84	-	13,205	P	61.7	13,205	0.6	80.0	22	61.7	63	0.0	1.8	1.7	1.7
Texas	15,965	13,282	0.4	83.2	61	-	10,001	P	62.6	10,001	0.4	75.3	47	62.6	54	0.0	0.6	1.1	2.4
Vernon	13,983	10,400	0.3	74.4	94	-	8,303	P	59.4	8,303	0.3	79.8	23	59.4	77	0.0	3.3	2.6	4.0
Warren	15,157	12,000	0.4	79.2	79	-	8,659	P	57.1	8,659	0.4	72.2	68	57.1	94	0.0	1.2	1.8	2.5
Washington	14,954	12,308	0.4	82.3	65	-	8,010	P	53.6	8,010	0.3	65.1	105	53.6	104	0.0	3.5	3.9	6.1
Wayne	8,897	8,500	0.3	95.5	18	-	6,019	P	67.7	6,019	0.3	70.8	78	67.7	17	0.0	3.9	2.9	4.6
Webster	17,807	14,388	0.5	80.8	72	-	10,640	P	59.8	10,640	0.4	74.0	57	59.8	73	0.0	2.3	2.5	6.5
Worth	1,765	1,850	<.1	104.8	6	-	1,413	P	80.1	1,413	<.1	76.4	42	80.1	1	0.0	3.4	3.2	2.2
Wright	12,326	10,250	0.3	83.2	62	-	7,684	P	62.3	7,684	0.3	75.0	53	62.3	59	0.0	1.0	1.2	2.5
St. Louis City	289,776	206,000	6.7	71.1	106	-	147,404	P	50.9	147,404	6.2	71.6	74	50.9	110	0.0	1.6	2.1	0.9
MISSOURI[2]	**3,858,000**	**3,067,955**	**100.0**	**79.5**		**-**	**2,391,568**		**62.0**	**2,391,568**	**100.0**	**78.0**		**62.0**		**0.0**	**1.5**	**2.0**	**1.8**

[1]Percent drop-off is zero for any office used as highest office turnout.   [2]Highest office turnout includes 295 write in votes for president reported only at the state level.

Table E. — Vote for President: November 3, 1992, General Election

County	Total	Clinton (DEM)	Bush (REP)	Perot (IND)	Marrou (LIB)[1]	Plurality Total	Party	DEM	REP	IND	Other	Rank DEM	Rank REP	Rank IND	Total	DEM	REP	IND	DEM	REP
Adair	10,640	4,232	4,141	2,224	43	91	D	39.8	38.9	20.9	0.4	65	35	66	0.4	0.4	0.5	0.4	50.5	49.5
Andrew	7,489	2,675	2,652	2,151	11	23	D	35.7	35.4	28.7	0.1	94	50	12	0.3	0.3	0.3	0.4	50.2	49.8
Atchison	3,199	1,208	1,140	840	11	68	D	37.8	35.6	26.3	0.3	78	49	26	0.1	0.1	0.1	0.2	51.4	48.6
Audrain	10,654	4,731	3,798	2,099	26	933	D	44.4	35.6	19.7	0.2	37	48	81	0.4	0.4	0.5	0.4	55.5	44.5
Barry	12,757	4,791	5,565	2,381	20	774	R	37.6	43.6	18.7	0.2	80	16	88	0.5	0.5	0.7	0.5	46.3	53.7
Barton	5,194	1,433	2,775	971	15	1,342	R	27.6	53.4	18.7	0.3	115	1	87	0.2	0.1	0.3	0.2	34.1	65.9
Bates	7,730	2,993	2,499	2,225	13	494	D	38.7	32.3	28.8	0.2	73	78	11	0.3	0.3	0.3	0.4	54.5	45.5
Benton	7,276	3,195	2,511	1,551	19	684	D	43.9	34.5	21.3	0.3	42	60	63	0.3	0.3	0.3	0.3	56.0	44.0
Bollinger	5,363	2,150	2,289	909	15	139	R	40.1	42.7	16.9	0.3	64	19	99	0.2	0.2	0.3	0.2	48.4	51.6
Boone	57,890	26,176	19,405	12,040	269	6,771	D	45.2	33.5	20.8	0.5	33	73	68	2.4	2.5	2.4	2.3	57.4	42.6
Buchanan	37,365	16,570	11,275	9,404	116	5,295	D	44.3	30.2	25.2	0.3	38	95	31	1.6	1.6	1.4	1.8	59.5	40.5
Butler	15,272	6,602	6,450	2,189	31	152	D	43.2	42.2	14.3	0.2	46	22	108	0.6	0.6	0.8	0.4	50.6	49.4
Caldwell	4,055	1,456	1,295	1,283	21	161	D	35.9	31.9	31.6	0.5	93	82	1	0.2	0.1	0.2	0.2	52.9	47.1
Callaway	13,981	5,799	4,880	3,266	36	919	D	41.5	34.9	23.4	0.3	57	55	44	0.6	0.6	0.6	0.6	54.3	45.7
Camden	14,627	5,140	5,554	3,891	42	414	R	35.1	38.0	26.6	0.3	98	38	22	0.6	0.5	0.7	0.8	48.1	51.9
Cape Girardeau	28,355	9,605	13,464	5,199	87	3,859	R	33.9	47.5	18.3	0.3	104	5	92	1.2	0.9	1.7	1.0	41.6	58.4
Carroll	5,378	2,100	1,774	1,495	9	326	D	39.0	33.0	27.8	0.2	69	76	16	0.2	0.2	0.2	0.3	54.2	45.8
Carter	2,686	1,169	1,101	405	11	68	D	43.5	41.0	15.1	0.4	44	27	106	0.1	0.1	0.1	< .1	51.5	48.5
Cass	29,905	10,246	10,349	9,216	94	103	R	34.3	34.6	30.8	0.3	102	57	2	1.3	1.0	1.3	1.8	49.7	50.3
Cedar	5,339	2,064	2,085	1,173	17	21	R	38.7	39.1	22.0	0.3	75	34	59	0.2	0.2	0.3	0.2	49.7	50.3
Chariton	4,601	2,141	1,378	1,067	15	763	D	46.5	30.0	23.2	0.3	25	96	47	0.2	0.2	0.2	0.2	60.8	39.2
Christian	17,145	6,242	7,422	3,422	59	1,180	R	36.4	43.3	20.0	0.3	91	18	77	0.7	0.6	0.9	0.7	45.7	54.3
Clark	3,584	1,815	1,039	725	5	776	D	50.6	29.0	20.2	0.1	13	103	74	0.1	0.2	0.1	0.1	63.6	36.4
Clay	75,778	30,565	23,798	20,951	464	6,767	D	40.3	31.4	27.6	0.6	63	88	18	3.2	2.9	2.9	4.0	56.2	43.8
Clinton	8,228	3,400	2,391	2,423	14	977	D	41.3	29.1	29.4	0.2	58	102	7	0.3	0.3	0.3	0.5	58.7	41.3
Cole	31,304	10,201	15,270	5,770	63	5,069	R	32.6	48.8	18.4	0.2	109	3	91	1.3	1.0	1.9	1.1	40.0	60.0
Cooper	7,339	2,709	2,867	1,735	28	158	R	36.9	39.1	23.6	0.4	86	33	41	0.3	0.3	0.4	0.3	48.6	51.4
Crawford	8,385	3,515	2,831	2,002	37	684	D	41.9	33.8	23.9	0.4	55	70	37	0.4	0.3	0.3	0.4	55.4	44.6
Dade	3,751	1,332	1,577	834	8	245	R	35.5	42.0	22.2	0.2	95	24	58	0.2	0.1	0.2	0.2	45.8	54.2
Dallas	6,051	2,533	2,116	1,392	10	417	D	41.9	35.0	23.0	0.2	56	53	51	0.3	0.2	0.3	0.3	54.5	45.5
Daviess	3,732	1,477	1,107	1,143	5	334	D	39.6	29.7	30.6	0.1	67	97	4	0.2	0.1	0.1	0.2	57.2	42.8
DeKalb	4,171	1,630	1,318	1,207	16	312	D	39.1	31.6	28.9	0.4	68	86	8	0.2	0.2	0.2	0.2	55.3	44.7
Dent	5,877	2,689	2,125	1,049	14	564	D	45.8	36.2	17.8	0.2	29	46	96	0.2	0.3	0.3	0.2	55.9	44.1
Douglas	5,792	2,126	2,569	1,081	16	443	R	36.7	44.4	18.7	0.3	87	10	89	0.2	0.2	0.3	0.2	45.3	54.7
Dunklin	11,479	6,277	4,024	1,166	12	2,253	D	54.7	35.1	10.2	0.1	6	52	114	0.5	0.6	0.5	0.2	60.9	39.1
Franklin	36,064	13,431	11,477	11,043	113	1,954	D	37.2	31.8	30.6	0.3	82	84	5	1.5	1.3	1.4	2.1	53.9	46.1
Gasconade	6,334	1,952	2,690	1,672	20	738	R	30.8	42.5	26.4	0.3	112	20	25	0.3	0.2	0.3	0.3	42.1	57.9
Gentry	3,724	1,519	1,272	921	12	247	D	40.8	34.2	24.7	0.3	61	66	34	0.2	0.1	0.2	0.2	54.4	45.6
Greene	105,713	41,137	46,457	17,770	349	5,320	R	38.9	43.9	16.8	0.3	71	13	100	4.4	3.9	5.7	3.4	47.0	53.0
Grundy	5,105	1,968	1,749	1,372	16	219	D	38.6	34.3	26.9	0.3	76	63	20	0.2	0.2	0.2	0.3	52.9	47.1
Harrison	4,222	1,590	1,563	1,059	10	27	D	37.7	37.0	25.1	0.2	79	43	32	0.2	0.2	0.2	0.2	50.4	49.6
Henry	9,740	4,232	2,681	2,807	20	1,425	D	43.4	27.5	28.8	0.2	45	108	9	0.4	0.4	0.3	0.5	61.2	38.8
Hickory	4,058	1,929	1,259	864	6	670	D	47.5	31.0	21.3	0.1	22	90	64	0.2	0.2	0.2	0.2	60.5	39.5
Holt	3,044	1,050	1,202	781	11	152	R	34.5	39.5	25.7	0.4	101	32	29	0.1	< .1	0.1	0.2	46.6	53.4
Howard	4,443	2,085	1,253	1,090	15	832	D	46.9	28.2	24.5	0.3	24	104	36	0.2	0.2	0.2	0.2	62.5	37.5
Howell	13,537	5,492	5,360	2,650	35	132	D	40.6	39.6	19.6	0.3	62	31	82	0.6	0.5	0.7	0.5	50.6	49.4
Iron	4,634	2,507	1,276	841	10	1,231	D	54.1	27.5	18.1	0.2	7	107	93	0.2	0.2	0.2	0.2	66.3	33.7
Jackson	291,595	145,999	78,611	66,142	843	67,388	D	50.1	27.0	22.7	0.3	14	109	54	12.2	13.9	9.7	12.8	65.0	35.0
Jasper	35,872	11,727	17,592	6,440	113	5,865	R	32.7	49.0	18.0	0.3	108	2	95	1.5	1.1	2.2	1.2	40.0	60.0
Jefferson	73,501	32,569	20,637	20,057	238	11,932	D	44.3	28.1	27.3	0.3	39	105	19	3.1	3.1	2.5	3.9	61.2	38.8
Johnson	15,203	5,546	5,032	4,578	47	514	D	36.5	33.1	30.1	0.3	90	74	6	0.6	0.5	0.6	0.9	52.4	47.6
Knox	2,262	1,010	724	523	5	286	D	44.7	32.0	23.1	0.2	35	80	50	< .1	< .1	< .1	0.1	58.2	41.8
Laclede	12,222	4,179	5,176	2,852	15	997	R	34.2	42.3	23.3	0.1	103	21	45	0.5	0.4	0.6	0.5	44.7	55.3
Lafayette	13,467	5,213	4,651	3,561	42	562	D	38.7	34.5	26.4	0.3	74	58	24	0.6	0.5	0.6	0.7	52.8	47.2
Lawrence	12,891	4,666	5,608	2,570	47	942	R	36.2	43.5	19.9	0.4	92	17	79	0.5	0.4	0.7	0.5	45.4	54.6
Lewis	4,562	2,196	1,461	892	13	735	D	48.1	32.0	19.6	0.3	21	79	83	0.2	0.2	0.2	0.2	60.0	40.0
Lincoln	12,765	5,453	3,718	3,572	22	1,735	D	42.7	29.1	28.0	0.2	50	101	15	0.5	0.5	0.5	0.7	59.5	40.5
Linn	6,436	2,916	1,967	1,524	29	949	D	45.3	30.6	23.7	0.5	32	94	40	0.3	0.3	0.2	0.3	59.7	40.3
Livingston	6,863	2,505	2,370	1,976	12	135	D	36.5	34.5	28.8	0.2	89	59	10	0.3	0.2	0.3	0.4	51.4	48.6
McDonald	6,875	2,281	3,010	1,551	33	729	R	33.2	43.8	22.6	0.5	106	15	55	0.3	0.2	0.4	0.3	43.1	56.9
Macon	7,164	3,194	2,256	1,697	17	938	D	44.6	31.5	23.7	0.2	36	87	39	0.3	0.3	0.3	0.3	58.6	41.4
Madison	5,082	2,501	1,673	899	9	828	D	49.2	32.9	17.7	0.2	16	77	97	0.2	0.2	0.2	0.2	59.9	40.1
Maries	4,015	1,732	1,356	915	12	376	D	43.1	33.8	22.8	0.3	47	69	52	0.2	0.2	0.2	0.2	56.1	43.9
Marion	11,783	5,156	4,762	1,841	24	394	D	43.8	40.4	15.6	0.2	43	29	104	0.5	0.5	0.6	0.4	52.0	48.0
Mercer	1,849	843	626	378	2	217	D	45.6	33.9	20.4	0.1	31	68	72	< .1	< .1	< .1	< .1	57.4	42.6
Miller	9,487	2,905	4,175	2,391	16	1,270	R	30.6	44.0	25.2	0.2	114	12	30	0.4	0.3	0.5	0.5	41.0	59.0
Mississippi	5,687	3,226	1,675	776	10	1,551	D	56.7	29.5	13.6	0.2	5	99	110	0.2	0.3	0.2	0.1	65.8	34.2
Moniteau	6,088	2,018	2,566	1,499	5	548	R	33.1	42.1	24.6	< .1	107	23	35	0.3	0.2	0.3	0.3	44.0	56.0
Monroe	4,187	2,060	1,153	969	5	907	D	49.2	27.5	23.1	0.1	17	106	49	0.2	0.2	0.1	0.2	64.1	35.9
Montgomery	5,319	2,063	1,974	1,266	16	89	D	38.8	37.1	23.8	0.3	72	42	38	0.2	0.2	0.2	0.2	51.1	48.9

[1] Libertarian candidate Marrou was only minor candidate besides Perot (only four candidates on ballot).

County	Total	Clinton (DEM)	Bush (REP)	Perot (IND)	Marrou (LIB)[1]	Plurality Total	Party	DEM	REP	IND	Other	Rank DEM	Rank REP	Rank IND	Total	DEM	REP	IND	DEM	REP
Morgan	7,770	2,906	2,819	2,028	17	87	D	37.4	36.3	26.1	0.2	81	45	27	0.3	0.3	0.3	0.4	50.8	49.2
New Madrid	8,289	4,883	2,431	962	13	2,452	D	58.9	29.3	11.6	0.2	3	100	113	0.3	0.5	0.3	0.2	66.8	33.2
Newton	18,479	5,987	8,804	3,567	121	2,817	R	32.4	47.6	19.3	0.7	110	4	84	0.8	0.6	1.1	0.7	40.5	59.5
Nodaway	9,388	3,723	3,147	2,484	34	576	D	39.7	33.5	26.5	0.4	66	72	23	0.4	0.4	0.4	0.5	54.2	45.8
Oregon	4,236	2,258	1,402	564	12	856	D	53.3	33.1	13.3	0.3	9	75	111	0.2	0.2	0.2	0.1	61.7	38.3
Osage	6,073	1,860	2,784	1,423	6	924	R	30.6	45.8	23.4	<.1	113	7	43	0.3	0.2	0.3	0.3	40.1	59.9
Ozark	4,271	1,581	1,772	906	12	191	R	37.0	41.5	21.2	0.3	85	25	65	0.2	0.2	0.2	0.2	47.2	52.8
Pemiscot	6,768	3,924	2,161	670	13	1,763	D	58.0	31.9	9.9	0.2	4	83	115	0.3	0.4	0.3	0.1	64.5	35.5
Perry	7,252	2,525	3,205	1,498	24	680	R	34.8	44.2	20.7	0.3	100	11	69	0.3	0.2	0.4	0.3	44.1	55.9
Pettis	16,470	5,314	6,823	4,278	55	1,509	R	32.3	41.4	26.0	0.3	111	26	28	0.7	0.5	0.8	0.8	43.8	56.2
Phelps	16,739	6,852	6,040	3,774	73	812	D	40.9	36.1	22.5	0.4	60	47	56	0.7	0.7	0.7	0.7	53.1	46.9
Pike	7,336	3,609	2,255	1,464	8	1,354	D	49.2	30.7	20.0	0.1	18	92	78	0.3	0.3	0.3	0.2	61.5	38.5
Platte	29,478	10,920	9,380	9,062	116	1,540	D	37.0	31.8	30.7	0.4	84	85	3	1.2	1.0	1.2	1.7	53.8	46.2
Polk	8,675	3,316	3,465	1,879	15	149	R	38.2	39.9	21.7	0.2	77	30	62	0.4	0.3	0.4	0.4	48.9	51.1
Pulaski	9,988	4,113	3,793	2,057	25	320	D	41.2	38.0	20.6	0.3	59	37	70	0.4	0.4	0.5	0.4	52.0	48.0
Putnam	2,503	838	1,143	522	0	305	R	33.5	45.7	20.9	0.0	105	8	67	0.1	<.1	0.1	0.1	42.3	57.7
Ralls	4,393	2,158	1,349	880	6	809	D	49.1	30.7	20.0	0.1	19	93	76	0.2	0.2	0.2	0.2	61.5	38.5
Randolph	10,210	4,951	3,025	2,212	22	1,926	D	48.5	29.6	21.7	0.2	20	98	61	0.4	0.5	0.4	0.4	62.1	37.9
Ray	9,620	4,457	2,563	2,567	33	1,890	D	46.3	26.6	26.7	0.3	27	111	21	0.4	0.4	0.3	0.5	63.5	36.5
Reynolds	3,325	2,014	776	532	3	1,238	D	60.6	23.3	16.0	<.1	2	114	103	0.1	0.2	<.1	0.1	72.2	27.8
Ripley	4,860	2,300	1,814	739	7	486	D	47.3	37.3	15.2	0.1	23	41	105	0.2	0.2	0.2	0.1	55.9	44.1
St. Charles	106,563	37,263	38,673	30,351	276	1,410	R	35.0	36.3	28.5	0.3	99	44	14	4.5	3.5	4.8	5.9	49.1	50.9
St. Clair	4,611	1,965	1,555	1,083	8	410	D	42.6	33.7	23.5	0.2	52	71	42	0.2	0.2	0.2	0.2	55.8	44.2
Ste. Genevieve	7,137	3,795	1,780	1,547	15	2,015	D	53.2	24.9	21.7	0.2	10	113	60	0.3	0.4	0.2	0.3	68.1	31.9
St. Francois	18,947	9,367	5,889	3,635	56	3,478	D	49.4	31.1	19.2	0.3	15	89	85	0.8	0.9	0.7	0.7	61.4	38.6
St. Louis	534,763	235,760	188,285	109,099	1,619	47,475	D	44.1	35.2	20.4	0.3	40	51	73	22.4	22.4	23.2	21.0	55.6	44.4
Saline	10,166	4,643	2,688	2,815	20	1,828	D	45.7	26.4	27.7	0.2	30	112	17	0.4	0.4	0.3	0.5	63.3	36.7
Schuyler	2,170	936	742	487	5	194	D	43.1	34.2	22.4	0.2	48	64	57	<.1	<.1	<.1	<.1	55.8	44.2
Scotland	2,494	1,070	798	617	9	272	D	42.9	32.0	24.7	0.4	49	81	33	0.1	0.1	<.1	0.1	57.3	42.7
Scott	16,507	7,452	6,265	2,763	27	1,187	D	45.1	38.0	16.7	0.2	34	39	101	0.7	0.7	0.8	0.5	54.3	45.7
Shannon	3,952	2,135	1,224	579	14	911	D	54.0	31.0	14.7	0.4	8	91	107	0.2	0.2	0.2	0.1	63.6	36.4
Shelby	3,394	1,435	1,169	786	4	266	D	42.3	34.4	23.2	0.1	54	61	48	0.1	0.1	0.1	0.2	55.1	44.9
Stoddard	12,308	5,720	4,608	1,977	3	1,112	D	46.5	37.4	16.1	<.1	26	40	102	0.5	0.5	0.6	0.4	55.4	44.6
Stone	9,196	3,256	4,035	1,884	21	779	R	35.4	43.9	20.5	0.2	97	14	71	0.4	0.3	0.5	0.4	44.7	55.3
Sullivan	3,436	1,510	1,326	596	4	184	D	43.9	38.6	17.3	0.1	41	36	98	0.1	0.1	0.2	0.1	53.2	46.8
Taney	13,205	4,682	6,081	2,395	47	1,399	R	35.5	46.1	18.1	0.4	96	6	94	0.6	0.4	0.7	0.5	43.5	56.5
Texas	10,001	4,597	3,470	1,900	34	1,127	D	46.0	34.7	19.0	0.4	28	56	86	0.4	0.4	0.4	0.4	57.0	43.0
Vernon	8,303	3,546	2,851	1,890	16	695	D	42.7	34.3	22.8	0.2	51	62	53	0.3	0.3	0.4	0.4	55.4	44.6
Warren	8,659	3,213	2,953	2,471	22	260	D	37.1	34.1	28.5	0.3	83	67	13	0.4	0.3	0.4	0.5	52.1	47.9
Washington	8,010	4,211	2,157	1,618	24	2,054	D	52.6	26.9	20.2	0.3	11	110	75	0.3	0.4	0.3	0.3	66.1	33.9
Wayne	6,019	3,073	2,101	837	8	972	D	51.1	34.9	13.9	0.1	12	54	109	0.3	0.3	0.3	0.2	59.4	40.6
Webster	10,640	4,149	4,361	2,108	22	212	R	39.0	41.0	19.8	0.2	70	28	80	0.4	0.4	0.5	0.4	48.8	51.2
Worth	1,413	599	483	328	3	116	D	42.4	34.2	23.2	0.2	53	65	46	<.1	<.1	<.1	<.1	55.4	44.6
Wright	7,684	2,814	3,427	1,425	18	613	R	36.6	44.6	18.5	0.2	88	9	90	0.3	0.3	0.4	0.3	45.1	54.9
St. Louis City	147,404	102,356	25,441	18,864	743	76,915	D	69.4	17.3	12.8	0.5	1	115	112	6.2	9.7	3.1	3.6	80.1	19.9
MISSOURI[2]	2,391,565	1,053,873	811,159	518,741	7,792	242,714	D	44.1	33.9	21.7	0.3				100.0	100.0	100.0	100.0	56.5	43.5

[1]Libertarian candidate Marrou was only minor candidate besides Perot (only four candidates on ballot). [2]Includes the following write-in votes reported only at the state level: 12 for Daniels, 17 for Fulani, 180 for Gritz, 64 for Hagelin, 13 for LaRouche, 1 for Messiah, 1 for Scott, 1 for Smith, and 6 for Warren; total of 295.

Table F. — Vote for U.S. Senator: November 3, 1992, General Election

County	Total	Rothman-Serot (DEM)	Bond (REP)	Bojarski (LIB)[1]	Plurality Total	Party	DEM	REP	LIB	Rank DEM	Rank REP	Rank LIB	Total	DEM	REP	LIB
Adair	10,414	3,759	6,329	326	2,570	R	36.1	60.8	3.1	96	24	56	0.4	0.4	0.5	0.4
Andrew	7,316	2,912	4,198	206	1,286	R	39.8	57.4	2.8	73	40	70	0.3	0.3	0.3	0.3
Atchison	3,183	1,143	1,935	105	792	R	35.9	60.8	3.3	97	23	46	0.1	0.1	0.2	0.1
Audrain	10,506	4,080	6,092	334	2,012	R	38.8	58.0	3.2	79	38	54	0.4	0.4	0.5	0.4
Barry	12,345	4,676	7,334	335	2,658	R	37.9	59.4	2.7	86	30	72	0.5	0.4	0.6	0.4
Barton	5,170	1,307	3,676	187	2,369	R	25.3	71.1	3.6	115	1	29	0.2	0.1	0.3	0.2
Bates	7,657	3,264	4,144	249	880	R	42.6	54.1	3.3	52	64	50	0.3	0.3	0.3	0.3
Benton	7,129	3,215	3,643	271	428	R	45.1	51.1	3.8	37	84	23	0.3	0.3	0.3	0.4
Bollinger	5,152	1,898	3,179	75	1,281	R	36.8	61.7	1.5	90	19	112	0.2	0.2	0.3	<.1
Boone	57,604	26,655	28,466	2,483	1,811	R	46.3	49.4	4.3	28	95	7	2.4	2.5	2.3	3.3
Buchanan	37,072	16,435	19,139	1,498	2,704	R	44.3	51.6	4.0	45	78	13	1.6	1.6	1.6	2.0
Butler	14,936	5,476	9,162	298	3,686	R	36.7	61.3	2.0	91	22	102	0.6	0.5	0.7	0.4
Caldwell	3,978	1,622	2,163	193	541	R	40.8	54.4	4.9	65	61	3	0.2	0.2	0.2	0.3
Callaway	13,874	6,410	6,911	553	501	R	46.2	49.8	4.0	29	92	16	0.6	0.6	0.6	0.7
Camden	14,398	5,706	8,127	565	2,421	R	39.6	56.4	3.9	74	48	19	0.6	0.5	0.7	0.8
Cape Girardeau	27,948	8,948	18,325	675	9,377	R	32.0	65.6	2.4	111	5	88	1.2	0.8	1.5	0.9
Carroll	5,237	2,178	2,951	108	773	R	41.6	56.3	2.1	58	49	100	0.2	0.2	0.2	0.1
Carter	2,569	917	1,603	49	686	R	35.7	62.4	1.9	100	11	105	0.1	<.1	0.1	<.1
Cass	29,529	11,800	16,254	1,475	4,454	R	40.0	55.0	5.0	71	57	1	1.3	1.1	1.3	2.0
Cedar	5,261	2,140	2,901	220	761	R	40.7	55.1	4.2	66	56	10	0.2	0.2	0.2	0.3
Chariton	4,378	2,181	2,099	98	82	D	49.8	47.9	2.2	10	102	94	0.2	0.2	0.2	0.1
Christian	17,034	6,557	9,932	545	3,375	R	38.5	58.3	3.2	82	35	52	0.7	0.6	0.8	0.7
Clark	3,452	1,738	1,621	93	117	D	50.3	47.0	2.7	8	107	75	0.1	0.2	0.1	0.1
Clay	71,689	31,630	37,057	3,002	5,427	R	44.1	51.7	4.2	46	77	9	3.0	3.0	3.0	4.0
Clinton	8,180	3,657	4,194	329	537	R	44.7	51.3	4.0	39	81	15	0.3	0.3	0.3	0.4
Cole	31,171	10,275	20,061	835	9,786	R	33.0	64.4	2.7	107	8	76	1.3	1.0	1.6	1.1
Cooper	7,300	2,875	4,161	264	1,286	R	39.4	57.0	3.6	77	45	30	0.3	0.3	0.3	0.4
Crawford	8,298	3,757	4,246	295	489	R	45.3	51.2	3.6	35	82	33	0.4	0.4	0.3	0.4
Dade	3,646	1,375	2,160	111	785	R	37.7	59.2	3.0	87	32	60	0.2	0.1	0.2	0.1
Dallas	5,808	2,535	3,107	166	572	R	43.6	53.5	2.9	47	68	67	0.2	0.2	0.3	0.2
Daviess	3,717	1,563	2,024	130	461	R	42.1	54.5	3.5	54	60	36	0.2	0.1	0.2	0.2
DeKalb	4,140	1,729	2,249	162	520	R	41.8	54.3	3.9	56	62	21	0.2	0.2	0.2	0.2
Dent	5,847	2,670	2,990	187	320	R	45.7	51.1	3.2	32	83	53	0.2	0.3	0.2	0.2
Douglas	5,556	1,984	3,434	138	1,450	R	35.7	61.8	2.5	99	18	80	0.2	0.2	0.3	0.2
Dunklin	10,715	4,820	5,723	172	903	R	45.0	53.4	1.6	38	69	110	0.5	0.5	0.5	0.2
Franklin	35,498	14,685	19,402	1,411	4,717	R	41.4	54.7	4.0	61	58	18	1.5	1.4	1.6	1.9
Gasconade	6,281	2,130	3,928	223	1,798	R	33.9	62.5	3.6	105	10	34	0.3	0.2	0.3	0.3
Gentry	3,612	1,506	2,028	78	522	R	41.7	56.1	2.2	57	51	99	0.2	0.1	0.2	0.1
Greene	104,655	42,060	59,685	2,910	17,625	R	40.2	57.0	2.8	68	44	71	4.4	4.0	4.9	3.9
Grundy	4,961	1,780	3,090	91	1,310	R	35.9	62.3	1.8	98	12	106	0.2	0.2	0.3	0.1
Harrison	4,049	1,477	2,491	81	1,014	R	36.5	61.5	2.0	93	20	101	0.2	0.1	0.2	0.1
Henry	9,537	4,596	4,513	428	83	D	48.2	47.3	4.5	19	106	5	0.4	0.4	0.4	0.6
Hickory	3,916	1,938	1,888	90	50	D	49.5	48.2	2.3	11	101	93	0.2	0.2	0.2	0.1
Holt	2,950	1,022	1,832	96	810	R	34.6	62.1	3.3	104	15	49	0.1	<.1	0.1	0.1
Howard	4,413	2,111	2,170	132	59	R	47.8	49.2	3.0	21	97	62	0.2	0.2	0.2	0.2
Howell	13,403	4,971	7,967	465	2,996	R	37.1	59.4	3.5	88	29	37	0.6	0.5	0.7	0.6
Iron	4,432	2,307	2,018	107	289	D	52.1	45.5	2.4	5	110	89	0.2	0.2	0.2	0.1
Jackson	287,173	146,449	129,016	11,708	17,433	D	51.0	44.9	4.1	6	111	12	12.2	13.8	10.6	15.6
Jasper	35,319	10,578	23,414	1,327	12,836	R	29.9	66.3	3.8	113	4	24	1.5	1.0	1.9	1.8
Jefferson	72,787	34,443	35,411	2,933	968	R	47.3	48.7	4.0	22	98	14	3.1	3.3	2.9	3.9
Johnson	15,097	5,957	8,426	714	2,469	R	39.5	55.8	4.7	76	54	4	0.6	0.6	0.7	1.0
Knox	2,186	1,029	1,115	42	86	R	47.1	51.0	1.9	23	86	104	<.1	<.1	<.1	<.1
Laclede	12,137	4,300	7,464	373	3,164	R	35.4	61.5	3.1	101	21	58	0.5	0.4	0.6	0.5
Lafayette	13,276	5,507	7,241	528	1,734	R	41.5	54.5	4.0	59	59	17	0.6	0.5	0.6	0.7
Lawrence	12,638	4,807	7,371	460	2,564	R	38.0	58.3	3.6	85	34	27	0.5	0.5	0.6	0.6
Lewis	4,372	2,335	1,933	104	402	D	53.4	44.2	2.4	4	112	91	0.2	0.2	0.2	0.1
Lincoln	12,680	5,622	6,638	420	1,016	R	44.3	52.4	3.3	44	74	44	0.5	0.5	0.5	0.6
Linn	6,304	2,886	3,208	210	322	R	45.8	50.9	3.3	31	89	43	0.3	0.3	0.3	0.3
Livingston	6,632	2,571	3,900	161	1,329	R	38.8	58.8	2.4	80	33	86	0.3	0.2	0.3	0.2
McDonald	6,732	2,244	4,192	296	1,948	R	33.3	62.3	4.4	106	13	6	0.3	0.2	0.3	0.4
Macon	6,994	2,860	3,897	237	1,037	R	40.9	55.7	3.4	63	55	40	0.3	0.3	0.3	0.3
Madison	5,037	2,179	2,732	126	553	R	43.3	54.2	2.5	48	63	79	0.2	0.2	0.2	0.2
Maries	3,965	1,767	2,033	165	266	R	44.6	51.3	4.2	41	80	11	0.2	0.2	0.2	0.2
Marion	11,639	5,442	5,937	260	495	R	46.8	51.0	2.2	25	85	95	0.5	0.5	0.5	0.3
Mercer	1,751	634	1,088	29	454	R	36.2	62.1	1.7	94	14	107	<.1	<.1	<.1	<.1
Miller	9,422	3,266	5,848	308	2,582	R	34.7	62.1	3.3	103	16	48	0.4	0.3	0.5	0.4
Mississippi	5,532	2,565	2,819	148	254	R	46.4	51.0	2.7	26	88	77	0.2	0.2	0.2	0.2
Moniteau	6,052	1,993	3,843	216	1,850	R	32.9	63.5	3.6	108	9	32	0.3	0.2	0.3	0.3
Monroe	4,151	2,028	2,002	121	26	D	48.9	48.2	2.9	14	100	65	0.2	0.2	0.2	0.2
Montgomery	5,170	2,094	2,949	127	855	R	40.5	57.0	2.5	67	43	82	0.2	0.2	0.2	0.2

[1]Libertarian candidate Bojarski was the only minor candidate (only three candidates on ballot).

Table F. — Vote for U.S. Senator: November 3, 1992, General Election (cont)

County	Total	Rothman-Serot (DEM)	Bond (REP)	Bojarski (LIB)[1]	Plurality Total	Party	DEM	REP	LIB	Rank DEM	Rank REP	Rank LIB	Total	DEM	REP	LIB
Morgan	7,696	3,078	4,330	288	1,252	R	40.0	56.3	3.7	70	50	25	0.3	0.3	0.4	0.4
New Madrid	7,874	3,863	3,899	112	36	R	49.1	49.5	1.4	12	93	113	0.3	0.4	0.3	0.1
Newton	17,150	5,548	11,179	423	5,631	R	32.3	65.2	2.5	110	6	81	0.7	0.5	0.9	0.6
Nodaway	9,270	3,557	5,376	337	1,819	R	38.4	58.0	3.6	83	37	28	0.4	0.3	0.4	0.4
Oregon	4,178	2,008	2,068	102	60	R	48.1	49.5	2.4	20	94	85	0.2	0.2	0.2	0.1
Osage	5,972	1,939	3,863	170	1,924	R	32.5	64.7	2.8	109	7	69	0.3	0.2	0.3	0.2
Ozark	4,176	1,544	2,491	141	947	R	37.0	59.7	3.4	89	27	41	0.2	0.1	0.2	0.2
Pemiscot	6,555	3,311	3,118	126	193	D	50.5	47.6	1.9	7	105	103	0.3	0.3	0.3	0.2
Perry	7,179	2,211	4,774	194	2,563	R	30.8	66.5	2.7	112	3	74	0.3	0.2	0.4	0.3
Pettis	16,266	5,886	9,758	622	3,872	R	36.2	60.0	3.8	95	26	22	0.7	0.6	0.8	0.8
Phelps	16,526	7,131	8,747	648	1,616	R	43.2	52.9	3.9	49	71	20	0.7	0.7	0.7	0.9
Pike	7,248	3,393	3,669	186	276	R	46.8	50.6	2.6	24	91	78	0.3	0.3	0.3	0.2
Platte	29,411	12,516	15,452	1,443	2,936	R	42.6	52.5	4.9	53	73	2	1.2	1.2	1.3	1.9
Polk	8,585	3,436	4,901	248	1,465	R	40.0	57.1	2.9	69	42	66	0.4	0.3	0.4	0.3
Pulaski	9,894	4,238	5,325	331	1,087	R	42.8	53.8	3.3	51	66	42	0.4	0.4	0.4	0.4
Putnam	2,372	659	1,674	39	1,015	R	27.8	70.6	1.6	114	2	108	0.1	<.1	0.1	<.1
Ralls	4,357	2,361	1,891	105	470	D	54.2	43.4	2.4	3	113	90	0.2	0.2	0.2	0.1
Randolph	10,112	4,922	4,827	363	95	D	48.7	47.7	3.6	16	103	31	0.4	0.5	0.4	0.5
Ray	9,488	4,646	4,443	399	203	D	49.0	46.8	4.2	13	108	8	0.4	0.4	0.4	0.5
Reynolds	3,151	1,719	1,363	69	356	D	54.6	43.3	2.2	2	114	98	0.1	0.2	0.1	<.1
Ripley	4,756	1,812	2,834	110	1,022	R	38.1	59.6	2.3	84	28	92	0.2	0.2	0.2	0.1
St. Charles	105,609	40,887	61,322	3,400	20,435	R	38.7	58.1	3.2	81	36	51	4.5	3.9	5.0	4.5
St. Clair	4,505	2,068	2,296	141	228	R	45.9	51.0	3.1	30	87	57	0.2	0.2	0.2	0.2
Ste. Genevieve	7,053	3,534	3,258	261	276	D	50.1	46.2	3.7	9	109	26	0.3	0.3	0.3	0.3
St. Francois	18,715	9,084	9,068	563	16	R	48.5	48.5	3.0	17	99	61	0.8	0.9	0.7	0.8
St. Louis	530,931	241,350	276,715	12,866	35,365	R	45.5	52.1	2.4	33	75	87	22.5	22.8	22.6	17.1
Saline	10,073	4,572	5,168	333	596	R	45.4	51.3	3.3	34	79	45	0.4	0.4	0.4	0.4
Schuyler	2,085	925	1,109	51	184	R	44.4	53.2	2.4	43	70	84	<.1	<.1	<.1	<.1
Scotland	2,309	1,070	1,173	66	103	R	46.3	50.8	2.9	27	90	68	<.1	0.1	<.1	<.1
Scott	15,823	6,563	9,001	259	2,438	R	41.5	56.9	1.6	60	46	109	0.7	0.6	0.7	0.3
Shannon	3,716	1,796	1,829	91	33	R	48.3	49.2	2.4	18	96	83	0.2	0.2	0.1	0.1
Shelby	3,384	1,527	1,782	75	255	R	45.1	52.7	2.2	36	72	96	0.1	0.1	0.1	<.1
Stoddard	11,731	4,632	6,958	141	2,326	R	39.5	59.3	1.2	75	31	115	0.5	0.4	0.6	0.2
Stone	9,054	3,560	5,185	309	1,625	R	39.3	57.3	3.4	78	41	39	0.4	0.3	0.4	0.4
Sullivan	3,332	1,395	1,895	42	500	R	41.9	56.9	1.3	55	47	114	0.1	0.1	0.2	<.1
Taney	12,962	4,740	7,795	427	3,055	R	36.6	60.1	3.3	92	25	47	0.6	0.4	0.6	0.6
Texas	9,944	4,425	5,178	341	753	R	44.5	52.1	3.4	42	76	38	0.4	0.4	0.4	0.5
Vernon	8,030	3,457	4,334	239	877	R	43.1	54.0	3.0	50	65	63	0.3	0.3	0.4	0.3
Warren	8,555	3,496	4,790	269	1,294	R	40.9	56.0	3.1	64	52	55	0.4	0.3	0.4	0.4
Washington	7,729	3,771	3,685	273	86	D	48.8	47.7	3.5	15	104	35	0.3	0.4	0.3	0.4
Wayne	5,784	2,585	3,111	88	526	R	44.7	53.8	1.5	40	67	111	0.2	0.2	0.3	0.1
Webster	10,390	4,254	5,817	319	1,563	R	40.9	56.0	3.1	62	53	59	0.4	0.4	0.5	0.4
Worth	1,365	544	791	30	247	R	39.9	57.9	2.2	72	39	97	<.1	<.1	<.1	<.1
Wright	7,605	2,671	4,711	223	2,040	R	35.1	61.9	2.9	102	17	64	0.3	0.3	0.4	0.3
St. Louis City	145,054	97,257	43,869	3,928	53,388	D	67.0	30.2	2.7	1	115	73	6.2	9.2	3.6	5.2
MISSOURI[2]	**2,354,925**	**1,057,967**	**1,221,901**	**75,057**	**163,934**	**R**	**44.9**	**51.9**	**3.2**				**100.0**	**100.0**	**100.0**	**100.0**

[1]Libertarian candidate Bojarski was the only minor candidate (only three candidates on ballot).   [2]Includes the following write-in votes reported only at the state level: 6 for Peacock and 3 for Sandor; total of 9.

Table G. — Vote for Governor: November 3, 1992, General Election

County	Total	Carnahan (DEM)	Webster (REP)	Other	Plurality Total	Plurality Party	Percent of total vote DEM	Percent of total vote REP	Percent of total vote Other	Rank DEM	Rank REP	Rank Other	Percent contribution to state vote Total	Percent contribution to state vote DEM	Percent contribution to state vote REP	Percent contribution to state vote Other
Adair	10,420	5,489	4,931	0	558	D	52.7	47.3	0	77	39	-	0.4	0.4	0.5	0
Andrew	7,314	3,657	3,657	0	0	D	50.0	50.0	0	91	25	-	0.3	0.3	0.4	0
Atchison	3,164	1,560	1,604	0	44	R	49.3	50.7	0	93	23	-	0.1	0.1	0.2	0
Audrain	10,431	5,927	4,504	0	1,423	D	56.8	43.2	0	42	74	-	0.4	0.4	0.5	0
Barry	12,422	5,893	6,529	0	636	R	47.4	52.6	0	98	18	-	0.5	0.4	0.7	0
Barton	5,141	1,811	3,330	0	1,519	R	35.2	64.8	0	114	2	-	0.2	0.1	0.3	0
Bates	7,618	4,414	3,204	0	1,210	D	57.9	42.1	0	35	81	-	0.3	0.3	0.3	0
Benton	7,104	3,859	3,245	0	614	D	54.3	45.7	0	64	52	-	0.3	0.3	0.3	0
Bollinger	5,212	2,345	2,867	0	522	R	45.0	55.0	0	107	9	-	0.2	0.2	0.3	0
Boone	56,975	35,141	21,834	0	13,307	D	61.7	38.3	0	13	103	-	2.4	2.6	2.3	0
Buchanan	36,813	21,139	15,674	0	5,465	D	57.4	42.6	0	38	78	-	1.6	1.5	1.6	0
Butler	14,916	7,581	7,335	0	246	D	50.8	49.2	0	88	28	-	0.6	0.6	0.8	0
Caldwell	3,931	2,127	1,804	0	323	D	54.1	45.9	0	68	48	-	0.2	0.2	0.2	0
Callaway	13,842	8,389	5,453	0	2,936	D	60.6	39.4	0	21	95	-	0.6	0.6	0.6	0
Camden	14,334	7,416	6,918	0	498	D	51.7	48.3	0	85	31	-	0.6	0.5	0.7	0
Cape Girardeau	27,716	12,636	15,080	0	2,444	R	45.6	54.4	0	105	11	-	1.2	0.9	1.6	0
Carroll	5,238	2,749	2,489	0	260	D	52.5	47.5	0	79	37	-	0.2	0.2	0.3	0
Carter	2,614	1,470	1,144	0	326	D	56.2	43.8	0	47	69	-	0.1	0.1	0.1	0
Cass	29,258	16,129	13,129	0	3,000	D	55.1	44.9	0	59	57	-	1.2	1.2	1.4	0
Cedar	5,231	2,518	2,713	0	195	R	48.1	51.9	0	96	20	-	0.2	0.2	0.3	0
Chariton	4,391	2,657	1,734	0	923	D	60.5	39.5	0	23	93	-	0.2	0.2	0.2	0
Christian	16,936	7,997	8,939	0	942	R	47.2	52.8	0	100	16	-	0.7	0.6	0.9	0
Clark	3,460	1,942	1,518	0	424	D	56.1	43.9	0	49	67	-	0.1	0.1	0.2	0
Clay	72,415	43,055	29,360	0	13,695	D	59.5	40.5	0	31	85	-	3.1	3.1	3.0	0
Clinton	8,132	4,836	3,296	0	1,540	D	59.5	40.5	0	30	86	-	0.3	0.4	0.3	0
Cole	31,010	16,810	14,200	0	2,610	D	54.2	45.8	0	66	50	-	1.3	1.2	1.5	0
Cooper	7,267	3,773	3,494	0	279	D	51.9	48.1	0	81	35	-	0.3	0.3	0.4	0
Crawford	8,228	4,758	3,470	0	1,288	D	57.8	42.2	0	36	80	-	0.4	0.3	0.4	0
Dade	3,644	1,700	1,944	0	244	R	46.7	53.3	0	103	13	-	0.2	0.1	0.2	0
Dallas	5,859	2,988	2,871	0	117	D	51.0	49.0	0	86	30	-	0.2	0.2	0.3	0
Daviess	3,688	2,092	1,596	0	496	D	56.7	43.3	0	43	73	-	0.2	0.2	0.2	0
DeKalb	4,119	2,266	1,853	0	413	D	55.0	45.0	0	60	56	-	0.2	0.2	0.2	0
Dent	5,824	3,242	2,582	0	660	D	55.7	44.3	0	53	63	-	0.2	0.2	0.3	0
Douglas	5,606	2,403	3,203	0	800	R	42.9	57.1	0	111	5	-	0.2	0.2	0.3	0
Dunklin	10,949	6,640	4,309	0	2,331	D	60.6	39.4	0	20	96	-	0.5	0.5	0.4	0
Franklin	35,103	20,191	14,912	0	5,279	D	57.5	42.5	0	37	79	-	1.5	1.5	1.5	0
Gasconade	6,227	2,945	3,282	0	337	R	47.3	52.7	0	99	17	-	0.3	0.2	0.3	0
Gentry	3,626	2,017	1,609	0	408	D	55.6	44.4	0	54	62	-	0.2	0.1	0.2	0
Greene	104,107	52,816	51,291	0	1,525	D	50.7	49.3	0	89	27	-	4.4	3.8	5.3	0
Grundy	4,958	2,681	2,277	0	404	D	54.1	45.9	0	69	47	-	0.2	0.2	0.2	0
Harrison	4,009	2,078	1,931	0	147	D	51.8	48.2	0	82	34	-	0.2	0.2	0.2	0
Henry	9,470	6,085	3,385	0	2,700	D	64.3	35.7	0	6	110	-	0.4	0.4	0.3	0
Hickory	3,959	2,344	1,615	0	729	D	59.2	40.8	0	32	84	-	0.2	0.2	0.2	0
Holt	2,927	1,324	1,603	0	279	R	45.2	54.8	0	106	10	-	0.1	<.1	0.2	0
Howard	4,385	2,645	1,740	0	905	D	60.3	39.7	0	25	91	-	0.2	0.2	0.2	0
Howell	13,263	6,862	6,401	0	461	D	51.7	48.3	0	84	32	-	0.6	0.5	0.7	0
Iron	4,459	2,806	1,653	0	1,153	D	62.9	37.1	0	10	106	-	0.2	0.2	0.2	0
Jackson	286,241	186,324	99,917	0	86,407	D	65.1	34.9	0	5	111	-	12.2	13.5	10.3	0
Jasper	35,484	12,400	23,084	0	10,684	R	34.9	65.1	0	115	1	-	1.5	0.9	2.4	0
Jefferson	72,209	45,667	26,542	0	19,125	D	63.2	36.8	0	9	107	-	3.1	3.3	2.7	0
Johnson	14,953	8,558	6,395	0	2,163	D	57.2	42.8	0	41	75	-	0.6	0.6	0.7	0
Knox	2,202	1,237	965	0	272	D	56.2	43.8	0	48	68	-	<.1	<.1	<.1	0
Laclede	12,089	5,687	6,402	0	715	R	47.0	53.0	0	101	15	-	0.5	0.4	0.7	0
Lafayette	13,213	7,252	5,961	0	1,291	D	54.9	45.1	0	61	55	-	0.6	0.5	0.6	0
Lawrence	12,589	6,105	6,484	0	379	R	48.5	51.5	0	95	21	-	0.5	0.4	0.7	0
Lewis	4,364	2,473	1,891	0	582	D	56.7	43.3	0	44	72	-	0.2	0.2	0.2	0
Lincoln	12,574	7,555	5,019	0	2,536	D	60.1	39.9	0	27	89	-	0.5	0.5	0.5	0
Linn	6,266	3,701	2,565	0	1,136	D	59.1	40.9	0	33	83	-	0.3	0.3	0.3	0
Livingston	6,645	3,724	2,921	0	803	D	56.0	44.0	0	50	66	-	0.3	0.3	0.3	0
McDonald	6,702	2,821	3,881	0	1,060	R	42.1	57.9	0	112	4	-	0.3	0.2	0.4	0
Macon	6,966	4,153	2,813	0	1,340	D	59.6	40.4	0	28	88	-	0.3	0.3	0.3	0
Madison	5,017	2,728	2,289	0	439	D	54.4	45.6	0	63	53	-	0.2	0.2	0.2	0
Maries	3,967	2,388	1,579	0	809	D	60.2	39.8	0	26	90	-	0.2	0.2	0.2	0
Marion	11,562	6,379	5,183	0	1,196	D	55.2	44.8	0	58	58	-	0.5	0.5	0.5	0
Mercer	1,753	973	780	0	193	D	55.5	44.5	0	56	60	-	<.1	<.1	<.1	0
Miller	9,392	4,459	4,933	0	474	R	47.5	52.5	0	97	19	-	0.4	0.3	0.5	0
Mississippi	5,519	3,204	2,315	0	889	D	58.1	41.9	0	34	82	-	0.2	0.2	0.2	0
Moniteau	6,009	3,109	2,900	0	209	D	51.7	48.3	0	83	33	-	0.3	0.2	0.3	0
Monroe	4,130	2,620	1,510	0	1,110	D	63.4	36.6	0	8	108	-	0.2	0.2	0.2	0
Montgomery	5,165	2,738	2,427	0	311	D	53.0	47.0	0	75	41	-	0.2	0.2	0.3	0

Table G. — Vote for Governor: November 3, 1992, General Election (cont)

County	Total	Carnahan (DEM)	Webster (REP)	Other	Plurality Total	Party	DEM	REP	Other	Rank DEM	Rank REP	Rank Other	Total	DEM	REP	Other
Morgan	7,647	3,872	3,775	0	97	D	50.6	49.4	0	90	26	-	0.3	0.3	0.4	0
New Madrid	7,917	4,830	3,087	0	1,743	D	61.0	39.0	0	17	99	-	0.3	0.4	0.3	0
Newton	17,342	6,756	10,586	0	3,830	R	39.0	61.0	0	113	3	-	0.7	0.5	1.1	0
Nodaway	9,219	5,001	4,218	0	783	D	54.2	45.8	0	65	51	-	0.4	0.4	0.4	0
Oregon	4,164	2,529	1,635	0	894	D	60.7	39.3	0	19	97	-	0.2	0.2	0.2	0
Osage	5,979	3,189	2,790	0	399	D	53.3	46.7	0	73	43	-	0.3	0.2	0.3	0
Ozark	4,176	1,954	2,222	0	268	R	46.8	53.2	0	102	14	-	0.2	0.1	0.2	0
Pemiscot	6,542	4,267	2,275	0	1,992	D	65.2	34.8	0	4	112	-	0.3	0.3	0.2	0
Perry	7,096	3,076	4,020	0	944	R	43.3	56.7	0	109	7	-	0.3	0.2	0.4	0
Pettis	16,159	8,509	7,650	0	859	D	52.7	47.3	0	78	38	-	0.7	0.6	0.8	0
Phelps	16,547	9,860	6,687	0	3,173	D	59.6	40.4	0	29	87	-	0.7	0.7	0.7	0
Pike	7,182	4,420	2,762	0	1,658	D	61.5	38.5	0	15	101	-	0.3	0.3	0.3	0
Platte	29,309	16,779	12,530	0	4,249	D	57.2	42.8	0	40	76	-	1.3	1.2	1.3	0
Polk	8,562	4,273	4,289	0	16	R	49.9	50.1	0	92	24	-	0.4	0.3	0.4	0
Pulaski	9,848	5,308	4,540	0	768	D	53.9	46.1	0	71	45	-	0.4	0.4	0.5	0
Putnam	2,371	1,019	1,352	0	333	R	43.0	57.0	0	110	6	-	0.1	<.1	0.1	0
Ralls	4,364	2,694	1,670	0	1,024	D	61.7	38.3	0	12	104	-	0.2	0.2	0.2	0
Randolph	10,049	6,175	3,874	0	2,301	D	61.4	38.6	0	16	100	-	0.4	0.4	0.4	0
Ray	9,515	5,937	3,578	0	2,359	D	62.4	37.6	0	11	105	-	0.4	0.4	0.4	0
Reynolds	3,192	2,158	1,034	0	1,124	D	67.6	32.4	0	2	114	-	0.1	0.2	0.1	0
Ripley	4,739	2,584	2,155	0	429	D	54.5	45.5	0	62	54	-	0.2	0.2	0.2	0
St. Charles	104,597	58,012	46,585	0	11,427	D	55.5	44.5	0	57	59	-	4.5	4.2	4.8	0
St. Clair	4,500	2,547	1,953	0	594	D	56.6	43.4	0	45	71	-	0.2	0.2	0.2	0
Ste. Genevieve	6,982	4,610	2,372	0	2,238	D	66.0	34.0	0	3	113	-	0.3	0.3	0.2	0
St. Francois	18,637	11,287	7,350	0	3,937	D	60.6	39.4	0	22	94	-	0.8	0.8	0.8	0
St. Louis	526,368	320,213	206,155	0	114,058	D	60.8	39.2	0	18	98	-	22.5	23.3	21.3	0
Saline	10,031	6,428	3,603	0	2,825	D	64.1	35.9	0	7	109	-	0.4	0.5	0.4	0
Schuyler	2,093	1,164	929	0	235	D	55.6	44.4	0	55	61	-	<.1	<.1	<.1	0
Scotland	2,344	1,307	1,037	0	270	D	55.8	44.2	0	52	64	-	0.1	<.1	0.1	0
Scott	15,986	8,422	7,564	0	858	D	52.7	47.3	0	76	40	-	0.7	0.6	0.8	0
Shannon	3,791	2,338	1,453	0	885	D	61.7	38.3	0	14	102	-	0.2	0.2	0.2	0
Shelby	3,385	1,891	1,494	0	397	D	55.9	44.1	0	51	65	-	0.1	0.1	0.2	0
Stoddard	11,752	6,265	5,487	0	778	D	53.3	46.7	0	74	42	-	0.5	0.5	0.6	0
Stone	8,985	4,370	4,615	0	245	R	48.6	51.4	0	94	22	-	0.4	0.3	0.5	0
Sullivan	3,329	1,741	1,588	0	153	D	52.3	47.7	0	80	36	-	0.1	0.1	0.2	0
Taney	12,974	5,996	6,978	0	982	R	46.2	53.8	0	104	12	-	0.6	0.4	0.7	0
Texas	9,887	5,343	4,544	0	799	D	54.0	46.0	0	70	46	-	0.4	0.4	0.5	0
Vernon	8,087	4,558	3,529	0	1,029	D	56.4	43.6	0	46	70	-	0.4	0.3	0.4	0
Warren	8,503	4,602	3,901	0	701	D	54.1	45.9	0	67	49	-	0.4	0.3	0.4	0
Washington	7,700	4,651	3,049	0	1,602	D	60.4	39.6	0	24	92	-	0.3	0.3	0.3	0
Wayne	5,845	3,352	2,493	0	859	D	57.3	42.7	0	39	77	-	0.2	0.2	0.3	0
Webster	10,376	5,274	5,102	0	172	D	50.8	49.2	0	87	29	-	0.4	0.4	0.5	0
Worth	1,368	730	638	0	92	D	53.4	46.6	0	72	44	-	<.1	<.1	<.1	0
Wright	7,594	3,314	4,280	0	966	R	43.6	56.4	0	108	8	-	0.3	0.2	0.4	0
St. Louis City	144,240	111,362	32,878	0	78,484	D	77.2	22.8	0	1	115	-	6.2	8.1	3.4	0
MISSOURI[1]	2,344,121	1,375,425	968,574	122	406,851	D	58.7	41.3	<.1				100.0	100.0	100.0	100.0

[1]Includes the following write-in votes reported only at the state level: 42 for Branscrum, 5 for Clement, 66 for Dow, 2 for Garrison, 1 for Kolocotronis, and 6 for Smith; total of 122.

550 Missouri

Table H. — Vote for U.S. Representative in Congress: November 3, 1992, General Election

Congressional district and county	Total	Democrat (DEM)	Republican (REP)	Other	Plurality Total	Plurality Party	Percent of total vote DEM	REP	Other	Rank within district DEM	REP	Other	Percent contribution to district vote Total	DEM	REP	Other
District 1	**233,175**	**158,693**	**74,482**	-	**84,211**	**D**	**68.1**	**31.9**	**-**				**100.0**	**100.0**	**100.0**	**-**
St. Louis (pt)	160,689	95,680	65,009	-	30,671	D	59.5	40.5	-	2	1	-	68.9	60.3	87.3	-
St. Louis City (pt)	72,486	63,013	9,473	-	53,540	D	86.9	13.1	-	1	2	-	31.1	39.7	12.7	-
District 2[1]	**312,445**	**148,729**	**157,594**	**6,122**	**8,865**	**R**	**47.6**	**50.4**	**2.0**				**100.0**	**100.0**	**100.0**	**100.0**
St. Charles (pt)	62,607	31,463	29,537	1,607	1,926	D	50.3	47.2	2.6	1	2	1	20.0	21.2	18.7	26.2
St. Louis (pt)	249,835	117,266	128,057	4,512	10,791	R	46.9	51.3	1.8	2	1	2	80.0	78.8	81.3	73.7
District 3	**271,834**	**174,000**	**90,006**	**7,828**	**83,994**	**D**	**64.0**	**33.1**	**2.9**				**100.0**	**100.0**	**100.0**	**100.0**
Jefferson	72,835	46,922	23,265	2,648	23,657	D	64.4	31.9	3.6	3	2	1	26.8	27.0	25.8	33.8
Ste. Genevieve	7,091	5,223	1,653	215	3,570	D	73.7	23.3	3.0	1	4	3	2.6	3.0	1.8	2.7
St. Louis (pt)	118,296	69,401	46,179	2,716	23,222	D	58.7	39.0	2.3	4	1	4	43.5	39.9	51.3	34.7
St. Louis City (pt)	73,612	52,454	18,909	2,249	33,545	D	71.3	25.7	3.1	2	3	2	27.1	30.1	21.0	28.7
District 4	**251,452**	**176,977**	**74,475**	-	**102,502**	**D**	**70.4**	**29.6**	**-**				**100.0**	**100.0**	**100.0**	**-**
Bates	7,628	5,670	1,958	-	3,712	D	74.3	25.7	-	5	19	-	3.0	3.2	2.6	-
Benton	7,166	5,123	2,043	-	3,080	D	71.5	28.5	-	11	13	-	2.8	2.9	2.7	-
Camden	14,266	9,021	5,245	-	3,776	D	63.2	36.8	-	21	3	-	5.7	5.1	7.0	-
Cass	29,163	19,852	9,311	-	10,541	D	68.1	31.9	-	19	5	-	11.6	11.2	12.5	-
Cole	30,819	21,616	9,203	-	12,413	D	70.1	29.9	-	14	10	-	12.3	12.2	12.4	-
Dallas	5,605	3,541	2,064	-	1,477	D	63.2	36.8	-	22	2	-	2.2	2.0	2.8	-
Henry	9,509	7,225	2,284	-	4,941	D	76.0	24.0	-	3	21	-	3.8	4.1	3.1	-
Hickory	3,854	2,678	1,176	-	1,502	D	69.5	30.5	-	15	9	-	1.5	1.5	1.6	-
Jackson (pt)	12,068	8,247	3,821	-	4,426	D	68.3	31.7	-	17	7	-	4.8	4.7	5.1	-
Johnson	14,936	11,181	3,755	-	7,426	D	74.9	25.1	-	4	20	-	5.9	6.3	5.0	-
Laclede	11,974	8,173	3,801	-	4,372	D	68.3	31.7	-	18	6	-	4.8	4.6	5.1	-
Lafayette	13,312	9,776	3,536	-	6,240	D	73.4	26.6	-	6	18	-	5.3	5.5	4.7	-
Maries	3,931	2,864	1,067	-	1,797	D	72.9	27.1	-	8	16	-	1.6	1.6	1.4	-
Miller	9,324	6,058	3,266	-	2,792	D	65.0	35.0	-	20	4	-	3.7	3.4	4.4	-
Moniteau	5,986	4,290	1,696	-	2,594	D	71.7	28.3	-	10	14	-	2.4	2.4	2.3	-
Morgan	7,609	5,337	2,272	-	3,065	D	70.1	29.9	-	13	11	-	3.0	3.0	3.1	-
Osage	5,879	4,021	1,858	-	2,163	D	68.4	31.6	-	16	8	-	2.3	2.3	2.5	-
Pettis	16,258	11,803	4,455	-	7,348	D	72.6	27.4	-	9	15	-	6.5	6.7	6.0	-
Pulaski	9,804	7,579	2,225	-	5,354	D	77.3	22.7	-	2	22	-	3.9	4.3	3.0	-
St. Clair	4,434	3,115	1,319	-	1,796	D	70.3	29.7	-	12	12	-	1.8	1.8	1.8	-
Saline	10,006	7,993	2,013	-	5,980	D	79.9	20.1	-	1	23	-	4.0	4.5	2.7	-
Vernon	7,973	5,834	2,139	-	3,695	D	73.2	26.8	-	7	17	-	3.2	3.3	2.9	-
Webster	9,948	5,980	3,968	-	2,012	D	60.1	39.9	-	23	1	-	4.0	3.4	5.3	-
District 5	**255,312**	**151,014**	**93,562**	**10,736**	**57,452**	**D**	**59.1**	**36.6**	**4.2**				**100.0**	**100.0**	**100.0**	**100.0**
Jackson (pt)	255,312	151,014	93,562	10,736	57,452	D	59.1	36.6	4.2	1	1	1	100.0	100.0	100.0	100.0
District 6	**268,524**	**148,887**	**119,637**	-	**29,250**	**D**	**55.4**	**44.6**	**-**				**100.0**	**100.0**	**100.0**	**-**
Andrew	7,335	4,179	3,156	-	1,023	D	57.0	43.0	-	14	14	-	2.7	2.8	2.6	-
Atchison	3,194	1,802	1,392	-	410	D	56.4	43.6	-	16	12	-	1.2	1.2	1.2	-
Buchanan	36,898	21,988	14,910	-	7,078	D	59.6	40.4	-	10	18	-	13.7	14.8	12.5	-
Caldwell	3,998	2,379	1,619	-	760	D	59.5	40.5	-	11	17	-	1.5	1.6	1.4	-
Carroll	5,241	2,962	2,279	-	683	D	56.5	43.5	-	15	13	-	2.0	2.0	1.9	-
Chariton	4,428	2,624	1,804	-	820	D	59.3	40.7	-	12	16	-	1.6	1.8	1.5	-
Clay	72,262	38,054	34,208	-	3,846	D	52.7	47.3	-	21	7	-	26.9	25.6	28.6	-
Clinton	8,168	5,298	2,870	-	2,428	D	64.9	35.1	-	2	26	-	3.0	3.6	2.4	-
Cooper	7,207	3,341	3,866	-	525	R	46.4	53.6	-	26	2	-	2.7	2.2	3.2	-
Daviess	3,696	2,211	1,485	-	726	D	59.8	40.2	-	8	20	-	1.4	1.5	1.2	-
DeKalb	4,144	2,576	1,568	-	1,008	D	62.2	37.8	-	6	22	-	1.5	1.7	1.3	-
Gentry	3,657	2,279	1,378	-	901	D	62.3	37.7	-	4	24	-	1.4	1.5	1.2	-
Grundy	4,989	2,532	2,457	-	75	D	50.8	49.2	-	24	4	-	1.9	1.7	2.1	-
Harrison	4,130	2,186	1,944	-	242	D	52.9	47.1	-	20	8	-	1.5	1.5	1.6	-
Holt	2,976	1,791	1,185	-	606	D	60.2	39.8	-	7	21	-	1.1	1.2	1.0	-
Howard	4,361	2,453	1,908	-	545	D	56.2	43.8	-	17	11	-	1.6	1.6	1.6	-
Jackson (pt)	19,808	9,813	9,995	-	182	R	49.5	50.5	-	25	3	-	7.4	6.6	8.4	-
Linn	6,334	3,788	2,546	-	1,242	D	59.8	40.2	-	9	19	-	2.4	2.5	2.1	-
Livingston	6,691	3,512	3,179	-	333	D	52.5	47.5	-	23	5	-	2.5	2.4	2.7	-
Mercer	1,797	1,049	748	-	301	D	58.4	41.6	-	13	15	-	0.7	0.7	0.6	-
Nodaway	9,305	5,793	3,512	-	2,281	D	62.3	37.7	-	5	23	-	3.5	3.9	2.9	-
Platte	29,174	15,340	13,834	-	1,506	D	52.6	47.4	-	22	6	-	10.9	10.3	11.6	-
Putnam	2,352	975	1,377	-	402	R	41.5	58.5	-	27	1	-	0.9	0.7	1.2	-
Ray	9,588	6,132	3,456	-	2,676	D	64.0	36.0	-	3	25	-	3.6	4.1	2.9	-
Schuyler	2,070	1,153	917	-	236	D	55.7	44.3	-	18	10	-	0.8	0.8	0.8	-
Sullivan	3,339	1,779	1,560	-	219	D	53.3	46.7	-	19	9	-	1.2	1.2	1.3	-
Worth	1,382	898	484	-	414	D	65.0	35.0	-	1	27	-	0.5	0.6	0.4	-
District 7	**260,065**	**99,762**	**160,303**	-	**60,541**	**R**	**38.4**	**61.6**	**-**				**100.0**	**100.0**	**100.0**	**-**
Barry	12,299	4,672	7,627	-	2,955	R	38.0	62.0	-	7	9	-	4.7	4.7	4.8	-
Barton	5,136	1,614	3,522	-	1,908	R	31.4	68.6	-	15	1	-	2.0	1.6	2.2	-
Cedar	5,288	2,130	3,158	-	1,028	R	40.3	59.7	-	2	14	-	2.0	2.1	2.0	-
Christian	16,952	6,805	10,147	-	3,342	R	40.1	59.9	-	3	13	-	6.5	6.8	6.3	-

[1] Includes the three (3) write-in votes reported only at the district level for Kaplan.

Congressional district and county	Total	Democrat (DEM)	Republican (REP)	Other	Plurality Total	Plurality Party	Percent of total vote DEM	REP	Other	Rank within district DEM	REP	Other	Percent contribution to district vote Total	DEM	REP	Other
District 7 (cont)																
Dade	3,653	1,358	2,295	-	937	R	37.2	62.8	-	11	5	-	1.4	1.4	1.4	-
Douglas	5,623	1,951	3,672	-	1,721	R	34.7	65.3	-	12	4	-	2.2	2.0	2.3	-
Greene	103,943	42,283	61,660	-	19,377	R	40.7	59.3	-	1	15	-	40.0	42.4	38.5	-
Jasper	35,478	12,276	23,202	-	10,926	R	34.6	65.4	-	13	3	-	13.6	12.3	14.5	-
Lawrence	12,752	5,010	7,742	-	2,732	R	39.3	60.7	-	5	11	-	4.9	5.0	4.8	-
McDonald	6,773	2,545	4,228	-	1,683	R	37.6	62.4	-	9	7	-	2.6	2.6	2.6	-
Newton	17,348	5,822	11,526	-	5,704	R	33.6	66.4	-	14	2	-	6.7	5.8	7.2	-
Ozark	4,176	1,621	2,555	-	934	R	38.8	61.2	-	6	10	-	1.6	1.6	1.6	-
Polk	8,618	3,408	5,210	-	1,802	R	39.5	60.5	-	4	12	-	3.3	3.4	3.3	-
Stone	9,040	3,409	5,631	-	2,222	R	37.7	62.3	-	8	8	-	3.5	3.4	3.5	-
Taney	12,986	4,858	8,128	-	3,270	R	37.4	62.6	-	10	6	-	5.0	4.9	5.1	-
District 8[1]	234,418	86,730	147,398	290	60,668	R	37.0	62.9	-				100.0	100.0	100.0	-
Bollinger	5,083	1,685	3,398	-	1,713	R	33.1	66.9	-	22	5	-	2.2	1.9	2.3	-
Butler	15,087	5,347	9,740	-	4,393	R	35.4	64.6	-	19	8	-	6.4	6.2	6.6	-
Cape Girardeau	27,587	7,720	19,867	-	12,147	R	28.0	72.0	-	26	1	-	11.8	8.9	13.5	-
Carter	2,591	860	1,731	-	871	R	33.2	66.8	-	21	6	-	1.1	1.0	1.2	-
Crawford	8,171	3,194	4,977	-	1,783	R	39.1	60.9	-	11	16	-	3.5	3.7	3.4	-
Dent	5,828	2,350	3,478	-	1,128	R	40.3	59.7	-	10	17	-	2.5	2.7	2.4	-
Dunklin	10,854	4,476	6,378	-	1,902	R	41.2	58.8	-	8	19	-	4.6	5.2	4.3	-
Howell	13,295	4,132	9,163	-	5,031	R	31.1	68.9	-	23	4	-	5.7	4.8	6.2	-
Iron	4,391	2,052	2,339	-	287	R	46.7	53.3	-	2	25	-	1.9	2.4	1.6	-
Madison	5,036	1,899	3,137	-	1,238	R	37.7	62.3	-	14	13	-	2.1	2.2	2.1	-
Mississippi	5,558	2,252	3,306	-	1,054	R	40.5	59.5	-	9	18	-	2.4	2.6	2.2	-
New Madrid	7,863	3,463	4,400	-	937	R	44.0	56.0	-	5	22	-	3.4	4.0	3.0	-
Oregon	4,164	1,801	2,363	-	562	R	43.3	56.7	-	7	20	-	1.8	2.1	1.6	-
Pemiscot	6,665	3,066	3,599	-	533	R	46.0	54.0	-	3	24	-	2.8	3.5	2.4	-
Perry	7,137	2,092	5,045	-	2,953	R	29.3	70.7	-	25	2	-	3.0	2.4	3.4	-
Phelps	16,273	6,066	10,207	-	4,141	R	37.3	62.7	-	15	12	-	6.9	7.0	6.9	-
Reynolds	3,131	1,562	1,569	-	7	R	49.9	50.1	-	1	26	-	1.3	1.8	1.1	-
Ripley	4,770	1,749	3,021	-	1,272	R	36.7	63.3	-	17	10	-	2.0	2.0	2.0	-
St. Francois	18,713	8,304	10,409	-	2,105	R	44.4	55.6	-	4	23	-	8.0	9.6	7.1	-
Scott	15,873	5,724	10,149	-	4,425	R	36.1	63.9	-	18	9	-	6.8	6.6	6.9	-
Shannon	3,696	1,361	2,335	-	974	R	36.8	63.2	-	16	11	-	1.6	1.6	1.6	-
Stoddard	11,841	4,075	7,766	-	3,691	R	34.4	65.6	-	20	7	-	5.1	4.7	5.3	-
Texas	9,761	3,796	5,965	-	2,169	R	38.9	61.1	-	12	15	-	4.2	4.4	4.0	-
Washington	7,524	3,255	4,269	-	1,014	R	43.3	56.7	-	6	21	-	3.2	3.8	2.9	-
Wayne	5,744	2,210	3,534	-	1,324	R	38.5	61.5	-	13	14	-	2.5	2.5	2.4	-
Wright	7,492	2,239	5,253	-	3,014	R	29.9	70.1	-	24	3	-	3.2	2.6	3.6	-
District 9	261,335	124,694	118,811	17,830	5,883	D	47.7	45.5	6.8				100.0	100.0	100.0	100.0
Adair	10,347	4,105	5,447	795	1,342	R	39.7	52.6	7.7	20	2	3	4.0	3.3	4.6	4.5
Audrain	10,547	5,074	5,085	388	11	R	48.1	48.2	3.7	18	4	8	4.0	4.1	4.3	2.2
Boone	57,063	16,520	31,625	8,918	15,105	R	29.0	55.4	15.6	21	1	1	21.8	13.2	26.6	50.0
Callaway	13,813	6,252	6,458	1,103	206	R	45.3	46.8	8.0	19	7	2	5.3	5.0	5.4	6.2
Clark	3,510	2,002	1,439	69	563	D	57.0	41.0	2.0	3	18	20	1.3	1.6	1.2	0.4
Franklin	34,991	20,810	12,454	1,727	8,356	D	59.5	35.6	4.9	2	21	5	13.4	16.7	10.5	9.7
Gasconade	6,208	3,005	2,986	217	19	D	48.4	48.1	3.5	17	5	10	2.4	2.4	2.5	1.2
Knox	2,201	1,100	1,055	46	45	D	50.0	47.9	2.1	15	6	18	0.8	0.9	0.9	0.3
Lewis	4,382	2,420	1,863	99	557	D	55.2	42.5	2.3	6	14	17	1.7	1.9	1.6	0.6
Lincoln	12,523	7,619	4,491	413	3,128	D	60.8	35.9	3.3	1	20	11	4.8	6.1	3.8	2.3
Macon	7,049	3,647	3,154	248	493	D	51.7	44.7	3.5	11	11	9	2.7	2.9	2.7	1.4
Marion	11,723	5,950	5,430	343	520	D	50.8	46.3	2.9	14	9	13	4.5	4.8	4.6	1.9
Monroe	4,150	2,152	1,876	122	276	D	51.9	45.2	2.9	10	10	12	1.6	1.7	1.6	0.7
Montgomery	5,150	2,642	2,401	107	241	D	51.3	46.6	2.1	13	8	19	2.0	2.1	2.0	0.6
Pike	7,213	4,059	2,961	193	1,098	D	56.3	41.1	2.7	4	17	14	2.8	3.3	2.5	1.1
Ralls	4,374	2,369	1,896	109	473	D	54.2	43.3	2.5	8	13	16	1.7	1.9	1.6	0.6
Randolph	10,100	5,612	4,093	395	1,519	D	55.6	40.5	3.9	5	19	7	3.9	4.5	3.4	2.2
St. Charles (pt)	41,776	22,040	17,664	2,072	4,376	D	52.8	42.3	5.0	9	15	4	16.0	17.7	14.9	11.6
Scotland	2,377	1,309	1,005	63	304	D	55.1	42.3	2.7	7	16	15	0.9	1.0	0.8	0.4
Shelby	3,397	1,672	1,662	63	10	D	49.2	48.9	1.9	16	3	21	1.3	1.3	1.4	0.4
Warren	8,441	4,335	3,766	340	569	D	51.4	44.6	4.0	12	12	6	3.2	3.5	3.2	1.9
MISSOURI	2,348,560	1,269,486	1,036,268	42,806	233,218	D	54.1	44.1	1.8							

[1]Includes the following write-in votes reported only at the district level: 8 for Baugh and 282 for Reed; total of 290.

1992 Vote for President
Percent for Clinton (D), by County

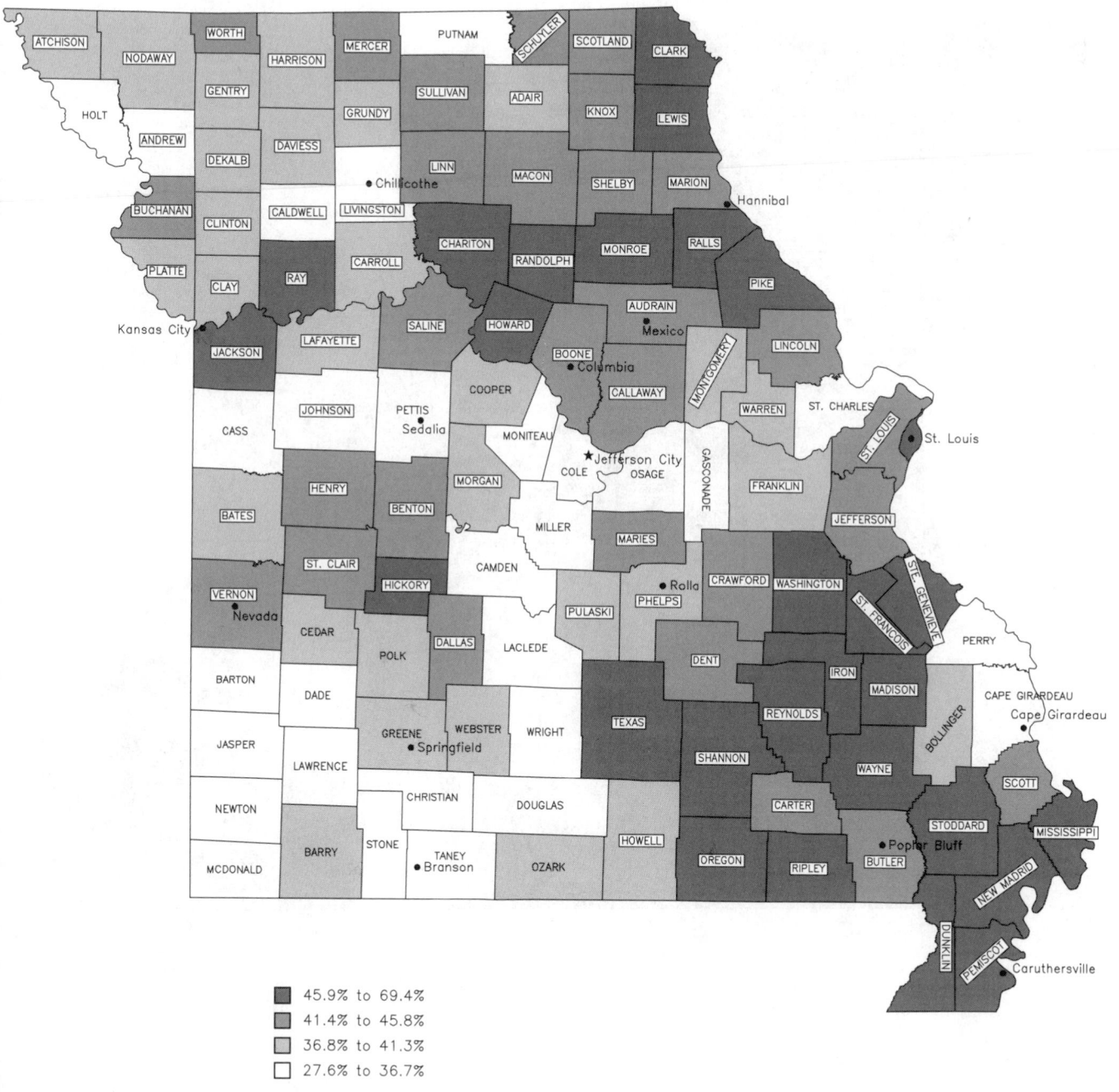

45.9% to 69.4%
41.4% to 45.8%
36.8% to 41.3%
27.6% to 36.7%

Clinton (D) received 44.1% statewide.

A framed county name indicates
a county carried by the winner.

opyright © 1993 by Election Data Services, Inc.

1992 Vote for U.S. Senator
Percent for Bond (R), by County

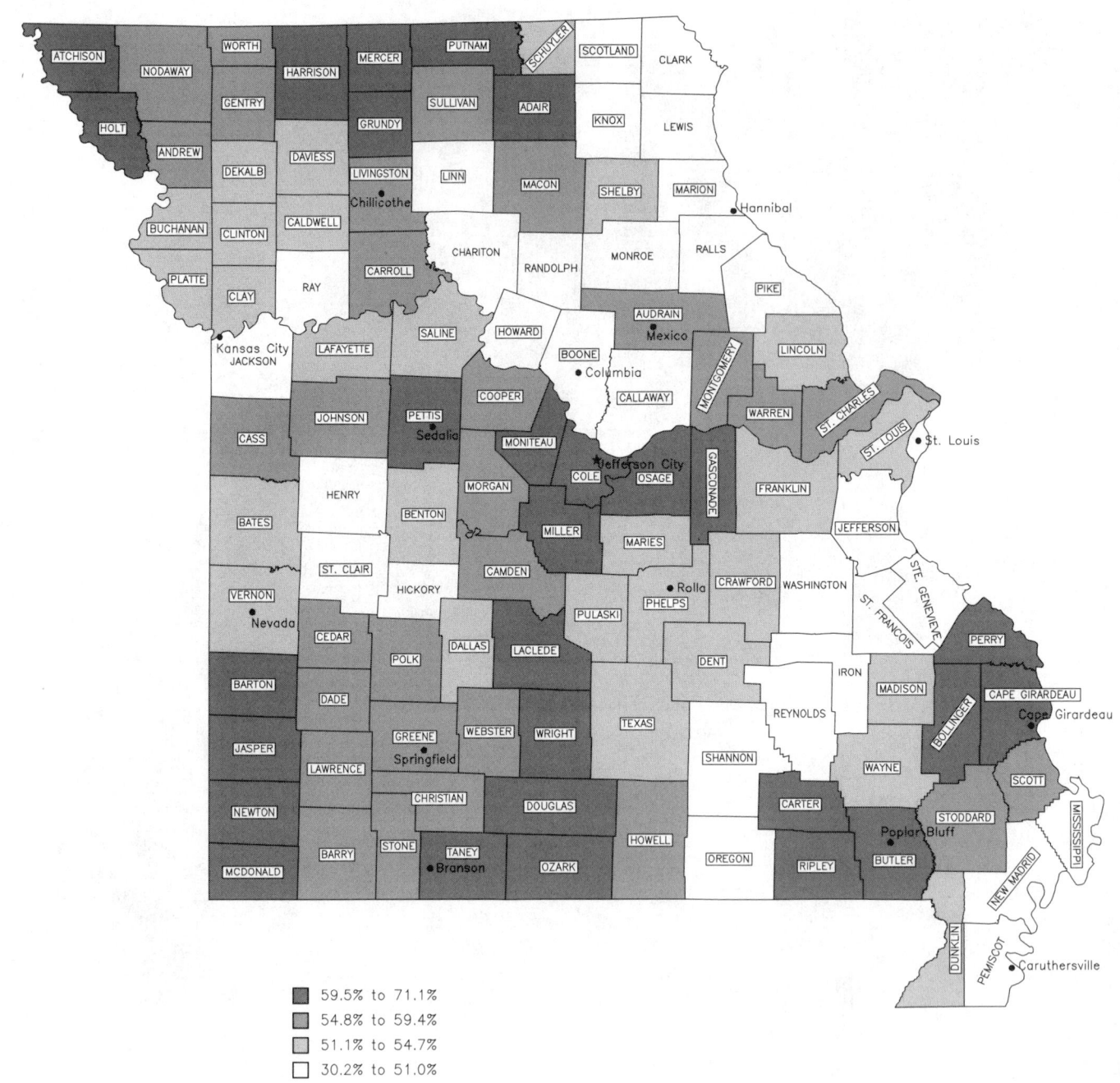

■ 59.5% to 71.1%

▨ 54.8% to 59.4%

▧ 51.1% to 54.7%

□ 30.2% to 51.0%

Bond (R) received 51.9% statewide.

A framed county name indicates
a county carried by the winner.

554 Missouri

1992 Vote for Governor
Percent for Carnahan (D), by County

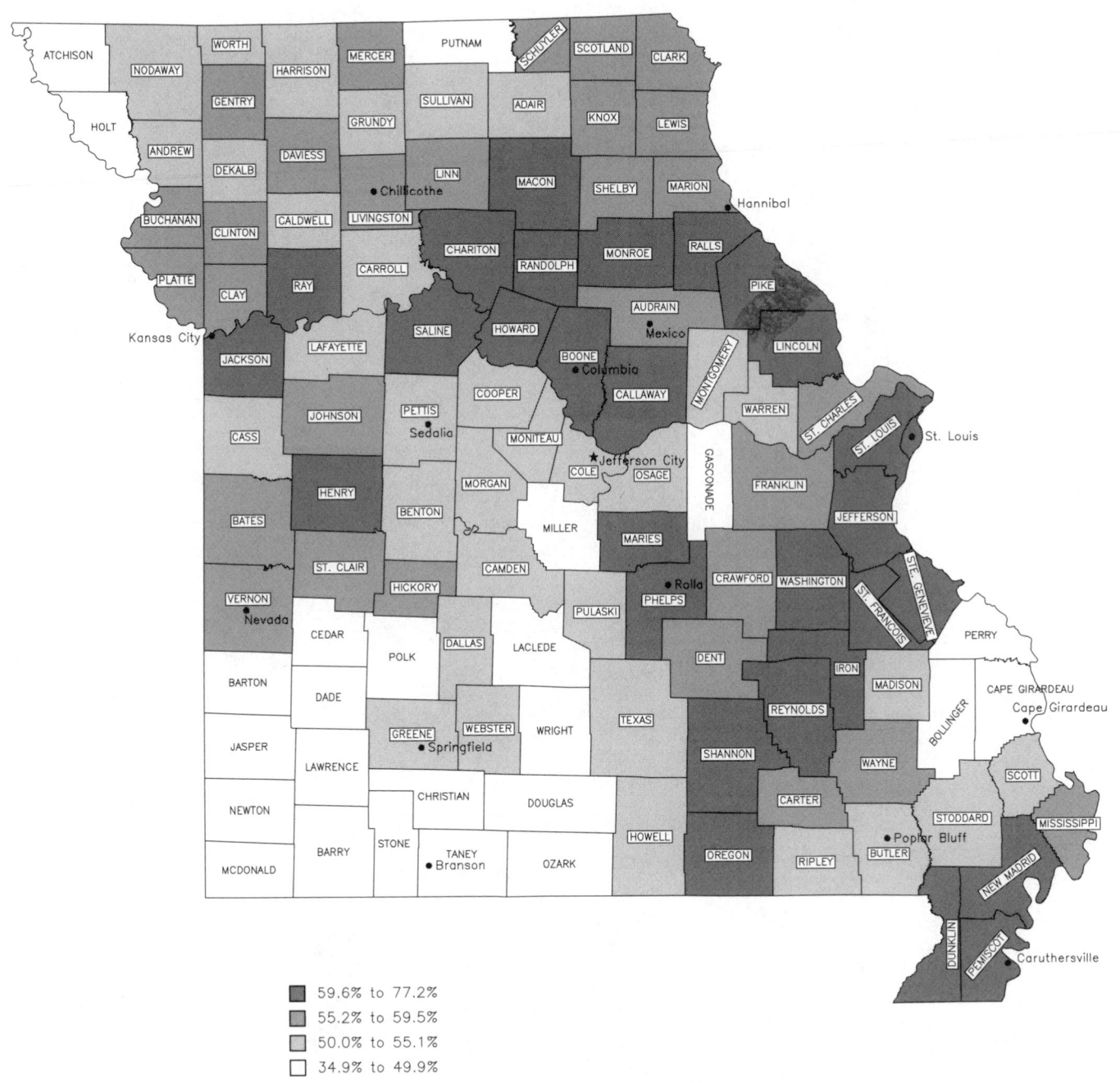

59.6% to 77.2%
55.2% to 59.5%
50.0% to 55.1%
34.9% to 49.9%

Carnahan (D) received 58.7% statewide.

A framed county name indicates
a county carried by the winner.

MONTANA

Alternative Registration Methods:
.......................Deputized Registrars, Mail-in, Motor-voter

Registration Deadline (Days before Election) 30

Voting Equipment Use (Counties)[2]

Datavote Punch Card	0	Paper Ballot	21
Electronic	0	Other Punch Card	16
Lever Machine	1	Mixed Systems	0
Optical Scanner	18		

Party Control	DEM	REP	IND	VAC
1993 State Senate	30	20	0	0
1992 State Senate	29	21	0	0
1993 State House	47	53	0	0
1992 State House	61	39	0	0

Population Statistics 1990

Race/ Ethnicity	Total Population		Voting Age Population		Voting Age Population % of total population
	Number	%	Number	%	
Non-Hispanic					
White	733,878	91.8	538,434	93.3	73.4
Black	2,242	0.3	1,437	0.2	64.1
Asian/Pacific Islander	4,123	0.5	2,716	0.5	65.9
Native American	46,475	5.8	27,236	4.7	58.6
Other	173	<.1	80	<.1	46.2
All Hispanic	12,174	1.5	7,058	1.2	58.0
TOTAL	799,065	100.0	576,961	100.0	72.2

Estimated Voting Age Population 1992 (VAP) 586,000
Number of Registered Voters................................... 529,822
   % of estimated VAP.. 90.4
Voter Turnout (Actual) 417,564
   % of VAP 71.3
   % of Registration 78.8
Persons Not Voting—of Voting Age 168,436
   % of VAP 28.7
Persons Not Voting—of Registered 112,258
   % of Registration 21.2
Straight Ticket Voting .... No

State Officials and Members of Congress

Governor:
Marc Racicot (R) 1992, elected to a four-year term in 1992.

U.S. Senators:
Max Baucus (D) 1978, elected to a six-year term in 1990.
Conrad Burns (R) 1988, elected to a six-year term in 1988.

U.S. Representative in Congress:
(District, Name, Party, Date first elected)

At-Large. Williams (D) 1978

---

[1]Includes part of Yellowstone National Park. [2]Less than total number of counties because Yellowstone National Park is combined with Park and Gallatin counties for election administration purposes.

Candidates: General Election, November 3, 1992

Candidate(s)	Total vote	Percent	Party	Status	First elected
President/Vice President					
Clinton/Gore	154,507	37.63%	Democrat	Challenger	1992
Bush/Quayle	144,207	35.12%	Republican	Incumbent	1988
Perot/Stockdale	107,225	26.11%	Independent	Challenger	
Gritz/Minett	3,658	0.89%	Independent	Challenger	
Marrou/Lord	986	0.24%	Libertarian	Challenger	
Write ins	28	<.01%	Write in	Challenger	
U.S. Senator (No Contest)					
Governor					
Racicot/Rehberg	209,401	51.35%	Republican	Challenger	1992
Bradley/Halligan	198,421	48.65%	Democrat	Challenger	
U.S. Representative in Congress					
District At-Large					
Pat Williams	203,711	50.46%	Democrat	Incumbent	1978
Ron Marlenee	189,570	46.95%	Republican	Incumbent	1976
Jerome Wilverding	10,454	2.59%	Libertarian	Challenger	

Candidates: June 2, 1992, Primary Election

Candidate	Total vote	Percent	Candidate	Total vote	Percent
Presidential Preference, Democratic			**Presidential Preference, Republican**		
Bill Clinton	54,989	46.81%	George Bush	65,176	71.64%
No Preference	28,164	23.98%	No Preference	15,098	16.60%
Jerry Brown	21,704	18.48%	Patrick Buchanan	10,701	11.76%
Paul Tsongas	12,614	10.74%			

Voter Registration and Turnout, 1948-1992 Elections

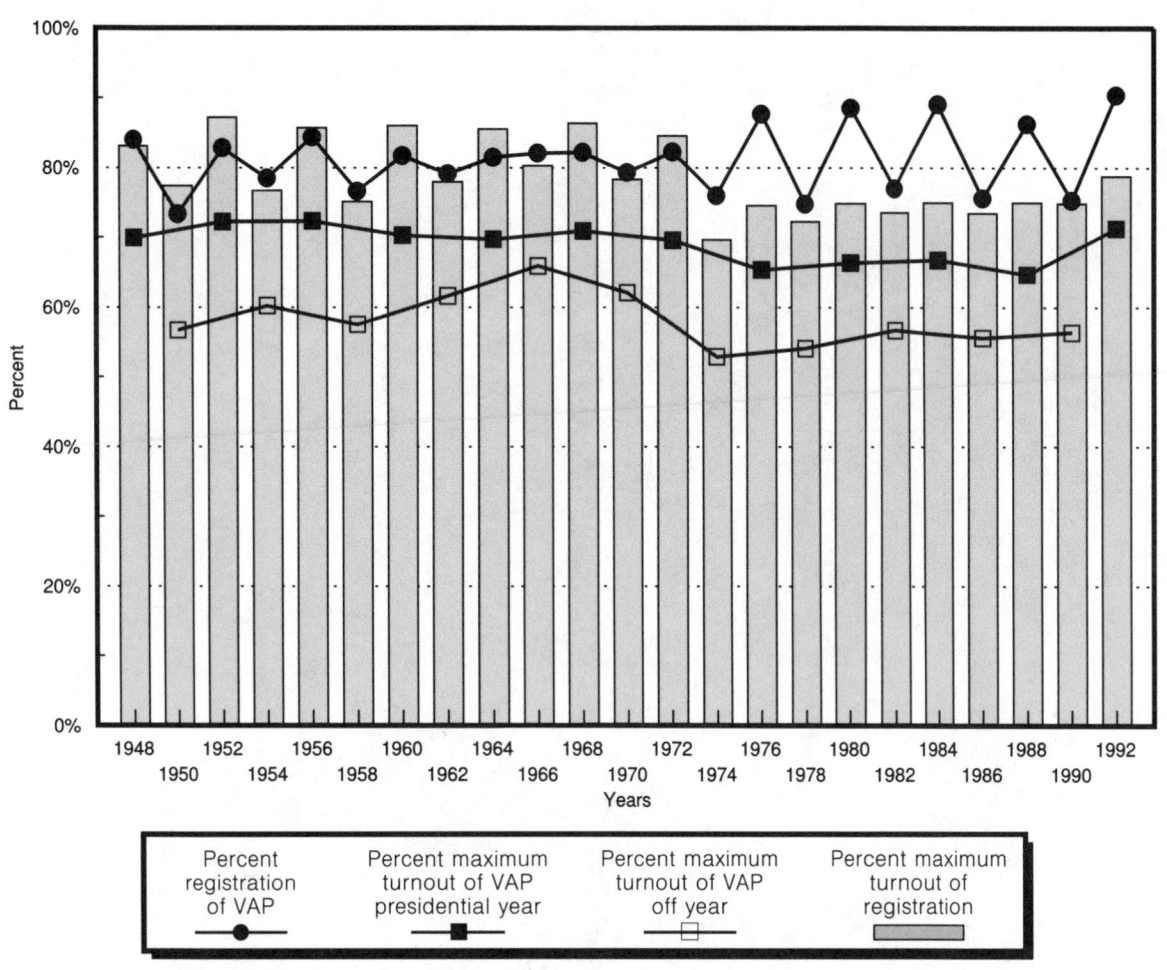

		Voter registration (REG)			Voter turnout												
							Highest office						Maximum vote				
Year	Estimated Voting Age Population (VAP)	Total	Percent of VAP	Rank by percent of VAP	Actual	Total	Office	Percent total REG	Rank by percent of REG	Percent of VAP	Rank by percent of VAP	Total	Percent total REG	Rank by percent of REG	Percent total VAP	Rank by percent of VAP
1992	586,000	529,822	90.4	4	417,564	410,611	P	77.5	25	70.1	3	417,564	78.8	24	71.3	3
1990	579,000	435,900	75.3	15	326,652	319,336	S	73.3	3	55.2	3	326,652	74.9	4	56.4	3
1988	586,000	505,541	86.3	6	378,981	365,674	P	72.3	22	62.4	2	378,981	75.0	21	64.7	2
1986	587,000	443,935	75.6	12	326,436	317,862	C	71.6	2	54.2	4	326,436	73.5	2	55.6	4
1984	591,000	526,841	89.1	5	395,006	384,377	P	73.0	26	65.0	2	395,006	75.0	25	66.8	2
1982	579,000	445,888	77.0	10	328,082	321,062	S	72.0	5	55.5	4	328,082	73.6	5	56.7	3
1980	560,000	496,402	88.6	6	371,976	363,952	P	73.3	30	65.0	5	371,976	74.9	28	66.4	6
1978	548,000	410,046	74.8	16	296,521	287,942	S	70.2	3	52.5	3	296,521	72.3	3	54.1	2
1976	519,000	454,924	87.7	6	339,346	328,734	P	72.3	30	63.3	7	339,346	74.6	29	65.4	5
1974	492,000	373,889	76.0	13	260,496	254,146	C	68.0	8	51.7	5	260,496	69.7	6	52.9	5
1972	470,000	386,867	82.3	10	327,176	317,603	P	82.1	6	67.6	5	327,176	84.6	7	69.6	4
1970	410,000	325,315	79.3	12	254,790	247,869	S	76.2	6	60.5	6	254,790	78.3	5	62.1	3
1968	403,000	331,078	82.2	14	285,892	274,404	P	82.9	16	68.1	13	285,892	86.4	6	70.9	8
1966	402,000	330,182	82.1	12	264,971	259,863	S	78.7	3	64.6	3	264,971	80.3	3	65.9	2
1964	402,000	327,477	81.5	18	280,010	278,628	P	85.1	11	69.3	18	280,010	85.5	13	69.7	17
1962	403,000	318,721	79.1	18	248,441	248,441	C	77.9	5	61.6	8	248,441	77.9	6	61.6	9
1960	395,000	322,876	81.7	15	276,612	277,579	P	86.0	17	70.3	26	277,579	86.0	18	70.3	26
1958	399,000	305,614	76.6	16	229,483	229,483	S	75.1	9	57.5	13	229,483	75.1	11	57.5	16
1956	375,000	316,444	84.4	11	263,204	271,171	P	85.7	9	72.3	11	271,171	85.7	11	72.3	12
1954	378,000	296,611	78.5	11	227,454	227,454	S	76.7	5	60.2	8	227,454	76.7	6	60.2	9
1952	367,000	304,053	82.8	12	260,469	265,037	P	87.2	8	72.2	22	265,037	87.2	8	72.2	22
1950	371,000	272,103	73.3	11	210,527	210,527	C	77.4	5	56.7	10	210,527	77.4	6	56.7	10
1948	321,000	269,779	84.0	5	221,003	224,278	P	83.1	6	69.9	4	224,278	83.1	6	69.9	4

MONTANA

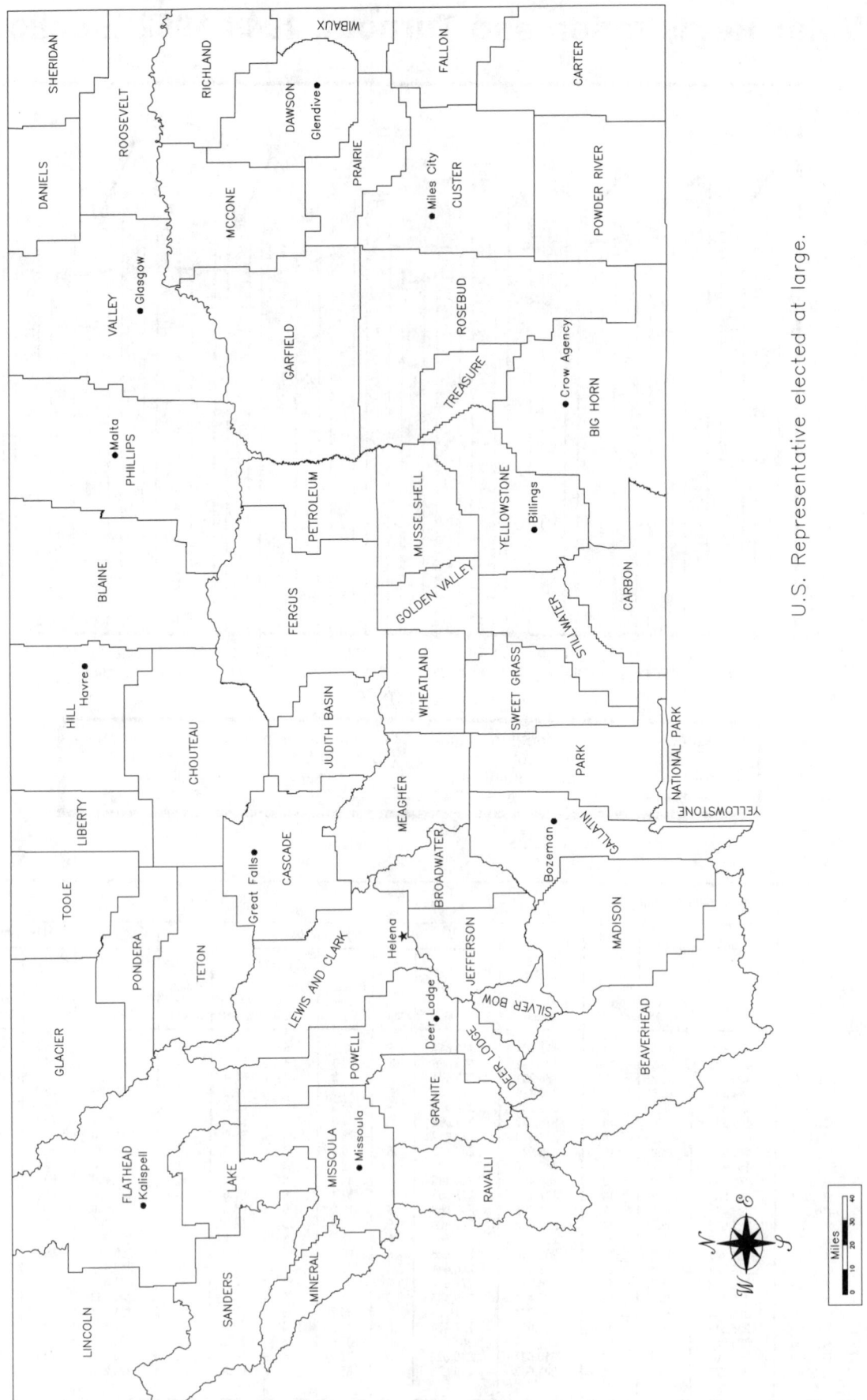

U.S. Representative elected at large.

Copyright © 1993 by Election Data Services, Inc.

Table A. — 1990 Population by Race and Ethnic Origin

State/ county code	County	Total persons	Percent of total persons						Rank				Percent contribution to state population			
			Non-Hispanic						Percent of total persons				Non-Hispanic			
										Non-Hispanic						
			White	Black	Asian and Pacific Islander	Native American	Other	Hispanic	Total	White	Black	Native American¹	Total	White	Black	Native American¹
30 001	Beaverhead	8,424	96.6	<.1	0.3	1.4	0.0	1.6	23	34	18	28	1.1	1.1	0.4	0.2
30 003	Big Horn	11,337	42.3	0.1	0.4	54.5	0.0	2.6	16	57	10	2	1.4	0.7	0.7	13.3
30 005	Blaine	6,728	59.8	<.1	<.1	39.2	0.0	0.8	27	54	24	4	0.8	0.5	0.3	5.7
30 007	Broadwater	3,318	97.5	<.1	0.2	1.3	<.1	1.0	38	24	39	30	0.4	0.4	<.1	<.1
30 009	Carbon	8,080	98.1	<.1	0.2	0.5	<.1	1.1	25	16	38	49	1.0	1.1	0.1	<.1
30 011	Carter	1,503	98.5	0.0	0.1	0.6	0.0	0.8	51	11	41	47	0.2	0.2	0.0	<.1
30 013	Cascade	77,691	92.1	1.3	1.0	3.8	<.1	1.8	3	47	1	14	9.7	9.8	45.4	6.3
30 015	Chouteau	5,452	95.5	<.1	0.1	3.9	0.0	0.5	33	42	27	12	0.7	0.7	0.2	0.5
30 017	Custer	11,697	96.7	<.1	0.2	1.6	0.0	1.4	15	32	19	22	1.5	1.5	0.5	0.4
30 019	Daniels	2,266	98.4	0.0	0.8	0.3	0.0	0.5	46	12	42	54	0.3	0.3	0.0	<.1
30 021	Dawson	9,505	98.3	0.0	0.3	0.8	0.0	0.7	21	13	43	40	1.2	1.3	0.0	0.2
30 023	Deer Lodge	10,278	95.5	0.3	0.2	2.4	<.1	1.5	20	41	5	16	1.3	1.3	1.3	0.5
30 025	Fallon	3,103	99.1	0.0	0.4	0.3	0.0	0.2	41	6	44	53	0.4	0.4	0.0	<.1
30 027	Fergus	12,083	98.3	<.1	0.1	1.0	<.1	0.6	14	14	29	36	1.5	1.6	0.4	0.2
30 029	Flathead	59,218	97.0	<.1	0.4	1.5	<.1	1.0	4	28	21	26	7.4	7.8	2.5	1.9
30 031	Gallatin	50,463	96.6	0.2	0.9	1.2	<.1	1.2	5	33	8	31	6.3	6.6	3.5	1.3
30 033	Garfield	1,589	99.6	0.0	0.1	0.3	0.0	0.0	50	2	45	55	0.2	0.2	0.0	<.1
30 035	Glacier	12,121	43.3	<.1	<.1	55.9	<.1	0.6	13	56	22	1	1.5	0.7	0.5	14.6
30 037	Golden Valley	912	97.6	0.0	0.4	1.1	0.0	0.9	54	22	46	33	0.1	0.1	0.0	<.1
30 039	Granite	2,548	98.7	0.0	0.2	0.8	0.0	0.4	42	10	47	39	0.3	0.3	0.0	<.1
30 041	Hill	17,654	83.0	0.1	0.5	15.4	<.1	1.0	10	51	16	7	2.2	2.0	0.8	5.9
30 043	Jefferson	7,939	97.2	<.1	0.2	1.5	<.1	1.0	26	26	32	24	1.0	1.1	0.2	0.3
30 045	Judith Basin	2,282	99.1	0.0	0.2	0.3	0.0	0.4	44	5	48	52	0.3	0.3	0.0	<.1
30 047	Lake	21,041	77.3	<.1	0.1	20.5	<.1	1.9	9	52	28	6	2.6	2.2	0.6	9.3
30 049	Lewis and Clark	47,495	96.0	0.1	0.5	2.1	<.1	1.2	6	38	13	20	5.9	6.2	2.8	2.2
30 051	Liberty	2,295	99.1	0.1	0.1	0.5	0.0	0.2	43	7	14	51	0.3	0.3	0.1	<.1
30 053	Lincoln	17,481	96.9	<.1	0.3	1.6	<.1	1.1	11	30	30	23	2.2	2.3	0.5	0.6
30 055	McCone	2,276	98.7	<.1	<.1	0.7	0.0	0.4	45	9	36	42	0.3	0.3	<.1	<.1
30 057	Madison	5,989	97.6	0.0	0.2	0.7	0.0	1.5	32	21	49	45	0.7	0.8	0.0	<.1
30 059	Meagher	1,819	97.5	0.0	0.1	0.9	0.0	1.4	49	23	50	37	0.2	0.2	0.0	<.1
30 061	Mineral	3,315	95.7	<.1	0.7	2.2	<.1	1.2	39	40	23	18	0.4	0.4	0.1	0.2
30 063	Missoula	78,687	95.3	0.2	1.0	2.2	<.1	1.2	2	43	7	19	9.8	10.2	3.7	3.7
30 065	Musselshell	4,106	98.2	<.1	0.2	0.6	0.0	0.9	37	15	33	46	0.5	0.5	<.1	<.1
30 067	Park	14,562	96.8	0.4	0.5	0.8	<.1	1.6	12	31	2	41	1.8	1.9	2.7	0.2
30 069	Petroleum	519	99.4	0.0	0.0	0.6	0.0	0.0	56	4	51	48	<.1	<.1	0.0	<.1
30 071	Phillips	5,163	91.4	<.1	0.3	7.5	<.1	0.9	34	48	37	10	0.6	0.6	<.1	0.8
30 073	Pondera	6,433	88.2	<.1	0.3	10.9	0.0	0.5	30	50	25	8	0.8	0.8	0.2	1.5
30 075	Powder River	2,090	97.1	0.0	0.1	1.8	0.0	1.0	48	27	52	21	0.3	0.3	0.0	<.1
30 077	Powell	6,620	94.2	0.3	0.4	3.8	<.1	1.2	28	44	4	13	0.8	0.9	1.0	0.5
30 079	Prairie	1,383	97.5	0.0	0.3	1.1	0.0	1.2	52	25	53	34	0.2	0.2	0.0	<.1
30 081	Ravalli	25,010	97.0	0.1	0.3	1.1	<.1	1.5	8	29	12	32	3.1	3.3	1.5	0.6
30 083	Richland	10,716	96.2	<.1	0.2	1.3	<.1	2.2	18	36	40	29	1.3	1.4	0.1	0.3
30 085	Roosevelt	10,999	50.4	0.2	0.4	48.1	<.1	0.9	17	55	9	3	1.4	0.8	0.8	11.4
30 087	Rosebud	10,505	71.1	0.2	0.5	26.0	0.0	2.1	19	53	6	5	1.3	1.0	1.1	5.9
30 089	Sanders	8,669	93.0	0.1	0.4	5.3	0.0	1.2	22	46	11	11	1.1	1.1	0.5	1.0
30 091	Sheridan	4,732	97.9	0.0	0.3	1.1	0.0	0.8	36	17	54	35	0.6	0.6	0.0	0.1
30 093	Silver Bow	33,941	95.8	<.1	0.4	1.4	<.1	2.4	7	39	20	27	4.2	4.4	1.4	1.0
30 095	Stillwater	6,536	97.7	<.1	0.1	0.7	0.0	1.4	29	20	26	43	0.8	0.9	0.2	0.1
30 097	Sweet Grass	3,154	99.0	<.1	0.2	0.5	<.1	0.2	40	8	31	50	0.4	0.4	<.1	<.1
30 099	Teton	6,271	97.7	<.1	0.1	1.5	<.1	0.6	31	19	34	25	0.8	0.8	0.1	0.2
30 101	Toole	5,046	96.5	<.1	0.3	2.3	0.0	0.7	35	35	17	17	0.6	0.7	0.2	0.3
30 103	Treasure	874	96.1	0.0	0.2	0.7	0.0	3.0	55	37	55	44	0.1	0.1	0.0	<.1
30 105	Valley	8,239	89.7	0.1	0.2	9.2	<.1	0.8	24	49	15	9	1.0	1.0	0.4	1.6
30 107	Wheatland	2,246	97.8	<.1	0.4	0.8	0.0	1.0	47	18	35	38	0.3	0.3	<.1	<.1
30 109	Wibaux	1,191	99.5	0.0	0.2	0.2	0.0	0.2	53	3	56	56	0.1	0.2	0.0	<.1
30 111	Yellowstone	113,419	93.5	0.4	0.5	2.7	<.1	2.8	1	45	3	15	14.2	14.5	20.7	6.6
30 113	Yellowstone National Park	52	100.0	0.0	0.0	0.0	0.0	0.0	57	1	57	57	<.1	<.1	0.0	0.0
30	MONTANA	799,065	91.8	0.3	0.5	5.8	<.1	1.5					100.0	100.0	100.0	100.0
	CONGRESSIONAL District At-Large	799,065	91.8	0.3	0.5	5.8	<.1	1.5								

¹Non-Hispanic Native American.

Table B. – 1990 Voting Age Population (VAP) by Race and Ethnic Origin

County	Total Voting Age Population	Percent of total VAP — Non-Hispanic — White	Black	Asian and Pacific Islander	Native American	Other	Hispanic	Rank Percent of total VAP — Total	Non-Hispanic White	Black	Native American¹	Percent contribution to state VAP — Total	Non-Hispanic White	Black	Native American¹	VAP percent of total population — Total	Non-Hispanic White	Black	Asian and Pacific Islander	Native American	Other	Hispanic
Beaverhead	6,083	97.1	<.1	0.3	1.2	0.0	1.3	23	33	32	28	1.1	1.1	0.1	0.3	72.2	72.6	25.0	65.5	62.1	0.0	60.9
Big Horn	7,181	49.4	0.1	0.4	47.8	0.0	2.3	18	56	10	2	1.2	0.7	0.6	12.6	63.3	73.8	56.3	63.0	55.6	0.0	56.5
Blaine	4,494	66.4	<.1	<.1	32.9	0.0	0.6	29	54	20	4	0.8	0.6	0.2	5.4	66.8	74.1	50.0	33.3	56.0	0.0	53.7
Broadwater	2,363	98.0	0.0	<.1	1.3	<.1	0.6	38	22	35	26	0.4	0.4	0.0	0.1	71.2	71.6	0.0	40.0	71.4	100.0	39.4
Carbon	5,903	98.6	<.1	0.2	0.5	0.0	0.7	25	14	34	50	1.0	1.1	<.1	0.1	73.1	73.4	33.3	76.5	68.3	0.0	47.8
Carter	1,117	98.7	0.0	<.1	0.7	0.0	0.4	50	11	36	42	0.2	0.2	0.0	<.1	74.3	74.5	0.0	50.0	88.9	0.0	41.7
Cascade	56,135	93.4	1.2	0.9	3.0	<.1	1.5	3	47	1	14	9.7	9.7	47.0	6.2	72.3	73.2	66.3	69.0	58.2	38.2	59.1
Chouteau	3,913	96.0	0.1	<.1	3.6	0.0	0.3	33	42	12	13	0.7	0.7	0.3	0.5	71.8	72.1	100.0	37.5	66.2	0.0	48.0
Custer	8,484	97.4	<.1	0.2	1.1	0.0	1.1	14	28	25	29	1.5	1.5	0.3	0.4	72.5	73.1	45.5	73.1	50.3	0.0	60.6
Daniels	1,688	98.9	0.0	0.5	0.2	0.0	0.4	44	10	37	55	0.3	0.3	0.0	<.1	74.5	74.9	0.0	44.4	66.7	0.0	50.0
Dawson	6,877	98.5	0.0	0.2	0.7	0.0	0.6	20	15	38	44	1.2	1.3	0.0	0.2	72.4	72.6	0.0	46.4	66.7	0.0	60.9
Deer Lodge	7,887	95.9	0.3	0.2	2.3	<.1	1.3	15	43	5	15	1.4	1.4	1.7	0.7	76.7	77.1	82.8	57.1	73.6	60.0	63.7
Fallon	2,154	99.2	0.0	0.4	0.3	0.0	0.2	41	6	39	53	0.4	0.4	0.0	<.1	69.4	69.5	0.0	61.5	66.7	0.0	66.7
Fergus	8,861	98.4	<.1	<.1	1.0	0.0	0.5	13	17	26	34	1.5	1.6	0.3	0.3	73.3	73.4	50.0	53.8	75.7	0.0	61.1
Flathead	42,469	97.4	<.1	0.4	1.4	<.1	0.8	4	30	18	25	7.4	7.7	2.2	2.1	71.7	72.0	58.2	68.0	66.4	50.0	57.1
Gallatin	38,195	96.9	0.2	0.9	1.0	<.1	1.0	5	36	8	32	6.6	6.9	4.0	1.4	75.7	75.9	74.4	73.9	65.2	57.1	66.9
Garfield	1,108	99.7	0.0	0.0	0.3	0.0	0.0	51	2	40	54	0.2	0.2	0.0	<.1	69.7	69.8	0.0	0.0	75.0	0.0	0.0
Glacier	7,625	48.7	0.1	<.1	50.6	0.0	0.5	16	57	11	1	1.3	0.7	0.6	14.2	62.9	70.8	72.7	70.0	57.0	0.0	47.4
Golden Valley	659	98.3	0.0	0.5	0.9	0.0	0.3	54	19	41	36	0.1	0.1	0.0	<.1	72.3	72.8	0.0	75.0	60.0	0.0	25.0
Granite	1,870	98.7	0.0	0.1	0.7	0.0	0.5	42	13	42	40	0.3	0.3	0.0	<.1	73.4	73.4	0.0	50.0	66.7	0.0	100.0
Hill	12,243	86.4	<.1	0.5	12.3	<.1	0.8	11	51	17	7	2.1	2.0	0.7	5.5	69.3	72.2	52.6	69.8	55.1	100.0	54.0
Jefferson	5,601	97.4	<.1	0.2	1.5	<.1	0.9	26	29	31	22	1.0	1.0	0.1	0.3	70.6	70.7	50.0	60.0	70.1	40.0	60.2
Judith Basin	1,701	99.1	0.0	0.1	0.4	0.0	0.4	43	7	43	52	0.3	0.3	0.0	<.1	74.5	74.5	0.0	40.0	100.0	0.0	75.0
Lake	14,692	80.4	<.1	0.1	18.1	<.1	1.3	9	52	29	6	2.5	2.2	0.4	9.7	69.8	72.6	42.9	58.1	61.5	54.5	48.8
Lewis and Clark	34,351	96.6	<.1	0.4	1.9	<.1	0.9	6	38	15	17	6.0	6.2	2.3	2.4	72.3	72.8	52.4	66.1	64.8	41.7	55.0
Liberty	1,563	99.1	0.0	<.1	0.7	0.0	0.1	47	8	44	43	0.3	0.3	0.0	<.1	68.1	68.1	0.0	33.3	100.0	0.0	50.0
Lincoln	12,252	97.3	<.1	0.3	1.5	<.1	0.9	10	31	30	21	2.1	2.2	0.3	0.7	70.1	70.3	45.5	59.3	67.4	100.0	57.9
McCone	1,619	99.0	<.1	<.1	0.7	0.0	0.2	46	9	23	41	0.3	0.3	<.1	<.1	71.1	71.3	100.0	50.0	70.6	0.0	30.0
Madison	4,460	97.8	0.0	0.2	0.6	0.0	1.3	30	26	45	47	0.8	0.8	0.0	0.1	74.5	74.6	0.0	61.5	68.3	0.0	68.2
Meagher	1,335	98.1	0.0	0.1	0.7	0.0	1.1	49	21	46	46	0.2	0.2	0.0	<.1	73.4	73.8	0.0	100.0	52.9	0.0	57.7
Mineral	2,334	97.0	0.0	0.5	1.7	0.0	0.8	39	35	47	20	0.4	0.4	0.0	0.1	70.4	71.3	0.0	54.5	52.7	0.0	46.3
Missoula	58,454	96.0	0.2	0.9	1.9	<.1	1.0	2	41	6	19	10.1	10.4	8.8	4.0	74.3	74.8	73.3	65.8	64.0	55.6	61.9
Musselshell	3,063	98.7	0.0	0.2	0.6	0.0	0.6	37	12	48	49	0.5	0.6	0.0	<.1	74.6	75.0	0.0	62.5	65.4	0.0	47.2
Park	10,879	97.1	0.4	0.4	0.6	<.1	1.4	12	34	3	48	1.9	2.0	3.0	0.2	74.7	75.0	71.7	69.7	61.8	66.7	66.4
Petroleum	378	99.2	0.0	0.0	0.8	0.0	0.0	56	5	49	39	<.1	<.1	0.0	<.1	72.8	72.7	0.0	0.0	100.0	0.0	0.0
Phillips	3,602	92.0	<.1	0.1	7.2	0.0	0.6	34	48	23	10	0.6	0.6	<.1	0.9	69.3	70.3	50.0	38.5	67.0	0.0	52.3
Pondera	4,460	90.3	<.1	0.4	8.8	0.0	0.4	31	50	21	8	0.8	0.7	0.2	1.4	69.3	71.0	60.0	85.0	55.9	0.0	61.3
Powder River	1,514	97.9	0.0	0.1	1.4	0.0	0.6	48	25	50	24	0.3	0.3	0.0	<.1	72.4	73.0	0.0	66.7	56.8	0.0	45.0
Powell	5,134	93.9	0.4	0.3	4.4	<.1	1.0	27	45	2	12	0.9	0.9	1.5	0.8	77.6	77.2	95.5	56.0	88.9	100.0	66.2
Prairie	1,056	98.2	0.0	0.2	0.9	0.0	0.7	52	20	51	35	0.2	0.2	0.0	<.1	76.4	76.9	0.0	50.0	66.7	0.0	43.8
Ravalli	18,159	97.5	<.1	0.2	1.0	<.1	1.2	8	27	19	33	3.1	3.3	0.9	0.7	72.6	73.0	38.2	56.3	65.5	100.0	58.8
Richland	7,330	96.8	0.0	0.2	1.1	0.0	2.0	17	37	52	30	1.3	1.3	0.0	0.3	68.4	68.8	0.0	54.2	56.1	0.0	60.4
Roosevelt	7,123	56.5	<.1	0.3	42.4	<.1	0.6	19	55	13	3	1.2	0.7	0.5	11.1	64.8	72.6	41.2	57.5	57.1	100.0	42.7
Rosebud	6,670	76.0	0.2	0.4	21.9	0.0	1.5	21	53	7	5	1.2	0.9	0.8	5.4	63.5	67.9	48.0	48.0	53.5	0.0	44.8
Sanders	6,185	93.9	0.1	0.2	4.9	0.0	0.9	22	46	9	11	1.1	1.1	0.6	1.1	71.3	72.0	75.0	38.9	65.4	0.0	54.8
Sheridan	3,484	98.4	0.0	0.1	1.1	0.0	0.4	36	16	53	31	0.6	0.6	0.0	0.1	73.6	74.0	0.0	41.7	74.0	0.0	34.2
Silver Bow	25,503	96.4	<.1	0.4	1.2	<.1	1.9	7	39	14	27	4.4	4.6	1.7	1.1	75.1	75.6	78.1	72.8	64.6	20.0	61.4
Stillwater	4,713	98.4	0.0	<.1	0.7	0.0	0.9	28	18	54	45	0.8	0.9	0.0	0.1	72.1	72.6	0.0	12.5	66.7	0.0	47.8
Sweet Grass	2,316	99.3	<.1	0.1	0.4	<.1	<.1	40	4	28	51	0.4	0.4	<.1	<.1	73.4	73.7	50.0	60.0	62.5	66.7	14.3
Teton	4,447	98.0	<.1	<.1	1.4	<.1	0.4	32	23	27	23	0.8	0.8	0.1	0.2	70.9	71.1	66.7	44.4	68.5	33.3	54.1
Toole	3,569	97.2	<.1	0.3	1.9	0.0	0.6	35	32	16	18	0.6	0.6	0.2	0.2	70.7	71.2	60.0	68.8	56.8	0.0	55.6
Treasure	629	96.0	0.0	0.3	0.8	0.0	2.9	55	40	55	38	0.1	0.1	0.0	<.1	72.0	71.9	0.0	100.0	83.3	0.0	69.2
Valley	5,990	91.6	<.1	0.2	7.4	<.1	0.6	24	49	22	9	1.0	1.0	0.3	1.6	72.7	74.3	44.4	73.7	58.8	100.0	59.7
Wheatland	1,637	97.9	<.1	0.3	0.9	0.0	0.9	45	24	24	37	0.3	0.3	<.1	<.1	72.9	73.0	100.0	62.5	73.7	0.0	63.6
Wibaux	861	99.4	0.0	0.2	0.1	0.0	0.2	53	3	56	56	0.1	0.2	0.0	<.1	72.3	72.2	0.0	100.0	50.0	0.0	100.0
Yellowstone	82,546	94.8	0.3	0.5	2.2	<.1	2.2	1	44	4	16	14.3	14.5	19.8	6.6	72.8	73.8	61.1	64.7	57.9	39.5	57.5
Yellowstone National Park	42	100.0	0.0	0.0	0.0	0.0	0.0	57	1	57	57	<.1	<.1	0.0	0.0	80.8	80.8	0.0	0.0	0.0	0.0	0.0
MONTANA	**576,961**	**93.3**	**0.2**	**0.5**	**4.7**	**<.1**	**1.2**					**100.0**	**100.0**	**100.0**	**100.0**	**72.2**	**73.4**	**64.1**	**65.9**	**58.6**	**46.2**	**58.0**
CONGRESSIONAL District At-Large	576,961	93.3	0.2	0.5	4.7	<.1	1.2									72.2	73.4	64.1	65.9	58.6	46.2	58.0

¹Non-Hispanic Native American.

Table C. — Voter Participation: November 3, 1992, General Election

| County | Estimated Voting Age Population (VAP), 1992 | Voter registration (REG) | | | | Voter turnout | | | | | | | | | | | | | |
| | | Total | % contribution to state REG | % of 1992 VAP | Rank by % of 1992 VAP | Highest office | | | | Maximum vote | | | | | | Percent drop-off, by office | | | |
						Actual	Total	Office	% of 1992 VAP	Total	% contribution to state turnout	% of REG	Rank by % of REG	% of 1992 VAP	Rank by % 1992 VAP	President	Senator	Governor	Representative
Beaverhead	6,139	5,286	1.0	86.1	47	4,210	4,160	P	67.8	4,210	1.0	79.6	30	68.6	45	1.2	-	2.1	1.8
Big Horn	7,380	6,268	1.2	84.9	51	4,516	4,403	C	59.7	4,516	1.1	72.0	53	61.2	52	2.7	-	3.5	2.5
Blaine	4,510	4,297	0.8	95.3	20	3,073	3,046	P	67.5	3,073	0.7	71.5	54	68.1	47	0.9	-	2.3	1.8
Broadwater	2,417	2,388	0.5	98.8	8	1,878	1,842	P	76.2	1,878	0.4	78.6	37	77.7	17	1.9	-	3.5	2.5
Carbon	6,107	6,013	1.1	98.5	11	4,837	4,754	C	77.8	4,837	1.2	80.4	24	79.2	12	4.5	-	3.2	1.7
Carter	1,093	1,126	0.2	103.0	4	892	874	P	80.0	892	0.2	79.2	34	81.6	7	2.0	-	4.5	4.4
Cascade	56,037	46,129	8.7	82.3	53	36,990	36,580	P	65.3	36,990	8.9	80.2	28	66.0	51	1.1	-	2.1	1.6
Chouteau	3,916	3,814	0.7	97.4	14	3,268	3,236	P	82.6	3,268	0.8	85.7	1	83.5	6	1.0	-	2.3	1.9
Custer	8,429	7,170	1.4	85.1	49	5,760	5,636	C	66.9	5,760	1.4	80.3	26	68.3	46	2.6	-	2.9	2.2
Daniels	1,649	1,622	0.3	98.4	12	1,385	1,363	P	82.7	1,385	0.3	85.4	2	84.0	5	1.6	-	2.5	1.9
Dawson	6,624	6,400	1.2	96.6	16	5,016	4,929	C	74.4	5,016	1.2	78.4	39	75.7	21	3.3	-	3.4	1.7
Deer Lodge	7,625	6,519	1.2	85.5	48	5,362	5,269	P	69.1	5,362	1.3	82.3	12	70.3	41	1.7	-	3.3	2.1
Fallon	2,108	2,011	0.4	95.4	19	1,655	1,608	P	76.3	1,655	0.4	82.3	11	78.5	13	2.8	-	5.0	12.4
Fergus	8,781	8,130	1.5	92.6	25	6,622	6,491	P	73.9	6,622	1.6	81.5	18	75.4	22	2.0	-	2.1	8.0
Flathead	44,641	39,749	7.5	89.0	39	31,924	31,417	P	70.4	31,924	7.6	80.3	27	71.5	37	1.6	-	2.3	9.7
Gallatin[1]	39,112	37,750	7.1	96.5	17	29,145	28,787	P	73.6	29,145	7.0	77.2	45	74.5	26	1.2	-	1.8	1.5
Garfield	1,135	1,049	0.2	92.4	29	822	819	P	72.2	822	0.2	78.4	40	72.4	31	0.4	-	1.9	0.9
Glacier	8,009	6,559	1.2	81.9	54	4,458	4,343	G	54.2	4,458	1.1	68.0	56	55.7	56	3.0	-	2.6	7.6
Golden Valley	671	631	0.1	94.0	21	503	496	P	73.9	503	0.1	79.7	29	75.0	23	1.4	-	2.6	1.8
Granite	1,893	1,726	0.3	91.2	36	1,349	1,323	P	69.9	1,349	0.3	78.2	42	71.3	38	1.9	-	3.0	2.4
Hill	12,293	10,657	2.0	86.7	44	8,279	8,082	P	65.7	8,279	2.0	77.7	43	67.3	48	2.4	-	3.0	2.5
Jefferson	5,896	5,542	1.0	94.0	22	4,352	4,281	C	72.6	4,352	1.0	78.5	38	73.8	30	2.9	-	3.0	1.6
Judith Basin	1,688	1,819	0.3	107.8	1	1,476	1,462	C	86.6	1,476	0.4	81.1	20	87.4	2	2.0	-	3.0	0.9
Lake	15,280	13,180	2.5	86.3	45	10,692	10,553	P	69.1	10,692	2.6	81.1	21	70.0	42	1.3	-	2.0	2.7
Lewis and Clark	35,406	33,003	6.2	93.2	24	26,527	26,181	P	73.9	26,527	6.4	80.4	25	74.9	24	1.3	-	1.6	1.7
Liberty	1,582	1,439	0.3	91.0	37	1,226	1,216	C	76.9	1,226	0.3	85.2	3	77.5	18	1.2	-	1.1	0.8
Lincoln	12,459	11,482	2.2	92.2	31	8,567	8,378	P	67.2	8,567	2.1	74.6	51	68.8	43	2.2	-	3.9	4.4
McCone	1,627	1,622	0.3	99.7	7	1,368	1,354	P	83.2	1,368	0.3	84.3	8	84.1	4	1.0	-	1.5	2.5
Madison	4,659	4,133	0.8	88.7	40	3,348	3,299	P	70.8	3,348	0.8	81.0	22	71.9	34	1.5	-	2.7	2.2
Meagher	1,335	1,287	0.2	96.4	18	1,021	1,002	P	75.1	1,021	0.2	79.3	33	76.5	20	1.9	-	3.5	7.9
Mineral	2,352	2,175	0.4	92.5	27	1,666	1,635	P	69.5	1,666	0.4	76.6	47	70.8	39	1.9	-	3.1	7.1
Missoula	58,721	57,490	10.9	97.9	13	43,614	43,307	P	73.8	43,614	10.4	75.9	49	74.3	28	0.7	-	1.4	1.4
Musselshell	3,118	2,882	0.5	92.4	28	2,253	2,228	P	71.5	2,253	0.5	78.2	41	72.3	32	1.1	-	2.2	1.2
Park[1]	11,384	9,808	1.9	86.2	46	7,548	7,483	P	65.7	7,548	1.8	77.0	46	66.3	50	0.9	-	1.4	1.2
Petroleum	378	367	<.1	97.1	15	300	298	C	78.8	300	<.1	81.7	16	79.4	11	1.3	-	1.3	0.7
Phillips	3,692	3,258	0.6	88.2	41	2,652	2,625	P	71.1	2,652	0.6	81.4	19	71.8	35	1.0	-	1.8	1.9
Pondera	4,505	3,955	0.7	87.8	42	3,240	3,175	G	70.5	3,240	0.8	81.9	14	71.9	33	2.3	-	2.0	6.6
Powder River	1,480	1,482	0.3	100.1	6	1,176	1,156	P	78.1	1,176	0.3	79.4	32	79.5	10	1.7	-	12.6	2.6
Powell	5,124	3,675	0.7	71.7	56	3,019	2,969	C	57.9	3,019	0.7	82.1	13	58.9	53	2.7	-	2.4	1.7
Prairie	996	1,040	0.2	104.4	2	886	856	P	85.9	886	0.2	85.2	4	89.0	1	3.4	-	4.7	3.7
Ravalli	18,895	19,134	3.6	101.3	5	15,125	15,020	P	79.5	15,125	3.6	79.0	35	80.0	9	0.7	-	1.8	1.5
Richland	7,304	6,100	1.2	83.5	52	4,850	4,748	P	65.0	4,850	1.2	79.5	31	66.4	49	2.1	-	2.5	8.2
Roosevelt	7,348	6,249	1.2	85.0	50	4,284	4,193	P	57.1	4,284	1.0	68.6	55	58.3	54	2.1	-	3.0	7.1
Rosebud	6,990	5,533	1.0	79.2	55	4,063	4,007	C	57.3	4,063	1.0	73.4	52	58.1	55	3.6	-	3.0	1.4
Sanders	6,347	5,961	1.1	93.9	23	4,558	4,506	P	71.0	4,558	1.1	76.5	48	71.8	36	1.1	-	2.8	3.0
Sheridan	3,464	3,206	0.6	92.6	26	2,705	2,663	P	76.9	2,705	0.6	84.4	7	78.1	14	1.6	-	3.0	2.3
Silver Bow	25,024	22,827	4.3	91.2	34	18,665	18,146	P	72.5	18,665	4.5	81.8	15	74.6	25	2.8	-	3.6	8.8
Stillwater	5,003	4,597	0.9	91.9	32	3,720	3,670	C	73.4	3,720	0.9	80.9	23	74.4	27	2.2	-	2.5	1.3
Sweet Grass	2,349	2,169	0.4	92.3	30	1,826	1,802	P	76.7	1,826	0.4	84.2	9	77.7	16	1.3	-	2.8	2.5
Teton	4,484	4,105	0.8	91.5	33	3,493	3,405	P	75.9	3,493	0.8	85.1	5	77.9	15	2.5	-	3.8	3.2
Toole	3,601	3,273	0.6	90.9	38	2,766	2,717	P	75.5	2,766	0.7	84.5	6	76.8	19	1.8	-	2.4	7.6
Treasure	642	664	0.1	103.4	3	549	547	P	85.2	549	0.1	82.7	10	85.5	3	0.4	-	0.9	0.5
Valley	5,785	5,707	1.1	98.7	9	4,663	4,568	P	79.0	4,663	1.1	81.7	17	80.6	8	2.0	-	7.0	10.4
Wheatland	1,648	1,503	0.3	91.2	35	1,166	1,150	P	69.8	1,166	0.3	77.6	44	70.8	40	1.4	-	2.4	2.0
Wibaux	850	837	0.2	98.5	10	628	609	C	71.6	628	0.2	75.0	50	73.9	29	3.3	-	4.8	3.0
Yellowstone	84,015	73,024	13.8	86.9	43	57,628	56,538	G	67.3	57,628	13.8	78.9	36	68.6	44	2.0	-	1.9	2.0
MONTANA	586,000	529,822	100.0	90.4		417,564	411,205		70.2	417,564	100.0	78.8		71.3		1.7	-	2.3	3.3

[1]Includes Yellowstone National Park (part), except estimated VAP (all of Yellowstone Park's total estimated VAP has been added to Gallatin's VAP).

Table E. — Vote for President: November 3, 1992, General Election

County	Total	Clinton (DEM)	Bush (REP)	Perot (IND)	Other	Plurality Total	Party	Percent of total vote DEM	REP	IND	Other	Rank DEM	Rank REP	Rank IND	Pct contr. to state vote Total	DEM	REP	IND	Major party DEM	REP
Beaverhead	4,160	1,098	1,746	1,202	114	544	R	26.4	42.0	28.9	2.7	47	16	28	1.0	0.7	1.2	1.1	38.6	61.4
Big Horn	4,394	2,154	1,377	840	23	777	D	49.0	31.3	19.1	0.5	3	46	56	1.1	1.4	1.0	0.8	61.0	39.0
Blaine	3,046	1,355	971	699	21	384	D	44.5	31.9	22.9	0.7	7	45	51	0.7	0.9	0.7	0.7	58.3	41.7
Broadwater	1,842	491	830	505	16	325	R	26.7	45.1	27.4	0.9	45	8	36	0.4	0.3	0.6	0.5	37.2	62.8
Carbon	4,620	1,549	1,562	1,482	27	13	R	33.5	33.8	32.1	0.6	22	42	8	1.1	1.0	1.1	1.4	49.8	50.2
Carter	874	154	497	220	3	277	R	17.6	56.9	25.2	0.3	55	1	45	0.2	<.1	0.3	0.2	23.7	76.3
Cascade	36,580	14,719	12,494	9,151	216	2,225	D	40.2	34.2	25.0	0.6	13	40	46	8.9	9.5	8.7	8.5	54.1	45.9
Chouteau	3,236	959	1,380	870	27	421	R	29.6	42.6	26.9	0.8	38	10	39	0.8	0.6	1.0	0.8	41.0	59.0
Custer	5,611	1,968	2,105	1,505	33	137	R	35.1	37.5	26.8	0.6	19	30	40	1.4	1.3	1.5	1.4	48.3	51.7
Daniels	1,363	457	496	402	8	39	R	33.5	36.4	29.5	0.6	21	34	19	0.3	0.3	0.3	0.4	48.0	52.0
Dawson	4,850	1,785	1,679	1,370	16	106	D	36.8	34.6	28.2	0.3	17	39	32	1.2	1.2	1.2	1.3	51.5	48.5
Deer Lodge	5,269	3,174	832	1,207	56	1,967	D	60.2	15.8	22.9	1.1	1	56	52	1.3	2.1	0.6	1.1	79.2	20.8
Fallon	1,608	446	731	427	4	285	R	27.7	45.5	26.6	0.2	43	7	42	0.4	0.3	0.5	0.4	37.9	62.1
Fergus	6,491	1,615	2,736	1,934	206	802	R	24.9	42.2	29.8	3.2	49	13	17	1.6	1.0	1.9	1.8	37.1	62.9
Flathead	31,417	9,746	11,699	9,109	863	1,953	R	31.0	37.2	29.0	2.7	32	31	26	7.7	6.3	8.1	8.5	45.4	54.6
Gallatin[1]	28,787	9,535	11,109	7,711	432	1,574	R	33.1	38.6	26.8	1.5	25	25	41	7.0	6.2	7.7	7.2	46.2	53.8
Garfield	819	125	403	281	10	122	R	15.3	49.2	34.3	1.2	56	2	2	0.2	<.1	0.3	0.3	23.7	76.3
Glacier	4,323	2,076	1,222	997	28	854	D	48.0	28.3	23.1	0.6	4	53	50	1.1	1.3	0.8	0.9	62.9	37.1
Golden Valley	496	142	192	157	5	35	R	28.6	38.7	31.7	1.0	41	24	9	0.1	<.1	0.1	0.1	42.5	57.5
Granite	1,323	358	556	386	23	170	R	27.1	42.0	29.2	1.7	44	15	22	0.3	0.2	0.4	0.4	39.2	60.8
Hill	8,082	3,618	2,408	2,017	39	1,210	D	44.8	29.8	25.0	0.5	6	49	47	2.0	2.3	1.7	1.9	60.0	40.0
Jefferson	4,225	1,415	1,541	1,172	97	126	R	33.5	36.5	27.7	2.3	23	33	35	1.0	0.9	1.1	1.1	47.9	52.1
Judith Basin	1,447	409	610	415	13	195	R	28.3	42.2	28.7	0.9	42	12	29	0.4	0.3	0.4	0.4	40.1	59.9
Lake	10,553	3,938	3,596	2,878	141	342	D	37.3	34.1	27.3	1.3	16	41	37	2.6	2.5	2.5	2.7	52.3	47.7
Lewis and Clark	26,181	11,117	9,351	5,560	153	1,766	D	42.5	35.7	21.2	0.6	10	37	54	6.4	7.2	6.5	5.2	54.3	45.7
Liberty	1,211	321	512	363	15	149	R	26.5	42.3	30.0	1.2	46	11	16	0.3	0.2	0.4	0.3	38.5	61.5
Lincoln	8,378	2,765	2,799	2,637	177	34	R	33.0	33.4	31.5	2.1	27	43	11	2.0	1.8	1.9	2.5	49.7	50.3
McCone	1,354	424	528	395	7	104	R	31.3	39.0	29.2	0.5	31	23	23	0.3	0.3	0.4	0.4	44.5	55.5
Madison	3,299	779	1,415	1,043	62	372	R	23.6	42.9	31.6	1.9	51	9	10	0.8	0.5	1.0	1.0	35.5	64.5
Meagher	1,002	260	422	310	10	112	R	25.9	42.1	30.9	1.0	48	14	13	0.2	0.2	0.3	0.3	38.1	61.9
Mineral	1,635	664	403	543	25	121	D	40.6	24.6	33.2	1.5	11	54	4	0.4	0.4	0.3	0.5	62.2	37.8
Missoula	43,307	20,347	12,898	9,735	327	7,449	D	47.0	29.8	22.5	0.8	5	50	53	10.5	13.2	8.9	9.1	61.2	38.8
Musselshell	2,228	648	876	691	13	185	R	29.1	39.3	31.0	0.6	39	21	12	0.5	0.4	0.6	0.6	42.5	57.5
Park[1]	7,483	2,258	2,846	2,182	197	588	R	30.2	38.0	29.2	2.6	37	28	24	1.8	1.5	2.0	2.0	44.2	55.8
Petroleum	296	61	135	95	5	40	R	20.6	45.6	32.1	1.7	54	6	7	<.1	<.1	<.1	<.1	31.1	68.9
Phillips	2,625	634	1,026	949	16	77	R	24.2	39.1	36.2	0.6	50	22	1	0.6	0.4	0.7	0.9	38.2	61.8
Pondera	3,165	1,046	1,252	855	12	206	R	33.0	39.6	27.0	0.4	26	20	38	0.8	0.7	0.9	0.8	45.5	54.5
Powder River	1,156	258	547	340	11	207	R	22.3	47.3	29.4	1.0	52	5	20	0.3	0.2	0.4	0.3	32.0	68.0
Powell	2,938	989	1,058	872	19	69	R	33.7	36.0	29.7	0.6	20	35	18	0.7	0.6	0.7	0.8	48.3	51.7
Prairie	856	260	412	179	5	152	R	30.4	48.1	20.9	0.6	35	4	55	0.2	0.2	0.3	0.2	38.7	61.3
Ravalli	15,020	4,644	5,392	4,573	411	748	R	30.9	35.9	30.4	2.7	33	36	15	3.7	3.0	3.7	4.3	46.3	53.7
Richland	4,748	1,440	1,760	1,525	23	235	R	30.3	37.1	32.1	0.5	36	32	6	1.2	0.9	1.2	1.4	45.0	55.0
Roosevelt	4,193	1,827	1,212	1,089	65	615	D	43.6	28.9	26.0	1.6	8	51	43	1.0	1.2	0.8	1.0	60.1	39.9
Rosebud	3,918	1,669	1,130	1,099	20	539	D	42.6	28.8	28.1	0.5	9	52	34	1.0	1.1	0.8	1.0	59.6	40.4
Sanders	4,506	1,689	1,361	1,378	78	311	D	37.5	30.2	30.6	1.7	15	47	14	1.1	1.1	0.9	1.3	55.4	44.6
Sheridan	2,663	1,077	795	782	9	282	D	40.4	29.9	29.4	0.3	12	48	21	0.6	0.7	0.6	0.7	57.5	42.5
Silver Bow	18,146	9,960	3,491	4,570	125	5,390	D	54.9	19.2	25.2	0.7	2	55	44	4.4	6.4	2.4	4.3	74.0	26.0
Stillwater	3,640	1,178	1,390	1,056	16	212	R	32.4	38.2	29.0	0.4	28	27	25	0.9	0.8	1.0	1.0	45.9	54.1
Sweet Grass	1,802	395	880	507	20	373	R	21.9	48.8	28.1	1.1	53	3	33	0.4	0.3	0.6	0.5	31.0	69.0
Teton	3,405	1,043	1,364	969	29	321	R	30.6	40.1	28.5	0.9	34	19	31	0.8	0.7	0.9	0.9	43.3	56.7
Toole	2,717	854	943	903	17	40	R	31.4	34.7	33.2	0.6	30	38	5	0.7	0.6	0.7	0.8	47.5	52.5
Treasure	547	157	206	178	6	28	R	28.7	37.7	32.5	1.1	40	29	5	0.1	0.1	0.1	0.2	43.3	56.7
Valley	4,568	1,715	1,497	1,320	36	218	D	37.5	32.8	28.9	0.8	14	44	27	1.1	1.1	1.0	1.2	53.4	46.6
Wheatland	1,150	384	478	284	4	94	R	33.4	41.6	24.7	0.3	24	17	48	0.3	0.2	0.3	0.3	44.5	55.5
Wibaux	607	195	234	173	5	39	R	32.1	38.6	28.5	0.8	29	26	30	0.1	0.1	0.2	0.2	45.5	54.5
Yellowstone	56,451	20,163	22,822	13,133	333	2,659	R	35.7	40.4	23.3	0.6	18	18	49	13.7	13.0	15.8	12.2	46.9	53.1
MONTANA	410,611	154,507	144,207	107,225	4,672	10,300	D	37.6	35.1	26.1	1.1				100.0	100.0	100.0	100.0	51.7	48.3

[1]Includes part of Yellowstone National Park.

Table G. – Vote for Governor: November 3, 1992, General Election

County	Total	Bradley (DEM)	Racicot (REP)		Plurality Total	Party	DEM	REP		Rank DEM	Rank REP		Total	DEM	REP	
Beaverhead	4,122	1,569	2,553	-	984	R	38.1	61.9	-	39	18	-	1.0	0.8	1.2	-
Big Horn	4,358	2,531	1,827	-	704	D	58.1	41.9	-	4	53	-	1.1	1.3	0.9	-
Blaine	3,001	1,682	1,319	-	363	D	56.0	44.0	-	10	47	-	0.7	0.8	0.6	-
Broadwater	1,812	657	1,155	-	498	R	36.3	63.7	-	47	10	-	0.4	0.3	0.6	-
Carbon	4,681	2,115	2,566	-	451	R	45.2	54.8	-	23	34	-	1.1	1.1	1.2	-
Carter	852	215	637	-	422	R	25.2	74.8	-	55	2	-	0.2	0.1	0.3	-
Cascade	36,224	19,405	16,819	-	2,586	D	53.6	46.4	-	12	45	-	8.9	9.8	8.0	-
Chouteau	3,194	1,376	1,818	-	442	R	43.1	56.9	-	26	31	-	0.8	0.7	0.9	-
Custer	5,594	2,658	2,936	-	278	R	47.5	52.5	-	15	42	-	1.4	1.3	1.4	-
Daniels	1,351	531	820	-	289	R	39.3	60.7	-	37	20	-	0.3	0.3	0.4	-
Dawson	4,845	2,238	2,607	-	369	R	46.2	53.8	-	21	36	-	1.2	1.1	1.2	-
Deer Lodge	5,187	3,677	1,510	-	2,167	D	70.9	29.1	-	1	56	-	1.3	1.9	0.7	-
Fallon	1,572	592	980	-	388	R	37.7	62.3	-	41	16	-	0.4	0.3	0.5	-
Fergus	6,485	2,512	3,973	-	1,461	R	38.7	61.3	-	38	19	-	1.6	1.3	1.9	-
Flathead	31,190	13,652	17,538	-	3,886	R	43.8	56.2	-	25	32	-	7.6	6.9	8.4	-
Gallatin[1]	28,623	12,969	15,654	-	2,685	R	45.3	54.7	-	22	35	-	7.0	6.5	7.5	-
Garfield	806	199	607	-	408	R	24.7	75.3	-	56	1	-	0.2	0.1	0.3	-
Glacier	4,343	2,642	1,701	-	941	D	60.8	39.2	-	3	54	-	1.1	1.3	0.8	-
Golden Valley	490	182	308	-	126	R	37.1	62.9	-	45	12	-	0.1	<.1	0.1	-
Granite	1,309	488	821	-	333	R	37.3	62.7	-	43	14	-	0.3	0.2	0.4	-
Hill	8,029	4,582	3,447	-	1,135	D	57.1	42.9	-	7	50	-	2.0	2.3	1.6	-
Jefferson	4,221	1,990	2,231	-	241	R	47.1	52.9	-	17	40	-	1.0	1.0	1.1	-
Judith Basin	1,432	536	896	-	360	R	37.4	62.6	-	42	15	-	0.4	0.3	0.4	-
Lake	10,473	4,998	5,475	-	477	R	47.7	52.3	-	14	43	-	2.6	2.5	2.6	-
Lewis and Clark	26,103	12,988	13,115	-	127	R	49.8	50.2	-	13	44	-	6.4	6.5	6.3	-
Liberty	1,212	457	755	-	298	R	37.7	62.3	-	40	17	-	0.3	0.2	0.4	-
Lincoln	8,236	3,648	4,588	-	940	R	44.3	55.7	-	24	33	-	2.0	1.8	2.2	-
McCone	1,347	539	808	-	269	R	40.0	60.0	-	35	22	-	0.3	0.3	0.4	-
Madison	3,259	1,111	2,148	-	1,037	R	34.1	65.9	-	50	7	-	0.8	0.6	1.0	-
Meagher	985	406	579	-	173	R	41.2	58.8	-	31	26	-	0.2	0.2	0.3	-
Mineral	1,615	933	682	-	251	D	57.8	42.2	-	5	52	-	0.4	0.5	0.3	-
Missoula	42,984	24,453	18,531	-	5,922	D	56.9	43.1	-	8	49	-	10.5	12.3	8.8	-
Musselshell	2,204	721	1,483	-	762	R	32.7	67.3	-	52	5	-	0.5	0.4	0.7	-
Park[1]	7,444	3,156	4,288	-	1,132	R	42.4	57.6	-	29	28	-	1.8	1.6	2.0	-
Petroleum	296	92	204	-	112	R	31.1	68.9	-	53	4	-	<.1	<.1	<.1	-
Phillips	2,604	884	1,720	-	836	R	33.9	66.1	-	51	6	-	0.6	0.4	0.8	-
Pondera	3,175	1,283	1,892	-	609	R	40.4	59.6	-	34	23	-	0.8	0.6	0.9	-
Powder River	1,028	382	646	-	264	R	37.2	62.8	-	44	13	-	0.3	0.2	0.3	-
Powell	2,948	1,386	1,562	-	176	R	47.0	53.0	-	18	39	-	0.7	0.7	0.7	-
Prairie	844	305	539	-	234	R	36.1	63.9	-	48	9	-	0.2	0.2	0.3	-
Ravalli	14,854	6,040	8,814	-	2,774	R	40.7	59.3	-	33	24	-	3.6	3.0	4.2	-
Richland	4,730	2,008	2,722	-	714	R	42.5	57.5	-	28	29	-	1.2	1.0	1.3	-
Roosevelt	4,156	2,391	1,765	-	626	D	57.5	42.5	-	6	51	-	1.0	1.2	0.8	-
Rosebud	3,940	2,224	1,716	-	508	D	56.4	43.6	-	9	48	-	1.0	1.1	0.8	-
Sanders	4,432	2,080	2,352	-	272	R	46.9	53.1	-	19	38	-	1.1	1.0	1.1	-
Sheridan	2,623	1,462	1,161	-	301	D	55.7	44.3	-	11	46	-	0.6	0.7	0.6	-
Silver Bow	17,998	11,470	6,528	-	4,942	D	63.7	36.3	-	2	55	-	4.4	5.8	3.1	-
Stillwater	3,626	1,513	2,113	-	600	R	41.7	58.3	-	30	27	-	0.9	0.8	1.0	-
Sweet Grass	1,774	541	1,233	-	692	R	30.5	69.5	-	54	3	-	0.4	0.3	0.6	-
Teton	3,359	1,341	2,018	-	677	R	39.9	60.1	-	36	21	-	0.8	0.7	1.0	-
Toole	2,699	1,160	1,539	-	379	R	43.0	57.0	-	27	30	-	0.7	0.6	0.7	-
Treasure	544	200	344	-	144	R	36.8	63.2	-	46	11	-	0.1	0.1	0.2	-
Valley	4,335	2,057	2,278	-	221	R	47.5	52.5	-	16	41	-	1.1	1.0	1.1	-
Wheatland	1,138	466	672	-	206	R	40.9	59.1	-	32	25	-	0.3	0.2	0.3	-
Wibaux	598	215	383	-	168	R	36.0	64.0	-	49	8	-	0.1	0.1	0.2	-
Yellowstone	56,538	26,513	30,025	-	3,512	R	46.9	53.1	-	20	37	-	13.9	13.4	14.3	-
MONTANA	**407,822**	**198,421**	**209,401**	-	**10,980**	**R**	**48.7**	**51.3**	-			-	**100.0**	**100.0**	**100.0**	-

[1]Includes part of Yellowstone National Park.

Table H. — Vote for U.S. Representative in Congress: November 3, 1992, General Election

Congressional district and county	Total	Democrat (DEM)	Republican (REP)	Other	Plurality Total	Plurality Party	Percent of total vote DEM	Percent of total vote REP	Percent of total vote Other	Rank within district DEM	Rank within district REP	Rank within district Other	Percent contribution to district vote Total	Percent contribution to district vote DEM	Percent contribution to district vote REP	Percent contribution to district vote Other
District At-Large	403,735	203,711	189,570	10,454	14,141	D	50.5	47.0	2.6				100.0	100.0	100.0	100.0
Beaverhead	4,135	1,531	2,509	95	978	R	37.0	60.7	2.3	33	23	31	1.0	0.8	1.3	0.9
Big Horn	4,403	2,542	1,783	78	759	D	57.7	40.5	1.8	7	50	47	1.1	1.2	0.9	0.7
Blaine	3,017	1,518	1,442	57	76	D	50.3	47.8	1.9	14	43	41	0.7	0.7	0.8	0.5
Broadwater	1,831	706	1,068	57	362	R	38.6	58.3	3.1	31	28	11	0.5	0.3	0.6	0.5
Carbon	4,754	2,279	2,376	99	97	R	47.9	50.0	2.1	18	38	37	1.2	1.1	1.3	0.9
Carter	853	160	677	16	517	R	18.8	79.4	1.9	55	2	42	0.2	0.1	0.4	0.2
Cascade	36,397	18,031	17,413	953	618	D	49.5	47.8	2.6	15	42	25	9.0	8.9	9.2	9.1
Chouteau	3,207	1,050	2,098	59	1,048	R	32.7	65.4	1.8	43	10	45	0.8	0.5	1.1	0.6
Custer	5,636	2,350	3,163	123	813	R	41.7	56.1	2.2	26	30	35	1.4	1.2	1.7	1.2
Daniels	1,359	359	986	14	627	R	26.4	72.6	1.0	52	5	55	0.3	0.2	0.5	0.1
Dawson	4,929	2,239	2,593	97	354	R	45.4	52.6	2.0	22	34	39	1.2	1.1	1.4	0.9
Deer Lodge	5,247	4,151	989	107	3,162	D	79.1	18.8	2.0	1	56	38	1.3	2.0	0.5	1.0
Fallon	1,450	448	975	27	527	R	30.9	67.2	1.9	49	8	44	0.4	0.2	0.5	0.3
Fergus	6,095	2,026	3,871	198	1,845	R	33.2	63.5	3.2	42	16	7	1.5	1.0	2.0	1.9
Flathead	28,822	12,327	15,232	1,263	2,905	R	42.8	52.8	4.4	24	33	1	7.1	6.1	8.0	12.1
Gallatin[1]	28,716	14,628	13,441	647	1,187	D	50.9	46.8	2.3	12	44	33	7.1	7.2	7.1	6.2
Garfield	815	129	678	8	549	R	15.8	83.2	1.0	56	1	56	0.2	0.1	0.4	0.1
Glacier	4,118	2,401	1,611	106	790	D	58.3	39.1	2.6	6	51	26	1.0	1.2	0.8	1.0
Golden Valley	494	156	323	15	167	R	31.6	65.4	3.0	48	11	12	0.1	0.1	0.2	0.1
Granite	1,316	507	768	41	261	R	38.5	58.4	3.1	32	27	10	0.3	0.2	0.4	0.4
Hill	8,076	4,267	3,594	215	673	D	52.8	44.5	2.7	9	47	21	2.0	2.1	1.9	2.1
Jefferson	4,281	2,178	1,984	119	194	D	50.9	46.3	2.8	13	45	17	1.1	1.1	1.0	1.1
Judith Basin	1,462	472	944	46	472	R	32.3	64.6	3.1	47	14	9	0.4	0.2	0.5	0.4
Lake	10,401	5,046	5,077	278	31	R	48.5	48.8	2.7	17	40	20	2.6	2.5	2.7	2.7
Lewis and Clark	26,069	15,904	9,473	692	6,431	D	61.0	36.3	2.7	4	53	22	6.5	7.8	5.0	6.6
Liberty	1,216	397	787	32	390	R	32.6	64.7	2.6	44	13	23	0.3	0.2	0.4	0.3
Lincoln	8,187	3,531	4,304	352	773	R·	43.1	52.6	4.3	23	35	2	2.0	1.7	2.3	3.4
McCone	1,334	458	858	18	400	R	34.3	64.3	1.3	41	15	52	0.3	0.2	0.5	0.2
Madison	3,276	1,212	1,969	95	757	R	37.0	60.1	2.9	34	24	14	0.8	0.6	1.0	0.9
Meagher	940	305	609	26	304	R	32.4	64.8	2.8	46	12	18	0.2	0.1	0.3	0.2
Mineral	1,548	925	570	53	355	D	59.8	36.8	3.4	5	52	4	0.4	0.5	0.3	0.5
Missoula	42,996	27,783	14,206	1,007	13,577	D	64.6	33.0	2.3	3	54	30	10.6	13.6	7.5	9.6
Musselshell	2,227	787	1,404	36	617	R	35.3	63.0	1.6	38	18	49	0.6	0.4	0.7	0.3
Park[1]	7,457	3,418	3,843	196	425	R	45.8	51.5	2.6	21	36	24	1.8	1.7	2.0	1.9
Petroleum	298	69	219	10	150	R	23.2	73.5	3.4	54	3	5	0.1	0.0	0.1	0.1
Phillips	2,602	663	1,892	47	1,229	R	25.5	72.7	1.8	53	4	46	0.6	0.3	1.0	0.4
Pondera	3,025	1,171	1,769	85	598	R	38.7	58.5	2.8	30	26	16	0.7	0.6	0.9	0.8
Powder River	1,145	310	809	26	499	R	27.1	70.7	2.3	51	6	32	0.3	0.2	0.4	0.2
Powell	2,969	1,390	1,498	81	108	R	46.8	50.5	2.7	20	37	19	0.7	0.7	0.8	0.8
Prairie	853	278	566	9	288	R	32.6	66.4	1.1	45	9	54	0.2	0.1	0.3	0.1
Ravalli	14,902	7,098	7,378	426	280	R	47.6	49.5	2.9	19	39	15	3.7	3.5	3.9	4.1
Richland	4,452	1,641	2,716	95	1,075	R	36.9	61.0	2.1	35	22	36	1.1	0.8	1.4	0.9
Roosevelt	3,978	2,069	1,780	129	289	D	52.0	44.7	3.2	11	46	8	1.0	1.0	0.9	1.2
Rosebud	4,007	2,145	1,764	98	381	D	53.5	44.0	2.4	8	49	28	1.0	1.1	0.9	0.9
Sanders	4,419	2,317	1,954	148	363	D	52.4	44.2	3.3	10	48	6	1.1	1.1	1.0	1.4
Sheridan	2,644	1,035	1,580	29	545	R	39.1	59.8	1.1	29	25	53	0.7	0.5	0.8	0.3
Silver Bow	17,031	12,643	3,988	400	8,655	D	74.2	23.4	2.3	2	55	29	4.2	6.2	2.1	3.8
Stillwater	3,670	1,567	2,039	64	472	R	42.7	55.6	1.7	25	32	48	0.9	0.8	1.1	0.6
Sweet Grass	1,780	522	1,223	35	701	R	29.3	68.7	2.0	50	7	40	0.4	0.3	0.6	0.3
Teton	3,381	1,193	2,125	63	932	R	35.3	62.9	1.9	40	19	43	0.8	0.6	1.1	0.6
Toole	2,556	1,043	1,425	88	382	R	40.8	55.8	3.4	28	31	3	0.6	0.5	0.8	0.8
Treasure	546	195	335	16	140	R	35.7	61.4	2.9	37	21	13	0.1	0.1	0.2	0.2
Valley	4,178	1,710	2,361	107	651	R	40.9	56.5	2.6	27	29	27	1.0	0.8	1.2	1.0
Wheatland	1,143	413	714	16	301	R	36.1	62.5	1.4	36	20	51	0.3	0.2	0.4	0.2
Wibaux	609	215	385	9	170	R	35.3	63.2	1.5	39	17	50	0.2	0.1	0.2	0.1
Yellowstone	56,483	27,803	27,432	1,248	371	D	49.2	48.6	2.2	16	41	34	14.0	13.6	14.5	11.9
MONTANA	403,735	203,711	189,570	10,454	14,141	D	50.5	47.0	2.6							

[1]Includes part of Yellowstone National Park.

Table I. — Vote for Presidential Preference: June 2, 1992, Democratic Primary Election

| County | Top candidates | | | | | | | | | Top three candidates (state vote) | | | | | | | | | |
| | | | | | | | | | | Percent of total vote | | | Rank | | | Percent contribution to state vote | | | |
	Total	Clinton	No Pre-ference	Brown	Tsongas					Clinton	No Pre-ference	Brown	Clinton	No Pre-ference	Brown	Total	Clinton	No Pre-ference	Brown
Beaverhead	502	313	0	104	85	-	-	-	-	62.4	0.0	20.7	6	52	10	0.4	0.6	0.0	0.5
Big Horn	1,246	629	213	246	158	-	-	-	-	50.5	17.1	19.7	27	41	13	1.1	1.1	0.8	1.1
Blaine	1,192	626	260	183	123	-	-	-	-	52.5	21.8	15.4	20	33	39	1.0	1.1	0.9	0.8
Broadwater	381	221	8	69	83	-	-	-	-	58.0	2.1	18.1	15	50	21	0.3	0.4	<.1	0.3
Carbon	1,245	559	285	263	138	-	-	-	-	44.9	22.9	21.1	43	30	8	1.1	1.0	1.0	1.2
Carter	98	58	13	19	8	-	-	-	-	59.2	13.3	19.4	12	47	15	<.1	0.1	<.1	<.1
Cascade	11,287	5,522	2,689	1,994	1,082	-	-	-	-	48.9	23.8	17.7	30	27	25	9.6	10.0	9.5	9.2
Chouteau	929	454	232	137	106	-	-	-	-	48.9	25.0	14.7	31	22	41	0.8	0.8	0.8	0.6
Custer	1,462	895	0	331	236	-	-	-	-	61.2	0.0	22.6	8	53	4	1.2	1.6	0.0	1.5
Daniels	265	156	43	37	29	-	-	-	-	58.9	16.2	14.0	13	43	44	0.2	0.3	0.2	0.2
Dawson	1,331	903	0	239	189	-	-	-	-	67.8	0.0	18.0	2	54	23	1.1	1.6	0.0	1.1
Deer Lodge	2,626	1,384	528	493	221	-	-	-	-	52.7	20.1	18.8	19	36	16	2.2	2.5	1.9	2.3
Fallon	379	179	121	42	37	-	-	-	-	47.2	31.9	11.1	36	5	54	0.3	0.3	0.4	0.2
Fergus	1,606	741	434	251	180	-	-	-	-	46.1	27.0	15.6	40	16	38	1.4	1.3	1.5	1.2
Flathead	7,691	3,105	2,354	1,421	811	-	-	-	-	40.4	30.6	18.5	53	6	18	6.5	5.6	8.4	6.5
Gallatin[1]	6,682	2,394	2,029	1,445	814	-	-	-	-	35.8	30.4	21.6	55	7	6	5.7	4.4	7.2	6.7
Garfield	131	72	28	14	17	-	-	-	-	55.0	21.4	10.7	17	34	56	0.1	0.1	<.1	<.1
Glacier	1,967	880	561	335	191	-	-	-	-	44.7	28.5	17.0	44	12	29	1.7	1.6	2.0	1.5
Golden Valley	114	64	18	21	11	-	-	-	-	56.1	15.8	18.4	16	44	19	<.1	0.1	<.1	<.1
Granite	300	138	87	45	30	-	-	-	-	46.0	29.0	15.0	41	11	40	0.3	0.3	0.3	0.2
Hill	3,712	1,748	1,044	600	320	-	-	-	-	47.1	28.1	16.2	37	13	35	3.2	3.2	3.7	2.8
Jefferson	1,488	647	388	262	191	-	-	-	-	43.5	26.1	17.6	47	18	26	1.3	1.2	1.4	1.2
Judith Basin	383	252	0	71	60	-	-	-	-	65.8	0.0	18.5	3	55	17	0.3	0.5	0.0	0.3
Lake	2,318	1,076	651	375	216	-	-	-	-	46.4	28.1	16.2	39	14	34	2.0	2.0	2.3	1.7
Lewis and Clark	9,513	4,431	1,955	1,987	1,140	-	-	-	-	46.6	20.6	20.9	38	35	9	8.1	8.1	6.9	9.2
Liberty	378	195	90	49	44	-	-	-	-	51.6	23.8	13.0	25	28	49	0.3	0.4	0.3	0.2
Lincoln	3,136	1,298	1,079	405	354	-	-	-	-	41.4	34.4	12.9	51	2	50	2.7	2.4	3.8	1.9
McCone	338	197	53	60	28	-	-	-	-	58.3	15.7	17.8	14	45	24	0.3	0.4	0.2	0.3
Madison	601	247	193	110	51	-	-	-	-	41.1	32.1	18.3	52	4	20	0.5	0.4	0.7	0.5
Meagher	198	121	0	47	30	-	-	-	-	61.1	0.0	23.7	9	56	3	0.2	0.2	0.0	0.2
Mineral	792	341	261	104	86	-	-	-	-	43.1	33.0	13.1	50	3	47	0.7	0.6	0.9	0.5
Missoula	12,320	5,549	2,725	2,777	1,269	-	-	-	-	45.0	22.1	22.5	42	32	5	10.5	10.1	9.7	12.8
Musselshell	490	253	111	72	54	-	-	-	-	51.6	22.7	14.7	24	31	42	0.4	0.5	0.4	0.3
Park[1]	1,565	677	398	321	169	-	-	-	-	43.3	25.4	20.5	48	20	11	1.3	1.2	1.4	1.5
Petroleum	63	25	16	17	5	-	-	-	-	39.7	25.4	27.0	54	21	1	<.1	<.1	<.1	<.1
Phillips	314	198	52	38	26	-	-	-	-	63.1	16.6	12.1	5	42	52	0.3	0.4	0.2	0.2
Pondera	1,398	661	389	221	127	-	-	-	-	47.3	27.8	15.8	35	15	36	1.2	1.2	1.4	1.0
Powder River	88	56	9	12	11	-	-	-	-	63.6	10.2	13.6	4	48	45	<.1	0.1	<.1	<.1
Powell	770	375	191	125	79	-	-	-	-	48.7	24.8	16.2	33	23	32	0.7	0.7	0.7	0.6
Prairie	190	118	37	21	14	-	-	-	-	62.1	19.5	11.1	7	37	55	0.2	0.2	0.1	<.1
Ravalli	3,149	1,362	930	548	309	-	-	-	-	43.3	29.5	17.4	49	10	28	2.7	2.5	3.3	2.5
Richland	1,012	526	242	122	122	-	-	-	-	52.0	23.9	12.1	22	25	53	0.9	1.0	0.9	0.6
Roosevelt	1,559	697	470	253	139	-	-	-	-	44.7	30.1	16.2	45	9	33	1.3	1.3	1.7	1.2
Rosebud	1,087	528	252	180	127	-	-	-	-	48.6	23.2	16.6	34	29	30	0.9	1.0	0.9	0.8
Sanders	1,360	830	71	272	187	-	-	-	-	61.0	5.2	20.0	10	49	12	1.2	1.5	0.3	1.3
Sheridan	1,138	600	272	146	120	-	-	-	-	52.7	23.9	12.8	18	26	51	1.0	1.1	1.0	0.7
Silver Bow	10,410	4,543	3,149	1,826	892	-	-	-	-	43.6	30.2	17.5	46	8	27	8.9	8.3	11.2	8.4
Stillwater	876	453	213	115	95	-	-	-	-	51.7	24.3	13.1	23	24	48	0.7	0.8	0.8	0.5
Sweet Grass	249	125	48	53	23	-	-	-	-	50.2	19.3	21.3	28	38	7	0.2	0.2	0.2	0.2
Teton	1,194	588	315	175	116	-	-	-	-	49.2	26.4	14.7	29	17	43	1.0	1.1	1.1	0.8
Toole	695	351	181	92	71	-	-	-	-	50.5	26.0	13.2	26	19	46	0.6	0.6	0.6	0.4
Treasure	270	95	97	44	34	-	-	-	-	35.2	35.9	16.3	56	1	31	0.2	0.2	0.3	0.2
Valley	1,257	747	185	197	128	-	-	-	-	59.4	14.7	15.7	11	46	37	1.1	1.4	0.7	0.9
Wheatland	243	174	5	64	0	-	-	-	-	71.6	2.1	26.3	1	51	2	0.2	0.3	<.1	0.3
Wibaux	167	87	32	30	18	-	-	-	-	52.1	19.2	18.0	21	39	22	0.1	0.2	0.1	0.1
Yellowstone	11,316	5,525	2,157	2,224	1,410	-	-	-	-	48.8	19.1	19.7	32	40	14	9.6	10.0	7.7	10.2
MONTANA	**117,471**	**54,989**	**28,164**	**21,704**	**12,614**	-	-	-	-	**46.8**	**24.0**	**18.5**				**100.0**	**100.0**	**100.0**	**100.0**

[1]Includes part of Yellowstone National Park.

Table J. — Vote for Presidential Preference: June 2, 1992, Republican Primary Election

County	Top candidates					Top four candidates (state vote)												
						Percent of total vote				Rank				Percent contribution to state vote				
	Total	Bush	No Preference	Buchanan		Bush	No Preference	Buchanan		Bush	No Preference	Buchanan		Total	Bush	No Preference	Buchanan	
Beaverhead	1,526	1,246	0	280	-	81.7	0.0	18.3	-	3	52	6	-	1.7	1.9	0.0	2.6	-
Big Horn	693	558	68	67	-	80.5	9.8	9.7	-	5	48	51	-	0.8	0.9	0.5	0.6	-
Blaine	549	425	74	50	-	77.4	13.5	9.1	-	13	39	55	-	0.6	0.7	0.5	0.5	-
Broadwater	705	550	8	147	-	78.0	1.1	20.9	-	11	51	1	-	0.8	0.8	<.1	1.4	-
Carbon	1,388	965	259	164	-	69.5	18.7	11.8	-	36	17	33	-	1.5	1.5	1.7	1.5	-
Carter	454	321	75	58	-	70.7	16.5	12.8	-	31	25	25	-	0.5	0.5	0.5	0.5	-
Cascade	6,915	5,212	1,060	643	-	75.4	15.3	9.3	-	16	32	53	-	7.6	8.0	7.0	6.0	-
Chouteau	1,032	774	161	97	-	75.0	15.6	9.4	-	18	29	52	-	1.1	1.2	1.1	0.9	-
Custer	1,412	1,207	0	205	-	85.5	0.0	14.5	-	1	53	14	-	1.6	1.9	0.0	1.9	-
Daniels	523	323	106	94	-	61.8	20.3	18.0	-	51	14	7	-	0.6	0.5	0.7	0.9	-
Dawson	1,248	1,008	0	240	-	80.8	0.0	19.2	-	4	54	4	-	1.4	1.5	0.0	2.2	-
Deer Lodge	442	318	61	63	-	71.9	13.8	14.3	-	29	38	18	-	0.5	0.5	0.4	0.6	-
Fallon	528	386	82	60	-	73.1	15.5	11.4	-	26	30	35	-	0.6	0.6	0.5	0.6	-
Fergus	2,007	1,412	324	271	-	70.4	16.1	13.5	-	34	27	23	-	2.2	2.2	2.1	2.5	-
Flathead	8,181	4,911	2,141	1,129	-	60.0	26.2	13.8	-	55	4	21	-	9.0	7.5	14.2	10.6	-
Gallatin[1]	5,906	4,046	1,219	641	-	68.5	20.6	10.9	-	39	12	40	-	6.5	6.2	8.1	6.0	-
Garfield	344	220	69	55	-	64.0	20.1	16.0	-	49	15	10	-	0.4	0.3	0.5	0.5	-
Glacier	669	434	141	94	-	64.9	21.1	14.1	-	47	10	20	-	0.7	0.7	0.9	0.9	-
Golden Valley	161	106	27	28	-	65.8	16.8	17.4	-	45	24	8	-	0.2	0.2	0.2	0.3	-
Granite	457	306	103	48	-	67.0	22.5	10.5	-	42	8	43	-	0.5	0.5	0.7	0.4	-
Hill	1,357	958	251	148	-	70.6	18.5	10.9	-	32	18	39	-	1.5	1.5	1.7	1.4	-
Jefferson	1,007	736	153	118	-	73.1	15.2	11.7	-	27	34	34	-	1.1	1.1	1.0	1.1	-
Judith Basin	408	344	0	64	-	84.3	0.0	15.7	-	2	55	11	-	0.4	0.5	0.0	0.6	-
Lake	2,406	1,627	490	289	-	67.6	20.4	12.0	-	41	13	31	-	2.6	2.5	3.2	2.7	-
Lewis and Clark	6,263	4,962	770	531	-	79.2	12.3	8.5	-	8	43	56	-	6.9	7.6	5.1	5.0	-
Liberty	387	291	58	38	-	75.2	15.0	9.8	-	17	36	50	-	0.4	0.4	0.4	0.4	-
Lincoln	1,447	880	384	183	-	60.8	26.5	12.6	-	54	2	26	-	1.6	1.4	2.5	1.7	-
McCone	355	276	37	42	-	77.7	10.4	11.8	-	12	47	32	-	0.4	0.4	0.2	0.4	-
Madison	1,451	891	383	177	-	61.4	26.4	12.2	-	53	3	27	-	1.6	1.4	2.5	1.7	-
Meagher	400	319	0	81	-	79.8	0.0	20.3	-	7	56	2	-	0.4	0.5	0.0	0.8	-
Mineral	176	117	40	19	-	66.5	22.7	10.8	-	43	7	42	-	0.2	0.2	0.3	0.2	-
Missoula	6,659	4,828	1,224	607	-	72.5	18.4	9.1	-	28	19	54	-	7.3	7.4	8.1	5.7	-
Musselshell	609	447	70	92	-	73.4	11.5	15.1	-	25	45	13	-	0.7	0.7	0.5	0.9	-
Park[1]	1,858	1,188	312	358	-	63.9	16.8	19.3	-	50	23	3	-	2.0	1.8	2.1	3.3	-
Petroleum	105	78	16	11	-	74.3	15.2	10.5	-	21	33	44	-	0.1	0.1	0.1	0.1	-
Phillips	1,197	738	286	173	-	61.7	23.9	14.5	-	52	6	16	-	1.3	1.1	1.9	1.6	-
Pondera	879	618	155	106	-	70.3	17.6	12.1	-	35	22	29	-	1.0	0.9	1.0	1.0	-
Powder River	591	400	107	84	-	67.7	18.1	14.2	-	40	21	19	-	0.6	0.6	0.7	0.8	-
Powell	953	633	213	107	-	66.4	22.4	11.2	-	44	9	37	-	1.0	1.0	1.4	1.0	-
Prairie	338	249	45	44	-	73.7	13.3	13.0	-	23	40	24	-	0.4	0.4	0.3	0.4	-
Ravalli	3,185	2,062	807	316	-	64.7	25.3	9.9	-	48	5	48	-	3.5	3.2	5.3	3.0	-
Richland	1,050	726	162	162	-	69.1	15.4	15.4	-	37	31	12	-	1.2	1.1	1.1	1.5	-
Roosevelt	662	473	109	80	-	71.5	16.5	12.1	-	30	26	28	-	0.7	0.7	0.7	0.7	-
Rosebud	665	491	94	80	-	73.8	14.1	12.0	-	22	37	30	-	0.7	0.8	0.6	0.7	-
Sanders	745	586	21	138	-	78.7	2.8	18.5	-	10	49	5	-	0.8	0.9	0.1	1.3	-
Sheridan	517	397	64	56	-	76.8	12.4	10.8	-	14	42	41	-	0.6	0.6	0.4	0.5	-
Silver Bow	2,101	1,451	437	213	-	69.1	20.8	10.1	-	38	11	47	-	2.3	2.2	2.9	2.0	-
Stillwater	1,161	855	186	120	-	73.6	16.0	10.3	-	24	28	45	-	1.3	1.3	1.2	1.1	-
Sweet Grass	804	609	107	88	-	75.7	13.3	10.9	-	15	41	38	-	0.9	0.9	0.7	0.8	-
Teton	1,031	726	188	117	-	70.4	18.2	11.3	-	33	20	36	-	1.1	1.1	1.2	1.1	-
Toole	1,066	629	284	153	-	59.0	26.6	14.4	-	56	1	17	-	1.2	1.0	1.9	1.4	-
Treasure	95	71	11	13	-	74.7	11.6	13.7	-	19	44	22	-	0.1	0.1	<.1	0.1	-
Valley	1,324	871	261	192	-	65.8	19.7	14.5	-	46	16	15	-	1.5	1.3	1.7	1.8	-
Wheatland	346	278	9	59	-	80.3	2.6	17.1	-	6	50	9	-	0.4	0.4	<.1	0.6	-
Wibaux	146	109	22	15	-	74.7	15.1	10.3	-	20	35	46	-	0.2	0.2	0.1	0.1	-
Yellowstone	12,091	9,534	1,364	1,193	-	78.9	11.3	9.9	-	9	46	49	-	13.3	14.6	9.0	11.1	-
MONTANA	90,975	65,176	15,098	10,701	-	71.6	16.6	11.8	-					100.0	100.0	100.0	100.0	-

[1]Includes part of Yellowstone National Park.

1992 Vote for President
Percent for Clinton (D), by County

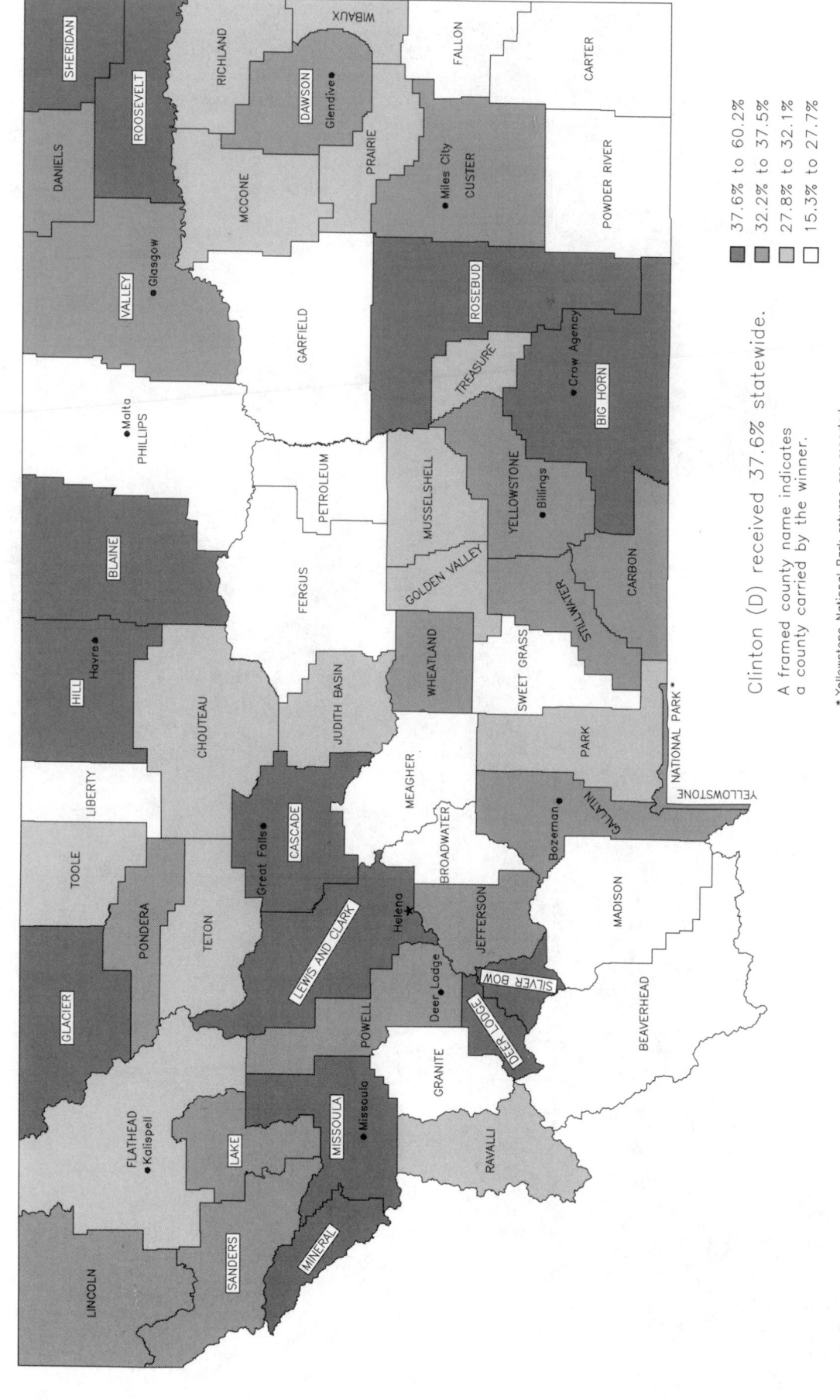

37.6% to 60.2%
32.2% to 37.5%
27.8% to 32.1%
15.3% to 27.7%

Clinton (D) received 37.6% statewide.

A framed county name indicates
a county carried by the winner.

*Yellowstone National Park returns are reported
with the returns of Gallatin county.

Montana 569

1992 Vote for Governor
Percent for Racicot (R), by County

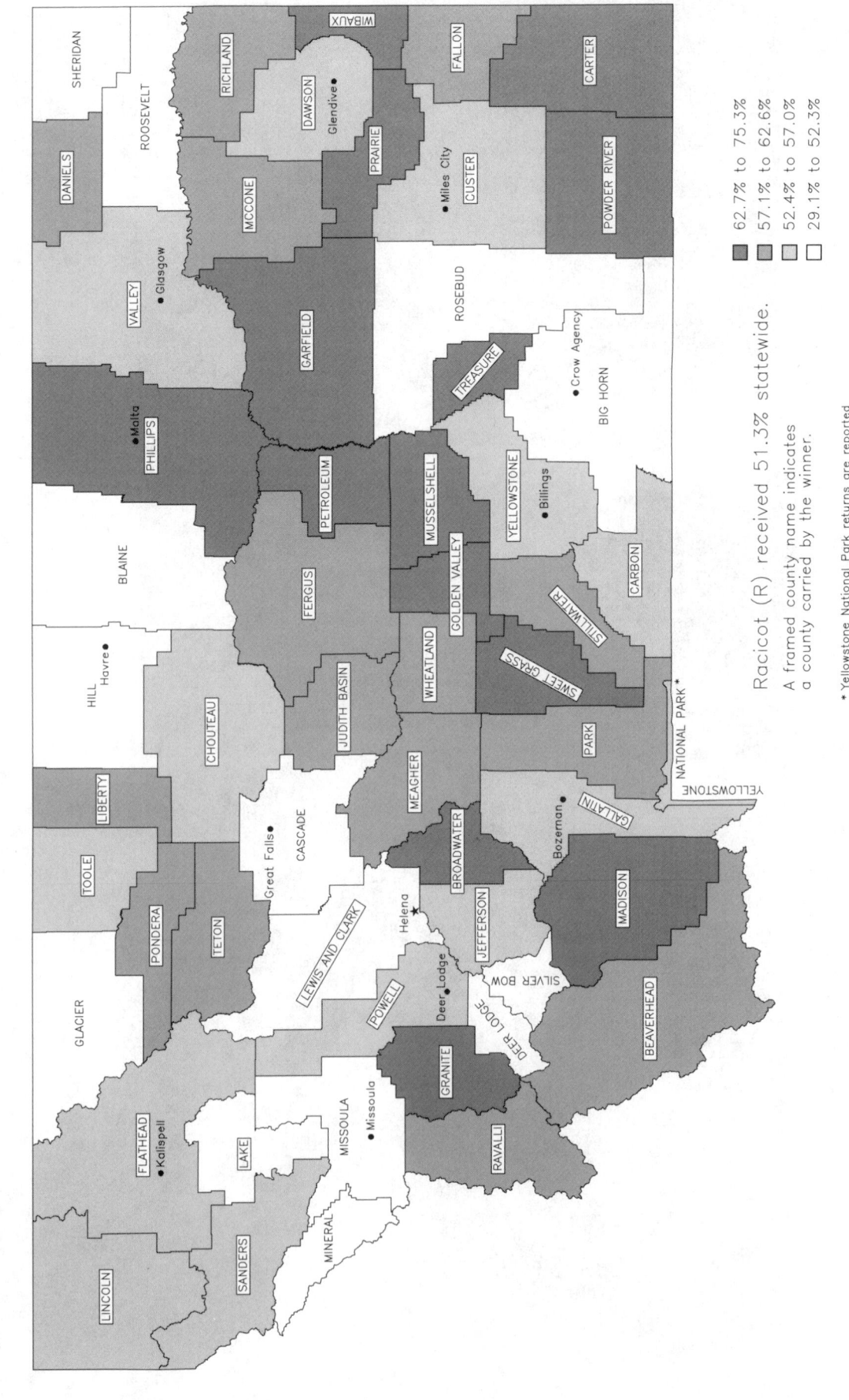

Racicot (R) received 51.3% statewide.

A framed county name indicates
a county carried by the winner.

* Yellowstone National Park returns are reported
with the returns of Gallatin county.

62.7% to 75.3%
57.1% to 62.6%
52.4% to 57.0%
29.1% to 52.3%

NEBRASKA

Congressional Districts 3
   Average Population 526,128
State Senate Districts[1].......................................49
   Average Population 32,212
State House Districts[1] ....N/A
   Average Population ....N/A

Electoral College Votes..5
Counties 93
Voting Precincts 1,836

Alternative Registration Methods:
....Deputized Registrars, Mail-in

Registration Deadline (Days before Election) 10

Voting Equipment Use (Counties)

Datavote Punch Card	0	Paper Ballot	65
Electronic	0	Other Punch Card	2
Lever Machine	0	Mixed Systems	0
Optical Scanner	26		

Party Control[1]	DEM	REP	IND	VAC
1993 State Senate	0	0	0	0
1992 State Senate	0	0	0	0
1993 State House	0	0	0	0
1992 State House	0	0	0	0

Population Statistics 1990

Race/ Ethnicity	Total Population		Voting Age Population		Voting Age Population % of total population
	Number	%	Number	%	
Non-Hispanic					
White	1,460,095	92.5	1,075,770	93.6	73.7
Black	56,711	3.6	36,075	3.1	63.6
Asian/Pacific Islander	12,026	0.8	8,131	0.7	67.6
Native American	11,719	0.7	6,873	0.6	58.6
Other	865	<.1	258	<.1	29.8
All Hispanic	36,969	2.3	22,266	1.9	60.2
TOTAL	1,578,385	100.0	1,149,373	100.0	72.8

Estimated Voting Age Population 1992 (VAP) 1,167,000
Number of Registered Voters................................... 951,395
   % of estimated VAP...................................... 81.5
Voter Turnout (Actual) 744,548
   % of VAP 63.8
   % of Registration 78.3
Persons Not Voting—of Voting Age 422,452
   % of VAP 36.2
Persons Not Voting—of Registered 206,847
   % of Registration 21.7
Straight Ticket Voting .... No

State Officials and Members of Congress

Governor:
Benjamin Nelson (D) 1990, elected to a four-year term in 1990.

U.S. Senators:
Jim Exon (D) 1978, elected to a six-year term in 1990.
Bob Kerrey (D) 1988, elected to a six-year term in 1988.

U.S. Representative in Congress:
(District, Name, Party, Date first elected)

1. Bereuter (R) 1978   2. Hoagland (D) 1988   3. Barrett (R) 1990

[1]Nebraska has a unicameral state legislature with members elected on a nonpartisan basis.

Candidates: General Election, November 3, 1992

Candidate(s)	Total vote	Percent	Party	Status	First elected
President/Vice President					
Bush/Quayle	343,678	46.60%	Republican	Incumbent	1988
Clinton/Gore	216,864	29.40%	Democrat	Challenger	1992
Perot/Stockdale	174,104	23.61%	Independent	Challenger	
Marrou/Lord	1,340	0.18%	Libertarian	Challenger	
Fulani/Munoz	846	0.11%	Independent	Challenger	
Hagelin/Tompkins	714	0.10%	Independent	Challenger	
U.S. Senator (No Contest)					
Governor (No Contest)					
U.S. Representative in Congress					
District 1					
Doug Bereuter	142,713	59.69%	Republican	Incumbent	1978
Gerry Finnegan	96,309	40.28%	Democrat	Challenger	
Write ins	86	0.04%	Write in	Challenger	
District 2					
Peter Hoagland	119,512	51.21%	Democrat	Incumbent	1988
Ronald Staskiewicz	113,828	48.78%	Republican	Challenger	
Write ins	32	0.01%	Write in	Challenger	
District 3					
Bill Barrett	170,857	71.68%	Republican	Incumbent	1990
Lowell Fisher	67,457	28.30%	Democrat	Challenger	
Write ins	41	0.02%	Write in	Challenger	

Candidates: May 12, 1992, Primary Election

Candidate	Total vote	Percent	Candidate	Total vote	Percent
Presidential Preference, Democratic			**Presidential Preference, Republican**		
Bill Clinton	68,562	45.53%	George Bush	156,346	81.39%
Jerry Brown	31,673	21.03%	Patrick Buchanan	25,847	13.46%
Uncommitted	24,714	16.41%	Write ins	5,033	2.62%
Paul Tsongas	10,707	7.11%	David Duke	2,808	1.46%
Write ins	7,259	4.82%	George Zimmermann	1,313	0.68%
Tom Harkin	4,239	2.81%	Tennie Rogers	751	0.39%
Eugene McCarthy	1,520	1.01%			
Lyndon LaRouche, Jr.	1,148	0.76%			
Charles Woods	485	0.32%			
Larry Agran	280	0.19%			

Voter Registration and Turnout, 1948-1992 Elections

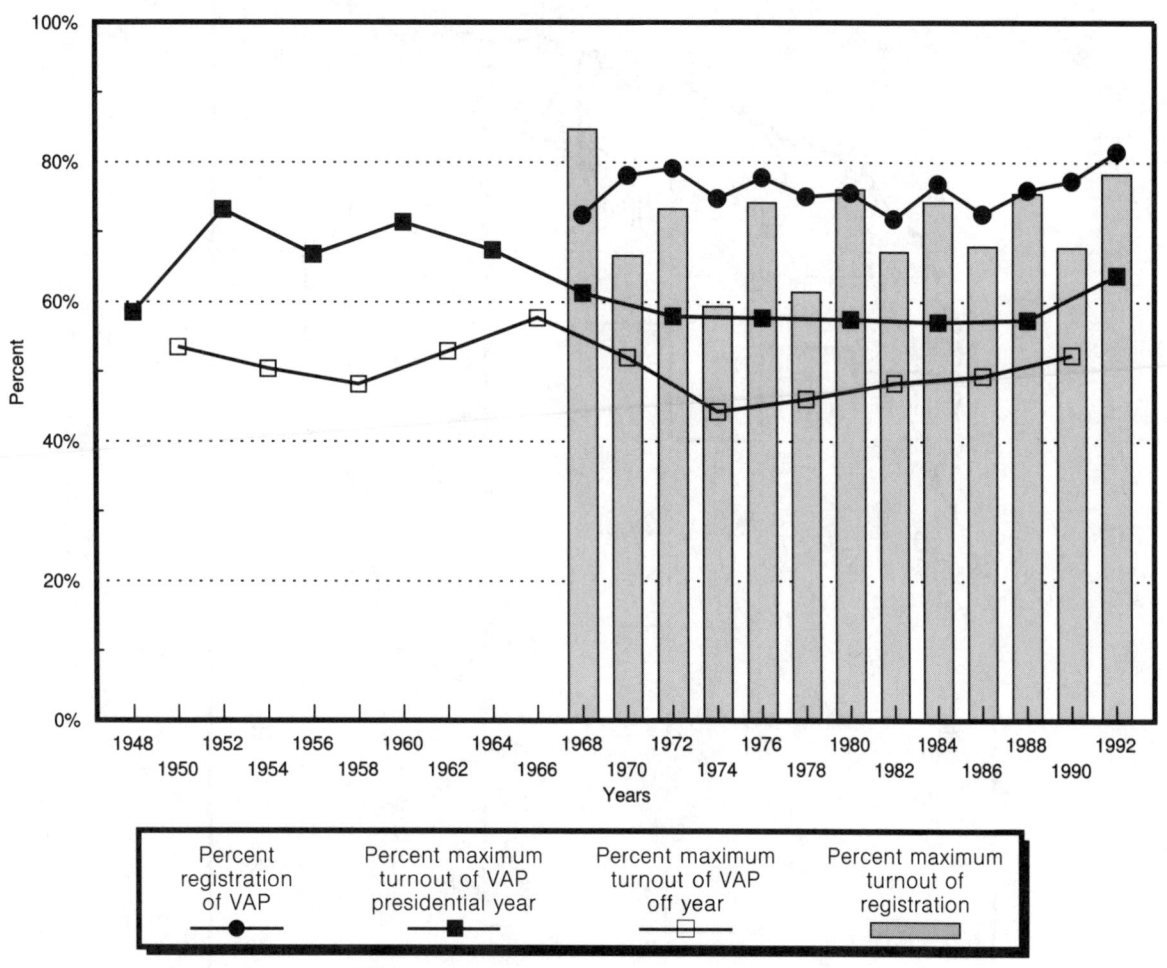

		Voter registration (REG)				Voter turnout												
							Highest office							Maximum vote				
Year	Estimated Voting Age Population (VAP)	Total	Percent of VAP	Rank by percent of VAP	Actual	Total	Office	Percent total REG	Rank by percent of REG	Percent of VAP	Rank by percent of VAP	Total	Percent total REG	Rank by percent of REG	Percent total VAP	Rank by percent of VAP
1992	1,167,000	951,395	81.5	12	744,548	737,546	P	77.5	26	63.2	14	744,548	78.3	26	63.8	16
1990	1,152,000	890,579	77.3	12	604,195	593,828	S	66.7	8	51.5	6	604,195	67.8	8	52.4	5
1988	1,183,000	898,959	76.0	17	678,669	661,465	P	73.6	19	55.9	15	678,669	75.5	20	57.4	15
1986	1,171,000	849,762	72.6	19	577,916	564,422	G	66.4	9	48.2	9	577,916	68.0	9	49.4	8
1984	1,174,000	902,626	76.9	17	670,781	652,090	P	72.2	28	55.5	25	670,781	74.3	29	57.1	22
1982	1,157,000	832,121	71.9	19	559,422	547,902	G	65.8	16	47.4	14	559,422	67.2	18	48.4	13
1980	1,133,000	856,182	75.6	20	651,281	640,854	P	74.9	26	56.6	23	651,281	76.1	24	57.5	23
1978	1,108,000	832,628	75.1	13	511,010	494,838	S	59.4	18	44.7	14	511,010	61.4	15	46.1	13
1976	1,081,000	840,666	77.8	18	623,764	607,668	P	72.3	31	56.2	26	623,764	74.2	30	57.7	24
1974	1,053,000	787,850	74.8	16	466,956	451,306	G	57.3	26	42.9	22	466,956	59.3	24	44.3	21
1972	1,021,000	807,267	79.1	15	591,616	576,289	P	71.4	31	56.4	31	591,616	73.3	30	57.9	30
1970	906,000	707,558	78.1	14	471,055	461,619	G	65.2	27	51.0	23	471,055	66.6	26	52.0	22
1968	881,000	637,719	72.4	29	540,176	536,851	P	84.2	13	60.9	31	540,176	84.7	13	61.3	32
1966	863,000	-	-	-	497,955	486,396	G	-	-	56.4	18	497,955	-	-	57.7	14
1964	879,000	-	-	-	592,673	584,154	P	-	-	66.5	27	592,673	-	-	67.4	26
1962	893,000	-	-	-	472,249	464,585	G	-	-	52.0	24	472,249	-	-	52.9	23
1960	868,000	-	-	-	619,399	613,095	P	-	-	70.6	25	619,399	-	-	71.4	24
1958	894,000	-	-	-	430,769	421,067	G	-	-	47.1	33	430,769	-	-	48.2	33
1956	876,000	-	-	-	584,786	577,137	P	-	-	65.9	26	584,786	-	-	66.8	25
1954	857,000	-	-	-	431,917	418,691	S	-	-	48.9	29	431,917	-	-	50.4	25
1952	842,000	-	-	-	616,239	609,660	P	-	-	72.4	18	616,239	-	-	73.2	18
1950	858,000	-	-	-	459,319	449,720	G	-	-	52.4	19	459,319	-	-	53.5	20
1948	849,000	-	-	-	497,084	488,940	P	-	-	57.6	26	497,084	-	-	58.5	27

NEBRASKA

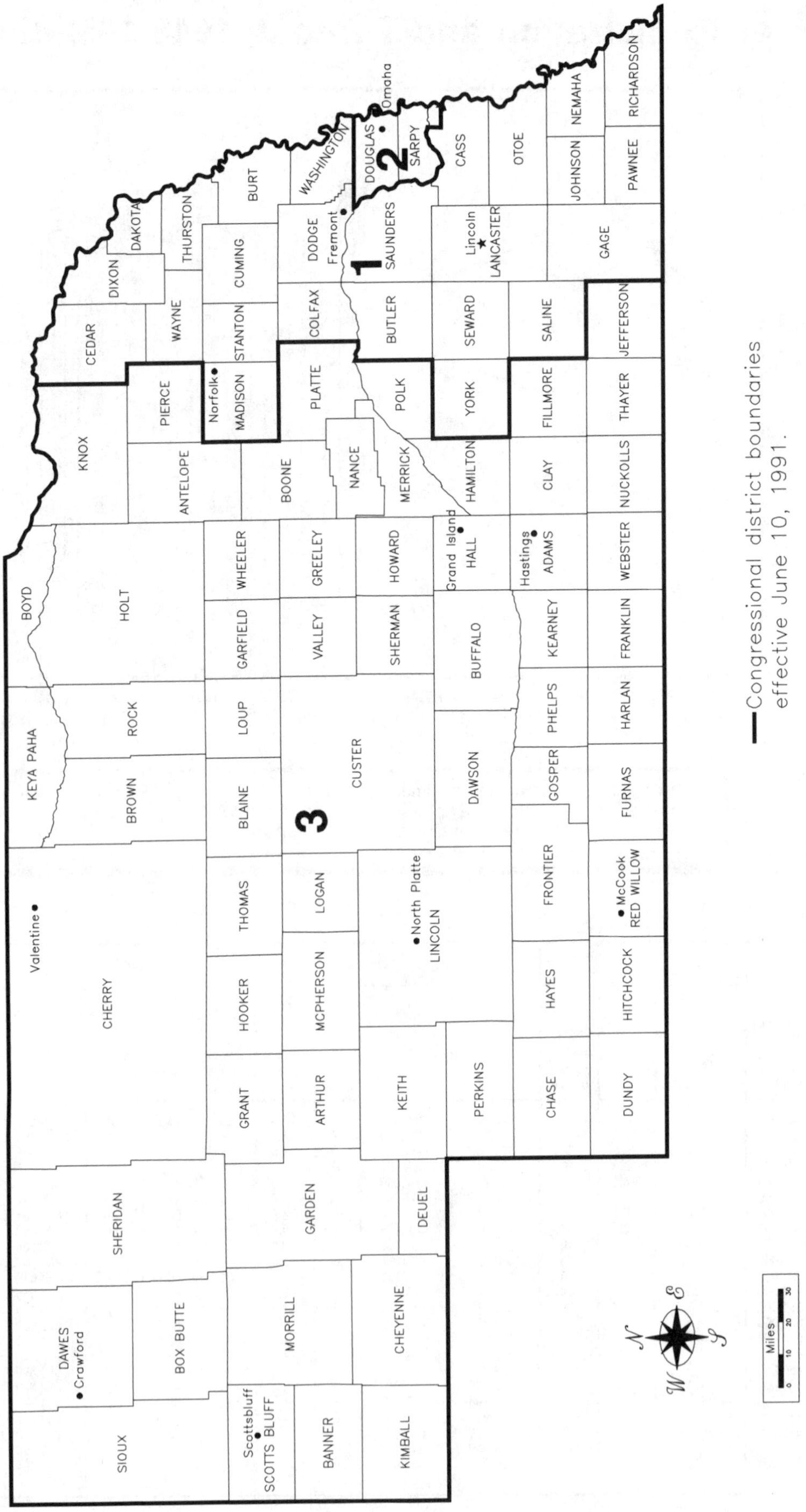

Valentine •

Crawford •

Scottsbluff •

Norfolk •

Fremont •

Omaha •

Lincoln ★

Grand Island •
Hastings •

North Platte •

McCook •

Counties

SIOUX, DAWES, SHERIDAN, CHERRY, KEYA PAHA, BOYD, BROWN, ROCK, HOLT, KNOX, CEDAR, DIXON, DAKOTA, THURSTON, BURT, WASHINGTON, DOUGLAS, SARPY, CASS, OTOE, NEMAHA, RICHARDSON, PAWNEE, JOHNSON, GAGE, JEFFERSON, THAYER, NUCKOLLS, WEBSTER, FRANKLIN, HARLAN, FURNAS, RED WILLOW, HITCHCOCK, DUNDY, CHASE, HAYES, FRONTIER, GOSPER, PHELPS, KEARNEY, ADAMS, CLAY, FILLMORE, SALINE, SEWARD, YORK, HAMILTON, MERRICK, NANCE, POLK, BUTLER, SAUNDERS, DODGE, COLFAX, PLATTE, BOONE, WHEELER, GREELEY, VALLEY, SHERMAN, HOWARD, HALL, BUFFALO, DAWSON, LINCOLN, LOGAN, CUSTER, BLAINE, LOUP, GARFIELD, VALLEY, THOMAS, HOOKER, GRANT, ARTHUR, MCPHERSON, KEITH, PERKINS, DEUEL, CHEYENNE, GARDEN, MORRILL, BANNER, KIMBALL, SCOTTS BLUFF, BOX BUTTE, ANTELOPE, PIERCE, MADISON, STANTON, CUMING, WAYNE

1
2
3

—Congressional district boundaries
effective June 10, 1991.

N
W E
S

Miles
0   10   20   30

Copyright © 1993 by Election Data Services, Inc.

574 Nebraska

Table A. — 1990 Population by Race and Ethnic Origin

State/ county code	County	Total persons	Percent of total persons — Non-Hispanic White	Black	Asian and Pacific Islander	Native American	Other	Hispanic	Rank — Percent of total persons Total	Non-Hispanic White	Black	Hispanic	Percent contribution to state population Total	Non-Hispanic White	Black	Hispanic
31 001	Adams	29,625	97.6	0.6	0.4	0.3	<.1	1.0	11	67	6	27	1.9	2.0	0.3	0.8
31 003	Antelope	7,965	99.5	<.1	0.1	0.3	<.1	<.1	41	11	57	89	0.5	0.5	<.1	<.1
31 005	Arthur	462	99.4	0.0	0.0	0.4	0.2	0.0	93	21	72	90	<.1	<.1	0.0	0.0
31 007	Banner	852	97.3	0.1	0.0	0.4	0.0	2.2	86	69	30	17	<.1	<.1	<.1	<.1
31 009	Blaine	675	99.4	0.1	0.0	0.1	0.3	0.0	91	18	26	91	<.1	<.1	<.1	0.0
31 011	Boone	6,667	99.5	<.1	<.1	0.2	0.1	0.3	48	12	70	71	0.4	0.5	<.1	<.1
31 013	Box Butte	13,130	91.6	0.4	0.4	2.1	<.1	5.5	21	86	13	4	0.8	0.8	<.1	2.0
31 015	Boyd	2,835	99.0	0.0	<.1	0.8	0.0	0.2	74	33	73	76	0.2	0.2	0.0	<.1
31 017	Brown	3,657	98.9	<.1	0.2	0.3	0.0	0.6	69	37	56	53	0.2	0.2	<.1	<.1
31 019	Buffalo	37,447	96.1	0.4	0.4	0.3	<.1	2.7	5	75	11	14	2.4	2.5	0.3	2.8
31 021	Burt	7,868	98.0	0.1	0.2	0.8	<.1	0.9	42	63	36	30	0.5	0.5	<.1	0.2
31 023	Butler	8,601	99.3	0.1	0.2	0.2	0.0	0.2	37	23	31	74	0.5	0.6	<.1	<.1
31 025	Cass	21,318	98.1	0.2	0.3	0.5	<.1	0.9	13	61	19	33	1.4	1.4	<.1	0.5
31 027	Cedar	10,131	99.5	<.1	<.1	0.1	0.0	0.2	26	10	44	80	0.6	0.7	<.1	<.1
31 029	Chase	4,381	97.7	<.1	<.1	0.1	<.1	2.0	61	65	61	18	0.3	0.3	<.1	0.2
31 031	Cherry	6,307	96.6	<.1	0.2	2.8	0.0	0.4	51	73	53	63	0.4	0.4	<.1	<.1
31 033	Cheyenne	9,494	95.7	<.1	0.2	0.7	<.1	3.3	31	78	42	10	0.6	0.6	<.1	0.9
31 035	Clay	7,123	99.0	<.1	0.2	0.2	0.0	0.6	44	34	71	50	0.5	0.5	<.1	0.1
31 037	Colfax	9,139	97.1	<.1	<.1	0.3	<.1	2.5	33	70	52	16	0.6	0.6	<.1	0.6
31 039	Cuming	10,117	99.5	<.1	0.2	<.1	0.0	0.1	27	15	39	81	0.6	0.7	<.1	<.1
31 041	Custer	12,270	98.6	<.1	<.1	0.6	0.0	0.7	24	50	59	42	0.8	0.8	<.1	0.2
31 043	Dakota	16,742	89.6	0.4	2.0	1.8	0.2	6.1	16	89	10	3	1.1	1.0	0.1	2.7
31 045	Dawes	9,021	93.2	0.6	0.8	3.7	<.1	1.6	34	85	8	24	0.6	0.6	<.1	0.4
31 047	Dawson	19,940	96.1	<.1	0.2	0.3	<.1	3.3	14	76	45	11	1.3	1.3	<.1	1.8
31 049	Deuel	2,237	94.7	<.1	0.3	0.4	0.0	4.6	77	80	50	6	0.1	0.1	<.1	0.3
31 051	Dixon	6,143	99.6	<.1	<.1	0.2	0.0	<.1	53	8	41	88	0.4	0.4	<.1	<.1
31 053	Dodge	34,500	98.5	0.2	0.3	0.3	<.1	0.6	7	56	20	44	2.2	2.3	0.1	0.6
31 055	Douglas	416,444	84.9	10.8	0.9	0.5	<.1	2.7	1	91	1	15	26.4	24.2	79.5	30.8
31 057	Dundy	2,582	99.1	0.0	0.2	0.1	<.1	0.6	75	29	74	52	0.2	0.2	0.0	<.1
31 059	Fillmore	7,103	98.7	0.2	<.1	0.5	<.1	0.5	45	41	21	58	0.5	0.5	<.1	<.1
31 061	Franklin	3,938	99.2	0.2	0.2	0.3	0.0	0.2	65	25	25	77	0.2	0.3	<.1	<.1
31 063	Frontier	3,101	98.7	<.1	0.3	0.1	0.2	0.6	72	42	54	47	0.2	0.2	<.1	<.1
31 065	Furnas	5,553	98.9	<.1	0.1	0.3	0.0	0.7	57	39	51	43	0.4	0.4	<.1	0.1
31 067	Gage	22,794	98.5	0.2	0.3	0.4	<.1	0.5	12	53	18	60	1.4	1.5	<.1	0.3
31 069	Garden	2,460	99.4	0.0	0.0	0.0	0.0	0.6	76	19	75	49	0.2	0.2	0.0	<.1
31 071	Garfield	2,141	99.5	0.0	0.2	0.1	0.0	0.1	78	13	76	83	0.1	0.1	0.0	<.1
31 073	Gosper	1,928	99.5	0.0	<.1	0.0	0.0	0.5	80	14	77	61	0.1	0.1	0.0	<.1
31 075	Grant	769	98.7	0.0	0.4	0.7	0.0	0.3	89	45	78	69	<.1	<.1	0.0	<.1
31 077	Greeley	3,006	99.7	0.0	<.1	0.1	0.0	<.1	73	5	79	87	0.2	0.2	0.0	<.1
31 079	Hall	48,925	94.0	0.3	1.1	0.3	<.1	4.3	4	83	17	7	3.1	3.1	0.2	5.7
31 081	Hamilton	8,862	98.9	0.1	0.2	<.1	0.0	0.6	35	36	37	45	0.6	0.6	<.1	0.2
31 083	Harlan	3,810	99.7	<.1	<.1	<.1	0.0	0.1	66	3	46	84	0.2	0.3	<.1	<.1
31 085	Hayes	1,222	99.2	0.0	0.2	0.2	0.0	0.5	82	27	80	59	<.1	<.1	0.0	<.1
31 087	Hitchcock	3,750	99.1	0.0	<.1	0.2	<.1	0.6	67	32	81	48	0.2	0.3	0.0	<.1
31 089	Holt	12,599	99.4	<.1	0.1	0.2	0.0	0.2	23	17	60	78	0.8	0.9	<.1	<.1
31 091	Hooker	793	98.2	0.0	0.0	0.0	0.0	1.8	88	58	82	21	<.1	<.1	0.0	<.1
31 093	Howard	6,055	99.1	<.1	<.1	0.2	0.0	0.7	54	30	68	41	0.4	0.4	<.1	0.1
31 095	Jefferson	8,759	98.7	<.1	<.1	0.3	0.0	0.9	36	43	62	32	0.6	0.6	<.1	0.2
31 097	Johnson	4,673	96.8	<.1	2.2	0.0	<.1	1.0	60	72	65	29	0.3	0.3	<.1	0.1
31 099	Kearney	6,629	98.1	0.0	<.1	<.1	<.1	1.7	50	60	83	23	0.4	0.4	0.0	0.3
31 101	Keith	8,584	95.4	0.1	0.2	0.4	<.1	3.9	38	79	32	8	0.5	0.6	<.1	0.9
31 103	Keya Paha	1,029	99.8	0.0	0.0	<.1	0.0	<.1	83	2	84	85	<.1	<.1	0.0	<.1
31 105	Kimball	4,108	96.1	<.1	0.1	0.2	0.0	3.6	64	77	49	9	0.3	0.3	<.1	0.4
31 107	Knox	9,534	94.7	0.0	0.2	5.1	<.1	<.1	30	81	85	86	0.6	0.6	0.0	<.1
31 109	Lancaster	213,641	93.9	2.1	1.6	0.5	<.1	1.8	2	84	3	19	13.5	13.7	8.1	10.7
31 111	Lincoln	32,508	94.0	0.3	0.3	0.3	<.1	5.0	9	82	16	5	2.1	2.1	0.2	4.4
31 113	Logan	878	99.3	0.3	0.0	0.0	0.0	0.3	85	22	15	65	<.1	<.1	<.1	<.1
31 115	Loup	683	99.7	0.0	0.1	0.0	0.0	0.1	90	4	86	82	<.1	<.1	0.0	<.1
31 117	McPherson	546	99.8	0.2	0.0	0.0	0.0	0.0	92	1	22	92	<.1	<.1	<.1	0.0
31 119	Madison	32,655	96.5	0.7	0.3	0.7	<.1	1.7	8	74	5	22	2.1	2.2	0.4	1.5
31 121	Merrick	8,042	98.7	<.1	0.2	0.1	<.1	0.9	39	44	58	37	0.5	0.5	<.1	0.2
31 123	Morrill	5,423	91.3	<.1	0.1	0.5	<.1	8.0	58	88	66	2	0.3	0.3	<.1	1.2
31 125	Nance	4,275	98.8	<.1	0.2	<.1	0.0	0.9	63	40	63	35	0.3	0.3	<.1	0.1
31 127	Nemaha	7,980	98.5	0.9	0.2	0.2	0.0	0.3	40	54	4	72	0.5	0.5	0.1	<.1
31 129	Nuckolls	5,786	99.6	<.1	0.0	0.1	0.0	0.3	55	9	69	68	0.4	0.4	<.1	<.1
31 131	Otoe	14,252	98.7	0.2	0.2	0.2	<.1	0.7	20	48	24	40	0.9	1.0	<.1	0.3
31 133	Pawnee	3,317	99.2	<.1	0.1	<.1	<.1	0.5	71	26	38	57	0.2	0.2	<.1	<.1
31 135	Perkins	3,367	98.0	0.0	0.2	0.2	<.1	1.6	70	62	87	25	0.2	0.2	0.0	0.1
31 137	Phelps	9,715	98.7	<.1	0.2	0.2	<.1	0.9	29	47	47	31	0.6	0.7	<.1	0.2
31 139	Pierce	7,827	99.4	0.0	0.1	0.3	0.0	0.2	43	20	88	79	0.5	0.5	0.0	<.1

Table A. – 1990 Population by Race and Ethnic Origin (cont)

State/ county code	County	Total persons	Percent of total persons						Rank				Percent contribution to state population			
			Non-Hispanic							Percent of total persons				Non-Hispanic		
			White	Black	Asian and Pacific Islander	Native American	Other	Hispanic	Total	Non-Hispanic		Hispanic	Total	White	Black	Hispanic
										White	Black					
31 141	Platte	29,820	98.5	0.2	0.2	0.2	<.1	0.9	10	55	23	38	1.9	2.0	<.1	0.7
31 143	Polk	5,675	99.1	<.1	0.2	0.2	0.0	0.5	56	31	67	55	0.4	0.4	<.1	<.1
31 145	Red Willow	11,705	97.7	0.1	0.2	0.2	<.1	1.8	25	66	35	20	0.7	0.8	<.1	0.6
31 147	Richardson	9,937	97.6	<.1	0.1	1.8	0.0	0.4	28	68	48	62	0.6	0.7	<.1	0.1
31 149	Rock	2,019	99.7	0.0	0.0	<.1	0.0	0.3	79	7	89	67	0.1	0.1	0.0	<.1
31 151	Saline	12,715	98.2	0.1	0.9	0.2	<.1	0.6	22	59	29	51	0.8	0.9	<.1	0.2
31 153	Sarpy	102,583	89.4	5.1	1.8	0.4	<.1	3.3	3	90	2	12	6.5	6.3	9.2	9.2
31 155	Saunders	18,285	98.9	<.1	0.2	0.2	<.1	0.6	15	35	40	54	1.2	1.2	<.1	0.3
31 157	Scotts Bluff	36,025	83.1	0.1	0.5	1.6	0.1	14.5	6	92	27	1	2.3	2.1	<.1	14.2
31 159	Seward	15,450	98.9	0.1	0.2	0.2	<.1	0.5	18	38	28	56	1.0	1.0	<.1	0.2
31 161	Sheridan	6,750	91.4	<.1	0.2	7.3	<.1	1.0	47	87	55	28	0.4	0.4	<.1	0.2
31 163	Sherman	3,718	99.4	0.0	0.3	<.1	<.1	0.2	68	16	90	75	0.2	0.3	0.0	<.1
31 165	Sioux	1,549	96.9	0.0	0.1	<.1	<.1	2.8	81	71	91	13	<.1	0.1	0.0	0.1
31 167	Stanton	6,244	98.6	0.4	<.1	0.6	0.0	0.4	52	51	14	64	0.4	0.4	<.1	<.1
31 169	Thayer	6,635	98.7	<.1	0.1	0.3	<.1	0.9	49	49	43	36	0.4	0.4	<.1	0.2
31 171	Thomas	851	98.6	0.0	0.0	0.1	0.0	1.3	87	52	92	26	<.1	<.1	0.0	<.1
31 173	Thurston	6,936	55.6	0.1	0.1	43.3	0.0	0.9	46	93	34	34	0.4	0.3	<.1	0.2
31 175	Valley	5,169	99.2	0.1	0.2	0.2	0.0	0.3	59	28	33	66	0.3	0.4	<.1	<.1
31 177	Washington	16,607	98.4	0.5	0.2	0.2	<.1	0.6	17	57	9	46	1.1	1.1	0.1	0.3
31 179	Wayne	9,364	98.7	0.4	0.4	0.3	0.0	0.2	32	46	12	73	0.6	0.6	<.1	<.1
31 181	Webster	4,279	99.3	<.1	0.3	0.1	0.0	0.3	62	24	64	70	0.3	0.3	<.1	<.1
31 183	Wheeler	948	99.7	0.0	0.3	0.0	0.0	0.0	84	6	93	93	<.1	<.1	0.0	0.0
31 185	York	14,428	98.0	0.6	0.3	0.3	<.1	0.8	19	64	7	39	0.9	1.0	0.2	0.3
31	**NEBRASKA**	**1,578,385**	**92.5**	**3.6**	**0.8**	**0.7**	**<.1**	**2.3**					**100.0**	**100.0**	**100.0**	**100.0**
	CONGRESSIONAL															
	District 1	526,297	95.7	1.0	0.9	1.0	<.1	1.4	2	2	2	3	33.3	34.5	9.6	19.2
	District 2	526,567	85.9	9.6	1.1	0.5	<.1	2.8	1	3	1	2	33.4	31.0	88.8	40.2
	District 3	525,521	96.0	0.2	0.3	0.7	<.1	2.9	3	1	3	1	33.3	34.5	1.6	40.6

Table B. — 1990 Voting Age Population (VAP) by Race and Ethnic Origin

County	Total Voting Age Population	Percent of total VAP Non-Hispanic White	Black	Asian and Pacific Islander	Native American	Other	Hispanic	Rank Total	Non-Hispanic White	Black	Hispanic	Pct contribution to state VAP Total	Non-Hispanic White	Black	Hispanic	VAP pct of total pop Total	Non-Hispanic White	Black	Asian and Pacific Islander	Native American	Other	Hispanic
Adams	22,257	97.9	0.7	0.3	0.3	0.0	0.8	10	69	6	26	1.9	2.0	0.4	0.8	75.1	75.3	81.8	54.5	66.3	0.0	62.4
Antelope	5,529	99.7	<.1	<.1	0.2	0.0	<.1	43	7	57	88	0.5	0.5	<.1	<.1	69.4	69.5	50.0	22.2	50.0	0.0	60.0
Arthur	343	99.7	0.0	0.0	0.3	0.0	0.0	93	8	60	90	<.1	<.1	0.0	0.0	74.2	74.5	0.0	0.0	50.0	0.0	0.0
Banner	599	98.0	0.0	0.0	0.2	0.0	1.8	85	68	61	17	<.1	<.1	0.0	<.1	70.3	70.8	0.0	0.0	33.3	0.0	57.9
Blaine	487	99.6	0.2	0.0	0.2	0.0	0.0	91	17	19	91	<.1	<.1	<.1	0.0	72.1	72.3	100.0	0.0	100.0	0.0	0.0
Boone	4,722	99.7	0.0	<.1	0.1	0.0	0.2	49	9	62	77	0.4	0.4	0.0	<.1	70.8	70.9	0.0	100.0	45.5	0.0	47.1
Box Butte	8,882	93.1	0.4	0.4	1.7	<.1	4.3	23	88	12	4	0.8	0.8	<.1	1.7	67.6	68.8	71.4	67.9	54.2	50.0	53.2
Boyd	2,068	99.5	0.0	<.1	0.3	0.0	<.1	74	21	63	83	0.2	0.2	0.0	<.1	72.9	73.3	0.0	100.0	31.8	0.0	33.3
Brown	2,676	99.0	0.0	0.1	0.3	0.0	0.6	67	48	64	37	0.2	0.2	0.0	<.1	73.2	73.3	0.0	57.1	63.6	0.0	71.4
Buffalo	27,817	96.8	0.3	0.4	0.2	<.1	2.3	5	77	13	16	2.4	2.5	0.3	2.8	74.3	74.8	58.4	70.5	53.5	64.3	61.5
Burt	5,749	98.5	<.1	<.1	0.6	0.0	0.7	41	57	33	28	0.5	0.5	<.1	0.2	73.1	73.5	62.5	21.4	55.6	0.0	55.4
Butler	6,191	99.5	<.1	0.1	0.2	0.0	0.2	38	26	37	78	0.5	0.6	<.1	<.1	72.0	72.1	40.0	53.8	75.0	0.0	50.0
Cass	15,183	98.5	0.1	0.2	0.4	<.1	0.7	13	59	25	30	1.3	1.4	<.1	0.5	71.2	71.5	56.4	59.7	54.2	66.7	55.4
Cedar	6,988	99.6	<.1	<.1	0.2	0.0	0.2	31	18	53	76	0.6	0.6	<.1	<.1	69.0	69.0	33.3	44.4	92.9	0.0	70.6
Chase	3,115	98.2	<.1	0.0	0.2	<.1	1.5	62	64	51	21	0.3	0.3	<.1	0.2	71.1	71.5	100.0	0.0	83.3	100.0	52.3
Cherry	4,533	97.2	<.1	0.3	2.3	0.0	0.2	50	74	56	70	0.4	0.4	<.1	<.1	71.9	72.3	50.0	92.9	59.7	0.0	37.5
Cheyenne	6,880	96.8	<.1	0.2	0.6	0.0	2.4	32	76	35	13	0.6	0.6	<.1	0.8	72.5	73.3	83.3	73.3	59.4	0.0	52.7
Clay	5,183	99.2	0.0	0.2	0.2	0.0	0.4	45	40	65	49	0.5	0.5	0.0	<.1	72.8	72.9	0.0	69.2	68.8	0.0	51.2
Colfax	6,611	97.2	<.1	<.1	0.2	<.1	2.5	34	72	42	12	0.6	0.6	<.1	0.7	72.3	72.4	100.0	28.6	61.5	100.0	72.3
Cuming	7,297	99.6	<.1	<.1	0.1	0.0	0.2	27	15	39	79	0.6	0.7	<.1	<.1	72.1	72.2	50.0	25.0	90.0	0.0	73.3
Custer	8,956	99.1	<.1	<.1	0.4	0.0	0.4	22	43	44	51	0.8	0.8	<.1	0.2	73.0	73.3	100.0	45.5	54.4	0.0	44.0
Dakota	11,669	91.4	0.4	1.7	1.4	0.1	4.9	17	89	11	3	1.0	1.0	0.1	2.6	69.7	71.1	66.2	60.7	56.1	65.4	62.0
Dawes	6,741	94.8	0.6	0.7	2.6	<.1	1.3	33	84	9	24	0.6	0.6	0.1	0.4	74.7	76.0	71.7	60.8	51.9	37.5	62.0
Dawson	14,368	97.0	<.1	0.2	0.3	<.1	2.6	14	75	41	10	1.3	1.3	<.1	1.7	72.1	72.7	63.6	60.5	58.1	50.0	55.7
Deuel	1,649	95.9	0.0	0.4	0.4	0.0	3.3	77	81	66	7	0.1	0.1	0.0	0.2	73.7	74.6	0.0	100.0	66.7	0.0	53.9
Dixon	4,412	99.7	<.1	<.1	0.1	0.0	<.1	52	4	32	89	0.4	0.4	<.1	<.1	71.8	71.9	100.0	33.3	54.5	0.0	25.0
Dodge	25,496	98.7	0.2	0.3	0.3	<.1	0.5	7	54	20	39	2.2	2.3	0.1	0.6	73.9	74.1	77.8	61.3	58.7	28.6	59.6
Douglas	304,546	86.9	9.4	0.9	0.5	<.1	2.4	1	91	1	14	26.5	24.6	79.0	32.3	73.1	74.9	63.2	66.9	62.5	25.4	63.3
Dundy	1,939	99.4	0.0	0.1	0.2	0.0	0.3	75	28	67	61	0.2	0.2	0.0	<.1	75.1	75.3	0.0	50.0	100.0	0.0	40.0
Fillmore	5,222	99.2	<.1	<.1	0.3	<.1	0.4	44	41	38	50	0.5	0.5	<.1	<.1	73.5	73.8	23.1	50.0	45.5	25.0	62.9
Franklin	3,015	99.3	0.1	0.2	0.2	0.0	0.1	64	32	26	80	0.3	0.3	<.1	<.1	76.6	76.6	66.7	83.3	70.0	0.0	50.0
Frontier	2,238	99.2	<.1	0.2	<.1	<.1	0.4	72	39	43	48	0.2	0.2	<.1	<.1	72.2	72.5	100.0	50.0	50.0	14.3	52.6
Furnas	4,237	99.3	<.1	<.1	0.3	0.0	0.4	55	31	54	58	0.4	0.4	<.1	<.1	76.3	76.7	50.0	16.7	61.1	0.0	40.5
Gage	17,227	98.7	0.2	0.3	0.4	<.1	0.4	12	56	15	55	1.5	1.6	0.1	0.3	75.6	75.7	86.7	68.4	63.4	33.3	62.7
Garden	1,889	99.0	0.0	0.0	0.0	0.0	0.6	76	30	68	35	0.2	0.2	0.0	<.1	76.8	76.8	0.0	0.0	0.0	0.0	80.0
Garfield	1,587	99.7	0.0	0.1	<.1	0.0	0.1	78	12	69	82	0.1	0.1	0.0	<.1	76.0	74.3	0.0	40.0	33.3	0.0	66.7
Gosper	1,458	99.5	0.0	<.1	0.0	0.0	0.4	79	20	70	52	0.1	0.1	0.0	<.1	75.6	75.7	0.0	100.0	0.0	0.0	66.7
Grant	544	98.7	0.0	0.4	0.6	0.0	0.4	89	55	71	57	<.1	<.1	0.0	<.1	70.7	70.8	0.0	66.7	60.0	0.0	100.0
Greeley	2,082	99.7	0.0	<.1	<.1	0.0	<.1	73	6	72	84	0.2	0.2	0.0	<.1	69.3	69.3	0.0	66.7	50.0	0.0	100.0
Hall	35,052	95.1	0.2	0.8	0.2	<.1	3.6	4	83	17	6	3.0	3.1	0.2	5.7	71.6	72.5	54.5	55.1	55.4	48.3	59.9
Hamilton	6,289	99.2	<.1	0.2	<.1	0.0	0.5	36	38	59	41	0.5	0.6	<.1	0.1	71.0	71.2	11.1	63.6	37.5	0.0	56.1
Harlan	2,871	99.7	<.1	<.1	<.1	0.0	0.2	66	10	47	75	0.2	0.3	<.1	<.1	75.4	75.3	50.0	100.0	100.0	0.0	100.0
Hayes	891	99.0	0.0	0.2	0.1	0.0	0.4	82	37	73	47	<.1	<.1	0.0	<.1	72.9	72.9	0.0	100.0	50.0	0.0	66.7
Hitchcock	2,667	99.4	0.0	<.1	0.2	0.0	0.2	69	27	74	62	0.2	0.2	0.0	<.1	71.1	71.4	0.0	33.3	75.0	0.0	34.8
Holt	8,790	99.5	<.1	<.1	0.2	0.0	0.2	24	22	48	71	0.8	0.8	<.1	<.1	69.8	69.8	100.0	35.3	56.7	0.0	73.9
Hooker	598	98.5	0.0	0.0	0.0	0.0	1.5	86	58	75	20	<.1	<.1	0.0	<.1	75.4	75.6	0.0	0.0	0.0	0.0	64.3
Howard	4,330	99.3	0.0	<.1	0.2	0.0	0.5	53	34	76	45	0.4	0.4	0.0	<.1	71.5	71.7	0.0	50.0	80.0	0.0	50.0
Jefferson	6,605	99.0	0.0	<.1	0.2	0.0	0.7	35	47	77	29	0.6	0.6	0.0	0.2	75.4	75.7	0.0	57.1	56.5	0.0	58.0
Johnson	3,528	97.7	0.0	1.5	0.0	<.1	0.8	60	70	78	27	0.3	0.3	0.0	0.1	75.5	76.2	0.0	53.5	0.0	50.0	57.4
Kearney	4,840	98.4	0.0	<.1	<.1	<.1	1.5	48	62	79	22	0.4	0.4	0.0	0.3	73.2	73.2	0.0	50.0	100.0	100.0	62.3
Keith	6,197	96.5	<.1	0.2	0.4	<.1	2.8	37	79	31	9	0.5	0.6	<.1	0.8	72.2	73.1	60.0	66.7	69.4	50.0	52.1
Keya Paha	760	99.7	0.0	0.0	0.1	0.0	0.1	83	3	80	81	<.1	<.1	0.0	<.1	73.9	73.8	0.0	0.0	100.0	0.0	100.0
Kimball	3,015	97.2	0.0	<.1	0.2	0.0	2.5	65	73	81	11	0.3	0.3	0.0	0.3	73.4	74.3	0.0	50.0	100.0	0.0	50.7
Knox	7,032	95.9	0.0	<.1	3.9	0.0	<.1	30	80	82	86	0.6	0.6	0.0	<.1	73.8	74.7	0.0	35.3	57.5	0.0	66.7
Lancaster	162,593	94.7	1.9	1.5	0.4	<.1	1.5	2	85	3	19	14.1	14.3	8.4	11.3	76.1	76.8	66.4	71.3	64.8	25.3	63.7
Lincoln	23,128	95.2	0.2	0.3	0.3	<.1	4.0	9	82	18	5	2.0	2.0	0.1	4.1	71.1	72.0	53.3	64.0	64.8	13.3	56.7
Logan	585	99.5	0.2	0.0	0.0	0.0	0.3	87	24	22	60	<.1	<.1	<.1	<.1	66.6	66.7	33.3	0.0	0.0	0.0	66.7
Loup	495	99.8	0.0	0.0	0.0	0.0	0.2	90	1	83	69	<.1	<.1	0.0	<.1	72.5	72.5	0.0	0.0	0.0	0.0	100.0
McPherson	386	99.7	0.3	0.0	0.0	0.0	0.0	92	2	14	92	<.1	<.1	<.1	0.0	70.7	70.6	100.0	0.0	0.0	0.0	0.0
Madison	23,344	96.8	0.7	0.2	0.6	0.0	1.7	8	78	7	18	2.0	2.1	0.4	1.8	71.5	71.7	65.1	65.1	63.5	0.0	69.9
Merrick	5,805	99.2	<.1	0.2	0.1	0.0	0.5	40	42	58	42	0.5	0.5	<.1	0.1	72.2	72.5	50.0	55.6	66.7	0.0	40.8
Morrill	3,903	93.3	0.0	0.1	0.3	<.1	6.3	58	86	84	2	0.3	0.3	0.0	1.1	72.0	73.5	0.0	71.4	46.2	33.3	56.2
Nance	3,046	99.2	<.1	0.1	<.1	0.0	0.5	63	36	50	43	0.3	0.3	<.1	0.1	71.3	71.6	100.0	50.0	75.0	0.0	39.5
Nemaha	6,028	98.4	0.9	0.2	0.2	0.0	0.2	39	61	4	66	0.5	0.6	0.2	<.1	75.5	75.5	78.9	92.9	100.0	0.0	70.0
Nuckolls	4,288	99.0	0.0	0.0	0.2	0.0	0.5	54	13	85	72	0.4	0.4	0.0	<.1	74.1	74.2	0.0	0.0	87.5	0.0	47.1
Otoe	10,525	99.1	0.1	0.1	0.2	0.0	0.5	19	45	27	38	0.9	1.0	<.1	0.2	73.8	74.1	56.0	45.8	61.3	0.0	51.9
Pawnee	2,549	99.5	0.0	<.1	<.1	<.1	0.4	70	23	86	59	0.2	0.2	0.0	<.1	76.8	77.1	0.0	50.0	100.0	50.0	52.9
Perkins	2,365	98.8	0.0	0.1	0.1	<.1	0.9	71	53	87	25	0.2	0.2	0.0	<.1	72.7	72.8	0.0	42.9	42.9	100.0	41.5
Phelps	7,059	99.0	<.1	0.1	0.1	0.0	0.7	29	46	44	32	0.6	0.6	<.1	0.2	72.7	72.9	60.0	50.0	60.0	0.0	52.7
Pierce	5,538	99.6	0.0	<.1	0.3	0.0	<.1	42	16	88	85	0.5	0.5	0.0	<.1	70.8	70.9	0.0	33.3	56.0	0.0	35.7

Nebraska 577

Table B. – 1990 Voting Age Population (VAP) by Race and Ethnic Origin (cont)

County	Total Voting Age Population	Percent of total VAP						Rank Percent of total VAP				Percent contribution to state VAP				VAP percent of total population						
				Non-Hispanic					Non-Hispanic				Non-Hispanic					Non-Hispanic				
		White	Black	Asian and Pacific Islander	Native American	Other	Hispanic	Total	White	Black	Hispanic	Total	White	Black	Hispanic	Total	White	Black	Asian and Pacific Islander	Native American	Other	Hispanic
Platte	20,563	98.8	0.2	0.2	0.2	<.1	0.7	11	51	23	33	1.8	1.9	<.1	0.6	69.0	69.2	64.2	55.4	54.1	66.7	54.1
Polk	4,161	99.4	<.1	<.1	0.2	0.0	0.3	57	29	55	64	0.4	0.4	<.1	<.1	73.3	73.6	100.0	27.3	90.0	0.0	40.0
Red Willow	8,527	98.1	0.1	0.2	0.2	0.0	1.4	25	65	28	23	0.7	0.8	<.1	0.5	72.8	73.2	76.9	72.0	75.0	0.0	55.2
Richardson	7,464	98.0	<.1	0.1	1.4	0.0	0.3	26	67	36	63	0.6	0.7	<.1	<.1	75.1	75.4	100.0	100.0	61.4	0.0	50.0
Rock	1,436	99.7	0.0	0.0	<.1	0.0	0.2	80	5	89	68	0.1	0.1	0.0	<.1	71.1	71.2	0.0	0.0	100.0	0.0	50.0
Saline	9,552	98.4	0.1	0.9	0.2	<.1	0.5	21	63	29	46	0.8	0.9	<.1	0.2	75.1	75.3	68.8	74.8	78.3	20.0	58.1
Sarpy	69,513	90.1	4.8	1.8	0.3	<.1	3.0	3	90	2	8	6.0	5.8	9.2	9.2	67.8	68.3	63.1	68.1	61.9	21.4	60.9
Saunders	13,066	99.3	<.1	<.1	0.2	<.1	0.4	15	35	40	56	1.1	1.2	<.1	0.2	71.5	71.7	50.0	37.9	60.0	25.0	50.0
Scotts Bluff	25,962	86.4	0.2	0.5	1.2	<.1	11.6	6	92	24	1	2.3	2.1	0.1	13.5	72.1	74.9	82.4	77.5	54.6	51.1	57.5
Seward	11,341	99.1	0.1	0.2	0.2	<.1	0.4	18	44	30	54	1.0	1.0	<.1	0.2	73.4	73.5	65.0	68.6	64.5	25.0	57.5
Sheridan	4,868	93.3	<.1	0.2	6.0	<.1	0.4	47	87	45	53	0.4	0.4	<.1	<.1	72.1	73.6	100.0	80.0	59.0	100.0	29.4
Sherman	2,668	99.6	0.0	0.2	<.1	<.1	<.1	68	14	90	87	0.2	0.2	0.0	<.1	71.8	71.9	0.0	50.0	100.0	100.0	25.0
Sioux	1,142	97.5	0.0	<.1	0.0	<.1	2.3	81	71	91	15	<.1	0.1	0.0	0.1	73.7	74.2	0.0	50.0	0.0	0.0	59.1
Stanton	4,182	98.9	0.2	<.1	0.5	0.0	0.3	56	50	16	65	0.4	0.4	<.1	<.1	67.0	67.2	39.1	100.0	56.8	0.0	52.2
Thayer	4,998	99.0	<.1	<.1	0.2	0.0	0.7	46	49	46	31	0.4	0.5	<.1	0.2	75.3	75.6	50.0	28.6	61.1	0.0	59.3
Thomas	582	99.3	0.0	0.0	0.2	0.0	0.5	88	33	92	40	<.1	<.1	0.0	<.1	68.4	68.9	0.0	0.0	100.0	0.0	27.3
Thurston	4,504	63.5	0.2	0.1	35.6	0.0	0.6	51	93	21	36	0.4	0.3	<.1	0.1	64.9	74.2	100.0	85.7	53.4	0.0	43.5
Valley	3,829	99.5	<.1	0.2	<.1	0.0	0.2	59	19	34	74	0.3	0.4	<.1	<.1	74.1	74.3	50.0	60.0	20.0	0.0	41.2
Washington	12,053	98.5	0.6	0.2	0.3	0.0	0.5	16	60	8	44	1.0	1.1	0.2	0.3	72.6	72.6	85.4	64.7	81.6	0.0	56.7
Wayne	7,107	98.8	0.5	0.3	0.2	0.0	0.2	28	52	10	67	0.6	0.7	<.1	<.1	75.9	76.0	92.3	58.8	57.1	0.0	68.2
Webster	3,265	99.5	<.1	0.2	0.2	0.0	0.2	61	25	52	73	0.3	0.3	<.1	<.1	76.3	76.5	100.0	38.5	83.3	0.0	54.5
Wheeler	638	99.7	0.0	0.3	0.0	0.0	0.0	84	11	93	93	<.1	<.1	0.0	0.0	67.3	67.3	0.0	66.7	0.0	0.0	0.0
York	10,465	98.1	0.7	0.2	0.3	<.1	0.7	20	66	5	34	0.9	1.0	0.2	0.3	72.5	72.6	85.2	43.2	75.0	66.7	62.5
NEBRASKA	**1,149,373**	**93.6**	**3.1**	**0.7**	**0.6**	**<.1**	**1.9**					**100.0**	**100.0**	**100.0**	**100.0**	**72.8**	**73.7**	**63.6**	**67.6**	**58.6**	**29.8**	**60.2**
CONGRESSIONAL																						
District 1	389,852	96.3	0.9	0.8	0.8	<.1	1.1	1	2	2	3	33.9	34.9	10.2	19.8	74.1	74.6	67.3	68.5	57.9	29.6	62.2
District 2	379,331	87.6	8.4	1.1	0.4	<.1	2.5	3	3	1	1	33.0	30.9	88.2	41.9	72.0	73.5	63.2	69.0	62.2	25.4	62.7
District 3	380,190	96.8	0.2	0.3	0.5	<.1	2.2	2	1	3	2	33.1	34.2	1.6	38.3	72.3	73.0	64.5	60.3	57.1	42.0	56.9

Table C. — Voter Participation: November 3, 1992, General Election

County	Estimated Voting Age Population (VAP), 1992	Voter registration (REG) Total	% contribution to state REG	% of 1992 VAP	Rank by % of 1992 VAP	Voter turnout Highest office Actual	Total	Office	% of 1992 VAP	Maximum vote Total	% contribution to state turnout	% of REG	Rank by % of REG	% of 1992 VAP	Rank by % 1992 VAP	Percent drop-off, by office President	Senator	Governor	Representative
Adams	22,132	16,619	1.7	75.1	89	13,188	13,110	P	59.2	13,188	1.8	79.4	26	59.6	86	0.6	-	-	2.6
Antelope	5,606	5,121	0.5	91.3	32	3,841	3,776	P	67.4	3,841	0.5	75.0	62	68.5	35	1.7	-	-	5.4
Arthur	344	325	<.1	94.5	17	267	263	P	76.5	267	<.1	82.2	9	77.6	9	1.5	-	-	3.4
Banner	619	578	<.1	93.4	20	491	480	P	77.5	491	<.1	84.9	2	79.3	7	2.2	-	-	3.7
Blaine	488	506	<.1	103.7	4	457	453	P	92.8	457	<.1	90.3	1	93.6	1	0.9	-	-	2.8
Boone	4,729	4,183	0.4	88.5	51	3,214	3,162	P	66.9	3,214	0.4	76.8	46	68.0	42	1.6	-	-	5.4
Box Butte	9,103	8,336	0.9	91.6	29	5,797	5,670	P	62.3	5,797	0.8	69.5	91	63.7	74	2.2	-	-	3.7
Boyd	2,067	2,077	0.2	100.5	9	1,604	1,571	P	76.0	1,604	0.2	77.2	41	77.6	10	2.1	-	-	3.4
Brown	2,603	2,383	0.3	91.5	30	1,877	1,846	P	70.9	1,877	0.3	78.8	30	72.1	19	1.7	-	-	4.5
Buffalo	27,768	21,808	2.3	78.5	84	17,724	17,617	P	63.4	17,724	2.4	81.3	14	63.8	71	0.6	-	-	3.4
Burt	5,796	5,203	0.5	89.8	42	3,952	3,912	P	67.5	3,952	0.5	76.0	54	68.2	39	1.0	-	-	7.2
Butler	6,280	5,767	0.6	91.8	28	4,237	4,147	P	66.0	4,237	0.6	73.5	69	67.5	49	2.1	-	-	5.6
Cass	15,693	13,505	1.4	86.1	64	10,029	9,979	P	63.6	10,029	1.3	74.3	67	63.9	70	0.5	-	-	5.0
Cedar	6,953	6,161	0.6	88.6	49	4,612	4,518	P	65.0	4,612	0.6	74.9	63	66.3	56	2.0	-	-	4.9
Chase	3,125	2,791	0.3	89.3	44	2,115	2,082	P	66.6	2,115	0.3	75.8	57	67.7	45	1.6	-	-	5.1
Cherry	4,542	4,243	0.4	93.4	19	3,034	3,008	P	66.2	3,034	0.4	71.5	81	66.8	51	0.9	-	-	4.6
Cheyenne	6,910	5,757	0.6	83.3	72	4,292	4,241	P	61.4	4,292	0.4	74.6	65	62.1	80	1.2	-	-	3.4
Clay	5,195	4,838	0.5	93.1	22	3,642	3,581	P	68.9	3,642	0.5	75.3	60	70.1	28	1.7	-	-	4.2
Colfax	6,638	5,452	0.6	82.1	75	4,179	4,144	P	62.4	4,179	0.6	76.7	48	63.0	76	0.8	-	-	5.9
Cuming	7,201	6,617	0.7	91.9	27	4,806	4,746	P	65.9	4,806	0.6	72.6	76	66.7	53	1.2	-	-	5.6
Custer	8,895	8,612	0.9	96.8	14	6,011	5,820	P	65.4	6,011	0.8	69.8	88	67.6	48	3.2	-	-	4.2
Dakota	11,903	8,635	0.9	72.5	91	6,441	6,414	P	53.9	6,441	0.9	74.6	64	54.1	92	0.4	-	-	4.0
Dawes	6,566	5,153	0.5	78.5	85	4,098	4,068	P	62.0	4,098	0.6	79.5	24	62.4	77	0.7	-	-	6.2
Dawson	14,338	11,212	1.2	78.2	86	8,908	8,781	P	61.2	8,908	1.2	79.5	25	62.1	79	1.4	-	-	1.8
Deuel	1,652	1,498	0.2	90.7	39	1,139	1,120	P	67.8	1,139	0.2	76.0	53	68.9	34	1.7	-	-	7.4
Dixon	4,391	4,001	0.4	91.1	33	3,086	3,054	P	69.6	3,086	0.4	77.1	43	70.3	24	1.0	-	-	3.7
Dodge	25,497	20,223	2.1	79.3	82	16,648	16,408	P	64.4	16,648	2.2	82.3	8	65.3	63	1.4	-	-	4.7
Douglas	311,513	252,367	26.5	81.0	78	201,546	199,880	P	64.2	201,546	27.1	79.9	22	64.7	67	0.8	-	-	5.0
Dundy	1,967	1,575	0.2	80.1	80	1,276	1,252	P	63.7	1,276	0.2	81.0	16	64.9	66	1.9	-	-	10.7
Fillmore	5,268	4,438	0.5	84.2	69	3,521	3,483	P	66.1	3,521	0.5	79.3	27	66.8	50	1.1	-	-	6.0
Franklin	3,026	2,823	0.3	93.3	21	2,009	1,980	P	65.4	2,009	0.3	71.2	83	66.4	55	1.4	-	-	5.3
Frontier	2,220	2,074	0.2	93.4	18	1,601	1,571	P	70.8	1,601	0.2	77.2	42	72.1	18	1.9	-	-	4.0
Furnas	4,214	3,664	0.4	86.9	61	2,849	2,801	P	66.5	2,849	0.4	77.8	37	67.6	47	1.7	-	-	5.7
Gage	17,080	13,950	1.5	81.7	76	10,129	10,073	P	59.0	10,129	1.4	72.6	78	59.3	87	0.6	-	-	3.2
Garden	1,874	1,888	0.2	100.7	8	1,326	1,303	P	69.5	1,326	0.2	70.2	86	70.8	23	1.7	-	-	7.0
Garfield	1,602	1,544	0.2	96.4	15	1,105	1,087	P	67.9	1,105	0.1	71.6	80	69.0	33	1.6	-	-	4.4
Gosper	1,472	1,302	0.1	88.5	52	1,062	1,048	P	71.2	1,062	0.1	81.6	13	72.1	17	1.3	-	-	1.8
Grant	539	548	<.1	101.7	5	455	449	P	83.3	455	<.1	83.0	6	84.4	3	1.3	-	-	4.4
Greeley	2,121	1,891	0.2	89.2	46	1,446	1,418	P	66.9	1,446	0.2	76.5	51	68.2	40	1.9	-	-	5.6
Hall	35,951	26,303	2.8	73.2	90	20,838	20,692	P	57.6	20,838	2.8	79.2	28	58.0	89	0.7	-	-	3.0
Hamilton	6,372	5,801	0.6	91.0	35	4,631	4,599	P	72.2	4,631	0.6	79.8	23	72.7	15	0.7	-	-	4.2
Harlan	2,883	2,916	0.3	101.1	6	2,134	2,112	P	73.3	2,134	0.3	73.2	74	74.0	12	1.0	-	-	4.7
Hayes	905	798	<.1	88.2	54	658	654	P	72.3	658	<.1	82.5	7	72.7	13	0.6	-	-	7.9
Hitchcock	2,730	2,222	0.2	81.4	77	1,746	1,731	P	63.4	1,746	0.2	78.6	32	64.0	69	0.9	-	-	7.7
Holt	8,807	7,944	0.8	90.2	40	5,797	5,703	P	64.8	5,797	0.8	73.0	75	65.8	60	1.6	-	-	4.2
Hooker	573	650	<.1	113.4	1	472	455	P	79.4	472	<.1	72.6	77	82.4	5	3.6	-	-	3.6
Howard	4,357	4,024	0.4	92.4	24	2,905	2,868	P	65.8	2,905	0.4	72.2	79	66.7	54	1.3	-	-	4.1
Jefferson	6,571	5,972	0.6	90.9	37	4,589	4,491	P	68.3	4,589	0.6	76.8	45	69.8	29	2.1	-	-	5.8
Johnson	3,534	3,441	0.4	97.4	13	2,393	2,360	P	66.8	2,393	0.3	69.5	90	67.7	43	1.4	-	-	8.2
Kearney	4,859	4,226	0.4	87.0	60	3,288	3,254	P	67.0	3,288	0.4	77.8	36	67.7	46	1.0	-	-	3.0
Keith	6,218	5,348	0.6	86.0	65	3,987	3,897	P	62.7	3,987	0.5	74.6	66	64.1	68	2.3	-	-	4.5
Keya Paha	745	834	<.1	111.9	2	641	631	P	84.7	641	<.1	76.9	44	86.0	2	1.6	-	-	6.7
Kimball	2,949	2,723	0.3	92.3	25	1,809	1,788	P	60.6	1,809	0.2	66.4	92	61.3	83	1.2	-	-	3.7
Knox	6,868	6,256	0.7	91.1	34	4,383	4,263	P	62.1	4,383	0.6	70.1	87	63.8	72	2.7	-	-	5.9
Lancaster	165,564	128,428	13.5	77.6	87	105,449	104,843	P	63.3	105,449	14.2	82.1	10	63.7	73	0.6	-	-	3.8
Lincoln	23,024	20,304	2.1	88.2	53	15,766	15,593	P	67.7	15,766	2.1	77.6	38	68.5	37	1.1	-	-	2.3
Logan	598	589	<.1	98.5	11	459	451	P	75.4	459	<.1	77.9	34	76.8	11	1.7	-	-	2.6
Loup	489	525	<.1	107.4	3	402	389	P	79.6	402	<.1	76.6	50	82.2	6	3.2	-	-	5.5
McPherson	397	395	<.1	99.5	10	332	329	P	82.9	332	<.1	84.1	4	83.6	4	0.9	-	-	2.7
Madison	23,776	18,846	2.0	79.3	83	13,832	13,736	P	57.8	13,832	1.9	73.4	71	58.2	88	0.7	-	-	3.0
Merrick	5,828	5,127	0.5	88.0	55	3,856	3,811	P	65.4	3,856	0.5	75.2	61	66.2	58	1.2	-	-	3.4
Morrill	3,898	3,492	0.4	89.6	43	2,565	2,525	P	64.8	2,565	0.3	73.5	70	65.8	61	1.6	-	-	4.9
Nance	3,081	2,663	0.3	86.4	62	2,020	1,987	P	64.5	2,020	0.3	75.9	55	65.6	62	1.6	-	-	8.2
Nemaha	5,965	4,905	0.5	82.2	74	3,927	3,854	P	64.6	3,927	0.5	80.1	20	65.8	59	1.9	-	-	6.5
Nuckolls	4,260	3,957	0.4	92.9	23	2,990	2,956	P	69.4	2,990	0.4	75.6	58	70.2	27	1.1	-	-	3.9
Otoe	10,608	9,135	1.0	86.1	63	6,899	6,838	P	64.5	6,899	0.9	75.5	59	65.0	64	0.9	-	-	15.3
Pawnee	2,524	2,294	0.2	90.9	36	1,833	1,808	P	71.6	1,833	0.2	79.9	21	72.6	16	1.4	-	-	3.3
Perkins	2,414	2,075	0.2	86.0	67	1,679	1,666	P	69.0	1,679	0.2	80.9	17	69.6	31	0.8	-	-	4.5
Phelps	7,218	6,429	0.7	89.1	47	4,932	4,894	P	67.8	4,932	0.7	76.7	47	68.3	38	0.8	-	-	2.1
Pierce	5,528	4,856	0.5	87.8	56	3,592	3,562	P	64.4	3,592	0.5	74.0	68	65.0	65	0.8	-	-	5.8

Table C. – Voter Participation: November 3, 1992, General Election (cont)

County	Estimated Voting Age Population (VAP), 1992	Voter registration (REG)				Voter turnout													
						Highest office				Maximum vote						Percent drop-off, by office			
		Total	% contribution to state REG	% of 1992 VAP	Rank by % of 1992 VAP	Actual	Total	Office	% of 1992 VAP	Total	% contribution to state turnout	% of REG	Rank by % of REG	% of 1992 VAP	Rank by % 1992 VAP	President	Senator	Governor	Representative
Platte	21,095	17,897	1.9	84.8	68	13,987	13,823	P	65.5	13,987	1.9	78.2	33	66.3	57	1.2	-	-	5.7
Polk	4,189	3,652	0.4	87.2	59	2,941	2,916	P	69.6	2,941	0.4	80.5	18	70.2	26	0.9	-	-	5.2
Red Willow	8,475	7,626	0.8	90.0	41	5,380	5,323	P	62.8	5,380	0.7	70.5	85	63.5	75	1.1	-	-	3.0
Richardson	7,390	7,084	0.7	95.9	16	5,028	4,940	P	66.8	5,028	0.7	71.0	84	68.0	41	1.8	-	-	9.2
Rock	1,431	1,274	0.1	89.0	48	1,005	987	P	69.0	1,005	0.1	78.9	29	70.2	25	1.8	-	-	5.1
Saline	9,492	8,329	0.9	87.7	57	5,802	5,765	P	60.7	5,802	0.8	69.7	89	61.1	84	0.6	-	-	2.4
Sarpy	74,433	52,312	5.5	70.3	92	40,726	40,604	P	54.6	40,726	5.5	77.9	35	54.7	91	0.3	-	-	4.4
Saunders	13,314	12,097	1.3	90.9	38	9,248	9,152	P	68.7	9,248	1.2	76.4	52	69.5	32	1.0	-	-	4.3
Scotts Bluff	26,054	17,894	1.9	68.7	93	15,069	14,947	P	57.4	15,069	2.0	84.2	3	57.8	90	0.8	-	-	2.9
Seward	11,215	8,534	0.9	76.1	88	6,970	6,908	P	61.6	6,970	0.9	81.7	12	62.1	78	0.9	-	-	3.0
Sheridan	4,871	3,945	0.4	81.0	79	3,023	2,996	P	61.5	3,023	0.4	76.6	49	62.1	81	0.9	-	-	4.2
Sherman	2,700	2,367	0.2	87.7	58	1,943	1,899	P	70.3	1,943	0.3	82.1	11	72.0	21	2.3	-	-	4.9
Sioux	1,126	1,135	0.1	100.8	7	811	802	P	71.2	811	0.1	71.5	82	72.0	20	1.1	-	-	4.2
Stanton	4,268	3,551	0.4	83.2	73	2,602	2,563	P	60.1	2,602	0.3	73.3	73	61.0	85	1.5	-	-	4.5
Thayer	4,937	4,244	0.4	86.0	66	3,440	3,403	P	68.9	3,440	0.5	81.1	15	69.7	30	1.1	-	-	4.4
Thomas	612	599	<.1	97.9	12	481	468	P	76.5	481	<.1	80.3	19	78.6	8	2.7	-	-	4.4
Thurston	4,531	3,800	0.4	83.9	71	2,287	2,257	P	49.8	2,287	0.3	60.2	93	50.5	93	1.3	-	-	6.8
Valley	3,863	3,422	0.4	88.6	50	2,646	2,590	P	67.0	2,646	0.4	77.3	40	68.5	36	2.1	-	-	4.3
Washington	12,487	9,936	1.0	79.6	81	8,340	8,307	P	66.5	8,340	1.1	83.9	5	66.8	52	0.4	-	-	7.2
Wayne	6,739	5,652	0.6	83.9	70	4,147	4,102	P	60.9	4,147	0.6	73.4	72	61.5	82	1.1	-	-	6.6
Webster	3,240	2,960	0.3	91.4	31	2,298	2,262	P	69.8	2,298	0.3	77.6	39	70.9	22	1.6	-	-	4.6
Wheeler	648	598	<.1	92.3	26	471	464	P	71.6	471	<.1	78.8	31	72.7	14	1.5	-	-	5.1
York	10,466	9,341	1.0	89.3	45	7,085	7,012	P	67.0	7,085	1.0	75.8	56	67.7	44	1.0	-	-	3.5
NEBRASKA	1,167,000	951,395	100.0	81.5		744,548	737,546		63.2	744,548	100.0	78.3		63.8		0.9	-	-	4.5

Table D. – Voter Registration by Political Party Affiliation: November 3, 1992, General Election

County	Total voter registration	Democrat (DEM)	Republican (REP)	Independent (IND)	Plurality Total	Plurality Party	Percent of total registration DEM	REP	IND	Rank DEM	REP	IND	Percent contribution to state registration Total	DEM	REP	IND
Adams	16,619	6,124	8,896	1,597	2,772	R	36.9	53.5	9.6	41	57	16	1.7	1.6	1.9	1.6
Antelope	5,121	1,713	3,063	345	1,350	R	33.5	59.8	6.7	53	38	55	0.5	0.4	0.7	0.4
Arthur	325	68	245	12	177	R	20.9	75.4	3.7	88	5	85	<.1	<.1	<.1	<.1
Banner	578	104	436	38	332	R	18.0	75.4	6.6	89	4	56	<.1	<.1	<.1	<.1
Blaine	506	114	373	19	259	R	22.5	73.7	3.8	84	8	84	<.1	<.1	<.1	<.1
Boone	4,183	1,720	2,174	289	454	R	41.1	52.0	6.9	23	64	50	0.4	0.4	0.5	0.3
Box Butte	8,336	3,168	4,213	953	1,045	R	38.0	50.6	11.4	36	70	8	0.9	0.8	0.9	1.0
Boyd	2,077	655	1,313	109	658	R	31.5	63.2	5.2	62	26	73	0.2	0.2	0.3	0.1
Brown	2,383	615	1,603	165	988	R	25.8	67.3	6.9	80	17	48	0.3	0.2	0.3	0.2
Buffalo	21,808	7,365	12,064	2,369	4,699	R	33.8	55.3	10.9	52	53	11	2.3	1.9	2.6	2.4
Burt	5,203	2,006	2,727	470	721	R	38.6	52.4	9.0	34	63	22	0.5	0.5	0.6	0.5
Butler	5,767	3,279	1,968	518	1,311	D	56.9	34.1	9.0	5	92	23	0.6	0.8	0.4	0.5
Cass	13,505	5,696	6,221	1,584	525	R	42.2	46.1	11.7	18	80	7	1.4	1.5	1.3	1.6
Cedar	6,161	3,222	2,503	436	719	D	52.3	40.6	7.1	7	86	44	0.6	0.8	0.5	0.4
Chase	2,791	1,022	1,615	153	593	R	36.6	57.9	5.5	43	43	71	0.3	0.3	0.3	0.2
Cherry	4,243	1,152	2,911	179	1,759	R	27.2	68.6	4.2	76	13	81	0.4	0.3	0.6	0.2
Cheyenne	5,757	1,923	3,416	418	1,493	R	33.4	59.3	7.3	54	41	41	0.6	0.5	0.7	0.4
Clay	4,838	1,608	2,783	447	1,175	R	33.2	57.5	9.2	56	45	20	0.5	0.4	0.6	0.5
Colfax	5,452	2,639	2,439	374	200	D	48.4	44.7	6.9	10	81	52	0.6	0.7	0.5	0.4
Cuming	6,617	2,097	4,193	327	2,096	R	31.7	63.4	4.9	60	25	77	0.7	0.5	0.9	0.3
Custer	8,612	2,704	5,376	532	2,672	R	31.4	62.4	6.2	63	30	63	0.9	0.7	1.2	0.5
Dakota	8,635	3,944	3,500	1,190	444	D	45.7	40.5	13.8	12	87	2	0.9	1.0	0.8	1.2
Dawes	5,153	1,444	3,211	498	1,767	R	28.0	62.3	9.7	75	31	15	0.5	0.4	0.7	0.5
Dawson	11,212	3,583	6,671	956	3,088	R	32.0	59.5	8.5	58	39	29	1.2	0.9	1.4	1.0
Deuel	1,498	268	1,091	139	823	R	17.9	72.8	9.3	90	10	19	0.2	<.1	0.2	0.1
Dixon	4,001	1,638	2,108	255	470	R	40.9	52.7	6.4	25	60	62	0.4	0.4	0.5	0.3
Dodge	20,223	8,106	9,886	2,227	1,780	R	40.1	48.9	11.0	28	75	10	2.1	2.1	2.1	2.3
Douglas	252,367	116,908	105,780	29,610	11,128	D	46.3	41.9	11.7	11	85	6	26.5	30.0	22.8	30.5
Dundy	1,575	454	1,031	90	577	R	28.8	65.5	5.7	72	18	69	0.2	0.1	0.2	<.1
Fillmore	4,438	1,844	2,264	330	420	R	41.6	51.0	7.4	20	69	38	0.5	0.5	0.5	0.3
Franklin	2,823	985	1,613	225	628	R	34.9	57.1	8.0	47	46	32	0.3	0.3	0.3	0.2
Frontier	2,074	618	1,323	133	705	R	29.8	63.8	6.4	67	22	60	0.2	0.2	0.3	0.1
Furnas	3,664	1,253	2,265	146	1,012	R	34.2	61.8	4.0	51	32	82	0.4	0.3	0.5	0.2
Gage	13,950	5,768	6,964	1,213	1,196	R	41.4	49.9	8.7	21	73	27	1.5	1.5	1.5	1.2
Garden	1,888	541	1,234	113	693	R	28.7	65.4	6.0	74	19	64	0.2	0.1	0.3	0.1
Garfield	1,544	342	1,145	57	803	R	22.2	74.2	3.7	85	7	86	0.2	<.1	0.2	<.1
Gosper	1,302	453	781	68	328	R	34.8	60.0	5.2	49	37	75	0.1	0.1	0.2	<.1
Grant	548	117	407	24	290	R	21.4	74.3	4.4	86	6	79	<.1	<.1	<.1	<.1
Greeley	1,891	1,191	643	57	548	D	63.0	34.0	3.0	1	93	90	0.2	0.3	0.1	<.1
Hall	26,303	9,841	13,178	3,281	3,337	R	37.4	50.1	12.5	38	71	3	2.8	2.5	2.8	3.4
Hamilton	5,801	1,722	3,660	419	1,938	R	29.7	63.1	7.2	68	27	42	0.6	0.4	0.8	0.4
Harlan	2,916	1,174	1,592	150	418	R	40.3	54.6	5.1	27	56	76	0.3	0.3	0.3	0.2
Hayes	798	210	545	43	335	R	26.3	68.3	5.4	78	15	72	<.1	<.1	0.1	<.1
Hitchcock	2,222	818	1,279	125	461	R	36.8	57.6	5.6	42	44	70	0.2	0.2	0.3	0.1
Holt	7,944	2,511	4,884	549	2,373	R	31.6	61.5	6.9	61	34	49	0.8	0.6	1.1	0.6
Hooker	650	87	548	15	461	R	13.4	84.3	2.3	93	1	91	<.1	<.1	0.1	<.1
Howard	4,024	1,974	1,762	288	212	D	49.1	43.8	7.2	9	82	43	0.4	0.5	0.4	0.3
Jefferson	5,972	2,307	3,133	532	826	R	38.6	52.5	8.9	33	62	26	0.6	0.6	0.7	0.5
Johnson	3,441	1,508	1,672	261	164	R	43.8	48.6	7.6	15	77	35	0.4	0.4	0.4	0.3
Kearney	4,226	1,526	2,400	298	874	R	36.1	56.8	7.1	45	48	46	0.4	0.4	0.5	0.3
Keith	5,348	1,565	3,221	562	1,656	R	29.3	60.2	10.5	70	36	12	0.6	0.4	0.7	0.6
Keya Paha	834	291	526	17	235	R	34.9	63.1	2.0	48	28	92	<.1	<.1	0.1	<.1
Kimball	2,723	851	1,769	103	918	R	31.3	65.0	3.8	64	20	83	0.3	0.2	0.4	0.1
Knox	6,256	2,559	3,216	481	657	R	40.9	51.4	7.7	26	67	34	0.7	0.7	0.7	0.5
Lancaster	128,428	57,326	55,070	15,989	2,256	D	44.7	42.9	12.5	14	83	4	13.5	14.7	11.8	16.5
Lincoln	20,304	8,783	10,129	1,386	1,346	R	43.3	49.9	6.8	17	74	53	2.1	2.3	2.2	1.4
Logan	589	99	465	25	366	R	16.8	78.9	4.2	92	2	80	<.1	<.1	0.1	<.1
Loup	525	133	374	18	241	R	25.3	71.2	3.4	82	12	87	<.1	<.1	<.1	<.1
McPherson	395	97	291	7	194	R	24.6	73.7	1.8	83	9	93	<.1	<.1	<.1	<.1
Madison	18,846	5,476	11,948	1,422	6,472	R	29.1	63.4	7.5	71	24	36	2.0	1.4	2.6	1.5
Merrick	5,127	1,800	3,028	299	1,228	R	35.1	59.1	5.8	46	42	67	0.5	0.5	0.7	0.3
Morrill	3,492	1,059	2,137	294	1,078	R	30.3	61.2	8.4	66	35	30	0.4	0.3	0.5	0.3
Nance	2,663	1,417	1,071	175	346	D	53.2	40.2	6.6	6	88	57	0.3	0.4	0.2	0.2
Nemaha	4,905	1,913	2,547	445	634	R	39.0	51.9	9.1	31	65	21	0.5	0.5	0.5	0.5
Nuckolls	3,957	1,773	1,930	254	157	R	44.8	48.8	6.4	13	76	59	0.4	0.5	0.4	0.3
Otoe	9,135	3,597	4,723	814	1,126	R	39.4	51.7	8.9	29	66	25	1.0	0.9	1.0	0.8
Pawnee	2,294	948	1,209	137	261	R	41.3	52.7	6.0	22	59	65	0.2	0.2	0.3	0.1
Perkins	2,075	711	1,178	186	467	R	34.3	56.8	9.0	50	49	24	0.2	0.2	0.3	0.2
Phelps	6,429	1,900	4,085	443	2,185	R	29.6	63.6	6.9	69	23	51	0.7	0.5	0.9	0.5
Pierce	4,856	1,586	2,992	278	1,406	R	32.7	61.6	5.7	57	33	68	0.5	0.4	0.6	0.3

County	Total voter registration	Political party affiliation					Percent of total registration						Percent contribution to state registration			
		Democrat (DEM)	Republican (REP)	Independent (IND)	Plurality		DEM	REP	IND	Rank			Total	DEM	REP	IND
					Total	Party				DEM	REP	IND				
Platte...............	17,897	7,356	9,192	1,345	1,836	R	41.1	51.4	7.5	24	68	37	1.9	1.9	2.0	1.4
Polk.................	3,652	1,362	2,023	267	661	R	37.3	55.4	7.3	40	52	40	0.4	0.4	0.4	0.3
Red Willow.......................	7,626	2,431	4,340	855	1,909	R	31.9	56.9	11.2	59	47	9	0.8	0.6	0.9	0.9
Richardson	7,084	3,090	3,539	454	449	R	43.6	50.0	6.4	16	72	61	0.7	0.8	0.8	0.5
Rock	1,274	271	921	82	650	R	21.3	72.3	6.4	87	11	58	0.1	< .1	0.2	< .1
Saline	8,329	4,741	2,872	715	1,869	D	56.9	34.5	8.6	4	91	28	0.9	1.2	0.6	0.7
Sarpy	52,312	19,961	24,505	7,833	4,544	R	38.2	46.9	15.0	35	79	1	5.5	5.1	5.3	8.1
Saunders	12,097	5,974	5,171	949	803	D	49.4	42.8	7.8	8	84	33	1.3	1.5	1.1	1.0
Scotts Bluff....................	17,894	6,537	9,512	1,844	2,975	R	36.5	53.2	10.3	44	58	14	1.9	1.7	2.0	1.9
Seward	8,534	3,573	4,142	819	569	R	41.9	48.5	9.6	19	78	17	0.9	0.9	0.9	0.8
Sheridan.......................	3,945	1,054	2,706	184	1,652	R	26.7	68.6	4.7	77	14	78	0.4	0.3	0.6	0.2
Sherman.......................	2,367	1,466	819	80	647	D	62.0	34.6	3.4	2	90	88	0.2	0.4	0.2	< .1
Sioux.............	1,135	294	734	107	440	R	25.9	64.7	9.4	65	21	18	0.1	< .1	0.2	0.1
Stanton	3,551	1,078	2,222	251	1,144	R	30.4	62.6	7.1	65	29	45	0.4	0.3	0.5	0.3
Thayer	4,244	1,592	2,341	311	749	R	37.5	55.2	7.3	37	55	39	0.4	0.4	0.5	0.3
Thomas.......................	599	107	472	20	365	R	17.9	78.8	3.3	91	3	89	< .1	< .1	0.1	< .1
Thurston	3,800	2,209	1,392	199	817	D	58.1	36.6	5.2	3	89	74	0.4	0.6	0.3	0.2
Valley	3,422	1,278	1,906	238	628	R	37.3	55.7	7.0	39	51	47	0.4	0.3	0.4	0.2
Washington....................	9,936	3,316	5,576	1,041	2,260	R	33.4	56.1	10.5	55	50	13	1.0	0.9	1.2	1.1
Wayne.............	5,652	1,621	3,354	675	1,733	R	28.7	59.4	11.9	73	40	5	0.6	0.4	0.7	0.7
Webster	2,960	1,157	1,559	243	402	R	39.1	52.7	8.2	30	61	31	0.3	0.3	0.3	0.3
Wheeler	598	233	330	35	97	R	39.0	55.2	5.9	32	54	66	< .1	< .1	< .1	< .1
York	9,341	2,388	6,316	636	3,928	R	25.6	67.6	6.8	81	16	54	1.0	0.6	1.4	0.7
NEBRASKA[1]	**951,395**	**389,102**	**464,955**	**97,144**	**75,853**	**R**	**40.9**	**48.9**	**10.2**				**100.0**	**100.0**	**100.0**	**100.0**

[1]Total voter registration also includes 194 for Libertarian party.

Table E. — Vote for President: November 3, 1992, General Election

County	Total	Clinton (DEM)	Bush (REP)	Perot (IND)	Other	Plurality Total	Party	DEM	REP	IND	Other	Rank DEM	Rank REP	Rank IND	Total	DEM	REP	IND	DEM	REP
Adams	13,110	3,445	6,346	3,273	46	2,901	R	26.3	48.4	25.0	0.4	33	52	74	1.8	1.6	1.8	1.9	35.2	64.8
Antelope	3,776	650	1,979	1,134	13	845	R	17.2	52.4	30.0	0.3	76	31	17	0.5	0.3	0.6	0.7	24.7	75.3
Arthur	263	18	148	97	0	51	R	6.8	56.3	36.9	0.0	93	14	1	<.1	<.1	<.1	<.1	10.8	89.2
Banner	480	68	284	128	0	156	R	14.2	59.2	26.7	0.0	90	7	49	<.1	<.1	<.1	<.1	19.3	80.7
Blaine	453	64	256	130	3	126	R	14.1	56.5	28.7	0.7	91	13	27	<.1	<.1	<.1	<.1	20.0	80.0
Boone	3,162	604	1,588	956	14	632	R	19.1	50.2	30.2	0.4	66	41	15	0.4	0.3	0.5	0.5	27.6	72.4
Box Butte	5,670	1,935	2,198	1,508	29	263	R	34.1	38.8	26.6	0.5	6	89	52	0.8	0.9	0.6	0.9	46.8	53.2
Boyd	1,571	353	744	468	6	276	R	22.5	47.4	29.8	0.4	47	57	18	0.2	0.2	0.2	0.3	32.2	67.8
Brown	1,846	311	999	525	11	474	R	16.8	54.1	28.4	0.6	80	24	30	0.3	0.1	0.3	0.3	23.7	76.3
Buffalo	17,617	3,742	9,708	4,083	84	5,625	R	21.2	55.1	23.2	0.5	54	19	84	2.4	1.7	2.8	2.3	27.8	72.2
Burt	3,912	1,224	1,667	1,009	12	443	R	31.3	42.6	25.8	0.3	12	80	65	0.5	0.6	0.5	0.6	42.3	57.7
Butler	4,147	1,087	1,881	1,157	22	724	R	26.2	45.4	27.9	0.5	34	64	36	0.6	0.5	0.5	0.7	36.6	63.4
Cass	9,979	2,949	4,314	2,657	59	1,365	R	29.6	43.2	26.6	0.6	18	74	50	1.4	1.4	1.3	1.5	40.6	59.4
Cedar	4,518	1,007	1,981	1,507	23	474	R	22.3	43.8	33.4	0.5	50	72	2	0.6	0.5	0.6	0.9	33.7	66.3
Chase	2,082	398	1,000	674	10	326	R	19.1	48.0	32.4	0.5	65	55	4	0.3	0.2	0.3	0.4	28.5	71.5
Cherry	3,008	563	1,707	730	8	977	R	18.7	56.7	24.3	0.3	69	11	80	0.4	0.3	0.5	0.4	24.8	75.2
Cheyenne	4,241	967	2,197	1,061	16	1,136	R	22.8	51.8	25.0	0.4	43	35	73	0.6	0.4	0.6	0.6	30.6	69.4
Clay	3,581	802	1,818	952	9	866	R	22.4	50.8	26.6	0.3	49	38	53	0.5	0.4	0.5	0.5	30.6	69.4
Colfax	4,144	1,011	1,915	1,197	21	718	R	24.4	46.2	28.9	0.5	36	63	25	0.6	0.5	0.6	0.7	34.6	65.4
Cuming	4,746	835	2,711	1,192	8	1,519	R	17.6	57.1	25.1	0.2	74	10	70	0.6	0.4	0.8	0.7	23.5	76.5
Custer	5,820	1,126	3,180	1,492	22	1,688	R	19.3	54.6	25.6	0.4	63	23	67	0.8	0.5	0.9	0.9	26.1	73.9
Dakota	6,414	2,322	2,771	1,307	14	449	R	36.2	43.2	20.4	0.2	4	75	91	0.9	1.1	0.8	0.8	45.6	54.4
Dawes	4,068	987	1,961	1,103	17	858	R	24.3	48.2	27.1	0.4	37	54	45	0.6	0.5	0.6	0.6	33.5	66.5
Dawson	8,781	1,739	4,710	2,305	27	2,405	R	19.8	53.6	26.2	0.4	58	27	60	1.2	0.8	1.4	1.3	27.0	73.0
Deuel	1,120	232	558	327	3	231	R	20.7	49.8	29.2	0.3	56	43	22	0.2	0.1	0.2	0.2	29.4	70.6
Dixon	3,054	830	1,484	726	14	654	R	27.2	48.6	23.8	0.5	28	50	81	0.4	0.4	0.4	0.4	35.9	64.1
Dodge	16,408	4,665	7,269	4,432	42	2,604	R	28.4	44.3	27.0	0.3	20	68	47	2.2	2.2	2.1	2.5	39.1	60.9
Douglas	199,880	67,003	93,421	38,641	815	26,418	R	33.5	46.7	19.3	0.4	8	62	92	27.1	30.9	27.2	22.2	41.8	58.2
Dundy	1,252	244	664	332	12	332	R	19.5	53.0	26.5	1.0	61	29	55	0.2	0.1	0.2	0.2	26.9	73.1
Fillmore	3,483	988	1,495	993	7	502	R	28.4	42.9	28.5	0.2	21	78	29	0.5	0.5	0.4	0.6	39.8	60.2
Franklin	1,980	477	967	527	9	440	R	24.1	48.8	26.6	0.5	39	47	51	0.3	0.2	0.3	0.3	33.0	67.0
Frontier	1,571	302	785	479	5	306	R	19.2	50.0	30.5	0.3	64	42	13	0.2	0.1	0.2	0.3	27.8	72.2
Furnas	2,801	624	1,365	804	8	561	R	22.3	48.7	28.7	0.3	51	48	26	0.4	0.3	0.4	0.5	31.4	68.6
Gage	10,073	3,309	3,995	2,726	43	686	R	32.9	39.7	27.1	0.4	10	87	46	1.4	1.5	1.2	1.6	45.3	54.7
Garden	1,303	212	697	385	9	312	R	16.3	53.5	29.5	0.7	84	28	20	0.2	<.1	0.2	0.2	23.3	76.7
Garfield	1,087	221	595	270	1	325	R	20.3	54.7	24.8	<.1	57	22	76	0.1	0.1	0.2	0.2	27.1	72.9
Gosper	1,048	254	492	297	5	195	R	24.2	46.9	28.3	0.5	38	58	31	0.1	0.1	0.1	0.2	34.0	66.0
Grant	449	75	247	124	3	123	R	16.7	55.0	27.6	0.7	81	20	39	<.1	<.1	<.1	<.1	23.3	76.7
Greeley	1,418	435	587	395	1	152	R	30.7	41.4	27.9	<.1	13	82	37	0.2	0.2	0.2	0.2	42.6	57.4
Hall	20,692	5,519	9,264	5,822	87	3,442	R	26.7	44.8	28.1	0.4	31	67	32	2.8	2.5	2.7	3.3	37.3	62.7
Hamilton	4,599	992	2,379	1,213	15	1,166	R	21.6	51.7	26.4	0.3	53	37	58	0.6	0.5	0.7	0.7	29.4	70.6
Harlan	2,112	488	991	623	10	368	R	23.1	46.9	29.5	0.5	40	59	21	0.3	0.2	0.3	0.4	33.0	67.0
Hayes	654	85	362	207	0	155	R	13.0	55.4	31.7	0.0	92	18	5	<.1	<.1	0.1	0.1	19.0	81.0
Hitchcock	1,731	359	824	540	8	284	R	20.7	47.6	31.2	0.5	55	56	9	0.2	0.2	0.2	0.3	30.3	69.7
Holt	5,703	835	3,131	1,714	23	1,417	R	14.6	54.9	30.1	0.4	89	21	16	0.8	0.4	0.9	1.0	21.1	78.9
Hooker	455	70	283	102	0	181	R	15.4	62.2	22.4	0.0	85	2	86	<.1	<.1	<.1	<.1	19.8	80.2
Howard	2,868	778	1,138	940	12	198	R	27.1	39.7	32.8	0.4	29	86	3	0.4	0.4	0.3	0.5	40.6	59.4
Jefferson	4,491	1,506	1,783	1,177	25	277	R	33.5	39.7	26.2	0.6	7	85	61	0.6	0.7	0.5	0.7	45.8	54.2
Johnson	2,360	822	885	642	11	63	R	34.8	37.5	27.2	0.5	5	91	44	0.3	0.4	0.3	0.4	48.2	51.8
Kearney	3,254	644	1,751	844	15	907	R	19.8	53.8	25.9	0.5	59	26	63	0.4	0.3	0.5	0.5	26.9	73.1
Keith	3,897	731	2,019	1,130	17	889	R	18.8	51.8	29.0	0.4	68	34	24	0.5	0.3	0.6	0.6	26.6	73.4
Keya Paha	631	105	368	158	0	210	R	16.6	58.3	25.0	0.0	82	8	72	<.1	<.1	0.1	<.1	22.2	77.8
Kimball	1,788	408	931	440	9	491	R	22.8	52.1	24.6	0.5	42	32	78	0.2	0.2	0.3	0.3	30.5	69.5
Knox	4,263	968	2,112	1,166	17	946	R	22.7	49.5	27.4	0.4	44	45	42	0.6	0.4	0.6	0.7	31.4	68.6
Lancaster	104,843	41,207	41,400	21,783	453	193	R	39.3	39.5	20.8	0.4	2	88	90	14.2	19.0	12.0	12.5	49.9	50.1
Lincoln	15,593	5,142	7,025	3,384	42	1,883	R	33.0	45.1	21.7	0.3	9	66	88	2.1	2.4	2.0	1.9	42.3	57.7
Logan	451	80	271	98	2	173	R	17.7	60.1	21.7	0.4	73	4	87	<.1	<.1	<.1	<.1	22.8	77.2
Loup	389	58	233	96	2	137	R	14.9	59.9	24.7	0.5	86	5	77	<.1	<.1	<.1	<.1	19.9	80.1
McPherson	329	49	217	62	1	155	R	14.9	66.0	18.8	0.3	87	1	93	<.1	<.1	<.1	<.1	18.4	81.6
Madison	13,736	2,352	7,851	3,486	47	4,365	R	17.1	57.2	25.4	0.3	78	9	69	1.9	1.1	2.3	2.0	23.1	76.9
Merrick	3,811	864	1,854	1,072	21	782	R	22.7	48.6	28.1	0.6	45	49	33	0.5	0.4	0.5	0.6	31.8	68.2
Morrill	2,525	577	1,184	752	12	432	R	22.9	46.9	29.8	0.5	41	60	19	0.3	0.3	0.3	0.4	32.8	67.2
Nance	1,987	559	851	569	8	282	R	28.1	42.8	28.6	0.4	23	79	28	0.3	0.3	0.2	0.3	39.6	60.4
Nemaha	3,854	1,110	1,696	1,020	28	586	R	28.8	44.0	26.5	0.7	19	71	56	0.5	0.5	0.5	0.6	39.6	60.4
Nuckolls	2,956	834	1,277	825	20	443	R	28.2	43.2	27.9	0.7	22	76	35	0.4	0.4	0.4	0.5	39.5	60.5
Otoe	6,838	2,038	2,960	1,800	40	922	R	29.8	43.3	26.3	0.6	17	73	59	0.9	0.9	0.9	1.0	40.8	59.2
Pawnee	1,808	566	670	565	7	104	R	31.3	37.1	31.3	0.4	11	92	8	0.2	0.3	0.2	0.3	45.8	54.2
Perkins	1,666	300	842	522	2	320	R	18.0	50.5	31.3	0.1	71	39	7	0.2	0.1	0.2	0.3	26.3	73.7
Phelps	4,894	829	2,748	1,298	19	1,450	R	16.9	56.2	26.5	0.4	79	15	54	0.7	0.4	0.8	0.7	23.2	76.8
Pierce	3,562	611	1,853	1,084	14	769	R	17.2	52.0	30.4	0.4	77	33	14	0.5	0.3	0.5	0.6	24.8	75.2

Nebraska 583

Table E. – Vote for President: November 3, 1992, General Election (cont)

County	Total	Clinton (DEM)	Bush (REP)	Perot (IND)	Other	Plurality Total	Party	DEM	REP	IND	Other	Rank DEM	Rank REP	Rank IND	Total	DEM	REP	IND	DEM	REP
Platte	13,823	2,409	7,712	3,656	46	4,056	R	17.4	55.8	26.4	0.3	75	16	57	1.9	1.1	2.2	2.1	23.8	76.2
Polk	2,916	661	1,435	812	8	623	R	22.7	49.2	27.8	0.3	46	46	38	0.4	0.3	0.4	0.5	31.5	68.5
Red Willow	5,323	1,164	2,488	1,660	11	828	R	21.9	46.7	31.2	0.2	52	61	10	0.7	0.5	0.7	1.0	31.9	68.1
Richardson	4,940	1,513	2,050	1,356	21	537	R	30.6	41.5	27.4	0.4	15	81	40	0.7	0.7	0.6	0.8	42.5	57.5
Rock	987	162	588	233	4	355	R	16.4	59.6	23.6	0.4	83	6	82	0.1	<.1	0.2	0.1	21.6	78.4
Saline	5,765	2,425	1,740	1,576	24	685	D	42.1	30.2	27.3	0.4	1	93	43	0.8	1.1	0.5	0.9	58.2	41.8
Sarpy	40,604	10,720	20,482	9,270	132	9,762	R	26.4	50.4	22.8	0.3	32	40	85	5.5	4.9	6.0	5.3	34.4	65.6
Saunders	9,152	2,509	4,037	2,567	39	1,470	R	27.4	44.1	28.0	0.4	27	69	34	1.2	1.2	1.2	1.5	38.3	61.7
Scotts Bluff	14,947	4,173	7,213	3,514	47	3,040	R	27.9	48.3	23.5	0.3	24	53	83	2.0	1.9	2.1	2.0	36.7	63.3
Seward	6,908	2,118	3,044	1,722	24	926	R	30.7	44.1	24.9	0.3	14	70	75	0.9	1.0	0.9	1.0	41.0	59.0
Sheridan	2,996	535	1,698	751	12	947	R	17.9	56.7	25.1	0.4	72	12	71	0.4	0.2	0.5	0.4	24.0	76.0
Sherman	1,899	568	736	582	13	154	R	29.9	38.8	30.6	0.7	16	90	12	0.3	0.3	0.2	0.3	43.6	56.4
Sioux	802	148	445	206	3	239	R	18.5	55.5	25.7	0.4	70	17	66	0.1	<.1	0.1	0.1	25.0	75.0
Stanton	2,563	496	1,274	786	7	488	R	19.4	49.7	30.7	0.3	62	44	11	0.3	0.2	0.4	0.5	28.0	72.0
Thayer	3,403	923	1,387	1,077	16	310	R	27.1	40.8	31.6	0.5	30	83	6	0.5	0.4	0.4	0.6	40.0	60.0
Thomas	468	69	283	115	1	168	R	14.7	60.5	24.6	0.2	88	3	79	<.1	<.1	<.1	<.1	19.6	80.4
Thurston	2,257	865	898	487	7	33	R	38.3	39.8	21.6	0.3	3	84	89	0.3	0.4	0.3	0.3	49.1	50.9
Valley	2,590	716	1,173	693	8	457	R	27.6	45.3	26.8	0.3	25	65	48	0.4	0.3	0.3	0.4	37.9	62.1
Washington	8,307	2,108	4,035	2,148	16	1,887	R	25.4	48.6	25.9	0.2	35	51	64	1.1	1.0	1.2	1.2	34.3	65.7
Wayne	4,102	921	2,122	1,047	12	1,075	R	22.5	51.7	25.5	0.3	48	36	68	0.6	0.4	0.6	0.6	30.3	69.7
Webster	2,262	624	972	657	9	315	R	27.6	43.0	29.0	0.4	26	77	23	0.3	0.3	0.3	0.4	39.1	60.9
Wheeler	464	88	246	127	3	119	R	19.0	53.0	27.4	0.6	67	30	41	<.1	<.1	<.1	<.1	26.3	73.7
York	7,012	1,385	3,783	1,825	19	1,958	R	19.8	54.0	26.0	0.3	60	25	62	1.0	0.6	1.1	1.0	26.8	73.2
NEBRASKA	737,546	216,864	343,678	174,104	2,900	126,814	R	29.4	46.6	23.6	0.4				100.0	100.0	100.0	100.0	38.7	61.3

Table H. — Vote for U.S. Representative in Congress: November 3, 1992, General Election

Congressional district and county	Total	Democrat (DEM)	Republican (REP)	Other	Plurality Total	Plurality Party	Percent of total vote DEM	REP	Other	Rank within district DEM	REP	Other	Percent contribution to district vote Total	DEM	REP	Other
District 1	239,108	96,309	142,713	86	46,404	R	40.3	59.7	<.1				100.0	100.0	100.0	100.0
Burt	3,667	1,239	2,428	0	1,189	R	33.8	66.2	0.0	15	11	13	1.5	1.3	1.7	0.0
Butler	4,000	1,497	2,503	0	1,006	R	37.4	62.6	0.0	9	17	14	1.7	1.6	1.8	0.0
Cass (pt)	6,489	2,316	4,165	8	1,849	R	35.7	64.2	0.1	12	14	3	2.7	2.4	2.9	9.3
Cedar	4,388	1,358	3,030	0	1,672	R	30.9	69.1	0.0	20	6	15	1.8	1.4	2.1	0.0
Colfax	3,933	1,288	2,645	0	1,357	R	32.7	67.3	0.0	18	8	16	1.6	1.3	1.9	0.0
Cuming	4,537	1,067	3,465	5	2,398	R	23.5	76.4	0.1	25	1	5	1.9	1.1	2.4	5.8
Dakota	6,182	2,136	4,046	0	1,910	R	34.6	65.4	0.0	14	12	17	2.6	2.2	2.8	0.0
Dixon	2,973	895	2,078	0	1,183	R	30.1	69.9	0.0	22	4	18	1.2	0.9	1.5	0.0
Dodge	15,864	5,328	10,520	16	5,192	R	33.6	66.3	0.1	16	10	6	6.6	5.5	7.4	18.6
Gage	9,802	4,535	5,267	0	732	R	46.3	53.7	0.0	3	23	19	4.1	4.7	3.7	0.0
Johnson	2,197	949	1,247	1	298	R	43.2	56.8	<.1	5	21	11	0.9	1.0	0.9	1.2
Lancaster	101,462	47,361	54,101	0	6,740	R	46.7	53.3	0.0	2	24	20	42.4	49.2	37.9	0.0
Madison	13,418	4,266	9,137	15	4,871	R	31.8	68.1	0.1	19	7	4	5.6	4.4	6.4	17.4
Nemaha	3,670	1,230	2,438	2	1,208	R	33.5	66.4	<.1	17	9	10	1.5	1.3	1.7	2.3
Otoe	5,844	2,191	3,649	4	1,458	R	37.5	62.4	<.1	8	18	9	2.4	2.3	2.6	4.7
Pawnee	1,772	770	1,002	0	232	R	43.5	56.5	0.0	4	22	21	0.7	0.8	0.7	0.0
Richardson	4,567	1,735	2,830	2	1,095	R	38.0	62.0	<.1	7	19	12	1.9	1.8	2.0	2.3
Saline	5,662	2,940	2,722	0	218	D	51.9	48.1	0.0	1	25	22	2.4	3.1	1.9	0.0
Saunders	8,848	3,206	5,630	12	2,424	R	36.2	63.6	0.1	11	15	2	3.7	3.3	3.9	14.0
Seward	6,762	2,635	4,121	6	1,486	R	39.0	60.9	<.1	6	20	8	2.8	2.7	2.9	7.0
Stanton	2,484	761	1,723	0	962	R	30.6	69.4	0.0	21	5	23	1.0	0.8	1.2	0.0
Thurston	2,131	749	1,380	2	631	R	35.1	64.8	<.1	13	13	7	0.9	0.8	1.0	2.3
Washington	7,743	2,275	5,468	0	3,193	R	29.4	70.6	0.0	23	3	24	3.2	2.4	3.8	0.0
Wayne	3,875	1,086	2,789	0	1,703	R	28.0	72.0	0.0	24	2	25	1.6	1.1	2.0	0.0
York	6,838	2,496	4,329	13	1,833	R	36.5	63.3	0.2	10	16	1	2.9	2.6	3.0	15.1
District 2	233,372	119,512	113,828	32	5,684	D	51.2	48.8	<.1				100.0	100.0	100.0	100.0
Cass (pt)	3,035	1,634	1,369	32	265	D	53.8	45.1	1.1	1	3	1	1.3	1.4	1.2	100.0
Douglas	191,391	99,309	92,082	0	7,227	D	51.9	48.1	0.0	2	2	2	82.0	83.1	80.9	0.0
Sarpy	38,946	18,569	20,377	0	1,808	R	47.7	52.3	0.0	3	1	3	16.7	15.5	17.9	0.0
District 3	238,355	67,457	170,857	41	103,400	R	28.3	71.7	<.1				100.0	100.0	100.0	100.0
Adams	12,847	3,512	9,317	18	5,805	R	27.3	72.5	0.1	24	43	2	5.4	5.2	5.5	43.9
Antelope	3,634	1,303	2,331	0	1,028	R	35.9	64.1	0.0	9	58	9	1.5	1.9	1.4	0.0
Arthur	258	34	224	0	190	R	13.2	86.8	0.0	66	1	10	0.1	0.1	0.1	0.0
Banner	473	101	372	0	271	R	21.4	78.6	0.0	48	19	11	0.2	0.1	0.2	0.0
Blaine	444	66	378	0	312	R	14.9	85.1	0.0	64	3	12	0.2	0.1	0.2	0.0
Boone	3,042	868	2,174	0	1,306	R	28.5	71.5	0.0	22	45	13	1.3	1.3	1.3	0.0
Box Butte	5,583	2,321	3,262	0	941	R	41.6	58.4	0.0	3	64	14	2.3	3.4	1.9	0.0
Boyd	1,549	900	649	0	251	D	58.1	41.9	0.0	1	66	15	0.6	1.3	0.4	0.0
Brown	1,792	355	1,437	0	1,082	R	19.8	80.2	0.0	53	14	16	0.8	0.5	0.8	0.0
Buffalo	17,126	3,961	13,165	0	9,204	R	23.1	76.9	0.0	41	26	17	7.2	5.9	7.7	0.0
Chase	2,008	465	1,543	0	1,078	R	23.2	76.8	0.0	40	27	18	0.8	0.7	0.9	0.0
Cherry	2,893	598	2,295	0	1,697	R	20.7	79.3	0.0	51	16	19	1.2	0.9	1.3	0.0
Cheyenne	4,146	988	3,158	0	2,170	R	23.8	76.2	0.0	37	30	20	1.7	1.5	1.8	0.0
Clay	3,488	944	2,543	1	1,599	R	27.1	72.9	<.1	25	42	6	1.5	1.4	1.5	2.4
Custer	5,756	1,313	4,443	0	3,130	R	22.8	77.2	0.0	42	25	21	2.4	1.9	2.6	0.0
Dawes	3,843	1,003	2,839	1	1,836	R	26.1	73.9	<.1	29	38	7	1.6	1.5	1.7	2.4
Dawson	8,752	1,818	6,934	0	5,116	R	20.8	79.2	0.0	50	17	22	3.7	2.7	4.1	0.0
Deuel	1,055	236	818	1	582	R	22.4	77.5	<.1	43	24	3	0.4	0.3	0.5	2.4
Dundy	1,139	289	850	0	561	R	25.4	74.6	0.0	32	35	23	0.5	0.4	0.5	0.0
Fillmore	3,308	997	2,311	0	1,314	R	30.1	69.9	0.0	20	47	24	1.4	1.5	1.4	0.0
Franklin	1,902	560	1,342	0	782	R	29.4	70.6	0.0	21	46	25	0.8	0.8	0.8	0.0
Frontier	1,537	289	1,248	0	959	R	18.8	81.2	0.0	55	12	26	0.6	0.4	0.7	0.0
Furnas	2,686	647	2,039	0	1,392	R	24.1	75.9	0.0	36	31	27	1.1	1.0	1.2	0.0
Garden	1,233	254	979	0	725	R	20.6	79.4	0.0	52	15	28	0.5	0.4	0.6	0.0
Garfield	1,056	247	809	0	562	R	23.4	76.6	0.0	39	28	29	0.4	0.4	0.5	0.0
Gosper	1,043	218	825	0	607	R	20.9	79.1	0.0	49	18	30	0.4	0.3	0.5	0.0
Grant	435	78	357	0	279	R	17.9	82.1	0.0	59	8	31	0.2	0.1	0.2	0.0
Greeley	1,365	436	929	0	493	R	31.9	68.1	0.0	14	53	32	0.6	0.6	0.5	0.0
Hall	20,220	6,444	13,776	0	7,332	R	31.9	68.1	0.0	15	52	33	8.5	9.6	8.1	0.0
Hamilton	4,438	1,168	3,270	0	2,102	R	26.3	73.7	0.0	28	39	34	1.9	1.7	1.9	0.0
Harlan	2,034	672	1,362	0	690	R	33.0	67.0	0.0	12	55	35	0.9	1.0	0.8	0.0
Hayes	606	112	494	0	382	R	18.5	81.5	0.0	57	10	36	0.3	0.2	0.3	0.0
Hitchcock	1,612	409	1,203	0	794	R	25.4	74.6	0.0	33	34	37	0.7	0.6	0.7	0.0
Holt	5,555	2,029	3,526	0	1,497	R	36.5	63.5	0.0	7	60	38	2.3	3.0	2.1	0.0
Hooker	455	60	395	0	335	R	13.2	86.8	0.0	65	2	39	0.2	0.1	0.2	0.0
Howard	2,787	1,151	1,636	0	485	R	41.3	58.7	0.0	4	63	40	1.2	1.7	1.0	0.0
Jefferson	4,323	1,556	2,767	0	1,211	R	36.0	64.0	0.0	8	59	41	1.8	2.3	1.6	0.0
Kearney	3,189	829	2,360	0	1,531	R	26.0	74.0	0.0	30	37	42	1.3	1.2	1.4	0.0
Keith	3,806	832	2,974	0	2,142	R	21.9	78.1	0.0	47	20	43	1.6	1.2	1.7	0.0
Keya Paha	598	142	456	0	314	R	23.7	76.3	0.0	38	29	44	0.3	0.2	0.3	0.0
Kimball	1,742	341	1,401	0	1,060	R	19.6	80.4	0.0	54	13	45	0.7	0.5	0.8	0.0
Knox	4,124	2,156	1,968	0	188	D	52.3	47.7	0.0	2	65	46	1.7	3.2	1.2	0.0
Lincoln	15,409	4,883	10,516	10	5,633	R	31.7	68.2	<.1	16	51	4	6.5	7.2	6.2	24.4

Congressional district and county	Total	Democrat (DEM)	Republican (REP)	Other	Plurality Total	Plurality Party	Percent of total vote DEM	Percent of total vote REP	Percent of total vote Other	Rank within district DEM	Rank within district REP	Rank within district Other	Percent contribution to district vote Total	Percent contribution to district vote DEM	Percent contribution to district vote REP	Percent contribution to district vote Other
District 3 (cont)																
Logan	447	73	374	0	301	R	16.3	83.7	0.0	62	5	47	0.2	0.1	0.2	0.0
Loup	380	84	296	0	212	R	22.1	77.9	0.0	45	22	48	0.2	0.1	0.2	0.0
McPherson	323	60	263	0	203	R	18.6	81.4	0.0	56	11	49	0.1	0.1	0.2	0.0
Merrick	3,723	981	2,742	0	1,761	R	26.3	73.7	0.0	27	40	50	1.6	1.5	1.6	0.0
Morrill	2,440	599	1,841	0	1,242	R	24.5	75.5	0.0	35	32	51	1.0	0.9	1.1	0.0
Nance	1,854	619	1,235	0	616	R	33.4	66.6	0.0	11	56	52	0.8	0.9	0.7	0.0
Nuckolls	2,872	1,082	1,790	0	708	R	37.7	62.3	0.0	6	61	53	1.2	1.6	1.0	0.0
Perkins	1,603	351	1,252	0	901	R	21.9	78.1	0.0	46	21	54	0.7	0.5	0.7	0.0
Phelps	4,827	1,074	3,753	0	2,679	R	22.2	77.8	0.0	44	23	55	2.0	1.6	2.2	0.0
Pierce	3,383	1,376	2,007	0	631	R	40.7	59.3	0.0	5	62	56	1.4	2.0	1.2	0.0
Platte	13,187	3,630	9,554	3	5,924	R	27.5	72.5	<.1	23	44	8	5.5	5.4	5.6	7.3
Polk	2,787	751	2,032	4	1,281	R	26.9	72.9	0.1	26	41	1	1.2	1.1	1.2	9.8
Red Willow	5,216	1,286	3,927	3	2,641	R	24.7	75.3	<.1	34	33	5	2.2	1.9	2.3	7.3
Rock	954	160	794	0	634	R	16.8	83.2	0.0	61	6	57	0.4	0.2	0.5	0.0
Scotts Bluff	14,629	3,754	10,875	0	7,121	R	25.7	74.3	0.0	31	36	58	6.1	5.6	6.4	0.0
Sheridan	2,896	513	2,383	0	1,870	R	17.7	82.3	0.0	60	7	59	1.2	0.8	1.4	0.0
Sherman	1,847	623	1,224	0	601	R	33.7	66.3	0.0	10	57	60	0.8	0.9	0.7	0.0
Sioux	777	143	634	0	491	R	18.4	81.6	0.0	58	9	61	0.3	0.2	0.4	0.0
Thayer	3,288	1,012	2,276	0	1,264	R	30.8	69.2	0.0	17	50	62	1.4	1.5	1.3	0.0
Thomas	460	72	388	0	316	R	15.7	84.3	0.0	63	4	63	0.2	0.1	0.2	0.0
Valley	2,532	775	1,757	0	982	R	30.6	69.4	0.0	18	49	64	1.1	1.1	1.0	0.0
Webster	2,192	718	1,474	0	756	R	32.8	67.2	0.0	13	54	65	0.9	1.1	0.9	0.0
Wheeler	447	136	311	0	175	R	30.4	69.6	0.0	19	48	66	0.2	0.2	0.2	0.0
NEBRASKA	710,835	283,278	427,398	159	144,120	R	39.9	60.1	<.1							

Table I. — Vote for Presidential Preference: May 12, 1992, Democratic Primary Election

County	Top candidates									Top three candidates (state vote)								
										Percent of total vote			Rank			Percent contribution to state vote		
	Total	Clinton	Brown	Uncom-mitted	Tsongas	Write ins	Harkin	McCarthy	Other	Clinton	Brown	Uncom-mitted	Clinton	Brown	Uncom-mitted	Total	Clinton	Brown	Uncom-mitted
Adams	2,258	1,121	388	419	175	70	28	27	30	49.6	17.2	18.6	55	37	25	1.5	1.6	1.2	1.7
Antelope	758	397	108	116	41	28	40	16	12	52.4	14.2	15.3	33	63	57	0.5	0.6	0.3	0.5
Arthur	31	10	4	8	4	1	0	2	2	32.3	12.9	25.8	93	75	1	<.1	<.1	<.1	<.1
Banner	39	19	6	9	2	3	0	0	0	48.7	15.4	23.1	64	56	3	<.1	<.1	<.1	<.1
Blaine	71	34	10	6	6	11	3	1	0	47.9	14.1	8.5	69	65	91	<.1	<.1	<.1	<.1
Boone	712	343	139	113	51	0	44	9	13	48.2	19.5	15.9	68	22	50	0.5	0.5	0.4	0.5
Box Butte	1,186	673	206	138	63	60	21	6	19	56.7	17.4	11.6	11	33	85	0.8	1.0	0.7	0.6
Boyd	321	189	50	27	20	6	10	8	11	58.9	15.6	8.4	6	54	92	0.2	0.3	0.2	0.1
Brown	270	141	37	61	18	0	5	2	6	52.2	13.7	22.6	35	66	4	0.2	0.2	0.1	0.2
Buffalo	2,609	1,077	595	544	223	0	61	41	68	41.3	22.8	20.9	89	6	9	1.7	1.6	1.9	2.2
Burt	843	465	146	115	48	14	41	6	8	55.2	17.3	13.6	14	34	74	0.6	0.7	0.5	0.5
Butler	1,500	662	364	226	90	22	86	21	29	44.1	24.3	15.1	84	3	61	1.0	1.0	1.1	0.9
Cass	2,064	946	401	369	127	101	69	14	37	45.8	19.4	17.9	75	23	32	1.4	1.4	1.3	1.5
Cedar	1,380	668	159	206	129	31	129	14	44	48.4	11.5	14.9	67	79	62	0.9	1.0	0.5	0.8
Chase	431	222	42	97	28	14	12	6	10	51.5	9.7	22.5	37	87	5	0.3	0.3	0.1	0.4
Cherry	436	236	53	93	28	0	11	2	13	54.1	12.2	21.3	24	77	6	0.3	0.3	0.2	0.4
Cheyenne	702	376	95	145	52	0	11	4	19	53.6	13.5	20.7	27	67	10	0.5	0.5	0.3	0.6
Clay	659	345	112	97	40	28	20	9	8	52.4	17.0	14.7	34	40	63	0.4	0.5	0.4	0.4
Colfax	1,143	555	226	145	81	28	77	18	13	48.6	19.8	12.7	66	20	81	0.8	0.8	0.7	0.6
Cuming	718	316	146	117	46	32	50	3	8	44.0	20.3	16.3	85	18	44	0.5	0.5	0.5	0.5
Custer	997	626	189	0	120	0	31	12	19	62.8	19.0	0.0	1	25	93	0.7	0.9	0.6	0.0
Dakota	958	551	67	149	53	51	58	10	19	57.5	7.0	15.6	9	90	54	0.6	0.8	0.2	0.6
Dawes	596	299	98	92	47	24	20	3	13	50.2	16.4	15.4	47	47	55	0.4	0.4	0.3	0.4
Dawson	1,349	660	203	264	116	44	29	17	16	48.9	15.0	19.6	61	58	16	0.9	1.0	0.6	1.1
Deuel	96	48	7	18	7	11	2	1	2	50.0	7.3	18.8	51	89	23	<.1	<.1	<.1	<.1
Dixon	701	412	39	107	47	4	78	2	12	58.8	5.6	15.3	7	93	58	0.5	0.6	0.1	0.4
Dodge	3,924	1,748	800	682	255	236	130	27	46	44.5	20.4	17.4	81	16	38	2.6	2.5	2.5	2.8
Douglas	40,431	16,481	10,194	6,726	2,865	2,458	970	373	364	40.8	25.2	16.6	90	1	42	26.8	24.0	32.2	27.2
Dundy	250	153	22	35	16	9	4	4	7	61.2	8.8	14.0	5	88	71	0.2	0.2	<.1	0.1
Fillmore	912	459	149	146	64	52	25	6	11	50.3	16.3	16.0	46	48	49	0.6	0.7	0.5	0.6
Franklin	420	228	71	58	29	16	6	3	9	54.3	16.9	13.8	22	42	73	0.3	0.3	0.2	0.2
Frontier	335	167	45	66	31	12	6	5	3	49.9	13.4	19.7	53	70	14	0.2	0.2	0.1	0.3
Furnas	493	308	50	72	33	0	17	5	8	62.5	10.1	14.6	2	84	69	0.3	0.4	0.2	0.3
Gage	1,894	966	407	339	104	0	39	15	24	51.0	21.5	17.9	38	13	31	1.3	1.4	1.3	1.4
Garden	225	103	30	46	20	16	1	5	4	45.8	13.3	20.4	76	73	12	0.1	0.2	<.1	0.2
Garfield	180	99	28	23	12	7	3	3	5	55.0	15.6	12.8	17	55	79	0.1	0.1	<.1	<.1
Gosper	196	108	36	23	13	7	5	0	4	55.1	18.4	11.7	15	27	84	0.1	0.1	<.1	<.1
Grant	59	31	6	10	4	7	0	0	1	52.5	10.2	16.9	31	83	41	<.1	<.1	<.1	<.1
Greeley	559	282	91	105	28	12	15	15	11	50.4	16.3	18.8	43	50	22	0.4	0.4	0.3	0.4
Hall	4,163	1,914	700	877	316	194	84	40	38	46.0	16.8	21.1	74	43	7	2.8	2.8	2.2	3.5
Hamilton	717	364	107	145	41	26	18	9	7	50.8	14.9	20.2	41	60	13	0.5	0.5	0.3	0.6
Harlan	534	277	76	104	34	17	10	6	10	51.9	14.2	19.5	36	64	17	0.4	0.4	0.2	0.4
Hayes	129	65	8	30	12	11	1	2	0	50.4	6.2	23.3	45	92	2	<.1	<.1	<.1	0.1
Hitchcock	397	210	40	83	39	6	2	6	11	52.9	10.1	20.9	28	86	8	0.3	0.3	0.1	0.3
Holt	994	489	159	187	62	11	46	12	28	49.2	16.0	18.8	58	51	21	0.7	0.7	0.5	0.8
Hooker	51	26	10	8	1	6	0	0	0	51.0	19.6	15.7	39	21	53	<.1	<.1	<.1	<.1
Howard	726	360	121	128	49	39	11	8	10	49.6	16.7	17.6	56	45	37	0.5	0.5	0.4	0.5
Jefferson	1,120	634	186	128	62	51	24	7	28	56.6	16.6	11.4	12	46	86	0.7	0.9	0.6	0.5
Johnson	592	276	128	87	46	18	18	10	9	46.6	21.6	14.7	70	12	65	0.4	0.4	0.4	0.4
Kearney	657	329	104	112	51	21	22	5	13	50.1	15.8	17.0	50	52	39	0.4	0.5	0.3	0.5
Keith	553	298	82	81	43	26	9	5	9	53.9	14.8	14.6	26	61	67	0.4	0.4	0.3	0.3
Keya Paha	164	82	18	31	16	4	10	1	2	50.0	11.0	18.9	52	80	20	0.1	0.1	<.1	0.1
Kimball	290	157	39	42	33	9	3	2	5	54.1	13.4	14.5	23	69	70	0.2	0.2	0.1	0.2
Knox	947	466	110	169	72	34	66	12	18	49.2	11.6	17.8	57	78	33	0.6	0.7	0.3	0.7
Lancaster	24,094	10,202	6,013	3,525	1,810	1,594	448	311	191	42.3	25.0	14.6	87	2	68	16.0	14.9	19.0	14.3
Lincoln	4,754	2,326	969	766	306	220	60	40	67	48.9	20.4	16.1	60	17	47	3.2	3.4	3.1	3.1
Logan	47	29	8	5	1	1	1	2	0	61.7	17.0	10.6	3	38	87	<.1	<.1	<.1	<.1
Loup	62	26	14	8	4	3	3	2	2	41.9	22.6	12.9	88	7	78	<.1	<.1	<.1	<.1
McPherson	56	31	8	5	2	7	0	0	3	55.4	14.3	8.9	12	62	89	<.1	<.1	<.1	<.1
Madison	1,659	769	271	316	129	32	102	19	21	46.4	16.3	19.0	71	49	19	1.1	1.1	0.9	1.3
Merrick	603	307	110	107	32	15	18	8	6	50.9	18.2	17.7	40	29	35	0.4	0.4	0.3	0.4
Morrill	384	203	68	51	30	19	7	2	4	52.9	17.7	13.3	29	31	76	0.3	0.3	0.2	0.2
Nance	564	298	96	83	33	26	15	6	7	52.8	17.0	14.7	30	39	64	0.4	0.4	0.3	0.3
Nemaha	777	360	163	93	60	38	36	10	17	46.3	21.0	12.0	72	14	83	0.5	0.5	0.5	0.4
Nuckolls	689	398	93	96	45	25	10	9	13	57.8	13.5	13.9	8	68	72	0.5	0.6	0.3	0.4
Otoe	1,701	853	312	277	99	32	73	17	38	50.1	18.3	16.3	48	28	46	1.1	1.2	1.0	1.1
Pawnee	447	219	77	76	27	20	18	3	7	49.0	17.2	17.0	59	36	40	0.3	0.3	0.2	0.3
Perkins	331	150	56	65	30	8	6	5	11	45.3	16.9	19.6	79	41	15	0.2	0.2	0.2	0.3
Phelps	736	402	123	118	54	0	16	8	15	54.6	16.7	16.0	20	44	48	0.5	0.6	0.4	0.5
Pierce	676	329	88	120	54	19	42	9	15	48.7	13.0	17.8	65	74	34	0.4	0.5	0.3	0.5

County	Total	Clinton	Brown	Uncom-mitted	Tsongas	Write ins	Harkin	McCarthy	Other	Clinton	Brown	Uncom-mitted	Rank Clinton	Rank Brown	Rank Uncom-mitted	Total	Clinton	Brown	Uncom-mitted
Platte	2,557	1,041	559	459	203	114	105	26	50	40.7	21.9	18.0	91	10	30	1.7	1.5	1.8	1.9
Polk	624	269	145	103	41	29	26	4	7	43.1	23.2	16.5	86	5	43	0.4	0.4	0.5	0.4
Red Willow	1,095	597	117	205	63	68	11	14	20	54.5	10.7	18.7	21	82	24	0.7	0.9	0.4	0.8
Richardson	1,269	724	170	135	83	85	31	14	27	57.1	13.4	10.6	10	72	88	0.8	1.1	0.5	0.5
Rock	145	64	25	23	14	9	5	1	4	44.1	17.2	15.9	83	35	51	<.1	<.1	<.1	<.1
Saline	1,856	1,014	375	231	93	56	47	15	25	54.6	20.2	12.4	19	19	82	1.2	1.5	1.2	0.9
Sarpy	6,935	2,796	1,560	1,419	467	401	192	38	62	40.3	22.5	20.5	92	8	11	4.6	4.1	4.9	5.7
Saunders	2,874	1,306	625	443	194	113	119	24	50	45.4	21.7	15.4	78	11	56	1.9	1.9	2.0	1.8
Scotts Bluff	2,640	1,331	474	401	205	151	37	17	24	50.4	18.0	15.2	44	30	59	1.8	1.9	1.5	1.6
Seward	1,540	712	339	226	102	65	64	17	15	46.2	22.0	14.7	73	9	66	1.0	1.0	1.1	0.9
Sheridan	394	207	49	53	48	19	7	3	8	52.5	12.4	13.5	32	76	75	0.3	0.3	0.2	0.2
Sherman	575	281	106	87	53	21	14	5	8	48.9	18.4	15.1	63	26	60	0.4	0.4	0.3	0.4
Sioux	109	60	11	20	7	0	8	2	1	55.0	10.1	18.3	16	85	27	<.1	<.1	<.1	<.1
Stanton	372	182	57	59	29	20	18	0	7	48.9	15.3	15.9	62	57	52	0.2	0.3	0.2	0.2
Thayer	797	430	107	145	65	8	24	8	10	54.0	13.4	18.2	25	71	28	0.5	0.6	0.3	0.6
Thomas	47	29	3	4	9	2	0	0	0	61.7	6.4	8.5	4	91	90	<.1	<.1	<.1	<.1
Thurston	623	312	68	110	44	13	58	5	13	50.1	10.9	17.7	49	81	36	0.4	0.5	0.2	0.4
Valley	541	297	103	69	36	9	12	5	10	54.9	19.0	12.8	18	24	80	0.4	0.4	0.3	0.3
Washington	1,325	589	277	239	85	67	50	10	8	44.5	20.9	18.0	82	15	29	0.9	0.9	0.9	1.0
Wayne	534	244	84	87	51	17	37	5	9	45.7	15.7	16.3	77	53	45	0.4	0.4	0.3	0.4
Webster	482	244	72	93	27	16	13	4	13	50.6	14.9	19.3	42	59	18	0.3	0.4	0.2	0.4
Wheeler	91	41	22	12	8	3	4	0	1	45.1	24.2	13.2	80	4	77	<.1	<.1	<.1	<.1
York	842	419	149	156	51	26	21	12	8	49.8	17.7	18.5	54	32	26	0.6	0.6	0.5	0.6
NEBRASKA	150,587	68,562	31,673	24,714	10,707	7,259	4,239	1,520	1,913	45.5	21.0	16.4				100.0	100.0	100.0	100.0

County	Total	Bush	Bu-chanan	Write ins	Other	Bush	Bu-chanan	Write ins	Other	Bush	Bu-chanan	Write ins	Other	Total	Bush	Bu-chanan	Write ins	Other
Adams	3,658	3,052	456	57	93	83.4	12.5	1.6	2.5	18	64	63	62	1.9	2.0	1.8	1.1	1.9
Antelope	1,540	1,276	201	27	36	82.9	13.1	1.8	2.3	26	59	57	75	0.8	0.8	0.8	0.5	0.7
Arthur	149	126	14	6	3	84.6	9.4	4.0	2.0	12	92	6	87	< .1	< .1	< .1	0.1	< .1
Banner	228	181	42	0	5	79.4	18.4	0.0	2.2	71	7	81	83	0.1	0.1	0.2	0.0	0.1
Blaine	253	204	32	6	11	80.6	12.6	2.4	4.3	58	62	33	8	0.1	0.1	0.1	0.1	0.2
Boone	944	764	142	0	38	80.9	15.0	0.0	4.0	54	23	82	13	0.5	0.5	0.5	0.0	0.8
Box Butte	1,592	1,200	336	0	56	75.4	21.1	0.0	3.5	89	3	83	20	0.8	0.8	1.3	0.0	1.1
Boyd	756	490	201	16	49	64.8	26.6	2.1	6.5	93	1	42	2	0.4	0.3	0.8	0.3	1.0
Brown	944	807	104	0	33	85.5	11.0	0.0	3.5	7	82	84	22	0.5	0.5	0.4	0.0	0.7
Buffalo	4,617	3,889	586	0	142	84.2	12.7	0.0	3.1	15	60	85	39	2.4	2.5	2.3	0.0	2.9
Burt	1,278	1,045	169	23	41	81.8	13.2	1.8	3.2	40	53	55	32	0.7	0.7	0.7	0.5	0.8
Butler	876	726	107	16	27	82.9	12.2	1.8	3.1	25	67	54	36	0.5	0.5	0.4	0.3	0.6
Cass	2,215	1,729	353	74	59	78.1	15.9	3.3	2.7	82	13	17	54	1.2	1.1	1.4	1.5	1.2
Cedar	1,161	944	177	16	24	81.3	15.2	1.4	2.1	50	21	69	85	0.6	0.6	0.7	0.3	0.5
Chase	732	585	115	11	21	79.9	15.7	1.5	2.9	65	15	66	44	0.4	0.4	0.4	0.2	0.4
Cherry	1,426	1,229	157	0	40	86.2	11.0	0.0	2.8	2	83	86	47	0.7	0.8	0.6	0.0	0.8
Cheyenne	1,311	1,070	199	0	42	81.6	15.2	0.0	3.2	46	22	87	33	0.7	0.7	0.8	0.0	0.9
Clay	1,402	1,146	190	19	47	81.7	13.6	1.4	3.4	41	51	70	26	0.7	0.7	0.7	0.4	1.0
Colfax	1,185	951	173	18	43	80.3	14.6	1.5	3.6	60	28	65	18	0.6	0.6	0.7	0.4	0.9
Cuming	1,616	1,343	185	48	40	83.1	11.4	3.0	2.5	22	78	22	66	0.8	0.9	0.7	1.0	0.8
Custer	2,483	2,133	279	0	71	85.9	11.2	0.0	2.9	4	80	88	45	1.3	1.4	1.1	0.0	1.5
Dakota	1,132	907	168	29	28	80.1	14.8	2.6	2.5	62	26	28	67	0.6	0.6	0.7	0.6	0.6
Dawes	1,559	1,202	263	46	48	77.1	16.9	3.0	3.1	87	10	23	38	0.8	0.8	1.0	0.9	1.0
Dawson	2,793	2,395	283	60	55	85.8	10.1	2.1	2.0	6	89	41	89	1.5	1.5	1.1	1.2	1.1
Deuel	467	371	64	20	12	79.4	13.7	4.3	2.6	70	48	3	61	0.2	0.2	0.2	0.4	0.2
Dixon	1,026	857	107	35	27	83.5	10.4	3.4	2.6	17	85	16	55	0.5	0.5	0.4	0.7	0.6
Dodge	5,097	4,181	671	126	119	82.0	13.2	2.5	2.3	35	56	31	76	2.7	2.7	2.6	2.5	2.4
Douglas	37,855	31,063	4,427	1,589	776	82.1	11.7	4.2	2.0	34	77	5	86	19.7	19.9	17.1	31.6	15.9
Dundy	606	478	87	21	20	78.9	14.4	3.5	3.3	77	36	15	29	0.3	0.3	0.3	0.4	0.4
Fillmore	1,195	983	166	26	20	82.3	13.9	2.2	1.7	32	44	40	92	0.6	0.6	0.6	0.5	0.4
Franklin	739	586	101	17	35	79.3	13.7	2.3	4.7	73	49	35	6	0.4	0.4	0.4	0.3	0.7
Frontier	729	599	100	12	18	82.2	13.7	1.6	2.5	33	46	58	68	0.4	0.4	0.4	0.2	0.4
Furnas	928	760	135	0	33	81.9	14.5	0.0	3.6	38	32	89	19	0.5	0.5	0.5	0.0	0.7
Gage	2,505	1,974	448	0	83	78.8	17.9	0.0	3.3	78	8	90	28	1.3	1.3	1.7	0.0	1.7
Garden	599	495	71	16	17	82.6	11.9	2.7	2.8	28	73	26	46	0.3	0.3	0.3	0.3	0.3
Garfield	588	471	92	12	13	80.1	15.6	2.0	2.2	63	17	44	82	0.3	0.3	0.4	0.2	0.3
Gosper	372	305	41	14	12	82.0	11.0	3.8	3.2	36	81	10	31	0.2	0.2	0.2	0.3	0.2
Grant	230	188	28	8	6	81.7	12.2	3.5	2.6	42	70	14	57	0.1	0.1	0.1	0.2	0.1
Greeley	328	272	41	4	11	82.9	12.5	1.2	3.4	24	63	72	25	0.2	0.2	0.2	< .1	0.2
Hall	5,962	4,970	705	149	138	83.4	11.8	2.5	2.3	21	74	29	78	3.1	3.2	2.7	3.0	2.8
Hamilton	1,650	1,415	172	20	43	85.8	10.4	1.2	2.6	5	86	73	58	0.9	0.9	0.7	0.4	0.9
Harlan	761	598	111	32	20	78.6	14.6	4.2	2.6	79	30	4	56	0.4	0.4	0.4	0.6	0.4
Hayes	324	259	41	6	18	79.9	12.7	1.9	5.6	64	61	53	3	0.2	0.2	0.2	0.1	0.4
Hitchcock	670	546	91	13	20	81.5	13.6	1.9	3.0	48	50	50	40	0.3	0.3	0.4	0.3	0.4
Holt	2,162	1,724	343	35	60	79.7	15.9	1.6	2.8	68	14	60	49	1.1	1.1	1.3	0.7	1.2
Hooker	251	207	27	10	7	82.5	10.8	4.0	2.8	30	84	7	48	0.1	0.1	0.1	0.2	0.1
Howard	729	600	90	14	25	82.3	12.3	1.9	3.4	31	66	51	24	0.4	0.4	0.3	0.3	0.5
Jefferson	1,681	1,310	270	33	68	77.9	16.1	2.0	4.0	83	12	47	12	0.9	0.8	1.0	0.7	1.4
Johnson	729	558	143	8	20	76.5	19.6	1.1	2.7	88	5	75	50	0.4	0.4	0.6	0.2	0.4
Kearney	1,076	879	134	32	31	81.7	12.5	3.0	2.9	44	65	21	43	0.6	0.6	0.5	0.6	0.6
Keith	1,298	1,062	175	21	40	81.8	13.5	1.6	3.1	39	52	62	37	0.7	0.7	0.7	0.4	0.8
Keya Paha	308	263	37	0	8	85.4	12.0	0.0	2.6	8	72	91	59	0.2	0.2	0.1	0.0	0.2
Kimball	811	631	117	30	33	77.8	14.4	3.7	4.1	84	34	11	11	0.4	0.4	0.5	0.6	0.7
Knox	1,372	1,124	181	27	40	81.9	13.2	2.0	2.9	37	55	46	41	0.7	0.7	0.7	0.5	0.8
Lancaster	22,478	17,782	3,367	877	452	79.1	15.0	3.9	2.0	75	24	8	88	11.7	11.4	13.0	17.4	9.3
Lincoln	5,476	4,434	724	182	136	81.0	13.2	3.3	2.5	53	54	18	65	2.9	2.8	2.8	3.6	2.8
Logan	249	193	47	5	4	77.5	18.9	2.0	1.6	86	6	45	93	0.1	0.1	0.2	< .1	< .1
Loup	205	175	21	4	5	85.4	10.2	2.0	2.4	9	87	49	70	0.1	0.1	< .1	< .1	0.1
McPherson	206	177	19	5	5	85.9	9.2	2.4	2.4	3	93	32	73	0.1	0.1	< .1	< .1	0.1
Madison	4,292	3,648	523	25	96	85.0	12.2	0.6	2.2	10	69	79	81	2.2	2.3	2.0	0.5	2.0
Merrick	1,194	991	157	8	38	83.0	13.1	0.7	3.2	23	57	77	34	0.6	0.6	0.6	0.2	0.8
Morrill	887	623	194	27	43	70.2	21.9	3.0	4.8	92	2	19	5	0.5	0.4	0.8	0.5	0.9
Nance	443	376	45	10	12	84.9	10.2	2.3	2.7	11	88	39	51	0.2	0.2	0.2	0.2	0.2
Nemaha	1,121	891	172	23	35	79.5	15.3	2.1	3.1	69	19	43	35	0.6	0.6	0.7	0.5	0.7
Nuckolls	740	597	108	11	24	80.7	14.6	1.5	3.2	57	29	67	30	0.4	0.4	0.4	0.2	0.5
Otoe	2,320	1,914	331	8	67	82.5	14.3	0.3	2.9	29	37	80	42	1.2	1.2	1.3	0.2	1.4
Pawnee	592	418	123	21	30	70.6	20.8	3.5	5.1	91	4	13	4	0.3	0.3	0.5	0.4	0.6
Perkins	613	501	87	10	15	81.7	14.2	1.6	2.4	43	38	59	69	0.3	0.3	0.3	0.2	0.3
Phelps	1,746	1,508	205	0	33	86.4	11.7	0.0	1.9	1	76	92	90	0.9	1.0	0.8	0.0	0.7
Pierce	1,327	1,098	182	17	30	82.7	13.7	1.3	2.3	27	47	71	80	0.7	0.7	0.7	0.3	0.6

Table J. – Vote for Presidential Preference: May 12, 1992, Republican Primary Election (cont)

| County | Top candidates | | | | | Top four candidates (state vote) | | | | | | | | | | | | |
| | | | | | | Percent of total vote | | | | Rank | | | | Percent contribution to state vote | | | | |
	Total	Bush	Bu-chanan	Write ins	Other	Bush	Bu-chanan	Write ins	Other	Bush	Bu-chanan	Write ins	Other	Total	Bush	Bu-chanan	Write ins	Other
Platte	3,466	2,891	420	62	93	83.4	12.1	1.8	2.7	19	71	56	53	1.8	1.8	1.6	1.2	1.9
Polk	989	797	144	14	34	80.6	14.6	1.4	3.4	59	31	68	23	0.5	0.5	0.6	0.3	0.7
Red Willow	1,882	1,485	267	67	63	78.9	14.2	3.6	3.3	76	39	12	27	1.0	0.9	1.0	1.3	1.3
Richardson	1,566	1,218	246	47	55	77.8	15.7	3.0	3.5	85	16	20	21	0.8	0.8	1.0	0.9	1.1
Rock	534	450	61	10	13	84.3	11.4	1.9	2.4	13	79	52	71	0.3	0.3	0.2	0.2	0.3
Saline	1,018	760	181	39	38	74.7	17.8	3.8	3.7	90	9	9	16	0.5	0.5	0.7	0.8	0.8
Sarpy	8,117	6,769	990	216	142	83.4	12.2	2.7	1.7	20	68	27	91	4.2	4.3	3.8	4.3	2.9
Saunders	2,356	1,918	325	54	59	81.4	13.8	2.3	2.5	49	45	36	64	1.2	1.2	1.3	1.1	1.2
Scotts Bluff	4,370	3,427	650	191	102	78.4	14.9	4.4	2.3	80	25	2	77	2.3	2.2	2.5	3.8	2.1
Seward	1,833	1,469	266	52	46	80.1	14.5	2.8	2.5	61	33	25	63	1.0	0.9	1.0	1.0	0.9
Sheridan	1,225	996	161	35	33	81.3	13.1	2.9	2.7	51	58	24	52	0.6	0.6	0.6	0.7	0.7
Sherman	322	257	45	8	12	79.8	14.0	2.5	3.7	67	43	30	17	0.2	0.2	0.2	0.2	0.2
Sioux	368	300	54	0	14	81.5	14.7	0.0	3.8	47	27	93	14	0.2	0.2	0.2	0.0	0.3
Stanton	856	679	120	20	37	79.3	14.0	2.3	4.3	72	41	34	9	0.4	0.4	0.5	0.4	0.8
Thayer	1,167	943	182	12	30	80.8	15.6	1.0	2.6	56	18	76	60	0.6	0.6	0.7	0.2	0.6
Thomas	264	222	26	6	10	84.1	9.8	2.3	3.8	16	90	38	15	0.1	0.1	0.1	0.1	0.2
Thurston	583	462	89	7	25	79.2	15.3	1.2	4.3	74	20	74	10	0.3	0.3	0.3	0.1	0.5
Valley	917	742	148	6	21	80.9	16.1	0.7	2.3	55	11	78	79	0.5	0.5	0.6	0.1	0.4
Washington	2,461	2,009	344	56	52	81.6	14.0	2.3	2.1	45	42	37	84	1.3	1.3	1.3	1.1	1.1
Wayne	1,421	1,197	167	23	34	84.2	11.8	1.6	2.4	14	75	61	74	0.7	0.8	0.6	0.5	0.7
Webster	707	565	100	11	31	79.9	14.1	1.6	4.4	66	40	64	7	0.4	0.4	0.4	0.2	0.6
Wheeler	175	137	17	9	12	78.3	9.7	5.1	6.9	81	91	1	1	<.1	<.1	<.1	0.2	0.2
York	2,714	2,204	391	53	66	81.2	14.4	2.0	2.4	52	35	48	72	1.4	1.4	1.5	1.1	1.4
NEBRASKA	192,098	156,346	25,847	5,033	4,872	81.4	13.5	2.6	2.5					100.0	100.0	100.0	100.0	100.0

1992 Vote for President
Percent for Bush (R), by County

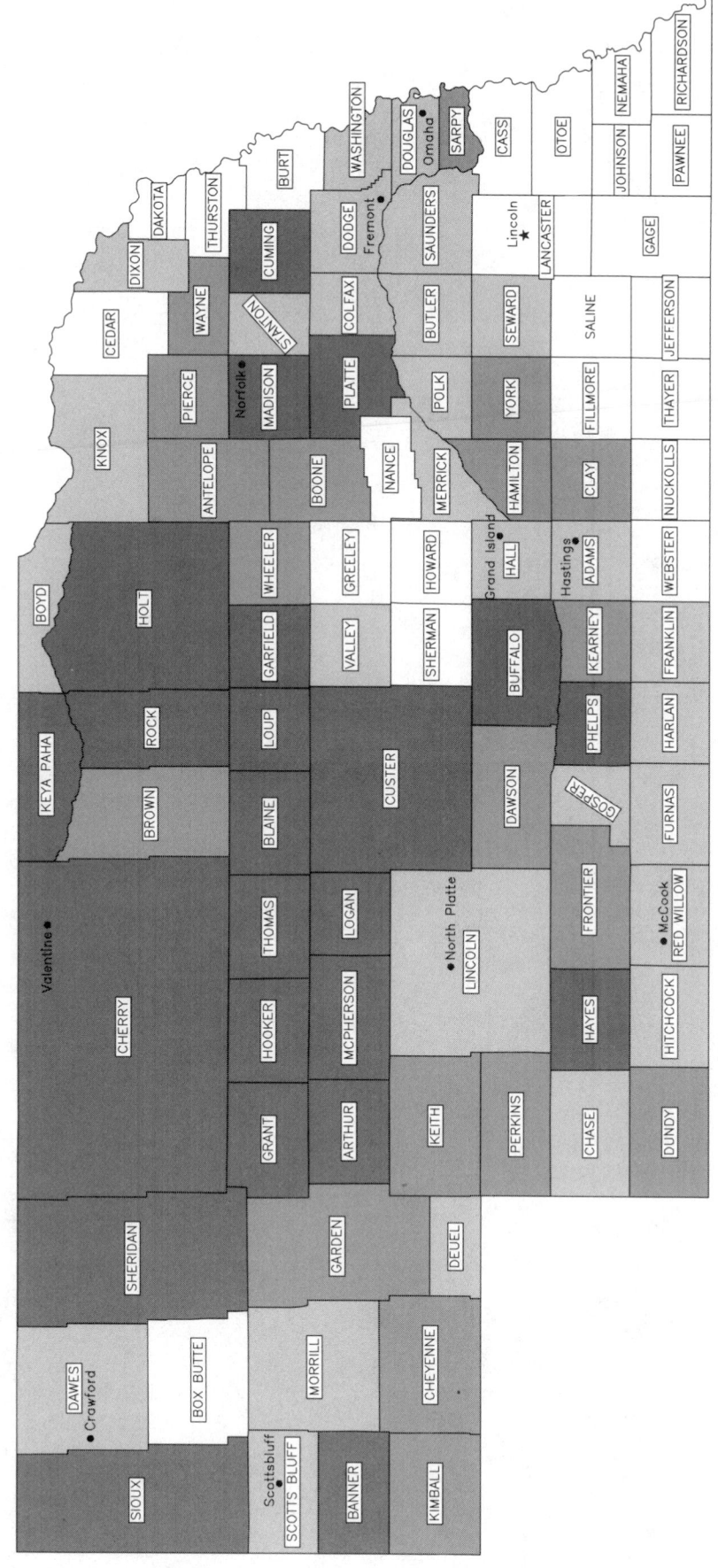

54.2% to 66.0%
50.0% to 54.1%
44.1% to 49.9%
30.2% to 44.0%

Bush (R) received 46.6% statewide.

A framed county name indicates
a county carried by the winner.

Copyright © 1993 by Election Data Services, Inc.

Nebraska 591

NEVADA

Congressional Districts 2
    Average Population 600,917
State Senate Districts 21
    Average Population 57,230
State House Districts 42
    Average Population 28,615

Electoral College Votes...4
Counties[1] 17
Voting Precincts 906

Alternative Registration Methods:
    ....Deputized Registrars, Mail-in, Motor-voter

Registration Deadline (Days before Election) 30

Voting Equipment Use (Counties)[1]

Datavote Punch Card	2	Paper Ballot	0
Electronic	1	Other Punch Card	2
Lever Machine	0	Mixed Systems	0
Optical Scanner	12		

Party Control	DEM	REP	IND	VAC
1993 State Senate	10	11	0	0
1992 State Senate	10	10	0	1
1993 State House	29	13	0	0
1992 State House	22	19	0	1

Population Statistics 1990

Race/ Ethnicity	Total Population		Voting Age Population		Voting Age Population % of total population
	Number	%	Number	%	
Non-Hispanic					
White	946,357	78.7	732,480	80.9	77.4
Black	76,503	6.4	50,836	5.6	66.4
Asian/Pacific Islander	35,897	3.0	26,800	3.0	74.7
Native American	17,480	1.5	12,091	1.3	69.2
Other	1,177	<.1	610	<.1	51.8
All Hispanic	124,419	10.4	82,068	9.1	66.0
TOTAL	1,201,833	100.0	904,885	100.0	75.3

Estimated Voting Age Population 1992 (VAP) 1,013,000
Number of Registered Voters.................................. 649,913
    % of estimated VAP...................................... 64.2
Voter Turnout (Actual) 513,387
    % of VAP 50.7
    % of Registration 79.0
Persons Not Voting—of Voting Age 499,613
    % of VAP 49.3
Persons Not Voting—of Registered 136,526
    % of Registration 21.0
Straight Ticket Voting .... No

State Officials and Members of Congress

Governor:
Robert J. Miller (D) 1989, elected to a four-year term in 1990.

U.S. Senators:
Harry Reid (D) 1986, elected to a six-year term in 1992.
Richard H. Bryon (D) 1988, elected to a six-year term in 1988.

U.S. Representative in Congress:
(District, Name, Party, Date first elected)

1. Bilbray (D) 1986   2. Vucanovich (R) 1982

---

[1]Includes Carson City.

Candidates: General Election, November 3, 1992

Candidate(s)	Total vote	Percent	Party	Status	First elected
President/Vice President					
Clinton/Gore	189,148	37.36%	Democrat	Challenger	1992
Bush/Quayle	175,828	34.73%	Republican	Incumbent	1988
Perot/Stockdale	132,580	26.19%	Independent	Challenger	
Gritz/Minett	2,892	0.57%	Populist	Challenger	
None Of These Candidates	2,537	0.50%	None	Unknown/NA	
Marrou/Lord	1,835	0.36%	Libertarian	Challenger	
Phillips/Knight	677	0.13%	Independent American	Challenger	
Fulani/Munoz	483	0.10%	Independent	Challenger	
Hagelin/Tompkins	338	0.07%	Natural Law	Challenger	
U.S. Senator					
Harry Reid	253,150	51.05%	Democrat	Incumbent	1986
Demar Dahl	199,413	40.21%	Republican	Challenger	
None of these Candidates	13,154	2.65%	None	Unknown/NA	
Joe Garcia, Jr.	11,240	2.27%	Independent American	Challenger	
Lois Avery	7,279	1.47%	Natural Law	Challenger	
H. Kent Cromwell	7,222	1.46%	Libertarian	Challenger	
Harry Tootle	4,429	0.89%	Populist	Challenger	
Governor (No Contest)					
U.S. Representative in Congress					
District 1					
James Bilbray	128,278	57.92%	Democrat	Incumbent	1986
J. Coy Pettyjohn	84,217	38.02%	Republican	Challenger	
Scott Kjar	8,993	4.06%	Libertarian	Challenger	
District 2					
Barbara Vucanovich	129,575	47.91%	Republican	Incumbent	1982
Pete Sferrazza	117,199	43.33%	Democrat	Challenger	
Daniel Hansen	13,285	4.91%	Independent American	Challenger	
Dan Becan	7,552	2.79%	Libertarian	Challenger	
Don Golden	2,850	1.05%	Populist	Challenger	

Voter Registration and Turnout, 1948-1992 Elections

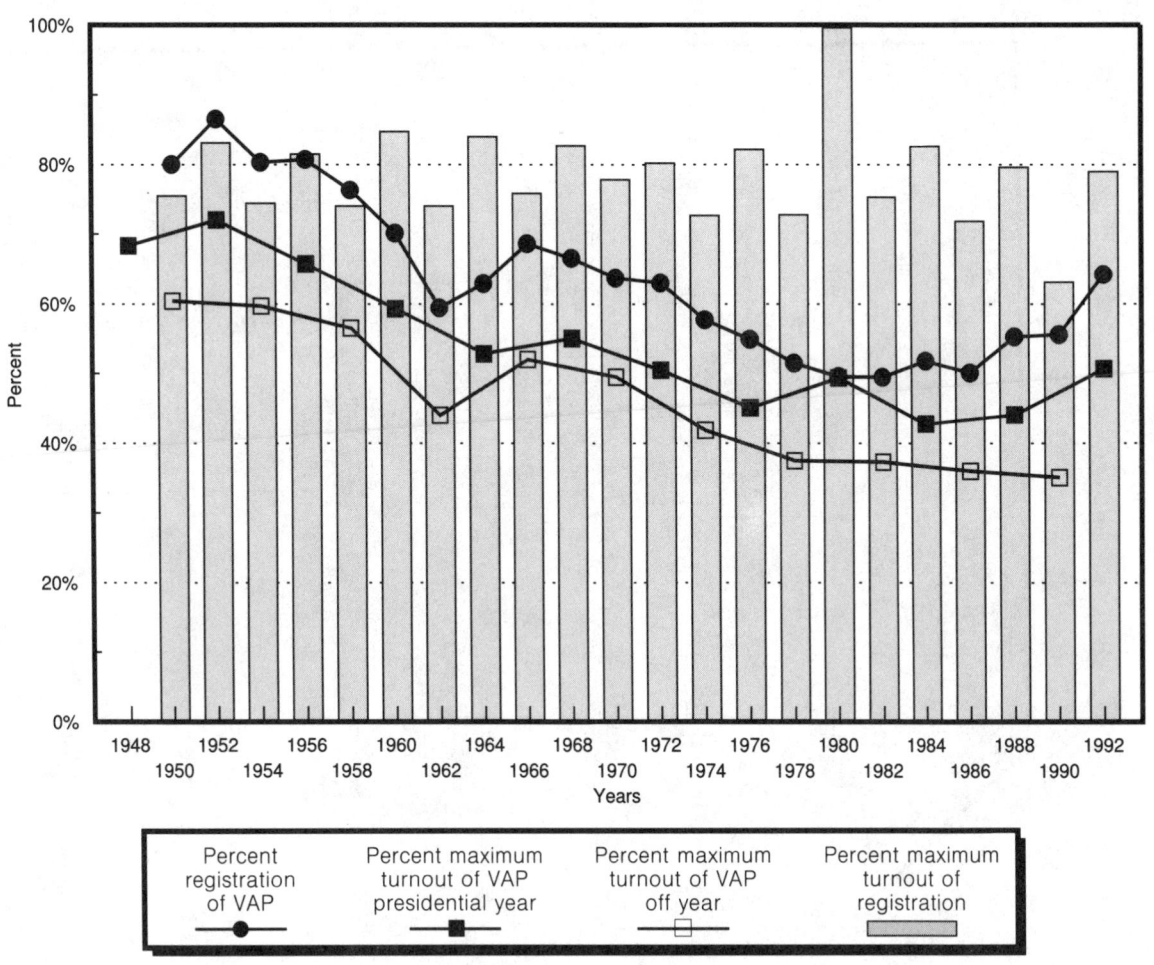

Legend:
- Percent registration of VAP (●)
- Percent maximum turnout of VAP presidential year (■)
- Percent maximum turnout of VAP off year (□)
- Percent maximum turnout of registration (bar)

Year	Estimated Voting Age Population (VAP)	Voter registration (REG)			Voter turnout												
						Highest office						Maximum vote					
		Total	Percent of VAP	Rank by percent of VAP	Actual	Total	Office	Percent total REG	Rank by percent of REG	Percent of VAP	Rank by percent of VAP	Total	Percent total REG	Rank by percent of REG	Percent total VAP	Rank by percent of VAP
1992	1,013,000	649,913	64.2	44	513,387	506,318	P	77.9	24	50.0	45	513,387	79.0	23	50.7	43
1990	929,000	516,409	55.6	47	325,959	320,743	G	62.1	15	34.5	39	325,959	63.1	15	35.1	38
1988	804,000	444,931	55.3	48	354,261	350,067	P	78.7	6	43.5	48	354,261	79.6	8	44.1	47
1986	734,000	367,579	50.1	49	264,365	261,932	S	71.3	3	35.7	36	264,365	71.9	4	36.0	36
1984	688,000	356,384	51.8	49	294,413	286,667	P	80.4	3	41.7	50	294,413	82.6	3	42.8	49
1982	651,000	322,154	49.5	49	242,578	240,394	S	74.6	2	36.9	39	242,578	75.3	2	37.3	39
1980	602,000	298,385	49.6	49	297,318	247,885	P	83.1	1	41.2	49	297,318	99.6	1	49.4	39
1978	520,000	267,698	51.5	48	195,013	192,445	G	71.9	1	37.0	32	195,013	72.8	2	37.5	32
1976	457,000	250,958	54.9	48	206,234	201,876	P	80.4	5	44.2	47	206,234	82.2	7	45.1	47
1974	411,000	236,948	57.7	46	172,355	169,473	S	71.5	2	41.2	28	172,355	72.7	2	41.9	31
1972	367,000	231,045	63.0	44	185,400	181,766	P	78.7	12	49.5	35	185,400	80.2	12	50.5	35
1970	303,000	192,933	63.7	36	150,078	147,768	S	76.6	5	48.8	31	150,078	77.8	6	49.5	31
1968	284,000	188,811	66.5	36	156,217	154,218	P	81.7	19	54.3	36	156,217	82.7	19	55.0	34
1966	268,000	183,863	68.6	30	139,355	137,677	G	74.9	8	51.4	25	139,355	75.8	9	52.0	27
1964	260,000	163,475	62.9	35	137,378	135,433	P	82.8	17	52.1	38	137,378	84.0	16	52.8	38
1962	226,000	134,350	59.4	29	99,430	97,192	S	72.3	12	43.0	36	99,430	74.0	12	44.0	36
1960	184,000	128,898	70.1	25	109,132	107,267	P	83.2	22	58.3	34	109,132	84.7	20	59.3	34
1958	154,000	117,568	76.3	17	87,026	84,889	G	72.2	13	55.1	22	87,026	74.0	12	56.5	20
1956	150,000	120,984	80.7	14	98,554	96,689	P	79.9	16	64.5	32	98,554	81.5	16	65.7	30
1954	135,000	108,373	80.3	10	80,609	78,462	G	72.4	8	58.1	11	80,609	74.4	7	59.7	11
1952	117,000	101,248	86.5	9	84,185	82,190	P	81.2	16	70.2	26	84,185	83.1	15	72.0	24
1950	105,000	83,950	80.0	5	63,402	61,773	G	73.6	8	58.8	8	63,402	75.5	7	60.4	8
1948	91,000	-	-	-	-	62,117	P	-	-	68.3	5	62,117	-	-	68.3	7

Nevada 595

NEVADA

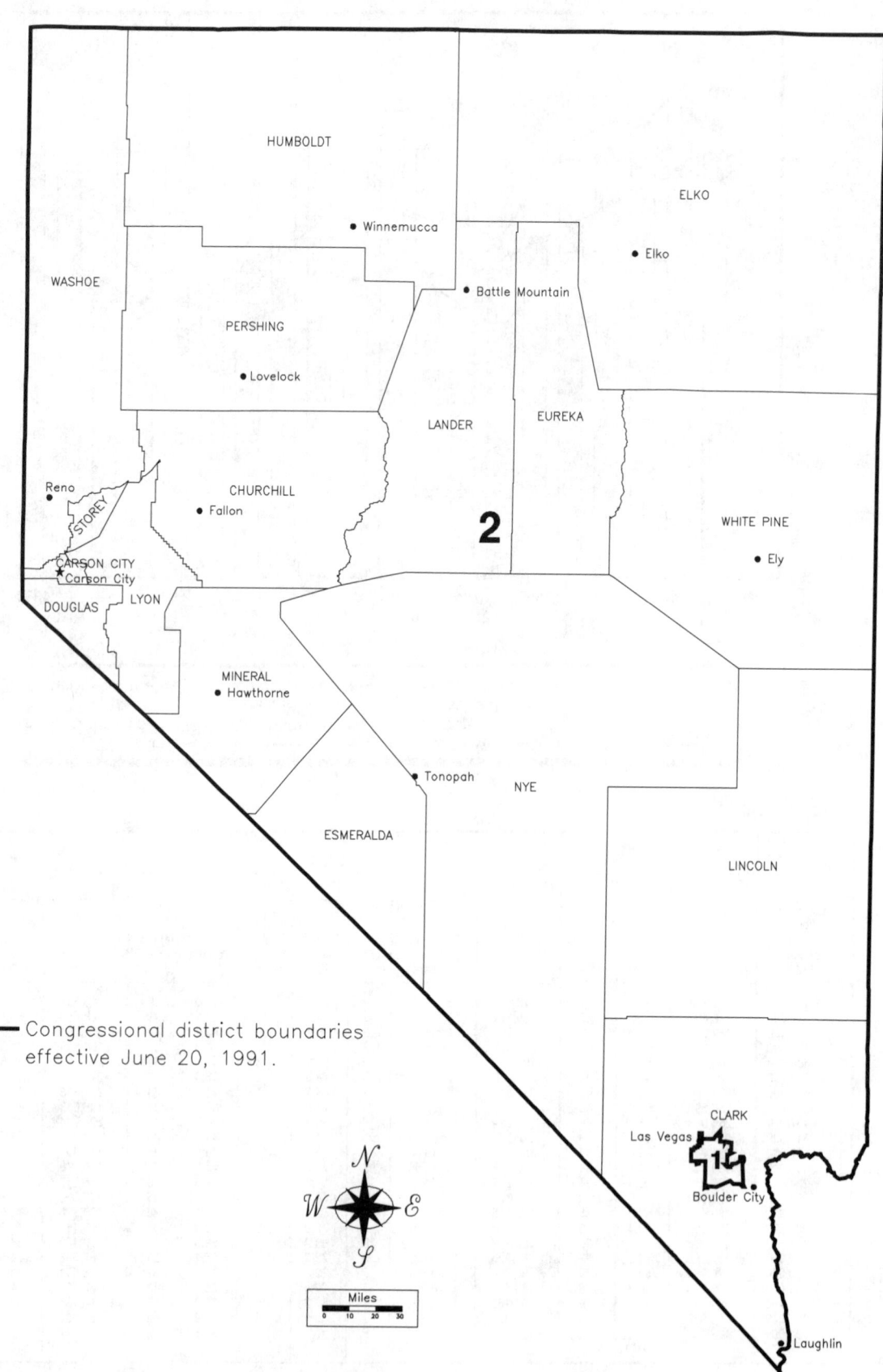

Congressional district boundaries effective June 20, 1991.

Miles
0 10 20 30

Table A. — 1990 Population by Race and Ethnic Origin

State/county code	County	Total persons	Percent of total persons — Non-Hispanic White	Black	Asian and Pacific Islander	Native American	Other	Hispanic	Rank — Total	Non-Hispanic White	Black	Hispanic	Percent contribution to state population — Total	Non-Hispanic White	Black	Hispanic
32 001	Churchill	17,938	86.0	1.1	2.5	4.7	<.1	5.6	7	8	8	15	1.5	1.6	0.3	0.8
32 003	Clark	741,459	75.4	9.3	3.3	0.7	0.1	11.2	1	16	1	5	61.7	59.1	90.0	66.6
32 005	Douglas	27,637	90.5	0.3	1.2	1.9	<.1	6.0	5	3	16	14	2.3	2.6	0.1	1.3
32 007	Elko	33,530	79.7	0.7	0.8	5.7	<.1	12.9	4	13	9	3	2.8	2.8	0.3	3.5
32 009	Esmeralda	1,344	84.6	0.5	0.6	5.0	0.0	9.3	17	10	11	6	0.1	0.1	<.1	0.1
32 011	Eureka	1,547	87.5	0.3	0.6	2.6	0.0	8.9	16	6	13	9	0.1	0.1	<.1	0.1
32 013	Humboldt	12,844	75.7	0.5	0.4	5.1	<.1	18.2	9	15	10	1	1.1	1.0	<.1	1.9
32 015	Lander	6,266	83.0	0.1	0.2	4.0	<.1	12.6	12	12	17	4	0.5	0.5	<.1	0.6
32 017	Lincoln	3,775	91.7	2.1	0.4	1.5	<.1	4.1	14	2	4	16	0.3	0.4	0.1	0.1
32 019	Lyon	20,001	88.5	0.3	0.7	2.9	<.1	7.6	6	4	12	12	1.7	1.9	<.1	1.2
32 021	Mineral	6,475	75.2	5.3	1.0	10.0	<.1	8.4	11	17	2	10	0.5	0.5	0.4	0.4
32 023	Nye	17,781	87.9	1.5	0.8	2.7	<.1	7.0	8	5	7	13	1.5	1.7	0.4	1.0
32 027	Pershing	4,336	79.4	0.3	0.6	4.4	<.1	15.3	13	14	15	2	0.4	0.4	<.1	0.5
32 029	Storey	2,526	92.8	0.3	1.1	1.8	0.1	3.8	15	1	14	17	0.2	0.2	<.1	<.1
32 031	Washoe	254,667	83.4	2.1	3.6	1.7	<.1	9.0	2	11	3	8	21.2	22.4	7.1	18.5
32 033	White Pine	9,264	85.6	1.9	0.4	2.8	0.1	9.2	10	9	5	7	0.8	0.8	0.2	0.7
32 510	Carson City	40,443	86.7	1.6	1.4	2.5	<.1	7.7	3	7	6	11	3.4	3.7	0.8	2.5
32	**NEVADA**	1,201,833	78.7	6.4	3.0	1.5	<.1	10.4					100.0	100.0	100.0	100.0
	CONGRESSIONAL															
	District 1	600,957	73.3	10.2	3.6	0.7	0.1	12.2	1	2	1	1	50.0	46.5	79.9	58.8
	District 2	600,876	84.2	2.6	2.4	2.2	<.1	8.5	2	1	2	2	50.0	53.5	20.1	41.2

Table B. — 1990 Voting Age Population (VAP) by Race and Ethnic Origin

County	Total Voting Age Population	Percent of total VAP — Non-Hispanic White	Black	Asian and Pacific Islander	Native American	Other	Hispanic	Rank — Total	Non-Hispanic White	Black	Hispanic	Percent contribution to state VAP — Total	Non-Hispanic White	Black	Hispanic	VAP percent of total population — Total	Non-Hispanic White	Black	Asian and Pacific Islander	Native American	Other	Hispanic
Churchill	12,883	87.6	1.1	2.2	4.1	<.1	4.9	8	8	8	15	1.4	1.5	0.3	0.8	71.8	73.2	69.5	64.0	62.9	57.1	62.9
Clark	559,650	78.0	8.1	3.3	0.7	<.1	9.9	1	17	1	5	61.8	59.6	88.9	67.4	75.5	78.1	65.7	74.9	73.5	49.7	66.7
Douglas	20,565	91.6	0.3	1.3	1.7	<.1	5.1	5	3	14	14	2.3	2.6	0.1	1.3	74.4	75.3	65.4	76.8	66.5	42.9	63.7
Elko	22,720	81.7	0.7	0.7	5.4	<.1	11.4	4	14	10	3	2.5	2.5	0.3	3.1	67.8	69.5	63.9	61.9	64.1	50.0	59.5
Esmeralda	1,021	86.7	0.3	0.5	4.3	0.0	8.2	17	10	12	6	0.1	0.1	<.1	0.1	76.0	77.8	42.9	62.5	65.7	0.0	67.2
Eureka	1,122	88.3	0.3	0.7	2.6	0.0	8.1	16	6	13	7	0.1	0.1	<.1	0.1	72.5	73.2	60.0	80.0	72.5	0.0	65.9
Humboldt	8,949	78.0	0.7	0.4	4.9	<.1	15.8	9	16	9	1	1.0	1.0	0.1	1.7	69.7	71.8	94.3	67.9	67.4	66.7	60.6
Lander	4,125	85.0	0.1	0.3	4.1	<.1	10.4	12	11	17	4	0.5	0.5	<.1	0.5	65.8	67.4	66.7	78.6	68.1	33.3	54.6
Lincoln	2,493	93.1	2.2	0.3	1.6	<.1	2.6	14	2	4	17	0.3	0.3	0.1	<.1	66.0	67.0	70.9	50.0	70.7	66.7	42.3
Lyon	14,539	90.4	0.2	0.6	2.6	<.1	6.2	6	4	16	12	1.6	1.8	<.1	1.1	72.7	74.2	46.2	63.6	65.4	16.7	59.7
Mineral	4,600	78.8	4.8	0.8	9.3	<.1	6.3	11	15	2	11	0.5	0.5	0.4	0.4	71.0	74.4	63.8	56.1	66.4	50.0	53.3
Nye	13,369	89.3	1.8	0.8	2.4	<.1	5.6	7	5	7	13	1.5	1.6	0.5	0.9	75.2	76.4	89.8	70.3	68.2	58.3	60.5
Pershing	3,016	82.7	0.2	0.7	4.1	<.1	12.3	13	13	15	2	0.3	0.3	<.1	0.5	69.6	72.5	53.8	84.0	64.1	50.0	55.9
Storey	1,940	93.7	0.4	1.0	1.5	0.2	3.2	15	1	11	16	0.2	0.2	<.1	<.1	76.8	77.5	100.0	65.5	66.7	100.0	65.6
Washoe	195,788	85.0	2.0	3.6	1.6	<.1	7.9	2	12	5	8	21.6	22.7	7.6	18.8	76.9	78.3	71.1	75.5	69.4	56.1	67.2
White Pine	6,699	86.9	2.6	0.3	2.3	<.1	7.7	10	9	3	9	0.7	0.8	0.3	0.6	72.3	73.4	99.4	69.7	59.2	54.5	60.9
Carson City	31,406	87.9	1.9	1.3	2.3	<.1	6.5	3	7	6	10	3.5	3.8	1.2	2.5	77.7	78.7	92.8	73.7	70.4	80.8	66.1
NEVADA	904,885	80.9	5.6	3.0	1.3	<.1	9.1					100.0	100.0	100.0	100.0	75.3	77.4	66.4	74.7	69.2	51.8	66.0
CONGRESSIONAL																						
District 1	456,138	76.2	8.8	3.5	0.7	<.1	10.8	1	2	1	1	50.4	47.5	78.5	59.8	75.9	79.0	65.3	75.1	73.7	49.7	67.1
District 2	448,747	85.8	2.4	2.4	2.0	<.1	7.4	2	1	2	2	49.6	52.5	21.5	40.2	74.7	76.1	71.1	74.0	67.7	55.1	64.4

Nevada 597

Table C. — Voter Participation: November 3, 1992, General Election

County	Estimated Voting Age Population (VAP), 1992	Voter registration (REG) Total	% contribution to state REG	% of 1992 VAP	Rank by % of 1992 VAP	Voter turnout — Highest office Actual	Total	Office	% of 1992 VAP	Maximum vote Total	% contribution to state turnout	% of REG	Rank by % of REG	% of 1992 VAP	Rank by % of 1992 VAP	Percent drop-off, by office Pres-ident	Sen-ator	Gov-ernor	Repre-sent-ative
Churchill	13,816	9,469	1.5	68.5	8	7,744	7,663	P	55.5	7,744	1.5	81.8	11	56.1	8	1.0	2.6	-	4.6
Clark	639,285	396,628	61.0	62.0	12	306,387	302,782	P	47.4	306,387	59.7	77.2	17	47.9	14	1.2	3.8	-	4.6
Douglas	22,567	18,470	2.8	81.8	3	15,300	15,145	P	67.1	15,300	3.0	82.8	6	67.8	3	1.0	2.6	-	5.1
Elko	27,226	15,557	2.4	57.1	16	12,060	11,926	P	43.8	12,060	2.3	77.5	15	44.3	17	1.1	2.3	-	2.2
Esmeralda	1,179	716	0.1	60.7	13	590	584	P	49.5	590	0.1	82.4	8	50.0	12	1.0	2.0	-	2.7
Eureka	1,184	832	0.1	70.3	6	702	690	P	58.3	702	0.1	84.4	4	59.3	4	1.7	2.3	-	2.6
Humboldt	9,848	5,546	0.9	56.3	17	4,691	4,586	S	46.6	4,691	0.9	84.6	3	47.6	15	24.9	2.2	-	2.9
Lander	4,744	2,718	0.4	57.3	15	2,253	2,225	S	46.9	2,253	0.4	82.9	5	47.5	16	11.6	1.2	-	2.2
Lincoln	2,582	2,182	0.3	84.5	2	1,888	1,857	P	71.9	1,888	0.4	86.5	1	73.1	1	1.6	1.6	-	4.4
Lyon	16,162	11,487	1.8	71.1	5	9,311	9,204	P	56.9	9,311	1.8	81.1	13	57.6	5	1.1	2.7	-	2.7
Mineral	4,662	3,455	0.5	74.1	4	2,679	2,641	P	56.6	2,679	0.5	77.5	14	57.5	6	1.4	2.7	-	2.6
Nye	15,811	10,778	1.7	68.2	9	8,343	8,022	P	50.7	8,343	1.6	77.4	16	52.8	11	3.8	5.5	-	6.1
Pershing	3,192	1,844	0.3	57.8	14	1,590	1,566	P	49.1	1,590	0.3	86.2	2	49.8	13	1.5	2.1	-	2.1
Storey	2,194	1,888	0.3	86.1	1	1,531	1,519	P	69.2	1,531	0.3	81.1	12	69.8	2	0.8	2.5	-	3.9
Washoe	208,460	140,701	21.6	67.5	10	115,511	114,671	P	55.0	115,511	22.5	82.1	10	55.4	9	0.7	3.0	-	3.1
White Pine	6,951	4,607	0.7	66.3	11	3,794	3,730	P	53.7	3,794	0.7	82.4	9	54.6	10	1.7	2.8	-	3.8
Carson City	33,137	23,035	3.5	69.5	7	19,013	18,803	P	56.7	19,013	3.7	82.5	7	57.4	7	1.1	1.7	-	5.3
NEVADA	**1,013,000**	**649,913**	**100.0**	**64.2**		**513,387**	**507,614**		**50.1**	**513,387**	**100.0**	**79.0**		**50.7**		**1.4**	**3.4**	**-**	**4.2**

Table D. — Voter Registration by Political Party Affiliation: November 3, 1992, General Election

County	Total voter registration	Political party affiliation Democrat (DEM)[1]	Republican (REP)[1]	Independent (IND)[1]	Plurality Total	Party	Percent of total registration DEM	REP	IND	Rank DEM	REP	IND	Percent contribution to state registration Total	DEM	REP	IND
Churchill	9,469	3,301	4,845	1,299	1,544	R	34.9	51.3	13.8	16	3	10	1.5	1.1	1.9	1.4
Clark	396,628	194,171	141,240	59,492	52,931	D	49.2	35.8	15.1	5	14	4	61.0	65.8	55.2	62.0
Douglas	18,470	5,869	9,929	2,580	4,060	R	31.9	54.0	14.0	17	1	9	2.8	2.0	3.9	2.7
Elko	15,557	6,016	6,707	2,771	691	R	38.8	43.3	17.9	13	10	1	2.4	2.0	2.6	2.9
Esmeralda	716	359	274	77	85	D	50.6	38.6	10.8	4	12	14	0.1	0.1	0.1	<.1
Eureka	832	312	431	65	119	R	38.6	53.3	8.0	14	2	16	0.1	0.1	0.2	<.1
Humboldt	5,546	2,232	2,449	841	217	R	40.4	44.3	15.2	10	8	3	0.9	0.8	1.0	0.9
Lander	2,718	1,007	1,216	480	209	R	37.3	45.0	17.8	15	7	2	0.4	0.3	0.5	0.5
Lincoln	2,182	1,302	725	154	577	D	59.7	33.2	7.1	1	15	17	0.3	0.4	0.3	0.2
Lyon	11,487	4,771	5,021	1,659	250	R	41.7	43.8	14.5	8	9	6	1.8	1.6	2.0	1.7
Mineral	3,455	1,968	1,119	362	849	D	57.1	32.4	10.5	3	16	15	0.5	0.7	0.4	0.4
Nye	10,778	5,081	4,109	1,544	972	D	47.3	38.3	14.4	6	13	7	1.7	1.7	1.6	1.6
Pershing	1,844	860	722	261	138	D	46.7	39.2	14.2	7	11	8	0.3	0.3	0.3	0.3
Storey	1,888	783	847	229	64	R	42.1	45.6	12.3	9	6	12	0.3	0.3	0.3	0.2
Washoe	140,701	55,466	63,915	20,480	8,449	R	39.7	45.7	14.6	11	5	5	21.6	18.8	25.0	21.4
White Pine	4,607	2,654	1,439	502	1,215	D	57.8	31.3	10.9	2	17	13	0.7	0.9	0.6	0.5
Carson City	23,035	8,959	10,909	3,092	1,950	R	39.0	47.5	13.5	12	4	11	3.5	3.0	4.3	3.2
NEVADA[2]	**649,913**	**295,111**	**255,897**	**95,888**	**39,214**	**D**	**45.6**	**39.6**	**14.8**				**100.0**	**100.0**	**100.0**	**100.0**

[1]Data from report dated October 3, 1992; sum of registrants by party differs slightly from total voter registration reported with November 1992 general election returns.
[2]Total voter registration also includes 2,315 for Libertarian party, 485 for Independent American party, 164 for Populist party, and 5 for Natural Law party, as reported October 3, 1992.

Table E. — Vote for President: November 3, 1992, General Election

County	Total	Clinton (DEM)	Bush (REP)	Perot (IND)	Other	Plurality Total	Party	DEM	REP	IND	Other	Rank DEM	Rank REP	Rank IND	Total	DEM	REP	IND	DEM	REP
Churchill	7,663	1,770	3,789	1,964	140	1,825	R	23.1	49.4	25.6	1.8	13	1	15	1.5	0.9	2.2	1.5	31.8	68.2
Clark	302,782	124,586	97,403	75,364	5,429	27,183	D	41.1	32.2	24.9	1.8	1	16	16	59.8	65.9	55.4	56.8	56.1	43.9
Douglas	15,145	3,928	6,182	4,814	221	1,368	R	25.9	40.8	31.8	1.5	11	8	5	3.0	2.1	3.5	3.6	38.9	61.1
Elko	11,926	2,782	5,208	3,628	308	1,580	R	23.3	43.7	30.4	2.6	12	5	8	2.4	1.5	3.0	2.7	34.8	65.2
Esmeralda	584	118	221	220	25	1	R	20.2	37.8	37.7	4.3	16	11	1	0.1	<.1	0.1	0.2	34.8	65.2
Eureka	690	129	330	214	17	116	R	18.7	47.8	31.0	2.5	17	3	7	0.1	<.1	0.2	0.2	28.1	71.9
Humboldt	3,523	810	1,505	1,149	59	356	R	23.0	42.7	32.6	1.7	14	6	4	0.7	0.4	0.9	0.9	35.0	65.0
Lander	1,992	423	885	652	32	233	R	21.2	44.4	32.7	1.6	15	4	3	0.4	0.2	0.5	0.5	32.3	67.7
Lincoln	1,857	511	890	394	62	379	R	27.5	47.9	21.2	3.3	10	2	17	0.4	0.3	0.5	0.3	36.5	63.5
Lyon	9,204	2,777	3,509	2,716	202	732	R	30.2	38.1	29.5	2.2	8	10	9	1.8	1.5	2.0	2.0	44.2	55.8
Mineral	2,641	909	918	746	68	9	R	34.4	34.8	28.2	2.6	4	13	11	0.5	0.5	0.5	0.6	49.8	50.2
Nye	8,022	2,561	2,743	2,501	217	182	R	31.9	34.2	31.2	2.7	7	14	6	1.6	1.4	1.6	1.9	48.3	51.7
Pershing	1,566	467	643	429	27	176	R	29.8	41.1	27.4	1.7	9	7	13	0.3	0.2	0.4	0.3	42.1	57.9
Storey	1,519	488	458	550	23	62	I	32.1	30.2	36.2	1.5	5	17	2	0.3	0.3	0.3	0.4	51.6	48.4
Washoe	114,671	39,500	42,636	30,974	1,561	3,136	R	34.4	37.2	27.0	1.4	3	12	14	22.6	20.9	24.2	23.4	48.1	51.9
White Pine	3,730	1,354	1,206	1,070	100	148	D	36.3	32.3	28.7	2.7	2	15	10	0.7	0.7	0.7	0.8	52.9	47.1
Carson City	18,803	6,035	7,302	5,195	271	1,267	R	32.1	38.8	27.6	1.4	6	9	12	3.7	3.2	4.2	3.9	45.3	54.7
NEVADA	506,318	189,148	175,828	132,580	8,762	13,320	D	37.4	34.7	26.2	1.7				100.0	100.0	100.0	100.0	51.8	48.2

Table F. — Vote for U.S. Senator: November 3, 1992, General Election

County	Total	Reid (DEM)	Dahl (REP)	Other	Plurality Total	Party	DEM	REP	Other	Rank DEM	Rank REP	Rank Other	Total	DEM	REP	Other
Churchill	7,546	1,812	4,968	766	3,156	R	24.0	65.8	10.2	17	1	7	1.5	0.7	2.5	1.8
Clark	294,737	159,721	109,510	25,506	50,211	D	54.2	37.2	8.7	1	17	13	59.4	63.1	54.9	58.9
Douglas	14,909	6,423	7,198	1,288	775	R	43.1	48.3	8.6	9	6	14	3.0	2.5	3.6	3.0
Elko	11,782	3,227	7,404	1,151	4,177	R	27.4	62.8	9.8	15	3	8	2.4	1.3	3.7	2.7
Esmeralda	578	223	277	78	54	R	38.6	47.9	13.5	12	8	3	0.1	<.1	0.1	0.2
Eureka	686	181	433	72	252	R	26.4	63.1	10.5	16	2	5	0.1	<.1	0.2	0.2
Humboldt	4,586	2,076	2,085	425	9	R	45.3	45.5	9.3	6	9	11	0.9	0.8	1.0	1.0
Lander	2,225	678	1,333	214	655	R	30.5	59.9	9.6	14	4	9	0.4	0.3	0.7	0.5
Lincoln	1,857	601	1,089	167	488	R	32.4	58.6	9.0	13	5	12	0.4	0.2	0.5	0.4
Lyon	9,061	4,089	4,105	867	16	R	45.1	45.3	9.6	7	10	10	1.8	1.6	2.1	2.0
Mineral	2,608	1,309	1,016	283	293	D	50.2	39.0	10.9	4	15	4	0.5	0.5	0.5	0.7
Nye	7,886	3,162	3,550	1,174	388	R	40.1	45.0	14.9	11	11	2	1.6	1.2	1.8	2.7
Pershing	1,557	681	751	125	70	R	43.7	48.2	8.0	8	7	15	0.3	0.3	0.4	0.3
Storey	1,492	762	576	154	186	D	51.1	38.6	10.3	3	16	6	0.3	0.3	0.3	0.4
Washoe	111,999	57,578	45,440	8,981	12,138	D	51.4	40.6	8.0	2	14	16	22.6	22.7	22.8	20.7
White Pine	3,687	1,570	1,513	604	57	D	42.6	41.0	16.4	10	13	1	0.7	0.6	0.8	1.4
Carson City	18,691	9,057	8,165	1,469	892	D	48.5	43.7	7.9	5	12	17	3.8	3.6	4.1	3.4
NEVADA	495,887	253,150	199,413	43,324	53,737	D	51.0	40.2	8.7				100.0	100.0	100.0	100.0

Table H. – Vote for U.S. Representative in Congress: November 3, 1992, General Election

Congressional district and county	Total	Democrat (DEM)	Republican (REP)	Other	Plurality Total	Plurality Party	Percent of total vote DEM	Percent of total vote REP	Percent of total vote Other	Rank within district DEM	Rank within district REP	Rank within district Other	Percent contribution to district vote Total	Percent contribution to district vote DEM	Percent contribution to district vote REP	Percent contribution to district vote Other
District 1	**221,488**	**128,278**	**84,217**	**8,993**	**44,061**	**D**	**57.9**	**38.0**	**4.1**				**100.0**	**100.0**	**100.0**	**100.0**
Clark (pt)	221,488	128,278	84,217	8,993	44,061	D	57.9	38.0	4.1	1	1	1	100.0	100.0	100.0	100.0
District 2	**270,461**	**117,199**	**129,575**	**23,687**	**12,376**	**R**	**43.3**	**47.9**	**8.8**				**100.0**	**100.0**	**100.0**	**100.0**
Churchill	7,389	2,634	4,044	711	1,410	R	35.6	54.7	9.6	12	6	5	2.7	2.2	3.1	3.0
Clark (pt)	70,785	32,502	34,061	4,222	1,559	R	45.9	48.1	6.0	3	12	15	26.2	27.7	26.3	17.8
Douglas	14,519	5,384	7,898	1,237	2,514	R	37.1	54.4	8.5	11	7	8	5.4	4.6	6.1	5.2
Elko	11,797	3,816	7,201	780	3,385	R	32.3	61.0	6.6	16	2	14	4.4	3.3	5.6	3.3
Esmeralda	574	225	292	57	67	R	39.2	50.9	9.9	10	8	4	0.2	0.2	0.2	0.2
Eureka	684	203	448	33	245	R	29.7	65.5	4.8	17	1	17	0.3	0.2	0.3	0.1
Humboldt	4,555	1,622	2,662	271	1,040	R	35.6	58.4	5.9	13	4	16	1.7	1.4	2.1	1.1
Lander	2,204	777	1,242	185	465	R	35.3	56.4	8.4	14	5	10	0.8	0.7	1.0	0.8
Lincoln	1,805	606	1,077	122	471	R	33.6	59.7	6.8	15	3	13	0.7	0.5	0.8	0.5
Lyon	9,057	3,912	4,182	963	270	R	43.2	46.2	10.6	6	13	3	3.3	3.3	3.2	4.1
Mineral	2,610	1,249	1,170	191	79	D	47.9	44.8	7.3	2	14	11	1.0	1.1	0.9	0.8
Nye	7,832	3,822	3,284	726	538	D	48.8	41.9	9.3	1	16	6	2.9	3.3	2.5	3.1
Pershing	1,557	666	782	109	116	R	42.8	50.2	7.0	7	9	12	0.6	0.6	0.6	0.5
Storey	1,472	669	588	215	81	D	45.4	39.9	14.6	4	17	1	0.5	0.6	0.5	0.9
Washoe	111,961	49,882	50,147	11,932	265	R	44.6	44.8	10.7	5	15	2	41.4	42.6	38.7	50.4
White Pine	3,650	1,539	1,801	310	262	R	42.2	49.3	8.5	9	10	9	1.3	1.3	1.4	1.3
Carson City	18,010	7,691	8,696	1,623	1,005	R	42.7	48.3	9.0	8	11	7	6.7	6.6	6.7	6.9
NEVADA	**491,949**	**245,477**	**213,792**	**32,680**	**31,685**	**D**	**49.9**	**43.5**	**6.6**							

1992 Vote for President
Percent for Clinton (D), by County

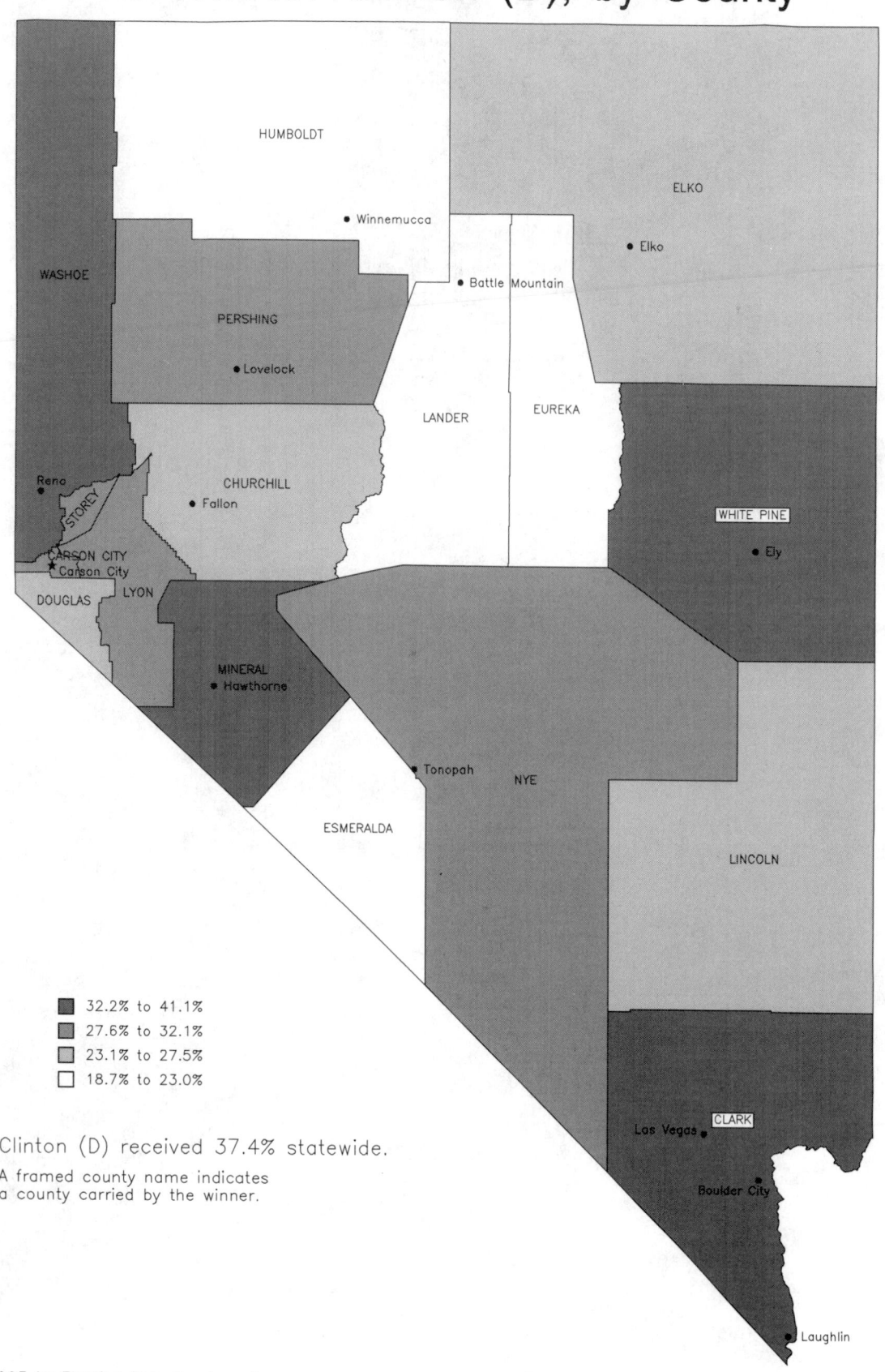

HUMBOLDT

ELKO

• Winnemucca

• Elko

WASHOE

• Battle Mountain

PERSHING

LANDER

EUREKA

• Lovelock

WHITE PINE

Reno
•

CHURCHILL

• Ely

STOREY

• Fallon

CARSON CITY
★ Carson City

DOUGLAS

LYON

MINERAL
• Hawthorne

NYE

LINCOLN

• Tonopah

ESMERALDA

■ 32.2% to 41.1%
■ 27.6% to 32.1%
▨ 23.1% to 27.5%
□ 18.7% to 23.0%

CLARK

Las Vegas
•

Clinton (D) received 37.4% statewide.

Boulder City
•

A framed county name indicates
a county carried by the winner.

Laughlin
•

Copyright © 1993 by Election Data Services, Inc.

Nevada 601

1992 Vote for U.S. Senator
Percent for Reid (D), by County

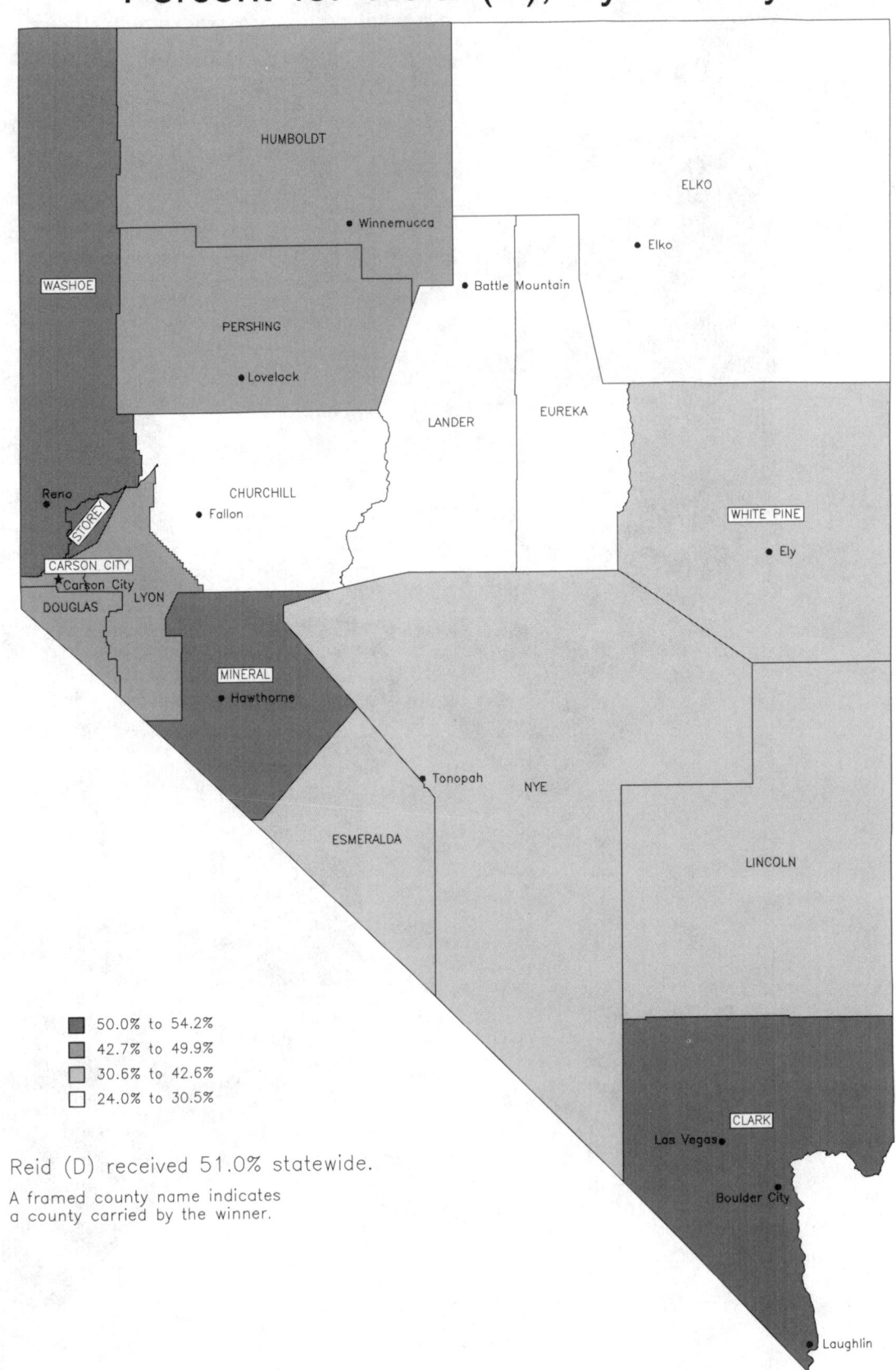

HUMBOLDT

ELKO

• Winnemucca

• Elko

WASHOE

• Battle Mountain

PERSHING

LANDER

EUREKA

• Lovelock

Reno •

STOREY

WHITE PINE

CHURCHILL

CARSON CITY

• Fallon

• Ely

★ Carson City

DOUGLAS   LYON

MINERAL

• Hawthorne

• Tonopah

NYE

LINCOLN

ESMERALDA

50.0% to 54.2%

42.7% to 49.9%

30.6% to 42.6%

24.0% to 30.5%

CLARK

Reid (D) received 51.0% statewide.

Las Vegas •

A framed county name indicates
a county carried by the winner.

Boulder City •

Laughlin •

602 Nevada

NEW HAMPSHIRE

Congressional Districts 2
   Average Population 554,626
State Senate Districts 24
   Average Population 46,219
State House Districts 400
   Average Population 2,773

Electoral College Votes...4
Counties[1] 10
Voting Precincts 301

Alternative Registration Methods:
   ....Deputized Registrars

Registration Deadline (Days before Election) 10

Voting Equipment Use (Cities and Towns)[2]

Datavote Punch Card	0	Paper Ballot	218
Electronic	0	Other Punch Card	0
Lever Machine	4	Mixed Systems	0
Optical Scanner	16		

Party Control	DEM	REP	IND[3]	VAC
1993 State Senate	11	13	0	0
1992 State Senate	11	13	0	0
1993 State House	136	258	5	1
1992 State House	123	267	2	8

Population Statistics 1990

Race/ Ethnicity	Total Population		Voting Age Population		Voting Age Population % of total population
	Number	%	Number	%	
Non-Hispanic					
White	1,079,484	97.3	810,298	97.6	75.1
Black	6,749	0.6	4,624	0.6	68.5
Asian/Pacific Islander	9,197	0.8	6,493	0.8	70.6
Native American	2,042	0.2	1,525	0.2	74.7
Other	447	<.1	164	<.1	36.7
All Hispanic	11,333	1.0	7,393	0.9	65.2
TOTAL	1,109,252	100.0	830,497	100.0	74.9

Estimated Voting Age Population 1992 (VAP) 852,000
Number of Registered Voters.................................... 660,985
   % of estimated VAP.. 77.6
Voter Turnout (Actual) 545,197
   % of VAP 64.0
   % of Registration 82.5
Persons Not Voting—of Voting Age 306,803
   % of VAP 36.0
Persons Not Voting—of Registered 115,788
   % of Registration 17.5
Straight Ticket Voting .... Yes, Exception

State Officials and Members of Congress

Governor:
Steve Merrill (R) 1992, elected to a two-year term in 1992.

U.S. Senators:
Robert Smith (R) 1990, elected to a six-year term in 1990.
Judd Gregg (R) 1992, elected to a six-year term in 1992.

U.S. Representative in Congress:
(District, Name, Party, Date first elected)

1. Zeliff (R) 1990   2. Swett (D) 1990

---

[1]Elections administered by 238 cities and towns rather than counties. Data presented for counties and 13 cities and towns with more than one voting precinct. [2]Reported for all 238 cities and towns, including those with a single voting precinct. [3]1993 State House includes four members of minor parties.

Candidates: General Election, November 3, 1992

Candidate(s)	Total vote	Percent	Party	Status	First elected
President/Vice President					
Clinton/Gore	209,040	38.86%	Democrat	Challenger	1992
Bush/Quayle	202,484	37.64%	Republican	Incumbent	1988
Perot/Stockdale	121,337	22.56%	Independent	Challenger	
Marrou/Lord	3,548	0.66%	Libertarian	Challenger	
Scattering (other)	730	0.14%	Composited Others	Challenger	
Fulani/Munoz	512	0.10%	New Alliance	Challenger	
Hagelin/Tompkins	292	0.05%	Natural Law	Challenger	
U.S. Senator					
Judd Gregg	249,591	48.14%	Republican	Challenger	1992
John Rauh	234,982	45.33%	Democrat	Challenger	
Katherine Alexander	18,214	3.51%	Libertarian	Challenger	
Larry Brady	9,340	1.80%	Independent	Challenger	
Kenneth Blevens	4,752	0.92%	Independent	Challenger	
David Haight	1,284	0.25%	Natural Law	Challenger	
Miscellaneous	232	0.04%	Composited Others	Challenger	
Sullivan	21	<.01%	Unknown	Challenger	
Governor					
Steve Merrill	289,170	56.02%	Republican	Challenger	1992
Deborah Arnesen	206,232	39.95%	Democrat	Challenger	
Miriam Luce	20,663	4.00%	Libertarian	Challenger	
Scattering (other)	105	0.02%	Composited Others	Challenger	
U.S. Representative in Congress					
District 1					
Bill Zeliff	135,936	53.13%	Republican	Incumbent	1990
Bob Preston	108,578	42.44%	Democrat	Challenger	
Knox Bickford	5,633	2.20%	Libertarian	Challenger	
Richard Bosa	3,537	1.38%	Independent	Challenger	
Linda Spitzfaden	1,997	0.78%	Natural Law	Challenger	
Scattering (other)	172	0.07%	Composited Others	Challenger	
District 2					
Dick Swett	157,328	61.65%	Democrat	Incumbent	1990
Bill Hatch	91,126	35.71%	Republican	Challenger	
John Lewicke	5,977	2.34%	Libertarian	Challenger	
James Bingham	657	0.26%	Natural Law	Challenger	
Scattering	97	0.04%	Composited Others	Challenger	

Candidates: February 18, 1992, Primary Election

Candidate	Total vote	Percent	Candidate	Total vote	Percent
Presidential Preference, Democratic			**Presidential Preference, Republican**		
Paul Tsongas	55,638	33.16%	George Bush	92,233	52.96%
Bill Clinton	41,522	24.74%	Patrick Buchanan	65,087	37.37%
Bob Kerrey	18,575	11.07%	Others	3,686	2.12%
Tom Harkin	17,057	10.17%	Paul Tsongas	3,677	2.11%
Jerry Brown	13,654	8.14%	Ralph Nader	3,257	1.87%
Mario Cuomo	6,577	3.92%	Bill Clinton	1,696	0.97%
Tom Laughlin	3,251	1.94%	Jim Lenanne	1,684	0.97%
Ralph Nader	3,054	1.82%	Mario Cuomo	798	0.46%
Charles Woods	2,862	1.71%	Jerry Brown	772	0.44%
Others[1]	2,693	1.60%	Bob Kerrey	735	0.42%
George Bush	1,433	0.85%	Tom Harkin	542	0.31%
Patrick Buchanan	1,248	0.74%			
Scattering	236	0.14%			

[1]Does not include votes reported as "scattering".

Voter Registration and Turnout, 1948-1992 Elections

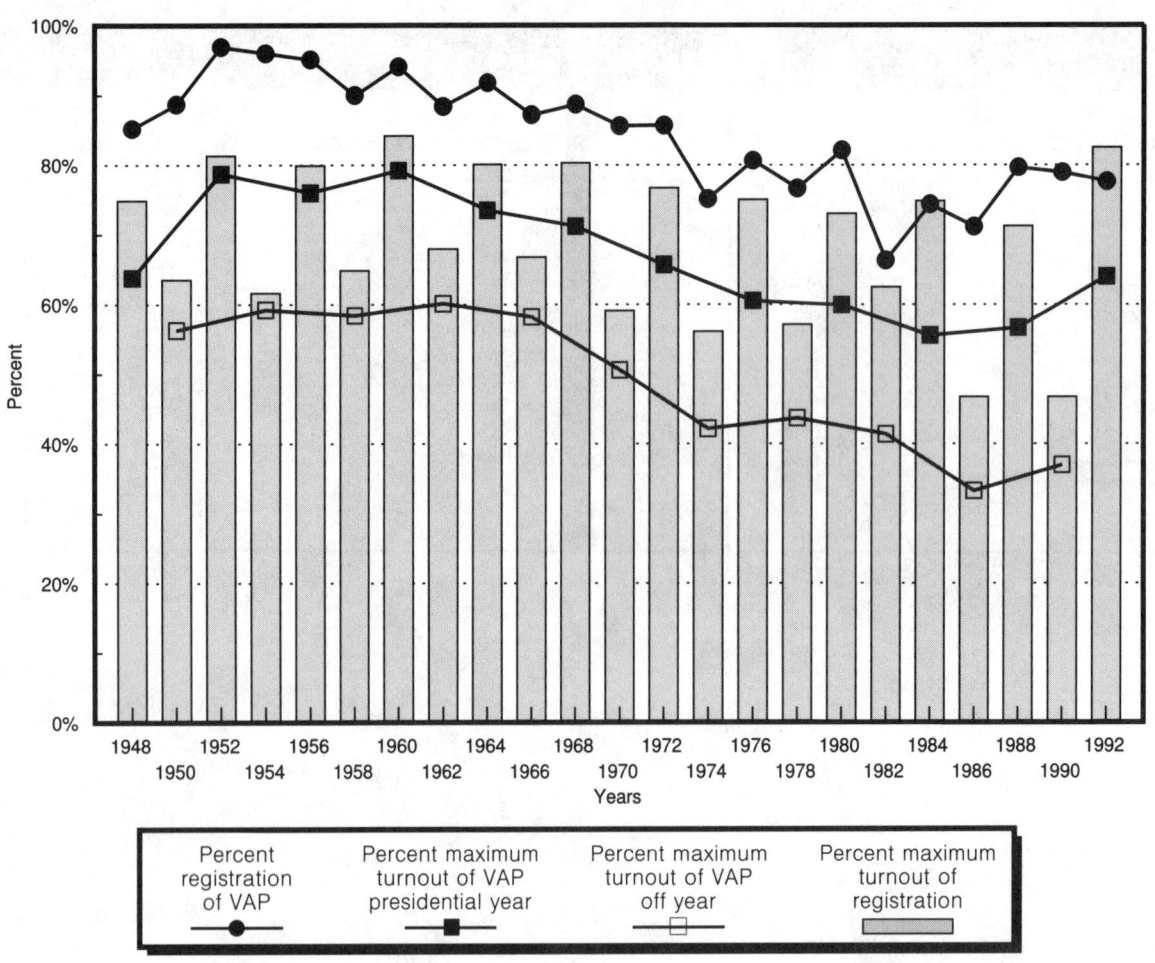

Year	Estimated Voting Age Population (VAP)	Voter registration (REG)			Voter turnout											
						Highest office						Maximum vote				
		Total	Percent of VAP	Rank by percent of VAP	Actual	Total	Office	Percent total REG	Rank by percent of REG	Percent of VAP	Rank by percent of VAP	Total	Percent total REG	Rank by percent of REG	Percent total VAP	Rank by percent of VAP
1992	852,000	660,985	77.6	18	545,197	537,943	P	81.4	12	63.1	15	545,197	82.5	13	64.0	14
1990	835,000	658,716	78.9	10	307,700	294,819	G	44.8	45	35.3	35	307,700	46.7	43	36.9	33
1988	817,000	649,924	79.6	13	462,503	451,074	P	69.4	32	55.2	17	462,503	71.2	29	56.6	17
1986	775,000	551,257	71.1	22	257,410	250,966	G	45.5	42	32.4	41	257,410	46.7	43	33.2	42
1984	732,000	543,790	74.3	23	406,608	388,904	P	71.5	33	53.1	30	406,608	74.8	27	55.5	27
1982	698,000	462,457	66.3	30	289,057	282,588	G	61.1	28	40.5	32	289,057	62.5	28	41.4	31
1980	672,000	551,432	82.1	12	402,415	383,990	P	69.6	38	57.1	21	402,415	73.0	34	59.9	14
1978	638,000	488,871	76.6	10	279,113	269,587	G	55.1	27	42.3	21	279,113	57.1	29	43.7	20
1976	593,000	478,188	80.6	14	358,663	339,618	P	71.0	33	57.3	23	358,663	75.0	28	60.5	17
1974	560,000	420,774	75.1	15	236,140	226,665	G	53.9	32	40.5	32	236,140	56.1	29	42.2	29
1972	525,000	449,714	85.7	8	345,013	334,055	P	74.3	25	63.6	9	345,013	76.7	24	65.7	8
1970	452,000	386,894	85.6	9	228,670	222,441	G	57.5	35	49.2	30	228,670	59.1	35	50.6	27
1968	427,000	378,660	88.7	8	304,051	297,298	P	78.5	28	69.6	9	304,051	80.3	25	71.2	6
1966	408,000	355,626	87.2	6	237,409	233,642	G	65.7	20	57.3	13	237,409	66.8	22	58.2	13
1964	398,000	365,224	91.8	6	292,638	288,093	P	78.9	27	72.4	10	292,638	80.1	22	73.5	10
1962	391,000	345,809	88.4	5	235,122	230,048	S	66.5	20	58.8	14	235,122	68.0	19	60.1	12
1960	376,000	353,717	94.1	3	297,951	295,761	P	83.6	20	78.7	2	297,951	84.2	21	79.2	4
1958	361,000	324,887	90.0	2	210,783	206,745	G	63.6	21	57.3	14	210,783	64.9	21	58.4	13
1956	355,000	337,591	95.1	3	269,791	266,994	P	79.1	19	75.2	5	269,791	79.9	20	76.0	6
1954	341,000	327,329	96.0	3	201,756	194,631	G	59.5	18	57.1	13	201,756	61.6	18	59.2	12
1952	349,000	338,204	96.9	2	274,797	272,950	P	80.7	17	78.2	4	274,797	81.3	17	78.7	4
1950	351,000	311,294	88.7	3	197,718	191,239	G	61.4	14	54.5	16	197,718	63.5	15	56.3	14
1948	367,000	312,644	85.2	4	234,080	231,440	P	74.0	12	63.1	16	234,080	74.9	12	63.8	17

NEW HAMPSHIRE

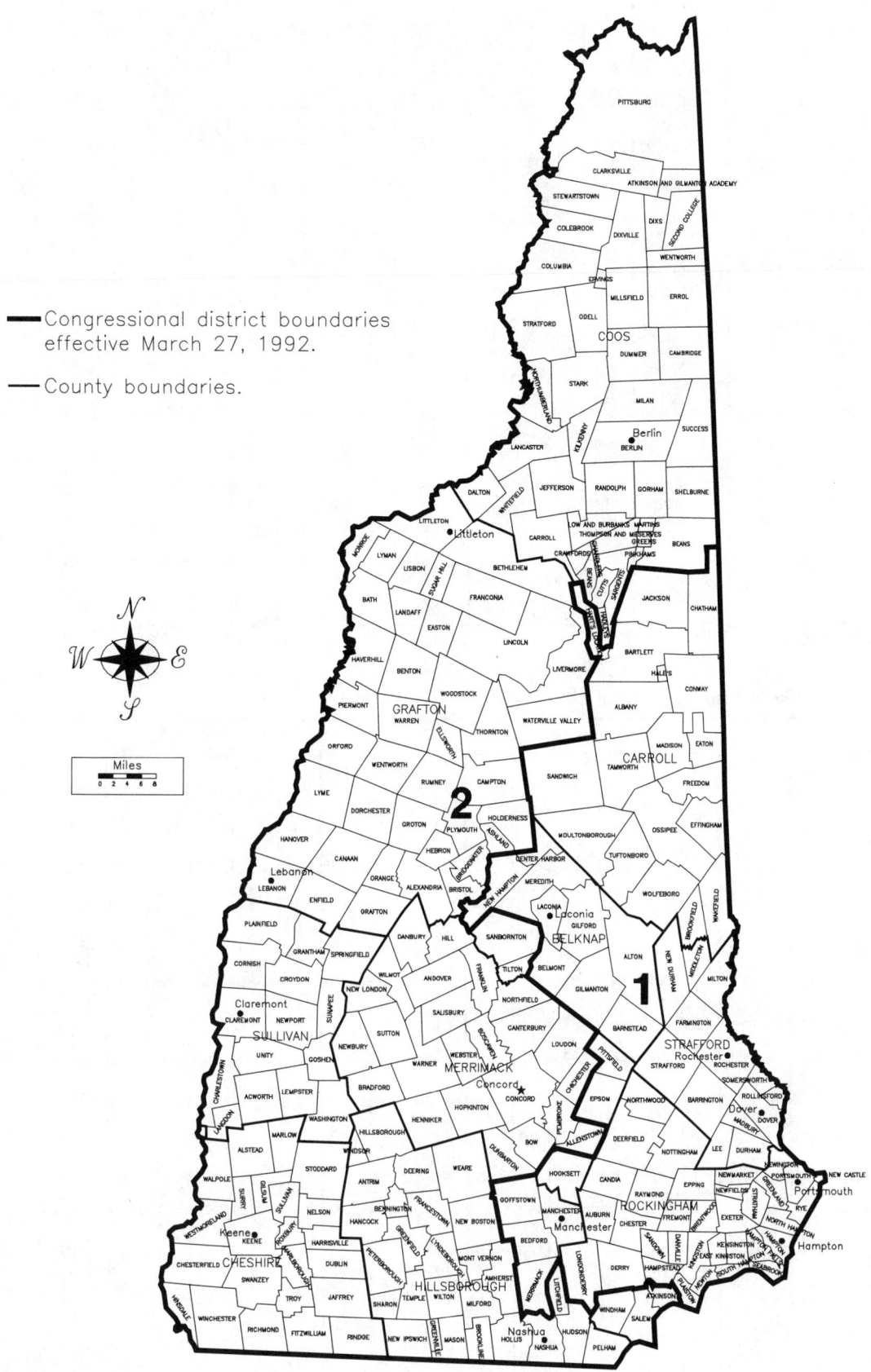

▬ Congressional district boundaries
effective March 27, 1992.

— County boundaries.

N E W S

Miles
0 2 4 6 8

2

1

New Hampshire 607

Table A. — 1990 Population by Race and Ethnic Origin

State/ county code	County	Total persons	Percent of total persons						Rank[1]				Percent contribution to state population			
			Non-Hispanic					Hispanic	Total	Percent of total persons		Hispanic	Total	Non-Hispanic		Hispanic
			White	Black	Asian and Pacific Islander	Native American	Other			Non-Hispanic				White	Black	
										White	Black					
33 001	Belknap	49,216	98.7	0.1	0.4	0.2	<.1	0.5	7	3	9	6	4.4	4.5	0.9	2.2
33 003	Carroll	35,410	99.0	0.2	0.3	0.2	<.1	0.4	9	1	7	10	3.2	3.2	0.9	1.2
33 005	Cheshire	70,121	98.6	0.3	0.4	0.2	<.1	0.5	6	5	6	7	6.3	6.4	3.0	2.9
33 007	Coos	34,828	98.9	<.1	0.4	0.2	<.1	0.4	10	2	10	8	3.1	3.2	0.5	1.3
33 009	Grafton	74,929	97.3	0.5	1.1	0.2	<.1	0.8	5	8	4	4	6.8	6.8	5.7	5.3
33 011	Hillsborough	336,073	96.1	0.8	1.1	0.2	<.1	1.7	1	10	2	1	30.3	29.9	40.6	50.3
33 013	Merrimack	120,005	98.3	0.3	0.5	0.2	<.1	0.7	3	6	5	5	10.8	10.9	6.1	6.9
33 015	Rockingham	245,845	97.0	0.9	0.9	0.2	<.1	1.0	2	9	1	2	22.2	22.1	33.1	21.1
33 017	Strafford	104,233	97.5	0.5	0.9	0.2	<.1	0.8	4	7	3	3	9.4	9.4	8.3	7.4
33 019	Sullivan	38,592	98.7	0.2	0.4	0.3	<.1	0.4	8	4	8	9	3.5	3.5	0.9	1.5
33	NEW HAMPSHIRE	1,109,252	97.3	0.6	0.8	0.2	<.1	1.0					100.0	100.0	100.0	100.0
	CITIES AND TOWNS															
33 007	Berlin city	11,824	98.7	0.1	0.5	0.2	<.1	0.5	11	1	12	12	1.1	1.1	0.2	0.5
33 019	Claremont city	13,902	98.1	0.2	0.6	0.6	<.1	0.5	9	6	10	13	1.3	1.3	0.5	0.6
33 013	Concord city	36,006	97.5	0.6	0.7	0.3	<.1	1.0	3	7	6	5	3.2	3.3	3.1	3.1
33 017	Dover city	25,042	96.6	1.0	1.1	0.2	<.1	1.0	6	10	3	4	2.3	2.2	3.9	2.2
33 013	Franklin city	8,304	98.7	0.2	0.4	0.1	0.0	0.6	13	2	11	9	0.7	0.8	0.2	0.5
33 005	Keene city	22,430	98.4	0.3	0.6	0.2	<.1	0.6	7	3	9	11	2.0	2.0	0.9	1.2
33 001	Laconia city	15,743	98.2	0.1	0.8	0.2	<.1	0.6	8	4	13	10	1.4	1.4	0.3	0.9
33 009	Lebanon city	12,183	96.8	0.4	1.6	0.3	<.1	0.9	10	9	7	6	1.1	1.1	0.7	1.0
33 011	Manchester city	99,567	95.6	0.9	1.1	0.2	<.1	2.1	1	11	4	2	9.0	8.8	13.4	18.7
33 011	Nashua city	79,662	93.3	1.4	1.9	0.2	0.1	3.0	2	12	2	1	7.2	6.9	16.9	21.2
33 015	Portsmouth city	25,925	91.4	4.5	1.7	0.3	0.1	2.0	5	13	1	3	2.3	2.2	17.3	4.6
33 017	Rochester city	26,630	98.2	0.3	0.5	0.2	<.1	0.7	4	5	8	8	2.4	2.4	1.2	1.7
33 017	Somersworth city	11,249	97.0	0.7	1.1	0.2	0.1	0.9	12	8	5	7	1.0	1.0	1.2	0.9
	CONGRESSIONAL															
	District 1	554,360	97.2	0.7	0.8	0.2	<.1	1.0	2	2	1	1	50.0	49.9	57.4	50.9
	District 2	554,892	97.4	0.5	0.9	0.2	<.1	1.0	1	1	2	2	50.0	50.1	42.6	49.1

[1]Separate rankings for 10 counties and for 13 cities and towns.

Table B. — 1990 Voting Age Population (VAP) by Race and Ethnic Origin

County	Total Voting Age Population	Percent of total VAP						Rank[1]				Percent contribution to state VAP				VAP percent of total population					
		Non-Hispanic					Hispanic	Total	Percent of total VAP		Hispanic	Total	Non-Hispanic		Hispanic	Total	Non-Hispanic				Hispanic
		White	Black	Asian and Pacific Islander	Native American	Other			Non-Hispanic				White	Black			White	Black	Asian and Pacific Islander	Native American	Other	
									White	Black												
Belknap	36,608	98.9	0.1	0.4	0.2	<.1	0.4	7	4	8	7	4.4	4.5	0.9	2.1	74.4	74.5	64.5	65.9	70.6	50.0	63.3
Carroll	26,932	99.1	0.2	0.2	0.1	<.1	0.3	9	2	7	9	3.2	3.3	0.9	1.2	76.1	76.2	65.6	58.5	67.8	60.0	68.9
Cheshire	53,055	98.7	0.3	0.4	0.2	<.1	0.4	6	5	6	6	6.4	6.5	3.2	3.2	75.7	75.8	74.6	65.1	70.3	50.0	70.4
Coos	26,261	99.2	<.1	0.3	0.2	<.1	0.3	10	1	10	10	3.2	3.2	0.3	1.1	75.4	75.6	45.5	57.4	75.8	60.0	56.0
Grafton	57,744	97.2	0.6	1.2	0.3	<.1	0.7	5	9	3	3	7.0	6.9	7.1	5.6	77.1	77.0	85.7	84.5	82.1	47.6	69.4
Hillsborough	249,875	96.5	0.7	1.1	0.2	<.1	1.5	1	10	2	1	30.1	29.8	39.7	50.3	74.4	74.6	67.1	71.2	73.2	37.0	65.3
Merrimack	89,644	98.5	0.3	0.4	0.2	<.1	0.6	3	6	5	5	10.8	10.9	6.3	7.1	74.7	74.8	70.4	69.6	76.8	10.0	66.9
Rockingham	181,874	97.3	0.8	0.8	0.2	<.1	0.8	2	8	1	2	21.9	21.8	32.4	20.6	74.0	74.2	67.1	67.2	80.9	39.2	63.6
Strafford	79,785	97.8	0.5	0.8	0.2	<.1	0.7	4	7	4	4	9.6	9.6	8.4	7.3	76.5	76.8	69.8	72.3	70.6	24.5	64.3
Sullivan	28,719	98.9	0.1	0.3	0.3	<.1	0.4	8	3	9	8	3.5	3.5	0.6	1.4	74.4	74.6	49.2	58.7	65.4	55.6	64.8
NEW HAMPSHIRE	830,497	97.6	0.6	0.8	0.2	<.1	0.9					100.0	100.0	100.0	100.0	74.9	75.1	68.5	70.6	74.7	36.7	65.2
CITIES AND TOWNS																						
Berlin city	9,209	99.0	<.1	0.3	0.2	<.1	0.4	11	1	13	13	1.1	1.1	0.2	0.5	77.9	78.2	46.7	49.1	81.0	50.0	59.0
Claremont city	10,460	98.5	0.2	0.4	0.5	<.1	0.4	9	6	10	12	1.3	1.3	0.4	0.6	75.2	75.6	55.9	55.7	57.8	75.0	63.4
Concord city	27,772	97.6	0.5	0.7	0.3	<.1	0.9	3	7	6	4	3.3	3.3	3.3	3.5	77.1	77.2	72.9	75.1	80.9	11.1	72.8
Dover city	19,987	97.0	0.9	1.0	0.2	<.1	0.9	5	9	3	5	2.4	2.4	4.0	2.3	79.8	80.2	70.2	69.1	87.8	12.5	68.1
Franklin city	6,064	99.0	0.1	0.3	0.1	0.0	0.4	13	2	11	11	0.7	0.7	0.2	0.4	73.0	73.3	60.0	52.9	70.0	0.0	50.9
Keene city	17,683	98.6	0.2	0.5	0.2	<.1	0.5	7	3	9	10	2.1	2.2	0.9	1.3	78.8	79.0	69.4	64.1	82.9	66.7	70.5
Laconia city	11,700	98.5	<.1	0.7	0.2	<.1	0.5	8	5	12	9	1.4	1.4	0.2	0.9	74.3	74.5	61.1	63.6	70.6	14.3	64.3
Lebanon city	9,377	96.9	0.4	1.5	0.3	<.1	0.9	10	10	7	6	1.1	1.1	0.8	1.1	77.0	77.0	78.0	75.7	83.9	66.7	73.0
Manchester city	76,631	96.2	0.8	1.0	0.2	<.1	1.8	1	11	4	2	9.2	9.1	12.8	18.8	77.0	77.4	65.9	75.0	72.5	37.5	65.7
Nashua city	60,462	94.0	1.3	1.8	0.2	<.1	2.6	2	12	2	1	7.3	7.0	16.9	21.5	75.9	76.5	68.4	72.5	73.3	36.4	66.1
Portsmouth city	20,111	92.7	3.8	1.5	0.3	<.1	1.6	4	13	1	3	2.4	2.3	16.7	4.4	77.6	78.6	66.3	69.7	79.7	33.3	63.1
Rochester city	19,669	98.5	0.3	0.5	0.2	<.1	0.6	6	4	8	8	2.4	2.4	1.1	1.5	73.9	74.1	64.2	63.6	68.5	16.7	59.4
Somersworth city	8,391	97.5	0.6	1.0	0.2	<.1	0.7	12	8	5	7	1.0	1.0	1.1	0.8	74.6	75.0	66.7	69.7	70.8	7.1	55.9
CONGRESSIONAL																						
District 1	415,884	97.5	0.6	0.8	0.2	<.1	0.9	1	2	1	1	50.1	50.1	56.5	50.3	75.0	75.2	67.4	70.1	75.8	35.9	64.4
District 2	414,613	97.6	0.5	0.8	0.2	<.1	0.9	2	1	2	2	49.9	49.9	43.5	49.7	74.7	74.9	70.0	71.0	73.7	37.5	66.1

[1]Separate rankings for 10 counties and 13 cities and towns.

608 New Hampshire

Table C. – Voter Participation: November 3, 1992, General Election

County	Estimated Voting Age Population (VAP), 1992	Voter registration (REG) Total	% contribution to state REG	% of 1992 VAP	Rank by % of 1992 VAP	Voter turnout Highest office Actual	Total	Office	% of 1992 VAP	Maximum vote Total	% contribution to state turnout	% of REG	Rank by % of REG[1]	% of 1992 VAP	Rank by % 1992 VAP	Percent drop-off, by office President	Senator	Governor	Representative
Belknap	37,565	30,312	4.6	80.7	2	25,354	25,121	P	66.9	25,354	4.7	83.6	2	67.5	2	0.9	2.9	2.9	4.0
Carroll	28,040	27,077	4.1	96.6	1	22,143	21,715	P	77.4	22,143	4.1	81.8	7	79.0	1	1.9	6.1	5.8	7.2
Cheshire	52,847	39,550	6.0	74.8	9	32,909	32,505	P	61.5	32,909	6.0	83.2	3	62.3	8	1.2	5.0	4.7	6.4
Coos	25,860	19,810	3.0	76.6	6	16,135	15,817	P	61.2	16,135	3.0	81.4	9	62.4	7	2.0	6.8	7.5	7.5
Grafton	57,300	45,223	6.8	78.9	4	36,898	36,429	P	63.6	36,898	6.8	81.6	8	64.4	5	1.3	5.6	4.8	7.3
Hillsborough	257,710	193,170	29.2	75.0	8	158,924	158,056	P	61.3	158,924	29.1	82.3	6	61.7	9	0.5	4.3	6.0	5.4
Merrimack	92,609	71,334	10.8	77.0	5	61,485	58,904	P	63.6	61,485	11.3	86.2	1	66.4	3	4.2	6.5	6.3	7.3
Rockingham	191,353	154,117	23.3	80.5	3	125,006	123,965	P	64.8	125,006	22.9	81.1	10	65.3	4	0.8	4.2	4.2	6.1
Strafford	79,978	58,612	8.9	73.3	10	48,321	47,595	P	59.5	48,321	8.9	82.4	5	60.4	10	1.5	6.2	6.1	8.0
Sullivan	28,738	21,780	3.3	75.8	7	18,022	17,836	P	62.1	18,022	3.3	82.7	4	62.7	6	1.0	4.6	4.9	5.4
NEW HAMPSHIRE	**852,000**	**660,985**	**100.0**	**77.6**		**545,197**	**537,943**		**63.1**	**545,197**	**100.0**	**82.5**		**64.0**		**1.3**	**4.9**	**5.3**	**6.3**
CITIES AND TOWNS																			
Berlin city	-	6,175	0.9	-	-	5,259	5,143	P	-	5,259	1.0	85.2	5	-	-	2.2	6.9	7.5	7.9
Claremont city	-	6,839	1.0	-	-	5,529	5,418	P	-	5,529	1.0	80.8	10	-	-	2.0	6.5	6.3	6.7
Concord city	-	20,951	3.2	-	-	18,979	16,944	P	-	18,979	3.5	90.6	1	-	-	10.7	11.8	12.1	12.1
Dover city	-	15,513	2.3	-	-	12,348	11,999	P	-	12,348	2.3	79.6	11	-	-	2.8	6.1	6.2	8.6
Franklin city	-	4,000	0.6	-	-	3,096	3,100	P	-	3,100	0.6	77.5	12	-	-	0.0	5.5	4.3	1.5
Keene city	-	12,817	1.9	-	-	10,486	10,247	P	-	10,486	1.9	81.8	6	-	-	2.3	6.6	5.0	6.3
Laconia city	-	8,145	1.2	-	-	7,015	6,952	P	-	7,015	1.3	86.1	4	-	-	0.9	2.4	2.5	3.2
Lebanon city	-	6,508	1.0	-	-	5,318	5,302	P	-	5,318	1.0	81.7	7	-	-	0.3	3.3	3.6	5.5
Manchester city	-	50,889	7.7	-	-	41,163	40,670	P	-	41,163	7.5	80.9	9	-	-	1.2	4.2	7.0	5.9
Nashua city	-	44,684	6.8	-	-	36,397	36,295	P	-	36,397	6.7	81.5	8	-	-	0.3	7.2	11.0	6.7
Portsmouth city	-	15,585	2.4	-	-	11,990	11,889	P	-	11,990	2.2	76.9	13	-	-	0.8	3.0	3.0	4.9
Rochester city	-	13,218	2.0	-	-	11,433	11,474	P	-	11,474	2.1	86.8	2	-	-	0.0	4.1	5.0	5.9
Somersworth city	-	5,746	0.9	-	-	4,953	4,716	P	-	4,953	0.9	86.2	3	-	-	4.8	9.6	10.1	10.9

[1]Separate rankings for 10 counties and for 13 cities and towns.

Table D. – Voter Registration by Political Party Affiliation: November 3, 1992, General Election

County	Total voter registration	Political party affiliation Democrat (DEM)	Republican (REP)	Independent (IND)	Plurality Total	Party	Percent of total registration DEM	REP	IND	Rank[1] DEM	REP	IND	Percent contribution to state registration Total	DEM	REP	IND
Belknap	30,312	8,261	14,250	7,695	5,989	R	27.3	47.2	25.5	9	2	7	4.6	3.8	5.5	4.3
Carroll	27,077	5,304	13,805	7,840	5,965	R	19.7	51.2	29.1	10	1	3	4.1	2.4	5.4	4.3
Cheshire	39,550	13,708	14,417	11,310	709	R	34.8	36.6	28.7	5	8	5	6.0	6.2	5.6	6.3
Coos	19,810	7,479	7,008	4,949	471	D	38.5	36.1	25.5	2	9	8	3.0	3.4	2.7	2.7
Grafton	45,223	13,204	18,311	13,593	4,718	R	29.3	40.6	30.1	8	4	2	6.8	6.0	7.1	7.5
Hillsborough	193,170	71,148	73,688	47,234	2,540	R	37.0	38.4	24.6	3	5	10	29.2	32.4	28.6	26.2
Merrimack	71,334	22,589	30,623	17,745	8,034	R	31.8	43.2	25.0	6	3	9	10.8	10.3	11.9	9.8
Rockingham	154,117	47,537	58,260	47,345	10,723	R	31.0	38.0	30.9	7	7	1	23.3	21.6	22.6	26.3
Strafford	58,612	22,752	18,660	16,886	4,092	D	39.0	32.0	29.0	1	10	4	8.9	10.4	7.3	9.4
Sullivan	21,780	7,787	8,290	5,670	503	R	35.8	38.1	26.1	4	6	6	3.3	3.5	3.2	3.1
NEW HAMPSHIRE[2]	**660,985**	**219,769**	**257,312**	**180,267**	**37,543**	**R**	**33.4**	**39.1**	**27.4**				**100.0**	**100.0**	**100.0**	**100.0**
CITIES AND TOWNS																
Berlin city	6,175	3,499	1,392	-	2,107	D	71.5	28.5	-	1	13	-	0.9	1.6	0.5	-
Claremont city	6,839	3,087	2,296	-	791	D	57.3	42.7	-	4	6	-	1.0	1.4	0.9	-
Concord city	20,951	7,639	8,763	-	1,124	R	46.6	53.4	-	11	2	-	3.2	3.5	3.4	-
Dover city	15,513	6,266	5,046	-	1,220	D	55.4	44.6	-	6	9	-	2.3	2.9	2.0	-
Franklin city	4,000	1,336	1,301	-	35	D	50.7	49.3	-	12	10	-	0.6	0.6	0.5	-
Keene city	12,817	5,238	4,466	-	772	D	54.0	46.0	-	5	5	-	1.9	2.4	1.7	-
Laconia city	8,145	2,501	3,689	-	1,188	R	40.4	59.6	-	13	1	-	1.2	1.1	1.4	-
Lebanon city	6,508	2,513	2,327	-	186	D	51.9	48.1	-	9	3	-	1.0	1.1	0.9	-
Manchester city	50,889	24,711	17,756	-	6,955	D	58.2	41.8	-	2	4	-	7.7	11.2	6.9	-
Nashua city	44,684	17,657	14,845	-	2,812	D	54.3	45.7	-	8	8	-	6.8	8.0	5.8	-
Portsmouth city	15,585	6,202	4,096	-	2,106	D	60.2	39.8	-	7	11	-	2.4	2.8	1.6	-
Rochester city	13,218	5,026	4,417	-	609	D	53.2	46.8	-	10	7	-	2.0	2.3	1.7	-
Somersworth city	5,746	2,671	1,363	-	1,308	D	66.2	33.8	-	3	12	-	0.9	1.2	0.5	-

[1]Separate rankings for 10 counties for 13 cities and towns.   [2]Total voter registration also includes 3,637 for the Libertarian party.

Table E. — Vote for President: November 3, 1992, General Election

County	Total	Clinton (DEM)	Bush (REP)	Perot (IND)	Other	Plurality Total	Party	DEM	REP	IND	Other	Rank DEM	Rank REP	Rank IND	Contrib Total	Contrib DEM	Contrib REP	Contrib IND	Major DEM	Major REP
Belknap	25,121	8,405	10,578	5,970	168	2,173	R	33.5	42.1	23.8	0.7	9	1	4	4.7	4.0	5.2	4.9	44.3	55.7
Carroll	21,715	7,258	8,715	5,546	196	1,457	R	33.4	40.1	25.5	0.9	10	2	1	4.0	3.5	4.3	4.6	45.4	54.6
Cheshire	32,505	15,037	11,037	6,195	236	4,000	D	46.3	34.0	19.1	0.7	1	8	10	6.0	7.2	5.5	5.1	57.7	42.3
Coos	15,817	6,559	5,271	3,868	119	1,288	D	41.5	33.3	24.5	0.8	6	10	3	2.9	3.1	2.6	3.2	55.4	44.6
Grafton	36,429	15,389	13,450	7,296	294	1,939	D	42.2	36.9	20.0	0.8	4	6	8	6.8	7.4	6.6	6.0	53.4	46.6
Hillsborough	158,056	58,470	61,620	36,067	1,899	3,150	R	37.0	39.0	22.8	1.2	7	3	5	29.4	28.0	30.4	29.7	48.7	51.3
Merrimack	58,904	24,437	22,114	11,860	493	2,323	D	41.5	37.5	20.1	0.8	5	5	7	10.9	11.7	10.9	9.8	52.5	47.5
Rockingham	123,965	44,317	47,353	31,192	1,103	3,036	R	35.7	38.2	25.2	0.9	8	4	2	23.0	21.2	23.4	25.7	48.3	51.7
Strafford	47,595	21,247	16,028	9,920	400	5,219	D	44.6	33.7	20.8	0.8	2	9	6	8.8	10.2	7.9	8.2	57.0	43.0
Sullivan	17,836	7,921	6,318	3,423	174	1,603	D	44.4	35.4	19.2	1.0	3	7	9	3.3	3.8	3.1	2.8	55.6	44.4
NEW HAMPSHIRE	**537,943**	**209,040**	**202,484**	**121,337**	**5,082**	**6,556**	**D**	**38.9**	**37.6**	**22.6**	**0.9**					**100.0**	**100.0**	**100.0**	**50.8**	**49.2**
CITIES AND TOWNS																				
Berlin city	5,143	2,680	1,272	1,162	29	1,408	D	52.1	24.7	22.6	0.6	1	13	2	1.0	1.3	0.6	1.0	67.8	32.2
Claremont city	5,418	2,650	1,822	904	42	828	D	48.9	33.6	16.7	0.8	5	8	12	1.0	1.3	0.9	0.7	59.3	40.7
Concord city	16,944	8,325	5,651	2,843	125	2,674	D	49.1	33.4	16.8	0.7	4	9	11	3.1	4.0	2.8	2.3	59.6	40.4
Dover city	11,999	5,449	4,197	2,246	107	1,252	D	45.4	35.0	18.7	0.9	8	5	7	2.2	2.6	2.1	1.9	56.5	43.5
Franklin city	3,100	1,252	1,139	691	18	113	D	40.4	36.7	22.3	0.6	11	4	3	0.6	0.6	0.6	0.6	52.4	47.6
Keene city	10,247	5,210	3,257	1,736	44	1,953	D	50.8	31.8	16.9	0.4	3	10	10	1.9	2.5	1.6	1.4	61.5	38.5
Laconia city	6,952	2,390	3,033	1,496	33	643	R	34.4	43.6	21.5	0.5	13	1	5	1.3	1.1	1.5	1.2	44.1	55.9
Lebanon city	5,302	2,579	1,849	827	47	730	D	48.6	34.9	15.6	0.9	6	6	13	1.0	1.2	0.9	0.7	58.2	41.8
Manchester city	40,670	16,627	16,298	7,441	304	329	D	40.9	40.1	18.3	0.7	9	2	8	7.6	8.0	8.0	6.1	50.5	49.5
Nashua city	36,295	14,777	12,514	8,306	698	2,263	D	40.7	34.5	22.9	1.9	10	7	1	6.7	7.1	6.2	6.8	54.1	45.9
Portsmouth city	11,889	6,132	3,563	2,088	106	2,569	D	51.6	30.0	17.6	0.9	2	12	9	2.2	2.9	1.8	1.7	63.2	36.8
Rochester city	11,474	4,588	4,272	2,541	73	316	D	40.0	37.2	22.1	0.6	12	3	4	2.1	2.2	2.1	2.1	51.8	48.2
Somersworth city	4,716	2,249	1,450	974	43	799	D	47.7	30.7	20.7	0.9	7	11	6	0.9	1.1	0.7	0.8	60.8	39.2

[1] Separate rankings for 10 counties and for 13 cities and towns.

Table F. — Vote for U.S. Senator: November 3, 1992, General Election

County	Total	Rauh (DEM)	Gregg (REP)	Other	Plurality Total	Party	DEM	REP	Other	Rank DEM	Rank REP	Rank Other	Contrib Total	Contrib DEM	Contrib REP	Contrib Other
Belknap	24,628	10,390	12,316	1,922	1,926	R	42.2	50.0	7.8	7	5	2	4.8	4.4	4.9	5.7
Carroll	20,793	7,898	11,250	1,645	3,352	R	38.0	54.1	7.9	10	1	1	4.0	3.4	4.5	4.9
Cheshire	31,258	17,422	12,219	1,617	5,203	D	55.7	39.1	5.2	1	10	9	6.0	7.4	4.9	4.8
Coos	15,033	6,188	7,724	1,121	1,536	R	41.2	51.4	7.5	9	3	3	2.9	2.6	3.1	3.3
Grafton	34,830	16,461	16,373	1,996	88	D	47.3	47.0	5.7	5	6	8	6.7	7.0	6.6	5.9
Hillsborough	152,152	63,890	78,430	9,832	14,540	R	42.0	51.5	6.5	8	2	5	29.3	27.2	31.4	29.1
Merrimack	57,472	30,489	23,390	3,593	7,099	D	53.1	40.7	6.3	2	9	6	11.1	13.0	9.4	10.6
Rockingham	119,739	50,773	60,374	8,592	9,601	R	42.4	50.4	7.2	6	4	4	23.1	21.6	24.2	25.4
Strafford	45,327	22,614	19,956	2,757	2,658	D	49.9	44.0	6.1	4	7	7	8.7	9.6	8.0	8.1
Sullivan	17,184	8,857	7,559	768	1,298	D	51.5	44.0	4.5	3	8	10	3.3	3.8	3.0	2.3
NEW HAMPSHIRE	**518,416**	**234,982**	**249,591**	**33,843**	**14,609**	**R**	**45.3**	**48.1**	**6.5**				**100.0**	**100.0**	**100.0**	**100.0**
CITIES AND TOWNS																
Berlin city	4,894	2,327	2,295	272	32	D	47.5	46.9	5.6	9	6	7	0.9	1.0	0.9	0.8
Claremont city	5,168	2,777	2,208	183	569	D	53.7	42.7	3.5	4	10	13	1.0	1.2	0.9	0.5
Concord city	16,748	10,251	5,520	977	4,731	D	61.2	33.0	5.8	2	13	4	3.2	4.4	2.2	2.9
Dover city	11,598	5,865	5,117	616	748	D	50.6	44.1	5.3	6	7	9	2.2	2.5	2.1	1.8
Franklin city	2,930	1,412	1,379	139	33	D	48.2	47.1	4.7	8	5	10	0.6	0.6	0.6	0.4
Keene city	9,792	6,038	3,297	457	2,741	D	61.7	33.7	4.7	1	12	11	1.9	2.6	1.3	1.4
Laconia city	6,847	3,022	3,348	477	326	R	44.1	48.9	7.0	12	3	1	1.3	1.3	1.3	1.4
Lebanon city	5,145	2,691	2,254	200	437	D	52.3	43.8	3.9	5	8	12	1.0	1.1	0.9	0.6
Manchester city	39,440	16,936	20,022	2,482	3,086	R	42.9	50.8	6.3	13	1	3	7.6	7.2	8.0	7.3
Nashua city	33,764	15,402	16,436	1,926	1,034	R	45.6	48.7	5.7	10	4	6	6.5	6.6	6.6	5.7
Portsmouth city	11,633	6,759	4,114	760	2,645	D	58.1	35.4	6.5	3	11	2	2.2	2.9	1.6	2.2
Rochester city	10,999	4,964	5,430	605	466	R	45.1	49.4	5.5	11	2	8	2.1	2.1	2.2	1.8
Somersworth city	4,478	2,264	1,957	257	307	D	50.6	43.7	5.7	7	9	5	0.9	1.0	0.8	0.8

[1] Separate rankings for 10 counties and for 13 cities and towns.

County	Total	Arnesen (DEM)	Merrill (REP)	Other	Plurality Total	Party	DEM	REP	Other	Rank¹ DEM	Rank¹ REP	Rank¹ Other	Total	DEM	REP	Other
Belknap	24,626	8,705	14,795	1,126	6,090	R	35.3	60.1	4.6	8	3	1	4.8	4.2	5.1	5.4
Carroll	20,862	7,226	12,797	839	5,571	R	34.6	61.3	4.0	10	1	4	4.0	3.5	4.4	4.0
Cheshire	31,352	16,005	14,399	948	1,606	D	51.0	45.9	3.0	1	10	8	6.1	7.8	5.0	4.6
Coos	14,923	6,301	8,287	335	1,986	R	42.2	55.5	2.2	6	5	10	2.9	3.1	2.9	1.6
Grafton	35,136	16,096	18,121	919	2,025	R	45.8	51.6	2.6	3	7	9	6.8	7.8	6.3	4.4
Hillsborough	149,371	52,260	90,441	6,670	38,181	R	35.0	60.5	4.5	9	2	3	28.9	25.3	31.3	32.1
Merrimack	57,608	25,697	29,617	2,294	3,920	R	44.6	51.4	4.0	4	8	5	11.2	12.5	10.2	11.0
Rockingham	119,748	45,173	69,135	5,440	23,962	R	37.7	57.7	4.5	7	4	2	23.2	21.9	23.9	26.2
Strafford	45,397	20,246	23,475	1,676	3,229	R	44.6	51.7	3.7	5	6	6	8.8	9.8	8.1	8.1
Sullivan	17,147	8,523	8,103	521	420	D	49.7	47.3	3.0	2	9	7	3.3	4.1	2.8	2.5
NEW HAMPSHIRE	**516,170**	**206,232**	**289,170**	**20,768**	**82,938**	**R**	**40.0**	**56.0**	**4.0**				**100.0**	**100.0**	**100.0**	**100.0**
CITIES AND TOWNS																
Berlin city	4,866	2,269	2,519	78	250	R	46.6	51.8	1.6	6	7	13	0.9	1.1	0.9	0.4
Claremont city	5,178	2,700	2,351	127	349	D	52.1	45.4	2.5	4	10	11	1.0	1.3	0.8	0.6
Concord city	16,689	8,943	7,115	631	1,828	D	53.6	42.6	3.8	2	11	5	3.2	4.3	2.5	3.0
Dover city	11,582	5,189	5,981	412	792	R	44.8	51.6	3.6	7	8	7	2.2	2.5	2.1	2.0
Franklin city	2,967	1,124	1,758	85	634	R	37.9	59.3	2.9	10	4	9	0.6	0.5	0.6	0.4
Keene city	9,965	5,547	4,145	273	1,402	D	55.7	41.6	2.7	1	13	10	1.9	2.7	1.4	1.3
Laconia city	6,843	2,530	4,058	255	1,528	R	37.0	59.3	3.7	11	3	6	1.3	1.2	1.4	1.2
Lebanon city	5,126	2,461	2,555	110	94	R	48.0	49.8	2.1	5	9	12	1.0	1.2	0.9	0.5
Manchester city	38,277	12,813	23,978	1,486	11,165	R	33.5	62.6	3.9	13	1	4	7.4	6.2	8.3	7.2
Nashua city	32,399	13,007	17,937	1,455	4,930	R	40.1	55.4	4.5	9	5	2	6.3	6.3	6.2	7.0
Portsmouth city	11,635	6,195	4,895	545	1,300	D	53.2	42.1	4.7	3	12	1	2.3	3.0	1.7	2.6
Rochester city	10,898	3,991	6,545	362	2,554	R	36.6	60.1	3.3	12	2	8	2.1	1.9	2.3	1.7
Somersworth city	4,455	1,913	2,361	181	448	R	42.9	53.0	4.1	8	6	3	0.9	0.9	0.8	0.9

¹Separate rankings for 10 counties and for 13 cities and towns.

Congressional district and county	Total	Democrat (DEM)	Republican (REP)	Other	Plurality Total	Party	DEM	REP	Other	Rank within district DEM	Rank within district REP	Rank within district Other	Total	DEM	REP	Other
District 1	**255,853**	**108,578**	**135,936**	**11,339**	**27,358**	**R**	**42.4**	**53.1**	**4.4**				**100.0**	**100.0**	**100.0**	**100.0**
Belknap (pt)	21,686	7,391	13,179	1,116	5,788	R	34.1	60.8	5.1	6	1	1	8.5	6.8	9.7	9.8
Carroll	20,549	7,219	12,308	1,022	5,089	R	35.1	59.9	5.0	5	2	3	8.0	6.6	9.1	9.0
Hillsborough (pt)	63,935	27,731	33,781	2,423	6,050	R	43.4	52.8	3.8	3	4	4	25.0	25.5	24.9	21.4
Merrimack (pt)	7,377	2,747	4,358	272	1,611	R	37.2	59.1	3.7	4	3	5	2.9	2.5	3.2	2.4
Rockingham (pt)	97,869	42,852	50,101	4,916	7,249	R	43.8	51.2	5.0	2	5	2	38.3	39.5	36.9	43.4
Strafford	44,437	20,638	22,209	1,590	1,571	R	46.4	50.0	3.6	1	6	6	17.4	19.0	16.3	14.0
District 2	**255,185**	**157,328**	**91,126**	**6,731**	**66,202**	**D**	**61.7**	**35.7**	**2.6**				**100.0**	**100.0**	**100.0**	**100.0**
Belknap (pt)	2,646	1,643	920	83	723	D	62.1	34.8	3.1	6	4	3	1.0	1.0	1.0	1.2
Cheshire	30,794	19,729	10,402	663	9,327	D	64.1	33.8	2.2	4	5	5	12.1	12.5	11.4	9.8
Coos	14,926	10,268	4,429	229	5,839	D	68.8	29.7	1.5	1	8	8	5.8	6.5	4.9	3.4
Grafton	34,196	21,323	12,213	660	9,110	D	62.4	35.7	1.9	5	3	6	13.4	13.6	13.4	9.8
Hillsborough (pt)	86,434	48,914	34,550	2,970	14,364	D	56.6	40.0	3.4	8	2	1	33.9	31.1	37.9	44.1
Merrimack (pt)	49,630	33,269	15,167	1,194	18,102	D	67.0	30.6	2.4	2	7	4	19.4	21.1	16.6	17.7
Rockingham (pt)	19,513	11,064	7,813	636	3,251	D	56.7	40.0	3.3	7	1	2	7.6	7.0	8.6	9.4
Sullivan	17,046	11,118	5,632	296	5,486	D	65.2	33.0	1.7	3	6	7	6.7	7.1	6.2	4.4
NEW HAMPSHIRE	**511,038**	**265,906**	**227,062**	**18,070**	**38,844**	**D**	**52.0**	**44.4**	**3.5**							

Table I. — Vote for Presidential Preference: February 18, 1992, Democratic Primary Election

County	Total	Tsongas	Clinton	Kerrey	Harkin	Brown	Cuomo	Laughlin	Other	Tsongas	Clinton	Kerrey	Tsongas	Clinton	Kerrey	Total	Tsongas	Clinton	Kerrey
			Top candidates							Percent of total vote			Rank[1]			Percent contribution to state vote			
Belknap	6,362	1,842	1,626	845	606	607	246	96	494	29.0	25.6	13.3	5	5	2	3.8	3.3	3.9	4.5
Carroll	3,996	1,454	794	366	264	564	255	36	263	36.4	19.9	9.2	2	10	10	2.4	2.6	1.9	2.0
Cheshire	10,432	2,806	2,811	1,149	871	1,322	523	40	910	26.9	26.9	11.0	8	4	5	6.2	5.0	6.8	6.2
Coos	4,948	922	1,494	611	912	302	222	20	465	18.6	30.2	12.3	10	2	3	2.9	1.7	3.6	3.3
Grafton	9,481	3,292	2,326	943	812	1,022	451	29	606	34.7	24.5	9.9	4	7	9	5.7	5.9	5.6	5.1
Hillsborough	53,923	19,521	13,114	5,862	4,938	3,676	1,766	1,534	3,512	36.2	24.3	10.9	3	8	6	32.1	35.1	31.6	31.6
Merrimack	18,673	5,177	5,099	2,026	2,408	1,624	672	321	1,346	27.7	27.3	10.8	7	3	7	11.1	9.3	12.3	10.9
Rockingham	37,088	14,403	8,071	3,790	3,494	2,801	1,500	868	2,161	38.8	21.8	10.2	1	9	8	22.1	25.9	19.4	20.4
Strafford	17,056	4,901	4,358	2,266	1,993	1,261	716	288	1,273	28.7	25.6	13.3	6	6	1	10.2	8.8	10.5	12.2
Sullivan	5,841	1,320	1,829	717	759	475	226	19	496	22.6	31.3	12.3	9	1	4	3.5	2.4	4.4	3.9
NEW HAMPSHIRE	167,800	55,638	41,522	18,575	17,057	13,654	6,577	3,251	11,526	33.2	24.7	11.1				100.0	100.0	100.0	100.0
CITIES AND TOWNS																			
Berlin city	2,425	396	738	271	535	100	144	10	231	16.3	30.4	11.2	12	4	8	1.4	0.7	1.8	1.5
Claremont city	2,240	337	857	309	356	115	85	3	178	15.0	38.3	13.8	13	1	4	1.3	0.6	2.1	1.7
Concord city	6,237	1,747	1,837	636	864	473	269	90	321	28.0	29.5	10.2	6	6	10	3.7	3.1	4.4	3.4
Dover city	4,293	1,304	1,082	496	516	295	200	53	347	30.4	25.2	11.6	3	13	7	2.6	2.3	2.6	2.7
Franklin city	1,104	208	363	129	150	95	20	43	96	18.8	32.9	11.7	11	3	6	0.7	0.4	0.9	0.7
Keene city	3,851	943	1,101	376	317	558	218	7	331	24.5	28.6	9.8	9	7	12	2.3	1.7	2.7	2.0
Laconia city	1,960	554	500	308	217	138	78	19	146	28.3	25.5	15.7	5	12	2	1.2	1.0	1.2	1.7
Lebanon city	1,470	444	446	146	133	127	68	4	102	30.2	30.3	9.9	4	5	11	0.9	0.8	1.1	0.8
Manchester city	17,506	4,776	4,647	2,321	2,360	1,043	588	449	1,322	27.3	26.5	13.3	7	11	5	10.4	8.6	11.2	12.5
Nashua city	13,297	5,368	3,757	1,261	867	742	360	442	500	40.4	28.3	9.5	1	10	13	7.9	9.6	9.0	6.8
Portsmouth city	4,564	1,418	1,292	504	503	369	201	46	231	31.1	28.3	11.0	2	9	9	2.7	2.5	3.1	2.7
Rochester city	3,959	981	1,127	585	415	239	165	104	343	24.8	28.5	14.8	8	8	3	2.4	1.8	2.7	3.1
Somersworth city	1,946	418	648	324	247	80	106	31	92	21.5	33.3	16.6	10	2	1	1.2	0.8	1.6	1.7

[1]Separate rankings for 10 counties and for 13 cities and towns.

Table J. — Vote for Presidential Preference: February 18, 1992, Republican Primary Election

County	Total	Bush	Other	Buchanan	Other	Bush	Other	Buchanan	Other	Bush	Other	Buchanan	Other	Total	Bush	Other	Buchanan	Other
		Top candidates				Percent of total vote				Rank[1]				Percent contribution to state vote				
Belknap	9,725	5,098	228	3,571	828	52.4	2.3	36.7	8.5	5	4	7	3	5.6	5.5	6.2	5.5	6.3
Carroll	8,732	4,739	166	3,278	549	54.3	1.9	37.5	6.3	3	9	6	8	5.0	5.1	4.5	5.0	4.2
Cheshire	10,202	5,295	217	3,426	1,264	51.9	2.1	33.6	12.4	6	6	10	1	5.9	5.7	5.9	5.3	9.6
Coos	4,506	2,100	107	2,059	240	46.6	2.4	45.7	5.3	10	3	1	9	2.6	2.3	2.9	3.2	1.8
Grafton	12,230	6,333	295	4,729	873	51.8	2.4	38.7	7.1	8	2	4	6	7.0	6.9	8.0	7.3	6.6
Hillsborough	49,797	25,833	957	19,350	3,657	51.9	1.9	38.9	7.3	7	8	3	5	28.6	28.0	26.0	29.7	27.8
Merrimack	21,509	11,353	534	7,252	2,370	52.8	2.5	33.7	11.0	4	1	9	2	12.3	12.3	14.5	11.1	18.0
Rockingham	39,298	21,606	816	14,801	2,075	55.0	2.1	37.7	5.3	2	7	5	10	22.6	23.4	22.1	22.7	15.8
Strafford	12,532	7,175	279	4,240	838	57.3	2.2	33.8	6.7	1	5	8	7	7.2	7.8	7.6	6.5	6.4
Sullivan	5,636	2,701	87	2,381	467	47.9	1.5	42.2	8.3	9	10	2	4	3.2	2.9	2.4	3.7	3.5
NEW HAMPSHIRE	174,167	92,233	3,686	65,087	13,161	53.0	2.1	37.4	7.6					100.0	100.0	100.0	100.0	100.0
CITIES AND TOWNS																		
Berlin city	1,020	450	24	471	75	44.1	2.4	46.2	7.4	13	6	1	7	0.6	0.5	0.7	0.7	0.6
Claremont city	1,510	709	17	653	131	47.0	1.1	43.2	8.7	11	13	3	4	0.9	0.8	0.5	1.0	1.0
Concord city	5,677	2,996	167	1,727	787	52.8	2.9	30.4	13.9	8	2	12	2	3.3	3.2	4.5	2.7	6.0
Dover city	3,164	1,827	61	1,068	208	57.7	1.9	33.8	6.6	4	9	8	9	1.8	2.0	1.7	1.6	1.6
Franklin city	990	509	15	373	93	51.4	1.5	37.7	9.4	10	11	5	3	0.6	0.6	0.4	0.6	0.7
Keene city	3,191	1,715	76	954	446	53.7	2.4	29.9	14.0	7	4	13	1	1.8	1.9	2.1	1.5	3.4
Laconia city	2,619	1,377	60	1,007	175	52.6	2.3	38.4	6.7	9	7	4	8	1.5	1.5	1.6	1.5	1.3
Lebanon city	1,347	788	18	429	112	58.5	1.3	31.8	8.3	3	12	10	5	0.8	0.9	0.5	0.7	0.9
Manchester city	11,532	5,285	274	5,090	883	45.8	2.4	44.1	7.7	12	5	2	6	6.6	5.7	7.4	7.8	6.7
Nashua city	9,926	5,598	214	3,578	536	56.4	2.2	36.0	5.4	5	8	7	12	5.7	6.1	5.8	5.5	4.1
Portsmouth city	2,513	1,517	85	774	137	60.4	3.4	30.8	5.5	2	1	11	11	1.4	1.6	2.3	1.2	1.0
Rochester city	3,085	1,702	57	1,127	199	55.2	1.8	36.5	6.5	6	10	6	10	1.8	1.8	1.5	1.7	1.5
Somersworth city	882	533	22	284	43	60.4	2.5	32.2	4.9	1	3	9	13	0.5	0.6	0.6	0.4	0.3

[1]Separate rankings for 10 counties and for 13 cities and towns.

1992 Vote for President
Percent for Clinton (D), by Minor Civil Division

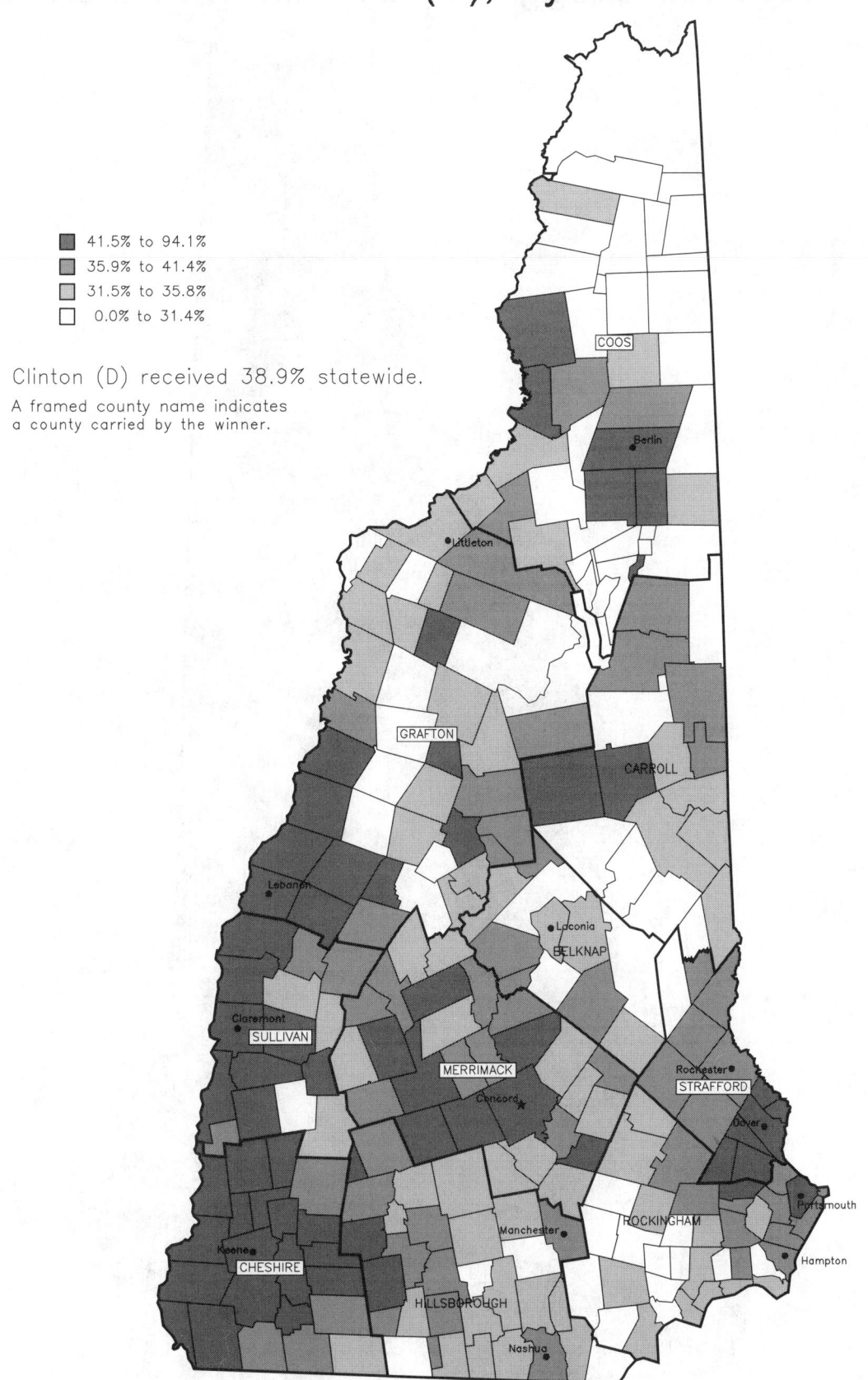

■ 41.5% to 94.1%
▨ 35.9% to 41.4%
▨ 31.5% to 35.8%
□ 0.0% to 31.4%

Clinton (D) received 38.9% statewide.

A framed county name indicates
a county carried by the winner.

COOS

Berlin

Littleton

GRAFTON

CARROLL

Lebanon

Laconia
BELKNAP

Claremont
SULLIVAN

MERRIMACK

Rochester
STRAFFORD

Concord

Dover

Portsmouth

ROCKINGHAM

Manchester

Hampton

Keene
CHESHIRE

HILLSBOROUGH

Nashua

New Hampshire 613

1992 Vote for U.S. Senator
Percent for Gregg (R), by Minor Civil Division

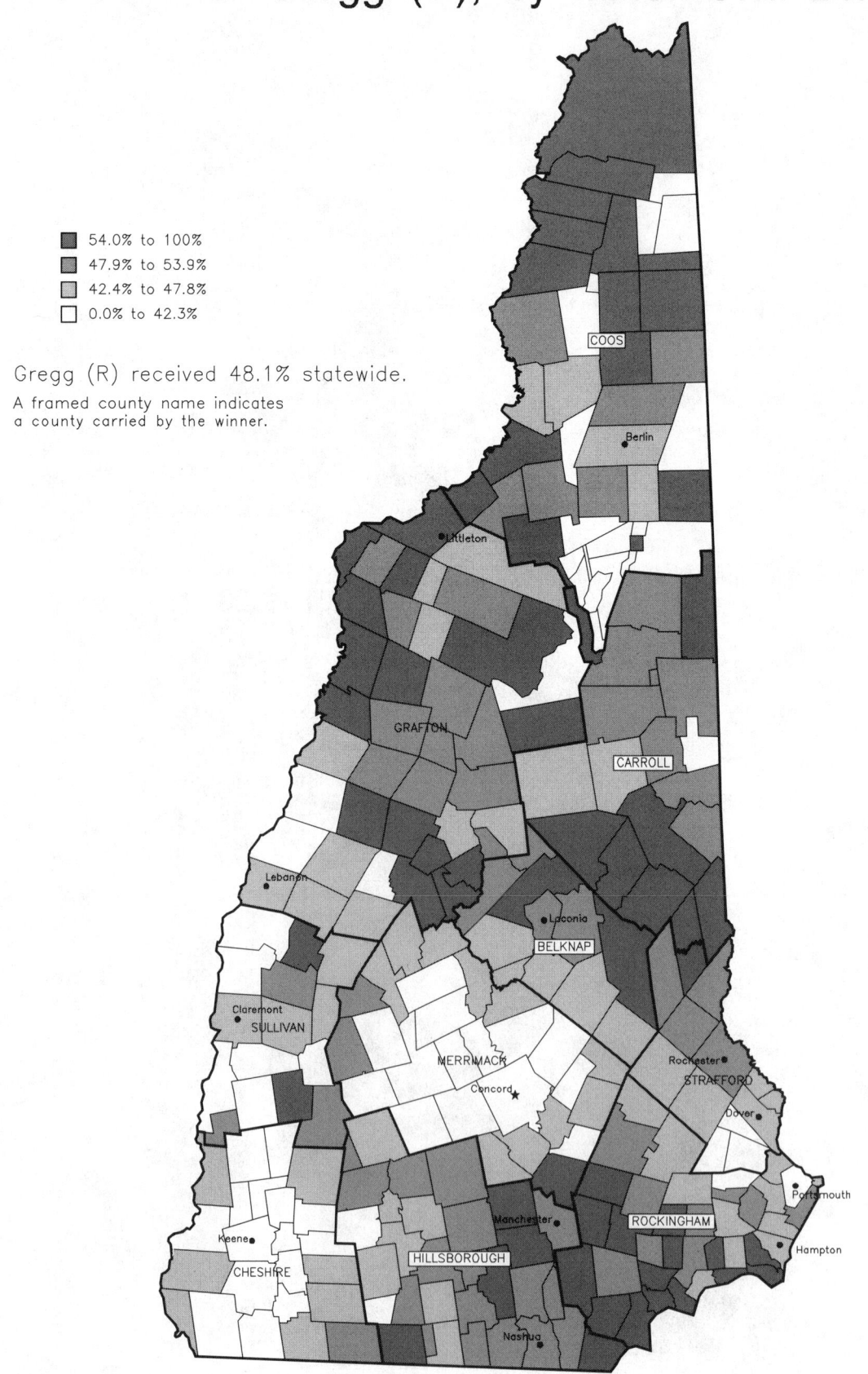

54.0% to 100%

47.9% to 53.9%

42.4% to 47.8%

0.0% to 42.3%

Gregg (R) received 48.1% statewide.

A framed county name indicates
a county carried by the winner.

COOS

Berlin

Littleton

GRAFTON

CARROLL

Lebanon

Laconia

BELKNAP

Claremont
SULLIVAN

MERRIMACK

Rochester

STRAFFORD

Concord

Dover

Portsmouth

Manchester

ROCKINGHAM

Keene

Hampton

HILLSBOROUGH

CHESHIRE

Nashua

614 New Hampshire

1992 Vote for Governor
Percent for Merrill (R), by Minor Civil Division

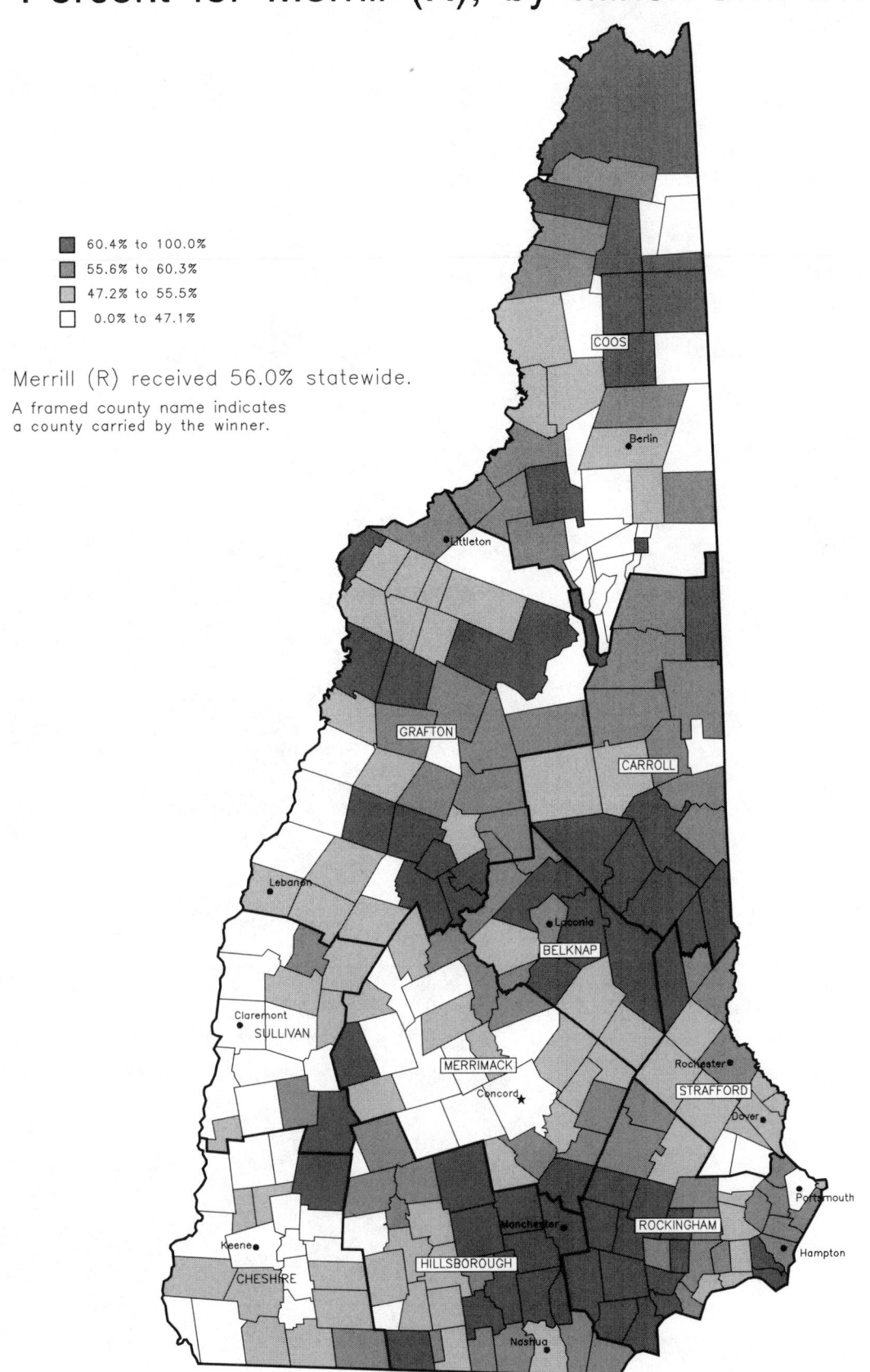

■ 60.4% to 100.0%
▨ 55.6% to 60.3%
▧ 47.2% to 55.5%
□ 0.0% to 47.1%

Merrill (R) received 56.0% statewide.

A framed county name indicates
a county carried by the winner.

COOS

• Berlin

• Littleton

GRAFTON

CARROLL

• Lebanon

• Laconia

BELKNAP

Claremont
• SULLIVAN

MERRIMACK

Rochester •

STRAFFORD

Concord ★

Dover •

Portsmouth

Manchester •

ROCKINGHAM

Keene •

HILLSBOROUGH

Hampton

CHESHIRE

Nashua •

New Hampshire 615

NEW JERSEY

Congressional Districts 13
   Average Population 594,630
State Senate Districts 40
   Average Population 193,255
State House Districts 80
   Average Population 96,627

Electoral College Votes.. 15
Counties 21
Voting Precincts 5,962

Alternative Registration Methods:
.... Agency-based, Mail-in, Motor-voter

Registration Deadline (Days before Election) 29

Voting Equipment Use (Counties)

Datavote Punch Card	2	Paper Ballot	0
Electronic	1	Other Punch Card	2
Lever Machine	16	Mixed Systems	0
Optical Scanner	0		

Party Control	DEM	REP	IND	VAC
1993 State Senate	13	27	0	0
1992 State Senate	13	27	0	0
1993 State House	22	58	0	0
1992 State House	22	58	0	0

Population Statistics 1990

Race/ Ethnicity	Total Population		Voting Age Population		Voting Age Population % of total population
	Number	%	Number	%	
Non-Hispanic					
White	5,718,966	74.0	4,514,331	76.1	78.9
Black	984,845	12.7	698,130	11.8	70.9
Asian/Pacific Islander	264,341	3.4	186,577	3.1	70.6
Native American	12,490	0.2	9,358	0.2	74.9
Other	9,685	0.1	5,028	<.1	51.9
All Hispanic	739,861	9.6	517,302	8.7	69.9
TOTAL	7,730,188	100.0	5,930,726	100.0	76.7

Estimated Voting Age Population 1992 (VAP) 5,943,000
Number of Registered Voters................................. 4,059,472
   % of estimated VAP...................................... 68.3
Voter Turnout (Maximum Vote)[1]........................... 3,366,794
   % of VAP 56.7
   % of Registration 82.9
Persons Not Voting—of Voting Age 2,576,206
   % of VAP 43.3
Persons Not Voting—of Registered 692,678
   % of Registration 17.1
Straight Ticket Voting .... No

State Officials and Members of Congress

Governor:
James J. Florio (D) 1989, elected to a four-year term in 1989.

U.S. Senators:
Bill Bradley (D) 1978, elected to a six-year term in 1990.
Frank Lautenberg (D) 1982, elected to a six-year term in 1988.

U.S. Representative in Congress:
(District, Name, Party, Date first elected)

1. Andrews (D) 1990
2. Hughes (D) 1974
3. Saxton (R) 1984
4. Smith (R) 1980

5. Roukema (R) 1980
6. Pallone (D) 1988
7. Franks (R) 1992

8. Klein (D) 1992
9. Torricelli (D) 1982
10. Payne (D) 1988

11. Gallo (R) 1984
12. Zimmer (R) 1990
13. Menendez (D) 1992

---

[1]Maximum vote turnout from Table C exceeds reported statewide actual voter turnout because in one or more counties the vote for highest office is greater than reported actual turnout.

Candidates: General Election, November 3, 1992

Candidate(s)	Total vote	Percent	Party	Status	First elected
President/Vice President					
Clinton/Gore	1,436,206	42.95%	Democrat	Challenger	1992
Bush/Quayle	1,356,865	40.58%	Republican	Incumbent	1988
Perot/Stockdale	521,829	15.61%	Independent	Challenger	
Marrou/Lord	6,822	0.20%	Libertarian	Challenger	
Drew Bradford	4,749	0.14%	Independent	Challenger	
Fulani/Munoz	3,513	0.11%	New Alliance	Challenger	
Phillips/Knight	2,670	0.08%	Taxpayers	Challenger	
LaRouche/Greenspan	2,095	0.06%	6 Million Jobs	Challenger	
Warren/Debates	2,011	0.06%	Socialist Workers	Challenger	
Daniels/Tupahache	1,996	0.06%	Ron Daniels Ind.	Challenger	
Gritz/Minett	1,867	0.06%	Amer. 1st Populist	Challenger	
Halyard/Mazelis	1,618	0.05%	Worker's League	Challenger	
Hagelin/Tomkins	1,353	0.04%	Natural Law	Challenger	
U.S. Senator (No Contest)					
Governor (No Contest)					
U.S. Representative in Congress					
District 1					
Robert Andrews	153,525	67.31%	Democrat	Incumbent	1990
Lee Solomon	65,123	28.55%	Republican	Challenger	
James Smith	3,761	1.65%	Pro-Life Pro-Family	Challenger	
Jerry Zeldin	2,641	1.16%	Libertarian	Challenger	
Kenneth Lowndes	2,163	0.95%	Pro-Life Independent	Challenger	
Nicholas Pastuch	859	0.38%	Amer. 1st Populist	Challenger	
District 2					
William Hughes	132,465	55.89%	Democrat	Incumbent	1974
Frank LoBiondo	98,315	41.48%	Republican	Challenger	
Roger Bacon	2,575	1.09%	Libertarian	Challenger	
Joseph Ponczek	2,067	0.87%	Anti-Tax	Challenger	
Andrea Lippi	1,605	0.68%	Freedom Equal. Prosp.	Challenger	
District 3					
James Saxton	151,368	59.17%	Republican	Incumbent	1984
Timothy Ryan	94,012	36.75%	Democrat	Challenger	
Helen Radder	2,711	1.06%	Libertarian	Challenger	
Joseph Plonski	2,309	0.90%	Amer. 1st Populist	Challenger	
Michael Permuko	1,728	0.68%	Conservative	Challenger	
James Reilly	915	0.36%	Independent	Challenger	
William McMahon	901	0.35%	Donald of Moorestown	Challenger	
Anthony Verderese	749	0.29%	Independent Party	Challenger	
Martin King	593	0.23%	Independent	Challenger	
Frank Burke	512	0.20%	Basic Ref. Gov't	Challenger	
District 4					
Christopher Smith	149,095	61.81%	Republican	Incumbent	1980
Brian Hughes	84,514	35.04%	Democrat	Challenger	
Benjamin Grindlinger	2,984	1.24%	Libertarian	Challenger	
Patrick Pasculli	2,137	0.89%	Independent	Challenger	
Agnes James	1,630	0.68%	Conservative	Challenger	
Joseph Notarangelo	865	0.36%	Amer. 1st Populist	Challenger	

Candidate(s)	Total vote	Percent	Party	Status	First elected
U.S. Representative in Congress (cont)					
District 5					
Marge Roukema	196,198	71.51%	Republican	Incumbent	1980
Frank Lucas	67,579	24.63%	Democrat	Challenger	
William Leonard	6,182	2.25%	Independent	Challenger	
Michael Pierone	2,636	0.96%	Libertarian	Challenger	
George Lahood	994	0.36%	Equal Brother. Just.	Challenger	
Stuart Bacha	782	0.29%	Amer. 1st Populist	Challenger	
District 6					
Frank Pallone, Jr.	118,266	52.31%	Democrat	Incumbent	1988
Joseph Kyrillos	100,949	44.65%	Republican	Challenger	
Joseph Spalletta	2,153	0.95%	The People's Cand.	Challenger	
Bill Stewart	1,404	0.62%	Libertarian	Challenger	
Peter Cerrato	1,073	0.47%	Ind. for Freedom	Challenger	
George Predham	951	0.42%	You Gotta Believe	Challenger	
Simone Berg	613	0.27%	Socialist Workers	Challenger	
Kenneth Matto	411	0.18%	Amer. 1st Populist	Challenger	
Charles Dickson	273	0.12%	Capitalist	Challenger	
District 7					
Bob Franks	132,174	53.28%	Republican	Challenger	1992
Leonard Sendelsky	105,761	42.63%	Democrat	Challenger	
Eugene Gillespie, Jr.	4,043	1.63%	Independent	Challenger	
Bill Campbell	2,612	1.05%	No Nonsense Gov't.	Challenger	
Spencer Layman	1,964	0.79%	Libertarian	Challenger	
John Kucek	844	0.34%	Amer. 1st Populist	Challenger	
Kevin Criss	684	0.28%	People's Cong. Pref.	Challenger	
District 8					
Herbert Klein	96,742	47.00%	Democrat	Challenger	1992
Joseph Bubba	84,674	41.14%	Republican	Challenger	
Gloria Kolodziej	16,170	7.86%	Ind. for Change	Challenger	
Thomas Caslander	2,916	1.42%	Ind. for Change	Challenger	
Carmine Pellosie	2,135	1.04%	Ind. People's Network	Challenger	
Louis Stefanelli	1,109	0.54%	Libertarian	Challenger	
Rob Dominianni	1,099	0.53%	Restore Public Trust	Challenger	
Jason Redrup	392	0.19%	Socialist Workers	Challenger	
Gregory Dzula	316	0.15%	Amer. 1st Populist	Challenger	
Neal Gorfinkle	275	0.13%	NJ Independents	Challenger	
District 9					
Robert Torricelli	139,188	58.31%	Democrat	Incumbent	1982
Patrick Roma	88,179	36.94%	Republican	Challenger	
Peter Russo	4,491	1.88%	Clean up Congress	Challenger	
Gary Novosielski	2,257	0.95%	NJ Independents	Challenger	
Joseph D'Alessio	1,606	0.67%	Amer. 1st Populist	Challenger	
Herbert Shaw	1,369	0.57%	Pol. Are Crooks	Challenger	
Daniel Karlan	1,099	0.46%	Libertarian	Challenger	
Shel Haas	515	0.22%	An Independent Voice	Challenger	
District 10					
Donald Payne	117,287	78.38%	Democrat	Incumbent	1988
Alfred Palermo	30,160	20.16%	Republican	Challenger	
Roberto Caraballo	1,272	0.85%	Libertarian	Challenger	
William Leonard	913	0.61%	Socialist Workers	Challenger	
District 11					
Dean Gallo	188,165	70.10%	Republican	Incumbent	1984
Ona Spiridellis	68,871	25.66%	Democrat	Challenger	
Richard Roth	3,538	1.32%	Libertarian	Challenger	
Barry Fitzpatrick	3,127	1.16%	Time For Change	Challenger	
David Karlen	1,882	0.70%	Independent	Challenger	
Howard Safier	1,711	0.64%	Independent	Challenger	
Richard Hrazanek	1,142	0.43%	Amer. 1st Populist	Challenger	

Candidate(s)	Total vote	Percent	Party	Status	First elected
U.S. Representative in Congress (cont)					
District 12					
Dick Zimmer	174,216	63.87%	Republican	Incumbent	1990
Frank Abate	83,035	30.44%	Democrat	Challenger	
Carl Mayer	11,051	4.05%	Independent	Challenger	
Carl Peters	1,906	0.70%	Libertarian	Challenger	
Edward Eggert	1,804	0.66%	Independent	Challenger	
Compton Pakenham	745	0.27%	Amer. 1st Populist	Challenger	
District 13					
Robert Menendez	93,670	64.28%	Democrat	Challenger	1992
Fred Theemling, Jr.	44,529	30.56%	Republican	Challenger	
Joseph Bonacci	2,363	1.62%	Stop Tax Increases	Challenger	
Len Flynn	1,539	1.06%	Libertarian	Challenger	
John Rummel	1,525	1.05%	Communist	Challenger	
Jane Harris	1,406	0.96%	Socialist Workers	Challenger	
Donald Stoveken	682	0.47%	Amer. 1st Populist	Challenger	

Candidates: June 2, 1992, Primary Election

Candidate	Total vote	Percent	Candidate	Total vote	Percent
Presidential Preference, Democratic			**Presidential Preference, Republican**		
Bill Clinton	256,337	65.27%	George Bush	240,535	83.82%
Jerry Brown	79,877	20.34%	Patrick Buchanan	46,432	16.18%
Paul Tsongas	45,191	11.51%			
Lyndon LaRouche, Jr.	7,799	1.99%			
George Ballard	2,067	0.53%			
Robert Hanson	1,473	0.38%			

Voter Registration and Turnout, 1948-1992 Elections

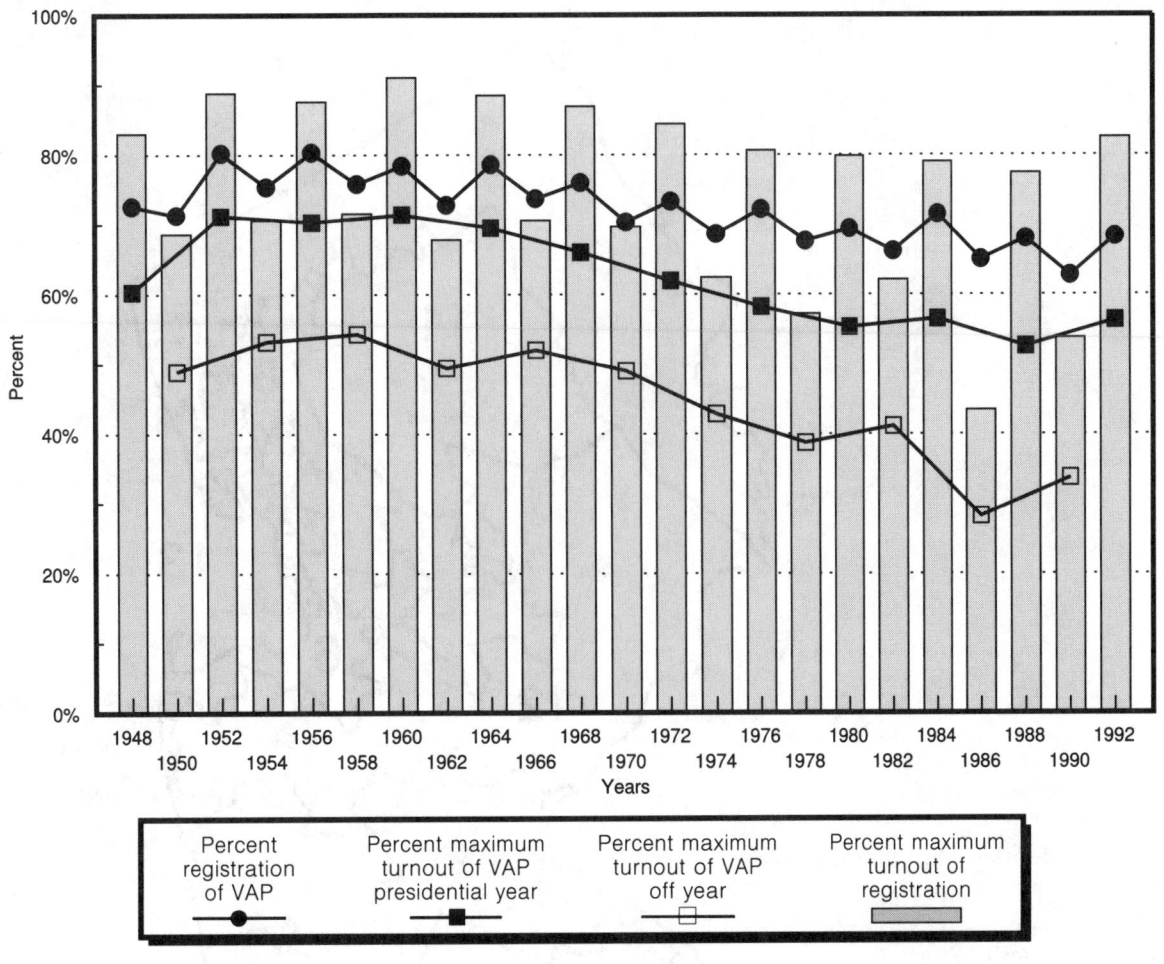

Year	Estimated Voting Age Population (VAP)	Voter registration (REG)			Voter turnout													
						Highest office						Maximum vote					
		Total	Percent of VAP	Rank by percent of VAP	Actual	Total	Office	Percent total REG	Rank by percent of REG	Percent of VAP	Rank by percent of VAP	Total	Percent total REG	Rank by percent of REG	Percent total VAP	Rank by percent of VAP
1992	5,943,000	4,059,472	68.3	36	3,348,312	3,343,594	P	82.4	8	56.3	28	3,348,312	82.5	14	56.3	28
1990	5,927,000	3,717,536	62.7	36	1,998,894	1,938,454	S	52.1	36	32.7	42	1,998,894	53.8	36	33.7	40
1988	5,894,000	4,010,790	68.0	34	3,102,502	3,099,553	P	77.3	10	52.6	26	3,102,502	77.4	13	52.6	27
1986	5,811,000	3,777,278	65.0	35	1,639,330	1,553,545	C	41.1	47	26.7	49	1,639,330	43.4	46	28.2	47
1984[1]	5,695,000	4,072,739	71.5	30	3,215,941	3,217,862	P	79.0	8	56.5	21	3,217,862	79.0	12	56.5	25
1982	5,562,000	3,681,211	66.2	31	2,286,925	2,193,945	S	59.6	32	39.4	36	2,286,925	62.1	29	41.1	34
1980	5,422,000	3,761,428	69.4	31	2,999,879	2,975,684	P	79.1	8	54.9	26	2,999,879	79.8	9	55.3	27
1978	5,326,000	3,602,225	67.6	29	2,059,724	1,957,515	S	54.3	32	36.8	35	2,059,724	57.2	27	38.7	29
1976	5,220,000	3,769,558	72.2	26	3,037,151	3,014,472	P	80.0	9	57.7	21	3,037,151	80.6	13	58.2	23
1974	5,108,000	3,502,175	68.6	30	2,183,962	2,083,557	C	59.5	22	40.8	30	2,183,962	62.4	20	42.8	27
1972	5,010,000	3,672,606	73.3	26	3,100,207	2,997,229	P	81.6	7	59.8	22	3,100,207	84.4	8	61.9	19
1970	4,507,000	3,167,532	70.3	31	2,209,298	2,142,105	S	67.6	19	47.5	32	2,209,298	69.7	16	49.0	32
1968	4,358,000	3,310,043	76.0	23	2,873,489	2,875,395	P	86.9	4	66.0	20	2,875,395	86.9	5	66.0	21
1966	4,232,000	3,117,575	73.7	26	2,200,177	2,131,188	S	68.4	17	50.4	30	2,200,177	70.6	17	52.0	28
1964	4,142,000	3,253,603	78.6	23	2,879,201	2,847,663	P	87.5	7	68.8	21	2,879,201	88.5	8	69.5	18
1962	4,089,000	2,977,333	72.8	22	2,018,321	1,958,960	C	65.8	21	47.9	31	2,018,321	67.8	20	49.4	29
1960	3,919,000	3,073,894	78.4	17	2,799,095	2,773,111	P	90.2	8	70.8	23	2,799,095	91.1	8	71.4	25
1958	3,660,000	2,774,295	75.8	19	1,986,880	1,881,329	S	67.8	17	51.4	26	1,986,880	71.6	14	54.3	26
1956	3,546,000	2,846,794	80.3	15	2,493,774	2,484,312	P	87.3	8	70.1	15	2,493,774	87.6	8	70.3	17
1954	3,497,000	2,635,441	75.4	15	1,859,814	1,770,557	S	67.2	12	50.6	23	1,859,814	70.6	10	53.2	19
1952	3,421,000	2,744,165	80.2	14	2,435,613	2,418,554	P	88.1	7	70.7	25	2,435,613	88.8	6	71.2	26
1950	3,331,000	2,374,680	71.3	12	1,629,032	1,571,263	C	66.2	13	47.2	30	1,629,032	68.6	13	48.9	29
1948	3,279,000	2,380,295	72.6	12	1,976,213	1,949,555	P	81.9	7	59.5	22	1,976,213	83.0	7	60.3	22

[1]Vote for President (highest office turnout) exceeds actual voter turnout reported by New Jersey Secretary of State.

NEW JERSEY

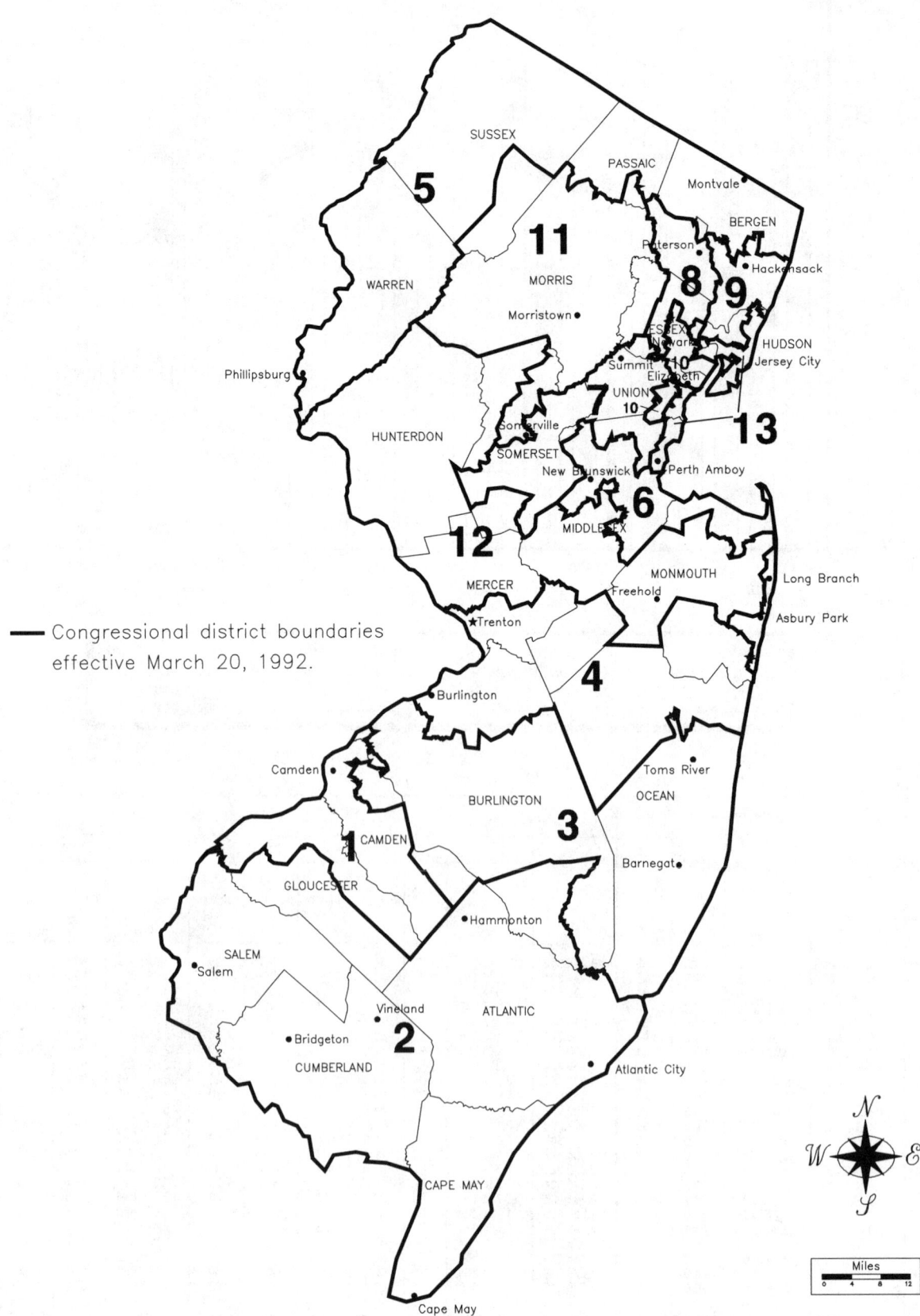

Congressional district boundaries effective March 20, 1992.

Copyright © 1993 by Election Data Services, Inc.

622 New Jersey

Table A. — 1990 Population by Race and Ethnic Origin

State/ county code	County	Total persons	Percent of total persons						Rank				Percent contribution to state population			
				Non-Hispanic					Total	Percent of total persons		Hispanic	Total	Non-Hispanic		Hispanic
			White	Black	Asian and Pacific Islander	Native American	Other	Hispanic		Non-Hispanic				White	Black	
										White	Black					
34 001	Atlantic	224,327	73.7	16.8	2.0	0.2	<.1	7.2	15	15	4	7	2.9	2.9	3.8	2.2
34 003	Bergen	825,380	82.7	4.6	6.5	0.1	<.1	6.0	1	10	16	10	10.7	11.9	3.9	6.7
34 005	Burlington	395,066	80.5	13.9	2.0	0.2	<.1	3.2	11	12	8	14	5.1	5.6	5.6	1.7
34 007	Camden	502,824	74.8	15.5	2.2	0.2	<.1	7.2	6	14	6	8	6.5	6.6	7.9	4.9
34 009	Cape May	95,089	91.7	5.5	0.6	0.2	<.1	2.0	19	5	15	18	1.2	1.5	0.5	0.3
34 011	Cumberland	138,053	68.9	16.1	0.8	0.9	0.1	13.3	16	17	5	4	1.8	1.7	2.3	2.5
34 013	Essex	778,206	45.1	39.3	2.6	0.2	0.2	12.6	2	21	1	5	10.1	6.1	31.0	13.2
34 015	Gloucester	230,082	88.2	8.5	1.2	0.2	<.1	1.8	14	7	11	20	3.0	3.5	2.0	0.6
34 017	Hudson	553,099	47.4	12.6	6.3	0.2	0.3	33.2	5	20	10	1	7.2	4.6	7.1	24.8
34 019	Hunterdon	107,776	95.0	2.0	1.3	<.1	<.1	1.6	18	3	19	21	1.4	1.8	0.2	0.2
34 021	Mercer	325,824	72.5	18.2	3.0	0.1	0.1	6.0	12	16	2	9	4.2	4.1	6.0	2.7
34 023	Middlesex	671,780	77.0	7.4	6.5	0.1	0.1	8.9	3	13	13	6	8.7	9.0	5.0	8.1
34 025	Monmouth	553,124	84.8	8.3	2.7	0.1	<.1	4.1	4	9	12	13	7.2	8.2	4.6	3.0
34 027	Morris	421,353	88.4	2.8	3.9	<.1	<.1	4.7	10	6	17	11	5.5	6.5	1.2	2.7
34 029	Ocean	433,203	93.1	2.6	0.9	0.1	<.1	3.2	9	4	18	15	5.9	7.1	1.2	1.9
34 031	Passaic	453,060	62.7	12.7	2.5	0.2	0.2	21.7	8	19	9	2	5.9	5.0	5.9	13.3
34 033	Salem	65,294	82.5	14.4	0.6	0.3	<.1	2.2	21	11	7	17	0.8	0.9	1.0	0.2
34 035	Somerset	240,279	85.2	6.0	4.3	<.1	<.1	4.2	13	8	14	12	3.1	3.6	1.5	1.4
34 037	Sussex	130,943	95.8	0.9	0.9	0.1	<.1	2.2	17	1	21	16	1.7	2.2	0.1	0.4
34 039	Union	493,819	65.3	18.1	2.7	0.1	0.1	13.7	7	18	3	3	6.4	5.6	9.1	9.2
34 041	Warren	91,607	95.7	1.4	0.8	0.1	<.1	1.9	20	2	20	19	1.2	1.5	0.1	0.2
34	NEW JERSEY	7,730,188	74.0	12.7	3.4	0.2	0.1	9.6					100.0	100.0	100.0	100.0
	CONGRESSIONAL															
	District 1	594,630	76.7	15.1	1.6	0.2	<.1	6.3	1	9	2	6	7.7	8.0	9.1	5.0
	District 2	594,630	78.1	13.6	1.2	0.4	<.1	6.6	6	8	3	5	7.7	8.1	8.2	5.3
	District 3	594,630	87.3	7.8	2.0	0.2	<.1	2.6	7	4	9	13	7.7	9.1	4.7	2.1
	District 4	594,630	81.0	12.0	1.5	0.1	<.1	5.2	8	5	4	8	7.7	8.4	7.3	4.2
	District 5	594,630	91.3	1.3	4.4	0.2	<.1	2.8	9	1	13	11	7.7	9.5	0.8	2.2
	District 6	594,630	78.2	10.8	4.6	0.1	<.1	6.1	10	7	7	7	7.7	8.1	6.5	4.9
	District 7	594,629	80.4	9.9	4.5	0.1	<.1	5.0	12	6	8	9	7.7	8.4	6.0	4.0
	District 8	594,629	67.0	11.5	3.4	0.1	0.2	17.8	13	11	5	2	7.7	7.0	7.0	14.3
	District 9	594,630	75.9	6.0	6.4	0.1	0.1	11.4	11	10	10	4	7.7	7.9	3.6	9.2
	District 10	594,630	26.4	58.6	2.3	0.2	0.2	12.3	2	13	1	3	7.7	2.7	35.4	9.9
	District 11	594,630	89.3	2.6	3.9	<.1	<.1	4.1	3	2	12	10	7.7	9.3	1.6	3.3
	District 12	594,630	87.8	5.1	4.3	<.1	<.1	2.7	4	3	11	12	7.7	9.1	3.1	2.1
	District 13	594,630	42.3	11.4	4.2	0.2	0.4	41.5	5	12	6	1	7.7	4.4	6.9	33.3

Table B. — 1990 Voting Age Population (VAP) by Race and Ethnic Origin

County	Total Voting Age Population	Percent of total VAP — Non-Hispanic White	Black	Asian and Pacific Islander	Native American	Other	Hispanic	Rank Percent of total VAP Total	Non-Hispanic White	Black	Hispanic	Percent contribution to state VAP Total	Non-Hispanic White	Black	Hispanic	VAP percent of total population Total	Non-Hispanic White	Black	Asian and Pacific Islander	Native American	Other	Hispanic
Atlantic	172,891	76.1	15.6	1.9	0.2	<.1	6.1	14	15	4	7	2.9	2.9	3.9	2.1	77.1	79.6	71.3	73.2	75.2	55.6	65.8
Bergen	657,012	84.1	4.4	5.6	0.1	<.1	5.7	1	11	16	9	11.1	12.2	4.2	7.3	79.6	81.0	76.8	68.6	72.1	48.2	75.4
Burlington	296,830	81.8	13.2	1.9	0.2	<.1	2.9	11	12	8	14	5.0	5.4	5.6	1.7	75.1	76.3	70.9	71.5	76.8	39.7	67.2
Camden	369,757	77.9	14.0	2.0	0.2	<.1	5.8	7	14	6	8	6.2	6.4	7.4	4.2	73.5	76.5	66.6	67.5	73.4	51.7	59.7
Cape May	74,027	92.8	4.8	0.5	0.2	<.1	1.6	19	5	15	20	1.2	1.5	0.5	0.2	77.9	78.8	68.3	69.3	78.4	37.9	63.8
Cumberland	102,104	72.4	14.5	0.8	0.9	<.1	11.4	16	17	5	4	1.7	1.6	2.1	2.2	74.0	77.7	66.8	72.7	75.4	58.7	63.2
Essex	589,569	48.8	37.0	2.5	0.2	0.2	11.3	2	21	1	5	9.9	6.4	31.3	12.9	75.8	81.9	71.4	72.3	75.5	64.3	68.2
Gloucester	168,544	88.9	8.1	1.1	0.2	<.1	1.7	15	7	11	19	2.8	3.3	2.0	0.5	73.3	73.8	70.0	65.3	75.0	32.9	67.3
Hudson	430,616	50.9	11.3	6.1	0.2	0.2	31.3	4	20	10	1	7.3	4.9	7.0	26.1	77.9	83.6	69.6	75.1	73.2	50.7	73.6
Hunterdon	81,835	94.9	2.3	1.1	<.1	<.1	1.6	18	3	18	21	1.4	1.7	0.3	0.2	75.9	75.8	88.4	66.4	77.9	43.8	74.0
Mercer	252,478	75.2	16.6	2.7	0.1	<.1	5.3	12	16	3	10	4.3	4.2	6.0	2.6	77.5	80.4	70.4	69.5	80.3	50.8	68.5
Middlesex	527,149	78.9	7.0	5.9	0.1	<.1	7.9	3	13	13	6	8.9	9.2	5.3	8.1	78.5	80.5	74.2	71.4	75.4	53.9	70.0
Monmouth	418,310	86.0	7.8	2.4	0.1	<.1	3.6	5	9	12	13	7.1	8.0	4.7	2.9	75.6	76.7	71.1	68.5	76.9	45.1	67.4
Morris	325,062	89.2	2.8	3.5	<.1	<.1	4.4	10	6	17	11	5.5	6.4	1.3	2.8	77.1	77.9	75.4	68.3	78.0	44.5	72.5
Ocean	335,038	94.1	2.2	0.8	0.1	<.1	2.7	9	4	19	15	5.6	7.0	1.1	1.8	77.3	78.2	65.5	68.8	68.8	42.7	65.3
Passaic	344,317	66.6	11.6	2.3	0.2	0.1	19.2	8	19	9	2	5.8	5.1	5.7	12.8	76.0	80.6	69.1	71.2	75.2	49.7	67.4
Salem	48,557	84.1	13.3	0.5	0.3	<.1	1.8	21	10	7	17	0.8	0.9	0.9	0.2	74.4	75.8	68.8	61.4	74.3	42.4	59.7
Somerset	187,390	86.6	5.5	3.9	<.1	<.1	3.9	13	8	14	12	3.2	3.6	1.5	1.4	78.0	79.2	71.4	69.4	77.1	47.0	72.1
Sussex	94,557	96.0	1.0	0.8	0.1	<.1	2.1	17	2	21	16	1.6	2.0	0.1	0.4	72.2	72.4	76.1	64.3	71.7	35.6	67.9
Union	385,731	68.0	16.6	2.4	0.1	<.1	12.7	6	18	2	3	6.5	5.8	9.2	9.5	78.1	81.4	71.9	71.7	74.3	49.9	72.4
Warren	68,952	96.1	1.3	0.7	0.1	<.1	1.8	20	1	20	18	1.2	1.5	0.1	0.2	75.3	75.6	69.6	69.0	75.9	33.3	67.9
NEW JERSEY	**5,930,726**	**76.1**	**11.8**	**3.1**	**0.2**	**<.1**	**8.7**					**100.0**	**100.0**	**100.0**	**100.0**	**76.7**	**78.9**	**70.9**	**70.6**	**74.9**	**51.9**	**69.9**
CONGRESSIONAL																						
District 1	435,857	79.3	13.9	1.5	0.2	<.1	5.1	13	9	2	7	7.3	7.7	8.7	4.3	73.3	75.8	67.2	67.8	72.9	48.0	59.6
District 2	450,384	80.3	12.5	1.1	0.4	<.1	5.6	11	7	3	5	7.6	8.0	8.1	4.9	75.7	77.9	69.5	71.8	75.4	50.6	64.4
District 3	451,821	88.5	7.2	1.8	0.2	<.1	2.3	10	3	9	13	7.6	8.9	4.6	2.0	76.0	77.0	70.0	69.1	74.1	38.2	67.3
District 4	451,927	83.0	10.9	1.3	0.2	<.1	4.6	9	5	4	9	7.6	8.3	7.1	4.0	76.0	77.8	69.1	68.5	77.2	48.5	66.4
District 5	452,587	92.1	1.2	3.8	0.2	<.1	2.7	8	1	13	11	7.6	9.2	0.8	2.3	76.1	76.8	74.8	65.7	70.8	43.7	72.5
District 6	465,699	80.1	9.9	4.4	0.1	<.1	5.5	3	8	7	6	7.9	8.3	6.6	5.0	78.3	80.2	71.8	73.4	76.9	52.6	70.3
District 7	467,393	82.0	9.2	4.0	0.1	<.1	4.6	2	6	8	8	7.9	8.5	6.1	4.2	78.6	80.2	73.2	69.5	74.4	47.4	72.7
District 8	461,457	70.7	10.4	3.1	0.1	0.1	15.6	4	11	5	2	7.8	7.2	6.9	13.9	77.6	81.9	70.1	71.4	75.3	53.4	67.9
District 9	480,677	77.9	5.7	5.7	0.1	<.1	10.5	1	10	10	4	8.1	8.3	3.9	9.7	80.8	83.0	76.9	71.8	76.0	51.5	74.2
District 10	444,087	30.0	55.8	2.3	0.2	0.2	11.5	12	13	1	3	7.5	3.0	35.5	9.8	74.7	84.8	71.2	74.9	75.0	62.5	.69.8
District 11	458,657	90.0	2.6	3.4	<.1	<.1	3.9	5	2	12	10	7.7	9.1	1.7	3.4	77.1	77.8	76.6	67.9	77.6	46.5	72.5
District 12	455,824	88.5	5.1	3.8	<.1	<.1	2.5	6	4	11	12	7.7	8.9	3.3	2.2	76.7	77.3	76.1	68.1	77.3	48.2	72.2
District 13	454,356	46.1	10.4	4.2	0.1	0.3	38.9	7	12	6	1	7.7	4.6	6.7	34.2	76.4	83.2	69.3	76.0	73.7	52.9	71.7

Table C. — Voter Participation: November 3, 1992, General Election

| County | Estimated Voting Age Population (VAP), 1992 | Voter registration (REG) | | | | Voter turnout | | | | | | | | | | | | | |
| | | Total | % contribution to state REG | % of 1992 VAP | Rank by % of 1992 VAP | Actual | Highest office | | | Maximum vote | | | | | | Percent drop-off, by office | | | |
							Total	Office	% of 1992 VAP	Total	% contribution to state turnout	% of REG	Rank by % of REG	% of 1992 VAP	Rank by % 1992 VAP	President	Senator	Governor	Representative
Atlantic	177,113	113,854	2.8	64.3	18	92,263	90,298	P	51.0	92,263	2.7	81.0	16	52.1	17	2.1	-	-	7.9
Bergen	646,293	475,151	11.7	73.5	5	406,143	403,137	P	62.4	406,143	12.1	85.5	7	62.8	5	0.7	-	-	7.3
Burlington	299,301	204,525	5.0	68.3	13	174,422	173,357	P	57.9	174,422	5.2	85.3	8	58.3	13	0.6	-	-	11.1
Camden	371,586	258,320	6.4	69.5	11	212,551	210,886	P	56.8	212,551	6.3	82.3	14	57.2	14	0.8	-	-	8.5
Cape May	75,572	59,232	1.5	78.4	1	49,731	48,856	P	64.6	49,731	1.5	84.0	10	65.8	1	1.8	-	-	6.9
Cumberland	102,224	66,776	1.7	65.3	17	50,207	52,116	P	51.0	52,116	1.5	78.0	20	51.0	18	0.0	-	-	8.0
Essex	575,211	355,973	8.8	61.9	19	267,483	276,858	P	48.1	276,858	8.2	77.8	21	48.1	20	0.0	-	-	14.5
Gloucester	172,688	126,146	3.1	73.0	6	106,094	104,619	P	60.6	106,094	3.2	84.1	9	61.4	8	1.4	-	-	8.8
Hudson	426,417	237,996	5.9	55.8	21	187,944	185,057	P	43.4	187,944	5.6	79.0	19	44.1	21	1.5	-	-	20.1
Hunterdon	85,847	62,089	1.5	72.3	7	54,541	53,974	P	62.9	54,541	1.6	87.8	2	63.5	3	1.0	-	-	10.7
Mercer	250,886	177,889	4.4	70.9	9	146,360	145,260	P	57.9	146,360	4.3	82.3	15	58.3	12	0.8	-	-	11.7
Middlesex	532,156	360,115	8.9	67.7	14	278,199	285,271	P	53.6	285,271	8.5	79.2	17	53.6	16	0.0	-	-	13.1
Monmouth	424,552	313,740	7.7	73.9	4	268,409	266,116	P	62.7	268,409	8.0	85.6	6	63.2	4	0.9	-	-	9.9
Morris	324,571	241,313	5.9	74.3	3	211,310	209,232	P	64.5	211,310	6.3	87.6	3	65.1	2	1.0	-	-	10.9
Ocean	349,423	251,518	6.1	72.0	8	216,117	216,243	P	61.9	216,243	6.4	86.0	5	61.9	7	0.0	-	-	10.5
Passaic	341,512	210,432	5.2	61.6	20	166,422	164,888	P	48.3	166,422	4.9	79.1	18	48.7	19	0.9	-	-	14.0
Salem	48,513	34,013	0.8	70.1	10	28,465	27,935	P	57.6	28,465	0.8	83.7	11	58.7	11	1.9	-	-	3.6
Somerset	193,915	144,947	3.6	74.7	2	120,862	120,813	P	62.3	120,862	3.6	83.4	13	62.3	6	0.0	-	-	11.9
Sussex	96,790	66,268	1.6	68.5	12	57,766	57,064	P	59.0	57,766	1.7	87.2	4	59.7	10	1.2	-	-	4.5
Union	379,041	252,399	6.2	66.6	16	210,752	210,112	P	55.4	210,752	6.3	83.5	12	55.6	15	0.3	-	-	13.6
Warren	69,389	46,776	1.2	67.4	15	42,271	41,502	P	59.8	42,271	1.3	90.4	1	60.9	9	1.8	-	-	7.0
NEW JERSEY	5,943,000	4,059,472	100.0	68.3		3,348,312	3,343,594		56.3	3,366,794	100.0	82.9		56.7		0.7	-	-	11.1

Table D. — Voter Registration by Political Party Affiliation: November 3, 1992, General Election

County	Total voter registration	Political party affiliation			Plurality		Percent of total registration			Rank			Percent contribution to state registration			
		Democrat (DEM)[1]	Republican (REP)[1]	Independent (IND)[1]	Total	Party	DEM	REP	IND	DEM	REP	IND	Total	DEM	REP	IND
Atlantic	113,854	22,371	32,514	182	10,143	R	40.6	59.0	0.3	15	6	10	2.8	1.9	4.0	2.8
Bergen	475,151	122,306	101,159	1,287	21,147	D	54.4	45.0	0.6	11	9	6	11.7	10.4	12.4	19.9
Burlington	204,525	49,193	41,516	452	7,677	D	54.0	45.5	0.5	12	12	7	5.0	4.2	5.1	7.0
Camden	258,320	91,764	39,418	531	52,346	D	69.7	29.9	0.4	4	17	8	6.4	7.8	4.8	8.2
Cape May	59,232	9,545	24,271	194	14,726	R	28.1	71.4	0.6	18	1	4	1.5	0.8	3.0	3.0
Cumberland	66,776	18,769	13,461	112	5,308	D	58.0	41.6	0.3	9	13	9	1.6	1.6	1.6	1.7
Essex	355,973	143,847	48,374	272	95,473	D	74.7	25.1	0.1	2	19	16	8.8	12.2	5.9	4.2
Gloucester	126,146	40,156	24,288	540	15,868	D	61.8	37.4	0.8	7	15	2	3.1	3.4	3.0	8.3
Hudson	237,996	122,049	24,032	89	98,017	D	83.5	16.4	<.1	1	21	17	5.9	10.4	2.9	1.4
Hunterdon	62,089	9,759	20,687	0	10,928	R	32.1	67.9	0.0	19	4	18	1.5	0.8	2.5	0.0
Mercer	177,889	59,171	25,033	647	34,138	D	69.7	29.5	0.8	5	18	3	4.4	5.0	3.1	10.0
Middlesex	360,115	118,876	42,168	486	76,708	D	73.6	26.1	0.3	6	20	11	8.9	10.1	5.2	7.5
Monmouth	313,740	74,555	64,471	337	10,084	D	53.5	46.3	0.2	13	10	15	7.7	6.3	7.9	5.2
Morris	241,313	40,855	81,377	0	40,522	R	33.4	66.6	0.0	17	3	19	5.9	3.5	10.0	0.0
Ocean	251,518	48,232	65,777	0	17,545	R	42.3	57.7	0.0	16	7	20	6.2	4.1	8.0	0.0
Passaic	210,432	59,737	42,336	923	17,401	D	58.0	41.1	0.9	8	14	1	5.2	5.1	5.2	14.3
Salem	34,013	8,974	6,968	95	2,006	D	56.0	43.4	0.6	10	11	5	0.8	0.8	0.9	1.5
Somerset	144,947	22,484	34,567	176	12,083	R	39.3	60.4	0.3	20	8	14	3.6	1.9	4.2	2.7
Sussex	66,268	9,440	24,647	85	15,207	R	27.6	72.1	0.2	21	2	13	1.6	0.8	3.0	1.3
Union	252,399	92,697	46,395	0	46,302	D	66.6	33.4	0.0	3	16	21	6.2	7.9	5.7	0.0
Warren	46,776	10,261	14,378	62	4,117	R	41.5	58.2	0.3	14	5	12	1.2	0.9	1.8	1.0
NEW JERSEY[2]	**4,059,472**	**1,175,041**	**817,837**	**6,470**	**357,204**	**D**	**58.8**	**40.9**	**0.3**				**100.0**	**100.0**	**100.0**	**100.0**

[1]Data from report dated Nov. 1992; sum of registrants by party differs slightly from total voter registration reported with November 3, 1992, general election returns.
[2]Total voter registration also includes 2,060,989 undeclared, as reported Nov. 1992.

Table E. — Vote for President: November 3, 1992, General Election

County	All candidates					Plurality		Percent of total vote				Rank			Percent contribution to state vote				Major party Percent of vote	
	Total	Clinton (DEM)	Bush (REP)	Perot (IND)	Other	Total	Party	DEM	REP	IND	Other	DEM	REP	IND	Total	DEM	REP	IND	DEM	REP
Atlantic	90,298	39,633	34,279	15,890	496	5,354	D	43.9	38.0	17.6	0.5	7	13	11	2.7	2.8	2.5	3.0	53.6	46.4
Bergen	403,137	171,104	178,223	52,082	1,728	7,119	R	42.4	44.2	12.9	0.4	10	8	18	12.1	11.9	13.1	10.0	49.0	51.0
Burlington	173,357	72,845	63,709	35,322	1,481	9,136	D	42.0	36.8	20.4	0.9	11	16	6	5.2	5.1	4.7	6.8	53.3	46.7
Camden	210,886	104,915	67,205	37,144	1,622	37,710	D	49.7	31.9	17.6	0.8	3	21	10	6.3	7.3	5.0	7.1	61.0	39.0
Cape May	48,856	17,324	21,502	9,798	232	4,178	R	35.5	44.0	20.1	0.5	16	9	7	1.5	1.2	1.6	1.9	44.6	55.4
Cumberland	52,116	22,220	19,253	9,901	742	2,967	D	42.6	36.9	19.0	1.4	8	15	9	1.6	1.5	1.4	1.9	53.6	46.4
Essex	276,858	158,130	89,146	26,961	2,621	68,984	D	57.1	32.2	9.7	0.9	1	20	20	8.3	11.0	6.6	5.2	63.9	36.1
Gloucester	104,619	42,425	37,335	24,132	727	5,090	D	40.6	35.7	23.1	0.7	12	18	4	3.1	3.0	2.8	4.6	53.2	46.8
Hudson	185,057	99,799	66,505	14,569	4,184	33,294	D	53.9	35.9	7.9	2.3	2	17	21	5.5	6.9	4.9	2.8	60.0	40.0
Hunterdon	53,974	15,423	25,130	12,736	685	9,707	R	28.6	46.6	23.6	1.3	20	3	3	1.6	1.1	1.9	2.4	38.0	62.0
Mercer	145,260	71,383	50,473	22,503	901	20,910	D	49.1	34.7	15.5	0.6	4	19	16	4.3	5.0	3.7	4.3	58.6	41.4
Middlesex	285,271	128,824	108,701	45,055	2,691	20,123	D	45.2	38.1	15.8	0.9	6	12	14	8.5	9.0	8.0	8.6	54.2	45.8
Monmouth	266,116	101,750	117,715	45,445	1,206	15,965	R	38.2	44.2	17.1	0.5	13	7	13	8.0	7.1	8.7	8.7	46.4	53.6
Morris	209,232	67,593	108,431	32,447	761	40,838	R	32.3	51.8	15.5	0.4	18	1	15	6.3	4.7	8.0	6.2	38.4	61.6
Ocean	216,243	75,431	95,984	41,668	3,160	20,553	R	34.9	44.4	19.3	1.5	17	6	8	6.5	5.3	7.1	8.0	44.0	56.0
Passaic	164,888	70,030	71,147	21,494	2,217	1,117	R	42.5	43.1	13.0	1.3	9	10	17	4.9	4.9	5.2	4.1	49.6	50.4
Salem	27,935	10,062	10,363	7,274	236	301	R	36.0	37.1	26.0	0.8	14	14	1	0.8	0.7	0.8	1.4	49.3	50.7
Somerset	120,813	42,867	56,044	21,014	888	13,177	R	35.5	46.4	17.4	0.7	15	4	12	3.6	3.0	4.1	4.0	43.3	56.7
Sussex	57,064	14,775	29,510	12,537	242	14,735	R	25.9	51.7	22.0	0.4	21	2	5	1.7	1.0	2.2	2.4	33.4	66.6
Union	210,112	96,671	87,742	23,991	1,708	8,929	D	46.0	41.8	11.4	0.8	5	11	19	6.3	6.7	6.5	4.6	52.4	47.6
Warren	41,502	13,002	18,468	9,866	166	5,466	R	31.3	44.5	23.8	0.4	19	5	2	1.2	0.9	1.4	1.9	41.3	58.7
NEW JERSEY	3,343,594	1,436,206	1,356,865	521,829	28,694	79,341	D	43.0	40.6	15.6	0.9				100.0	100.0	100.0	100.0	51.4	48.6

Table H. — Vote for U.S. Representative in Congress: November 3, 1992, General Election

Congressional district and county	Total	Democrat (DEM)	Republican (REP)	Other	Plurality Total	Party	Percent of total vote DEM	REP	Other	Rank within district DEM	REP	Other	Percent contribution to district vote Total	DEM	REP	Other
District 1	**228,072**	**153,525**	**65,123**	**9,424**	**88,402**	**D**	**67.3**	**28.6**	**4.1**				**100.0**	**100.0**	**100.0**	**100.0**
Burlington (pt)	12,066	8,068	3,601	397	4,467	D	66.9	29.8	3.3	2	2	3	5.3	5.3	5.5	4.2
Camden (pt)	149,356	103,432	40,087	5,837	63,345	D	69.3	26.8	3.9	1	3	2	65.5	67.4	61.6	61.9
Gloucester (pt)	66,650	42,025	21,435	3,190	20,590	D	63.1	32.2	4.8	3	1	1	29.2	27.4	32.9	33.8
District 2	**237,027**	**132,465**	**98,315**	**6,247**	**34,150**	**D**	**55.9**	**41.5**	**2.6**				**100.0**	**100.0**	**100.0**	**100.0**
Atlantic	84,936	53,087	30,396	1,453	22,691	D	62.5	35.8	1.7	1	6	6	35.8	40.1	30.9	23.3
Burlington (pt)	333	142	183	8	41	R	42.6	55.0	2.4	6	1	4	0.1	0.1	0.2	0.1
Cape May	46,299	26,911	18,473	915	8,438	D	58.1	39.9	2.0	2	5	5	19.5	20.3	18.8	14.6
Cumberland	47,959	23,761	22,618	1,580	1,143	D	49.5	47.2	3.3	4	3	2	20.2	17.9	23.0	25.3
Gloucester (pt)	30,069	14,326	14,315	1,428	11	D	47.6	47.6	4.7	5	2	1	12.7	10.8	14.6	22.9
Salem	27,431	14,238	12,330	863	1,908	D	51.9	44.9	3.1	3	4	3	11.6	10.7	12.5	13.8
District 3	**255,798**	**94,012**	**151,368**	**10,418**	**57,356**	**R**	**36.8**	**59.2**	**4.1**				**100.0**	**100.0**	**100.0**	**100.0**
Burlington (pt)	112,601	41,245	67,760	3,596	26,515	R	36.6	60.2	3.2	2	1	3	44.0	43.9	44.8	34.5
Camden (pt)	45,147	17,355	26,084	1,708	8,729	R	38.4	57.8	3.8	1	3	2	17.6	18.5	17.2	16.4
Ocean (pt)	98,050	35,412	57,524	5,114	22,112	R	36.1	58.7	5.2	3	2	1	38.3	37.7	38.0	49.1
District 4	**241,225**	**84,514**	**149,095**	**7,616**	**64,581**	**R**	**35.0**	**61.8**	**3.2**				**100.0**	**100.0**	**100.0**	**100.0**
Burlington (pt)	30,140	10,948	18,560	632	7,612	R	36.3	61.6	2.1	2	3	3	12.5	13.0	12.4	8.3
Mercer (pt)	75,622	31,344	42,611	1,667	11,267	R	41.4	56.3	2.2	1	4	2	31.3	37.1	28.6	21.9
Monmouth (pt)	40,079	10,873	28,400	806	17,527	R	27.1	70.9	2.0	4	1	4	16.6	12.9	19.0	10.6
Ocean (pt)	95,384	31,349	59,524	4,511	28,175	R	32.9	62.4	4.7	3	2	1	39.5	37.1	39.9	59.2
District 5	**274,371**	**67,579**	**196,198**	**10,594**	**128,619**	**R**	**24.6**	**71.5**	**3.9**				**100.0**	**100.0**	**100.0**	**100.0**
Bergen (pt)	173,674	41,245	127,759	4,670	86,514	R	23.7	73.6	2.7	3	1	4	63.3	61.0	65.1	44.1
Passaic (pt)	26,037	6,261	18,863	913	12,602	R	24.0	72.4	3.5	2	2	3	9.5	9.3	9.6	8.6
Sussex (pt)	35,368	7,253	25,608	2,507	18,355	R	20.5	72.4	7.1	4	3	1	12.9	10.7	13.1	23.7
Warren	39,292	12,820	23,968	2,504	11,148	R	32.6	61.0	6.4	1	4	2	14.3	19.0	12.2	23.6
District 6	**226,093**	**118,266**	**100,949**	**6,878**	**17,317**	**D**	**52.3**	**44.6**	**3.0**				**100.0**	**100.0**	**100.0**	**100.0**
Middlesex (pt)	124,354	64,622	54,427	5,305	10,195	D	52.0	43.8	4.3	2	2	1	55.0	54.6	53.9	77.1
Monmouth (pt)	101,739	53,644	46,522	1,573	7,122	D	52.7	45.7	1.5	1	1	2	45.0	45.4	46.1	22.9
District 7	**248,082**	**105,761**	**132,174**	**10,147**	**26,413**	**R**	**42.6**	**53.3**	**4.1**				**100.0**	**100.0**	**100.0**	**100.0**
Essex (pt)	10,985	3,818	6,685	482	2,867	R	34.8	60.9	4.4	4	1	2	4.4	3.6	5.1	4.8
Middlesex (pt)	53,512	25,688	25,888	1,936	200	R	48.0	48.4	3.6	1	4	4	21.6	24.3	19.6	19.1
Somerset (pt)	61,417	24,703	33,551	3,163	8,848	R	40.2	54.6	5.2	3	2	1	24.8	23.4	25.4	31.2
Union (pt)	122,168	51,552	66,050	4,566	14,498	R	42.2	54.1	3.7	2	3	3	49.2	48.7	50.0	45.0
District 8	**205,828**	**96,742**	**84,674**	**24,412**	**12,068**	**D**	**47.0**	**41.1**	**11.9**				**100.0**	**100.0**	**100.0**	**100.0**
Essex (pt)	91,685	45,262	39,560	6,863	5,702	D	49.4	43.1	7.5	1	1	2	44.5	46.8	46.7	28.1
Passaic (pt)	114,143	51,480	45,114	17,549	6,366	D	45.1	39.5	15.4	2	2	1	55.5	53.2	53.3	71.9
District 9	**238,704**	**139,188**	**88,179**	**11,337**	**51,009**	**D**	**58.3**	**36.9**	**4.7**				**100.0**	**100.0**	**100.0**	**100.0**
Bergen (pt)	202,641	117,581	75,961	9,099	41,620	D	58.0	37.5	4.5	2	1	2	84.9	84.5	86.1	80.3
Hudson (pt)	36,063	21,607	12,218	2,238	9,389	D	59.9	33.9	6.2	1	2	1	15.1	15.5	13.9	19.7
District 10	**149,632**	**117,287**	**30,160**	**2,185**	**87,127**	**D**	**78.4**	**20.2**	**1.5**				**100.0**	**100.0**	**100.0**	**100.0**
Essex (pt)	86,028	76,269	8,757	1,002	67,512	D	88.7	10.2	1.2	1	3	3	57.5	65.0	29.0	45.9
Hudson (pt)	12,850	8,822	3,500	528	5,322	D	68.7	27.2	4.1	2	2	1	8.6	7.5	11.6	24.2
Union (pt)	50,754	32,196	17,903	655	14,293	D	63.4	35.3	1.3	3	1	2	33.9	27.5	59.4	30.0
District 11	**268,436**	**68,871**	**188,165**	**11,400**	**119,294**	**R**	**25.7**	**70.1**	**4.2**				**100.0**	**100.0**	**100.0**	**100.0**
Essex (pt)	32,102	8,904	21,977	1,221	13,073	R	27.7	68.5	3.8	3	3	4	12.0	12.9	11.7	10.7
Morris	188,234	47,262	133,990	6,982	86,728	R	25.1	71.2	3.7	4	1	5	70.1	68.6	71.2	61.2
Passaic (pt)	2,873	866	1,876	131	1,010	R	30.1	65.3	4.6	1	5	3	1.1	1.3	1.0	1.1
Somerset (pt)	25,428	7,532	16,712	1,184	9,180	R	29.6	65.7	4.7	2	4	2	9.5	10.9	8.9	10.4
Sussex (pt)	19,799	4,307	13,610	1,882	9,303	R	21.8	68.7	9.5	5	2	1	7.4	6.3	7.2	16.5
District 12	**272,757**	**83,035**	**174,216**	**15,506**	**91,181**	**R**	**30.4**	**63.9**	**5.7**				**100.0**	**100.0**	**100.0**	**100.0**
Hunterdon	48,697	9,164	36,956	2,577	27,792	R	18.8	75.9	5.3	5	1	2	17.9	11.0	21.2	16.6
Mercer (pt)	53,676	18,327	29,466	5,883	11,139	R	34.1	54.9	11.0	2	5	1	19.7	22.1	16.9	37.9
Middlesex (pt)	50,689	19,168	28,875	2,646	9,707	R	37.8	57.0	5.2	1	4	3	18.6	23.1	16.6	17.1
Monmouth (pt)	100,095	32,511	64,165	3,419	31,654	R	32.5	64.1	3.4	3	3	5	36.7	39.2	36.8	22.0
Somerset (pt)	19,600	3,865	14,754	981	10,889	R	19.7	75.3	5.0	4	2	4	7.2	4.7	8.5	6.3
District 13	**145,714**	**93,670**	**44,529**	**7,515**	**49,141**	**D**	**64.3**	**30.6**	**5.2**				**100.0**	**100.0**	**100.0**	**100.0**
Essex (pt)	15,871	10,104	4,253	1,514	5,851	D	63.7	26.8	9.5	3	3	1	10.9	10.8	9.6	20.1
Hudson (pt)	101,269	65,071	31,213	4,985	33,858	D	64.3	30.8	4.9	2	2	2	69.5	69.5	70.1	66.3
Middlesex (pt)	19,316	11,937	6,722	657	5,215	D	61.8	34.8	3.4	4	1	4	13.3	12.7	15.1	8.7
Union (pt)	9,258	6,558	2,341	359	4,217	D	70.8	25.3	3.9	1	4	3	6.4	7.0	5.3	4.8
NEW JERSEY	**2,991,739**	**1,354,915**	**1,503,145**	**133,679**	**148,230**	**R**	**45.3**	**50.2**	**4.5**							

Table I. — Vote for Presidential Preference: June 2, 1992, Democratic Primary Election

County	Top candidates									Top three candidates (state vote)									
										Percent of total vote			Rank			Percent contribution to state vote			
	Total	Clinton	Brown	Tsongas	LaRouche	Ballard	Hanson			Clinton	Brown	Tsongas	Clinton	Brown	Tsongas	Total	Clinton	Brown	Tsongas
Atlantic	8,349	5,312	1,719	1,089	86	114	29	-	-	63.6	20.6	13.0	9	13	12	2.1	2.1	2.2	2.4
Bergen	35,539	23,517	6,002	5,071	783	64	102	-	-	66.2	16.9	14.3	5	18	7	9.0	9.2	7.5	11.2
Burlington	19,823	12,110	5,186	1,861	216	85	365	-	-	61.1	26.2	9.4	13	5	18	5.0	4.7	6.5	4.1
Camden	25,641	15,595	6,658	2,691	466	138	93	-	-	60.8	26.0	10.5	15	6	15	6.5	6.1	8.3	6.0
Cape May	3,710	2,158	825	492	148	29	58	-	-	58.2	22.2	13.3	16	10	11	0.9	0.8	1.0	1.1
Cumberland	4,694	3,176	807	583	96	22	10	-	-	67.7	17.2	12.4	4	17	14	1.2	1.2	1.0	1.3
Essex	63,261	49,545	7,555	5,222	736	59	144	-	-	78.3	11.9	8.3	1	21	19	16.1	19.3	9.5	11.6
Gloucester	12,758	8,283	2,801	1,317	300	38	19	-	-	64.9	22.0	10.3	7	11	16	3.2	3.2	3.5	2.9
Hudson	46,917	30,640	10,538	4,556	813	169	201	-	-	65.3	22.5	9.7	6	9	17	11.9	12.0	13.2	10.1
Hunterdon	3,060	1,625	828	562	29	4	12	-	-	53.1	27.1	18.4	20	3	2	0.8	0.6	1.0	1.2
Mercer	14,778	9,003	2,677	2,164	199	631	104	-	-	60.9	18.1	14.6	14	16	6	3.8	3.5	3.4	4.8
Middlesex	36,764	22,772	10,037	3,013	863	31	48	-	-	61.9	27.3	8.2	11	2	20	9.4	8.9	12.6	6.7
Monmouth	25,621	14,677	6,170	4,165	216	328	65	-	-	57.3	24.1	16.3	18	7	4	6.5	5.7	7.7	9.2
Morris	13,375	7,145	3,152	2,519	431	83	45	-	-	53.4	23.6	18.8	19	8	1	3.4	2.8	3.9	5.6
Ocean	16,073	11,891	2,597	1,109	436	23	17	-	-	74.0	16.2	6.9	2	19	21	4.1	4.6	3.3	2.5
Passaic	17,588	11,111	3,359	2,439	437	203	39	-	-	63.2	19.1	13.9	10	14	9	4.5	4.3	4.2	5.4
Salem	1,913	1,297	288	270	51	4	3	-	-	67.8	15.1	14.1	3	20	8	0.5	0.5	0.4	0.6
Somerset	8,045	4,925	1,664	1,183	254	13	6	-	-	61.2	20.7	14.7	12	12	5	2.0	1.9	2.1	2.6
Sussex	2,810	1,294	918	512	70	2	14	-	-	46.0	32.7	18.2	21	1	3	0.7	0.5	1.1	1.1
Union	28,919	18,461	5,272	3,978	1,100	21	87	-	-	63.8	18.2	13.8	8	15	10	7.4	7.2	6.6	8.8
Warren	3,106	1,800	824	395	69	6	12	-	-	58.0	26.5	12.7	17	4	13	0.8	0.7	1.0	0.9
NEW JERSEY	**392,744**	**256,337**	**79,877**	**45,191**	**7,799**	**2,067**	**1,473**	**-**	**-**	**65.3**	**20.3**	**11.5**				**100.0**	**100.0**	**100.0**	**100.0**

Table J. — Vote for Presidential Preference: June 2, 1992, Republican Primary Election

County	Top candidates					Top four candidates (state vote)								Percent contribution to state vote				
						Percent of total vote				Rank								
	Total	Bush	Bu-chanan			Bush	Bu-chanan		Other	Bush	Bu-chanan			Total	Bush	Bu-chanan		
Atlantic	8,128	6,413	1,715	-	-	78.9	21.1	-	-	21	1	-	-	2.8	2.7	3.7	-	-
Bergen	32,180	26,737	5,443	-	-	83.1	16.9	-	-	14	8	-	-	11.2	11.1	11.7	-	-
Burlington	19,078	15,495	3,583	-	-	81.2	18.8	-	-	19	3	-	-	6.6	6.4	7.7	-	-
Camden	10,423	8,574	1,849	-	-	82.3	17.7	-	-	15	7	-	-	3.6	3.6	4.0	-	-
Cape May	8,252	6,610	1,642	-	-	80.1	19.9	-	-	20	2	-	-	2.9	2.7	3.5	-	-
Cumberland	3,997	3,327	670	-	-	83.2	16.8	-	-	13	9	-	-	1.4	1.4	1.4	-	-
Essex	18,037	15,620	2,417	-	-	86.6	13.4	-	-	2	20	-	-	6.3	6.5	5.2	-	-
Gloucester	7,071	5,899	1,172	-	-	83.4	16.6	-	-	12	10	-	-	2.5	2.5	2.5	-	-
Hudson	9,747	8,003	1,744	-	-	82.1	17.9	-	-	18	4	-	-	3.4	3.3	3.8	-	-
Hunterdon	8,402	7,180	1,222	-	-	85.5	14.5	-	-	6	16	-	-	2.9	3.0	2.6	-	-
Mercer	6,723	5,733	990	-	-	85.3	14.7	-	-	7	15	-	-	2.3	2.4	2.1	-	-
Middlesex	14,705	12,430	2,275	-	-	84.5	15.5	-	-	9	13	-	-	5.1	5.2	4.9	-	-
Monmouth	20,632	17,833	2,799	-	-	86.4	13.6	-	-	3	19	-	-	7.2	7.4	6.0	-	-
Morris	35,197	28,935	6,262	-	-	82.2	17.8	-	-	16	6	-	-	12.3	12.0	13.5	-	-
Ocean	23,640	20,062	3,578	-	-	84.9	15.1	-	-	8	14	-	-	8.2	8.3	7.7	-	-
Passaic	15,960	13,329	2,631	-	-	83.5	16.5	-	-	10	12	-	-	5.6	5.5	5.7	-	-
Salem	1,725	1,418	307	-	-	82.2	17.8	-	-	17	5	-	-	0.6	0.6	0.7	-	-
Somerset	11,525	9,898	1,627	-	-	85.9	14.1	-	-	4	18	-	-	4.0	4.1	3.5	-	-
Sussex	10,079	8,626	1,453	-	-	85.6	14.4	-	-	5	17	-	-	3.5	3.6	3.1	-	-
Union	15,627	13,538	2,089	-	-	86.6	13.4	-	-	1	21	-	-	5.4	5.6	4.5	-	-
Warren	5,839	4,875	964	-	-	83.5	16.5	-	-	11	11	-	-	2.0	2.0	2.1	-	-
NEW JERSEY	**286,967**	**240,535**	**46,432**	**-**	**-**	**83.8**	**16.2**	**-**	**-**					**100.0**	**100.0**	**100.0**	**-**	**-**

1992 Vote for President
Percent for Clinton (D), by County

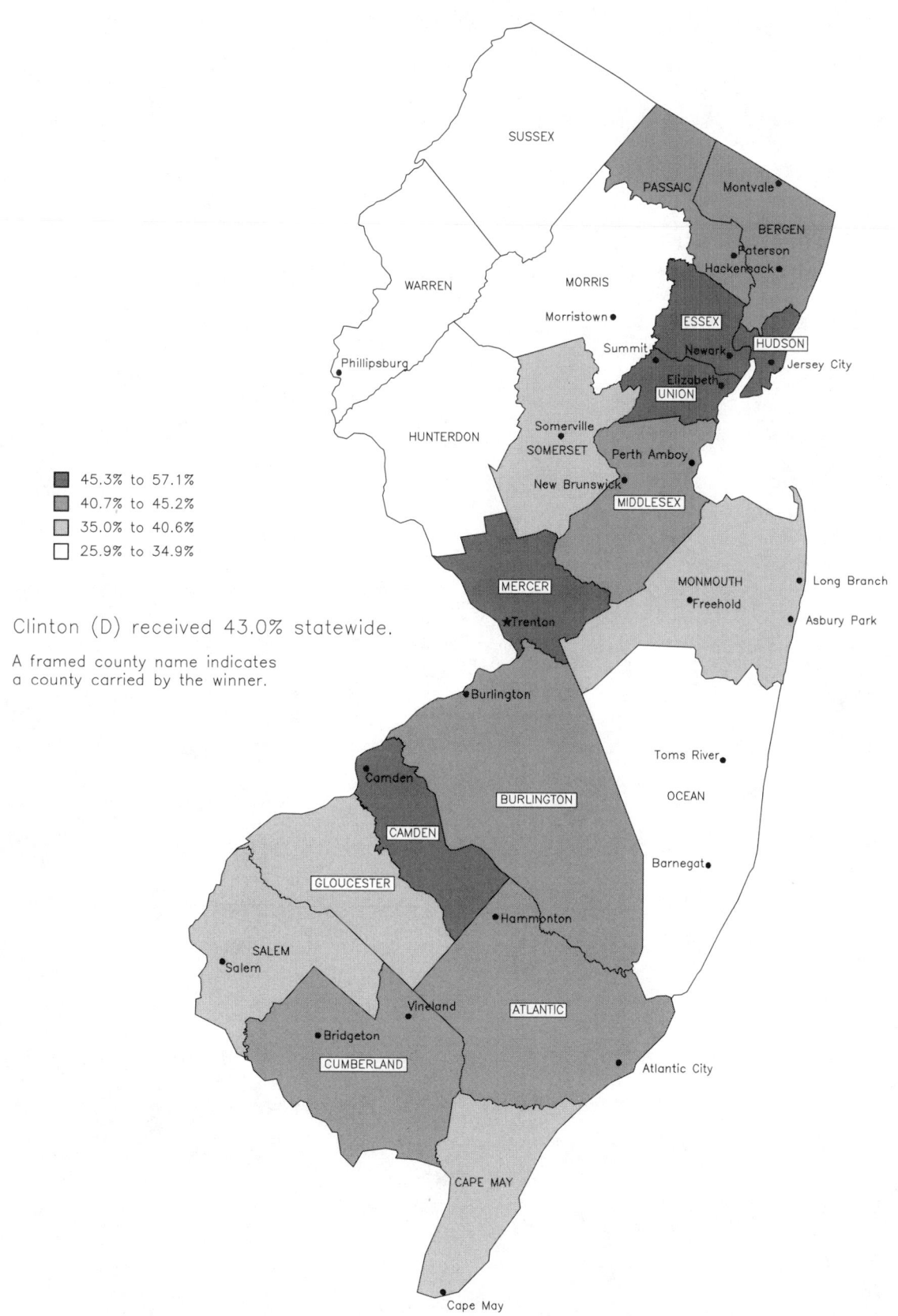

45.3% to 57.1%
40.7% to 45.2%
35.0% to 40.6%
25.9% to 34.9%

Clinton (D) received 43.0% statewide.

A framed county name indicates
a county carried by the winner.

SUSSEX

PASSAIC
Montvale

BERGEN
Paterson
Hackensack

WARREN

MORRIS

Morristown

ESSEX
HUDSON

Summit
Newark
Jersey City

Phillipsburg

Elizabeth
UNION

HUNTERDON

Somerville
SOMERSET
Perth Amboy

New Brunswick
MIDDLESEX

MONMOUTH
Long Branch
Freehold
Asbury Park

MERCER

Trenton

Burlington

Toms River

Camden
OCEAN

BURLINGTON

CAMDEN

Barnegat

GLOUCESTER

Hammonton

SALEM
Salem

Vineland

ATLANTIC

Bridgeton

Atlantic City

CUMBERLAND

CAPE MAY

Cape May

New Jersey 631

NEW MEXICO

Alternative Registration Methods:
....Deputized Registrars, Motor-voter

Registration Deadline (Days before Election) 28

Voting Equipment Use (Counties)

Datavote Punch Card	0	Paper Ballot	0
Electronic	8	Other Punch Card	0
Lever Machine	18	Mixed Systems	5
Optical Scanner	2		

Party Control	DEM	REP	IND	VAC
1993 State Senate	27	15	0	0
1992 State Senate	26	16	0	0
1993 State House	52	18	0	0
1992 State House	49	21	0	0

Population Statistics 1990

Race/ Ethnicity	Total Population		Voting Age Population		Voting Age Population % of total population
	Number	%	Number	%	
Non-Hispanic					
White	764,164	50.4	586,192	54.9	76.7
Black	27,642	1.8	18,590	1.7	67.3
Asian/Pacific Islander	12,587	0.8	8,833	0.8	70.2
Native American	128,068	8.5	76,720	7.2	59.9
Other	3,384	0.2	2,226	0.2	65.8
All Hispanic	579,224	38.2	375,767	35.2	64.9
TOTAL	1,515,069	100.0	1,068,328	100.0	70.5

Estimated Voting Age Population 1992 (VAP) 1,104,000
Number of Registered Voters 706,966
  % of estimated VAP 64.0
Voter Turnout (Actual) 590,901
  % of VAP 53.5
  % of Registration 83.6
Persons Not Voting—of Voting Age 513,099
  % of VAP 46.5
Persons Not Voting—of Registered 116,065
  % of Registration 16.4
Straight Ticket Voting .... Yes, Exception

State Officials and Members of Congress

Governor:
Bruce King (D) 1970, elected to a four-year term in 1990.

U.S. Senators:
Pete V. Domenici (R) 1972, elected to a six-year term in 1990.
Jeff Bingaman (D) 1982, elected to a six-year term in 1988.

U.S. Representative in Congress:
(District, Name, Party, Date first elected)

1. Schiff (R) 1988   2. Skeen (R) 1980   3. Richardson (D) 1982

Candidates: General Election, November 3, 1992

Candidate(s)	Total vote	Percent	Party	Status	First elected
President/Vice President					
Clinton/Gore	261,617	45.90%	Democrat	Challenger	1992
Bush/Quayle	212,824	37.34%	Republican	Incumbent	1988
Perot/Stockdale	91,895	16.12%	Independent	Challenger	
Marrou/Lord	1,615	0.28%	Libertarian	Challenger	
Phillips/Knight	620	0.11%	Taxpayers	Challenger	
Hagelin/Tompkins	562	0.10%	Natural Law	Challenger	
Fulani/Munoz	369	0.06%	New Alliance	Challenger	
Warren/Reid	183	0.03%	Socialist Workers	Challenger	
La Riva/Holmes	181	0.03%	Workers World	Challenger	
Dodge/Ormsby	120	0.02%	Prohibition	Challenger	
U.S. Senator (No Contest)					
Governor (No Contest)					
U.S. Representative in Congress					
District 1					
Steven Schiff	128,426	62.58%	Republican	Incumbent	1988
Robert Aragon	76,600	37.33%	Democrat	Challenger	
Orlin Cole	188	0.09%	Write in	Challenger	
District 2					
Joe Skeen	94,838	56.39%	Republican	Incumbent	1980
Dan Sosa, Jr.	73,157	43.50%	Democrat	Challenger	
David Pilley	175	0.10%	Write in	Challenger	
District 3					
Bill Richardson	122,850	67.42%	Democrat	Incumbent	1982
F. Gregg Bemis, Jr.	54,569	29.95%	Republican	Challenger	
Ed Nagel	4,798	2.63%	Libertarian	Challenger	

Candidates: June 2, 1992, Primary Election

Candidate	Total vote	Percent	Candidate	Total vote	Percent
Presidential Preference, Democratic			**Presidential Preference, Republican**		
Bill Clinton	95,933	52.84%	George Bush	55,522	63.84%
Uncommitted	35,269	19.43%	Uncommitted	23,574	27.11%
Jerry Brown	30,705	16.91%	Patrick Buchanan	7,871	9.05%
Paul Tsongas	11,409	6.28%			
Tom Harkin	3,233	1.78%			
Larry Agran	2,573	1.42%			
Lyndon LaRouche, Jr.	2,415	1.33%			

Voter Registration and Turnout, 1948-1992 Elections

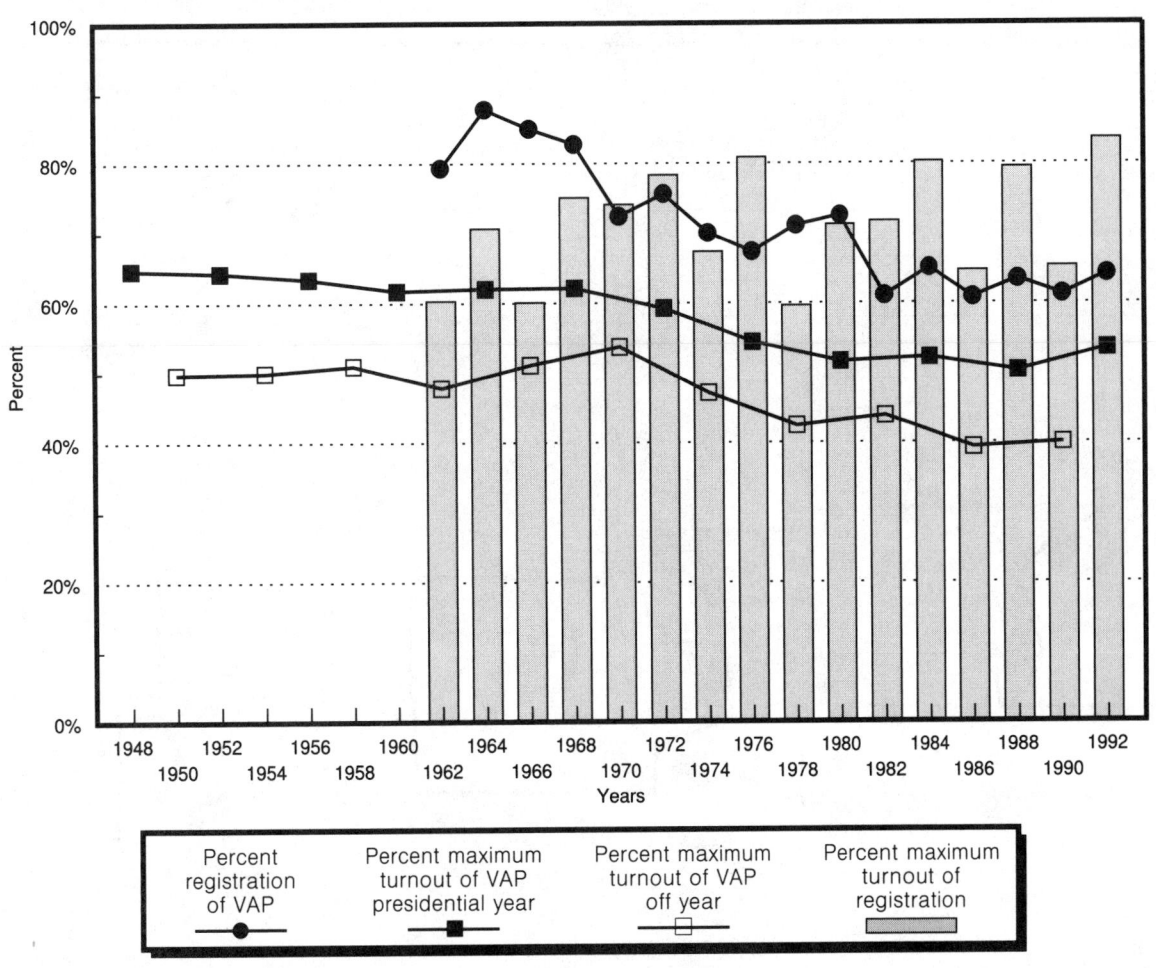

Legend:
- Percent registration of VAP
- Percent maximum turnout of VAP presidential year
- Percent maximum turnout of VAP off year
- Percent maximum turnout of registration

Year	Estimated Voting Age Population (VAP)	Voter registration (REG)			Voter turnout												
						Highest office						Maximum vote					
		Total	Percent of VAP	Rank by percent of VAP	Actual	Total	Office	Percent total REG	Rank by percent of REG	Percent of VAP	Rank by percent of VAP	Total	Percent total REG	Rank by percent of REG	Percent total VAP	Rank by percent of VAP
1992	1,104,000	706,966	64.0	45	590,901	569,986	P	80.6	16	51.6	40	590,901	83.6	8	53.5	38
1990	1,075,000	658,374	61.2	38	429,509	411,236	G	62.5	13	38.3	28	429,509	65.2	10	40.0	28
1988	1,065,000	674,826	63.4	43	535,694	521,287	P	77.2	11	48.9	34	535,694	79.4	9	50.3	32
1986	1,041,000	632,787	60.8	42	408,621	394,833	G	62.4	11	37.9	28	408,621	64.6	10	39.3	27
1984	1,001,000	650,929	65.0	42	522,328	514,370	P	79.0	9	51.4	36	522,328	80.2	7	52.2	34
1982	955,000	582,646	61.0	39	417,945	407,466	G	69.9	8	42.7	28	417,945	71.7	6	43.8	28
1980	900,000	652,687	72.5	27	464,848	456,971	P	70.0	37	50.8	35	464,848	71.2	36	51.6	34
1978	841,000	597,754	71.1	20	356,509	345,577	G	57.8	21	41.1	24	356,509	59.6	20	42.4	24
1976	783,000	527,278	67.3	36	426,265	418,409	P	79.4	14	53.4	31	426,265	80.8	12	54.4	30
1974	720,000	504,197	70.0	26	339,074	328,742	G	65.2	13	45.7	17	339,074	67.3	13	47.1	15
1972	669,000	505,432	75.6	22	395,911	386,241	P	76.4	21	57.7	27	395,911	78.3	18	59.2	27
1970	561,000	406,277	72.4	26	301,104	290,375	G	71.5	12	51.8	18	301,104	74.1	11	53.7	17
1968	539,000	445,776	82.7	13	334,867	327,350	P	73.4	38	60.7	32	334,867	75.1	37	62.1	31
1966	532,000	451,540	84.9	10	271,592	260,232	G	57.6	31	48.9	31	271,592	60.1	31	51.1	29
1964	530,000	464,931	87.7	11	-	328,645	P	70.7	35	62.0	33	328,645	70.7	36	62.0	33
1962	517,000	409,998	79.3	16	-	247,135	G	60.3	25	47.8	32	247,135	60.3	26	47.8	32
1960	504,000	-	-	-	-	311,107	P	-	-	61.7	33	311,107	-	-	61.7	33
1958	414,000	-	-	-	211,295	205,048	G	-	-	49.5	31	211,295	-	-	51.0	27
1956	409,000	-	-	-	259,496	253,926	P	-	-	62.1	34	259,496	-	-	63.4	34
1954	396,000	-	-	-	198,082	194,422	S	-	-	49.1	28	198,082	-	-	50.0	28
1952	380,000	-	-	-	244,502	238,608	P	-	-	62.8	34	244,502	-	-	64.3	33
1950	366,000	-	-	-	182,329	180,205	G	-	-	49.2	27	182,329	-	-	49.8	28
1948	301,000	-	-	-	194,652	187,063	P	-	-	62.1	17	194,652	-	-	64.7	14

NEW MEXICO

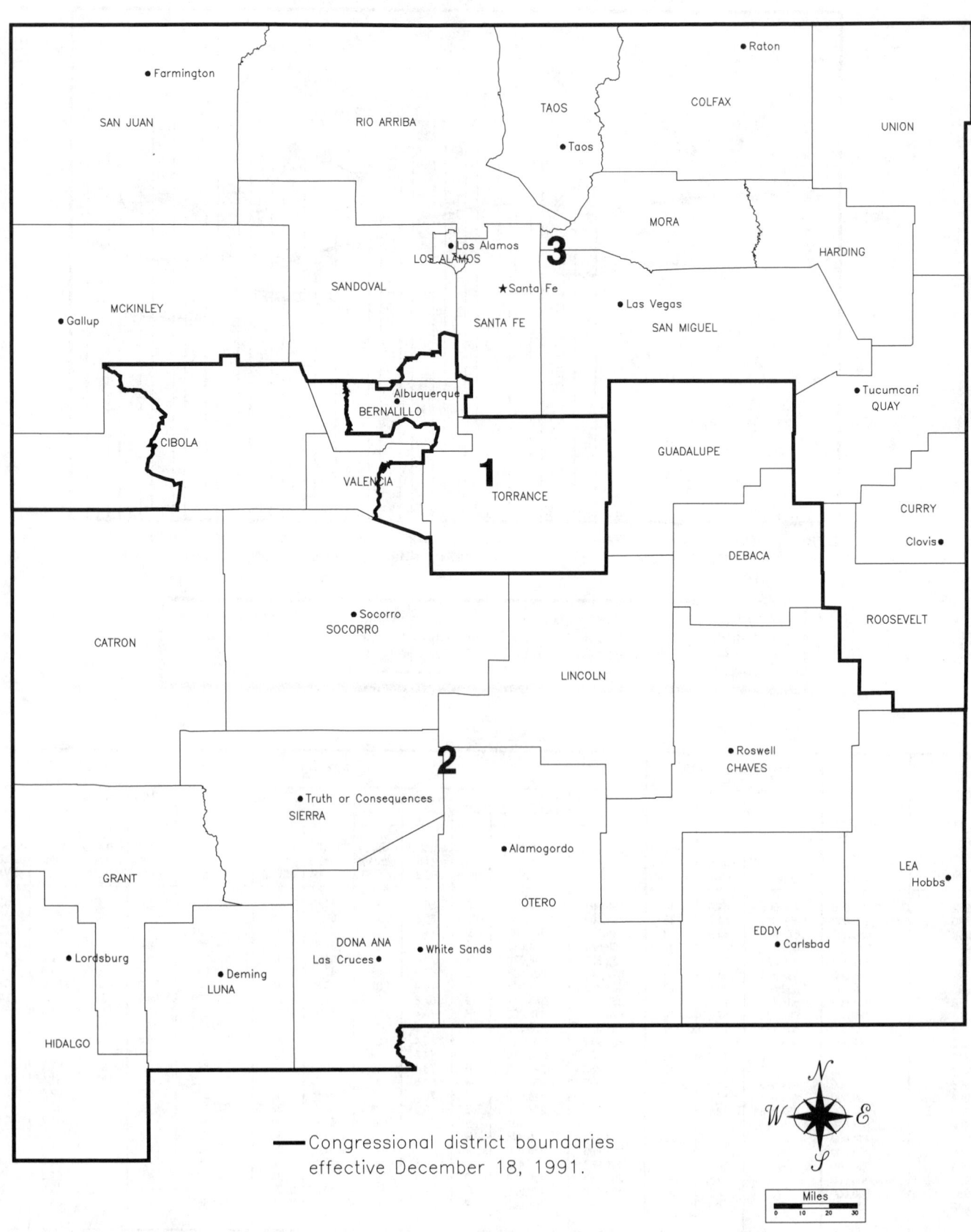

—Congressional district boundaries
effective December 18, 1991.

Copyright © 1993 by Election Data Services, Inc.

Table A. — 1990 Population by Race and Ethnic Origin

State/ county code	County	Total persons	Percent of total persons — Non-Hispanic White	Black	Asian and Pacific Islander	Native American	Other	Hispanic	Rank Total	Rank Non-Hispanic White	Black	Hispanic	Percent contribution to state population Total	Non-Hispanic White	Black	Hispanic
35 001	Bernalillo	480,577	55.8	2.5	1.4	3.0	0.3	37.1	1	15	4	17	31.7	35.1	42.9	30.8
35 003	Catron	2,563	70.5	0.3	<.1	0.7	0.0	28.4	31	3	25	24	0.2	0.2	<.1	0.1
35 005	Chaves	57,849	60.1	1.9	0.4	0.5	0.3	36.8	7	13	5	18	3.8	4.6	4.0	3.7
35 006	Cibola	23,794	27.3	0.8	0.3	37.6	<.1	34.1	16	28	13	20	1.6	0.8	0.6	1.4
35 007	Colfax	12,925	50.8	0.2	0.1	0.5	0.4	47.9	22	18	26	11	0.9	0.9	0.1	1.1
35 009	Curry	42,207	67.1	6.6	1.7	0.6	0.3	23.7	12	6	1	30	2.8	3.7	10.0	1.7
35 011	DeBaca	2,252	65.7	<.1	0.0	1.3	0.2	32.7	32	8	31	22	0.1	0.2	<.1	0.1
35 013	Dona Ana	135,510	40.7	1.5	0.7	0.6	<.1	56.4	2	25	7	6	8.9	7.2	7.1	13.2
35 015	Eddy	48,605	62.2	1.5	0.3	0.4	0.2	35.3	10	11	6	19	3.2	4.0	2.7	3.0
35 017	Grant	27,676	47.8	0.4	0.2	0.7	<.1	50.8	14	22	21	7	1.8	1.7	0.4	2.4
35 019	Guadalupe	4,156	14.4	0.2	0.6	0.4	0.1	84.3	29	32	29	2	0.3	<.1	<.1	0.6
35 021	Harding	987	52.4	0.2	0.1	0.5	0.1	46.7	33	16	27	14	<.1	<.1	<.1	<.1
35 023	Hidalgo	5,958	49.0	0.2	0.5	0.3	0.0	50.1	27	21	30	9	0.4	0.4	<.1	0.5
35 025	Lea	55,765	64.7	4.6	0.3	0.6	<.1	29.8	8	9	3	23	3.7	4.7	9.2	2.9
35 027	Lincoln	12,219	70.3	0.5	0.2	1.0	<.1	28.0	23	4	17	25	0.8	1.1	0.2	0.6
35 028	Los Alamos	18,115	85.4	0.5	2.3	0.6	0.1	11.1	18	1	18	33	1.2	2.0	0.3	0.3
35 029	Luna	18,110	50.3	1.2	0.3	0.5	0.1	47.6	19	19	10	13	1.2	1.2	0.8	1.5
35 031	McKinley	60,686	15.8	0.5	0.4	70.4	0.2	12.8	6	30	19	32	4.0	1.3	1.0	1.3
35 033	Mora	4,264	14.4	<.1	<.1	0.3	0.3	85.0	28	31	33	1	0.3	<.1	<.1	0.6
35 035	Otero	51,928	64.1	5.1	1.7	5.2	0.1	23.8	9	10	2	29	3.4	4.4	9.6	2.1
35 037	Quay	10,823	60.0	1.1	0.3	0.7	0.3	37.5	24	14	11	16	0.7	0.9	0.4	0.7
35 039	Rio Arriba	34,365	12.7	0.3	0.1	14.1	0.1	72.6	13	33	22	4	2.3	0.6	0.4	4.3
35 041	Roosevelt	16,702	70.1	1.3	0.5	0.7	0.2	27.2	20	5	9	27	1.1	1.5	0.8	0.8
35 043	Sandoval	63,319	51.2	1.3	0.7	19.2	0.1	27.4	5	17	8	26	4.2	4.2	3.1	3.0
35 045	San Juan	91,605	50.0	0.4	0.2	36.1	<.1	13.1	4	20	20	31	6.0	6.0	1.5	2.1
35 047	San Miguel	25,743	18.2	0.6	0.5	0.7	0.5	79.6	15	29	15	3	1.7	0.6	0.5	3.5
35 049	Santa Fe	98,928	47.0	0.5	0.4	2.3	0.3	49.5	3	23	16	10	6.5	6.1	1.8	8.4
35 051	Sierra	9,912	74.8	0.3	0.1	0.6	<.1	24.0	26	2	24	28	0.7	1.0	0.1	0.4
35 053	Socorro	14,764	40.4	0.7	1.3	9.6	<.1	47.8	21	26	14	12	1.0	0.8	0.4	1.2
35 055	Taos	23,118	27.7	0.2	0.3	6.4	0.5	64.9	17	27	28	5	1.5	0.8	0.2	2.6
35 057	Torrance	10,285	60.5	0.3	0.2	1.1	<.1	37.8	25	12	23	15	0.7	0.8	0.1	0.7
35 059	Union	4,124	65.9	<.1	<.1	0.2	<.1	33.7	30	7	32	21	0.3	0.4	<.1	0.2
35 061	Valencia	45,235	45.7	1.0	0.3	2.6	0.2	50.3	11	24	12	8	3.0	2.7	1.6	3.9
35	**NEW MEXICO**	1,515,069	50.4	1.8	0.8	8.5	0.2	38.2					100.0	100.0	100.0	100.0
	CONGRESSIONAL															
	District 1	505,491	55.6	2.4	1.3	2.3	0.3	38.1	1	1	1	2	33.4	36.8	43.7	33.2
	District 2	504,659	51.7	2.0	0.6	3.5	0.1	42.1	3	2	2	1	33.3	34.2	36.1	36.7
	District 3	504,919	44.0	1.1	0.6	19.6	0.2	34.6	2	3	3	3	33.3	29.1	20.2	30.1

Table B. – 1990 Voting Age Population (VAP) by Race and Ethnic Origin

County	Total Voting Age Population	Percent of total VAP — Non-Hispanic White	Black	Asian and Pacific Islander	Native American	Other	Hispanic	Rank Pct of total VAP Total	Non-Hispanic White	Black	Hispanic	Pct contribution to state VAP Total	Non-Hispanic White	Black	Hispanic	VAP pct of total pop Total	Non-Hispanic White	Black	Asian and Pacific Islander	Native American	Other	Hispanic
Bernalillo	354,978	59.5	2.3	1.3	2.7	0.3	33.9	1	15	4	16	33.2	36.1	43.7	32.0	73.9	78.9	68.4	70.8	66.5	66.9	67.4
Catron	1,881	73.4	0.2	0.1	0.6	0.0	25.7	31	4	26	23	0.2	0.2	<.1	0.1	73.4	76.3	57.1	100.0	61.1	0.0	66.5
Chaves	40,137	65.8	1.8	0.4	0.5	0.3	31.2	6	12	5	19	3.8	4.5	4.0	3.3	69.4	75.9	67.3	65.7	70.9	61.2	58.9
Cibola	15,720	31.1	0.8	0.2	34.8	<.1	33.1	17	27	13	18	1.5	0.8	0.7	1.4	66.1	75.2	74.3	58.1	61.1	87.5	64.1
Colfax	9,226	55.5	0.1	0.1	0.4	0.4	43.5	22	18	29	13	0.9	0.9	<.1	1.1	71.4	77.9	37.9	66.7	56.9	63.6	64.8
Curry	29,246	71.6	5.9	1.6	0.5	0.3	20.1	12	6	1	30	2.7	3.6	9.3	1.6	69.3	73.9	62.5	63.8	65.7	67.9	58.6
DeBaca	1,684	67.9	0.1	0.0	1.1	0.1	30.7	32	9	30	21	0.2	0.2	<.1	0.1	74.8	77.3	100.0	0.0	63.3	50.0	70.2
Dona Ana	94,310	46.1	1.4	0.8	0.7	<.1	50.9	2	25	7	6	8.8	7.4	7.3	12.8	69.6	78.8	68.8	75.4	76.9	72.9	62.8
Eddy	33,949	66.6	1.5	0.3	0.5	0.2	30.8	10	11	6	20	3.2	3.9	2.8	2.8	69.8	74.8	69.8	67.5	75.6	64.5	61.1
Grant	19,270	52.1	0.4	0.2	0.7	<.1	46.5	14	20	20	10	1.8	1.7	0.4	2.4	69.6	75.8	66.7	70.2	70.6	66.7	63.8
Guadalupe	2,882	15.9	0.2	0.7	0.3	0.1	82.9	30	32	27	2	0.3	<.1	<.1	0.6	69.3	76.7	71.4	73.1	50.0	60.0	68.2
Harding	709	52.0	0.3	0.0	0.4	0.1	47.1	33	21	22	8	<.1	<.1	<.1	<.1	71.8	71.4	100.0	0.0	60.0	100.0	72.5
Hidalgo	3,985	51.5	0.1	0.6	0.4	0.0	47.5	27	22	31	7	0.4	0.3	<.1	0.5	66.9	70.3	44.4	79.3	73.7	0.0	63.4
Lea	37,234	70.5	4.2	0.3	0.6	<.1	24.4	7	7	3	26	3.5	4.5	8.5	2.4	66.8	72.7	62.0	61.8	69.6	50.0	54.7
Lincoln	9,114	73.0	0.5	0.1	0.9	<.1	25.3	23	5	17	24	0.9	1.1	0.3	0.6	74.6	77.5	81.7	57.1	69.5	87.5	67.3
Los Alamos	13,398	86.8	0.4	2.3	0.5	<.1	9.9	18	1	21	33	1.3	2.0	0.3	0.4	74.0	75.2	60.2	72.0	65.2	57.9	66.3
Luna	12,835	57.7	1.1	0.3	0.5	0.1	40.4	19	16	10	14	1.2	1.3	0.8	1.4	70.9	81.2	67.5	72.5	71.3	59.1	60.0
McKinley	37,130	19.3	0.5	0.4	66.7	0.2	12.9	8	30	16	31	3.5	1.2	1.1	1.3	61.2	74.5	71.3	67.9	58.0	51.9	61.9
Mora	3,020	15.9	<.1	<.1	0.3	0.3	83.4	28	31	33	1	0.3	<.1	<.1	0.7	70.8	78.0	100.0	100.0	75.0	90.9	69.5
Otero	36,041	67.7	4.9	1.7	4.2	0.1	21.4	9	10	2	28	3.4	4.2	9.5	2.1	69.4	73.4	67.0	68.5	56.0	58.0	62.3
Quay	7,845	63.6	1.1	0.3	0.7	0.3	34.0	25	14	11	15	0.7	0.9	0.5	0.7	72.5	76.8	69.4	60.0	69.7	83.9	65.7
Rio Arriba	23,222	14.3	0.3	0.1	12.8	0.1	72.3	13	33	24	4	2.2	0.6	0.3	4.5	67.6	76.2	53.8	75.0	61.5	60.4	67.3
Roosevelt	12,170	74.4	1.2	0.6	0.8	0.1	22.9	20	3	9	27	1.1	1.5	0.8	0.7	72.9	77.4	71.9	76.9	80.7	40.5	61.3
Sandoval	43,040	55.6	1.3	0.7	17.0	0.1	25.3	5	17	8	25	4.0	4.1	3.0	2.9	68.0	73.9	67.1	64.4	60.3	54.9	62.6
San Juan	58,265	54.8	0.4	0.2	32.4	0.1	12.0	4	19	19	32	5.5	5.4	1.4	1.9	63.6	69.7	63.4	69.9	57.1	74.4	58.2
San Miguel	17,944	20.5	0.6	0.5	0.7	0.6	77.2	15	29	14	3	1.7	0.6	0.6	3.7	69.7	78.5	78.6	70.7	70.8	73.9	67.6
Santa Fe	73,231	50.7	0.5	0.4	2.1	0.3	46.0	3	23	18	11	6.9	6.3	2.1	9.0	74.0	79.9	76.2	72.2	67.4	64.0	68.8
Sierra	7,958	78.8	0.2	0.1	0.6	<.1	20.2	24	2	25	29	0.7	1.1	<.1	0.4	80.3	84.5	62.1	66.7	73.4	77.8	67.7
Socorro	10,288	45.4	0.6	1.6	8.1	<.1	44.2	21	26	15	12	1.0	0.8	0.3	1.2	69.7	78.3	60.4	82.6	58.3	70.0	64.5
Taos	16,390	30.5	0.2	0.2	6.2	0.5	62.4	16	28	28	5	1.5	0.9	0.1	2.7	70.9	78.1	58.7	48.6	69.1	68.3	68.2
Torrance	6,982	64.8	0.3	0.2	0.9	<.1	33.8	26	13	23	17	0.7	0.8	0.1	0.6	67.9	72.7	55.9	75.0	54.1	100.0	60.6
Union	2,959	69.2	<.1	0.1	0.3	<.1	30.3	29	8	32	22	0.3	0.3	<.1	0.2	71.8	75.3	100.0	100.0	80.0	100.0	64.6
Valencia	31,285	49.3	1.1	0.3	2.5	0.2	46.7	11	24	12	9	2.9	2.6	1.8	3.9	69.2	74.6	76.3	72.7	65.7	69.0	64.2
NEW MEXICO	1,068,328	54.9	1.7	0.8	7.2	0.2	35.2					100.0	100.0	100.0	100.0	70.5	76.7	67.3	70.2	59.9	65.8	64.9
CONGRESSIONAL																						
District 1	371,875	59.4	2.2	1.3	2.1	0.3	34.7	1	1	1	2	34.8	37.7	44.5	34.3	73.6	78.6	68.5	70.7	67.4	66.9	67.0
District 2	350,557	56.6	1.9	0.6	3.1	0.1	37.6	2	2	2	1	32.8	33.8	35.8	35.1	69.5	76.0	66.7	71.3	62.5	64.8	62.1
District 3	345,896	48.2	1.1	0.6	16.7	0.2	33.2	3	3	3	3	32.4	28.5	19.7	30.6	68.5	75.1	65.5	67.8	58.6	64.8	65.8

Table C. — Voter Participation: November 3, 1992, General Election

County	Estimated Voting Age Population (VAP), 1992	Voter registration (REG) Total	% contri- bution to state REG	% of 1992 VAP	Rank by % of 1992 VAP	Highest office Actual	Total	Office	% of 1992 VAP	Maximum vote Total	% contri- bution to state turnout	% of REG	Rank by % of REG	% of 1992 VAP	Rank by % 1992 VAP	President	Senator	Governor	Representative
Bernalillo	361,303	240,661	34.0	66.6	19	207,370	200,698	P	55.5	207,370	35.1	86.2	6	57.4	15	3.2	-	-	6.0
Catron	1,845	1,938	0.3	105.0	3	1,599	1,553	P	84.2	1,599	0.3	82.5	18	86.7	2	2.9	-	-	5.1
Chaves	41,033	23,735	3.4	57.8	27	19,578	18,898	P	46.1	19,578	3.3	82.5	19	47.7	27	3.5	-	-	4.7
Cibola	14,965	7,655	1.1	51.2	33	6,672	6,284	P	42.0	6,672	1.1	87.2	5	44.6	30	5.8	-	-	9.1
Colfax	9,093	6,323	0.9	69.5	14	5,386	5,228	P	57.5	5,386	0.9	85.2	10	59.2	11	2.9	-	-	3.0
Curry	29,118	15,390	2.2	52.9	32	12,867	12,633	P	43.4	12,867	2.2	83.6	15	44.2	32	1.8	-	-	3.7
DeBaca	1,656	1,424	0.2	86.0	6	1,222	1,185	P	71.6	1,222	0.2	85.8	8	73.8	6	3.0	-	-	4.0
Dona Ana	101,636	59,666	8.4	58.7	25	45,842	44,217	P	43.5	45,842	7.8	76.8	31	45.1	29	3.5	-	-	6.3
Eddy	33,909	21,932	3.1	64.7	21	18,851	18,202	P	53.7	18,851	3.2	86.0	7	55.6	19	3.4	-	-	3.9
Grant	19,437	13,315	1.9	68.5	17	10,787	10,277	P	52.9	10,787	1.8	81.0	25	55.5	20	4.7	-	-	7.3
Guadalupe	2,857	2,850	0.4	99.8	4	2,234	2,102	P	73.6	2,234	0.4	78.4	28	78.2	5	5.9	-	-	8.5
Harding	712	797	0.1	111.9	1	696	678	P	95.2	696	0.1	87.3	4	97.8	1	2.6	-	-	4.0
Hidalgo	4,055	2,906	0.4	71.7	12	2,391	2,315	P	57.1	2,391	0.4	82.3	21	59.0	12	3.2	-	-	4.6
Lea	37,354	20,768	2.9	55.6	30	17,122	16,311	P	43.7	17,122	2.9	82.4	20	45.8	28	4.7	-	-	8.5
Lincoln	9,234	6,618	0.9	71.7	11	6,034	5,857	P	63.4	6,034	1.0	91.2	2	65.3	8	2.9	-	-	3.7
Los Alamos	13,416	11,597	1.6	86.4	5	10,730	10,642	P	79.3	10,730	1.8	92.5	1	80.0	4	0.8	-	-	2.7
Luna	13,252	7,653	1.1	57.7	28	6,473	6,272	P	47.3	6,473	1.1	84.6	12	48.8	26	3.1	-	-	4.3
McKinley	37,915	21,236	3.0	56.0	29	16,302	15,531	P	41.0	16,302	2.8	76.8	32	43.0	33	4.7	-	-	7.3
Mora	3,046	3,285	0.5	107.8	2	2,553	2,421	P	79.5	2,553	0.4	77.7	29	83.8	3	5.2	-	-	9.5
Otero	37,014	19,857	2.8	53.6	31	16,493	16,203	P	43.8	16,493	2.8	83.1	16	44.6	31	1.8	-	-	4.6
Quay	7,947	5,094	0.7	64.1	22	4,474	4,289	P	54.0	4,474	0.8	87.8	3	56.3	17	4.1	-	-	5.7
Rio Arriba	24,102	15,972	2.3	66.3	20	12,067	11,542	P	47.9	12,067	2.0	75.6	33	50.1	23	4.4	-	-	7.3
Roosevelt	11,894	7,994	1.1	67.2	18	6,637	6,513	P	54.8	6,637	1.1	83.0	17	55.8	18	1.9	-	-	4.2
Sandoval	49,702	29,886	4.2	60.1	24	24,436	23,574	P	47.4	24,436	4.1	81.8	22	49.2	25	3.5	-	-	6.3
San Juan	60,419	36,770	5.2	60.9	23	31,498	30,281	P	50.1	31,498	5.3	85.7	9	52.1	22	3.9	-	-	5.5
San Miguel	18,242	12,777	1.8	70.0	13	9,860	9,387	P	51.5	9,860	1.7	77.2	30	54.1	21	4.8	-	-	7.8
Santa Fe	77,715	53,550	7.6	68.9	16	45,124	42,917	P	55.2	45,124	7.6	84.3	13	58.1	14	4.9	-	-	7.7
Sierra	8,126	5,648	0.8	69.5	15	4,589	4,418	P	54.4	4,589	0.8	81.3	24	56.5	16	3.7	-	-	6.6
Socorro	10,589	7,987	1.1	75.4	9	6,297	6,088	P	57.5	6,297	1.1	78.8	27	59.5	10	3.3	-	-	7.5
Taos	17,021	13,391	1.9	78.7	8	10,947	10,681	P	62.8	10,947	1.9	81.7	23	64.3	9	2.4	-	-	3.2
Torrance	7,690	5,618	0.8	73.1	10	4,482	4,167	P	54.2	4,482	0.8	79.8	26	58.3	13	7.0	-	-	8.2
Union	2,841	2,271	0.3	79.9	7	1,910	1,854	P	65.3	1,910	0.3	84.1	14	67.2	7	2.9	-	-	4.4
Valencia	34,862	20,402	2.9	58.5	26	17,378	16,768	P	48.1	17,378	2.9	85.2	11	49.8	24	3.5	-	-	4.7
NEW MEXICO	1,104,000	706,966	100.0	64.0		590,901	569,986		51.6	590,901	100.0	83.6		53.5		3.5	-	-	6.0

Table D. — Voter Registration by Political Party Affiliation: November 3, 1992, General Election

County	Total voter registration	Democrat (DEM)	Republican (REP)	Independent (IND)	Plurality Total	Plurality Party	DEM	REP	IND	Rank DEM	Rank REP	Rank IND	Total	DEM	REP	IND
Bernalillo	240,661	123,892	94,228	21,533	29,664	D	51.7	39.3	9.0	29	8	3	34.0	30.1	39.3	45.2
Catron	1,938	1,014	823	73	191	D	53.1	43.1	3.8	27	5	18	0.3	0.2	0.3	0.2
Chaves	23,735	10,757	11,249	1,200	492	R	46.4	48.5	5.2	31	2	14	3.4	2.6	4.7	2.5
Cibola	7,655	5,532	1,810	219	3,722	D	73.2	23.9	2.9	9	23	22	1.1	1.3	0.8	0.5
Colfax	6,323	4,427	1,615	275	2,812	D	70.1	25.6	4.4	12	21	16	0.9	1.1	0.7	0.6
Curry	15,390	8,948	5,568	849	3,380	D	58.2	36.2	5.5	20	11	11	2.2	2.2	2.3	1.8
DeBaca	1,424	1,190	218	3	972	D	84.3	15.5	0.2	2	32	33	0.2	0.3	<.1	<.1
Dona Ana	59,666	32,713	20,230	6,571	12,483	D	55.0	34.0	11.0	24	15	1	8.4	8.0	8.4	13.8
Eddy	21,932	15,205	6,053	642	9,152	D	69.4	27.6	2.9	14	20	21	3.1	3.7	2.5	1.3
Grant	13,315	9,593	2,875	796	6,718	D	72.3	21.7	6.0	10	25	8	1.9	2.3	1.2	1.7
Guadalupe	2,850	2,293	526	12	1,767	D	81.0	18.6	0.4	4	29	30	0.4	0.6	0.2	<.1
Harding	797	408	363	5	45	D	52.6	46.8	0.6	30	4	29	0.1	<.1	0.2	<.1
Hidalgo	2,906	2,333	512	23	1,821	D	81.3	17.9	0.8	5	30	28	0.4	0.6	0.2	<.1
Lea	20,768	12,246	7,477	1,010	4,769	D	59.1	36.1	4.9	19	12	15	2.9	3.0	3.1	2.1
Lincoln	6,618	2,694	3,669	187	975	R	41.1	56.0	2.9	33	1	23	0.9	0.7	1.5	0.4
Los Alamos	11,597	5,001	5,303	1,274	302	R	43.2	45.8	11.0	32	3	2	1.6	1.2	2.2	2.7
Luna	7,653	4,851	2,380	397	2,471	D	63.6	31.2	5.2	16	18	13	1.1	1.2	1.0	0.8
McKinley	21,236	15,379	4,203	1,417	11,176	D	73.2	20.0	6.7	8	27	6	3.0	3.7	1.8	3.0
Mora	3,285	2,390	805	12	1,585	D	74.5	25.1	0.4	7	22	31	0.5	0.6	0.3	<.1
Otero	19,857	10,417	8,053	1,282	2,364	D	52.7	40.8	6.5	26	7	7	2.8	2.5	3.4	2.7
Quay	5,094	3,852	1,122	116	2,730	D	75.7	22.0	2.3	6	24	24	0.7	0.9	0.5	0.2
Rio Arriba	15,972	13,741	1,864	56	11,877	D	87.7	11.9	0.4	1	33	32	2.3	3.3	0.8	0.1
Roosevelt	7,994	4,718	2,636	629	2,082	D	59.1	33.0	7.9	18	17	4	1.1	1.1	1.1	1.3
Sandoval	29,886	16,661	10,356	1,638	6,305	D	58.1	36.1	5.7	23	14	12	4.2	4.1	4.3	3.4
San Juan	36,770	19,030	15,468	2,054	3,562	D	52.1	42.3	5.6	28	6	10	5.2	4.6	6.5	4.3
San Miguel	12,777	10,312	2,001	167	8,311	D	82.6	16.0	1.3	3	31	26	1.8	2.5	0.8	0.4
Santa Fe	53,550	37,244	10,946	3,189	26,298	D	72.5	21.3	6.2	13	26	9	7.6	9.1	4.6	6.7
Sierra	5,648	3,055	2,156	415	899	D	54.3	38.3	7.4	25	9	5	0.8	0.7	0.9	0.9
Socorro	7,987	4,454	2,836	252	1,618	D	59.1	37.6	3.3	22	13	19	1.1	1.1	1.2	0.5
Taos	13,391	9,641	2,588	569	7,053	D	75.3	20.2	4.4	11	28	17	1.9	2.3	1.1	1.2
Torrance	5,618	3,247	2,131	112	1,116	D	59.1	38.8	2.0	21	10	25	0.8	0.8	0.9	0.2
Union	2,271	1,530	677	26	853	D	68.5	30.3	1.2	15	19	27	0.3	0.4	0.3	<.1
Valencia	20,402	12,495	6,732	642	5,763	D	62.9	33.9	3.2	17	16	20	2.9	3.0	2.8	1.3
NEW MEXICO[1]	**706,966**	**411,263**	**239,473**	**47,645**	**171,790**	**D**	**58.9**	**34.3**	**6.8**				**100.0**	**100.0**	**100.0**	**100.0**

[1]Total voter registration also includes 8,666 for other parties.

Table E. — Vote for President: November 3, 1992, General Election

County	Total	Clinton (DEM)	Bush (REP)	Perot (IND)	Other	Plurality Total	Plurality Party	Pct DEM	Pct REP	Pct IND	Pct Other	Rank DEM	Rank REP	Rank IND	Contrib Total	Contrib DEM	Contrib REP	Contrib IND	Major DEM	Major REP
Bernalillo	200,698	90,863	77,304	31,241	1,290	13,559	D	45.3	38.5	15.6	0.6	13	16	23	35.2	34.7	36.3	34.0	54.0	46.0
Catron	1,553	465	771	289	28	306	R	29.9	49.6	18.6	1.8	30	3	12	0.3	0.2	0.4	0.3	37.6	62.4
Chaves	18,898	6,360	8,872	3,590	76	2,512	R	33.7	46.9	19.0	0.4	26	6	10	3.3	2.4	4.2	3.9	41.8	58.2
Cibola	6,284	3,334	2,051	847	52	1,283	D	53.1	32.6	13.5	0.8	9	26	26	1.1	1.3	1.0	0.9	61.9	38.1
Colfax	5,228	2,607	1,730	871	20	877	D	49.9	33.1	16.7	0.4	10	24	19	0.9	1.0	0.8	0.9	60.1	39.9
Curry	12,633	3,699	6,831	2,056	47	3,132	R	29.3	54.1	16.3	0.4	32	1	22	2.2	1.4	3.2	2.2	35.1	64.9
DeBaca	1,185	451	526	204	4	75	R	38.1	44.4	17.2	0.3	23	10	17	0.2	0.2	0.2	0.2	46.2	53.8
Dona Ana	44,217	19,894	16,308	7,682	333	3,586	D	45.0	36.9	17.4	0.8	14	19	15	7.8	7.6	7.7	8.4	55.0	45.0
Eddy	18,202	7,409	7,313	3,430	50	96	D	40.7	40.2	18.8	0.3	19	14	11	3.2	2.8	3.4	3.7	50.3	49.7
Grant	10,277	5,603	2,917	1,685	72	2,686	D	54.5	28.4	16.4	0.7	8	28	21	1.8	2.1	1.4	1.8	65.8	34.2
Guadalupe	2,102	1,225	691	173	13	534	D	58.3	32.9	8.2	0.6	7	25	32	0.4	0.5	0.3	0.2	63.9	36.1
Harding	678	268	312	98	0	44	R	39.5	46.0	14.5	0.0	22	8	25	0.1	0.1	0.1	0.1	46.2	53.8
Hidalgo	2,315	995	871	442	7	124	R	43.0	37.6	19.1	0.3	16	17	9	0.4	0.4	0.4	0.5	53.3	46.7
Lea	16,311	5,047	7,921	3,233	110	2,874	R	30.9	48.6	19.8	0.7	29	5	6	2.9	1.9	3.7	3.5	38.9	61.1
Lincoln	5,857	1,730	2,669	1,431	27	939	R	29.5	45.6	24.4	0.5	31	9	1	1.0	0.7	1.3	1.6	39.3	60.7
Los Alamos	10,642	3,897	4,320	2,339	86	423	R	36.6	40.6	22.0	0.8	25	13	4	1.9	1.5	2.0	2.5	47.4	52.6
Luna	6,272	2,637	2,166	1,445	24	471	D	42.0	34.5	23.0	0.4	17	23	3	1.1	1.0	1.0	1.6	54.9	45.1
McKinley	15,531	9,405	4,720	1,304	102	4,685	D	60.6	30.4	8.4	0.7	6	27	31	2.7	3.6	2.2	1.4	66.6	33.4
Mora	2,421	1,555	668	188	10	887	D	64.2	27.6	7.8	0.4	4	29	33	0.4	0.6	0.3	0.2	70.0	30.0
Otero	16,203	5,377	7,481	3,257	88	2,104	R	33.2	46.2	20.1	0.5	28	7	5	2.8	2.1	3.5	3.5	41.8	58.2
Quay	4,289	1,758	1,759	755	17	1	R	41.0	41.0	17.6	0.4	18	12	14	0.8	0.7	0.8	0.8	50.0	50.0
Rio Arriba	11,542	7,832	2,680	984	46	5,152	D	67.9	23.2	8.5	0.4	1	31	30	2.0	3.0	1.3	1.1	74.5	25.5
Roosevelt	6,513	2,172	3,215	1,085	41	1,043	R	33.3	49.4	16.7	0.6	27	4	20	1.1	0.8	1.5	1.2	40.3	59.7
Sandoval	23,574	10,951	8,491	3,954	178	2,460	D	46.5	36.0	16.8	0.8	12	20	18	4.1	4.2	4.0	4.3	56.3	43.7
San Juan	30,281	11,302	13,415	5,351	213	2,113	R	37.3	44.3	17.7	0.7	24	11	13	5.3	4.3	6.3	5.8	45.7	54.3
San Miguel	9,387	6,186	2,183	965	53	4,003	D	65.9	23.3	10.3	0.6	3	30	29	1.6	2.4	1.0	1.1	73.9	26.1
Santa Fe	42,917	27,189	9,684	5,656	388	17,505	D	63.4	22.6	13.2	0.9	5	32	27	7.5	10.4	4.6	6.2	73.7	26.3
Sierra	4,418	1,771	1,562	1,055	30	209	D	40.1	35.4	23.9	0.7	20	22	2	0.8	0.7	0.7	1.1	53.1	46.9
Socorro	6,088	2,908	2,186	918	76	722	D	47.8	35.9	15.1	1.2	11	21	24	1.1	1.1	1.0	1.0	57.1	42.9
Taos	10,681	7,051	2,260	1,300	70	4,791	D	66.0	21.2	12.2	0.7	2	33	28	1.9	2.7	1.1	1.4	75.7	24.3
Torrance	4,167	1,662	1,667	810	28	5	R	39.9	40.0	19.4	0.7	21	15	7	0.7	0.6	0.8	0.9	49.9	50.1
Union	1,854	519	975	355	5	456	R	28.0	52.6	19.1	0.3	33	2	8	0.3	0.2	0.5	0.4	34.7	65.3
Valencia	16,768	7,495	6,305	2,902	66	1,190	D	44.7	37.6	17.3	0.4	15	18	16	2.9	2.9	3.0	3.2	54.3	45.7
NEW MEXICO	569,986	261,617	212,824	91,895	3,650	48,793	D	45.9	37.3	16.1	0.6				100.0	100.0	100.0	100.0	55.1	44.9

Congressional district and county	Total	Democrat (DEM)	Republican (REP)	Other	Plurality Total	Plurality Party	Percent of total vote DEM	Percent of total vote REP	Percent of total vote Other	Rank within district DEM	Rank within district REP	Rank within district Other	Percent contribution to district vote Total	Percent contribution to district vote DEM	Percent contribution to district vote REP	Percent contribution to district vote Other
District 1	**205,214**	**76,600**	**128,426**	188	**51,826**	**R**	**37.3**	**62.6**	**<.1**				**100.0**	**100.0**	**100.0**	**100.0**
Bernalillo (pt)	190,996	70,523	120,294	179	49,771	R	36.9	63.0	<.1	4	3	2	93.1	92.1	93.7	95.2
Sandoval (pt)	4,799	2,433	2,363	3	70	D	50.7	49.2	<.1	1	5	3	2.3	3.2	1.8	1.6
Santa Fe (pt)	654	180	474	0	294	R	27.5	72.5	0.0	5	1	4	0.3	0.2	0.4	0.0
Torrance	4,114	1,521	2,593	0	1,072	R	37.0	63.0	0.0	3	2	5	2.0	2.0	2.0	0.0
Valencia (pt)	4,651	1,943	2,702	6	759	R	41.8	58.1	0.1	2	4	1	2.3	2.5	2.1	3.2
District 2	**168,170**	**73,157**	**94,838**	175	**21,681**	**R**	**43.5**	**56.4**	**0.1**				**100.0**	**100.0**	**100.0**	**100.0**
Bernalillo (pt)	433	256	177	0	79	D	59.1	40.9	0.0	1	17	13	0.3	0.3	0.2	0.0
Catron	1,517	513	1,004	0	491	R	33.8	66.2	0.0	17	1	14	0.9	0.7	1.1	0.0
Chaves	18,651	7,102	11,511	38	4,409	R	38.1	61.7	0.2	12	6	2	11.1	9.7	12.1	21.7
Cibola (pt)	5,576	2,865	2,710	1	155	D	51.4	48.6	<.1	4	14	12	3.3	3.9	2.9	0.6
DeBaca	1,173	436	737	0	301	R	37.2	62.8	0.0	13	5	15	0.7	0.6	0.8	0.0
Dona Ana	42,954	20,585	22,324	45	1,739	R	47.9	52.0	0.1	7	11	5	25.5	28.1	23.5	25.7
Eddy	18,110	7,453	10,643	14	3,190	R	41.2	58.8	<.1	11	7	8	10.8	10.2	11.2	8.0
Grant	9,997	5,347	4,644	6	703	D	53.5	46.5	<.1	3	15	10	5.9	7.3	4.9	3.4
Guadalupe	2,045	1,182	863	0	319	D	57.8	42.2	0.0	2	16	16	1.2	1.6	0.9	0.0
Hidalgo	2,281	1,066	1,215	0	149	R	46.7	53.3	0.0	9	9	17	1.4	1.5	1.3	0.0
Lea	15,672	5,318	10,334	20	5,016	R	33.9	65.9	0.1	16	2	3	9.3	7.3	10.9	11.4
Lincoln	5,813	2,110	3,691	12	1,581	R	36.3	63.5	0.2	14	4	1	3.5	2.9	3.9	6.9
Luna	6,192	2,966	3,221	5	255	R	47.9	52.0	<.1	8	10	7	3.7	4.1	3.4	2.9
Otero	15,738	5,522	10,197	19	4,675	R	35.1	64.8	0.1	15	3	4	9.4	7.5	10.8	10.9
Sierra	4,284	1,847	2,433	4	586	R	43.1	56.8	<.1	10	8	6	2.5	2.5	2.6	2.3
Socorro	5,822	2,818	3,001	3	183	R	48.4	51.5	<.1	6	12	11	3.5	3.9	3.2	1.7
Valencia (pt)	11,912	5,771	6,133	8	362	R	48.4	51.5	<.1	5	13	9	7.1	7.9	6.5	4.6
District 3	**182,217**	**122,850**	**54,569**	4,798	**68,281**	**D**	**67.4**	**29.9**	**2.6**				**100.0**	**100.0**	**100.0**	**100.0**
Bernalillo (pt)	3,454	1,788	1,565	101	223	D	51.8	45.3	2.9	17	1	5	1.9	1.5	2.9	2.1
Cibola (pt)	487	383	92	12	291	D	78.6	18.9	2.5	4	14	8	0.3	0.3	0.2	0.3
Colfax	5,225	3,748	1,403	74	2,345	D	71.7	26.9	1.4	9	9	15	2.9	3.1	2.6	1.5
Curry	12,389	7,192	4,995	202	2,197	D	58.1	40.3	1.6	14	4	13	6.8	5.9	9.2	4.2
Harding	668	477	180	11	297	D	71.4	26.9	1.6	10	8	12	0.4	0.4	0.3	0.2
Los Alamos	10,444	5,547	4,490	407	1,057	D	53.1	43.0	3.9	16	2	1	5.7	4.5	8.2	8.5
McKinley	15,116	11,827	3,054	235	8,773	D	78.2	20.2	1.6	5	13	14	8.3	9.6	5.6	4.9
Mora	2,310	1,805	479	26	1,326	D	78.1	20.7	1.1	6	12	17	1.3	1.5	0.9	0.5
Quay	4,219	3,098	1,047	74	2,051	D	73.4	24.8	1.8	7	10	10	2.3	2.5	1.9	1.5
Rio Arriba	11,187	8,966	2,069	152	6,897	D	80.1	18.5	1.4	2	15	16	6.1	7.3	3.8	3.2
Roosevelt	6,355	4,039	2,180	136	1,859	D	63.6	34.3	2.1	12	6	9	3.5	3.3	4.0	2.8
Sandoval (pt)	18,104	10,530	7,031	543	3,499	D	58.2	38.8	3.0	13	5	4	9.9	8.6	12.9	11.3
San Juan	29,760	16,273	12,655	832	3,618	D	54.7	42.5	2.8	15	3	6	16.3	13.2	23.2	17.3
San Miguel	9,087	7,477	1,451	159	6,026	D	82.3	16.0	1.7	1	17	11	5.0	6.1	2.7	3.3
Santa Fe (pt)	40,984	30,076	9,522	1,386	20,554	D	73.4	23.2	3.4	8	11	3	22.5	24.5	17.4	28.9
Taos	10,602	8,428	1,772	402	6,656	D	79.5	16.7	3.8	3	16	2	5.8	6.9	3.2	8.4
Union	1,826	1,196	584	46	612	D	65.5	32.0	2.5	11	7	7	1.0	1.0	1.1	1.0
NEW MEXICO	**555,601**	**272,607**	**277,833**	**5,161**	**5,226**	**R**	**49.1**	**50.0**	**0.9**							

Table I. — Vote for Presidential Preference: June 2, 1992, Democratic Primary Election

County	Top candidates									Top three candidates (state vote)									
										Percent of total vote			Rank			Percent contribution to state vote			
	Total	Clinton	Uncom-mitted	Brown	Tsongas	Harkin	Agran	LaRouche		Clinton	Uncom-mitted	Brown	Clinton	Uncom-mitted	Brown	Total	Clinton	Uncom-mitted	Brown
Bernalillo	50,477	23,949	11,726	10,348	3,155	399	505	395	-	47.4	23.2	20.5	30	8	3	27.8	25.0	33.2	33.7
Catron	484	246	66	72	49	15	21	15	-	50.8	13.6	14.9	26	25	13	0.3	0.3	0.2	0.2
Chaves	3,931	1,989	914	438	308	129	54	99	-	50.6	23.3	11.1	27	7	25	2.2	2.1	2.6	1.4
Cibola	3,079	1,891	380	420	200	26	68	94	-	61.4	12.3	13.6	7	26	18	1.7	2.0	1.1	1.4
Colfax	2,497	1,399	359	449	177	66	24	23	-	56.0	14.4	18.0	17	23	5	1.4	1.5	1.0	1.5
Curry	3,418	2,070	710	296	222	62	20	38	-	60.6	20.8	8.7	8	13	31	1.9	2.2	2.0	1.0
DeBaca	768	439	161	70	52	15	16	15	-	57.2	21.0	9.1	14	12	29	0.4	0.5	0.5	0.2
Dona Ana	12,555	6,925	2,306	1,786	1,013	227	123	175	-	55.2	18.4	14.2	18	20	16	6.9	7.2	6.5	5.8
Eddy	6,452	3,342	1,473	580	540	171	193	153	-	51.8	22.8	9.0	23	9	30	3.6	3.5	4.2	1.9
Grant	4,649	2,762	933	544	259	75	22	54	-	59.4	20.1	11.7	9	14	22	2.6	2.9	2.6	1.8
Guadalupe	1,582	1,121	86	250	71	17	22	15	-	70.9	5.4	15.8	2	32	9	0.9	1.2	0.2	0.8
Harding	247	166	26	28	12	7	8	0	-	67.2	10.5	11.3	3	27	24	0.1	0.2	<.1	<.1
Hidalgo	1,344	780	229	128	123	43	19	22	-	58.0	17.0	9.5	11	22	26	0.7	0.8	0.6	0.4
Lea	3,984	2,292	864	337	246	62	102	81	-	57.5	21.7	8.5	13	11	33	2.2	2.4	2.4	1.1
Lincoln	1,311	632	343	197	82	28	12	17	-	48.2	26.2	15.0	29	4	12	0.7	0.7	1.0	0.6
Los Alamos	2,315	829	701	337	365	40	26	17	-	35.8	30.3	14.6	33	2	15	1.3	0.9	2.0	1.1
Luna	1,952	871	594	271	114	40	23	39	-	44.6	30.4	13.9	32	1	17	1.1	0.9	1.7	0.9
McKinley	7,777	4,830	695	1,010	483	312	204	243	-	62.1	8.9	13.0	6	31	19	4.3	5.0	2.0	3.3
Mora	1,550	1,122	71	230	60	28	19	20	-	72.4	4.6	14.8	1	33	14	0.9	1.2	0.2	0.7
Otero	4,866	2,532	1,396	416	295	105	45	77	-	52.0	28.7	8.5	22	3	32	2.7	2.6	4.0	1.4
Quay	2,428	1,397	483	230	165	44	80	29	-	57.5	19.9	9.5	12	16	27	1.3	1.5	1.4	0.7
Rio Arriba	7,715	5,069	755	1,171	321	174	128	97	-	65.7	9.8	15.2	5	29	11	4.2	5.3	2.1	3.8
Roosevelt	1,526	888	362	143	73	31	8	21	-	58.2	23.7	9.4	10	6	28	0.8	0.9	1.0	0.5
Sandoval	7,440	3,840	1,440	1,453	420	99	77	111	-	51.6	19.4	19.5	25	19	4	4.1	4.0	4.1	4.7
San Juan	7,570	4,160	1,499	868	482	350	102	109	-	55.0	19.8	11.5	19	17	23	4.2	4.3	4.3	2.8
San Miguel	6,111	4,025	612	985	225	153	64	47	-	65.9	10.0	16.1	4	28	8	3.4	4.2	1.7	3.2
Santa Fe	16,186	7,352	3,148	4,474	848	165	94	105	-	45.4	19.4	27.6	31	18	1	8.9	7.7	8.9	14.6
Sierra	1,323	742	322	157	44	19	17	22	-	56.1	24.3	11.9	16	5	21	0.7	0.8	0.9	0.5
Socorro	1,975	1,059	271	311	185	41	69	39	-	53.6	13.7	15.7	20	24	10	1.1	1.1	0.8	1.0
Taos	5,407	2,795	512	1,326	334	138	169	133	-	51.7	9.5	24.5	24	30	2	3.0	2.9	1.5	4.3
Torrance	1,609	909	321	272	56	18	15	18	-	56.5	20.0	16.9	15	15	6	0.9	0.9	0.9	0.9
Union	781	415	140	97	62	16	31	20	-	53.1	17.9	12.4	21	21	20	0.4	0.4	0.4	0.3
Valencia	6,228	3,095	1,371	1,011	368	118	193	72	-	49.7	22.0	16.2	28	10	7	3.4	3.2	3.9	3.3
NEW MEXICO	**181,537**	**95,933**	**35,269**	**30,705**	**11,409**	**3,233**	**2,573**	**2,415**	**-**	**52.8**	**19.4**	**16.9**				**100.0**	**100.0**	**100.0**	**100.0**

Table J. — Vote for Presidential Preference: June 2, 1992, Republican Primary Election

County	Top candidates Total	Bush	Uncommitted	Buchanan		Percent of total vote Bush	Uncommitted	Buchanan		Rank Bush	Uncommitted	Buchanan		Percent contribution to state vote Total	Bush	Uncommitted	Buchanan	
Bernalillo	34,609	22,118	9,799	2,692	-	63.9	28.3	7.8	-	21	11	26	-	39.8	39.8	41.6	34.2	-
Catron	413	246	113	54	-	59.6	27.4	13.1	-	29	13	3	-	0.5	0.4	0.5	0.7	-
Chaves	4,852	3,005	1,430	417	-	61.9	29.5	8.6	-	23	8	23	-	5.6	5.4	6.1	5.3	-
Cibola	815	566	153	96	-	69.4	18.8	11.8	-	12	25	11	-	0.9	1.0	0.6	1.2	-
Colfax	682	451	142	89	-	66.1	20.8	13.0	-	19	22	4	-	0.8	0.8	0.6	1.1	-
Curry	1,446	1,057	206	183	-	73.1	14.2	12.7	-	6	28	7	-	1.7	1.9	0.9	2.3	-
DeBaca	103	76	24	3	-	73.8	23.3	2.9	-	4	15	33	-	0.1	0.1	0.1	<.1	-
Dona Ana	5,801	3,518	1,698	585	-	60.6	29.3	10.1	-	27	9	19	-	6.7	6.3	7.2	7.4	-
Eddy	1,903	1,172	586	145	-	61.6	30.8	7.6	-	24	6	27	-	2.2	2.1	2.5	1.8	-
Grant	1,077	605	383	89	-	56.2	35.6	8.3	-	31	4	24	-	1.2	1.1	1.6	1.1	-
Guadalupe	291	229	26	36	-	78.7	8.9	12.4	-	1	32	10	-	0.3	0.4	0.1	0.5	-
Harding	224	161	29	34	-	71.9	12.9	15.2	-	9	31	1	-	0.3	0.3	0.1	0.4	-
Hidalgo	263	186	57	20	-	70.7	21.7	7.6	-	11	20	28	-	0.3	0.3	0.2	0.3	-
Lea	2,058	1,400	474	184	-	68.0	23.0	8.9	-	15	16	20	-	2.4	2.5	2.0	2.3	-
Lincoln	1,888	1,224	465	199	-	64.8	24.6	10.5	-	20	14	14	-	2.2	2.2	2.0	2.5	-
Los Alamos	1,995	1,128	723	144	-	56.5	36.2	7.2	-	30	3	32	-	2.3	2.0	3.1	1.8	-
Luna	882	471	322	89	-	53.4	36.5	10.1	-	33	2	18	-	1.0	0.8	1.4	1.1	-
McKinley	1,720	1,268	229	223	-	73.7	13.3	13.0	-	5	29	5	-	2.0	2.3	1.0	2.8	-
Mora	463	363	41	59	-	78.4	8.9	12.7	-	2	33	6	-	0.5	0.7	0.2	0.7	-
Otero	3,166	1,922	1,015	229	-	60.7	32.1	7.2	-	26	5	31	-	3.6	3.5	4.3	2.9	-
Quay	475	329	109	37	-	69.3	22.9	7.8	-	13	17	25	-	0.5	0.6	0.5	0.5	-
Rio Arriba	719	523	105	91	-	72.7	14.6	12.7	-	8	27	8	-	0.8	0.9	0.4	1.2	-
Roosevelt	875	623	162	90	-	71.2	18.5	10.3	-	10	26	17	-	1.0	1.1	0.7	1.1	-
Sandoval	3,441	2,096	953	392	-	60.9	27.7	11.4	-	25	12	13	-	4.0	3.8	4.0	5.0	-
San Juan	5,452	3,669	1,154	629	-	67.3	21.2	11.5	-	16	21	12	-	6.3	6.6	4.9	8.0	-
San Miguel	855	634	113	108	-	74.2	13.2	12.6	-	3	30	9	-	1.0	1.1	0.5	1.4	-
Santa Fe	3,510	1,959	1,294	257	-	55.8	36.9	7.3	-	32	1	30	-	4.0	3.5	5.5	3.3	-
Sierra	990	591	296	103	-	59.7	29.9	10.4	-	28	7	15	-	1.1	1.1	1.3	1.3	-
Socorro	1,152	771	262	119	-	66.9	22.7	10.3	-	18	18	16	-	1.3	1.4	1.1	1.5	-
Taos	1,017	682	193	142	-	67.1	19.0	14.0	-	17	24	2	-	1.2	1.2	0.8	1.8	-
Torrance	996	688	220	88	-	69.1	22.1	8.8	-	14	19	21	-	1.1	1.2	0.9	1.1	-
Union	224	163	44	17	-	72.8	19.6	7.6	-	7	23	29	-	0.3	0.3	0.2	0.2	-
Valencia	2,610	1,628	754	228	-	62.4	28.9	8.7	-	22	10	22	-	3.0	2.9	3.2	2.9	-
NEW MEXICO	86,967	55,522	23,574	7,871	-	63.8	27.1	9.1	-					100.0	100.0	100.0	100.0	-

1992 Vote for President
Percent for Clinton (D), by County

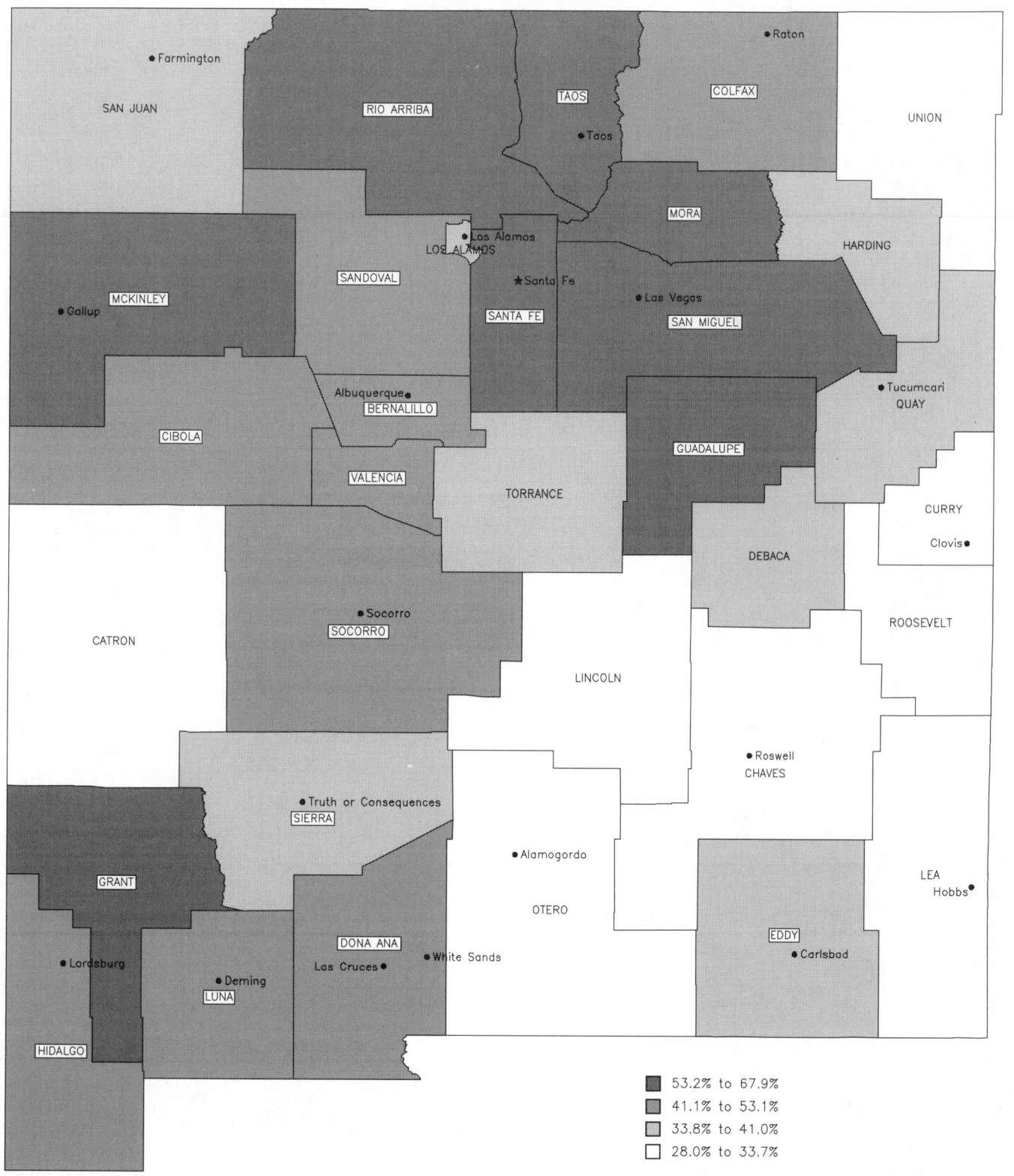

53.2% to 67.9%
41.1% to 53.1%
33.8% to 41.0%
28.0% to 33.7%

Clinton (D) received 45.9% statewide.

A framed county name indicates
a county carried by the winner.

Copyright © 1993 by Election Data Services, Inc.

New Mexico 645

NEW YORK

Congressional Districts 31
 Average Population 580,337
State Senate Districts 61
 Average Population 294,925
State House Districts 150
 Average Population 119,936

Electoral College Votes.....................................33
Counties 62
Voting Precincts 14,942

Alternative Registration Methods:
.... Agency-based, Mail-in, Motor-voter

Registration Deadline (Days before Election) 25

Population Statistics 1990

Race/Ethnicity	Total Population		Voting Age Population		Voting Age Population % of total population
	Number	%	Number	%	
Non-Hispanic					
White	12,460,189	69.3	9,816,664	71.5	78.8
Black	2,569,126	14.3	1,823,478	13.3	71.0
Asian/Pacific Islander	666,843	3.7	501,729	3.7	75.2
Native American	50,540	0.3	35,649	0.3	70.5
Other	29,731	0.2	15,330	0.1	51.6
All Hispanic	2,214,026	12.3	1,538,056	11.2	69.5
TOTAL	17,990,455	100.0	13,730,906	100.0	76.3

Voting Equipment Use (Counties)

Datavote Punch Card	0	Paper Ballot	0
Electronic	0	Other Punch Card	0
Lever Machine	61	Mixed Systems	1
Optical Scanner	0		

Party Control	DEM	REP	IND	VAC
1993 State Senate	26	35	0	0
1992 State Senate	26	35	0	0
1993 State House	101	49	0	0
1992 State House	95	55	0	0

Estimated Voting Age Population 1992 (VAP) 13,609,000
Number of Registered Voters................................. 9,193,391
 % of estimated VAP..................................... 67.6
Voter Turnout (Actual) 7,068,630
 % of VAP 51.9
 % of Registration 76.9
Persons Not Voting—of Voting Age 6,540,370
 % of VAP 48.1
Persons Not Voting—of Registered 2,124,761
 % of Registration 23.1
Straight Ticket Voting .... No

State Officials and Members of Congress

Governor:
Mario M. Cuomo (D) 1982, elected to a four-year term in 1990.

U.S. Senators:
Daniel Patrick Moynihan (D) 1976, elected to a six-year term in 1988.
Alfonse M. D'Amato (R) 1980, elected to a six-year term in 1992.

U.S. Representative in Congress:
(District, Name, Party, Date first elected)

1. Hochbrueckner (D) 1986
2. Lazio (R) 1992
3. King (R) 1992
4. Levy (R) 1992
5. Ackerman (D) 1983
6. Flake (D) 1986
7. Manton (D) 1984
8. Nadler (D) 1992
9. Schumer (D) 1980
10. Towns (D) 1982
11. Owens (D) 1982
12. Velazquez (D) 1992
13. Molinari (R) 1990
14. Maloney (D) 1992
15. Rangel (D) 1970
16. Serrano (D) 1990
17. Engel (D) 1988
18. Lowey (D) 1988
19. Fish Jr. (R) 1968
20. Gilman (R) 1972
21. McNulty (D) 1988
22. Solomon (R) 1978
23. Boehlert (R) 1982
24. McHugh (R) 1992
25. Walsh (R) 1988
26. Hinchey (D) 1992
27. Paxon (R) 1988
28. Slaughter (D) 1986
29. LaFalce (D) 1974
30. Quinn (R) 1992
31. Houghton (R) 1986

Candidates: General Election, November 3, 1992

Candidate(s)	Total vote	Percent	Party	Status	First elected
President/Vice President					
Clinton/Gore	3,444,450	49.73%	Total	Challenger	1992
	(3,346,894)	(97.17)	Democrat		
	(97,556)	(2.83)	Liberal		
Bush/Quayle	2,346,649	33.88%	Total	Incumbent	1988
	(2,041,690)	(87.00)	Republican		
	(177,000)	(7.54)	Conservative		
	(127,959)	(5.45)	Right to Life		
Perot/Stockdale	1,090,721	15.75%	No Party	Challenger	
Warren/Debates	15,472	0.22%	Socialist Workers	Challenger	
Marrou/Lord	13,451	0.19%	Libertarian	Challenger	
Fulani/Munoz	11,318	0.16%	New Alliance	Challenger	
Hagelin/Tompkins	4,420	0.06%	Natural Law	Challenger	
Daniels/Tupahache	385	<.01%	Write in	Challenger	
Gritz/Minett	23	<.01%	Write in	Challenger	
LaRouche/Bevel	20	<.01%	Write in	Challenger	
Brisben/Garson	16	<.01%	Write in	Challenger	
U.S. Senator					
Alfonse M. D'Amato	3,166,994	49.03%	Total	Incumbent	1980
	(2,652,822)	(83.76)	Republican		
	(289,258)	(9.13)	Conservative		
	(224,914)	(7.10)	Right to Life		
Robert Abrams	3,086,200	47.78%	Total	Challenger	
	(2,943,001)	(95.36)	Democrat		
	(143,199)	(4.64)	Liberal		
Norma Segal	108,530	1.68%	Libertarian	Challenger	
Mohammad Mehdi	56,631	0.88%	New Alliance	Challenger	
Stanley Nelson	23,747	0.37%	Natural Law	Challenger	
Ed Warren	16,724	0.26%	Socialist Workers	Challenger	
Governor (No Contest)					
U.S. Representative in Congress					
District 1					
George Hochbrueckner	117,940	51.73%	Total	Incumbent	1986
	(111,908)	(94.89)	Democrat		
	(6,032)	(5.11)	Long Island First		
Edward Romaine	110,043	48.27%	Total	Challenger	
	(87,248)	(79.29)	Republican		
	(11,785)	(10.71)	Conservative		
	(11,010)	(10.01)	Right to Life		
District 2					
Rick Lazio	109,386	53.17%	Total	Challenger	1992
	(94,208)	(86.12)	Republican		
	(15,178)	(13.88)	Conservative		
Thomas Downey	96,328	46.83%	Total	Incumbent	1974
	(91,320)	(94.80)	Democrat		
	(5,008)	(5.20)	Long Island First		
District 3					
Peter King	124,727	49.57%	Total	Challenger	1992
	(108,574)	(87.05)	Republican		
	(16,153)	(12.95)	Conservative		
Steve Orlins	116,915	46.46%	Democrat	Challenger	
Louis Roccanova	6,888	2.74%	Right to Life	Challenger	
Ben-Zion Heyman	3,092	1.23%	Liberal	Challenger	

Candidate(s)	Total vote	Percent	Party	Status	First elected
U.S. Representative in Congress (cont)					
District 4					
David Levy	110,710	50.18%	Total	Challenger	1992
	(98,723)	(89.17)	Republican		
	(11,987)	(10.83)	Conservative		
Philip Schiliro	100,386	45.50%	Total	Challenger	
	(97,007)	(96.63)	Democrat		
	(3,379)	(3.37)	Liberal		
Vincent Garbitelli	9,548	4.33%	Right to Life	Challenger	
District 5					
Gary Ackerman	110,476	52.40%	Total	Incumbent	1983
	(105,953)	(95.91)	Democrat		
	(4,523)	(4.09)	Liberal		
Allan Binder	94,907	45.02%	Total	Challenger	
	(82,883)	(87.33)	Republican		
	(12,024)	(12.67)	Conservative		
Andrew Duff	5,448	2.58%	Right to Life	Challenger	
District 6					
Floyd Flake	96,972	81.04%	Democrat	Incumbent	1986
Dianand Bhagwandin	22,687	18.96%	Total	Challenger	
	(18,725)	(82.54)	Republican		
	(3,962)	(17.46)	Conservative		
District 7					
Thomas Manton	72,280	56.95%	Democrat	Incumbent	1984
Dennis Shea	54,639	43.05%	Total	Challenger	
	(46,218)	(84.59)	Republican		
	(8,421)	(15.41)	Conservative		
District 8					
Jerrold Nadler	138,296	81.23%	Total	Challenger	1992
	(132,172)	(95.57)	Democrat		
	(6,124)	(4.43)	Liberal		
David Askren	25,548	15.01%	Republican	Challenger	
Margaret Byrnes	5,180	3.04%	Conservative	Challenger	
Arthur Block	1,224	0.72%	New Alliance	Challenger	
District 9					
Charles Schumer	116,545	88.61%	Total	Incumbent	1980
	(111,424)	(95.61)	Democrat		
	(5,121)	(4.39)	Liberal		
Alice Gaffney	14,985	11.39%	Conservative	Challenger	
District 10					
Edolphus Towns	97,509	95.76%	Total	Incumbent	1982
	(93,801)	(96.20)	Democrat		
	(3,708)	(3.80)	Liberal		
Owen Augustin	4,315	4.24%	Conservative	Challenger	
District 11					
Major Owens	80,028	93.61%	Total	Incumbent	1982
	(76,724)	(95.87)	Democrat		
	(3,304)	(4.13)	Liberal		
Michael Gaffney	4,287	5.01%	Conservative	Challenger	
Ernest Foster	1,179	1.38%	New Alliance	Challenger	
District 12					
Nydia Velazquez	55,926	76.54%	Democrat	Challenger	1992
Angel Diaz	14,976	20.50%	Total	Challenger	
	(12,288)	(82.05)	Republican		
	(1,535)	(10.25)	Conservative		
	(1,153)	(7.70)	Right to Life		
Ruben Franco	1,556	2.13%	Liberal	Challenger	
Rafael Mendez	609	0.83%	New Alliance	Challenger	

Candidate(s)	Total vote	Percent	Party	Status	First elected
U.S. Representative in Congress (cont)					
District 13					
Susan Molinari	107,903	56.13%	Total	Incumbent	1990
	(92,144)	(85.40)	Republican		
	(15,759)	(14.60)	Conservative		
Sal Albanese	73,520	38.24%	Total	Challenger	
	(68,738)	(93.50)	Democrat		
	(4,782)	(6.50)	Liberal		
Kathleen Murphy	10,825	5.63%	Right to Life	Challenger	
District 14					
Carolyn Maloney	101,652	50.36%	Total	Challenger	1992
	(97,059)	(95.48)	Democrat		
	(4,593)	(4.52)	Liberal		
Bill Green	97,215	48.17%	Republican	Incumbent	
	(92,034)	(94.67)	Republican		
	(5,181)	(5.33)	Independent Neighbors		
Abraham Hirschfeld	2,970	1.47%	Independent Fusion	Challenger	
District 15					
Charles Rangel	105,011	94.87%	Total	Incumbent	1970
	(101,229)	(96.40)	Democrat		
	(3,782)	(3.60)	Liberal		
Jose Suero	4,345	3.93%	Total	Challenger	
	(3,425)	(78.83)	Conservative		
	(920)	(21.17)	Independent Fusion		
Jessie Fields	1,337	1.21%	New Alliance	Challenger	
District 16					
Jose Serrano	85,222	91.44%	Total	Incumbent	1990
	(80,927)	(94.96)	Democrat		
	(4,295)	(5.04)	Liberal		
Michael Walters	7,975	8.56%	Total	Challenger	
	(6,741)	(84.53)	Republican		
	(1,234)	(15.47)	Conservative		
District 17					
Eliot Engel	98,068	80.13%	Total	Incumbent	1988
	(94,758)	(96.62)	Democrat		
	(3,310)	(3.38)	Liberal		
Martin Richman	16,511	13.49%	Republican	Challenger	
Kevin Brawley	3,143	2.57%	Conservative	Challenger	
Martin O'Grady	3,067	2.51%	Right to Life	Challenger	
Nana LaLuz	1,592	1.30%	Natural Law	Challenger	
District 18					
Nita Lowey	115,841	55.55%	Democrat	Incumbent	1988
Joseph DioGuardi	92,687	44.45%	Total	Challenger	
	(74,076)	(79.92)	Republican		
	(11,027)	(11.90)	Conservative		
	(7,584)	(8.18)	Right to Life		
District 19					
Hamilton Fish, Jr.	139,610	60.06%	Total	Incumbent	1968
	(119,047)	(85.27)	Republican		
	(20,563)	(14.73)	Conservative		
Neil McCarthy	92,854	39.94%	Democrat	Challenger	
District 20					
Benjamin Gilman	150,301	66.12%	Republican	Incumbent	1972
Jonathan Levine	66,826	29.40%	Democrat	Challenger	
Robert Garrison	10,204	4.49%	Right to Life	Challenger	

Candidate(s)	Total vote	Percent	Party	Status	First elected
U.S. Representative in Congress (cont)					
District 21					
Michael McNulty	166,371	62.72%	Total	Incumbent	1988
	(149,319)	(89.75)	Democrat		
	(17,052)	(10.25)	Conservative		
Nancy Norman	91,184	34.37%	Total	Challenger	
	(83,845)	(91.95)	Republican		
	(7,339)	(8.05)	Liberal		
William Donnelly	7,723	2.91%	Right to Life	Challenger	
District 22					
Gerald Solomon	164,436	65.43%	Total	Incumbent	1978
	(136,909)	(83.26)	Republican		
	(16,085)	(9.78)	Conservative		
	(11,442)	(6.96)	Right to Life		
David Roberts	86,896	34.57%	Democrat	Challenger	
District 23					
Sherwood Boehlert	139,774	63.63%	Republican	Incumbent	1982
Paula DiPerna	61,835	28.15%	Democrat	Challenger	
Randall Terry	8,688	3.96%	Right to Life	Challenger	
Geoffrey Grace	8,011	3.65%	Conservative	Challenger	
Ted Janowski	1,354	0.62%	Natural Law	Challenger	
District 24					
John McHugh	122,257	60.80%	Total	Challenger	1992
	(113,408)	(92.76)	Republican		
	(8,849)	(7.24)	Voter Rights		
Margaret Ravenscroft	47,675	23.71%	Democrat	Challenger	
Morrison Hosley, Jr.	26,763	13.31%	Total	Challenger	
	(17,484)	(65.33)	Conservative		
	(9,279)	(34.67)	Right to Life		
Stephen Burke	4,374	2.18%	Liberal	Challenger	
District 25					
James Walsh	135,076	55.73%	Total	Incumbent	1988
	(119,282)	(88.31)	Republican		
	(15,794)	(11.69)	Conservative		
Rhea Jezer	107,310	44.27%	Total	Challenger	
	(101,422)	(94.51)	Democrat		
	(5,888)	(5.49)	Common Sense		
District 26					
Maurice Hinchey	119,557	50.42%	Total	Challenger	1992
	(112,763)	(94.32)	Democrat		
	(6,794)	(5.68)	Liberal		
Bob Moppert	110,738	46.70%	Total	Challenger	
	(98,389)	(88.85)	Republican		
	(12,349)	(11.15)	Conservative		
Mary Dixon	6,821	2.88%	Right to Life	Challenger	
District 27					
Bill Paxon	156,596	63.53%	Total	Incumbent	1988
	(126,997)	(81.10)	Republican		
	(17,386)	(11.10)	Conservative		
	(12,213)	(7.80)	Right to Life		
W. Douglas Call	89,906	36.47%	Democrat	Challenger	
District 28					
Louise Slaughter	140,908	55.24%	Democrat	Incumbent	1986
William Polito	112,273	44.02%	Total	Challenger	
	(93,806)	(83.55)	Republican		
	(18,467)	(16.45)	Conservative		
Keith Perez	1,897	0.74%	Economic Justice	Challenger	

Candidate(s)	Total vote	Percent	Party	Status	First elected
U.S. Representative in Congress (cont)					
District 29					
John LaFalce	128,230	54.46%	Total	Incumbent	1974
	(120,758)	(94.17)	Democrat		
	(7,472)	(5.83)	Liberal		
William Miller, Jr.	98,031	41.63%	Total	Challenger	
	(85,294)	(87.01)	Republican		
	(12,737)	(12.99)	Conservative		
Kenneth Kowalski	7,367	3.13%	Right to Life	Challenger	
John Basar, Jr.	1,830	0.78%	Economic Justice	Challenger	
District 30					
Jack Quinn	125,734	51.70%	Total	Challenger	1992
	(114,921)	(91.40)	Republican		
	(10,813)	(8.60)	Change Congress		
Dennis Gorski	111,445	45.82%	Total	Challenger	
	(102,519)	(91.99)	Democrat		
	(8,926)	(8.01)	Conservative		
Mary Refermat	6,025	2.48%	Right to Life	Challenger	
District 31					
Amo Houghton	150,696	70.57%	Total	Incumbent	1986
	(133,758)	(88.76)	Republican		
	(16,938)	(11.24)	Conservative		
Joseph Leahey	52,010	24.35%	Democrat	Challenger	
Gretchen McManus	10,848	5.08%	Right to Life	Challenger	

Candidates: April 7, 1992, Primary Election

Candidate	Total vote	Percent	Candidate	Total vote	Percent
Presidential Preference, Democratic			**Presidential Preference, Republican**		
Bill Clinton	412,349	40.92%	(No Contest)		
Paul Tsongas	288,330	28.61%			
Jerry Brown	264,278	26.23%			
Tom Harkin	11,535	1.14%			
Bob Kerrey	11,147	1.11%			
Larry Agran	10,733	1.07%			
Eugene McCarthy	9,354	0.93%			

Voter Registration and Turnout, 1948-1992 Elections

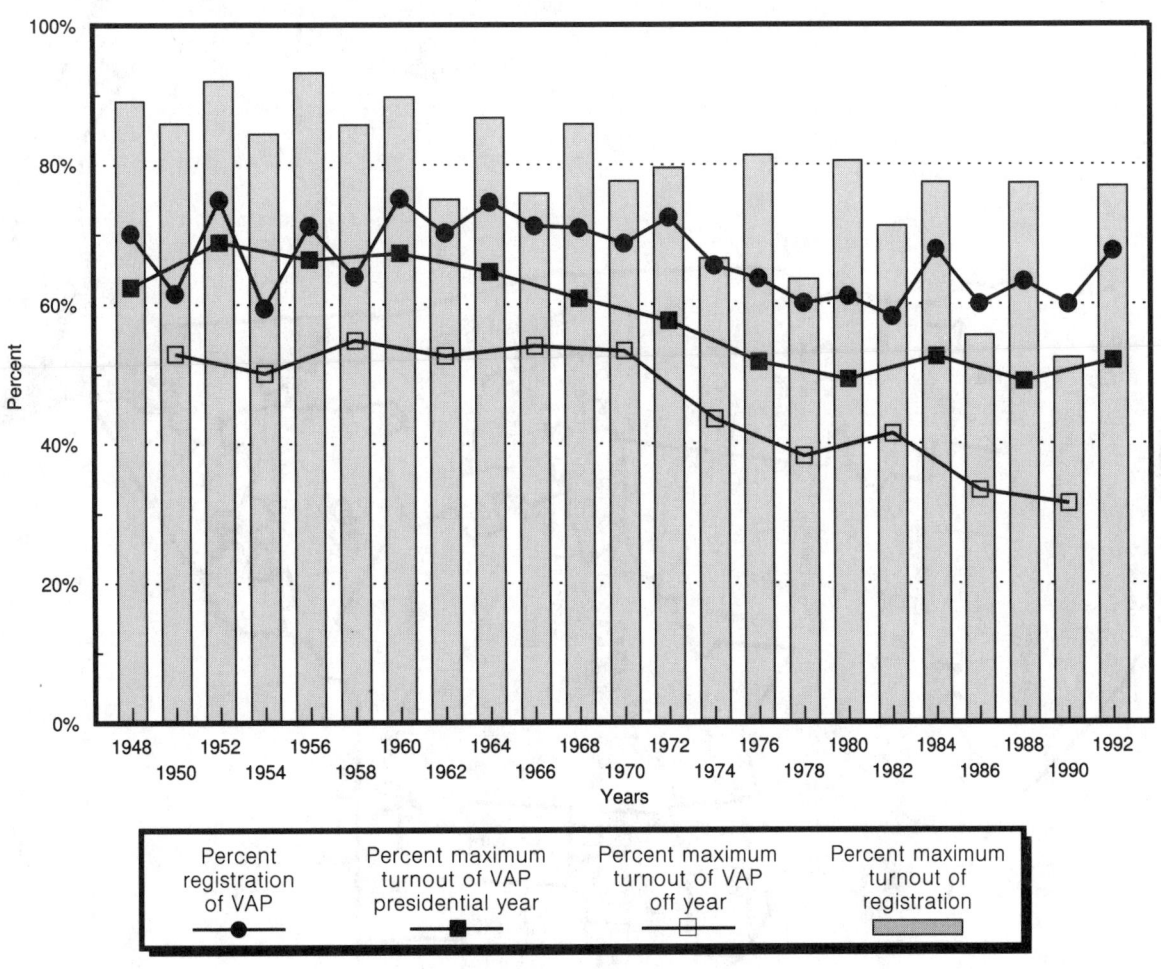

		Voter registration (REG)			Voter turnout											
						Highest office						Maximum vote				
Year	Estimated Voting Age Population (VAP)	Total	Percent of VAP	Rank by percent of VAP	Actual	Total	Office	Percent total REG	Rank by percent of REG	Percent of VAP	Rank by percent of VAP	Total	Percent total REG	Rank by percent of REG	Percent total VAP	Rank by percent of VAP
1992	13,609,000	9,193,391	67.6	37	7,068,630	6,926,925	P	75.3	32	50.9	41	7,068,630	76.9	31	51.9	41
1990	13,683,000	8,201,532	59.9	41	4,290,261	4,056,896	G	49.5	40	29.6	47	4,290,261	52.3	38	31.4	45
1988	13,574,000	8,581,276	63.2	44	6,636,310	6,485,683	P	75.6	15	47.8	37	6,636,310	77.3	14	48.9	35
1986	13,447,000	8,071,004	60.0	43	4,481,718	4,293,971	G	53.2	32	31.9	42	4,481,718	55.5	31	33.3	41
1984	13,331,000	9,044,208	67.8	39	7,000,828	6,806,810	P	75.3	20	51.1	37	7,000,828	77.4	18	52.5	32
1982	13,129,000	7,634,992	58.2	43	5,437,367	5,254,891	G	68.8	9	40.0	33	5,437,367	71.2	9	41.4	32
1980	12,933,000	7,897,555	61.1	43	6,359,218	6,201,959	P	78.5	10	48.0	42	6,359,218	80.5	7	49.2	40
1978	12,912,000	7,764,171	60.1	42	4,929,426	4,768,820	G	61.4	13	36.9	34	4,929,426	63.5	10	38.2	31
1976	12,892,000	8,198,950	63.6	41	6,668,262	6,534,170	P	79.7	12	50.7	33	6,668,262	81.3	11	51.7	33
1974	12,734,000	8,341,198	65.5	34	5,543,654	5,293,176	G	63.5	14	41.6	27	5,543,654	66.5	14	43.5	23
1972	12,717,000	9,207,363	72.4	27	7,323,471	7,165,919	P	77.8	18	56.3	32	7,323,471	79.5	15	57.6	31
1970	11,543,000	7,930,768	68.7	32	6,150,477	6,013,064	G	75.8	7	52.1	17	6,150,477	77.6	7	53.3	19
1968	11,450,000	8,113,216	70.9	31	6,961,690	6,791,688	P	83.7	15	59.3	33	6,961,690	85.8	8	60.8	33
1966	11,403,000	8,117,944	71.2	27	6,159,578	6,031,585	G	74.3	9	52.9	23	6,159,578	75.9	8	54.0	23
1964	11,324,000	8,443,430	74.6	25	7,317,586	7,166,275	P	84.9	13	63.3	32	7,317,586	86.7	12	64.6	31
1962	11,247,000	7,892,002	70.2	24	5,921,503	5,805,631	G	73.6	10	51.6	26	5,921,503	75.0	9	52.6	24
1960	10,965,000	8,231,203	75.1	21	7,380,075	7,291,079	P	88.6	11	66.5	30	7,380,075	89.7	9	67.3	30
1958	10,584,000	6,759,343	63.9	24	5,795,981	5,712,665	G	84.5	2	54.0	23	5,795,981	85.7	2	54.8	25
1956	10,832,000	7,715,154	71.2	19	7,187,408	7,095,971	P	92.0	4	65.5	27	7,187,408	93.2	4	66.4	27
1954	10,470,000	6,218,297	59.4	20	5,248,177	5,161,942	G	83.0	2	49.3	27	5,248,177	84.4	2	50.1	27
1952	10,476,000	7,841,613	74.9	16	7,216,054	7,128,239	P	90.9	4	68.0	28	7,216,054	92.0	4	68.9	28
1950	10,354,000	6,368,995	61.5	17	5,473,048	5,228,403	S	82.1	3	50.5	25	5,473,048	85.9	2	52.9	21
1948	10,053,000	7,044,676	70.1	13	6,274,527	6,177,337	P	87.7	2	61.4	18	6,274,527	89.1	2	62.4	18

NEW YORK

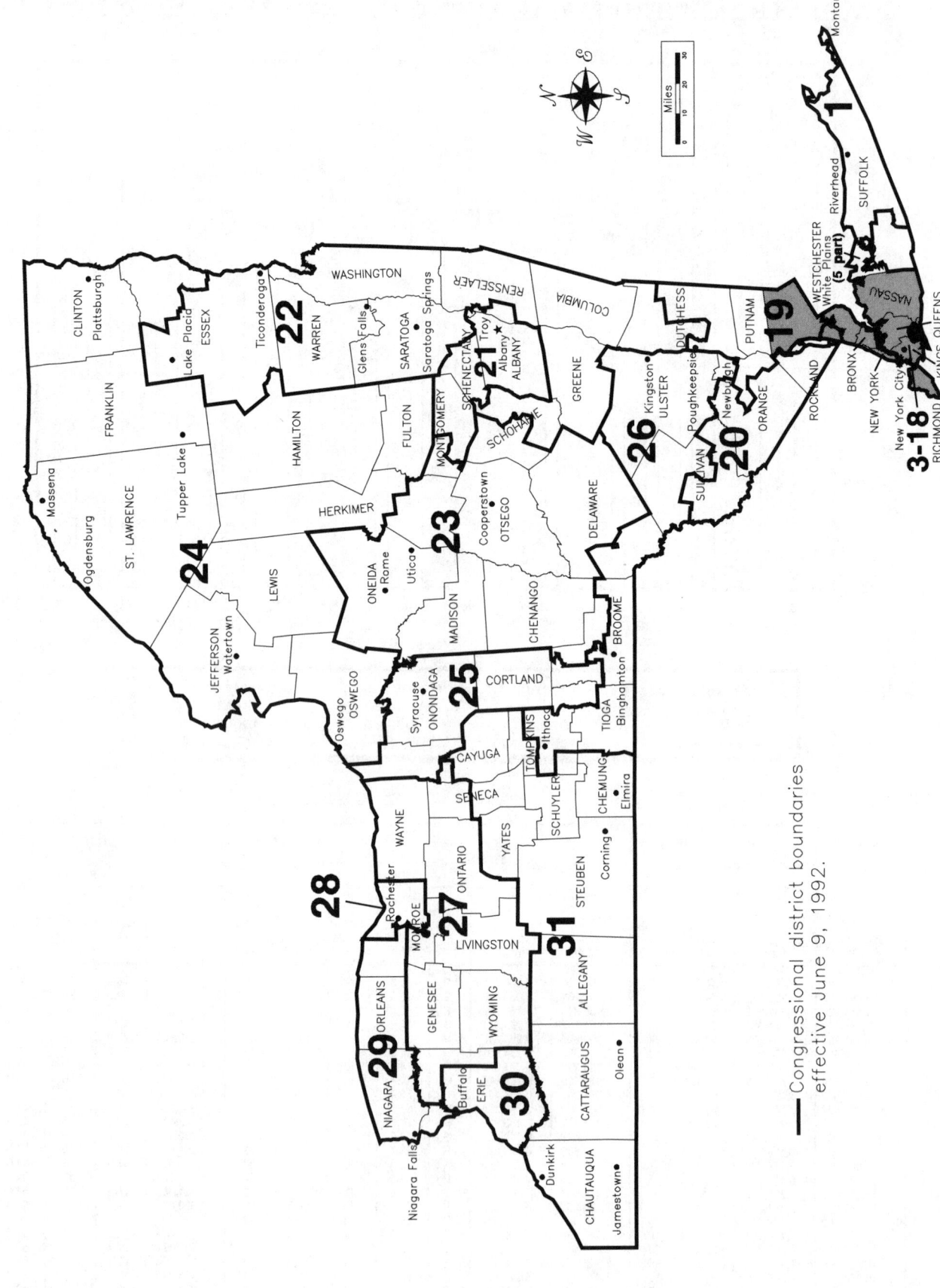

— Congressional district boundaries effective June 9, 1992.

New York City Metropolitan Area, New York

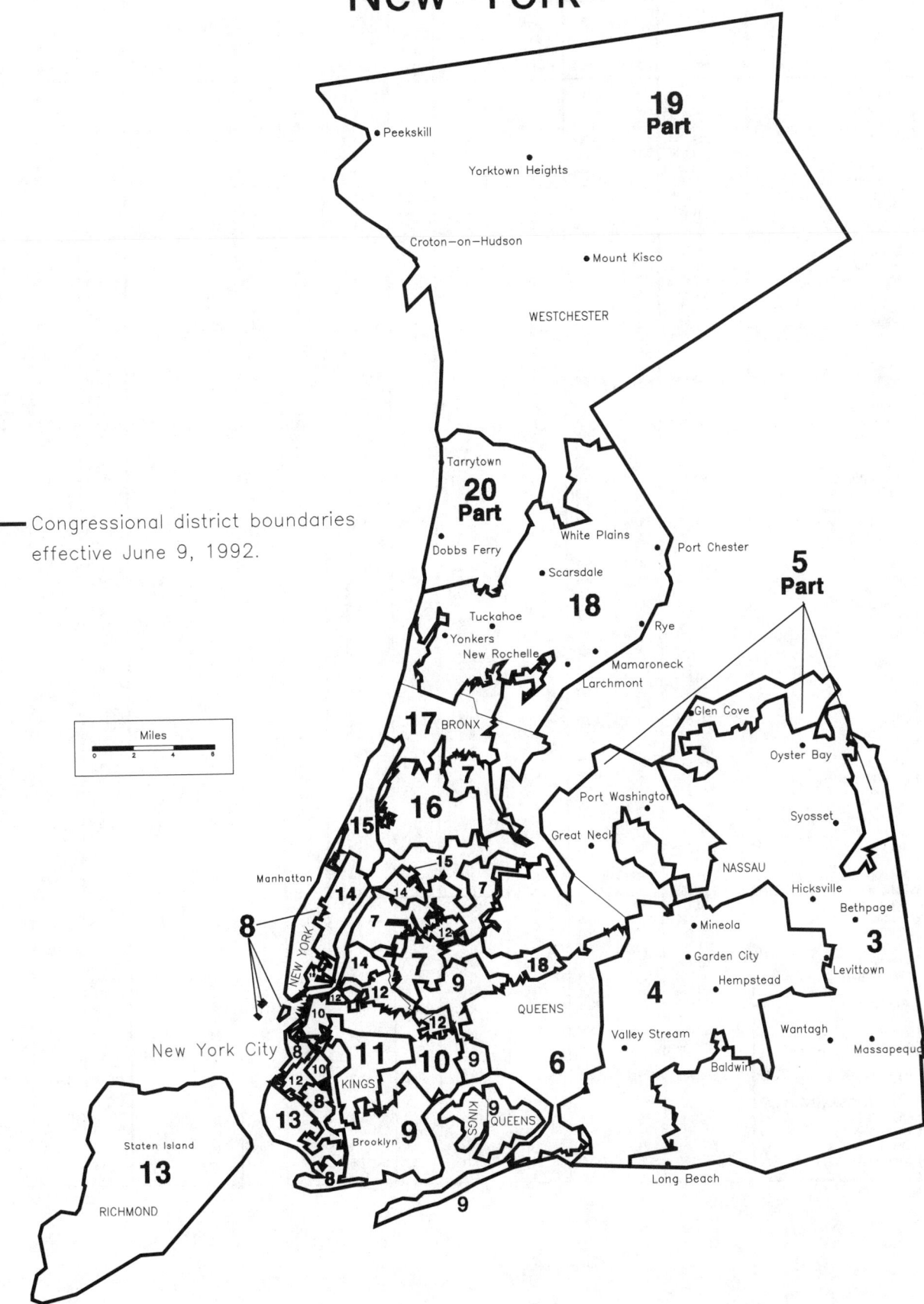

—Congressional district boundaries effective June 9, 1992.

19 Part

• Peekskill

• Yorktown Heights

Croton-on-Hudson

• Mount Kisco

WESTCHESTER

Miles
0 2 4 6

• Tarrytown

20 Part

• Dobbs Ferry

White Plains

• Scarsdale

• Port Chester

5 Part

• Tuckahoe

• Yonkers

New Rochelle

18

• Rye

Mamaroneck

Larchmont

• Glen Cove

• Oyster Bay

Port Washington

• Syosset

17 BRONX

7

Great Neck

NASSAU

• Hicksville

16

• Bethpage

15

• Mineola

• Garden City

Levittown

3

Manhattan

15

7

• Hempstead

8

14

14

7

18

NEW YORK

7

7

9

QUEENS

4

Valley Stream

• Wantagh

• Massapequa

12

12

• Baldwin

10

12

New York City

8

10

11

10

9

6

KINGS

12

9

QUEENS

8

13

Brooklyn

9

Long Beach

8

Staten Island

13

RICHMOND

9

Copyright © 1993 by Election Data Services, Inc.

New York 655

Table A. — 1990 Population by Race and Ethnic Origin

State/county code	County	Total persons	Percent of total persons						Rank				Percent contribution to state population			
			Non-Hispanic					Hispanic	Percent of total persons				Non-Hispanic			Hispanic
			White	Black	Asian and Pacific Islander	Native American	Other		Total	Non-Hispanic		Hispanic	Total	White	Black	
										White	Black					
36 001	Albany	292,594	88.0	8.2	1.7	0.2	0.1	1.8	13	48	9	29	1.6	2.1	0.9	0.2
36 003	Allegany	50,470	98.0	0.6	0.6	0.2	<.1	0.6	49	5	56	58	0.3	0.4	<.1	<.1
36 005	Bronx	1,203,789	22.6	30.7	2.6	0.3	0.4	43.5	6	62	2	1	6.7	2.2	14.4	23.6
36 007	Broome	212,160	94.9	1.9	1.7	0.2	<.1	1.2	18	26	36	41	1.2	1.6	0.2	0.1
36 009	Cattaraugus	84,234	95.9	0.9	0.4	2.2	<.1	0.6	33	23	50	57	0.5	0.6	<.1	<.1
36 011	Cayuga	82,313	94.4	3.4	0.4	0.3	<.1	1.5	35	31	28	37	0.5	0.6	0.1	<.1
36 013	Chautauqua	141,895	94.7	1.6	0.4	0.4	<.1	2.9	23	28	39	17	0.8	1.1	<.1	0.2
36 015	Chemung	95,195	92.2	5.2	0.7	0.2	0.2	1.5	28	39	20	36	0.5	0.7	0.2	<.1
36 017	Chenango	51,768	97.8	0.7	0.3	0.3	<.1	0.9	48	10	52	49	0.3	0.4	<.1	<.1
36 019	Clinton	85,969	92.6	3.9	0.8	0.2	<.1	2.4	32	37	26	21	0.5	0.6	0.1	<.1
36 021	Columbia	62,982	94.1	3.6	0.4	0.2	0.1	1.6	39	32	27	33	0.4	0.5	<.1	<.1
36 023	Cortland	48,963	97.7	0.6	0.4	0.3	<.1	0.9	50	11	54	50	0.3	0.4	<.1	<.1
36 025	Delaware	47,225	97.3	0.9	0.4	0.2	<.1	1.1	51	14	49	43	0.3	0.4	<.1	<.1
36 027	Dutchess	259,462	85.9	7.9	2.2	0.1	<.1	3.8	15	49	12	14	1.4	1.8	0.8	0.4
36 029	Erie	968,532	84.9	11.2	1.0	0.6	<.1	2.3	7	51	7	25	5.4	6.6	4.2	1.0
36 031	Essex	37,152	94.8	2.5	0.4	0.2	<.1	2.0	56	27	34	28	0.2	0.3	<.1	<.1
36 033	Franklin	46,540	89.0	3.2	0.3	5.0	<.1	2.4	52	45	30	22	0.3	0.3	<.1	<.1
36 035	Fulton	54,191	97.5	1.1	0.4	0.2	<.1	0.8	45	13	46	54	0.3	0.4	<.1	<.1
36 037	Genesee	60,060	96.0	1.7	0.3	1.1	<.1	0.8	42	22	37	55	0.3	0.5	<.1	<.1
36 039	Greene	44,739	91.4	4.4	0.4	0.3	0.1	3.4	53	41	22	16	0.2	0.3	<.1	<.1
36 041	Hamilton	5,279	98.9	0.2	0.1	0.2	<.1	0.6	62	1	62	59	<.1	<.1	<.1	<.1
36 043	Herkimer	65,797	98.8	0.3	0.2	0.2	<.1	0.6	38	2	61	60	0.4	0.5	<.1	<.1
36 045	Jefferson	110,943	90.3	5.6	0.8	0.4	<.1	2.8	26	43	18	18	0.6	0.8	0.2	0.1
36 047	Kings	2,300,664	40.1	34.7	4.6	0.2	0.3	20.1	1	61	1	3	12.8	7.4	31.1	20.9
36 049	Lewis	26,796	98.5	0.4	0.3	0.2	<.1	0.5	59	3	60	62	0.1	0.2	<.1	<.1
36 051	Livingston	62,372	95.4	2.2	0.5	0.3	<.1	1.6	40	24	35	34	0.3	0.5	<.1	<.1
36 053	Madison	69,120	97.1	1.0	0.6	0.4	<.1	0.8	37	15	47	52	0.4	0.5	<.1	<.1
36 055	Monroe	713,968	82.6	11.6	1.7	0.3	<.1	3.7	9	55	6	15	4.0	4.7	3.2	1.2
36 057	Montgomery	51,981	93.5	0.7	0.4	0.2	<.1	5.2	47	34	53	12	0.3	0.4	<.1	0.1
36 059	Nassau	1,287,348	82.6	8.2	3.0	<.1	<.1	6.0	5	54	10	11	7.2	8.5	4.1	3.5
36 061	New York	1,487,536	48.9	17.6	7.1	0.2	0.3	26.0	3	59	4	2	8.3	5.8	10.2	17.5
36 063	Niagara	220,756	92.3	5.4	0.4	0.9	<.1	1.0	17	38	19	48	1.2	1.6	0.5	<.1
36 065	Oneida	250,836	91.5	5.0	0.8	0.2	<.1	2.3	16	40	21	24	1.4	1.8	0.5	0.3
36 067	Onondaga	468,973	88.4	7.9	1.4	0.7	0.1	1.5	10	47	13	35	2.6	3.3	1.4	0.3
36 069	Ontario	95,101	96.2	1.7	0.5	0.2	<.1	1.3	29	20	38	38	0.5	0.7	<.1	<.1
36 071	Orange	307,647	84.8	6.7	1.1	0.2	<.1	7.0	12	52	15	7	1.7	2.1	0.8	1.0
36 073	Orleans	41,846	90.5	6.2	0.3	0.4	<.1	2.5	55	42	16	20	0.2	0.3	0.1	<.1
36 075	Oswego	121,771	97.8	0.5	0.4	0.3	<.1	1.0	24	8	59	47	0.7	1.0	<.1	<.1
36 077	Otsego	60,517	96.8	1.3	0.5	0.2	<.1	1.2	41	17	41	40	0.3	0.5	<.1	<.1
36 079	Putnam	83,941	95.3	1.0	0.9	0.1	<.1	2.7	34	25	48	19	0.5	0.6	<.1	0.1
36 081	Queens	1,951,598	48.0	20.0	11.8	0.3	0.3	19.5	2	60	3	4	10.8	7.5	15.2	17.2
36 083	Rensselaer	154,429	93.9	3.3	1.4	0.2	<.1	1.2	21	33	29	39	0.9	1.2	0.2	<.1
36 085	Richmond	378,977	80.0	7.4	4.3	0.2	0.1	8.0	11	56	14	6	2.1	2.4	1.1	1.4
36 087	Rockland	265,475	79.9	9.2	4.0	0.2	0.1	6.7	14	57	8	9	1.5	1.7	0.9	0.8
36 089	St. Lawrence	111,974	96.2	1.2	0.7	0.7	<.1	1.1	25	21	42	42	0.6	0.9	<.1	<.1
36 091	Saratoga	181,276	96.8	1.2	0.7	0.1	<.1	1.1	19	16	43	45	1.0	1.4	<.1	<.1
36 093	Schenectady	149,285	92.7	4.1	1.2	0.2	0.1	1.7	22	36	25	32	0.8	1.1	0.2	0.1
36 095	Schoharie	31,859	96.6	1.2	0.3	0.2	<.1	1.7	58	18	44	31	0.2	0.2	<.1	<.1
36 097	Schuyler	18,662	97.8	0.8	0.2	0.3	<.1	0.9	61	9	51	51	0.1	0.1	<.1	<.1
36 099	Seneca	33,683	96.5	1.5	0.6	0.2	<.1	1.1	57	19	40	44	0.2	0.3	<.1	<.1
36 101	Steuben	99,088	97.5	1.1	0.5	0.2	<.1	0.5	27	12	45	61	0.6	0.8	<.1	<.1
36 103	Suffolk	1,321,864	85.5	5.8	1.7	0.2	<.1	6.6	4	50	17	10	7.3	9.1	3.0	4.0
36 105	Sullivan	69,277	84.1	8.0	0.8	0.2	0.1	6.9	36	53	11	8	0.4	0.5	0.2	0.2
36 107	Tioga	52,337	97.9	0.6	0.6	0.2	<.1	0.7	46	6	57	56	0.3	0.4	<.1	<.1
36 109	Tompkins	94,097	88.7	3.2	5.4	0.3	0.2	2.2	30	46	31	26	0.5	0.7	0.1	0.3
36 111	Ulster	165,304	90.0	4.4	1.2	0.3	<.1	4.1	20	44	23	13	0.9	1.2	0.3	0.3
36 113	Warren	59,209	98.1	0.5	0.5	0.2	<.1	0.8	44	4	58	53	0.3	0.5	<.1	<.1
36 115	Washington	59,330	94.6	2.9	0.2	0.2	<.1	2.2	43	29	33	27	0.3	0.5	<.1	<.1
36 117	Wayne	89,123	94.5	3.1	0.4	0.3	<.1	1.7	31	30	32	30	0.5	0.7	0.1	<.1
36 119	Westchester	874,866	73.2	13.1	3.6	0.1	0.1	9.9	8	58	5	5	4.9	5.1	4.4	3.9
36 121	Wyoming	42,507	92.8	4.3	0.3	0.2	<.1	2.4	54	35	24	23	0.2	0.3	<.1	<.1
36 123	Yates	22,810	97.9	0.6	0.3	0.2	<.1	1.0	60	7	55	46	0.1	0.2	<.1	<.1
36	**NEW YORK**	**17,990,455**	**69.3**	**14.3**	**3.7**	**0.3**	**0.2**	**12.3**					**100.0**	**100.0**	**100.0**	**100.0**
	CONGRESSIONAL															
	District 1	580,338	89.4	3.9	1.7	0.2	<.1	4.7	2	10	22	19	3.2	4.2	0.9	1.2
	District 2	580,337	79.4	9.0	1.6	0.2	0.1	9.7	16	19	10	12	3.2	3.7	2.0	2.5
	District 3	580,337	91.1	1.9	2.5	<.1	<.1	4.4	24	7	31	20	3.2	4.2	0.4	1.2
	District 4	580,338	73.7	15.5	3.1	0.1	0.1	7.5	7	22	8	14	3.2	3.4	3.5	2.0

Table A. — 1990 Population by Race and Ethnic Origin (cont)

State/ county code	County	Total persons	Percent of total persons						Rank				Percent contribution to state population			
			Non-Hispanic							Percent of total persons				Non-Hispanic		
			White	Black	Asian and Pacific Islander	Native American	Other	Hispanic	Total	Non-Hispanic		Hispanic	Total	White	Black	Hispanic
										White	Black					
District 5		580,337	78.8	3.2	10.5	<.1	<.1	7.3	27	20	24	16	3.2	3.7	0.7	1.9
District 6		580,337	22.8	53.3	6.0	0.6	0.4	16.9	28	26	3	7	3.2	1.1	12.0	4.4
District 7		580,337	58.2	8.9	11.1	0.2	0.4	21.3	29	24	11	5	3.2	2.7	2.0	5.6
District 8		580,337	73.5	7.3	6.1	0.2	0.2	12.7	30	23	14	8	3.2	3.4	1.7	3.3
District 9		580,338	82.3	2.9	6.1	0.1	0.1	8.5	8	14	25	13	3.2	3.8	0.7	2.2
District 10		580,335	21.0	56.6	2.2	0.3	0.3	19.7	31	27	2	6	3.2	1.0	12.8	5.2
District 11		580,337	15.8	69.4	2.7	0.3	0.2	11.5	9	28	1	9	3.2	0.7	15.7	3.0
District 12		580,340	14.0	8.7	18.7	0.3	0.5	57.9	1	30	12	2	3.2	0.7	2.0	15.2
District 13		580,337	81.8	5.1	5.4	0.1	0.1	7.5	10	15	20	15	3.2	3.8	1.2	2.0
District 14		580,337	79.5	3.9	5.4	0.1	0.2	10.9	11	18	23	10	3.2	3.7	0.9	2.9
District 15		580,337	14.0	36.8	2.1	0.2	0.4	46.4	12	29	5	3	3.2	0.7	8.3	12.2
District 16		580,338	4.2	33.2	1.7	0.3	0.5	60.2	3	31	6	1	3.2	0.2	7.5	15.8
District 17		580,337	29.1	37.8	3.4	0.3	0.3	29.1	13	25	4	4	3.2	1.4	8.5	7.6
District 18		580,337	74.4	7.0	8.0	0.1	0.1	10.4	14	21	15	11	3.2	3.5	1.6	2.7
District 19		580,337	85.5	6.8	2.2	0.1	<.1	5.2	15	12	16	18	3.2	4.0	1.5	1.4
District 20		580,338	82.8	7.6	3.3	0.2	<.1	6.1	4	13	13	17	3.2	3.9	1.7	1.6
District 21		580,337	90.1	6.1	1.5	0.2	0.1	2.1	17	9	18	24	3.2	4.2	1.4	0.5
District 22		580,337	95.7	2.0	0.6	0.2	<.1	1.5	18	1	30	28	3.2	4.5	0.4	0.4
District 23		580,337	95.0	2.6	0.6	0.2	<.1	1.5	19	3	26	26	3.2	4.4	0.6	0.4
District 24		580,338	94.6	2.4	0.6	0.8	<.1	1.6	5	5	28	25	3.2	4.4	0.5	0.4
District 25		580,337	90.2	6.5	1.2	0.6	<.1	1.4	20	8	17	30	3.2	4.2	1.5	0.4
District 26		580,338	88.1	5.4	1.9	0.2	0.1	4.3	6	11	19	21	3.2	4.1	1.2	1.1
District 27		580,337	94.8	2.4	1.1	0.3	<.1	1.3	21	4	27	31	3.2	4.4	0.5	0.3
District 28		580,337	79.8	13.6	1.9	0.3	<.1	4.3	22	17	9	22	3.2	3.7	3.1	1.1
District 29		580,337	91.4	4.3	0.7	0.7	<.1	2.8	23	6	21	23	3.2	4.3	1.0	0.7
District 30		580,337	80.8	16.6	0.6	0.5	<.1	1.5	25	16	7	27	3.2	3.8	3.7	0.4
District 31		580,337	95.1	2.2	0.6	0.5	<.1	1.5	26	2	29	29	3.2	4.4	0.5	0.4

New York 657

Table B. — 1990 Voting Age Population (VAP) by Race and Ethnic Origin

County	Total Voting Age Population	Percent of total VAP						Rank: Percent of total VAP				Percent contribution to state VAP				VAP percent of total population						
		Non-Hispanic White	NH Black	NH Asian and Pacific Islander	NH Native American	NH Other	Hispanic	Total	NH White	NH Black	Hispanic	Total	NH White	NH Black	Hispanic	Total	NH White	NH Black	NH Asian and Pacific Islander	NH Native American	NH Other	Hispanic
Albany	229,974	89.4	7.2	1.6	0.2	<.1	1.6	12	46	12	30	1.7	2.1	0.9	0.2	78.6	79.8	68.7	73.6	77.8	36.7	70.6
Allegany	37,471	98.0	0.6	0.6	0.2	<.1	0.6	48	9	53	55	0.3	0.4	<.1	<.1	74.2	74.2	81.7	72.5	70.5	37.5	73.5
Bronx	872,141	27.0	29.9	2.6	0.3	0.3	40.0	6	62	2	1	6.4	2.4	14.3	22.7	72.4	86.4	70.6	73.4	68.8	51.4	66.6
Broome	163,579	95.4	1.7	1.7	0.2	<.1	1.1	18	26	36	40	1.2	1.6	0.1	0.1	77.1	77.5	66.1	74.1	73.4	29.9	70.9
Cattaraugus	60,935	96.6	0.7	0.3	1.9	<.1	0.5	34	22	54	59	0.4	0.6	<.1	<.1	72.3	72.9	56.5	62.0	62.6	20.7	59.9
Cayuga	60,732	94.0	3.7	0.3	0.3	<.1	1.7	35	32	28	29	0.4	0.6	0.1	<.1	73.8	73.5	80.8	58.9	63.7	15.0	85.1
Chautauqua	105,963	95.5	1.6	0.3	0.3	<.1	2.3	23	25	37	25	0.8	1.0	<.1	0.2	74.7	75.3	71.6	59.3	61.4	29.9	60.5
Chemung	71,057	92.4	5.1	0.6	0.2	<.1	1.6	30	37	20	32	0.5	0.7	0.2	<.1	74.6	74.8	74.1	65.8	73.5	19.7	77.6
Chenango	37,436	97.9	0.7	0.2	0.3	<.1	0.8	49	10	50	49	0.3	0.4	<.1	<.1	72.3	72.4	78.2	58.1	76.9	15.0	65.5
Clinton	64,532	91.9	4.4	0.7	0.2	<.1	2.7	31	39	24	20	0.5	0.6	0.2	0.1	75.1	74.5	85.1	72.4	68.3	55.1	83.5
Columbia	47,541	94.8	3.2	0.3	0.1	<.1	1.5	39	30	30	34	0.3	0.5	<.1	<.1	75.5	76.1	67.2	56.0	65.7	25.0	68.5
Cortland	36,822	97.8	0.6	0.4	0.2	<.1	0.9	50	11	55	46	0.3	0.4	<.1	<.1	75.2	75.3	73.8	71.0	67.9	43.5	70.9
Delaware	35,345	97.8	0.7	0.3	0.2	<.1	0.9	51	13	51	44	0.3	0.4	<.1	<.1	74.8	75.2	55.3	65.0	76.6	55.6	60.3
Dutchess	197,496	86.6	7.5	2.1	0.1	<.1	3.7	14	50	11	14	1.4	1.7	0.8	0.5	76.1	76.8	71.9	70.4	81.3	23.6	74.1
Erie	743,065	86.6	10.1	1.0	0.5	<.1	1.9	7	51	6	28	5.4	6.6	4.1	0.9	76.7	78.2	69.2	72.9	66.5	45.3	62.1
Essex	28,133	93.7	3.2	0.4	0.2	<.1	2.5	56	34	31	24	0.2	0.3	<.1	<.1	75.7	74.9	95.8	76.8	67.0	69.2	92.8
Franklin	34,642	88.0	4.2	0.2	4.5	<.1	3.0	52	48	25	16	0.3	0.3	<.1	<.1	74.4	73.6	96.8	66.1	66.6	58.3	93.9
Fulton	40,134	98.1	0.8	0.4	0.2	<.1	0.5	45	7	49	57	0.3	0.4	<.1	<.1	74.1	74.6	52.3	64.3	69.0	28.0	52.3
Genesee	44,158	96.6	1.6	0.2	1.0	<.1	0.6	43	21	38	56	0.3	0.4	<.1	<.1	73.5	74.0	66.0	50.2	68.1	16.1	57.9
Greene	34,345	90.8	4.9	0.4	0.2	<.1	3.6	53	41	21	15	0.3	0.3	<.1	<.1	76.8	76.3	85.3	68.0	71.4	47.9	81.0
Hamilton	4,137	98.7	0.3	0.1	0.2	0.0	0.7	62	3	61	54	<.1	<.1	<.1	<.1	78.4	78.3	91.7	83.3	100.0	0.0	87.1
Herkimer	48,957	99.0	0.2	0.2	0.2	<.1	0.4	38	1	62	61	0.4	0.5	<.1	<.1	74.4	74.6	65.9	63.0	78.3	18.2	57.0
Jefferson	80,427	90.4	5.6	0.8	0.4	<.1	2.8	26	44	18	19	0.6	0.7	0.2	0.1	72.5	72.6	72.7	68.1	68.2	40.0	73.0
Kings	1,695,110	43.8	32.8	4.7	0.2	0.2	18.2	1	61	1	3	12.3	7.6	30.5	20.1	73.7	80.5	69.7	75.6	71.5	57.9	66.8
Lewis	18,635	98.7	0.4	0.3	0.2	<.1	0.4	59	2	60	62	0.1	0.2	<.1	<.1	69.5	69.7	63.6	60.2	60.7	16.7	57.0
Livingston	47,179	95.0	2.6	0.4	0.3	<.1	1.6	40	28	35	31	0.3	0.5	<.1	<.1	75.6	75.4	89.1	64.0	75.8	56.3	78.2
Madison	51,686	96.9	1.2	0.6	0.4	<.1	0.8	37	17	43	48	0.4	0.5	<.1	<.1	74.8	74.6	87.0	78.7	73.9	45.2	76.2
Monroe	538,518	85.5	9.7	1.5	0.3	<.1	3.0	9	53	7	18	3.9	4.7	2.9	1.0	75.4	78.0	63.3	66.9	71.6	34.0	60.3
Montgomery	39,120	94.9	0.5	0.3	0.2	<.1	4.1	46	29	57	12	0.3	0.4	<.1	0.1	75.3	76.3	60.6	63.4	74.4	41.9	58.9
Nassau	1,006,650	84.0	7.6	2.6	<.1	<.1	5.6	4	55	10	11	7.3	8.6	4.2	3.7	78.2	79.5	72.3	68.3	76.1	47.8	73.4
New York	1,240,709	53.7	16.2	7.2	0.2	0.2	22.6	3	59	4	2	9.0	6.8	11.0	18.2	83.4	91.7	77.1	83.6	79.8	52.6	72.4
Niagara	165,754	93.5	4.6	0.3	0.8	<.1	0.8	17	35	23	52	1.2	1.6	0.4	<.1	75.1	76.1	63.7	63.4	63.3	25.2	62.7
Oneida	190,080	92.2	4.7	0.7	0.2	<.1	2.2	16	38	22	27	1.4	1.8	0.5	0.3	75.8	76.3	70.1	67.3	75.1	31.0	71.1
Onondaga	354,128	90.2	6.5	1.3	0.6	<.1	1.3	10	45	13	38	2.6	3.3	1.3	0.3	75.5	77.1	62.8	70.2	63.2	29.7	64.2
Ontario	71,310	96.9	1.5	0.4	0.2	<.1	1.1	29	19	40	41	0.5	0.7	<.1	<.1	75.0	75.5	64.8	59.1	68.1	22.2	60.2
Orange	222,586	85.9	6.4	1.1	0.2	<.1	6.4	13	52	15	8	1.6	1.9	0.8	0.9	72.4	73.3	68.3	68.9	75.2	47.5	66.1
Orleans	30,586	90.4	6.3	0.3	0.5	<.1	2.5	55	43	16	23	0.2	0.3	0.1	<.1	73.1	73.0	74.6	62.2	77.0	9.7	75.2
Oswego	87,860	98.0	0.5	0.3	0.3	<.1	0.8	24	8	58	50	0.6	0.9	<.1	<.1	72.2	72.3	72.7	65.6	63.8	35.5	62.6
Otsego	46,480	97.2	1.1	0.5	0.2	<.1	1.0	41	15	45	43	0.3	0.5	<.1	<.1	76.8	77.1	67.8	73.1	73.5	33.3	67.4
Putnam	62,308	95.6	0.9	0.8	0.1	<.1	2.6	33	24	48	22	0.5	0.6	<.1	0.1	74.2	74.5	69.5	66.5	79.6	35.1	71.0
Queens	1,542,971	51.4	18.5	11.3	0.3	0.3	18.2	2	60	3	4	11.2	8.1	15.6	18.3	79.1	84.7	72.9	76.2	74.6	59.9	73.8
Rensselaer	117,587	94.4	2.9	1.5	0.2	<.1	1.1	21	31	32	39	0.9	1.1	0.2	<.1	76.1	76.6	67.6	78.7	75.8	24.2	68.6
Richmond	284,915	82.2	6.4	4.1	0.2	<.1	7.1	11	56	14	6	2.1	2.4	1.0	1.3	75.2	77.3	64.8	70.9		49.6	67.0
Rockland	196,516	81.5	8.4	3.6	0.2	<.1	6.1	15	57	8	9	1.4	1.6	0.9	0.8	75.0	75.5	68.1	67.8	71.9	49.3	68.0
St. Lawrence	83,759	95.8	1.5	0.7	0.7	<.1	1.3	25	23	39	37	0.6	0.8	<.1	<.1	74.8	74.5	92.4	76.6	70.7	59.3	86.0
Saratoga	134,781	97.0	1.2	0.6	0.1	<.1	1.0	19	16	44	42	1.0	1.3	<.1	<.1	74.4	74.5	75.6	63.3	73.9	34.5	72.3
Schenectady	115,032	93.9	3.5	1.0	0.2	<.1	1.4	22	33	29	36	0.8	1.1	0.2	0.1	77.1	78.0	65.4	66.3	73.6	20.0	63.6
Schoharie	24,111	96.6	1.3	0.2	0.2	<.1	1.6	58	20	42	33	0.2	0.2	<.1	<.1	75.7	75.7	84.0	54.9	83.8	66.7	70.1
Schuyler	13,624	97.7	0.9	0.2	0.3	0.0	0.9	61	14	47	47	<.1	0.1	<.1	<.1	73.0	72.9	85.8	64.1	83.7	0.0	70.9
Seneca	24,973	96.9	1.4	0.5	0.3	0.0	0.9	57	18	41	45	0.2	0.2	<.1	<.1	74.1	74.4	68.8	63.7	79.8	0.0	62.8
Steuben	72,121	97.8	1.1	0.4	0.2	<.1	0.4	28	12	46	60	0.5	0.7	<.1	<.1	72.8	73.0	67.8	60.0	74.1	10.0	62.5
Suffolk	995,276	86.8	5.3	1.6	0.2	<.1	6.1	5	49	19	10	7.2	8.8	2.9	3.9	75.3	76.4	68.6	70.3	70.8	49.0	68.9
Sullivan	52,142	84.7	7.9	0.7	0.2	<.1	6.4	36	54	9	7	0.4	0.5	0.2	0.2	75.3	75.8	73.9	72.8	78.2	43.7	70.5
Tioga	37,512	98.2	0.6	0.5	0.2	<.1	0.5	47	5	56	58	0.3	0.4	<.1	<.1	71.7	71.9	70.5	63.6	64.8	35.0	54.8
Tompkins	75,861	88.9	2.8	5.7	0.3	<.1	2.2	27	47	33	26	0.6	0.7	0.1	0.1	80.6	80.8	69.9	85.4	80.6	46.6	79.3
Ulster	126,695	90.6	4.2	1.1	0.2	<.1	3.8	20	42	26	13	0.9	1.2	0.3	0.3	76.6	77.2	74.0	73.6	70.7	46.0	70.3
Warren	44,461	98.2	0.5	0.4	0.2	<.1	0.7	42	4	59	53	0.3	0.4	<.1	<.1	75.2	75.2	69.6	65.2	75.8	11.1	68.5
Washington	44,022	93.3	3.7	0.1	0.2	<.1	2.7	44	36	27	21	0.3	0.4	<.1	<.1	74.2	73.2	95.7	58.7	78.5	66.7	89.0
Wayne	64,189	95.3	2.7	0.3	0.2	<.1	1.4	32	27	34	35	0.5	0.6	<.1	<.1	72.0	72.6	63.9	52.0	66.8	23.3	60.0
Westchester	684,597	75.5	12.1	3.2	0.1	<.1	9.0	8	58	5	5	5.0	5.3	4.6	4.0	78.3	80.7	72.7	68.9	78.9	52.3	71.2
Wyoming	31,286	90.9	5.7	0.2	0.2	<.1	3.0	54	40	17	17	0.2	0.3	<.1	<.1	73.6	72.1	97.0	53.0	73.6	52.9	93.1
Yates	16,754	98.2	0.6	0.2	0.2	<.1	0.8	60	6	54	51	0.1	0.2	<.1	<.1	73.5	73.7	77.0	45.3	65.2	100.0	59.6
NEW YORK	13,730,906	71.5	13.3	3.7	0.3	0.1	11.2					100.0	100.0	100.0	100.0	76.3	78.8	71.0	75.2	70.5	51.6	69.5
CONGRESSIONAL																						
District 1	433,173	90.2	3.6	1.6	0.2	<.1	4.3	23	10	23	19	3.2	4.0	0.8	1.2	74.6	75.3	68.6	73.4	69.3	47.3	69.0
District 2	437,435	81.3	8.2	1.4	0.2	<.1	8.8	18	18	11	12	3.2	3.6	2.0	2.5	75.4	77.2	68.4	72.2		50.7	68.7
District 3	455,840	91.7	1.8	2.2	<.1	<.1	4.2	7	7	31	20	3.3	4.3	0.4	1.2	78.5	79.1	74.5	68.9	77.9	48.4	74.9
District 4	450,745	75.8	14.3	2.7	0.1	<.1	7.0	9	22	8	14	3.3	3.5	3.5	2.1	77.7	79.9	71.8	68.4	75.2	46.8	72.4

Table B. — 1990 Voting Age Population (VAP) by Race and Ethnic Origin (cont)

County	Total Voting Age Population	Percent of total VAP — Non-Hispanic White	Black	Asian and Pacific Islander	Native American	Other	Hispanic	Rank — Percent of total VAP Total	Non-Hispanic White	Black	Hispanic	Percent contribution to state VAP Total	Non-Hispanic White	Black	Hispanic	VAP percent of total population Total	Non-Hispanic White	Black	Asian and Pacific Islander	Native American	Other	Hispanic
District 5	462,505	80.5	3.0	9.5	<.1	<.1	6.8	6	20	24	15	3.4	3.8	0.8	2.1	79.7	81.4	75.0	72.4	75.1	52.6	74.5
District 6	432,187	25.5	51.8	5.9	0.6	0.3	16.0	24	26	3	7	3.1	1.1	12.3	4.5	74.5	83.3	72.3	73.0	74.1	60.5	70.3
District 7	472,528	61.2	8.1	10.6	0.2	0.3	19.6	3	24	12	5	3.4	2.9	2.1	6.0	81.4	85.6	74.6	78.1	74.8	67.0	75.0
District 8	486,296	75.6	6.6	6.0	0.2	0.1	11.5	2	23	15	8	3.5	3.7	1.8	3.6	83.8	86.1	75.5	81.9	85.2	66.2	76.1
District 9	469,579	83.6	2.7	5.8	0.1	0.1	7.7	4	15	25	13	3.4	4.0	0.7	2.3	80.9	82.3	76.1	76.4	75.1	63.5	73.1
District 10	414,610	23.1	55.5	2.3	0.3	0.2	18.5	29	27	2	6	3.0	1.0	12.6	5.0	71.4	78.6	70.1	77.0	72.1	57.9	67.3
District 11	414,564	17.7	67.8	2.9	0.3	0.2	11.1	30	28	1	9	3.0	0.7	15.4	3.0	71.4	79.9	69.8	76.5	71.7	60.6	68.6
District 12	417,930	16.5	8.3	20.2	0.2	0.4	54.3	28	29	10	2	3.0	0.7	1.9	14.8	72.0	84.7	69.1	78.1	69.5	51.7	67.6
District 13	449,571	83.8	4.3	5.0	0.1	<.1	6.6	10	14	20	16	3.3	3.8	1.1	1.9	77.5	79.4	65.0	72.6	73.2	55.2	68.8
District 14	515,981	81.1	3.7	5.2	0.1	0.1	9.7	1	19	22	10	3.8	4.3	1.1	3.2	88.9	90.7	85.4	86.5	83.0	67.4	78.8
District 15	437,484	16.5	37.0	2.4	0.2	0.2	43.6	17	30	4	3	3.2	0.7	8.9	12.4	75.4	88.5	75.9	84.3	72.0	43.8	70.9
District 16	385,188	5.3	33.6	1.8	0.3	0.3	58.7	31	31	6	1	2.8	0.2	7.1	14.7	66.4	83.9	67.1	71.9	65.8	48.1	64.8
District 17	438,290	33.7	36.4	3.4	0.3	0.2	26.1	16	25	5	4	3.2	1.5	8.7	7.4	75.5	87.5	72.7	73.6	77.6	58.9	75.0
District 18	467,381	76.3	6.5	7.3	0.1	0.1	9.7	5	21	16	11	3.4	3.6	1.7	2.9	80.5	82.5	75.7	73.6	80.6	34.2	75.1
District 19	444,315	86.0	6.6	2.0	0.1	<.1	5.1	12	12	14	18	3.2	3.9	1.6	1.5	76.6	77.1	74.2	70.0	72.9	50.1	68.4
District 20	429,329	83.9	7.2	3.0	0.2	<.1	5.6	25	13	13	17	3.1	3.7	1.7	1.6	74.0	75.0	70.6	67.8	76.0	30.2	66.3
District 21	451,775	91.3	5.3	1.4	0.2	<.1	1.8	8	9	18	24	3.3	4.2	1.3	0.5	77.8	78.9	67.9	73.7	76.0	30.2	76.0
District 22	434,538	95.7	2.1	0.5	0.2	<.1	1.5	21	1	30	26	3.2	4.2	0.5	0.4	75.2	75.4	70.8	68.2	76.2	32.9	69.6
District 23	436,162	95.3	2.5	0.5	0.2	<.1	1.4	19	3	27	27	3.2	4.2	0.6	0.5	75.2	75.4	70.8	68.2	76.2	32.9	69.6
District 24	426,525	94.5	2.6	0.5	0.7	<.1	1.7	27	5	26	25	3.1	4.1	0.6	0.5	73.5	73.4	79.3	70.2	67.3	43.1	77.2
District 25	435,923	91.7	5.4	1.1	0.5	<.1	1.2	20	8	17	31	3.2	4.1	1.3	0.3	75.1	76.4	62.8	69.8	63.1	29.8	64.5
District 26	446,405	89.2	4.8	2.0	0.2	<.1	3.8	11	11	19	21	3.3	4.1	1.2	1.1	76.9	77.8	68.7	78.9	73.3	40.7	68.5
District 27	433,948	95.1	2.4	1.0	0.3	<.1	1.2	22	4	28	30	3.2	4.2	0.6	0.3	74.8	75.0	74.4	67.5	68.7	40.0	69.6
District 28	439,156	83.2	11.4	1.7	0.3	<.1	3.4	15	16	9	22	3.2	3.7	2.7	1.0	75.7	78.9	63.1	67.6	71.5	34.7	59.9
District 29	441,716	92.6	3.9	0.6	0.6	<.1	2.2	13	6	21	23	3.2	4.2	0.9	0.6	76.1	77.1	68.1	67.4	65.1	32.5	60.9
District 30	441,308	82.7	14.9	0.6	0.5	<.1	1.3	14	17	7	29	3.2	3.7	3.6	0.4	76.0	77.9	68.6	74.9	67.6	40.3	64.9
District 31	428,519	95.5	2.2	0.5	0.5	<.1	1.4	26	2	29	28	3.1	4.2	0.5	0.4	73.8	74.1	73.9	64.2	65.4	21.9	67.5

Table C. – Voter Participation: November 3, 1992, General Election

County	Estimated Voting Age Population (VAP), 1992	Voter registration (REG) Total	% contribution to state REG	% of 1992 VAP	Rank by % of 1992 VAP	Highest office Actual	Total	Office	% of 1992 VAP	Maximum vote Total	% contribution to state turnout	% of REG	Rank by % of REG	% of 1992 VAP	Rank by % 1992 VAP	President	Senator	Governor	Representative
Albany	224,834	192,816	2.1	85.8	2	157,471	155,363	P	69.1	157,471	2.2	81.7	48	70.0	2	1.3	6.1	-	8.9
Allegany	35,378	22,120	0.2	62.5	56	18,979	18,719	P	52.9	18,979	0.3	85.8	27	53.6	53	1.4	9.5	-	11.7
Bronx	868,620	521,102	5.7	60.0	59	319,771	305,460	P	35.2	319,771	4.5	61.4	62	36.8	61	4.5	13.4	-	28.4
Broome	159,058	115,123	1.3	72.4	24	101,627	99,846	P	62.8	101,627	1.4	88.3	6	63.9	11	1.8	8.6	-	9.7
Cattaraugus	59,909	41,851	0.5	69.9	34	35,425	35,092	P	58.6	35,425	0.5	84.6	35	59.1	37	0.9	9.4	-	14.1
Cayuga	60,326	41,246	0.4	68.4	41	36,155	35,671	P	59.1	36,155	0.5	87.7	8	59.9	33	1.3	11.7	-	18.6
Chautauqua	103,107	77,513	0.8	75.2	10	63,283	62,789	P	60.9	63,283	0.9	81.6	49	61.4	24	0.8	9.4	-	14.9
Chemung	69,427	45,860	0.5	66.1	51	39,814	39,135	P	56.4	39,814	0.6	86.8	15	57.3	48	1.7	8.4	-	11.1
Chenango	37,596	25,410	0.3	67.6	46	21,881	21,787	P	58.0	21,881	0.3	86.1	26	58.2	45	0.4	9.2	-	13.0
Clinton	63,892	39,363	0.4	61.6	57	32,335	31,988	P	50.1	32,335	0.5	82.1	47	50.6	57	1.1	9.8	-	16.3
Columbia	47,627	33,800	0.4	71.0	30	29,338	29,056	P	61.0	29,338	0.4	86.8	17	61.6	23	1.0	7.3	-	11.9
Cortland	35,474	24,429	0.3	68.9	39	21,084	20,851	P	58.8	21,084	0.3	86.3	23	59.4	35	1.1	9.8	-	11.1
Delaware	34,477	23,313	0.3	67.6	45	20,780	20,530	P	59.5	20,780	0.3	89.1	2	60.3	31	1.2	10.0	-	15.4
Dutchess	196,079	137,918	1.5	70.3	32	116,113	115,328	P	58.8	116,113	1.6	84.2	36	59.2	36	0.7	6.4	-	12.6
Erie	723,152	540,215	5.9	74.7	12	455,943	451,496	P	62.4	455,943	6.5	84.4	36	63.0	14	1.0	10.3	-	9.1
Essex	28,013	22,911	0.2	81.8	3	19,187	18,973	P	67.7	19,187	0.3	83.7	42	68.5	4	1.1	12.7	-	21.4
Franklin	34,335	23,403	0.3	68.2	43	18,730	18,365	P	53.5	18,730	0.3	80.0	54	54.6	51	1.9	11.8	-	14.6
Fulton	39,740	26,635	0.3	67.0	48	23,248	22,845	P	57.5	23,248	0.3	87.3	11	58.5	42	1.7	8.3	-	19.4
Genesee	43,581	30,316	0.3	69.6	37	26,460	26,225	P	60.2	26,460	0.4	87.3	12	60.7	28	0.9	10.3	-	7.7
Greene	34,658	25,042	0.3	72.3	25	21,411	21,191	P	61.1	21,411	0.3	85.5	30	61.8	20	1.0	6.8	-	11.6
Hamilton	4,157	4,569	<.1	109.9	1	3,893	3,817	P	91.8	3,893	<.1	85.2	31	93.6	1	2.0	10.2	-	10.7
Herkimer	47,977	35,710	0.4	74.4	13	30,277	29,939	P	62.4	30,277	0.4	84.8	34	63.1	13	1.1	11.2	-	16.7
Jefferson	83,845	45,696	0.5	54.5	61	37,711	37,426	P	44.6	37,711	0.5	82.5	46	45.0	58	0.8	9.0	-	7.3
Kings	1,695,073	967,539	10.5	57.1	60	607,629	581,594	P	34.3	607,629	8.6	62.8	61	35.8	62	4.3	11.7	-	31.6
Lewis	18,880	13,816	0.2	73.2	19	11,223	11,032	P	58.4	11,223	0.2	81.2	51	59.4	34	1.7	10.0	-	11.4
Livingston	46,475	30,531	0.3	65.7	52	27,060	26,814	P	57.7	27,060	0.4	88.6	5	58.2	44	0.9	11.6	-	10.4
Madison	49,937	33,730	0.4	67.5	47	29,271	29,034	P	58.1	29,271	0.4	86.8	18	58.6	41	0.8	10.5	-	18.2
Monroe	529,254	386,876	4.2	73.1	20	343,347	340,369	P	64.3	343,347	4.9	88.7	3	64.9	8	0.9	9.8	-	8.5
Montgomery	38,420	27,458	0.3	71.5	27	23,783	23,443	P	61.0	23,783	0.3	86.6	21	61.9	18	1.4	9.0	-	17.3
Nassau	990,390	760,028	8.3	76.7	8	618,369	609,326	P	61.5	618,369	8.7	81.4	50	62.4	17	1.5	5.1	-	14.9
New York	1,233,244	859,861	9.4	69.7	36	550,085	532,118	P	43.1	550,085	7.8	64.0	60	44.6	59	3.3	8.8	-	20.6
Niagara	161,956	113,550	1.2	70.1	33	97,377	96,584	P	59.6	97,377	1.4	85.8	28	60.1	32	0.8	10.1	-	8.2
Oneida	185,745	136,626	1.5	73.6	17	109,689	108,342	P	58.3	109,689	1.6	80.3	53	59.1	38	1.2	8.9	-	10.2
Onondaga	345,758	250,388	2.7	72.4	23	216,272	214,907	P	62.2	216,272	3.1	86.4	22	62.6	16	0.6	8.2	-	7.7
Ontario	70,986	51,775	0.6	72.9	21	45,242	44,889	P	63.2	45,242	0.6	87.4	10	63.7	12	0.8	10.0	-	11.5
Orange	228,061	149,018	1.6	65.3	53	123,341	122,520	P	53.7	123,341	1.7	82.8	44	54.1	52	0.7	7.8	-	14.4
Orleans	30,906	20,040	0.2	64.8	54	16,912	16,754	P	54.2	16,912	0.2	84.4	37	54.7	50	0.9	12.5	-	12.0
Oswego	87,664	64,541	0.7	73.6	16	51,389	50,931	P	58.1	51,389	0.7	79.6	55	58.6	40	0.9	9.8	-	12.9
Otsego	44,698	31,214	0.3	69.8	35	27,050	26,606	P	59.5	27,050	0.4	86.7	20	60.5	29	1.6	9.7	-	13.0
Putnam	63,019	49,444	0.5	78.5	7	43,335	41,263	P	65.5	43,335	0.6	87.6	9	68.8	3	4.8	9.3	-	16.6
Queens	1,536,113	821,019	8.9	53.4	62	575,104	555,956	P	36.2	575,104	8.1	70.0	59	37.4	60	3.3	9.0	-	27.2
Rensselaer	115,150	87,283	0.9	75.8	9	75,742	74,580	P	64.8	75,742	1.1	86.8	19	65.8	6	1.5	6.8	-	11.0
Richmond	286,772	196,811	2.1	68.6	40	152,131	147,760	P	51.5	152,131	2.2	77.3	58	53.0	55	2.9	7.5	-	10.1
Rockland	195,908	143,691	1.6	73.3	18	123,067	121,831	P	62.2	123,067	1.7	85.6	29	62.8	15	1.0	5.5	-	13.9
St. Lawrence	80,509	51,511	0.6	64.0	55	42,843	42,318	P	52.6	42,843	0.6	83.2	43	53.2	54	1.2	11.1	-	10.0
Saratoga	138,507	110,227	1.2	79.6	4	91,055	89,811	P	64.8	91,055	1.3	82.6	45	65.7	7	1.4	7.7	-	10.6
Schenectady	112,775	89,553	1.0	79.4	5	75,098	73,870	P	65.5	75,098	1.1	83.9	41	66.6	5	1.6	7.5	-	12.7
Schoharie	23,477	17,065	0.2	72.7	22	14,315	14,147	P	60.3	14,315	0.2	83.9	40	61.0	26	1.2	6.7	-	14.0
Schuyler	13,722	9,125	<.1	66.5	49	8,298	8,199	P	59.8	8,298	0.1	90.9	1	60.5	30	1.2	11.0	-	12.6
Seneca	24,680	17,039	0.2	69.0	38	15,117	14,974	P	60.7	15,117	0.2	88.7	4	61.3	25	0.9	10.7	-	19.2
Steuben	71,625	48,498	0.5	67.7	44	41,797	41,410	P	57.8	41,797	0.6	86.2	24	58.4	43	0.9	10.2	-	9.8
Suffolk	990,909	730,094	7.9	73.7	15	573,006	567,955	P	57.3	573,006	8.1	78.5	57	57.8	46	0.9	5.6	-	12.0
Sullivan	52,020	40,968	0.4	78.8	6	32,185	31,635	P	60.8	32,185	0.5	78.6	56	61.9	19	1.7	8.5	-	17.4
Tioga	37,706	26,790	0.3	71.0	28	23,255	23,065	P	61.2	23,255	0.3	86.8	16	61.7	21	0.8	9.6	-	10.4
Tompkins	71,521	47,557	0.5	66.5	50	41,961	41,660	P	58.2	41,961	0.6	88.2	7	58.7	39	0.7	9.8	-	14.0
Ulster	125,795	93,435	1.0	74.3	14	81,540	80,821	P	64.2	81,540	1.2	87.3	13	64.8	9	0.9	8.2	-	9.8
Warren	44,729	33,621	0.4	75.2	11	28,954	28,767	P	64.3	28,954	0.4	86.1	25	64.7	10	0.6	9.0	-	8.1
Washington	44,447	30,299	0.3	68.2	42	25,436	25,135	P	56.6	25,436	0.4	84.0	39	57.2	49	1.2	9.8	-	8.7
Wayne	64,238	45,494	0.5	70.8	31	39,615	39,306	P	61.2	39,615	0.6	87.1	14	61.7	22	0.8	10.9	-	16.1
Westchester	674,399	479,127	5.2	71.0	29	389,129	378,840	P	56.2	389,129	5.5	81.2	52	57.7	47	2.6	6.9	-	13.0
Wyoming	31,567	19,391	0.2	61.4	58	16,517	16,375	P	51.9	16,517	0.2	85.2	32	52.3	56	0.9	10.6	-	7.5
Yates	16,703	11,997	0.1	71.8	26	10,175	10,092	P	60.4	10,175	0.1	84.8	33	60.9	27	0.8	10.0	-	15.0
NEW YORK	13,609,000	9,193,391	100.0	67.6		7,068,630	6,926,925		50.9	7,068,630	100.0	76.9		51.9		2.0	8.6	-	16.2

Table E. — Vote for President: November 3, 1992, General Election

County	Total	Clinton (DEM)[1]	Bush (REP)[2]	Perot (IND)	Other	Plurality Total	Party	DEM	REP	IND	Other	Rank DEM	Rank REP	Rank IND	Total	DEM	REP	IND	DEM	REP
Albany	155,363	80,641	49,452	24,064	1,206	31,189	D	51.9	31.8	15.5	0.8	6	55	54	2.2	2.3	2.1	2.2	62.0	38.0
Allegany	18,719	4,848	8,976	4,703	192	4,128	R	25.9	48.0	25.1	1.0	60	2	13	0.3	0.1	0.4	0.4	35.1	64.9
Bronx	305,460	225,038	63,310	15,115	1,997	161,728	D	73.7	20.7	4.9	0.7	2	61	62	4.4	6.5	2.7	1.4	78.0	22.0
Broome	99,846	43,444	34,653	21,280	469	8,791	D	43.5	34.7	21.3	0.5	11	51	36	1.4	1.3	1.5	2.0	55.6	44.4
Cattaraugus	35,092	10,150	13,944	10,662	336	3,282	R	28.9	39.7	30.4	1.0	59	33	2	0.5	0.3	0.6	1.0	42.1	57.9
Cayuga	35,671	13,088	12,065	10,279	239	1,023	D	36.7	33.8	28.8	0.7	35	52	6	0.5	0.4	0.5	0.9	52.0	48.0
Chautauqua	62,789	22,645	21,222	18,455	467	1,423	D	36.1	33.8	29.4	0.7	38	53	4	0.9	0.7	0.9	1.7	51.6	48.4
Chemung	39,135	15,099	16,088	7,493	455	989	R	38.6	41.1	19.1	1.2	26	19	49	0.6	0.4	0.7	0.7	48.4	51.6
Chenango	21,787	8,017	8,114	5,356	300	97	R	36.8	37.2	24.6	1.4	32	42	15	0.3	0.2	0.3	0.5	49.7	50.3
Clinton	31,988	12,881	13,455	5,389	263	574	R	40.3	42.1	16.8	0.8	20	18	52	0.5	0.4	0.6	0.5	48.9	51.1
Columbia	29,056	11,368	11,568	5,829	291	200	R	39.1	39.8	20.1	1.0	23	32	44	0.4	0.3	0.5	0.5	49.6	50.4
Cortland	20,851	7,815	7,782	5,098	156	33	D	37.5	37.3	24.4	0.7	30	41	16	0.3	0.2	0.3	0.5	50.1	49.9
Delaware	20,530	7,152	8,829	4,404	145	1,677	R	34.8	43.0	21.5	0.7	44	15	33	0.3	0.2	0.4	0.4	44.8	55.2
Dutchess	115,328	41,655	46,709	26,320	644	5,054	R	36.1	40.5	22.8	0.6	37	24	25	1.7	1.2	2.0	2.4	47.1	52.9
Erie	451,496	196,233	129,444	123,358	2,461	66,789	D	43.5	28.7	27.3	0.5	12	57	8	6.5	5.7	5.5	11.3	60.3	39.7
Essex	18,973	6,717	8,278	3,784	194	1,561	R	35.4	43.6	19.9	1.0	41	13	46	0.3	0.2	0.4	0.3	44.8	55.2
Franklin	18,365	7,654	6,635	3,857	219	1,019	D	41.7	36.1	21.0	1.2	16	47	39	0.3	0.2	0.3	0.4	53.6	46.4
Fulton	22,845	8,400	9,137	5,120	188	737	R	36.8	40.0	22.4	0.8	33	31	27	0.3	0.2	0.4	0.5	47.9	52.1
Genesee	26,225	8,071	11,663	6,192	299	3,592	R	30.8	44.5	23.6	1.1	55	10	19	0.4	0.2	0.5	0.6	40.9	59.1
Greene	21,191	6,924	9,390	4,689	188	2,466	R	32.7	44.3	22.1	0.9	52	11	30	0.3	0.2	0.4	0.4	42.4	57.6
Hamilton	3,817	963	2,038	793	23	1,075	R	25.2	53.4	20.8	0.6	61	1	41	<.1	<.1	<.1	<.1	32.1	67.9
Herkimer	29,939	10,880	12,052	6,866	141	1,172	R	36.3	40.3	22.9	0.5	36	28	24	0.4	0.3	0.5	0.6	47.4	52.6
Jefferson	37,426	13,380	14,227	9,461	358	847	R	35.8	38.0	25.3	1.0	40	39	12	0.5	0.4	0.6	0.9	48.5	51.5
Kings	581,594	411,183	133,344	33,014	4,053	277,839	D	70.7	22.9	5.7	0.7	3	60	60	8.4	11.9	5.7	3.0	75.5	24.5
Lewis	11,032	3,676	4,101	3,164	91	425	R	33.3	37.2	28.7	0.8	51	43	7	0.2	0.1	0.2	0.3	47.3	52.7
Livingston	26,814	8,648	12,122	5,775	269	3,474	R	32.3	45.2	21.5	1.0	53	7	32	0.4	0.3	0.5	0.5	41.6	58.4
Madison	29,034	10,099	11,293	7,391	251	1,194	R	34.8	38.9	25.5	0.9	45	36	10	0.4	0.3	0.5	0.7	47.2	52.8
Monroe	340,369	141,502	134,021	63,229	1,617	7,481	D	41.6	39.4	18.6	0.5	17	34	50	4.9	4.1	5.7	5.8	51.4	48.6
Montgomery	23,443	9,509	8,802	5,020	112	707	D	40.6	37.5	21.4	0.5	19	40	34	0.3	0.3	0.4	0.5	51.9	48.1
Nassau	609,326	282,593	246,881	77,097	2,755	35,712	D	46.4	40.5	12.7	0.5	9	23	56	8.8	8.2	10.5	7.1	53.4	46.6
New York	532,118	416,142	84,501	27,689	3,786	331,641	D	78.2	15.9	5.2	0.7	1	62	61	7.7	12.1	3.6	2.5	83.1	16.9
Niagara	96,584	35,649	30,401	30,126	408	5,248	D	36.9	31.5	31.2	0.4	31	56	1	1.4	1.0	1.3	2.8	54.0	46.0
Oneida	108,342	40,966	43,806	22,717	853	2,840	R	37.8	40.4	21.0	0.8	28	25	40	1.6	1.2	1.9	2.1	48.3	51.7
Onondaga	214,907	90,645	77,642	45,175	1,445	13,003	D	42.2	36.1	21.0	0.7	15	48	38	3.1	2.6	3.3	4.1	53.9	46.1
Ontario	44,889	16,064	18,995	9,571	259	2,931	R	35.8	42.3	21.3	0.6	39	17	35	0.6	0.5	0.8	0.9	45.8	54.2
Orange	122,520	45,946	53,493	22,499	582	7,547	R	37.5	43.7	18.4	0.5	29	12	51	1.8	1.3	2.3	2.1	46.2	53.8
Orleans	16,754	4,927	7,468	4,275	84	2,541	R	29.4	44.6	25.5	0.5	57	9	9	0.2	0.1	0.3	0.4	39.7	60.3
Oswego	50,931	16,990	18,530	14,853	558	1,540	R	33.4	36.4	29.2	1.1	50	44	5	0.7	0.5	0.8	1.4	47.8	52.2
Otsego	26,606	10,471	10,141	5,841	153	330	D	39.4	38.1	22.0	0.6	22	38	31	0.4	0.3	0.4	0.5	50.8	49.2
Putnam	41,263	14,048	18,934	8,011	270	4,886	R	34.0	45.9	19.4	0.7	47	5	48	0.6	0.4	0.8	0.7	42.6	57.4
Queens	555,956	349,520	157,561	46,014	2,861	191,959	D	62.9	28.3	8.3	0.5	4	58	59	8.0	10.1	6.7	4.2	68.9	31.1
Rensselaer	74,580	29,793	28,937	15,198	652	856	D	39.9	38.8	20.4	0.9	21	37	42	1.1	0.9	1.2	1.4	50.7	49.3
Richmond	147,760	56,901	70,707	19,678	474	13,806	R	38.5	47.9	13.3	0.3	27	3	55	2.1	1.7	3.0	1.8	44.6	55.4
Rockland	121,831	56,759	49,608	15,026	438	7,151	D	46.6	40.7	12.3	0.4	8	22	57	1.8	1.6	2.1	1.4	53.4	46.6
St. Lawrence	42,318	18,197	13,901	9,758	462	4,296	D	43.0	32.8	23.1	1.1	14	54	23	0.6	0.5	0.6	0.9	56.7	43.3
Saratoga	89,811	33,011	36,917	19,091	792	3,906	R	36.8	41.1	21.3	0.9	34	20	37	1.3	1.0	1.6	1.8	47.2	52.8
Schenectady	73,870	32,335	26,258	14,838	439	6,077	D	43.8	35.5	20.1	0.6	10	50	43	1.1	0.9	1.1	1.4	55.2	44.8
Schoharie	14,147	4,997	5,678	3,327	145	681	R	35.3	40.1	23.5	1.0	42	29	20	0.2	0.1	0.2	0.3	46.8	53.2
Schuyler	8,199	2,859	3,226	2,051	63	367	R	34.9	39.3	25.0	0.8	43	35	14	0.1	<.1	0.1	0.2	47.0	53.0
Seneca	14,974	5,810	5,432	3,660	72	378	D	38.8	36.3	24.4	0.5	25	45	17	0.2	0.2	0.2	0.3	51.7	48.3
Steuben	41,410	12,043	19,761	9,378	228	7,718	R	29.1	47.7	22.6	0.6	58	4	26	0.6	0.3	0.8	0.9	37.9	62.1
Suffolk	567,955	220,811	229,467	112,973	4,704	8,656	R	38.9	40.4	19.9	0.8	24	26	47	8.2	6.4	9.8	10.4	49.0	51.0
Sullivan	31,635	13,717	11,396	6,336	186	2,321	D	43.4	36.0	20.0	0.6	13	49	45	0.5	0.4	0.5	0.6	54.6	45.4
Tioga	23,065	7,791	9,287	5,867	120	1,496	R	33.8	40.3	25.4	0.5	48	27	11	0.3	0.2	0.4	0.5	45.6	54.4
Tompkins	41,660	23,197	11,520	6,704	239	11,677	D	55.7	27.7	16.1	0.6	5	59	53	0.6	0.7	0.5	0.6	66.8	33.2
Ulster	80,821	32,886	29,223	17,952	760	3,663	D	40.7	36.2	22.2	0.9	18	46	29	1.2	1.0	1.2	1.6	52.9	47.1
Warren	28,767	9,820	12,260	6,401	286	2,440	R	34.1	42.6	22.3	1.0	46	16	28	0.4	0.3	0.5	0.6	44.5	55.5
Washington	25,135	8,429	10,305	6,143	258	1,876	R	33.5	41.0	24.4	1.0	49	21	18	0.4	0.2	0.4	0.6	45.0	55.0
Wayne	39,306	11,866	18,019	9,188	233	6,153	R	30.2	45.8	23.4	0.6	56	6	21	0.6	0.3	0.8	0.8	39.7	60.3
Westchester	378,840	184,300	151,990	39,933	2,617	32,310	D	48.6	40.1	10.5	0.7	7	30	58	5.5	5.4	6.5	3.7	54.8	45.2
Wyoming	16,375	4,045	7,324	4,837	169	2,487	R	24.7	44.7	29.5	1.0	62	8	3	0.2	0.1	0.3	0.4	35.6	64.4
Yates	10,092	3,242	4,366	2,354	130	1,124	R	32.1	43.3	23.3	1.3	54	14	22	0.1	<.1	0.2	0.2	42.6	57.4
NEW YORK	6,926,925	3,444,450	2,346,649	1,090,721	45,105	1,097,801	D	49.7	33.9	15.7	0.7				100.0	100.0	100.0	100.0	59.5	40.5

[1]Includes votes cast for Clinton-Gore as the nominee of Democratic and Liberal parties.   [2]Includes votes cast for Bush-Quayle as the nominee of Republican, Conservative, and Right to Life parties.

Table F. — Vote for U.S. Senator: November 3, 1992, General Election

County	Total	Abrams (DEM)[1]	D'Amato (REP)[2]	Other	Plurality Total	Plurality Party	Percent of total vote DEM	REP	Other	Rank DEM	REP	Other	Percent contribution to state vote Total	DEM	REP	Other
Albany	147,922	78,275	64,073	5,574	14,202	D	52.9	43.3	3.8	5	58	45	2.3	2.5	2.0	2.7
Allegany	17,177	6,005	10,229	943	4,224	R	35.0	59.6	5.5	55	12	13	0.3	0.2	0.3	0.5
Bronx	276,922	184,619	87,215	5,088	97,404	D	66.7	31.5	1.8	2	61	59	4.3	6.0	2.8	2.5
Broome	92,888	39,163	51,049	2,676	11,886	R	42.2	55.0	2.9	19	40	51	1.4	1.3	1.6	1.3
Cattaraugus	32,094	12,641	17,011	2,442	4,370	R	39.4	53.0	7.6	31	47	2	0.5	0.4	0.5	1.2
Cayuga	31,909	12,066	17,743	2,100	5,677	R	37.8	55.6	6.6	37	34	4	0.5	0.4	0.6	1.0
Chautauqua	57,346	25,596	28,465	3,285	2,869	R	44.6	49.6	5.7	12	54	10	0.9	0.8	0.9	1.6
Chemung	36,450	12,092	23,243	1,115	11,151	R	33.2	63.8	3.1	59	3	50	0.6	0.4	0.7	0.5
Chenango	19,870	7,172	11,553	1,145	4,381	R	36.1	58.1	5.8	46	21	9	0.3	0.2	0.4	0.6
Clinton	29,172	11,824	16,066	1,282	4,242	R	40.5	55.1	4.4	22	39	33	0.5	0.4	0.5	0.6
Columbia	27,183	10,925	15,042	1,216	4,117	R	40.2	55.3	4.5	26	37	31	0.4	0.4	0.5	0.6
Cortland	19,018	7,043	10,938	1,037	3,895	R	37.0	57.5	5.5	43	27	15	0.3	0.2	0.3	0.5
Delaware	18,707	7,367	10,590	750	3,223	R	39.4	56.6	4.0	32	29	40	0.3	0.2	0.3	0.4
Dutchess	108,648	43,477	61,406	3,765	17,929	R	40.0	56.5	3.5	27	31	47	1.7	1.4	1.9	1.8
Erie	409,036	200,284	186,314	22,438	13,970	D	49.0	45.5	5.5	7	57	14	6.3	6.5	5.9	10.9
Essex	16,748	6,637	9,283	828	2,646	R	39.6	55.4	4.9	30	36	21	0.3	0.2	0.3	0.4
Franklin	16,518	6,949	8,791	778	1,842	R	42.1	53.2	4.7	20	45	27	0.3	0.2	0.3	0.4
Fulton	21,330	8,115	12,328	887	4,213	R	38.0	57.8	4.2	36	23	36	0.3	0.3	0.4	0.4
Genesee	23,747	8,830	13,715	1,202	4,885	R	37.2	57.8	5.1	42	24	19	0.4	0.3	0.4	0.6
Greene	19,945	6,827	12,222	896	5,395	R	34.2	61.3	4.5	57	6	30	0.3	0.2	0.4	0.4
Hamilton	3,495	1,149	2,206	140	1,057	R	32.9	63.1	4.0	60	4	41	<.1	<.1	<.1	<.1
Herkimer	26,874	9,917	15,849	1,108	5,932	R	36.9	59.0	4.1	44	15	39	0.4	0.3	0.5	0.5
Jefferson	34,300	12,196	20,199	1,905	8,003	R	35.6	58.9	5.6	48	17	12	0.5	0.4	0.6	0.9
Kings	536,460	315,709	210,643	10,108	105,066	D	58.9	39.3	1.9	3	59	58	8.3	10.2	6.7	4.9
Lewis	10,106	3,573	5,990	543	2,417	R	35.4	59.3	5.4	50	14	16	0.2	0.1	0.2	0.3
Livingston	23,926	8,976	13,813	1,137	4,837	R	37.5	57.7	4.8	39	25	25	0.4	0.3	0.4	0.6
Madison	26,204	9,882	14,596	1,726	4,714	R	37.7	55.7	6.6	38	33	3	0.4	0.3	0.5	0.8
Monroe	309,744	139,163	158,382	12,199	19,219	R	44.9	51.1	3.9	11	51	43	4.8	4.5	5.0	5.9
Montgomery	21,646	9,255	11,634	757	2,379	R	42.8	53.7	3.5	16	42	46	0.3	0.3	0.4	0.4
Nassau	586,959	237,692	337,715	11,552	100,023	R	40.5	57.5	2.0	23	26	56	9.1	7.7	10.7	5.6
New York	501,926	382,877	110,023	9,026	272,854	D	76.3	21.9	1.8	1	62	60	7.8	12.4	3.5	4.4
Niagara	87,512	40,232	42,386	4,894	2,154	R	46.0	48.4	5.6	9	55	11	1.4	1.3	1.3	2.4
Oneida	99,961	37,411	58,671	3,879	21,260	R	37.4	58.7	3.9	40	18	44	1.5	1.2	1.9	1.9
Onondaga	198,537	79,954	106,654	11,929	26,700	R	40.3	53.7	6.0	25	43	8	3.1	2.6	3.4	5.8
Ontario	40,715	16,167	22,605	1,943	6,438	R	39.7	55.5	4.8	29	35	23	0.6	0.5	0.7	0.9
Orange	113,765	42,568	67,921	3,276	25,353	R	37.4	59.7	2.9	41	10	52	1.8	1.4	2.1	1.6
Orleans	14,798	5,298	8,716	784	3,418	R	35.8	58.9	5.3	47	16	17	0.2	0.2	0.3	0.4
Oswego	46,375	16,310	26,242	3,823	9,932	R	35.2	56.6	8.2	52	30	1	0.7	0.5	0.8	1.9
Otsego	24,418	10,766	12,576	1,076	1,810	R	44.1	51.5	4.4	13	50	32	0.4	0.3	0.4	0.5
Putnam	39,303	13,560	24,616	1,127	11,056	R	34.5	62.6	2.9	56	5	53	0.6	0.4	0.8	0.5
Queens	523,149	275,737	238,407	9,005	37,330	D	52.7	45.6	1.7	6	56	61	8.1	8.9	7.5	4.4
Rensselaer	70,603	30,104	37,288	3,211	7,184	R	42.6	52.8	4.5	18	48	29	1.1	1.0	1.2	1.6
Richmond	140,780	43,783	94,825	2,172	51,042	R	31.1	67.4	1.5	61	1	62	2.2	1.4	3.0	1.1
Rockland	116,287	46,265	67,829	2,193	21,564	R	39.8	58.3	1.9	28	20	57	1.8	1.5	2.1	1.1
St. Lawrence	38,085	16,786	18,916	2,383	2,130	R	44.1	49.7	6.3	14	53	6	0.6	0.5	0.6	1.2
Saratoga	84,041	33,988	46,375	3,678	12,387	R	40.4	55.2	4.4	24	38	34	1.3	1.1	1.5	1.8
Schenectady	69,500	31,840	34,790	2,870	2,950	R	45.8	50.1	4.1	10	52	38	1.1	1.0	1.1	1.4
Schoharie	13,358	5,132	7,590	636	2,458	R	38.4	56.8	4.8	35	28	24	0.2	0.2	0.2	0.3
Schuyler	7,382	2,596	4,433	353	1,837	R	35.2	60.1	4.8	53	8	22	0.1	<.1	0.1	0.2
Seneca	13,496	4,791	8,067	638	3,276	R	35.5	59.8	4.7	49	9	26	0.2	0.2	0.3	0.3
Steuben	37,532	11,472	24,350	1,710	12,878	R	30.6	64.9	4.6	62	2	28	0.6	0.4	0.8	0.8
Suffolk	541,191	212,688	313,515	14,988	100,827	R	39.3	57.9	2.8	33	22	54	8.4	6.9	9.9	7.3
Sullivan	29,464	12,886	15,665	913	2,779	R	43.7	53.2	3.1	15	46	49	0.5	0.4	0.5	0.4
Tioga	21,021	7,689	12,492	840	4,803	R	36.6	59.4	4.0	45	13	42	0.3	0.2	0.4	0.4
Tompkins	37,852	22,094	14,536	1,222	7,558	D	58.4	38.4	3.2	4	60	48	0.6	0.7	0.5	0.6
Ulster	74,835	31,912	39,830	3,093	7,918	R	42.6	53.2	4.1	17	44	37	1.2	1.0	1.3	1.5
Warren	26,337	10,755	14,453	1,129	3,698	R	40.8	54.9	4.3	21	41	35	0.4	0.3	0.5	0.5
Washington	22,933	8,815	12,959	1,159	4,144	R	38.4	56.5	5.1	34	32	20	0.4	0.3	0.4	0.6
Wayne	35,280	12,392	21,044	1,844	8,652	R	35.1	59.6	5.2	54	11	18	0.5	0.4	0.7	0.9
Westchester	362,127	167,719	186,675	7,733	18,956	R	46.3	51.5	2.1	8	49	55	5.6	5.4	5.9	3.8
Wyoming	14,759	4,962	8,870	927	3,908	R	33.6	60.1	6.3	58	7	5	0.2	0.2	0.3	0.5
Yates	9,160	3,232	5,372	556	2,140	R	35.3	58.6	6.1	51	19	7	0.1	0.1	0.2	0.3
NEW YORK	6,458,826	3,086,200	3,166,994	205,632	80,794	R	47.8	49.0	3.2				100.0	100.0	100.0	100.0

[1]Includes votes cast for Robert Abrams as the nominee of Democratic and Liberal parties. [2]Includes votes cast for Alfonse M. D'Amato as the nominee of Republican, Conservative, and Right to Life parties.

Table H. — Vote for U.S. Representative in Congress: November 3, 1992, General Election

Congressional district and county	Total	Democrat (DEM)[1]	Republican (REP)[1]	Other	Plurality Total	Plurality Party	Percent of total vote DEM	REP	Other	Rank within district DEM	REP	Other	Percent contribution to district vote Total	DEM	REP	Other
District 1	227,983	117,940	110,043	-	7,897	D	51.7	48.3	-				100.0	100.0	100.0	-
Suffolk (pt)	227,983	117,940	110,043	-	7,897	D	51.7	48.3	-	1	1	-	100.0	100.0	100.0	-
District 2	205,714	96,328	109,386	-	13,058	R	46.8	53.2	-				100.0	100.0	100.0	-
Suffolk (pt)	205,714	96,328	109,386	-	13,058	R	46.8	53.2	-	1	1	-	100.0	100.0	100.0	-
District 3	251,622	116,915	124,727	9,980	7,812	R	46.5	49.6	4.0				100.0	100.0	100.0	100.0
Nassau (pt)	251,622	116,915	124,727	9,980	7,812	R	46.5	49.6	4.0	1	1	1	100.0	100.0	100.0	100.0
District 4	220,644	100,386	110,710	9,548	10,324	R	45.5	50.2	4.3				100.0	100.0	100.0	100.0
Nassau (pt)	220,644	100,386	110,710	9,548	10,324	R	45.5	50.2	4.3	1	1	1	100.0	100.0	100.0	100.0
District 5	210,831	110,476	94,907	5,448	15,569	D	52.4	45.0	2.6				100.0	100.0	100.0	100.0
Nassau (pt)	53,773	31,558	21,277	938	10,281	D	58.7	39.6	1.7	2	2	2	25.5	28.6	22.4	17.2
Queens (pt)	86,435	52,387	32,610	1,438	19,777	D	60.6	37.7	1.7	1	3	3	41.0	47.4	34.4	26.4
Suffolk (pt)	70,623	26,531	41,020	3,072	14,489	R	37.6	58.1	4.3	3	1	1	33.5	24.0	43.2	56.4
District 6	119,659	96,972	22,687	-	74,285	D	81.0	19.0	-				100.0	100.0	100.0	-
Queens (pt)	119,659	96,972	22,687	-	74,285	D	81.0	19.0	-	1	1	-	100.0	100.0	100.0	-
District 7	126,919	72,280	54,639	-	17,641	D	56.9	43.1	-				100.0	100.0	100.0	-
Bronx (pt)	32,434	16,838	15,596	-	1,242	D	51.9	48.1	-	2	1	-	25.6	23.3	28.5	-
Queens (pt)	94,485	55,442	39,043	-	16,399	D	58.7	41.3	-	1	2	-	74.4	76.7	71.5	-
District 8	170,248	138,296	25,548	6,404	112,748	D	81.2	15.0	3.8				100.0	100.0	100.0	100.0
Kings (pt)	41,522	30,452	8,857	2,213	21,595	D	73.3	21.3	5.3	2	1	1	24.4	22.0	34.7	34.6
New York (pt)	128,726	107,844	16,691	4,191	91,153	D	83.8	13.0	3.3	1	2	2	75.6	78.0	65.3	65.4
District 9	131,530	116,545	-	14,985	101,560	D	88.6	-	11.4				100.0	100.0	-	100.0
Kings (pt)	82,318	75,309	-	7,009	68,300	D	91.5	-	8.5	1	-	2	62.6	64.6	-	46.8
Queens (pt)	49,212	41,236	-	7,976	33,260	D	83.8	-	16.2	2	-	1	37.4	35.4	-	53.2
District 10	101,824	97,509	-	4,315	93,194	D	95.8	-	4.2				100.0	100.0	-	100.0
Kings (pt)	101,824	97,509	-	4,315	93,194	D	95.8	-	4.2	1	-	1	100.0	100.0	-	100.0
District 11	85,494	80,028	-	5,466	74,562	D	93.6	-	6.4				100.0	100.0	-	100.0
Kings (pt)	85,494	80,028	-	5,466	74,562	D	93.6	-	6.4	1	-	1	100.0	100.0	-	100.0
District 12	73,067	55,926	14,976	2,165	40,950	D	76.5	20.5	3.0				100.0	100.0	100.0	100.0
Kings (pt)	39,107	30,953	7,173	981	23,780	D	79.1	18.3	2.5	2	2	3	53.5	55.3	47.9	45.3
New York (pt)	19,640	15,680	3,280	680	12,400	D	79.8	16.7	3.5	1	3	2	26.9	28.0	21.9	31.4
Queens (pt)	14,320	9,293	4,523	504	4,770	D	64.9	31.6	3.5	3	1	1	19.6	16.6	30.2	23.3
District 13	192,248	73,520	107,903	10,825	34,383	R	38.2	56.1	5.6				100.0	100.0	100.0	100.0
Kings (pt)	55,501	28,402	24,534	2,565	3,868	D	51.2	44.2	4.6	1	2	2	28.9	38.6	22.7	23.7
Richmond	136,747	45,118	83,369	8,260	38,251	R	33.0	61.0	6.0	2	1	1	71.1	61.4	77.3	76.3
District 14	201,837	101,652	97,215	2,970	4,437	D	50.4	48.2	1.5				100.0	100.0	100.0	100.0
Kings (pt)	9,597	5,718	3,716	163	2,002	D	59.6	38.7	1.7	2	2	1	4.8	5.6	3.8	5.5
New York (pt)	177,774	86,627	88,482	2,665	1,855	R	48.7	49.8	1.5	3	1	2	88.1	85.2	91.0	89.7
Queens (pt)	14,466	9,307	5,017	142	4,290	D	64.3	34.7	1.0	1	3	3	7.2	9.2	5.2	4.8
District 15	110,693	105,011	-	5,682	99,329	D	94.9	-	5.1				100.0	100.0	-	100.0
Bronx (pt)[2]	0	0	-	0	0	D	0.0	-	0.0	2	-	2	0.0	0.0	-	0.0
New York (pt)	110,693	105,011	-	5,682	99,329	D	94.9	-	5.1	1	-	1	100.0	100.0	-	100.0
District 16	93,197	85,222	7,975	-	77,247	D	91.4	8.6	-				100.0	100.0	100.0	-
Bronx (pt)	93,197	85,222	7,975	-	77,247	D	91.4	8.6	-	1	1	-	100.0	100.0	100.0	-
District 17	122,381	98,068	16,511	7,802	81,557	D	80.1	13.5	6.4				100.0	100.0	100.0	100.0
Bronx (pt)	97,024	78,392	12,476	6,156	65,916	D	80.8	12.9	6.3	1	2	2	79.3	79.9	75.6	78.9
Westchester (pt)	25,357	19,676	4,035	1,646	15,641	D	77.6	15.9	6.5	2	1	1	20.7	20.1	24.4	21.1
District 18	208,528	115,841	92,687	-	23,154	D	55.6	44.4	-				100.0	100.0	100.0	-
Bronx (pt)	6,385	2,293	4,092	-	1,799	R	35.9	64.1	-	3	1	-	3.1	2.0	4.4	-
Queens (pt)	40,036	28,237	11,799	-	16,438	D	70.5	29.5	-	1	3	-	19.2	24.4	12.7	-
Westchester (pt)	162,107	85,311	76,796	-	8,515	D	52.6	47.4	-	2	2	-	77.7	73.6	82.9	-
District 19	232,464	92,854	139,610	-	46,756	R	39.9	60.1	-				100.0	100.0	100.0	-
Dutchess (pt)	65,962	22,925	43,037	-	20,112	R	34.8	65.2	-	2	3	-	28.4	24.7	30.8	-
Orange (pt)	16,785	5,479	11,306	-	5,827	R	32.6	67.4	-	4	1	-	7.2	5.9	8.1	-
Putnam	36,158	12,273	23,885	-	11,612	R	33.9	66.1	-	3	2	-	15.6	13.2	17.1	-
Westchester (pt)	113,559	52,177	61,382	-	9,205	R	45.9	54.1	-	1	4	-	48.9	56.2	44.0	-
District 20	227,331	66,826	150,301	10,204	83,475	R	29.4	66.1	4.5				100.0	100.0	100.0	100.0
Orange (pt)	74,033	17,315	52,940	3,778	35,625	R	23.4	71.5	5.1	4	1	1	32.6	25.9	35.2	37.0

[1] Also includes votes cast for candidates as nominees of minor political parties.   [2] No registered voters—Rikers Island corrections facility.

Congressional district and county	Total	Democrat (DEM)[1]	Republican (REP)[1]	Other	Plurality Total	Party	Percent of total vote DEM	REP	Other	Rank within district DEM	REP	Other	Percent contribution to district vote Total	DEM	REP	Other
District 20 (cont)																
Rockland	106,020	30,204	71,053	4,763	40,849	R	28.5	67.0	4.5	2	3	2	46.6	45.2	47.3	46.7
Sullivan (pt)	9,715	2,535	6,772	408	4,237	R	26.1	69.7	4.2	3	2	3	4.3	3.8	4.5	4.0
Westchester (pt)	37,563	16,772	19,536	1,255	2,764	R	44.7	52.0	3.3	1	4	4	16.5	25.1	13.0	12.3
District 21	**265,278**	**166,371**	**91,184**	**7,723**	**75,187**	**D**	**62.7**	**34.4**	**2.9**				**100.0**	**100.0**	**100.0**	**100.0**
Albany	143,457	93,077	46,806	3,574	46,271	D	64.9	32.6	2.5	1	5	5	54.1	55.9	51.3	46.3
Montgomery (pt)	16,532	9,833	6,149	550	3,684	D	59.5	37.2	3.3	3	3	3	6.2	5.9	6.7	7.1
Rensselaer (pt)	35,750	22,168	12,198	1,384	9,970	D	62.0	34.1	3.9	2	4	2	13.5	13.3	13.4	17.9
Saratoga (pt)	3,982	2,316	1,497	169	819	D	58.2	37.6	4.2	5	1	1	1.5	1.4	1.6	2.2
Schenectady	65,557	38,977	24,534	2,046	14,443	D	59.5	37.4	3.1	4	2	4	24.7	23.4	26.9	26.5
District 22	**251,332**	**86,896**	**164,436**	**-**	**77,540**	**R**	**34.6**	**65.4**	**-**				**100.0**	**100.0**	**100.0**	**-**
Columbia	25,853	8,924	16,929	-	8,005	R	34.5	65.5	-	5	5	-	10.3	10.3	10.3	-
Dutchess (pt)	31,289	11,237	20,052	-	8,815	R	35.9	64.1	-	3	7	-	12.4	12.9	12.2	-
Essex (pt)	10,701	3,725	6,976	-	3,251	R	34.8	65.2	-	4	6	-	4.3	4.3	4.2	-
Greene	18,924	5,782	13,142	-	7,360	R	30.6	69.4	-	9	1	-	7.5	6.7	8.0	-
Rensselaer (pt)	31,681	10,428	21,253	-	10,825	R	32.9	67.1	-	8	2	-	12.6	12.0	12.9	-
Saratoga (pt)	77,446	28,051	49,395	-	21,344	R	36.2	63.8	-	2	8	-	30.8	32.3	30.0	-
Schoharie (pt)	5,620	2,151	3,469	-	1,318	R	38.3	61.7	-	1	9	-	2.2	2.5	2.1	-
Warren	26,604	8,851	17,753	-	8,902	R	33.3	66.7	-	7	3	-	10.6	10.2	10.8	-
Washington	23,214	7,747	15,467	-	7,720	R	33.4	66.6	-	6	4	-	9.2	8.9	9.4	-
District 23	**219,662**	**61,835**	**139,774**	**18,053**	**77,939**	**R**	**28.2**	**63.6**	**8.2**				**100.0**	**100.0**	**100.0**	**100.0**
Broome (pt)	7,427	2,010	4,635	782	2,625	R	27.1	62.4	10.5	6	5	3	3.4	3.3	3.3	4.3
Chenango	19,038	4,645	12,707	1,686	8,062	R	24.4	66.7	8.9	9	1	5	8.7	7.5	9.1	9.3
Delaware (pt)	15,385	4,054	9,639	1,692	5,585	R	26.4	62.7	11.0	8	4	1	7.0	6.6	6.9	9.4
Herkimer (pt)	22,027	6,468	13,911	1,648	7,443	R	29.4	63.2	7.5	5	3	8	10.0	10.5	10.0	9.1
Madison	23,944	7,598	13,951	2,395	6,353	R	31.7	58.3	10.0	2	8	4	10.9	12.3	10.0	13.3
Montgomery (pt)	3,134	947	1,916	271	969	R	30.2	61.1	8.6	3	6	6	1.4	1.5	1.4	1.5
Oneida	98,501	26,136	65,459	6,906	39,323	R	26.5	66.5	7.0	7	2	9	44.8	42.3	46.8	38.3
Otsego	23,522	7,998	13,580	1,944	5,582	R	34.0	57.7	8.3	1	9	7	10.7	12.9	9.7	10.8
Schoharie (pt)	6,684	1,979	3,976	729	1,997	R	29.6	59.5	10.9	4	7	2	3.0	3.2	2.8	4.0
District 24	**201,069**	**47,675**	**122,257**	**31,137**	**74,582**	**R**	**23.7**	**60.8**	**15.5**				**100.0**	**100.0**	**100.0**	**100.0**
Clinton	27,049	8,182	14,366	4,501	6,184	R	30.2	53.1	16.6	2	7	5	13.5	17.2	11.8	14.5
Essex (pt)	4,380	1,090	2,597	693	1,507	R	24.9	59.3	15.8	5	5	6	2.2	2.3	2.1	2.2
Franklin	16,001	5,023	7,713	3,265	2,690	R	31.4	48.2	20.4	1	9	3	8.0	10.5	6.3	10.5
Fulton	18,740	5,613	9,170	3,957	3,557	R	30.0	48.9	21.1	3	8	2	9.3	11.8	7.5	12.7
Hamilton	3,478	532	1,304	1,642	338	O	15.3	37.5	47.2	10	10	1	1.7	1.1	1.1	5.3
Herkimer (pt)	3,202	813	1,777	612	964	R	25.4	55.5	19.1	4	6	4	1.6	1.7	1.5	2.0
Jefferson	34,971	6,026	24,759	4,186	18,733	R	17.2	70.8	12.0	9	1	10	17.4	12.6	20.3	13.4
Lewis	9,940	1,993	6,739	1,208	4,746	R	20.1	67.8	12.2	8	2	9	4.9	4.2	5.5	3.9
Oswego	44,767	9,396	29,665	5,706	20,269	R	21.0	66.3	12.7	7	3	8	22.3	19.7	24.3	18.3
St. Lawrence	38,541	9,007	24,167	5,367	15,160	R	23.4	62.7	13.9	6	4	7	19.2	18.9	19.8	17.2
District 25	**242,386**	**107,310**	**135,076**	**-**	**27,766**	**R**	**44.3**	**55.7**	**-**				**100.0**	**100.0**	**100.0**	**-**
Broome (pt)	3,526	1,077	2,449	-	1,372	R	30.5	69.5	-	5	1	-	1.5	1.0	1.8	-
Cayuga (pt)	18,103	8,003	10,100	-	2,097	R	44.2	55.8	-	3	3	-	7.5	7.5	7.5	-
Cortland	18,745	8,350	10,395	-	2,045	R	44.5	55.5	-	2	4	-	7.7	7.8	7.7	-
Onondaga	199,699	89,034	110,665	-	21,631	R	44.6	55.4	-	1	5	-	82.4	83.0	81.9	-
Tioga (pt)	2,313	846	1,467	-	621	R	36.6	63.4	-	4	2	-	1.0	0.8	1.1	-
District 26	**237,116**	**119,557**	**110,738**	**6,821**	**8,819**	**D**	**50.4**	**46.7**	**2.9**				**100.0**	**100.0**	**100.0**	**100.0**
Broome (pt)	80,849	34,262	44,916	1,671	10,654	R	42.4	55.6	2.1	6	3	8	34.1	28.7	40.6	24.5
Delaware (pt)	2,193	752	1,357	84	605	R	34.3	61.9	3.8	8	1	3	0.9	0.6	1.2	1.2
Dutchess (pt)	4,248	2,152	1,904	192	248	D	50.7	44.8	4.5	4	5	2	1.8	1.8	1.7	2.8
Orange (pt)	14,701	7,223	6,685	793	538	D	49.1	45.5	5.4	5	4	1	6.2	6.0	6.0	11.6
Sullivan (pt)	16,872	9,489	6,817	566	2,672	D	56.2	40.4	3.4	3	6	5	7.1	7.9	6.2	8.3
Tioga (pt)	18,516	6,572	11,292	652	4,720	R	35.5	61.0	3.5	7	2	4	7.8	5.5	10.2	9.6
Tompkins (pt)	26,211	16,660	8,986	565	7,674	D	63.6	34.3	2.2	1	8	7	11.1	13.9	8.1	8.3
Ulster	73,526	42,447	28,781	2,298	13,666	D	57.7	39.1	3.1	2	7	6	31.0	35.5	26.0	33.7
District 27	**246,502**	**89,906**	**156,596**	**-**	**66,690**	**R**	**36.5**	**63.5**	**-**				**100.0**	**100.0**	**100.0**	**-**
Cayuga (pt)	1,413	612	801	-	189	R	43.3	56.7	-	2	8	-	0.6	0.7	0.5	-
Erie (pt)	76,102	27,925	48,177	-	20,252	R	36.7	63.3	-	4	6	-	30.9	31.1	30.8	-
Genesee	24,433	12,177	12,256	-	79	R	49.8	50.2	-	1	9	-	9.9	13.5	7.8	-
Livingston	24,256	8,613	15,643	-	7,030	R	35.5	64.5	-	7	3	-	9.8	9.6	10.0	-
Monroe (pt)	23,172	8,571	14,601	-	6,030	R	37.0	63.0	-	3	7	-	9.4	9.5	9.3	-
Ontario	40,058	14,570	25,488	-	10,918	R	36.4	63.6	-	5	5	-	16.3	16.2	16.3	-
Seneca (pt)	8,577	3,062	5,515	-	2,453	R	35.7	64.3	-	6	4	-	3.5	3.4	3.5	-
Wayne	33,219	9,805	23,414	-	13,609	R	29.5	70.5	-	9	1	-	13.5	10.9	15.0	-
Wyoming	15,272	4,571	10,701	-	6,130	R	29.9	70.1	-	8	2	-	6.2	5.1	6.8	-
District 28	**255,078**	**140,908**	**112,273**	**1,897**	**28,635**	**D**	**55.2**	**44.0**	**0.7**				**100.0**	**100.0**	**100.0**	**100.0**
Monroe (pt)	255,078	140,908	112,273	1,897	28,635	D	55.2	44.0	0.7	1	1	1	100.0	100.0	100.0	100.0

[1]Also includes votes cast for candidates as nominees of minor political parties.

Congressional district and county	Total	Democrat (DEM)[1]	Republican (REP)[1]	Other	Plurality Total	Plurality Party	Percent of total vote DEM	REP	Other	Rank within district DEM	REP	Other	Percent contribution to district vote Total	DEM	REP	Other
District 29	**235,458**	**128,230**	**98,031**	**9,197**	**30,199**	**D**	**54.5**	**41.6**	**3.9**				**100.0**	**100.0**	**100.0**	**100.0**
Erie (pt)	95,300	57,604	34,396	3,300	23,208	D	60.4	36.1	3.5	1	4	4	40.5	44.9	35.1	35.9
Monroe (pt)	35,923	18,514	15,703	1,706	2,811	D	51.5	43.7	4.7	2	3	1	15.3	14.4	16.0	18.5
Niagara	89,344	44,624	41,140	3,580	3,484	D	49.9	46.0	4.0	4	1	3	37.9	34.8	42.0	38.9
Orleans	14,891	7,488	6,792	611	696	D	50.3	45.6	4.1	3	2	2	6.3	5.8	6.9	6.6
District 30	**243,204**	**111,445**	**125,734**	**6,025**	**14,289**	**R**	**45.8**	**51.7**	**2.5**				**100.0**	**100.0**	**100.0**	**100.0**
Erie (pt)	243,204	111,445	125,734	6,025	14,289	R	45.8	51.7	2.5	1	1	1	100.0	100.0	100.0	100.0
District 31	**213,554**	**52,010**	**150,696**	**10,848**	**98,686**	**R**	**24.4**	**70.6**	**5.1**				**100.0**	**100.0**	**100.0**	**100.0**
Allegany	16,766	2,994	12,843	929	9,849	R	17.9	76.6	5.5	9	2	3	7.9	5.8	8.5	8.6
Cattaraugus	30,447	9,081	19,566	1,800	10,485	R	29.8	64.3	5.9	3	8	2	14.3	17.5	13.0	16.6
Cayuga (pt)	9,932	3,253	6,150	529	2,897	R	32.8	61.9	5.3	2	9	4	4.7	6.3	4.1	4.9
Chautauqua	53,885	15,712	35,911	2,262	20,199	R	29.2	66.6	4.2	4	6	10	25.2	30.2	23.8	20.9
Chemung	35,380	6,885	26,885	1,610	20,000	R	19.5	76.0	4.6	8	3	9	16.6	13.2	17.8	14.8
Schuyler	7,253	1,651	5,256	346	3,605	R	22.8	72.5	4.8	7	4	7	3.4	3.2	3.5	3.2
Seneca (pt)	3,638	1,059	2,401	178	1,342	R	29.1	66.0	4.9	5	7	6	1.7	2.0	1.6	1.6
Steuben	37,718	5,806	29,626	2,286	23,820	R	15.4	78.5	6.1	10	1	1	17.7	11.2	19.7	21.1
Tompkins (pt)	9,891	3,443	5,992	456	2,549	R	34.8	60.6	4.6	1	10	8	4.6	6.6	4.0	4.2
Yates	8,644	2,126	6,066	452	3,940	R	24.6	70.2	5.2	6	5	5	4.0	4.1	4.0	4.2
NEW YORK	**5,924,853**	**3,050,738**	**2,686,620**	**187,495**	**364,118**	**D**	**51.5**	**45.3**	**3.2**							

[1]Also includes votes cast for candidates as nominees of minor political parties.

Table I. — Vote for Presidential Preference: April 7, 1992, Democratic Primary Election

County	Total	Clinton	Tsongas	Brown	Harkin	Kerrey	Agran	McCarthy		Clinton	Tsongas	Brown	Clinton	Tsongas	Brown	Total	Clinton	Tsongas	Brown
			Top candidates							Top three candidates (state vote)									
										Percent of total vote			Rank			Percent contribution to state vote			
Albany	26,587	6,901	9,565	8,799	529	324	268	201	-	26.0	36.0	33.1	60	11	16	2.6	1.7	3.3	3.3
Allegany	1,132	397	346	329	12	8	11	29	-	35.1	30.6	29.1	33	37	33	0.1	<.1	0.1	0.1
Bronx	71,235	36,274	12,219	18,540	929	1,240	1,222	811	-	50.9	17.2	26.0	1	62	47	7.1	8.8	4.2	7.0
Broome	9,091	3,048	3,154	2,557	90	86	76	80	-	33.5	34.7	28.1	35	20	39	0.9	0.7	1.1	1.0
Cattaraugus	2,689	991	760	781	40	43	33	41	-	36.9	28.3	29.0	19	48	34	0.3	0.2	0.3	0.3
Cayuga	3,279	1,317	860	990	25	33	32	22	-	40.2	26.2	30.2	8	53	29	0.3	0.3	0.3	0.4
Chautauqua	5,426	1,958	1,539	1,706	75	48	55	45	-	36.1	28.4	31.4	26	47	22	0.5	0.5	0.5	0.6
Chemung	3,127	1,148	1,172	681	35	30	40	21	-	36.7	37.5	21.8	20	5	58	0.3	0.3	0.4	0.3
Chenango	1,454	487	452	456	15	24	7	13	-	33.5	31.1	31.4	37	34	24	0.1	0.1	0.2	0.2
Clinton	2,174	793	766	512	35	34	12	22	-	36.5	35.2	23.6	21	15	56	0.2	0.2	0.3	0.2
Columbia	2,629	755	805	959	49	20	17	24	-	28.7	30.6	36.5	53	36	4	0.3	0.2	0.3	0.4
Cortland	1,710	559	474	621	15	11	18	12	-	32.7	27.7	36.3	44	50	5	0.2	0.1	0.2	0.2
Delaware	1,624	544	498	491	32	26	16	17	-	33.5	30.7	30.2	36	35	28	0.2	0.1	0.2	0.2
Dutchess	9,920	2,708	3,746	3,155	84	63	94	70	-	27.3	37.8	31.8	56	3	20	1.0	0.7	1.3	1.2
Erie	65,297	25,366	16,159	19,139	1,767	1,177	923	766	-	38.8	24.7	29.3	11	57	32	6.5	6.2	5.6	7.2
Essex	1,269	407	488	309	17	21	12	15	-	32.1	38.5	24.3	46	2	54	0.1	<.1	0.2	0.1
Franklin	1,531	585	511	350	15	28	14	28	-	38.2	33.4	22.9	13	24	57	0.2	0.1	0.2	0.1
Fulton	1,855	673	483	642	24	14	10	9	-	36.3	26.0	34.6	23	54	8	0.2	0.2	0.2	0.2
Genesee	1,756	578	510	563	49	13	23	20	-	32.9	29.0	32.1	42	45	19	0.2	0.1	0.2	0.2
Greene	1,305	378	394	478	21	9	11	14	-	29.0	30.2	36.6	52	39	3	0.1	<.1	0.1	0.2
Hamilton	307	99	84	105	5	2	6	6	-	32.2	27.4	34.2	45	52	12	<.1	<.1	<.1	<.1
Herkimer	2,165	724	738	621	24	27	16	15	-	33.4	34.1	28.7	38	21	38	0.2	0.2	0.3	0.2
Jefferson	2,863	1,069	688	989	35	34	35	13	-	37.3	24.0	34.5	18	58	9	0.3	0.3	0.2	0.4
Kings	140,965	70,198	31,296	33,350	1,385	1,688	1,666	1,382	-	49.8	22.2	23.7	2	60	55	14.0	17.0	10.9	12.6
Lewis	678	243	144	260	16	7	5	3	-	35.8	21.2	38.3	27	61	2	<.1	<.1	<.1	<.1
Livingston	1,696	634	568	422	23	25	13	11	-	37.4	33.5	24.9	17	23	53	0.2	0.2	0.2	0.2
Madison	2,131	758	699	599	33	18	9	15	-	35.6	32.8	28.1	30	29	40	0.2	0.2	0.2	0.2
Monroe	31,790	11,565	11,132	7,995	260	332	262	244	-	36.4	35.0	25.1	22	18	50	3.2	2.8	3.9	3.0
Montgomery	2,750	908	799	944	43	28	16	12	-	33.0	29.1	34.3	41	44	10	0.3	0.2	0.3	0.4
Nassau	62,662	24,530	24,413	11,629	740	326	619	405	-	39.1	39.0	18.6	10	1	62	6.2	5.9	8.5	4.4
New York	165,295	70,669	40,947	47,703	1,072	1,751	1,648	1,505	-	42.8	24.8	28.9	4	56	36	16.4	17.1	14.2	18.1
Niagara	10,740	3,895	2,454	3,683	292	164	153	99	-	36.3	22.8	34.3	24	59	11	1.1	0.9	0.9	1.4
Oneida	8,242	2,944	2,741	2,184	129	103	78	63	-	35.7	33.3	26.5	29	25	44	0.8	0.7	1.0	0.8
Onondaga	18,039	6,381	5,709	5,369	229	101	105	145	-	35.4	31.6	29.8	32	32	31	1.8	1.5	2.0	2.0
Ontario	2,914	966	1,059	792	21	22	23	31	-	33.2	36.3	27.2	40	10	42	0.3	0.2	0.4	0.3
Orange	10,468	3,638	3,132	3,287	128	95	109	79	-	34.8	29.9	31.4	34	40	23	1.0	0.9	1.1	1.2
Orleans	899	375	268	225	6	7	9	9	-	41.7	29.8	25.0	6	41	51	<.1	<.1	<.1	<.1
Oswego	2,972	1,075	876	902	39	23	24	33	-	36.2	29.5	30.3	25	43	27	0.3	0.3	0.3	0.3
Otsego	2,284	648	798	761	24	19	9	25	-	28.4	34.9	33.3	54	19	14	0.2	0.2	0.3	0.3
Putnam	2,963	882	1,050	941	35	22	13	20	-	29.8	35.4	31.8	49	13	21	0.3	0.2	0.4	0.4
Queens	129,477	58,098	38,408	28,115	1,057	1,310	1,166	1,323	-	44.9	29.7	21.7	3	42	59	12.8	14.1	13.3	10.6
Rensselaer	6,223	1,565	2,323	2,060	119	49	50	57	-	25.1	37.3	33.1	61	6	15	0.6	0.4	0.8	0.8
Richmond	18,485	6,570	6,100	5,093	119	297	134	172	-	35.5	33.0	27.6	31	27	41	1.8	1.6	2.1	1.9
Rockland	19,420	7,529	7,160	4,092	131	155	191	162	-	38.8	36.9	21.1	12	8	60	1.9	1.8	2.5	1.5
St. Lawrence	3,240	1,081	902	968	85	137	38	29	-	33.4	27.8	29.9	39	49	30	0.3	0.3	0.3	0.4
Saratoga	6,121	1,497	2,269	2,130	85	58	38	44	-	24.5	37.1	34.8	62	7	7	0.6	0.4	0.8	0.8
Schenectady	7,706	2,086	2,754	2,596	122	59	41	48	-	27.1	35.7	33.7	58	12	13	0.8	0.5	1.0	1.0
Schoharie	1,066	350	351	328	15	7	6	9	-	32.8	32.9	30.8	43	28	26	0.1	<.1	0.1	0.1
Schuyler	654	194	214	213	8	4	12	9	-	29.7	32.7	32.6	50	30	17	<.1	<.1	<.1	<.1
Seneca	1,164	441	367	308	19	6	13	10	-	37.9	31.5	26.5	14	33	45	0.1	0.1	0.1	0.1
Steuben	2,795	1,117	845	723	25	26	32	27	-	40.0	30.2	25.9	9	38	48	0.3	0.3	0.3	0.3
Suffolk	39,385	12,557	13,850	11,330	616	240	411	381	-	31.9	35.2	28.8	47	17	37	3.9	3.0	4.8	4.3
Sullivan	3,191	1,353	883	833	30	34	29	29	-	42.4	27.7	26.1	5	51	46	0.3	0.3	0.3	0.3
Tioga	1,825	565	685	494	28	21	18	14	-	31.0	37.5	27.1	48	4	43	0.2	0.1	0.2	0.2
Tompkins	7,900	2,153	2,574	2,798	58	42	207	68	-	27.3	32.6	35.4	57	31	6	0.8	0.5	0.9	1.1
Ulster	8,218	2,213	2,066	3,621	117	59	57	85	-	26.9	25.1	44.1	59	55	1	0.8	0.5	0.7	1.4
Warren	2,058	564	754	644	30	17	30	19	-	27.4	36.6	31.3	55	9	25	0.2	0.1	0.3	0.2
Washington	1,510	446	508	487	27	10	20	12	-	29.5	33.6	32.3	51	22	18	0.1	0.1	0.2	0.2
Wayne	1,813	681	599	464	17	15	15	22	-	37.6	33.0	25.6	16	26	49	0.2	0.2	0.2	0.2
Westchester	56,020	22,651	19,737	11,743	409	543	498	439	-	40.4	35.2	21.0	7	16	61	5.6	5.5	6.8	4.4
Wyoming	872	330	248	252	17	6	8	11	-	37.8	28.4	28.9	15	46	35	<.1	<.1	<.1	<.1
Yates	670	240	237	167	4	6	7	9	-	35.8	35.4	24.9	28	14	52	<.1	<.1	<.1	<.1
NEW YORK	1,007,726	412,349	288,330	264,278	11,535	11,147	10,733	9,354	-	40.9	28.6	26.2				100.0	100.0	100.0	100.0

1992 Vote for President
Percent for Clinton (D), by County

Clinton (D) received 49.7% statewide.

A framed county name indicates a county carried by the winner.

Legend:
- 41.8% to 78.2%
- 36.9% to 41.7%
- 34.1% to 36.8%
- 24.7% to 34.0%

New York 667

1992 Vote for U.S. Senator
Percent for D'Amato (R), by County

Legend:
- 59.0% to 67.4%
- 56.6% to 58.9%
- 53.1% to 56.5%
- 21.9% to 53.0%

D'Amato (R) received 49.0% statewide.

A framed county name indicates a county carried by the winner.

NORTH CAROLINA

Congressional Districts 12
   Average Population 552,386
State Senate Districts 50
   Average Population 132,573
State House Districts 120
   Average Population 55,239

Electoral College Votes 14
Counties 100
Voting Precincts 2,458

Alternative Registration Methods:
  .... Deputized Registrars, Motor-voter

Registration Deadline (Days before Election) 21

Voting Equipment Use (Counties)

Datavote Punch Card	0	Paper Ballot	16
Electronic	9	Other Punch Card	18
Lever Machine	20	Mixed Systems	0
Optical Scanner	37		

Party Control	DEM	REP	IND	VAC
1993 State Senate	39	11	0	0
1992 State Senate	36	14	0	0
1993 State House	78	42	0	0
1992 State House	81	39	0	0

Population Statistics 1990

Race/ Ethnicity	Total Population		Voting Age Population		Voting Age Population % of total population
	Number	%	Number	%	
Non-Hispanic					
White	4,971,127	75.0	3,876,739	77.2	78.0
Black	1,449,142	21.9	1,003,427	20.0	69.2
Asian/Pacific Islander	50,593	0.8	35,773	0.7	70.7
Native American	78,930	1.2	52,923	1.1	67.1
Other	2,119	<.1	857	<.1	40.4
All Hispanic	76,726	1.2	52,769	1.1	68.8
TOTAL	6,628,637	100.0	5,022,488	100.0	75.8

Estimated Voting Age Population 1992 (VAP) 5,217,000
Number of Registered Voters 3,817,380
   % of estimated VAP 73.2
Voter Turnout (Highest Office) 2,625,045
   % of VAP 50.3
   % of Registration 68.8
Persons Not Voting—of Voting Age 2,591,955
   % of VAP 49.7
Persons Not Voting—of Registered 1,192,335
   % of Registration 31.2
Straight Ticket Voting .... Yes, Exception

State Officials and Members of Congress

Governor:
James B. Hunt, Jr. (D) 1976, elected to a four-year term in 1992.

U.S. Senators:
Jesse Helms (R) 1972, elected to a six-year term in 1990.
Lauch Faircloth (R) 1992, elected to a six-year term in 1992.

U.S. Representative in Congress:
(District, Name, Party, Date first elected)

1. Clayton (D) 1992
2. Valentine (D) 1982
3. Lancaster (D) 1986

4. Price (D) 1986
5. Neal (D) 1974
6. Coble (R) 1984

7. Rose (D) 1972
8. Hefner (D) 1974
9. McMillan (R) 1984

10. Ballenger (R) 1986
11. Taylor (R) 1990
12. Watt (D) 1992

[1]Deadline is 21 *business* days before election.

Candidates: General Election, November 3, 1992

Candidate(s)	Total vote	Percent	Party	Status	First elected
President/Vice President					
Bush/Quayle	1,134,661	43.44%	Republican	Incumbent	1988
Clinton/Gore	1,114,042	42.65%	Democrat	Challenger	1992
Perot/Stockdale	357,864	13.70%	Unaffiliated	Challenger	
Marrou/Lord	5,171	0.20%	Libertarian	Challenger	
Fulani/Munoz	59	<.01%	New Alliance	Challenger	
Hagelin/Tompkins	41	<.01%	Natural Law	Challenger	
Warren/Debates	12	<.01%	Socialist Workers	Challenger	
U.S. Senator					
Lauch Faircloth	1,297,892	50.35%	Republican	Challenger	1992
Terry Sanford	1,194,015	46.32%	Democrat	Incumbent	1986
Bobby Emory	85,948	3.33%	Libertarian	Challenger	
Bruce Kimball	23	<.01%	Socialist Workers	Challenger	
Mary Ann Zakutney	13	<.01%	Natural Law	Challenger	
Governor					
James Hunt, Jr.	1,368,246	52.72%	Democrat	Challenger	1992
Jim Gardner	1,121,955	43.23%	Republican	Challenger	
Scott McLaughlin	104,983	4.05%	Libertarian	Challenger	
U.S. Representative in Congress					
District 1[1]					
Eva Clayton	116,078	67.00%	Democrat	Challenger	1992
Ted Tyler	54,457	31.43%	Republican	Challenger	
C. Barry Williams	2,727	1.57%	Libertarian	Challenger	
District 2					
I. T. (Tim) Valentine, Jr.	113,693	53.74%	Democrat	Incumbent	1982
Don Davis	93,893	44.38%	Republican	Challenger	
Dennis Lubahn	3,983	1.88%	Libertarian	Challenger	
District 3					
Martin Lancaster	101,739	54.39%	Democrat	Incumbent	1986
Tommy Pollard	80,759	43.18%	Republican	Challenger	
Mark Jackson	4,552	2.43%	Libertarian	Challenger	
District 4					
David Price	171,299	64.63%	Democrat	Incumbent	1986
Lavinia Goudie	89,345	33.71%	Republican	Challenger	
Eugene Paczelt	4,416	1.67%	Libertarian	Challenger	
District 5					
Steve Neal	117,835	52.68%	Democrat	Incumbent	1974
Richard Burr	102,086	45.64%	Republican	Challenger	
Gary Albrecht	3,758	1.68%	Libertarian	Challenger	
Norris Weathers	4	<.01%	Write in	Challenger	
District 6					
J. Howard Coble	162,822	70.79%	Republican	Incumbent	1984
Robin Hood	67,200	29.21%	Democrat	Challenger	
District 7					
Charles Rose III	92,414	56.66%	Democrat	Incumbent	1972
Robert Anderson	66,536	40.79%	Republican	Challenger	
Marc Kelley	4,151	2.55%	Libertarian	Challenger	
District 8					
W.G. (Bill) Hefner	113,162	59.26%	Democrat	Incumbent	1974
Coy Privette	71,842	37.62%	Republican	Challenger	
J. Wendell Drye	5,947	3.11%	Libertarian	Challenger	

[1]Special election also held November 3, 1992, to fill unexpired term of Rep. Walter B. Jones (D) with same three candidates; votes in the special election include 118,324 for Clayton (D); 86,273 for Tyler (R); and 4,121 for Williams (L).

Candidate(s)	Total vote	Percent	Party	Status	First elected
U.S. Representative in Congress (cont)					
District 9					
J. Alex McMillan	153,650	67.32%	Republican	Incumbent	1984
Rory Blake	74,583	32.68%	Democrat	Challenger	
Wendy Russell	12	<.01%	Write in	Challenger	
District 10					
T. Cass Ballenger	148,999	63.38%	Republican	Incumbent	1986
Ben Neill	79,206	33.69%	Democrat	Challenger	
Jeffrey Brown	6,886	2.93%	Libertarian	Challenger	
District 11					
Charles Taylor	130,158	54.65%	Republican	Incumbent	1990
John Stevens	108,003	45.35%	Democrat	Challenger	
District 12					
Melvin Watt	127,262	70.38%	Democrat	Challenger	1992
Barbara Washington	49,402	27.32%	Republican	Challenger	
Curtis Krumel	4,160	2.30%	Libertarian	Challenger	

Candidates: May 5, 1992, Primary Election

Candidate	Total vote	Percent	Candidate	Total vote	Percent
Presidential Preference, Democratic			**Presidential Preference, Republican**		
Bill Clinton	443,498	64.10%	George Bush	200,387	70.67%
No Preference	106,697	15.42%	Patrick Buchanan	55,420	19.54%
Jerry Brown	71,984	10.40%	No Preference	27,764	9.79%
Paul Tsongas	57,589	8.32%			
Bob Kerrey	6,216	0.90%			
Tom Harkin	5,891	0.85%			

Voter Registration and Turnout, 1948-1992 Elections

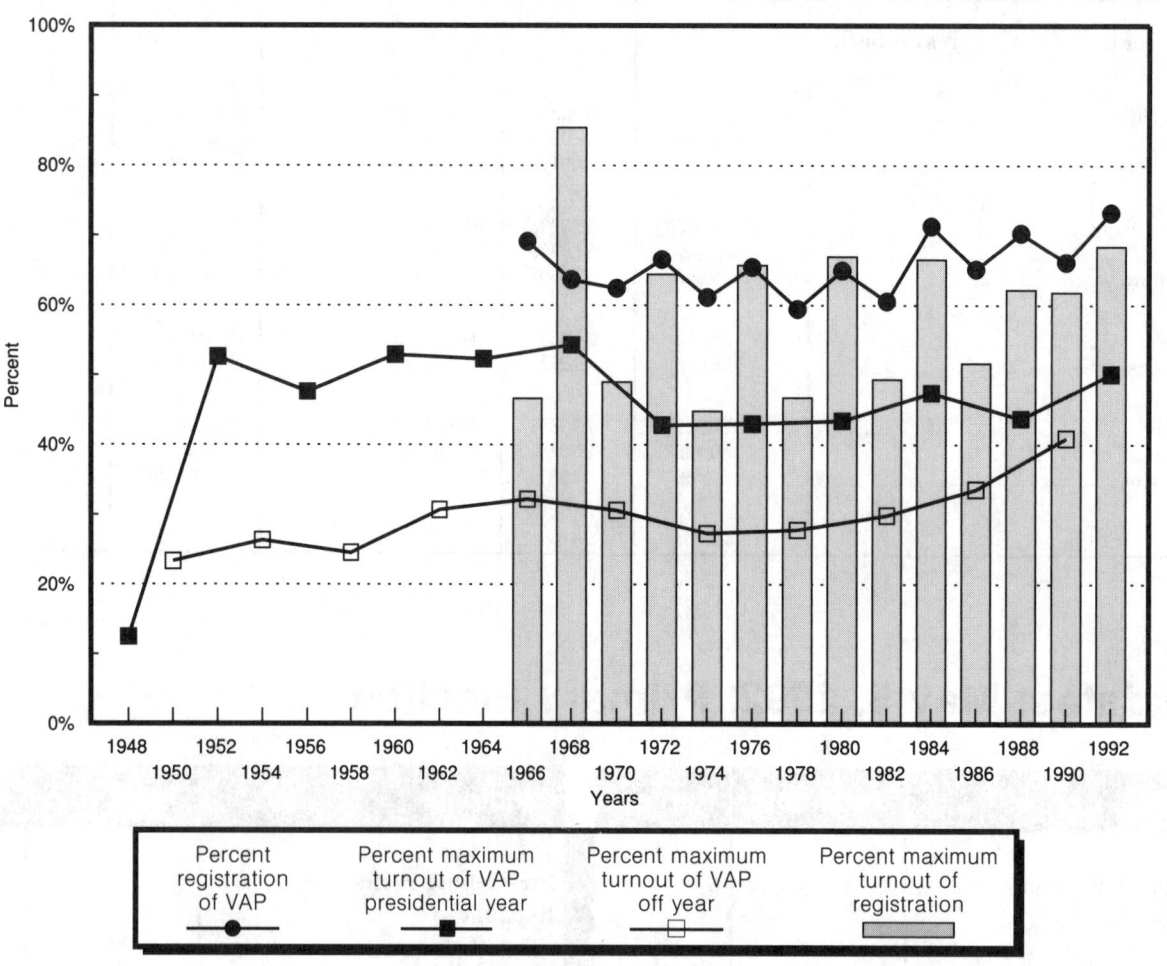

Legend	
Percent registration of VAP ●——	Percent maximum turnout of VAP presidential year ■——
Percent maximum turnout of VAP off year □——	Percent maximum turnout of registration ▨

Year	Estimated Voting Age Population (VAP)	Voter registration (REG)			Voter turnout											
							Highest office						Maximum vote			
		Total	Percent of VAP	Rank by percent of VAP	Actual	Total	Office	Percent total REG	Rank by percent of REG	Percent of VAP	Rank by percent of VAP	Total	Percent total REG	Rank by percent of REG	Percent total VAP	Rank by percent of VAP
1992	5,217,000	3,817,380	73.2	29	-	2,611,850	P	68.4	46	50.1	44	2,611,850	68.4	46	50.1	47
1990	5,061,000	3,347,635	66.1	31	-	2,069,585	S	61.8	16	40.9	21	2,069,585	61.8	18	40.9	22
1988	4,880,000	3,432,042	70.3	28	-	2,134,370	P	62.2	44	43.7	46	2,134,370	62.2	45	43.7	48
1986	4,731,000	3,080,990	65.1	34	-	1,591,330	S	51.7	37	33.6	39	1,591,330	51.7	37	33.6	40
1984	4,586,000	3,270,933	71.3	31	-	2,175,361	P	66.5	43	47.4	44	2,175,361	66.5	43	47.4	44
1982	4,421,000	2,674,787	60.5	40	-	1,321,080	C	49.4	45	29.9	45	1,321,080	49.4	45	29.9	45
1980	4,274,000	2,774,844	64.9	39	-	1,855,833	P	66.9	44	43.4	47	1,855,833	66.9	44	43.4	46
1978	4,088,000	2,430,306	59.4	44	-	1,135,814	S	46.7	42	27.8	46	1,135,814	46.7	42	27.8	46
1976	3,907,000	2,553,717	65.4	39	-	1,678,914	P	65.7	44	43.0	48	1,678,914	65.7	44	43.0	48
1974	3,734,000	2,279,646	61.1	40	-	1,020,367	S	44.8	42	27.3	45	1,020,367	44.8	42	27.3	45
1972	3,548,000	2,357,645	66.5	38	-	1,518,612	P	64.4	40	42.8	48	1,518,612	64.4	41	42.8	48
1970	3,043,000	1,899,090	62.4	40	-	929,948	C	49.0	41	30.6	47	929,948	49.0	41	30.6	47
1968	2,921,000	1,858,987	63.6	39	-	1,587,493	P	85.4	7	54.3	37	1,587,493	85.4	10	54.3	38
1966	2,798,000	1,933,763	69.1	29	-	901,978	S	46.6	40	32.2	46	901,978	46.6	40	32.2	46
1964	2,723,000	-	-	-	-	1,424,983	P	-	-	52.3	37	1,424,983	-	-	52.3	39
1962	2,647,000	-	-	-	-	813,155	S	-	-	30.7	40	813,155	-	-	30.7	40
1960	2,585,000	-	-	-	-	1,368,556	P	-	-	52.9	37	1,368,556	-	-	52.9	38
1958	2,517,000	-	-	-	-	616,469	S	-	-	24.5	39	616,469	-	-	24.5	39
1956	2,447,000	-	-	-	-	1,165,592	P	-	-	47.6	39	1,165,592	-	-	47.6	39
1954	2,352,000	-	-	-	-	619,634	S	-	-	26.3	39	619,634	-	-	26.3	39
1952	2,301,000	-	-	-	-	1,210,910	P	-	-	52.6	37	1,210,910	-	-	52.6	38
1950	2,278,000	-	-	-	-	548,276	S	-	-	24.1	39	531,131	-	-	23.3	39
1948	2,074,000	-	-	-	-	258,572	P	-	-	12.5	48	258,572	-	-	12.5	48

NORTH CAROLINA

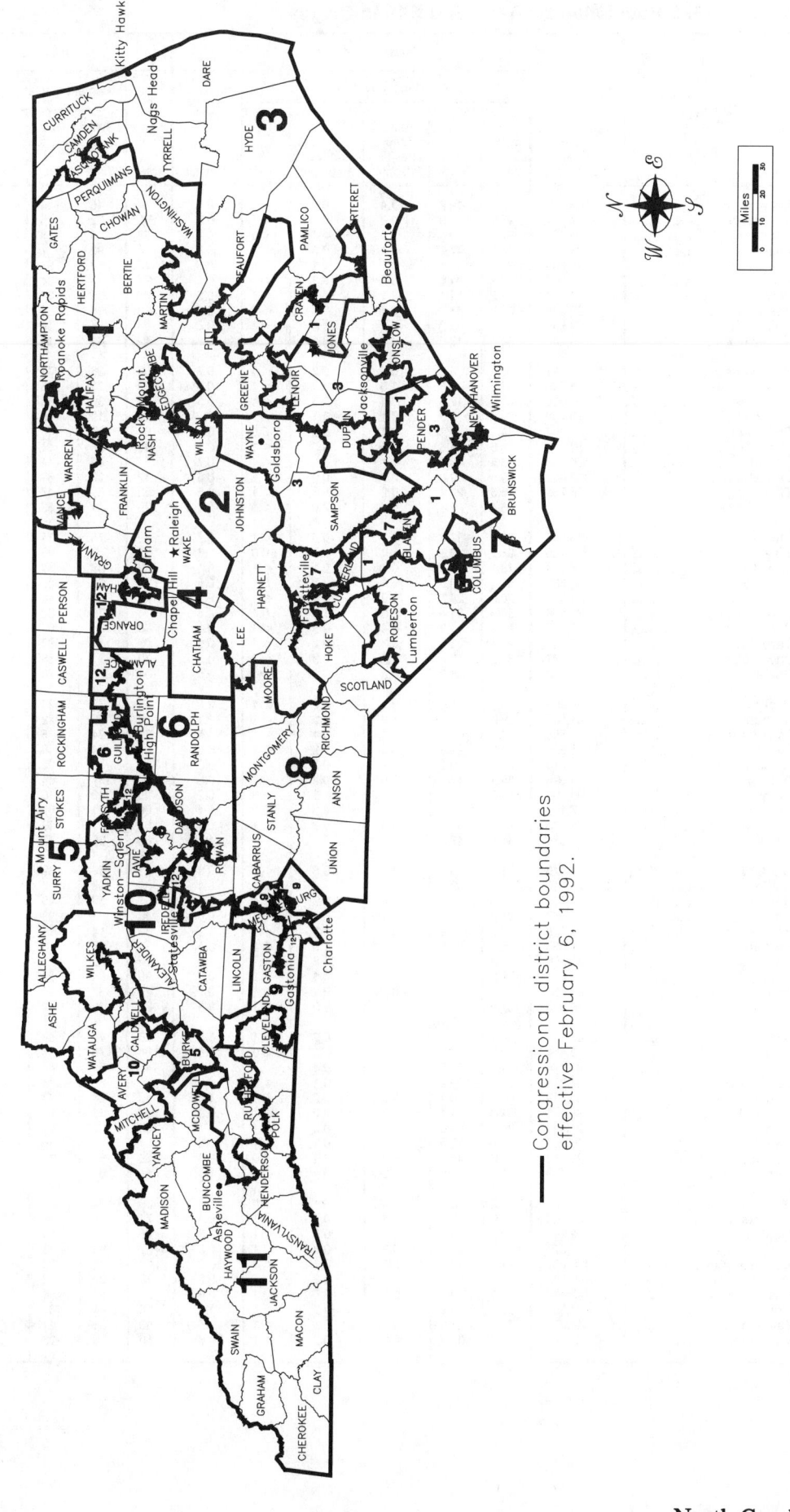

Congressional district boundaries effective February 6, 1992.

North Carolina 673

Table A. — 1990 Population by Race and Ethnic Origin

State/county code	County	Total persons	Percent of total persons — Non-Hispanic White	Black	Asian and Pacific Islander	Native American	Other	Hispanic	Rank Total	Rank NH White	Rank NH Black	Rank Hispanic	Pct contribution Total	Pct contribution NH White	NH Black	Hispanic
37 001	Alamance	108,213	79.4	19.2	0.4	0.3	<.1	0.7	14	45	55	54	1.6	1.7	1.4	1.0
37 003	Alexander	27,544	92.9	6.0	0.2	0.2	<.1	0.7	65	22	76	58	0.4	0.5	0.1	0.2
37 005	Alleghany	9,590	97.1	1.8	<.1	<.1	0.0	0.9	93	8	88	26	0.1	0.2	<.1	0.1
37 007	Anson	23,474	52.1	47.2	0.1	0.3	<.1	0.3	70	92	7	96	0.4	0.2	0.8	<.1
37 009	Ashe	22,209	98.7	0.6	0.1	<.1	<.1	0.5	75	2	97	83	0.3	0.4	<.1	0.1
37 011	Avery	14,867	97.9	1.0	0.1	0.1	<.1	0.8	84	6	94	39	0.2	0.3	<.1	0.2
37 013	Beaufort	42,283	68.2	31.1	0.1	<.1	<.1	0.5	48	65	34	80	0.6	0.6	0.9	0.3
37 015	Bertie	20,388	38.2	61.4	<.1	0.2	<.1	0.2	78	98	1	100	0.3	0.2	0.9	<.1
37 017	Bladen	28,663	58.8	39.0	<.1	1.6	<.1	0.5	63	84	18	73	0.4	0.3	0.8	0.2
37 019	Brunswick	50,985	80.7	18.0	0.1	0.5	<.1	0.7	42	41	57	45	0.8	0.8	0.6	0.5
37 021	Buncombe	174,821	90.4	8.2	0.4	0.3	<.1	0.7	8	26	72	56	2.6	3.2	1.0	1.5
37 023	Burke	75,744	91.5	6.8	1.0	0.2	<.1	0.5	28	25	75	84	1.1	1.4	0.4	0.4
37 025	Cabarrus	98,935	85.9	12.9	0.4	0.3	<.1	0.5	19	36	63	77	1.5	1.7	0.9	0.6
37 027	Caldwell	70,709	93.8	5.5	0.1	0.1	<.1	0.4	29	19	79	86	1.1	1.3	0.3	0.4
37 029	Camden	5,904	74.1	25.1	0.1	0.3	0.0	0.4	98	53	44	89	<.1	<.1	0.1	<.1
37 031	Carteret	52,556	89.8	8.3	0.5	0.5	<.1	0.9	40	29	71	28	0.8	0.9	0.3	0.6
37 033	Caswell	20,693	58.5	40.6	<.1	0.1	<.1	0.7	77	85	14	60	0.3	0.2	0.6	0.2
37 035	Catawba	118,412	89.3	9.0	0.7	0.2	<.1	0.8	12	30	69	43	1.8	2.1	0.7	1.2
37 037	Chatham	38,759	75.3	22.7	0.2	0.3	<.1	1.5	52	50	47	10	0.6	0.6	0.6	0.7
37 039	Cherokee	20,170	95.4	1.8	0.2	2.0	<.1	0.6	79	11	89	61	0.3	0.4	<.1	0.2
37 041	Chowan	13,506	61.6	37.3	0.2	0.2	<.1	0.7	89	75	21	48	0.2	0.2	0.3	0.1
37 043	Clay	7,155	98.2	0.6	<.1	0.5	0.0	0.6	97	5	98	70	0.1	0.1	<.1	<.1
37 045	Cleveland	84,714	78.1	20.9	0.4	0.1	<.1	0.4	23	48	50	87	1.3	1.3	1.2	0.5
37 047	Columbus	49,587	66.2	30.5	0.1	2.7	<.1	0.5	44	69	35	78	0.7	0.7	1.0	0.3
37 049	Craven	81,613	70.8	25.7	0.9	0.4	<.1	2.2	25	59	42	5	1.2	1.2	1.4	2.4
37 051	Cumberland	274,566	60.1	31.4	2.0	1.5	0.1	4.8	4	79	32	2	4.1	3.3	5.9	17.3
37 053	Currituck	13,736	87.1	11.2	0.4	0.5	<.1	0.8	88	35	67	34	0.2	0.2	0.1	0.3
37 055	Dare	22,746	95.1	3.5	0.3	0.2	<.1	0.9	73	12	85	27	0.3	0.4	<.1	0.3
37 057	Davidson	126,677	89.2	9.7	0.4	0.3	<.1	0.5	10	31	68	79	1.9	2.3	0.8	0.8
37 059	Davie	27,859	90.2	8.9	0.2	0.3	<.1	0.5	64	27	70	82	0.4	0.5	0.2	0.2
37 061	Duplin	39,995	64.1	33.0	0.1	0.2	<.1	2.5	50	72	28	3	0.6	0.5	0.9	1.3
37 063	Durham	181,835	59.8	37.1	1.8	0.2	<.1	1.1	6	80	22	18	2.7	2.2	4.7	2.7
37 065	Edgecombe	56,558	43.5	55.8	0.1	0.1	<.1	0.5	38	94	5	85	0.9	0.5	2.2	0.3
37 067	Forsyth	265,878	73.6	24.8	0.6	0.2	<.1	0.8	5	54	46	40	4.0	3.9	4.5	2.7
37 069	Franklin	36,414	63.7	35.1	0.1	0.2	<.1	0.8	56	73	25	36	0.5	0.5	0.9	0.4
37 071	Gaston	175,093	85.8	12.9	0.5	0.2	<.1	0.5	7	37	64	76	2.6	3.0	1.6	1.1
37 073	Gates	9,305	54.7	44.9	0.1	<.1	0.0	0.2	95	89	10	99	0.1	0.1	0.3	<.1
37 075	Graham	7,196	93.2	<.1	<.1	6.3	0.0	0.4	96	21	100	90	0.1	0.1	<.1	<.1
37 077	Granville	38,345	59.8	38.8	0.3	0.2	<.1	0.9	53	81	19	24	0.6	0.5	1.0	0.5
37 079	Greene	15,384	56.5	42.3	<.1	0.1	<.1	1.1	83	86	13	19	0.2	0.2	0.4	0.2
37 081	Guilford	347,420	71.4	26.3	1.0	0.5	<.1	0.8	3	57	39	29	5.2	5.0	6.3	3.8
37 083	Halifax	55,516	46.7	49.5	0.3	3.1	<.1	0.4	39	93	6	88	0.8	0.5	1.9	0.3
37 085	Harnett	67,822	74.5	22.4	0.4	0.9	<.1	1.7	31	52	49	7	1.0	1.0	1.1	1.5
37 087	Haywood	46,942	97.6	1.4	0.1	0.4	<.1	0.5	46	7	93	74	0.7	0.9	<.1	0.3
37 089	Henderson	69,285	94.7	3.4	0.4	0.3	<.1	1.2	30	14	86	16	1.0	1.3	0.2	1.1
37 091	Hertford	22,523	40.7	57.5	0.4	1.0	<.1	0.4	74	96	3	92	0.3	0.2	0.9	0.1
37 093	Hoke	22,856	41.8	43.1	0.4	13.8	<.1	1.0	72	95	12	21	0.3	0.2	0.7	0.3
37 095	Hyde	5,411	66.2	32.9	<.1	<.1	<.1	0.8	99	68	29	38	<.1	<.1	0.1	<.1
37 097	Iredell	92,931	82.7	15.9	0.4	0.2	<.1	0.7	21	38	60	46	1.4	1.5	1.0	0.9
37 099	Jackson	26,846	87.6	1.6	0.4	9.9	<.1	0.6	66	33	92	67	0.4	0.5	<.1	0.2
37 101	Johnston	81,306	80.4	17.6	0.2	0.2	<.1	1.6	26	42	58	8	1.2	1.3	1.0	1.6
37 103	Jones	9,414	60.2	39.0	0.2	<.1	0.0	0.6	94	78	17	69	0.1	0.1	0.3	<.1
37 105	Lee	41,374	74.8	22.5	0.4	0.4	<.1	1.9	49	51	48	6	0.6	0.6	0.6	1.0
37 107	Lenoir	57,274	59.6	39.2	0.2	0.1	<.1	0.8	36	82	16	32	0.9	0.7	1.5	0.6
37 109	Lincoln	50,319	90.1	8.1	0.3	0.2	<.1	1.1	43	28	73	17	0.8	0.9	0.3	0.7
37 111	McDowell	35,681	94.8	4.1	0.5	0.2	<.1	0.3	57	13	84	94	0.5	0.7	0.1	0.1
37 113	Macon	23,499	97.1	1.6	0.2	0.3	<.1	0.7	69	9	91	49	0.4	0.5	<.1	0.2
37 115	Madison	16,953	98.4	0.8	0.2	0.1	<.1	0.5	81	4	96	75	0.3	0.3	<.1	0.1
37 117	Martin	25,078	54.9	44.5	0.2	<.1	0.0	0.4	68	88	11	91	0.4	0.3	0.8	0.1
37 119	Mecklenburg	511,433	70.5	26.2	1.6	0.4	<.1	1.3	1	60	40	12	7.7	7.3	9.2	8.7
37 121	Mitchell	14,433	99.2	0.2	0.1	0.1	0.0	0.3	85	1	99	93	0.2	0.3	<.1	<.1
37 123	Montgomery	23,346	71.0	25.6	0.6	0.4	<.1	2.4	71	58	43	4	0.4	0.3	0.4	0.7
37 125	Moore	59,013	80.1	18.4	0.2	0.5	<.1	0.8	35	43	56	37	0.9	1.0	0.7	0.6
37 127	Nash	76,677	67.2	31.4	0.3	0.3	<.1	0.8	27	66	33	41	1.2	1.0	1.7	0.8
37 129	New Hanover	120,284	78.4	19.9	0.5	0.4	<.1	0.8	11	47	53	44	1.8	1.9	1.7	1.2
37 131	Northampton	20,798	40.2	58.9	<.1	0.2	<.1	0.6	76	97	2	71	0.3	0.2	0.8	0.2
37 133	Onslow	149,838	72.7	19.4	1.8	0.6	0.1	5.4	9	56	54	1	2.3	2.2	2.0	10.5
37 135	Orange	93,851	80.0	15.8	2.5	0.3	<.1	1.4	20	44	62	11	1.4	1.5	1.0	1.7
37 137	Pamlico	11,372	73.1	25.9	0.2	0.3	<.1	0.5	90	55	41	72	0.2	0.2	0.2	<.1
37 139	Pasquotank	31,298	61.5	36.9	0.6	0.2	<.1	0.8	59	76	23	42	0.5	0.4	0.8	0.3

674 North Carolina

Table A. — 1990 Population by Race and Ethnic Origin (cont)

State/county code	County	Total persons	Non-Hispanic White	Non-Hispanic Black	Non-Hispanic Asian and Pacific Islander	Non-Hispanic Native American	Non-Hispanic Other	Hispanic	Rank Total	Rank Non-Hispanic White	Rank Non-Hispanic Black	Rank Hispanic	Pct contrib Total	Pct contrib Non-Hispanic White	Pct contrib Non-Hispanic Black	Pct contrib Hispanic
37 141	Pender	28,855	68.4	30.3	0.1	0.3	<.1	0.9	62	64	36	22	0.4	0.4	0.6	0.4
37 143	Perquimans	10,447	66.6	32.7	0.2	0.2	<.1	0.3	92	67	30	98	0.2	0.1	0.2	<.1
37 145	Person	30,180	68.4	30.1	<.1	0.6	<.1	0.8	61	63	37	30	0.5	0.4	0.6	0.3
37 147	Pitt	107,924	65.1	33.2	0.6	0.2	<.1	0.9	15	71	26	25	1.6	1.4	2.5	1.3
37 149	Polk	14,416	91.6	7.3	0.2	0.1	<.1	0.8	86	24	74	35	0.2	0.3	<.1	0.1
37 151	Randolph	106,546	92.6	6.0	0.3	0.4	<.1	0.7	16	23	77	52	1.6	2.0	0.4	1.0
37 153	Richmond	44,518	69.0	28.7	0.4	1.1	<.1	0.7	47	62	38	59	0.7	0.6	0.9	0.4
37 155	Robeson	105,179	36.0	24.8	0.2	38.3	<.1	0.7	17	100	45	57	1.6	0.8	1.8	0.9
37 157	Rockingham	86,064	78.5	20.3	0.2	0.2	<.1	0.7	22	46	52	47	1.3	1.4	1.2	0.8
37 159	Rowan	110,605	82.7	16.0	0.4	0.2	<.1	0.6	13	39	59	66	1.7	1.8	1.2	0.8
37 161	Rutherford	56,918	87.7	11.4	0.2	0.2	<.1	0.6	37	32	66	64	0.9	1.0	0.4	0.4
37 163	Sampson	47,297	63.5	33.0	0.1	1.8	<.1	1.5	45	74	27	9	0.7	0.6	1.1	0.9
37 165	Scotland	33,754	55.9	35.8	0.2	7.1	<.1	0.9	58	87	24	23	0.5	0.4	0.8	0.4
37 167	Stanly	51,765	87.1	11.5	0.5	0.3	<.1	0.6	41	34	65	65	0.8	0.9	0.4	0.4
37 169	Stokes	37,223	93.5	5.5	0.2	0.1	<.1	0.7	54	20	78	53	0.6	0.7	0.1	0.3
37 171	Surry	61,704	94.3	4.5	0.1	0.1	<.1	1.0	33	17	82	20	0.9	1.2	0.2	0.8
37 173	Swain	11,268	70.4	1.7	0.2	27.0	<.1	0.7	91	61	90	51	0.2	0.2	<.1	0.1
37 175	Transylvania	25,520	94.1	4.6	0.4	0.3	<.1	0.6	67	18	81	63	0.4	0.5	<.1	0.2
37 177	Tyrrell	3,856	59.5	40.0	0.1	0.1	0.0	0.3	100	83	15	97	<.1	<.1	0.1	<.1
37 179	Union	84,211	82.7	15.9	0.3	0.3	<.1	0.8	24	40	61	33	1.3	1.4	0.9	0.9
37 181	Vance	38,892	54.0	44.9	0.1	0.2	<.1	0.7	51	90	9	50	0.6	0.4	1.2	0.4
37 183	Wake	423,380	75.8	20.7	1.9	0.3	<.1	1.3	2	49	51	14	6.4	6.5	6.0	7.0
37 185	Warren	17,265	38.1	56.9	<.1	4.4	<.1	0.6	80	99	4	68	0.3	0.1	0.7	0.1
37 187	Washington	13,997	53.8	45.4	0.2	<.1	<.1	0.5	87	91	8	81	0.2	0.2	0.4	<.1
37 189	Watauga	36,952	96.7	2.1	0.4	0.2	<.1	0.7	55	10	87	55	0.6	0.7	<.1	0.3
37 191	Wayne	104,666	65.5	32.2	0.8	0.2	<.1	1.3	18	70	31	13	1.6	1.4	2.3	1.8
37 193	Wilkes	59,393	94.4	4.7	0.2	0.1	<.1	0.6	34	15	80	62	0.9	1.1	0.2	0.5
37 195	Wilson	66,061	61.2	37.6	0.2	<.1	<.1	0.8	32	77	20	31	1.0	0.8	1.7	0.7
37 197	Yadkin	30,488	94.3	4.2	<.1	<.1	<.1	1.3	60	16	83	15	0.5	0.6	<.1	0.5
37 199	Yancey	15,419	98.5	1.0	<.1	0.2	0.0	0.3	82	3	95	95	0.2	0.3	<.1	<.1
37	**NORTH CAROLINA**	**6,628,637**	**75.0**	**21.9**	**0.8**	**1.2**	**<.1**	**1.2**					**100.0**	**100.0**	**100.0**	**100.0**
	CONGRESSIONAL															
	District 1	552,394	41.4	57.1	0.2	0.6	<.1	0.7	1	12	1	9	8.3	4.6	21.7	5.3
	District 2	552,378	75.7	21.8	0.7	0.6	<.1	1.2	12	8	4	5	8.3	8.4	8.3	8.4
	District 3	552,387	75.9	21.4	0.7	0.4	<.1	1.6	4	7	5	2	8.3	8.4	8.1	11.3
	District 4	552,387	76.5	20.0	1.9	0.3	<.1	1.3	5	6	6	4	8.3	8.5	7.6	9.4
	District 5	552,386	83.5	15.1	0.4	0.2	<.1	0.8	9	5	8	8	8.3	9.3	5.8	5.6
	District 6	552,385	90.9	7.4	0.6	0.3	<.1	0.7	11	2	10	11	8.3	10.1	2.8	4.9
	District 7	552,386	70.3	18.5	1.0	7.2	<.1	2.9	10	10	7	1	8.3	7.8	7.0	21.2
	District 8	552,387	72.3	23.1	0.7	2.5	<.1	1.4	6	9	3	3	8.3	8.0	8.8	10.1
	District 9	552,387	88.4	8.9	1.3	0.3	<.1	1.1	7	4	9	6	8.3	9.8	3.4	7.6
	District 10	552,386	93.3	5.4	0.4	0.2	<.1	0.7	8	1	12	10	8.3	10.4	2.1	5.2
	District 11	552,387	90.4	7.2	0.3	1.4	<.1	0.7	2	3	11	12	8.3	10.0	2.7	4.7
	District 12	552,387	41.4	56.4	0.9	0.4	<.1	0.9	3	11	2	7	8.3	4.6	21.5	6.2

Table B. — 1990 Voting Age Population (VAP) by Race and Ethnic Origin

County	Total Voting Age Population	Percent of total VAP — Non-Hispanic White	Black	Asian and Pacific Islander	Native American	Other	Hispanic	Rank Percent of total VAP — Total	Non-Hispanic White	Black	Hispanic	Percent contribution to state VAP — Total	Non-Hispanic White	Black	Hispanic	VAP percent of total population — Total	Non-Hispanic White	Black	Asian and Pacific Islander	Native American	Other	Hispanic
Alamance	84,538	80.8	17.9	0.4	0.3	<.1	0.6	13	45	54	60	1.7	1.8	1.5	0.9	78.1	79.5	73.0	66.4	79.1	30.4	64.3
Alexander	20,771	93.5	5.6	0.1	0.2	0.0	0.6	66	22	76	49	0.4	0.5	0.1	0.2	75.4	75.8	70.4	50.0	65.4	0.0	69.6
Alleghany	7,535	97.2	1.8	<.1	0.1	0.0	0.8	93	9	88	23	0.2	0.2	<.1	0.1	78.6	78.6	79.0	40.0	100.0	0.0	75.3
Anson	17,130	56.0	43.3	0.1	0.3	<.1	0.6	73	92	7	95	0.3	0.2	0.7	<.1	73.0	78.4	67.0	74.1	68.1	100.0	74.6
Ashe	17,406	98.6	0.6	0.1	<.1	<.1	0.5	71	2	97	65	0.3	0.4	<.1	0.2	78.4	78.3	78.5	74.2	71.4	100.0	92.2
Avery	11,529	97.7	1.2	0.1	0.1	<.1	0.8	84	7	94	27	0.2	0.3	<.1	0.2	77.5	77.4	87.2	80.0	72.2	100.0	79.7
Beaufort	31,328	71.4	28.0	0.1	<.1	<.1	0.4	48	63	35	85	0.6	0.6	0.9	0.2	74.1	77.5	66.7	75.0	89.3	70.0	62.4
Bertie	14,547	42.3	57.3	<.1	0.2	0.0	0.2	79	98	1	100	0.3	0.2	0.8	<.1	71.4	79.0	66.6	78.6	63.6	0.0	78.1
Bladen	21,057	61.8	36.1	<.1	1.5	<.1	0.5	65	83	18	73	0.4	0.3	0.8	0.2	73.5	77.2	68.1	76.2	67.5	100.0	64.7
Brunswick	38,960	82.9	15.9	0.2	0.4	<.1	0.6	42	41	58	47	0.8	0.8	0.6	0.5	76.4	78.6	67.4	78.7	71.8	12.5	64.6
Buncombe	135,886	91.4	7.4	0.4	0.3	<.1	0.6	7	27	71	56	2.7	3.2	1.0	1.5	77.7	78.6	70.0	69.4	71.2	17.9	67.2
Burke	57,937	92.4	6.4	0.7	0.2	<.1	0.4	27	25	75	83	1.2	1.4	0.4	0.4	76.5	77.3	71.4	48.0	71.0	21.4	67.4
Cabarrus	75,038	87.2	11.8	0.3	0.3	<.1	0.4	19	37	63	78	1.5	1.7	0.9	0.6	75.8	77.0	69.0	70.8	68.6	40.0	68.3
Caldwell	54,022	94.4	5.0	0.1	0.1	<.1	0.4	30	20	79	86	1.1	1.3	0.3	0.4	76.7	76.9	69.5	74.3	77.6	40.0	66.0
Camden	4,469	74.8	24.3	0.2	0.2	0.0	0.4	98	56	40	82	<.1	<.1	0.1	<.1	75.7	76.4	73.5	100.0	68.8	0.0	75.0
Carteret	40,749	91.1	7.1	0.5	0.5	<.1	0.7	38	28	72	35	0.8	1.0	0.3	0.6	77.5	78.7	66.5	78.0	76.5	33.3	64.7
Caswell	15,774	59.2	40.0	0.1	0.1	<.1	0.5	76	87	13	64	0.3	0.2	0.6	0.2	76.2	77.2	75.0	94.7	75.0	66.7	63.2
Catawba	90,127	90.6	7.9	0.6	0.2	<.1	0.7	12	30	70	37	1.8	2.1	0.7	1.2	76.1	77.2	67.1	62.7	75.4	46.7	68.3
Chatham	30,073	76.9	21.2	0.2	0.3	<.1	1.4	51	51	47	8	0.6	0.6	0.6	0.8	77.6	79.3	72.6	70.6	69.1	31.3	73.2
Cherokee	15,599	95.5	1.7	0.2	2.1	<.1	0.5	77	12	90	69	0.3	0.4	<.1	0.1	77.3	77.5	75.1	79.5	79.2	20.0	60.3
Chowan	9,970	64.8	34.2	0.2	0.2	0.0	0.6	89	76	22	52	0.2	0.2	0.3	0.1	73.8	77.7	67.7	79.3	78.3	0.0	63.2
Clay	5,540	98.2	0.6	<.1	0.6	0.0	0.6	96	5	98	61	0.1	0.1	<.1	<.1	77.4	77.4	78.0	57.1	87.2	0.0	77.5
Cleveland	63,940	80.3	18.8	0.4	0.1	<.1	0.4	23	47	52	80	1.3	1.3	1.2	0.5	75.5	77.6	67.9	64.7	79.6	11.1	70.5
Columbus	35,986	69.4	27.5	0.1	2.6	<.1	0.4	45	68	37	77	0.7	0.6	1.0	0.3	72.6	76.1	65.4	78.4	68.7	33.3	65.7
Craven	59,570	73.2	23.6	0.9	0.4	<.1	2.0	26	61	43	5	1.2	1.1	1.4	2.2	73.0	75.4	67.1	76.1	69.9	34.0	64.4
Cumberland	197,792	62.7	29.3	2.0	1.5	<.1	4.4	5	79	32	2	3.9	3.2	5.8	16.3	72.0	75.1	67.3	73.8	70.0	40.8	64.8
Currituck	10,242	87.7	10.9	0.4	0.4	0.0	0.6	87	35	65	50	0.2	0.2	0.1	0.1	74.6	75.0	72.3	76.5	70.8	0.0	57.3
Dare	17,657	95.5	3.2	0.3	0.2	<.1	0.8	70	13	85	28	0.4	0.4	<.1	0.3	77.6	78.0	70.6	65.8	86.5	100.0	71.4
Davidson	96,357	90.1	8.9	0.3	0.3	<.1	0.4	10	31	68	79	1.9	2.2	0.9	0.8	76.1	76.9	69.9	60.8	72.6	17.4	67.9
Davie	21,333	90.7	8.5	0.1	0.2	<.1	0.4	64	29	69	87	0.4	0.5	0.2	0.2	76.6	77.1	73.5	57.7	56.5	20.0	63.6
Duplin	29,441	66.7	30.6	0.1	0.2	<.1	2.4	52	72	28	3	0.6	0.5	0.9	1.4	73.6	76.6	68.2	72.7	63.9	75.0	70.2
Durham	140,425	62.3	34.6	1.8	0.2	<.1	1.1	6	81	21	15	2.8	2.3	4.8	3.0	77.2	80.4	72.2	77.3	74.9	40.5	75.9
Edgecombe	40,539	47.3	52.0	<.1	0.1	<.1	0.4	39	94	5	75	0.8	0.5	2.1	0.3	71.7	78.0	66.7	62.5	76.4	76.2	71.0
Forsyth	205,470	75.8	22.7	0.6	0.2	<.1	0.7	4	53	46	36	4.1	4.0	4.7	2.8	77.3	79.6	70.9	72.8	74.2	27.4	69.3
Franklin	27,577	66.0	32.9	0.1	0.2	<.1	0.7	56	74	24	32	0.5	0.5	0.9	0.4	75.7	78.5	70.9	75.9	67.6	25.0	70.7
Gaston	130,910	87.4	11.5	0.5	0.2	<.1	0.5	8	36	64	74	2.6	3.0	1.5	1.1	76.8	78.1	66.5	66.4	72.6	37.5	69.1
Gates	6,932	56.6	43.0	0.1	0.1	0.0	0.2	94	91	8	99	0.1	0.1	0.3	<.1	74.5	77.2	71.3	53.8	100.0	0.0	57.1
Graham	5,499	94.5	<.1	<.1	5.1	0.0	0.4	97	19	100	88	0.1	0.1	<.1	<.1	76.4	77.4	100.0	83.3	61.4	0.0	72.4
Granville	29,108	61.0	37.5	0.2	0.3	<.1	1.0	53	84	15	18	0.6	0.5	1.1	0.5	75.9	77.5	73.4	63.6	81.7	66.7	78.7
Greene	11,391	59.8	39.1	<.1	<.1	<.1	0.9	85	85	14	20	0.2	0.2	0.4	0.2	74.0	78.4	68.5	100.0	62.5	100.0	63.9
Guilford	269,703	73.4	24.5	0.9	0.4	<.1	0.8	3	59	39	31	5.4	5.1	6.6	3.9	77.6	79.9	72.2	68.5	73.5	34.5	72.1
Halifax	40,191	50.9	45.6	0.2	2.9	<.1	0.4	40	93	6	84	0.8	0.5	1.8	0.3	72.4	78.9	66.7	65.7	67.3	61.5	67.1
Harnett	50,536	76.8	20.4	0.4	0.8	<.1	1.6	31	52	48	7	1.0	1.0	1.0	1.5	74.5	76.8	67.8	72.9	66.8	50.0	67.6
Haywood	37,196	97.8	1.3	0.1	0.4	0.0	0.4	44	6	93	81	0.7	0.9	<.1	0.3	79.2	79.4	74.3	77.4	77.8	0.0	64.4
Henderson	54,708	95.6	2.9	0.3	0.2	<.1	1.0	29	11	86	17	1.1	1.3	0.2	1.0	79.0	79.7	67.2	64.0	65.6	33.3	64.4
Hertford	16,416	44.8	53.4	0.5	0.9	<.1	0.3	74	96	4	92	0.3	0.2	0.9	0.1	72.9	80.3	67.7	81.9	68.5	100.0	67.9
Hoke	15,878	46.0	40.8	0.4	12.0	<.1	0.6	75	95	12	22	0.3	0.2	0.6	0.3	69.5	76.4	65.8	70.6	60.3	57.1	62.8
Hyde	4,052	68.1	31.2	<.1	0.0	0.0	0.6	99	70	26	55	<.1	<.1	0.1	<.1	74.9	77.0	71.2	100.0	0.0	0.0	55.8
Iredell	70,496	84.7	14.1	0.3	0.2	<.1	0.7	21	38	61	42	1.4	1.5	1.0	0.9	75.9	77.6	67.3	66.1	75.7	42.9	69.3
Jackson	21,434	89.3	1.7	0.4	8.0	<.1	0.5	63	32	89	70	0.4	0.5	<.1	0.2	78.0	81.4	88.0	78.3	65.0	66.7	69.7
Johnston	61,203	82.3	16.0	0.2	0.2	<.1	1.3	24	43	57	9	1.2	1.3	1.0	1.6	75.3	77.0	68.2	77.5	73.6	22.2	65.1
Jones	6,911	62.0	37.2	0.2	0.1	0.0	0.5	95	82	16	72	0.1	0.1	0.3	<.1	73.4	75.7	70.0	77.8	87.5	0.0	60.4
Lee	30,618	77.4	20.1	0.4	0.4	<.1	1.8	50	49	49	6	0.6	0.6	0.6	1.0	74.0	76.6	66.0	73.4	66.3	75.0	68.9
Lenoir	42,389	63.2	35.7	0.2	0.1	<.1	0.7	37	78	19	33	0.8	0.7	1.5	0.6	74.0	78.5	67.4	68.3	84.1	37.5	62.9
Lincoln	37,809	91.4	7.1	0.3	0.2	<.1	1.0	43	26	73	19	0.8	0.9	0.3	0.7	75.1	76.2	65.7	62.2	64.4	50.0	63.5
McDowell	27,153	95.1	4.0	0.4	0.2	<.1	0.3	57	14	83	93	0.5	0.7	0.1	0.2	76.1	76.3	73.5	58.2	72.2	40.0	78.1
Macon	18,834	97.4	1.5	0.2	0.3	0.0	0.6	68	8	92	57	0.4	0.5	<.1	0.2	80.1	80.4	73.4	65.5	80.8	0.0	66.1
Madison	13,256	98.4	0.9	0.2	0.1	<.1	0.4	80	4	96	76	0.3	0.3	<.1	0.1	78.2	78.2	88.9	69.0	94.1	100.0	68.6
Martin	18,384	58.2	41.1	0.2	<.1	0.0	0.4	69	88	11	91	0.4	0.3	0.8	0.1	73.3	77.7	67.9	81.6	80.0	0.0	67.7
Mecklenburg	387,980	73.2	23.7	1.5	0.4	<.1	1.3	1	60	42	11	7.7	7.3	9.2	9.3	75.9	78.7	68.8	68.4	72.9	38.9	73.3
Mitchell	11,324	99.3	0.2	<.1	0.2	0.0	0.3	86	1	99	98	0.2	0.3	<.1	<.1	78.5	78.5	87.0	64.7	89.5	0.0	62.0
Montgomery	17,325	73.8	23.2	0.4	0.4	<.1	2.1	72	58	44	4	0.3	0.3	0.4	0.7	74.2	77.2	67.2	51.4	84.4	12.5	65.6
Moore	45,677	82.7	16.0	0.2	0.4	<.1	0.8	34	42	56	39	0.9	1.0	0.7	0.6	77.4	79.9	67.6	61.4	66.7	66.7	66.2
Nash	57,107	69.9	28.7	0.3	0.3	<.1	0.8	28	66	33	29	1.1	1.0	1.6	0.8	74.5	77.4	68.2	72.4	76.1	63.6	73.6
New Hanover	92,923	80.7	17.7	0.5	0.4	<.1	0.7	11	46	55	34	1.9	1.9	1.6	1.3	77.3	79.5	68.6	73.2	76.8	43.1	72.5
Northampton	15,595	43.7	55.4	<.1	0.2	0.0	0.6	78	97	2	58	0.3	0.2	0.9	0.2	75.0	81.5	70.5	63.6	90.0	0.0	76.7
Onslow	113,534	73.8	18.7	1.7	0.6	<.1	5.1	9	57	53	1	2.3	2.2	2.1	10.9	75.8	77.0	72.9	70.1	80.0	52.7	71.6
Orange	76,104	81.2	14.8	2.4	0.3	<.1	1.2	18	44	59	12	1.5	1.6	1.1	1.8	81.1	82.3	76.1	77.9	85.3	44.4	73.8
Pamlico	8,662	75.2	24.0	0.2	0.3	0.0	0.4	90	54	41	89	0.2	0.2	0.2	<.1	76.2	78.3	70.6	75.0	72.7	0.0	54.1
Pasquotank	22,829	63.3	35.3	0.5	0.2	<.1	0.6	60	77	20	44	0.5	0.4	0.8	0.3	72.9	75.1	69.8	66.5	78.2	20.0	59.3

Table B. – 1990 Voting Age Population (VAP) by Race and Ethnic Origin (cont)

County	Total Voting Age Population	Percent of total VAP						Rank				Percent contribution to state VAP				VAP percent of total population						
		Non-Hispanic					Hispanic	Percent of total VAP				Non-Hispanic				Non-Hispanic						
		White	Black	Asian and Pacific Islander	Native American	Other	Hispanic	Total	White	Black	Hispanic	Total	White	Black	Hispanic	Total	White	Black	Asian and Pacific Islander	Native American	Other	Hispanic
Pender	21,742	71.2	27.5	0.2	0.3	<.1	0.8	62	64	36	25	0.4	0.4	0.6	0.3	75.3	78.5	68.5	78.6	74.3	25.0	67.4
Perquimans	7,875	69.4	29.9	0.2	0.2	0.0	0.3	92	67	29	96	0.2	0.1	0.2	<.1	75.4	78.6	68.8	75.0	88.9	0.0	82.1
Person	22,761	70.2	28.4	<.1	0.6	<.1	0.7	61	65	34	40	0.5	0.4	0.6	0.3	75.4	77.4	71.2	78.6	82.1	100.0	62.2
Pitt	81,820	68.9	29.4	0.6	0.2	<.1	0.8	15	69	31	24	1.6	1.5	2.4	1.3	75.8	80.3	67.3	73.7	78.1	33.3	71.1
Polk	11,623	92.7	6.4	0.1	0.1	0.0	0.6	83	24	74	43	0.2	0.3	<.1	0.1	80.6	81.6	70.7	60.0	94.1	0.0	65.2
Randolph	80,829	93.0	5.6	0.3	0.4	<.1	0.6	16	23	77	45	1.6	1.9	0.5	1.0	75.9	76.2	71.6	72.0	71.8	42.9	69.2
Richmond	32,745	71.9	26.1	0.3	1.0	<.1	0.6	47	62	38	46	0.7	0.6	0.9	0.4	73.6	76.7	66.7	55.2	67.1	50.0	70.0
Robeson	72,903	40.4	23.1	0.2	35.7	<.1	0.6	20	100	45	51	1.5	0.8	1.7	0.8	69.3	77.7	64.4	71.4	64.7	41.2	63.2
Rockingham	65,632	80.0	19.0	0.2	0.2	<.1	0.6	22	48	51	54	1.3	1.4	1.2	0.7	76.3	77.7	71.3	64.5	76.9	21.7	62.7
Rowan	84,409	84.2	14.7	0.4	0.2	<.1	0.5	14	40	60	67	1.7	1.8	1.2	0.8	76.3	77.7	69.9	71.0	72.0	25.0	68.4
Rutherford	43,037	89.0	10.2	0.1	0.2	<.1	0.6	36	33	66	62	0.9	1.0	0.4	0.4	75.6	76.7	67.4	70.3	70.5	33.3	69.3
Sampson	34,852	66.3	30.6	0.1	1.6	<.1	1.3	46	73	27	10	0.7	0.6	1.1	0.9	73.7	77.0	68.2	72.9	67.7	14.3	63.3
Scotland	23,823	59.8	32.4	0.2	6.6	<.1	0.9	58	86	25	21	0.5	0.4	0.8	0.4	70.6	75.5	64.0	72.8	65.5	65.7	65.7
Stanly	39,064	88.7	10.1	0.4	0.2	<.1	0.5	41	34	67	63	0.8	0.9	0.4	0.4	75.5	76.8	66.6	59.3	59.5	25.0	69.3
Stokes	28,146	93.8	5.4	0.2	0.1	<.1	0.5	55	21	78	66	0.6	0.7	0.2	0.3	75.6	75.9	73.7	61.6	75.6	100.0	59.1
Surry	47,583	94.8	4.1	0.1	0.1	<.1	0.8	33	16	81	26	0.9	1.2	0.2	0.7	77.1	77.5	71.0	77.4	77.6	58.6	65.0
Swain	8,413	75.1	1.6	0.2	22.6	0.0	0.5	91	55	91	68	0.2	0.2	<.1	<.1	74.7	79.7	70.7	68.2	62.3	0.0	56.4
Transylvania	19,948	94.8	4.0	0.4	0.3	<.1	0.6	67	15	84	59	0.4	0.5	<.1	0.2	78.2	78.8	67.2	76.5	66.7	100.0	72.7
Tyrrell	2,792	62.5	37.0	0.1	0.1	0.0	0.3	100	80	17	97	<.1	<.1	0.1	<.1	72.4	76.0	67.0	60.0	100.0	0.0	72.7
Union	61,201	84.6	14.0	0.3	0.3	<.1	0.8	25	39	62	30	1.2	1.3	0.9	0.9	72.7	74.3	64.3	64.7	72.8	33.3	70.1
Vance	28,497	57.5	41.5	0.1	0.2	<.1	0.7	54	90	9	41	0.6	0.4	1.2	0.4	73.3	77.9	67.7	72.4	80.6	100.0	69.7
Wake	325,565	77.2	20.0	1.8	0.3	<.1	1.2	2	50	50	13	6.5	6.5	6.3	7.3	76.9	78.3	72.6	72.1	80.1	45.9	71.9
Warren	12,916	41.5	53.8	<.1	4.2	<.1	0.5	81	99	3	71	0.3	0.1	0.7	0.1	74.8	81.5	70.7	64.3	71.0	100.0	63.3
Washington	10,116	57.8	41.5	0.2	<.1	<.1	0.4	88	89	10	90	0.2	0.2	0.4	<.1	72.3	77.7	66.1	64.7	87.5	25.0	56.9
Watauga	30,630	96.5	2.2	0.4	0.2	<.1	0.6	49	10	87	48	0.6	0.8	<.1	0.4	82.9	82.8	89.4	86.8	85.7	75.0	75.9
Wayne	77,296	68.1	29.8	0.7	0.2	<.1	1.1	17	71	30	14	1.5	1.4	2.3	1.7	73.9	76.8	68.4	69.4	80.1	28.6	64.9
Wilkes	45,423	94.7	4.5	0.1	0.1	<.1	0.6	35	17	80	53	0.9	1.1	0.2	0.5	76.5	76.7	71.9	69.1	80.6	50.0	75.1
Wilson	48,833	64.9	34.1	0.2	<.1	<.1	0.7	32	75	23	38	1.0	0.8	1.7	0.6	73.9	78.3	67.1	74.8	63.5	40.0	63.5
Yadkin	23,648	94.7	4.1	<.1	<.1	<.1	1.0	59	18	82	16	0.5	0.6	<.1	0.5	77.6	77.9	74.9	84.6	95.5	66.7	63.9
Yancey	11,985	98.5	1.0	<.1	0.1	0.0	0.3	82	3	95	94	0.2	0.3	<.1	<.1	77.7	77.7	78.8	72.7	63.0	0.0	77.6
NORTH CAROLINA	5,022,488	77.2	20.0	0.7	1.1	<.1	1.1					100.0	100.0	100.0	100.0	75.8	78.0	69.2	70.7	67.1	40.4	68.8
CONGRESSIONAL																						
District 1	399,878	45.3	53.2	0.2	0.6	<.1	0.7	12	11	1	8	8.0	4.7	21.2	5.1	72.4	79.2	67.6	74.5	70.5	43.0	66.0
District 2	420,178	77.7	20.0	0.7	0.5	<.1	1.1	7	8	4	5	8.4	8.4	8.4	8.6	76.1	78.1	69.6	75.5	69.0	46.5	70.3
District 3	413,256	78.0	19.6	0.7	0.4	<.1	1.4	9	6	5	2	8.2	8.3	8.1	10.7	74.8	76.8	68.5	72.5	72.8	32.7	65.1
District 4	428,984	77.8	18.8	1.8	0.3	<.1	1.2	2	7	6	4	8.5	8.6	8.1	9.9	77.7	79.1	73.1	73.4	80.2	44.9	72.3
District 5	428,782	84.8	14.0	0.4	0.2	<.1	0.7	3	5	8	9	8.5	9.4	6.0	5.4	77.6	78.8	71.8	67.3	76.5	37.7	67.5
District 6	428,096	91.5	7.0	0.5	0.3	<.1	0.6	4	3	10	11	8.5	10.1	3.0	5.0	77.5	78.0	73.1	68.9	72.6	39.3	70.2
District 7	414,413	73.0	17.0	1.0	6.3	<.1	2.7	8	10	7	1	8.3	7.8	7.0	21.5	75.0	77.8	68.8	72.5	66.0	50.7	69.7
District 8	403,678	75.1	20.8	0.7	2.1	<.1	1.2	11	9	3	3	8.0	7.8	8.4	9.5	76.3	76.0	65.7	69.9	63.2	30.9	64.7
District 9	421,623	89.5	8.0	1.2	0.3	<.1	1.0	5	4	9	6	8.4	9.7	3.4	8.0	76.2	77.3	68.7	68.7	73.8	43.8	72.2
District 10	421,456	93.9	4.9	0.3	0.2	<.1	0.6	6	1	12	10	8.4	10.2	2.1	5.1	76.3	76.8	69.1	62.9	74.7	48.5	67.9
District 11	430,457	91.6	6.4	0.3	1.2	<.1	0.6	1	2	11	12	8.6	10.2	2.7	4.6	77.9	78.9	69.0	69.2	65.7	26.6	67.4
District 12	411,687	44.8	53.2	0.8	0.4	<.1	0.8	10	12	2	7	8.2	4.8	21.8	6.5	74.5	80.7	70.2	67.1	73.6	28.2	71.6

Table C. — Voter Participation: November 3, 1992, General Election

| County | Estimated Voting Age Population (VAP), 1992 | Voter registration (REG) | | | | | Voter turnout | | | | | | | | | | | | |
		Total	% contribution to state REG	% of 1992 VAP	Rank by % of 1992 VAP	Actual	Highest office Total	Office	% of 1992 VAP	Maximum vote Total	% contribution to state turnout	% of REG	Rank by % of REG	% of 1992 VAP	Rank by % 1992 VAP	President	Senator	Governor	Representative
Alamance	86,188	63,270	1.7	73.4	58	-	43,140	G	50.1	43,140	1.6	68.2	61	50.1	56	1.0	2.1	0.0	4.7
Alexander	21,621	19,233	0.5	89.0	10	-	13,843	G	64.0	13,843	0.5	72.0	18	64.0	5	1.6	1.0	0.0	1.0
Alleghany	7,656	6,480	0.2	84.6	17	-	4,730	P	61.8	4,730	0.2	73.0	9	61.8	9	0.0	2.8	3.6	1.7
Anson	17,260	12,030	0.3	69.7	77	-	8,539	P	49.5	8,539	0.3	71.0	25	49.5	60	0.0	4.8	2.8	5.2
Ashe	17,596	15,421	0.4	87.6	13	-	11,070	P	62.9	11,070	0.4	71.8	20	62.9	8	0.0	1.3	0.9	1.0
Avery	11,522	9,794	0.3	85.0	16	-	6,787	P	58.9	6,787	0.3	69.3	46	58.9	15	0.0	2.6	2.8	4.8
Beaufort	32,304	22,712	0.6	70.3	73	-	15,980	P	49.5	15,980	0.6	70.4	33	49.5	61	0.0	1.9	0.2	1.0
Bertie	14,859	11,716	0.3	78.8	32	-	6,743	P	45.4	6,743	0.3	57.6	96	45.4	85	0.0	6.3	6.5	6.5
Bladen	21,294	16,465	0.4	77.3	44	-	10,177	P	47.8	10,177	0.4	61.8	90	47.8	68	0.0	5.2	3.1	10.7
Brunswick	43,253	32,769	0.9	75.8	48	-	22,400	P	51.8	22,400	0.9	68.4	59	51.8	50	0.0	2.9	0.9	1.7
Buncombe	139,626	109,805	2.9	78.6	34	-	75,492	P	54.1	75,492	2.9	68.8	56	54.1	35	0.0	2.9	1.7	3.6
Burke	59,286	41,850	1.1	70.6	72	-	30,632	G	51.7	30,632	1.2	73.2	8	51.7	51	1.7	1.7	0.0	1.7
Cabarrus	78,628	60,252	1.6	76.6	47	-	41,568	C	52.9	41,568	1.6	69.0	51	52.9	45	1.1	0.9	0.1	0.0
Caldwell	55,288	38,196	1.0	69.1	79	-	26,185	G	47.4	26,185	1.0	68.6	58	47.4	70	2.3	0.6	0.0	1.7
Camden	4,571	3,829	0.1	83.8	20	-	2,675	P	58.5	2,675	0.1	69.9	40	58.5	16	0.0	2.3	1.8	4.8
Carteret	43,665	30,526	0.8	69.9	76	-	21,986	P	50.4	21,986	0.8	72.0	17	50.4	54	0.8	0.6	0.0	1.5
Caswell	15,978	11,900	0.3	74.5	54	-	8,363	P	52.3	8,363	0.3	70.3	35	52.3	48	0.0	6.8	4.2	6.6
Catawba	94,009	68,487	1.8	72.9	61	-	49,409	P	52.6	49,409	1.9	72.1	14	52.6	47	0.0	0.4	0.1	1.1
Chatham	31,259	24,907	0.7	79.7	30	-	18,577	P	59.4	18,577	0.7	74.6	6	59.4	13	0.0	3.0	0.9	3.3
Cherokee	16,024	14,394	0.4	89.8	9	-	8,783	G	54.8	8,783	0.3	61.0	94	54.8	32	0.3	2.1	0.0	2.3
Chowan	10,268	7,412	0.2	72.2	63	-	4,610	G	44.9	4,610	0.2	62.2	88	44.9	87	2.3	4.6	0.0	12.4
Clay	5,730	5,715	0.1	99.7	3	-	3,960	P	69.1	3,960	0.2	69.3	47	69.1	3	0.0	2.7	1.1	2.6
Cleveland	64,899	43,359	1.1	66.8	86	-	30,522	P	47.0	30,522	1.2	70.4	31	47.0	74	0.0	1.3	0.4	4.2
Columbus	36,654	31,344	0.8	85.5	15	-	19,377	P	52.9	19,377	0.7	61.8	89	52.9	46	2.4	0.6	0.0	1.5
Craven	62,147	39,362	1.0	63.3	94	-	25,287	P	40.7	25,287	1.0	64.2	83	40.7	94	0.0	2.3	0.7	5.1
Cumberland	202,610	104,468	2.7	51.6	99	-	66,683	G	32.9	66,683	2.5	63.8	86	32.9	99	3.3	0.5	0.0	1.7
Currituck	10,920	7,311	0.2	67.0	85	-	5,297	P	48.5	5,297	0.2	72.5	12	48.5	67	0.0	3.0	1.1	4.7
Dare	20,155	14,941	0.4	74.1	55	-	10,696	P	53.1	10,696	0.4	71.6	21	53.1	43	0.0	1.5	0.1	2.3
Davidson	100,297	69,608	1.8	69.4	78	-	49,725	P	49.6	49,725	1.9	71.4	22	49.6	59	0.0	0.5	0.1	2.4
Davie	22,269	16,369	0.4	73.5	57	-	12,387	P	55.6	12,387	0.5	75.7	2	55.6	27	0.0	2.6	0.6	4.7
Duplin	29,861	21,182	0.6	70.9	66	-	14,138	P	47.3	14,138	0.5	66.7	71	47.3	71	2.8	0.7	0.0	2.2
Durham	146,109	117,678	3.1	80.5	27	-	83,257	S	57.0	83,257	3.2	70.7	28	57.0	20	0.7	0.0	2.8	6.0
Edgecombe	41,556	31,927	0.8	76.8	45	-	19,657	P	47.3	19,657	0.7	61.6	91	47.3	72	0.0	0.7	0.5	2.3
Forsyth	210,291	161,423	4.2	76.8	46	-	116,274	P	55.3	116,274	4.4	72.0	16	55.3	30	0.0	0.8	0.4	2.2
Franklin	29,111	19,860	0.5	68.2	81	-	13,481	P	46.3	13,481	0.5	67.9	62	46.3	78	1.6	0.7	0.0	1.9
Gaston	135,247	87,728	2.3	64.9	93	-	61,532	G	45.5	61,532	2.3	70.1	37	45.5	84	0.2	0.5	0.0	2.5
Gates	7,098	5,546	0.1	78.1	37	-	3,834	P	54.0	3,834	0.1	69.1	49	54.0	36	0.0	6.2	3.5	7.4
Graham	5,576	5,730	0.2	102.8	1	-	3,876	P	69.5	3,876	0.1	67.6	63	69.5	2	0.0	3.7	1.7	2.8
Granville	30,402	18,327	0.5	60.3	95	-	12,609	G	41.5	12,609	0.5	68.8	54	41.5	91	3.8	0.9	0.0	3.8
Greene	11,493	8,136	0.2	70.8	69	-	5,732	P	49.9	5,732	0.2	70.5	30	49.9	57	0.0	5.5	1.7	6.9
Guilford	275,376	229,000	6.0	83.2	23	-	147,043	G	53.4	147,043	5.6	64.2	84	53.4	41	0.4	0.7	0.0	1.6
Halifax	41,008	27,839	0.7	67.9	82	-	18,556	S	45.2	18,556	0.7	66.7	72	45.2	76	4.1	0.0	4.6	6.9
Harnett	52,376	29,552	0.8	56.4	97	-	20,932	P	40.0	20,932	0.8	70.8	27	40.0	95	0.0	1.4	1.3	3.0
Haywood	37,546	30,910	0.8	82.3	25	-	21,258	G	56.6	21,258	0.8	68.8	55	56.6	22	1.2	1.4	0.0	0.6
Henderson	57,363	45,893	1.2	80.0	28	-	33,072	P	57.7	33,072	1.3	72.1	15	57.7	19	0.0	2.8	0.9	2.7
Hertford	16,359	14,019	0.4	85.7	14	-	7,672	P	46.9	7,672	0.3	54.7	98	46.9	75	0.0	5.2	2.7	3.9
Hoke	16,607	9,741	0.3	58.7	96	-	6,337	P	38.2	6,337	0.2	65.1	80	38.2	96	0.0	3.7	2.6	6.1
Hyde	4,048	3,388	<.1	83.7	21	-	2,288	P	56.5	2,288	<.1	67.5	65	56.5	23	0.0	6.6	2.6	5.6
Iredell	73,515	55,014	1.4	74.8	53	-	38,980	P	53.0	38,980	1.5	70.9	26	53.0	44	0.0	0.5	0.6	2.5
Jackson	20,924	17,529	0.5	83.8	19	-	11,633	G	55.6	11,633	0.4	66.4	73	55.6	28	0.6	1.2	0.0	2.3
Johnston	64,383	44,429	1.2	69.0	80	-	31,679	P	49.2	31,679	1.2	71.3	23	49.2	63	0.0	2.3	1.3	3.8
Jones	6,952	5,467	0.1	78.6	35	-	3,846	P	55.3	3,846	0.1	70.3	34	55.3	29	0.0	1.6	0.6	2.1
Lee	31,830	21,035	0.6	66.1	90	-	14,659	P	46.1	14,659	0.6	69.7	42	46.1	82	0.0	1.3	0.9	4.3
Lenoir	43,023	28,335	0.7	65.9	91	-	19,842	P	46.1	19,842	0.8	70.0	39	46.1	81	0.0	5.3	2.3	6.4
Lincoln	39,921	30,871	0.8	77.3	43	-	22,355	P	56.0	22,355	0.9	72.4	13	56.0	24	0.0	1.1	0.8	3.7
McDowell	27,745	19,608	0.5	70.7	70	-	13,541	C	48.8	13,541	0.5	69.1	50	48.8	66	1.8	2.0	1.0	0.0
Macon	19,489	16,417	0.4	84.2	18	-	11,282	G	57.9	11,282	0.4	68.7	57	57.9	18	0.0	0.3	0.0	0.1
Madison	13,295	12,435	0.3	93.5	6	-	7,989	P	60.1	7,989	0.3	64.2	82	60.1	12	0.0	8.5	6.7	8.3
Martin	18,621	13,282	0.3	71.3	65	-	8,073	G	43.4	8,073	0.3	60.8	95	43.4	90	0.7	3.4	0.0	10.3
Mecklenburg	413,552	326,005	8.5	78.8	33	-	228,375	P	55.2	228,375	8.7	70.1	38	55.2	31	0.0	4.3	5.8	10.3
Mitchell	11,412	10,782	0.3	94.5	5	-	7,015	P	61.5	7,015	0.3	65.1	79	61.5	10	3.3	1.6	0.0	7.5
Montgomery	17,822	13,153	0.3	73.8	56	-	9,161	P	51.4	9,161	0.3	69.6	43	51.4	52	0.0	4.2	2.2	3.3
Moore	47,791	37,001	1.0	77.4	41	-	26,591	P	55.6	26,591	1.0	71.9	19	55.6	26	0.0	1.0	0.8	5.9
Nash	60,097	42,600	1.1	70.9	67	-	29,886	P	49.7	29,886	1.1	70.2	36	49.7	58	0.0	1.0	0.8	1.8
New Hanover	96,666	77,169	2.0	79.8	29	-	52,154	P	54.0	52,154	2.0	67.6	64	54.0	38	0.0	2.0	1.2	2.8
Northampton	15,505	12,951	0.3	83.5	22	-	7,967	P	51.4	7,967	0.3	61.5	92	51.4	53	0.0	7.4	2.6	7.9
Onslow	118,521	36,947	1.0	31.2	100	-	24,318	P	20.5	24,318	0.9	65.8	75	20.5	100	0.0	1.9	0.9	2.9
Orange	77,566	68,606	1.8	88.4	12	-	47,300	P	61.0	47,300	1.8	68.9	52	61.0	11	0.0	1.4	2.1	3.7
Pamlico	8,902	7,000	0.2	78.6	36	-	4,975	P	55.9	4,975	0.2	71.1	24	55.9	25	0.0	2.3	1.5	2.5
Pasquotank	23,375	15,609	0.4	66.8	87	-	9,581	P	41.0	9,581	0.4	61.4	93	41.0	93	0.0	2.9	0.0	4.6

[1] Percent drop-off is zero for any office used as highest office turnout.

Table C. – **Voter Participation: November 3, 1992, General Election (cont)**

County	Estimated Voting Age Population (VAP), 1992	Voter registration (REG)				Actual	Voter turnout												
							Highest office			Maximum vote							Percent drop-off, by office[1]			
		Total	% contribution to state REG	% of 1992 VAP	Rank by % of 1992 VAP		Total	Office	% of 1992 VAP	Total	% contribution to state turnout	% of REG	Rank by % of REG	% of 1992 VAP	Rank by % 1992 VAP	President	Senator	Governor	Representative
Pender	23,607	17,757	0.5	75.2	50	-	12,546	G	53.1	12,546	0.5	70.7	29	53.1	42	0.9	0.6	0.0	2.0
Perquimans	8,125	5,948	0.2	73.2	59	-	3,878	P	47.7	3,878	0.1	65.2	77	47.7	69	0.0	5.2	2.4	7.9
Person	23,274	15,235	0.4	65.5	92	-	10,230	P	44.0	10,230	0.4	67.1	69	44.0	89	0.0	5.2	2.3	23.8
Pitt	84,598	59,372	1.6	70.2	75	-	39,895	P	47.2	39,895	1.5	67.2	68	47.2	73	0.0	2.7	1.2	4.2
Polk	11,935	11,040	0.3	92.5	7	-	7,533	P	63.1	7,533	0.3	68.2	60	63.1	7	0.0	6.2	3.9	9.3
Randolph	84,742	56,783	1.5	67.0	84	-	39,101	G	46.1	39,101	1.5	68.9	53	46.1	80	0.5	2.3	0.0	3.7
Richmond	33,252	24,316	0.6	73.1	60	-	15,553	P	46.8	15,553	0.6	64.0	85	46.8	76	0.0	2.3	3.4	3.2
Robeson	75,510	56,869	1.5	75.3	49	-	31,295	G	41.4	31,295	1.2	55.0	97	41.4	92	2.6	0.7	0.0	1.1
Rockingham	67,006	44,424	1.2	66.3	88	-	31,269	P	46.7	31,269	1.2	70.4	32	46.7	77	0.0	1.4	0.4	0.7
Rowan	87,079	61,716	1.6	70.9	68	-	42,732	P	49.1	42,732	1.6	69.2	48	49.1	64	0.0	0.7	0.3	2.9
Rutherford	44,165	29,280	0.8	66.3	89	-	20,390	G	46.2	20,390	0.8	69.6	44	46.2	79	0.3	1.1	0.0	2.0
Sampson	35,236	28,074	0.7	79.7	31	-	18,925	S	53.7	18,925	0.7	67.4	66	53.7	39	1.9	0.0	0.1	1.7
Scotland	24,732	17,997	0.5	72.8	62	-	9,360	P	37.8	9,360	0.4	52.0	99	37.8	97	0.2	6.5	5.5	14.5
Stanly	39,919	29,884	0.8	74.9	52	-	21,710	C	54.4	21,710	0.8	72.6	11	54.4	34	0.2	0.4	0.0	0.0
Stokes	29,456	23,012	0.6	78.1	38	-	16,775	G	56.9	16,775	0.6	72.9	10	56.9	21	0.7	1.1	0.0	0.0
Surry	48,678	34,164	0.9	70.2	74	-	23,834	G	49.0	23,834	0.9	69.8	41	49.0	65	1.6	1.8	0.0	1.1
Swain	8,625	8,568	0.2	99.3	4	-	4,341	G	50.3	4,341	0.2	50.7	100	50.3	55	0.3	1.5	0.0	0.3
Transylvania	20,182	17,868	0.5	88.5	11	-	13,137	P	65.1	13,137	0.5	73.5	7	65.1	4	0.0	2.2	1.9	1.6
Tyrrell	2,836	2,213	<.1	78.0	39	-	1,674	P	59.0	1,674	<.1	75.6	3	59.0	14	0.0	7.9	4.0	9.1
Union	64,770	48,511	1.3	74.9	51	-	31,992	P	49.4	31,992	1.2	65.9	74	49.4	62	0.0	2.8	2.2	3.3
Vance	29,329	19,862	0.5	67.7	83	-	12,978	G	44.2	12,978	0.5	65.3	76	44.2	88	1.4	0.3	0.0	1.5
Wake	357,313	278,030	7.3	77.8	40	-	207,893	G	58.2	207,893	7.9	74.8	5	58.2	17	0.2	0.5	0.0	2.4
Warren	13,247	10,987	0.3	82.9	24	-	7,150	G	54.0	7,150	0.3	65.1	78	54.0	37	0.3	1.6	0.0	1.7
Washington	10,188	7,882	0.2	77.4	42	-	5,277	G	51.8	5,277	0.2	67.0	70	51.8	49	0.5	3.3	0.0	4.3
Watauga	30,158	27,705	0.7	91.9	8	-	19,225	P	63.7	19,225	0.7	69.4	45	63.7	6	0.0	2.5	1.4	3.8
Wayne	79,827	42,720	1.1	53.5	98	-	27,532	P	34.5	27,532	1.0	64.4	81	34.5	98	0.0	3.9	2.2	5.2
Wilkes	46,355	37,484	1.0	80.9	26	-	25,232	G	54.4	25,232	1.0	67.3	67	54.4	33	5.4	0.8	0.0	4.5
Wilson	50,179	36,212	0.9	72.2	64	-	23,030	G	45.9	23,030	0.9	63.6	87	45.9	83	0.4	4.3	0.0	7.3
Yadkin	24,282	17,144	0.4	70.6	71	-	12,977	P	53.4	12,977	0.5	75.7	1	53.4	40	0.0	2.6	1.5	3.9
Yancey	12,225	12,274	0.3	100.4	2	-	9,208	P	75.3	9,208	0.4	75.0	4	75.3	1	0.0	2.0	1.2	1.5
NORTH CAROLINA[2]	**5,217,000**	**3,817,380**	**100.0**	**73.2**		**-**	**2,625,045**		**50.3**	**2,625,045**	**100.0**	**68.8**		**50.3**		**0.5**	**1.8**	**1.1**	**3.7**

[1]Percent drop-off is zero for any office used as highest office turnout. [2]North Carolina reports voter registration by political party affiliation (see Table D) and by race. State voter registration by race is 3,064,242 (80.3%) for white, 710,209 (18.6%) for black, 27,725 (0.7%) for (American) Indian, and 15,204 (0.4%) for other.

Table D. — Voter Registration by Political Party Affiliation: November 3, 1992, General Election

County	Total voter registration	Political party affiliation					Percent of total registration						Percent contribution to state registration			
		Democrat (DEM)	Republican (REP)	Independent (IND)	Plurality		DEM	REP	IND	Rank			Total	DEM	REP	IND
					Total	Party				DEM	REP	IND				
Alamance	63,270	38,720	19,737	4,801	18,983	D	61.2	31.2	7.6	59	41	33	1.7	1.7	1.6	1.7
Alexander	19,233	8,897	8,810	1,525	87	D	46.3	45.8	7.9	89	9	26	0.5	0.4	0.7	0.5
Alleghany	6,480	4,613	1,616	251	2,997	D	71.2	24.9	3.9	39	56	69	0.2	0.2	0.1	<.1
Anson	12,030	10,665	1,143	222	9,522	D	88.7	9.5	1.8	10	93	93	0.3	0.5	<.1	<.1
Ashe	15,421	7,757	6,886	775	871	D	50.3	44.7	5.0	83	13	58	0.4	0.3	0.6	0.3
Avery	9,794	1,820	7,380	594	5,560	R	18.6	75.4	6.1	99	2	47	0.3	<.1	0.6	0.2
Beaufort	22,712	16,663	5,174	872	11,489	D	73.4	22.8	3.8	34	64	70	0.6	0.7	0.4	0.3
Bertie	11,716	10,791	769	156	10,022	D	92.1	6.6	1.3	3	98	97	0.3	0.5	<.1	<.1
Bladen	16,465	14,380	1,665	420	12,715	D	87.3	10.1	2.6	13	88	84	0.4	0.6	0.1	0.1
Brunswick	32,769	18,995	11,761	2,007	7,234	D	58.0	35.9	6.1	64	36	46	0.9	0.8	1.0	0.7
Buncombe	109,805	64,746	36,469	8,573	28,277	D	59.0	33.2	7.8	61	39	30	2.9	2.8	3.0	3.0
Burke	41,850	23,094	15,304	3,448	7,790	D	55.2	36.6	8.2	70	32	23	1.1	1.0	1.3	1.2
Cabarrus	60,252	32,143	23,259	4,836	8,884	D	53.4	38.6	8.0	77	23	24	1.6	1.4	1.9	1.7
Caldwell	38,196	18,330	16,443	3,420	1,887	D	48.0	43.1	9.0	88	15	17	1.0	0.8	1.4	1.2
Camden	3,829	3,207	423	199	2,784	D	83.8	11.0	5.2	20	84	56	0.1	0.1	<.1	<.1
Carteret	30,526	16,541	11,144	2,837	5,397	D	54.2	36.5	9.3	74	34	13	0.8	0.7	0.9	1.0
Caswell	11,900	10,381	1,257	262	9,124	D	87.2	10.6	2.2	14	85	89	0.3	0.4	0.1	<.1
Catawba	68,487	29,645	31,527	7,294	1,882	R	43.3	46.0	10.7	93	8	7	1.8	1.3	2.6	2.5
Chatham	24,907	16,968	6,224	1,709	10,744	D	68.1	25.0	6.9	47	55	40	0.7	0.7	0.5	0.6
Cherokee	14,394	7,690	5,697	1,006	1,993	D	53.4	39.6	7.0	76	22	38	0.4	0.3	0.5	0.4
Chowan	7,412	5,720	1,348	343	4,372	D	77.2	18.2	4.6	29	72	63	0.2	0.2	0.1	0.1
Clay	5,715	2,617	2,426	670	191	D	45.8	42.5	11.7	90	17	3	0.1	0.1	0.2	0.2
Cleveland	43,359	30,420	10,302	2,627	20,118	D	70.2	23.8	6.1	40	62	48	1.1	1.3	0.8	0.9
Columbus	31,344	26,276	4,391	676	21,885	D	83.8	14.0	2.2	19	78	91	0.8	1.1	0.4	0.2
Craven	39,362	24,279	11,708	3,373	12,571	D	61.7	29.7	8.6	57	44	21	1.0	1.0	1.0	1.2
Cumberland	104,468	69,229	26,022	9,205	43,207	D	66.3	24.9	8.8	51	57	19	2.7	3.0	2.1	3.2
Currituck	7,311	5,344	1,317	648	4,027	D	73.1	18.0	8.9	35	73	18	0.2	0.2	0.1	0.2
Dare	14,941	8,663	4,579	1,698	4,084	D	58.0	30.6	11.4	63	43	4	0.4	0.4	0.4	0.6
Davidson	69,608	34,223	31,213	4,164	3,010	D	49.2	44.8	6.0	87	12	50	1.8	1.5	2.6	1.5
Davie	16,369	6,086	9,330	953	3,244	R	37.2	57.0	5.8	97	4	52	0.4	0.3	0.8	0.3
Duplin	21,182	16,945	3,939	297	13,006	D	80.0	18.6	1.4	26	71	96	0.6	0.7	0.3	0.1
Durham	117,678	80,334	25,405	11,905	54,929	D	68.3	21.6	10.1	46	67	12	3.1	3.5	2.1	4.2
Edgecombe	31,927	26,735	4,254	938	22,481	D	83.7	13.3	2.9	21	81	79	0.8	1.2	0.3	0.3
Forsyth	161,423	89,374	57,270	14,759	32,104	D	55.4	35.5	9.1	69	37	15	4.2	3.9	4.7	5.2
Franklin	19,860	14,931	4,186	743	10,745	D	75.2	21.1	3.7	30	68	71	0.5	0.6	0.3	0.3
Gaston	87,728	49,323	32,467	5,927	16,856	D	56.2	37.0	6.8	67	30	41	2.3	2.1	2.7	2.1
Gates	5,546	5,013	382	151	4,631	D	90.4	6.9	2.7	5	97	83	0.1	0.2	<.1	<.1
Graham	5,730	2,856	2,578	296	278	D	49.8	45.0	5.2	86	11	57	0.2	0.1	0.2	0.1
Granville	18,327	15,420	2,318	587	13,102	D	84.1	12.6	3.2	18	82	77	0.5	0.7	0.2	0.2
Greene	8,136	7,166	785	184	6,381	D	88.1	9.6	2.3	11	92	87	0.2	0.3	<.1	<.1
Guilford	229,000	133,448	76,114	19,376	57,334	D	58.3	33.2	8.5	62	38	22	6.0	5.8	6.3	6.8
Halifax	27,839	24,233	2,818	788	21,415	D	87.0	10.1	2.8	16	87	81	0.7	1.0	0.2	0.3
Harnett	29,552	21,117	7,494	941	13,623	D	71.5	25.4	3.2	38	53	78	0.8	0.9	0.6	0.3
Haywood	30,910	21,186	7,731	1,992	13,455	D	68.5	25.0	6.4	45	54	43	0.8	0.9	0.6	0.7
Henderson	45,893	18,113	23,568	4,210	5,455	R	39.5	51.4	9.2	94	7	14	1.2	0.8	1.9	1.5
Hertford	14,019	12,457	1,362	199	11,095	D	88.9	9.7	1.4	9	91	95	0.4	0.5	0.1	<.1
Hoke	9,741	8,237	1,148	355	7,089	D	84.6	11.8	3.6	17	83	72	0.3	0.4	<.1	0.1
Hyde	3,388	3,049	264	75	2,785	D	90.0	7.8	2.2	6	96	88	<.1	0.1	<.1	<.1
Iredell	55,014	30,478	20,700	3,831	9,778	D	55.4	37.6	7.0	68	28	39	1.4	1.3	1.7	1.3
Jackson	17,529	10,744	5,402	1,383	5,342	D	61.3	30.8	7.9	58	42	27	0.5	0.5	0.4	0.5
Johnston	44,429	30,021	12,395	2,009	17,626	D	67.6	27.9	4.5	48	50	66	1.2	1.3	1.0	0.7
Jones	5,467	4,863	532	72	4,331	D	89.0	9.7	1.3	8	90	98	0.1	0.2	<.1	<.1
Lee	21,035	15,224	4,847	962	10,377	D	72.4	23.0	4.6	36	63	65	0.6	0.7	0.4	0.3
Lenoir	28,335	22,160	5,531	642	16,629	D	78.2	19.5	2.3	27	69	86	0.7	1.0	0.5	0.2
Lincoln	30,871	16,639	11,803	2,425	4,836	D	53.9	38.2	7.9	75	25	28	0.8	0.7	1.0	0.8
McDowell	19,608	12,993	5,480	1,135	7,513	D	66.3	27.9	5.8	52	49	53	0.5	0.6	0.5	0.4
Macon	16,417	8,372	6,562	1,483	1,810	D	51.0	40.0	9.0	82	19	16	0.4	0.4	0.5	0.5
Madison	12,435	8,054	3,640	739	4,414	D	64.8	29.3	5.9	55	45	51	0.3	0.3	0.3	0.3
Martin	13,282	11,071	1,823	388	9,248	D	83.4	13.7	2.9	22	79	80	0.3	0.5	0.1	0.1
Mecklenburg	326,005	168,846	122,671	34,409	46,175	D	51.8	37.6	10.6	80	27	8	8.5	7.3	10.1	12.0
Mitchell	10,782	1,738	8,188	856	6,450	R	16.1	75.9	7.9	100	1	25	0.3	<.1	0.7	0.3
Montgomery	13,153	9,035	3,484	633	5,551	D	68.7	26.5	4.8	44	52	61	0.3	0.4	0.3	0.2
Moore	37,001	16,523	16,698	3,779	175	R	44.7	45.1	10.2	91	10	9	1.0	0.7	1.4	1.3
Nash	42,600	28,342	12,340	1,918	16,002	D	66.5	29.0	4.5	50	46	67	1.1	1.2	1.0	0.7
New Hanover	77,169	42,536	28,805	5,785	13,731	D	55.2	37.3	7.5	71	29	35	2.0	1.8	2.4	2.0
Northampton	12,951	12,388	476	87	11,912	D	95.7	3.7	0.7	1	100	100	0.3	0.5	<.1	<.1
Onslow	36,947	23,619	10,503	2,820	13,116	D	63.9	28.4	7.6	56	47	31	1.0	1.0	0.9	1.0
Orange	68,606	44,856	15,255	8,456	29,601	D	65.4	22.2	12.3	54	65	2	1.8	1.9	1.3	3.0
Pamlico	7,000	5,406	1,252	341	4,154	D	77.2	17.9	4.9	28	74	60	0.2	0.2	0.1	0.1
Pasquotank	15,609	11,673	2,938	994	8,735	D	74.8	18.8	6.4	31	70	44	0.4	0.5	0.2	0.3

680 North Carolina

County	Total voter registration	Democrat (DEM)	Republican (REP)	Independent (IND)	Plurality Total	Plurality Party	DEM	REP	IND	Rank DEM	Rank REP	Rank IND	Total	DEM	REP	IND
Pender	17,757	12,411	4,403	940	8,008	D	69.9	24.8	5.3	41	58	55	0.5	0.5	0.4	0.3
Perquimans	5,948	4,853	811	284	4,042	D	81.6	13.6	4.8	24	80	62	0.2	0.2	<.1	<.1
Person	15,235	12,227	2,457	547	9,770	D	80.3	16.1	3.6	25	75	73	0.4	0.5	0.2	0.2
Pitt	59,372	41,057	14,388	3,927	26,669	D	69.2	24.2	6.6	42	61	42	1.6	1.8	1.2	1.4
Polk	11,040	5,506	4,409	1,123	1,097	D	49.9	39.9	10.2	85	20	11	0.3	0.2	0.4	0.4
Randolph	56,783	22,013	30,537	4,222	8,524	R	38.8	53.8	7.4	95	6	36	1.5	1.0	2.5	1.5
Richmond	24,316	20,029	3,497	787	16,532	D	82.4	14.4	3.2	23	77	76	0.6	0.9	0.3	0.3
Robeson	56,869	50,733	5,064	1,071	45,669	D	89.2	8.9	1.9	7	94	92	1.5	2.2	0.4	0.4
Rockingham	44,424	30,719	10,929	2,775	19,790	D	69.2	24.6	6.2	43	60	45	1.2	1.3	0.9	1.0
Rowan	61,716	31,027	25,840	4,842	5,187	D	50.3	41.9	7.8	84	18	29	1.6	1.3	2.1	1.7
Rutherford	29,280	19,683	8,243	1,353	11,440	D	67.2	28.2	4.6	49	48	64	0.8	0.9	0.7	0.5
Sampson	28,074	16,984	10,311	778	6,673	D	60.5	36.7	2.8	60	31	82	0.7	0.7	0.8	0.3
Scotland	17,997	13,397	2,764	1,834	10,633	D	74.4	15.4	10.2	33	76	10	0.5	0.6	0.2	0.6
Stanly	29,884	15,733	11,873	2,277	3,860	D	52.6	39.7	7.6	78	21	32	0.8	0.7	1.0	0.8
Stokes	23,012	12,023	9,858	1,129	2,165	D	52.3	42.8	4.9	79	16	59	0.6	0.5	0.8	0.4
Surry	34,164	19,784	12,324	2,056	7,460	D	57.9	36.1	6.0	65	35	49	0.9	0.9	1.0	0.7
Swain	8,568	5,604	2,316	648	3,288	D	65.4	27.0	7.6	53	51	34	0.2	0.2	0.2	0.2
Transylvania	17,868	9,148	6,751	1,966	2,397	D	51.2	37.8	11.0	81	26	5	0.5	0.4	0.6	0.7
Tyrrell	2,213	2,012	178	23	1,834	D	90.9	8.0	1.0	4	95	99	<.1	<.1	<.1	<.1
Union	48,511	26,631	17,712	4,166	8,919	D	54.9	36.5	8.6	72	33	20	1.3	1.2	1.5	1.5
Vance	19,862	17,451	1,975	434	15,476	D	87.9	9.9	2.2	12	89	90	0.5	0.8	0.2	0.2
Wake	278,030	156,350	91,598	29,938	64,752	D	56.3	33.0	10.8	66	40	6	7.3	6.8	7.5	10.5
Warren	10,987	10,202	618	167	9,584	D	92.9	5.6	1.5	2	99	94	0.3	0.4	<.1	<.1
Washington	7,882	6,862	819	200	6,043	D	87.1	10.4	2.5	15	86	85	0.2	0.3	<.1	<.1
Watauga	27,705	12,067	11,982	3,647	85	D	43.6	43.3	13.2	92	14	1	0.7	0.5	1.0	1.3
Wayne	42,720	30,698	10,580	1,438	20,118	D	71.9	24.8	3.4	37	59	75	1.1	1.3	0.9	0.5
Wilkes	37,484	14,116	21,215	2,151	7,099	R	37.7	56.6	5.7	96	5	54	1.0	0.6	1.7	0.8
Wilson	36,212	26,976	7,963	1,264	19,013	D	74.5	22.0	3.5	32	66	74	0.9	1.2	0.7	0.4
Yadkin	17,144	6,140	10,252	752	4,112	R	35.8	59.8	4.4	98	3	68	0.4	0.3	0.8	0.3
Yancey	12,274	6,663	4,715	896	1,948	D	54.3	38.4	7.3	73	24	37	0.3	0.3	0.4	0.3
NORTH CAROLINA[1]	**3,817,380**	**2,313,520**	**1,217,114**	**286,069**	**1,096,406**	**D**	**60.6**	**31.9**	**7.5**				**100.0**	**100.0**	**100.0**	**100.0**

State total voter registration also includes 677 for Libertarian party.

North Carolina 681

Table E. – Vote for President: November 3, 1992, General Election

County	Total	Clinton (DEM)	Bush (REP)	Perot (IND)	Other	Plurality Total	Party	DEM	REP	IND	Other	Rank DEM	Rank REP	Rank IND	Total	DEM	REP	IND	DEM	REP
Alamance	42,701	15,521	20,637	6,444	99	5,116	R	36.3	48.3	15.1	0.2	79	24	28	1.6	1.4	1.8	1.8	42.9	57.1
Alexander	13,626	4,849	6,764	2,002	11	1,915	R	35.6	49.6	14.7	<.1	84	17	35	0.5	0.4	0.6	0.6	41.8	58.2
Alleghany	4,730	2,271	1,853	600	6	418	D	48.0	39.2	12.7	0.1	35	61	64	0.2	0.2	0.2	0.2	55.1	44.9
Anson	8,539	5,269	2,334	921	15	2,935	D	61.7	27.3	10.8	0.2	5	95	86	0.3	0.5	0.2	0.3	69.3	30.7
Ashe	11,070	4,624	5,200	1,220	26	576	R	41.8	47.0	11.0	0.2	58	29	84	0.4	0.4	0.5	0.3	47.1	52.9
Avery	6,787	1,755	3,895	1,123	14	2,140	R	25.9	57.4	16.5	0.2	99	2	8	0.3	0.2	0.3	0.3	31.1	68.9
Beaufort	15,980	6,445	7,337	2,174	24	892	R	40.3	45.9	13.6	0.2	63	34	49	0.6	0.6	0.6	0.6	46.8	53.2
Bertie	6,743	4,382	1,756	600	5	2,626	D	65.0	26.0	8.9	<.1	3	97	100	0.3	0.4	0.2	0.2	71.4	28.6
Bladen	10,177	5,700	3,214	1,248	15	2,486	D	56.0	31.6	12.3	0.1	15	89	68	0.4	0.5	0.3	0.3	63.9	36.1
Brunswick	22,400	10,177	8,833	3,349	41	1,344	D	45.4	39.4	15.0	0.2	42	60	32	0.9	0.9	0.8	0.9	53.5	46.5
Buncombe	75,492	32,955	30,892	11,481	164	2,063	D	43.7	40.9	15.2	0.2	49	57	25	2.9	3.0	2.7	3.2	51.6	48.4
Burke	30,122	12,565	13,397	4,124	36	832	R	41.7	44.5	13.7	0.1	59	44	47	1.2	1.1	1.2	1.2	48.4	51.6
Cabarrus	41,123	13,513	21,281	6,251	78	7,768	R	32.9	51.7	15.2	0.2	93	9	27	1.6	1.2	1.9	1.7	38.8	61.2
Caldwell	25,576	9,033	12,543	3,965	35	3,510	R	35.3	49.0	15.5	0.1	85	20	21	1.0	0.8	1.1	1.1	41.9	58.1
Camden	2,675	1,153	1,039	479	4	114	D	43.1	38.8	17.9	0.1	50	64	4	0.1	0.1	<.1	0.1	52.6	47.4
Carteret	21,819	8,028	10,334	3,401	56	2,306	R	36.8	47.4	15.6	0.3	75	28	18	0.8	0.7	0.9	1.0	43.7	56.3
Caswell	8,363	4,725	2,793	827	18	1,932	D	56.5	33.4	9.9	0.2	14	82	97	0.3	0.4	0.2	0.2	62.8	37.2
Catawba	49,409	16,334	25,466	7,523	86	9,132	R	33.1	51.5	15.2	0.2	92	11	24	1.9	1.5	2.2	2.1	39.1	60.9
Chatham	18,577	9,520	6,568	2,425	64	2,952	D	51.2	35.4	13.1	0.3	22	78	59	0.7	0.9	0.6	0.7	59.2	40.8
Cherokee	8,758	3,686	4,021	1,040	11	335	R	42.1	45.9	11.9	0.1	57	35	73	0.3	0.3	0.4	0.3	47.8	52.2
Chowan	4,506	2,136	1,661	700	9	475	D	47.4	36.9	15.5	0.2	36	75	20	0.2	0.2	0.1	0.2	56.3	43.7
Clay	3,960	1,600	1,890	465	5	290	R	40.4	47.7	11.7	0.1	62	27	74	0.2	0.1	0.2	0.1	45.8	54.2
Cleveland	30,522	13,037	13,650	3,784	51	613	R	42.7	44.7	12.4	0.2	53	43	66	1.2	1.2	1.2	1.1	48.9	51.1
Columbus	18,916	11,469	5,462	1,963	22	6,007	D	60.6	28.9	10.4	0.1	6	91	80	0.7	1.0	0.5	0.5	67.7	32.3
Craven	25,287	9,998	11,575	3,679	35	1,577	R	39.5	45.8	14.5	0.1	68	37	36	1.0	0.9	1.0	1.0	46.3	53.7
Cumberland	64,470	30,291	27,139	6,792	248	3,152	D	47.0	42.1	10.5	0.4	37	51	91	2.5	2.7	2.4	1.9	52.7	47.3
Currituck	5,297	1,935	2,188	1,163	11	253	R	36.5	41.3	22.0	0.2	77	54	2	0.2	0.2	0.2	0.3	46.9	53.1
Dare	10,696	3,925	4,357	2,388	26	432	R	36.7	40.7	22.3	0.2	76	58	1	0.4	0.4	0.4	0.7	47.4	52.6
Davidson	49,725	16,462	24,869	8,324	70	8,407	R	33.1	50.0	16.7	0.1	90	14	6	1.9	1.5	2.2	2.3	39.8	60.2
Davie	12,387	3,675	6,796	1,903	13	3,121	R	29.7	54.9	15.4	0.1	97	5	22	0.5	0.3	0.6	0.5	35.1	64.9
Duplin	13,747	6,816	5,286	1,636	9	1,530	D	49.6	38.5	11.9	<.1	28	67	72	0.5	0.6	0.5	0.5	56.3	43.7
Durham	82,682	47,331	27,581	7,504	266	19,750	D	57.2	33.4	9.1	0.3	12	83	99	3.2	4.2	2.4	2.1	63.2	36.8
Edgecombe	19,657	11,174	6,275	2,175	33	4,899	D	56.8	31.9	11.1	0.2	13	87	82	0.8	1.0	0.6	0.6	64.0	36.0
Forsyth	116,274	49,006	52,787	14,262	219	3,781	R	42.1	45.4	12.3	0.2	56	41	67	4.5	4.4	4.7	4.0	48.1	51.9
Franklin	13,266	6,517	4,669	2,062	18	1,848	D	49.1	35.2	15.5	0.1	31	79	19	0.5	0.6	0.4	0.6	58.3	41.7
Gaston	61,435	19,121	34,714	7,490	110	15,593	R	31.1	56.5	12.2	0.2	95	3	70	2.4	1.7	3.1	2.1	35.5	64.5
Gates	3,834	2,206	1,158	466	4	1,048	D	57.5	30.2	12.2	0.1	11	90	71	0.1	0.2	0.1	0.1	65.6	34.4
Graham	3,876	1,551	1,919	403	3	368	R	40.0	49.5	10.4	<.1	65	18	92	0.1	0.1	0.2	0.1	44.7	55.3
Granville	12,128	6,178	4,538	1,321	91	1,640	D	50.9	37.4	10.9	0.8	24	70	85	0.5	0.6	0.4	0.4	57.7	42.3
Greene	5,732	2,768	2,180	780	4	588	D	48.3	38.0	13.6	<.1	33	68	48	0.2	0.2	0.2	0.2	55.9	44.1
Guilford	146,399	66,319	60,140	19,601	339	6,179	D	45.3	41.1	13.4	0.2	43	56	51	5.6	6.0	5.3	5.5	52.4	47.6
Halifax	17,804	9,960	5,769	2,047	28	4,191	D	55.9	32.4	11.5	0.2	16	85	77	0.7	0.9	0.5	0.6	63.3	36.7
Harnett	20,932	8,473	9,751	2,684	24	1,278	R	40.5	46.6	12.8	0.1	61	32	62	0.8	0.8	0.9	0.8	46.5	53.5
Haywood	21,009	10,385	7,292	3,303	29	3,093	D	49.4	34.7	15.7	0.1	29	80	15	0.8	0.9	0.6	0.9	58.7	41.3
Henderson	33,072	10,747	17,010	5,260	55	6,263	R	32.5	51.4	15.9	0.2	94	12	14	1.3	1.0	1.5	1.5	38.7	61.3
Hertford	7,672	4,609	2,208	846	9	2,401	D	60.1	28.8	11.0	0.1	8	92	83	0.3	0.4	0.2	0.2	67.6	32.4
Hoke	6,337	3,730	1,711	887	9	2,019	D	58.9	27.0	14.0	0.1	10	96	42	0.2	0.3	0.2	0.2	68.6	31.4
Hyde	2,288	1,206	740	340	2	466	D	52.7	32.3	14.9	<.1	20	86	34	<.1	0.1	<.1	<.1	62.0	38.0
Iredell	38,980	13,263	19,411	6,204	102	6,148	R	34.0	49.8	15.9	0.3	86	16	13	1.5	1.2	1.7	1.7	40.6	59.4
Jackson	11,558	5,753	4,275	1,516	14	1,478	D	49.8	37.0	13.1	0.1	27	73	57	0.4	0.5	0.4	0.4	57.4	42.6
Johnston	31,679	11,284	15,418	4,939	38	4,134	R	35.6	48.7	15.6	0.1	83	22	17	1.2	1.0	1.4	1.4	42.3	57.7
Jones	3,846	1,962	1,438	444	2	524	D	51.0	37.4	11.5	<.1	23	71	76	0.1	0.2	0.1	0.1	57.7	42.3
Lee	14,659	5,852	6,658	2,125	24	806	R	39.9	45.4	14.5	0.2	67	40	37	0.6	0.5	0.6	0.6	46.8	53.2
Lenoir	19,842	8,793	8,932	2,107	10	139	R	44.3	45.0	10.6	<.1	47	42	90	0.8	0.8	0.8	0.6	49.6	50.4
Lincoln	22,355	8,150	11,018	3,142	45	2,868	R	36.5	49.3	14.1	0.2	78	19	41	0.9	0.7	1.0	0.9	42.5	57.5
McDowell	13,295	5,309	6,090	1,881	15	781	R	39.9	45.8	14.1	0.1	66	36	40	0.5	0.5	0.5	0.5	46.6	53.4
Macon	11,279	4,624	4,797	1,829	29	173	R	41.0	42.5	16.2	0.3	60	50	11	0.4	0.4	0.4	0.5	49.1	50.9
Madison	7,989	3,980	3,121	857	31	859	D	49.8	39.1	10.7	0.4	26	63	88	0.3	0.4	0.3	0.2	56.0	44.0
Martin	8,016	4,069	2,958	981	8	1,111	D	50.8	36.9	12.2	<.1	25	74	69	0.3	0.4	0.3	0.3	57.9	42.1
Mecklenburg	228,375	97,065	99,496	31,283	531	2,431	R	42.5	43.6	13.7	0.2	54	47	46	8.7	8.7	8.8	8.7	49.4	50.6
Mitchell	7,015	1,727	4,405	877	6	2,678	R	24.6	62.8	12.5	<.1	100	1	65	0.3	0.2	0.4	0.2	28.2	71.8
Montgomery	9,161	4,422	3,543	1,185	11	879	D	48.3	38.7	12.9	0.1	34	66	61	0.4	0.4	0.3	0.3	55.5	44.5
Moore	26,591	9,649	12,448	4,448	46	2,799	R	36.3	46.8	16.7	0.2	80	30	7	1.0	0.9	1.1	1.2	43.7	56.3
Nash	29,886	10,809	14,446	4,544	87	3,637	R	36.2	48.3	15.2	0.3	81	23	26	1.1	1.0	1.3	1.3	42.8	57.2
New Hanover	52,154	20,291	24,338	7,401	124	4,047	R	38.9	46.7	14.2	0.2	71	31	39	2.0	1.8	2.1	2.1	45.5	54.5
Northampton	7,967	5,195	1,845	916	11	3,350	D	65.2	23.2	11.5	0.1	2	100	78	0.3	0.5	0.2	0.3	73.8	26.2
Onslow	24,318	8,045	11,842	4,387	44	3,797	R	33.1	48.7	18.0	0.2	91	21	3	0.9	0.7	1.0	1.2	40.5	59.5
Orange	47,300	28,595	13,009	5,535	161	15,586	D	60.5	27.5	11.7	0.3	7	94	75	1.8	2.6	1.1	1.5	68.7	31.3
Pamlico	4,975	2,229	1,929	809	8	300	D	44.8	38.8	16.3	0.2	45	65	10	0.2	0.2	0.2	0.2	53.6	46.4
Pasquotank	9,581	4,709	3,419	1,434	19	1,290	D	49.1	35.7	15.0	0.2	30	77	31	0.4	0.4	0.3	0.4	57.9	42.1

Table E. — Vote for President: November 3, 1992, General Election (cont)

County	Total	Clinton (DEM)	Bush (REP)	Perot (IND)	Other	Plurality Total	Party	DEM	REP	IND	Other	Rank DEM	Rank REP	Rank IND	Total	DEM	REP	IND	DEM	REP
Pender	12,430	5,825	4,857	1,725	23	968	D	46.9	39.1	13.9	0.2	39	62	44	0.5	0.5	0.4	0.5	54.5	45.5
Perquimans	3,878	1,818	1,429	624	7	389	D	46.9	36.8	16.1	0.2	38	76	12	0.1	0.2	0.1	0.2	56.0	44.0
Person	10,230	4,323	4,460	1,431	16	137	R	42.3	43.6	14.0	0.2	55	46	43	0.4	0.4	0.4	0.4	49.2	50.8
Pitt	39,895	17,959	16,609	5,262	65	1,350	D	45.0	41.6	13.2	0.2	44	53	54	1.5	1.6	1.5	1.5	52.0	48.0
Polk	7,533	2,939	3,448	1,134	12	509	R	39.0	45.8	15.1	0.2	69	38	29	0.3	0.3	0.3	0.3	46.0	54.0
Randolph	38,902	11,274	20,697	6,870	61	9,423	R	29.0	53.2	17.7	0.2	98	6	5	1.5	1.0	1.8	1.9	35.3	64.7
Richmond	15,553	9,163	4,356	2,015	19	4,807	D	58.9	28.0	13.0	0.1	9	93	60	0.6	0.8	0.4	0.6	67.8	32.2
Robeson	30,474	19,378	7,777	3,277	42	11,601	D	63.6	25.5	10.8	0.1	4	98	87	1.2	1.7	0.7	0.9	71.4	28.6
Rockingham	31,269	13,880	12,678	4,671	40	1,202	D	44.4	40.5	14.9	0.1	46	59	33	1.2	1.2	1.1	1.3	52.3	47.7
Rowan	42,732	14,308	21,297	7,053	74	6,989	R	33.5	49.8	16.5	0.2	88	15	9	1.6	1.3	1.9	2.0	40.2	59.8
Rutherford	20,329	7,855	9,748	2,695	31	1,893	R	38.6	48.0	13.3	0.2	73	25	53	0.8	0.7	0.9	0.8	44.6	55.4
Sampson	18,568	8,698	8,007	1,852	11	691	D	46.8	43.1	10.0	<.1	40	49	95	0.7	0.8	0.7	0.5	52.1	47.9
Scotland	9,360	5,175	2,980	1,196	9	2,195	D	55.3	31.8	12.8	<.1	18	88	63	0.4	0.5	0.3	0.3	63.5	36.5
Stanly	21,664	7,735	11,030	2,855	44	3,295	R	35.7	50.9	13.2	0.2	82	13	55	0.8	0.7	1.0	0.8	41.2	58.8
Stokes	16,657	6,463	7,979	2,183	32	1,516	R	38.8	47.9	13.1	0.2	72	26	58	0.6	0.6	0.7	0.6	44.8	55.2
Surry	23,453	9,392	10,866	3,164	31	1,474	R	40.0	46.3	13.5	0.1	64	33	50	0.9	0.8	1.0	0.9	46.4	53.6
Swain	4,330	2,117	1,640	568	5	477	D	48.9	37.9	13.1	0.1	32	69	56	0.2	0.2	0.1	0.2	56.3	43.7
Transylvania	13,137	5,120	5,984	2,006	27	864	R	39.0	45.6	15.3	0.2	70	39	23	0.5	0.5	0.5	0.6	46.1	53.9
Tyrrell	1,674	928	553	189	4	375	D	55.4	33.0	11.3	0.2	17	84	80	<.1	<.1	<.1	<.1	62.7	37.3
Union	31,992	10,789	16,542	4,601	60	5,753	R	33.7	51.7	14.4	0.2	87	10	38	1.2	1.0	1.5	1.3	39.5	60.5
Vance	12,800	6,598	4,747	1,444	11	1,851	D	51.5	37.1	11.3	<.1	21	72	81	0.5	0.6	0.4	0.4	58.2	41.8
Wake	207,467	88,979	86,798	31,140	550	2,181	D	42.9	41.8	15.0	0.3	52	52	30	7.9	8.0	7.6	8.7	50.6	49.4
Warren	7,125	4,656	1,767	693	9	2,889	D	65.3	24.8	9.7	0.1	1	99	98	0.3	0.4	0.2	0.2	72.5	27.5
Washington	5,253	2,902	1,780	563	8	1,122	D	55.2	33.9	10.7	0.2	19	81	89	0.2	0.3	0.2	0.2	62.0	38.0
Watauga	19,225	8,262	7,899	3,007	57	363	D	43.0	41.1	15.6	0.3	51	55	16	0.7	0.7	0.7	0.8	51.1	48.9
Wayne	27,532	10,307	14,397	2,798	30	4,090	R	37.4	52.3	10.2	0.1	74	8	94	1.1	0.9	1.3	0.8	41.7	58.3
Wilkes	23,868	7,991	12,547	3,307	23	4,556	R	33.5	52.6	13.9	<.1	89	7	45	0.9	0.7	1.1	0.9	38.9	61.1
Wilson	22,937	10,105	10,176	2,630	26	71	R	44.1	44.4	11.5	0.1	48	45	79	0.9	0.9	0.9	0.7	49.8	50.2
Yadkin	12,977	3,913	7,311	1,725	28	3,398	R	30.2	56.3	13.3	0.2	96	4	52	0.5	0.4	0.6	0.5	34.9	65.1
Yancey	9,208	4,285	3,994	917	12	291	D	46.5	43.4	10.0	0.1	41	48	96	0.4	0.4	0.4	0.3	51.8	48.2
NORTH CAROLINA	2,611,850	1,114,042	1,134,661	357,864	5,283	20,619	R	42.7	43.4	13.7	0.2				100.0	100.0	100.0	100.0	49.5	50.5

County	Total	Sanford (DEM)	Faircloth (REP)	Other	Plurality Total	Party	DEM	REP	Other	Rank DEM	Rank REP	Rank Other	Total	DEM	REP	Other
Alamance	42,214	17,573	23,299	1,342	5,726	R	41.6	55.2	3.2	75	28	40	1.6	1.5	1.8	1.6
Alexander	13,700	5,392	7,885	423	2,493	R	39.4	57.6	3.1	82	16	42	0.5	0.5	0.6	0.5
Alleghany	4,597	2,198	2,259	140	61	R	47.8	49.1	3.0	49	52	43	0.2	0.2	0.2	0.2
Anson	8,131	5,473	2,532	126	2,941	D	67.3	31.1	1.5	5	96	80	0.3	0.5	0.2	0.1
Ashe	10,926	4,580	6,077	269	1,497	R	41.9	55.6	2.5	72	26	58	0.4	0.4	0.5	0.3
Avery	6,612	1,879	4,507	226	2,628	R	28.4	68.2	3.4	99	2	32	0.3	0.2	0.3	0.3
Beaufort	15,677	6,564	8,717	396	2,153	R	41.9	55.6	2.5	74	27	54	0.6	0.5	0.7	0.5
Bertie	6,319	4,165	2,083	71	2,082	D	65.9	33.0	1.1	7	92	93	0.2	0.3	0.2	<.1
Bladen	9,643	6,064	3,436	143	2,628	D	62.9	35.6	1.5	13	87	83	0.4	0.5	0.3	0.2
Brunswick	21,750	10,015	10,617	1,118	602	R	46.0	48.8	5.1	54	55	5	0.8	0.8	0.8	1.3
Buncombe	73,295	34,458	37,250	1,587	2,792	R	47.0	50.8	2.2	51	46	65	2.8	2.9	2.9	1.8
Burke	30,105	13,080	15,833	1,192	2,753	R	43.4	52.6	4.0	67	39	17	1.2	1.1	1.2	1.4
Cabarrus	41,210	15,115	24,051	2,044	8,936	R	36.7	58.4	5.0	89	13	8	1.6	1.3	1.9	2.4
Caldwell	26,029	9,517	15,341	1,171	5,824	R	36.6	58.9	4.5	90	11	12	1.0	0.8	1.2	1.4
Camden	2,613	1,405	1,159	49	246	D	53.8	44.4	1.9	27	72	72	0.1	0.1	<.1	<.1
Carteret	21,848	9,041	11,934	873	2,893	R	41.4	54.6	4.0	77	30	15	0.8	0.8	0.9	1.0
Caswell	7,794	4,950	2,732	112	2,218	D	63.5	35.1	1.4	11	88	85	0.3	0.4	0.2	0.1
Catawba	49,190	16,754	29,829	2,607	13,075	R	34.1	60.6	5.3	94	9	2	1.9	1.4	2.3	3.0
Chatham	18,024	9,830	7,599	595	2,231	D	54.5	42.2	3.3	24	78	36	0.7	0.8	0.6	0.7
Cherokee	8,597	4,000	4,533	64	533	R	46.5	52.7	0.7	52	38	100	0.3	0.3	0.3	<.1
Chowan	4,397	2,440	1,867	90	573	D	55.5	42.5	2.0	23	77	68	0.2	0.2	0.1	0.1
Clay	3,854	1,749	2,064	41	315	R	45.4	53.6	1.1	58	36	95	0.1	0.1	0.2	<.1
Cleveland	30,125	13,353	15,575	1,197	2,222	R	44.3	51.7	4.0	63	44	16	1.2	1.1	1.2	1.4
Columbus	19,252	12,163	6,610	479	5,553	D	63.2	34.3	2.5	12	90	57	0.7	1.0	0.5	0.6
Craven	24,702	10,257	13,901	544	3,644	R	41.5	56.3	2.2	76	24	64	1.0	0.9	1.1	0.6
Cumberland	66,338	34,076	29,654	2,608	4,422	D	51.4	44.7	3.9	34	71	18	2.6	2.9	2.3	3.0
Currituck	5,136	2,546	2,457	133	89	D	49.6	47.8	2.6	41	61	52	0.2	0.2	0.2	0.2
Dare	10,540	5,121	5,121	298	0		48.6	48.6	2.8	45	56	45	0.4	0.4	0.4	0.3
Davidson	49,496	18,053	29,413	2,030	11,360	R	36.5	59.4	4.1	91	10	14	1.9	1.5	2.3	2.4
Davie	12,065	3,841	7,812	412	3,971	R	31.8	64.7	3.4	96	4	33	0.5	0.3	0.6	0.5
Duplin	14,032	7,120	6,589	323	531	D	50.7	47.0	2.3	37	63	62	0.5	0.6	0.5	0.4
Durham	83,257	51,016	29,970	2,271	21,046	D	61.3	36.0	2.7	14	86	48	3.2	4.3	2.3	2.6
Edgecombe	19,525	11,856	7,264	405	4,592	D	60.7	37.2	2.1	15	85	67	0.8	1.0	0.6	0.5
Forsyth	115,393	52,080	59,574	3,739	7,494	R	45.1	51.6	3.2	59	45	38	4.5	4.4	4.6	4.3
Franklin	13,392	6,810	6,117	465	693	D	50.9	45.7	3.5	36	68	31	0.5	0.6	0.5	0.5
Gaston	61,233	19,133	38,774	3,326	19,641	R	31.2	63.3	5.4	97	6	1	2.4	1.6	3.0	3.9
Gates	3,598	2,530	1,014	54	1,516	D	70.3	28.2	1.5	2	99	81	0.1	0.2	<.1	<.1
Graham	3,734	1,618	2,081	35	463	R	43.3	55.7	0.9	68	25	96	0.1	0.1	0.2	<.1
Granville	12,493	6,712	5,336	445	1,376	D	53.7	42.7	3.6	28	76	28	0.5	0.6	0.4	0.5
Greene	5,417	2,683	2,653	81	30	D	49.5	49.0	1.5	42	53	82	0.2	0.2	0.2	<.1
Guilford	145,964	71,511	69,752	4,701	1,759	D	49.0	47.8	3.2	44	62	39	5.7	6.0	5.4	5.5
Halifax	18,556	10,919	7,173	464	3,746	D	58.8	38.7	2.5	19	84	56	0.7	0.9	0.6	0.5
Harnett	20,633	9,088	10,785	760	1,697	R	44.0	52.3	3.7	64	43	24	0.8	0.8	0.8	0.9
Haywood	20,952	10,871	9,530	551	1,341	D	51.9	45.5	2.6	33	69	51	0.8	0.9	0.7	0.6
Henderson	32,158	11,202	20,073	883	8,871	R	34.8	62.4	2.7	92	7	47	1.2	0.9	1.5	1.0
Hertford	7,271	4,860	2,350	61	2,510	D	66.8	32.3	0.8	6	94	99	0.3	0.4	0.2	<.1
Hoke	6,101	3,961	2,000	140	1,961	D	64.9	32.8	2.3	10	93	63	0.2	0.3	0.2	0.2
Hyde	2,137	1,260	834	43	426	D	59.0	39.0	2.0	18	83	69	<.1	0.1	<.1	<.1
Iredell	38,799	14,266	22,514	2,019	8,248	R	36.8	58.0	5.2	88	15	4	1.5	1.2	1.7	2.3
Jackson	11,495	6,236	5,093	166	1,143	D	54.2	44.3	1.4	26	74	84	0.4	0.5	0.4	0.2
Johnston	30,948	12,003	17,755	1,190	5,752	R	38.8	57.4	3.8	83	18	20	1.2	1.0	1.4	1.4
Jones	3,784	2,017	1,677	90	340	D	53.3	44.3	2.4	29	73	61	0.1	0.2	0.1	0.1
Lee	14,471	6,361	7,578	532	1,217	R	44.0	52.4	3.7	65	42	25	0.6	0.5	0.6	0.6
Lenoir	18,793	9,048	9,477	268	429	R	48.1	50.4	1.4	46	48	86	0.7	0.8	0.7	0.3
Lincoln	22,099	8,332	12,669	1,098	4,337	R	37.7	57.3	5.0	84	19	7	0.9	0.7	1.0	1.3
McDowell	13,267	5,950	6,977	340	1,027	R	44.8	52.6	2.6	60	40	53	0.5	0.5	0.5	0.4
Macon	11,244	5,030	5,940	274	910	R	44.7	52.8	2.4	61	37	60	0.4	0.4	0.5	0.3
Madison	7,312	3,857	3,364	91	493	D	52.7	46.0	1.2	31	67	91	0.3	0.3	0.3	0.1
Martin	7,797	4,249	3,450	98	799	D	54.5	44.2	1.3	25	75	90	0.3	0.4	0.3	0.1
Mecklenburg	218,643	104,373	105,867	8,403	1,494	R	47.7	48.4	3.8	50	59	21	8.5	8.7	8.2	9.8
Mitchell	6,784	1,811	4,784	189	2,973	R	26.7	70.5	2.8	100	1	46	0.3	0.2	0.4	0.2
Montgomery	8,772	4,486	4,065	221	421	D	51.1	46.3	2.5	35	66	55	0.3	0.4	0.3	0.3
Moore	26,320	10,674	15,004	642	4,330	R	40.6	57.0	2.4	79	20	59	1.0	0.9	1.2	0.7
Nash	29,597	11,971	16,826	800	4,855	R	40.4	56.9	2.7	80	22	49	1.1	1.0	1.3	0.9
New Hanover	51,100	20,976	27,540	2,584	6,564	R	41.0	53.9	5.1	78	33	6	2.0	1.8	2.1	3.0
Northampton	7,378	5,211	2,076	91	3,135	D	70.6	28.1	1.2	1	100	92	0.3	0.4	0.2	0.1
Onslow	23,861	8,873	13,878	1,110	5,005	R	37.2	58.2	4.7	87	14	10	0.9	0.7	1.1	1.3
Orange	46,655	30,320	14,805	1,530	15,515	D	65.0	31.7	3.3	9	95	37	1.8	2.5	1.1	1.8
Pamlico	4,860	2,414	2,262	184	152	D	49.7	46.5	3.8	39	64	22	0.2	0.2	0.2	0.2
Pasquotank	9,305	5,387	3,832	86	1,555	D	57.9	41.2	0.9	20	81	97	0.4	0.5	0.3	0.1

County	Total	Sanford (DEM)	Faircloth (REP)	Other	Plurality Total	Party	Percent of total vote DEM	REP	Other	Rank DEM	REP	Other	Percent contribution to state vote Total	DEM	REP	Other
Pender	12,474	5,729	6,177	568	448	R	45.9	49.5	4.6	55	51	11	0.5	0.5	0.5	0.7
Perquimans	3,675	1,947	1,666	62	281	D	53.0	45.3	1.7	30	70	77	0.1	0.2	0.1	<.1
Person	9,698	4,417	4,926	355	509	R	45.5	50.8	3.7	57	47	26	0.4	0.4	0.4	0.4
Pitt	38,810	19,299	18,827	684	472	D	49.7	48.5	1.8	38	57	75	1.5	1.6	1.5	0.8
Polk	7,067	3,100	3,835	132	735	R	43.9	54.3	1.9	66	31	73	0.3	0.3	0.3	0.2
Randolph	38,213	12,454	24,467	1,292	12,013	R	32.6	64.0	3.4	95	5	34	1.5	1.0	1.9	1.5
Richmond	15,195	9,177	5,310	708	3,867	D	60.4	34.9	4.7	16	89	9	0.6	0.8	0.4	0.8
Robeson	31,070	21,308	9,098	664	12,210	D	68.6	29.3	2.1	3	98	66	1.2	1.8	0.7	0.8
Rockingham	30,838	14,800	14,885	1,153	85	R	48.0	48.3	3.7	48	60	23	1.2	1.2	1.1	1.3
Rowan	42,431	15,847	24,344	2,240	8,497	R	37.3	57.4	5.3	86	17	3	1.6	1.3	1.9	2.6
Rutherford	20,168	8,628	10,830	710	2,202	R	42.8	53.7	3.5	69	35	29	0.8	0.7	0.8	0.8
Sampson	18,925	8,740	9,945	240	1,205	R	46.2	52.5	1.3	53	41	88	0.7	0.7	0.8	0.3
Scotland	8,753	5,690	2,924	139	2,766	D	65.0	33.4	1.6	8	91	79	0.3	0.5	0.2	0.2
Stanly	21,614	8,529	12,297	788	3,768	R	39.5	56.9	3.6	81	21	27	0.8	0.7	0.9	0.9
Stokes	16,596	6,983	9,133	480	2,150	R	42.1	55.0	2.9	71	29	44	0.6	0.6	0.7	0.6
Surry	23,396	10,387	12,566	443	2,179	R	44.4	53.7	1.9	62	34	71	0.9	0.9	1.0	0.5
Swain	4,275	2,237	1,984	54	253	D	52.3	46.4	1.3	32	65	89	0.2	0.2	0.2	<.1
Transylvania	12,848	5,483	6,940	425	1,457	R	42.7	54.0	3.3	70	32	35	0.5	0.5	0.5	0.5
Tyrrell	1,541	911	605	25	306	D	59.1	39.3	1.6	17	82	78	<.1	<.1	<.1	<.1
Union	31,086	11,716	18,165	1,205	6,449	R	37.7	58.4	3.9	85	12	19	1.2	1.0	1.4	1.4
Vance	12,941	7,281	5,407	253	1,874	D	56.3	41.8	2.0	22	80	70	0.5	0.6	0.4	0.3
Wake	206,897	99,315	100,311	7,271	996	R	48.0	48.5	3.5	47	58	30	8.0	8.3	7.7	8.5
Warren	7,038	4,762	2,152	124	2,610	D	67.7	30.6	1.8	4	97	76	0.3	0.4	0.2	0.1
Washington	5,101	2,908	2,138	55	770	D	57.0	41.9	1.1	21	79	94	0.2	0.2	0.2	<.1
Watauga	18,743	8,577	9,372	794	795	R	45.8	50.0	4.2	56	49	13	0.7	0.7	0.7	0.9
Wayne	26,452	11,082	14,899	471	3,817	R	41.9	56.3	1.8	73	23	74	1.0	0.9	1.1	0.5
Wilkes	25,026	8,717	15,515	794	6,798	R	34.8	62.0	3.2	93	8	41	1.0	0.7	1.2	0.9
Wilson	22,048	10,941	10,797	310	144	D	49.6	49.0	1.4	40	54	87	0.9	0.9	0.8	0.4
Yadkin	12,635	3,871	8,431	333	4,560	R	30.6	66.7	2.6	98	3	50	0.5	0.3	0.6	0.4
Yancey	9,028	4,452	4,497	79	45	R	49.3	49.8	0.9	43	50	98	0.4	0.4	0.3	<.1
NORTH CAROLINA	**2,577,891**	**1,194,015**	**1,297,892**	**85,984**	**103,877**	**R**	**46.3**	**50.3**	**3.3**				**100.0**	**100.0**	**100.0**	**100.0**

Table G. — Vote for Governor: November 3, 1992, General Election

County	Total	Hunt (DEM)	Gardner (REP)	McLaughlin (LIB)[1]	Plurality Total	Plurality Party	Percent of total vote DEM	Percent of total vote REP	Percent of total vote LIB	Rank DEM	Rank REP	Rank LIB	Percent contribution to state vote Total	Percent contribution to state vote DEM	Percent contribution to state vote REP	Percent contribution to state vote LIB
Alamance	43,140	20,599	20,711	1,830	112	R	47.7	48.0	4.2	76	33	26	1.7	1.5	1.8	1.7
Alexander	13,843	6,144	7,262	437	1,118	R	44.4	52.5	3.2	86	11	45	0.5	0.4	0.6	0.4
Alleghany	4,559	2,404	2,019	136	385	D	52.7	44.3	3.0	52	45	50	0.2	0.2	0.2	0.1
Anson	8,304	5,850	2,316	138	3,534	D	70.4	27.9	1.7	5	96	81	0.3	0.4	0.2	0.1
Ashe	10,975	5,376	5,363	236	13	D	49.0	48.9	2.2	68	29	69	0.4	0.4	0.5	0.2
Avery	6,597	2,322	4,054	221	1,732	R	35.2	61.5	3.4	99	2	40	0.3	0.2	0.4	0.2
Beaufort	15,955	8,093	7,379	483	714	D	50.7	46.2	3.0	59	40	48	0.6	0.6	0.7	0.5
Bertie	6,304	4,251	1,966	87	2,285	D	67.4	31.2	1.4	10	89	87	0.2	0.3	0.2	0.1
Bladen	9,860	6,424	3,275	161	3,149	D	65.2	33.2	1.6	14	86	82	0.4	0.5	0.3	0.2
Brunswick	22,207	11,520	9,442	1,245	2,078	D	51.9	42.5	5.6	56	53	7	0.9	0.8	0.8	1.2
Buncombe	74,243	38,748	33,659	1,836	5,089	D	52.2	45.3	2.5	55	43	61	2.9	2.8	3.0	1.7
Burke	30,632	15,356	14,104	1,172	1,252	D	50.1	46.0	3.8	62	42	35	1.2	1.1	1.3	1.1
Cabarrus	41,534	18,841	20,305	2,388	1,464	R	45.4	48.9	5.7	83	28	3	1.6	1.4	1.8	2.3
Caldwell	26,185	11,593	13,333	1,259	1,740	R	44.3	50.9	4.8	87	16	15	1.0	0.8	1.2	1.2
Camden	2,627	1,483	1,077	67	406	D	56.5	41.0	2.6	38	61	58	0.1	0.1	<.1	<.1
Carteret	21,986	10,806	10,187	993	619	D	49.1	46.3	4.5	65	39	21	0.8	0.8	0.9	0.9
Caswell	8,014	5,311	2,579	124	2,732	D	66.3	32.2	1.5	12	88	85	0.3	0.4	0.2	0.1
Catawba	49,338	20,760	26,121	2,457	5,361	R	42.1	52.9	5.0	92	10	12	1.9	1.5	2.3	2.3
Chatham	18,412	10,912	6,690	810	4,222	D	59.3	36.3	4.4	29	75	23	0.7	0.8	0.6	0.8
Cherokee	8,783	4,306	4,412	65	106	R	49.0	50.2	0.7	67	19	100	0.3	0.3	0.4	<.1
Chowan	4,610	2,851	1,666	93	1,185	D	61.8	36.1	2.0	23	76	75	0.2	0.2	0.1	<.1
Clay	3,918	1,871	2,004	43	133	R	47.8	51.1	1.1	75	14	95	0.2	0.1	0.2	<.1
Cleveland	30,396	16,333	12,824	1,239	3,509	D	53.7	42.2	4.1	48	54	28	1.2	1.2	1.1	1.2
Columbus	19,377	13,240	5,654	483	7,586	D	68.3	29.2	2.5	9	91	59	0.7	1.0	0.5	0.5
Craven	25,114	11,955	12,550	609	595	R	47.6	50.0	2.4	78	22	62	1.0	0.9	1.1	0.6
Cumberland	66,683	38,327	25,645	2,711	12,682	D	57.5	38.5	4.1	33	69	29	2.6	2.8	2.3	2.6
Currituck	5,237	2,805	2,287	145	518	D	53.6	43.7	2.8	49	49	55	0.2	0.2	0.2	0.1
Dare	10,681	5,927	4,434	320	1,493	D	55.5	41.5	3.0	44	59	49	0.4	0.4	0.4	0.3
Davidson	49,658	20,964	25,901	2,793	4,937	R	42.2	52.2	5.6	91	12	6	1.9	1.5	2.3	2.7
Davie	12,309	4,630	7,188	491	2,558	R	37.6	58.4	4.0	97	4	31	0.5	0.3	0.6	0.5
Duplin	14,138	8,146	5,698	294	2,448	D	57.6	40.3	2.1	31	64	73	0.5	0.6	0.5	0.3
Durham	83,127	54,278	25,817	3,032	28,461	D	65.3	31.1	3.6	13	90	36	3.2	4.0	2.3	2.9
Edgecombe	19,550	12,519	6,571	460	5,948	D	64.0	33.6	2.4	18	83	64	0.8	0.9	0.6	0.4
Forsyth	115,823	58,904	51,448	5,471	7,456	D	50.9	44.4	4.7	58	44	18	4.5	4.3	4.6	5.2
Franklin	13,481	7,662	5,232	587	2,430	D	56.8	38.8	4.4	36	68	24	0.5	0.6	0.5	0.6
Gaston	61,532	25,382	32,627	3,523	7,245	R	41.3	53.0	5.7	93	9	4	2.4	1.9	2.9	3.4
Gates	3,698	2,762	907	29	1,855	D	74.7	24.5	0.8	1	100	99	0.1	0.2	<.1	<.1
Graham	3,812	1,866	1,911	35	45	R	49.0	50.1	0.9	69	21	97	0.1	0.1	0.2	<.1
Granville	12,609	7,527	4,524	558	3,003	D	59.7	35.9	4.4	27	78	22	0.5	0.6	0.4	0.5
Greene	5,632	3,347	2,209	76	1,138	D	59.4	39.2	1.3	28	67	91	0.2	0.2	0.2	<.1
Guilford	147,043	83,458	55,422	8,163	28,036	D	56.8	37.7	5.6	37	73	8	5.7	6.1	4.9	7.8
Halifax	17,710	11,070	6,128	512	4,942	D	62.5	34.6	2.9	22	81	52	0.7	0.8	0.5	0.5
Harnett	20,670	10,399	9,549	722	850	D	50.3	46.2	3.5	60	41	39	0.8	0.8	0.9	0.7
Haywood	21,258	11,831	8,764	663	3,067	D	55.7	41.2	3.1	43	60	46	0.8	0.9	0.8	0.6
Henderson	32,784	13,414	18,617	753	5,203	R	40.9	56.8	2.3	95	5	65	1.3	1.0	1.7	0.7
Hertford	7,464	5,302	2,096	66	3,206	D	71.0	28.1	0.9	4	95	98	0.3	0.4	0.2	<.1
Hoke	6,173	4,296	1,737	140	2,559	D	69.6	28.1	2.3	7	94	66	0.2	0.3	0.2	0.1
Hyde	2,228	1,433	746	49	687	D	64.3	33.5	2.2	17	85	67	<.1	0.1	<.1	<.1
Iredell	38,746	16,667	20,035	2,044	3,368	R	43.0	51.7	5.3	90	13	9	1.5	1.2	1.8	1.9
Jackson	11,633	6,687	4,722	224	1,965	D	57.5	40.6	1.9	32	62	77	0.4	0.5	0.4	0.2
Johnston	31,283	14,782	15,171	1,330	389	R	47.3	48.5	4.3	79	32	25	1.2	1.1	1.4	1.3
Jones	3,823	2,263	1,468	92	795	D	59.2	38.4	2.4	30	70	63	0.1	0.2	0.1	<.1
Lee	14,528	7,736	6,216	576	1,520	D	53.2	42.8	4.0	51	51	33	0.6	0.6	0.6	0.5
Lenoir	19,388	10,931	8,129	328	2,802	D	56.4	41.9	1.7	39	56	80	0.7	0.8	0.7	0.3
Lincoln	22,187	9,929	11,160	1,098	1,231	R	44.8	50.3	4.9	85	18	13	0.9	0.7	1.0	1.0
McDowell	13,402	6,654	6,320	428	334	D	49.6	47.2	3.2	63	36	44	0.5	0.5	0.6	0.4
Macon	11,282	5,490	5,577	215	87	R	48.7	49.4	1.9	71	23	78	0.4	0.4	0.5	0.2
Madison	7,457	4,170	3,185	102	985	D	55.9	42.7	1.4	41	52	90	0.3	0.3	0.3	<.1
Martin	8,073	4,916	3,058	99	1,858	D	60.9	37.9	1.2	26	72	92	0.3	0.4	0.3	<.1
Mecklenburg	215,036	114,568	89,277	11,191	25,291	D	53.3	41.5	5.2	50	58	10	8.3	8.4	8.0	10.7
Mitchell	6,904	2,196	4,536	172	2,340	R	31.8	65.7	2.5	100	1	60	0.3	0.2	0.4	0.2
Montgomery	8,964	5,137	3,576	251	1,561	D	57.3	39.9	2.8	34	66	54	0.3	0.4	0.3	0.2
Moore	26,376	12,415	13,235	726	820	R	47.1	50.2	2.8	80	20	56	1.0	0.9	1.2	0.7
Nash	29,635	12,848	15,839	948	2,991	R	43.4	53.4	3.2	89	8	43	1.1	0.9	1.4	0.9
New Hanover	51,517	25,394	22,344	3,779	3,050	D	49.3	43.4	7.3	64	50	1	2.0	1.9	2.0	3.6
Northampton	7,758	5,585	2,066	107	3,519	D	72.0	26.6	1.4	2	98	88	0.3	0.4	0.2	0.1
Onslow	24,102	11,069	11,862	1,171	793	R	45.9	49.2	4.9	81	26	14	0.9	0.8	1.1	1.1
Orange	46,318	31,999	12,476	1,843	19,523	D	69.1	26.9	4.0	8	97	32	1.8	2.3	1.1	1.8
Pamlico	4,900	2,753	1,958	189	795	D	56.2	40.0	3.9	40	65	34	0.2	0.2	0.2	0.2
Pasquotank	9,581	6,058	3,416	107	2,642	D	63.2	35.7	1.1	20	80	94	0.4	0.4	0.3	0.1

[1]Libertarian candidate McLaughlin was the only minor candidate (only three candidates on ballot).

686 North Carolina

Table G. — Vote for Governor: November 3, 1992, General Election (cont)

County	Total	Hunt (DEM)	Gardner (REP)	McLaughlin (LIB)[1]	Plurality Total	Party	Percent of total vote DEM	REP	LIB	Rank DEM	Rank REP	Rank LIB	Percent contribution to state vote Total	DEM	REP	LIB
Pender	12,546	6,578	5,237	731	1,341	D	52.4	41.7	5.8	54	57	2	0.5	0.5	0.5	0.7
Perquimans	3,786	2,372	1,359	55	1,013	D	62.7	35.9	1.5	21	77	86	0.1	0.2	0.1	<.1
Person	9,992	4,870	4,703	419	167	D	48.7	47.1	4.2	70	37	27	0.4	0.4	0.4	0.4
Pitt	39,422	22,021	16,572	829	5,449	D	55.9	42.0	2.1	42	55	71	1.5	1.6	1.5	0.8
Polk	7,239	3,555	3,537	147	18	D	49.1	48.9	2.0	66	30	74	0.3	0.3	0.3	0.1
Randolph	39,101	15,552	21,678	1,871	6,126	R	39.8	55.4	4.8	96	7	16	1.5	1.1	1.9	1.8
Richmond	15,017	10,119	4,368	530	5,751	D	67.4	29.1	3.5	11	92	38	0.6	0.7	0.4	0.5
Robeson	31,295	22,431	8,194	670	14,237	D	71.7	26.2	2.1	3	99	70	1.2	1.6	0.7	0.6
Rockingham	31,156	17,043	12,561	1,552	4,482	D	54.7	40.3	5.0	46	63	11	1.2	1.2	1.1	1.5
Rowan	42,625	18,618	21,584	2,423	2,966	R	43.7	50.6	5.7	88	17	5	1.6	1.4	1.9	2.3
Rutherford	20,390	9,882	9,693	815	189	D	48.5	47.5	4.0	73	35	30	0.8	0.7	0.9	0.8
Sampson	18,900	10,216	8,333	351	1,883	D	54.1	44.1	1.9	47	47	79	0.7	0.7	0.7	0.3
Scotland	8,844	6,174	2,531	139	3,643	D	69.8	28.6	1.6	6	93	83	0.3	0.5	0.2	0.1
Stanly	21,703	9,838	11,075	790	1,237	R	45.3	51.0	3.6	84	15	37	0.8	0.7	1.0	0.8
Stokes	16,775	7,997	8,217	561	220	R	47.7	49.0	3.3	77	27	41	0.6	0.6	0.7	0.5
Surry	23,834	11,967	11,352	515	615	D	50.2	47.6	2.2	61	34	68	0.9	0.9	1.0	0.5
Swain	4,341	2,392	1,897	52	495	D	55.1	43.7	1.2	45	48	93	0.2	0.2	0.2	<.1
Transylvania	12,885	6,195	6,269	421	74	R	48.1	48.7	3.3	74	31	42	0.5	0.5	0.6	0.4
Tyrrell	1,607	1,036	540	31	496	D	64.5	33.6	1.9	16	84	76	<.1	<.1	<.1	<.1
Union	31,299	14,354	15,462	1,483	1,108	R	45.9	49.4	4.7	82	24	17	1.2	1.0	1.4	1.4
Vance	12,978	8,009	4,636	333	3,373	D	61.7	35.7	2.6	24	79	57	0.5	0.6	0.4	0.3
Wake	207,893	118,345	79,808	9,740	38,537	D	56.9	38.4	4.7	35	71	19	8.0	8.6	7.1	9.3
Warren	7,150	4,638	2,308	204	2,330	D	64.9	32.3	2.9	15	87	53	0.3	0.3	0.2	0.2
Washington	5,277	3,371	1,824	82	1,547	D	63.9	34.6	1.6	19	82	84	0.2	0.2	0.2	<.1
Watauga	18,949	9,702	8,361	886	1,341	D	51.2	44.1	4.7	57	46	20	0.7	0.7	0.7	0.8
Wayne	26,936	13,104	13,267	565	163	R	48.6	49.3	2.1	72	25	72	1.0	1.0	1.2	0.5
Wilkes	25,232	10,369	14,077	786	3,708	R	41.1	55.8	3.1	94	6	47	1.0	0.8	1.3	0.7
Wilson	23,030	14,205	8,508	317	5,697	D	61.7	36.9	1.4	25	74	89	0.9	1.0	0.8	0.3
Yadkin	12,780	4,659	7,749	372	3,090	R	36.5	60.6	2.9	98	3	51	0.5	0.3	0.7	0.4
Yancey	9,096	4,789	4,219	88	570	D	52.6	46.4	1.0	53	38	96	0.4	0.4	0.4	<.1
NORTH CAROLINA	**2,595,184**	**1,368,246**	**1,121,955**	**104,983**	**246,291**	**D**	**52.7**	**43.2**	**4.0**				**100.0**	**100.0**	**100.0**	**100.0**

[1]Libertarian candidate McLaughlin was the only minor candidate (only three candidates on ballot).

Table H. — Vote for U.S. Representative in Congress: November 3, 1992, General Election

Congressional district and county	Total	Democrat (DEM)	Republican (REP)	Other	Plurality Total	Plurality Party	Percent of total vote DEM	REP	Other	Rank within district DEM	REP	Other	Percent contribution to district vote Total	DEM	REP	Other
District 1	173,262	116,078	54,457	2,727	61,621	D	67.0	31.4	1.6				100.0	100.0	100.0	100.0
Beaufort (pt)	7,774	3,938	3,683	153	255	D	50.7	47.4	2.0	26	3	8	4.5	3.4	6.8	5.6
Bertie	6,307	4,081	2,141	85	1,940	D	64.7	33.9	1.3	17	12	18	3.6	3.5	3.9	3.1
Bladen (pt)	5,223	3,944	1,211	68	2,733	D	75.5	23.2	1.3	5	23	21	3.0	3.4	2.2	2.5
Chowan	4,039	2,326	1,624	89	702	D	57.6	40.2	2.2	21	8	5	2.3	2.0	3.0	3.3
Columbus (pt)	5,413	4,047	1,234	132	2,813	D	74.8	22.8	2.4	6	25	4	3.1	3.5	2.3	4.8
Craven (pt)	7,996	4,983	2,854	159	2,129	D	62.3	35.7	2.0	18	11	7	4.6	4.3	5.2	5.8
Cumberland (pt)	9,333	7,492	1,701	140	5,791	D	80.3	18.2	1.5	3	26	15	5.4	6.5	3.1	5.1
Duplin (pt)	4,716	3,057	1,560	99	1,497	D	64.8	33.1	2.1	16	13	6	2.7	2.6	2.9	3.6
Edgecombe (pt)	9,404	7,782	1,516	106	6,266	D	82.8	16.1	1.1	1	27	24	5.4	6.7	2.8	3.9
Gates	3,549	2,364	1,138	47	1,226	D	66.6	32.1	1.3	14	15	19	2.0	2.0	2.1	1.7
Greene	5,334	2,486	2,773	75	287	R	46.6	52.0	1.4	27	2	16	3.1	2.1	5.1	2.8
Halifax (pt)	9,391	6,671	2,573	147	4,098	D	71.0	27.4	1.6	10	19	14	5.4	5.7	4.7	5.4
Hertford	7,370	4,898	2,403	69	2,495	D	66.5	32.6	0.9	15	14	26	4.3	4.2	4.4	2.5
Jones (pt)	1,881	1,118	702	61	416	D	59.4	37.3	3.2	20	9	2	1.1	1.0	1.3	2.2
Lenoir (pt)	7,600	5,627	1,899	74	3,728	D	74.0	25.0	1.0	7	21	25	4.4	4.8	3.5	2.7
Martin (pt)	4,757	2,716	1,978	63	738	D	57.1	41.6	1.3	23	6	20	2.7	2.3	3.6	2.3
Nash (pt)	4,524	2,751	1,688	85	1,063	D	60.8	37.3	1.9	19	10	9	2.6	2.4	3.1	3.1
New Hanover (pt)	6,470	5,347	916	207	4,431	D	82.6	14.2	3.2	2	28	3	3.7	4.6	1.7	7.6
Northampton	7,341	5,140	2,110	91	3,030	D	70.0	28.7	1.2	12	17	22	4.2	4.4	3.9	3.3
Pasquotank (pt)	4,352	3,061	1,262	29	1,799	D	70.3	29.0	0.7	11	16	28	2.5	2.6	2.3	1.1
Pender (pt)	2,317	1,693	539	85	1,154	D	73.1	23.3	3.7	8	22	1	1.3	1.5	1.0	3.1
Perquimans	3,573	1,968	1,544	61	424	D	55.1	43.2	1.7	25	4	12	2.1	1.7	2.8	2.2
Pitt (pt)	18,863	10,742	7,890	231	2,852	D	56.9	41.8	1.2	24	5	23	10.9	9.3	14.5	8.5
Vance (pt)	6,249	4,449	1,691	109	2,758	D	71.2	27.1	1.7	9	20	11	3.6	3.8	3.1	4.0
Warren	7,029	4,893	2,009	127	2,884	D	69.6	28.6	1.8	13	18	10	4.1	4.2	3.7	4.7
Washington	5,052	2,895	2,088	69	807	D	57.3	41.3	1.4	22	7	17	2.9	2.5	3.8	2.5
Wayne (pt)	62	24	37	1	13	R	38.7	59.7	1.6	28	1	13	0.0	0.0	0.1	0.0
Wilson (pt)	7,343	5,585	1,693	65	3,892	D	76.1	23.1	0.9	4	24	27	4.2	4.8	3.1	2.4
District 2	211,569	113,693	93,893	3,983	19,800	D	53.7	44.4	1.9				100.0	100.0	100.0	100.0
Durham (pt)	41,123	25,068	14,972	1,083	10,096	D	61.0	36.4	2.6	5	9	1	19.4	22.0	15.9	27.2
Edgecombe (pt)	9,794	5,632	4,006	156	1,626	D	57.5	40.9	1.6	6	8	11	4.6	5.0	4.3	3.9
Franklin	13,228	8,288	4,723	217	3,565	D	62.7	35.7	1.6	4	10	8	6.3	7.3	5.0	5.4
Granville (pt)	9,747	6,732	2,834	181	3,898	D	69.1	29.1	1.9	1	13	4	4.6	5.9	3.0	4.5
Halifax (pt)	7,876	5,111	2,617	148	2,494	D	64.9	33.2	1.9	2	12	3	3.7	4.5	2.8	3.7
Harnett	20,303	9,945	9,983	375	38	R	49.0	49.2	1.8	8	6	5	9.6	8.7	10.6	9.4
Johnston	30,484	14,490	15,455	539	965	R	47.5	50.7	1.8	10	4	7	14.4	12.7	16.5	13.5
Lee	14,032	7,392	6,341	299	1,051	D	52.7	45.2	2.1	7	7	2	6.6	6.5	6.8	7.5
Moore (pt)	19,382	8,256	10,775	351	2,519	R	42.6	55.6	1.8	12	2	6	9.2	7.3	11.5	8.8
Nash (pt)	24,811	12,063	12,341	407	278	R	48.6	49.7	1.6	9	5	9	11.7	10.6	13.1	10.2
Vance (pt)	6,537	4,131	2,301	105	1,830	D	63.2	35.2	1.6	3	11	10	3.1	3.6	2.5	2.6
Wake (pt)	253	95	155	3	60	R	37.5	61.3	1.2	13	1	12	0.1	0.1	0.2	0.1
Wilson (pt)	13,999	6,490	7,390	119	900	R	46.4	52.8	0.9	11	3	13	6.6	5.7	7.9	3.0
District 3	187,050	101,739	80,759	4,552	20,980	D	54.4	43.2	2.4				100.0	100.0	100.0	100.0
Beaufort (pt)	8,042	4,125	3,704	213	421	D	51.3	46.1	2.6	15	6	7	4.3	4.1	4.6	4.7
Camden	2,547	1,446	1,041	60	405	D	56.8	40.9	2.4	10	12	9	1.4	1.4	1.3	1.3
Carteret	21,662	11,600	9,161	901	2,439	D	53.6	42.3	4.2	13	9	1	11.6	11.4	11.3	19.8
Craven (pt)	16,011	7,816	7,834	361	18	R	48.8	48.9	2.3	18	2	11	8.6	7.7	9.7	7.9
Currituck	5,047	2,532	2,344	171	188	D	50.2	46.4	3.4	17	5	5	2.7	2.5	2.9	3.8
Dare	10,445	5,611	4,510	324	1,101	D	53.7	43.2	3.1	12	7	6	5.6	5.5	5.6	7.1
Duplin (pt)	9,114	5,483	3,450	181	2,033	D	60.2	37.9	2.0	6	13	12	4.9	5.4	4.3	4.0
Hyde	2,161	1,521	598	42	923	D	70.4	27.7	1.9	1	19	13	1.2	1.5	0.7	0.9
Jones (pt)	1,883	1,164	675	44	489	D	61.8	35.8	2.3	3	16	10	1.0	1.1	0.8	1.0
Lenoir (pt)	10,979	5,564	5,233	182	331	D	50.7	47.7	1.7	16	3	15	5.9	5.5	6.5	4.0
Martin (pt)	2,482	1,534	908	40	626	D	61.8	36.6	1.6	4	15	16	1.3	1.5	1.1	0.9
Onslow (pt)	14,798	6,744	7,541	513	797	R	45.6	51.0	3.5	19	1	3	7.9	6.6	9.3	11.3
Pamlico	4,852	2,978	1,673	201	1,305	D	61.4	34.5	4.1	5	17	2	2.6	2.9	2.1	4.4
Pasquotank (pt)	4,785	2,493	2,235	57	258	D	52.1	46.7	1.2	14	4	18	2.6	2.5	2.8	1.3
Pender (pt)	6,712	4,012	2,469	231	1,543	D	59.8	36.8	3.4	7	14	4	3.6	3.9	3.1	5.1
Pitt (pt)	19,374	10,578	8,315	481	2,263	D	54.6	42.9	2.5	11	8	8	10.4	10.4	10.3	10.6
Sampson	18,599	10,616	7,752	231	2,864	D	57.1	41.7	1.2	9	11	17	9.9	10.4	9.6	5.1
Tyrrell	1,522	1,043	452	27	591	D	68.5	29.7	1.8	2	18	14	0.8	1.0	0.6	0.6
Wayne (pt)	26,035	14,879	10,864	292	4,015	D	57.2	41.7	1.1	8	10	19	13.9	14.6	13.5	6.4
District 4	265,060	171,299	89,345	4,416	81,954	D	64.6	33.7	1.7				100.0	100.0	100.0	100.0
Chatham	17,969	12,220	5,430	319	6,790	D	68.0	30.2	1.8	2	2	2	6.8	7.1	6.1	7.2
Orange (pt)	44,395	33,147	10,186	1,062	22,961	D	74.7	22.9	2.4	1	3	1	16.7	19.4	11.4	24.0
Wake (pt)	202,696	125,932	73,729	3,035	52,203	D	62.1	36.4	1.5	3	1	3	76.5	73.5	82.5	68.7
District 5	223,683	117,835	102,086	3,762	15,749	D	52.7	45.6	1.7				100.0	100.0	100.0	100.0
Alleghany	4,650	2,591	1,995	64	596	D	55.7	42.9	1.4	6	9	9	2.1	2.2	2.0	1.7
Ashe	10,960	5,608	5,229	123	379	D	51.2	47.7	1.1	9	5	13	4.9	4.8	5.1	3.3
Burke (pt)	18,105	9,955	7,813	337	2,142	D	55.0	43.2	1.9	7	8	5	8.1	8.4	7.7	9.0
Caldwell (pt)	7,100	3,811	3,127	162	684	D	53.7	44.0	2.3	8	7	3	3.2	3.2	3.1	4.3

Congressional district and county	Total	Democrat (DEM)	Republican (REP)	Other	Plurality		Percent of total vote			Rank within district			Percent contribution to district vote			
					Total	Party	DEM	REP	Other	DEM	REP	Other	Total	DEM	REP	Other
District 5 (cont)																
Caswell	7,807	5,164	2,553	90	2,611	D	66.1	32.7	1.2	2	13	12	3.5	4.4	2.5	2.4
Forsyth (pt)	67,113	33,160	32,738	1,215	422	D	49.4	48.8	1.8	14	1	6	30.0	28.1	32.1	32.3
Granville (pt)	2,379	1,727	618	34	1,109	D	72.6	26.0	1.4	1	14	8	1.1	1.5	0.6	0.9
Guilford (pt)	1,483	836	616	31	220	D	56.4	41.5	2.1	4	12	4	0.7	0.7	0.6	0.8
Person	7,797	4,355	3,258	184	1,097	D	55.9	41.8	2.4	5	10	2	3.5	3.7	3.2	4.9
Rockingham	31,042	17,616	12,914	512	4,702	D	56.7	41.6	1.6	3	11	7	13.9	14.9	12.7	13.6
Stokes	16,770	8,463	8,088	219	375	D	50.5	48.2	1.3	12	4	11	7.5	7.2	7.9	5.8
Surry	23,581	11,928	11,407	246	521	D	50.6	48.4	1.0	11	3	14	10.5	10.1	11.2	6.5
Watauga	18,501	9,429	8,615	457	814	D	51.0	46.6	2.5	10	6	1	8.3	8.0	8.4	12.1
Wilkes (pt)	6,395	3,192	3,115	88	77	D	49.9	48.7	1.4	13	2	10	2.9	2.7	3.1	2.3
District 6	230,022	67,200	162,822	-	95,622	R	29.2	70.8	-				100.0	100.0	100.0	-
Alamance (pt)	33,624	10,357	23,267	-	12,910	R	30.8	69.2	-	4	3	-	14.6	15.4	14.3	-
Davidson (pt)	40,502	11,774	28,728	-	16,954	R	29.1	70.9	-	5	2	-	17.6	17.5	17.6	-
Davie (pt)	6,722	2,278	4,444	-	2,166	R	33.9	66.1	-	1	6	-	2.9	3.4	2.7	-
Guilford (pt)	97,648	26,409	71,239	-	44,830	R	27.0	73.0	-	6	1	-	42.5	39.3	43.8	-
Randolph	37,673	12,032	25,641	-	13,609	R	31.9	68.1	-	2	5	-	16.4	17.9	15.7	-
Rowan (pt)	13,853	4,350	9,503	-	5,153	R	31.4	68.6	-	3	4	-	6.0	6.5	5.8	-
District 7	163,101	92,414	66,536	4,151	25,878	D	56.7	40.8	2.5				100.0	100.0	100.0	100.0
Bladen (pt)	3,863	2,599	1,211	53	1,388	D	67.3	31.3	1.4	3	6	6	2.4	2.8	1.8	1.3
Brunswick	22,017	12,538	8,868	611	3,670	D	56.9	40.3	2.8	4	5	4	13.5	13.6	13.3	14.7
Columbus (pt)	13,675	10,257	3,235	183	7,022	D	75.0	23.7	1.3	2	7	7	8.4	11.1	4.9	4.4
Cumberland (pt)	42,972	22,031	19,914	1,027	2,117	D	51.3	46.3	2.4	5	4	5	26.3	23.8	29.9	24.7
New Hanover (pt)	44,233	20,856	21,862	1,515	1,006	R	47.2	49.4	3.4	6	3	3	27.1	22.6	32.9	36.5
Onslow (pt)	8,822	3,824	4,681	317	857	R	43.3	53.1	3.6	7	2	2	5.4	4.1	7.0	7.6
Pender (pt)	3,267	1,377	1,764	126	387	R	42.1	54.0	3.9	8	1	1	2.0	1.5	2.7	3.0
Robeson (pt)	24,252	18,932	5,001	319	13,931	D	78.1	20.6	1.3	1	8	8	14.9	20.5	7.5	7.7
District 8	190,951	113,162	71,842	5,947	41,320	D	59.3	37.6	3.1				100.0	100.0	100.0	100.0
Anson	8,095	6,208	1,796	91	4,412	D	76.7	22.2	1.1	2	13	14	4.2	5.5	2.5	1.5
Cabarrus	41,568	24,272	15,663	1,633	8,609	D	58.4	37.7	3.9	7	8	3	21.8	21.4	21.8	27.5
Cumberland (pt)	13,240	8,488	4,366	386	4,122	D	64.1	33.0	2.9	6	9	7	6.9	7.5	6.1	6.5
Hoke	5,950	4,400	1,427	123	2,973	D	73.9	24.0	2.1	3	12	10	3.1	3.9	2.0	2.1
Iredell (pt)	4,097	2,248	1,683	166	565	D	54.9	41.1	4.1	10	4	2	2.1	2.0	2.3	2.8
Mecklenburg (pt)	1,657	924	670	63	254	D	55.8	40.4	3.8	9	6	4	0.9	0.8	0.9	1.1
Montgomery	8,855	5,117	3,493	245	1,624	D	57.8	39.4	2.8	8	7	8	4.6	4.5	4.9	4.1
Moore (pt)	5,633	2,646	2,905	82	259	R	47.0	51.6	1.5	14	1	13	3.0	2.3	4.0	1.4
Richmond	15,051	10,820	3,735	496	7,085	D	71.9	24.8	3.3	5	11	5	7.9	9.6	5.2	8.3
Robeson (pt)	6,700	5,244	1,334	122	3,910	D	78.3	19.9	1.8	1	14	11	3.5	4.6	1.9	2.1
Rowan (pt)	19,446	10,614	7,926	906	2,688	D	54.6	40.8	4.7	11	5	1	10.2	9.4	11.0	15.2
Scotland	8,006	5,829	2,044	133	3,785	D	72.8	25.5	1.7	4	10	12	4.2	5.2	2.8	2.2
Stanly	21,710	11,046	10,077	587	969	D	50.9	46.4	2.7	12	3	9	11.4	9.8	14.0	9.9
Union	30,943	15,306	14,723	914	583	D	49.5	47.6	3.0	13	2	6	16.2	13.5	20.5	15.4
District 9	228,245	74,583	153,650	12	79,067	R	32.7	67.3	<.1				100.0	100.0	100.0	100.0
Cleveland (pt)	14,085	5,993	8,090	2	2,097	R	42.5	57.4	<.1	1	3	1	6.2	8.0	5.3	16.7
Gaston (pt)	57,168	19,365	37,803	0	18,438	R	33.9	66.1	0.0	2	2	3	25.0	26.0	24.6	0.0
Mecklenburg (pt)	156,992	49,225	107,757	10	58,532	R	31.4	68.6	<.1	3	1	2	68.8	66.0	70.1	83.3
District 10	235,091	79,206	148,999	6,886	69,793	R	33.7	63.4	2.9				100.0	100.0	100.0	100.0
Alexander	13,705	5,531	7,862	312	2,331	R	40.4	57.4	2.3	1	16	15	5.8	7.0	5.3	4.5
Avery	6,460	1,563	4,706	191	3,143	R	24.2	72.8	3.0	16	2	8	2.7	2.0	3.2	2.8
Buncombe (pt)	6,582	2,291	4,111	180	1,820	R	34.8	62.5	2.7	6	11	11	2.8	2.9	2.8	2.6
Burke (pt)	11,997	4,035	7,619	343	3,584	R	33.6	63.5	2.9	9	9	9	5.1	5.1	5.1	5.0
Caldwell (pt)	18,648	5,803	12,418	427	6,615	R	31.1	66.6	2.3	12	6	14	7.9	7.3	8.3	6.2
Catawba	48,866	15,814	31,468	1,584	15,654	R	32.4	64.4	3.2	11	8	6	20.8	20.0	21.1	23.0
Davie (pt)	5,083	1,410	3,498	175	2,088	R	27.7	68.8	3.4	14	4	4	2.2	1.8	2.3	2.5
Forsyth (pt)	29,264	9,555	18,924	785	9,369	R	32.7	64.7	2.7	10	7	12	12.4	12.1	12.7	11.4
Henderson (pt)	2,711	776	1,839	96	1,063	R	28.6	67.8	3.5	13	5	1	1.2	1.0	1.2	1.4
Iredell (pt)	26,903	9,611	16,396	896	6,785	R	35.7	60.9	3.3	5	14	5	11.4	12.1	11.0	13.0
Lincoln	21,521	8,242	12,517	762	4,275	R	38.3	58.2	3.5	3	15	2	9.2	10.4	8.4	11.1
McDowell (pt)	2,746	1,090	1,573	83	483	R	39.7	57.3	3.0	2	17	7	1.2	1.4	1.1	1.2
Mitchell	6,490	1,484	4,849	157	3,365	R	22.9	74.7	2.4	17	1	13	2.8	1.9	3.3	2.3
Polk (pt)	464	128	326	10	198	R	27.6	70.3	2.2	15	3	17	0.2	0.2	0.2	0.1
Rutherford (pt)	3,469	1,186	2,162	121	976	R	34.2	62.3	3.5	8	12	3	1.5	1.5	1.5	1.8
Wilkes (pt)	17,709	6,129	11,092	488	4,963	R	34.6	62.6	2.8	7	10	10	7.5	7.7	7.4	7.1
Yadkin	12,473	4,558	7,639	276	3,081	R	36.5	61.2	2.2	4	13	16	5.3	5.8	5.1	4.0
District 11	238,161	108,003	130,158	-	22,155	R	45.3	54.7	-				100.0	100.0	100.0	-
Buncombe (pt)	66,206	31,875	34,331	-	2,456	R	48.1	51.9	-	7	10	-	27.8	29.5	26.4	-
Cherokee	8,580	3,846	4,734	-	888	R	44.8	55.2	-	8	9	-	3.6	3.6	3.6	-
Clay	3,857	1,697	2,160	-	463	R	44.0	56.0	-	9	8	-	1.6	1.6	1.7	-
Cleveland (pt)	15,169	7,671	7,498	-	173	D	50.6	49.4	-	3	14	-	6.4	7.1	5.8	-
Graham	3,766	1,563	2,203	-	640	R	41.5	58.5	-	14	3	-	1.6	1.4	1.7	-
Haywood	21,135	10,182	10,953	-	771	R	48.2	51.8	-	6	11	-	8.9	9.4	8.4	-

North Carolina 689

Congressional district and county	Total	Democrat (DEM)	Republican (REP)	Other	Plurality Total	Plurality Party	Percent of total vote DEM	Percent of total vote REP	Percent of total vote Other	Rank within district DEM	Rank within district REP	Rank within district Other	Percent contribution to district vote Total	Percent contribution to district vote DEM	Percent contribution to district vote REP	Percent contribution to district vote Other
District 11 (cont)																
Henderson (pt)	29,481	10,582	18,899	-	8,317	R	35.9	64.1	-	16	1	-	12.4	9.8	14.5	-
Jackson	11,369	5,992	5,377	-	615	D	52.7	47.3	-	1	16	-	4.8	5.5	4.1	-
McDowell (pt)	10,795	4,575	6,220	-	1,645	R	42.4	57.6	-	12	5	-	4.5	4.2	4.8	-
Macon	11,275	4,928	6,347	-	1,419	R	43.7	56.3	-	11	6	-	4.7	4.6	4.9	-
Madison	7,326	3,722	3,604	-	118	D	50.8	49.2	-	2	15	-	3.1	3.4	2.8	-
Polk (pt)	6,368	2,682	3,686	-	1,004	R	42.1	57.9	-	13	4	-	2.7	2.5	2.8	-
Rutherford (pt)	16,517	6,567	9,950	-	3,383	R	39.8	60.2	-	15	2	-	6.9	6.1	7.6	-
Swain	4,326	2,089	2,237	-	148	R	48.3	51.7	-	5	12	-	1.8	1.9	1.7	-
Transylvania	12,923	5,649	7,274	-	1,625	R	43.7	56.3	-	10	7	-	5.4	5.2	5.6	-
Yancey	9,068	4,383	4,685	-	302	R	48.3	51.7	-	4	13	-	3.8	4.1	3.6	-
District 12	180,824	127,262	49,402	4,160	77,860	D	70.4	27.3	2.3				100.0	100.0	100.0	100.0
Alamance (pt)	7,483	4,511	2,750	222	1,761	D	60.3	36.8	3.0	6	5	4	4.1	3.5	5.6	5.3
Davidson (pt)	8,038	4,568	3,237	233	1,331	D	56.8	40.3	2.9	7	4	5	4.4	3.6	6.6	5.6
Durham (pt)	37,112	26,253	9,982	877	16,271	D	70.7	26.9	2.4	4	8	6	20.5	20.6	20.2	21.1
Forsyth (pt)	17,377	12,302	4,738	337	7,564	D	70.8	27.3	1.9	3	7	8	9.6	9.7	9.6	8.1
Gaston (pt)	2,839	2,196	597	46	1,599	D	77.4	21.0	1.6	2	9	10	1.6	1.7	1.2	1.1
Guilford (pt)	45,500	31,437	13,087	976	18,350	D	69.1	28.8	2.1	5	6	7	25.2	24.7	26.5	23.5
Iredell (pt)	6,994	3,738	3,012	244	726	D	53.4	43.1	3.5	9	2	2	3.9	2.9	6.1	5.9
Mecklenburg (pt)	46,158	37,270	8,018	870	29,252	D	80.7	17.4	1.9	1	10	9	25.5	29.3	16.2	20.9
Orange (pt)	1,145	496	613	36	117	R	43.3	53.5	3.1	10	1	3	0.6	0.4	1.2	0.9
Rowan (pt)	8,178	4,491	3,368	319	1,123	D	54.9	41.2	3.9	8	3	1	4.5	3.5	6.8	7.7
NORTH CAROLINA	2,527,019	1,282,474	1,203,949	40,596	78,525	D	50.8	47.6	1.6							

Table I. — Vote for Presidential Preference: May 5, 1992, Democratic Primary Election

County	Total	Clinton	No Pre-ference	Brown	Tsongas	Kerrey	Harkin			Clinton	No Pre-ference	Brown	Clinton	No Pre-ference	Brown	Total	Clinton	No Pre-ference	Brown
Alamance	11,639	6,522	2,081	1,508	1,281	137	110	-	-	56.0	17.9	13.0	95	27	4	1.7	1.5	2.0	2.1
Alexander	1,801	1,401	155	125	96	10	14	-	-	77.8	8.6	6.9	6	98	92	0.3	0.3	0.1	0.2
Alleghany	1,774	1,290	206	132	108	20	18	-	-	72.7	11.6	7.4	16	80	85	0.3	0.3	0.2	0.2
Anson	3,591	2,498	533	262	185	50	63	-	-	69.6	14.8	7.3	34	52	87	0.5	0.6	0.5	0.4
Ashe	2,297	1,713	302	137	115	16	14	-	-	74.6	13.1	6.0	12	66	97	0.3	0.4	0.3	0.2
Avery	531	381	59	58	29	3	1	-	-	71.8	11.1	10.9	21	86	22	<.1	<.1	<.1	<.1
Beaufort	7,309	4,085	1,707	861	536	57	63	-	-	55.9	23.4	11.8	96	5	11	1.1	0.9	1.6	1.2
Bertie	3,444	2,543	384	336	124	31	26	-	-	73.8	11.1	9.8	13	85	43	0.5	0.6	0.4	0.5
Bladen	5,623	4,084	682	419	326	47	65	-	-	72.6	12.1	7.5	17	78	84	0.8	0.9	0.6	0.6
Brunswick	7,046	4,981	919	545	482	60	59	-	-	70.7	13.0	7.7	30	68	79	1.0	1.1	0.9	0.8
Buncombe	18,768	11,521	2,817	2,102	1,984	187	157	-	-	61.4	15.0	11.2	79	48	20	2.7	2.6	2.6	2.9
Burke	5,383	3,683	674	554	382	48	42	-	-	68.4	12.5	10.3	39	72	35	0.8	0.8	0.6	0.8
Cabarrus	7,798	4,701	1,335	901	692	88	81	-	-	60.3	17.1	11.6	82	31	15	1.1	1.1	1.3	1.3
Caldwell	3,537	2,506	438	326	214	28	25	-	-	70.9	12.4	9.2	27	74	50	0.5	0.6	0.4	0.5
Camden	1,320	737	368	105	82	11	17	-	-	55.8	27.9	8.0	97	1	74	0.2	0.2	0.3	0.1
Carteret	5,451	3,408	812	567	526	66	72	-	-	62.5	14.9	10.4	70	50	32	0.8	0.8	0.8	0.8
Caswell	4,298	2,641	943	365	255	55	39	-	-	61.4	21.9	8.5	78	9	64	0.6	0.6	0.9	0.5
Catawba	6,359	4,199	856	667	517	67	53	-	-	66.0	13.5	10.5	52	62	28	0.9	0.9	0.8	0.9
Chatham	5,587	3,630	675	707	494	36	45	-	-	65.0	12.1	12.7	55	79	7	0.8	0.8	0.6	1.0
Cherokee	1,824	1,423	136	147	96	11	11	-	-	78.0	7.5	8.1	5	99	69	0.3	0.3	0.1	0.2
Chowan	1,857	1,252	324	141	112	12	16	-	-	67.4	17.4	7.6	44	30	81	0.3	0.3	0.3	0.2
Clay	714	560	62	48	37	4	3	-	-	78.4	8.7	6.7	4	97	94	0.1	0.1	<.1	<.1
Cleveland	8,814	5,365	1,855	784	656	84	70	-	-	60.9	21.0	8.9	81	13	57	1.3	1.2	1.7	1.1
Columbus	10,627	7,945	1,195	804	524	68	91	-	-	74.8	11.2	7.6	11	83	82	1.5	1.8	1.1	1.1
Craven	7,538	4,643	1,189	920	650	66	70	-	-	61.6	15.8	12.2	76	42	10	1.1	1.0	1.1	1.3
Cumberland	21,859	13,612	4,195	2,077	1,619	189	167	-	-	62.3	19.2	9.5	73	21	48	3.2	3.1	3.9	2.9
Currituck	2,143	1,137	566	229	162	25	24	-	-	53.1	26.4	10.7	99	2	25	0.3	0.3	0.5	0.3
Dare	3,480	1,739	876	470	327	40	28	-	-	50.0	25.2	13.5	100	3	2	0.5	0.4	0.8	0.7
Davidson	8,339	5,334	1,418	712	674	68	133	-	-	64.0	17.0	8.5	62	32	62	1.2	1.2	1.3	1.0
Davie	1,724	1,148	285	135	129	16	11	-	-	66.6	16.5	7.8	49	35	78	0.2	0.3	0.3	0.2
Duplin	5,947	4,095	857	518	381	45	51	-	-	68.9	14.4	8.7	36	55	58	0.9	0.9	0.8	0.7
Durham	30,642	19,230	4,603	3,587	2,875	173	174	-	-	62.8	15.0	11.7	68	47	13	4.4	4.3	4.3	5.0
Edgecombe	9,775	6,685	1,350	1,015	523	93	109	-	-	68.4	13.8	10.4	41	60	33	1.4	1.5	1.3	1.4
Forsyth	22,571	13,475	3,574	2,566	2,562	216	178	-	-	59.7	15.8	11.4	86	40	19	3.3	3.0	3.3	3.6
Franklin	5,265	3,757	529	552	337	45	45	-	-	71.4	10.0	10.5	24	91	29	0.8	0.8	0.5	0.8
Gaston	14,114	8,309	2,890	1,410	1,213	163	129	-	-	58.9	20.5	10.0	90	16	40	2.0	1.9	2.7	2.0
Gates	1,978	1,239	442	151	103	27	16	-	-	62.6	22.3	7.6	69	8	80	0.3	0.3	0.4	0.2
Graham	891	726	83	44	31	4	3	-	-	81.5	9.3	4.9	2	93	100	0.1	0.2	<.1	<.1
Granville	6,501	4,045	1,276	681	395	49	55	-	-	62.2	19.6	10.5	74	19	30	0.9	0.9	1.2	0.9
Greene	3,251	2,012	705	267	187	47	33	-	-	61.9	21.7	8.2	75	10	67	0.5	0.5	0.7	0.4
Guilford	31,598	20,134	4,270	3,364	3,359	238	233	-	-	63.7	13.5	10.6	64	61	26	4.6	4.5	4.0	4.7
Halifax	8,083	5,186	1,368	877	496	72	84	-	-	64.2	16.9	10.8	59	34	23	1.2	1.2	1.3	1.2
Harnett	8,074	5,164	1,443	783	510	88	86	-	-	64.0	17.9	9.7	63	28	45	1.2	1.2	1.4	1.1
Haywood	7,884	5,555	1,010	643	566	54	56	-	-	70.5	12.8	8.2	31	70	68	1.1	1.3	0.9	0.9
Henderson	4,352	2,787	567	454	482	43	19	-	-	64.0	13.0	10.4	61	69	31	0.6	0.6	0.5	0.6
Hertford	2,997	2,086	370	349	146	26	20	-	-	69.6	12.3	11.6	33	75	14	0.4	0.5	0.3	0.5
Hoke	3,326	2,161	659	245	151	50	60	-	-	65.0	19.8	7.4	54	17	86	0.5	0.5	0.6	0.3
Hyde	1,445	885	325	116	84	13	22	-	-	61.2	22.5	8.0	80	7	71	0.2	0.2	0.3	0.2
Iredell	9,053	5,367	1,906	926	689	94	71	-	-	59.3	21.1	10.2	88	12	36	1.3	1.2	1.8	1.3
Jackson	3,838	2,820	347	331	286	31	23	-	-	73.5	9.0	8.6	14	96	60	0.6	0.6	0.3	0.5
Johnston	10,237	6,157	2,140	1,000	742	104	94	-	-	60.1	20.9	9.8	83	14	42	1.5	1.4	2.0	1.4
Jones	1,804	1,289	268	124	85	16	22	-	-	71.5	14.9	6.9	23	51	93	0.3	0.3	0.3	0.2
Lee	5,548	3,187	1,284	512	490	34	41	-	-	57.4	23.1	9.2	93	6	49	0.8	0.7	1.2	0.7
Lenoir	7,842	5,077	1,202	813	577	86	87	-	-	64.7	15.3	10.4	57	44	34	1.1	1.1	1.1	1.1
Lincoln	4,014	2,856	489	315	274	37	43	-	-	71.2	12.2	7.8	26	77	77	0.6	0.6	0.5	0.4
McDowell	3,734	2,411	687	337	244	29	26	-	-	64.6	18.4	9.0	58	22	54	0.5	0.5	0.6	0.5
Macon	2,968	2,173	306	237	205	22	25	-	-	73.2	10.3	8.0	15	88	73	0.4	0.5	0.3	0.3
Madison	1,935	1,644	60	136	87	5	3	-	-	85.0	3.1	7.0	1	100	91	0.3	0.4	<.1	0.2
Martin	3,946	2,793	521	354	207	37	34	-	-	70.8	13.2	9.0	28	65	55	0.6	0.6	0.5	0.5
Mecklenburg	41,157	27,389	4,653	4,717	3,793	326	279	-	-	66.5	11.3	11.5	50	82	16	5.9	6.2	4.4	6.6
Mitchell	463	322	52	37	39	7	6	-	-	69.5	11.2	8.0	35	84	72	<.1	<.1	<.1	<.1
Montgomery	3,019	2,136	485	192	147	27	32	-	-	70.8	16.1	6.4	29	38	96	0.4	0.5	0.5	0.3
Moore	4,749	3,259	580	484	360	43	23	-	-	68.6	12.2	10.2	37	76	37	0.7	0.7	0.5	0.7
Nash	8,299	5,111	1,342	948	708	88	102	-	-	61.6	16.2	11.4	77	37	18	1.2	1.2	1.3	1.3
New Hanover	12,821	7,585	2,334	1,284	1,420	111	87	-	-	59.2	18.2	10.0	89	23	39	1.9	1.7	2.2	1.8
Northampton	4,210	2,880	684	445	153	21	27	-	-	68.4	16.2	10.6	40	36	27	0.6	0.6	0.6	0.6
Onslow	7,205	4,042	1,554	847	610	96	56	-	-	56.1	21.6	11.8	94	11	12	1.0	0.9	1.5	1.2
Orange	13,262	7,380	1,651	2,261	1,719	105	146	-	-	55.6	12.4	17.0	98	73	1	1.9	1.7	1.5	3.1
Pamlico	1,941	1,130	383	239	140	27	22	-	-	58.2	19.7	12.3	91	18	9	0.3	0.3	0.4	0.3
Pasquotank	3,708	2,538	566	369	199	18	18	-	-	68.4	15.3	10.0	38	45	41	0.5	0.6	0.5	0.5

Table I. — Vote for Presidential Preference: May 5, 1992, Democratic Primary Election (cont)

County	Top candidates									Top three candidates (state vote)									
										Percent of total vote			Rank			Percent contribution to state vote			
	Total	Clinton	No Preference	Brown	Tsongas	Kerrey	Harkin			Clinton	No Preference	Brown	Clinton	No Preference	Brown	Total	Clinton	No Preference	Brown
Pender	4,968	3,328	729	483	349	38	41	-	-	67.0	14.7	9.7	47	54	44	0.7	0.8	0.7	0.7
Perquimans	1,723	1,030	420	123	106	26	18	-	-	59.8	24.4	7.1	85	4	89	0.2	0.2	0.4	0.2
Person	4,050	2,673	641	407	242	38	49	-	-	66.0	15.8	10.0	53	41	38	0.6	0.6	0.6	0.6
Pitt	14,043	8,995	2,094	1,516	1,201	129	108	-	-	64.1	14.9	10.8	60	49	24	2.0	2.0	2.0	2.1
Polk	1,719	1,305	174	98	120	8	14	-	-	75.9	10.1	5.7	9	90	98	0.2	0.3	0.2	0.1
Randolph	4,417	2,982	671	381	309	43	31	-	-	67.5	15.2	8.6	43	46	59	0.6	0.7	0.6	0.5
Richmond	5,889	3,949	940	542	351	54	53	-	-	67.1	16.0	9.2	46	39	52	0.9	0.9	0.9	0.8
Robeson	17,367	12,122	2,497	1,551	847	169	181	-	-	69.8	14.4	8.9	32	56	56	2.5	2.7	2.3	2.2
Rockingham	7,953	5,004	1,445	732	654	59	59	-	-	62.9	18.2	9.2	67	24	53	1.1	1.1	1.4	1.0
Rowan	8,209	4,900	1,479	1,022	636	82	90	-	-	59.7	18.0	12.4	87	26	8	1.2	1.1	1.4	1.4
Rutherford	4,705	3,130	828	387	299	28	33	-	-	66.5	17.6	8.2	51	29	65	0.7	0.7	0.8	0.5
Sampson	4,701	3,656	436	334	225	21	29	-	-	77.8	9.3	7.1	7	95	90	0.7	0.8	0.4	0.5
Scotland	3,752	2,516	680	268	238	18	32	-	-	67.1	18.1	7.1	45	25	88	0.5	0.6	0.6	0.4
Stanly	3,965	2,697	531	365	285	40	47	-	-	68.0	13.4	9.2	42	63	51	0.6	0.6	0.5	0.5
Stokes	3,245	2,455	330	258	163	22	17	-	-	75.7	10.2	8.0	10	89	75	0.5	0.6	0.3	0.4
Surry	4,260	3,086	464	350	289	39	32	-	-	72.4	10.9	8.2	18	87	66	0.6	0.7	0.4	0.5
Swain	1,085	867	105	60	41	8	4	-	-	79.9	9.7	5.5	3	92	99	0.2	0.2	<.1	<.1
Transylvania	2,640	1,768	367	227	230	26	22	-	-	67.0	13.9	8.6	48	59	61	0.4	0.4	0.3	0.3
Tyrrell	1,086	678	211	105	64	19	9	-	-	62.4	19.4	9.7	71	20	46	0.2	0.2	0.2	0.1
Union	6,345	4,004	1,075	611	542	66	47	-	-	63.1	16.9	9.6	65	33	47	0.9	0.9	1.0	0.8
Vance	6,046	3,634	1,251	664	386	49	62	-	-	60.1	20.7	11.0	84	15	21	0.9	0.8	1.2	0.9
Wake	48,676	28,041	6,884	6,266	6,624	494	367	-	-	57.6	14.1	12.9	92	57	5	7.0	6.3	6.5	8.7
Warren	4,048	2,883	571	344	188	26	36	-	-	71.2	14.1	8.5	25	58	63	0.6	0.7	0.5	0.5
Washington	2,301	1,665	265	174	137	36	24	-	-	72.4	11.5	7.6	19	81	83	0.3	0.4	0.2	0.2
Watauga	2,849	1,795	378	380	261	15	20	-	-	63.0	13.3	13.3	66	64	3	0.4	0.4	0.4	0.5
Wayne	9,286	5,784	1,213	1,179	844	140	126	-	-	62.3	13.1	12.7	72	67	6	1.3	1.3	1.1	1.6
Wilkes	3,736	2,678	470	300	234	28	26	-	-	71.7	12.6	8.0	22	71	70	0.5	0.6	0.4	0.4
Wilson	7,594	4,926	1,181	868	502	55	62	-	-	64.9	15.6	11.4	56	43	17	1.1	1.1	1.1	1.2
Yadkin	1,969	1,413	289	132	113	13	9	-	-	71.8	14.7	6.7	20	53	95	0.3	0.3	0.3	0.2
Yancey	2,326	1,775	216	183	120	17	15	-	-	76.3	9.3	7.9	8	94	76	0.3	0.4	0.2	0.3
NORTH CAROLINA	**691,875**	**443,498**	**106,697**	**71,984**	**57,589**	**6,216**	**5,891**	**-**	**-**	**64.1**	**15.4**	**10.4**				**100.0**	**100.0**	**100.0**	**100.0**

Table J. — Vote for Presidential Preference: May 5, 1992, Republican Primary Election

County	Top candidates					Top four candidates (state vote)													
						Percent of total vote								Percent contribution to state vote					
										Rank									
	Total	Bush	Bu-chanan	No Pre-ference		Bush	Bu-chanan	No Pre-ference		Bush	Bu-chanan	No Pre-ference		Total	Bush	Bu-chanan	No Pre-ference	
Alamance	5,277	3,696	1,126	455	-	70.0	21.3	8.6	-	74	20	56	-	1.9	1.8	2.0	1.6	-
Alexander	1,263	963	230	70	-	76.2	18.2	5.5	-	21	50	90	-	0.4	0.5	0.4	0.3	-
Alleghany	297	234	43	20	-	78.8	14.5	6.7	-	12	81	80	-	0.1	0.1	<.1	<.1	-
Anson	245	198	35	12	-	80.8	14.3	4.9	-	8	83	98	-	<.1	<.1	<.1	<.1	-
Ashe	1,572	1,269	190	113	-	80.7	12.1	7.2	-	9	93	75	-	0.6	0.6	0.3	0.4	-
Avery	3,106	2,135	477	494	-	68.7	15.4	15.9	-	84	72	2	-	1.1	1.1	0.9	1.8	-
Beaufort	1,482	1,076	290	116	-	72.6	19.6	7.8	-	52	32	69	-	0.5	0.5	0.5	0.4	-
Bertie	185	124	44	17	-	67.0	23.8	9.2	-	92	6	44	-	<.1	<.1	<.1	<.1	-
Bladen	372	271	65	36	-	72.8	17.5	9.7	-	47	58	37	-	0.1	0.1	0.1	0.1	-
Brunswick	2,797	1,946	468	383	-	69.6	16.7	13.7	-	78	63	6	-	1.0	1.0	0.8	1.4	-
Buncombe	7,528	5,494	1,209	825	-	73.0	16.1	11.0	-	45	66	22	-	2.7	2.7	2.2	3.0	-
Burke	2,729	2,009	508	212	-	73.6	18.6	7.8	-	39	43	70	-	1.0	1.0	0.9	0.8	-
Cabarrus	4,723	3,284	1,011	428	-	69.5	21.4	9.1	-	79	18	49	-	1.7	1.6	1.8	1.5	-
Caldwell	3,511	2,497	689	325	-	71.1	19.6	9.3	-	68	31	42	-	1.2	1.2	1.2	1.2	-
Camden	101	72	23	6	-	71.3	22.8	5.9	-	64	10	87	-	<.1	<.1	<.1	<.1	-
Carteret	3,389	2,501	555	333	-	73.8	16.4	9.8	-	37	65	35	-	1.2	1.2	1.0	1.2	-
Caswell	239	163	47	29	-	68.2	19.7	12.1	-	89	30	15	-	<.1	<.1	<.1	0.1	-
Catawba	6,842	4,963	1,255	624	-	72.5	18.3	9.1	-	53	48	47	-	2.4	2.5	2.3	2.2	-
Chatham	1,387	991	255	141	-	71.4	18.4	10.2	-	61	46	32	-	0.5	0.5	0.5	0.5	-
Cherokee	1,053	828	117	108	-	78.6	11.1	10.3	-	13	96	28	-	0.4	0.4	0.2	0.4	-
Chowan	467	337	68	62	-	72.2	14.6	13.3	-	56	80	9	-	0.2	0.2	0.1	0.2	-
Clay	623	520	60	43	-	83.5	9.6	6.9	-	4	98	78	-	0.2	0.3	0.1	0.2	-
Cleveland	1,826	1,288	342	196	-	70.5	18.7	10.7	-	71	41	26	-	0.6	0.6	0.6	0.7	-
Columbus	1,169	852	211	106	-	72.9	18.0	9.1	-	46	53	48	-	0.4	0.4	0.4	0.4	-
Craven	3,001	2,092	602	307	-	69.7	20.1	10.2	-	76	27	29	-	1.1	1.0	1.1	1.1	-
Cumberland	6,109	4,423	1,067	619	-	72.4	17.5	10.1	-	55	59	33	-	2.2	2.2	1.9	2.2	-
Currituck	239	172	45	22	-	72.0	18.8	9.2	-	58	38	43	-	<.1	<.1	<.1	<.1	-
Dare	1,463	1,041	222	200	-	71.2	15.2	13.7	-	66	75	7	-	0.5	0.5	0.4	0.7	-
Davidson	6,250	4,438	1,276	536	-	71.0	20.4	8.6	-	69	26	57	-	2.2	2.2	2.3	1.9	-
Davie	3,385	2,541	575	269	-	75.1	17.0	7.9	-	30	61	68	-	1.2	1.3	1.0	1.0	-
Duplin	1,138	885	191	62	-	77.8	16.8	5.4	-	20	62	92	-	0.4	0.4	0.3	0.2	-
Durham	7,941	5,586	1,444	911	-	70.3	18.2	11.5	-	72	51	18	-	2.8	2.8	2.6	3.3	-
Edgecombe	859	588	186	85	-	68.5	21.7	9.9	-	88	17	34	-	0.3	0.3	0.3	0.3	-
Forsyth	13,368	8,619	3,528	1,221	-	64.5	26.4	9.1	-	98	3	45	-	4.7	4.3	6.4	4.4	-
Franklin	912	592	271	49	-	64.9	29.7	5.4	-	95	1	93	-	0.3	0.3	0.5	0.2	-
Gaston	8,271	6,057	1,553	661	-	73.2	18.8	8.0	-	42	40	64	-	2.9	3.0	2.8	2.4	-
Gates	72	56	9	7	-	77.8	12.5	9.7	-	19	92	36	-	<.1	<.1	<.1	<.1	-
Graham	733	639	48	46	-	87.2	6.5	6.3	-	1	100	86	-	0.3	0.3	<.1	0.2	-
Granville	480	330	101	49	-	68.8	21.0	10.2	-	83	23	30	-	0.2	0.2	0.2	0.2	-
Greene	213	162	39	12	-	76.1	18.3	5.6	-	22	49	89	-	<.1	<.1	<.1	<.1	-
Guilford	16,533	11,318	3,531	1,684	-	68.5	21.4	10.2	-	86	19	31	-	5.8	5.6	6.4	6.1	-
Halifax	539	363	114	62	-	67.3	21.2	11.5	-	91	22	17	-	0.2	0.2	0.2	0.2	-
Harnett	1,834	1,339	399	96	-	73.0	21.8	5.2	-	44	16	95	-	0.6	0.7	0.7	0.3	-
Haywood	1,558	1,178	244	136	-	75.6	15.7	8.7	-	27	68	54	-	0.5	0.6	0.4	0.5	-
Henderson	5,481	3,986	825	670	-	72.7	15.1	12.2	-	51	78	13	-	1.9	2.0	1.5	2.4	-
Hertford	251	186	45	20	-	74.1	17.9	8.0	-	34	54	66	-	<.1	<.1	<.1	<.1	-
Hoke	313	244	44	25	-	78.0	14.1	8.0	-	16	84	65	-	0.1	0.1	<.1	<.1	-
Hyde	86	62	16	8	-	72.1	18.6	9.3	-	57	44	41	-	<.1	<.1	<.1	<.1	-
Iredell	5,087	3,634	968	485	-	71.4	19.0	9.5	-	62	36	39	-	1.8	1.8	1.7	1.7	-
Jackson	1,199	937	157	105	-	78.1	13.1	8.8	-	15	91	53	-	0.4	0.5	0.3	0.4	-
Johnston	2,694	1,902	614	178	-	70.6	22.8	6.6	-	70	9	81	-	1.0	0.9	1.1	0.6	-
Jones	110	79	23	8	-	71.8	20.9	7.3	-	59	24	73	-	<.1	<.1	<.1	<.1	-
Lee	1,293	983	207	103	-	76.0	16.0	8.0	-	23	67	67	-	0.5	0.5	0.4	0.4	-
Lenoir	969	705	202	62	-	72.8	20.8	6.4	-	49	25	84	-	0.3	0.4	0.4	0.2	-
Lincoln	2,215	1,663	391	161	-	75.1	17.7	7.3	-	29	57	74	-	0.8	0.8	0.7	0.6	-
McDowell	1,018	793	154	71	-	77.9	15.1	7.0	-	17	77	76	-	0.4	0.4	0.3	0.3	-
Macon	1,678	1,275	254	149	-	76.0	15.1	8.9	-	25	76	52	-	0.6	0.6	0.5	0.5	-
Madison	414	338	50	26	-	81.6	12.1	6.3	-	7	94	85	-	0.1	0.2	<.1	<.1	-
Martin	545	403	97	45	-	73.9	17.8	8.3	-	36	56	62	-	0.2	0.2	0.2	0.2	-
Mecklenburg	27,086	17,664	5,914	3,508	-	65.2	21.8	13.0	-	94	15	10	-	9.6	8.8	10.7	12.6	-
Mitchell	3,438	2,502	467	469	-	72.8	13.6	13.6	-	48	87	8	-	1.2	1.2	0.8	1.7	-
Montgomery	823	658	122	43	-	80.0	14.8	5.2	-	10	79	96	-	0.3	0.3	0.2	0.2	-
Moore	6,841	5,199	896	746	-	76.0	13.1	10.9	-	24	90	23	-	2.4	2.6	1.6	2.7	-
Nash	2,564	1,654	745	165	-	64.5	29.1	6.4	-	97	2	83	-	0.9	0.8	1.3	0.6	-
New Hanover	6,201	4,295	1,139	767	-	69.3	18.4	12.4	-	80	47	12	-	2.2	2.1	2.1	2.8	-
Northampton	114	67	28	19	-	58.8	24.6	16.7	-	100	5	1	-	<.1	<.1	<.1	<.1	-
Onslow	2,251	1,568	427	256	-	69.7	19.0	11.4	-	77	37	19	-	0.8	0.8	0.8	0.9	-
Orange	2,738	1,715	610	413	-	62.6	22.3	15.1	-	99	12	4	-	1.0	0.9	1.1	1.5	-
Pamlico	404	297	73	34	-	73.5	18.1	8.4	-	40	52	60	-	0.1	0.1	0.1	0.1	-
Pasquotank	615	421	115	79	-	68.5	18.7	12.8	-	87	42	11	-	0.2	0.2	0.2	0.3	-

County	Top candidates					Top four candidates (state vote)									Percent contribution to state vote				
						Percent of total vote				Rank									
	Total	Bush	Bu-chanan	No Pre-ference		Bush	Bu-chanan	No Pre-ference		Bush	Bu-chanan	No Pre-ference		Total	Bush	Bu-chanan	No Pre-ference	
Pender	1,204	819	239	146	-	68.0	19.9	12.1	-	90	29	16	-	0.4	0.4	0.4	0.5	-
Perquimans	205	135	40	30	-	65.9	19.5	14.6	-	93	34	5	-	<.1	<.1	<.1	0.1	-
Person	530	388	83	59	-	73.2	15.7	11.1	-	43	69	21	-	0.2	0.2	0.1	0.2	-
Pitt	3,360	2,403	673	284	-	71.5	20.0	8.5	-	60	28	58	-	1.2	1.2	1.2	1.0	-
Polk	1,402	1,041	190	171	-	74.3	13.6	12.2	-	33	88	14	-	0.5	0.5	0.3	0.6	-
Randolph	6,683	4,862	1,258	563	-	72.8	18.8	8.4	-	50	39	59	-	2.4	2.4	2.3	2.0	-
Richmond	626	446	112	68	-	71.2	17.9	10.9	-	65	55	24	-	0.2	0.2	0.2	0.2	-
Robeson	964	688	188	88	-	71.4	19.5	9.1	-	63	35	46	-	0.3	0.3	0.3	0.3	-
Rockingham	2,092	1,435	468	189	-	68.6	22.4	9.0	-	85	11	50	-	0.7	0.7	0.8	0.7	-
Rowan	6,770	4,725	1,435	610	-	69.8	21.2	9.0	-	75	21	51	-	2.4	2.4	2.6	2.2	-
Rutherford	1,390	1,045	214	131	-	75.2	15.4	9.4	-	28	71	40	-	0.5	0.5	0.4	0.5	-
Sampson	2,415	2,031	278	106	-	84.1	11.5	4.4	-	3	95	99	-	0.9	1.0	0.5	0.4	-
Scotland	500	351	70	79	-	70.2	14.0	15.8	-	73	86	3	-	0.2	0.2	0.1	0.3	-
Stanly	2,085	1,653	317	115	-	79.3	15.2	5.5	-	11	74	91	-	0.7	0.8	0.6	0.4	-
Stokes	1,978	1,539	341	98	-	77.8	17.2	5.0	-	18	60	97	-	0.7	0.8	0.6	0.4	-
Surry	1,518	1,118	297	103	-	73.6	19.6	6.8	-	38	33	79	-	0.5	0.6	0.5	0.4	-
Swain	316	258	34	24	-	81.6	10.8	7.6	-	6	97	72	-	0.1	0.1	<.1	<.1	-
Transylvania	1,588	1,165	243	180	-	73.4	15.3	11.3	-	41	73	20	-	0.6	0.6	0.4	0.6	-
Tyrrell	57	48	8	1	-	84.2	14.0	1.8	-	2	85	100	-	<.1	<.1	<.1	<.1	-
Union	3,668	2,539	811	318	-	69.2	22.1	8.7	-	82	14	55	-	1.3	1.3	1.5	1.1	-
Vance	411	308	76	27	-	74.9	18.5	6.6	-	31	45	82	-	0.1	0.2	0.1	<.1	-
Wake	22,653	14,616	5,853	2,184	-	64.5	25.8	9.6	-	96	4	38	-	8.0	7.3	10.6	7.9	-
Warren	222	166	32	24	-	74.8	14.4	10.8	-	32	82	25	-	<.1	<.1	<.1	<.1	-
Washington	187	133	43	11	-	71.1	23.0	5.9	-	67	8	88	-	<.1	<.1	<.1	<.1	-
Watauga	2,144	1,586	335	223	-	74.0	15.6	10.4	-	35	70	27	-	0.8	0.8	0.6	0.8	-
Wayne	1,980	1,436	439	105	-	72.5	22.2	5.3	-	54	13	94	-	0.7	0.7	0.8	0.4	-
Wilkes	6,592	5,172	891	529	-	78.5	13.5	8.0	-	14	89	63	-	2.3	2.6	1.6	1.9	-
Wilson	1,766	1,223	420	123	-	69.3	23.8	7.0	-	81	7	77	-	0.6	0.6	0.8	0.4	-
Yadkin	3,423	2,592	570	261	-	75.7	16.7	7.6	-	26	64	71	-	1.2	1.3	1.0	0.9	-
Yancey	1,333	1,106	116	111	-	83.0	8.7	8.3	-	5	99	61	-	0.5	0.6	0.2	0.4	-
NORTH CAROLINA	283,571	200,387	55,420	27,764	-	70.7	19.5	9.8	-					100.0	100.0	100.0	100.0	-

1992 Vote for President
Percent for Bush (R), by County

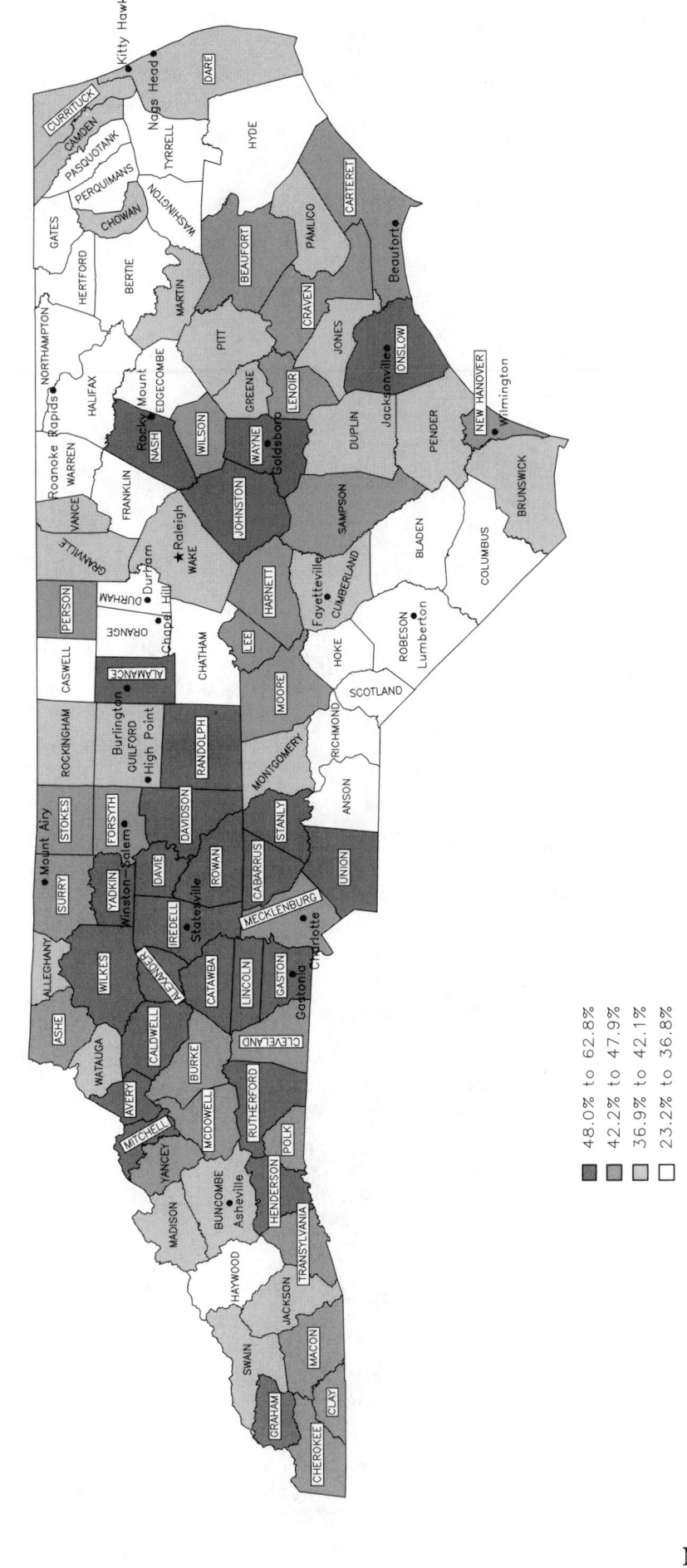

48.0% to 62.8%

42.2% to 47.9%

36.9% to 42.1%

23.2% to 36.8%

Bush (R) received 43.4% statewide.

A framed county name indicates a county carried by the winner.

North Carolina 695

1992 Vote for U.S. Senator
Percent for Faircloth (R), by County

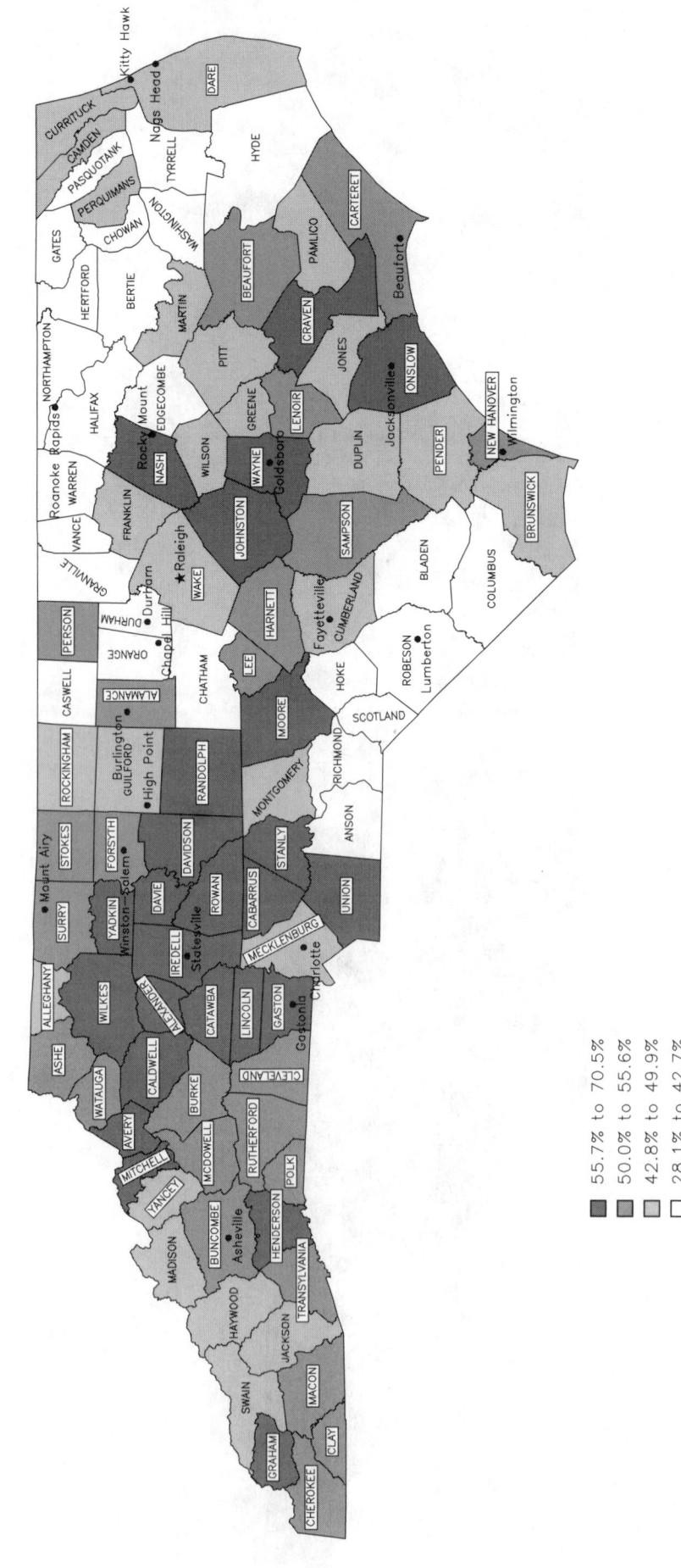

Faircloth (R) received 50.3% statewide.

- 55.7% to 70.5%
- 50.0% to 55.6%
- 42.8% to 49.9%
- 28.1% to 42.7%

A framed county name indicates
a county carried by the winner.

696 North Carolina

1992 Vote for Governor
Percent for Hunter (D), by County

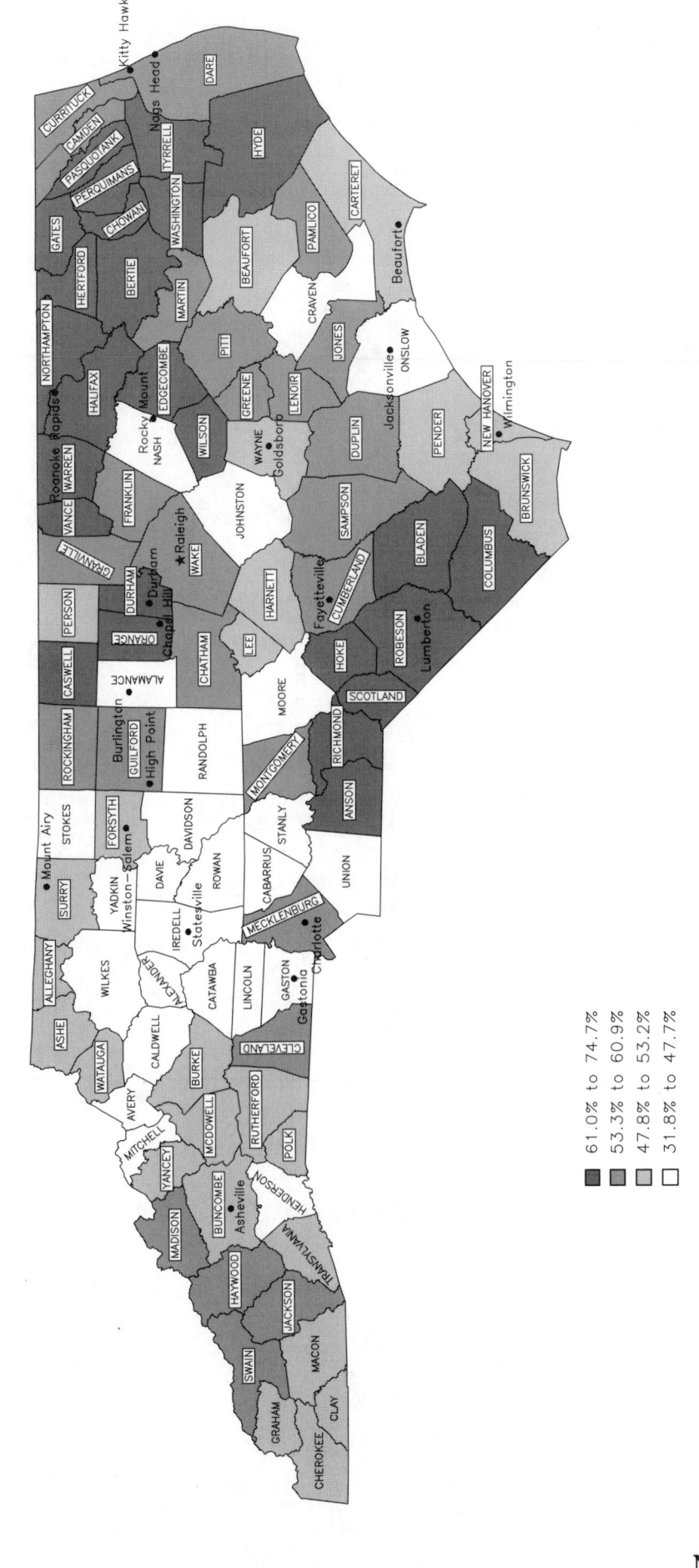

Hunter (D) received 52.7% statewide.

A framed county name indicates
a county carried by the winner.

61.0% to 74.7%
53.3% to 60.9%
47.8% to 53.2%
31.8% to 47.7%

North Carolina 697

NORTH DAKOTA

Congressional Districts 1
    Average Population 638,800
State Senate Districts 49
    Average Population 13,037
State House Districts 98
    Average Population 6,518

Electoral College Votes..3
Counties 53
Voting Precincts 784

Alternative Registration Methods:[1]
....N/A

Registration Deadline[1] (Days before Election)...............N/A

Voting Equipment Use (Counties)

Datavote Punch Card	0	Paper Ballot	21
Electronic	0	Other Punch Card	13
Lever Machine	1	Mixed Systems	0
Optical Scanner	18		

Party Control	DEM	REP	IND	VAC
1993 State Senate	25	24	0	0
1992 State Senate	27	26	0	0
1993 State House	33	65	0	0
1992 State House	48	58	0	0

Population Statistics 1990

Race/ Ethnicity	Total Population		Voting Age Population		Voting Age Population % of total population
	Number	%	Number	%	
Non-Hispanic					
White	601,592	94.2	442,126	95.4	73.5
Black	3,451	0.5	2,170	0.5	62.9
Asian/Pacific Islander	3,345	0.5	2,316	0.5	69.2
Native American	25,590	4.0	14,166	3.1	55.4
Other	157	<.1	62	<.1	39.5
All Hispanic	4,665	0.7	2,575	0.6	55.2
TOTAL	638,800	100.0	463,415	100.0	72.5

Estimated Voting Age Population 1992 (VAP) 458,000
Number of Registered Voters[1] ....N/A
    % of estimated VAP...N/A
Voter Turnout (Actual) 315,199
    % of VAP 68.8
    % of Registration ....N/A
Persons Not Voting—of Voting Age 142,801
    % of VAP 31.2
Persons Not Voting—of Registered[1] ....N/A
    % of Registration ....N/A
Straight Ticket Voting .... No

State Officials and Members of Congress

Governor:
Edward T. Schafer (R) 1992, elected to a four-year term in 1992.

U.S. Senators:
Kent Conrad (D) 1986, elected to a two-year term in 1992.
Bryon L. Dorgan (D) 1992, elected to a six-year term in 1992.

U.S. Representative in Congress:
(District, Name, Party, Date first elected)

At-Large. Pomeroy (D) 1992

---

[1]No voter registration requirement.

Candidates: General Election, November 3, 1992

Candidate(s)	Total vote	Percent	Party	Status	First elected
President/Vice President					
George Bush	136,244	44.22%	Republican	Incumbent	1988
Bill Clinton	99,168	32.18%	Democrat	Challenger	1992
Ross Perot	71,084	23.07%	Independent	Challenger	
Lyndon LaRouche, Jr.	642	0.21%	Independent	Challenger	
Andre Marrou	416	0.14%	Independent	Challenger	
John Hagelin	240	0.08%	Independent	Challenger	
James Warren	193	0.06%	Independent	Challenger	
Lenora Fulani	143	0.05%	Independent	Challenger	
Earl Dodge	3	<.01%	Independent	Challenger	
U.S. Senator					
Byron Dorgan	179,347	59.00%	Democrat	Challenger	1992
Steve Sydness	118,162	38.87%	Republican	Challenger	
Tom Asbridge	6,448	2.12%	Independent	Challenger	
U.S. Senator (Special Election, December 4, 1992)[1]					
Kent Conrad	103,246	63.22%	Democrat	Challenger	1992
Jack Dalrymple	55,194	33.80%	Republican	Challenger	
Darold Larson	4,871	2.98%	Independent	Challenger	
Governor					
Schafer/Myrdal	176,398	57.86%	Republican	Challenger	1992
Spaeth/Hill	123,845	40.62%	Democrat	Challenger	
McLain/Sandry	2,614	0.86%	Independent	Challenger	
DuPaul/Scott	2,004	0.66%	Independent	Challenger	
U.S. Representative in Congress					
District At-Large					
Earl Pomeroy	169,273	56.82%	Democrat	Challenger	1992
John Korsmo	117,442	39.42%	Republican	Challenger	
Anna Bourcois	7,394	2.48%	Independent	Challenger	
Grady Blount	3,789	1.27%	Independent	Challenger	

[1]For remaining two years of term of the late Senator Quentin Burdick (D).

Candidates: June 9, 1992, Primary Election

Candidate	Total vote	Percent	Candidate	Total vote	Percent
Presidential Preference, Democratic			**Presidential Preference, Republican**		
Ross Perot	9,516	29.02%	George Bush	39,863	80.65%
Lyndon LaRouche, Jr.	7,003	21.36%	Pat Paulsen	4,093	8.28%
Charles Woods	6,641	20.26%	Ross Perot	3,852	7.79%
Tom Shiekman	4,866	14.84%	Others	1,620	3.28%
Bill Clinton	4,760	14.52%			

Voter Registration and Turnout, 1948-1992 Elections

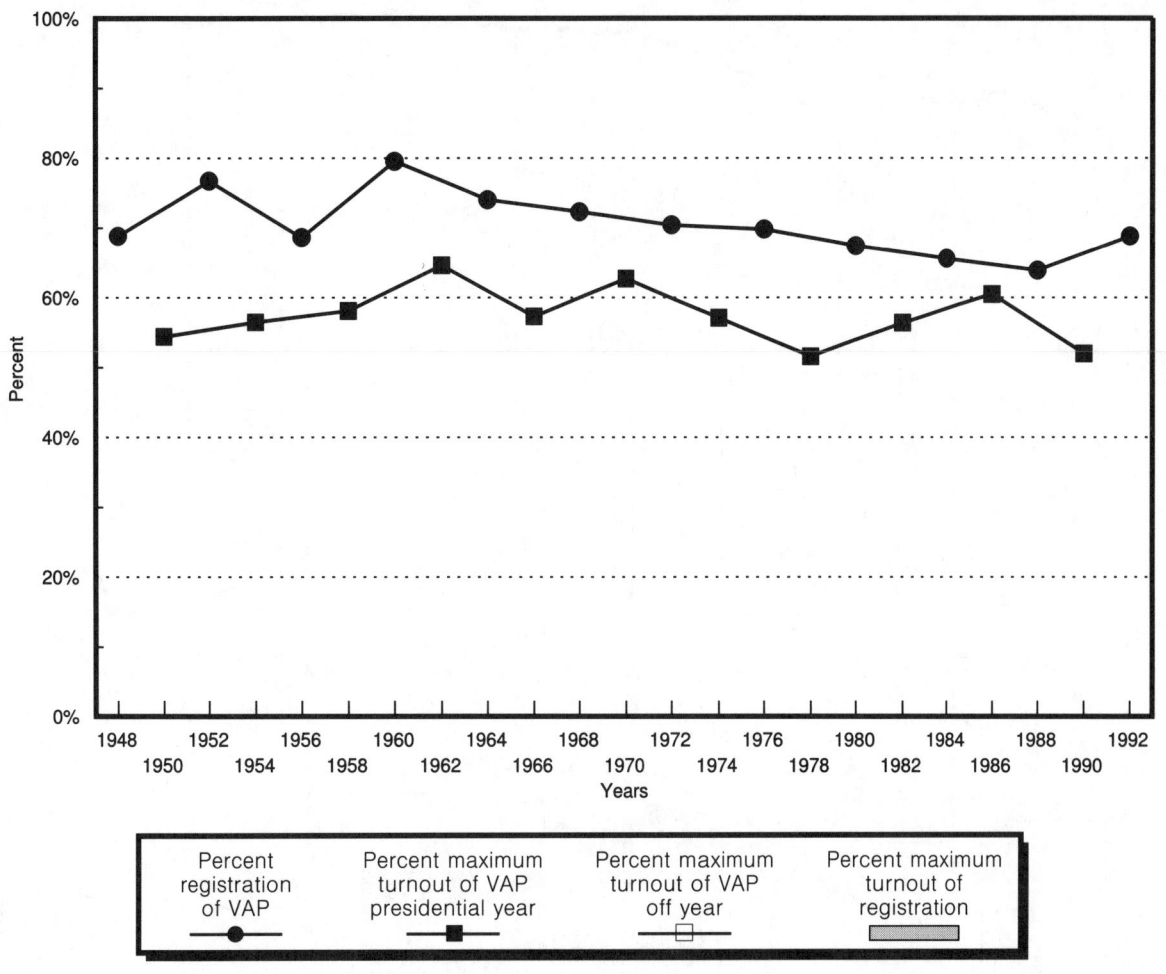

Year	Estimated Voting Age Population (VAP)	Voter registration (REG)[1]			Voter turnout												
						Highest office						Maximum vote					
		Total	Percent of VAP	Rank by percent of VAP	Actual	Total	Office	Percent total REG	Rank by percent of REG	Percent of VAP	Rank by percent of VAP	Total	Percent total REG	Rank by percent of REG	Percent total VAP	Rank by percent of VAP
1992........	458,000	-	-	-	315,199	308,133	P	-	-	67.3	6	315,199	-	-	68.8	5
1990........	462,000	-	-	-	240,301	233,973	C	-	-	50.6	8	240,301	-	-	52.0	7
1988........	484,000	-	-	-	309,100	297,261	P	-	-	61.4	3	309,100	-	-	63.9	4
1986........	488,000	-	-	-	295,177	289,013	S	-	-	59.2	1	295,177	-	-	60.5	1
1984........	494,000	-	-	-	324,179	308,971	P	-	-	62.5	5	324,179	-	-	65.6	3
1982........	484,000	-	-	-	272,876	262,465	S	-	-	54.2	6	272,876	-	-	56.4	4
1980........	467,000	-	-	-	314,525	301,545	P	-	-	64.6	6	314,525	-	-	67.4	3
1978........	455,000	-	-	-	234,712	220,348	C	-	-	48.4	5	234,712	-	-	51.6	5
1976........	442,000	-	-	-	308,684	297,188	P	-	-	67.2	3	308,684	-	-	69.8	2
1974........	424,000	-	-	-	242,065	235,661	S	-	-	55.6	3	242,065	-	-	57.1	3
1972........	411,000	-	-	-	289,205	280,514	P	-	-	68.3	4	289,205	-	-	70.4	1
1970........	360,000	-	-	-	225,859	219,560	S	-	-	61.0	3	225,859	-	-	62.7	2
1968........	354,000	-	-	-	256,093	247,882	P	-	-	70.0	7	256,093	-	-	72.3	5
1966........	358,000	-	-	-	204,986	197,499	C	-	-	55.2	19	204,986	-	-	57.3	17
1964........	362,000	-	-	-	267,910	258,389	P	-	-	71.4	13	267,910	-	-	74.0	8
1962........	359,000	-	-	-	231,856	228,509	G	-	-	63.7	2	231,856	-	-	64.6	2
1960........	357,000	-	-	-	283,797	278,431	P	-	-	78.0	4	283,797	-	-	79.5	3
1958........	373,000	-	-	-	216,734	210,599	G	-	-	56.5	17	216,734	-	-	58.1	15
1956........	379,000	-	-	-	259,980	253,926	P	-	-	67.0	24	259,980	-	-	68.6	20
1954........	367,000	-	-	-	207,423	193,501	G	-	-	52.7	19	207,423	-	-	56.5	17
1952[2]......	362,000	-	-	-	277,568	270,127	P	-	-	74.6	13	277,568	-	-	76.7	9
1950........	367,000	-	-	-	199,652	186,716	S	-	-	50.9	21	199,652	-	-	54.4	17
1948........	332,000	-	-	-	228,453	220,716	P	-	-	66.5	9	228,453	-	-	68.8	6

[1]No voter registration requirement.   [2]Voter registration requirement repealed 1951.

NORTH DAKOTA

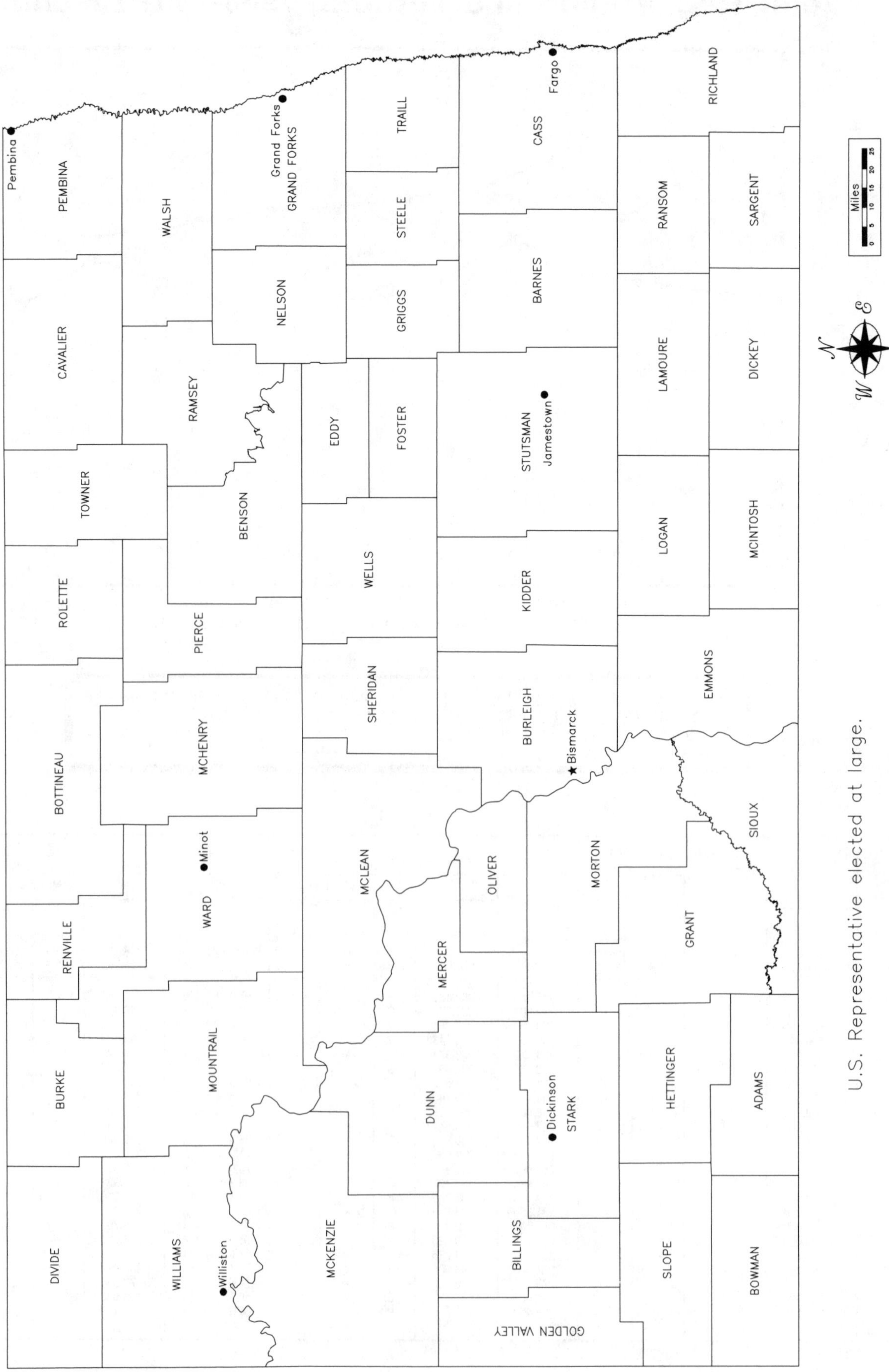

DIVIDE

BURKE

RENVILLE

BOTTINEAU

ROLETTE

TOWNER

CAVALIER

PEMBINA

● Pembina

WILLIAMS

●Williston

MOUNTRAIL

WARD

●Minot

MCHENRY

PIERCE

BENSON

RAMSEY

WALSH

NELSON

Grand Forks ●
GRAND FORKS

MCKENZIE

DUNN

MERCER

MCLEAN

SHERIDAN

WELLS

EDDY

FOSTER

GRIGGS

STEELE

TRAILL

CASS

Fargo ●

RICHLAND

SARGENT

RANSOM

BARNES

STUTSMAN
Jamestown ●

LAMOURE

DICKEY

GOLDEN VALLEY

BILLINGS

● Dickinson
STARK

HETTINGER

SLOPE

BOWMAN

ADAMS

GRANT

MORTON

OLIVER

BURLEIGH

Bismarck ★

EMMONS

SIOUX

KIDDER

LOGAN

MCINTOSH

U.S. Representative elected at large.

702 North Dakota

Miles
0 5 10 15 20 25

Table A. — 1990 Population by Race and Ethnic Origin

State/ county code	County	Total persons	Percent of total persons						Rank				Percent contribution to state population			
			Non-Hispanic							Percent of total persons				Non-Hispanic		
											Non-Hispanic					
			White	Black	Asian and Pacific Islander	Native American	Other	Hispanic	Total	White	Black	Native American[1]	Total	White	Black	Native American[1]
38 001	Adams	3,174	99.6	<.1	0.0	0.3	0.0	<.1	42	8	16	37	0.5	0.5	<.1	<.1
38 003	Barnes	12,545	98.8	0.2	0.3	0.5	0.0	0.3	13	27	6	32	2.0	2.1	0.8	0.2
38 005	Benson	7,198	61.2	0.0	<.1	38.3	<.1	0.3	19	51	38	3	1.1	0.7	0.0	10.8
38 007	Billings	1,108	99.7	0.0	0.0	0.3	0.0	0.0	52	1	39	39	0.2	0.2	0.0	<.1
38 009	Bottineau	8,011	98.8	<.1	0.2	0.7	0.0	0.2	18	25	19	24	1.3	1.3	0.2	0.2
38 011	Bowman	3,596	99.6	0.0	0.1	0.1	<.1	0.2	37	10	40	48	0.6	0.6	0.0	<.1
38 013	Burke	3,002	98.9	<.1	0.2	0.4	0.0	0.5	44	24	32	34	0.5	0.5	<.1	<.1
38 015	Burleigh	60,131	96.3	0.1	0.4	2.6	<.1	0.6	3	41	15	10	9.4	9.6	1.9	6.1
38 017	Cass	102,874	97.2	0.3	0.9	0.9	<.1	0.7	1	37	4	21	16.1	16.6	7.9	3.6
38 019	Cavalier	6,064	99.0	<.1	<.1	0.7	0.0	0.1	24	22	22	22	0.9	1.0	0.1	0.2
38 021	Dickey	6,107	98.8	0.1	0.2	0.3	0.0	0.5	23	26	11	35	1.0	1.0	0.2	<.1
38 023	Divide	2,899	99.2	<.1	0.2	0.3	0.0	0.2	46	18	30	38	0.5	0.5	<.1	<.1
38 025	Dunn	4,005	89.8	0.0	0.1	9.4	0.0	0.6	33	48	41	6	0.6	0.6	0.0	1.5
38 027	Eddy	2,951	98.2	0.0	<.1	1.7	0.0	0.1	45	34	42	15	0.5	0.5	0.0	0.2
38 029	Emmons	4,830	99.7	0.0	<.1	0.1	0.0	0.1	29	5	43	49	0.8	0.8	0.0	<.1
38 031	Foster	3,983	99.1	0.0	<.1	0.6	0.0	0.3	34	21	44	29	0.6	0.7	0.0	<.1
38 033	Golden Valley	2,108	99.0	0.0	0.4	0.6	0.0	<.1	51	23	45	28	0.3	0.3	0.0	<.1
38 035	Grand Forks	70,683	93.6	2.0	1.2	1.7	<.1	1.5	2	46	2	13	11.1	11.0	40.9	4.7
38 037	Grant	3,549	98.6	<.1	0.1	0.9	0.0	0.3	38	28	35	20	0.6	0.6	<.1	0.1
38 039	Griggs	3,303	99.5	0.0	0.2	0.2	0.0	0.1	41	14	46	40	0.5	0.5	0.0	<.1
38 041	Hettinger	3,445	99.5	0.0	0.2	0.2	<.1	<.1	39	12	47	43	0.5	0.6	0.0	<.1
38 043	Kidder	3,332	99.7	0.0	0.1	0.0	0.0	0.2	40	4	48	53	0.5	0.6	0.0	0.0
38 045	LaMoure	5,383	99.7	0.0	<.1	<.1	0.0	0.1	27	2	49	51	0.8	0.9	0.0	<.1
38 047	Logan	2,847	99.5	<.1	<.1	0.1	0.0	0.3	47	15	29	46	0.4	0.5	<.1	<.1
38 049	McHenry	6,528	99.5	<.1	<.1	0.2	0.0	0.2	21	16	23	44	1.0	1.1	0.1	<.1
38 051	McIntosh	4,021	99.5	0.0	0.1	0.1	0.0	0.1	32	11	36	45	0.6	0.7	<.1	<.1
38 053	McKenzie	6,383	85.0	<.1	<.1	14.1	0.0	0.8	22	49	33	5	1.0	0.9	<.1	3.5
38 055	McLean	10,457	94.3	<.1	<.1	5.3	<.1	0.4	14	45	34	7	1.6	1.6	<.1	2.1
38 057	Mercer	9,808	96.8	0.1	0.4	2.3	<.1	0.4	15	40	13	11	1.5	1.6	0.3	0.9
38 059	Morton	23,700	97.8	<.1	0.2	1.7	0.0	0.3	5	36	26	14	3.7	3.9	0.3	1.6
38 061	Mountrail	7,021	79.6	<.1	0.2	19.8	0.0	0.4	20	50	24	4	1.1	0.9	0.1	5.4
38 063	Nelson	4,410	99.6	<.1	<.1	0.1	0.0	0.2	31	7	27	47	0.7	0.7	<.1	<.1
38 065	Oliver	2,381	98.2	0.0	0.0	1.6	0.0	0.2	49	33	50	16	0.4	0.4	0.0	0.2
38 067	Pembina	9,238	97.2	0.2	0.1	1.6	<.1	0.9	16	38	9	18	1.4	1.5	0.4	0.6
38 069	Pierce	5,052	99.2	<.1	0.3	0.5	0.0	<.1	28	19	28	31	0.8	0.8	<.1	<.1
38 071	Ramsey	12,681	94.6	0.2	0.2	4.6	<.1	0.4	12	43	8	9	2.0	2.0	0.6	2.3
38 073	Ransom	5,921	99.2	<.1	0.1	0.2	<.1	0.4	25	20	21	41	0.9	1.0	0.1	<.1
38 075	Renville	3,160	98.3	0.4	0.3	0.7	0.0	0.2	43	31	3	23	0.5	0.5	0.6	<.1
38 077	Richland	18,148	97.0	0.1	0.5	2.2	<.1	0.3	9	39	14	12	2.8	2.9	0.6	1.6
38 079	Rolette	12,772	32.9	0.2	0.1	66.2	<.1	0.5	11	52	5	2	2.0	0.7	0.8	33.0
38 081	Sargent	4,549	99.4	<.1	0.1	0.2	0.0	0.2	30	17	37	42	0.7	0.8	<.1	<.1
38 083	Sheridan	2,148	99.5	0.0	<.1	0.4	0.0	<.1	50	13	51	33	0.3	0.4	0.0	<.1
38 085	Sioux	3,761	24.1	<.1	0.3	74.8	0.0	0.8	35	53	18	1	0.6	0.2	<.1	11.0
38 087	Slope	907	99.6	0.0	0.0	0.3	0.0	0.1	53	9	52	36	0.1	0.2	0.0	<.1
38 089	Stark	22,832	98.4	<.1	0.3	0.6	<.1	0.6	6	29	20	27	3.6	3.7	0.5	0.5
38 091	Steele	2,420	99.6	0.0	<.1	<.1	0.0	0.2	48	6	53	52	0.4	0.4	0.0	<.1
38 093	Stutsman	22,241	98.3	0.2	0.4	0.6	<.1	0.4	7	30	7	26	3.5	3.6	1.3	0.5
38 095	Towner	3,627	98.2	<.1	0.1	1.5	0.0	0.1	36	32	25	19	0.6	0.6	<.1	0.2
38 097	Traill	8,752	97.9	0.1	0.3	0.5	<.1	1.2	17	35	10	30	1.4	1.4	0.3	0.2
38 099	Walsh	13,840	95.6	0.1	0.4	0.7	0.0	3.2	10	42	12	25	2.2	2.2	0.5	0.4
38 101	Ward	57,921	93.5	2.4	1.0	1.6	<.1	1.5	4	47	1	17	9.1	9.0	40.1	3.7
38 103	Wells	5,864	99.7	<.1	<.1	0.1	0.0	0.1	26	3	31	50	0.9	1.0	<.1	<.1
38 105	Williams	21,129	94.4	<.1	0.2	4.8	<.1	0.5	8	44	17	8	3.3	3.3	0.5	3.9
38	**NORTH DAKOTA**	**638,800**	**94.2**	**0.5**	**0.5**	**4.0**	**<.1**	**0.7**					**100.0**	**100.0**	**100.0**	**100.0**
	CONGRESSIONAL District At-Large	638,800	94.2	0.5	0.5	4.0	<.1	0.7								

[1]Non-Hispanic Native American.

Table B. — 1990 Voting Age Population (VAP) by Race and Ethnic Origin

County	Total Voting Age Population	Percent of total VAP — White	Black	Asian and Pacific Islander	Native American	Other	Hispanic	Rank — Percent of total VAP — Total	White	Black	Native American[1]	Percent contribution to state VAP — Total	White	Black	Native American[1]	VAP percent of total population — Total	White	Black	Asian and Pacific Islander	Native American	Other	Hispanic
Adams	2,347	99.7	0.1	0.0	0.2	0.0	<.1	41	11	10	39	0.5	0.5	0.1	<.1	73.9	74.0	100.0	0.0	40.0	0.0	100.0
Barnes	9,453	98.9	0.2	0.3	0.4	0.0	0.2	11	27	5	30	2.0	2.1	0.9	0.3	75.4	75.5	70.4	68.4	68.4	0.0	47.1
Benson	4,696	70.4	0.0	<.1	29.4	<.1	0.2	21	51	31	3	1.0	0.7	0.0	9.7	65.2	75.0	0.0	33.3	50.0	33.3	37.5
Billings	744	99.6	0.0	0.0	0.4	0.0	0.0	52	13	32	32	0.2	0.2	0.0	<.1	67.1	67.1	0.0	0.0	100.0	0.0	0.0
Bottineau	5,948	98.9	<.1	0.2	0.7	0.0	<.1	18	28	17	20	1.3	1.3	0.2	0.3	74.2	74.3	83.3	73.3	74.1	0.0	31.3
Bowman	2,587	99.7	0.0	0.2	0.2	0.0	0.0	37	10	33	43	0.6	0.6	0.0	<.1	72.0	72.0	0.0	100.0	100.0	0.0	0.0
Burke	2,260	99.5	<.1	<.1	0.2	0.0	0.0	43	19	23	37	0.5	0.5	<.1	<.1	75.3	75.7	100.0	33.3	45.5	0.0	28.6
Burleigh	43,387	97.1	0.1	0.3	2.0	<.1	0.5	3	41	12	10	9.4	9.5	2.2	6.1	72.2	72.7	72.7	64.5	55.5	36.8	54.6
Cass	77,184	97.6	0.2	0.9	0.7	<.1	0.5	1	38	4	21	16.7	17.0	7.4	3.9	75.0	75.4	58.8	72.1	60.5	47.8	58.3
Cavalier	4,431	99.1	<.1	<.1	0.7	0.0	0.1	23	24	28	24	1.0	1.0	<.1	0.2	73.1	73.2	25.0	66.7	66.7	0.0	75.0
Dickey	4,580	99.0	0.2	0.1	0.3	0.0	0.4	22	26	7	34	1.0	1.0	0.4	<.1	75.0	75.2	100.0	46.2	66.7	0.0	51.5
Divide	2,207	99.6	0.0	0.2	0.1	0.0	<.1	45	14	34	44	0.5	0.5	0.0	<.1	76.1	76.4	0.0	83.3	33.3	0.0	14.3
Dunn	2,768	91.4	0.0	0.2	7.9	0.0	0.5	34	48	35	6	0.6	0.6	0.0	1.5	69.1	70.4	0.0	83.3	57.8	0.0	57.7
Eddy	2,213	98.3	0.0	<.1	1.6	0.0	<.1	44	35	36	13	0.5	0.5	0.0	0.3	75.0	75.1	0.0	100.0	73.5	0.0	25.0
Emmons	3,587	99.9	0.0	<.1	<.1	0.0	<.1	29	1	37	50	0.8	0.8	0.0	<.1	74.3	74.4	0.0	25.0	40.0	0.0	28.6
Foster	2,889	99.4	0.0	<.1	0.4	0.0	0.1	33	20	38	33	0.6	0.6	0.0	<.1	72.5	72.8	0.0	50.0	50.0	0.0	40.0
Golden Valley	1,457	99.2	0.0	0.4	0.4	0.0	0.0	51	23	39	31	0.3	0.3	0.0	<.1	69.1	69.2	0.0	75.0	50.0	0.0	0.0
Grand Forks	52,306	94.4	1.7	1.2	1.4	<.1	1.2	2	47	2	15	11.3	11.2	41.5	5.1	74.0	74.7	63.7	76.2	60.4	45.2	60.7
Grant	2,607	99.1	0.0	0.1	0.7	0.0	0.1	36	25	40	23	0.6	0.6	0.0	0.1	73.5	73.8	0.0	60.0	56.3	0.0	30.0
Griggs	2,446	99.6	0.0	0.1	0.2	0.0	0.1	39	15	41	41	0.5	0.6	0.0	<.1	74.1	74.1	0.0	60.0	50.0	0.0	75.0
Hettinger	2,545	99.8	0.0	<.1	<.1	0.0	<.1	38	3	42	52	0.5	0.6	0.0	<.1	73.9	74.1	0.0	16.7	14.3	0.0	66.7
Kidder	2,416	99.8	0.0	<.1	0.0	0.0	0.2	40	7	43	53	0.5	0.5	0.0	0.0	72.5	72.6	0.0	50.0	0.0	0.0	57.1
LaMoure	3,918	99.8	0.0	0.0	<.1	0.0	<.1	27	2	44	49	0.8	0.9	0.0	<.1	72.8	72.9	0.0	0.0	60.0	0.0	37.5
Logan	2,141	99.6	<.1	<.1	<.1	0.0	0.2	46	12	22	47	0.5	0.5	<.1	<.1	75.2	75.3	100.0	100.0	50.0	0.0	44.4
McHenry	4,758	99.6	<.1	<.1	0.2	0.0	0.1	20	16	18	40	1.0	1.1	0.2	<.1	72.9	73.0	100.0	60.0	61.5	0.0	46.2
McIntosh	3,148	99.6	<.1	0.1	0.1	0.0	0.2	32	17	26	46	0.7	0.7	<.1	<.1	78.3	78.3	100.0	66.7	66.7	0.0	83.3
McKenzie	4,272	88.0	<.1	<.1	11.3	0.0	0.6	26	49	29	5	0.9	0.9	<.1	3.4	66.9	69.3	50.0	66.7	53.9	0.0	48.1
McLean	7,404	95.4	<.1	<.1	4.3	<.1	0.2	14	45	27	7	1.6	1.6	<.1	2.2	70.8	71.7	66.7	33.3	57.4	100.0	44.7
Mercer	6,629	97.5	<.1	0.3	1.9	0.0	0.2	16	39	16	11	1.4	1.5	0.3	0.9	67.6	68.1	50.0	55.6	54.9	0.0	35.7
Morton	16,539	98.4	<.1	0.2	1.2	0.0	0.2	5	34	30	18	3.6	3.7	0.1	1.4	69.8	70.2	25.0	68.1	50.9	0.0	43.2
Mountrail	4,913	83.2	<.1	0.2	16.4	0.0	0.2	19	50	25	4	1.1	0.9	<.1	5.7	70.0	73.1	50.0	57.1	58.0	0.0	36.0
Nelson	3,383	99.8	0.0	<.1	<.1	0.0	<.1	30	6	45	48	0.7	0.8	0.0	<.1	76.7	76.9	0.0	33.3	50.0	0.0	37.5
Oliver	1,581	98.2	0.0	0.0	1.6	0.0	0.1	50	36	46	12	0.3	0.4	0.0	0.2	66.4	66.4	0.0	0.0	66.7	0.0	50.0
Pembina	6,647	97.4	0.2	<.1	1.5	0.0	0.8	15	40	9	14	1.4	1.5	0.5	0.7	72.0	72.1	71.4	50.0	67.1	0.0	64.4
Pierce	3,765	99.3	<.1	0.2	0.4	0.0	<.1	28	21	21	29	0.8	0.8	<.1	0.1	74.5	74.6	100.0	40.0	69.6	0.0	100.0
Ramsey	9,336	96.0	<.1	0.2	3.4	<.1	0.3	12	43	15	9	2.0	2.0	0.4	2.2	73.6	74.7	75.0	72.4	54.6	40.0	53.1
Ransom	4,390	99.3	<.1	<.1	0.2	0.0	0.4	25	22	19	38	0.9	1.0	0.1	<.1	74.1	74.3	75.0	28.6	69.2	0.0	66.7
Renville	2,287	98.6	0.3	0.3	0.7	0.0	0.1	42	30	3	22	0.5	0.5	0.3	0.1	72.9	72.6	42.9	72.7	69.6	0.0	50.0
Richland	13,231	98.1	0.1	0.4	1.1	<.1	0.2	9	37	11	19	2.9	2.9	0.8	1.0	72.9	73.8	81.0	72.0	35.8	25.0	63.0
Rolette	7,895	39.3	0.2	0.1	60.1	<.1	0.3	13	52	6	2	1.7	0.7	0.6	33.5	61.8	73.8	50.0	61.5	56.1	20.0	40.0
Sargent	3,325	99.5	0.0	<.1	0.3	0.0	0.1	31	18	47	35	0.7	0.7	0.0	<.1	73.1	73.2	0.0	40.0	90.0	0.0	40.0
Sheridan	1,632	99.7	0.0	<.1	0.2	0.0	0.0	49	9	48	36	0.4	0.4	0.0	<.1	76.0	76.1	0.0	100.0	44.4	0.0	0.0
Sioux	2,140	30.9	0.0	0.4	68.2	0.0	0.5	47	53	49	1	0.5	0.1	0.0	10.3	56.9	73.1	0.0	66.7	51.9	0.0	37.9
Slope	635	99.8	0.0	0.0	0.2	0.0	0.0	53	4	50	42	0.1	0.1	0.0	<.1	70.0	70.2	0.0	0.0	33.3	0.0	0.0
Stark	16,059	98.8	<.1	0.2	0.5	<.1	0.4	7	29	24	27	3.5	3.6	0.3	0.6	70.3	70.6	41.2	50.6	56.5	100.0	47.6
Steele	1,788	99.8	0.0	0.0	<.1	0.0	0.1	48	5	51	51	0.4	0.4	0.0	<.1	73.9	74.0	0.0	0.0	50.0	0.0	40.0
Stutsman	16,456	98.5	<.1	0.4	0.6	<.1	0.4	6	32	14	25	3.6	3.7	0.7	0.7	74.0	74.1	34.8	70.8	75.7	50.0	69.0
Towner	2,652	98.5	0.0	<.1	1.4	0.0	<.1	35	31	52	16	0.6	0.6	0.0	0.3	73.1	73.3	0.0	40.0	67.9	0.0	40.0
Traill	6,508	98.4	0.2	0.2	0.5	<.1	0.7	17	33	8	28	1.4	1.4	0.5	0.2	74.4	74.7	91.7	59.1	69.8	50.0	47.5
Walsh	10,023	96.8	<.1	0.3	0.6	0.0	2.1	10	42	13	26	2.2	2.2	0.5	0.4	72.4	73.4	58.8	63.0	61.9	0.0	48.3
Ward	41,669	94.5	2.1	0.9	1.3	<.1	1.2	4	46	1	17	9.0	8.9	41.1	3.8	71.9	72.7	64.3	64.8	56.7	27.8	59.2
Wells	4,430	99.7	0.0	<.1	0.1	0.0	<.1	24	8	53	45	1.0	1.0	0.0	<.1	75.5	75.6	0.0	66.7	100.0	0.0	57.1
Williams	14,803	95.6	<.1	0.2	3.8	<.1	0.3	8	44	20	8	3.2	3.2	0.4	4.0	70.1	70.9	44.4	69.0	56.2	100.0	45.5
NORTH DAKOTA	**463,415**	**95.4**	**0.5**	**0.5**	**3.1**	**<.1**	**0.6**					**100.0**	**100.0**	**100.0**	**100.0**	**72.5**	**73.5**	**62.9**	**69.2**	**55.4**	**39.5**	**55.2**
CONGRESSIONAL District At-Large	463,415	95.4	0.5	0.5	3.1	<.1	0.6									72.5	73.5	62.9	69.2	55.4	39.5	55.2

[1]Non-Hispanic Native American.

Table C. — Voter Participation: November 3, 1992, General Election

County	Estimated Voting Age Population (VAP), 1992	Voter registration (REG)[1]				Voter turnout													
							Highest office			Maximum vote						Percent drop-off, by office			
		Total	% contribution to state REG	% of 1992 VAP	Rank by % of 1992 VAP	Actual	Total	Office	% of 1992 VAP	Total	% contribution to state turnout	% of REG	Rank by % of REG	% of 1992 VAP	Rank by % 1992 VAP	President	Senator	Governor	Representative
Adams	2,295	-	-	-	-	1,685	1,626	P	70.8	1,685	0.5	-	-	73.4	27	3.5	6.4	4.6	7.9
Barnes	9,123	-	-	-	-	6,641	6,518	S	71.4	6,641	2.1	-	-	72.8	30	2.9	1.9	3.0	2.5
Benson	4,589	-	-	-	-	2,745	2,625	P	57.2	2,745	0.9	-	-	59.8	51	4.4	5.8	5.2	9.0
Billings	762	-	-	-	-	691	678	P	89.0	691	0.2	-	-	90.7	1	1.9	2.2	2.0	3.3
Bottineau	5,691	-	-	-	-	4,214	4,104	P	72.1	4,214	1.3	-	-	74.0	22	2.6	3.9	3.4	5.9
Bowman	2,526	-	-	-	-	1,938	1,907	P	75.5	1,938	0.6	-	-	76.7	13	1.6	2.7	2.6	4.5
Burke	2,184	-	-	-	-	1,554	1,524	P	69.8	1,554	0.5	-	-	71.2	33	1.9	3.7	2.7	5.2
Burleigh	43,927	-	-	-	-	33,680	32,384	P	73.7	33,680	10.7	-	-	76.7	14	3.8	7.8	8.0	12.3
Cass	78,398	-	-	-	-	53,611	53,116	P	67.8	53,611	17.0	-	-	68.4	43	0.9	2.2	1.4	2.4
Cavalier	4,232	-	-	-	-	3,179	3,126	P	73.9	3,179	1.0	-	-	75.1	20	1.7	2.5	3.9	5.5
Dickey	4,364	-	-	-	-	3,177	3,060	P	70.1	3,177	1.0	-	-	72.8	29	3.7	6.4	5.8	9.0
Divide	2,144	-	-	-	-	1,662	1,620	P	75.6	1,662	0.5	-	-	77.5	11	2.5	2.6	3.5	5.2
Dunn	2,659	-	-	-	-	2,146	2,108	S	79.3	2,146	0.7	-	-	80.7	4	1.9	1.8	1.9	3.6
Eddy	2,131	-	-	-	-	1,662	1,618	S	75.9	1,662	0.5	-	-	78.0	9	2.8	2.6	3.6	4.2
Emmons	3,414	-	-	-	-	2,508	2,441	S	71.5	2,508	0.8	-	-	73.5	26	3.1	2.7	3.7	5.5
Foster	2,783	-	-	-	-	1,989	1,940	P	69.7	1,989	0.6	-	-	71.5	31	2.5	4.9	3.4	6.6
Golden Valley	1,454	-	-	-	-	1,137	1,114	P	76.6	1,137	0.4	-	-	78.2	7	2.0	3.6	3.1	7.5
Grand Forks	51,482	-	-	-	-	31,412	31,104	P	60.4	31,412	10.0	-	-	61.0	50	1.0	3.5	2.8	5.4
Grant	2,504	-	-	-	-	1,997	1,959	P	78.2	1,997	0.6	-	-	79.8	5	1.9	2.5	2.9	4.4
Griggs	2,415	-	-	-	-	1,853	1,766	G	73.1	1,853	0.6	-	-	76.7	12	5.2	6.2	4.7	8.1
Hettinger	2,430	-	-	-	-	1,900	1,853	G	76.3	1,900	0.6	-	-	78.2	8	3.3	3.6	2.5	5.5
Kidder	2,367	-	-	-	-	1,749	1,719	S	72.6	1,749	0.6	-	-	73.9	25	2.2	1.7	3.1	3.7
LaMoure	3,810	-	-	-	-	2,818	2,763	P	72.5	2,818	0.9	-	-	74.0	24	2.0	2.8	2.4	4.9
Logan	2,058	-	-	-	-	1,553	1,497	S	72.7	1,553	0.5	-	-	75.5	17	4.3	3.6	5.0	6.3
McHenry	4,633	-	-	-	-	3,507	3,401	G	73.4	3,507	1.1	-	-	75.7	16	3.2	5.0	3.0	6.6
McIntosh	3,006	-	-	-	-	2,132	2,054	P	68.3	2,132	0.7	-	-	70.9	35	3.7	4.6	4.0	8.1
McKenzie	4,205	-	-	-	-	3,158	3,090	P	73.5	3,158	1.0	-	-	75.1	21	2.2	4.0	2.7	5.8
McLean	7,235	-	-	-	-	5,505	5,370	S	74.2	5,505	1.7	-	-	76.1	15	3.7	2.5	3.3	5.0
Mercer	6,752	-	-	-	-	5,087	5,017	P	74.3	5,087	1.6	-	-	75.3	19	1.4	2.7	2.2	2.5
Morton	16,404	-	-	-	-	11,945	11,670	S	71.1	11,945	3.8	-	-	72.8	28	3.5	2.3	3.1	6.0
Mountrail	4,864	-	-	-	-	3,389	3,289	P	67.6	3,389	1.1	-	-	69.7	39	3.0	3.8	3.4	5.8
Nelson	3,264	-	-	-	-	2,296	2,223	S	68.1	2,296	0.7	-	-	70.3	36	3.9	3.2	4.1	6.6
Oliver	1,613	-	-	-	-	1,256	1,245	S	77.2	1,256	0.4	-	-	77.9	10	2.2	0.9	1.4	1.4
Pembina	6,568	-	-	-	-	4,247	4,146	S	63.1	4,247	1.3	-	-	64.7	47	2.8	2.4	2.9	5.6
Pierce	3,587	-	-	-	-	2,505	2,431	P	67.8	2,505	0.8	-	-	69.8	37	3.0	4.4	3.8	6.9
Ramsey	9,166	-	-	-	-	6,216	6,054	P	66.0	6,216	2.0	-	-	67.8	44	2.6	3.7	3.0	4.1
Ransom	4,259	-	-	-	-	2,956	2,903	P	68.2	2,956	0.9	-	-	69.4	41	1.8	2.7	2.1	4.2
Renville	2,273	-	-	-	-	1,714	1,670	P	73.5	1,714	0.5	-	-	75.4	18	2.6	4.0	3.9	5.8
Richland	12,645	-	-	-	-	8,436	8,301	P	65.6	8,436	2.7	-	-	66.7	45	1.6	3.8	2.9	6.4
Rolette	8,031	-	-	-	-	3,743	3,643	S	45.4	3,743	1.2	-	-	46.6	52	3.7	2.7	5.0	7.3
Sargent	3,207	-	-	-	-	2,284	2,254	P	70.3	2,284	0.7	-	-	71.2	32	1.3	2.5	1.8	3.7
Sheridan	1,551	-	-	-	-	1,221	1,175	P	75.8	1,221	0.4	-	-	78.7	6	3.8	5.2	5.1	4.3
Sioux	2,204	-	-	-	-	1,013	987	S	44.8	1,013	0.3	-	-	46.0	53	2.9	2.6	3.3	4.6
Slope	633	-	-	-	-	552	543	S	85.8	552	0.2	-	-	87.2	2	3.1	1.6	3.3	4.0
Stark	15,733	-	-	-	-	10,793	10,678	P	67.9	10,793	3.4	-	-	68.6	42	1.1	1.3	1.9	2.9
Steele	1,721	-	-	-	-	1,414	1,383	G	80.4	1,414	0.4	-	-	82.2	3	3.1	4.0	2.2	5.9
Stutsman	15,987	-	-	-	-	10,356	10,001	P	62.6	10,356	3.3	-	-	64.8	46	3.4	3.8	4.1	6.9
Towner	2,605	-	-	-	-	1,816	1,757	P	67.4	1,816	0.6	-	-	69.7	38	3.2	5.2	4.8	8.6
Traill	6,321	-	-	-	-	4,678	4,558	G	72.1	4,678	1.5	-	-	74.0	23	2.7	3.2	2.6	5.2
Walsh	9,825	-	-	-	-	6,077	5,937	S	60.4	6,077	1.9	-	-	61.9	49	2.8	2.3	2.8	5.4
Ward	41,036	-	-	-	-	26,181	25,852	P	63.0	26,181	8.3	-	-	63.8	48	1.3	3.6	2.0	3.6
Wells	4,273	-	-	-	-	3,035	2,916	P	68.2	3,035	1.0	-	-	71.0	34	3.9	5.1	4.0	7.1
Williams	14,657	-	-	-	-	10,186	9,946	S	67.9	10,186	3.2	-	-	69.5	40	2.6	2.4	2.8	5.2
NORTH DAKOTA	**458,000**	-	-	-	-	**315,199**	**308,664**		**67.4**	**315,199**	**100.0**	-		**68.8**		**2.2**	**3.6**	**3.3**	**5.5**

[1]No voter registration requirement.

Table E. – Vote for President: November 3, 1992, General Election

County	Total	Clinton (DEM)	Bush (REP)	Perot (IND)	Other	Plurality Total	Party	DEM	REP	IND	Other	Rank DEM	Rank REP	Rank IND	Total	DEM	REP	IND	DEM	REP
Adams	1,626	469	647	499	11	148	R	28.8	39.8	30.7	0.7	35	36	10	0.5	0.5	0.5	0.7	42.0	58.0
Barnes	6,449	2,124	2,728	1,568	29	604	R	32.9	42.3	24.3	0.4	21	26	32	2.1	2.1	2.0	2.2	43.8	56.2
Benson	2,625	1,126	874	610	15	252	D	42.9	33.3	23.2	0.6	4	49	36	0.9	1.1	0.6	0.9	56.3	43.7
Billings	678	123	279	270	6	9	R	18.1	41.2	39.8	0.9	53	31	1	0.2	0.1	0.2	0.4	30.6	69.4
Bottineau	4,104	1,266	1,787	1,036	15	521	R	30.8	43.5	25.2	0.4	27	21	27	1.3	1.3	1.3	1.5	41.5	58.5
Bowman	1,907	506	712	678	11	34	R	26.5	37.3	35.6	0.6	42	41	2	0.6	0.5	0.5	1.0	41.5	58.5
Burke	1,524	458	551	506	9	45	R	30.1	36.2	33.2	0.6	31	47	3	0.5	0.5	0.4	0.7	45.4	54.6
Burleigh	32,384	8,940	16,484	6,780	180	7,544	R	27.6	50.9	20.9	0.6	39	2	44	10.5	9.0	12.1	9.5	35.2	64.8
Cass	53,116	18,077	25,312	9,513	214	7,235	R	34.0	47.7	17.9	0.4	18	6	53	17.2	18.2	18.6	13.4	41.7	58.3
Cavalier	3,126	866	1,527	723	10	661	R	27.7	48.8	23.1	0.3	38	5	37	1.0	0.9	1.1	1.0	36.2	63.8
Dickey	3,060	918	1,514	616	12	596	R	30.0	49.5	20.1	0.4	32	4	48	1.0	0.9	1.1	0.9	37.7	62.3
Divide	1,620	634	515	456	15	119	D	39.1	31.8	28.1	0.9	9	50	17	0.5	0.6	0.4	0.6	55.2	44.8
Dunn	2,105	667	784	637	17	117	R	31.7	37.2	30.3	0.8	24	42	12	0.7	0.7	0.6	0.9	46.0	54.0
Eddy	1,615	575	591	432	17	16	R	35.6	36.6	26.7	1.1	13	45	20	0.5	0.6	0.4	0.6	49.3	50.7
Emmons	2,430	595	1,047	774	14	273	R	24.5	43.1	31.9	0.6	48	24	7	0.8	0.6	0.8	1.1	36.2	63.8
Foster	1,940	565	803	556	16	238	R	29.1	41.4	28.7	0.8	33	30	15	0.6	0.6	0.6	0.8	41.3	58.7
Golden Valley	1,114	255	503	352	4	151	R	22.9	45.2	31.6	0.4	50	16	8	0.4	0.3	0.4	0.5	33.6	66.4
Grand Forks	31,104	10,930	13,705	6,349	120	2,775	R	35.1	44.1	20.4	0.4	14	18	47	10.1	11.0	10.1	8.9	44.4	55.6
Grant	1,959	415	900	629	15	271	R	21.2	45.9	32.1	0.8	52	13	5	0.6	0.4	0.7	0.9	31.6	68.4
Griggs	1,756	647	773	330	6	126	R	36.8	44.0	18.8	0.3	11	19	51	0.6	0.7	0.6	0.5	45.6	54.4
Hettinger	1,838	465	854	500	19	354	R	25.3	46.5	27.2	1.0	46	10	19	0.6	0.5	0.6	0.7	35.3	64.7
Kidder	1,711	468	739	489	15	250	R	27.4	43.2	28.6	0.9	40	22	16	0.6	0.5	0.5	0.7	38.8	61.2
LaMoure	2,763	797	1,270	679	17	473	R	28.8	46.0	24.6	0.6	34	12	31	0.9	0.8	0.9	1.0	38.6	61.4
Logan	1,486	383	703	390	10	313	R	25.8	47.3	26.2	0.7	44	7	21	0.5	0.4	0.5	0.5	35.3	64.7
McHenry	3,396	1,173	1,321	886	16	148	R	34.5	38.9	26.1	0.5	16	39	23	1.1	1.2	1.0	1.2	47.0	53.0
McIntosh	2,054	450	1,134	454	16	680	R	21.9	55.2	22.1	0.8	51	1	41	0.7	0.5	0.8	0.6	28.4	71.6
McKenzie	3,090	787	1,324	969	10	355	R	25.5	42.8	31.4	0.3	45	25	9	1.0	0.8	1.0	1.4	37.3	62.7
McLean	5,303	1,808	2,124	1,330	41	316	R	34.1	40.1	25.1	0.8	17	35	28	1.7	1.8	1.6	1.9	46.0	54.0
Mercer	5,017	1,323	2,274	1,378	42	896	R	26.4	45.3	27.5	0.8	43	14	18	1.6	1.3	1.7	1.9	36.8	63.2
Morton	11,522	3,594	5,042	2,787	99	1,448	R	31.2	43.8	24.2	0.9	26	20	33	3.7	3.6	3.7	3.9	41.6	58.4
Mountrail	3,289	1,393	1,017	861	18	376	D	42.4	30.9	26.2	0.5	7	51	22	1.1	1.4	0.7	1.2	57.8	42.2
Nelson	2,206	841	864	486	15	23	R	38.1	39.2	22.0	0.7	10	38	42	0.7	0.8	0.6	0.7	49.3	50.7
Oliver	1,228	306	503	407	12	96	R	24.9	41.0	33.1	1.0	47	32	4	0.4	0.3	0.4	0.6	37.8	62.2
Pembina	4,127	1,186	1,917	991	33	731	R	28.7	46.5	24.0	0.8	36	11	34	1.3	1.2	1.4	1.4	38.2	61.8
Pierce	2,431	761	1,099	554	17	338	R	31.3	45.2	22.8	0.7	25	15	39	0.8	0.8	0.8	0.8	40.9	59.1
Ramsey	6,054	2,008	2,516	1,507	23	508	R	33.2	41.6	24.9	0.4	19	29	29	2.0	2.0	1.8	2.1	44.4	55.6
Ransom	2,903	1,166	1,102	625	10	64	D	40.2	38.0	21.5	0.3	8	40	43	0.9	1.2	0.8	0.9	51.4	48.6
Renville	1,670	580	655	429	6	75	R	34.7	39.2	25.7	0.4	15	37	26	0.5	0.6	0.5	0.6	47.0	53.0
Richland	8,301	2,688	3,873	1,698	42	1,185	R	32.4	46.7	20.5	0.5	23	8	46	2.7	2.7	2.8	2.4	41.0	59.0
Rolette	3,606	2,002	895	660	49	1,107	D	55.5	24.8	18.3	1.4	1	53	52	1.2	2.0	0.7	0.9	69.1	30.9
Sargent	2,254	961	816	463	14	145	D	42.6	36.2	20.5	0.6	5	46	45	0.7	1.0	0.6	0.7	54.1	45.9
Sheridan	1,175	276	589	304	6	285	R	23.5	50.1	25.9	0.5	49	3	24	0.4	0.3	0.4	0.4	31.9	68.1
Sioux	984	463	264	244	13	199	D	47.1	26.8	24.8	1.3	2	52	30	0.3	0.5	0.2	0.3	63.7	36.3
Slope	535	145	226	162	2	64	R	27.1	42.2	30.3	0.4	41	27	11	0.2	0.1	0.2	0.2	39.1	60.9
Stark	10,678	3,003	4,491	3,123	61	1,368	R	28.1	42.1	29.2	0.6	37	28	13	3.5	3.0	3.3	4.4	40.1	59.9
Steele	1,370	598	503	267	2	95	D	43.6	36.7	19.5	0.1	3	44	49	0.4	0.6	0.4	0.4	54.3	45.7
Stutsman	10,001	3,313	4,039	2,580	69	726	R	33.1	40.4	25.8	0.7	20	33	25	3.2	3.3	3.0	3.6	45.1	54.9
Towner	1,757	748	600	402	7	148	D	42.6	34.1	22.9	0.4	6	48	38	0.6	0.8	0.4	0.6	55.5	44.5
Traill	4,553	1,638	2,019	875	21	381	R	36.0	44.3	19.2	0.5	12	17	50	1.5	1.7	1.5	1.2	44.8	55.2
Walsh	5,904	1,936	2,544	1,384	40	608	R	32.8	43.1	23.4	0.7	22	23	35	1.9	2.0	1.9	1.9	43.2	56.8
Ward	25,852	7,856	12,056	5,856	84	4,200	R	30.4	46.6	22.7	0.3	29	9	40	8.4	7.9	8.8	8.2	39.5	60.5
Wells	2,916	888	1,171	850	7	283	R	30.5	40.2	29.1	0.2	28	34	14	0.9	0.9	0.9	1.2	43.1	56.9
Williams	9,917	3,008	3,664	3,180	65	484	R	30.3	36.9	32.1	0.7	30	43	6	3.2	3.0	2.7	4.5	45.1	54.9
NORTH DAKOTA	**308,133**	**99,168**	**136,244**	**71,084**	**1,637**	**37,076**	**R**	**32.2**	**44.2**	**23.1**	**0.5**				**100.0**	**100.0**	**100.0**	**100.0**	**42.1**	**57.9**

Table F. — Vote for U.S. Senator: November 3, 1992, General Election

County	Total	Dorgan (DEM)	Sydness (REP)	Asbridge (IND)¹	Plurality Total	Plurality Party	Percent of total vote DEM	REP	IND	Rank DEM	REP	IND	% contribution Total	DEM	REP	IND
Adams	1,578	928	594	56	334	D	58.8	37.6	3.5	28	33	7	0.5	0.5	0.5	0.9
Barnes	6,518	3,957	2,452	109	1,505	D	60.7	37.6	1.7	18	34	34	2.1	2.2	2.1	1.7
Benson	2,585	1,756	792	37	964	D	67.9	30.6	1.4	7	46	48	0.9	1.0	0.7	0.6
Billings	676	363	280	33	83	D	53.7	41.4	4.9	48	13	2	0.2	0.2	0.2	0.5
Bottineau	4,049	2,473	1,511	65	962	D	61.1	37.3	1.6	17	36	40	1.3	1.4	1.3	1.0
Bowman	1,885	1,098	716	71	382	D	58.2	38.0	3.8	30	32	6	0.6	0.6	0.6	1.1
Burke	1,497	986	486	25	500	D	65.9	32.5	1.7	12	42	35	0.5	0.5	0.4	0.4
Burleigh	31,065	16,916	13,277	872	3,639	D	54.5	42.7	2.8	45	6	13	10.2	9.4	11.2	13.5
Cass	52,414	31,179	20,420	815	10,759	D	59.5	39.0	1.6	24	25	44	17.2	17.4	17.3	12.6
Cavalier	3,100	1,845	1,197	58	648	D	59.5	38.6	1.9	23	28	31	1.0	1.0	1.0	0.9
Dickey	2,975	1,600	1,332	43	268	D	53.8	44.8	1.4	47	5	47	1.0	0.9	1.1	0.7
Divide	1,618	1,127	460	31	667	D	69.7	28.4	1.9	6	49	30	0.5	0.6	0.4	0.5
Dunn	2,108	1,247	813	48	434	D	59.2	38.6	2.3	27	29	21	0.7	0.7	0.7	0.7
Eddy	1,618	939	628	51	311	D	58.0	38.8	3.2	32	26	9	0.5	0.5	0.5	0.8
Emmons	2,441	1,258	1,099	84	159	D	51.5	45.0	3.4	50	4	8	0.8	0.7	0.9	1.3
Foster	1,892	1,091	762	39	329	D	57.7	40.3	2.1	35	16	28	0.6	0.6	0.6	0.6
Golden Valley	1,096	612	458	26	154	D	55.8	41.8	2.4	43	8	16	0.4	0.3	0.4	0.4
Grand Forks	30,305	17,506	12,201	598	5,305	D	57.8	40.3	2.0	33	17	29	10.0	9.8	10.3	9.3
Grant	1,948	1,002	813	133	189	D	51.4	41.7	6.8	51	9	1	0.6	0.6	0.7	2.1
Griggs	1,738	1,069	647	22	422	D	61.5	37.2	1.3	15	38	51	0.6	0.6	0.5	0.3
Hettinger	1,832	1,068	725	39	343	D	58.3	39.6	2.1	29	22	25	0.6	0.6	0.6	0.6
Kidder	1,719	926	710	83	216	D	53.9	41.3	4.8	46	14	3	0.6	0.5	0.6	1.3
LaMoure	2,740	1,555	1,141	44	414	D	56.8	41.6	1.6	39	11	39	0.9	0.9	1.0	0.7
Logan	1,497	776	676	45	100	D	51.8	45.2	3.0	49	3	12	0.5	0.4	0.6	0.7
McHenry	3,332	2,121	1,161	50	960	D	63.7	34.8	1.5	13	41	46	1.1	1.2	1.0	0.8
McIntosh	2,034	868	1,123	43	255	R	42.7	55.2	2.1	53	1	26	0.7	0.5	1.0	0.7
McKenzie	3,033	1,746	1,218	69	528	D	57.6	40.2	2.3	37	19	22	1.0	1.0	1.0	1.1
McLean	5,370	3,202	2,041	127	1,161	D	59.6	38.0	2.4	20	31	17	1.8	1.8	1.7	2.0
Mercer	4,949	2,835	1,998	116	837	D	57.3	40.4	2.3	38	15	19	1.6	1.6	1.7	1.8
Morton	11,670	6,930	4,389	351	2,541	D	59.4	37.6	3.0	25	35	11	3.8	3.9	3.7	5.4
Mountrail	3,259	2,273	914	72	1,359	D	69.7	28.0	2.2	5	51	23	1.1	1.3	0.8	1.1
Nelson	2,223	1,508	684	31	824	D	67.8	30.8	1.4	9	45	49	0.7	0.8	0.6	0.5
Oliver	1,245	743	464	38	279	D	59.7	37.3	3.1	19	37	10	0.4	0.4	0.4	0.6
Pembina	4,146	2,390	1,667	89	723	D	57.6	40.2	2.1	36	18	24	1.4	1.3	1.4	1.4
Pierce	2,394	1,334	1,022	38	312	D	55.7	42.7	1.6	44	7	41	0.8	0.7	0.9	0.6
Ramsey	5,989	3,675	2,220	94	1,455	D	61.4	37.1	1.6	16	39	43	2.0	2.0	1.9	1.5
Ransom	2,876	1,952	876	48	1,076	D	67.9	30.5	1.7	8	47	36	0.9	1.1	0.7	0.7
Renville	1,646	1,104	516	26	588	D	67.1	31.3	1.6	10	44	42	0.5	0.6	0.4	0.4
Richland	8,116	4,838	3,144	134	1,694	D	59.6	38.7	1.7	21	27	37	2.7	2.7	2.7	2.1
Rolette	3,643	2,789	789	65	2,000	D	76.6	21.7	1.8	1	53	32	1.2	1.6	0.7	1.0
Sargent	2,226	1,470	718	38	752	D	66.0	32.3	1.7	11	43	33	0.7	0.8	0.6	0.6
Sheridan	1,158	527	612	19	85	R	45.5	52.8	1.6	52	2	38	0.4	0.3	0.5	0.3
Sioux	987	708	239	40	469	D	71.7	24.2	4.1	2	52	4	0.3	0.4	0.2	0.6
Slope	543	306	215	22	91	D	56.4	39.6	4.1	40	21	5	0.2	0.2	0.2	0.3
Stark	10,649	6,199	4,186	264	2,013	D	58.2	39.3	2.5	31	23	14	3.5	3.5	3.5	4.1
Steele	1,358	955	385	18	570	D	70.3	28.4	1.3	4	50	50	0.4	0.5	0.3	0.3
Stutsman	9,960	5,594	4,127	239	1,467	D	56.2	41.4	2.4	41	12	15	3.3	3.1	3.5	3.7
Towner	1,722	1,211	490	21	721	D	70.3	28.5	1.2	3	48	52	0.6	0.7	0.4	0.3
Traill	4,530	2,883	1,595	52	1,288	D	63.6	35.2	1.1	14	40	53	1.5	1.6	1.3	0.8
Walsh	5,937	3,520	2,325	92	1,195	D	59.3	39.2	1.5	26	24	45	2.0	2.0	2.0	1.4
Ward	25,243	15,040	9,676	527	5,364	D	59.6	38.3	2.1	22	30	27	8.3	8.4	8.2	8.2
Wells	2,879	1,612	1,199	68	413	D	56.0	41.6	2.4	42	10	18	0.9	0.9	1.0	1.1
Williams	9,946	5,737	3,979	230	1,758	D	57.7	40.0	2.3	34	20	20	3.3	3.2	3.4	3.6
NORTH DAKOTA	303,957	179,347	118,162	6,448	61,185	D	59.0	38.9	2.1				100.0	100.0	100.0	100.0

¹Independent candidate Asbridge was the only minor candidate (only three candidates on ballot).

Table F2. — Vote for U.S. Senator, December 4, 1992, Special Election[1]

County	Total	Conrad (DEM)	Dalrymple (REP)	Larson (IND)[2]	Plurality Total	Party	DEM	REP	IND	Rank DEM	Rank REP	Rank IND	Total	DEM	REP	IND
Adams	787	503	281	3	222	D	63.9	35.7	0.4	24	21	53	0.5	0.5	0.5	<.1
Barnes	3,742	2,402	1,206	134	1,196	D	64.2	32.2	3.6	23	31	13	2.3	2.3	2.2	2.8
Benson	1,666	1,192	411	63	781	D	71.5	24.7	3.8	5	50	12	1.0	1.2	0.7	1.3
Billings	381	182	184	15	2	R	47.8	48.3	3.9	51	3	10	0.2	0.2	0.3	0.3
Bottineau	2,336	1,500	770	66	730	D	64.2	33.0	2.8	22	29	24	1.4	1.5	1.4	1.4
Bowman	989	627	339	23	288	D	63.4	34.3	2.3	26	25	34	0.6	0.6	0.6	0.5
Burke	916	620	287	9	333	D	67.7	31.3	1.0	15	34	52	0.6	0.6	0.5	0.2
Burleigh	17,318	9,587	7,364	367	2,223	D	55.4	42.5	2.1	46	7	41	10.6	9.3	13.3	7.5
Cass	26,502	16,053	9,600	849	6,453	D	60.6	36.2	3.2	37	18	14	16.2	15.5	17.4	17.4
Cavalier	2,133	1,276	681	176	595	D	59.8	31.9	8.3	39	32	1	1.3	1.2	1.2	3.6
Dickey	1,674	968	641	65	327	D	57.8	38.3	3.9	43	13	11	1.0	0.9	1.2	1.3
Divide	1,016	741	252	23	489	D	72.9	24.8	2.3	3	49	37	0.6	0.7	0.5	0.5
Dunn	1,249	759	467	23	292	D	60.8	37.4	1.8	36	15	45	0.8	0.7	0.8	0.5
Eddy	1,024	653	311	60	342	D	63.8	30.4	5.9	25	37	2	0.6	0.6	0.6	1.2
Emmons	1,422	790	596	36	194	D	55.6	41.9	2.5	45	9	31	0.9	0.8	1.1	0.7
Foster	1,273	698	552	23	146	D	54.8	43.4	1.8	47	6	46	0.8	0.7	1.0	0.5
Golden Valley	609	378	217	14	161	D	62.1	35.6	2.3	31	23	35	0.4	0.4	0.4	0.3
Grand Forks	15,692	10,737	4,480	475	6,257	D	68.4	28.5	3.0	13	41	20	9.6	10.4	8.1	9.8
Grant	1,197	631	532	34	99	D	52.7	44.4	2.8	49	5	23	0.7	0.6	1.0	0.7
Griggs	1,216	761	407	48	354	D	62.6	33.5	3.9	29	27	9	0.7	0.7	0.7	1.0
Hettinger	1,069	629	417	23	212	D	58.8	39.0	2.2	41	12	40	0.7	0.6	0.8	0.5
Kidder	1,054	575	447	32	128	D	54.6	42.4	3.0	48	8	19	0.6	0.6	0.8	0.7
LaMoure	1,784	1,068	659	57	409	D	59.9	36.9	3.2	38	16	15	1.1	1.0	1.2	1.2
Logan	964	505	437	22	68	D	52.4	45.3	2.3	50	4	36	0.6	0.5	0.8	0.5
McHenry	2,155	1,537	553	65	984	D	71.3	25.7	3.0	7	46	22	1.3	1.5	1.0	1.3
McIntosh	1,195	530	640	25	110	R	44.4	53.6	2.1	52	2	42	0.7	0.5	1.2	0.5
McKenzie	1,675	1,050	597	28	453	D	62.7	35.6	1.7	28	22	48	1.0	1.0	1.1	0.6
McLean	3,468	2,133	1,245	90	888	D	61.5	35.9	2.6	34	20	29	2.1	2.1	2.3	1.8
Mercer	2,610	1,556	997	57	559	D	59.6	38.2	2.2	40	14	39	1.6	1.5	1.8	1.2
Morton	5,510	3,397	1,979	134	1,418	D	61.7	35.9	2.4	33	19	33	3.4	3.3	3.6	2.8
Mountrail	1,845	1,394	399	52	995	D	75.6	21.6	2.8	2	52	25	1.1	1.4	0.7	1.1
Nelson	1,590	1,124	417	49	707	D	70.7	26.2	3.1	10	45	16	1.0	1.1	0.8	1.0
Oliver	709	410	287	12	123	D	57.8	40.5	1.7	42	10	47	0.4	0.4	0.5	0.2
Pembina	2,275	1,413	760	102	653	D	62.1	33.4	4.5	30	28	7	1.4	1.4	1.4	2.1
Pierce	1,396	920	411	65	509	D	65.9	29.4	4.7	18	40	6	0.9	0.9	0.7	1.3
Ramsey	3,131	2,128	857	146	1,271	D	68.0	27.4	4.7	14	42	5	1.9	2.1	1.6	3.0
Ransom	1,769	1,258	472	39	786	D	71.1	26.7	2.2	9	44	38	1.1	1.2	0.9	0.8
Renville	1,092	792	267	33	525	D	72.5	24.5	3.0	4	51	21	0.7	0.8	0.5	0.7
Richland	4,268	2,608	1,442	218	1,166	D	61.1	33.8	5.1	35	26	3	2.6	2.5	2.6	4.5
Rolette	1,709	1,321	336	52	985	D	77.3	19.7	3.0	1	53	18	1.0	1.3	0.6	1.1
Sargent	1,490	1,001	465	24	536	D	67.2	31.2	1.6	17	35	50	0.9	1.0	0.8	0.5
Sheridan	828	359	448	21	89	R	43.4	54.1	2.5	53	1	30	0.5	0.3	0.8	0.4
Sioux	374	256	113	5	143	D	68.4	30.2	1.3	12	38	51	0.2	0.2	0.2	0.1
Slope	344	216	119	9	97	D	62.8	34.6	2.6	27	24	28	0.2	0.2	0.2	0.2
Stark	4,822	2,979	1,747	96	1,232	D	61.8	36.2	2.0	32	17	43	3.0	2.9	3.2	2.0
Steele	1,021	729	275	17	454	D	71.4	26.9	1.7	6	43	49	0.6	0.7	0.5	0.3
Stutsman	5,330	3,511	1,678	141	1,833	D	65.9	31.5	2.6	19	33	27	3.3	3.4	3.0	2.9
Towner	1,110	783	279	48	504	D	70.5	25.1	4.3	11	48	8	0.7	0.8	0.5	1.0
Traill	2,824	1,827	927	70	900	D	64.7	32.8	2.5	21	30	32	1.7	1.8	1.7	1.4
Walsh	3,098	2,022	923	153	1,099	D	65.3	29.8	4.9	20	39	4	1.9	2.0	1.7	3.1
Ward	11,399	8,128	2,922	349	5,206	D	71.3	25.6	3.1	8	47	17	7.0	7.9	5.3	7.2
Wells	1,814	1,032	733	49	299	D	56.9	40.4	2.7	44	11	26	1.1	1.0	1.3	1.0
Williams	4,447	2,997	1,368	82	1,629	D	67.4	30.8	1.8	16	36	44	2.7	2.9	2.5	1.7
NORTH DAKOTA	163,311	103,246	55,194	4,871	48,052	D	63.2	33.8	3.0				100.0	100.0	100.0	100.0

[1]For remaining two years of term of the late Senator Quentin Burdick (D).   [2]Independent candidate Larson was the only minor candidate (only three candidates on ballot).

Table G. – **Vote for Governor: November 3, 1992, General Election**

County	Total	Spaeth (DEM)	Schafer (REP)	Other	Plurality Total	Party	DEM	REP	Other	Rank DEM	Rank REP	Rank Other	Total	DEM	REP	Other
Adams	1,608	638	948	22	310	R	39.7	59.0	1.4	37	17	37	0.5	0.5	0.5	0.5
Barnes	6,442	2,795	3,453	194	658	R	43.4	53.6	3.0	23	37	2	2.1	2.3	2.0	4.2
Benson	2,603	1,225	1,328	50	103	R	47.1	51.0	1.9	10	44	7	0.9	1.0	0.8	1.1
Billings	677	295	364	18	69	R	43.6	53.8	2.7	19	36	3	0.2	0.2	0.2	0.4
Bottineau	4,070	1,769	2,242	59	473	R	43.5	55.1	1.4	20	32	34	1.3	1.4	1.3	1.3
Bowman	1,887	769	1,082	36	313	R	40.8	57.3	1.9	34	23	8	0.6	0.6	0.6	0.8
Burke	1,512	704	781	27	77	R	46.6	51.7	1.8	11	42	14	0.5	0.6	0.4	0.6
Burleigh	30,977	9,452	21,144	381	11,692	R	30.5	68.3	1.2	52	3	44	10.2	7.6	12.0	8.3
Cass	52,843	22,338	29,948	557	7,610	R	42.3	56.7	1.1	26	27	50	17.3	18.0	17.0	12.1
Cavalier	3,056	1,013	1,985	58	972	R	33.1	65.0	1.9	47	8	10	1.0	0.8	1.1	1.3
Dickey	2,994	1,223	1,727	44	504	R	40.8	57.7	1.5	33	21	33	1.0	1.0	1.0	1.0
Divide	1,603	826	756	21	70	D	51.5	47.2	1.3	6	48	42	0.5	0.7	0.4	0.5
Dunn	2,105	861	1,212	32	351	R	40.9	57.6	1.5	32	22	28	0.7	0.7	0.7	0.7
Eddy	1,602	696	887	19	191	R	43.4	55.4	1.2	21	29	47	0.5	0.6	0.5	0.4
Emmons	2,415	912	1,470	33	558	R	37.8	60.9	1.4	40	13	38	0.6	0.6	0.7	0.7
Foster	1,922	733	1,158	31	425	R	38.1	60.2	1.6	39	15	22	0.6	0.6	0.7	0.7
Golden Valley	1,102	447	638	17	191	R	40.6	57.9	1.5	35	19	25	0.4	0.4	0.4	0.4
Grand Forks	30,525	11,790	18,279	456	6,489	R	38.6	59.9	1.5	38	16	31	10.0	9.5	10.4	9.9
Grant	1,940	617	1,289	34	672	R	31.8	66.4	1.8	50	6	16	0.6	0.5	0.7	0.7
Griggs	1,766	822	923	21	101	R	46.5	52.3	1.2	12	41	46	0.6	0.7	0.5	0.5
Hettinger	1,853	765	1,072	16	307	R	41.3	57.9	0.9	31	20	52	0.6	0.6	0.6	0.3
Kidder	1,694	564	1,104	26	540	R	33.3	65.2	1.5	45	7	26	0.6	0.5	0.6	0.6
LaMoure	2,750	1,140	1,569	41	429	R	41.5	57.1	1.5	30	24	32	0.9	0.9	0.9	0.9
Logan	1,475	476	983	16	507	R	32.3	66.6	1.1	48	4	48	0.5	0.4	0.6	0.3
McHenry	3,401	1,663	1,678	60	15	R	48.9	49.3	1.8	8	46	15	1.1	1.3	1.0	1.3
McIntosh	2,046	633	1,397	16	764	R	30.9	68.3	0.8	51	2	53	0.7	0.5	0.8	0.3
McKenzie	3,072	1,288	1,751	33	463	R	41.9	57.0	1.1	27	25	49	1.0	1.0	1.0	0.7
McLean	5,323	2,291	2,942	90	651	R	43.0	55.3	1.7	25	30	20	1.7	1.8	1.7	1.9
Mercer	4,974	1,719	3,177	78	1,458	R	34.6	63.9	1.6	44	10	23	1.6	1.4	1.8	1.7
Morton	11,580	4,074	7,351	155	3,277	R	35.2	63.5	1.3	43	11	40	3.8	3.3	4.2	3.4
Mountrail	3,273	1,734	1,473	66	261	D	53.0	45.0	2.0	4	51	5	1.1	1.4	0.8	1.4
Nelson	2,202	1,001	1,172	29	171	R	45.5	53.2	1.3	14	39	41	0.7	0.8	0.7	0.6
Oliver	1,238	412	803	23	391	R	33.3	64.9	1.9	46	9	12	0.4	0.3	0.5	0.5
Pembina	4,122	1,324	2,747	51	1,423	R	32.1	66.6	1.2	49	5	43	1.4	1.1	1.6	1.1
Pierce	2,410	1,047	1,330	33	283	R	43.4	55.2	1.4	22	31	36	0.8	0.8	0.8	0.7
Ramsey	6,029	2,519	3,418	92	899	R	41.8	56.7	1.5	28	26	27	2.0	2.0	1.9	2.0
Ransom	2,893	1,444	1,410	39	34	D	49.9	48.7	1.3	7	47	39	0.9	1.2	0.8	0.8
Renville	1,648	765	850	33	85	R	46.4	51.6	2.0	13	43	6	0.5	0.6	0.5	0.7
Richland	8,193	3,653	4,413	127	760	R	44.6	53.9	1.6	17	35	24	2.7	2.9	2.5	2.8
Rolette	3,557	2,243	1,206	108	1,037	D	63.1	33.9	3.0	1	53	1	1.2	1.8	0.7	2.3
Sargent	2,243	1,197	1,012	34	185	D	53.4	45.1	1.5	3	50	29	0.7	1.0	0.6	0.7
Sheridan	1,159	337	808	14	471	R	29.1	69.7	1.2	53	1	45	0.4	0.3	0.5	0.3
Sioux	980	569	394	17	175	D	58.1	40.2	1.7	2	52	18	0.3	0.5	0.2	0.4
Slope	534	234	290	10	56	R	43.8	54.3	1.9	18	34	11	0.2	0.2	0.2	0.2
Stark	10,592	4,413	5,999	180	1,586	R	41.7	56.6	1.7	29	28	19	3.5	3.6	3.4	3.9
Steele	1,383	726	638	19	88	D	52.5	46.1	1.4	5	49	35	0.5	0.6	0.4	0.4
Stutsman	9,936	3,959	5,755	222	1,796	R	39.8	57.9	2.2	36	18	4	3.3	3.2	3.3	4.8
Towner	1,728	825	877	26	52	R	47.7	50.8	1.5	9	45	30	0.6	0.7	0.5	0.6
Traill	4,558	2,040	2,442	76	402	R	44.8	53.6	1.7	16	38	21	1.5	1.6	1.4	1.6
Walsh	5,904	2,217	3,627	60	1,410	R	37.6	61.4	1.0	42	12	51	1.9	1.8	2.1	1.3
Ward	25,652	11,053	14,111	488	3,058	R	43.1	55.0	1.9	24	33	9	8.4	8.9	8.0	10.6
Wells	2,913	1,099	1,763	51	664	R	37.7	60.5	1.8	41	14	17	1.0	0.9	1.0	1.1
Williams	9,897	4,496	5,222	179	726	R	45.4	52.8	1.8	15	40	13	3.2	3.6	3.0	3.9
NORTH DAKOTA	304,861	123,845	176,398	4,618	52,553	R	40.6	57.9	1.5				100.0	100.0	100.0	100.0

Table H. – Vote for U.S. Representative in Congress: November 3, 1992, General Election

Congressional district and county	Total	Democrat (DEM)	Republican (REP)	Other	Plurality Total	Party	Percent of total vote DEM	REP	Other	Rank within district DEM	REP	Other	Percent contribution to district vote Total	DEM	REP	Other
District At-Large	**297,898**	**169,273**	**117,442**	**11,183**	**51,831**	**D**	**56.8**	**39.4**	**3.8**				**100.0**	**100.0**	**100.0**	**100.0**
Adams	1,552	875	615	62	260	D	56.4	39.6	4.0	37	18	21	0.5	0.5	0.5	0.6
Barnes	6,478	4,602	1,734	142	2,868	D	71.0	26.8	2.2	3	51	53	2.2	2.7	1.5	1.3
Benson	2,499	1,568	854	77	714	D	62.7	34.2	3.1	12	41	40	0.8	0.9	0.7	0.7
Billings	668	326	302	40	24	D	48.8	45.2	6.0	51	7	3	0.2	0.2	0.3	0.4
Bottineau	3,965	2,352	1,497	116	855	D	59.3	37.8	2.9	23	28	42	1.3	1.4	1.3	1.0
Bowman	1,851	1,041	712	98	329	D	56.2	38.5	5.3	38	21	6	0.6	0.6	0.6	0.9
Burke	1,473	945	476	52	469	D	64.2	32.3	3.5	11	45	31	0.5	0.6	0.4	0.5
Burleigh	29,542	15,468	12,921	1,153	2,547	D	52.4	43.7	3.9	45	9	23	9.9	9.1	11.0	10.3
Cass	52,326	26,883	24,168	1,275	2,715	D	51.4	46.2	2.4	47	4	47	17.6	15.9	20.6	11.4
Cavalier	3,005	1,683	1,226	96	457	D	56.0	40.8	3.2	39	12	36	1.0	1.0	1.0	0.9
Dickey	2,892	1,465	1,319	108	146	D	50.7	45.6	3.7	48	6	26	1.0	0.9	1.1	1.0
Divide	1,575	1,064	461	50	603	D	67.6	29.3	3.2	5	49	37	0.5	0.6	0.4	0.4
Dunn	2,068	1,230	761	77	469	D	59.5	36.8	3.7	20	32	28	0.7	0.7	0.6	0.7
Eddy	1,593	942	582	69	360	D	59.1	36.5	4.3	25	34	14	0.5	0.6	0.5	0.6
Emmons	2,371	1,286	967	118	319	D	54.2	40.8	5.0	42	13	11	0.8	0.8	0.8	1.1
Foster	1,858	1,095	686	77	409	D	58.9	36.9	4.1	26	31	18	0.6	0.6	0.6	0.7
Golden Valley	1,052	524	486	42	38	D	49.8	46.2	4.0	50	3	22	0.4	0.3	0.4	0.4
Grand Forks	29,710	15,986	12,046	1,678	3,940	D	53.8	40.5	5.6	43	15	4	10.0	9.4	10.3	15.0
Grant	1,909	954	873	82	81	D	50.0	45.7	4.3	49	5	16	0.6	0.6	0.7	0.7
Griggs	1,703	1,014	645	44	369	D	59.5	37.9	2.6	19	27	46	0.6	0.6	0.5	0.4
Hettinger	1,795	1,044	689	62	355	D	58.2	38.4	3.5	29	22	32	0.6	0.6	0.6	0.6
Kidder	1,684	870	710	104	160	D	51.7	42.2	6.2	46	10	2	0.6	0.5	0.6	0.9
LaMoure	2,680	1,515	1,092	73	423	D	56.5	40.7	2.7	36	14	44	0.9	0.9	0.9	0.7
Logan	1,455	763	653	39	110	D	52.4	44.9	2.7	44	8	45	0.5	0.5	0.6	0.3
McHenry	3,274	2,035	1,137	102	898	D	62.2	34.7	3.1	14	39	39	1.1	1.2	1.0	0.9
McIntosh	1,959	867	1,005	87	138	R	44.3	51.3	4.4	53	1	13	0.7	0.5	0.9	0.8
McKenzie	2,976	1,695	1,131	150	564	D	57.0	38.0	5.0	34	24	10	1.0	1.0	1.0	1.3
McLean	5,229	3,064	1,970	195	1,094	D	58.6	37.7	3.7	28	29	27	1.8	1.8	1.7	1.7
Mercer	4,962	2,988	1,583	391	1,405	D	60.2	31.9	7.9	16	46	1	1.7	1.8	1.3	3.5
Morton	11,231	6,677	4,095	459	2,582	D	59.5	36.5	4.1	21	35	20	3.8	3.9	3.5	4.1
Mountrail	3,193	2,221	862	110	1,359	D	69.6	27.0	3.4	4	50	33	1.1	1.3	0.7	1.0
Nelson	2,145	1,337	757	51	580	D	62.3	35.3	2.4	13	38	50	0.7	0.8	0.6	0.5
Oliver	1,238	675	500	63	175	D	54.5	40.4	5.1	41	16	9	0.4	0.4	0.4	0.6
Pembina	4,010	2,190	1,689	131	501	D	54.6	42.1	3.3	40	11	35	1.3	1.3	1.4	1.2
Pierce	2,333	1,400	845	88	555	D	60.0	36.2	3.8	17	37	24	0.8	0.8	0.7	0.8
Ramsey	5,962	3,556	2,182	224	1,374	D	59.6	36.6	3.8	18	33	25	2.0	2.1	1.9	2.0
Ransom	2,831	1,844	919	68	925	D	65.1	32.5	2.4	8	44	49	1.0	1.1	0.8	0.6
Renville	1,614	1,077	486	51	591	D	66.7	30.1	3.2	6	48	38	0.5	0.6	0.4	0.5
Richland	7,898	4,537	3,076	285	1,461	D	57.4	38.9	3.6	32	20	30	2.7	2.7	2.6	2.5
Rolette	3,468	2,665	639	164	2,026	D	76.8	18.4	4.7	1	53	12	1.2	1.6	0.5	1.5
Sargent	2,199	1,421	729	49	692	D	64.6	33.2	2.2	9	42	52	0.7	0.8	0.6	0.4
Sheridan	1,169	536	571	62	35	R	45.9	48.8	5.3	52	2	5	0.4	0.3	0.5	0.6
Sioux	966	698	217	51	481	D	72.3	22.5	5.3	2	52	8	0.3	0.4	0.2	0.5
Slope	530	301	201	28	100	D	56.8	37.9	5.3	35	25	7	0.2	0.2	0.2	0.3
Stark	10,480	6,418	3,611	451	2,807	D	61.2	34.5	4.3	15	40	15	3.5	3.8	3.1	4.0
Steele	1,330	877	421	32	456	D	65.9	31.7	2.4	7	47	48	0.4	0.5	0.4	0.3
Stutsman	9,638	5,655	3,585	398	2,070	D	58.7	37.2	4.1	27	30	19	3.2	3.3	3.1	3.6
Towner	1,659	1,067	543	49	524	D	64.3	32.7	3.0	10	43	41	0.6	0.6	0.5	0.4
Traill	4,436	2,548	1,786	102	762	D	57.4	40.3	2.3	33	17	51	1.5	1.5	1.5	0.9
Walsh	5,751	3,408	2,180	163	1,228	D	59.3	37.9	2.8	24	26	43	1.9	2.0	1.9	1.5
Ward	25,235	14,669	9,631	935	5,038	D	58.1	38.2	3.7	30	23	29	8.5	8.7	8.2	8.4
Wells	2,821	1,622	1,103	96	519	D	57.5	39.1	3.4	31	19	34	0.9	1.0	0.9	0.9
Williams	9,657	5,730	3,513	414	2,217	D	59.3	36.4	4.3	22	36	17	3.2	3.4	3.0	3.7
NORTH DAKOTA	**297,898**	**169,273**	**117,442**	**11,183**	**51,831**	**D**	**56.8**	**39.4**	**3.8**							

Table I. — Vote for Presidential Preference: June 9, 1992, Democratic Primary Election

County	Top candidates									Top three candidates (state vote)									
										Percent of total vote						Percent contribution to state vote			
														Rank					
	Total	Perot	La-Rouche	Woods	Shiek-man	Clinton	-	-	-	Perot	La-Rouche	Woods	Perot	La-Rouche	Woods	Total	Perot	La-Rouche	Woods
Adams	268	81	67	43	37	40	-	-	-	30.2	25.0	16.0	34	20	29	0.8	0.9	1.0	0.6
Barnes	648	207	162	145	109	25	-	-	-	31.9	25.0	22.4	31	21	13	2.0	2.2	2.3	2.2
Benson	465	134	114	90	61	66	-	-	-	28.8	24.5	19.4	37	24	17	1.4	1.4	1.6	1.4
Billings	149	91	19	12	12	15	-	-	-	61.1	12.8	8.1	1	51	53	0.5	1.0	0.3	0.2
Bottineau	417	126	83	78	65	65	-	-	-	30.2	19.9	18.7	35	33	21	1.3	1.3	1.2	1.2
Bowman	289	103	63	47	45	31	-	-	-	35.6	21.8	16.3	24	28	28	0.9	1.1	0.9	0.7
Burke	251	111	34	39	26	41	-	-	-	44.2	13.5	15.5	6	48	33	0.8	1.2	0.5	0.6
Burleigh	2,779	0	876	1,086	698	119	-	-	-	0.0	31.5	39.1	53	8	1	8.5	0.0	12.5	16.4
Cass	5,327	2,090	683	616	426	1,512	-	-	-	39.2	12.8	11.6	18	50	51	16.2	22.0	9.8	9.3
Cavalier	518	98	137	148	101	34	-	-	-	18.9	26.4	28.6	43	17	10	1.6	1.0	2.0	2.2
Dickey	440	167	103	62	64	44	-	-	-	38.0	23.4	14.1	21	26	42	1.3	1.8	1.5	0.9
Divide	196	104	48	25	19	0	-	-	-	53.1	24.5	12.8	2	25	45	0.6	1.1	0.7	0.4
Dunn	353	161	65	41	33	53	-	-	-	45.6	18.4	11.6	5	38	50	1.1	1.7	0.9	0.6
Eddy	258	83	47	53	33	42	-	-	-	32.2	18.2	20.5	30	39	15	0.8	0.9	0.7	0.8
Emmons	383	143	106	64	51	19	-	-	-	37.3	27.7	16.7	23	16	27	1.2	1.5	1.5	1.0
Foster	313	149	48	36	31	49	-	-	-	47.6	15.3	11.5	4	47	52	1.0	1.6	0.7	0.5
Golden Valley	136	54	26	21	12	23	-	-	-	39.7	19.1	15.4	16	35	34	0.4	0.6	0.4	0.3
Grand Forks	2,684	845	351	418	476	594	-	-	-	31.5	13.1	15.6	32	49	32	8.2	8.9	5.0	6.3
Grant	314	122	65	49	48	30	-	-	-	38.9	20.7	15.6	20	31	31	1.0	1.3	0.9	0.7
Griggs	232	96	45	28	24	39	-	-	-	41.4	19.4	12.1	12	34	49	0.7	1.0	0.6	0.4
Hettinger	307	121	80	44	36	26	-	-	-	39.4	26.1	14.3	17	18	41	0.9	1.3	1.1	0.7
Kidder	215	84	49	40	23	19	-	-	-	39.1	22.8	18.6	19	27	22	0.7	0.9	0.7	0.6
LaMoure	375	157	58	54	55	51	-	-	-	41.9	15.5	14.4	10	45	40	1.1	1.6	0.8	0.8
Logan	169	52	53	34	30	0	-	-	-	30.8	31.4	20.1	33	9	16	0.5	0.5	0.8	0.5
McHenry	480	144	118	73	51	94	-	-	-	30.0	24.6	15.2	36	23	35	1.5	1.5	1.7	1.1
McIntosh	167	48	50	32	18	19	-	-	-	28.7	29.9	19.2	38	11	18	0.5	0.5	0.7	0.5
McKenzie	358	150	64	44	38	62	-	-	-	41.9	17.9	12.3	8	40	48	1.1	1.6	0.9	0.7
McLean	578	52	214	180	126	6	-	-	-	9.0	37.0	31.1	48	2	8	1.8	0.5	3.1	2.7
Mercer	678	284	126	99	66	103	-	-	-	41.9	18.6	14.6	9	37	38	2.1	3.0	1.8	1.5
Morton	1,109	128	363	365	232	21	-	-	-	11.5	32.7	32.9	46	6	6	3.4	1.3	5.2	5.5
Mountrail	575	216	115	72	66	106	-	-	-	37.6	20.0	12.5	22	32	47	1.8	2.3	1.6	1.1
Nelson	248	39	71	65	61	12	-	-	-	15.7	28.6	26.2	44	15	12	0.8	0.4	1.0	1.0
Oliver	174	86	45	26	17	0	-	-	-	49.4	25.9	14.9	3	19	37	0.5	0.9	0.6	0.4
Pembina	319	8	94	123	85	9	-	-	-	2.5	29.5	38.6	51	12	2	1.0	<.1	1.3	1.9
Pierce	203	55	64	38	24	22	-	-	-	27.1	31.5	18.7	41	7	20	0.6	0.6	0.9	0.6
Ramsey	638	209	133	118	96	82	-	-	-	32.8	20.8	18.5	29	30	23	1.9	2.2	1.9	1.8
Ransom	429	147	74	62	58	88	-	-	-	34.3	17.2	14.5	28	41	39	1.3	1.5	1.1	0.9
Renville	229	79	48	41	27	34	-	-	-	34.5	21.0	17.9	27	29	25	0.7	0.8	0.7	0.6
Richland	596	19	203	220	133	21	-	-	-	3.2	34.1	36.9	50	4	3	1.8	0.2	2.9	3.3
Rolette	482	10	196	142	127	7	-	-	-	2.1	40.7	29.5	52	1	9	1.5	0.1	2.8	2.1
Sargent	216	21	62	68	45	20	-	-	-	9.7	28.7	31.5	47	14	7	0.7	0.2	0.9	1.0
Sheridan	178	50	52	24	18	34	-	-	-	28.1	29.2	13.5	39	13	44	0.5	0.5	0.7	0.4
Sioux	259	72	89	49	39	10	-	-	-	27.8	34.4	18.9	40	3	19	0.8	0.8	1.3	0.7
Slope	94	39	11	15	14	15	-	-	-	41.5	11.7	16.0	11	53	30	0.3	0.4	0.2	0.2
Stark	1,111	450	171	141	121	228	-	-	-	40.5	15.4	12.7	14	46	46	3.4	4.7	2.4	2.1
Steele	240	105	38	33	17	47	-	-	-	43.8	15.8	13.8	7	44	43	0.7	1.1	0.5	0.5
Stutsman	1,007	234	250	276	191	56	-	-	-	23.2	24.8	27.4	42	22	11	3.1	2.5	3.6	4.2
Towner	277	97	45	57	37	41	-	-	-	35.0	16.2	20.6	25	43	14	0.8	1.0	0.6	0.9
Traill	582	233	74	101	68	106	-	-	-	40.0	12.7	17.4	15	52	26	1.8	2.4	1.1	1.5
Walsh	538	23	178	182	144	11	-	-	-	4.3	33.1	33.8	49	5	5	1.6	0.2	2.5	2.7
Ward	2,626	910	443	480	285	508	-	-	-	34.7	16.9	18.3	26	42	24	8.0	9.6	6.3	7.2
Wells	406	165	77	61	42	61	-	-	-	40.6	19.0	15.0	13	36	36	1.2	1.7	1.1	0.9
Williams	503	64	153	181	105	0	-	-	-	12.7	30.4	36.0	45	10	4	1.5	0.7	2.2	2.7
NORTH DAKOTA	32,786	9,516	7,003	6,641	4,866	4,760	-	-	-	29.0	21.4	20.3				100.0	100.0	100.0	100.0

Table J. — Vote for Presidential Preference: June 9, 1992, Republican Primary Election

County	Top candidates					Top four candidates (state vote)												
						Percent of total vote				Rank				Percent contribution to state vote				
	Total	Bush	Paulsen	Perot	Other	Bush	Paulsen	Perot	Other	Bush	Paulsen	Perot	Other	Total	Bush	Paulsen	Perot	Other
Adams	515	380	58	77	0	73.8	11.3	15.0	0.0	44	10	8	31	1.0	1.0	1.4	2.0	0.0
Barnes	920	794	62	64	0	86.3	6.7	7.0	0.0	3	44	39	32	1.9	2.0	1.5	1.7	0.0
Benson	389	303	29	57	0	77.9	7.5	14.7	0.0	31	37	9	33	0.8	0.8	0.7	1.5	0.0
Billings	172	93	22	51	6	54.1	12.8	29.7	3.5	53	6	1	11	0.3	0.2	0.5	1.3	0.4
Bottineau	790	679	50	61	0	85.9	6.3	7.7	0.0	6	47	37	34	1.6	1.7	1.2	1.6	0.0
Bowman	625	470	74	81	0	75.2	11.8	13.0	0.0	40	9	17	35	1.3	1.2	1.8	2.1	0.0
Burke	290	218	20	47	5	75.2	6.9	16.2	1.7	41	42	6	18	0.6	0.5	0.5	1.2	0.3
Burleigh	5,311	4,035	439	0	837	76.0	8.3	0.0	15.8	37	31	53	1	10.7	10.1	10.7	0.0	51.7
Cass	6,627	5,484	371	772	0	82.8	5.6	11.6	0.0	20	50	22	36	13.4	13.8	9.1	20.0	0.0
Cavalier	462	385	37	23	17	83.3	8.0	5.0	3.7	17	35	42	9	0.9	1.0	0.9	0.6	1.0
Dickey	572	468	42	62	0	81.8	7.3	10.8	0.0	22	40	24	37	1.2	1.2	1.0	1.6	0.0
Divide	288	248	13	27	0	86.1	4.5	9.4	0.0	4	52	27	38	0.6	0.6	0.3	0.7	0.0
Dunn	442	317	48	71	6	71.7	10.9	16.1	1.4	50	13	7	22	0.9	0.8	1.2	1.8	0.4
Eddy	299	205	28	52	14	68.6	9.4	17.4	4.7	51	23	5	7	0.6	0.5	0.7	1.3	0.9
Emmons	778	583	120	70	5	74.9	15.4	9.0	0.6	43	3	29	24	1.6	1.5	2.9	1.8	0.3
Foster	320	241	12	62	5	75.3	3.8	19.4	1.6	39	53	3	20	0.6	0.6	0.3	1.6	0.3
Golden Valley	277	214	24	38	1	77.3	8.7	13.7	0.4	33	27	14	28	0.6	0.5	0.6	1.0	<.1
Grand Forks	4,115	3,468	303	344	0	84.3	7.4	8.4	0.0	10	39	32	39	8.3	8.7	7.4	8.9	0.0
Grant	520	398	58	64	0	76.5	11.2	12.3	0.0	34	11	20	40	1.1	1.0	1.4	1.7	0.0
Griggs	424	350	36	38	0	82.5	8.5	9.0	0.0	21	29	30	41	0.9	0.9	0.9	1.0	0.0
Hettinger	407	305	39	56	7	74.9	9.6	13.8	1.7	42	20	13	19	0.8	0.8	1.0	1.5	0.4
Kidder	510	375	62	73	0	73.5	12.2	14.3	0.0	45	8	11	42	1.0	0.9	1.5	1.9	0.0
LaMoure	521	435	33	52	1	83.5	6.3	10.0	0.2	16	46	26	30	1.1	1.1	0.8	1.3	<.1
Logan	607	440	89	78	0	72.5	14.7	12.9	0.0	48	4	18	43	1.2	1.1	2.2	2.0	0.0
McHenry	634	517	66	51	0	81.5	10.4	8.0	0.0	23	14	35	44	1.3	1.3	1.6	1.3	0.0
McIntosh	812	681	69	59	3	83.9	8.5	7.3	0.4	13	28	38	27	1.6	1.7	1.7	1.5	0.2
McKenzie	620	497	38	85	0	80.2	6.1	13.7	0.0	26	48	16	45	1.3	1.2	0.9	2.2	0.0
McLean	865	735	82	18	30	85.0	9.5	2.1	3.5	7	22	46	12	1.8	1.8	2.0	0.5	1.9
Mercer	827	652	73	102	0	78.8	8.8	12.3	0.0	29	26	19	46	1.7	1.6	1.8	2.6	0.0
Morton	1,549	1,263	172	49	65	81.5	11.1	3.2	4.2	24	12	44	8	3.1	3.2	4.2	1.3	4.0
Mountrail	476	343	46	87	0	72.1	9.7	18.3	0.0	49	18	4	47	1.0	0.9	1.1	2.3	0.0
Nelson	325	270	31	6	18	83.1	9.5	1.8	5.5	19	21	47	6	0.7	0.7	0.8	0.2	1.1
Oliver	213	155	27	31	0	72.8	12.7	14.6	0.0	47	7	10	48	0.4	0.4	0.7	0.8	0.0
Pembina	607	534	49	5	19	88.0	8.1	0.8	3.1	2	33	50	14	1.2	1.3	1.2	0.1	1.2
Pierce	379	322	27	30	0	85.0	7.1	7.9	0.0	8	41	36	49	0.8	0.8	0.7	0.8	0.0
Ramsey	779	658	66	45	10	84.5	8.5	5.8	1.3	9	30	41	23	1.6	1.7	1.6	1.2	0.6
Ransom	439	352	33	54	0	80.2	7.5	12.3	0.0	25	36	21	50	0.9	0.9	0.8	1.4	0.0
Renville	273	229	18	22	4	83.9	6.6	8.1	1.5	12	45	34	21	0.6	0.6	0.4	0.6	0.2
Richland	1,233	1,031	85	10	107	83.6	6.9	0.8	8.7	14	43	51	4	2.5	2.6	2.1	0.3	6.6
Rolette	281	236	29	6	10	84.0	10.3	2.1	3.6	11	15	45	10	0.6	0.6	0.7	0.2	0.6
Sargent	352	280	26	6	40	79.5	7.4	1.7	11.4	27	38	48	2	0.7	0.7	0.6	0.2	2.5
Sheridan	455	353	60	42	0	77.6	13.2	9.2	0.0	32	5	28	51	0.9	0.9	1.5	1.1	0.0
Sioux	136	99	26	11	0	72.8	19.1	8.1	0.0	46	1	33	52	0.3	0.2	0.6	0.3	0.0
Slope	122	75	20	24	3	61.5	16.4	19.7	2.5	52	2	2	15	0.2	0.2	0.5	0.6	0.2
Stark	1,609	1,212	160	186	51	75.3	9.9	11.6	3.2	38	16	23	13	3.3	3.0	3.9	4.8	3.1
Steele	220	173	20	22	5	78.6	9.1	10.0	2.3	30	24	25	16	0.4	0.4	0.5	0.6	0.3
Stutsman	1,780	1,413	172	72	123	79.4	9.7	4.0	6.9	28	19	43	5	3.6	3.5	4.2	1.9	7.6
Towner	226	172	22	31	1	76.1	9.7	13.7	0.4	36	17	15	26	0.5	0.4	0.5	0.8	<.1
Traill	658	566	35	57	0	86.0	5.3	8.7	0.0	5	51	31	53	1.3	1.4	0.9	1.5	0.0
Walsh	838	765	68	3	2	91.3	8.1	0.4	0.2	1	32	52	29	1.7	1.9	1.7	<.1	0.1
Ward	4,291	3,584	345	277	85	83.5	8.0	6.5	2.0	15	34	40	17	8.7	9.0	8.4	7.2	5.2
Wells	891	680	79	127	5	76.3	8.9	14.3	0.6	35	25	12	25	1.8	1.7	1.9	3.3	0.3
Williams	1,357	1,128	80	14	135	83.1	5.9	1.0	9.9	18	49	49	3	2.7	2.8	2.0	0.4	8.3
NORTH DAKOTA	49,428	39,863	4,093	3,852	1,620	80.6	8.3	7.8	3.3					100.0	100.0	100.0	100.0	100.0

1992 Vote for President
Percent for Bush (R), by County

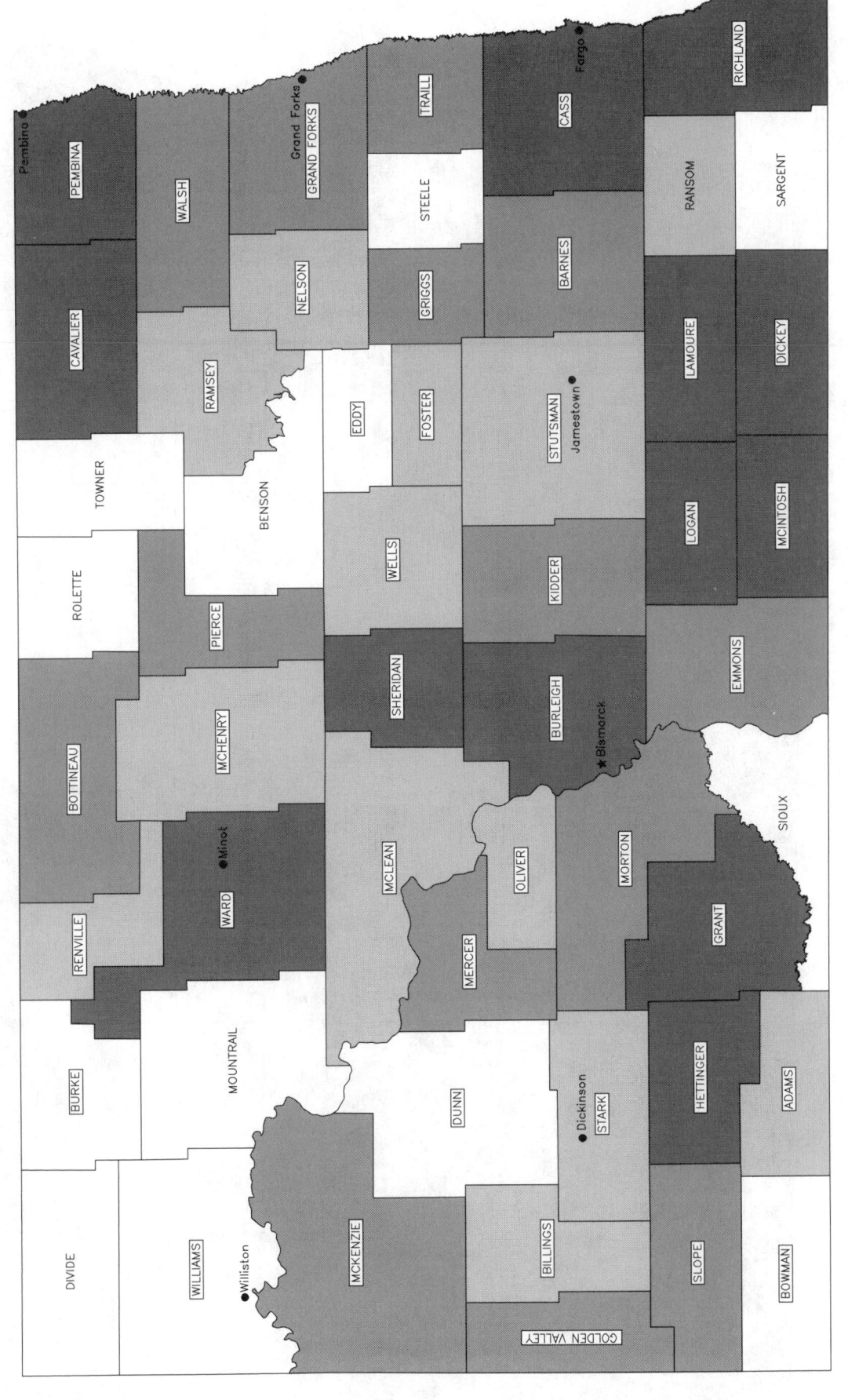

45.4% to 55.2%
42.2% to 45.3%
37.4% to 42.1%
24.8% to 37.3%

Bush (R) received 44.2% statewide.

A framed county name indicates a county carried by the winner.

Copyright © 1993 by Election Data Services, Inc.

North Dakota 713

1992 Vote for U.S. Senator
Percent for Dorgan (D), by County

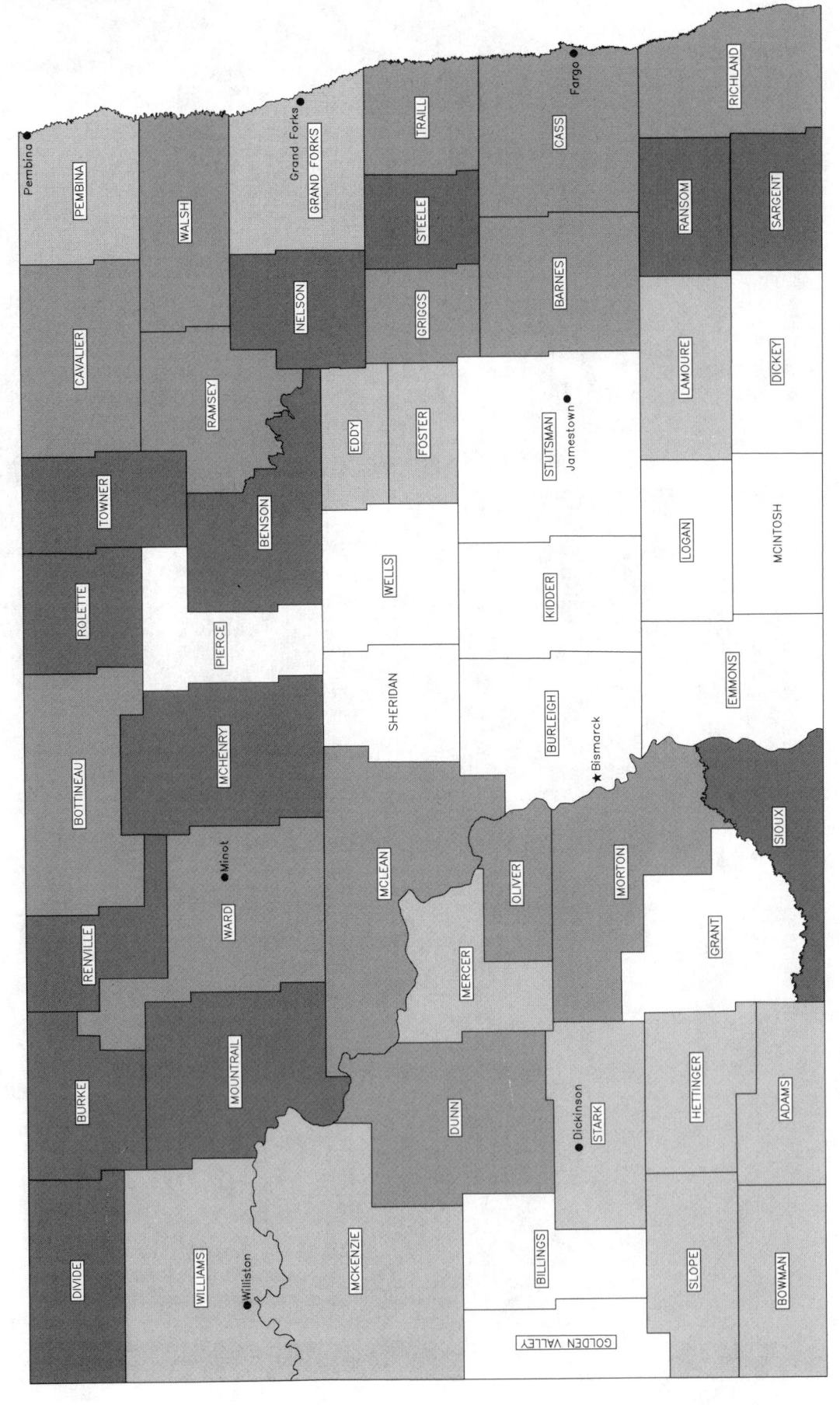

63.7% to 76.6%
58.9% to 63.6%
56.3% to 58.8%
42.7% to 56.2%

Dorgan (D) received 59.0% statewide.

A framed county name indicates
a county carried by the winner.

714 North Dakota

1992 Vote for U.S. Senator*
Percent for Conrad (D), by County

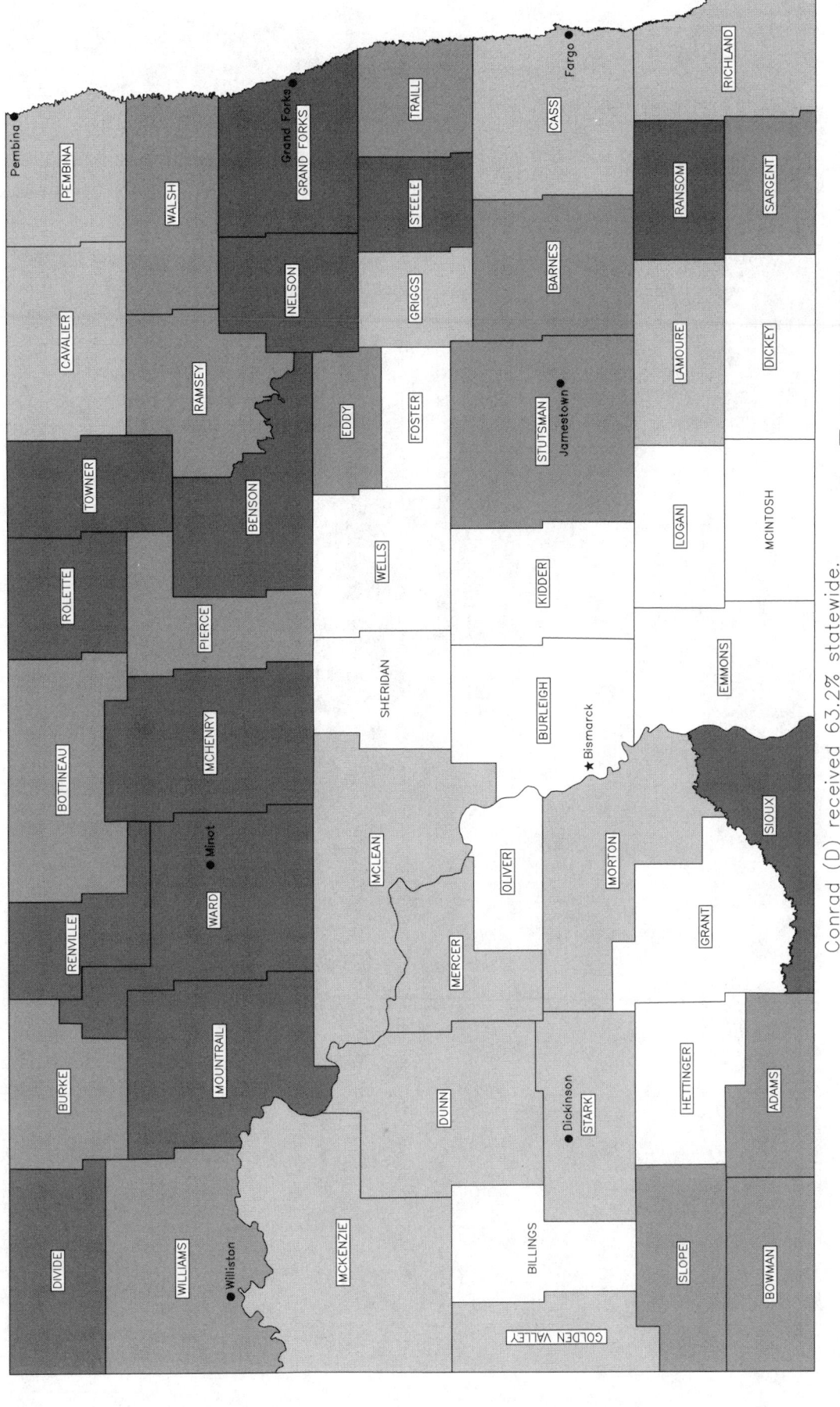

Conrad (D) received 63.2% statewide.

A framed county name indicates a county carried by the winner.

* Special election held December 4, 1992, for the remaining two years of the term of the late Senator Quentin Burdick (D).

68.1% to 77.3%
62.8% to 68.0%
58.9% to 62.7%
43.4% to 58.8%

Copyright © 1993 by Election Data Services, Inc.

North Dakota 715

1992 Vote for Governor
Percent for Schafer (R), by County

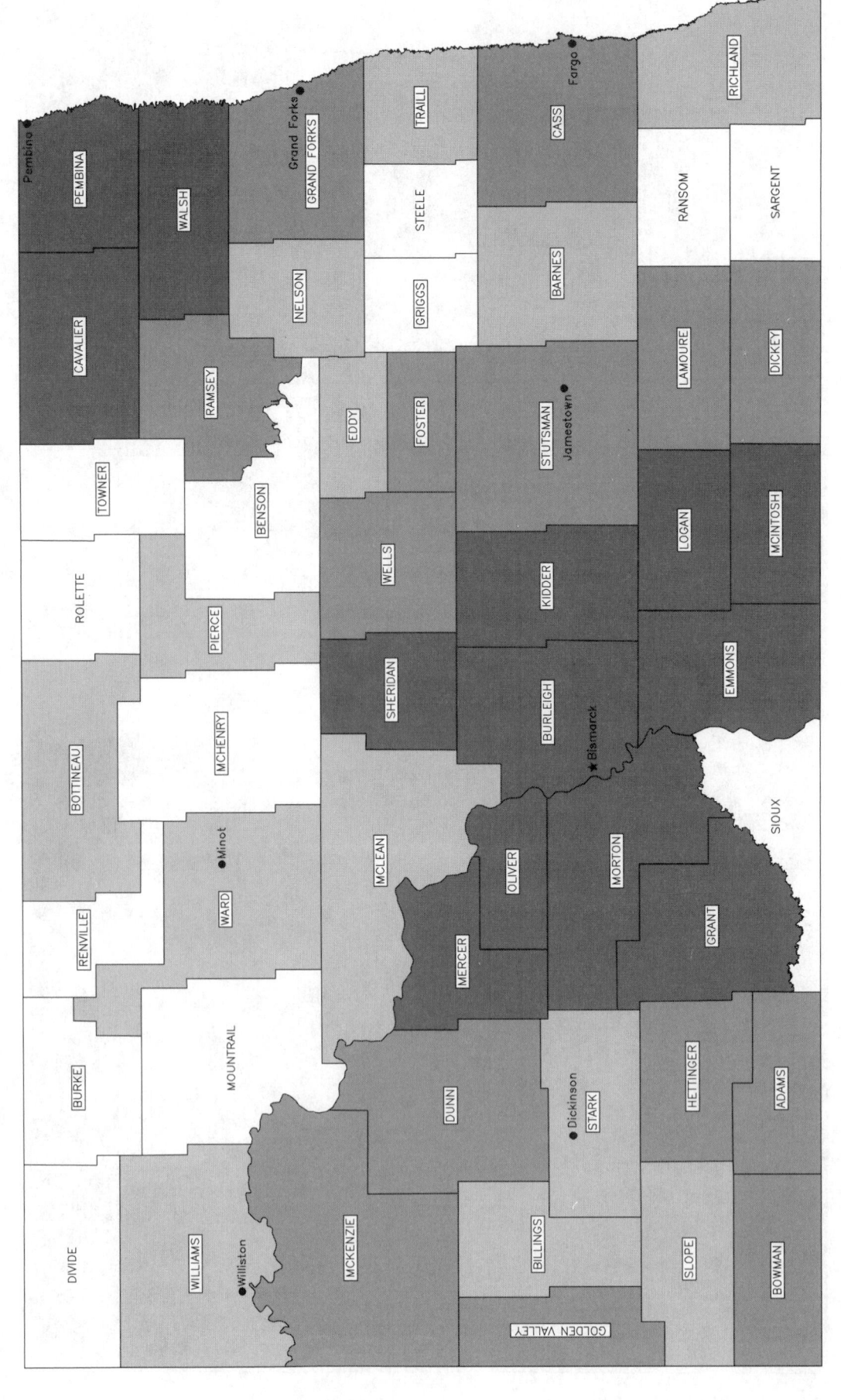

Schafer (R) received 57.9% statewide.

A framed county name indicates a county carried by the winner.

- 60.6% to 69.7%
- 56.7% to 60.5%
- 52.4% to 56.6%
- 33.9% to 52.3%

716 North Dakota

OHIO

Congressional Districts 19
   Average Population 570,901
State Senate Districts 33
   Average Population 328,700
State House Districts 99
   Average Population 109,567

Electoral College Votes.. 21
Counties 88
Voting Precincts 13,738

Alternative Registration Methods:
   .... Agency-based, Mail-in, Motor-voter

Registration Deadline (Days before Election) 30

Voting Equipment Use (Counties)

Datavote Punch Card	3	Paper Ballot	0
Electronic	0	Other Punch Card	69
Lever Machine	11	Mixed Systems	0
Optical Scanner	5		

Party Control	DEM	REP	IND	VAC
1993 State Senate	13	20	0	0
1992 State Senate	12	21	0	0
1993 State House	53	46	0	0
1992 State House	61	38	0	0

Population Statistics 1990

Race/ Ethnicity	Total Population		Voting Age Population		Voting Age Population % of total population
	Number	%	Number	%	
Non-Hispanic					
White	9,444,622	87.1	7,098,470	88.2	75.2
Black	1,147,440	10.6	781,957	9.7	68.1
Asian/Pacific Islander	89,195	0.8	63,524	0.8	71.2
Native American	19,137	0.2	14,205	0.2	74.2
Other	7,025	<.1	2,088	<.1	29.7
All Hispanic	139,696	1.3	87,127	1.1	62.4
TOTAL	10,847,115	100.0	8,047,371	100.0	74.2

Estimated Voting Age Population 1992 (VAP) 8,146,000
Number of Registered Voters................................... 6,542,931
   % of estimated VAP... 80.3
Voter Turnout (Actual) 5,043,094
   % of VAP 61.9
   % of Registration 77.1
Persons Not Voting—of Voting Age 3,102,906
   % of VAP 38.1
Persons Not Voting—of Registered 1,499,837
   % of Registration 22.9
Straight Ticket Voting .... No

State Officials and Members of Congress

Governor:
George V. Voinovich (R) 1990, elected to a four-year term in 1990.

U.S. Senators:
John Glenn (D) 1974, elected to a six-year term in 1992.
Howard Metzenbaum (D) 1976, elected to a six-year term in 1988.

U.S. Representative in Congress:
(District, Name, Party, Date first elected)

1. Mann (D) 1992
2. Portman (R) 1993[1]
3. Hall (D) 1978
4. Oxley (R) 1981
5. Gillmor (R) 1988

6. Strickland (D) 1992
7. Hobson (R) 1990
8. Boehner (R) 1990
9. Kaptur (D) 1982
10. Hoke (R) 1992

11. Stokes (D) 1968
12. Kasich (R) 1982
13. Brown (D) 1992
14. Sawyer (D) 1986
15. Pryce (R) 1992

16. Regula (R) 1972
17. Traficant (D) 1984
18. Applegate (D) 1976
19. Fingerhut (D) 1992

[1]Elected from May 4, 1993, special election to replace Bill Gradison (R), who resigned.

Candidates: General Election, November 3, 1992

Candidate(s)	Total vote	Percent	Party	Status	First elected
President/Vice President					
Clinton/Gore	1,984,942	40.18%	Democrat	Challenger	1992
Bush/Quayle	1,894,310	38.35%	Republican	Incumbent	1988
Perot/Stockdale	1,036,426	20.98%	Independent	Challenger	
Marrou/Lord	7,252	0.15%	Independent	Challenger	
Fulani/Munoz	6,413	0.13%	Independent	Challenger	
Gritz/Minett	4,699	0.10%	Independent	Challenger	
Hagelin/Tompkins	3,437	0.07%	Independent	Challenger	
LaRouche/Bevel	2,446	0.05%	Independent	Challenger	
Warren/Debates	32	<.01%	Write in	Challenger	
King	10	<.01%	Write in	Challenger	
U.S. Senator					
John Glenn	2,444,419	50.99%	Democrat	Incumbent	1974
Mike DeWine	2,028,300	42.31%	Republican	Challenger	
Martha Grevatt	321,234	6.70%	Independent	Challenger	
Governor (No Contest)					
U.S. Representative in Congress					
District 1					
David Mann	120,190	51.27%	Democrat	Challenger	1992
Steve Grote	101,498	43.30%	Independent	Challenger	
James Berns	12,734	5.43%	Independent	Challenger	
Mayberry	6	<.01%	Write in	Challenger	
Taylor	5	<.01%	Write in	Challenger	
District 2					
Bill Gradison, Jr.[1]	177,720	70.06%	Republican	Incumbent	1974
Thomas Chandler	75,924	29.93%	Democrat	Challenger	
Wood	7	<.01%	Write in	Challenger	
District 3					
Tony Hall	146,072	59.67%	Democrat	Incumbent	1978
Peter Davis	98,733	40.33%	Republican	Challenger	
McDonald	6	<.01%	Write in	Challenger	
District 4					
Michael Oxley	147,346	61.28%	Republican	Incumbent	1981
Raymond Ball	92,608	38.52%	Democrat	Challenger	
James Stahl	486	0.20%	Write in	Challenger	
District 5					
Paul Gillmor	187,860	100.00%	Republican	Incumbent	1988
District 6					
Ted Strickland	122,720	50.72%	Democrat	Challenger	1992
Bob McEwen	119,252	49.28%	Republican	Incumbent	1980
District 7					
David Hobson	164,195	71.26%	Republican	Incumbent	1990
Clifford Heskett	66,237	28.74%	Democrat	Challenger	
District 8					
John Boehner	176,362	73.98%	Republican	Incumbent	1990
Fred Sennet	62,033	26.02%	Democrat	Challenger	
District 9					
Marcy Kaptur	178,879	73.58%	Democrat	Incumbent	1982
Ken Brown	53,011	21.81%	Republican	Challenger	
Ed Howard	11,162	4.59%	Independent	Challenger	
Haupricht	50	0.02%	Write in	Challenger	

[1]Resigned; Rob Portman (R) elected at May 4, 1993, special election to fill vacancy.

Candidate(s)	Total vote	Percent	Party	Status	First elected
U.S. Representative in Congress (cont)					
District 10					
Martin Hoke	136,433	56.79%	Republican	Challenger	1992
Mary Rose Oakar	103,788	43.20%	Democrat	Incumbent	1976
Thierjung	12	<.01%	Write in	Challenger	
Black	6	<.01%	Write in	Challenger	
District 11					
Louis Stokes	154,718	69.19%	Democrat	Incumbent	1968
Beryl Rothschild	43,866	19.62%	Republican	Challenger	
Edmund Gudenas	19,773	8.84%	Independent	Challenger	
Gerald Henley	5,267	2.36%	Independent	Challenger	
District 12					
John Kasich	170,297	71.24%	Republican	Incumbent	1982
Bob Fitrakis	68,761	28.76%	Democrat	Challenger	
District 13					
Sherrod Brown	134,486	53.31%	Democrat	Challenger	1992
Margaret Mueller	88,889	35.24%	Republican	Challenger	
Mark Miller	20,320	8.06%	Independent	Challenger	
Tom Lawson	4,719	1.87%	Independent	Challenger	
Werner Lange	3,844	1.52%	Independent	Challenger	
District 14					
Tom Sawyer	165,335	67.76%	Democrat	Incumbent	1986
Robert Morgan	78,659	32.24%	Republican	Challenger	
District 15					
Deborah Pryce	110,390	44.12%	Republican	Challenger	1992
Richard Cordray	94,907	37.93%	Democrat	Challenger	
Linda Reidelbach	44,906	17.95%	Independent	Challenger	
Oliver	2	<.01%	Write in	Challenger	
District 16					
Ralph Regula	158,489	63.72%	Republican	Incumbent	1972
Warner Mendenhall	90,224	36.28%	Democrat	Challenger	
District 17					
James Traficant, Jr.	216,503	84.16%	Democrat	Incumbent	1984
Salvatore Pansino	40,743	15.84%	Republican	Challenger	
District 18					
Douglas Applegate	166,189	68.27%	Democrat	Incumbent	1976
Bill Ress	77,229	31.73%	Republican	Challenger	
District 19					
Eric Fingerhut	138,465	52.63%	Democrat	Challenger	1992
Robert Gardner	124,606	47.36%	Republican	Challenger	
Mononen	7	<.01%	Write in	Challenger	
Mackle	5	<.01%	Write in	Challenger	

Candidates: June 2, 1992, Primary Election

Candidate	Total vote	Percent	Candidate	Total vote	Percent
Presidential Preference, Democratic			**Presidential Preference, Republican**		
Bill Clinton	638,347	61.24%	George Bush	716,766	83.30%
Jerry Brown	197,449	18.94%	Patrick Buchanan	143,687	16.70%
Paul Tsongas	110,773	10.63%			
Louis Stokes	29,983	2.88%			
Tom Harkin	25,395	2.44%			
Bob Kerrey	22,976	2.20%			
Lyndon LaRouche, Jr.	17,412	1.67%			

Voter Registration and Turnout, 1948-1992 Elections

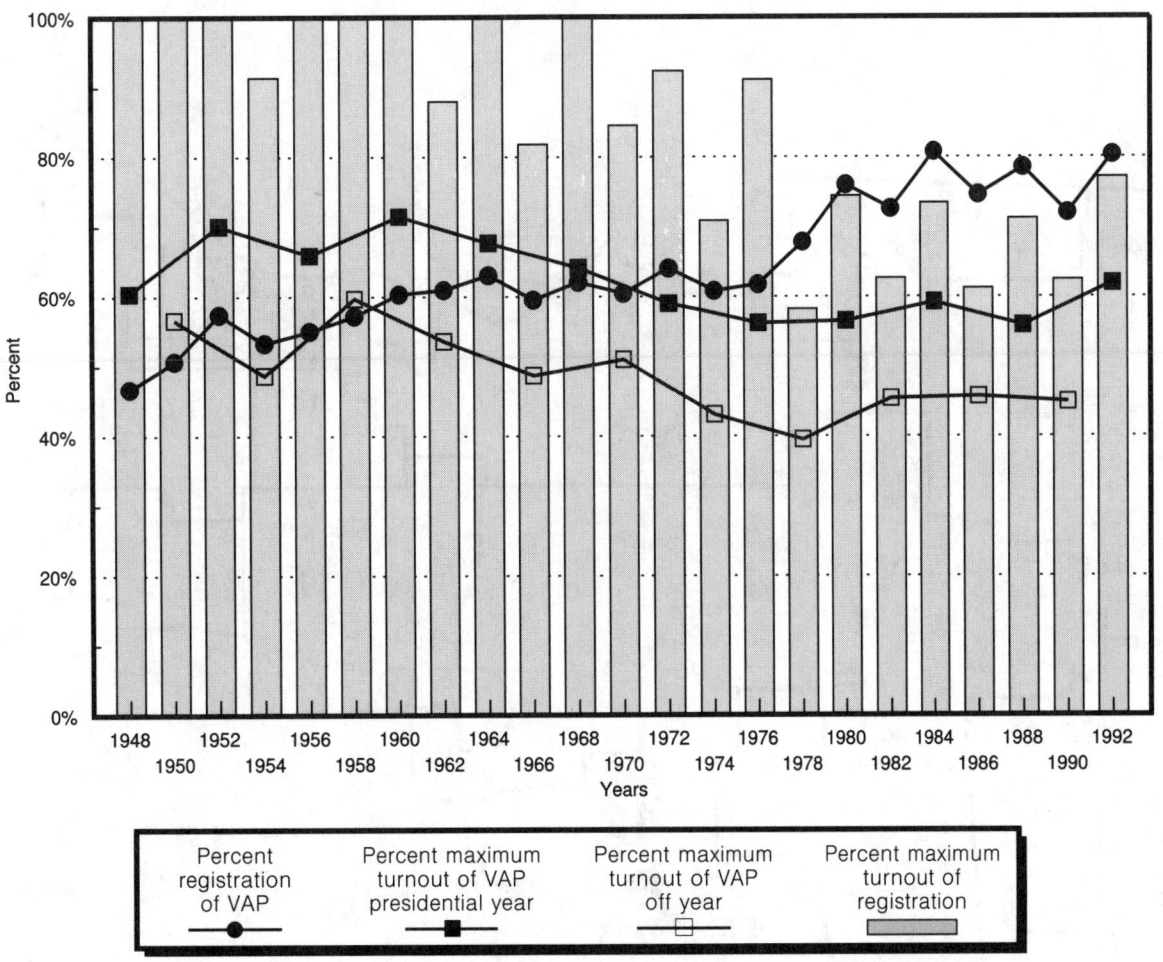

Year	Estimated Voting Age Population (VAP)	Voter registration (REG)			Voter turnout											
						Highest office						Maximum vote				
		Total	Percent of VAP	Rank by percent of VAP	Actual	Total	Office	Percent total REG	Rank by percent of REG	Percent of VAP	Rank by percent of VAP	Total	Percent total REG	Rank by percent of REG	Percent total VAP	Rank by percent of VAP
1992.......	8,146,000	6,542,931	80.3	13	5,043,094	4,939,967	P	75.5	31	60.6	21	5,043,094	77.1	30	61.9	22
1990.......	8,066,000	5,804,659	72.0	18	3,620,469	3,477,650	G	59.9	21	43.1	18	3,620,469	62.4	16	44.9	17
1988.......	8,059,000	6,323,352	78.5	15	4,505,284	4,393,585	P	69.5	31	54.5	19	4,505,284	71.2	30	55.9	18
1986.......	7,946,000	5,924,746	74.6	14	3,628,870	3,121,189	S	52.7	33	39.3	24	3,628,870	61.2	16	45.7	13
1984.......	7,875,000	6,358,558	80.7	15	4,664,223	4,547,619	P	71.5	34	57.7	16	4,664,223	73.4	30	59.2	15
1982.......	7,816,000	5,674,128	72.6	18	3,551,995	3,395,463	S	59.8	31	43.4	23	3,551,995	62.6	26	45.4	22
1980.......	7,744,000	5,887,488	76.0	17	4,378,937	4,283,603	P	72.8	32	55.3	25	4,378,937	74.4	31	56.5	25
1978.......	7,638,000	5,181,910	67.8	28	3,017,700	2,843,351	G	54.9	28	37.2	31	3,017,700	58.2	24	39.5	27
1976.......	7,461,000	4,602,237	61.7	43	4,194,557	4,111,873	P	89.3	1	55.1	28	4,194,557	91.1	1	56.2	28
1974.......	7,311,000	4,441,795	60.8	41	3,151,406	3,072,010	G	69.2	7	42.0	25	3,151,406	70.9	5	43.1	26
1972.......	7,149,000	4,572,709	64.0	43	4,219,645	4,094,787	P	89.5	1	57.3	29	4,219,645	92.3	2	59.0	28
1970.......	6,419,000	3,879,300	60.4	43	3,276,231	3,184,133	G	82.1	3	49.6	28	3,276,231	84.5	3	51.0	26
1968[1]......	6,252,000	3,873,426	62.0	43	4,010,480	3,959,698	P	102.2	1	63.3	28	4,010,480	103.5	1	64.1	28
1966.......	6,080,000	3,618,582	59.5	39	2,960,147	2,887,331	G	79.8	2	47.5	32	2,960,147	81.8	2	48.7	32
1964[1]......	5,962,000	3,756,252	63.0	34	4,034,494	3,969,196	P	105.7	1	66.6	26	4,034,494	107.4	1	67.7	25
1962.......	5,989,000	3,647,556	60.9	27	3,210,972	3,116,711	G	85.4	2	52.0	25	3,210,972	88.0	2	53.6	22
1960[1]......	5,888,000	3,549,211	60.3	29	4,208,811	4,161,859	P	117.3	1	70.7	24	4,208,811	118.6	1	71.5	23
1958[1]......	5,693,000	3,258,086	57.2	26	3,395,910	3,284,134	G	100.8	1	57.7	11	3,395,910	104.2	1	59.7	10
1956[1]......	5,704,000	3,137,821	55.0	27	3,761,322	3,702,265	P	118.0	1	64.9	30	3,761,322	119.9	1	65.9	29
1954.......	5,469,000	2,914,355	53.3	23	2,663,509	2,597,790	G	89.1	1	47.5	31	2,663,509	91.4	1	48.7	31
1952[1]......	5,349,000	3,072,372	57.4	21	3,749,828	3,700,758	P	120.5	1	69.2	27	3,749,828	122.0	1	70.1	27
1950[1]......	5,274,000	2,673,516	50.7	20	2,987,424	2,892,819	G	108.2	1	54.9	14	2,987,424	111.7	1	56.6	11
1948[1]......	5,196,000	2,428,145	46.7	19	3,138,468	2,936,071	P	120.9	1	56.5	27	3,138,468	129.3	1	60.4	21

[1]Voter turnout exceeds total voter registration because voter registration reports are missing from several counties. Counties were not required to report voter registration to Ohio Secretary of State until 1979.

OHIO

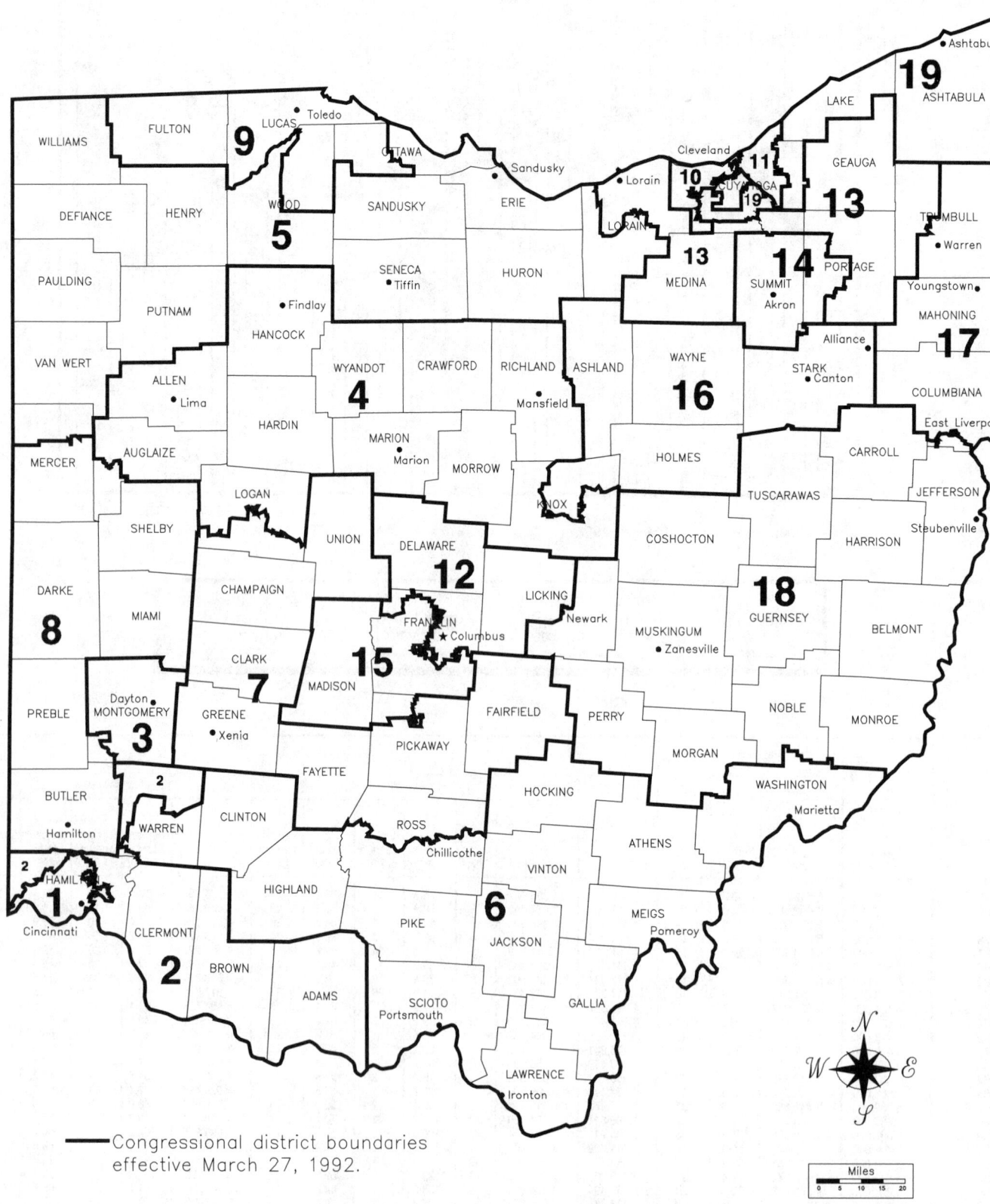

Congressional district boundaries
effective March 27, 1992.

Miles
0 5 10 15 20

Copyright © 1993 by Election Data Services, Inc.

722 Ohio

Table A. — 1990 Population by Race and Ethnic Origin

State/ county code	County	Total persons	Percent of total persons — Non-Hispanic White	Black	Asian and Pacific Islander	Native American	Other	Hispanic	Rank — Percent of total persons Total	Non-Hispanic White	Black	Hispanic	Percent contribution to state population Total	Non-Hispanic White	Black	Hispanic
39 001	Adams	25,371	99.1	0.2	0.1	0.3	<.1	0.4	79	8	78	66	0.2	0.3	<.1	<.1
39 003	Allen	109,755	87.0	11.1	0.5	0.2	0.1	1.1	22	80	8	20	1.0	1.0	1.1	0.9
39 005	Ashland	47,507	98.0	1.0	0.6	0.1	<.1	0.4	48	25	59	56	0.4	0.5	<.1	0.1
39 007	Ashtabula	99,821	94.7	3.1	0.3	0.2	<.1	1.5	26	61	25	18	0.9	1.0	0.3	1.1
39 009	Athens	59,549	93.8	2.8	2.3	0.3	<.1	0.7	43	67	27	26	0.5	0.6	0.1	0.3
39 011	Auglaize	44,585	98.8	0.1	0.4	<.1	<.1	0.5	51	9	81	41	0.4	0.5	<.1	0.2
39 013	Belmont	71,074	97.6	1.8	0.2	0.1	<.1	0.3	34	31	42	78	0.7	0.7	0.1	0.1
39 015	Brown	34,966	98.5	1.2	<.1	<.1	<.1	0.1	65	18	54	88	0.3	0.4	<.1	<.1
39 017	Butler	291,479	94.0	4.5	0.9	0.1	<.1	0.5	8	66	20	45	2.7	2.9	1.1	1.1
39 019	Carroll	26,521	98.8	0.5	0.1	0.2	<.1	0.4	77	12	72	61	0.2	0.3	<.1	<.1
39 021	Champaign	36,019	96.0	2.7	0.3	0.2	0.1	0.7	61	50	29	30	0.3	0.4	<.1	0.2
39 023	Clark	147,548	89.9	8.8	0.4	0.2	<.1	0.7	14	78	9	33	1.4	1.4	1.1	0.7
39 025	Clermont	150,187	98.2	0.8	0.3	0.1	<.1	0.5	13	21	62	49	1.4	1.6	0.1	0.5
39 027	Clinton	35,415	97.1	2.0	0.4	0.2	<.1	0.3	64	39	37	67	0.3	0.4	<.1	<.1
39 029	Columbiana	108,276	98.0	1.3	0.2	0.2	<.1	0.4	23	26	50	59	1.0	1.1	0.1	0.3
39 031	Coshocton	35,427	98.0	1.2	0.3	0.2	<.1	0.3	63	24	53	75	0.3	0.4	<.1	<.1
39 033	Crawford	47,870	98.6	0.5	0.2	0.1	<.1	0.5	47	17	71	43	0.4	0.5	<.1	0.2
39 035	Cuyahoga	1,412,140	71.6	24.7	1.3	0.2	<.1	2.2	1	88	1	15	13.0	10.7	30.3	22.5
39 037	Darke	53,619	98.6	0.3	0.2	0.2	<.1	0.6	45	15	75	34	0.5	0.6	<.1	0.2
39 039	Defiance	39,350	91.5	1.2	0.3	0.2	<.1	6.8	56	74	52	1	0.4	0.4	<.1	1.9
39 041	Delaware	66,929	96.6	2.1	0.6	0.2	<.1	0.5	36	48	35	46	0.6	0.7	0.1	0.2
39 043	Erie	76,779	89.7	8.2	0.3	0.2	0.1	1.5	33	79	10	19	0.7	0.7	0.5	0.8
39 045	Fairfield	103,461	97.9	1.1	0.4	0.2	<.1	0.5	24	28	55	50	1.0	1.1	<.1	0.4
39 047	Fayette	27,466	96.6	2.4	0.4	0.2	0.1	0.3	76	47	34	71	0.3	0.3	<.1	<.1
39 049	Franklin	961,437	80.9	15.8	2.0	0.2	0.1	1.0	2	84	4	22	8.9	8.2	13.2	6.6
39 051	Fulton	38,498	94.5	0.2	0.3	0.1	<.1	4.8	58	63	77	4	0.4	0.4	<.1	1.3
39 053	Gallia	30,954	96.0	2.8	0.4	0.2	<.1	0.5	71	49	28	44	0.3	0.3	<.1	0.1
39 055	Geauga	81,129	97.8	1.3	0.4	<.1	<.1	0.4	30	30	49	63	0.7	0.8	<.1	0.2
39 057	Greene	136,731	90.1	7.0	1.5	0.3	0.1	1.0	16	77	14	21	1.3	1.3	0.8	1.0
39 059	Guernsey	39,024	97.5	1.6	0.3	0.2	<.1	0.3	57	32	45	68	0.4	0.4	<.1	<.1
39 061	Hamilton	866,228	77.3	20.8	1.0	0.1	<.1	0.6	3	87	2	36	8.0	7.1	15.7	3.7
39 063	Hancock	65,536	95.8	0.9	0.6	0.1	<.1	2.6	37	52	61	11	0.6	0.7	<.1	1.2
39 065	Hardin	31,111	98.2	0.7	0.4	0.2	<.1	0.5	70	20	65	52	0.3	0.3	<.1	0.1
39 067	Harrison	16,085	97.0	2.4	<.1	0.1	<.1	0.3	84	40	32	80	0.1	0.2	<.1	<.1
39 069	Henry	29,108	94.4	0.5	0.3	0.2	<.1	4.6	74	64	73	5	0.3	0.3	<.1	1.0
39 071	Highland	35,728	97.4	1.9	0.2	0.2	<.1	0.3	62	35	38	73	0.3	0.4	<.1	<.1
39 073	Hocking	25,533	98.4	0.9	<.1	0.2	<.1	0.4	78	19	60	62	0.2	0.3	<.1	<.1
39 075	Holmes	32,849	99.3	0.2	0.1	<.1	<.1	0.4	67	5	80	60	0.3	0.3	<.1	<.1
39 077	Huron	56,240	96.7	1.0	0.3	0.1	<.1	1.8	44	45	56	16	0.5	0.6	<.1	0.7
39 079	Jackson	30,230	98.7	0.7	0.1	0.2	<.1	0.3	73	14	67	77	0.3	0.3	<.1	<.1
39 081	Jefferson	80,298	93.3	5.6	0.3	0.2	<.1	0.5	32	68	19	42	0.7	0.8	0.4	0.3
39 083	Knox	47,473	98.2	0.8	0.4	0.2	<.1	0.4	49	22	63	65	0.4	0.5	<.1	0.1
39 085	Lake	215,499	96.9	1.6	0.7	0.1	<.1	0.7	12	43	44	31	2.0	2.2	0.3	1.1
39 087	Lawrence	61,834	97.0	2.5	0.1	<.1	<.1	0.2	41	41	31	85	0.6	0.6	0.1	<.1
39 089	Licking	128,300	97.2	1.7	0.4	0.2	<.1	0.5	17	38	43	51	1.2	1.3	0.2	0.4
39 091	Logan	42,310	97.0	1.9	0.6	0.1	<.1	0.4	52	42	41	58	0.4	0.4	<.1	0.1
39 093	Lorain	271,126	85.9	7.6	0.5	0.3	<.1	5.6	9	82	12	3	2.5	2.5	1.8	10.9
39 095	Lucas	462,361	80.6	14.7	1.1	0.2	<.1	3.4	6	85	6	8	4.3	3.9	5.9	11.2
39 097	Madison	37,068	91.3	7.4	0.4	0.2	0.1	0.6	59	75	13	38	0.3	0.4	0.2	0.2
39 099	Mahoning	264,806	82.4	14.8	0.4	0.2	<.1	2.2	10	83	5	13	2.4	2.3	3.4	4.3
39 101	Marion	64,274	94.4	4.2	0.4	0.2	<.1	0.8	38	65	22	24	0.6	0.6	0.2	0.3
39 103	Medina	122,354	98.0	0.7	0.6	0.1	<.1	0.6	19	23	68	39	1.1	1.3	<.1	0.5
39 105	Meigs	22,987	98.7	0.8	<.1	0.2	<.1	0.3	81	13	64	82	0.2	0.2	<.1	<.1
39 107	Mercer	39,443	98.8	<.1	0.2	0.2	<.1	0.7	55	10	88	29	0.4	0.4	<.1	0.2
39 109	Miami	93,182	96.9	1.9	0.6	0.2	<.1	0.4	27	44	40	57	0.9	1.0	0.2	0.3
39 111	Monroe	15,497	99.5	0.1	<.1	0.2	<.1	0.2	85	3	82	87	0.1	0.2	<.1	<.1
39 113	Montgomery	573,809	80.3	17.7	1.0	0.2	<.1	0.8	4	86	3	23	5.3	4.9	8.8	3.2
39 115	Morgan	14,194	95.1	4.0	<.1	0.4	0.1	0.3	86	59	23	84	0.1	0.1	<.1	<.1
39 117	Morrow	27,749	99.1	0.2	0.1	0.2	<.1	0.3	75	6	76	69	0.3	0.3	<.1	<.1
39 119	Muskingum	82,068	95.0	4.2	0.2	0.3	<.1	0.3	29	60	21	74	0.8	0.8	0.3	0.2
39 121	Noble	11,336	99.5	<.1	<.1	0.1	0.0	0.2	87	1	85	86	0.1	0.1	<.1	<.1
39 123	Ottawa	40,029	95.3	0.7	0.2	0.1	<.1	3.7	54	58	69	7	0.4	0.4	<.1	1.1
39 125	Paulding	20,488	95.6	1.0	<.1	0.2	<.1	3.1	83	54	57	9	0.2	0.2	<.1	0.4
39 127	Perry	31,557	99.3	0.2	<.1	0.1	<.1	0.3	69	4	79	83	0.3	0.3	<.1	<.1
39 129	Pickaway	48,255	92.7	6.2	0.2	0.2	<.1	0.7	46	69	18	32	0.4	0.5	0.3	0.2
39 131	Pike	24,249	97.9	1.3	0.2	0.3	<.1	0.3	80	27	48	72	0.2	0.3	<.1	<.1
39 133	Portage	142,585	95.7	2.7	0.8	0.2	<.1	0.6	15	53	30	40	1.3	1.4	0.3	0.6
39 135	Preble	40,113	99.1	0.4	0.2	0.1	<.1	0.3	53	7	74	81	0.4	0.4	<.1	<.1
39 137	Putnam	33,819	95.5	<.1	<.1	<.1	<.1	4.2	66	55	84	6	0.3	0.3	<.1	1.0
39 139	Richland	126,137	90.7	7.9	0.5	0.2	<.1	0.7	18	76	11	28	1.2	1.2	0.9	0.6

Table A. — 1990 Population by Race and Ethnic Origin (cont)

State/ county code	County	Total persons	Percent of total persons						Rank				Percent contribution to state population			
				Non-Hispanic						Percent of total persons				Non-Hispanic		
											Non-Hispanic					
			White	Black	Asian and Pacific Islander	Native American	Other	Hispanic	Total	White	Black	Hispanic	Total	White	Black	Hispanic
39 141	Ross	69,330	92.5	6.4	0.4	0.2	<.1	0.5	35	70	17	47	0.6	0.7	0.4	0.2
39 143	Sandusky	61,963	91.5	2.4	0.2	0.1	<.1	5.7	40	73	33	2	0.6	0.6	0.1	2.5
39 145	Scioto	80,327	96.0	3.0	0.2	0.5	<.1	0.3	31	51	26	70	0.7	0.8	0.2	0.2
39 147	Seneca	59,733	94.7	1.9	0.4	0.1	<.1	2.8	42	62	39	10	0.6	0.6	<.1	1.2
39 149	Shelby	44,915	97.2	1.4	0.9	0.1	<.1	0.4	50	36	47	55	0.4	0.5	<.1	0.1
39 151	Stark	367,585	91.7	6.8	0.4	0.3	<.1	0.7	7	72	15	25	3.4	3.6	2.2	2.0
39 153	Summit	514,990	86.4	11.8	1.0	0.2	<.1	0.6	5	81	7	37	4.7	4.7	5.3	2.2
39 155	Trumbull	227,813	92.1	6.6	0.4	0.1	<.1	0.6	11	71	16	35	2.1	2.2	1.3	1.0
39 157	Tuscarawas	84,090	98.6	0.7	0.2	0.2	<.1	0.3	28	16	66	79	0.8	0.9	<.1	0.2
39 159	Union	31,969	95.3	3.6	0.4	0.2	<.1	0.5	68	57	24	48	0.3	0.3	0.1	0.1
39 161	Van Wert	30,464	97.4	0.6	0.3	<.1	<.1	1.6	72	33	70	17	0.3	0.3	<.1	0.3
39 163	Vinton	11,098	99.5	<.1	<.1	0.1	0.0	0.3	88	2	87	76	0.1	0.1	<.1	<.1
39 165	Warren	113,909	96.7	2.1	0.5	0.2	<.1	0.5	20	46	36	53	1.1	1.2	0.2	0.4
39 167	Washington	62,254	97.9	1.2	0.3	0.2	<.1	0.4	39	29	51	64	0.6	0.6	<.1	0.2
39 169	Wayne	101,461	97.4	1.5	0.5	0.1	<.1	0.4	25	34	46	54	0.9	1.0	0.1	0.3
39 171	Williams	36,956	97.2	<.1	0.3	0.1	<.1	2.2	60	37	86	14	0.3	0.4	<.1	0.6
39 173	Wood	113,269	95.3	1.0	0.9	0.2	<.1	2.5	21	56	58	12	1.0	1.1	0.1	2.1
39 175	Wyandot	22,254	98.8	<.1	0.3	<.1	<.1	0.7	82	11	83	27	0.2	0.2	<.1	0.1
39	OHIO	10,847,115	87.1	10.6	0.8	0.2	<.1	1.3					100.0	100.0	100.0	100.0
	CONGRESSIONAL															
	District 1	570,900	68.2	30.0	0.9	0.1	0.1	0.6	15	18	2	14	5.3	4.1	14.9	2.4
	District 2	570,902	96.3	2.2	0.8	0.1	<.1	0.5	5	3	15	16	5.3	5.8	1.1	2.1
	District 3	570,901	80.2	17.8	1.0	0.2	<.1	0.8	9	16	4	11	5.3	4.8	8.8	3.2
	District 4	570,901	93.9	4.6	0.4	0.2	<.1	0.9	10	8	11	8	5.3	5.7	2.3	3.8
	District 5	570,901	94.3	2.1	0.3	0.1	<.1	3.1	11	6	17	3	5.3	5.7	1.0	12.6
	District 6	570,901	96.8	2.1	0.5	0.2	<.1	0.4	12	2	16	18	5.3	5.9	1.0	1.6
	District 7	570,902	93.1	5.3	0.7	0.2	<.1	0.7	6	9	8	12	5.3	5.6	2.6	2.7
	District 8	570,901	95.9	2.8	0.7	0.1	<.1	0.5	13	5	13	17	5.3	5.8	1.4	2.0
	District 9	570,901	83.3	12.1	1.0	0.2	<.1	3.4	14	15	5	2	5.3	5.0	6.0	13.8
	District 10	570,903	92.3	2.0	1.4	0.2	<.1	4.0	1	10	18	1	5.3	5.6	1.0	16.4
	District 11	570,901	39.3	58.3	1.0	0.2	0.1	1.1	7	19	1	6	5.3	2.4	29.0	4.6
	District 12	570,902	74.4	23.1	1.3	0.2	0.1	0.8	2	17	3	10	5.3	4.5	11.5	3.5
	District 13	570,894	91.9	4.5	0.5	0.2	<.1	2.9	19	11	12	4	5.3	5.6	2.2	11.9
	District 14	570,900	87.3	10.9	1.0	0.2	<.1	0.6	16	14	6	15	5.3	5.3	5.4	2.4
	District 15	570,902	91.8	4.8	2.1	0.2	<.1	1.0	3	12	9	7	5.3	5.5	2.4	3.9
	District 16	570,902	93.9	4.8	0.4	0.2	<.1	0.6	4	7	10	13	5.3	5.7	2.4	2.6
	District 17	570,900	88.4	9.7	0.4	0.2	<.1	1.3	17	13	7	5	5.3	5.3	4.8	5.5
	District 18	570,900	96.9	2.3	0.2	0.2	<.1	0.3	18	1	14	19	5.3	5.9	1.2	1.4
	District 19	570,901	96.2	1.8	1.0	<.1	<.1	0.9	8	4	19	9	5.3	5.8	0.9	3.6

Table B. — 1990 Voting Age Population (VAP) by Race and Ethnic Origin

County	Total Voting Age Population	Percent of total VAP — Non-Hispanic White	Black	Asian and Pacific Islander	Native American	Other	Hispanic	Rank — Percent of total VAP Total	Non-Hispanic White	Black	Hispanic	Percent contribution to state VAP Total	Non-Hispanic White	Black	Hispanic	VAP percent of total population Total	Non-Hispanic White	Black	Asian and Pacific Islander	Native American	Other	Hispanic
Adams	18,013	99.1	0.2	<.1	0.3	0.0	0.3	79	8	78	60	0.2	0.3	<.1	<.1	71.0	71.0	68.1	53.6	76.1	0.0	63.3
Allen	79,749	88.3	10.0	0.4	0.2	<.1	1.0	22	80	8	20	1.0	1.0	1.0	0.9	72.7	73.8	65.3	64.3	80.0	11.7	64.6
Ashland	34,518	98.3	0.8	0.5	0.1	<.1	0.3	49	22	64	58	0.4	0.5	<.1	0.1	72.7	72.9	58.3	67.8	83.3	42.9	58.1
Ashtabula	72,503	95.5	2.8	0.3	0.2	<.1	1.2	26	60	27	19	0.9	1.0	0.3	1.0	72.6	73.2	65.2	68.6	75.0	22.9	56.0
Athens	47,418	93.6	2.8	2.5	0.3	<.1	0.7	38	68	26	24	0.6	0.6	0.2	0.4	79.6	79.4	81.6	87.9	82.9	52.1	77.6
Auglaize	31,541	99.0	0.1	0.3	0.1	<.1	0.4	50	10	81	46	0.4	0.4	<.1	0.2	70.7	70.9	64.6	64.8	82.5	28.6	56.8
Belmont	54,228	97.8	1.7	0.2	0.1	<.1	0.2	34	31	42	77	0.7	0.7	0.1	0.2	76.3	76.5	70.4	70.9	76.0	6.5	67.5
Brown	24,954	98.5	1.2	<.1	<.1	0.0	0.1	65	18	54	88	0.3	0.3	<.1	<.1	71.4	71.4	72.3	73.3	82.1	0.0	57.1
Butler	215,198	94.5	4.1	0.8	0.1	<.1	0.5	8	64	22	45	2.7	2.9	1.1	1.1	73.8	74.3	67.0	69.2	77.7	15.7	66.7
Carroll	19,269	98.9	0.5	<.1	0.2	0.0	0.3	77	12	70	62	0.2	0.3	<.1	<.1	72.7	72.7	71.6	65.5	67.7	0.0	59.6
Champaign	26,448	96.2	2.7	0.3	0.2	<.1	0.6	61	51	29	31	0.3	0.4	<.1	0.2	73.4	73.6	72.8	61.3	85.3	22.7	63.8
Clark	109,624	90.9	8.0	0.4	0.2	<.1	0.5	13	76	10	36	1.4	1.4	1.1	0.7	74.3	75.1	67.8	68.3	71.8	26.3	61.5
Clermont	106,141	98.3	0.8	0.3	0.2	<.1	0.4	15	20	62	47	1.3	1.5	0.1	0.5	70.7	70.8	66.3	65.6	74.8	35.3	63.2
Clinton	25,737	97.3	1.9	0.4	0.1	<.1	0.3	64	41	36	64	0.3	0.4	<.1	<.1	72.7	72.8	68.3	67.4	63.0	60.0	63.9
Columbiana	79,471	98.1	1.2	0.2	0.1	<.1	0.3	23	26	51	65	1.0	1.1	0.1	0.3	73.4	73.5	69.3	71.6	70.9	10.7	59.5
Coshocton	25,748	98.2	1.1	0.3	0.2	0.0	0.2	63	25	55	78	0.3	0.4	<.1	<.1	72.7	72.8	68.4	70.5	67.2	0.0	57.5
Crawford	35,090	98.7	0.5	0.2	0.1	<.1	0.5	48	15	72	44	0.4	0.5	<.1	0.2	73.3	73.4	62.7	66.7	75.8	14.3	65.4
Cuyahoga	1,073,957	74.2	22.6	1.2	0.2	<.1	1.8	1	88	1	13	13.3	11.2	31.0	22.6	76.1	78.8	69.6	71.9	72.1	38.2	62.7
Darke	38,813	98.8	0.3	0.2	0.2	<.1	0.5	45	14	74	41	0.5	0.5	<.1	0.2	72.4	72.5	71.6	66.1	80.0	50.0	56.6
Defiance	28,071	92.9	1.2	0.3	0.2	<.1	5.4	56	71	52	1	0.3	0.4	<.1	1.7	71.3	72.4	71.2	69.5	77.8	40.0	57.0
Delaware	48,523	97.0	1.8	0.6	0.2	<.1	0.4	36	46	37	52	0.6	0.7	0.1	0.2	72.5	72.8	62.7	75.6	79.2	23.5	56.3
Erie	56,677	91.2	7.1	0.3	0.2	<.1	1.3	33	75	15	18	0.7	0.7	0.5	0.8	73.8	75.0	64.1	64.5	70.0	14.1	60.8
Fairfield	75,467	97.8	1.3	0.3	0.2	<.1	0.4	24	32	48	49	0.9	1.0	0.1	0.4	72.9	72.9	85.0	69.8	66.5	72.7	63.0
Fayette	20,221	96.7	2.5	0.3	0.1	<.1	0.3	75	47	32	69	0.3	0.3	<.1	<.1	73.6	73.7	77.1	65.3	59.2	29.0	65.2
Franklin	724,671	82.8	14.2	1.9	0.2	<.1	0.9	2	85	4	22	9.0	8.5	13.1	7.5	74.7	77.1	67.6	71.8	75.9	30.9	70.8
Fulton	27,173	95.4	0.1	0.3	0.2	<.1	4.0	59	62	80	4	0.3	0.4	<.1	1.2	70.6	71.3	43.5	60.4	78.9	61.5	58.6
Gallia	22,688	96.0	2.8	0.5	0.3	<.1	0.4	69	54	28	50	0.3	0.3	<.1	0.1	73.3	73.3	73.8	85.7	83.3	40.0	57.7
Geauga	57,882	98.0	1.3	0.3	<.1	<.1	0.3	32	28	49	68	0.7	0.8	<.1	0.2	71.3	71.5	68.7	65.4	63.3	13.3	57.8
Greene	101,603	90.0	7.3	1.5	0.3	<.1	0.9	16	78	14	21	1.3	1.3	0.9	1.1	74.3	74.3	77.4	70.4	76.8	34.6	67.2
Guernsey	28,547	97.8	1.5	0.3	0.2	0.0	0.3	55	33	44	74	0.4	0.4	<.1	<.1	73.2	73.3	69.2	62.9	67.1	0.0	60.8
Hamilton	641,298	79.5	18.8	1.0	0.1	<.1	0.5	3	87	2	35	8.0	7.2	15.4	4.0	74.0	76.1	66.6	73.1	76.4	25.2	67.6
Hancock	47,894	96.4	0.8	0.5	0.1	<.1	2.1	37	48	63	11	0.6	0.7	<.1	1.2	73.1	73.5	66.2	67.6	72.8	36.4	61.0
Hardin	23,125	98.2	0.8	0.4	0.2	<.1	0.4	67	24	60	53	0.3	0.3	<.1	0.1	74.3	74.3	82.8	80.4	68.4	90.0	60.7
Harrison	12,018	97.4	2.2	<.1	0.2	0.0	0.2	84	40	34	83	0.1	0.2	<.1	<.1	74.7	75.0	68.8	40.0	86.4	0.0	58.1
Henry	20,656	95.7	0.2	0.3	0.1	<.1	3.7	44	57	79	5	0.3	0.3	<.1	0.9	71.0	71.9	24.5	58.2	68.2	72.7	57.0
Highland	25,936	97.6	1.8	0.2	0.2	<.1	0.3	62	36	39	72	0.3	0.4	<.1	<.1	72.6	72.8	66.3	66.2	73.6	14.3	67.6
Hocking	18,740	98.3	1.1	<.1	0.2	<.1	0.3	78	21	57	59	0.2	0.3	<.1	<.1	73.4	73.3	84.2	62.5	78.2	33.3	64.5
Holmes	21,076	99.3	0.2	0.1	<.1	<.1	0.3	73	5	77	63	0.3	0.3	<.1	<.1	64.2	64.2	82.7	53.5	95.2	66.7	52.0
Huron	39,778	97.1	1.0	0.2	0.2	<.1	1.4	44	45	59	16	0.5	0.5	<.1	0.7	70.7	71.1	67.1	55.4	79.8	8.7	57.3
Jackson	21,927	98.7	0.7	0.1	0.2	<.1	0.2	72	16	65	79	0.3	0.3	<.1	<.1	72.5	72.6	75.6	63.9	76.9	25.0	57.3
Jefferson	61,351	93.9	5.1	0.3	0.2	<.1	0.5	29	67	19	39	0.8	0.8	0.4	0.4	76.4	76.9	69.3	73.0	72.4	10.3	73.0
Knox	35,637	98.3	0.8	0.4	0.2	<.1	0.3	47	19	61	70	0.4	0.5	<.1	0.1	75.1	75.2	76.7	70.3	69.2	13.0	59.6
Lake	161,755	97.2	1.5	0.6	0.1	<.1	0.6	12	44	45	28	2.0	2.2	0.3	1.1	75.1	75.3	68.9	69.4	71.7	20.5	67.0
Lawrence	45,127	97.2	2.4	0.1	<.1	<.1	0.2	41	42	33	86	0.6	0.6	0.1	0.1	73.0	73.1	68.8	71.4	78.9	30.0	63.3
Licking	94,530	97.5	1.6	0.3	0.2	<.1	0.4	17	37	43	51	1.2	1.3	0.2	0.4	73.7	73.9	69.4	66.4	70.1	10.3	61.8
Logan	30,628	97.4	1.7	0.5	0.1	<.1	0.3	52	39	41	57	0.4	0.4	<.1	0.1	72.4	72.7	64.3	62.8	74.1	13.3	62.9
Lorain	196,710	87.8	6.8	0.5	0.2	<.1	4.6	10	82	16	3	2.4	2.4	1.7	10.4	73.6	74.2	64.5	71.8	68.4	35.6	59.2
Lucas	340,046	83.1	12.9	1.1	0.2	<.1	2.7	6	84	5	8	4.2	4.0	5.6	10.4	73.5	75.8	64.8	75.1	72.4	37.0	57.9
Madison	27,886	89.8	8.9	0.4	0.3	<.1	0.6	57	79	9	32	0.3	0.4	0.3	0.2	75.2	74.0	90.7	69.6	95.6	39.5	73.6
Mahoning	199,887	84.8	12.8	0.3	0.1	<.1	1.8	9	83	6	14	2.5	2.4	3.3	4.2	75.5	77.7	65.5	71.9	72.6	31.2	61.7
Marion	47,108	94.2	4.5	0.4	0.2	<.1	0.7	39	66	21	27	0.6	0.6	0.3	0.4	73.3	73.2	78.0	65.8	76.3	18.9	64.7
Medina	87,487	98.2	0.6	0.5	0.1	<.1	0.5	19	23	68	40	1.1	1.2	<.1	0.5	71.5	71.7	66.8	60.6	71.5	16.7	62.0
Meigs	16,805	98.8	0.7	<.1	0.2	<.1	0.2	81	13	66	76	0.2	0.2	<.1	<.1	73.1	73.2	67.8	52.6	78.0	100.0	69.5
Mercer	27,203	99.0	<.1	0.2	0.2	<.1	0.6	58	9	88	33	0.3	0.4	<.1	0.2	69.0	69.1	75.0	59.2	62.2	14.3	55.4
Miami	68,190	97.2	1.7	0.6	0.2	<.1	0.3	27	43	40	56	0.8	0.9	0.2	0.3	73.2	73.4	66.3	65.5	74.5	25.0	60.9
Monroe	11,510	99.6	<.1	<.1	0.1	0.0	0.2	85	1	84	87	0.1	0.2	<.1	<.1	74.3	74.3	47.4	50.0	65.4	0.0	75.0
Montgomery	431,169	82.1	16.0	0.9	0.2	<.1	0.7	4	86	3	25	5.4	5.0	8.8	3.5	75.1	76.9	68.1	69.8	78.5	22.4	67.7
Morgan	10,124	95.4	3.8	<.1	0.4	<.1	0.2	86	63	23	85	0.1	0.1	<.1	<.1	71.3	71.6	68.1	66.7	69.8	30.0	55.6
Morrow	19,687	99.2	0.2	0.1	0.2	0.0	0.3	76	7	75	61	0.2	0.3	<.1	<.1	70.9	71.0	73.0	57.9	73.5	0.0	66.3
Muskingum	60,147	95.5	3.8	0.2	0.2	<.1	0.3	30	61	24	75	0.7	0.8	0.3	0.2	73.3	73.7	66.5	72.8	69.7	37.0	61.5
Noble	8,054	99.5	<.1	<.1	0.1	0.0	0.2	87	3	85	82	0.1	0.1	<.1	<.1	71.0	71.0	85.7	77.8	80.0	0.0	73.9
Ottawa	30,089	96.1	0.6	0.2	0.1	<.1	2.9	53	53	69	7	0.4	0.4	<.1	1.0	75.2	75.8	70.9	70.1	82.6	83.3	68.7
Paulding	14,376	96.2	1.0	<.1	0.3	<.1	2.4	83	52	58	9	0.2	0.2	<.1	0.4	70.2	70.6	70.0	64.7	88.4	30.0	56.1
Perry	22,409	99.3	0.2	<.1	0.2	<.1	0.2	70	4	76	80	0.3	0.3	<.1	<.1	71.0	71.0	86.0	66.7	86.7	45.5	63.0
Pickaway	36,542	90.8	7.9	0.2	0.3	<.1	0.8	46	77	11	23	0.5	0.5	0.4	0.3	75.7	74.3	97.0	63.3	86.6	40.9	85.1
Pike	17,284	98.1	1.2	0.1	0.3	0.0	0.3	80	27	50	73	0.2	0.2	<.1	<.1	71.3	71.4	66.1	62.5	63.4	0.0	64.9
Portage	107,612	95.9	2.6	0.8	0.2	<.1	0.5	14	55	30	43	1.3	1.5	0.4	0.6	75.5	75.7	71.0	77.7	73.0	31.6	67.2
Preble	29,047	99.2	0.3	0.1	0.1	0.0	0.2	54	6	73	84	0.4	0.4	<.1	<.1	72.4	72.5	71.6	66.7	75.5	0.0	56.2
Putnam	23,109	96.3	<.1	<.1	<.1	<.1	3.4	68	50	82	6	0.3	0.3	<.1	0.9	68.3	68.9	76.0	75.0	67.7	87.5	55.1
Richland	93,176	91.4	7.5	0.4	0.2	<.1	0.6	18	74	12	30	1.2	1.2	0.9	0.6	73.9	74.4	70.1	57.7	77.0	31.0	62.2

Table B. — 1990 Voting Age Population (VAP) by Race and Ethnic Origin (cont)

County	Total Voting Age Population	Percent of total VAP — Non-Hispanic White	Black	Asian and Pacific Islander	Native American	Other	Hispanic	Rank — Percent of total VAP Total	Non-Hispanic White	Black	Hispanic	Percent contribution to state VAP Total	Non-Hispanic White	Black	Hispanic	VAP percent of total population Total	Non-Hispanic White	Black	Asian and Pacific Islander	Native American	Other	Hispanic
Ross....................	51,997	91.6	7.3	0.4	0.2	<.1	0.5	35	73	13	38	0.6	0.7	0.5	0.3	75.0	74.3	85.5	69.8	76.7	50.0	76.3
Sandusky................	44,602	92.9	2.0	0.2	0.1	<.1	4.7	42	70	35	2	0.6	0.6	0.1	2.4	72.0	73.1	60.1	72.7	68.2	30.8	59.3
Scioto..................	58,827	95.6	3.5	0.1	0.5	<.1	0.3	31	58	25	71	0.7	0.8	0.3	0.2	73.2	73.0	83.6	70.2	71.5	27.8	64.4
Seneca..................	42,716	95.5	1.8	0.4	0.1	<.1	2.2	43	59	38	10	0.5	0.6	<.1	1.1	71.5	72.1	66.1	69.3	66.7	26.5	56.4
Shelby..................	31,472	97.5	1.3	0.8	0.1	<.1	0.4	51	38	47	54	0.4	0.4	<.1	0.1	70.1	70.2	65.6	63.1	72.3	26.7	61.1
Stark...................	275,119	92.8	5.9	0.4	0.2	<.1	0.7	7	72	18	26	3.4	3.6	2.1	2.2	74.8	75.7	64.9	68.9	69.5	30.9	69.1
Summit..................	389,201	87.9	10.4	0.9	0.2	<.1	0.5	5	81	7	37	4.8	4.8	5.2	2.3	75.6	76.9	66.8	69.4	75.2	22.2	67.0
Trumbull	170,416	93.0	5.9	0.4	0.2	<.1	0.6	11	69	17	34	2.1	2.2	1.3	1.1	74.8	75.5	66.3	68.2	78.4	21.6	64.8
Tuscarawas	61,938	98.7	0.7	0.2	0.2	<.1	0.2	28	17	67	81	0.8	0.9	<.1	0.2	73.7	73.7	70.8	62.0	73.5	37.5	59.2
Union..................	23,436	94.3	4.7	0.4	0.2	<.1	0.5	66	65	20	42	0.3	0.3	0.1	0.1	73.3	72.5	94.9	65.9	76.9	58.3	73.6
Van Wert	22,030	97.8	0.5	0.2	0.1	<.1	1.3	71	30	71	17	0.3	0.3	<.1	0.3	72.3	72.6	58.3	59.7	85.7	25.0	60.4
Vinton	8,021	99.5	<.1	<.1	0.1	0.0	0.3	88	2	87	67	<.1	0.1	<.1	<.1	72.3	72.3	75.0	33.3	75.0	0.0	72.7
Warren..................	83,253	96.3	2.5	0.5	0.2	<.1	0.4	21	49	31	48	1.0	1.1	0.3	0.4	73.1	72.8	88.4	69.0	70.0	18.5	66.0
Washington	46,286	98.0	1.2	0.3	0.2	<.1	0.3	40	29	53	66	0.6	0.6	<.1	0.2	74.4	74.4	71.7	72.4	81.1	51.7	61.8
Wayne..................	72,662	97.6	1.4	0.5	0.1	<.1	0.3	25	35	46	55	0.9	1.0	0.1	0.3	71.6	71.8	65.3	70.5	74.4	26.7	59.2
Williams................	26,496	97.8	<.1	0.3	0.1	<.1	1.8	60	34	86	15	0.3	0.4	<.1	0.5	71.7	72.1	75.0	56.8	75.0	28.6	57.0
Wood...................	85,692	95.8	1.1	0.9	0.2	<.1	2.1	20	56	56	12	1.1	1.2	0.1	2.0	75.7	76.0	80.8	74.4	82.8	34.4	61.5
Wyandot................	16,131	98.9	<.1	0.3	0.1	<.1	0.6	82	11	83	29	0.2	0.2	<.1	0.1	72.5	72.6	68.4	64.6	95.0	100.0	60.5
OHIO	**8,047,371**	**88.2**	**9.7**	**0.8**	**0.2**	**<.1**	**1.1**					**100.0**	**100.0**	**100.0**	**100.0**	**74.2**	**75.2**	**68.1**	**71.2**	**74.2**	**29.7**	**62.4**
CONGRESSIONAL																						
District 1	420,468	71.2	27.1	1.0	0.1	<.1	0.6	12	18	2	14	5.2	4.2	14.6	2.7	73.7	76.9	66.5	77.0	74.1	23.6	68.6
District 2	417,784	96.4	2.2	0.7	0.1	<.1	0.5	14	4	14	16	5.2	5.7	1.2	2.2	73.2	73.3	72.8	67.8	79.0	31.8	65.3
District 3	429,073	82.0	16.1	0.9	0.2	<.1	0.7	5	16	4	11	5.3	5.0	8.8	3.5	75.2	76.9	68.1	69.8	78.8	22.4	67.7
District 4	417,141	94.4	4.3	0.4	0.2	<.1	0.8	15	8	10	8	5.2	5.5	2.3	3.8	73.1	73.4	68.6	64.5	77.5	24.6	62.5
District 5	411,006	95.2	1.9	0.3	0.2	<.1	2.5	19	6	17	3	5.1	5.5	1.0	11.7	72.0	72.6	65.5	66.5	74.3	30.4	57.9
District 6	421,059	96.8	2.1	0.5	0.2	<.1	0.3	11	2	16	18	5.2	5.7	1.2	1.7	73.8	73.7	75.1	78.9	73.9	41.8	66.0
District 7	421,456	93.2	5.4	0.6	0.2	<.1	0.6	9	10	8	12	5.2	5.5	2.9	2.8	73.8	73.9	75.1	68.6	74.0	34.0	65.9
District 8	415,676	96.3	2.5	0.6	0.1	<.1	0.4	17	5	13	17	5.2	5.6	1.4	2.0	72.8	73.1	66.9	67.7	75.5	21.3	62.9
District 9	421,341	85.5	10.6	1.0	0.2	<.1	2.7	10	15	5	2	5.2	5.1	5.7	13.0	73.8	75.7	65.0	75.1	73.8	37.3	58.4
District 10	435,467	93.6	1.7	1.2	0.2	<.1	3.2	3	9	18	1	5.4	5.7	1.0	16.0	76.3	77.3	65.2	68.9	68.0	40.5	60.8
District 11	424,718	43.1	54.6	1.1	0.2	<.1	1.0	7	19	1	6	5.3	2.6	29.7	4.9	74.4	81.5	69.7	79.1	75.1	37.0	67.1
District 12	416,053	76.5	21.3	1.2	0.2	<.1	0.8	16	17	3	9	5.2	4.5	11.3	3.7	72.9	75.0	67.0	66.6	75.0	27.5	66.1
District 13	413,086	92.9	4.0	0.5	0.2	<.1	2.4	18	11	12	4	5.1	5.4	2.1	11.3	72.4	73.2	64.9	68.1	68.8	32.1	59.4
District 14	433,423	88.7	9.6	0.9	0.2	<.1	0.5	4	14	6	15	5.4	5.4	5.3	2.7	75.9	77.2	67.0	70.9	75.3	23.1	67.8
District 15	443,164	92.0	4.7	2.1	0.2	<.1	0.9	1	12	9	7	5.5	5.7	2.7	4.7	77.6	77.9	75.5	75.2	78.8	35.2	75.1
District 16	419,742	94.6	4.2	0.4	0.2	<.1	0.6	13	7	11	13	5.2	5.6	2.3	2.8	73.5	74.1	65.0	69.0	70.5	29.9	66.4
District 17	428,405	89.9	8.5	0.3	0.1	<.1	1.1	6	13	7	5	5.3	5.4	4.6	5.5	75.0	76.3	65.7	70.4	73.9	23.7	62.2
District 18	421,743	97.1	2.2	0.2	0.2	<.1	0.3	8	1	15	19	5.2	5.8	1.2	1.4	73.9	74.1	68.6	67.1	71.8	20.2	63.3
District 19	436,566	96.6	1.6	0.9	<.1	<.1	0.7	2	3	19	10	5.4	5.9	0.9	3.7	76.5	76.8	69.0	68.5	76.3	26.8	64.8

Table C. — Voter Participation: November 3, 1992, General Election

County	Estimated Voting Age Population (VAP), 1992	Voter registration (REG)				Voter turnout — Highest office				Voter turnout — Maximum vote						Percent drop-off, by office			
		Total	% contribution to state REG	% of 1992 VAP	Rank by % of 1992 VAP	Actual	Total	Office	% of 1992 VAP	Total	% contribution to state turnout	% of REG	Rank by % of REG	% of 1992 VAP	Rank by % 1992 VAP	President	Senator	Governor	Representative
Adams	18,747	14,904	0.2	79.5	45	11,085	10,758	P	57.4	11,085	0.2	74.4	79	59.1	71	2.9	5.2	-	14.0
Allen	80,026	60,797	0.9	76.0	68	48,264	47,350	P	59.2	48,264	1.0	79.4	35	60.3	60	1.9	3.1	-	3.2
Ashland	35,058	25,906	0.4	73.9	79	21,100	20,855	P	59.5	21,100	0.4	81.4	10	60.2	64	1.2	2.4	-	6.4
Ashtabula	73,037	57,224	0.9	78.3	50	44,164	43,028	P	58.9	44,164	0.9	77.2	65	60.5	58	2.6	4.8	-	6.4
Athens	45,760	39,542	0.6	86.4	8	26,322	25,793	P	56.4	26,322	0.5	66.6	87	57.5	82	2.0	3.8	-	5.6
Auglaize	32,403	26,031	0.4	80.3	39	20,569	20,306	P	62.7	20,569	0.4	79.0	46	63.5	35	1.3	2.6	-	4.7
Belmont	53,041	45,824	0.7	86.4	9	34,212	33,421	P	63.0	34,212	0.7	74.7	78	64.5	22	2.3	4.0	-	4.0
Brown	25,993	19,984	0.3	76.9	61	15,466	15,186	P	58.4	15,466	0.3	77.4	63	59.5	70	1.8	4.3	-	10.8
Butler	221,979	173,780	2.7	78.3	51	133,209	131,112	P	59.1	133,209	2.6	76.7	67	60.0	66	1.6	3.9	-	9.3
Carroll	19,781	16,328	0.2	82.5	28	12,727	12,463	P	63.0	12,727	0.3	77.9	55	64.3	25	2.1	4.0	-	6.3
Champaign	27,372	21,337	0.3	78.0	55	16,542	16,252	P	59.4	16,542	0.3	77.5	59	60.4	59	1.8	3.1	-	9.1
Clark	110,277	83,007	1.3	75.3	73	64,892	63,538	P	57.6	64,892	1.3	78.2	52	58.8	74	2.1	3.0	-	7.9
Clermont	112,452	81,930	1.3	72.9	81	66,299	64,142	P	57.0	66,299	1.3	80.9	13	59.0	73	3.3	4.4	-	9.4
Clinton	26,263	20,048	0.3	76.3	67	15,635	15,391	P	58.6	15,635	0.3	78.0	54	59.5	69	1.6	3.4	-	6.4
Columbiana	80,159	63,496	1.0	79.2	47	48,609	47,554	P	59.3	48,609	1.0	76.6	68	60.6	55	2.2	3.8	-	4.6
Coshocton	26,042	20,638	0.3	79.2	46	16,587	16,173	P	62.1	16,587	0.3	80.4	21	63.7	31	2.5	5.1	-	9.7
Crawford	35,209	27,506	0.4	78.1	54	21,306	20,835	P	59.2	21,306	0.4	77.5	61	60.5	57	2.2	4.0	-	6.3
Cuyahoga	1,069,718	932,611	14.3	87.2	7	656,034	640,241	P	59.9	656,034	13.0	70.3	85	61.3	47	2.4	5.4	-	9.1
Darke	39,258	31,057	0.5	79.1	48	24,949	24,426	P	62.2	24,949	0.5	80.3	22	63.6	34	2.1	3.8	-	7.3
Defiance	28,583	21,940	0.3	76.8	62	17,595	17,211	P	60.2	17,595	0.3	80.2	25	61.6	44	2.2	4.1	-	28.2
Delaware	51,849	46,760	0.7	90.2	4	37,291	36,873	P	71.1	37,291	0.7	79.7	30	71.9	3	1.1	2.8	-	4.2
Erie	57,123	46,549	0.7	81.5	31	36,629	35,828	P	62.7	36,629	0.7	78.7	47	64.1	27	2.2	3.7	-	33.9
Fairfield	78,710	63,661	1.0	80.9	34	51,456	50,789	P	64.5	51,456	1.0	80.8	17	65.4	17	1.3	2.4	-	11.5
Fayette	20,545	13,274	0.2	64.6	85	10,287	10,086	P	49.1	10,287	0.2	77.5	60	50.1	86	2.0	2.7	-	11.7
Franklin	744,450	582,202	8.9	78.2	52	450,833	444,801	P	59.7	450,833	8.9	77.4	62	60.6	56	1.3	6.8	-	10.1
Fulton	27,946	23,613	0.4	84.5	13	19,067	18,804	P	67.3	19,067	0.4	80.7	18	68.2	6	1.4	3.7	-	3.7
Gallia	23,104	19,657	0.3	85.1	11	14,147	13,738	P	59.5	14,147	0.3	72.0	83	61.2	51	0.7	9.2	-	9.5
Geauga	60,087	50,445	0.8	84.0	15	40,821	40,518	P	67.4	40,821	0.8	80.9	14	67.9	8	0.7	9.2	-	13.3
Greene	103,080	82,837	1.3	80.4	38	65,644	59,708	S	57.9	65,644	1.3	79.2	41	63.7	32	9.4	9.0	-	14.9
Guernsey	28,565	22,317	0.3	78.1	53	16,730	16,348	P	57.2	16,730	0.3	75.0	77	58.6	75	2.3	3.7	-	5.2
Hamilton	644,767	536,386	8.2	83.2	23	413,357	403,420	P	62.6	413,357	8.2	77.1	66	64.1	28	2.4	4.7	-	8.0
Hancock	48,694	39,692	0.6	81.5	30	32,153	31,963	P	65.6	32,153	0.6	81.0	12	66.0	12	0.6	4.7	-	9.8
Hardin	22,840	16,812	0.3	73.6	80	13,305	13,215	P	57.9	13,305	0.3	79.1	45	58.3	78	0.7	2.7	-	4.2
Harrison	11,953	10,000	0.2	83.7	17	8,032	7,827	P	65.5	8,032	0.2	80.3	23	67.2	10	2.6	4.4	-	4.7
Henry	21,178	16,932	0.3	80.0	42	13,538	13,359	P	63.1	13,538	0.3	80.0	28	63.9	29	1.3	3.0	-	22.1
Highland	26,912	20,426	0.3	75.9	70	15,551	15,242	P	56.6	15,551	0.3	76.1	70	57.8	81	2.0	2.9	-	3.1
Hocking	19,275	14,406	0.2	74.7	77	10,847	10,574	P	54.9	10,847	0.2	75.3	73	56.3	83	2.5	4.0	-	5.9
Holmes	22,086	13,588	0.2	61.5	88	10,824	9,056	P	41.0	10,824	0.2	79.7	31	49.0	88	16.3	20.7	-	20.6
Huron	40,948	31,666	0.5	77.3	57	24,652	24,471	P	59.8	24,652	0.5	77.9	57	60.2	62	0.7	3.5	-	36.8
Jackson	22,442	20,210	0.3	90.1	5	13,233	12,883	P	57.4	13,233	0.3	65.5	88	59.0	72	2.6	5.2	-	5.3
Jefferson	60,477	50,591	0.8	83.7	18	39,673	38,798	P	64.2	39,673	0.8	78.4	50	65.6	15	2.2	4.4	-	4.2
Knox	35,878	26,996	0.4	75.2	74	21,877	21,745	P	60.6	21,877	0.4	81.0	11	65.2	52	0.6	5.5	-	15.0
Lake	164,040	135,000	2.1	82.3	29	106,989	105,990	P	64.6	106,989	2.1	79.3	40	65.2	19	0.9	8.3	-	9.9
Lawrence	45,930	38,530	0.6	83.9	16	27,700	27,021	P	58.8	27,700	0.5	71.9	84	60.3	61	2.5	4.9	-	6.0
Licking	96,819	78,024	1.2	80.6	37	61,350	60,434	P	62.4	61,350	1.2	78.6	48	63.4	36	1.5	2.1	-	6.6
Logan	31,859	26,424	0.4	82.9	26	19,151	18,787	P	59.0	19,151	0.4	72.5	82	60.1	65	1.9	2.8	-	10.7
Lorain	199,436	161,238	2.5	80.8	35	121,267	118,605	P	59.5	121,267	2.4	75.2	74	60.8	54	2.2	3.5	-	4.6
Lucas	342,014	262,219	4.0	76.7	63	204,182	203,019	P	59.4	204,182	4.0	77.9	56	59.7	68	0.6	10.5	-	4.6
Madison	29,082	17,925	0.3	61.6	87	14,297	14,071	P	49.2	14,297	0.3	79.8	29	49.2	87	1.6	2.9	-	5.4
Mahoning	198,373	165,241	2.5	83.3	21	129,485	125,650	P	63.3	129,485	2.6	78.4	51	65.3	18	3.0	3.4	-	3.4
Marion	47,155	35,444	0.5	75.2	75	28,175	27,715	P	58.8	28,175	0.6	79.5	33	59.7	67	1.6	2.5	-	7.7
Medina	91,005	75,769	1.2	83.3	22	61,255	60,601	P	66.6	61,255	1.2	80.8	16	67.3	9	1.1	2.9	-	5.6
Meigs	17,090	14,419	0.2	84.4	14	10,597	10,286	P	60.2	10,597	0.2	73.5	81	62.0	41	2.9	5.1	-	6.2
Mercer	27,810	23,199	0.4	83.4	19	18,930	18,548	P	66.7	18,930	0.4	81.6	7	68.1	7	2.0	3.3	-	12.7
Miami	69,937	53,070	0.8	75.9	71	43,745	43,006	P	61.5	43,745	0.9	82.4	3	62.5	38	1.7	2.9	-	11.6
Monroe	11,434	10,034	0.2	87.8	6	7,874	7,591	P	66.4	7,874	0.2	78.5	49	68.9	4	3.6	6.3	-	8.1
Montgomery	434,739	343,172	5.2	78.9	49	266,432	261,720	P	60.2	266,432	5.3	77.6	58	61.3	49	1.8	3.4	-	7.6
Morgan	10,407	8,672	0.1	83.3	20	6,865	6,707	P	64.4	6,865	0.1	79.2	43	66.0	14	2.3	4.3	-	15.4
Morrow	20,386	17,300	0.3	84.9	12	12,998	12,791	P	62.7	12,998	0.3	75.1	76	63.8	30	1.6	3.1	-	11.1
Muskingum	60,720	45,354	0.7	74.7	78	35,456	34,720	P	57.2	35,456	0.7	78.2	53	58.4	76	2.1	3.4	-	10.5
Noble	8,205	7,667	0.1	93.4	2	6,078	5,883	P	71.7	6,078	0.1	79.3	38	74.1	1	3.2	6.2	-	9.0
Ottawa	30,585	24,766	0.4	81.0	33	20,195	19,795	P	64.7	20,195	0.4	81.5	9	66.0	13	2.0	2.8	-	16.0
Paulding	14,578	12,114	0.2	83.1	25	9,702	9,510	P	65.2	9,702	0.2	80.1	26	66.6	11	2.0	4.1	-	31.0
Perry	23,043	18,454	0.3	80.1	41	13,869	13,547	P	58.8	13,869	0.3	75.2	75	60.2	63	2.3	3.6	-	14.5
Pickaway	37,820	24,657	0.4	65.2	84	19,055	18,930	P	50.1	19,055	0.4	77.3	64	50.4	85	0.7	3.2	-	13.2
Pike	18,069	17,163	0.3	95.0	1	11,737	11,393	P	63.1	11,737	0.2	68.4	86	65.0	20	2.9	5.7	-	4.7
Portage	107,838	82,388	1.3	76.4	65	62,946	62,135	P	57.6	62,946	1.2	76.4	69	58.4	77	1.3	2.7	-	6.4
Preble	29,997	22,969	0.4	76.6	64	18,440	18,098	P	60.3	18,440	0.4	80.3	24	61.5	45	1.9	3.2	-	8.0
Putnam	23,651	20,236	0.3	85.6	10	17,313	17,004	P	71.9	17,313	0.3	85.6	1	73.2	2	1.8	3.0	-	24.1
Richland	93,808	70,300	1.1	74.9	76	57,797	56,697	P	60.4	57,797	1.1	82.2	4	61.6	43	1.9	3.3	-	10.8

Table C. – **Voter Participation: November 3, 1992, General Election (cont)**

County	Estimated Voting Age Population (VAP), 1992	Voter registration (REG)				Voter turnout													
							Highest office			Maximum vote							Percent drop-off, by office			
		Total	% contribution to state REG	% of 1992 VAP	Rank by % of 1992 VAP	Actual	Total	Office	% of 1992 VAP	Total	% contribution to state turnout	% of REG	Rank by % of REG	% of 1992 VAP	Rank by % of 1992 VAP	President	Senator	Governor	Representative
Ross	53,815	34,759	0.5	64.6	86	27,579	27,173	P	50.5	27,579	0.5	79.3	36	51.2	84	1.5	11.0	-	11.6
Sandusky	45,175	32,704	0.5	72.4	82	27,935	27,472	P	60.8	27,935	0.6	85.4	2	61.8	42	1.7	4.1	-	30.3
Scioto	59,459	45,756	0.7	77.0	60	34,508	33,624	P	56.5	34,508	0.7	75.4	72	58.0	79	2.6	4.1	-	3.0
Seneca	43,013	33,397	0.5	77.6	56	26,744	26,150	P	60.8	26,744	0.5	80.1	27	62.2	40	2.2	3.7	-	24.6
Shelby	32,527	24,847	0.4	76.4	66	20,344	20,011	P	61.5	20,344	0.4	81.9	5	62.5	39	1.6	18.3	-	8.5
Stark	276,013	220,522	3.4	79.9	43	177,986	175,092	P	63.4	177,986	3.5	80.7	19	64.5	23	1.6	2.6	-	3.1
Summit	390,612	313,004	4.8	80.1	40	248,247	241,492	P	61.8	248,247	4.9	79.3	37	63.6	33	2.7	5.0	-	9.3
Trumbull	170,571	138,776	2.1	81.4	32	109,842	107,606	P	63.1	109,842	2.2	79.2	44	64.4	24	2.0	3.8	-	10.6
Tuscarawas	62,871	48,419	0.7	77.0	59	38,537	36,894	P	58.7	38,537	0.8	79.6	32	61.3	48	4.3	8.8	-	9.1
Union	24,407	18,542	0.3	76.0	69	14,994	14,777	P	60.5	14,994	0.3	80.9	15	61.4	46	1.4	15.9	-	9.2
Van Wert	22,514	18,185	0.3	80.8	36	14,441	14,217	P	63.1	14,441	0.3	79.4	34	64.1	26	1.6	2.8	-	24.8
Vinton	8,175	7,586	0.1	92.8	3	5,583	5,363	P	65.6	5,583	0.1	73.6	80	68.3	5	3.9	7.4	-	8.9
Warren	87,463	67,574	1.0	77.3	58	53,567	52,802	P	60.4	53,567	1.1	79.3	39	61.2	50	1.4	2.7	-	11.9
Washington	46,539	35,218	0.5	75.7	72	28,342	28,073	P	60.3	28,342	0.6	80.5	20	60.9	53	0.9	5.1	-	6.1
Wayne	74,125	52,549	0.8	70.9	83	42,880	41,982	P	56.6	42,880	0.9	81.6	6	57.8	80	2.1	4.1	-	5.0
Williams	27,076	22,391	0.3	82.7	27	17,730	17,464	P	64.5	17,730	0.4	79.2	42	65.5	16	1.5	4.1	-	27.4
Wood	85,403	71,030	1.1	83.2	24	53,827	53,203	P	62.3	53,827	1.1	75.8	71	63.0	37	1.2	3.5	-	21.3
Wyandot	16,345	13,014	0.2	79.6	44	10,615	10,443	P	63.9	10,615	0.2	81.6	8	64.9	21	1.6	3.3	-	4.9
OHIO	8,146,000	6,542,931	100.0	80.3		5,043,094	4,940,173		60.6	5,043,094	100.0	77.1		61.9		2.0	4.9	-	9.2

Table E. — Vote for President: November 3, 1992, General Election

County	Total	Clinton (DEM)	Bush (REP)	Perot (IND)	Other	Plurality Total	Party	DEM	REP	IND	Other	Rank DEM	Rank REP	Rank IND	Total	DEM	REP	IND	DEM	REP
Adams	10,758	3,998	4,722	1,993	45	724	R	37.2	43.9	18.5	0.4	36	32	80	0.2	0.2	0.2	0.2	45.8	54.2
Allen	47,350	13,777	25,322	8,131	120	11,545	R	29.1	53.5	17.2	0.3	69	3	86	1.0	0.7	1.3	0.8	35.2	64.8
Ashland	20,855	5,985	9,864	4,950	56	3,879	R	28.7	47.3	23.7	0.3	72	18	43	0.4	0.3	0.5	0.5	37.8	62.2
Ashtabula	43,028	18,843	13,254	10,765	166	5,589	D	43.8	30.8	25.0	0.4	13	79	25	0.9	0.9	0.7	1.0	58.7	41.3
Athens	25,793	13,423	7,184	5,074	112	6,239	D	52.0	27.9	19.7	0.4	5	83	72	0.5	0.7	0.4	0.5	65.1	34.9
Auglaize	20,306	4,960	10,455	4,840	51	5,495	R	24.4	51.5	23.8	0.3	85	7	39	0.4	0.2	0.6	0.5	32.2	67.8
Belmont	33,421	18,527	8,614	6,142	138	9,913	D	55.4	25.8	18.4	0.4	2	85	81	0.7	0.9	0.5	0.6	68.3	31.7
Brown	15,186	5,540	5,912	3,676	58	372	R	36.5	38.9	24.2	0.4	40	53	37	0.3	0.3	0.3	0.4	48.4	51.6
Butler	131,112	39,682	63,375	27,527	528	23,693	R	30.3	48.3	21.0	0.4	63	14	66	2.7	2.0	3.3	2.7	38.5	61.5
Carroll	12,463	4,731	4,224	3,434	74	507	D	38.0	33.9	27.6	0.6	33	74	9	0.3	0.2	0.2	0.3	52.8	47.2
Champaign	16,252	5,201	7,004	3,992	55	1,803	R	32.0	43.1	24.6	0.3	55	36	28	0.3	0.3	0.4	0.4	42.6	57.4
Clark	63,538	26,692	24,011	12,571	264	2,681	D	42.0	37.8	19.8	0.4	18	59	71	1.3	1.3	1.3	1.2	52.6	47.4
Clermont	64,142	17,558	32,065	14,279	240	14,507	R	27.4	50.0	22.3	0.4	77	9	54	1.3	0.9	1.7	1.4	35.4	64.6
Clinton	15,391	4,638	7,290	3,402	61	2,652	R	30.1	47.4	22.1	0.4	64	17	55	0.3	0.2	0.4	0.3	38.9	61.1
Columbiana	47,554	19,765	15,016	12,611	162	4,749	D	41.6	31.6	26.5	0.3	19	76	13	1.0	1.0	0.8	1.2	56.8	43.2
Coshocton	16,173	6,212	5,705	4,081	175	507	D	38.4	35.3	25.2	1.1	32	69	21	0.3	0.3	0.3	0.4	52.1	47.9
Crawford	20,835	6,351	8,618	5,764	102	2,267	R	30.5	41.4	27.7	0.5	61	45	7	0.4	0.3	0.5	0.6	42.4	57.6
Cuyahoga	640,241	337,548	187,186	112,352	3,155	150,362	D	52.7	29.2	17.5	0.5	4	82	85	13.0	17.0	9.9	10.8	64.3	35.7
Darke	24,426	7,016	11,098	6,217	95	4,082	R	28.7	45.4	25.5	0.4	71	25	19	0.5	0.4	0.6	0.6	38.7	61.3
Defiance	17,211	5,735	7,195	4,187	94	1,460	R	33.3	41.8	24.3	0.5	51	42	32	0.3	0.3	0.4	0.4	44.4	55.6
Delaware	36,873	9,263	18,225	9,244	141	8,962	R	25.1	49.4	25.1	0.4	83	11	24	0.7	0.5	1.0	0.9	33.7	66.3
Erie	35,828	14,531	12,449	8,720	118	2,072	D	40.6	34.8	24.3	0.3	23	72	31	0.7	0.7	0.7	0.8	53.8	46.2
Fairfield	50,789	14,249	24,125	12,246	169	9,876	R	28.1	47.5	24.1	0.3	75	16	38	1.0	0.7	1.3	1.2	37.1	62.9
Fayette	10,086	2,976	4,916	2,162	32	1,940	R	29.5	48.7	21.4	0.3	66	13	64	0.2	0.1	0.3	0.2	37.7	62.3
Franklin	444,801	176,656	186,324	79,049	2,772	9,668	R	39.7	41.9	17.8	0.6	26	41	84	9.0	8.9	9.8	7.6	48.7	51.3
Fulton	18,804	5,576	8,358	4,798	72	2,782	R	29.7	44.4	25.5	0.4	65	28	18	0.4	0.3	0.4	0.5	40.0	60.0
Gallia	13,738	5,350	5,776	2,549	63	426	R	38.9	42.0	18.6	0.5	29	40	78	0.3	0.3	0.3	0.2	48.1	51.9
Geauga	40,518	11,466	18,200	10,577	275	6,734	R	28.3	44.9	26.1	0.7	74	26	16	0.8	0.6	1.0	1.0	38.7	61.3
Greene	59,502	20,139	27,651	11,459	253	7,512	R	33.8	46.5	19.3	0.4	48	20	75	1.2	1.0	1.5	1.1	42.1	57.9
Guernsey	16,348	6,428	5,749	4,103	68	679	D	39.3	35.2	25.1	0.4	27	70	23	0.3	0.3	0.3	0.4	52.8	47.2
Hamilton	403,420	148,409	192,447	60,145	2,419	44,038	R	36.8	47.7	14.9	0.6	38	15	88	8.2	7.5	10.2	5.8	43.5	56.5
Hancock	31,963	7,944	16,821	7,002	196	8,877	R	24.9	52.6	21.9	0.6	84	6	57	0.6	0.4	0.9	0.7	32.1	67.9
Hardin	13,215	4,364	5,851	2,867	133	1,487	R	33.0	44.3	21.7	1.0	53	30	60	0.3	0.2	0.3	0.3	42.7	57.3
Harrison	7,827	3,830	2,289	1,679	29	1,541	D	48.9	29.2	21.5	0.4	9	81	63	0.2	0.2	0.1	0.2	62.6	37.4
Henry	13,359	3,933	6,196	3,178	52	2,263	R	29.4	46.4	23.8	0.4	67	21	42	0.3	0.2	0.3	0.3	38.8	61.2
Highland	15,242	4,866	7,020	3,315	41	2,154	R	31.9	46.1	21.7	0.3	56	22	59	0.3	0.2	0.4	0.3	40.9	59.1
Hocking	10,574	3,935	3,761	2,831	47	174	D	37.2	35.6	26.8	0.4	35	66	11	0.2	0.2	0.2	0.3	51.1	48.9
Holmes	9,056	1,969	5,079	1,945	63	3,110	R	21.7	56.1	21.5	0.7	88	1	61	0.2	<.1	0.3	0.2	27.9	72.1
Huron	24,471	7,930	9,480	6,751	310	1,550	R	32.4	38.7	27.6	1.3	54	54	8	0.5	0.4	0.5	0.7	45.5	54.5
Jackson	12,883	5,016	5,422	2,389	56	406	R	38.9	42.1	18.5	0.4	30	39	79	0.3	0.3	0.3	0.2	48.1	51.9
Jefferson	38,798	20,978	10,764	6,910	146	10,214	D	54.1	27.7	17.8	0.4	3	84	83	0.8	1.1	0.6	0.7	66.1	33.9
Knox	21,745	7,259	9,044	5,282	160	1,785	R	33.4	41.6	24.3	0.7	50	43	34	0.4	0.4	0.5	0.5	44.5	55.5
Lake	105,990	37,682	40,766	26,878	664	3,084	R	35.6	38.5	25.4	0.6	43	56	20	2.1	1.9	2.2	2.6	48.0	52.0
Lawrence	27,021	12,325	10,044	4,536	116	2,281	D	45.6	37.2	16.8	0.4	10	62	87	0.5	0.6	0.5	0.4	55.1	44.9
Licking	60,434	18,898	26,918	13,806	812	8,020	R	31.3	44.5	22.8	1.3	58	27	49	1.2	1.0	1.4	1.3	41.2	58.8
Logan	18,787	4,889	9,364	4,472	62	4,475	R	26.0	49.8	23.8	0.3	81	10	41	0.4	0.2	0.5	0.4	34.3	65.7
Lorain	118,605	50,962	36,803	30,425	415	14,159	D	43.0	31.0	25.7	0.3	16	78	17	2.4	2.6	1.9	2.9	58.1	41.9
Lucas	203,019	99,989	63,297	38,108	1,625	36,692	D	49.3	31.2	18.8	0.8	8	77	77	4.1	5.0	3.3	3.7	61.2	38.8
Madison	14,071	3,998	6,865	3,170	38	2,867	R	28.4	48.8	22.5	0.3	73	12	53	0.3	0.2	0.4	0.3	36.8	63.2
Mahoning	125,650	64,731	31,191	29,417	311	33,540	D	51.5	24.8	23.4	0.2	6	86	45	2.5	3.3	1.6	2.8	67.5	32.5
Marion	27,715	9,444	11,675	6,471	125	2,231	R	34.1	42.1	23.3	0.5	47	38	46	0.6	0.5	0.6	0.6	44.7	55.3
Medina	60,601	18,995	24,090	17,290	226	5,095	R	31.3	39.8	28.5	0.4	57	51	2	1.2	1.0	1.3	1.7	44.1	55.9
Meigs	10,286	4,226	3,916	2,098	46	310	D	41.1	38.1	20.4	0.4	21	58	69	0.2	0.2	0.2	0.2	51.9	48.1
Mercer	18,548	4,883	8,683	4,913	69	3,770	R	26.3	46.8	26.5	0.4	79	19	14	0.4	0.2	0.5	0.5	36.0	64.0
Miami	43,006	12,547	19,741	10,544	174	7,194	R	29.2	45.9	24.5	0.4	68	24	29	0.9	0.6	1.0	1.0	38.9	61.1
Monroe	7,591	4,235	1,823	1,505	28	2,412	D	55.8	24.0	19.8	0.4	1	87	70	0.2	0.2	<.1	0.1	69.9	30.1
Montgomery	261,720	108,017	104,751	47,854	1,098	3,266	D	41.3	40.0	18.3	0.4	20	49	82	5.3	5.4	5.5	4.6	50.8	49.2
Morgan	6,707	2,402	2,719	1,551	35	317	R	35.8	40.5	23.1	0.5	42	48	48	0.1	0.1	0.1	0.1	46.9	53.1
Morrow	12,791	3,907	5,208	3,623	53	1,301	R	30.5	40.7	28.3	0.4	60	47	3	0.3	0.2	0.3	0.3	42.9	57.1
Muskingum	34,720	11,670	14,168	8,731	151	2,498	R	33.6	40.8	25.1	0.4	49	46	22	0.7	0.6	0.7	0.8	45.2	54.8
Noble	5,883	2,201	2,223	1,429	30	22	R	37.4	37.8	24.3	0.5	34	60	35	0.1	0.1	0.1	0.1	49.8	50.2
Ottawa	19,795	8,128	6,782	4,832	53	1,346	D	41.1	34.3	24.4	0.3	22	73	30	0.4	0.4	0.4	0.5	54.5	45.5
Paulding	9,510	3,293	3,652	2,510	55	359	R	34.6	38.4	26.4	0.6	45	57	15	0.2	0.2	0.2	0.2	47.4	52.6
Perry	13,547	4,972	4,712	3,810	53	260	D	36.7	34.8	28.1	0.4	39	71	4	0.3	0.3	0.3	0.4	51.3	48.7
Pickaway	18,930	5,765	8,690	4,319	156	2,925	R	30.5	45.9	22.8	0.8	62	23	51	0.4	0.3	0.5	0.4	39.9	60.1
Pike	11,393	5,057	4,094	2,192	50	963	D	44.4	35.9	19.2	0.4	12	64	76	0.2	0.3	0.2	0.2	55.3	44.7
Portage	62,135	26,325	18,447	17,065	298	7,878	D	42.4	29.7	27.5	0.5	17	80	10	1.3	1.3	1.0	1.6	58.8	41.2
Preble	18,098	5,557	8,023	4,460	58	2,466	R	30.7	44.3	24.6	0.3	59	29	27	0.4	0.3	0.4	0.4	40.9	59.1
Putnam	17,004	3,962	9,338	3,648	56	5,376	R	23.3	54.9	21.5	0.3	87	2	62	0.3	0.2	0.5	0.4	29.8	70.2
Richland	56,697	19,606	23,532	13,370	189	3,926	R	34.6	41.5	23.6	0.3	46	44	44	1.1	1.0	1.2	1.3	45.4	54.6

Ohio 729

County	Total	Clinton (DEM)	Bush (REP)	Perot (IND)	Other	Plurality Total	Party	DEM	REP	IND	Other	Rank DEM	Rank REP	Rank IND	Total	DEM	REP	IND	DEM	REP
Ross	27,173	10,452	10,825	5,616	280	373	R	38.5	39.8	20.7	1.0	31	50	67	0.6	0.5	0.6	0.5	49.1	50.9
Sandusky	27,472	9,878	10,772	6,682	140	894	R	36.0	39.2	24.3	0.5	41	52	33	0.6	0.5	0.6	0.6	47.8	52.2
Scioto	33,624	14,715	11,931	6,860	118	2,784	D	43.8	35.5	20.4	0.4	14	67	68	0.7	0.7	0.6	0.7	55.2	44.8
Seneca	26,150	9,280	9,763	6,967	140	483	R	35.5	37.3	26.6	0.5	44	61	12	0.5	0.5	0.5	0.7	48.7	51.3
Shelby	20,011	5,262	8,854	5,835	60	3,019	R	26.3	44.2	29.2	0.3	80	31	1	0.4	0.3	0.5	0.6	37.3	62.7
Stark	175,092	70,064	61,863	42,413	752	8,201	D	40.0	35.3	24.2	0.4	25	68	36	3.5	3.5	3.3	4.1	53.1	46.9
Summit	241,492	107,881	77,530	55,151	930	30,351	D	44.7	32.1	22.8	0.4	11	75	50	4.9	5.4	4.1	5.3	58.2	41.8
Trumbull	107,606	54,591	25,831	26,791	393	27,800	D	50.7	24.0	24.9	0.4	7	88	26	2.2	2.8	1.4	2.6	67.9	32.1
Tuscarawas	36,894	14,787	13,179	8,785	143	1,608	D	40.1	35.7	23.8	0.4	24	65	40	0.7	0.7	0.7	0.8	52.9	47.1
Union	14,777	3,465	7,818	3,433	61	4,353	R	23.4	52.9	23.2	0.4	86	5	47	0.3	0.2	0.4	0.3	30.7	69.3
Van Wert	14,217	3,822	7,227	3,102	66	3,405	R	26.9	50.8	21.8	0.5	78	8	58	0.3	0.2	0.4	0.3	34.6	65.4
Vinton	5,363	2,308	1,975	1,050	30	333	D	43.0	36.8	19.6	0.6	15	63	73	0.1	0.1	0.1	0.1	53.9	46.1
Warren	52,802	13,542	27,998	11,115	147	14,456	R	25.6	53.0	21.1	0.3	82	4	65	1.1	0.7	1.5	1.1	32.6	67.4
Washington	28,073	10,380	12,204	5,415	74	1,824	R	37.0	43.5	19.3	0.3	37	35	74	0.6	0.5	0.6	0.5	46.0	54.0
Wayne	41,982	13,953	18,350	9,482	197	4,397	R	33.2	43.7	22.6	0.5	52	33	52	0.8	0.7	1.0	0.9	43.2	56.8
Williams	17,464	4,862	7,614	4,902	86	2,712	R	27.8	43.6	28.1	0.5	76	34	5	0.4	0.2	0.4	0.5	39.0	61.0
Wood	53,203	20,754	20,579	11,682	188	175	D	39.0	38.7	22.0	0.4	28	55	56	1.1	1.0	1.1	1.1	50.2	49.8
Wyandot	10,443	3,031	4,411	2,929	72	1,380	R	29.0	42.2	28.0	0.7	70	37	6	0.2	0.2	0.2	0.3	40.7	59.3
OHIO	**4,939,967**	**1,984,942**	**1,894,310**	**1,036,426**	**24,289**	**90,632**	**D**	**40.2**	**38.3**	**21.0**	**0.5**				**100.0**	**100.0**	**100.0**	**100.0**	**51.2**	**48.8**

Table F. — Vote for U.S. Senator: November 3, 1992, General Election

County	Total	Glenn (DEM)	DeWine (REP)	Grevatt (IND)[1]	Plurality Total	Party	Percent of total vote DEM	REP	IND	Rank DEM	REP	IND	Percent contribution to state vote Total	DEM	REP	IND
Adams	10,507	4,792	5,152	563	360	R	45.6	49.0	5.4	42	37	79	0.2	0.2	0.3	0.2
Allen	46,744	15,580	28,464	2,700	12,884	R	33.3	60.9	5.8	84	5	73	1.0	0.6	1.4	0.8
Ashland	20,595	7,684	11,433	1,478	3,749	R	37.3	55.5	7.2	79	9	52	0.4	0.3	0.6	0.5
Ashtabula	42,032	21,958	16,751	3,323	5,207	D	52.2	39.9	7.9	20	71	33	0.9	0.9	0.8	1.0
Athens	25,320	14,967	8,870	1,483	6,097	D	59.1	35.0	5.9	9	79	71	0.5	0.6	0.4	0.5
Auglaize	20,042	6,337	12,362	1,343	6,025	R	31.6	61.7	6.7	87	2	61	0.4	0.3	0.6	0.4
Belmont	32,834	21,977	8,166	2,691	13,811	D	66.9	24.9	8.2	2	88	29	0.7	0.9	0.4	0.8
Brown	14,795	7,041	6,497	1,257	544	D	47.6	43.9	8.5	32	60	20	0.3	0.3	0.3	0.4
Butler	128,022	54,848	63,798	9,376	8,950	R	42.8	49.8	7.3	53	31	50	2.7	2.2	3.1	2.9
Carroll	12,224	6,225	4,939	1,060	1,286	D	50.9	40.4	8.7	23	70	17	0.3	0.3	0.2	0.3
Champaign	16,033	6,550	8,687	796	2,137	R	40.9	54.2	5.0	65	13	82	0.3	0.3	0.4	0.2
Clark	62,952	30,871	29,431	2,650	1,440	D	49.0	46.8	4.2	26	48	87	1.3	1.3	1.5	0.8
Clermont	63,357	25,744	32,350	5,263	6,606	R	40.6	51.1	8.3	67	29	26	1.3	1.1	1.6	1.6
Clinton	15,096	6,166	7,983	947	1,817	R	40.8	52.9	6.3	66	19	65	0.3	0.3	0.4	0.3
Columbiana	46,740	25,353	17,454	3,933	7,899	D	54.2	37.3	8.4	15	77	22	1.0	1.0	0.9	1.2
Coshocton	15,747	7,151	7,271	1,325	120	R	45.4	46.2	8.4	44	51	23	0.3	0.3	0.4	0.4
Crawford	20,446	8,180	10,121	2,145	1,941	R	40.0	49.5	10.5	69	34	3	0.4	0.3	0.5	0.7
Cuyahoga	620,903	390,743	197,776	32,384	192,967	D	62.9	31.9	5.2	6	81	81	13.0	16.0	9.8	10.1
Darke	23,997	10,074	12,102	1,821	2,028	R	42.0	50.4	7.6	57	30	43	0.5	0.4	0.6	0.6
Defiance	16,876	7,036	8,280	1,560	1,244	R	41.7	49.1	9.2	59	36	11	0.4	0.3	0.4	0.5
Delaware	36,254	13,697	19,407	3,150	5,710	R	37.8	53.5	8.7	78	14	16	0.8	0.6	1.0	1.0
Erie	35,272	18,091	14,716	2,465	3,375	D	51.3	41.7	7.0	22	66	55	0.7	0.7	0.7	0.8
Fairfield	50,226	20,537	25,925	3,764	5,388	R	40.9	51.6	7.5	64	26	46	1.0	0.8	1.3	1.2
Fayette	10,013	3,649	5,878	486	2,229	R	36.4	58.7	4.9	81	7	84	0.2	0.1	0.3	0.2
Franklin	420,009	201,716	188,979	29,314	12,737	D	48.0	45.0	7.0	30	57	56	8.8	8.3	9.3	9.1
Fulton	18,368	8,863	7,890	1,615	973	D	48.3	43.0	8.8	29	63	15	0.4	0.4	0.4	0.5
Gallia	13,403	6,391	6,231	781	160	D	47.7	46.5	5.8	31	49	72	0.3	0.3	0.3	0.2
Geauga	37,069	15,767	19,236	2,066	3,469	R	42.5	51.9	5.6	55	24	76	0.8	0.6	0.9	0.6
Greene	59,708	25,643	31,231	2,834	5,588	R	42.9	52.3	4.7	51	23	86	1.2	1.0	1.5	0.9
Guernsey	16,106	7,399	7,201	1,506	198	D	45.9	44.7	9.4	40	59	10	0.3	0.3	0.4	0.5
Hamilton	394,049	185,201	180,880	27,968	4,321	D	47.0	45.9	7.1	35	53	53	8.2	7.6	8.9	8.7
Hancock	30,647	12,037	16,312	2,298	4,275	R	39.3	53.2	7.5	73	16	45	0.6	0.5	0.8	0.7
Hardin	12,947	5,309	6,625	1,013	1,316	R	41.0	51.2	7.8	63	27	34	0.3	0.2	0.3	0.3
Harrison	7,675	4,814	2,224	637	2,590	D	62.7	29.0	8.3	7	85	27	0.2	0.2	0.1	0.2
Henry	13,129	6,036	5,994	1,099	42	D	46.0	45.7	8.4	39	55	24	0.3	0.2	0.3	0.3
Highland	15,095	6,470	7,819	806	1,349	R	42.9	51.8	5.3	52	25	80	0.3	0.3	0.4	0.3
Hocking	10,410	4,890	4,674	846	216	D	47.0	44.9	8.1	36	58	30	0.2	0.2	0.2	0.3
Holmes	8,580	2,972	5,070	538	2,098	R	34.6	59.1	6.3	82	6	66	0.2	0.1	0.3	0.2
Huron	23,785	11,029	10,921	1,835	108	D	46.4	45.9	7.7	37	52	37	0.5	0.5	0.5	0.6
Jackson	12,550	5,558	6,253	739	695	R	44.3	49.8	5.9	47	32	69	0.3	0.2	0.3	0.2
Jefferson	37,932	24,839	9,712	3,381	15,127	D	65.5	25.6	8.9	3	87	12	0.8	1.0	0.5	1.1
Knox	20,673	8,512	10,220	1,941	1,708	R	41.2	49.4	9.4	62	35	9	0.4	0.3	0.5	0.6
Lake	98,148	46,441	46,213	5,494	228	D	47.3	47.1	5.6	33	46	74	2.0	1.9	2.3	1.7
Lawrence	26,347	13,668	10,995	1,684	2,673	D	51.9	41.7	6.4	21	65	64	0.5	0.6	0.5	0.5
Licking	60,079	25,259	29,170	5,650	3,911	R	42.0	48.6	9.4	56	42	8	1.3	1.0	1.4	1.8
Logan	18,617	6,400	10,924	1,293	4,524	R	34.4	58.7	6.9	83	8	58	0.4	0.3	0.5	0.4
Lorain	116,990	64,362	43,928	8,700	20,434	D	55.0	37.5	7.4	12	76	48	2.4	2.6	2.2	2.7
Lucas	182,686	124,867	55,274	2,545	69,593	D	68.4	30.3	1.4	1	83	88	3.8	5.1	2.7	0.8
Madison	13,887	5,271	7,548	1,068	2,277	R	38.0	54.4	7.7	76	12	39	0.3	0.2	0.4	0.3
Mahoning	125,058	79,530	37,178	8,350	42,352	D	63.6	29.7	6.7	4	84	62	2.6	3.3	1.8	2.6
Marion	27,475	10,857	14,527	2,091	3,670	R	39.5	52.9	7.6	72	20	42	0.6	0.4	0.7	0.7
Medina	59,456	27,410	27,247	4,799	163	D	46.1	45.8	8.1	38	54	32	1.2	1.1	1.3	1.5
Meigs	10,056	4,596	4,783	677	187	R	45.7	47.6	6.7	41	44	60	0.2	0.2	0.2	0.2
Mercer	18,298	6,015	11,161	1,122	5,146	R	32.9	61.0	6.1	85	3	68	0.4	0.2	0.6	0.3
Miami	42,461	18,267	20,694	3,500	2,427	R	43.0	48.7	8.2	50	40	28	0.9	0.7	1.0	1.1
Monroe	7,375	4,676	2,123	576	2,553	D	63.4	28.8	7.8	5	86	35	0.2	0.2	0.1	0.2
Montgomery	257,265	139,234	105,444	12,587	33,790	D	54.1	41.0	4.9	16	68	83	5.4	5.7	5.2	3.9
Morgan	6,572	2,642	3,487	443	845	R	40.2	53.1	6.7	68	18	59	0.1	0.1	0.2	0.1
Morrow	12,595	5,218	6,082	1,295	864	R	41.4	48.3	10.3	61	43	4	0.3	0.2	0.3	0.4
Muskingum	34,251	13,688	18,072	2,491	4,384	R	40.0	52.8	7.3	70	21	51	0.7	0.6	0.9	0.8
Noble	5,699	2,549	2,667	483	118	R	44.7	46.8	8.5	46	47	21	0.1	0.1	0.1	0.2
Ottawa	19,634	11,230	6,729	1,675	4,501	D	57.2	34.3	8.5	10	80	19	0.4	0.5	0.3	0.5
Paulding	9,301	3,705	4,897	699	1,192	R	39.8	52.7	7.5	71	22	44	0.2	0.2	0.2	0.2
Perry	13,374	6,484	5,805	1,085	679	D	48.5	43.4	8.1	28	62	31	0.3	0.3	0.3	0.3
Pickaway	18,447	7,062	10,201	1,184	3,139	R	38.3	55.3	6.4	75	10	63	0.4	0.3	0.5	0.4
Pike	11,068	6,025	4,512	531	1,513	D	54.4	40.8	4.8	14	69	85	0.2	0.2	0.2	0.2
Portage	61,277	32,328	23,150	5,799	9,178	D	52.8	37.8	9.5	19	74	7	1.3	1.3	1.1	1.8
Preble	17,848	8,113	8,248	1,487	135	R	45.5	46.2	8.3	43	50	25	0.4	0.3	0.4	0.5
Putnam	16,789	5,326	10,228	1,235	4,902	R	31.7	60.9	7.4	86	4	49	0.4	0.2	0.5	0.4
Richland	55,889	24,666	27,265	3,958	2,599	R	44.1	48.8	7.1	48	38	54	1.2	1.0	1.3	1.2

[1]Independent candidate Grevatt was the only minor candidate (only three candidates on ballot).

Table F. – Vote for U.S. Senator: November 3, 1992, General Election (cont)

County	Total	Glenn (DEM)	DeWine (REP)	Grevatt (IND)[1]	Plurality Total	Plurality Party	DEM	REP	IND	Rank DEM	Rank REP	Rank IND	Total	DEM	REP	IND
Ross	24,557	11,043	11,975	1,539	932	R	45.0	48.8	6.3	45	39	67	0.5	0.5	0.6	0.5
Sandusky	26,776	13,422	10,365	2,989	3,057	D	50.1	38.7	11.2	24	72	1	0.6	0.5	0.5	0.9
Scioto	33,091	17,517	13,796	1,778	3,721	D	52.9	41.7	5.4	18	67	78	0.7	0.7	0.7	0.6
Seneca	25,753	12,165	11,020	2,568	1,145	D	47.2	42.8	10.0	34	64	5	0.5	0.5	0.5	0.8
Shelby	16,614	6,301	8,835	1,478	2,534	R	37.9	53.2	8.9	77	17	13	0.3	0.3	0.4	0.5
Stark	173,359	84,543	75,847	12,969	8,696	D	48.8	43.8	7.5	27	61	47	3.6	3.5	3.7	4.0
Summit	235,740	128,438	89,168	18,134	39,270	D	54.5	37.8	7.7	13	73	38	4.9	5.3	4.4	5.6
Trumbull	105,648	65,970	32,316	7,362	33,654	D	62.4	30.6	7.0	8	82	57	2.2	2.7	1.6	2.3
Tuscarawas	35,163	18,824	13,237	3,102	5,587	D	53.5	37.6	8.8	17	75	14	0.7	0.8	0.7	1.0
Union	12,611	4,655	6,871	1,085	2,216	R	36.9	54.5	8.6	80	11	18	0.3	0.2	0.3	0.3
Van Wert	14,041	4,211	9,007	823	4,796	R	30.0	64.1	5.9	88	1	70	0.3	0.2	0.4	0.3
Vinton	5,168	2,538	2,347	283	191	D	49.1	45.4	5.5	25	56	77	0.1	0.1	0.1	<.1
Warren	52,112	20,184	27,862	4,066	7,678	R	38.7	53.5	7.8	74	15	36	1.1	0.8	1.4	1.3
Washington	26,910	11,643	13,765	1,502	2,122	R	43.3	51.2	5.6	49	28	75	0.6	0.5	0.7	0.5
Wayne	41,111	17,576	20,400	3,135	2,824	R	42.8	49.6	7.6	54	33	41	0.9	0.7	1.0	1.0
Williams	16,998	7,068	8,263	1,667	1,195	R	41.6	48.6	9.8	60	41	6	0.4	0.3	0.4	0.5
Wood	51,934	29,435	18,517	3,982	10,918	D	56.7	35.7	7.7	11	78	40	1.1	1.2	0.9	1.2
Wyandot	10,263	4,300	4,872	1,091	572	R	41.9	47.5	10.6	58	45	2	0.2	0.2	0.2	0.3
OHIO	**4,793,953**	**2,444,419**	**2,028,300**	**321,234**	**416,119**	**D**	**51.0**	**42.3**	**6.7**				**100.0**	**100.0**	**100.0**	**100.0**

[1]Independent candidate Grevatt was the only minor candidate (only three candidates on ballot).

Table H. — Vote for U.S. Representative in Congress: November 3, 1992, General Election

Congressional district and county	Total	Democrat (DEM)	Republican (REP)	Other	Plurality Total	Plurality Party	Percent of total vote DEM	Percent of total vote REP	Percent of total vote Other	Rank within district DEM	Rank within district REP	Rank within district Other	Percent contribution to district vote Total	Percent contribution to district vote DEM	Percent contribution to district vote REP	Percent contribution to district vote Other
District 1	**234,433**	**120,190**	**-**	**114,243**	**5,947**	**D**	**51.3**	**-**	**48.7**				**100.0**	**100.0**	**-**	**100.0**
Hamilton (pt)	234,433	120,190	-	114,243	5,947	D	51.3	-	48.7	1	-	1	100.0	100.0	-	100.0
District 2	**253,651**	**75,924**	**177,720**	**7**	**101,796**	**R**	**29.9**	**70.1**	**<.1**				**100.0**	**100.0**	**100.0**	**100.0**
Adams	9,531	4,166	5,365	0	1,199	R	43.7	56.3	0.0	1	5	3	3.8	5.5	3.0	0.0
Brown	13,789	5,986	7,799	4	1,813	R	43.4	56.6	<.1	2	4	1	5.4	7.9	4.4	57.1
Clermont	60,094	19,888	40,206	0	20,318	R	33.1	66.9	0.0	4	2	4	23.7	26.2	22.6	0.0
Hamilton (pt)	145,778	36,854	108,921	3	72,067	R	25.3	74.7	<.1	5	1	2	57.5	48.5	61.3	42.9
Warren (pt)	24,459	9,030	15,429	0	6,399	R	36.9	63.1	0.0	3	3	5	9.6	11.9	8.7	0.0
District 3	**244,811**	**146,072**	**98,733**	**6**	**47,339**	**D**	**59.7**	**40.3**	**<.1**				**100.0**	**100.0**	**100.0**	**100.0**
Montgomery (pt)	244,811	146,072	98,733	6	47,339	D	59.7	40.3	<.1	1	1	1	100.0	100.0	100.0	100.0
District 4	**240,440**	**92,608**	**147,346**	**486**	**54,738**	**R**	**38.5**	**61.3**	**0.2**				**100.0**	**100.0**	**100.0**	**100.0**
Allen	46,721	16,057	30,654	10	14,597	R	34.4	65.6	<.1	6	6	4	19.4	17.3	20.8	2.1
Auglaize (pt)	15,300	4,821	10,479	0	5,658	R	31.5	68.5	0.0	10	2	7	6.4	5.2	7.1	0.0
Crawford	19,961	6,795	13,166	0	6,371	R	34.0	66.0	0.0	8	4	8	8.3	7.3	8.9	0.0
Hancock	29,012	11,981	16,567	464	4,586	R	41.3	57.1	1.6	2	10	1	12.1	12.9	11.2	95.5
Hardin	12,745	4,555	8,189	1	3,634	R	35.7	64.3	<.1	5	7	5	5.3	4.9	5.6	0.2
Knox (pt)	9,588	3,170	6,418	0	3,248	R	33.1	66.9	0.0	9	3	9	4.0	3.4	4.4	0.0
Logan (pt)	7,892	2,372	5,520	0	3,148	R	30.1	69.9	0.0	11	1	10	3.3	2.6	3.7	0.0
Marion	26,000	10,581	15,419	0	4,838	R	40.7	59.3	0.0	3	9	11	10.8	11.4	10.5	0.0
Morrow	11,553	4,691	6,859	3	2,168	R	40.6	59.4	<.1	4	8	3	4.8	5.1	4.7	0.6
Richland	51,577	24,140	27,434	3	3,294	R	46.8	53.2	<.1	1	11	6	21.5	26.1	18.6	0.6
Wyandot	10,091	3,445	6,641	5	3,196	R	34.1	65.8	<.1	7	5	2	4.2	3.7	4.5	1.0
District 5	**187,860**	**-**	**187,860**	**-**	**187,860**	**R**	**-**	**100.0**	**-**				**100.0**	**-**	**100.0**	**-**
Defiance	12,626	-	12,626	-	12,626	R	-	100.0	-	-	1	-	6.7	-	6.7	-
Erie	24,199	-	24,199	-	24,199	R	-	100.0	-	-	2	-	12.9	-	12.9	-
Henry	10,548	-	10,548	-	10,548	R	-	100.0	-	-	3	-	5.6	-	5.6	-
Huron	15,578	-	15,578	-	15,578	R	-	100.0	-	-	4	-	8.3	-	8.3	-
Lorain (pt)	10,387	-	10,387	-	10,387	R	-	100.0	-	-	5	-	5.5	-	5.5	-
Mercer (pt)	1,888	-	1,888	-	1,888	R	-	100.0	-	-	6	-	1.0	-	1.0	-
Ottawa (pt)	10,068	-	10,068	-	10,068	R	-	100.0	-	-	7	-	5.4	-	5.4	-
Paulding	6,692	-	6,692	-	6,692	R	-	100.0	-	-	8	-	3.6	-	3.6	-
Putnam	13,135	-	13,135	-	13,135	R	-	100.0	-	-	9	-	7.0	-	7.0	-
Sandusky	19,457	-	19,457	-	19,457	R	-	100.0	-	-	10	-	10.4	-	10.4	-
Seneca	20,154	-	20,154	-	20,154	R	-	100.0	-	-	11	-	10.7	-	10.7	-
Van Wert	10,863	-	10,863	-	10,863	R	-	100.0	-	-	12	-	5.8	-	5.8	-
Williams	12,876	-	12,876	-	12,876	R	-	100.0	-	-	13	-	6.9	-	6.9	-
Wood (pt)	19,389	-	19,389	-	19,389	R	-	100.0	-	-	14	-	10.3	-	10.3	-
District 6	**241,972**	**122,720**	**119,252**	**-**	**3,468**	**D**	**50.7**	**49.3**	**-**				**100.0**	**100.0**	**100.0**	**-**
Athens	24,836	16,184	8,652	-	7,532	D	65.2	34.8	-	1	14	-	10.3	13.2	7.3	-
Clinton	14,632	4,565	10,067	-	5,502	R	31.2	68.8	-	13	2	-	6.0	3.7	8.4	-
Gallia	12,809	6,893	5,916	-	977	D	53.8	46.2	-	6	9	-	5.3	5.6	5.0	-
Highland	15,065	5,803	9,262	-	3,459	R	38.5	61.5	-	12	3	-	6.2	4.7	7.8	-
Hocking	10,205	5,525	4,680	-	845	D	54.1	45.9	-	5	10	-	4.2	4.5	3.9	-
Jackson	12,532	5,806	6,726	-	920	R	46.3	53.7	-	10	5	-	5.2	4.7	5.6	-
Lawrence	26,045	15,292	10,753	-	4,539	D	58.7	41.3	-	3	12	-	10.8	12.5	9.0	-
Meigs	9,941	5,214	4,727	-	487	D	52.4	47.6	-	7	8	-	4.1	4.2	4.0	-
Pike	11,186	5,812	5,374	-	438	D	52.0	48.0	-	8	7	-	4.6	4.7	4.5	-
Ross (pt)	16,791	7,386	9,405	-	2,019	R	44.0	56.0	-	11	4	-	6.9	6.0	7.9	-
Scioto	33,475	19,493	13,982	-	5,511	D	58.2	41.8	-	4	11	-	13.8	15.9	11.7	-
Vinton	5,085	2,426	2,659	-	233	R	47.7	52.3	-	9	6	-	2.1	2.0	2.2	-
Warren (pt)	22,754	6,494	16,260	-	9,766	R	28.5	71.5	-	14	1	-	9.4	5.3	13.6	-
Washington	26,616	15,827	10,789	-	5,038	D	59.5	40.5	-	2	13	-	11.0	12.9	9.0	-
District 7	**230,432**	**66,237**	**164,195**	**-**	**97,958**	**R**	**28.7**	**71.3**	**-**				**100.0**	**100.0**	**100.0**	**-**
Champaign	15,044	4,099	10,945	-	6,846	R	27.2	72.8	-	5	5	-	6.5	6.2	6.7	-
Clark	59,773	17,226	42,547	-	25,321	R	28.8	71.2	-	4	6	-	25.9	26.0	25.9	-
Fairfield	45,541	15,088	30,453	-	15,365	R	33.1	66.9	-	3	7	-	19.8	22.8	18.5	-
Fayette	9,082	2,193	6,889	-	4,696	R	24.1	75.9	-	7	3	-	3.9	3.3	4.2	-
Greene	55,840	14,555	41,285	-	26,730	R	26.1	73.9	-	6	4	-	24.2	22.0	25.1	-
Logan (pt)	9,205	2,081	7,124	-	5,043	R	22.6	77.4	-	9	1	-	4.0	3.1	4.3	-
Pickaway (pt)	14,752	4,940	9,812	-	4,872	R	33.5	66.5	-	2	8	-	6.4	7.5	6.0	-
Ross (pt)	7,585	2,782	4,803	-	2,021	R	36.7	63.3	-	1	9	-	3.3	4.2	2.9	-
Union	13,610	3,273	10,337	-	7,064	R	24.0	76.0	-	8	2	-	5.9	4.9	6.3	-
District 8	**238,395**	**62,033**	**176,362**	**-**	**114,329**	**R**	**26.0**	**74.0**	**-**				**100.0**	**100.0**	**100.0**	**-**
Auglaize (pt)	4,309	973	3,336	-	2,363	R	22.6	77.4	-	8	1	-	1.8	1.6	1.9	-
Butler	120,802	31,427	89,375	-	57,948	R	26.0	74.0	-	4	5	-	50.7	50.7	50.7	-
Darke	23,117	5,268	17,849	-	12,581	R	22.8	77.2	-	7	2	-	9.7	8.5	10.1	-
Mercer (pt)	14,646	3,677	10,969	-	7,292	R	25.1	74.9	-	6	3	-	6.1	5.9	6.2	-
Miami	38,692	9,959	28,733	-	18,774	R	25.7	74.3	-	5	4	-	16.2	16.1	16.3	-
Montgomery (pt)	1,257	395	862	-	467	R	31.4	68.6	-	1	8	-	0.5	0.6	0.5	-

Ohio 733

Table H. — Vote for U.S. Representative in Congress: November 3, 1992, General Election (cont)

Congressional district and county	Total	Democrat (DEM)	Republican (REP)	Other	Plurality Total	Party	DEM	REP	Other	Rank within district DEM	REP	Other	Total	DEM	REP	Other
District 8 (cont)																
Preble	16,959	4,897	12,062	-	7,165	R	28.9	71.1	-	3	6	-	7.1	7.9	6.8	-
Shelby	18,613	5,437	13,176	-	7,739	R	29.2	70.8	-	2	7	-	7.8	8.8	7.5	-
District 9	243,102	178,879	53,011	11,212	125,868	D	73.6	21.8	4.6				100.0	100.0	100.0	100.0
Fulton	18,364	11,960	5,749	655	6,211	D	65.1	31.3	3.6	4	1	3	7.6	6.7	10.8	5.8
Lucas	194,856	145,003	40,424	9,429	104,579	D	74.4	20.7	4.8	1	4	1	80.2	81.1	76.3	84.1
Ottawa (pt)	6,888	5,057	1,594	237	3,463	D	73.4	23.1	3.4	2	2	4	2.8	2.8	3.0	2.1
Wood (pt)	22,994	16,859	5,244	891	11,615	D	73.3	22.8	3.9	3	3	2	9.5	9.4	9.9	7.9
District 10	240,239	103,788	136,433	18	32,645	R	43.2	56.8	<.1				100.0	100.0	100.0	100.0
Cuyahoga (pt)	240,239	103,788	136,433	18	32,645	R	43.2	56.8	<.1	1	1	1	100.0	100.0	100.0	100.0
District 11	223,624	154,718	43,866	25,040	110,852	D	69.2	19.6	11.2				100.0	100.0	100.0	100.0
Cuyahoga (pt)	223,624	154,718	43,866	25,040	110,852	D	69.2	19.6	11.2	1	1	1	100.0	100.0	100.0	100.0
District 12	239,058	68,761	170,297	-	101,536	R	28.8	71.2	-				100.0	100.0	100.0	-
Delaware	35,708	5,978	29,730	-	23,752	R	16.7	83.3	-	3	1	-	14.9	8.7	17.5	-
Franklin (pt)	170,501	55,174	115,327	-	60,153	R	32.4	67.6	-	1	3	-	71.3	80.2	67.7	-
Licking (pt)	32,849	7,609	25,240	-	17,631	R	23.2	76.8	-	2	2	-	13.7	11.1	14.8	-
District 13	252,258	134,486	88,889	28,883	45,597	D	53.3	35.2	11.4				100.0	100.0	100.0	100.0
Cuyahoga (pt)	7,440	3,360	3,273	807	87	D	45.2	44.0	10.8	6	2	6	2.9	2.5	3.7	2.8
Geauga	35,373	15,447	15,579	4,347	132	R	43.7	44.0	12.3	7	1	3	14.0	11.5	17.5	15.1
Lorain (pt)	97,873	59,851	27,874	10,148	31,977	D	61.2	28.5	10.4	1	7	7	38.8	44.5	31.4	35.1
Medina	57,796	28,038	23,427	6,331	4,611	D	48.5	40.5	11.0	4	3	5	22.9	20.8	26.4	21.9
Portage (pt)	24,604	11,876	8,990	3,738	2,886	D	48.3	36.5	15.2	5	4	1	9.8	8.8	10.1	12.9
Summit (pt)	17,328	9,091	6,237	2,000	2,854	D	52.5	36.0	11.5	3	5	4	6.9	6.8	7.0	6.9
Trumbull (pt)	11,844	6,823	3,509	1,512	3,314	D	57.6	29.6	12.8	2	6	2	4.7	5.1	3.9	5.2
District 14	243,994	165,335	78,659	-	86,676	D	67.8	32.2	-				100.0	100.0	100.0	-
Portage (pt)	34,324	23,679	10,645	-	13,034	D	69.0	31.0	-	1	3	-	14.1	14.3	13.5	-
Stark (pt)	1,885	1,200	685	-	515	D	63.7	36.3	-	3	1	-	0.8	0.7	0.9	-
Summit (pt)	207,785	140,456	67,329	-	73,127	D	67.6	32.4	-	2	2	-	85.2	85.0	85.6	-
District 15	250,205	94,907	110,390	44,908	15,483	R	37.9	44.1	17.9				100.0	100.0	100.0	100.0
Franklin (pt)	234,887	89,931	103,021	41,935	13,090	R	38.3	43.9	17.9	1	2	3	93.9	94.8	93.3	93.4
Madison	13,524	4,329	6,647	2,548	2,318	R	32.0	49.1	18.8	3	1	2	5.4	4.6	6.0	5.7
Pickaway (pt)	1,794	647	722	425	75	R	36.1	40.2	23.7	2	3	1	0.7	0.7	0.7	0.9
District 16	248,713	90,224	158,489	-	68,265	R	36.3	63.7	-				100.0	100.0	100.0	-
Ashland	19,750	6,811	12,939	-	6,128	R	34.5	65.5	-	4	2	-	7.9	7.5	8.2	-
Holmes	8,596	2,275	6,321	-	4,046	R	26.5	73.5	-	5	1	-	3.5	2.5	4.0	-
Knox (pt)	9,017	3,925	5,092	-	1,167	R	43.5	56.5	-	1	5	-	3.6	4.4	3.2	-
Stark (pt)	170,605	62,521	108,084	-	45,563	R	36.6	63.4	-	2	4	-	68.6	69.3	68.2	-
Wayne	40,745	14,692	26,053	-	11,361	R	36.1	63.9	-	3	3	-	16.4	16.3	16.4	-
District 17	257,246	216,503	40,743	-	175,760	D	84.2	15.8	-				100.0	100.0	100.0	-
Columbiana (pt)	45,819	35,900	9,919	-	25,981	D	78.4	21.6	-	3	1	-	17.8	16.6	24.3	-
Mahoning	125,021	106,174	18,847	-	87,327	D	84.9	15.1	-	2	2	-	48.6	49.0	46.3	-
Trumbull (pt)	86,406	74,429	11,977	-	62,452	D	86.1	13.9	-	1	3	-	33.6	34.4	29.4	-
District 18	243,418	166,189	77,229	-	88,960	D	68.3	31.7	-				100.0	100.0	100.0	-
Belmont	32,838	26,590	6,248	-	20,342	D	81.0	19.0	-	2	13	-	13.5	16.0	8.1	-
Carroll	11,930	7,900	4,030	-	3,870	D	66.2	33.8	-	9	6	-	4.9	4.8	5.2	-
Columbiana (pt)	533	429	104	-	325	D	80.5	19.5	-	3	12	-	0.2	0.3	0.1	-
Coshocton	14,972	9,734	5,238	-	4,496	D	65.0	35.0	-	10	5	-	6.2	5.9	6.8	-
Guernsey	15,854	11,465	4,389	-	7,076	D	72.3	27.7	-	6	9	-	6.5	6.9	5.7	-
Harrison	7,653	5,815	1,838	-	3,977	D	76.0	24.0	-	5	10	-	3.1	3.5	2.4	-
Jefferson	38,009	30,294	7,715	-	22,579	D	79.7	20.3	-	4	11	-	15.6	18.2	10.0	-
Licking (pt)	24,451	13,317	11,134	-	2,183	D	54.5	45.5	-	12	3	-	10.0	8.0	14.4	-
Monroe	7,238	6,089	1,149	-	4,940	D	84.1	15.9	-	1	14	-	3.0	3.7	1.5	-
Morgan	5,808	2,906	2,902	-	4	D	50.0	50.0	-	14	1	-	2.4	1.7	3.8	-
Muskingum	31,723	17,137	14,586	-	2,551	D	54.0	46.0	-	13	2	-	13.0	10.3	18.9	-
Noble	5,532	3,860	1,672	-	2,188	D	69.8	30.2	-	7	8	-	2.3	2.3	2.2	-
Perry	11,853	6,851	5,002	-	1,849	D	57.8	42.2	-	11	4	-	4.9	4.1	6.5	-
Tuscarawas	35,024	23,802	11,222	-	12,580	D	68.0	32.0	-	8	7	-	14.4	14.3	14.5	-
District 19	263,083	138,465	124,606	12	13,859	D	52.6	47.4	<.1				100.0	100.0	100.0	100.0
Ashtabula	41,335	21,886	19,437	12	2,449	D	52.9	47.0	<.1	2	2	1	15.7	15.8	15.6	100.0
Cuyahoga (pt)	125,328	70,709	54,619	0	16,090	D	56.4	43.6	0.0	1	3	2	47.6	51.1	43.8	0.0
Lake	96,420	45,870	50,550	0	4,680	R	47.6	52.4	0.0	3	1	3	36.7	33.1	40.6	0.0
OHIO	4,576,934	2,198,039	2,154,080	224,815	43,959	D	48.0	47.1	4.9							

Table I. — Vote for Presidential Preference: June 2, 1992, Democratic Primary Election

County	Top candidates									Top three candidates (state vote)									
										Percent of total vote			Rank			Percent contribution to state vote			
	Total	Clinton	Brown	Tsongas	Stokes	Harkin	Kerrey	LaRouche		Clinton	Brown	Tsongas	Clinton	Brown	Tsongas	Total	Clinton	Brown	Tsongas
Adams	1,794	1,330	246	134	0	46	38	0	–	74.1	13.7	7.5	2	76	80	0.2	0.2	0.1	0.1
Allen	7,740	4,879	1,263	974	0	214	236	174	–	63.0	16.3	12.6	57	60	16	0.7	0.8	0.6	0.9
Ashland	2,906	1,973	496	263	0	74	51	49	–	67.9	17.1	9.1	28	55	65	0.3	0.3	0.3	0.2
Ashtabula	11,387	7,194	2,273	1,170	0	288	234	228	–	63.2	20.0	10.3	56	27	37	1.1	1.1	1.2	1.1
Athens	6,984	4,302	1,622	697	0	148	137	78	–	61.6	23.2	10.0	68	4	49	0.7	0.7	0.8	0.6
Auglaize	2,613	1,634	555	240	0	78	46	60	–	62.5	21.2	9.2	64	14	63	0.3	0.3	0.3	0.2
Belmont	16,328	10,577	2,937	1,671	0	315	338	490	–	64.8	18.0	10.2	44	45	41	1.6	1.7	1.5	1.5
Brown	3,149	2,146	549	255	0	54	71	74	–	68.1	17.4	8.1	26	51	77	0.3	0.3	0.3	0.2
Butler	12,902	8,453	2,379	1,354	0	280	243	193	–	65.5	18.4	10.5	39	42	34	1.2	1.3	1.2	1.2
Carroll	2,755	1,810	485	264	0	64	55	77	–	65.7	17.6	9.6	37	50	57	0.3	0.3	0.2	0.2
Champaign	2,293	1,615	349	183	0	50	46	50	–	70.4	15.2	8.0	16	74	78	0.2	0.3	0.2	0.2
Clark	12,759	8,672	1,989	1,261	0	248	327	262	–	68.0	15.6	9.9	27	70	52	1.2	1.4	1.0	1.1
Clermont	6,485	4,140	1,270	652	0	155	118	150	–	63.8	19.6	10.1	50	31	48	0.6	0.6	0.6	0.6
Clinton	5,389	3,131	1,039	920	0	131	168	0	–	58.1	19.3	17.1	84	39	7	0.5	0.5	0.5	0.8
Columbiana	12,182	7,663	2,640	1,158	0	228	264	229	–	62.9	21.7	9.5	59	10	60	1.2	1.2	1.3	1.0
Coshocton	3,107	1,943	447	402	0	117	124	74	–	62.5	14.4	12.9	63	75	15	0.3	0.3	0.2	0.4
Crawford	3,822	2,347	817	423	0	117	101	17	–	61.4	21.4	11.1	70	13	26	0.4	0.4	0.4	0.4
Cuyahoga	220,143	117,753	39,147	22,188	29,983	3,769	3,619	3,684	–	53.5	17.8	10.1	88	46	46	21.1	18.4	19.8	20.0
Darke	3,113	1,985	601	307	0	87	63	70	–	63.8	19.3	9.9	51	38	53	0.3	0.3	0.3	0.3
Defiance	2,589	1,765	0	523	0	182	119	0	–	68.2	0.0	20.2	25	80	3	0.2	0.3	0.0	0.5
Delaware	3,371	1,933	752	479	0	90	62	55	–	57.3	22.3	14.2	86	7	12	0.3	0.3	0.4	0.4
Erie	6,301	4,691	0	1,020	0	290	300	0	–	74.4	0.0	16.2	1	81	10	0.6	0.7	0.0	0.9
Fairfield	7,492	4,705	1,478	788	0	208	167	146	–	62.8	19.7	10.5	60	29	33	0.7	0.7	0.7	0.7
Fayette	1,419	985	236	119	0	43	25	11	–	69.4	16.6	8.4	23	59	71	0.1	0.2	0.1	0.1
Franklin	54,005	32,773	10,872	6,194	0	1,601	1,375	1,190	–	60.7	20.1	11.5	76	23	21	5.2	5.1	5.5	5.6
Fulton	1,818	1,232	238	221	0	59	41	27	–	67.8	13.1	12.2	29	78	17	0.2	0.2	0.1	0.2
Gallia	3,692	2,616	596	259	0	92	55	74	–	70.9	16.1	7.0	13	63	85	0.4	0.4	0.3	0.2
Geauga	7,401	4,167	1,593	1,031	0	260	175	175	–	56.3	21.5	13.9	87	11	13	0.7	0.7	0.8	0.9
Greene	8,829	5,718	1,737	906	0	174	182	112	–	64.8	19.7	10.3	46	30	39	0.8	0.9	0.9	0.8
Guernsey	4,463	2,714	1,042	396	0	88	107	116	–	60.8	23.3	8.9	75	3	67	0.4	0.4	0.5	0.4
Hamilton	32,155	19,615	7,229	3,654	0	569	538	550	–	61.0	22.5	11.4	73	6	24	3.1	3.1	3.7	3.3
Hancock	2,693	1,578	477	369	0	111	87	71	–	58.6	17.7	13.7	82	47	14	0.3	0.2	0.2	0.3
Hardin	1,977	1,213	302	233	0	66	91	72	–	61.4	15.3	11.8	71	73	20	0.2	0.2	0.2	0.2
Harrison	3,128	2,033	611	275	0	71	62	76	–	65.0	19.5	8.8	41	32	68	0.3	0.3	0.3	0.2
Henry	1,740	1,215	0	326	0	110	89	0	–	69.8	0.0	18.7	20	82	5	0.2	0.2	0.0	0.3
Highland	1,968	1,394	313	168	0	51	42	0	–	70.8	15.9	8.5	14	68	69	0.2	0.2	0.2	0.2
Hocking	2,931	1,986	538	299	0	51	57	0	–	67.8	18.4	10.2	30	43	42	0.3	0.3	0.3	0.3
Holmes	1,877	1,160	378	189	0	72	45	33	–	61.8	20.1	10.1	67	22	47	0.2	0.2	0.2	0.2
Huron	3,993	2,589	641	471	0	123	96	73	–	64.8	16.1	11.8	43	64	19	0.4	0.4	0.3	0.4
Jackson	2,211	1,596	341	155	0	63	56	0	–	72.2	15.4	7.0	10	71	86	0.2	0.3	0.2	0.1
Jefferson	19,539	12,213	3,923	2,066	0	421	441	475	–	62.5	20.1	10.6	65	25	31	1.9	1.9	2.0	1.9
Knox	2,688	1,741	525	267	0	59	49	47	–	64.8	19.5	9.9	45	33	51	0.3	0.3	0.3	0.2
Lake	23,888	14,585	4,863	2,486	0	734	559	661	–	61.1	20.4	10.4	72	21	35	2.3	2.3	2.5	2.2
Lawrence	4,422	3,245	740	261	0	49	73	54	–	73.4	16.7	5.9	5	58	88	0.4	0.5	0.4	0.2
Licking	9,510	5,794	1,966	1,050	0	252	253	195	–	60.9	20.7	11.0	74	19	27	0.9	0.9	1.0	0.9
Logan	2,001	1,315	354	194	0	53	41	44	–	65.7	17.7	9.7	36	48	54	0.2	0.2	0.2	0.2
Lorain	35,495	22,560	7,408	3,214	0	953	744	616	–	63.6	20.9	9.1	53	18	64	3.4	3.5	3.8	2.9
Lucas	27,324	16,819	5,093	2,940	0	967	873	632	–	61.6	18.6	10.8	69	40	30	2.6	2.6	2.6	2.7
Madison	1,415	979	243	117	0	29	24	23	–	69.2	17.2	8.3	24	54	73	0.1	0.2	0.1	0.1
Mahoning	51,171	30,552	13,188	4,606	0	854	1,103	868	–	59.7	25.8	9.0	80	1	66	4.9	4.8	6.7	4.2
Marion	6,167	4,113	1,035	593	0	177	131	118	–	66.7	16.8	9.6	34	57	56	0.6	0.6	0.5	0.5
Medina	12,274	7,669	2,527	1,348	0	294	214	222	–	62.5	20.6	11.0	66	20	29	1.2	1.2	1.3	1.2
Meigs	1,804	1,303	286	130	0	27	32	26	–	72.2	15.9	7.2	9	69	84	0.2	0.2	0.1	0.1
Mercer	3,953	2,334	831	453	0	117	106	112	–	59.0	21.0	11.5	81	16	22	0.4	0.4	0.4	0.4
Miami	5,296	3,408	1,023	540	0	127	103	95	–	64.4	19.3	10.2	48	36	43	0.5	0.5	0.5	0.5
Monroe	3,677	2,573	589	269	0	90	84	72	–	70.0	16.0	7.3	19	66	82	0.4	0.4	0.3	0.2
Montgomery	55,323	36,524	9,765	6,221	0	1,380	1,433	0	–	66.0	17.7	11.2	35	49	25	5.3	5.7	4.9	5.6
Morgan	1,072	748	182	78	0	26	21	17	–	69.8	17.0	7.3	21	56	83	0.1	0.1	<.1	<.1
Morrow	2,373	1,519	441	193	0	100	43	77	–	64.0	18.6	8.1	49	41	76	0.2	0.2	0.2	0.2
Muskingum	4,985	3,239	908	496	0	144	110	88	–	65.0	18.2	9.9	42	44	50	0.5	0.5	0.5	0.4
Noble	1,668	1,079	335	136	0	38	40	40	–	64.7	20.1	8.2	47	24	75	0.2	0.2	0.2	0.1
Ottawa	4,241	2,952	0	884	0	227	178	0	–	69.6	0.0	20.8	22	83	2	0.4	0.5	0.0	0.8
Paulding	2,088	1,547	0	325	0	105	111	0	–	74.1	0.0	15.6	3	84	11	0.2	0.2	0.0	0.3
Perry	3,382	2,218	653	278	0	92	64	77	–	65.6	19.3	8.2	38	37	74	0.3	0.3	0.3	0.3
Pickaway	3,078	2,056	534	293	0	77	56	62	–	66.8	17.3	9.5	32	52	59	0.3	0.3	0.3	0.3
Pike	2,720	2,015	359	231	0	64	51	0	–	74.1	13.2	8.5	4	77	70	0.3	0.3	0.2	0.2
Portage	17,667	10,207	4,079	2,106	0	515	407	353	–	57.8	23.1	11.9	85	5	18	1.7	1.6	2.1	1.9
Preble	2,391	1,676	383	176	0	69	47	40	–	70.1	16.0	7.4	18	67	81	0.2	0.3	0.2	0.2
Putnam	4,355	2,775	0	1,002	0	323	255	0	–	63.7	0.0	23.0	52	85	1	0.4	0.4	0.0	0.9
Richland	13,850	8,691	2,964	1,326	0	354	273	242	–	62.8	21.4	9.6	61	12	58	1.3	1.4	1.5	1.2

Table I. — **Vote for Presidential Preference: June 2, 1992, Democratic Primary Election (cont)**

County	Top candidates									Top three candidates(state vote)									
										Percent of total vote			Rank			Percent contribution to state vote			
	Total	Clinton	Brown	Tsongas	Stokes	Harkin	Kerrey	LaRouche		Clinton	Brown	Tsongas	Clinton	Brown	Tsongas	Total	Clinton	Brown	Tsongas
Ross	4,545	3,194	741	424	0	103	83	0	-	70.3	16.3	9.3	17	61	61	0.4	0.5	0.4	0.4
Sandusky	4,164	3,041	0	716	0	226	181	0	-	73.0	0.0	17.2	6	86	6	0.4	0.5	0.0	0.6
Scioto	7,304	5,203	1,171	546	0	208	176	0	-	71.2	16.0	7.5	11	65	79	0.7	0.8	0.6	0.5
Seneca	4,838	3,498	0	813	0	293	234	0	-	72.3	0.0	16.8	8	87	9	0.5	0.5	0.0	0.7
Shelby	4,117	2,480	902	415	0	115	105	100	-	60.2	21.9	10.1	79	8	45	0.4	0.4	0.5	0.4
Stark	44,412	28,198	8,849	4,560	0	1,050	834	921	-	63.5	19.9	10.3	54	28	38	4.3	4.4	4.5	4.1
Summit	59,487	37,425	11,885	6,549	0	1,377	1,291	960	-	62.9	20.0	11.0	58	26	28	5.7	5.9	6.0	5.9
Trumbull	42,894	25,095	10,625	4,367	0	1,021	934	852	-	58.5	24.8	10.2	83	2	44	4.1	3.9	5.4	3.9
Tuscarawas	12,143	7,334	2,543	1,388	0	332	278	268	-	60.4	20.9	11.4	77	17	23	1.2	1.1	1.3	1.3
Union	1,555	1,012	301	144	0	40	28	30	-	65.1	19.4	9.3	40	35	62	0.1	0.2	0.2	0.1
Van Wert	1,829	1,147	388	176	0	42	51	25	-	62.7	21.2	9.6	62	15	55	0.2	0.2	0.2	0.2
Vinton	1,638	1,193	251	108	0	52	34	0	-	72.8	15.3	6.6	7	72	87	0.2	0.2	0.1	<.1
Warren	5,488	3,664	943	566	0	167	148	0	-	66.8	17.2	10.3	33	53	36	0.5	0.6	0.5	0.5
Washington	5,473	3,861	890	457	0	100	94	71	-	70.5	16.3	8.4	15	62	72	0.5	0.6	0.5	0.4
Wayne	7,091	4,495	1,376	748	0	199	149	124	-	63.4	19.4	10.5	55	34	32	0.7	0.7	0.7	0.7
Williams	2,201	1,566	0	420	0	107	108	0	-	71.1	0.0	19.1	12	88	4	0.2	0.2	0.0	0.4
Wood	7,905	5,343	574	1,349	0	361	248	30	-	67.6	7.3	17.1	31	79	8	0.8	0.8	0.3	1.2
Wyandot	1,530	924	335	157	0	48	31	35	-	60.4	21.9	10.3	78	9	40	0.1	0.1	0.2	0.1
OHIO	**1,042,335**	**638,347**	**197,449**	**110,773**	**29,983**	**25,395**	**22,976**	**17,412**	**-**	**61.2**	**18.9**	**10.6**				**100.0**	**100.0**	**100.0**	**100.0**

736 Ohio

Table J. — Vote for Presidential Preference: June 2, 1992, Republican Primary Election

County	Top candidates					Top four candidates (state vote)								Percent contribution to state vote				
						Percent of total vote				Rank								
	Total	Bush	Bu-chanan			Bush	Bu-chanan			Bush	Bu-chanan			Total	Bush	Bu-chanan		
Adams	3,331	2,808	523	-	-	84.3	15.7	-	-	30	59	-	-	0.4	0.4	0.4	-	-
Allen	17,613	14,162	3,451	-	-	80.4	19.6	-	-	76	13	-	-	2.0	2.0	2.4	-	-
Ashland	5,029	4,255	774	-	-	84.6	15.4	-	-	24	65	-	-	0.6	0.6	0.5	-	-
Ashtabula	6,840	5,610	1,230	-	-	82.0	18.0	-	-	60	29	-	-	0.8	0.8	0.9	-	-
Athens	3,706	3,145	561	-	-	84.9	15.1	-	-	19	70	-	-	0.4	0.4	0.4	-	-
Auglaize	4,461	3,805	656	-	-	85.3	14.7	-	-	15	74	-	-	0.5	0.5	0.5	-	-
Belmont	3,221	2,695	526	-	-	83.7	16.3	-	-	39	50	-	-	0.4	0.4	0.4	-	-
Brown	2,055	1,750	305	-	-	85.2	14.8	-	-	17	72	-	-	0.2	0.2	0.2	-	-
Butler	24,870	21,072	3,798	-	-	84.7	15.3	-	-	23	66	-	-	2.9	2.9	2.6	-	-
Carroll	4,130	3,119	1,011	-	-	75.5	24.5	-	-	88	1	-	-	0.5	0.4	0.7	-	-
Champaign	4,438	3,787	651	-	-	85.3	14.7	-	-	14	75	-	-	0.5	0.5	0.5	-	-
Clark	13,788	11,485	2,303	-	-	83.3	16.7	-	-	44	45	-	-	1.6	1.6	1.6	-	-
Clermont	12,759	10,462	2,297	-	-	82.0	18.0	-	-	61	28	-	-	1.5	1.5	1.6	-	-
Clinton	5,931	4,967	964	-	-	83.7	16.3	-	-	38	51	-	-	0.7	0.7	0.7	-	-
Columbiana	8,029	6,521	1,508	-	-	81.2	18.8	-	-	73	16	-	-	0.9	0.9	1.0	-	-
Coshocton	3,326	2,745	581	-	-	82.5	17.5	-	-	57	32	-	-	0.4	0.4	0.4	-	-
Crawford	4,502	3,726	776	-	-	82.8	17.2	-	-	52	37	-	-	0.5	0.5	0.5	-	-
Cuyahoga	81,614	68,655	12,959	-	-	84.1	15.9	-	-	31	58	-	-	9.5	9.6	9.0	-	-
Darke	7,061	5,647	1,414	-	-	80.0	20.0	-	-	80	9	-	-	0.8	0.8	1.0	-	-
Defiance	4,055	3,216	839	-	-	79.3	20.7	-	-	84	5	-	-	0.5	0.4	0.6	-	-
Delaware	10,024	8,407	1,617	-	-	83.9	16.1	-	-	36	53	-	-	1.2	1.2	1.1	-	-
Erie	6,210	5,177	1,033	-	-	83.4	16.6	-	-	42	47	-	-	0.7	0.7	0.7	-	-
Fairfield	12,967	10,791	2,176	-	-	83.2	16.8	-	-	46	43	-	-	1.5	1.5	1.5	-	-
Fayette	3,947	3,339	608	-	-	84.6	15.4	-	-	25	64	-	-	0.5	0.5	0.4	-	-
Franklin	62,212	53,450	8,762	-	-	85.9	14.1	-	-	8	81	-	-	7.2	7.5	6.1	-	-
Fulton	5,125	4,234	891	-	-	82.6	17.4	-	-	55	34	-	-	0.6	0.6	0.6	-	-
Gallia	4,919	4,108	811	-	-	83.5	16.5	-	-	41	48	-	-	0.6	0.6	0.6	-	-
Geauga	10,673	9,190	1,483	-	-	86.1	13.9	-	-	5	84	-	-	1.2	1.3	1.0	-	-
Greene	13,595	11,586	2,009	-	-	85.2	14.8	-	-	16	73	-	-	1.6	1.6	1.4	-	-
Guernsey	4,635	3,734	901	-	-	80.6	19.4	-	-	75	14	-	-	0.5	0.5	0.6	-	-
Hamilton	54,075	44,863	9,212	-	-	83.0	17.0	-	-	50	39	-	-	6.3	6.3	6.4	-	-
Hancock	10,382	8,251	2,131	-	-	79.5	20.5	-	-	82	7	-	-	1.2	1.2	1.5	-	-
Hardin	3,903	3,246	657	-	-	83.2	16.8	-	-	47	42	-	-	0.5	0.5	0.5	-	-
Harrison	1,480	1,229	251	-	-	83.0	17.0	-	-	48	41	-	-	0.2	0.2	0.2	-	-
Henry	4,224	3,519	705	-	-	83.3	16.7	-	-	43	46	-	-	0.5	0.5	0.5	-	-
Highland	3,165	2,720	445	-	-	85.9	14.1	-	-	6	83	-	-	0.4	0.4	0.3	-	-
Hocking	1,901	1,624	277	-	-	85.4	14.6	-	-	11	78	-	-	0.2	0.2	0.2	-	-
Holmes	2,565	2,167	398	-	-	84.5	15.5	-	-	27	62	-	-	0.3	0.3	0.3	-	-
Huron	4,464	3,670	794	-	-	82.2	17.8	-	-	58	31	-	-	0.5	0.5	0.6	-	-
Jackson	5,228	4,182	1,046	-	-	80.0	20.0	-	-	79	10	-	-	0.6	0.6	0.7	-	-
Jefferson	4,273	3,585	688	-	-	83.9	16.1	-	-	35	54	-	-	0.5	0.5	0.5	-	-
Knox	5,948	4,747	1,201	-	-	79.8	20.2	-	-	81	8	-	-	0.7	0.7	0.8	-	-
Lake	19,984	16,380	3,604	-	-	82.0	18.0	-	-	63	26	-	-	2.3	2.3	2.5	-	-
Lawrence	5,141	4,194	947	-	-	81.6	18.4	-	-	67	22	-	-	0.6	0.6	0.7	-	-
Licking	12,060	10,200	1,860	-	-	84.6	15.4	-	-	26	63	-	-	1.4	1.4	1.3	-	-
Logan	5,662	4,842	820	-	-	85.5	14.5	-	-	10	79	-	-	0.7	0.7	0.6	-	-
Lorain	18,115	14,984	3,131	-	-	82.7	17.3	-	-	53	36	-	-	2.1	2.1	2.2	-	-
Lucas	17,776	15,181	2,595	-	-	85.4	14.6	-	-	13	76	-	-	2.1	2.1	1.8	-	-
Madison	3,318	2,841	477	-	-	85.6	14.4	-	-	9	80	-	-	0.4	0.4	0.3	-	-
Mahoning	11,567	9,761	1,806	-	-	84.4	15.6	-	-	29	60	-	-	1.3	1.4	1.3	-	-
Marion	7,461	6,298	1,163	-	-	84.4	15.6	-	-	28	61	-	-	0.9	0.9	0.8	-	-
Medina	14,250	11,956	2,294	-	-	83.9	16.1	-	-	34	55	-	-	1.7	1.7	1.6	-	-
Meigs	3,885	3,013	872	-	-	77.6	22.4	-	-	86	3	-	-	0.5	0.4	0.6	-	-
Mercer	2,622	2,191	431	-	-	83.6	16.4	-	-	40	49	-	-	0.3	0.3	0.3	-	-
Miami	10,611	8,912	1,699	-	-	84.0	16.0	-	-	32	57	-	-	1.2	1.2	1.2	-	-
Monroe	644	536	108	-	-	83.2	16.8	-	-	45	44	-	-	<.1	<.1	<.1	-	-
Montgomery	39,737	33,942	5,795	-	-	85.4	14.6	-	-	12	77	-	-	4.6	4.7	4.0	-	-
Morgan	2,504	1,986	518	-	-	79.3	20.7	-	-	83	6	-	-	0.3	0.3	0.4	-	-
Morrow	3,627	3,008	619	-	-	82.9	17.1	-	-	51	38	-	-	0.4	0.4	0.4	-	-
Muskingum	7,833	6,421	1,412	-	-	82.0	18.0	-	-	62	27	-	-	0.9	0.9	1.0	-	-
Noble	2,017	1,632	385	-	-	80.9	19.1	-	-	74	15	-	-	0.2	0.2	0.3	-	-
Ottawa	2,337	1,989	348	-	-	85.1	14.9	-	-	18	71	-	-	0.3	0.3	0.2	-	-
Paulding	2,207	1,709	498	-	-	77.4	22.6	-	-	87	2	-	-	0.3	0.2	0.3	-	-
Perry	4,257	3,370	887	-	-	79.2	20.8	-	-	85	4	-	-	0.5	0.5	0.6	-	-
Pickaway	3,971	3,477	494	-	-	87.6	12.4	-	-	2	87	-	-	0.5	0.5	0.3	-	-
Pike	1,700	1,497	203	-	-	88.1	11.9	-	-	1	88	-	-	0.2	0.2	0.1	-	-
Portage	8,358	6,911	1,447	-	-	82.7	17.3	-	-	54	35	-	-	1.0	1.0	1.0	-	-
Preble	5,550	4,543	1,007	-	-	81.9	18.1	-	-	65	24	-	-	0.6	0.6	0.7	-	-
Putnam	3,688	3,128	560	-	-	84.8	15.2	-	-	21	68	-	-	0.4	0.4	0.4	-	-
Richland	14,773	12,081	2,692	-	-	81.8	18.2	-	-	66	23	-	-	1.7	1.7	1.9	-	-

Table J. — Vote for Presidential Preference: June 2, 1992, Republican Primary Election (cont)

County	Top candidates					Top four candidates (state vote)								Percent contribution to state vote				
						Percent of total vote				Rank								
	Total	Bush	Bu-chanan			Bush	Bu-chanan			Bush	Bu-chanan			Total	Bush	Bu-chanan		
Ross	4,749	4,028	721	-	-	84.8	15.2	-	-	20	69	-	-	0.6	0.6	0.5	-	-
Sandusky	5,813	4,667	1,146	-	-	80.3	19.7	-	-	77	12	-	-	0.7	0.7	0.8	-	-
Scioto	5,665	4,803	862	-	-	84.8	15.2	-	-	22	67	-	-	0.7	0.7	0.6	-	-
Seneca	5,690	4,562	1,128	-	-	80.2	19.8	-	-	78	11	-	-	0.7	0.6	0.8	-	-
Shelby	3,647	3,163	484	-	-	86.7	13.3	-	-	3	86	-	-	0.4	0.4	0.3	-	-
Stark	36,483	29,663	6,820	-	-	81.3	18.7	-	-	69	20	-	-	4.2	4.1	4.7	-	-
Summit	30,496	24,778	5,718	-	-	81.3	18.8	-	-	72	17	-	-	3.5	3.5	4.0	-	-
Trumbull	12,332	10,020	2,312	-	-	81.3	18.7	-	-	71	18	-	-	1.4	1.4	1.6	-	-
Tuscarawas	4,540	3,805	735	-	-	83.8	16.2	-	-	37	52	-	-	0.5	0.5	0.5	-	-
Union	4,107	3,540	567	-	-	86.2	13.8	-	-	4	85	-	-	0.5	0.5	0.4	-	-
Van Wert	4,497	3,657	840	-	-	81.3	18.7	-	-	68	21	-	-	0.5	0.5	0.6	-	-
Vinton	1,632	1,354	278	-	-	83.0	17.0	-	-	49	40	-	-	0.2	0.2	0.2	-	-
Warren	14,227	11,937	2,290	-	-	83.9	16.1	-	-	33	56	-	-	1.7	1.7	1.6	-	-
Washington	7,270	6,247	1,023	-	-	85.9	14.1	-	-	7	82	-	-	0.8	0.9	0.7	-	-
Wayne	9,774	7,944	1,830	-	-	81.3	18.7	-	-	70	19	-	-	1.1	1.1	1.3	-	-
Williams	5,232	4,288	944	-	-	82.0	18.0	-	-	64	25	-	-	0.6	0.6	0.7	-	-
Wood	9,317	7,697	1,620	-	-	82.6	17.4	-	-	56	33	-	-	1.1	1.1	1.1	-	-
Wyandot	2,653	2,179	474	-	-	82.1	17.9	-	-	59	30	-	-	0.3	0.3	0.3	-	-
OHIO	**860,453**	**716,766**	**143,687**	-	-	**83.3**	**16.7**	-	-					**100.0**	**100.0**	**100.0**	-	-

1992 Vote for President
Percent for Clinton (D), by County

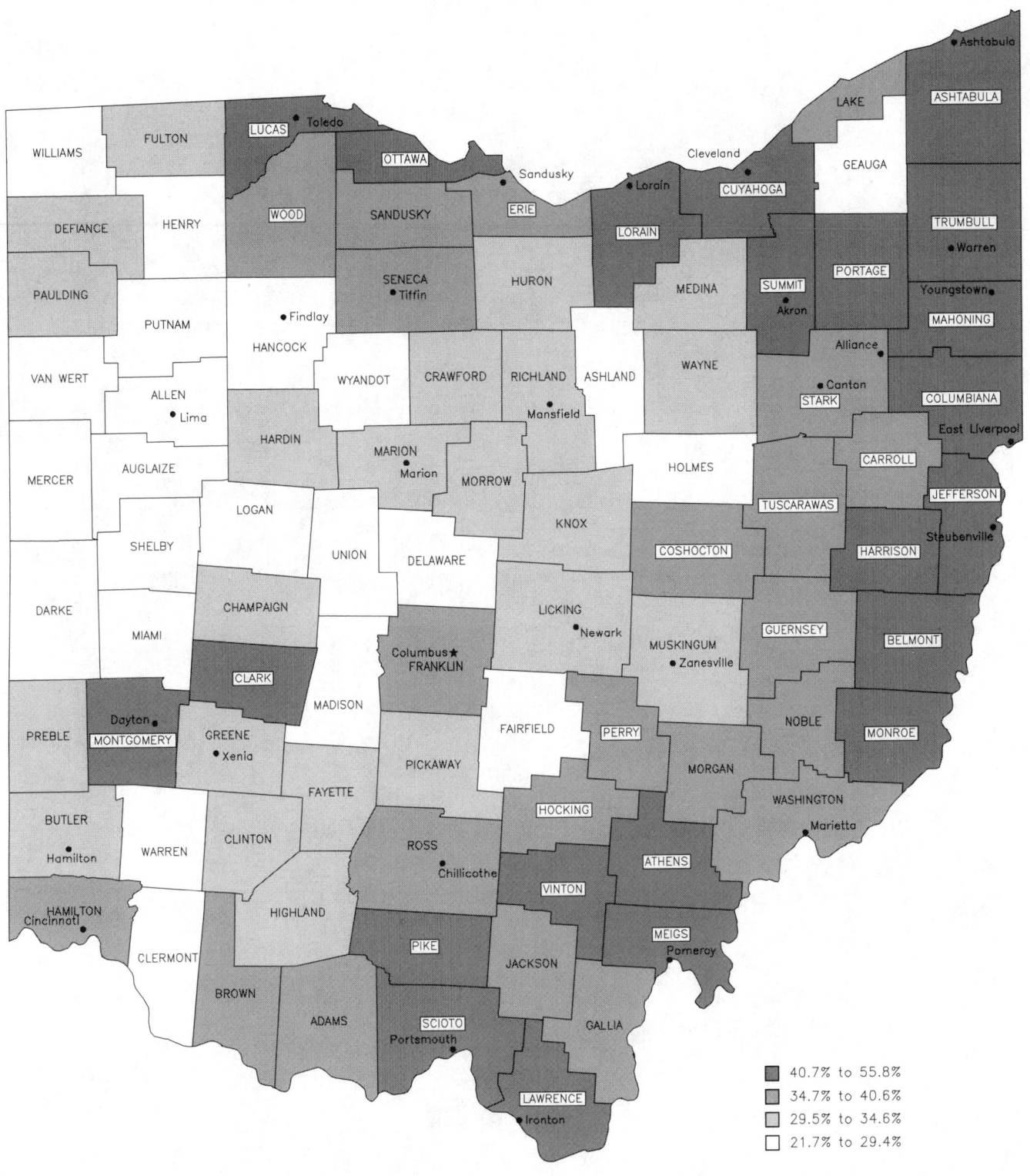

Legend:
- 40.7% to 55.8%
- 34.7% to 40.6%
- 29.5% to 34.6%
- 21.7% to 29.4%

Clinton (D) received 40.2% statewide.

A framed county name indicates a county carried by the winner.

Ohio 739

1992 Vote for U.S. Senator
Percent for Glenn (D), by County

Legend:
- 50.0% to 68.4%
- 45.1% to 49.9%
- 40.7% to 45.0%
- 30.0% to 40.6%

Glenn (D) received 51.0% statewide.

A framed county name indicates
a county carried by the winner.

OKLAHOMA

Congressional Districts 6
  Average Population 524,264
State Senate Districts 48
  Average Population 65,533
State House Districts 101
  Average Population 31,144

Electoral College Votes..8
Counties 77
Voting Precincts 2,146

Alternative Registration Methods:
....Deputized Registrars

Registration Deadline (Days before Election) 10

Voting Equipment Use (Counties)

Datavote Punch Card	0	Paper Ballot	0
Electronic	0	Other Punch Card	0
Lever Machine	0	Mixed Systems	0
Optical Scanner	77		

Party Control	DEM	REP	IND	VAC
1993 State Senate	37	11	0	0
1992 State Senate	37	11	0	0
1993 State House	68	33	0	0
1992 State House	68	32	0	1

Population Statistics 1990

Race/ Ethnicity	Total Population		Voting Age Population		Voting Age Population % of total population
	Number	%	Number	%	
Non-Hispanic					
White	2,547,588	81.0	1,925,439	83.4	75.6
Black	231,462	7.4	152,235	6.6	65.8
Asian/Pacific Islander	32,366	1.0	23,073	1.0	71.3
Native American	246,631	7.8	155,626	6.7	63.1
Other	1,378	<.1	663	<.1	48.1
All Hispanic	86,160	2.7	51,542	2.2	59.8
TOTAL	3,145,585	100.0	2,308,578	100.0	73.4

Estimated Voting Age Population 1992 (VAP) 2,328,000
Number of Registered Voters................................. 2,302,279
  % of estimated VAP... 98.9
Voter Turnout (Actual) 1,455,635
  % of VAP 62.5
  % of Registration 63.2
Persons Not Voting—of Voting Age 872,365
  % of VAP 37.5
Persons Not Voting—of Registered 846,644
  % of Registration 36.8
Straight Ticket Voting .... Yes, Exception

State Officials and Members of Congress

Governor:
David Walters (D) 1990, elected to a four-year term in 1990.

U.S. Senators:
David L. Boren (D) 1978, elected to a six-year term in 1990.
Don Nickles (R) 1980, elected to a six-year term in 1992.

U.S. Representative in Congress:
(District, Name, Party, Date first elected)

1. Inhofe (R) 1986
2. Synar (D) 1978

3. Brewster (D) 1990
4. McCurdy (D) 1980

5. Istook (R) 1992

6. English (D) 1974

Candidates: General Election, November 3, 1992

Candidate(s)	Total vote	Percent	Party	Status	First elected
President/Vice President					
Bush/Quayle	592,929	42.65%	Republican	Incumbent	1988
Clinton/Gore	473,066	34.02%	Democrat	Challenger	1992
Perot/Stockdale	319,878	23.01%	Independent	Challenger	
Marrou/Lord	4,486	0.32%	Libertarian	Challenger	
U.S. Senator					
Don Nickles	757,876	58.55%	Republican	Incumbent	1980
Steve Lewis	494,350	38.19%	Democrat	Challenger	
Roy V. Edwards	21,225	1.64%	Independent	Challenger	
Thomas Ledgerwood II	20,972	1.62%	Independent	Challenger	
Governor (No Contest)					
U.S. Representative in Congress					
District 1					
James Inhofe	119,211	52.79%	Republican	Incumbent	1986
John Selph	106,619	47.21%	Democrat	Challenger	
District 2					
Mike Synar	118,542	55.52%	Democrat	Incumbent	1978
Jerry Hill	87,657	41.05%	Republican	Challenger	
William Vardeman	7,314	3.43%	Independent	Challenger	
District 3					
Bill Brewster	155,934	75.09%	Democrat	Incumbent	1990
Robert Stokes	51,725	24.91%	Republican	Challenger	
District 4					
Dave McCurdy	140,841	70.75%	Democrat	Incumbent	1980
Howard Bell	58,235	29.25%	Republican	Challenger	
District 5					
Ernest Jim Istook	123,237	53.39%	Republican	Challenger	1992
Laurie Williams	107,579	46.61%	Democrat	Challenger	
District 6					
Glenn English	134,734	67.77%	Democrat	Incumbent	1974
Bob Anthony	64,068	32.23%	Republican	Challenger	

Candidates: March 10, 1992, Primary Election

Candidate	Total vote	Percent	Candidate	Total vote	Percent
Presidential Preference, Democratic			**Presidential Preference, Republican**		
Bill Clinton	293,266	70.47%	George Bush	151,612	69.64%
Jerry Brown	69,624	16.73%	Patrick Buchanan	57,933	26.61%
Charles Woods	16,828	4.04%	David Duke	5,672	2.61%
Tom Harkin	14,015	3.37%	Isabell Masters	1,830	0.84%
Bob Kerrey	13,252	3.18%	Tennie Rogers	674	0.31%
Lyndon LaRouche, Jr.	6,474	1.56%			
J. Louis McAlpine	2,670	0.64%			

Voter Registration and Turnout, 1948-1992 Elections

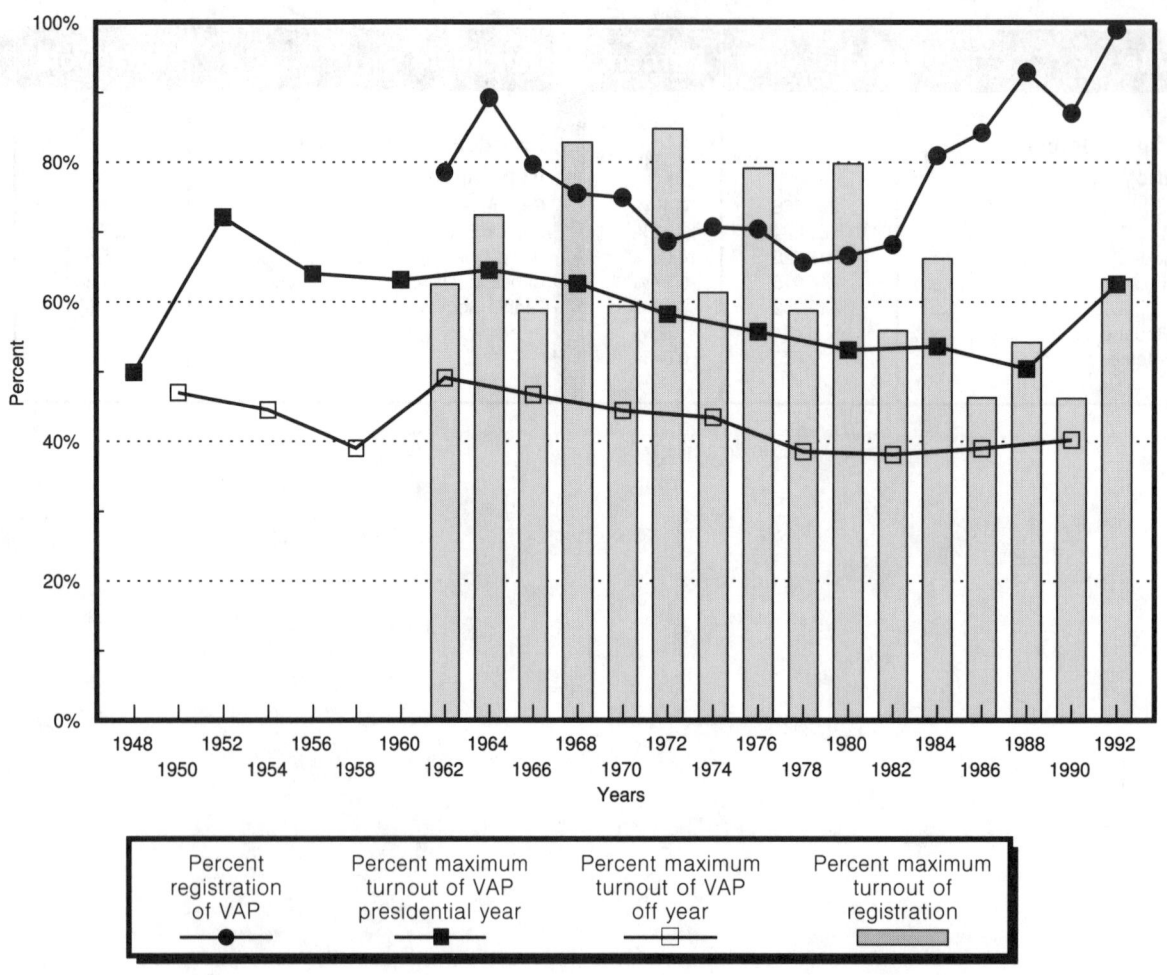

Year	Estimated Voting Age Population (VAP)	Voter registration (REG)			Voter turnout										
						Highest office						Maximum vote			
		Total	Percent of VAP	Rank by percent of VAP	Actual	Total	Office	Percent total REG	Rank by percent of REG	Percent of VAP	Rank by percent of VAP	Total	Percent total REG	Rank by percent of REG	Percent total VAP	Rank by percent of VAP
1992	2,328,000	2,302,279	98.9	2	1,455,635	1,390,359	P	60.4	48	59.7	25	1,455,635	63.2	48	62.5	20
1990	2,310,000	2,010,684	87.0	4	929,639	911,314	G	45.3	44	39.5	25	929,639	46.2	44	40.2	26
1988	2,366,000	2,199,014	92.9	2	1,192,815	1,171,036	P	53.3	49	49.5	31	1,192,815	54.2	49	50.4	31
1986	2,396,000	2,018,401	84.2	4	934,447	909,925	G	45.1	43	38.0	27	934,447	46.3	44	39.0	30
1984	2,410,000	1,949,989	80.9	14	1,290,555	1,255,676	P	64.4	47	52.1	32	1,290,555	66.2	45	53.6	31
1982	2,367,000	1,613,827	68.2	26	901,488	883,130	G	54.7	37	37.3	37	901,488	55.9	37	38.1	37
1980	2,207,000	1,469,320	66.6	35	1,172,303	1,149,708	P	78.2	11	52.1	31	1,172,303	79.8	10	53.1	30
1978	2,081,000	1,366,019	65.6	35	801,190	777,414	G	56.9	23	37.4	29	801,190	58.7	22	38.5	30
1976	1,990,000	1,401,094	70.4	33	1,108,463	1,092,251	P	78.0	17	54.9	29	1,108,463	79.1	17	55.7	29
1974	1,896,000	1,341,209	70.7	25	822,026	804,848	G	60.0	20	42.4	24	822,026	61.3	21	43.4	24
1972	1,818,000	1,247,157	68.6	35	1,057,396	1,029,900	P	82.6	5	56.7	30	1,057,396	84.8	6	58.2	29
1970	1,605,000	1,201,666	74.9	20	712,425	698,790	G	58.2	34	43.5	37	712,425	59.3	34	44.4	36
1968	1,540,000	1,163,328	75.5	24	963,728	943,086	P	81.1	22	61.2	30	963,728	82.8	18	62.6	30
1966	1,489,000	1,185,225	79.6	16	695,518	677,258	G	57.1	32	45.5	35	695,518	58.7	32	46.7	35
1964	1,471,000	1,311,864	89.2	10	949,330	932,499	P	71.1	34	63.4	31	949,330	72.4	34	64.5	32
1962	1,478,000	1,160,515	78.5	19	724,974	709,763	G	61.2	23	48.0	30	724,974	62.5	23	49.1	31
1960	1,431,000	-	-	-	-	903,150	P	-	-	63.1	32	903,150	-	-	63.1	32
1958	1,382,000	-	-	-	-	538,839	G	-	-	39.0	36	538,839	-	-	39.0	36
1956	1,342,000	-	-	-	-	859,350	P	-	-	64.0	33	859,350	-	-	64.0	33
1954	1,368,000	-	-	-	-	609,194	G	-	-	44.5	33	609,194	-	-	44.5	33
1952	1,317,000	-	-	-	-	948,984	P	-	-	72.1	23	948,984	-	-	72.1	23
1950	1,372,000	-	-	-	-	644,726	G	-	-	47.0	31	644,726	-	-	47.0	31
1948	1,445,000	-	-	-	-	721,599	P	-	-	49.9	33	721,599	-	-	49.9	33

OKLAHOMA

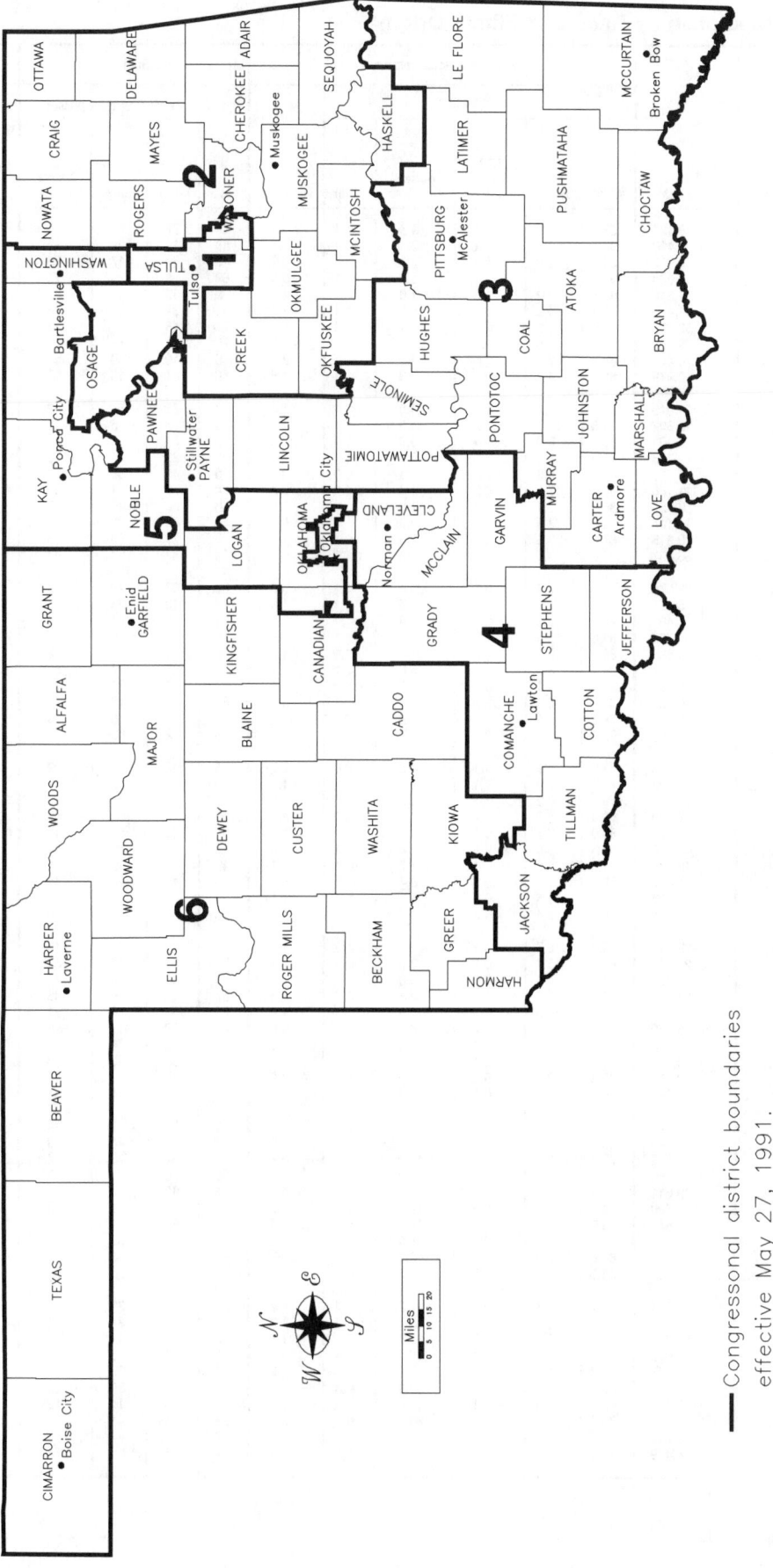

— Congressonal district boundaries
effective May 27, 1991.

Copyright © 1993 by Election Data Services, Inc.

Oklahoma 745

Table A. — 1990 Population by Race and Ethnic Origin

State/ county code	County	Total persons	Percent of total persons — Non-Hispanic White	Black	Asian and Pacific Islander	Native American	Other	Hispanic	Rank Total	Rank Non-Hispanic White	Black	Native American[1]	Pct contrib Total	Non-Hispanic White	Black	Native American[1]
40 001	Adair	18,421	55.2	<.1	<.1	43.3	<.1	1.3	40	77	75	1	0.6	0.4	<.1	3.2
40 003	Alfalfa	6,416	92.6	3.1	<.1	2.4	0.1	1.6	68	11	29	62	0.2	0.2	<.1	<.1
40 005	Atoka	12,778	80.8	5.9	0.1	12.3	<.1	0.9	48	54	17	26	0.4	0.4	0.3	0.6
40 007	Beaver	6,023	93.9	<.1	<.1	1.0	<.1	5.0	69	8	76	73	0.2	0.2	<.1	<.1
40 009	Beckham	18,812	91.8	2.0	0.2	1.8	<.1	4.2	39	13	47	67	0.6	0.7	0.2	0.1
40 011	Blaine	11,470	84.5	4.2	0.2	8.5	<.1	2.5	51	39	21	35	0.4	0.4	0.2	0.4
40 013	Bryan	32,089	82.7	1.3	0.4	14.1	<.1	1.4	27	43	53	22	1.0	1.0	0.2	1.8
40 015	Caddo	29,550	71.2	2.5	0.2	21.2	<.1	4.8	29	72	38	4	0.9	0.8	0.3	2.5
40 017	Canadian	74,409	89.3	2.4	1.6	4.1	<.1	2.6	5	19	39	55	2.4	2.6	0.8	1.2
40 019	Carter	42,919	81.2	8.3	0.4	8.3	<.1	1.8	16	51	13	37	1.4	1.4	1.5	1.4
40 021	Cherokee	34,049	64.3	1.1	0.2	33.0	<.1	1.4	23	76	54	2	1.1	0.9	0.2	4.6
40 023	Choctaw	15,302	70.8	12.8	0.2	14.9	<.1	1.3	44	73	5	18	0.5	0.4	0.8	0.9
40 025	Cimarron	3,301	86.4	0.0	0.4	0.7	<.1	12.5	77	31	77	77	0.1	0.1	0.0	<.1
40 027	Cleveland	174,253	87.0	3.0	2.3	5.0	<.1	2.7	3	29	31	49	5.5	6.0	2.2	3.5
40 029	Coal	5,780	82.1	0.8	<.1	16.3	0.0	0.7	70	49	58	13	0.2	0.2	<.1	0.4
40 031	Comanche	111,486	69.2	17.5	2.6	4.3	0.1	6.2	4	74	1	53	3.5	3.0	8.4	2.0
40 033	Cotton	6,651	86.8	2.1	<.1	7.5	<.1	3.5	66	30	46	40	0.2	0.2	<.1	0.2
40 035	Craig	14,104	76.7	3.3	0.2	19.0	<.1	0.7	45	59	28	7	0.4	0.4	0.2	1.1
40 037	Creek	60,915	87.2	3.1	0.2	8.3	<.1	1.1	8	27	30	36	1.9	2.1	0.8	2.1
40 039	Custer	26,897	84.0	3.5	0.6	5.9	<.1	6.0	34	41	27	47	0.9	0.9	0.4	0.6
40 041	Delaware	28,070	73.9	<.1	0.1	25.1	<.1	0.8	33	67	70	3	0.9	0.8	<.1	2.9
40 043	Dewey	5,551	93.0	<.1	0.1	5.5	<.1	1.3	72	10	68	48	0.2	0.2	<.1	0.1
40 045	Ellis	4,497	95.2	<.1	0.2	1.4	<.1	3.1	73	5	73	70	0.1	0.2	<.1	<.1
40 047	Garfield	56,735	91.5	3.5	1.0	2.1	<.1	1.9	10	14	26	65	1.8	2.0	0.9	0.5
40 049	Garvin	26,605	88.8	2.7	0.2	7.0	<.1	1.2	35	21	34	42	0.8	0.9	0.3	0.8
40 051	Grady	41,747	89.3	3.7	0.3	5.0	<.1	1.7	18	20	24	50	1.3	1.5	0.7	0.8
40 053	Grant	5,689	97.4	<.1	0.2	1.3	0.0	1.0	71	1	71	72	0.2	0.2	<.1	<.1
40 055	Greer	6,559	85.5	6.9	0.2	2.1	<.1	5.1	67	34	16	64	0.2	0.2	0.2	<.1
40 057	Harmon	3,793	74.3	7.4	0.2	0.9	0.0	17.3	76	66	15	75	0.1	0.1	0.1	<.1
40 059	Harper	4,063	97.3	<.1	0.1	0.7	0.0	1.8	75	2	69	76	0.1	0.2	<.1	<.1
40 061	Haskell	10,940	83.9	0.9	<.1	14.5	0.0	0.7	56	42	57	20	0.3	0.4	<.1	0.6
40 063	Hughes	13,023	79.0	2.9	<.1	16.9	<.1	1.0	47	58	32	11	0.4	0.4	0.2	0.9
40 065	Jackson	28,764	76.2	9.2	1.3	1.6	0.2	11.6	32	60	12	69	0.9	0.9	1.1	0.2
40 067	Jefferson	7,010	90.0	0.6	0.2	4.8	0.0	4.4	65	16	63	52	0.2	0.2	<.1	0.1
40 069	Johnston	10,032	81.0	2.1	0.1	15.5	<.1	1.2	60	52	45	15	0.3	0.3	<.1	0.6
40 071	Kay	48,056	88.5	1.8	0.5	7.4	<.1	1.8	13	23	49	41	1.5	1.7	0.4	1.4
40 073	Kingfisher	13,212	91.8	2.3	<.1	2.7	<.1	3.1	46	12	42	61	0.4	0.5	0.1	0.1
40 075	Kiowa	11,347	82.5	5.4	0.3	6.4	<.1	5.3	53	46	18	44	0.4	0.4	0.3	0.3
40 077	Latimer	10,333	82.1	1.5	0.2	15.1	<.1	1.1	59	48	52	16	0.3	0.3	<.1	0.6
40 079	Le Flore	43,270	84.8	2.4	0.2	11.7	<.1	1.0	15	37	40	29	1.4	1.4	0.4	2.0
40 081	Lincoln	29,216	89.9	2.7	0.2	6.2	<.1	1.1	30	18	35	46	0.9	1.0	0.3	0.7
40 083	Logan	29,011	80.8	13.7	0.3	3.2	<.1	1.9	31	53	4	59	0.9	0.9	1.7	0.4
40 085	Love	8,157	84.7	4.4	0.1	6.6	<.1	4.1	63	38	20	43	0.3	0.3	0.2	0.2
40 087	McClain	22,795	89.9	1.0	0.2	6.4	<.1	2.5	37	17	56	45	0.7	0.8	<.1	0.6
40 089	McCurtain	33,433	73.8	10.3	0.3	14.4	<.1	1.4	25	68	8	21	1.1	1.0	1.5	1.9
40 091	McIntosh	16,779	75.5	5.2	0.2	18.1	<.1	0.9	41	62	19	8	0.5	0.5	0.4	1.2
40 093	Major	8,055	96.6	<.1	0.1	1.6	<.1	1.6	64	3	74	68	0.3	0.3	<.1	<.1
40 095	Marshall	10,829	85.8	1.7	0.1	9.8	<.1	2.5	57	33	50	33	0.3	0.4	<.1	0.4
40 097	Mayes	33,366	80.8	0.2	0.2	17.9	<.1	0.9	26	55	66	10	1.1	1.1	<.1	2.4
40 099	Murray	12,042	85.8	1.7	0.1	10.9	<.1	1.4	49	32	51	31	0.4	0.4	<.1	0.5
40 101	Muskogee	68,078	71.2	13.9	0.4	13.1	<.1	1.3	6	71	3	24	2.2	1.9	4.1	3.6
40 103	Noble	11,045	88.6	1.8	0.2	8.3	<.1	1.1	54	22	48	38	0.4	0.4	<.1	0.4
40 105	Nowata	9,992	79.4	3.6	<.1	16.2	<.1	0.7	61	57	25	14	0.3	0.3	0.2	0.7
40 107	Okfuskee	11,551	67.2	11.5	0.1	20.0	<.1	1.2	50	75	7	6	0.4	0.3	0.6	0.9
40 109	Oklahoma	599,611	75.3	14.6	1.9	3.8	<.1	4.2	1	63	2	58	19.1	17.7	37.8	9.4
40 111	Okmulgee	36,490	74.4	12.1	0.2	12.0	<.1	1.3	21	64	6	28	1.2	1.1	1.9	1.8
40 113	Osage	41,645	73.7	10.0	0.2	14.5	<.1	1.6	19	69	9	19	1.3	1.2	1.8	2.5
40 115	Ottawa	30,561	79.8	0.6	0.3	18.0	<.1	1.2	28	56	62	9	1.0	1.0	<.1	2.2
40 117	Pawnee	15,575	88.0	0.8	0.2	10.4	<.1	0.7	43	26	60	32	0.5	0.5	<.1	0.7
40 119	Payne	61,507	88.5	2.9	2.8	4.3	<.1	1.5	7	24	33	54	2.0	2.1	0.8	1.1
40 121	Pittsburg	40,581	82.7	3.7	0.2	12.2	<.1	1.2	20	45	23	27	1.3	1.3	0.6	2.0
40 123	Pontotoc	34,119	82.3	2.5	0.3	13.7	<.1	1.2	22	47	37	23	1.1	1.1	0.4	1.9
40 125	Pottawatomie	58,760	84.2	2.2	0.5	11.3	<.1	1.7	9	40	43	30	1.9	1.9	0.6	2.7
40 127	Pushmataha	10,997	82.7	1.0	<.1	15.0	<.1	1.2	55	44	55	17	0.3	0.4	<.1	0.7
40 129	Roger Mills	4,147	94.3	<.1	<.1	3.9	0.0	1.8	74	6	72	57	0.1	0.2	<.1	<.1
40 131	Rogers	55,170	85.0	0.8	0.3	12.8	<.1	1.1	11	36	59	25	1.8	1.8	0.2	2.9
40 133	Seminole	25,412	74.3	7.5	0.1	16.7	<.1	1.3	36	65	14	12	0.8	0.7	0.8	1.7
40 135	Sequoyah	33,828	76.0	2.3	0.2	20.5	<.1	0.9	24	61	41	5	1.1	1.0	0.3	2.8
40 137	Stephens	42,299	91.1	2.2	0.4	4.0	<.1	2.2	17	15	44	56	1.3	1.5	0.4	0.7
40 139	Texas	16,419	88.4	0.4	0.2	1.0	<.1	10.0	42	25	65	74	0.5	0.6	<.1	<.1

[1] Non-Hispanic Native American.

Table A. – 1990 Population by Race and Ethnic Origin (cont)

State/county code	County	Total persons	Percent of total persons						Rank				Percent contribution to state population			
			Non-Hispanic							Percent of total persons			Non-Hispanic			
			White	Black	Asian and Pacific Islander	Native American	Other	Hispanic	Total	Non-Hispanic		Native American[1]	Total	White	Black	Native American[1]
										White	Black					
40 141	Tillman	10,384	72.6	9.8	0.2	3.1	0.2	14.1	58	70	10	60	0.3	0.3	0.4	0.1
40 143	Tulsa	503,341	81.7	9.8	1.2	4.9	<.1	2.4	2	50	11	51	16.0	16.1	21.2	10.0
40 145	Wagoner	47,883	85.1	4.1	0.4	9.1	<.1	1.3	14	35	22	34	1.5	1.6	0.9	1.8
40 147	Washington	48,066	87.1	2.6	0.8	7.7	<.1	1.6	12	28	36	39	1.5	1.6	0.5	1.5
40 149	Washita	11,441	94.0	0.2	0.2	2.1	<.1	3.5	52	7	67	66	0.4	0.4	<.1	<.1
40 151	Woods	9,103	96.2	0.5	0.3	1.4	0.0	1.5	62	4	64	71	0.3	0.3	<.1	<.1
40 153	Woodward	18,976	93.6	0.7	0.4	2.3	<.1	3.0	38	9	61	63	0.6	0.7	<.1	0.2
40	**OKLAHOMA**	**3,145,585**	**81.0**	**7.4**	**1.0**	**7.8**	**<.1**	**2.7**					**100.0**	**100.0**	**100.0**	**100.0**
	CONGRESSIONAL															
	District 1	524,264	82.0	9.5	1.1	5.0	<.1	2.3	2	4	2	3	16.7	16.9	21.5	10.7
	District 2	524,264	76.6	5.0	0.2	17.0	<.1	1.1	3	6	5	1	16.7	15.8	11.4	36.2
	District 3	524,264	82.7	4.0	0.6	11.3	<.1	1.4	4	2	6	2	16.7	17.0	9.1	23.9
	District 4	524,265	82.6	7.1	1.6	4.6	<.1	4.0	1	3	3	5	16.7	17.0	16.0	9.8
	District 5	524,264	85.2	5.5	1.6	4.5	<.1	3.2	5	1	4	6	16.7	17.5	12.5	9.5
	District 6	524,264	76.9	13.0	1.0	4.7	<.1	4.4	6	5	1	4	16.7	15.8	29.6	9.9

[1]Non-Hispanic Native American.

Table B. — 1990 Voting Age Population (VAP) by Race and Ethnic Origin

County	Total Voting Age Population	Percent of total VAP — Non-Hispanic White	Black	Asian and Pacific Islander	Native American	Other	Hispanic	Rank Percent of total VAP — Total	Non-Hispanic White	Black	Native American[1]	Percent contribution to state VAP — Total	Non-Hispanic White	Black	Native American[1]	VAP percent of total population — Total	Non-Hispanic White	Black	Asian and Pacific Islander	Native American	Other	Hispanic
Adair	12,770	60.6	0.0	<.1	38.4	<.1	0.9	41	77	75	1	0.6	0.4	0.0	3.2	69.3	76.1	0.0	75.0	61.4	25.0	46.9
Alfalfa	5,064	92.2	3.9	<.1	2.2	0.1	1.4	67	15	21	62	0.2	0.2	0.1	<.1	78.9	78.6	98.5	83.3	70.7	87.5	70.6
Atoka	9,462	82.6	5.9	0.2	10.4	<.1	0.9	47	55	16	26	0.4	0.4	0.4	0.6	74.0	75.7	74.8	93.8	62.5	100.0	73.7
Beaver	4,353	95.4	<.1	<.1	0.8	<.1	3.7	69	8	73	75	0.2	0.2	<.1	<.1	72.3	73.4	100.0	66.7	54.1	60.0	54.3
Beckham	13,525	93.9	1.5	0.1	1.3	<.1	3.1	39	11	49	68	0.6	0.7	0.1	0.1	71.9	73.5	55.2	47.6	53.9	60.0	53.6
Blaine	8,301	87.9	3.8	0.2	6.2	<.1	1.8	54	33	22	40	0.4	0.4	0.2	0.3	72.4	75.2	66.0	72.2	52.9	50.0	53.0
Bryan	24,015	85.2	1.3	0.5	12.0	<.1	1.1	26	48	53	22	1.0	1.1	0.2	1.8	74.8	77.1	76.3	78.6	63.6	83.3	55.3
Caddo	21,110	75.8	2.4	0.2	17.7	<.1	3.8	31	71	36	5	0.9	0.8	0.3	2.4	71.4	76.1	69.4	65.7	59.6	60.0	56.6
Canadian	51,949	90.4	2.4	1.4	3.5	<.1	2.3	5	24	37	56	2.3	2.4	0.8	1.2	69.8	70.6	71.3	60.5	60.0	40.6	61.4
Carter	31,198	84.1	7.2	0.3	7.0	<.1	1.4	17	50	13	36	1.4	1.4	1.5	1.4	72.7	75.3	63.0	59.5	61.3	66.7	55.7
Cherokee	24,818	69.4	1.0	0.2	28.4	0.0	1.0	23	76	54	2	1.1	0.9	0.2	4.5	72.9	78.7	68.4	66.7	62.6	0.0	53.4
Choctaw	10,994	74.7	11.3	0.1	12.7	<.1	1.0	44	72	6	18	0.5	0.4	0.8	0.9	71.8	75.8	63.6	66.7	61.2	83.3	58.5
Cimarron	2,391	88.7	0.0	0.3	0.8	0.0	10.2	77	29	76	74	0.1	0.1	0.0	<.1	72.4	74.4	0.0	58.3	82.6	0.0	59.0
Cleveland	128,274	87.9	2.9	2.4	4.5	<.1	2.3	3	34	31	48	5.6	5.9	2.5	3.7	73.6	74.3	72.3	77.3	66.1	50.7	63.1
Coal	4,243	85.4	0.9	<.1	13.2	0.0	0.6	71	44	57	14	0.2	0.2	<.1	0.4	73.4	76.3	77.1	50.0	59.2	0.0	61.5
Comanche	79,971	71.8	16.2	2.6	3.8	<.1	5.5	4	74	1	53	3.5	3.0	8.5	2.0	71.7	74.4	66.1	71.8	63.8	42.8	63.6
Cotton	4,952	88.4	1.8	<.1	7.0	<.1	2.7	68	31	46	37	0.2	0.2	<.1	0.2	74.5	75.8	66.7	66.7	69.1	75.0	58.0
Craig	10,803	79.2	3.4	0.2	16.5	0.0	0.7	45	62	25	6	0.5	0.4	0.2	1.1	76.6	79.1	78.9	80.6	66.4	0.0	70.3
Creek	43,822	88.8	3.0	0.2	7.2	<.1	0.9	8	28	30	35	1.9	2.0	0.9	2.0	71.9	73.2	68.0	63.9	62.0	22.2	58.6
Custer	19,782	86.8	3.1	0.6	4.8	<.1	4.6	35	40	28	47	0.9	0.9	0.4	0.6	73.5	76.1	66.6	74.8	60.2	73.3	55.5
Delaware	21,264	78.3	<.1	0.1	20.9	0.0	0.6	29	65	69	3	0.9	0.9	<.1	2.9	75.8	80.3	70.0	60.0	63.0	0.0	58.1
Dewey	4,088	94.5	<.1	0.1	4.2	<.1	1.0	72	9	68	51	0.2	0.2	<.1	0.1	73.6	74.9	60.0	83.3	56.5	100.0	57.5
Ellis	3,319	96.3	0.0	0.2	1.2	<.1	2.3	73	5	77	69	0.1	0.2	0.0	<.1	73.8	74.6	0.0	45.5	63.5	100.0	55.8
Garfield	41,857	92.7	3.1	0.9	1.7	<.1	1.6	10	14	29	65	1.8	2.0	0.9	0.5	73.8	74.7	65.1	69.1	61.4	62.5	60.6
Garvin	19,842	90.5	2.4	0.2	5.9	<.1	1.0	34	22	35	42	0.9	0.9	0.3	0.8	74.6	76.0	67.3	70.2	62.8	100.0	58.3
Grady	29,931	90.8	3.3	0.2	4.3	<.1	1.3	20	19	26	50	1.3	1.4	0.7	0.8	71.7	72.9	65.0	63.2	61.7	100.0	54.4
Grant	4,257	98.0	<.1	0.2	1.0	0.0	0.7	70	2	74	72	0.2	0.2	<.1	<.1	74.8	75.3	33.3	71.4	59.7	0.0	53.4
Greer	5,247	87.1	6.6	0.2	2.1	<.1	3.8	66	35	15	64	0.2	0.2	0.2	<.1	80.0	81.5	77.3	81.3	78.0	80.0	59.5
Harmon	2,752	80.5	5.8	0.1	0.7	0.0	12.9	76	59	17	76	0.1	0.1	0.1	<.1	72.6	78.6	56.8	66.7	57.6	0.0	54.1
Harper	3,031	98.0	<.1	<.1	0.6	0.0	1.2	74	1	70	77	0.1	0.2	<.1	<.1	74.6	75.2	66.7	50.0	60.0	0.0	51.4
Haskell	8,100	86.4	0.8	<.1	12.3	0.0	0.4	56	42	59	20	0.4	0.4	<.1	0.6	74.0	76.2	67.3	62.5	63.0	0.0	48.6
Hughes	9,824	82.2	2.7	<.1	14.2	<.1	0.8	46	57	32	11	0.4	0.4	0.2	0.9	75.4	78.5	70.1	69.2	63.1	40.0	58.8
Jackson	20,286	80.1	7.9	1.2	1.4	0.1	9.2	33	60	12	67	0.9	0.8	1.1	0.2	70.5	74.1	60.9	68.4	65.0	50.9	55.8
Jefferson	5,278	91.7	0.5	0.2	4.1	<.1	3.4	65	16	64	52	0.2	0.3	<.1	0.1	75.3	76.8	72.5	75.0	64.5	0.0	57.4
Johnston	7,353	83.9	2.1	0.1	13.1	0.0	0.9	61	51	43	15	0.3	0.3	<.1	0.6	73.3	75.9	70.9	64.3	61.8	0.0	53.3
Kay	35,303	90.6	1.5	0.4	6.0	<.1	1.4	13	20	48	41	1.5	1.7	0.4	1.4	73.5	75.2	63.8	58.9	59.7	37.5	57.7
Kingfisher	9,428	93.1	2.3	<.1	2.2	<.1	2.2	38	12	41	61	0.4	0.5	0.1	0.1	71.4	72.4	70.4	61.5	59.7	100.0	51.6
Kiowa	8,322	86.2	4.0	0.3	5.3	<.1	4.2	53	43	20	45	0.4	0.4	0.2	0.3	73.3	76.6	54.5	60.0	60.4	83.3	57.5
Latimer	7,537	84.8	1.5	0.1	12.8	0.0	0.8	58	49	51	17	0.3	0.3	<.1	0.6	72.9	75.3	73.3	50.0	61.9	0.0	55.7
Le Flore	31,346	86.9	2.3	0.2	9.8	<.1	0.8	15	39	39	29	1.4	1.4	0.5	2.0	72.4	74.3	70.5	58.7	61.1	60.0	56.8
Lincoln	20,997	91.2	2.6	0.2	5.3	<.1	0.8	32	18	34	46	0.9	1.0	0.4	0.7	71.9	72.9	69.0	70.9	61.0	100.0	53.7
Logan	21,121	80.8	14.6	0.3	2.8	<.1	1.5	30	58	2	59	0.9	0.9	2.0	0.4	72.8	72.8	77.4	70.8	64.5	50.0	55.6
Love	6,110	86.5	4.6	0.1	5.7	0.0	3.1	63	41	19	44	0.3	0.3	0.2	0.2	74.9	76.5	78.1	66.7	64.3	0.0	57.0
McClain	16,489	92.1	1.0	0.1	5.7	<.1	1.9	37	17	55	43	0.7	0.8	0.1	0.6	72.3	73.4	72.9	60.0	64.5	40.0	54.7
McCurtain	23,539	77.6	9.1	0.2	12.0	<.1	1.2	27	67	9	21	1.0	0.9	1.4	1.8	70.4	74.0	62.3	59.5	58.8	20.0	59.5
McIntosh	12,861	79.8	4.8	0.2	14.6	<.1	0.6	40	61	18	10	0.6	0.5	0.4	1.2	76.6	81.0	69.7	80.8	61.8	18.2	54.7
Major	5,881	97.5	<.1	0.1	1.1	0.0	1.2	64	3	71	71	0.3	0.3	<.1	<.1	73.0	73.7	66.7	80.0	50.8	0.0	55.3
Marshall	8,370	88.2	1.5	0.1	8.2	<.1	1.9	51	32	50	33	0.4	0.4	<.1	0.4	77.3	79.4	67.4	69.2	65.1	50.0	58.9
Mayes	24,289	83.7	0.2	0.2	15.1	<.1	0.8	24	53	66	9	1.1	1.1	<.1	2.4	72.8	75.5	76.5	63.8	61.3	100.0	61.0
Murray	8,975	88.6	1.4	0.1	8.8	<.1	1.0	49	30	52	32	0.4	0.4	<.1	0.5	74.5	77.0	63.1	68.8	60.0	83.3	53.3
Muskogee	49,457	74.3	13.0	0.3	11.3	<.1	1.1	6	73	3	23	2.1	1.9	4.2	3.6	72.6	75.8	67.6	61.9	62.6	57.9	60.1
Noble	8,060	90.5	1.6	0.2	6.9	<.1	0.9	57	21	47	38	0.3	0.4	<.1	0.4	73.0	74.5	64.8	58.3	60.6	100.0	55.6
Nowata	7,472	82.5	3.3	<.1	13.6	0.0	0.6	60	56	27	13	0.3	0.3	0.2	0.7	74.8	77.7	68.5	33.3	62.9	0.0	60.3
Okfuskee	8,527	70.8	11.9	0.1	16.1	<.1	1.1	50	75	5	7	0.4	0.3	0.7	0.9	73.8	77.8	76.8	70.6	59.4	100.0	65.0
Oklahoma	442,921	78.5	12.7	1.9	3.5	<.1	3.4	1	64	4	55	19.2	18.0	36.9	10.0	73.9	76.9	64.1	71.9	67.3	43.4	59.9
Okmulgee	26,724	77.3	11.2	0.2	10.2	<.1	1.1	21	69	7	27	1.2	1.1	2.0	1.8	73.2	76.1	67.6	72.0	62.3	50.0	62.2
Osage	30,096	76.8	9.3	0.1	12.5	<.1	1.3	19	70	8	19	1.3	1.2	1.8	2.4	72.3	75.3	67.3	62.9	62.1	40.0	58.2
Ottawa	23,229	82.8	0.7	0.3	15.2	<.1	1.0	28	54	61	8	1.0	1.0	0.1	2.3	76.0	78.9	91.5	63.9	64.2	66.7	58.9
Pawnee	11,377	89.7	0.7	0.1	8.9	<.1	0.6	43	25	62	31	0.5	0.5	<.1	0.6	73.0	74.5	69.2	62.5	62.6	100.0	55.8
Payne	48,510	89.4	2.6	3.1	3.6	<.1	1.4	7	26	33	54	2.1	2.3	0.8	1.1	78.9	79.6	70.8	85.5	66.6	48.6	72.8
Pittsburg	30,517	85.2	3.6	0.2	10.1	<.1	0.9	18	46	24	28	1.3	1.4	0.7	2.0	75.2	77.5	72.5	61.0	62.4	83.3	59.1
Pontotoc	25,588	85.2	2.3	0.3	11.3	<.1	0.9	22	47	40	24	1.1	1.1	0.4	1.9	75.0	77.7	68.8	81.5	61.6	50.0	56.2
Pottawatomie	42,908	87.0	2.0	0.5	9.2	<.1	1.3	9	36	44	30	1.9	1.9	0.6	2.5	73.0	75.4	64.0	70.7	59.6	62.9	57.0
Pushmataha	8,193	85.2	1.0	<.1	12.8	<.1	0.9	55	45	56	16	0.4	0.4	<.1	0.7	74.5	76.8	71.4	66.7	63.8	100.0	53.7
Roger Mills	2,994	95.4	<.1	<.1	3.1	0.0	1.4	75	6	72	58	0.1	0.1	<.1	<.1	72.2	73.1	50.0	33.3	58.8	0.0	57.5
Rogers	39,498	86.9	0.8	0.3	11.1	<.1	0.9	11	38	60	25	1.7	1.8	0.2	2.8	71.6	73.2	70.1	71.5	62.0	54.5	57.6
Seminole	18,647	78.2	6.9	0.1	13.8	<.1	0.9	36	66	14	12	0.8	0.8	0.8	1.7	73.4	77.2	67.3	73.0	60.9	100.0	51.5
Sequoyah	24,200	78.7	2.1	0.2	18.2	<.1	0.8	25	63	42	4	1.0	1.0	0.3	2.8	71.5	74.0	65.0	68.9	63.5	50.0	61.9
Stephens	31,306	92.9	1.9	0.3	3.4	<.1	1.6	16	13	45	57	1.4	1.5	0.4	0.7	74.0	75.4	62.0	57.9	62.3	57.1	53.3
Texas	11,797	90.4	0.5	0.1	0.9	<.1	8.0	42	23	65	73	0.5	0.6	<.1	<.1	71.8	73.5	81.2	50.0	66.2	50.0	58.1

[1] Non-Hispanic Native American.

Table B. — 1990 Voting Age Population (VAP) by Race and Ethnic Origin (cont)

County	Total Voting Age Population	Percent of total VAP						Rank				Percent contribution to state VAP				VAP percent of total population						
		Non-Hispanic							Percent of total VAP				Non-Hispanic				Non-Hispanic					
										Non-Hispanic												
		White	Black	Asian and Pacific Islander	Native American	Other	Hispanic	Total	White	Black	Native American[1]	Total	White	Black	Native American[1]	Total	White	Black	Asian and Pacific Islander	Native American	Other	Hispanic
Tillman..............................	7,489	77.4	8.5	0.2	2.7	0.1	11.1	59	68	11	60	0.3	0.3	0.4	0.1	72.1	76.9	62.4	78.3	62.8	44.4	56.7
Tulsa	371,847	83.8	8.6	1.1	4.4	<.1	2.0	2	52	10	49	16.1	16.2	21.0	10.6	73.9	75.8	65.1	68.6	66.4	43.7	63.2
Wagoner	33,654	86.9	3.8	0.3	7.9	<.1	1.1	14	37	23	34	1.5	1.5	0.8	1.7	70.3	71.8	65.1	57.3	60.9	29.4	56.9
Washington	35,641	88.8	2.3	0.7	6.7	<.1	1.4	12	27	38	39	1.5	1.6	0.5	1.5	74.2	75.6	65.5	60.3	64.7	33.3	63.3
Washita	8,352	95.4	0.2	0.2	1.6	0.0	2.7	52	7	67	66	0.4	0.4	<.1	<.1	73.0	74.1	85.0	48.1	56.6	0.0	54.7
Woods	7,140	96.7	0.6	0.3	1.1	0.0	1.3	62	4	63	70	0.3	0.4	<.1	<.1	78.4	78.8	85.7	64.3	65.1	0.0	66.7
Woodward	13,640	94.3	0.9	0.3	2.1	<.1	2.3	38	10	58	63	0.6	0.7	<.1	0.2	71.9	72.5	88.6	64.7	66.1	100.0	54.4
OKLAHOMA	**2,308,578**	**83.4**	**6.6**	**1.0**	**6.7**	**<.1**	**2.2**					**100.0**	**100.0**	**100.0**	**100.0**	**73.4**	**75.6**	**65.8**	**71.3**	**63.1**	**48.1**	**59.8**
CONGRESSIONAL																						
District 1	386,158	84.0	8.4	1.0	4.5	<.1	2.0	3	4	2	3	16.7	16.9	21.2	11.2	73.7	75.5	65.0	68.4	66.1	43.6	63.1
District 2	382,426	79.6	4.7	0.2	14.6	<.1	0.9	4	6	5	1	16.6	15.8	11.9	35.8	72.9	75.8	68.5	65.5	62.4	42.1	58.4
District 3	388,310	85.3	3.6	0.6	9.4	<.1	1.1	1	2	6	2	16.8	17.2	9.2	23.4	74.1	76.3	66.9	78.3	61.6	60.8	58.8
District 4	381,702	84.5	6.4	1.7	4.1	<.1	3.3	6	3	3	4	16.5	16.7	16.0	10.1	72.8	74.5	65.7	73.7	64.7	48.2	60.4
District 5	388,030	87.2	4.8	1.5	3.9	<.1	2.6	2	1	4	6	16.8	17.6	12.1	9.8	74.0	75.8	64.1	69.7	65.1	42.4	59.4
District 6	381,952	79.7	11.8	0.9	4.0	<.1	3.5	5	5	1	5	16.5	15.8	29.5	9.8	72.9	75.6	65.7	70.4	62.4	52.6	58.5

[1]Non-Hispanic Native American.

Table C. — Voter Participation: November 3, 1992, General Election

County	Estimated Voting Age Population (VAP), 1992	Voter registration (REG)				Voter turnout										Percent drop-off, by office			
						Highest office				Maximum vote									
		Total	% contribution to state REG	% of 1992 VAP	Rank by % of 1992 VAP	Actual	Total	Office	% of 1992 VAP	Total	% contribution to state turnout	% of REG	Rank by % of REG	% of 1992 VAP	Rank by % 1992 VAP	President	Senator	Governor	Representative
Adair	12,999	12,679	0.6	97.5	46	6,700	6,583	P	50.6	6,700	0.5	52.8	76	51.5	74	1.7	9.6	-	9.6
Alfalfa	4,938	4,591	0.2	93.0	66	3,292	3,045	P	61.7	3,292	0.2	71.7	7	66.7	19	7.5	12.2	-	12.5
Atoka	9,539	8,727	0.4	91.5	68	5,290	5,167	P	54.2	5,290	0.4	60.6	52	55.5	68	2.3	7.1	-	10.1
Beaver	4,358	4,283	0.2	98.3	44	2,877	2,850	P	65.4	2,877	0.2	67.2	20	66.0	24	0.9	8.3	-	8.2
Beckham	13,554	13,067	0.6	96.4	49	7,926	7,820	P	57.7	7,926	0.5	60.7	51	58.5	62	1.3	6.2	-	6.7
Blaine	7,992	7,892	0.3	98.7	40	5,118	5,052	P	63.2	5,118	0.4	64.9	33	64.0	29	1.3	6.2	-	7.4
Bryan	24,173	23,269	1.0	96.3	50	13,654	13,468	P	55.7	13,654	0.9	58.7	59	56.5	66	1.4	8.9	-	11.2
Caddo	21,066	18,741	0.8	89.0	74	11,674	11,488	P	54.5	11,674	0.8	62.3	44	55.4	69	1.6	7.4	-	8.7
Canadian	56,392	49,438	2.1	87.7	75	33,233	33,050	P	58.6	33,233	2.3	67.2	18	58.9	59	0.6	6.3	-	7.7
Carter	31,275	30,343	1.3	97.0	48	18,705	18,368	P	58.7	18,705	1.3	61.6	46	59.8	50	1.8	7.8	-	9.1
Cherokee	25,119	25,506	1.1	101.5	28	15,298	15,111	P	60.2	15,298	1.1	60.0	53	60.9	43	1.2	6.0	-	6.1
Choctaw	10,820	12,074	0.5	111.6	9	6,459	6,377	P	58.9	6,459	0.4	53.5	73	59.7	52	1.3	8.7	-	11.4
Cimarron	2,371	2,454	0.1	103.5	20	1,650	1,624	P	68.5	1,650	0.1	67.2	17	69.6	12	1.6	9.5	-	9.3
Cleveland	136,041	126,852	5.5	93.2	64	81,732	80,629	P	59.3	81,732	5.6	64.4	34	60.1	48	1.3	8.3	-	10.1
Coal	4,300	4,842	0.2	112.6	7	3,699	2,800	P	65.1	3,699	0.3	76.4	3	86.0	3	24.3	30.7	-	33.0
Comanche	78,489	56,827	2.5	72.4	77	35,864	35,520	P	45.3	35,864	2.5	63.1	40	45.7	77	1.0	6.9	-	8.9
Cotton	4,894	4,837	0.2	98.8	38	3,140	3,091	P	63.2	3,140	0.2	64.9	31	64.2	28	1.6	7.9	-	10.9
Craig	10,684	10,256	0.4	96.0	53	6,319	6,219	P	58.2	6,319	0.4	61.6	47	59.1	58	1.6	7.5	-	7.2
Creek	44,586	39,753	1.7	89.2	72	25,576	25,238	P	56.6	25,576	1.8	64.3	35	57.4	64	1.3	7.0	-	7.7
Custer	19,453	20,418	0.9	105.0	16	11,811	11,694	P	60.1	11,811	0.8	57.8	67	60.7	44	1.0	5.0	-	5.7
Delaware	22,139	21,856	0.9	98.7	41	12,578	12,426	P	56.1	12,578	0.9	57.5	68	56.8	65	1.2	8.3	-	8.3
Dewey	4,079	4,268	0.2	104.6	17	2,824	2,782	P	68.2	2,824	0.2	66.2	24	69.2	14	1.5	6.6	-	7.0
Ellis	3,212	3,437	0.1	107.0	14	2,320	2,307	P	71.8	2,320	0.2	67.5	15	72.2	9	0.6	6.0	-	6.2
Garfield	40,783	38,067	1.7	93.3	63	25,808	25,485	P	62.5	25,808	1.8	67.8	11	63.3	31	1.3	6.5	-	7.4
Garvin	19,732	18,971	0.8	96.1	51	12,064	11,863	P	60.1	12,064	0.8	63.6	38	61.1	40	1.7	8.1	-	11.7
Grady	30,582	28,869	1.3	94.4	61	19,747	17,757	P	58.1	19,747	1.4	68.4	8	64.6	26	10.1	16.4	-	18.8
Grant	4,179	4,575	0.2	109.5	10	3,094	3,056	P	73.1	3,094	0.2	67.6	13	74.0	8	1.2	6.5	-	7.3
Greer	5,170	4,903	0.2	94.8	60	2,843	2,779	P	53.8	2,843	0.2	58.0	66	55.0	71	2.3	9.2	-	10.8
Harmon	2,681	2,707	0.1	101.0	31	1,646	1,611	P	60.1	1,646	0.1	60.8	49	61.4	38	2.1	10.9	-	12.6
Harper	2,956	3,039	0.1	102.8	22	2,059	2,035	P	68.8	2,059	0.1	67.8	12	69.7	11	1.2	7.0	-	8.8
Haskell	8,120	10,570	0.5	130.2	1	5,647	5,546	P	68.3	5,647	0.4	53.4	74	69.5	13	1.8	8.1	-	7.4
Hughes	9,670	9,736	0.4	100.7	33	5,668	5,554	P	57.4	5,668	0.4	58.2	61	58.6	60	2.0	9.1	-	12.5
Jackson	19,966	16,045	0.7	80.4	76	9,530	9,420	P	47.2	9,530	0.7	59.4	56	47.7	76	1.2	7.0	-	9.1
Jefferson	5,105	5,227	0.2	102.4	24	3,092	3,019	P	59.1	3,092	0.2	59.2	57	60.6	45	2.4	10.3	-	13.3
Johnston	7,338	8,213	0.4	111.9	8	4,421	4,339	P	59.1	4,421	0.3	53.8	72	60.2	47	1.9	6.9	-	8.8
Kay	34,823	35,856	1.6	103.0	21	26,416	22,828	P	65.6	26,416	1.8	73.7	4	75.9	6	13.6	18.6	-	20.0
Kingfisher	9,388	9,490	0.4	101.1	30	6,472	6,411	P	68.3	6,472	0.4	68.2	9	68.9	15	0.9	5.5	-	7.2
Kiowa	8,202	8,077	0.4	98.5	43	5,009	4,910	P	59.9	5,009	0.3	62.0	45	61.1	41	2.0	8.6	-	9.9
Latimer	7,476	8,536	0.4	114.2	5	4,956	4,885	P	65.3	4,956	0.3	58.1	65	66.3	23	1.4	7.0	-	10.6
Le Flore	32,050	29,211	1.3	91.1	70	16,984	16,763	P	52.3	16,984	1.2	58.1	63	53.0	73	1.3	9.2	-	11.7
Lincoln	21,734	19,354	0.8	89.0	73	12,963	12,423	P	57.2	12,963	0.9	67.0	21	59.6	53	4.2	9.6	-	13.5
Logan	21,409	24,538	1.1	114.6	4	16,646	13,806	P	64.5	16,646	1.1	67.8	10	77.8	5	17.1	21.7	-	22.8
Love	6,244	6,341	0.3	101.6	27	3,746	3,679	P	58.9	3,746	0.3	59.1	58	60.0	49	1.8	8.3	-	8.4
McClain	17,168	16,368	0.7	95.3	59	10,863	10,776	P	62.8	10,863	0.7	66.4	22	63.3	32	0.8	7.4	-	9.2
McCurtain	23,343	25,098	1.1	107.5	13	11,657	11,494	P	49.2	11,657	0.8	46.4	77	49.9	75	1.4	7.9	-	10.6
McIntosh	13,066	13,410	0.6	102.6	23	8,043	7,893	P	60.4	8,043	0.6	60.0	54	61.6	36	1.9	7.1	-	7.0
Major	5,820	5,578	0.2	95.8	54	4,092	3,755	P	64.5	4,092	0.3	73.4	5	70.3	10	8.2	12.5	-	13.4
Marshall	8,375	8,811	0.4	105.2	15	5,580	5,498	P	65.6	5,580	0.4	63.3	39	66.6	20	1.5	7.4	-	8.9
Mayes	24,611	23,556	1.0	95.7	55	15,354	15,171	P	61.6	15,354	1.1	65.2	28	62.4	34	1.2	7.4	-	7.6
Murray	9,007	9,083	0.4	100.8	32	5,673	5,588	P	62.0	5,673	0.4	62.5	43	63.0	33	1.5	7.9	-	9.9
Muskogee	49,875	45,619	2.0	91.5	69	29,064	27,932	P	56.0	29,064	2.0	63.7	37	58.3	63	3.9	8.8	-	8.1
Noble	8,046	8,072	0.4	100.3	36	5,347	5,283	P	65.7	5,347	0.4	66.2	23	66.5	21	1.2	5.9	-	7.5
Nowata	7,226	7,503	0.3	103.8	19	4,582	4,524	P	62.6	4,582	0.3	61.1	48	63.4	30	1.3	7.8	-	7.6
Okfuskee	8,581	7,887	0.3	91.9	67	4,705	4,630	P	54.0	4,705	0.3	59.7	55	54.8	72	1.6	8.9	-	9.8
Oklahoma	446,028	481,012	20.9	107.8	12	263,850	259,923	P	58.3	263,850	18.1	54.9	71	59.2	57	1.5	9.0	-	10.5
Okmulgee	26,284	26,772	1.2	101.9	25	15,656	15,421	P	58.7	15,656	1.1	58.5	60	59.6	55	1.5	7.3	-	7.7
Osage	30,749	27,511	1.2	89.5	71	18,196	17,322	P	56.3	18,196	1.3	66.1	25	59.2	56	4.8	11.2	-	12.3
Ottawa	22,371	21,342	0.9	95.4	58	13,362	13,209	P	59.0	13,362	0.9	62.6	42	59.7	51	1.1	10.4	-	9.8
Pawnee	11,492	11,640	0.5	101.3	29	7,068	6,973	P	60.7	7,068	0.5	60.7	50	61.5	37	1.3	6.9	-	10.9
Payne	46,183	58,235	2.5	126.1	2	31,096	30,880	P	66.9	31,096	2.1	53.4	75	67.3	18	0.7	6.4	-	9.4
Pittsburg	30,707	32,043	1.4	104.4	18	26,740	18,827	P	61.3	26,740	1.8	83.5	2	87.1	2	29.6	33.7	-	35.5
Pontotoc	25,592	24,130	1.0	94.3	62	15,700	15,521	P	60.6	15,700	1.1	65.1	29	61.3	39	1.1	6.8	-	9.4
Pottawatomie	43,465	40,424	1.8	93.0	65	25,902	25,572	P	58.8	25,902	1.8	64.1	36	59.6	54	1.3	7.0	-	10.8
Pushmataha	8,148	8,890	0.4	109.1	11	4,976	4,897	P	60.1	4,976	0.3	56.0	70	61.1	42	1.6	8.9	-	11.8
Roger Mills	2,942	3,389	0.1	115.2	3	2,204	2,173	P	73.9	2,204	0.2	65.0	30	74.9	7	1.4	6.5	-	7.5
Rogers	41,461	41,613	1.8	100.4	35	28,091	27,892	P	67.3	28,091	1.9	67.5	14	67.8	16	0.7	6.2	-	6.5
Seminole	18,389	17,853	0.8	97.1	47	10,387	10,240	P	55.7	10,387	0.7	58.2	62	56.5	67	1.4	8.2	-	11.3
Sequoyah	24,992	23,995	1.0	96.0	52	13,776	13,556	P	54.2	13,776	0.9	57.4	69	55.1	70	1.6	10.1	-	9.6
Stephens	31,137	31,667	1.4	101.7	26	20,674	20,471	P	65.7	20,674	1.4	65.3	26	66.4	22	1.0	5.5	-	7.5
Texas	11,651	11,147	0.5	95.7	56	7,034	6,980	P	59.9	7,034	0.5	63.1	41	60.4	46	0.8	8.5	-	8.7

Table C. – **Voter Participation: November 3, 1992, General Election (cont)**

County	Estimated Voting Age Population (VAP), 1992	Voter registration (REG)				Voter turnout													
							Highest office			Maximum vote							Percent drop-off, by office		
		Total	% contribution to state REG	% of 1992 VAP	Rank by % of 1992 VAP	Actual	Total	Office	% of 1992 VAP	Total	% contribution to state turnout	% of REG	Rank by % of REG	% of 1992 VAP	Rank by % 1992 VAP	President	Senator	Governor	Representative
Tillman	7,230	7,275	0.3	100.6	34	4,229	4,178	P	57.8	4,229	0.3	58.1	64	58.5	61	1.2	8.0	-	10.3
Tulsa	375,076	366,145	15.9	97.6	45	245,971	239,068	P	63.7	245,971	16.9	67.2	19	65.6	25	2.8	11.3	-	11.7
Wagoner	35,211	33,605	1.5	95.4	57	21,795	21,529	P	61.1	21,795	1.5	64.9	32	61.9	35	1.2	6.5	-	6.7
Washington	35,586	35,059	1.5	98.5	42	47,941	23,663	P	66.5	47,941	3.3	136.7	1	134.7	1	50.6	54.7	-	55.9
Washita	8,029	8,041	0.3	100.1	37	5,419	5,339	P	66.5	5,419	0.4	67.4	16	67.5	17	1.5	7.1	-	6.8
Woods	6,712	7,563	0.3	112.7	6	5,445	4,777	P	71.2	5,445	0.4	72.0	6	81.1	4	12.3	17.2	-	18.3
Woodward	13,366	13,208	0.6	98.8	39	8,613	8,526	P	63.8	8,613	0.6	65.2	27	64.4	27	1.0	4.4	-	5.4
OKLAHOMA	**2,328,000**	**2,302,279**	**100.0**	**98.9**		**1,455,635**	**1,390,359**		**59.7**	**1,455,635**	**100.0**	**63.2**		**62.5**		**4.5**	**11.1**	**-**	**12.4**

Oklahoma 751

Table D. — Voter Registration by Political Party Affiliation: November 3, 1992, General Election

County	Total voter registration	Democrat (DEM)	Republican (REP)	Independent (IND)	Plurality Total	Plurality Party	DEM	REP	IND	Rank DEM	Rank REP	Rank IND	Total	DEM	REP	IND
Adair	12,679	8,407	4,095	177	4,312	D	66.3	32.3	1.4	51	24	44	0.6	0.6	0.5	0.2
Alfalfa	4,591	2,168	2,350	73	182	R	47.2	51.2	1.6	73	4	37	0.2	0.1	0.3	<.1
Atoka	8,727	8,088	563	76	7,525	D	92.7	6.5	0.9	9	69	62	0.4	0.6	<.1	0.1
Beaver	4,283	2,128	2,100	55	28	D	49.7	49.0	1.3	69	5	49	0.2	0.1	0.3	<.1
Beckham	13,067	10,302	2,536	229	7,766	D	78.8	19.4	1.8	37	41	29	0.6	0.7	0.3	0.3
Blaine	7,892	4,387	3,366	139	1,021	D	55.6	42.7	1.8	63	13	28	0.3	0.3	0.4	0.2
Bryan	23,269	20,806	2,171	292	18,635	D	89.4	9.3	1.3	21	58	50	1.0	1.4	0.3	0.4
Caddo	18,741	15,622	2,884	235	12,738	D	83.4	15.4	1.3	29	51	51	0.8	1.1	0.4	0.3
Canadian	49,438	26,276	21,434	1,728	4,842	D	53.1	43.4	3.5	67	12	7	2.1	1.8	2.8	2.3
Carter	30,343	24,570	5,356	417	19,214	D	81.0	17.7	1.4	32	46	46	1.3	1.7	0.7	0.6
Cherokee	25,506	19,155	5,628	723	13,527	D	75.1	22.1	2.8	40	38	12	1.1	1.3	0.7	1.0
Choctaw	12,074	11,447	533	94	10,914	D	94.8	4.4	0.8	5	73	67	0.5	0.8	<.1	0.1
Cimarron	2,454	1,705	715	34	990	D	69.5	29.1	1.4	47	30	45	0.1	0.1	<.1	<.1
Cleveland	126,852	68,204	52,061	6,587	16,143	D	53.8	41.0	5.2	65	17	1	5.5	4.7	6.7	9.0
Coal	4,842	4,641	192	9	4,449	D	95.8	4.0	0.2	1	76	77	0.2	0.3	<.1	<.1
Comanche	56,827	39,106	15,893	1,828	23,213	D	68.8	28.0	3.2	49	31	9	2.5	2.7	2.0	2.5
Cotton	4,837	4,443	356	38	4,087	D	91.9	7.4	0.8	13	65	66	0.2	0.3	<.1	<.1
Craig	10,256	8,228	1,864	164	6,364	D	80.2	18.2	1.6	34	44	36	0.4	0.6	0.2	0.2
Creek	39,753	25,971	12,826	956	13,145	D	65.3	32.3	2.4	53	25	17	1.7	1.8	1.7	1.3
Custer	20,418	13,660	6,355	403	7,305	D	66.9	31.1	2.0	50	28	23	0.9	0.9	0.8	0.5
Delaware	21,856	15,564	5,923	369	9,641	D	71.2	27.1	1.7	46	32	34	0.9	1.1	0.8	0.5
Dewey	4,268	3,080	1,154	34	1,926	D	72.2	27.0	0.8	44	33	65	0.2	0.2	0.1	<.1
Ellis	3,437	1,924	1,439	74	485	D	56.0	41.9	2.2	62	14	20	0.1	0.1	0.2	0.1
Garfield	38,067	16,845	20,173	1,049	3,328	R	44.3	53.0	2.8	75	2	13	1.7	1.2	2.6	1.4
Garvin	18,971	16,213	2,480	278	13,733	D	85.5	13.1	1.5	25	53	41	0.8	1.1	0.3	0.4
Grady	28,869	21,264	7,102	503	14,162	D	73.7	24.6	1.7	42	36	30	1.3	1.5	0.9	0.7
Grant	4,575	2,591	1,906	78	685	D	56.6	41.7	1.7	61	15	33	0.2	0.2	0.2	0.1
Greer	4,903	4,516	349	38	4,167	D	92.1	7.1	0.8	12	67	68	0.2	0.3	<.1	<.1
Harmon	2,707	2,564	127	16	2,437	D	94.7	4.7	0.6	6	72	73	0.1	0.2	<.1	<.1
Harper	3,039	1,760	1,245	34	515	D	57.9	41.0	1.1	60	18	54	0.1	0.1	0.2	<.1
Haskell	10,570	10,094	417	59	9,677	D	95.5	3.9	0.6	2	77	74	0.5	0.7	<.1	<.1
Hughes	9,736	8,993	702	41	8,291	D	92.4	7.2	0.4	11	66	76	0.4	0.6	<.1	<.1
Jackson	16,045	12,816	2,982	247	9,834	D	79.9	18.6	1.5	35	42	39	0.7	0.9	0.4	0.3
Jefferson	5,227	4,977	216	34	4,761	D	95.2	4.1	0.7	3	75	72	0.2	0.3	<.1	<.1
Johnston	8,213	7,651	519	43	7,132	D	93.2	6.3	0.5	8	70	75	0.4	0.5	<.1	<.1
Kay	35,856	17,808	16,741	1,307	1,067	D	49.7	46.7	3.6	70	9	6	1.6	1.2	2.2	1.8
Kingfisher	9,490	4,751	4,600	139	151	D	50.1	48.5	1.5	68	8	42	0.4	0.3	0.6	0.2
Kiowa	8,077	7,060	904	113	6,156	D	87.4	11.2	1.4	23	55	43	0.4	0.5	0.1	0.2
Latimer	8,536	7,891	588	57	7,303	D	92.4	6.9	0.7	10	68	71	0.4	0.5	<.1	<.1
Le Flore	29,211	25,317	3,339	555	21,978	D	86.7	11.4	1.9	24	54	25	1.3	1.7	0.4	0.8
Lincoln	19,354	12,800	6,211	343	6,589	D	66.1	32.1	1.8	52	26	27	0.8	0.9	0.8	0.5
Logan	24,538	14,556	9,222	760	5,334	D	59.3	37.6	3.1	57	21	10	1.1	1.0	1.2	1.0
Love	6,341	5,737	540	64	5,197	D	90.5	8.5	1.0	17	62	58	0.3	0.4	<.1	<.1
McClain	16,368	12,614	3,440	314	9,174	D	77.1	21.0	1.9	38	40	24	0.7	0.9	0.4	0.4
McCurtain	25,098	23,461	1,325	312	22,136	D	93.5	5.3	1.2	7	71	52	1.1	1.6	0.2	0.4
McIntosh	13,410	12,077	1,210	123	10,867	D	90.1	9.0	0.9	19	59	59	0.6	0.8	0.2	0.2
Major	5,578	1,965	3,502	111	1,537	R	35.2	62.8	2.0	77	1	22	0.2	0.1	0.5	0.2
Marshall	8,811	7,983	751	77	7,232	D	90.6	8.5	0.9	16	61	61	0.4	0.5	<.1	0.1
Mayes	23,556	17,458	5,778	320	11,680	D	74.1	24.5	1.4	41	37	47	1.0	1.2	0.7	0.4
Murray	9,083	8,295	706	82	7,589	D	91.3	7.8	0.9	14	64	60	0.4	0.6	<.1	0.1
Muskogee	45,619	36,410	8,422	787	27,988	D	79.8	18.5	1.7	36	43	31	2.0	2.5	1.1	1.1
Noble	8,072	4,741	3,187	144	1,554	D	58.7	39.5	1.8	59	19	26	0.4	0.3	0.4	0.2
Nowata	7,503	5,186	2,202	115	2,984	D	69.1	29.3	1.5	48	29	40	0.3	0.4	0.3	0.2
Okfuskee	7,887	7,121	679	87	6,442	D	90.3	8.6	1.1	18	60	55	0.3	0.5	<.1	0.1
Oklahoma	481,012	261,197	197,568	22,247	63,629	D	54.3	41.1	4.6	64	16	3	20.9	18.0	25.5	30.2
Okmulgee	26,772	21,691	4,620	461	17,071	D	81.0	17.3	1.7	31	47	32	1.2	1.5	0.6	0.6
Osage	27,511	19,614	7,193	704	12,421	D	71.3	26.1	2.6	45	34	15	1.2	1.3	0.9	1.0
Ottawa	21,342	16,356	4,705	281	11,651	D	76.6	22.0	1.3	39	39	48	0.9	1.1	0.6	0.4
Pawnee	11,640	7,484	3,886	270	3,598	D	64.3	33.4	2.3	55	23	19	0.5	0.5	0.5	0.4
Payne	58,235	28,814	26,425	2,996	2,389	D	49.5	45.4	5.1	71	10	2	2.5	2.0	3.4	4.1
Pittsburg	32,043	28,480	3,059	504	25,421	D	88.9	9.5	1.6	22	56	38	1.4	2.0	0.4	0.7
Pontotoc	24,130	20,181	3,744	205	16,437	D	83.6	15.5	0.8	28	49	63	1.0	1.4	0.5	0.3
Pottawatomie	40,424	29,354	10,082	988	19,272	D	72.6	24.9	2.4	43	35	16	1.8	2.0	1.3	1.3
Pushmataha	8,890	8,440	387	63	8,053	D	94.9	4.4	0.7	4	74	70	0.4	0.6	<.1	<.1
Roger Mills	3,389	3,034	320	35	2,714	D	89.5	9.4	1.0	20	57	57	0.1	0.2	<.1	<.1
Rogers	41,613	27,160	13,243	1,210	13,917	D	65.3	31.8	2.9	54	27	11	1.8	1.9	1.7	1.6
Seminole	17,853	15,051	2,503	299	12,548	D	84.3	14.0	1.7	26	52	35	0.8	1.0	0.3	0.4
Sequoyah	23,995	19,965	3,745	285	16,220	D	83.2	15.6	1.2	30	48	53	1.0	1.4	0.5	0.4
Stephens	31,667	25,625	5,712	330	19,913	D	80.9	18.0	1.0	33	45	56	1.4	1.8	0.7	0.4
Texas	11,147	6,580	4,338	229	2,242	D	59.0	38.9	2.1	58	20	21	0.5	0.5	0.6	0.3

County	Total voter registration	Political party affiliation					Percent of total registration						Percent contribution to state registration			
		Democrat (DEM)	Republican (REP)	Independent (IND)	Plurality		DEM	REP	IND	Rank			Total	DEM	REP	IND
					Total	Party				DEM	REP	IND				
Tillman	7,275	6,626	590	59	6,036	D	91.1	8.1	0.8	15	63	64	0.3	0.5	< .1	< .1
Tulsa............................	366,145	170,721	179,240	16,184	8,519	R	46.6	49.0	4.4	74	6	4	15.9	11.8	23.1	22.0
Wagoner........................	33,605	20,656	11,797	1,152	8,859	D	61.5	35.1	3.4	56	22	8	1.5	1.4	1.5	1.6
Washington....................	35,059	15,019	18,516	1,524	3,497	R	42.8	52.8	4.3	76	3	5	1.5	1.0	2.4	2.1
Washita.........................	8,041	6,736	1,245	60	5,491	D	83.8	15.5	0.7	27	50	69	0.3	0.5	0.2	< .1
Woods...........................	7,563	3,715	3,669	179	46	D	49.1	48.5	2.4	72	7	18	0.3	0.3	0.5	0.2
Woodward	13,208	7,053	5,808	347	1,245	D	53.4	44.0	2.6	66	11	14	0.6	0.5	0.7	0.5
OKLAHOMA	**2,302,279**	**1,452,949**	**775,754**	**73,576**	**677,195**	**D**	**63.1**	**33.7**	**3.2**				**100.0**	**100.0**	**100.0**	**100.0**

Oklahoma 753

Table E. – Vote for President: November 3, 1992, General Election

County	Total	Clinton (DEM)	Bush (REP)	Perot (IND)	Other	Plurality Total	Party	DEM	REP	IND	Other	Rank DEM	Rank REP	Rank IND	Total	DEM	REP	IND	DEM	REP
Adair	6,583	2,645	2,994	914	30	349	R	40.2	45.5	13.9	0.5	36	18	77	0.5	0.6	0.5	0.3	46.9	53.1
Alfalfa	3,045	741	1,567	722	15	826	R	24.3	51.5	23.7	0.5	69	6	41	0.2	0.2	0.3	0.2	32.1	67.9
Atoka	5,167	2,336	1,561	1,255	15	775	D	45.2	30.2	24.3	0.3	21	61	36	0.4	0.5	0.3	0.4	59.9	40.1
Beaver	2,850	580	1,699	565	6	1,119	R	20.4	59.6	19.8	0.2	76	1	68	0.2	0.1	0.3	0.2	25.4	74.6
Beckham	7,820	2,947	2,913	1,929	31	34	D	37.7	37.3	24.7	0.4	40	38	31	0.6	0.6	0.5	0.6	50.3	49.7
Blaine	5,052	1,564	2,209	1,258	21	645	R	31.0	43.7	24.9	0.4	55	24	28	0.4	0.3	0.4	0.4	41.5	58.5
Bryan	13,468	6,259	3,452	3,713	44	2,546	D	46.5	25.6	27.6	0.3	15	73	9	1.0	1.3	0.6	1.2	64.5	35.5
Caddo	11,488	4,861	3,664	2,911	52	1,197	D	42.3	31.9	25.3	0.5	30	55	23	0.8	1.0	0.6	0.9	57.0	43.0
Canadian	33,050	7,215	16,756	8,985	94	7,771	R	21.8	50.7	27.2	0.3	73	9	13	2.4	1.5	2.8	2.8	30.1	69.9
Carter	18,368	7,171	5,947	5,188	62	1,224	D	39.0	32.4	28.2	0.3	38	54	4	1.3	1.5	1.0	1.6	54.7	45.3
Cherokee	15,111	6,794	4,977	3,297	43	1,817	D	45.0	32.9	21.8	0.3	23	53	53	1.1	1.4	0.8	1.0	57.7	42.3
Choctaw	6,377	3,413	1,641	1,298	25	1,772	D	53.5	25.7	20.4	0.4	2	72	65	0.5	0.7	0.3	0.4	67.5	32.5
Cimarron	1,624	395	965	254	10	570	R	24.3	59.4	15.6	0.6	70	2	76	0.1	<.1	0.2	<.1	29.0	71.0
Cleveland	80,629	24,404	35,561	20,352	312	11,157	R	30.3	44.1	25.2	0.4	58	22	24	5.8	5.2	6.0	6.4	40.7	59.3
Coal	2,800	1,448	714	618	20	734	D	51.7	25.5	22.1	0.7	7	74	52	0.2	0.3	0.1	0.2	67.0	33.0
Comanche	35,520	12,237	15,704	7,463	116	3,467	R	34.5	44.2	21.0	0.3	48	21	60	2.6	2.6	2.6	2.3	43.8	56.2
Cotton	3,091	1,314	910	853	14	404	D	42.5	29.4	27.6	0.5	28	64	8	0.2	0.3	0.2	0.3	59.1	40.9
Craig	6,219	2,780	2,106	1,316	17	674	D	44.7	33.9	21.2	0.3	25	47	59	0.4	0.6	0.4	0.4	56.9	43.1
Creek	25,238	9,118	10,055	5,984	81	937	R	36.1	39.8	23.7	0.3	44	34	42	1.8	1.9	1.7	1.9	47.6	52.4
Custer	11,694	3,540	5,362	2,741	51	1,822	R	30.3	45.9	23.4	0.4	57	17	46	0.8	0.7	0.9	0.9	39.8	60.2
Delaware	12,426	4,842	4,840	2,689	55	2	D	39.0	39.0	21.6	0.4	39	36	55	0.9	1.0	0.8	0.8	50.0	50.0
Dewey	2,782	845	1,244	684	9	399	R	30.4	44.7	24.6	0.3	56	19	33	0.2	0.2	0.2	0.2	40.5	59.6
Ellis	2,307	594	1,072	632	9	440	R	25.7	46.5	27.4	0.4	67	16	12	0.2	0.1	0.2	0.2	35.7	64.3
Garfield	25,485	6,720	13,095	5,559	111	6,375	R	26.4	51.4	21.8	0.4	66	7	54	1.8	1.4	2.2	1.7	33.9	66.1
Garvin	11,863	4,811	3,983	3,014	55	828	D	40.6	33.6	25.4	0.5	35	49	22	0.9	1.0	0.7	0.9	54.7	45.3
Grady	17,757	6,177	6,997	4,528	55	820	R	34.8	39.4	25.5	0.3	46	35	17	1.3	1.3	1.2	1.4	46.9	53.1
Grant	3,056	864	1,311	871	10	440	R	28.3	42.9	28.5	0.3	64	25	2	0.2	0.2	0.2	0.3	39.7	60.3
Greer	2,779	1,162	964	640	13	198	D	41.8	34.7	23.0	0.5	33	43	48	0.2	0.2	0.2	0.2	54.7	45.3
Harmon	1,611	783	496	326	6	287	D	48.6	30.8	20.2	0.4	11	59	67	0.1	0.2	<.1	0.1	61.2	38.8
Harper	2,035	486	1,038	501	10	537	R	23.9	51.0	24.6	0.5	72	8	32	0.1	0.1	0.2	0.2	31.9	68.1
Haskell	5,546	3,069	1,461	995	21	1,608	D	55.3	26.3	17.9	0.4	1	71	75	0.4	0.6	0.2	0.3	67.7	32.3
Hughes	5,554	2,850	1,522	1,158	24	1,328	D	51.3	27.4	20.8	0.4	8	68	61	0.4	0.6	0.3	0.4	65.2	34.8
Jackson	9,420	3,273	3,893	2,227	27	620	R	34.7	41.3	23.6	0.3	47	29	43	0.7	0.7	0.7	0.7	45.7	54.3
Jefferson	3,019	1,580	671	758	10	822	D	52.3	22.2	25.1	0.3	5	77	26	0.2	0.3	0.1	0.2	70.2	29.8
Johnston	4,339	2,096	1,191	1,040	12	905	D	48.3	27.4	24.0	0.3	12	67	37	0.3	0.4	0.2	0.3	63.8	36.2
Kay	22,828	6,643	9,115	6,984	86	2,131	R	29.1	39.9	30.6	0.4	62	33	1	1.6	1.4	1.5	2.2	42.2	57.8
Kingfisher	6,411	1,379	3,479	1,534	19	1,945	R	21.5	54.3	23.9	0.3	74	5	39	0.5	0.3	0.6	0.5	28.4	71.6
Kiowa	4,910	2,143	1,635	1,114	18	508	D	43.6	33.3	22.7	0.4	27	51	51	0.4	0.5	0.3	0.3	56.7	43.3
Latimer	4,885	2,606	1,212	1,049	18	1,394	D	53.3	24.8	21.5	0.4	3	76	57	0.4	0.6	0.2	0.3	68.3	31.7
Le Flore	16,763	7,843	5,850	3,021	49	1,993	D	46.8	34.9	18.0	0.3	14	42	74	1.2	1.7	1.0	0.9	57.3	42.7
Lincoln	12,423	3,904	5,315	3,160	44	1,411	R	31.4	42.8	25.4	0.4	53	26	20	0.9	0.8	0.9	1.0	42.3	57.7
Logan	13,806	4,453	6,071	3,239	43	1,618	R	32.3	44.0	23.5	0.3	51	23	45	1.0	0.9	1.0	1.0	42.3	57.7
Love	3,679	1,708	922	1,033	16	675	D	46.4	25.1	28.1	0.4	16	75	5	0.3	0.4	0.2	0.3	64.9	35.1
McClain	10,776	3,378	4,377	2,996	25	999	R	31.3	40.6	27.8	0.2	54	31	7	0.8	0.7	0.7	0.9	43.6	56.4
McCurtain	11,494	5,082	3,519	2,852	41	1,563	D	44.2	30.6	24.8	0.4	26	60	30	0.8	1.1	0.6	0.9	59.1	40.9
McIntosh	7,893	4,184	2,225	1,469	15	1,959	D	53.0	28.2	18.6	0.2	4	65	72	0.6	0.9	0.4	0.5	65.3	34.7
Major	3,755	731	2,154	857	13	1,297	R	19.5	57.4	22.8	0.3	77	4	49	0.3	0.2	0.4	0.3	25.3	74.7
Marshall	5,498	2,519	1,478	1,486	15	1,033	D	45.8	26.9	27.0	0.3	19	70	14	0.4	0.5	0.2	0.5	63.0	37.0
Mayes	15,171	6,432	5,445	3,235	59	987	D	42.4	35.9	21.3	0.4	29	40	58	1.1	1.4	0.9	1.0	54.2	45.8
Murray	5,588	2,594	1,536	1,447	11	1,058	D	46.4	27.5	25.9	0.2	17	66	15	0.4	0.5	0.3	0.5	62.8	37.2
Muskogee	27,932	13,619	8,782	5,454	77	4,837	D	48.8	31.4	19.5	0.3	10	57	70	2.0	2.9	1.5	1.7	60.8	39.2
Noble	5,283	1,333	2,474	1,449	27	1,025	R	25.2	46.8	27.4	0.5	68	14	11	0.4	0.3	0.4	0.5	35.0	65.0
Nowata	4,524	1,912	1,531	1,063	18	381	D	42.3	33.8	23.5	0.4	31	48	44	0.3	0.4	0.3	0.3	55.5	44.5
Okfuskee	4,630	2,141	1,580	889	20	561	D	46.2	34.1	19.2	0.4	18	45	71	0.3	0.5	0.3	0.3	57.5	42.5
Oklahoma	259,923	76,271	126,788	56,139	725	50,517	R	29.3	48.8	21.6	0.3	61	11	56	18.7	16.1	21.4	17.6	37.6	62.4
Okmulgee	15,421	7,767	4,586	3,013	55	3,181	D	50.4	29.7	19.5	0.4	9	63	69	1.1	1.6	0.8	0.9	62.9	37.1
Osage	17,322	6,894	5,891	4,477	60	1,003	D	39.8	34.0	25.8	0.3	37	46	16	1.2	1.5	1.0	1.4	53.9	46.1
Ottawa	13,209	6,304	4,141	2,721	43	2,163	D	47.7	31.3	20.6	0.3	13	58	63	1.0	1.3	0.7	0.9	60.4	39.6
Pawnee	6,973	2,612	2,675	1,656	30	63	R	37.5	38.4	23.7	0.4	41	37	40	0.5	0.6	0.5	0.5	49.4	50.6
Payne	30,880	9,886	13,032	7,852	110	3,146	R	32.0	42.2	25.4	0.4	52	27	21	2.2	2.1	2.2	2.5	43.1	56.9
Pittsburg	18,827	8,523	5,659	4,594	51	2,864	D	45.3	30.1	24.4	0.3	20	62	35	1.4	1.8	1.0	1.4	60.1	39.9
Pontotoc	15,521	6,350	5,206	3,916	49	1,144	D	40.9	33.5	25.2	0.3	34	50	25	1.1	1.3	0.9	1.2	54.9	45.1
Pottawatomie	25,572	8,616	10,350	6,520	86	1,734	R	33.7	40.5	25.5	0.3	49	32	18	1.8	1.8	1.7	2.0	45.4	54.6
Pushmataha	4,897	2,553	1,319	1,000	25	1,234	D	52.1	26.9	20.4	0.5	6	69	64	0.4	0.5	0.2	0.3	65.9	34.1
Roger Mills	2,173	767	890	505	11	123	R	35.3	41.0	23.2	0.5	45	30	47	0.2	0.2	0.2	0.2	46.3	53.7
Rogers	27,892	8,257	12,455	7,101	79	4,198	R	29.6	44.7	25.5	0.3	60	20	19	2.0	1.7	2.1	2.2	39.9	60.1
Seminole	10,240	4,624	3,253	2,330	33	1,371	D	45.2	31.8	22.8	0.3	22	56	50	0.7	1.0	0.5	0.7	58.7	41.3
Sequoyah	13,556	6,092	4,925	2,486	53	1,167	D	44.9	36.3	18.3	0.4	24	39	73	1.0	1.3	0.8	0.8	55.3	44.7
Stephens	20,471	7,644	7,085	5,692	50	559	D	37.3	34.6	27.8	0.2	42	44	6	1.5	1.6	1.2	1.8	51.9	48.1
Texas	6,980	1,487	4,059	1,417	17	2,572	R	21.3	58.2	20.3	0.2	75	3	66	0.5	0.3	0.7	0.4	26.8	73.2

Table E. – **Vote for President: November 3, 1992, General Election (cont)**

County	All candidates					Plurality		Percent of total vote				Rank			Percent contribution to state vote				Major party Percent of vote	
	Total	Clinton (DEM)	Bush (REP)	Perot (IND)	Other	Total	Party	DEM	REP	IND	Other	DEM	REP	IND	Total	DEM	REP	IND	DEM	REP
Tillman	4,178	1,749	1,377	1,039	13	372	D	41.9	33.0	24.9	0.3	32	52	29	0.3	0.4	0.2	0.3	56.0	44.0
Tulsa	239,068	71,165	117,465	49,760	678	46,300	R	29.8	49.1	20.8	0.3	59	10	62	17.2	15.0	19.8	15.6	37.7	62.3
Wagoner	21,529	7,041	9,053	5,381	54	2,012	R	32.7	42.1	25.0	0.3	50	28	27	1.5	1.5	1.5	1.7	43.7	56.3
Washington	23,663	6,593	11,342	5,664	64	4,749	R	27.9	47.9	23.9	0.3	65	12	38	1.7	1.4	1.9	1.8	36.8	63.2
Washita	5,339	1,929	1,912	1,468	30	17	D	36.1	35.8	27.5	0.6	43	41	10	0.4	0.4	0.3	0.5	50.2	49.8
Woods	4,777	1,361	2,225	1,167	24	864	R	28.5	46.6	24.4	0.5	63	15	34	0.3	0.3	0.4	0.4	38.0	62.0
Woodward	8,526	2,063	4,006	2,411	46	1,595	R	24.2	47.0	28.3	0.5	71	13	3	0.6	0.4	0.7	0.8	34.0	66.0
OKLAHOMA	**1,390,359**	**473,066**	**592,929**	**319,878**	**4,486**	**119,863**	**R**	**34.0**	**42.6**	**23.0**	**0.3**				**100.0**	**100.0**	**100.0**	**100.0**	**44.4**	**55.6**

Table F. — Vote for U.S. Senator: November 3, 1992, General Election

County	Total	Lewis (DEM)	Nickles (REP)	Other	Plurality Total	Party	DEM	REP	Other	Rank DEM	Rank REP	Rank Other	Total	DEM	REP	Other
Adair	6,054	2,377	3,526	151	1,149	R	39.3	58.2	2.5	44	31	67	0.5	0.5	0.5	0.4
Alfalfa	2,890	819	1,986	85	1,167	R	28.3	68.7	2.9	72	6	42	0.2	0.2	0.3	0.2
Atoka	4,916	2,476	2,311	129	165	D	50.4	47.0	2.6	18	58	63	0.4	0.5	0.3	0.3
Beaver	2,637	614	1,945	78	1,331	R	23.3	73.8	3.0	76	3	41	0.2	0.1	0.3	0.2
Beckham	7,435	3,003	4,194	238	1,191	R	40.4	56.4	3.2	41	38	27	0.6	0.6	0.6	0.6
Blaine	4,799	1,453	3,189	157	1,736	R	30.3	66.5	3.3	67	10	25	0.4	0.3	0.4	0.4
Bryan	12,438	6,720	5,388	330	1,332	D	54.0	43.3	2.7	6	71	60	1.0	1.4	0.7	0.8
Caddo	10,813	4,774	5,707	332	933	R	44.2	52.8	3.1	33	45	34	0.8	1.0	0.8	0.8
Canadian	31,132	8,660	21,231	1,241	12,571	R	27.8	68.2	4.0	73	7	5	2.4	1.8	2.8	2.9
Carter	17,237	7,962	8,659	616	697	R	46.2	50.2	3.6	26	53	17	1.3	1.6	1.1	1.5
Cherokee	14,385	7,196	6,716	473	480	D	50.0	46.7	3.3	19	60	24	1.1	1.5	0.9	1.1
Choctaw	5,899	3,447	2,323	129	1,124	D	58.4	39.4	2.2	1	77	73	0.5	0.7	0.3	0.3
Cimarron	1,493	434	1,032	27	598	R	29.1	69.1	1.8	70	5	76	0.1	<.1	0.1	<.1
Cleveland	74,967	26,998	44,271	3,698	17,273	R	36.0	59.1	4.9	51	29	1	5.8	5.5	5.8	8.8
Coal	2,565	1,415	1,081	69	334	D	55.2	42.1	2.7	4	74	58	0.2	0.3	0.1	0.2
Comanche	33,401	10,948	21,574	879	10,626	R	32.8	64.6	2.6	60	16	62	2.6	2.2	2.8	2.1
Cotton	2,892	1,303	1,504	85	201	R	45.1	52.0	2.9	32	47	43	0.2	0.3	0.2	0.2
Craig	5,843	2,819	2,865	159	46	R	48.2	49.0	2.7	24	54	55	0.5	0.6	0.4	0.4
Creek	23,783	9,704	13,296	783	3,592	R	40.8	55.9	3.3	39	41	23	1.8	2.0	1.8	1.9
Custer	11,216	3,695	7,193	328	3,498	R	32.9	64.1	2.9	59	17	45	0.9	0.7	0.9	0.8
Delaware	11,529	4,885	6,263	381	1,378	R	42.4	54.3	3.3	35	43	22	0.9	1.0	0.8	0.9
Dewey	2,639	836	1,739	64	903	R	31.7	65.9	2.4	64	13	69	0.2	0.2	0.2	0.2
Ellis	2,181	705	1,423	53	718	R	32.3	65.2	2.4	63	15	68	0.2	0.1	0.2	0.1
Garfield	24,126	7,238	16,004	884	8,766	R	30.0	66.3	3.7	68	11	14	1.9	1.5	2.1	2.1
Garvin	11,087	4,839	5,830	418	991	R	43.6	52.6	3.8	34	46	13	0.9	1.0	0.8	1.0
Grady	16,505	6,479	9,341	685	2,862	R	39.3	56.6	4.2	45	37	3	1.3	1.3	1.2	1.6
Grant	2,894	885	1,898	111	1,013	R	30.6	65.6	3.8	66	14	10	0.2	0.2	0.3	0.3
Greer	2,582	1,062	1,449	71	387	R	41.1	56.1	2.7	37	40	53	0.2	0.2	0.2	0.2
Harmon	1,467	668	778	21	110	R	45.5	53.0	1.4	30	44	77	0.1	0.1	0.1	<.1
Harper	1,915	556	1,304	55	748	R	29.0	68.1	2.9	71	8	47	0.1	0.1	0.2	0.1
Haskell	5,190	2,953	2,089	148	864	D	56.9	40.3	2.9	2	76	49	0.4	0.6	0.3	0.4
Hughes	5,151	2,615	2,401	135	214	D	50.8	46.6	2.6	15	62	64	0.4	0.5	0.3	0.3
Jackson	8,865	2,984	5,653	228	2,669	R	33.7	63.8	2.6	57	20	65	0.7	0.6	0.7	0.5
Jefferson	2,774	1,495	1,204	75	291	D	53.9	43.4	2.7	7	70	56	0.2	0.3	0.2	0.2
Johnston	4,115	2,126	1,874	115	252	D	51.7	45.5	2.8	13	65	51	0.3	0.4	0.2	0.3
Kay	21,499	7,350	13,500	649	6,150	R	34.2	62.8	3.0	55	22	37	1.7	1.5	1.8	1.5
Kingfisher	6,118	1,439	4,517	162	3,078	R	23.5	73.8	2.6	75	2	61	0.5	0.3	0.6	0.4
Kiowa	4,577	1,897	2,576	104	679	R	41.4	56.3	2.3	36	39	71	0.4	0.4	0.3	0.2
Latimer	4,610	2,569	1,886	155	683	D	55.7	40.9	3.4	3	75	19	0.4	0.5	0.2	0.4
Le Flore	15,428	7,815	7,196	417	619	D	50.7	46.6	2.7	16	61	57	1.2	1.6	0.9	1.0
Lincoln	11,716	4,001	7,237	478	3,236	R	34.1	61.8	4.1	56	24	4	0.9	0.8	1.0	1.1
Logan	13,039	4,639	7,894	506	3,255	R	35.6	60.5	3.9	52	26	8	1.0	0.9	1.0	1.2
Love	3,435	1,885	1,453	97	432	D	54.9	42.3	2.8	5	73	50	0.3	0.4	0.2	0.2
McClain	10,056	3,720	5,893	443	2,173	R	37.0	58.6	4.4	50	30	2	0.8	0.8	0.8	1.0
McCurtain	10,741	5,497	5,001	243	496	D	51.2	46.6	2.3	14	63	72	0.8	1.1	0.7	0.6
McIntosh	7,471	3,891	3,376	204	515	D	52.1	45.2	2.7	12	67	54	0.6	0.8	0.4	0.5
Major	3,581	815	2,653	113	1,838	R	22.8	74.1	3.2	77	1	31	0.3	0.2	0.4	0.3
Marshall	5,166	2,612	2,396	158	216	D	50.6	46.4	3.1	17	64	35	0.4	0.5	0.3	0.4
Mayes	14,211	6,568	7,211	432	643	R	46.2	50.7	3.0	25	52	36	1.1	1.3	1.0	1.0
Murray	5,226	2,607	2,445	174	162	D	49.9	46.8	3.3	20	59	21	0.4	0.5	0.3	0.4
Muskogee	26,494	13,082	12,742	670	340	D	49.4	48.1	2.5	22	55	66	2.0	2.6	1.7	1.6
Noble	5,030	1,473	3,373	184	1,900	R	29.3	67.1	3.7	69	9	15	0.4	0.3	0.4	0.4
Nowata	4,226	1,906	2,185	135	279	R	45.1	51.7	3.2	31	48	28	0.3	0.4	0.3	0.3
Okfuskee	4,287	1,976	2,192	119	216	R	46.1	51.1	2.8	27	51	52	0.3	0.4	0.3	0.3
Oklahoma	240,062	78,643	152,261	9,158	73,618	R	32.8	63.4	3.8	62	21	12	18.5	15.9	20.1	21.7
Okmulgee	14,506	7,740	6,377	389	1,363	D	53.4	44.0	2.7	9	69	59	1.1	1.6	0.8	0.9
Osage	16,165	7,395	8,273	497	878	R	45.7	51.2	3.1	28	50	32	1.2	1.5	1.1	1.2
Ottawa	11,969	6,409	5,170	390	1,239	D	53.5	43.2	3.3	8	72	26	0.9	1.3	0.7	0.9
Pawnee	6,582	2,704	3,670	208	966	R	41.1	55.8	3.2	38	42	30	0.5	0.5	0.5	0.5
Payne	29,120	10,786	17,282	1,052	6,496	R	37.0	59.3	3.6	49	28	16	2.2	2.2	2.3	2.5
Pittsburg	17,718	9,317	7,803	598	1,514	D	52.6	44.0	3.4	10	68	18	1.4	1.9	1.0	1.4
Pontotoc	14,625	6,689	7,511	425	822	R	45.7	51.4	2.9	29	49	46	1.1	1.4	1.0	1.0
Pottawatomie	24,089	9,474	13,656	959	4,182	R	39.3	56.7	4.0	43	36	6	1.9	1.9	1.8	2.3
Pushmataha	4,535	2,377	2,061	97	316	D	52.4	45.4	2.1	11	66	74	0.4	0.5	0.3	0.2
Roger Mills	2,061	813	1,169	79	356	R	39.4	56.7	3.8	42	35	11	0.2	0.2	0.2	0.2
Rogers	26,340	9,862	15,643	835	5,781	R	37.4	59.4	3.2	48	27	29	2.0	2.0	2.1	2.0
Seminole	9,539	4,650	4,514	375	136	D	48.7	47.3	3.9	23	57	7	0.7	0.9	0.6	0.9
Sequoyah	12,387	6,123	5,895	369	228	D	49.4	47.6	3.0	21	56	38	1.0	1.2	0.8	0.9
Stephens	19,529	7,430	11,343	756	3,913	R	38.0	58.1	3.9	47	32	9	1.5	1.5	1.5	1.8
Texas	6,434	1,674	4,569	191	2,895	R	26.0	71.0	3.0	74	4	40	0.5	0.3	0.6	0.5

County	Total	Lewis (DEM)	Nickles (REP)	Other	Plurality		Percent of total vote						Percent contribution to state vote			
					Total	Party	DEM	REP	Other	DEM (Rank)	REP (Rank)	Other (Rank)	Total	DEM	REP	Other
Tillman	3,890	1,583	2,226	81	643	R	40.7	57.2	2.1	40	34	75	0.3	0.3	0.3	0.2
Tulsa	218,291	76,893	136,405	4,993	59,512	R	35.2	62.5	2.3	54	23	70	16.9	15.6	18.0	11.8
Wagoner	20,374	7,938	11,810	626	3,872	R	39.0	58.0	3.1	46	33	33	1.6	1.6	1.6	1.5
Washington	21,703	7,112	13,864	727	6,752	R	32.8	63.9	3.3	61	18	20	1.7	1.4	1.8	1.7
Washita	5,035	1,789	3,096	150	1,307	R	35.5	61.5	3.0	53	25	39	0.4	0.4	0.4	0.4
Woods	4,506	1,499	2,875	132	1,376	R	33.3	63.8	2.9	58	19	44	0.3	0.3	0.4	0.3
Woodward	8,237	2,565	5,436	236	2,871	R	31.1	66.0	2.9	65	12	48	0.6	0.5	0.7	0.6
OKLAHOMA	**1,294,423**	**494,350**	**757,876**	**42,197**	**263,526**	**R**	**38.2**	**58.5**	**3.3**				**100.0**	**100.0**	**100.0**	**100.0**

Table H. — Vote for U.S. Representative in Congress: November 3, 1992, General Election

Congressional district and county	Total	Democrat (DEM)	Republican (REP)	Other	Plurality Total	Plurality Party	Percent of total vote DEM	REP	Other	Rank within district DEM	REP	Other	Percent contribution to district vote Total	DEM	REP	Other
District 1	**225,830**	**106,619**	**119,211**	-	**12,592**	**R**	**47.2**	**52.8**	-				**100.0**	**100.0**	**100.0**	-
Tulsa	217,093	102,833	114,260	-	11,427	R	47.4	52.6	-	1	2	-	96.1	96.4	95.8	-
Wagoner (pt)..............	8,737	3,786	4,951	-	1,165	R	43.3	56.7	-	2	1	-	3.9	3.6	4.2	-
District 2	**213,513**	**118,542**	**87,657**	**7,314**	**30,885**	**D**	**55.5**	**41.1**	**3.4**				**100.0**	**100.0**	**100.0**	**100.0**
Adair	6,058	3,410	2,496	152	914	D	56.3	41.2	2.5	11	6	18	2.8	2.9	2.8	2.1
Cherokee	14,367	8,090	5,705	572	2,385	D	56.3	39.7	4.0	10	9	4	6.7	6.8	6.5	7.8
Craig	5,863	3,451	2,217	195	1,234	D	58.9	37.8	3.3	6	13	13	2.7	2.9	2.5	2.7
Creek	23,598	13,416	9,345	837	4,071	D	56.9	39.6	3.5	9	11	9	11.1	11.3	10.7	11.4
Delaware	11,538	5,817	5,246	475	571	D	50.4	45.5	4.1	16	3	2	5.4	4.9	6.0	6.5
Haskell	5,228	3,713	1,358	157	2,355	D	71.0	26.0	3.0	1	18	15	2.4	3.1	1.5	2.1
McIntosh	7,481	4,636	2,571	274	2,065	D	62.0	34.4	3.7	4	15	7	3.5	3.9	2.9	3.7
Mayes	14,181	7,914	5,826	441	2,088	D	55.8	41.1	3.1	12	7	14	6.6	6.7	6.6	6.0
Muskogee	26,720	14,109	11,939	672	2,170	D	52.8	44.7	2.5	14	5	17	12.5	11.9	13.6	9.2
Nowata	4,232	2,461	1,624	147	837	D	58.2	38.4	3.5	7	12	11	2.0	2.1	1.9	2.0
Okfuskee	4,242	2,752	1,334	156	1,418	D	64.9	31.4	3.7	2	17	6	2.0	2.3	1.5	2.1
Okmulgee	14,444	9,279	4,639	526	4,640	D	64.2	32.1	3.6	3	16	8	6.8	7.8	5.3	7.2
Osage (pt)	12,478	7,670	4,389	419	3,281	D	61.5	35.2	3.4	5	14	12	5.8	6.5	5.0	5.7
Ottawa	12,052	6,700	4,857	495	1,843	D	55.6	40.3	4.1	13	8	3	5.6	5.7	5.5	6.8
Pawnee (pt)	727	348	347	32	1	D	47.9	47.7	4.4	17	2	1	0.3	0.3	0.4	0.4
Rogers	26,257	11,702	13,569	986	1,867	R	44.6	51.7	3.8	18	1	5	12.3	9.9	15.5	13.5
Sequoyah	12,450	7,138	4,942	370	2,196	D	57.3	39.7	3.0	8	10	16	5.8	6.0	5.6	5.1
Wagoner (pt)..............	11,597	5,936	5,253	408	683	D	51.2	45.3	3.5	15	4	10	5.4	5.0	6.0	5.6
District 3	**207,659**	**155,934**	**51,725**	-	**104,209**	**D**	**75.1**	**24.9**	-				**100.0**	**100.0**	**100.0**	-
Atoka......................	4,754	3,972	782	-	3,190	D	83.6	16.4	-	4	18	-	2.3	2.5	1.5	-
Bryan	12,130	10,074	2,056	-	8,018	D	83.1	16.9	-	6	16	-	5.8	6.5	4.0	-
Carter	17,012	13,180	3,832	-	9,348	D	77.5	22.5	-	16	6	-	8.2	8.5	7.4	-
Choctaw	5,724	4,910	814	-	4,096	D	85.8	14.2	-	1	21	-	2.8	3.1	1.6	-
Coal.......................	2,480	2,048	432	-	1,616	D	82.6	17.4	-	8	14	-	1.2	1.3	0.8	-
Hughes	4,959	4,071	888	-	3,183	D	82.1	17.9	-	10	12	-	2.4	2.6	1.7	-
Johnston	4,032	3,450	582	-	2,868	D	85.6	14.4	-	3	19	-	1.9	2.2	1.1	-
Latimer	4,433	3,641	792	-	2,849	D	82.1	17.9	-	9	13	-	2.1	2.3	1.5	-
Le Flore	14,990	11,139	3,851	-	7,288	D	74.3	25.7	-	17	5	-	7.2	7.1	7.4	-
Lincoln	11,211	7,592	3,619	-	3,973	D	67.7	32.3	-	19	3	-	5.4	4.9	7.0	-
Love	3,430	2,845	585	-	2,260	D	82.9	17.1	-	7	15	-	1.7	1.8	1.1	-
McCurtain	10,421	8,111	2,310	-	5,801	D	77.8	22.2	-	14	8	-	5.0	5.2	4.5	-
Marshall	5,081	4,074	1,007	-	3,067	D	80.2	19.8	-	12	10	-	2.4	2.6	1.9	-
Murray	5,109	4,255	854	-	3,401	D	83.3	16.7	-	5	17	-	2.5	2.7	1.7	-
Pawnee (pt)	5,568	3,654	1,914	-	1,740	D	65.6	34.4	-	20	2	-	2.7	2.3	3.7	-
Payne	28,167	17,129	11,038	-	6,091	D	60.8	39.2	-	21	1	-	13.6	11.0	21.3	-
Pittsburg	17,242	13,757	3,485	-	10,272	D	79.8	20.2	-	13	9	-	8.3	8.8	6.7	-
Pontotoc	14,226	11,481	2,745	-	8,736	D	80.7	19.3	-	11	11	-	6.9	7.4	5.3	-
Pottawatomie	23,092	15,647	7,445	-	8,202	D	67.8	32.2	-	18	4	-	11.1	10.0	14.4	-
Pushmataha	4,389	3,758	631	-	3,127	D	85.6	14.4	-	2	20	-	2.1	2.4	1.2	-
Seminole..................	9,209	7,146	2,063	-	5,083	D	77.6	22.4	-	15	7	-	4.4	4.6	4.0	-
District 4	**199,076**	**140,841**	**58,235**	-	**82,606**	**D**	**70.7**	**29.3**	-				**100.0**	**100.0**	**100.0**	-
Cleveland	73,446	49,106	24,340	-	24,766	D	66.9	33.1	-	10	2	-	36.9	34.9	41.8	-
Comanche	32,684	23,482	9,202	-	14,280	D	71.8	28.2	-	8	4	-	16.4	16.7	15.8	-
Cotton	2,797	2,210	587	-	1,623	D	79.0	21.0	-	3	9	-	1.4	1.6	1.0	-
Garvin	10,655	8,405	2,250	-	6,155	D	78.9	21.1	-	4	8	-	5.4	6.0	3.9	-
Grady	16,039	11,479	4,560	-	6,919	D	71.6	28.4	-	9	3	-	8.1	8.2	7.8	-
Jackson...................	8,661	6,480	2,181	-	4,299	D	74.8	25.2	-	6	6	-	4.4	4.6	3.7	-
Jefferson..................	2,681	2,187	494	-	1,693	D	81.6	18.4	-	1	11	-	1.3	1.6	0.8	-
McClain	9,863	7,337	2,526	-	4,811	D	74.4	25.6	-	7	5	-	5.0	5.2	4.3	-
Oklahoma (pt)............	19,342	12,765	6,577	-	6,188	D	66.0	34.0	-	11	1	-	9.7	9.1	11.3	-
Stephens	19,114	14,381	4,733	-	9,648	D	75.2	24.8	-	5	7	-	9.6	10.2	8.1	-
Tillman	3,794	3,009	785	-	2,224	D	79.3	20.7	-	2	10	-	1.9	2.1	1.3	-
District 5	**230,816**	**107,579**	**123,237**	-	**15,658**	**R**	**46.6**	**53.4**	-				**100.0**	**100.0**	**100.0**	-
Canadian (pt)	17,314	7,698	9,616	-	1,918	R	44.5	55.5	-	6	2	-	7.5	7.2	7.8	-
Kay	21,137	11,596	9,541	-	2,055	D	54.9	45.1	-	3	5	-	9.2	10.8	7.7	-
Logan	12,856	6,937	5,919	-	1,018	D	54.0	46.0	-	4	4	-	5.6	6.4	4.8	-
Noble......................	4,948	2,756	2,192	-	564	D	55.7	44.3	-	2	6	-	2.1	2.6	1.8	-
Oklahoma (pt)............	149,923	67,422	82,501	-	15,079	R	45.0	55.0	-	5	3	-	65.0	62.7	66.9	-
Osage (pt)................	3,481	2,115	1,366	-	749	D	60.8	39.2	-	1	7	-	1.5	2.0	1.1	-
Washington	21,157	9,055	12,102	-	3,047	R	42.8	57.2	-	7	1	-	9.2	8.4	9.8	-
District 6	**198,802**	**134,734**	**64,068**	-	**70,666**	**D**	**67.8**	**32.2**	-				**100.0**	**100.0**	**100.0**	-
Alfalfa	2,882	1,943	939	-	1,004	D	67.4	32.6	-	13	12	-	1.4	1.4	1.5	-
Beaver	2,642	1,504	1,138	-	366	D	56.9	43.1	-	24	1	-	1.3	1.1	1.8	-
Beckham..................	7,396	5,567	1,829	-	3,738	D	75.3	24.7	-	6	19	-	3.7	4.1	2.9	-
Blaine	4,739	3,460	1,279	-	2,181	D	73.0	27.0	-	9	16	-	2.4	2.6	2.0	-
Caddo	10,655	8,019	2,636	-	5,383	D	75.3	24.7	-	7	18	-	5.4	6.0	4.1	-
Canadian (pt)	13,373	8,517	4,856	-	3,661	D	63.7	36.3	-	19	6	-	6.7	6.3	7.6	-

Table H. — Vote for U.S. Representative in Congress: November 3, 1992, General Election (cont)

Congressional district and county	Total	Democrat (DEM)	Republican (REP)	Other	Plurality Total	Party	Percent of total vote DEM	REP	Other	Rank within district DEM	REP	Other	Percent contribution to district vote Total	DEM	REP	Other
District 6 (cont)																
Cimarron	1,496	900	596	–	304	D	60.2	39.8	–	22	3	–	0.8	0.7	0.9	–
Custer	11,133	7,742	3,391	–	4,351	D	69.5	30.5	–	11	14	–	5.6	5.7	5.3	–
Dewey	2,625	1,971	654	–	1,317	D	75.1	24.9	–	8	17	–	1.3	1.5	1.0	–
Ellis	2,176	1,490	686	–	804	D	68.5	31.5	–	12	13	–	1.1	1.1	1.1	–
Garfield	23,900	15,811	8,089	–	7,722	D	66.2	33.8	–	16	9	–	12.0	11.7	12.6	–
Grant	2,867	2,068	799	–	1,269	D	72.1	27.9	–	10	15	–	1.4	1.5	1.2	–
Greer	2,536	1,980	556	–	1,424	D	78.1	21.9	–	2	23	–	1.3	1.5	0.9	–
Harmon	1,438	1,173	265	–	908	D	81.6	18.4	–	1	24	–	0.7	0.9	0.4	–
Harper	1,878	1,211	667	–	544	D	64.5	35.5	–	18	7	–	0.9	0.9	1.0	–
Kingfisher	6,008	4,032	1,976	–	2,056	D	67.1	32.9	–	14	11	–	3.0	3.0	3.1	–
Kiowa	4,513	3,472	1,041	–	2,431	D	76.9	23.1	–	4	21	–	2.3	2.6	1.6	–
Major	3,543	2,218	1,325	–	893	D	62.6	37.4	–	20	5	–	1.8	1.6	2.1	–
Oklahoma (pt)	66,899	44,518	22,381	–	22,137	D	66.5	33.5	–	15	10	–	33.7	33.0	34.9	–
Roger Mills	2,038	1,540	498	–	1,042	D	75.6	24.4	–	5	20	–	1.0	1.1	0.8	–
Texas	6,421	3,694	2,727	–	967	D	57.5	42.5	–	23	2	–	3.2	2.7	4.3	–
Washita	5,051	3,914	1,137	–	2,777	D	77.5	22.5	–	3	22	–	2.5	2.9	1.8	–
Woods	4,447	2,718	1,729	–	989	D	61.1	38.9	–	21	4	–	2.2	2.0	2.7	–
Woodward	8,146	5,272	2,874	–	2,398	D	64.7	35.3	–	17	8	–	4.1	3.9	4.5	–
OKLAHOMA	1,275,696	764,249	504,133	7,314	260,116	D	59.9	39.5	0.6							

Table I. — Vote for Presidential Preference: March 10, 1992, Democratic Primary Election

County	Total	Clinton	Brown	Woods	Harkin	Kerrey	LaRouche	McAlpine		Clinton	Brown	Woods	Rank Clinton	Rank Brown	Rank Woods	Total	Clinton	Brown	Woods
		Top candidates								Top three candidates (state vote)									
										Percent of total vote						Percent contribution to state vote			
Adair	2,071	1,677	231	43	45	38	20	17	-	81.0	11.2	2.1	3	60	70	0.5	0.6	0.3	0.3
Alfalfa	889	653	122	32	32	29	12	9	-	73.5	13.7	3.6	39	36	43	0.2	0.2	0.2	0.2
Atoka	2,569	1,752	238	382	54	80	39	24	-	68.2	9.3	14.9	67	68	1	0.6	0.6	0.3	2.3
Beaver	785	531	115	34	47	32	22	4	-	67.6	14.6	4.3	70	35	30	0.2	0.2	0.2	0.2
Beckham	3,095	2,352	399	101	81	102	50	10	-	76.0	12.9	3.3	18	47	46	0.7	0.8	0.6	0.6
Blaine	1,571	1,173	212	58	60	39	19	10	-	74.7	13.5	3.7	28	38	42	0.4	0.4	0.3	0.3
Bryan	5,269	3,929	520	500	117	127	64	12	-	74.6	9.9	9.5	29	66	9	1.3	1.3	0.7	3.0
Caddo	5,136	3,802	676	247	148	164	69	30	-	74.0	13.2	4.8	34	44	25	1.2	1.3	1.0	1.5
Canadian	8,779	5,599	1,716	485	411	341	165	62	-	63.8	19.5	5.5	75	5	18	2.1	1.9	2.5	2.9
Carter	6,792	4,833	747	623	211	233	106	39	-	71.2	11.0	9.2	50	61	10	1.6	1.6	1.1	3.7
Cherokee	5,175	3,904	806	138	115	133	46	33	-	75.4	15.6	2.7	21	21	59	1.2	1.3	1.2	0.8
Choctaw	2,698	2,028	215	292	68	45	40	10	-	75.2	8.0	10.8	23	76	7	0.6	0.7	0.3	1.7
Cimarron	585	428	72	25	24	29	4	3	-	73.2	12.3	4.3	40	52	33	0.1	0.1	0.1	0.1
Cleveland	21,296	13,103	5,016	914	1,028	796	301	138	-	61.5	23.6	4.3	77	1	32	5.1	4.5	7.2	5.4
Coal	1,274	894	127	158	27	39	19	10	-	70.2	10.0	12.4	56	64	4	0.3	0.3	0.2	0.9
Comanche	12,178	8,572	1,989	494	390	449	171	113	-	70.4	16.3	4.1	54	17	39	2.9	2.9	2.9	2.9
Cotton	1,417	1,104	140	88	31	28	17	9	-	77.9	9.9	6.2	10	65	12	0.3	0.4	0.2	0.5
Craig	2,511	2,008	276	57	55	66	35	14	-	80.0	11.0	2.3	5	62	69	0.6	0.7	0.4	0.3
Creek	7,712	5,746	1,184	198	180	217	123	64	-	74.5	15.4	2.6	30	25	62	1.9	2.0	1.7	1.2
Custer	4,070	3,006	536	167	142	142	57	20	-	73.9	13.2	4.1	36	43	37	1.0	1.0	0.8	1.0
Delaware	3,552	2,702	482	91	97	101	56	23	-	76.1	13.6	2.6	16	37	63	0.9	0.9	0.7	0.5
Dewey	1,269	868	188	75	57	51	23	7	-	68.4	14.8	5.9	66	30	13	0.3	0.3	0.3	0.4
Ellis	837	589	123	36	31	33	17	8	-	70.4	14.7	4.3	55	34	31	0.2	0.2	0.2	0.2
Garfield	6,336	4,342	1,168	267	232	195	94	38	-	68.5	18.4	4.2	64	8	34	1.5	1.5	1.7	1.6
Garvin	5,461	3,951	700	314	199	166	80	51	-	72.3	12.8	5.7	45	48	15	1.3	1.3	1.0	1.9
Grady	7,120	4,949	1,054	400	289	219	139	70	-	69.5	14.8	5.6	58	31	17	1.7	1.7	1.5	2.4
Grant	1,107	762	190	34	56	45	12	8	-	68.8	17.2	3.1	62	15	48	0.3	0.3	0.3	0.2
Greer	1,365	1,026	178	27	51	42	22	19	-	75.2	13.0	2.0	24	46	72	0.3	0.3	0.3	0.2
Harmon	747	583	85	14	30	24	9	2	-	78.0	11.4	1.9	9	59	73	0.2	0.2	0.1	< .1
Harper	782	524	141	32	35	25	20	5	-	67.0	18.0	4.1	73	10	38	0.2	0.2	0.2	0.2
Haskell	2,245	1,871	197	51	58	32	23	13	-	83.3	8.8	2.3	1	70	68	0.5	0.6	0.3	0.3
Hughes	2,819	2,175	327	117	72	71	46	11	-	77.2	11.6	4.2	13	57	35	0.7	0.7	0.5	0.7
Jackson	3,948	2,864	523	118	160	147	73	63	-	72.5	13.2	3.0	43	41	50	0.9	1.0	0.8	0.7
Jefferson	1,377	1,033	112	151	23	32	19	7	-	75.0	8.1	11.0	25	75	6	0.3	0.4	0.2	0.9
Johnston	2,407	1,702	198	317	64	73	32	21	-	70.7	8.2	13.2	52	74	2	0.6	0.6	0.3	1.9
Kay	5,790	3,999	1,070	144	228	218	92	39	-	69.1	18.5	2.5	61	7	65	1.4	1.4	1.5	0.9
Kingfisher	1,815	1,184	313	107	100	60	36	15	-	65.2	17.2	5.9	74	14	14	0.4	0.4	0.4	0.6
Kiowa	2,211	1,651	271	84	88	65	31	21	-	74.7	12.3	3.8	27	53	41	0.5	0.6	0.4	0.5
Latimer	2,317	1,916	193	58	59	31	40	20	-	82.7	8.3	2.5	2	72	64	0.6	0.7	0.3	0.3
Le Flore	6,255	4,621	818	110	338	231	104	33	-	73.9	13.1	1.8	35	45	75	1.5	1.6	1.2	0.7
Lincoln	4,397	3,055	682	228	173	149	65	45	-	69.5	15.5	5.2	59	22	21	1.1	1.0	1.0	1.4
Logan	3,940	2,703	690	163	153	123	76	32	-	68.6	17.5	4.1	63	13	36	0.9	0.9	1.0	1.0
Love	1,465	1,069	111	191	38	35	16	5	-	73.0	7.6	13.0	41	77	3	0.4	0.4	0.2	1.1
McClain	4,301	2,900	694	245	192	154	81	35	-	67.4	16.1	5.7	71	18	16	1.0	1.0	1.0	1.5
McCurtain	4,479	3,532	400	226	117	105	62	37	-	78.9	8.9	5.0	8	69	22	1.1	1.2	0.6	1.3
McIntosh	3,942	3,134	460	115	86	82	52	13	-	79.5	11.7	2.9	6	56	52	0.9	1.1	0.7	0.7
Major	838	597	127	40	28	33	8	5	-	71.2	15.2	4.8	49	26	28	0.2	0.2	0.2	0.2
Marshall	2,382	1,728	199	250	71	83	37	14	-	72.5	8.4	10.5	42	71	8	0.6	0.6	0.3	1.5
Mayes	5,408	4,206	674	110	147	156	86	29	-	77.8	12.5	2.0	11	51	71	1.3	1.4	1.0	0.7
Murray	2,595	1,910	297	194	66	73	40	15	-	73.6	11.4	7.5	37	58	11	0.6	0.7	0.4	1.2
Muskogee	10,398	8,203	1,328	185	247	255	131	49	-	78.9	12.8	1.8	7	49	74	2.5	2.8	1.9	1.1
Noble	1,784	1,214	316	49	88	81	26	10	-	68.0	17.7	2.7	68	12	56	0.4	0.4	0.5	0.3
Nowata	1,530	1,183	195	41	44	32	26	9	-	77.3	12.7	2.7	12	50	58	0.4	0.4	0.3	0.2
Okfuskee	2,163	1,591	286	104	83	56	27	16	-	73.6	13.2	4.8	38	42	26	0.5	0.5	0.4	0.6
Oklahoma	62,629	39,804	13,750	2,226	2,641	2,570	1,226	412	-	63.6	22.0	3.6	76	2	44	15.1	13.6	19.7	13.2
Okmulgee	6,140	4,628	905	160	134	153	127	33	-	75.4	14.7	2.6	22	33	60	1.5	1.6	1.3	1.0
Osage	6,183	4,588	954	150	152	161	112	66	-	74.2	15.4	2.4	33	24	67	1.5	1.6	1.4	0.9
Ottawa	4,203	3,380	564	58	69	81	36	15	-	80.4	13.4	1.4	4	39	77	1.0	1.2	0.8	0.3
Pawnee	2,463	1,830	389	69	51	56	42	26	-	74.3	15.8	2.8	32	20	55	0.6	0.6	0.6	0.4
Payne	7,259	4,885	1,527	211	258	254	99	25	-	67.3	21.0	2.9	72	4	53	1.7	1.7	2.2	1.3
Pittsburg	8,244	6,269	1,103	278	218	182	118	76	-	76.0	13.4	3.4	17	40	45	2.0	2.1	1.6	1.7
Pontotoc	6,556	4,646	1,090	311	187	195	107	20	-	70.9	16.6	4.7	51	16	29	1.6	1.6	1.6	1.8
Pottawatomie	9,905	6,917	1,779	475	267	254	159	54	-	69.8	18.0	4.8	57	11	27	2.4	2.4	2.6	2.8
Pushmataha	2,257	1,705	188	250	34	39	34	7	-	75.5	8.3	11.1	20	73	5	0.5	0.6	0.3	1.5
Roger Mills	1,061	790	129	31	43	38	20	10	-	74.5	12.2	2.9	31	54	51	0.3	0.3	0.2	0.2
Rogers	8,034	5,662	1,494	231	235	212	154	46	-	70.5	18.6	2.9	53	6	54	1.9	1.9	2.1	1.4
Seminole	4,564	3,309	707	225	120	135	57	11	-	72.5	15.5	4.9	44	23	23	1.1	1.1	1.0	1.3
Sequoyah	4,894	3,665	729	78	190	144	66	22	-	74.9	14.9	1.6	26	29	76	1.2	1.2	1.0	0.5
Stephens	8,264	6,374	861	434	263	206	89	37	-	77.1	10.4	5.3	14	63	20	2.0	2.2	1.2	2.6
Texas	2,404	1,646	291	127	148	120	57	15	-	68.5	12.1	5.3	65	55	19	0.6	0.6	0.4	0.8

County	Top candidates								Top three candidates(state vote)									
									Percent of total vote						Percent contribution to state vote			
												Rank						
	Total	Clinton	Brown	Woods	Harkin	Kerrey	LaRouche	McAlpine		Clinton	Brown	Woods	Clinton	Brown	Woods	Total	Clinton	Brown	Woods
Tillman	1,872	1,440	176	92	60	65	27	12	-	76.9	9.4	4.9	15	67	24	0.4	0.5	0.3	0.5
Tulsa..........................	45,572	30,921	9,914	1,176	1,283	1,449	568	261	-	67.9	21.8	2.6	69	3	61	11.0	10.5	14.2	7.0
Wagoner	6,079	4,609	897	148	158	140	96	31	-	75.8	14.8	2.4	19	32	66	1.5	1.6	1.3	0.9
Washington....................	5,599	4,003	1,020	151	145	177	79	24	-	71.5	18.2	2.7	48	9	57	1.3	1.4	1.5	0.9
Washita........................	2,608	1,874	392	84	100	83	52	23	-	71.9	15.0	3.2	46	27	47	0.6	0.6	0.6	0.5
Woods.........................	1,604	1,110	241	64	95	59	26	9	-	69.2	15.0	4.0	60	28	40	0.4	0.4	0.3	0.4
Woodward	2,481	1,780	397	75	98	72	43	16	-	71.7	16.0	3.0	47	19	49	0.6	0.6	0.6	0.4
OKLAHOMA	**416,129**	**293,266**	**69,624**	**16,828**	**14,015**	**13,252**	**6,474**	**2,670**	-	**70.5**	**16.7**	**4.0**				**100.0**	**100.0**	**100.0**	**100.0**

Table J. — Vote for Presidential Preference: March 10, 1992, Republican Primary Election

| County | Top candidates | | | | | Top four candidates (state vote) | | | | | | | | | | | | |
| | Total | Bush | Bu-chanan | Duke | Other | Percent of total vote | | | | Rank | | | | Percent contribution to state vote | | | | |
						Bush	Bu-chanan	Duke	Other	Bush	Bu-chanan	Duke	Other	Total	Bush	Bu-chanan	Duke	Other
Adair	811	625	156	20	10	77.1	19.2	2.5	1.2	4	75	40	30	0.4	0.4	0.3	0.4	0.4
Alfalfa	1,055	738	273	26	18	70.0	25.9	2.5	1.7	39	38	41	12	0.5	0.5	0.5	0.5	0.7
Atoka	163	122	34	6	1	74.8	20.9	3.7	0.6	6	73	15	64	<.1	<.1	<.1	0.1	<.1
Beaver	795	576	199	16	4	72.5	25.0	2.0	0.5	18	49	69	69	0.4	0.4	0.3	0.3	0.2
Beckham	649	417	207	17	8	64.3	31.9	2.6	1.2	75	3	34	31	0.3	0.3	0.4	0.3	0.3
Blaine	1,248	843	356	39	10	67.5	28.5	3.1	0.8	64	15	25	57	0.6	0.6	0.6	0.7	0.4
Bryan	390	274	102	9	5	70.3	26.2	2.3	1.3	35	33	52	27	0.2	0.2	0.2	0.2	0.2
Caddo	815	581	200	27	7	71.3	24.5	3.3	0.9	27	51	21	53	0.4	0.4	0.3	0.5	0.3
Canadian	6,799	4,769	1,772	189	69	70.1	26.1	2.8	1.0	37	34	32	49	3.1	3.1	3.1	3.3	2.8
Carter	1,329	948	343	30	8	71.3	25.8	2.3	0.6	26	40	54	65	0.6	0.6	0.6	0.5	0.3
Cherokee	1,306	975	280	31	20	74.7	21.4	2.4	1.5	7	71	48	15	0.6	0.6	0.5	0.5	0.8
Choctaw	99	72	24	2	1	72.7	24.2	2.0	1.0	16	55	67	50	<.1	<.1	<.1	<.1	<.1
Cimarron	280	177	98	3	2	63.2	35.0	1.1	0.7	77	1	75	63	0.1	0.1	0.2	<.1	<.1
Cleveland	13,569	9,272	3,766	340	191	68.3	27.8	2.5	1.4	57	23	38	19	6.2	6.1	6.5	6.0	7.6
Coal	69	51	15	1	2	73.9	21.7	1.4	2.9	8	70	74	2	<.1	<.1	<.1	<.1	<.1
Comanche	3,949	2,898	909	113	29	73.4	23.0	2.9	0.7	12	65	29	59	1.8	1.9	1.6	2.0	1.2
Cotton	96	62	32	2	0	64.6	33.3	2.1	0.0	74	2	63	74	<.1	<.1	<.1	<.1	0.0
Craig	505	360	129	11	5	71.3	25.5	2.2	1.0	28	44	56	51	0.2	0.2	0.2	0.2	0.2
Creek	3,488	2,396	921	135	36	68.7	26.4	3.9	1.0	54	28	12	48	1.6	1.6	1.6	2.4	1.4
Custer	1,503	1,099	354	32	18	73.1	23.6	2.1	1.2	13	60	61	35	0.7	0.7	0.6	0.6	0.7
Delaware	1,433	1,058	325	30	20	73.8	22.7	2.1	1.4	9	67	62	21	0.7	0.7	0.6	0.5	0.8
Dewey	468	334	109	16	9	71.4	23.3	3.4	1.9	25	63	17	8	0.2	0.2	0.2	0.3	0.4
Ellis	637	431	180	15	11	67.7	28.3	2.4	1.7	63	18	49	10	0.3	0.3	0.3	0.3	0.4
Garfield	7,634	5,352	2,005	190	87	70.1	26.3	2.5	1.1	38	31	39	38	3.5	3.5	3.5	3.3	3.5
Garvin	786	514	234	29	9	65.4	29.8	3.7	1.1	71	7	14	37	0.4	0.3	0.4	0.5	0.4
Grady	2,137	1,477	570	60	30	69.1	26.7	2.8	1.4	49	26	30	20	1.0	1.0	1.0	1.1	1.2
Grant	774	504	241	19	10	65.1	31.1	2.5	1.3	73	4	44	26	0.4	0.3	0.4	0.3	0.4
Greer	122	94	26	2	0	77.0	21.3	1.6	0.0	5	72	71	75	<.1	<.1	<.1	<.1	0.0
Harmon	35	28	6	0	1	80.0	17.1	0.0	2.9	2	76	77	3	<.1	<.1	<.1	0.0	<.1
Harper	501	328	149	14	10	65.5	29.7	2.8	2.0	70	8	31	7	0.2	0.2	0.3	0.2	0.4
Haskell	121	84	28	8	1	69.4	23.1	6.6	0.8	43	64	1	55	<.1	<.1	<.1	0.1	<.1
Hughes	166	117	42	5	2	70.5	25.3	3.0	1.2	34	48	26	34	<.1	<.1	<.1	<.1	<.1
Jackson	697	501	177	15	4	71.9	25.4	2.2	0.6	21	45	60	66	0.3	0.3	0.3	0.3	0.2
Jefferson	49	38	10	1	0	77.6	20.4	2.0	0.0	3	74	66	76	<.1	<.1	<.1	<.1	0.0
Johnston	92	76	11	2	3	82.6	12.0	2.2	3.3	1	77	58	1	<.1	<.1	<.1	<.1	0.1
Kay	5,447	3,703	1,575	112	57	68.0	28.9	2.1	1.0	59	12	65	46	2.5	2.4	2.7	2.0	2.3
Kingfisher	1,928	1,360	501	42	25	70.5	26.0	2.2	1.3	33	36	57	24	0.9	0.9	0.9	0.7	1.0
Kiowa	273	188	65	13	7	68.9	23.8	4.8	2.6	53	57	6	5	0.1	0.1	0.1	0.2	0.3
Latimer	139	95	36	7	1	68.3	25.9	5.0	0.7	56	37	4	62	<.1	<.1	<.1	0.1	<.1
Le Flore	635	459	155	16	5	72.3	24.4	2.5	0.8	19	53	36	58	0.3	0.3	0.3	0.3	0.2
Lincoln	2,042	1,467	476	70	29	71.8	23.3	3.4	1.4	22	62	16	18	0.9	1.0	0.8	1.2	1.2
Logan	3,087	2,134	815	98	40	69.1	26.4	3.2	1.3	48	29	23	25	1.4	1.4	1.4	1.7	1.6
Love	137	98	36	2	1	71.5	26.3	1.5	0.7	24	30	73	61	<.1	<.1	<.1	<.1	<.1
McClain	1,026	695	298	24	9	67.7	29.0	2.3	0.9	61	10	51	52	0.5	0.5	0.5	0.4	0.4
McCurtain	192	133	45	12	2	69.3	23.4	6.3	1.0	45	61	2	47	<.1	<.1	<.1	0.2	<.1
McIntosh	301	217	69	14	1	72.1	22.9	4.7	0.3	20	66	8	73	0.1	0.1	0.1	0.2	<.1
Major	1,454	975	421	38	20	67.1	29.0	2.6	1.4	66	11	35	22	0.7	0.6	0.7	0.7	0.8
Marshall	221	161	54	5	1	72.9	24.4	2.3	0.5	15	52	53	71	0.1	0.1	<.1	<.1	<.1
Mayes	1,595	1,112	438	32	13	69.7	27.5	2.0	0.8	41	25	70	56	0.7	0.7	0.8	0.6	0.5
Murray	201	141	51	8	1	70.1	25.4	4.0	0.5	36	46	11	70	<.1	<.1	<.1	0.1	<.1
Muskogee	2,040	1,416	539	68	17	69.4	26.4	3.3	0.8	44	27	20	54	0.9	0.9	0.9	1.2	0.7
Noble	1,158	854	252	32	20	73.7	21.8	2.8	1.7	10	69	33	11	0.5	0.6	0.4	0.6	0.8
Nowata	686	440	207	28	11	64.1	30.2	4.1	1.6	76	6	9	14	0.3	0.3	0.4	0.5	0.4
Okfuskee	181	125	44	11	1	69.1	24.3	6.1	0.6	50	54	3	67	<.1	<.1	<.1	0.2	<.1
Oklahoma	53,627	37,868	13,835	1,318	606	70.6	25.8	2.5	1.1	32	41	43	39	24.6	25.0	23.9	23.2	24.2
Okmulgee	1,035	685	287	50	13	66.2	27.7	4.8	1.3	68	24	5	28	0.5	0.5	0.5	0.9	0.5
Osage	2,084	1,389	589	83	23	66.7	28.3	4.0	1.1	67	17	10	42	1.0	0.9	1.0	1.5	0.9
Ottawa	1,066	759	270	25	12	71.2	25.3	2.3	1.1	29	47	50	41	0.5	0.5	0.5	0.4	0.5
Pawnee	1,217	864	302	29	22	71.0	24.8	2.4	1.8	31	50	47	9	0.6	0.6	0.5	0.5	0.9
Payne	4,990	3,623	1,176	120	71	72.6	23.6	2.4	1.4	17	59	46	17	2.3	2.4	2.0	2.1	2.8
Pittsburg	735	523	178	25	9	71.2	24.2	3.4	1.2	30	56	18	32	0.3	0.3	0.3	0.4	0.4
Pontotoc	1,021	714	266	30	11	69.9	26.1	2.9	1.1	40	35	27	44	0.5	0.5	0.5	0.5	0.4
Pottawatomie	2,789	1,943	719	93	34	69.7	25.8	3.3	1.2	42	42	19	33	1.3	1.3	1.2	1.6	1.4
Pushmataha	84	58	22	4	0	69.0	26.2	4.8	0.0	51	32	7	77	<.1	<.1	<.1	<.1	0.0
Roger Mills	115	78	33	1	3	67.8	28.7	0.9	2.6	60	13	76	4	<.1	<.1	<.1	<.1	0.1
Rogers	3,630	2,439	1,032	118	41	67.2	28.4	3.3	1.1	65	16	22	40	1.7	1.6	1.8	2.1	1.6
Seminole	742	532	190	16	4	71.7	25.6	2.2	0.5	23	43	59	68	0.3	0.4	0.3	0.3	0.2
Sequoyah	677	498	153	17	9	73.6	22.6	2.5	1.3	11	68	37	23	0.3	0.3	0.3	0.3	0.4
Stephens	1,555	1,021	478	49	7	65.7	30.7	3.2	0.5	69	5	24	72	0.7	0.7	0.8	0.9	0.3
Texas	1,500	1,037	421	31	11	69.1	28.1	2.1	0.7	46	20	64	60	0.7	0.7	0.7	0.5	0.4

County	Top candidates					Top four candidates (state vote)											
						Percent of total vote				Rank				Percent contribution to state vote			
	Total	Bush	Bu-chanan	Duke	Other	Bush	Bu-chanan	Duke	Other	Bush	Bu-chanan	Duke	Other	Total	Bush	Bu-chanan	Duke	Other
Tillman	133	90	38	3	2	67.7	28.6	2.3	1.5	62	14	55	16	<.1	<.1	<.1	<.1	<.1
Tulsa	49,436	33,729	13,949	1,217	541	68.2	28.2	2.5	1.1	58	19	42	43	22.7	22.2	24.1	21.5	21.6
Wagoner	2,982	1,948	886	113	35	65.3	29.7	3.8	1.2	72	9	13	36	1.4	1.3	1.5	2.0	1.4
Washington	6,990	5,100	1,662	141	87	73.0	23.8	2.0	1.2	14	58	68	29	3.2	3.4	2.9	2.5	3.5
Washita	373	257	104	6	6	68.9	27.9	1.6	1.6	52	22	72	13	0.2	0.2	0.2	0.1	0.2
Woods	1,542	1,066	398	45	33	69.1	25.8	2.9	2.1	47	39	28	6	0.7	0.7	0.7	0.8	1.3
Woodward	2,085	1,427	585	51	22	68.4	28.1	2.4	1.1	55	21	45	45	1.0	0.9	1.0	0.9	0.9
OKLAHOMA	**217,721**	**151,612**	**57,933**	**5,672**	**2,504**	**69.6**	**26.6**	**2.6**	**1.2**					**100.0**	**100.0**	**100.0**	**100.0**	**100.0**

1992 Vote for President
Percent for Bush (R), by County

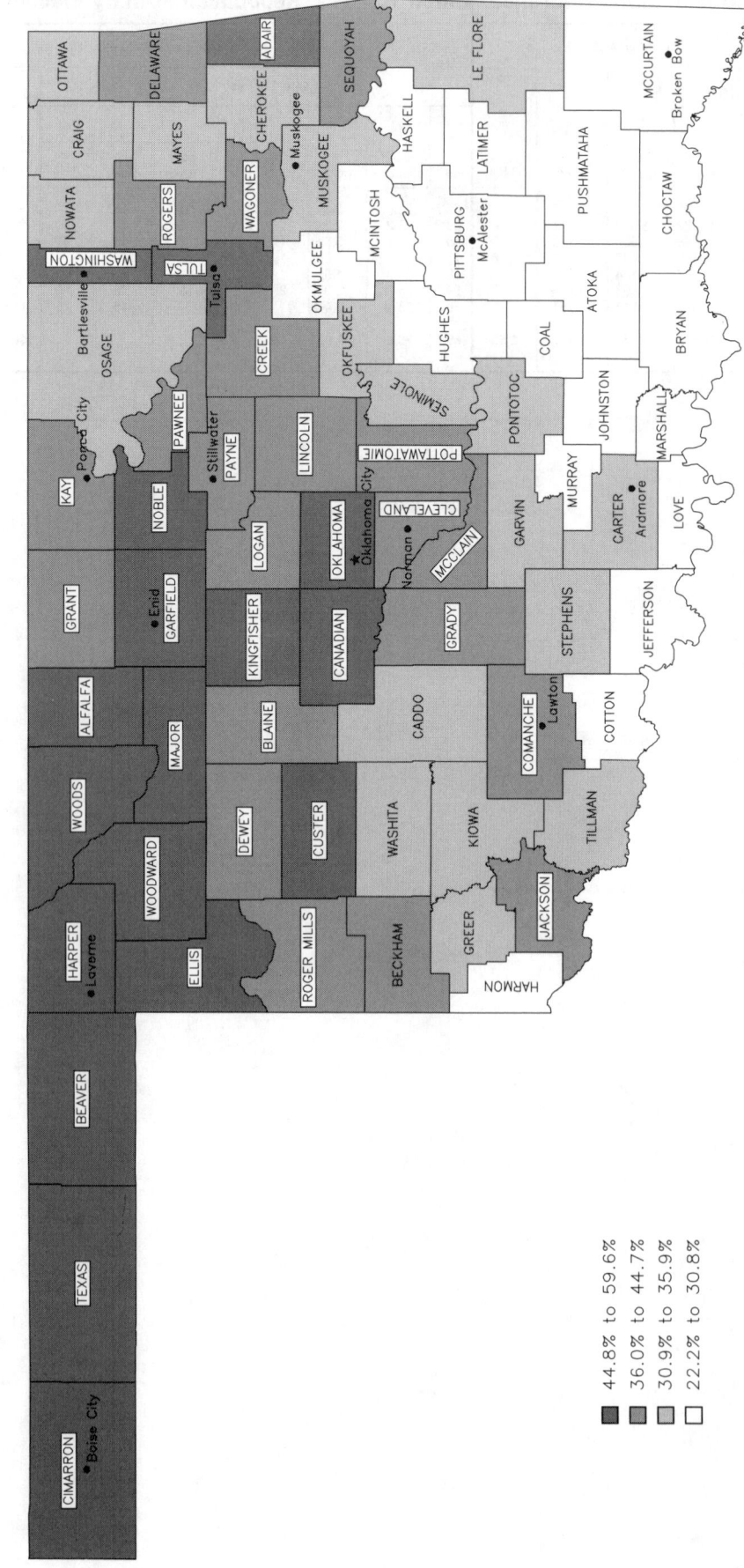

Bush (R) received 42.6% statewide.

A framed county name indicates
a county carried by the winner.

44.8% to 59.6%
36.0% to 44.7%
30.9% to 35.9%
22.2% to 30.8%

1992 Vote for U.S. Senator
Percent for Nickles (R), by County

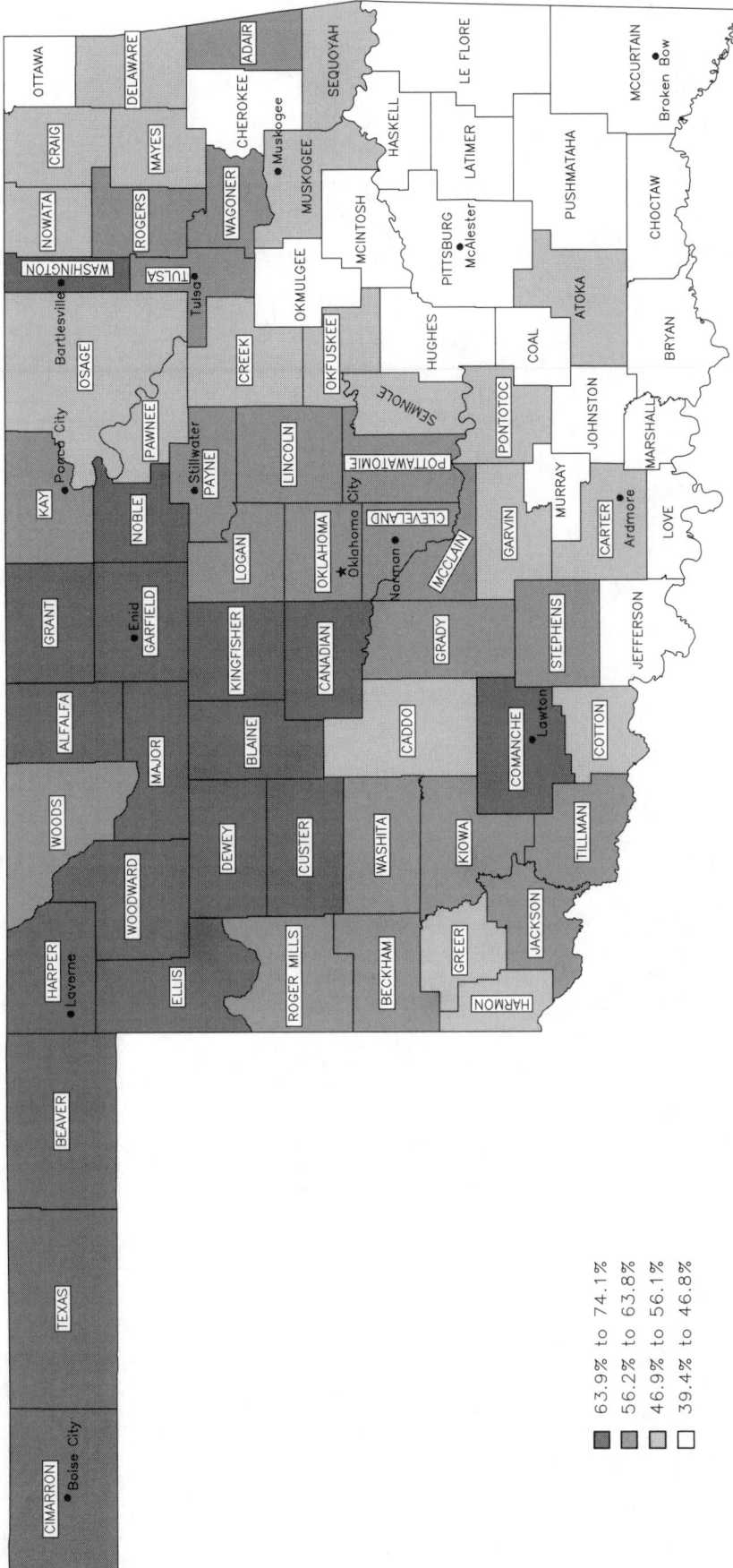

63.9% to 74.1%
56.2% to 63.8%
46.9% to 56.1%
39.4% to 46.8%

Nickles (R) received 58.5% statewide.

A framed county name indicates
a county carried by the winner.

Oklahoma 765

OREGON

Congressional Districts 5
   Average Population 568,464
State Senate Districts 30
   Average Population 94,744
State House Districts 60
   Average Population 47,372

Electoral College Votes..7
Counties 36
Voting Precincts 2,329

Alternative Registration Methods:
   ....Mail-in, Motor-voter

Registration Deadline (Days before Election) 20

Voting Equipment Use (Counties)

Datavote Punch Card	2	Paper Ballot	13
Electronic	0	Other Punch Card	16
Lever Machine	0	Mixed Systems	0
Optical Scanner	5		

Party Control	DEM	REP	IND	VAC
1993 State Senate	16	14	0	0
1992 State Senate	20	10	0	0
1993 State House	28	32	0	0
1992 State House	28	32	0	0

Population Statistics 1990

Race/ Ethnicity	Total Population		Voting Age Population		Voting Age Population % of total population
	Number	%	Number	%	
Non-Hispanic					
White	2,579,732	90.8	1,948,020	92.0	75.5
Black	44,982	1.6	29,279	1.4	65.1
Asian/Pacific Islander	67,422	2.4	47,427	2.2	70.3
Native American	35,749	1.3	23,713	1.1	66.3
Other	1,729	<.1	753	<.1	43.6
All Hispanic	112,707	4.0	68,999	3.3	61.2
TOTAL	2,842,321	100.0	2,118,191	100.0	74.5

Estimated Voting Age Population 1992 (VAP) 2,226,000
Number of Registered Voters.............................. 1,775,416
   % of estimated VAP.. 79.8
Voter Turnout (Actual) 1,498,959
   % of VAP 67.3
   % of Registration 84.4
Persons Not Voting—of Voting Age 727,041
   % of VAP 32.7
Persons Not Voting—of Registered 276,457
   % of Registration 15.6
Straight Ticket Voting .... No

State Officials and Members of Congress

Governor:
Barbara Roberts (D) 1990, elected to a four-year term in 1990.

U.S. Senators:
Mark O. Hatfield (R) 1966, elected to a six-year term in 1990.
Bob Packwood (R) 1968, elected to a six-year term in 1992.

U.S. Representative in Congress:
(District, Name, Party, Date first elected)

1. Furse (D) 1992
2. Smith (R) 1982
3. Wyden (D) 1980
4. DeFazio (D) 1986
5. Kopetski (D) 1990

Candidates: General Election, November 3, 1992

Candidate(s)	Total vote	Percent	Party	Status	First elected
President/Vice President					
Clinton/Gore	621,314	42.48%	Democrat	Challenger	1992
Bush/Quayle	475,757	32.53%	Republican	Incumbent	1988
Perot/Stockdale	354,091	24.21%	Independent Init. OR	Challenger	
Marrou/Lord	4,277	0.29%	Libertarian	Challenger	
Fulani/Munoz	3,030	0.21%	New Alliance	Challenger	
Miscellaneous	2,609	0.18%	Write in	Challenger	
James (Bo) Gritz	1,470	0.10%	Write in	Challenger	
John Hagelin	91	<.1%	Write in	Challenger	
J. Quinn Brisben	4	<.01%	Write in	Challenger	
U.S. Senator					
Bob Packwood	717,455	52.14%	Republican	Incumbent	1968
Les AuCoin	639,851	46.50%	Democrat	Challenger	
Miscellaneous	12,934	0.94%	Write in	Challenger	
Harry Lonsdale	5,793	0.42%	Write in	Challenger	

Governor (No Contest)

U.S. Representative in Congress

Candidate(s)	Total vote	Percent	Party	Status	First elected
District 1					
Elizabeth Furse	152,917	51.99%	Democrat	Challenger	1992
Tony Meeker	140,986	47.93%	Republican	Challenger	
Miscellaneous	251	0.09%	Write in	Challenger	
District 2					
Robert Smith	184,163	67.10%	Republican	Incumbent	1982
Denzel Ferguson	90,036	32.80%	Democrat	Challenger	
Miscellaneous	279	0.10%	Write in	Challenger	
District 3					
Ron Wyden	208,028	77.08%	Democrat	Incumbent	1980
Al Ritter	50,235	18.61%	Republican	Challenger	
Blair Bobier	11,413	4.23%	Libertarian	Challenger	
Miscellaneous	203	0.08%	Write in	Challenger	
District 4					
Peter DeFazio	199,372	71.38%	Democrat	Incumbent	1986
Richard Schulz	79,733	28.55%	Republican	Challenger	
Miscellaneous	194	0.07%	Write in	Challenger	
District 5					
Mike Kopetski	174,443	63.91%	Democrat	Incumbent	1990
Jim Seagraves	97,984	35.90%	Republican	Challenger	
Miscellaneous	517	0.19%	Write in	Challenger	

Candidates: May 19, 1992, Primary Election

Candidate	Total vote	Percent	Candidate	Total vote	Percent
Presidential Preference, Democratic			**Presidential Preference, Republican**		
Bill Clinton	159,802	45.10%	George Bush	203,957	67.06%
Jerry Brown	110,494	31.18%	Patrick Buchanan	57,730	18.98%
Paul Tsongas	37,139	10.48%	Miscellaneous	35,805	11.77%
Miscellaneous	33,540	9.47%	David Duke	6,667	2.19%
Eugene McCarthy	6,714	1.89%			
Lyndon LaRouche, Jr.	3,096	0.87%			
Charles Woods	1,895	0.53%			
Larry Agran	1,652	0.47%			

Voter Registration and Turnout, 1948-1992 Elections

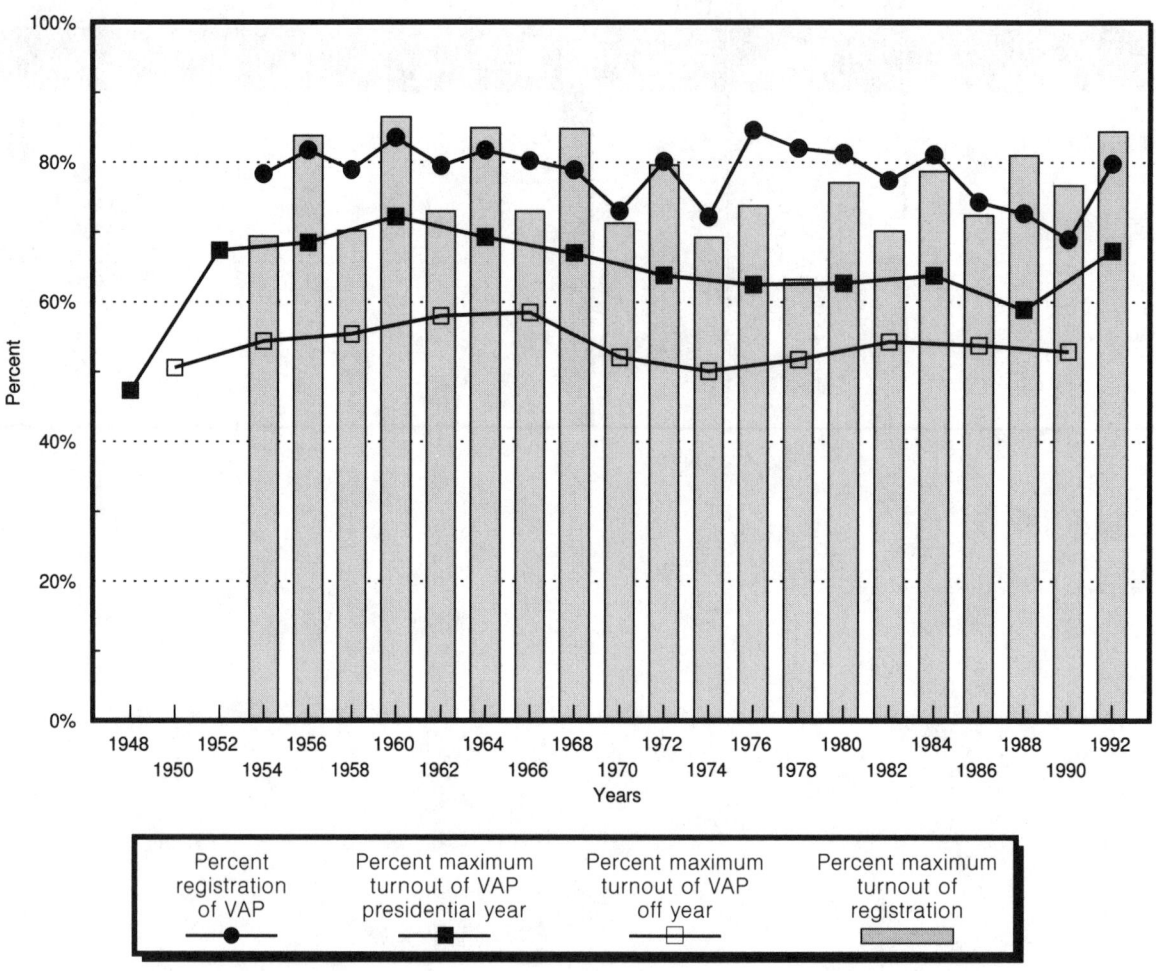

		Voter registration (REG)				Voter turnout										
						Highest office						Maximum vote				
Year	Estimated Voting Age Population (VAP)	Total	Percent of VAP	Rank by percent of VAP	Actual	Total	Office	Percent total REG	Rank by percent of REG	Percent of VAP	Rank by percent of VAP	Total	Percent total REG	Rank by percent of REG	Percent total VAP	Rank by percent of VAP
1992........	2,226,000	1,775,416	79.8	16	1,498,959	1,462,643	P	82.4	9	65.7	8	1,498,959	84.4	4	67.3	8
1990........	2,140,000	1,476,500	69.0	25	1,133,125	1,112,847	G	75.4	2	52.0	4	1,133,125	76.7	2	52.9	4
1988........	2,096,000	1,524,446	72.7	21	1,235,199	1,201,694	P	78.8	5	57.3	13	1,235,199	81.0	6	58.9	12
1986[1].....	2,022,000	1,502,244	74.3	15	1,088,086	1,059,630	G	70.5	5	52.4	5	1,088,086	72.4	3	53.8	5
1984........	1,984,000	1,608,693	81.1	12	1,265,824	1,226,527	P	76.2	17	61.8	8	1,265,824	78.7	13	63.8	5
1982........	1,959,000	1,516,589	77.4	9	1,063,913	1,042,009	G	68.7	10	53.2	8	1,063,913	70.2	11	54.3	8
1980[2].....	1,929,000	1,569,222	81.3	13	1,209,691	1,181,516	P	75.3	25	61.3	10	1,209,691	77.1	20	62.7	10
1978........	1,808,000	1,482,339	82.0	6	937,423	911,143	G	61.5	12	50.4	4	937,423	63.2	12	51.8	4
1976........	1,679,000	1,420,146	84.6	7	1,048,561	1,029,876	P	72.5	29	61.3	11	1,048,561	73.8	32	62.5	12
1974........	1,583,000	1,143,073	72.2	21	792,557	770,574	G	67.4	11	48.7	11	792,557	69.3	9	50.1	10
1972........	1,495,000	1,197,676	80.1	14	953,376	927,946	P	77.5	19	62.1	16	953,376	79.6	14	63.8	13
1970........	1,308,000	955,459	73.0	25	681,381	666,394	G	69.7	13	50.9	25	681,381	71.3	14	52.1	21
1968........	1,231,000	971,851	78.9	18	824,562	821,118	P	84.5	11	66.7	17	824,562	84.8	11	67.0	17
1966........	1,185,000	949,825	80.2	15	693,796	685,067	S	72.1	13	57.8	11	693,796	73.0	13	58.5	11
1964........	1,141,000	932,461	81.7	17	791,245	786,305	P	84.3	14	68.9	20	791,245	84.9	14	69.3	20
1962........	1,111,000	883,690	79.5	13	644,772	637,407	G	72.1	13	57.4	17	644,772	73.0	14	58.0	17
1960........	1,079,000	900,616	83.5	12	779,159	776,421	P	86.2	15	72.0	19	779,159	86.5	15	72.2	20
1958........	1,084,000	855,044	78.9	13	-	599,994	G	70.2	15	55.4	20	599,994	70.2	17	55.4	22
1956........	1,075,000	877,952	81.7	13	-	736,132	P	83.8	14	68.5	19	736,132	83.8	14	68.5	21
1954........	1,046,000	819,539	78.3	12	-	569,088	S	69.4	10	54.4	16	569,088	69.4	12	54.4	18
1952........	1,031,000	-	-	-	-	695,059	P	-	-	67.4	29	695,059	-	-	67.4	30
1950........	1,000,000	-	-	-	-	505,910	G	-	-	50.6	24	505,910	-	-	50.6	26
1948........	1,109,000	-	-	-	-	524,080	P	-	-	47.3	34	524,080	-	-	47.3	35

[1]Voter registration deadline of one day before election day enacted 1985. Initiative measure approved at November 1986 general election moving deadline to 20 days before election day.   [2]Election day voter registration law enacted 1979.

OREGON

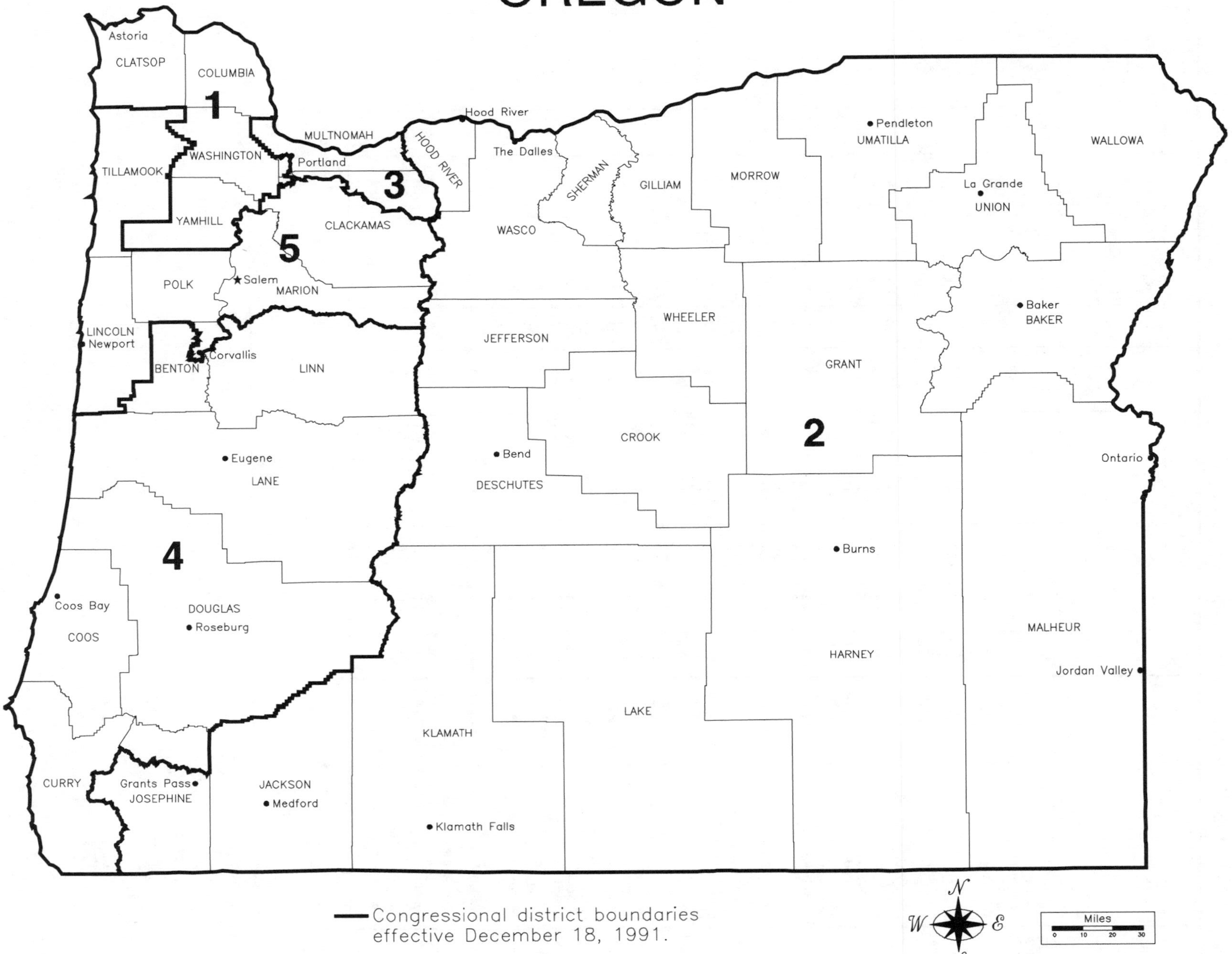

WALLOWA

Ontario

MALHEUR

Jordan Valley

Baker
BAKER

La Grande
UNION

Pendleton
UMATILLA

GRANT

2

Burns

HARNEY

MORROW

GILLIAM

WHEELER

CROOK

LAKE

SHERMAN

The Dalles

WASCO

JEFFERSON

Bend
DESCHUTES

KLAMATH

Klamath Falls

Hood River

HOOD RIVER

MULTNOMAH

Portland

3

CLACKAMAS

5

MARION

Salem

LINN

Eugene
LANE

JACKSON
Medford

COLUMBIA

WASHINGTON

YAMHILL

TILLAMOOK

POLK

Corvallis
BENTON

DOUGLAS

Roseburg

Astoria
CLATSOP

1

LINCOLN
Newport

4

Grants Pass
JOSEPHINE

Coos Bay
COOS

CURRY

Congressional district boundaries
effective December 18, 1991.

Copyright © 1993 by Election Data Services, Inc.

Miles
0 10 20 30

N
W E
S

Oregon 771

Table A. — 1990 Population by Race and Ethnic Origin

State/county code	County	Total persons	Percent of total persons						Rank				Percent contribution to state population			
			Non-Hispanic					Hispanic	Total	Percent of total persons			Total	Non-Hispanic		Hispanic
			White	Black	Asian and Pacific Islander	Native American	Other			Non-Hispanic		Hispanic		White	Black	
										White	Black					
41 001	Baker	15,317	96.8	0.2	0.3	0.9	<.1	1.8	26	4	19	29	0.5	0.6	<.1	0.2
41 003	Benton	70,811	90.5	0.8	5.4	0.7	<.1	2.5	10	26	3	19	2.5	2.5	1.3	1.5
41 005	Clackamas	278,850	94.7	0.4	1.7	0.7	<.1	2.6	4	18	10	18	9.8	10.2	2.5	6.3
41 007	Clatsop	33,301	95.4	0.3	1.3	1.1	<.1	1.9	19	12	12	25	1.2	1.2	0.2	0.6
41 009	Columbia	37,557	96.0	<.1	0.7	1.3	<.1	1.8	18	9	28	28	1.3	1.4	<.1	0.6
41 011	Coos	60,273	94.4	0.2	0.9	2.2	<.1	2.2	13	19	15	23	2.1	2.2	0.3	1.2
41 013	Crook	14,111	95.4	<.1	0.3	1.5	<.1	2.7	27	13	30	17	0.5	0.5	<.1	0.3
41 015	Curry	19,327	95.0	0.2	0.6	2.3	<.1	1.8	24	16	23	27	0.7	0.7	<.1	0.3
41 017	Deschutes	74,958	96.5	0.1	0.6	0.8	<.1	2.0	9	7	27	24	2.6	2.8	0.2	1.4
41 019	Douglas	94,649	95.3	0.1	0.7	1.5	<.1	2.4	7	14	24	22	3.3	3.5	0.3	2.0
41 021	Gilliam	1,717	97.1	0.0	0.5	0.6	0.0	1.7	35	3	35	30	<.1	<.1	0.0	<.1
41 023	Grant	7,853	96.7	<.1	0.2	1.1	0.0	1.9	29	5	31	26	0.3	0.3	<.1	0.1
41 025	Harney	7,060	92.7	<.1	0.6	3.6	<.1	3.1	32	23	34	15	0.2	0.3	<.1	0.2
41 027	Hood River	16,903	80.6	0.2	1.7	1.1	0.1	16.3	25	34	17	2	0.6	0.5	<.1	2.4
41 029	Jackson	146,389	93.6	0.2	0.9	1.2	<.1	4.1	6	21	16	12	5.2	5.3	0.7	5.3
41 031	Jefferson	13,676	70.1	0.1	0.5	18.7	<.1	10.6	28	36	25	4	0.5	0.4	<.1	1.3
41 033	Josephine	62,649	95.0	0.2	0.7	1.3	<.1	2.8	12	17	18	16	2.2	2.3	0.3	1.6
41 035	Klamath	57,702	89.6	0.6	0.8	3.8	<.1	5.2	15	29	6	9	2.0	2.0	0.8	2.6
41 037	Lake	7,186	93.1	<.1	0.6	2.5	<.1	3.8	31	22	33	13	0.3	0.3	<.1	0.2
41 039	Lane	282,912	93.8	0.7	1.9	1.1	<.1	2.4	3	20	4	20	10.0	10.3	4.5	6.1
41 041	Lincoln	38,889	95.0	0.2	0.8	2.4	<.1	1.5	17	15	22	34	1.4	1.4	0.1	0.5
41 043	Linn	91,227	95.5	0.2	0.8	1.1	<.1	2.4	8	11	20	21	3.2	3.4	0.4	1.9
41 045	Malheur	26,038	76.2	0.2	3.0	0.7	<.1	19.8	20	35	14	1	0.9	0.8	0.1	4.6
41 047	Marion	228,483	88.1	0.9	1.7	1.3	<.1	8.0	5	30	2	6	8.0	7.8	4.5	16.2
41 049	Morrow	7,625	87.7	0.1	0.4	0.9	0.1	10.8	30	31	26	3	0.3	0.3	<.1	0.7
41 051	Multnomah	583,887	85.2	5.9	4.6	1.0	0.1	3.1	1	33	1	14	20.5	19.3	76.5	16.3
41 053	Polk	49,541	91.1	0.4	1.3	1.4	<.1	5.7	16	24	11	8	1.7	1.8	0.4	2.5
41 055	Sherman	1,918	96.6	0.0	0.7	1.3	0.0	1.5	34	6	36	35	<.1	<.1	0.0	<.1
41 057	Tillamook	21,570	96.3	0.2	0.7	1.1	<.1	1.7	23	8	21	31	0.8	0.8	<.1	0.3
41 059	Umatilla	59,249	86.6	0.6	0.8	2.9	<.1	9.0	14	32	7	5	2.1	2.0	0.8	4.7
41 061	Union	23,598	95.8	0.4	1.1	1.0	<.1	1.6	21	10	9	33	0.8	0.9	0.2	0.3
41 063	Wallowa	6,911	97.5	<.1	0.3	0.4	0.0	1.6	33	2	29	32	0.2	0.3	<.1	0.1
41 065	Wasco	21,683	89.8	0.3	1.1	3.9	<.1	4.9	22	28	13	10	0.8	0.8	0.1	0.9
41 067	Washington	311,554	89.9	0.6	4.2	0.5	<.1	4.6	2	27	5	11	11.0	10.9	4.4	12.8
41 069	Wheeler	1,396	98.1	<.1	0.1	0.8	0.0	0.9	36	1	32	36	<.1	<.1	<.1	<.1
41 071	Yamhill	65,551	90.8	0.5	1.2	1.2	<.1	6.3	11	25	8	7	2.3	2.3	0.8	3.7
41	OREGON	2,842,321	90.8	1.6	2.4	1.3	<.1	4.0					100.0	100.0	100.0	100.0
	CONGRESSIONAL															
	District 1	568,461	91.2	0.8	3.3	0.7	<.1	4.0	5	4	2	3	20.0	20.1	9.6	20.0
	District 2	568,464	91.3	0.3	0.9	2.1	<.1	5.4	4	2	5	1	20.0	20.1	3.4	27.0
	District 3	568,465	85.5	5.8	4.4	1.1	0.1	3.2	2	5	1	4	20.0	18.8	73.4	15.9
	District 4	568,465	94.5	0.5	1.3	1.3	<.1	2.4	3	1	4	5	20.0	20.8	5.7	11.9
	District 5	568,466	91.3	0.6	2.0	1.1	<.1	5.0	1	3	3	2	20.0	20.1	7.8	25.1

Table B. — 1990 Voting Age Population (VAP) by Race and Ethnic Origin

County	Total Voting Age Population	Percent of total VAP — Non-Hispanic White	Black	Asian and Pacific Islander	Native American	Other	Hispanic	Rank Total	Rank Non-Hispanic White	Black	Hispanic	Percent contribution to state VAP Total	Non-Hispanic White	Black	Hispanic	VAP percent of total population Total	Non-Hispanic White	Black	Asian and Pacific Islander	Native American	Other	Hispanic
Baker	11,303	97.3	0.2	0.2	0.8	0.0	1.4	26	4	14	29	0.5	0.6	<.1	0.2	73.8	74.2	93.1	57.8	67.9	0.0	56.2
Benton	55,041	90.5	0.7	5.9	0.6	<.1	2.2	10	29	3	18	2.6	2.6	1.4	1.7	77.7	77.7	70.7	84.0	68.9	53.2	68.8
Clackamas	204,447	95.3	0.3	1.5	0.6	<.1	2.2	4	19	10	17	9.7	10.0	2.4	6.4	73.3	73.8	62.4	65.9	69.8	48.0	62.2
Clatsop	24,741	95.8	0.3	1.2	1.0	<.1	1.6	19	16	12	26	1.2	1.2	0.2	0.6	74.3	74.7	73.7	71.4	68.4	61.1	62.0
Columbia	26,761	96.7	<.1	0.6	1.2	<.1	1.4	18	9	28	27	1.3	1.3	<.1	0.6	71.3	71.8	56.8	56.0	63.7	45.5	56.3
Coos	45,138	95.4	0.2	0.8	1.9	<.1	1.8	13	18	17	24	2.1	2.2	0.2	1.1	74.9	75.7	54.1	64.6	64.6	28.6	58.4
Crook	10,247	96.3	<.1	0.2	1.3	<.1	2.2	27	10	32	19	0.5	0.5	<.1	0.3	72.6	73.3	27.3	48.9	63.3	66.7	57.2
Curry	15,337	96.1	0.1	0.6	1.9	<.1	1.4	24	13	23	28	0.7	0.8	<.1	0.3	79.4	80.2	64.5	71.1	64.0	40.0	59.6
Deschutes	55,633	97.0	<.1	0.5	0.8	<.1	1.6	9	7	30	25	2.6	2.8	0.1	1.3	74.2	74.7	52.6	61.7	71.6	62.5	59.4
Douglas	69,189	96.0	0.1	0.6	1.4	<.1	1.9	7	14	24	21	3.3	3.4	0.3	1.9	73.1	73.6	60.0	61.0	67.6	51.6	60.4
Gilliam	1,256	97.9	0.0	0.4	0.4	0.0	1.4	35	3	34	30	<.1	<.1	0.0	<.1	73.2	73.7	0.0	55.6	50.0	0.0	56.7
Grant	5,724	96.9	<.1	0.2	1.1	0.0	1.8	29	8	31	23	0.3	0.3	<.1	0.2	72.9	73.0	50.0	71.4	70.9	0.0	68.4
Harney	5,087	93.5	<.1	0.6	2.9	<.1	2.9	32	23	33	13	0.2	0.2	<.1	0.2	72.1	72.7	50.0	71.8	59.5	100.0	67.9
Hood River	12,283	82.7	0.2	1.9	1.1	<.1	14.1	25	34	16	2	0.6	0.5	<.1	2.5	72.7	74.5	63.9	82.0	69.9	70.6	62.8
Jackson	109,684	94.7	0.2	0.9	1.1	<.1	3.2	6	21	18	12	5.2	5.3	0.6	5.0	74.9	75.8	54.5	67.4	71.0	50.0	58.1
Jefferson	9,394	76.1	0.1	0.5	14.9	<.1	8.3	28	36	21	4	0.4	0.4	<.1	1.1	68.7	74.6	65.0	80.6	54.8	40.0	53.9
Josephine	47,453	95.8	0.1	0.6	1.2	<.1	2.2	11	17	19	16	2.2	2.3	0.2	1.5	75.7	76.3	56.9	71.0	71.4	60.0	60.1
Klamath	42,333	91.5	0.5	0.7	3.1	<.1	4.1	15	27	7	9	2.0	2.0	0.8	2.5	73.4	74.9	65.3	71.0	60.4	55.6	57.7
Lake	5,164	94.9	<.1	0.6	2.0	0.0	2.5	31	20	29	15	0.2	0.3	<.1	0.2	71.9	73.2	80.0	70.7	56.7	0.0	48.5
Lane	213,712	94.5	0.6	1.9	1.0	<.1	2.0	3	22	6	20	10.1	10.4	4.2	6.3	75.5	76.1	60.5	75.8	67.7	40.9	63.6
Lincoln	29,809	95.9	<.1	0.7	1.9	<.1	1.3	17	15	26	32	1.4	1.5	<.1	0.6	76.7	77.4	42.9	64.1	62.2	72.7	65.4
Linn	66,862	96.2	0.1	0.7	1.1	<.1	1.9	8	11	20	22	3.2	3.3	0.3	1.9	73.3	73.9	57.3	59.3	70.9	21.9	58.9
Malheur	18,079	79.7	0.2	3.4	0.6	<.1	16.0	20	35	15	1	0.9	0.7	0.1	4.2	69.4	72.6	66.7	79.6	61.0	52.4	55.9
Marion	168,195	89.8	0.9	1.6	1.2	<.1	6.5	5	30	2	6	7.9	7.8	4.9	15.9	73.6	75.1	70.5	67.9	66.3	51.0	60.1
Morrow	5,313	89.6	<.1	0.3	0.9	<.1	9.0	30	31	25	3	0.3	0.2	<.1	0.7	69.7	71.2	62.5	56.7	72.3	33.3	58.1
Multnomah	448,967	87.1	5.0	4.2	1.0	<.1	2.7	1	33	1	14	21.2	20.1	76.6	17.7	76.9	78.5	65.2	71.1	70.2	38.3	66.4
Polk	36,437	92.7	0.3	1.3	1.2	<.1	4.4	16	24	11	8	1.7	1.7	0.4	2.3	73.5	74.8	60.9	72.4	62.4	55.6	57.0
Sherman	1,385	97.3	0.0	0.4	1.3	0.0	1.1	34	5	35	35	<.1	<.1	0.0	<.1	72.2	72.7	0.0	38.5	75.0	0.0	53.6
Tillamook	16,495	97.1	0.1	0.6	0.9	<.1	1.3	22	6	22	34	0.8	0.8	<.1	0.3	76.5	77.1	57.9	61.0	67.5	25.0	55.9
Umatilla	42,743	88.8	0.6	0.7	2.6	<.1	7.1	14	32	4	5	2.0	1.9	0.9	4.4	72.1	74.0	78.6	63.0	64.2	62.5	57.2
Union	17,053	96.2	0.4	1.1	0.9	<.1	1.3	21	12	9	31	0.8	0.8	0.3	0.3	72.3	72.5	74.7	72.8	67.3	41.7	59.6
Wallowa	5,068	97.9	<.1	0.3	0.5	0.0	1.3	33	2	27	33	0.2	0.3	<.1	<.1	73.3	73.6	66.7	60.9	74.2	0.0	57.5
Wasco	15,826	92.2	0.2	0.9	3.1	<.1	3.6	23	25	13	11	0.7	0.7	0.1	0.8	73.0	74.9	66.1	58.3	58.6	16.7	53.5
Washington	227,968	91.1	0.5	3.9	0.5	<.1	3.9	2	28	8	10	10.8	10.7	4.2	13.0	73.2	74.1	61.8	67.3	71.7	41.1	62.3
Wheeler	1,087	98.3	0.0	0.2	0.7	0.0	0.8	36	1	36	36	<.1	<.1	0.0	<.1	77.9	78.0	0.0	100.0	72.7	0.0	75.0
Yamhill	46,977	91.8	0.6	1.1	1.1	<.1	5.4	12	26	5	7	2.2	2.2	1.0	3.7	71.7	72.5	82.0	67.0	66.8	20.8	61.4
OREGON	**2,118,191**	**92.0**	**1.4**	**2.2**	**1.1**	**<.1**	**3.3**					**100.0**	**100.0**	**100.0**	**100.0**	**74.5**	**75.5**	**65.1**	**70.3**	**66.3**	**43.6**	**61.2**
CONGRESSIONAL																						
District 1	425,695	92.1	0.7	3.1	0.7	<.1	3.4	2	4	2	3	20.1	20.1	10.6	20.9	74.9	75.6	71.9	69.9	71.7	47.2	63.9
District 2	418,063	92.9	0.2	0.8	1.8	<.1	4.2	5	2	5	1	19.7	19.9	3.5	25.5	73.5	74.8	65.8	69.5	62.9	53.3	57.8
District 3	428,542	87.3	5.0	4.0	1.0	<.1	2.7	1	5	1	4	20.2	19.2	72.5	16.7	75.4	77.0	64.3	69.3	68.4	36.0	64.3
District 4	424,702	95.2	0.4	1.3	1.2	<.1	1.9	3	1	4	5	20.1	20.8	5.2	12.0	74.7	75.3	59.8	71.8	67.2	40.0	61.6
District 5	421,189	92.4	0.6	1.9	1.0	<.1	4.1	4	3	3	2	19.9	20.0	8.1	24.9	74.1	75.0	68.0	72.7	66.4	50.9	60.7

Table C. — **Voter Participation: November 3, 1992, General Election**

County	Estimated Voting Age Population (VAP), 1992	Voter registration (REG) Total	% contribution to state REG	% of 1992 VAP	Rank by % of 1992 VAP	Highest office Actual	Total	Office	% of 1992 VAP	Maximum vote Total	% contribution to state turnout	% of REG	Rank by % of REG	% of 1992 VAP	Rank by % 1992 VAP	Pres-ident	Sen-ator	Gov-ernor	Repre-sent-ative
Baker	11,563	9,303	0.5	80.5	17	7,735	7,530	P	65.1	7,735	0.5	83.1	25	66.9	25	2.7	6.3	-	6.7
Benton	55,461	45,593	2.6	82.2	14	38,190	37,923	P	68.4	38,190	2.5	83.8	23	68.9	14	0.7	4.3	-	5.7
Clackamas	220,603	183,631	10.3	83.2	8	156,806	154,538	P	70.1	156,806	10.5	85.4	14	71.1	7	1.4	9.2	-	9.3
Clatsop	25,679	19,681	1.1	76.6	30	17,360	16,812	P	65.5	17,360	1.2	88.2	2	67.6	23	3.2	6.9	-	10.5
Columbia	28,366	22,587	1.3	79.6	22	19,617	19,402	P	68.4	19,617	1.3	86.9	5	69.2	12	1.1	4.7	-	3.2
Coos	46,115	36,469	2.1	79.1	25	30,024	29,659	P	64.3	30,024	2.0	82.3	30	65.1	28	1.2	5.3	-	3.5
Crook	10,802	8,671	0.5	80.3	19	7,488	7,271	P	67.3	7,488	0.5	86.4	10	69.3	11	2.9	7.3	-	7.6
Curry	16,132	13,607	0.8	84.3	7	11,132	11,050	P	68.5	11,132	0.7	81.8	33	69.0	13	0.7	4.4	-	4.0
Deschutes	60,180	52,836	3.0	87.8	5	44,744	43,918	P	73.0	44,744	3.0	84.7	19	74.4	5	1.8	5.8	-	4.7
Douglas	71,782	56,729	3.2	79.0	26	46,905	45,860	P	63.9	46,905	3.1	82.7	28	65.3	27	2.2	6.6	-	5.9
Gilliam	1,248	1,201	<.1	96.2	1	1,042	1,038	P	83.2	1,042	<.1	86.8	7	83.5	1	0.4	6.2	-	4.3
Grant	5,915	4,906	0.3	82.9	9	4,066	3,986	P	67.4	4,066	0.3	82.9	26	68.7	15	2.0	4.8	-	4.2
Harney	5,093	4,047	0.2	79.5	23	3,465	3,372	P	66.2	3,465	0.2	85.6	13	68.0	19	2.7	7.1	-	3.8
Hood River	12,889	9,401	0.5	72.9	33	8,080	7,841	P	60.8	8,080	0.5	85.9	12	62.7	32	3.0	6.6	-	10.4
Jackson	115,901	92,633	5.2	79.9	20	78,634	77,096	P	66.5	78,634	5.2	84.9	17	67.8	20	2.0	25.2	-	5.8
Jefferson	10,023	7,181	0.4	71.6	34	6,060	5,906	P	58.9	6,060	0.4	84.4	21	60.5	34	2.5	4.5	-	3.4
Josephine	49,576	39,323	2.2	79.3	24	33,861	33,559	P	67.7	33,861	2.3	86.1	11	68.3	17	0.9	5.8	-	5.0
Klamath	43,532	34,375	1.9	79.0	27	27,531	26,593	P	61.1	27,531	1.8	80.1	35	63.2	31	3.4	5.4	-	3.8
Lake	5,347	4,690	0.3	87.7	6	3,851	3,802	P	71.1	3,851	0.3	82.1	31	72.0	6	1.3	11.3	-	3.0
Lane	220,068	182,020	10.3	82.7	12	154,508	151,862	P	69.0	154,508	10.3	84.9	18	70.2	8	1.7	6.0	-	5.5
Lincoln	31,429	25,884	1.5	82.4	13	22,041	21,623	P	68.8	22,041	1.5	85.2	16	70.1	9	1.9	6.7	-	18.3
Linn	69,428	54,651	3.1	78.7	28	46,151	45,287	P	65.2	46,151	3.1	84.4	20	66.5	26	1.9	14.8	-	14.8
Malheur	18,669	13,102	0.7	70.2	35	10,835	10,663	P	57.1	10,835	0.7	82.7	27	58.0	35	1.6	4.5	-	4.6
Marion	177,833	132,379	7.5	74.4	31	111,402	110,334	P	62.0	111,402	7.4	84.2	22	62.6	33	1.0	5.1	-	4.3
Morrow	5,556	4,533	0.3	81.6	15	3,540	3,474	P	62.5	3,540	0.2	78.1	36	63.7	29	1.9	4.9	-	4.7
Multnomah	464,666	374,471	21.1	80.6	16	311,752	298,291	P	64.2	311,752	20.8	83.3	24	67.1	24	4.3	6.7	-	7.4
Polk	38,243	31,666	1.8	82.8	11	25,928	25,614	P	67.0	25,928	1.7	81.9	32	67.8	21	1.2	16.6	-	20.1
Sherman	1,398	1,304	<.1	93.3	2	1,137	1,116	P	79.8	1,137	<.1	87.2	4	81.3	2	1.8	5.9	-	3.2
Tillamook	16,960	13,628	0.8	80.4	18	11,835	11,484	P	67.7	11,835	0.8	86.8	6	69.8	10	3.0	7.4	-	5.3
Umatilla	44,358	28,607	1.6	64.5	36	23,387	21,759	S	49.1	23,387	1.6	81.8	34	52.7	36	16.0	7.0	-	7.5
Union	17,605	14,584	0.8	82.8	10	12,048	11,588	P	65.8	12,048	0.8	82.6	29	68.4	16	3.8	8.3	-	8.1
Wallowa	5,217	4,755	0.3	91.1	3	4,163	4,074	P	78.1	4,163	0.3	87.5	3	79.8	4	2.1	6.9	-	5.7
Wasco	16,447	13,144	0.7	79.9	21	11,209	10,973	P	66.7	11,209	0.7	85.3	15	68.2	18	2.1	6.1	-	7.2
Washington	250,299	195,834	11.0	78.2	29	169,511	167,195	P	66.8	169,511	11.3	86.6	9	67.7	22	1.4	9.1	-	8.1
Wheeler	1,100	986	<.1	89.6	4	882	860	P	78.2	882	<.1	89.5	1	80.2	3	2.5	7.6	-	5.1
Yamhill	50,517	37,004	2.1	73.3	32	32,039	31,406	P	62.2	32,039	2.1	86.6	8	63.4	30	2.0	6.3	-	4.2
OREGON[1]	**2,226,000**	**1,775,416**	**100.0**	**79.8**		**1,498,959**	**1,464,759**		**65.8**	**1,498,959**	**100.0**	**84.4**		**67.3**		**2.4**	**8.2**	**-**	**7.2**

[1]Oregon reports voter registration and turnout by political party affiliation. See Table D-registration by party. State voter turnout by party is 662,500 (44.2%) for Democratic party, 542,237 (36.2%) for Republican party, 243,328 (16.2%) for nonaffiliated, and 14,249 (1.0%) for other. Not classified by party were 36,645 (2.4%) absentee ballots from Multnomah county.

Table D. — Voter Registration by Political Party Affiliation: November 3, 1992, General Election

County	Total voter registration	Political party affiliation Democrat (DEM)	Republican (REP)	Independent (IND)	Plurality Total	Party	Percent of total registration DEM	REP	IND	Rank DEM	REP	IND	Percent contribution to state registration Total	DEM	REP	IND
Baker	9,303	4,110	3,709	1,392	401	D	44.6	40.3	15.1	15	18	27	0.5	0.5	0.6	0.4
Benton	45,593	19,159	16,723	9,478	2,436	D	42.2	36.9	20.9	24	27	1	2.6	2.4	2.6	2.9
Clackamas	183,631	77,266	71,523	33,734	5,743	D	42.3	39.2	18.5	23	23	13	10.3	9.7	11.1	10.5
Clatsop	19,681	9,662	6,272	0	3,390	D	60.6	39.4	0.0	5	33	33	1.1	1.2	1.0	0.0
Columbia	22,587	12,617	6,347	3,545	6,270	D	56.1	28.2	15.7	1	35	26	1.3	1.6	1.0	1.1
Coos	36,469	19,116	11,139	5,957	7,977	D	52.8	30.8	16.5	3	34	21	2.1	2.4	1.7	1.9
Crook	8,671	3,918	3,251	1,378	667	D	45.8	38.0	16.1	11	25	24	0.5	0.5	0.5	0.4
Curry	13,607	5,641	5,547	2,346	94	D	41.7	41.0	17.3	25	12	16	0.8	0.7	0.9	0.7
Deschutes	52,836	20,659	21,314	10,446	655	R	39.4	40.7	19.9	33	17	4	3.0	2.6	3.3	3.2
Douglas	56,729	24,816	22,245	9,410	2,571	D	43.9	39.4	16.7	16	20	20	3.2	3.1	3.5	2.9
Gilliam	1,201	553	489	0	64	D	53.1	46.9	0.0	9	13	34	<.1	<.1	<.1	0.0
Grant	4,906	2,096	1,992	777	104	D	43.1	40.9	16.0	21	15	25	0.3	0.3	0.3	0.2
Harney	4,047	1,765	1,722	560	43	D	43.6	42.6	13.8	17	6	29	0.2	0.2	0.3	0.2
Hood River	9,401	4,035	3,461	1,759	574	D	43.6	37.4	19.0	20	26	8	0.5	0.5	0.5	0.5
Jackson	92,633	36,683	37,394	18,045	711	R	39.8	40.6	19.6	31	16	5	5.2	4.6	5.8	5.6
Jefferson	7,181	3,064	2,827	0	237	D	52.0	48.0	0.0	22	19	35	0.4	0.4	0.4	0.0
Josephine	39,323	14,477	17,751	6,671	3,274	R	37.2	45.6	17.1	35	2	18	2.2	1.8	2.8	2.1
Klamath	34,375	13,921	14,320	5,814	399	R	40.9	42.0	17.1	28	8	19	1.9	1.8	2.2	1.8
Lake	4,690	2,079	2,012	534	67	D	45.0	43.5	11.5	14	5	32	0.3	0.3	0.3	0.2
Lane	182,020	87,252	58,485	33,815	28,767	D	48.6	32.6	18.8	6	32	10	10.3	11.0	9.1	10.5
Lincoln	25,884	12,149	8,340	5,269	3,809	D	47.2	32.4	20.5	8	31	2	1.5	1.5	1.3	1.6
Linn	54,651	24,733	19,639	10,055	5,094	D	45.4	36.1	18.5	10	28	12	3.1	3.1	3.1	3.1
Malheur	13,102	4,571	6,528	1,883	1,957	R	35.2	50.3	14.5	36	1	28	0.7	0.6	1.0	0.6
Marion	132,379	53,410	54,880	23,589	1,470	R	40.5	41.6	17.9	29	9	14	7.5	6.7	8.5	7.3
Morrow	4,533	2,014	1,704	0	310	D	54.2	45.8	0.0	13	24	36	0.3	0.3	0.3	0.0
Multnomah	374,471	196,750	104,386	69,985	92,364	D	53.0	28.1	18.9	2	36	9	21.1	24.8	16.3	21.8
Polk	31,666	12,744	13,314	5,608	570	R	40.2	42.0	17.7	30	7	15	1.8	1.6	2.1	1.7
Sherman	1,304	567	563	168	4	D	43.7	43.4	12.9	18	3	31	<.1	<.1	<.1	<.1
Tillamook	13,628	6,770	4,666	2,192	2,104	D	49.7	34.2	16.1	4	30	23	0.8	0.9	0.7	0.7
Umatilla	28,607	11,779	11,168	5,524	611	D	41.4	39.2	19.4	26	22	6	1.6	1.5	1.7	1.7
Union	14,584	6,285	5,703	2,511	582	D	43.3	39.3	17.3	19	21	17	0.8	0.8	0.9	0.8
Wallowa	4,755	2,131	1,959	616	172	D	45.3	41.6	13.1	12	11	30	0.3	0.3	0.3	0.2
Wasco	13,144	6,190	4,526	2,428	1,664	D	47.1	34.4	18.5	7	29	11	0.7	0.8	0.7	0.8
Washington	195,834	74,544	80,858	38,828	6,314	R	38.4	41.6	20.0	34	10	3	11.0	9.4	12.6	12.1
Wheeler	986	402	423	159	21	R	40.9	43.0	16.2	27	4	22	<.1	<.1	<.1	<.1
Yamhill	37,004	14,623	15,026	7,056	403	R	39.8	40.9	19.2	32	14	7	2.1	1.8	2.3	2.2
OREGON[1]	**1,775,416**	**792,551**	**642,206**	**321,532**	**150,345**	**D**	**45.1**	**36.6**	**18.3**				**100.0**	**100.0**	**100.0**	**100.0**

[1]Total voter registration also includes 5,797 for Libertarian party and 13,330 for other parties. State voter turnout by party as a percentage of voter registration by party is 662,500 (83.6%) for Democrat; 542,237 (84.4%) for Republican; 243,328 (75.7%) for independent (nonaffiliated).

Table E. – Vote for President: November 3, 1992, General Election

County	Total	Clinton (DEM)	Bush (REP)	Perot (IND)	Other	Plurality Total	Party	DEM	REP	IND	Other	Rank DEM	Rank REP	Rank IND	Total	DEM	REP	IND	DEM	REP
Baker	7,530	2,395	2,862	2,191	82	467	R	31.8	38.0	29.1	1.1	28	11	10	0.5	0.4	0.6	0.6	45.6	54.4
Benton	37,923	17,966	11,550	8,103	304	6,416	D	47.4	30.5	21.4	0.8	3	29	35	2.6	2.9	2.4	2.3	60.9	39.1
Clackamas	154,538	60,310	53,724	39,776	728	6,586	D	39.0	34.8	25.7	0.5	12	22	25	10.6	9.7	11.3	11.2	52.9	47.1
Clatsop	16,812	7,700	4,683	4,316	113	3,017	D	45.8	27.9	25.7	0.7	4	32	26	1.1	1.2	1.0	1.2	62.2	37.8
Columbia	19,402	8,298	5,227	5,670	207	2,628	D	42.8	26.9	29.2	1.1	7	34	8	1.3	1.3	1.1	1.6	61.4	38.6
Coos	29,659	12,072	9,284	7,989	314	2,788	D	40.7	31.3	26.9	1.1	9	27	20	2.0	1.9	2.0	2.3	56.5	43.5
Crook	7,271	2,508	2,703	2,024	36	195	R	34.5	37.2	27.8	0.5	22	16	16	0.5	0.4	0.6	0.6	48.1	51.9
Curry	11,050	3,841	3,809	3,310	90	32	D	34.8	34.5	30.0	0.8	20	23	4	0.8	0.6	0.8	0.9	50.2	49.8
Deschutes	43,918	15,693	15,655	12,293	277	38	D	35.7	35.6	28.0	0.6	18	21	15	3.0	2.5	3.3	3.5	50.1	49.9
Douglas	45,860	14,137	19,011	12,377	335	4,874	R	30.8	41.5	27.0	0.7	30	5	19	3.1	2.3	4.0	3.5	42.6	57.4
Gilliam	1,038	374	377	283	4	3	R	36.0	36.3	27.3	0.4	17	19	18	<.1	<.1	<.1	<.1	49.8	50.2
Grant	3,986	1,135	1,496	1,302	53	194	R	28.5	37.5	32.7	1.3	34	13	1	0.3	0.2	0.3	0.4	43.1	56.9
Harney	3,372	973	1,350	1,024	25	326	R	28.9	40.0	30.4	0.7	33	6	3	0.2	0.2	0.3	0.3	41.9	58.1
Hood River	7,841	3,106	2,453	2,235	47	653	D	39.6	31.3	28.5	0.6	11	28	12	0.5	0.5	0.5	0.6	55.9	44.1
Jackson	77,096	29,146	28,704	18,633	613	442	D	37.8	37.2	24.2	0.8	13	14	31	5.3	4.7	6.0	5.3	50.4	49.6
Jefferson	5,906	2,161	1,962	1,741	42	199	D	36.6	33.2	29.5	0.7	16	26	6	0.4	0.3	0.4	0.5	52.4	47.6
Josephine	33,559	11,007	13,003	8,426	1,123	1,996	R	32.8	38.7	25.1	3.3	26	9	27	2.3	1.8	2.7	2.4	45.8	54.2
Klamath	26,593	7,918	11,864	6,636	175	3,946	R	29.8	44.6	25.0	0.7	31	3	28	1.8	1.3	2.5	1.9	40.0	60.0
Lake	3,802	1,019	1,791	980	12	772	R	26.8	47.1	25.8	0.3	35	2	24	0.3	0.2	0.4	0.3	36.3	63.7
Lane	151,862	74,083	41,789	34,906	1,084	32,294	D	48.8	27.5	23.0	0.7	2	33	33	10.4	11.9	8.8	9.9	63.9	36.1
Lincoln	21,623	9,603	5,716	6,127	177	3,476	D	44.4	26.4	28.3	0.8	5	35	14	1.5	1.5	1.2	1.7	62.7	37.3
Linn	45,287	15,399	16,461	13,256	171	1,062	R	34.0	36.3	29.3	0.4	24	18	7	3.1	2.5	3.5	3.7	48.3	51.7
Malheur	10,663	2,539	5,374	2,654	96	2,720	R	23.8	50.4	24.9	0.9	36	1	29	0.7	0.4	1.1	0.7	32.1	67.9
Marion	110,334	41,137	42,145	26,156	896	1,008	R	37.3	38.2	23.7	0.8	15	10	32	7.5	6.6	8.9	7.4	49.4	50.6
Morrow	3,474	1,174	1,187	1,089	24	13	R	33.8	34.2	31.3	0.7	25	25	2	0.2	0.2	0.2	0.3	49.7	50.3
Multnomah	298,291	165,081	72,326	58,236	2,648	92,755	D	55.3	24.2	19.5	0.9	1	36	36	20.4	26.6	15.2	16.4	69.5	30.5
Polk	25,614	9,551	10,082	5,818	163	531	R	37.3	39.4	22.7	0.6	14	8	34	1.8	1.5	2.1	1.6	48.6	51.4
Sherman	1,116	362	424	326	4	62	R	32.4	38.0	29.2	0.4	27	12	9	<.1	<.1	<.1	<.1	46.1	53.9
Tillamook	11,484	5,040	3,359	2,997	88	1,681	D	43.9	29.2	26.1	0.8	6	31	23	0.8	0.8	0.7	0.8	60.0	40.0
Umatilla	19,643	6,787	7,095	5,581	180	308	R	34.6	36.1	28.4	0.9	21	20	13	1.3	1.1	1.5	1.6	48.9	51.1
Union	11,588	3,990	4,223	3,305	70	233	R	34.4	36.4	28.5	0.6	23	17	11	0.8	0.6	0.9	0.9	48.6	51.4
Wallowa	4,074	1,203	1,630	1,209	32	421	R	29.5	40.0	29.7	0.8	32	7	5	0.3	0.2	0.3	0.3	42.5	57.5
Wasco	10,973	4,663	3,242	3,008	60	1,421	D	42.5	29.5	27.4	0.5	8	30	17	0.8	0.8	0.7	0.8	59.0	41.0
Washington	167,195	67,528	57,146	41,575	946	10,382	D	40.4	34.2	24.9	0.6	10	24	30	11.4	10.9	12.0	11.7	54.2	45.8
Wheeler	860	267	357	227	9	90	R	31.0	41.5	26.4	1.0	29	4	22	<.1	<.1	<.1	<.1	42.8	57.2
Yamhill	31,406	11,148	11,693	8,312	253	545	R	35.5	37.2	26.5	0.8	19	15	21	2.1	1.8	2.5	2.3	48.8	51.2
OREGON	1,462,643	621,314	475,757	354,091	11,481	145,557	D	42.5	32.5	24.2	0.8				100.0	100.0	100.0	100.0	56.6	43.4

Table F. — Vote for U.S. Senator: November 3, 1992, General Election

County	Total	AuCoin (DEM)	Packwood (REP)	Other	Plurality Total	Party	Percent of total vote DEM	REP	Other	Rank DEM	Rank REP	Rank Other	Percent contribution to state vote Total	DEM	REP	Other
Baker	7,249	2,283	4,847	119	2,564	R	31.5	66.9	1.6	30	7	11	0.5	0.4	0.7	0.6
Benton	36,532	18,300	17,405	827	895	D	50.1	47.6	2.3	6	31	7	2.7	2.9	2.4	4.4
Clackamas	142,305	63,998	77,210	1,097	13,212	R	45.0	54.3	0.8	10	27	20	10.3	10.0	10.8	5.9
Clatsop	16,170	8,927	7,173	70	1,754	D	55.2	44.4	0.4	2	35	29	1.2	1.4	1.0	0.4
Columbia	18,689	9,056	9,042	591	14	D	48.5	48.4	3.2	7	30	3	1.4	1.4	1.3	3.2
Coos	28,433	11,973	15,809	651	3,836	R	42.1	55.6	2.3	13	25	6	2.1	1.9	2.2	3.5
Crook	6,942	2,165	4,658	119	2,493	R	31.2	67.1	1.7	31	6	10	0.5	0.3	0.6	0.6
Curry	10,647	3,913	6,611	123	2,698	R	36.8	62.1	1.2	21	14	16	0.8	0.6	0.9	0.7
Deschutes	42,168	15,395	25,920	853	10,525	R	36.5	61.5	2.0	23	17	8	3.1	2.4	3.6	4.6
Douglas	43,819	15,023	28,663	133	13,640	R	34.3	65.4	0.3	26	11	31	3.2	2.3	4.0	0.7
Gilliam	977	374	591	12	217	R	38.3	60.5	1.2	18	20	14	<.1	<.1	<.1	<.1
Grant	3,869	1,287	2,574	8	1,287	R	33.3	66.5	0.2	27	8	34	0.3	0.2	0.4	<.1
Harney	3,220	880	2,340	0	1,460	R	27.3	72.7	0.0	34	3	35	0.2	0.1	0.3	0.0
Hood River	7,547	3,179	4,334	34	1,155	R	42.1	57.4	0.5	12	22	28	0.5	0.5	0.6	0.2
Jackson	58,836	25,470	33,046	320	7,576	R	43.3	56.2	0.5	11	23	25	4.3	4.0	4.6	1.7
Jefferson	5,785	2,148	3,502	135	1,354	R	37.1	60.5	2.3	20	19	5	0.4	0.3	0.5	0.7
Josephine	31,912	11,361	19,742	809	8,381	R	35.6	61.9	2.5	24	15	4	2.3	1.8	2.8	4.3
Klamath	26,055	7,585	18,283	187	10,698	R	29.1	70.2	0.7	32	5	23	1.9	1.2	2.5	1.0
Lake	3,416	826	2,590	0	1,764	R	24.2	75.8	0.0	36	1	36	0.2	0.1	0.4	0.0
Lane	145,264	77,296	67,268	700	10,028	D	53.2	46.3	0.5	3	33	27	10.6	12.1	9.4	3.7
Lincoln	20,563	10,692	9,746	125	946	D	52.0	47.4	0.6	5	32	24	1.5	1.7	1.4	0.7
Linn	39,326	15,101	23,823	402	8,722	R	38.4	60.6	1.0	17	18	18	2.9	2.4	3.3	2.1
Malheur	10,351	2,953	7,362	36	4,409	R	28.5	71.1	0.3	33	4	30	0.8	0.5	1.0	0.2
Marion	105,741	42,748	59,302	3,691	16,554	R	40.4	56.1	3.5	15	24	2	7.7	6.7	8.3	19.7
Morrow	3,366	1,281	2,078	7	797	R	38.1	61.7	0.2	19	16	33	0.2	0.2	0.3	<.1
Multnomah	291,020	170,839	115,905	4,276	54,934	D	58.7	39.8	1.5	1	36	13	21.1	26.7	16.2	22.8
Polk	21,621	8,693	12,697	231	4,004	R	40.2	58.7	1.1	16	21	17	1.6	1.4	1.8	1.2
Sherman	1,070	393	669	8	276	R	36.7	62.5	0.7	22	13	21	<.1	<.1	<.1	<.1
Tillamook	10,957	5,698	5,067	192	631	D	52.0	46.2	1.8	4	34	9	0.8	0.9	0.7	1.0
Umatilla	21,759	7,677	13,921	161	6,244	R	35.3	64.0	0.7	25	12	22	1.6	1.2	1.9	0.9
Union	11,045	3,671	7,317	57	3,646	R	33.2	66.2	0.5	28	10	26	0.8	0.6	1.0	0.3
Wallowa	3,875	1,041	2,823	11	1,782	R	26.9	72.9	0.3	35	2	32	0.3	0.2	0.4	<.1
Wasco	10,525	4,811	5,547	167	736	R	45.7	52.7	1.6	8	29	12	0.8	0.8	0.8	0.9
Washington	154,143	70,299	82,392	1,452	12,093	R	45.6	53.5	0.9	9	28	19	11.2	11.0	11.5	7.8
Wheeler	815	263	542	10	279	R	32.3	66.5	1.2	29	9	15	<.1	<.1	<.1	<.1
Yamhill	30,021	12,252	16,656	1,113	4,404	R	40.8	55.5	3.7	14	26	1	2.2	1.9	2.3	5.9
OREGON	1,376,033	639,851	717,455	18,727	77,604	R	46.5	52.1	1.4				100.0	100.0	100.0	100.0

Table H. — Vote for U.S. Representative in Congress: November 3, 1992, General Election

Congressional district and county	Total	Democrat (DEM)	Republican (REP)	Other	Plurality Total	Plurality Party	Percent of total vote DEM	Percent of total vote REP	Percent of total vote Other	Rank within district DEM	Rank within district REP	Rank within district Other	Percent contribution to district vote Total	Percent contribution to district vote DEM	Percent contribution to district vote REP	Percent contribution to district vote Other
District 1	**294,154**	**152,917**	**140,986**	**251**	**11,931**	**D**	**52.0**	**47.9**	**<.1**				**100.0**	**100.0**	**100.0**	**100.0**
Clackamas (pt)	19,412	9,549	9,861	2	312	R	49.2	50.8	<.1	5	2	5	6.6	6.2	7.0	0.8
Clatsop	15,534	8,458	7,076	0	1,382	D	54.4	45.6	0.0	2	5	6	5.3	5.5	5.0	0.0
Columbia	18,980	9,625	9,285	70	340	D	50.7	48.9	0.4	3	4	2	6.5	6.3	6.6	27.9
Multnomah (pt)	53,768	35,917	17,813	38	18,104	D	66.8	33.1	<.1	1	6	3	18.3	23.5	12.6	15.1
Washington	155,762	76,871	78,867	24	1,996	R	49.4	50.6	<.1	4	3	4	53.0	50.3	55.9	9.6
Yamhill	30,698	12,497	18,084	117	5,587	R	40.7	58.9	0.4	6	1	1	10.4	8.2	12.8	46.6
District 2	**274,478**	**90,036**	**184,163**	**279**	**94,127**	**R**	**32.8**	**67.1**	**0.1**				**100.0**	**100.0**	**100.0**	**100.0**
Baker	7,219	1,917	5,287	15	3,370	R	26.6	73.2	0.2	13	8	3	2.6	2.1	2.9	5.4
Crook	6,922	1,939	4,972	11	3,033	R	28.0	71.8	0.2	11	10	4	2.5	2.2	2.7	3.9
Deschutes	42,648	15,869	26,751	28	10,882	R	37.2	62.7	<.1	1	20	9	15.5	17.6	14.5	10.0
Gilliam	997	245	751	1	506	R	24.6	75.3	0.1	14	7	7	0.4	0.3	0.4	0.4
Grant	3,894	886	3,008	0	2,122	R	22.8	77.2	0.0	17	4	16	1.4	1.0	1.6	0.0
Harney	3,333	541	2,792	0	2,251	R	16.2	83.8	0.0	20	1	17	1.2	0.6	1.5	0.0
Hood River	7,239	2,548	4,691	0	2,143	R	35.2	64.8	0.0	4	17	18	2.6	2.8	2.5	0.0
Jackson	74,106	27,516	46,579	11	19,063	R	37.1	62.9	<.1	2	19	15	27.0	30.6	25.3	3.9
Jefferson	5,851	1,871	3,973	7	2,102	R	32.0	67.9	0.1	7	14	6	2.1	2.1	2.2	2.5
Josephine (pt)	29,366	9,428	19,850	88	10,422	R	32.1	67.6	0.3	6	15	2	10.7	10.5	10.8	31.5
Klamath	26,490	7,531	18,953	6	11,422	R	28.4	71.5	<.1	9	12	13	9.7	8.4	10.3	2.2
Lake	3,737	846	2,891	0	2,045	R	22.6	77.4	0.0	18	3	19	1.4	0.9	1.6	0.0
Malheur	10,341	2,380	7,959	2	5,579	R	23.0	77.0	<.1	16	5	14	3.8	2.6	4.3	0.7
Morrow	3,373	950	2,421	2	1,471	R	28.2	71.8	<.1	10	11	10	1.2	1.1	1.3	0.7
Sherman	1,101	299	801	1	502	R	27.2	72.8	<.1	12	9	8	0.4	0.3	0.4	0.4
Umatilla	21,625	6,848	14,691	86	7,843	R	31.7	67.9	0.4	8	13	1	7.9	7.6	8.0	30.8
Union	11,075	3,613	7,456	6	3,843	R	32.6	67.3	<.1	5	16	11	4.0	4.0	4.0	2.2
Wallowa	3,924	768	3,154	2	2,386	R	19.6	80.4	<.1	19	2	12	1.4	0.9	1.7	0.7
Wasco	10,400	3,846	6,541	13	2,695	R	37.0	62.9	0.1	3	18	5	3.8	4.3	3.6	4.7
Wheeler	837	195	642	0	447	R	23.3	76.7	0.0	15	6	20	0.3	0.2	0.3	0.0
District 3	**269,879**	**208,028**	**50,235**	**11,616**	**157,793**	**D**	**77.1**	**18.6**	**4.3**				**100.0**	**100.0**	**100.0**	**100.0**
Clackamas (pt)	34,872	24,173	9,255	1,444	14,918	D	69.3	26.5	4.1	2	1	2	12.9	11.6	18.4	12.4
Multnomah (pt)	235,007	183,855	40,980	10,172	142,875	D	78.2	17.4	4.3	1	2	1	87.1	88.4	81.6	87.6
District 4	**279,299**	**199,372**	**79,733**	**194**	**119,639**	**D**	**71.4**	**28.5**	**<.1**				**100.0**	**100.0**	**100.0**	**100.0**
Benton (pt)	7,438	5,172	2,260	6	2,912	D	69.5	30.4	<.1	3	5	4	2.7	2.6	2.8	3.1
Coos	28,982	20,794	8,136	52	12,658	D	71.7	28.1	0.2	2	6	2	10.4	10.4	10.2	26.8
Curry	10,684	6,737	3,929	18	2,808	D	63.1	36.8	0.2	6	2	3	3.8	3.4	4.9	9.3
Douglas	44,137	28,085	16,050	2	12,035	D	63.6	36.4	<.1	5	3	6	15.8	14.1	20.1	1.0
Josephine (pt)	2,808	1,570	1,202	36	368	D	55.9	42.8	1.3	7	1	1	1.0	0.8	1.5	18.6
Lane	145,947	111,821	34,046	80	77,775	D	76.6	23.3	<.1	1	7	5	52.3	56.1	42.7	41.2
Linn	39,303	25,193	14,110	0	11,083	D	64.1	35.9	0.0	4	4	7	14.1	12.6	17.7	0.0
District 5	**272,944**	**174,443**	**97,984**	**517**	**76,459**	**D**	**63.9**	**35.9**	**0.2**				**100.0**	**100.0**	**100.0**	**100.0**
Benton (pt)	28,566	19,932	8,550	84	11,382	D	69.8	29.9	0.3	2	5	2	10.5	11.4	8.7	16.2
Clackamas (pt)	87,883	55,597	32,272	14	23,325	D	63.3	36.7	<.1	4	3	5	32.2	31.9	32.9	2.7
Lincoln	18,003	12,033	5,970	0	6,063	D	66.8	33.2	0.0	3	4	6	6.6	6.9	6.1	0.0
Marion	106,585	66,339	39,848	398	26,491	D	62.2	37.4	0.4	5	2	1	39.1	38.0	40.7	77.0
Polk	20,704	12,451	8,240	13	4,211	D	60.1	39.8	<.1	6	1	4	7.6	7.1	8.4	2.5
Tillamook	11,203	8,091	3,104	8	4,987	D	72.2	27.7	<.1	1	6	3	4.1	4.6	3.2	1.5
OREGON	**1,390,754**	**824,796**	**553,101**	**12,857**	**271,695**	**D**	**59.3**	**39.8**	**0.9**							

Table I. – **Vote for Presidential Preference: May 19, 1992, Democratic Primary Election**

County	Total	Clinton	Brown	Tsongas	Miscellaneous	McCarthy	LaRouche	Woods	Agran	Clinton	Brown	Tsongas	Rank Clinton	Rank Brown	Rank Tsongas	Total	Clinton	Brown	Tsongas
Baker	1,914	956	344	210	324	24	28	14	14	49.9	18.0	11.0	10	30	14	0.5	0.6	0.3	0.6
Benton	9,832	3,762	4,078	1,365	206	229	71	46	75	38.3	41.5	13.9	35	1	2	2.8	2.4	3.7	3.7
Clackamas	31,678	14,221	10,159	4,029	1,897	685	314	222	151	44.9	32.1	12.7	25	7	5	8.9	8.9	9.2	10.8
Clatsop	4,675	2,222	1,406	540	299	103	52	24	29	47.5	30.1	11.6	14	11	10	1.3	1.4	1.3	1.5
Columbia	6,014	2,775	1,276	579	1,176	98	52	35	23	46.1	21.2	9.6	18	25	26	1.7	1.7	1.2	1.6
Coos	8,965	3,986	2,187	668	1,811	132	74	71	36	44.5	24.4	7.5	26	18	36	2.5	2.5	2.0	1.8
Crook	1,772	840	323	161	398	16	18	11	5	47.4	18.2	9.1	15	29	28	0.5	0.5	0.3	0.4
Curry	2,727	1,187	634	207	626	34	20	7	12	43.5	23.2	7.6	32	21	35	0.8	0.7	0.6	0.6
Deschutes	9,990	3,741	3,128	986	1,886	129	59	29	32	37.4	31.3	9.9	36	9	24	2.8	2.3	2.8	2.7
Douglas	9,805	4,938	2,705	1,067	610	173	140	99	73	50.4	27.6	10.9	9	14	16	2.8	3.1	2.4	2.9
Gilliam	262	135	59	32	27	3	4	1	1	51.5	22.5	12.2	4	23	7	<.1	<.1	<.1	<.1
Grant	1,114	563	190	123	172	24	22	12	8	50.5	17.1	11.0	6	33	13	0.3	0.4	0.2	0.3
Harney	806	407	149	72	143	10	14	9	2	50.5	18.5	8.9	7	28	30	0.2	0.3	0.1	0.2
Hood River	2,219	1,120	656	259	86	42	29	13	14	50.5	29.6	11.7	8	12	9	0.6	0.7	0.6	0.7
Jackson	14,828	6,763	5,637	1,268	732	192	101	66	69	45.6	38.0	8.6	21	2	32	4.2	4.2	5.1	3.4
Jefferson	1,477	650	343	149	286	22	12	10	5	44.0	23.2	10.1	29	22	21	0.4	0.4	0.3	0.4
Josephine	7,237	3,074	2,302	620	1,049	83	64	20	25	42.5	31.8	8.6	33	8	31	2.0	1.9	2.1	1.7
Klamath	6,858	3,290	1,668	613	1,049	90	78	34	36	48.0	24.3	8.9	13	19	29	1.9	2.1	1.5	1.7
Lake	1,110	615	222	112	94	28	25	9	5	55.4	20.0	10.1	1	26	20	0.3	0.4	0.2	0.3
Lane	41,647	19,413	15,076	3,391	2,260	873	260	186	188	46.6	36.2	8.1	17	3	34	11.8	12.1	13.6	9.1
Lincoln	5,913	2,694	1,795	590	574	125	68	28	39	45.6	30.4	10.0	22	10	22	1.7	1.7	1.6	1.6
Linn	10,459	5,449	2,785	1,141	495	246	170	111	62	52.1	26.6	10.9	3	15	15	3.0	3.4	2.5	3.1
Malheur	1,989	898	321	242	417	40	38	17	16	45.1	16.1	12.2	24	35	8	0.6	0.6	0.3	0.7
Marion	22,791	10,072	6,501	2,305	3,175	407	164	90	77	44.2	28.5	10.1	28	13	19	6.4	6.3	5.9	6.2
Morrow	805	396	141	113	131	16	4	2	2	49.2	17.5	14.0	11	31	1	0.2	0.2	0.1	0.3
Multnomah	88,369	38,716	29,519	9,033	8,062	1,752	602	338	347	43.8	33.4	10.2	31	4	18	24.9	24.2	26.7	24.3
Polk	5,118	2,356	1,645	645	262	96	37	41	36	46.0	32.1	12.6	20	6	6	1.4	1.5	1.5	1.7
Sherman	355	161	62	47	67	5	8	1	4	45.4	17.5	13.2	23	32	4	0.1	0.1	<.1	0.1
Tillamook	4,016	1,900	858	341	770	78	36	15	18	47.3	21.4	8.5	16	24	33	1.1	1.2	0.8	0.9
Umatilla	4,624	2,448	879	528	400	94	175	64	36	52.9	19.0	11.4	2	27	11	1.3	1.5	0.8	1.4
Union	2,931	1,229	687	285	614	40	33	25	18	41.9	23.4	9.7	34	20	25	0.8	0.8	0.6	0.8
Wallowa	1,175	541	184	121	263	26	18	13	9	46.0	15.7	10.3	19	36	17	0.3	0.3	0.2	0.3
Wasco	2,890	1,471	754	322	208	60	39	21	15	50.9	26.1	11.1	5	16	12	0.8	0.9	0.7	0.9
Washington	30,918	13,703	10,113	4,280	1,715	601	206	160	140	44.3	32.7	13.8	27	5	3	8.7	8.6	9.2	11.5
Wheeler	236	114	39	22	42	7	5	2	5	48.3	16.5	9.3	12	34	27	<.1	<.1	<.1	<.1
Yamhill	6,813	2,996	1,669	673	1,214	131	56	49	25	44.0	24.5	9.9	30	17	23	1.9	1.9	1.5	1.8
OREGON	354,332	159,802	110,494	37,139	33,540	6,714	3,096	1,895	1,652	45.1	31.2	10.5				100.0	100.0	100.0	100.0

Table J. — Vote for Presidential Preference: May 19, 1992, Republican Primary Election

County	Top candidates Total	Bush	Bu-chanan	Miscel-laneous	Duke	Percent of total vote Bush	Bu-chanan	Miscel-laneous	Duke	Rank Bush	Bu-chanan	Miscel-laneous	Duke	Percent contribution to state vote Total	Bush	Bu-chanan	Miscel-laneous	Duke
Baker	1,937	1,221	335	345	36	63.0	17.3	17.8	1.9	27	20	12	28	0.6	0.6	0.6	1.0	0.5
Benton	8,722	6,322	1,884	290	226	72.5	21.6	3.3	2.6	2	5	36	9	2.9	3.1	3.3	0.8	3.4
Clackamas	30,208	21,206	6,151	2,185	666	70.2	20.4	7.2	2.2	10	9	27	17	9.9	10.4	10.7	6.1	10.0
Clatsop	3,207	2,200	704	211	92	68.6	22.0	6.6	2.9	14	3	31	6	1.1	1.1	1.2	0.6	1.4
Columbia	3,226	1,945	570	634	77	60.3	17.7	19.7	2.4	31	18	7	14	1.1	1.0	1.0	1.8	1.2
Coos	5,941	3,444	931	1,451	115	58.0	15.7	24.4	1.9	35	28	2	25	2.0	1.7	1.6	4.1	1.7
Crook	1,812	1,207	230	354	21	66.6	12.7	19.5	1.2	18	36	8	36	0.6	0.6	0.4	1.0	0.3
Curry	3,136	1,706	549	823	58	54.4	17.5	26.2	1.8	36	19	1	29	1.0	0.8	1.0	2.3	0.9
Deschutes	10,866	6,750	1,508	2,461	147	62.1	13.9	22.6	1.4	28	33	4	35	3.6	3.3	2.6	6.9	2.2
Douglas	10,325	7,265	2,230	549	281	70.4	21.6	5.3	2.7	9	6	33	7	3.4	3.6	3.9	1.5	4.2
Gilliam	291	207	50	28	6	71.1	17.2	9.6	2.1	5	22	24	21	<.1	0.1	<.1	<.1	<.1
Grant	1,260	838	227	146	49	66.5	18.0	11.6	3.9	19	16	22	2	0.4	0.4	0.4	0.4	0.7
Harney	977	599	128	227	23	61.3	13.1	23.2	2.4	29	35	3	16	0.3	0.3	0.2	0.6	0.3
Hood River	2,142	1,542	397	147	56	72.0	18.5	6.9	2.6	3	15	30	8	0.7	0.8	0.7	0.4	0.8
Jackson	15,000	10,092	3,653	929	326	67.3	24.4	6.2	2.2	17	1	32	19	4.9	4.9	6.3	2.6	4.9
Jefferson	1,552	1,028	215	280	29	66.2	13.9	18.0	1.9	21	34	11	26	0.5	0.5	0.4	0.8	0.4
Josephine	10,461	6,226	2,263	1,764	208	59.5	21.6	16.9	2.0	32	4	14	24	3.4	3.1	3.9	4.9	3.1
Klamath	7,944	5,353	1,342	1,101	148	67.4	16.9	13.9	1.9	16	24	19	27	2.6	2.6	2.3	3.1	2.2
Lake	1,338	928	231	133	46	69.4	17.3	9.9	3.4	13	21	23	3	0.4	0.5	0.4	0.4	0.7
Lane	27,437	19,401	5,228	2,154	654	70.7	19.1	7.9	2.4	6	13	25	15	9.0	9.5	9.1	6.0	9.8
Lincoln	4,315	2,637	985	583	110	61.1	22.8	13.5	2.5	30	2	20	10	1.4	1.3	1.7	1.6	1.6
Linn	9,562	6,749	2,036	480	297	70.6	21.3	5.0	3.1	8	7	35	4	3.1	3.3	3.5	1.3	4.5
Malheur	3,463	2,419	490	492	62	69.9	14.1	14.2	1.8	12	32	18	30	1.1	1.2	0.8	1.4	0.9
Marion	25,613	17,297	3,850	4,015	451	67.5	15.0	15.7	1.8	15	30	15	31	8.4	8.5	6.7	11.2	6.8
Morrow	760	488	130	130	12	64.2	17.1	17.1	1.6	24	23	13	33	0.2	0.2	0.2	0.4	0.2
Multnomah	50,548	31,916	9,968	7,620	1,044	63.1	19.7	15.1	2.1	26	11	17	20	16.6	15.6	17.3	21.3	15.7
Polk	5,765	4,235	1,089	297	144	73.5	18.9	5.2	2.5	1	14	34	11	1.9	2.1	1.9	0.8	2.2
Sherman	444	295	69	67	13	66.4	15.5	15.1	2.9	20	29	16	5	0.1	0.1	0.1	0.2	0.2
Tillamook	2,806	1,647	498	604	57	58.7	17.7	21.5	2.0	34	17	6	22	0.9	0.8	0.9	1.7	0.9
Umatilla	4,668	3,270	787	361	250	70.1	16.9	7.7	5.4	11	25	26	1	1.5	1.6	1.4	1.0	3.7
Union	2,890	1,701	465	653	71	58.9	16.1	22.6	2.5	33	27	5	13	1.0	0.8	0.8	1.8	1.1
Wallowa	1,296	843	187	234	32	65.0	14.4	18.1	2.5	22	31	10	12	0.4	0.4	0.3	0.7	0.5
Wasco	2,460	1,739	494	173	54	70.7	20.1	7.0	2.2	7	10	29	18	0.8	0.9	0.9	0.5	0.8
Washington	33,611	24,043	6,520	2,375	673	71.5	19.4	7.1	2.0	4	12	28	23	11.1	11.8	11.3	6.6	10.1
Wheeler	331	213	69	44	5	64.4	20.8	13.3	1.5	23	8	21	34	0.1	0.1	0.1	0.1	<.1
Yamhill	7,845	4,985	1,267	1,465	128	63.5	16.2	18.7	1.6	25	26	9	32	2.6	2.4	2.2	4.1	1.9
OREGON	304,159	203,957	57,730	35,805	6,667	67.1	19.0	11.8	2.2					100.0	100.0	100.0	100.0	100.0

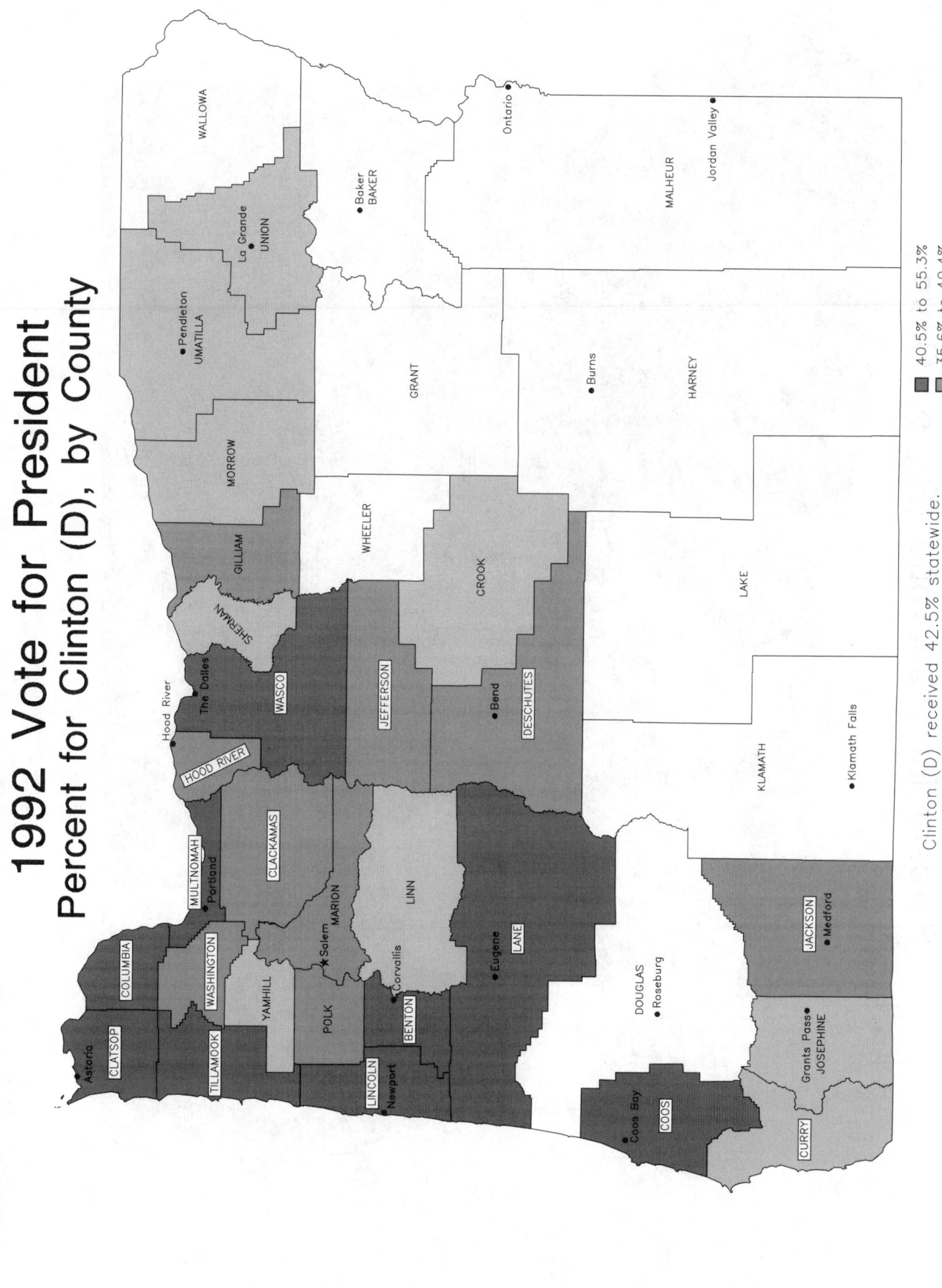

1992 Vote for President
Percent for Clinton (D), by County

Clinton (D) received 42.5% statewide.

A framed county name indicates a county carried by the winner.

40.5% to 55.3%
35.6% to 40.4%
31.9% to 35.5%
23.8% to 31.8%

Copyright © 1993 by Election Data Services, Inc.

Oregon 781

1992 Vote for U.S. Senator
Percent for Packwood (R), by County

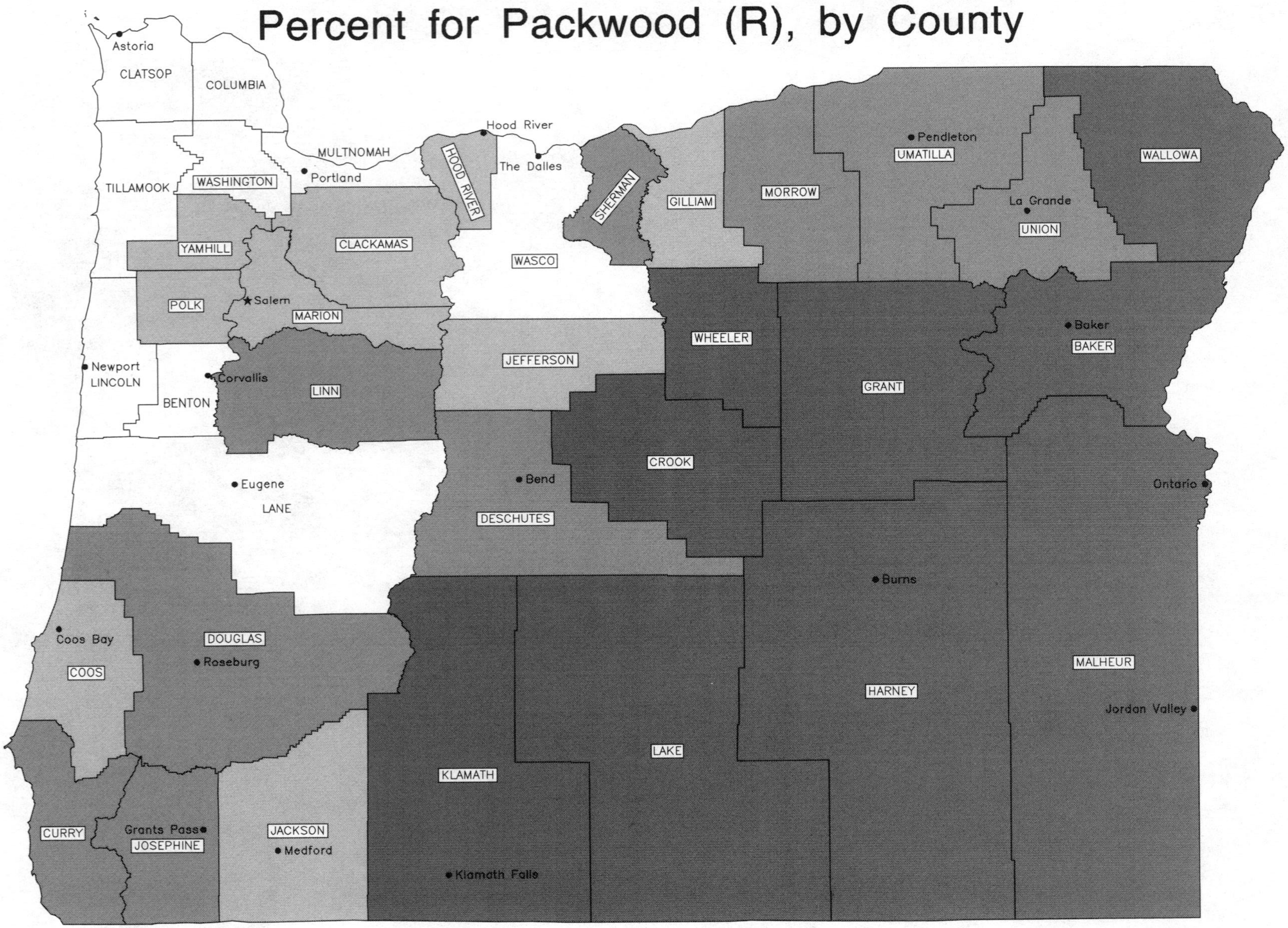

WALLOWA

UNION
La Grande

BAKER
Baker

Ontario

MALHEUR
Jordan Valley

UMATILLA
Pendleton

MORROW

GRANT

HARNEY
Burns

GILLIAM

WHEELER

CROOK

LAKE

SHERMAN

WASCO

JEFFERSON

DESCHUTES
Bend

KLAMATH
Klamath Falls

Hood River
The Dalles

HOOD RIVER

MULTNOMAH
Portland

CLACKAMAS

MARION
Salem

LINN

LANE
Eugene

Corvallis

DOUGLAS
Roseburg

JACKSON
Medford

COLUMBIA

CLATSOP
Astoria

WASHINGTON

TILLAMOOK

YAMHILL

POLK

BENTON

LINCOLN
Newport

COOS
Coos Bay

JOSEPHINE
Grants Pass

CURRY

Packwood (R) received 52.1% statewide.

A framed county name indicates
a county carried by the winner.

- 66.3% to 75.8%
- 60.6% to 66.2%
- 53.6% to 60.5%
- 39.8% to 53.5%

782 Oregon

PENNSYLVANIA

Congressional Districts 21
   Average Population 565,793
State Senate Districts 50
   Average Population 237,633
State House Districts 203
   Average Population 58,530

Electoral College Votes..23
Counties 67
Voting Precincts 9,431

Alternative Registration Methods:
   ....Deputized Registrars, Mail-in

Registration Deadline (Days before Election) 30

Voting Equipment Use (Counties)

Datavote Punch Card	0	Paper Ballot	8
Electronic	2	Other Punch Card	0
Lever Machine	28	Mixed Systems	0
Optical Scanner	29		

Party Control	DEM	REP	IND	VAC
1993 State Senate	25	24	0	1
1992 State Senate	24	26	0	0
1993 State House	105	98	0	0
1992 State House	107	96	0	0

Population Statistics 1990

Race/ Ethnicity	Total Population		Voting Age Population		Voting Age Population % of total population
	Number	%	Number	%	
Non-Hispanic					
White	10,422,058	87.7	8,076,128	88.9	77.5
Black	1,072,459	9.0	758,770	8.4	70.8
Asian/Pacific Islander	134,056	1.1	93,242	1.0	69.6
Native American	13,505	0.1	10,114	0.1	74.9
Other	7,303	<.1	2,539	<.1	34.8
All Hispanic	232,262	2.0	146,040	1.6	62.9
TOTAL	11,881,643	100.0	9,086,833	100.0	76.5

Estimated Voting Age Population 1992 (VAP) 9,129,000
Number of Registered Voters................................. 5,993,002
   % of estimated VAP.. 65.6
Voter Turnout (Highest Office) 4,960,233
   % of VAP 54.3
   % of Registration 82.8
Persons Not Voting—of Voting Age 4,168,767
   % of VAP 45.7
Persons Not Voting—of Registered 1,032,769
   % of Registration 17.2
Straight Ticket Voting .... Yes, Exception

State Officials and Members of Congress

Governor:
Robert Casey (D) 1986, elected to a four-year term in 1990.

U.S. Senators:
Arlen Specter (R) 1980, elected to a six-year term in 1992.
Harris Wofford (D) 1991, elected to a three-year term in 1991.

U.S. Representative in Congress:
(District, Name, Party, Date first elected)

1. Foglietta (D) 1980
2. Blackwell (D) 1991
3. Borski (D) 1982
4. Klink (D) 1992
5. Clinger (R) 1978
6. Holden (D) 1992
7. Weldon (R) 1986
8. Greenwood (R) 1992
9. Shuster (R) 1972
10. McDade (R) 1962
11. Kanjorski (D) 1984
12. Murtha (D) 1974
13. Margolies-Mezvinsky (D) 1992
14. Coyne (D) 1980
15. McHale (D) 1992
16. Walker (R) 1976
17. Gekas (R) 1982
18. Santorum (R) 1990
19. Goodling (R) 1974
20. Murphy (D) 1976
21. Ridge (R) 1982

Candidates: General Election, November 3, 1992

Candidate(s)	Total vote	Percent	Party	Status	First elected
President/Vice President					
Clinton/Gore..	2,239,164	45.15%	Democrat	Challenger	1992
Bush/Quayle...	1,791,841	36.13%	Republican	Incumbent	1988
Perot/Stockdale......................................	902,667	18.20%	Penn. for Perot	Challenger	
Marrou/Lord..	21,477	0.43%	Libertarian	Challenger	
Fulani/Munoz..	4,661	0.09%	New Alliance	Challenger	
U.S. Senator					
Arlen Specter...	2,358,125	49.10%	Republican	Incumbent	1980
Lynn Yeakel	2,224,966	46.33%	Democrat	Challenger	
John Perry	219,319	4.57%	Libertarian	Challenger	
U.S. Senator (Special Election, November 5, 1991):[1]					
Harrison Wofford.....................................	1,860,760	55.01%	Democrat	Incumbent	1991
Richard Thornburgh	1,521,986	44.99%	Republican	Challenger	
Governor (No Contest)					
U.S. Representative in Congress					
District 1					
Thomas Foglietta	150,172	80.92%	Democrat	Incumbent	1980
Craig Snyder	35,419	19.08%	Republican	Challenger	
District 2					
Lucien Blackwell.....................................	164,355	76.83%	Democrat	Incumbent	1991
Larry Hollin	47,906	22.39%	Republican	Challenger	
Mark Wyatt	1,666	0.78%	Socialist Workers	Challenger	
District 3					
Robert Borski	130,828	58.94%	Democrat	Incumbent	1982
Charles Dougherty	86,787	39.10%	Republican	Challenger	
John Hughes	4,356	1.96%	Independent	Challenger	
District 4					
Ron Klink..	186,684	78.46%	Democrat	Challenger	
Gordon Johnston....................................	48,484	20.38%	Republican	Challenger	
Drew Ley	2,754	1.16%	None of Above	Challenger	
District 5					
Bill Clinger[2]	188,911	100.00%	Republican	Incumbent	1978
District 6					
Tim Holden...	108,312	52.07%	Democrat	Challenger	
John E. Jones	99,694	47.93%	Republican	Challenger	
District 7					
Curt Weldon..	180,648	65.95%	Republican	Incumbent	1986
Frank Daly	91,623	33.45%	Democrat	Challenger	
William Hickman......................................	1,627	0.59%	Natural Law	Challenger	
District 8					
Jim Greenwood.......................................	129,593	51.93%	Republican	Challenger	
Peter Kostmayer	114,095	45.72%	Democrat	Incumbent	1976
William Magerman	5,850	2.34%	Independent	Challenger	
District 9					
Bud Shuster[2]	182,406	100.00%	Republican	Incumbent	1972
District 10					
Joseph McDade[2]	189,414	90.39%	Republican	Incumbent	1962
Albert Smith	20,134	9.61%	Libertarian	Challenger	

[1]For remaining three years of term of the late Senator John Heinz (R). Incumbent Harris Wofford (D) appointed as interim senator in May 1991. [2]Candidate's name appears on ballot with the party designation Democrat and Republican.

Candidate(s)	Total vote	Percent	Party	Status	First elected
U.S. Representative in Congress (cont)					
District 11					
Paul Kanjorski	138,875	67.09%	Democrat	Incumbent	1984
Michael Fescina	68,112	32.91%	Republican	Challenger	
District 12					
John P. Murtha	166,916	100.00%	Democrat	Incumbent	1974
District 13					
Marjorie Margolies-Mezvinsky	127,685	50.27%	Democrat	Challenger	
Jon D. Fox	126,312	49.73%	Republican	Challenger	
District 14					
William Coyne	165,633	72.32%	Democrat	Incumbent	1980
Byron King	61,311	26.77%	Republican	Challenger	
Joanne Kuniansky	1,300	0.57%	Socialist Workers	Challenger	
Paul Scherrer	794	0.35%	Workers League	Challenger	
District 15					
Paul McHale	111,419	52.23%	Democrat	Challenger	
Don Ritter	99,520	46.65%	Republican	Incumbent	1978
Eugene Nau	2,385	1.12%	Natural Law	Challenger	
District 16					
Robert S. Walker	137,823	64.84%	Republican	Incumbent	1976
Robert Peters	74,741	35.16%	Democrat	Challenger	
District 17					
George Gekas	150,158	69.51%	Republican	Incumbent	1982
Bill Sturges	65,881	30.49%	Democrat	Challenger	
District 18					
Rick Santorum	154,024	60.56%	Republican	Incumbent	1990
Frank Pecora	96,655	38.00%	Democrat	Challenger	
Denise Edwards	3,650	1.44%	New Independent	Challenger	
District 19					
Bill Goodling	98,599	45.31%	Republican	Incumbent	1974
Paul Kilker	74,798	34.38%	Democrat	Challenger	
Thomas Humbert	44,190	20.31%	Independent	Challenger	
District 20					
Austin Murphy	114,898	50.73%	Democrat	Incumbent	1976
Bill Townsend	111,591	49.27%	Republican	Challenger	
District 21					
Tom Ridge	150,729	68.04%	Republican	Incumbent	1982
John Harkins	70,802	31.96%	Democrat	Challenger	

Candidates: April 28, 1992, Primary Election

Candidate	Total vote	Percent	Candidate	Total vote	Percent
Presidential Preference, Democratic			**Presidential Preference, Republican**		
Bill Clinton	715,031	56.50%	George Bush	774,865	76.81%
Jerry Brown	325,543	25.72%	Patrick Buchanan	233,912	23.19%
Paul Tsongas	161,572	12.77%			
Lyndon LaRouche, Jr.	21,534	1.70%			
Tom Harkin	21,013	1.66%			
Bob Kerrey	20,802	1.64%			

Voter Registration and Turnout, 1948-1992 Elections

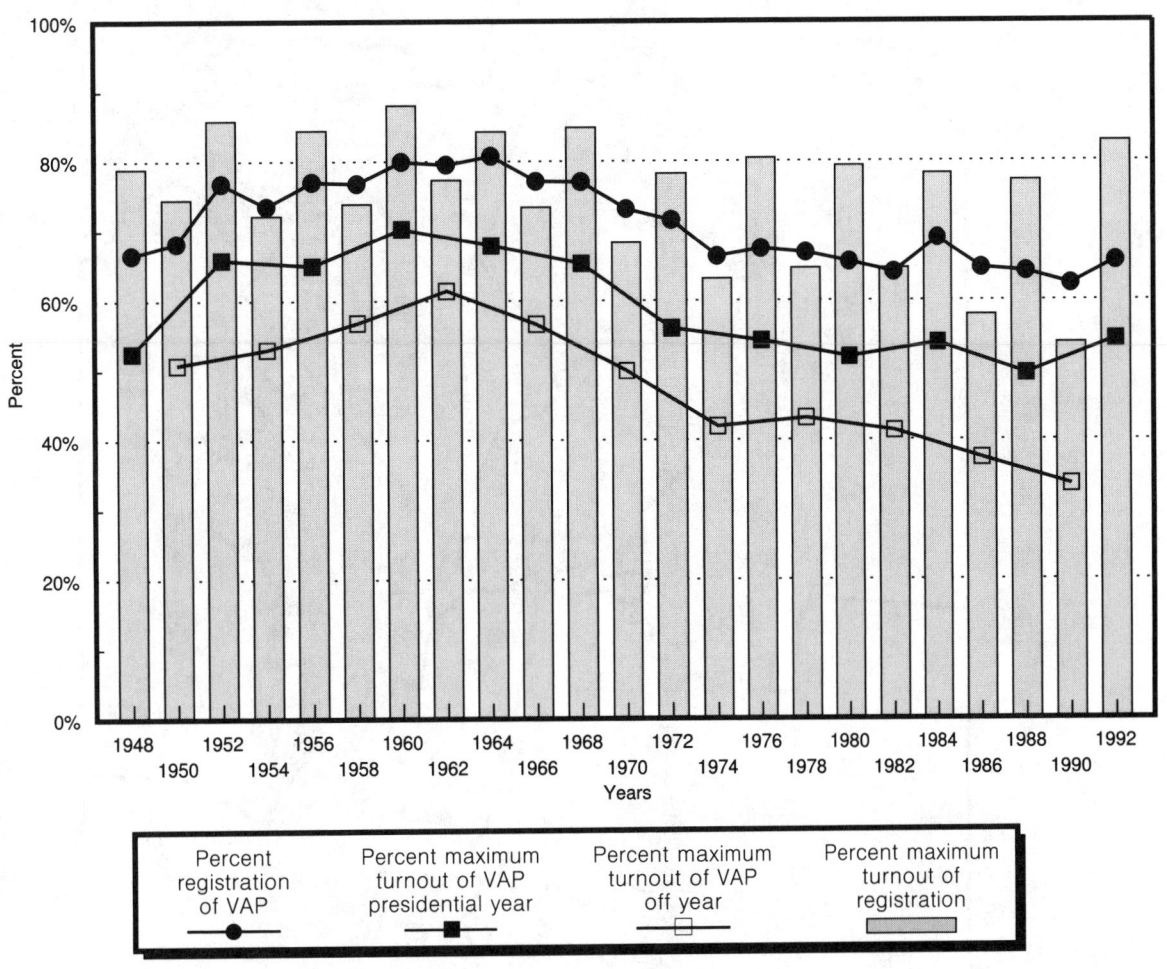

Year	Estimated Voting Age Population (VAP)	Voter registration (REG)				Voter turnout									
						Highest office						Maximum vote			
		Total	Percent of VAP	Rank by percent of VAP	Actual	Total	Office	Percent total REG	Rank by percent of REG	Percent of VAP	Rank by percent of VAP	Total	Percent total REG	Rank by percent of REG	Percent total VAP	Rank by percent of VAP
1992	9,129,000	5,993,002	65.6	41	-	4,959,810	P	82.8	5	54.3	32	4,959,810	82.8	11	54.3	33
1990	9,091,000	5,659,189	62.3	37	-	3,052,760	G	53.9	33	33.6	40	3,052,760	53.9	35	33.6	41
1988	9,171,000	5,875,943	64.1	39	-	4,536,251	P	77.2	12	49.5	32	4,536,251	77.2	15	49.5	34
1986	9,057,000	5,846,975	64.6	36	-	3,388,275	G	57.9	21	37.4	31	3,388,275	57.9	25	37.4	33
1984	8,989,000	6,193,702	68.9	35	-	4,844,903	P	78.2	12	53.9	28	4,844,903	78.2	15	53.9	30
1982	8,910,000	5,702,557	64.0	36	-	3,683,985	G	64.6	21	41.3	31	3,683,985	64.6	24	41.3	33
1980	8,787,000	5,754,087	65.5	37	- .	4,561,501	P	79.3	7	51.9	32	4,561,501	79.3	12	51.9	32
1978	8,673,000	5,796,510	66.8	31	-	3,741,969	G	64.6	8	43.1	19	3,741,969	64.6	9	43.1	22
1976	8,531,000	5,749,660	67.4	35	-	4,620,787	P	80.4	6	54.2	30	4,620,787	80.4	14	54.2	31
1974	8,342,000	5,529,047	66.3	33	-	3,491,234	G	63.1	16	41.9	26	3,491,234	63.1	18	41.9	32
1972	8,207,000	5,871,902	71.5	30	-	4,592,106	P	78.2	16	56.0	33	4,592,106	78.2	20	56.0	33
1970	7,412,000	5,419,551	73.1	23	-	3,700,060	G	68.3	16	49.9	27	3,700,060	68.3	19	49.9	29
1968	7,273,000	5,599,364	77.0	22	-	4,747,928	P	84.8	8	65.3	23	4,747,928	84.8	12	65.3	23
1966	7,159,000	5,519,001	77.1	20	-	4,050,668	S	73.4	11	56.6	16	4,050,668	73.4	12	56.6	18
1964	7,100,000	5,728,359	80.7	19	-	4,822,690	P	84.2	15	67.9	24	4,822,690	84.2	15	67.9	24
1962	7,135,000	5,673,497	79.5	14	-	4,383,475	S	77.3	7	61.4	10	4,383,475	77.3	7	61.4	11
1960	7,122,000	5,687,837	79.9	16	-	5,006,541	P	88.0	12	70.3	27	5,006,541	88.0	14	70.3	27
1958	7,028,000	5,397,407	76.8	15	-	3,988,622	S	73.9	12	56.8	16	3,988,622	73.9	13	56.8	18
1956	7,046,000	5,422,150	77.0	16	-	4,576,503	P	84.4	12	65.0	29	4,576,503	84.4	12	65.0	31
1954	7,017,000	5,154,734	73.5	16	-	3,720,457	G	72.2	9	53.0	18	3,720,457	72.2	9	53.0	21
1952	6,957,000	5,341,970	76.8	15	-	4,580,969	P	85.8	10	65.8	32	4,580,969	85.8	12	65.8	32
1950	6,985,000	4,761,660	68.2	14	-	3,548,703	S	74.5	7	50.8	22	3,548,703	74.5	8	50.8	24
1948	7,119,000	4,736,973	66.5	15	-	3,735,348	P	78.9	10	52.5	30	3,735,348	78.9	10	52.5	30

PENNSYLVANIA

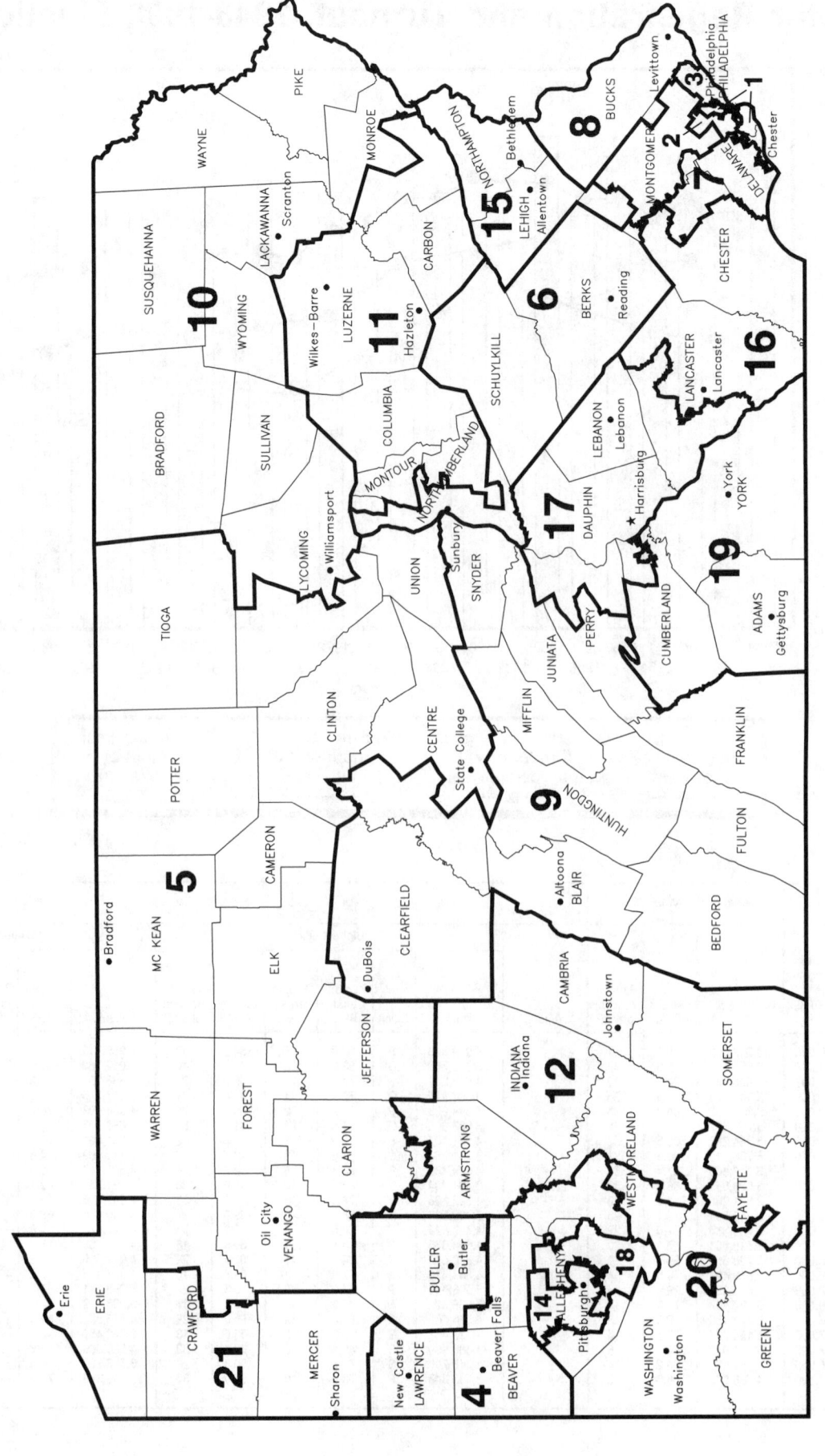

Congressional district boundaries effective March 3, 1992.

Table A. — 1990 Population by Race and Ethnic Origin

State/county code	County	Total persons	Percent of total persons Non-Hispanic White	Black	Asian and Pacific Islander	Native American	Other	Hispanic	Rank Total	Rank Non-Hispanic White	Black	Hispanic	Percent contribution to state population Total	Non-Hispanic White	Black	Hispanic
42 001	Adams	78,274	96.8	1.1	0.5	<.1	<.1	1.6	35	40	31	13	0.7	0.7	<.1	0.5
42 003	Allegheny	1,336,449	87.0	11.1	1.0	<.1	<.1	0.7	2	64	3	25	11.2	11.2	13.9	3.8
42 005	Armstrong	73,478	98.8	0.8	0.1	<.1	<.1	0.2	38	17	40	64	0.6	0.7	<.1	<.1
42 007	Beaver	186,093	93.4	5.6	0.2	0.1	<.1	0.6	19	55	7	27	1.6	1.7	1.0	0.5
42 009	Bedford	47,919	99.2	0.3	0.2	<.1	<.1	0.2	43	8	54	60	0.4	0.5	<.1	<.1
42 011	Berks	336,523	91.3	2.7	0.7	<.1	<.1	5.1	10	61	16	3	2.8	2.9	0.9	7.4
42 013	Blair	130,542	98.5	0.8	0.3	<.1	<.1	0.3	24	27	39	53	1.1	1.2	<.1	0.2
42 015	Bradford	60,967	98.8	0.2	0.3	0.2	<.1	0.4	40	16	55	49	0.5	0.6	<.1	<.1
42 017	Bucks	541,174	93.9	2.8	1.5	<.1	<.1	1.6	5	54	15	12	4.6	4.9	1.4	3.8
42 019	Butler	152,013	98.6	0.5	0.4	<.1	<.1	0.4	22	18	44	47	1.3	1.4	<.1	0.2
42 021	Cambria	163,029	96.8	2.3	0.2	<.1	<.1	0.6	20	39	19	28	1.4	1.5	0.3	0.4
42 023	Cameron	5,913	99.4	0.1	0.1	0.2	<.1	<.1	66	3	64	67	<.1	<.1	<.1	<.1
42 025	Carbon	56,846	98.5	0.2	0.3	<.1	<.1	0.9	42	25	59	21	0.5	0.5	<.1	0.2
42 027	Centre	123,786	93.4	2.2	3.1	0.1	<.1	1.1	25	56	21	18	1.0	1.1	0.3	0.6
42 029	Chester	376,396	90.2	6.2	1.1	0.1	<.1	2.3	7	63	5	9	3.2	3.3	2.2	3.7
42 031	Clarion	41,699	98.6	0.5	0.5	0.2	<.1	0.3	49	24	48	57	0.4	0.4	<.1	<.1
42 033	Clearfield	78,097	99.2	0.2	0.2	0.1	<.1	0.3	37	9	57	59	0.7	0.7	<.1	<.1
42 035	Clinton	37,182	98.9	0.4	0.3	0.1	<.1	0.2	55	13	52	61	0.3	0.4	<.1	<.1
42 037	Columbia	63,202	98.6	0.4	0.4	<.1	<.1	0.5	39	22	50	31	0.5	0.6	<.1	0.1
42 039	Crawford	86,169	97.9	1.2	0.3	0.1	<.1	0.4	34	34	29	50	0.7	0.8	<.1	0.1
42 041	Cumberland	195,257	96.3	1.5	1.3	0.1	<.1	0.7	18	42	27	23	1.6	1.8	0.3	0.6
42 043	Dauphin	237,813	81.4	14.7	1.1	0.1	0.1	2.5	15	66	2	6	2.0	1.9	3.2	2.6
42 045	Delaware	547,651	85.9	11.1	1.8	0.1	<.1	1.1	4	65	4	17	4.6	4.5	5.7	2.6
42 047	Elk	34,878	99.4	<.1	0.3	<.1	<.1	0.2	58	1	67	66	0.3	0.3	<.1	<.1
42 049	Erie	275,572	93.0	5.1	0.5	0.2	<.1	1.2	13	57	8	16	2.3	2.5	1.3	1.4
42 051	Fayette	145,351	95.9	3.5	0.2	<.1	<.1	0.3	23	47	11	54	1.2	1.3	0.5	0.2
42 053	Forest	4,802	98.3	0.9	<.1	0.2	0.0	0.5	67	28	36	36	<.1	<.1	<.1	<.1
42 055	Franklin	121,082	96.2	2.2	0.5	0.1	<.1	0.9	26	45	20	22	1.0	1.1	0.3	0.5
42 057	Fulton	13,837	98.6	0.9	0.1	0.2	<.1	0.2	64	23	35	63	0.1	0.1	<.1	<.1
42 059	Greene	39,550	98.1	0.9	0.3	0.2	<.1	0.5	54	30	33	33	0.3	0.4	<.1	<.1
42 061	Huntingdon	44,164	94.8	4.4	0.2	0.1	<.1	0.4	48	51	10	39	0.4	0.4	0.2	<.1
42 063	Indiana	89,994	97.5	1.3	0.6	<.1	<.1	0.4	33	36	28	42	0.8	0.8	0.1	0.2
42 065	Jefferson	46,083	99.4	0.1	0.2	<.1	<.1	0.2	46	2	66	65	0.4	0.4	<.1	<.1
42 067	Juniata	20,625	99.3	0.1	0.2	<.1	<.1	0.2	61	5	62	62	0.2	0.2	<.1	<.1
42 069	Lackawanna	219,039	98.1	0.7	0.6	<.1	<.1	0.5	16	31	41	34	1.8	2.1	0.1	0.5
42 071	Lancaster	422,822	92.9	2.2	1.1	0.1	<.1	3.7	6	58	22	5	3.6	3.8	0.9	6.7
42 073	Lawrence	96,246	96.3	3.0	0.3	<.1	<.1	0.4	31	43	14	46	0.8	0.9	0.3	0.2
42 075	Lebanon	113,744	96.3	0.5	0.8	<.1	<.1	2.3	29	44	43	7	1.0	1.1	<.1	1.1
42 077	Lehigh	291,130	91.3	2.1	1.2	<.1	<.1	5.2	12	60	23	2	2.5	2.6	0.6	6.5
42 079	Luzerne	328,149	97.7	1.2	0.4	<.1	<.1	0.6	11	35	30	26	2.8	3.1	0.4	0.9
42 081	Lycoming	118,710	96.5	2.3	0.4	0.2	<.1	0.5	28	41	18	32	1.0	1.1	0.3	0.3
42 083	Mc Kean	47,131	97.4	1.0	0.3	0.2	<.1	1.1	44	37	32	19	0.4	0.4	<.1	0.2
42 085	Mercer	121,003	94.3	4.8	0.3	<.1	<.1	0.4	27	53	9	41	1.0	1.1	0.5	0.2
42 087	Mifflin	46,197	99.2	0.2	0.2	<.1	<.1	0.3	45	6	58	56	0.4	0.4	<.1	<.1
42 089	Monroe	95,709	95.3	1.7	0.7	0.1	<.1	2.1	32	49	26	10	0.8	0.9	0.2	0.9
42 091	Montgomery	678,111	90.6	5.6	2.3	<.1	<.1	1.2	3	62	6	15	5.7	5.9	3.6	3.6
42 093	Montour	17,735	98.1	0.4	0.8	<.1	<.1	0.7	62	29	49	24	0.1	0.2	<.1	<.1
42 095	Northampton	247,105	92.1	2.0	1.1	<.1	<.1	4.7	14	59	24	4	2.1	2.2	0.5	5.0
42 097	Northumberland	96,771	98.9	0.3	0.2	<.1	<.1	0.5	30	15	53	30	0.8	0.9	<.1	0.2
42 099	Perry	41,172	99.0	0.2	0.2	0.1	<.1	0.5	50	11	56	37	0.3	0.4	<.1	<.1
42 101	Philadelphia	1,585,577	52.1	39.3	2.7	0.2	0.1	5.6	1	67	1	1	13.3	7.9	58.1	38.4
42 103	Pike	27,966	96.2	0.9	0.5	0.2	<.1	2.3	60	46	37	8	0.2	0.3	<.1	0.3
42 105	Potter	16,717	99.1	0.1	0.2	0.1	0.0	0.4	63	10	63	40	0.1	0.2	<.1	<.1
42 107	Schuylkill	152,585	98.6	0.5	0.3	<.1	<.1	0.4	21	20	45	38	1.3	1.4	<.1	0.3
42 109	Snyder	36,680	98.9	0.4	0.3	<.1	<.1	0.4	56	14	51	44	0.3	0.3	<.1	<.1
42 111	Somerset	78,218	99.3	0.1	0.2	<.1	<.1	0.3	36	4	61	55	0.7	0.7	<.1	<.1
42 113	Sullivan	6,104	98.1	0.9	0.1	0.5	0.0	0.4	65	32	34	43	<.1	<.1	<.1	<.1
42 115	Susquehanna	40,380	99.0	0.2	0.2	0.2	<.1	0.4	52	12	60	45	0.3	0.4	<.1	<.1
42 117	Tioga	41,126	98.6	0.5	0.3	0.3	<.1	0.3	51	21	46	51	0.3	0.4	<.1	<.1
42 119	Union	36,176	95.0	2.4	0.6	0.2	<.1	1.8	57	50	17	11	0.3	0.3	<.1	0.3
42 121	Venango	59,381	98.5	0.8	0.2	<.1	<.1	0.3	41	26	38	52	0.5	0.6	<.1	<.1
42 123	Warren	45,050	99.2	0.1	0.2	0.2	<.1	0.3	47	7	65	58	0.4	0.4	<.1	<.1
42 125	Washington	204,584	95.7	3.3	0.3	<.1	<.1	0.6	17	48	12	29	1.7	1.9	0.6	0.5
42 127	Wayne	39,944	98.0	0.7	0.2	0.1	<.1	0.9	53	33	42	20	0.3	0.4	<.1	0.2
42 129	Westmoreland	370,321	97.2	1.8	0.4	<.1	<.1	0.4	8	38	25	48	3.1	3.5	0.6	0.6
42 131	Wyoming	28,076	98.6	0.5	0.3	<.1	<.1	0.5	59	19	47	35	0.2	0.3	<.1	<.1
42 133	York	339,574	94.6	3.1	0.6	0.1	<.1	1.5	9	52	13	14	2.9	3.1	1.0	2.2
42	**PENNSYLVANIA**	11,881,643	87.7	9.0	1.1	0.1	<.1	2.0					100.0	100.0	100.0	100.0

Table A. – 1990 Population by Race and Ethnic Origin (cont)

State/county code	County	Total persons	Percent of total persons						Rank				Percent contribution to state population			
			Non-Hispanic					Hispanic	Total	Percent of total persons			Total	Non-Hispanic		Hispanic
			White	Black	Asian and Pacific Islander	Native American	Other			Non-Hispanic		Hispanic		White	Black	
										White	Black					
	CONGRESSIONAL															
	District 1	565,842	36.0	51.5	2.3	0.2	0.1	9.9	3	20	2	1	4.8	2.0	27.1	24.1
	District 2	565,650	34.1	61.8	2.1	0.2	0.1	1.6	21	21	1	8	4.8	1.9	32.6	3.8
	District 3	565,866	87.3	4.6	3.1	0.1	<.1	4.7	2	18	8	3	4.8	4.7	2.4	11.4
	District 4	565,792	95.9	3.2	0.3	<.1	<.1	0.5	13	6	11	19	4.8	5.2	1.7	1.1
	District 5	565,813	97.4	0.9	0.9	0.1	<.1	0.6	7	5	20	16	4.8	5.3	0.5	1.5
	District 6	565,760	93.7	2.3	0.5	<.1	<.1	3.3	17	11	15	5	4.8	5.1	1.2	8.1
	District 7	565,746	93.1	3.8	2.0	<.1	<.1	0.9	18	12	10	11	4.8	5.1	2.0	2.3
	District 8	565,787	93.9	2.8	1.6	<.1	<.1	1.6	15	10	13	7	4.8	5.1	1.5	3.9
	District 9	565,803	98.0	1.2	0.3	0.1	<.1	0.4	9	1	18	20	4.8	5.3	0.6	1.1
	District 10	565,681	97.5	1.1	0.5	0.1	<.1	0.8	20	4	19	14	4.8	5.3	0.6	1.9
	District 11	565,913	97.9	0.9	0.4	<.1	<.1	0.7	1	3	21	15	4.8	5.3	0.5	1.8
	District 12	565,794	98.0	1.3	0.3	<.1	<.1	0.4	11	2	17	21	4.8	5.3	0.7	0.9
	District 13	565,793	90.2	2.5	2.5	<.1	<.1	1.2	12	16	6	10	4.8	4.9	3.1	2.9
	District 14	565,787	80.0	17.7	1.3	0.1	0.1	0.8	14	19	3	13	4.8	4.3	9.3	1.9
	District 15	565,810	92.0	2.0	1.1	<.1	<.1	4.7	8	13	16	2	4.8	5.0	1.0	11.5
	District 16	565,835	89.9	5.0	1.1	0.1	<.1	3.8	4	17	7	4	4.8	4.9	2.6	9.3
	District 17	565,742	90.4	6.5	1.0	0.1	<.1	1.9	19	15	5	6	4.8	4.9	3.4	4.6
	District 18	565,781	90.8	7.7	0.7	<.1	<.1	0.6	16	14	4	17	4.8	4.9	4.1	1.4
	District 19	565,831	95.3	2.5	0.7	0.1	<.1	1.3	5	8	14	9	4.8	5.2	1.3	3.2
	District 20	565,815	95.8	3.1	0.5	<.1	<.1	0.5	6	7	12	18	4.8	5.2	1.7	1.2
	District 21	565,802	94.8	3.8	0.4	0.1	<.1	0.8	10	9	9	12	4.8	5.1	2.0	1.9

Table B. — 1990 Voting Age Population (VAP) by Race and Ethnic Origin

County	Total Voting Age Population	Percent of total VAP						Rank Percent of total VAP				Percent contribution to state VAP				VAP percent of total population						
		Non-Hispanic					Hispanic	Total	Non-Hispanic		Hispanic	Total	Non-Hispanic		Hispanic	Total	Non-Hispanic					Hispanic
		White	Black	Asian and Pacific Islander	Native American	Other			White	Black			White	Black			White	Black	Asian and Pacific Islander	Native American	Other	
Adams	58,679	97.3	1.0	0.4	0.1	<.1	1.3	35	38	33	14	0.6	0.7	<.1	0.5	75.0	75.4	65.3	61.4	83.3	4.8	60.8
Allegheny	1,054,266	88.4	9.9	0.9	<.1	<.1	0.6	2	64	4	24	11.6	11.5	13.8	4.3	78.9	80.1	70.3	73.8	74.6	22.8	72.4
Armstrong	55,796	98.9	0.7	<.1	<.1	<.1	0.2	38	20	37	64	0.6	0.7	<.1	<.1	75.9	76.0	73.2	67.9	79.7	21.4	63.4
Beaver	142,671	94.3	4.9	0.2	<.1	<.1	0.5	19	54	8	28	1.6	1.7	0.9	0.5	76.7	77.4	66.6	69.5	67.9	12.8	68.6
Bedford	35,903	99.3	0.3	0.1	<.1	0.0	0.2	43	7	52	65	0.4	0.4	<.1	<.1	74.9	75.1	67.1	55.1	70.0	0.0	55.1
Berks	258,077	93.1	2.4	0.6	<.1	<.1	3.8	9	61	18	3	2.8	3.0	0.8	6.8	76.7	78.2	66.5	66.3	69.8	34.2	57.4
Blair	98,722	98.6	0.7	0.2	<.1	<.1	0.3	25	28	36	50	1.1	1.2	<.1	0.2	75.6	75.8	70.1	58.6	74.8	16.3	66.4
Bradford	44,420	99.0	0.2	0.3	0.2	<.1	0.3	40	14	56	54	0.5	0.5	<.1	<.1	72.9	73.0	65.5	59.4	73.7	22.7	55.5
Bucks	402,235	94.5	2.5	1.4	0.1	<.1	1.4	5	52	15	12	4.4	4.7	1.3	4.0	74.3	74.8	68.0	67.1	78.5	36.1	65.1
Butler	114,398	98.8	0.5	0.3	<.1	<.1	0.3	22	22	44	44	1.3	1.4	<.1	0.3	75.3	75.3	72.6	70.3	79.4	24.4	65.2
Cambria	125,059	97.0	2.1	0.2	<.1	<.1	0.6	20	39	19	25	1.4	1.5	0.3	0.5	76.7	76.9	72.1	72.1	78.6	22.1	71.1
Cameron	4,400	99.6	<.1	<.1	0.2	<.1	<.1	66	2	66	67	<.1	<.1	<.1	<.1	74.4	74.5	42.9	50.0	50.0	80.0	66.7
Carbon	43,842	98.8	0.2	0.3	<.1	<.1	0.8	42	23	59	21	0.5	0.5	<.1	0.2	77.1	77.3	60.2	65.9	72.7	27.3	65.2
Centre	101,167	93.3	2.4	3.1	0.1	<.1	1.1	24	59	17	17	1.1	1.2	0.3	0.8	81.7	81.6	88.9	81.4	83.6	59.7	82.4
Chester	282,371	90.9	6.0	0.9	0.1	<.1	2.1	8	63	5	6	3.1	3.2	2.2	4.0	75.0	75.5	71.8	66.6	72.2	39.5	68.5
Clarion	32,014	98.6	0.5	0.5	<.1	<.1	0.3	49	29	43	53	0.4	0.4	<.1	<.1	76.8	76.8	86.8	77.7	66.7	20.0	76.7
Clearfield	58,451	99.3	0.2	0.2	0.1	<.1	0.2	37	9	55	60	0.6	0.7	<.1	<.1	74.8	74.9	76.6	60.2	68.6	50.0	62.0
Clinton	28,529	98.9	0.4	0.3	0.1	<.1	0.3	55	19	50	55	0.3	0.3	<.1	<.1	76.7	76.7	80.4	77.6	73.5	100.0	82.4
Columbia	49,413	98.7	0.4	0.3	<.1	<.1	0.5	39	26	48	32	0.5	0.6	<.1	0.2	78.2	78.3	80.8	73.5	75.7	42.1	67.7
Crawford	63,831	98.1	1.1	0.3	0.1	<.1	0.3	34	32	31	47	0.7	0.8	<.1	0.1	74.1	74.2	66.6	72.1	70.4	19.1	65.3
Cumberland	152,329	96.7	1.5	1.1	0.1	<.1	0.6	18	45	27	23	1.7	1.8	0.3	0.7	78.0	78.3	76.8	66.5	76.2	30.2	70.8
Dauphin	182,188	83.8	13.1	1.0	0.1	<.1	1.9	15	66	2	9	2.0	1.9	3.1	2.4	76.6	78.8	68.3	67.8	79.8	37.9	58.6
Delaware	421,041	87.2	10.1	1.6	0.1	<.1	1.0	4	65	3	18	4.6	4.5	5.6	2.8	76.9	78.1	70.0	69.2	77.4	38.9	67.3
Elk	25,924	99.6	<.1	0.2	<.1	0.0	<.1	58	1	67	66	0.3	0.3	<.1	<.1	74.3	74.4	46.7	63.3	75.9	0.0	35.7
Erie	204,135	94.3	4.2	0.5	0.1	<.1	0.9	13	55	10	19	2.2	2.4	1.1	1.3	74.1	75.1	60.7	68.6	65.5	17.2	55.7
Fayette	110,268	96.4	3.1	0.1	<.1	<.1	0.3	23	47	11	52	1.2	1.3	0.5	0.2	75.9	76.2	67.6	72.1	75.4	12.3	69.7
Forest	3,685	98.9	0.5	<.1	0.2	0.0	0.2	67	15	45	56	<.1	<.1	<.1	<.1	76.7	77.2	41.9	100.0	81.8	0.0	39.1
Franklin	91,551	96.8	2.0	0.4	0.1	<.1	0.7	27	44	21	22	1.0	1.1	0.2	0.4	75.6	76.0	68.1	66.3	69.4	22.0	58.3
Fulton	10,131	98.9	0.7	<.1	0.2	0.0	0.2	64	18	38	62	0.1	0.1	<.1	<.1	73.2	73.4	53.2	52.9	77.3	0.0	64.5
Greene	29,415	98.0	1.1	0.3	0.2	<.1	0.5	54	34	32	30	0.3	0.4	<.1	0.1	74.4	74.3	86.6	70.1	69.1	41.7	72.7
Huntingdon	33,777	94.1	5.1	0.2	0.1	<.1	0.4	47	57	7	33	0.4	0.4	0.2	0.1	76.5	75.9	88.9	72.2	75.0	17.6	75.9
Indiana	69,001	97.4	1.4	0.7	<.1	<.1	0.4	33	37	28	39	0.8	0.8	0.1	0.2	76.7	76.6	82.2	83.2	76.1	51.5	71.4
Jefferson	34,388	99.5	<.1	<.1	<.1	<.1	0.2	46	4	64	63	0.4	0.4	<.1	<.1	74.6	74.7	67.3	48.6	73.9	20.0	68.4
Juniata	15,302	99.5	0.1	0.1	<.1	0.0	0.2	61	3	65	61	0.2	0.2	<.1	<.1	74.2	74.3	42.3	43.9	70.6	0.0	65.3
Lackawanna	171,088	98.4	0.6	0.5	<.1	<.1	0.4	16	30	42	36	1.9	2.1	0.1	0.5	78.1	78.4	61.7	65.1	72.2	20.4	65.4
Lancaster	310,886	94.2	1.9	0.9	<.1	<.1	2.9	6	56	22	5	3.4	3.6	0.8	6.1	73.5	74.6	63.2	62.9	68.9	32.9	57.2
Lawrence	73,636	97.0	2.4	0.2	<.1	<.1	0.3	31	40	16	48	0.8	0.9	0.2	0.2	76.5	77.1	61.9	60.7	72.2	10.3	63.3
Lebanon	85,982	97.0	0.5	0.6	<.1	<.1	1.8	29	41	47	10	0.9	1.0	<.1	1.1	75.6	76.2	67.0	61.0	73.9	33.3	59.1
Lehigh	225,186	93.2	1.8	1.0	<.1	<.1	3.8	12	60	23	2	2.5	2.6	0.5	5.9	77.3	79.0	64.9	65.5	73.3	30.6	57.7
Luzerne	257,965	97.9	1.1	0.4	<.1	<.1	0.6	10	35	30	26	2.8	3.1	0.4	1.0	78.6	78.7	77.0	67.1	84.8	18.8	71.4
Lycoming	89,154	96.9	2.1	0.3	0.2	<.1	0.5	28	43	20	29	1.0	1.1	0.2	0.3	75.1	75.4	67.4	56.8	70.6	31.3	73.0
Mc Kean	35,476	97.0	1.2	0.3	0.2	<.1	1.3	44	42	29	13	0.4	0.4	<.1	0.3	75.3	75.0	92.4	72.7	73.6	37.5	88.3
Mercer	92,625	95.0	4.3	0.3	<.1	<.1	0.4	26	51	9	40	1.0	1.1	0.5	0.2	76.5	77.1	67.4	68.2	75.0	21.9	65.6
Mifflin	34,685	99.4	0.2	0.2	<.1	0.0	0.2	45	6	57	58	0.4	0.4	<.1	<.1	75.2	75.2	61.9	59.4	74.2	0.0	62.9
Monroe	71,907	95.8	1.6	0.6	0.1	<.1	1.8	32	49	26	11	0.8	0.9	0.2	0.9	75.1	75.6	69.1	67.7	73.4	36.8	63.1
Montgomery	525,206	91.2	5.4	2.1	<.1	<.1	1.1	3	62	6	16	5.8	5.9	3.7	4.1	77.5	78.0	74.3	68.8	81.6	41.9	71.5
Montour	13,414	98.7	0.3	0.6	<.1	<.1	0.5	62	27	53	31	0.1	0.2	<.1	<.1	75.6	76.1	47.4	54.4	80.0	20.0	56.0
Northampton	189,779	93.5	1.7	1.0	<.1	<.1	3.7	14	58	24	4	2.1	2.2	0.4	4.8	76.8	78.0	64.7	69.9	77.0	28.5	60.3
Northumberland	74,340	99.1	0.3	0.1	<.1	<.1	0.4	30	13	54	34	0.8	0.9	<.1	0.2	76.8	77.0	63.0	64.7	64.9	16.0	59.6
Perry	30,074	99.2	0.1	0.1	0.1	<.1	0.4	51	11	63	37	0.3	0.4	<.1	<.1	73.0	73.2	32.6	53.6	71.4	71.4	63.4
Philadelphia	1,206,156	55.6	36.9	2.5	0.2	<.1	4.6	1	67	1	1	13.3	8.3	58.7	38.3	76.1	81.3	71.5	71.4	76.2	55.4	62.7
Pike	20,903	96.5	0.9	0.4	0.1	<.1	2.0	59	46	34	8	0.2	0.2	<.1	0.3	74.7	75.0	75.6	69.0	66.7	80.0	63.9
Potter	12,126	99.2	0.1	0.1	0.2	0.0	0.3	63	10	60	42	0.1	0.1	<.1	<.1	72.5	72.6	80.0	66.7	76.0	0.0	55.6
Schuylkill	118,927	98.7	0.6	0.3	<.1	<.1	0.4	21	25	41	38	1.3	1.5	<.1	0.3	77.9	78.0	82.0	65.2	75.7	39.1	70.9
Snyder	27,363	98.9	0.4	0.2	<.1	<.1	0.3	57	16	49	41	0.3	0.3	<.1	<.1	74.6	74.7	81.1	67.7	53.3	16.7	63.5
Somerset	58,665	99.4	0.1	0.2	<.1	<.1	0.3	36	5	61	51	0.6	0.7	<.1	0.1	75.0	75.0	74.3	65.9	65.9	16.7	73.2
Sullivan	4,694	98.4	0.6	0.1	0.4	0.0	0.4	65	31	39	35	<.1	<.1	<.1	<.1	76.9	77.2	53.6	55.6	72.4	0.0	80.0
Susquehanna	29,542	99.1	0.2	0.2	0.2	<.1	0.3	53	12	58	43	0.3	0.4	<.1	<.1	74.7	73.3	63.3	59.8	79.5	37.5	59.9
Tioga	30,732	98.8	0.5	0.2	0.2	<.1	0.3	50	24	46	49	0.3	0.4	<.1	<.1	74.7	74.8	70.3	65.7	65.1	63.6	64.7
Union	27,876	94.3	2.8	0.7	0.2	<.1	2.0	56	53	13	7	0.3	0.3	0.1	0.4	77.1	76.5	90.4	81.3	85.9	50.0	87.8
Venango	43,991	98.9	0.6	0.2	<.1	<.1	0.2	41	21	40	57	0.5	0.5	<.1	<.1	74.1	74.4	57.4	61.5	65.4	14.3	53.2
Warren	33,706	99.3	0.1	0.2	0.2	<.1	0.2	48	8	62	59	0.4	0.4	<.1	<.1	74.8	74.9	73.6	56.4	74.6	69.2	67.2
Washington	158,629	96.1	3.0	0.2	<.1	<.1	0.6	17	48	12	27	1.7	1.9	0.6	0.6	77.5	77.8	71.5	64.9	72.0	23.3	74.5
Wayne	29,892	98.0	0.8	0.2	0.1	<.1	0.9	52	33	35	20	0.3	0.4	<.1	0.2	74.8	74.9	86.2	55.3	81.0	37.5	69.3
Westmoreland	287,201	97.6	1.6	0.3	<.1	<.1	0.3	7	36	25	46	3.2	3.5	0.6	0.6	77.0	77.9	69.2	62.6	79.4	11.0	66.5
Wyoming	20,338	98.9	0.3	0.3	<.1	<.1	0.3	60	17	51	45	0.2	0.2	<.1	<.1	72.4	72.7	49.6	76.5	80.0	27.3	48.1
York	257,310	95.6	2.6	0.5	0.1	<.1	1.2	11	50	14	15	2.8	3.0	0.9	2.0	75.8	76.6	63.5	62.2	71.9	27.3	57.6
PENNSYLVANIA	9,086,833	88.9	8.4	1.0	0.1	<.1	1.6					100.0	100.0	100.0	100.0	76.5	77.5	70.8	69.6	74.9	34.8	62.9

Table B. – 1990 Voting Age Population (VAP) by Race and Ethnic Origin (cont)

County	Total Voting Age Population	Percent of total VAP — Non-Hispanic White	Black	Asian and Pacific Islander	Native American	Other	Hispanic	Rank Percent of total VAP — Total	Non-Hispanic White	Black	Hispanic	Percent contribution to state VAP — Total	Non-Hispanic White	Black	Hispanic	VAP percent of total population — Total	Non-Hispanic White	Black	Asian and Pacific Islander	Native American	Other	Hispanic
CONGRESSIONAL																						
District 1	412,698	40.5	49.0	2.2	0.2	<.1	8.0	21	20	2	1	4.5	2.1	26.6	22.7	72.9	82.0	69.4	69.5	75.1	52.7	59.3
District 2	439,005	38.0	58.0	2.1	0.3	<.1	1.5	6	21	1	6	4.8	2.1	33.6	4.5	77.6	86.5	72.8	78.7	80.7	51.9	74.2
District 3	437,241	88.8	4.3	2.8	0.1	<.1	4.0	7	18	8	2	4.8	4.8	2.5	12.0	77.3	78.6	71.6	68.0	70.6	56.5	65.8
District 4	431,946	96.5	2.7	0.3	<.1	<.1	0.4	12	6	12	19	4.8	5.2	1.5	1.2	76.3	76.8	65.6	63.8	74.2	14.0	65.2
District 5	431,688	97.2	1.0	0.9	0.1	<.1	0.6	14	5	19	14	4.8	5.2	0.6	1.9	76.3	76.2	84.6	78.3	73.8	47.6	78.8
District 6	435,113	94.9	2.0	0.5	<.1	<.1	2.5	9	10	15	5	4.8	5.1	1.2	7.5	76.9	77.9	67.1	65.7	71.2	32.2	58.1
District 7	440,847	93.6	3.6	1.8	<.1	<.1	0.9	4	13	9	11	4.9	5.1	2.1	2.6	77.9	78.3	74.2	69.4	78.1	43.0	72.0
District 8	421,078	94.5	2.5	1.4	0.1	<.1	1.4	19	11	13	8	4.6	4.9	1.4	4.1	74.4	74.9	68.4	67.2	78.3	35.5	65.3
District 9	425,600	98.2	1.1	0.2	<.1	<.1	0.4	17	1	18	20	4.7	5.2	0.6	1.1	75.2	75.3	74.1	62.	71.5	19.2	62.3
District 10	429,001	97.9	0.9	0.4	0.1	<.1	0.7	15	4	20	13	4.7	5.2	0.5	1.9	75.8	76.1	66.6	63.8	73.2	28.8	65.2
District 11	441,076	98.1	0.9	0.4	<.1	<.1	0.6	3	3	21	15	4.9	5.4	0.5	1.9	77.9	78.1	75.3	67.1	79.9	23.3	67.2
District 12	431,900	98.1	1.2	0.3	<.1	<.1	0.4	13	2	17	21	4.8	5.2	0.7	1.0	76.3	76.4	73.0	73.6	75.6	23.2	70.1
District 13	439,030	90.8	5.7	2.2	<.1	<.1	1.1	5	17	6	9	4.8	4.9	3.3	3.4	77.6	78.1	74.8	68.8	82.1	44.3	72.6
District 14	449,602	82.0	15.8	1.3	0.1	<.1	0.7	1	19	3	12	4.9	4.6	9.4	2.2	79.5	81.5	70.9	78.4	75.0	27.4	74.7
District 15	434,900	93.6	1.7	1.0	<.1	<.1	3.6	10	12	16	3	4.8	5.0	1.0	10.8	76.9	78.2	64.7	67.1	75.1	29.7	58.9
District 16	416,963	91.1	4.7	0.9	0.1	<.1	3.2	20	16	7	4	4.6	4.7	2.6	9.0	73.7	74.6	69.1	64.6	69.1	37.7	60.9
District 17	427,231	91.7	5.9	0.8	0.1	<.1	1.5	16	15	5	7	4.7	4.8	3.3	4.3	75.5	76.5	68.2	63.9	75.0	39.2	59.0
District 18	447,925	92.0	6.7	0.6	<.1	<.1	0.5	2	14	4	17	4.9	5.1	4.0	1.6	79.2	80.2	68.7	69.2	73.2	16.9	71.8
District 19	432,114	96.0	2.2	0.6	0.1	<.1	1.0	11	8	14	10	4.8	5.1	1.2	3.1	76.4	77.0	66.3	64.4	75.6	24.7	60.2
District 20	436,817	96.1	2.9	0.4	<.1	<.1	0.5	8	7	11	18	4.8	5.2	1.7	1.4	77.2	77.5	71.5	65.4	74.1	18.7	71.5
District 21	425,058	95.7	3.2	0.4	0.1	<.1	0.6	18	9	10	16	4.7	5.0	1.8	1.8	75.1	75.8	63.3	69.7	69.5	19.6	58.3

Table C. — Voter Participation: November 3, 1992, General Election

County	Estimated Voting Age Population (VAP), 1992	Voter registration (REG) Total	% contribution to state REG	% of 1992 VAP	Rank by % of 1992 VAP	Actual	Highest office Total	Office	% of 1992 VAP	Maximum vote Total	% contribution to state turnout	% of REG	Rank by % of REG	% of 1992 VAP	Rank by % 1992 VAP	President	Senator	Governor	Representative
Adams	60,568	33,436	0.6	55.2	62	-	29,501	P	48.7	29,501	0.6	88.2	2	48.7	52	0.0	1.5	-	1.8
Allegheny	1,037,739	730,613	12.2	70.4	7	-	614,187	P	59.2	614,187	12.4	84.1	39	59.2	6	0.0	3.3	-	6.9
Armstrong	55,800	33,272	0.6	59.6	42	-	28,333	P	50.8	28,333	0.6	85.2	28	50.8	39	0.0	0.8	-	19.4
Beaver	140,114	95,851	1.6	68.4	11	-	82,340	P	58.8	82,340	1.7	85.9	14	58.8	7	0.0	0.9	-	1.5
Bedford	36,614	22,754	0.4	62.1	30	-	18,817	P	51.4	18,817	0.4	82.7	57	51.4	35	0.0	1.0	-	11.3
Berks	263,151	153,654	2.6	58.4	50	-	131,407	P	49.9	131,407	2.6	85.5	20	49.9	44	0.0	2.8	-	6.4
Blair	98,300	54,496	0.9	55.4	60	-	44,758	P	45.5	44,758	0.9	82.1	59	45.5	63	0.0	0.1	-	10.1
Bradford	44,692	26,909	0.4	60.2	40	-	22,628	P	50.6	22,628	0.5	84.1	38	50.6	40	0.0	1.9	-	4.9
Bucks	417,766	290,841	4.9	69.6	9	-	248,507	P	59.5	248,507	5.0	85.4	22	59.5	5	0.0	3.4	-	3.7
Butler	115,280	71,599	1.2	62.1	31	-	61,130	P	53.0	61,130	1.2	85.4	24	53.0	31	0.0	0.9	-	2.7
Cambria	122,519	78,652	1.3	64.2	21	-	66,349	P	54.2	66,349	1.3	84.4	36	54.2	23	0.0	0.2	-	18.2
Cameron	4,320	3,506	<.1	81.2	1	-	2,678	P	62.0	2,678	<.1	76.4	65	62.0	3	0.0	2.5	-	9.2
Carbon	44,983	25,552	0.4	56.8	55	-	22,079	C	49.1	22,079	0.4	86.4	7	49.1	50	1.9	6.2	-	0.0
Centre	99,887	60,414	1.0	60.5	38	-	51,225	P	51.3	51,225	1.0	84.8	33	51.3	36	0.0	1.2	-	14.3
Chester	295,713	198,172	3.3	67.0	14	-	169,208	P	57.2	169,208	3.4	85.4	23	57.2	13	0.0	1.2	-	4.4
Clarion	31,206	18,543	0.3	59.4	43	-	15,718	P	50.4	15,718	0.3	84.8	34	50.4	41	0.0	0.9	-	10.1
Clearfield	58,198	36,004	0.6	61.9	32	-	30,847	P	53.0	30,847	0.6	85.7	17	53.0	32	0.0	0.8	-	10.9
Clinton	28,067	15,103	0.3	53.8	64	-	12,569	P	44.8	12,569	0.3	83.2	50	44.8	65	0.0	2.3	-	14.2
Columbia	48,761	30,622	0.5	62.8	28	-	23,739	P	48.7	23,739	0.5	77.5	64	48.7	53	0.0	0.8	-	1.8
Crawford	63,913	41,738	0.7	65.3	18	-	34,628	P	54.2	34,628	0.7	83.0	53	54.2	22	0.0	4.8	-	7.7
Cumberland	154,694	98,528	1.6	63.7	25	-	84,573	P	54.7	84,573	1.7	85.8	16	54.7	18	0.0	3.3	-	5.0
Dauphin	184,454	117,846	2.0	63.9	24	-	98,910	P	53.6	98,910	2.0	83.9	44	53.6	27	0.0	1.9	-	3.0
Delaware	418,349	324,241	5.4	77.5	3	-	266,074	P	63.6	266,074	5.4	82.1	60	63.6	2	0.0	3.7	-	5.9
Elk	25,710	16,469	0.3	64.1	23	-	13,832	P	53.8	13,832	0.3	84.0	42	53.8	25	0.0	0.6	-	8.7
Erie	203,385	136,847	2.3	67.3	13	-	117,804	P	57.9	117,804	2.4	86.1	11	57.9	8	0.0	4.5	-	6.6
Fayette	109,375	64,580	1.1	59.0	47	-	53,861	P	49.2	53,861	1.1	83.4	49	49.2	47	0.0	4.5	-	18.0
Forest	3,732	2,640	<.1	70.7	6	-	2,147	S	57.5	2,147	<.1	81.3	61	57.5	10	0.1	0.0	-	12.8
Franklin	93,618	51,282	0.9	54.8	63	-	43,834	P	46.8	43,834	0.9	85.5	21	46.8	60	0.0	1.6	-	10.2
Fulton	10,538	6,042	0.1	57.3	54	-	5,023	P	47.7	5,023	0.1	83.1	52	47.7	59	0.0	1.7	-	10.3
Greene	29,646	17,533	0.3	59.1	45	-	15,135	P	51.1	15,135	0.3	86.3	8	51.1	37	0.0	1.7	-	2.1
Huntingdon	34,183	18,926	0.3	55.4	61	-	15,700	P	45.9	15,700	0.3	83.0	54	45.9	62	0.0	1.7	-	12.6
Indiana	67,686	39,090	0.7	57.8	51	-	33,314	P	49.2	33,314	0.7	85.2	26	49.2	48	0.0	0.9	-	20.6
Jefferson	34,410	21,186	0.4	61.6	34	-	17,711	P	51.5	17,711	0.4	83.6	48	51.5	34	0.0	0.4	-	8.4
Juniata	15,767	9,704	0.2	61.5	35	-	8,420	P	53.4	8,420	0.2	86.8	5	53.4	29	0.0	1.2	-	10.3
Lackawanna	169,553	124,822	2.1	73.6	4	-	94,968	P	56.0	94,968	1.9	76.1	66	56.0	14	0.0	2.9	-	10.2
Lancaster	323,408	186,386	3.1	57.6	52	-	160,180	P	49.5	160,180	3.2	85.9	13	49.5	46	0.0	4.8	-	7.7
Lawrence	71,970	48,794	0.8	67.8	12	-	41,203	P	57.3	41,203	0.8	84.4	35	57.3	12	0.0	1.6	-	2.7
Lebanon	87,727	48,704	0.8	55.5	59	-	43,021	P	49.0	43,021	0.9	88.3	1	49.0	51	0.0	3.4	-	7.8
Lehigh	229,285	137,326	2.3	59.9	41	-	114,836	P	50.1	114,836	2.3	83.6	46	50.1	43	0.0	3.6	-	3.9
Luzerne	255,799	151,277	2.5	59.1	46	-	127,146	P	49.7	127,146	2.6	84.0	40	49.7	45	0.0	4.8	-	6.7
Lycoming	89,705	50,739	0.8	56.6	56	-	43,172	P	48.1	43,172	0.9	85.1	30	48.1	56	0.0	2.7	-	11.5
Mc Kean	35,137	19,591	0.3	55.8	58	-	16,400	P	46.7	16,400	0.3	83.7	45	46.7	61	0.0	8.7	-	15.1
Mercer	91,483	57,945	1.0	63.3	27	-	49,836	P	54.5	49,836	1.0	86.0	12	54.5	19	0.0	8.3	-	7.5
Mifflin	34,840	17,490	0.3	50.2	67	-	14,688	P	42.2	14,688	0.3	84.0	43	42.2	67	0.0	3.9	-	14.3
Monroe	78,230	48,052	0.8	61.4	36	-	37,500	P	47.9	37,500	0.8	78.0	63	47.9	58	0.0	4.7	-	11.7
Montgomery	533,160	371,118	6.2	69.6	10	-	318,576	P	59.8	318,576	6.4	85.8	15	59.8	4	0.0	2.9	-	7.2
Montour	13,758	8,496	0.1	61.8	33	-	6,646	P	48.3	6,646	0.1	78.2	62	48.3	55	0.0	0.6	-	2.1
Northampton	193,823	114,681	1.9	59.2	44	-	97,525	P	50.3	97,525	2.0	85.0	31	50.3	42	0.0	4.4	-	4.2
Northumberland	74,389	41,795	0.7	56.2	57	-	35,792	P	48.1	35,792	0.7	85.6	19	48.1	57	0.0	4.1	-	7.6
Perry	31,625	18,174	0.3	57.5	53	-	15,327	P	48.5	15,327	0.3	84.3	37	48.5	54	0.0	1.0	-	6.1
Philadelphia	1,192,586	874,181	14.6	73.3	5	-	638,058	P	53.5	638,058	12.9	73.0	67	53.5	28	0.0	4.1	-	8.7
Pike	23,686	15,713	0.3	66.3	15	-	13,603	P	57.4	13,603	0.3	86.6	6	57.4	11	0.0	6.9	-	12.5
Potter	12,166	8,509	0.1	69.9	8	-	7,044	P	57.9	7,044	0.1	82.8	55	57.9	9	0.0	3.4	-	13.0
Schuylkill	118,636	71,492	1.2	60.3	39	-	63,029	P	53.1	63,029	1.3	88.2	3	53.1	30	0.0	1.0	-	1.6
Snyder	27,804	14,703	0.2	52.9	65	-	12,596	P	45.3	12,596	0.3	85.7	18	45.3	64	0.0	1.4	-	11.9
Somerset	58,993	38,978	0.7	66.1	17	-	32,759	P	55.5	32,759	0.7	84.0	41	55.5	15	0.0	1.0	-	25.2
Sullivan	4,650	3,723	<.1	80.1	2	-	3,113	P	66.9	3,113	<.1	83.6	47	66.9	1	0.0	1.0	-	6.0
Susquehanna	30,277	19,609	0.3	64.8	20	-	16,709	P	55.2	16,709	0.3	85.2	27	55.2	16	0.0	1.8	-	4.5
Tioga	30,659	19,429	0.3	63.4	26	-	16,543	P	54.0	16,543	0.3	85.1	29	54.0	24	0.0	4.0	-	16.6
Union	27,843	14,238	0.2	51.1	66	-	12,265	P	44.1	12,265	0.2	86.1	10	44.1	66	0.0	0.9	-	14.0
Venango	43,908	25,903	0.4	59.0	48	-	21,554	P	49.1	21,554	0.4	83.2	51	49.1	49	0.0	0.6	-	9.6
Warren	33,661	22,264	0.4	66.1	16	-	18,426	P	54.7	18,426	0.4	82.8	56	54.7	17	0.0	5.3	-	13.8
Washington	157,123	102,501	1.7	65.2	19	-	84,364	P	53.7	84,364	1.7	82.3	58	53.7	26	0.0	1.1	-	1.6
Wayne	31,043	19,316	0.3	62.2	29	-	16,822	P	54.2	16,822	0.3	87.1	4	54.2	21	0.0	4.7	-	13.2
Westmoreland	283,857	182,109	3.0	64.2	22	-	154,451	P	54.4	154,451	3.1	84.8	32	54.4	20	0.0	4.2	-	14.2
Wyoming	20,855	12,720	0.2	61.0	37	-	10,850	P	52.0	10,850	0.2	85.3	25	52.0	33	0.0	1.2	-	4.4
York	264,223	155,579	2.6	58.9	49	-	134,245	P	50.8	134,245	2.7	86.3	9	50.8	38	0.0	4.3	-	3.6
PENNSYLVANIA	9,129,000	5,993,002	100.0	65.6	-	-	4,960,233		54.3	4,960,233	100.0	82.8		54.3		0.0	3.2	-	7.5

[1]Percent drop-off is zero for any office used as highest office turnout.

Table D. — Voter Registration by Political Party Affiliation: November 3, 1992, General Election

County	Total voter registration	Political party affiliation			Plurality		Percent of total registration			Rank			Percent contribution to state registration			
		Democrat (DEM)	Republican (REP)	Other Parties	Total	Party	DEM	REP	Other	DEM	REP	Other	Total	DEM	REP	Other
Adams	33,436	12,777	18,394	2,265	5,617	R	38.2	55.0	6.8	47	23	16	0.6	0.4	0.7	0.6
Allegheny	730,613	486,861	198,827	44,925	288,034	D	66.6	27.2	6.1	7	62	24	12.2	16.0	7.7	11.8
Armstrong	33,272	17,607	14,539	1,126	3,068	D	52.9	43.7	3.4	16	49	57	0.6	0.6	0.6	0.3
Beaver	95,851	64,894	25,883	5,074	39,011	D	67.7	27.0	5.3	6	63	32	1.6	2.1	1.0	1.3
Bedford	22,754	9,113	12,947	694	3,834	R	40.1	56.9	3.1	42	20	63	0.4	0.3	0.5	0.2
Berks	153,654	78,049	64,537	11,068	13,512	D	50.8	42.0	7.2	20	51	14	2.6	2.6	2.5	2.9
Blair	54,496	19,893	31,565	3,038	11,672	R	36.5	57.9	5.6	50	17	28	0.9	0.7	1.2	0.8
Bradford	26,909	7,836	17,607	1,466	9,771	R	29.1	65.4	5.4	61	4	31	0.4	0.3	0.7	0.4
Bucks	290,841	113,978	148,566	28,297	34,588	R	39.2	51.1	9.7	45	33	5	4.9	3.7	5.8	7.4
Butler	71,599	32,610	33,518	5,471	908	R	45.5	46.8	7.6	30	44	13	1.2	1.1	1.3	1.4
Cambria	78,652	51,894	24,425	2,333	27,469	D	66.0	31.1	3.0	9	59	64	1.3	1.7	1.0	0.6
Cameron	3,506	1,649	1,730	127	81	R	47.0	49.3	3.6	27	36	54	<.1	<.1	<.1	<.1
Carbon	25,552	13,615	10,592	1,345	3,023	D	53.3	41.5	5.3	15	52	33	0.4	0.4	0.4	0.4
Centre	60,414	24,749	29,173	6,492	4,424	R	41.0	48.3	10.7	40	41	4	1.0	0.8	1.1	1.7
Chester	198,172	53,950	120,778	23,444	66,828	R	27.2	60.9	11.8	64	12	3	3.3	1.8	4.7	6.1
Clarion	18,543	8,592	9,103	848	511	R	46.3	49.1	4.6	28	38	43	0.3	0.3	0.4	0.2
Clearfield	36,004	18,447	16,078	1,479	2,369	D	51.2	44.7	4.1	18	47	49	0.6	0.6	0.6	0.4
Clinton	15,103	7,342	7,100	661	242	D	48.6	47.0	4.4	23	42	46	0.3	0.2	0.3	0.2
Columbia	30,622	15,644	13,147	1,831	2,497	D	51.1	42.9	6.0	19	50	26	0.5	0.5	0.5	0.5
Crawford	41,738	18,152	21,800	1,786	3,648	R	43.5	52.2	4.3	32	32	47	0.7	0.6	0.8	0.5
Cumberland	98,528	32,022	58,784	7,722	26,762	R	32.5	59.7	7.8	55	15	11	1.6	1.1	2.3	2.0
Dauphin	117,846	43,754	66,257	7,835	22,503	R	37.1	56.2	6.6	49	21	18	2.0	1.4	2.6	2.1
Delaware	324,241	82,771	218,770	22,700	135,999	R	25.5	67.5	7.0	65	3	15	5.4	2.7	8.5	5.9
Elk	16,469	9,541	6,023	905	3,518	D	57.9	36.6	5.5	12	56	29	0.3	0.3	0.2	0.2
Erie	136,847	79,200	51,005	6,642	28,195	D	57.9	37.3	4.9	13	54	41	2.3	2.6	2.0	1.7
Fayette	64,580	50,057	12,645	1,878	37,412	D	77.5	19.6	2.9	2	67	65	1.1	1.6	0.5	0.5
Forest	2,640	1,112	1,422	106	310	R	42.1	53.9	4.0	35	28	50	<.1	<.1	<.1	<.1
Franklin	51,282	18,299	29,537	3,446	11,238	R	35.7	57.6	6.7	51	18	17	0.9	0.6	1.2	0.9
Fulton	6,042	2,899	2,970	173	71	R	48.0	49.2	2.9	25	37	66	0.1	<.1	0.1	<.1
Greene	17,533	13,723	3,471	339	10,252	D	78.3	19.8	1.9	1	66	67	0.3	0.5	0.1	<.1
Huntingdon	18,926	7,190	10,858	878	3,668	R	38.0	57.4	4.6	48	19	42	0.3	0.2	0.4	0.2
Indiana	39,090	19,116	17,566	2,408	1,550	D	48.9	44.9	6.2	22	46	23	0.7	0.6	0.7	0.6
Jefferson	21,186	9,710	10,771	705	1,061	R	45.8	50.8	3.3	29	35	59	0.4	0.3	0.4	0.2
Juniata	9,704	4,060	5,335	309	1,275	R	41.8	55.0	3.2	36	24	62	0.2	0.1	0.2	<.1
Lackawanna	124,822	84,720	36,031	4,071	48,689	D	67.9	28.9	3.3	5	60	60	2.1	2.8	1.4	1.1
Lancaster	186,386	47,206	121,190	17,990	73,984	R	25.3	65.0	9.7	66	6	7	3.1	1.6	4.7	4.7
Lawrence	48,794	29,031	17,312	2,451	11,719	D	59.5	35.5	5.0	11	58	39	0.8	1.0	0.7	0.6
Lebanon	48,704	14,625	30,935	3,144	16,310	R	30.0	63.5	6.5	58	9	21	0.8	0.5	1.2	0.8
Lehigh	137,326	65,571	61,117	10,638	4,454	D	47.7	44.5	7.7	26	48	12	2.3	2.2	2.4	2.8
Luzerne	151,277	90,327	56,087	4,863	34,240	D	59.7	37.1	3.2	10	55	61	2.5	3.0	2.2	1.3
Lycoming	50,739	20,839	27,606	2,294	6,767	R	41.1	54.4	4.5	39	26	44	0.8	0.7	1.1	0.6
Mc Kean	19,591	6,469	12,117	1,005	5,648	R	33.0	61.8	5.1	53	11	35	0.3	0.2	0.5	0.3
Mercer	57,945	30,478	23,921	3,546	6,557	D	52.6	41.3	6.1	17	53	25	1.0	1.0	0.9	0.9
Mifflin	17,490	7,492	9,252	746	1,760	R	42.8	52.9	4.3	33	31	48	0.3	0.2	0.4	0.2
Monroe	48,052	20,344	21,983	5,725	1,639	R	42.3	45.7	11.9	34	45	2	0.8	0.7	0.9	1.5
Montgomery	371,118	111,653	223,246	36,039	111,773	R	30.1	60.2	9.7	57	13	6	6.2	3.7	8.7	9.4
Montour	8,496	3,811	4,122	563	311	R	44.9	48.5	6.6	31	39	19	0.1	0.1	0.2	0.1
Northampton	114,681	64,085	40,994	9,602	23,091	D	55.9	35.7	8.4	14	57	9	1.9	2.1	1.6	2.5
Northumberland	41,795	20,600	19,633	1,562	967	D	49.3	47.0	3.7	21	43	52	0.7	0.7	0.8	0.4
Perry	18,174	5,391	11,769	1,014	6,378	R	29.7	64.8	5.6	59	7	27	0.3	0.2	0.5	0.3
Philadelphia	874,181	629,067	212,771	32,343	416,296	D	72.0	24.3	3.7	3	65	53	14.6	20.7	8.3	8.5
Pike	15,713	5,176	8,428	2,109	3,252	R	32.9	53.6	13.4	54	29	1	0.3	0.2	0.3	0.6
Potter	8,509	3,278	4,929	302	1,651	R	38.5	57.9	3.5	46	16	55	0.1	0.1	0.2	<.1
Schuylkill	71,492	29,797	39,020	2,675	9,223	R	41.7	54.6	3.7	37	25	51	1.2	1.0	1.5	0.7
Snyder	14,703	3,676	10,271	756	6,595	R	25.0	69.9	5.1	67	1	34	0.2	0.1	0.4	0.2
Somerset	38,978	18,795	18,876	1,307	81	R	48.2	48.4	3.4	24	40	58	0.7	0.6	0.7	0.3
Sullivan	3,723	1,539	2,020	164	481	R	41.3	54.3	4.4	38	27	45	<.1	<.1	<.1	<.1
Susquehanna	19,609	6,844	11,779	986	4,935	R	34.9	60.1	5.0	52	14	38	0.3	0.2	0.5	0.3
Tioga	19,429	5,538	13,216	675	7,678	R	28.5	68.0	3.5	63	2	56	0.3	0.2	0.5	0.2
Union	14,238	4,196	8,866	1,176	4,670	R	29.5	62.3	8.3	60	10	10	0.2	0.1	0.3	0.3
Venango	25,903	10,278	14,302	1,323	4,024	R	39.7	55.2	5.1	44	22	36	0.4	0.3	0.6	0.3
Warren	22,264	9,008	11,797	1,459	2,789	R	40.5	53.0	6.6	41	30	20	0.4	0.3	0.5	0.4
Washington	102,501	70,466	26,815	5,220	43,651	D	68.7	26.2	5.1	4	64	37	1.7	2.3	1.0	1.4
Wayne	19,316	5,522	12,582	1,212	7,060	R	28.6	65.1	6.3	62	5	22	0.3	0.2	0.5	0.3
Westmoreland	182,109	120,916	51,252	9,941	69,664	D	66.4	28.1	5.5	8	61	30	3.0	4.0	2.0	2.6
Wyoming	12,720	3,997	8,104	619	4,107	R	31.4	63.7	4.9	56	8	40	0.2	0.1	0.3	0.2
York	155,579	61,916	79,397	14,266	17,481	R	39.8	51.0	9.2	43	34	8	2.6	2.0	3.1	3.7
PENNSYLVANIA	5,993,002	3,043,757	2,567,643	381,602	476,114	D	50.8	42.8	6.4				100.0	100.0	100.0	100.0

County	Total	Clinton (DEM)	Bush (REP)	Perot (IND)	Other	Plurality Total	Party	DEM	REP	IND	Other	Rank DEM	Rank REP	Rank IND	Total	DEM	REP	IND	Major party DEM	Major party REP
Adams	29,501	9,576	13,552	6,313	60	3,976	R	32.5	45.9	21.4	0.2	47	20	30	0.6	0.4	0.8	0.7	41.4	58.6
Allegheny	614,187	324,004	183,035	103,470	3,678	140,969	D	52.8	29.8	16.8	0.6	6	62	59	12.4	14.5	10.2	11.5	63.9	36.1
Armstrong	28,333	12,995	9,122	6,166	50	3,873	D	45.9	32.2	21.8	0.2	12	58	24	0.6	0.6	0.5	0.7	58.8	41.2
Beaver	82,340	44,877	21,361	15,954	148	23,516	D	54.5	25.9	19.4	0.2	5	64	47	1.7	2.0	1.2	1.8	67.8	32.2
Bedford	18,817	5,840	9,216	3,731	30	3,376	R	31.0	49.0	19.8	0.2	53	10	46	0.4	0.3	0.5	0.4	38.8	61.2
Berks	131,407	46,031	52,939	31,663	774	6,908	R	35.0	40.3	24.1	0.6	38	38	9	2.6	2.1	3.0	3.5	46.5	53.5
Blair	44,758	14,857	21,447	8,284	170	6,590	R	33.2	47.9	18.5	0.4	43	12	52	0.9	0.7	1.2	0.9	40.9	59.1
Bradford	22,628	6,903	10,221	5,452	52	3,318	R	30.5	45.2	24.1	0.2	58	21	10	0.5	0.3	0.6	0.6	40.3	59.7
Bucks	248,507	97,902	94,584	53,931	2,090	3,318	D	39.4	38.1	21.7	0.8	25	45	27	5.0	4.4	5.3	6.0	50.9	49.1
Butler	61,130	22,303	23,656	15,013	158	1,353	R	36.5	38.7	24.6	0.3	32	44	6	1.2	1.0	1.3	1.7	48.5	51.5
Cambria	66,349	34,334	20,770	11,070	175	13,564	D	51.7	31.3	16.7	0.3	7	59	61	1.3	1.5	1.2	1.2	62.3	37.7
Cameron	2,678	824	1,173	676	5	349	R	30.8	43.8	25.2	0.2	56	25	3	<.1	<.1	<.1	<.1	41.3	58.7
Carbon	21,659	9,072	7,243	5,222	122	1,829	D	41.9	33.4	24.1	0.6	19	54	8	0.4	0.4	0.4	0.6	55.6	44.4
Centre	51,225	21,177	20,478	9,356	214	699	D	41.3	40.0	18.3	0.4	22	39	54	1.0	0.9	1.1	1.0	50.8	49.2
Chester	169,208	59,643	74,002	34,536	1,027	14,359	R	35.2	43.7	20.4	0.6	37	26	45	3.4	2.7	4.1	3.8	44.6	55.4
Clarion	15,718	5,584	6,477	3,619	38	893	R	35.5	41.2	23.0	0.2	36	32	18	0.3	0.2	0.4	0.4	46.3	53.7
Clearfield	30,847	12,247	11,553	6,989	58	694	D	39.7	37.5	22.7	0.2	24	46	20	0.6	0.5	0.6	0.8	51.5	48.5
Clinton	12,569	5,397	4,471	2,654	47	926	D	42.9	35.6	21.1	0.4	17	50	36	0.3	0.2	0.3	0.3	54.7	45.3
Columbia	23,739	8,261	9,742	5,683	53	1,481	R	34.8	41.0	23.9	0.2	39	34	13	0.5	0.4	0.5	0.6	45.9	54.1
Crawford	34,628	12,813	14,112	7,392	311	1,299	R	37.0	40.8	21.3	0.9	31	37	31	0.7	0.6	0.8	0.8	47.6	52.4
Cumberland	84,573	26,635	43,447	14,344	147	16,812	R	31.5	51.4	17.0	0.2	52	5	57	1.7	1.2	2.4	1.6	38.0	62.0
Dauphin	98,910	36,990	45,479	16,063	378	8,489	R	37.4	46.0	16.2	0.4	30	19	65	2.0	1.7	2.5	1.8	44.9	55.1
Delaware	266,074	111,210	108,587	43,728	2,549	2,623	D	41.8	40.8	16.4	1.0	20	36	64	5.4	5.0	6.1	4.8	50.6	49.4
Elk	13,832	5,016	4,908	3,885	23	108	D	36.3	35.5	28.1	0.2	33	51	1	0.3	0.2	0.3	0.4	50.5	49.5
Erie	117,804	56,381	39,283	21,510	630	17,098	D	47.9	33.3	18.3	0.5	9	55	55	2.4	2.5	2.2	2.4	58.9	41.1
Fayette	53,861	30,577	12,820	10,162	302	17,757	D	56.8	23.8	18.9	0.6	2	65	51	1.1	1.4	0.7	1.1	70.5	29.5
Forest	2,144	890	801	448	5	89	D	41.5	37.4	20.9	0.2	21	47	39	<.1	<.1	<.1	<.1	52.6	47.4
Franklin	43,834	13,440	23,387	6,941	66	9,947	R	30.7	53.4	15.8	0.2	57	3	66	0.9	0.6	1.3	0.8	36.5	63.5
Fulton	5,023	1,588	2,558	869	8	970	R	31.6	50.9	17.3	0.2	51	7	56	0.1	<.1	0.1	<.1	38.3	61.7
Greene	15,135	8,438	3,482	3,186	29	4,956	D	55.8	23.0	21.1	0.2	3	66	37	0.3	0.4	0.2	0.4	70.8	29.2
Huntingdon	15,700	5,153	7,249	3,273	25	2,096	R	32.8	46.2	20.8	0.2	45	18	40	0.3	0.2	0.4	0.4	41.5	58.5
Indiana	33,314	15,194	10,966	7,089	65	4,228	D	45.6	32.9	21.3	0.2	13	56	33	0.7	0.7	0.6	0.8	58.1	41.9
Jefferson	17,711	5,998	7,271	4,403	39	1,273	R	33.9	41.1	24.9	0.2	41	33	4	0.4	0.3	0.4	0.5	45.2	54.8
Juniata	8,420	2,601	3,980	1,819	20	1,379	R	30.9	47.3	21.6	0.2	54	16	29	0.2	0.1	0.2	0.2	39.5	60.5
Lackawanna	94,968	45,054	33,443	15,667	804	11,611	D	47.4	35.2	16.5	0.8	10	53	63	1.9	2.0	1.9	1.7	57.4	42.6
Lancaster	160,180	44,255	88,447	26,807	671	44,192	R	27.6	55.2	16.7	0.4	64	1	60	3.2	2.0	4.9	3.0	33.3	66.7
Lawrence	41,203	20,830	12,359	7,950	64	8,471	D	50.6	30.0	19.3	0.2	8	61	49	0.8	0.9	0.7	0.9	62.8	37.2
Lebanon	43,021	12,350	21,512	9,005	154	9,162	R	28.7	50.0	20.9	0.4	62	8	38	0.9	0.6	1.2	1.0	36.5	63.5
Lehigh	114,836	46,711	42,631	24,853	641	4,080	D	40.7	37.1	21.6	0.6	23	48	28	2.3	2.1	2.4	2.8	52.3	47.7
Luzerne	127,146	56,623	49,285	21,007	231	7,338	D	44.5	38.8	16.5	0.2	15	43	62	2.6	2.5	2.8	2.3	53.5	46.5
Lycoming	43,172	13,315	20,536	9,170	151	7,221	R	30.8	47.6	21.2	0.3	55	13	35	0.9	0.6	1.1	1.0	39.3	60.7
Mc Kean	16,400	5,331	6,965	4,019	85	1,634	R	32.5	42.5	24.5	0.5	46	29	7	0.3	0.2	0.4	0.4	43.4	56.6
Mercer	49,836	23,264	16,081	10,277	214	7,183	D	46.7	32.3	20.6	0.4	11	57	44	1.0	1.0	0.9	1.1	59.1	40.9
Mifflin	14,688	4,946	6,300	3,382	60	1,354	R	33.7	42.9	23.0	0.4	42	28	17	0.3	0.2	0.4	0.4	44.0	56.0
Monroe	37,500	13,468	14,557	9,257	218	1,089	R	35.9	38.8	24.7	0.6	34	42	5	0.8	0.6	0.8	1.0	48.1	51.9
Montgomery	318,576	136,572	125,704	53,738	2,562	10,868	D	42.9	39.5	16.9	0.8	18	41	58	6.4	6.1	7.0	6.0	52.1	47.9
Montour	6,646	2,150	3,096	1,373	27	946	R	32.4	46.6	20.7	0.4	48	17	43	0.1	<.1	0.2	0.2	41.0	59.0
Northampton	97,525	42,203	34,429	20,234	659	7,774	D	43.3	35.3	20.7	0.7	16	52	19	2.0	1.9	1.9	2.2	55.1	44.9
Northumberland	35,792	12,814	15,057	7,782	139	2,243	R	35.8	42.1	21.7	0.4	35	31	26	0.7	0.6	0.8	0.9	46.0	54.0
Perry	15,327	4,086	7,871	3,334	36	3,785	R	26.7	51.4	21.8	0.2	66	6	25	0.3	0.2	0.4	0.4	34.2	65.8
Philadelphia	638,058	434,904	133,328	65,455	4,371	301,576	D	68.2	20.9	10.3	0.7	1	67	67	12.9	19.4	7.4	7.3	76.5	23.5
Pike	13,603	4,382	6,084	3,019	118	1,702	R	32.2	44.7	22.2	0.9	49	23	21	0.3	0.2	0.3	0.3	41.9	58.1
Potter	7,044	1,892	3,452	1,687	13	1,560	R	26.9	49.0	23.9	0.2	65	9	12	0.1	<.1	0.2	0.2	35.4	64.6
Schuylkill	63,029	23,679	25,780	13,398	172	2,101	R	37.6	40.9	21.3	0.3	29	35	34	1.3	1.1	1.4	1.5	47.9	52.1
Snyder	12,596	2,952	6,934	2,686	24	3,982	R	23.4	55.0	21.3	0.2	67	2	32	0.3	0.1	0.4	0.3	29.9	70.1
Somerset	32,759	12,493	13,858	6,333	75	1,365	R	38.1	42.3	19.3	0.2	27	30	48	0.7	0.6	0.8	0.7	47.4	52.6
Sullivan	3,113	1,030	1,340	731	12	310	R	33.1	43.0	23.5	0.4	44	27	15	<.1	<.1	<.1	<.1	43.5	56.5
Susquehanna	16,709	5,368	7,356	3,946	39	1,988	R	32.1	44.0	23.6	0.2	50	24	14	0.3	0.2	0.4	0.4	42.2	57.8
Tioga	16,543	4,868	7,823	3,804	48	2,955	R	29.4	47.3	23.0	0.3	60	15	19	0.3	0.2	0.4	0.4	38.4	61.6
Union	12,265	3,623	6,362	2,255	25	2,739	R	29.5	51.9	18.4	0.2	59	4	53	0.2	0.2	0.4	0.2	36.3	63.7
Venango	21,554	8,230	8,545	4,695	84	315	R	38.2	39.6	21.8	0.4	26	40	23	0.4	0.4	0.5	0.5	49.1	50.9
Warren	18,426	6,972	6,585	4,795	74	387	D	37.8	35.7	26.0	0.4	28	49	2	0.4	0.3	0.4	0.5	51.4	48.6
Washington	84,364	46,143	21,977	16,083	161	24,166	D	54.7	26.1	19.1	0.2	4	63	50	1.7	2.1	1.2	1.8	67.7	32.3
Wayne	16,822	4,817	8,184	3,727	94	3,367	R	28.6	48.7	22.2	0.6	63	11	22	0.3	0.2	0.5	0.4	37.1	62.9
Westmoreland	154,451	69,817	47,315	37,036	283	22,502	D	45.2	30.6	24.0	0.2	14	60	11	3.1	3.1	2.6	4.1	59.6	40.4
Wyoming	10,850	3,158	5,143	2,525	24	1,985	R	29.1	47.4	23.3	0.2	61	14	16	0.2	0.1	0.3	0.3	38.0	62.0
York	134,245	46,113	60,130	27,743	259	14,017	R	34.3	44.8	20.7	0.2	40	22	42	2.7	2.1	3.4	3.1	43.4	56.6
PENNSYLVANIA	4,959,810	2,239,164	1,791,841	902,667	26,138	447,323	D	45.1	36.1	18.2	0.5				100.0	100.0	100.0	100.0	55.5	44.5

Table F. — Vote for U.S. Senator: November 3, 1992, General Election

County	Total	Yeakel (DEM)	Specter (REP)	Perry (LIB)[1]	Plurality Total	Party	Percent of total vote DEM	REP	LIB	Rank DEM	REP	LIB	Percent contribution to state vote Total	DEM	REP	LIB
Adams	29,057	12,141	14,925	1,991	2,784	R	41.8	51.4	6.9	42	30	23	0.6	0.5	0.6	0.9
Allegheny	593,862	277,191	293,156	23,515	15,965	R	46.7	49.4	4.0	21	44	55	12.4	12.5	12.4	10.7
Armstrong	28,101	12,206	13,979	1,916	1,773	R	43.4	49.7	6.8	31	42	24	0.6	0.5	0.6	0.9
Beaver	81,568	43,716	32,418	5,434	11,298	D	53.6	39.7	6.7	3	66	26	1.7	2.0	1.4	2.5
Bedford	18,637	6,848	10,251	1,538	3,403	R	36.7	55.0	8.3	60	10	9	0.4	0.3	0.4	0.7
Berks	127,759	56,993	64,062	6,704	7,069	R	44.6	50.1	5.2	27	39	42	2.7	2.6	2.7	3.1
Blair	44,714	16,960	24,337	3,417	7,377	R	37.9	54.4	7.6	57	15	13	0.9	0.8	1.0	1.6
Bradford	22,199	8,951	11,667	1,581	2,716	R	40.3	52.6	7.1	49	22	20	0.5	0.4	0.5	0.7
Bucks	240,050	109,859	121,763	8,428	11,904	R	45.8	50.7	3.5	24	34	59	5.0	4.9	5.2	3.8
Butler	60,555	24,901	30,929	4,725	6,028	R	41.1	51.1	7.8	48	33	12	1.3	1.1	1.3	2.2
Cambria	66,239	31,589	30,988	3,662	601	D	47.7	46.8	5.5	16	53	37	1.4	1.4	1.3	1.7
Cameron	2,610	1,126	1,290	194	164	R	43.1	49.4	7.4	34	43	16	<.1	<.1	<.1	<.1
Carbon	20,705	10,571	9,500	634	1,071	D	51.1	45.9	3.1	9	55	64	0.4	0.5	0.4	0.3
Centre	50,595	23,863	23,626	3,106	237	D	47.2	46.7	6.1	17	54	30	1.1	1.1	1.0	1.4
Chester	167,121	70,948	86,581	9,592	15,633	R	42.5	51.8	5.7	39	26	33	3.5	3.2	3.7	4.4
Clarion	15,583	6,431	7,895	1,257	1,464	R	41.3	50.7	8.1	44	35	11	0.3	0.3	0.3	0.6
Clearfield	30,609	14,248	13,756	2,605	492	D	46.5	44.9	8.5	22	57	8	0.6	0.6	0.6	1.2
Clinton	12,278	6,025	5,151	1,102	874	D	49.1	42.0	9.0	11	63	5	0.3	0.3	0.2	0.5
Columbia	23,558	10,814	11,512	1,232	698	R	45.9	48.9	5.2	23	47	43	0.5	0.5	0.5	0.6
Crawford	32,956	13,972	16,580	2,404	2,608	R	42.4	50.3	7.3	40	37	18	0.7	0.6	0.7	1.1
Cumberland	81,757	30,245	48,377	3,135	18,132	R	37.0	59.2	3.8	59	2	57	1.7	1.4	2.1	1.4
Dauphin	97,010	37,178	54,399	5,433	17,221	R	38.3	56.1	5.6	54	7	35	2.0	1.7	2.3	2.5
Delaware	256,229	111,242	136,228	8,759	24,986	R	43.4	53.2	3.4	32	20	60	5.3	5.0	5.8	4.0
Elk	13,750	6,607	6,135	1,008	472	D	48.1	44.6	7.3	13	58	17	0.3	0.3	0.3	0.5
Erie	112,474	54,095	51,555	6,824	2,540	D	48.1	45.8	6.1	12	56	31	2.3	2.4	2.2	3.1
Fayette	51,439	27,261	21,812	2,366	5,449	D	53.0	42.4	4.6	5	62	49	1.1	1.2	0.9	1.1
Forest	2,147	944	1,101	102	157	R	44.0	51.3	4.8	28	31	47	<.1	<.1	<.1	<.1
Franklin	43,111	15,773	23,665	3,673	7,892	R	36.6	54.9	8.5	62	12	7	0.9	0.7	1.0	1.7
Fulton	4,937	1,888	2,786	263	898	R	38.2	56.4	5.3	55	6	39	0.1	<.1	0.1	0.1
Greene	14,878	8,248	5,996	634	2,252	D	55.4	40.3	4.3	2	65	52	0.3	0.4	0.3	0.3
Huntingdon	15,432	5,990	8,181	1,261	2,191	R	38.8	53.0	8.2	52	21	10	0.3	0.3	0.3	0.6
Indiana	33,011	14,998	15,976	2,037	978	R	45.4	48.4	6.2	25	51	29	0.7	0.7	0.7	0.9
Jefferson	17,646	7,107	8,923	1,616	1,816	R	40.3	50.6	9.2	50	36	3	0.4	0.3	0.4	0.7
Juniata	8,316	3,120	4,663	533	1,543	R	37.5	56.1	6.4	58	8	28	0.2	0.1	0.2	0.2
Lackawanna	92,189	45,349	44,009	2,831	1,340	D	49.2	47.7	3.1	10	52	63	1.9	2.0	1.9	1.3
Lancaster	152,489	49,815	87,828	14,846	38,013	R	32.7	57.6	9.7	66	5	1	3.2	2.2	3.7	6.8
Lawrence	40,557	21,718	16,707	2,132	5,011	D	53.5	41.2	5.3	4	64	41	0.8	1.0	0.7	1.0
Lebanon	41,572	14,708	24,527	2,337	9,819	R	35.4	59.0	5.6	64	3	34	0.9	0.7	1.0	1.1
Lehigh	110,647	53,125	53,763	3,759	638	R	48.0	48.6	3.4	15	49	61	2.3	2.4	2.3	1.7
Luzerne	121,048	58,125	59,642	3,281	1,517	R	48.0	49.3	2.7	14	45	66	2.5	2.6	2.5	1.5
Lycoming	41,989	17,285	21,986	2,718	4,701	R	41.2	52.4	6.5	45	23	27	0.9	0.8	0.9	1.2
Mc Kean	14,967	6,455	7,768	744	1,313	R	43.1	51.9	5.0	35	25	45	0.3	0.3	0.3	0.3
Mercer	45,717	24,113	19,749	1,855	4,364	D	52.7	43.2	4.1	6	61	54	1.0	1.1	0.8	0.8
Mifflin	14,122	6,077	7,280	765	1,203	R	43.0	51.6	5.4	37	27	38	0.3	0.3	0.3	0.3
Monroe	35,727	16,792	17,580	1,355	788	R	47.0	49.2	3.8	20	46	58	0.7	0.8	0.7	0.6
Montgomery	309,423	128,961	168,323	12,139	39,362	R	41.7	54.4	3.9	43	16	56	6.4	5.8	7.1	5.5
Montour	6,606	2,888	3,320	398	432	R	43.7	50.3	6.0	29	38	32	0.1	0.1	0.1	0.2
Northampton	93,258	48,641	41,455	3,162	7,186	D	52.2	44.5	3.4	7	59	62	1.9	2.2	1.8	1.4
Northumberland	34,313	15,476	17,076	1,761	1,600	R	45.1	49.8	5.1	26	41	44	0.7	0.7	0.7	0.8
Perry	15,178	4,747	9,044	1,387	4,297	R	31.3	59.6	9.1	67	1	4	0.3	0.2	0.4	0.6
Philadelphia	611,965	361,993	240,440	9,532	121,553	D	59.2	39.3	1.6	1	67	67	12.7	16.3	10.2	4.3
Pike	12,660	5,456	6,834	370	1,378	R	43.1	54.0	2.9	36	18	65	0.3	0.2	0.3	0.2
Potter	6,805	2,426	3,734	645	1,308	R	35.7	54.9	9.5	63	13	2	0.1	0.1	0.2	0.3
Schuylkill	62,401	27,188	32,493	2,720	5,305	R	43.6	52.1	4.4	30	24	51	1.3	1.2	1.4	1.2
Snyder	12,422	4,101	7,248	1,073	3,147	R	33.0	58.3	8.6	65	4	6	0.3	0.2	0.3	0.5
Somerset	32,419	13,335	16,669	2,415	3,334	R	41.1	51.4	7.4	47	29	15	0.7	0.6	0.7	1.1
Sullivan	3,082	1,334	1,585	163	251	R	43.3	51.4	5.3	33	28	40	<.1	<.1	<.1	<.1
Susquehanna	16,412	6,914	8,396	1,102	1,482	R	42.1	51.2	6.7	41	32	25	0.3	0.3	0.4	0.5
Tioga	15,889	5,831	8,853	1,205	3,022	R	36.7	55.7	7.6	61	9	14	0.3	0.3	0.4	0.5
Union	12,154	4,631	6,653	870	2,022	R	38.1	54.7	7.2	56	14	19	0.3	0.2	0.3	0.4
Venango	21,426	9,184	10,731	1,511	1,547	R	42.9	50.1	7.1	38	40	22	0.4	0.4	0.5	0.7
Warren	17,448	8,211	8,471	766	260	R	47.1	48.6	4.4	19	50	50	0.4	0.4	0.4	0.3
Washington	83,457	42,842	36,739	3,876	6,103	D	51.3	44.0	4.6	8	60	48	1.7	1.9	1.6	1.8
Wayne	16,028	6,437	8,806	785	2,369	R	40.2	54.9	4.9	51	11	46	0.3	0.3	0.4	0.4
Westmoreland	148,002	69,777	72,024	6,201	2,247	R	47.1	48.7	4.2	18	48	53	3.1	3.1	3.1	2.8
Wyoming	10,722	4,154	5,805	763	1,651	R	38.7	54.1	7.1	53	17	21	0.2	0.2	0.2	0.3
York	128,423	52,828	68,424	7,171	15,596	R	41.1	53.3	5.6	46	19	36	2.7	2.4	2.9	3.3
PENNSYLVANIA	**4,802,410**	**2,224,966**	**2,358,125**	**219,319**	**133,159**	**R**	**46.3**	**49.1**	**4.6**				**100.0**	**100.0**	**100.0**	**100.0**

[1]Libertarian candidate Perry was the only minor candidate (only three candidates on ballot).

County	Total	Wofford (DEM)	Thornburgh (REP)		Plurality Total	Party	Percent of total vote DEM	REP		Rank DEM	Rank REP		Percent contribution to state vote Total	DEM	REP	
Adams	19,855	8,745	11,110	-	2,365	R	44.0	56.0	-	44	24	-	0.6	0.5	0.7	-
Allegheny	425,363	257,482	167,881	-	89,601	D	60.5	39.5	-	9	59	-	12.6	13.8	11.0	-
Armstrong	23,125	13,369	9,756	-	3,613	D	57.8	42.2	-	14	54	-	0.7	0.7	0.6	-
Beaver	61,073	42,400	18,673	-	23,727	D	69.4	30.6	-	3	65	-	1.8	2.3	1.2	-
Bedford	15,054	5,865	9,189	-	3,324	R	39.0	61.0	-	58	10	-	0.4	0.3	0.6	-
Berks	82,723	35,447	47,276	-	11,829	R	42.9	57.1	-	49	19	-	2.4	1.9	3.1	-
Blair	32,289	14,132	18,157	-	4,025	R	43.8	56.2	-	46	22	-	1.0	0.8	1.2	-
Bradford	16,035	6,433	9,602	-	3,169	R	40.1	59.9	-	54	14	-	0.5	0.3	0.6	-
Bucks	148,353	75,844	72,509	-	3,335	D	51.1	48.9	-	25	43	-	4.4	4.1	4.8	-
Butler	42,463	20,054	22,409	-	2,355	R	47.2	52.8	-	32	36	-	1.3	1.1	1.5	-
Cambria	52,503	31,442	21,061	-	10,381	D	59.9	40.1	-	11	57	-	1.6	1.7	1.4	-
Cameron	2,398	947	1,451	-	504	R	39.5	60.5	-	57	11	-	<.1	<.1	<.1	-
Carbon	16,270	9,443	6,827	-	2,616	D	58.0	42.0	-	13	55	-	0.5	0.5	0.4	-
Centre	31,630	14,380	17,250	-	2,870	R	45.5	54.5	-	38	30	-	0.9	0.8	1.1	-
Chester	98,382	43,393	54,989	-	11,596	R	44.1	55.9	-	43	25	-	2.9	2.3	3.6	-
Clarion	11,991	5,625	6,366	-	741	R	46.9	53.1	-	34	34	-	0.4	0.3	0.4	-
Clearfield	23,506	12,027	11,479	-	548	D	51.2	48.8	-	24	44	-	0.7	0.6	0.8	-
Clinton	9,551	5,408	4,143	-	1,265	D	56.6	43.4	-	15	53	-	0.3	0.3	0.3	-
Columbia	16,414	7,509	8,905	-	1,396	R	45.7	54.3	-	36	32	-	0.5	0.4	0.6	-
Crawford	24,947	13,178	11,769	-	1,409	D	52.8	47.2	-	20	48	-	0.7	0.7	0.8	-
Cumberland	56,404	21,101	35,303	-	14,202	R	37.4	62.6	-	61	7	-	1.7	1.1	2.3	-
Dauphin	67,111	30,313	36,798	-	6,485	R	45.2	54.8	-	39	29	-	2.0	1.6	2.4	-
Delaware	179,805	90,613	89,192	-	1,421	D	50.4	49.6	-	26	42	-	5.3	4.9	5.9	-
Elk	10,982	5,534	5,448	-	86	D	50.4	49.6	-	27	41	-	0.3	0.3	0.4	-
Erie	81,190	44,251	36,939	-	7,312	D	54.5	45.5	-	18	50	-	2.4	2.4	2.4	-
Fayette	39,404	28,185	11,219	-	16,966	D	71.5	28.5	-	2	66	-	1.2	1.5	0.7	-
Forest	1,713	807	906	-	99	R	47.1	52.9	-	33	35	-	<.1	<.1	<.1	-
Franklin	28,400	10,841	17,559	-	6,718	R	38.2	61.8	-	59	9	-	0.8	0.6	1.2	-
Fulton	3,948	1,566	2,382	-	816	R	39.7	60.3	-	56	12	-	0.1	<.1	0.2	-
Greene	12,071	8,342	3,729	-	4,613	D	69.1	30.9	-	4	64	-	0.4	0.4	0.2	-
Huntingdon	12,443	5,080	7,363	-	2,283	R	40.8	59.2	-	53	15	-	0.4	0.3	0.5	-
Indiana	23,879	13,041	10,838	-	2,203	D	54.6	45.4	-	16	52	-	0.7	0.7	0.7	-
Jefferson	14,310	6,445	7,865	-	1,420	R	45.0	55.0	-	40	28	-	0.4	0.3	0.5	-
Juniata	6,738	2,765	3,973	-	1,208	R	41.0	59.0	-	51	17	-	0.2	0.1	0.3	-
Lackawanna	72,175	46,145	26,030	-	20,115	D	63.9	36.1	-	6	62	-	2.1	2.5	1.7	-
Lancaster	96,343	29,779	66,564	-	36,785	R	30.9	69.1	-	67	1	-	2.8	1.6	4.4	-
Lawrence	30,674	19,301	11,373	-	7,928	D	62.9	37.1	-	7	61	-	0.9	1.0	0.7	-
Lebanon	28,895	10,686	18,209	-	7,523	R	37.0	63.0	-	62	6	-	0.9	0.6	1.2	-
Lehigh	71,560	37,071	34,489	-	2,582	D	51.8	48.2	-	21	47	-	2.1	2.0	2.3	-
Luzerne	96,699	59,991	36,708	-	23,283	D	62.0	38.0	-	8	60	-	2.9	3.2	2.4	-
Lycoming	31,021	13,294	17,727	-	4,433	R	42.9	57.1	-	48	20	-	0.9	0.7	1.2	-
Mc Kean	10,936	4,472	6,464	-	1,992	R	40.9	59.1	-	52	16	-	0.3	0.2	0.4	-
Mercer	33,647	20,150	13,497	-	6,653	D	59.9	40.1	-	10	58	-	1.0	1.1	0.9	-
Mifflin	10,460	4,616	5,844	-	1,228	R	44.1	55.9	-	42	26	-	0.3	0.2	0.4	-
Monroe	22,976	11,506	11,470	-	36	D	50.1	49.9	-	28	40	-	0.7	0.6	0.8	-
Montgomery	202,284	104,215	98,069	-	6,146	D	51.5	48.5	-	23	45	-	6.0	5.6	6.4	-
Montour	4,686	2,178	2,508	-	330	R	46.5	53.5	-	35	33	-	0.1	0.1	0.2	-
Northampton	60,205	32,461	27,744	-	4,717	D	53.9	46.1	-	19	49	-	1.8	1.7	1.8	-
Northumberland	27,686	14,306	13,380	-	926	D	51.7	48.3	-	22	46	-	0.8	0.8	0.9	-
Perry	11,163	3,768	7,395	-	3,627	R	33.8	66.2	-	65	3	-	0.3	0.2	0.5	-
Philadelphia	445,655	331,638	114,017	-	217,621	D	74.4	25.6	-	1	67	-	13.2	17.8	7.5	-
Pike	7,851	3,486	4,365	-	879	R	44.4	55.6	-	41	27	-	0.2	0.2	0.3	-
Potter	5,562	1,973	3,589	-	1,616	R	35.5	64.5	-	64	4	-	0.2	0.1	0.2	-
Schuylkill	48,383	26,387	21,996	-	4,391	D	54.5	45.5	-	17	51	-	1.4	1.4	1.4	-
Snyder	9,399	2,973	6,426	-	3,453	R	31.6	68.4	-	66	2	-	0.3	0.2	0.4	-
Somerset	25,568	12,416	13,152	-	736	R	48.6	51.4	-	30	38	-	0.8	0.7	0.9	-
Sullivan	2,802	1,233	1,569	-	336	R	44.0	56.0	-	45	23	-	<.1	<.1	0.1	-
Susquehanna	12,747	5,831	6,916	-	1,085	R	45.7	54.3	-	37	31	-	0.4	0.3	0.5	-
Tioga	12,624	4,551	8,073	-	3,522	R	36.1	63.9	-	63	5	-	0.4	0.2	0.5	-
Union	8,821	3,335	5,486	-	2,151	R	37.8	62.2	-	60	8	-	0.3	0.2	0.4	-
Venango	15,066	7,504	7,562	-	58	R	49.8	50.2	-	29	39	-	0.4	0.4	0.5	-
Warren	12,947	6,263	6,684	-	421	R	48.4	51.6	-	31	37	-	0.4	0.3	0.4	-
Washington	62,027	40,415	21,612	-	18,803	D	65.2	34.8	-	5	63	-	1.8	2.2	1.4	-
Wayne	11,783	4,682	7,101	-	2,419	R	39.7	60.3	-	55	13	-	0.3	0.3	0.5	-
Westmoreland	108,501	63,873	44,628	-	19,245	D	58.9	41.1	-	12	56	-	3.2	3.4	2.9	-
Wyoming	7,388	3,090	4,298	-	1,208	R	41.8	58.2	-	50	18	-	0.2	0.2	0.3	-
York	81,889	35,164	46,725	-	11,561	R	42.9	57.1	-	47	21	-	2.4	1.9	3.1	-
PENNSYLVANIA	**3,382,746**	**1,860,760**	**1,521,986**	-	**338,774**	**D**	**55.0**	**45.0**	-			-	**100.0**	**100.0**	**100.0**	-

[1]For remaining three years of term of the late Senator John Heinz (R). Incumbent Harris Wofford (D) appointed as interim senator in May 1991.

Table H. — Vote for U.S. Representative in Congress: November 3, 1992, General Election

Congressional district and county	Total	Democrat (DEM)	Republican (REP)	Other	Plurality Total	Plurality Party	Percent of total vote DEM	Percent of total vote REP	Percent of total vote Other	Rank within district DEM	Rank within district REP	Rank within district Other	Percent contribution to district vote Total	Percent contribution to district vote DEM	Percent contribution to district vote REP	Percent contribution to district vote Other
District 1	**185,591**	**150,172**	**35,419**	-	**114,753**	**D**	**80.9**	**19.1**	**-**				**100.0**	**100.0**	**100.0**	**-**
Delaware (pt)	24,999	14,352	10,647	-	3,705	D	57.4	42.6	-	2	1	-	13.5	9.6	30.1	-
Philadelphia (pt)	160,592	135,820	24,772	-	111,048	D	84.6	15.4	-	1	2	-	86.5	90.4	69.9	-
District 2	**213,927**	**164,355**	**47,906**	**1,666**	**116,449**	**D**	**76.8**	**22.4**	**0.8**				**100.0**	**100.0**	**100.0**	**100.0**
Delaware (pt)	14,084	7,184	6,826	74	358	D	51.0	48.5	0.5	2	1	2	6.6	4.4	14.2	4.4
Philadelphia (pt)	199,843	157,171	41,080	1,592	116,091	D	78.6	20.6	0.8	1	2	1	93.4	95.6	85.8	95.6
District 3	**221,971**	**130,828**	**86,787**	**4,356**	**44,041**	**D**	**58.9**	**39.1**	**2.0**				**100.0**	**100.0**	**100.0**	**100.0**
Philadelphia (pt)	221,971	130,828	86,787	4,356	44,041	D	58.9	39.1	2.0	1	1	1	100.0	100.0	100.0	100.0
District 4	**237,922**	**186,684**	**48,484**	**2,754**	**138,200**	**D**	**78.5**	**20.4**	**1.2**				**100.0**	**100.0**	**100.0**	**100.0**
Allegheny (pt)	34,195	25,843	8,021	331	17,822	D	75.6	23.5	1.0	4	2	4	14.4	13.8	16.5	12.0
Beaver	81,144	65,493	14,592	1,059	50,901	D	80.7	18.0	1.3	2	4	3	34.1	35.1	30.1	38.5
Butler (pt)	18,923	12,679	5,615	629	7,064	D	67.0	29.7	3.3	5	1	1	8.0	6.8	11.6	22.8
Lawrence	40,100	30,733	8,840	527	21,893	D	76.6	22.0	1.3	3	3	2	16.9	16.5	18.2	19.1
Westmoreland (pt)	63,560	51,936	11,416	208	40,520	D	81.7	18.0	0.3	1	5	5	26.7	27.8	23.5	7.6
District 5[1]	**188,911**	**-**	**188,911**	**-**	**188,911**	**R**	**-**	**100.0**	**-**				**100.0**	**-**	**100.0**	**-**
Armstrong (pt)	259	-	259	-	259	R	-	100.0	-	-	1	-	0.1	-	0.1	-
Cameron	2,432	-	2,432	-	2,432	R	-	100.0	-	-	2	-	1.3	-	1.3	-
Centre (pt)	38,632	-	38,632	-	38,632	R	-	100.0	-	-	3	-	20.4	-	20.4	-
Clarion (pt)	13,779	-	13,779	-	13,779	R	-	100.0	-	-	4	-	7.3	-	7.3	-
Clearfield (pt)	15	-	15	-	15	R	-	100.0	-	-	5	-	0.0	-	0.0	-
Clinton	10,783	-	10,783	-	10,783	R	-	100.0	-	-	6	-	5.7	-	5.7	-
Crawford (pt)	7,147	-	7,147	-	7,147	R	-	100.0	-	-	7	-	3.8	-	3.8	-
Elk	12,628	-	12,628	-	12,628	R	-	100.0	-	-	8	-	6.7	-	6.7	-
Forest	1,872	-	1,872	-	1,872	R	-	100.0	-	-	9	-	1.0	-	1.0	-
Jefferson	16,222	-	16,222	-	16,222	R	-	100.0	-	-	10	-	8.6	-	8.6	-
Lycoming (pt)	5,377	-	5,377	-	5,377	R	-	100.0	-	-	11	-	2.8	-	2.8	-
Mc Kean	13,926	-	13,926	-	13,926	R	-	100.0	-	-	12	-	7.4	-	7.4	-
Potter	6,128	-	6,128	-	6,128	R	-	100.0	-	-	13	-	3.2	-	3.2	-
Tioga	13,805	-	13,805	-	13,805	R	-	100.0	-	-	14	-	7.3	-	7.3	-
Union	10,544	-	10,544	-	10,544	R	-	100.0	-	-	15	-	5.6	-	5.6	-
Venango	19,487	-	19,487	-	19,487	R	-	100.0	-	-	16	-	10.3	-	10.3	-
Warren	15,875	-	15,875	-	15,875	R	-	100.0	-	-	17	-	8.4	-	8.4	-
District 6	**208,006**	**108,312**	**99,694**	**-**	**8,618**	**D**	**52.1**	**47.9**	**-**				**100.0**	**100.0**	**100.0**	**-**
Berks	123,061	60,806	62,255	-	1,449	D	49.4	50.6	-	3	2	-	59.2	56.1	62.4	-
Montgomery (pt)	7,420	4,040	3,380	-	660	D	54.4	45.6	-	2	3	-	3.6	3.7	3.4	-
Northumberland (pt)	15,504	5,878	9,626	-	3,748	R	37.9	62.1	-	4	1	-	7.5	5.4	9.7	-
Schuylkill	62,021	37,588	24,433	-	13,155	D	60.6	39.4	-	1	4	-	29.8	34.7	24.5	-
District 7	**273,898**	**91,623**	**180,648**	**1,627**	**89,025**	**R**	**33.5**	**66.0**	**0.6**				**100.0**	**100.0**	**100.0**	**100.0**
Chester (pt)	48,211	15,232	32,019	960	16,787	R	31.6	66.4	2.0	3	1	1	17.6	16.6	17.7	59.0
Delaware (pt)	211,318	70,837	139,884	597	69,047	R	33.5	66.2	0.3	2	2	3	77.2	77.3	77.4	36.7
Montgomery (pt)	14,369	5,554	8,745	70	3,191	R	38.7	60.9	0.5	1	3	2	5.2	6.1	4.8	4.3
District 8	**249,538**	**114,095**	**129,593**	**5,850**	**15,498**	**R**	**45.7**	**51.9**	**2.3**				**100.0**	**100.0**	**100.0**	**100.0**
Bucks	239,217	110,107	123,462	5,648	13,355	R	46.0	51.6	2.4	1	2	1	95.9	96.5	95.3	96.5
Montgomery (pt)	10,321	3,988	6,131	202	2,143	R	38.6	59.4	2.0	2	1	2	4.1	3.5	4.7	3.5
District 9[1]	**182,406**	**-**	**182,406**	**-**	**182,406**	**R**	**-**	**100.0**	**-**				**100.0**	**-**	**100.0**	**-**
Bedford	16,698	-	16,698	-	16,698	R	-	100.0	-	-	1	-	9.2	-	9.2	-
Blair	40,237	-	40,237	-	40,237	R	-	100.0	-	-	2	-	22.1	-	22.1	-
Centre (pt)	5,263	-	5,263	-	5,263	R	-	100.0	-	-	3	-	2.9	-	2.9	-
Clearfield (pt)	27,477	-	27,477	-	27,477	R	-	100.0	-	-	4	-	15.1	-	15.1	-
Franklin	39,351	-	39,351	-	39,351	R	-	100.0	-	-	5	-	21.6	-	21.6	-
Fulton	4,505	-	4,505	-	4,505	R	-	100.0	-	-	6	-	2.5	-	2.5	-
Huntingdon	13,720	-	13,720	-	13,720	R	-	100.0	-	-	7	-	7.5	-	7.5	-
Juniata	7,556	-	7,556	-	7,556	R	-	100.0	-	-	8	-	4.1	-	4.1	-
Mifflin	12,585	-	12,585	-	12,585	R	-	100.0	-	-	9	-	6.9	-	6.9	-
Perry (pt)	3,917	-	3,917	-	3,917	R	-	100.0	-	-	10	-	2.1	-	2.1	-
Snyder	11,097	-	11,097	-	11,097	R	-	100.0	-	-	11	-	6.1	-	6.1	-
District 10[1]	**209,548**	**-**	**189,414**	**20,134**	**169,280**	**R**	**-**	**90.4**	**9.6**				**100.0**	**-**	**100.0**	**100.0**
Bradford	21,530	-	18,702	2,828	15,874	R	-	86.9	13.1	-	7	3	10.3	-	9.9	14.0
Lackawanna	85,234	-	79,852	5,382	74,470	R	-	93.7	6.3	-	1	9	40.7	-	42.2	26.7
Lycoming (pt)	32,828	-	28,955	3,873	25,082	R	-	88.2	11.8	-	6	4	15.7	-	15.3	19.2
Monroe (pt)	14,180	-	12,595	1,585	11,010	R	-	88.8	11.2	-	4	6	6.8	-	6.6	7.9
Pike	11,907	-	10,839	1,068	9,771	R	-	91.0	9.0	-	2	8	5.7	-	5.7	5.3
Sullivan	2,925	-	2,589	336	2,253	R	-	88.5	11.5	-	5	5	1.4	-	1.4	1.7
Susquehanna	15,963	-	13,729	2,234	11,495	R	-	86.0	14.0	-	9	1	7.6	-	7.2	11.1
Wayne	14,606	-	13,159	1,447	11,712	R	-	90.1	9.9	-	3	7	7.0	-	6.9	7.2
Wyoming	10,375	-	8,994	1,381	7,613	R	-	86.7	13.3	-	8	2	5.0	-	4.7	6.9

[1]Republican candidate's name appears on ballot with the party designation Democrat and Republican.

Congressional district and county	Total	Democrat (DEM)	Republican (REP)	Other	Plurality Total	Plurality Party	Percent of total vote DEM	Percent of total vote REP	Percent of total vote Other	Rank within district DEM	Rank within district REP	Rank within district Other	Percent contribution to district vote Total	Percent contribution to district vote DEM	Percent contribution to district vote REP	Percent contribution to district vote Other
District 11	**206,987**	**138,875**	**68,112**	-	**70,763**	D	67.1	32.9	-				100.0	100.0	100.0	-
Carbon	22,079	14,231	7,848	-	6,383	D	64.5	35.5	-	5	2	-	10.7	10.2	11.5	-
Columbia	23,314	15,640	7,674	-	7,966	D	67.1	32.9	-	3	4	-	11.3	11.3	11.3	-
Luzerne	118,594	81,016	37,578	-	43,438	D	68.3	31.7	-	2	5	-	57.3	58.3	55.2	-
Monroe (pt)	18,927	10,980	7,947	-	3,033	D	58.0	42.0	-	6	1	-	9.1	7.9	11.7	-
Montour	6,504	4,256	2,248	-	2,008	D	65.4	34.6	-	4	3	-	3.1	3.1	3.3	-
Northumberland (pt)	17,569	12,752	4,817	-	7,935	D	72.6	27.4	-	1	6	-	8.5	9.2	7.1	-
District 12	**166,916**	**166,916**	-	-	**166,916**	D	100.0	-	-				100.0	100.0	-	-
Armstrong (pt)	22,583	22,583	-	-	22,583	D	100.0	-	-	1	-	-	13.5	13.5	-	-
Cambria	54,242	54,242	-	-	54,242	D	100.0	-	-	2	-	-	32.5	32.5	-	-
Clarion (pt)	357	357	-	-	357	D	100.0	-	-	3	-	-	0.2	0.2	-	-
Fayette (pt)	11,642	11,642	-	-	11,642	D	100.0	-	-	4	-	-	7.0	7.0	-	-
Indiana	26,443	26,443	-	-	26,443	D	100.0	-	-	5	-	-	15.8	15.8	-	-
Somerset	24,508	24,508	-	-	24,508	D	100.0	-	-	6	-	-	14.7	14.7	-	-
Westmoreland (pt)	27,141	27,141	-	-	27,141	D	100.0	-	-	7	-	-	16.3	16.3	-	-
District 13	**253,997**	**127,685**	**126,312**	-	**1,373**	D	50.3	49.7	-				100.0	100.0	100.0	-
Montgomery (pt)	253,997	127,685	126,312	-	1,373	D	50.3	49.7	-	1	1	-	100.0	100.0	100.0	-
District 14	**229,038**	**165,633**	**61,311**	**2,094**	**104,322**	D	72.3	26.8	0.9				100.0	100.0	100.0	100.0
Allegheny (pt)	229,038	165,633	61,311	2,094	104,322	D	72.3	26.8	0.9	1	1	1	100.0	100.0	100.0	100.0
District 15	**213,324**	**111,419**	**99,520**	**2,385**	**11,899**	D	52.2	46.7	1.1				100.0	100.0	100.0	100.0
Lehigh	110,326	57,153	52,032	1,141	5,121	D	51.8	47.2	1.0	2	2	2	51.7	51.3	52.3	47.8
Montgomery (pt)	9,570	3,896	5,630	44	1,734	R	40.7	58.8	0.5	3	1	3	4.5	3.5	5.7	1.8
Northampton	93,428	50,370	41,858	1,200	8,512	D	53.9	44.8	1.3	1	3	1	43.8	45.2	42.1	50.3
District 16	**212,564**	**74,741**	**137,823**	-	**63,082**	R	35.2	64.8	-				100.0	100.0	100.0	-
Chester (pt)	113,490	41,751	71,739	-	29,988	R	36.8	63.2	-	1	2	-	53.4	55.9	52.1	-
Lancaster (pt)	99,074	32,990	66,084	-	33,094	R	33.3	66.7	-	2	1	-	46.6	44.1	47.9	-
District 17	**216,039**	**65,881**	**150,158**	-	**84,277**	R	30.5	69.5	-				100.0	100.0	100.0	-
Cumberland (pt)	21,139	6,003	15,136	-	9,133	R	28.4	71.6	-	4	2	-	9.8	9.1	10.1	-
Dauphin	95,934	29,561	66,373	-	36,812	R	30.8	69.2	-	2	4	-	44.4	44.9	44.2	-
Lancaster (pt)	48,830	14,451	34,379	-	19,928	R	29.6	70.4	-	3	3	-	22.6	21.9	22.9	-
Lebanon	39,667	13,385	26,282	-	12,897	R	33.7	66.3	-	1	5	-	18.4	20.3	17.5	-
Perry (pt)	10,469	2,481	7,988	-	5,507	R	23.7	76.3	-	5	1	-	4.8	3.8	5.3	-
District 18	**254,329**	**96,655**	**154,024**	**3,650**	**57,369**	R	38.0	60.6	1.4				100.0	100.0	100.0	100.0
Allegheny (pt)	254,329	96,655	154,024	3,650	57,369	R	38.0	60.6	1.4	1	1	1	100.0	100.0	100.0	100.0
District 19	**217,587**	**74,798**	**98,599**	**44,190**	**23,801**	R	34.4	45.3	20.3				100.0	100.0	100.0	100.0
Adams	28,975	8,930	12,305	7,740	3,375	R	30.8	42.5	26.7	3	3	1	13.3	11.9	12.5	17.5
Cumberland (pt)	59,190	20,432	26,992	11,766	6,560	R	34.5	45.6	19.9	2	2	2	27.2	27.3	27.4	26.6
York	129,422	45,436	59,302	24,684	13,866	R	35.1	45.8	19.1	1	1	3	59.5	60.7	60.1	55.9
District 20	**226,489**	**114,898**	**111,591**	-	**3,307**	D	50.7	49.3	-				100.0	100.0	100.0	-
Allegheny (pt)	54,422	22,425	31,997	-	9,572	R	41.2	58.8	-	5	1	-	24.0	19.5	28.7	-
Fayette (pt)	32,512	21,196	11,316	-	9,880	D	65.2	34.8	-	1	5	-	14.4	18.4	10.1	-
Greene	14,819	8,306	6,513	-	1,793	D	56.0	44.0	-	2	4	-	6.5	7.2	5.8	-
Washington	82,984	40,957	42,027	-	1,070	R	49.4	50.6	-	4	2	-	36.6	35.6	37.7	-
Westmoreland (pt)	41,752	22,014	19,738	-	2,276	D	52.7	47.3	-	3	3	-	18.4	19.2	17.7	-
District 21	**221,531**	**70,802**	**150,729**	-	**79,927**	R	32.0	68.0	-				100.0	100.0	100.0	-
Butler (pt)	40,544	16,966	23,578	-	6,612	R	41.8	58.2	-	1	4	-	18.3	24.0	15.6	-
Crawford (pt)	24,831	6,062	18,769	-	12,707	R	24.4	75.6	-	4	1	-	11.2	8.6	12.5	-
Erie	110,070	32,026	78,044	-	46,018	R	29.1	70.9	-	3	2	-	49.7	45.2	51.8	-
Mercer	46,086	15,748	30,338	-	14,590	R	34.2	65.8	-	2	3	-	20.8	22.2	20.1	-
PENNSYLVANIA	**4,590,519**	**2,154,372**	**2,347,441**	**88,706**	**193,069**	R	46.9	51.1	1.9							

Table I. — Vote for Presidential Preference: April 28, 1992, Democratic Primary Election

County	Total	Clinton	Brown	Tsongas	LaRouche	Harkin	Kerrey	-	-	% Clinton	% Brown	% Tsongas	Rank Clinton	Rank Brown	Rank Tsongas	Contrib Total	Contrib Clinton	Contrib Brown	Contrib Tsongas
Adams	4,453	2,439	975	850	53	75	61	-	-	54.8	21.9	19.1	39	45	5	0.4	0.3	0.3	0.5
Allegheny	229,900	129,145	55,134	30,016	4,114	6,573	4,918	-	-	56.2	24.0	13.1	36	32	34	18.2	18.1	16.9	18.6
Armstrong	8,258	5,433	1,815	671	123	136	80	-	-	65.8	22.0	8.1	10	44	65	0.7	0.8	0.6	0.4
Beaver	35,899	23,644	8,427	2,652	498	416	262	-	-	65.9	23.5	7.4	9	34	67	2.8	3.3	2.6	1.6
Bedford	3,393	2,416	538	317	47	43	32	-	-	71.2	15.9	9.3	2	64	59	0.3	0.3	0.2	0.2
Berks	33,146	17,797	8,627	5,114	437	590	581	-	-	53.7	26.0	15.4	41	27	21	2.6	2.5	2.7	3.2
Blair	7,995	4,154	2,293	1,038	210	196	104	-	-	52.0	28.7	13.0	48	15	36	0.6	0.6	0.7	0.6
Bradford	2,648	1,543	604	395	32	39	35	-	-	58.3	22.8	14.9	31	38	25	0.2	0.2	0.2	0.2
Bucks	41,085	20,064	11,729	7,382	792	500	618	-	-	48.8	28.5	18.0	55	17	9	3.2	2.8	3.6	4.6
Butler	14,372	8,210	3,794	1,711	249	251	157	-	-	57.1	26.4	11.9	35	24	42	1.1	1.1	1.2	1.1
Cambria	27,170	16,734	5,360	3,564	651	534	327	-	-	61.6	19.7	13.1	24	57	32	2.1	2.3	1.6	2.2
Cameron	541	339	110	68	5	12	7	-	-	62.7	20.3	12.6	19	52	38	<.1	<.1	<.1	<.1
Carbon	5,263	2,767	1,612	610	100	70	104	-	-	52.6	30.6	11.6	46	10	45	0.4	0.4	0.5	0.4
Centre	10,408	5,252	3,068	1,716	109	163	100	-	-	50.5	29.5	16.5	52	13	16	0.8	0.7	0.9	1.1
Chester	19,712	9,514	6,239	3,469	189	180	121	-	-	48.3	31.7	17.6	57	8	11	1.6	1.3	1.9	2.1
Clarion	4,388	2,875	868	482	61	56	46	-	-	65.5	19.8	11.0	11	56	48	0.3	0.4	0.3	0.3
Clearfield	8,102	5,265	1,704	837	89	120	87	-	-	65.0	21.0	10.3	13	50	51	0.6	0.7	0.5	0.5
Clinton	3,002	1,889	638	322	58	52	43	-	-	62.9	21.3	10.7	17	48	50	0.2	0.3	0.2	0.2
Columbia	6,551	3,401	1,961	786	171	129	103	-	-	51.9	29.9	12.0	49	11	41	0.5	0.5	0.6	0.5
Crawford	7,065	3,683	2,068	922	122	138	132	-	-	52.1	29.3	13.1	47	14	35	0.6	0.5	0.6	0.6
Cumberland	12,984	6,653	2,813	2,830	178	240	270	-	-	51.2	21.7	21.8	50	47	2	1.0	0.9	0.9	1.8
Dauphin	17,196	9,504	3,741	3,243	193	268	247	-	-	55.3	21.8	18.9	38	46	6	1.4	1.3	1.1	2.0
Delaware	33,318	15,746	9,959	5,818	663	524	608	-	-	47.3	29.9	17.5	59	12	12	2.6	2.2	3.1	3.6
Elk	4,150	2,386	1,070	505	75	60	54	-	-	57.5	25.8	12.2	32	28	40	0.3	0.3	0.3	0.3
Erie	37,188	16,271	12,575	6,209	408	900	825	-	-	43.8	33.8	16.7	64	7	15	2.9	2.3	3.9	3.8
Fayette	26,563	18,865	4,526	2,279	309	342	242	-	-	71.0	17.0	8.6	3	59	62	2.1	2.6	1.4	1.4
Forest	525	361	89	48	15	8	4	-	-	68.8	17.0	9.1	5	60	60	<.1	<.1	<.1	<.1
Franklin	5,590	3,511	912	958	66	74	69	-	-	62.8	16.3	17.1	18	62	13	0.4	0.5	0.3	0.6
Fulton	964	669	122	130	17	15	11	-	-	69.4	12.7	13.5	4	67	29	<.1	<.1	<.1	<.1
Greene	7,299	5,357	1,083	592	81	115	71	-	-	73.4	14.8	8.1	1	66	66	0.6	0.7	0.3	0.4
Huntingdon	2,959	1,848	616	340	56	52	47	-	-	62.5	20.8	11.5	21	51	46	0.2	0.3	0.2	0.2
Indiana	8,196	5,353	1,834	699	106	136	68	-	-	65.3	22.4	8.5	12	41	63	0.6	0.7	0.6	0.4
Jefferson	3,705	2,401	819	356	43	51	35	-	-	64.8	22.1	9.6	14	43	57	0.3	0.3	0.3	0.2
Juniata	1,572	1,054	239	204	24	28	23	-	-	67.0	15.2	13.0	8	65	37	0.1	0.1	<.1	0.1
Lackawanna	31,271	13,058	13,923	2,953	567	329	441	-	-	41.8	44.5	9.4	66	2	58	2.5	1.8	4.3	1.8
Lancaster	16,847	8,017	4,670	3,138	319	289	414	-	-	47.6	27.7	18.6	58	19	7	1.3	1.1	1.4	1.9
Lawrence	13,986	8,968	3,269	1,183	205	218	143	-	-	64.1	23.4	8.5	15	36	64	1.1	1.3	1.0	0.7
Lebanon	5,699	2,880	1,299	1,158	102	118	142	-	-	50.5	22.8	20.3	51	39	4	0.5	0.4	0.4	0.7
Lehigh	24,854	11,543	8,407	3,779	334	374	417	-	-	46.4	33.8	15.2	61	6	22	2.0	1.6	2.6	2.3
Luzerne	36,380	14,863	16,488	3,517	597	471	444	-	-	40.9	45.3	9.7	67	1	55	2.9	2.1	5.1	2.2
Lycoming	7,624	4,036	2,178	1,056	111	140	103	-	-	52.9	28.6	13.9	45	16	28	0.6	0.6	0.7	0.7
Mc Kean	2,374	1,328	595	373	28	29	21	-	-	55.9	25.1	15.7	37	29	19	0.2	0.2	0.2	0.2
Mercer	11,946	7,058	2,768	1,482	171	208	259	-	-	59.1	23.2	12.4	30	37	39	0.9	1.0	0.9	0.9
Mifflin	2,891	1,718	573	433	39	84	44	-	-	59.4	19.8	15.0	28	54	23	0.2	0.2	0.2	0.3
Monroe	6,131	2,830	1,923	991	131	105	151	-	-	46.2	31.4	16.2	63	9	18	0.5	0.4	0.6	0.6
Montgomery	47,247	25,303	12,484	8,363	399	423	275	-	-	53.6	26.4	17.7	42	23	10	3.7	3.5	3.8	5.2
Montour	1,343	673	372	219	29	31	19	-	-	50.1	27.7	16.3	53	20	17	0.1	<.1	0.1	0.1
Northampton	25,043	11,746	8,694	3,289	386	453	475	-	-	46.9	34.7	13.1	60	5	31	2.0	1.6	2.7	2.0
Northumberland	8,204	4,390	2,165	1,226	132	151	140	-	-	53.5	26.4	14.9	43	25	24	0.6	0.6	0.7	0.8
Perry	2,356	1,354	470	402	44	52	34	-	-	57.5	19.9	17.1	33	53	14	0.2	0.2	0.1	0.2
Philadelphia	217,497	137,129	48,287	21,006	4,864	1,871	4,340	-	-	63.0	22.2	9.7	16	42	56	17.2	19.2	14.8	13.0
Pike	1,367	586	382	319	26	21	33	-	-	42.9	27.9	23.3	65	18	1	0.1	<.1	0.1	0.2
Potter	1,202	738	253	158	18	18	17	-	-	61.4	21.0	13.1	25	49	30	<.1	0.1	<.1	<.1
Schuylkill	13,226	7,889	3,470	1,330	204	184	149	-	-	59.6	26.2	10.1	27	26	52	1.0	1.1	1.1	0.8
Snyder	1,293	801	252	186	17	18	19	-	-	61.9	19.5	14.4	23	58	26	0.1	0.1	<.1	0.1
Somerset	8,355	5,736	1,349	974	88	127	81	-	-	68.7	16.1	11.7	6	63	44	0.7	0.8	0.4	0.6
Sullivan	629	390	148	63	11	6	11	-	-	62.0	23.5	10.0	22	33	53	<.1	<.1	<.1	<.1
Susquehanna	2,534	1,456	694	279	43	35	27	-	-	57.5	27.4	11.0	34	21	47	0.2	0.2	0.2	0.2
Tioga	2,462	1,542	408	386	32	56	38	-	-	62.6	16.6	15.7	20	61	20	0.2	0.2	0.1	0.2
Union	1,604	778	431	331	14	29	21	-	-	48.5	26.9	20.6	56	22	3	0.1	0.1	0.1	0.2
Venango	4,917	2,908	1,153	575	93	111	77	-	-	59.1	23.4	11.7	29	35	43	0.4	0.4	0.4	0.4
Warren	3,123	1,691	772	447	64	83	66	-	-	54.1	24.7	14.3	40	31	27	0.2	0.2	0.2	0.3
Washington	36,218	24,598	7,168	3,139	499	488	326	-	-	67.9	19.8	8.7	7	55	61	2.9	3.4	2.2	1.9
Wayne	2,203	1,018	786	288	38	36	37	-	-	46.2	35.7	13.1	62	4	33	0.2	0.1	0.2	0.2
Westmoreland	62,883	37,518	15,612	6,782	1,101	913	957	-	-	59.7	24.8	10.8	26	30	49	5.0	5.2	4.8	4.2
Wyoming	1,508	752	542	150	20	28	16	-	-	49.9	35.9	9.9	54	3	54	0.1	0.1	0.2	<.1
York	24,718	13,193	5,596	4,464	464	428	573	-	-	53.4	22.6	18.1	44	40	8	2.0	1.8	1.7	2.8
PENNSYLVANIA	**1,265,495**	**715,031**	**325,543**	**161,572**	**21,534**	**21,013**	**20,802**	**-**	**-**	**56.5**	**25.7**	**12.8**				**100.0**	**100.0**	**100.0**	**100.0**

Table J. — Vote for Presidential Preference: April 28, 1992, Republican Primary Election

County	Top candidates					Top four candidates (state vote)											
						Percent of total vote								Percent contribution to state vote			
										Rank							
	Total	Bush	Bu-chanan			Bush	Bu-chanan			Bush	Bu-chanan			Total	Bush	Bu-chanan	
Adams	6,819	5,680	1,139	-	-	83.3	16.7	-	-	4	64	-	-	0.7	0.7	0.5	-	-
Allegheny	82,617	63,670	18,947	-	-	77.1	22.9	-	-	41	27	-	-	8.2	8.2	8.1	-	-
Armstrong	6,181	4,236	1,945	-	-	68.5	31.5	-	-	67	1	-	-	0.6	0.5	0.8	-	-
Beaver	11,545	8,472	3,073	-	-	73.4	26.6	-	-	61	7	-	-	1.1	1.1	1.3	-	-
Bedford	4,970	4,078	892	-	-	82.1	17.9	-	-	10	58	-	-	0.5	0.5	0.4	-	-
Berks	26,703	21,061	5,642	-	-	78.9	21.1	-	-	30	38	-	-	2.6	2.7	2.4	-	-
Blair	14,991	11,855	3,136	-	-	79.1	20.9	-	-	28	40	-	-	1.5	1.5	1.3	-	-
Bradford	7,127	5,679	1,448	-	-	79.7	20.3	-	-	23	45	-	-	0.7	0.7	0.6	-	-
Bucks	48,602	36,048	12,554	-	-	74.2	25.8	-	-	59	9	-	-	4.8	4.7	5.4	-	-
Butler	14,455	10,333	4,122	-	-	71.5	28.5	-	-	66	2	-	-	1.4	1.3	1.8	-	-
Cambria	11,289	8,237	3,052	-	-	73.0	27.0	-	-	63	5	-	-	1.1	1.1	1.3	-	-
Cameron	736	604	132	-	-	82.1	17.9	-	-	9	59	-	-	<.1	<.1	<.1	-	-
Carbon	3,718	2,812	906	-	-	75.6	24.4	-	-	52	16	-	-	0.4	0.4	0.4	-	-
Centre	11,451	9,055	2,396	-	-	79.1	20.9	-	-	29	39	-	-	1.1	1.2	1.0	-	-
Chester	47,519	37,098	10,421	-	-	78.1	21.9	-	-	35	33	-	-	4.7	4.8	4.5	-	-
Clarion	4,639	3,515	1,124	-	-	75.8	24.2	-	-	49	19	-	-	0.5	0.5	0.5	-	-
Clearfield	7,042	5,362	1,680	-	-	76.1	23.9	-	-	48	20	-	-	0.7	0.7	0.7	-	-
Clinton	3,063	2,370	693	-	-	77.4	22.6	-	-	39	29	-	-	0.3	0.3	0.3	-	-
Columbia	5,646	4,623	1,023	-	-	81.9	18.1	-	-	11	57	-	-	0.6	0.6	0.4	-	-
Crawford	8,741	6,699	2,042	-	-	76.6	23.4	-	-	45	23	-	-	0.9	0.9	0.9	-	-
Cumberland	26,403	21,751	4,652	-	-	82.4	17.6	-	-	7	61	-	-	2.6	2.8	2.0	-	-
Dauphin	27,658	22,589	5,069	-	-	81.7	18.3	-	-	12	56	-	-	2.7	2.9	2.2	-	-
Delaware	88,004	64,254	23,750	-	-	73.0	27.0	-	-	62	6	-	-	8.7	8.3	10.2	-	-
Elk	2,751	2,064	687	-	-	75.0	25.0	-	-	55	13	-	-	0.3	0.3	0.3	-	-
Erie	22,618	17,380	5,238	-	-	76.8	23.2	-	-	43	25	-	-	2.2	2.2	2.2	-	-
Fayette	5,571	4,180	1,391	-	-	75.0	25.0	-	-	54	14	-	-	0.6	0.5	0.6	-	-
Forest	666	519	147	-	-	77.9	22.1	-	-	38	30	-	-	<.1	<.1	<.1	-	-
Franklin	10,226	8,515	1,711	-	-	83.3	16.7	-	-	5	63	-	-	1.0	1.1	0.7	-	-
Fulton	1,116	916	200	-	-	82.1	17.9	-	-	8	60	-	-	0.1	0.1	<.1	-	-
Greene	1,551	1,233	318	-	-	79.5	20.5	-	-	25	43	-	-	0.2	0.2	0.1	-	-
Huntingdon	5,342	4,300	1,042	-	-	80.5	19.5	-	-	19	49	-	-	0.5	0.6	0.4	-	-
Indiana	7,061	5,269	1,792	-	-	74.6	25.4	-	-	57	11	-	-	0.7	0.7	0.8	-	-
Jefferson	4,732	3,614	1,118	-	-	76.4	23.6	-	-	46	22	-	-	0.5	0.5	0.5	-	-
Juniata	2,141	1,794	347	-	-	83.8	16.2	-	-	2	66	-	-	0.2	0.2	0.1	-	-
Lackawanna	11,510	9,021	2,489	-	-	78.4	21.6	-	-	34	34	-	-	1.1	1.2	1.1	-	-
Lancaster	49,280	40,159	9,121	-	-	81.5	18.5	-	-	13	55	-	-	4.9	5.2	3.9	-	-
Lawrence	7,779	5,750	2,029	-	-	73.9	26.1	-	-	60	8	-	-	0.8	0.7	0.9	-	-
Lebanon	13,297	10,596	2,701	-	-	79.7	20.3	-	-	22	46	-	-	1.3	1.4	1.2	-	-
Lehigh	19,927	15,091	4,836	-	-	75.7	24.3	-	-	51	17	-	-	2.0	1.9	2.1	-	-
Luzerne	21,249	16,298	4,951	-	-	76.7	23.3	-	-	44	24	-	-	2.1	2.1	2.1	-	-
Lycoming	10,577	8,379	2,198	-	-	79.2	20.8	-	-	27	41	-	-	1.0	1.1	0.9	-	-
Mc Kean	4,844	3,806	1,038	-	-	78.6	21.4	-	-	32	36	-	-	0.5	0.5	0.4	-	-
Mercer	10,125	7,830	2,295	-	-	77.3	22.7	-	-	40	28	-	-	1.0	1.0	1.0	-	-
Mifflin	3,678	2,941	737	-	-	80.0	20.0	-	-	21	47	-	-	0.4	0.4	0.3	-	-
Monroe	5,782	4,511	1,271	-	-	78.0	22.0	-	-	37	31	-	-	0.6	0.6	0.5	-	-
Montgomery	85,495	64,426	21,069	-	-	75.4	24.6	-	-	53	15	-	-	8.5	8.3	9.0	-	-
Montour	1,477	1,196	281	-	-	81.0	19.0	-	-	16	52	-	-	0.1	0.2	0.1	-	-
Northampton	12,989	9,986	3,003	-	-	76.9	23.1	-	-	42	26	-	-	1.3	1.3	1.3	-	-
Northumberland	8,055	6,150	1,905	-	-	76.4	23.6	-	-	47	21	-	-	0.8	0.8	0.8	-	-
Perry	6,246	5,050	1,196	-	-	80.9	19.1	-	-	17	51	-	-	0.6	0.7	0.5	-	-
Philadelphia	67,199	48,409	18,790	-	-	72.0	28.0	-	-	65	3	-	-	6.7	6.2	8.0	-	-
Pike	2,276	1,789	487	-	-	78.6	21.4	-	-	31	37	-	-	0.2	0.2	0.2	-	-
Potter	2,509	2,035	474	-	-	81.1	18.9	-	-	15	53	-	-	0.2	0.3	0.2	-	-
Schuylkill	16,834	12,749	4,085	-	-	75.7	24.3	-	-	50	18	-	-	1.7	1.6	1.7	-	-
Snyder	3,912	3,301	611	-	-	84.4	15.6	-	-	1	67	-	-	0.4	0.4	0.3	-	-
Somerset	7,858	6,288	1,570	-	-	80.0	20.0	-	-	20	48	-	-	0.8	0.8	0.7	-	-
Sullivan	863	719	144	-	-	83.3	16.7	-	-	3	65	-	-	<.1	<.1	<.1	-	-
Susquehanna	4,495	3,578	917	-	-	79.6	20.4	-	-	24	44	-	-	0.4	0.5	0.4	-	-
Tioga	7,558	6,087	1,471	-	-	80.5	19.5	-	-	18	50	-	-	0.7	0.8	0.6	-	-
Union	3,572	2,943	629	-	-	82.4	17.6	-	-	6	62	-	-	0.4	0.4	0.3	-	-
Venango	7,655	5,538	2,117	-	-	72.3	27.7	-	-	64	4	-	-	0.8	0.7	0.9	-	-
Warren	4,387	3,423	964	-	-	78.0	22.0	-	-	36	32	-	-	0.4	0.4	0.4	-	-
Washington	10,729	8,039	2,690	-	-	74.9	25.1	-	-	56	12	-	-	1.1	1.0	1.2	-	-
Wayne	5,121	4,020	1,101	-	-	78.5	21.5	-	-	33	35	-	-	0.5	0.5	0.5	-	-
Westmoreland	21,854	16,265	5,589	-	-	74.4	25.6	-	-	58	10	-	-	2.2	2.1	2.4	-	-
Wyoming	3,485	2,830	655	-	-	81.2	18.8	-	-	14	54	-	-	0.3	0.4	0.3	-	-
York	32,466	25,797	6,669	-	-	79.5	20.5	-	-	26	42	-	-	3.2	3.3	2.9	-	-
PENNSYLVANIA	**1,008,777**	**774,865**	**233,912**	**-**	**-**	**76.8**	**23.2**	**-**	**-**					**100.0**	**100.0**	**100.0**	**-**	**-**

1992 Vote for President
Percent for Clinton (D), by County

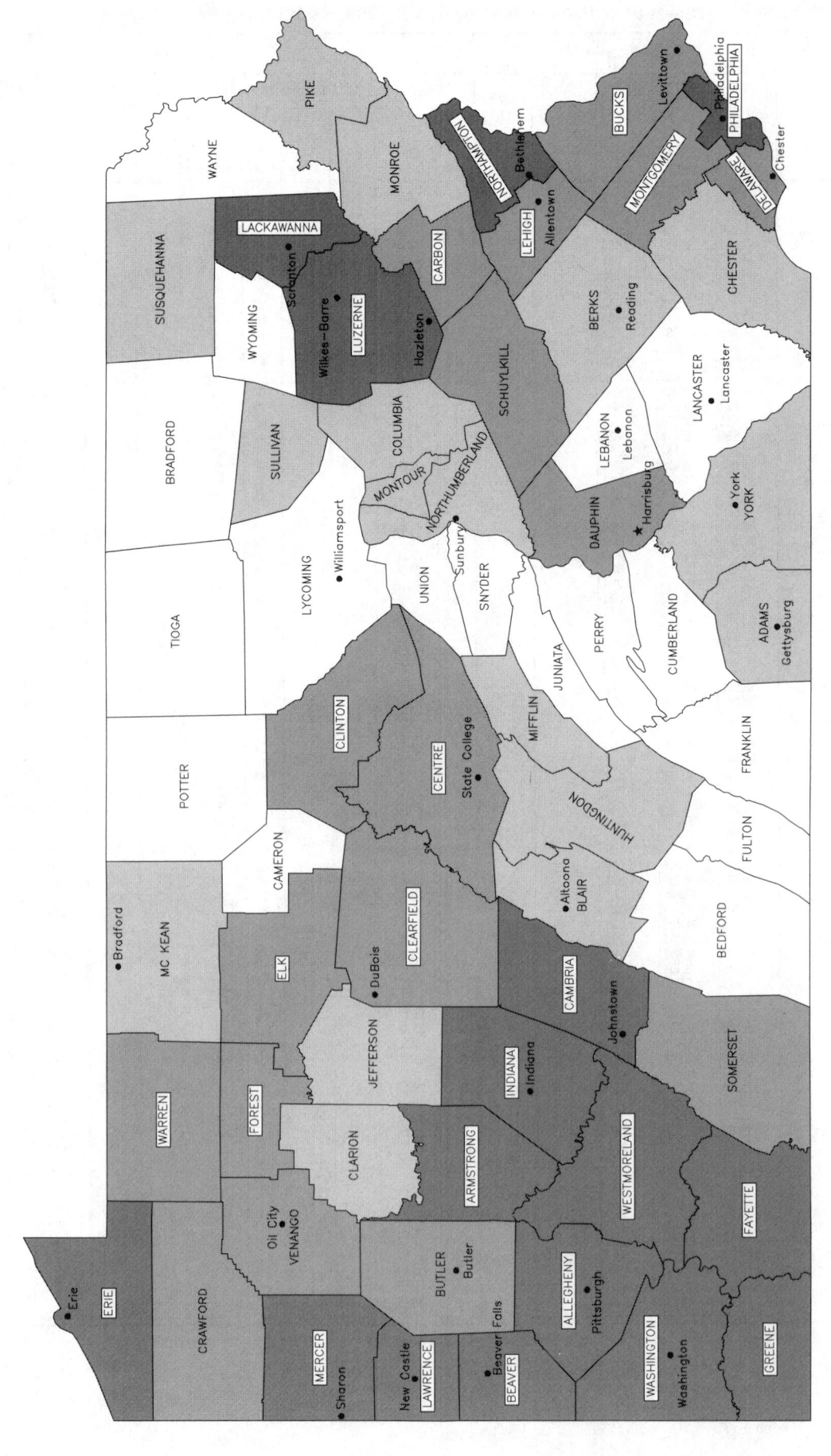

Clinton (D) received 45.1% statewide.

A framed county name indicates a county carried by the winner.

- 43.0% to 68.2%
- 36.0% to 42.9%
- 31.7% to 35.9%
- 23.4% to 31.6%

1992 Vote for U.S. Senator
Percent for Specter (R), by County

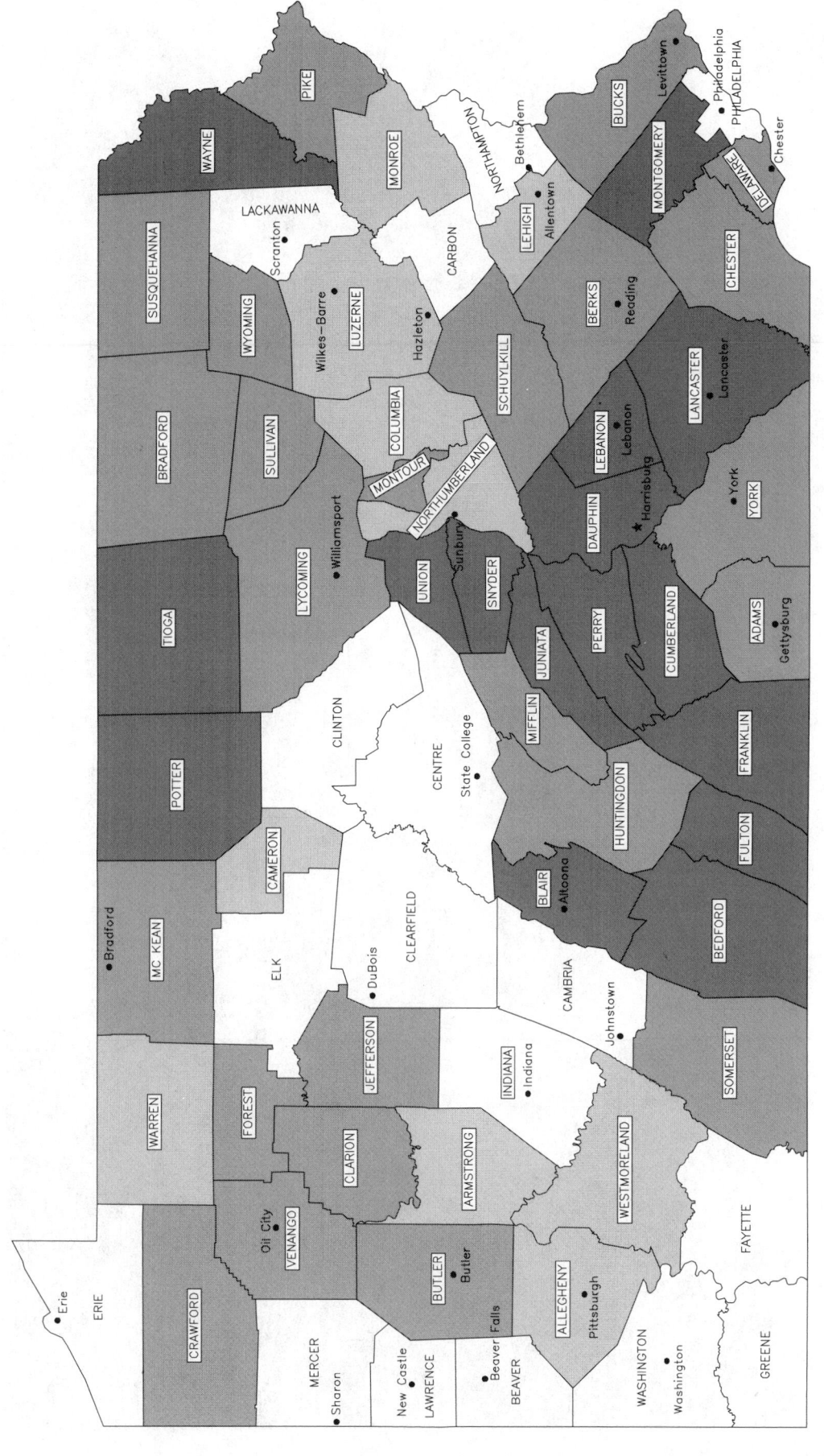

Specter (R) received 49.1% statewide.

A framed county name indicates a county carried by the winner.

54.2% to 59.6%
50.0% to 54.1%
48.5% to 49.9%
39.3% to 48.4%

1991 Vote for U.S. Senator*
Percent for Wofford (D), by County

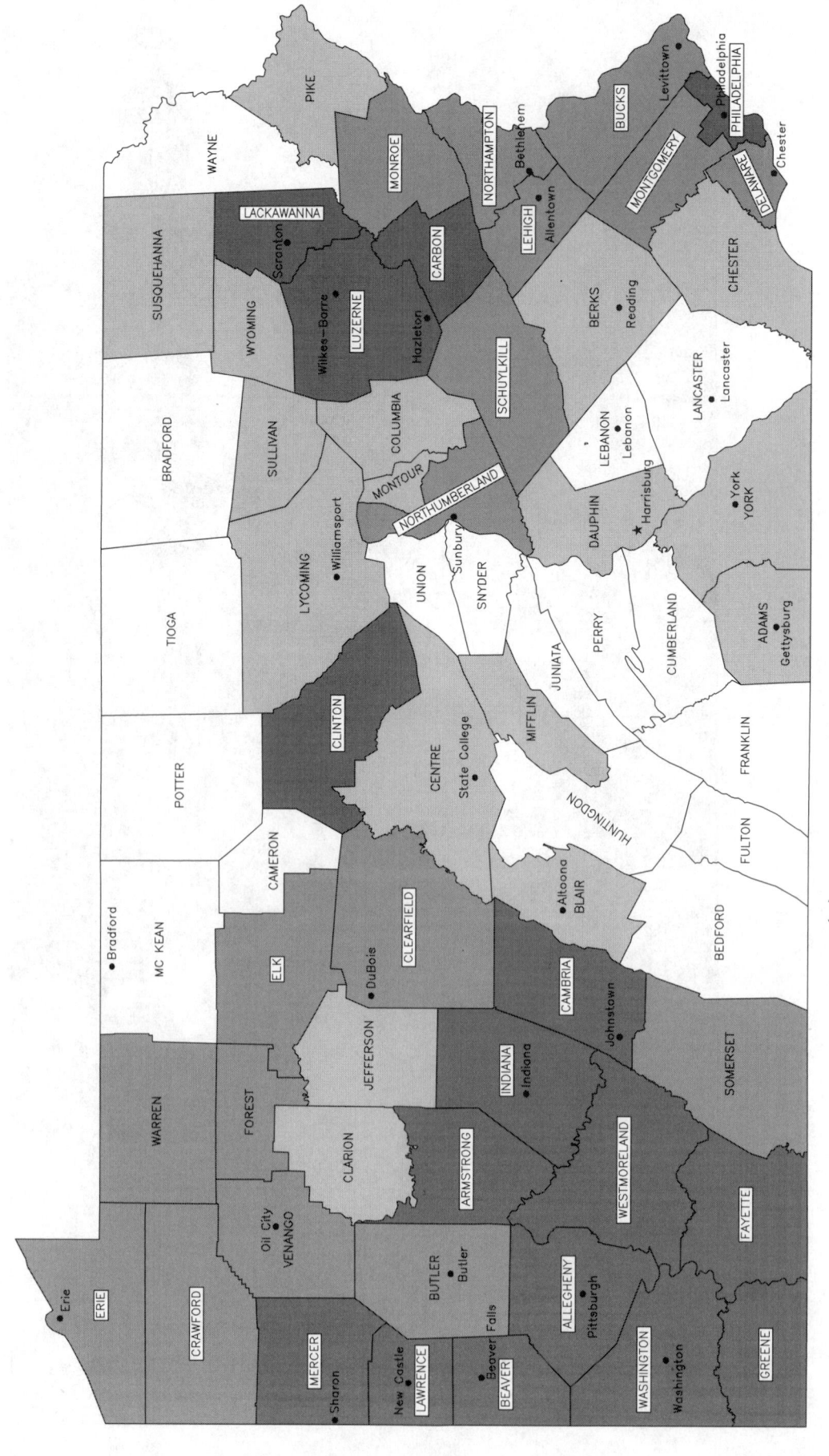

Wofford (D) received 55.0% statewide.

A framed county name indicates
a county carried by the winner.

* Special election held November 5, 1991, for the
remaining three years of the term of the late
Senator John Heinz (R).

Legend:
- 54.6% to 74.4%
- 47.0% to 54.5%
- 41.1% to 46.9%
- 30.9% to 41.0%

RHODE ISLAND

Congressional Districts 2
    Average Population 501,732
State Senate Districts 50
    Average Population 20,069
State House Districts 100
    Average Population 10,035

Electoral College Votes...4
Counties[1] 5
Voting Precincts 545

Alternative Registration Methods:
    .... Agency-based, Deputized Registrars, Motor-voter

Registration Deadline (Days before Election) 30

Voting Equipment Use (Cities and Towns)[2]

Datavote Punch Card	0	Paper Ballot	1
Electronic	0	Other Punch Card	0
Lever Machine	38	Mixed Systems	0
Optical Scanner	0		

Party Control	DEM	REP	IND	VAC
1993 State Senate	39	11	0	0
1992 State Senate	45	5	0	0
1993 State House	85	15	0	0
1992 State House	84	16	0	0

Population Statistics 1990

Race/ Ethnicity	Total Population		Voting Age Population		Voting Age Population % of total population
	Number	%	Number	%	
Non-Hispanic					
White	896,109	89.3	707,286	90.9	78.9
Black	34,283	3.4	22,896	2.9	66.8
Asian/Pacific Islander	17,584	1.8	11,553	1.5	65.7
Native American	3,629	0.4	2,460	0.3	67.8
Other	6,107	0.6	3,934	0.5	64.4
All Hispanic	45,752	4.6	29,645	3.8	64.8
TOTAL	1,003,464	100.0	777,774	100.0	77.5

Estimated Voting Age Population 1992 (VAP) 776,000
Number of Registered Voters..................................... 554,664
    % of estimated VAP.. 71.5
Voter Turnout (Highest Office) 453,471
    % of VAP 58.4
    % of Registration 81.8
Persons Not Voting—of Voting Age 322,529
    % of VAP 41.6
Persons Not Voting—of Registered 101,193
    % of Registration 18.2
Straight Ticket Voting .... Yes, Exception

State Officials and Members of Congress

Governor:
Bruce Sundlun (D) 1990, elected to a two-year term in 1992.

U.S. Senators:
Claiborne Pell (D) 1960, elected to a six-year term in 1990.
John H. Chafee (R) 1976, elected to a six-year term in 1988.

U.S. Representative in Congress:
(District, Name, Party, Date first elected)

1. Machtley (R) 1988   2. Reed (D) 1990

---

[1]Elections administered by 39 cities and towns rather than counties. Data presented for counties and 35 cities and towns with more than one voting precinct. [2]Reported for all 39 cities and towns, including those with a single voting precinct.

Candidates: General Election, November 3, 1992

Candidate(s)	Total vote	Percent	Party	Status	First elected
President/Vice President					
Clinton/Gore	213,299	47.04%	Democrat	Challenger	1992
Bush/Quayle	131,601	29.02%	Republican	Incumbent	1988
Perot/Stockdale	105,045	23.16%	Perot for Pres.	Challenger	
Fulani/Munoz	1,878	0.41%	New Alliance	Challenger	
Marrou/Lord	571	0.13%	Libertarian	Challenger	
LaRouche/Bevel	494	0.11%	Ind. for LaRouche	Challenger	
Hagelin/Tompkins	262	0.06%	Natural Law	Challenger	
Phillips/Knight	215	0.05%	Taxpayers	Challenger	
Other	106	0.02%	Write in	Challenger	
U.S. Senator (No Contest)					
Governor					
Bruce Sundlun	261,484	61.55%	Democrat	Incumbent	1990
Elizabeth Leonard	145,590	34.27%	Republican	Challenger	
Joseph Devine	14,511	3.42%	Reform 92	Challenger	
Jack Potter	1,698	0.40%	Populist	Challenger	
John Staradumsky	1,535	0.36%	Independent	Challenger	
U.S. Representative in Congress					
District 1					
Ronald Machtley	135,982	70.06%	Republican	Incumbent	1988
David Carlin	48,092	24.78%	Democrat	Challenger	
Fredrick Dick	6,012	3.10%	Ross Perot	Challenger	
Norman Jacques	4,003	2.06%	Independent	Challenger	
District 2					
John Reed	144,450	70.67%	Democrat	Incumbent	1990
James Bell	49,998	24.46%	Republican	Challenger	
Thomas Ricci	6,715	3.29%	Independent	Challenger	
John Turnbell	3,250	1.59%	Independent	Challenger	

Candidates: March 10, 1992, Primary Election

Candidate	Total vote	Percent	Candidate	Total vote	Percent
Presidential Preference, Democratic			**Presidential Preference, Republican**		
Paul Tsongas	26,825	52.90%	George Bush	9,853	63.01%
Bill Clinton	10,762	21.22%	Patrick Buchanan	4,967	31.77%
Jerry Brown	9,541	18.82%	Uncommitted	444	2.84%
Uncommitted	703	1.39%	David Duke	326	2.08%
Bob Kerrey	469	0.92%	Others	46	0.29%
Charles Woods	408	0.80%			
Tom Harkin	319	0.63%			
Susan Fey	308	0.61%			
Others	307	0.61%			
Lyndon LaRouche, Jr.	300	0.59%			
Eugene McCarthy	235	0.46%			
John Staradumsky	168	0.33%			
Thomas Laughlin	94	0.19%			
Ray Rollinson	91	0.18%			
Larry Agran	79	0.16%			
Curly Thornton	52	0.10%			
Steve Burke	48	0.09%			

Voter Registration and Turnout, 1948-1992 Elections

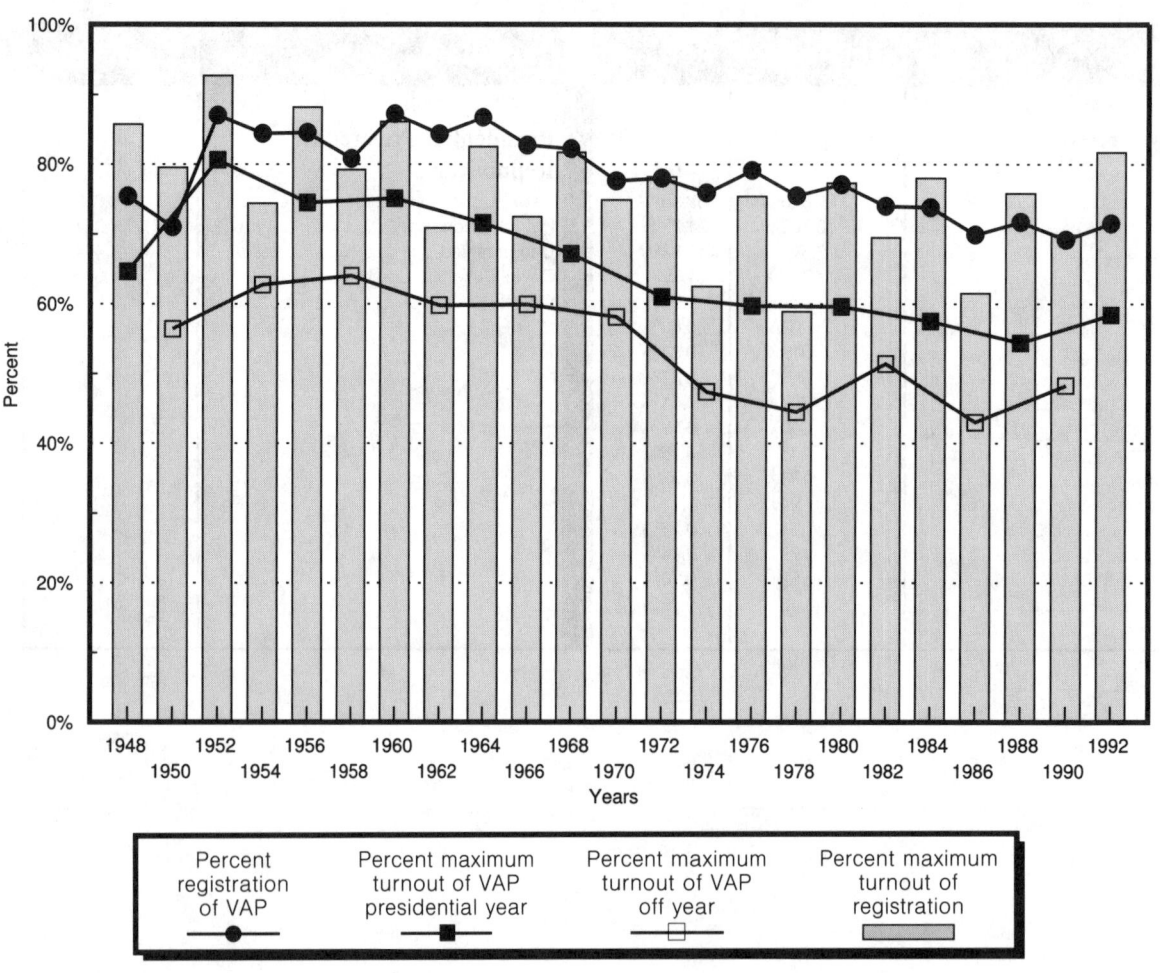

Percent registration of VAP	Percent maximum turnout of VAP presidential year	Percent maximum turnout of VAP off year	Percent maximum turnout of registration

Year	Estimated Voting Age Population (VAP)	Voter registration (REG)				Voter turnout										
						Highest office						Maximum vote				
		Total	Percent of VAP	Rank by percent of VAP	Actual	Total	Office	Percent total REG	Rank by percent of REG	Percent of VAP	Rank by percent of VAP	Total	Percent total REG	Rank by percent of REG	Percent total VAP	Rank by percent of VAP
1992	776,000	554,664	71.5	34	-	453,471	P	81.8	11	58.4	27	453,471	81.8	16	58.4	27
1990	776,000	536,773	69.2	23	375,188	364,052	S	67.8	6	46.9	13	375,188	69.9	6	48.3	13
1988	765,000	548,758	71.7	25	415,963	404,620	P	73.7	18	52.9	23	415,963	75.8	18	54.4	24
1986	751,000	524,664	69.9	24	322,724	322,724	G	61.5	13	43.0	17	322,724	61.5	14	43.0	19
1984	735,000	542,216	73.8	25	422,851	410,492	P	75.7	18	55.8	23	422,851	78.0	16	57.5	19
1982	721,000	533,853	74.0	16	370,928	342,779	S	64.2	22	47.5	11	370,928	69.5	14	51.4	9
1980	710,000	547,469	77.1	16	423,349	416,072	P	76.0	19	58.6	15	423,349	77.3	18	59.6	15
1978	707,000	533,843	75.5	12	-	314,363	G	58.9	19	44.5	16	314,363	58.9	21	44.5	18
1976	689,000	544,992	79.1	16	-	411,070	P	75.4	24	59.7	15	411,070	75.4	26	59.7	20
1974	678,000	514,334	75.9	14	-	321,660	G	62.5	18	47.4	14	321,660	62.5	19	47.4	14
1972	682,000	531,847	78.0	18	-	415,808	P	78.2	17	61.0	18	415,808	78.2	21	61.0	21
1970	596,000	462,252	77.6	15	-	346,342	G	74.9	8	58.1	9	346,342	74.9	10	58.1	10
1968	573,000	471,112	82.2	15	-	385,000	P	81.7	20	67.2	15	385,000	81.7	22	67.2	16
1966	554,000	458,260	82.7	11	-	332,064	G	72.5	12	59.9	6	332,064	72.5	14	59.9	8
1964	545,000	472,659	86.7	14	-	390,091	P	82.5	18	71.6	12	390,091	82.5	19	71.6	13
1962	548,000	462,165	84.3	7	-	327,506	G	70.9	16	59.8	12	327,506	70.9	16	59.8	13
1960	540,000	471,114	87.2	9	-	405,535	P	86.1	16	75.1	13	405,535	86.1	17	75.1	13
1958	542,000	437,810	80.8	11	-	346,780	G	79.2	5	64.0	3	346,780	79.2	6	64.0	3
1956	520,000	439,575	84.5	10	-	387,609	P	88.2	6	74.5	6	387,609	88.2	7	74.5	7
1954	524,000	442,039	84.4	7	-	328,670	G	74.4	7	62.7	5	328,670	74.4	8	62.7	5
1952	514,000	447,249	87.0	7	-	414,498	P	92.7	2	80.6	3	414,498	92.7	3	80.6	3
1950	526,000	373,375	71.0	13	-	296,809	G	79.5	4	56.4	12	296,809	79.5	4	56.4	13
1948	507,000	382,340	75.4	9	-	327,702	P	85.7	3	64.6	12	327,702	85.7	5	64.6	15

RHODE ISLAND

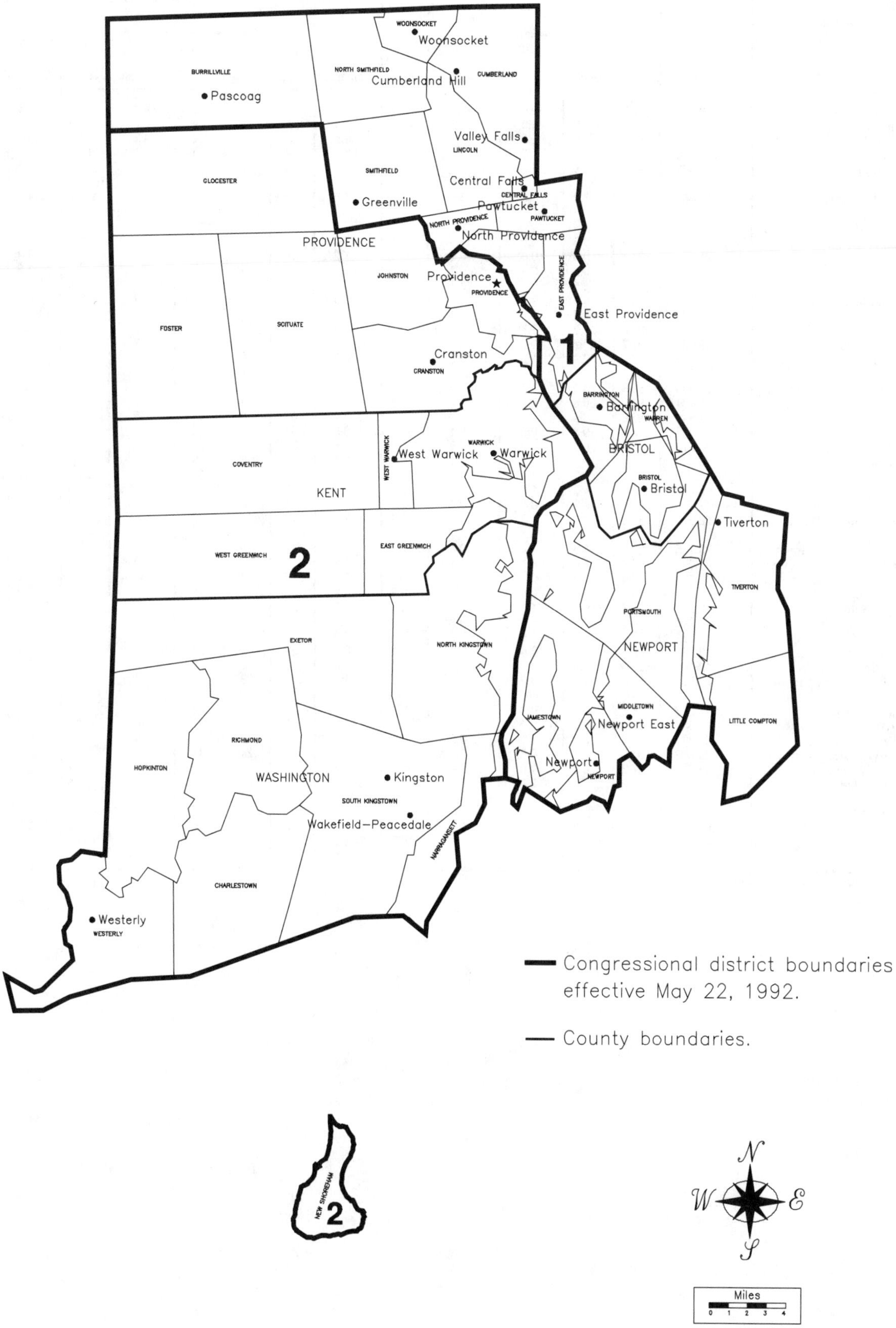

WOONSOCKET
● Woonsocket

BURRILLVILLE
● Pascoag

NORTH SMITHFIELD
Cumberland Hill
CUMBERLAND

Valley Falls

LINCOLN

GLOCESTER

SMITHFIELD

Central Falls
CENTRAL FALLS
● Greenville
Pawtucket
PAWTUCKET

NORTH PROVIDENCE
North Providence

PROVIDENCE

JOHNSTON

Providence ★
PROVIDENCE

East Providence
EAST PROVIDENCE

FOSTER

SCITUATE

● Cranston
CRANSTON

BARRINGTON
● Barrington
WARREN

WARWICK
WEST WARWICK
West Warwick ● Warwick
WARWICK

BRISTOL

BRISTOL
● Bristol

COVENTRY

KENT

● Tiverton

EAST GREENWICH

TIVERTON

WEST GREENWICH

2

PORTSMOUTH

NORTH KINGSTOWN

NEWPORT

EXETOR

JAMESTOWN
MIDDLETOWN
Newport East

LITTLE COMPTON

RICHMOND

Newport
NEWPORT

HOPKINTON

WASHINGTON
● Kingston

SOUTH KINGSTOWN
Wakefield—Peacedale

NARRAGANSETT

CHARLESTOWN

● Westerly
WESTERLY

── Congressional district boundaries
effective May 22, 1992.

── County boundaries.

NEW SHOREHAM
2

N
W E
S

Miles
0 1 2 3 4

Rhode Island 809

Table A. — 1990 Population by Race and Ethnic Origin

State/county code	County	Total persons	White	Black	Asian and Pacific Islander	Native American	Other	Hispanic	Total	White	Black	Hispanic	Total	White	Black	Hispanic
			Percent of total persons (Non-Hispanic)						Rank[1] (Percent of total persons, Non-Hispanic)				Percent contribution to state population (Non-Hispanic)			
44 001	Bristol	48,859	97.5	0.4	0.6	<.1	<.1	1.4	5	1	5	3	4.9	5.3	0.5	1.5
44 003	Kent	161,135	97.3	0.6	0.8	0.2	<.1	1.1	2	2	4	4	16.1	17.5	2.9	3.8
44 005	Newport	87,194	92.6	3.8	1.2	0.4	0.2	2.0	4	4	2	2	8.7	9.0	9.5	3.7
44 007	Providence	596,270	84.8	4.8	2.3	0.3	1.0	6.8	1	5	1	1	59.4	56.4	84.0	88.7
44 009	Washington	110,006	95.9	0.9	1.3	0.9	<.1	1.0	3	3	3	5	11.0	11.8	3.0	2.3
44	**RHODE ISLAND**	**1,003,464**	**89.3**	**3.4**	**1.8**	**0.4**	**0.6**	**4.6**					**100.0**	**100.0**	**100.0**	**100.0**
	CITIES AND TOWNS															
44 001	Barrington town	15,849	97.8	0.3	1.0	<.1	<.1	0.8	23	12	26	24	1.6	1.7	0.1	0.3
44 001	Bristol town	21,625	97.1	0.4	0.5	0.1	<.1	1.9	15	20	21	8	2.2	2.3	0.3	0.9
44 007	Burrillville town	16,230	99.2	0.1	0.1	0.1	<.1	0.4	22	1	35	34	1.6	1.8	<.1	0.2
44 007	Central Falls city	17,637	64.8	2.8	0.5	0.1	2.7	29.0	20	34	6	1	1.8	1.3	1.4	11.2
44 009	Charlestown town	6,478	96.6	0.6	0.6	1.6	<.1	0.6	32	22	17	29	0.6	0.7	0.1	<.1
44 003	Coventry town	31,083	98.4	0.3	0.4	0.1	<.1	0.8	8	6	29	22	3.1	3.4	0.2	0.6
44 007	Cranston city	76,060	93.8	2.2	1.7	0.2	0.1	2.0	3	27	8	7	7.6	8.0	4.8	3.3
44 007	Cumberland town	29,038	97.7	0.2	0.4	<.1	0.1	1.5	10	13	30	12	2.9	3.2	0.2	1.0
44 003	East Greenwich town	11,865	97.4	0.4	1.3	0.2	<.1	0.6	26	16	24	27	1.2	1.3	0.1	0.2
44 007	East Providence city	50,380	90.9	4.3	0.6	0.5	2.1	1.7	5	30	4	11	5.0	5.1	6.3	1.8
44 009	Exeter town	5,461	97.7	0.8	0.3	0.7	<.1	0.5	33	14	15	30	0.5	0.6	0.1	<.1
44 007	Foster town	4,316	98.6	0.4	0.3	0.3	0.0	0.4	35	4	23	35	0.4	0.5	<.1	<.1
44 007	Glocester town	9,227	98.8	0.3	0.2	0.1	<.1	0.5	30	2	25	33	0.9	1.0	<.1	<.1
44 009	Hopkinton town	6,873	98.1	0.3	0.2	0.8	0.0	0.7	31	9	28	26	0.7	0.8	<.1	0.1
44 007	Johnston town	26,542	98.1	0.6	0.6	<.1	<.1	0.7	12	8	19	25	2.6	2.9	0.4	0.4
44 007	Lincoln town	18,045	97.5	0.2	1.0	<.1	0.1	1.0	19	15	31	19	1.8	2.0	0.1	0.4
44 005	Middletown town	19,460	90.4	4.5	1.9	0.3	0.2	2.7	17	31	3	5	1.9	2.0	2.5	1.2
44 009	Narragansett town	14,985	96.4	0.8	0.9	0.9	<.1	1.0	24	23	13	18	1.5	1.6	0.3	0.3
44 005	Newport city	28,227	87.0	7.8	1.3	0.7	0.4	2.8	11	32	2	4	2.8	2.7	6.4	1.7
44 009	North Kingstown town	23,786	96.2	1.3	1.0	0.4	<.1	1.1	14	25	10	16	2.4	2.6	0.9	0.6
44 007	North Providence town	32,090	95.8	1.0	1.1	<.1	0.2	1.8	7	26	11	10	3.2	3.4	1.0	1.2
44 007	North Smithfield town	10,497	98.6	0.2	0.7	<.1	<.1	0.5	28	5	34	32	1.0	1.2	<.1	0.1
44 007	Pawtucket city	72,644	85.4	3.2	0.6	0.2	3.4	7.2	4	33	5	3	7.2	6.9	6.8	11.4
44 005	Portsmouth town	16,857	96.7	0.9	1.1	0.2	0.1	1.0	21	21	12	17	1.7	1.8	0.4	0.4
44 007	Providence city	160,728	64.5	12.6	5.6	0.8	0.9	15.5	1	35	1	2	16.0	11.6	59.1	54.6
44 009	Richmond town	5,351	97.3	0.4	0.6	0.7	<.1	0.9	34	17	22	21	0.5	0.6	<.1	0.1
44 007	Scituate town	9,796	98.8	0.2	0.4	<.1	<.1	0.5	29	3	33	31	1.0	1.1	<.1	0.1
44 007	Smithfield town	19,163	98.0	0.5	0.7	0.1	<.1	0.6	18	10	20	28	1.9	2.1	0.3	0.2
44 009	South Kingstown town	24,631	92.5	1.4	3.0	1.8	0.1	1.2	13	28	9	13	2.5	2.5	1.0	0.7
44 005	Tiverton town	14,312	98.2	0.2	0.3	0.1	<.1	1.1	25	7	32	15	1.4	1.6	<.1	0.4
44 001	Warren town	11,385	97.9	0.3	0.4	<.1	<.1	1.2	27	11	27	14	1.1	1.2	<.1	0.3
44 003	Warwick city	85,427	97.2	0.8	0.8	0.2	<.1	1.0	2	19	14	20	8.5	9.3	1.9	1.8
44 003	West Warwick town	29,268	96.2	0.7	0.9	0.2	<.1	1.9	9	24	16	9	2.9	3.1	0.6	1.2
44 009	Westerly town	21,605	97.2	0.6	1.0	0.4	<.1	0.8	16	18	18	23	2.2	2.3	0.4	0.4
44 007	Woonsocket city	43,877	91.6	2.6	2.9	0.2	0.1	2.6	6	29	7	6	4.4	4.5	3.3	2.5
	CONGRESSIONAL															
	District 1	501,677	90.7	3.0	1.2	0.2	1.0	3.8	2	1	2	2	50.0	50.8	44.3	41.5
	District 2	501,787	87.9	3.8	2.3	0.5	0.2	5.3	1	2	1	1	50.0	49.2	55.7	58.5

[1]Separate rankings for five counties and for 35 cities and towns.

810 Rhode Island

Table B. — 1990 Voting Age Population (VAP) by Race and Ethnic Origin

County	Total Voting Age Population	Percent of total VAP — Non-Hispanic White	Black	Asian and Pacific Islander	Native American	Other	Hispanic	Rank[1] Percent of total VAP — Total	Non-Hispanic White	Black	Hispanic	Percent contribution to state VAP — Total	Non-Hispanic White	Black	Hispanic	VAP percent of total population — Total	Non-Hispanic White	Black	Asian and Pacific Islander	Native American	Other	Hispanic
Bristol	38,115	97.8	0.3	0.6	<.1	<.1	1.2	5	1	5	3	4.9	5.3	0.6	1.6	78.0	78.2	73.6	73.2	68.4	44.4	69.2
Kent	124,799	97.6	0.6	0.7	0.2	<.1	0.9	2	2	4	4	16.0	17.2	3.1	4.0	77.5	77.7	70.9	68.9	71.0	56.8	67.9
Newport	67,548	93.2	3.4	1.1	0.3	0.2	1.8	4	4	2	2	8.7	8.9	10.2	4.1	77.5	78.0	71.2	71.8	66.0	59.0	70.3
Providence	462,672	87.3	4.1	1.9	0.3	0.8	5.6	1	5	1	1	59.5	57.1	82.9	87.9	77.6	79.9	65.9	63.6	67.3	64.9	64.2
Washington	84,640	96.1	0.9	1.3	0.8	<.1	0.9	3	3	3	5	10.9	11.5	3.2	2.5	76.9	77.2	71.6	76.8	68.4	55.0	70.1
RHODE ISLAND	**777,774**	**90.9**	**2.9**	**1.5**	**0.3**	**0.5**	**3.8**					**100.0**	**100.0**	**100.0**	**100.0**	**77.5**	**78.9**	**66.8**	**65.7**	**67.8**	**64.4**	**64.8**
CITIES AND TOWNS																						
Barrington town	11,937	98.1	0.3	0.9	<.1	<.1	0.7	23	12	26	23	1.5	1.7	0.2	0.3	75.3	75.5	72.5	67.1	60.0	57.1	65.6
Bristol town	17,245	97.3	0.4	0.5	<.1	<.1	1.7	15	20	20	8	2.2	2.4	0.3	1.0	79.7	80.0	77.4	80.6	59.1	42.9	70.2
Burrillville town	11,751	99.2	<.1	0.1	0.2	<.1	0.4	24	1	35	33	1.5	1.6	<.1	0.2	72.4	72.4	58.8	75.0	90.5	40.0	67.6
Central Falls city	12,827	69.4	2.2	0.5	0.1	2.1	25.7	20	35	7	1	1.6	1.3	1.2	11.1	72.7	77.9	57.6	66.3	58.3	56.6	64.4
Charlestown town	4,903	97.0	0.5	0.6	1.4	0.0	0.5	32	22	17	29	0.6	0.7	0.1	<.1	75.7	76.0	66.7	77.5	66.7	0.0	64.9
Coventry town	23,457	98.6	0.2	0.3	<.1	<.1	0.8	8	6	31	21	3.0	3.3	0.2	0.6	75.5	75.6	59.0	67.0	59.4	54.5	69.6
Cranston city	61,387	94.2	2.2	1.4	0.2	<.1	1.9	3	27	6	7	7.9	8.2	6.0	3.9	80.7	81.1	82.6	65.2	79.7	58.2	75.5
Cumberland town	22,611	97.9	0.2	0.4	<.1	0.1	1.4	10	14	29	12	2.9	3.1	0.2	1.1	77.9	78.0	68.2	71.6	100.0	64.9	72.3
East Greenwich town	8,952	97.7	0.5	1.1	0.2	<.1	0.6	26	16	19	24	1.2	1.2	0.2	0.2	75.4	75.6	83.7	61.3	63.6	50.0	74.0
East Providence city	39,723	91.6	3.9	0.6	0.5	1.9	1.6	5	30	4	11	5.1	5.1	6.8	2.1	78.8	79.5	72.3	77.7	74.6	71.4	72.9
Exeter town	3,940	97.6	0.8	0.4	0.7	<.1	0.4	33	17	13	32	0.5	0.5	0.1	<.1	72.1	72.1	73.2	82.4	80.6	75.0	56.7
Foster town	3,131	99.0	0.4	0.1	0.2	0.0	0.3	35	4	24	35	0.4	0.4	<.1	<.1	72.5	72.8	61.1	30.8	58.3	0.0	62.5
Glocester town	6,701	99.2	0.2	0.1	0.1	0.0	0.3	30	2	32	34	0.9	0.9	<.1	<.1	72.6	72.9	40.6	62.5	69.2	0.0	50.0
Hopkinton town	5,034	98.2	0.3	0.3	0.7	0.0	0.5	31	8	25	31	0.6	0.7	<.1	<.1	73.2	73.4	88.9	82.4	69.8	0.0	51.1
Johnston town	21,210	98.5	0.4	0.5	<.1	<.1	0.6	12	7	21	27	2.7	3.0	0.4	0.4	79.9	80.2	57.0	68.9	82.6	66.7	68.0
Lincoln town	14,155	97.9	0.2	0.9	<.1	0.1	0.9	19	13	28	19	1.8	2.0	0.1	0.4	78.4	78.7	77.5	65.1	70.0	75.0	66.7
Middletown town	14,784	91.0	4.3	1.7	0.3	0.1	2.5	18	31	3	4	1.9	1.9	2.8	1.2	76.0	76.5	73.1	68.5	78.7	66.7	68.7
Narragansett town	12,116	96.7	0.7	0.9	0.6	<.1	0.9	22	23	14	16	1.6	1.7	0.4	0.4	80.9	81.2	73.9	83.8	60.2	54.5	74.2
Newport city	22,471	88.7	6.8	1.3	0.5	0.3	2.5	11	32	2	5	2.9	2.8	6.7	1.9	79.6	81.1	70.1	74.6	58.8	58.1	70.1
North Kingstown town	17,710	96.7	1.1	0.9	0.4	<.1	0.9	14	25	10	17	2.3	2.4	0.9	0.5	74.5	74.9	63.7	67.2	65.3	45.5	62.8
North Providence town	26,435	96.2	1.0	1.0	<.1	0.1	1.6	7	26	11	10	3.4	3.6	1.2	1.4	82.4	82.7	81.9	72.9	82.1	62.3	73.4
North Smithfield town	8,165	98.7	0.1	0.6	<.1	<.1	0.5	28	5	33	28	1.0	1.1	<.1	0.1	77.8	77.9	75.0	65.2	80.0	100.0	73.2
Pawtucket city	55,925	87.6	2.6	0.5	0.2	2.8	6.3	4	33	5	3	7.2	6.9	6.4	11.8	77.0	78.9	63.0	66.7	66.0	65.0	67.1
Portsmouth town	12,682	97.0	0.9	1.0	0.2	<.1	0.9	21	21	12	18	1.6	1.7	0.5	0.4	75.2	75.5	73.5	69.7	63.4	57.9	64.6
Providence city	122,756	70.5	10.7	4.6	0.6	0.8	12.7	1	34	1	2	15.8	12.2	57.3	52.7	76.4	83.5	64.8	62.7	63.3	63.6	62.5
Richmond town	3,786	97.8	0.4	0.6	0.6	0.0	0.6	34	15	22	26	0.5	0.5	<.1	<.1	70.8	71.2	65.2	61.8	60.0	0.0	47.9
Scituate town	7,370	99.0	0.1	0.4	<.1	<.1	0.5	29	3	34	30	0.9	1.0	<.1	0.1	75.2	75.4	60.0	61.4	100.0	100.0	64.2
Smithfield town	15,265	98.2	0.4	0.6	0.1	<.1	0.6	17	9	23	25	2.0	2.1	0.3	0.3	79.7	79.8	57.3	71.9	91.7	66.7	85.0
South Kingstown town	19,861	92.6	1.4	3.0	1.6	<.1	1.3	13	29	9	13	2.6	2.6	1.2	0.8	80.6	80.8	80.9	81.0	71.2	66.7	82.0
Tiverton town	11,146	98.1	0.2	0.3	0.1	<.1	1.2	25	11	30	14	1.4	1.5	<.1	0.4	77.9	77.8	71.0	82.6	78.9	50.0	82.0
Warren town	8,933	98.2	0.2	0.4	0.1	<.1	1.1	27	10	27	15	1.1	1.2	<.1	0.3	78.5	78.6	64.7	77.8	90.9	25.0	69.3
Warwick city	67,105	97.5	0.7	0.7	0.2	<.1	0.8	2	19	15	20	8.6	9.2	2.1	1.9	78.6	78.8	72.7	70.5	75.9	65.5	66.9
West Warwick town	22,708	96.7	0.6	0.8	0.2	<.1	1.6	9	24	16	9	2.9	3.1	0.6	1.2	77.6	78.0	67.0	70.0	66.0	23.1	67.7
Westerly town	16,617	97.5	0.5	0.9	0.3	<.1	0.8	16	18	18	22	2.1	2.3	0.4	0.4	76.9	77.2	62.8	70.4	69.7	25.0	69.4
Woonsocket city	33,260	93.7	1.9	2.3	0.1	<.1	1.9	6	28	8	6	4.3	4.4	2.8	2.1	75.8	77.5	57.3	59.0	63.0	51.0	54.7
CONGRESSIONAL																						
District 1	392,873	91.9	2.7	1.2	0.2	0.8	3.2	1	1	2	2	50.5	51.0	45.9	42.8	78.3	79.3	69.1	74.2	70.2	66.0	66.9
District 2	384,901	90.0	3.2	1.8	0.4	0.2	4.4	2	2	1	1	49.5	49.0	54.1	57.2	76.7	78.5	64.9	61.0	66.6	57.0	63.3

[1]Separate rankings for five counties and for 35 cities and towns.

Table C. — Voter Participation: November 3, 1992, General Election

County	Estimated Voting Age Population (VAP), 1992	Voter registration (REG)				Voter turnout													
							Highest office			Maximum vote						Percent drop-off, by office			
		Total	% contribution to state REG	% of 1992 VAP	Rank by % of 1992 VAP	Actual	Total	Office	% of 1992 VAP	Total	% contribution to state turnout	% of REG	Rank by % of REG[1]	% of 1992 VAP	Rank by % 1992 VAP	President	Senator	Governor	Representative
Bristol	37,646	28,073	5.1	74.6	2	-	24,911	P	66.2	24,911	5.5	88.7	1	66.2	1	0.0	-	6.7	12.0
Kent	125,124	95,722	17.3	76.5	1	-	82,425	P	65.9	82,425	18.2	86.1	2	65.9	2	0.0	-	4.7	10.0
Newport	67,635	46,397	8.4	68.6	5	-	39,644	P	58.6	39,644	8.7	85.4	3	58.6	4	0.0	-	9.7	11.9
Providence	459,983	321,253	57.9	69.8	4	-	253,441	P	55.1	253,441	55.9	78.9	5	55.1	5	0.0	-	6.3	12.8
Washington	85,612	63,219	11.4	73.8	3	-	52,944	P	61.8	52,944	11.7	83.7	4	61.8	3	0.0	-	6.0	12.4
RHODE ISLAND	**776,000**	**554,664**	**100.0**	**71.5**		-	**453,471**		**58.4**	**453,471**	**100.0**	**81.8**		**58.4**		**0.0**	-	**6.3**	**12.1**
CITIES AND TOWNS																			
Barrington town	-	11,142	2.0	-	-	-	9,565	P	-	9,565	2.1	85.8	16	-	-	0.0	-	6.4	10.1
Bristol town	-	11,166	2.0	-	-	-	10,068	P	-	10,068	2.2	90.2	4	-	-	0.0	-	6.8	14.1
Burrillville town	-	7,697	1.4	-	-	-	6,423	P	-	6,423	1.4	83.4	25	-	-	0.0	-	7.5	13.7
Central Falls city	-	6,004	1.1	-	-	-	4,086	P	-	4,086	0.9	68.1	34	-	-	0.0	-	10.6	17.7
Charlestown town	-	3,964	0.7	-	-	-	3,183	P	-	3,183	0.7	80.3	32	-	-	0.0	-	3.3	10.7
Coventry town	-	17,311	3.1	-	-	-	15,080	P	-	15,080	3.3	87.1	10	-	-	0.0	-	6.0	11.1
Cranston city	-	52,176	9.4	-	-	-	39,606	P	-	39,606	8.7	75.9	33	-	-	0.0	-	4.1	10.2
Cumberland town	-	17,213	3.1	-	-	-	15,345	P	-	15,345	3.4	89.1	9	-	-	0.0	-	5.4	12.0
East Greenwich town	-	7,944	1.4	-	-	-	6,762	P	-	6,762	1.5	85.1	21	-	-	0.0	-	4.6	10.1
East Providence city	-	25,046	4.5	-	-	-	22,361	P	-	22,361	4.9	89.3	7	-	-	0.0	-	5.8	13.1
Exeter town	-	3,133	0.6	-	-	-	2,694	P	-	2,694	0.6	86.0	14	-	-	0.0	-	5.9	11.5
Foster town	-	2,395	0.4	-	-	-	2,138	P	-	2,138	0.5	89.3	8	-	-	0.0	-	4.2	5.6
Glocester town	-	5,165	0.9	-	-	-	4,613	P	-	4,613	1.0	89.3	6	-	-	0.0	-	6.1	12.1
Hopkinton town	-	4,036	0.7	-	-	-	3,285	P	-	3,285	0.7	81.4	30	-	-	0.0	-	9.0	16.9
Johnston town	-	16,868	3.0	-	-	-	14,540	P	-	14,540	3.2	86.2	12	-	-	0.0	-	5.5	12.1
Lincoln town	-	11,835	2.1	-	-	-	10,111	P	-	10,111	2.2	85.4	18	-	-	0.0	-	5.2	8.7
Middletown town	-	7,819	1.4	-	-	-	7,327	P	-	7,327	1.6	93.7	1	-	-	0.0	-	11.8	13.2
Narragansett town	-	9,321	1.7	-	-	-	7,642	P	-	7,642	1.7	82.0	29	-	-	0.0	-	7.4	13.7
Newport city	-	13,772	2.5	-	-	-	11,118	P	-	11,118	2.5	80.7	31	-	-	0.0	-	10.7	12.2
North Kingstown town	-	14,448	2.6	-	-	-	12,303	P	-	12,303	2.7	85.2	20	-	-	0.0	-	1.9	8.0
North Providence town	-	22,692	4.1	-	-	-	18,657	P	-	18,657	4.1	82.2	27	-	-	0.0	-	6.1	13.5
North Smithfield town	-	6,689	1.2	-	-	-	5,747	P	-	5,747	1.3	85.9	15	-	-	0.0	-	5.9	10.7
Pawtucket city	-	32,868	5.9	-	-	-	26,962	P	-	26,962	5.9	82.0	28	-	-	0.0	-	7.6	13.7
Portsmouth town	-	10,253	1.8	-	-	-	8,712	P	-	8,712	1.9	85.0	22	-	-	0.0	-	7.0	9.5
Providence city	-	79,093	14.3	-	-	-	52,288	P	-	52,288	11.5	66.1	35	-	-	0.0	-	7.7	15.3
Richmond town	-	3,461	0.6	-	-	-	2,915	P	-	2,915	0.6	84.2	23	-	-	0.0	-	8.1	14.6
Scituate town	-	5,904	1.1	-	-	-	5,316	P	-	5,316	1.2	90.0	5	-	-	0.0	-	5.5	11.6
Smithfield town	-	10,833	2.0	-	-	-	9,773	P	-	9,773	2.2	90.2	3	-	-	0.0	-	5.4	11.2
South Kingstown town	-	12,232	2.2	-	-	-	10,251	P	-	10,251	2.3	83.8	24	-	-	0.0	-	5.5	10.2
Tiverton town	-	8,572	1.5	-	-	-	7,356	P	-	7,356	1.6	85.8	17	-	-	0.0	-	8.8	14.4
Warren town	-	5,765	1.0	-	-	-	5,278	P	-	5,278	1.2	91.6	2	-	-	0.0	-	7.3	11.5
Warwick city	-	51,821	9.3	-	-	-	44,692	P	-	44,692	9.9	86.2	11	-	-	0.0	-	3.7	9.1
West Warwick town	-	15,900	2.9	-	-	-	13,542	P	-	13,542	3.0	85.2	19	-	-	0.0	-	6.3	11.7
Westerly town	-	11,451	2.1	-	-	-	9,856	P	-	9,856	2.2	86.1	13	-	-	0.0	-	10.0	18.0
Woonsocket city	-	18,775	3.4	-	-	-	15,475	P	-	15,475	3.4	82.4	26	-	-	0.0	-	8.2	13.4

[1]Separate rankings for five counties and for 35 cities and towns.

Table E. — Vote for President: November 3, 1992, General Election

County	All candidates																			Major party	
						Plurality		Percent of total vote				Rank¹			Percent contribution to state vote				Percent of vote	
	Total	Clinton (DEM)	Bush (REP)	Perot (IND)	Other	Total	Party	DEM	REP	IND	Other	DEM	REP	IND	Total	DEM	REP	IND	DEM	REP
Bristol	24,911	11,414	8,208	5,132	157	3,206	D	45.8	32.9	20.6	0.6	2	1	5	5.5	5.4	6.2	4.9	58.2	41.8
Kent	82,425	35,934	25,217	20,690	584	10,717	D	43.6	30.6	25.1	0.7	4	4	1	18.2	16.8	19.2	19.7	58.8	41.2
Newport	39,644	17,584	12,386	9,366	308	5,198	D	44.4	31.2	23.6	0.8	3	2	3	8.7	8.2	9.4	8.9	58.7	41.3
Providence	253,441	125,358	69,579	56,575	1,929	55,779	D	49.5	27.5	22.3	0.8	1	5	4	55.9	58.8	52.9	53.9	64.3	35.7
Washington	52,944	23,009	16,211	13,282	442	6,798	D	43.5	30.6	25.1	0.8	5	3	2	11.7	10.8	12.3	12.6	58.7	41.3
RHODE ISLAND²	**453,471**	**213,299**	**131,601**	**105,045**	**3,526**	**81,698**	**D**	**47.0**	**29.0**	**23.2**	**0.8**				**100.0**	**100.0**	**100.0**	**100.0**	**61.8**	**38.2**
CITIES AND TOWNS																				
Barrington town	9,565	3,968	3,846	1,689	62	122	D	41.5	40.2	17.7	0.6	21	2	34	2.1	1.9	2.9	1.6	50.8	49.2
Bristol town	10,068	5,018	2,818	2,178	54	2,200	D	49.8	28.0	21.6	0.5	5	27	29	2.2	2.4	2.1	2.1	64.0	36.0
Burrillville town	6,423	2,454	1,880	2,018	71	436	D	38.2	29.3	31.4	1.1	29	22	3	1.4	1.2	1.4	1.9	56.6	43.4
Central Falls city	4,086	2,269	955	831	31	1,314	D	55.5	23.4	20.3	0.8	2	34	33	0.9	1.1	0.7	0.8	70.4	29.6
Charlestown town	3,183	1,249	1,063	839	32	186	D	39.2	33.4	26.4	1.0	28	7	12	0.7	0.6	0.8	0.8	54.0	46.0
Coventry town	15,080	6,086	4,466	4,415	113	1,620	D	40.4	29.6	29.3	0.7	26	20	8	3.3	2.9	3.4	4.2	57.7	42.3
Cranston city	39,606	18,589	12,450	8,331	236	6,139	D	46.9	31.4	21.0	0.6	10	13	30	8.7	8.7	9.5	7.9	59.9	40.1
Cumberland town	15,345	6,406	4,869	3,971	99	1,537	D	41.7	31.7	25.9	0.6	20	10	14	3.4	3.0	3.7	3.8	56.8	43.2
East Greenwich town	6,762	2,400	2,838	1,489	35	438	R	35.5	42.0	22.0	0.5	34	1	27	1.5	1.1	2.2	1.4	45.8	54.2
East Providence city	22,361	11,701	5,843	4,661	156	5,858	D	52.3	26.1	20.8	0.7	4	30	31	4.9	5.5	4.4	4.4	66.7	33.3
Exeter town	2,694	1,004	842	824	24	162	D	37.3	31.3	30.6	0.9	31	14	5	0.6	0.5	0.6	0.8	54.4	45.6
Foster town	2,138	848	627	648	15	200	D	39.7	29.3	30.3	0.7	27	21	6	0.5	0.4	0.5	0.6	57.5	42.5
Glocester town	4,613	1,699	1,451	1,420	43	248	D	36.8	31.5	30.8	0.9	32	12	4	1.0	0.8	1.1	1.4	53.9	46.1
Hopkinton town	3,285	1,186	1,000	1,055	44	131	D	36.1	30.4	32.1	1.3	33	16	2	0.7	0.6	0.8	1.0	54.3	45.7
Johnston town	14,540	6,655	4,230	3,538	117	2,425	D	45.8	29.1	24.3	0.8	13	24	19	3.2	3.1	3.2	3.4	61.1	38.9
Lincoln town	10,111	4,158	3,361	2,518	74	797	D	41.1	33.2	24.9	0.7	24	8	18	2.2	1.9	2.6	2.4	55.3	44.7
Middletown town	7,327	3,147	2,452	1,672	56	695	D	43.0	33.5	22.8	0.8	18	6	25	1.6	1.5	1.9	1.6	56.2	43.8
Narragansett town	7,642	3,606	2,309	1,690	37	1,297	D	47.2	30.2	22.1	0.5	9	17	26	1.7	1.7	1.8	1.6	61.0	39.0
Newport city	11,118	5,363	3,412	2,278	65	1,951	D	48.2	30.7	20.5	0.6	8	15	32	2.5	2.5	2.6	2.2	61.1	38.9
North Kingstown town	12,303	5,070	4,199	2,929	105	871	D	41.2	34.1	23.8	0.9	22	4	21	2.7	2.4	3.2	2.8	54.7	45.3
North Providence town	18,657	9,111	5,108	4,310	128	4,003	D	48.8	27.4	23.1	0.7	6	28	24	4.1	4.3	3.9	4.1	64.1	35.9
North Smithfield town	5,747	2,187	1,886	1,626	48	301	D	38.1	32.8	28.3	0.8	30	9	9	1.3	1.0	1.4	1.5	53.7	46.3
Pawtucket city	26,962	14,177	6,322	6,244	219	7,855	D	52.6	23.4	23.2	0.8	3	33	23	5.9	6.6	4.8	5.9	69.2	30.8
Portsmouth town	8,712	3,528	2,921	2,193	70	607	D	40.5	33.5	25.2	0.8	25	5	16	1.9	1.7	2.2	2.1	54.7	45.3
Providence city	52,288	32,536	11,519	7,816	417	21,017	D	62.2	22.0	14.9	0.8	1	35	35	11.5	15.3	8.8	7.4	73.9	26.1
Richmond town	2,915	1,199	737	952	27	247	D	41.1	25.3	32.7	0.9	23	32	1	0.6	0.6	0.6	0.9	61.9	38.1
Scituate town	5,316	1,759	1,996	1,493	68	237	R	33.1	37.5	28.1	1.3	35	3	10	1.2	0.8	1.5	1.4	46.8	53.2
Smithfield town	9,773	4,155	3,086	2,460	72	1,069	D	42.5	31.6	25.2	0.7	19	11	17	2.2	1.9	2.3	2.3	57.4	42.6
South Kingstown town	10,251	4,988	2,940	2,241	82	2,048	D	48.7	28.7	21.9	0.8	7	25	28	2.3	2.3	2.2	2.1	62.9	37.1
Tiverton town	7,356	3,279	1,997	2,021	59	1,258	D	44.6	27.1	27.5	0.8	15	29	11	1.6	1.5	1.5	1.9	62.1	37.9
Warren town	5,278	2,428	1,544	1,265	41	884	D	46.0	29.3	24.0	0.8	11	23	20	1.2	1.1	1.2	1.2	61.1	38.9
Warwick city	44,692	20,504	13,348	10,526	314	7,156	D	45.9	29.9	23.6	0.7	12	18	22	9.9	9.6	10.1	10.0	60.6	39.4
West Warwick town	13,542	6,134	3,792	3,516	100	2,342	D	45.3	28.0	26.0	0.7	14	26	13	3.0	2.9	2.9	3.3	61.8	38.2
Westerly town	9,856	4,293	2,935	2,542	86	1,358	D	43.6	29.8	25.8	0.9	16	19	15	2.2	2.0	2.2	2.4	59.4	40.6
Woonsocket city	15,475	6,654	3,996	4,690	135	1,964	D	43.0	25.8	30.3	0.9	17	31	7	3.4	3.1	3.0	4.5	62.5	37.5

¹Separate rankings for five counties and for 35 cities and towns. ²Includes 106 scattered write in votes reported only at the state level.

Table H. — Vote for U.S. Representative in Congress: November 3, 1992, General Election

Congressional district and county	Total	Democrat (DEM)	Republican (REP)	Other	Plurality Total	Party	Percent of total vote DEM	REP	Other	Rank within district DEM	REP	Other	Percent contribution to district vote Total	DEM	REP	Other
District 1	**194,089**	**48,092**	**135,982**	**10,015**	**87,890**	**R**	**24.8**	**70.1**	**5.2**				**100.0**	**100.0**	**100.0**	**100.0**
Bristol	21,915	4,815	16,232	868	11,417	R	22.0	74.1	4.0	2	2	2	11.3	10.0	11.9	8.7
Newport	34,929	7,425	26,358	1,146	18,933	R	21.3	75.5	3.3	3	1	3	18.0	15.4	19.4	11.4
Providence (pt)	137,245	35,852	93,392	8,001	57,540	R	26.1	68.0	5.8	1	3	1	70.7	74.5	68.7	79.9
District 2	**204,413**	**144,450**	**49,998**	**9,965**	**94,452**	**D**	**70.7**	**24.5**	**4.9**				**100.0**	**100.0**	**100.0**	**100.0**
Kent	74,147	50,916	20,167	3,064	30,749	D	68.7	27.2	4.1	2	2	2	36.3	35.2	40.3	30.7
Providence (pt)	83,864	61,745	16,909	5,210	44,836	D	73.6	20.2	6.2	1	3	1	41.0	42.7	33.8	52.3
Washington	46,402	31,789	12,922	1,691	18,867	D	68.5	27.8	3.6	3	1	3	22.7	22.0	25.8	17.0
RHODE ISLAND	**398,502**	**192,542**	**185,980**	**19,980**	**6,562**	**D**	**48.3**	**46.7**	**5.0**							

Table G. — Vote for Governor: November 3, 1992, General Election

County	Total	Sundlun (DEM)	Leonard (REP)	Other	Plurality Total	Party	Percent of total vote DEM	REP	Other	Rank¹ DEM	REP	Other	Percent contribution to state vote Total	DEM	REP	Other
Bristol	23,230	14,223	8,410	597	5,813	D	61.2	36.2	2.6	3	1	4	5.5	5.4	5.8	3.4
Kent	78,566	47,746	27,145	3,675	20,601	D	60.8	34.6	4.7	5	2	1	18.5	18.3	18.6	20.7
Newport	35,782	22,886	12,015	881	10,871	D	64.0	33.6	2.5	1	5	5	8.4	8.8	8.3	5.0
Providence	237,449	145,250	81,276	10,923	63,974	D	61.2	34.2	4.6	4	3	2	55.9	55.5	55.8	61.6
Washington	49,791	31,379	16,744	1,668	14,635	D	63.0	33.6	3.4	2	4	3	11.7	12.0	11.5	9.4
RHODE ISLAND	**424,818**	**261,484**	**145,590**	**17,744**	**115,894**	**D**	**61.6**	**34.3**	**4.2**				**100.0**	**100.0**	**100.0**	**100.0**
CITIES AND TOWNS																
Barrington town	8,954	5,168	3,569	217	1,599	D	57.7	39.9	2.4	28	5	29	2.1	2.0	2.4	1.3
Bristol town	9,384	6,058	3,123	203	2,935	D	64.6	33.3	2.2	7	25	32	2.2	2.3	2.1	1.3
Burrillville town	5,941	3,641	2,082	218	1,559	D	61.3	35.0	3.7	19	18	13	1.4	1.4	1.4	1.3
Central Falls city	3,654	2,452	1,092	110	1,360	D	67.1	29.9	3.0	3	33	24	0.9	0.9	0.7	0.7
Charlestown town	3,078	1,896	1,092	90	804	D	61.6	35.5	2.9	17	16	26	0.7	0.7	0.7	0.6
Coventry town	14,173	8,611	4,979	583	3,632	D	60.8	35.1	4.1	21	17	11	3.3	3.3	3.4	3.6
Cranston city	37,998	21,889	14,407	1,702	7,482	D	57.6	37.9	4.5	29	8	8	8.9	8.4	9.8	10.5
Cumberland town	14,517	9,185	4,854	478	4,331	D	63.3	33.4	3.3	14	24	20	3.4	3.5	3.3	2.9
East Greenwich town	6,448	4,016	2,237	195	1,779	D	62.3	34.7	3.0	15	22	23	1.5	1.5	1.5	1.2
East Providence city	21,070	11,909	8,335	826	3,574	D	56.5	39.6	3.9	31	6	12	5.0	4.6	5.7	5.1
Exeter town	2,535	1,357	1,085	93	272	D	53.5	42.8	3.7	34	2	14	0.6	0.5	0.7	0.6
Foster town	2,049	1,180	775	94	405	D	57.6	37.8	4.6	30	9	6	0.5	0.5	0.5	0.6
Glocester town	4,331	2,405	1,734	192	671	D	55.5	40.0	4.4	32	4	9	1.0	0.9	1.2	1.2
Hopkinton town	2,988	1,766	1,134	88	632	D	59.1	38.0	2.9	26	7	25	0.7	0.7	0.8	0.5
Johnston town	13,744	7,366	5,603	775	1,763	D	53.6	40.8	5.6	33	3	2	3.2	2.8	3.8	4.8
Lincoln town	9,583	5,820	3,414	349	2,406	D	60.7	35.6	3.6	22	14	15	2.3	2.2	2.3	2.2
Middletown town	6,460	4,136	2,225	99	1,911	D	64.0	34.4	1.5	9	23	35	1.5	1.6	1.5	0.6
Narragansett town	7,080	4,537	2,291	252	2,246	D	64.1	32.4	3.6	8	28	17	1.7	1.7	1.6	1.6
Newport city	9,926	6,649	3,039	238	3,610	D	67.0	30.6	2.4	4	31	30	2.3	2.5	2.1	1.5
North Kingstown town	12,068	7,208	4,421	439	2,787	D	59.7	36.6	3.6	24	10	16	2.8	2.8	3.0	2.7
North Providence town	17,512	10,245	6,377	890	3,868	D	58.5	36.4	5.1	27	11	4	4.1	3.9	4.3	5.5
North Smithfield town	5,406	3,449	1,786	171	1,663	D	63.8	33.0	3.2	10	27	22	1.3	1.3	1.2	1.1
Pawtucket city	24,902	15,780	8,273	849	7,507	D	63.4	33.2	3.4	12	26	18	5.9	6.0	5.6	5.2
Portsmouth town	8,098	5,127	2,823	148	2,304	D	63.3	34.9	1.8	13	20	34	1.9	2.0	1.9	0.9
Providence city	48,264	32,200	14,015	2,049	18,185	D	66.7	29.0	4.2	5	34	10	11.4	12.3	9.5	12.6
Richmond town	2,680	1,654	935	91	719	D	61.7	34.9	3.4	16	19	19	0.6	0.6	0.6	0.6
Scituate town	5,024	2,595	2,160	269	435	D	51.7	43.0	5.4	35	1	3	1.2	1.0	1.5	1.7
Smithfield town	9,244	5,472	3,219	553	2,253	D	59.2	34.8	6.0	25	21	1	2.2	2.1	2.2	3.4
South Kingstown town	9,689	6,414	3,013	262	3,401	D	66.2	31.1	2.7	6	30	27	2.3	2.5	2.0	1.6
Tiverton town	6,710	4,121	2,435	154	1,686	D	61.4	36.3	2.3	18	12	31	1.6	1.6	1.7	1.0
Warren town	4,892	2,997	1,772	123	1,225	D	61.3	36.2	2.5	20	13	28	1.2	1.1	1.2	0.8
Warwick city	43,054	25,794	15,322	1,938	10,472	D	59.9	35.6	4.5	23	15	7	10.1	9.9	10.4	12.0
West Warwick town	12,692	8,090	3,983	619	4,107	D	63.7	31.4	4.9	11	29	5	3.0	3.1	2.7	3.8
Westerly town	8,871	6,030	2,668	173	3,362	D	68.0	30.1	2.0	2	32	33	2.1	2.3	1.8	1.1
Woonsocket city	14,210	9,662	4,092	456	5,570	D	68.0	28.8	3.2	1	35	21	3.3	3.7	2.8	2.8

¹Separate rankings for five counties and for 35 cities and towns.

814 Rhode Island

Table I. — Vote for Presidential Preference: March 10, 1992, Democratic Primary Election

County	Total	Tsongas	Clinton	Brown	Uncom-mitted	Kerrey	Woods	Harkin	Other	Tsongas	Clinton	Brown	Tsongas	Clinton	Brown	Total	Tsongas	Clinton	Brown
											Percent of total vote			**Rank[1]**			**Percent contribution to state vote**		
Bristol	2,635	1,559	567	379	25	26	14	4	61	59.2	21.5	14.4	1	3	5	5.2	5.8	5.3	4.0
Kent	8,144	4,264	1,857	1,461	107	38	78	67	272	52.4	22.8	17.9	4	1	4	16.1	15.9	17.3	15.3
Newport	4,559	2,577	813	836	92	58	40	18	125	56.5	17.8	18.3	2	5	3	9.0	9.6	7.6	8.8
Providence	30,556	15,871	6,655	5,738	421	323	237	198	1,113	51.9	21.8	18.8	5	2	2	60.3	59.2	61.8	60.1
Washington	4,815	2,554	870	1,127	58	24	39	32	111	53.0	18.1	23.4	3	4	1	9.5	9.5	8.1	11.8
RHODE ISLAND	**50,709**	**26,825**	**10,762**	**9,541**	**703**	**469**	**408**	**319**	**1,682**	**52.9**	**21.2**	**18.8**				**100.0**	**100.0**	**100.0**	**100.0**
CITIES AND TOWNS																			
Barrington town	1,080	761	119	163	6	5	3	4	19	70.5	11.0	15.1	1	34	30	2.1	2.8	1.1	1.7
Bristol town	1,090	525	332	165	14	14	9	0	31	48.2	30.5	15.1	27	3	29	2.1	2.0	3.1	1.7
Burrillville town	466	258	83	86	10	5	5	5	14	55.4	17.8	18.5	12	25	17	0.9	1.0	0.8	0.9
Central Falls city	817	324	280	110	13	21	14	2	53	39.7	34.3	13.5	35	1	34	1.6	1.2	2.6	1.2
Charlestown town	194	112	18	58	1	0	0	2	3	57.7	9.3	29.9	7	35	2	0.4	0.4	0.2	0.6
Coventry town	1,113	487	314	224	19	7	13	9	40	43.8	28.2	20.1	33	4	13	2.2	1.8	2.9	2.3
Cranston city	3,150	1,722	629	625	21	17	30	11	95	54.7	20.0	19.8	15	19	14	6.2	6.4	5.8	6.6
Cumberland town	1,904	1,099	323	357	29	14	5	9	68	57.7	17.0	18.8	8	28	16	3.8	4.1	3.0	3.7
East Greenwich town	615	405	80	102	8	0	3	4	13	65.9	13.0	16.6	2	33	25	1.2	1.5	0.7	1.1
East Providence city	2,689	1,462	576	463	27	44	19	14	84	54.4	21.4	17.2	16	15	24	5.3	5.5	5.4	4.9
Exeter town	227	107	57	49	4	0	5	1	4	47.1	25.1	21.6	29	8	10	0.4	0.4	0.5	0.5
Foster town	172	72	31	61	1	0	3	3	1	41.9	18.0	35.5	34	23	1	0.3	0.3	0.3	0.6
Glocester town	339	182	48	84	2	2	3	7	11	53.7	14.2	24.8	19	31	5	0.7	0.7	0.4	0.9
Hopkinton town	210	96	46	52	3	0	3	3	7	45.7	21.9	24.8	30	14	6	0.4	0.4	0.4	0.5
Johnston town	1,508	713	425	240	30	19	11	20	50	47.3	28.2	15.9	28	5	26	3.0	2.7	3.9	2.5
Lincoln town	963	522	168	210	7	10	6	2	38	54.2	17.4	21.8	18	26	9	1.9	1.9	1.6	2.2
Middletown town	699	374	149	127	14	7	12	0	16	53.5	21.3	18.2	20	16	19	1.4	1.4	1.4	1.3
Narragansett town	807	449	125	192	14	2	3	9	13	55.6	15.5	23.8	11	29	7	1.6	1.7	1.2	2.0
Newport city	1,486	833	266	284	36	17	10	5	35	56.1	17.9	19.1	10	24	15	2.9	3.1	2.5	3.0
North Kingstown town	1,356	766	245	284	14	10	7	3	27	56.5	18.1	20.9	9	22	12	2.7	2.9	2.3	3.0
North Providence town	2,239	1,194	544	355	35	22	13	9	67	53.3	24.3	15.9	21	10	27	4.4	4.5	5.1	3.7
North Smithfield town	501	305	94	68	4	10	5	5	10	60.9	18.8	13.6	3	21	33	1.0	1.1	0.9	0.7
Pawtucket city	4,344	2,218	986	780	77	52	34	15	182	51.1	22.7	18.0	24	11	21	8.6	8.3	9.2	8.2
Portsmouth town	870	508	151	154	16	13	6	2	20	58.4	17.4	17.7	6	27	23	1.7	1.9	1.4	1.6
Providence city	8,227	4,123	1,714	1,755	113	56	72	77	317	50.1	20.8	21.3	25	18	11	16.2	15.4	15.9	18.4
Richmond town	233	121	45	60	2	0	2	1	2	51.9	19.3	25.8	23	20	4	0.5	0.5	0.4	0.6
Scituate town	283	168	38	67	2	4	2	0	2	59.4	13.4	23.7	4	32	8	0.6	0.6	0.4	0.7
Smithfield town	919	504	205	163	7	9	4	4	23	54.8	22.3	17.7	14	13	22	1.8	1.9	1.9	1.7
South Kingstown town	1,119	588	165	301	10	5	12	7	31	52.5	14.7	26.9	22	30	3	2.2	2.2	1.5	3.2
Tiverton town	757	418	169	113	9	12	4	9	23	55.2	22.3	14.9	13	12	31	1.5	1.6	1.6	1.2
Warren town	465	273	116	51	5	7	2	0	11	58.7	24.9	11.0	5	9	35	0.9	1.0	1.1	0.5
Warwick city	5,343	2,897	1,115	965	68	27	53	42	176	54.2	20.9	18.1	17	17	20	10.5	10.8	10.4	10.1
West Warwick town	939	415	315	135	11	4	8	11	40	44.2	33.5	14.4	32	2	32	1.9	1.5	2.9	1.4
Westerly town	550	251	154	100	10	7	6	3	19	45.6	28.0	18.2	31	6	18	1.1	0.9	1.4	1.0
Woonsocket city	2,035	1,005	511	314	43	38	11	15	98	49.4	25.1	15.4	26	7	28	4.0	3.7	4.7	3.3

[1]Separate rankings for five counties and for 35 cities and towns.

Rhode Island 815

Table J. — **Vote for Presidential Preference: March 10, 1992, Republican Primary Election**

County	Top candidates					Top four candidates (state vote)												
	Total	Bush	Bu-chanan	Uncom-mitted	Other	Percent of total vote				Rank[1]				Percent contribution to state vote				
						Bush	Bu-chanan	Uncom-mitted	Other	Bush	Bu-chanan	Uncom-mitted	Other	Total	Bush	Bu-chanan	Uncom-mitted	Other
Bristol	1,491	1,043	387	35	26	70.0	26.0	2.3	1.7	1	5	4	4	9.5	10.6	7.8	7.9	7.0
Kent	2,833	1,699	1,016	75	43	60.0	35.9	2.6	1.5	5	1	3	5	18.1	17.2	20.5	16.9	11.6
Newport	2,169	1,444	578	94	53	66.6	26.6	4.3	2.4	2	4	1	3	13.9	14.7	11.6	21.2	14.2
Providence	6,746	4,122	2,282	151	191	61.1	33.8	2.2	2.8	4	2	5	1	43.1	41.8	45.9	34.0	51.3
Washington	2,397	1,545	704	89	59	64.5	29.4	3.7	2.5	3	3	2	2	15.3	15.7	14.2	20.0	15.9
RHODE ISLAND	**15,636**	**9,853**	**4,967**	**444**	**372**	**63.0**	**31.8**	**2.8**	**2.4**					**100.0**	**100.0**	**100.0**	**100.0**	**100.0**
CITIES AND TOWNS																		
Barrington town	855	625	196	24	10	73.1	22.9	2.8	1.2	1	34	15	33	5.5	6.3	3.9	5.4	2.7
Bristol town	469	319	135	7	8	68.0	28.8	1.5	1.7	5	26	32	29	3.0	3.2	2.7	1.6	2.2
Burrillville town	144	84	47	6	7	58.3	32.6	4.2	4.9	26	15	8	2	0.9	0.9	0.9	1.4	1.9
Central Falls city	85	56	26	2	1	65.9	30.6	2.4	1.2	10	17	21	32	0.5	0.6	0.5	0.5	0.3
Charlestown town	191	137	41	9	4	71.7	21.5	4.7	2.1	2	35	6	23	1.2	1.4	0.8	2.0	1.1
Coventry town	468	260	183	14	11	55.6	39.1	3.0	2.4	28	8	12	20	3.0	2.6	3.7	3.2	3.0
Cranston city	1,513	990	456	39	28	65.4	30.1	2.6	1.9	12	20	17	28	9.7	10.0	9.2	8.8	7.5
Cumberland town	385	231	142	3	9	60.0	36.9	0.8	2.3	24	10	35	21	2.5	2.3	2.9	0.7	2.4
East Greenwich town	403	265	117	19	2	65.8	29.0	4.7	0.5	11	24	5	35	2.6	2.7	2.4	4.3	0.5
East Providence city	758	463	259	14	22	61.1	34.2	1.8	2.9	23	12	28	14	4.8	4.7	5.2	3.2	5.9
Exeter town	144	96	41	3	4	66.7	28.5	2.1	2.8	7	27	27	16	0.9	1.0	0.8	0.7	1.1
Foster town	126	84	35	3	4	66.7	27.8	2.4	3.2	8	29	20	12	0.8	0.9	0.7	0.7	1.1
Glocester town	167	90	68	3	6	53.9	40.7	1.8	3.6	31	6	29	8	1.1	0.9	1.4	0.7	1.6
Hopkinton town	147	91	39	7	10	61.9	26.5	4.8	6.8	20	30	4	1	0.9	0.9	0.8	1.6	2.7
Johnston town	231	121	100	5	5	52.4	43.3	2.2	2.2	32	4	25	22	1.5	1.2	2.0	1.1	1.3
Lincoln town	428	262	140	14	12	61.2	32.7	3.3	2.8	22	14	10	15	2.7	2.7	2.8	3.2	3.2
Middletown town	388	268	101	14	5	69.1	26.0	3.6	1.3	4	32	9	31	2.5	2.7	2.0	3.2	1.3
Narragansett town	256	163	80	4	9	63.7	31.3	1.6	3.5	17	16	31	9	1.6	1.7	1.6	0.9	2.4
Newport city	590	379	156	32	23	64.2	26.4	5.4	3.9	15	31	2	6	3.8	3.8	3.1	7.2	6.2
North Kingstown town	678	449	206	17	6	66.2	30.4	2.5	0.9	9	19	18	34	4.3	4.6	4.1	3.8	1.6
North Providence town	180	87	84	4	5	48.3	46.7	2.2	2.8	34	1	22	17	1.2	0.9	1.7	0.9	1.3
North Smithfield town	265	179	75	3	8	67.5	28.3	1.1	3.0	6	28	34	13	1.7	1.8	1.5	0.7	2.2
Pawtucket city	557	307	220	9	21	55.1	39.5	1.6	3.8	29	7	30	7	3.6	3.1	4.4	2.0	5.6
Portsmouth town	458	290	138	21	9	63.3	30.1	4.6	2.0	19	21	7	25	2.9	2.9	2.8	4.7	2.4
Providence city	947	603	288	25	31	63.7	30.4	2.6	3.3	16	18	16	11	6.1	6.1	5.8	5.6	8.3
Richmond town	120	55	52	8	5	45.8	43.3	6.7	4.2	35	3	1	5	0.8	0.6	1.0	1.8	1.3
Scituate town	319	224	77	7	11	70.2	24.1	2.2	3.4	3	33	23	10	2.0	2.3	1.6	1.6	3.0
Smithfield town	291	146	130	9	6	50.2	44.7	3.1	2.1	33	2	11	24	1.9	1.5	2.6	2.0	1.6
South Kingstown town	368	240	107	11	10	65.2	29.1	3.0	2.7	13	23	13	18	2.4	2.4	2.2	2.5	2.7
Tiverton town	307	200	92	9	6	65.1	30.0	2.9	2.0	14	22	14	26	2.0	2.0	1.9	2.0	1.6
Warren town	167	99	56	4	8	59.3	33.5	2.4	4.8	25	13	19	3	1.1	1.0	1.1	0.9	2.2
Warwick city	1,556	954	546	33	23	61.3	35.1	2.1	1.5	21	11	26	30	10.0	9.7	11.0	7.4	6.2
West Warwick town	323	175	135	7	6	54.2	41.8	2.2	1.9	30	5	24	27	2.1	1.8	2.7	1.6	1.6
Westerly town	426	271	123	21	11	63.6	28.9	4.9	2.6	18	25	3	19	2.7	2.8	2.5	4.7	3.0
Woonsocket city	350	195	135	5	15	55.7	38.6	1.4	4.3	27	9	33	4	2.2	2.0	2.7	1.1	4.0

[1]Separate rankings for five counties and for 35 cities and towns.

816 Rhode Island

1992 Vote for President
Percent for Clinton (D), by Minor Civil Division

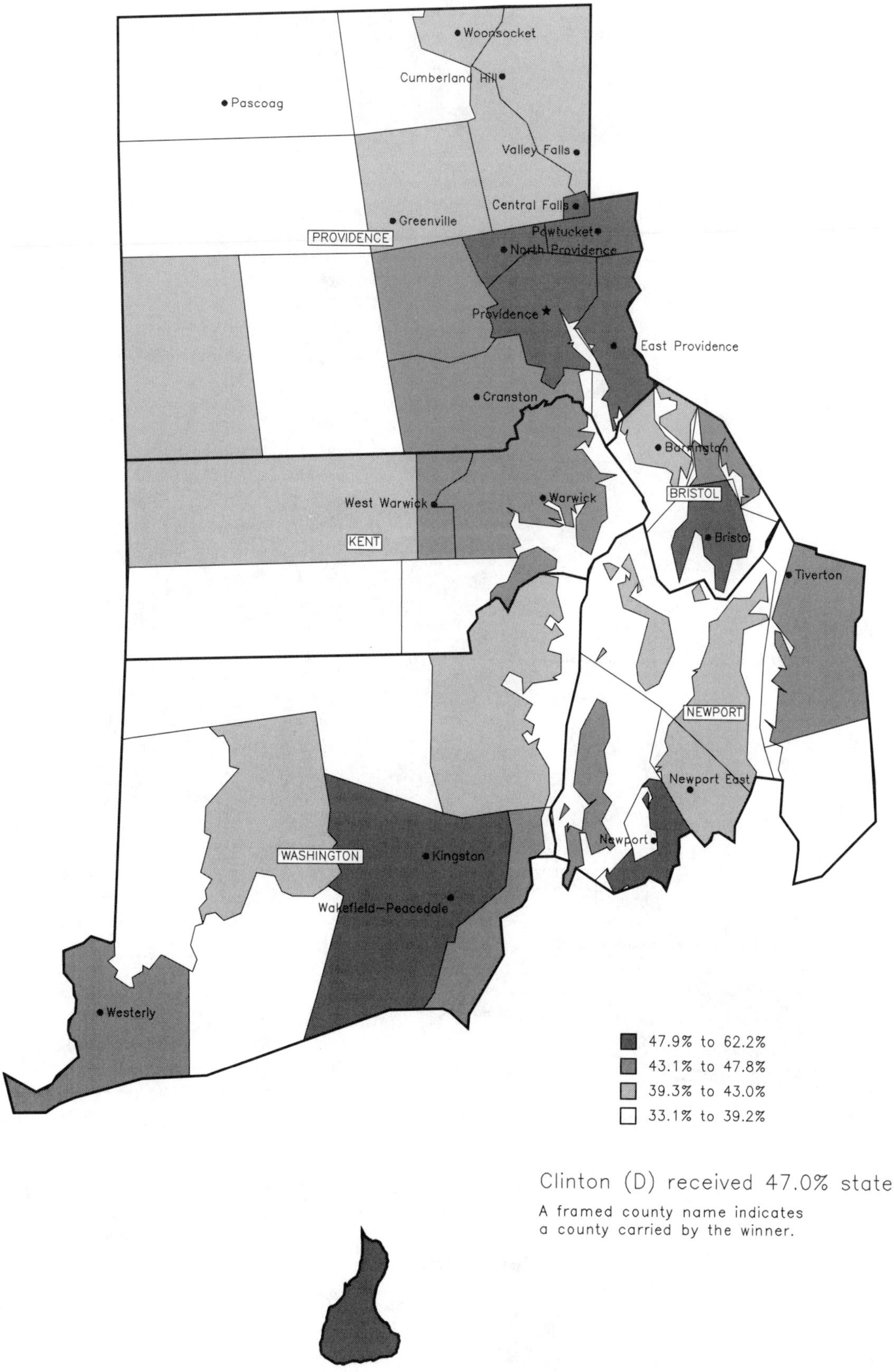

Woonsocket

Cumberland Hill

Pascoag

Valley Falls

Central Falls

Greenville

PROVIDENCE

Pawtucket

North Providence

Providence ★

East Providence

Cranston

Barrington

BRISTOL

Bristol

West Warwick

Warwick

Tiverton

KENT

NEWPORT

Newport East

WASHINGTON

Kingston

Newport

Wakefield–Peacedale

Westerly

■	47.9% to 62.2%
▨	43.1% to 47.8%
▨	39.3% to 43.0%
□	33.1% to 39.2%

Clinton (D) received 47.0% statewide.

A framed county name indicates
a county carried by the winner.

Rhode Island 817

1992 Vote for Governor
Percent for Sundlun (D), by Minor Civil Division

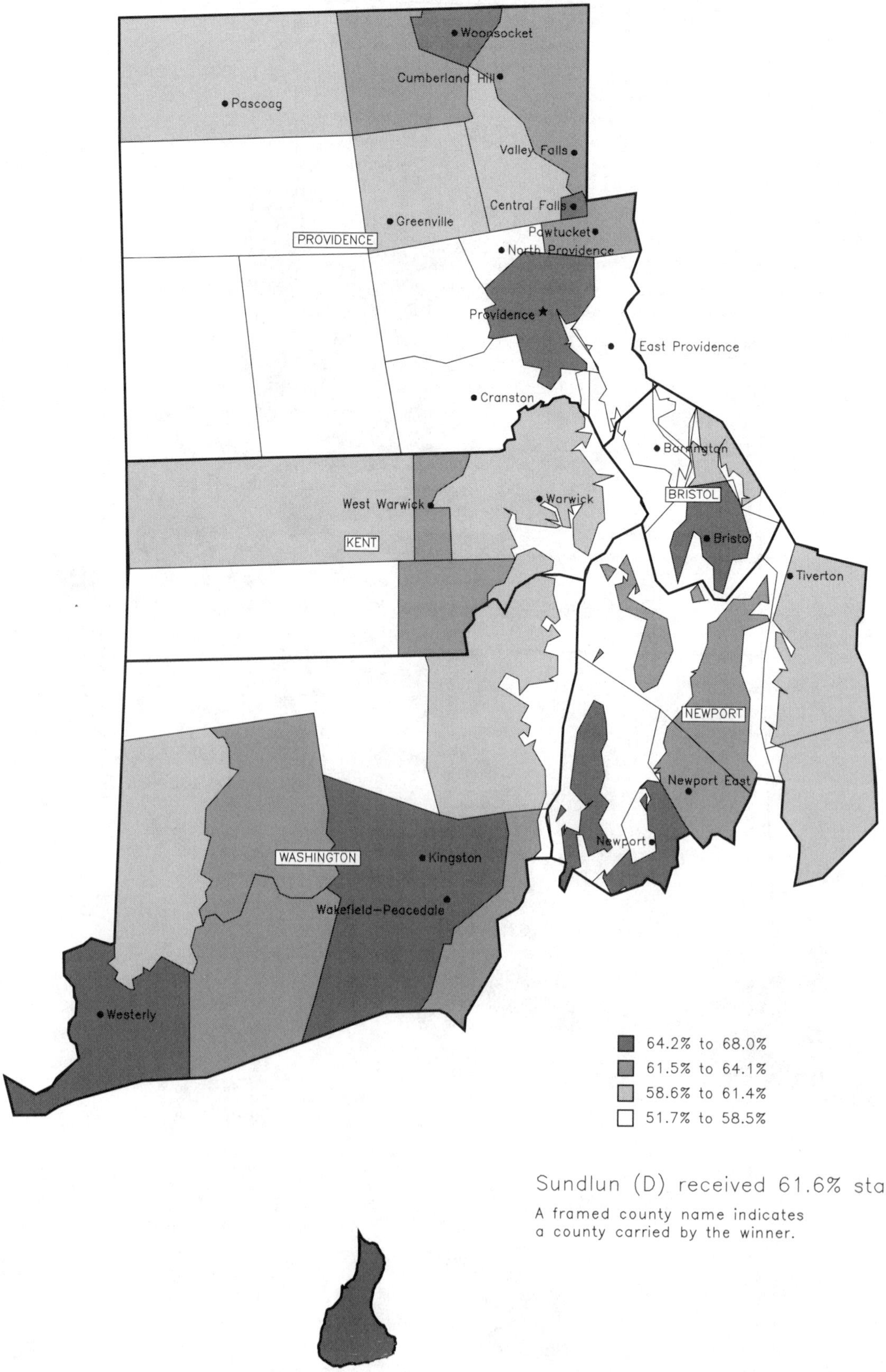

Woonsocket

Cumberland Hill

Pascoag

Valley Falls

Central Falls

Greenville

PROVIDENCE

Pawtucket

North Providence

Providence ★

East Providence

Cranston

Barrington

BRISTOL

West Warwick

Warwick

Bristol

KENT

Tiverton

NEWPORT

Newport East

WASHINGTON

Kingston

Newport

Wakefield-Peacedale

Westerly

■ 64.2% to 68.0%

■ 61.5% to 64.1%

▨ 58.6% to 61.4%

□ 51.7% to 58.5%

Sundlun (D) received 61.6% statewide.

A framed county name indicates
a county carried by the winner.

SOUTH CAROLINA

Congressional Districts 6
    Average Population 581,117
State Senate Districts 46
    Average Population 75,798
State House Districts 124
    Average Population 28,119

Electoral College Votes...8
Counties 46
Voting Precincts 1,704

Alternative Registration Methods:
    ....Deputized Registrars, Mail-in

Registration Deadline (Days before Election) 30

Voting Equipment Use (Counties)

Datavote Punch Card	0	Paper Ballot	10
Electronic	15	Other Punch Card	14
Lever Machine	2	Mixed Systems	0
Optical Scanner	5		

Party Control	DEM	REP	IND	VAC
1993 State Senate	30	16	0	0
1992 State Senate	33	12	0	1
1993 State House	73	50	1	0
1992 State House	79	44	1	0

Population Statistics 1990

Race/ Ethnicity	Total Population		Voting Age Population		Voting Age Population % of total population
	Number	%	Number	%	
Non-Hispanic					
White	2,390,056	68.5	1,835,914	71.5	76.8
Black	1,035,947	29.7	688,580	26.8	66.5
Asian/Pacific Islander	21,304	0.6	15,095	0.6	70.9
Native American	8,004	0.2	5,745	0.2	71.8
Other	841	<.1	353	<.1	42.0
All Hispanic	30,551	0.9	20,809	0.8	68.1
TOTAL	3,486,703	100.0	2,566,496	100.0	73.6

Estimated Voting Age Population 1992 (VAP) 2,672,000
Number of Registered Voters................................. 1,537,140
    % of estimated VAP.. 57.5
Voter Turnout (Maximum Vote)[1]........................... 1,235,798
    % of VAP 46.2
    % of Registration 80.4
Persons Not Voting—of Voting Age 1,436,202
    % of VAP 53.8
Persons Not Voting—of Registered 301,342
    % of Registration 19.6
Straight Ticket Voting .... Yes, Exception

State Officials and Members of Congress

Governor:
Carroll Campbell, Jr. (R) 1986, elected to a four-year term in 1990.

U.S. Senators:
Strom Thurmond (R) 1954, elected to a six-year term in 1990.
Ernest F. Hollings (D) 1966, elected to a six-year term in 1992.

U.S. Representative in Congress:
(District, Name, Party, Date first elected)

1. Ravenel (R) 1986
2. Spence (R) 1970
3. Derrick (D) 1974
4. Inglis (R) 1992
5. Spratt (D) 1982
6. Clyburn (D) 1992

---

[1]Maximum vote turnout from Table C exceeds reported statewide actual voter turnout because in one or more counties the vote for highest office is greater than reported actual turnout.

Candidates: General Election, November 3, 1992

Candidate(s)	Total vote	Percent	Party	Status	First elected
President/Vice President					
Bush/Quayle	577,507	48.02%	Republican	Incumbent	1988
Clinton/Gore	479,514	39.88%	Democrat	Challenger	1992
Perot/Stockdale	138,872	11.55%	Petition	Challenger	
Marrou/Lord	2,719	0.23%	Libertarian	Challenger	
Phillips/Knight	2,680	0.22%	American	Challenger	
Fulani/Munoz	1,235	0.10%	United Citizens	Challenger	
U.S. Senator					
Fritz Hollings	591,030	50.07%	Democrat	Incumbent	1966
Tommy Harnett	554,175	46.95%	Republican	Challenger	
Mark Johnson	22,962	1.95%	Libertarian	Challenger	
Robert Clarkson II	11,568	0.98%	American	Challenger	
Write ins	703	0.06%	Write in	Challenger	
Governor (No Contest)					
U.S. Representative in Congress					
District 1					
Arthur Ravenel, Jr.	121,938	66.07%	Republican	Incumbent	1986
Bill Oberst	59,908	32.46%	Democrat	Challenger	
John R. Peeples	2,608	1.41%	American	Challenger	
Write ins	95	0.05%	Write in	Challenger	
District 2					
Floyd Spence	148,667	87.62%	Republican	Incumbent	1970
Geb Sommer	20,816	12.27%	Libertarian	Challenger	
Write ins	187	0.11%	Write in	Challenger	
District 3					
Butler Derrick	119,119	61.13%	Democrat	Incumbent	1974
Jim Bland	75,660	38.83%	Republican	Challenger	
Write ins	85	0.04%	Write in	Challenger	
District 4					
Bob Inglis	99,879	50.34%	Republican	Challenger	1992
Liz J. Patterson	94,182	47.47%	Democrat	Incumbent	1986
Jo Jorgensen	4,286	2.16%	Libertarian	Challenger	
Write ins	63	0.03%	Write in	Challenger	
District 5					
John Spratt	112,031	61.19%	Democrat	Incumbent	1982
Bill Horne	70,866	38.71%	Republican	Challenger	
Write ins	189	0.10%	Write in	Challenger	
District 6					
James Clyburn	120,647	65.26%	Democrat	Challenger	1992
John Chase	64,149	34.70%	Republican	Challenger	
Write ins	75	0.04%	Write in	Challenger	

Candidates: March 7, 1992, Primary Election

Candidate	Total vote	Percent	Candidate	Total vote	Percent
Presidential Preference, Democratic			**Presidential Preference, Republican**		
Bill Clinton	73,221	62.90%	George Bush	99,558	66.89%
Paul Tsongas	21,338	18.33%	Patrick Buchanan	38,247	25.70%
Tom Harkin	7,657	6.58%	David Duke	10,553	7.09%
Jerry Brown	6,961	5.98%	Paul Daugherty	482	0.32%
Uncommitted	3,640	3.13%			
Bob Cunningham	1,369	1.18%			
Charles Woods	854	0.73%			
Bob Kerrey	566	0.49%			
William Kreml	336	0.29%			
Angus McDonald	268	0.23%			
Lyndon LaRouche, Jr.	204	0.18%			

Voter Registration and Turnout, 1948-1992 Elections

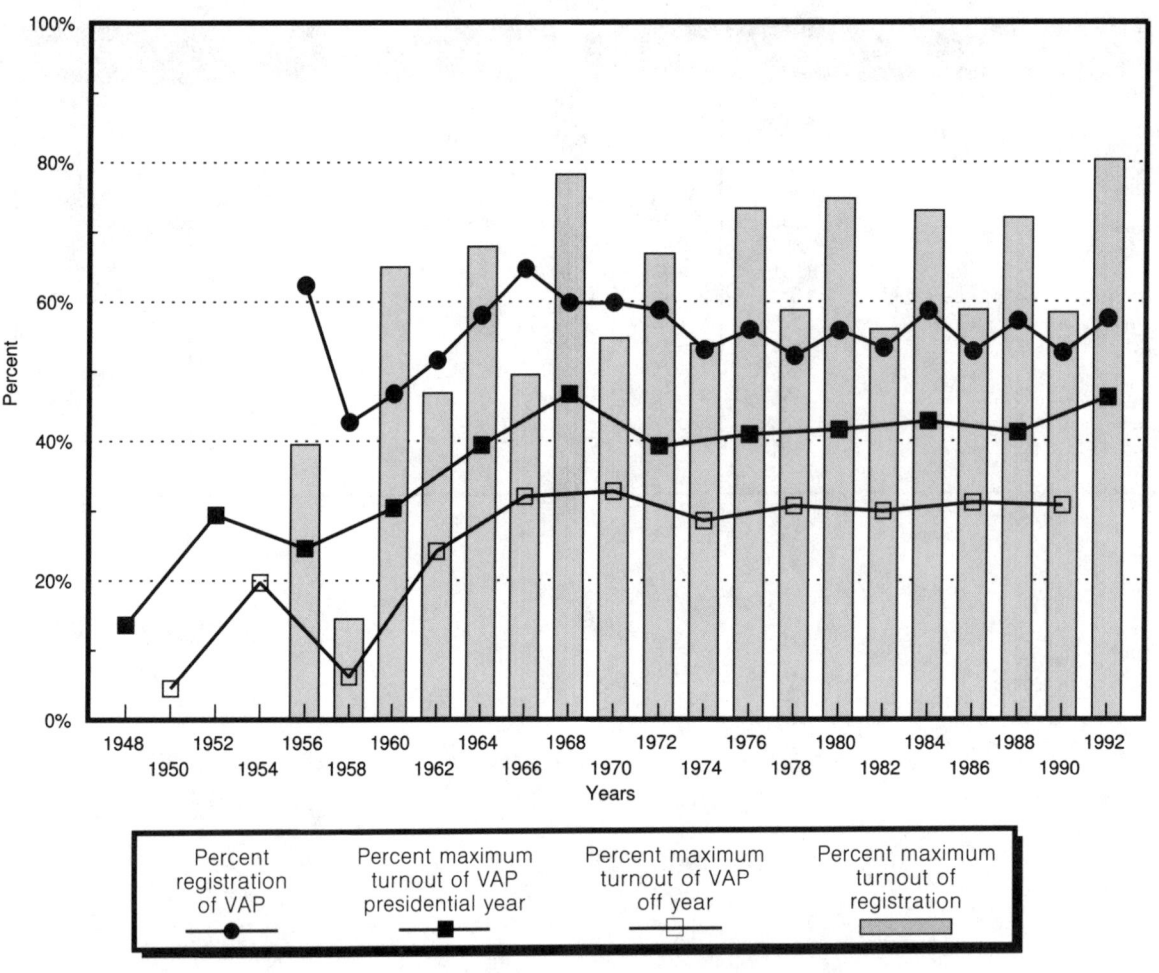

| | | Percent registration of VAP | Percent maximum turnout of VAP presidential year | Percent maximum turnout of VAP off year | Percent maximum turnout of registration |

Year	Estimated Voting Age Population (VAP)	Voter registration (REG)			Voter turnout											
						Highest office						Maximum vote				
		Total	Percent of VAP	Rank by percent of VAP	Actual	Total	Office	Percent total REG	Rank by percent of REG	Percent of VAP	Rank by percent of VAP	Total	Percent total REG	Rank by percent of REG	Percent total VAP	Rank by percent of VAP
1992	2,672,000	1,537,140	57.5	48	1,234,712	1,202,527	P	78.2	21	45.0	50	1,234,712	80.3	21	46.2	50
1990	2,587,000	1,360,082	52.6	49	793,614	760,965	G	55.9	29	29.4	48	793,614	58.4	29	30.7	46
1988	2,531,000	1,447,151	57.2	47	1,041,846	986,009	P	68.1	35	39.0	51	1,041,846	72.0	28	41.2	50
1986	2,458,000	1,298,857	52.8	48	763,493	753,751	G	58.0	20	30.7	43	763,493	58.8	22	31.1	44
1984	2,382,000	1,395,714	58.6	46	1,018,701	968,529	P	69.4	38	40.7	51	1,018,701	73.0	32	42.8	50
1982	2,305,000	1,229,319	53.3	48	688,300	671,625	G	54.6	38	29.1	47	688,300	56.0	36	29.9	46
1980	2,215,000	1,235,521	55.8	48	922,397	894,071	P	72.4	33	40.4	50	922,397	74.7	29	41.6	49
1978	2,104,000	1,097,001	52.1	47	644,448	632,852	S	57.7	22	30.1	44	644,448	58.7	23	30.6	44
1976	1,993,000	1,113,361	55.9	47	816,007	802,583	P	72.1	32	40.3	50	816,007	73.3	33	40.9	50
1974	1,883,000	997,808	53.0	47	537,364	523,199	G	52.4	36	27.8	44	537,364	53.9	35	28.5	43
1972	1,762,000	1,033,688	58.7	46	690,534	673,960	P	65.2	39	38.2	49	690,534	66.8	38	39.2	49
1970	1,487,000	888,894	59.8	44	485,976	484,857	G	54.5	36	32.6	46	485,976	54.7	36	32.7	46
1968	1,427,000	853,014	59.8	44	-	666,978	P	78.2	30	46.7	49	666,978	78.2	31	46.7	49
1966	1,373,000	888,090	64.7	35	-	439,942	S	49.5	37	32.0	47	439,942	49.5	37	32.0	47
1964	1,333,000	772,572	58.0	37	-	524,779	P	67.9	39	39.4	48	524,779	67.9	39	39.4	48
1962	1,293,000	666,694	51.6	34	-	312,647	S	46.9	32	24.2	45	312,647	46.9	32	24.2	45
1960	1,272,000	595,289	46.8	33	-	386,688	P	65.0	34	30.4	48	386,688	65.0	34	30.4	48
1958	1,257,000	536,205	42.7	30	-	77,740	G	14.5	30	6.2	47	77,740	14.5	30	6.2	47
1956	1,222,000	761,162	62.3	25	-	300,583	P	39.5	29	24.6	47	300,583	39.5	29	24.6	47
1954	1,156,000	-	-	-	-	227,232	S	-	-	19.7	40	227,232	-	-	19.7	40
1952	1,159,000	-	-	-	-	341,087	P	-	-	29.4	46	341,087	-	-	29.4	46
1950	1,136,000	-	-	-	-	50,642	G	-	-	4.5	48	50,642	-	-	4.5	48
1948	1,049,000	-	-	-	-	142,571	P	-	-	13.6	47	142,571	-	-	13.6	47

SOUTH CAROLINA

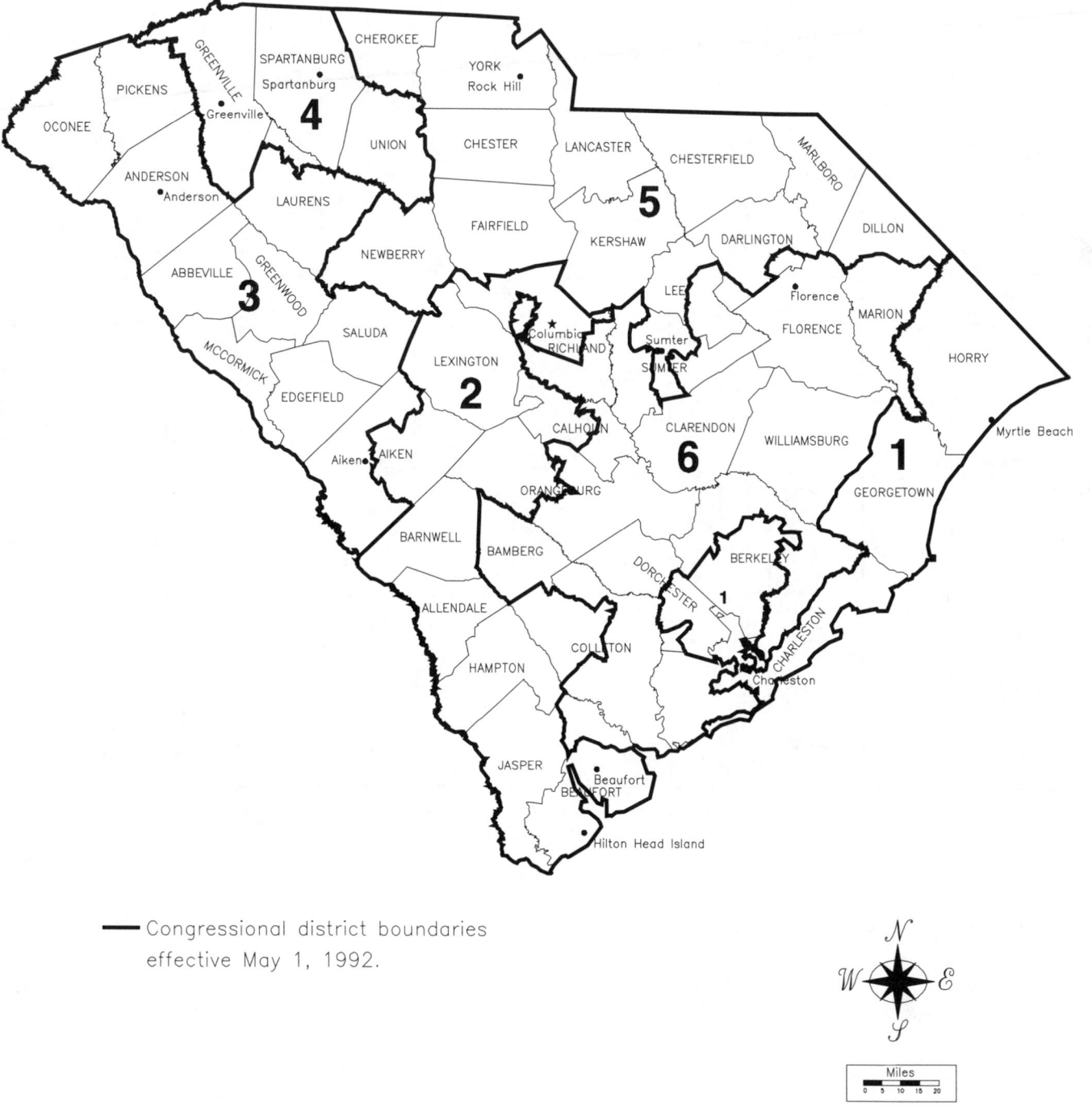

Congressional district boundaries
effective May 1, 1992.

N W E S

Miles
0 5 10 15 20

South Carolina 823

Table A. — 1990 Population by Race and Ethnic Origin

State/ county code	County	Total persons	Percent of total persons						Rank				Percent contribution to state population			
			Non-Hispanic							Percent of total persons				Non-Hispanic		
			White	Black	Asian and Pacific Islander	Native American	Other	Hispanic	Total	Non-Hispanic		Hispanic	Total	White	Black	Hispanic
										White	Black					
45 001	Abbeville	23,862	67.9	31.4	0.2	<.1	<.1	0.4	35	19	28	30	0.7	0.7	0.7	0.3
45 003	Aiken	120,940	74.5	24.1	0.4	0.2	<.1	0.7	10	10	35	13	3.5	3.8	2.8	2.8
45 005	Allendale	11,722	30.7	67.7	<.1	<.1	<.1	1.4	45	46	1	4	0.3	0.2	0.8	0.5
45 007	Anderson	145,196	82.7	16.6	0.2	0.1	<.1	0.4	6	4	43	36	4.2	5.0	2.3	1.8
45 009	Bamberg	16,902	38.0	61.3	0.1	0.1	<.1	0.4	41	43	4	24	0.5	0.3	1.0	0.2
45 011	Barnwell	20,293	56.3	42.8	<.1	0.2	<.1	0.7	37	28	19	12	0.6	0.5	0.8	0.5
45 013	Beaufort	86,425	68.1	28.2	0.8	0.3	<.1	2.5	14	18	31	1	2.5	2.5	2.4	7.1
45 015	Berkeley	128,776	71.8	24.0	1.9	0.3	<.1	2.0	9	13	36	2	3.7	3.9	3.0	8.5
45 017	Calhoun	12,753	48.1	51.5	<.1	<.1	0.0	0.3	44	35	12	41	0.4	0.3	0.6	0.1
45 019	Charleston	295,039	62.8	34.7	0.9	0.2	<.1	1.3	2	23	24	5	8.5	7.8	9.9	12.7
45 021	Cherokee	44,506	78.4	20.5	0.4	0.1	<.1	0.6	23	7	39	16	1.3	1.5	0.9	0.8
45 023	Chester	32,170	59.5	39.9	0.1	0.2	0.0	0.2	30	25	22	45	0.9	0.8	1.2	0.3
45 025	Chesterfield	38,577	66.1	33.2	<.1	0.2	<.1	0.4	25	21	26	29	1.1	1.1	1.2	0.5
45 027	Clarendon	28,450	43.0	56.3	<.1	0.1	<.1	0.5	34	38	9	21	0.8	0.5	1.5	0.5
45 029	Colleton	34,377	54.1	44.8	0.1	0.5	<.1	0.5	27	32	15	20	1.0	0.8	1.5	0.6
45 031	Darlington	61,851	59.5	38.6	0.1	0.1	<.1	0.3	17	26	21	39	1.8	1.5	2.4	0.7
45 033	Dillon	29,114	54.4	43.6	0.2	1.5	<.1	0.3	33	31	16	44	0.8	0.7	1.2	0.2
45 035	Dorchester	83,060	74.3	22.9	0.9	0.7	<.1	1.3	16	11	37	6	2.4	2.6	1.8	3.4
45 037	Edgefield	18,375	53.1	46.2	0.2	<.1	<.1	0.4	39	33	14	27	0.5	0.4	0.8	0.3
45 039	Fairfield	22,295	41.3	58.1	0.1	<.1	0.0	0.5	36	40	6	22	0.6	0.4	1.2	0.3
45 041	Florence	114,344	60.6	38.6	0.2	0.1	<.1	0.4	11	24	23	25	3.3	2.9	4.3	1.7
45 043	Georgetown	46,302	56.3	43.0	0.1	0.1	<.1	0.4	22	27	17	32	1.3	1.1	1.9	0.6
45 045	Greenville	320,167	80.3	18.0	0.7	0.1	<.1	0.9	1	6	41	8	9.2	10.8	5.5	9.9
45 047	Greenwood	59,567	69.0	30.1	0.4	<.1	<.1	0.4	18	17	29	28	1.7	1.7	1.7	0.8
45 049	Hampton	18,191	45.4	54.1	<.1	<.1	0.0	0.4	40	36	11	33	0.5	0.3	1.0	0.2
45 051	Horry	144,053	80.7	17.4	0.8	0.2	<.1	0.9	7	5	42	10	4.1	4.9	2.4	4.1
45 053	Jasper	15,487	41.9	57.3	0.2	0.1	0.0	0.4	43	39	8	23	0.4	0.3	0.9	0.2
45 055	Kershaw	43,599	70.8	28.2	0.2	0.2	<.1	0.6	24	15	32	17	1.3	1.3	1.2	0.8
45 057	Lancaster	54,516	74.1	25.3	0.1	0.1	<.1	0.4	21	12	34	35	1.6	1.7	1.3	0.7
45 059	Laurens	58,092	71.2	28.2	0.2	<.1	<.1	0.4	19	14	33	37	1.7	1.7	1.6	0.7
45 061	Lee	18,437	37.1	62.3	0.1	<.1	0.0	0.4	38	44	3	31	0.5	0.3	1.1	0.2
45 063	Lexington	167,611	87.4	11.0	0.6	0.2	<.1	0.8	5	3	44	11	4.8	6.1	1.8	4.3
45 065	McCormick	8,868	41.0	58.4	0.1	<.1	<.1	0.3	46	42	5	42	0.3	0.2	0.5	<.1
45 067	Marion	33,899	44.5	54.5	0.4	0.3	<.1	0.3	28	37	10	40	1.0	0.6	1.8	0.4
45 069	Marlboro	29,361	48.7	48.4	<.1	2.5	<.1	0.3	32	34	13	43	0.8	0.6	1.4	0.3
45 071	Newberry	33,172	64.6	34.6	0.2	0.1	<.1	0.4	29	22	25	26	1.0	0.9	1.1	0.5
45 073	Oconee	57,494	89.9	8.7	0.3	0.1	<.1	0.9	20	2	45	9	1.6	2.2	0.5	1.7
45 075	Orangeburg	84,803	41.1	57.9	0.4	0.2	<.1	0.4	15	41	7	34	2.4	1.5	4.7	1.1
45 077	Pickens	93,894	91.2	7.2	0.8	0.2	<.1	0.6	13	1	46	15	2.7	3.6	0.7	1.9
45 079	Richland	285,720	55.3	41.5	1.3	0.2	<.1	1.6	3	29	20	3	8.2	6.6	11.5	15.2
45 081	Saluda	16,357	66.3	33.1	<.1	<.1	0.0	0.5	42	20	27	19	0.5	0.5	0.5	0.3
45 083	Spartanburg	226,800	77.8	20.6	0.7	0.1	<.1	0.7	4	9	38	14	6.5	7.4	4.5	5.0
45 085	Sumter	102,637	54.7	43.0	0.9	0.2	<.1	1.2	12	30	18	7	2.9	2.3	4.3	4.1
45 087	Union	30,337	69.7	29.9	<.1	<.1	<.1	0.2	31	16	30	46	0.9	0.9	0.9	0.2
45 089	Williamsburg	36,815	35.5	64.0	<.1	<.1	<.1	0.4	26	45	2	38	1.1	0.5	2.3	0.4
45 091	York	131,497	78.3	20.0	0.5	0.6	<.1	0.6	8	8	40	18	3.8	4.3	2.5	2.4
45	**SOUTH CAROLINA**	**3,486,703**	**68.5**	**29.7**	**0.6**	**0.2**	**<.1**	**0.9**					**100.0**	**100.0**	**100.0**	**100.0**
	CONGRESSIONAL															
	District 1	581,125	77.1	20.0	1.1	0.3	<.1	1.4	2	3	5	2	16.7	18.8	11.2	26.3
	District 2	581,111	72.2	25.2	0.9	0.2	<.1	1.4	5	4	3	1	16.7	17.5	14.2	27.1
	District 3	581,104	78.3	20.7	0.4	0.1	<.1	0.5	6	2	4	6	16.7	19.0	11.6	10.2
	District 4	581,113	78.8	19.6	0.6	0.1	<.1	0.8	4	1	6	3	16.7	19.2	11.0	15.2
	District 5	581,131	67.9	30.7	0.4	0.4	<.1	0.6	1	5	2	5	16.7	16.5	17.2	10.6
	District 6	581,119	37.1	61.9	0.2	0.2	<.1	0.6	3	6	1	4	16.7	9.0	34.7	10.6

Table B. — 1990 Voting Age Population (VAP) by Race and Ethnic Origin

County	Total Voting Age Population	Percent of total VAP — Non-Hispanic: White	Black	Asian and Pacific Islander	Native American	Other	Hispanic	Rank — Percent of total VAP: Total	Non-Hispanic: White	Black	Hispanic	Percent contribution to state VAP: Total	Non-Hispanic: White	Black	Hispanic	VAP percent of total population: Total	Non-Hispanic: White	Black	Asian and Pacific Islander	Native American	Other	Hispanic
Abbeville	17,697	70.6	28.7	0.2	<.1	0.0	0.4	35	19	28	33	0.7	0.7	0.7	0.3	74.2	77.2	67.8	72.0	88.2	0.0	64.3
Aiken	87,921	76.8	21.9	0.4	0.2	<.1	0.6	9	11	37	13	3.4	3.7	2.8	2.7	72.7	75.0	66.0	72.3	74.2	38.5	64.2
Allendale	8,263	35.1	63.0	<.1	<.1	<.1	1.6	45	46	1	3	0.3	0.2	0.8	0.6	70.5	80.7	65.6	100.0	72.7	83.3	81.4
Anderson	109,116	84.3	15.1	0.2	0.1	<.1	0.4	7	4	42	34	4.3	5.0	2.4	1.8	75.2	76.6	68.2	68.9	69.9	36.7	68.3
Bamberg	11,996	41.0	58.3	0.1	0.2	<.1	0.4	42	44	3	24	0.5	0.3	1.0	0.2	71.0	76.6	67.5	60.0	86.4	100.0	66.7
Barnwell	14,118	60.1	38.9	<.1	0.2	0.0	0.8	37	28	17	11	0.6	0.5	0.8	0.5	69.6	74.2	63.3	76.5	90.3	0.0	74.0
Beaufort	64,607	72.0	24.6	0.8	0.3	<.1	2.3	14	18	33	1	2.5	2.5	2.3	7.2	74.8	79.0	65.2	69.6	74.2	58.3	69.2
Berkeley	87,025	73.6	22.4	1.9	0.3	<.1	1.8	10	13	34	2	3.4	3.5	2.8	7.4	67.6	69.3	63.2	67.4	69.3	46.5	59.0
Calhoun	9,282	51.5	48.0	<.1	0.1	0.0	0.3	44	35	12	37	0.4	0.3	0.6	0.1	72.8	77.9	67.9	100.0	91.7	0.0	79.5
Charleston	221,434	66.8	30.8	0.8	0.2	<.1	1.3	2	23	25	5	8.6	8.1	9.9	13.6	75.1	79.8	66.5	74.3	80.4	48.0	72.9
Cherokee	32,812	81.2	17.8	0.3	0.2	0.0	0.5	22	7	40	20	1.3	1.5	0.8	0.8	73.7	76.4	64.1	51.1	79.4	0.0	61.8
Chester	23,182	63.7	35.9	0.1	0.2	0.0	0.2	30	25	22	46	0.9	0.8	1.2	0.2	72.1	77.1	64.8	77.1	57.7	0.0	52.5
Chesterfield	27,963	69.2	30.3	<.1	0.1	<.1	0.3	25	21	26	38	1.1	1.1	1.2	0.4	72.5	75.9	66.0	71.4	65.1	14.3	56.9
Clarendon	20,022	46.8	52.5	0.1	0.1	<.1	0.5	33	38	9	22	0.8	0.5	1.5	0.5	70.4	76.7	65.6	77.8	77.4	50.0	65.3
Colleton	24,271	57.6	41.4	0.1	0.5	0.0	0.5	28	31	15	18	0.9	0.8	1.5	0.6	70.6	75.1	65.2	71.4	67.3	0.0	69.3
Darlington	44,382	63.3	36.2	<.1	0.1	<.1	0.3	17	26	21	40	1.7	1.5	2.3	0.6	71.8	76.3	65.1	60.0	67.6	66.7	64.0
Dillon	19,929	59.6	38.6	0.2	1.3	<.1	0.3	34	29	18	43	0.8	0.6	1.1	0.2	68.5	75.0	60.6	60.0	62.9	100.0	67.1
Dorchester	58,492	75.4	22.0	0.9	0.6	<.1	1.2	16	12	36	6	2.3	2.4	1.9	3.2	70.4	71.5	67.5	70.0	68.3	31.0	64.9
Edgefield	13,082	56.4	42.9	0.1	<.1	<.1	0.5	38	33	14	21	0.5	0.4	0.8	0.3	71.2	75.6	66.0	65.5	90.9	75.0	78.5
Fairfield	15,952	45.1	54.2	0.1	<.1	0.0	0.5	36	40	7	23	0.6	0.4	1.3	0.4	71.5	78.3	66.8	71.4	78.6	0.0	70.5
Florence	81,888	64.4	34.8	0.2	0.1	<.1	0.4	11	24	23	26	3.2	2.9	4.1	1.6	71.6	76.2	64.5	68.6	69.5	22.2	66.9
Georgetown	32,484	61.7	37.7	0.1	0.1	<.1	0.3	23	27	20	35	1.3	1.1	1.8	0.5	70.2	76.9	61.4	68.5	69.4	23.5	59.4
Greenville	241,338	82.3	16.1	0.6	0.1	<.1	0.9	1	6	41	8	9.4	10.8	5.7	10.0	75.4	77.2	67.7	68.3	74.3	34.4	69.0
Greenwood	44,363	72.2	27.0	0.4	<.1	0.0	0.4	18	17	30	27	1.7	1.7	1.7	0.9	74.5	77.9	66.8	68.1	84.0	0.0	72.1
Hampton	12,382	50.7	48.8	<.1	<.1	0.0	0.4	40	36	11	29	0.5	0.3	0.9	0.2	68.1	76.0	61.4	52.9	66.7	0.0	67.6
Horry	109,742	83.8	14.5	0.7	0.2	<.1	0.8	6	5	43	10	4.3	5.0	2.3	4.1	76.2	79.1	63.6	70.7	70.9	23.1	67.5
Jasper	10,582	46.0	53.2	0.2	<.1	0.0	0.4	43	39	8	25	0.4	0.3	0.8	0.2	68.3	75.0	63.5	76.7	45.0	0.0	63.8
Kershaw	31,788	72.7	26.5	0.2	0.1	<.1	0.5	24	15	31	19	1.2	1.3	1.2	0.7	72.9	74.9	68.3	63.9	67.6	33.3	63.7
Lancaster	39,871	77.0	22.4	0.1	0.1	<.1	0.4	21	10	35	28	1.6	1.7	1.3	0.8	73.1	76.0	64.7	75.9	76.7	25.0	74.5
Laurens	43,345	73.3	26.1	0.1	<.1	<.1	0.3	20	14	32	36	1.7	1.7	1.6	0.7	74.6	76.8	69.2	62.6	77.8	64.3	68.7
Lee	12,782	42.2	57.2	0.1	0.1	0.0	0.4	39	43	4	32	0.5	0.3	1.1	0.2	69.3	78.9	63.6	72.0	82.4	0.0	61.3
Lexington	123,054	88.6	9.9	0.6	0.2	<.1	0.7	5	3	44	12	4.8	5.9	1.8	4.2	73.4	74.4	66.0	69.8	77.3	34.5	67.2
McCormick	6,729	43.9	55.6	0.1	<.1	<.1	0.3	46	42	5	39	0.3	0.2	0.5	0.1	75.9	81.2	72.2	81.8	83.3	40.0	80.8
Marion	23,320	49.3	49.8	0.4	0.2	0.0	0.3	29	37	10	41	0.9	0.6	1.7	0.3	68.8	76.1	62.9	69.1	55.3	0.0	63.6
Marlboro	20,831	52.3	45.0	<.1	2.2	<.1	0.3	32	34	13	44	0.8	0.6	1.4	0.3	70.9	76.3	66.0	60.0	63.9	62.5	67.1
Newberry	24,796	67.8	31.5	0.2	0.1	<.1	0.4	27	22	24	30	1.0	0.9	1.1	0.4	74.7	78.5	68.0	60.8	77.5	10.0	62.6
Oconee	43,436	90.8	8.0	0.3	0.1	<.1	0.8	19	2	45	9	1.7	2.1	0.5	1.7	75.5	76.3	69.4	65.1	72.5	25.0	66.7
Orangeburg	60,921	44.1	54.9	0.3	0.3	<.1	0.4	15	41	6	31	2.4	1.5	4.9	1.1	71.8	77.2	68.1	66.3	74.8	87.5	67.7
Pickens	73,116	91.4	6.9	0.9	0.2	<.1	0.6	13	1	46	15	2.8	3.6	0.7	2.1	77.9	78.1	74.8	82.7	74.3	33.3	76.9
Richland	216,951	58.9	38.0	1.3	0.2	<.1	1.5	3	30	19	4	8.5	7.0	12.0	15.8	75.9	80.9	69.5	76.8	81.6	45.2	70.6
Saluda	12,032	70.1	29.2	<.1	<.1	0.0	0.5	41	20	27	16	0.5	0.5	0.5	0.3	73.6	77.8	64.9	100.0	60.0	0.0	76.7
Spartanburg	170,933	80.0	18.7	0.6	0.1	<.1	0.6	4	9	38	14	6.7	7.4	4.6	5.0	75.4	77.4	68.3	65.5	74.8	46.2	68.2
Sumter	73,220	57.5	40.3	0.9	0.2	<.1	1.1	12	32	16	7	2.9	2.3	4.3	4.0	71.3	75.0	66.8	72.7	70.2	64.7	66.7
Union	22,786	72.6	27.0	<.1	0.1	<.1	0.2	31	16	29	45	0.9	0.9	0.9	0.2	75.1	78.2	67.9	63.3	92.3	100.0	69.6
Williamsburg	24,835	40.3	59.3	<.1	<.1	<.1	0.3	26	45	2	42	1.0	0.5	2.1	0.3	67.5	76.4	62.6	76.0	60.0	50.0	53.5
York	97,425	80.2	18.3	0.4	0.5	<.1	0.5	8	8	39	17	3.8	4.3	2.6	2.4	74.1	75.9	67.8	62.5	66.8	42.1	67.9
SOUTH CAROLINA	**2,566,496**	**71.5**	**26.8**	**0.6**	**0.2**	**<.1**	**0.8**					**100.0**	**100.0**	**100.0**	**100.0**	**73.6**	**76.8**	**66.5**	**70.9**	**71.8**	**42.0**	**68.1**
CONGRESSIONAL																						
District 1	427,603	79.8	17.6	1.1	0.3	<.1	1.2	4	3	6	2	16.7	18.6	10.9	25.5	73.6	76.1	64.6	70.6	72.6	39.0	66.2
District 2	431,032	74.9	22.6	0.9	0.2	<.1	1.3	3	4	3	1	16.8	17.6	14.2	27.8	74.2	77.0	66.4	73.2	78.6	47.8	70.1
District 3	435,406	80.3	18.7	0.4	0.1	<.1	0.5	2	2	4	6	17.0	19.0	11.9	10.5	74.9	76.8	67.9	74.1	74.1	36.0	69.8
District 4	437,837	80.8	17.7	0.6	0.1	<.1	0.7	1	1	5	3	17.1	19.3	11.3	15.4	75.3	77.3	68.0	67.0	75.1	40.4	68.7
District 5	422,575	71.0	27.8	0.3	0.4	<.1	0.5	5	5	2	5	16.5	16.3	17.0	10.2	72.7	76.0	65.7	65.9	66.0	45.0	65.7
District 6	412,043	40.9	58.1	0.3	0.2	<.1	0.5	6	6	1	4	16.1	9.2	34.8	10.6	70.9	78.3	66.5	76.3	71.8	42.9	67.8

Table C. — Voter Participation: November 3, 1992, General Election

County	Estimated Voting Age Population (VAP), 1992	Voter registration (REG)				Voter turnout													
						Highest office				Maximum vote						Percent drop-off, by office			
		Total	% contribution to state REG	% of 1992 VAP	Rank by % of 1992 VAP	Actual	Total	Office	% of 1992 VAP	Total	% contribution to state turnout	% of REG	Rank by % of REG	% of 1992 VAP	Rank by % 1992 VAP	President	Senator	Governor	Representative
Abbeville	18,061	10,665	0.7	59.0	25	8,260	8,343	P	46.2	8,343	0.7	78.2	30	46.2	24	0.0	6.0	-	5.0
Aiken	92,255	58,458	3.8	63.4	15	47,954	46,778	P	50.7	47,954	3.9	82.0	11	52.0	12	2.5	2.8	-	5.9
Allendale	8,513	4,781	0.3	56.2	31	3,490	3,455	P	40.6	3,490	0.3	73.0	42	41.0	40	1.0	3.2	-	58.2
Anderson	112,994	58,978	3.8	52.2	39	49,364	47,971	P	42.5	49,364	4.0	83.7	6	43.7	32	2.8	3.3	-	3.8
Bamberg	11,973	7,684	0.5	64.2	12	5,917	5,727	P	47.8	5,917	0.5	77.0	37	49.4	16	3.2	5.5	-	7.6
Barnwell	14,536	10,085	0.7	69.4	7	8,357	8,177	P	56.3	8,357	0.7	82.9	7	57.5	4	2.2	5.1	-	34.8
Beaufort	68,116	41,238	2.7	60.5	20	31,617	31,287	P	45.9	31,617	2.6	76.7	39	46.4	23	1.0	1.5	-	23.3
Berkeley	96,106	44,945	2.9	46.8	46	36,700	35,479	P	36.9	36,700	3.0	81.7	13	38.2	45	3.3	5.3	-	6.4
Calhoun	9,540	7,071	0.5	74.1	3	5,769	5,778	P	60.6	5,778	0.5	81.7	12	60.6	1	0.0	4.9	-	38.4
Charleston	224,024	134,152	8.7	59.9	23	102,760	98,749	P	44.1	102,760	8.3	76.6	40	45.9	27	3.9	6.8	-	7.8
Cherokee	34,153	18,910	1.2	55.4	34	15,069	14,674	S	43.0	15,069	1.2	79.7	23	44.1	31	3.4	2.6	-	3.6
Chester	24,020	14,780	1.0	61.5	18	10,478	10,322	C	43.0	10,478	0.8	70.9	46	43.6	33	1.8	2.3	-	1.5
Chesterfield	28,654	14,758	1.0	51.5	41	11,608	11,254	S	39.3	11,608	0.9	78.7	27	40.5	42	3.4	3.0	-	3.4
Clarendon	20,582	14,242	0.9	69.2	9	11,276	11,044	S	53.7	11,276	0.9	79.2	26	54.8	7	2.2	2.1	-	2.5
Colleton	25,407	14,911	1.0	58.7	27	11,930	11,314	P	44.5	11,930	1.0	80.0	22	47.0	22	5.2	7.2	-	20.5
Darlington	45,583	24,786	1.6	54.4	37	20,345	20,253	P	44.4	20,345	1.6	82.1	10	44.6	29	0.5	7.4	-	12.0
Dillon	20,351	12,884	0.8	63.3	16	9,295	9,390	P	46.1	9,390	0.8	72.9	43	46.1	25	0.0	3.4	-	10.1
Dorchester	65,163	36,428	2.4	55.9	32	28,031	28,029	P	43.0	28,031	2.3	76.9	38	43.0	37	0.0	4.4	-	4.5
Edgefield	13,519	9,449	0.6	69.9	6	7,585	7,396	P	54.7	7,585	0.6	80.3	19	56.1	6	2.5	6.1	-	5.0
Fairfield	16,633	10,345	0.7	62.2	17	8,290	8,091	P	48.6	8,290	0.7	80.1	21	49.8	15	2.4	5.8	-	7.6
Florence	84,615	50,192	3.3	59.3	24	40,430	39,429	S	46.6	40,430	3.3	80.6	17	47.8	20	3.5	2.5	-	2.8
Georgetown	34,027	21,788	1.4	64.0	13	17,283	16,656	S	48.9	17,283	1.4	79.3	25	50.8	14	5.8	3.6	-	3.7
Greenville	249,246	140,040	9.1	56.2	30	117,243	115,127	C	46.2	117,243	9.5	83.7	5	47.0	21	2.8	2.2	-	1.8
Greenwood	45,168	23,895	1.6	52.9	38	19,176	18,923	P	41.9	19,176	1.6	80.3	20	42.5	38	1.3	4.7	-	5.0
Hampton	12,784	9,793	0.6	76.6	2	7,640	7,361	P	57.6	7,640	0.6	78.0	31	59.8	3	3.7	10.9	-	57.7
Horry	122,106	66,616	4.3	54.6	35	52,936	51,204	P	41.9	52,936	4.3	79.5	24	43.4	35	3.3	9.3	-	13.9
Jasper	10,934	7,568	0.5	69.2	8	5,858	5,763	P	52.7	5,858	0.5	77.4	34	53.6	11	1.6	6.1	-	63.2
Kershaw	33,423	21,620	1.4	64.7	10	18,108	17,535	S	52.5	18,108	1.5	83.8	4	54.2	9	4.5	3.2	-	13.5
Lancaster	40,787	22,225	1.4	54.5	36	18,613	18,655	P	45.7	18,655	1.5	83.9	3	45.7	28	0.0	3.6	-	1.5
Laurens	45,087	22,050	1.4	48.9	44	17,279	17,200	P	38.1	17,279	1.4	78.4	29	38.3	44	0.5	4.4	-	8.4
Lee	13,100	10,043	0.7	76.7	1	7,878	7,822	P	59.7	7,878	0.6	78.4	28	60.1	2	0.7	6.2	-	9.0
Lexington	131,052	84,399	5.5	64.4	11	70,916	69,435	S	53.0	70,916	5.7	84.0	2	54.1	10	2.7	2.1	-	12.6
McCormick	7,077	4,127	0.3	58.3	28	3,036	3,052	P	43.1	3,052	0.2	74.0	41	43.1	36	0.0	4.7	-	3.1
Marion	24,177	14,552	0.9	60.2	22	10,482	10,376	P	42.9	10,482	0.8	72.0	44	43.4	34	1.0	4.9	-	5.3
Marlboro	21,148	12,041	0.8	56.9	29	8,395	8,570	P	40.5	8,570	0.7	71.2	45	40.5	41	0.0	6.8	-	21.5
Newberry	25,461	15,357	1.0	60.3	21	12,528	12,329	P	48.4	12,528	1.0	81.6	14	49.2	18	1.6	4.4	-	7.7
Oconee	46,087	25,709	1.7	55.8	33	21,242	20,752	S	45.0	21,242	1.7	82.6	9	46.1	26	3.6	2.3	-	2.4
Orangeburg	61,881	43,393	2.8	70.1	5	33,831	32,421	S	52.4	33,831	2.7	78.0	32	54.7	8	4.7	4.2	-	13.4
Pickens	74,583	38,092	2.5	51.1	42	28,828	29,494	P	39.5	29,494	2.4	77.4	33	39.5	43	0.0	0.1	-	1.1
Richland	219,393	132,980	8.7	60.6	19	108,001	106,250	P	48.4	108,001	8.7	81.2	15	49.2	17	1.6	6.4	-	26.7
Saluda	12,304	7,833	0.5	63.7	14	6,298	6,214	C	50.5	6,298	0.5	80.4	18	51.2	13	1.4	1.9	-	1.3
Spartanburg	177,790	89,779	5.8	50.5	43	74,324	72,635	P	40.9	74,324	6.0	82.8	8	41.8	39	2.3	5.2	-	4.1
Sumter	77,165	37,443	2.4	48.5	45	28,875	27,689	S	35.9	28,875	2.3	77.1	35	37.4	46	7.9	4.1	-	5.3
Union	23,151	13,656	0.9	59.0	26	11,068	11,013	C	47.6	11,068	0.9	81.0	16	47.8	19	3.5	1.5	-	0.5
Williamsburg	25,629	18,777	1.2	73.3	4	14,471	14,277	P	55.7	14,471	1.2	77.1	36	56.5	5	1.3	8.5	-	8.8
York	103,642	53,622	3.5	51.7	40	45,878	43,694	P	42.2	45,878	3.7	85.6	1	44.3	30	4.8	6.2	-	5.7
SOUTH CAROLINA[1]	2,672,000	1,537,140	100.0	57.5		1,234,712	1,207,387		45.2	1,235,798	100.0	80.4		46.2		2.7	4.5	-	9.7

[1]South Carolina does not report voter registration by political party, but does report registration and voter turnout by race. State voter registration by race is 1,149,516 (74.8%) for white; 381,524 (24.8%) for black; 3,053 (0.2%) for Oriental; 1,592 (0.1%) for Indian; 1,359 (<.1%) for Hispanic; and 96 (<.1%) unknown. Voter turnout by race is 948,385 (76.8%) for white and 286,327 (23.2%) for non-white.

Table E. — Vote for President: November 3, 1992, General Election

County	Total	Clinton (DEM)	Bush (REP)	Perot (IND)	Other	Plurality Total	Party	DEM	REP	IND	Other	Rank DEM	Rank REP	Rank IND	Total	DEM	REP	IND	DEM	REP
Abbeville	8,343	3,968	3,317	1,036	22	651	D	47.6	39.8	12.4	0.3	19	31	18	0.7	0.8	0.6	0.7	54.5	45.5
Aiken	46,778	14,802	25,731	6,056	189	10,929	R	31.6	55.0	12.9	0.4	43	4	13	3.9	3.1	4.5	4.4	36.5	63.5
Allendale	3,455	2,159	1,049	212	35	1,110	D	62.5	30.4	6.1	1.0	1	43	45	0.3	0.5	0.2	0.2	67.3	32.7
Anderson	47,971	16,072	24,793	6,966	140	8,721	R	33.5	51.7	14.5	0.3	40	7	6	4.0	3.4	4.3	5.0	39.3	60.7
Bamberg	5,727	3,426	1,906	360	35	1,520	D	59.8	33.3	6.3	0.6	5	40	44	0.5	0.7	0.3	0.3	64.3	35.7
Barnwell	8,177	3,344	4,026	752	55	682	R	40.9	49.2	9.2	0.7	26	11	32	0.7	0.7	0.7	0.5	45.4	54.6
Beaufort	31,287	11,466	14,735	4,966	120	3,269	R	36.6	47.1	15.9	0.4	36	21	3	2.6	2.4	2.6	3.6	43.8	56.2
Berkeley	35,479	12,533	18,048	4,632	266	5,515	R	35.3	50.9	13.1	0.7	38	8	11	3.0	2.6	3.1	3.3	41.0	59.0
Calhoun	5,778	2,770	2,418	564	26	352	D	47.9	41.8	9.8	0.5	18	27	28	0.5	0.6	0.4	0.4	53.4	46.6
Charleston	98,749	40,095	47,403	10,354	897	7,308	R	40.6	48.0	10.5	0.9	27	16	26	8.2	8.4	8.2	7.5	45.8	54.2
Cherokee	14,557	5,453	6,887	2,186	31	1,434	R	37.5	47.3	15.0	0.2	34	19	4	1.2	1.1	1.2	1.6	44.2	55.8
Chester	10,288	5,458	3,451	1,350	29	2,007	D	53.1	33.5	13.1	0.3	13	39	10	0.9	1.1	0.6	1.0	61.3	38.7
Chesterfield	11,212	5,691	4,183	1,315	23	1,508	D	50.8	37.3	11.7	0.2	15	34	21	0.9	1.2	0.7	0.9	57.6	42.4
Clarendon	10,945	6,033	4,147	744	21	1,886	D	55.1	37.9	6.8	0.2	12	33	43	0.9	1.3	0.7	0.5	59.3	40.7
Colleton	11,314	5,455	4,545	1,245	69	910	D	48.2	40.2	11.0	0.6	17	30	25	0.9	1.1	0.8	0.9	54.6	45.5
Darlington	20,253	9,090	8,912	1,863	388	178	D	44.9	44.0	9.2	1.9	22	24	31	1.7	1.9	1.5	1.3	50.5	49.5
Dillon	9,390	4,953	3,575	831	31	1,378	D	52.7	38.1	8.8	0.3	14	32	34	0.8	1.0	0.6	0.6	58.1	41.9
Dorchester	28,029	9,160	15,004	3,648	217	5,844	R	32.7	53.5	13.0	0.8	41	5	12	2.3	1.9	2.6	2.6	37.9	62.1
Edgefield	7,396	3,433	3,339	596	28	94	D	46.4	45.1	8.1	0.4	20	23	35	0.6	0.7	0.6	0.4	50.7	49.3
Fairfield	8,091	4,867	2,518	652	54	2,349	D	60.2	31.1	8.1	0.7	3	42	36	0.7	1.0	0.4	0.5	65.9	34.1
Florence	39,003	15,569	19,802	3,499	133	4,233	R	39.9	50.8	9.0	0.3	29	9	33	3.2	3.2	3.4	2.5	44.0	56.0
Georgetown	16,272	7,494	6,870	1,840	68	624	D	46.1	42.2	11.3	0.4	21	26	22	1.4	1.6	1.2	1.3	52.2	47.8
Greenville	113,907	34,651	65,066	13,699	491	30,415	R	30.4	57.1	12.0	0.4	44	3	20	9.5	7.2	11.3	9.9	34.7	65.3
Greenwood	18,923	7,621	9,079	2,101	122	1,458	R	40.3	48.0	11.1	0.6	28	17	24	1.6	1.6	1.6	1.5	45.6	54.4
Hampton	7,361	4,332	2,402	564	63	1,930	D	58.9	32.6	7.7	0.9	7	41	40	0.6	0.9	0.4	0.4	64.3	35.7
Horry	51,204	18,896	23,489	8,472	347	4,593	R	36.9	45.9	16.5	0.7	35	22	2	4.3	3.9	4.1	6.1	44.6	55.4
Jasper	5,763	3,453	1,725	549	36	1,728	D	59.9	29.9	9.5	0.6	4	44	30	0.5	0.7	0.3	0.4	66.7	33.3
Kershaw	17,301	6,585	8,499	2,150	67	1,914	R	38.1	49.1	12.4	0.4	33	12	17	1.4	1.4	1.5	1.5	43.7	56.3
Lancaster	18,655	8,307	7,757	2,563	28	550	D	44.5	41.6	13.7	0.2	24	28	8	1.6	1.7	1.3	1.8	51.7	48.3
Laurens	17,200	6,638	8,347	2,157	58	1,709	R	38.6	48.5	12.5	0.3	31	14	15	1.4	1.4	1.4	1.6	44.3	55.7
Lee	7,822	4,454	2,730	611	27	1,724	D	56.9	34.9	7.8	0.3	9	38	38	0.7	0.9	0.5	0.4	62.0	38.0
Lexington	69,022	18,312	41,759	8,652	299	23,447	R	26.5	60.5	12.5	0.4	46	1	16	5.7	3.8	7.2	6.2	30.5	69.5
McCormick	3,052	1,846	899	295	12	947	D	60.5	29.5	9.7	0.4	2	46	29	0.3	0.4	0.2	0.2	67.2	32.8
Marion	10,376	5,843	3,647	822	64	2,196	D	56.3	35.1	7.9	0.6	11	36	37	0.9	1.2	0.6	0.6	61.6	38.4
Marlboro	8,570	5,111	2,526	895	38	2,585	D	59.6	29.5	10.4	0.4	6	45	27	0.7	1.1	0.4	0.6	66.9	33.1
Newberry	12,329	4,896	5,980	1,393	60	1,084	R	39.7	48.5	11.3	0.5	30	15	23	1.0	1.0	1.0	1.0	45.0	55.0
Oconee	20,479	6,617	10,379	3,405	78	3,762	R	32.3	50.7	16.6	0.4	42	10	1	1.7	1.4	1.8	2.5	38.9	61.1
Orangeburg	32,234	18,440	11,328	2,383	83	7,112	D	57.2	35.1	7.4	0.3	8	37	42	2.7	3.8	2.0	1.7	61.9	38.1
Pickens	29,494	8,275	17,008	4,128	83	8,733	R	28.1	57.7	14.0	0.3	45	2	7	2.5	1.7	2.9	3.0	32.7	67.3
Richland	106,250	53,648	43,744	7,918	940	9,904	D	50.5	41.2	7.5	0.9	16	29	41	8.8	11.2	7.6	5.7	55.1	44.9
Saluda	6,209	2,393	2,968	833	15	575	R	38.5	47.8	13.4	0.2	32	18	9	0.5	0.5	0.5	0.6	44.6	55.4
Spartanburg	72,635	25,488	37,707	8,900	540	12,219	R	35.1	51.9	12.3	0.7	39	6	19	6.0	5.3	6.5	6.4	40.3	59.7
Sumter	26,596	11,852	12,576	2,062	106	724	R	44.6	47.3	7.8	0.4	23	20	39	2.2	2.5	2.2	1.5	48.5	51.5
Union	10,680	4,644	4,647	1,371	18	3	R	43.5	43.5	12.8	0.2	25	25	14	0.9	1.0	0.8	1.0	50.0	50.0
Williamsburg	14,277	8,077	5,289	864	47	2,788	D	56.6	37.0	6.1	0.3	10	35	46	1.2	1.7	0.9	0.6	60.4	39.6
York	43,694	15,844	21,297	6,418	135	5,453	R	36.3	48.7	14.7	0.3	37	13	5	3.6	3.3	3.7	4.6	42.7	57.3
SOUTH CAROLINA	**1,202,527**	**479,514**	**577,507**	**138,872**	**6,634**	**97,993**	**R**	**39.9**	**48.0**	**11.5**	**0.6**				**100.0**	**100.0**	**100.0**	**100.0**	**45.4**	**54.6**

Table F. — Vote for U.S. Senator: November 3, 1992, General Election

County	Total	Hollings (DEM)	Harnett (REP)	Other	Plurality Total	Party	DEM	REP	Other	Rank DEM	Rank REP	Rank Other	Total	DEM	REP	Other
Abbeville	7,844	4,821	2,869	154	1,952	D	61.5	36.6	2.0	14	32	37	0.7	0.8	0.5	0.4
Aiken	46,606	20,934	23,923	1,749	2,989	R	44.9	51.3	3.8	40	9	6	3.9	3.5	4.3	5.0
Allendale	3,377	2,416	880	81	1,536	D	71.5	26.1	2.4	3	44	26	0.3	0.4	0.2	0.2
Anderson	47,737	21,485	24,864	1,388	3,379	R	45.0	52.1	2.9	39	7	18	4.0	3.6	4.5	3.9
Bamberg	5,589	3,959	1,536	94	2,423	D	70.8	27.5	1.7	4	43	41	0.5	0.7	0.3	0.3
Barnwell	7,931	4,457	3,252	222	1,205	D	56.2	41.0	2.8	22	26	21	0.7	0.8	0.6	0.6
Beaufort	31,133	13,479	16,681	973	3,202	R	43.3	53.6	3.1	42	5	12	2.6	2.3	3.0	2.8
Berkeley	34,755	16,471	17,264	1,020	793	R	47.4	49.7	2.9	35	12	16	2.9	2.8	3.1	2.9
Calhoun	5,492	3,305	2,049	138	1,256	D	60.2	37.3	2.5	16	31	24	0.5	0.6	0.4	0.4
Charleston	95,772	50,923	42,400	2,449	8,523	D	53.2	44.3	2.6	28	18	23	8.1	8.6	7.7	7.0
Cherokee	14,674	7,563	6,698	413	865	D	51.5	45.6	2.8	31	16	20	1.2	1.3	1.2	1.2
Chester	10,239	6,184	3,713	342	2,471	D	60.4	36.3	3.3	15	34	10	0.9	1.0	0.7	1.0
Chesterfield	11,254	6,510	4,500	244	2,010	D	57.8	40.0	2.2	19	28	34	1.0	1.1	0.8	0.7
Clarendon	11,044	6,869	4,005	170	2,864	D	62.2	36.3	1.5	12	33	43	0.9	1.2	0.7	0.5
Colleton	11,076	6,265	4,558	253	1,707	D	56.6	41.2	2.3	21	25	29	0.9	1.1	0.8	0.7
Darlington	18,837	10,148	7,993	696	2,155	D	53.9	42.4	3.7	25	24	7	1.6	1.7	1.4	2.0
Dillon	9,073	5,838	3,108	127	2,730	D	64.3	34.3	1.4	10	37	44	0.8	1.0	0.6	0.4
Dorchester	26,804	12,158	13,958	688	1,800	R	45.4	52.1	2.6	38	8	22	2.3	2.1	2.5	2.0
Edgefield	7,119	4,150	2,818	151	1,332	D	58.3	39.6	2.1	17	29	35	0.6	0.7	0.5	0.4
Fairfield	7,812	5,410	2,178	224	3,232	D	69.3	27.9	2.9	6	42	19	0.7	0.9	0.4	0.6
Florence	39,429	19,517	19,158	754	359	D	49.5	48.6	1.9	32	13	38	3.3	3.3	3.5	2.1
Georgetown	16,656	9,184	7,086	386	2,098	D	55.1	42.5	2.3	23	23	27	1.4	1.6	1.3	1.1
Greenville	114,664	45,761	65,508	3,395	19,747	R	39.9	57.1	3.0	44	2	15	9.7	7.7	11.8	9.6
Greenwood	18,280	8,894	8,852	534	42	D	48.7	48.4	2.9	34	14	17	1.5	1.5	1.6	1.5
Hampton	6,807	4,484	2,186	137	2,298	D	65.9	32.1	2.0	8	39	36	0.6	0.8	0.4	0.4
Horry	48,011	22,058	24,133	1,820	2,075	R	45.9	50.3	3.8	37	11	4	4.1	3.7	4.4	5.2
Jasper	5,500	3,414	1,964	122	1,450	D	62.1	35.7	2.2	13	35	33	0.5	0.6	0.4	0.3
Kershaw	17,535	8,635	8,238	662	397	D	49.2	47.0	3.8	33	15	5	1.5	1.5	1.5	1.9
Lancaster	17,986	9,613	7,931	442	1,682	D	53.4	44.1	2.5	27	19	25	1.5	1.6	1.4	1.3
Laurens	16,526	9,081	7,161	284	1,920	D	54.9	43.3	1.7	24	22	40	1.4	1.5	1.3	0.8
Lee	7,389	5,147	2,164	78	2,983	D	69.7	29.3	1.1	5	41	46	0.6	0.9	0.4	0.2
Lexington	69,435	26,194	39,712	3,529	13,518	R	37.7	57.2	5.1	46	1	1	5.9	4.4	7.2	10.0
McCormick	2,908	2,110	752	46	1,358	D	72.6	25.9	1.6	1	45	42	0.2	0.4	0.1	0.1
Marion	9,968	6,340	3,454	174	2,886	D	63.6	34.7	1.7	11	36	39	0.8	1.1	0.6	0.5
Marlboro	7,987	5,786	2,021	180	3,765	D	72.4	25.3	2.3	2	46	32	0.7	1.0	0.4	0.5
Newberry	11,981	6,202	5,362	417	840	D	51.8	44.8	3.5	30	17	9	1.0	1.0	1.0	1.2
Oconee	20,752	8,840	11,123	789	2,283	R	42.6	53.6	3.8	43	4	3	1.8	1.5	2.0	2.2
Orangeburg	32,421	21,365	10,318	738	11,047	D	65.9	31.8	2.3	7	40	30	2.7	3.6	1.9	2.1
Pickens	29,470	11,722	16,583	1,165	4,861	R	39.8	56.3	4.0	45	3	2	2.5	2.0	3.0	3.3
Richland	101,085	58,841	39,118	3,126	19,723	D	58.2	38.7	3.1	18	30	13	8.6	10.0	7.1	8.9
Saluda	6,180	3,265	2,693	222	572	D	52.8	43.6	3.6	29	21	8	0.5	0.6	0.5	0.6
Spartanburg	70,428	32,594	35,500	2,334	2,906	R	46.3	50.4	3.3	36	10	11	6.0	5.5	6.4	6.6
Sumter	27,689	14,877	12,176	636	2,701	D	53.7	44.0	2.3	26	20	28	2.3	2.5	2.2	1.8
Union	10,903	6,197	4,459	247	1,738	D	56.8	40.9	2.3	20	27	31	0.9	1.0	0.8	0.7
Williamsburg	13,238	8,593	4,492	153	4,101	D	64.9	33.9	1.2	9	38	45	1.1	1.5	0.8	0.4
York	43,042	18,971	22,784	1,287	3,813	R	44.1	52.9	3.0	41	6	14	3.6	3.2	4.1	3.7
SOUTH CAROLINA	**1,180,438**	**591,030**	**554,175**	**35,233**	**36,855**	**D**	**50.1**	**46.9**	**3.0**				**100.0**	**100.0**	**100.0**	**100.0**

Congressional district and county	Total	Democrat (DEM)	Republican (REP)	Other	Plurality Total	Party	DEM	REP	Other	Rank within district DEM	REP	Other	Total	DEM	REP	Other
District 1	**184,549**	**59,908**	**121,938**	**2,703**	**62,030**	**R**	**32.5**	**66.1**	**1.5**				**100.0**	**100.0**	**100.0**	**100.0**
Berkeley (pt)	28,309	7,131	20,520	658	13,389	R	25.2	72.5	2.3	3	3	1	15.3	11.9	16.8	24.3
Charleston (pt)	72,358	17,757	53,351	1,250	35,594	R	24.5	73.7	1.7	4	2	3	39.2	29.6	43.8	46.2
Dorchester (pt)	21,658	5,190	16,041	427	10,851	R	24.0	74.1	2.0	5	1	2	11.7	8.7	13.2	15.8
Georgetown	16,649	9,329	7,177	143	2,152	D	56.0	43.1	0.9	1	5	4	9.0	15.6	5.9	5.3
Horry	45,575	20,501	24,849	225	4,348	R	45.0	54.5	0.5	2	4	5	24.7	34.2	20.4	8.3
District 2	**169,670**	**-**	**148,667**	**21,003**	**127,664**	**R**	**-**	**87.6**	**12.4**				**100.0**	**-**	**100.0**	**100.0**
Aiken (pt)	4,968	-	4,294	674	3,620	R	-	86.4	13.6	-	9	3	2.9	-	2.9	3.2
Allendale	1,458	-	1,348	110	1,238	R	-	92.5	7.5	-	3	9	0.9	-	0.9	0.5
Barnwell	5,448	-	5,037	411	4,626	R	-	92.5	7.5	-	2	10	3.2	-	3.4	2.0
Beaufort (pt)	23,239	-	20,084	3,155	16,929	R	-	86.4	13.6	-	10	2	13.7	-	13.5	15.0
Calhoun (pt)	2,249	-	2,106	143	1,963	R	-	93.6	6.4	-	1	11	1.3	-	1.4	0.7
Colleton (pt)	3,249	-	2,971	278	2,693	R	-	91.4	8.6	-	4	8	1.9	-	2.0	1.3
Hampton	3,229	-	2,932	297	2,635	R	-	90.8	9.2	-	5	7	1.9	-	2.0	1.4
Jasper	2,156	-	1,898	258	1,640	R	-	88.0	12.0	-	7	5	1.3	-	1.3	1.2
Lexington	62,013	-	53,541	8,472	45,069	R	-	86.3	13.7	-	11	1	36.5	-	36.0	40.3
Orangeburg (pt)	11,308	-	10,201	1,107	9,094	R	-	90.2	9.8	-	6	6	6.7	-	6.9	5.3
Richland (pt)	50,353	-	44,255	6,098	38,157	R	-	87.9	12.1	-	8	4	29.7	-	29.8	29.0
District 3	**194,864**	**119,119**	**75,660**	**85**	**43,459**	**D**	**61.1**	**38.8**	**<.1**				**100.0**	**100.0**	**100.0**	**100.0**
Abbeville	7,925	5,729	2,196	0	3,533	D	72.3	27.7	0.0	2	9	6	4.1	4.8	2.9	0.0
Aiken (pt)	40,138	21,512	18,552	74	2,960	D	53.6	46.2	0.2	10	1	1	20.6	18.1	24.5	87.1
Anderson	47,508	30,831	16,673	4	14,158	D	64.9	35.1	<.1	6	5	4	24.4	25.9	22.0	4.7
Edgefield	7,204	4,894	2,310	0	2,584	D	67.9	32.1	0.0	3	8	7	3.7	4.1	3.1	0.0
Greenwood	18,214	10,908	7,303	3	3,605	D	59.9	40.1	<.1	8	3	3	9.3	9.2	9.7	3.5
Laurens (pt)	14,824	9,890	4,933	1	4,957	D	66.7	33.3	<.1	4	7	5	7.6	8.3	6.5	1.2
McCormick	2,956	2,311	645	0	1,666	D	78.2	21.8	0.0	1	10	8	1.5	1.9	0.9	0.0
Oconee	20,724	12,751	7,973	0	4,778	D	61.5	38.5	0.0	7	4	9	10.6	10.7	10.5	0.0
Pickens	29,157	16,170	12,987	0	3,183	D	55.5	44.5	0.0	9	2	10	15.0	13.6	17.2	0.0
Saluda	6,214	4,123	2,088	3	2,035	D	66.4	33.6	<.1	5	6	2	3.2	3.5	2.8	3.5
District 4	**198,410**	**94,182**	**99,879**	**4,349**	**5,697**	**R**	**47.5**	**50.3**	**2.2**				**100.0**	**100.0**	**100.0**	**100.0**
Greenville	115,127	46,775	65,480	2,872	18,705	R	40.6	56.9	2.5	4	1	1	58.0	49.7	65.6	66.0
Laurens (pt)	999	456	526	17	70	R	45.6	52.7	1.7	3	2	3	0.5	0.5	0.5	0.4
Spartanburg	71,271	39,405	30,539	1,327	8,866	D	55.3	42.8	1.9	2	3	2	35.9	41.8	30.6	30.5
Union	11,013	7,546	3,334	133	4,212	D	68.5	30.3	1.2	1	4	4	5.6	8.0	3.3	3.1
District 5	**183,086**	**112,031**	**70,866**	**189**	**41,165**	**D**	**61.2**	**38.7**	**0.1**				**100.0**	**100.0**	**100.0**	**100.0**
Cherokee	14,520	8,895	5,624	1	3,271	D	61.3	38.7	<.1	7	7	4	7.9	7.9	7.9	0.5
Chester	10,322	7,123	3,199	0	3,924	D	69.0	31.0	0.0	5	9	6	5.6	6.4	4.5	0.0
Chesterfield	11,216	7,570	3,632	14	3,938	D	67.5	32.4	0.1	6	8	2	6.1	6.8	5.1	7.4
Darlington (pt)	14,288	8,186	6,101	1	2,085	D	57.3	42.7	<.1	10	4	5	7.8	7.3	8.6	0.5
Dillon	8,445	5,828	2,617	0	3,211	D	69.0	31.0	0.0	4	10	7	4.6	5.2	3.7	0.0
Fairfield	7,659	5,817	1,841	1	3,976	D	75.9	24.0	<.1	1	13	3	4.2	5.2	2.6	0.5
Kershaw	15,655	8,439	7,044	172	1,395	D	53.9	45.0	1.1	13	1	1	8.6	7.5	9.9	91.0
Lancaster	18,369	11,212	7,157	0	4,055	D	61.0	39.0	0.0	8	6	8	10.0	10.0	10.1	0.0
Lee (pt)	4,159	2,883	1,276	0	1,607	D	69.3	30.7	0.0	3	11	9	2.3	2.6	1.8	0.0
Marlboro	6,729	4,901	1,828	0	3,073	D	72.8	27.2	0.0	2	12	10	3.7	4.4	2.6	0.0
Newberry	11,560	6,941	4,619	0	2,322	D	60.0	40.0	0.0	9	5	11	6.3	6.2	6.5	0.0
Sumter (pt)	16,916	9,661	7,255	0	2,406	D	57.1	42.9	0.0	11	3	12	9.2	8.6	10.2	0.0
York	43,248	24,575	18,673	0	5,902	D	56.8	43.2	0.0	12	2	13	23.6	21.9	26.3	0.0
District 6	**184,871**	**120,647**	**64,149**	**75**	**56,498**	**D**	**65.3**	**34.7**	**<.1**				**100.0**	**100.0**	**100.0**	**100.0**
Bamberg	5,465	3,569	1,894	2	1,675	D	65.3	34.7	<.1	8	9	5	3.0	3.0	3.0	2.7
Beaufort (pt)	1,014	797	217	0	580	D	78.6	21.4	0.0	2	15	10	0.5	0.7	0.3	0.0
Berkeley (pt)	6,057	4,560	1,497	0	3,063	D	75.3	24.7	0.0	5	12	11	3.3	3.8	2.3	0.0
Calhoun (pt)	1,312	743	569	0	174	D	56.6	43.4	0.0	15	2	12	0.7	0.6	0.9	0.0
Charleston (pt)	22,422	17,495	4,926	1	12,569	D	78.0	22.0	<.1	3	14	8	12.1	14.5	7.7	1.3
Clarendon	10,999	6,718	4,267	14	2,451	D	61.1	38.8	0.1	11	6	2	5.9	5.6	6.7	18.7
Colleton (pt)	6,234	3,996	2,237	1	1,759	D	64.1	35.9	<.1	10	7	7	3.4	3.3	3.5	1.3
Darlington (pt)	3,611	2,334	1,276	1	1,058	D	64.6	35.3	<.1	9	8	6	2.0	1.9	2.0	1.3
Dorchester (pt)	5,113	2,994	2,116	3	878	D	58.6	41.4	<.1	14	3	3	2.8	2.5	3.3	4.0
Florence	39,295	15,827	23,468	0	7,641	R	40.3	59.7	0.0	16	1	13	21.3	13.1	36.6	0.0
Lee (pt)	3,009	2,346	663	0	1,683	D	78.0	22.0	0.0	4	13	14	1.6	1.9	1.0	0.0
Marion	9,924	5,949	3,971	4	1,978	D	59.9	40.0	<.1	12	5	4	5.4	4.9	6.2	5.3
Orangeburg (pt)	18,002	13,096	4,858	48	8,238	D	72.7	27.0	0.3	6	11	1	9.7	10.9	7.6	64.0
Richland (pt)	28,776	24,768	4,007	1	20,761	D	86.1	13.9	<.1	1	16	9	15.6	20.5	6.2	1.3
Sumter (pt)	10,436	7,552	2,884	0	4,668	D	72.4	27.6	0.0	7	10	15	5.6	6.3	4.5	0.0
Williamsburg	13,202	7,903	5,299	0	2,604	D	59.9	40.1	0.0	13	4	16	7.1	6.6	8.3	0.0
SOUTH CAROLINA	**1,115,450**	**505,887**	**581,159**	**28,404**	**75,272**	**R**	**45.4**	**52.1**	**2.5**							

Table I. — Vote for Presidential Preference: March 7, 1992, Democratic Primary Election

| County | Top candidates | | | | | | | | | Top three candidates (state vote) | | | | | | | | | |
| | | | | | | | | | | Percent of total vote | | | Rank | | | Percent contribution to state vote | | | |
	Total	Clinton	Tsongas	Harkin	Brown	Uncom-mitted	Cunning-ham	Woods	Other	Clinton	Tsongas	Harkin	Clinton	Tsongas	Harkin	Total	Clinton	Tsongas	Harkin
Abbeville	1,013	729	131	26	39	62	12	4	10	72.0	12.9	2.6	19	22	38	0.9	1.0	0.6	0.3
Aiken	2,821	1,861	539	78	200	70	32	8	33	66.0	19.1	2.8	27	14	36	2.4	2.5	2.5	1.0
Allendale	508	370	35	14	38	24	17	4	6	72.8	6.9	2.8	13	38	37	0.4	0.5	0.2	0.2
Anderson	4,125	2,631	885	135	257	116	26	40	35	63.8	21.5	3.3	32	9	32	3.5	3.6	4.1	1.8
Bamberg	688	515	55	23	45	17	21	3	9	74.9	8.0	3.3	8	33	30	0.6	0.7	0.3	0.3
Barnwell	582	383	65	29	51	17	22	1	14	65.8	11.2	5.0	29	25	19	0.5	0.5	0.3	0.4
Beaufort	2,190	1,028	804	61	210	54	14	3	16	46.9	36.7	2.8	45	1	35	1.9	1.4	3.8	0.8
Berkeley	5,702	3,725	579	510	448	166	145	41	88	65.3	10.2	8.9	31	28	10	4.9	5.1	2.7	6.7
Calhoun	584	447	58	25	21	14	12	3	4	76.5	9.9	4.3	7	30	27	0.5	0.6	0.3	0.3
Charleston	9,074	4,897	2,419	901	517	212	51	20	57	54.0	26.7	9.9	42	4	8	7.8	6.7	11.3	11.8
Cherokee	1,366	985	149	30	47	115	6	18	16	72.1	10.9	2.2	18	26	41	1.2	1.3	0.7	0.4
Chester	1,209	889	125	49	60	44	10	6	26	73.5	10.3	4.1	12	27	28	1.0	1.2	0.6	0.6
Chesterfield	1,336	964	134	49	56	89	11	16	17	72.2	10.0	3.7	17	29	29	1.1	1.3	0.6	0.6
Clarendon	1,697	1,189	91	262	61	41	18	11	24	70.1	5.4	15.4	21	43	3	1.5	1.6	0.4	3.4
Colleton	1,579	1,180	122	73	68	85	19	11	21	74.7	7.7	4.6	9	35	23	1.4	1.6	0.6	1.0
Darlington	1,899	1,276	224	143	71	120	23	24	18	67.2	11.8	7.5	24	23	14	1.6	1.7	1.0	1.9
Dillon	954	683	83	46	25	84	14	3	16	71.6	8.7	4.8	20	31	21	0.8	0.9	0.4	0.6
Dorchester	1,831	1,095	392	144	104	27	27	27	15	59.8	21.4	7.9	36	10	12	1.6	1.5	1.8	1.9
Edgefield	774	631	50	12	42	9	22	2	6	81.5	6.5	1.6	2	39	43	0.7	0.9	0.2	0.2
Fairfield	1,696	1,128	108	291	71	42	22	14	20	66.5	6.4	17.2	25	40	1	1.5	1.5	0.5	3.8
Florence	3,220	2,124	430	373	108	121	22	16	26	66.0	13.4	11.6	28	17	5	2.8	2.9	2.0	4.9
Georgetown	1,925	1,043	266	319	108	152	18	10	9	54.2	13.8	16.6	41	16	2	1.7	1.4	1.2	4.2
Greenville	8,349	4,396	2,653	244	656	263	37	44	56	52.7	31.8	2.9	43	3	33	7.2	6.0	12.4	3.2
Greenwood	1,403	919	287	31	77	56	14	6	13	65.5	20.5	2.2	30	12	40	1.2	1.3	1.3	0.4
Hampton	892	564	116	64	51	54	23	4	16	63.2	13.0	7.2	33	20	16	0.8	0.8	0.5	0.8
Horry	3,583	2,152	731	200	275	104	33	38	50	60.1	20.4	5.6	35	13	17	3.1	2.9	3.4	2.6
Jasper	767	637	26	4	50	12	18	8	12	83.1	3.4	0.5	1	46	46	0.7	0.9	0.1	<.1
Kershaw	2,333	1,731	307	118	91	35	15	22	14	74.2	13.2	5.1	10	18	18	2.0	2.4	1.4	1.5
Lancaster	1,701	1,157	220	76	76	127	12	15	18	68.0	12.9	4.5	22	21	24	1.5	1.6	1.0	1.0
Laurens	1,561	965	320	30	82	115	8	25	16	61.8	20.5	1.9	34	11	42	1.3	1.3	1.5	0.4
Lee	1,125	862	44	107	46	32	11	10	13	76.6	3.9	9.5	6	45	9	1.0	1.2	0.2	1.4
Lexington	4,925	2,777	1,263	239	347	118	30	106	45	56.4	25.6	4.9	39	5	20	4.2	3.8	5.9	3.1
McCormick	468	339	36	4	28	30	15	7	9	72.4	7.7	0.9	15	36	45	0.4	0.5	0.2	<.1
Marion	930	423	55	100	37	12	290	2	11	45.5	5.9	10.8	46	41	6	0.8	0.6	0.3	1.3
Marlboro	962	744	55	46	26	55	6	11	19	77.3	5.7	4.8	4	42	22	0.8	1.0	0.3	0.6
Newberry	1,231	896	161	35	63	26	16	13	21	72.8	13.1	2.8	14	19	34	1.1	1.2	0.8	0.5
Oconee	2,298	1,341	541	53	140	149	23	29	22	58.4	23.5	2.3	38	7	39	2.0	1.8	2.5	0.7
Orangeburg	4,006	3,072	314	325	141	78	30	20	26	76.7	7.8	8.1	5	34	11	3.4	4.2	1.5	4.2
Pickens	2,101	1,027	691	92	166	65	11	24	25	48.9	32.9	4.4	44	2	25	1.8	1.4	3.2	1.2
Richland	15,861	9,366	3,492	1,199	1,069	249	62	85	339	59.1	22.0	7.6	37	8	13	13.6	12.8	16.4	15.7
Saluda	694	502	58	30	32	47	7	7	11	72.3	8.4	4.3	16	32	26	0.6	0.7	0.3	0.4
Spartanburg	5,117	3,458	921	170	359	73	35	39	62	67.6	18.0	3.3	23	15	31	4.4	4.7	4.3	2.2
Sumter	3,388	2,249	381	472	136	62	35	20	33	66.4	11.2	13.9	26	24	4	2.9	3.1	1.8	6.2
Union	1,162	947	86	17	34	39	9	18	12	81.5	7.4	1.5	3	37	44	1.0	1.3	0.4	0.2
Williamsburg	1,680	1,242	68	176	67	54	46	5	22	73.9	4.0	10.5	11	44	7	1.4	1.7	0.3	2.3
York	3,104	1,682	768	232	265	104	19	11	23	54.2	24.7	7.5	40	6	15	2.7	2.3	3.6	3.0
SOUTH CAROLINA	**116,414**	**73,221**	**21,338**	**7,657**	**6,961**	**3,640**	**1,369**	**854**	**1,374**	**62.9**	**18.3**	**6.6**				**100.0**	**100.0**	**100.0**	**100.0**

Table J. — Vote for Presidential Preference: March 7, 1992, Republican Primary Election

| County | Top candidates | | | | | Top four candidates (state vote) | | | | | | | | | | | | |
| | | | | | | Percent of total vote | | | | Rank | | | | Percent contribution to state vote | | | | |
	Total	Bush	Bu-chanan	Duke	Daugh-erty	Bush	Bu-chanan	Duke	Daugh-erty	Bush	Bu-chanan	Duke	Daugh-erty	Total	Bush	Bu-chanan	Duke	Daugh-erty
Abbeville	576	379	132	65	0	65.8	22.9	11.3	0.0	32	24	9	41	0.4	0.4	0.3	0.6	0.0
Aiken	7,045	4,371	2,076	534	64	62.0	29.5	7.6	0.9	39	4	30	1	4.7	4.4	5.4	5.1	13.3
Allendale	190	140	33	17	0	73.7	17.4	8.9	0.0	6	39	18	42	0.1	0.1	< .1	0.2	0.0
Anderson	5,864	3,618	1,576	649	21	61.7	26.9	11.1	0.4	40	9	10	15	3.9	3.6	4.1	6.1	4.4
Bamberg	550	435	87	28	0	79.1	15.8	5.1	0.0	2	45	41	43	0.4	0.4	0.2	0.3	0.0
Barnwell	862	581	218	62	1	67.4	25.3	7.2	0.1	26	13	33	40	0.6	0.6	0.6	0.6	0.2
Beaufort	5,510	4,032	1,307	150	21	73.2	23.7	2.7	0.4	9	22	46	13	3.7	4.0	3.4	1.4	4.4
Berkeley	4,596	2,722	1,257	611	6	59.2	27.3	13.3	0.1	45	8	6	38	3.1	2.7	3.3	5.8	1.2
Calhoun	625	472	105	47	1	75.5	16.8	7.5	0.2	3	42	31	32	0.4	0.5	0.3	0.4	0.2
Charleston	12,910	8,717	3,067	1,109	17	67.5	23.8	8.6	0.1	25	21	23	37	8.7	8.8	8.0	10.5	3.5
Cherokee	876	497	252	124	3	56.7	28.8	14.2	0.3	46	5	4	18	0.6	0.5	0.7	1.2	0.6
Chester	766	526	144	95	1	68.7	18.8	12.4	0.1	21	35	7	39	0.5	0.5	0.4	0.9	0.2
Chesterfield	595	407	135	53	0	68.4	22.7	8.9	0.0	23	25	19	44	0.4	0.4	0.4	0.5	0.0
Clarendon	856	620	145	88	3	72.4	16.9	10.3	0.4	12	41	12	16	0.6	0.6	0.4	0.8	0.6
Colleton	877	525	212	135	5	59.9	24.2	15.4	0.6	42	20	2	3	0.6	0.5	0.6	1.3	1.0
Darlington	1,456	1,015	294	142	5	69.7	20.2	9.8	0.3	19	31	15	17	1.0	1.0	0.8	1.3	1.0
Dillon	494	320	122	51	1	64.8	24.7	10.3	0.2	34	17	11	28	0.3	0.3	0.3	0.5	0.2
Dorchester	3,695	2,455	858	365	17	66.4	23.2	9.9	0.5	31	23	14	10	2.5	2.5	2.2	3.5	3.5
Edgefield	915	547	300	63	5	59.8	32.8	6.9	0.5	43	1	37	4	0.6	0.5	0.8	0.6	1.0
Fairfield	929	697	154	76	2	75.0	16.6	8.2	0.2	5	43	26	27	0.6	0.7	0.4	0.7	0.4
Florence	3,551	2,372	862	312	5	66.8	24.3	8.8	0.1	29	19	22	35	2.4	2.4	2.3	3.0	1.0
Georgetown	1,291	866	314	105	6	67.1	24.3	8.1	0.5	27	18	27	9	0.9	0.9	0.8	1.0	1.2
Greenville	18,385	11,746	5,717	882	40	63.9	31.1	4.8	0.2	37	3	42	26	12.4	11.8	14.9	8.4	8.3
Greenwood	2,024	1,476	404	141	3	72.9	20.0	7.0	0.1	10	32	36	34	1.4	1.5	1.1	1.3	0.6
Hampton	328	237	61	29	1	72.3	18.6	8.8	0.3	14	36	21	19	0.2	0.2	0.2	0.3	0.2
Horry	6,161	3,979	1,728	422	32	64.6	28.0	6.8	0.5	35	7	38	5	4.1	4.0	4.5	4.0	6.6
Jasper	303	241	49	13	0	79.5	16.2	4.3	0.0	1	44	44	45	0.2	0.2	0.1	0.1	0.0
Kershaw	2,823	2,046	596	176	5	72.5	21.1	6.2	0.2	11	28	39	30	1.9	2.1	1.6	1.7	1.0
Lancaster	999	649	247	101	2	65.0	24.7	10.1	0.2	33	16	13	29	0.7	0.7	0.6	1.0	0.4
Laurens	1,270	863	285	120	2	68.0	22.4	9.4	0.2	24	27	16	33	0.9	0.9	0.7	1.1	0.4
Lee	395	279	67	48	1	70.6	17.0	12.2	0.3	17	40	8	23	0.3	0.3	0.2	0.5	0.2
Lexington	12,877	8,840	3,393	596	48	68.6	26.3	4.6	0.4	22	10	43	14	8.7	8.9	8.9	5.6	10.0
McCormick	138	82	36	19	1	59.4	26.1	13.8	0.7	44	11	5	2	< .1	< .1	< .1	0.2	0.2
Marion	575	411	118	45	1	71.5	20.5	7.8	0.2	15	30	28	31	0.4	0.4	0.3	0.4	0.2
Marlboro	191	140	34	17	0	73.3	17.8	8.9	0.0	8	37	20	46	0.1	0.1	< .1	0.2	0.0
Newberry	1,713	1,261	300	144	8	73.6	17.5	8.4	0.5	7	38	24	8	1.2	1.3	0.8	1.4	1.7
Oconee	2,740	1,904	619	210	7	69.5	22.6	7.7	0.3	20	26	29	22	1.8	1.9	1.6	2.0	1.5
Orangeburg	3,420	2,476	650	284	10	72.4	19.0	8.3	0.3	13	33	25	20	2.3	2.5	1.7	2.7	2.1
Pickens	3,990	2,660	1,027	283	20	66.7	25.7	7.1	0.5	30	12	35	6	2.7	2.7	2.7	2.7	4.1
Richland	15,296	10,794	3,835	605	62	70.6	25.1	4.0	0.4	18	15	45	12	10.3	10.8	10.0	5.7	12.9
Saluda	625	403	130	89	3	64.5	20.8	14.2	0.5	36	29	3	7	0.4	0.4	0.3	0.8	0.6
Spartanburg	10,072	6,090	3,238	720	24	60.5	32.1	7.1	0.2	41	2	34	24	6.8	6.1	8.5	6.8	5.0
Sumter	3,747	2,817	706	219	5	75.2	18.8	5.8	0.1	4	34	40	36	2.5	2.8	1.8	2.1	1.0
Union	720	449	203	66	2	62.4	28.2	9.2	0.3	38	6	17	21	0.5	0.5	0.5	0.6	0.4
Williamsburg	857	611	106	138	2	71.3	12.4	16.1	0.2	16	46	1	25	0.6	0.6	0.3	1.3	0.4
York	4,162	2,790	1,048	305	19	67.0	25.2	7.3	0.5	28	14	32	11	2.8	2.8	2.7	2.9	3.9
SOUTH CAROLINA	148,840	99,558	38,247	10,553	482	66.9	25.7	7.1	0.3					100.0	100.0	100.0	100.0	100.0

1992 Vote for President
Percent for Bush (R), by County

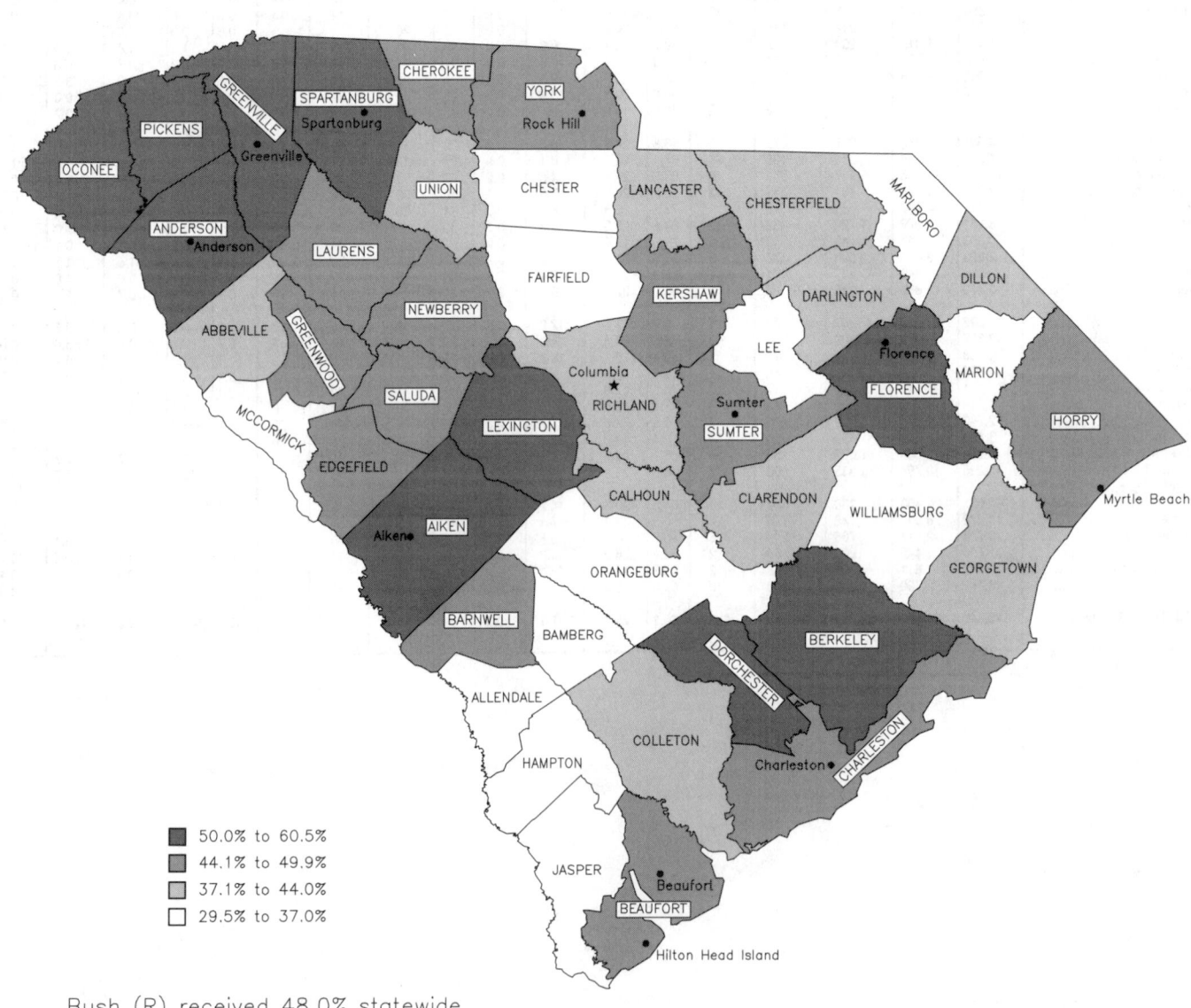

Legend:

- ■ 50.0% to 60.5%
- ■ 44.1% to 49.9%
- ■ 37.1% to 44.0%
- □ 29.5% to 37.0%

Bush (R) received 48.0% statewide.

A framed county name indicates
a county carried by the winner.

1992 Vote for U.S. Senator
Percent for Hollings (D), by County

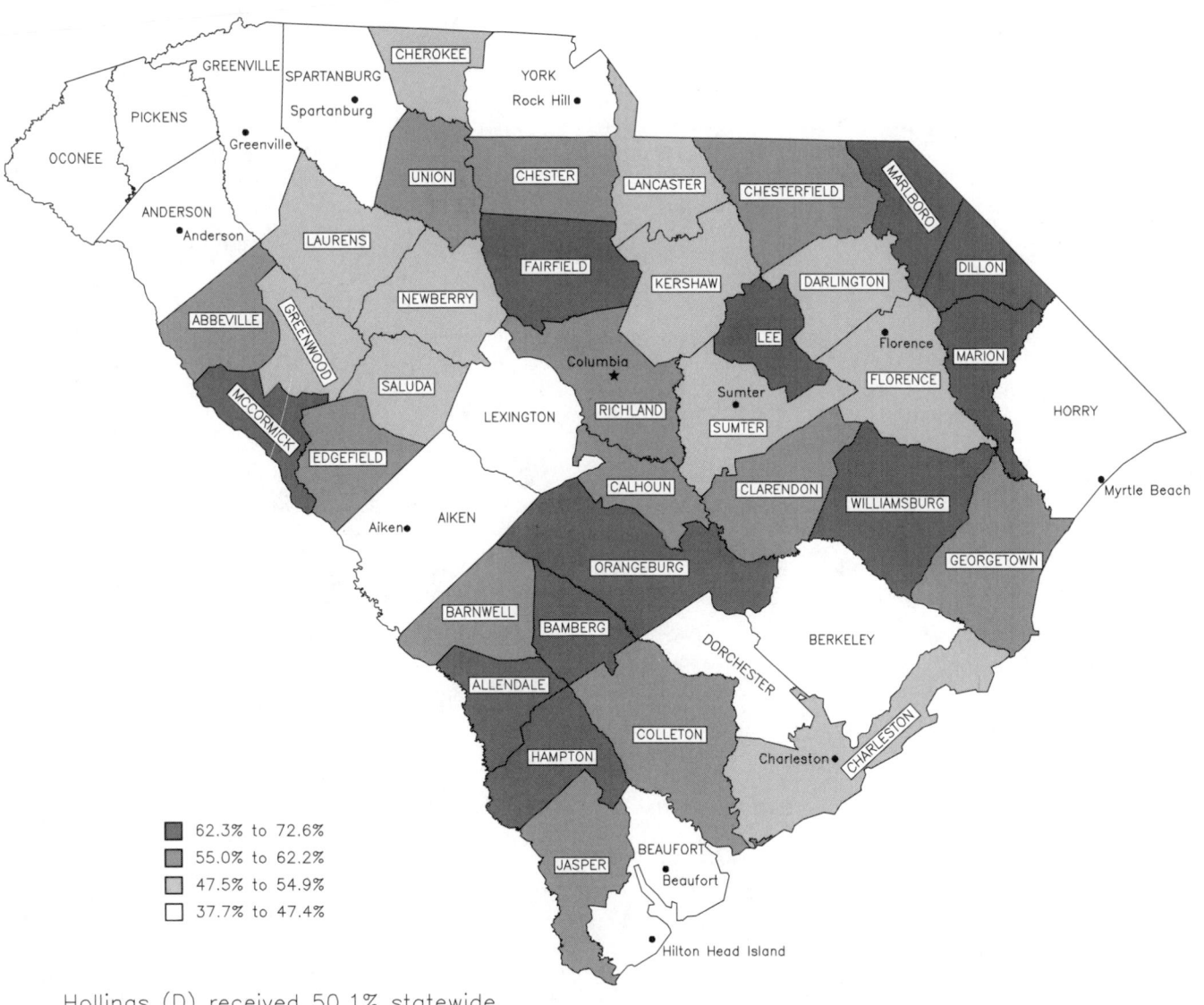

62.3% to 72.6%
55.0% to 62.2%
47.5% to 54.9%
37.7% to 47.4%

Hollings (D) received 50.1% statewide.

A framed county name indicates
a county carried by the winner.

SOUTH DAKOTA

Congressional Districts 1
    Average Population 696,004
State Senate Districts 35
    Average Population 19,886
State House Districts 70
    Average Population 9,943

Electoral College Votes 3
Counties 66
Voting Precincts 1,019

Alternative Registration Methods:
    .... Deputized Registrars

Registration Deadline (Days before Election) 15

Voting Equipment Use (Counties)

Datavote Punch Card	0	Paper Ballot	32
Electronic	0	Other Punch Card	16
Lever Machine	0	Mixed Systems	0
Optical Scanner	18		

Party Control	DEM	REP	IND	VAC
1993 State Senate	20	15	0	0
1992 State Senate	17	18	0	0
1993 State House	29	41	0	0
1992 State House	25	45	0	0

Population Statistics 1990

Race/ Ethnicity	Total Population		Voting Age Population		Voting Age Population % of total population
	Number	%	Number	%	
Non-Hispanic					
White	634,788	91.2	463,954	93.2	73.1
Black	3,176	0.5	1,979	0.4	62.3
Asian/Pacific Islander	3,013	0.4	1,937	0.4	64.3
Native American	49,648	7.1	26,691	5.4	53.8
Other	127	<.1	47	<.1	37.0
All Hispanic	5,252	0.8	2,934	0.6	55.9
TOTAL	696,004	100.0	497,542	100.0	71.5

Estimated Voting Age Population 1992 (VAP) 502,000
Number of Registered Voters 448,292
    % of estimated VAP 89.3
Voter Turnout (Highest Office) 336,409
    % of VAP 67.0
    % of Registration 75.0
Persons Not Voting—of Voting Age 165,591
    % of VAP 33.0
Persons Not Voting—of Registered 111,883
    % of Registration 25.0
Straight Ticket Voting .... Yes, Exception

State Officials and Members of Congress

Governor:
Walter D. Miller (R), succeeded to office April 1993.[1]

U.S. Senators:
Larry Pressler (R) 1978, elected to a six-year term in 1990.
Tom Daschle (D) 1986, elected to a six-year term in 1992.

U.S. Representative in Congress:
(District, Name, Party, Date first elected)

At-Large. Johnson (D) 1986

---

[1]For the remainder of the unexpired term of the late George Mickelson (R) 1986, elected to a four-year term in 1990.

Candidates: General Election, November 3, 1992

Candidate(s)	Total vote	Percent	Party	Status	First elected
President/Vice President					
Bush/Quayle	136,718	40.66%	Republican	Incumbent	1988
Clinton/Gore	124,888	37.14%	Democrat	Challenger	1992
Perot/Stockdale	73,295	21.80%	Independent	Challenger	
Marrou/Lord	814	0.24%	Libertarian	Challenger	
Hagelin/Tompkins	429	0.13%	Independent	Challenger	
Fulani/Munoz	110	0.03%	Independent	Challenger	
U.S. Senator					
Tom Daschle	217,095	64.90%	Democrat	Incumbent	1986
Charlene Haar	108,733	32.51%	Republican	Challenger	
Gus Hercules	4,353	1.30%	Libertarian	Challenger	
Kent Hyde	4,314	1.29%	Natural Law	Challenger	
Governor (No Contest)					
U.S. Representative in Congress					
District At-Large					
Tim Johnson	230,070	69.11%	Democrat	Incumbent	1986
John Timmer	89,375	26.85%	Republican	Challenger	
Ronald Wieczorek	6,746	2.03%	Independent	Challenger	
Robert Newland	3,931	1.18%	Libertarian	Challenger	
Ann Balakier	2,780	0.84%	Independent	Challenger	

Candidates: February 25, 1992, Primary Election

Candidate	Total vote	Percent	Candidate	Total vote	Percent
Presidential Preference, Democratic			**Presidential Preference, Republican**		
Bob Kerrey	23,892	40.15%	George Bush	30,964	69.32%
Tom Harkin	15,023	25.25%	Uncommitted	13,707	30.68%
Bill Clinton	11,375	19.12%			
Paul Tsongas	5,729	9.63%			
Jerry Brown	2,300	3.87%			
Larry Agran	606	1.02%			
Lyndon LaRouche, Jr.	441	0.74%			
Lawrence Wilder	137	0.23%			

Voter Registration and Turnout, 1948-1992 Elections

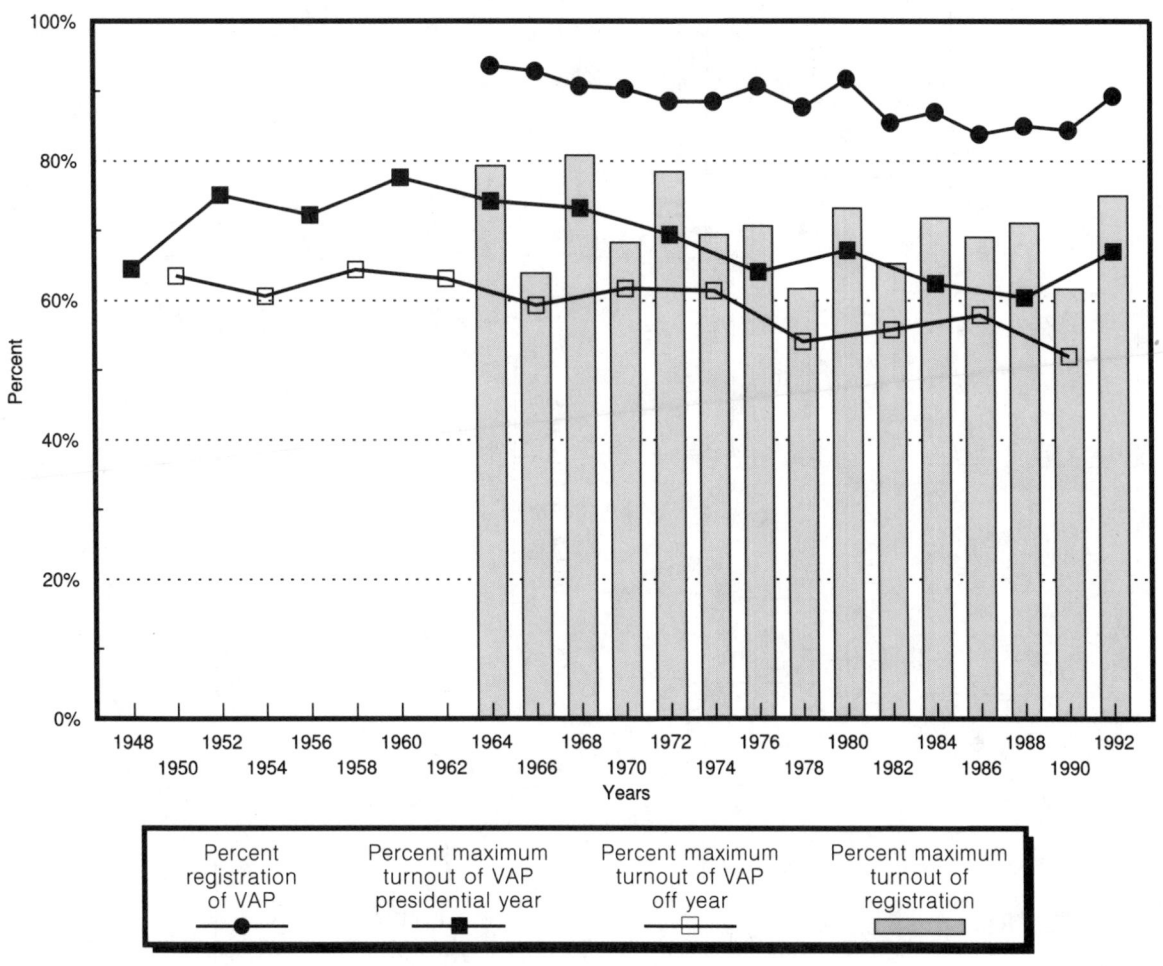

		Voter registration (REG)				Voter turnout										
							Highest office						Maximum vote			
Year	Estimated Voting Age Population (VAP)	Total	Percent of VAP	Rank by percent of VAP	Actual	Total	Office	Percent total REG	Rank by percent of REG	Percent of VAP	Rank by percent of VAP	Total	Percent total REG	Rank by percent of REG	Percent total VAP	Rank by percent of VAP
1992	502,000	448,292	89.3	6	-	336,254	P	75.0	33	67.0	7	336,254	75.0	35	67.0	9
1990	498,000	420,351	84.4	6	-	258,976	S	61.6	17	52.0	5	258,976	61.6	19	52.0	8
1988	518,000	440,301	85.0	7	-	312,991	P	71.1	28	60.4	7	312,991	71.1	33	60.4	8
1986	511,000	428,097	83.8	6	-	295,830	S	69.1	8	57.9	2	295,830	69.1	8	57.9	2
1984	509,000	442,790	87.0	7	-	317,867	P	71.8	30	62.4	6	317,867	71.8	35	62.4	9
1982	499,000	426,511	85.5	4	-	278,562	G	65.3	19	55.8	3	278,562	65.3	21	55.8	5
1980	488,000	447,508	91.7	4	-	327,703	P	73.2	31	67.2	4	327,703	73.2	33	67.2	5
1978	480,000	420,818	87.7	3	-	259,795	G	61.7	11	54.1	2	259,795	61.7	14	54.1	3
1976	469,000	425,532	90.7	4	-	300,678	P	70.7	34	64.1	5	300,678	70.7	35	64.1	6
1974	454,000	401,651	88.5	1	-	278,884	S	69.4	5	61.4	1	278,884	69.4	8	61.4	1
1972	443,000	392,256	88.5	5	-	307,415	P	78.4	13	69.4	1	307,415	78.4	17	69.4	5
1970	389,000	351,316	90.3	3	-	239,963	G	68.3	17	61.7	2	239,963	68.3	20	61.7	6
1968	384,000	348,254	90.7	6	-	281,264	P	80.8	23	73.2	4	281,264	80.8	24	73.2	4
1966	385,000	357,291	92.8	3	-	228,214	G	63.9	24	59.3	7	228,214	63.9	25	59.3	9
1964	395,000	369,782	93.6	4	-	293,118	P	79.3	24	74.2	6	293,118	79.3	26	74.2	7
1962	406,000	-	-	-	-	256,120	G	-	-	63.1	5	256,120	-	-	63.1	6
1960	395,000	-	-	-	-	306,487	P	-	-	77.6	6	306,487	-	-	77.6	8
1958	401,000	-	-	-	-	258,281	G	-	-	64.4	2	258,281	-	-	64.4	2
1956	407,000	-	-	-	-	293,857	P	-	-	72.2	12	293,857	-	-	72.2	14
1954	390,000	-	-	-	-	236,255	G	-	-	60.6	7	236,255	-	-	60.6	8
1952	392,000	-	-	-	-	294,283	P	-	-	75.1	12	294,283	-	-	75.1	14
1950	399,000	-	-	-	-	253,316	G	-	-	63.5	3	253,316	-	-	63.5	3
1948	388,000	-	-	-	-	250,105	P	-	-	64.5	13	250,105	-	-	64.5	16

South Dakota 837

SOUTH DAKOTA

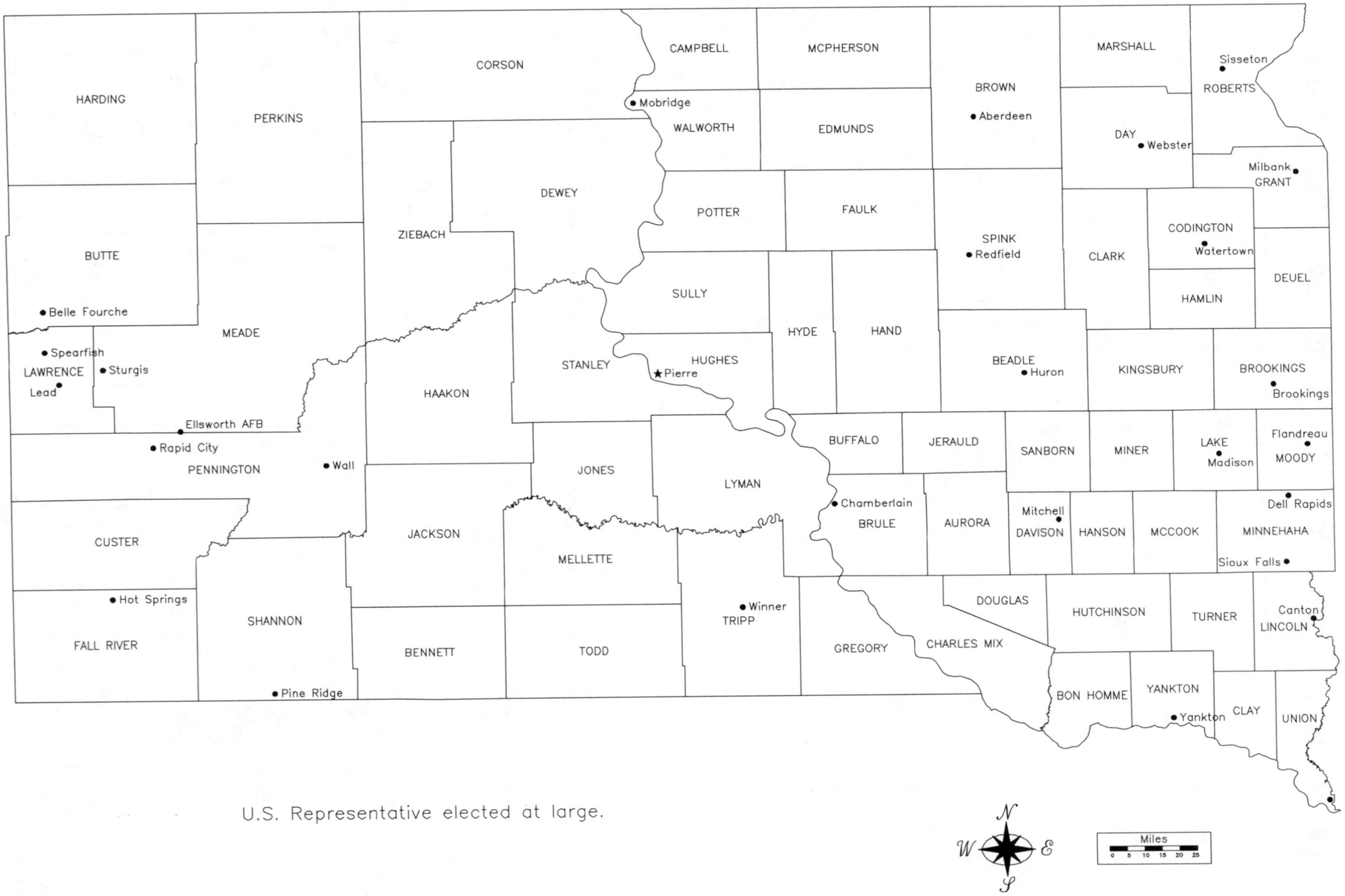

MARSHALL

Sisseton
ROBERTS

Milbank
GRANT

DEUEL

DAY
• Webster

CODINGTON
• Watertown

HAMLIN

BROOKINGS

• Brookings

Flandreau
MOODY

Dell Rapids

MINNEHAHA

• Sioux Falls

Canton
LINCOLN

UNION

CLARK

KINGSBURY

LAKE
• Madison

MCCOOK

TURNER

YANKTON

CLAY

• Yankton

BROWN

• Aberdeen

SPINK
• Redfield

BEADLE
• Huron

MINER

SANBORN

HANSON

HUTCHINSON

BON HOMME

MCPHERSON

EDMUNDS

FAULK

HAND

JERAULD

AURORA

Mitchell
DAVISON

DOUGLAS

CHARLES MIX

HYDE

BUFFALO

Chamberlain
BRULE

GREGORY

CAMPBELL

WALWORTH

POTTER

SULLY

HUGHES
★ Pierre

LYMAN

• Winner
TRIPP

• Mobridge

CORSON

DEWEY

STANLEY

JONES

MELLETTE

TODD

ZIEBACH

HAAKON

JACKSON

BENNETT

PERKINS

MEADE

Ellsworth AFB

• Rapid City
PENNINGTON

• Wall

SHANNON

• Pine Ridge

HARDING

BUTTE

• Belle Fourche

Spearfish
LAWRENCE
Lead

Sturgis

CUSTER

• Hot Springs

FALL RIVER

U.S. Representative elected at large.

Copyright © 1993 by Election Data Services, Inc.

Miles
0 5 10 15 20 25

838 South Dakota

Table A. — 1990 Population by Race and Ethnic Origin

State/county code	County	Total persons	Percent of total persons — Non-Hispanic: White	Black	Asian and Pacific Islander	Native American	Other	Hispanic	Rank — Percent of total persons: Total	Non-Hispanic: White	Black	Native American[1]	Percent contribution to state population: Total	Non-Hispanic: White	Black	Native American[1]
46 003	Aurora	3,135	98.4	0.0	<.1	1.3	0.0	0.2	51	27	53	37	0.5	0.5	0.0	<.1
46 005	Beadle	18,253	98.1	0.4	0.3	0.9	<.1	0.4	9	29	7	41	2.6	2.8	2.1	0.3
46 007	Bennett	3,206	53.0	0.2	<.1	45.6	<.1	1.1	49	59	12	8	0.5	0.3	0.3	2.9
46 009	Bon Homme	7,089	97.0	0.3	<.1	2.2	<.1	0.5	26	34	8	29	1.0	1.1	0.7	0.3
46 011	Brookings	25,207	97.6	0.3	1.2	0.6	<.1	0.3	4	33	10	44	3.6	3.9	2.3	0.3
46 013	Brown	35,580	96.4	0.1	0.4	2.7	<.1	0.3	3	38	24	26	5.1	5.4	1.4	2.0
46 015	Brule	5,485	92.2	0.1	0.2	6.9	0.0	0.6	35	49	28	16	0.8	0.8	0.2	0.8
46 017	Buffalo	1,759	22.3	0.0	0.0	77.5	0.0	0.2	62	64	54	3	0.3	<.1	0.0	2.7
46 019	Butte	7,914	95.4	0.3	0.2	1.4	0.0	2.8	24	41	11	33	1.1	1.2	0.7	0.2
46 021	Campbell	1,965	99.7	0.1	0.0	0.2	0.0	0.0	61	2	30	62	0.3	0.3	<.1	<.1
46 023	Charles Mix	9,131	77.8	<.1	<.1	21.7	0.0	0.4	18	55	39	12	1.3	1.1	0.1	4.0
46 025	Clark	4,403	99.2	0.1	0.2	0.2	<.1	0.3	40	19	20	61	0.6	0.7	0.2	<.1
46 027	Clay	13,186	94.8	0.4	1.1	2.9	<.1	0.8	13	42	5	25	1.9	2.0	1.8	0.8
46 029	Codington	22,698	98.2	<.1	0.3	1.1	0.0	0.2	5	28	33	38	3.3	3.5	0.5	0.5
46 031	Corson	4,195	51.1	<.1	<.1	47.7	0.0	1.1	43	61	45	6	0.6	0.3	<.1	4.0
46 033	Custer	6,179	96.5	0.1	0.1	2.5	0.0	0.7	30	37	18	27	0.9	0.9	0.3	0.3
46 035	Davison	17,503	97.9	0.1	0.3	1.4	<.1	0.2	10	30	23	35	2.5	2.7	0.7	0.5
46 037	Day	6,978	93.1	<.1	<.1	6.7	<.1	0.2	27	47	51	18	1.0	1.0	<.1	0.9
46 039	Deuel	4,522	99.2	<.1	0.2	0.2	<.1	0.3	39	18	47	56	0.6	0.7	<.1	<.1
46 041	Dewey	5,523	32.9	0.2	<.1	66.0	0.0	0.8	34	63	13	4	0.8	0.3	0.3	7.3
46 043	Douglas	3,746	99.3	0.0	<.1	0.6	<.1	<.1	45	14	55	45	0.5	0.6	0.0	<.1
46 045	Edmunds	4,356	99.3	<.1	<.1	0.4	0.0	0.1	41	11	46	48	0.6	0.7	<.1	<.1
46 047	Fall River	7,353	91.5	0.4	0.4	6.0	<.1	1.6	25	51	6	21	1.1	1.1	0.9	0.9
46 049	Faulk	2,744	99.6	0.0	<.1	0.2	0.0	0.1	55	5	56	57	0.4	0.4	0.0	<.1
46 051	Grant	8,372	99.2	<.1	0.2	0.4	0.0	0.1	20	17	42	49	1.2	1.3	<.1	<.1
46 053	Gregory	5,359	94.1	<.1	<.1	5.2	<.1	0.5	36	44	49	23	0.8	0.8	<.1	0.6
46 055	Haakon	2,624	97.6	0.2	0.5	1.4	0.0	0.4	56	32	17	34	0.4	0.4	0.1	<.1
46 057	Hamlin	4,974	99.3	<.1	0.1	0.2	0.0	0.3	37	13	32	59	0.7	0.8	0.1	<.1
46 059	Hand	4,272	99.3	<.1	0.3	0.1	0.0	0.3	42	15	34	64	0.6	0.7	<.1	<.1
46 061	Hanson	2,994	99.7	0.0	0.0	0.2	0.0	<.1	52	3	57	55	0.4	0.5	0.0	<.1
46 063	Harding	1,669	98.5	0.3	0.0	1.0	<.1	0.2	64	26	9	39	0.2	0.3	0.2	<.1
46 065	Hughes	14,817	92.4	0.1	0.2	6.5	0.0	0.8	12	48	25	19	2.1	2.2	0.6	1.9
46 067	Hutchinson	8,262	99.4	<.1	0.1	0.2	0.0	0.2	22	8	52	54	1.2	1.3	<.1	<.1
46 069	Hyde	1,696	96.1	<.1	<.1	3.4	0.0	0.4	63	39	36	24	0.2	0.3	<.1	0.1
46 071	Jackson	2,811	57.2	0.1	0.2	42.0	0.0	0.5	54	58	29	9	0.4	0.3	<.1	2.4
46 073	Jerauld	2,425	99.5	0.0	0.3	0.2	0.0	<.1	58	7	58	58	0.3	0.4	0.0	<.1
46 075	Jones	1,324	99.3	0.0	<.1	0.5	0.0	<.1	66	12	59	46	0.2	0.2	0.0	<.1
46 077	Kingsbury	5,925	99.6	0.0	0.1	0.2	0.0	<.1	32	6	60	60	0.9	0.9	0.0	<.1
46 079	Lake	10,550	99.0	0.1	0.2	0.3	<.1	0.3	14	21	27	51	1.5	1.6	0.4	<.1
46 081	Lawrence	20,655	95.5	0.1	0.3	2.5	<.1	1.6	7	40	19	28	3.0	3.1	0.9	1.0
46 083	Lincoln	15,427	99.1	0.1	0.3	0.4	<.1	0.1	11	20	21	50	2.2	2.4	0.7	0.1
46 085	Lyman	3,638	70.8	<.1	<.1	28.6	0.0	0.5	46	57	31	10	0.5	0.4	<.1	2.1
46 087	McCook	5,688	99.3	0.0	0.1	0.5	0.0	0.1	33	16	61	47	0.8	0.9	0.0	<.1
46 089	McPherson	3,228	99.8	<.1	<.1	<.1	0.0	0.0	48	1	43	65	0.5	0.5	<.1	<.1
46 091	Marshall	4,844	94.2	<.1	<.1	5.5	0.0	0.3	38	43	48	22	0.7	0.7	<.1	0.5
46 093	Meade	21,878	93.4	2.3	0.8	1.7	<.1	1.8	6	45	1	31	3.1	3.2	16.0	0.8
46 095	Mellette	2,137	52.7	<.1	<.1	46.4	<.1	0.7	60	60	37	7	0.3	0.2	<.1	2.0
46 097	Miner	3,272	99.7	0.0	0.0	0.1	<.1	0.2	47	4	62	63	0.5	0.5	0.0	<.1
46 099	Minnehaha	123,809	97.0	0.6	0.6	1.3	<.1	0.5	1	35	3	36	17.8	18.9	23.3	3.3
46 101	Moody	6,507	91.4	0.2	0.2	8.1	0.0	0.2	29	52	15	14	0.9	0.9	0.3	1.1
46 103	Pennington	81,343	88.4	1.5	1.1	6.8	<.1	2.2	2	54	2	17	11.7	11.3	39.3	11.1
46 105	Perkins	3,932	97.9	0.2	<.1	1.4	0.0	0.4	44	31	16	32	0.6	0.6	0.2	0.1
46 107	Potter	3,190	99.0	0.0	<.1	0.8	0.0	0.2	50	22	63	42	0.5	0.5	0.0	<.1
46 109	Roberts	9,914	76.8	0.0	0.1	22.9	0.0	0.3	16	56	64	11	1.4	1.2	0.0	4.6
46 111	Sanborn	2,833	99.4	0.0	0.1	0.0	0.0	0.5	53	10	65	66	0.4	0.4	0.0	0.0
46 113	Shannon	9,902	5.0	<.1	<.1	93.1	<.1	1.8	17	66	41	1	1.4	<.1	0.1	18.6
46 115	Spink	7,981	99.0	<.1	<.1	0.8	0.0	0.2	23	23	44	43	1.1	1.2	<.1	0.1
46 117	Stanley	2,453	93.2	<.1	0.0	6.3	<.1	0.4	57	46	40	20	0.4	0.4	<.1	0.3
46 119	Sully	1,589	98.7	<.1	0.0	0.9	<.1	0.2	65	24	35	40	0.2	0.2	<.1	<.1
46 121	Todd	8,352	17.0	0.1	<.1	81.3	0.0	1.5	21	65	26	2	1.2	0.2	0.3	13.7
46 123	Tripp	6,924	90.1	0.0	0.1	9.7	0.0	0.1	28	53	66	13	1.0	1.0	0.0	1.3
46 125	Turner	8,576	99.4	<.1	<.1	0.3	0.0	0.2	19	9	38	52	1.2	1.3	0.1	<.1
46 127	Union	10,189	98.6	0.2	0.3	0.3	<.1	0.7	15	25	14	53	1.5	1.6	0.6	<.1
46 129	Walworth	6,087	91.8	<.1	0.2	7.6	0.0	0.4	31	50	50	15	0.9	0.9	<.1	0.9
46 135	Yankton	19,252	96.6	0.6	0.3	2.1	<.1	0.5	8	36	4	30	2.8	2.9	3.5	0.8
46 137	Ziebach	2,220	35.5	0.1	0.2	62.8	0.0	1.3	59	62	22	5	0.3	0.1	<.1	2.8
46	**SOUTH DAKOTA**	**696,004**	**91.2**	**0.5**	**0.4**	**7.1**	**<.1**	**0.8**					**100.0**	**100.0**	**100.0**	**100.0**
	CONGRESSIONAL District At-Large	696,004	91.2	0.5	0.4	7.1	<.1	0.8								

[1]Non-Hispanic Native American.

South Dakota 839

Table B. – 1990 Voting Age Population (VAP) by Race and Ethnic Origin

County	Total Voting Age Population	Percent of total VAP — Non-Hispanic White	Black	Asian and Pacific Islander	Native American	Other	Hispanic	Rank Percent of total VAP Total	Non-Hispanic White	Black	Native American[1]	Percent contribution to state VAP Total	Non-Hispanic White	Black	Native American[1]	VAP percent of total population Total	Non-Hispanic White	Black	Asian and Pacific Islander	Native American	Other	Hispanic
Aurora	2,214	99.7	0.0	<.1	0.1	0.0	0.1	50	7	48	59	0.4	0.5	0.0	<.1	70.6	71.5	0.0	33.3	7.5	0.0	42.9
Beadle	13,362	98.5	0.3	0.3	0.6	0.0	0.3	9	29	6	43	2.7	2.8	2.3	0.3	73.2	73.5	68.2	72.5	52.2	0.0	53.9
Bennett	2,059	62.0	0.2	<.1	37.2	<.1	0.6	52	59	12	8	0.4	0.3	0.2	2.9	64.2	75.1	50.0	50.0	52.3	100.0	34.3
Bon Homme	5,314	97.0	0.3	<.1	2.4	<.1	0.3	25	37	7	25	1.1	1.1	0.9	0.5	75.0	74.9	77.3	25.0	82.5	100.0	47.1
Brookings	19,460	97.7	0.2	1.2	0.5	<.1	0.3	4	33	10	44	3.9	4.1	2.3	0.4	77.2	77.3	63.0	78.4	64.9	50.0	75.0
Brown	26,412	97.3	<.1	0.3	2.1	<.1	0.2	3	35	26	27	5.3	5.5	1.3	2.0	74.2	74.9	59.1	63.3	56.0	33.3	52.3
Brule	3,669	96.6	0.1	<.1	2.8	0.0	0.5	35	39	21	24	0.7	0.8	0.2	0.4	66.9	70.0	66.7	18.2	27.0	0.0	58.1
Buffalo	973	27.9	0.0	0.0	71.9	0.0	0.2	65	64	49	3	0.2	<.1	0.0	2.6	55.3	69.0	0.0	0.0	51.4	0.0	66.7
Butte	5,603	96.4	0.2	0.1	1.1	0.0	2.2	22	41	11	35	1.1	1.2	0.7	0.2	70.8	71.5	61.9	41.2	56.9	0.0	55.7
Campbell	1,464	99.9	0.0	0.0	<.1	0.0	0.0	59	1	50	63	0.3	0.3	0.0	<.1	74.5	74.6	0.0	0.0	33.3	0.0	0.0
Charles Mix	6,203	83.0	<.1	<.1	16.8	0.0	0.2	18	55	38	12	1.2	1.1	0.1	3.9	67.9	72.4	50.0	50.0	52.4	0.0	41.2
Clark	3,153	99.6	<.1	<.1	0.1	<.1	0.2	41	12	39	61	0.6	0.7	<.1	<.1	71.6	71.9	16.7	28.6	50.0	100.0	46.2
Clay	10,550	95.8	0.5	1.1	1.9	<.1	0.7	12	44	5	29	2.1	2.2	2.6	0.8	80.0	80.8	91.1	83.8	52.9	33.3	75.0
Codington	16,194	98.6	<.1	0.3	0.9	0.0	0.2	5	28	40	37	3.3	3.4	0.3	0.5	71.3	71.6	31.3	58.3	55.3	0.0	60.0
Corson	2,597	59.7	<.1	<.1	39.4	0.0	0.8	45	61	36	7	0.5	0.3	<.1	3.8	72.2	72.6	66.7	55.6	65.6	0.0	48.9
Custer	4,464	97.0	0.1	0.1	2.3	0.0	0.5	31	36	19	26	0.9	0.9	0.3	0.2	72.5	72.8	59.1	63.3	54.6	50.0	68.4
Davison	12,681	98.4	0.1	0.3	1.0	<.1	0.2	10	30	23	36	2.5	2.7	0.7	0.5	72.9	74.7	100.0	100.0	48.4	100.0	45.5
Day	5,086	95.4	<.1	<.1	4.4	<.1	<.1	26	46	44	20	1.0	1.0	<.1	0.8	73.3	73.5	100.0	55.6	50.0	0.0	28.6
Deuel	3,315	99.5	<.1	0.2	0.2	0.0	0.1	38	13	42	55	0.7	0.7	<.1	<.1	73.3	73.5	100.0	55.6	53.5	0.0	41.3
Dewey	3,301	40.0	0.2	<.1	59.1	0.0	0.6	39	63	9	4	0.7	0.3	0.4	7.3	59.8	72.8	72.7	60.0	53.5	0.0	41.3
Douglas	2,608	99.7	0.0	<.1	0.2	0.0	<.1	44	5	51	54	0.5	0.6	0.0	<.1	69.6	69.9	0.0	100.0	19.0	0.0	100.0
Edmunds	3,191	99.5	<.1	<.1	0.3	0.0	0.1	40	16	41	47	0.6	0.7	<.1	<.1	73.3	73.4	100.0	25.0	57.9	0.0	80.0
Fall River	5,562	92.6	0.3	0.4	5.4	<.1	1.3	23	53	8	15	1.1	1.1	0.8	1.1	75.6	76.5	55.6	73.3	68.0	100.0	60.0
Faulk	2,009	99.7	0.0	<.1	0.1	0.0	<.1	54	10	52	56	0.4	0.4	0.0	<.1	73.2	73.2	0.0	100.0	50.0	0.0	100.0
Grant	5,886	99.4	<.1	<.1	0.4	0.0	0.1	20	19	45	46	1.2	1.3	<.1	<.1	70.3	70.4	33.3	47.1	66.7	0.0	45.5
Gregory	3,816	95.7	0.0	<.1	3.9	<.1	0.3	34	45	53	21	0.8	0.8	0.0	0.6	64.5	64.8	25.0	66.7	58.3	0.0	36.4
Haakon	1,693	98.0	<.1	0.5	1.2	0.0	0.2	57	32	33	32	0.3	0.4	<.1	<.1	71.1	71.3	75.0	42.9	58.3	0.0	46.2
Hamlin	3,537	99.5	<.1	<.1	0.1	0.0	0.2	37	15	29	58	0.7	0.8	0.2	<.1	71.1	71.3	75.0	42.9	50.0	0.0	27.3
Hand	3,095	99.6	<.1	0.2	<.1	0.0	<.1	42	11	27	65	0.6	0.7	0.2	<.1	72.4	72.7	100.0	45.5	20.0	0.0	50.0
Hanson	2,072	99.8	0.0	0.0	0.1	0.0	<.1	51	3	54	57	0.4	0.4	0.0	<.1	69.2	69.3	0.0	0.0	42.9	0.0	50.0
Harding	1,115	98.8	0.2	0.0	0.8	0.0	0.2	64	27	14	38	0.2	0.2	0.1	<.1	66.8	67.0	40.0	0.0	56.3	0.0	66.7
Hughes	10,393	94.1	<.1	0.2	5.1	0.0	0.5	13	50	32	18	2.1	2.1	0.4	2.0	70.1	71.5	44.4	55.9	54.7	0.0	50.9
Hutchinson	6,181	99.7	<.1	<.1	0.1	0.0	0.1	19	6	46	60	1.2	1.3	<.1	<.1	74.8	75.0	100.0	9.1	40.0	0.0	64.3
Hyde	1,250	96.5	<.1	<.1	3.0	0.0	0.3	62	40	31	23	0.3	0.3	<.1	0.1	64.2	72.4	100.0	100.0	66.7	0.0	57.1
Jackson	1,806	64.4	0.2	0.2	34.8	0.0	0.4	55	58	16	9	0.4	0.3	0.2	2.4	73.8	73.9	0.0	42.9	53.2	0.0	50.0
Jerauld	1,789	99.7	0.0	0.2	0.1	0.0	<.1	56	9	55	62	0.4	0.4	0.0	<.1	73.8	73.9	0.0	42.9	40.0	0.0	100.0
Jones	952	99.2	0.0	0.1	0.6	0.0	0.1	66	23	56	42	0.9	0.9	0.0	<.1	74.0	74.1	0.0	57.1	81.8	0.0	20.0
Kingsbury	4,385	99.7	0.0	<.1	0.2	0.0	<.1	32	8	57	52	0.9	0.9	0.0	<.1	73.4	73.5	83.3	77.3	54.5	14.3	63.0
Lake	7,746	99.2	0.1	0.2	0.2	<.1	0.2	14	22	20	51	1.6	1.7	0.5	<.1	73.4	73.5	83.3	77.3	54.5	14.3	63.0
Lawrence	15,043	96.3	0.2	0.2	2.0	<.1	1.3	6	42	18	28	3.0	3.1	1.2	1.2	72.8	73.4	79.3	64.3	59.9	66.7	58.7
Lincoln	10,682	99.3	0.1	0.2	0.3	0.0	<.1	11	20	24	48	2.1	2.3	0.6	0.1	69.2	69.4	52.4	50.0	60.3	0.0	43.5
Lyman	2,424	77.8	<.1	<.1	21.7	0.0	0.3	47	57	30	10	0.5	0.4	0.1	2.0	66.6	73.3	66.7	50.0	50.6	0.0	44.4
McCook	4,103	99.4	<.1	0.1	0.4	0.0	<.1	33	18	59	45	0.8	0.9	0.0	<.1	72.1	72.2	0.0	50.0	64.3	0.0	37.5
McPherson	2,503	99.9	<.1	0.0	<.1	0.0	0.0	46	2	35	64	0.5	0.5	<.1	<.1	77.5	77.6	100.0	0.0	50.0	0.0	0.0
Marshall	3,550	96.0	0.0	0.0	3.9	0.0	0.1	36	43	58	22	0.7	0.7	0.0	0.5	73.3	74.7	0.0	0.0	51.7	0.0	38.5
Meade	14,786	94.2	2.1	0.7	1.5	<.1	1.5	7	49	1	31	3.0	3.0	15.8	0.8	67.6	68.2	61.6	60.2	58.1	60.0	56.8
Mellette	1,368	59.9	0.0	<.1	39.7	0.0	0.4	60	60	60	6	0.3	0.2	0.0	2.0	64.0	72.7	0.0	50.0	54.7	0.0	33.3
Miner	2,384	99.8	0.0	0.0	0.2	0.0	<.1	48	4	61	53	0.5	0.5	0.0	<.1	72.9	73.0	0.0	0.0	100.0	0.0	16.7
Minnehaha	90,362	97.5	0.5	0.5	1.1	<.1	0.4	1	34	4	34	18.2	19.0	22.6	3.8	73.0	73.4	60.5	60.1	61.7	22.0	59.4
Moody	4,504	92.9	0.2	0.1	6.6	0.0	0.2	30	51	15	14	0.9	0.9	0.4	1.1	69.2	70.4	80.0	38.5	56.7	0.0	53.8
Pennington	57,562	90.5	1.3	1.0	5.3	<.1	1.8	2	54	2	16	11.6	11.2	38.7	11.4	70.8	72.5	61.2	67.0	55.2	45.5	57.6
Perkins	2,906	98.3	0.1	<.1	1.1	0.0	0.4	43	31	25	33	0.6	0.6	0.2	0.1	73.9	74.2	50.0	100.0	58.9	0.0	64.7
Potter	2,306	99.2	0.0	<.1	0.7	0.0	<.1	49	21	62	41	0.5	0.5	0.0	<.1	72.3	72.5	0.0	100.0	57.7	0.0	20.0
Roberts	6,918	81.7	0.0	<.1	18.0	0.0	0.2	16	56	63	11	1.4	1.2	0.0	4.7	69.8	74.3	0.0	30.0	55.1	0.0	57.1
Sanborn	2,020	99.5	0.0	0.1	0.0	0.0	0.4	53	17	64	66	0.4	0.4	0.0	0.0	71.3	71.4	0.0	100.0	0.0	0.0	53.3
Shannon	5,462	7.7	<.1	<.1	90.6	<.1	1.6	24	66	34	1	1.1	<.1	0.2	18.5	55.2	86.0	75.0	80.0	53.6	100.0	47.5
Spink	5,809	99.0	<.1	<.1	0.8	0.0	0.1	21	24	37	39	1.2	1.2	0.1	0.2	72.8	72.8	100.0	50.0	71.9	0.0	53.3
Stanley	1,679	94.9	0.0	0.0	4.8	0.0	0.3	58	47	65	19	0.3	0.3	0.0	0.3	68.4	69.7	0.0	0.0	52.6	0.0	50.0
Sully	1,146	99.0	<.1	0.0	0.8	<.1	<.1	63	25	28	40	0.2	0.2	<.1	<.1	72.1	72.3	100.0	0.0	60.0	100.0	33.3
Todd	4,585	22.3	0.1	0.1	76.4	0.0	1.1	28	65	22	2	0.9	0.2	0.3	13.1	54.9	71.7	50.0	83.3	51.6	0.0	42.3
Tripp	4,840	92.6	0.0	<.1	7.2	0.0	0.1	27	52	66	13	1.0	1.0	0.0	1.3	69.9	71.9	0.0	28.6	52.9	0.0	55.6
Turner	6,287	99.5	<.1	<.1	0.3	0.0	0.1	17	14	47	49	1.3	1.3	<.1	<.1	73.3	73.4	25.0	25.0	73.1	0.0	44.4
Union	7,209	98.9	0.2	0.2	0.3	<.1	0.4	15	26	13	50	1.4	1.5	0.7	<.1	70.8	71.0	65.0	40.7	77.8	100.0	47.8
Walworth	4,510	94.3	<.1	0.1	5.2	0.0	0.3	29	48	43	17	0.9	0.9	<.1	0.9	74.1	76.1	100.0	54.5	51.1	0.0	53.8
Yankton	14,158	96.9	0.6	0.2	1.9	<.1	0.4	8	38	3	30	2.8	3.0	4.3	1.0	73.5	73.8	77.3	58.5	65.9	33.3	58.4
Ziebach	1,276	44.8	0.2	0.2	54.1	0.0	0.8	61	62	17	5	0.3	0.1	0.1	2.6	57.5	72.5	66.7	50.0	49.5	0.0	34.5
SOUTH DAKOTA	**497,542**	**93.2**	**0.4**	**0.4**	**5.4**	**<.1**	**0.6**					**100.0**	**100.0**	**100.0**	**100.0**	**71.5**	**73.1**	**62.3**	**64.3**	**53.8**	**37.0**	**55.9**
CONGRESSIONAL District At-Large	497,542	93.2	0.4	0.4	5.4	<.1	0.6									71.5	73.1	62.3	64.3	53.8	37.0	55.9

[1]Non-Hispanic Native American.

Table C. — Voter Participation: November 3, 1992, General Election

| County | Estimated Voting Age Population (VAP), 1992 | Voter registration (REG) | | | | Voter turnout | | | | | | | | | | | | | |
| | | Total | % contribution to state REG | % of 1992 VAP | Rank by % of 1992 VAP | Actual | Highest office | | | Maximum vote | | | | | | Percent drop-off, by office[1] | | | |
							Total	Office	% of 1992 VAP	Total	% contribution to state turnout	% of REG	Rank by % of REG	% of 1992 VAP	Rank by % 1992 VAP	President	Senator	Governor	Representative
Aurora	2,271	2,232	0.5	98.3	15	-	1,717	S	75.6	1,717	0.5	76.9	30	75.6	14	0.3	0.0	-	0.6
Beadle	13,245	12,063	2.7	91.1	39	-	9,170	S	69.2	9,170	2.7	76.0	34	69.2	33	0.4	0.0	-	0.5
Bennett	2,120	2,017	0.4	95.1	23	-	1,198	S	56.5	1,198	0.4	59.4	61	56.5	60	0.1	0.0	-	0.8
Bon Homme	5,187	4,810	1.1	92.7	31	-	3,384	S	65.2	3,384	1.0	70.4	57	65.2	50	0.5	0.0	-	0.1
Brookings	18,790	15,933	3.6	84.8	56	-	12,002	P	63.9	12,002	3.6	75.3	38	63.9	53	0.0	0.3	-	0.6
Brown	25,960	22,866	5.1	88.1	51	-	18,056	S	69.6	18,056	5.4	79.0	14	69.6	32	0.0	0.0	-	0.4
Brule	3,786	3,448	0.8	91.1	40	-	2,676	P	70.7	2,676	0.8	77.6	28	70.7	28	0.0	0.4	-	0.9
Buffalo	1,001	1,016	0.2	101.5	7	-	496	P	49.6	496	0.1	48.8	64	49.6	63	0.0	0.2	-	1.2
Butte	5,581	4,719	1.1	84.6	57	-	3,700	P	66.3	3,700	1.1	78.4	22	66.3	46	0.0	2.1	-	1.7
Campbell	1,467	1,469	0.3	100.1	8	-	1,053	P	71.8	1,053	0.3	71.7	51	71.8	25	0.0	2.0	-	3.7
Charles Mix	6,206	5,746	1.3	92.6	32	-	4,107	S	66.2	4,107	1.2	71.5	53	66.2	48	0.2	0.0	-	0.7
Clark	3,205	2,937	0.7	91.6	37	-	2,375	P	74.1	2,375	0.7	80.9	4	74.1	16	0.0	0.8	-	1.3
Clay	9,710	8,028	1.8	82.7	62	-	6,036	P	62.2	6,036	1.8	75.2	40	62.2	56	0.0	0.8	-	0.6
Codington	16,701	13,953	3.1	83.5	61	-	10,943	P	65.5	10,943	3.3	78.4	21	65.5	49	0.0	0.2	-	1.0
Corson	2,550	2,171	0.5	85.1	55	-	1,251	P	49.1	1,251	0.4	57.6	62	49.1	64	0.0	3.2	-	4.4
Custer	4,592	4,358	1.0	94.9	24	-	3,363	P	73.2	3,363	1.0	77.2	29	73.2	21	0.0	0.8	-	1.9
Davison	12,638	10,646	2.4	84.2	58	-	8,146	P	64.5	8,146	2.4	76.5	32	64.5	52	0.0	0.3	-	0.4
Day	4,959	4,861	1.1	98.0	17	-	3,725	P	75.1	3,725	1.1	76.6	31	75.1	15	0.0	1.2	-	1.6
Deuel	3,271	3,092	0.7	94.5	26	-	2,423	P	74.1	2,423	0.7	78.4	23	74.1	17	0.0	0.2	-	1.0
Dewey	3,407	3,112	0.7	91.3	38	-	1,752	P	51.4	1,752	0.5	56.3	63	51.4	62	0.0	1.7	-	1.3
Douglas	2,590	2,563	0.6	99.0	12	-	2,067	P	79.8	2,067	0.6	80.6	5	79.8	8	0.0	0.5	-	0.9
Edmunds	3,108	3,067	0.7	98.7	13	-	2,260	P	72.7	2,260	0.7	73.7	45	72.7	24	0.0	0.5	-	2.0
Fall River	5,506	5,250	1.2	95.4	22	-	3,754	P	68.2	3,754	1.1	71.5	52	68.2	40	0.0	1.3	-	2.4
Faulk	1,957	1,818	0.4	92.9	30	-	1,434	P	73.3	1,434	0.4	78.9	16	73.3	20	0.0	0.6	-	1.9
Grant	5,950	5,210	1.2	87.6	52	-	4,110	P	69.1	4,110	1.2	78.9	15	69.1	34	0.0	0.9	-	0.9
Gregory	3,756	3,529	0.8	94.0	28	-	2,615	P	69.6	2,615	0.8	74.1	43	69.6	31	0.0	0.1	-	0.7
Haakon	1,738	1,604	0.4	92.3	33	-	1,318	P	75.8	1,318	0.4	82.2	2	75.8	13	0.0	0.8	-	1.5
Hamlin	3,573	3,442	0.8	96.3	20	-	2,742	S	76.7	2,742	0.8	79.7	9	76.7	10	0.1	0.0	-	0.8
Hand	3,054	3,161	0.7	103.5	4	-	2,548	S	83.4	2,548	0.8	80.6	6	83.4	2	0.1	0.0	-	1.2
Hanson	2,101	2,032	0.5	96.7	19	-	1,437	S	68.4	1,437	0.4	70.7	56	68.4	38	0.1	0.0	-	0.3
Harding	1,160	1,109	0.2	95.6	21	-	881	P	75.9	881	0.3	79.4	11	75.9	12	0.0	2.2	-	2.7
Hughes	10,647	10,313	2.3	96.9	18	-	8,121	P	76.3	8,121	2.4	78.7	19	76.3	11	0.0	1.5	-	1.1
Hutchinson	6,077	5,759	1.3	94.8	25	-	4,181	S	68.8	4,181	1.2	72.6	49	68.8	36	0.6	0.0	-	0.5
Hyde	1,189	1,211	0.3	101.9	6	-	955	P	80.3	955	0.3	78.9	18	80.3	6	0.0	1.4	-	2.5
Jackson	1,759	1,725	0.4	98.1	16	-	1,168	P	66.4	1,168	0.3	67.7	59	66.4	44	0.0	1.1	-	2.0
Jerauld	1,781	1,770	0.4	99.4	9	-	1,474	S	82.8	1,474	0.4	83.3	1	82.8	4	0.5	0.0	-	0.3
Jones	940	961	0.2	102.2	5	-	779	P	82.9	779	0.2	81.1	3	82.9	3	0.0	0.3	-	0.4
Kingsbury	4,324	3,986	0.9	92.2	35	-	3,150	S	72.8	3,150	0.9	79.0	13	72.8	22	0.2	0.0	-	0.5
Lake	7,683	6,978	1.6	90.8	42	-	5,590	P	72.8	5,590	1.7	80.1	7	72.8	23	0.0	0.0	-	0.3
Lawrence	15,472	13,006	2.9	84.1	59	-	9,659	P	62.4	9,659	2.9	74.3	42	62.4	55	0.0	0.5	-	0.8
Lincoln	11,167	10,045	2.2	90.0	44	-	7,923	P	71.0	7,923	2.4	78.9	17	71.0	27	0.0	0.9	-	1.2
Lyman	2,438	1,979	0.4	81.2	65	-	1,488	S	61.0	1,488	0.4	75.2	39	61.0	58	0.5	0.0	-	1.3
McCook	4,047	3,822	0.9	94.4	27	-	2,984	P	73.7	2,984	0.9	78.1	25	73.7	18	0.0	0.4	-	1.1
McPherson	2,387	2,370	0.5	99.3	11	-	1,752	P	73.4	1,752	0.5	73.9	44	73.4	19	0.0	3.8	-	5.0
Marshall	3,529	3,046	0.7	86.3	54	-	2,297	P	65.1	2,297	0.7	75.4	37	65.1	51	0.0	0.9	-	1.2
Meade	15,121	13,948	3.1	92.2	34	-	10,075	P	66.6	10,075	3.0	72.2	50	66.6	43	0.0	0.5	-	1.2
Mellette	1,391	1,237	0.3	88.9	47	-	856	S	61.5	856	0.3	69.2	58	61.5	57	1.8	0.0	-	0.2
Miner	2,374	2,093	0.5	88.2	49	-	1,584	P	66.7	1,584	0.5	75.7	36	66.7	42	0.0	0.1	-	1.3
Minnehaha	93,081	82,012	18.3	88.1	50	-	63,786	P	68.5	63,786	19.0	77.8	27	68.5	37	0.0	0.6	-	1.2
Moody	4,587	3,990	0.9	87.0	53	-	3,110	S	67.8	3,110	0.9	77.9	26	67.8	41	0.2	0.0	-	0.3
Pennington	59,700	52,982	11.8	88.7	48	-	37,669	P	63.1	37,669	11.2	71.1	54	63.1	54	0.0	0.5	-	0.5
Perkins	2,819	2,801	0.6	99.4	10	-	1,991	P	70.6	1,991	0.6	71.1	55	70.6	29	0.0	0.7	-	0.8
Potter	2,300	2,262	0.5	98.3	14	-	1,778	P	77.3	1,778	0.5	78.6	20	77.3	9	0.0	0.0	-	1.1
Roberts	6,914	5,676	1.3	82.1	63	-	4,121	P	59.6	4,121	1.2	72.6	48	59.6	59	0.0	5.1	-	6.1
Sanborn	2,010	2,113	0.5	105.1	3	-	1,610	P	80.1	1,610	0.5	76.2	33	80.1	7	0.0	0.4	-	1.6
Shannon	5,399	4,404	1.0	81.6	64	-	1,651	P	30.6	1,651	0.5	37.5	66	30.6	66	0.0	1.1	-	2.8
Spink	5,754	5,147	1.1	89.5	46	-	4,112	P	71.5	4,112	1.2	79.9	8	71.5	26	0.0	1.1	-	1.5
Stanley	1,708	1,883	0.4	110.2	2	-	1,399	P	81.9	1,399	0.4	74.3	41	81.9	5	0.0	0.1	-	0.9
Sully	1,138	1,271	0.3	111.7	1	-	1,010	P	88.8	1,010	0.3	79.5	10	88.8	1	0.0	0.0	-	0.4
Todd	4,865	3,411	0.8	70.1	66	-	1,630	P	33.5	1,630	0.5	47.8	65	33.5	65	0.0	0.2	-	0.4
Tripp	4,880	4,435	1.0	90.9	41	-	3,365	C	69.0	3,365	1.0	75.9	35	69.0	35	0.1	0.1	-	0.0
Turner	6,299	5,883	1.3	93.4	29	-	4,295	S	68.2	4,295	1.3	73.0	47	68.2	39	0.1	0.0	-	0.4
Union	7,251	6,516	1.5	89.9	45	-	5,097	P	70.3	5,097	1.5	78.2	24	70.3	30	0.0	2.0	-	1.8
Walworth	4,389	3,954	0.9	90.1	43	-	2,908	P	66.3	2,908	0.9	73.5	46	66.3	47	0.0	1.2	-	2.5
Yankton	14,132	11,842	2.6	83.8	60	-	9,372	P	66.3	9,372	2.8	79.1	12	66.3	45	0.0	0.7	-	0.6
Ziebach	1,308	1,199	0.3	91.7	36	-	730	P	55.8	730	0.2	60.9	60	55.8	61	0.0	4.4	-	6.6
SOUTH DAKOTA	502,000	448,292	100.0	89.3		-	336,409		67.0	336,409	100.0	75.0		67.0		0.0	0.6	-	1.0

[1]Percent drop-off is zero for any office used as highest office turnout.

Table D. — Voter Registration by Political Party Affiliation: November 3, 1992, General Election

County	Total voter registration	Political party affiliation			Plurality		Percent of total registration			Rank			Percent contribution to state registration			
		Democrat (DEM)	Republican (REP)	Independent (IND)	Total	Party	DEM	REP	IND	DEM	REP	IND	Total	DEM	REP	IND
Aurora	2,232	1,294	843	95	451	D	58.0	37.8	4.3	7	57	53	0.5	0.7	0.4	0.2
Beadle	12,063	6,166	4,661	1,229	1,505	D	51.1	38.7	10.2	15	55	17	2.7	3.2	2.2	2.9
Bennett	2,017	1,099	810	108	289	D	54.5	40.2	5.4	12	50	47	0.4	0.6	0.4	0.3
Bon Homme	4,810	2,167	2,405	237	238	R	45.1	50.0	4.9	28	33	48	1.1	1.1	1.1	0.6
Brookings	15,933	5,680	7,618	2,624	1,938	R	35.7	47.8	16.5	49	37	1	3.6	3.0	3.5	6.1
Brown	22,866	11,407	9,409	2,045	1,998	D	49.9	41.2	8.9	19	49	22	5.1	6.0	4.4	4.8
Brule	3,448	2,011	1,239	198	772	D	58.3	35.9	5.7	6	60	42	0.8	1.1	0.6	0.5
Buffalo	1,016	759	220	37	539	D	74.7	21.7	3.6	1	64	56	0.2	0.4	0.1	<.1
Butte	4,719	1,269	3,151	288	1,882	R	27.0	66.9	6.1	61	9	38	1.1	0.7	1.5	0.7
Campbell	1,469	209	1,233	27	1,024	R	14.2	83.9	1.8	66	1	66	0.3	0.1	0.6	<.1
Charles Mix	5,746	3,463	2,001	281	1,462	D	60.3	34.8	4.9	4	61	49	1.3	1.8	0.9	0.7
Clark	2,937	1,140	1,657	140	517	R	38.8	56.4	4.8	43	18	52	0.7	0.6	0.8	0.3
Clay	8,028	3,692	3,176	1,157	516	D	46.0	39.6	14.4	23	51	3	1.8	1.9	1.5	2.7
Codington	13,953	6,293	5,766	1,884	527	D	45.1	41.4	13.5	27	47	5	3.1	3.3	2.7	4.4
Corson	2,171	1,110	920	141	190	D	51.1	42.4	6.5	14	45	33	0.5	0.6	0.4	0.3
Custer	4,358	1,336	2,407	607	1,071	R	30.7	55.3	14.0	55	21	4	1.0	0.7	1.1	1.4
Davison	10,646	4,917	4,621	1,105	296	D	46.2	43.4	10.4	22	44	14	2.4	2.6	2.1	2.6
Day	4,861	2,661	1,921	279	740	D	54.7	39.5	5.7	11	52	43	1.1	1.4	0.9	0.7
Deuel	3,092	1,363	1,402	327	39	R	44.1	45.3	10.6	31	42	13	0.7	0.7	0.7	0.8
Dewey	3,112	1,837	1,051	224	786	D	59.0	33.8	7.2	5	63	29	0.7	1.0	0.5	0.5
Douglas	2,563	588	1,896	79	1,308	R	22.9	74.0	3.1	64	3	64	0.6	0.3	0.9	0.2
Edmunds	3,067	1,404	1,488	175	84	R	45.8	48.5	5.7	24	36	44	0.7	0.7	0.7	0.4
Fall River	5,250	1,921	2,752	577	831	R	36.6	52.4	11.0	47	25	11	1.2	1.0	1.3	1.4
Faulk	1,818	805	961	52	156	R	44.3	52.9	2.9	29	24	65	0.4	0.4	0.4	0.1
Grant	5,210	2,270	2,461	479	191	R	43.6	47.2	9.2	34	39	21	1.2	1.2	1.1	1.1
Gregory	3,529	1,741	1,654	134	87	D	49.3	46.9	3.8	20	40	55	0.8	0.9	0.8	0.3
Haakon	1,604	445	1,101	58	656	R	27.7	68.6	3.6	59	6	58	0.4	0.2	0.5	0.1
Hamlin	3,442	1,242	1,971	229	729	R	36.1	57.3	6.7	48	16	31	0.8	0.7	0.9	0.5
Hand	3,161	1,357	1,630	174	273	R	42.9	51.6	5.5	36	29	45	0.7	0.7	0.8	0.4
Hanson	2,032	972	744	316	228	D	47.8	36.6	15.6	21	58	2	0.5	0.5	0.3	0.7
Harding	1,109	295	760	54	465	R	26.6	68.5	4.9	62	7	50	0.2	0.2	0.4	0.1
Hughes	10,313	3,152	6,211	950	3,059	R	30.6	60.2	9.2	56	12	20	2.3	1.7	2.9	2.2
Hutchinson	5,759	1,436	4,129	193	2,693	R	24.9	71.7	3.4	63	4	63	1.3	0.8	1.9	0.5
Hyde	1,211	519	618	74	99	R	42.9	51.0	6.1	37	30	37	0.3	0.3	0.3	0.2
Jackson	1,725	642	981	100	339	R	37.3	56.9	5.8	45	17	41	0.4	0.3	0.5	0.2
Jerauld	1,770	767	891	111	124	R	43.4	50.4	6.3	35	32	35	0.4	0.4	0.4	0.3
Jones	961	260	666	34	406	R	27.1	69.4	3.5	60	5	59	0.2	0.1	0.3	<.1
Kingsbury	3,986	1,376	2,365	245	989	R	34.5	59.3	6.1	51	13	36	0.9	0.7	1.1	0.6
Lake	6,978	3,065	3,450	462	385	R	43.9	49.4	6.6	33	35	32	1.6	1.6	1.6	1.1
Lawrence	13,006	4,481	7,097	1,390	2,616	R	34.6	54.7	10.7	52	23	12	2.9	2.4	3.3	3.3
Lincoln	10,045	3,911	5,109	1,024	1,198	R	38.9	50.9	10.2	42	31	16	2.2	2.1	2.4	2.4
Lyman	1,979	748	1,161	68	413	R	37.8	58.7	3.4	44	14	62	0.4	0.4	0.5	0.2
McCook	3,822	1,689	1,822	309	133	R	44.2	47.7	8.1	30	38	27	0.9	0.9	0.8	0.7
McPherson	2,370	453	1,834	83	1,381	R	19.1	77.4	3.5	65	2	61	0.5	0.2	0.9	0.3
Marshall	3,046	1,668	1,259	119	409	D	54.8	41.3	3.9	10	46	54	0.7	0.9	0.6	0.3
Meade	13,948	4,596	7,759	1,577	3,163	R	33.0	55.3	11.3	54	20	8	3.1	2.4	3.6	3.7
Mellette	1,237	562	616	59	54	R	45.4	49.8	4.8	25	34	51	0.3	0.3	0.3	0.1
Miner	2,093	1,174	754	165	420	D	56.1	36.0	7.9	9	59	28	0.5	0.6	0.4	0.4
Minnehaha	82,012	37,041	37,173	7,726	132	R	45.2	45.4	9.4	26	43	19	18.3	19.5	17.3	18.1
Moody	3,990	2,039	1,543	408	496	D	51.1	38.7	10.2	16	54	15	0.9	1.1	0.7	1.0
Pennington	52,982	18,340	27,582	6,921	9,242	R	34.7	52.2	13.1	50	26	7	11.8	9.7	12.8	16.2
Perkins	2,801	1,030	1,605	164	575	R	36.8	57.3	5.9	46	15	40	0.6	0.5	0.7	0.4
Potter	2,262	643	1,539	80	896	R	28.4	68.0	3.5	58	8	60	0.5	0.3	0.7	0.2
Roberts	5,676	3,258	1,952	466	1,306	D	57.4	34.4	8.2	8	62	26	1.3	1.7	0.9	1.1
Sanborn	2,113	902	1,095	115	193	R	42.7	51.8	5.4	38	28	46	0.5	0.5	0.5	0.3
Shannon	4,404	3,142	680	582	2,462	D	71.3	15.4	13.2	2	66	6	1.0	1.7	0.3	1.4
Spink	5,147	2,577	2,126	441	451	D	50.1	41.3	8.6	18	48	25	1.1	1.4	1.0	1.0
Stanley	1,883	738	979	166	241	R	39.2	52.0	8.8	41	27	24	0.4	0.4	0.5	0.4
Sully	1,271	509	716	46	207	R	40.0	56.3	3.6	39	19	57	0.3	0.3	0.3	0.1
Todd	3,411	2,301	727	383	1,574	D	67.5	21.3	11.2	3	65	9	0.8	1.2	0.3	0.9
Tripp	4,435	1,743	2,432	260	689	R	39.3	54.8	5.9	40	22	39	1.0	0.9	1.1	0.6
Turner	5,883	1,941	3,550	392	1,609	R	33.0	60.3	6.7	53	11	30	1.3	1.0	1.6	0.9
Union	6,516	3,318	2,480	718	838	D	50.9	38.1	11.0	17	56	10	1.5	1.7	1.2	1.7
Walworth	3,954	1,168	2,532	254	1,364	R	29.5	64.0	6.4	57	10	34	0.9	0.6	1.2	0.6
Yankton	11,842	5,211	5,452	1,175	241	R	44.0	46.1	9.9	32	41	18	2.6	2.7	2.5	2.7
Ziebach	1,199	622	471	106	151	D	51.9	39.3	8.8	13	53	23	0.3	0.3	0.2	0.2
SOUTH DAKOTA[1]	448,292	189,935	215,285	42,726	25,350	R	42.4	48.1	9.5				100.0	100.0	100.0	100.0

[1]Total voter registration also includes 346 for Libertarian party.

Table E. — Vote for President: November 3, 1992, General Election

County	Total	Clinton (DEM)	Bush (REP)	Perot (IND)	Other	Plurality Total	Party	DEM	REP	IND	Other	Rank DEM	Rank REP	Rank IND	Total	DEM	REP	IND	DEM	REP
Aurora	1,712	680	594	435	3	86	D	39.7	34.7	25.4	0.2	21	55	15	0.5	0.5	0.4	0.6	53.4	46.6
Beadle	9,136	3,925	3,363	1,819	29	562	D	43.0	36.8	19.9	0.3	10	44	47	2.7	3.1	2.5	2.5	53.9	46.1
Bennett	1,197	413	556	221	7	143	R	34.5	46.4	18.5	0.6	37	17	54	0.4	0.3	0.4	0.3	42.6	57.4
Bon Homme	3,367	1,294	1,212	836	25	82	D	38.4	36.0	24.8	0.7	28	49	18	1.0	1.0	0.9	1.1	51.6	48.4
Brookings	12,002	4,645	4,698	2,614	45	53	R	38.7	39.1	21.8	0.4	27	35	32	3.6	3.7	3.4	3.6	49.7	50.3
Brown	18,047	7,521	6,665	3,812	49	856	D	41.7	36.9	21.1	0.3	15	43	37	5.4	6.0	4.9	5.2	53.0	47.0
Brule	2,676	1,060	908	687	21	152	D	39.6	33.9	25.7	0.8	22	57	12	0.8	0.8	0.7	0.9	53.9	46.1
Buffalo	496	282	137	72	5	145	D	56.9	27.6	14.5	1.0	2	65	64	0.1	0.2	0.1	<.1	67.3	32.7
Butte	3,700	973	1,674	1,039	14	635	R	26.3	45.2	28.1	0.4	61	20	5	1.1	0.8	1.2	1.4	36.8	63.2
Campbell	1,053	222	574	252	5	322	R	21.1	54.5	23.9	0.5	64	6	21	0.3	0.2	0.4	0.3	27.9	72.1
Charles Mix	4,099	1,639	1,570	886	4	69	D	40.0	38.3	21.6	<.1	20	39	33	1.2	1.3	1.1	1.2	51.1	48.9
Clark	2,375	799	803	761	12	4	R	33.6	33.8	32.0	0.5	40	58	1	0.7	0.6	0.6	1.0	49.9	50.1
Clay	6,036	2,826	1,869	1,303	38	957	D	46.8	31.0	21.6	0.6	5	62	35	1.8	2.3	1.4	1.8	60.2	39.8
Codington	10,943	3,701	3,943	3,262	37	242	R	33.8	36.0	29.8	0.3	39	48	3	3.3	3.0	2.9	4.5	48.4	51.6
Corson	1,251	444	483	321	3	39	R	35.5	38.6	25.7	0.2	35	38	13	0.4	0.4	0.4	0.4	47.9	52.1
Custer	3,363	1,078	1,422	845	18	344	R	32.1	42.3	25.1	0.5	45	28	17	1.0	0.9	1.0	1.2	43.1	56.9
Davison	8,146	3,285	3,111	1,706	44	174	D	40.3	38.2	20.9	0.5	18	40	42	2.4	2.6	2.3	2.3	51.4	48.6
Day	3,725	1,578	1,161	973	13	417	D	42.4	31.2	26.1	0.3	12	61	10	1.1	1.3	0.8	1.3	57.6	42.4
Deuel	2,423	880	778	761	4	102	D	36.3	32.1	31.4	0.2	33	60	2	0.7	0.7	0.6	1.0	53.1	46.9
Dewey	1,752	766	642	340	4	124	D	43.7	36.6	19.4	0.2	8	45	51	0.5	0.6	0.5	0.5	54.4	45.6
Douglas	2,067	481	1,175	403	8	694	R	23.3	56.8	19.5	0.4	62	4	50	0.6	0.4	0.9	0.5	29.0	71.0
Edmunds	2,260	894	944	415	7	50	R	39.6	41.8	18.4	0.3	23	29	56	0.7	0.7	0.7	0.6	48.6	51.4
Fall River	3,754	1,416	1,533	792	13	117	R	37.7	40.8	21.1	0.3	30	31	38	1.1	1.1	1.1	1.1	48.0	52.0
Faulk	1,434	488	658	281	7	170	R	34.0	45.9	19.6	0.5	38	19	49	0.4	0.4	0.5	0.4	42.6	57.4
Grant	4,110	1,484	1,595	1,018	13	111	R	36.1	38.8	24.8	0.3	34	37	19	1.2	1.2	1.2	1.4	48.2	51.8
Gregory	2,615	879	1,027	688	21	148	R	33.6	39.3	26.3	0.8	41	34	9	0.8	0.7	0.8	0.9	46.1	53.9
Haakon	1,318	209	860	245	4	615	R	15.9	65.3	18.6	0.3	65	1	52	0.4	0.2	0.6	0.3	19.6	80.4
Hamlin	2,740	826	1,133	774	7	307	R	30.1	41.4	28.2	0.3	51	30	4	0.8	0.7	0.8	1.1	42.2	57.8
Hand	2,546	785	1,130	624	7	345	R	30.8	44.4	24.5	0.3	49	24	20	0.8	0.6	0.8	0.9	41.0	59.0
Hanson	1,435	566	522	341	6	44	D	39.4	36.4	23.8	0.4	24	47	22	0.4	0.5	0.4	0.5	52.0	48.0
Harding	881	139	515	225	2	290	R	15.8	58.5	25.5	0.2	66	2	14	0.3	0.1	0.4	0.3	21.3	78.7
Hughes	8,121	2,578	4,325	1,160	58	1,747	R	31.7	53.3	14.3	0.7	46	9	65	2.4	2.1	3.2	1.6	37.3	62.7
Hutchinson	4,156	1,211	2,002	920	23	791	R	29.1	48.2	22.1	0.6	54	14	30	1.2	1.0	1.5	1.3	37.7	62.3
Hyde	955	301	440	211	3	139	R	31.5	46.1	22.1	0.3	47	18	31	0.3	0.2	0.3	0.3	40.6	59.4
Jackson	1,168	351	627	184	6	276	R	30.1	53.7	15.8	0.5	52	8	62	0.3	0.3	0.5	0.3	35.9	64.1
Jerauld	1,467	600	518	346	3	82	D	40.9	35.3	23.6	0.2	17	51	24	0.4	0.5	0.4	0.5	53.7	46.3
Jones	779	166	454	154	5	288	R	21.3	58.3	19.8	0.6	63	3	48	0.2	0.1	0.3	0.2	26.8	73.2
Kingsbury	3,143	1,267	1,113	744	19	154	D	40.3	35.4	23.7	0.6	19	50	23	0.9	1.0	0.8	1.0	53.2	46.8
Lake	5,590	2,388	1,890	1,299	13	498	D	42.7	33.8	23.2	0.2	11	59	26	1.7	1.9	1.4	1.8	55.8	44.2
Lawrence	9,659	3,157	3,770	2,673	59	613	R	32.7	39.0	27.7	0.6	44	36	6	2.9	2.5	2.8	3.6	45.6	54.4
Lincoln	7,923	2,943	3,365	1,593	22	422	R	37.1	42.5	20.1	0.3	31	27	46	2.4	2.4	2.5	2.2	46.7	53.3
Lyman	1,480	486	669	311	14	183	R	32.8	45.2	21.0	0.9	43	21	40	0.4	0.4	0.5	0.4	42.1	57.9
McCook	2,984	1,167	1,177	617	23	10	R	39.1	39.4	20.7	0.8	26	32	43	0.9	0.9	0.9	0.8	49.8	50.2
McPherson	1,752	478	945	322	7	467	R	27.3	53.9	18.4	0.4	58	7	55	0.5	0.4	0.7	0.4	33.6	66.4
Marshall	2,297	1,056	810	427	4	246	D	46.0	35.3	18.6	0.2	6	52	53	0.7	0.8	0.6	0.6	56.6	43.4
Meade	10,075	2,694	4,724	2,611	46	2,030	R	26.7	46.9	25.9	0.5	60	16	11	3.0	2.2	3.5	3.6	36.3	63.7
Mellette	841	277	417	140	7	140	R	32.9	49.6	16.6	0.8	42	12	59	0.3	0.2	0.3	0.2	39.9	60.1
Miner	1,584	698	543	332	11	155	D	44.1	34.3	21.0	0.7	7	56	41	0.5	0.6	0.4	0.5	56.2	43.8
Minnehaha	63,786	27,016	25,081	11,496	193	1,935	D	42.4	39.3	18.0	0.3	13	33	57	19.0	21.6	18.3	15.7	51.9	48.1
Moody	3,104	1,473	898	715	18	575	D	47.5	28.9	23.0	0.6	4	63	28	0.9	1.2	0.7	1.0	62.1	37.9
Pennington	37,669	11,106	18,052	8,358	153	6,946	R	29.5	47.9	22.2	0.4	53	15	29	11.2	8.9	13.2	11.4	38.1	61.9
Perkins	1,991	566	872	541	12	306	R	28.4	43.8	27.2	0.6	56	25	7	0.6	0.5	0.6	0.7	39.4	60.6
Potter	1,778	493	901	375	9	408	R	27.7	50.7	21.1	0.5	57	11	39	0.5	0.4	0.7	0.5	35.4	64.6
Roberts	4,121	1,716	1,437	954	14	279	D	41.6	34.9	23.1	0.3	16	54	27	1.2	1.4	1.1	1.3	54.4	45.6
Sanborn	1,610	632	595	376	7	37	D	39.3	37.0	23.4	0.4	25	42	25	0.5	0.5	0.4	0.5	51.5	48.5
Shannon	1,651	1,267	225	137	22	1,042	D	76.7	13.6	8.3	1.3	1	66	66	0.5	1.0	0.2	0.2	84.9	15.1
Spink	4,112	1,732	1,527	839	14	205	D	42.1	37.1	20.4	0.3	14	41	44	1.2	1.4	1.1	1.1	53.1	46.9
Stanley	1,399	427	719	240	13	292	R	30.5	51.4	17.2	0.9	50	10	58	0.4	0.3	0.5	0.3	37.3	62.7
Sully	1,010	273	565	167	5	292	R	27.0	55.9	16.5	0.5	59	5	60	0.3	0.2	0.4	0.2	32.6	67.4
Todd	1,630	915	456	246	13	459	D	56.1	28.0	15.1	0.8	3	64	63	0.5	0.7	0.3	0.3	66.7	33.3
Tripp	3,363	1,046	1,459	848	10	413	R	31.1	43.4	25.2	0.3	48	26	16	1.0	0.8	1.1	1.2	41.8	58.2
Turner	4,290	1,507	1,906	867	10	399	R	35.1	44.4	20.2	0.2	36	23	45	1.3	1.2	1.4	1.2	44.2	55.8
Union	5,097	2,210	1,784	1,085	18	426	D	43.4	35.0	21.3	0.4	9	53	36	1.5	1.8	1.3	1.5	55.3	44.7
Walworth	2,908	829	1,439	628	12	610	R	28.5	49.5	21.6	0.4	55	13	34	0.9	0.7	1.1	0.9	36.6	63.4
Yankton	9,372	3,404	3,430	2,511	27	26	R	36.3	36.6	26.8	0.3	32	46	8	2.8	2.7	2.5	3.4	49.8	50.2
Ziebach	730	280	328	117	5	48	R	38.4	44.9	16.0	0.7	29	22	61	0.2	0.2	0.2	0.2	46.1	53.9
SOUTH DAKOTA	336,254	124,888	136,718	73,295	1,353	11,830	R	37.1	40.7	21.8	0.4				100.0	100.0	100.0	100.0	47.7	52.3

Table F. — Vote for U.S. Senator: November 3, 1992, General Election

County	Total	Daschle (DEM)	Haar (REP)	Other	Plurality Total	Party	DEM	REP	Other	Rank DEM	Rank REP	Rank Other	Total	DEM	REP	Other
Aurora	1,717	1,147	540	30	607	D	66.8	31.5	1.7	25	39	57	0.5	0.5	0.5	0.3
Beadle	9,170	6,014	2,953	203	3,061	D	65.6	32.2	2.2	32	33	33	2.7	2.8	2.7	2.3
Bennett	1,198	782	384	32	398	D	65.3	32.1	2.7	34	34	18	0.4	0.4	0.4	0.4
Bon Homme	3,384	2,419	910	55	1,509	D	71.5	26.9	1.6	6	60	61	1.0	1.1	0.8	0.6
Brookings	11,963	8,101	3,551	311	4,550	D	67.7	29.7	2.6	19	49	20	3.6	3.7	3.3	3.6
Brown	18,056	12,867	4,317	872	8,550	D	71.3	23.9	4.8	7	65	1	5.4	5.9	4.0	10.1
Brule	2,666	1,748	843	75	905	D	65.6	31.6	2.8	33	37	16	0.8	0.8	0.8	0.9
Buffalo	495	352	134	9	218	D	71.1	27.1	1.8	8	58	51	0.1	0.2	0.1	0.1
Butte	3,621	1,911	1,632	78	279	D	52.8	45.1	2.2	60	6	35	1.1	0.9	1.5	0.9
Campbell	1,032	581	429	22	152	D	56.3	41.6	2.1	52	11	38	0.3	0.3	0.4	0.3
Charles Mix	4,107	2,826	1,213	68	1,613	D	68.8	29.5	1.7	15	50	60	1.2	1.3	1.1	0.8
Clark	2,355	1,547	738	70	809	D	65.7	31.3	3.0	31	42	14	0.7	0.7	0.7	0.8
Clay	5,986	4,318	1,483	185	2,835	D	72.1	24.8	3.1	4	63	10	1.8	2.0	1.4	2.1
Codington	10,926	6,908	3,752	266	3,156	D	63.2	34.3	2.4	38	30	27	3.3	3.2	3.5	3.1
Corson	1,211	621	534	56	87	D	51.3	44.1	4.6	64	7	2	1.0	0.9	1.2	1.6
Custer	3,337	1,903	1,297	137	606	D	57.0	38.9	4.1	51	19	3	2.4	2.5	2.3	1.6
Davison	8,120	5,467	2,510	143	2,957	D	67.3	30.9	1.8	23	44	54	2.4	2.5	2.3	1.6
Day	3,680	2,597	992	91	1,605	D	70.6	27.0	2.5	9	59	25	1.1	1.2	0.9	1.1
Deuel	2,418	1,598	757	63	841	D	66.1	31.3	2.6	30	43	19	0.7	0.7	0.7	0.7
Dewey	1,723	1,065	622	36	443	D	61.8	36.1	2.1	40	26	42	0.5	0.5	0.6	0.4
Douglas	2,056	1,021	999	36	22	D	49.7	48.6	1.8	65	2	56	0.6	0.5	0.9	0.4
Edmunds	2,249	1,530	663	56	867	D	68.0	29.5	2.5	18	52	24	0.7	0.7	0.6	0.6
Fall River	3,706	2,250	1,329	127	921	D	60.7	35.9	3.4	42	28	7	1.1	1.0	1.2	1.5
Faulk	1,426	950	450	26	500	D	66.6	31.6	1.8	27	38	50	0.4	0.4	0.4	0.3
Grant	4,085	2,531	1,467	87	1,064	D	62.0	35.9	2.1	39	27	39	1.2	1.2	1.3	1.0
Gregory	2,613	1,577	990	46	587	D	60.4	37.9	1.8	43	22	55	0.8	0.7	0.9	0.5
Haakon	1,307	634	645	28	11	R	48.5	49.3	2.1	66	1	37	0.4	0.3	0.6	0.3
Hamlin	2,742	1,648	1,008	86	640	D	60.1	36.8	3.1	44	25	9	0.8	0.8	0.9	1.0
Hand	2,548	1,695	813	40	882	D	66.5	31.9	1.6	28	35	62	0.8	0.8	0.7	0.5
Hanson	1,437	973	439	25	534	D	67.7	30.5	1.7	20	45	58	0.4	0.4	0.4	0.3
Harding	862	452	394	16	58	D	52.4	45.7	1.9	61	5	48	0.3	0.2	0.4	0.2
Hughes	8,001	4,751	3,042	208	1,709	D	59.4	38.0	2.6	45	21	21	2.4	2.2	2.8	2.4
Hutchinson	4,181	2,565	1,568	48	997	D	61.3	37.5	1.1	41	24	65	1.2	1.2	1.4	0.6
Hyde	942	549	373	20	176	D	58.3	39.6	2.1	48	16	40	0.3	0.3	0.3	0.2
Jackson	1,155	597	529	29	68	D	51.7	45.8	2.5	62	4	23	0.3	0.3	0.5	0.3
Jerauld	1,474	1,018	435	21	583	D	69.1	29.5	1.4	13	51	63	0.4	0.5	0.4	0.2
Jones	777	400	359	18	41	D	51.5	46.2	2.3	63	3	32	0.2	0.2	0.3	0.2
Kingsbury	3,150	2,117	957	76	1,160	D	67.2	30.4	2.4	24	46	29	0.9	1.0	0.9	0.9
Lake	5,589	3,728	1,754	107	1,974	D	66.7	31.4	1.9	26	41	47	1.7	1.7	1.6	1.2
Lawrence	9,608	5,651	3,606	351	2,045	D	58.8	37.5	3.7	47	23	6	2.9	2.6	3.3	4.0
Lincoln	7,850	5,360	2,346	144	3,014	D	68.3	29.9	1.8	17	48	49	2.3	2.5	2.2	1.7
Lyman	1,488	836	614	38	222	D	56.2	41.3	2.6	53	14	22	0.4	0.4	0.6	0.4
McCook	2,972	1,975	946	51	1,029	D	66.5	31.8	1.7	29	36	59	0.9	0.9	0.9	0.6
McPherson	1,686	946	689	51	257	D	56.1	40.9	3.0	54	15	12	0.5	0.4	0.6	0.6
Marshall	2,276	1,634	597	45	1,037	D	71.8	26.2	2.0	5	61	45	0.7	0.8	0.5	0.5
Meade	10,024	5,578	4,146	300	1,432	D	55.6	41.4	3.0	57	13	13	3.0	2.6	3.8	3.5
Mellette	856	579	269	8	310	D	67.6	31.4	0.9	21	40	66	0.3	0.3	0.2	<.1
Miner	1,582	1,093	456	33	637	D	69.1	28.8	2.1	12	54	43	0.5	0.5	0.4	0.4
Minnehaha	63,380	44,541	17,561	1,278	26,980	D	70.3	27.7	2.0	10	57	44	18.9	20.5	16.2	14.7
Moody	3,110	2,255	789	66	1,466	D	72.5	25.4	2.1	3	62	41	0.9	1.0	0.7	0.8
Pennington	37,659	21,679	14,560	1,420	7,119	D	57.6	38.7	3.8	49	20	4	11.3	10.0	13.4	16.4
Perkins	1,978	1,074	848	56	226	D	54.3	42.9	2.8	59	8	15	0.6	0.5	0.8	0.6
Potter	1,778	1,023	701	54	322	D	57.5	39.4	3.0	50	17	11	0.5	0.5	0.6	0.6
Roberts	3,910	2,545	1,296	69	1,249	D	65.1	33.1	1.8	35	32	53	1.2	1.2	1.2	0.8
Sanborn	1,604	1,080	486	38	594	D	67.3	30.3	2.4	22	47	31	0.5	0.5	0.4	0.4
Shannon	1,633	1,416	165	52	1,251	D	86.7	10.1	3.2	1	66	8	0.5	0.7	0.2	0.6
Spink	4,067	2,805	1,164	98	1,641	D	69.0	28.6	2.4	14	55	30	1.2	1.3	1.1	1.1
Stanley	1,398	884	475	39	409	D	63.2	34.0	2.8	37	31	17	0.4	0.4	0.4	0.5
Sully	1,010	566	422	22	144	D	56.0	41.8	2.2	55	9	34	0.3	0.3	0.4	0.3
Todd	1,626	1,197	394	35	803	D	73.6	24.2	2.2	2	64	36	0.5	0.6	0.4	0.4
Tripp	3,363	1,994	1,308	61	686	D	59.3	38.9	1.8	46	18	52	1.0	0.9	1.2	0.7
Turner	4,295	2,750	1,491	54	1,259	D	64.0	34.7	1.3	36	29	64	1.3	1.3	1.4	0.6
Union	4,997	3,491	1,385	121	2,106	D	69.9	27.7	2.4	11	56	28	1.5	1.6	1.3	1.4
Walworth	2,873	1,607	1,195	71	412	D	55.9	41.6	2.5	56	10	26	0.9	0.7	1.1	0.8
Yankton	9,309	6,396	2,729	184	3,667	D	68.7	29.3	2.0	16	53	46	2.8	2.9	2.5	2.1
Ziebach	698	382	290	26	92	D	54.7	41.5	3.7	58	12	5	0.2	0.2	0.3	0.3
SOUTH DAKOTA	334,495	217,095	108,733	8,667	108,362	D	64.9	32.5	2.6				100.0	100.0	100.0	100.0

Table H. — Vote for U.S. Representative in Congress: November 3, 1992, General Election

Congressional district and county	Total	Democrat (DEM)	Republican (REP)	Other	Plurality Total	Party	Percent of total vote DEM	REP	Other	Rank within district DEM	REP	Other	Percent contribution to district vote Total	DEM	REP	Other
District At-Large	**332,902**	**230,070**	**89,375**	**13,457**	**140,695**	**D**	**69.1**	**26.8**	**4.0**				**100.0**	**100.0**	**100.0**	**100.0**
Aurora	1,707	1,165	400	142	765	D	68.2	23.4	8.3	39	43	3	0.5	0.5	0.4	1.1
Beadle	9,125	6,797	1,992	336	4,805	D	74.5	21.8	3.7	13	52	48	2.7	3.0	2.2	2.5
Bennett	1,189	799	311	79	488	D	67.2	26.2	6.6	43	31	10	0.4	0.3	0.3	0.6
Bon Homme	3,379	2,671	587	121	2,084	D	79.0	17.4	3.6	3	63	50	1.0	1.2	0.7	0.9
Brookings	11,926	8,493	3,021	412	5,472	D	71.2	25.3	3.5	27	35	52	3.6	3.7	3.4	3.1
Brown	17,991	13,875	3,601	515	10,274	D	77.1	20.0	2.9	5	60	58	5.4	6.0	4.0	3.8
Brule	2,652	1,940	526	186	1,414	D	73.2	19.8	7.0	17	61	9	0.8	0.8	0.6	1.4
Buffalo	490	369	89	32	280	D	75.3	18.2	6.5	10	62	12	0.1	0.2	0.1	0.2
Butte	3,636	2,100	1,248	288	852	D	57.8	34.3	7.9	62	7	4	1.1	0.9	1.4	2.1
Campbell	1,014	636	341	37	295	D	62.7	33.6	3.6	54	8	49	0.3	0.3	0.4	0.3
Charles Mix	4,080	3,060	848	172	2,212	D	75.0	20.8	4.2	11	57	36	1.2	1.3	0.9	1.3
Clark	2,343	1,678	583	82	1,095	D	71.6	24.9	3.5	24	38	51	0.7	0.7	0.7	0.6
Clay	5,997	4,752	964	281	3,788	D	79.2	16.1	4.7	2	65	28	1.8	2.1	1.1	2.1
Codington	10,831	7,476	2,921	434	4,555	D	69.0	27.0	4.0	38	28	41	3.3	3.2	3.3	3.2
Corson	1,196	677	386	133	291	D	56.6	32.3	11.1	64	12	1	0.4	0.3	0.4	1.0
Custer	3,299	2,072	1,025	202	1,047	D	62.8	31.1	6.1	53	16	16	1.0	0.9	1.1	1.5
Davison	8,114	5,605	1,936	573	3,669	D	69.1	23.9	7.1	37	41	8	2.4	2.4	2.2	4.3
Day	3,665	2,822	746	97	2,076	D	77.0	20.4	2.6	6	59	60	1.1	1.2	0.8	0.7
Deuel	2,398	1,764	518	116	1,246	D	73.6	21.6	4.8	15	53	26	0.7	0.8	0.6	0.9
Dewey	1,729	1,248	394	87	854	D	72.2	22.8	5.0	21	47	21	0.5	0.5	0.4	0.6
Douglas	2,049	1,122	716	211	406	D	54.8	34.9	10.3	66	5	2	0.6	0.5	0.8	1.6
Edmunds	2,214	1,598	558	58	1,040	D	72.2	25.2	2.6	22	36	61	0.7	0.7	0.6	0.4
Fall River	3,664	2,437	985	242	1,452	D	66.5	26.9	6.6	45	29	11	1.1	1.1	1.1	1.8
Faulk	1,407	1,006	338	63	668	D	71.5	24.0	4.5	25	40	32	0.4	0.4	0.4	0.5
Grant	4,075	2,744	1,171	160	1,573	D	67.3	28.7	3.9	42	23	42	1.2	1.2	1.3	1.2
Gregory	2,597	1,805	665	127	1,140	D	69.5	25.6	4.9	35	33	25	0.8	0.8	0.7	0.9
Haakon	1,298	737	508	53	229	D	56.8	39.1	4.1	63	1	39	0.4	0.3	0.6	0.4
Hamlin	2,720	1,779	829	112	950	D	65.4	30.5	4.1	48	19	38	0.8	0.8	0.9	0.8
Hand	2,517	1,838	573	106	1,265	D	73.0	22.8	4.2	18	48	37	0.8	0.8	0.6	0.8
Hanson	1,432	1,022	329	81	693	D	71.4	23.0	5.7	26	45	18	0.4	0.4	0.4	0.6
Harding	857	481	333	43	148	D	56.1	38.9	5.0	65	2	22	0.3	0.2	0.4	0.3
Hughes	8,030	5,267	2,519	244	2,748	D	65.6	31.4	3.0	47	14	55	2.4	2.3	2.8	1.8
Hutchinson	4,161	2,825	1,176	160	1,649	D	67.9	28.3	3.8	41	25	44	1.2	1.2	1.3	1.2
Hyde	931	634	243	54	391	D	68.1	26.1	5.8	40	32	17	0.3	0.3	0.3	0.4
Jackson	1,145	696	405	44	291	D	60.8	35.4	3.8	57	4	45	0.3	0.3	0.5	0.3
Jerauld	1,470	1,071	344	55	727	D	72.9	23.4	3.7	20	44	47	0.4	0.5	0.4	0.4
Jones	776	474	269	33	205	D	61.1	34.7	4.3	56	6	35	0.2	0.2	0.3	0.2
Kingsbury	3,135	2,369	672	94	1,697	D	75.6	21.4	3.0	9	55	57	0.9	1.0	0.8	0.7
Lake	5,572	4,119	1,324	129	2,795	D	73.9	23.8	2.3	14	42	62	1.7	1.8	1.5	1.0
Lawrence	9,585	6,030	2,942	613	3,088	D	62.9	30.7	6.4	52	18	13	2.9	2.6	3.3	4.6
Lincoln	7,831	5,436	2,224	171	3,212	D	69.4	28.4	2.2	36	24	65	2.4	2.4	2.5	1.3
Lyman	1,469	970	431	68	539	D	66.0	29.3	4.6	46	22	30	0.4	0.4	0.5	0.5
McCook	2,950	2,080	740	130	1,340	D	70.5	25.1	4.4	30	37	34	0.9	0.9	0.8	1.0
McPherson	1,665	981	634	50	347	D	58.9	38.1	3.0	61	3	56	0.5	0.4	0.7	0.4
Marshall	2,269	1,738	486	45	1,252	D	76.6	21.4	2.0	8	56	66	0.7	0.8	0.5	0.3
Meade	9,956	5,997	3,337	622	2,660	D	60.2	33.5	6.2	59	9	15	3.0	2.6	3.7	4.6
Mellette	854	595	217	42	378	D	69.7	25.4	4.9	33	34	24	0.3	0.3	0.2	0.3
Miner	1,564	1,141	351	72	790	D	73.0	22.4	4.6	19	49	31	0.5	0.5	0.4	0.5
Minnehaha	63,021	43,850	17,735	1,436	26,115	D	69.6	28.1	2.3	34	26	64	18.9	19.1	19.8	10.7
Moody	3,101	2,377	640	84	1,737	D	76.7	20.6	2.7	7	58	59	0.9	1.0	0.7	0.6
Pennington	37,486	23,478	12,256	1,752	11,222	D	62.6	32.7	4.7	55	11	29	11.3	10.2	13.7	13.0
Perkins	1,976	1,166	660	150	506	D	59.0	33.4	7.6	60	10	6	0.6	0.5	0.7	1.1
Potter	1,758	1,138	526	94	612	D	64.7	29.9	5.3	50	20	19	0.5	0.5	0.6	0.7
Roberts	3,869	2,735	962	172	1,773	D	70.7	24.9	4.4	29	39	33	1.2	1.2	1.1	1.3
Sanborn	1,585	1,123	340	122	783	D	70.9	21.5	7.7	28	54	5	0.5	0.5	0.4	0.9
Shannon	1,605	1,373	130	102	1,243	D	85.5	8.1	6.4	1	66	14	0.5	0.6	0.1	0.8
Spink	4,050	3,032	891	127	2,141	D	74.9	22.0	3.1	12	51	53	1.2	1.3	1.0	0.9
Stanley	1,387	977	367	43	610	D	70.4	26.5	3.1	31	30	54	0.4	0.4	0.4	0.3
Sully	1,006	654	313	39	341	D	65.0	31.1	3.9	49	15	43	0.3	0.3	0.4	0.3
Todd	1,624	1,268	278	78	990	D	78.1	17.1	4.8	4	64	27	0.5	0.6	0.3	0.6
Tripp	3,365	2,241	996	128	1,245	D	66.6	29.6	3.8	44	21	46	1.0	1.0	1.1	1.0
Turner	4,277	2,984	1,195	98	1,789	D	69.8	27.9	2.3	32	27	63	1.3	1.3	1.3	0.7
Union	5,005	3,608	1,148	249	2,460	D	72.1	22.9	5.0	23	46	23	1.5	1.6	1.3	1.9
Walworth	2,835	1,810	878	147	932	D	63.8	31.0	5.2	51	17	20	0.9	0.8	1.0	1.1
Yankton	9,316	6,852	2,084	380	4,768	D	73.6	22.4	4.1	16	50	40	2.8	3.0	2.3	2.8
Ziebach	682	413	220	49	193	D	60.6	32.3	7.2	58	13	7	0.2	0.2	0.2	0.4
SOUTH DAKOTA	**332,902**	**230,070**	**89,375**	**13,457**	**140,695**	**D**	**69.1**	**26.8**	**4.0**							

Table I. — Vote for Presidential Preference: February 25, 1992, Democratic Primary Election

County	Total	Kerrey	Harkin	Clinton	Tsongas	Brown	Agran	LaRouche	Wilder	Pct Kerrey	Pct Harkin	Pct Clinton	Rank Kerrey	Rank Harkin	Rank Clinton	Contrib Total	Contrib Kerrey	Contrib Harkin	Contrib Clinton
Aurora	485	168	147	69	60	23	2	12	4	34.6	30.3	14.2	47	22	56	0.8	0.7	1.0	0.6
Beadle	2,293	689	833	508	181	64	6	5	7	30.0	36.3	22.2	61	4	8	3.9	2.9	5.5	4.5
Bennett	309	176	45	50	26	7	3	0	2	57.0	14.6	16.2	6	60	49	0.5	0.7	0.3	0.4
Bon Homme	605	264	183	88	38	23	2	5	2	43.6	30.2	14.5	19	23	54	1.0	1.1	1.2	0.8
Brookings	1,579	497	414	294	266	63	29	14	2	31.5	26.2	18.6	58	35	30	2.7	2.1	2.8	2.6
Brown	4,071	1,400	1,254	785	421	159	19	25	8	34.4	30.8	19.3	48	19	24	6.8	5.9	8.3	6.9
Brule	680	249	207	114	48	45	4	12	1	36.6	30.4	16.8	41	20	46	1.1	1.0	1.4	1.0
Buffalo	123	44	36	22	5	9	7	0	0	35.8	29.3	17.9	44	26	36	0.2	0.2	0.2	0.2
Butte	417	241	63	70	29	10	2	1	1	57.8	15.1	16.8	5	57	45	0.7	1.0	0.4	0.6
Campbell	85	26	17	30	10	1	0	1	0	30.6	20.0	35.3	60	54	1	0.1	0.1	0.1	0.3
Charles Mix	1,184	717	258	114	61	12	10	11	1	60.6	21.8	9.6	2	49	65	2.0	3.0	1.7	1.0
Clark	473	190	147	89	16	16	3	10	2	40.2	31.1	18.8	29	18	28	0.8	0.8	1.0	0.8
Clay	1,058	378	223	218	168	56	9	3	3	35.7	21.1	20.6	45	51	14	1.8	1.6	1.5	1.9
Codington	1,643	467	546	378	154	67	12	16	3	28.4	33.2	23.0	65	14	7	2.8	2.0	3.6	3.3
Corson	244	83	55	41	21	28	6	6	4	34.0	22.5	16.8	50	45	44	0.4	0.3	0.4	0.4
Custer	488	274	65	79	40	20	8	1	1	56.1	13.3	16.2	8	61	48	0.8	1.1	0.4	0.7
Davison	1,509	581	344	327	167	60	5	24	1	38.5	22.8	21.7	36	44	12	2.5	2.4	2.3	2.9
Day	964	307	344	192	64	39	4	13	1	31.8	35.7	19.9	56	6	21	1.6	1.3	2.3	1.7
Deuel	505	170	179	101	33	13	5	3	1	33.7	35.4	20.0	53	8	19	0.8	0.7	1.2	0.9
Dewey	404	177	61	58	58	30	15	3	2	43.8	15.1	14.4	18	58	55	0.7	0.7	0.4	0.5
Douglas	230	90	63	35	29	9	0	4	0	39.1	27.4	15.2	34	30	53	0.4	0.4	0.4	0.3
Edmunds	597	242	181	110	37	22	0	5	0	40.5	30.3	18.4	27	21	32	1.0	1.0	1.2	1.0
Fall River	706	409	86	130	53	20	4	3	1	57.9	12.2	18.4	4	63	33	1.2	1.7	0.6	1.1
Faulk	370	157	83	75	30	23	1	1	0	42.4	22.4	20.3	23	46	18	0.6	0.7	0.6	0.7
Grant	663	198	241	121	59	30	2	9	3	29.9	36.3	18.3	62	3	34	1.1	0.8	1.6	1.1
Gregory	661	251	176	129	47	26	8	20	4	38.0	26.6	19.5	38	34	22	1.1	1.1	1.2	1.1
Haakon	184	95	42	19	19	6	1	1	1	51.6	22.8	10.3	12	43	64	0.3	0.4	0.3	0.2
Hamlin	477	136	164	98	38	26	1	13	1	28.5	34.4	20.5	64	11	15	0.8	0.6	1.1	0.9
Hand	490	141	174	100	35	28	7	4	1	28.8	35.5	20.4	63	7	16	0.8	0.6	1.2	0.9
Hanson	318	107	114	61	20	9	4	3	0	33.6	35.8	19.2	54	5	25	0.5	0.4	0.8	0.5
Harding	113	55	18	18	17	3	0	1	1	48.7	15.9	15.9	14	56	51	0.2	0.2	0.1	0.2
Hughes	1,106	404	223	263	151	40	16	7	2	36.5	20.2	23.8	43	53	6	1.9	1.7	1.5	2.3
Hutchinson	444	174	156	62	28	15	1	8	0	39.2	35.1	14.0	33	9	58	0.7	0.7	1.0	0.5
Hyde	218	83	68	41	10	10	2	3	1	38.1	31.2	18.8	37	16	29	0.4	0.3	0.5	0.4
Jackson	211	112	43	30	16	5	2	3	0	53.1	20.4	14.2	11	52	57	0.4	0.5	0.3	0.3
Jerauld	297	100	118	53	14	10	0	2	0	33.7	39.7	17.8	52	2	37	0.5	0.4	0.8	0.5
Jones	110	52	26	22	5	5	0	0	0	47.3	23.6	20.0	15	41	20	0.2	0.2	0.2	0.2
Kingsbury	516	158	219	83	28	16	1	9	2	30.6	42.4	16.1	59	1	50	0.9	0.7	1.5	0.7
Lake	943	319	231	241	94	39	7	10	2	33.8	24.5	25.6	51	37	5	1.6	1.3	1.5	2.1
Lawrence	1,361	592	324	234	129	52	20	8	2	43.5	23.8	17.2	20	40	42	2.3	2.5	2.2	2.1
Lincoln	1,142	486	291	232	83	37	5	6	2	42.6	25.5	20.3	22	36	17	1.9	2.0	1.9	2.0
Lyman	257	97	59	50	22	19	6	4	0	37.7	23.0	19.5	40	42	23	0.4	0.4	0.4	0.4
McCook	586	232	157	112	52	21	1	8	3	39.6	26.8	19.1	31	32	26	1.0	1.0	1.0	1.0
McPherson	157	64	38	27	17	5	1	3	2	40.8	24.2	17.2	25	38	41	0.3	0.3	0.3	0.2
Marshall	669	272	148	177	45	19	3	3	2	40.7	22.1	26.5	26	47	4	1.1	1.1	1.0	1.6
Meade	1,428	805	208	243	101	47	10	6	8	56.4	14.6	17.0	7	59	43	2.4	3.4	1.4	2.1
Mellette	171	85	48	23	6	5	2	2	0	49.7	28.1	13.5	13	29	60	0.3	0.4	0.3	0.2
Miner	400	139	140	65	37	12	5	1	1	34.8	35.0	16.3	46	10	47	0.7	0.6	0.9	0.6
Minnehaha	11,011	4,027	2,640	2,422	1,296	466	102	39	19	36.6	24.0	22.0	42	39	9	18.5	16.9	17.6	21.3
Moody	654	257	204	116	40	25	12	0	0	39.3	31.2	17.7	32	17	39	1.1	1.1	1.4	1.0
Pennington	5,090	2,799	648	804	574	139	106	15	5	55.0	12.7	15.8	9	62	52	8.6	11.7	4.3	7.1
Perkins	354	193	65	61	24	3	3	3	2	54.5	18.4	17.2	10	55	40	0.6	0.8	0.4	0.5
Potter	282	114	84	52	20	5	1	5	1	40.4	29.8	18.4	28	25	31	0.5	0.5	0.6	0.5
Roberts	1,045	283	280	317	80	56	11	14	4	27.1	26.8	30.3	66	31	2	1.8	1.2	1.9	2.8
Sanborn	346	118	115	72	24	11	2	4	0	34.1	33.2	20.8	49	13	13	0.6	0.5	0.8	0.6
Shannon	539	356	37	50	30	27	35	2	2	66.0	6.9	9.3	1	66	66	0.9	1.5	0.2	0.4
Spink	954	379	274	171	83	31	8	6	2	39.7	28.7	17.9	30	27	35	1.6	1.6	1.8	1.5
Stanley	242	77	53	69	30	10	2	1	0	31.8	21.9	28.5	57	48	3	0.4	0.3	0.4	0.6
Sully	216	69	65	47	19	9	2	4	1	31.9	30.1	21.8	55	24	11	0.4	0.3	0.4	0.4
Todd	513	307	46	61	29	39	20	8	3	59.8	9.0	11.9	3	65	63	0.9	1.3	0.3	0.5
Tripp	642	264	216	87	44	20	3	7	1	41.1	33.6	13.6	24	12	59	1.1	1.1	1.4	0.8
Turner	643	282	140	140	57	19	2	2	1	43.9	21.8	21.8	17	50	10	1.1	1.2	0.9	1.2
Union	861	368	242	115	85	31	8	8	4	42.7	28.1	13.4	21	28	61	1.4	1.5	1.6	1.0
Walworth	404	153	108	72	44	22	0	4	1	37.9	26.7	17.8	39	33	38	0.7	0.6	0.7	0.6
Yankton	1,605	619	529	208	153	71	14	7	4	38.6	33.0	13.0	35	15	62	2.7	2.6	3.5	1.8
Ziebach	158	74	17	30	9	12	14	0	2	46.8	10.8	19.0	16	64	27	0.3	0.3	0.1	0.3
SOUTH DAKOTA	59,503	23,892	15,023	11,375	5,729	2,300	606	441	137	40.2	25.2	19.1				100.0	100.0	100.0	100.0

Table J. — Vote for Presidential Preference: February 25, 1992, Republican Primary Election

County	Top candidates					Top four candidates (state vote)								Percent contribution to state vote				
						Percent of total vote				Rank								
	Total	Bush	Uncom-mitted			Bush	Uncom-mitted			Bush	Uncom-mitted			Total	Bush	Uncom-mitted		
Aurora	190	127	63	-	-	66.8	33.2	-	-	44	23	-	-	0.4	0.4	0.5	-	-
Beadle	1,050	816	234	-	-	77.7	22.3	-	-	5	62	-	-	2.4	2.6	1.7	-	-
Bennett	181	135	46	-	-	74.6	25.4	-	-	10	57	-	-	0.4	0.4	0.3	-	-
Bon Homme	465	338	127	-	-	72.7	27.3	-	-	15	52	-	-	1.0	1.1	0.9	-	-
Brookings	1,374	913	461	-	-	66.4	33.6	-	-	49	18	-	-	3.1	2.9	3.4	-	-
Brown	2,240	1,593	647	-	-	71.1	28.9	-	-	26	41	-	-	5.0	5.1	4.7	-	-
Brule	258	168	90	-	-	65.1	34.9	-	-	55	12	-	-	0.6	0.5	0.7	-	-
Buffalo	61	48	13	-	-	78.7	21.3	-	-	4	63	-	-	0.1	0.2	<.1	-	-
Butte	797	525	272	-	-	65.9	34.1	-	-	51	16	-	-	1.8	1.7	2.0	-	-
Campbell	315	165	150	-	-	52.4	47.6	-	-	66	1	-	-	0.7	0.5	1.1	-	-
Charles Mix	415	311	104	-	-	74.9	25.1	-	-	9	58	-	-	0.9	1.0	0.8	-	-
Clark	469	301	168	-	-	64.2	35.8	-	-	56	11	-	-	1.0	1.0	1.2	-	-
Clay	521	345	176	-	-	66.2	33.8	-	-	50	17	-	-	1.2	1.1	1.3	-	-
Codington	1,148	807	341	-	-	70.3	29.7	-	-	32	35	-	-	2.6	2.6	2.5	-	-
Corson	219	159	60	-	-	72.6	27.4	-	-	16	51	-	-	0.5	0.5	0.4	-	-
Custer	543	341	202	-	-	62.8	37.2	-	-	58	9	-	-	1.2	1.1	1.5	-	-
Davison	805	588	217	-	-	73.0	27.0	-	-	13	54	-	-	1.8	1.9	1.6	-	-
Day	460	290	170	-	-	63.0	37.0	-	-	57	10	-	-	1.0	0.9	1.2	-	-
Deuel	365	218	147	-	-	59.7	40.3	-	-	63	4	-	-	0.8	0.7	1.1	-	-
Dewey	243	173	70	-	-	71.2	28.8	-	-	24	43	-	-	0.5	0.6	0.5	-	-
Douglas	451	317	134	-	-	70.3	29.7	-	-	33	34	-	-	1.0	1.0	1.0	-	-
Edmunds	392	280	112	-	-	71.4	28.6	-	-	22	44	-	-	0.9	0.9	0.8	-	-
Fall River	702	469	233	-	-	66.8	33.2	-	-	46	21	-	-	1.6	1.5	1.7	-	-
Faulk	305	183	122	-	-	60.0	40.0	-	-	62	5	-	-	0.7	0.6	0.9	-	-
Grant	600	401	199	-	-	66.8	33.2	-	-	45	22	-	-	1.3	1.3	1.5	-	-
Gregory	383	261	122	-	-	68.1	31.9	-	-	41	26	-	-	0.9	0.8	0.9	-	-
Haakon	306	213	93	-	-	69.6	30.4	-	-	37	30	-	-	0.7	0.7	0.7	-	-
Hamlin	581	358	223	-	-	61.6	38.4	-	-	60	7	-	-	1.3	1.2	1.6	-	-
Hand	475	344	131	-	-	72.4	27.6	-	-	17	50	-	-	1.1	1.1	1.0	-	-
Hanson	142	116	26	-	-	81.7	18.3	-	-	1	66	-	-	0.3	0.4	0.2	-	-
Harding	229	169	60	-	-	73.8	26.2	-	-	12	55	-	-	0.5	0.5	0.4	-	-
Hughes	1,510	1,126	384	-	-	74.6	25.4	-	-	11	56	-	-	3.4	3.6	2.8	-	-
Hutchinson	835	579	256	-	-	69.3	30.7	-	-	38	29	-	-	1.9	1.9	1.9	-	-
Hyde	197	140	57	-	-	71.1	28.9	-	-	28	39	-	-	0.4	0.5	0.4	-	-
Jackson	256	198	58	-	-	77.3	22.7	-	-	6	61	-	-	0.6	0.6	0.4	-	-
Jerauld	153	116	37	-	-	75.8	24.2	-	-	8	59	-	-	0.3	0.4	0.3	-	-
Jones	174	122	52	-	-	70.1	29.9	-	-	34	33	-	-	0.4	0.4	0.4	-	-
Kingsbury	722	431	291	-	-	59.7	40.3	-	-	64	3	-	-	1.6	1.4	2.1	-	-
Lake	633	421	212	-	-	66.5	33.5	-	-	48	19	-	-	1.4	1.4	1.5	-	-
Lawrence	1,534	1,068	466	-	-	69.6	30.4	-	-	36	31	-	-	3.4	3.4	3.4	-	-
Lincoln	766	540	226	-	-	70.5	29.5	-	-	30	37	-	-	1.7	1.7	1.6	-	-
Lyman	242	159	83	-	-	65.7	34.3	-	-	53	14	-	-	0.5	0.5	0.6	-	-
McCook	368	268	100	-	-	72.8	27.2	-	-	14	53	-	-	0.8	0.9	0.7	-	-
McPherson	491	349	142	-	-	71.1	28.9	-	-	27	40	-	-	1.1	1.1	1.0	-	-
Marshall	339	259	80	-	-	76.4	23.6	-	-	7	60	-	-	0.8	0.8	0.6	-	-
Meade	1,546	1,010	536	-	-	65.3	34.7	-	-	54	13	-	-	3.5	3.3	3.9	-	-
Mellette	140	100	40	-	-	71.4	28.6	-	-	23	45	-	-	0.3	0.3	0.3	-	-
Miner	164	108	56	-	-	65.9	34.1	-	-	52	15	-	-	0.4	0.3	0.4	-	-
Minnehaha	6,651	4,731	1,920	-	-	71.1	28.9	-	-	25	42	-	-	14.9	15.3	14.0	-	-
Moody	226	163	63	-	-	72.1	27.9	-	-	18	49	-	-	0.5	0.5	0.5	-	-
Pennington	5,072	3,548	1,524	-	-	70.0	30.0	-	-	35	32	-	-	11.4	11.5	11.1	-	-
Perkins	393	283	110	-	-	72.0	28.0	-	-	20	47	-	-	0.9	0.9	0.8	-	-
Potter	411	238	173	-	-	57.9	42.1	-	-	65	2	-	-	0.9	0.8	1.3	-	-
Roberts	488	329	159	-	-	67.4	32.6	-	-	42	25	-	-	1.1	1.1	1.2	-	-
Sanborn	223	152	71	-	-	68.2	31.8	-	-	40	27	-	-	0.5	0.5	0.5	-	-
Shannon	83	50	33	-	-	60.2	39.8	-	-	61	6	-	-	0.2	0.2	0.2	-	-
Spink	498	341	157	-	-	68.5	31.5	-	-	39	28	-	-	1.1	1.1	1.1	-	-
Stanley	179	144	35	-	-	80.4	19.6	-	-	2	65	-	-	0.4	0.5	0.3	-	-
Sully	177	125	52	-	-	70.6	29.4	-	-	29	38	-	-	0.4	0.4	0.4	-	-
Todd	143	103	40	-	-	72.0	28.0	-	-	19	48	-	-	0.3	0.3	0.3	-	-
Tripp	519	365	154	-	-	70.3	29.7	-	-	31	36	-	-	1.2	1.2	1.1	-	-
Turner	652	467	185	-	-	71.6	28.4	-	-	21	46	-	-	1.5	1.5	1.3	-	-
Union	361	241	120	-	-	66.8	33.2	-	-	47	20	-	-	0.8	0.8	0.9	-	-
Walworth	618	385	233	-	-	62.3	37.7	-	-	59	8	-	-	1.4	1.2	1.7	-	-
Yankton	1,113	746	367	-	-	67.0	33.0	-	-	43	24	-	-	2.5	2.4	2.7	-	-
Ziebach	109	87	22	-	-	79.8	20.2	-	-	3	64	-	-	0.2	0.3	0.2	-	-
SOUTH DAKOTA	44,671	30,964	13,707	-	-	69.3	30.7	-	-					100.0	100.0	100.0	-	-

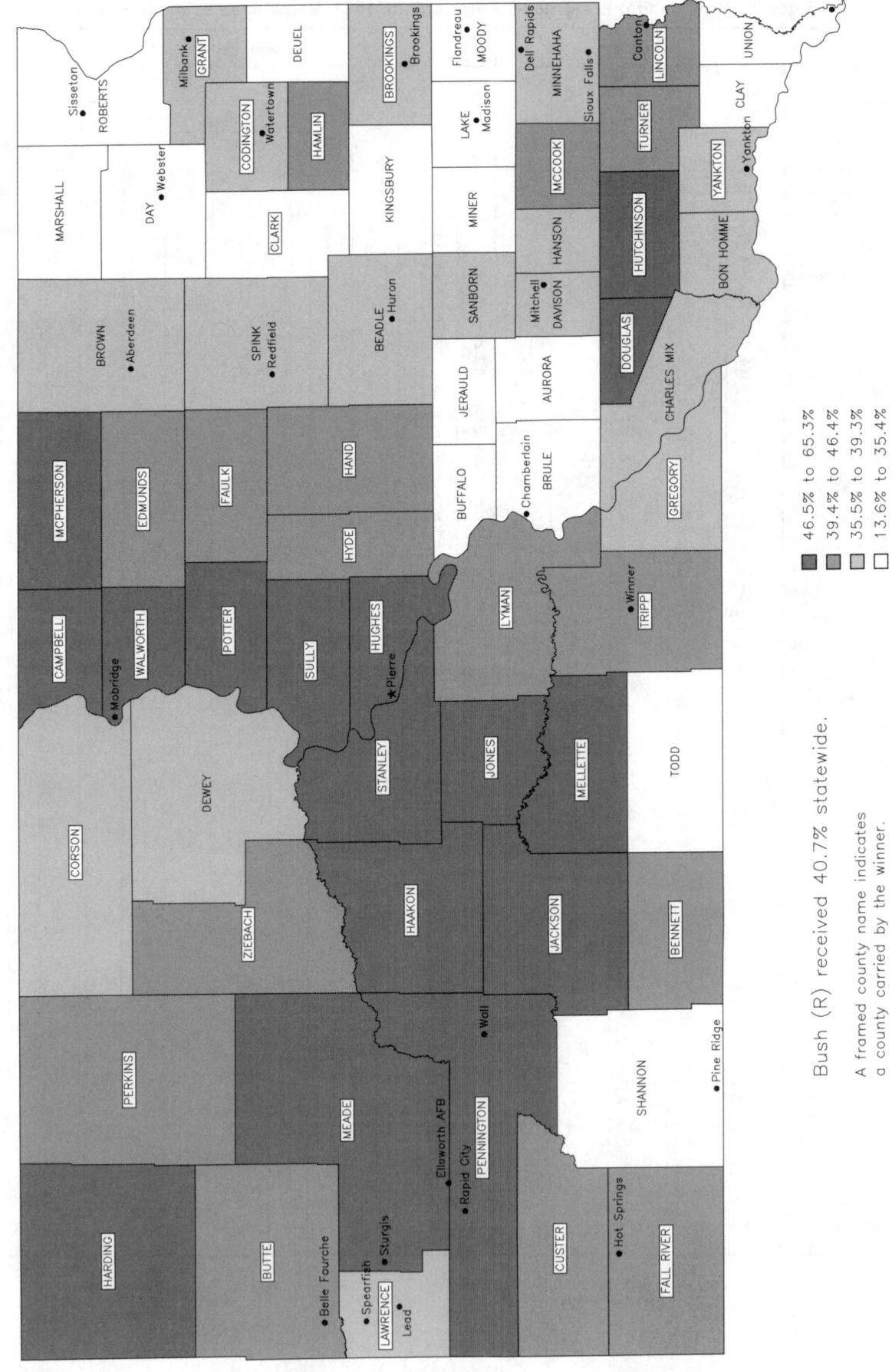

1992 Vote for President
Percent for Bush (R), by County

- 46.5% to 65.3%
- 39.4% to 46.4%
- 35.5% to 39.3%
- 13.6% to 35.4%

Bush (R) received 40.7% statewide.

A framed county name indicates
a county carried by the winner.

Copyright © 1993 by Election Data Services, Inc.

848 South Dakota

1992 Vote for U.S. Senator
Percent for Daschle (D), by County

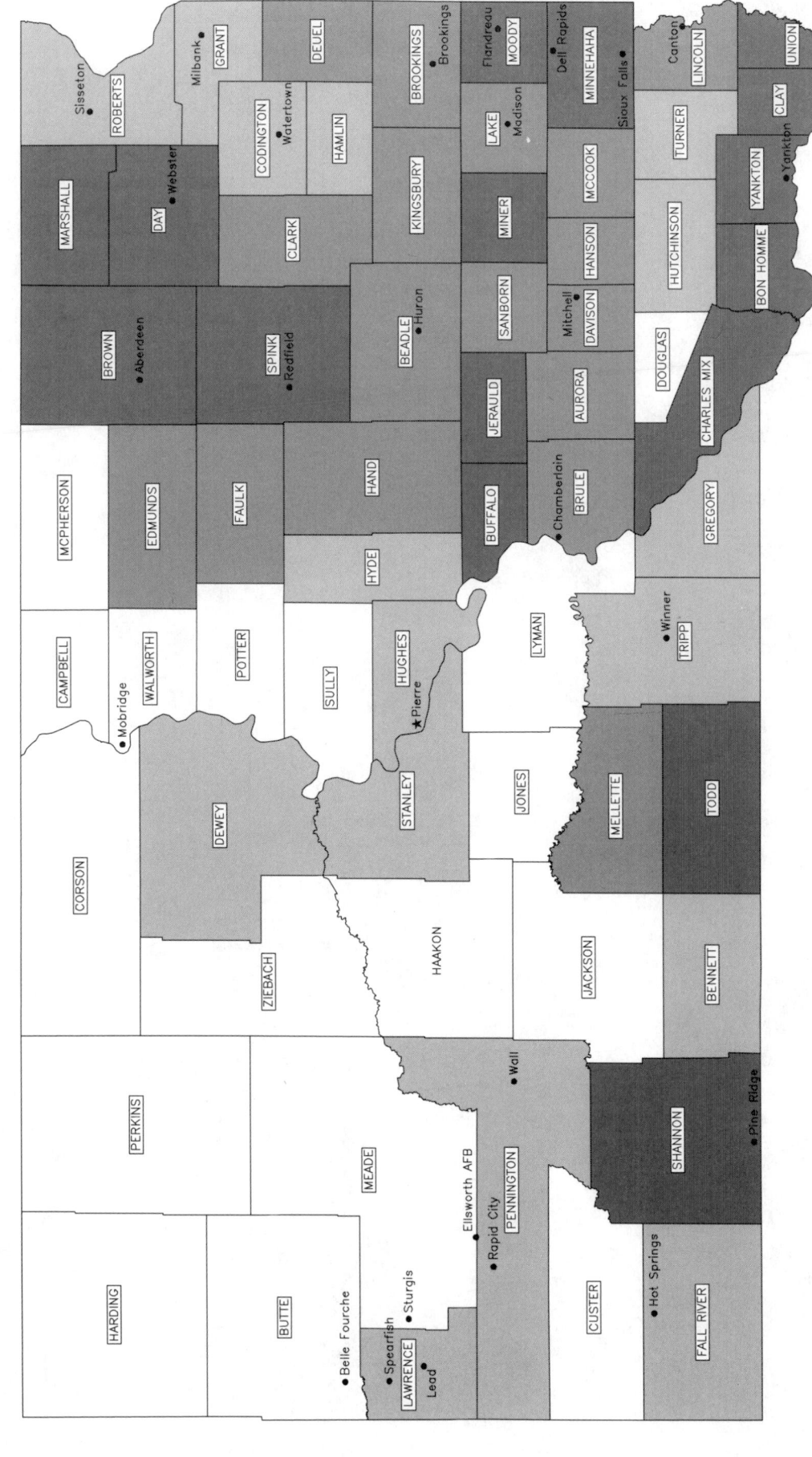

Legend:
- 68.4% to 86.7%
- 65.4% to 68.3%
- 57.6% to 65.3%
- 48.5% to 57.5%

Daschle (D) received 64.9% statewide.

A framed county name indicates a county carried by the winner.

South Dakota 849

TENNESSEE

Congressional Districts 9
    Average Population 541,909
State Senate Districts 33
    Average Population 147,793
State House Districts 99
    Average Population 49,264

Electoral College Votes...11
Counties 95
Voting Precincts 2,423

Alternative Registration Methods:
    ....Mail-in

Registration Deadline (Days before Election) 29

Voting Equipment Use (Counties)

Datavote Punch Card	0	Paper Ballot	0
Electronic	9	Other Punch Card	15
Lever Machine	66	Mixed Systems	4
Optical Scanner	1		

Party Control	DEM	REP	IND	VAC
1993 State Senate	19	14	0	0
1992 State Senate	20	13	0	0
1993 State House	63	36	0	0
1992 State House	57	42	0	0

Population Statistics 1990

Race/ Ethnicity	Total Population		Voting Age Population		Voting Age Population % of total population
	Number	%	Number	%	
Non-Hispanic					
White	4,027,631	82.6	3,084,908	84.3	76.6
Black	774,925	15.9	523,791	14.3	67.6
Asian/Pacific Islander	30,938	0.6	21,630	0.6	69.9
Native American	9,685	0.2	7,318	0.2	75.6
Other	1,265	<.1	468	<.1	37.0
All Hispanic	32,741	0.7	22,466	0.6	68.6
TOTAL	4,877,185	100.0	3,660,581	100.0	75.1

Estimated Voting Age Population 1992 (VAP) 3,783,000
Number of Registered Voters................................. 2,726,449
    % of estimated VAP... 72.1
Voter Turnout (Highest Office) 1,986,635
    % of VAP 52.5
    % of Registration 72.9
Persons Not Voting—of Voting Age 1,796,365
    % of VAP 47.5
Persons Not Voting—of Registered 739,814
    % of Registration 27.1
Straight Ticket Voting .... No

State Officials and Members of Congress

Governor:
Ned McWherter (D) 1986, elected to a four-year term in 1990.

U.S. Senators:
Jim Sasser (D) 1976, elected to a six-year term in 1988.
Harlan Matthews (D) 1992, appointed to a two-year term in 1992.[1]

U.S. Representative in Congress:
(District, Name, Party, Date first elected)

1. Quillen (R) 1962
2. Duncan (R) 1988
3. Lloyd (D) 1974
4. Cooper (D) 1982
5. Clement (D) 1988
6. Gordon (D) 1984
7. Sundquist (R) 1982
8. Tanner (D) 1988
9. Ford (D) 1974

---

[1]Appointed to replace Al Gore (D), who was elected Vice President of the United States.

Candidates: General Election, November 3, 1992

Candidate(s)	Total vote	Percent	Party	Status	First elected
President/Vice President					
Clinton/Gore	933,521	47.08%	Democrat	Challenger	1992
Bush/Quayle	841,300	42.43%	Republican	Incumbent	1988
Perot/Stockdale	199,968	10.09%	Independent	Challenger	
Marrou/Lord	1,847	0.09%	Independent	Challenger	
Brisben/Edwards	1,356	0.07%	Independent	Challenger	
Gritz/Minett	756	0.04%	Independent	Challenger	
Fulani/Munoz	727	0.04%	Independent	Challenger	
Hagelin/Tompkins	599	0.03%	Independent	Challenger	
Phillips/Knight	579	0.03%	Independent	Challenger	
Daniels/Tupahache	511	0.03%	Independent	Challenger	
LaRouche/Bevel	460	0.02%	Independent	Challenger	
Dodge/Ormsby	343	0.02%	Independent	Challenger	
Warren/Reid	277	0.01%	Independent	Challenger	
Yiamouyiannis/McCone	233	0.01%	Independent	Challenger	
Write ins	161	<.01%	Independent	Challenger	

U.S. Senator (No Contest)

Governor (No Contest)

U.S. Representative in Congress

District 1					
James Quillen	114,797	67.46%	Republican	Incumbent	1962
J. Carr Christian	47,809	28.10%	Democrat	Challenger	
Don Fox	4,126	2.42%	Independent	Challenger	
Fred Hartley	3,416	2.01%	Independent	Challenger	
Write ins	10	<.01%	Write in	Challenger	
District 2					
John Duncan Jr.	148,377	72.24%	Republican	Incumbent	1988
Troy Goodale	52,887	25.75%	Democrat	Challenger	
Randon Krieg	4,134	2.01%	Independent	Challenger	
Write ins	3	<.01%	Write in	Challenger	
District 3					
Marilyn Lloyd	105,693	48.81%	Democrat	Incumbent	1974
Zach Wamp	102,763	47.46%	Republican	Challenger	
Carol Hagan	4,433	2.05%	Independent	Challenger	
Pete Melcher	2,048	0.95%	Independent	Challenger	
Marjorie Martin	1,593	0.74%	Independent	Challenger	
Write ins	3	<.01%	Write in	Challenger	
District 4					
Jim Cooper	98,984	64.06%	Democrat	Incumbent	1982
Dale Johnson	50,340	32.58%	Republican	Challenger	
Ginnia Fox	3,970	2.57%	Independent	Challenger	
Kieven Parks	1,210	0.78%	Independent	Challenger	
Write ins	7	<.01%	Write in	Challenger	
District 5					
Bob Clement	125,233	66.76%	Democrat	Incumbent	1988
Tom Stone	49,417	26.34%	Republican	Challenger	
Steven Edmondson	6,724	3.58%	Independent	Challenger	
Richard Wyatt	3,507	1.87%	Independent	Challenger	
John Haury	1,685	0.90%	Independent	Challenger	
Ben Tomeo	1,002	0.53%	Independent	Challenger	
Write ins	22	<.01%	Write in	Challenger	

Candidate(s)	Total vote	Percent	Party	Status	First elected
U.S. Representative in Congress (cont)					
District 6					
Bart Gordon	120,177	56.57%	Democrat	Incumbent	1984
Marsha Blackburn	86,289	40.62%	Republican	Challenger	
H. Scott Benson	5,952	2.80%	Independent	Challenger	
Write ins	10	<.01%	Write in	Challenger	
District 7					
Don Sundquist	125,101	61.67%	Republican	Incumbent	1982
David Davis	72,062	35.52%	Democrat	Challenger	
Rickey Boyette	2,290	1.13%	Independent	Challenger	
Jim Osburn	1,831	0.90%	Independent	Challenger	
Francis Tapp	1,573	0.78%	Independent	Challenger	
Write ins	9	<.01%	Write in	Challenger	
District 8					
John Tanner	136,852	83.74%	Democrat	Incumbent	1988
Lawrence Barnes	9,605	5.88%	Independent	Challenger	
David Ward	6,930	4.24%	Independent	Challenger	
John Vinson	5,435	3.33%	Independent	Challenger	
Millard McKissack II	4,600	2.81%	Independent	Challenger	
Write ins	10	<.01%	Write in	Challenger	
District 9					
Harold Ford	123,276	57.94%	Democrat	Incumbent	1974
Charles Black	60,606	28.49%	Republican	Challenger	
Richard Liptock	14,075	6.62%	Independent	Challenger	
James Vandergriff	12,265	5.76%	Independent	Challenger	
William Rolen	2,517	1.18%	Independent	Challenger	
Write ins	16	<.01%	Write in	Challenger	

Candidates: March 10, 1992, Primary Election

Candidate	Total vote	Percent	Candidate	Total vote	Percent
Presidential Preference, Democratic			**Presidential Preference, Republican**		
Bill Clinton	214,485	67.35%	George Bush	178,219	72.55%
Paul Tsongas	61,717	19.38%	Patrick Buchanan	54,585	22.22%
Jerry Brown	25,560	8.03%	David Duke	7,709	3.14%
Uncommitted	12,551	3.94%	Uncommitted	5,022	2.04%
Tom Harkin	2,099	0.66%	Write ins	118	0.05%
Bob Kerrey	1,638	0.51%			
Write ins	432	0.14%			

Voter Registration and Turnout, 1948-1992 Elections

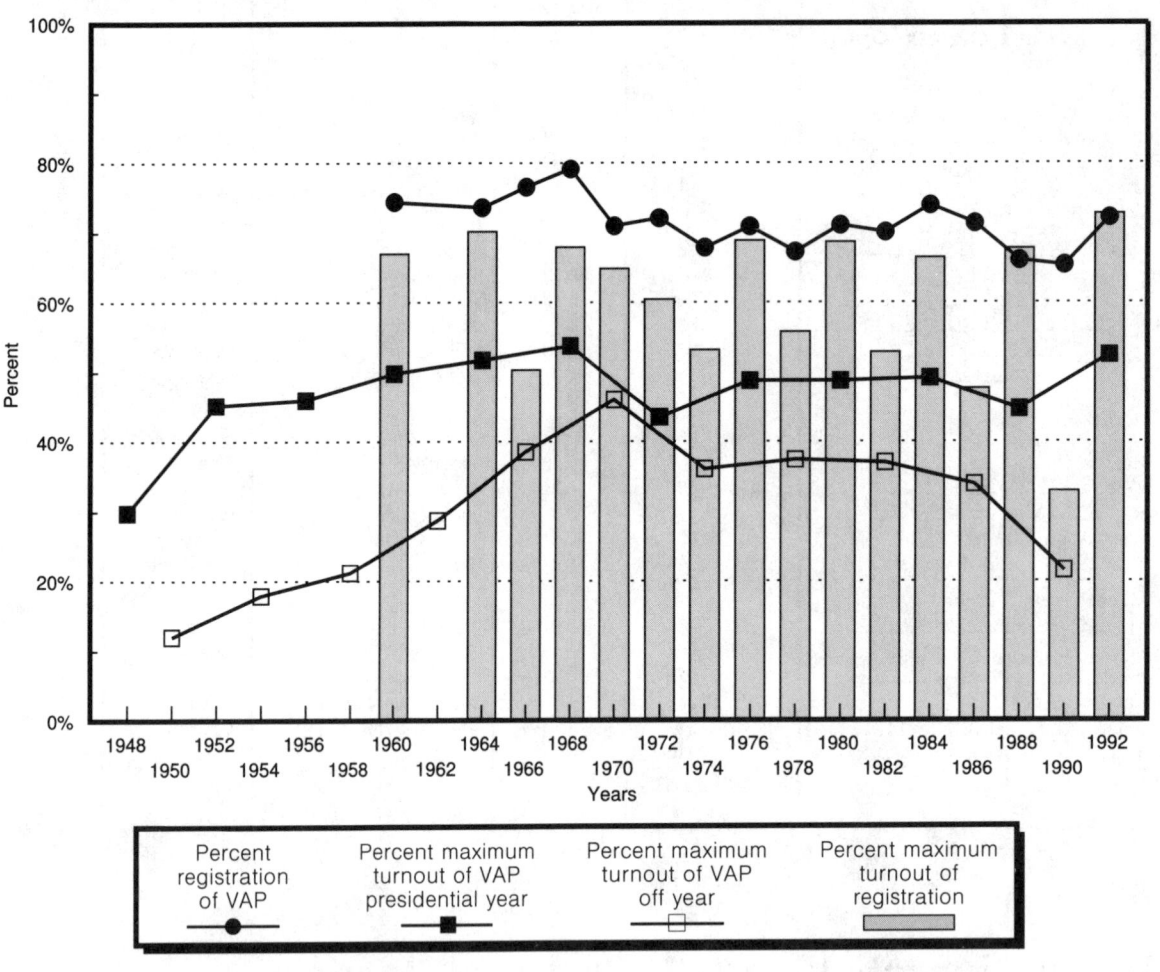

Year	Estimated Voting Age Population (VAP)	Voter registration (REG)				Voter turnout										
						Highest office						Maximum vote				
		Total	Percent of VAP	Rank by percent of VAP	Actual	Total	Office	Percent total REG	Rank by percent of REG	Percent of VAP	Rank by percent of VAP	Total	Percent total REG	Rank by percent of REG	Percent total VAP	Rank by percent of VAP
1992	3,783,000	2,726,449	72.1	32	-	1,982,638	P	72.7	38	52.4	39	1,982,638	72.7	39	52.4	40
1990	3,685,000	2,405,154	65.3	33	-	790,441	G	32.9	48	21.5	50	790,441	32.9	48	21.5	50
1988	3,660,000	2,417,033	66.0	38	-	1,636,250	P	67.7	36	44.7	45	1,636,250	67.7	37	44.7	46
1986	3,569,000	2,543,597	71.3	21	-	1,210,339	G	47.6	39	33.9	37	1,210,339	47.6	40	33.9	39
1984	3,489,000	2,579,504	73.9	24	-	1,711,994	P	66.4	44	49.1	42	1,711,994	66.4	44	49.1	42
1982	3,408,000	2,385,885	70.0	21	-	1,259,785	S	52.8	42	37.0	38	1,259,785	52.8	42	37.0	40
1980	3,323,000	2,358,809	71.0	28	-	1,617,616	P	68.6	40	48.7	41	1,617,616	68.6	42	48.7	43
1978	3,179,000	2,137,789	67.2	30	-	1,189,695	G	55.7	25	37.4	30	1,189,695	55.7	32	37.4	33
1976	3,033,000	2,147,380	70.8	31	-	1,476,345	P	68.8	38	48.7	38	1,476,345	68.8	38	48.7	40
1974	2,890,000	1,960,158	67.8	31	-	1,040,714	G	53.1	35	36.0	38	1,040,714	53.1	36	36.0	38
1972	2,763,000	1,990,026	72.0	28	-	1,201,182	P	60.4	43	43.5	46	1,201,182	60.4	43	43.5	46
1970	2,410,000	1,709,433	70.9	27	-	1,108,247	G	64.8	28	46.0	34	1,108,247	64.8	28	46.0	35
1968	2,325,000	1,840,077	79.1	17	-	1,248,617	P	67.9	44	53.7	40	1,248,617	67.9	44	53.7	40
1966	2,254,000	1,723,664	76.5	22	-	866,961	S	50.3	35	38.5	41	866,961	50.3	35	38.5	41
1964	2,212,000	1,628,825	73.6	26	-	1,143,946	P	70.2	36	51.7	39	1,143,946	70.2	37	51.7	40
1962	2,165,000	-	-	-	-	621,064	G	-	-	28.7	42	621,064	-	-	28.7	42
1960	2,110,000	1,569,118	74.4	22	-	1,051,792	P	67.0	33	49.8	40	1,051,792	67.0	33	49.8	40
1958	2,038,000	-	-	-	-	432,545	G	-	-	21.2	40	432,545	-	-	21.2	40
1956	2,042,000	-	-	-	-	939,404	P	-	-	46.0	40	939,404	-	-	46.0	40
1954	1,989,000	-	-	-	-	356,094	S	-	-	17.9	42	356,094	-	-	17.9	42
1952	1,976,000	-	-	-	-	892,553	P	-	-	45.2	40	892,553	-	-	45.2	40
1950	1,971,000	-	-	-	-	236,194	G	-	-	12.0	43	236,194	-	-	12.0	43
1948	1,846,000	-	-	-	-	550,283	P	-	-	29.8	39	550,283	-	-	29.8	39

TENNESSEE

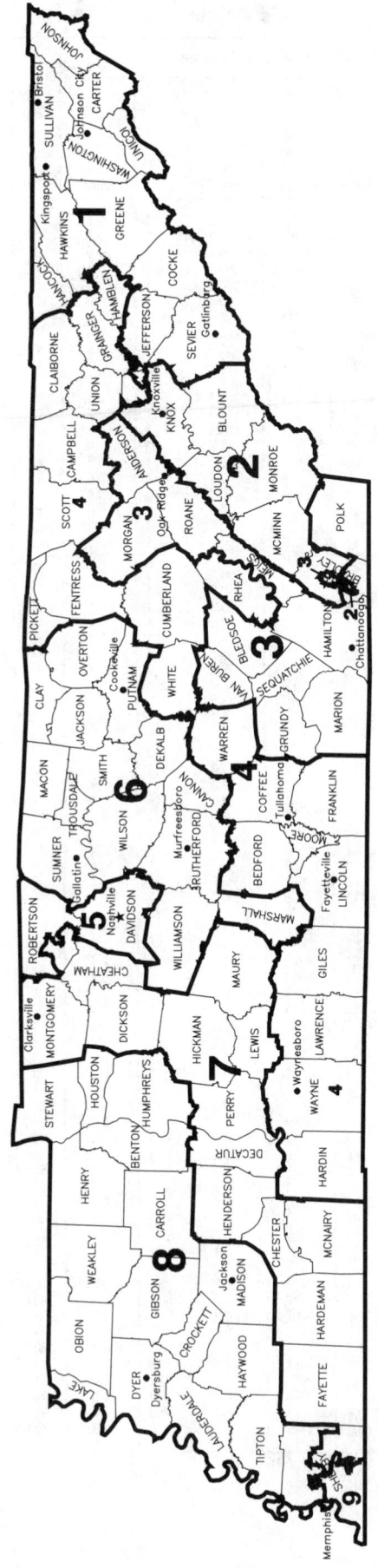

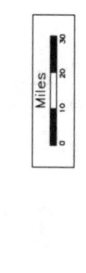

— Congressional district boundaries
effective May 7, 1992.

Copyright © 1993 by Election Data Services, Inc.

Tennessee 855

Table A. — 1990 Population by Race and Ethnic Origin

State/ county code	County	Total persons	Percent of total persons — Non-Hispanic: White	Black	Asian and Pacific Islander	Native American	Other	Hispanic	Rank — Percent of total persons: Total	Non-Hispanic: White	Black	Hispanic	Percent contribution to state population: Total	Non-Hispanic: White	Black	Hispanic
47 001	Anderson	68,250	94.2	4.0	0.8	0.3	<.1	0.6	14	59	41	22	1.4	1.6	0.4	1.2
47 003	Bedford	30,411	88.8	10.0	0.5	0.1	<.1	0.6	41	74	23	21	0.6	0.7	0.4	0.5
47 005	Benton	14,524	96.7	2.4	0.2	0.2	<.1	0.5	69	38	56	35	0.3	0.3	<.1	0.2
47 007	Bledsoe	9,669	95.3	3.9	<.1	0.4	0.0	0.4	81	50	44	62	0.2	0.2	<.1	0.1
47 009	Blount	85,969	95.6	3.2	0.5	0.2	<.1	0.4	10	47	52	46	1.8	2.0	0.4	1.1
47 011	Bradley	73,712	94.6	3.9	0.3	0.3	<.1	1.0	13	57	43	2	1.5	1.7	0.4	2.2
47 013	Campbell	35,079	98.7	0.4	<.1	0.5	<.1	0.3	30	16	82	79	0.7	0.9	<.1	0.4
47 015	Cannon	10,467	97.6	1.8	0.1	0.1	0.0	0.4	80	30	65	67	0.2	0.3	<.1	0.1
47 017	Carroll	27,514	88.0	11.4	<.1	0.1	<.1	0.5	45	78	18	42	0.6	0.6	0.4	0.4
47 019	Carter	51,505	98.3	0.9	0.2	0.2	<.1	0.4	18	19	78	70	1.1	1.3	<.1	0.6
47 021	Cheatham	27,140	97.1	2.0	0.1	0.3	<.1	0.5	46	36	60	29	0.6	0.7	<.1	0.4
47 023	Chester	12,819	88.4	10.8	0.2	0.2	<.1	0.4	78	76	20	53	0.3	0.3	0.2	0.2
47 025	Claiborne	26,137	98.1	0.9	0.4	0.2	<.1	0.3	47	21	77	80	0.5	0.6	<.1	0.3
47 027	Clay	7,238	97.9	1.6	<.1	0.2	0.0	0.4	87	23	68	68	0.1	0.2	<.1	<.1
47 029	Cocke	29,141	97.0	2.1	<.1	0.3	<.1	0.5	42	37	59	36	0.6	0.7	<.1	0.4
47 031	Coffee	40,339	94.8	3.7	0.6	0.2	<.1	0.6	27	55	46	12	0.8	0.9	0.2	0.8
47 033	Crockett	13,378	82.7	16.8	<.1	<.1	<.1	0.4	76	83	13	72	0.3	0.3	0.3	0.1
47 035	Cumberland	34,736	99.0	0.1	0.1	0.4	<.1	0.4	33	14	86	74	0.7	0.9	<.1	0.4
47 037	Davidson	510,784	74.2	23.3	1.4	0.2	<.1	0.9	2	89	9	3	10.5	9.4	15.3	14.6
47 039	Decatur	10,472	95.1	4.0	0.2	0.2	<.1	0.5	79	53	42	39	0.2	0.2	<.1	0.1
47 041	DeKalb	14,360	97.8	1.5	<.1	0.1	<.1	0.4	70	25	70	45	0.3	0.3	<.1	0.2
47 043	Dickson	35,061	94.1	5.0	0.2	0.2	<.1	0.5	31	61	36	34	0.7	0.8	0.2	0.5
47 045	Dyer	34,854	87.4	11.9	0.2	0.2	<.1	0.4	32	79	17	63	0.7	0.8	0.5	0.4
47 047	Fayette	25,559	55.4	43.9	<.1	0.1	<.1	0.5	49	93	2	31	0.5	0.4	1.4	0.4
47 049	Fentress	14,669	99.5	<.1	0.1	<.1	<.1	0.3	68	3	93	87	0.3	0.4	<.1	0.1
47 051	Franklin	34,725	93.0	6.0	0.3	0.1	<.1	0.5	34	63	33	26	0.7	0.8	0.3	0.6
47 053	Gibson	46,315	80.1	19.3	0.1	<.1	<.1	0.4	23	84	10	64	0.9	0.9	1.2	0.6
47 055	Giles	25,741	85.9	13.2	0.2	0.2	<.1	0.4	48	80	16	50	0.5	0.5	0.4	0.3
47 057	Grainger	17,095	98.9	0.6	<.1	0.2	0.0	0.2	63	15	79	91	0.4	0.4	<.1	0.1
47 059	Greene	55,853	97.3	2.2	0.1	0.2	<.1	0.3	16	35	58	83	1.1	1.3	0.2	0.5
47 061	Grundy	13,362	99.1	0.1	<.1	0.2	0.0	0.5	77	12	85	32	0.3	0.3	<.1	0.2
47 063	Hamblen	50,480	94.6	4.6	0.2	0.2	<.1	0.3	21	56	38	75	1.0	1.2	0.3	0.5
47 065	Hamilton	285,536	79.2	19.0	0.8	0.2	<.1	0.7	4	85	11	10	5.9	5.6	7.0	5.9
47 067	Hancock	6,739	97.4	1.8	<.1	0.3	<.1	0.5	90	33	64	28	0.1	0.2	<.1	0.1
47 069	Hardeman	23,377	61.6	37.3	0.3	<.1	<.1	0.7	53	92	4	9	0.5	0.4	1.1	0.5
47 071	Hardin	22,633	94.9	4.4	0.2	0.2	<.1	0.4	54	54	39	65	0.5	0.5	0.1	0.3
47 073	Hawkins	44,565	97.7	1.7	0.1	0.2	<.1	0.3	24	27	67	82	0.9	1.1	<.1	0.4
47 075	Haywood	19,437	49.5	49.5	<.1	0.1	<.1	0.8	59	95	1	6	0.4	0.2	1.2	0.5
47 077	Henderson	21,844	91.1	8.2	<.1	<.1	<.1	0.5	56	68	28	41	0.4	0.5	0.2	0.3
47 079	Henry	27,888	89.1	10.1	0.2	0.2	<.1	0.4	44	72	22	61	0.6	0.6	0.4	0.3
47 081	Hickman	16,754	94.2	5.1	<.1	0.2	<.1	0.4	64	60	35	58	0.3	0.4	0.1	0.2
47 083	Houston	7,018	95.5	3.8	<.1	0.1	0.0	0.6	89	48	45	17	0.1	0.2	<.1	0.1
47 085	Humphreys	15,795	95.7	3.5	0.2	0.2	<.1	0.4	67	45	49	60	0.3	0.4	<.1	0.2
47 087	Jackson	9,297	99.1	<.1	0.2	0.2	<.1	0.4	83	13	88	56	0.2	0.2	<.1	0.1
47 089	Jefferson	33,016	96.5	2.8	0.1	0.2	<.1	0.3	35	41	54	81	0.7	0.8	0.1	0.3
47 091	Johnson	13,766	99.1	0.4	0.1	0.1	<.1	0.2	73	11	80	92	0.3	0.3	<.1	<.1
47 093	Knox	335,749	89.4	8.8	1.0	0.2	<.1	0.6	3	71	26	14	6.9	7.4	3.8	6.3
47 095	Lake	7,129	75.9	23.7	<.1	<.1	0.0	0.4	88	87	7	66	0.1	0.1	0.2	<.1
47 097	Lauderdale	23,491	67.7	30.9	<.1	0.5	<.1	0.8	52	91	5	8	0.5	0.4	0.9	0.5
47 099	Lawrence	35,303	97.9	1.4	0.2	0.2	0.0	0.4	29	24	72	54	0.7	0.9	<.1	0.4
47 101	Lewis	9,247	97.7	1.3	<.1	0.3	<.1	0.6	84	28	73	18	0.2	0.2	<.1	0.2
47 103	Lincoln	28,157	90.6	8.6	0.2	0.1	<.1	0.5	43	69	27	37	0.6	0.6	0.3	0.4
47 105	Loudon	31,255	98.1	1.3	0.2	0.2	<.1	0.3	39	20	74	88	0.6	0.8	<.1	0.3
47 107	McMinn	42,383	94.3	4.8	0.3	0.2	<.1	0.4	25	58	37	55	0.9	1.0	0.3	0.5
47 109	McNairy	22,422	92.9	6.4	0.2	<.1	0.0	0.4	55	64	32	48	0.5	0.5	0.2	0.3
47 111	Macon	15,906	99.2	0.3	<.1	0.2	<.1	0.2	66	10	83	90	0.3	0.4	<.1	0.1
47 113	Madison	77,982	68.2	30.9	0.3	<.1	<.1	0.5	12	90	6	38	1.6	1.3	3.1	1.1
47 115	Marion	24,860	95.2	4.1	0.1	0.1	<.1	0.3	50	51	40	77	0.5	0.6	0.1	0.3
47 117	Marshall	21,539	90.4	8.8	0.2	0.1	<.1	0.4	57	70	25	47	0.4	0.5	0.2	0.3
47 119	Maury	54,812	83.3	15.7	0.3	0.1	<.1	0.6	17	82	14	15	1.1	1.1	1.1	1.0
47 121	Meigs	8,033	97.9	1.5	<.1	0.3	0.0	0.2	86	22	71	93	0.2	0.2	<.1	<.1
47 123	Monroe	30,541	96.5	2.7	0.2	0.2	<.1	0.4	40	42	55	57	0.6	0.7	0.1	0.4
47 125	Montgomery	100,498	77.1	17.5	1.7	0.4	<.1	3.2	8	86	12	1	2.1	1.9	2.3	9.9
47 127	Moore	4,721	95.7	3.7	<.1	0.1	0.0	0.4	94	46	47	49	<.1	0.1	<.1	<.1
47 129	Morgan	17,300	97.7	1.5	0.1	0.3	<.1	0.3	62	26	69	76	0.4	0.4	<.1	0.2
47 131	Obion	31,717	89.0	10.2	0.1	0.1	<.1	0.4	38	73	21	44	0.7	0.7	0.4	0.4
47 133	Overton	17,636	99.3	0.2	<.1	<.1	0.0	0.4	61	6	84	52	0.4	0.4	<.1	0.2
47 135	Perry	6,612	97.4	1.8	0.1	0.1	0.0	0.5	91	32	62	24	0.1	0.2	<.1	0.1
47 137	Pickett	4,548	99.6	0.0	<.1	<.1	0.0	0.3	95	2	94	84	<.1	0.1	0.0	<.1
47 139	Polk	13,643	99.2	0.0	0.3	0.2	0.0	0.3	75	8	95	89	0.3	0.3	0.0	0.1

Table A. — 1990 Population by Race and Ethnic Origin (cont)

State/county code	County	Total persons	Percent of total persons						Rank				Percent contribution to state population			
			Non-Hispanic							Percent of total persons				Non-Hispanic		
			White	Black	Asian and Pacific Islander	Native American	Other	Hispanic	Total	Non-Hispanic			Total	White	Black	Hispanic
										White	Black	Hispanic				
47 141	Putnam	51,373	96.7	1.7	0.9	0.2	<.1	0.6	19	39	66	19	1.1	1.2	0.1	0.9
47 143	Rhea	24,344	96.6	2.4	0.2	0.2	<.1	0.5	51	40	57	25	0.5	0.6	<.1	0.4
47 145	Roane	47,227	95.9	3.1	0.4	0.2	<.1	0.4	22	44	53	43	1.0	1.1	0.2	0.6
47 147	Robertson	41,494	88.4	10.9	0.1	0.1	<.1	0.4	26	77	19	51	0.9	0.9	0.6	0.5
47 149	Rutherford	118,570	88.7	8.9	1.4	0.2	<.1	0.8	6	75	24	7	2.4	2.6	1.4	2.8
47 151	Scott	18,358	99.3	<.1	<.1	0.4	<.1	0.2	60	7	89	94	0.4	0.5	<.1	0.1
47 153	Sequatchie	8,863	99.6	<.1	<.1	<.1	0.0	0.3	85	1	90	85	0.2	0.2	<.1	<.1
47 155	Sevier	51,043	98.5	0.4	0.4	0.3	<.1	0.5	20	17	81	40	1.0	1.2	<.1	0.7
47 157	Shelby	826,330	54.6	43.4	0.9	0.2	<.1	0.9	1	94	3	4	16.9	11.2	46.3	21.7
47 159	Smith	14,143	96.1	3.2	<.1	0.3	<.1	0.3	71	43	51	78	0.3	0.3	<.1	0.1
47 161	Stewart	9,479	97.6	1.0	0.3	0.6	<.1	0.5	82	29	75	33	0.2	0.2	<.1	0.1
47 163	Sullivan	143,596	97.3	1.8	0.3	0.2	<.1	0.4	5	34	63	73	2.9	3.5	0.3	1.6
47 165	Sumner	103,281	93.6	5.4	0.3	0.2	<.1	0.5	7	62	34	23	2.1	2.4	0.7	1.7
47 167	Tipton	37,568	75.3	23.5	0.3	0.3	<.1	0.7	28	88	8	11	0.8	0.7	1.1	0.8
47 169	Trousdale	5,920	84.7	14.4	0.1	0.2	<.1	0.5	92	81	15	27	0.1	0.1	0.1	<.1
47 171	Unicoi	16,549	99.2	<.1	<.1	<.1	<.1	0.6	65	9	92	16	0.3	0.4	<.1	0.3
47 173	Union	13,694	99.5	<.1	<.1	0.2	<.1	0.3	74	4	91	86	0.3	0.3	<.1	0.1
47 175	Van Buren	4,846	99.4	0.1	0.0	0.3	0.0	0.2	93	5	87	95	<.1	0.1	<.1	<.1
47 177	Warren	32,992	95.2	3.4	0.3	0.2	<.1	0.8	36	52	50	5	0.7	0.8	0.1	0.8
47 179	Washington	92,315	95.4	3.5	0.4	0.2	<.1	0.5	9	49	48	30	1.9	2.2	0.4	1.4
47 181	Wayne	13,935	98.4	1.0	<.1	0.1	<.1	0.4	72	18	76	69	0.3	0.3	<.1	0.2
47 183	Weakley	31,972	91.6	6.9	0.9	0.1	<.1	0.4	37	67	29	59	0.7	0.7	0.3	0.4
47 185	White	20,090	97.5	1.9	0.1	0.1	<.1	0.4	58	31	61	71	0.4	0.5	<.1	0.2
47 187	Williamson	81,021	92.0	6.6	0.6	0.2	<.1	0.6	11	66	31	13	1.7	1.9	0.7	1.6
47 189	Wilson	67,675	92.0	6.8	0.4	0.3	<.1	0.6	15	65	30	20	1.4	1.5	0.6	1.2
47	**TENNESSEE**	**4,877,185**	**82.6**	**15.9**	**0.6**	**0.2**	**<.1**	**0.7**					**100.0**	**100.0**	**100.0**	**100.0**
	CONGRESSIONAL															
	District 1	541,875	97.2	1.9	0.3	0.2	<.1	0.4	6	1	9	9	11.1	13.1	1.3	6.5
	District 2	541,864	91.9	6.6	0.7	0.2	<.1	0.6	9	4	6	7	11.1	12.4	4.6	9.1
	District 3	541,866	87.0	11.5	0.6	0.2	<.1	0.6	8	5	5	5	11.1	11.7	8.1	10.3
	District 4	541,868	95.5	3.6	0.2	0.2	<.1	0.4	7	2	8	8	11.1	12.8	2.5	7.3
	District 5	541,910	74.9	22.7	1.3	0.2	<.1	0.9	4	8	2	2	11.1	10.1	15.9	15.0
	District 6	541,977	92.9	5.7	0.6	0.2	<.1	0.6	2	3	7	6	11.1	12.5	4.0	9.6
	District 7	541,937	85.5	12.3	0.9	0.2	<.1	1.1	3	6	4	1	11.1	11.5	8.6	18.9
	District 8	541,907	79.1	19.6	0.4	0.2	<.1	0.7	5	7	3	4	11.1	10.6	13.7	11.6
	District 9	541,981	39.3	59.0	0.7	0.1	<.1	0.7	1	9	1	3	11.1	5.3	41.3	11.7

Table B. — 1990 Voting Age Population (VAP) by Race and Ethnic Origin

County	Total Voting Age Population	Percent of total VAP — Non-Hispanic: White	Black	Asian and Pacific Islander	Native American	Other	Hispanic	Rank — Percent of total VAP: Total	Non-Hispanic White	Non-Hispanic Black	Hispanic	Percent contribution to state VAP: Total	Non-Hispanic White	Non-Hispanic Black	Hispanic	VAP percent of total population: Total	Non-Hispanic White	Black	Asian and Pacific Islander	Native American	Other	Hispanic
Anderson	51,916	94.9	3.5	0.7	0.3	<.1	0.5	14	57	45	22	1.4	1.6	0.3	1.1	76.1	76.6	66.6	70.6	76.3	13.0	64.6
Bedford	22,696	89.4	9.5	0.4	0.1	0.0	0.5	41	75	20	19	0.6	0.7	0.4	0.5	74.6	75.1	70.9	69.5	79.4	0.0	65.1
Benton	11,184	97.1	2.2	0.2	0.2	<.1	0.4	68	36	58	46	0.3	0.4	<.1	0.2	77.0	77.3	69.9	58.1	87.0	66.7	58.3
Bledsoe	7,301	95.1	4.1	<.1	0.4	0.0	0.4	82	55	39	48	0.2	0.2	<.1	0.1	75.5	75.4	79.6	66.7	69.0	0.0	71.1
Blount	66,307	95.9	3.0	0.4	0.2	<.1	0.4	10	46	52	43	1.8	2.1	0.4	1.1	77.1	77.4	72.1	67.9	77.9	36.8	69.6
Bradley	55,464	95.0	3.6	0.3	0.2	<.1	0.8	13	56	44	5	1.5	1.7	0.4	2.1	75.2	75.6	69.3	75.7	66.5	33.3	65.9
Campbell	26,076	98.8	0.4	<.1	0.5	0.0	0.3	32	16	82	74	0.7	0.8	<.1	0.3	74.3	74.4	73.8	65.7	69.1	0.0	65.0
Cannon	7,830	97.9	1.7	0.1	0.1	0.0	0.3	80	26	66	85	0.2	0.2	<.1	<.1	74.8	75.0	70.7	57.1	66.7	0.0	51.3
Carroll	20,983	89.0	10.5	<.1	0.1	<.1	0.4	45	78	17	52	0.6	0.6	0.4	0.3	76.3	77.1	70.4	88.9	79.4	33.3	60.8
Carter	40,116	98.4	0.9	0.2	0.2	<.1	0.3	19	18	78	64	1.1	1.3	<.1	0.6	77.9	78.0	74.9	67.2	83.5	83.3	68.1
Cheatham	19,534	97.0	2.1	0.1	0.4	<.1	0.4	46	37	59	29	0.5	0.6	<.1	0.4	72.0	71.9	77.3	67.6	86.3	18.2	62.6
Chester	9,805	90.0	9.3	0.1	0.2	<.1	0.3	77	74	21	57	0.3	0.3	0.2	0.2	76.5	77.8	66.0	61.9	95.0	20.0	64.2
Claiborne	19,469	98.3	0.9	0.2	0.2	<.1	0.3	47	20	76	68	0.5	0.6	<.1	0.3	74.5	74.7	73.8	35.2	75.0	100.0	73.5
Clay	5,564	97.8	1.7	<.1	0.2	0.0	0.3	87	27	65	73	0.2	0.2	<.1	<.1	76.9	76.8	80.2	100.0	90.9	0.0	63.0
Cocke	22,157	97.2	2.0	<.1	0.2	0.0	0.4	42	35	60	42	0.6	0.7	<.1	0.4	76.0	76.2	73.7	75.0	70.1	0.0	61.8
Coffee	29,960	95.4	3.3	0.5	0.2	<.1	0.5	27	51	47	16	0.8	0.9	0.2	0.7	74.3	74.7	66.6	65.3	70.4	33.3	60.9
Crockett	10,121	84.3	15.3	<.1	<.1	0.0	0.3	75	83	13	63	0.3	0.3	0.3	0.2	75.7	75.4	68.8	50.0	100.0	0.0	69.4
Cumberland	26,615	99.1	0.1	0.1	0.4	<.1	0.3	28	14	86	81	0.7	0.9	<.1	0.3	76.6	76.7	90.5	58.7	79.4	50.0	59.7
Davidson	394,243	76.7	20.9	1.2	0.2	<.1	0.9	2	88	9	3	10.8	9.8	15.8	15.0	77.2	79.8	69.5	70.2	77.4	41.0	70.6
Decatur	8,080	95.4	3.8	0.2	0.3	0.0	0.4	79	52	43	40	0.2	0.2	<.1	0.1	77.2	77.4	72.9	71.4	95.7	0.0	67.3
DeKalb	10,898	98.0	1.4	<.1	0.1	<.1	0.4	69	24	71	55	0.3	0.3	<.1	0.2	75.9	76.0	72.1	75.0	84.2	33.3	62.9
Dickson	25,485	94.7	4.5	0.2	0.2	0.0	0.4	35	60	36	33	0.7	0.8	0.2	0.5	72.7	73.1	66.3	66.2	79.4	0.0	63.3
Dyer	25,947	88.9	10.5	0.2	0.2	<.1	0.2	33	79	18	72	0.7	0.7	0.5	0.4	74.4	75.7	65.8	74.1	73.8	40.0	58.4
Fayette	17,918	59.1	40.2	<.1	0.1	0.0	0.5	51	93	2	23	0.5	0.3	1.4	0.4	70.1	74.8	64.2	66.7	78.1	0.0	65.4
Fentress	10,840	99.5	<.1	0.1	<.1	<.1	0.3	70	4	91	79	0.3	0.3	<.1	0.1	73.9	73.9	100.0	83.3	88.9	100.0	79.5
Franklin	26,195	93.4	5.7	0.3	0.2	<.1	0.3	29	64	33	25	0.7	0.8	0.3	0.5	75.4	75.8	71.3	73.7	84.3	35.7	64.7
Gibson	35,264	82.2	17.2	0.1	<.1	<.1	0.3	23	84	10	60	1.0	0.9	1.2	0.5	76.1	78.1	68.1	66.1	78.4	0.0	66.3
Giles	19,312	86.7	12.4	0.3	0.2	<.1	0.4	48	80	16	37	0.5	0.5	0.5	0.4	75.7	75.7	70.6	82.0	78.4	100.0	74.3
Grainger	12,924	98.8	0.7	<.1	0.2	0.0	0.3	63	15	79	88	0.4	0.4	<.1	0.1	75.6	75.6	85.3	37.5	76.2	0.0	75.6
Greene	43,056	97.5	2.0	0.1	0.2	<.1	0.2	16	33	62	86	1.2	1.4	0.2	0.5	77.1	77.3	70.5	63.8	78.7	28.6	65.0
Grundy	9,644	99.1	0.1	<.1	0.2	0.0	0.5	78	12	85	27	0.3	0.3	<.1	0.2	72.2	72.2	77.8	66.7	81.5	0.0	64.7
Hamblen	38,398	94.9	4.4	0.2	0.1	<.1	0.3	21	58	37	80	1.0	1.2	0.3	0.5	76.1	76.3	73.8	73.8	67.5	15.4	62.3
Hamilton	216,526	81.3	17.1	0.8	0.2	<.1	0.7	4	85	11	10	5.9	5.7	7.1	6.4	75.8	77.8	68.3	67.9	76.5	28.8	73.3
Hancock	5,038	96.9	2.3	0.0	0.3	<.1	0.5	90	39	56	15	0.1	0.2	<.1	0.1	74.8	74.4	96.6	0.0	72.2	100.0	77.1
Hardeman	16,756	65.6	33.4	0.2	<.1	<.1	0.8	55	92	4	6	0.5	0.4	1.1	0.6	71.7	76.3	64.1	69.5	58.8	33.3	72.0
Hardin	16,981	95.3	4.1	0.1	0.1	<.1	0.4	53	54	40	44	0.5	0.5	0.1	0.3	75.0	75.3	69.8	67.6	67.6	50.0	73.6
Hawkins	33,971	97.8	1.6	0.1	0.1	<.1	0.3	24	28	68	78	0.9	1.1	0.1	0.4	76.2	76.3	75.5	66.1	63.6	50.0	73.1
Haywood	13,799	53.1	45.9	<.1	0.1	<.1	0.7	59	95	1	7	0.4	0.2	1.2	0.5	71.0	76.2	65.9	46.2	83.3	100.0	65.4
Henderson	16,392	91.6	7.9	<.1	<.1	0.0	0.4	56	68	28	36	0.4	0.5	0.2	0.3	75.0	75.4	71.6	56.3	75.0	0.0	69.0
Henry	21,517	90.1	9.2	0.2	0.2	<.1	0.3	43	73	22	61	0.6	0.6	0.4	0.3	77.2	78.0	70.6	78.4	76.0	33.3	66.4
Hickman	12,735	93.5	5.9	<.1	0.2	0.0	0.3	65	63	32	66	0.3	0.4	0.1	0.2	76.0	75.4	88.1	75.0	73.7	0.0	61.2
Houston	5,327	95.8	3.5	<.1	0.1	0.0	0.5	89	47	46	17	0.1	0.2	<.1	0.1	75.9	76.2	70.1	75.0	87.5	0.0	68.3
Humphreys	11,824	96.1	3.2	0.2	0.2	<.1	0.3	67	45	51	67	0.3	0.4	<.1	0.2	74.9	75.1	68.7	78.1	92.3	100.0	60.3
Jackson	7,183	99.1	<.1	0.1	0.2	<.1	0.4	83	11	88	38	0.2	0.2	<.1	0.1	77.3	77.3	100.0	52.6	68.4	100.0	78.9
Jefferson	25,778	96.7	2.7	0.1	0.2	<.1	0.3	34	41	55	75	0.7	0.8	0.1	0.3	78.1	78.2	74.7	67.5	84.0	46.2	75.0
Johnson	10,575	99.1	0.5	<.1	0.1	0.0	0.2	72	13	80	94	0.3	0.3	<.1	<.1	76.8	76.8	86.9	71.4	100.0	0.0	62.5
Knox	260,637	90.4	7.9	0.9	0.2	<.1	0.5	3	72	26	13	7.1	7.6	3.9	6.4	77.6	78.5	69.9	72.0	77.8	28.1	69.0
Lake	5,564	76.2	23.4	<.1	<.1	0.0	0.4	88	89	7	45	0.2	0.1	0.2	<.1	78.0	78.4	77.0	100.0	75.0	0.0	77.8
Lauderdale	17,088	70.5	28.2	<.1	0.5	0.0	0.7	52	91	5	8	0.5	0.4	0.9	0.5	72.7	75.7	66.6	50.0	63.0	0.0	68.0
Lawrence	26,088	98.0	1.3	0.2	0.2	0.0	0.3	30	23	72	59	0.7	0.8	<.1	0.4	73.9	74.0	71.0	61.1	79.7	0.0	62.1
Lewis	6,768	97.9	1.3	<.1	0.3	<.1	0.5	84	25	73	26	0.2	0.2	<.1	0.1	73.2	73.3	71.4	42.9	75.0	75.0	57.4
Lincoln	21,177	91.3	7.9	0.2	0.1	<.1	0.4	44	69	27	35	0.6	0.6	0.3	0.4	75.2	75.8	69.2	71.4	78.9	100.0	66.4
Loudon	23,923	98.3	1.2	0.1	0.2	0.0	0.3	38	21	74	90	0.7	0.8	<.1	0.2	76.5	76.7	71.8	55.1	80.8	0.0	62.7
McMinn	32,009	94.8	4.4	0.2	0.2	<.1	0.4	25	59	38	49	0.9	1.0	0.3	0.5	75.5	76.0	68.4	63.3	80.0	25.0	67.8
McNairy	16,919	93.8	5.6	0.1	0.1	0.0	0.4	54	62	34	53	0.5	0.5	0.2	0.3	75.6	76.1	66.6	62.5	90.5	0.0	64.2
Macon	11,882	99.3	0.3	<.1	0.2	<.1	0.3	66	10	83	93	0.3	0.4	<.1	0.1	74.7	74.7	77.3	70.0	67.6	100.0	59.0
Madison	57,657	71.4	27.7	0.3	<.1	<.1	0.4	11	90	6	31	1.6	1.3	3.1	1.1	73.9	77.4	66.5	71.4	76.6	61.5	67.6
Marion	18,333	95.4	4.0	0.1	0.1	0.0	0.2	49	50	41	87	0.5	0.6	0.1	0.2	73.7	73.9	72.1	77.4	72.2	0.0	52.9
Marshall	16,085	90.9	8.5	0.2	0.1	0.0	0.5	57	70	24	65	0.4	0.5	0.3	0.2	74.7	75.1	71.4	69.8	75.0	0.0	56.5
Maury	40,534	84.4	14.8	0.2	0.1	<.1	0.5	17	82	14	24	1.1	1.1	1.1	0.9	74.0	74.9	69.7	64.7	65.7	28.6	59.1
Meigs	6,036	98.0	1.5	<.1	0.3	0.0	0.2	86	22	70	95	0.2	0.2	<.1	<.1	75.1	75.2	75.4	100.0	64.3	0.0	64.7
Monroe	22,810	96.5	2.7	0.2	0.1	<.1	0.3	40	42	54	58	0.6	0.7	0.1	0.4	74.7	74.7	74.5	78.6	72.3	50.0	64.2
Montgomery	73,865	78.4	16.6	1.7	0.4	<.1	2.9	8	86	12	1	2.0	1.9	2.3	9.5	73.5	74.7	69.7	73.1	75.1	29.9	66.0
Moore	3,518	95.6	3.9	<.1	0.2	0.0	0.3	94	49	42	69	<.1	0.1	<.1	<.1	74.4	74.4	79.3	50.0	85.7	0.0	66.0
Morgan	12,838	97.3	2.0	0.1	0.2	<.1	0.3	64	34	61	84	0.4	0.4	<.1	0.1	74.2	73.9	98.5	70.8	71.1	100.0	55.0
Obion	23,880	90.4	8.9	0.1	0.2	<.1	0.4	39	71	23	50	0.7	0.7	0.4	0.4	75.5	76.5	65.8	59.6	76.6	16.7	62.0
Overton	13,394	99.4	0.2	<.1	<.1	0.0	0.3	60	7	84	39	0.4	0.4	<.1	0.2	75.9	76.0	73.3	50.0	70.0	0.0	75.3
Perry	4,952	97.7	1.6	0.1	0.1	0.0	0.5	91	30	69	18	0.1	0.2	<.1	0.1	74.9	75.1	64.7	85.7	75.0	0.0	72.2
Pickett	3,431	99.5	0.0	<.1	0.1	0.0	0.3	95	3	93	76	<.1	0.1	0.0	<.1	75.4	75.4	0.0	100.0	100.0	0.0	76.9
Polk	10,349	99.3	0.0	0.3	0.2	0.0	0.3	74	9	94	83	0.3	0.3	0.0	0.1	75.9	75.9	0.0	64.3	72.0	0.0	75.0

Table B. — 1990 Voting Age Population (VAP) by Race and Ethnic Origin (cont)

County	Total Voting Age Population	Percent of total VAP (Non-Hispanic) White	Black	Asian and Pacific Islander	Native American	Other	Hispanic	Rank Total	Rank White (NH)	Rank Black (NH)	Rank Hispanic	Pct contrib to state VAP Total	White (NH)	Black (NH)	Hispanic	VAP pct of total pop Total	White (NH)	Black	Asian and Pacific Islander	Native American	Other	Hispanic
Putnam	40,128	96.7	1.7	0.9	0.1	<.1	0.5	18	40	64	14	1.1	1.3	0.1	1.0	78.1	78.1	78.7	79.5	74.7	61.5	73.8
Rhea	18,186	96.9	2.2	0.2	0.2	<.1	0.4	50	38	57	41	0.5	0.6	<.1	0.3	74.7	74.9	70.2	76.9	72.2	63.6	56.1
Roane	36,120	96.2	2.8	0.4	0.2	<.1	0.4	22	43	53	56	1.0	1.1	0.2	0.6	76.5	76.8	70.0	69.4	81.1	75.0	60.4
Robertson	30,109	89.0	10.3	0.1	0.2	<.1	0.4	26	77	19	54	0.8	0.9	0.6	0.5	72.6	73.1	68.6	73.8	81.4	33.3	62.4
Rutherford	86,797	89.4	8.4	1.2	0.2	<.1	0.7	6	76	25	9	2.4	2.5	1.4	2.7	73.2	73.8	69.2	65.4	80.3	38.8	65.3
Scott	12,977	99.3	<.1	<.1	0.3	<.1	0.2	61	8	89	91	0.4	0.4	<.1	0.1	70.7	70.7	100.0	81.8	67.2	100.0	68.4
Sequatchie	6,577	99.6	0.0	<.1	<.1	0.0	0.3	85	1	95	77	0.2	0.2	0.0	<.1	74.2	74.2	0.0	60.0	75.0	0.0	76.0
Sevier	38,834	98.7	0.4	0.4	0.2	<.1	0.4	20	17	81	47	1.1	1.2	<.1	0.6	76.1	76.2	69.3	70.5	71.1	50.0	61.6
Shelby	600,023	58.5	39.5	0.9	0.2	<.1	0.9	1	94	3	2	16.4	11.4	45.3	23.1	72.6	77.8	66.1	70.5	75.4	36.3	73.1
Smith	10,604	96.1	3.3	<.1	0.2	<.1	0.3	71	44	49	70	0.3	0.3	<.1	0.1	75.0	75.0	75.8	33.3	69.4	50.0	68.8
Stewart	7,373	97.8	0.9	0.3	0.6	<.1	0.4	81	29	77	34	0.2	0.2	<.1	0.1	77.8	77.9	71.9	80.0	73.2	50.0	66.7
Sullivan	111,342	97.5	1.6	0.3	0.2	<.1	0.3	5	32	67	71	3.0	3.5	0.4	1.5	77.5	77.7	71.9	66.6	70.4	11.1	66.2
Sumner	74,833	94.0	5.0	0.3	0.2	<.1	0.5	7	61	35	21	2.0	2.3	0.7	1.6	69.4	71.7	62.4	64.3	73.5	26.7	64.2
Tipton	26,081	77.8	21.1	0.3	0.3	<.1	0.6	31	87	8	12	0.7	0.7	1.1	0.7	72.5	72.8	67.6	68.8	67.0	25.0	60.5
Trousdale	4,499	85.0	14.3	<.1	0.2	0.0	0.4	92	81	15	30	0.1	0.1	0.1	<.1	76.0	76.2	75.6	50.0	71.4	0.0	64.5
Unicoi	12,952	99.4	<.1	0.1	<.1	<.1	0.4	62	6	90	32	0.4	0.4	<.1	0.3	78.3	78.4	100.0	92.9	50.0	50.0	58.8
Union	10,025	99.5	<.1	<.1	0.2	<.1	0.2	76	2	92	89	0.3	0.3	<.1	<.1	73.2	73.2	33.3	100.0	73.9	100.0	57.9
Van Buren	3,573	99.4	0.1	0.0	0.3	0.0	0.2	93	5	87	92	<.1	0.1	<.1	<.1	73.7	73.8	80.0	0.0	62.5	0.0	70.0
Warren	24,698	95.4	3.3	0.3	0.2	<.1	0.9	37	53	48	4	0.7	0.8	0.2	0.9	74.9	75.0	72.4	66.1	76.5	54.5	76.1
Washington	72,230	95.8	3.2	0.4	0.2	<.1	0.4	9	48	50	28	2.0	2.2	0.4	1.4	78.2	78.6	70.8	77.5	79.5	35.7	68.4
Wayne	10,359	98.4	1.0	<.1	0.1	<.1	0.3	73	19	75	62	0.3	0.3	<.1	0.2	74.3	74.3	78.8	88.9	73.3	100.0	67.3
Weakley	24,935	91.7	6.8	1.0	0.1	<.1	0.4	36	67	29	51	0.7	0.7	0.3	0.4	78.0	78.0	76.1	90.2	92.3	43.8	71.9
White	15,286	97.6	1.9	0.1	0.1	<.1	0.3	58	31	63	82	0.4	0.5	<.1	0.2	76.1	76.1	77.0	76.0	79.2	100.0	56.8
Williamson	57,463	92.3	6.5	0.5	0.1	<.1	0.6	12	66	31	11	1.6	1.7	0.7	1.5	70.9	71.2	69.5	58.8	65.4	27.3	65.9
Wilson	49,136	92.4	6.5	0.3	0.3	<.1	0.5	15	65	30	20	1.3	1.5	0.6	1.1	72.6	72.9	69.7	60.7	77.0	25.0	62.7
TENNESSEE	3,660,581	84.3	14.3	0.6	0.2	<.1	0.6					100.0	100.0	100.0	100.0	75.1	76.6	67.6	69.9	75.6	37.0	68.6
CONGRESSIONAL																						
District 1	418,894	97.5	1.8	0.2	0.2	<.1	0.3	1	1	9	9	11.4	13.2	1.4	6.3	77.3	77.5	72.5	70.4	74.2	37.3	66.6
District 2	416,775	92.6	6.0	0.7	0.2	<.1	0.5	2	4	6	7	11.4	12.5	4.8	9.1	76.9	77.5	70.0	71.3	77.2	31.5	68.5
District 3	410,195	88.2	10.5	0.6	0.2	<.1	0.6	4	5	5	5	11.2	11.7	8.2	10.4	75.7	76.8	68.5	68.8	74.6	26.9	69.4
District 4	405,759	95.7	3.4	0.2	0.2	<.1	0.4	5	2	8	8	11.1	12.6	2.7	7.0	74.9	75.1	71.3	66.8	74.8	52.9	65.9
District 5	416,547	77.2	20.5	1.2	0.2	<.1	0.8	3	8	2	2	11.4	10.4	16.3	15.4	76.9	79.3	69.5	70.2	77.7	41.0	70.3
District 6	399,124	93.3	5.4	0.5	0.2	<.1	0.5	7	3	7	6	10.9	12.1	4.1	9.2	73.6	74.0	69.8	65.9	74.5	38.5	65.7
District 7	396,773	86.5	11.5	0.8	0.2	<.1	1.0	8	6	4	1	10.8	11.1	8.7	18.4	73.2	74.1	68.3	69.1	75.8	34.1	66.9
District 8	402,139	81.5	17.3	0.4	0.2	<.1	0.6	6	7	3	4	11.0	10.6	13.3	11.4	74.2	76.5	65.5	73.2	74.3	36.7	67.3
District 9	394,375	44.5	53.9	0.7	0.2	<.1	0.7	9	9	1	3	10.8	5.7	40.6	12.8	72.8	82.3	66.4	72.5	77.3	35.7	75.2

Table C. — Voter Participation: November 3, 1992, General Election

| County | Estimated Voting Age Population (VAP), 1992 | Voter registration (REG) | | | | Voter turnout | | | | | | | | | | | | | |
| | | Total | % contribution to state REG | % of 1992 VAP | Rank by % of 1992 VAP | Highest office | | | | Maximum vote | | | | | | Percent drop-off, by office[1] | | | |
						Actual	Total	Office	% of 1992 VAP	Total	% contribution to state turnout	% of REG	Rank by % of REG	% of 1992 VAP	Rank by % 1992 VAP	President	Senator	Governor	Representative
Anderson	53,081	36,402	1.3	68.6	68	-	28,611	P	53.9	28,611	1.4	78.6	8	53.9	30	0.0	-	-	8.5
Bedford	23,738	15,324	0.6	64.6	83	-	11,421	P	48.1	11,421	0.6	74.5	29	48.1	71	0.0	-	-	17.4
Benton	11,394	9,290	0.3	81.5	18	-	6,114	P	53.7	6,114	0.3	65.8	67	53.7	34	0.0	-	-	24.1
Bledsoe	7,468	6,357	0.2	85.1	13	-	4,018	P	53.8	4,018	0.2	63.2	82	53.8	32	0.0	-	-	0.3
Blount	69,084	51,642	1.9	74.8	37	-	37,651	P	54.5	37,651	1.9	72.9	40	54.5	25	0.0	-	-	9.4
Bradley	57,787	39,687	1.5	68.7	67	-	29,696	P	51.4	29,696	1.5	74.8	27	51.4	49	0.0	-	-	5.7
Campbell	26,947	19,817	0.7	73.5	44	-	12,931	P	48.0	12,931	0.7	65.3	70	48.0	72	0.0	-	-	39.9
Cannon	8,035	5,783	0.2	72.0	48	-	4,331	P	53.9	4,331	0.2	74.9	26	53.9	29	0.0	-	-	8.3
Carroll	21,117	16,080	0.6	76.1	35	-	11,799	P	55.9	11,799	0.6	73.4	35	55.9	17	0.0	-	-	38.1
Carter	40,976	25,473	0.9	62.2	90	-	19,190	P	46.8	19,190	1.0	75.3	21	46.8	81	0.0	-	-	24.9
Cheatham	21,311	12,470	0.5	58.5	94	-	9,788	P	45.9	9,788	0.5	78.5	9	45.9	86	0.0	-	-	12.8
Chester	9,741	7,806	0.3	80.1	24	-	5,596	P	57.4	5,596	0.3	71.7	47	57.4	10	0.0	-	-	16.4
Claiborne	20,297	14,861	0.5	73.2	45	-	9,485	P	46.7	9,485	0.5	63.8	79	46.7	82	0.0	-	-	31.2
Clay	5,636	4,954	0.2	87.9	8	-	3,226	P	57.2	3,226	0.2	65.1	72	57.2	12	0.0	-	-	20.8
Cocke	22,849	15,879	0.6	69.5	62	-	10,000	P	43.8	10,000	0.5	63.0	84	43.8	92	0.0	-	-	24.4
Coffee	30,927	22,084	0.8	71.4	52	-	17,044	P	55.1	17,044	0.9	77.2	13	55.1	24	0.0	-	-	26.3
Crockett	10,051	8,230	0.3	81.9	17	-	5,357	P	53.3	5,357	0.3	65.1	73	53.3	36	0.0	-	-	20.4
Cumberland	28,401	21,120	0.8	74.4	40	-	15,792	P	55.6	15,792	0.8	74.8	28	55.6	21	0.0	-	-	25.4
Davidson	404,308	278,359	10.2	68.8	66	-	203,807	P	50.4	203,807	10.3	73.2	36	50.4	54	0.0	-	-	12.5
Decatur	8,205	6,737	0.2	82.1	15	-	4,661	P	56.8	4,661	0.2	69.2	60	56.8	13	0.0	-	-	13.1
DeKalb	11,343	9,730	0.4	85.8	12	-	6,722	P	59.3	6,722	0.3	69.1	61	59.3	5	0.0	-	-	14.5
Dickson	27,195	18,754	0.7	69.0	65	-	14,093	P	51.8	14,093	0.7	75.1	23	51.8	44	0.0	-	-	20.1
Dyer	26,557	19,550	0.7	73.6	43	-	12,787	P	48.1	12,787	0.6	65.4	69	48.1	70	0.0	-	-	14.9
Fayette	18,531	12,780	0.5	69.0	64	-	8,609	P	46.5	8,609	0.4	67.4	64	46.5	84	0.0	-	-	9.1
Fentress	11,169	9,160	0.3	82.0	16	-	5,759	P	51.6	5,759	0.3	62.9	85	51.6	47	0.0	-	-	34.0
Franklin	27,068	19,373	0.7	71.6	50	-	14,176	P	52.4	14,176	0.7	73.2	38	52.4	42	0.0	-	-	24.2
Gibson	35,430	24,231	0.9	68.4	71	-	18,332	P	51.7	18,332	0.9	75.7	18	51.7	45	0.0	-	-	35.4
Giles	19,871	15,161	0.6	76.3	34	-	9,781	P	49.2	9,781	0.5	64.5	77	49.2	60	0.0	-	-	23.5
Grainger	13,289	8,767	0.3	66.0	78	-	5,553	P	41.8	5,553	0.3	63.3	81	41.8	93	0.0	-	-	29.5
Greene	44,332	27,845	1.0	62.8	87	-	20,875	P	47.1	20,875	1.1	75.0	25	47.1	77	0.0	-	-	18.8
Grundy	9,902	6,187	0.2	62.5	89	-	4,386	P	44.3	4,386	0.2	70.9	49	44.3	91	0.0	-	-	12.2
Hamblen	39,516	26,190	1.0	66.3	76	-	17,854	P	45.2	17,854	0.9	68.2	62	45.2	89	0.0	-	-	10.1
Hamilton	219,655	162,534	6.0	74.0	42	-	118,395	C	53.9	118,395	6.0	72.8	42	53.9	31	2.8	-	-	0.0
Hancock	5,132	5,007	0.2	97.6	4	-	2,449	P	47.7	2,449	0.1	48.9	95	47.7	75	0.0	-	-	33.6
Hardeman	17,064	13,281	0.5	77.8	29	-	8,627	P	50.6	8,627	0.4	65.0	74	50.6	52	0.0	-	-	28.5
Hardin	17,495	12,206	0.4	69.8	59	-	8,592	P	49.1	8,592	0.4	70.4	51	49.1	61	0.0	-	-	37.1
Hawkins	34,962	22,954	0.8	65.7	79	-	16,285	P	46.6	16,285	0.8	70.9	48	46.6	83	0.0	-	-	17.0
Haywood	14,038	10,019	0.4	71.4	53	-	6,376	P	45.4	6,376	0.3	63.6	80	45.4	88	0.0	-	-	21.5
Henderson	16,849	13,473	0.5	80.0	26	-	9,024	P	53.6	9,024	0.5	67.0	65	53.6	35	0.0	-	-	20.1
Henry	21,739	15,352	0.6	70.6	55	-	12,095	P	55.6	12,095	0.6	78.8	5	55.6	19	0.0	-	-	32.4
Hickman	13,325	9,626	0.4	72.2	47	-	6,727	P	50.5	6,727	0.3	69.9	55	50.5	53	0.0	-	-	12.9
Houston	5,440	3,892	0.1	71.5	51	-	2,951	P	54.2	2,951	0.1	75.8	17	54.2	27	0.0	-	-	41.6
Humphreys	12,081	9,454	0.3	78.3	28	-	6,135	P	50.8	6,135	0.3	64.9	75	50.8	50	0.0	-	-	30.9
Jackson	7,318	6,422	0.2	87.8	9	-	4,258	P	58.2	4,258	0.2	66.3	66	58.2	9	0.0	-	-	12.0
Jefferson	26,367	15,592	0.6	59.1	93	-	12,362	P	46.9	12,362	0.6	79.3	4	46.9	80	0.0	-	-	25.8
Johnson	10,822	7,633	0.3	70.5	56	-	5,563	P	51.4	5,563	0.3	72.9	41	51.4	48	0.0	-	-	17.8
Knox	265,389	187,762	6.9	70.7	54	-	142,476	P	53.7	142,476	7.2	75.9	16	53.7	33	0.0	-	-	10.4
Lake	5,618	3,517	0.1	62.6	88	-	2,306	P	41.0	2,306	0.1	65.6	68	41.0	94	0.0	-	-	30.3
Lauderdale	17,370	13,308	0.5	76.6	33	-	7,958	P	45.8	7,958	0.4	59.8	90	45.8	87	0.0	-	-	16.8
Lawrence	26,853	18,367	0.7	68.4	70	-	13,864	P	51.6	13,864	0.7	75.5	20	51.6	46	0.0	-	-	30.4
Lewis	6,854	5,986	0.2	87.3	10	-	4,152	P	60.6	4,152	0.2	69.4	59	60.6	4	0.0	-	-	24.5
Lincoln	21,936	13,554	0.5	61.8	92	-	10,302	P	47.0	10,302	0.5	76.0	15	47.0	79	0.0	-	-	22.1
Loudon	25,058	18,787	0.7	75.0	36	-	13,510	P	53.9	13,510	0.7	71.9	44	53.9	28	0.0	-	-	14.9
McMinn	32,830	21,787	0.8	66.4	74	-	15,990	P	48.7	15,990	0.8	73.4	34	48.7	67	0.0	-	-	7.9
McNairy	17,327	12,879	0.5	74.3	41	-	9,595	P	55.4	9,595	0.5	74.5	30	55.4	22	0.0	-	-	14.3
Macon	12,187	9,363	0.3	76.8	31	-	5,726	P	47.0	5,726	0.3	61.2	86	47.0	78	0.0	-	-	16.6
Madison	59,040	43,129	1.6	73.1	46	-	31,196	P	52.8	31,196	1.6	72.3	43	52.8	38	0.0	-	-	11.8
Marion	19,024	20,116	0.7	105.7	1	-	10,323	C	54.3	10,323	0.5	51.3	94	54.3	26	2.5	-	-	0.0
Marshall	16,911	10,643	0.4	62.9	86	-	8,098	P	47.9	8,098	0.4	76.1	14	47.9	74	0.0	-	-	7.0
Maury	42,126	27,635	1.0	65.6	80	-	20,459	P	48.6	20,459	1.0	74.0	31	48.6	66	0.0	-	-	17.5
Meigs	6,303	5,788	0.2	91.8	6	-	3,484	P	55.3	3,484	0.2	60.2	89	55.3	23	0.0	-	-	8.5
Monroe	23,635	19,044	0.7	80.6	22	-	12,411	P	52.5	12,411	0.6	65.2	71	52.5	40	0.0	-	-	14.8
Montgomery	77,994	39,461	1.4	50.6	95	-	31,341	P	40.2	31,341	1.6	79.4	3	40.2	95	0.0	-	-	9.3
Moore	3,650	2,934	0.1	80.4	23	-	2,145	P	58.8	2,145	0.1	73.1	39	58.8	7	0.0	-	-	25.6
Morgan	13,384	8,872	0.3	66.3	75	-	6,184	P	46.2	6,184	0.3	69.7	57	46.2	85	0.0	-	-	16.8
Obion	24,486	17,098	0.6	69.8	58	-	12,864	P	52.5	12,864	0.6	75.2	22	52.5	39	0.0	-	-	25.5
Overton	13,771	9,551	0.4	69.4	63	-	6,651	P	48.3	6,651	0.3	69.6	58	48.3	69	0.0	-	-	14.1
Perry	5,152	4,175	0.2	81.0	20	-	2,919	P	56.7	2,919	0.1	69.9	54	56.7	14	0.0	-	-	17.6
Pickett	3,510	3,688	0.1	105.1	2	-	2,368	P	67.5	2,368	0.1	64.2	78	67.5	1	0.0	-	-	40.3
Polk	10,697	8,300	0.3	77.6	30	-	5,042	C	47.1	5,042	0.3	60.7	88	47.1	76	8.6	-	-	0.0

[1]Percent drop-off is zero for any office used as highest office turnout.

Table C. – Voter Participation: November 3, 1992, General Election (cont)

County	Estimated Voting Age Population (VAP), 1992	Voter registration (REG)				Voter turnout — Highest office				Voter turnout — Maximum vote						Percent drop-off, by office[1]			
		Total	% contribution to state REG	% of 1992 VAP	Rank by % of 1992 VAP	Actual	Total	Office	% of 1992 VAP	Total	% contribution to state turnout	% of REG	Rank by % of REG	% of 1992 VAP	Rank by % 1992 VAP	President	Senator	Governor	Representative
Putnam	40,609	27,279	1.0	67.2	73	-	21,482	P	52.9	21,482	1.1	78.7	6	52.9	37	0.0	-	-	9.7
Rhea	18,604	14,827	0.5	79.7	27	-	10,348	P	55.6	10,348	0.5	69.8	56	55.6	20	0.0	-	-	27.7
Roane	36,646	36,240	1.3	98.9	3	-	20,999	P	57.3	20,999	1.1	57.9	93	57.3	11	0.0	-	-	7.7
Robertson	31,665	20,436	0.7	64.5	84	-	15,779	P	49.8	15,779	0.8	77.2	12	49.8	57	0.0	-	-	10.5
Rutherford	96,374	62,389	2.3	64.7	82	-	47,140	P	48.9	47,140	2.4	75.6	19	48.9	62	0.0	-	-	4.1
Scott	13,377	10,852	0.4	81.1	19	-	6,418	P	48.0	6,418	0.3	59.1	92	48.0	73	0.0	-	-	32.9
Sequatchie	6,783	5,068	0.2	74.7	38	-	3,559	P	52.5	3,559	0.2	70.2	52	52.5	41	0.0	-	-	2.5
Sevier	41,958	28,772	1.1	68.6	69	-	21,266	P	50.7	21,266	1.1	73.9	32	50.7	51	0.0	-	-	15.6
Shelby	618,812	498,719	18.3	80.6	21	-	366,110	P	59.2	366,110	18.4	73.4	33	59.2	6	0.0	-	-	8.9
Smith	10,688	9,797	0.4	91.7	7	-	7,044	P	65.9	7,044	0.4	71.9	45	65.9	2	0.0	-	-	13.8
Stewart	7,738	5,764	0.2	74.5	39	-	4,323	P	55.9	4,323	0.2	75.0	24	55.9	18	0.0	-	-	39.2
Sullivan	113,238	72,494	2.7	64.0	85	-	56,980	P	50.3	56,980	2.9	78.6	7	50.3	55	0.0	-	-	12.9
Sumner	80,656	52,600	1.9	65.2	81	-	42,132	P	52.2	42,132	2.1	80.1	2	52.2	43	0.0	-	-	10.1
Tipton	27,671	19,403	0.7	70.1	57	-	13,717	P	49.6	13,717	0.7	70.7	50	49.6	59	0.0	-	-	14.5
Trousdale	4,548	3,915	0.1	86.1	11	-	2,664	P	58.6	2,664	0.1	68.0	63	58.6	8	0.0	-	-	13.9
Unicoi	13,254	8,973	0.3	67.7	72	-	6,447	P	48.6	6,447	0.3	71.8	46	48.6	65	0.0	-	-	14.3
Union	10,704	9,025	0.3	84.3	14	-	5,354	P	50.0	5,354	0.3	59.3	91	50.0	56	0.0	-	-	35.8
Van Buren	3,689	3,420	0.1	92.7	5	-	2,080	P	56.4	2,080	0.1	60.8	87	56.4	16	0.0	-	-	30.0
Warren	25,289	17,616	0.6	69.7	60	-	12,355	P	48.9	12,355	0.6	70.1	53	48.9	63	0.0	-	-	23.7
Washington	73,366	45,354	1.7	61.8	91	-	35,483	P	48.4	35,483	1.8	78.2	10	48.4	68	0.0	-	-	20.4
Wayne	10,622	8,147	0.3	76.7	32	-	5,266	P	49.6	5,266	0.3	64.6	76	49.6	58	0.0	-	-	34.2
Weakley	24,478	16,215	0.6	66.2	77	-	11,869	P	48.5	11,869	0.6	73.2	37	48.5	67	0.0	-	-	11.1
White	15,670	11,229	0.4	71.7	49	-	7,074	P	45.1	7,074	0.4	63.0	83	45.1	90	0.0	-	-	12.4
Williamson	64,650	51,756	1.9	80.1	25	-	40,195	P	62.2	40,195	2.0	77.7	11	62.2	3	0.0	-	-	3.8
Wilson	52,963	36,887	1.4	69.6	61	-	29,903	P	56.5	29,903	1.5	81.1	1	56.5	15	0.0	-	-	11.2
TENNESSEE	**3,783,000**	**2,726,449**	**100.0**	**72.1**		-	**1,986,635**		**52.5**	**1,986,635**	**100.0**	**72.9**		**52.5**		**0.2**	-	-	**13.1**

[1]Percent drop-off is zero for any office used as highest office turnout.

Table E. — Vote for President: November 3, 1992, General Election

County	Total	Clinton (DEM)	Bush (REP)	Perot (IND)	Other	Plurality Total	Party	DEM	REP	IND	Other	Rank DEM	Rank REP	Rank IND	Contribution Total	Contribution DEM	Contribution REP	Contribution IND	Major DEM	Major REP
Anderson	28,611	13,482	11,838	3,149	142	1,644	D	47.1	41.4	11.0	0.5	57	42	43	1.4	1.4	1.4	1.6	53.2	46.8
Bedford	11,421	5,978	3,836	1,541	66	2,142	D	52.3	33.6	13.5	0.6	33	68	8	0.6	0.6	0.5	0.8	60.9	39.1
Benton	6,114	3,896	1,625	559	34	2,271	D	63.7	26.6	9.1	0.6	11	86	67	0.3	0.4	0.2	0.3	70.6	29.4
Bledsoe	4,018	1,884	1,776	352	6	108	D	46.9	44.2	8.8	0.1	58	33	72	0.2	0.2	0.2	0.2	51.5	48.5
Blount	37,651	14,655	18,415	4,468	113	3,760	R	38.9	48.9	11.9	0.3	82	18	23	1.9	1.6	2.2	2.2	44.3	55.7
Bradley	29,696	9,889	16,528	3,212	67	6,639	R	33.3	55.7	10.8	0.2	92	4	48	1.5	1.1	2.0	1.6	37.4	62.6
Campbell	12,931	6,756	4,897	1,240	38	1,859	D	52.2	37.9	9.6	0.3	35	55	61	0.7	0.7	0.6	0.6	58.0	42.0
Cannon	4,331	2,593	1,229	495	14	1,364	D	59.9	28.4	11.4	0.3	16	82	32	0.2	0.3	0.1	0.2	67.8	32.2
Carroll	11,799	5,741	4,842	1,139	77	899	D	48.7	41.0	9.7	0.7	51	44	60	0.6	0.6	0.6	0.6	54.2	45.8
Carter	19,190	6,502	10,712	1,898	78	4,210	R	33.9	55.8	9.9	0.4	91	3	57	1.0	0.7	1.3	0.9	37.8	62.2
Cheatham	9,788	4,817	3,496	1,433	42	1,321	D	49.2	35.7	14.6	0.4	45	65	3	0.5	0.5	0.4	0.7	57.9	42.1
Chester	5,596	2,317	2,834	439	6	517	R	41.4	50.6	7.8	0.1	73	12	80	0.3	0.2	0.3	0.2	45.0	55.0
Claiborne	9,485	4,509	4,065	860	51	444	D	47.5	42.9	9.1	0.5	55	35	70	0.5	0.5	0.5	0.4	52.6	47.4
Clay	3,226	1,922	1,072	223	9	850	D	59.6	33.2	6.9	0.3	17	70	88	0.2	0.2	0.1	0.1	64.2	35.8
Cocke	10,000	3,495	5,298	1,124	83	1,803	R	35.0	53.0	11.2	0.8	90	7	40	0.5	0.4	0.6	0.6	39.7	60.3
Coffee	17,044	8,534	6,047	2,420	43	2,487	D	50.1	35.5	14.2	0.3	42	66	4	0.9	0.9	0.7	1.2	58.5	41.5
Crockett	5,357	2,657	2,180	507	13	477	D	49.6	40.7	9.5	0.2	43	45	63	0.3	0.3	0.3	0.3	54.9	45.1
Cumberland	15,792	6,393	7,116	2,200	83	723	R	40.5	45.1	13.9	0.5	78	31	6	0.8	0.7	0.8	1.1	47.3	52.7
Davidson	203,807	106,355	76,567	20,184	701	29,788	D	52.2	37.6	9.9	0.3	36	56	56	10.3	11.4	9.1	10.1	58.1	41.9
Decatur	4,661	2,633	1,667	351	10	966	D	56.5	35.8	7.5	0.2	21	64	85	0.2	0.3	0.2	0.2	61.2	38.8
DeKalb	6,722	4,382	1,714	608	18	2,668	D	65.2	25.5	9.0	0.3	7	87	71	0.3	0.5	0.2	0.3	71.9	28.1
Dickson	14,093	7,863	4,450	1,730	50	3,413	D	55.8	31.6	12.3	0.4	26	73	21	0.7	0.8	0.5	0.9	63.9	36.1
Dyer	12,787	5,845	5,668	1,241	33	177	D	45.7	44.3	9.7	0.3	64	32	59	0.6	0.6	0.7	0.6	50.8	49.2
Fayette	8,609	4,211	3,713	657	28	498	D	48.9	43.1	7.6	0.3	48	34	83	0.4	0.5	0.4	0.3	53.1	46.9
Fentress	5,759	2,730	2,391	606	32	339	D	47.4	41.5	10.5	0.6	56	40	50	0.3	0.3	0.3	0.3	53.3	46.7
Franklin	14,176	7,773	4,507	1,837	59	3,266	D	54.8	31.8	13.0	0.4	30	72	15	0.7	0.8	0.5	0.9	63.3	36.7
Gibson	18,332	9,555	7,161	1,536	80	2,394	D	52.1	39.1	8.4	0.4	37	52	76	0.9	1.0	0.9	0.8	57.2	42.8
Giles	9,781	5,601	2,827	1,309	44	2,774	D	57.3	28.9	13.4	0.4	20	81	9	0.5	0.6	0.3	0.7	66.5	33.5
Grainger	5,553	2,242	2,772	513	26	530	R	40.4	49.9	9.2	0.5	79	15	65	0.3	0.2	0.3	0.3	44.7	55.3
Greene	20,875	7,857	9,912	2,930	176	2,055	R	37.6	47.5	14.0	0.8	85	23	5	1.1	0.8	1.2	1.5	44.2	55.8
Grundy	4,386	2,997	1,004	366	19	1,993	D	68.3	22.9	8.3	0.4	4	91	77	0.2	0.3	0.1	0.2	74.9	25.1
Hamblen	17,854	7,114	8,898	1,760	82	1,784	R	39.8	49.8	9.9	0.5	81	16	58	0.9	0.8	1.1	0.9	44.4	55.6
Hamilton	115,085	46,770	53,476	14,400	439	6,706	R	40.6	46.5	12.5	0.4	77	28	18	5.8	5.0	6.4	7.2	46.7	53.3
Hancock	2,449	1,000	1,274	151	24	274	R	40.8	52.0	6.2	1.0	75	9	92	0.1	0.1	0.2	<.1	44.0	56.0
Hardeman	8,627	4,832	3,122	594	79	1,710	D	56.0	36.2	6.9	0.9	24	63	90	0.4	0.5	0.4	0.3	60.7	39.3
Hardin	8,592	3,922	3,875	734	61	47	D	45.6	45.1	8.5	0.7	65	30	74	0.4	0.4	0.5	0.4	50.3	49.7
Hawkins	16,285	6,623	7,758	1,847	57	1,135	R	40.7	47.6	11.3	0.4	76	22	36	0.8	0.7	0.9	0.9	46.1	53.9
Haywood	6,376	3,511	2,518	331	16	993	D	55.1	39.5	5.2	0.3	29	51	94	0.3	0.4	0.3	0.2	58.2	41.8
Henderson	9,024	3,502	4,719	785	18	1,217	R	38.8	52.3	8.7	0.2	83	8	73	0.5	0.4	0.6	0.4	42.6	57.4
Henry	12,095	6,797	3,661	1,588	49	3,136	D	56.2	30.3	13.1	0.4	22	76	11	0.6	0.7	0.4	0.8	65.0	35.0
Hickman	6,727	4,093	1,820	795	19	2,273	D	60.8	27.1	11.8	0.3	14	83	25	0.3	0.4	0.2	0.4	69.2	30.8
Houston	2,951	2,012	648	280	11	1,364	D	68.2	22.0	9.5	0.4	5	92	62	0.1	0.2	<.1	0.1	75.6	24.4
Humphreys	6,135	3,875	1,641	609	10	2,234	D	63.2	26.7	9.9	0.2	12	84	55	0.3	0.4	0.2	0.3	70.3	29.7
Jackson	4,258	3,208	708	332	10	2,500	D	75.3	16.6	7.8	0.2	1	95	81	0.2	0.3	<.1	0.2	81.9	18.1
Jefferson	12,362	4,740	6,184	1,385	53	1,444	R	38.3	50.0	11.2	0.4	84	14	42	0.6	0.5	0.7	0.7	43.4	56.6
Johnson	5,563	1,781	3,170	574	38	1,389	R	32.0	57.0	10.3	0.7	94	1	52	0.3	0.2	0.4	0.3	36.0	64.0
Knox	142,476	59,702	66,607	15,669	498	6,905	R	41.9	46.7	11.0	0.3	70	26	44	7.2	6.4	7.9	7.8	47.3	52.7
Lake	2,306	1,449	680	151	26	769	D	62.8	29.5	6.5	1.1	13	79	91	0.1	0.2	<.1	<.1	68.1	31.9
Lauderdale	7,958	4,452	2,928	561	17	1,524	D	55.9	36.8	7.0	0.2	25	61	86	0.4	0.5	0.3	0.3	60.3	39.7
Lawrence	13,864	6,816	5,608	1,403	37	1,208	D	49.2	40.5	10.1	0.3	46	46	53	0.7	0.7	0.7	0.7	54.9	45.1
Lewis	4,152	2,491	1,218	434	9	1,273	D	60.0	29.3	10.5	0.2	15	80	51	0.2	0.3	0.1	0.2	67.2	32.8
Lincoln	10,302	5,063	3,814	1,371	54	1,249	D	49.1	37.0	13.3	0.5	47	60	10	0.5	0.5	0.5	0.7	57.0	43.0
Loudon	13,510	5,414	6,444	1,602	50	1,030	R	40.1	47.7	11.9	0.4	80	20	24	0.7	0.6	0.8	0.8	45.7	54.3
McMinn	15,990	6,682	7,453	1,812	43	771	R	41.8	46.6	11.3	0.3	71	27	37	0.8	0.7	0.9	0.9	47.3	52.7
McNairy	9,595	4,691	4,093	774	37	598	D	48.9	42.7	8.1	0.4	49	36	78	0.5	0.5	0.5	0.4	53.4	46.6
Macon	5,726	2,961	2,299	443	23	662	D	51.7	40.2	7.7	0.4	38	49	82	0.3	0.3	0.3	0.2	56.3	43.7
Madison	31,196	13,629	14,869	2,634	64	1,240	R	43.7	47.7	8.4	0.2	67	21	75	1.6	1.5	1.8	1.3	47.8	52.2
Marion	10,068	5,589	3,262	1,186	31	2,327	D	55.5	32.4	11.8	0.3	27	71	27	0.5	0.6	0.4	0.6	63.1	36.9
Marshall	8,098	4,491	2,516	1,050	41	1,975	D	55.5	31.1	13.0	0.5	28	74	14	0.4	0.5	0.3	0.5	64.1	35.9
Maury	20,459	9,997	7,440	2,821	201	2,557	D	48.9	36.4	13.8	1.0	50	62	7	1.0	1.1	0.9	1.4	57.3	42.7
Meigs	3,484	1,673	1,355	453	3	318	D	48.0	38.9	13.0	<.1	53	53	12	0.2	0.2	0.2	0.2	55.3	44.7
Monroe	12,411	5,384	6,025	936	66	641	R	43.4	48.5	7.5	0.5	68	19	84	0.6	0.6	0.7	0.5	47.2	52.8
Montgomery	31,341	14,507	13,011	3,753	70	1,496	D	46.3	41.5	12.0	0.2	61	41	22	1.6	1.6	1.5	1.9	52.7	47.3
Moore	2,145	1,151	661	327	6	490	D	53.7	30.8	15.2	0.3	32	75	1	0.1	0.1	<.1	0.2	63.5	36.5
Morgan	6,184	3,190	2,306	658	30	884	D	51.6	37.3	10.6	0.5	39	58	49	0.3	0.3	0.3	0.3	58.0	42.0
Obion	12,864	6,497	4,812	1,494	61	1,685	D	50.5	37.4	11.6	0.5	41	57	28	0.6	0.7	0.6	0.7	57.4	42.6
Overton	6,651	4,489	1,657	468	37	2,832	D	67.5	24.9	7.0	0.6	6	88	87	0.3	0.5	0.2	0.2	73.0	27.0
Perry	2,919	1,889	708	317	5	1,181	D	64.7	24.3	10.9	0.2	8	89	46	0.1	0.2	<.1	0.2	72.7	27.3
Pickett	2,368	1,144	1,094	121	9	50	D	48.3	46.2	5.1	0.4	52	29	95	0.1	0.1	0.1	<.1	51.1	48.9
Polk	4,610	2,583	1,584	419	24	999	D	56.0	34.4	9.1	0.5	23	67	69	0.2	0.3	0.2	0.2	62.0	38.0

County	Total	Clinton (DEM)	Bush (REP)	Perot (IND)	Other	Plurality Total	Party	DEM	REP	IND	Other	Rank DEM	Rank REP	Rank IND	Total	DEM	REP	IND	DEM	REP
Putnam	21,482	10,858	7,998	2,473	153	2,860	D	50.5	37.2	11.5	0.7	40	59	30	1.1	1.2	1.0	1.2	57.6	42.4
Rhea	10,348	4,289	4,860	1,163	36	571	R	41.4	47.0	11.2	0.3	72	24	41	0.5	0.5	0.6	0.6	46.9	53.1
Roane	20,999	9,812	8,719	2,396	72	1,093	D	46.7	41.5	11.4	0.3	59	39	34	1.1	1.1	1.0	1.2	52.9	47.1
Robertson	15,779	8,498	5,271	1,978	32	3,227	D	53.9	33.4	12.5	0.2	31	69	17	0.8	0.9	0.6	1.0	61.7	38.3
Rutherford	47,140	21,084	18,877	7,005	174	2,207	D	44.7	40.0	14.9	0.4	66	50	2	2.4	2.3	2.2	3.5	52.8	47.2
Scott	6,418	2,730	3,011	643	34	281	R	42.5	46.9	10.0	0.5	69	25	54	0.3	0.3	0.4	0.3	47.6	52.4
Sequatchie	3,559	1,754	1,381	405	19	373	D	49.3	38.8	11.4	0.5	44	54	35	0.2	0.2	0.2	0.2	55.9	44.1
Sevier	21,266	6,719	11,714	2,760	73	4,995	R	31.6	55.1	13.0	0.3	95	5	13	1.1	0.7	1.4	1.4	36.5	63.5
Shelby	366,110	191,322	153,310	20,223	1,255	38,012	D	52.3	41.9	5.5	0.3	34	38	93	18.5	20.5	18.2	10.1	55.5	44.5
Smith	7,044	5,061	1,482	486	15	3,579	D	71.8	21.0	6.9	0.2	2	94	89	0.4	0.5	0.2	0.2	77.3	22.7
Stewart	4,323	2,779	1,046	487	11	1,733	D	64.3	24.2	11.3	0.3	9	90	39	0.2	0.3	0.1	0.2	72.7	27.3
Sullivan	56,980	20,935	28,801	6,730	514	7,866	R	36.7	50.5	11.8	0.9	88	13	26	2.9	2.2	3.4	3.4	42.1	57.9
Sumner	42,132	19,387	17,401	5,177	167	1,986	D	46.0	41.3	12.3	0.4	63	43	20	2.1	2.1	2.1	2.6	52.7	47.3
Tipton	13,717	5,652	6,757	1,279	29	1,105	R	41.2	49.3	9.3	0.2	74	17	64	0.7	0.6	0.8	0.6	45.5	54.5
Trousdale	2,664	1,846	565	243	10	1,281	D	69.3	21.2	9.1	0.4	3	93	68	0.1	0.2	<.1	0.1	76.6	23.4
Unicoi	6,447	2,375	3,344	709	19	969	R	36.8	51.9	11.0	0.4	86	10	45	0.3	0.3	0.4	0.4	41.5	58.5
Union	5,354	2,478	2,274	580	22	204	D	46.3	42.5	10.8	0.4	62	37	47	0.3	0.3	0.3	0.3	52.1	47.9
Van Buren	2,080	1,329	555	191	5	774	D	63.9	26.7	9.2	0.2	10	85	66	0.1	0.1	<.1	<.1	70.5	29.5
Warren	12,355	7,189	3,704	1,415	47	3,485	D	58.2	30.0	11.5	0.4	18	77	31	0.6	0.8	0.4	0.7	66.0	34.0
Washington	35,483	13,071	18,206	4,002	204	5,135	R	36.8	51.3	11.3	0.6	87	11	38	1.8	1.4	2.2	2.0	41.8	58.2
Wayne	5,266	1,868	2,955	424	19	1,087	R	35.5	56.1	8.1	0.4	89	2	79	0.3	0.2	0.4	0.2	38.7	61.3
Weakley	11,869	5,691	4,800	1,355	23	891	D	47.9	40.4	11.4	0.2	54	47	33	0.6	0.6	0.6	0.7	54.2	45.8
White	7,074	4,102	2,118	821	33	1,984	D	58.0	29.9	11.6	0.5	19	78	29	0.4	0.4	0.3	0.4	65.9	34.1
Williamson	40,195	13,053	22,015	5,026	101	8,962	R	32.5	54.8	12.5	0.3	93	6	19	2.0	1.4	2.6	2.5	37.2	62.8
Wilson	29,903	13,861	12,061	3,848	133	1,800	D	46.4	40.3	12.9	0.4	60	48	16	1.5	1.5	1.4	1.9	53.5	46.5
TENNESSEE	1,982,638	933,521	841,300	199,968	7,849	92,221	D	47.1	42.4	10.1	0.4				100.0	100.0	100.0	100.0	52.6	47.4

Table H. — Vote for U.S. Representative in Congress: November 3, 1992, General Election

Congressional district and county	Total	Democrat (DEM)	Republican (REP)	Other	Plurality Total	Party	DEM	REP	Other	DEM	REP	Other	Total	DEM	REP	Other
							Percent of total vote			Rank within district			Percent contribution to district vote			
District 1	170,158	47,809	114,797	7,552	66,988	R	28.1	67.5	4.4				100.0	100.0	100.0	100.0
Carter	14,407	3,125	10,603	679	7,478	R	21.7	73.6	4.7	10	5	5	8.5	6.5	9.2	9.0
Cocke	7,557	1,245	6,008	304	4,763	R	16.5	79.5	4.0	12	1	6	4.4	2.6	5.2	4.0
Greene	16,949	4,895	11,538	516	6,643	R	28.9	68.1	3.0	4	8	10	10.0	10.2	10.1	6.8
Hancock	1,626	376	1,201	49	825	R	23.1	73.9	3.0	7	4	11	1.0	0.8	1.0	0.6
Hawkins	13,520	5,189	8,022	309	2,833	R	38.4	59.3	2.3	1	12	12	7.9	10.9	7.0	4.1
Jefferson	9,169	2,140	6,669	360	4,529	R	23.3	72.7	3.9	6	6	7	5.4	4.5	5.8	4.8
Johnson	4,572	1,005	3,423	144	2,418	R	22.0	74.9	3.1	9	3	9	2.7	2.1	3.0	1.9
Knox (pt)	979	336	593	50	257	R	34.3	60.6	5.1	2	11	3	0.6	0.7	0.5	0.7
Sevier	17,947	4,042	12,977	928	8,935	R	22.5	72.3	5.2	8	7	2	10.5	8.5	11.3	12.3
Sullivan	49,651	16,404	30,718	2,529	14,314	R	33.0	61.9	5.1	3	10	4	29.2	34.3	26.8	33.5
Unicoi	5,524	1,186	4,148	190	2,962	R	21.5	75.1	3.4	11	2	8	3.2	2.5	3.6	2.5
Washington	28,257	7,866	18,897	1,494	11,031	R	27.8	66.9	5.3	5	9	1	16.6	16.5	16.5	19.8
District 2	205,401	52,887	148,377	4,137	95,490	R	25.7	72.2	2.0				100.0	100.0	100.0	100.0
Blount	34,099	7,059	26,320	720	19,261	R	20.7	77.2	2.1	6	1	3	16.6	13.3	17.7	17.4
Bradley (pt)	11,928	3,154	8,301	473	5,147	R	26.4	69.6	4.0	3	5	1	5.8	6.0	5.6	11.4
Knox (pt)	122,583	33,126	87,033	2,424	53,907	R	27.0	71.0	2.0	2	4	4	59.7	62.6	58.7	58.6
Loudon	11,499	2,903	8,596	0	5,693	R	25.2	74.8	0.0	4	2	6	5.6	5.5	5.8	0.0
McMinn	14,719	3,359	10,964	396	7,605	R	22.8	74.5	2.7	5	3	2	7.2	6.4	7.4	9.6
Monroe	10,573	3,286	7,163	124	3,877	R	31.1	67.7	1.2	1	6	5	5.1	6.2	4.8	3.0
District 3	216,533	105,693	102,763	8,077	2,930	D	48.8	47.5	3.7				100.0	100.0	100.0	100.0
Anderson	26,185	15,802	9,520	863	6,282	D	60.3	36.4	3.3	2	11	6	12.1	15.0	9.3	10.7
Bledsoe	4,007	1,753	2,112	142	359	R	43.7	52.7	3.5	11	2	4	1.9	1.7	2.1	1.8
Bradley (pt)	16,086	6,072	9,415	599	3,343	R	37.7	58.5	3.7	12	1	3	7.4	5.7	9.2	7.4
Grundy	3,852	2,735	1,003	114	1,732	D	71.0	26.0	3.0	1	12	8	1.8	2.6	1.0	1.4
Hamilton	118,395	52,649	60,755	4,991	8,106	R	44.5	51.3	4.2	10	3	2	54.7	49.8	59.1	61.8
Marion	10,323	5,883	4,156	284	1,727	D	57.0	40.3	2.8	5	8	9	4.8	5.6	4.0	3.5
Meigs	3,188	1,570	1,540	78	30	D	49.2	48.3	2.4	9	4	11	1.5	1.5	1.5	1.0
Morgan	5,142	3,063	1,968	111	1,095	D	59.6	38.3	2.2	3	9	12	2.4	2.9	1.9	1.4
Polk	5,042	2,730	2,145	167	585	D	54.1	42.5	3.3	7	6	5	2.3	2.6	2.1	2.1
Roane	19,387	10,776	8,036	575	2,740	D	55.6	41.5	3.0	6	7	7	9.0	10.2	7.8	7.1
Sequatchie	3,469	1,797	1,583	89	214	D	51.8	45.6	2.6	8	5	10	1.6	1.7	1.5	1.1
Van Buren	1,457	863	530	64	333	D	59.2	36.4	4.4	4	10	1	0.7	0.8	0.5	0.8
District 4	154,511	98,984	50,340	5,187	48,644	D	64.1	32.6	3.4				100.0	100.0	100.0	100.0
Bedford	9,431	7,319	1,876	236	5,443	D	77.6	19.9	2.5	1	22	18	6.1	7.4	3.7	4.5
Campbell	7,775	5,535	2,009	231	3,526	D	71.2	25.8	3.0	9	15	15	5.0	5.6	4.0	4.5
Claiborne	6,530	4,409	1,916	205	2,493	D	67.5	29.3	3.1	11	12	11	4.2	4.5	3.8	4.0
Coffee	12,562	8,556	3,556	450	5,000	D	68.1	28.3	3.6	10	13	5	8.1	8.6	7.1	8.7
Cumberland	11,783	6,982	4,439	362	2,543	D	59.3	37.7	3.1	15	8	13	7.6	7.1	8.8	7.0
Fentress	3,800	2,782	926	92	1,856	D	73.2	24.4	2.4	5	17	20	2.5	2.8	1.8	1.8
Franklin	10,752	7,666	2,746	340	4,920	D	71.3	25.5	3.2	8	16	10	7.0	7.7	5.5	6.6
Giles	7,480	5,646	1,582	252	4,064	D	75.5	21.1	3.4	2	21	8	4.8	5.7	3.1	4.9
Grainger	3,915	2,178	1,615	122	563	D	55.6	41.3	3.1	17	6	12	2.5	2.2	3.2	2.4
Hamblen	16,050	7,184	8,387	479	1,203	R	44.8	52.3	3.0	22	1	14	10.4	7.3	16.7	9.2
Hardin	5,404	2,504	2,533	367	29	R	46.3	46.9	6.8	21	3	2	3.5	2.5	5.0	7.1
Knox (pt)	4,026	1,948	1,761	317	187	D	48.4	43.7	7.9	19	5	1	2.6	2.0	3.5	6.1
Lawrence	9,656	6,911	2,514	231	4,397	D	71.6	26.0	2.4	7	14	21	6.2	7.0	5.0	4.5
Lincoln	8,027	5,385	2,387	255	2,998	D	67.1	29.7	3.2	12	11	9	5.2	5.4	4.7	4.9
Moore	1,595	1,170	358	67	812	D	73.4	22.4	4.2	4	18	4	1.0	1.2	0.7	1.3
Pickett	1,413	808	582	23	226	D	57.2	41.2	1.6	16	7	22	0.9	0.8	1.2	0.4
Rhea	7,484	3,810	3,490	184	320	D	50.9	46.6	2.5	18	4	19	4.8	3.8	6.9	3.5
Scott	4,309	2,839	1,361	109	1,478	D	65.9	31.6	2.5	13	10	17	2.8	2.9	2.7	2.1
Union	3,435	2,165	1,150	120	1,015	D	63.0	33.5	3.5	14	9	7	2.2	2.2	2.3	2.3
Warren	9,421	7,029	2,055	337	4,974	D	74.6	21.8	3.6	3	19	6	6.1	7.1	4.1	6.5
Wayne	3,467	1,622	1,748	97	126	R	46.8	50.4	2.8	20	2	16	2.2	1.6	3.5	1.9
White	6,196	4,536	1,349	311	3,187	D	73.2	21.8	5.0	6	20	3	4.0	4.6	2.7	6.0
District 5	187,590	125,233	49,417	12,940	75,816	D	66.8	26.3	6.9				100.0	100.0	100.0	100.0
Davidson (pt)	175,960	116,731	46,863	12,366	69,868	D	66.3	26.6	7.0	2	1	1	93.8	93.2	94.8	95.6
Robertson (pt)	11,630	8,502	2,554	574	5,948	D	73.1	22.0	4.9	1	2	2	6.2	6.8	5.2	4.4
District 6	212,428	120,177	86,289	5,962	33,888	D	56.6	40.6	2.8				100.0	100.0	100.0	100.0
Cannon	3,970	2,817	1,078	75	1,739	D	71.0	27.2	1.9	6	10	9	1.9	2.3	1.2	1.3
Clay	2,556	1,874	643	39	1,231	D	73.3	25.2	1.5	4	12	13	1.2	1.6	0.7	0.7
Davidson (pt)	2,302	906	1,347	49	441	R	39.4	58.5	2.1	15	1	7	1.1	0.8	1.6	0.8
DeKalb	5,747	4,052	1,572	123	2,480	D	70.5	27.4	2.1	7	9	6	2.7	3.4	1.8	2.1
Jackson	3,749	3,055	629	65	2,426	D	81.5	16.8	1.7	1	15	11	1.8	2.5	0.7	1.1
Macon	4,778	2,940	1,781	57	1,159	D	61.5	37.3	1.2	9	7	15	2.2	2.4	2.1	1.0
Marshall	7,532	4,907	2,492	133	2,415	D	65.1	33.1	1.8	8	8	10	3.5	4.1	2.9	2.2
Overton	5,714	4,358	1,275	81	3,083	D	76.3	22.3	1.4	2	14	14	2.7	3.6	1.5	1.4
Putnam	19,408	11,210	7,648	550	3,562	D	57.8	39.4	2.8	11	5	5	9.1	9.3	8.9	9.2
Rutherford	45,204	26,551	17,267	1,386	9,284	D	58.7	38.2	3.1	10	6	2	21.3	22.1	20.0	23.2
Smith	6,072	4,349	1,628	95	2,721	D	71.6	26.8	1.6	5	11	12	2.9	3.6	1.9	1.6

Table H. — Vote for U.S. Representative in Congress: November 3, 1992, General Election (cont)

Congressional district and county	Total	Democrat (DEM)	Republican (REP)	Other	Plurality Total	Plurality Party	Percent of total vote DEM	Percent of total vote REP	Percent of total vote Other	Rank within district DEM	Rank within district REP	Rank within district Other	Percent contribution to district vote Total	Percent contribution to district vote DEM	Percent contribution to district vote REP	Percent contribution to district vote Other
District 6 (cont)																
Sumner	37,862	21,600	15,110	1,152	6,490	D	57.0	39.9	3.0	12	4	3	17.8	18.0	17.5	19.3
Trousdale	2,295	1,734	517	44	1,217	D	75.6	22.5	1.9	3	13	8	1.1	1.4	0.6	0.7
Williamson	38,685	15,273	22,280	1,132	7,007	R	39.5	57.6	2.9	14	2	4	18.2	12.7	25.8	19.0
Wilson	26,554	14,551	11,022	981	3,529	D	54.8	41.5	3.7	13	3	1	12.5	12.1	12.8	16.5
District 7	202,866	72,062	125,101	5,703	53,039	R	35.5	61.7	2.8				100.0	100.0	100.0	100.0
Cheatham	8,532	5,225	3,109	198	2,116	D	61.2	36.4	2.3	2	14	7	4.2	7.3	2.5	3.5
Chester	4,678	1,661	2,954	63	1,293	R	35.5	63.1	1.3	13	3	14	2.3	2.3	2.4	1.1
Decatur	4,049	2,227	1,774	48	453	D	55.0	43.8	1.2	4	11	15	2.0	3.1	1.4	0.8
Dickson	11,261	6,108	4,924	229	1,184	D	54.2	43.7	2.0	5	12	9	5.6	8.5	3.9	4.0
Fayette	7,829	3,254	4,352	223	1,098	R	41.6	55.6	2.8	10	6	6	3.9	4.5	3.5	3.9
Hardeman	6,171	2,641	3,331	199	690	R	42.8	54.0	3.2	9	7	4	3.0	3.7	2.7	3.5
Henderson	7,212	2,340	4,771	101	2,431	R	32.4	66.2	1.4	14	2	12	3.6	3.2	3.8	1.8
Hickman	5,858	3,004	2,747	107	257	D	51.3	46.9	1.8	7	9	10	2.9	4.2	2.2	1.9
Lewis	3,135	1,881	1,211	43	670	D	60.0	38.6	1.4	3	13	13	1.5	2.6	1.0	0.8
McNairy	8,226	3,259	4,630	337	1,371	R	39.6	56.3	4.1	11	5	1	4.1	4.5	3.7	5.9
Maury	16,877	9,065	7,431	381	1,634	D	53.7	44.0	2.3	6	10	8	8.3	12.6	5.9	6.7
Montgomery	28,420	10,702	16,571	1,147	5,869	R	37.7	58.3	4.0	12	4	2	14.0	14.9	13.2	20.1
Perry	2,406	1,513	850	43	663	D	62.9	35.3	1.8	1	15	11	1.2	2.1	0.7	0.8
Robertson (pt)	2,496	1,231	1,173	92	58	D	49.3	47.0	3.7	8	8	3	1.2	1.7	0.9	1.6
Shelby (pt)	85,716	17,951	65,273	2,492	47,322	R	20.9	76.2	2.9	15	1	5	42.3	24.9	52.2	43.7
District 8	163,432	136,852	-	26,580	110,272	D	83.7	-	16.3				100.0	100.0	-	100.0
Benton	4,640	4,009	-	631	3,378	D	86.4	-	13.6	9	-	9	2.8	2.9	-	2.4
Carroll	7,303	6,673	-	630	6,043	D	91.4	-	8.6	4	-	14	4.5	4.9	-	2.4
Crockett	4,263	3,689	-	574	3,115	D	86.5	-	13.5	8	-	10	2.6	2.7	-	2.2
Dyer	10,884	9,300	-	1,584	7,716	D	85.4	-	14.6	11	-	7	6.7	6.8	-	6.0
Gibson	11,842	11,141	-	701	10,440	D	94.1	-	5.9	2	-	16	7.2	8.1	-	2.6
Haywood	5,005	4,337	-	668	3,669	D	86.7	-	13.3	7	-	11	3.1	3.2	-	2.5
Henry	8,171	7,443	-	728	6,715	D	91.1	-	8.9	5	-	13	5.0	5.4	-	2.7
Houston	1,723	1,448	-	275	1,173	D	84.0	-	16.0	13	-	5	1.1	1.1	-	1.0
Humphreys	4,237	3,392	-	845	2,547	D	80.1	-	19.9	16	-	2	2.6	2.5	-	3.2
Lake	1,607	1,528	-	79	1,449	D	95.1	-	4.9	1	-	17	1.0	1.1	-	0.3
Lauderdale	6,624	5,819	-	805	5,014	D	87.8	-	12.2	6	-	12	4.1	4.3	-	3.0
Madison	27,517	22,756	-	4,761	17,995	D	82.7	-	17.3	14	-	4	16.8	16.6	-	17.9
Obion	9,589	8,964	-	625	8,339	D	93.5	-	6.5	3	-	15	5.9	6.6	-	2.4
Shelby (pt)	35,114	25,696	-	9,418	16,278	D	73.2	-	26.8	17	-	1	21.5	18.8	-	35.4
Stewart	2,629	2,270	-	359	1,911	D	86.3	-	13.7	10	-	8	1.6	1.7	-	1.4
Tipton	11,729	9,453	-	2,276	7,177	D	80.6	-	19.4	15	-	3	7.2	6.9	-	8.6
Weakley	10,555	8,934	-	1,621	7,313	D	84.6	-	15.4	12	-	6	6.5	6.5	-	6.1
District 9	212,755	123,276	60,606	28,873	62,670	D	57.9	28.5	13.6				100.0	100.0	100.0	100.0
Shelby (pt)	212,755	123,276	60,606	28,873	62,670	D	57.9	28.5	13.6	1	1	1	100.0	100.0	100.0	100.0
TENNESSEE	1,725,674	882,973	737,690	105,011	145,283	D	51.2	42.7	6.1							

Table I. — Vote for Presidential Preference: March 10, 1992, Democratic Primary Election

County	Total	Clinton	Tsongas	Brown	Uncom-mitted	Harkin	Kerrey	Write ins		Clinton	Tsongas	Brown	Clinton (Rank)	Tsongas (Rank)	Brown (Rank)	Total	Clinton	Tsongas	Brown
Anderson	6,060	3,148	2,257	455	123	53	21	3	–	51.9	37.2	7.5	92	1	28	1.9	1.5	3.7	1.8
Bedford	4,842	2,841	875	347	683	48	40	8	–	58.7	18.1	7.2	86	27	41	1.5	1.3	1.4	1.4
Benton	1,601	1,267	197	82	35	14	6	0	–	79.1	12.3	5.1	30	55	75	0.5	0.6	0.3	0.3
Bledsoe	1,385	1,033	142	107	77	10	16	0	–	74.6	10.3	7.7	47	70	26	0.4	0.5	0.2	0.4
Blount	4,150	2,489	1,099	428	89	23	19	3	–	60.0	26.5	10.3	85	5	7	1.3	1.2	1.8	1.7
Bradley	4,111	2,704	732	362	262	22	29	0	–	65.8	17.8	8.8	74	29	21	1.3	1.3	1.2	1.4
Campbell	2,507	1,853	349	145	101	36	19	4	–	73.9	13.9	5.8	50	45	65	0.8	0.9	0.6	0.6
Cannon	1,828	1,203	306	98	176	16	29	0	–	65.8	16.7	5.4	73	32	70	0.6	0.6	0.5	0.4
Carroll	1,617	1,302	185	76	32	10	7	5	–	80.5	11.4	4.7	24	61	81	0.5	0.6	0.3	0.3
Carter	1,398	967	253	126	30	10	9	3	–	69.2	18.1	9.0	62	26	18	0.4	0.5	0.4	0.5
Cheatham	1,467	980	293	132	42	7	6	7	–	66.8	20.0	9.0	70	19	19	0.5	0.5	0.5	0.5
Chester	758	669	48	31	6	1	2	1	–	88.3	6.3	4.1	4	91	87	0.2	0.3	<.1	0.1
Claiborne	1,139	867	174	62	24	9	3	0	–	76.1	15.3	5.4	40	38	68	0.4	0.4	0.3	0.2
Clay	433	360	36	27	7	1	1	1	–	83.1	8.3	6.2	14	79	55	0.1	0.2	<.1	0.1
Cocke	695	513	105	59	5	10	2	1	–	73.8	15.1	8.5	52	41	24	0.2	0.2	0.2	0.2
Coffee	2,923	1,885	666	216	113	27	14	2	–	64.5	22.8	7.4	80	13	33	0.9	0.9	1.1	0.8
Crockett	794	711	44	26	7	5	1	0	–	89.5	5.5	3.3	3	93	93	0.2	0.3	<.1	0.1
Cumberland	4,051	2,507	794	358	320	39	33	0	–	61.9	19.6	8.8	83	22	20	1.3	1.2	1.3	1.4
Davidson	37,186	19,248	12,349	4,123	1,035	147	153	131	–	51.8	33.2	11.1	93	4	6	11.7	9.0	20.0	16.1
Decatur	1,026	858	85	44	26	4	7	2	–	83.6	8.3	4.3	13	80	86	0.3	0.4	0.1	0.2
DeKalb	2,347	1,660	320	171	155	20	21	0	–	70.7	13.6	7.3	58	49	35	0.7	0.8	0.5	0.7
Dickson	2,402	1,760	401	179	42	12	8	0	–	73.3	16.7	7.5	54	33	30	0.8	0.8	0.6	0.7
Dyer	1,667	1,405	153	61	29	12	5	2	–	84.3	9.2	3.7	11	75	89	0.5	0.7	0.2	0.2
Fayette	3,138	2,379	254	173	278	25	29	0	–	75.8	8.1	5.5	44	82	66	1.0	1.1	0.4	0.7
Fentress	628	485	86	38	8	8	2	1	–	77.2	13.7	6.1	36	48	61	0.2	0.2	0.1	0.1
Franklin	6,136	3,514	1,216	591	705	51	48	11	–	57.3	19.8	9.6	91	21	10	1.9	1.6	2.0	2.3
Gibson	3,402	2,923	228	161	59	13	13	5	–	85.9	6.7	4.7	9	88	80	1.1	1.4	0.4	0.6
Giles	1,392	1,051	212	85	24	12	7	1	–	75.5	15.2	6.1	45	39	60	0.4	0.5	0.3	0.3
Grainger	540	423	65	39	9	3	1	0	–	78.3	12.0	7.2	32	57	39	0.2	0.2	0.1	0.2
Greene	2,624	1,791	415	250	119	29	20	0	–	68.3	15.8	9.5	64	35	11	0.8	0.8	0.7	1.0
Grundy	2,255	1,724	190	118	183	25	10	5	–	76.5	8.4	5.2	38	78	72	0.7	0.8	0.3	0.5
Hamblen	1,993	1,274	447	183	47	22	20	0	–	63.9	22.4	9.2	81	14	16	0.6	0.6	0.7	0.7
Hamilton	16,359	11,147	3,099	1,493	426	101	76	17	–	68.1	18.9	9.1	66	24	17	5.1	5.2	5.0	5.8
Hancock	106	84	9	10	2	1	0	0	–	79.2	8.5	9.4	28	77	12	<.1	<.1	<.1	<.1
Hardeman	2,512	2,004	190	137	141	26	14	0	–	79.8	7.6	5.5	25	86	67	0.8	0.9	0.3	0.5
Hardin	1,275	1,098	90	49	24	6	5	3	–	86.1	7.1	3.8	8	87	88	0.4	0.5	0.1	0.2
Hawkins	2,270	1,577	313	219	126	10	24	1	–	69.5	13.8	9.6	61	47	9	0.7	0.7	0.5	0.9
Haywood	943	831	63	34	10	4	1	0	–	88.1	6.7	3.6	6	89	91	0.3	0.4	0.1	0.1
Henderson	770	658	60	38	3	4	7	0	–	85.5	7.8	4.9	10	84	77	0.2	0.3	<.1	0.1
Henry	4,638	3,115	688	315	451	37	22	10	–	67.2	14.8	6.8	69	43	43	1.5	1.5	1.1	1.2
Hickman	1,085	801	182	71	23	4	3	1	–	73.8	16.8	6.5	51	31	50	0.3	0.4	0.3	0.3
Houston	577	443	75	37	12	3	5	2	–	76.8	13.0	6.4	37	52	51	0.2	0.2	0.1	0.1
Humphreys	1,269	1,002	166	66	22	4	9	0	–	79.0	13.1	5.2	31	51	73	0.4	0.5	0.3	0.3
Jackson	883	727	86	48	16	4	0	2	–	82.3	9.7	5.4	15	73	69	0.3	0.3	0.1	0.2
Jefferson	1,001	681	208	75	22	7	4	4	–	68.0	20.8	7.5	67	18	29	0.3	0.3	0.3	0.3
Johnson	407	304	63	25	11	4	0	0	–	74.7	15.5	6.1	46	36	58	0.1	0.1	0.1	<.1
Knox	20,133	10,156	7,113	2,339	282	101	106	36	–	50.4	35.3	11.6	94	3	5	6.3	4.7	11.5	9.2
Lake	327	283	21	15	5	2	1	0	–	86.5	6.4	4.6	7	90	83	0.1	0.1	<.1	<.1
Lauderdale	1,250	1,122	63	38	19	7	1	0	–	89.8	5.0	3.0	2	95	94	0.4	0.5	0.1	0.1
Lawrence	1,984	1,618	206	105	33	14	8	0	–	81.6	10.4	5.3	19	68	71	0.6	0.8	0.3	0.4
Lewis	1,384	1,023	143	136	66	7	9	0	–	73.9	10.3	9.8	49	69	8	0.4	0.5	0.2	0.5
Lincoln	2,667	1,861	404	198	174	18	10	2	–	69.8	15.1	7.4	60	40	31	0.8	0.9	0.7	0.8
Loudon	1,540	998	389	111	23	10	8	1	–	64.8	25.3	7.2	78	7	40	0.5	0.5	0.6	0.4
McMinn	1,923	1,460	259	139	40	14	9	2	–	75.9	13.5	7.2	43	50	37	0.6	0.7	0.4	0.5
McNairy	1,402	1,262	75	38	18	4	4	1	–	90.0	5.3	2.7	1	94	95	0.4	0.6	0.1	0.1
Macon	439	355	50	20	4	3	7	0	–	80.9	11.4	4.6	22	62	84	0.1	0.2	<.1	<.1
Madison	4,053	3,297	446	186	90	17	10	7	–	81.3	11.0	4.6	20	65	82	1.3	1.5	0.7	0.7
Marion	3,386	2,640	273	214	213	24	22	0	–	78.0	8.1	6.3	33	83	53	1.1	1.2	0.4	0.8
Marshall	1,244	899	212	78	32	15	8	0	–	72.3	17.0	6.3	57	30	54	0.4	0.4	0.3	0.3
Maury	2,852	1,855	696	188	58	31	18	6	–	65.0	24.4	6.6	77	9	49	0.9	0.9	1.1	0.7
Meigs	505	408	41	30	18	2	6	0	–	80.8	8.1	5.9	23	81	64	0.2	0.2	<.1	0.1
Monroe	1,372	1,044	211	83	20	9	3	2	–	76.1	15.4	6.0	41	37	62	0.4	0.5	0.3	0.3
Montgomery	3,957	2,636	880	268	108	32	26	7	–	66.6	22.2	6.8	71	16	44	1.2	1.2	1.4	1.0
Moore	300	219	55	15	11	0	0	0	–	73.0	18.3	5.0	55	25	76	<.1	0.1	<.1	<.1
Morgan	1,005	782	142	49	19	7	6	0	–	77.8	14.1	4.9	34	44	79	0.3	0.4	0.2	0.2
Obion	3,012	2,196	295	192	273	39	15	2	–	72.9	9.8	6.4	56	72	52	0.9	1.0	0.5	0.8
Overton	2,253	1,680	269	140	122	26	16	0	–	74.6	11.9	6.2	48	58	56	0.7	0.8	0.4	0.5
Perry	1,802	1,236	211	143	177	18	8	9	–	68.6	11.7	7.9	63	59	25	0.6	0.6	0.3	0.6
Pickett	184	155	14	14	1	0	0	0	–	84.2	7.6	7.6	12	85	27	<.1	<.1	<.1	<.1
Polk	2,551	1,946	287	132	133	31	22	0	–	76.3	11.3	5.2	39	63	74	0.8	0.9	0.5	0.5

Table I. — Vote for Presidential Preference: March 10, 1992, Democratic Primary Election (cont)

County	Top candidates									Top three candidates (state vote)									
										Percent of total vote			Rank			Percent contribution to state vote			
	Total	Clinton	Tsongas	Brown	Uncom-mitted	Harkin	Kerrey	Write ins		Clinton	Tsongas	Brown	Clinton	Tsongas	Brown	Total	Clinton	Tsongas	Brown
Putnam	7,549	4,396	1,474	696	806	73	82	22	-	58.2	19.5	9.2	88	23	15	2.4	2.0	2.4	2.7
Rhea	1,243	984	134	82	26	9	6	2	-	79.2	10.8	6.6	29	67	48	0.4	0.5	0.2	0.3
Roane	3,940	2,541	970	266	102	33	20	8	-	64.5	24.6	6.8	79	8	46	1.2	1.2	1.6	1.0
Robertson	2,378	1,621	474	175	81	18	6	3	-	68.2	19.9	7.4	65	20	34	0.7	0.8	0.8	0.7
Rutherford	9,722	5,699	2,324	916	629	74	61	19	-	58.6	23.9	9.4	87	11	13	3.1	2.7	3.8	3.6
Scott	795	585	119	59	18	8	6	0	-	73.6	15.0	7.4	53	42	32	0.2	0.3	0.2	0.2
Sequatchie	546	443	66	24	8	2	2	1	-	81.1	12.1	4.4	21	56	85	0.2	0.2	0.1	<.1
Sevier	1,350	775	356	165	42	4	7	1	-	57.4	26.4	12.2	90	6	3	0.4	0.4	0.6	0.6
Shelby	41,524	34,114	3,966	2,784	390	168	84	18	-	82.2	9.6	6.7	16	74	47	13.0	15.9	6.4	10.9
Smith	997	770	129	61	25	5	3	4	-	77.2	12.9	6.1	35	53	59	0.3	0.4	0.2	0.2
Stewart	803	610	111	58	13	8	3	0	-	76.0	13.8	7.2	42	46	38	0.3	0.3	0.2	0.2
Sullivan	8,549	5,310	1,910	735	408	106	73	7	-	62.1	22.3	8.6	82	15	23	2.7	2.5	3.1	2.9
Sumner	5,890	3,841	1,350	511	122	21	29	16	-	65.2	22.9	8.7	75	12	22	1.8	1.8	2.2	2.0
Tipton	2,140	1,887	130	78	31	9	5	0	-	88.2	6.1	3.6	5	92	90	0.7	0.9	0.2	0.3
Trousdale	523	428	47	38	6	1	3	0	-	81.8	9.0	7.3	17	76	36	0.2	0.2	<.1	0.1
Unicoi	440	268	79	63	19	6	2	3	-	60.9	18.0	14.3	84	28	1	0.1	0.1	0.1	0.2
Union	656	523	76	39	9	5	4	0	-	79.7	11.6	5.9	26	60	63	0.2	0.2	0.1	0.1
Van Buren	759	621	83	26	17	6	5	1	-	81.8	10.9	3.4	18	66	92	0.2	0.3	0.1	0.1
Warren	3,084	2,181	506	191	164	21	19	2	-	70.7	16.4	6.2	59	34	57	1.0	1.0	0.8	0.7
Washington	3,247	1,881	778	406	124	21	29	8	-	57.9	24.0	12.5	89	10	2	1.0	0.9	1.3	1.6
Wayne	468	371	46	44	5	2	0	0	-	79.3	9.8	9.4	27	71	14	0.1	0.2	<.1	0.2
Weakley	3,373	2,294	372	228	423	35	21	0	-	68.0	11.0	6.8	68	64	45	1.1	1.1	0.6	0.9
White	3,411	2,262	441	168	474	41	25	0	-	66.3	12.9	4.9	72	54	78	1.1	1.1	0.7	0.7
Williamson	2,935	1,439	1,069	350	57	11	9	0	-	49.0	36.4	11.9	95	2	4	0.9	0.7	1.7	1.4
Wilson	8,045	5,244	1,684	556	473	42	40	6	-	65.2	20.9	6.9	76	17	42	2.5	2.4	2.7	2.2
TENNESSEE	318,482	214,485	61,717	25,560	12,551	2,099	1,638	432	-	67.3	19.4	8.0				100.0	100.0	100.0	100.0

County	Top candidates					Top four candidates (state vote)												
						Percent of total vote				Rank				Percent contribution to state vote				
	Total	Bush	Bu-chanan	Duke	Other	Bush	Bu-chanan	Duke	Other	Bush	Bu-chanan	Duke	Other	Total	Bush	Bu-chanan	Duke	Other
Anderson	3,441	2,621	654	116	50	76.2	19.0	3.4	1.5	25	68	67	60	1.4	1.5	1.2	1.5	1.0
Bedford	336	229	82	19	6	68.2	24.4	5.7	1.8	72	30	27	45	0.1	0.1	0.2	0.2	0.1
Benton	332	218	88	25	1	65.7	26.5	7.5	0.3	83	12	14	92	0.1	0.1	0.2	0.3	<.1
Bledsoe	806	662	108	23	13	82.1	13.4	2.9	1.6	2	92	78	51	0.3	0.4	0.2	0.3	0.3
Blount	7,991	5,947	1,673	177	194	74.4	20.9	2.2	2.4	33	52	90	21	3.3	3.3	3.1	2.3	3.8
Bradley	6,071	4,323	1,346	230	172	71.2	22.2	3.8	2.8	46	46	55	15	2.5	2.4	2.5	3.0	3.3
Campbell	2,701	1,863	606	125	107	69.0	22.4	4.6	4.0	68	44	43	7	1.1	1.0	1.1	1.6	2.1
Cannon	149	98	35	13	3	65.8	23.5	8.7	2.0	81	36	4	31	<.1	<.1	<.1	0.2	<.1
Carroll	1,026	750	180	81	15	73.1	17.5	7.9	1.5	39	78	9	59	0.4	0.4	0.3	1.1	0.3
Carter	3,258	2,185	859	113	101	67.1	26.4	3.5	3.1	75	13	63	11	1.3	1.2	1.6	1.5	2.0
Cheatham	826	529	237	47	13	64.0	28.7	5.7	1.6	89	7	26	52	0.3	0.3	0.4	0.6	0.3
Chester	536	380	108	46	2	70.9	20.1	8.6	0.4	50	60	6	91	0.2	0.2	0.2	0.6	<.1
Claiborne	859	660	165	22	12	76.8	19.2	2.6	1.4	19	67	84	64	0.3	0.4	0.3	0.3	0.2
Clay	157	124	27	3	3	79.0	17.2	1.9	1.9	8	79	93	36	<.1	<.1	<.1	<.1	<.1
Cocke	1,997	1,574	300	66	57	78.8	15.0	3.3	2.9	9	87	70	13	0.8	0.9	0.5	0.9	1.1
Coffee	1,410	997	339	54	20	70.7	24.0	3.8	1.4	51	33	54	63	0.6	0.6	0.6	0.7	0.4
Crockett	317	249	38	24	6	78.5	12.0	7.6	1.9	11	94	13	37	0.1	0.1	<.1	0.3	0.1
Cumberland	3,219	2,449	608	84	78	76.1	18.9	2.6	2.4	26	72	82	22	1.3	1.4	1.1	1.1	1.5
Davidson	19,742	14,037	4,928	468	309	71.1	25.0	2.4	1.6	47	26	88	54	8.0	7.9	9.0	6.1	6.0
Decatur	482	373	71	29	9	77.4	14.7	6.0	1.9	17	88	23	40	0.2	0.2	0.1	0.4	0.2
DeKalb	255	189	51	9	6	74.1	20.0	3.5	2.4	35	61	60	25	0.1	0.1	<.1	0.1	0.1
Dickson	1,010	698	246	54	12	69.1	24.4	5.3	1.2	67	31	32	73	0.4	0.4	0.5	0.7	0.2
Dyer	848	636	161	30	21	75.0	19.0	3.5	2.5	31	70	59	20	0.3	0.4	0.3	0.4	0.4
Fayette	594	438	122	23	11	73.7	20.5	3.9	1.9	37	57	52	41	0.2	0.2	0.2	0.3	0.2
Fentress	439	331	81	17	10	75.4	18.5	3.9	2.3	27	74	53	26	0.2	0.2	0.1	0.2	0.2
Franklin	455	318	113	18	6	69.9	24.8	4.0	1.3	59	28	49	67	0.2	0.2	0.2	0.2	0.1
Gibson	1,230	873	245	95	17	71.0	19.9	7.7	1.4	48	63	11	66	0.5	0.5	0.4	1.2	0.3
Giles	458	280	141	31	6	61.1	30.8	6.8	1.3	94	4	20	68	0.2	0.2	0.3	0.4	0.1
Grainger	845	665	138	26	16	78.7	16.3	3.1	1.9	10	82	74	38	0.3	0.4	0.3	0.3	0.3
Greene	5,920	4,260	1,250	202	208	72.0	21.1	3.4	3.5	43	51	64	8	2.4	2.4	2.3	2.6	4.0
Grundy	116	72	36	3	5	62.1	31.0	2.6	4.3	91	2	83	6	<.1	<.1	<.1	<.1	<.1
Hamblen	2,316	1,788	440	59	29	77.2	19.0	2.5	1.3	18	69	85	71	0.9	1.0	0.8	0.8	0.6
Hamilton	18,046	12,037	5,073	610	326	66.7	28.1	3.4	1.8	76	8	66	44	7.3	6.8	9.3	7.9	6.3
Hancock	1,406	1,009	276	57	64	71.8	19.6	4.1	4.6	44	64	48	4	0.6	0.6	0.5	0.7	1.2
Hardeman	427	277	116	30	4	64.9	27.2	7.0	0.9	87	10	18	83	0.2	0.2	0.2	0.4	<.1
Hardin	773	564	172	30	7	73.0	22.3	3.9	0.9	40	45	51	86	0.3	0.3	0.3	0.4	0.1
Hawkins	4,265	3,261	775	122	107	76.5	18.2	2.9	2.5	21	75	77	19	1.7	1.8	1.4	1.6	2.1
Haywood	495	396	72	23	4	80.0	14.5	4.6	0.8	4	89	42	88	0.2	0.2	0.1	0.3	<.1
Henderson	909	720	121	68	0	79.2	13.3	7.5	0.0	6	93	15	94	0.4	0.4	0.2	0.9	0.0
Henry	425	336	67	14	8	79.1	15.8	3.3	1.9	7	83	71	39	0.2	0.2	0.1	0.2	0.2
Hickman	434	299	102	25	8	68.9	23.5	5.8	1.8	69	35	25	42	0.2	0.2	0.2	0.3	0.2
Houston	179	98	62	14	5	54.7	34.6	7.8	2.8	95	1	10	17	<.1	<.1	0.1	0.2	<.1
Humphreys	384	239	119	20	6	62.2	31.0	5.2	1.6	90	3	36	55	0.2	0.1	0.2	0.3	0.1
Jackson	189	124	46	13	6	65.6	24.3	6.9	3.2	84	32	19	10	<.1	<.1	<.1	0.2	0.1
Jefferson	4,257	2,993	888	138	238	70.3	20.9	3.2	5.6	56	53	72	1	1.7	1.7	1.6	1.8	4.6
Johnson	717	558	110	32	17	77.8	15.3	4.5	2.4	14	85	44	23	0.3	0.3	0.2	0.4	0.3
Knox	21,640	16,253	4,648	416	323	75.1	21.5	1.9	1.5	29	49	92	58	8.8	9.1	8.5	5.4	6.3
Lake	126	88	29	9	0	69.8	23.0	7.1	0.0	60	39	17	95	<.1	<.1	<.1	0.1	0.0
Lauderdale	452	315	104	25	8	69.7	23.0	5.5	1.8	64	40	29	46	0.2	0.2	0.2	0.3	0.2
Lawrence	1,024	801	184	29	10	78.2	18.0	2.8	1.0	13	76	79	79	0.4	0.4	0.3	0.4	0.2
Lewis	390	298	65	21	6	76.4	16.7	5.4	1.5	23	80	30	56	0.2	0.2	0.1	0.3	0.1
Lincoln	1,374	986	309	51	28	71.8	22.5	3.7	2.0	45	43	56	30	0.6	0.6	0.6	0.7	0.5
Loudon	2,156	1,647	398	60	51	76.4	18.5	2.8	2.4	24	73	81	24	0.9	0.9	0.7	0.8	1.0
McMinn	3,501	2,546	723	136	96	72.7	20.6	3.9	2.7	42	55	50	18	1.4	1.4	1.3	1.8	1.9
McNairy	881	621	201	49	10	70.5	22.8	5.6	1.1	54	42	28	76	0.4	0.3	0.4	0.6	0.2
Macon	506	357	116	27	6	70.6	22.9	5.3	1.2	53	41	33	74	0.2	0.2	0.2	0.4	0.1
Madison	2,929	2,007	741	153	28	68.5	25.3	5.2	1.0	71	19	35	81	1.2	1.1	1.4	2.0	0.5
Marion	1,440	971	367	71	31	67.4	25.5	4.9	2.2	74	17	38	27	0.6	0.5	0.7	0.9	0.6
Marshall	576	402	135	31	8	69.8	23.4	5.4	1.4	62	37	31	65	0.2	0.2	0.2	0.4	0.2
Maury	1,592	1,111	398	67	16	69.8	25.0	4.2	1.0	63	25	46	78	0.6	0.6	0.7	0.9	0.3
Meigs	888	547	233	77	31	61.6	26.2	8.7	3.5	93	14	5	9	0.4	0.3	0.4	1.0	0.6
Monroe	2,399	1,934	327	88	50	80.6	13.6	3.7	2.1	3	90	58	29	1.0	1.1	0.6	1.1	1.0
Montgomery	2,413	1,681	609	81	42	69.7	25.2	3.4	1.7	65	20	69	47	1.0	0.9	1.1	1.1	0.8
Moore	159	104	35	18	2	65.4	22.0	11.3	1.3	85	47	1	69	<.1	<.1	<.1	0.2	<.1
Morgan	519	387	107	22	3	74.6	20.6	4.2	0.6	32	56	45	90	0.2	0.2	0.2	0.3	<.1
Obion	469	303	121	36	9	64.6	25.8	7.7	1.9	88	16	12	35	0.2	0.2	0.2	0.5	0.2
Overton	191	130	48	10	3	68.1	25.1	5.2	1.6	73	22	34	53	<.1	<.1	<.1	0.1	<.1
Perry	103	80	12	9	2	77.7	11.7	8.7	1.9	15	95	3	33	<.1	<.1	<.1	0.1	<.1
Pickett	326	268	44	8	6	82.2	13.5	2.5	1.8	1	91	87	43	0.1	0.2	<.1	0.1	0.1
Polk	562	441	87	27	7	78.5	15.5	4.8	1.2	12	84	40	72	0.2	0.2	0.2	0.4	0.1

Table J. — Vote for Presidential Preference: March 10, 1992, Republican Primary Election (cont)

County	Total	Bush	Bu-chanan	Duke	Other	Bush	Bu-chanan	Duke	Other	Bush	Bu-chanan	Duke	Other	Total	Bush	Bu-chanan	Duke	Other
Putnam	857	602	202	29	24	70.2	23.6	3.4	2.8	57	34	65	16	0.3	0.3	0.4	0.4	0.5
Rhea	3,089	2,032	776	193	88	65.8	25.1	6.2	2.8	80	23	21	14	1.3	1.1	1.4	2.5	1.7
Roane	2,841	2,178	537	80	46	76.7	18.9	2.8	1.6	20	71	80	50	1.2	1.2	1.0	1.0	0.9
Robertson	1,110	736	304	54	16	66.3	27.4	4.9	1.4	79	9	39	62	0.5	0.4	0.6	0.7	0.3
Rutherford	4,054	2,853	1,007	143	51	70.4	24.8	3.5	1.3	55	27	62	70	1.7	1.6	1.8	1.9	1.0
Scott	775	582	155	23	15	75.1	20.0	3.0	1.9	30	62	76	34	0.3	0.3	0.3	0.3	0.3
Sequatchie	339	209	100	29	1	61.7	29.5	8.6	0.3	92	6	7	93	0.1	0.1	0.2	0.4	<.1
Sevier	8,080	5,730	1,745	190	415	70.9	21.6	2.4	5.1	49	48	89	2	3.3	3.2	3.2	2.5	8.1
Shelby	34,050	26,019	6,886	856	289	76.4	20.2	2.5	0.8	22	59	86	87	13.9	14.6	12.6	11.1	5.6
Smith	310	219	72	16	3	70.6	23.2	5.2	1.0	52	38	37	80	0.1	0.1	0.1	0.2	<.1
Stewart	301	211	59	25	6	70.1	19.6	8.3	2.0	58	65	8	32	0.1	0.1	0.1	0.3	0.1
Sullivan	8,651	6,699	1,672	130	150	77.4	19.3	1.5	1.7	16	66	95	48	3.5	3.8	3.1	1.7	2.9
Sumner	3,988	2,757	1,069	120	42	69.1	26.8	3.0	1.1	66	11	75	77	1.6	1.5	2.0	1.6	0.8
Tipton	1,409	1,038	292	66	13	73.7	20.7	4.7	0.9	38	54	41	85	0.6	0.6	0.5	0.9	0.3
Trousdale	138	92	36	8	2	66.7	26.1	5.8	1.4	77	15	24	61	<.1	<.1	<.1	0.1	<.1
Unicoi	2,272	1,509	564	84	115	66.4	24.8	3.7	5.1	78	29	57	3	0.9	0.8	1.0	1.1	2.2
Union	528	398	93	32	5	75.4	17.6	6.1	0.9	28	77	22	82	0.2	0.2	0.2	0.4	<.1
Van Buren	216	160	33	21	2	74.1	15.3	9.7	0.9	36	86	2	84	<.1	<.1	<.1	0.3	<.1
Warren	656	431	166	49	10	65.7	25.3	7.5	1.5	82	18	16	57	0.3	0.2	0.3	0.6	0.2
Washington	4,916	3,433	1,230	101	152	69.8	25.0	2.1	3.1	61	24	91	12	2.0	1.9	2.3	1.3	3.0
Wayne	446	355	73	15	3	79.6	16.4	3.4	0.7	5	81	68	89	0.2	0.2	0.1	0.2	<.1
Weakley	537	391	115	22	9	72.8	21.4	4.1	1.7	41	50	47	49	0.2	0.2	0.2	0.3	0.2
White	170	111	51	6	2	65.3	30.0	3.5	1.2	86	5	61	75	<.1	<.1	<.1	<.1	<.1
Williamson	10,713	7,345	2,703	194	471	68.6	25.2	1.8	4.4	70	21	94	5	4.4	4.1	5.0	2.5	9.2
Wilson	5,543	4,124	1,129	174	116	74.4	20.4	3.1	2.1	34	58	73	28	2.3	2.3	2.1	2.3	2.3
TENNESSEE	245,653	178,219	54,585	7,709	5,140	72.5	22.2	3.1	2.1					100.0	100.0	100.0	100.0	100.0

1992 Vote for President
Percent for Clinton (D), by County

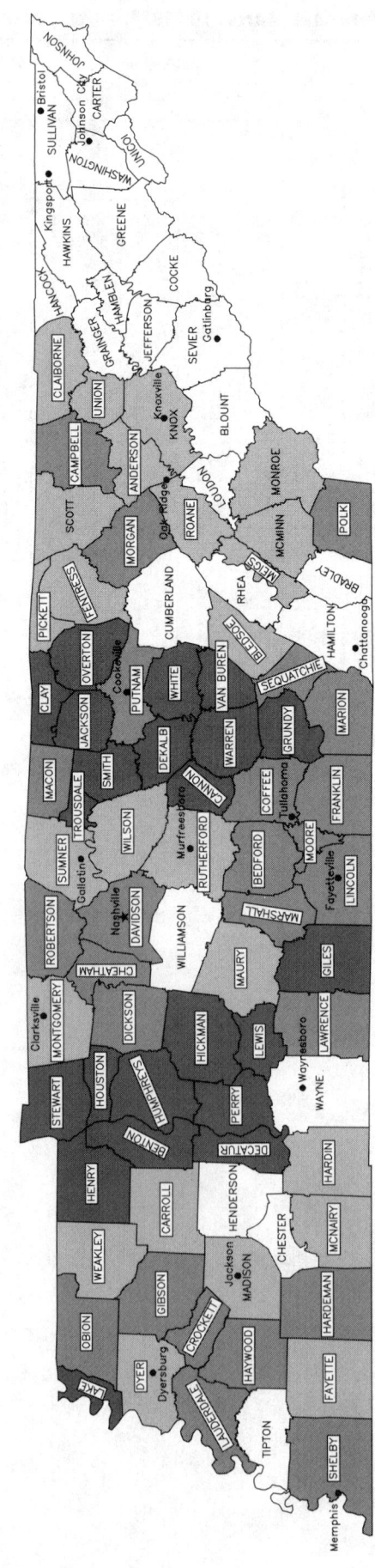

56.1% to 75.3%
49.0% to 56.0%
41.5% to 48.9%
31.6% to 41.4%

Clinton (D) received 47.1% statewide.

A framed county name indicates
a county carried by the winner.

TEXAS

Congressional Districts 30
   Average Population 566,217
State Senate Districts 31
   Average Population 547,952
State House Districts 150
   Average Population 113,243

Electoral College Votes 32
Counties 254
Voting Precincts 8,282

Alternative Registration Methods:
   ....Deputized Registrars, Mail-in, Motor-voter

Registration Deadline (Days before Election) 30

Voting Equipment Use (Counties)

Datavote Punch Card	0	Paper Ballot	136
Electronic	0	Other Punch Card	29
Lever Machine	7	Mixed Systems	0
Optical Scanner	82		

Party Control	DEM	REP	IND	VAC
1993 State Senate	18	13	0	0
1992 State Senate	22	9	0	0
1993 State House	92	58	0	0
1992 State House	93	57	0	0

Population Statistics 1990

Race/ Ethnicity	Total Population		Voting Age Population		Voting Age Population % of total population
	Number	%	Number	%	
Non-Hispanic					
White	10,291,680	60.6	7,828,352	64.4	76.1
Black	1,976,360	11.6	1,336,688	11.0	67.6
Asian/Pacific Islander	303,825	1.8	213,294	1.8	70.2
Native American	52,803	0.3	39,316	0.3	74.5
Other	21,937	0.1	13,435	0.1	61.2
All Hispanic	4,339,905	25.5	2,719,586	22.4	62.7
TOTAL	16,986,510	100.0	12,150,671	100.0	71.5

Estimated Voting Age Population 1992 (VAP) 12,524,000
Number of Registered Voters 8,440,143
   % of estimated VAP 67.4
Voter Turnout (Highest Office) 6,154,088
   % of VAP 49.1
   % of Registration 72.9
Persons Not Voting—of Voting Age 6,369,912
   % of VAP 50.9
Persons Not Voting—of Registered 2,286,055
   % of Registration 27.1
Straight Ticket Voting .... Yes, Exception

State Officials and Members of Congress

Governor:
Ann W. Richards (D) 1990, elected to a four-year term in 1990.

U.S. Senators:
Phil Gramm (R) 1984, elected to a six-year term in 1990.
Kay Bailey Hutchison (R) 1993, elected to a two-year term in 1993.[1]

U.S. Representative in Congress:
(District, Name, Party, Date first elected)

1. Chapman (D) 1985
2. Wilson (D) 1972
3. Johnson (R) 1991
4. Hall (D) 1980
5. Bryant (D) 1982
6. Barton (R) 1984
7. Archer (R) 1970
8. Fields (R) 1980
9. Brooks (D) 1952
10. Pickle (D) 1963
11. Edwards (D) 1990
12. Geren (D) 1989
13. Sarpalius (D) 1988
14. Laughlin (D) 1988
15. de la Garza (D) 1964
16. Coleman (D) 1982
17. Stenholm (D) 1978
18. Washington (D) 1989
19. Combest (R) 1984
20. Gonzalez (D) 1961
21. Smith (R) 1986
22. DeLay (R) 1984
23. Bonilla (R) 1992
24. Frost (D) 1978
25. Andrews (D) 1982
26. Armey (R) 1984
27. Ortiz (D) 1982
28. Tejeda (D) 1992
29. Green (D) 1992
30. Johnson (D) 1992

[1]Elected from June 5, 1993, special election for remaining two years of term vacated by Lloyd Bentsen (D), who was appointed as U.S. Secretary of the Treasury; defeated interim appointee Robert Krueger (D).

Candidates: General Election, November 3, 1992

Candidate(s)	Total vote	Percent	Party	Status	First elected
President/Vice President					
Bush/Quayle	2,496,071	40.56%	Republican	Incumbent	1988
Clinton/Gore	2,281,815	37.08%	Democrat	Challenger	1992
Perot/Stockdale	1,354,781	22.01%	Independent	Challenger	
Marrou/Lord	19,699	0.32%	Libertarian	Challenger	
Gritz/Minett	505	<.01%	Write in	Challenger	
Phillips/Knight	359	<.01%	Write in	Challenger	
Fulani/Munoz	301	<.01%	Write in	Challenger	
Hagelin/Tompkins	217	<.01%	Write in	Challenger	
LaRouche/Bevel	169	<.01%	Write in	Challenger	
Brisben/Garson	78	<.01%	Write in	Challenger	
Wright/Cunningham	23	<.01%	Write in	Challenger	

U.S. Senator (No Contest)

Governor (No Contest)

U.S. Representative in Congress

Candidate(s)	Total vote	Percent	Party	Status	First elected
District 1					
Jim Chapman	152,209	100.00%	Democrat	Incumbent	1985
District 2					
Charles Wilson	118,625	56.13%	Democrat	Incumbent	1972
Donna Peterson	92,176	43.61%	Republican	Challenger	
Roger Northen	549	0.26%	Write in	Challenger	
District 3					
Sam Johnson	201,569	86.09%	Republican	Incumbent	1991
Noel Kopala	32,570	13.91%	Libertarian	Challenger	
District 4					
Ralph Hall	128,008	58.10%	Democrat	Incumbent	1980
David Bridges	83,875	38.07%	Republican	Challenger	
Steven Rothacker	8,450	3.84%	Libertarian	Challenger	
District 5					
John Bryant	98,567	58.91%	Democrat	Incumbent	1982
Richard Stokley	62,419	37.30%	Republican	Challenger	
William Walker	6,344	3.79%	Libertarian	Challenger	
District 6					
Joe Barton	189,140	71.90%	Republican	Incumbent	1984
John Dietrich	73,933	28.10%	Democrat	Challenger	
District 7					
Bill Archer	169,407	100.00%	Republican	Incumbent	1970
District 8					
Jack Fields, Jr.	179,349	77.03%	Republican	Incumbent	1980
Chas. Robinson	53,473	22.97%	Democrat	Challenger	
District 9					
Jack Brooks	118,690	53.62%	Democrat	Incumbent	1952
Steve Stockman	96,270	43.49%	Republican	Challenger	
Billy Joe Crawford	6,401	2.89%	Libertarian	Challenger	
District 10					
J.J. "Jake" Pickle	177,233	67.67%	Democrat	Incumbent	1963
Herbert Spiro	68,646	26.21%	Republican	Challenger	
Terry Blum	6,353	2.43%	Libertarian	Challenger	
Jeff Davis	6,056	2.31%	Independent	Challenger	
Stephen Hopkins	3,510	1.34%	Write in	Challenger	
Robert Shaw	94	0.04%	Write in	Challenger	

Candidate(s)	Total vote	Percent	Party	Status	First elected
U.S. Representative in Congress (cont)					
District 11					
Chet Edwards	119,999	67.40%	Democrat	Incumbent	1990
James Broyles	58,033	32.60%	Republican	Challenger	
District 12					
Pete Geren	125,492	62.77%	Democrat	Incumbent	1989
David Hobbs	74,432	37.23%	Republican	Challenger	
District 13					
Bill Sarpalius	117,892	60.33%	Democrat	Incumbent	1988
Beau Boulter	77,514	39.67%	Republican	Challenger	
District 14					
Greg Laughlin	135,930	68.08%	Democrat	Incumbent	1988
Humberto Garza	54,412	27.25%	Republican	Challenger	
Vic Vreeland	9,329	4.67%	Independent	Challenger	
District 15					
E "Kika" Garza	86,351	60.43%	Democrat	Incumbent	1964
Tom Haughey	56,549	39.57%	Republican	Challenger	
District 16					
Ronald Coleman	66,731	51.89%	Democrat	Incumbent	1982
Chip Taberski	61,870	48.11%	Republican	Challenger	
District 17					
Charles Stenholm	136,213	66.07%	Democrat	Incumbent	1978
Jeannie Sadowski	69,958	33.93%	Republican	Challenger	
District 18					
Craig Washington	111,422	64.70%	Democrat	Incumbent	1989
Edward Blum	56,080	32.57%	Republican	Challenger	
Gregg Lassen	4,706	2.73%	Libertarian	Challenger	
District 19					
Larry Combest	162,057	77.40%	Republican	Incumbent	1984
Terry Moser	47,325	22.60%	Democrat	Challenger	
District 20					
Henry Gonzalez	103,755	100.00%	Democrat	Incumbent	1961
District 21					
Lamar Smith	190,979	72.16%	Republican	Incumbent	1986
James Gaddy	62,827	23.74%	Democrat	Challenger	
William Grisham	10,847	4.10%	Libertarian	Challenger	
District 22					
Tom DeLay	150,221	68.90%	Republican	Incumbent	1984
Richard Konrad	67,812	31.10%	Democrat	Challenger	
District 23					
Henry Bonilla	98,259	59.07%	Republican	Challenger	1992
Albert Bustamante	63,797	38.35%	Democrat	Incumbent	1984
David Alter	4,291	2.58%	Libertarian	Challenger	
District 24					
Martin Frost	104,174	59.80%	Democrat	Incumbent	1978
Steve Masterson	70,042	40.20%	Republican	Challenger	
District 25					
Mike Andrews	98,975	55.96%	Democrat	Incumbent	1982
Dolly McKenna	73,192	41.38%	Republican	Challenger	
Richard Mauk	4,710	2.66%	Libertarian	Challenger	
District 26					
Dick Armey	150,209	73.08%	Republican	Incumbent	1984
John Wayne Caton	55,237	26.88%	Democrat	Challenger	
Steve Love	85	0.04%	Write in	Challenger	

Candidate(s)	Total vote	Percent	Party	Status	First elected
U.S. Representative in Congress (cont)					
District 27					
Solomon Ortiz	87,022	55.48%	Democrat	Incumbent	1982
Jay Kimbrough	66,853	42.62%	Republican	Challenger	
Charles Schoonover	2,969	1.89%	Libertarian	Challenger	
District 28					
Frank Tejeda	122,457	87.11%	Democrat	Challenger	1992
David Slatter	18,128	12.89%	Libertarian	Challenger	
District 29					
Gene Green	64,064	64.93%	Democrat	Challenger	1992
Clark Ervin	34,609	35.07%	Republican	Challenger	
District 30					
Eddie Johnson	107,831	71.53%	Democrat	Challenger	1992
Lucy Cain	37,853	25.11%	Republican	Challenger	
Ken Ashby	5,063	3.36%	Libertarian	Challenger	

Candidates: March 10, 1992, Primary Election

Candidate	Total vote	Percent
Presidential Preference, Democratic		
Bill Clinton	972,151	65.55%
Paul Tsongas	285,191	19.23%
Jerry Brown	118,923	8.02%
Charles Woods	30,092	2.03%
Bob Kerrey	20,298	1.37%
Tom Harkin	19,617	1.32%
Lyndon LaRouche, Jr.	12,220	0.82%
George Benns	7,876	0.53%
Rufus Higginbotham	7,674	0.52%
Tod Hawks	4,924	0.33%
J. Louis McAlpine	4,009	0.27%

Candidate	Total vote	Percent
Presidential Preference, Republican		
George Bush	556,280	69.78%
Patrick Buchanan	190,572	23.91%
Uncommitted	27,936	3.50%
David Duke	20,255	2.54%
George Zimmermann	1,349	0.17%
Tennie Rogers	754	0.09%

Voter Registration and Turnout, 1948-1992 Elections

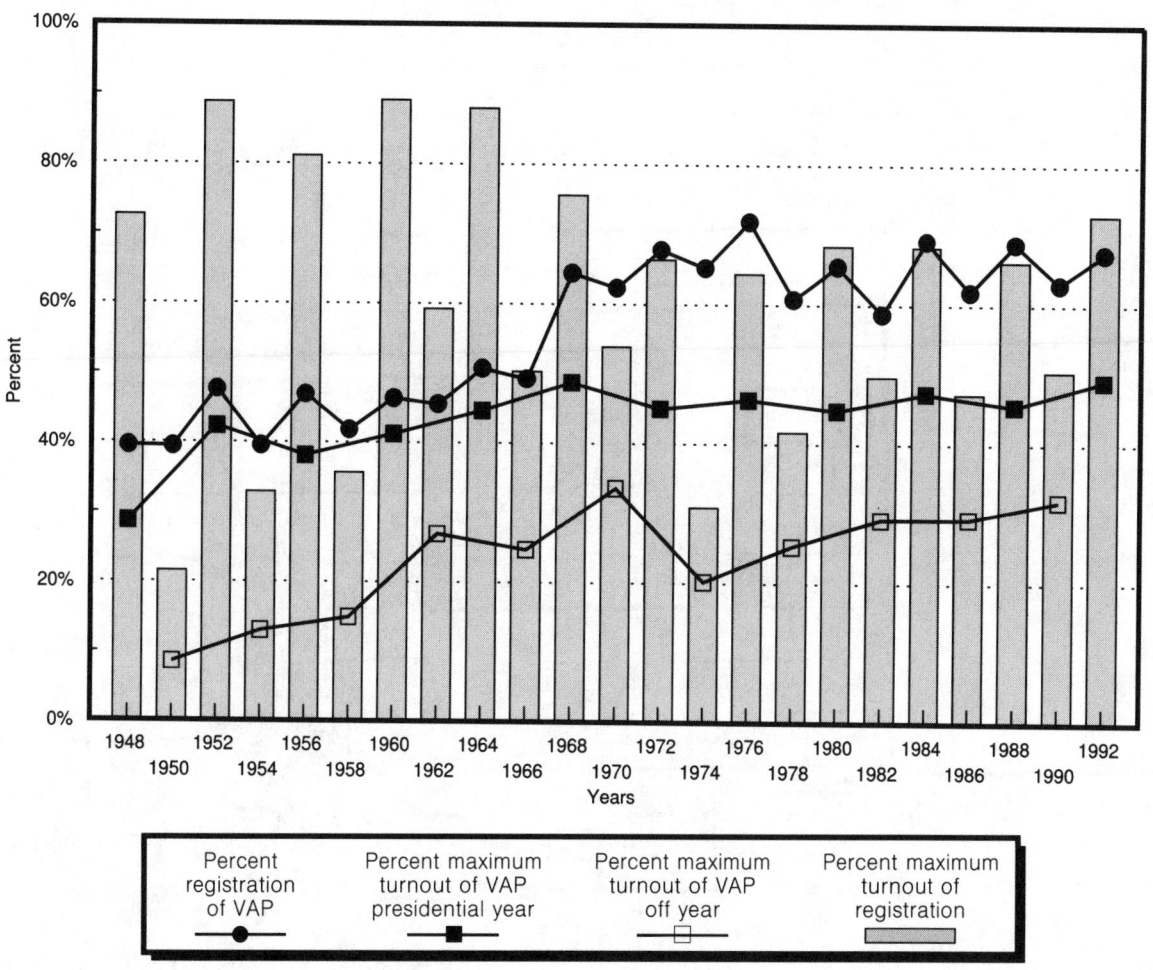

Percent registration of VAP	Percent maximum turnout of VAP presidential year	Percent maximum turnout of VAP off year	Percent maximum turnout of registration

Year	Estimated Voting Age Population (VAP)	Voter registration (REG)				Voter turnout										
						Highest office						Maximum vote				
		Total	Percent of VAP	Rank by percent of VAP	Actual	Total	Office	Percent total REG	Rank by percent of REG	Percent of VAP	Rank by percent of VAP	Total	Percent total REG	Rank by percent of REG	Percent total VAP	Rank by percent of VAP
1992	12,524,000	8,440,143	67.4	38	-	6,154,018	P	72.9	37	49.1	48	6,154,018	72.9	38	49.1	48
1990	12,222,000	7,701,499	63.0	35	-	3,892,746	G	50.5	39	31.9	43	3,892,746	50.5	40	31.9	44
1988	11,919,000	8,201,856	68.8	31	-	5,427,410	P	66.2	39	45.5	43	5,427,410	66.2	40	45.5	43
1986	11,764,000	7,287,173	61.9	40	-	3,442,368	G	47.2	40	29.3	44	3,442,368	47.2	42	29.3	45
1984	11,420,000	7,900,167	69.2	32	-	5,397,571	P	68.3	39	47.3	45	5,397,571	68.3	40	47.3	45
1982	10,924,000	6,414,988	58.7	42	-	3,191,091	G	49.7	44	29.2	46	3,191,091	49.7	44	29.2	47
1980	10,130,000	6,639,661	65.5	38	-	4,541,636	P	68.4	41	44.8	44	4,541,636	68.4	43	44.8	47
1978	9,350,000	5,681,875	60.8	40	-	2,369,764	G	41.7	44	25.3	47	2,369,764	41.7	44	25.3	47
1976	8,789,000	6,319,293	71.9	28	-	4,071,884	P	64.4	45	46.3	45	4,071,884	64.4	45	46.3	46
1974	8,198,000	5,348,393	65.2	36	-	1,654,984	G	30.9	47	20.2	49	1,654,984	30.9	47	20.2	49
1972	7,719,000	5,230,521	67.8	36	-	3,471,281	P	66.4	38	45.0	42	3,471,281	66.4	39	45.0	42
1970	6,658,000	4,149,250	62.3	41	-	2,235,847	G	53.9	37	33.6	44	2,235,847	53.9	37	33.6	44
1968	6,327,000	4,073,576	64.4	37	-	3,079,216	P	75.6	36	48.7	48	3,079,216	75.6	36	48.7	48
1966	6,035,000	2,970,966	49.2	41	-	1,493,182	S	50.3	36	24.7	50	1,493,182	50.3	36	24.7	50
1964	5,889,000	2,984,766	50.7	39	-	2,626,811	P	88.0	6	44.6	44	2,626,811	88.0	10	44.6	45
1962	5,832,000	2,651,211	45.5	35	-	1,569,181	P	59.2	28	26.9	44	1,569,181	59.2	28	26.9	44
1960	5,605,000	2,594,254	46.3	34	-	2,311,084	P	89.1	10	41.2	44	2,311,084	89.1	11	41.2	44
1958	5,298,000	2,213,514	41.8	31	-	789,133	G	35.7	28	14.9	44	789,133	35.7	28	14.9	44
1956	5,135,000	2,410,188	46.9	28	-	1,955,168	P	81.1	15	38.1	42	1,955,168	81.1	17	38.1	42
1954	4,905,000	1,935,319	39.5	25	-	636,892	G	32.9	23	13.0	46	636,892	32.9	23	13.0	46
1952	4,909,000	2,338,261	47.6	22	-	2,075,946	P	88.8	6	42.3	41	2,075,946	88.8	7	42.3	41
1950	4,650,000	1,832,475	39.4	21	-	394,747	G	21.5	22	8.5	46	394,747	21.5	22	8.5	46
1948	4,360,000	1,720,093	39.5	20	-	1,249,577	P	72.6	14	28.7	40	1,249,577	72.6	14	28.7	40

TEXAS

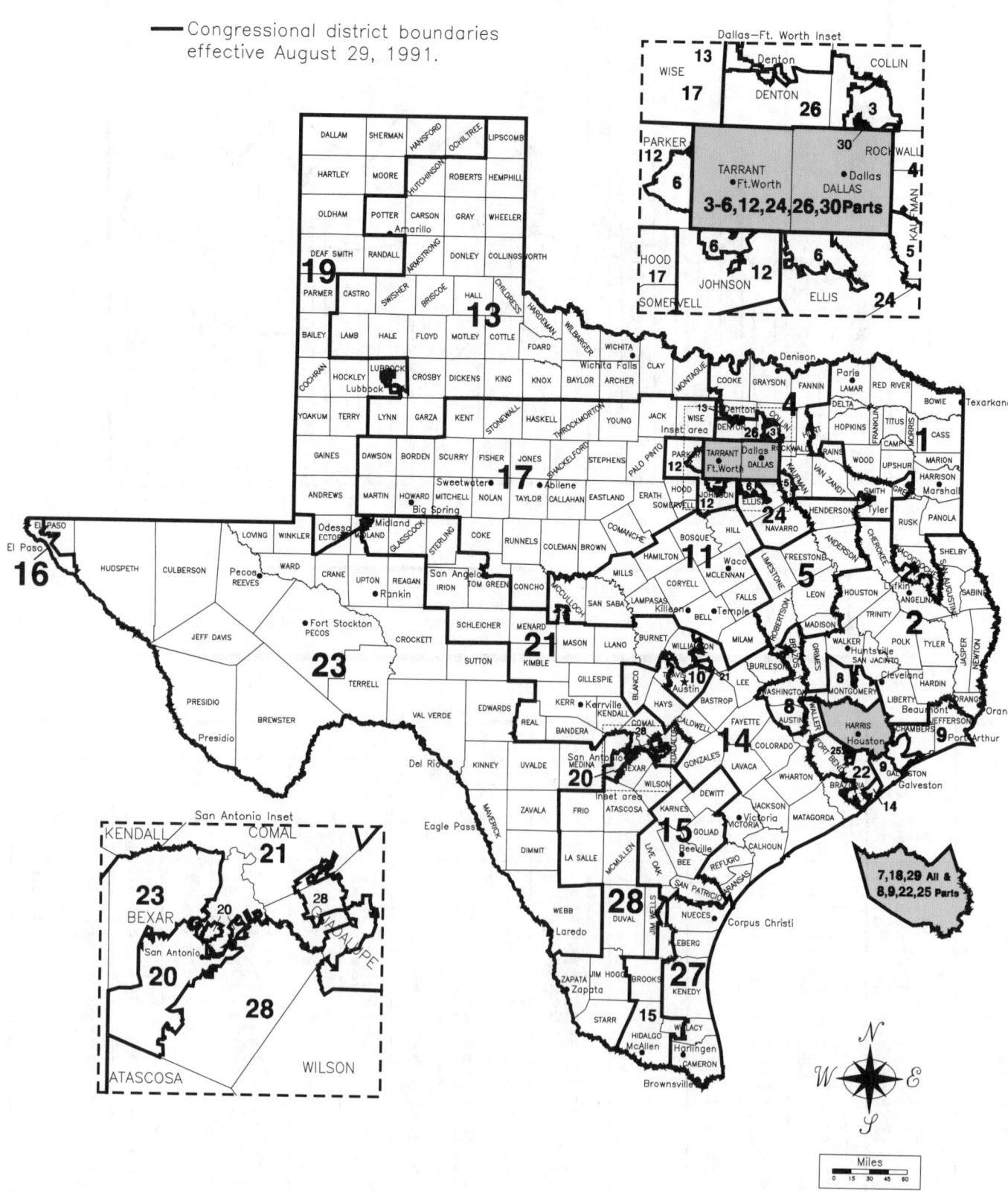

Congressional district boundaries effective August 29, 1991.

Copyright © 1993 by Election Data Services, Inc.

Tarrant & Dallas Counties, Texas

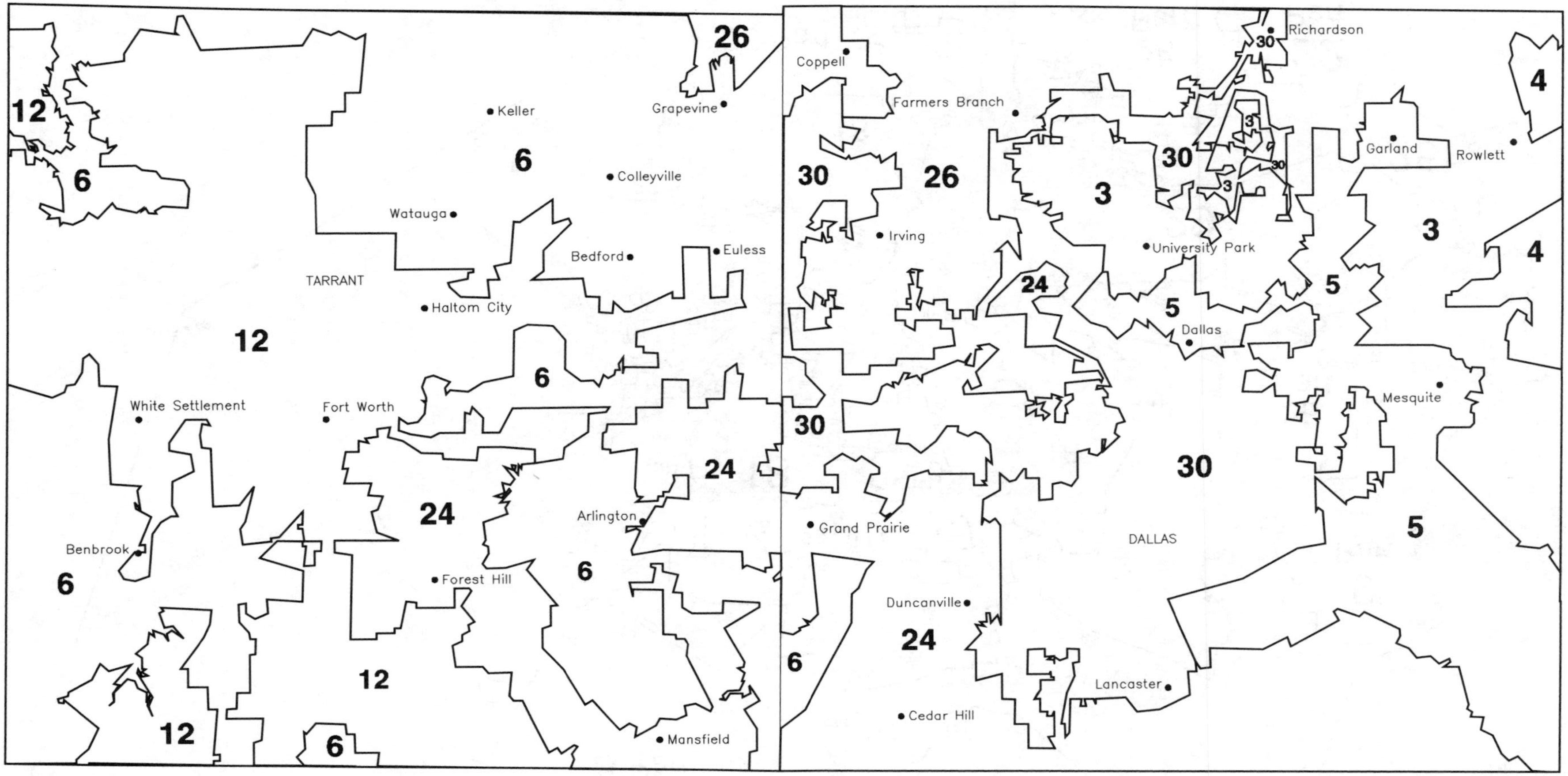

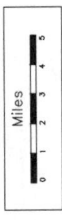

— Congressional district boundaries effective August 29, 1991.

All districts are partial. Each district extends beyond the county boundary.

Texas 877

Harris County, Texas

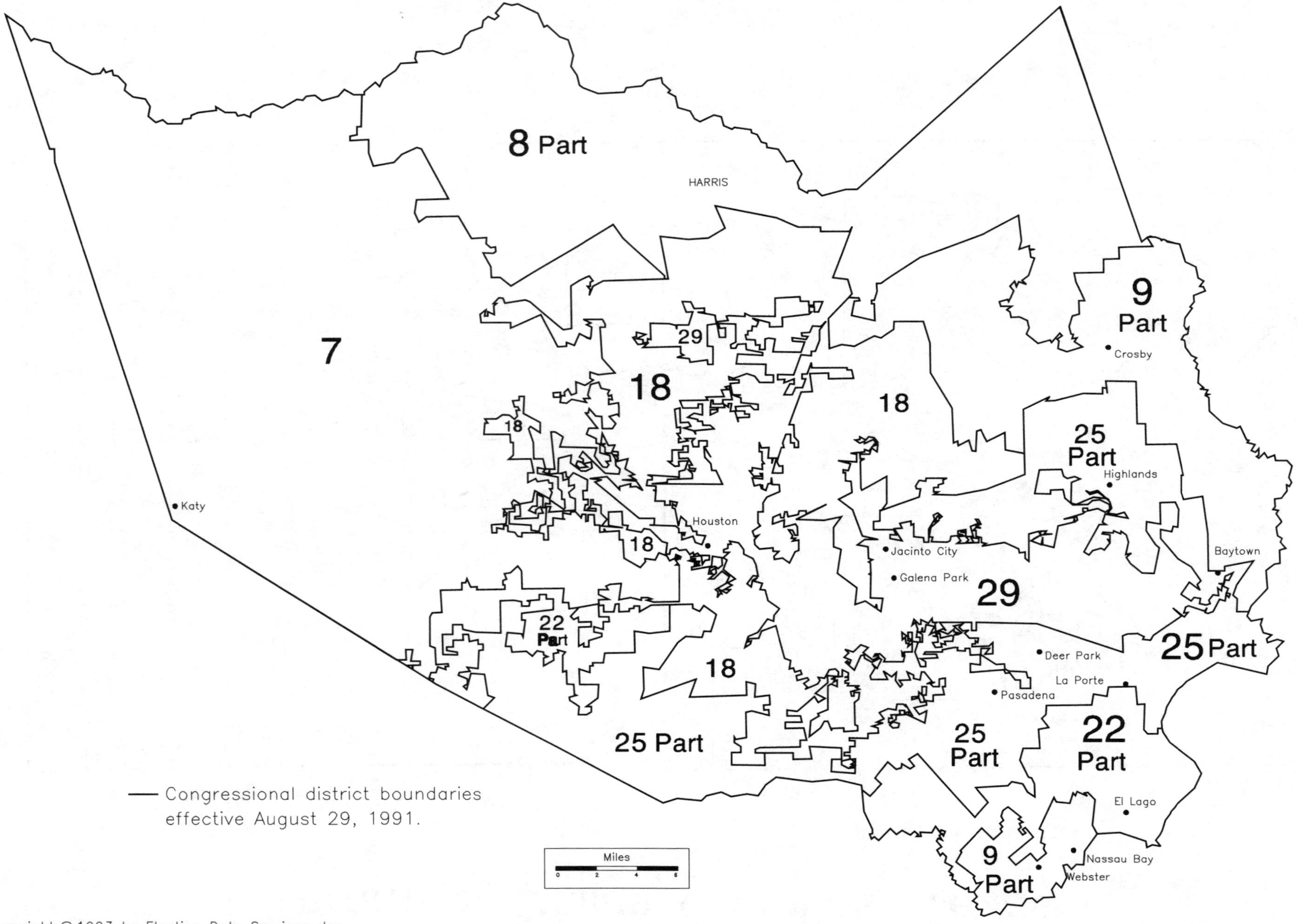

HARRIS

8 Part

7

9 Part
• Crosby

25 Part
• Highlands

18

29

18

18

18

18

29

• Katy

• Houston

• Jacinto City
• Galena Park

• Deer Park
• La Porte
• Pasadena

22 Part

25 Part

18

25 Part

• Baytown

25 Part

22 Part

• El Lago

• Nassau Bay
• Webster

9 Part

Miles

— Congressional district boundaries
effective August 29, 1991.

Table A. — 1990 Population by Race and Ethnic Origin

State/ county code	County	Total persons	Percent of total persons — Non-Hispanic White	Black	Asian and Pacific Islander	Native American	Other	Hispanic	Rank Total	Rank Non-Hispanic White	Black	Hispanic	Percent contribution to state population Total	Non-Hispanic White	Black	Hispanic
48 001	Anderson	48,024	68.0	23.1	0.2	0.2	0.2	8.2	52	154	14	178	0.3	0.3	0.6	<.1
48 003	Andrews	14,338	64.7	1.8	1.0	0.4	0.3	31.7	135	169	160	73	<.1	<.1	<.1	0.1
48 005	Angelina	69,884	75.5	15.1	0.4	0.2	0.1	8.7	38	117	42	173	0.4	0.5	0.5	0.1
48 007	Aransas	17,892	74.4	1.7	3.2	0.5	0.2	20.1	115	124	166	104	0.1	0.1	<.1	<.1
48 009	Archer	7,973	97.0	0.1	<.1	0.5	0.0	2.4	180	1	219	236	<.1	<.1	<.1	<.1
48 011	Armstrong	2,021	96.5	0.0	0.2	0.4	<.1	2.7	237	2	242	229	<.1	<.1	0.0	<.1
48 013	Atascosa	30,533	46.5	0.4	0.2	0.2	0.2	52.6	75	225	197	27	0.2	0.1	<.1	0.4
48 015	Austin	19,832	76.3	12.9	0.1	0.2	<.1	10.5	105	107	50	165	0.1	0.1	0.1	<.1
48 017	Bailey	7,064	59.2	1.7	0.2	0.1	<.1	38.8	184	192	167	55	<.1	<.1	<.1	<.1
48 019	Bandera	10,562	87.8	0.2	0.2	0.6	<.1	11.1	157	40	208	155	<.1	<.1	<.1	<.1
48 021	Bastrop	38,263	69.7	11.4	0.3	0.4	0.1	18.1	61	146	59	115	0.2	0.3	0.2	0.2
48 023	Baylor	4,385	87.8	4.1	0.3	0.2	<.1	7.6	211	41	116	184	<.1	<.1	<.1	<.1
48 025	Bee	25,135	44.6	2.7	0.8	0.2	0.3	51.4	88	227	145	30	0.1	0.1	<.1	0.3
48 027	Bell	191,088	65.4	18.3	2.7	0.4	0.1	13.1	17	164	33	141	1.1	1.2	1.8	0.6
48 029	Bexar	1,185,394	41.9	6.9	1.2	0.2	0.2	49.7	3	230	87	33	7.0	4.8	4.1	13.6
48 031	Blanco	5,972	84.4	0.9	0.3	0.3	<.1	14.1	192	63	181	136	<.1	<.1	<.1	<.1
48 033	Borden	799	83.7	0.0	0.0	1.3	0.0	15.0	251	67	243	127	<.1	<.1	0.0	<.1
48 035	Bosque	15,125	88.1	2.1	0.2	0.2	<.1	9.5	129	38	157	168	<.1	0.1	<.1	<.1
48 037	Bowie	81,665	75.9	21.7	0.3	0.5	<.1	1.6	35	114	16	247	0.5	0.6	0.9	<.1
48 039	Brazoria	191,707	72.9	8.0	1.0	0.4	0.1	17.6	16	132	80	117	1.1	1.4	0.8	0.8
48 041	Brazos	121,862	71.5	11.0	3.5	0.2	0.1	13.7	24	137	60	138	0.7	0.8	0.7	0.4
48 043	Brewster	8,681	55.7	0.9	0.6	0.2	<.1	42.6	172	203	182	42	<.1	<.1	<.1	<.1
48 045	Briscoe	1,971	77.7	3.5	0.0	0.2	0.0	18.6	239	99	132	112	<.1	<.1	<.1	<.1
48 047	Brooks	8,204	10.0	<.1	<.1	<.1	0.3	89.4	175	249	235	5	<.1	<.1	<.1	0.2
48 049	Brown	34,371	83.8	4.5	0.2	0.3	<.1	11.1	69	66	107	158	0.2	0.3	<.1	<.1
48 051	Burleson	13,625	70.0	17.6	<.1	0.3	0.1	11.9	138	144	34	149	<.1	<.1	0.1	<.1
48 053	Burnet	22,677	87.4	1.1	0.2	0.4	<.1	10.8	97	44	175	162	0.1	0.2	<.1	<.1
48 055	Caldwell	26,392	51.3	10.1	0.3	0.2	0.2	37.8	84	216	64	56	0.2	0.1	0.1	0.2
48 057	Calhoun	19,053	57.8	2.8	2.9	0.2	<.1	36.2	107	197	142	62	0.1	0.1	<.1	0.2
48 059	Callahan	11,859	95.2	<.1	0.3	0.4	<.1	4.1	152	8	240	216	<.1	0.1	<.1	<.1
48 061	Cameron	260,120	17.4	0.2	0.2	<.1	0.2	81.9	11	244	209	11	1.5	0.4	<.1	4.9
48 063	Camp	9,904	70.8	23.7	<.1	0.3	<.1	5.1	161	140	11	207	<.1	<.1	0.1	<.1
48 065	Carson	6,576	93.6	0.2	0.1	0.6	<.1	5.4	190	12	216	202	<.1	<.1	<.1	<.1
48 067	Cass	29,982	78.3	20.1	<.1	0.3	<.1	1.2	77	97	23	250	0.2	0.2	0.3	<.1
48 069	Castro	9,070	50.4	2.9	0.2	<.1	0.3	46.2	168	218	141	37	<.1	<.1	<.1	<.1
48 071	Chambers	20,088	80.5	12.6	0.6	0.2	0.1	5.9	104	86	51	197	0.1	0.2	0.1	<.1
48 073	Cherokee	41,049	76.0	16.7	0.4	0.2	<.1	6.6	56	112	36	193	0.2	0.3	0.3	<.1
48 075	Childress	5,953	79.6	5.3	0.3	0.4	<.1	14.3	193	90	96	132	<.1	<.1	<.1	<.1
48 077	Clay	10,024	96.2	0.3	0.2	0.8	0.0	2.4	159	5	200	233	<.1	0.1	<.1	<.1
48 079	Cochran	4,377	52.0	5.3	<.1	0.3	<.1	42.4	212	215	99	44	<.1	<.1	<.1	<.1
48 081	Coke	3,424	86.9	0.1	<.1	0.5	<.1	12.3	221	48	222	145	<.1	<.1	<.1	<.1
48 083	Coleman	9,710	85.4	2.5	<.1	0.3	<.1	11.7	163	57	149	152	<.1	<.1	<.1	<.1
48 085	Collin	264,036	85.8	4.1	2.8	0.4	<.1	6.9	10	56	121	191	1.6	2.2	0.5	0.4
48 087	Collingsworth	3,573	77.0	6.4	<.1	0.8	0.1	15.7	220	102	91	124	<.1	<.1	0.2	<.1
48 089	Colorado	18,383	67.7	16.6	<.1	0.1	<.1	15.4	113	156	37	125	0.1	0.1	0.2	<.1
48 091	Comal	51,832	75.7	0.8	0.3	0.2	0.1	22.9	50	115	184	95	0.3	0.4	<.1	0.3
48 093	Comanche	13,381	83.0	<.1	<.1	0.2	0.1	16.5	142	71	223	121	<.1	0.1	<.1	<.1
48 095	Concho	3,044	60.0	0.5	0.1	0.1	<.1	39.2	227	188	192	53	<.1	<.1	<.1	<.1
48 097	Cooke	30,777	90.5	3.7	0.4	0.7	<.1	4.6	73	22	126	211	0.2	0.3	<.1	<.1
48 099	Coryell	64,213	66.5	20.7	2.3	0.6	0.1	9.7	43	160	19	167	0.4	0.4	0.7	0.1
48 101	Cottle	2,247	74.6	8.7	0.1	0.2	<.1	16.3	236	123	71	123	<.1	<.1	<.1	<.1
48 103	Crane	4,652	62.8	2.8	0.2	0.2	0.1	33.9	207	179	144	69	<.1	<.1	<.1	<.1
48 105	Crockett	4,078	49.4	0.8	<.1	0.2	0.0	49.6	215	219	186	34	<.1	<.1	<.1	<.1
48 107	Crosby	7,304	53.0	4.1	0.1	<.1	0.2	42.6	183	211	120	43	<.1	<.1	<.1	<.1
48 109	Culberson	3,407	27.9	<.1	0.7	0.3	0.0	71.0	223	234	226	19	<.1	<.1	<.1	<.1
48 111	Dallam	5,461	76.1	1.9	0.3	0.6	0.1	21.1	196	109	159	101	<.1	<.1	<.1	<.1
48 113	Dallas	1,852,810	60.2	19.5	2.7	0.4	0.1	17.0	2	187	26	118	10.9	10.8	18.3	7.3
48 115	Dawson	14,349	52.7	4.2	0.1	<.1	0.1	42.7	134	212	112	41	<.1	<.1	<.1	0.1
48 117	Deaf Smith	19,153	49.2	1.5	0.2	0.2	0.1	48.8	106	221	170	35	0.1	<.1	<.1	0.2
48 119	Delta	4,857	89.4	8.2	0.1	0.8	0.0	1.4	204	30	77	249	<.1	<.1	<.1	<.1
48 121	Denton	273,525	85.1	4.9	2.5	0.5	<.1	7.0	9	60	101	190	1.6	2.3	0.7	0.4
48 123	DeWitt	18,840	65.1	10.4	<.1	<.1	0.2	24.2	108	168	63	90	0.1	0.1	<.1	0.1
48 125	Dickens	2,571	76.4	4.3	<.1	0.5	0.1	18.6	231	106	111	111	<.1	<.1	<.1	<.1
48 127	Dimmit	10,433	15.9	0.5	<.1	0.1	0.2	83.3	158	245	191	10	<.1	<.1	<.1	0.2
48 129	Donley	3,696	92.4	3.4	<.1	0.4	0.0	3.8	218	15	133	223	<.1	<.1	<.1	<.1
48 131	Duval	12,918	12.4	<.1	<.1	<.1	0.2	87.2	147	248	225	7	<.1	<.1	<.1	0.3
48 133	Eastland	18,488	89.8	2.1	0.2	0.2	<.1	7.6	112	26	155	185	0.1	0.2	<.1	<.1
48 135	Ector	118,934	62.9	4.5	0.5	0.5	0.2	31.4	26	178	104	75	0.7	0.7	0.3	0.9
48 137	Edwards	2,266	47.5	0.0	0.2	0.2	0.0	52.2	234	222	244	29	<.1	<.1	0.0	<.1
48 139	Ellis	85,167	76.2	9.9	0.2	0.4	0.1	13.2	34	108	65	139	0.5	0.6	0.4	0.3

State/county code	County	Total persons	White	Black	Asian and Pacific Islander	Native American	Other	Hispanic	Total	White	Black	Hispanic	Total	White	Black	Hispanic
			\<Percent of total persons — Non-Hispanic\>						\<Rank — Percent of total persons; Non-Hispanic\>				\<Percent contribution to state population — Non-Hispanic\>			
48 141	El Paso	591,610	25.6	3.5	1.0	0.3	0.1	69.6	5	238	131	21	3.5	1.5	1.0	9.5
48 143	Erath	27,991	89.8	0.7	0.4	0.3	<.1	8.8	81	28	188	171	0.2	0.2	<.1	<.1
48 145	Falls	17,712	61.2	26.7	0.1	0.2	<.1	11.7	117	183	8	153	0.1	0.1	0.2	<.1
48 147	Fannin	24,804	90.6	6.5	0.2	0.7	<.1	2.0	90	21	89	241	0.1	0.2	<.1	<.1
48 149	Fayette	20,095	83.0	8.3	<.1	0.1	<.1	8.5	103	72	76	177	0.1	0.2	<.1	<.1
48 151	Fisher	4,842	75.4	3.8	0.0	0.1	<.1	20.6	205	119	124	102	<.1	<.1	<.1	<.1
48 153	Floyd	8,497	56.0	3.7	0.1	0.2	0.2	39.8	174	202	127	48	<.1	<.1	<.1	<.1
48 155	Foard	1,794	82.4	4.1	0.2	0.3	<.1	13.0	242	76	119	142	<.1	<.1	<.1	<.1
48 157	Fort Bend	225,421	53.8	20.3	6.2	0.2	<.1	19.5	13	210	22	107	1.3	1.2	2.3	1.0
48 159	Franklin	7,802	90.2	4.5	0.2	0.5	<.1	4.6	181	24	106	210	<.1	<.1	<.1	<.1
48 161	Freestone	15,818	76.6	19.0	0.2	0.3	<.1	3.9	127	104	27	221	<.1	0.1	0.2	<.1
48 163	Frio	13,472	26.0	1.0	0.2	<.1	0.3	72.4	141	237	177	17	<.1	<.1	<.1	0.2
48 165	Gaines	14,123	64.4	2.3	<.1	0.2	0.4	32.6	137	173	153	70	<.1	<.1	<.1	0.1
48 167	Galveston	217,399	66.6	17.2	1.5	0.3	<.1	14.2	15	159	35	133	1.3	1.4	1.9	0.7
48 169	Garza	5,143	65.2	5.9	0.4	<.1	<.1	28.3	201	165	95	80	<.1	<.1	<.1	<.1
48 171	Gillespie	17,204	85.3	0.2	0.1	0.2	<.1	14.1	121	58	215	135	0.1	0.1	<.1	<.1
48 173	Glasscock	1,447	70.4	0.0	0.0	0.0	0.3	29.3	245	141	245	79	<.1	<.1	0.0	<.1
48 175	Goliad	5,980	57.2	6.5	<.1	0.2	0.2	35.9	191	199	90	63	<.1	<.1	<.1	<.1
48 177	Gonzales	17,205	54.6	9.2	0.1	<.1	0.3	35.7	120	205	66	64	0.1	<.1	<.1	0.1
48 179	Gray	23,967	87.0	3.7	0.5	0.8	0.1	7.9	93	47	128	181	0.1	0.2	<.1	<.1
48 181	Grayson	95,021	88.7	6.9	0.4	1.1	<.1	2.9	32	34	88	228	0.6	0.8	0.3	<.1
48 183	Gregg	104,948	76.6	18.9	0.5	0.4	<.1	3.6	28	105	28	224	0.6	0.8	1.0	<.1
48 185	Grimes	18,828	61.4	24.2	<.1	0.2	<.1	14.1	109	182	10	134	0.1	0.1	0.2	<.1
48 187	Guadalupe	64,873	63.9	5.3	0.6	0.3	0.2	29.7	40	174	97	78	0.4	0.4	0.2	0.4
48 189	Hale	34,671	52.4	5.1	0.3	0.3	0.2	41.6	68	213	100	46	0.2	0.2	<.1	0.3
48 191	Hall	3,905	73.0	7.7	0.2	0.4	0.1	18.6	216	130	81	113	<.1	<.1	<.1	<.1
48 193	Hamilton	7,733	94.2	<.1	0.3	0.2	<.1	5.2	182	9	234	205	<.1	<.1	<.1	<.1
48 195	Hansford	5,848	79.3	0.0	0.1	0.4	0.1	20.1	195	92	246	103	<.1	<.1	0.0	<.1
48 197	Hardeman	5,283	82.0	6.0	0.2	0.5	0.1	11.1	199	78	94	154	<.1	<.1	<.1	<.1
48 199	Hardin	41,320	89.6	8.4	0.1	0.3	<.1	1.6	55	29	74	246	0.2	0.4	0.2	<.1
48 201	Harris	2,818,199	54.2	18.7	3.8	0.2	0.2	22.9	1	209	31	96	16.6	14.8	26.7	14.9
48 203	Harrison	57,483	69.4	27.8	0.2	0.3	<.1	2.2	46	148	6	238	0.3	0.4	0.8	<.1
48 205	Hartley	3,634	93.2	0.2	0.2	0.8	<.1	5.5	219	13	205	200	<.1	<.1	<.1	<.1
48 207	Haskell	6,820	76.7	3.5	0.2	0.2	0.1	19.2	186	103	130	108	<.1	<.1	<.1	<.1
48 209	Hays	65,614	68.1	3.2	0.6	0.2	<.1	27.8	39	153	138	81	0.4	0.4	0.1	0.4
48 211	Hemphill	3,720	88.0	0.2	0.1	0.6	0.0	11.1	217	39	211	157	<.1	<.1	<.1	<.1
48 213	Henderson	58,543	87.3	8.1	0.2	0.3	<.1	4.0	45	45	79	217	0.3	0.5	0.2	<.1
48 215	Hidalgo	383,545	14.1	0.1	0.2	<.1	0.2	85.3	7	247	220	8	2.3	0.5	<.1	7.5
48 217	Hill	27,146	82.2	9.2	0.1	0.2	<.1	8.2	83	77	67	179	0.2	0.2	0.1	<.1
48 219	Hockley	24,199	63.7	4.1	0.1	0.3	0.2	31.6	91	175	115	74	0.1	0.1	<.1	0.2
48 221	Hood	28,981	94.0	0.2	0.6	0.5	<.1	4.7	79	11	213	209	0.2	0.3	<.1	<.1
48 223	Hopkins	28,833	85.9	8.6	0.2	0.4	<.1	4.9	80	55	73	208	0.2	0.2	0.1	<.1
48 225	Houston	21,375	65.7	29.3	0.2	0.1	0.1	4.5	101	161	4	212	0.1	0.1	0.3	<.1
48 227	Howard	32,343	68.7	3.6	0.5	0.4	0.2	26.6	70	150	129	82	0.2	0.2	<.1	0.2
48 229	Hudspeth	2,915	32.8	0.3	<.1	0.3	0.2	66.4	229	233	202	22	<.1	<.1	<.1	<.1
48 231	Hunt	64,343	84.1	10.5	0.5	0.4	<.1	4.5	42	64	62	213	0.4	0.5	0.3	<.1
48 233	Hutchinson	25,689	86.0	2.6	0.3	1.3	<.1	9.8	86	54	147	166	0.2	0.2	<.1	<.1
48 235	Irion	1,629	76.1	0.1	0.0	<.1	<.1	23.6	243	111	221	93	<.1	<.1	<.1	<.1
48 237	Jack	6,981	95.5	0.7	0.1	0.3	<.1	3.3	185	6	187	225	<.1	<.1	<.1	<.1
48 239	Jackson	13,039	69.4	9.2	<.1	<.1	<.1	21.3	146	149	68	99	<.1	<.1	<.1	<.1
48 241	Jasper	31,102	78.9	18.8	0.1	0.2	<.1	1.9	72	95	30	242	0.2	0.2	0.3	<.1
48 243	Jeff Davis	1,946	59.3	0.3	0.2	0.6	0.0	39.6	240	190	203	50	<.1	<.1	<.1	<.1
48 245	Jefferson	239,397	61.5	30.8	2.1	0.2	<.1	5.3	12	181	3	203	1.4	1.4	3.7	0.3
48 247	Jim Hogg	5,109	8.3	<.1	<.1	0.1	0.3	91.2	202	250	227	4	<.1	<.1	<.1	0.1
48 249	Jim Wells	37,679	26.8	0.5	0.1	<.1	0.3	72.2	63	236	190	18	0.2	<.1	<.1	0.6
48 251	Johnson	97,165	89.0	2.5	0.4	0.4	<.1	7.7	31	31	148	183	0.6	0.8	0.1	0.2
48 253	Jones	16,490	78.7	3.9	0.2	0.2	<.1	16.9	124	96	123	119	<.1	0.1	<.1	<.1
48 255	Karnes	12,455	49.3	2.8	<.1	0.1	0.3	47.5	150	220	143	36	<.1	<.1	<.1	0.1
48 257	Kaufman	52,220	78.9	13.9	0.4	0.3	<.1	6.4	49	94	45	196	0.3	0.4	0.4	<.1
48 259	Kendall	14,589	82.6	0.3	0.2	0.5	0.0	16.4	133	75	199	122	<.1	0.1	<.1	<.1
48 261	Kenedy	460	20.2	0.0	0.0	0.0	1.1	78.7	252	241	247	14	<.1	<.1	0.0	<.1
48 263	Kent	1,010	87.4	0.6	0.0	<.1	0.0	11.9	249	43	189	150	<.1	<.1	<.1	<.1
48 265	Kerr	36,304	80.7	2.1	0.4	0.3	<.1	16.5	66	84	156	120	0.2	0.3	<.1	0.1
48 267	Kimble	4,122	80.8	<.1	<.1	0.1	0.3	18.7	214	82	229	110	<.1	<.1	<.1	<.1
48 269	King	354	85.0	0.0	0.0	0.0	0.0	15.0	253	61	248	128	<.1	<.1	0.0	<.1
48 271	Kinney	3,119	46.9	1.5	0.2	0.7	0.3	50.3	226	224	169	32	<.1	<.1	<.1	<.1
48 273	Kleberg	30,274	34.0	3.2	1.3	0.2	0.3	61.2	76	232	139	23	0.2	<.1	<.1	0.4
48 275	Knox	4,837	70.2	6.9	0.1	0.1	0.1	22.5	206	142	86	97	<.1	<.1	<.1	<.1
48 277	Lamar	43,949	83.2	14.5	0.3	0.9	<.1	1.1	53	70	43	253	0.3	0.4	0.3	<.1
48 279	Lamb	15,072	57.7	5.3	0.1	0.2	<.1	36.6	131	198	98	61	<.1	<.1	<.1	0.1

Table A. — 1990 Population by Race and Ethnic Origin (cont)

State/county code	County	Total persons	Percent of total persons						Rank				Percent contribution to state population			
			Non-Hispanic							Percent of total persons				Non-Hispanic		
			White	Black	Asian and Pacific Islander	Native American	Other	Hispanic	Total	Non-Hispanic		Hispanic	Total	White	Black	Hispanic
										White	Black					
48 281	Lampasas	13,521	83.7	1.8	0.9	0.5	<.1	13.0	140	68	162	143	<.1	0.1	<.1	<.1
48 283	La Salle	5,254	21.0	1.0	<.1	0.1	0.4	77.4	200	240	179	15	<.1	<.1	<.1	<.1
48 285	Lavaca	18,690	84.1	7.0	<.1	<.1	0.2	8.5	110	65	85	175	0.1	0.2	<.1	<.1
48 287	Lee	12,854	75.1	13.6	<.1	0.1	0.1	11.0	148	122	46	159	<.1	<.1	<.1	<.1
48 289	Leon	12,665	83.0	12.6	<.1	0.3	<.1	4.0	149	73	52	218	<.1	0.1	<.1	<.1
48 291	Liberty	52,726	81.0	12.9	0.2	0.3	0.1	5.5	48	80	49	201	0.3	0.4	0.3	<.1
48 293	Limestone	20,946	72.8	19.7	0.2	0.2	0.2	7.0	102	133	25	189	0.1	0.1	0.2	<.1
48 295	Lipscomb	3,143	86.6	<.1	0.4	0.9	0.0	12.1	225	51	231	147	<.1	<.1	<.1	<.1
48 297	Live Oak	9,556	64.4	<.1	0.2	0.3	0.3	34.8	165	172	232	67	<.1	<.1	<.1	<.1
48 299	Llano	11,631	95.4	0.2	0.2	0.3	<.1	3.9	153	7	210	222	<.1	0.1	<.1	<.1
48 301	Loving	107	86.9	0.0	0.0	0.0	0.0	13.1	254	49	249	140	<.1	<.1	0.0	<.1
48 303	Lubbock	222,636	68.0	7.5	1.2	0.3	0.2	22.9	14	155	84	94	1.3	1.5	0.8	1.2
48 305	Lynn	6,758	54.5	3.3	<.1	0.3	0.2	41.7	187	206	137	45	<.1	<.1	<.1	<.1
48 307	McCulloch	8,778	71.6	1.7	<.1	0.2	0.0	26.4	171	136	165	83	<.1	<.1	<.1	<.1
48 309	McLennan	189,123	71.1	15.4	0.7	0.2	<.1	12.5	18	138	41	144	1.1	1.3	1.5	0.5
48 311	McMullen	817	60.3	0.0	0.0	0.4	0.1	39.2	250	186	250	54	<.1	<.1	0.0	<.1
48 313	Madison	10,931	65.2	23.3	0.1	0.5	0.1	10.8	156	166	13	161	<.1	<.1	0.1	<.1
48 315	Marion	9,984	67.1	31.0	<.1	0.4	<.1	1.5	160	158	2	248	<.1	<.1	0.2	<.1
48 317	Martin	4,956	58.1	1.8	0.1	0.2	0.2	39.5	203	196	164	51	<.1	<.1	<.1	<.1
48 319	Mason	3,423	79.9	0.2	<.1	0.3	0.0	19.6	222	89	214	106	<.1	<.1	<.1	<.1
48 321	Matagorda	36,928	59.2	13.6	2.2	0.2	0.2	24.6	64	191	47	88	0.2	0.2	0.3	0.2
48 323	Maverick	36,378	4.3	<.1	0.1	1.9	0.1	93.5	65	253	230	3	0.2	<.1	<.1	0.8
48 325	Medina	27,312	54.7	0.3	0.2	0.3	0.2	44.4	82	204	204	39	0.2	0.1	<.1	0.3
48 327	Menard	2,252	67.1	0.3	0.0	0.2	0.2	32.2	235	157	201	71	<.1	<.1	<.1	<.1
48 329	Midland	106,611	69.9	7.5	0.8	0.3	0.1	21.4	27	145	83	98	0.6	0.7	0.4	0.5
48 331	Milam	22,946	72.0	12.6	0.1	0.2	<.1	15.1	96	135	53	126	0.1	0.2	0.1	<.1
48 333	Mills	4,531	88.9	0.2	<.1	<.1	<.1	10.7	208	32	207	163	<.1	<.1	<.1	<.1
48 335	Mitchell	8,016	65.4	4.5	<.1	0.2	<.1	29.8	177	163	105	77	<.1	<.1	<.1	<.1
48 337	Montague	17,274	96.3	<.1	<.1	0.4	<.1	3.2	119	4	237	227	0.1	0.2	<.1	<.1
48 339	Montgomery	182,201	87.5	4.2	0.6	0.4	<.1	7.3	19	42	114	186	1.1	1.5	0.4	0.3
48 341	Moore	17,865	65.5	0.4	1.4	0.6	0.1	31.9	116	162	193	72	0.1	0.1	<.1	0.1
48 343	Morris	13,200	73.2	24.4	<.1	0.5	<.1	1.8	144	129	9	244	<.1	<.1	0.2	<.1
48 345	Motley	1,532	86.1	4.4	0.3	0.3	0.0	8.9	244	53	108	170	<.1	<.1	<.1	<.1
48 347	Nacogdoches	54,753	77.8	16.3	0.5	0.2	<.1	5.1	47	98	38	206	0.3	0.4	0.5	<.1
48 349	Navarro	39,926	72.9	18.8	0.6	0.3	<.1	7.2	59	131	29	187	0.2	0.3	0.4	<.1
48 351	Newton	13,569	76.1	22.3	<.1	0.3	<.1	1.1	139	110	15	252	<.1	0.1	0.2	<.1
48 353	Nolan	16,594	69.4	4.4	0.1	0.2	0.2	25.6	123	147	109	85	<.1	0.1	<.1	<.1
48 355	Nueces	291,145	42.5	4.1	0.7	0.3	0.2	52.2	8	228	117	28	1.7	1.2	0.6	3.5
48 357	Ochiltree	9,128	80.8	<.1	<.1	1.0	0.2	18.0	167	83	238	116	<.1	<.1	<.1	<.1
48 359	Oldham	2,278	88.7	0.4	0.7	1.3	0.1	8.8	233	35	195	172	<.1	<.1	<.1	<.1
48 361	Orange	80,509	88.4	8.4	0.6	0.2	<.1	2.4	36	36	75	234	0.5	0.7	0.3	<.1
48 363	Palo Pinto	25,055	86.6	3.1	0.7	0.3	<.1	9.2	89	52	140	169	0.1	0.2	<.1	<.1
48 365	Panola	22,035	79.1	18.3	0.1	0.3	<.1	2.2	99	93	32	239	0.1	0.2	0.2	<.1
48 367	Parker	64,785	94.1	0.9	0.3	0.5	<.1	4.2	41	10	183	215	0.4	0.6	<.1	<.1
48 369	Parmer	9,863	56.8	1.1	0.2	0.2	0.1	41.5	162	200	174	47	<.1	<.1	<.1	<.1
48 371	Pecos	14,675	42.3	0.3	0.1	0.2	0.2	56.8	132	229	198	25	<.1	<.1	<.1	0.2
48 373	Polk	30,687	79.9	12.5	0.2	2.1	<.1	5.2	74	88	54	204	0.2	0.2	0.2	<.1
48 375	Potter	97,874	68.3	8.6	2.5	0.7	0.2	19.7	30	152	72	105	0.6	0.6	0.4	0.4
48 377	Presidio	6,637	18.0	<.1	0.2	0.2	0.0	81.6	189	243	233	12	<.1	<.1	<.1	0.1
48 379	Rains	6,715	92.8	4.2	0.1	0.4	<.1	2.4	188	14	113	237	<.1	<.1	<.1	<.1
48 381	Randall	89,673	90.7	1.2	0.7	0.5	<.1	6.9	33	20	173	192	0.5	0.8	<.1	0.1
48 383	Reagan	4,514	54.5	2.4	0.0	0.2	0.0	43.0	209	207	151	40	<.1	<.1	<.1	<.1
48 385	Real	2,412	75.2	0.0	0.0	1.0	<.1	23.8	232	121	251	92	<.1	<.1	0.0	<.1
48 387	Red River	14,317	77.6	20.0	<.1	0.4	<.1	1.9	136	101	24	243	<.1	0.1	0.1	<.1
48 389	Reeves	15,852	24.7	2.1	0.2	0.2	<.1	72.8	126	239	154	16	<.1	<.1	<.1	0.3
48 391	Refugio	7,976	52.4	7.6	<.1	0.2	<.1	39.7	179	214	82	49	<.1	<.1	<.1	<.1
48 393	Roberts	1,025	96.4	0.0	0.2	<.1	0.0	3.3	248	3	252	226	<.1	<.1	0.0	<.1
48 395	Robertson	15,511	60.4	27.1	<.1	0.1	<.1	12.3	128	185	7	146	<.1	<.1	0.2	<.1
48 397	Rockwall	25,604	89.8	3.3	0.6	0.4	<.1	5.9	87	27	134	199	0.2	0.2	<.1	<.1
48 399	Runnels	11,294	73.8	1.6	0.1	<.1	<.1	24.3	155	127	168	89	<.1	<.1	<.1	<.1
48 401	Rusk	43,735	75.2	20.4	0.1	0.3	<.1	4.0	54	120	21	220	0.3	0.3	0.5	<.1
48 403	Sabine	9,586	87.0	11.6	0.1	0.1	<.1	1.2	164	46	58	251	<.1	<.1	<.1	<.1
48 405	San Augustine	7,999	70.1	28.0	<.1	0.1	<.1	1.7	178	143	5	245	<.1	0.1	0.1	<.1
48 407	San Jacinto	16,372	81.4	15.5	<.1	0.4	<.1	2.6	125	79	39	231	<.1	0.1	0.1	<.1
48 409	San Patricio	58,749	47.1	1.5	0.2	0.3	0.2	50.7	44	223	171	31	0.3	0.3	<.1	0.7
48 411	San Saba	5,401	81.0	0.2	<.1	0.1	0.1	18.5	197	81	206	114	<.1	<.1	<.1	<.1
48 413	Schleicher	2,990	63.5	0.8	0.0	<.1	0.1	35.5	228	176	185	66	<.1	<.1	<.1	<.1
48 415	Scurry	18,634	70.9	4.6	0.2	0.3	<.1	23.9	111	139	103	91	0.1	0.1	<.1	0.1
48 417	Shackelford	3,316	91.0	0.4	<.1	0.3	0.2	8.2	224	19	196	180	<.1	<.1	<.1	<.1
48 419	Shelby	22,034	75.9	21.4	0.1	0.2	<.1	2.4	100	113	17	232	0.1	0.2	0.2	<.1

Table A. — 1990 Population by Race and Ethnic Origin (cont)

State/ county code	County	Total persons	Percent of total persons — Non-Hispanic — White	Black	Asian and Pacific Islander	Native American	Other	Hispanic	Rank — Percent of total persons — Total	Non-Hispanic White	Black	Hispanic	Percent contribution to state population — Total	Non-Hispanic White	Black	Hispanic
48 421	Sherman	2,858	80.5	0.1	0.2	0.2	0.0	18.8	230	85	218	109	<.1	<.1	<.1	<.1
48 423	Smith	151,309	72.6	20.7	0.4	0.3	<.1	5.9	20	134	20	198	0.9	1.1	1.6	0.2
48 425	Somervell	5,360	84.8	0.2	0.3	0.6	<.1	14.0	198	62	212	137	<.1	<.1	<.1	<.1
48 427	Starr	40,518	2.5	<.1	<.1	<.1	0.2	97.2	57	254	239	1	0.2	<.1	<.1	0.9
48 429	Stephens	9,010	88.2	2.6	0.3	0.3	<.1	8.5	169	37	146	176	<.1	<.1	<.1	<.1
48 431	Sterling	1,438	74.2	0.0	0.0	0.3	<.1	25.5	246	125	253	86	<.1	<.1	0.0	<.1
48 433	Stonewall	2,013	83.3	4.4	0.3	<.1	<.1	11.8	238	69	110	151	<.1	<.1	<.1	<.1
48 435	Sutton	4,135	54.3	<.1	0.1	0.3	<.1	45.1	213	208	236	38	<.1	<.1	<.1	<.1
48 437	Swisher	8,133	64.6	4.1	0.2	0.3	0.1	30.7	176	170	118	76	<.1	<.1	<.1	<.1
48 439	Tarrant	1,170,103	73.3	11.8	2.5	0.4	<.1	12.0	4	128	57	148	6.9	8.3	7.0	3.2
48 441	Taylor	119,655	77.7	6.1	1.1	0.3	0.1	14.6	25	100	93	129	0.7	0.9	0.4	0.4
48 443	Terrell	1,410	46.2	<.1	0.1	0.2	0.1	53.3	247	226	224	26	<.1	<.1	<.1	<.1
48 445	Terry	13,218	56.6	3.3	0.2	0.2	0.3	39.3	143	201	135	52	<.1	<.1	<.1	0.1
48 447	Throckmorton	1,880	92.1	0.0	0.4	0.4	0.0	7.2	241	16	254	188	<.1	<.1	0.0	<.1
48 449	Titus	24,009	75.5	13.3	<.1	0.4	<.1	10.6	92	118	48	164	0.1	0.2	0.2	<.1
48 451	Tom Green	98,458	68.7	4.0	1.0	0.3	0.1	25.9	29	151	122	84	0.6	0.7	0.2	0.6
48 453	Travis	576,407	65.1	10.6	2.8	0.3	0.2	21.1	6	167	61	100	3.4	3.6	3.1	2.8
48 455	Trinity	11,445	82.9	14.3	0.2	0.2	<.1	2.4	154	74	44	235	<.1	<.1	<.1	<.1
48 457	Tyler	16,646	86.7	11.9	<.1	0.3	0.0	1.1	122	50	56	254	<.1	0.1	0.1	<.1
48 459	Upshur	31,370	85.2	12.3	<.1	0.4	<.1	2.0	71	59	55	240	0.2	0.3	0.2	<.1
48 461	Upton	4,447	60.0	2.0	<.1	0.4	0.1	37.5	210	189	158	57	<.1	<.1	<.1	<.1
48 463	Uvalde	23,340	38.7	0.2	0.2	0.1	0.4	60.4	95	231	217	24	0.1	0.1	<.1	0.3
48 465	Val Verde	38,721	26.9	1.8	0.6	0.2	0.1	70.5	60	235	163	20	0.2	0.1	<.1	0.6
48 467	Van Zandt	37,944	91.7	3.8	0.1	0.4	<.1	4.0	62	17	125	219	0.2	0.3	<.1	<.1
48 469	Victoria	74,361	58.9	6.2	0.3	0.2	0.2	34.1	37	193	92	68	0.4	0.4	0.2	0.6
48 471	Walker	50,917	64.5	23.7	0.6	0.3	0.1	10.8	51	171	12	160	0.3	0.3	0.6	0.1
48 473	Waller	23,390	51.1	37.4	0.3	<.1	<.1	11.1	94	217	1	156	0.1	0.1	0.4	<.1
48 475	Ward	13,115	58.9	3.3	0.2	0.5	0.3	36.8	145	194	136	58	<.1	<.1	<.1	0.1
48 477	Washington	26,154	73.9	20.8	0.7	0.1	0.1	4.4	85	126	18	214	0.2	0.2	0.3	<.1
48 479	Webb	133,239	5.6	<.1	0.3	<.1	0.2	93.9	22	252	228	2	0.8	<.1	<.1	2.9
48 481	Wharton	39,955	58.8	15.4	0.3	<.1	0.2	25.3	58	195	40	87	0.2	0.2	0.3	0.2
48 483	Wheeler	5,879	90.1	2.5	0.4	0.6	<.1	6.4	194	25	150	194	<.1	<.1	<.1	<.1
48 485	Wichita	122,378	80.2	9.0	1.5	0.7	<.1	8.6	23	87	69	174	0.7	1.0	0.6	0.2
48 487	Wilbarger	15,121	75.6	8.8	0.5	0.5	0.1	14.5	130	116	70	130	<.1	0.1	<.1	<.1
48 489	Willacy	17,705	15.0	0.4	<.1	<.1	0.2	84.4	118	246	194	9	0.1	<.1	<.1	0.3
48 491	Williamson	139,551	79.3	4.7	1.3	0.3	<.1	14.3	21	91	102	131	0.8	1.1	0.3	0.5
48 493	Wilson	22,650	63.0	1.0	<.1	0.1	0.2	35.6	98	177	178	65	0.1	0.1	<.1	0.2
48 495	Winkler	8,626	60.7	1.8	<.1	0.5	0.2	36.8	173	184	161	59	<.1	<.1	<.1	<.1
48 497	Wise	34,679	90.4	1.1	0.2	0.5	<.1	7.7	67	23	176	182	0.2	0.3	<.1	<.1
48 499	Wood	29,380	88.7	8.1	0.1	0.4	<.1	2.7	78	33	78	230	0.2	0.3	0.1	<.1
48 501	Yoakum	8,786	61.9	1.0	0.1	0.3	<.1	36.6	170	180	180	60	<.1	<.1	<.1	<.1
48 503	Young	18,126	91.6	1.4	0.2	0.3	<.1	6.4	114	18	172	195	0.1	0.2	<.1	<.1
48 505	Zapata	9,279	18.6	<.1	<.1	<.1	0.2	81.0	166	242	241	13	<.1	<.1	<.1	0.2
48 507	Zavala	12,162	7.8	2.3	0.0	<.1	0.4	89.4	151	251	152	6	<.1	<.1	<.1	0.3
48	**TEXAS**	16,986,510	**60.6**	**11.6**	**1.8**	**0.3**	**0.1**	**25.5**					**100.0**	**100.0**	**100.0**	**100.0**
	CONGRESSIONAL															
	District 1	566,217	78.1	18.0	0.3	0.4	<.1	3.2	1	8	6	30	3.3	4.3	5.2	0.4
	District 2	566,217	77.1	16.5	0.3	0.3	<.1	5.6	12	9	7	27	3.3	4.2	4.7	0.7
	District 3	566,217	85.9	4.3	3.3	0.3	<.1	6.0	23	3	22	26	3.3	4.7	1.2	0.8
	District 4	566,217	86.3	8.3	0.4	0.6	<.1	4.3	25	2	13	29	3.3	4.7	2.4	0.6
	District 5	566,217	64.3	16.0	1.3	0.4	0.1	17.9	26	19	8	13	3.3	3.5	4.6	2.3
	District 6	566,217	87.6	4.3	2.1	0.4	<.1	5.4	27	1	21	28	3.3	4.8	1.2	0.7
	District 7	566,217	76.6	5.7	5.4	0.2	0.1	11.9	28	11	18	22	3.3	4.2	1.6	1.6
	District 8	566,217	85.4	5.2	1.9	0.3	<.1	7.2	29	4	20	25	3.3	4.7	1.5	0.9
	District 9	566,217	66.9	21.4	2.0	0.3	<.1	9.4	30	16	4	23	3.3	3.7	6.1	1.2
	District 10	566,217	64.6	10.8	2.8	0.3	0.2	21.4	2	18	10	10	3.3	3.6	3.1	2.8
	District 11	566,217	70.2	15.6	1.5	0.3	<.1	12.3	3	14	9	21	3.3	3.9	4.5	1.6
	District 12	566,217	73.6	7.8	1.8	0.5	<.1	16.3	4	12	15	17	3.3	4.0	2.2	2.1
	District 13	566,217	71.0	7.8	1.1	0.5	0.1	19.4	5	13	16	12	3.3	3.9	2.2	2.5
	District 14	566,217	65.1	10.3	0.6	0.2	0.1	23.6	6	17	11	8	3.3	3.6	3.0	3.1
	District 15	566,217	23.9	1.0	0.3	0.1	0.2	74.5	7	30	30	1	3.3	1.3	0.3	9.7
	District 16	566,217	25.0	3.3	0.9	0.3	0.1	70.4	8	29	25	2	3.3	1.4	1.0	9.2
	District 17	566,217	78.5	3.4	0.5	0.3	0.1	17.2	9	7	24	14	3.3	4.3	1.0	2.2
	District 18	566,217	31.3	50.2	2.9	0.2	0.1	15.3	10	25	1	19	3.3	1.7	14.4	2.0
	District 19	566,217	76.6	2.5	0.8	0.4	0.1	19.6	11	10	27	11	3.3	4.2	0.7	2.6
	District 20	566,217	32.2	5.5	1.2	0.2	0.2	60.7	13	23	19	5	3.3	1.8	1.6	7.9
	District 21	566,217	82.2	2.4	1.0	0.3	<.1	14.1	14	6	28	20	3.3	4.5	0.7	1.8
	District 22	566,217	69.2	7.6	6.8	0.2	0.1	16.1	15	15	17	18	3.3	3.8	2.2	2.1

Table A. — 1990 Population by Race and Ethnic Origin (cont)

State/county code	County	Total persons	Percent of total persons							Rank				Percent contribution to state population			
			Non-Hispanic					Hispanic	Total	Percent of total persons			Non-Hispanic			Hispanic
			White	Black	Asian and Pacific Islander	Native American	Other			Non-Hispanic		Hispanic	Total	White	Black	
										White	Black					
	District 23........................	566,217	33.6	2.8	0.6	0.3	0.2	62.5	16	22	26	4	3.3	1.8	0.8	8.2
	District 24........................	566,217	56.7	18.8	2.1	0.5	0.2	21.8	17	20	5	9	3.3	3.1	5.4	2.8
	District 25........................	566,217	53.0	26.3	3.6	0.3	0.1	16.7	18	21	3	16	3.3	2.9	7.5	2.2
	District 26........................	566,217	82.4	4.1	3.8	0.4	<.1	9.2	19	5	23	24	3.3	4.5	1.2	1.2
	District 27........................	566,217	30.7	2.3	0.5	0.2	0.2	66.2	20	26	29	3	3.3	1.7	0.6	8.6
	District 28........................	566,217	30.4	8.2	0.6	0.2	0.2	60.4	21	27	14	7	3.3	1.7	2.4	7.9
	District 29........................	566,217	27.8	9.6	1.5	0.2	0.3	60.6	22	28	12	6	3.3	1.5	2.7	7.9
	District 30........................	566,217	31.4	49.2	1.9	0.3	0.1	17.1	24	24	2	15	3.3	1.7	14.1	2.2

Table B. — 1990 Voting Age Population (VAP) by Race and Ethnic Origin

County	Total Voting Age Population	Percent of total VAP — Non-Hispanic White	Black	Asian and Pacific Islander	Native American	Other	Hispanic	Rank — Percent of total VAP Total	Non-Hispanic White	Black	Hispanic	Percent contribution to state VAP Total	Non-Hispanic White	Black	Hispanic	VAP percent of total population Total	Non-Hispanic White	Black	Asian and Pacific Islander	Native American	Other	Hispanic
Anderson	36,744	67.0	24.3	0.2	0.3	0.2	8.1	52	177	9	166	0.3	0.3	0.7	0.1	76.5	75.3	80.4	69.2	82.1	96.7	75.1
Andrews	9,375	70.5	1.8	0.9	0.5	0.3	26.0	143	160	162	76	<.1	<.1	<.1	<.1	65.4	71.2	64.5	59.9	75.0	62.5	53.6
Angelina	49,869	78.9	13.7	0.3	0.2	<.1	6.8	38	113	41	176	0.4	0.5	0.5	0.1	71.4	74.6	64.7	67.2	71.5	48.1	55.5
Aransas	13,386	78.9	1.6	2.2	0.5	0.1	16.7	112	115	166	104	0.1	0.1	<.1	<.1	74.8	79.3	72.1	51.0	73.7	53.6	62.3
Archer	5,741	97.1	0.1	<.1	0.4	0.0	2.3	179	3	215	227	<.1	<.1	<.1	<.1	72.0	72.1	63.6	100.0	69.4	0.0	69.3
Armstrong	1,459	96.9	0.0	0.3	0.5	<.1	2.3	237	4	240	228	<.1	<.1	0.0	<.1	72.2	72.5	0.0	80.0	77.8	100.0	60.0
Atascosa	20,441	50.7	0.4	0.2	0.2	0.2	48.3	81	225	197	27	0.2	0.1	<.1	0.4	66.9	73.0	69.4	72.4	87.0	69.8	61.5
Austin	14,519	79.3	11.8	0.1	0.2	<.1	8.6	104	107	52	161	0.1	0.1	0.1	<.1	73.2	76.1	67.1	65.4	60.9	66.7	63.3
Bailey	4,814	65.5	1.7	0.1	0.1	<.1	32.6	187	180	163	57	<.1	<.1	<.1	<.1	68.1	75.3	68.4	50.0	77.8	100.0	57.2
Bandera	8,054	89.1	0.1	0.3	0.6	<.1	9.9	156	46	214	152	<.1	<.1	<.1	<.1	76.3	77.3	43.5	84.0	75.8	75.0	68.2
Bastrop	27,242	72.6	11.1	0.3	0.4	0.1	15.5	61	149	55	111	0.2	0.3	0.2	0.2	71.2	74.1	69.7	68.9	76.8	58.0	60.9
Baylor	3,406	90.8	3.2	0.3	0.2	<.1	5.4	207	31	133	193	<.1	<.1	<.1	<.1	77.7	80.4	60.0	84.6	77.8	100.0	55.4
Bee	17,210	48.8	2.6	0.8	0.3	0.2	47.2	92	227	144	29	0.1	0.1	<.1	0.3	68.5	75.0	65.9	70.0	75.4	59.4	62.9
Bell	136,055	68.5	16.8	2.8	0.4	<.1	11.4	17	170	32	135	1.1	1.2	1.7	0.6	71.2	74.6	65.3	73.5	76.6	49.6	61.9
Bexar	839,453	46.0	6.8	1.2	0.2	0.2	45.6	4	230	84	32	6.9	4.9	4.2	14.1	70.8	77.8	69.8	75.1	77.3	63.4	65.0
Blanco	4,482	87.3	0.9	0.2	0.2	<.1	11.4	191	58	183	134	<.1	<.1	<.1	<.1	75.1	77.6	71.4	52.6	58.8	50.0	60.7
Borden	575	88.3	0.0	0.0	1.0	0.0	10.6	251	53	241	143	<.1	<.1	0.0	<.1	72.0	75.9	0.0	0.0	60.0	0.0	50.8
Bosque	11,563	90.7	1.8	0.2	0.2	<.1	7.1	125	36	161	172	<.1	0.1	<.1	<.1	76.4	78.7	66.3	78.1	84.0	83.3	57.6
Bowie	59,471	78.3	19.2	0.3	0.5	<.1	1.6	34	120	18	241	0.5	0.6	0.9	<.1	72.8	73.2	64.6	69.8	77.6	45.5	71.7
Brazoria	135,462	75.0	8.3	0.9	0.4	0.1	15.3	18	138	68	112	1.1	1.3	0.8	0.8	70.7	72.7	72.9	67.4	75.7	66.2	61.3
Brazos	95,689	74.9	9.3	3.6	0.2	0.1	11.9	22	139	64	131	0.8	0.9	0.7	0.4	78.5	82.3	66.1	81.8	83.9	73.8	68.0
Brewster	6,629	59.4	1.0	0.6	0.2	<.1	38.6	165	209	180	40	<.1	<.1	<.1	<.1	76.4	81.5	85.7	89.6	88.2	100.0	69.2
Briscoe	1,420	82.8	2.7	0.0	0.3	0.0	14.2	240	89	143	117	<.1	<.1	<.1	<.1	72.0	76.8	55.9	0.0	100.0	0.0	55.0
Brooks	5,490	11.6	<.1	0.1	<.1	0.3	87.8	182	249	231	5	<.1	<.1	<.1	0.2	66.9	77.5	100.0	75.0	100.0	66.7	65.7
Brown	25,134	87.0	3.6	0.2	0.3	<.1	8.7	65	61	119	160	0.2	0.3	<.1	<.1	73.1	75.9	59.0	70.6	74.8	71.4	57.7
Burleson	9,912	73.3	16.0	<.1	0.3	<.1	10.2	135	144	34	150	<.1	0.1	0.1	<.1	72.7	76.2	66.4	88.9	82.5	35.3	62.1
Burnet	17,101	90.3	1.0	0.2	0.4	<.1	8.1	94	38	182	165	0.1	0.2	<.1	<.1	75.4	77.9	63.9	72.0	71.4	55.0	56.7
Caldwell	18,562	55.5	10.1	0.4	0.2	0.2	33.6	86	218	58	53	0.2	0.1	0.1	0.2	70.3	76.0	70.4	85.0	79.2	74.1	62.4
Calhoun	13,435	62.4	2.9	2.2	0.2	<.1	32.2	111	199	140	59	0.1	0.1	<.1	0.2	70.5	76.1	71.2	53.6	77.4	72.2	62.8
Callahan	8,601	95.9	<.1	0.3	0.4	<.1	3.4	153	8	234	215	<.1	0.1	<.1	<.1	72.5	73.1	100.0	69.7	75.0	50.0	59.7
Cameron	168,280	22.0	0.2	0.3	<.1	0.1	77.2	12	243	203	12	1.4	0.5	<.1	4.8	64.7	81.7	70.4	74.4	81.0	60.3	61.0
Camp	7,297	72.5	22.8	<.1	0.3	<.1	4.3	162	150	13	204	<.1	<.1	0.1	<.1	73.7	75.4	70.8	100.0	72.7	100.0	62.9
Carson	4,609	94.9	0.2	0.1	0.6	<.1	4.1	189	11	210	207	<.1	<.1	<.1	<.1	70.1	71.0	72.7	66.7	70.7	100.0	53.7
Cass	21,785	80.5	18.1	<.1	0.3	<.1	1.0	76	104	24	250	0.2	0.2	0.3	<.1	72.7	74.7	65.6	56.5	68.3	100.0	60.1
Castro	5,774	57.6	2.6	0.2	0.1	0.3	39.2	177	213	146	39	<.1	<.1	<.1	<.1	63.7	72.7	57.9	64.3	75.0	67.9	54.0
Chambers	14,113	81.6	12.5	0.5	0.3	0.1	5.0	106	95	49	196	0.1	0.1	0.1	<.1	70.3	71.2	69.3	63.7	79.6	85.7	59.6
Cherokee	30,290	78.2	15.3	0.5	0.3	<.1	5.7	55	121	37	191	0.2	0.3	0.3	<.1	73.8	75.9	67.6	83.3	78.4	50.0	64.0
Childress	4,400	84.4	4.7	0.2	0.3	<.1	10.4	192	78	101	145	<.1	<.1	<.1	<.1	73.9	78.4	65.1	41.2	60.0	75.0	53.5
Clay	7,383	96.7	0.3	0.2	0.9	0.0	2.0	160	5	198	234	<.1	<.1	<.1	<.1	73.1	74.0	75.8	52.2	77.4	0.0	59.5
Cochran	2,918	58.7	4.9	0.0	0.3	<.1	36.1	212	210	98	48	<.1	<.1	<.1	<.1	66.7	75.3	62.2	0.0	72.7	66.7	56.7
Coke	2,632	89.5	<.1	<.1	0.5	<.1	9.8	218	44	220	153	<.1	<.1	<.1	<.1	76.9	79.1	50.0	100.0	76.5	100.0	61.1
Coleman	7,382	88.1	2.1	<.1	0.3	<.1	9.4	161	57	153	155	<.1	<.1	<.1	<.1	76.0	78.4	63.9	85.7	85.2	40.0	60.9
Collin	187,534	87.1	3.8	2.6	0.4	<.1	6.2	10	59	116	184	1.5	2.1	0.5	0.4	72.0	72.6	66.6	71.5	42.1	50.0	63.6
Collingsworth	2,622	82.2	5.5	<.1	0.8	<.1	11.4	219	93	93	133	<.1	<.1	0.2	<.1	73.4	78.4	63.0	33.3	75.0	50.0	53.5
Colorado	13,490	71.1	15.7	<.1	0.1	<.1	13.0	110	156	36	124	0.1	0.1	0.2	<.1	73.4	77.1	69.1	92.3	69.2	64.3	61.8
Comal	38,576	78.9	0.8	0.3	0.2	0.1	19.7	49	112	186	95	0.3	0.4	<.1	0.3	74.4	77.6	71.7	73.8	81.5	70.5	63.9
Comanche	10,242	86.7	<.1	<.1	0.2	<.1	13.0	134	63	230	125	0.1	0.1	<.1	<.1	76.5	79.9	40.0	62.5	60.6	37.5	60.2
Concho	2,344	62.0	0.6	0.2	0.1	<.1	37.1	224	200	190	42	<.1	<.1	<.1	<.1	77.0	79.6	92.9	100.0	75.0	100.0	72.8
Cooke	22,068	92.7	2.9	0.4	0.7	<.1	3.4	75	20	139	216	0.2	0.3	<.1	<.1	71.7	73.4	55.2	69.8	59.5	69.7	62.3
Coryell	47,273	67.0	21.1	2.3	0.6	0.1	8.9	41	176	15	157	0.4	0.4	0.7	0.2	73.6	74.2	74.9	73.5	71.3	60.9	67.3
Cottle	1,669	81.0	6.9	0.2	0.2	<.1	11.7	234	99	82	132	<.1	<.1	<.1	<.1	74.3	80.7	58.7	100.0	75.0	100.0	53.1
Crane	3,038	68.6	2.6	0.3	0.2	<.1	28.2	210	169	145	70	<.1	<.1	<.1	<.1	65.3	71.3	61.7	100.0	63.6	33.3	54.3
Crockett	2,822	53.6	1.0	<.1	0.2	0.0	45.1	216	221	179	33	<.1	<.1	<.1	<.1	69.2	75.0	93.5	50.0	87.5	0.0	63.0
Crosby	5,022	60.2	4.2	<.1	<.1	0.2	35.2	186	203	106	49	<.1	<.1	<.1	0.2	65.1	78.2	71.4	50.0	80.0	57.1	56.9
Culberson	2,219	33.1	<.1	0.7	0.2	0.0	65.9	227	234	226	19	<.1	<.1	<.1	<.1	69.6	72.4	56.9	78.6	83.9	66.7	60.1
Dallam	3,801	79.2	1.5	0.3	0.7	0.1	18.2	198	108	168	99	<.1	<.1	<.1	<.1	65.1	77.4	50.0	60.0	45.5	0.0	60.5
Dallas	1,357,162	64.3	18.0	2.6	0.4	0.1	14.7	2	187	26	116	11.2	11.1	18.2	7.3	73.2	78.2	67.4	69.7	74.1	60.5	63.0
Dawson	9,807	59.6	4.0	0.1	0.1	0.1	36.1	136	207	110	47	<.1	<.1	0.1	0.1	68.3	77.2	65.0	57.9	85.7	63.2	57.8
Deaf Smith	12,387	55.7	1.5	0.2	0.2	<.1	42.3	119	216	171	36	0.1	<.1	<.1	0.2	64.7	73.3	63.4	59.4	75.8	75.0	56.0
Delta	3,680	91.0	7.1	0.2	0.7	0.0	1.0	199	30	80	251	<.1	<.1	<.1	<.1	75.8	77.1	65.5	85.7	69.2	0.0	53.7
Denton	199,880	86.1	4.7	2.4	0.5	<.1	6.3	9	66	102	181	1.6	2.2	0.7	0.5	73.1	73.9	70.6	70.5	73.7	57.7	65.8
DeWitt	13,783	68.7	9.8	<.1	<.1	0.1	21.2	109	167	61	90	0.1	0.1	0.1	0.1	73.2	77.2	69.2	100.0	86.7	60.0	64.0
Dickens	1,960	80.9	3.7	0.0	0.4	0.1	14.9	231	101	118	114	<.1	<.1	<.1	<.1	76.2	80.8	64.9	0.0	61.5	66.7	61.0
Dimmit	6,642	18.1	0.4	<.1	0.2	0.2	81.1	164	247	196	8	<.1	<.1	<.1	0.2	63.7	72.8	52.0	50.0	85.7	54.5	62.0
Donley	2,895	94.1	2.9	<.1	0.2	0.0	2.7	213	14	137	224	<.1	<.1	<.1	<.1	78.3	79.8	66.1	50.0	53.8	0.0	56.1
Duval	8,690	13.9	<.1	<.1	<.1	0.2	85.7	151	248	223	7	<.1	<.1	<.1	0.3	67.3	75.6	75.0	41.7	100.0	53.8	66.1
Eastland	14,185	91.3	2.3	0.2	0.3	<.1	5.9	105	29	150	187	0.1	0.2	<.1	<.1	76.7	78.0	82.0	84.8	83.7	50.0	59.5
Ector	81,223	68.3	4.3	0.5	0.5	0.2	26.2	26	171	104	75	0.7	0.7	0.3	0.8	67.1	71.6	65.5	67.1	75.8	60.2	57.9
Edwards	1,520	54.7	0.0	0.1	0.2	0.0	45.0	235	220	242	34	<.1	<.1	0.0	<.1	67.1	77.2	0.0	50.0	75.0	0.0	57.9
Ellis	58,765	79.0	9.1	0.2	0.4	0.1	11.1	35	111	65	137	0.5	0.6	0.4	0.2	69.0	71.6	63.8	64.2	74.0	66.0	58.1

Table B. — 1990 Voting Age Population (VAP) by Race and Ethnic Origin (cont)

County	Total Voting Age Population	Percent of total VAP — Non-Hispanic White	Black	Asian and Pacific Islander	Native American	Other	Hispanic	Rank — % of total VAP NH Total	White	Black	Hispanic	Percent contribution to state VAP NH Total	White	Black	Hispanic	VAP percent of total population NH Total	White	Black	Asian and Pacific Islander	Native American	Other	Hispanic
El Paso	398,798	29.3	3.6	1.1	0.3	0.1	65.6	6	238	120	21	3.3	1.5	1.1	9.6	67.4	77.3	69.4	76.1	71.7	60.4	63.5
Erath	21,294	91.7	0.8	0.3	0.3	<.1	6.9	79	25	187	175	0.2	0.2	<.1	<.1	76.1	77.7	85.9	67.0	72.2	73.7	59.4
Falls	13,188	64.0	25.3	0.1	0.2	<.1	10.3	116	188	6	146	0.1	0.1	0.2	<.1	74.5	77.8	70.5	90.0	80.0	80.0	65.7
Fannin	18,832	91.7	5.9	0.2	0.6	<.1	1.5	85	24	90	242	0.2	0.2	<.1	<.1	75.9	76.9	68.7	71.7	62.2	80.0	60.0
Fayette	15,271	85.1	7.6	<.1	0.1	<.1	7.0	103	76	75	173	0.1	0.2	<.1	<.1	76.0	77.9	69.8	61.5	78.3	64.7	63.2
Fisher	3,590	79.1	3.5	0.0	0.2	<.1	17.2	201	110	126	103	<.1	<.1	<.1	<.1	74.1	77.7	67.2	0.0	100.0	100.0	62.1
Floyd	5,811	63.9	3.6	0.2	0.1	0.2	32.1	175	189	121	61	<.1	<.1	<.1	<.1	68.4	78.0	66.1	75.0	53.8	57.9	55.2
Foard	1,365	85.4	3.4	0.1	0.4	<.1	10.6	241	73	129	142	<.1	<.1	<.1	<.1	76.1	78.9	63.0	50.0	100.0	100.0	62.2
Fort Bend	150,599	56.7	19.1	6.0	0.2	<.1	17.9	15	215	19	101	1.2	1.1	2.2	1.0	66.8	70.4	63.1	64.2	70.6	58.5	61.5
Franklin	5,815	91.5	4.1	0.2	0.5	0.0	3.7	173	27	109	212	<.1	<.1	<.1	<.1	74.5	75.6	67.6	61.1	78.4	0.0	60.5
Freestone	11,531	78.1	18.3	0.2	0.2	<.1	3.2	126	122	23	221	<.1	0.1	0.2	<.1	72.9	74.3	70.3	71.9	62.8	100.0	58.8
Frio	8,787	30.2	1.5	0.2	<.1	0.3	67.7	148	236	167	18	<.1	<.1	<.1	0.2	65.2	75.6	96.5	62.1	75.0	72.2	61.0
Gaines	8,982	68.7	2.0	0.1	0.2	0.4	28.6	146	168	155	69	<.1	<.1	<.1	<.1	63.6	67.8	56.8	64.3	64.5	68.0	55.7
Galveston	157,498	69.5	15.9	1.4	0.3	<.1	12.8	14	163	35	126	1.3	1.4	1.9	0.7	72.4	74.6	65.5	65.7	73.0	58.0	56.6
Garza	3,515	71.0	5.1	0.3	0.1	0.1	23.4	202	157	96	81	<.1	<.1	<.1	<.1	68.3	74.4	58.5	47.6	100.0	100.0	56.6
Gillespie	13,196	88.5	0.1	<.1	0.2	<.1	11.0	115	52	216	138	0.1	0.1	<.1	<.1	76.7	79.6	48.3	37.5	72.1	83.3	60.1
Glasscock	936	73.3	0.0	0.0	0.0	0.3	26.4	247	145	243	74	<.1	<.1	0.0	<.1	64.7	67.4	0.0	0.0	0.0	60.0	58.3
Goliad	4,343	60.1	6.6	0.1	0.2	0.2	32.8	193	204	86	54	<.1	<.1	<.1	<.1	72.6	76.3	73.9	100.0	58.3	90.9	66.4
Gonzales	12,250	59.9	9.0	<.1	<.1	0.3	30.6	120	205	67	64	0.1	<.1	<.1	0.1	71.2	78.1	70.0	63.2	73.3	74.0	61.0
Gray	17,630	89.5	3.2	0.4	0.9	0.1	5.9	90	42	131	188	0.1	0.2	<.1	<.1	73.6	75.7	64.5	62.3	77.1	52.9	54.6
Grayson	70,913	90.1	6.1	0.4	1.0	<.1	2.4	30	39	84	225	0.6	0.8	0.3	<.1	74.6	75.8	66.9	70.6	69.3	29.3	61.2
Gregg	76,227	78.9	17.2	0.4	0.5	<.1	3.0	27	114	29	223	0.6	0.8	1.0	<.1	72.6	74.8	66.1	67.1	75.8	51.1	60.2
Grimes	13,889	63.5	23.5	<.1	0.3	<.1	12.7	108	193	10	127	0.1	0.1	0.2	<.1	73.8	76.3	71.6	78.6	90.0	90.9	66.2
Guadalupe	46,382	67.8	5.3	0.6	0.3	0.2	25.8	43	174	95	77	0.4	0.4	0.2	0.4	71.5	75.9	70.8	74.4	74.3	56.1	62.3
Hale	23,507	59.5	4.7	0.4	0.3	0.2	34.8	69	208	100	50	0.2	0.2	<.1	0.3	67.8	77.0	63.1	78.6	68.9	53.1	56.8
Hall	2,978	79.1	6.8	0.2	0.3	<.1	13.6	211	109	83	122	<.1	<.1	<.1	<.1	76.3	82.7	67.4	71.4	53.3	40.0	55.6
Hamilton	6,007	95.9	<.1	0.2	0.2	<.1	3.7	172	9	237	213	<.1	<.1	<.1	<.1	77.1	79.1	50.0	50.0	73.7	100.0	54.8
Hansford	4,028	82.8	0.0	0.1	0.4	<.1	16.5	195	88	244	105	<.1	<.1	0.0	<.1	68.9	71.9	0.0	83.3	73.9	50.0	56.7
Hardeman	3,904	85.9	5.4	0.2	0.5	<.1	7.9	197	71	94	167	<.1	<.1	<.1	<.1	73.9	77.4	66.0	69.2	76.9	33.3	52.5
Hardin	29,206	90.8	7.4	0.1	0.3	<.1	1.4	56	32	77	247	0.2	0.3	0.2	<.1	70.7	71.6	62.8	66.7	79.5	40.0	58.2
Harris	2,013,190	57.9	17.8	3.7	0.2	0.1	20.2	1	212	27	93	16.6	14.9	26.9	14.9	71.4	76.3	68.0	69.9	76.3	62.1	62.9
Harrison	40,928	71.4	26.2	0.2	0.3	<.1	1.8	47	155	5	238	0.3	0.4	0.8	<.1	71.2	73.2	67.3	67.4	69.2	61.1	58.8
Hartley	2,581	94.2	0.2	0.3	0.8	<.1	4.5	221	13	209	202	<.1	<.1	<.1	<.1	71.0	71.8	55.6	100.0	71.4	100.0	57.7
Haskell	5,117	81.3	3.0	0.2	0.2	<.1	15.3	183	97	136	113	<.1	<.1	<.1	<.1	75.0	79.5	65.3	56.3	73.3	11.1	59.5
Hays	49,624	70.9	3.4	0.7	0.3	<.1	24.6	39	158	128	79	0.4	0.4	0.1	0.4	75.6	78.8	81.0	82.3	80.9	72.7	67.0
Hemphill	2,570	90.7	0.2	<.1	0.7	0.0	8.3	222	34	207	162	<.1	<.1	<.1	<.1	69.1	71.2	71.4	50.0	81.8	0.0	51.7
Henderson	44,481	89.0	7.2	0.2	0.3	<.1	3.3	44	47	78	219	0.4	0.5	0.2	<.1	76.0	77.4	67.6	73.6	83.4	60.0	61.6
Hidalgo	243,124	18.3	0.1	0.2	<.1	0.2	81.0	7	246	212	9	2.0	0.6	<.1	7.2	63.4	82.1	68.7	71.2	75.5	63.6	60.2
Hill	20,292	85.0	8.0	0.2	0.3	<.1	6.6	82	77	72	177	0.2	0.2	0.1	<.1	74.8	77.3	64.8	88.9	78.8	50.0	60.3
Hockley	16,386	69.1	3.8	0.1	0.3	0.1	26.6	96	164	115	73	0.1	0.1	<.1	0.2	67.7	73.5	62.2	67.7	73.0	54.5	56.9
Hood	21,579	95.0	0.1	0.5	0.5	<.1	3.8	77	10	213	210	0.2	0.3	<.1	<.1	74.5	75.3	59.6	63.9	77.6	58.3	60.0
Hopkins	21,172	87.0	8.1	0.2	0.4	<.1	4.2	80	60	71	206	0.2	0.2	0.1	<.1	73.4	74.4	69.6	67.2	72.7	71.4	62.7
Houston	15,991	68.2	27.1	0.2	0.2	<.1	4.2	98	172	4	205	0.1	0.1	0.3	<.1	74.8	77.7	69.2	72.3	92.3	56.5	69.5
Howard	23,626	72.2	3.5	0.5	0.4	0.1	23.3	68	151	125	82	0.2	0.2	<.1	0.2	73.0	76.7	71.0	71.0	75.0	52.8	63.9
Hudspeth	1,987	36.9	0.5	<.1	0.2	0.3	62.1	230	233	192	22	<.1	<.1	<.1	<.1	68.2	76.8	100.0	50.0	50.0	100.0	63.8
Hunt	47,338	89.3	5.3	0.5	0.4	<.1	3.8	40	69	63	209	0.4	0.5	0.3	<.1	73.6	75.2	65.5	75.1	71.1	57.1	62.8
Hutchinson	18,216	88.3	2.3	0.3	1.3	<.1	7.7	88	54	151	168	0.1	0.2	<.1	<.1	70.9	72.8	62.2	78.3	71.5	68.4	56.2
Irion	1,167	77.7	<.1	0.0	<.1	<.1	22.0	244	126	218	87	<.1	<.1	<.1	<.1	71.6	73.1	50.0	0.0	100.0	100.0	66.8
Jack	5,110	96.6	0.7	0.1	0.2	<.1	2.3	184	6	188	226	<.1	<.1	<.1	<.1	73.2	74.0	70.6	60.0	55.6	50.0	51.7
Jackson	9,363	72.0	9.1	<.1	0.1	<.1	18.7	144	152	66	97	<.1	<.1	<.1	<.1	74.5	74.5	71.4	63.6	76.9	100.0	63.1
Jasper	22,293	81.6	16.5	<.1	0.2	<.1	1.5	74	94	33	243	0.2	0.2	0.3	<.1	71.7	74.2	62.8	55.6	68.9	41.2	56.7
Jeff Davis	1,433	61.8	<.1	0.3	0.8	0.0	37.1	239	201	222	43	<.1	<.1	<.1	<.1	73.6	76.8	16.7	100.0	91.7	0.0	69.0
Jefferson	174,707	65.3	28.0	1.7	0.2	<.1	4.7	11	182	3	200	1.4	1.5	3.7	0.3	73.0	77.4	66.4	59.7	72.8	62.7	65.6
Jim Hogg	3,441	9.3	<.1	<.1	0.2	0.3	90.1	206	251	217	4	<.1	<.1	<.1	0.1	67.4	75.5	100.0	66.7	85.7	76.9	66.5
Jim Wells	25,425	29.6	0.5	0.1	0.1	0.3	69.4	63	237	191	16	0.2	<.1	<.1	0.6	67.5	74.6	64.9	66.7	83.8	68.3	64.8
Johnson	68,829	90.3	2.3	0.4	0.4	<.1	6.6	32	37	149	178	0.6	0.8	0.1	0.2	70.8	71.9	64.6	65.5	68.9	61.2	61.1
Jones	11,939	82.2	3.6	0.2	0.3	<.1	13.7	124	92	121	121	<.1	0.1	<.1	<.1	72.4	75.7	65.1	72.4	82.1	60.0	58.7
Karnes	8,657	55.1	2.7	<.1	0.1	0.2	41.8	152	219	142	37	<.1	<.1	<.1	0.1	69.5	77.7	67.6	58.3	68.8	59.4	61.2
Kaufman	36,858	80.9	13.0	0.4	0.3	<.1	5.3	51	102	45	194	0.3	0.4	0.4	<.1	70.6	72.3	66.5	65.6	71.2	48.5	58.2
Kendall	10,759	85.2	0.3	0.2	0.6	0.0	13.8	131	74	202	119	<.1	0.1	<.1	<.1	73.7	76.1	57.1	84.6	85.7	0.0	62.0
Kenedy	322	22.7	0.0	0.0	0.0	1.6	75.8	252	242	245	13	<.1	<.1	0.0	<.1	70.0	78.5	0.0	0.0	0.0	100.0	67.4
Kent	749	89.2	0.7	0.0	0.1	0.0	10.0	248	45	189	151	<.1	<.1	0.0	<.1	74.2	75.7	83.3	0.0	100.0	0.0	62.5
Kerr	27,873	83.8	1.8	0.3	0.3	<.1	13.7	60	82	160	120	0.2	0.3	<.1	0.1	76.8	79.7	68.4	66.4	79.8	56.5	63.8
Kimble	3,070	84.1	<.1	<.1	0.2	<.1	15.5	209	79	224	110	<.1	<.1	<.1	<.1	74.5	77.5	100.0	100.0	100.0	27.3	61.8
King	245	86.9	0.0	0.0	0.0	0.0	13.1	253	62	246	123	<.1	<.1	0.0	<.1	69.2	70.8	0.0	0.0	0.0	0.0	64.7
Kinney	2,334	51.6	1.2	0.2	0.9	0.2	46.0	225	223	176	31	<.1	<.1	<.1	<.1	74.8	82.3	56.3	71.4	90.9	55.6	68.3
Kleberg	21,429	37.2	3.3	1.5	0.2	0.2	57.6	78	232	130	23	0.2	0.1	<.1	0.5	70.8	77.5	73.6	84.3	85.7	63.0	66.6
Knox	3,507	76.2	5.6	<.1	0.2	0.1	17.9	204	129	91	102	<.1	<.1	<.1	<.1	72.5	78.7	58.5	60.0	100.0	71.4	57.5
Lamar	32,510	85.2	12.8	0.4	0.8	<.1	0.9	53	75	46	253	0.3	0.4	0.3	<.1	71.6	75.8	65.2	78.2	63.3	33.3	61.3
Lamb	10,558	64.7	4.8	<.1	0.2	<.1	30.2	132	185	99	68	<.1	<.1	<.1	0.1	70.1	78.5	63.2	52.6	72.2	64.3	57.8

Table B. — 1990 Voting Age Population (VAP) by Race and Ethnic Origin (cont)

County	Total Voting Age Population	Percent of total VAP — Non-Hispanic — White	Black	Asian and Pacific Islander	Native American	Other	Hispanic	Rank — Total	Non-Hispanic White	Black	Hispanic	Pct contribution to state VAP — Total	Non-Hispanic White	Black	Hispanic	VAP percent of total population — Total	Non-Hispanic White	Black	Asian and Pacific Islander	Native American	Other	Hispanic
Lampasas	9,774	86.0	1.6	1.0	0.5	<.1	10.8	137	68	164	140	<.1	0.1	<.1	<.1	72.3	74.3	66.8	78.6	67.6	66.7	60.1
La Salle	3,509	23.8	1.5	0.1	0.2	0.2	74.2	203	241	170	15	<.1	<.1	<.1	<.1	66.8	75.7	100.0	80.0	100.0	38.1	64.0
Lavaca	14,087	85.9	6.4	<.1	<.1	0.1	7.4	107	70	87	169	0.1	0.2	<.1	<.1	75.4	77.0	68.8	78.6	80.0	48.5	65.2
Lee	9,040	78.3	13.2	<.1	0.1	<.1	8.2	145	119	44	163	<.1	0.1	<.1	<.1	70.3	73.4	68.0	58.3	84.6	52.9	52.5
Leon	9,390	83.6	12.6	<.1	0.4	0.0	3.3	142	84	47	217	<.1	0.1	<.1	<.1	74.1	74.7	73.9	100.0	84.6	0.0	61.5
Liberty	37,323	82.3	12.6	0.2	0.3	0.1	4.5	50	91	48	201	0.3	0.4	0.4	<.1	70.8	71.9	68.7	64.7	74.3	71.2	58.7
Limestone	15,438	76.0	18.0	0.2	0.2	0.2	5.4	102	132	25	192	0.1	0.1	0.2	<.1	73.7	77.0	67.4	62.5	73.7	88.6	57.6
Lipscomb	2,228	89.8	<.1	0.3	1.0	0.0	8.8	226	40	227	158	<.1	<.1	<.1	<.1	70.9	73.5	100.0	53.8	85.2	0.0	51.7
Live Oak	6,941	68.8	<.1	0.1	0.4	0.2	30.4	163	165	229	67	<.1	<.1	<.1	<.1	72.6	77.5	100.0	52.9	83.3	70.8	63.5
Llano	9,729	96.2	0.2	0.2	0.3	<.1	3.1	138	7	208	222	<.1	0.1	<.1	<.1	83.6	84.3	86.4	90.0	91.4	100.0	65.8
Loving	79	86.1	0.0	0.0	0.0	0.0	13.9	254	67	247	118	<.1	<.1	0.0	<.1	73.8	73.1	0.0	0.0	0.0	0.0	78.6
Lubbock	163,771	72.7	6.6	1.3	0.3	0.1	19.0	13	148	85	96	1.3	1.5	0.8	1.1	73.6	78.6	65.2	78.7	74.9	67.7	61.1
Lynn	4,706	59.8	3.2	<.1	0.2	0.3	36.5	188	206	132	45	<.1	<.1	<.1	<.1	69.6	76.4	67.6	100.0	58.8	87.5	61.0
McCulloch	6,410	75.9	1.6	<.1	0.2	0.0	22.3	168	133	165	84	<.1	<.1	<.1	<.1	73.0	77.3	69.5	57.1	78.6	0.0	61.6
McLennan	139,885	75.1	13.6	0.8	0.2	<.1	10.3	16	137	42	148	1.2	1.3	1.4	0.5	74.0	78.1	65.5	79.8	73.5	58.5	60.9
McMullen	615	63.3	0.0	0.0	0.3	0.0	36.4	250	196	248	46	<.1	<.1	0.0	<.1	75.3	78.9	0.0	0.0	66.7	0.0	70.0
Madison	8,579	65.2	23.2	<.1	0.5	0.1	10.9	154	183	11	139	<.1	<.1	0.1	<.1	78.5	78.5	78.3	50.0	72.2	69.2	79.4
Marion	7,513	70.2	28.2	<.1	0.3	0.0	1.3	159	162	2	248	<.1	<.1	0.2	<.1	75.3	78.7	68.4	57.1	60.0	0.0	65.3
Martin	3,262	63.3	1.9	0.2	0.2	0.2	34.2	208	195	158	52	<.1	<.1	<.1	<.1	65.8	71.7	70.1	85.7	63.6	50.0	57.0
Mason	2,618	83.7	<.1	<.1	0.3	0.0	15.9	220	83	221	107	<.1	<.1	<.1	<.1	76.5	80.1	33.3	66.7	88.9	0.0	61.8
Matagorda	25,325	63.4	13.4	1.6	0.2	0.1	21.3	64	194	43	89	0.2	0.2	0.3	0.2	68.6	73.4	67.4	51.1	77.0	50.0	59.2
Maverick	22,544	5.5	<.1	0.2	2.0	0.1	92.2	72	253	228	3	0.2	<.1	<.1	0.8	62.0	78.6	76.9	76.5	66.6	70.0	61.1
Medina	19,209	58.6	0.3	0.1	0.3	0.1	40.5	84	211	201	38	0.2	0.1	<.1	0.3	70.3	75.4	76.1	74.5	73.5	55.1	64.1
Menard	1,703	71.5	0.3	0.0	0.2	0.2	27.8	233	153	200	71	<.1	<.1	<.1	<.1	75.6	80.5	71.4	0.0	100.0	75.0	65.3
Midland	73,168	73.7	7.1	0.7	0.3	0.1	18.0	28	143	79	100	0.6	0.7	0.4	0.5	68.6	72.4	65.1	64.6	72.6	58.3	57.7
Milam	16,471	76.1	11.2	0.1	0.2	<.1	12.4	95	130	54	129	0.1	0.2	<.1	<.1	71.8	75.8	63.8	73.9	71.7	88.9	59.0
Mills	3,448	91.5	0.2	<.1	<.1	<.1	8.1	205	28	204	164	<.1	<.1	<.1	<.1	76.1	78.3	80.0	100.0	50.0	33.3	58.1
Mitchell	5,813	70.3	4.1	<.1	0.2	<.1	25.2	174	161	107	78	<.1	<.1	<.1	<.1	72.5	78.0	66.6	100.0	76.9	83.3	61.3
Montague	13,028	97.3	<.1	<.1	0.4	<.1	2.2	117	2	235	229	0.1	0.2	<.1	<.1	75.4	76.2	75.0	53.8	70.4	66.7	52.6
Montgomery	128,109	88.9	3.8	0.6	0.4	<.1	6.2	19	49	113	182	1.1	1.5	0.4	0.3	70.3	71.4	64.4	67.5	74.5	56.3	60.5
Moore	11,963	70.9	0.4	1.3	0.7	0.1	26.6	123	159	194	72	<.1	0.1	<.1	0.1	67.0	72.4	65.8	62.0	76.1	59.1	55.8
Morris	9,577	75.7	22.3	<.1	0.5	<.1	1.4	140	134	14	245	<.1	0.1	0.2	<.1	72.6	75.0	66.4	63.6	72.5	100.0	56.9
Motley	1,175	88.3	4.3	0.3	0.3	0.0	6.9	243	55	105	174	<.1	<.1	<.1	<.1	76.7	78.6	73.5	75.0	80.0	0.0	59.6
Nacogdoches	42,069	80.3	14.6	0.5	0.2	<.1	4.3	45	105	39	203	0.3	0.4	0.5	<.1	76.8	79.3	68.5	76.3	81.6	61.8	65.3
Navarro	29,168	75.6	17.2	0.7	0.3	<.1	6.2	57	135	30	183	0.2	0.3	0.4	<.1	73.1	75.7	66.6	77.2	76.9	61.9	62.3
Newton	9,560	78.4	20.1	<.1	0.3	<.1	1.1	141	117	16	249	<.1	0.1	0.1	<.1	70.5	72.6	63.5	81.8	67.4	66.7	66.7
Nolan	11,976	74.3	4.1	0.1	0.2	0.2	21.2	122	141	108	91	<.1	0.1	<.1	<.1	72.2	77.2	66.7	72.2	70.7	54.5	59.7
Nueces	202,321	46.5	4.0	0.7	0.3	0.2	48.3	8	229	111	28	1.7	1.2	0.6	3.6	69.5	76.1	67.9	70.6	73.1	64.9	64.2
Ochiltree	6,306	84.1	<.1	0.1	1.0	0.1	14.7	169	80	233	115	<.1	<.1	<.1	<.1	69.1	71.9	100.0	71.4	70.1	44.4	62.6
Oldham	1,338	91.6	0.0	0.8	1.3	0.0	6.3	242	26	249	180	<.1	<.1	0.0	<.1	58.7	60.6	0.0	64.7	62.1	0.0	42.0
Orange	57,508	89.6	7.6	0.5	0.2	<.1	2.1	36	41	76	232	0.5	0.7	0.3	<.1	71.4	72.4	64.5	59.3	75.8	68.3	62.8
Palo Pinto	18,445	88.9	2.8	0.6	0.3	<.1	7.3	87	50	141	170	0.2	0.2	<.1	<.1	73.6	75.5	66.2	65.9	77.2	73.3	58.8
Panola	15,896	81.0	16.8	0.1	0.3	<.1	1.8	99	100	31	239	0.1	0.2	0.2	<.1	72.1	73.9	66.2	82.6	75.4	14.3	59.5
Parker	46,641	94.8	0.8	0.3	0.5	<.1	3.5	42	12	185	214	0.4	0.6	<.1	<.1	72.0	72.6	66.8	70.8	70.0	83.3	60.3
Parmer	6,601	63.5	1.2	0.2	0.2	0.1	34.7	166	192	175	51	<.1	<.1	<.1	<.1	66.9	74.9	71.7	70.0	71.4	53.8	56.0
Pecos	9,609	47.0	0.3	0.1	0.2	0.2	52.1	139	228	199	25	<.1	<.1	<.1	0.2	65.5	72.8	58.8	61.9	77.4	56.3	60.1
Polk	23,083	83.1	10.8	0.2	1.9	<.1	4.1	70	87	57	208	0.2	0.2	0.2	<.1	75.2	78.2	64.7	65.5	68.0	50.0	58.2
Potter	69,734	73.2	7.7	2.2	0.7	0.1	16.1	31	146	74	106	0.6	0.7	0.4	0.4	71.2	76.3	63.6	62.2	71.9	60.9	58.3
Presidio	4,494	21.2	<.1	0.2	0.2	0.0	78.4	190	244	236	11	<.1	<.1	<.1	0.1	67.7	79.7	50.0	90.0	72.7	0.0	65.0
Rains	5,031	93.6	3.9	<.1	0.4	<.1	1.9	185	15	112	236	<.1	<.1	<.1	<.1	74.9	75.6	69.7	50.0	78.6	33.3	60.8
Randall	65,169	91.9	1.1	0.7	0.5	<.1	5.8	33	22	177	190	0.5	0.8	<.1	0.1	72.7	73.6	67.8	72.0	77.1	46.5	61.2
Reagan	2,798	60.3	2.4	0.0	0.3	0.0	37.0	217	202	147	44	<.1	<.1	<.1	<.1	62.0	68.6	63.0	0.0	100.0		53.4
Real	1,847	78.0	0.0	0.0	0.7	<.1	21.3	232	124	250	88	<.1	<.1	0.0	<.1	76.6	79.4	0.0	0.0	56.5	100.0	68.5
Red River	10,874	80.5	17.6	<.1	0.4	<.1	1.4	130	103	28	244	<.1	0.1	0.1	<.1	76.0	78.8	67.0	64.3	63.9	40.0	57.1
Reeves	10,537	29.3	2.2	0.2	0.2	<.1	68.1	133	239	152	17	<.1	<.1	<.1	0.3	66.5	78.9	68.5	74.2	92.3	100.0	62.1
Refugio	5,782	55.5	7.0	<.1	0.2	<.1	37.3	176	217	81	41	<.1	<.1	<.1	<.1	72.5	76.7	66.1	60.0	75.0	33.3	68.2
Roberts	718	97.8	0.0	0.1	0.1	0.0	1.9	249	1	251	235	<.1	<.1	0.0	<.1	70.0	71.1	0.0	50.0	100.0	0.0	41.2
Robertson	11,075	64.9	24.7	<.1	<.1	<.1	10.2	129	184	7	149	<.1	<.1	0.2	<.1	71.4	76.7	65.1	58.3	57.9	50.0	59.5
Rockwall	18,082	90.7	3.2	0.6	0.4	<.1	5.1	89	35	134	195	0.1	0.2	<.1	<.1	70.6	71.4	67.2	65.4	77.8	71.4	61.4
Runnels	8,206	78.0	1.5	0.1	<.1	<.1	20.2	155	123	169	92	<.1	<.1	<.1	<.1	72.7	76.8	69.1	60.0	72.7	71.4	60.5
Rusk	31,567	77.8	18.6	0.1	0.3	<.1	3.2	54	125	21	220	0.3	0.3	0.4	<.1	72.2	74.6	66.0	71.4	70.4	50.0	58.3
Sabine	7,572	89.0	10.1	0.1	0.1	<.1	0.7	158	48	59	254	<.1	<.1	<.1	<.1	79.0	80.8	69.0	72.7	80.0	16.7	47.7
San Augustine	6,046	73.8	24.6	<.1	0.2	0.0	1.4	171	142	8	246	<.1	<.1	0.1	<.1	75.6	79.6	66.4	83.3	90.9	0.0	60.9
San Jacinto	12,074	83.3	14.0	<.1	0.4	<.1	2.2	121	86	40	230	<.1	0.1	0.1	<.1	73.7	75.5	66.8	64.3	69.0	66.7	61.7
San Patricio	39,757	51.4	1.4	0.2	0.3	0.2	46.6	48	224	172	30	0.3	0.3	<.1	0.7	67.7	73.8	63.6	64.3	70.0	62.1	62.1
San Saba	4,001	83.9	0.2	<.1	0.1	0.1	15.7	196	81	205	109	<.1	<.1	<.1	<.1	74.1	76.7	61.5	100.0	62.5	62.5	62.8
Schleicher	2,017	68.1	1.0	0.0	<.1	<.1	30.7	229	173	181	63	<.1	<.1	<.1	<.1	67.5	72.4	83.3	0.0	100.0	50.0	58.3
Scurry	13,319	74.5	5.1	0.1	0.3	<.1	20.0	113	140	97	94	0.1	0.1	<.1	<.1	71.5	75.7	78.2	64.3	64.3	62.5	59.7
Shackelford	2,428	93.3	0.5	<.1	0.2	0.1	5.8	223	16	193	189	<.1	<.1	<.1	<.1	73.2	75.1	91.7	100.0	44.4	60.0	52.2
Shelby	16,269	78.8	18.8	0.1	0.2	0.0	2.1	97	116	20	233	0.1	0.2	0.2	<.1	73.8	76.6	65.1	66.7	73.5	0.0	63.6

Table B. — 1990 Voting Age Population (VAP) by Race and Ethnic Origin (cont)

County	Total Voting Age Population	Percent of total VAP — Non-Hispanic: White	Black	Asian and Pacific Islander	Native American	Other	Hispanic	Rank: Total	Non-Hisp. White	Non-Hisp. Black	Hispanic	Pct contribution to state VAP: Total	Non-Hisp. White	Non-Hisp. Black	Hispanic	VAP pct of total pop: Total	Non-Hisp. White	Black	Asian and Pacific Islander	Native American	Other	Hispanic
Sherman	2,022	83.6	0.1	0.2	0.2	0.0	15.8	228	85	211	108	<.1	<.1	<.1	<.1	70.7	73.5	75.0	57.1	71.4	0.0	59.3
Smith	111,026	75.2	19.3	0.4	0.3	<.1	4.8	20	136	17	199	0.9	1.1	1.6	0.2	73.4	76.0	68.5	69.3	70.5	46.3	59.0
Somervell	3,643	88.2	<.1	0.4	0.5	<.1	10.8	200	56	219	141	0.2	<.1	<.1	<.1	68.0	70.7	30.0	77.8	55.9	100.0	52.3
Starr	24,553	2.9	<.1	<.1	<.1	0.2	96.7	67	254	239	1	0.2	<.1	<.1	0.9	60.6	72.1	44.4	100.0	66.7	55.6	60.3
Stephens	6,550	90.7	2.4	0.2	0.3	<.1	6.3	167	33	148	179	<.1	<.1	<.1	<.1	72.7	74.8	67.9	57.1	58.6	50.0	53.8
Sterling	955	76.6	0.0	0.0	0.4	0.0	22.9	246	128	252	83	<.1	<.1	0.0	<.1	66.4	68.6	0.0	0.0	100.0	0.0	59.8
Stonewall	1,501	86.5	3.5	0.3	<.1	<.1	9.6	236	64	124	154	<.1	<.1	<.1	<.1	74.6	77.4	60.2	57.1	50.0	50.0	60.8
Sutton	2,866	56.7	<.1	0.2	0.3	0.1	42.6	214	214	232	35	<.1	<.1	<.1	<.1	69.3	72.4	100.0	100.0	71.4	100.0	65.4
Swisher	5,675	71.4	3.7	0.2	0.3	<.1	24.4	181	154	117	80	<.1	<.1	<.1	<.1	69.8	77.1	63.6	69.2	61.5	41.7	55.4
Tarrant	852,582	76.1	10.8	2.3	0.4	<.1	10.3	3	131	56	147	7.0	8.3	6.9	3.2	72.9	75.6	66.8	68.0	75.9	56.3	62.9
Taylor	87,053	81.0	5.5	1.1	0.3	<.1	12.0	24	98	92	130	0.7	0.9	0.4	0.4	72.8	75.9	65.4	70.5	74.9	50.3	59.5
Terrell	993	50.1	0.0	0.0	0.3	0.2	49.4	245	226	253	26	<.1	<.1	0.0	<.1	70.4	76.3	0.0	0.0	100.0	100.0	65.4
Terry	8,844	63.7	2.9	0.1	0.3	0.2	32.8	147	191	138	55	<.1	<.1	<.1	0.1	66.9	75.2	58.4	45.8	80.6	44.4	55.9
Throckmorton	1,435	93.3	0.0	0.3	0.3	0.0	6.1	238	17	254	186	<.1	<.1	0.0	<.1	76.3	77.3	0.0	62.5	100.0	0.0	64.0
Titus	17,157	78.4	12.0	0.1	0.4	<.1	9.1	93	118	51	156	0.1	0.2	0.2	<.1	71.5	74.2	64.7	91.3	65.6	50.0	60.9
Tom Green	71,840	72.8	3.8	0.9	0.3	<.1	22.0	29	147	114	86	0.6	0.7	0.2	0.6	73.0	77.3	69.4	68.3	82.1	50.4	62.1
Travis	438,196	68.7	9.6	2.9	0.3	0.1	18.4	5	166	62	98	3.6	3.8	3.1	3.0	76.0	80.2	68.7	80.2	80.3	62.8	66.2
Trinity	8,765	85.4	12.4	0.1	0.2	0.0	1.8	150	72	50	237	<.1	<.1	<.1	<.1	76.6	79.0	66.2	47.6	70.8	0.0	59.6
Tyler	12,493	88.9	9.8	<.1	0.2	0.0	1.0	118	51	60	252	0.1	0.1	0.1	<.1	75.1	77.0	61.9	83.3	68.9	0.0	68.9
Upshur	22,704	86.2	11.6	<.1	0.4	<.1	1.7	71	65	53	240	0.2	0.3	0.2	<.1	72.4	73.3	68.3	78.6	79.1	28.6	58.8
Upton	2,859	64.6	2.1	<.1	0.4	0.1	32.7	215	186	154	56	<.1	<.1	<.1	<.1	64.3	69.3	68.2	100.0	57.9	66.7	56.1
Uvalde	15,848	43.8	0.2	0.2	0.1	0.3	55.4	100	231	206	24	0.1	<.1	<.1	0.3	67.9	76.9	88.6	69.8	67.9	52.2	62.2
Val Verde	25,965	31.3	1.8	0.6	0.2	0.1	65.9	62	235	159	20	0.2	0.1	<.1	0.6	67.1	78.1	70.6	76.3	72.1	63.6	62.7
Van Zandt	28,223	92.8	3.4	<.1	0.4	<.1	3.3	58	19	127	218	0.2	0.3	<.1	<.1	74.4	75.3	67.1	65.9	73.6	33.3	61.5
Victoria	51,824	62.6	6.3	0.3	0.2	0.2	30.5	37	198	88	66	0.4	0.4	0.2	0.6	69.7	74.0	69.9	67.6	78.7	58.7	62.3
Walker	41,231	65.4	23.1	0.6	0.3	0.1	10.4	46	181	12	144	0.3	0.3	0.7	0.2	81.0	82.1	79.2	79.4	87.1	84.3	77.9
Waller	17,460	51.6	39.2	0.3	<.1	<.1	8.8	91	222	1	159	0.1	0.1	0.5	<.1	74.6	75.4	78.4	68.2	75.0	55.6	59.0
Ward	8,769	63.9	3.1	0.1	0.5	0.3	32.2	149	190	135	60	<.1	<.1	<.1	0.1	66.9	72.5	62.0	65.0	64.1	63.4	58.4
Washington	19,501	76.8	18.6	0.6	0.1	<.1	3.7	83	127	22	211	0.2	0.2	0.3	<.1	74.6	77.5	66.7	68.0	73.0	76.7	63.1
Webb	84,362	6.5	<.1	0.3	<.1	0.2	92.9	25	252	225	2	0.7	<.1	<.1	2.9	63.3	74.0	79.4	68.8	68.2	66.7	62.6
Wharton	28,013	62.6	14.8	0.3	<.1	<.1	22.2	59	197	38	85	0.2	0.2	0.4	0.3	70.1	74.7	67.0	69.9	82.4	56.9	61.5
Wheeler	4,312	92.3	1.9	0.3	0.6	<.1	4.8	194	21	157	198	<.1	<.1	<.1	<.1	73.3	75.1	56.6	57.1	80.0	66.7	55.0
Wichita	90,399	82.6	8.2	1.3	0.7	<.1	7.2	23	90	69	171	0.7	1.0	0.6	0.2	73.9	76.1	67.2	66.8	72.8	58.0	61.4
Wilbarger	11,130	79.7	8.2	0.4	0.5	<.1	11.2	128	106	70	136	<.1	0.1	<.1	<.1	73.6	77.6	68.0	67.1	73.2	50.0	56.8
Willacy	11,231	18.7	0.4	<.1	<.1	0.2	80.6	127	245	195	6	<.1	<.1	<.1	0.3	63.4	79.3	63.0	81.8	87.5	64.3	60.6
Williamson	96,362	81.4	4.4	1.3	0.3	<.1	12.6	21	96	103	128	0.8	1.0	0.3	0.4	69.1	70.8	65.5	68.5	67.5	59.8	60.6
Wilson	15,637	66.1	1.0	<.1	0.2	0.2	32.4	101	179	178	58	0.1	0.1	<.1	0.2	69.0	72.4	69.4	76.5	80.0	80.5	63.0
Winkler	5,757	66.8	1.9	0.1	0.6	<.1	30.6	178	178	156	65	<.1	<.1	<.1	<.1	66.7	73.4	71.0	87.5	80.0	26.7	55.5
Wise	24,869	91.8	1.3	0.2	0.5	<.1	6.1	66	23	173	185	0.2	0.3	<.1	<.1	71.7	72.8	82.4	65.8	69.3	66.7	57.3
Wood	22,317	89.5	7.9	0.1	0.3	<.1	2.2	73	43	73	231	0.2	0.3	0.1	<.1	76.0	76.6	73.9	69.2	71.4	40.0	61.9
Yoakum	5,725	67.2	0.9	0.1	0.3	<.1	31.5	180	175	184	62	<.1	<.1	<.1	<.1	65.2	70.7	60.0	88.9	63.3	33.3	56.0
Young	13,302	93.2	1.1	0.2	0.4	<.1	5.0	114	18	174	197	0.1	0.2	<.1	<.1	73.4	74.7	63.1	56.8	69.8	37.5	57.6
Zapata	6,051	23.9	<.1	<.1	0.1	0.2	75.7	170	240	238	14	<.1	<.1	<.1	0.2	65.2	84.0	100.0	100.0	100.0	54.5	60.9
Zavala	7,815	10.0	3.5	0.0	<.1	0.3	86.1	157	250	123	6	<.1	<.1	<.1	0.2	64.3	81.9	97.5	0.0	66.7	58.7	61.9
TEXAS	12,150,671	64.4	11.0	1.8	0.3	0.1	22.4					100.0	100.0	100.0	100.0	71.5	76.1	67.6	70.2	74.5	61.2	62.7
CONGRESSIONAL																						
District 1	416,554	80.3	16.3	0.3	0.4	<.1	2.7	5	9	6	30	3.4	4.3	5.1	0.4	73.6	75.7	66.6	72.6	71.4	47.6	62.3
District 2	414,273	79.1	15.2	0.3	0.3	<.1	4.9	7	10	7	27	3.4	4.2	4.7	0.7	73.2	75.1	67.7	69.0	73.3	62.7	63.6
District 3	419,571	87.4	3.8	3.0	0.3	<.1	5.4	4	3	23	26	3.5	4.7	1.2	0.8	74.1	75.3	65.6	67.8	72.7	52.3	66.5
District 4	413,296	87.9	7.6	0.4	0.5	<.1	3.6	10	2	14	29	3.4	4.6	2.4	0.5	73.0	74.3	66.8	67.7	70.8	48.8	59.9
District 5	414,181	67.9	15.0	1.2	0.4	0.1	15.3	8	19	8	13	3.4	3.6	4.6	2.3	73.1	77.3	68.6	66.7	74.5	65.8	62.8
District 6	411,725	88.8	4.0	2.0	0.4	<.1	4.9	14	1	21	28	3.4	4.7	1.2	0.7	72.7	73.6	66.7	67.1	75.3	52.5	64.8
District 7	412,822	78.7	5.1	5.0	0.2	<.1	10.9	11	11	19	21	3.4	4.1	1.6	1.6	72.9	74.9	65.2	67.5	74.9	54.8	66.3
District 8	408,226	86.6	4.7	1.9	0.3	<.1	6.5	17	4	20	25	3.4	4.5	1.4	1.0	72.1	73.1	65.3	72.5	75.8	66.9	64.9
District 9	410,971	69.9	19.6	1.7	0.3	<.1	8.5	15	16	4	23	3.4	3.7	6.0	1.3	72.6	75.8	66.5	64.4	76.7	64.2	65.0
District 10	430,148	68.2	9.7	3.0	0.3	0.1	18.7	1	18	11	10	3.5	3.7	3.1	3.0	76.0	80.2	68.7	80.2	80.2	62.8	66.2
District 11	413,528	73.4	14.3	1.5	0.3	<.1	10.4	9	14	9	22	3.4	3.9	4.4	1.6	73.0	76.3	67.0	74.6	74.4	56.3	61.8
District 12	412,814	76.8	7.2	1.6	0.5	<.1	13.8	12	12	15	18	3.4	4.1	2.2	2.1	72.9	76.2	67.2	65.8	73.8	59.9	61.8
District 13	409,490	75.4	7.2	1.1	0.5	0.1	15.7	16	13	17	12	3.4	3.9	2.2	2.4	72.3	76.8	66.3	69.7	72.7	61.1	58.6
District 14	407,375	68.6	10.5	0.5	0.2	0.1	20.4	19	17	10	8	3.4	3.6	3.1	3.1	71.9	75.9	70.3	61.6	76.8	61.6	62.2
District 15	369,299	28.7	1.0	0.3	0.1	0.2	69.6	30	30	30	1	3.0	1.4	0.3	9.5	65.2	78.3	69.0	73.7	75.5	63.8	60.9
District 16	382,985	28.7	3.4	1.1	0.3	0.1	66.4	25	29	24	2	3.2	1.4	1.0	9.3	67.6	77.7	70.3	76.5	72.2	60.9	63.8
District 17	412,570	81.8	3.2	0.5	0.3	<.1	14.1	13	7	25	17	3.4	4.3	1.0	2.1	72.9	76.0	67.1	67.8	73.7	55.3	60.1
District 18	414,418	35.2	47.9	2.9	0.2	0.1	13.7	6	26	1	19	3.4	1.9	14.9	2.1	73.2	82.4	69.9	72.7	78.3	63.7	65.2
District 19	403,001	80.5	2.2	0.9	0.4	0.1	16.0	22	8	29	11	3.3	4.1	0.7	2.4	71.2	74.8	63.0	73.1	75.0	61.2	58.1
District 20	398,984	36.7	5.5	1.3	0.2	0.2	56.1	23	23	18	6	3.3	1.9	1.6	8.2	70.5	80.3	70.9	77.2	77.8	64.3	65.1
District 21	420,498	84.2	2.2	0.9	0.3	<.1	12.3	3	5	28	20	3.5	4.5	0.7	1.9	74.3	76.0	68.2	72.2	76.1	58.7	65.1
District 22	406,687	71.7	7.2	6.4	0.3	0.1	14.4	20	15	16	16	3.3	3.7	2.2	2.1	71.8	74.4	68.5	67.7	76.4	61.8	64.2

Table B. — **1990 Voting Age Population (VAP) by Race and Ethnic Origin (cont)**

County	Total Voting Age Population	Percent of total VAP — Non-Hispanic White	Black	Asian and Pacific Islander	Native American	Other	Hispanic	Rank Percent of total VAP Total	Non-Hispanic White	Black	Hispanic	Percent contribution to state VAP Total	Non-Hispanic White	Black	Hispanic	VAP percent of total population Total	Non-Hispanic White	Black	Asian and Pacific Islander	Native American	Other	Hispanic
District 23	374,947	37.8	2.8	0.6	0.3	0.2	58.3	29	22	26	4	3.1	1.8	0.8	8.0	66.2	74.5	67.4	70.6	70.7	60.6	61.7
District 24	396,176	60.9	17.6	2.1	0.5	0.1	18.8	24	20	5	9	3.3	3.1	5.2	2.7	70.0	75.2	65.4	70.6	73.4	58.8	60.3
District 25	405,030	56.8	24.3	3.6	0.3	0.1	14.9	21	21	3	15	3.3	2.9	7.4	2.2	71.5	76.6	66.1	72.7	74.9	58.0	63.7
District 26	422,747	83.9	3.9	3.5	0.4	<.1	8.2	2	6	22	24	3.5	4.5	1.2	1.3	74.7	76.0	70.5	69.3	75.7	62.7	66.6
District 27	380,622	35.4	2.3	0.5	0.2	0.2	61.4	27	25	27	3	3.1	1.7	0.6	8.6	67.2	77.5	68.0	71.5	74.8	62.9	62.4
District 28	382,636	34.0	8.4	0.7	0.2	0.2	56.5	26	27	13	5	3.1	1.7	2.4	7.9	67.6	75.6	69.3	73.1	77.3	62.3	63.2
District 29	377,455	33.4	9.2	1.5	0.2	0.3	55.4	28	28	12	7	3.1	1.6	2.6	7.7	66.7	80.1	64.0	68.6	76.6	64.8	60.9
District 30	407,638	36.1	46.4	1.9	0.3	0.1	15.1	18	24	2	14	3.4	1.9	14.1	2.3	72.0	82.9	67.9	72.9	76.0	58.9	63.7

Table C. – Voter Participation: November 3, 1992, General Election

County	Estimated Voting Age Population (VAP), 1992	Voter registration (REG) Total	% contri-bution to state REG	% of 1992 VAP	Rank by % of 1992 VAP	Highest office Actual	Total	Office	% of 1992 VAP	Maximum vote Total	% contri-bution to state turnout	% of REG	Rank by % of REG	% of 1992 VAP	Rank by % 1992 VAP	Percent drop-off, by office[1] Pres-ident	Sen-ator	Gov-ernor	Repre-sent-ative
Anderson	38,091	20,747	0.2	54.5	249	-	14,466	P	38.0	14,466	0.2	69.7	164	38.0	246	0.0	-	-	3.1
Andrews	9,577	6,057	<.1	63.2	234	-	4,228	P	44.1	4,228	<.1	69.8	162	44.1	235	0.0	-	-	2.1
Angelina	50,201	35,811	0.4	71.3	177	-	26,281	P	52.4	26,281	0.4	73.4	93	52.4	153	0.0	-	-	1.0
Aransas	13,897	8,814	0.1	63.4	232	-	6,770	P	48.7	6,770	0.1	76.8	46	48.7	203	0.0	-	-	4.9
Archer	5,823	5,128	<.1	88.1	52	-	3,967	P	68.1	3,967	<.1	77.4	41	68.1	21	0.0	-	-	2.3
Armstrong	1,443	1,301	<.1	90.2	38	-	1,028	P	71.2	1,028	<.1	79.0	22	71.2	14	0.0	-	-	3.3
Atascosa	21,452	15,751	0.2	73.4	162	-	9,658	P	45.0	9,658	0.2	61.3	231	45.0	230	0.0	-	-	11.8
Austin	14,739	10,633	0.1	72.1	168	-	7,890	P	53.5	7,890	0.1	74.2	80	53.5	143	0.0	-	-	3.9
Bailey	4,648	3,437	<.1	73.9	159	-	2,365	P	50.9	2,365	<.1	68.8	174	50.9	180	0.0	-	-	4.0
Bandera	8,735	6,776	<.1	77.6	121	-	5,322	P	60.9	5,322	<.1	78.5	28	60.9	56	0.0	-	-	3.8
Bastrop	30,583	20,624	0.2	67.4	213	-	14,474	P	47.3	14,474	0.2	70.2	156	47.3	214	0.0	-	-	5.3
Baylor	3,223	3,055	<.1	94.8	24	-	2,132	P	66.1	2,132	<.1	69.8	163	66.1	31	0.0	-	-	4.1
Bee	16,849	15,071	0.2	89.4	42	-	9,108	P	54.1	9,108	0.1	60.4	234	54.1	135	0.0	-	-	4.1
Bell	138,973	73,966	0.9	53.2	251	-	55,077	P	39.6	55,077	0.9	74.5	78	39.6	243	0.0	-	-	6.0
Bexar	863,383	584,335	6.9	67.7	210	-	415,276	P	48.1	415,276	6.7	71.1	130	48.1	209	0.0	-	-	23.2
Blanco	4,710	3,831	<.1	81.3	86	-	3,109	P	66.0	3,109	<.1	81.2	9	66.0	33	0.0	-	-	9.3
Borden	566	501	<.1	88.5	48	-	378	P	66.8	378	<.1	75.4	64	66.8	27	0.0	-	-	9.0
Bosque	11,676	8,710	0.1	74.6	154	-	6,489	P	55.6	6,489	0.1	74.5	77	55.6	109	0.0	-	-	4.7
Bowie	60,083	43,047	0.5	71.6	171	-	30,365	P	50.5	30,365	0.5	70.5	142	50.5	186	0.0	-	-	28.4
Brazoria	137,871	95,022	1.1	68.9	201	-	71,467	P	51.8	71,467	1.2	75.2	68	51.8	164	0.0	-	-	3.0
Brazos	94,637	60,915	0.7	64.4	227	-	49,340	P	52.1	49,340	0.8	81.0	11	52.1	158	0.0	-	-	7.6
Brewster	6,571	5,117	<.1	77.9	118	-	3,247	P	49.4	3,247	<.1	63.5	218	49.4	195	0.0	-	-	3.6
Briscoe	1,314	1,328	<.1	101.1	15	-	957	P	72.8	957	<.1	72.1	116	72.8	12	0.0	-	-	1.8
Brooks	5,408	6,236	<.1	115.3	3	-	3,765	P	69.6	3,765	<.1	60.4	235	69.6	17	0.0	-	-	0.8
Brown	24,982	17,815	0.2	71.3	179	-	12,630	P	50.6	12,630	0.2	70.9	133	50.6	185	0.0	-	-	3.1
Burleson	10,070	8,120	<.1	80.6	94	-	5,711	P	56.7	5,711	<.1	70.3	153	56.7	96	0.0	-	-	11.4
Burnet	17,941	13,844	0.2	77.2	126	-	10,807	P	60.2	10,807	0.2	78.1	36	60.2	63	0.0	-	-	6.7
Caldwell	18,695	12,299	0.1	65.8	221	-	8,344	P	44.6	8,344	0.1	67.8	185	44.6	233	0.0	-	-	9.3
Calhoun	13,181	10,126	0.1	76.8	131	-	6,779	P	51.4	6,779	0.1	66.9	193	51.4	168	0.0	-	-	2.8
Callahan	8,623	7,037	<.1	81.6	83	-	5,285	P	61.3	5,285	<.1	75.1	70	61.3	53	0.0	-	-	3.4
Cameron	178,397	100,193	1.2	56.2	247	-	59,057	P	33.1	59,057	1.0	58.9	243	33.1	249	0.0	-	-	8.5
Camp	7,293	5,786	<.1	79.3	104	-	3,980	P	54.6	3,980	<.1	68.8	175	54.6	124	0.0	-	-	25.4
Carson	4,596	3,986	<.1	86.7	57	-	3,057	P	66.5	3,057	<.1	76.7	49	66.5	29	0.0	-	-	1.7
Cass	21,709	17,352	0.2	79.9	99	-	11,660	P	53.7	11,660	0.2	67.2	191	53.7	140	0.0	-	-	30.7
Castro	5,594	4,453	<.1	79.6	103	-	2,910	P	52.0	2,910	<.1	65.3	208	52.0	161	0.0	-	-	7.7
Chambers	14,428	11,575	0.1	80.2	96	-	8,366	P	58.0	8,366	0.1	72.3	112	58.0	84	0.0	-	-	3.5
Cherokee	30,215	20,525	0.2	67.9	205	-	14,138	P	46.8	14,138	0.2	68.9	173	46.8	217	0.0	-	-	2.4
Childress	4,186	3,306	<.1	79.0	108	-	2,338	P	55.9	2,338	<.1	70.7	136	55.9	107	0.0	-	-	2.0
Clay	7,434	6,357	<.1	85.5	63	-	4,910	P	66.0	4,910	<.1	77.2	45	66.0	32	0.0	-	-	2.7
Cochran	2,844	2,189	<.1	77.0	129	-	1,461	P	51.4	1,461	<.1	66.7	194	51.4	169	0.0	-	-	7.1
Coke	2,611	2,171	<.1	83.1	77	-	1,614	P	61.8	1,614	<.1	74.3	79	61.8	51	0.0	-	-	6.9
Coleman	7,144	6,001	<.1	84.0	72	-	4,138	P	57.9	4,138	<.1	69.0	170	57.9	86	0.0	-	-	3.9
Collin	214,595	153,736	1.8	71.6	172	-	128,833	P	60.0	128,833	2.1	83.8	4	60.0	68	0.0	-	-	10.0
Collingsworth	2,443	2,159	<.1	88.4	51	-	1,600	P	65.5	1,600	<.1	74.1	82	65.5	38	0.0	-	-	3.1
Colorado	13,212	10,171	0.1	77.0	128	-	7,162	P	54.2	7,162	0.1	70.4	150	54.2	131	0.0	-	-	4.7
Comal	41,743	31,616	0.4	75.7	142	-	24,941	P	59.7	24,941	0.4	78.9	25	59.7	71	0.0	-	-	5.2
Comanche	10,104	7,204	<.1	71.3	180	-	5,248	P	51.9	5,248	<.1	72.8	101	51.9	163	0.0	-	-	6.7
Concho	2,316	1,732	<.1	74.8	152	-	1,236	P	53.4	1,236	<.1	71.4	126	53.4	144	0.0	-	-	9.5
Cooke	22,374	17,388	0.2	77.7	119	-	13,084	P	58.5	13,084	0.2	75.2	66	58.5	79	0.0	-	-	11.0
Coryell	46,526	19,591	0.2	42.1	254	-	14,312	P	30.8	14,312	0.2	73.1	98	30.8	253	0.0	-	-	2.6
Cottle	1,553	1,562	<.1	100.6	16	-	1,025	P	66.0	1,025	<.1	65.6	205	66.0	34	0.0	-	-	3.9
Crane	3,079	2,530	<.1	82.2	80	-	1,845	P	59.9	1,845	<.1	72.9	100	59.9	69	0.0	-	-	5.4
Crockett	2,721	2,626	<.1	96.5	22	-	1,645	P	60.5	1,645	<.1	62.6	223	60.5	61	0.0	-	-	12.9
Crosby	4,745	3,736	<.1	78.7	112	-	2,335	P	49.2	2,335	<.1	62.5	224	49.2	198	0.0	-	-	6.6
Culberson	2,232	1,730	<.1	77.5	123	-	847	P	37.9	847	<.1	49.0	253	37.9	247	0.0	-	-	9.2
Dallam	3,606	2,328	<.1	64.6	226	-	1,683	P	46.7	1,683	<.1	72.3	111	46.7	219	0.0	-	-	8.7
Dallas	1,389,477	879,137	10.4	63.3	233	-	661,252	P	47.6	661,252	10.7	75.2	67	47.6	213	0.0	-	-	9.1
Dawson	9,473	7,427	0.1	78.4	113	-	4,855	P	51.3	4,855	<.1	65.4	206	51.3	172	0.0	-	-	10.6
Deaf Smith	12,002	8,277	<.1	69.0	200	-	5,559	P	46.3	5,559	<.1	67.2	192	46.3	223	0.0	-	-	3.1
Delta	3,623	2,857	<.1	78.9	110	-	2,015	P	55.6	2,015	<.1	70.5	144	55.6	108	0.0	-	-	27.3
Denton	228,481	148,476	1.8	65.0	223	-	116,576	P	51.0	116,576	1.9	78.5	29	51.0	177	0.0	-	-	33.4
DeWitt	13,545	10,139	0.1	74.9	151	-	6,730	P	49.7	6,730	0.1	66.4	198	49.7	192	0.0	-	-	11.6
Dickens	1,798	1,687	<.1	93.8	27	-	1,160	P	64.5	1,160	<.1	68.8	176	64.5	40	0.0	-	-	5.3
Dimmit	6,580	7,376	<.1	112.1	5	-	4,380	P	66.6	4,380	<.1	59.4	241	66.6	28	0.0	-	-	1.0
Donley	2,744	2,289	<.1	83.4	75	-	1,735	P	63.2	1,735	<.1	75.8	56	63.2	46	0.0	-	-	2.1
Duval	8,781	9,178	0.1	104.5	11	-	5,035	P	57.3	5,035	<.1	54.9	249	57.3	93	0.0	-	-	16.5
Eastland	13,569	10,130	0.1	74.7	153	-	7,281	P	53.7	7,281	0.1	71.9	118	53.7	141	0.0	-	-	2.5
Ector	80,528	49,865	0.6	61.9	235	-	36,073	P	44.8	36,073	0.6	72.3	110	44.8	231	0.0	-	-	4.2
Edwards	1,578	1,333	<.1	84.5	68	-	887	P	56.2	887	<.1	66.5	195	56.2	103	0.0	-	-	7.4
Ellis	64,441	44,756	0.5	69.5	197	-	33,495	P	52.0	33,495	0.5	74.8	73	52.0	162	0.0	-	-	2.2

[1]Percent drop-off is zero for any office used as highest office turnout.

Table C. – **Voter Participation: November 3, 1992, General Election (cont)**

County	Estimated Voting Age Population (VAP), 1992	Voter registration (REG)					Voter turnout									Percent drop-off, by office[1]			
							Highest office			Maximum vote									
		Total	% contribution to state REG	% of 1992 VAP	Rank by % of 1992 VAP	Actual	Total	Office	% of 1992 VAP	Total	% contribution to state turnout	% of REG	Rank by % of REG	% of 1992 VAP	Rank by % 1992 VAP	President	Senator	Governor	Representative
El Paso	417,093	210,125	2.5	50.4	253	-	135,163	P	32.4	135,163	2.2	64.3	213	32.4	251	0.0	-	-	1.4
Erath	21,633	13,128	0.2	60.7	241	-	10,431	P	48.2	10,431	0.2	79.5	18	48.2	206	0.0	-	-	3.4
Falls	12,928	9,075	0.1	70.2	191	-	5,773	P	44.7	5,773	<.1	63.6	216	44.7	232	0.0	-	-	3.2
Fannin	18,634	13,338	0.2	71.6	174	-	9,615	P	51.6	9,615	0.2	72.1	115	51.6	167	0.0	-	-	2.2
Fayette	15,225	11,514	0.1	75.6	145	-	8,823	P	58.0	8,823	0.1	76.6	50	58.0	85	0.0	-	-	3.4
Fisher	3,394	3,103	<.1	91.4	31	-	2,225	P	65.6	2,225	<.1	71.7	123	65.6	37	0.0	-	-	7.1
Floyd	5,485	4,764	<.1	86.9	56	-	3,009	P	54.9	3,009	<.1	63.2	220	54.9	120	0.0	-	-	4.7
Foard	1,279	1,178	<.1	92.1	28	-	796	P	62.2	796	<.1	67.6	187	62.2	50	0.0	-	-	1.5
Fort Bend	170,203	101,368	1.2	59.6	242	-	88,031	P	51.7	88,031	1.4	86.8	1	51.7	166	0.0	-	-	2.4
Franklin	5,909	4,468	<.1	75.6	146	-	3,342	P	56.6	3,342	<.1	74.8	74	56.6	98	0.0	-	-	36.6
Freestone	11,644	9,024	0.1	77.5	124	-	6,365	P	54.7	6,365	0.1	70.5	143	54.7	123	0.0	-	-	2.8
Frio	8,783	8,081	<.1	92.0	29	-	4,319	P	49.2	4,319	<.1	53.4	252	49.2	199	0.0	-	-	11.8
Gaines	9,154	5,627	<.1	61.5	237	-	3,933	P	43.0	3,933	<.1	69.9	159	43.0	239	0.0	-	-	3.9
Galveston	159,079	122,859	1.5	77.2	125	-	90,242	P	56.7	90,242	1.5	73.5	92	56.7	95	0.0	-	-	2.4
Garza	3,487	2,863	<.1	82.1	82	-	1,888	P	54.1	1,888	<.1	65.9	203	54.1	134	0.0	-	-	13.8
Gillespie	13,765	10,548	0.1	76.6	135	-	8,372	P	60.8	8,372	0.1	79.4	19	60.8	59	0.0	-	-	3.0
Glasscock	956	729	<.1	76.3	139	-	574	P	60.0	574	<.1	78.7	26	60.0	67	0.0	-	-	8.9
Goliad	4,423	3,776	<.1	85.4	64	-	2,831	P	64.0	2,831	<.1	75.0	71	64.0	43	0.0	-	-	11.7
Gonzales	12,048	9,757	0.1	81.0	89	-	5,557	P	46.1	5,557	<.1	57.0	246	46.1	224	0.0	-	-	8.0
Gray	16,994	13,272	0.2	78.1	117	-	10,372	P	61.0	10,372	0.2	78.1	34	61.0	54	0.0	-	-	1.4
Grayson	70,367	51,204	0.6	72.8	166	-	38,332	P	54.5	38,332	0.6	74.9	72	54.5	126	0.0	-	-	3.7
Gregg	75,398	57,718	0.7	76.6	136	-	41,829	P	55.5	41,829	0.7	72.5	105	55.5	110	0.0	-	-	14.5
Grimes	14,850	8,810	0.1	59.3	243	-	6,217	P	41.9	6,217	0.1	70.6	141	41.9	240	0.0	-	-	7.2
Guadalupe	49,813	32,208	0.4	64.7	225	-	23,120	P	46.4	23,120	0.4	71.8	119	46.4	222	0.0	-	-	6.3
Hale	22,695	15,412	0.2	67.9	206	-	10,234	P	45.1	10,234	0.2	66.4	197	45.1	229	0.0	-	-	1.6
Hall	2,718	2,783	<.1	102.4	13	-	1,714	P	63.1	1,714	<.1	61.6	230	63.1	47	0.0	-	-	2.8
Hamilton	5,794	4,454	<.1	76.9	130	-	3,259	P	56.2	3,259	<.1	73.2	94	56.2	102	0.0	-	-	5.6
Hansford	3,942	3,036	<.1	77.0	127	-	2,403	P	61.0	2,403	<.1	79.2	21	61.0	55	0.0	-	-	10.6
Hardeman	3,676	2,820	<.1	76.7	134	-	1,991	C	54.2	1,991	<.1	70.6	140	54.2	132	2.8	-	-	0.0
Hardin	29,164	26,140	0.3	89.6	39	-	16,793	P	57.6	16,793	0.3	64.2	214	57.6	91	0.0	-	-	1.5
Harris	2,057,565	1,315,010	15.6	63.9	228	-	942,947	P	45.8	942,947	15.3	71.7	122	45.8	227	0.0	-	-	11.6
Harrison	41,582	31,776	0.4	76.4	137	-	22,683	P	54.6	22,683	0.4	71.4	125	54.6	125	0.0	-	-	31.0
Hartley	2,538	2,296	<.1	90.5	36	-	1,797	P	70.8	1,797	<.1	78.3	32	70.8	15	0.0	-	-	5.5
Haskell	4,898	4,138	<.1	84.5	67	-	2,853	P	58.2	2,853	<.1	68.9	172	58.2	81	0.0	-	-	10.5
Hays	52,188	36,020	0.4	69.0	199	-	27,267	P	52.2	27,267	0.4	75.7	58	52.2	156	0.0	-	-	9.0
Hemphill	2,379	2,103	<.1	88.4	50	-	1,700	P	71.5	1,700	<.1	80.8	12	71.5	13	0.0	-	-	2.4
Henderson	47,375	33,193	0.4	70.1	192	-	24,261	P	51.2	24,261	0.4	73.1	95	51.2	173	0.0	-	-	3.7
Hidalgo	264,140	152,141	1.8	57.6	245	-	88,160	P	33.4	88,160	1.4	57.9	245	33.4	248	0.0	-	-	6.8
Hill	20,401	14,202	0.2	69.6	196	-	10,376	P	50.9	10,376	0.2	73.1	97	50.9	182	0.0	-	-	3.8
Hockley	16,172	11,497	0.1	71.1	184	-	7,868	P	48.7	7,868	0.1	68.4	179	48.7	204	0.0	-	-	3.2
Hood	23,808	17,354	0.2	72.9	165	-	14,162	P	59.5	14,162	0.2	81.6	7	59.5	72	0.0	-	-	4.6
Hopkins	21,535	13,763	0.2	63.9	229	-	10,643	P	49.4	10,643	0.2	77.3	42	49.4	194	0.0	-	-	32.0
Houston	15,633	11,895	0.1	76.1	141	-	8,020	P	51.3	8,020	0.1	67.4	188	51.3	170	0.0	-	-	1.3
Howard	22,977	15,557	0.2	67.7	208	-	10,873	P	47.3	10,873	0.2	69.9	160	47.3	215	0.0	-	-	2.2
Hudspeth	2,014	1,367	<.1	67.9	207	-	869	P	43.1	869	<.1	63.6	217	43.1	238	0.0	-	-	17.6
Hunt	48,239	32,609	0.4	67.6	212	-	24,650	P	51.1	24,650	0.4	75.6	62	51.1	176	0.0	-	-	19.0
Hutchinson	17,986	14,192	0.2	78.9	109	-	10,888	P	60.5	10,888	0.2	76.7	47	60.5	60	0.0	-	-	0.9
Irion	1,197	1,146	<.1	95.7	23	-	831	P	69.4	831	<.1	72.5	104	69.4	18	0.0	-	-	8.1
Jack	4,936	4,332	<.1	87.8	54	-	3,347	P	67.8	3,347	<.1	77.3	43	67.8	23	0.0	-	-	8.3
Jackson	9,168	7,241	<.1	79.0	107	-	5,152	P	56.2	5,152	<.1	71.2	128	56.2	104	0.0	-	-	9.7
Jasper	22,244	20,259	0.2	91.1	33	-	12,087	P	54.3	12,087	0.2	59.7	239	54.3	129	0.0	-	-	1.2
Jeff Davis	1,496	1,210	<.1	80.9	91	-	876	P	58.6	876	<.1	72.4	107	58.6	78	0.0	-	-	7.5
Jefferson	169,541	135,220	1.6	79.8	101	-	95,543	P	56.4	95,543	1.6	70.7	138	56.4	100	0.0	-	-	1.9
Jim Hogg	3,364	3,735	<.1	111.0	7	-	2,110	P	62.7	2,110	<.1	56.5	247	62.7	48	0.0	-	-	10.6
Jim Wells	25,436	21,207	0.3	83.4	76	-	12,561	P	49.4	12,561	0.2	59.2	242	49.4	196	0.0	-	-	7.8
Johnson	75,271	49,801	0.6	66.2	219	-	37,202	P	49.4	37,202	0.6	74.7	75	49.4	193	0.0	-	-	2.3
Jones	11,705	8,043	<.1	68.7	202	-	5,932	P	50.7	5,932	<.1	73.8	88	50.7	184	0.0	-	-	2.7
Karnes	8,298	7,100	<.1	85.6	62	-	4,700	P	56.6	4,700	<.1	66.2	199	56.6	97	0.0	-	-	7.6
Kaufman	39,755	25,771	0.3	64.8	224	-	19,060	P	47.9	19,060	0.3	74.0	83	47.9	210	0.0	-	-	5.1
Kendall	11,568	9,248	0.1	79.9	98	-	7,354	P	63.6	7,354	0.1	79.5	17	63.6	45	0.0	-	-	3.1
Kenedy	302	297	<.1	98.3	19	-	174	P	57.6	174	<.1	58.6	244	57.6	89	0.0	-	-	1.7
Kent	732	801	<.1	109.4	8	-	610	P	83.3	610	<.1	76.2	54	83.3	4	0.0	-	-	7.5
Kerr	28,985	21,370	0.3	73.7	161	-	16,358	P	56.4	16,358	0.3	76.5	51	56.4	99	0.0	-	-	2.8
Kimble	3,024	2,264	<.1	74.9	150	-	1,613	P	53.3	1,613	<.1	71.2	127	53.3	145	0.0	-	-	6.0
King	245	223	<.1	91.0	34	-	189	P	77.1	189	<.1	84.8	3	77.1	7	0.0	-	-	4.8
Kinney	2,490	1,930	<.1	77.5	122	-	1,539	P	61.8	1,539	<.1	79.7	16	61.8	52	0.0	-	-	4.0
Kleberg	20,256	14,996	0.2	74.0	158	-	10,564	P	52.2	10,564	0.2	70.4	146	52.2	157	0.0	-	-	7.8
Knox	3,416	2,669	<.1	78.1	116	-	1,815	P	53.1	1,815	<.1	68.0	183	53.1	148	0.0	-	-	5.1
Lamar	32,151	23,556	0.3	73.3	163	-	16,242	P	50.5	16,242	0.3	69.0	171	50.5	187	0.0	-	-	25.0
Lamb	9,900	8,340	<.1	84.2	71	-	5,451	P	55.1	5,451	<.1	65.4	207	55.1	117	0.0	-	-	5.6

[1]Percent drop-off is zero for any office used as highest office turnout.

Table C. — **Voter Participation: November 3, 1992, General Election (cont)**

County	Estimated Voting Age Population (VAP), 1992	Voter registration (REG)				Voter turnout												
							Highest office			Maximum vote						Percent drop-off, by office[1]		
		Total	% contribution to state REG	% of 1992 VAP	Rank by % of 1992 VAP	Actual	Total	Office	% of 1992 VAP	Total	% contribution to state turnout	% of REG	Rank by % of REG	% of 1992 VAP	Rank by % 1992 VAP	President	Senator	Governor	Representative
Lampasas	9,915	7,101	<.1	71.6	173	-	5,185	P	52.3	5,185	<.1	73.0	99	52.3	155	0.0	-	-	4.0
La Salle	3,433	3,897	<.1	113.5	4	-	2,319	P	67.6	2,319	<.1	59.5	240	67.6	24	0.0	-	-	24.5
Lavaca	13,811	10,791	0.1	78.1	115	-	7,776	P	56.3	7,776	0.1	72.1	117	56.3	101	0.0	-	-	8.2
Lee	9,406	6,708	<.1	71.3	178	-	5,058	P	53.8	5,058	<.1	75.4	65	53.8	137	0.0	-	-	8.2
Leon	10,002	8,348	<.1	83.5	74	-	5,508	P	55.1	5,508	<.1	66.0	202	55.1	116	0.0	-	-	10.1
Liberty	38,047	26,497	0.3	69.6	195	-	18,339	P	48.2	18,339	0.3	69.2	167	48.2	207	0.0	-	-	2.2
Limestone	15,354	10,712	0.1	69.8	194	-	7,060	P	46.0	7,060	0.1	65.9	204	46.0	225	0.0	-	-	3.2
Lipscomb	2,135	1,834	<.1	85.9	60	-	1,453	P	68.1	1,453	<.1	79.2	20	68.1	22	0.0	-	-	3.2
Live Oak	6,867	6,265	<.1	91.2	32	-	3,965	P	57.7	3,965	<.1	63.3	219	57.7	87	0.0	-	-	4.2
Llano	9,758	8,723	0.1	89.4	43	-	7,283	P	74.6	7,283	0.1	83.5	5	74.6	9	0.0	-	-	3.6
Loving	77	116	<.1	150.6	1	-	96	P	124.7	96	<.1	82.8	6	124.7	1	0.0	-	-	10.4
Lubbock	159,951	109,552	1.3	68.5	204	-	82,858	P	51.8	82,858	1.3	75.6	61	51.8	165	0.0	-	-	2.2
Lynn	4,403	4,001	<.1	90.9	35	-	2,428	P	55.1	2,428	<.1	60.7	233	55.1	114	0.0	-	-	6.1
McCulloch	6,363	4,778	<.1	75.1	148	-	3,491	P	54.9	3,491	<.1	73.1	96	54.9	119	0.0	-	-	16.8
McLennan	138,643	98,807	1.2	71.3	181	-	70,016	P	50.5	70,016	1.1	70.9	134	50.5	188	0.0	-	-	1.4
McMullen	602	631	<.1	104.8	10	-	443	P	73.6	443	<.1	70.2	155	73.6	10	0.0	-	-	45.6
Madison	8,288	5,585	<.1	67.4	215	-	3,883	P	46.9	3,883	<.1	69.5	166	46.9	216	0.0	-	-	5.1
Marion	7,386	6,565	<.1	88.9	46	-	4,288	P	58.1	4,288	<.1	65.3	209	58.1	83	0.0	-	-	34.3
Martin	3,304	2,744	<.1	83.1	78	-	1,988	P	60.2	1,988	<.1	72.4	106	60.2	64	0.0	-	-	14.6
Mason	2,551	2,274	<.1	89.1	45	-	1,722	P	67.5	1,722	<.1	75.7	57	67.5	25	0.0	-	-	5.6
Matagorda	24,964	18,513	0.2	74.2	157	-	13,165	P	52.7	13,165	0.2	71.1	129	52.7	151	0.0	-	-	3.8
Maverick	23,789	13,343	0.2	56.1	248	-	7,339	P	30.9	7,339	0.1	55.0	248	30.9	252	0.0	-	-	2.7
Medina	19,816	15,209	0.2	76.8	133	-	10,785	P	54.4	10,785	0.2	70.9	132	54.4	127	0.0	-	-	1.1
Menard	1,649	1,643	<.1	99.6	18	-	1,277	P	77.4	1,277	<.1	77.7	39	77.4	6	0.0	-	-	12.8
Midland	76,697	51,714	0.6	67.4	214	-	41,347	P	53.9	41,347	0.7	80.0	15	53.9	136	0.0	-	-	2.9
Milam	16,279	11,919	0.1	73.2	164	-	7,468	P	45.9	7,468	0.1	62.7	222	45.9	226	0.0	-	-	1.5
Mills	3,411	2,569	<.1	75.3	147	-	1,990	P	58.3	1,990	<.1	77.5	40	58.3	80	0.0	-	-	5.9
Mitchell	5,585	4,542	<.1	81.3	87	-	3,093	P	55.4	3,093	<.1	68.1	182	55.4	111	0.0	-	-	5.8
Montague	12,840	10,227	0.1	79.6	102	-	7,526	P	58.6	7,526	0.1	73.6	89	58.6	76	0.0	-	-	5.3
Montgomery	139,430	99,354	1.2	71.3	182	-	77,958	P	55.9	77,958	1.3	78.5	30	55.9	105	0.0	-	-	3.2
Moore	12,083	7,472	<.1	61.8	236	-	5,498	P	45.5	5,498	<.1	73.6	90	45.5	228	0.0	-	-	4.5
Morris	9,230	8,173	<.1	88.5	47	-	5,569	P	60.3	5,569	<.1	68.1	181	60.3	62	0.0	-	-	23.7
Motley	1,093	1,099	<.1	100.5	17	-	819	P	74.9	819	<.1	74.5	76	74.9	8	0.0	-	-	4.6
Nacogdoches	41,277	30,727	0.4	74.4	155	-	21,643	P	52.4	21,643	0.4	70.4	147	52.4	152	0.0	-	-	29.6
Navarro	29,492	20,821	0.2	70.6	189	-	14,721	P	49.9	14,721	0.2	70.7	137	49.9	191	0.0	-	-	2.8
Newton	9,585	8,473	0.1	88.4	49	-	5,523	C	57.6	5,523	<.1	65.2	210	57.6	88	0.3	-	-	0.0
Nolan	11,644	8,222	<.1	70.6	187	-	5,952	P	51.1	5,952	<.1	72.4	109	51.1	175	0.0	-	-	2.7
Nueces	204,663	144,844	1.7	70.8	186	-	100,791	P	49.2	100,791	1.6	69.6	165	49.2	197	0.0	-	-	3.1
Ochiltree	6,175	4,561	<.1	73.9	160	-	3,554	P	57.6	3,554	<.1	77.9	37	57.6	92	0.0	-	-	8.7
Oldham	1,441	1,290	<.1	89.5	40	-	987	P	68.5	987	<.1	76.5	52	68.5	19	0.0	-	-	8.4
Orange	56,396	43,821	0.5	77.7	120	-	32,490	P	57.6	32,490	0.5	74.1	81	57.6	90	0.0	-	-	1.2
Palo Pinto	18,264	13,164	0.2	72.1	169	-	9,275	P	50.8	9,275	0.2	70.5	145	50.8	183	0.0	-	-	3.6
Panola	15,936	12,966	0.2	81.1	88	-	9,332	P	58.6	9,332	0.2	72.2	113	58.6	77	0.0	-	-	29.1
Parker	51,189	34,020	0.4	66.5	216	-	27,494	P	53.7	27,494	0.4	80.8	13	53.7	139	0.0	-	-	2.3
Parmer	6,357	3,861	<.1	60.7	240	-	3,033	P	47.7	3,033	<.1	78.6	27	47.7	211	0.0	-	-	5.9
Pecos	9,669	7,323	<.1	75.7	143	-	4,523	P	46.8	4,523	<.1	61.8	229	46.8	218	0.0	-	-	1.6
Polk	24,027	20,799	0.2	86.6	59	-	14,254	P	59.3	14,254	0.2	68.5	177	59.3	74	0.0	-	-	2.4
Potter	67,849	36,395	0.4	53.6	250	-	27,775	P	40.9	27,775	0.5	76.3	53	40.9	242	0.0	-	-	1.5
Presidio	4,795	3,050	<.1	63.6	231	-	1,891	P	39.4	1,891	<.1	62.0	227	39.4	244	0.0	-	-	6.3
Rains	5,450	3,941	<.1	72.3	167	-	2,983	P	54.7	2,983	<.1	75.7	59	54.7	122	0.0	-	-	7.4
Randall	66,587	49,960	0.6	75.0	149	-	40,537	P	60.9	40,537	0.7	81.1	10	60.9	58	0.0	-	-	6.1
Reagan	2,881	1,840	<.1	63.9	230	-	1,250	P	43.4	1,250	<.1	67.9	184	43.4	237	0.0	-	-	5.1
Real	1,797	2,123	<.1	118.1	2	-	1,640	P	91.3	1,640	<.1	77.2	44	91.3	2	0.0	-	-	13.5
Red River	10,403	8,544	0.1	82.1	81	-	5,655	P	54.4	5,655	<.1	66.2	200	54.4	128	0.0	-	-	29.7
Reeves	10,444	7,371	<.1	70.6	190	-	4,557	P	43.6	4,557	<.1	61.8	228	43.6	236	0.0	-	-	1.7
Refugio	5,540	5,201	<.1	93.9	26	-	3,732	P	67.4	3,732	<.1	71.8	120	67.4	26	0.0	-	-	5.9
Roberts	700	781	<.1	111.6	6	-	617	P	88.1	617	<.1	79.0	23	88.1	3	0.0	-	-	1.9
Robertson	11,114	8,968	0.1	80.7	93	-	5,604	P	50.4	5,604	<.1	62.5	225	50.4	189	0.0	-	-	6.1
Rockwall	20,559	16,277	0.2	79.2	106	-	13,269	P	64.5	13,269	0.2	81.5	8	64.5	39	0.0	-	-	2.5
Runnels	8,013	6,278	<.1	78.3	114	-	4,340	P	54.2	4,340	<.1	69.1	168	54.2	133	0.0	-	-	6.6
Rusk	31,692	25,103	0.3	79.2	105	-	16,574	P	52.3	16,574	0.3	66.0	201	52.3	154	0.0	-	-	39.2
Sabine	7,500	6,699	<.1	89.3	44	-	4,678	P	62.4	4,678	<.1	69.8	161	62.4	49	0.0	-	-	3.1
San Augustine	5,738	6,109	<.1	106.5	9	-	3,649	P	63.6	3,649	<.1	59.7	238	63.6	44	0.0	-	-	2.5
San Jacinto	13,155	9,784	0.1	74.4	156	-	7,011	P	53.3	7,011	0.1	71.7	124	53.3	146	*0.0	-	-	5.1
San Patricio	39,684	30,302	0.4	76.4	138	-	18,887	P	47.6	18,887	0.3	62.3	226	47.6	212	0.0	-	-	3.8
San Saba	3,827	3,167	<.1	82.8	79	-	2,103	P	55.0	2,103	<.1	66.4	196	55.0	118	0.0	-	-	12.4
Schleicher	2,046	1,669	<.1	81.6	84	-	1,231	P	60.2	1,231	<.1	73.8	87	60.2	65	0.0	-	-	8.0
Scurry	13,134	8,724	0.1	66.4	217	-	6,121	P	46.6	6,121	<.1	70.2	157	46.6	220	0.0	-	-	2.1
Shackelford	2,305	2,362	<.1	102.5	12	-	1,533	P	66.5	1,533	<.1	64.9	211	66.5	30	0.0	-	-	5.8
Shelby	15,884	13,616	0.2	85.7	61	-	8,705	P	54.8	8,705	0.1	63.9	215	54.8	121	0.0	-	-	2.1

[1]Percent drop-off is zero for any office used as highest office turnout.

Table C. – Voter Participation: November 3, 1992, General Election (cont)

County	Estimated Voting Age Population (VAP), 1992	Voter registration (REG)				Voter turnout										Percent drop-off, by office[1]			
							Highest office			Maximum vote									
		Total	% contribution to state REG	% of 1992 VAP	Rank by % of 1992 VAP	Actual	Total	Office	% of 1992 VAP	Total	% contribution to state turnout	% of REG	Rank by % of REG	% of 1992 VAP	Rank by % 1992 VAP	President	Senator	Governor	Representative
Sherman	1,957	1,704	<.1	87.1	55	-	1,369	P	70.0	1,369	<.1	80.3	14	70.0	16	0.0	-	-	9.6
Smith	113,259	79,968	0.9	70.6	188	-	59,006	P	52.1	59,006	1.0	73.8	86	52.1	159	0.0	-	-	3.2
Somervell	3,905	3,495	<.1	89.5	41	-	2,568	P	65.8	2,568	<.1	73.5	91	65.8	35	0.0	-	-	13.2
Starr	27,983	17,030	0.2	60.9	239	-	9,261	P	33.1	9,261	0.2	54.4	250	33.1	250	0.0	-	-	13.4
Stephens	6,283	5,349	<.1	85.1	65	-	3,756	P	59.8	3,756	<.1	70.2	154	59.8	70	0.0	-	-	6.3
Sterling	987	838	<.1	84.9	66	-	634	P	64.2	634	<.1	75.7	60	64.2	42	0.0	-	-	13.1
Stonewall	1,423	1,441	<.1	101.3	14	-	1,125	P	79.1	1,125	<.1	78.1	35	79.1	5	0.0	-	-	6.2
Sutton	2,744	2,317	<.1	84.4	69	-	1,598	P	58.2	1,598	<.1	69.0	169	58.2	82	0.0	-	-	10.8
Swisher	5,341	4,315	<.1	80.8	92	-	2,949	P	55.2	2,949	<.1	68.3	180	55.2	113	0.0	-	-	4.2
Tarrant	905,365	596,958	7.1	65.9	220	-	471,396	P	52.1	471,396	7.7	79.0	24	52.1	160	0.0	-	-	3.9
Taylor	85,806	58,096	0.7	67.7	209	-	45,454	P	53.0	45,454	0.7	78.2	33	53.0	149	0.0	-	-	3.8
Terrell	979	896	<.1	91.5	30	-	631	P	64.5	631	<.1	70.4	149	64.5	41	0.0	-	-	10.6
Terry	8,585	6,998	<.1	81.5	85	-	4,395	P	51.2	4,395	<.1	62.8	221	51.2	174	0.0	-	-	6.6
Throckmorton	1,389	1,347	<.1	97.0	21	-	1,018	P	73.3	1,018	<.1	75.6	63	73.3	11	0.0	-	-	8.0
Titus	17,294	12,283	0.1	71.0	185	-	8,810	P	50.9	8,810	0.1	71.7	121	50.9	178	0.0	-	-	27.3
Tom Green	72,158	47,892	0.6	66.4	218	-	36,739	P	50.9	36,739	0.6	76.7	48	50.9	179	0.0	-	-	3.8
Travis	459,450	352,737	4.2	76.8	132	-	276,235	P	60.1	276,235	4.5	78.3	31	60.1	66	0.0	-	-	2.8
Trinity	8,998	8,791	0.1	97.7	20	-	5,909	P	65.7	5,909	<.1	67.2	190	65.7	36	0.0	-	-	0.7
Tyler	12,403	10,749	0.1	86.7	58	-	7,360	P	59.3	7,360	0.1	68.5	178	59.3	73	0.0	-	-	1.6
Upshur	22,758	17,348	0.2	76.2	140	-	12,208	P	53.6	12,208	0.2	70.4	152	53.6	142	0.0	-	-	30.4
Upton	2,883	2,419	<.1	83.9	73	-	1,756	P	60.9	1,756	<.1	72.6	103	60.9	57	0.0	-	-	9.9
Uvalde	15,745	13,279	0.2	84.3	70	-	8,543	P	54.3	8,543	0.1	64.3	212	54.3	130	0.0	-	-	0.8
Val Verde	26,307	15,545	0.2	59.1	244	-	10,996	P	41.8	10,996	0.2	70.7	135	41.8	241	0.0	-	-	2.3
Van Zandt	29,325	23,102	0.3	78.8	111	-	16,396	P	55.9	16,396	0.3	71.0	131	55.9	106	0.0	-	-	3.6
Victoria	51,948	37,179	0.4	71.6	175	-	26,037	P	50.1	26,037	0.4	70.0	158	50.1	190	0.0	-	-	7.4
Walker	41,061	21,558	0.3	52.5	252	-	15,924	P	38.8	15,924	0.3	73.9	85	38.8	245	0.0	-	-	2.7
Waller	17,109	15,041	0.2	87.9	53	-	9,058	P	52.9	9,058	0.1	60.2	236	52.9	150	0.0	-	-	4.9
Ward	8,693	6,261	<.1	72.0	170	-	4,422	P	50.9	4,422	<.1	70.6	139	50.9	181	0.0	-	-	1.8
Washington	19,690	14,899	0.2	75.7	144	-	10,853	P	55.1	10,853	0.2	72.8	102	55.1	115	0.0	-	-	3.6
Webb	90,831	52,178	0.6	57.4	246	-	24,866	P	27.4	24,866	0.4	47.7	254	27.4	254	0.0	-	-	0.9
Wharton	27,523	19,017	0.2	69.1	198	-	12,797	P	46.5	12,797	0.2	67.3	189	46.5	221	0.0	-	-	2.6
Wheeler	4,060	3,822	<.1	94.1	25	-	2,767	P	68.2	2,767	<.1	72.4	108	68.2	20	0.0	-	-	1.9
Wichita	87,488	59,926	0.7	68.5	203	-	46,608	P	53.3	46,608	0.8	77.8	38	53.3	147	0.0	-	-	2.4
Wilbarger	10,866	7,586	<.1	69.8	193	-	5,340	P	49.1	5,340	<.1	70.4	151	49.1	200	0.0	-	-	2.9
Willacy	11,447	9,158	0.1	80.0	97	-	5,510	P	48.1	5,510	<.1	60.2	237	48.1	208	0.0	-	-	5.9
Williamson	110,646	72,005	0.9	65.1	222	-	61,254	P	55.4	61,254	1.0	85.1	2	55.4	112	0.0	-	-	6.1
Wilson	16,878	13,666	0.2	81.0	90	-	9,625	P	57.0	9,625	0.2	70.4	148	57.0	94	0.0	-	-	28.9
Winkler	5,600	3,990	<.1	71.3	183	-	2,702	P	48.3	2,702	<.1	67.7	186	48.3	205	0.0	-	-	2.2
Wise	26,466	17,895	0.2	67.6	211	-	13,568	P	51.3	13,568	0.2	75.8	55	51.3	171	0.0	-	-	4.4
Wood	22,909	16,378	0.2	71.5	176	-	12,318	P	53.8	12,318	0.2	75.2	69	53.8	138	0.0	-	-	33.9
Yoakum	5,827	3,572	<.1	61.3	238	-	2,575	P	44.2	2,575	<.1	72.1	114	44.2	234	0.0	-	-	0.8
Young	13,002	10,379	0.1	79.8	100	-	7,675	P	59.0	7,675	0.1	73.9	84	59.0	75	0.0	-	-	5.8
Zapata	6,646	5,342	<.1	80.4	95	-	3,249	P	48.9	3,249	<.1	60.8	232	48.9	202	0.0	-	-	30.4
Zavala	7,901	7,128	<.1	90.2	37	-	3,868	P	49.0	3,868	<.1	54.3	251	49.0	201	0.0	-	-	1.5
TEXAS	**12,524,000**	**8,440,143**	**100.0**	**67.4**		**-**	**6,154,088**		**49.1**	**6,154,088**	**100.0**	**72.9**		**49.1**		**0.0**	**-**	**-**	**8.6**

[1]Percent drop-off is zero for any office used as highest office turnout.

892 Texas

Table E. — Vote for President: November 3, 1992, General Election

County	Total	Clinton (DEM)	Bush (REP)	Perot (IND)	Other	Plurality Total	Party	DEM	REP	IND	Other	Rank DEM	Rank REP	Rank IND	Total	DEM	REP	IND	DEM	REP
Anderson	14,466	5,322	5,598	3,519	27	276	R	36.8	38.7	24.3	0.2	124	135	75	0.2	0.2	0.2	0.3	48.7	51.3
Andrews	4,228	1,081	2,266	875	6	1,185	R	25.6	53.6	20.7	0.1	227	35	131	<.1	<.1	<.1	<.1	32.3	67.7
Angelina	26,281	10,318	9,722	6,204	37	596	D	39.3	37.0	23.6	0.1	96	154	85	0.4	0.5	0.4	0.5	51.5	48.5
Aransas	6,770	2,246	2,826	1,676	22	580	R	33.2	41.7	24.8	0.3	160	101	66	0.1	<.1	0.1	0.1	44.3	55.7
Archer	3,967	1,284	1,560	1,106	17	276	R	32.4	39.3	27.9	0.4	171	128	42	<.1	<.1	<.1	<.1	45.1	54.9
Armstrong	1,028	278	561	187	2	283	R	27.0	54.6	18.2	0.2	219	28	190	<.1	<.1	<.1	<.1	33.1	66.9
Atascosa	9,658	3,766	3,806	2,035	51	40	R	39.0	39.4	21.1	0.5	99	126	126	0.2	0.2	0.2	0.2	49.7	50.3
Austin	7,890	2,278	4,015	1,585	12	1,737	R	28.9	50.9	20.1	0.2	204	45	148	0.1	<.1	0.2	0.1	36.2	63.8
Bailey	2,365	677	1,308	376	4	631	R	28.6	55.3	15.9	0.2	208	25	219	<.1	<.1	<.1	<.1	34.1	65.9
Bandera	5,322	1,059	2,674	1,537	52	1,137	R	19.9	50.2	28.9	1.0	245	51	30	<.1	<.1	0.1	0.1	28.4	71.6
Bastrop	14,474	6,252	4,980	3,240	2	1,272	D	43.2	34.4	22.4	<.1	66	182	104	0.2	0.3	0.2	0.2	55.7	44.3
Baylor	2,132	990	611	529	2	379	D	46.4	28.7	24.8	<.1	50	232	65	<.1	<.1	<.1	<.1	61.8	38.2
Bee	9,108	4,083	3,633	1,367	25	450	D	44.8	39.9	15.0	0.3	57	119	225	0.1	0.2	0.1	0.1	52.9	47.1
Bell	55,077	18,684	24,936	11,026	431	6,252	R	33.9	45.3	20.0	0.8	146	74	150	0.9	0.8	1.0	0.8	42.8	57.2
Bexar	415,276	172,513	168,816	72,110	1,837	3,697	D	41.5	40.7	17.4	0.4	77	109	200	6.7	7.6	6.8	5.3	50.5	49.5
Blanco	3,109	891	1,370	830	18	479	R	28.7	44.1	26.7	0.6	206	79	52	<.1	<.1	<.1	<.1	39.4	60.6
Borden	378	106	184	87	1	78	R	28.0	48.7	23.0	0.3	214	57	95	<.1	<.1	<.1	<.1	36.6	63.4
Bosque	6,489	2,173	2,300	1,999	17	127	R	33.5	35.4	30.8	0.3	156	169	19	0.1	<.1	0.1	0.1	48.6	51.4
Bowie	30,365	11,825	11,776	6,659	105	49	D	38.9	38.8	21.9	0.3	101	133	111	0.5	0.5	0.5	0.5	50.1	49.9
Brazoria	71,467	21,861	30,384	18,954	268	8,523	R	30.6	42.5	26.5	0.4	190	94	56	1.2	1.0	1.2	1.4	41.8	58.2
Brazos	49,340	14,819	23,943	10,372	206	9,124	R	30.0	48.5	21.0	0.4	194	59	127	0.8	0.6	1.0	0.8	38.2	61.8
Brewster	3,247	1,383	1,127	712	25	256	D	42.6	34.7	21.9	0.8	70	178	112	<.1	<.1	<.1	<.1	55.1	44.9
Briscoe	957	430	360	164	3	70	D	44.9	37.6	17.1	0.3	56	148	204	<.1	<.1	<.1	<.1	54.4	45.6
Brooks	3,765	2,856	585	318	6	2,271	D	75.9	15.5	8.4	0.2	4	251	249	0.1	0.1	<.1	<.1	83.0	17.0
Brown	12,630	4,264	5,313	3,034	19	1,049	R	33.8	42.1	24.0	0.2	152	96	82	0.2	0.2	0.2	0.2	44.5	55.5
Burleson	5,711	2,511	2,013	1,179	8	498	D	44.0	35.2	20.6	0.1	59	174	132	<.1	0.1	<.1	<.1	55.5	44.5
Burnet	10,807	3,638	4,272	2,865	32	634	R	33.7	39.5	26.5	0.3	155	123	57	0.2	0.2	0.2	0.2	46.0	54.0
Caldwell	8,344	3,794	2,749	1,776	25	1,045	D	45.5	32.9	21.3	0.3	54	198	123	0.1	0.2	0.1	0.1	58.0	42.0
Calhoun	6,779	2,550	2,640	1,579	10	90	R	37.6	38.9	23.3	0.1	116	130	91	0.1	0.1	0.1	0.1	49.1	50.9
Callahan	5,285	1,694	2,134	1,452	5	440	R	32.1	40.4	27.5	0.1	176	116	48	<.1	<.1	<.1	0.1	44.3	55.7
Cameron	59,057	29,435	20,123	9,286	213	9,312	D	49.8	34.1	15.7	0.4	31	186	220	1.0	1.3	0.8	0.7	59.4	40.6
Camp	3,980	1,938	1,219	821	2	719	D	48.7	30.6	20.6	<.1	34	220	133	<.1	<.1	<.1	<.1	61.4	38.6
Carson	3,057	825	1,647	578	7	822	R	27.0	53.9	18.9	0.2	220	32	172	<.1	<.1	<.1	<.1	33.4	66.6
Cass	11,660	5,476	3,999	2,168	17	1,477	D	47.0	34.3	18.6	0.1	48	185	179	0.2	0.2	0.2	0.2	57.8	42.2
Castro	2,910	1,113	1,307	485	5	194	R	38.2	44.9	16.7	0.2	109	77	209	<.1	<.1	<.1	<.1	46.0	54.0
Chambers	8,366	2,832	3,398	2,122	14	566	R	33.9	40.6	25.4	0.2	149	111	61	0.1	0.1	0.1	0.2	45.5	54.5
Cherokee	14,138	5,003	5,847	3,273	15	844	R	35.4	41.4	23.2	0.1	134	104	93	0.2	0.2	0.2	0.2	46.1	53.9
Childress	2,338	881	1,033	421	3	152	R	37.7	44.2	18.0	0.1	115	78	192	<.1	<.1	<.1	<.1	46.0	54.0
Clay	4,910	1,919	1,586	1,397	8	333	D	39.1	32.3	28.5	0.2	98	201	35	<.1	<.1	<.1	0.1	54.8	45.2
Cochran	1,461	454	750	255	2	296	R	31.1	51.3	17.5	0.1	185	43	198	<.1	<.1	<.1	<.1	37.7	62.3
Coke	1,614	580	640	393	1	60	R	35.9	39.7	24.3	<.1	133	122	74	<.1	<.1	<.1	<.1	47.5	52.5
Coleman	4,138	1,579	1,462	1,095	2	117	D	38.2	35.3	26.5	<.1	111	172	58	<.1	<.1	<.1	<.1	51.9	48.1
Collin	128,833	24,508	60,514	43,287	524	17,227	R	19.0	47.0	33.6	0.4	248	66	7	2.1	1.1	2.4	3.2	28.8	71.2
Collingsworth	1,600	635	697	265	3	62	R	39.7	43.6	16.6	0.2	92	82	211	<.1	<.1	<.1	<.1	47.7	52.3
Colorado	7,162	2,442	3,286	1,421	13	844	R	34.1	45.9	19.8	0.2	142	69	154	0.1	0.1	0.1	0.1	42.6	57.4
Comal	24,941	6,312	12,651	5,841	137	6,339	R	25.3	50.7	23.4	0.5	228	48	89	0.4	0.3	0.5	0.4	33.3	66.7
Comanche	5,248	2,296	1,666	1,281	5	630	D	43.8	31.7	24.4	0.1	60	210	72	<.1	0.1	<.1	<.1	58.0	42.0
Concho	1,236	489	414	329	4	75	D	39.6	33.5	26.6	0.3	93	194	54	<.1	<.1	<.1	<.1	54.2	45.8
Cooke	13,084	3,105	5,299	4,658	22	641	R	23.7	40.5	35.6	0.2	232	113	2	0.2	0.1	0.2	0.3	36.9	63.1
Coryell	14,312	4,157	6,144	3,974	37	1,987	R	29.0	42.9	27.8	0.3	202	91	44	0.2	0.2	0.2	0.3	40.4	59.6
Cottle	1,025	542	245	235	3	297	D	52.9	23.9	22.9	0.3	21	245	98	<.1	<.1	<.1	<.1	68.9	31.1
Crane	1,845	514	918	412	1	404	R	27.9	49.8	22.3	<.1	215	52	106	<.1	<.1	<.1	<.1	35.9	64.1
Crockett	1,645	653	623	368	1	30	D	39.7	37.9	22.4	<.1	91	144	105	<.1	<.1	<.1	<.1	51.2	48.8
Crosby	2,335	1,010	1,006	313	6	4	D	43.3	43.1	13.4	0.3	65	86	234	<.1	<.1	<.1	<.1	50.1	49.9
Culberson	847	424	251	171	1	173	D	50.1	29.6	20.2	0.1	28	227	144	<.1	<.1	<.1	<.1	62.8	37.2
Dallam	1,683	434	922	325	2	488	R	25.8	54.8	19.3	0.1	226	27	161	<.1	<.1	<.1	<.1	32.0	68.0
Dallas	661,252	231,412	256,007	170,571	3,262	24,595	R	35.0	38.7	25.8	0.5	136	134	60	10.7	10.1	10.3	12.6	47.5	52.5
Dawson	4,855	1,639	2,691	518	7	1,052	R	33.8	55.4	10.7	0.1	153	23	243	<.1	<.1	<.1	<.1	37.9	62.1
Deaf Smith	5,559	1,642	3,137	772	8	1,495	R	29.5	56.4	13.9	0.1	198	20	232	0.1	<.1	0.1	<.1	34.4	65.6
Delta	2,015	864	599	551	1	265	D	42.9	29.7	27.3	<.1	68	226	49	<.1	<.1	<.1	<.1	59.1	40.9
Denton	116,576	27,891	48,492	39,653	540	8,839	R	23.9	41.6	34.0	0.5	230	103	6	1.9	1.2	1.9	2.9	36.5	63.5
DeWitt	6,730	2,127	3,238	1,346	19	1,111	R	31.6	48.1	20.0	0.3	180	61	152	0.1	<.1	0.1	<.1	39.6	60.4
Dickens	1,160	536	373	250	1	163	D	46.2	32.2	21.6	<.1	51	203	117	<.1	<.1	<.1	<.1	59.0	41.0
Dimmit	4,380	3,172	844	361	3	2,328	D	72.4	19.3	8.2	<.1	5	250	250	<.1	0.1	<.1	<.1	79.0	21.0
Donley	1,735	578	893	260	4	315	R	33.3	51.5	15.0	0.2	158	42	226	<.1	<.1	<.1	<.1	39.3	60.7
Duval	5,035	4,006	698	326	5	3,308	D	79.6	13.9	6.5	<.1	2	253	251	<.1	0.2	<.1	<.1	85.2	14.8
Eastland	7,281	2,738	2,830	1,698	15	92	R	37.6	38.9	23.3	0.2	117	132	90	0.1	0.1	0.1	0.1	49.2	50.8
Ector	36,073	11,130	18,161	6,668	114	7,031	R	30.9	50.3	18.5	0.3	186	49	181	0.6	0.5	0.7	0.5	38.0	62.0
Edwards	887	254	460	171	2	206	R	28.6	51.9	19.3	0.2	207	40	162	<.1	<.1	<.1	<.1	35.6	64.4
Ellis	33,495	9,537	13,564	10,303	91	3,261	R	28.5	40.5	30.8	0.3	210	114	20	0.5	0.4	0.5	0.8	41.3	58.7

Table E. — Vote for President: November 3, 1992, General Election (cont)

County	Total	Clinton (DEM)	Bush (REP)	Perot (IND)	Other	Plurality Total	Party	Percent of total vote DEM	REP	IND	Other	Rank DEM	REP	IND	Percent contribution to state vote Total	DEM	REP	IND	Major party Percent of vote DEM	REP
El Paso	135,163	67,715	47,224	19,738	486	20,491	D	50.1	34.9	14.6	0.4	27	177	227	2.2	3.0	1.9	1.5	58.9	41.1
Erath	10,431	3,531	3,835	3,046	19	304	R	33.9	36.8	29.2	0.2	150	159	29	0.2	0.2	0.2	0.2	47.9	52.1
Falls	5,773	2,761	1,826	1,185	1	935	D	47.8	31.6	20.5	<.1	37	214	135	<.1	0.1	<.1	<.1	60.2	39.8
Fannin	9,615	4,164	2,510	2,919	22	1,245	D	43.3	26.1	30.4	0.2	63	240	21	0.2	0.2	0.1	0.2	62.4	37.6
Fayette	8,823	2,923	3,789	2,088	23	866	R	33.1	42.9	23.7	0.3	163	90	84	0.1	0.1	0.2	0.2	43.5	56.5
Fisher	2,225	1,242	539	442	2	703	D	55.8	24.2	19.9	<.1	17	244	153	<.1	<.1	<.1	<.1	69.7	30.3
Floyd	3,009	947	1,676	385	1	729	R	31.5	55.7	12.8	<.1	182	22	238	<.1	<.1	<.1	<.1	36.1	63.9
Foard	796	435	207	152	2	228	D	54.6	26.0	19.1	0.3	19	241	168	<.1	<.1	<.1	<.1	67.8	32.2
Fort Bend	88,031	29,992	41,039	16,853	147	11,047	R	34.1	46.6	19.1	0.2	144	68	166	1.4	1.3	1.6	1.2	42.2	57.8
Franklin	3,342	1,338	1,058	942	4	280	D	40.0	31.7	28.2	0.1	87	213	40	<.1	<.1	<.1	<.1	55.8	44.2
Freestone	6,365	2,445	2,316	1,596	8	129	D	38.4	36.4	25.1	0.1	104	165	64	0.1	0.1	<.1	0.1	51.4	48.6
Frio	4,319	2,377	1,275	654	13	1,102	D	55.0	29.5	15.1	0.3	18	228	224	<.1	0.1	<.1	<.1	65.1	34.9
Gaines	3,933	1,095	2,138	696	4	1,043	R	27.8	54.4	17.7	0.1	217	30	197	<.1	<.1	<.1	<.1	33.9	66.1
Galveston	90,242	38,623	31,303	20,103	213	7,320	D	42.8	34.7	22.3	0.2	69	179	107	1.5	1.7	1.3	1.5	55.2	44.8
Garza	1,888	558	982	345	3	424	R	29.6	52.0	18.3	0.2	197	39	188	<.1	<.1	<.1	<.1	36.2	63.8
Gillespie	8,372	1,600	4,712	2,018	42	2,694	R	19.1	56.3	24.1	0.5	246	21	81	0.1	<.1	0.2	0.1	25.3	74.7
Glasscock	574	100	379	93	2	279	R	17.4	66.0	16.2	0.3	252	3	215	<.1	<.1	<.1	<.1	20.9	79.1
Goliad	2,831	1,069	1,236	521	5	167	R	37.8	43.7	18.4	0.2	114	80	182	<.1	<.1	<.1	<.1	46.4	53.6
Gonzales	5,557	2,006	2,502	1,018	31	496	R	36.1	45.0	18.3	0.6	131	76	185	<.1	<.1	0.1	<.1	44.5	55.5
Gray	10,372	2,426	6,105	1,810	31	3,679	R	23.4	58.9	17.5	0.3	233	13	199	0.2	0.1	0.2	0.1	28.4	71.6
Grayson	38,332	12,547	12,322	13,327	136	780	I	32.7	32.1	34.8	0.4	168	204	5	0.6	0.5	0.5	1.0	50.5	49.5
Gregg	41,829	12,797	20,542	8,437	53	7,745	R	30.6	49.1	20.2	0.1	189	55	145	0.7	0.6	0.8	0.6	38.4	61.6
Grimes	6,217	2,594	2,402	1,213	8	192	D	41.7	38.6	19.5	0.1	75	136	159	0.1	0.1	<.1	<.1	51.9	48.1
Guadalupe	23,120	6,567	10,818	5,618	117	4,251	R	28.4	46.8	24.3	0.5	211	67	76	0.4	0.3	0.4	0.4	37.8	62.2
Hale	10,234	2,761	6,098	1,357	18	3,337	R	27.0	59.6	13.3	0.2	221	10	236	0.2	0.1	0.2	0.1	31.2	68.8
Hall	1,714	819	631	263	1	188	D	47.8	36.8	15.3	<.1	38	158	222	<.1	<.1	<.1	<.1	56.5	43.5
Hamilton	3,259	1,100	1,232	921	6	132	R	33.8	37.8	28.3	0.2	154	146	38	<.1	<.1	<.1	<.1	47.2	52.8
Hansford	2,403	345	1,660	398	0	1,262	R	14.4	69.1	16.6	0.0	254	1	210	<.1	<.1	<.1	<.1	17.2	82.8
Hardeman	1,936	954	614	362	6	340	D	49.3	31.7	18.7	0.3	32	212	176	<.1	<.1	<.1	<.1	60.8	39.2
Hardin	16,793	6,753	5,885	4,129	26	868	D	40.2	35.0	24.6	0.2	86	176	70	0.3	0.3	0.2	0.3	53.4	46.6
Harris	942,947	360,171	406,778	172,922	3,076	46,607	R	38.2	43.1	18.3	0.3	110	85	184	15.3	15.8	16.3	12.8	47.0	53.0
Harrison	22,683	9,538	8,733	4,371	41	805	D	42.0	38.5	19.3	0.2	72	138	163	0.4	0.4	0.3	0.3	52.2	47.8
Hartley	1,797	406	1,081	308	2	675	R	22.6	60.2	17.1	0.1	238	9	203	<.1	<.1	<.1	<.1	27.3	72.7
Haskell	2,853	1,438	852	562	1	586	D	50.4	29.9	19.7	<.1	25	225	157	<.1	<.1	<.1	<.1	62.8	37.2
Hays	27,267	10,842	10,008	6,252	165	834	D	39.8	36.7	22.9	0.6	90	161	97	0.4	0.5	0.4	0.5	52.0	48.0
Hemphill	1,700	479	989	232	0	510	R	28.2	58.2	13.6	0.0	213	15	233	<.1	<.1	<.1	<.1	32.6	67.4
Henderson	24,261	9,105	8,368	6,746	42	737	D	37.5	34.5	27.8	0.2	118	181	43	0.4	0.4	0.3	0.5	52.1	47.9
Hidalgo	88,160	51,205	26,976	9,757	222	24,229	D	58.1	30.6	11.1	0.3	15	222	242	1.4	2.2	1.1	0.7	65.5	34.5
Hill	10,376	3,929	3,669	2,752	26	260	D	37.9	35.4	26.5	0.3	112	171	55	0.2	0.2	0.1	0.2	51.7	48.3
Hockley	7,868	2,301	4,261	1,291	15	1,960	R	29.2	54.2	16.4	0.2	199	31	212	0.1	0.1	0.2	<.1	35.1	64.9
Hood	14,162	4,359	5,313	4,457	33	856	R	30.8	37.5	31.5	0.2	188	150	13	0.2	0.2	0.2	0.3	45.1	54.9
Hopkins	10,643	4,085	3,398	3,147	13	687	D	38.4	31.9	29.6	0.1	105	207	27	0.2	0.2	0.1	0.2	54.6	45.4
Houston	8,020	3,250	3,067	1,690	13	183	D	40.5	38.2	21.1	0.2	83	139	125	0.1	0.1	0.1	0.1	51.4	48.6
Howard	10,873	3,735	5,129	1,984	25	1,394	R	34.4	47.2	18.2	0.2	139	64	189	0.2	0.2	0.2	0.1	42.1	57.9
Hudspeth	869	364	325	178	2	39	D	41.9	37.4	20.5	0.2	73	151	137	<.1	<.1	<.1	<.1	52.8	47.2
Hunt	24,650	7,452	9,739	7,387	72	2,287	R	30.2	39.5	30.0	0.3	193	124	23	0.4	0.3	0.4	0.5	43.3	56.7
Hutchinson	10,888	2,833	6,034	1,993	28	3,201	R	26.0	55.4	18.3	0.3	225	24	186	0.2	0.1	0.2	0.1	31.9	68.1
Irion	831	256	283	290	2	7	I	30.8	34.1	34.9	0.2	187	188	4	<.1	<.1	<.1	<.1	47.5	52.5
Jack	3,347	1,254	1,041	1,045	7	209	D	37.5	31.1	31.2	0.2	119	216	15	<.1	<.1	<.1	<.1	54.6	45.4
Jackson	5,152	1,722	2,451	976	3	729	R	33.4	47.6	18.9	<.1	157	63	171	<.1	<.1	<.1	<.1	41.3	58.7
Jasper	12,087	5,658	3,870	2,539	20	1,788	D	46.8	32.0	21.0	0.2	49	206	128	0.2	0.2	0.2	0.2	59.4	40.6
Jeff Davis	876	321	360	187	8	39	R	36.6	41.1	21.3	0.9	125	106	121	<.1	<.1	<.1	<.1	47.1	52.9
Jefferson	95,543	48,405	29,622	17,242	274	18,783	D	50.7	31.0	18.0	0.3	24	217	191	1.6	2.1	1.2	1.3	62.0	38.0
Jim Hogg	2,110	1,520	478	107	5	1,042	D	72.0	22.7	5.1	0.2	6	246	253	<.1	<.1	<.1	<.1	76.1	23.9
Jim Wells	12,561	7,812	3,311	1,413	25	4,501	D	62.2	26.4	11.2	0.2	10	239	241	0.2	0.3	0.1	0.1	70.2	29.8
Johnson	37,202	12,030	13,473	11,573	126	1,443	R	32.3	36.2	31.1	0.3	172	166	16	0.6	0.5	0.5	0.9	47.2	52.8
Jones	5,932	2,400	2,088	1,436	8	312	D	40.5	35.2	24.2	0.1	84	175	78	0.1	0.1	<.1	0.1	53.5	46.5
Karnes	4,700	1,897	1,990	802	11	93	R	40.4	42.3	17.1	0.2	85	95	206	<.1	<.1	<.1	<.1	48.8	51.2
Kaufman	19,060	6,498	6,578	5,913	71	80	R	34.1	34.5	31.0	0.4	143	180	17	0.3	0.3	0.3	0.4	49.7	50.3
Kendall	7,354	1,374	4,162	1,773	45	2,389	R	18.7	56.6	24.1	0.6	249	19	80	0.1	<.1	0.2	0.1	24.8	75.2
Kenedy	174	87	69	18	0	18	D	50.0	39.7	10.3	0.0	29	121	245	<.1	<.1	<.1	<.1	55.8	44.2
Kent	610	271	175	163	1	96	D	44.4	28.7	26.7	0.2	58	231	51	<.1	<.1	<.1	<.1	60.8	39.2
Kerr	16,358	3,707	8,787	3,790	74	4,997	R	22.7	53.7	23.2	0.5	237	33	92	0.3	0.2	0.4	0.3	29.7	70.3
Kimble	1,613	467	790	354	2	323	R	29.0	49.0	21.9	0.1	203	56	110	<.1	<.1	<.1	<.1	37.2	62.8
King	189	54	79	56	0	23	R	28.6	41.8	29.6	0.0	209	100	26	<.1	<.1	<.1	<.1	40.6	59.4
Kinney	1,539	598	634	299	8	36	R	38.9	41.2	19.4	0.5	102	105	160	<.1	<.1	<.1	<.1	48.5	51.5
Kleberg	10,564	5,109	3,897	1,470	88	1,212	D	48.4	36.9	13.9	0.8	35	157	231	0.2	0.2	0.2	0.1	56.7	43.3
Knox	1,815	854	521	438	2	333	D	47.1	28.7	24.1	0.1	47	230	79	<.1	<.1	<.1	<.1	62.1	37.9
Lamar	16,242	6,328	5,778	4,093	43	550	D	39.0	35.6	25.2	0.3	100	167	62	0.3	0.3	0.2	0.3	52.3	47.7
Lamb	5,451	1,737	2,998	709	7	1,261	R	31.9	55.0	13.0	0.1	178	26	237	<.1	<.1	0.1	<.1	36.7	63.3

County	All candidates					Plurality		Percent of total vote				Rank			Percent contribution to state vote				Major party Percent of vote	
	Total	Clinton (DEM)	Bush (REP)	Perot (IND)	Other	Total	Party	DEM	REP	IND	Other	DEM	REP	IND	Total	DEM	REP	IND	DEM	REP
Lampasas	5,185	1,508	2,233	1,432	12	725	R	29.1	43.1	27.6	0.2	201	87	45	< .1	< .1	< .1	0.1	40.3	59.7
La Salle	2,319	1,522	586	211	0	936	D	65.6	25.3	9.1	0.0	7	242	248	< .1	< .1	< .1	< .1	72.2	27.8
Lavaca	7,776	2,700	3,362	1,696	18	662	R	34.7	43.2	21.8	0.2	138	84	114	0.1	0.1	0.1	0.1	44.5	55.5
Lee	5,058	1,847	2,108	1,088	15	261	R	36.5	41.7	21.5	0.3	128	102	119	< .1	< .1	< .1	< .1	46.7	53.3
Leon	5,508	2,042	2,212	1,251	3	170	R	37.1	40.2	22.7	< .1	122	117	101	< .1	< .1	< .1	< .1	48.0	52.0
Liberty	18,339	7,036	6,959	4,311	33	77	D	38.4	37.9	23.5	0.2	106	143	88	0.3	0.3	0.3	0.3	50.3	49.7
Limestone	7,060	3,188	2,358	1,505	9	830	D	45.2	33.4	21.3	0.1	55	196	122	0.1	0.1	0.1	0.1	57.5	42.5
Lipscomb	1,453	338	839	270	6	501	R	23.3	57.7	18.6	0.4	234	16	180	< .1	< .1	< .1	< .1	28.7	71.3
Live Oak	3,965	1,345	1,805	806	9	460	R	33.9	45.5	20.3	0.2	147	73	141	< .1	< .1	< .1	< .1	42.7	57.3
Llano	7,283	2,409	3,056	1,799	19	647	R	33.1	42.0	24.7	0.3	165	97	67	0.1	0.1	0.1	0.1	44.1	55.9
Loving	96	20	31	45	0	14	I	20.8	32.3	46.9	0.0	242	202	1	< .1	< .1	< .1	< .1	39.2	60.8
Lubbock	82,858	22,240	48,847	11,618	153	26,607	R	26.8	59.0	14.0	0.2	223	12	230	1.3	1.0	2.0	0.9	31.3	68.7
Lynn	2,428	902	1,233	291	2	331	R	37.1	50.8	12.0	< .1	120	47	239	< .1	< .1	< .1	< .1	42.2	57.8
McCulloch	3,491	1,393	1,108	986	4	285	D	39.9	31.7	28.2	0.1	89	211	39	< .1	< .1	< .1	< .1	55.7	44.3
McLennan	70,016	25,903	28,473	15,505	135	2,570	R	37.0	40.7	22.1	0.2	123	108	109	1.1	1.1	1.1	1.1	47.6	52.4
McMullen	443	78	274	89	2	185	R	17.6	61.9	20.1	0.5	251	6	147	< .1	< .1	< .1	< .1	22.2	77.8
Madison	3,883	1,553	1,544	778	8	9	D	40.0	39.8	20.0	0.2	88	120	149	< .1	< .1	< .1	< .1	50.1	49.9
Marion	4,288	2,156	1,245	882	5	911	D	50.3	29.0	20.6	0.1	26	229	134	< .1	< .1	< .1	< .1	63.4	36.6
Martin	1,988	641	986	356	5	345	R	32.2	49.6	17.9	0.3	174	54	194	< .1	< .1	< .1	< .1	39.4	60.6
Mason	1,722	570	776	364	12	206	R	33.1	45.1	21.1	0.7	164	75	124	< .1	< .1	< .1	< .1	42.3	57.7
Matagorda	13,165	4,759	5,328	3,045	33	569	R	36.1	40.5	23.1	0.3	130	115	94	0.2	0.2	0.2	0.2	47.2	52.8
Maverick	7,339	4,540	2,002	771	26	2,538	D	61.9	27.3	10.5	0.4	11	236	244	0.1	0.2	< .1	< .1	69.4	30.6
Medina	10,785	3,650	4,912	2,167	56	1,262	R	33.8	45.5	20.1	0.5	151	72	146	0.2	0.2	0.2	0.2	42.6	57.4
Menard	1,277	553	354	367	3	186	D	43.3	27.7	28.7	0.2	64	234	32	< .1	< .1	< .1	< .1	61.0	39.0
Midland	41,347	9,160	24,143	7,880	164	14,983	R	22.2	58.4	19.1	0.4	240	14	169	0.7	0.4	1.0	0.6	27.5	72.5
Milam	7,468	3,542	2,414	1,495	17	1,128	D	47.4	32.3	20.0	0.2	41	200	151	0.1	0.2	0.1	0.1	59.5	40.5
Mills	1,990	753	702	530	5	51	D	37.8	35.3	26.6	0.3	113	173	53	< .1	< .1	< .1	< .1	51.8	48.2
Mitchell	3,093	1,353	1,128	604	8	225	D	43.7	36.5	19.5	0.3	61	164	158	< .1	< .1	< .1	< .1	54.5	45.5
Montague	7,526	2,885	2,304	2,330	7	555	D	38.3	30.6	31.0	< .1	107	221	18	0.1	0.1	< .1	0.2	55.6	44.4
Montgomery	77,958	18,551	39,976	19,203	228	20,773	R	23.8	51.3	24.6	0.3	231	44	68	1.3	0.8	1.6	1.4	31.7	68.3
Moore	5,498	1,361	3,147	976	14	1,786	R	24.8	57.2	17.8	0.3	229	18	196	< .1	< .1	0.1	< .1	30.2	69.8
Morris	5,569	3,028	1,400	1,138	3	1,628	D	54.4	25.1	20.4	< .1	20	243	138	0.1	0.1	< .1	< .1	68.4	31.6
Motley	819	256	446	117	0	190	R	31.3	54.5	14.3	0.0	183	29	228	< .1	< .1	< .1	< .1	36.5	63.5
Nacogdoches	21,643	6,937	9,864	4,803	39	2,927	R	32.1	45.6	22.2	0.2	177	71	108	0.4	0.3	0.4	0.4	41.3	58.7
Navarro	14,721	6,006	4,897	3,800	18	1,109	D	40.8	33.3	25.8	0.1	80	197	59	0.2	0.3	0.2	0.3	55.1	44.9
Newton	5,508	3,249	1,212	1,032	15	2,037	D	59.0	22.0	18.7	0.3	13	247	174	< .1	0.1	< .1	< .1	72.8	27.2
Nolan	5,952	2,490	1,993	1,455	14	497	D	41.8	33.5	24.4	0.2	74	195	71	< .1	0.1	< .1	< .1	55.5	44.5
Nueces	100,791	46,317	36,781	17,374	319	9,536	D	46.0	36.5	17.2	0.3	52	163	201	1.6	2.0	1.5	1.3	55.7	44.3
Ochiltree	3,554	557	2,419	576	2	1,843	R	15.7	68.1	16.2	< .1	253	2	214	< .1	< .1	< .1	< .1	18.7	81.3
Oldham	987	225	583	177	2	358	R	22.8	59.1	17.9	0.2	236	11	193	< .1	< .1	< .1	< .1	27.8	72.2
Orange	32,490	15,305	9,793	7,321	71	5,512	D	47.1	30.1	22.5	0.2	45	224	102	0.5	0.7	0.4	0.5	61.0	39.0
Palo Pinto	9,275	3,392	2,852	3,010	21	382	D	36.6	30.7	32.5	0.2	126	218	11	0.2	0.1	0.1	0.2	54.3	45.7
Panola	9,332	3,950	3,473	1,906	3	477	D	42.3	37.2	20.4	< .1	71	153	139	0.2	0.2	0.1	0.1	53.2	46.8
Parker	27,494	7,934	10,321	9,148	91	1,173	R	28.9	37.5	33.3	0.3	205	149	8	0.4	0.3	0.4	0.7	43.5	56.5
Parmer	3,033	637	1,829	564	3	1,192	R	21.0	60.3	18.6	< .1	241	8	178	< .1	< .1	< .1	< .1	25.8	74.2
Pecos	4,523	1,778	1,836	895	14	58	R	39.3	40.6	19.8	0.3	95	112	155	< .1	< .1	< .1	< .1	49.2	50.8
Polk	14,254	5,942	5,390	2,884	38	552	D	41.7	37.8	20.2	0.3	76	145	143	0.2	0.3	0.2	0.2	52.4	47.6
Potter	27,775	9,527	13,510	4,655	83	3,983	R	34.3	48.6	16.8	0.3	140	58	208	0.5	0.4	0.5	0.3	41.4	58.6
Presidio	1,891	1,189	400	290	12	789	D	62.9	21.2	15.3	0.6	9	249	223	< .1	< .1	< .1	< .1	74.8	25.2
Rains	2,983	1,108	975	890	10	133	D	37.1	32.7	29.8	0.3	121	199	24	< .1	< .1	< .1	< .1	53.2	46.8
Randall	40,537	9,119	24,971	6,340	107	15,852	R	22.5	61.6	15.6	0.3	239	7	221	0.7	0.4	1.0	0.5	26.7	73.3
Reagan	1,250	337	651	259	3	314	R	27.0	52.1	20.7	0.2	222	38	130	< .1	< .1	< .1	< .1	34.1	65.9
Real	1,640	463	787	386	4	324	R	28.2	48.0	23.5	0.2	212	62	87	< .1	< .1	< .1	< .1	37.0	63.0
Red River	5,655	2,686	1,735	1,228	6	951	D	47.5	30.7	21.7	0.1	40	219	115	< .1	0.1	< .1	< .1	60.8	39.2
Reeves	4,557	2,569	1,244	734	10	1,325	D	56.4	27.3	16.1	0.2	16	235	216	< .1	0.1	< .1	< .1	67.4	32.6
Refugio	3,732	1,531	1,469	716	16	62	D	41.0	39.4	19.2	0.4	79	127	164	< .1	< .1	< .1	< .1	51.0	49.0
Roberts	617	126	391	99	1	265	R	20.4	63.4	16.0	0.2	243	4	217	< .1	< .1	< .1	< .1	24.4	75.6
Robertson	5,604	2,927	1,707	963	7	1,220	D	52.2	30.5	17.2	0.1	22	223	202	< .1	0.1	< .1	< .1	63.2	36.8
Rockwall	13,269	2,397	6,427	4,393	52	2,034	R	18.1	48.4	33.1	0.4	250	60	9	0.2	0.1	0.3	0.3	27.2	72.8
Runnels	4,340	1,401	1,653	1,279	7	252	R	32.3	38.1	29.5	0.2	173	142	28	< .1	< .1	< .1	< .1	45.9	54.1
Rusk	16,574	5,391	7,560	3,575	48	2,169	R	32.5	45.6	21.6	0.3	169	70	116	0.3	0.2	0.3	0.3	41.6	58.4
Sabine	4,678	2,288	1,490	894	6	798	D	48.9	31.9	19.1	0.1	33	209	161	< .1	0.1	< .1	< .1	60.6	39.4
San Augustine	3,649	1,737	1,243	667	2	494	D	47.6	34.1	18.3	< .1	39	187	187	< .1	0.1	< .1	< .1	58.3	41.7
San Jacinto	7,011	2,846	2,494	1,653	18	352	D	40.6	35.6	23.6	0.3	82	168	86	0.1	0.1	< .1	0.1	53.3	46.7
San Patricio	18,887	8,202	7,456	3,178	51	746	D	43.4	39.5	16.8	0.3	62	125	207	0.3	0.4	0.3	0.2	52.4	47.6
San Saba	2,103	716	723	660	4	7	R	34.0	34.4	31.4	0.2	145	183	14	< .1	< .1	< .1	< .1	49.8	50.2
Schleicher	1,231	420	452	355	4	32	R	34.1	36.7	28.8	0.3	141	160	31	< .1	< .1	< .1	< .1	48.2	51.8
Scurry	6,121	1,609	2,670	1,826	16	844	R	26.3	43.6	29.8	0.3	224	81	25	< .1	< .1	0.1	0.1	37.6	62.4
Shackelford	1,533	484	623	422	4	139	R	31.6	40.6	27.5	0.3	181	110	47	< .1	< .1	< .1	< .1	43.7	56.3
Shelby	8,705	3,986	3,217	1,487	15	769	D	45.8	37.0	17.1	0.2	53	155	205	0.1	0.2	0.1	0.1	55.3	44.7

Texas 895

Table E. — Vote for President: November 3, 1992, General Election (cont)

County	Total	Clinton (DEM)	Bush (REP)	Perot (IND)	Other	Plurality Total	Party	DEM	REP	IND	Other	Rank DEM	Rank REP	Rank IND	Total	DEM	REP	IND	DEM	REP
Sherman	1,369	261	851	256	1	590	R	19.1	62.2	18.7	<.1	247	5	175	<.1	<.1	<.1	<.1	23.5	76.5
Smith	59,006	17,514	27,753	13,569	170	10,239	R	29.7	47.0	23.0	0.3	196	65	96	1.0	0.8	1.1	1.0	38.7	61.3
Somervell	2,568	782	872	903	11	31	I	30.5	34.0	35.2	0.4	191	189	3	<.1	<.1	<.1	<.1	47.3	52.7
Starr	9,261	7,668	1,209	345	39	6,459	D	82.8	13.1	3.7	0.4	1	254	254	0.2	0.3	<.1	<.1	86.4	13.6
Stephens	3,756	1,115	1,573	1,062	6	458	R	29.7	41.9	28.3	0.2	195	98	37	<.1	<.1	<.1	<.1	41.5	58.5
Sterling	634	127	322	182	3	140	R	20.0	50.8	28.7	0.5	244	46	33	<.1	<.1	<.1	<.1	28.3	71.7
Stonewall	1,125	561	242	322	0	239	D	49.9	21.5	28.6	0.0	30	248	34	<.1	<.1	<.1	<.1	69.9	30.1
Sutton	1,598	524	687	387	0	163	R	32.8	43.0	24.2	0.0	167	89	77	<.1	<.1	<.1	<.1	43.3	56.7
Swisher	2,949	1,413	989	541	6	424	D	47.9	33.5	18.3	0.2	36	193	183	<.1	<.1	<.1	<.1	58.8	41.2
Tarrant	471,396	156,230	183,387	129,998	1,781	27,157	R	33.1	38.9	27.6	0.4	162	131	46	7.7	6.8	7.3	9.6	46.0	54.0
Taylor	45,454	12,382	22,614	10,331	127	10,232	R	27.2	49.8	22.7	0.3	218	53	99	0.7	0.5	0.9	0.8	35.4	64.6
Terrell	631	325	176	128	2	149	D	51.5	27.9	20.3	0.3	23	233	142	<.1	<.1	<.1	<.1	64.9	35.1
Terry	4,395	1,461	2,309	619	6	848	R	33.2	52.5	14.1	0.1	159	37	229	<.1	<.1	<.1	<.1	38.8	61.2
Throckmorton	1,018	401	389	228	0	12	D	39.4	38.2	22.4	0.0	94	141	103	<.1	<.1	<.1	<.1	50.8	49.2
Titus	8,810	3,625	3,024	2,146	15	601	D	41.1	34.3	24.4	0.2	78	184	73	0.1	0.2	0.1	0.2	54.5	45.5
Tom Green	36,739	11,437	14,989	10,244	69	3,552	R	31.1	40.8	27.9	0.2	184	107	41	0.6	0.5	0.6	0.8	43.3	56.7
Travis	276,235	130,546	88,105	56,158	1,426	42,441	D	47.3	31.9	20.3	0.5	42	208	140	4.5	5.7	3.5	4.1	59.7	40.3
Trinity	5,909	2,784	1,988	1,133	4	796	D	47.1	33.6	19.2	<.1	44	191	165	0.1	0.1	<.1	0.1	58.3	41.7
Tyler	7,360	3,465	2,357	1,529	9	1,108	D	47.1	32.0	20.8	0.1	46	205	129	0.1	0.2	<.1	0.1	59.5	40.5
Upshur	12,208	4,776	4,511	2,896	25	265	D	39.1	37.0	23.7	0.2	97	156	83	0.2	0.2	0.2	0.2	51.4	48.6
Upton	1,756	489	908	313	46	419	R	27.8	51.7	17.8	2.6	216	41	195	<.1	<.1	<.1	<.1	35.0	65.0
Uvalde	8,543	3,482	3,635	1,387	39	153	R	40.8	42.5	16.2	0.5	81	93	213	0.1	0.2	0.1	0.1	48.9	51.1
Val Verde	10,996	4,748	4,102	2,093	53	646	D	43.2	37.3	19.0	0.5	67	152	170	0.2	0.2	0.2	0.2	53.6	46.4
Van Zandt	16,396	5,310	5,810	5,239	37	500	R	32.4	35.4	32.0	0.2	170	170	12	0.3	0.2	0.2	0.4	47.8	52.2
Victoria	26,037	7,604	13,086	5,136	211	5,482	R	29.2	50.3	19.7	0.8	200	50	156	0.4	0.3	0.5	0.4	36.8	63.2
Walker	15,924	5,619	6,662	3,619	24	1,043	R	35.3	41.8	22.7	0.2	135	99	100	0.3	0.2	0.3	0.3	45.8	54.2
Waller	9,058	4,270	3,065	1,692	31	1,205	D	47.1	33.8	18.7	0.3	43	190	177	0.1	0.2	0.1	0.1	58.2	41.8
Ward	4,422	1,695	1,769	948	10	74	R	38.3	40.0	21.4	0.2	108	118	120	<.1	<.1	<.1	<.1	48.9	51.1
Washington	10,853	3,283	5,817	1,738	15	2,534	R	30.2	53.6	16.0	0.1	192	34	218	0.2	0.1	0.2	0.1	36.1	63.9
Webb	24,866	14,509	7,789	2,517	51	6,720	D	58.3	31.3	10.1	0.2	14	215	246	0.4	0.6	0.3	0.2	65.1	34.9
Wharton	12,797	4,643	5,503	2,624	27	860	R	36.3	43.0	20.5	0.2	129	88	136	0.2	0.2	0.2	0.2	45.8	54.2
Wheeler	2,767	938	1,458	367	4	520	R	33.9	52.7	13.3	0.1	148	36	235	<.1	<.1	<.1	<.1	39.1	60.9
Wichita	46,608	17,021	17,956	11,478	153	935	R	36.5	38.5	24.6	0.3	127	137	69	0.8	0.7	0.7	0.8	48.7	51.3
Wilbarger	5,340	1,924	1,959	1,453	4	35	R	36.0	36.7	27.2	<.1	132	162	50	<.1	<.1	0.1	<.1	49.5	50.5
Willacy	5,510	3,359	1,490	652	9	1,869	D	61.0	27.0	11.8	0.2	12	237	240	<.1	0.1	<.1	<.1	69.3	30.7
Williamson	61,254	19,437	26,208	15,415	194	6,771	R	31.7	42.8	25.2	0.3	179	92	63	1.0	0.9	1.1	1.1	42.6	57.4
Wilson	9,625	3,711	3,766	2,105	43	55	R	38.6	39.1	21.9	0.4	103	129	113	0.2	0.2	0.2	0.2	49.6	50.4
Winkler	2,702	942	1,173	582	5	231	R	34.9	43.4	21.5	0.2	137	83	118	<.1	<.1	<.1	<.1	44.5	55.5
Wise	13,568	4,478	4,555	4,485	50	70	R	33.0	33.6	33.1	0.4	166	192	10	0.2	0.2	0.2	0.3	49.6	50.4
Wood	12,318	4,084	4,708	3,494	32	624	R	33.2	38.2	28.4	0.3	161	140	36	0.2	0.2	0.2	0.3	46.5	53.5
Yoakum	2,575	595	1,486	484	10	891	R	23.1	57.7	18.8	0.4	235	17	173	<.1	<.1	<.1	<.1	28.6	71.4
Young	7,675	2,464	2,894	2,302	15	430	R	32.1	37.7	30.0	0.2	175	147	22	0.1	0.1	0.1	0.2	46.0	54.0
Zapata	3,249	2,052	866	326	5	1,186	D	63.2	26.7	10.0	0.2	8	238	247	<.1	<.1	<.1	<.1	70.3	29.7
Zavala	3,868	3,058	571	237	2	2,487	D	79.1	14.8	6.1	<.1	3	252	252	<.1	0.1	<.1	<.1	84.3	15.7
TEXAS	6,154,018	2,281,815	2,496,071	1,354,781	21,351	214,256	R	37.1	40.6	22.0	0.3				100.0	100.0	100.0	100.0	47.8	52.2

Table H. — Vote for U.S. Representative in Congress: November 3, 1992, General Election

Congressional district and county	Total	Democrat (DEM)	Republican (REP)	Other	Plurality Total	Party	Percent of total vote DEM	REP	Other	Rank within district DEM	REP	Other	Percent contribution to district vote Total	DEM	REP	Other
District 1	**152,209**	**152,209**	**-**	**-**	**152,209**	**D**	**100.0**	**-**	**-**				**100.0**	**100.0**	**-**	**-**
Bowie	21,744	21,744	-	-	21,744	D	100.0	-	-	1	-	-	14.3	14.3	-	-
Camp	2,971	2,971	-	-	2,971	D	100.0	-	-	2	-	-	2.0	2.0	-	-
Cass	8,077	8,077	-	-	8,077	D	100.0	-	-	3	-	-	5.3	5.3	-	-
Delta	1,465	1,465	-	-	1,465	D	100.0	-	-	4	-	-	1.0	1.0	-	-
Franklin	2,118	2,118	-	-	2,118	D	100.0	-	-	5	-	-	1.4	1.4	-	-
Gregg (pt)	9,039	9,039	-	-	9,039	D	100.0	-	-	6	-	-	5.9	5.9	-	-
Harrison	15,659	15,659	-	-	15,659	D	100.0	-	-	7	-	-	10.3	10.3	-	-
Hopkins	7,232	7,232	-	-	7,232	D	100.0	-	-	8	-	-	4.8	4.8	-	-
Hunt (pt)	9,021	9,021	-	-	9,021	D	100.0	-	-	9	-	-	5.9	5.9	-	-
Lamar	12,179	12,179	-	-	12,179	D	100.0	-	-	10	-	-	8.0	8.0	-	-
Marion	2,816	2,816	-	-	2,816	D	100.0	-	-	11	-	-	1.9	1.9	-	-
Morris	4,251	4,251	-	-	4,251	D	100.0	-	-	12	-	-	2.8	2.8	-	-
Nacogdoches (pt)	11,909	11,909	-	-	11,909	D	100.0	-	-	13	-	-	7.8	7.8	-	-
Panola	6,613	6,613	-	-	6,613	D	100.0	-	-	14	-	-	4.3	4.3	-	-
Red River	3,977	3,977	-	-	3,977	D	100.0	-	-	15	-	-	2.6	2.6	-	-
Rusk	10,081	10,081	-	-	10,081	D	100.0	-	-	16	-	-	6.6	6.6	-	-
Titus	6,409	6,409	-	-	6,409	D	100.0	-	-	17	-	-	4.2	4.2	-	-
Upshur	8,501	8,501	-	-	8,501	D	100.0	-	-	18	-	-	5.6	5.6	-	-
Wood	8,147	8,147	-	-	8,147	D	100.0	-	-	19	-	-	5.4	5.4	-	-
District 2	**211,350**	**118,625**	**92,176**	**549**	**26,449**	**D**	**56.1**	**43.6**	**0.3**				**100.0**	**100.0**	**100.0**	**100.0**
Angelina	26,023	16,743	9,246	34	7,497	D	64.3	35.5	0.1	3	17	10	12.3	14.1	10.0	6.2
Cherokee	13,803	6,724	6,871	208	147	R	48.7	49.8	1.5	18	2	1	6.5	5.7	7.5	37.9
Grimes	5,770	3,033	2,737	0	296	D	52.6	47.4	0.0	11	9	17	2.7	2.6	3.0	0.0
Hardin	16,540	8,500	7,954	86	546	D	51.4	48.1	0.5	15	5	2	7.8	7.2	8.6	15.7
Houston	7,912	4,137	3,775	0	362	D	52.3	47.7	0.0	12	8	18	3.7	3.5	4.1	0.0
Jasper	11,946	7,174	4,763	9	2,411	D	60.1	39.9	<.1	6	14	14	5.7	6.0	5.2	1.6
Liberty	17,934	9,326	8,590	18	736	D	52.0	47.9	0.1	14	6	12	8.5	7.9	9.3	3.3
Montgomery (pt)	4,688	2,442	2,238	8	204	D	52.1	47.7	0.2	13	7	8	2.2	2.1	2.4	1.5
Nacogdoches (pt)	3,337	2,198	1,136	3	1,062	D	65.9	34.0	<.1	2	18	13	1.6	1.9	1.2	0.5
Newton	5,523	3,853	1,656	14	2,197	D	69.8	30.0	0.3	1	19	3	2.6	3.2	1.8	2.6
Orange	32,099	19,281	12,743	75	6,538	D	60.1	39.7	0.2	5	15	6	15.2	16.3	13.8	13.7
Polk	13,913	7,051	6,829	33	222	D	50.7	49.1	0.2	16	4	5	6.6	5.9	7.4	6.0
Sabine	4,531	2,648	1,872	11	776	D	58.4	41.3	0.2	8	12	4	2.1	2.2	2.0	2.0
San Augustine	3,556	2,041	1,511	4	530	D	57.4	42.5	0.1	9	11	11	1.7	1.7	1.6	0.7
San Jacinto	6,652	3,358	3,293	1	65	D	50.5	49.5	<.1	17	3	16	3.1	2.8	3.6	0.2
Shelby	8,519	4,661	3,844	14	817	D	54.7	45.1	0.2	10	10	9	4.0	3.9	4.2	2.6
Trinity	5,865	3,647	2,218	0	1,429	D	62.2	37.8	0.0	4	16	19	2.8	3.1	2.4	0.0
Tyler	7,240	4,287	2,949	4	1,338	D	59.2	40.7	<.1	7	13	15	3.4	3.6	3.2	0.7
Walker	15,499	7,521	7,951	27	430	R	48.5	51.3	0.2	19	1	7	7.3	6.3	8.6	4.9
District 3	**234,139**	**-**	**201,569**	**32,570**	**168,999**	**R**	**-**	**86.1**	**13.9**				**100.0**	**-**	**100.0**	**100.0**
Collin (pt)	60,984	-	53,126	7,858	45,268	R	-	87.1	12.9	-	1	2	26.0	-	26.4	24.1
Dallas (pt)	173,155	-	148,443	24,712	123,731	R	-	85.7	14.3	-	2	1	74.0	-	73.6	75.9
District 4	**220,333**	**128,008**	**83,875**	**8,450**	**44,133**	**D**	**58.1**	**38.1**	**3.8**				**100.0**	**100.0**	**100.0**	**100.0**
Collin (pt)	15,095	8,333	5,823	939	2,510	D	55.2	38.6	6.2	9	8	2	6.9	6.5	6.9	11.1
Cooke (pt)	11,509	6,399	4,747	363	1,652	D	55.6	41.2	3.2	8	5	10	5.2	5.0	5.7	4.3
Dallas (pt)	3,055	1,044	1,784	227	740	R	34.2	58.4	7.4	13	1	1	1.4	0.8	2.1	2.7
Denton (pt)	12,774	6,241	5,782	751	459	D	48.9	45.3	5.9	12	2	3	5.8	4.9	6.9	8.9
Fannin	9,402	7,169	1,933	300	5,236	D	76.2	20.6	3.2	1	13	9	4.3	5.6	2.3	3.6
Grayson	36,899	23,823	11,512	1,564	12,311	D	64.6	31.2	4.2	2	12	7	16.7	18.6	13.7	18.5
Gregg (pt)	26,707	15,615	10,507	585	5,108	D	58.5	39.3	2.2	5	7	13	12.1	12.2	12.5	6.9
Hunt (pt)	10,950	6,294	4,183	473	2,111	D	57.5	38.2	4.3	6	9	6	5.0	4.9	5.0	5.6
Kaufman (pt)	15,358	9,805	4,842	711	4,963	D	63.8	31.5	4.6	3	11	4	7.0	7.7	5.8	8.4
Rains	2,763	1,551	1,150	62	401	D	56.1	41.6	2.2	7	4	12	1.3	1.2	1.4	0.7
Rockwall	12,932	7,020	5,316	596	1,704	D	54.3	41.1	4.6	10	6	5	5.9	5.5	6.3	7.1
Smith (pt)	47,087	24,772	21,050	1,265	3,722	D	52.6	44.7	2.7	11	3	11	21.4	19.4	25.1	15.0
Van Zandt	15,802	9,942	5,246	614	4,696	D	62.9	33.2	3.9	4	10	8	7.2	7.8	6.3	7.3
District 5	**167,330**	**98,567**	**62,419**	**6,344**	**36,148**	**D**	**58.9**	**37.3**	**3.8**				**100.0**	**100.0**	**100.0**	**100.0**
Anderson	14,020	8,223	5,429	368	2,794	D	58.7	38.7	2.6	6	6	6	8.4	8.3	8.7	5.8
Brazos (pt)	4,306	3,117	1,027	162	2,090	D	72.4	23.9	3.8	2	11	3	2.6	3.2	1.6	2.6
Dallas (pt)	85,960	48,544	33,344	4,072	15,200	D	56.5	38.8	4.7	8	5	1	51.4	49.2	53.4	64.2
Freestone	6,184	3,446	2,594	144	852	D	55.7	41.9	2.3	9	3	8	3.7	3.5	4.2	2.3
Henderson	23,368	13,706	8,871	791	4,835	D	58.7	38.0	3.4	5	7	4	14.0	13.9	14.2	12.5
Kaufman (pt)	2,734	1,408	1,205	121	203	D	51.5	44.1	4.4	11	1	2	1.6	1.4	1.9	1.9
Leon	4,949	2,732	2,138	79	594	D	55.2	43.2	1.6	10	2	10	3.0	2.8	3.4	1.2
Limestone	6,833	4,518	2,160	155	2,358	D	66.1	31.6	2.3	4	8	9	4.1	4.6	3.5	2.4
Madison	3,686	2,093	1,501	92	592	D	56.8	40.7	2.5	7	4	7	2.2	2.1	2.4	1.5
Robertson	5,262	3,815	1,380	67	2,435	D	72.5	26.2	1.3	1	10	11	3.1	3.9	2.2	1.1
Smith (pt)	10,028	6,965	2,770	293	4,195	D	69.5	27.6	2.9	3	9	5	6.0	7.1	4.4	4.6
District 6	**263,073**	**73,933**	**189,140**	**-**	**115,207**	**R**	**28.1**	**71.9**	**-**				**100.0**	**100.0**	**100.0**	**-**
Dallas (pt)	7,782	1,887	5,895	-	4,008	R	24.2	75.8	-	4	2	-	3.0	2.6	3.1	-

Texas 897

Congressional district and county	Total	Democrat (DEM)	Republican (REP)	Other	Plurality Total	Party	Percent of total vote DEM	REP	Other	Rank within district DEM	REP	Other	Percent contribution to district vote Total	DEM	REP	Other
District 6 (cont)																
Ellis (pt)	12,961	2,992	9,969	-	6,977	R	23.1	76.9	-	5	1	-	4.9	4.0	5.3	-
Johnson (pt)	12,043	3,450	8,593	-	5,143	R	28.6	71.4	-	2	4	-	4.6	4.7	4.5	-
Parker (pt)	7,642	2,316	5,326	-	3,010	R	30.3	69.7	-	1	5	-	2.9	3.1	2.8	-
Tarrant (pt)	222,645	63,288	159,357	-	96,069	R	28.4	71.6	-	3	3	-	84.6	85.6	84.3	-
District 7	**169,407**	**-**	**169,407**	**-**	**169,407**	**R**	**-**	**100.0**	**-**				**100.0**	**-**	**100.0**	**-**
Harris (pt)	169,407	-	169,407	-	169,407	R	-	100.0	-	-	1	-	100.0	-	100.0	-
District 8	**232,822**	**53,473**	**179,349**	**-**	**125,876**	**R**	**23.0**	**77.0**	**-**				**100.0**	**100.0**	**100.0**	
Austin (pt)	6,031	1,619	4,412	-	2,793	R	26.8	73.2	-	3	4	-	2.6	3.0	2.5	-
Brazos (pt)	41,300	10,346	30,954	-	20,608	R	25.1	74.9	-	5	2	-	17.7	19.3	17.3	-
Harris (pt)	102,477	20,077	82,400	-	62,323	R	19.6	80.4	-	6	1	-	44.0	37.5	45.9	-
Montgomery (pt)	70,812	17,793	53,019	-	35,226	R	25.1	74.9	-	4	3	-	30.4	33.3	29.6	-
Waller (pt)	1,737	521	1,216	-	695	R	30.0	70.0	-	1	6	-	0.7	1.0	0.7	-
Washington	10,465	3,117	7,348	-	4,231	R	29.8	70.2	-	2	5	-	4.5	5.8	4.1	-
District 9	**221,361**	**118,690**	**96,270**	**6,401**	**22,420**	**D**	**53.6**	**43.5**	**2.9**				**100.0**	**100.0**	**100.0**	**100.0**
Chambers	8,075	4,314	3,435	326	879	D	53.4	42.5	4.0	2	3	1	3.6	3.6	3.6	5.1
Galveston	88,055	46,767	38,711	2,577	8,056	D	53.1	44.0	2.9	3	2	3	39.8	39.4	40.2	40.3
Harris (pt)	31,527	11,078	19,489	960	8,411	R	35.1	61.8	3.0	4	1	2	14.2	9.3	20.2	15.0
Jefferson	93,704	56,531	34,635	2,538	21,896	D	60.3	37.0	2.7	1	4	4	42.3	47.6	36.0	39.7
District 10	**261,892**	**177,233**	**68,646**	**16,013**	**108,587**	**D**	**67.7**	**26.2**	**6.1**				**100.0**	**100.0**	**100.0**	**100.0**
Travis (pt)	261,892	177,233	68,646	16,013	108,587	D	67.7	26.2	6.1	1	1	1	100.0	100.0	100.0	100.0
District 11	**178,032**	**119,999**	**58,033**	**-**	**61,966**	**D**	**67.4**	**32.6**	**-**				**100.0**	**100.0**	**100.0**	
Bell	51,758	32,830	18,928	-	13,902	D	63.4	36.6	-	11	2	-	29.1	27.4	32.6	-
Bosque	6,184	4,137	2,047	-	2,090	D	66.9	33.1	-	7	6	-	3.5	3.4	3.5	-
Coryell	13,946	9,260	4,686	-	4,574	D	66.4	33.6	-	9	4	-	7.8	7.7	8.1	-
Falls	5,590	4,344	1,246	-	3,098	D	77.7	22.3	-	3	10	-	3.1	3.6	2.1	-
Hamilton	3,077	1,901	1,176	-	725	D	61.8	38.2	-	12	1	-	1.7	1.6	2.0	-
Hill	9,983	6,867	3,116	-	3,751	D	68.8	31.2	-	5	8	-	5.6	5.7	5.4	-
Lampasas	4,980	3,313	1,667	-	1,646	D	66.5	33.5	-	8	5	-	2.8	2.8	2.9	-
McCulloch (pt)	2,412	1,599	813	-	786	D	66.3	33.7	-	10	3	-	1.4	1.3	1.4	-
McLennan	69,031	47,165	21,866	-	25,299	D	68.3	31.7	-	6	7	-	38.8	39.3	37.7	-
Milam	7,356	5,781	1,575	-	4,206	D	78.6	21.4	-	1	12	-	4.1	4.8	2.7	-
Mills	1,873	1,462	411	-	1,051	D	78.1	21.9	-	2	11	-	1.1	1.2	0.7	-
San Saba	1,842	1,340	502	-	838	D	72.7	27.3	-	4	9	-	1.0	1.1	0.9	-
District 12	**199,924**	**125,492**	**74,432**	**-**	**51,060**	**D**	**62.8**	**37.2**	**-**				**100.0**	**100.0**	**100.0**	
Johnson (pt)	24,318	14,829	9,489	-	5,340	D	61.0	39.0	-	2	2	-	12.2	11.8	12.7	-
Parker (pt)	19,208	11,246	7,962	-	3,284	D	58.5	41.5	-	3	1	-	9.6	9.0	10.7	-
Tarrant (pt)	156,398	99,417	56,981	-	42,436	D	63.6	36.4	-	1	3	-	78.2	79.2	76.6	-
District 13	**195,406**	**117,892**	**77,514**	**-**	**40,378**	**D**	**60.3**	**39.7**	**-**				**100.0**	**100.0**	**100.0**	
Archer	3,874	2,453	1,421	-	1,032	D	63.3	36.7	-	17	22	-	2.0	2.1	1.8	-
Armstrong	994	539	455	-	84	D	54.2	45.8	-	31	8	-	0.5	0.5	0.6	-
Baylor	2,044	1,412	632	-	780	D	69.1	30.9	-	11	28	-	1.0	1.2	0.8	-
Briscoe	940	654	286	-	368	D	69.6	30.4	-	10	29	-	0.5	0.6	0.4	-
Carson	3,005	1,694	1,311	-	383	D	56.4	43.6	-	26	13	-	1.5	1.4	1.7	-
Castro	2,686	1,639	1,047	-	592	D	61.0	39.0	-	23	16	-	1.4	1.4	1.4	-
Childress	2,291	1,419	872	-	547	D	61.9	38.1	-	22	17	-	1.2	1.2	1.1	-
Clay	4,776	3,155	1,621	-	1,534	D	66.1	33.9	-	13	26	-	2.4	2.7	2.1	-
Collingsworth	1,550	1,013	537	-	476	D	65.4	34.6	-	15	24	-	0.8	0.9	0.7	-
Cooke (pt)	135	87	48	-	39	D	64.4	35.6	-	16	23	-	0.1	0.1	0.1	-
Cottle	985	787	198	-	589	D	79.9	20.1	-	3	36	-	0.5	0.7	0.3	-
Crosby	2,180	1,425	755	-	670	D	65.4	34.6	-	14	25	-	1.1	1.2	1.0	-
Denton (pt)	13,561	7,522	6,039	-	1,483	D	55.5	44.5	-	28	11	-	6.9	6.4	7.8	-
Dickens	1,099	796	303	-	493	D	72.4	27.6	-	6	33	-	0.6	0.7	0.4	-
Donley	1,698	918	780	-	138	D	54.1	45.9	-	32	7	-	0.9	0.8	1.0	-
Floyd	2,867	1,604	1,263	-	341	D	55.9	44.1	-	27	12	-	1.5	1.4	1.6	-
Foard	784	665	119	-	546	D	84.8	15.2	-	1	38	-	0.4	0.6	0.2	-
Garza	1,628	952	676	-	276	D	58.5	41.5	-	24	15	-	0.8	0.8	0.9	-
Gray	10,226	4,788	5,438	-	650	R	46.8	53.2	-	36	3	-	5.2	4.1	7.0	-
Hale	10,070	5,346	4,724	-	622	D	53.1	46.9	-	34	5	-	5.2	4.5	6.1	-
Hall	1,666	1,175	491	-	684	D	70.5	29.5	-	8	31	-	0.9	1.0	0.6	-
Hardeman	1,991	1,622	369	-	1,253	D	81.5	18.5	-	2	37	-	1.0	1.4	0.5	-
Hemphill	1,659	796	863	-	67	R	48.0	52.0	-	35	4	-	0.8	0.7	1.1	-
Hutchinson	10,788	5,948	4,840	-	1,108	D	55.1	44.9	-	29	10	-	5.5	5.0	6.2	-
King	180	126	54	-	72	D	70.0	30.0	-	9	30	-	0.1	0.1	0.1	-
Knox	1,722	1,222	500	-	722	D	71.0	29.0	-	7	32	-	0.9	1.0	0.6	-
Lamb	5,148	3,196	1,952	-	1,244	D	62.1	37.9	-	20	19	-	2.6	2.7	2.5	-
Lipscomb	1,407	633	774	-	141	R	45.0	55.0	-	37	2	-	0.7	0.5	1.0	-
Lubbock (pt)	9,100	6,932	2,168	-	4,764	D	76.2	23.8	-	4	35	-	4.7	5.9	2.8	-
Lynn	2,281	1,433	848	-	585	D	62.8	37.2	-	18	21	-	1.2	1.2	1.1	-
Montague	7,128	4,416	2,712	-	1,704	D	62.0	38.0	-	21	18	-	3.6	3.7	3.5	-

Congressional district and county	Total	Democrat (DEM)	Republican (REP)	Other	Plurality Total	Party	Percent of total vote DEM	REP	Other	Rank within district DEM	REP	Other	Percent contribution to district vote Total	DEM	REP	Other
District 13 (cont)																
Motley	781	429	352	-	77	D	54.9	45.1	-	30	9	-	0.4	0.4	0.5	-
Potter	27,361	15,467	11,894	-	3,573	D	56.5	43.5	-	25	14	-	14.0	13.1	15.3	-
Roberts	605	258	347	-	89	R	42.6	57.4	-	38	1	-	0.3	0.2	0.4	-
Swisher	2,824	2,078	746	-	1,332	D	73.6	26.4	-	5	34	-	1.4	1.8	1.0	-
Wheeler	2,715	1,442	1,273	-	169	D	53.1	46.9	-	33	6	-	1.4	1.2	1.6	-
Wichita	45,473	28,370	17,103	-	11,267	D	62.4	37.6	-	19	20	-	23.3	24.1	22.1	-
Wilbarger	5,184	3,481	1,703	-	1,778	D	67.1	32.9	-	12	27	-	2.7	3.0	2.2	-
District 14	**199,671**	**135,930**	**54,412**	**9,329**	**81,518**	**D**	**68.1**	**27.3**	**4.7**				**100.0**	**100.0**	**100.0**	**100.0**
Aransas	6,439	3,826	2,201	412	1,625	D	59.4	34.2	6.4	20	3	2	3.2	2.8	4.0	4.4
Austin (pt)	1,549	1,071	433	45	638	D	69.1	28.0	2.9	15	6	19	0.8	0.8	0.8	0.5
Bastrop	13,706	8,222	3,716	1,768	4,506	D	60.0	27.1	12.9	19	8	1	6.9	6.0	6.8	19.0
Blanco	2,819	1,736	936	147	800	D	61.6	33.2	5.2	18	4	6	1.4	1.3	1.7	1.6
Brazoria (pt)	19,518	12,891	5,585	1,042	7,306	D	66.0	28.6	5.3	17	5	4	9.8	9.5	10.3	11.2
Burleson	5,060	3,847	1,019	194	2,828	D	76.0	20.1	3.8	4	19	11	2.5	2.8	1.9	2.1
Caldwell	7,572	5,100	2,087	385	3,013	D	67.4	27.6	5.1	16	7	7	3.8	3.8	3.8	4.1
Calhoun	6,587	5,109	1,281	197	3,828	D	77.6	19.4	3.0	2	20	18	3.3	3.8	2.4	2.1
Colorado	6,826	5,095	1,521	210	3,574	D	74.6	22.3	3.1	5	17	16	3.4	3.7	2.8	2.3
Fayette	8,526	6,316	1,857	353	4,459	D	74.1	21.8	4.1	7	18	8	4.3	4.6	3.4	3.8
Gonzales	5,112	3,630	1,314	168	2,316	D	71.0	25.7	3.3	13	11	14	2.6	2.7	2.4	1.8
Hays	24,803	14,399	9,026	1,378	5,373	D	58.1	36.4	5.6	21	2	3	12.4	10.6	16.6	14.8
Jackson	4,654	3,451	1,093	110	2,358	D	74.2	23.5	2.4	6	15	21	2.3	2.5	2.0	1.2
Lavaca	7,138	5,823	1,121	194	4,702	D	81.6	15.7	2.7	1	22	20	3.6	4.3	2.1	2.1
Lee	4,641	3,365	1,111	165	2,254	D	72.5	23.9	3.6	9	13	13	2.3	2.5	2.0	1.8
Matagorda	12,661	9,145	3,020	496	6,125	D	72.2	23.9	3.9	11	14	10	6.3	6.7	5.6	5.3
Refugio	3,512	2,698	672	142	2,026	D	76.8	19.1	4.0	3	21	9	1.8	2.0	1.2	1.5
Travis (pt)	6,582	2,513	3,724	345	1,211	R	38.2	56.6	5.2	22	1	5	3.3	1.8	6.8	3.7
Victoria	24,121	17,771	5,623	727	12,148	D	73.7	23.3	3.0	8	16	17	12.1	13.1	10.3	7.8
Waller (pt)	6,874	4,952	1,778	144	3,174	D	72.0	25.9	2.1	12	10	22	3.4	3.6	3.3	1.5
Wharton	12,460	9,005	3,071	384	5,934	D	72.3	24.6	3.1	10	12	15	6.2	6.6	5.6	4.1
Williamson (pt)	8,511	5,965	2,223	323	3,742	D	70.1	26.1	3.8	14	9	12	4.3	4.4	4.1	3.5
District 15	**142,900**	**86,351**	**56,549**	**-**	**29,802**	**D**	**60.4**	**39.6**	**-**				**100.0**	**100.0**	**100.0**	**-**
Bee	8,737	4,962	3,775	-	1,187	D	56.8	43.2	-	6	6	-	6.1	5.7	6.7	-
Brooks	3,734	3,261	473	-	2,788	D	87.3	12.7	-	1	11	-	2.6	3.8	0.8	-
DeWitt	5,946	2,569	3,377	-	808	R	43.2	56.8	-	11	1	-	4.2	3.0	6.0	-
Goliad	2,501	1,361	1,140	-	221	D	54.4	45.6	-	8	4	-	1.8	1.6	2.0	-
Hidalgo	82,197	51,282	30,915	-	20,367	D	62.4	37.6	-	4	8	-	57.5	59.4	54.7	-
Jim Wells (pt)	3,555	1,960	1,595	-	365	D	55.1	44.9	-	7	5	-	2.5	2.3	2.8	-
Karnes	4,342	2,699	1,643	-	1,056	D	62.2	37.8	-	5	7	-	3.0	3.1	2.9	-
Kleberg (pt)	5,845	3,692	2,153	-	1,539	D	63.2	36.8	-	3	9	-	4.1	4.3	3.8	-
Live Oak	3,799	1,798	2,001	-	203	R	47.3	52.7	-	10	2	-	2.7	2.1	3.5	-
San Patricio	18,161	9,638	8,523	-	1,115	D	53.1	46.9	-	9	3	-	12.7	11.2	15.1	-
Willacy (pt)	4,083	3,129	954	-	2,175	D	76.6	23.4	-	2	10	-	2.9	3.6	1.7	-
District 16	**128,601**	**66,731**	**61,870**	**-**	**4,861**	**D**	**51.9**	**48.1**	**-**				**100.0**	**100.0**	**100.0**	**-**
El Paso (pt)	128,601	66,731	61,870	-	4,861	D	51.9	48.1	-	1	1	-	100.0	100.0	100.0	-
District 17	**206,171**	**136,213**	**69,958**	**-**	**66,255**	**D**	**66.1**	**33.9**	**-**				**100.0**	**100.0**	**100.0**	**-**
Borden	344	252	92	-	160	D	73.3	26.7	-	10	23	-	0.2	0.2	0.1	-
Brown	12,239	8,265	3,974	-	4,291	D	67.5	32.5	-	20	13	-	5.9	6.1	5.7	-
Callahan	5,104	3,343	1,761	-	1,582	D	65.5	34.5	-	24	9	-	2.5	2.5	2.5	-
Coke	1,503	1,113	390	-	723	D	74.1	25.9	-	8	25	-	0.7	0.8	0.6	-
Coleman	3,978	2,843	1,135	-	1,708	D	71.5	28.5	-	12	21	-	1.9	2.1	1.6	-
Comanche	4,895	3,377	1,518	-	1,859	D	69.0	31.0	-	16	17	-	2.4	2.5	2.2	-
Concho	1,118	889	229	-	660	D	79.5	20.5	-	3	30	-	0.5	0.7	0.3	-
Dawson	4,342	2,946	1,396	-	1,550	D	67.8	32.2	-	19	14	-	2.1	2.2	2.0	-
Eastland	7,097	4,767	2,330	-	2,437	D	67.2	32.8	-	22	11	-	3.4	3.5	3.3	-
Erath	10,078	6,911	3,167	-	3,744	D	68.6	31.4	-	17	16	-	4.9	5.1	4.5	-
Fisher	2,067	1,652	415	-	1,237	D	79.9	20.1	-	1	32	-	1.0	1.2	0.6	-
Haskell	2,553	2,040	513	-	1,527	D	79.9	20.1	-	2	31	-	1.2	1.5	0.7	-
Hood	13,508	6,979	6,529	-	450	D	51.7	48.3	-	32	1	-	6.6	5.1	9.3	-
Howard	10,637	6,740	3,897	-	2,843	D	63.4	36.6	-	29	4	-	5.2	4.9	5.6	-
Jack	3,068	2,344	724	-	1,620	D	76.4	23.6	-	4	29	-	1.5	1.7	1.0	-
Jones	5,769	4,019	1,750	-	2,269	D	69.7	30.3	-	14	19	-	2.8	3.0	2.5	-
Kent	564	424	140	-	284	D	75.2	24.8	-	6	27	-	0.3	0.3	0.2	-
Martin	1,697	1,081	616	-	465	D	63.7	36.3	-	28	5	-	0.8	0.8	0.9	-
Mitchell	2,915	2,194	721	-	1,473	D	75.3	24.7	-	5	28	-	1.4	1.6	1.0	-
Nolan	5,791	4,308	1,483	-	2,825	D	74.4	25.6	-	7	26	-	2.8	3.2	2.1	-
Palo Pinto	8,942	6,190	2,752	-	3,438	D	69.2	30.8	-	15	18	-	4.3	4.5	3.9	-
Runnels	4,053	2,910	1,143	-	1,767	D	71.8	28.2	-	11	22	-	2.0	2.1	1.6	-
Scurry	5,994	3,911	2,083	-	1,828	D	65.2	34.8	-	25	8	-	2.9	2.9	3.0	-
Shackelford	1,444	940	504	-	436	D	65.1	34.9	-	26	7	-	0.7	0.7	0.7	-
Somervell	2,229	1,411	818	-	593	D	63.3	36.7	-	30	3	-	1.1	1.0	1.2	-
Stephens	3,518	2,321	1,197	-	1,124	D	66.0	34.0	-	23	10	-	1.7	1.7	1.7	-
Stonewall	1,055	748	307	-	441	D	70.9	29.1	-	13	20	-	0.5	0.5	0.4	-

Congressional district and county	Total	Democrat (DEM)	Republican (REP)	Other	Plurality Total	Party	Percent of total vote DEM	REP	Other	Rank within district DEM	REP	Other	Percent contribution to district vote Total	DEM	REP	Other
District 17 (cont)																
Taylor	43,734	27,222	16,512	-	10,710	D	62.2	37.8	-	31	2	-	21.2	20.0	23.6	-
Throckmorton	937	690	247	-	443	D	73.6	26.4	-	9	24	-	0.5	0.5	0.4	-
Tom Green (pt)	14,792	10,069	4,723	-	5,346	D	68.1	31.9	-	18	15	-	7.2	7.4	6.8	-
Wise	12,974	8,433	4,541	-	3,892	D	65.0	35.0	-	27	6	-	6.3	6.2	6.5	-
Young	7,232	4,881	2,351	-	2,530	D	67.5	32.5	-	21	12	-	3.5	3.6	3.4	-
District 18	**172,208**	**111,422**	**56,080**	**4,706**	**55,342**	**D**	**64.7**	**32.6**	**2.7**				**100.0**	**100.0**	**100.0**	**100.0**
Harris (pt)	172,208	111,422	56,080	4,706	55,342	D	64.7	32.6	2.7	1	1	1	100.0	100.0	100.0	100.0
District 19	**209,382**	**47,325**	**162,057**	**-**	**114,732**	**R**	**22.6**	**77.4**	**-**				**100.0**	**100.0**	**100.0**	**-**
Andrews	4,139	1,080	3,059	-	1,979	R	26.1	73.9	-	9	12	-	2.0	2.3	1.9	-
Bailey	2,270	547	1,723	-	1,176	R	24.1	75.9	-	14	7	-	1.1	1.2	1.1	-
Cochran	1,357	336	1,021	-	685	R	24.8	75.2	-	12	9	-	0.6	0.7	0.6	-
Dallam	1,536	539	997	-	458	R	35.1	64.9	-	1	20	-	0.7	1.1	0.6	-
Deaf Smith	5,386	1,744	3,642	-	1,898	R	32.4	67.6	-	3	18	-	2.6	3.7	2.2	-
Ector (pt)	28,620	6,518	22,102	-	15,584	R	22.8	77.2	-	16	5	-	13.7	13.8	13.6	-
Gaines	3,778	1,056	2,722	-	1,666	R	28.0	72.0	-	6	15	-	1.8	2.2	1.7	-
Hansford	2,149	432	1,717	-	1,285	R	20.1	79.9	-	18	3	-	1.0	0.9	1.1	-
Hartley	1,698	492	1,206	-	714	R	29.0	71.0	-	5	16	-	0.8	1.0	0.7	-
Hockley	7,615	1,893	5,722	-	3,829	R	24.9	75.1	-	11	10	-	3.6	4.0	3.5	-
Lubbock (pt)	71,911	13,366	58,545	-	45,179	R	18.6	81.4	-	20	1	-	34.3	28.2	36.1	-
Midland (pt)	20,710	4,211	16,499	-	12,288	R	20.3	79.7	-	17	4	-	9.9	8.9	10.2	-
Moore	5,250	1,823	3,427	-	1,604	R	34.7	65.3	-	2	19	-	2.5	3.9	2.1	-
Ochiltree	3,245	648	2,597	-	1,949	R	20.0	80.0	-	19	2	-	1.5	1.4	1.6	-
Oldham	904	279	625	-	346	R	30.9	69.1	-	4	17	-	0.4	0.6	0.4	-
Parmer	2,854	704	2,150	-	1,446	R	24.7	75.3	-	13	8	-	1.4	1.5	1.3	-
Randall	38,065	9,636	28,429	-	18,793	R	25.3	74.7	-	10	11	-	18.2	20.4	17.5	-
Sherman	1,237	329	908	-	579	R	26.6	73.4	-	7	14	-	0.6	0.7	0.6	-
Terry	4,104	1,085	3,019	-	1,934	R	26.4	73.6	-	8	13	-	2.0	2.3	1.9	-
Yoakum	2,554	607	1,947	-	1,340	R	23.8	76.2	-	15	6	-	1.2	1.3	1.2	-
District 20	**103,755**	**103,755**	**-**	**-**	**103,755**	**D**	**100.0**	**-**	**-**				**100.0**	**100.0**	**-**	**-**
Bexar (pt)	103,755	103,755	-	-	103,755	D	100.0	-	-	1	-	-	100.0	100.0	-	-
District 21	**264,653**	**62,827**	**190,979**	**10,847**	**128,152**	**R**	**23.7**	**72.2**	**4.1**				**100.0**	**100.0**	**100.0**	**100.0**
Bandera	5,118	942	3,868	308	2,926	R	18.4	75.6	6.0	17	9	1	1.9	1.5	2.0	2.8
Bexar (pt)	81,980	15,596	63,351	3,033	47,755	R	19.0	77.3	3.7	16	7	9	31.0	24.8	33.2	28.0
Burnet	10,087	4,011	5,651	425	1,640	R	39.8	56.0	4.2	1	21	7	3.8	6.4	3.0	3.9
Comal (pt)	20,462	3,954	15,491	1,017	11,537	R	19.3	75.7	5.0	15	8	4	7.7	6.3	8.1	9.4
Gillespie	8,125	1,438	6,378	309	4,940	R	17.7	78.5	3.8	18	4	8	3.1	2.3	3.3	2.8
Glasscock	523	90	415	18	325	R	17.2	79.3	3.4	19	3	10	0.2	0.1	0.2	0.2
Guadalupe (pt)	15,476	4,105	10,600	771	6,495	R	26.5	68.5	5.0	7	17	3	5.8	6.5	5.6	7.1
Irion	764	195	557	12	362	R	25.5	72.9	1.6	9	13	19	0.3	0.3	0.3	0.1
Kendall	7,129	1,097	5,706	326	4,609	R	15.4	80.0	4.6	20	2	6	2.7	1.7	3.0	3.0
Kerr	15,894	3,369	11,751	774	8,382	R	21.2	73.9	4.9	12	10	5	6.0	5.4	6.2	7.1
Kimble	1,517	381	1,116	20	735	R	25.1	73.6	1.3	10	11	21	0.6	0.6	0.6	0.2
Llano	7,021	2,334	4,465	222	2,131	R	33.2	63.6	3.2	4	18	11	2.7	3.7	2.3	2.0
McCulloch (pt)	491	133	351	7	218	R	27.1	71.5	1.4	6	14	20	0.2	0.2	0.2	0.1
Mason	1,626	467	1,126	33	659	R	28.7	69.2	2.0	5	16	16	0.6	0.7	0.6	0.3
Menard	1,114	392	698	24	306	R	35.2	62.7	2.2	3	19	15	0.4	0.6	0.4	0.2
Midland (pt)	14,638	2,083	12,160	395	10,077	R	14.2	83.1	2.7	21	1	13	5.5	3.3	6.4	3.6
Real	1,418	365	1,012	41	647	R	25.7	71.4	2.9	8	15	12	0.5	0.6	0.5	0.4
Schleicher	1,133	282	831	20	549	R	24.9	73.3	1.8	11	12	17	0.4	0.4	0.4	0.2
Sterling	551	114	428	9	314	R	20.7	77.7	1.6	13	6	18	0.2	0.2	0.2	0.1
Tom Green (pt)	20,564	4,015	16,083	466	12,068	R	19.5	78.2	2.3	14	5	14	7.8	6.4	8.4	4.3
Williamson (pt)	49,022	17,464	28,941	2,617	11,477	R	35.6	59.0	5.3	2	20	2	18.5	27.8	15.2	24.1
District 22	**218,033**	**67,812**	**150,221**	**-**	**82,409**	**R**	**31.1**	**68.9**	**-**				**100.0**	**100.0**	**100.0**	**-**
Brazoria (pt)	49,830	17,400	32,430	-	15,030	R	34.9	65.1	-	1	3	-	22.9	25.7	21.6	-
Fort Bend (pt)	71,215	20,376	50,839	-	30,463	R	28.6	71.4	-	3	1	-	32.7	30.0	33.8	-
Harris (pt)	96,988	30,036	66,952	-	36,916	R	31.0	69.0	-	2	2	-	44.5	44.3	44.6	-
District 23	**166,347**	**63,797**	**98,259**	**4,291**	**34,462**	**R**	**38.4**	**59.1**	**2.6**				**100.0**	**100.0**	**100.0**	**100.0**
Bexar (pt)	47,716	7,699	38,723	1,294	31,024	R	16.1	81.2	2.7	29	1	15	28.7	12.1	39.4	30.2
Brewster	3,131	1,220	1,799	112	579	R	39.0	57.5	3.6	16	15	11	1.9	1.9	1.8	2.6
Crane	1,746	434	1,236	76	802	R	24.9	70.8	4.4	27	3	8	1.0	0.7	1.3	1.8
Crockett	1,433	657	704	72	47	R	45.8	49.1	5.0	11	18	4	0.9	1.0	0.7	1.7
Culberson	769	305	446	18	141	R	39.7	58.0	2.3	15	14	19	0.5	0.5	0.5	0.4
Dimmit	4,338	2,585	1,740	13	845	D	59.6	40.1	0.3	3	25	29	2.6	4.1	1.8	0.3
Ector (pt)	5,922	3,338	2,373	211	965	D	56.4	40.1	3.6	6	26	12	3.6	5.2	2.4	4.9
Edwards	821	260	548	13	288	R	31.7	66.7	1.6	23	6	25	0.5	0.4	0.6	0.3
El Paso (pt)	4,673	2,100	2,208	365	108	R	44.9	47.3	7.8	12	19	2	2.8	3.3	2.2	8.5
Hudspeth	716	370	306	40	64	D	51.7	42.7	5.6	10	22	3	0.4	0.6	0.3	0.9
Jeff Davis	810	279	502	29	223	R	34.4	62.0	3.6	20	9	10	0.5	0.4	0.5	0.7
Kinney	1,477	432	1,018	27	586	R	29.2	68.9	1.8	24	5	22	0.9	0.7	1.0	0.6
Loving	86	28	51	7	23	R	32.6	59.3	8.1	22	12	1	0.1	0.0	0.1	0.2

Congressional district and county	Total	Democrat (DEM)	Republican (REP)	Other	Plurality Total	Plurality Party	Percent of total vote DEM	REP	Other	Rank within district DEM	REP	Other	Percent contribution to district vote Total	DEM	REP	Other
District 23 (cont)																
Maverick	7,142	3,902	3,140	100	762	D	54.6	44.0	1.4	8	21	26	4.3	6.1	3.2	2.3
Medina	10,666	2,866	7,544	256	4,678	R	26.9	70.7	2.4	26	4	18	6.4	4.5	7.7	6.0
Midland (pt)	4,793	2,706	1,937	150	769	D	56.5	40.4	3.1	5	24	14	2.9	4.2	2.0	3.5
Pecos	4,452	1,782	2,522	148	740	R	40.0	56.6	3.3	14	16	13	2.7	2.8	2.6	3.4
Presidio	1,771	1,049	684	38	365	D	59.2	38.6	2.1	4	27	20	1.1	1.6	0.7	0.9
Reagan	1,186	230	937	19	707	R	19.4	79.0	1.6	28	2	24	0.7	0.4	1.0	0.4
Reeves	4,481	2,449	1,913	119	536	D	54.7	42.7	2.7	7	23	16	2.7	3.8	1.9	2.8
Sutton	1,426	638	726	62	88	R	44.7	50.9	4.3	13	17	9	0.9	1.0	0.7	1.4
Terrell	564	299	251	14	48	D	53.0	44.5	2.5	9	20	17	0.3	0.5	0.3	0.3
Upton	1,582	457	1,046	79	589	R	28.9	66.1	5.0	25	7	5	1.0	0.7	1.1	1.8
Uvalde	8,475	3,088	5,246	141	2,158	R	36.4	61.9	1.7	18	10	23	5.1	4.8	5.3	3.3
Val Verde	10,748	3,956	6,564	228	2,608	R	36.8	61.1	2.1	17	11	21	6.5	6.2	6.7	5.3
Ward	4,341	1,566	2,571	204	1,005	R	36.1	59.2	4.7	19	13	7	2.6	2.5	2.6	4.8
Webb	24,631	15,548	8,778	305	6,770	D	63.1	35.6	1.2	2	28	27	14.8	24.4	8.9	7.1
Winkler	2,642	870	1,641	131	771	R	32.9	62.1	5.0	21	8	6	1.6	1.4	1.7	3.1
Zavala	3,809	2,684	1,105	20	1,579	D	70.5	29.0	0.5	1	29	28	2.3	4.2	1.1	0.5
District 24	174,216	104,174	70,042	-	34,132	D	59.8	40.2	-				100.0	100.0	100.0	-
Dallas (pt)	68,373	35,904	32,469	-	3,435	D	52.5	47.5	-	4	1	-	39.2	34.5	46.4	-
Ellis (pt)	19,801	11,681	8,120	-	3,561	D	59.0	41.0	-	2	3	-	11.4	11.2	11.6	-
Navarro	14,311	7,847	6,464	-	1,383	D	54.8	45.2	-	3	2	-	8.2	7.5	9.2	-
Tarrant (pt)	71,731	48,742	22,989	-	25,753	D	68.0	32.0	-	1	4	-	41.2	46.8	32.8	-
District 25	176,877	98,975	73,192	4,710	25,783	D	56.0	41.4	2.7				100.0	100.0	100.0	100.0
Fort Bend (pt)	14,695	11,317	3,126	252	8,191	D	77.0	21.3	1.7	1	2	2	8.3	11.4	4.3	5.4
Harris (pt)	162,182	87,658	70,066	4,458	17,592	D	54.0	43.2	2.7	2	1	1	91.7	88.6	95.7	94.6
District 26	205,531	55,237	150,209	85	94,972	R	26.9	73.1	<.1				100.0	100.0	100.0	100.0
Collin (pt)	39,073	8,193	30,876	4	22,683	R	21.0	79.0	<.1	4	1	3	19.0	14.8	20.6	4.7
Dallas (pt)	113,301	32,002	81,292	7	49,290	R	28.2	71.7	<.1	2	2	4	55.1	57.9	54.1	8.2
Denton (pt)	51,361	14,535	36,753	73	22,218	R	28.3	71.6	0.1	1	4	1	25.0	26.3	24.5	85.9
Tarrant (pt)	1,796	507	1,288	1	781	R	28.2	71.7	<.1	3	3	2	0.9	0.9	0.9	1.2
District 27	156,844	87,022	66,853	2,969	20,169	D	55.5	42.6	1.9				100.0	100.0	100.0	100.0
Cameron	54,013	33,977	18,828	1,208	15,149	D	62.9	34.9	2.2	3	3	1	34.4	39.0	28.2	40.7
Kenedy	171	116	55	0	61	D	67.8	32.2	0.0	2	4	5	0.1	0.1	0.1	0.0
Kleberg (pt)	3,898	2,302	1,535	61	767	D	59.1	39.4	1.6	4	2	4	2.5	2.6	2.3	2.1
Nueces	97,659	49,870	46,111	1,678	3,759	D	51.1	47.2	1.7	5	1	3	62.3	57.3	69.0	56.5
Willacy (pt)	1,103	757	324	22	433	D	68.6	29.4	2.0	1	5	2	0.7	0.9	0.5	0.7
District 28	140,585	122,457	-	18,128	104,329	D	87.1	-	12.9				100.0	100.0	-	100.0
Atascosa	8,518	6,643	-	1,875	4,768	D	78.0	-	22.0	11	-	3	6.1	5.4	-	10.3
Bexar (pt)	85,668	75,416	-	10,252	65,164	D	88.0	-	12.0	6	-	8	60.9	61.6	-	56.6
Comal (pt)	3,170	2,534	-	636	1,898	D	79.9	-	20.1	10	-	4	2.3	2.1	-	3.5
Duval	4,205	4,044	-	161	3,883	D	96.2	-	3.8	1	-	13	3.0	3.3	-	0.9
Frio	3,811	3,275	-	536	2,739	D	85.9	-	14.1	8	-	6	2.7	2.7	-	3.0
Guadalupe (pt)	6,182	4,380	-	1,802	2,578	D	70.9	-	29.1	13	-	1	4.4	3.6	-	9.9
Jim Hogg	1,886	1,783	-	103	1,680	D	94.5	-	5.5	4	-	10	1.3	1.5	-	0.6
Jim Wells (pt)	8,024	7,035	-	989	6,046	D	87.7	-	12.3	7	-	7	5.7	5.7	-	5.5
La Salle	1,752	1,672	-	80	1,592	D	95.4	-	4.6	3	-	11	1.2	1.4	-	0.4
McMullen	241	186	-	55	131	D	77.2	-	22.8	12	-	2	0.2	0.2	-	0.3
Starr	8,020	7,710	-	310	7,400	D	96.1	-	3.9	2	-	12	5.7	6.3	-	1.7
Wilson	6,847	5,662	-	1,185	4,477	D	82.7	-	17.3	9	-	5	4.9	4.6	-	6.5
Zapata	2,261	2,117	-	144	1,973	D	93.6	-	6.4	5	-	9	1.6	1.7	-	0.8
District 29	98,673	64,064	34,609	-	29,455	D	64.9	35.1	-				100.0	100.0	100.0	-
Harris (pt)	98,673	64,064	34,609	-	29,455	D	64.9	35.1	-	1	1	-	100.0	100.0	100.0	-
District 30	150,747	107,831	37,853	5,063	69,978	D	71.5	25.1	3.4				100.0	100.0	100.0	100.0
Collin (pt)	829	421	340	68	81	D	50.8	41.0	8.2	3	1	1	0.5	0.4	0.9	1.3
Dallas (pt)	149,557	107,097	37,473	4,987	69,624	D	71.6	25.1	3.3	2	2	2	99.2	99.3	99.0	98.5
Tarrant (pt)	361	313	40	8	273	D	86.7	11.1	2.2	1	3	3	0.2	0.3	0.1	0.2
TEXAS	5,622,472	2,806,044	2,685,973	130,455	120,071	D	49.9	47.8	2.3							

Table I. — Vote for Presidential Preference: March 10, 1992, Democratic Primary Election

County	Total	Clinton	Tsongas	Brown	Woods	Kerrey	Harkin	LaRouche	Other	Clinton	Tsongas	Brown	Clinton Rank	Tsongas Rank	Brown Rank	Total	Clinton	Tsongas	Brown
Anderson	7,819	5,532	1,381	326	125	141	93	102	119	70.8	17.7	4.2	90	94	194	0.5	0.6	0.5	0.3
Andrews	1,971	1,138	416	125	94	58	36	31	73	57.7	21.1	6.3	233	36	69	0.1	0.1	0.1	0.1
Angelina	11,248	8,438	1,558	573	66	187	198	74	154	75.0	13.9	5.1	39	186	135	0.8	0.9	0.5	0.5
Aransas	1,201	786	225	90	52	20	12	10	6	65.4	18.7	7.5	174	69	44	<.1	<.1	<.1	<.1
Archer	1,673	1,224	198	76	114	23	8	12	18	73.2	11.8	4.5	55	226	174	0.1	0.1	<.1	<.1
Armstrong	497	334	67	25	29	15	10	4	13	67.2	13.5	5.0	145	196	143	<.1	<.1	<.1	<.1
Atascosa	3,739	2,233	823	266	99	67	75	62	114	59.7	22.0	7.1	223	26	55	0.3	0.2	0.3	0.2
Austin	2,052	1,430	362	132	13	27	19	21	48	69.7	17.6	6.4	104	96	68	0.1	0.1	0.1	0.1
Bailey	864	576	134	63	39	12	11	17	12	66.7	15.5	7.3	149	146	52	<.1	<.1	<.1	<.1
Bandera	618	387	135	57	2	14	9	11	3	62.6	21.8	9.2	206	29	26	<.1	<.1	<.1	<.1
Bastrop	6,817	4,329	1,187	821	122	126	87	41	104	63.5	17.4	12.0	193	101	10	0.5	0.4	0.4	0.7
Baylor	1,484	1,032	208	91	64	30	26	12	21	69.5	14.0	6.1	107	179	80	0.1	0.1	<.1	<.1
Bee	3,165	2,089	565	169	96	58	60	50	78	66.0	17.9	5.3	163	88	116	0.2	0.2	0.2	0.1
Bell	8,733	5,952	1,675	510	78	220	122	58	118	68.2	19.2	5.8	128	65	94	0.6	0.6	0.6	0.4
Bexar	68,568	37,490	18,550	6,734	986	992	803	1,015	1,998	54.7	27.1	9.8	246	7	20	4.6	3.9	6.5	5.7
Blanco	421	261	74	55	8	6	9	2	6	62.0	17.6	13.1	211	99	7	<.1	<.1	<.1	<.1
Borden	210	143	35	6	18	2	3	1	2	68.1	16.7	2.9	129	122	245	<.1	<.1	<.1	<.1
Bosque	2,598	1,871	412	145	61	29	20	17	43	72.0	15.9	5.6	68	139	108	0.2	0.2	0.1	0.1
Bowie	15,194	12,075	1,543	490	421	131	300	81	153	79.5	10.2	3.2	7	243	236	1.0	1.2	0.5	0.4
Brazoria	10,768	7,138	2,075	1,058	81	84	139	83	110	66.3	19.3	9.8	157	62	19	0.7	0.7	0.7	0.9
Brazos	5,835	3,294	1,724	576	17	45	106	16	57	56.5	29.5	9.9	239	3	17	0.4	0.3	0.6	0.5
Brewster	986	554	212	103	37	13	20	15	32	56.2	21.5	10.4	240	32	13	<.1	<.1	<.1	<.1
Briscoe	572	436	68	20	30	2	5	3	8	76.2	11.9	3.5	29	224	222	<.1	<.1	<.1	<.1
Brooks	3,221	2,403	343	110	99	36	67	50	113	74.6	10.6	3.4	42	239	229	0.2	0.2	0.1	<.1
Brown	6,397	4,226	1,210	383	152	154	98	63	111	66.1	18.9	6.0	162	67	86	0.4	0.4	0.4	0.3
Burleson	3,455	2,514	480	206	60	43	53	57	42	72.8	13.9	6.0	62	185	88	0.2	0.3	0.2	0.2
Burnet	4,632	3,076	796	386	102	117	66	44	45	66.4	17.2	8.3	154	107	32	0.3	0.3	0.3	0.3
Caldwell	3,168	2,104	547	258	96	55	31	34	43	66.4	17.3	8.1	153	104	34	0.2	0.2	0.2	0.2
Calhoun	2,362	1,599	465	114	40	36	33	42	33	67.7	19.7	4.8	140	55	156	0.2	0.2	0.2	<.1
Callahan	3,043	2,165	471	118	116	67	29	34	43	71.1	15.5	3.9	79	149	208	0.2	0.2	0.2	<.1
Cameron	21,699	13,887	3,986	1,263	402	563	287	310	1,001	64.0	18.4	5.8	191	75	97	1.5	1.4	1.4	1.1
Camp	2,097	1,614	224	90	63	29	29	16	32	77.0	10.7	4.3	23	237	189	0.1	0.2	<.1	<.1
Carson	1,098	736	180	82	47	11	23	6	13	67.0	16.4	7.5	146	128	46	<.1	<.1	<.1	<.1
Cass	5,263	4,356	392	153	209	36	29	28	60	82.8	7.4	2.9	2	254	244	0.4	0.4	0.1	0.1
Castro	1,568	1,110	212	65	76	25	28	13	39	70.8	13.5	4.1	88	192	196	0.1	0.1	<.1	<.1
Chambers	3,943	2,618	661	228	82	91	69	74	120	66.4	16.8	5.8	156	120	101	0.3	0.3	0.2	0.2
Cherokee	7,253	5,156	1,205	339	119	94	146	77	117	71.1	16.6	4.7	84	125	166	0.5	0.5	0.4	0.3
Childress	1,336	942	216	39	48	15	25	9	42	70.5	16.2	2.9	94	134	243	<.1	<.1	<.1	<.1
Clay	2,966	2,109	395	116	197	61	36	21	31	71.1	13.3	3.9	83	201	206	0.2	0.2	0.1	<.1
Cochran	1,004	686	103	53	101	16	14	6	25	68.3	10.3	5.3	124	242	124	<.1	<.1	<.1	<.1
Coke	741	535	103	38	23	10	7	10	15	72.2	13.9	5.1	66	183	132	<.1	<.1	<.1	<.1
Coleman	2,232	1,647	287	70	100	23	27	20	58	73.8	12.9	3.1	46	209	240	0.2	0.2	0.1	<.1
Collin	10,380	5,175	3,506	1,293	123	92	114	27	50	49.9	33.8	12.5	251	1	8	0.7	0.5	1.2	1.1
Collingsworth	1,130	782	154	60	57	19	16	13	29	69.2	13.6	5.3	111	190	118	<.1	<.1	<.1	<.1
Colorado	3,776	2,495	794	210	39	57	59	46	76	66.1	21.0	5.6	160	37	111	0.3	0.3	0.3	0.2
Comal	2,847	1,631	724	344	29	38	27	23	31	57.3	25.4	12.1	236	9	9	0.2	0.2	0.3	0.3
Comanche	3,377	2,321	551	176	88	52	58	28	103	68.7	16.3	5.2	120	132	128	0.2	0.2	0.2	0.1
Concho	838	596	112	30	36	17	8	22	17	71.1	13.4	3.6	81	200	220	<.1	<.1	<.1	<.1
Cooke	6,531	3,865	1,502	498	302	90	130	43	101	59.2	23.0	7.6	228	15	37	0.4	0.4	0.5	0.4
Coryell	4,393	3,016	801	271	63	63	80	32	67	68.7	18.2	6.2	121	76	77	0.3	0.3	0.3	0.2
Cottle	627	489	61	21	21	9	12	7	7	78.0	9.7	3.3	10	248	232	<.1	<.1	<.1	<.1
Crane	1,294	709	254	58	92	52	52	22	55	54.8	19.6	4.5	245	58	181	<.1	<.1	<.1	<.1
Crockett	1,027	646	174	53	36	24	45	17	32	62.9	16.9	5.2	204	115	131	<.1	<.1	<.1	<.1
Crosby	813	566	115	28	73	1	10	7	13	69.6	14.1	3.4	106	176	226	<.1	<.1	<.1	<.1
Culberson	653	361	146	34	30	18	17	14	33	55.3	22.4	5.2	243	21	129	<.1	<.1	<.1	<.1
Dallam	415	292	73	24	14	2	4	2	4	70.4	17.6	5.8	99	97	100	<.1	<.1	<.1	<.1
Dallas	108,681	69,688	24,577	10,380	1,384	560	919	320	853	64.1	22.6	9.6	189	19	23	7.3	7.2	8.6	8.7
Dawson	2,257	1,466	384	106	125	65	31	33	47	65.0	17.0	4.7	178	112	164	0.2	0.2	0.1	<.1
Deaf Smith	1,976	1,185	394	109	92	49	48	43	56	60.0	19.9	5.5	222	50	112	0.1	0.1	0.1	<.1
Delta	1,135	855	142	46	48	2	13	10	19	75.3	12.5	4.1	34	219	200	<.1	<.1	<.1	<.1
Denton	10,423	5,516	3,068	1,409	120	117	119	16	58	52.9	29.4	13.5	248	4	5	0.7	0.6	1.1	1.2
DeWitt	2,782	1,840	577	140	31	37	69	50	38	66.1	20.7	5.0	159	40	142	0.2	0.2	0.2	0.1
Dickens	820	580	92	49	56	11	7	6	19	70.7	11.2	6.0	91	232	87	<.1	<.1	<.1	<.1
Dimmit	2,767	1,954	311	131	75	45	64	30	157	70.6	11.2	4.7	93	231	162	0.2	0.2	0.1	0.1
Donley	656	498	70	30	18	11	9	11	9	75.9	10.7	4.6	31	238	173	<.1	<.1	<.1	<.1
Duval	4,287	2,793	545	161	106	133	286	114	149	65.2	12.7	3.8	175	215	213	0.3	0.3	0.2	0.1
Eastland	3,156	2,254	478	138	87	58	37	37	67	71.4	15.1	4.4	78	156	184	0.2	0.2	0.2	0.1
Ector	5,049	3,708	717	283	147	71	53	23	47	73.4	14.2	5.6	50	174	107	0.3	0.4	0.3	0.2
Edwards	323	192	67	13	5	9	11	9	17	59.4	20.7	4.0	225	39	202	<.1	<.1	<.1	<.1
Ellis	5,273	3,772	864	381	100	49	53	26	28	71.5	16.4	7.2	76	129	54	0.4	0.4	0.3	0.3

Table I. — Vote for Presidential Preference: March 10, 1992, Democratic Primary Election (cont)

County	Top candidates: Total	Clinton	Tsongas	Brown	Woods	Kerrey	Harkin	LaRouche	Other	Percent of total vote: Clinton	Tsongas	Brown	Rank: Clinton	Tsongas	Brown	Percent contribution to state vote: Total	Clinton	Tsongas	Brown
El Paso	42,655	21,821	11,398	6,064	254	801	528	413	1,376	51.2	26.7	14.2	250	8	4	2.9	2.2	4.0	5.1
Erath	4,166	2,640	892	260	126	69	81	22	76	63.4	21.4	6.2	195	33	73	0.3	0.3	0.3	0.2
Falls	3,351	2,460	427	201	69	51	56	34	53	73.4	12.7	6.0	51	213	85	0.2	0.3	0.1	0.2
Fannin	5,149	3,763	682	250	238	63	72	33	48	73.1	13.2	4.9	56	202	155	0.3	0.4	0.2	0.2
Fayette	3,732	2,685	578	241	55	55	29	43	46	71.9	15.5	6.5	70	148	66	0.3	0.3	0.2	0.2
Fisher	1,275	930	212	53	22	16	23	3	16	72.9	16.6	4.2	59	124	195	<.1	<.1	<.1	<.1
Floyd	1,228	837	159	58	106	20	11	9	28	68.2	12.9	4.7	127	207	163	<.1	<.1	<.1	<.1
Foard	546	379	71	25	28	25	6	3	9	69.4	13.0	4.6	109	204	172	<.1	<.1	<.1	<.1
Fort Bend	11,736	8,078	2,323	849	79	113	92	65	137	68.8	19.8	7.2	116	52	53	0.8	0.8	0.8	0.7
Franklin	1,868	1,451	208	86	56	20	10	17	20	77.7	11.1	4.6	13	234	170	0.1	0.1	<.1	<.1
Freestone	2,998	2,179	514	118	61	43	35	16	32	72.7	17.1	3.9	63	109	205	0.2	0.2	0.2	<.1
Frio	3,193	2,219	458	149	64	76	53	44	130	69.5	14.3	4.7	108	170	168	0.2	0.2	0.2	0.1
Gaines	1,665	1,065	246	97	136	34	24	23	40	64.0	14.8	5.8	192	161	96	0.1	0.1	0.1	0.1
Galveston	18,473	12,512	3,801	1,352	120	167	268	128	125	67.7	20.6	7.3	137	42	50	1.2	1.3	1.3	1.1
Garza	1,245	771	191	58	110	38	24	16	37	61.9	15.3	4.7	213	152	169	<.1	<.1	<.1	<.1
Gillespie	614	389	130	71	0	16	5	1	2	63.4	21.2	11.6	197	35	12	<.1	<.1	<.1	<.1
Glasscock	167	101	28	16	10	1	3	4	4	60.5	16.8	9.6	219	119	22	<.1	<.1	<.1	<.1
Goliad	1,153	740	236	52	40	18	24	15	28	64.2	20.5	4.5	188	44	178	<.1	<.1	<.1	<.1
Gonzales	2,597	1,646	570	137	56	65	34	37	52	63.4	21.9	5.3	194	27	126	0.2	0.2	0.2	0.1
Gray	2,360	1,649	343	120	89	35	50	24	50	69.9	14.5	5.1	102	163	136	0.2	0.2	0.1	0.1
Grayson	10,654	7,243	2,010	649	368	134	110	71	69	68.0	18.9	6.1	133	68	81	0.7	0.7	0.7	0.5
Gregg	6,638	5,132	905	281	98	67	67	29	59	77.3	13.6	4.2	19	189	190	0.4	0.5	0.3	0.2
Grimes	2,846	2,196	413	105	30	37	18	15	32	77.2	14.5	3.7	21	165	216	0.2	0.2	0.1	<.1
Guadalupe	3,541	2,035	898	364	54	47	87	31	25	57.5	25.4	10.3	235	10	16	0.2	0.2	0.3	0.3
Hale	4,130	2,461	793	260	296	70	83	63	104	59.6	19.2	6.3	224	64	72	0.3	0.3	0.3	0.2
Hall	1,064	779	151	38	32	13	18	10	23	73.2	14.2	3.6	54	175	221	<.1	<.1	<.1	<.1
Hamilton	1,506	1,099	242	69	20	16	11	12	37	73.0	16.1	4.6	58	138	171	0.1	0.1	<.1	<.1
Hansford	514	337	80	32	29	11	12	5	8	65.6	15.6	6.2	171	145	75	<.1	<.1	<.1	<.1
Hardeman	1,372	1,008	172	58	68	11	12	15	28	73.5	12.5	4.2	49	218	191	<.1	0.1	<.1	<.1
Hardin	7,930	5,724	1,139	393	184	98	178	68	146	72.2	14.4	5.0	67	169	147	0.5	0.6	0.4	0.3
Harris	139,481	90,260	32,030	12,158	779	961	1,155	879	1,259	64.7	23.0	8.7	180	16	29	9.4	9.3	11.2	10.2
Harrison	8,753	7,291	805	49	280	104	75	49	100	83.3	9.2	0.6	1	251	254	0.6	0.8	0.3	<.1
Hartley	762	500	124	30	38	19	17	13	21	65.6	16.3	3.9	170	133	204	<.1	<.1	<.1	<.1
Haskell	1,859	1,443	225	60	54	16	16	15	30	77.6	12.1	3.2	16	223	235	0.1	0.1	<.1	<.1
Hays	6,577	3,621	1,453	1,123	83	112	83	37	65	55.1	22.1	17.1	244	24	2	0.4	0.4	0.5	0.9
Hemphill	534	373	75	31	33	6	6	3	7	69.9	14.0	5.8	103	177	98	<.1	<.1	<.1	<.1
Henderson	8,456	6,387	1,187	407	179	71	103	44	78	75.5	14.0	4.8	32	178	159	0.6	0.7	0.4	0.3
Hidalgo	35,631	25,951	4,543	1,985	377	875	453	290	1,157	72.8	12.8	5.6	61	212	109	2.4	2.7	1.6	1.7
Hill	5,160	3,689	789	290	89	75	71	40	117	71.5	15.3	5.6	77	153	106	0.3	0.4	0.3	0.2
Hockley	3,043	1,794	567	159	307	67	41	43	65	59.0	18.6	5.2	229	72	127	0.2	0.2	0.2	0.1
Hood	3,785	2,585	743	246	77	34	47	19	34	68.3	19.6	6.5	126	57	64	0.3	0.3	0.3	0.2
Hopkins	5,509	4,109	813	258	108	39	66	54	62	74.6	14.8	4.7	43	162	165	0.4	0.4	0.3	0.2
Houston	4,543	3,462	614	180	61	54	38	55	79	76.2	13.5	4.0	30	193	203	0.3	0.4	0.2	0.2
Howard	4,043	2,774	686	195	92	79	94	47	76	68.6	17.0	4.8	122	114	157	0.3	0.3	0.2	0.2
Hudspeth	686	434	117	64	7	12	18	10	24	63.3	17.1	9.3	198	110	24	<.1	<.1	<.1	<.1
Hunt	7,102	5,005	1,294	403	135	70	82	52	61	70.5	18.2	5.7	96	79	105	0.5	0.5	0.5	0.3
Hutchinson	1,977	1,418	318	75	77	20	37	7	25	71.7	16.1	3.8	73	137	211	0.1	0.1	0.1	<.1
Irion	408	282	74	13	14	6	3	6	10	69.1	18.1	3.2	113	82	237	<.1	<.1	<.1	<.1
Jack	2,169	1,543	282	128	113	18	38	9	38	71.1	13.0	5.9	82	205	91	0.1	0.2	<.1	0.1
Jackson	2,767	1,831	545	141	32	64	36	46	72	66.2	19.7	5.1	158	54	134	0.2	0.2	0.2	0.1
Jasper	7,180	5,401	882	310	163	112	114	60	138	75.2	12.3	4.3	36	221	187	0.5	0.6	0.3	0.3
Jeff Davis	462	215	130	36	17	16	7	21	20	46.5	28.1	7.8	253	6	35	<.1	<.1	<.1	<.1
Jefferson	29,207	21,003	4,433	1,549	365	559	452	359	487	71.9	15.2	5.3	71	155	120	2.0	2.2	1.6	1.3
Jim Hogg	1,953	1,431	253	68	45	34	33	20	69	73.3	13.0	3.5	53	206	223	0.1	0.1	<.1	<.1
Jim Wells	6,820	4,803	869	477	246	99	115	69	142	70.4	12.7	7.0	97	214	57	0.5	0.5	0.3	0.4
Johnson	10,008	6,733	1,969	658	239	139	130	59	81	67.3	19.7	6.6	143	56	63	0.7	0.7	0.7	0.6
Jones	2,275	1,687	307	88	81	30	37	12	33	74.2	13.5	3.9	44	195	209	0.2	0.2	0.1	<.1
Karnes	3,106	1,999	557	228	67	77	48	64	66	64.4	17.9	7.3	185	83	49	0.2	0.2	0.2	0.2
Kaufman	5,670	4,080	879	286	107	85	84	32	117	72.0	15.5	5.0	69	147	139	0.4	0.4	0.3	0.2
Kendall	395	208	116	53	1	6	8	3	0	52.7	29.4	13.4	249	5	6	<.1	<.1	<.1	<.1
Kenedy	130	73	23	8	6	5	7	0	8	56.2	17.7	6.2	241	92	79	<.1	<.1	<.1	<.1
Kent	521	334	73	18	56	15	12	4	9	64.1	14.0	3.5	190	180	224	<.1	<.1	<.1	<.1
Kerr	1,441	878	339	150	11	16	26	9	12	60.9	23.5	10.4	217	13	15	<.1	<.1	0.1	0.1
Kimble	537	361	73	40	11	13	8	10	21	67.2	13.6	7.4	144	191	47	<.1	<.1	<.1	<.1
King	131	96	16	3	3	1	8	1	3	73.3	12.2	2.3	52	222	252	<.1	<.1	<.1	<.1
Kinney	752	474	119	63	15	23	10	19	29	63.0	15.8	8.4	202	140	31	<.1	<.1	<.1	<.1
Kleberg	5,008	3,104	936	276	162	74	214	54	188	62.0	18.7	5.5	212	70	113	0.3	0.3	0.3	0.2
Knox	1,128	867	145	32	31	22	11	5	15	76.9	12.9	2.8	24	210	246	<.1	<.1	<.1	<.1
Lamar	7,676	5,282	1,201	367	507	75	101	42	101	68.8	15.6	4.8	117	143	160	0.5	0.5	0.4	0.3
Lamb	2,657	1,748	405	98	256	45	33	18	54	65.8	15.2	3.7	166	154	217	0.2	0.2	0.1	<.1

County	Total	Clinton	Tsongas	Brown	Woods	Kerrey	Harkin	LaRouche	Other	Clinton	Tsongas	Brown	Clinton	Tsongas	Brown	Total	Clinton	Tsongas	Brown
														Rank					
										Percent of total vote						Percent contribution to state vote			
Lampasas	1,743	1,180	292	128	31	27	35	21	29	67.7	16.8	7.3	139	121	48	0.1	0.1	0.1	0.1
La Salle	1,654	1,244	186	54	25	24	30	36	55	75.2	11.2	3.3	37	230	233	0.1	0.1	<.1	<.1
Lavaca	3,883	2,681	680	214	70	65	65	40	68	69.0	17.5	5.5	115	100	114	0.3	0.3	0.2	0.2
Lee	2,919	2,076	393	222	67	34	44	24	59	71.1	13.5	7.6	82	197	39	0.2	0.2	0.1	0.2
Leon	2,622	2,093	286	90	35	36	25	21	36	79.8	10.9	3.4	5	235	227	0.2	0.2	0.1	<.1
Liberty	7,314	5,375	1,103	364	100	91	61	73	147	73.5	15.1	5.0	48	157	145	0.5	0.6	0.4	0.3
Limestone	3,119	2,385	369	158	62	32	41	31	41	76.5	11.8	5.1	27	227	138	0.2	0.2	0.1	0.1
Lipscomb	446	316	62	26	23	7	5	4	3	70.9	13.9	5.8	86	182	95	<.1	<.1	<.1	<.1
Live Oak	1,439	895	293	87	93	9	17	16	29	62.2	20.4	6.0	209	47	83	<.1	<.1	0.1	<.1
Llano	2,971	2,101	506	210	42	40	41	13	18	70.7	17.0	7.1	92	111	56	0.2	0.2	0.2	0.2
Loving	73	32	22	3	10	1	1	1	3	43.8	30.1	4.1	254	2	199	<.1	<.1	<.1	<.1
Lubbock	10,114	6,164	2,076	888	597	151	95	50	93	60.9	20.5	8.8	216	43	28	0.7	0.6	0.7	0.7
Lynn	1,541	1,027	208	39	147	27	23	27	43	66.6	13.5	2.5	150	194	250	0.1	0.1	<.1	<.1
McCulloch	2,155	1,464	347	120	69	47	42	19	47	67.9	16.1	5.6	135	136	110	0.1	0.1	0.2	0.1
McLennan	19,934	13,705	3,832	1,228	208	383	284	120	174	68.8	19.2	6.2	119	63	78	1.3	1.4	1.3	1.0
McMullen	307	163	67	23	12	12	15	7	8	53.1	21.8	7.5	247	30	45	<.1	<.1	<.1	<.1
Madison	1,940	1,511	227	81	18	21	30	16	36	77.9	11.7	4.2	11	229	192	0.1	0.2	<.1	<.1
Marion	2,446	1,935	236	93	93	16	21	18	34	79.1	9.6	3.8	8	249	210	0.2	0.2	<.1	<.1
Martin	1,038	671	175	50	50	14	32	8	38	64.6	16.9	4.8	182	118	158	<.1	<.1	<.1	<.1
Mason	597	402	132	32	10	6	7	7	1	67.3	22.1	5.4	142	23	115	<.1	<.1	<.1	<.1
Matagorda	7,550	4,913	1,563	402	76	167	131	100	198	65.1	20.7	5.3	176	41	117	0.5	0.5	0.5	0.3
Maverick	3,731	2,340	647	178	114	121	103	52	176	62.7	17.3	4.8	205	102	161	0.3	0.2	0.2	0.1
Medina	3,426	2,055	793	261	91	61	46	56	63	60.0	23.1	7.6	221	14	38	0.2	0.2	0.3	0.2
Menard	695	465	101	24	42	9	12	14	28	66.9	14.5	3.5	148	164	225	<.1	<.1	<.1	<.1
Midland	2,815	1,779	576	294	49	42	23	17	35	63.2	20.5	10.4	199	46	14	0.2	0.2	0.2	0.2
Milam	4,256	3,077	672	247	71	51	43	34	61	72.3	15.8	5.8	64	141	99	0.3	0.3	0.2	0.2
Mills	1,362	960	213	78	44	19	21	13	14	70.5	15.6	5.7	95	144	104	<.1	<.1	<.1	<.1
Mitchell	1,992	1,397	326	73	70	29	34	31	32	70.1	16.4	3.7	101	130	218	0.1	0.1	0.1	<.1
Montague	3,578	2,515	513	176	232	38	30	27	47	70.3	14.3	4.9	100	171	149	0.2	0.3	0.2	0.1
Montgomery	7,790	5,427	1,394	692	45	61	81	45	45	69.7	17.9	8.9	105	86	27	0.5	0.6	0.5	0.6
Moore	1,453	937	260	73	57	35	43	11	37	64.5	17.9	5.0	184	87	144	<.1	<.1	<.1	<.1
Morris	3,721	2,991	342	93	133	27	49	36	50	80.4	9.2	2.5	4	252	251	0.3	0.3	0.1	<.1
Motley	473	304	66	21	35	7	15	5	20	64.3	14.0	4.4	186	181	182	<.1	<.1	<.1	<.1
Nacogdoches	6,128	4,339	1,053	358	90	70	73	75	70	70.8	17.2	5.8	87	108	93	0.4	0.4	0.4	0.3
Navarro	5,132	3,738	838	265	115	49	51	33	43	72.8	16.3	5.2	60	131	130	0.3	0.4	0.3	0.2
Newton	2,456	1,907	260	101	88	21	30	16	33	77.6	10.6	4.1	14	240	198	0.2	0.2	<.1	<.1
Nolan	3,692	2,399	721	181	68	118	75	38	92	65.0	19.5	4.9	177	61	151	0.2	0.2	0.3	0.2
Nueces	35,107	20,812	7,119	4,080	813	461	458	254	1,110	59.3	20.3	11.6	227	48	11	2.4	2.1	2.5	3.4
Ochiltree	1,019	635	203	50	53	22	13	19	24	62.3	19.9	4.9	208	51	150	<.1	<.1	<.1	<.1
Oldham	603	350	118	32	48	9	11	11	24	58.0	19.6	5.3	232	60	119	<.1	<.1	<.1	<.1
Orange	14,119	10,129	2,173	847	263	163	263	104	177	71.7	15.4	6.0	72	150	84	1.0	1.0	0.8	0.7
Palo Pinto	3,721	2,520	660	236	114	27	73	37	54	67.7	17.7	6.3	138	91	70	0.3	0.3	0.2	0.2
Panola	4,982	3,866	486	153	277	43	63	30	64	77.6	9.8	3.1	17	246	241	0.3	0.4	0.2	0.1
Parker	7,674	5,219	1,375	581	177	87	104	61	70	68.0	17.9	7.6	132	84	40	0.5	0.5	0.5	0.5
Parmer	953	627	209	30	36	15	11	11	14	65.8	21.9	3.1	164	28	239	<.1	<.1	<.1	<.1
Pecos	2,152	1,208	489	93	145	47	80	27	63	56.1	22.7	4.3	242	18	186	0.1	0.1	0.2	<.1
Polk	6,215	4,536	978	280	73	71	88	74	115	73.0	15.7	4.5	57	142	179	0.4	0.5	0.3	0.2
Potter	5,739	3,881	989	398	240	71	61	34	65	67.6	17.2	6.9	141	105	59	0.4	0.4	0.3	0.3
Presidio	1,152	726	186	87	43	30	22	18	40	63.0	16.1	7.6	203	135	42	<.1	<.1	<.1	<.1
Rains	1,483	1,120	215	67	33	14	0	12	22	75.5	14.5	4.5	33	166	177	0.1	0.1	<.1	<.1
Randall	4,412	2,854	916	363	116	58	56	20	29	64.7	20.8	8.2	181	38	33	0.3	0.3	0.3	0.3
Reagan	673	442	93	42	33	13	8	4	38	65.7	13.8	6.2	168	187	74	<.1	<.1	<.1	<.1
Real	536	338	106	41	8	8	9	14	12	63.1	19.8	7.6	200	53	36	<.1	<.1	<.1	<.1
Red River	3,656	2,838	454	103	129	44	38	14	36	77.6	12.4	2.8	15	220	247	0.2	0.3	0.2	<.1
Reeves	3,094	1,819	535	188	133	95	86	53	185	58.8	17.3	6.1	230	103	82	0.2	0.2	0.2	0.2
Refugio	1,256	823	209	95	62	17	18	16	16	65.5	16.6	7.6	173	123	41	<.1	<.1	<.1	<.1
Roberts	379	258	54	20	24	3	4	4	12	68.1	14.2	5.3	130	172	125	<.1	<.1	<.1	<.1
Robertson	2,475	2,023	277	66	28	17	20	18	26	81.7	11.2	2.7	3	233	249	0.2	0.2	<.1	<.1
Rockwall	1,645	1,015	375	152	30	37	18	8	10	61.7	22.8	9.2	214	17	25	0.1	0.1	0.1	0.1
Runnels	2,584	1,732	437	117	92	41	68	38	59	67.0	16.9	4.5	147	117	176	0.2	0.2	0.2	<.1
Rusk	6,334	4,375	849	262	315	145	151	65	172	69.1	13.4	4.1	114	198	197	0.4	0.5	0.3	0.2
Sabine	3,676	2,878	359	109	124	62	52	24	68	78.3	9.8	3.0	9	245	242	0.2	0.3	0.1	<.1
San Augustine	2,888	2,168	281	124	90	49	34	44	98	75.1	9.7	4.3	38	247	188	0.2	0.2	<.1	0.1
San Jacinto	3,404	2,564	443	166	45	33	33	52	68	75.3	13.0	4.9	35	203	153	0.2	0.3	0.2	0.1
San Patricio	6,731	3,996	1,035	356	666	90	150	91	347	59.4	15.4	5.3	226	151	122	0.5	0.4	0.4	0.3
San Saba	1,469	1,034	241	74	41	14	11	32	22	70.4	16.4	5.0	98	127	141	<.1	0.1	<.1	<.1
Schleicher	743	487	107	38	44	14	24	12	17	65.5	14.4	5.1	172	168	133	<.1	<.1	<.1	<.1
Scurry	1,988	1,320	361	105	59	45	38	19	41	66.4	18.2	5.3	155	81	123	0.1	0.1	0.1	<.1
Shackelford	1,035	735	170	29	21	23	21	12	24	71.0	16.4	2.8	85	126	248	<.1	<.1	<.1	<.1
Shelby	6,516	5,024	582	211	301	77	63	64	194	77.1	8.9	3.2	22	253	234	0.4	0.5	0.2	0.2

Table I. — Vote for Presidential Preference: March 10, 1992, Democratic Primary Election (cont)

| County | Top candidates | | | | | | | | | Top three candidates (state vote) | | | | | | | | | |
| | | | | | | | | | | Percent of total vote | | | Rank | | | Percent contribution to state vote | | | |
	Total	Clinton	Tsongas	Brown	Woods	Kerrey	Harkin	LaRouche	Other	Clinton	Tsongas	Brown	Clinton	Tsongas	Brown	Total	Clinton	Tsongas	Brown
Sherman	372	231	71	22	15	10	15	3	5	62.1	19.1	5.9	210	66	90	<.1	<.1	<.1	<.1
Smith	8,219	6,370	1,037	409	117	58	75	47	106	77.5	12.6	5.0	18	216	146	0.6	0.7	0.4	0.3
Somervell	1,362	906	244	95	39	21	22	17	18	66.5	17.9	7.0	151	85	58	<.1	<.1	<.1	<.1
Starr	4,483	3,209	623	167	68	79	133	83	121	71.6	13.9	3.7	75	184	215	0.3	0.3	0.2	0.1
Stephens	2,310	1,517	412	154	57	39	69	19	43	65.7	17.8	6.7	169	89	62	0.2	0.2	0.1	0.1
Sterling	197	134	35	3	12	3	2	5	3	68.0	17.8	1.5	131	90	253	<.1	<.1	<.1	<.1
Stonewall	743	574	87	30	17	7	11	4	13	77.3	11.7	4.0	20	228	201	<.1	<.1	<.1	<.1
Sutton	554	368	101	27	12	13	10	2	21	66.4	18.2	4.9	152	77	154	<.1	<.1	<.1	<.1
Swisher	1,473	1,083	219	55	46	12	14	21	23	73.5	14.9	3.7	47	160	214	<.1	0.1	<.1	<.1
Tarrant	67,710	43,466	14,952	6,665	846	509	604	333	335	64.2	22.1	9.8	187	25	18	4.6	4.5	5.2	5.6
Taylor	10,320	6,789	2,248	547	170	213	156	88	109	65.8	21.8	5.3	167	31	121	0.7	0.7	0.8	0.5
Terrell	412	258	88	26	5	9	14	7	5	62.6	21.4	6.3	207	34	71	<.1	<.1	<.1	<.1
Terry	2,276	1,476	340	77	212	57	40	22	52	64.9	14.9	3.4	179	159	230	0.2	0.2	0.1	<.1
Throckmorton	767	524	91	29	64	25	11	5	18	68.3	11.9	3.8	125	225	212	<.1	<.1	<.1	<.1
Titus	5,189	4,041	664	164	153	39	52	36	40	77.9	12.8	3.2	12	211	238	0.3	0.4	0.2	0.1
Tom Green	10,881	7,019	2,227	795	253	134	183	92	178	64.5	20.5	7.3	183	45	51	0.7	0.7	0.8	0.7
Travis	70,784	33,959	17,800	15,947	494	1,035	989	180	380	48.0	25.1	22.5	252	11	1	4.8	3.5	6.2	13.4
Trinity	3,360	2,582	333	151	59	62	45	57	71	76.8	9.9	4.5	25	244	180	0.2	0.3	0.1	0.1
Tyler	4,046	3,000	508	205	97	71	67	36	62	74.1	12.6	5.1	45	217	137	0.3	0.3	0.2	0.2
Upshur	4,986	3,963	468	208	121	38	56	47	85	79.5	9.4	4.2	6	250	193	0.3	0.4	0.2	0.2
Upton	1,178	717	208	55	69	36	36	19	38	60.9	17.7	4.7	218	95	167	<.1	<.1	<.1	<.1
Uvalde	4,660	2,657	1,044	321	105	141	97	112	183	57.0	22.4	6.9	237	20	60	0.3	0.3	0.4	0.3
Val Verde	3,265	1,851	805	318	48	71	47	41	84	56.7	24.7	9.7	238	12	21	0.2	0.2	0.3	0.3
Van Zandt	6,757	5,052	978	307	187	51	60	51	71	74.8	14.5	4.5	41	167	175	0.5	0.5	0.3	0.3
Victoria	5,414	3,413	1,087	466	39	108	96	64	141	63.0	20.1	8.6	201	49	30	0.4	0.4	0.4	0.4
Walker	3,926	2,714	694	244	89	61	49	27	48	69.1	17.7	6.2	112	93	76	0.3	0.3	0.2	0.2
Waller	3,649	2,636	519	210	81	60	45	39	59	72.2	14.2	5.8	65	173	102	0.2	0.3	0.2	0.2
Ward	2,602	1,569	448	127	158	77	75	49	99	60.3	17.2	4.9	220	106	152	0.2	0.2	0.2	0.1
Washington	3,385	2,329	617	219	25	33	42	46	74	68.8	18.2	6.5	118	78	65	0.2	0.2	0.2	0.2
Webb	15,214	10,414	2,273	981	401	325	205	163	452	68.5	14.9	6.4	123	158	67	1.0	1.1	0.8	0.8
Wharton	6,533	4,426	1,218	387	47	131	103	95	126	67.7	18.6	5.9	136	71	89	0.4	0.5	0.4	0.3
Wheeler	1,659	1,174	229	72	83	31	33	16	21	70.8	13.8	4.3	89	188	185	0.1	0.1	<.1	<.1
Wichita	10,924	7,563	1,850	627	514	168	76	45	81	69.2	16.9	5.7	110	116	103	0.7	0.8	0.6	0.5
Wilbarger	2,660	1,750	452	134	124	68	49	26	57	65.8	17.0	5.0	165	113	140	0.2	0.2	0.2	0.1
Willacy	3,280	2,351	439	119	97	72	49	50	103	71.7	13.4	3.6	74	199	219	0.2	0.2	0.2	0.1
Williamson	11,074	6,486	2,463	1,653	80	157	137	40	58	58.6	22.2	14.9	231	22	3	0.7	0.7	0.9	1.4
Wilson	3,993	2,530	782	234	103	81	91	75	97	63.4	19.6	5.9	196	59	92	0.3	0.3	0.3	0.2
Winkler	1,392	803	256	105	60	77	28	14	49	57.7	18.4	7.5	234	74	43	<.1	<.1	<.1	<.1
Wise	5,552	3,774	1,026	379	123	62	56	45	87	68.0	18.5	6.8	134	73	61	0.4	0.4	0.4	0.3
Wood	4,444	3,404	574	219	93	51	42	27	34	76.6	12.9	4.9	26	208	148	0.3	0.4	0.2	0.2
Yoakum	891	544	162	39	96	20	11	7	12	61.1	18.2	4.4	215	80	183	<.1	<.1	<.1	<.1
Young	4,168	2,754	733	162	246	100	54	44	75	66.1	17.6	3.9	161	98	207	0.3	0.3	0.3	0.1
Zapata	1,811	1,357	189	62	57	24	29	14	79	74.9	10.4	3.4	40	241	228	0.1	0.1	<.1	<.1
Zavala	2,317	1,771	248	78	49	33	36	25	77	76.4	10.7	3.4	28	236	231	0.2	0.2	<.1	<.1
TEXAS	1,482,975	972,151	285,191	118,923	30,092	20,298	19,617	12,220	24,483	65.6	19.2	8.0				100.0	100.0	100.0	100.0

Table J. — Vote for Presidential Preference: March 10, 1992, Republican Primary Election

County	Total	Bush	Bu-chanan	Uncom-mitted	Other	Bush	Bu-chanan	Uncom-mitted	Other	Rank Bush	Rank Bu-chanan	Rank Uncom-mitted	Rank Other	Total	Bush	Bu-chanan	Uncom-mitted	Other
Anderson	639	430	159	15	35	67.3	24.9	2.3	5.5	168	90	113	24	<.1	<.1	<.1	<.1	0.2
Andrews	250	170	65	10	5	68.0	26.0	4.0	2.0	156	76	46	161	<.1	<.1	<.1	<.1	<.1
Angelina	1,755	1,161	419	35	140	66.2	23.9	2.0	8.0	179	113	133	5	0.2	0.2	0.2	0.1	0.6
Aransas	2,022	1,327	482	164	49	65.6	23.8	8.1	2.4	181	114	3	133	0.3	0.2	0.3	0.6	0.2
Archer	126	75	44	4	3	59.5	34.9	3.2	2.4	220	13	70	136	<.1	<.1	<.1	<.1	<.1
Armstrong	70	37	32	0	1	52.9	45.7	0.0	1.4	229	3	208	189	<.1	<.1	<.1	0.0	<.1
Atascosa	543	393	124	12	14	72.4	22.8	2.2	2.6	83	131	120	121	<.1	<.1	<.1	<.1	<.1
Austin	779	546	185	12	36	70.1	23.7	1.5	4.6	122	119	151	40	<.1	<.1	<.1	<.1	0.2
Bailey	146	97	45	2	2	66.4	30.8	1.4	1.4	178	32	164	191	<.1	<.1	<.1	<.1	<.1
Bandera	1,939	1,262	453	150	74	65.1	23.4	7.7	3.8	186	124	5	60	0.2	0.2	0.2	0.5	0.3
Bastrop	868	564	264	23	17	65.0	30.4	2.6	2.0	188	35	99	164	0.1	0.1	0.1	<.1	<.1
Baylor	30	27	3	0	0	90.0	10.0	0.0	0.0	3	226	209	204	<.1	<.1	<.1	0.0	0.0
Bee	907	701	168	26	12	77.3	18.5	2.9	1.3	28	192	82	193	0.1	0.1	<.1	<.1	<.1
Bell	6,341	4,376	1,529	263	173	69.0	24.1	4.1	2.7	139	109	42	113	0.8	0.8	0.8	0.9	0.8
Bexar	56,333	40,671	12,720	1,800	1,142	72.2	22.6	3.2	2.0	87	134	69	159	7.1	7.3	6.7	6.4	5.1
Blanco	361	259	89	7	6	71.7	24.7	1.9	1.7	98	96	137	180	<.1	<.1	<.1	<.1	<.1
Borden	13	5	8	0	0	38.5	61.5	0.0	0.0	230	2	210	228	<.1	<.1	<.1	0.0	0.0
Bosque	442	346	71	12	13	78.3	16.1	2.7	2.9	24	209	93	99	<.1	<.1	<.1	<.1	<.1
Bowie	1,284	925	262	33	64	72.0	20.4	2.6	5.0	94	171	105	31	0.2	0.2	0.1	0.1	0.3
Brazoria	8,661	6,060	1,930	267	404	70.0	22.3	3.1	4.7	124	139	74	39	1.1	1.1	1.0	1.0	1.8
Brazos	7,206	5,223	1,560	249	174	72.5	21.6	3.5	2.4	82	147	59	134	0.9	0.9	0.8	0.9	0.8
Brewster	325	198	104	13	10	60.9	32.0	4.0	3.1	215	26	47	95	<.1	<.1	<.1	<.1	<.1
Briscoe	21	18	2	1	0	85.7	9.5	4.8	0.0	6	227	23	229	<.1	<.1	<.1	<.1	0.0
Brooks	0	0	0	0	0	0.0	0.0	0.0	0.0	232	228	185	204	0.0	0.0	0.0	0.0	0.0
Brown	697	506	176	0	15	72.6	25.3	0.0	2.2	80	82	211	152	<.1	<.1	<.1	0.0	<.1
Burleson	100	73	21	0	6	73.0	21.0	0.0	6.0	76	162	212	16	<.1	<.1	<.1	0.0	<.1
Burnet	1,116	848	228	18	22	76.0	20.4	1.6	2.0	39	170	149	163	0.1	0.2	0.1	<.1	<.1
Caldwell	501	327	151	11	12	65.3	30.1	2.2	2.4	184	36	123	135	<.1	<.1	<.1	<.1	<.1
Calhoun	392	287	75	6	24	73.2	19.1	1.5	6.1	74	188	152	15	<.1	<.1	<.1	<.1	0.1
Callahan	174	120	43	9	2	69.0	24.7	5.2	1.1	140	94	19	197	<.1	<.1	<.1	<.1	<.1
Cameron	4,150	2,546	1,434	79	91	61.3	34.6	1.9	2.2	211	15	140	149	0.5	0.5	0.8	0.3	0.4
Camp	0	0	0	0	0	0.0	0.0	0.0	0.0	233	229	186	205	0.0	0.0	0.0	0.0	0.0
Carson	394	268	106	10	10	68.0	26.9	2.5	2.5	155	65	108	124	<.1	<.1	<.1	<.1	<.1
Cass	448	345	70	7	26	77.0	15.6	1.6	5.8	31	211	150	19	<.1	<.1	<.1	<.1	0.1
Castro	182	123	51	4	4	67.6	28.0	2.2	2.2	162	55	122	147	<.1	<.1	<.1	<.1	<.1
Chambers	276	185	69	3	19	67.0	25.0	1.1	6.9	172	86	172	10	<.1	<.1	<.1	<.1	<.1
Cherokee	596	454	126	0	16	76.2	21.1	0.0	2.7	37	155	213	114	<.1	<.1	<.1	0.0	<.1
Childress	97	80	16	1	0	82.5	16.5	1.0	0.0	12	207	175	230	<.1	<.1	<.1	<.1	0.0
Clay	90	71	15	0	4	78.9	16.7	0.0	4.4	20	205	214	46	<.1	<.1	<.1	0.0	<.1
Cochran	68	47	18	1	2	69.1	26.5	1.5	2.9	135	70	154	100	<.1	<.1	<.1	<.1	<.1
Coke	0	0	0	0	0	0.0	0.0	0.0	0.0	234	230	187	206	0.0	0.0	0.0	0.0	0.0
Coleman	152	110	32	4	6	72.4	21.1	2.6	3.9	84	157	101	57	<.1	<.1	<.1	<.1	<.1
Collin	25,489	17,084	6,432	1,413	560	67.0	25.2	5.5	2.2	173	83	13	148	3.2	3.1	3.4	5.1	2.5
Collingsworth	0	0	0	0	0	0.0	0.0	0.0	0.0	235	231	188	207	0.0	0.0	0.0	0.0	0.0
Colorado	353	268	57	10	18	75.9	16.1	2.8	5.1	41	208	85	27	<.1	<.1	<.1	<.1	<.1
Comal	6,557	4,611	1,562	294	90	70.3	23.8	4.5	1.4	118	117	31	190	0.8	0.8	0.8	1.1	0.4
Comanche	0	0	0	0	0	0.0	0.0	0.0	0.0	236	232	189	208	0.0	0.0	0.0	0.0	0.0
Concho	15	13	0	1	1	86.7	0.0	6.7	6.7	5	251	7	13	<.1	<.1	0.0	<.1	<.1
Cooke	615	464	132	0	19	75.4	21.5	0.0	3.1	44	152	215	93	<.1	<.1	<.1	0.0	<.1
Coryell	1,095	743	289	31	32	67.9	26.4	2.8	2.9	157	72	86	101	0.1	0.1	0.2	0.1	0.1
Cottle	0	0	0	0	0	0.0	0.0	0.0	0.0	237	233	190	209	0.0	0.0	0.0	0.0	0.0
Crane	28	9	19	0	0	32.1	67.9	0.0	0.0	231	1	216	231	<.1	<.1	<.1	0.0	0.0
Crockett	0	0	0	0	0	0.0	0.0	0.0	0.0	238	234	191	210	0.0	0.0	0.0	0.0	0.0
Crosby	101	70	27	3	1	69.3	26.7	3.0	1.0	132	66	80	199	<.1	<.1	<.1	<.1	<.1
Culberson	0	0	0	0	0	0.0	0.0	0.0	0.0	239	235	192	211	0.0	0.0	0.0	0.0	0.0
Dallam	267	164	90	12	1	61.4	33.7	4.5	0.4	209	18	30	203	<.1	<.1	<.1	<.1	<.1
Dallas	106,867	73,855	26,710	3,322	2,980	69.1	25.0	3.1	2.8	136	88	72	109	13.4	13.3	14.0	11.9	13.3
Dawson	223	183	31	5	4	82.1	13.9	2.2	1.8	13	220	115	174	<.1	<.1	<.1	<.1	<.1
Deaf Smith	449	302	135	6	6	67.3	30.1	1.3	1.3	169	40	166	192	<.1	<.1	<.1	<.1	<.1
Delta	47	36	8	1	2	76.6	17.0	2.1	4.3	33	203	127	54	<.1	<.1	<.1	<.1	<.1
Denton	17,615	10,821	5,402	943	449	61.4	30.7	5.4	2.5	208	34	16	123	2.2	1.9	2.8	3.4	2.0
DeWitt	524	395	90	24	15	75.4	17.2	4.6	2.9	45	202	27	107	<.1	<.1	<.1	<.1	<.1
Dickens	0	0	0	0	0	0.0	0.0	0.0	0.0	240	236	193	212	0.0	0.0	0.0	0.0	0.0
Dimmit	16	12	4	0	0	75.0	25.0	0.0	0.0	48	87	217	232	<.1	<.1	<.1	0.0	0.0
Donley	158	119	35	0	4	75.3	22.2	0.0	2.5	46	140	218	125	<.1	<.1	<.1	0.0	<.1
Duval	0	0	0	0	0	0.0	0.0	0.0	0.0	241	237	194	213	0.0	0.0	0.0	0.0	0.0
Eastland	410	252	143	5	10	61.5	34.9	1.2	2.4	207	14	169	132	<.1	<.1	<.1	<.1	<.1
Ector	10,111	6,980	2,312	614	205	69.0	22.9	6.1	2.0	138	130	10	160	1.3	1.3	1.2	2.2	0.9
Edwards	117	81	32	0	4	69.2	27.4	0.0	3.4	133	62	219	78	<.1	<.1	<.1	0.0	<.1
Ellis	4,517	3,041	1,183	126	167	67.3	26.2	2.8	3.7	166	73	88	63	0.6	0.5	0.6	0.5	0.7

Table J. — Vote for Presidential Preference: March 10, 1992, Republican Primary Election (cont)

County	Total	Bush	Bu-chanan	Uncom-mitted	Other	Bush	Bu-chanan	Uncom-mitted	Other	Bush	Bu-chanan	Uncom-mitted	Other	Total	Bush	Bu-chanan	Uncom-mitted	Other
El Paso	15,842	11,788	3,127	636	291	74.4	19.7	4.0	1.8	61	185	45	173	2.0	2.1	1.6	2.3	1.3
Erath	569	415	119	14	21	72.9	20.9	2.5	3.7	77	164	110	64	<.1	<.1	<.1	<.1	<.1
Falls	114	75	32	5	2	65.8	28.1	4.4	1.8	180	53	33	176	<.1	<.1	<.1	<.1	<.1
Fannin	262	164	84	6	8	62.6	32.1	2.3	3.1	203	25	114	96	<.1	<.1	<.1	<.1	<.1
Fayette	1,014	732	203	35	44	72.2	20.0	3.5	4.3	88	177	60	50	0.1	0.1	0.1	0.1	0.2
Fisher	12	7	5	0	0	58.3	41.7	0.0	0.0	222	4	220	233	<.1	<.1	<.1	0.0	0.0
Floyd	143	93	43	2	5	65.0	30.1	1.4	3.5	187	39	159	73	<.1	<.1	<.1	<.1	<.1
Foard	0	0	0	0	0	0.0	0.0	0.0	0.0	242	238	195	214	0.0	0.0	0.0	0.0	0.0
Fort Bend	13,181	9,533	2,791	415	442	72.3	21.2	3.1	3.4	85	154	71	81	1.7	1.7	1.5	1.5	2.0
Franklin	163	122	30	4	7	74.8	18.4	2.5	4.3	54	195	111	52	<.1	<.1	<.1	<.1	<.1
Freestone	348	256	76	5	11	73.6	21.8	1.4	3.2	69	145	157	88	<.1	<.1	<.1	<.1	<.1
Frio	29	16	12	1	0	55.2	41.4	3.4	0.0	226	6	61	234	<.1	<.1	<.1	<.1	0.0
Gaines	189	135	45	2	7	71.4	23.8	1.1	3.7	104	118	173	62	<.1	<.1	<.1	<.1	<.1
Galveston	6,936	4,832	1,491	145	468	69.7	21.5	2.1	6.7	127	151	130	12	0.9	0.9	0.8	0.5	2.1
Garza	36	23	12	0	1	63.9	33.3	0.0	2.8	197	20	221	110	<.1	<.1	<.1	0.0	<.1
Gillespie	3,283	2,350	733	131	69	71.6	22.3	4.0	2.1	103	138	48	154	0.4	0.4	0.4	0.5	0.3
Glasscock	131	75	50	4	2	57.3	38.2	3.1	1.5	224	10	76	184	<.1	<.1	<.1	<.1	<.1
Goliad	63	47	13	0	3	74.6	20.6	0.0	4.8	58	168	222	35	<.1	<.1	<.1	0.0	<.1
Gonzales	202	130	54	2	16	64.4	26.7	1.0	7.9	192	67	176	6	<.1	<.1	<.1	<.1	<.1
Gray	3,573	2,481	870	147	75	69.4	24.3	4.1	2.1	131	107	43	155	0.4	0.4	0.5	0.5	0.3
Grayson	2,552	1,797	608	68	79	70.4	23.8	2.7	3.1	116	116	97	92	0.3	0.3	0.3	0.2	0.4
Gregg	6,404	4,663	1,300	164	277	72.8	20.3	2.6	4.3	78	174	107	51	0.8	0.8	0.7	0.6	1.2
Grimes	470	357	79	13	21	76.0	16.8	2.8	4.5	40	204	92	45	<.1	<.1	<.1	<.1	<.1
Guadalupe	3,862	2,749	894	130	89	71.2	23.1	3.4	2.3	108	128	63	140	0.5	0.5	0.5	0.5	0.4
Hale	780	540	227	0	13	69.2	29.1	0.0	1.7	134	46	223	179	<.1	<.1	0.1	0.0	<.1
Hall	34	24	10	0	0	70.6	29.4	0.0	0.0	113	44	224	235	<.1	<.1	<.1	0.0	0.0
Hamilton	162	111	42	4	5	68.5	25.9	2.5	3.1	149	78	109	94	<.1	<.1	<.1	<.1	<.1
Hansford	660	465	156	36	3	70.5	23.6	5.5	0.5	115	121	15	202	<.1	<.1	<.1	0.1	<.1
Hardeman	31	20	7	2	2	64.5	22.6	6.5	6.5	191	133	9	14	<.1	<.1	<.1	<.1	<.1
Hardin	492	301	165	7	19	61.2	33.5	1.4	3.9	212	19	158	59	<.1	<.1	<.1	<.1	<.1
Harris	135,145	99,394	27,562	3,641	4,548	73.5	20.4	2.7	3.4	70	172	95	80	17.0	17.9	14.5	13.0	20.3
Harrison	1,362	1,008	272	22	60	74.0	20.0	1.6	4.4	64	181	148	47	0.2	0.2	0.1	<.1	0.3
Hartley	230	167	54	6	3	72.6	23.5	2.6	1.3	79	123	103	194	<.1	<.1	<.1	<.1	<.1
Haskell	0	0	0	0	0	0.0	0.0	0.0	0.0	243	239	196	215	0.0	0.0	0.0	0.0	0.0
Hays	2,898	1,961	753	112	72	67.7	26.0	3.9	2.5	160	77	52	128	0.4	0.4	0.4	0.4	0.3
Hemphill	417	258	124	23	12	61.9	29.7	5.5	2.9	205	41	14	105	<.1	<.1	<.1	<.1	<.1
Henderson	2,421	1,709	556	71	85	70.6	23.0	2.9	3.5	112	129	81	71	0.3	0.3	0.3	0.3	0.4
Hidalgo	3,549	2,424	1,027	26	72	68.3	28.9	0.7	2.0	152	47	180	157	0.4	0.4	0.5	<.1	0.3
Hill	557	410	111	10	26	73.6	19.9	1.8	4.7	67	182	143	38	<.1	<.1	<.1	<.1	0.1
Hockley	324	231	79	9	5	71.3	24.4	2.8	1.5	106	105	89	183	<.1	<.1	<.1	<.1	<.1
Hood	2,069	1,488	445	82	54	71.9	21.5	4.0	2.6	95	150	50	118	0.3	0.3	0.2	0.3	0.2
Hopkins	507	363	120	6	18	71.6	23.7	1.2	3.6	102	120	170	69	<.1	<.1	<.1	<.1	<.1
Houston	358	246	89	7	16	68.7	24.9	2.0	4.5	147	91	136	44	<.1	<.1	<.1	<.1	<.1
Howard	650	444	192	9	5	68.3	29.5	1.4	0.8	151	42	160	200	<.1	<.1	0.1	<.1	<.1
Hudspeth	4	3	0	1	0	75.0	0.0	25.0	0.0	49	252	1	236	<.1	<.1	0.0	<.1	0.0
Hunt	3,046	2,153	733	68	92	70.7	24.1	2.2	3.0	111	110	117	97	0.4	0.4	0.4	0.2	0.4
Hutchinson	3,393	2,339	829	142	83	68.9	24.4	4.2	2.4	142	102	41	131	0.4	0.4	0.4	0.5	0.4
Irion	25	20	5	0	0	80.0	20.0	0.0	0.0	17	178	225	237	<.1	<.1	<.1	0.0	0.0
Jack	69	46	14	7	2	66.7	20.3	10.1	2.9	176	175	2	104	<.1	<.1	<.1	<.1	<.1
Jackson	171	128	36	1	6	74.9	21.1	0.6	3.5	53	158	182	72	<.1	<.1	<.1	<.1	<.1
Jasper	345	264	69	5	7	76.5	20.0	1.4	2.0	34	179	155	158	<.1	<.1	<.1	<.1	<.1
Jeff Davis	0	0	0	0	0	0.0	0.0	0.0	0.0	244	240	197	216	0.0	0.0	0.0	0.0	0.0
Jefferson	6,306	4,338	1,674	80	214	68.8	26.5	1.3	3.4	145	69	168	79	0.8	0.8	0.9	0.3	1.0
Jim Hogg	32	27	5	0	0	84.4	15.6	0.0	0.0	9	212	226	238	<.1	<.1	<.1	0.0	0.0
Jim Wells	283	212	56	6	9	74.9	19.8	2.1	3.2	51	184	128	87	<.1	<.1	<.1	<.1	<.1
Johnson	3,690	2,367	1,078	110	135	64.1	29.2	3.0	3.7	196	45	79	67	0.5	0.4	0.6	0.4	0.6
Jones	310	195	82	11	22	62.9	26.5	3.5	7.1	201	71	57	7	<.1	<.1	<.1	<.1	<.1
Karnes	0	0	0	0	0	0.0	0.0	0.0	0.0	245	241	198	217	0.0	0.0	0.0	0.0	0.0
Kaufman	1,676	1,055	505	23	93	62.9	30.1	1.4	5.5	200	37	162	23	0.2	0.2	0.3	<.1	0.4
Kendall	2,997	2,108	630	182	77	70.3	21.0	6.1	2.6	117	161	11	122	0.4	0.4	0.3	0.7	0.3
Kenedy	4	4	0	0	0	100.0	0.0	0.0	0.0	1	253	227	239	<.1	<.1	0.0	0.0	0.0
Kent	2	2	0	0	0	100.0	0.0	0.0	0.0	2	254	228	240	<.1	<.1	0.0	0.0	0.0
Kerr	6,703	4,477	1,604	478	144	66.8	23.9	7.1	2.1	175	111	6	153	0.8	0.8	0.8	1.7	0.6
Kimble	134	96	32	0	6	71.6	23.9	0.0	4.5	101	112	229	43	<.1	<.1	<.1	0.0	<.1
King	0	0	0	0	0	0.0	0.0	0.0	0.0	246	242	199	218	0.0	0.0	0.0	0.0	0.0
Kinney	93	61	28	4	0	65.6	30.1	4.3	0.0	183	38	36	241	<.1	<.1	<.1	<.1	0.0
Kleberg	489	374	99	8	8	76.5	20.2	1.6	1.6	35	176	147	181	<.1	<.1	<.1	<.1	<.1
Knox	45	33	11	0	1	73.3	24.4	0.0	2.2	72	99	230	144	<.1	<.1	<.1	0.0	<.1
Lamar	684	509	144	15	16	74.4	21.1	2.2	2.3	60	159	124	138	<.1	<.1	<.1	<.1	<.1
Lamb	106	82	22	0	2	77.4	20.8	0.0	1.9	27	166	231	169	<.1	<.1	<.1	0.0	<.1

Table J. — Vote for Presidential Preference: March 10, 1992, Republican Primary Election (cont)

County	Top candidates					Top four candidates (state vote)											
						Percent of total vote				Rank				Percent contribution to state vote			
	Total	Bush	Bu-chanan	Uncom-mitted	Other	Bush	Bu-chanan	Uncom-mitted	Other	Bush	Bu-chanan	Uncom-mitted	Other	Total	Bush	Bu-chanan	Uncom-mitted	Other
Lampasas	406	280	99	17	10	69.0	24.4	4.2	2.5	141	104	40	130	<.1	<.1	<.1	<.1	<.1
La Salle	0	0	0	0	0	0.0	0.0	0.0	0.0	247	243	200	219	0.0	0.0	0.0	0.0	0.0
Lavaca	389	275	87	10	17	70.7	22.4	2.6	4.4	110	136	104	49	<.1	<.1	<.1	<.1	<.1
Lee	234	187	33	0	14	79.9	14.1	0.0	6.0	18	219	232	18	<.1	<.1	<.1	0.0	<.1
Leon	377	305	51	0	21	80.9	13.5	0.0	5.6	14	221	233	22	<.1	<.1	<.1	0.0	<.1
Liberty	1,003	691	234	21	57	68.9	23.3	2.1	5.7	143	125	129	21	0.1	0.1	0.1	<.1	0.3
Limestone	361	273	65	16	7	75.6	18.0	4.4	1.9	43	197	32	165	<.1	<.1	<.1	<.1	<.1
Lipscomb	359	233	98	19	9	64.9	27.3	5.3	2.5	189	63	18	126	<.1	<.1	<.1	<.1	<.1
Live Oak	159	107	44	3	5	67.3	27.7	1.9	3.1	167	57	141	90	<.1	<.1	<.1	<.1	<.1
Llano	1,705	1,296	304	68	37	76.0	17.8	4.0	2.2	38	198	49	151	0.2	0.2	0.2	0.2	0.2
Loving	0	0	0	0	0	0.0	0.0	0.0	0.0	248	244	201	220	0.0	0.0	0.0	0.0	0.0
Lubbock	20,480	14,867	4,432	758	423	72.6	21.6	3.7	2.1	81	148	56	156	2.6	2.7	2.3	2.7	1.9
Lynn	39	26	13	0	0	66.7	33.3	0.0	0.0	177	21	234	242	<.1	<.1	<.1	0.0	0.0
McCulloch	70	54	11	3	2	77.1	15.7	4.3	2.9	29	210	37	108	<.1	<.1	<.1	<.1	<.1
McLennan	7,303	5,271	1,698	141	193	72.2	23.3	1.9	2.6	89	126	138	115	0.9	0.9	0.9	0.5	0.9
McMullen	0	0	0	0	0	0.0	0.0	0.0	0.0	249	245	202	221	0.0	0.0	0.0	0.0	0.0
Madison	217	161	38	10	8	74.2	17.5	4.6	3.7	62	200	26	65	<.1	<.1	<.1	<.1	<.1
Marion	61	44	9	1	7	72.1	14.8	1.6	11.5	91	217	146	3	<.1	<.1	<.1	<.1	<.1
Martin	60	32	25	0	3	53.3	41.7	0.0	5.0	227	5	235	28	<.1	<.1	<.1	0.0	<.1
Mason	188	127	59	1	1	67.6	31.4	0.5	0.5	163	29	183	201	<.1	<.1	<.1	<.1	<.1
Matagorda	438	312	83	18	25	71.2	18.9	4.1	5.7	107	189	44	20	<.1	<.1	<.1	<.1	0.1
Maverick	120	95	18	4	3	79.2	15.0	3.3	2.5	19	214	65	127	<.1	<.1	<.1	<.1	<.1
Medina	809	594	177	14	24	73.4	21.9	1.7	3.0	71	144	144	98	0.1	0.1	<.1	<.1	0.1
Menard	26	22	4	0	0	84.6	15.4	0.0	0.0	8	213	236	243	<.1	<.1	<.1	0.0	0.0
Midland	19,334	11,613	6,089	1,266	366	60.1	31.5	6.5	1.9	216	27	8	168	2.4	2.1	3.2	4.5	1.6
Milam	452	330	97	12	13	73.0	21.5	2.7	2.9	75	153	98	106	<.1	<.1	<.1	<.1	<.1
Mills	29	22	6	0	1	75.9	20.7	0.0	3.4	42	167	237	77	<.1	<.1	<.1	0.0	<.1
Mitchell	76	61	14	1	0	80.3	18.4	1.3	0.0	16	194	167	244	<.1	<.1	<.1	<.1	0.0
Montague	107	73	30	2	2	68.2	28.0	1.9	1.9	153	54	142	172	<.1	<.1	<.1	<.1	<.1
Montgomery	18,966	12,808	4,399	1,008	751	67.5	23.2	5.3	4.0	164	127	17	56	2.4	2.3	2.3	3.6	3.4
Moore	964	677	235	41	11	70.2	24.4	4.3	1.1	119	106	39	198	0.1	0.1	0.1	0.1	<.1
Morris	103	65	20	5	13	63.1	19.4	4.9	12.6	199	187	21	1	<.1	<.1	<.1	<.1	<.1
Motley	23	18	5	0	0	78.3	21.7	0.0	0.0	25	146	238	245	<.1	<.1	<.1	0.0	0.0
Nacogdoches	1,669	1,187	407	37	38	71.1	24.4	2.2	2.3	109	103	119	142	0.2	0.2	0.2	0.1	0.2
Navarro	1,265	830	366	27	42	65.6	28.9	2.1	3.3	182	48	126	84	0.2	0.1	0.2	<.1	0.2
Newton	156	98	43	4	11	62.8	27.6	2.6	7.1	202	59	106	8	<.1	<.1	<.1	<.1	<.1
Nolan	135	100	33	0	2	74.1	24.4	0.0	1.5	63	100	239	186	<.1	<.1	<.1	0.0	<.1
Nueces	9,297	6,495	2,341	282	179	69.9	25.2	3.0	1.9	125	85	77	166	1.2	1.2	1.2	1.0	0.8
Ochiltree	938	635	268	21	14	67.7	28.6	2.2	1.5	159	50	116	185	0.1	0.1	0.1	<.1	<.1
Oldham	0	0	0	0	0	0.0	0.0	0.0	0.0	250	246	203	222	0.0	0.0	0.0	0.0	0.0
Orange	992	620	326	11	35	62.5	32.9	1.1	3.5	204	24	171	70	0.1	0.1	0.2	<.1	0.2
Palo Pinto	500	343	124	15	18	68.6	24.8	3.0	3.6	148	93	78	68	<.1	<.1	<.1	<.1	<.1
Panola	114	68	43	0	3	59.6	37.7	0.0	2.6	219	11	240	117	<.1	<.1	<.1	0.0	<.1
Parker	3,166	2,033	916	111	106	64.2	28.9	3.5	3.3	194	49	58	82	0.4	0.4	0.5	0.4	0.5
Parmer	236	139	95	2	0	58.9	40.3	0.8	0.0	221	7	178	246	<.1	<.1	<.1	<.1	0.0
Pecos	163	120	36	5	2	73.6	22.1	3.1	1.2	66	142	75	195	<.1	<.1	<.1	<.1	<.1
Polk	900	649	180	25	46	72.1	20.0	2.8	5.1	93	180	90	26	0.1	0.1	<.1	<.1	0.2
Potter	5,835	3,969	1,483	288	95	68.0	25.4	4.9	1.6	154	81	20	182	0.7	0.7	0.8	1.0	0.4
Presidio	64	34	17	5	8	53.1	26.6	7.8	12.5	228	68	4	2	<.1	<.1	<.1	<.1	<.1
Rains	102	71	22	2	7	69.6	21.6	2.0	6.9	129	149	135	11	<.1	<.1	<.1	<.1	<.1
Randall	10,030	6,780	2,718	386	146	67.6	27.1	3.8	1.5	161	64	53	188	1.3	1.2	1.4	1.4	0.7
Reagan	61	47	12	0	2	77.0	19.7	0.0	3.3	30	186	241	85	<.1	<.1	<.1	0.0	<.1
Real	135	97	34	2	2	71.9	25.2	1.5	1.5	96	84	153	187	<.1	<.1	<.1	<.1	<.1
Red River	80	54	22	0	4	67.5	27.5	0.0	5.0	165	61	242	29	<.1	<.1	<.1	0.0	<.1
Reeves	0	0	0	0	0	0.0	0.0	0.0	0.0	251	247	204	223	0.0	0.0	0.0	0.0	0.0
Refugio	103	80	19	1	3	77.7	18.4	1.0	2.9	26	193	177	103	<.1	<.1	<.1	<.1	<.1
Roberts	38	24	13	1	0	63.2	34.2	2.6	0.0	198	16	102	247	<.1	<.1	<.1	<.1	0.0
Robertson	258	193	54	8	3	74.8	20.9	3.1	1.2	55	163	73	196	<.1	<.1	<.1	<.1	<.1
Rockwall	3,497	2,250	965	160	122	64.3	27.6	4.6	3.5	193	58	28	74	0.4	0.4	0.5	0.6	0.5
Runnels	95	71	20	1	3	74.7	21.1	1.1	3.2	57	160	174	89	<.1	<.1	<.1	<.1	<.1
Rusk	1,017	762	191	14	50	74.9	18.8	1.4	4.9	50	191	161	32	0.1	0.1	0.1	<.1	0.2
Sabine	70	55	9	3	3	78.6	12.9	4.3	4.3	21	223	38	53	<.1	<.1	<.1	<.1	<.1
San Augustine	34	24	7	0	3	70.6	20.6	0.0	8.8	114	169	243	4	<.1	<.1	<.1	0.0	<.1
San Jacinto	257	179	67	1	10	69.6	26.1	0.4	3.9	128	74	184	58	<.1	<.1	<.1	<.1	<.1
San Patricio	1,150	807	298	22	23	70.2	25.9	1.9	2.0	120	79	139	162	0.1	0.1	0.2	<.1	0.1
San Saba	42	29	13	0	0	69.0	31.0	0.0	0.0	137	31	244	248	<.1	<.1	<.1	0.0	0.0
Schleicher	61	44	15	0	2	72.1	24.6	0.0	3.3	92	97	245	86	<.1	<.1	<.1	0.0	<.1
Scurry	365	273	77	5	10	74.8	21.1	1.4	2.7	56	156	165	112	<.1	<.1	<.1	<.1	<.1
Shackelford	45	27	16	1	1	60.0	35.6	2.2	2.2	217	12	118	145	<.1	<.1	<.1	<.1	<.1
Shelby	75	62	10	0	3	82.7	13.3	0.0	4.0	11	222	246	55	<.1	<.1	<.1	0.0	<.1

Table J. — Vote for Presidential Preference: March 10, 1992, Republican Primary Election (cont)

County	Top candidates					Top four candidates (state vote)												
						Percent of total vote				Rank				Percent contribution to state vote				
	Total	Bush	Bu-chanan	Uncom-mitted	Other	Bush	Bu-chanan	Uncom-mitted	Other	Bush	Bu-chanan	Uncom-mitted	Other	Total	Bush	Bu-chanan	Uncom-mitted	Other
Sherman	169	113	53	0	3	66.9	31.4	0.0	1.8	174	30	247	175	<.1	<.1	<.1	0.0	<.1
Smith	14,325	9,803	3,534	462	526	68.4	24.7	3.2	3.7	150	95	66	66	1.8	1.8	1.9	1.7	2.4
Somervell	116	78	23	7	8	67.2	19.8	6.0	6.9	170	183	12	9	<.1	<.1	<.1	<.1	<.1
Starr	14	10	4	0	0	71.4	28.6	0.0	0.0	105	51	248	249	<.1	<.1	<.1	0.0	0.0
Stephens	64	57	7	0	0	89.1	10.9	0.0	0.0	4	225	249	250	<.1	<.1	<.1	0.0	0.0
Sterling	53	37	15	0	1	69.8	28.3	0.0	1.9	126	52	250	170	<.1	<.1	<.1	0.0	<.1
Stonewall	14	12	2	0	0	85.7	14.3	0.0	0.0	7	218	251	251	<.1	<.1	<.1	0.0	0.0
Sutton	96	66	25	2	3	68.8	26.0	2.1	3.1	146	75	131	91	<.1	<.1	<.1	<.1	<.1
Swisher	54	33	21	0	0	61.1	38.9	0.0	0.0	213	9	252	252	<.1	<.1	<.1	0.0	0.0
Tarrant	70,527	45,965	19,430	3,187	1,945	65.2	27.5	4.5	2.8	185	60	29	111	8.8	8.3	10.2	11.4	8.7
Taylor	9,191	6,738	1,922	359	172	73.3	20.9	3.9	1.9	73	165	51	171	1.2	1.2	1.0	1.3	0.8
Terrell	0	0	0	0	0	0.0	0.0	0.0	0.0	252	248	205	224	0.0	0.0	0.0	0.0	0.0
Terry	181	136	41	4	0	75.1	22.7	2.2	0.0	47	132	121	253	<.1	<.1	<.1	<.1	0.0
Throckmorton	0	0	0	0	0	0.0	0.0	0.0	0.0	253	249	206	225	0.0	0.0	0.0	0.0	0.0
Titus	210	169	31	0	10	80.5	14.8	0.0	4.8	15	216	253	36	<.1	<.1	<.1	0.0	<.1
Tom Green	4,833	3,360	1,181	181	111	69.5	24.4	3.7	2.3	130	101	55	141	0.6	0.6	0.6	0.6	0.5
Travis	32,371	23,237	7,713	854	567	71.8	23.8	2.6	1.8	97	115	100	177	4.1	4.2	4.0	3.1	2.5
Trinity	269	211	40	9	9	78.4	14.9	3.3	3.3	23	215	64	83	<.1	<.1	<.1	<.1	<.1
Tyler	155	112	38	1	4	72.3	24.5	0.6	2.6	86	98	181	120	<.1	<.1	<.1	<.1	<.1
Upshur	505	354	122	10	19	70.1	24.2	2.0	3.8	121	108	134	61	<.1	<.1	<.1	<.1	<.1
Upton	42	24	14	2	2	57.1	33.3	4.8	4.8	225	22	24	37	<.1	<.1	<.1	<.1	<.1
Uvalde	296	190	91	8	7	64.2	30.7	2.7	2.4	195	33	94	137	<.1	<.1	<.1	<.1	<.1
Val Verde	787	564	173	27	23	71.7	22.0	3.4	2.9	99	143	62	102	<.1	0.1	<.1	<.1	0.1
Van Zandt	1,123	762	280	30	51	67.9	24.9	2.7	4.5	158	89	96	42	0.1	0.1	0.1	0.1	0.2
Victoria	2,991	2,350	496	41	104	78.6	16.6	1.4	3.5	22	206	163	75	0.4	0.4	0.3	0.1	0.5
Walker	1,660	1,243	300	34	83	74.9	18.1	2.0	5.0	52	196	132	30	0.2	0.2	0.2	0.1	0.4
Waller	456	340	86	10	20	74.6	18.9	2.2	4.4	59	190	125	48	<.1	<.1	<.1	<.1	<.1
Ward	162	100	51	7	4	61.7	31.5	4.3	2.5	206	28	35	129	<.1	<.1	<.1	<.1	<.1
Washington	1,180	901	205	33	41	76.4	17.4	2.8	3.5	36	201	87	76	0.1	0.2	0.1	0.1	0.2
Webb	368	307	45	9	7	83.4	12.2	2.4	1.9	10	224	112	167	<.1	<.1	<.1	<.1	<.1
Wharton	650	500	115	5	30	76.9	17.7	0.8	4.6	32	199	179	41	<.1	<.1	<.1	<.1	0.1
Wheeler	176	118	49	5	4	67.0	27.8	2.8	2.3	171	56	84	143	<.1	<.1	<.1	<.1	<.1
Wichita	4,557	3,289	1,018	130	120	72.2	22.3	2.9	2.6	90	137	83	116	0.6	0.6	0.5	0.5	0.5
Wilbarger	187	134	38	6	9	71.7	20.3	3.2	4.8	100	173	68	34	<.1	<.1	<.1	<.1	<.1
Willacy	50	30	20	0	0	60.0	40.0	0.0	0.0	218	8	254	254	<.1	<.1	<.1	0.0	0.0
Williamson	9,152	6,298	2,347	294	213	68.8	25.6	3.2	2.3	144	80	67	139	1.1	1.1	1.2	1.1	1.0
Wilson	538	396	119	9	14	73.6	22.1	1.7	2.6	68	141	145	119	<.1	<.1	<.1	<.1	<.1
Winkler	124	71	41	6	6	57.3	33.1	4.8	4.8	223	23	22	33	<.1	<.1	<.1	<.1	<.1
Wise	686	421	202	26	37	61.4	29.4	3.8	5.4	210	43	54	25	<.1	<.1	0.1	<.1	0.2
Wood	1,650	1,069	410	72	99	64.8	24.8	4.4	6.0	190	92	34	17	0.2	0.2	0.2	0.3	0.4
Yoakum	138	102	31	2	3	73.9	22.5	1.4	2.2	65	135	156	150	<.1	<.1	<.1	<.1	<.1
Young	180	110	61	5	4	61.1	33.9	2.8	2.2	214	17	91	146	<.1	<.1	<.1	<.1	<.1
Zapata	344	241	81	16	6	70.1	23.5	4.7	1.7	123	122	25	178	<.1	<.1	<.1	<.1	<.1
Zavala	0	0	0	0	0	0.0	0.0	0.0	0.0	254	250	207	226	0.0	0.0	0.0	0.0	0.0
TEXAS	797,146	556,280	190,572	27,936	22,358	69.8	23.9	3.5	2.8					100.0	100.0	100.0	100.0	100.0

1992 Vote for President
Percent for Bush (R), by County

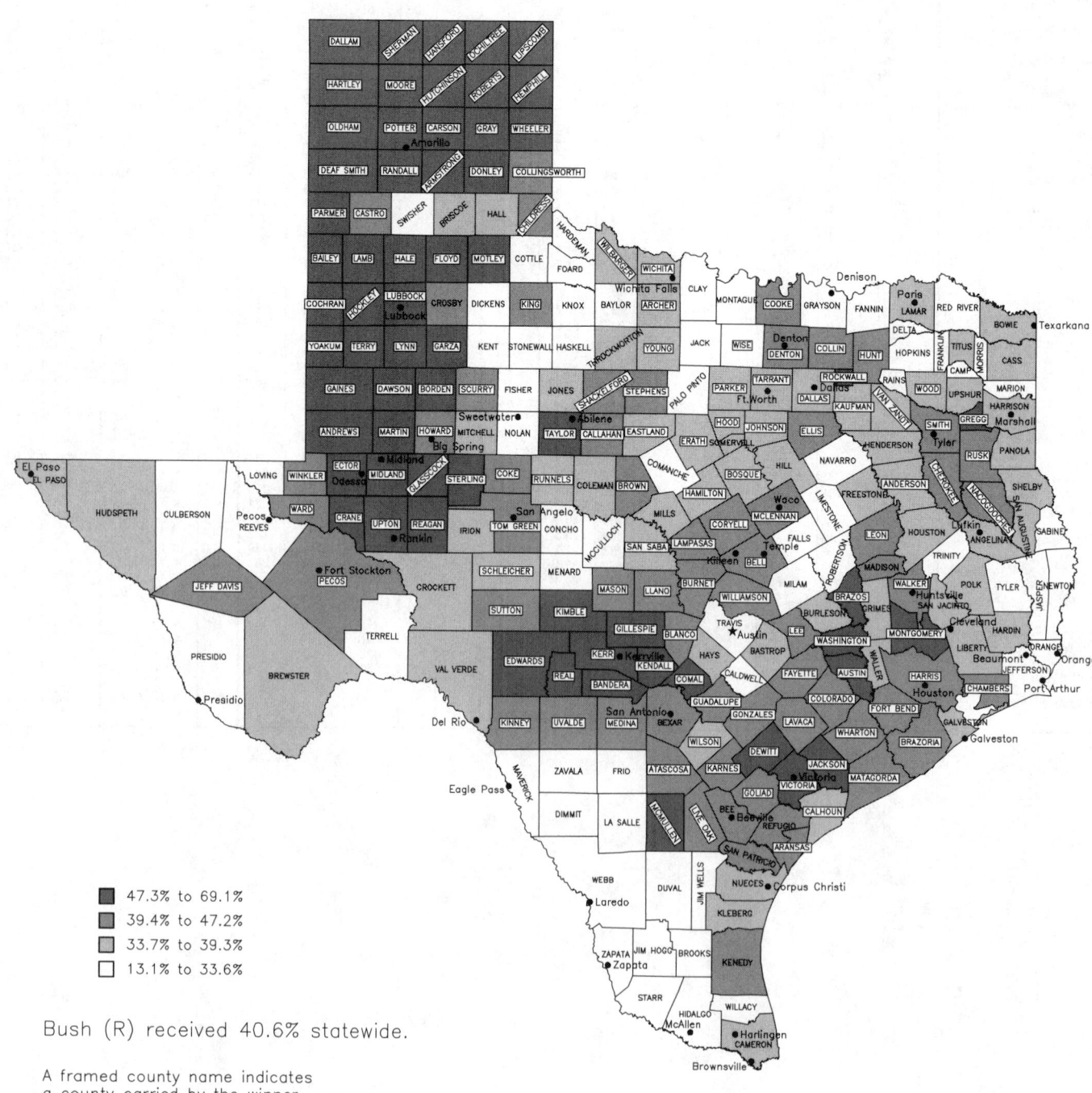

- ▓ 47.3% to 69.1%
- ▒ 39.4% to 47.2%
- ░ 33.7% to 39.3%
- ☐ 13.1% to 33.6%

Bush (R) received 40.6% statewide.

A framed county name indicates
a county carried by the winner.

910 Texas

UTAH

Congressional Districts 3
  Average Population 574,283
State Senate Districts 29
  Average Population 59,409
State House Districts 75
  Average Population 22,971

Electoral College Votes...5
Counties 29
Voting Precincts 1,661

Alternative Registration Methods:
....Mail-in

Registration Deadline (Days before Election) 5

Voting Equipment Use (Counties)

Datavote Punch Card	0	Paper Ballot	10
Electronic	0	Other Punch Card	19
Lever Machine	0	Mixed Systems	0
Optical Scanner	0		

Party Control	DEM	REP	IND	VAC
1993 State Senate	11	18	0	0
1992 State Senate	10	19	0	0
1993 State House	26	49	0	0
1992 State House	31	44	0	0

Population Statistics 1990

Race/ Ethnicity	Total Population		Voting Age Population		Voting Age Population % of total population
	Number	%	Number	%	
Non-Hispanic					
White	1,571,254	91.2	1,004,607	91.7	63.9
Black	10,868	0.6	7,060	0.6	65.0
Asian/Pacific Islander	32,490	1.9	21,132	1.9	65.0
Native American	22,748	1.3	12,654	1.2	55.6
Other	893	<.1	464	<.1	52.0
All Hispanic	84,597	4.9	49,489	4.5	58.5
TOTAL	1,722,850	100.0	1,095,406	100.0	63.6

Estimated Voting Age Population 1992 (VAP) 1,142,000
Number of Registered Voters................................... 965,211
  % of estimated VAP... 84.5
Voter Turnout (Actual) 784,988
  % of VAP 68.7
  % of Registration 81.3
Persons Not Voting—of Voting Age 357,012
  % of VAP 31.3
Persons Not Voting—of Registered 180,223
  % of Registration 18.7
Straight Ticket Voting ....Yes, Separate

State Officials and Members of Congress

Governor:
Mike Leavitt (R) 1992, elected to a four-year term in 1992.

U.S. Senators:
Orrin G. Hatch (R) 1976, elected to a six-year term in 1988.
Robert F. Bennett (R) 1992, elected to a six-year term in 1992.

U.S. Representative in Congress:
(District, Name, Party, Date first elected)

1. Hansen (R) 1980   2. Shepherd (D) 1992   3. Orton (D) 1990

Candidates: General Election, November 3, 1992

Candidate(s)	Total vote	Percent	Party	Status	First elected
President/Vice President					
Bush/Quayle	322,632	43.36%	Republican	Incumbent	1988
Perot/Stockdale	203,400	27.34%	Independent	Challenger	
Clinton/Gore	183,429	24.65%	Democrat	Challenger	1992
Gritz/Minett	28,602	3.84%	Populist	Challenger	
Marrou/Lord	1,900	0.26%	Libertarian	Challenger	
Hagelin/Tompkins	1,319	0.18%	Natural Law	Challenger	
LaRouche/Bevel	1,089	0.15%	Ind. Econ. Recovery	Challenger	
Fulani/Munoz	414	0.06%	New Alliance	Challenger	
Phillips/Knight	393	0.05%	Taxpayers	Challenger	
Smith/Feimer	292	0.04%	American	Challenger	
Warren/Reid	200	0.03%	Socialist Workers	Challenger	
Ron Daniels	177	0.02%	Campaign New Tomorrow	Challenger	
Brisben/Garson	151	0.02%	Socialists	Challenger	
Others	1	<.01%	Write in	Challenger	
U.S. Senator					
Robert Bennett	420,069	55.38%	Republican	Challenger	1992
Wayne Owens	301,228	39.71%	Democrat	Challenger	
Anita Morrow	17,549	2.31%	Populist	Challenger	
Maury Modine	14,341	1.89%	Libertarian	Challenger	
Patricia Grogan	5,292	0.70%	Socialist Workers	Challenger	
Governor					
Leavitt/Walker	321,713	42.19%	Republican	Challenger	1992
Cook/Merrill	255,753	33.54%	Independent	Challenger	
Hanson/Julander	177,181	23.24%	Democrat	Challenger	
Gum/West	3,593	0.47%	Populist	Challenger	
Van Horn/Pedersen	1,492	0.20%	Independent American	Challenger	
Garcia/Arth	1,158	0.15%	Socialist Workers	Challenger	
Linda Metzgeragin	917	0.12%	Independent	Challenger	
Frank Richins	729	0.10%	Independent American	Challenger	
U.S. Representative in Congress					
District 1					
James V. Hansen	160,037	65.25%	Republican	Incumbent	1980
Ron Holt	68,712	28.02%	Democrat	Challenger	
William Lawrence	16,505	6.73%	Independent	Challenger	
District 2					
Karen Shepard	127,738	50.50%	Democrat	Challenger	1992
Enid Greene	118,307	46.77%	Republican	Challenger	
A. Peter Crane	6,274	2.48%	Independent	Challenger	
Eileen Koschak	650	0.26%	Socialist Workers	Challenger	
District 3					
Bill Orton	135,029	58.95%	Democrat	Incumbent	1990
Richard Harrington	84,019	36.68%	Republican	Challenger	
Wayne Hill	5,764	2.52%	Independent	Challenger	
Charles Wilson	2,068	0.90%	Independent	Challenger	
Doug Jones	1,797	0.78%	Libertarian	Challenger	
Nels J'Anthony	384	0.17%	Socialist Workers	Challenger	

Voter Registration and Turnout, 1948-1992 Elections

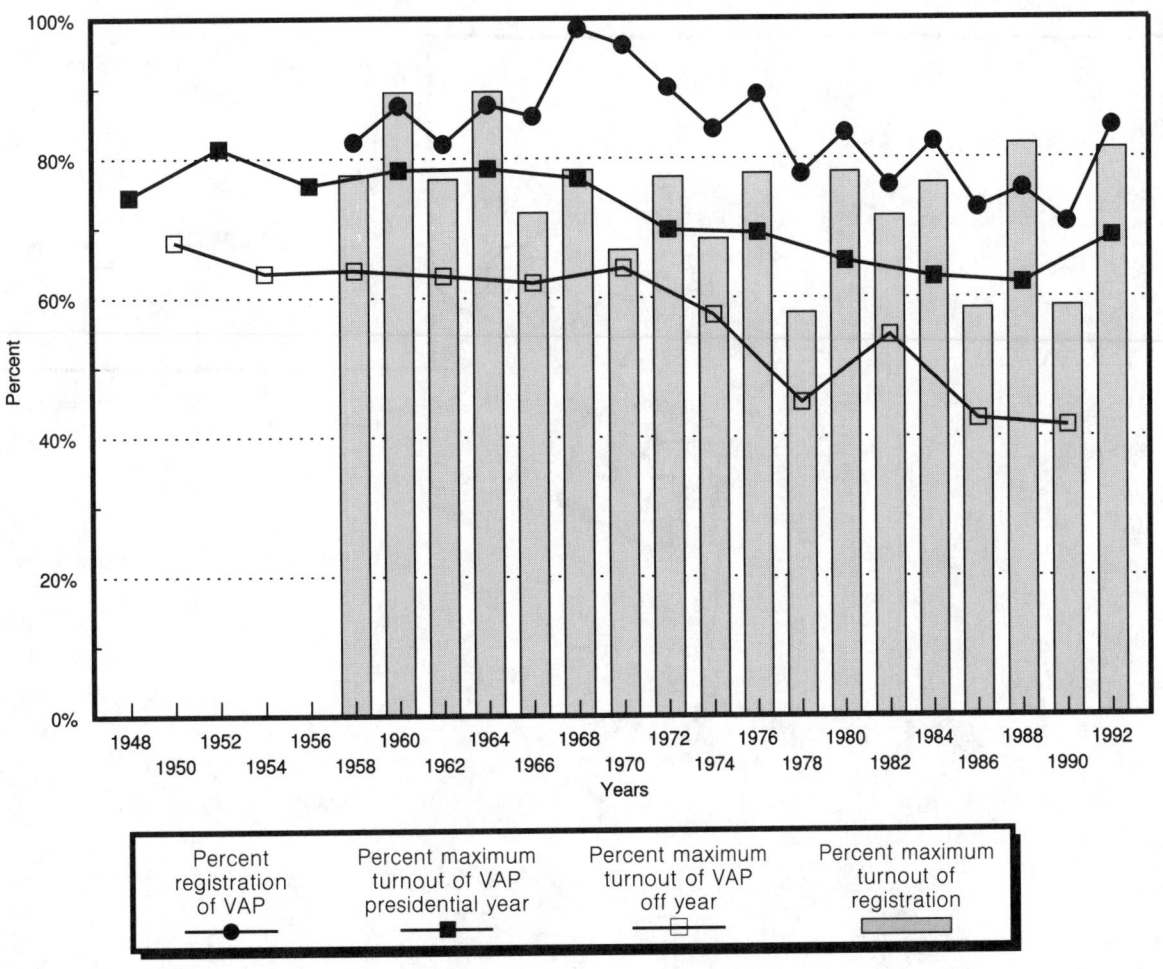

Year	Estimated Voting Age Population (VAP)	Voter registration (REG)			Voter turnout											
						Highest office						Maximum vote				
		Total	Percent of VAP	Rank by percent of VAP	Actual	Total	Office	Percent total REG	Rank by percent of REG	Percent of VAP	Rank by percent of VAP	Total	Percent total REG	Rank by percent of REG	Percent total VAP	Rank by percent of VAP
1992[1]	1,142,000	965,211	84.5	9	784,988	743,999	P	77.1	27	65.1	12	784,988	81.3	17	68.7	6
1990	1,104,000	780,555	70.7	20	457,983	442,213	C	56.7	28	40.1	24	457,983	58.7	26	41.5	21
1988	1,067,000	806,934	75.6	18	661,546	647,008	P	80.2	3	60.6	6	661,546	82.0	4	62.0	5
1986	1,048,000	763,057	72.8	18	445,499	435,111	S	57.0	23	41.5	20	445,499	58.4	24	42.5	20
1984	1,021,000	840,416	82.3	10	641,846	629,656	P	74.9	22	61.7	9	641,846	76.4	20	62.9	8
1982	984,000	748,730	76.1	11	537,207	530,802	S	70.9	6	53.9	7	537,207	71.7	7	54.6	7
1980	935,000	781,711	83.6	10	609,691	604,222	P	77.3	14	64.6	7	609,691	78.0	16	65.2	7
1978	858,000	666,951	77.7	9	385,289	379,160	C	56.8	24	44.2	18	385,289	57.8	25	44.9	15
1976	791,000	704,839	89.1	5	548,329	541,198	P	76.8	19	68.4	2	548,329	77.8	19	69.3	3
1974	736,000	618,873	84.1	3	423,183	420,642	S	68.0	9	57.2	2	423,183	68.4	10	57.5	2
1972	689,000	621,014	90.1	2	480,217	478,476	P	77.0	20	69.4	2	480,217	77.3	22	69.7	3
1970[2]	583,000	560,650	96.2	2	372,861	374,303	S	66.8	24	64.2	1	374,303	66.8	25	64.2	1
1968	551,000	542,793	98.5	3	424,916	422,568	P	77.9	31	76.7	1	424,916	78.3	30	77.1	1
1966	530,000	455,985	86.0	9	329,362	307,437	C	67.4	19	58.0	10	329,362	72.2	15	62.1	5
1964	512,000	448,463	87.6	12	401,881	401,413	P	89.5	4	78.4	1	401,881	89.6	6	78.5	1
1962	506,000	414,879	82.0	9	319,398	318,411	S	76.7	8	62.9	6	319,398	77.0	8	63.1	7
1960	479,000	419,095	87.5	7	374,981	374,709	P	89.4	9	78.2	3	374,981	89.5	10	78.3	5
1958	458,000	376,798	82.3	9	292,579	291,311	S	77.3	7	63.6	5	292,579	77.6	7	63.9	4
1956	439,000	-	-	-	-	333,995	P	-	-	76.1	3	333,995	-	-	76.1	5
1954	414,000	-	-	-	-	262,851	C	-	-	63.5	2	262,851	-	-	63.5	3
1952	405,000	-	-	-	-	329,554	P	-	-	81.4	2	329,554	-	-	81.4	2
1950	389,000	-	-	-	-	264,440	S	-	-	68.0	1	264,440	-	-	68.0	1
1948	371,000	-	-	-	-	276,306	P	-	-	74.5	1	276,306	-	-	74.5	1

[1]Highest office voter turnout shows the vote for president even though the vote for senator (758,479) and the vote for governor (762,536) are higher. [2]Votes for U.S. senator (highest office turnout) exceeds actual voter turnout reported by Utah Secretary of State.

UTAH

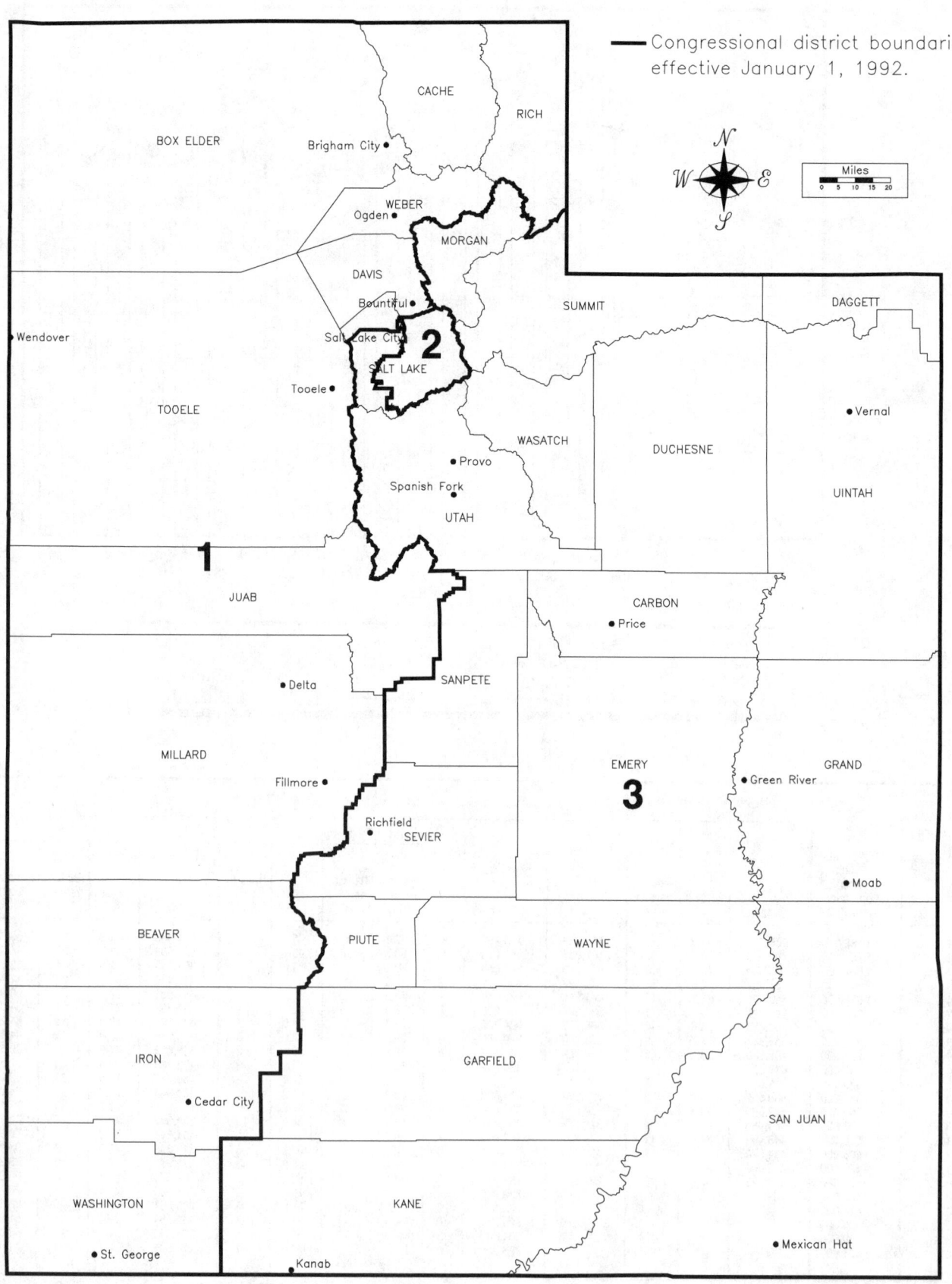

Table A. — 1990 Population by Race and Ethnic Origin

State/county code	County	Total persons	White	Black	Asian and Pacific Islander	Native American	Other	Hispanic	Rank Total	Rank White	Rank Black	Rank Hispanic	Total	White	Black	Hispanic
			Percent of total persons — Non-Hispanic						Rank — Percent of total persons — Non-Hispanic				Percent contribution to state population — Non-Hispanic			
49 001	Beaver	4,765	96.2	0.1	0.4	0.8	<.1	2.5	24	11	12	15	0.3	0.3	<.1	0.1
49 003	Box Elder	36,485	93.4	<.1	1.1	1.0	<.1	4.4	7	20	20	5	2.1	2.2	0.1	1.9
49 005	Cache	70,183	93.7	0.3	2.7	0.7	<.1	2.5	5	19	5	14	4.1	4.2	2.0	2.1
49 007	Carbon	20,228	87.4	0.3	0.5	0.6	0.1	11.1	11	26	6	2	1.2	1.1	0.5	2.7
49 009	Daggett	690	96.4	0.0	0.6	0.9	0.0	2.2	29	10	28	17	<.1	<.1	0.0	<.1
49 011	Davis	187,941	92.7	1.2	1.7	0.5	<.1	3.9	3	21	2	7	10.9	11.1	21.0	8.6
49 013	Duchesne	12,645	92.0	<.1	0.2	4.9	<.1	2.8	15	23	17	13	0.7	0.7	<.1	0.4
49 015	Emery	10,332	97.1	<.1	0.3	0.4	<.1	2.1	18	5	22	18	0.6	0.6	<.1	0.3
49 017	Garfield	3,980	97.2	<.1	0.2	1.7	0.0	0.9	25	4	26	29	0.2	0.2	<.1	<.1
49 019	Grand	6,620	92.3	<.1	0.3	2.9	<.1	4.4	20	22	14	6	0.4	0.4	<.1	0.3
49 021	Iron	20,789	94.6	0.2	0.4	2.9	<.1	1.8	10	15	7	22	1.2	1.3	0.4	0.5
49 023	Juab	5,817	97.0	<.1	0.2	1.4	0.1	1.3	21	6	23	25	0.3	0.4	<.1	<.1
49 025	Kane	5,169	96.0	<.1	0.5	1.5	0.0	2.0	23	13	13	20	0.3	0.3	<.1	0.1
49 027	Millard	11,333	93.9	<.1	0.9	1.6	0.0	3.5	17	18	27	8	0.7	0.7	<.1	0.5
49 029	Morgan	5,528	98.1	0.1	0.3	0.1	0.0	1.4	22	2	10	24	0.3	0.3	<.1	<.1
49 031	Piute	1,277	98.0	0.0	<.1	0.7	0.0	1.2	28	3	29	27	<.1	<.1	0.0	<.1
49 033	Rich	1,725	98.3	<.1	0.3	<.1	0.0	1.2	27	1	18	26	0.1	0.1	<.1	<.1
49 035	Salt Lake	725,956	89.8	0.7	2.7	0.8	<.1	6.0	1	24	4	4	42.1	41.5	47.9	51.6
49 037	San Juan	12,621	42.4	<.1	0.3	53.7	<.1	3.5	16	29	15	9	0.7	0.3	<.1	0.5
49 039	Sanpete	16,259	94.3	<.1	1.5	0.7	<.1	3.4	12	17	16	10	0.9	1.0	0.1	0.7
49 041	Sevier	15,431	95.9	<.1	0.2	2.0	<.1	1.9	14	14	24	21	0.9	0.9	<.1	0.3
49 043	Summit	15,518	96.9	0.1	0.5	0.4	0.0	2.1	13	7	11	19	0.9	1.0	0.2	0.4
49 045	Tooele	26,601	86.0	0.8	0.7	1.3	<.1	11.1	8	28	3	1	1.5	1.5	2.1	3.5
49 047	Uintah	22,211	86.3	<.1	0.4	10.1	<.1	3.1	9	27	21	12	1.3	1.2	<.1	0.8
49 049	Utah	263,590	94.5	0.1	1.5	0.7	<.1	3.2	2	16	8	11	15.3	15.9	3.3	10.0
49 051	Wasatch	10,089	96.7	<.1	0.2	0.6	<.1	2.5	19	9	25	16	0.6	0.6	<.1	0.3
49 053	Washington	48,560	96.1	0.1	0.6	1.4	<.1	1.8	6	12	9	23	2.8	3.0	0.6	1.0
49 055	Wayne	2,177	96.9	<.1	<.1	1.8	0.0	1.1	26	8	19	28	0.1	0.1	<.1	<.1
49 057	Weber	158,330	89.5	1.5	1.4	0.6	<.1	7.0	4	25	1	3	9.2	9.0	21.3	13.1
49	UTAH	1,722,850	91.2	0.6	1.9	1.3	<.1	4.9					100.0	100.0	100.0	100.0
	CONGRESSIONAL															
	District 1	574,286	92.1	0.9	1.5	0.8	<.1	4.7	2	1	1	3	33.3	33.7	47.8	31.6
	District 2	574,241	91.5	0.6	2.3	0.6	<.1	4.9	3	2	2	2	33.3	33.5	29.7	33.5
	District 3	574,323	90.0	0.4	1.9	2.5	<.1	5.1	1	3	3	1	33.3	32.9	22.5	34.9

Table B. — 1990 Voting Age Population (VAP) by Race and Ethnic Origin

County	Total Voting Age Population	Percent of total VAP — Non-Hispanic White	Black	Asian and Pacific Islander	Native American	Other	Hispanic	Rank Percent of total VAP — Total	Non-Hispanic White	Black	Hispanic	Percent contribution to state VAP — Total	Non-Hispanic White	Black	Hispanic	VAP percent of total population — Total	Non-Hispanic White	Black	Asian and Pacific Islander	Native American	Other	Hispanic
Beaver	3,035	97.0	<.1	0.5	0.6	<.1	1.9	24	10	12	17	0.3	0.3	<.1	0.1	63.7	64.2	60.0	73.7	47.2	100.0	47.5
Box Elder	21,678	93.6	<.1	1.2	1.0	<.1	4.1	7	20	21	5	2.0	2.0	0.1	1.8	59.4	59.6	50.0	67.6	57.3	87.5	55.0
Cache	44,560	93.5	0.4	3.1	0.7	<.1	2.3	5	21	5	13	4.1	4.1	2.2	2.0	63.5	63.4	73.2	73.6	60.2	51.4	56.8
Carbon	13,246	88.8	0.3	0.6	0.5	0.1	9.8	10	26	6	2	1.2	1.2	0.5	2.6	65.5	66.6	66.7	70.9	51.2	62.5	57.5
Daggett	451	96.0	0.0	0.7	1.1	0.0	2.2	29	14	27	15	<.1	<.1	0.0	<.1	65.4	65.1	0.0	75.0	83.3	0.0	66.7
Davis	112,515	92.8	1.3	1.7	0.5	<.1	3.7	3	23	2	6	10.3	10.4	20.7	8.4	59.9	59.9	63.9	62.6	57.8	36.7	56.8
Duchesne	7,207	93.0	<.1	0.2	4.5	<.1	2.2	15	22	16	14	0.7	0.7	<.1	0.3	57.0	57.6	62.5	45.2	52.2	66.7	46.0
Emery	5,885	97.2	<.1	0.3	0.4	<.1	2.0	19	9	17	16	0.5	0.6	<.1	0.2	57.0	57.0	100.0	54.5	64.1	100.0	52.5
Garfield	2,553	97.5	<.1	0.3	1.4	0.0	0.7	25	4	20	29	0.2	0.2	<.1	<.1	64.1	64.4	100.0	87.5	54.4	0.0	51.4
Grand	4,509	93.7	<.1	0.4	2.1	<.1	3.7	20	19	13	7	0.4	0.4	<.1	0.3	68.1	69.2	66.7	77.3	50.0	100.0	56.7
Iron	13,414	95.1	0.2	0.5	2.6	<.1	1.7	9	15	7	20	1.2	1.3	0.4	0.5	64.5	64.8	77.5	75.3	56.0	100.0	58.6
Juab	3,554	97.3	<.1	0.1	1.2	<.1	1.3	21	7	19	24	0.3	0.3	<.1	<.1	61.1	61.3	100.0	40.0	54.3	14.3	63.0
Kane	3,274	96.8	<.1	0.3	1.3	0.0	1.5	22	12	18	22	0.3	0.3	<.1	0.1	63.3	63.9	40.0	45.8	53.2	0.0	49.5
Millard	6,466	94.7	<.1	0.9	1.4	0.0	3.0	17	17	26	9	0.6	0.6	<.1	0.4	57.1	57.5	50.0	53.8	50.6	0.0	48.0
Morgan	3,255	98.6	<.1	0.1	<.1	0.0	1.1	23	2	22	26	0.3	0.3	<.1	<.1	58.9	59.2	14.3	26.7	28.6	0.0	47.4
Piute	862	98.6	0.0	0.0	0.6	0.0	0.8	28	3	28	28	<.1	<.1	0.0	<.1	67.5	67.9	0.0	0.0	55.6	0.0	46.7
Rich	981	98.8	0.0	0.1	0.1	0.0	1.0	27	1	29	27	<.1	<.1	0.0	<.1	56.9	57.1	0.0	16.7	100.0	0.0	47.6
Salt Lake	473,539	90.3	0.7	2.6	0.7	<.1	5.6	1	25	4	4	43.2	42.6	47.9	53.1	65.2	65.7	65.0	63.9	59.6	53.5	60.2
San Juan	7,150	45.3	0.1	0.2	51.0	<.1	3.4	16	29	10	8	0.7	0.3	0.1	0.5	56.7	60.6	80.0	33.3	53.8	16.7	55.2
Sanpete	10,075	94.1	0.1	2.1	0.7	<.1	3.0	13	18	11	10	0.9	0.9	0.2	0.6	62.0	61.9	100.0	86.9	60.6	40.0	53.6
Sevier	9,359	96.8	<.1	<.1	1.5	0.0	1.5	14	11	24	21	0.9	0.9	<.1	0.3	60.7	61.3	40.0	23.1	45.8	0.0	49.8
Summit	10,335	97.3	<.1	0.4	0.4	0.0	1.9	12	8	14	18	0.9	1.0	0.1	0.4	66.6	66.9	50.0	55.8	62.9	0.0	59.2
Tooele	16,980	87.2	0.8	0.7	1.3	<.1	10.0	8	28	3	1	1.6	1.5	1.9	3.4	63.8	64.7	58.9	62.0	63.3	57.1	57.5
Uintah	13,015	87.6	<.1	0.4	9.1	<.1	2.9	11	27	23	12	1.2	1.1	<.1	0.8	58.6	59.5	44.4	58.8	52.8	40.0	54.3
Utah	164,086	94.8	0.1	1.5	0.6	<.1	3.0	2	16	9	11	15.0	15.5	3.0	9.9	62.3	62.4	58.5	65.4	52.1	52.3	57.5
Wasatch	6,103	97.4	<.1	0.1	0.6	<.1	1.8	18	5	25	19	0.6	0.6	<.1	0.2	60.5	61.0	33.3	50.0	58.1	100.0	43.1
Washington	30,966	96.7	0.2	0.5	1.1	<.1	1.5	6	13	8	23	2.8	3.0	0.7	1.0	63.8	64.2	76.2	60.1	49.4	18.8	54.9
Wayne	1,356	97.3	<.1	<.1	1.3	0.0	1.3	26	6	15	25	0.1	0.1	<.1	<.1	62.3	62.6	100.0	50.0	42.5	0.0	68.0
Weber	104,997	90.4	1.5	1.5	0.6	<.1	6.0	4	24	1	3	9.6	9.4	21.8	12.8	66.3	67.0	66.6	71.1	62.9	58.8	57.4
UTAH	**1,095,406**	**91.7**	**0.6**	**1.9**	**1.2**	**<.1**	**4.5**					**100.0**	**100.0**	**100.0**	**100.0**	**63.6**	**63.9**	**65.0**	**65.0**	**55.6**	**52.0**	**58.5**
CONGRESSIONAL																						
District 1	360,394	92.4	0.9	1.6	0.8	<.1	4.2	2	1	1	3	32.9	33.2	48.2	30.8	62.8	63.0	65.4	67.3	57.7	48.9	56.9
District 2	379,147	91.8	0.6	2.3	0.6	<.1	4.6	1	2	2	2	34.6	34.7	31.0	35.3	66.0	66.2	67.8	67.4	61.5	55.8	61.8
District 3	355,865	90.8	0.4	1.9	2.1	<.1	4.7	3	3	3	1	32.5	32.2	20.8	33.9	62.0	62.5	60.2	60.4	53.4	50.8	56.8

916 Utah

Table C. — Voter Participation: November 3, 1992, General Election

County	Estimated Voting Age Population (VAP), 1992	Voter registration (REG)				Voter turnout													
							Highest office			Maximum vote						Percent drop-off, by office			
		Total	% contribution to state REG	% of 1992 VAP	Rank by % of 1992 VAP	Actual	Total	Office	% of 1992 VAP	Total	% contribution to state turnout	% of REG	Rank by % of REG	% of 1992 VAP	Rank by % 1992 VAP	President	Senator	Governor	Representative
Beaver	3,189	2,694	0.3	84.5	21	2,272	2,209	S	69.3	2,272	0.3	84.3	7	71.2	15	7.1	2.8	4.3	6.3
Box Elder	22,588	20,025	2.1	88.7	15	16,514	16,040	G	71.0	16,514	2.1	82.5	10	73.1	11	5.8	3.3	2.9	5.9
Cache	46,439	44,330	4.6	95.5	8	32,702	31,548	S	67.9	32,702	4.2	73.8	27	70.4	17	6.0	4.1	3.5	7.2
Carbon	13,121	11,447	1.2	87.2	18	9,370	9,087	S	69.3	9,370	1.2	81.9	12	71.4	13	5.9	3.0	3.5	4.2
Daggett	446	542	<.1	121.5	1	445	442	P	99.1	445	<.1	82.1	11	99.8	1	0.7	8.8	4.9	17.3
Davis	120,825	99,935	10.4	82.7	25	84,497	82,989	G	68.7	84,497	10.8	84.6	5	69.9	19	3.7	2.8	1.8	6.2
Duchesne	7,473	6,288	0.7	84.1	22	4,854	4,688	G	62.7	4,854	0.6	77.2	22	65.0	25	6.0	3.6	3.4	5.6
Emery	5,967	5,816	0.6	97.5	7	4,578	4,510	P	75.6	4,578	0.6	78.7	17	76.7	9	1.5	7.9	2.7	15.6
Garfield	2,621	2,263	0.2	86.3	19	2,004	1,983	P	75.7	2,004	0.3	88.6	2	76.5	10	1.0	6.4	2.4	17.4
Grand	4,357	4,688	0.5	107.6	3	3,532	3,376	G	77.5	3,532	0.4	75.3	26	81.1	7	5.4	4.4	4.4	6.1
Iron	13,930	13,118	1.4	94.2	10	9,903	9,635	G	69.2	9,903	1.3	75.5	25	71.1	16	5.3	3.2	2.7	6.6
Juab	3,687	3,422	0.4	92.8	11	2,905	2,895	P	78.5	2,905	0.4	84.9	3	78.8	8	0.3	5.2	1.5	16.6
Kane	3,539	2,881	0.3	81.4	27	2,328	2,233	G	63.1	2,328	0.3	80.8	15	65.8	24	6.7	11.1	4.1	6.8
Millard	7,079	6,248	0.6	88.3	16	5,045	4,902	G	69.2	5,045	0.6	80.7	16	71.3	14	5.5	3.0	2.8	6.4
Morgan	3,496	3,238	0.3	92.6	12	2,956	2,940	P	84.1	2,956	0.4	91.3	1	84.6	5	0.5	8.1	2.2	17.4
Piute	880	901	<.1	102.4	4	761	753	P	85.6	761	<.1	84.5	6	86.5	3	1.1	5.3	1.8	15.8
Rich	999	1,091	0.1	109.2	2	882	876	P	87.7	882	0.1	80.8	14	88.3	2	0.7	6.5	1.5	18.8
Salt Lake	491,386	397,534	41.2	80.9	28	336,195	326,308	G	66.4	336,195	42.8	84.6	4	68.4	21	5.2	3.1	2.9	8.9
San Juan	7,357	6,720	0.7	91.3	14	4,584	4,335	P	58.9	4,584	0.6	68.2	29	62.3	28	5.4	9.6	8.2	15.4
Sanpete	10,240	9,431	1.0	92.1	13	7,199	6,919	G	67.6	7,199	0.9	76.3	23	70.3	18	7.1	4.3	3.9	5.9
Sevier	9,795	8,235	0.9	84.1	23	6,711	6,464	G	66.0	6,711	0.9	81.5	13	68.5	20	6.8	4.1	3.7	5.3
Summit	11,737	11,921	1.2	101.6	6	9,840	9,537	G	81.3	9,840	1.3	82.5	9	83.8	6	4.5	3.4	3.1	6.6
Tooele	17,540	14,113	1.5	80.5	29	11,038	10,616	S	60.5	11,038	1.4	78.2	19	62.9	27	6.9	3.8	4.0	6.3
Uintah	13,637	11,406	1.2	83.6	24	8,242	8,042	S	59.0	8,242	1.1	72.3	28	60.4	29	5.7	2.4	3.4	4.8
Utah	168,670	145,465	15.1	86.2	20	113,425	110,780	G	65.7	113,425	14.4	78.0	20	67.2	23	4.6	3.1	2.3	4.5
Wasatch	6,548	6,172	0.6	94.3	9	4,704	4,701	C	71.8	4,704	0.6	76.2	24	71.8	12	7.8	3.7	2.7	0.1
Washington	35,601	29,081	3.0	81.7	26	22,876	22,130	G	62.2	22,876	2.9	78.7	18	64.3	26	6.1	4.2	3.3	7.6
Wayne	1,439	1,466	0.2	101.9	5	1,236	1,225	P	85.1	1,236	0.2	84.3	8	85.9	4	0.9	5.4	2.3	17.3
Weber	107,414	94,740	9.8	88.2	17	73,390	71,021	G	66.1	73,390	9.3	77.5	21	68.3	22	7.1	4.0	3.2	6.1
UTAH	**1,142,000**	**965,211**	**100.0**	**84.5**		**784,988**	**763,184**		**66.8**	**784,988**	**100.0**	**81.3**		**68.7**		**5.2**	**3.4**	**2.9**	**7.4**

Table E. – Vote for President: November 3, 1992, General Election

County	Total	Clinton (DEM)	Bush (REP)	Perot (IND)	Other	Plurality Total	Party	DEM	REP	IND	Other	Rank DEM	Rank REP	Rank IND	Total	DEM	REP	IND	DEM	REP
Beaver	2,111	668	1,040	330	73	372	R	31.6	49.3	15.6	3.5	6	13	28	0.3	0.4	0.3	0.2	39.1	60.9
Box Elder	15,555	2,186	7,712	4,507	1,150	3,205	R	14.1	49.6	29.0	7.4	27	12	6	2.1	1.2	2.4	2.2	22.1	77.9
Cache	30,725	4,973	15,971	8,032	1,749	7,939	R	16.2	52.0	26.1	5.7	23	10	14	4.1	2.7	5.0	3.9	23.7	76.3
Carbon	8,817	4,480	2,038	2,002	297	2,442	D	50.8	23.1	22.7	3.4	1	29	18	1.2	2.4	0.6	1.0	68.7	31.3
Daggett	442	122	172	117	31	50	R	27.6	38.9	26.5	7.0	10	23	13	<.1	<.1	<.1	<.1	41.5	58.5
Davis	81,350	14,924	39,087	24,105	3,234	14,982	R	18.3	48.0	29.6	4.0	16	14	4	10.9	8.1	12.1	11.9	27.6	72.4
Duchesne	4,565	772	1,983	1,229	581	754	R	16.9	43.4	26.9	12.7	20	19	11	0.6	0.4	0.6	0.6	28.0	72.0
Emery	4,510	1,349	1,643	1,138	380	294	R	29.9	36.4	25.2	8.4	8	25	16	0.6	0.7	0.5	0.6	45.1	54.9
Garfield	1,983	309	1,235	355	84	880	R	15.6	62.3	17.9	4.2	25	1	27	0.3	0.2	0.4	0.2	20.0	80.0
Grand	3,342	1,160	1,100	991	91	60	D	34.7	32.9	29.7	2.7	3	28	3	0.4	0.6	0.3	0.5	51.3	48.7
Iron	9,378	1,537	5,616	1,693	532	3,923	R	16.4	59.9	18.1	5.7	22	3	26	1.3	0.8	1.7	0.8	21.5	78.5
Juab	2,895	823	1,237	616	219	414	R	28.4	42.7	21.3	7.6	9	20	23	0.4	0.4	0.4	0.3	40.0	60.0
Kane	2,172	295	1,241	534	102	707	R	13.6	57.1	24.6	4.7	28	5	17	0.3	0.2	0.4	0.3	19.2	80.8
Millard	4,770	742	2,496	1,064	468	1,432	R	15.6	52.3	22.3	9.8	26	9	20	0.6	0.4	0.8	0.5	22.9	77.1
Morgan	2,940	520	1,339	851	230	488	R	17.7	45.5	28.9	7.8	17	16	7	0.4	0.3	0.4	0.4	28.0	72.0
Piute	753	169	429	146	9	260	R	22.4	57.0	19.4	1.2	13	6	25	0.1	<.1	0.1	<.1	28.3	71.7
Rich	876	154	525	187	10	338	R	17.6	59.9	21.3	1.1	19	2	22	0.1	<.1	0.2	<.1	22.7	77.3
Salt Lake	318,661	100,082	117,247	91,968	9,364	17,165	R	31.4	36.8	28.9	2.9	7	24	9	42.8	54.6	36.3	45.2	46.1	53.9
San Juan	4,335	1,639	2,004	576	116	365	R	37.8	46.2	13.3	2.7	2	15	29	0.6	0.9	0.6	0.3	45.0	55.0
Sanpete	6,685	1,302	2,995	1,742	646	1,253	R	19.5	44.8	26.1	9.7	14	18	15	0.9	0.7	0.9	0.9	30.3	69.7
Sevier	6,258	1,039	3,160	1,671	388	1,489	R	16.6	50.5	26.7	6.2	21	11	12	0.8	0.6	1.0	0.8	24.7	75.3
Summit	9,399	3,013	3,133	3,060	193	73	R	32.1	33.3	32.6	2.1	4	27	1	1.3	1.6	1.0	1.5	49.0	51.0
Tooele	10,271	3,270	3,676	3,011	314	406	R	31.8	35.8	29.3	3.1	5	26	5	1.4	1.8	1.1	1.5	47.1	52.9
Uintah	7,774	1,374	3,505	2,250	645	1,255	R	17.7	45.1	28.9	8.3	18	17	8	1.0	0.7	1.1	1.1	28.2	71.8
Utah	108,178	14,090	61,398	24,558	8,132	36,840	R	13.0	56.8	22.7	7.5	29	7	19	14.5	7.7	19.0	12.1	18.7	81.3
Wasatch	4,336	1,042	1,822	1,234	238	588	R	24.0	42.0	28.5	5.5	12	21	10	0.6	0.6	0.6	0.6	36.4	63.6
Washington	21,476	3,364	11,310	4,623	2,179	6,687	R	15.7	52.7	21.5	10.1	24	8	21	2.9	1.8	3.5	2.3	22.9	77.1
Wayne	1,225	236	706	251	32	455	R	19.3	57.6	20.5	2.6	15	4	24	0.2	0.1	0.2	0.1	25.1	74.9
Weber	68,216	17,795	26,812	20,559	3,050	6,253	R	26.1	39.3	30.1	4.5	11	22	2	9.2	9.7	8.3	10.1	39.9	60.1
UTAH[1]	743,999	183,429	322,632	203,400	34,538	119,232	R	24.7	43.4	27.3	4.6				100.0	100.0	100.0	100.0	36.2	63.8

[1]Includes 1 Write in vote reported only at the state level.

Table F. — Vote for U.S. Senator: November 3, 1992, General Election

County	Total	Owens (DEM)	Bennett (REP)	Other	Plurality Total	Party	Percent of total vote DEM	REP	Other	Rank DEM	REP	Other	Percent contribution to state vote Total	DEM	REP	Other
Beaver	2,209	802	1,351	56	549	R	36.3	61.2	2.5	11	17	25	0.3	0.3	0.3	0.2
Box Elder	15,970	5,171	9,777	1,022	4,606	R	32.4	61.2	6.4	15	16	4	2.1	1.7	2.3	2.7
Cache	31,368	10,212	19,575	1,581	9,363	D	32.6	62.4	5.0	14	14	11	4.1	3.4	4.7	4.3
Carbon	9,087	5,249	3,449	389	1,800	R	57.8	38.0	4.3	1	29	19	1.2	1.7	0.8	1.0
Daggett	406	164	224	18	60	R	40.4	55.2	4.4	9	23	17	<.1	<.1	<.1	<.1
Davis	82,092	28,318	49,415	4,359	21,097	R	34.5	60.2	5.3	13	18	9	10.8	9.4	11.8	11.7
Duchesne	4,678	1,292	3,132	254	1,840	R	27.6	67.0	5.4	20	12	7	0.6	0.4	0.7	0.7
Emery	4,216	1,167	2,846	203	1,679	R	27.7	67.5	4.8	19	11	12	0.6	0.4	0.7	0.5
Garfield	1,875	377	1,457	41	1,080	R	20.1	77.7	2.2	27	2	26	0.2	0.1	0.3	0.1
Grand	3,375	1,413	1,803	159	390	R	41.9	53.4	4.7	7	24	14	0.4	0.5	0.4	0.4
Iron	9,591	2,293	6,908	390	4,615	R	23.9	72.0	4.1	25	6	21	1.3	0.8	1.6	1.0
Juab	2,755	1,022	1,639	94	617	R	37.1	59.5	3.4	10	19	22	0.4	0.3	0.4	0.3
Kane	2,070	371	1,601	98	1,230	R	17.9	77.3	4.7	28	3	13	0.3	0.1	0.4	0.3
Millard	4,892	1,249	3,383	260	2,134	R	25.5	69.2	5.3	22	8	8	0.6	0.4	0.8	0.7
Morgan	2,717	981	1,588	148	607	R	36.1	58.4	5.4	12	20	6	0.4	0.3	0.4	0.4
Piute	721	171	537	13	366	R	23.7	74.5	1.8	26	4	27	<.1	<.1	0.1	<.1
Rich	825	202	602	21	400	R	24.5	73.0	2.5	24	5	24	0.1	<.1	0.1	<.1
Salt Lake	325,922	153,714	157,781	14,427	4,067	R	47.2	48.4	4.4	4	26	18	43.0	51.0	37.6	38.8
San Juan	4,146	1,794	2,304	48	510	R	43.3	55.6	1.2	6	22	29	0.5	0.6	0.5	0.1
Sanpete	6,890	2,205	4,308	377	2,103	R	32.0	62.5	5.5	16	13	5	0.9	0.7	1.0	1.0
Sevier	6,438	1,654	4,485	299	2,831	R	25.7	69.7	4.6	21	7	15	0.8	0.5	1.1	0.8
Summit	9,506	4,680	4,437	389	243	D	49.2	46.7	4.1	2	27	20	1.3	1.6	1.1	1.0
Tooele	10,616	5,180	4,877	559	303	D	48.8	45.9	5.3	3	28	10	1.4	1.7	1.2	1.5
Uintah	8,042	2,492	4,983	567	2,491	R	31.0	62.0	7.1	17	15	1	1.1	0.8	1.2	1.5
Utah	109,961	30,487	74,545	4,929	44,058	R	27.7	67.8	4.5	18	10	16	14.5	10.1	17.7	13.3
Wasatch	4,530	1,870	2,526	134	656	R	41.3	55.8	3.0	8	21	23	0.6	0.6	0.6	0.4
Washington	21,926	5,555	14,953	1,418	9,398	R	25.3	68.2	6.5	23	9	3	2.9	1.8	3.6	3.8
Wayne	1,169	195	960	14	765	R	16.7	82.1	1.2	29	1	28	0.2	<.1	0.2	<.1
Weber	70,486	30,948	34,623	4,915	3,675	R	43.9	49.1	7.0	5	25	2	9.3	10.3	8.2	13.2
UTAH	**758,479**	**301,228**	**420,069**	**37,182**	**118,841**	**R**	**39.7**	**55.4**	**4.9**				**100.0**	**100.0**	**100.0**	**100.0**

Table G. – Vote for Governor: November 3, 1992, General Election

County	Total[1]	Hanson (DEM)	Leavitt (REP)	Cook (IND)	Plurality Total	Party	DEM	REP	IND	Rank DEM	Rank REP	Rank IND	Total	DEM	REP	IND
Beaver	2,175	547	1,121	502	574	R	25.1	51.5	23.1	8	11	25	0.3	0.3	0.3	0.2
Box Elder	16,040	2,005	7,863	5,994	1,869	R	12.5	49.0	37.4	27	13	4	2.1	1.1	2.4	2.3
Cache	31,548	4,736	17,251	9,199	8,052	R	15.0	54.7	29.2	20	8	20	4.1	2.7	5.4	3.6
Carbon	9,039	3,850	2,149	2,956	894	D	42.6	23.8	32.7	1	29	15	1.2	2.2	0.7	1.2
Daggett	423	124	189	108	65	R	29.3	44.7	25.5	6	19	23	<.1	<.1	<.1	<.1
Davis	82,989	14,359	37,921	29,949	7,972	R	17.3	45.7	36.1	14	18	7	10.9	8.1	11.8	11.7
Duchesne	4,688	755	2,144	1,735	409	R	16.1	45.7	37.0	17	17	5	0.6	0.4	0.7	0.7
Emery	4,454	1,076	1,941	1,376	565	R	24.2	43.6	30.9	9	20	17	0.6	0.6	0.6	0.5
Garfield	1,956	248	1,289	409	880	R	12.7	65.9	20.9	26	1	27	0.3	0.1	0.4	0.2
Grand	3,376	1,117	1,163	1,057	46	R	33.1	34.4	31.3	4	27	16	0.4	0.6	0.4	0.4
Iron	9,635	1,241	6,167	2,125	4,042	R	12.9	64.0	22.1	25	2	26	1.3	0.7	1.9	0.8
Juab	2,862	597	1,225	1,009	216	R	20.9	42.8	35.3	12	21	9	0.4	0.3	0.4	0.4
Kane	2,233	300	1,253	660	593	R	13.4	56.1	29.6	23	5	19	0.3	0.2	0.4	0.3
Millard	4,902	644	2,510	1,703	807	R	13.1	51.2	34.7	24	12	11	0.6	0.4	0.8	0.7
Morgan	2,890	470	1,354	1,029	325	R	16.3	46.9	35.6	16	15	8	0.4	0.3	0.4	0.4
Piute	747	109	444	191	253	R	14.6	59.4	25.6	21	4	22	<.1	<.1	0.1	<.1
Rich	869	173	485	208	277	R	19.9	55.8	23.9	13	6	24	0.1	<.1	0.2	<.1
Salt Lake	326,308	100,570	115,583	107,549	8,034	R	30.8	35.4	33.0	5	25	14	42.8	56.8	35.9	42.1
San Juan	4,208	1,596	2,020	563	424	R	37.9	48.0	13.4	3	14	29	0.6	0.9	0.6	0.2
Sanpete	6,919	1,072	3,233	2,511	722	R	15.5	46.7	36.3	19	16	6	0.9	0.6	1.0	1.0
Sevier	6,464	754	3,389	2,275	1,114	R	11.7	52.4	35.2	28	10	10	0.8	0.4	1.1	0.9
Summit	9,537	3,645	3,194	2,629	451	D	38.2	33.5	27.6	2	28	21	1.3	2.1	1.0	1.0
Tooele	10,598	2,785	3,712	4,017	305	I	26.3	35.0	37.9	7	26	3	1.4	1.6	1.2	1.6
Uintah	7,959	1,308	3,328	3,224	104	R	16.4	41.8	40.5	15	23	1	1.0	0.7	1.0	1.3
Utah	110,780	12,414	59,933	37,067	22,866	R	11.2	54.1	33.5	29	9	12	14.5	7.0	18.6	14.5
Wasatch	4,578	1,063	1,952	1,521	431	R	23.2	42.6	33.2	10	22	13	0.6	0.6	0.6	0.6
Washington	22,130	3,037	12,113	6,590	5,523	R	13.7	54.7	29.8	22	7	18	2.9	1.7	3.8	2.6
Wayne	1,208	191	773	243	530	R	15.8	64.0	20.1	18	3	28	0.2	0.1	0.2	<.1
Weber	71,021	16,395	26,014	27,354	1,340	I	23.1	36.6	38.5	11	24	2	9.3	9.3	8.1	10.7
UTAH[2]	**762,536**	**177,181**	**321,713**	**255,753**	**65,960**	**R**	**23.2**	**42.2**	**33.5**				**100.0**	**100.0**	**100.0**	**100.0**

[1]Includes votes for minor party and other independent candidates.   [2]Total statewide vote for other candidates was 7,889.

Table H. — Vote for U.S. Representative in Congress: November 3, 1992, General Election

Congressional district and county	Total	Democrat (DEM)	Republican (REP)	Other	Plurality Total	Party	DEM	REP	Other	Rank within district DEM	REP	Other	Total	DEM	REP	Other
District 1	**245,254**	**68,712**	**160,037**	**16,505**	**91,325**	**R**	**28.0**	**65.3**	**6.7**				**100.0**	**100.0**	**100.0**	**100.0**
Beaver	2,128	621	1,442	65	821	R	29.2	67.8	3.1	5	7	11	0.9	0.9	0.9	0.4
Box Elder	15,547	3,840	10,626	1,081	6,786	R	24.7	68.3	7.0	7	6	4	6.3	5.6	6.6	6.5
Cache	30,359	6,739	22,385	1,235	15,646	R	22.2	73.7	4.1	8	5	8	12.4	9.8	14.0	7.5
Davis	79,289	20,386	52,028	6,875	31,642	R	25.7	65.6	8.7	6	9	1	32.3	29.7	32.5	41.7
Iron	9,246	1,680	7,257	309	5,577	R	18.2	78.5	3.3	11	3	10	3.8	2.4	4.5	1.9
Juab	2,424	722	1,617	85	895	R	29.8	66.7	3.5	4	8	9	1.0	1.1	1.0	0.5
Millard	4,723	778	3,719	226	2,941	R	16.5	78.7	4.8	12	2	7	1.9	1.1	2.3	1.4
Rich	716	135	572	9	437	R	18.9	79.9	1.3	9	1	12	0.3	0.2	0.4	0.1
Salt Lake (pt)	422	173	218	31	45	R	41.0	51.7	7.3	1	12	3	0.2	0.3	0.1	0.2
Tooele	10,346	3,220	6,360	766	3,140	R	31.1	61.5	7.4	3	10	2	4.2	4.7	4.0	4.6
Washington	21,148	3,919	16,069	1,160	12,150	R	18.5	76.0	5.5	10	4	6	8.6	5.7	10.0	7.0
Weber	68,906	26,499	37,744	4,663	11,245	R	38.5	54.8	6.8	2	11	5	28.1	38.6	23.6	28.3
District 2	**252,969**	**127,738**	**118,307**	**6,924**	**9,431**	**D**	**50.5**	**46.8**	**2.7**				**100.0**	**100.0**	**100.0**	**100.0**
Salt Lake (pt)	252,969	127,738	118,307	6,924	9,431	D	50.5	46.8	2.7	1	1	1	100.0	100.0	100.0	100.0
District 3	**229,061**	**135,029**	**84,019**	**10,013**	**51,010**	**D**	**58.9**	**36.7**	**4.4**				**100.0**	**100.0**	**100.0**	**100.0**
Carbon	8,972	7,208	1,442	322	5,766	D	80.3	16.1	3.6	1	18	10	3.9	5.3	1.7	3.2
Daggett	368	261	103	4	158	D	70.9	28.0	1.1	2	13	18	0.2	0.2	0.1	0.0
Duchesne	4,583	3,074	1,329	180	1,745	D	67.1	29.0	3.9	6	12	9	2.0	2.3	1.6	1.8
Emery	3,862	2,433	1,357	72	1,076	D	63.0	35.1	1.9	9	9	14	1.7	1.8	1.6	0.7
Garfield	1,656	792	845	19	53	R	47.8	51.0	1.1	17	1	17	0.7	0.6	1.0	0.2
Grand	3,315	2,172	881	262	1,291	D	65.5	26.6	7.9	8	15	1	1.4	1.6	1.0	2.6
Kane	2,170	1,006	1,046	118	40	R	46.4	48.2	5.4	18	3	5	0.9	0.7	1.2	1.2
Morgan	2,442	1,435	941	66	494	D	58.8	38.5	2.7	12	7	12	1.1	1.1	1.1	0.7
Piute	641	364	262	15	102	D	56.8	40.9	2.3	13	6	13	0.3	0.3	0.3	0.1
Salt Lake (pt)	52,938	36,917	12,687	3,334	24,230	D	69.7	24.0	6.3	3	17	3	23.1	27.3	15.1	33.3
San Juan	3,879	2,583	1,236	60	1,347	D	66.6	31.9	1.5	7	11	15	1.7	1.9	1.5	0.6
Sanpete	6,772	3,697	2,778	297	919	D	54.6	41.0	4.4	14	5	7	3.0	2.7	3.3	3.0
Sevier	6,352	3,749	2,351	252	1,398	D	59.0	37.0	4.0	11	8	8	2.8	2.8	2.8	2.5
Summit	9,190	6,218	2,448	524	3,770	D	67.7	26.6	5.7	5	14	4	4.0	4.6	2.9	5.2
Uintah	7,847	4,786	2,698	363	2,088	D	61.0	34.4	4.6	10	10	6	3.4	3.5	3.2	3.6
Utah	108,351	54,642	49,961	3,748	4,681	D	50.4	46.1	3.5	15	4	11	47.3	40.5	59.5	37.4
Wasatch	4,701	3,198	1,138	365	2,060	D	68.0	24.2	7.8	4	16	2	2.1	2.4	1.4	3.6
Wayne	1,022	494	516	12	22	R	48.3	50.5	1.2	16	2	16	0.4	0.4	0.6	0.1
UTAH	**727,284**	**331,479**	**362,363**	**33,442**	**30,884**	**R**	**45.6**	**49.8**	**4.6**							

1992 Vote for President
Percent for Bush (R), by County

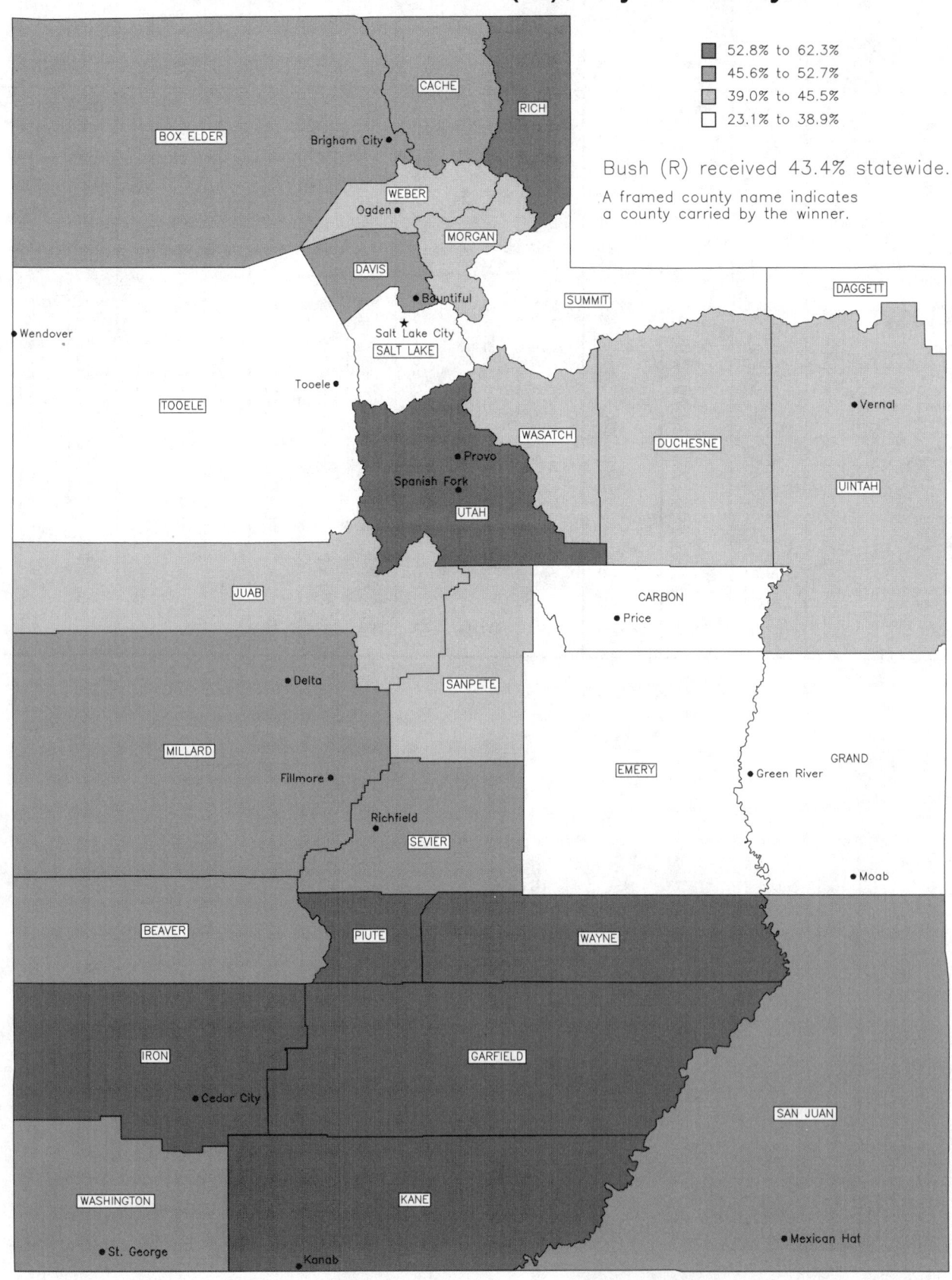

Legend:
- 52.8% to 62.3%
- 45.6% to 52.7%
- 39.0% to 45.5%
- 23.1% to 38.9%

Bush (R) received 43.4% statewide.
A framed county name indicates
a county carried by the winner.

CACHE
RICH
BOX ELDER
Brigham City
WEBER
Ogden
MORGAN
Wendover
DAVIS
Bountiful
Salt Lake City
SUMMIT
DAGGETT
SALT LAKE
Vernal
Tooele
TOOELE
WASATCH
DUCHESNE
UINTAH
Provo
Spanish Fork
UTAH
JUAB
CARBON
Price
Delta
SANPETE
MILLARD
EMERY
GRAND
Green River
Fillmore
Richfield
SEVIER
Moab
BEAVER
PIUTE
WAYNE
IRON
GARFIELD
Cedar City
SAN JUAN
WASHINGTON
KANE
Mexican Hat
St. George
Kanab

1992 Vote for U.S. Senator
Percent for Bennett (R), by County

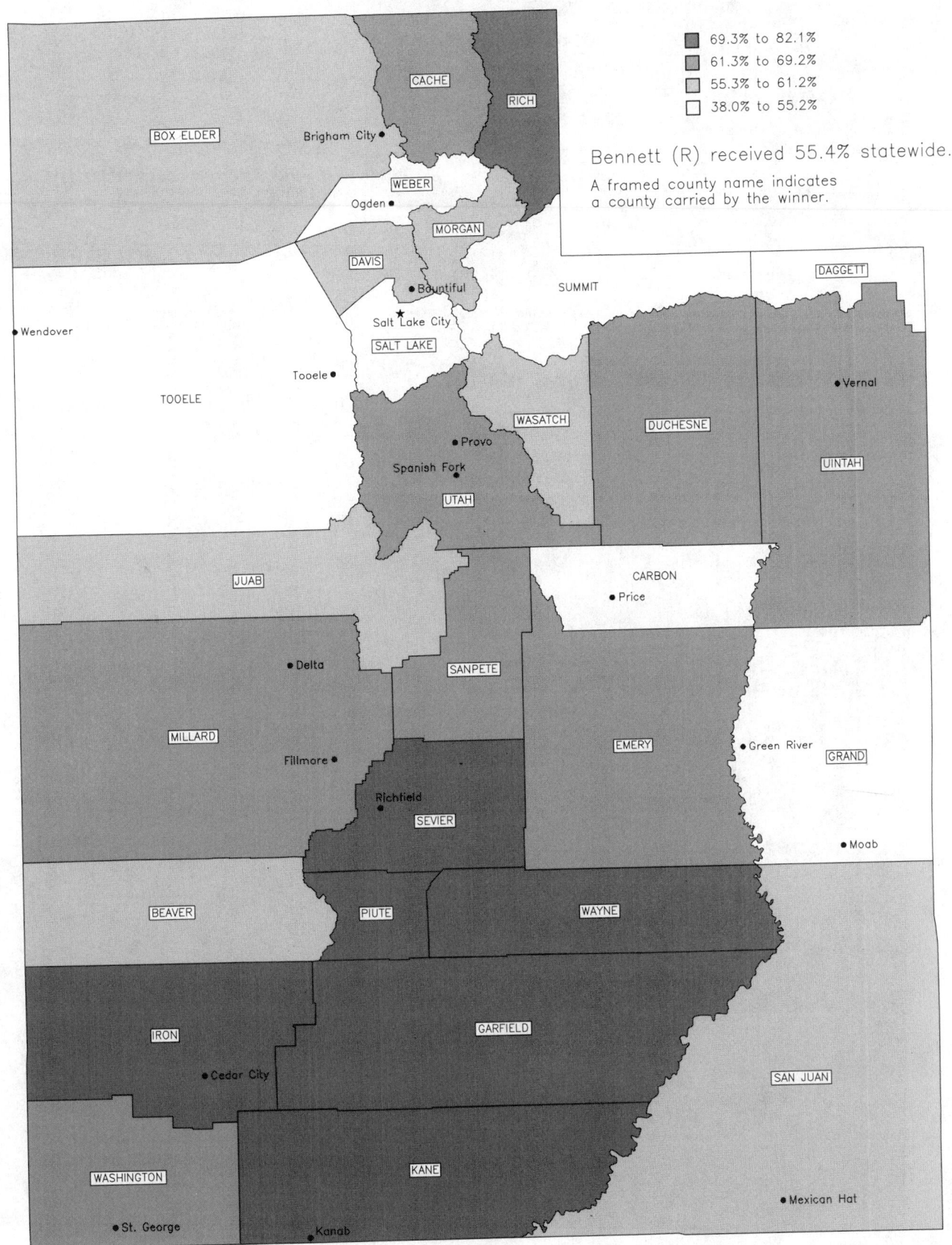

69.3% to 82.1%
61.3% to 69.2%
55.3% to 61.2%
38.0% to 55.2%

Bennett (R) received 55.4% statewide.

A framed county name indicates
a county carried by the winner.

CACHE

RICH

BOX ELDER

Brigham City

WEBER

Ogden

MORGAN

DAVIS

Bountiful

Salt Lake City

SUMMIT

DAGGETT

Wendover

SALT LAKE

Vernal

Tooele

WASATCH

DUCHESNE

UINTAH

TOOELE

Provo

Spanish Fork

UTAH

CARBON

Price

JUAB

Delta

SANPETE

EMERY

Green River

GRAND

MILLARD

Fillmore

Richfield

SEVIER

Moab

BEAVER

PIUTE

WAYNE

IRON

GARFIELD

Cedar City

SAN JUAN

WASHINGTON

KANE

Mexican Hat

St. George

Kanab

Utah 923

1992 Vote for Governor
Percent for Leavitt (R), by County

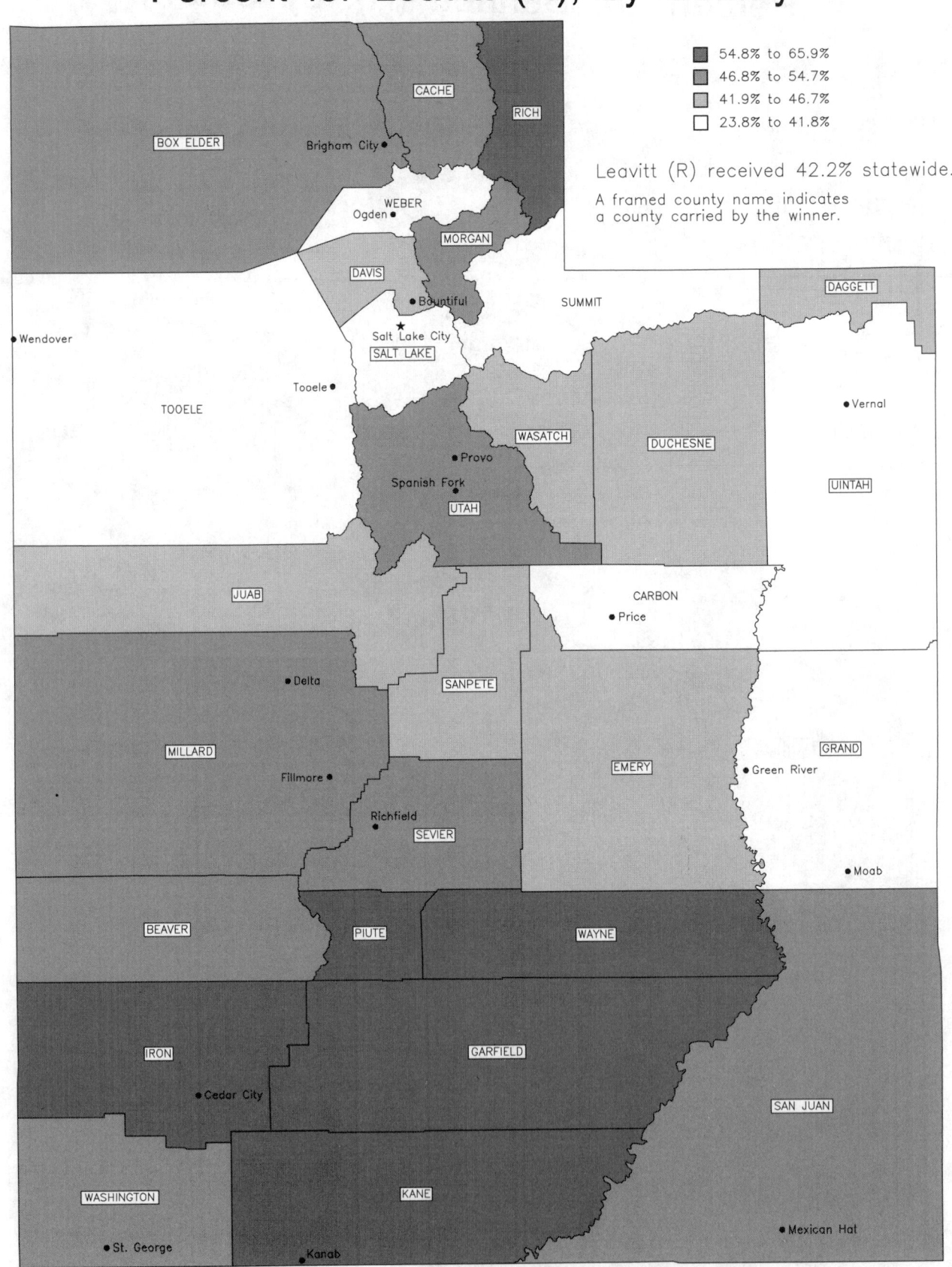

Legend:
- 54.8% to 65.9%
- 46.8% to 54.7%
- 41.9% to 46.7%
- 23.8% to 41.8%

Leavitt (R) received 42.2% statewide.

A framed county name indicates a county carried by the winner.

VERMONT

Voting Equipment Use (Cities and Towns)[2]

Datavote Punch Card	0	Paper Ballot	230
Electronic	0	Other Punch Card	0
Lever Machine	1	Mixed Systems	0
Optical Scanner	20		

Party Control	DEM	REP	IND[3]	VAC
1993 State Senate	14	16	0	0
1992 State Senate	15	15	0	0
1993 State House	87	57	6	0
1992 State House	73	75	2	0

Population Statistics 1990

Race/ Ethnicity	Total Population		Voting Age Population		Voting Age Population % of total population
	Number	%	Number	%	
Non-Hispanic					
White	552,184	98.1	412,537	98.3	74.7
Black	1,868	0.3	1,208	0.3	64.7
Asian/Pacific Islander	3,159	0.6	2,131	0.5	67.5
Native American	1,651	0.3	1,135	0.3	68.7
Other	235	<.1	106	<.1	45.1
All Hispanic	3,661	0.7	2,558	0.6	69.9
TOTAL	562,758	100.0	419,675	100.0	74.6

Estimated Voting Age Population 1992 (VAP) 429,000
Number of Registered Voters 383,371
    % of estimated VAP 89.4
Voter Turnout (Actual) 292,797
    % of VAP 68.3
    % of Registration 76.4
Persons Not Voting—of Voting Age 136,203
    % of VAP 31.7
Persons Not Voting—of Registered 90,574
    % of Registration 23.6
Straight Ticket Voting .... No

State Officials and Members of Congress

Governor:
Howard Dean (D) 1991, elected to a two-year term in 1992.

U.S. Senators:
Patrick J. Leahy (D) 1974, elected to a six-year term in 1992.
James M. Jeffords (R) 1988, elected to a six-year term in 1988.

U.S. Representative in Congress:
(District, Name, Party, Date first elected)

At-Large. Sanders (I) 1990

---

[1]Elections administered by 251 cities and towns rather than counties. Data presented for counties and 23 cities and towns with more than one voting precinct. [2]Reported for all 251 cities and towns, including those with a single voting precinct. [3]Two of the six independent members are members of minor parties.

Candidates: General Election, November 3, 1992

Candidate(s)	Total vote	Percent	Party	Status	First elected
President/Vice President					
Clinton/Gore	133,592	46.11%	Democrat	Challenger	1992
Bush/Quayle	88,122	30.42%	Republican	Incumbent	1988
Perot/Stockdale	65,991	22.78%	Independent	Challenger	
Marrou/Lord	501	0.17%	Libertarian	Challenger	
Write ins	488	0.17%	Unknown	Challenger	
Fulani/Munoz	329	0.11%	New Alliance	Challenger	
Hagelin/Tompkins	315	0.11%	Natural Law	Challenger	
Phillips/Knight	124	0.04%	Taxpayers	Challenger	
Fulani/Mulholland	100	0.03%	Liberty Union	Challenger	
Warren/Debates	82	0.03%	Socialist Workers	Challenger	
LaRouche/Bevel	57	0.02%	Freedom for LaRouche	Challenger	
U.S. Senator					
Patrick Leahy	154,762	54.16%	Democrat	Incumbent	1974
James Douglas	123,854	43.35%	Republican	Challenger	
Jerry Levy	5,121	1.79%	Liberty Union	Challenger	
Michael Godeck	1,780	0.62%	Freedom for LaRouche	Challenger	
Write ins	222	0.08%	Write in	Challenger	
Governor					
Howard Dean	213,523	74.73%	Democrat	Challenger	1992
John McClaughry	65,837	23.04%	Republican	Challenger	
Richard Gottlieb	3,120	1.09%	Liberty Union	Challenger	
August Jaccaci	2,834	0.99%	Natural Law	Challenger	
Write ins	414	0.14%	Write in	Challenger	
U.S. Representative in Congress					
District At-Large					
Bernie Sanders	162,724	57.78%	Independent	Incumbent	1990
Tim Philbin	86,901	30.86%	Republican	Challenger	
Lewis Young	22,279	7.91%	Democrat	Challenger	
Pete Diamondstone	3,660	1.30%	Liberty Union	Challenger	
John Dewey	3,549	1.26%	Natural Law	Challenger	
Douglas Miller	2,049	0.73%	Freedom for LaRouche	Challenger	
Write ins	464	0.16%	Write in	Challenger	

Voter Registration and Turnout, 1948-1992 Elections

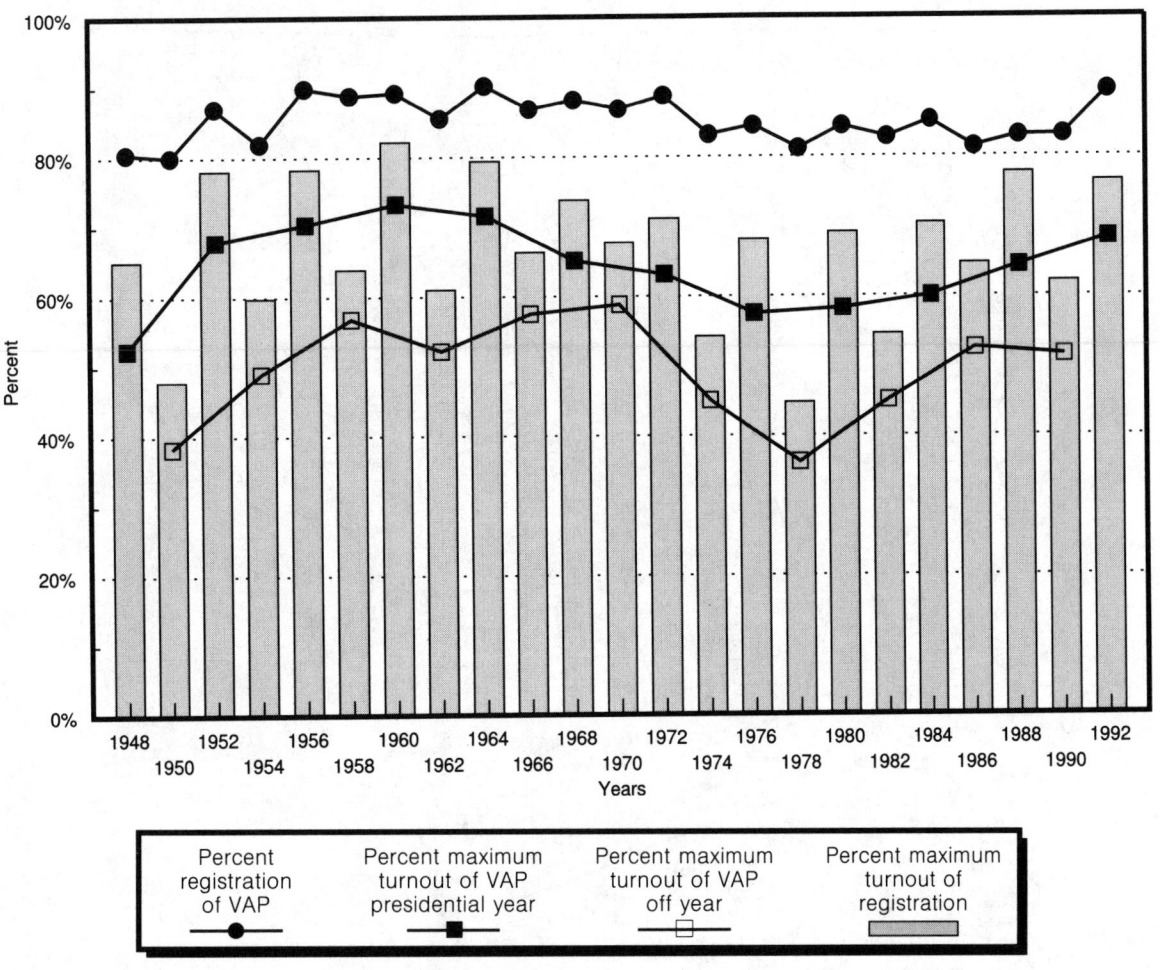

	Percent registration of VAP ●—	Percent maximum turnout of VAP presidential year ■—	Percent maximum turnout of VAP off year □—	Percent maximum turnout of registration

Year	Estimated Voting Age Population (VAP)	Voter registration (REG)			Voter turnout											
						Highest office						Maximum vote				
		Total	Percent of VAP	Rank by percent of VAP	Actual	Total	Office	Percent total REG	Rank by percent of REG	Percent of VAP	Rank by percent of VAP	Total	Percent total REG	Rank by percent of REG	Percent total VAP	Rank by percent of VAP
1992	429,000	383,371	89.4	5	292,797	289,701	P	75.6	30	67.5	5	292,797	76.4	32	68.3	7
1990	422,000	350,349	83.0	7	217,384	211,422	G	60.3	18	50.1	11	217,384	62.0	17	51.5	10
1988	420,000	348,312	82.9	9	270,148	243,328	P	69.9	30	57.9	10	270,148	77.6	12	64.3	3
1986	403,000	327,788	81.3	8	211,709	196,716	G	60.0	15	48.8	8	211,709	64.6	11	52.5	6
1984	392,000	333,778	85.1	8	235,140	234,561	P	70.3	36	59.8	12	235,140	70.4	38	60.0	13
1982	382,000	315,767	82.7	7	172,084	169,251	G	53.6	40	44.3	20	172,084	54.5	40	45.0	23
1980	370,000	311,919	84.3	9	215,500	213,299	P	68.4	42	57.6	18	215,500	69.1	40	58.2	21
1978	353,000	286,275	81.1	8	127,829	124,482	G	43.5	43	35.3	37	127,829	44.7	43	36.2	37
1976	337,000	284,294	84.4	8	193,655	187,765	P	66.0	43	55.7	27	193,655	68.1	42	57.5	25
1974	321,000	266,649	83.1	5	144,556	142,772	S	53.5	33	44.5	18	144,556	54.2	34	45.0	20
1972	308,000	273,056	88.7	4	194,215	186,947	P	68.5	34	60.7	20	194,215	71.1	32	63.1	16
1970	265,000	230,148	86.8	7	155,709	154,899	S	67.3	21	58.5	8	155,709	67.7	23	58.8	9
1968	252,000	222,024	88.1	9	163,955	161,404	P	72.7	40	64.0	27	163,955	73.8	39	65.1	24
1966	240,000	208,221	86.8	7	137,994	136,262	G	65.4	22	56.8	15	137,994	66.3	23	57.5	16
1964	232,000	209,225	90.2	7	166,049	163,089	P	77.9	29	70.3	15	166,049	79.4	25	71.6	14
1962	233,000	199,141	85.5	6	120,747	121,571	S	61.0	24	52.2	22	121,571	61.0	24	52.2	25
1960	231,000	206,034	89.2	5	169,438	167,324	P	81.2	25	72.4	16	169,438	82.2	25	73.3	15
1958	221,000	196,279	88.8	4	125,461	124,442	S	63.4	22	56.3	18	125,461	63.9	22	56.8	19
1956	223,000	200,381	89.9	6	156,973	152,978	P	76.3	22	68.6	18	156,973	78.3	23	70.4	16
1954	237,000	194,198	81.9	9	116,179	114,360	G	58.9	19	48.3	30	116,179	59.8	19	49.0	30
1952	231,000	201,000	87.0	8	156,923	153,557	P	76.4	20	66.5	30	156,923	78.1	21	67.9	29
1950	237,000	189,655	80.0	6	90,778	89,171	S	47.0	18	37.6	36	90,778	47.9	18	38.3	36
1948	238,000	191,521	80.5	6	124,749	123,382	P	64.4	19	51.8	31	124,749	65.1	19	52.4	31

VERMONT

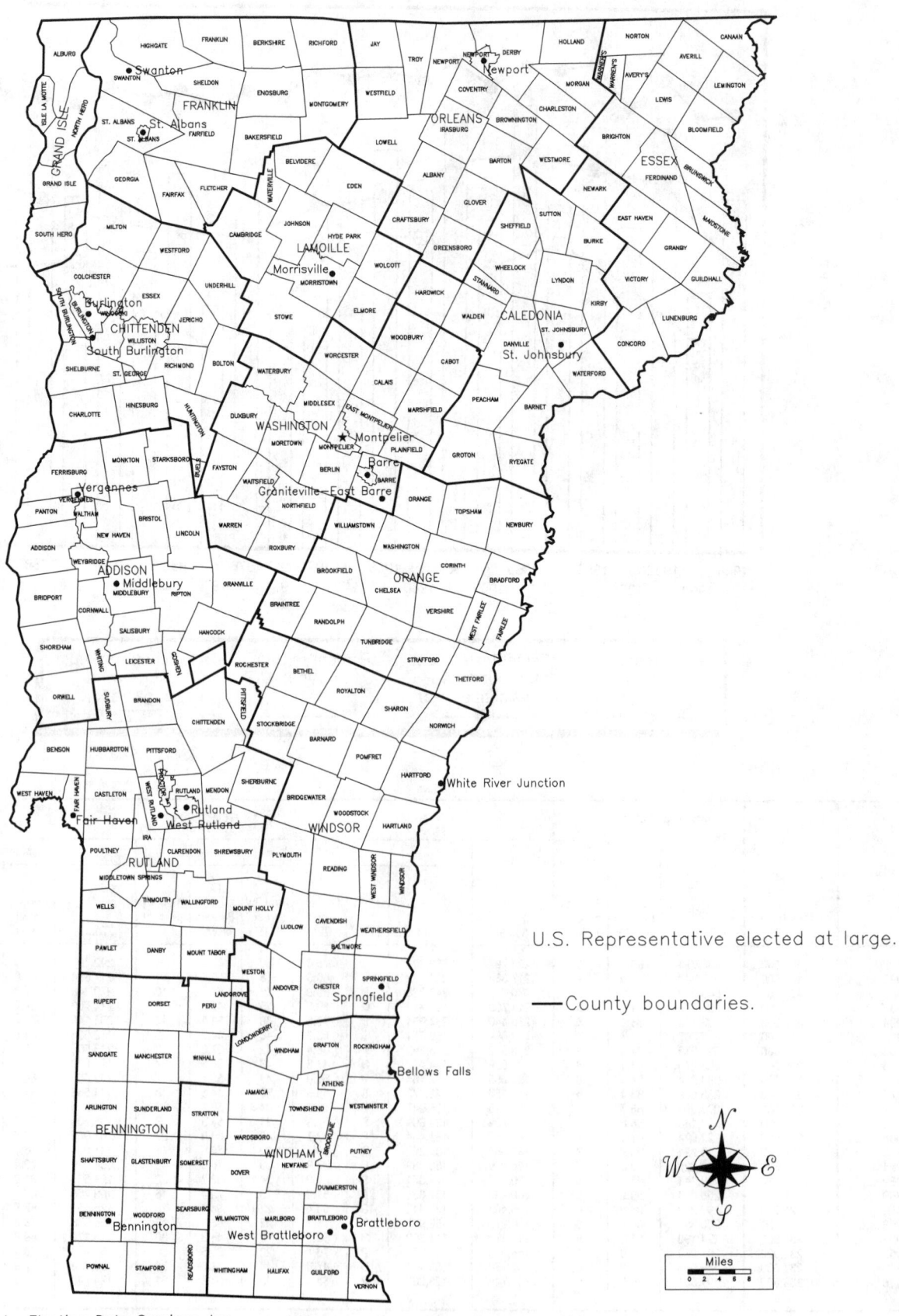

U.S. Representative elected at large.

—— County boundaries.

928 Vermont

Table A. — 1990 Population by Race and Ethnic Origin

State/ county code	County	Total persons	Percent of total persons						Rank[1]				Percent contribution to state population			
			Non-Hispanic				Other	Hispanic	Percent of total persons					Non-Hispanic		
			White	Black	Asian and Pacific Islander	Native American			Total	Non-Hispanic		Hispanic	Total	White	Black	Hispanic
										White	Black					
50 001	Addison	32,953	98.1	0.4	0.6	0.2	<.1	0.6	8	10	2	4	5.9	5.9	6.7	5.7
50 003	Bennington	35,845	98.4	0.3	0.5	0.1	<.1	0.6	7	9	4	5	6.4	6.4	6.1	6.0
50 005	Caledonia	27,846	98.9	0.2	0.2	0.3	<.1	0.3	9	2	11	14	4.9	5.0	2.8	2.5
50 007	Chittenden	131,761	97.1	0.6	1.1	0.2	<.1	0.9	1	14	1	2	23.4	23.2	41.9	32.2
50 009	Essex	6,405	98.8	0.2	0.2	0.3	<.1	0.5	13	5	9	7	1.1	1.1	0.7	0.8
50 011	Franklin	39,980	97.8	0.1	0.2	1.5	<.1	0.3	6	13	13	13	7.1	7.1	3.1	3.7
50 013	Grand Isle	5,318	98.7	0.3	0.2	0.4	<.1	0.4	14	7	6	12	0.9	1.0	0.8	0.5
50 015	Lamoille	19,735	98.8	0.1	0.3	0.2	<.1	0.5	12	6	14	8	3.5	3.5	1.4	2.4
50 017	Orange	26,149	98.9	0.2	0.3	0.2	<.1	0.4	10	3	12	10	4.6	4.7	2.4	2.8
50 019	Orleans	24,053	99.0	0.2	0.2	0.2	<.1	0.4	11	1	10	11	4.3	4.3	2.6	2.5
50 021	Rutland	62,142	98.9	0.2	0.3	0.1	<.1	0.4	2	4	8	9	11.0	11.1	7.8	7.5
50 023	Washington	54,928	97.9	0.3	0.4	0.2	<.1	1.2	3	12	5	1	9.8	9.7	8.8	18.1
50 025	Windham	41,588	98.1	0.4	0.6	0.2	<.1	0.7	5	11	3	3	7.4	7.4	8.0	8.3
50 027	Windsor	54,055	98.5	0.2	0.5	0.2	<.1	0.5	4	8	7	6	9.6	9.6	6.8	7.0
50	**VERMONT**	**562,758**	**98.1**	**0.3**	**0.6**	**0.3**	**<.1**	**0.7**					**100.0**	**100.0**	**100.0**	**100.0**
	CITIES AND TOWNS															
50 023	Barre city	9,482	97.3	0.2	0.2	0.2	<.1	2.0	9	16	15	1	1.7	1.7	1.2	5.2
50 019	Barton town	2,967	99.0	<.1	0.3	0.2	0.0	0.4	20	2	22	19	0.5	0.5	0.1	0.4
50 003	Bennington town	16,451	97.8	0.4	0.8	0.2	<.1	0.8	4	12	10	10	2.9	2.9	3.7	3.8
50 025	Brattleboro town	12,241	96.6	0.8	1.2	0.2	0.1	1.1	7	20	3	5	2.2	2.1	5.2	3.7
50 007	Burlington city	39,127	96.0	1.0	1.5	0.3	<.1	1.2	1	23	2	4	7.0	6.8	20.2	13.2
50 007	Colchester town	14,731	97.5	0.5	0.8	0.2	<.1	0.9	5	15	8	6	2.6	2.6	4.0	3.7
50 007	Essex town	16,498	96.9	0.6	1.4	0.1	<.1	0.9	3	19	5	9	2.9	2.9	5.6	3.9
50 027	Hartford town	9,404	97.7	0.5	0.9	0.3	<.1	0.6	10	13	6	14	1.7	1.7	2.7	1.5
50 009	Lunenburg town	1,176	98.4	0.2	0.3	0.5	0.0	0.7	23	9	19	12	0.2	0.2	0.1	0.2
50 001	Middlebury town	8,034	96.1	1.0	1.4	<.1	<.1	1.2	12	22	1	3	1.4	1.4	4.4	2.7
50 023	Montpelier city	8,247	96.9	0.4	0.9	0.3	<.1	1.4	11	18	9	2	1.5	1.4	1.9	3.2
50 017	Newbury town	1,985	98.9	0.2	0.2	0.5	0.0	0.3	22	3	20	22	0.4	0.4	0.2	0.2
50 017	Randolph town	4,764	98.7	0.2	0.4	0.2	0.1	0.3	17	5	16	23	0.8	0.9	0.6	0.4
50 021	Rutland city	18,230	98.6	0.4	0.5	0.1	<.1	0.4	2	6	11	18	3.2	3.3	3.5	2.2
50 021	Rutland town	3,781	98.5	0.3	0.4	<.1	0.0	0.7	19	7	13	11	0.7	0.7	0.6	0.7
50 007	Shelburne town	5,871	97.9	0.3	1.0	0.1	<.1	0.6	16	11	12	13	1.0	1.0	1.0	1.0
50 007	South Burlington city	12,809	96.3	0.5	1.9	0.3	<.1	0.9	6	21	7	7	2.3	2.2	3.5	3.2
50 027	Springfield town	9,579	98.5	<.1	0.6	0.3	0.0	0.5	8	8	21	16	1.7	1.7	0.4	1.3
50 011	St. Albans city	7,339	97.7	0.2	0.4	1.1	<.1	0.5	14	14	17	15	1.3	1.3	0.9	1.1
50 011	St. Albans town	4,606	98.3	0.3	0.3	0.7	<.1	0.4	18	10	14	21	0.8	0.8	0.7	0.5
50 005	St. Johnsbury town	7,608	98.7	0.2	0.3	0.2	<.1	0.5	13	4	18	17	1.4	1.4	0.8	1.0
50 017	Williamstown town	2,839	99.4	<.1	0.1	<.1	0.0	0.4	21	1	23	20	0.5	0.5	<.1	0.3
50 007	Winooski city	6,649	96.9	0.7	1.1	0.3	<.1	0.9	15	17	4	8	1.2	1.2	2.6	1.6
	CONGRESSIONAL															
	District At-Large	562,758	98.1	0.3	0.6	0.3	<.1	0.7								

[1]Separate rankings for 14 counties and for 23 cities and towns.

Table B. — 1990 Voting Age Population (VAP) by Race and Ethnic Origin

County	Total Voting Age Population	Percent of total VAP Non-Hispanic White	Black	Asian and Pacific Islander	Native American	Other	Hispanic	Rank Percent of total VAP Total	Non-Hispanic White	Black	Hispanic	Percent contribution to state VAP Total	Non-Hispanic White	Black	Hispanic	VAP percent of total population Total	Non-Hispanic White	Black	Asian and Pacific Islander	Native American	Other	Hispanic
Addison	24,352	98.2	0.4	0.6	0.2	<.1	0.6	8	11	2	3	5.8	5.8	8.0	6.2	73.9	73.9	77.0	73.8	55.3	62.5	76.0
Bennington	26,852	98.6	0.3	0.5	0.1	0.0	0.6	7	9	4	5	6.4	6.4	6.2	5.8	74.9	75.0	65.8	68.7	72.5	0.0	67.7
Caledonia	20,166	99.0	0.1	0.2	0.3	<.1	0.3	9	4	11	12	4.8	4.8	2.2	2.5	72.4	72.5	50.0	63.2	70.5	16.7	70.0
Chittenden	100,945	97.3	0.5	1.0	0.2	<.1	0.9	1	14	1	2	24.1	23.8	44.2	33.7	76.6	76.8	68.2	72.0	79.7	41.4	73.1
Essex	4,699	99.0	0.2	0.1	0.3	0.0	0.2	13	3	5	14	1.1	1.1	0.9	0.4	73.4	73.5	84.6	63.6	88.9	0.0	36.7
Franklin	28,204	98.0	0.1	0.2	1.3	<.1	0.3	6	13	12	11	6.7	6.7	3.0	3.6	70.5	70.7	62.1	53.1	64.0	60.0	66.9
Grand Isle	3,903	98.9	0.2	0.1	0.4	0.0	0.4	14	6	8	7	0.9	0.9	0.7	0.6	73.4	73.5	53.3	40.0	65.2	0.0	80.0
Lamoille	14,663	98.9	0.1	0.3	0.2	<.1	0.5	12	7	14	6	3.5	3.5	1.2	2.6	74.3	74.4	55.6	69.1	64.4	69.2	75.3
Orange	18,907	99.0	0.1	0.2	0.2	<.1	0.4	10	2	13	9	4.5	4.5	1.9	2.8	72.3	72.4	51.1	55.9	67.7	23.1	69.9
Orleans	17,227	99.2	0.2	0.1	0.2	<.1	0.3	11	1	10	13	4.1	4.1	2.2	1.9	71.6	71.8	54.2	40.0	76.8	40.0	52.2
Rutland	47,149	99.0	0.2	0.3	0.1	<.1	0.4	2	5	9	10	11.2	11.3	7.5	6.9	75.9	76.0	62.1	69.0	75.0	27.8	64.8
Washington	40,988	98.0	0.2	0.4	0.2	<.1	1.2	3	12	6	1	9.8	9.7	7.6	19.1	74.6	74.7	55.8	64.1	69.0	63.6	73.8
Windham	30,958	98.3	0.3	0.6	0.2	<.1	0.6	5	10	3	4	7.4	7.4	7.5	7.4	74.4	74.6	60.0	68.0	75.0	65.0	62.4
Windsor	40,662	98.8	0.2	0.4	0.2	<.1	0.4	4	8	7	8	9.7	9.7	7.0	6.5	75.2	75.4	66.9	54.3	60.7	50.0	65.1
VERMONT	**419,675**	**98.3**	**0.3**	**0.5**	**0.3**	**<.1**	**0.6**					**100.0**	**100.0**	**100.0**	**100.0**	**74.6**	**74.7**	**64.7**	**67.5**	**68.7**	**45.1**	**69.9**
CITIES AND TOWNS																						
Barre city	7,276	97.6	0.1	0.2	0.2	<.1	2.0	8	15	18	1	1.7	1.7	0.7	5.6	76.7	76.9	40.9	68.4	60.0	50.0	75.7
Barton town	2,153	99.4	<.1	<.1	0.2	0.0	0.3	20	2	23	22	0.5	0.5	<.1	0.2	72.6	72.9	50.0	12.5	71.4	0.0	46.2
Bennington town	12,287	97.9	0.4	0.7	0.2	0.0	0.8	3	14	9	10	2.9	2.9	4.1	3.7	74.7	74.8	72.5	69.3	72.4	0.0	67.6
Brattleboro town	9,339	97.1	0.6	1.1	0.2	0.1	0.9	7	19	4	6	2.2	2.2	4.4	3.4	76.3	76.7	54.6	70.8	85.0	71.4	62.8
Burlington city	32,887	96.3	0.8	1.4	0.3	<.1	1.2	1	22	2	4	7.8	7.7	21.7	15.5	84.0	84.3	69.3	81.4	75.8	43.8	82.0
Colchester town	11,290	97.5	0.5	0.8	0.2	<.1	0.9	5	16	6	5	2.7	2.7	4.7	4.1	76.6	76.6	77.0	74.4	92.3	20.0	77.9
Essex town	11,885	97.3	0.5	1.2	0.1	<.1	0.8	4	17	5	9	2.8	2.8	5.0	3.6	72.0	72.4	58.1	61.2	88.2	46.7	63.6
Hartford town	7,098	98.0	0.5	0.8	0.2	<.1	0.5	10	12	8	13	1.7	1.7	2.8	1.4	75.5	75.7	68.0	67.1	58.3	100.0	66.7
Lunenburg town	864	98.5	0.1	0.3	0.7	0.0	0.3	23	9	19	20	0.2	0.2	<.1	0.1	73.5	73.6	50.0	100.0	100.0	0.0	37.5
Middlebury town	6,515	95.8	1.1	1.6	<.1	<.1	1.4	11	23	1	3	1.6	1.5	6.0	3.5	81.1	80.8	87.8	88.7	50.0	85.7	90.0
Montpelier city	6,361	97.0	0.3	0.8	0.3	<.1	1.5	12	20	10	2	1.5	1.5	1.8	3.6	77.1	77.2	62.9	69.2	79.2	100.0	79.5
Newbury town	1,465	98.8	0.1	0.2	0.6	0.0	0.3	22	7	17	23	0.3	0.4	0.2	0.2	73.8	73.7	66.7	100.0	90.0	0.0	66.7
Randolph town	3,609	98.9	0.1	0.4	0.2	<.1	0.3	17	3	20	21	0.9	0.9	0.3	0.4	75.8	75.9	36.4	66.7	70.0	28.6	84.6
Rutland city	14,257	98.8	0.3	0.5	0.1	<.1	0.4	2	8	12	19	3.4	3.4	3.4	2.0	78.2	78.3	62.1	77.4	78.3	66.7	61.0
Rutland town	2,841	98.8	0.2	0.3	<.1	0.0	0.6	19	6	15	11	0.7	0.7	0.4	0.7	75.1	75.3	45.5	60.0	66.7	0.0	69.2
Shelburne town	4,320	98.1	0.3	0.8	0.1	<.1	0.6	16	11	7	12	1.0	1.0	1.1	1.0	73.6	73.8	72.2	60.0	85.7	50.0	67.6
South Burlington city	10,030	96.6	0.5	1.7	0.3	<.1	0.8	6	21	7	7	2.4	2.3	4.1	3.3	78.3	78.6	76.9	68.8	77.5	28.6	72.4
Springfield town	7,211	98.9	<.1	0.4	0.3	0.0	0.4	9	4	21	18	1.7	1.7	0.5	1.0	75.3	75.6	75.0	48.3	64.5	0.0	56.5
St. Albans city	5,443	97.9	0.2	0.3	1.1	<.1	0.4	14	13	14	17	1.3	1.3	1.0	0.9	74.2	74.3	75.0	65.4	71.6	60.0	55.0
St. Albans town	3,406	98.4	0.2	0.2	0.7	<.1	0.4	18	10	13	14	0.8	0.8	0.7	0.6	73.9	74.0	61.5	58.3	69.7	100.0	78.9
St. Johnsbury town	5,607	98.9	0.1	0.3	0.2	<.1	0.4	13	5	16	16	1.3	1.3	0.9	0.9	73.7	73.8	53.3	72.0	72.2	33.3	63.9
Williamstown town	2,044	99.4	<.1	<.1	<.1	0.0	0.4	21	1	22	15	0.5	0.5	<.1	0.4	72.0	72.0	100.0	25.0	100.0	0.0	75.0
Winooski city	5,257	97.1	0.7	1.1	0.3	<.1	0.8	15	18	3	8	1.3	1.2	2.9	1.6	79.1	79.2	71.4	77.8	88.2	60.0	68.3
CONGRESSIONAL																						
District At-Large	419,675	98.3	0.3	0.5	0.3	<.1	0.6									74.6	74.7	64.7	67.5	68.7	45.1	69.9

[1]Separate rankings for 14 counties and for 23 cities and towns.

Table C. — Voter Participation: November 3, 1992, General Election

County	Estimated Voting Age Population (VAP), 1992	Voter registration (REG)[1]				Voter turnout												
							Highest office			Maximum vote[2]						Percent drop-off, by office[3]		
		Total	% contribution to state REG	% of 1992 VAP	Rank by % of 1992 VAP	Actual[1]	Total	Office	% of 1992 VAP	Total	% contribution to state turnout	% of REG	Rank by % of REG	% of 1992 VAP	Rank by % 1992 VAP	President	Senator	Governor	Representative
Addison	24,765	-	-	-	-	-	17,026	P	68.8	17,026	5.9	-	-	68.8	4	0.0	0.9	1.4	2.1
Bennington	27,240	-	-	-	-	-	18,225	P	66.9	18,225	6.3	-	-	66.9	8	0.0	2.4	2.3	4.4
Caledonia	20,746	-	-	-	-	-	13,072	P	63.0	13,072	4.5	-	-	63.0	13	0.0	1.5	1.1	2.5
Chittenden	102,395	-	-	-	-	-	70,119	P	68.5	70,119	24.2	-	-	68.5	5	0.0	1.4	1.5	2.5
Essex	4,832	-	-	-	-	-	2,996	P	62.0	2,996	1.0	-	-	62.0	14	0.0	1.5	1.3	3.3
Franklin	29,693	-	-	-	-	-	18,752	P	63.2	18,752	6.5	-	-	63.2	12	0.0	0.9	0.7	2.1
Grand Isle	4,053	-	-	-	-	-	3,379	P	83.4	3,379	1.2	-	-	83.4	1	0.0	0.9	0.8	2.4
Lamoille	15,112	-	-	-	-	-	10,142	P	67.1	10,142	3.5	-	-	67.1	7	0.0	1.2	1.3	2.3
Orange	19,668	-	-	-	-	-	13,410	P	68.2	13,410	4.6	-	-	68.2	6	0.0	1.4	1.3	2.7
Orleans	17,620	-	-	-	-	-	11,513	P	65.3	11,513	4.0	-	-	65.3	10	0.0	1.0	0.9	2.0
Rutland	47,779	-	-	-	-	-	31,143	P	65.2	31,143	10.8	-	-	65.2	11	0.0	1.3	1.2	2.3
Washington	41,617	-	-	-	-	-	29,334	P	70.5	29,334	10.1	-	-	70.5	2	0.0	1.1	1.1	4.0
Windham	31,998	-	-	-	-	-	21,398	P	66.9	21,398	7.4	-	-	66.9	9	0.0	1.8	2.1	3.4
Windsor	41,482	-	-	-	-	-	29,192	P	70.4	29,192	10.1	-	-	70.4	3	0.0	1.4	1.3	2.8
VERMONT	429,000	383,371	100.0	89.4	-	292,797	289,701		67.5	292,747	100.0	76.4	-	68.3		1.1	2.5	2.5	3.9
CITIES AND TOWNS																			
Barre city	-	-	-	-	-	-	4,378	G	-	4,378	1.5	-	-	-	-	0.3	0.2	0.0	2.4
Barton town	-	-	-	-	-	-	1,318	P	-	1,318	0.5	-	-	-	-	0.0	0.6	0.0	1.4
Bennington town	-	-	-	-	-	-	7,381	P	-	7,381	2.5	-	-	-	-	0.0	2.8	2.6	5.1
Brattleboro town	-	-	-	-	-	-	5,845	P	-	5,845	2.0	-	-	-	-	0.0	1.6	2.4	3.8
Burlington city	-	-	-	-	-	-	20,400	P	-	20,400	7.0	-	-	-	-	0.0	1.8	2.5	2.8
Colchester town	-	-	-	-	-	-	6,737	P	-	6,737	2.3	-	-	-	-	0.0	2.3	1.3	3.0
Essex town	-	-	-	-	-	-	9,132	P	-	9,132	3.2	-	-	-	-	0.0	1.2	1.3	2.3
Hartford town	-	-	-	-	-	-	4,422	P	-	4,422	1.5	-	-	-	-	0.0	1.1	1.1	3.1
Lunenburg town	-	-	-	-	-	-	574	P	-	574	0.2	-	-	-	-	0.0	1.9	2.6	6.3
Middlebury town	-	-	-	-	-	-	3,837	P	-	3,837	1.3	-	-	-	-	0.0	2.5	3.4	3.4
Montpelier city	-	-	-	-	-	-	4,588	P	-	4,588	1.6	-	-	-	-	0.0	2.2	2.9	13.1
Newbury town	-	-	-	-	-	-	1,065	P	-	1,065	0.4	-	-	-	-	0.0	2.3	1.2	3.2
Randolph town	-	-	-	-	-	-	2,153	P	-	2,153	0.7	-	-	-	-	0.0	0.8	0.5	2.0
Rutland city	-	-	-	-	-	-	8,559	P	-	8,559	3.0	-	-	-	-	0.0	0.7	0.6	2.5
Rutland town	-	-	-	-	-	-	2,330	P	-	2,330	0.8	-	-	-	-	0.0	0.6	0.1	1.2
Shelburne town	-	-	-	-	-	-	3,786	P	-	3,786	1.3	-	-	-	-	0.0	0.8	0.9	2.7
South Burlington city	-	-	-	-	-	-	7,278	P	-	7,278	2.5	-	-	-	-	0.0	1.1	1.0	2.4
Springfield town	-	-	-	-	-	-	4,767	P	-	4,767	1.6	-	-	-	-	0.0	1.3	0.9	2.5
St. Albans city	-	-	-	-	-	-	3,120	P	-	3,120	1.1	-	-	-	-	0.0	1.2	0.7	2.3
St. Albans town	-	-	-	-	-	-	2,282	P	-	2,282	0.8	-	-	-	-	0.0	0.9	0.7	2.5
St. Johnsbury town	-	-	-	-	-	-	3,344	P	-	3,344	1.2	-	-	-	-	0.0	1.5	0.9	2.8
Williamstown town	-	-	-	-	-	-	1,307	P	-	1,307	0.5	-	-	-	-	0.0	0.6	1.0	1.5
Winooski city	-	-	-	-	-	-	2,868	P	-	2,868	1.0	-	-	-	-	0.0	2.2	3.0	3.6

[1]Officially certified county-level voter registration and voter turnout data were not available from the Vermont Secretary of State at the time of publication (state-level voter registration and turnout data are certified).   [2]Statewide total does not equal sum of county totals because actual voter turnout data is available at the state level only.   [3]Percent drop-off is zero for any office used as highest office turnout.

Table E. — Vote for President: November 3, 1992, General Election

County	Total	Clinton (DEM)	Bush (REP)	Perot (IND)	Other	Plurality Total	Party	DEM	REP	IND	Other	Rank¹ DEM	Rank¹ REP	Rank¹ IND	Total	DEM	REP	IND	DEM	REP
Addison	17,026	8,092	5,034	3,777	123	3,058	D	47.5	29.6	22.2	0.7	3	10	9	5.9	6.1	5.7	5.7	61.6	38.4
Bennington	18,225	8,178	5,895	4,023	129	2,283	D	44.9	32.3	22.1	0.7	6	4	10	6.3	6.1	6.7	6.1	58.1	41.9
Caledonia	13,072	4,948	4,571	3,468	85	377	D	37.9	35.0	26.5	0.7	13	2	4	4.5	3.7	5.2	5.3	52.0	48.0
Chittenden	70,119	35,314	19,093	15,202	510	16,221	D	50.4	27.2	21.7	0.7	2	13	11	24.2	26.4	21.7	23.0	64.9	35.1
Essex	2,996	1,092	1,038	845	21	54	D	36.4	34.6	28.2	0.7	14	3	1	1.0	0.8	1.2	1.3	51.3	48.7
Franklin	18,752	8,004	5,484	5,146	118	2,520	D	42.7	29.2	27.4	0.6	10	11	2	6.5	6.0	6.2	7.8	59.3	40.7
Grand Isle	3,379	1,444	1,012	893	30	432	D	42.7	29.9	26.4	0.9	9	9	5	1.2	1.1	1.1	1.4	58.8	41.2
Lamoille	10,142	4,459	2,936	2,674	73	1,523	D	44.0	28.9	26.4	0.7	7	12	6	3.5	3.3	3.3	4.1	60.3	39.7
Orange	13,410	5,774	4,249	3,283	104	1,525	D	43.1	31.7	24.5	0.8	8	6	7	4.6	4.3	4.8	5.0	57.6	42.4
Orleans	11,513	4,721	3,572	3,135	85	1,149	D	41.0	31.0	27.2	0.7	12	7	3	4.0	3.5	4.1	4.8	56.9	43.1
Rutland	31,143	12,829	10,963	7,190	161	1,866	D	41.2	35.2	23.1	0.5	11	1	8	10.8	9.6	12.4	10.9	53.9	46.1
Washington	29,334	13,452	9,424	6,274	184	4,028	D	45.9	32.1	21.4	0.6	5	5	12	10.1	10.1	10.7	9.5	58.8	41.2
Windham	21,398	11,414	5,816	4,004	164	5,598	D	53.3	27.2	18.7	0.8	1	14	14	7.4	8.5	6.6	6.1	66.2	33.8
Windsor	29,192	13,871	9,035	6,077	209	4,836	D	47.5	31.0	20.8	0.7	4	8	13	10.1	10.4	10.3	9.2	60.6	39.4
VERMONT	**289,701**	**133,592**	**88,122**	**65,991**	**1,996**	**45,470**	**D**	**46.1**	**30.4**	**22.8**	**0.7**				**100.0**	**100.0**	**100.0**	**100.0**	**60.3**	**39.7**
CITIES AND TOWNS																				
Barre city	4,363	1,807	1,508	1,035	13	299	D	41.4	34.6	23.7	0.3	16	4	11	1.5	1.4	1.7	1.6	54.5	45.5
Barton town	1,318	512	413	368	25	99	D	38.8	31.3	27.9	1.9	20	10	3	0.5	0.4	0.5	0.6	55.4	44.6
Bennington town	7,381	3,646	2,151	1,536	48	1,495	D	49.4	29.1	20.8	0.7	7	17	14	2.5	2.7	2.4	2.3	62.9	37.1
Brattleboro town	5,845	3,519	1,447	837	42	2,072	D	60.2	24.8	14.3	0.7	2	22	22	2.0	2.6	1.6	1.3	70.9	29.1
Burlington city	20,400	12,510	4,462	3,241	187	8,048	D	61.3	21.9	15.9	0.9	1	23	21	7.0	9.4	5.1	4.9	73.7	26.3
Colchester town	6,737	2,966	1,997	1,739	35	969	D	44.0	29.6	25.8	0.5	13	15	5	2.3	2.2	2.3	2.6	59.8	40.2
Essex town	9,132	3,825	2,960	2,302	45	865	D	41.9	32.4	25.2	0.5	15	8	7	3.2	2.9	3.4	3.5	56.4	43.6
Hartford town	4,422	2,034	1,564	793	31	470	D	46.0	35.4	17.9	0.7	10	3	19	1.5	1.5	1.8	1.2	56.5	43.5
Lunenburg town	574	227	188	157	2	39	D	39.5	32.8	27.4	0.3	17	7	4	0.2	0.2	0.2	0.2	54.7	45.3
Middlebury town	3,837	2,176	1,021	612	28	1,155	D	56.7	26.6	16.0	0.7	3	20	20	1.3	1.6	1.2	0.9	68.1	31.9
Montpelier city	4,588	2,490	1,407	657	34	1,083	D	54.3	30.7	14.3	0.7	4	14	23	1.6	1.9	1.6	1.0	63.9	36.1
Newbury town	1,065	420	366	274	5	54	D	39.4	34.4	25.7	0.5	18	5	6	0.4	0.3	0.4	0.4	53.4	46.6
Randolph town	2,153	924	672	533	24	252	D	42.9	31.2	24.8	1.1	14	11	9	0.7	0.7	0.8	0.8	57.9	42.1
Rutland city	8,559	3,888	2,915	1,722	34	973	D	45.4	34.1	20.1	0.4	12	6	16	3.0	2.9	3.3	2.6	57.2	42.8
Rutland town	2,330	855	984	479	12	129	R	36.7	42.2	20.6	0.5	23	1	15	0.8	0.6	1.1	0.7	46.5	53.5
Shelburne town	3,786	1,841	1,202	723	20	639	D	48.6	31.7	19.1	0.5	8	9	17	1.3	1.4	1.4	1.1	60.5	39.5
South Burlington city	7,278	3,730	2,131	1,359	58	1,599	D	51.3	29.3	18.7	0.8	5	16	18	2.5	2.8	2.4	2.1	63.6	36.4
Springfield town	4,767	2,179	1,468	1,091	29	711	D	45.7	30.8	22.9	0.6	11	12	12	1.6	1.6	1.7	1.7	59.7	40.3
St. Albans city	3,120	1,455	887	744	34	568	D	46.6	28.4	23.8	1.1	9	18	10	1.1	1.1	1.0	1.1	62.1	37.9
St. Albans town	2,282	892	700	676	14	192	D	39.1	30.7	29.6	0.6	19	13	2	0.8	0.7	0.8	1.0	56.0	44.0
St. Johnsbury town	3,344	1,249	1,243	836	16	6	D	37.4	37.2	25.0	0.5	22	2	8	1.2	0.9	1.4	1.3	50.1	49.9
Williamstown town	1,307	499	368	437	3	62	D	38.2	28.2	33.4	0.2	21	19	1	0.5	0.4	0.4	0.7	57.6	42.4
Winooski city	2,868	1,462	733	646	27	729	D	51.0	25.6	22.5	0.9	6	21	13	1.0	1.1	0.8	1.0	66.6	33.4

¹Separate rankings for 14 counties and for 23 cities and towns.

Table F. — Vote for U.S. Senator: November 3, 1992, General Election

County	Total	Leahy (DEM)	Douglas (REP)	Other	Plurality Total	Party	DEM	REP	Other	DEM	REP	Other	Total	DEM	REP	Other
							Percent of total vote			Rank[1]			Percent contribution to state vote			
Addison	16,866	8,414	8,103	349	311	D	49.9	48.0	2.1	12	3	13	5.9	5.4	6.5	4.9
Bennington	17,787	9,489	7,713	585	1,776	D	53.3	43.4	3.3	8	9	2	6.2	6.1	6.2	8.2
Caledonia	12,880	6,090	6,495	295	405	R	47.3	50.4	2.3	14	1	11	4.5	3.9	5.2	4.1
Chittenden	69,152	41,448	26,582	1,122	14,866	D	59.9	38.4	1.6	1	14	14	24.2	26.8	21.5	15.8
Essex	2,952	1,485	1,377	90	108	D	50.3	46.6	3.0	11	4	3	1.0	1.0	1.1	1.3
Franklin	18,574	10,304	7,812	458	2,492	D	55.5	42.1	2.5	2	12	7	6.5	6.7	6.3	6.4
Grand Isle	3,347	1,792	1,478	77	314	D	53.5	44.2	2.3	7	7	10	1.2	1.2	1.2	1.1
Lamoille	10,019	5,475	4,301	243	1,174	D	54.6	42.9	2.4	4	11	8	3.5	3.5	3.5	3.4
Orange	13,220	6,831	6,045	344	786	D	51.7	45.7	2.6	10	5	5	4.6	4.4	4.9	4.8
Orleans	11,400	6,171	4,941	288	1,230	D	54.1	43.3	2.5	5	10	6	4.0	4.0	4.0	4.0
Rutland	30,747	15,067	14,946	734	121	D	49.0	48.6	2.4	13	2	9	10.8	9.7	12.1	10.3
Washington	29,012	15,576	12,794	642	2,782	D	53.7	44.1	2.2	6	8	12	10.2	10.1	10.3	9.0
Windham	21,011	11,576	8,332	1,103	3,244	D	55.1	39.7	5.2	3	13	1	7.4	7.5	6.7	15.5
Windsor	28,772	15,044	12,935	793	2,109	D	52.3	45.0	2.8	9	6	4	10.1	9.7	10.4	11.1
VERMONT	**285,739**	**154,762**	**123,854**	**7,123**	**30,908**	**D**	**54.2**	**43.3**	**2.5**				**100.0**	**100.0**	**100.0**	**100.0**
CITIES AND TOWNS																
Barre city	4,371	2,189	2,097	85	92	D	50.1	48.0	1.9	19	4	14	1.5	1.4	1.7	1.2
Barton town	1,310	698	584	28	114	D	53.3	44.6	2.1	15	9	11	0.5	0.5	0.5	0.4
Bennington town	7,176	4,299	2,664	213	1,635	D	59.9	37.1	3.0	3	20	6	2.5	2.8	2.2	3.0
Brattleboro town	5,752	3,426	2,029	297	1,397	D	59.6	35.3	5.2	4	22	1	2.0	2.2	1.6	4.2
Burlington city	20,030	13,955	5,635	440	8,320	D	69.7	28.1	2.2	1	23	10	7.0	9.0	4.5	6.2
Colchester town	6,581	3,669	2,818	94	851	D	55.8	42.8	1.4	10	15	19	2.3	2.4	2.3	1.3
Essex town	9,026	4,705	4,224	97	481	D	52.1	46.8	1.1	16	6	22	3.2	3.0	3.4	1.4
Hartford town	4,373	2,273	2,017	83	256	D	52.0	46.1	1.9	17	7	15	1.5	1.5	1.6	1.2
Lunenburg town	563	321	229	13	92	D	57.0	40.7	2.3	8	16	8	0.2	0.2	0.2	0.2
Middlebury town	3,741	2,056	1,641	44	415	D	55.0	43.9	1.2	11	12	20	1.3	1.3	1.3	0.6
Montpelier city	4,486	2,592	1,802	92	790	D	57.8	40.2	2.1	7	17	12	1.6	1.7	1.5	1.3
Newbury town	1,041	531	475	35	56	D	51.0	45.6	3.4	18	8	2	0.4	0.3	0.4	0.5
Randolph town	2,136	1,145	942	49	203	D	53.6	44.1	2.3	14	10	9	0.7	0.7	0.8	0.7
Rutland city	8,497	4,641	3,708	148	933	D	54.6	43.6	1.7	12	13	16	3.0	3.0	3.0	2.1
Rutland town	2,316	1,051	1,228	37	177	R	45.4	53.0	1.6	22	2	18	0.8	0.7	1.0	0.5
Shelburne town	3,756	2,108	1,613	35	495	D	56.1	42.9	0.9	9	14	23	1.3	1.4	1.3	0.5
South Burlington city	7,200	4,288	2,832	80	1,456	D	59.6	39.3	1.1	5	18	21	2.5	2.8	2.3	1.1
Springfield town	4,704	2,355	2,203	146	152	D	50.1	46.8	3.1	20	5	4	1.6	1.5	1.8	2.0
St. Albans city	3,084	1,825	1,163	96	662	D	59.2	37.7	3.1	6	19	3	1.1	1.2	0.9	1.3
St. Albans town	2,262	1,222	995	45	227	D	54.0	44.0	2.0	13	11	13	0.8	0.8	0.8	0.6
St. Johnsbury town	3,295	1,413	1,803	79	390	R	42.9	54.7	2.4	23	1	7	1.2	0.9	1.5	1.1
Williamstown town	1,299	623	636	40	13	R	48.0	49.0	3.1	21	3	5	0.5	0.4	0.5	0.6
Winooski city	2,804	1,745	1,011	48	734	D	62.2	36.1	1.7	2	21	17	1.0	1.1	0.8	0.7

[1]Separate rankings for 14 counties and for 23 cities and towns.

Table G. — Vote for Governor: November 3, 1992, General Election

County	Total	Dean (DEM)	McClaughry (REP)	Other	Plurality Total	Party	Percent of total vote DEM	REP	Other	Rank[1] DEM	REP	Other	Percent contribution to state vote Total	DEM	REP	Other
Addison	16,796	13,058	3,413	325	9,645	D	77.7	20.3	1.9	2	13	9	5.9	6.1	5.2	5.1
Bennington	17,812	12,640	4,776	396	7,864	D	71.0	26.8	2.2	11	4	7	6.2	5.9	7.3	6.2
Caledonia	12,934	7,027	5,665	242	1,362	D	54.3	43.8	1.9	14	1	10	4.5	3.3	8.6	3.8
Chittenden	69,067	54,818	13,047	1,202	41,771	D	79.4	18.9	1.7	1	14	12	24.2	25.7	19.8	18.9
Essex	2,956	1,738	1,138	80	600	D	58.8	38.5	2.7	13	2	3	1.0	0.8	1.7	1.3
Franklin	18,617	14,258	4,045	314	10,213	D	76.6	21.7	1.7	4	10	13	6.5	6.7	6.1	4.9
Grand Isle	3,351	2,548	743	60	1,805	D	76.0	22.2	1.8	5	9	11	1.2	1.2	1.1	0.9
Lamoille	10,012	7,564	2,242	206	5,322	D	75.5	22.4	2.1	6	8	8	3.5	3.5	3.4	3.2
Orange	13,229	9,532	3,253	444	6,279	D	72.1	24.6	3.4	10	5	2	4.6	4.5	4.9	7.0
Orleans	11,406	7,990	3,154	262	4,836	D	70.1	27.7	2.3	12	3	6	4.0	3.7	4.8	4.1
Rutland	30,783	22,907	7,360	516	15,547	D	74.4	23.9	1.7	8	6	14	10.8	10.7	11.2	8.1
Washington	29,009	21,584	6,724	701	14,860	D	74.4	23.2	2.4	9	7	4	10.2	10.1	10.2	11.0
Windham	20,957	15,698	4,312	947	11,386	D	74.9	20.6	4.5	7	12	1	7.3	7.4	6.5	14.9
Windsor	28,799	22,161	5,965	673	16,196	D	77.0	20.7	2.3	3	11	5	10.1	10.4	9.1	10.6
VERMONT	**285,728**	**213,523**	**65,837**	**6,368**	**147,686**	**D**	**74.7**	**23.0**	**2.2**				**100.0**	**100.0**	**100.0**	**100.0**
CITIES AND TOWNS																
Barre city	4,378	3,176	1,133	69	2,043	D	72.5	25.9	1.6	18	6	15	1.5	1.5	1.7	1.1
Barton town	1,318	940	350	28	590	D	71.3	26.6	2.1	20	5	6	0.5	0.4	0.5	0.4
Bennington town	7,188	5,451	1,602	135	3,849	D	75.8	22.3	1.9	14	11	8	2.5	2.6	2.4	2.1
Brattleboro town	5,705	4,551	905	249	3,646	D	79.8	15.9	4.4	6	22	1	2.0	2.1	1.4	3.9
Burlington city	19,884	16,506	2,798	580	13,708	D	83.0	14.1	2.9	1	23	3	7.0	7.7	4.2	9.1
Colchester town	6,648	5,292	1,299	57	3,993	D	79.6	19.5	0.9	7	16	23	2.3	2.5	2.0	0.9
Essex town	9,017	6,778	2,157	82	4,621	D	75.2	23.9	0.9	16	8	22	3.2	3.2	3.3	1.3
Hartford town	4,373	3,317	978	78	2,339	D	75.9	22.4	1.8	13	10	9	1.5	1.6	1.5	1.2
Lunenburg town	559	290	253	16	37	D	51.9	45.3	2.9	22	2	4	0.2	0.1	0.4	0.3
Middlebury town	3,708	3,010	626	72	2,384	D	81.2	16.9	1.9	3	20	7	1.3	1.4	1.0	1.1
Montpelier city	4,457	3,454	878	125	2,576	D	77.5	19.7	2.8	10	15	5	1.6	1.6	1.3	2.0
Newbury town	1,052	689	324	39	365	D	65.5	30.8	3.7	21	3	2	0.4	0.3	0.5	0.6
Randolph town	2,142	1,658	447	37	1,211	D	77.4	20.9	1.7	11	13	11	0.7	0.8	0.7	0.6
Rutland city	8,508	6,639	1,766	103	4,873	D	78.0	20.8	1.2	9	14	19	3.0	3.1	2.7	1.6
Rutland town	2,327	1,667	638	22	1,029	D	71.6	27.4	0.9	19	4	21	0.8	0.8	1.0	0.3
Shelburne town	3,751	3,031	681	39	2,350	D	80.8	18.2	1.0	4	19	20	1.3	1.4	1.0	0.6
South Burlington city	7,208	5,783	1,330	95	4,453	D	80.2	18.5	1.3	5	18	17	2.5	2.7	2.0	1.5
Springfield town	4,726	3,725	919	82	2,806	D	78.8	19.4	1.7	8	17	10	1.7	1.7	1.4	1.3
St. Albans city	3,098	2,372	674	52	1,698	D	76.6	21.8	1.7	12	12	12	1.1	1.1	1.0	0.8
St. Albans town	2,265	1,710	519	36	1,191	D	75.5	22.9	1.6	15	9	14	0.8	0.8	0.8	0.6
St. Johnsbury town	3,313	1,637	1,622	54	15	D	49.4	49.0	1.6	23	1	13	1.2	0.8	2.5	0.8
Williamstown town	1,294	946	331	17	615	D	73.1	25.6	1.3	17	7	18	0.5	0.4	0.5	0.3
Winooski city	2,783	2,271	469	43	1,802	D	81.6	16.9	1.5	2	21	16	1.0	1.1	0.7	0.7

[1]Separate rankings for 14 counties and for 23 cities and towns.

Table H. — Vote for U.S. Representative in Congress: November 3, 1992, General Election

Congressional district and county	Total[1]	Democrat (DEM)	Republican (REP)	Sanders (IND)	Plurality Total	Plurality Party	DEM	REP	IND	Rank within district DEM	Rank within district REP	Rank within district IND	Total	DEM	REP	IND
District At-Large	**281,626**	**22,279**	**86,901**	**162,724**	**75,823**	**I**	**7.9**	**30.9**	**57.8**				**100.0**	**100.0**	**100.0**	**100.0**
Addison	16,667	932	4,899	10,402	5,503	I	5.6	29.4	62.4	13	11	2	5.9	4.2	5.6	6.4
Bennington	17,427	2,375	6,045	8,142	2,097	I	13.6	34.7	46.7	2	3	14	6.2	10.7	7.0	5.0
Caledonia	12,742	787	4,441	7,080	2,639	I	6.2	34.9	55.6	12	2	10	4.5	3.5	5.1	4.4
Chittenden	68,376	4,473	19,751	42,524	22,773	I	6.5	28.9	62.2	10	13	3	24.3	20.1	22.7	26.1
Essex	2,897	368	924	1,445	521	I	12.7	31.9	49.9	3	4	13	1.0	1.7	1.1	0.9
Franklin	18,363	1,408	5,585	10,793	5,208	I	7.7	30.4	58.8	5	5	7	6.5	6.3	6.4	6.6
Grand Isle	3,298	213	976	1,996	1,020	I	6.5	29.6	60.5	11	10	5	1.2	1.0	1.1	1.2
Lamoille	9,910	507	2,970	6,201	3,231	I	5.1	30.0	62.6	14	9	1	3.5	2.3	3.4	3.8
Orange	13,051	962	3,596	7,900	4,304	I	7.4	27.6	60.5	6	14	4	4.6	4.3	4.1	4.9
Orleans	11,285	820	3,415	6,642	3,227	I	7.3	30.3	58.9	7	6	6	4.0	3.7	3.9	4.1
Rutland	30,419	2,072	11,304	16,288	4,984	I	6.8	37.2	53.5	8	1	11	10.8	9.3	13.0	10.0
Washington	28,150	1,852	8,507	16,503	7,996	I	6.6	30.2	58.6	9	7	8	10.0	8.3	9.8	10.1
Windham	20,660	2,955	6,219	10,394	4,175	I	14.3	30.1	50.3	1	8	12	7.3	13.3	7.2	6.4
Windsor	28,381	2,555	8,269	16,414	8,145	I	9.0	29.1	57.8	4	12	9	10.1	11.5	9.5	10.1
VERMONT[2]	**281,626**	**22,279**	**86,901**	**162,724**	**75,823**	**I**	**7.9**	**30.9**	**57.8**							

[1]Includes votes for minor party and other independent candidates. [2]The statewide total for other candidates is 9,722.

1992 Vote for President
Percent for Clinton (D), by Minor Civil Division

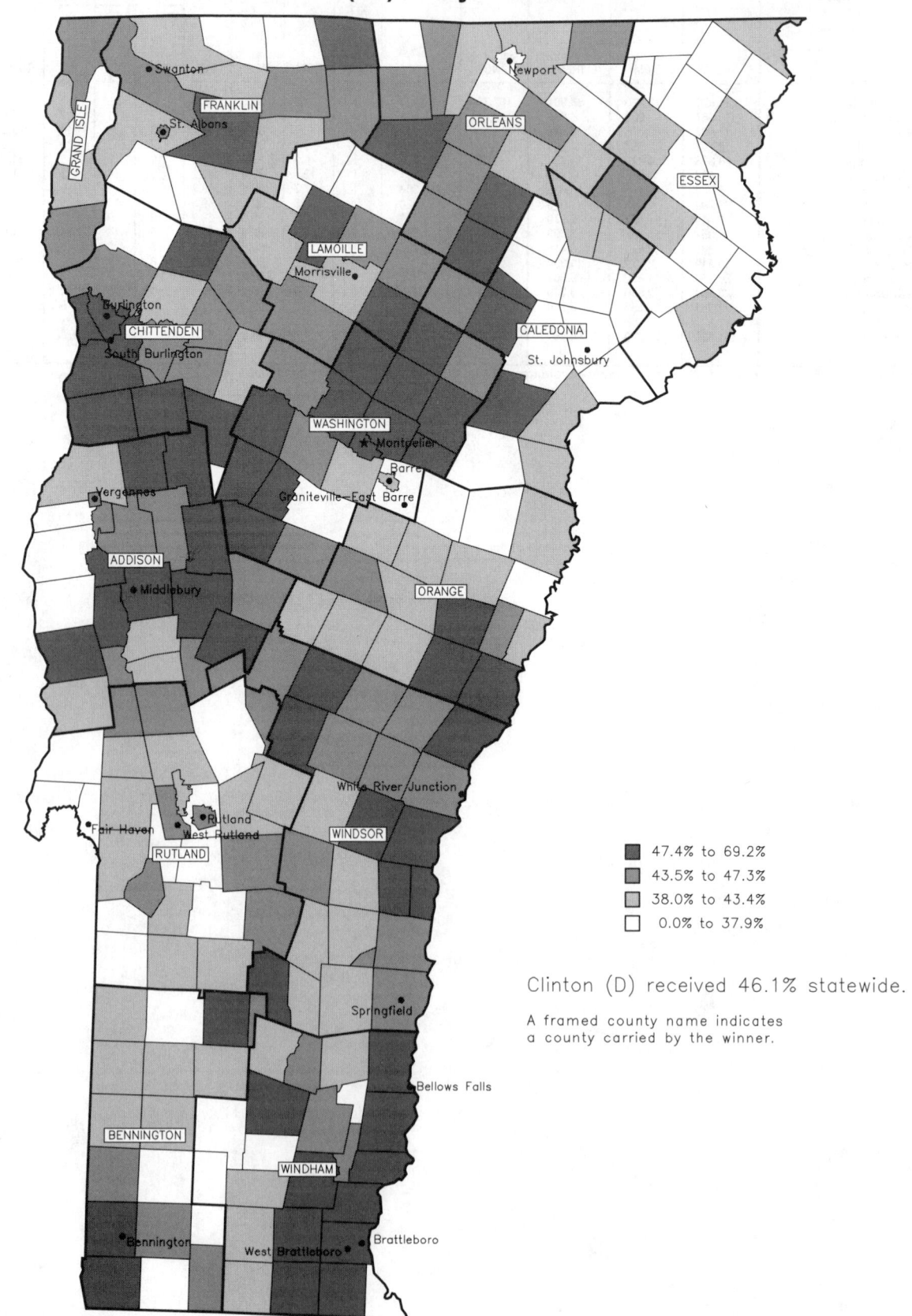

47.4% to 69.2%

43.5% to 47.3%

38.0% to 43.4%

0.0% to 37.9%

Clinton (D) received 46.1% statewide.

A framed county name indicates
a county carried by the winner.

936 Vermont

1992 Vote for U.S. Senator
Percent for Leahy (D), by Minor Civil Division

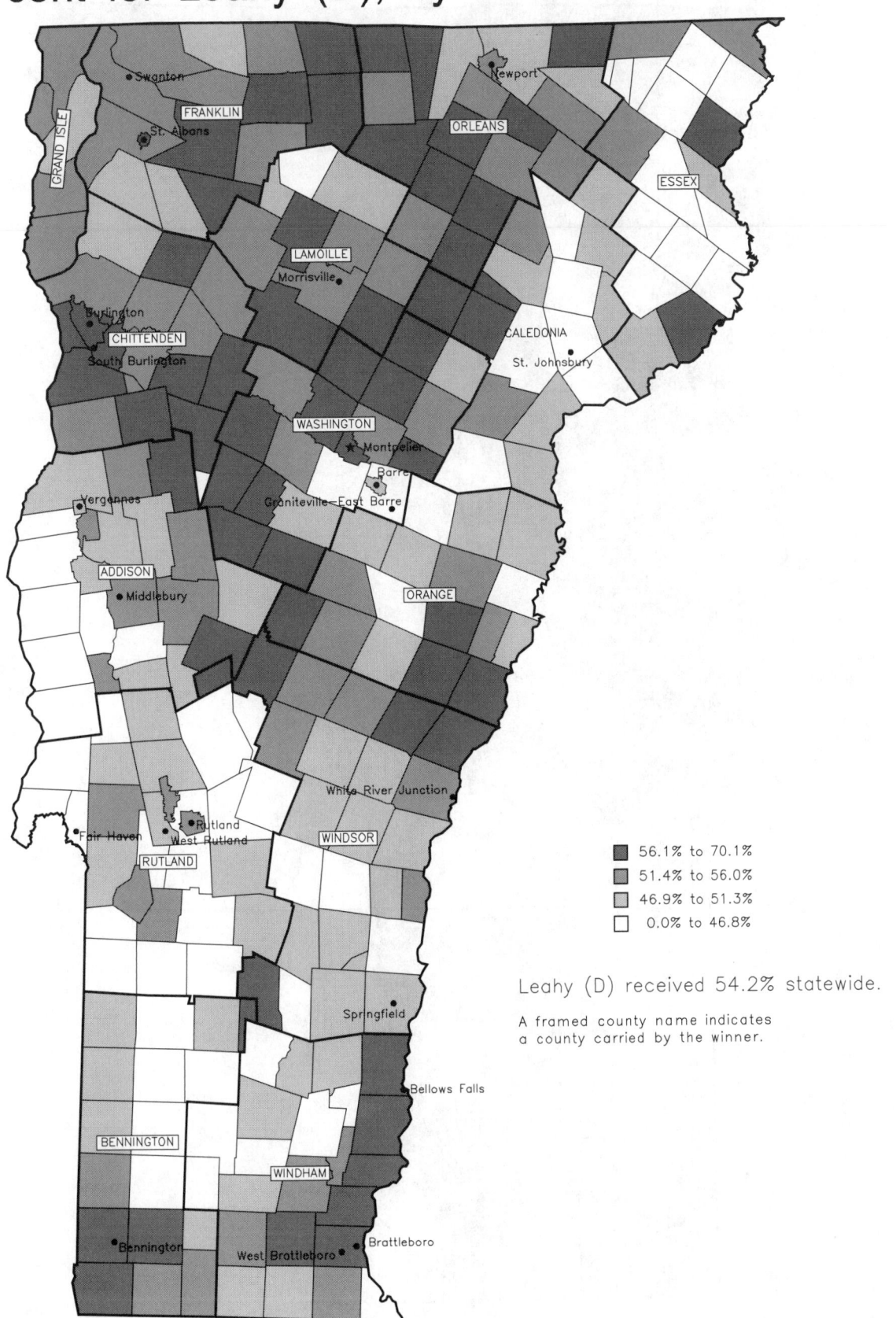

56.1% to 70.1%
51.4% to 56.0%
46.9% to 51.3%
0.0% to 46.8%

Leahy (D) received 54.2% statewide.

A framed county name indicates a county carried by the winner.

Vermont 937

1992 Vote for Governor
Percent for Dean (D), by Minor Civil Division

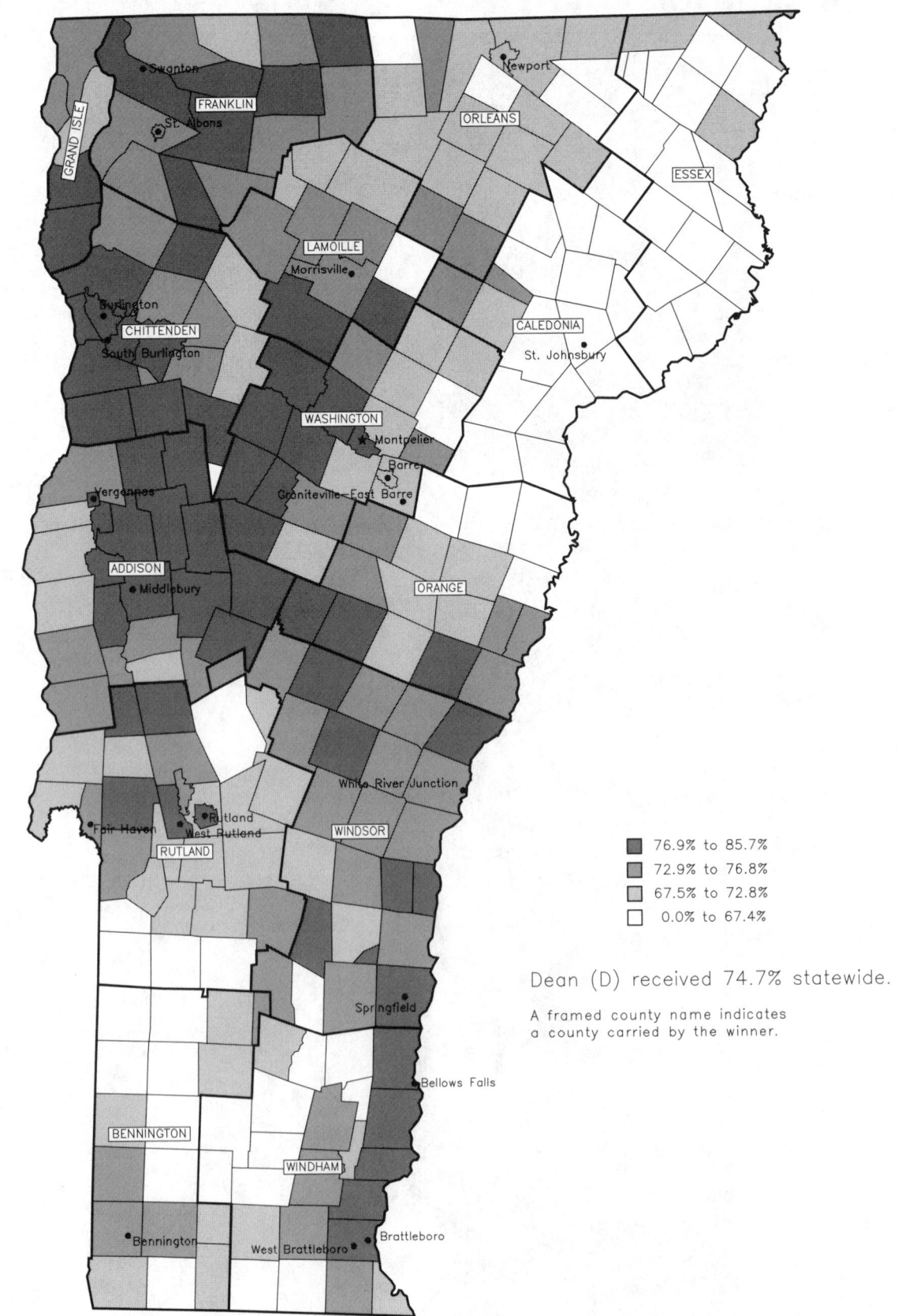

76.9% to 85.7%
72.9% to 76.8%
67.5% to 72.8%
0.0% to 67.4%

Dean (D) received 74.7% statewide.

A framed county name indicates
a county carried by the winner.

VIRGINIA

Alternative Registration Methods:
....Deputized Registrars

Registration Deadline (Days before Election) 30

Voting Equipment Use (Counties)[1]

Datavote Punch Card	0	Paper Ballot	2
Electronic	2	Other Punch Card	0
Lever Machine	124	Mixed Systems	0
Optical Scanner	8		

Party Control	DEM	REP	IND	VAC
1993 State Senate	22	18	0	0
1992 State Senate	22	18	0	0
1993 State House	58	41	1	0
1992 State House	58	41	1	0

Population Statistics 1990

Race/ Ethnicity	Total Population		Voting Age Population		Voting Age Population % of total population
	Number	%	Number	%	
Non-Hispanic					
White	4,701,650	76.0	3,629,183	77.5	77.2
Black	1,153,133	18.6	816,963	17.4	70.8
Asian/Pacific Islander	154,183	2.5	110,519	2.4	71.7
Native American	14,347	0.2	11,063	0.2	77.1
Other	3,757	<.1	1,552	<.1	41.3
All Hispanic	160,288	2.6	113,340	2.4	70.7
TOTAL	6,187,358	100.0	4,682,620	100.0	75.7

Estimated Voting Age Population 1992 (VAP) 4,842,000
Number of Registered Voters................................. 3,054,662
   % of estimated VAP....................................... 63.1
Voter Turnout (Highest Office) 2,558,665
   % of VAP 52.8
   % of Registration 83.8
Persons Not Voting—of Voting Age 2,283,335
   % of VAP 47.2
Persons Not Voting—of Registered 495,997
   % of Registration 16.2
Straight Ticket Voting .... No

State Officials and Members of Congress

Governor:
L. Douglas Wilder (D) 1989, elected to a four-year term in 1989.

U.S. Senators:
John W. Warner (R) 1978, elected to a six-year term in 1990.
Charles S. Robb (D) 1988, elected to a six-year term in 1988.

U.S. Representative in Congress:
(District, Name, Party, Date first elected)

1. Bateman (R) 1982
2. Pickett (D) 1986
3. Scott (D) 1992

4. Sisisky (D) 1982
5. Payne (D) 1988
6. Goodlatte (R) 1992

7. Bliley (R) 1980
8. Moran (D) 1990
9. Boucher (D) 1982

10. Wolf (R) 1980
11. Byrne (D) 1992

[1]Includes 41 independent cities.

Candidates: General Election, November 3, 1992

Candidate(s)	Total vote	Percent	Party	Status	First elected
President/Vice President					
Bush/Quayle	1,150,517	44.97%	Republican	Incumbent	1988
Clinton/Gore	1,038,650	40.59%	Democrat	Challenger	1992
Perot/Stockdale	348,639	13.63%	Independent	Challenger	
LaRouche/Bevel	11,937	0.47%	Independent	Challenger	
Marrou/Lord	5,730	0.22%	Libertarian	Challenger	
Fulani/Munoz	3,192	0.12%	Independent	Challenger	
U.S. Senator (No Contest)					
Governor (No Contest)					
U.S. Representative in Congress					
District 1					
Herbert Bateman	133,537	57.55%	Republican	Incumbent	1982
Andrew Fox	89,814	38.70%	Democrat	Challenger	
Donald Macleay, Jr.	8,677	3.74%	Independent	Challenger	
Write ins	23	<.01%	Write in	Challenger	
District 2					
Owen Pickett	99,253	56.03%	Democrat	Incumbent	1986
Jim Chapman	77,797	43.92%	Republican	Challenger	
Write ins	83	0.05%	Write in	Challenger	
District 3					
Robert Scott	132,432	78.61%	Democrat	Challenger	1992
Daniel Jenkins	35,780	21.24%	Republican	Challenger	
Write ins	261	0.15%	Write in	Challenger	
District 4					
Norman Sisisky	147,649	68.37%	Democrat	Incumbent	1982
Tony Zevgolis	68,286	31.62%	Republican	Challenger	
Write ins	25	0.01%	Write in	Challenger	
District 5					
Lewis F. Payne, Jr.	133,031	68.90%	Democrat	Incumbent	1988
Bill Hurlburt	60,030	31.09%	Republican	Challenger	
Write ins	23	0.01%	Write in	Challenger	
District 6					
Robert Goodlatte	127,309	60.03%	Republican	Challenger	1992
Stephen Musselwhite	84,618	39.90%	Democrat	Challenger	
Write ins	160	0.08%	Write in	Challenger	
District 7					
Thomas Bliley, Jr.	211,618	82.87%	Republican	Incumbent	1980
Gerald Berg	43,267	16.94%	Independent	Challenger	
Write ins	490	0.19%	Write in	Challenger	
District 8					
James Moran, Jr.	138,542	56.06%	Democrat	Incumbent	1990
Kyle McSlarrow	102,717	41.56%	Republican	Challenger	
Alvin West	5,601	2.27%	Independent	Challenger	
Write ins	266	0.11%	Write in	Challenger	
District 9					
Fredick Boucher	133,284	63.08%	Democrat	Incumbent	1982
L. Garrett Weddle	77,985	36.91%	Republican	Challenger	
Write ins	26	0.01%	Write in	Challenger	

Candidate(s)	Total vote	Percent	Party	Status	First elected
U.S. Representative in Congress (cont)					
District 10					
Frank Wolf	144,471	63.59%	Republican	Incumbent	1980
Raymond Vickery, Jr.	75,775	33.35%	Democrat	Challenger	
Alan Ogden	6,874	3.03%	Independent	Challenger	
Write ins	71	0.03%	Write in	Challenger	
District 11					
Leslie Byrne	114,172	50.02%	Democrat	Challenger	1992
Henry Butler	103,119	45.17%	Republican	Challenger	
Art Narro	6,681	2.93%	Independent	Challenger	
Perry Mitchell	4,155	1.82%	Independent	Challenger	
Write ins	145	0.06%	Write in	Challenger	

Voter Registration and Turnout, 1948-1992 Elections

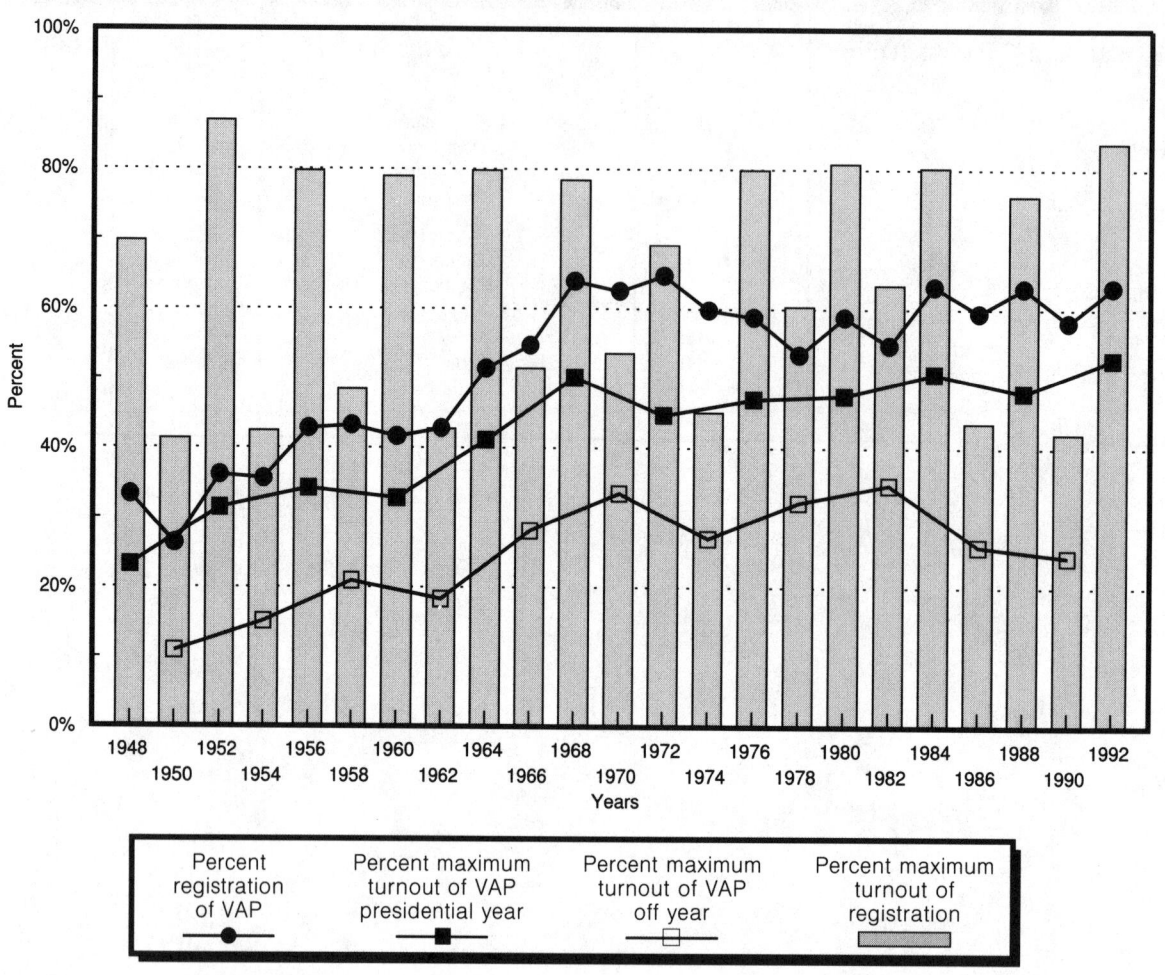

Percent registration of VAP	Percent maximum turnout of VAP presidential year	Percent maximum turnout of VAP off year	Percent maximum turnout of registration

Year	Estimated Voting Age Population (VAP)	Voter registration (REG)				Voter turnout									
						Highest office					Maximum vote				
		Total	Percent of VAP	Rank by percent of VAP	Actual	Total	Office	Percent total REG	Rank by percent of REG	Percent of VAP	Rank by percent of VAP	Total	Percent total REG	Rank by percent of REG	Percent total VAP	Rank by percent of VAP
1992	4,842,000	3,054,662	63.1	46	-	2,558,665	P	83.8	4	52.8	38	2,558,665	83.8	7	52.8	39
1990	4,716,000	2,738,029	58.1	45	-	1,152,874	C	42.1	47	24.4	49	1,152,854	42.1	47	24.4	49
1988	4,568,000	2,877,144	63.0	45	-	2,191,609	P	76.2	13	48.0	36	2,191,609	76.2	17	48.0	38
1986	4,392,000	2,609,698	59.4	44	-	1,137,768	C	43.6	44	25.9	50	1,137,768	43.6	45	25.9	50
1984	4,234,000	2,675,641	63.2	45	-	2,146,635	P	80.2	5	50.7	39	2,146,635	80.2	8	50.7	40
1982	4,077,000	2,234,011	54.8	46	-	1,415,622	S	63.4	24	34.7	43	1,415,622	63.4	25	34.7	43
1980	3,930,000	2,309,181	58.8	44	-	1,866,032	P	80.8	4	47.5	43	1,866,032	80.8	6	47.5	44
1978	3,794,000	2,026,515	53.4	46	-	1,222,256	S	60.3	15	32.2	42	1,222,256	60.3	16	32.2	42
1976	3,613,000	2,123,849	58.8	44	-	1,697,094	P	79.9	11	47.0	42	1,697,094	79.9	15	47.0	44
1974	3,429,000	2,050,809	59.8	44	-	924,186	C	45.1	40	27.0	46	924,186	45.1	40	27.0	46
1972	3,257,000	2,107,367	64.7	42	-	1,457,019	P	69.1	33	44.7	43	1,457,019	69.1	35	44.7	43
1970	2,823,000	1,765,078	62.5	39	-	946,751	S	53.6	38	33.5	45	946,751	53.6	38	33.5	45
1968	2,717,000	1,737,214	63.9	38	-	1,361,491	P	78.4	29	50.1	45	1,361,491	78.4	29	50.1	47
1966	2,608,000	1,427,037	54.7	40	-	733,879	S	51.4	34	28.1	48	733,879	51.4	34	28.1	48
1964	2,539,000	1,305,383	51.4	38	-	1,042,267	P	79.8	21	41.1	47	1,042,267	79.8	23	41.1	47
1962	2,456,000	1,052,255	42.8	36	-	448,952	C	42.7	34	18.3	48	448,952	42.7	34	18.3	48
1960	2,349,000	978,307	41.6	35	-	771,449	P	78.9	27	32.8	46	771,449	78.9	27	32.8	46
1958	2,186,000	944,627	43.2	29	-	457,640	S	48.4	26	20.9	41	457,640	48.4	26	20.9	41
1956	2,043,000	875,388	42.8	29	-	697,978	P	79.7	17	34.2	44	697,978	79.7	21	34.2	44
1954	2,031,000	723,126	35.6	26	-	306,510	S	42.4	22	15.1	45	306,510	42.4	22	15.1	45
1952	1,973,000	713,064	36.1	23	-	619,689	P	86.9	9	31.4	44	619,689	86.9	10	31.4	44
1950	1,949,000	513,070	26.3	22	-	211,830	C	41.3	19	10.9	44	211,830	41.3	19	10.9	44
1948	1,807,000	601,766	33.3	21	-	419,256	P	69.7	15	23.2	43	419,256	69.7	16	23.2	43

VIRGINIA

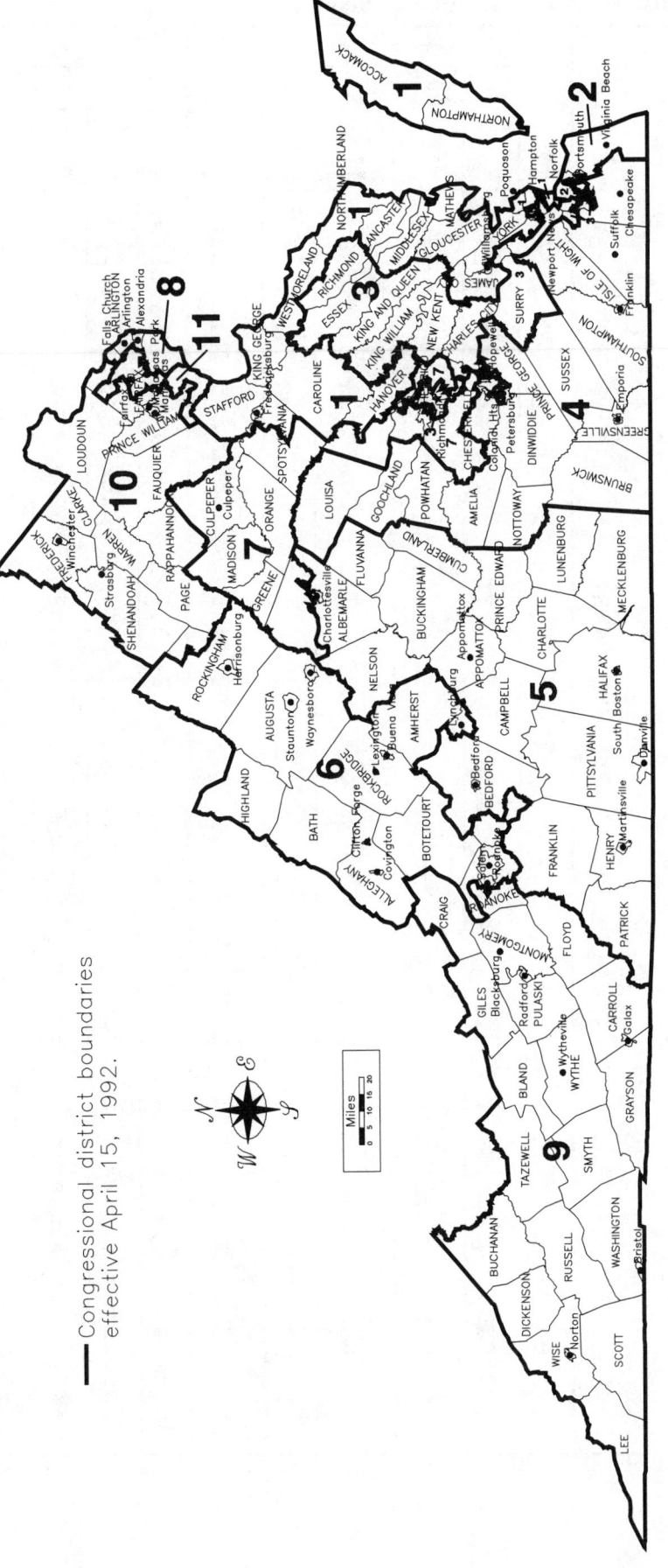

— Congressional district boundaries
effective April 15, 1992.

Miles
0 5 10 15 20

Copyright © 1993 by Election Data Services, Inc.

Virginia 943

Table A. — 1990 Population by Race and Ethnic Origin

State/ county code	County	Total persons	Percent of total persons Non-Hispanic White	Black	Asian and Pacific Islander	Native American	Other	Hispanic	Rank — Percent of total persons Total	Non-Hispanic White	Black	Hispanic	Percent contribution to state population Total	Non-Hispanic White	Black	Hispanic
51 001	Accomack	31,703	64.1	34.2	0.2	0.1	<.1	1.4	43	105	31	22	0.5	0.4	0.9	0.3
51 003	Albemarle	68,040	86.3	10.0	2.4	0.1	<.1	1.2	18	54	84	30	1.1	1.2	0.6	0.5
51 005	Alleghany	13,176	96.7	2.5	0.3	<.1	0.0	0.4	91	19	117	103	0.2	0.3	<.1	<.1
51 007	Amelia	8,787	67.2	32.0	0.1	0.2	<.1	0.5	112	100	34	88	0.1	0.1	0.2	<.1
51 009	Amherst	28,578	78.5	20.0	0.3	0.4	<.1	0.8	51	75	60	52	0.5	0.5	0.5	0.1
51 011	Appomattox	12,298	76.8	22.8	<.1	<.1	<.1	0.2	96	80	51	129	0.2	0.2	0.2	<.1
51 013	Arlington	170,936	69.5	10.1	6.5	0.3	0.2	13.5	8	96	83	1	2.8	2.5	1.5	14.4
51 015	Augusta	54,677	95.6	3.7	0.2	<.1	<.1	0.4	26	27	109	101	0.9	1.1	0.2	0.1
51 017	Bath	4,799	94.1	5.1	0.2	<.1	<.1	0.5	132	31	102	94	<.1	<.1	<.1	<.1
51 019	Bedford	45,656	91.4	7.9	0.2	0.1	<.1	0.4	34	39	88	104	0.7	0.9	0.3	0.1
51 021	Bland	6,514	95.9	3.5	0.1	<.1	0.0	0.4	125	24	110	110	0.1	0.1	<.1	<.1
51 023	Botetourt	24,992	94.6	4.5	0.3	<.1	<.1	0.6	59	29	105	76	0.4	0.5	<.1	<.1
51 025	Brunswick	15,987	41.2	58.3	<.1	<.1	<.1	0.3	84	134	3	123	0.3	0.1	0.8	<.1
51 027	Buchanan	31,333	98.8	0.2	0.1	<.1	<.1	0.8	45	7	135	50	0.5	0.7	<.1	0.2
51 029	Buckingham	12,873	58.7	40.7	0.2	0.1	<.1	0.3	93	119	16	122	0.2	0.2	0.5	<.1
51 031	Campbell	47,572	84.7	14.4	0.3	<.1	<.1	0.5	30	62	67	97	0.8	0.9	0.6	0.1
51 033	Caroline	19,217	60.5	37.6	0.2	1.1	<.1	0.5	71	117	22	85	0.3	0.2	0.6	<.1
51 035	Carroll	26,594	98.8	0.4	<.1	<.1	0.0	0.6	55	6	131	77	0.4	0.6	<.1	<.1
51 036	Charles City	6,282	28.6	63.1	0.2	7.8	<.1	0.4	128	135	2	107	0.1	<.1	0.3	<.1
51 037	Charlotte	11,688	63.1	36.4	<.1	0.2	<.1	0.3	100	107	27	127	0.2	0.2	0.4	<.1
51 041	Chesterfield	209,274	83.9	12.9	1.8	0.2	<.1	1.2	6	65	73	28	3.4	3.7	2.3	1.6
51 043	Clarke	12,101	90.2	8.7	0.2	0.1	<.1	0.7	97	43	87	65	0.2	0.2	<.1	<.1
51 045	Craig	4,372	99.5	0.2	<.1	0.1	0.0	0.1	134	2	134	136	<.1	<.1	<.1	<.1
51 047	Culpeper	27,791	80.8	17.1	1.0	0.3	<.1	0.7	53	67	63	60	0.4	0.5	0.4	0.1
51 049	Cumberland	7,825	60.5	38.6	0.1	0.1	<.1	0.6	117	116	19	75	0.1	0.1	0.3	<.1
51 051	Dickenson	17,620	99.1	0.4	<.1	<.1	0.0	0.3	76	3	132	116	0.3	0.4	<.1	<.1
51 053	Dinwiddie	20,960	63.4	35.6	0.3	0.1	<.1	0.6	68	106	30	74	0.3	0.3	0.6	<.1
51 057	Essex	8,689	61.1	37.5	0.5	0.5	<.1	0.3	113	114	23	115	0.1	0.1	0.3	<.1
51 059	Fairfax	818,584	77.4	7.6	8.3	0.2	0.1	6.3	1	78	89	3	13.2	13.5	5.4	32.4
51 061	Fauquier	48,741	86.8	11.1	0.6	0.2	<.1	1.2	29	52	77	26	0.8	0.9	0.5	0.4
51 063	Floyd	12,005	96.8	2.4	0.2	0.1	<.1	0.5	98	17	118	90	0.2	0.2	<.1	<.1
51 065	Fluvanna	12,429	76.2	22.9	0.1	0.2	<.1	0.6	95	83	50	79	0.2	0.2	0.2	<.1
51 067	Franklin	39,549	88.6	10.7	0.2	<.1	<.1	0.3	38	48	80	114	0.6	0.7	0.4	<.1
51 069	Frederick	45,723	96.9	1.8	0.5	0.1	<.1	0.6	33	16	121	70	0.7	0.9	<.1	0.2
51 071	Giles	16,366	97.7	1.7	0.1	<.1	0.0	0.3	80	10	123	112	0.3	0.3	<.1	<.1
51 073	Gloucester	30,131	87.1	11.1	0.6	0.2	<.1	1.0	47	51	78	41	0.5	0.6	0.3	0.2
51 075	Goochland	14,163	69.8	29.7	0.2	0.1	<.1	0.2	89	95	39	131	0.2	0.2	0.4	<.1
51 077	Grayson	16,278	96.4	3.0	0.1	<.1	0.0	0.5	81	21	113	96	0.3	0.3	<.1	<.1
51 079	Greene	10,297	92.6	6.4	0.3	0.1	<.1	0.5	108	36	96	87	0.2	0.2	<.1	<.1
51 081	Greensville	8,853	43.9	55.0	0.3	0.1	<.1	0.7	111	131	6	56	0.1	<.1	0.4	<.1
51 083	Halifax	29,033	60.1	39.0	<.1	0.2	<.1	0.6	49	118	17	78	0.5	0.4	1.0	0.1
51 085	Hanover	63,306	88.8	10.1	0.4	0.2	<.1	0.5	20	47	82	89	1.0	1.2	0.6	0.2
51 087	Henrico	217,881	76.7	20.0	2.0	0.3	<.1	1.0	4	81	59	39	3.5	3.6	3.8	1.4
51 089	Henry	56,942	76.2	23.0	0.2	0.1	<.1	0.4	24	84	49	100	0.9	0.9	1.1	0.2
51 091	Highland	2,635	99.6	0.1	<.1	0.0	0.0	0.2	136	1	136	134	<.1	<.1	<.1	<.1
51 093	Isle of Wight	25,053	67.4	31.4	0.3	0.2	<.1	0.7	58	99	35	64	0.4	0.4	0.7	0.1
51 095	James City	34,859	79.0	18.4	1.3	0.2	<.1	1.1	40	73	62	34	0.6	0.6	0.6	0.2
51 097	King and Queen	6,289	56.5	41.9	0.2	1.0	<.1	0.4	127	122	14	99	0.1	<.1	0.2	<.1
51 099	King George	13,527	77.5	20.1	0.9	0.3	<.1	1.2	90	77	58	31	0.2	0.2	0.2	<.1
51 101	King William	10,913	67.0	30.2	0.2	2.0	<.1	0.6	104	101	36	72	0.2	0.2	0.3	<.1
51 103	Lancaster	10,896	69.3	29.8	0.1	<.1	<.1	0.7	105	97	38	63	0.2	0.2	0.3	<.1
51 105	Lee	24,496	99.0	0.4	<.1	0.1	0.0	0.5	60	5	133	92	0.4	0.5	<.1	<.1
51 107	Loudoun	86,129	87.7	7.1	2.4	0.2	<.1	2.5	15	50	93	13	1.4	1.6	0.5	1.3
51 109	Louisa	20,325	73.3	25.6	0.2	0.3	<.1	0.5	69	89	45	84	0.3	0.3	0.5	<.1
51 111	Lunenburg	11,419	61.7	37.4	0.2	<.1	0.0	0.7	102	112	24	55	0.2	0.1	0.4	<.1
51 113	Madison	11,949	85.0	14.2	0.2	0.2	<.1	0.3	99	60	69	124	0.2	0.2	0.1	<.1
51 115	Mathews	8,348	85.2	13.9	0.2	0.1	<.1	0.6	115	59	70	73	0.1	0.2	0.1	<.1
51 117	Mecklenburg	29,241	61.1	38.3	0.2	<.1	<.1	0.4	48	115	21	109	0.5	0.4	1.0	<.1
51 119	Middlesex	8,653	74.8	24.4	0.1	<.1	<.1	0.6	114	87	47	80	0.1	0.1	0.2	<.1
51 121	Montgomery	73,913	91.2	3.8	3.8	<.1	<.1	1.1	17	40	108	35	1.2	1.4	0.2	0.5
51 125	Nelson	12,778	80.0	18.7	0.2	0.1	<.1	0.9	94	72	61	45	0.2	0.2	0.2	<.1
51 127	New Kent	10,445	77.0	20.5	0.3	1.3	0.2	0.7	107	79	57	53	0.2	0.2	0.2	<.1
51 131	Northampton	13,061	51.7	46.1	0.1	0.1	<.1	2.0	92	127	10	17	0.2	0.1	0.5	0.2
51 133	Northumberland	10,524	69.9	29.3	0.2	<.1	<.1	0.5	106	94	40	93	0.2	0.2	0.3	<.1
51 135	Nottoway	14,993	58.1	40.8	0.3	0.2	0.0	0.6	88	120	15	82	0.2	0.2	0.5	<.1
51 137	Orange	21,421	84.7	14.3	0.2	0.1	<.1	0.7	67	63	68	66	0.3	0.4	0.3	<.1
51 139	Page	21,690	97.1	2.0	0.3	<.1	<.1	0.5	66	15	120	91	0.4	0.4	<.1	<.1
51 141	Patrick	17,473	92.0	7.1	0.1	<.1	<.1	0.7	78	37	92	59	0.3	0.3	0.1	<.1
51 143	Pittsylvania	55,655	72.7	26.7	0.1	<.1	<.1	0.4	25	90	43	102	0.9	0.9	1.3	0.1
51 145	Powhatan	15,328	77.9	21.4	0.2	0.2	<.1	0.4	87	76	55	106	0.2	0.3	0.3	<.1

944 Virginia

Table A. — 1990 Population by Race and Ethnic Origin (cont)

State/county code	County	Total persons	Percent of total persons						Rank				Percent contribution to state population			
			Non-Hispanic							Percent of total persons				Non-Hispanic		
			White	Black	Asian and Pacific Islander	Native American	Other	Hispanic	Total	Non-Hispanic		Hispanic	Total	White	Black	Hispanic
										White	Black					
51 147	Prince Edward	17,320	62.7	36.0	0.4	0.2	<.1	0.7	79	108	29	67	0.3	0.2	0.5	<.1
51 149	Prince George	27,394	65.0	28.6	2.1	0.3	0.1	3.9	54	103	41	9	0.4	0.4	0.7	0.7
51 153	Prince William	215,686	80.7	11.4	3.0	0.3	0.1	4.5	5	68	76	8	3.5	3.7	2.1	6.0
51 155	Pulaski	34,496	93.4	5.8	0.2	0.1	<.1	0.4	41	33	100	98	0.6	0.7	0.2	<.1
51 157	Rappahannock	6,622	91.2	7.4	0.2	0.2	0.0	1.0	124	41	90	36	0.1	0.1	<.1	<.1
51 159	Richmond	7,273	68.8	30.1	0.3	0.1	0.0	0.7	118	98	37	58	0.1	0.1	0.2	<.1
51 161	Roanoke	79,332	96.0	2.5	0.8	<.1	<.1	0.6	16	23	116	81	1.3	1.6	0.2	0.3
51 163	Rockbridge	18,350	96.1	3.1	0.3	0.2	<.1	0.3	75	22	112	120	0.3	0.4	<.1	<.1
51 165	Rockingham	57,482	97.2	1.5	0.2	<.1	<.1	0.9	22	14	124	42	0.9	1.2	<.1	0.3
51 167	Russell	28,667	98.5	1.1	<.1	<.1	0.0	0.3	50	8	127	128	0.5	0.6	<.1	<.1
51 169	Scott	23,204	99.0	0.6	<.1	<.1	<.1	0.3	63	4	130	118	0.4	0.5	<.1	<.1
51 171	Shenandoah	31,636	97.5	1.1	0.3	<.1	<.1	0.9	44	11	126	46	0.5	0.7	<.1	0.2
51 173	Smyth	32,370	97.3	2.0	0.2	0.1	<.1	0.3	42	13	119	117	0.5	0.7	<.1	<.1
51 175	Southampton	17,550	54.7	44.7	<.1	<.1	<.1	0.4	77	124	12	108	0.3	0.2	0.7	<.1
51 177	Spotsylvania	57,403	86.4	10.7	1.0	0.3	<.1	1.5	23	53	79	21	0.9	1.1	0.5	0.5
51 179	Stafford	61,236	89.4	6.9	1.2	0.4	<.1	2.0	21	45	94	15	1.0	1.2	0.4	0.8
51 181	Surry	6,145	44.0	55.5	<.1	0.2	0.0	0.3	129	130	5	119	<.1	<.1	0.3	<.1
51 183	Sussex	10,248	41.4	58.1	0.2	0.1	<.1	0.2	109	133	4	132	0.2	<.1	0.5	<.1
51 185	Tazewell	45,960	96.5	2.6	0.5	0.1	<.1	0.3	31	20	115	125	0.7	0.9	0.1	<.1
51 187	Warren	26,142	93.7	4.9	0.3	0.2	<.1	0.9	56	32	103	43	0.4	0.5	0.1	0.2
51 191	Washington	45,887	98.0	1.5	0.2	<.1	<.1	0.3	32	9	125	121	0.7	1.0	<.1	<.1
51 193	Westmoreland	15,480	65.8	32.9	0.4	0.2	<.1	0.6	86	102	33	68	0.3	0.2	0.4	<.1
51 195	Wise	39,573	97.5	1.8	0.3	<.1	<.1	0.3	37	12	122	126	0.6	0.8	<.1	<.1
51 197	Wythe	25,466	95.9	3.5	0.2	0.1	<.1	0.2	57	25	111	130	0.4	0.5	<.1	<.1
51 199	York	42,422	80.3	15.5	2.2	0.2	<.1	1.7	35	71	64	19	0.7	0.7	0.6	0.5
51 510	Alexandria City	111,183	64.3	21.5	4.1	0.3	0.1	9.7	12	104	53	2	1.8	1.5	2.1	6.7
51 515	Bedford City	6,073	76.6	21.9	0.5	0.1	0.0	0.9	130	82	52	48	<.1	<.1	0.1	<.1
51 520	Bristol City	18,426	93.3	5.7	0.5	0.1	<.1	0.3	74	34	101	113	0.3	0.4	<.1	<.1
51 530	Buena Vista City	6,406	95.0	4.4	0.3	<.1	<.1	0.2	126	28	107	135	0.1	0.1	<.1	<.1
51 540	Charlottesville City	40,341	75.2	21.1	2.3	<.1	<.1	1.2	36	85	56	29	0.7	0.6	0.7	0.3
51 550	Chesapeake City	151,976	70.0	27.3	1.2	0.3	<.1	1.3	10	93	42	25	2.5	2.3	3.6	1.2
51 560	Clifton Forge City	4,679	84.4	14.8	0.1	<.1	<.1	0.5	133	64	66	83	<.1	<.1	<.1	<.1
51 570	Colonial Heights City	16,064	95.9	0.8	2.1	0.2	<.1	1.0	83	26	128	37	0.3	0.3	<.1	0.1
51 580	Covington City	6,991	84.9	13.9	0.7	<.1	0.1	0.4	120	61	71	105	0.1	0.1	<.1	<.1
51 590	Danville City	53,056	62.4	36.5	0.5	0.1	<.1	0.5	27	110	26	86	0.9	0.7	1.7	0.2
51 595	Emporia City	5,306	53.2	45.0	0.5	0.2	0.0	1.1	131	126	11	32	<.1	<.1	0.2	<.1
51 600	Fairfax City	19,622	82.1	4.8	7.0	0.2	<.1	5.9	70	66	104	5	0.3	0.3	<.1	0.7
51 610	Falls Church City	9,578	85.5	3.0	4.7	0.4	0.1	6.3	110	58	114	4	0.2	0.2	<.1	0.4
51 620	Franklin City	7,864	46.2	53.3	0.3	<.1	<.1	0.2	116	129	8	133	0.1	<.1	0.4	<.1
51 630	Fredericksburg City	19,027	74.9	21.4	1.1	0.1	<.1	2.4	72	86	54	14	0.3	0.3	0.4	0.3
51 640	Galax City	6,670	92.8	5.8	0.2	0.1	<.1	1.0	123	35	99	40	0.1	0.1	<.1	<.1
51 650	Hampton City	133,793	57.5	38.5	1.7	0.3	<.1	2.0	11	121	20	16	2.2	1.6	4.5	1.6
51 660	Harrisonburg City	30,707	90.2	6.5	1.5	0.1	0.1	1.6	46	44	95	20	0.5	0.6	0.2	0.3
51 670	Hopewell City	23,101	71.2	25.4	1.2	0.3	<.1	1.8	64	92	46	18	0.4	0.4	0.5	0.3
51 678	Lexington City	6,959	86.0	11.6	1.2	0.3	0.0	0.9	121	56	75	47	0.1	0.1	<.1	<.1
51 680	Lynchburg City	66,049	72.1	26.3	0.7	0.2	<.1	0.7	19	91	44	57	1.1	1.0	1.5	0.3
51 683	Manassas City	27,957	80.6	10.2	3.1	0.3	0.1	5.7	52	69	81	6	0.5	0.5	0.2	1.0
51 685	Manassas Park City	6,734	85.5	7.1	2.5	0.1	<.1	4.7	122	57	91	7	0.1	0.1	<.1	0.2
51 690	Martinsville City	16,162	62.6	36.7	0.2	0.1	<.1	0.4	82	109	25	111	0.3	0.2	0.5	<.1
51 700	Newport News City	170,045	61.4	33.2	2.2	0.3	<.1	2.8	9	113	32	12	2.7	2.2	4.9	2.9
51 710	Norfolk City	261,229	55.6	38.7	2.4	0.4	0.1	2.9	3	123	18	11	4.2	3.1	8.8	4.7
51 720	Norton City	4,247	91.8	6.3	0.8	0.3	0.0	0.7	135	38	97	54	<.1	<.1	<.1	<.1
51 730	Petersburg City	38,386	26.2	71.6	0.7	0.2	<.1	1.2	39	136	1	27	0.6	0.2	2.4	0.3
51 735	Poquoson City	11,005	96.7	0.7	1.4	0.2	<.1	0.9	103	18	129	49	0.2	0.2	<.1	<.1
51 740	Portsmouth City	103,907	50.6	47.0	0.7	0.3	<.1	1.3	13	128	9	23	1.7	1.1	4.2	0.9
51 750	Radford City	15,940	91.1	6.0	1.7	<.1	<.1	1.1	85	42	98	33	0.3	0.3	0.1	0.1
51 760	Richmond City	203,056	43.0	55.0	0.9	0.2	<.1	0.9	7	132	7	44	3.3	1.9	9.7	1.2
51 770	Roanoke City	96,397	74.2	24.1	0.7	0.2	<.1	0.7	14	88	48	62	1.6	1.5	2.0	0.4
51 775	Salem City	23,756	94.3	4.4	0.7	0.1	<.1	0.5	62	30	106	95	0.4	0.5	<.1	<.1
51 780	South Boston City	6,997	62.3	36.4	0.5	0.2	<.1	0.6	119	111	28	69	0.1	<.1	0.2	<.1
51 790	Staunton City	24,461	86.2	12.6	0.4	0.1	<.1	0.7	61	55	74	61	0.4	0.4	0.3	0.1
51 800	Suffolk City	52,141	54.4	44.4	0.4	0.2	<.1	0.6	28	125	13	71	0.8	0.6	2.0	0.2
51 810	Virginia Beach City	393,069	78.8	13.7	4.1	0.3	<.1	3.1	2	74	72	10	6.4	6.6	4.7	7.6
51 820	Waynesboro City	18,549	89.4	9.4	0.2	0.2	<.1	0.8	73	46	86	51	0.3	0.4	0.2	<.1
51 830	Williamsburg City	11,530	80.4	15.1	2.9	0.2	0.1	1.3	101	70	65	24	0.2	0.2	0.2	<.1
51 840	Winchester City	21,947	87.9	10.0	0.9	0.1	<.1	1.0	65	49	85	38	0.4	0.4	0.2	0.1
51	VIRGINIA	6,187,358	76.0	18.6	2.5	0.2	<.1	2.6					100.0	100.0	100.0	100.0

Table A. — 1990 Population by Race and Ethnic Origin (cont)

State/ county code	County	Total persons	Percent of total persons						Rank				Percent contribution to state population			
				Non-Hispanic					Total	Percent of total persons			Total	Non-Hispanic		
											Non-Hispanic					
			White	Black	Asian and Pacific Islander	Native American	Other	Hispanic		White	Black	Hispanic		White	Black	Hispanic
	CONGRESSIONAL															
	District 1.........................	562,677	79.1	17.8	1.3	0.3	<.1	1.6	1	5	4	5	9.1	9.5	8.7	5.6
	District 2.........................	562,276	76.5	16.3	3.5	0.4	<.1	3.3	10	6	5	3	9.1	9.1	8.0	11.5
	District 3.........................	562,431	33.4	63.7	1.0	0.4	<.1	1.4	8	11	1	6	9.1	4.0	31.1	4.8
	District 4.........................	562,466	65.6	31.9	1.1	0.2	<.1	1.1	7	10	2	7	9.1	7.8	15.6	4.0
	District 5.........................	562,268	74.0	24.7	0.6	0.1	<.1	0.6	11	8	3	10	9.1	8.9	12.0	2.0
	District 6.........................	562,572	87.1	11.4	0.6	0.1	<.1	0.7	4	3	7	9	9.1	10.4	5.6	2.4
	District 7.........................	562,643	87.1	9.9	1.6	0.2	<.1	1.0	3	4	8	8	9.1	10.4	4.9	3.6
	District 8.........................	562,484	71.3	13.1	6.5	0.3	0.1	8.7	6	9	6	1	9.1	8.5	6.4	30.6
	District 9.........................	562,380	96.2	2.5	0.7	<.1	<.1	0.5	9	1	11	11	9.1	11.5	1.2	1.8
	District 10.......................	562,664	89.2	5.7	2.6	0.2	<.1	2.2	2	2	10	4	9.1	10.7	2.8	7.9
	District 11.......................	562,497	76.3	8.0	7.9	0.2	0.1	7.4	5	7	9	2	9.1	9.1	3.9	25.9

Table B. — 1990 Voting Age Population (VAP) by Race and Ethnic Origin

County	Total Voting Age Population	Percent of total VAP — Non-Hispanic White	Black	Asian and Pacific Islander	Native American	Other	Hispanic	Rank Total	Rank White	Rank Black	Rank Hispanic	Pct contribution Total	White	Black	Hispanic	VAP % Total	White	Black	Asian and Pacific Islander	Native American	Other	Hispanic
Accomack	24,182	67.9	30.4	0.2	0.1	<.1	1.3	45	101	34	21	0.5	0.5	0.9	0.3	76.3	80.9	67.9	69.8	77.1	50.0	70.8
Albemarle	52,764	86.4	10.0	2.5	<.1	<.1	1.1	18	58	80	32	1.1	1.3	0.6	0.5	77.5	77.6	77.3	80.1	68.1	45.0	72.3
Alleghany	9,989	97.1	2.3	0.3	<.1	0.0	0.3	91	17	118	121	0.2	0.3	<.1	<.1	75.8	76.1	70.1	62.5	69.2	0.0	51.9
Amelia	6,491	67.1	32.2	0.2	0.2	<.1	0.4	114	104	29	95	0.1	0.1	0.3	<.1	73.9	73.7	74.3	84.6	78.6	100.0	60.0
Amherst	21,871	79.0	19.3	0.3	0.5	<.1	0.9	50	76	57	41	0.5	0.5	0.5	0.2	76.5	77.1	73.8	80.6	79.7	33.3	86.6
Appomattox	9,234	78.1	21.6	<.1	0.1	0.0	0.2	99	81	51	129	0.2	0.2	0.2	<.1	75.1	76.4	70.9	50.0	100.0	0.0	66.7
Arlington	145,058	72.1	9.4	6.1	0.3	0.1	12.0	8	95	84	1	3.1	2.9	1.7	15.4	84.9	88.0	79.3	79.3	83.2	63.1	75.7
Augusta	41,212	95.3	4.0	0.2	<.1	<.1	0.4	25	27	108	99	0.9	1.1	0.2	0.1	78.8	78.8	81.0	75.0	71.7	20.0	69.5
Bath	3,782	94.1	5.3	0.2	<.1	0.0	0.4	132	31	100	93	<.1	<.1	<.1	<.1	78.8	78.8	81.0	75.0	50.0	0.0	69.6
Bedford	34,757	91.6	7.7	0.2	0.1	0.0	0.4	32	40	89	106	0.7	0.9	0.3	0.1	76.1	76.3	74.4	66.7	72.9	0.0	67.2
Bland	5,070	95.1	4.3	0.1	<.1	0.0	0.3	124	28	106	108	0.1	0.1	<.1	<.1	77.8	77.2	96.1	75.0	100.0	0.0	70.8
Botetourt	19,186	94.5	4.7	0.3	<.1	<.1	0.5	59	29	104	72	0.4	0.5	0.1	<.1	76.8	76.7	80.7	67.6	73.3	0.0	71.3
Brunswick	12,152	43.2	56.3	<.1	<.1	<.1	0.3	85	134	3	118	0.3	0.1	0.8	<.1	72.5	79.7	73.4	83.3	66.7	75.0	76.6
Buchanan	22,724	99.3	<.1	<.1	<.1	<.1	0.4	46	3	136	89	0.5	0.6	<.1	<.1	72.5	72.9	9.1	54.1	80.8	50.0	39.7
Buckingham	9,838	59.5	39.9	0.2	0.1	<.1	0.2	92	119	15	127	0.2	0.2	0.5	<.1	76.4	77.5	75.0	63.0	82.4	33.3	57.9
Campbell	35,986	85.6	13.6	0.3	<.1	<.1	0.4	29	63	66	101	0.8	0.8	0.6	0.1	75.6	76.5	71.2	68.8	87.5	14.3	65.3
Caroline	14,202	60.8	37.3	0.2	1.1	<.1	0.5	74	118	19	77	0.3	0.2	0.6	<.1	73.9	74.3	73.3	68.8	77.2	16.7	72.0
Carroll	20,713	99.0	0.4	<.1	<.1	0.0	0.5	52	7	131	80	0.4	0.6	<.1	<.1	77.9	78.0	74.3	65.4	68.2	0.0	67.5
Charles City	4,775	29.5	61.8	0.1	8.1	<.1	0.3	127	136	2	109	0.1	<.1	0.4	<.1	75.2	78.7	74.5	50.0	79.9	20.0	66.7
Charlotte	8,795	65.6	33.9	<.1	0.1	0.0	0.3	101	109	26	114	0.2	0.2	0.4	<.1	75.2	78.2	70.1	100.0	66.7	0.0	84.8
Chesterfield	148,339	84.7	12.3	1.6	0.2	<.1	1.1	7	65	73	30	3.2	3.5	2.2	1.5	70.9	71.6	67.5	63.8	79.3	27.5	65.7
Clarke	9,340	90.1	8.8	0.3	0.1	0.0	0.7	96	45	86	51	0.2	0.2	0.1	<.1	77.2	77.1	78.0	80.0	100.0	0.0	81.7
Craig	3,365	99.6	0.2	<.1	<.1	0.0	0.1	134	2	134	135	<.1	<.1	<.1	<.1	77.0	77.0	75.0	25.0	60.0	0.0	100.0
Culpeper	20,416	81.4	16.6	1.0	0.3	<.1	0.6	53	71	63	56	0.4	0.5	0.4	0.1	73.5	74.0	71.2	72.7	69.8	50.0	67.2
Cumberland	5,775	61.9	37.4	0.1	0.1	<.1	0.5	117	117	17	82	0.1	<.1	0.3	<.1	72.7	75.5	71.4	66.7	75.0	0.0	62.2
Dickenson	12,818	99.1	0.4	<.1	<.1	0.0	0.3	80	4	133	113	0.3	0.4	<.1	<.1	72.7	72.8	67.6	78.6	92.3	0.0	70.7
Dinwiddie	15,867	64.0	35.2	0.3	0.1	<.1	0.5	68	112	25	84	0.3	0.3	0.7	<.1	76.5	76.3	74.8	70.0	75.0	33.3	62.3
Essex	6,649	62.5	36.1	0.5	0.6	<.1	0.4	113	115	21	110	0.1	0.1	0.3	<.1	76.5	78.3	73.6	85.0	80.4	66.7	73.3
Fairfax	618,516	78.7	7.2	7.8	0.2	<.1	6.0	1	77	90	3	13.2	13.4	5.4	32.8	75.6	76.8	71.6	70.9	75.5	49.2	71.6
Fauquier	35,675	86.8	11.3	0.5	0.2	<.1	1.1	30	53	76	31	0.8	0.9	0.5	0.3	73.2	73.3	74.3	67.8	74.3	16.0	64.0
Floyd	9,258	96.7	2.5	0.1	0.1	<.1	0.5	98	20	115	76	0.2	0.2	<.1	<.1	77.1	77.1	79.8	57.1	75.0	100.0	79.7
Fluvanna	9,292	77.1	22.1	0.2	0.2	0.0	0.5	97	84	49	78	0.2	0.2	0.3	<.1	74.8	75.6	72.3	83.3	71.4	0.0	66.7
Franklin	30,533	89.4	9.9	0.1	<.1	<.1	0.5	36	47	81	112	0.7	0.8	0.4	<.1	77.2	77.9	71.8	72.1	74.4	50.0	73.0
Frederick	33,526	97.2	1.7	0.4	0.1	<.1	0.6	34	16	123	62	0.7	0.9	<.1	0.2	73.3	73.5	68.8	60.0	80.6	23.1	67.7
Giles	12,750	97.7	1.7	0.1	<.1	0.0	0.3	81	11	121	111	0.3	0.3	<.1	<.1	77.9	77.9	78.8	75.0	87.5	0.0	73.7
Gloucester	21,907	86.9	11.4	0.5	0.2	<.1	0.8	49	52	75	45	0.5	0.5	0.3	0.2	72.7	72.6	74.9	63.2	77.6	80.0	63.4
Goochland	11,157	69.5	29.9	0.2	0.1	0.0	0.2	89	98	35	132	0.2	0.2	0.4	<.1	78.8	78.5	79.5	75.0	87.5	0.0	66.7
Grayson	12,610	96.7	2.8	<.1	<.1	0.0	0.3	82	21	113	107	0.3	0.3	<.1	<.1	72.9	75.7	72.6	55.0	100.0	0.0	57.3
Greene	7,508	93.3	5.8	0.2	0.2	0.0	0.4	110	36	96	85	0.2	0.2	<.1	<.1	72.9	73.5	66.0	61.5	92.3	0.0	67.9
Greensville	6,442	46.2	52.7	0.2	0.1	0.0	0.8	115	132	6	48	0.1	<.1	0.4	<.1	72.8	76.6	69.7	56.5	72.7	0.0	78.1
Halifax	21,954	62.4	36.8	<.1	0.3	<.1	0.5	48	116	20	75	0.5	0.4	1.0	<.1	75.6	78.6	71.2	73.9	77.5	50.0	68.3
Hanover	47,499	89.1	9.8	0.4	0.2	<.1	0.5	20	48	82	79	1.0	1.2	0.6	0.2	75.0	75.3	72.6	71.4	75.5	36.4	72.9
Henrico	167,843	78.7	18.4	1.7	0.3	<.1	0.9	4	78	59	39	3.6	3.6	3.8	1.4	76.7	79.0	70.7	68.0	76.8	27.7	71.3
Henry	43,671	77.8	21.5	0.2	<.1	0.0	0.4	21	82	52	102	0.9	0.9	1.2	0.1	76.7	78.3	71.7	68.0	60.0	0.0	66.0
Highland	2,073	99.6	0.1	<.1	0.0	0.0	0.1	136	1	135	136	<.1	<.1	<.1	<.1	78.7	78.7	100.0	100.0	0.0	0.0	60.0
Isle of Wight	18,538	68.0	30.9	0.2	0.2	<.1	0.6	61	100	32	58	0.4	0.3	0.7	0.1	75.0	74.7	72.8	65.7	66.0	37.5	68.0
James City	26,366	80.0	17.5	1.2	0.2	<.1	1.1	41	74	62	33	0.6	0.6	0.6	0.2	75.6	76.6	71.8	70.9	80.9	46.2	73.3
King and Queen	4,703	58.7	39.8	<.1	1.0	0.0	0.4	128	123	16	90	0.1	<.1	0.2	<.1	74.8	77.7	71.1	40.0	72.3	0.0	75.0
King George	9,727	78.1	19.8	0.8	0.3	<.1	1.0	94	79	54	35	0.2	0.2	0.2	<.1	71.9	72.4	70.6	68.4	81.1	66.7	59.6
King William	7,997	67.4	29.7	0.2	2.1	0.0	0.6	105	103	37	61	0.2	0.1	0.3	<.1	73.7	73.7	72.1	66.7	77.4	0.0	77.7
Lancaster	8,667	72.5	26.8	0.1	<.1	0.0	0.5	102	94	40	83	0.2	0.2	0.3	<.1	79.5	83.2	71.6	100.0	100.0	0.0	56.0
Lee	18,144	99.0	0.4	<.1	<.1	0.0	0.4	62	6	132	91	0.4	0.5	<.1	<.1	74.1	74.1	72.5	70.0	69.2	0.0	66.4
Loudoun	62,851	88.2	7.0	2.3	0.2	<.1	2.3	15	50	92	13	1.3	1.5	0.5	1.3	73.0	73.4	71.5	69.7	77.8	42.9	66.7
Louisa	15,202	74.1	24.9	0.1	0.4	<.1	0.5	71	92	44	88	0.3	0.3	0.5	<.1	74.8	75.6	72.8	60.0	85.9	42.9	68.7
Lunenburg	8,460	63.8	35.4	0.1	<.1	0.0	0.7	103	114	24	53	0.2	0.1	0.4	<.1	74.7	76.6	70.1	52.6	54.5	0.0	68.7
Madison	8,930	85.9	13.4	0.2	0.2	<.1	0.2	100	59	68	128	0.2	0.2	0.1	<.1	74.7	75.5	70.4	86.4	75.9	30.0	57.1
Mathews	6,659	85.8	13.3	0.1	0.1	<.1	0.6	112	60	69	68	0.1	0.2	0.1	<.1	76.6	76.6	74.6	46.7	81.8	100.0	75.5
Mecklenburg	22,402	63.9	35.5	0.1	<.1	0.0	0.4	47	113	23	103	0.5	0.4	1.0	<.1	76.6	80.1	71.1	68.1	90.0	0.0	78.7
Middlesex	6,884	76.2	23.0	0.1	<.1	0.0	0.5	111	87	47	71	0.1	0.1	0.2	<.1	79.6	81.1	75.1	77.8	100.0	0.0	77.1
Montgomery	60,672	91.1	3.7	4.0	<.1	<.1	1.1	17	41	110	28	1.3	1.5	0.3	0.6	82.1	82.0	80.0	86.5	90.5	55.3	85.9
Nelson	9,694	80.8	18.1	0.2	<.1	<.1	0.8	95	72	60	47	0.2	0.2	0.2	<.1	75.9	76.6	73.4	66.7	64.3	12.5	65.3
New Kent	7,818	77.0	20.7	0.2	1.3	<.1	0.7	107	85	53	54	0.2	0.2	0.2	<.1	74.8	74.9	75.7	59.4	75.7	35.0	66.7
Northampton	9,746	55.2	43.0	0.1	0.1	<.1	1.6	93	127	11	17	0.2	0.1	0.5	0.1	74.6	79.7	69.5	68.8	81.3	100.0	60.2
Northumberland	8,418	73.0	26.4	0.2	<.1	0.0	0.4	104	93	41	98	0.2	0.2	0.3	<.1	80.0	83.4	72.0	84.2	88.9	0.0	66.7
Nottoway	11,640	59.0	40.0	0.3	0.2	0.0	0.5	88	121	14	70	0.2	0.2	0.6	<.1	75.7	76.7	70.5	74.4	86.7	11.1	58.5
Orange	16,211	85.8	13.3	0.2	0.2	<.1	0.5	67	61	70	74	0.3	0.4	0.3	<.1	76.4	76.7	76.3	62.7	81.0	0.0	66.7
Page	16,574	97.2	2.0	0.3	0.1	<.1	0.4	66	15	119	94	0.3	0.3	<.1	<.1	76.4	76.5	70.4	73.7	92.3	100.0	61.0
Patrick	13,600	92.8	6.5	0.1	<.1	<.1	0.6	78	38	93	69	0.3	0.3	0.1	<.1	78.5	78.5	70.4	73.7	92.3	100.0	61.0
Pittsylvania	42,116	74.2	25.3	0.1	<.1	0.0	0.4	24	91	43	96	0.9	0.9	1.3	0.2	75.7	77.2	71.6	69.4	65.1	0.0	72.8
Powhatan	11,805	75.9	23.4	0.2	0.2	0.0	0.4	87	88	45	105	0.3	0.2	0.3	<.1	77.0	75.0	84.5	69.2	86.2	0.0	71.2

Table B. — 1990 Voting Age Population (VAP) by Race and Ethnic Origin (cont)

County	Total Voting Age Population	Percent of total VAP Non-Hispanic White	Black	Asian and Pacific Islander	Native American	Other	Hispanic	Rank – Percent of total VAP Total	Non-Hispanic White	Black	Hispanic	Percent contribution to state VAP Total	Non-Hispanic White	Black	Hispanic	VAP percent of total population Total	Non-Hispanic White	Black	Asian and Pacific Islander	Native American	Other	Hispanic
Prince Edward	13,724	67.0	31.8	0.5	0.2	<.1	0.6	77	105	31	63	0.3	0.3	0.5	<.1	79.2	84.7	70.0	81.8	79.3	66.7	70.2
Prince George	20,097	66.0	28.0	1.9	0.4	<.1	3.7	54	108	39	9	0.4	0.4	0.7	0.7	73.4	74.4	71.9	68.7	77.7	25.8	69.5
Prince William	149,823	81.8	10.8	2.9	0.3	<.1	4.2	6	68	78	8	3.2	3.4	2.0	5.5	69.5	70.4	65.4	68.0	72.8	41.3	64.7
Pulaski	26,806	93.7	5.5	0.2	0.1	<.1	0.4	40	34	98	97	0.6	0.7	0.2	<.1	77.7	78.0	74.5	69.2	85.0	20.0	71.4
Rappahannock	5,102	90.9	7.8	0.2	0.2	0.0	1.0	123	42	88	34	0.1	0.1	<.1	<.1	77.0	76.8	81.3	61.5	80.0	0.0	73.1
Richmond	5,586	70.4	28.6	0.4	<.1	0.0	0.6	119	97	38	59	0.1	0.1	0.2	<.1	76.8	78.5	73.1	87.0	50.0	0.0	67.3
Roanoke	61,505	96.3	2.5	0.7	<.1	<.1	0.5	16	23	116	86	1.3	1.6	0.2	0.3	77.5	77.7	76.3	67.6	82.6	10.0	66.4
Rockbridge	14,149	96.3	3.0	0.2	0.2	<.1	0.3	75	22	112	120	0.3	0.4	<.1	<.1	77.1	77.2	75.4	67.4	75.8	14.3	71.4
Rockingham	43,433	97.4	1.5	0.2	<.1	<.1	0.8	22	14	124	44	0.9	1.2	<.1	0.3	75.6	75.7	75.8	57.8	61.2	57.1	67.4
Russell	21,490	98.5	1.2	<.1	<.1	0.0	0.2	51	8	126	126	0.5	0.6	<.1	<.1	75.0	74.9	81.3	86.7	69.2	0.0	68.4
Scott	18,079	99.0	0.6	<.1	<.1	<.1	0.3	63	5	130	124	0.4	0.5	<.1	<.1	77.9	78.0	74.8	100.0	70.6	50.0	66.2
Shenandoah	24,630	97.8	1.1	0.2	<.1	<.1	0.8	44	10	127	49	0.5	0.7	<.1	0.2	77.9	78.0	75.7	62.2	96.0	100.0	64.7
Smyth	24,927	97.4	2.0	0.2	0.1	<.1	0.3	43	13	120	117	0.5	0.7	<.1	<.1	77.0	77.1	76.2	66.7	76.5	50.0	71.2
Southampton	13,447	55.7	43.7	<.1	<.1	0.0	0.4	79	126	9	100	0.3	0.2	0.7	<.1	76.6	78.0	74.9	68.8	86.7	0.0	79.1
Spotsylvania	39,975	86.7	10.6	1.1	0.4	<.1	1.3	27	55	79	23	0.9	1.0	0.5	0.4	69.6	69.9	68.7	72.0	76.6	17.4	59.4
Stafford	43,093	89.7	7.0	1.1	0.4	<.1	1.8	23	46	91	15	0.9	1.1	0.4	0.7	70.4	70.6	71.2	66.2	69.7	41.2	62.3
Surry	4,524	46.8	52.7	<.1	0.2	0.0	0.3	130	131	5	115	<.1	<.1	0.3	<.1	73.6	78.3	69.9	100.0	70.0	0.0	73.7
Sussex	7,712	43.7	55.8	0.2	0.1	<.1	0.2	109	133	4	133	0.2	<.1	0.5	<.1	75.3	79.3	72.4	81.3	90.9	33.3	65.2
Tazewell	34,301	96.8	2.4	0.4	<.1	<.1	0.3	33	19	117	122	0.7	0.9	0.1	<.1	74.6	74.9	69.6	60.7	73.9	66.7	71.6
Warren	19,686	94.0	4.7	0.2	<.1	<.1	0.9	56	32	103	43	0.4	0.5	0.1	0.2	75.3	75.6	71.9	70.6	68.9	66.7	69.0
Washington	35,656	98.0	1.5	0.2	<.1	<.1	0.2	31	9	125	125	0.8	1.0	<.1	<.1	77.7	77.7	78.0	77.8	75.0	100.0	63.0
Westmoreland	11,871	69.0	29.8	0.4	0.2	<.1	0.6	86	99	36	57	0.3	0.2	0.4	<.1	76.7	80.4	69.4	69.7	80.0	50.0	75.0
Wise	29,102	97.6	1.7	0.3	0.1	<.1	0.3	39	12	122	123	0.6	0.8	<.1	<.1	73.5	73.6	70.4	65.2	88.2	11.1	71.7
Wythe	19,521	96.2	3.3	0.2	0.1	0.0	0.2	57	24	111	130	0.4	0.5	<.1	<.1	76.7	76.9	72.3	70.5	79.4	0.0	65.0
York	30,040	81.6	14.7	2.0	0.2	<.1	1.4	37	69	64	19	0.6	0.7	0.5	0.4	70.8	72.0	67.2	63.2	74.0	44.4	59.1
Alexandria City	94,051	67.8	19.4	3.8	0.3	<.1	8.7	12	102	55	2	2.0	1.8	2.2	7.2	84.6	89.1	76.0	79.5	87.3	39.4	76.2
Bedford City	4,809	79.5	19.3	0.4	0.1	0.0	0.6	126	75	56	60	0.1	0.1	0.1	<.1	79.2	82.2	70.1	54.5	100.0	0.0	56.6
Bristol City	14,453	93.9	5.3	0.4	<.1	<.1	0.3	72	33	101	116	0.3	0.4	<.1	<.1	78.4	78.9	72.2	70.3	84.6	33.3	68.8
Buena Vista City	5,018	95.4	4.0	0.3	<.1	0.0	0.2	125	26	109	131	0.1	0.1	<.1	<.1	78.3	78.7	72.5	66.7	60.0	0.0	83.3
Charlottesville City	33,088	78.1	18.1	2.5	<.1	<.1	1.1	35	80	61	27	0.7	0.7	0.7	0.3	82.0	85.2	70.3	90.9	81.6	28.6	78.2
Chesapeake City	108,347	71.7	25.6	1.2	0.3	<.1	1.2	10	96	42	25	2.3	2.1	3.4	1.1	71.3	73.1	67.0	69.1	74.9	19.2	66.2
Clifton Forge City	3,685	85.2	14.2	0.1	<.1	0.0	0.4	133	64	65	92	<.1	<.1	<.1	<.1	78.8	79.5	75.3	71.4	100.0	0.0	64.0
Colonial Heights City	12,561	96.1	0.8	1.9	0.2	<.1	0.9	83	25	128	37	0.3	0.3	<.1	0.1	78.2	78.4	82.0	69.6	68.8	66.7	73.9
Covington City	5,577	85.7	13.4	0.4	<.1	<.1	0.4	120	62	67	104	0.1	0.1	<.1	<.1	79.8	80.5	77.2	50.0	33.3	57.1	74.1
Danville City	41,039	66.9	32.1	0.4	0.1	<.1	0.5	26	130	30	81	0.9	0.8	1.6	0.2	77.4	82.9	68.2	63.7	68.2	25.0	72.5
Emporia City	3,998	57.8	40.6	0.5	0.1	0.0	1.0	131	124	13	36	<.1	<.1	0.2	<.1	75.3	81.8	68.1	79.2	45.5	0.0	64.4
Fairfax City	15,863	83.8	4.3	6.4	0.2	<.1	5.2	69	66	107	6	0.3	0.4	<.1	0.7	80.8	82.6	73.3	73.9	75.6	50.0	71.6
Falls Church City	7,715	86.8	2.7	4.4	0.4	<.1	5.6	108	54	114	5	0.2	0.2	<.1	0.4	80.5	81.8	74.6	75.3	74.4	53.8	71.5
Franklin City	5,759	48.6	50.9	0.3	<.1	<.1	0.2	118	129	7	134	0.1	<.1	0.4	<.1	73.2	77.1	69.9	80.0	83.3	100.0	66.7
Fredericksburg City	15,485	77.5	19.2	1.0	0.2	<.1	2.1	70	83	58	14	0.3	0.3	0.4	0.3	81.4	84.3	73.0	75.5	92.6	72.7	69.1
Galax City	5,243	93.6	5.1	0.3	<.1	0.0	0.9	122	35	102	40	0.1	0.1	<.1	<.1	78.6	79.3	68.7	100.0	50.0	0.0	73.8
Hampton City	100,375	59.0	37.3	1.6	0.3	<.1	1.7	11	120	18	16	2.1	1.6	4.6	1.5	75.0	77.0	72.8	70.4	78.2	39.8	65.8
Harrisonburg City	25,918	90.8	6.3	1.4	0.1	<.1	1.4	42	43	94	20	0.6	0.6	0.2	0.3	84.4	85.0	81.2	75.9	88.6	52.9	75.9
Hopewell City	17,056	74.8	22.3	1.2	0.3	<.1	1.5	65	90	48	18	0.4	0.4	0.5	0.2	73.8	77.5	64.8	73.3	69.8	19.0	60.7
Lexington City	6,147	86.7	10.9	1.3	0.3	0.0	0.8	116	56	77	46	0.1	0.1	<.1	<.1	88.3	89.1	82.8	92.9	81.0	0.0	82.3
Lynchburg City	51,238	75.1	23.4	0.7	0.2	<.1	0.7	19	89	46	55	1.1	1.1	1.5	0.3	77.6	80.8	68.9	75.0	82.0	52.2	70.2
Manassas City	19,981	81.6	9.5	2.9	0.3	<.1	5.7	55	70	83	4	0.4	0.4	0.2	1.0	71.5	72.3	66.6	68.4	67.8	37.9	71.0
Manassas Park City	4,642	86.7	6.2	2.5	0.1	<.1	4.4	129	57	95	7	<.1	0.1	<.1	0.2	68.9	69.9	60.3	70.1	85.7	20.0	64.6
Martinsville City	12,540	66.2	33.3	0.2	0.1	<.1	0.3	84	107	28	119	0.3	0.2	0.5	<.1	77.6	82.0	70.4	62.5	70.0	33.3	61.0
Newport News City	123,379	64.4	30.6	2.2	0.3	<.1	2.4	9	111	33	12	2.6	2.2	4.6	2.6	72.6	76.1	66.9	71.0	72.1	35.4	63.3
Norfolk City	201,242	58.8	35.5	2.3	0.4	<.1	2.8	3	122	22	10	4.3	3.3	8.8	5.0	77.0	81.6	70.8	76.1	81.5	40.1	74.2
Norton City	3,137	93.0	5.6	0.6	0.2	0.0	0.6	135	37	97	66	<.1	<.1	<.1	<.1	73.9	74.8	66.0	51.4	46.2	0.0	58.1
Petersburg City	29,392	30.1	67.9	0.7	0.2	<.1	1.1	38	135	1	26	0.6	0.2	2.4	0.3	76.6	87.9	72.5	81.2	72.5	40.0	70.8
Poquoson City	7,977	97.0	0.8	1.2	0.2	<.1	0.8	106	18	129	65	0.2	0.2	<.1	<.1	72.5	72.7	78.0	59.7	79.2	100.0	62.5
Portsmouth City	76,050	54.2	43.6	0.7	0.3	<.1	1.2	13	128	10	24	1.6	1.1	4.1	0.8	73.2	78.5	67.8	73.7	73.4	38.1	65.2
Radford City	13,918	91.7	5.3	1.7	<.1	<.1	1.1	76	39	99	29	0.3	0.4	<.1	0.1	87.3	87.9	77.7	90.0	86.7	50.0	89.1
Richmond City	161,054	48.2	49.8	0.9	0.2	<.1	0.9	5	130	8	44	3.4	2.1	9.8	1.3	79.3	89.0	71.8	79.2	84.8	51.8	75.1
Roanoke City	75,223	76.9	21.7	0.6	0.2	<.1	0.6	14	86	50	65	1.6	1.6	2.0	0.4	78.0	80.9	70.1	65.3	76.7	30.0	65.4
Salem City	19,089	94.4	4.4	0.6	0.1	<.1	0.5	60	30	105	87	0.4	0.5	0.1	<.1	80.4	80.5	79.4	71.4	88.9	20.0	79.3
South Boston City	5,352	65.3	33.5	0.4	0.2	<.1	0.6	121	110	27	67	0.1	<.1	0.2	<.1	76.5	80.2	70.3	70.6	81.8	100.0	66.7
Staunton City	19,433	87.4	11.5	0.4	0.1	<.1	0.6	58	51	74	64	0.4	0.5	0.3	<.1	79.4	80.5	72.9	73.3	90.3	27.3	66.9
Suffolk City	37,998	56.8	42.1	0.3	0.2	<.1	0.5	28	125	12	73	0.8	0.6	2.0	0.2	72.9	76.0	69.1	70.4	87.9	33.3	62.1
Virginia Beach City	283,182	80.4	12.6	3.8	0.3	<.1	2.8	2	73	72	11	6.0	6.3	4.4	7.0	72.0	73.5	66.7	67.1	73.3	33.1	65.4
Waynesboro City	14,262	90.7	8.3	0.2	0.1	0.0	0.7	73	44	87	52	0.3	0.4	0.1	<.1	76.9	78.0	68.0	68.2	70.0	0.0	66.7
Williamsburg City	10,472	82.6	12.9	2.9	0.2	<.1	1.3	90	67	71	22	0.2	0.2	0.2	0.1	90.8	93.3	77.8	92.1	82.6	60.0	90.1
Winchester City	17,205	89.0	9.0	0.9	0.1	<.1	0.9	64	49	85	38	0.4	0.4	0.2	0.1	78.4	79.3	71.1	71.6	88.5	14.3	74.4
VIRGINIA	4,682,620	77.5	17.4	2.4	0.2	<.1	2.4					100.0	100.0	100.0	100.0	75.7	77.2	70.8	71.7	77.1	41.3	70.7

County	Total Voting Age Population	Percent of total VAP						Rank				Percent contribution to state VAP				VAP percent of total population						
		Non-Hispanic							Non-Hispanic			Non-Hispanic				Non-Hispanic						
		White	Black	Asian and Pacific Islander	Native American	Other	Hispanic	Total	White	Black	Hispanic	Total	White	Black	Hispanic	Total	White	Black	Asian and Pacific Islander	Native American	Other	Hispanic
CONGRESSIONAL																						
District 1	418,734	80.4	16.7	1.2	0.3	<.1	1.4	8	5	4	5	8.9	9.3	8.6	5.1	74.4	75.7	70.0	70.5	76.4	40.8	65.2
District 2	419,231	78.0	15.2	3.3	0.4	<.1	3.0	7	6	5	3	9.0	9.0	7.8	11.2	74.6	76.1	69.6	69.9	77.2	36.3	68.8
District 3	414,401	36.4	60.9	1.0	0.4	<.1	1.2	10	11	1	6	8.8	4.2	30.9	4.5	73.7	80.2	70.5	72.4	77.1	39.8	66.7
District 4	415,002	67.2	30.5	1.0	0.2	<.1	1.0	9	10	2	7	8.9	7.7	15.5	3.8	73.8	75.6	70.5	68.4	76.2	27.1	66.7
District 5	433,192	76.0	22.8	0.6	0.1	<.1	0.5	4	8	3	10	9.3	9.1	12.1	2.0	77.0	79.0	71.2	80.7	73.8	36.3	70.6
District 6	437,920	88.1	10.6	0.5	0.1	<.1	0.6	2	3	7	9	9.4	10.6	5.7	2.4	77.8	78.7	72.0	69.9	78.3	34.5	70.5
District 7	424,882	88.0	9.3	1.5	0.2	<.1	0.9	5	4	8	8	9.1	10.3	4.8	3.5	75.5	76.3	70.7	67.6	78.9	30.5	69.1
District 8	453,533	73.4	12.2	6.0	0.3	<.1	8.0	1	9	6	1	9.7	9.2	6.8	32.1	80.6	83.0	75.4	74.3	80.8	50.4	74.2
District 9	433,970	96.3	2.4	0.8	<.1	<.1	0.5	3	1	11	11	9.3	11.5	1.3	1.8	77.2	77.2	75.3	81.7	79.4	44.2	71.9
District 10	411,822	89.7	5.5	2.5	0.2	<.1	2.1	11	2	10	4	8.8	10.2	2.8	7.6	73.2	73.6	70.7	68.8	75.8	41.8	68.4
District 11	419,933	77.8	7.3	7.6	0.2	<.1	7.0	6	7	9	2	9.0	9.0	3.8	26.0	74.7	76.1	68.2	71.2	73.8	48.0	70.9

Table C. — Voter Participation: November 3, 1992, General Election

County	Estimated Voting Age Population (VAP), 1992	Voter registration (REG)				Voter turnout													
						Highest office				Maximum vote							Percent drop-off, by office[1]			
		Total	% contribution to state REG	% of 1992 VAP	Rank by % of 1992 VAP	Actual	Total	Office	% of 1992 VAP	Total	% contribution to state turnout	% of REG	Rank by % of REG	% of 1992 VAP	Rank by % 1992 VAP	President	Senator	Governor	Representative
Accomack	24,218	16,131	0.5	66.6	56	-	13,125	P	54.2	13,125	0.5	81.4	108	54.2	61	0.0	-	-	3.3
Albemarle	53,176	37,298	1.2	70.1	39	-	31,804	P	59.8	31,804	1.2	85.3	49	59.8	32	0.0	-	-	15.9
Alleghany	9,870	6,495	0.2	65.8	60	-	5,657	P	57.3	5,657	0.2	87.1	24	57.3	42	0.0	-	-	5.9
Amelia	6,598	5,011	0.2	75.9	11	-	4,224	P	64.0	4,224	0.2	84.3	64	64.0	16	0.0	-	-	7.5
Amherst	21,643	12,919	0.4	59.7	103	-	10,908	P	50.4	10,908	0.4	84.4	62	50.4	99	0.0	-	-	7.7
Appomattox	9,325	7,026	0.2	75.3	14	-	5,620	P	60.3	5,620	0.2	80.0	121	60.3	31	0.0	-	-	16.5
Arlington	147,323	97,902	3.2	66.5	59	-	82,584	P	56.1	82,584	3.2	84.4	63	56.1	49	0.0	-	-	4.5
Augusta	41,539	24,749	0.8	59.6	104	-	21,866	P	52.6	21,866	0.9	88.4	10	52.6	80	0.0	-	-	8.3
Bath	3,590	2,835	<.1	79.0	6	-	2,330	P	64.9	2,330	<.1	82.2	94	64.9	11	0.0	-	-	7.4
Bedford	37,252	23,929	0.8	64.2	68	-	20,756	P	55.7	20,756	0.8	86.7	32	55.7	50	0.0	-	-	13.1
Bland	5,127	3,486	0.1	68.0	48	-	2,832	P	55.2	2,832	0.1	81.2	111	55.2	54	0.0	-	-	9.8
Botetourt	19,627	14,112	0.5	71.9	30	-	12,209	P	62.2	12,209	0.5	86.5	37	62.2	22	0.0	-	-	5.7
Brunswick	12,155	8,744	0.3	71.9	29	-	6,718	P	55.3	6,718	0.3	76.8	134	55.3	53	0.0	-	-	10.6
Buchanan	22,382	15,178	0.5	67.8	49	-	11,704	P	52.3	11,704	0.5	77.1	132	52.3	83	0.0	-	-	5.4
Buckingham	9,971	6,263	0.2	62.8	80	-	5,103	P	51.2	5,103	0.2	81.5	107	51.2	95	0.0	-	-	11.9
Campbell	36,386	24,333	0.8	66.9	55	-	19,757	P	54.3	19,757	0.8	81.2	112	54.3	60	0.0	-	-	15.4
Caroline	14,385	9,416	0.3	65.5	61	-	7,753	P	53.9	7,753	0.3	82.3	89	53.9	67	0.0	-	-	5.6
Carroll	20,666	12,798	0.4	61.9	88	-	10,915	P	52.8	10,915	0.4	85.3	48	52.8	78	0.0	-	-	5.9
Charles City	4,687	3,614	0.1	77.1	9	-	3,014	P	64.3	3,014	0.1	83.4	76	64.3	13	0.0	-	-	10.2
Charlotte	8,697	6,353	0.2	73.0	23	-	5,111	P	58.8	5,111	0.2	80.5	119	58.8	38	0.0	-	-	15.7
Chesterfield	165,116	118,963	3.9	72.0	28	-	101,933	P	61.7	101,933	4.0	85.7	42	61.7	26	0.0	-	-	3.9
Clarke	9,743	5,344	0.2	54.8	122	-	4,648	P	47.7	4,648	0.2	87.0	27	47.7	116	0.0	-	-	6.9
Craig	3,437	2,636	<.1	76.7	10	-	2,297	P	66.8	2,297	<.1	87.1	21	66.8	9	0.0	-	-	1.5
Culpeper	21,444	12,511	0.4	58.3	109	-	10,466	P	48.8	10,466	0.4	83.7	73	48.8	111	0.0	-	-	38.7
Cumberland	5,803	4,264	0.1	73.5	19	-	3,384	P	58.3	3,384	0.1	79.4	125	58.3	39	0.0	-	-	22.5
Dickenson	12,708	10,287	0.3	80.9	2	-	8,143	P	64.1	8,143	0.3	79.2	128	64.1	15	0.0	-	-	2.6
Dinwiddie	15,638	10,110	0.3	64.7	65	-	8,597	P	55.0	8,597	0.3	85.0	51	55.0	56	0.0	-	-	6.4
Essex	6,583	4,494	0.1	68.3	46	-	3,904	P	59.3	3,904	0.2	86.9	30	59.3	35	0.0	-	-	17.4
Fairfax	669,856	459,102	15.0	68.5	45	-	385,280	P	57.5	385,280	15.1	83.9	70	57.5	41	0.0	-	-	6.0
Fauquier	38,531	23,211	0.8	60.2	99	-	20,759	P	53.9	20,759	0.8	89.4	6	53.9	68	0.0	-	-	12.5
Floyd	9,340	6,219	0.2	66.6	57	-	5,316	P	56.9	5,316	0.2	85.5	44	56.9	45	0.0	-	-	6.7
Fluvanna	9,651	6,718	0.2	69.6	44	-	5,852	P	60.6	5,852	0.2	87.1	23	60.6	30	0.0	-	-	10.9
Franklin	30,839	17,943	0.6	58.2	112	-	15,701	P	50.9	15,701	0.6	87.5	18	50.9	96	0.0	-	-	9.9
Frederick	36,110	20,939	0.7	58.0	114	-	17,468	P	48.4	17,468	0.7	83.4	75	48.4	113	0.0	-	-	7.7
Giles	12,469	9,155	0.3	73.4	20	-	7,632	P	61.2	7,632	0.3	83.4	77	61.2	29	0.0	-	-	7.1
Gloucester	24,624	15,552	0.5	63.2	75	-	13,345	P	54.2	13,345	0.5	85.8	41	54.2	62	0.0	-	-	6.1
Goochland	11,580	8,269	0.3	71.4	34	-	7,479	P	64.6	7,479	0.3	90.4	3	64.6	12	0.0	-	-	8.2
Grayson	12,593	8,463	0.3	67.2	52	-	6,939	P	55.1	6,939	0.3	82.0	98	55.1	55	0.0	-	-	5.4
Greene	8,049	5,239	0.2	65.1	64	-	4,331	P	53.8	4,331	0.2	82.7	86	53.8	69	0.0	-	-	33.8
Greensville	6,217	5,030	0.2	80.9	3	-	3,986	P	64.1	3,986	0.2	79.2	127	64.1	14	0.0	-	-	7.4
Halifax	21,778	13,716	0.4	63.0	78	-	11,262	P	51.7	11,262	0.4	82.1	97	51.7	91	0.0	-	-	17.3
Hanover	50,187	37,597	1.2	74.9	16	-	34,261	P	68.3	34,261	1.3	91.1	2	68.3	4	0.0	-	-	8.1
Henrico	175,147	122,698	4.0	70.1	40	-	108,868	P	62.2	108,868	4.3	88.7	7	62.2	23	0.0	-	-	6.0
Henry	43,346	26,574	0.9	61.3	94	-	21,825	P	50.4	21,825	0.9	82.1	96	50.4	100	0.0	-	-	14.3
Highland	2,010	1,598	<.1	79.5	5	-	1,400	P	69.7	1,400	<.1	87.6	16	69.7	3	0.0	-	-	2.4
Isle of Wight	19,117	13,520	0.4	70.7	37	-	11,387	P	59.6	11,387	0.4	84.2	66	59.6	34	0.0	-	-	6.6
James City	29,379	20,911	0.7	71.2	35	-	18,221	P	62.0	18,221	0.7	87.1	22	62.0	24	0.0	-	-	8.1
King and Queen	4,741	3,463	0.1	73.0	24	-	2,917	P	61.5	2,917	0.1	84.2	65	61.5	27	0.0	-	-	14.1
King George	10,355	6,148	0.2	59.4	106	-	5,324	P	51.4	5,324	0.2	86.6	36	51.4	93	0.0	-	-	3.4
King William	8,325	6,134	0.2	73.7	18	-	5,230	P	62.8	5,230	0.2	85.3	50	62.8	21	0.0	-	-	13.5
Lancaster	8,681	6,370	0.2	73.4	21	-	5,528	P	63.7	5,528	0.2	86.8	31	63.7	17	0.0	-	-	7.4
Lee	18,150	12,896	0.4	71.1	36	-	9,796	P	54.0	9,796	0.4	76.0	135	54.0	65	0.0	-	-	4.0
Loudoun	70,125	49,040	1.6	69.9	42	-	41,574	P	59.3	41,574	1.6	84.8	56	59.3	36	0.0	-	-	10.0
Louisa	15,701	9,607	0.3	61.2	95	-	8,307	P	52.9	8,307	0.3	86.5	39	52.9	75	0.0	-	-	13.5
Lunenburg	8,354	5,976	0.2	71.5	32	-	4,912	P	58.8	4,912	0.2	82.2	93	58.8	37	0.0	-	-	22.1
Madison	9,232	5,600	0.2	60.7	97	-	4,779	P	51.8	4,779	0.2	85.3	47	51.8	89	0.0	-	-	34.4
Mathews	6,698	5,224	0.2	78.0	7	-	4,525	P	67.6	4,525	0.2	86.6	35	67.6	6	0.0	-	-	4.0
Mecklenburg	22,433	13,457	0.4	60.0	102	-	10,970	P	48.9	10,970	0.4	81.5	105	48.9	109	0.0	-	-	19.9
Middlesex	6,944	5,407	0.2	77.9	8	-	4,685	P	67.5	4,685	0.2	86.6	34	67.5	7	0.0	-	-	5.9
Montgomery	58,465	29,343	1.0	50.2	130	-	24,935	P	42.6	24,935	1.0	85.0	53	42.6	130	0.0	-	-	3.7
Nelson	9,792	6,677	0.2	68.2	47	-	5,538	P	56.6	5,538	0.2	82.9	80	56.6	47	0.0	-	-	4.7
New Kent	8,199	6,214	0.2	75.8	12	-	5,483	P	66.9	5,483	0.2	88.2	11	66.9	8	0.0	-	-	7.8
Northampton	9,412	7,083	0.2	75.3	15	-	5,618	P	59.7	5,618	0.2	79.3	126	59.7	33	0.0	-	-	3.1
Northumberland	8,385	6,278	0.2	74.9	17	-	5,334	P	63.6	5,334	0.2	85.0	54	63.6	18	0.0	-	-	5.0
Nottoway	11,643	6,893	0.2	59.2	107	-	5,743	P	49.3	5,743	0.2	83.3	78	49.3	107	0.0	-	-	16.5
Orange	16,828	10,369	0.3	61.6	90	-	8,966	P	53.3	8,966	0.4	86.5	38	53.3	72	0.0	-	-	38.6
Page	16,912	10,373	0.3	61.3	93	-	8,460	P	50.0	8,460	0.3	81.6	104	50.0	103	0.0	-	-	13.0
Patrick	13,586	8,507	0.3	62.6	82	-	7,189	P	52.9	7,189	0.3	84.5	60	52.9	74	0.0	-	-	23.9
Pittsylvania	40,612	26,088	0.9	64.2	67	-	21,894	P	53.9	21,894	0.9	83.9	69	53.9	66	0.0	-	-	14.9
Powhatan	12,261	7,903	0.3	64.5	66	-	7,086	P	57.8	7,086	0.3	89.7	5	57.8	40	0.0	-	-	8.7

[1]Percent drop-off is zero for any office used as highest office turnout.

950 Virginia

Table C. — Voter Participation: November 3, 1992, General Election (cont)

County	Estimated Voting Age Population (VAP), 1992	REG Total	REG % contribution to state REG	REG % of 1992 VAP	REG Rank by % of 1992 VAP	Highest office Actual	Highest office Total	Highest office Office	Highest office % of 1992 VAP	Max vote Total	Max vote % contribution to state turnout	Max vote % of REG	Max vote Rank by % of REG	Max vote % of 1992 VAP	Max vote Rank by % 1992 VAP	Drop-off President	Drop-off Senator	Drop-off Governor	Drop-off Representative
Prince Edward	12,946	7,696	0.3	59.4	105	-	6,383	P	49.3	6,383	0.2	82.9	82	49.3	108	0.0	-	-	16.6
Prince George	20,172	10,799	0.4	53.5	125	-	9,412	P	46.7	9,412	0.4	87.2	20	46.7	120	0.0	-	-	6.7
Prince William	167,067	85,512	2.8	51.2	129	-	75,680	P	45.3	75,680	3.0	88.5	8	45.3	123	0.0	-	-	8.4
Pulaski	26,606	16,761	0.5	63.0	77	-	13,987	P	52.6	13,987	0.5	83.4	74	52.6	81	0.0	-	-	4.6
Rappahannock	5,173	3,621	0.1	70.0	41	-	3,181	P	61.5	3,181	0.1	87.8	15	61.5	28	0.0	-	-	3.2
Richmond	5,583	3,518	0.1	63.0	76	-	3,050	P	54.6	3,050	0.1	86.7	33	54.6	58	0.0	-	-	27.4
Roanoke	62,648	45,448	1.5	72.5	26	-	41,080	P	65.6	41,080	1.6	90.4	4	65.6	10	0.0	-	-	3.5
Rockbridge	14,247	8,617	0.3	60.5	98	-	7,503	P	52.7	7,503	0.3	87.1	25	52.7	79	0.0	-	-	7.3
Rockingham	43,059	24,378	0.8	56.6	115	-	21,493	P	49.9	21,493	0.8	88.2	12	49.9	104	0.0	-	-	9.5
Russell	21,274	14,423	0.5	67.8	50	-	11,484	P	54.0	11,484	0.4	79.6	122	54.0	64	0.0	-	-	4.3
Scott	17,883	11,987	0.4	67.0	54	-	9,690	P	54.2	9,690	0.4	80.8	117	54.2	63	0.0	-	-	4.9
Shenandoah	25,255	15,697	0.5	62.2	86	-	13,834	P	54.8	13,834	0.5	88.1	13	54.8	57	0.0	-	-	7.5
Smyth	24,841	15,258	0.5	61.4	92	-	12,931	P	52.1	12,931	0.5	84.7	57	52.1	85	0.0	-	-	5.1
Southampton	13,156	8,254	0.3	62.7	81	-	6,874	P	52.2	6,874	0.3	83.3	79	52.2	84	0.0	-	-	9.7
Spotsylvania	45,285	27,585	0.9	60.9	96	-	24,014	P	53.0	24,014	0.9	87.1	26	53.0	73	0.0	-	-	9.4
Stafford	48,469	29,113	1.0	60.1	101	-	24,871	P	51.3	24,871	1.0	85.4	46	51.3	94	0.0	-	-	5.3
Surry	4,538	3,977	0.1	87.6	1	-	3,275	P	72.2	3,275	0.1	82.3	88	72.2	1	0.0	-	-	12.0
Sussex	7,575	5,530	0.2	73.0	25	-	4,253	P	56.1	4,253	0.2	76.9	133	56.1	48	0.0	-	-	18.1
Tazewell	33,969	21,034	0.7	61.9	89	-	17,056	P	50.2	17,056	0.7	81.1	113	50.2	101	0.0	-	-	7.7
Warren	20,530	11,226	0.4	54.7	123	-	9,676	P	47.1	9,676	0.4	86.2	40	47.1	118	0.0	-	-	12.2
Washington	35,505	22,585	0.7	63.6	72	-	18,995	P	53.5	18,995	0.7	84.1	68	53.5	71	0.0	-	-	4.0
Westmoreland	12,033	7,564	0.2	62.9	79	-	6,223	P	51.7	6,223	0.2	82.3	92	51.7	90	0.0	-	-	11.6
Wise	28,692	18,717	0.6	65.2	63	-	14,857	P	51.8	14,857	0.6	79.4	124	51.8	88	0.0	-	-	3.9
Wythe	19,522	12,382	0.4	63.4	73	-	10,492	P	53.7	10,492	0.4	84.7	58	53.7	70	0.0	-	-	5.4
York	31,678	22,714	0.7	71.7	31	-	19,966	P	63.0	19,966	0.8	87.9	14	63.0	20	0.0	-	-	2.5
Alexandria City	94,618	67,596	2.2	71.4	33	-	52,675	P	55.7	52,675	2.1	77.9	131	55.7	51	0.0	-	-	4.7
Bedford City	4,754	2,949	<.1	62.0	87	-	2,409	P	50.7	2,409	<.1	81.7	101	50.7	97	0.0	-	-	15.0
Bristol City	14,114	9,020	0.3	63.9	69	-	7,462	P	52.9	7,462	0.3	82.7	85	52.9	76	0.0	-	-	4.3
Buena Vista City	4,870	2,697	<.1	55.4	120	-	2,200	P	45.2	2,200	<.1	81.6	102	45.2	124	0.0	-	-	8.0
Charlottesville City	32,104	17,147	0.6	53.4	127	-	14,899	P	46.4	14,899	0.6	86.9	29	46.4	122	0.0	-	-	10.5
Chesapeake City	117,124	77,883	2.5	66.5	58	-	61,868	P	52.8	61,868	2.4	79.4	123	52.8	77	0.0	-	-	2.9
Clifton Forge City	3,568	2,275	<.1	63.8	70	-	1,873	P	52.5	1,873	<.1	82.3	90	52.5	82	0.0	-	-	9.9
Colonial Heights City	12,371	9,892	0.3	80.0	4	-	8,400	P	67.9	8,400	0.3	84.9	55	67.9	5	0.0	-	-	3.7
Covington City	5,173	3,482	0.1	67.3	51	-	2,869	P	55.5	2,869	0.1	82.4	87	55.5	52	0.0	-	-	6.5
Danville City	42,171	23,470	0.8	55.7	117	-	19,661	P	46.6	19,661	0.8	83.8	72	46.6	121	0.0	-	-	10.8
Emporia City	4,078	2,880	<.1	70.6	38	-	2,319	P	56.9	2,319	<.1	80.5	118	56.9	46	0.0	-	-	6.9
Fairfax City	15,677	10,955	0.4	69.9	43	-	9,693	P	61.8	9,693	0.4	88.5	9	61.8	25	0.0	-	-	6.0
Falls Church City	7,694	5,829	0.2	75.8	13	-	5,404	P	70.2	5,404	0.2	92.7	1	70.2	2	0.0	-	-	4.0
Franklin City	5,837	4,219	0.1	72.3	27	-	3,339	P	57.2	3,339	0.1	79.1	129	57.2	44	0.0	-	-	9.0
Fredericksburg City	15,519	8,294	0.3	53.4	126	-	6,879	P	44.3	6,879	0.3	82.9	81	44.3	128	0.0	-	-	6.7
Galax City	5,191	2,881	<.1	55.5	119	-	2,344	P	45.2	2,344	<.1	81.4	109	45.2	125	0.0	-	-	5.0
Hampton City	100,819	60,715	2.0	60.2	100	-	49,878	P	49.5	49,878	1.9	82.2	95	49.5	106	0.0	-	-	7.5
Harrisonburg City	26,118	11,622	0.4	44.5	135	-	9,632	P	36.9	9,632	0.4	82.9	83	36.9	134	0.0	-	-	9.4
Hopewell City	16,900	9,835	0.3	58.2	111	-	8,042	P	47.6	8,042	0.3	81.8	100	47.6	117	0.0	-	-	8.5
Lexington City	5,384	2,665	<.1	49.5	131	-	2,277	P	42.3	2,277	<.1	85.4	45	42.3	131	0.0	-	-	8.3
Lynchburg City	49,419	30,804	1.0	62.3	84	-	24,969	P	50.5	24,969	1.0	81.1	114	50.5	98	0.0	-	-	8.8
Manassas City	22,851	13,253	0.4	58.0	113	-	11,154	P	48.8	11,154	0.4	84.2	67	48.8	110	0.0	-	-	13.8
Manassas Park City	4,698	2,031	<.1	43.2	136	-	1,720	P	36.6	1,720	<.1	84.7	59	36.6	135	0.0	-	-	14.2
Martinsville City	12,185	8,180	0.3	67.1	53	-	6,617	P	54.3	6,617	0.3	80.9	116	54.3	59	0.0	-	-	12.0
Newport News City	127,126	74,942	2.5	59.0	108	-	61,091	P	48.1	61,091	2.4	81.5	106	48.1	114	0.0	-	-	3.8
Norfolk City	193,457	92,304	3.0	47.7	132	-	69,027	P	35.7	69,027	2.7	74.8	136	35.7	136	0.0	-	-	3.5
Norton City	3,091	1,930	<.1	62.4	83	-	1,548	P	50.1	1,548	<.1	80.2	120	50.1	102	0.0	-	-	5.6
Petersburg City	28,522	16,107	0.5	56.5	116	-	12,717	P	44.6	12,717	0.5	79.0	130	44.6	127	0.0	-	-	14.9
Poquoson City	8,548	6,252	0.2	73.1	22	-	5,437	P	63.6	5,437	0.2	87.0	28	63.6	19	0.0	-	-	1.6
Portsmouth City	75,500	46,396	1.5	61.5	91	-	37,599	P	49.8	37,599	1.5	81.0	115	49.8	105	0.0	-	-	6.8
Radford City	12,717	5,706	0.2	44.9	134	-	4,785	P	37.6	4,785	0.2	83.9	71	37.6	133	0.0	-	-	4.0
Richmond City	154,790	96,283	3.2	62.2	85	-	79,735	P	51.5	79,735	3.1	82.8	84	51.5	92	0.0	-	-	15.3
Roanoke City	73,670	42,915	1.4	58.3	110	-	35,181	P	47.8	35,181	1.4	82.0	99	47.8	115	0.0	-	-	4.6
Salem City	18,626	12,191	0.4	65.5	62	-	10,669	P	57.3	10,669	0.4	87.5	17	57.3	43	0.0	-	-	4.4
South Boston City	5,309	3,380	0.1	63.7	71	-	2,757	P	51.9	2,757	0.1	81.6	103	51.9	87	0.0	-	-	12.7
Staunton City	19,703	10,861	0.4	55.1	121	-	9,232	P	46.9	9,232	0.4	85.0	52	46.9	119	0.0	-	-	10.3
Suffolk City	38,898	24,573	0.8	63.2	74	-	20,223	P	52.0	20,223	0.8	82.3	91	52.0	86	0.0	-	-	6.2
Virginia Beach City	313,943	169,556	5.6	54.0	124	-	137,785	P	43.9	137,785	5.4	81.3	110	43.9	129	0.0	-	-	1.7
Waynesboro City	14,737	8,196	0.3	55.6	118	-	7,149	P	48.5	7,149	0.3	87.2	19	48.5	112	0.0	-	-	9.7
Williamsburg City	9,474	4,401	0.1	46.5	133	-	3,719	P	39.3	3,719	0.1	84.5	61	39.3	132	0.0	-	-	8.1
Winchester City	17,200	8,994	0.3	52.3	128	-	7,701	P	44.8	7,701	0.3	85.6	43	44.8	126	0.0	-	-	8.2
VIRGINIA	4,842,000	3,054,662	100.0	63.1		-	2,558,665	P	52.8	2,558,665	100.0	83.8		52.8		0.0	-	-	7.4

[1] Percent drop-off is zero for any office used as highest office turnout.

Table E. — Vote for President: November 3, 1992, General Election

County	All candidates					Plurality		Percent of total vote				Rank			Percent contribution to state vote				Major party Percent of vote	
	Total	Clinton (DEM)	Bush (REP)	Perot (IND)	Other	Total	Party	DEM	REP	IND	Other	DEM	REP	IND	Total	DEM	REP	IND	DEM	REP
Accomack	13,125	4,950	5,666	2,304	205	716	R	37.7	43.2	17.6	1.6	78	89	9	0.5	0.5	0.5	0.7	46.6	53.4
Albemarle	31,804	13,886	13,894	3,855	169	8	R	43.7	43.7	12.1	0.5	41	88	89	1.2	1.3	1.2	1.1	50.0	50.0
Alleghany	5,657	2,396	2,294	926	41	102	D	42.4	40.6	16.4	0.7	47	104	24	0.2	0.2	0.2	0.3	51.1	48.9
Amelia	4,224	1,534	2,062	574	54	528	R	36.3	48.8	13.6	1.3	85	44	61	0.2	0.1	0.2	0.2	42.7	57.3
Amherst	10,908	4,101	5,482	1,268	57	1,381	R	37.6	50.3	11.6	0.5	80	29	96	0.4	0.4	0.5	0.4	42.8	57.2
Appomattox	5,620	1,919	2,830	801	70	911	R	34.1	50.4	14.3	1.2	105	27	51	0.2	0.2	0.2	0.2	40.4	59.6
Arlington	82,584	47,756	26,376	7,992	460	21,380	D	57.8	31.9	9.7	0.6	8	128	121	3.2	4.6	2.3	2.3	64.4	35.6
Augusta	21,866	5,190	12,896	3,397	383	7,706	R	23.7	59.0	15.5	1.8	133	5	30	0.9	0.5	1.1	1.0	28.7	71.3
Bath	2,330	855	1,075	354	46	220	R	36.7	46.1	15.2	2.0	83	73	34	<.1	<.1	<.1	0.1	44.3	55.7
Bedford	20,756	6,792	10,496	3,251	217	3,704	R	32.7	50.6	15.7	1.0	115	24	28	0.8	0.7	0.9	0.9	39.3	60.7
Bland	2,832	1,001	1,368	408	55	367	R	35.3	48.3	14.4	1.9	94	54	49	0.1	<.1	0.1	0.1	42.3	57.7
Botetourt	12,209	4,349	5,904	1,819	137	1,555	R	35.6	48.4	14.9	1.1	89	53	40	0.5	0.4	0.5	0.5	42.4	57.6
Brunswick	6,718	3,687	2,480	479	72	1,207	D	54.9	36.9	7.1	1.1	13	115	133	0.3	0.4	0.2	0.1	59.8	40.2
Buchanan	11,704	7,405	3,297	815	187	4,108	D	63.3	28.2	7.0	1.6	3	134	134	0.5	0.7	0.3	0.2	69.2	30.8
Buckingham	5,103	2,193	2,368	459	83	175	R	43.0	46.4	9.0	1.6	43	69	126	0.2	0.2	0.2	0.1	48.1	51.9
Campbell	19,757	5,999	10,931	2,553	274	4,932	R	30.4	55.3	12.9	1.4	127	8	78	0.8	0.6	1.0	0.7	35.4	64.6
Caroline	7,753	3,770	2,947	965	71	823	D	48.6	38.0	12.4	0.9	27	112	84	0.3	0.4	0.3	0.3	56.1	43.9
Carroll	10,915	3,790	5,664	1,388	73	1,874	R	34.7	51.9	12.7	0.7	101	18	79	0.4	0.4	0.5	0.4	40.1	59.9
Charles City	3,014	2,010	729	251	24	1,281	D	66.7	24.2	8.3	0.8	2	136	130	0.1	0.2	<.1	<.1	73.4	26.6
Charlotte	5,111	2,098	2,293	640	80	195	R	41.0	44.9	12.5	1.6	57	79	82	0.2	0.2	0.2	0.2	47.8	52.2
Chesterfield	101,933	28,028	56,626	16,898	381	28,598	R	27.5	55.6	16.6	0.4	131	7	21	4.0	2.7	4.9	4.8	33.1	66.9
Clarke	4,648	1,811	1,994	802	41	183	R	39.0	42.9	17.3	0.9	66	92	13	0.2	0.2	0.2	0.2	47.6	52.4
Craig	2,297	965	1,008	304	20	43	R	42.0	43.9	13.2	0.9	51	86	72	<.1	<.1	<.1	<.1	48.9	51.1
Culpeper	10,466	3,444	5,226	1,640	156	1,782	R	32.9	49.9	15.7	1.5	112	33	27	0.4	0.3	0.5	0.5	39.7	60.3
Cumberland	3,384	1,284	1,643	372	85	359	R	37.9	48.6	11.0	2.5	76	49	103	0.1	0.1	0.1	0.1	43.9	56.1
Dickenson	8,143	4,839	2,574	660	70	2,265	D	59.4	31.6	8.1	0.9	5	130	132	0.3	0.5	0.2	0.2	65.3	34.7
Dinwiddie	8,597	3,624	3,648	1,198	127	24	R	42.2	42.4	13.9	1.5	49	95	54	0.3	0.3	0.3	0.3	49.8	50.2
Essex	3,904	1,583	1,897	382	42	314	R	40.5	48.6	9.8	1.1	60	48	120	0.2	0.2	0.2	0.1	45.5	54.5
Fairfax	385,280	160,186	170,488	53,012	1,594	10,302	R	41.6	44.3	13.8	0.4	54	84	56	15.1	15.4	14.8	15.2	48.4	51.6
Fauquier	20,759	6,600	10,497	3,464	198	3,897	R	31.8	50.6	16.7	1.0	119	25	19	0.8	0.6	0.9	1.0	38.6	61.4
Floyd	5,316	2,026	2,575	672	43	549	R	38.1	48.4	12.6	0.8	73	51	81	0.2	0.2	0.2	0.2	44.0	56.0
Fluvanna	5,852	2,134	2,811	871	36	677	R	36.5	48.0	14.9	0.6	84	60	41	0.2	0.2	0.2	0.2	43.2	56.8
Franklin	15,701	6,590	6,724	2,232	155	134	R	42.0	42.8	14.2	1.0	53	93	52	0.6	0.6	0.6	0.6	49.5	50.5
Frederick	17,468	4,942	9,425	2,981	120	4,483	R	28.3	54.0	17.1	0.7	129	11	16	0.7	0.5	0.8	0.9	34.4	65.6
Giles	7,632	3,346	3,023	1,142	121	323	D	43.8	39.6	15.0	1.6	40	106	37	0.3	0.3	0.3	0.3	52.5	47.5
Gloucester	13,345	4,058	6,461	2,640	186	2,403	R	30.4	48.4	19.8	1.4	126	52	2	0.5	0.4	0.6	0.8	38.6	61.4
Goochland	7,479	2,589	3,834	994	62	1,245	R	34.6	51.3	13.3	0.8	102	20	71	0.3	0.2	0.3	0.3	40.3	59.7
Grayson	6,939	2,615	3,378	860	86	763	R	37.7	48.7	12.4	1.2	79	47	86	0.3	0.3	0.3	0.2	43.6	56.4
Greene	4,331	1,353	2,265	627	86	912	R	31.2	52.3	14.5	2.0	121	15	48	0.2	0.1	0.2	0.2	37.4	62.6
Greensville	3,986	2,237	1,335	360	54	902	D	56.1	33.5	9.0	1.4	11	124	125	0.2	0.2	0.1	0.1	62.6	37.4
Halifax	11,262	4,752	5,199	1,140	171	447	R	42.2	46.2	10.1	1.5	48	72	116	0.4	0.5	0.5	0.3	47.8	52.2
Hanover	34,261	8,021	20,336	5,674	230	12,315	R	23.4	59.4	16.6	0.7	134	4	22	1.3	0.8	1.8	1.6	28.3	71.7
Henrico	108,868	36,807	56,910	14,720	431	20,103	R	33.8	52.3	13.5	0.4	110	16	62	4.3	3.5	4.9	4.2	39.3	60.7
Henry	21,825	9,296	9,005	3,212	312	291	D	42.6	41.3	14.7	1.4	45	100	45	0.9	0.9	0.8	0.9	50.8	49.2
Highland	1,400	494	686	212	8	192	R	35.3	49.0	15.1	0.6	95	40	35	<.1	<.1	<.1	<.1	41.9	58.1
Isle of Wight	11,387	4,380	5,370	1,536	101	990	R	38.5	47.2	13.5	0.9	69	65	64	0.4	0.4	0.5	0.4	44.9	55.1
James City	18,221	6,536	8,781	2,675	229	2,245	R	35.9	48.2	14.7	1.3	87	57	46	0.7	0.6	0.8	0.8	42.7	57.3
King and Queen	2,917	1,363	1,206	323	25	157	D	46.7	41.3	11.1	0.9	30	99	102	0.1	0.1	0.1	<.1	53.1	46.9
King George	5,324	1,811	2,570	918	25	759	R	34.0	48.3	17.2	0.5	107	55	14	0.2	0.2	0.2	0.3	41.3	58.7
King William	5,230	1,822	2,591	758	59	769	R	34.8	49.5	14.5	1.1	99	36	47	0.2	0.2	0.2	0.2	41.3	58.7
Lancaster	5,528	1,812	2,841	739	136	1,029	R	32.8	51.4	13.4	2.5	114	19	69	0.2	0.2	0.2	0.2	38.9	61.1
Lee	9,796	5,215	3,504	1,002	75	1,711	D	53.2	35.8	10.2	0.8	16	118	114	0.4	0.5	0.3	0.3	59.8	40.2
Loudoun	41,574	14,462	19,290	7,391	431	4,828	R	34.8	46.4	17.8	1.0	100	70	6	1.6	1.4	1.7	2.1	42.8	57.2
Louisa	8,307	3,399	3,461	1,381	66	62	R	40.9	41.7	16.6	0.8	58	97	20	0.3	0.3	0.3	0.4	49.5	50.5
Lunenburg	4,912	2,082	2,227	505	98	145	R	42.4	45.3	10.3	2.0	46	77	113	0.2	0.2	0.2	0.1	48.3	51.7
Madison	4,779	1,700	2,341	653	85	641	R	35.6	49.0	13.7	1.8	92	41	59	0.2	0.2	0.2	0.2	42.1	57.9
Mathews	4,525	1,402	2,179	884	60	777	R	31.0	48.2	19.5	1.3	-124	59	3	0.2	0.1	0.2	0.3	39.2	60.8
Mecklenburg	10,970	4,273	5,401	1,128	168	1,128	R	39.0	49.2	10.3	1.5	67	39	112	0.4	0.4	0.5	0.3	44.2	55.8
Middlesex	4,685	1,597	2,224	768	96	627	R	34.1	47.5	16.4	2.0	106	62	23	0.2	0.2	0.2	0.2	41.8	58.2
Montgomery	24,935	10,658	10,606	3,449	222	52	D	42.7	42.5	13.8	0.9	44	94	55	1.0	1.0	0.9	1.0	50.1	49.9
Nelson	5,538	2,586	2,159	748	45	427	D	46.7	39.0	13.5	0.8	31	108	63	0.2	0.2	0.2	0.2	54.5	45.5
New Kent	5,483	1,738	2,708	1,017	20	970	R	31.7	49.4	18.5	0.4	120	37	4	0.2	0.2	0.2	0.3	39.1	60.9
Northampton	5,618	2,568	2,088	844	118	480	D	45.7	37.2	15.0	2.1	35	114	36	0.2	0.2	0.2	0.2	55.2	44.8
Northumberland	5,334	1,862	2,667	729	76	805	R	34.9	50.0	13.7	1.4	98	32	58	0.2	0.2	0.2	0.2	41.1	58.9
Nottoway	5,743	2,411	2,610	606	116	199	R	42.0	45.4	10.6	2.0	52	76	109	0.2	0.2	0.2	0.2	48.0	52.0
Orange	8,966	3,348	4,092	1,425	101	744	R	37.3	45.6	15.9	1.1	81	75	26	0.4	0.3	0.4	0.4	45.0	55.0
Page	8,460	3,010	4,203	1,163	84	1,193	R	35.6	49.7	13.7	1.0	91	35	57	0.3	0.3	0.4	0.3	41.7	58.3
Patrick	7,189	2,465	3,521	1,026	177	1,056	R	34.3	49.0	14.3	2.5	104	42	50	0.3	0.2	0.3	0.7	41.2	58.8
Pittsylvania	21,894	7,675	11,467	2,296	456	3,792	R	35.1	52.4	10.5	2.1	96	14	110	0.9	0.7	1.0	0.7	40.1	59.9
Powhatan	7,086	1,950	3,832	1,232	72	1,882	R	27.5	54.1	17.4	1.0	130	9	12	0.3	0.2	0.3	0.4	33.7	66.3

Table E. – Vote for President: November 3, 1992, General Election (cont)

County	Total	Clinton (DEM)	Bush (REP)	Perot (IND)	Other	Plurality Total	Party	DEM	REP	IND	Other	Rank DEM	Rank REP	Rank IND	Total	DEM	REP	IND	DEM	REP
Prince Edward	6,383	2,775	2,858	635	115	83	R	43.5	44.8	9.9	1.8	42	80	118	0.2	0.3	0.2	0.2	49.3	50.7
Prince George	9,412	3,087	4,799	1,459	67	1,712	R	32.8	51.0	15.5	0.7	113	23	31	0.4	0.3	0.4	0.4	39.1	60.9
Prince William	75,680	26,486	35,432	13,190	572	8,946	R	35.0	46.8	17.4	0.8	97	66	11	3.0	2.6	3.1	3.8	42.8	57.2
Pulaski	13,987	5,633	6,148	2,066	140	515	R	40.3	44.0	14.8	1.0	61	85	44	0.5	0.5	0.5	0.6	47.8	52.2
Rappahannock	3,181	1,273	1,410	487	11	137	R	40.0	44.3	15.3	0.3	63	83	32	0.1	0.1	0.1	0.1	47.4	52.6
Richmond	3,050	1,034	1,609	366	41	575	R	33.9	52.8	12.0	1.3	108	12	92	0.1	<.1	0.1	0.1	39.1	60.9
Roanoke	41,080	14,704	20,667	5,477	232	5,963	R	35.8	50.3	13.3	0.6	88	28	70	1.6	1.4	1.8	1.6	41.6	58.4
Rockbridge	7,503	2,908	3,228	1,254	113	320	R	38.8	43.0	16.7	1.5	68	90	18	0.3	0.3	0.3	0.4	47.4	52.6
Rockingham	21,493	5,407	13,016	2,839	231	7,609	R	25.2	60.6	13.2	1.1	132	3	74	0.8	0.5	1.1	0.8	29.3	70.7
Russell	11,484	6,480	3,891	958	155	2,589	D	56.4	33.9	8.3	1.3	9	122	129	0.4	0.6	0.3	0.3	62.5	37.5
Scott	9,690	3,979	4,515	957	239	536	R	41.1	46.6	9.9	2.5	56	68	119	0.4	0.4	0.4	0.3	46.8	53.2
Shenandoah	13,834	3,956	7,746	2,063	69	3,790	R	28.6	56.0	14.9	0.5	128	6	39	0.5	0.4	0.7	0.6	33.8	66.2
Smyth	12,931	4,924	6,128	1,618	261	1,204	R	38.1	47.4	12.5	2.0	74	63	83	0.5	0.5	0.5	0.5	44.6	55.4
Southampton	6,874	3,199	2,844	754	77	355	D	46.5	41.4	11.0	1.1	32	98	105	0.3	0.3	0.2	0.2	52.9	47.1
Spotsylvania	24,014	8,133	11,829	3,918	134	3,696	R	33.9	49.3	16.3	0.6	109	38	25	0.9	0.8	1.0	1.1	40.7	59.3
Stafford	24,871	7,718	12,528	4,481	144	4,810	R	31.0	50.4	18.0	0.6	123	26	5	1.0	0.7	1.1	1.3	38.1	61.9
Surry	3,275	1,823	1,046	364	42	777	D	55.7	31.9	11.1	1.3	12	127	100	0.1	0.2	<.1	0.1	63.5	36.5
Sussex	4,253	2,193	1,527	446	87	666	D	51.6	35.9	10.5	2.0	19	117	111	0.2	0.2	0.1	0.1	59.0	41.0
Tazewell	17,056	8,586	6,375	1,872	223	2,211	D	50.3	37.4	11.0	1.3	23	113	104	0.7	0.8	0.6	0.5	57.4	42.6
Warren	9,676	3,554	4,319	1,650	153	765	R	36.7	44.6	17.1	1.6	82	82	17	0.4	0.3	0.4	0.5	45.1	54.9
Washington	18,995	7,269	9,150	2,288	288	1,881	R	38.3	48.2	12.0	1.5	71	58	91	0.7	0.7	0.8	0.7	44.3	55.7
Westmoreland	6,223	2,758	2,554	818	93	204	D	44.3	41.0	13.1	1.5	39	101	76	0.2	0.3	0.2	0.2	51.9	48.1
Wise	14,857	7,681	5,144	1,835	197	2,537	D	51.7	34.6	12.4	1.3	18	121	87	0.6	0.7	0.4	0.5	59.9	40.1
Wythe	10,492	3,616	5,121	1,557	198	1,505	R	34.5	48.8	14.8	1.9	103	45	43	0.4	0.3	0.4	0.4	41.4	58.6
York	19,966	6,218	10,197	3,426	125	3,979	R	31.1	51.1	17.2	0.6	122	22	15	0.8	0.6	0.9	1.0	37.9	62.1
Alexandria City	52,675	30,784	16,700	4,934	257	14,084	D	58.4	31.7	9.4	0.5	6	129	123	2.1	3.0	1.5	1.4	64.8	35.2
Bedford City	2,409	963	1,091	313	42	128	R	40.0	45.3	13.0	1.7	64	78	77	<.1	<.1	<.1	<.1	46.9	53.1
Bristol City	7,462	2,948	3,616	851	47	668	R	39.5	48.5	11.4	0.6	65	50	98	0.3	0.3	0.3	0.2	44.9	55.1
Buena Vista City	2,200	1,023	849	291	37	174	D	46.5	38.6	13.2	1.7	33	109	73	<.1	<.1	<.1	<.1	54.6	45.4
Charlottesville City	14,899	8,685	4,705	1,397	112	3,980	D	58.3	31.6	9.4	0.8	7	131	122	0.6	0.8	0.4	0.4	64.9	35.1
Chesapeake City	61,868	23,495	28,909	9,237	227	5,414	R	38.0	46.7	14.9	0.4	75	67	38	2.4	2.3	2.5	2.6	44.8	55.2
Clifton Forge City	1,873	958	632	251	32	326	D	51.1	33.7	13.4	1.7	20	123	68	<.1	<.1	<.1	<.1	60.3	39.7
Colonial Heights City	8,400	1,721	5,298	1,312	69	3,577	R	20.5	63.1	15.6	0.8	135	1	29	0.3	0.2	0.5	0.4	24.5	75.5
Covington City	2,869	1,442	995	402	30	447	D	50.3	34.7	14.0	1.0	24	120	53	0.1	0.1	<.1	0.1	59.2	40.8
Danville City	19,661	8,134	9,584	1,679	264	1,450	R	41.4	48.7	8.5	1.3	55	46	133	0.8	0.8	0.8	0.5	45.9	54.1
Emporia City	2,319	1,048	1,094	157	20	46	R	45.2	47.2	6.8	0.9	38	64	135	<.1	0.1	<.1	<.1	48.9	51.1
Fairfax City	9,693	3,884	4,333	1,439	37	449	R	40.1	44.7	14.8	0.4	62	81	42	0.4	0.4	0.4	0.4	47.3	52.7
Falls Church City	5,404	2,864	1,912	599	29	952	D	53.0	35.4	11.1	0.5	17	119	101	0.2	0.3	0.2	0.2	60.0	40.0
Franklin City	3,339	1,696	1,347	272	24	349	D	50.8	40.3	8.1	0.7	21	105	131	0.1	0.2	0.1	<.1	55.7	44.3
Fredericksburg City	6,879	3,266	2,819	738	56	447	D	47.5	41.0	10.7	0.8	28	102	106	0.3	0.3	0.2	0.2	53.7	46.3
Galax City	2,344	957	1,087	276	24	130	R	40.8	46.4	11.8	1.0	59	71	94	<.1	<.1	<.1	<.1	46.8	53.2
Hampton City	49,878	23,395	19,219	6,581	683	4,176	D	46.9	38.5	13.2	1.4	29	110	75	1.9	2.3	1.7	1.9	54.9	45.1
Harrisonburg City	9,632	3,414	4,935	1,162	121	1,521	R	35.4	51.2	12.1	1.3	93	21	90	0.4	0.3	0.4	0.3	40.9	59.1
Hopewell City	8,042	2,863	3,818	1,227	134	955	R	35.6	47.5	15.3	1.7	90	61	33	0.3	0.3	0.3	0.4	42.9	57.1
Lexington City	2,277	1,128	894	228	27	234	D	49.5	39.3	10.0	1.2	26	107	117	<.1	0.1	<.1	<.1	55.8	44.2
Lynchburg City	24,969	9,587	12,518	2,545	319	2,931	R	38.4	50.1	10.2	1.3	70	30	115	1.0	0.9	1.1	0.7	43.4	56.6
Manassas City	11,154	3,647	5,453	1,971	83	1,806	R	32.7	48.9	17.7	0.7	116	43	7	0.4	0.4	0.5	0.6	40.1	59.9
Manassas Park City	1,720	567	792	356	5	225	R	33.0	46.0	20.7	0.3	111	74	1	<.1	<.1	<.1	0.1	41.7	58.3
Martinsville City	6,617	3,073	2,690	748	106	383	D	46.4	40.7	11.3	1.6	34	103	99	0.3	0.3	0.2	0.2	53.3	46.7
Newport News City	61,091	25,743	26,779	8,217	352	1,036	R	42.1	43.8	13.5	0.6	50	87	65	2.4	2.5	2.3	2.4	49.0	51.0
Norfolk City	69,027	37,602	22,362	8,732	331	15,240	D	54.5	32.4	12.7	0.5	14	126	80	2.7	3.6	1.9	2.5	62.7	37.3
Norton City	1,548	871	472	182	23	399	D	56.3	30.5	11.8	1.5	10	133	95	<.1	<.1	<.1	<.1	64.9	35.1
Petersburg City	12,717	8,671	3,125	834	87	5,546	D	68.2	24.6	6.6	0.7	1	135	136	0.5	0.8	0.3	0.2	73.5	26.5
Poquoson City	5,437	1,086	3,354	960	37	2,268	R	20.0	61.7	17.7	0.7	136	2	8	0.2	0.1	0.3	0.3	24.5	75.5
Portsmouth City	37,599	20,416	12,575	4,360	248	7,841	D	54.3	33.4	11.6	0.7	15	125	97	1.5	2.0	1.1	1.3	61.9	38.1
Radford City	4,785	2,183	1,996	582	24	187	D	45.6	41.7	12.2	0.5	36	96	88	0.2	0.2	0.2	0.2	52.2	47.8
Richmond City	79,735	47,642	24,341	6,992	760	23,301	D	59.8	30.5	8.8	1.0	4	132	127	3.1	4.6	2.1	2.0	66.2	33.8
Roanoke City	35,181	17,724	13,443	3,753	261	4,281	D	50.4	38.2	10.7	0.7	22	111	107	1.4	1.7	1.2	1.1	56.9	43.1
Salem City	10,669	4,028	5,143	1,430	68	1,115	R	37.8	48.2	13.4	0.6	77	56	67	0.4	0.4	0.4	0.4	43.9	56.1
South Boston City	2,757	1,051	1,435	252	19	384	R	38.1	52.0	9.1	0.7	72	17	124	0.1	0.1	0.1	<.1	42.3	57.7
Staunton City	9,232	2,851	4,989	1,146	246	2,138	R	30.9	54.0	12.4	2.7	125	10	85	0.4	0.3	0.4	0.3	36.4	63.6
Suffolk City	20,223	9,196	8,697	2,150	180	499	D	45.5	43.0	10.6	0.9	37	91	108	0.8	0.9	0.8	0.6	51.4	48.6
Virginia Beach City	137,785	44,294	68,936	24,087	468	24,642	R	32.1	50.0	17.5	0.3	118	31	10	5.4	4.3	6.0	6.9	39.1	60.9
Waynesboro City	7,149	2,302	3,758	961	128	1,456	R	32.2	52.6	13.4	1.8	117	13	66	0.3	0.2	0.3	0.3	38.0	62.0
Williamsburg City	3,719	1,856	1,349	445	69	507	D	49.9	36.3	12.0	1.9	25	116	93	0.1	0.2	0.1	0.1	57.9	42.1
Winchester City	7,701	2,768	3,833	1,048	52	1,065	R	35.9	49.8	13.6	0.7	86	34	60	0.3	0.3	0.3	0.3	41.9	58.1
VIRGINIA	**2,558,665**	**1,038,650**	**1,150,517**	**348,639**	**20,859**	**111,867**	**R**	**40.6**	**45.0**	**13.6**	**0.8**				**100.0**	**100.0**	**100.0**	**100.0**	**47.4**	**52.6**

Congressional district and county	Total	Democrat (DEM)	Republican (REP)	Other	Plurality Total	Plurality Party	Percent of total vote DEM	Percent of total vote REP	Percent of total vote Other	Rank within district DEM	Rank within district REP	Rank within district Other	Percent contribution to district vote Total	Percent contribution to district vote DEM	Percent contribution to district vote REP	Percent contribution to district vote Other
District 1	232,051	89,814	133,537	8,700	43,723	R	38.7	57.5	3.7				100.0	100.0	100.0	100.0
Accomack	12,698	5,694	6,613	391	919	R	44.8	52.1	3.1	6	13	13	5.5	6.3	5.0	4.5
Caroline	7,320	3,730	3,372	218	358	D	51.0	46.1	3.0	2	19	14	3.2	4.2	2.5	2.5
Gloucester	12,530	5,101	7,038	391	1,937	R	40.7	56.2	3.1	9	12	12	5.4	5.7	5.3	4.5
Hanover (pt)	17,608	5,685	11,316	607	5,631	R	32.3	64.3	3.4	18	3	7	7.6	6.3	8.5	7.0
James City (pt)	13,376	4,977	7,981	418	3,004	R	37.2	59.7	3.1	14	6	11	5.8	5.5	6.0	4.8
King George	5,145	2,039	2,932	174	893	R	39.6	57.0	3.4	12	9	8	2.2	2.3	2.2	2.0
Lancaster	5,119	1,889	3,049	181	1,160	R	36.9	59.6	3.5	15	7	6	2.2	2.1	2.3	2.1
Mathews	4,344	1,761	2,460	123	699	R	40.5	56.6	2.8	10	10	18	1.9	2.0	1.8	1.4
Middlesex	4,409	1,761	2,480	168	719	R	39.9	56.2	3.8	11	11	5	1.9	2.0	1.9	1.9
Northampton	5,446	2,790	2,418	238	372	D	51.2	44.4	4.4	1	20	4	2.3	3.1	1.8	2.7
Northumberland	5,067	1,953	2,945	169	992	R	38.5	58.1	3.3	13	8	9	2.2	2.2	2.2	1.9
Spotsylvania (pt)	13,966	6,215	7,030	721	815	R	44.5	50.3	5.2	7	15	2	6.0	6.9	5.3	8.3
Stafford	23,553	9,667	11,820	2,066	2,153	R	41.0	50.2	8.8	8	16	1	10.1	10.8	8.9	23.7
Westmoreland	5,501	2,575	2,747	179	172	R	46.8	49.9	3.3	4	17	10	2.4	2.9	2.1	2.1
York	19,474	6,836	12,077	561	5,241	R	35.1	62.0	2.9	17	4	17	8.4	7.6	9.0	6.4
Fredericksburg City	6,416	3,084	3,017	315	67	D	48.1	47.0	4.9	3	18	3	2.8	3.4	2.3	3.6
Hampton City (pt)	26,246	9,679	15,802	765	6,123	R	36.9	60.2	2.9	16	5	16	11.3	10.8	11.8	8.8
Newport News City (pt)	35,065	11,240	23,048	777	11,808	R	32.1	65.7	2.2	19	2	20	15.1	12.5	17.3	8.9
Poquoson City	5,352	1,582	3,633	137	2,051	R	29.6	67.9	2.6	20	1	19	2.3	1.8	2.7	1.6
Williamsburg City	3,416	1,556	1,759	101	203	R	45.6	51.5	3.0	5	14	15	1.5	1.7	1.3	1.2
District 2	177,133	99,253	77,797	83	21,456	D	56.0	43.9	<.1				100.0	100.0	100.0	100.0
Norfolk City (pt)	44,922	27,982	16,915	25	11,067	D	62.3	37.7	<.1	1	2	1	25.4	28.2	21.7	30.1
Virginia Beach City (pt)	132,211	71,271	60,882	58	10,389	D	53.9	46.0	<.1	2	1	2	74.6	71.8	78.3	69.9
District 3	168,473	132,432	35,780	261	96,652	D	78.6	21.2	0.2				100.0	100.0	100.0	100.0
Charles City	2,706	2,186	520	0	1,666	D	80.8	19.2	0.0	7	12	11	1.6	1.7	1.5	0.0
Essex	3,223	2,125	1,091	7	1,034	D	65.9	33.9	0.2	12	6	2	1.9	1.6	3.0	2.7
Henrico (pt)	18,967	13,578	5,358	31	8,220	D	71.6	28.2	0.2	10	9	4	11.3	10.3	15.0	11.9
James City (pt)	3,370	1,637	1,733	0	96	R	48.6	51.4	0.0	18	1	12	2.0	1.2	4.8	0.0
King and Queen	2,506	1,752	754	0	998	D	69.9	30.1	0.0	11	8	13	1.5	1.3	2.1	0.0
King William	4,524	2,558	1,965	1	593	D	56.5	43.4	<.1	17	2	6	2.7	1.9	5.5	0.4
New Kent	5,058	2,924	2,123	11	801	D	57.8	42.0	0.2	16	4	3	3.0	2.2	5.9	4.2
Prince George (pt)	799	462	337	0	125	D	57.8	42.2	0.0	15	3	14	0.5	0.3	0.9	0.0
Richmond	2,213	1,314	711	188	603	D	59.4	32.1	8.5	13	7	1	1.3	1.0	2.0	72.0
Surry	2,881	2,216	665	0	1,551	D	76.9	23.1	0.0	9	10	15	1.7	1.7	1.9	0.0
Hampton City (pt)	19,887	16,074	3,812	1	12,262	D	80.8	19.2	<.1	6	13	10	11.8	12.1	10.7	0.4
Hopewell City (pt)	690	612	78	0	534	D	88.7	11.3	0.0	2	17	16	0.4	0.5	0.2	0.0
Newport News City (pt)	23,678	18,397	5,279	2	13,118	D	77.7	22.3	<.1	8	11	8	14.1	13.9	14.8	0.8
Norfolk City (pt)	21,677	19,075	2,590	12	16,485	D	88.0	11.9	<.1	3	16	5	12.9	14.4	7.2	4.6
Petersburg City (pt)	5,690	4,804	886	0	3,918	D	84.4	15.6	0.0	4	15	17	3.4	3.6	2.5	0.0
Portsmouth City (pt)	12,184	11,108	1,075	1	10,033	D	91.2	8.8	<.1	1	18	9	7.2	8.4	3.0	0.4
Richmond City (pt)	37,675	31,170	6,498	7	24,672	D	82.7	17.2	<.1	5	14	7	22.4	23.5	18.2	2.7
Suffolk City (pt)	745	440	305	0	135	D	59.1	40.9	0.0	14	5	18	0.4	0.3	0.9	0.0
District 4	215,960	147,649	68,286	25	79,363	D	68.4	31.6	<.1				100.0	100.0	100.0	100.0
Amelia	3,909	2,372	1,537	0	835	D	60.7	39.3	0.0	19	4	8	1.8	1.6	2.3	0.0
Brunswick	6,009	4,874	1,135	0	3,739	D	81.1	18.9	0.0	6	17	9	2.8	3.3	1.7	0.0
Chesterfield (pt)	11,144	7,864	3,279	1	4,585	D	70.6	29.4	<.1	13	10	6	5.2	5.3	4.8	4.0
Dinwiddie	8,043	6,110	1,933	0	4,177	D	76.0	24.0	0.0	9	14	10	3.7	4.1	2.8	0.0
Goochland	6,868	4,400	2,468	0	1,932	D	64.1	35.9	0.0	15	8	11	3.2	3.0	3.6	0.0
Greensville	3,693	3,214	479	0	2,735	D	87.0	13.0	0.0	1	22	12	1.7	2.2	0.7	0.0
Isle of Wight	10,631	7,864	2,767	0	5,097	D	74.0	26.0	0.0	12	11	13	4.9	5.3	4.1	0.0
Louisa	7,186	5,354	1,830	2	3,524	D	74.5	25.5	<.1	11	12	3	3.3	3.6	2.7	8.0
Nottoway	4,793	3,756	1,037	0	2,719	D	78.4	21.6	0.0	7	16	14	2.2	2.5	1.5	0.0
Powhatan	6,466	3,964	2,502	0	1,462	D	61.3	38.7	0.0	17	6	15	3.0	2.7	3.7	0.0
Prince George (pt)	7,987	4,956	3,029	2	1,927	D	62.1	37.9	<.1	16	7	4	3.7	3.4	4.4	8.0
Southampton	6,204	5,242	962	0	4,280	D	84.5	15.5	0.0	2	21	16	2.9	3.6	1.4	0.0
Sussex	3,482	2,860	622	0	2,238	D	82.1	17.9	0.0	5	18	17	1.6	1.9	0.9	0.0
Chesapeake City	60,102	36,727	23,364	11	13,363	D	61.1	38.9	<.1	18	5	5	27.8	24.9	34.2	44.0
Colonial Heights City	8,088	4,518	3,570	0	948	D	55.9	44.1	0.0	20	3	18	3.7	3.1	5.2	0.0
Emporia City	2,158	1,773	385	0	1,388	D	82.2	17.8	0.0	4	19	19	1.0	1.2	0.6	0.0
Franklin City	3,039	2,501	538	0	1,963	D	82.3	17.7	0.0	3	20	20	1.4	1.7	0.8	0.0
Hopewell City (pt)	6,669	3,462	3,205	2	257	D	51.9	48.1	<.1	22	1	2	3.1	2.3	4.7	8.0
Petersburg City (pt)	5,134	3,847	1,287	0	2,560	D	74.9	25.1	0.0	10	13	21	2.4	2.6	1.9	0.0
Portsmouth City (pt)	22,864	17,599	5,264	1	12,335	D	77.0	23.0	<.1	8	15	7	10.6	11.9	7.7	4.0
Suffolk City (pt)	18,215	12,626	5,589	0	7,037	D	69.3	30.7	0.0	14	9	22	8.4	8.6	8.2	0.0
Virginia Beach City (pt)	3,276	1,766	1,504	6	262	D	53.9	45.9	0.2	21	2	1	1.5	1.2	2.2	24.0
District 5	193,084	133,031	60,030	23	73,001	D	68.9	31.1	<.1				100.0	100.0	100.0	100.0
Albemarle (pt)	11,045	7,614	3,427	4	4,187	D	68.9	31.0	<.1	13	10	2	5.7	5.7	5.7	17.4
Appomattox	4,690	3,522	1,168	0	2,354	D	75.1	24.9	0.0	5	18	10	2.4	2.6	1.9	0.0
Bedford (pt)	13,374	8,152	5,221	1	2,931	D	61.0	39.0	<.1	21	2	7	6.9	6.1	8.7	4.3
Buckingham	4,496	3,520	976	0	2,544	D	78.3	21.7	0.0	2	21	11	2.3	2.6	1.6	0.0
Campbell	16,715	11,094	5,619	2	5,475	D	66.4	33.6	<.1	18	5	6	8.7	8.3	9.4	8.7

Table H. – Vote for U.S. Representative in Congress: November 3, 1992, General Election (cont)

Congressional district and county	Total	Democrat (DEM)	Republican (REP)	Other	Plurality Total	Party	DEM	REP	Other	Rank within district DEM	REP	Other	Percent contribution Total	DEM	REP	Other
District 5 (cont)																
Charlotte	4,309	3,147	1,162	0	1,985	D	73.0	27.0	0.0	8	15	12	2.2	2.4	1.9	0.0
Cumberland	2,622	1,799	823	0	976	D	68.6	31.4	0.0	14	9	13	1.4	1.4	1.4	0.0
Fluvanna	5,212	3,738	1,474	0	2,264	D	71.7	28.3	0.0	9	14	14	2.7	2.8	2.5	0.0
Franklin	14,148	10,613	3,534	1	7,079	D	75.0	25.0	<.1	6	17	8	7.3	8.0	5.9	4.3
Halifax	9,311	6,451	2,857	3	3,594	D	69.3	30.7	<.1	12	11	3	4.8	4.8	4.8	13.0
Henry	18,709	12,820	5,889	0	6,931	D	68.5	31.5	0.0	15	8	15	9.7	9.6	9.8	0.0
Lunenburg	3,826	2,966	860	0	2,106	D	77.5	22.5	0.0	3	20	16	2.0	2.2	1.4	0.0
Mecklenburg	8,790	6,250	2,540	0	3,710	D	71.1	28.9	0.0	10	13	17	4.6	4.7	4.2	0.0
Nelson	5,275	4,280	995	0	3,285	D	81.1	18.9	0.0	1	22	18	2.7	3.2	1.7	0.0
Patrick	5,470	3,743	1,727	0	2,016	D	68.4	31.6	0.0	16	7	19	2.8	2.8	2.9	0.0
Pittsylvania	18,630	11,324	7,306	0	4,018	D	60.8	39.2	0.0	22	1	20	9.6	8.5	12.2	0.0
Prince Edward	5,325	3,900	1,424	1	2,476	D	73.2	26.7	<.1	7	16	4	2.8	2.9	2.4	4.3
Bedford City	2,047	1,355	692	0	663	D	66.2	33.8	0.0	19	4	21	1.1	1.0	1.2	0.0
Charlottesville City	13,329	10,168	3,152	9	7,016	D	76.3	23.6	<.1	4	19	1	6.9	7.6	5.3	39.1
Danville City	17,530	10,899	6,630	1	4,269	D	62.2	37.8	<.1	20	3	9	9.1	8.2	11.0	4.3
Martinsville City	5,823	4,058	1,764	1	2,294	D	69.7	30.3	<.1	11	12	5	3.0	3.1	2.9	4.3
South Boston City	2,408	1,618	790	0	828	D	67.2	32.8	0.0	17	6	22	1.2	1.2	1.3	0.0
District 6	212,087	84,618	127,309	160	42,691	R	39.9	60.0	<.1				100.0	100.0	100.0	100.0
Alleghany	5,321	2,670	2,651	0	19	D	50.2	49.8	0.0	6	15	14	2.5	3.2	2.1	0.0
Amherst	10,067	4,269	5,797	1	1,528	R	42.4	57.6	<.1	10	11	13	4.7	5.0	4.6	0.6
Augusta	20,047	5,246	14,795	6	9,549	R	26.2	73.8	<.1	19	2	10	9.5	6.2	11.6	3.8
Bath	2,158	944	1,213	1	269	R	43.7	56.2	<.1	7	14	8	1.0	1.1	1.0	0.6
Bedford (pt)	4,654	2,020	2,634	0	614	R	43.4	56.6	0.0	8	12	15	2.2	2.4	2.1	0.0
Botetourt	11,507	4,671	6,822	14	2,151	R	40.6	59.3	0.1	13	8	4	5.4	5.5	5.4	8.8
Highland	1,367	563	804	0	241	R	41.2	58.8	0.0	11	10	16	0.6	0.7	0.6	0.0
Roanoke (pt)	33,879	13,661	20,165	53	6,504	R	40.3	59.5	0.2	15	6	2	16.0	16.1	15.8	33.1
Rockbridge	6,954	3,014	3,929	11	915	R	43.3	56.5	0.2	9	13	1	3.3	3.6	3.1	6.9
Rockingham (pt)	17,656	4,488	13,165	3	8,677	R	25.4	74.6	<.1	20	1	11	8.3	5.3	10.3	1.9
Buena Vista City	2,024	1,119	905	0	214	D	55.3	44.7	0.0	2	19	17	1.0	1.3	0.7	0.0
Clifton Forge City	1,688	980	708	0	272	D	58.1	41.9	0.0	1	20	18	0.8	1.2	0.6	0.0
Covington City	2,683	1,425	1,258	0	167	D	53.1	46.9	0.0	3	18	19	1.3	1.7	1.0	0.0
Harrisonburg City	8,724	2,979	5,740	5	2,761	R	34.1	65.8	<.1	16	5	6	4.1	3.5	4.5	3.1
Lexington City	2,089	1,079	1,009	1	70	D	51.7	48.3	<.1	5	16	7	1.0	1.3	0.8	0.6
Lynchburg City	22,779	9,228	13,544	7	4,316	R	40.5	59.5	<.1	14	7	9	10.7	10.9	10.6	4.4
Roanoke City	33,559	17,366	16,144	49	1,222	D	51.7	48.1	0.1	4	17	3	15.8	20.5	12.7	30.6
Salem City	10,195	4,184	6,003	8	1,819	R	41.0	58.9	<.1	12	9	5	4.8	4.9	4.7	5.0
Staunton City	8,281	2,558	5,723	0	3,165	R	30.9	69.1	0.0	18	3	20	3.9	3.0	4.5	0.0
Waynesboro City	6,455	2,154	4,300	1	2,146	R	33.4	66.6	<.1	17	4	12	3.0	2.5	3.4	0.6
District 7	255,375	-	211,618	43,757	167,861	R	-	82.9	17.1				100.0	-	100.0	100.0
Albemarle (pt)	15,690	-	12,812	2,878	9,934	R	-	81.7	18.3	-	8	3	6.1	-	6.1	6.6
Chesterfield (pt)	86,845	-	72,076	14,769	57,307	R	-	83.0	17.0	-	7	4	34.0	-	34.1	33.8
Culpeper	6,417	-	5,403	1,014	4,389	R	-	84.2	15.8	-	5	6	2.5	-	2.6	2.3
Greene	2,868	-	2,451	417	2,034	R	-	85.5	14.5	-	1	10	1.1	-	1.2	1.0
Hanover	13,874	-	11,710	2,164	9,546	R	-	84.4	15.6	-	4	7	5.4	-	5.5	4.9
Henrico (pt)	83,405	-	70,054	13,351	56,703	R	-	84.0	16.0	-	6	5	32.7	-	33.1	30.5
Madison	3,133	-	2,677	456	2,221	R	-	85.4	14.6	-	2	9	1.2	-	1.3	1.0
Orange	5,509	-	4,687	822	3,865	R	-	85.1	14.9	-	3	8	2.2	-	2.2	1.9
Spotsylvania (pt)	7,801	-	6,046	1,755	4,291	R	-	77.5	22.5	-	10	1	3.1	-	2.9	4.0
Richmond City (pt)	29,833	-	23,702	6,131	17,571	R	-	79.4	20.6	-	9	2	11.7	-	11.2	14.0
District 8	247,126	138,542	102,717	5,867	35,825	D	56.1	41.6	2.4				100.0	100.0	100.0	100.0
Arlington	78,836	47,586	28,965	2,285	18,621	D	60.4	36.7	2.9	2	3	1	31.9	34.3	28.2	38.9
Fairfax (pt)	112,908	55,586	54,821	2,501	765	D	49.2	48.6	2.2	4	1	3	45.7	40.1	53.4	42.6
Alexandria City	50,193	32,500	16,750	943	15,750	D	64.8	33.4	1.9	1	4	4	20.3	23.5	16.3	16.1
Falls Church City	5,189	2,870	2,181	138	689	D	55.3	42.0	2.7	3	2	2	2.1	2.1	2.1	2.4
District 9	211,295	133,284	77,985	26	55,299	D	63.1	36.9	<.1				100.0	100.0	100.0	100.0
Bland	2,554	1,609	945	0	664	D	63.0	37.0	0.0	11	13	12	1.2	1.2	1.2	0.0
Buchanan	11,071	8,426	2,645	0	5,781	D	76.1	23.9	0.0	2	22	13	5.2	6.3	3.4	0.0
Carroll	10,273	5,157	5,116	0	41	D	50.2	49.8	0.0	23	1	14	4.9	3.9	6.6	0.0
Craig	2,262	1,659	603	0	1,056	D	73.3	26.7	0.0	4	20	15	1.1	1.2	0.8	0.0
Dickenson	7,933	5,790	2,142	1	3,648	D	73.0	27.0	<.1	5	19	8	3.8	4.3	2.7	3.8
Floyd	4,961	2,766	2,195	0	571	D	55.8	44.2	0.0	21	3	16	2.3	2.1	2.8	0.0
Giles	7,089	4,898	2,190	1	2,708	D	69.1	30.9	<.1	8	16	6	3.4	3.7	2.8	3.8
Grayson	6,566	3,859	2,707	0	1,152	D	58.8	41.2	0.0	16	8	17	3.1	2.9	3.5	0.0
Lee	9,405	7,009	2,396	0	4,613	D	74.5	25.5	0.0	3	21	18	4.5	5.3	3.1	0.0
Montgomery	24,000	14,029	9,967	4	4,062	D	58.5	41.5	<.1	18	7	5	11.4	10.5	12.8	15.4
Pulaski	13,344	8,482	4,862	0	3,620	D	63.6	36.4	0.0	10	14	19	6.3	6.4	6.2	0.0
Roanoke (pt)	5,763	3,431	2,329	3	1,102	D	59.5	40.4	<.1	14	10	2	2.7	2.6	3.0	11.5
Russell	10,985	7,852	3,133	0	4,719	D	71.5	28.5	0.0	7	17	20	5.2	5.9	4.0	0.0
Scott	9,213	5,423	3,788	2	1,635	D	58.9	41.1	<.1	15	9	3	4.4	4.1	4.9	7.7
Smyth	12,270	7,173	5,096	1	2,077	D	58.5	41.5	<.1	17	6	11	5.8	5.4	6.5	3.8
Tazewell	15,750	10,668	5,080	2	5,588	D	67.7	32.3	<.1	9	15	9	7.5	8.0	6.5	7.7
Washington	18,227	9,894	8,331	2	1,563	D	54.3	45.7	<.1	22	2	10	8.6	7.4	10.7	7.7

Table H. — Vote for U.S. Representative in Congress: November 3, 1992, General Election (cont)

Congressional district and county	Total	Democrat (DEM)	Republican (REP)	Other	Plurality Total	Party	DEM	REP	Other	Rank within district DEM	REP	Other	Total	DEM	REP	Other
District 9 (cont)																
Wise	14,282	10,248	4,032	2	6,216	D	71.8	28.2	<.1	6	18	7	6.8	7.7	5.2	7.7
Wythe	9,925	5,649	4,276	0	1,373	D	56.9	43.1	0.0	19	5	21	4.7	4.2	5.5	0.0
Bristol City	7,140	3,993	3,140	7	853	D	55.9	44.0	<.1	20	4	1	3.4	3.0	4.0	26.9
Galax City	2,226	1,391	835	0	556	D	62.5	37.5	0.0	12	12	22	1.1	1.0	1.1	0.0
Norton City	1,462	1,126	336	0	790	D	77.0	23.0	0.0	1	23	23	0.7	0.8	0.4	0.0
Radford City	4,594	2,752	1,841	1	911	D	59.9	40.1	<.1	13	11	4	2.2	2.1	2.4	3.8
District 10	227,191	75,775	144,471	6,945	68,696	R	33.4	63.6	3.1				100.0	100.0	100.0	100.0
Clarke	4,327	1,935	2,237	155	302	R	44.7	51.7	3.6	1	14	8	1.9	2.6	1.5	2.2
Fairfax (pt)	69,424	21,206	46,767	1,451	25,561	R	30.5	67.4	2.1	13	2	14	30.6	28.0	32.4	20.9
Fauquier	18,158	6,260	11,340	558	5,080	R	34.5	62.5	3.1	9	5	12	8.0	8.3	7.8	8.0
Frederick	16,119	5,777	9,681	661	3,904	R	35.8	60.1	4.1	6	8	5	7.1	7.6	6.7	9.5
Loudoun	37,436	11,728	24,823	885	13,095	R	31.3	66.3	2.4	12	3	13	16.5	15.5	17.2	12.7
Page	7,357	2,598	4,317	442	1,719	R	35.3	58.7	6.0	8	10	1	3.2	3.4	3.0	6.4
Prince William (pt)	30,034	9,991	18,929	1,114	8,938	R	33.3	63.0	3.7	10	4	7	13.2	13.2	13.1	16.0
Rappahannock	3,080	1,295	1,669	116	374	R	42.0	54.2	3.8	3	12	6	1.4	1.7	1.2	1.7
Rockingham (pt)	1,805	495	1,228	82	733	R	27.4	68.0	4.5	14	1	4	0.8	0.7	0.9	1.2
Shenandoah	12,801	4,257	7,921	623	3,664	R	33.3	61.9	4.9	11	6	2	5.6	5.6	5.5	9.0
Warren	8,496	3,668	4,556	272	888	R	43.2	53.6	3.2	2	13	9	3.7	4.8	3.2	3.9
Manassas City	9,611	3,407	5,908	296	2,501	R	35.4	61.5	3.1	7	7	11	4.2	4.5	4.1	4.3
Manassas Park City	1,476	542	866	68	324	R	36.7	58.7	4.6	5	11	3	0.6	0.7	0.6	1.0
Winchester City	7,067	2,616	4,229	222	1,613	R	37.0	59.8	3.1	4	9	10	3.1	3.5	2.9	3.2
District 11	228,272	114,172	103,119	10,981	11,053	D	50.0	45.2	4.8				100.0	100.0	100.0	100.0
Fairfax (pt)	179,868	90,773	80,381	8,714	10,392	D	50.5	44.7	4.8	1	3	2	78.8	79.5	77.9	79.4
Prince William (pt)	39,295	18,935	18,542	1,818	393	D	48.2	47.2	4.6	3	1	3	17.2	16.6	18.0	16.6
Fairfax City	9,109	4,464	4,196	449	268	D	49.0	46.1	4.9	2	2	1	4.0	3.9	4.1	4.1
VIRGINIA	2,368,047	1,148,570	1,142,649	76,828	5,921	D	48.5	48.3	3.2							

1992 Vote for President
Percent for Bush (R), by County

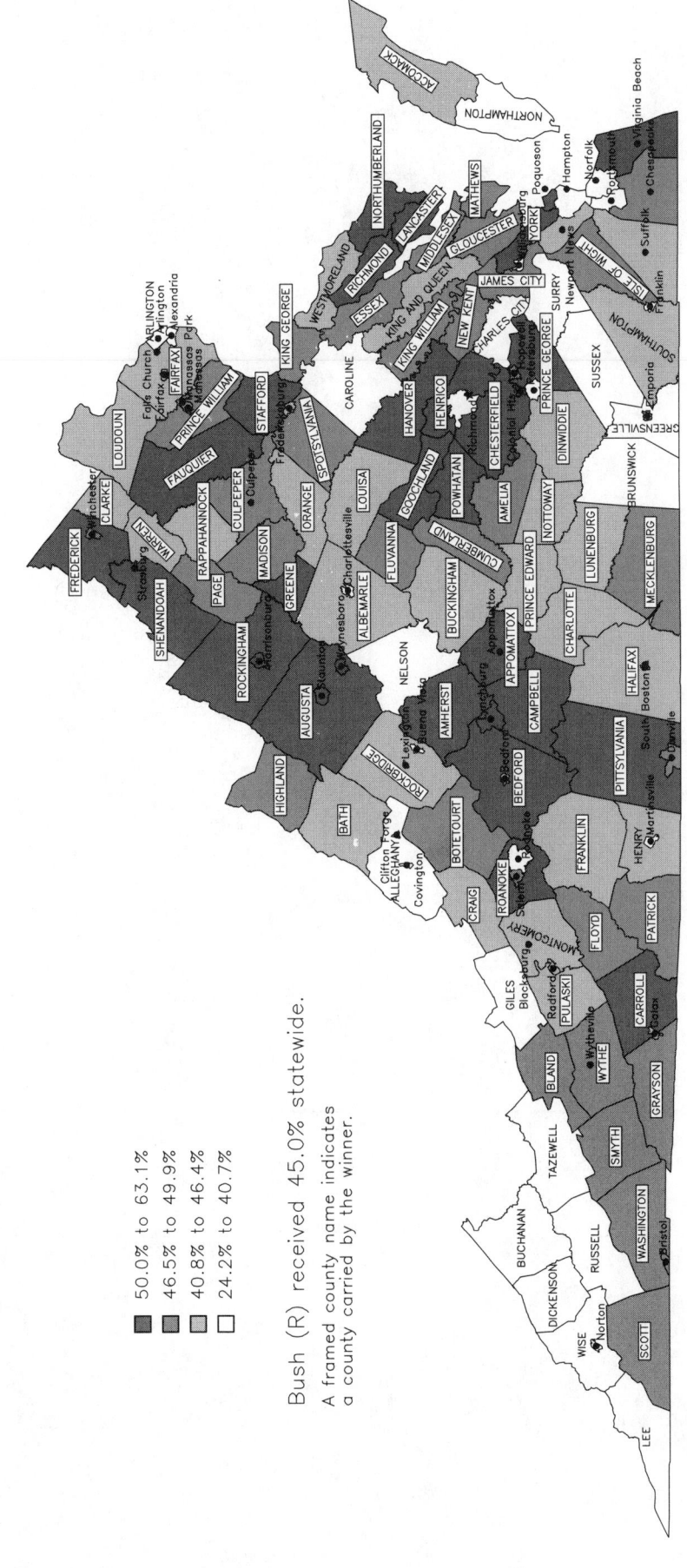

Bush (R) received 45.0% statewide.

A framed county name indicates a county carried by the winner.

Legend:
- 50.0% to 63.1%
- 46.5% to 49.9%
- 40.8% to 46.4%
- 24.2% to 40.7%

Virginia 957

WASHINGTON

Congressional Districts 9
    Average Population 540,744
State Senate Districts 49
    Average Population 99,320
State House Districts 98
    Average Population 49,660

Electoral College Votes..11
Counties 39
Voting Precincts 6,641

Alternative Registration Methods:
    .... Agency-based, Deputized Registrars, Motor-voter

Registration Deadline (Days before Election) 30

Voting Equipment Use (Counties)

Datavote Punch Card	1	Paper Ballot	8
Electronic	0	Other Punch Card	23
Lever Machine	3	Mixed Systems	0
Optical Scanner	4		

Party Control	DEM	REP	IND	VAC
1993 State Senate	28	21	0	0
1992 State Senate	24	25	0	0
1993 State House	65	33	0	0
1992 State House	58	40	0	0

Population Statistics 1990

Race/ Ethnicity	Total Population		Voting Age Population		Voting Age Population % of total population
	Number	%	Number	%	
Non-Hispanic					
White	4,221,622	86.7	3,186,190	88.4	75.5
Black	146,000	3.0	97,408	2.7	66.7
Asian/Pacific Islander	203,668	4.2	141,854	3.9	69.6
Native American	76,397	1.6	49,533	1.4	64.8
Other	4,435	<.1	1,923	<.1	43.4
All Hispanic	214,570	4.4	128,397	3.6	59.8
TOTAL	4,866,692	100.0	3,605,305	100.0	74.1

Estimated Voting Age Population 1992 (VAP) 3,818,000
Number of Registered Voters................................. 2,814,680
    % of estimated VAP 73.7
Voter Turnout (Maximum Vote)[1].......................... 2,324,974
    % of VAP 60.9
    % of Registration 82.6
Persons Not Voting—of Voting Age 1,493,026
    % of VAP 39.1
Persons Not Voting—of Registered 489,706
    % of Registration 17.4
Straight Ticket Voting .... No

State Officials and Members of Congress

Governor:
Mike Lowry (D) 1992, elected to a four-year term in 1992.

U.S. Senators:
Slade Gorton (R) 1988, elected to a six-year term in 1988.
Patty Murray (D) 1992, elected to a six-year term in 1992.

U.S. Representative in Congress:
(District, Name, Party, Date first elected)

1. Cantwell (D) 1992
2. Swift (D) 1978
3. Unsoeld (D) 1988
4. Inslee (D) 1992
5. Foley (D) 1964
6. Dicks (D) 1976
7. McDermott (D) 1988
8. Dunn (R) 1992
9. Kreidler (D) 1992

---

[1]Maximum vote turnout from Table C exceeds reported statewide actual voter turnout because in one or more counties the vote for highest office is greater than reported actual turnout.

Candidates: General Election, November 3, 1992

Candidate(s)	Total vote	Percent	Party	Status	First elected
President/Vice President					
Clinton/Gore	993,037	43.40%	Democrat	Challenger	1992
Bush/Quayle	731,234	31.96%	Republican	Incumbent	1988
Perot/Stockdale	541,780	23.68%	Independent	Challenger	
Marrou/Lord	7,533	0.33%	Libertarian	Challenger	
Gritz/Minett	4,854	0.21%	Populist	Challenger	
Hagelin/Tompkins	2,456	0.11%	Natural Law	Challenger	
Phillips/Knight	2,354	0.10%	Taxpayers	Challenger	
Fulani/Munoz	1,776	0.08%	New Alliance	Challenger	
Daniels/Tupahache	1,171	0.05%	Independent	Challenger	
LaRouche/Bevel	855	0.04%	Independent	Challenger	
Warren/DeBates	515	0.02%	Socialist Workers	Challenger	
Other	368	0.02%	Write in	Challenger	
Jack Kemp	168	<.01%	Write in	Challenger	
Paul Tsongas	129	<.01%	Write in	Challenger	
U.S. Senator					
Patty Murray	1,197,973	53.98%	Democrat	Challenger	1992
Rod Chandler	1,020,829	46.00%	Republican	Challenger	
Other	201	<.01%	Write in	Challenger	
William Goodloe	94	<.01%	Write in	Challenger	
Gary Gill	31	<.01%	Write in	Challenger	
Lee Thorness	24	<.01%	Write in	Challenger	
Brock Adams	10	<.01%	Write in	Challenger	
Governor					
Mike Lowry	1,184,315	52.15%	Democrat	Challenger	1992
Ken Eikenberry	1,086,216	47.83%	Republican	Challenger	
Other	142	<.01%	Write in	Challenger	
Sid Morrison	121	<.01%	Write in	Challenger	
Dan McDonald	32	<.01%	Write in	Challenger	
U.S. Representative in Congress					
District 1					
Maria Cantwell	148,844	54.87%	Democrat	Challenger	1992
Gary Nelson	113,897	41.99%	Republican	Challenger	
Patrick Ruckert	4,322	1.59%	Independent	Challenger	
Anne Fleming	4,211	1.55%	Natural Law	Challenger	
Other	4	<.01%	Write in	Challenger	
District 2					
Al Swift	133,207	52.05%	Democrat	Incumbent	1978
Jack Metcalf	107,365	41.95%	Republican	Challenger	
Robin Dexter	8,702	3.40%	Independent	Challenger	
Karen Leibrant	6,646	2.60%	Natural Law	Challenger	
Other	6	<.01%	Write in	Challenger	
District 3					
Jolene Unsoeld	138,043	55.97%	Democrat	Incumbent	1988
Pat Fiske	108,583	44.02%	Republican	Challenger	
Other	18	<.01%	Write in	Challenger	
District 4					
Jay Inslee	106,556	50.84%	Democrat	Challenger	1992
Richard Hastings	103,028	49.15%	Republican	Challenger	
Other	20	<.01%	Write in	Challenger	
District 5					
Thomas Foley	135,965	55.18%	Democrat	Incumbent	1964
John Sonneland	110,443	44.82%	Republican	Challenger	
Other	5	<.01%	Write in	Challenger	

Candidate(s)	Total vote	Percent	Party	Status	First elected
U.S. Representative in Congress (cont)					
District 6					
Norm Dicks	152,933	64.21%	Democrat	Incumbent	1976
Lauri Phillips	66,664	27.99%	Republican	Challenger	
Tom Donnelly	14,490	6.08%	Independent	Challenger	
Jim Horrigan	4,075	1.71%	Libertarian	Challenger	
Other	20	<.01%	Write in	Challenger	
District 7					
Jim McDermott	222,604	78.38%	Democrat	Incumbent	1988
Glenn Hampson	54,149	19.07%	Republican	Challenger	
Paul Glumaz	7,197	2.53%	Independent	Challenger	
Other	42	0.01%	Write in	Challenger	
District 8					
Jennifer Dunn	155,874	60.37%	Republican	Challenger	1992
George Tamblyn	87,611	33.93%	Democrat	Challenger	
Bob Adams	14,686	5.69%	Independent	Challenger	
Other	17	<.01%	Write in	Challenger	
District 9					
Mike Kreidler	110,902	52.08%	Democrat	Challenger	1992
Pete von Reichbauer	91,910	43.16%	Republican	Challenger	
Brian Wilson	6,585	3.09%	Independent	Challenger	
Timothy Brill	3,522	1.65%	Independent	Challenger	
Other	12	<.01%	Write in	Challenger	

Candidates: May 19, 1992, Primary Election

Candidate	Total vote	Percent	Candidate	Total vote	Percent
Presidential Preference, Democratic			**Presidential Preference, Republican**		
Bill Clinton	62,171	42.01%	George Bush	86,839	66.98%
Jerry Brown	34,111	23.05%	Ross Perot	25,423	19.61%
Ross Perot	28,311	19.13%	Patrick Buchanan	13,273	10.24%
Paul Tsongas	18,981	12.83%	Stephen Michael	2,619	2.02%
Tom Harkin	1,858	1.26%	David Duke	1,501	1.16%
Bob Kerrey	1,489	1.01%			
Lyndon LaRouche, Jr.	1,060	0.72%			

Voter Registration and Turnout, 1948-1992 Elections

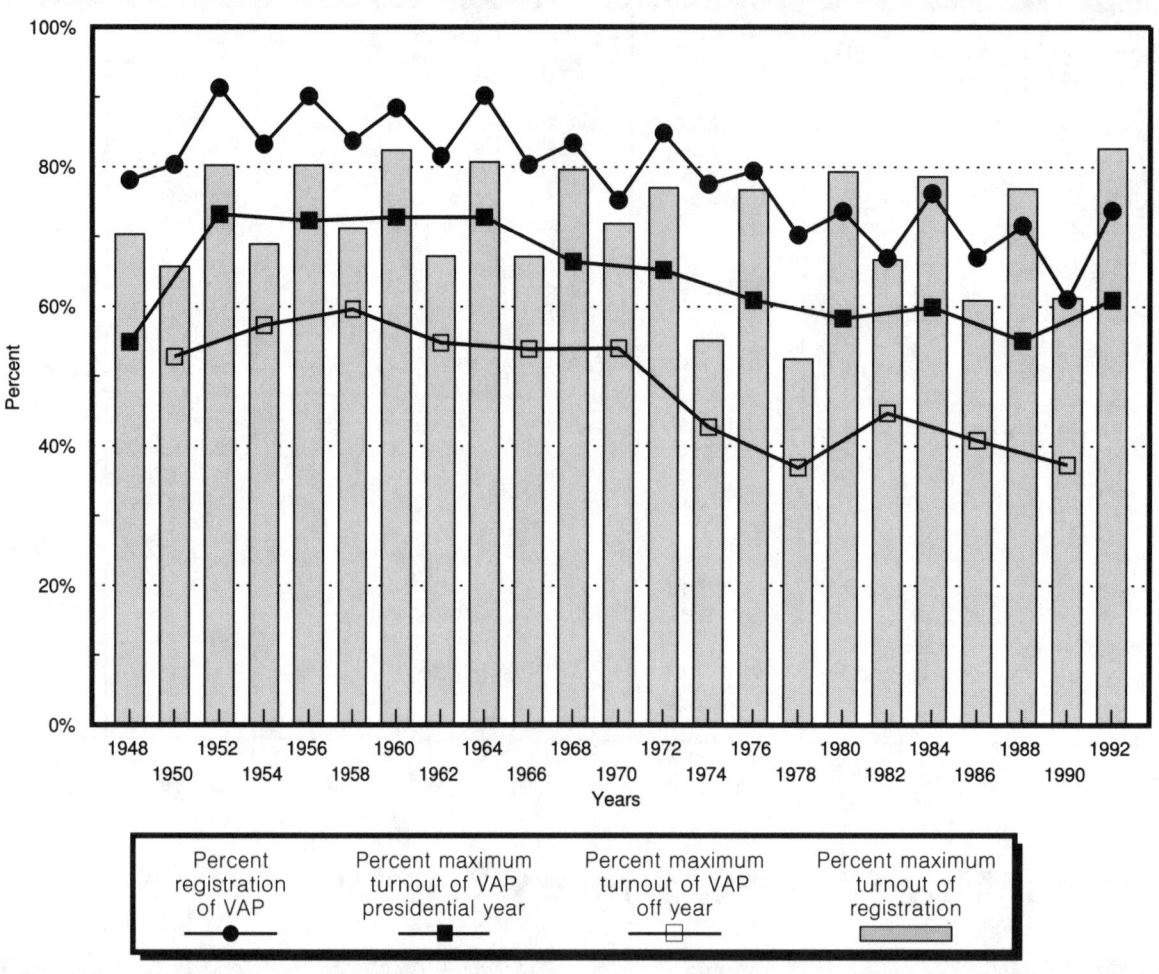

		Voter registration (REG)			Voter turnout											
							Highest office					Maximum vote				
Year	Estimated Voting Age Population (VAP)	Total	Percent of VAP	Rank by percent of VAP	Actual	Total	Office	Percent total REG	Rank by percent of REG	Percent of VAP	Rank by percent of VAP	Total	Percent total REG	Rank by percent of REG	Percent total VAP	Rank by percent of VAP
1992	3,818,000	2,814,680	73.7	28	2,324,907	2,288,230	P	81.3	13	59.9	23	2,324,907	82.6	12	60.9	24
1990	3,650,000	2,225,101	61.0	39	1,362,651	1,313,217	C	59.0	24	36.0	32	1,362,651	61.2	21	37.3	32
1988	3,491,000	2,499,309	71.6	26	1,923,043	1,865,253	P	74.6	16	53.4	22	1,923,043	76.9	16	55.1	19
1986	3,329,000	2,230,354	67.0	29	1,358,160	1,337,367	S	60.0	16	40.2	23	1,358,160	60.9	18	40.8	23
1984	3,226,000	2,457,667	76.2	20	1,931,546	1,883,910	P	76.7	14	58.4	14	1,931,546	78.6	14	59.9	14
1982	3,145,000	2,105,563	66.9	28	1,404,831	1,368,476	S	65.0	20	43.5	22	1,404,831	66.7	19	44.7	25
1980	3,040,000	2,236,603	73.6	25	1,772,904	1,742,394	P	77.9	13	57.3	19	1,772,904	79.3	13	58.3	20
1978	2,792,000	1,960,900	70.2	24	1,028,854	978,574	C	49.9	40	35.0	38	1,028,854	52.5	37	36.9	36
1976	2,601,000	2,065,378	79.4	15	1,584,590	1,555,534	P	75.3	25	59.8	14	1,584,590	76.7	23	60.9	15
1974	2,448,000	1,896,214	77.5	10	1,044,425	1,007,847	S	53.2	34	41.2	29	1,044,425	55.1	31	42.7	28
1972	2,330,000	1,974,849	84.8	9	1,519,771	1,470,847	P	74.5	24	63.1	11	1,519,771	77.0	23	65.2	9
1970	2,078,000	1,562,916	75.2	19	1,123,000	1,066,807	S	68.3	18	51.3	21	1,123,000	71.9	13	54.0	16
1968	1,975,000	1,646,831	83.4	12	1,310,942	1,304,281	P	79.2	26	66.0	21	1,310,942	79.6	27	66.4	20
1966	1,833,000	1,472,054	80.3	14	987,134	939,441	C	63.8	25	51.3	26	987,134	67.1	21	53.9	24
1964	1,754,000	1,582,046	90.2	8	1,276,956	1,258,556	P	79.6	23	71.8	11	1,276,956	80.7	21	72.8	12
1962	1,774,000	1,446,593	81.5	10	971,706	943,229	S	65.2	22	53.2	21	971,706	67.2	21	54.8	20
1960	1,727,000	1,527,516	88.4	6	1,257,952	1,241,572	P	81.3	24	71.9	20	1,257,952	82.4	24	72.8	17
1958	1,642,000	1,375,035	83.7	6	978,400	886,822	S	64.5	19	54.0	24	978,400	71.2	15	59.6	11
1956	1,611,000	1,451,375	90.1	5	1,164,104	1,150,889	P	79.3	18	71.4	14	1,164,104	80.2	19	72.3	13
1954	1,553,000	1,292,871	83.2	8	890,509	809,795	C	62.6	16	52.1	20	890,509	68.9	13	57.3	15
1952	1,525,000	1,392,594	91.3	4	1,116,414	1,102,708	P	79.2	18	72.3	21	1,116,414	80.2	20	73.2	19
1950	1,516,000	1,217,942	80.3	4	800,573	744,783	S	61.2	16	49.1	28	800,573	65.7	14	52.8	22
1948	1,671,000	1,304,406	78.1	7	917,518	905,058	P	69.4	16	54.2	28	917,518	70.3	15	54.9	28

WASHINGTON

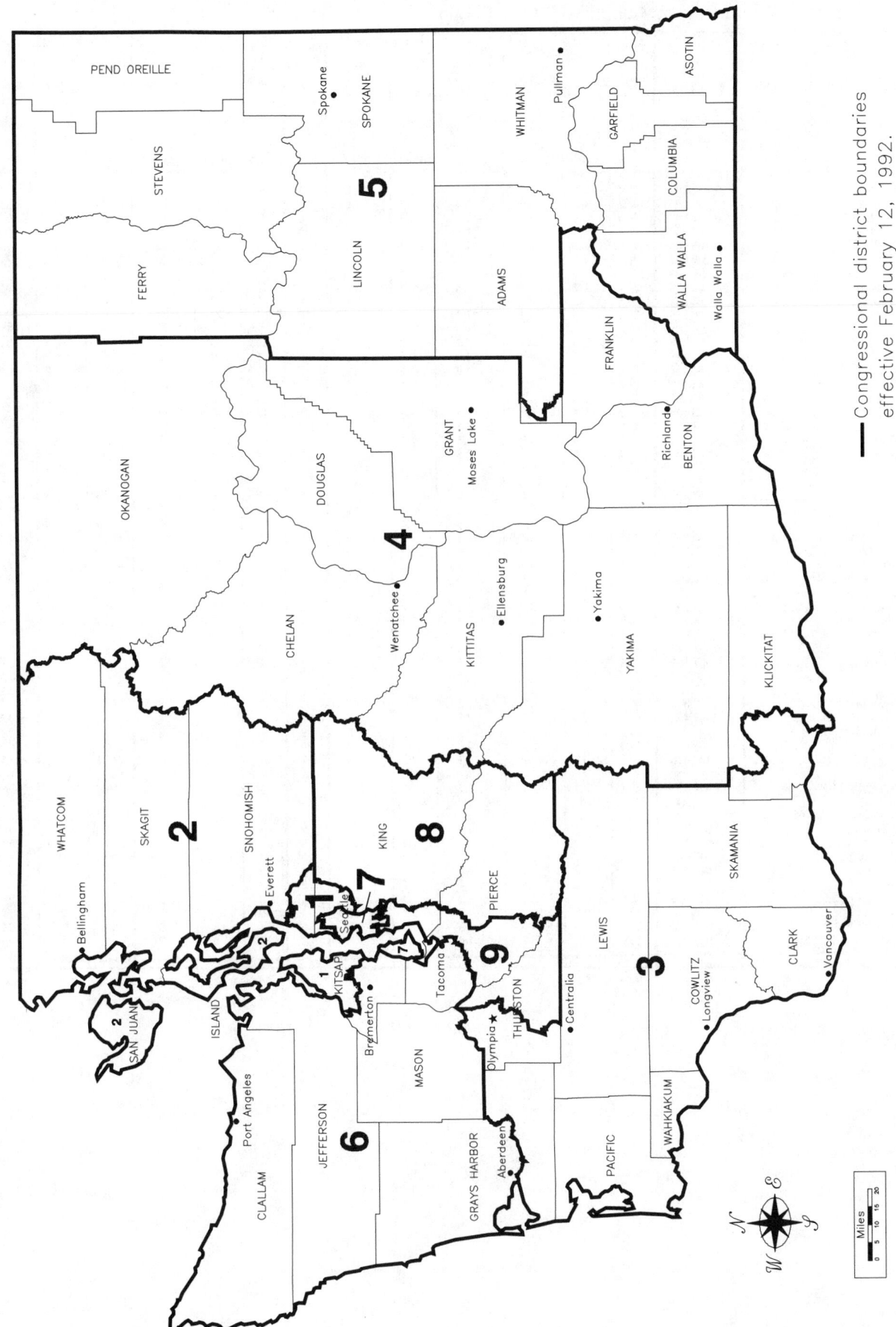

Congressional district boundaries
effective February 12, 1992.

Copyright © 1993 by Election Data Services, Inc.

Washington 963

Table A. — 1990 Population by Race and Ethnic Origin

State/ county code	County	Total persons	Percent of total persons						Rank				Percent contribution to state population			
			Non-Hispanic							Percent of total persons				Non-Hispanic		
			White	Black	Asian and Pacific Islander	Native American	Other	Hispanic	Total	Non-Hispanic		Hispanic	Total	White	Black	Hispanic
										White	Black					
53 001	Adams	13,603	65.7	0.2	0.7	0.5	0.1	32.8	31	38	26	1	0.3	0.2	<.1	2.1
53 003	Asotin	17,605	96.2	0.2	0.6	1.4	<.1	1.6	29	4	27	32	0.4	0.4	<.1	0.1
53 005	Benton	112,560	88.6	0.9	2.0	0.7	0.1	7.7	10	27	14	10	2.3	2.4	0.7	4.0
53 007	Chelan	52,250	89.1	0.1	0.7	0.9	<.1	9.2	18	26	31	8	1.1	1.1	<.1	2.2
53 009	Clallam	56,464	91.8	0.5	1.0	4.6	<.1	2.0	16	19	17	27	1.2	1.2	0.2	0.5
53 011	Clark	238,053	93.1	1.2	2.3	0.9	<.1	2.5	5	13	10	20	4.9	5.2	2.0	2.7
53 013	Columbia	4,024	87.4	<.1	0.4	0.6	<.1	11.5	37	30	38	5	<.1	<.1	<.1	0.2
53 015	Cowlitz	82,119	94.7	0.3	1.3	1.6	<.1	2.0	11	9	20	28	1.7	1.8	0.2	0.8
53 017	Douglas	26,205	88.1	0.2	0.6	0.8	<.1	10.4	26	29	30	6	0.5	0.5	<.1	1.3
53 019	Ferry	6,295	80.1	0.3	0.4	17.8	<.1	1.4	36	35	22	34	0.1	0.1	<.1	<.1
53 021	Franklin	37,473	63.5	3.3	2.1	0.6	0.3	30.2	22	39	3	2	0.8	0.6	0.9	5.3
53 023	Garfield	2,248	98.2	0.0	0.3	0.5	0.0	1.0	39	1	39	38	<.1	<.1	0.0	<.1
53 025	Grant	54,758	79.6	1.0	1.1	1.0	<.1	17.2	17	36	11	4	1.1	1.0	0.4	4.4
53 027	Grays Harbor	64,175	92.8	0.2	1.1	4.1	<.1	1.8	13	14	29	30	1.3	1.4	<.1	0.5
53 029	Island	60,195	89.5	2.4	4.0	0.8	<.1	3.3	14	25	5	14	1.2	1.3	1.0	0.9
53 031	Jefferson	20,146	94.7	0.4	0.9	2.8	<.1	1.2	27	10	19	37	0.4	0.5	<.1	0.1
53 033	King	1,507,319	83.3	5.0	7.7	1.1	0.1	2.9	1	33	2	17	31.0	29.7	51.1	20.7
53 035	Kitsap	189,731	88.5	2.6	4.0	1.6	<.1	3.3	6	28	4	15	3.9	4.0	3.4	2.9
53 037	Kittitas	26,725	94.4	0.6	1.7	0.8	<.1	2.6	25	11	16	19	0.5	0.6	0.1	0.3
53 039	Klickitat	16,616	90.0	0.1	0.7	3.4	<.1	5.6	30	24	32	11	0.3	0.4	<.1	0.4
53 041	Lewis	59,358	95.7	0.3	0.6	1.0	<.1	2.3	15	6	23	22	1.2	1.3	0.1	0.6
53 043	Lincoln	8,864	97.1	0.1	0.4	1.5	<.1	0.9	34	2	34	39	0.2	0.2	<.1	<.1
53 045	Mason	38,341	92.1	0.8	1.1	3.6	<.1	2.3	21	16	15	21	0.8	0.8	0.2	0.4
53 047	Okanogan	33,350	80.6	0.1	0.5	10.3	<.1	8.3	23	34	33	9	0.7	0.6	<.1	1.3
53 049	Pacific	18,882	92.3	0.3	2.5	2.6	<.1	2.3	28	15	24	23	0.4	0.4	<.1	0.2
53 051	Pend Oreille	8,915	96.1	0.1	0.3	2.2	0.0	1.3	33	5	35	35	0.2	0.2	<.1	<.1
53 053	Pierce	586,203	83.3	7.0	4.7	1.3	0.1	3.5	2	32	1	13	12.0	11.6	28.2	9.6
53 055	San Juan	10,035	96.9	0.2	0.8	0.8	<.1	1.2	32	3	25	36	0.2	0.2	<.1	<.1
53 057	Skagit	79,555	91.0	0.3	0.9	2.1	0.2	5.4	12	21	21	12	1.6	1.7	0.2	2.0
53 059	Skamania	8,289	94.9	<.1	0.6	2.4	<.1	2.1	35	8	37	26	0.2	0.2	<.1	<.1
53 061	Snohomish	465,642	91.9	1.0	3.4	1.3	<.1	2.3	3	18	12	24	9.6	10.1	3.2	5.0
53 063	Spokane	361,364	93.4	1.4	1.8	1.4	<.1	1.9	4	12	8	29	7.4	8.0	3.4	3.3
53 065	Stevens	30,948	92.0	0.2	0.5	5.6	<.1	1.6	24	17	28	33	0.6	0.7	<.1	0.2
53 067	Thurston	161,238	90.2	1.7	3.6	1.4	<.1	3.0	8	23	6	16	3.3	3.4	1.9	2.3
53 069	Wahkiakum	3,327	95.7	<.1	0.5	1.6	<.1	2.1	38	7	36	25	<.1	<.1	<.1	<.1
53 071	Walla Walla	48,439	86.8	1.4	1.2	0.7	<.1	9.7	19	31	7	7	1.0	1.0	0.5	2.2
53 073	Whatcom	127,780	91.7	0.5	1.8	3.0	<.1	2.9	9	20	18	18	2.6	2.8	0.4	1.7
53 075	Whitman	38,775	91.0	1.2	5.4	0.6	<.1	1.8	20	22	9	31	0.8	0.8	0.3	0.3
53 077	Yakima	188,823	70.0	0.9	0.9	4.1	0.2	23.9	7	37	13	3	3.9	3.1	1.2	21.0
53	**WASHINGTON**	**4,866,692**	**86.7**	**3.0**	**4.2**	**1.6**	**<.1**	**4.4**					**100.0**	**100.0**	**100.0**	**100.0**
	CONGRESSIONAL															
	District 1	540,745	90.2	1.3	5.2	0.9	<.1	2.3	2	5	5	8	11.1	11.6	4.7	5.9
	District 2	540,739	92.1	0.9	2.1	1.9	<.1	3.0	9	2	8	6	11.1	11.8	3.2	7.6
	District 3	540,745	93.3	0.9	2.1	1.2	<.1	2.5	3	1	9	7	11.1	11.9	3.2	6.3
	District 4	540,744	79.3	0.9	1.2	2.6	0.1	15.9	4	8	7	1	11.1	10.2	3.4	40.0
	District 5	540,744	91.9	1.2	1.8	1.7	<.1	3.4	5	3	6	4	11.1	11.8	4.3	8.5
	District 6	540,742	85.8	5.2	3.7	2.2	<.1	3.1	7	6	3	5	11.1	11.0	19.3	7.8
	District 7	540,747	73.9	9.8	11.3	1.3	0.1	3.5	1	9	1	3	11.1	9.5	36.2	8.9
	District 8	540,742	90.6	1.6	4.5	0.9	<.1	2.3	8	4	4	9	11.1	11.6	5.9	5.8
	District 9	540,744	83.7	5.3	5.9	1.4	<.1	3.7	6	7	2	2	11.1	10.7	19.7	9.2

Table B. — 1990 Voting Age Population (VAP) by Race and Ethnic Origin

County	Total Voting Age Population	Percent of total VAP — Non-Hispanic White	Black	Asian and Pacific Islander	Native American	Other	Hispanic	Rank — Total Percent of total VAP	Rank — Non-Hispanic White	Black	Hispanic	Percent contribution to state VAP — Total	Non-Hispanic White	Black	Hispanic	VAP percent of total population — Total	Non-Hispanic White	Black	Asian and Pacific Islander	Native American	Other	Hispanic
Adams	8,971	71.4	0.2	0.6	0.5	0.1	27.1	31	38	24	1	0.2	0.2	<.1	1.9	65.9	71.7	62.1	63.3	65.6	60.0	54.5
Asotin	12,731	97.2	0.2	0.5	1.1	<.1	1.1	29	4	26	33	0.4	0.4	<.1	0.1	72.3	73.0	56.8	56.3	56.6	33.3	51.4
Benton	78,827	90.6	0.8	1.8	0.7	<.1	6.0	10	27	15	10	2.2	2.2	0.7	3.7	70.0	71.6	61.5	64.3	71.2	50.0	54.5
Chelan	38,274	91.3	0.1	0.6	0.8	<.1	7.2	17	24	30	8	1.1	1.1	<.1	2.1	73.3	75.1	65.3	59.1	65.5	65.8	57.6
Clallam	42,775	93.1	0.6	0.9	3.7	<.1	1.7	15	18	16	24	1.2	1.3	0.3	0.6	75.8	76.8	85.8	67.3	61.2	50.0	61.7
Clark	170,365	94.1	1.0	2.0	0.8	<.1	2.0	5	15	10	20	4.7	5.0	1.8	2.6	71.6	72.4	60.4	63.0	66.8	32.2	57.6
Columbia	3,025	88.5	<.1	0.4	0.5	<.1	10.4	37	31	36	5	<.1	<.1	<.1	0.2	75.2	76.2	100.0	75.0	61.5	100.0	68.3
Cowlitz	59,711	95.7	0.3	1.1	1.4	<.1	1.6	11	10	21	28	1.7	1.8	0.2	0.7	72.7	73.5	55.3	58.4	65.9	32.6	55.7
Douglas	18,636	90.0	0.1	0.6	0.8	<.1	8.5	26	28	31	6	0.5	0.5	<.1	1.2	71.1	72.7	51.2	72.8	68.5	75.0	58.3
Ferry	4,310	82.5	0.3	0.3	15.9	<.1	1.0	36	36	22	34	0.1	0.1	<.1	<.1	68.5	70.5	55.0	60.9	61.2	50.0	51.8
Franklin	24,514	69.2	3.2	1.9	0.6	0.2	24.9	22	39	3	2	0.7	0.5	0.8	4.8	65.4	71.3	62.2	58.5	69.1	53.0	54.0
Garfield	1,661	99.0	0.0	0.2	0.2	0.0	0.5	39	1	39	39	<.1	<.1	0.0	<.1	73.9	74.5	0.0	42.9	33.3	0.0	40.9
Grant	37,576	82.6	1.0	1.1	0.9	<.1	14.4	13	35	11	4	1.0	1.0	0.4	4.2	68.6	71.2	66.6	70.4	60.7	46.9	57.3
Grays Harbor	46,871	94.1	0.1	0.9	3.4	<.1	1.4	13	14	27	30	1.3	1.4	<.1	0.5	73.0	74.1	60.3	58.5	61.4	47.4	57.3
Island	44,741	90.7	2.2	3.5	0.7	<.1	2.9	14	26	5	14	1.2	1.3	1.0	1.0	74.3	75.3	68.5	65.5	68.3	55.2	64.5
Jefferson	15,593	95.7	0.3	0.8	2.3	<.1	0.9	27	9	20	36	0.4	0.5	<.1	0.1	77.4	78.3	52.6	65.4	63.9	25.0	58.9
King	1,166,248	84.9	4.4	7.2	1.0	<.1	2.6	1	33	2	16	32.3	31.1	52.4	23.3	77.4	78.9	68.4	72.2	70.6	44.1	67.4
Kitsap	136,742	89.8	2.4	3.7	1.4	<.1	2.7	6	29	4	15	3.8	3.9	3.4	2.9	72.1	73.1	66.6	65.7	63.1	37.3	60.4
Kittitas	21,081	94.5	0.5	1.9	0.7	<.1	2.4	25	11	17	18	0.6	0.6	0.1	0.4	70.7	72.1	79.0	74.1	85.7	76.1	42.9
Klickitat	11,753	91.7	<.1	0.6	2.8	<.1	4.8	30	22	33	11	0.3	0.3	<.1	0.4	70.7	72.1	37.5	52.8	57.0	62.5	61.1
Lewis	42,522	96.6	0.2	0.5	1.0	<.1	1.7	16	7	23	25	1.2	1.3	0.1	0.5	71.6	72.3	54.4	60.3	68.0	40.0	51.5
Lincoln	6,507	97.7	<.1	0.3	1.2	<.1	0.8	33	2	38	38	0.2	0.2	<.1	<.1	73.4	73.9	16.7	53.1	59.1	100.0	59.0
Mason	28,706	93.2	0.9	0.9	3.0	<.1	1.9	21	17	12	22	0.8	0.8	0.3	0.4	74.9	75.8	85.1	61.3	61.6	52.6	62.9
Okanogan	23,763	83.3	0.1	0.4	8.9	<.1	7.1	23	34	32	9	0.7	0.6	<.1	1.3	71.3	73.6	55.3	64.6	61.8	51.5	60.8
Pacific	14,333	94.3	0.1	1.6	2.1	<.1	1.8	28	12	28	23	0.4	0.4	<.1	0.2	75.9	77.6	38.2	49.1	62.2	100.0	58.2
Pend Oreille	6,292	96.9	<.1	0.3	1.9	0.0	0.9	34	5	37	37	0.2	0.2	<.1	<.1	70.6	71.2	16.7	80.0	60.3	0.0	46.7
Pierce	426,554	85.2	6.3	4.3	1.2	<.1	2.9	2	32	1	13	11.8	11.4	27.5	9.9	72.8	74.4	65.2	66.1	65.4	32.2	61.7
San Juan	7,974	97.4	0.2	0.7	0.7	<.1	1.0	32	3	25	35	0.2	0.2	<.1	<.1	79.5	79.8	65.2	67.9	71.4	80.0	66.1
Skagit	58,711	92.8	0.3	0.8	1.8	0.1	4.2	12	21	19	12	1.6	1.7	0.2	1.9	73.8	75.2	61.4	65.4	63.0	58.7	57.1
Skamania	5,828	96.0	<.1	0.4	2.1	0.0	1.4	35	8	34	29	0.2	0.2	<.1	<.1	70.3	71.1	75.0	49.0	63.6	0.0	48.8
Snohomish	336,490	92.8	0.9	3.1	1.2	<.1	1.9	3	20	13	21	9.3	9.8	3.0	5.1	72.3	73.0	63.9	66.3	64.8	38.9	61.2
Spokane	266,078	94.3	1.2	1.6	1.2	<.1	1.6	4	13	9	26	7.4	7.9	3.3	3.3	73.6	74.3	64.0	68.7	63.4	29.7	61.1
Stevens	21,191	93.4	0.1	0.4	4.9	<.1	1.2	24	16	29	32	0.6	0.6	<.1	0.2	68.5	69.5	43.1	52.9	59.4	47.1	51.3
Thurston	117,794	91.6	1.4	3.2	1.3	<.1	2.5	8	23	7	17	3.3	3.4	1.7	2.3	73.1	74.2	59.7	64.3	65.7	45.2	60.3
Wahkiakum	2,503	96.7	<.1	0.4	1.4	<.1	1.3	38	6	35	31	<.1	<.1	<.1	<.1	75.2	76.0	33.3	73.3	69.2	100.0	46.5
Walla Walla	36,419	88.6	1.5	1.2	0.7	<.1	7.8	19	30	6	7	1.0	1.0	0.6	2.2	75.2	76.7	78.9	75.3	80.4	54.5	60.7
Whatcom	95,766	93.0	0.4	1.7	2.4	<.1	2.4	9	19	18	19	2.7	2.8	0.4	1.8	74.9	76.0	68.4	70.1	60.6	55.9	61.1
Whitman	31,884	91.0	1.2	5.6	0.6	<.1	1.6	20	25	8	27	0.9	0.9	0.4	0.4	82.8	82.3	81.6	85.2	78.3	47.6	74.4
Yakima	131,585	75.6	0.9	0.9	3.5	0.2	18.9	7	37	14	3	3.6	3.1	1.2	19.3	69.7	75.3	64.7	70.6	60.6	56.6	55.0
WASHINGTON	3,605,305	88.4	2.7	3.9	1.4	<.1	3.6					100.0	100.0	100.0	100.0	74.1	75.5	66.7	69.6	64.8	43.4	59.8
CONGRESSIONAL																						
District 1	401,047	91.2	1.1	4.8	0.8	<.1	2.0	3	5	5	7	11.1	11.5	4.7	6.3	74.2	75.0	65.8	68.2	68.1	35.8	63.9
District 2	396,004	93.2	0.8	1.8	1.6	<.1	2.5	6	2	8	6	11.0	11.6	3.2	7.6	73.2	74.2	65.8	65.5	62.2	52.6	59.9
District 3	392,267	94.4	0.7	1.8	1.1	<.1	2.0	7	1	9	8	10.9	11.6	2.9	6.1	72.5	73.4	60.3	62.3	66.2	37.5	57.9
District 4	380,303	83.1	0.8	1.1	2.3	0.1	12.6	9	8	7	1	10.5	9.9	3.3	37.2	70.3	73.7	63.6	67.1	62.0	55.1	55.6
District 5	398,869	93.0	1.1	1.7	1.5	<.1	2.7	4	3	6	4	11.1	11.6	4.3	8.5	73.8	74.6	66.5	72.2	63.0	36.8	59.5
District 6	403,037	87.6	4.6	3.3	1.8	<.1	2.6	2	6	2	5	11.2	11.1	19.2	8.1	74.5	76.1	66.4	66.8	63.7	32.6	62.1
District 7	447,790	77.1	8.3	10.4	1.2	<.1	3.1	1	9	1	3	12.4	10.8	38.0	10.8	82.8	86.3	70.0	75.8	74.3	46.7	72.2
District 8	388,671	91.6	1.4	4.2	0.8	<.1	1.9	8	4	4	9	10.8	11.2	5.6	5.9	71.9	72.6	63.3	67.0	65.3	43.8	60.7
District 9	397,317	85.6	4.6	5.3	1.2	<.1	3.1	5	7	3	2	11.0	10.7	18.9	9.7	73.5	75.2	64.1	66.7	65.2	39.0	62.7

Table C. — Voter Participation: November 3, 1992, General Election

County	Estimated Voting Age Population (VAP), 1992	Voter registration (REG) Total	% contribution to state REG	% of 1992 VAP	Rank by % of 1992 VAP	Voter turnout — Highest office Actual	Total	Office	% of 1992 VAP	Maximum vote Total	% contribution to state turnout	% of REG	Rank by % of REG	% of 1992 VAP	Rank by % 1992 VAP	Percent drop-off, by office President	Senator	Governor	Representative
Adams	9,262	5,886	0.2	63.6	37	4,712	4,585	P	49.5	4,712	0.2	80.1	32	50.9	37	2.7	3.8	3.3	2.7
Asotin	13,188	9,729	0.3	73.8	21	7,725	7,596	P	57.6	7,725	0.3	79.4	34	58.6	26	1.7	4.3	3.3	2.6
Benton	81,125	65,475	2.3	80.7	8	53,261	52,602	P	64.8	53,261	2.3	81.3	26	65.7	9	1.2	2.9	3.3	2.3
Chelan	40,343	28,505	1.0	70.7	27	23,690	23,476	P	58.2	23,690	1.0	83.1	14	58.7	24	0.9	5.6	2.7	7.9
Clallam	44,333	34,667	1.2	78.2	11	29,044	28,673	P	64.7	29,044	1.2	83.8	11	65.5	11	1.3	3.0	2.3	6.7
Clark	184,313	129,869	4.6	70.5	28	107,863	106,536	P	57.8	107,863	4.6	83.1	15	58.5	27	1.2	3.9	3.5	2.7
Columbia	3,119	2,452	<.1	78.6	9	1,953	1,914	P	61.4	1,953	<.1	79.6	33	62.6	16	2.0	5.0	2.1	5.0
Cowlitz	61,339	42,360	1.5	69.1	31	34,936	34,529	P	56.3	34,936	1.5	82.5	21	57.0	30	1.2	4.4	2.5	2.9
Douglas	19,866	13,561	0.5	68.3	33	11,220	11,048	P	55.6	11,220	0.5	82.7	18	56.5	32	1.5	3.5	2.6	4.0
Ferry	4,509	3,313	0.1	73.5	22	2,592	2,557	P	56.7	2,592	0.1	78.2	37	57.5	28	1.4	3.9	2.7	2.8
Franklin	25,690	15,483	0.6	60.3	38	12,398	12,005	G	46.7	12,398	0.5	80.1	31	48.3	38	11.8	4.1	3.2	3.3
Garfield	1,712	1,572	<.1	91.8	2	1,326	1,321	P	77.2	1,326	<.1	84.4	9	77.5	3	0.4	2.7	1.7	1.4
Grant	39,562	26,805	1.0	67.8	34	22,192	21,921	P	55.4	22,192	1.0	82.8	16	56.1	33	1.2	4.4	2.3	4.2
Grays Harbor	47,375	33,060	1.2	69.8	29	27,800	27,238	P	57.5	27,800	1.2	84.1	10	58.7	25	2.0	3.7	2.7	6.4
Island	49,123	33,014	1.2	67.2	36	27,884	27,168	P	55.3	27,884	1.2	84.5	7	56.8	31	2.6	3.0	2.7	3.7
Jefferson	16,837	15,136	0.5	89.9	5	13,050	12,942	P	76.9	13,050	0.6	86.2	3	77.5	2	0.8	3.4	1.4	5.0
King	1,229,788	943,396	33.5	76.7	14	788,511	778,593	P	63.3	788,511	33.9	83.6	12	64.1	13	1.3	2.6	2.1	5.2
Kitsap	148,986	108,470	3.9	72.8	25	89,755	88,568	P	59.4	89,755	3.9	82.7	17	60.2	21	1.3	3.1	2.6	5.0
Kittitas	20,931	15,366	0.5	73.4	23	12,586	12,385	P	59.2	12,586	0.5	81.9	24	60.1	22	1.6	3.4	3.0	4.9
Klickitat	12,269	8,843	0.3	72.1	26	6,996	6,849	P	55.8	6,996	0.3	79.1	36	57.0	29	2.1	6.3	5.2	7.6
Lewis	44,234	33,696	1.2	76.2	16	27,646	27,168	P	61.4	27,646	1.2	82.0	23	62.5	18	1.7	3.6	2.6	4.0
Lincoln	6,605	5,891	0.2	89.2	6	5,051	4,940	G	74.8	5,051	0.2	85.7	4	76.5	4	2.3	3.2	2.2	2.5
Mason	30,837	23,613	0.8	76.6	15	20,093	19,659	G	63.8	20,093	0.9	85.1	5	65.2	12	2.3	3.0	2.2	5.6
Okanogan	24,725	16,720	0.6	67.6	35	13,256	13,033	P	52.7	13,256	0.6	79.3	35	53.6	36	1.7	4.3	3.1	6.5
Pacific	14,897	11,248	0.4	75.5	19	9,488	9,252	P	62.1	9,488	0.4	84.4	8	63.7	15	2.5	4.7	3.2	4.2
Pend Oreille	6,590	5,986	0.2	90.8	4	4,804	4,716	P	71.6	4,804	0.2	80.3	30	72.9	6	1.8	5.7	3.3	2.7
Pierce	453,893	314,777	11.2	69.4	30	243,492	241,149	P	53.1	243,492	10.5	77.4	38	53.6	35	1.0	3.9	2.0	5.1
San Juan	8,581	7,932	0.3	92.4	1	7,050	7,117	P	82.9	7,117	0.3	89.7	1	82.9	1	0.0	4.0	3.3	4.9
Skagit	62,980	48,737	1.7	77.4	13	41,280	40,728	P	64.7	41,280	1.8	84.7	6	65.5	10	1.3	3.0	2.3	3.9
Skamania	6,074	4,626	0.2	76.2	17	3,733	3,680	P	60.6	3,733	0.2	80.7	28	61.5	19	1.4	7.2	5.2	3.9
Snohomish	372,092	272,621	9.7	73.3	24	227,721	225,430	P	60.6	227,721	9.8	83.5	13	61.2	20	1.0	13.5	2.0	4.3
Spokane	273,737	207,167	7.4	75.7	18	171,134	169,132	P	61.8	171,134	7.4	82.6	19	62.5	17	1.2	2.7	2.1	1.7
Stevens	22,369	18,309	0.7	81.8	7	15,102	14,787	P	66.1	15,102	0.6	82.5	20	67.5	7	2.1	6.9	2.9	8.3
Thurston	128,913	95,998	3.4	74.5	20	85,479	84,569	P	65.6	85,479	3.7	89.0	2	66.3	8	1.1	2.5	2.1	3.7
Wahkiakum	2,458	2,220	<.1	90.3	4	1,815	1,796	P	73.1	1,815	<.1	81.8	25	73.8	5	1.0	6.0	4.1	3.9
Walla Walla	36,653	25,062	0.9	68.4	32	20,149	19,881	P	54.2	20,149	0.9	80.4	29	55.0	34	1.3	4.9	2.4	2.0
Whatcom	101,198	79,501	2.8	78.6	10	64,463	63,679	P	62.9	64,463	2.8	81.1	27	63.7	14	1.2	11.9	2.5	3.8
Whitman	30,094	23,424	0.8	77.8	12	17,832	17,478	P	58.1	17,832	0.8	76.1	39	59.3	23	2.0	19.2	2.7	2.9
Yakima	137,400	80,190	2.8	58.4	39	65,825	63,819	C	46.4	65,825	2.8	82.1	22	47.9	39	11.9	4.0	3.2	3.0
WASHINGTON	3,818,000	2,814,680	100.0	73.7		2,324,907	2,294,519		60.1	2,324,974	100.0	82.6		60.9		1.6	4.6	2.3	4.4

Table E. – Vote for President: November 3, 1992, General Election

County	Total	Clinton (DEM)	Bush (REP)	Perot (IND)	Other	Plurality Total	Party	DEM	REP	IND	Other	Rank DEM	Rank REP	Rank IND	Total	DEM	REP	IND	DEM	REP
Adams	4,585	1,449	2,087	1,010	39	638	R	31.6	45.5	22.0	0.9	37	3	32	0.2	0.1	0.3	0.2	41.0	59.0
Asotin	7,596	3,239	2,425	1,849	83	814	D	42.6	31.9	24.3	1.1	10	26	24	0.3	0.3	0.3	0.3	57.2	42.8
Benton	52,602	16,459	22,883	12,878	382	6,424	R	31.3	43.5	24.5	0.7	38	8	21	2.3	1.7	3.1	2.4	41.8	58.2
Chelan	23,476	7,860	10,716	4,606	294	2,856	R	33.5	45.6	19.6	1.3	35	2	35	1.0	0.8	1.5	0.9	42.3	57.7
Clallam	28,673	10,820	9,765	7,775	313	1,055	D	37.7	34.1	27.1	1.1	24	19	11	1.3	1.1	1.3	1.4	52.6	47.4
Clark	106,536	42,648	36,906	26,163	819	5,742	D	40.0	34.6	24.6	0.8	17	18	20	4.7	4.3	5.0	4.8	53.6	46.4
Columbia	1,914	668	761	466	19	93	R	34.9	39.8	24.3	1.0	30	11	23	<.1	<.1	0.1	<.1	46.7	53.3
Cowlitz	34,529	15,052	10,000	9,246	231	5,052	D	43.6	29.0	26.8	0.7	9	33	14	1.5	1.5	1.4	1.7	60.1	39.9
Douglas	11,048	3,731	4,920	2,315	82	1,189	R	33.8	44.5	21.0	0.7	32	6	34	0.5	0.4	0.7	0.4	43.1	56.9
Ferry	2,557	963	773	762	59	190	D	37.7	30.2	29.8	2.3	25	30	2	0.1	<.1	0.1	0.1	55.5	44.5
Franklin	10,937	3,743	4,486	2,597	111	743	R	34.2	41.0	23.7	1.0	31	10	25	0.5	0.4	0.6	0.5	45.5	54.5
Garfield	1,321	473	620	222	6	147	R	35.8	46.9	16.8	0.5	28	1	39	<.1	<.1	<.1	<.1	43.3	56.7
Grant	21,921	7,278	9,503	4,898	242	2,225	R	33.2	43.4	22.3	1.1	36	9	30	1.0	0.7	1.3	0.9	43.4	56.6
Grays Harbor	27,238	12,599	6,904	7,460	275	5,139	D	46.3	25.3	27.4	1.0	5	38	9	1.2	1.3	0.9	1.4	64.6	35.4
Island	27,168	9,555	9,526	7,889	198	29	D	35.2	35.1	29.0	0.7	29	17	4	1.2	1.0	1.3	1.5	50.1	49.9
Jefferson	12,942	6,148	3,467	3,168	159	2,681	D	47.5	26.8	24.5	1.2	3	36	22	0.6	0.6	0.5	0.6	63.9	36.1
King	778,593	391,050	212,986	167,216	7,341	178,064	D	50.2	27.4	21.5	0.9	1	34	33	34.0	39.4	29.1	30.9	64.7	35.3
Kitsap	88,568	34,442	29,340	23,873	913	5,102	D	38.9	33.1	27.0	1.0	20	20	12	3.9	3.5	4.0	4.4	54.0	46.0
Kittitas	12,385	5,432	4,078	2,778	97	1,354	D	43.9	32.9	22.4	0.8	7	21	29	0.5	0.5	0.6	0.5	57.1	42.9
Klickitat	6,849	2,758	2,085	1,938	68	673	D	40.3	30.4	28.3	1.0	15	28	8	0.3	0.3	0.3	0.4	56.9	43.1
Lewis	27,168	7,810	12,316	6,684	358	4,506	R	28.7	45.3	24.6	1.3	39	4	19	1.2	0.8	1.7	1.2	38.8	61.2
Lincoln	4,937	1,653	2,152	1,098	34	499	R	33.5	43.6	22.2	0.7	34	7	31	0.2	0.2	0.3	0.2	43.4	56.6
Mason	19,626	8,076	5,776	5,577	197	2,300	D	41.1	29.4	28.4	1.0	13	32	6	0.9	0.8	0.8	1.0	58.3	41.7
Okanogan	13,033	5,015	4,265	3,541	212	750	D	38.5	32.7	27.2	1.6	22	23	10	0.6	0.5	0.6	0.7	54.0	46.0
Pacific	9,252	4,587	2,243	2,351	71	2,236	D	49.6	24.2	25.4	0.8	2	39	16	0.4	0.5	0.3	0.4	67.2	32.8
Pend Oreille	4,716	1,798	1,528	1,340	50	270	D	38.1	32.4	28.4	1.1	23	24	7	0.2	0.2	0.2	0.2	54.1	45.9
Pierce	241,149	102,243	77,410	59,523	1,973	24,833	D	42.4	32.1	24.7	0.8	11	25	18	10.5	10.3	10.6	11.0	56.9	43.1
San Juan	7,117	3,353	1,901	1,776	87	1,452	D	47.1	26.7	25.0	1.2	4	37	17	0.3	0.3	0.3	0.3	63.8	36.2
Skagit	40,728	15,936	13,388	10,973	431	2,548	D	39.1	32.9	26.9	1.1	19	22	13	1.8	1.6	1.8	2.0	54.3	45.7
Skamania	3,680	1,474	1,102	1,050	54	372	D	40.1	29.9	28.5	1.5	16	31	5	0.2	0.1	0.2	0.2	57.2	42.8
Snohomish	225,430	88,643	69,137	65,838	1,812	19,506	D	39.3	30.7	29.2	0.8	18	27	3	9.9	8.9	9.5	12.2	56.2	43.8
Spokane	169,132	69,526	59,984	38,251	1,371	9,542	D	41.1	35.5	22.6	0.8	14	16	28	7.4	7.0	8.2	7.1	53.7	46.3
Stevens	14,787	4,960	5,706	3,769	352	746	R	33.5	38.6	25.5	2.4	33	13	15	0.6	0.5	0.8	0.7	46.5	53.5
Thurston	84,569	38,293	25,643	19,551	1,082	12,650	D	45.3	30.3	23.1	1.3	6	29	26	3.7	3.9	3.5	3.6	59.9	40.1
Wahkiakum	1,796	696	488	584	28	112	D	38.8	27.2	32.5	1.6	21	35	1	<.1	<.1	<.1	0.1	58.8	41.2
Walla Walla	19,881	7,325	7,894	4,507	155	569	R	36.8	39.7	22.7	0.8	26	12	27	0.9	0.7	1.1	0.8	48.1	51.9
Whatcom	63,679	26,619	23,801	12,455	804	2,818	D	41.8	37.4	19.6	1.3	12	14	36	2.8	2.7	3.3	2.3	52.8	47.2
Whitman	17,478	7,637	6,428	3,220	193	1,209	D	43.7	36.8	18.4	1.1	8	15	37	0.8	0.8	0.9	0.6	54.3	45.7
Yakima	57,969	21,026	25,841	10,583	519	4,815	R	36.3	44.6	18.3	0.9	27	5	38	2.5	2.1	3.5	2.0	44.9	55.1
WASHINGTON¹	**2,288,230**	**993,037**	**731,234**	**541,780**	**22,179**	**261,803**	**D**	**43.4**	**32.0**	**23.7**	**1.0**				**100.0**	**100.0**	**100.0**	**100.0**	**57.6**	**42.4**

¹Includes the following write in votes reported only at the state level: 168 for Kemp, 129 for Tsongas, and 368 for other candidates, total of 665.

Table F. — Vote for U.S. Senator: November 3, 1992, General Election

County	Total	Murray (DEM)	Chandler (REP)	Other	Plurality Total	Party	DEM	REP	Other	Rank DEM	Rank REP	Rank Other	Total	DEM	REP	Other
Adams	4,535	1,656	2,879	0	1,223	R	36.5	63.5	0.0	37	3	–	0.2	0.1	0.3	0.0
Asotin	7,389	3,686	3,703	0	17	R	49.9	50.1	0.0	20	20	–	0.3	0.3	0.4	0.0
Benton	51,722	19,180	32,542	0	13,362	R	37.1	62.9	0.0	36	4	–	2.3	1.6	3.2	0.0
Chelan	22,369	9,174	13,195	0	4,021	R	41.0	59.0	0.0	30	10	–	1.0	0.8	1.3	0.0
Clallam	28,164	13,896	14,268	0	372	R	49.3	50.7	0.0	21	19	–	1.3	1.2	1.4	0.0
Clark..........................	103,690	57,767	45,923	0	11,844	D	55.7	44.3	0.0	9	31	–	4.7	4.8	4.5	0.0
Columbia	1,856	728	1,128	0	400	R	39.2	60.8	0.0	34	6	–	<.1	<.1	0.1	0.0
Cowlitz	33,412	18,955	14,457	0	4,498	D	56.7	43.3	0.0	8	32	–	1.5	1.6	1.4	0.0
Douglas	10,823	4,407	6,416	0	2,009	R	40.7	59.3	0.0	32	8	–	0.5	0.4	0.6	0.0
Ferry.........................	2,491	1,213	1,278	0	65	R	48.7	51.3	0.0	22	18	–	0.1	0.1	0.1	0.0
Franklin	11,894	4,852	7,042	0	2,190	R	40.8	59.2	0.0	31	9	–	0.5	0.4	0.7	0.0
Garfield......................	1,290	468	822	0	354	R	36.3	63.7	0.0	39	1	–	<.1	<.1	<.1	0.0
Grant.........................	21,226	8,485	12,741	0	4,256	R	40.0	60.0	0.0	33	7	–	1.0	0.7	1.2	0.0
Grays Harbor	26,760	15,265	11,495	0	3,770	D	57.0	43.0	0.0	6	34	–	1.2	1.3	1.1	0.0
Island	27,041	13,721	13,320	0	401	D	50.7	49.3	0.0	18	22	–	1.2	1.1	1.3	0.0
Jefferson	12,600	7,382	5,218	0	2,164	D	58.6	41.4	0.0	5	35	–	0.6	0.6	0.5	0.0
King	768,191	458,177	310,014	0	148,163	D	59.6	40.4	0.0	2	38	–	34.6	38.2	30.4	0.0
Kitsap	86,960	43,413	43,547	0	134	R	49.9	50.1	0.0	19	21	–	3.9	3.6	4.3	0.0
Kittitas	12,155	6,366	5,789	0	577	D	52.4	47.6	0.0	17	23	–	0.5	0.5	0.6	0.0
Klickitat.....................	6,553	3,547	3,006	0	541	D	54.1	45.9	0.0	14	26	–	0.3	0.3	0.3	0.0
Lewis	26,639	10,066	16,573	0	6,507	R	37.8	62.2	0.0	35	5	–	1.2	0.8	1.6	0.0
Lincoln	4,890	1,782	3,108	0	1,326	R	36.4	63.6	0.0	38	2	–	0.2	0.1	0.3	0.0
Mason........................	19,496	10,606	8,890	0	1,716	D	54.4	45.6	0.0	13	27	–	0.9	0.9	0.9	0.0
Okanogan	12,687	5,855	6,832	0	977	R	46.1	53.9	0.0	27	13	–	0.6	0.5	0.7	0.0
Pacific	9,043	5,464	3,579	0	1,885	D	60.4	39.6	0.0	1	39	–	0.4	0.5	0.4	0.0
Pend Oreille.................	4,529	2,158	2,371	0	213	R	47.6	52.4	0.0	23	17	–	0.2	0.2	0.2	0.0
Pierce........................	234,027	128,681	105,346	0	23,335	D	55.0	45.0	0.0	10	30	–	10.5	10.7	10.3	0.0
San Juan	6,835	4,008	2,827	0	1,181	D	58.6	41.4	0.0	4	36	–	0.3	0.3	0.3	0.0
Skagit	40,029	21,037	18,992	0	2,045	D	52.6	47.4	0.0	15	25	–	1.8	1.8	1.9	0.0
Skamania	3,465	2,059	1,406	0	653	D	59.4	40.6	0.0	3	37	–	0.2	0.2	0.1	0.0
Snohomish	196,906	107,217	89,689	0	17,528	D	54.5	45.5	0.0	12	28	–	8.9	8.9	8.8	0.0
Spokane	166,442	77,585	88,857	0	11,272	R	46.6	53.4	0.0	26	14	–	7.5	6.5	8.7	0.0
Stevens.......................	14,061	5,847	8,214	0	2,367	R	41.6	58.4	0.0	29	11	–	0.6	0.5	0.8	0.0
Thurston	83,375	47,337	36,038	0	11,299	D	56.8	43.2	0.0	7	33	–	3.8	4.0	3.5	0.0
Wahkiakum	1,707	932	775	0	157	D	54.6	45.4	0.0	11	29	–	<.1	<.1	<.1	0.0
Walla Walla	19,160	9,093	10,067	0	974	R	47.5	52.5	0.0	24	16	–	0.9	0.8	1.0	0.0
Whatcom......................	56,786	29,836	26,950	0	2,886	D	52.5	47.5	0.0	16	24	–	2.6	2.5	2.6	0.0
Whitman	14,408	6,610	7,798	0	1,188	R	45.9	54.1	0.0	28	12	–	0.6	0.6	0.8	0.0
Yakima	63,196	29,462	33,734	0	4,272	R	46.6	53.4	0.0	25	15	–	2.8	2.5	3.3	0.0
WASHINGTON¹.............	**2,219,162**	**1,197,973**	**1,020,829**	**360**	**177,144**	**D**	**54.0**	**46.0**	**<.1**				**100.0**	**100.0**	**100.0**	**100.0**

¹Includes the following write in votes reported only at the state level: 94 for Goodloe, 24 for Thorness, 10 for Adams, 31 for Gill, and 201 for other candidates; total of 360.

Table G. — Vote for Governor: November 3, 1992, General Election

County	Total	Lowry (DEM)	Eikenberry (REP)	Other	Plurality Total	Party	DEM	REP	Other	Rank DEM	Rank REP	Rank Other	Total	DEM	REP	Other
Adams	4,557	1,750	2,807	0	1,057	R	38.4	61.6	0.0	31	9	-	0.2	0.1	0.3	0.0
Asotin	7,471	3,436	4,035	0	599	R	46.0	54.0	0.0	19	21	-	0.3	0.3	0.4	0.0
Benton	51,486	21,872	29,614	0	7,742	R	42.5	57.5	0.0	25	15	-	2.3	1.8	2.7	0.0
Chelan	23,045	8,666	14,379	0	5,713	R	37.6	62.4	0.0	33	7	-	1.0	0.7	1.3	0.0
Clallam	28,379	12,049	16,330	0	4,281	R	42.5	57.5	0.0	26	14	-	1.2	1.0	1.5	0.0
Clark	104,072	48,292	55,780	0	7,488	R	46.4	53.6	0.0	18	22	-	4.6	4.1	5.1	0.0
Columbia	1,912	599	1,313	0	714	R	31.3	68.7	0.0	38	2	-	<.1	<.1	0.1	0.0
Cowlitz	34,058	16,677	17,381	0	704	R	49.0	51.0	0.0	11	29	-	1.5	1.4	1.6	0.0
Douglas	10,924	4,139	6,785	0	2,646	R	37.9	62.1	0.0	32	8	-	0.5	0.3	0.6	0.0
Ferry	2,521	1,062	1,459	0	397	R	42.1	57.9	0.0	28	12	-	0.1	<.1	0.1	0.0
Franklin	12,005	5,474	6,531	0	1,057	R	45.6	54.4	0.0	21	19	-	0.5	0.5	0.6	0.0
Garfield	1,304	426	878	0	452	R	32.7	67.3	0.0	37	3	-	<.1	<.1	<.1	0.0
Grant	21,679	7,991	13,688	0	5,697	R	36.9	63.1	0.0	35	5	-	1.0	0.7	1.3	0.0
Grays Harbor	27,046	14,986	12,060	0	2,926	D	55.4	44.6	0.0	3	37	-	1.2	1.3	1.1	0.0
Island	27,133	12,429	14,704	0	2,275	R	45.8	54.2	0.0	20	20	-	1.2	1.0	1.4	0.0
Jefferson	12,867	7,047	5,820	0	1,227	D	54.8	45.2	0.0	4	36	-	0.6	0.6	0.5	0.0
King	771,832	466,506	305,326	0	161,180	D	60.4	39.6	0.0	1	39	-	34.0	39.4	28.1	0.0
Kitsap	87,414	42,562	44,852	0	2,290	R	48.7	51.3	0.0	13	27	-	3.8	3.6	4.1	0.0
Kittitas	12,210	6,232	5,978	0	254	D	51.0	49.0	0.0	8	32	-	0.5	0.5	0.6	0.0
Klickitat	6,635	2,883	3,752	0	869	R	43.5	56.5	0.0	24	16	-	0.3	0.2	0.3	0.0
Lewis	26,941	7,938	19,003	0	11,065	R	29.5	70.5	0.0	39	1	-	1.2	0.7	1.7	0.0
Lincoln	4,940	1,717	3,223	0	1,506	R	34.8	65.2	0.0	36	4	-	0.2	0.1	0.3	0.0
Mason	19,659	9,548	10,111	0	563	R	48.6	51.4	0.0	14	26	-	0.9	0.8	0.9	0.0
Okanogan	12,851	5,139	7,712	0	2,573	R	40.0	60.0	0.0	30	10	-	0.6	0.4	0.7	0.0
Pacific	9,187	4,933	4,254	0	679	D	53.7	46.3	0.0	6	34	-	0.4	0.4	0.4	0.0
Pend Oreille	4,645	1,919	2,726	0	807	R	41.3	58.7	0.0	29	11	-	0.2	0.2	0.3	0.0
Pierce	238,591	120,968	117,623	0	3,345	D	50.7	49.3	0.0	9	31	-	10.5	10.2	10.8	0.0
San Juan	6,881	3,758	3,123	0	635	D	54.6	45.4	0.0	5	35	-	0.3	0.3	0.3	0.0
Skagit	40,344	18,784	21,560	0	2,776	R	46.6	53.4	0.0	17	23	-	1.8	1.6	2.0	0.0
Skamania	3,540	1,657	1,883	0	226	R	46.8	53.2	0.0	16	24	-	0.2	0.1	0.2	0.0
Snohomish	223,196	117,000	106,196	0	10,804	D	52.4	47.6	0.0	7	33	-	9.8	9.9	9.8	0.0
Spokane	167,531	74,262	93,269	0	19,007	R	44.3	55.7	0.0	23	17	-	7.4	6.3	8.6	0.0
Stevens	14,664	5,447	9,217	0	3,770	R	37.1	62.9	0.0	34	6	-	0.6	0.5	0.8	0.0
Thurston	83,704	46,666	37,038	0	9,628	D	55.8	44.2	0.0	2	38	-	3.7	3.9	3.4	0.0
Wahkiakum	1,741	775	966	0	191	R	44.5	55.5	0.0	22	18	-	<.1	<.1	<.1	0.0
Walla Walla	19,663	8,330	11,333	0	3,003	R	42.4	57.6	0.0	27	13	-	0.9	0.7	1.0	0.0
Whatcom	62,869	31,113	31,756	0	643	R	49.5	50.5	0.0	10	30	-	2.8	2.6	2.9	0.0
Whitman	17,342	8,459	8,883	0	424	R	48.8	51.2	0.0	12	28	-	0.8	0.7	0.8	0.0
Yakima	63,692	30,824	32,868	0	2,044	R	48.4	51.6	0.0	15	25	-	2.8	2.6	3.0	0.0
WASHINGTON[1]	**2,270,826**	**1,184,315**	**1,086,216**	**295**	**98,099**	**D**	**52.2**	**47.8**	**<.1**				**100.0**	**100.0**	**100.0**	**100.0**

[1]Includes the following write in votes reported only at the state level: 32 for McDonald, 121 for Morrison, and 142 for other candidates; total of 295.

Table H. — Vote for U.S. Representative in Congress: November 3, 1992, General Election

Congressional district and county	Total	Democrat (DEM)	Republican (REP)	Other	Plurality Total	Plurality Party	Percent of total vote DEM	REP	Other	Rank within district DEM	REP	Other	Percent contribution to district vote Total	DEM	REP	Other
District 1[1]	271,278	148,844	113,897	8,537	34,947	D	54.9	42.0	3.1				100.0	100.0	100.0	100.0
King (pt)	133,985	75,141	54,881	3,963	20,260	D	56.1	41.0	3.0	1	3	3	49.4	50.5	48.2	46.4
Kitsap (pt)	40,070	20,916	17,643	1,511	3,273	D	52.2	44.0	3.8	3	1	1	14.8	14.1	15.5	17.7
Snohomish (pt)	97,219	52,787	41,373	3,059	11,414	D	54.3	42.6	3.1	2	2	2	35.8	35.5	36.3	35.8
District 2[2]	255,926	133,207	107,365	15,354	25,842	D	52.0	42.0	6.0				100.0	100.0	100.0	100.0
Island	26,846	13,101	12,492	1,253	609	D	48.8	46.5	4.7	5	1	5	10.5	9.8	11.6	8.2
San Juan	6,768	3,751	2,568	449	1,183	D	55.4	37.9	6.6	1	5	1	2.6	2.8	2.4	2.9
Skagit	39,671	20,463	17,169	2,039	3,294	D	51.6	43.3	5.1	3	3	4	15.5	15.4	16.0	13.3
Snohomish (pt)	120,616	65,173	47,876	7,567	17,297	D	54.0	39.7	6.3	2	4	3	47.1	48.9	44.6	49.3
Whatcom	62,019	30,719	27,260	4,040	3,459	D	49.5	44.0	6.5	4	2	2	24.2	23.1	25.4	26.3
District 3[3]	246,644	138,043	108,583	18	29,460	D	56.0	44.0	<.1				100.0	100.0	100.0	100.0
Clark	104,939	58,088	46,851	0	11,237	D	55.4	44.6	0.0	8	2	-	42.5	42.1	43.1	0.0
Cowlitz	33,907	18,816	15,091	0	3,725	D	55.5	44.5	0.0	7	3	-	13.7	13.6	13.9	0.0
Grays Harbor (pt)	6,640	4,430	2,210	0	2,220	D	66.7	33.3	0.0	2	8	-	2.7	3.2	2.0	0.0
Klickitat (pt)	3,033	1,841	1,192	0	649	D	60.7	39.3	0.0	4	6	-	1.2	1.3	1.1	0.0
Lewis	26,549	10,870	15,679	0	4,809	R	40.9	59.1	0.0	9	1	-	10.8	7.9	14.4	0.0
Pacific	9,087	6,246	2,841	0	3,405	D	68.7	31.3	0.0	1	9	-	3.7	4.5	2.6	0.0
Skamania	3,588	2,189	1,399	0	790	D	61.0	39.0	0.0	3	7	-	1.5	1.6	1.3	0.0
Thurston (pt)	57,138	34,582	22,556	0	12,026	D	60.5	39.5	0.0	5	5	-	23.2	25.1	20.8	0.0
Wahkiakum	1,745	981	764	0	217	D	56.2	43.8	0.0	6	4	-	0.7	0.7	0.7	0.0
District 4[4]	209,604	106,556	103,028	20	3,528	D	50.8	49.2	<.1				100.0	100.0	100.0	100.0
Adams (pt)	100	23	77	0	54	R	23.0	77.0	0.0	10	1	-	0.0	0.0	0.1	0.0
Benton	52,033	22,837	29,196	0	6,359	R	43.9	56.1	0.0	8	3	-	24.8	21.4	28.3	0.0
Chelan	21,818	11,297	10,521	0	776	D	51.8	48.2	0.0	6	5	-	10.4	10.6	10.2	0.0
Douglas	10,776	6,024	4,752	0	1,272	D	55.9	44.1	0.0	2	9	-	5.1	5.7	4.6	0.0
Franklin	11,991	4,815	7,176	0	2,361	R	40.2	59.8	0.0	9	2	-	5.7	4.5	7.0	0.0
Grant	21,255	10,711	10,544	0	167	D	50.4	49.6	0.0	7	4	-	10.1	10.1	10.2	0.0
Kittitas	11,971	7,306	4,665	0	2,641	D	61.0	39.0	0.0	1	10	-	5.7	6.9	4.5	0.0
Klickitat (pt)	3,430	1,879	1,551	0	328	D	54.8	45.2	0.0	4	7	-	1.6	1.8	1.5	0.0
Okanogan	12,391	6,896	5,495	0	1,401	D	55.7	44.3	0.0	3	8	-	5.9	6.5	5.3	0.0
Yakima	63,819	34,768	29,051	0	5,717	D	54.5	45.5	0.0	5	6	-	30.4	32.6	28.2	0.0
District 5[5]	246,413	135,965	110,443	5	25,522	D	55.2	44.8	<.1				100.0	100.0	100.0	100.0
Adams (pt)	4,484	2,258	2,226	0	32	D	50.4	49.6	0.0	6	6	-	1.8	1.7	2.0	0.0
Asotin	7,527	3,844	3,683	0	161	D	51.1	48.9	0.0	5	7	-	3.1	2.8	3.3	0.0
Columbia	1,855	881	974	0	93	R	47.5	52.5	0.0	10	2	-	0.8	0.6	0.9	0.0
Ferry	2,520	1,234	1,286	0	52	R	49.0	51.0	0.0	8	4	-	1.0	0.9	1.2	0.0
Garfield	1,307	637	670	0	33	R	48.7	51.3	0.0	9	3	-	0.5	0.5	0.6	0.0
Lincoln	4,924	2,476	2,448	0	28	D	50.3	49.7	0.0	7	5	-	2.0	1.8	2.2	0.0
Pend Oreille	4,673	2,397	2,276	0	121	D	51.3	48.7	0.0	4	8	-	1.9	1.8	2.1	0.0
Spokane	168,210	95,594	72,616	0	22,978	D	56.8	43.2	0.0	1	11	-	68.3	70.3	65.7	0.0
Stevens	13,841	6,173	7,668	0	1,495	R	44.6	55.4	0.0	11	1	-	5.6	4.5	6.9	0.0
Walla Walla	19,754	10,960	8,794	0	2,166	D	55.5	44.5	0.0	2	10	-	8.0	8.1	8.0	0.0
Whitman	17,313	9,511	7,802	0	1,709	D	54.9	45.1	0.0	3	9	-	7.0	7.0	7.1	0.0
District 6[6]	238,182	152,933	66,664	18,585	86,269	D	64.2	28.0	7.8				100.0	100.0	100.0	100.0
Clallam	27,098	15,125	9,037	2,936	6,088	D	55.8	33.3	10.8	6	1	2	11.4	9.9	13.6	15.8
Grays Harbor (pt)	19,381	13,725	4,606	1,050	9,119	D	70.8	23.8	5.4	1	6	6	8.1	9.0	6.9	5.6
Jefferson	12,392	7,334	3,604	1,454	3,730	D	59.2	29.1	11.7	5	3	1	5.2	4.8	5.4	7.8
Kitsap (pt)	45,181	30,376	11,451	3,354	18,925	D	67.2	25.3	7.4	2	5	4	19.0	19.9	17.2	18.0
Mason	18,963	11,915	5,594	1,454	6,321	D	62.8	29.5	7.7	4	2	3	8.0	7.8	8.4	7.8
Pierce (pt)	115,147	74,458	32,372	8,317	42,086	D	64.7	28.1	7.2	3	4	5	48.3	48.7	48.6	44.8
District 7[7]	283,992	222,604	54,149	7,239	168,455	D	78.4	19.1	2.5				100.0	100.0	100.0	100.0
King (pt)	283,950	222,604	54,149	7,197	168,455	D	78.4	19.1	2.5	1	1	1	100.0	100.0	100.0	99.4
District 8[8]	258,188	87,611	155,874	14,703	68,263	R	33.9	60.4	5.7				100.0	100.0	100.0	100.0
King (pt)	216,377	73,329	131,249	11,799	57,920	R	33.9	60.7	5.5	2	1	2	83.8	83.7	84.2	80.2
Pierce (pt)	41,794	14,282	24,625	2,887	10,343	R	34.2	58.9	6.9	1	2	1	16.2	16.3	15.8	19.6
District 9[9]	212,931	110,902	91,910	10,119	18,992	D	52.1	43.2	4.8				100.0	100.0	100.0	100.0
King (pt)	113,586	59,251	49,306	5,029	9,945	D	52.2	43.4	4.4	2	2	3	53.3	53.4	53.6	49.7
Pierce (pt)	74,197	37,637	32,665	3,895	4,972	D	50.7	44.0	5.2	3	1	1	34.8	33.9	35.5	38.5
Thurston (pt)	25,136	14,014	9,939	1,183	4,075	D	55.8	39.5	4.7	1	3	2	11.8	12.6	10.8	11.7
WASHINGTON	2,223,158	1,236,665	911,913	74,580	324,752	D	55.6	41.0	3.4							

[1]Includes 4 write in votes for other candidates reported only at the district level. [2]Includes 6 write in votes for other candidates reported only at the district level.
[3]Includes 18 write in votes for other candidates reported only at the district level. [4]Includes 20 write in votes for other candidates reported only at the district level.
[5]Includes 5 write in votes for other candidates reported only at the district level. [6]Includes 20 write in votes for other candidates reported only at the district level.
[7]Includes 42 write in votes for other candidates reported only at the district level. [8]Includes 17 write in votes for other candidates reported only at the district level.
[9]Includes 12 write in votes for other candidates reported only at the district level.

Table I. — Vote for Presidential Preference: May 19, 1992, Democratic Primary Election

County	Top candidates									Top three candidates (state vote)								
										Percent of total vote			Rank			Percent contribution to state vote		
	Total	Clinton	Brown	Perot	Tsongas	Harkin	Kerrey	LaRouche		Clinton	Brown	Perot	Clinton	Brown	Perot	Total	Clinton	Brown	Perot
Adams	360	208	50	37	47	6	8	4	-	57.8	13.9	10.3	6	36	35	0.2	0.3	0.1	0.1
Asotin	359	211	49	57	32	5	1	4	-	58.8	13.6	15.9	4	37	25	0.2	0.3	0.1	0.2
Benton	2,536	1,313	432	138	529	53	46	25	-	51.8	17.0	5.4	9	31	39	1.7	2.1	1.3	0.5
Chelan	1,265	641	222	183	184	14	9	12	-	50.7	17.5	14.5	12	29	27	0.9	1.0	0.7	0.6
Clallam	2,121	843	400	550	262	28	27	11	-	39.7	18.9	25.9	29	22	5	1.4	1.4	1.2	1.9
Clark	7,684	3,431	2,218	1,038	797	77	68	55	-	44.7	28.9	13.5	23	2	30	5.2	5.5	6.5	3.7
Columbia	126	63	14	30	11	4	3	1	-	50.0	11.1	23.8	14	39	11	<.1	0.1	<.1	0.1
Cowlitz	4,322	2,090	767	1,038	290	65	39	33	-	48.4	17.7	24.0	16	27	9	2.9	3.4	2.2	3.7
Douglas	907	489	164	106	99	20	15	14	-	53.9	18.1	11.7	7	26	33	0.6	0.8	0.5	0.4
Ferry	347	148	66	83	39	5	2	4	-	42.7	19.0	23.9	26	21	10	0.2	0.2	0.2	0.3
Franklin	785	498	101	96	66	7	8	9	-	63.4	12.9	12.2	1	38	32	0.5	0.8	0.3	0.3
Garfield	63	37	9	7	5	5	0	0	-	58.7	14.3	11.1	5	35	34	<.1	<.1	<.1	<.1
Grant	1,885	946	326	368	182	17	20	26	-	50.2	17.3	19.5	13	30	17	1.3	1.5	1.0	1.3
Grays Harbor	2,296	1,009	426	568	208	29	38	18	-	43.9	18.6	24.7	24	23	8	1.6	1.6	1.2	2.0
Island	1,763	700	439	329	240	19	21	15	-	39.7	24.9	18.7	30	8	21	1.2	1.1	1.3	1.2
Jefferson	2,412	742	606	699	301	18	24	22	-	30.8	25.1	29.0	38	7	3	1.6	1.2	1.8	2.5
King	46,790	17,617	12,410	8,212	7,317	564	428	242	-	37.7	26.5	17.6	34	4	23	31.6	28.3	36.4	29.0
Kitsap	5,084	1,947	1,212	990	750	79	60	46	-	38.3	23.8	19.5	32	10	18	3.4	3.1	3.6	3.5
Kittitas	919	443	170	173	113	10	6	4	-	48.2	18.5	18.8	17	24	20	0.6	0.7	0.5	0.6
Klickitat	894	462	165	183	64	3	8	9	-	51.7	18.5	20.5	10	25	16	0.6	0.7	0.5	0.6
Lewis	1,652	808	425	136	217	24	22	20	-	48.9	25.7	8.2	15	6	36	1.1	1.3	1.2	0.5
Lincoln	448	269	72	29	52	10	6	10	-	60.0	16.1	6.5	3	32	37	0.3	0.4	0.2	0.1
Mason	1,561	630	347	365	178	15	12	14	-	40.4	22.2	23.4	28	13	13	1.1	1.0	1.0	1.3
Okanogan	946	444	190	170	92	16	22	12	-	46.9	20.1	18.0	21	16	22	0.6	0.7	0.6	0.6
Pacific	1,247	640	245	186	128	17	15	16	-	51.3	19.6	14.9	11	17	26	0.8	1.0	0.7	0.7
Pend Oreille	767	360	156	158	72	6	8	7	-	46.9	20.3	20.6	20	15	15	0.5	0.6	0.5	0.6
Pierce	14,226	6,049	2,771	3,588	1,503	145	91	79	-	42.5	19.5	25.2	27	18	7	9.6	9.7	8.1	12.7
San Juan	744	181	179	267	106	4	4	3	-	24.3	24.1	35.9	39	9	1	0.5	0.3	0.5	0.9
Skagit	1,970	750	459	464	233	22	27	15	-	38.1	23.3	23.6	33	11	12	1.3	1.2	1.3	1.6
Skamania	485	171	131	125	40	4	7	7	-	35.3	27.0	25.8	35	3	6	0.3	0.3	0.4	0.4
Snohomish	11,778	4,562	2,730	2,649	1,471	158	104	104	-	38.7	23.2	22.5	31	12	14	8.0	7.3	8.0	9.4
Spokane	8,814	3,949	1,374	2,489	753	116	83	50	-	44.8	15.6	28.2	22	34	4	6.0	6.4	4.0	8.8
Stevens	1,501	710	286	283	169	19	19	15	-	47.3	19.1	18.9	18	20	19	1.0	1.1	0.8	1.0
Thurston	7,238	2,511	2,233	1,241	1,013	112	69	59	-	34.7	30.9	17.1	37	1	24	4.9	4.0	6.5	4.4
Wahkiakum	483	170	85	158	56	5	3	6	-	35.2	17.6	32.7	36	28	2	0.3	0.3	0.2	0.6
Walla Walla	1,869	975	363	260	206	31	23	11	-	52.2	19.4	13.9	8	19	29	1.3	1.6	1.1	0.9
Whatcom	2,915	1,266	770	416	355	46	33	29	-	43.4	26.4	14.3	25	5	28	2.0	2.0	2.3	1.5
Whitman	683	323	145	89	108	6	11	1	-	47.3	21.2	13.0	19	14	31	0.5	0.5	0.4	0.3
Yakima	5,736	3,565	904	353	693	74	99	48	-	62.2	15.8	6.2	2	33	38	3.9	5.7	2.7	1.2
WASHINGTON	147,981	62,171	34,111	28,311	18,981	1,858	1,489	1,060	-	42.0	23.1	19.1				100.0	100.0	100.0	100.0

County	Top candidates					Top four candidates (state vote)												
						Percent of total vote								Percent contribution to state vote				
										Rank								
	Total	Bush	Perot	Bu-chanan	Other	Bush	Perot	Bu-chanan	Other	Bush	Perot	Bu-chanan	Other	Total	Bush	Perot	Bu-chanan	Other
Adams	557	427	38	78	14	76.7	6.8	14.0	2.5	9	35	6	18	0.4	0.5	0.1	0.6	0.3
Asotin	245	160	33	44	8	65.3	13.5	18.0	3.3	23	27	1	6	0.2	0.2	0.1	0.3	0.2
Benton	4,456	3,775	158	426	97	84.7	3.5	9.6	2.2	1	39	27	23	3.4	4.3	0.6	3.2	2.4
Chelan	1,968	1,529	190	219	30	77.7	9.7	11.1	1.5	5	33	17	36	1.5	1.8	0.7	1.7	0.7
Clallam	2,150	1,211	639	240	60	56.3	29.7	11.2	2.8	38	4	15	12	1.7	1.4	2.5	1.8	1.5
Clark	5,683	3,979	799	767	138	70.0	14.1	13.5	2.4	14	26	7	19	4.4	4.6	3.1	5.8	3.3
Columbia	168	105	36	22	5	62.5	21.4	13.1	3.0	32	18	8	9	0.1	0.1	0.1	0.2	0.1
Cowlitz	2,463	1,621	575	216	51	65.8	23.3	8.8	2.1	22	11	30	26	1.9	1.9	2.3	1.6	1.2
Douglas	1,431	1,158	124	125	24	80.9	8.7	8.7	1.7	3	34	31	34	1.1	1.3	0.5	0.9	0.6
Ferry	235	136	64	24	11	57.9	27.2	10.2	4.7	36	6	23	2	0.2	0.2	0.3	0.2	0.3
Franklin	734	565	78	70	21	77.0	10.6	9.5	2.9	8	32	28	11	0.6	0.7	0.3	0.5	0.5
Garfield	99	77	11	11	0	77.8	11.1	11.1	0.0	4	31	18	39	<.1	<.1	<.1	<.1	0.0
Grant	2,187	1,602	286	267	32	73.3	13.1	12.2	1.5	12	30	10	37	1.7	1.8	1.1	2.0	0.8
Grays Harbor	1,158	716	292	123	27	61.8	25.2	10.6	2.3	34	8	21	20	0.9	0.8	1.1	0.9	0.7
Island	2,690	2,000	413	222	55	74.3	15.4	8.3	2.0	11	22	33	29	2.1	2.3	1.6	1.7	1.3
Jefferson	2,037	1,162	691	151	33	57.0	33.9	7.4	1.6	37	2	37	35	1.6	1.3	2.7	1.1	0.8
King	35,769	22,384	7,924	3,593	1,868	62.6	22.2	10.0	5.2	31	16	24	1	27.6	25.8	31.2	27.1	45.3
Kitsap	4,556	2,902	1,058	470	126	63.7	23.2	10.3	2.8	26	12	22	13	3.5	3.3	4.2	3.5	3.1
Kittitas	728	465	182	66	15	63.9	25.0	9.1	2.1	25	9	29	27	0.6	0.5	0.7	0.5	0.4
Klickitat	630	395	171	55	9	62.7	27.1	8.7	1.4	29	7	32	38	0.5	0.5	0.7	0.4	0.2
Lewis	2,188	1,697	122	311	58	77.6	5.6	14.2	2.7	6	37	5	16	1.7	2.0	0.5	2.3	1.4
Lincoln	494	383	18	74	19	77.5	3.6	15.0	3.8	7	38	4	4	0.4	0.4	<.1	0.6	0.5
Mason	1,253	826	280	125	22	65.9	22.3	10.0	1.8	21	15	26	32	1.0	1.0	1.1	0.9	0.5
Okanogan	818	556	145	102	15	68.0	17.7	12.5	1.8	17	20	9	31	0.6	0.6	0.6	0.8	0.4
Pacific	554	385	83	66	20	69.5	15.0	11.9	3.6	15	23	11	5	0.4	0.4	0.3	0.5	0.5
Pend Oreille	581	396	99	68	18	68.2	17.0	11.7	3.1	16	21	13	8	0.4	0.5	0.4	0.5	0.4
Pierce	11,543	7,228	3,164	921	230	62.6	27.4	8.0	2.0	30	5	35	30	8.9	8.3	12.4	6.9	5.6
San Juan	868	370	446	37	15	42.6	51.4	4.3	1.7	39	1	39	33	0.7	0.4	1.8	0.3	0.4
Skagit	2,046	1,298	473	228	47	63.4	23.1	11.1	2.3	28	13	16	21	1.6	1.5	1.9	1.7	1.1
Skamania	340	211	83	39	7	62.1	24.4	11.5	2.1	33	10	14	28	0.3	0.2	0.3	0.3	0.2
Snohomish	9,889	6,291	2,238	1,098	262	63.6	22.6	11.1	2.6	27	14	19	17	7.6	7.2	8.8	8.3	6.4
Spokane	7,998	5,205	1,734	884	175	65.1	21.7	11.1	2.2	24	17	20	22	6.2	6.0	6.8	6.7	4.2
Stevens	1,676	1,125	250	255	46	67.1	14.9	15.2	2.7	19	24	3	14	1.3	1.3	1.0	1.9	1.1
Thurston	5,778	3,854	1,216	472	236	66.7	21.0	8.2	4.1	20	19	34	3	4.5	4.4	4.8	3.6	5.7
Wahkiakum	256	149	84	16	7	58.2	32.8	6.3	2.7	35	3	38	15	0.2	0.2	0.3	0.1	0.2
Walla Walla	2,277	1,723	327	179	48	75.7	14.4	7.9	2.1	10	25	36	25	1.8	2.0	1.3	1.3	1.2
Whatcom	2,506	1,801	333	294	78	71.9	13.3	11.7	3.1	13	29	12	7	1.9	2.1	1.3	2.2	1.9
Whitman	741	499	99	121	22	67.3	13.4	16.3	3.0	18	28	2	10	0.6	0.6	0.4	0.9	0.5
Yakima	7,905	6,473	467	794	171	81.9	5.9	10.0	2.2	2	36	25	24	6.1	7.5	1.8	6.0	4.2
WASHINGTON	**129,655**	**86,839**	**25,423**	**13,273**	**4,120**	**67.0**	**19.6**	**10.2**	**3.2**					**100.0**	**100.0**	**100.0**	**100.0**	**100.0**

1992 Vote for President
Percent for Clinton (D), by County

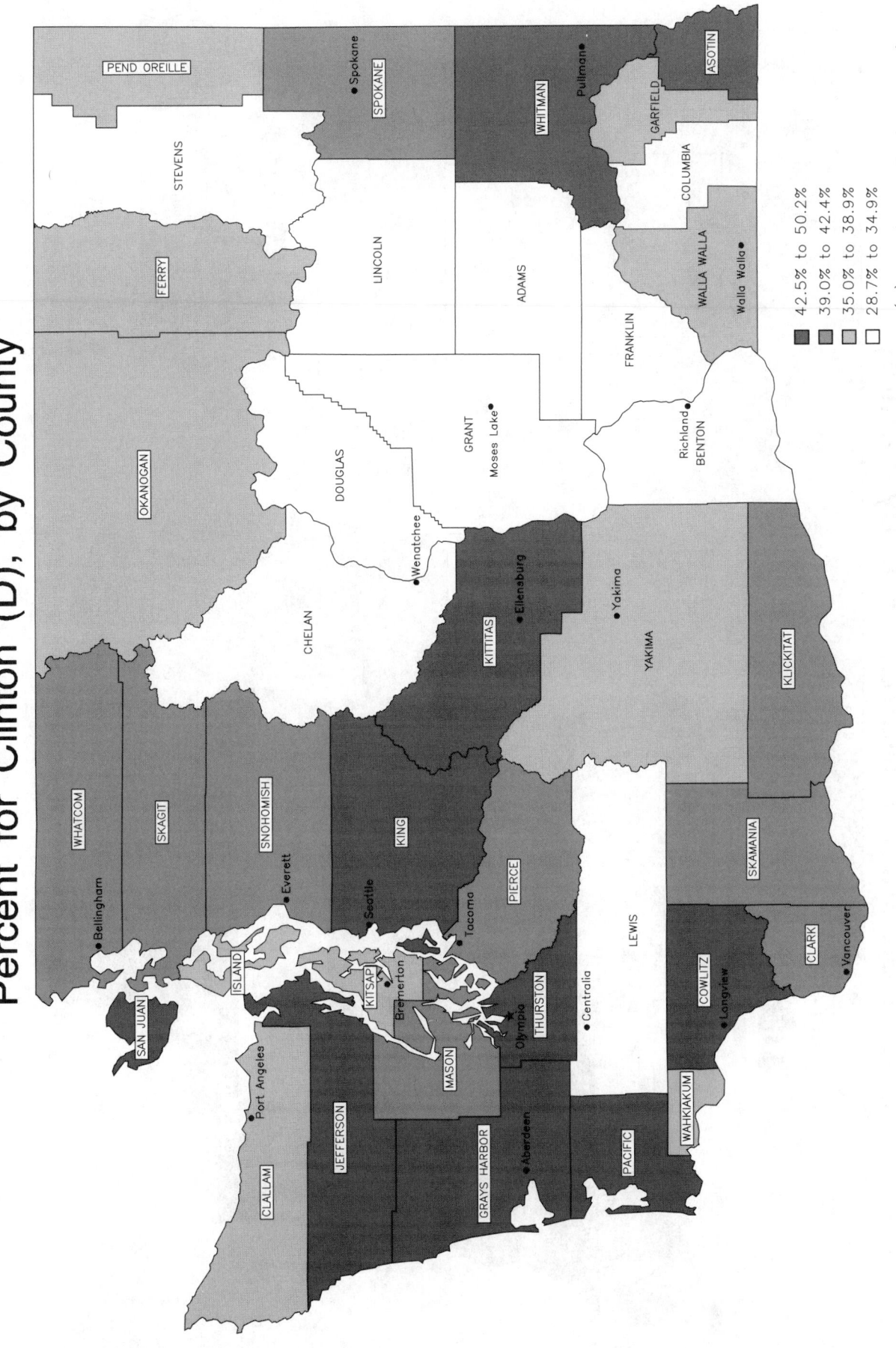

42.5% to 50.2%
39.0% to 42.4%
35.0% to 38.9%
28.7% to 34.9%

Clinton (D) received 43.4% statewide.

A framed county name indicates
a county carried by the winner.

Washington 973

1992 Vote for U.S. Senator
Percent for Murray (D), by County

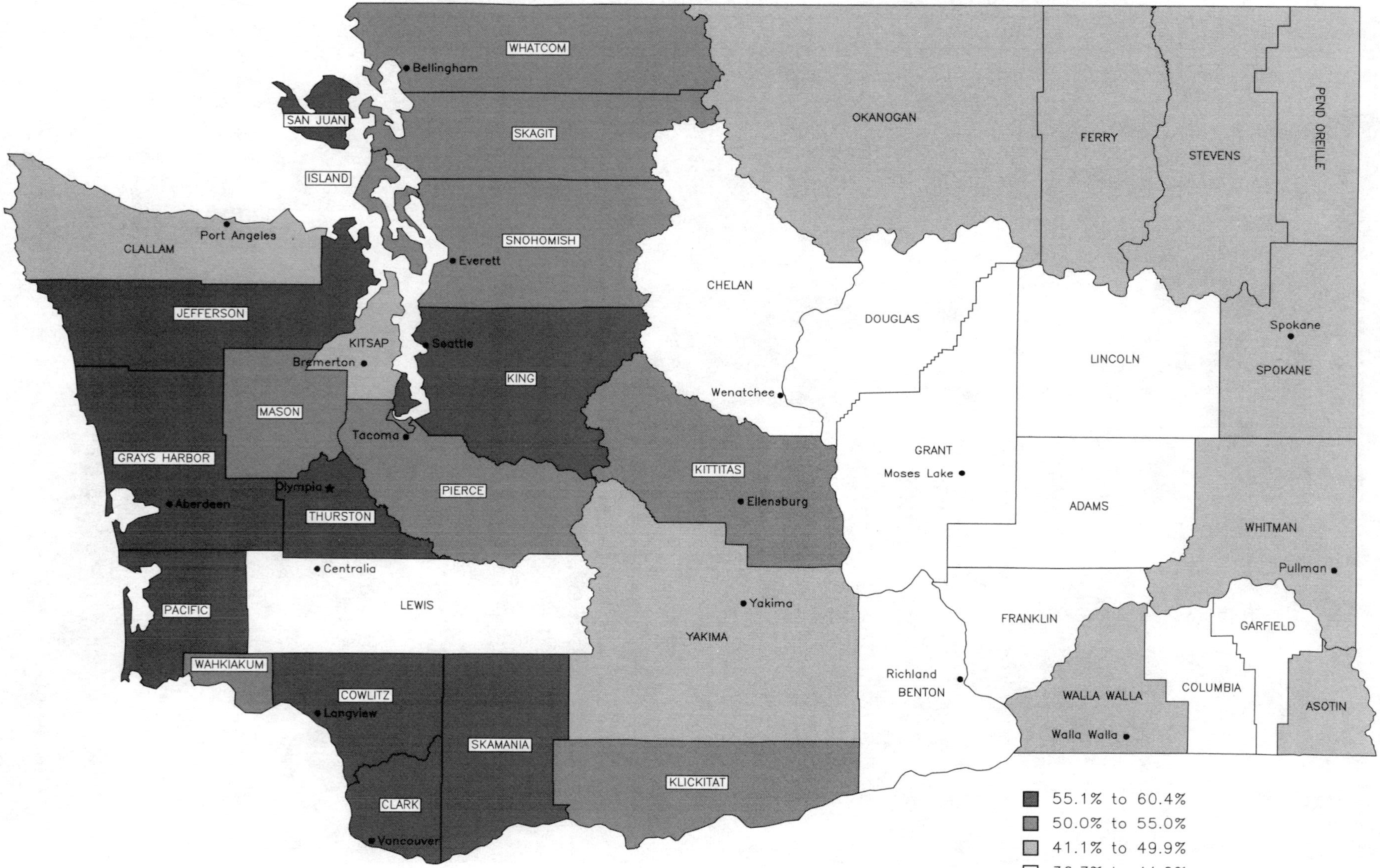

Legend:
- 55.1% to 60.4%
- 50.0% to 55.0%
- 41.1% to 49.9%
- 36.3% to 41.0%

Murray (D) received 54.0% statewide.

A framed county name indicates a county carried by the winner.

PEND OREILLE
STEVENS
FERRY
OKANOGAN
WHATCOM
SKAGIT
SNOHOMISH
SAN JUAN
ISLAND
CLALLAM
JEFFERSON
KITSAP
MASON
KING
GRAYS HARBOR
THURSTON
PACIFIC
WAHKIAKUM
PIERCE
LEWIS
COWLITZ
CLARK
SKAMANIA
KLICKITAT
YAKIMA
KITTITAS
CHELAN
DOUGLAS
LINCOLN
SPOKANE
GRANT
ADAMS
WHITMAN
GARFIELD
COLUMBIA
ASOTIN
FRANKLIN
WALLA WALLA
BENTON

Spokane
Pullman
Walla Walla
Moses Lake
Richland
Wenatchee
Ellensburg
Yakima
Bellingham
Everett
Seattle
Bremerton
Tacoma
Olympia
Centralia
Langview
Vancouver
Aberdeen
Port Angeles

Copyright © 1993 by Election Data Services, Inc.

974 Washington

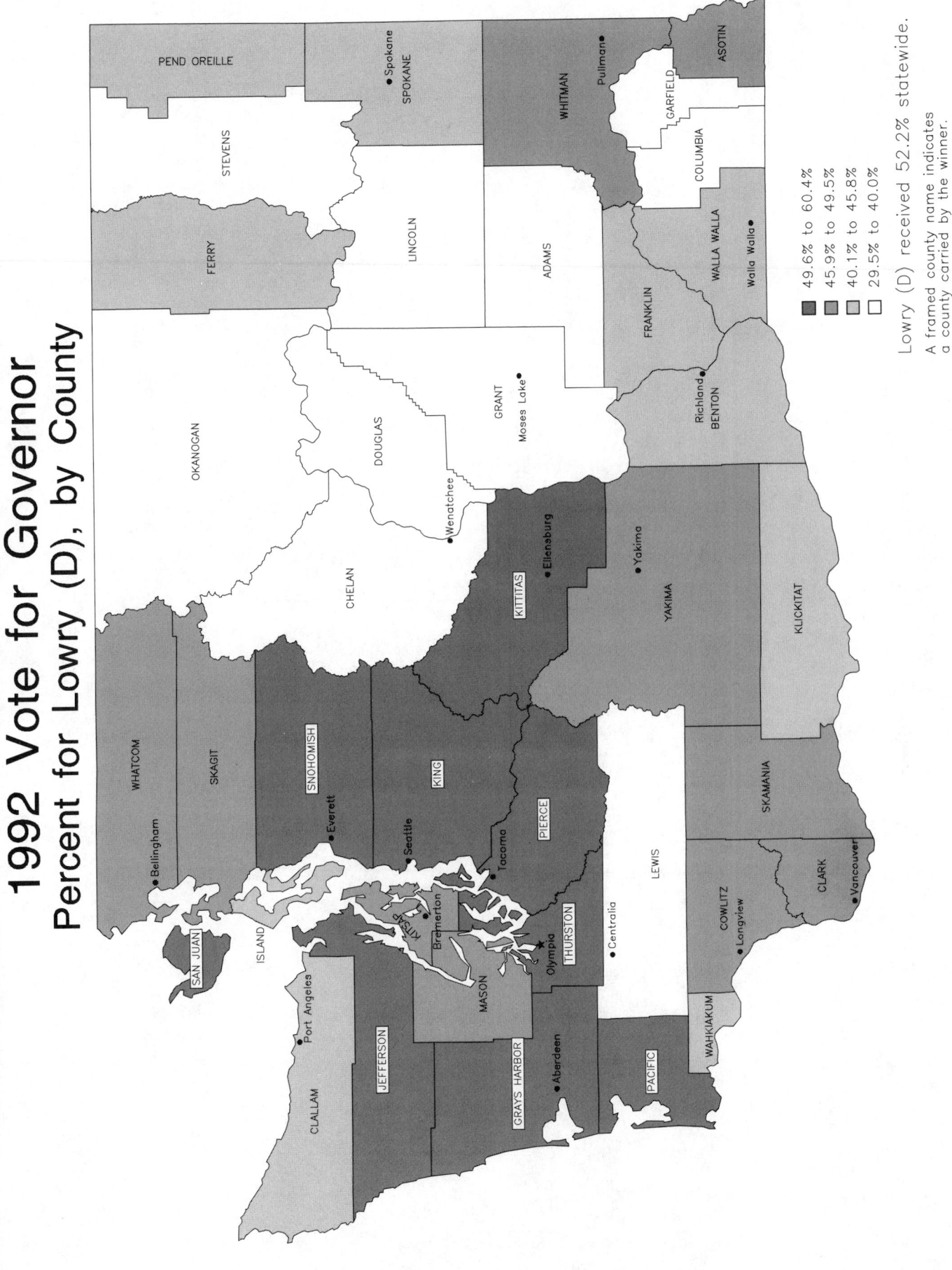

1992 Vote for Governor
Percent for Lowry (D), by County

Lowry (D) received 52.2% statewide.

A framed county name indicates
a county carried by the winner.

49.6% to 60.4%
45.9% to 49.5%
40.1% to 45.8%
29.5% to 40.0%

Washington 975

WEST VIRGINIA

Congressional Districts 3
    Average Population 592,826
State Senate Districts 34
    Average Population 52,749
State House Districts 100
    Average Population 17,935

Electoral College Votes 5
Counties 55
Voting Precincts 2,111

Alternative Registration Methods:
    .... Deputized Registrars, Mail-in, Motor-voter

Registration Deadline (Days before Election) 30

Population Statistics 1990

Race/ Ethnicity	Total Population		Voting Age Population		Voting Age Population % of total population
	Number	%	Number	%	
Non-Hispanic					
White	1,718,896	95.8	1,297,191	96.1	75.5
Black	55,986	3.1	39,762	2.9	71.0
Asian/Pacific Islander	7,252	0.4	5,128	0.4	70.7
Native American	2,363	0.1	1,801	0.1	76.2
Other	491	<.1	116	<.1	23.6
All Hispanic	8,489	0.5	5,902	0.4	69.5
TOTAL	1,793,477	100.0	1,349,900	100.0	75.3

Voting Equipment Use (Counties)

Datavote Punch Card	0	Paper Ballot	29
Electronic	0	Other Punch Card	22
Lever Machine	4	Mixed Systems	0
Optical Scanner	0		

Party Control	DEM	REP	IND	VAC
1993 State Senate	32	2	0	0
1992 State Senate	33	1	0	0
1993 State House	79	21	0	0
1992 State House	74	26	0	0

Estimated Voting Age Population 1992 (VAP) 1,350,000
Number of Registered Voters 956,172
    % of estimated VAP 70.8
Voter Turnout (Highest Office) 683,762
    % of VAP 50.6
    % of Registration 71.5
Persons Not Voting—of Voting Age 666,238
    % of VAP 49.4
Persons Not Voting—of Registered 272,410
    % of Registration 28.5
Straight Ticket Voting .... Yes, Exception

State Officials and Members of Congress

Governor:
Gaston Caperton (D) 1988, elected to a four-year term in 1992.

U.S. Senators:
Robert C. Byrd (D) 1958, elected to a six-year term in 1988.
John D. Rockfeller IV (D) 1984, elected to a six-year term in 1990.

U.S. Representative in Congress:
(District, Name, Party, Date first elected)

1. Mollohan (D) 1982   2. Wise (D) 1982   3. Rahall (D) 1976

Candidates: General Election, November 3, 1992

Candidate(s)	Total vote	Percent	Party	Status	First elected
President/Vice President					
Clinton/Gore	331,001	48.41%	Democrat	Challenger	1992
Bush/Quayle	241,974	35.39%	Republican	Incumbent	1988
Perot/Stockdale	108,829	15.92%	Independent	Challenger	
Marrou/Lord	1,873	0.27%	Libertarian	Challenger	
Write ins	85	0.01%	Write in	Challenger	
U.S. Senator (No Contest)					
Governor					
Gaston Caperton	368,302	56.04%	Democrat	Incumbent	1988
Cleve Benedict	240,390	36.58%	Republican	Challenger	
Charlotte Pritt	48,501	7.38%	Write in	Challenger	
U.S. Representative in Congress					
District 1					
Alan Mollohan	172,924	100.00%	Democrat	Incumbent	1982
District 2					
Bob Wise	143,988	70.90%	Democrat	Incumbent	1982
Samuel Cravotta	59,102	29.10%	Republican	Challenger	
District 3					
Nick Joe Rahall II	122,279	65.64%	Democrat	Incumbent	1976
Ben Waldman	64,012	34.36%	Republican	Challenger	

Candidates: May 12, 1992, Primary Election

Candidate	Total vote	Percent	Candidate	Total vote	Percent
Presidential Preference, Democratic			**Presidential Preference, Republican**		
Bill Clinton	227,815	74.24%	George Bush	99,994	80.54%
Jerry Brown	36,505	11.90%	Patrick Buchanan	18,067	14.55%
Paul Tsongas	21,271	6.93%	Jack Fellure	6,096	4.91%
Angus McDonald	9,632	3.14%			
Bob Kerrey	3,152	1.03%			
Lyndon LaRouche, Jr.	3,141	1.02%			
Tom Harkin	2,774	0.90%			
Charles Woods	1,487	0.48%			
Ralph Spelbring	1,089	0.35%			

Voter Registration and Turnout, 1948-1992 Elections

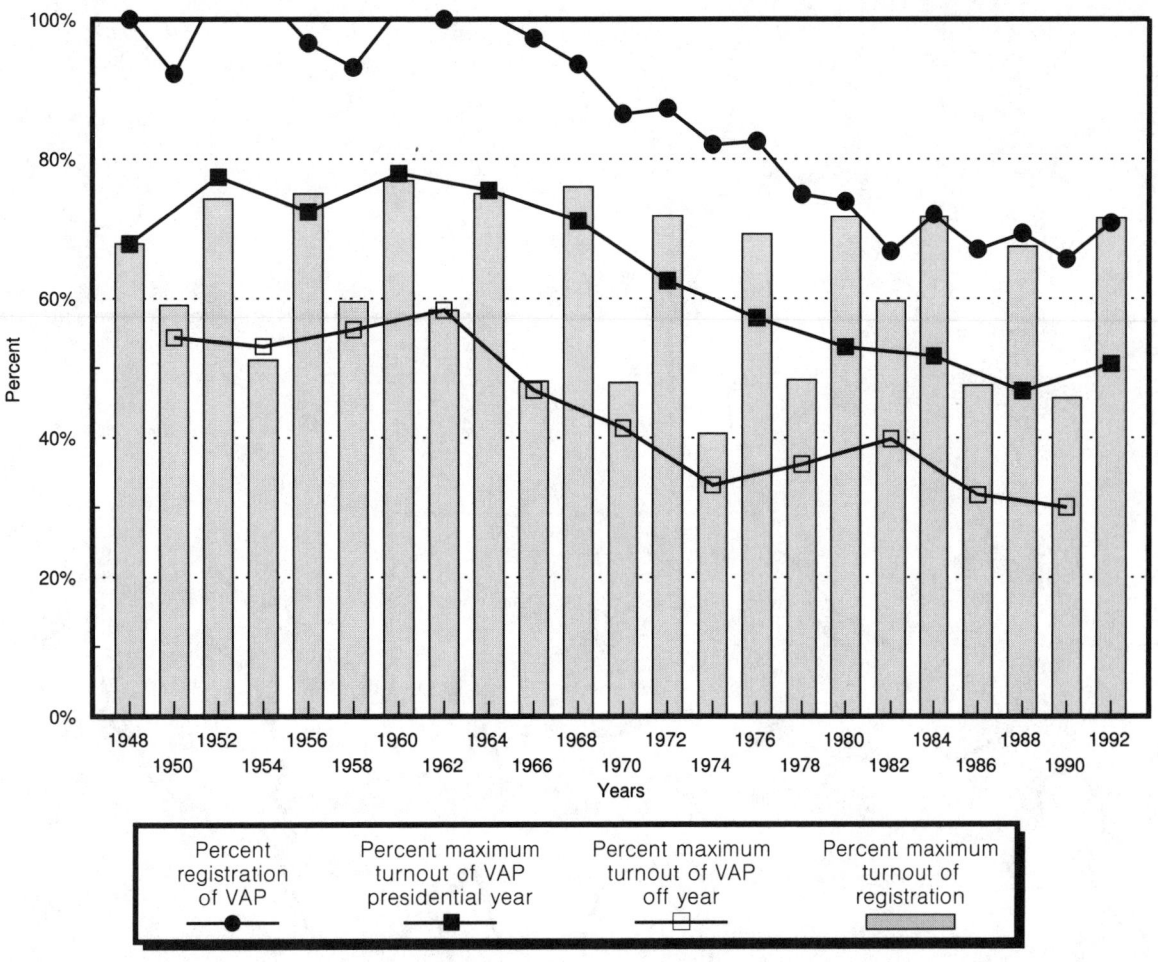

Percent registration of VAP	Percent maximum turnout of VAP presidential year	Percent maximum turnout of VAP off year	Percent maximum turnout of registration

Year	Estimated Voting Age Population (VAP)	Voter registration (REG)				Voter turnout										
						Highest office						Maximum vote				
		Total	Percent of VAP	Rank by percent of VAP	Actual	Total	Office	Percent total REG	Rank by percent of REG	Percent of VAP	Rank by percent of VAP	Total	Percent total REG	Rank by percent of REG	Percent total VAP	Rank by percent of VAP
1992	1,350,000	956,172	70.8	35	-	683,762	P	71.5	42	50.6	42	683,762	71.5	42	50.6	44
1990	1,349,000	884,839	65.6	32	-	404,305	S	45.7	43	30.0	46	404,305	45.7	45	30.0	48
1988	1,398,000	968,619	69.3	30	-	653,311	P	67.4	38	46.7	40	653,311	67.4	38	46.7	41
1986	1,412,000	946,039	67.0	30	449,249	410,131	R	43.4	45	29.0	45	449,249	47.5	41	31.8	43
1984	1,424,000	1,025,444	72.0	28	-	735,742	P	71.7	31	51.7	34	735,742	71.7	36	51.7	37
1982	1,422,000	948,329	66.7	29	-	565,314	S	59.6	33	39.8	35	565,314	59.6	34	39.8	36
1980	1,400,000	1,034,546	73.9	23	742,150	737,715	P	71.3	34	52.7	30	742,150	71.7	35	53.0	31
1978	1,363,000	1,020,892	74.9	14	-	493,351	S	48.3	41	36.2	36	493,351	48.3	41	36.2	38
1976	1,314,000	1,084,451	82.5	10	-	750,964	P	69.2	37	57.2	25	750,964	69.2	37	57.2	27
1974	1,250,000	1,024,688	82.0	6	-	415,518	C	40.6	43	33.2	40	415,514	40.6	43	33.2	40
1972	1,219,000	1,062,519	87.2	6	-	762,399	P	71.8	30	62.5	12	762,399	71.8	31	62.5	17
1970	1,077,000	930,968	86.4	8	-	445,623	S	47.9	42	41.4	39	445,623	47.9	42	41.4	39
1968	1,061,000	993,024	93.6	4	-	754,206	P	76.0	33	71.1	5	754,206	76.0	33	71.1	7
1966	1,049,000	1,020,723	97.3	2	-	491,216	S	48.1	39	46.8	34	491,216	48.1	39	46.8	34
1964[1]	1,049,000	1,055,429	100.6	2	-	792,040	P	75.0	30	75.5	4	792,040	75.0	30	75.5	4
1962[1]	1,051,000	1,051,139	100.0	2	-	613,018	C	58.3	30	58.3	15	613,018	58.3	30	58.3	16
1960[1]	1,075,000	1,090,042	101.4	1	-	837,781	P	76.9	29	77.9	5	837,781	76.9	29	77.9	7
1958	1,163,000	1,083,144	93.1	1	-	644,917	S	59.5	24	55.5	19	644,917	59.5	24	55.5	21
1956	1,147,000	1,107,453	96.6	2	-	830,831	P	75.0	23	72.4	10	830,831	75.0	24	72.4	11
1954[1]	1,118,000	1,160,434	103.8	1	-	593,329	S	51.1	21	53.1	17	593,329	51.1	21	53.1	20
1952[1]	1,128,000	1,176,428	104.3	1	-	873,548	P	74.3	22	77.4	5	873,548	74.3	22	77.4	6
1950	1,172,000	1,080,113	92.2	2	-	662,836	C	61.4	15	56.6	11	662,836	61.4	16	56.6	12
1948	1,104,000	1,103,928	100.0	1	-	748,750	P	67.8	18	67.8	6	748,750	67.8	18	67.8	8

[1]Total voter registration reported by West Virginia Secretary of State exceeds estimated voting age population (VAP).

WEST VIRGINIA

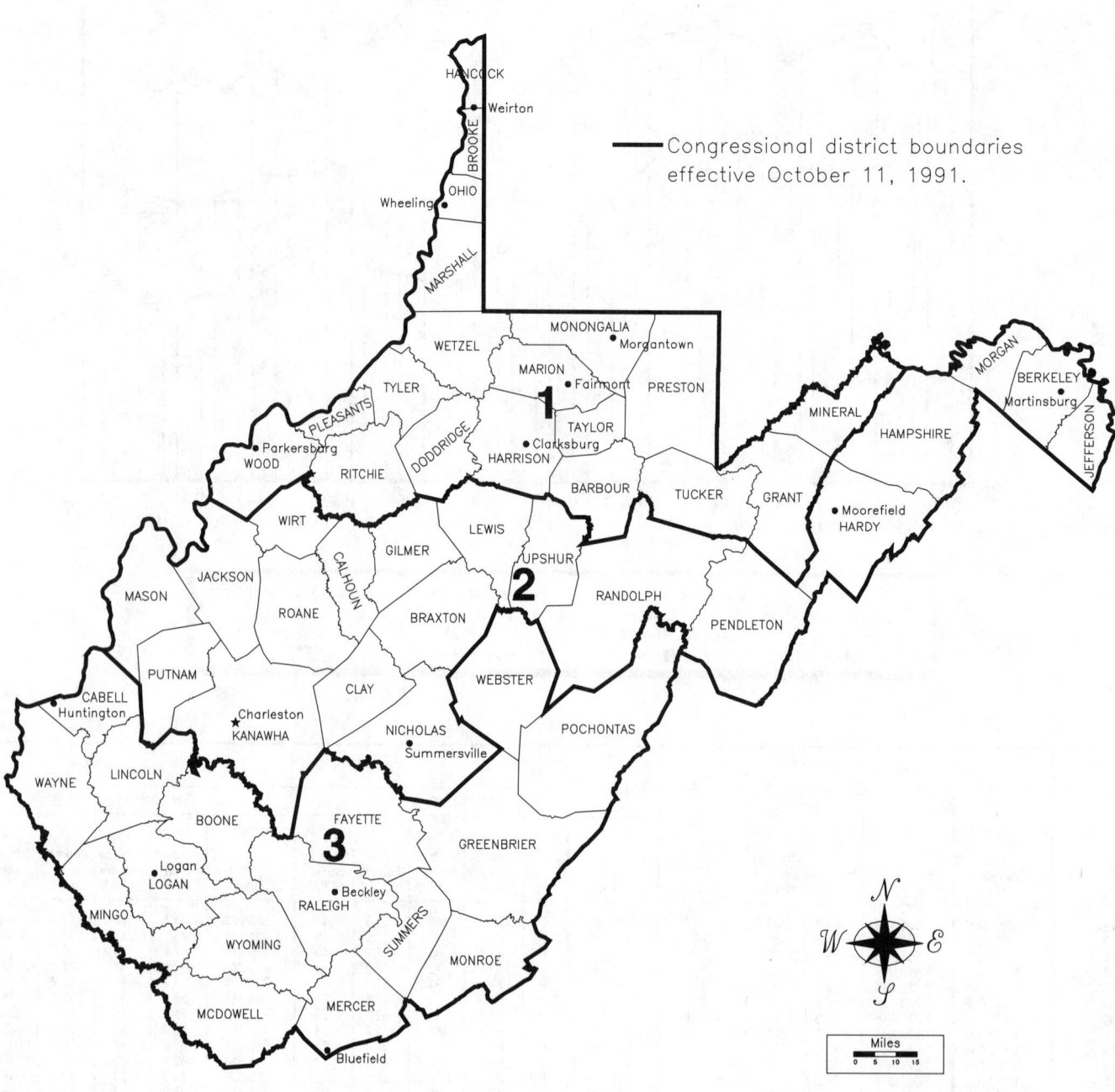

—Congressional district boundaries effective October 11, 1991.

Table A. — 1990 Population by Race and Ethnic Origin

State/county code	County	Total persons	Percent of total persons Non-Hispanic White	Black	Asian and Pacific Islander	Native American	Other	Hispanic	Rank Percent of total persons Total	Non-Hispanic White	Black	Hispanic	Percent contribution to state population Total	Non-Hispanic White	Black	Hispanic
54 001	Barbour	15,699	97.2	0.9	0.2	1.0	<.1	0.6	35	37	23	8	0.9	0.9	0.3	1.0
54 003	Berkeley	59,253	95.0	3.7	0.5	0.1	<.1	0.7	8	46	9	5	3.3	3.3	3.9	4.7
54 005	Boone	25,870	98.8	0.8	<.1	0.1	<.1	0.2	28	21	25	50	1.4	1.5	0.4	0.6
54 007	Braxton	12,998	99.0	0.4	0.2	0.1	<.1	0.3	39	17	37	37	0.7	0.7	<.1	0.4
54 009	Brooke	26,992	98.6	0.7	0.2	0.1	<.1	0.3	24	27	30	32	1.5	1.5	0.4	1.0
54 011	Cabell	96,827	94.8	4.1	0.5	0.1	<.1	0.5	2	47	8	17	5.4	5.3	7.1	5.2
54 013	Calhoun	7,885	99.2	<.1	0.4	0.2	<.1	0.2	50	16	53	43	0.4	0.5	<.1	0.2
54 015	Clay	9,983	99.7	<.1	<.1	<.1	0.0	0.1	46	3	55	52	0.6	0.6	<.1	0.2
54 017	Doddridge	6,994	99.2	<.1	0.1	0.4	0.0	0.2	54	15	49	51	0.4	0.4	<.1	0.1
54 019	Fayette	47,952	92.8	6.3	0.3	0.1	<.1	0.5	11	50	6	12	2.7	2.6	5.4	3.0
54 021	Gilmer	7,669	98.7	0.4	0.4	0.1	<.1	0.3	52	22	36	33	0.4	0.4	<.1	0.3
54 023	Grant	10,428	98.2	1.0	0.2	0.2	<.1	0.3	44	33	22	29	0.6	0.6	0.2	0.4
54 025	Greenbrier	34,693	95.7	3.6	0.2	0.1	<.1	0.4	19	45	10	23	1.9	1.9	2.3	1.6
54 027	Hampshire	16,498	98.5	0.7	<.1	0.2	<.1	0.6	34	29	31	10	0.9	0.9	0.2	1.1
54 029	Hancock	35,233	96.4	2.6	0.3	0.1	<.1	0.6	17	41	15	9	2.0	2.0	1.6	2.3
54 031	Hardy	10,977	97.4	1.9	<.1	0.1	<.1	0.5	42	36	19	15	0.6	0.6	0.4	0.6
54 033	Harrison	69,371	97.0	1.4	0.2	0.1	<.1	1.2	6	38	20	3	3.9	3.9	1.7	9.6
54 035	Jackson	25,938	99.3	<.1	0.2	0.1	0.0	0.3	27	13	45	41	1.4	1.5	<.1	0.8
54 037	Jefferson	35,926	90.9	7.3	0.4	0.2	<.1	1.2	16	54	3	2	2.0	1.9	4.7	5.0
54 039	Kanawha	207,619	92.2	6.6	0.6	0.1	<.1	0.4	1	52	4	18	11.6	11.1	24.5	10.6
54 041	Lewis	17,223	98.9	0.3	0.2	0.1	<.1	0.4	33	18	39	24	1.0	1.0	<.1	0.8
54 043	Lincoln	21,382	99.6	<.1	<.1	<.1	0.0	0.2	31	4	50	45	1.2	1.2	<.1	0.6
54 045	Logan	43,032	95.7	3.1	0.4	0.1	<.1	0.7	12	43	13	6	2.4	2.4	2.4	3.3
54 047	McDowell	35,233	85.9	13.4	<.1	<.1	<.1	0.5	18	55	1	14	2.0	1.8	8.5	2.1
54 049	Marion	57,249	95.7	3.2	0.3	0.2	<.1	0.5	9	42	12	11	3.2	3.2	3.3	3.7
54 051	Marshall	37,356	98.5	0.5	0.2	<.1	<.1	0.6	15	28	33	7	2.1	2.1	0.4	2.7
54 053	Mason	25,178	98.9	0.4	0.3	0.1	<.1	0.2	29	20	35	47	1.4	1.4	0.2	0.6
54 055	Mercer	64,980	92.6	6.3	0.5	0.1	<.1	0.4	7	51	5	21	3.6	3.5	7.4	3.2
54 057	Mineral	26,697	96.6	2.7	0.2	<.1	<.1	0.4	26	40	14	25	1.5	1.5	1.3	1.2
54 059	Mingo	33,739	96.9	2.4	0.2	<.1	<.1	0.4	20	39	16	26	1.9	1.9	1.5	1.5
54 061	Monongalia	75,509	94.5	2.4	2.1	0.2	<.1	0.8	5	48	17	4	4.2	4.1	3.2	7.5
54 063	Monroe	12,406	98.1	1.3	<.1	0.2	0.0	0.3	40	34	21	31	0.7	0.7	0.3	0.5
54 065	Morgan	12,128	98.5	0.8	0.1	0.2	<.1	0.4	41	30	29	22	0.7	0.7	0.2	0.6
54 067	Nicholas	26,775	99.5	<.1	0.2	0.1	<.1	0.2	25	9	54	46	1.5	1.5	<.1	0.7
54 069	Ohio	50,871	95.7	3.3	0.6	<.1	<.1	0.3	10	44	11	36	2.8	2.8	3.0	1.7
54 071	Pendleton	8,054	97.5	2.0	0.1	<.1	0.0	0.3	49	35	18	30	0.4	0.5	0.3	0.3
54 073	Pleasants	7,546	99.5	0.2	<.1	<.1	<.1	0.1	53	8	41	53	0.4	0.4	<.1	0.1
54 075	Pocahontas	9,008	98.7	0.8	<.1	0.1	0.0	0.3	48	23	28	27	0.5	0.5	0.1	0.4
54 077	Preston	29,037	99.3	0.3	<.1	<.1	<.1	0.3	21	14	40	40	1.6	1.7	0.1	0.9
54 079	Putnam	42,835	98.9	0.3	0.3	0.1	<.1	0.3	13	19	38	28	2.4	2.5	0.2	1.7
54 081	Raleigh	76,819	91.3	7.6	0.5	0.1	<.1	0.4	4	53	2	20	4.3	4.1	10.5	3.8
54 083	Randolph	27,803	98.3	0.8	0.3	0.1	<.1	0.5	23	31	27	13	1.6	1.6	0.4	1.7
54 085	Ritchie	10,233	99.7	<.1	<.1	<.1	<.1	<.1	45	2	44	54	0.6	0.6	<.1	<.1
54 087	Roane	15,120	99.4	<.1	0.2	0.2	<.1	0.2	37	12	52	42	0.8	0.9	<.1	0.4
54 089	Summers	14,204	93.1	4.9	0.2	0.2	<.1	1.5	38	49	7	1	0.8	0.8	1.2	2.5
54 091	Taylor	15,144	98.6	0.6	0.2	0.1	<.1	0.4	36	25	32	19	0.8	0.9	0.2	0.8
54 093	Tucker	7,728	99.5	<.1	0.2	<.1	<.1	0.2	51	6	46	48	0.4	0.4	<.1	0.2
54 095	Tyler	9,796	99.4	<.1	0.1	0.2	0.0	0.2	47	10	48	44	0.5	0.6	<.1	0.3
54 097	Upshur	22,867	98.6	0.5	0.2	0.2	0.0	0.5	30	26	34	16	1.3	1.3	0.2	1.3
54 099	Wayne	41,636	99.4	<.1	0.1	0.2	<.1	0.3	14	11	47	38	2.3	2.4	<.1	1.3
54 101	Webster	10,729	99.5	<.1	<.1	<.1	<.1	0.3	43	5	51	39	0.6	0.6	<.1	0.3
54 103	Wetzel	19,258	99.5	<.1	0.2	<.1	0.0	0.2	32	7	42	49	1.1	1.1	<.1	0.4
54 105	Wirt	5,192	99.8	<.1	<.1	0.0	0.0	<.1	55	1	43	55	0.3	0.3	<.1	<.1
54 107	Wood	86,915	98.2	0.9	0.4	0.1	<.1	0.3	3	32	24	35	4.8	5.0	1.4	3.0
54 109	Wyoming	28,990	98.7	0.8	<.1	0.1	<.1	0.3	22	24	26	34	1.6	1.7	0.4	1.0
54	**WEST VIRGINIA**	**1,793,477**	**95.8**	**3.1**	**0.4**	**0.1**	**<.1**	**0.5**					**100.0**	**100.0**	**100.0**	**100.0**
	CONGRESSIONAL															
	District 1	598,056	97.2	1.6	0.5	0.2	<.1	0.5	1	1	3	1	33.3	33.8	17.1	37.1
	District 2	597,921	95.7	3.3	0.4	0.1	<.1	0.5	2	2	2	2	33.3	33.3	35.5	32.1
	District 3	597,500	94.7	4.4	0.3	0.1	<.1	0.4	3	3	1	3	33.3	32.9	47.4	30.8

Table B. — 1990 Voting Age Population (VAP) by Race and Ethnic Origin

County	Total Voting Age Population	Percent of total VAP — White (Non-Hisp)	Black (Non-Hisp)	Asian and Pacific Islander (Non-Hisp)	Native American (Non-Hisp)	Other (Non-Hisp)	Hispanic	Rank Total	Rank White (Non-Hisp)	Rank Black (Non-Hisp)	Rank Hispanic	% contrib Total	White (Non-Hisp)	Black (Non-Hisp)	Hispanic	VAP % Total	White (Non-Hisp)	Black (Non-Hisp)	Asian and Pacific Islander (Non-Hisp)	Native American (Non-Hisp)	Other (Non-Hisp)	Hispanic
Barbour	11,733	97.3	1.0	0.2	0.9	<.1	0.5	35	37	23	8	0.9	0.9	0.3	1.1	74.7	74.8	76.9	62.9	68.8	63.6	71.9
Berkeley	43,794	95.3	3.5	0.4	0.1	<.1	0.6	9	46	10	7	3.2	3.2	3.9	4.3	73.9	74.2	70.5	65.2	76.5	21.4	63.2
Boone	18,864	98.9	0.8	<.1	0.1	<.1	0.2	28	21	29	47	1.4	1.4	0.4	0.5	72.9	73.0	66.4	78.9	79.3	12.5	62.5
Braxton	9,633	99.2	0.4	0.1	0.1	<.1	0.2	39	16	37	48	0.7	0.7	<.1	0.3	74.1	74.2	84.8	52.2	76.5	33.3	40.5
Brooke	20,902	98.6	0.7	0.2	<.1	<.1	0.3	23	26	30	29	1.5	1.6	0.4	1.1	77.4	77.5	76.1	78.3	62.1	33.3	72.9
Cabell	75,656	95.2	3.8	0.5	0.1	<.1	0.4	2	47	8	18	5.6	5.6	7.2	5.1	78.1	78.5	72.0	72.1	84.3	24.3	68.1
Calhoun	5,746	99.2	<.1	0.4	0.2	<.1	0.2	52	17	48	41	0.4	0.4	<.1	0.2	72.9	72.9	100.0	73.3	85.7	33.3	61.1
Clay	7,000	99.7	<.1	<.1	0.1	0.0	0.1	47	3	53	52	0.5	0.5	<.1	0.2	70.1	70.1	100.0	66.7	100.0	0.0	71.4
Doddridge	5,121	99.4	<.1	0.1	0.3	0.0	0.2	54	15	51	49	0.4	0.4	<.1	0.1	73.2	73.3	50.0	87.5	51.6	0.0	66.7
Fayette	35,866	93.0	6.1	0.3	0.1	<.1	0.5	11	50	4	14	2.7	2.6	5.5	2.8	74.8	74.9	73.1	84.7	75.0	14.3	66.7
Gilmer	5,896	98.6	0.5	0.5	0.1	0.0	0.3	50	27	35	32	0.4	0.4	<.1	0.3	76.9	76.8	84.4	96.8	100.0	0.0	70.8
Grant	7,784	98.3	1.0	0.1	0.2	0.0	0.3	44	32	22	33	0.6	0.6	0.2	0.4	74.6	74.7	76.4	52.6	77.3	0.0	62.9
Greenbrier	26,423	95.8	3.5	0.2	0.1	<.1	0.4	18	44	9	20	2.0	2.0	2.4	1.7	76.2	76.3	73.9	70.7	85.7	25.0	74.5
Hampshire	12,108	98.7	0.6	<.1	0.2	0.0	0.5	34	25	32	15	0.9	0.9	0.2	0.9	73.4	73.5	66.1	75.0	73.3	0.0	60.2
Hancock	27,158	96.6	2.5	0.3	0.1	<.1	0.5	16	41	15	11	2.0	2.0	1.7	2.3	77.1	77.2	75.3	69.6	72.5	12.5	67.8
Hardy	8,359	97.5	1.9	<.1	0.1	<.1	0.5	42	36	19	12	0.6	0.6	0.4	0.7	76.2	76.2	75.1	80.0	84.6	100.0	72.7
Harrison	52,329	97.2	1.3	0.2	0.1	<.1	1.2	6	38	21	2	3.9	3.9	1.7	10.3	75.4	75.5	71.0	65.3	78.2	35.7	74.1
Jackson	19,175	99.5	<.1	0.2	0.1	0.0	0.2	27	10	46	46	1.4	1.5	<.1	0.5	73.9	74.0	66.7	66.7	63.9	0.0	47.7
Jefferson	26,731	91.5	6.9	0.4	0.2	<.1	1.1	17	54	3	3	2.0	1.9	4.6	4.8	74.4	74.9	70.2	72.3	79.6	31.6	65.7
Kanawha	159,369	92.9	6.0	0.5	0.1	<.1	0.4	1	51	5	22	11.8	11.4	24.2	10.1	76.8	77.4	70.0	64.4	79.8	19.6	66.7
Lewis	13,063	99.0	0.3	0.2	0.2	<.1	0.4	33	20	38	24	1.0	1.0	0.1	0.8	75.8	75.9	85.4	58.1	87.5	33.3	70.1
Lincoln	15,403	99.6	<.1	<.1	0.1	<.1	0.2	31	5	50	40	1.1	1.2	<.1	0.6	72.0	72.0	66.7	56.3	81.3	0.0	70.8
Logan	31,063	95.7	3.2	0.4	0.1	0.0	0.6	13	45	11	5	2.3	2.3	2.5	3.2	72.2	72.2	73.3	62.1	73.9	0.0	66.5
McDowell	25,045	86.2	13.2	<.1	<.1	<.1	0.5	19	55	1	10	1.9	1.7	8.3	2.2	71.1	71.3	69.7	50.0	72.7	100.0	69.8
Marion	44,282	96.0	3.0	0.2	0.2	<.1	0.5	8	43	12	9	3.3	3.3	3.4	3.9	77.3	77.6	72.5	67.6	79.3	18.8	74.3
Marshall	28,229	98.5	0.6	0.2	<.1	<.1	0.6	15	28	34	6	2.1	2.1	0.4	2.8	75.6	75.6	77.8	73.2	71.9	30.0	72.9
Mason	18,658	99.0	0.4	0.3	0.1	0.0	0.1	29	19	36	50	1.4	1.4	0.2	0.5	74.1	74.2	72.3	71.3	76.9	0.0	50.9
Mercer	49,372	93.2	5.8	0.4	0.1	<.1	0.4	7	49	6	17	3.7	3.5	7.2	3.5	76.0	76.5	69.5	69.1	67.9	23.1	76.6
Mineral	20,007	96.8	2.6	0.2	<.1	0.0	0.3	25	40	14	25	1.5	1.5	1.3	1.2	74.9	75.1	72.0	57.4	75.0	0.0	67.3
Mingo	23,473	97.0	2.5	0.1	<.1	<.1	0.3	20	39	16	26	1.7	1.8	1.5	1.3	69.6	69.6	70.2	56.5	95.2	25.0	61.3
Monongalia	60,466	94.5	2.3	2.2	0.2	<.1	0.9	4	48	17	4	4.5	4.4	3.5	8.9	80.1	80.1	77.4	82.8	83.1	17.8	82.7
Monroe	9,359	98.1	1.3	<.1	0.2	0.0	0.3	40	34	20	35	0.7	0.7	0.3	0.4	75.4	75.4	79.2	100.0	64.0	0.0	61.0
Morgan	9,359	98.5	0.8	0.1	0.2	<.1	0.4	41	31	25	21	0.7	0.7	0.2	0.6	77.2	77.2	83.5	66.7	76.2	25.0	72.0
Nicholas	19,423	99.5	<.1	0.1	0.1	0.0	0.2	26	7	55	45	1.4	1.5	<.1	0.5	72.5	72.6	50.0	56.9	78.1	0.0	56.1
Ohio	39,709	96.3	2.8	0.6	<.1	0.0	0.3	10	42	13	34	2.9	2.9	2.8	1.9	78.1	78.6	65.8	69.9	83.9	0.0	76.0
Pendleton	6,117	97.6	1.9	<.1	<.1	0.0	0.3	49	35	18	28	0.5	0.5	0.3	0.3	75.9	76.1	71.5	50.0	100.0	0.0	70.4
Pleasants	5,613	99.5	0.3	<.1	<.1	<.1	0.1	53	9	39	53	0.4	0.4	<.1	0.1	74.4	74.4	88.2	50.0	71.4	16.7	77.8
Pocahontas	6,917	98.7	0.8	<.1	0.2	0.0	0.3	48	24	27	27	0.5	0.5	0.1	0.4	76.8	76.8	81.2	100.0	84.6	0.0	71.0
Preston	21,150	99.4	0.2	<.1	<.1	0.0	0.2	21	14	41	39	1.6	1.6	0.1	0.8	72.8	72.9	68.5	44.8	76.9	0.0	62.3
Putnam	31,373	99.1	0.3	0.3	0.1	0.0	0.3	12	18	40	30	2.3	2.4	0.2	1.6	73.2	73.4	64.3	57.9	64.0	0.0	64.1
Raleigh	56,761	91.9	7.1	0.5	0.1	<.1	0.4	5	53	2	19	4.2	4.0	10.1	3.8	73.9	74.4	68.5	67.7	81.7	29.2	69.7
Randolph	21,088	98.3	0.9	0.3	0.1	<.1	0.5	22	33	24	13	1.6	1.6	0.5	1.7	75.8	75.8	83.3	72.6	78.8	33.3	69.4
Ritchie	7,731	99.8	<.1	<.1	<.1	0.0	<.1	45	2	44	54	0.6	0.6	<.1	0.1	75.5	75.6	71.4	44.4	100.0	0.0	85.7
Roane	11,063	99.4	<.1	0.2	0.2	<.1	0.1	37	13	52	51	0.8	0.8	<.1	0.3	73.2	73.2	50.0	89.3	87.0	100.0	43.2
Summers	10,883	92.3	5.6	0.2	0.2	<.1	1.7	38	52	7	1	0.8	0.8	1.5	3.1	76.6	75.9	86.7	77.4	78.8	66.7	86.3
Taylor	11,301	98.7	0.7	0.1	0.1	<.1	0.4	36	22	31	23	0.8	0.9	0.2	0.7	74.6	74.7	80.0	51.9	88.9	100.0	65.6
Tucker	5,868	99.6	<.1	<.1	<.1	0.0	0.2	51	4	49	43	0.4	0.5	<.1	0.2	75.9	76.0	50.0	53.8	50.0	0.0	62.5
Tyler	7,298	99.4	<.1	0.2	0.2	0.0	0.2	46	12	45	42	0.5	0.6	<.1	0.2	74.5	74.5	100.0	78.6	81.3	0.0	59.1
Upshur	17,062	98.5	0.6	0.3	0.2	0.0	0.4	30	29	33	16	1.3	1.3	0.2	1.3	74.6	74.6	83.9	89.3	65.9	0.0	67.9
Wayne	30,947	99.4	<.1	0.1	0.1	0.0	0.3	14	11	47	36	2.3	2.4	<.1	1.4	74.3	74.4	73.7	76.6	58.9	0.0	70.2
Webster	7,795	99.6	<.1	<.1	<.1	<.1	0.2	43	6	54	37	0.6	0.6	<.1	0.3	72.7	72.7	33.3	75.0	62.5	40.0	62.1
Wetzel	14,301	99.5	<.1	0.2	<.1	0.0	0.2	32	8	43	44	1.1	1.1	<.1	0.4	74.3	74.3	68.8	69.2	83.3	0.0	64.9
Wirt	3,808	99.8	<.1	<.1	0.0	0.0	<.1	55	1	42	55	0.3	0.3	<.1	<.1	73.3	73.3	75.0	75.0	0.0	0.0	66.7
Wood	65,570	98.5	0.8	0.3	0.1	<.1	0.2	3	30	28	38	4.9	5.0	1.3	2.6	75.4	75.6	65.1	63.3	75.6	34.2	59.4
Wyoming	20,696	98.7	0.8	<.1	0.1	<.1	0.3	24	23	26	31	1.5	1.6	0.4	1.0	71.4	71.4	71.8	48.0	79.5	66.7	69.3
WEST VIRGINIA	**1,349,900**	**96.1**	**2.9**	**0.4**	**0.1**	**<.1**	**0.4**					**100.0**	**100.0**	**100.0**	**100.0**	**75.3**	**75.5**	**71.0**	**70.7**	**76.2**	**23.6**	**69.5**
CONGRESSIONAL																						
District 1	456,552	97.3	1.5	0.5	0.1	<.1	0.5	1	1	3	1	33.8	34.3	17.4	39.0	76.3	76.5	72.1	74.8	75.3	23.5	73.1
District 2	448,825	96.0	3.1	0.3	0.1	<.1	0.4	2	2	2	3	33.2	33.2	35.2	29.8	75.1	75.3	70.5	66.2	77.3	21.9	64.6
District 3	444,523	94.9	4.2	0.3	0.1	<.1	0.4	3	3	1	2	32.9	32.5	47.4	31.2	74.4	74.6	71.1	69.7	76.3	26.5	70.4

Table C. — Voter Participation: November 3, 1992, General Election

| County | Estimated Voting Age Population (VAP), 1992 | Voter registration (REG) | | | | Actual | Voter turnout | | | | | | | | | | | | |
| | | Total | % contribution to state REG | % of 1992 VAP | Rank by % of 1992 VAP | | Highest office | | | Maximum vote | | | | | | Percent drop-off, by office[1] | | | |
							Total	Office	% of 1992 VAP	Total	% contribution to state turnout	% of REG	Rank by % of REG	% of 1992 VAP	Rank by % 1992 VAP	President	Senator	Governor	Representative
Barbour	11,715	9,115	1.0	77.8	13	-	6,954	P	59.4	6,954	1.0	76.3	15	59.4	5	0.0	-	1.8	32.2
Berkeley	47,336	27,937	2.9	59.0	53	-	20,029	P	42.3	20,029	2.9	71.7	33	42.3	53	0.0	-	5.6	11.5
Boone	19,010	14,477	1.5	76.2	18	-	9,658	P	50.8	9,658	1.4	66.7	48	50.8	36	0.0	-	4.0	14.4
Braxton	9,707	7,778	0.8	80.1	9	-	5,765	P	59.4	5,765	0.8	74.1	25	59.4	4	0.0	-	2.8	11.3
Brooke	20,483	13,919	1.5	68.0	41	-	10,415	P	50.8	10,415	1.5	74.8	20	50.8	35	0.0	-	4.8	21.0
Cabell	74,207	49,310	5.2	66.4	44	-	33,725	P	45.4	33,725	4.9	68.4	44	45.4	47	0.0	-	3.9	13.9
Calhoun	5,846	4,678	0.5	80.0	10	-	3,268	P	55.9	3,268	0.5	69.9	39	55.9	15	0.0	-	4.3	14.5
Clay	7,042	5,678	0.6	80.6	5	-	3,657	P	51.9	3,657	0.5	64.4	51	51.9	33	0.0	-	2.9	11.2
Doddridge	5,170	3,937	0.4	76.2	19	-	2,992	P	57.9	2,992	0.4	76.0	18	57.9	10	0.0	-	2.5	37.5
Fayette	35,281	22,215	2.3	63.0	50	-	15,608	P	44.2	15,608	2.3	70.3	36	44.2	50	0.0	-	3.3	11.4
Gilmer	5,707	4,361	0.5	76.4	16	-	3,154	P	55.3	3,154	0.5	72.3	31	55.3	18	0.0	-	2.5	9.2
Grant	8,003	5,964	0.6	74.5	23	-	4,298	P	53.7	4,298	0.6	72.1	32	53.7	25	0.0	-	3.5	66.2
Greenbrier	26,324	16,308	1.7	62.0	51	-	12,187	P	46.3	12,187	1.8	74.7	21	46.3	45	0.0	-	4.4	8.2
Hampshire	12,681	7,773	0.8	61.3	52	-	6,171	P	48.7	6,171	0.9	79.4	4	48.7	40	0.0	-	3.4	17.7
Hancock	26,992	18,772	2.0	69.5	37	-	15,046	P	55.7	15,046	2.2	80.2	1	55.7	16	0.0	-	6.6	28.5
Hardy	8,682	6,067	0.6	69.9	36	-	4,671	P	53.8	4,671	0.7	77.0	10	53.8	24	0.0	-	3.0	13.6
Harrison	51,963	40,691	4.3	78.3	11	-	30,341	P	58.4	30,341	4.4	74.6	24	58.4	7	0.0	-	3.4	17.4
Jackson	19,594	14,506	1.5	74.0	25	-	11,229	P	57.3	11,229	1.6	77.4	6	57.3	14	0.0	-	2.7	11.7
Jefferson	28,033	16,506	1.7	58.9	54	-	12,189	P	43.5	12,189	1.8	73.8	27	43.5	52	0.0	-	5.8	13.4
Kanawha	157,036	117,569	12.3	74.9	22	-	81,683	P	52.0	81,683	11.9	69.5	42	52.0	32	0.0	-	3.6	12.0
Lewis	13,120	8,527	0.9	65.0	46	-	6,563	P	50.0	6,563	1.0	77.0	11	50.0	37	0.0	-	1.8	4.2
Lincoln	15,651	14,525	1.5	92.8	1	-	7,984	P	51.0	7,984	1.2	55.0	55	51.0	34	0.0	-	3.5	7.3
Logan	31,311	26,547	2.8	84.8	3	-	16,297	P	52.0	16,297	2.4	61.4	53	52.0	30	0.0	-	6.6	9.4
McDowell	24,327	15,682	1.6	64.5	48	-	9,781	P	40.2	9,781	1.4	62.4	52	40.2	55	0.0	-	5.1	7.0
Marion	43,358	32,866	3.4	75.8	20	-	25,194	P	58.1	25,194	3.7	76.7	14	58.1	9	0.0	-	2.1	18.1
Marshall	28,166	19,981	2.1	70.9	32	-	15,219	P	54.0	15,219	2.2	76.2	17	54.0	23	0.0	-	4.9	23.9
Mason	18,873	15,162	1.6	80.3	8	-	11,200	P	59.3	11,200	1.6	73.9	26	59.3	6	0.0	-	2.9	4.5
Mercer	48,920	28,047	2.9	57.3	55	-	20,290	P	41.4	20,290	3.0	72.3	30	41.4	54	0.0	-	5.1	5.3
Mineral	20,111	14,548	1.5	72.3	27	-	10,728	P	53.3	10,728	1.6	73.7	28	53.3	27	0.0	-	1.6	46.8
Mingo	24,002	19,292	2.0	80.4	6	-	10,873	P	45.3	10,873	1.6	56.4	54	45.3	48	0.0	-	4.8	12.4
Monongalia	58,327	37,760	3.9	64.7	47	-	28,634	P	49.1	28,634	4.2	75.8	19	49.1	38	0.0	-	2.5	31.1
Monroe	9,440	7,775	0.8	82.4	4	-	5,420	P	57.4	5,420	0.8	69.7	40	57.4	13	0.0	-	2.3	9.1
Morgan	9,769	6,703	0.7	68.6	38	-	5,346	P	54.7	5,346	0.8	79.8	3	54.7	20	0.0	-	3.4	22.3
Nicholas	19,781	13,982	1.5	70.7	33	-	9,531	P	48.2	9,531	1.4	68.2	45	48.2	43	0.0	-	4.0	16.3
Ohio	38,092	26,732	2.8	70.2	35	-	20,633	P	54.2	20,633	3.0	77.2	8	54.2	22	0.0	-	2.5	31.3
Pendleton	6,202	4,644	0.5	74.9	21	-	3,583	P	57.8	3,583	0.5	77.2	9	57.8	11	0.0	-	3.0	17.1
Pleasants	5,677	4,225	0.4	74.4	24	-	3,376	P	59.5	3,376	0.5	79.9	2	59.5	3	0.0	-	3.3	26.5
Pocahontas	6,813	4,916	0.5	72.2	28	-	3,781	P	55.5	3,781	0.6	76.9	13	55.5	17	0.0	-	2.2	8.4
Preston	21,527	13,585	1.4	63.1	49	-	10,495	P	48.8	10,495	1.5	77.3	7	48.8	39	0.0	-	2.5	39.4
Putnam	33,085	23,742	2.5	71.8	29	-	17,428	P	52.7	17,428	2.5	73.4	29	52.7	28	0.0	-	2.8	11.9
Raleigh	57,108	38,096	4.0	66.7	43	-	25,214	P	44.2	25,214	3.7	66.2	49	44.2	51	0.0	-	6.4	3.2
Randolph	21,175	14,871	1.6	70.2	34	-	10,222	P	48.3	10,222	1.5	68.7	43	48.3	42	0.0	-	3.7	20.3
Ritchie	7,672	5,919	0.6	77.2	14	-	4,416	P	57.6	4,416	0.6	74.6	23	57.6	12	0.0	-	3.1	36.8
Roane	11,260	8,178	0.9	72.6	26	-	5,857	P	52.0	5,857	0.9	71.6	34	52.0	31	0.0	-	4.9	6.9
Summers	10,790	7,202	0.8	66.7	42	-	4,882	P	45.2	4,882	0.7	67.8	46	45.2	49	0.0	-	13.3	7.4
Taylor	11,254	7,711	0.8	68.5	40	-	6,117	P	54.4	6,117	0.9	79.3	5	54.4	21	0.0	-	0.7	21.3
Tucker	5,849	5,177	0.5	88.5	2	-	3,625	P	62.0	3,625	0.5	70.0	37	62.0	1	0.0	-	2.3	35.1
Tyler	7,223	5,512	0.6	76.3	17	-	4,203	P	58.2	4,203	0.6	76.3	16	58.2	8	0.0	-	2.2	29.7
Upshur	16,976	11,647	1.2	68.6	39	-	8,253	P	48.6	8,253	1.2	70.9	35	48.6	41	0.0	-	2.4	20.2
Wayne	31,114	24,260	2.5	78.0	12	-	16,347	P	52.5	16,347	2.4	67.4	47	52.5	29	0.0	-	6.3	10.5
Webster	7,810	5,110	0.5	65.4	45	-	3,576	P	45.8	3,576	0.5	70.0	38	45.8	46	0.0	-	2.2	8.5
Wetzel	14,222	10,903	1.1	76.7	15	-	7,597	P	53.4	7,597	1.1	69.7	41	53.4	26	0.0	-	3.1	29.2
Wirt	3,967	3,188	0.3	80.4	7	-	2,382	P	60.0	2,382	0.3	74.7	22	60.0	2	0.0	-	3.3	5.9
Wood	65,547	46,889	4.9	71.5	30	-	36,068	P	55.0	36,068	5.3	76.9	12	55.0	19	0.0	-	4.3	39.3
Wyoming	20,669	14,707	1.5	71.2	31	-	9,607	P	46.5	9,607	1.4	65.3	50	46.5	44	0.0	-	2.8	8.6
WEST VIRGINIA	1,350,000	956,172	100.0	70.8		-	683,762		50.6	683,762	100.0	71.5		50.6		0.0	-	3.9	17.8

[1]Percent drop-off is zero for any office used as highest office turnout.

Table D. — Voter Registration by Political Party Affiliation: November 3, 1992, General Election

County	Total voter registration	Democrat (DEM)	Republican (REP)	Independent (IND)	Plurality Total	Plurality Party	DEM	REP	IND	Rank DEM	Rank REP	Rank IND	Total	DEM	REP	IND
Barbour	9,115	5,250	3,467	398	1,783	D	57.6	38.0	4.4	40	17	13	1.0	0.8	1.2	1.1
Berkeley	27,937	14,692	11,115	2,130	3,577	D	52.6	39.8	7.6	44	14	2	2.9	2.3	3.8	5.7
Boone	14,477	12,373	1,864	240	10,509	D	85.5	12.9	1.7	4	52	49	1.5	2.0	0.6	0.6
Braxton	7,778	6,241	1,465	72	4,776	D	80.2	18.8	0.9	9	46	55	0.8	1.0	0.5	0.2
Brooke	13,919	10,642	2,905	372	7,737	D	76.5	20.9	2.7	11	45	37	1.5	1.7	1.0	1.0
Cabell	49,310	30,583	16,684	2,043	13,899	D	62.0	33.8	4.1	32	24	19	5.2	4.9	5.7	5.5
Calhoun	4,678	3,403	1,142	133	2,261	D	72.7	24.4	2.8	20	37	34	0.5	0.5	0.4	0.4
Clay	5,678	4,249	1,298	131	2,951	D	74.8	22.9	2.3	14	40	43	0.6	0.7	0.4	0.4
Doddridge	3,937	1,351	2,418	168	1,067	R	34.3	61.4	4.3	54	2	17	0.4	0.2	0.8	0.5
Fayette	22,215	18,352	3,335	528	15,017	D	82.6	15.0	2.4	6	51	42	2.3	2.9	1.1	1.4
Gilmer	4,361	3,289	977	95	2,312	D	75.4	22.4	2.2	12	42	44	0.5	0.5	0.3	0.3
Grant	5,964	1,057	4,717	190	3,660	R	17.7	79.1	3.2	55	1	29	0.6	0.2	1.6	0.5
Greenbrier	16,308	11,245	4,385	678	6,860	D	69.0	26.9	4.2	24	32	18	1.7	1.8	1.5	1.8
Hampshire	7,773	5,229	2,097	447	3,132	D	67.3	27.0	5.8	26	31	7	0.8	0.8	0.7	1.2
Hancock	18,772	13,883	4,419	470	9,464	D	74.0	23.5	2.5	17	39	41	2.0	2.2	1.5	1.3
Hardy	6,067	4,522	1,372	173	3,150	D	74.5	22.6	2.9	16	41	33	0.6	0.7	0.5	0.5
Harrison	40,691	27,543	12,029	1,119	15,514	D	67.7	29.6	2.8	25	30	36	4.3	4.4	4.1	3.0
Jackson	14,506	7,377	6,649	480	728	D	50.9	45.8	3.3	45	7	28	1.5	1.2	2.3	1.3
Jefferson	16,506	10,159	4,963	1,384	5,196	D	61.5	30.1	8.4	34	29	1	1.7	1.6	1.7	3.7
Kanawha	117,569	73,150	38,856	5,563	34,294	D	62.2	33.0	4.7	30	25	12	12.3	11.7	13.3	15.0
Lewis	8,527	4,774	3,532	221	1,242	D	56.0	41.4	2.6	42	12	39	0.9	0.8	1.2	0.6
Lincoln	14,525	11,903	2,479	143	9,424	D	81.9	17.1	1.0	7	49	54	1.5	1.9	0.9	0.4
Logan	26,547	23,759	2,425	363	21,334	D	89.5	9.1	1.4	2	54	53	2.8	3.8	0.8	1.0
McDowell	15,682	14,040	1,405	237	12,635	D	89.5	9.0	1.5	1	55	50	1.6	2.2	0.5	0.6
Marion	32,866	24,081	7,789	996	16,292	D	73.3	23.7	3.0	19	38	30	3.4	3.8	2.7	2.7
Marshall	19,981	12,432	6,799	750	5,633	D	62.2	34.0	3.8	31	23	25	2.1	2.0	2.3	2.0
Mason	15,162	8,885	5,843	434	3,042	D	58.6	38.5	2.9	38	16	32	1.6	1.4	2.0	1.2
Mercer	28,047	19,642	7,370	1,035	12,272	D	70.0	26.3	3.7	23	33	27	2.9	3.1	2.5	2.8
Mineral	14,548	7,349	6,358	841	991	D	50.5	43.7	5.8	47	10	6	1.5	1.2	2.2	2.3
Mingo	19,292	17,133	1,888	271	15,245	D	88.8	9.8	1.4	3	53	51	2.0	2.7	0.6	0.7
Monongalia	37,760	23,500	11,573	2,687	11,927	D	62.2	30.6	7.1	29	28	3	3.9	3.7	4.0	7.2
Monroe	7,775	4,585	2,858	332	1,727	D	59.0	36.8	4.3	37	18	16	0.8	0.7	1.0	0.9
Morgan	6,703	2,847	3,427	429	580	R	42.5	51.1	6.4	50	6	4	0.7	0.5	1.2	1.2
Nicholas	13,982	10,166	3,514	302	6,652	D	72.7	25.1	2.2	21	35	46	1.5	1.6	1.2	0.8
Ohio	26,732	15,633	9,626	1,473	6,007	D	58.5	36.0	5.5	39	20	9	2.8	2.5	3.3	4.0
Pendleton	4,644	2,965	1,504	175	1,461	D	63.8	32.4	3.8	27	27	24	0.5	0.5	0.5	0.5
Pleasants	4,225	2,535	1,515	175	1,020	D	60.0	35.9	4.1	36	21	20	0.4	0.4	0.5	0.5
Pocahontas	4,916	3,067	1,597	252	1,470	D	62.4	32.5	5.1	28	26	10	0.5	0.5	0.5	0.7
Preston	13,585	6,859	6,224	502	635	D	50.5	45.8	3.7	48	8	26	1.4	1.1	2.1	1.4
Putnam	23,742	13,356	9,260	1,126	4,096	D	56.3	39.0	4.7	41	15	11	2.5	2.1	3.2	3.0
Raleigh	38,096	28,576	8,427	1,093	20,149	D	75.0	22.1	2.9	13	43	31	4.0	4.6	2.9	2.9
Randolph	14,871	11,120	3,151	600	7,969	D	74.8	21.2	4.0	15	44	21	1.6	1.8	1.1	1.6
Ritchie	5,919	2,222	3,470	227	1,248	R	37.5	58.6	3.8	53	3	23	0.6	0.4	1.2	0.6
Roane	8,178	4,152	3,572	454	580	D	50.8	43.7	5.6	46	11	8	0.9	0.7	1.2	1.2
Summers	7,202	5,708	1,338	156	4,370	D	79.3	18.6	2.2	10	47	45	0.8	0.9	0.5	0.4
Taylor	7,711	4,768	2,740	203	2,028	D	61.8	35.5	2.6	33	22	38	0.8	0.8	0.9	0.5
Tucker	5,177	3,133	1,898	146	1,235	D	60.5	36.7	2.8	35	19	35	0.5	0.5	0.7	0.4
Tyler	5,512	2,141	3,132	239	991	R	38.8	56.8	4.3	52	4	14	0.6	0.3	1.1	0.6
Upshur	11,647	4,732	6,448	467	1,716	R	40.6	55.4	4.0	51	5	22	1.2	0.8	2.2	1.3
Wayne	24,260	17,789	5,978	493	11,811	D	73.3	24.6	2.0	18	36	47	2.5	2.8	2.1	1.3
Webster	5,110	4,226	791	93	3,435	D	82.7	15.5	1.8	5	50	48	0.5	0.7	0.3	0.3
Wetzel	10,903	7,884	2,743	276	5,141	D	72.3	25.2	2.5	22	34	40	1.1	1.3	0.9	0.7
Wirt	3,188	1,762	1,289	137	473	D	55.3	40.4	4.3	43	13	15	0.3	0.3	0.4	0.4
Wood	46,889	23,565	20,587	2,737	2,978	D	50.3	43.9	5.8	49	9	5	4.9	3.8	7.1	7.4
Wyoming	14,707	11,957	2,546	204	9,411	D	81.3	17.3	1.4	8	48	52	1.5	1.9	0.9	0.6
WEST VIRGINIA	**956,172**	**627,836**	**291,253**	**37,083**	**336,583**	**D**	**65.7**	**30.5**	**3.9**				**100.0**	**100.0**	**100.0**	**100.0**

Table E. – Vote for President: November 3, 1992, General Election

County	Total	Clinton (DEM)	Bush (REP)	Perot (IND)	Other	Plurality Total	Party	DEM	REP	IND	Other	Rank DEM	Rank REP	Rank IND	Total	DEM	REP	IND	DEM	REP
Barbour	6,954	3,467	2,322	1,153	12	1,145	D	49.9	33.4	16.6	0.2	21	38	25	1.0	1.0	1.0	1.1	59.9	40.1
Berkeley	20,029	7,159	9,134	3,645	91	1,975	R	35.7	45.6	18.2	0.5	51	6	14	2.9	2.2	3.8	3.3	43.9	56.1
Boone	9,658	6,576	2,021	1,037	24	4,555	D	68.1	20.9	10.7	0.2	2	53	50	1.4	2.0	0.8	1.0	76.5	23.5
Braxton	5,765	3,396	1,535	823	11	1,861	D	58.9	26.6	14.3	0.2	8	46	38	0.8	1.0	0.6	0.8	68.9	31.1
Brooke	10,415	5,693	2,582	2,103	37	3,111	D	54.7	24.8	20.2	0.4	11	50	7	1.5	1.7	1.1	1.9	68.8	31.2
Cabell	33,725	15,111	13,203	5,311	100	1,908	D	44.8	39.1	15.7	0.3	36	16	31	4.9	4.6	5.5	4.9	53.4	46.6
Calhoun	3,268	1,627	1,095	537	9	532	D	49.8	33.5	16.4	0.3	23	37	29	0.5	0.5	0.5	0.5	59.8	40.2
Clay	3,657	1,928	1,255	462	12	673	D	52.7	34.3	12.6	0.3	14	33	45	0.5	0.6	0.5	0.4	60.6	39.4
Doddridge	2,992	968	1,500	515	9	532	R	32.4	50.1	17.2	0.3	54	2	19	0.4	0.3	0.6	0.5	39.2	60.8
Fayette	15,608	9,574	3,991	2,002	41	5,583	D	61.3	25.6	12.8	0.3	6	48	43	2.3	2.9	1.6	1.8	70.6	29.4
Gilmer	3,154	1,576	1,085	484	9	491	D	50.0	34.4	15.3	0.3	19	31	35	0.5	0.5	0.4	0.4	59.2	40.8
Grant	4,298	1,011	2,762	519	6	1,751	R	23.5	64.3	12.1	0.1	55	1	47	0.6	0.3	1.1	0.5	26.8	73.2
Greenbrier	12,187	5,784	4,442	1,898	63	1,342	D	47.5	36.4	15.6	0.5	28	26	33	1.8	1.7	1.8	1.7	56.6	43.4
Hampshire	6,171	2,365	2,767	1,022	17	402	R	38.3	44.8	16.6	0.3	45	8	27	0.9	0.7	1.1	0.9	46.1	53.9
Hancock	15,046	7,830	3,897	3,267	52	3,933	D	52.0	25.9	21.7	0.3	16	47	3	2.2	2.4	1.6	3.0	66.8	33.2
Hardy	4,671	1,917	2,144	602	8	227	R	41.0	45.9	12.9	0.2	43	5	41	0.7	0.6	0.9	0.6	47.2	52.8
Harrison	30,341	15,480	9,687	5,131	43	5,793	D	51.0	31.9	16.9	0.1	18	41	21	4.4	4.7	4.0	4.7	61.5	38.5
Jackson	11,229	5,102	4,192	1,908	27	910	D	45.4	37.3	17.0	0.2	34	22	20	1.6	1.5	1.7	1.8	54.9	45.1
Jefferson	12,189	5,363	4,656	2,114	56	707	D	44.0	38.2	17.3	0.5	40	19	17	1.8	1.6	1.9	1.9	53.5	46.5
Kanawha	81,683	38,315	31,358	11,778	232	6,957	D	46.9	38.4	14.4	0.3	29	18	37	11.9	11.6	13.0	10.8	55.0	45.0
Lewis	6,563	2,931	2,413	1,197	22	518	D	44.7	36.8	18.2	0.3	37	25	13	1.0	0.9	1.0	1.1	54.8	45.2
Lincoln	7,984	4,502	2,637	787	58	1,865	D	56.4	33.0	9.9	0.7	9	40	53	1.2	1.4	1.1	0.7	63.1	36.9
Logan	16,297	11,095	3,336	1,835	31	7,759	D	68.1	20.5	11.3	0.2	3	54	49	2.4	3.4	1.4	1.7	76.9	23.1
McDowell	9,781	7,019	1,941	803	18	5,078	D	71.8	19.8	8.2	0.2	1	55	55	1.4	2.1	0.8	0.7	78.3	21.7
Marion	25,194	14,042	6,380	4,736	36	7,662	D	55.7	25.3	18.8	0.1	10	49	11	3.7	4.2	2.6	4.4	68.8	31.2
Marshall	15,219	7,298	4,463	3,402	56	2,835	D	48.0	29.3	22.4	0.4	26	45	2	2.2	2.2	1.8	3.1	62.1	37.9
Mason	11,200	5,331	3,808	2,045	16	1,523	D	47.6	34.0	18.3	0.1	27	35	12	1.6	1.6	1.6	1.9	58.3	41.7
Mercer	20,290	9,511	7,888	2,817	74	1,623	D	46.9	38.9	13.9	0.4	30	17	39	3.0	2.9	3.3	2.6	54.7	45.3
Mineral	10,728	3,992	4,837	1,884	15	845	R	37.2	45.1	17.6	0.1	50	7	16	1.6	1.2	2.0	1.7	45.2	54.8
Mingo	10,873	7,342	2,584	915	32	4,758	D	67.5	23.8	8.4	0.3	4	51	54	1.6	2.2	1.1	0.8	74.0	26.0
Monongalia	28,634	14,142	9,831	4,576	85	4,311	D	49.4	34.3	16.0	0.3	25	32	30	4.2	4.3	4.1	4.2	59.0	41.0
Monroe	5,420	2,418	2,311	685	6	107	D	44.6	42.6	12.6	0.1	38	12	44	0.8	0.7	1.0	0.6	51.1	48.9
Morgan	5,346	1,854	2,585	886	21	731	R	34.7	48.4	16.6	0.4	52	4	26	0.8	0.6	1.1	0.8	41.8	58.2
Nicholas	9,531	5,042	2,959	1,495	35	2,083	D	52.9	31.0	15.7	0.4	13	42	32	1.4	1.5	1.2	1.4	63.0	37.0
Ohio	20,633	9,522	7,421	3,632	58	2,101	D	46.1	36.0	17.6	0.3	32	27	15	3.0	2.9	3.1	3.3	56.2	43.8
Pendleton	3,583	1,626	1,589	362	6	37	D	45.4	44.3	10.1	0.2	35	9	52	0.5	0.5	0.7	0.3	50.6	49.4
Pleasants	3,376	1,387	1,248	731	10	139	D	41.1	37.0	21.7	0.3	42	24	4	0.5	0.4	0.5	0.7	52.6	47.4
Pocahontas	3,781	1,741	1,401	627	12	340	D	46.0	37.1	16.6	0.3	33	23	24	0.6	0.5	0.6	0.6	55.4	44.6
Preston	10,495	3,933	4,429	2,109	24	496	R	37.5	42.2	20.1	0.2	49	14	8	1.5	1.2	1.8	1.9	47.0	53.0
Putnam	17,428	6,817	7,653	2,910	48	836	R	39.1	43.9	16.7	0.3	44	10	23	2.5	2.1	3.2	2.7	47.1	52.9
Raleigh	25,214	13,171	8,700	3,247	96	4,471	D	52.2	34.5	12.9	0.4	15	30	42	3.7	4.0	3.6	3.0	60.2	39.8
Randolph	10,222	5,097	3,496	1,582	47	1,601	D	49.9	34.2	15.5	0.5	20	34	34	1.5	1.5	1.4	1.5	59.3	40.7
Ritchie	4,416	1,474	2,184	745	13	710	R	33.4	49.5	16.9	0.3	53	3	22	0.6	0.4	0.9	0.7	40.3	59.7
Roane	5,857	2,607	2,207	1,009	34	400	D	44.5	37.7	17.2	0.6	39	21	18	0.9	0.8	0.9	0.9	54.2	45.8
Summers	4,882	2,650	1,652	565	15	998	D	54.3	33.8	11.6	0.3	12	36	48	0.7	0.8	0.7	0.5	61.6	38.4
Taylor	6,117	2,843	2,022	1,242	10	821	D	46.5	33.1	20.3	0.2	31	39	6	0.9	0.9	0.8	1.1	58.4	41.6
Tucker	3,625	1,805	1,261	550	9	544	D	49.8	34.8	15.2	0.2	22	29	36	0.5	0.5	0.5	0.5	58.9	41.1
Tyler	4,203	1,587	1,593	1,013	10	6	R	37.8	37.9	24.1	0.2	47	20	1	0.6	0.5	0.7	0.9	49.9	50.1
Upshur	8,253	3,161	3,505	1,558	29	344	R	38.3	42.5	18.9	0.4	46	13	10	1.2	1.0	1.4	1.4	47.4	52.6
Wayne	16,347	8,392	5,729	2,199	27	2,663	D	51.3	35.0	13.5	0.2	17	28	40	2.4	2.5	2.4	2.0	59.4	40.6
Webster	3,576	2,320	811	436	9	1,509	D	64.9	22.7	12.2	0.3	5	52	46	0.5	0.7	0.3	0.4	74.1	25.9
Wetzel	7,597	3,753	2,271	1,550	23	1,482	D	49.4	29.9	20.4	0.3	24	43	5	1.1	1.1	0.9	1.4	62.3	37.7
Wirt	2,382	1,043	939	394	6	104	D	43.8	39.4	16.5	0.3	41	15	28	0.3	0.3	0.4	0.4	52.6	47.4
Wood	36,068	13,529	15,441	6,998	100	1,912	R	37.5	42.8	19.4	0.3	48	11	9	5.3	4.1	6.4	6.4	46.7	53.3
Wyoming	9,607	5,782	2,821	996	8	2,961	D	60.2	29.4	10.4	< .1	7	44	51	1.4	1.7	1.2	0.9	67.2	32.8
WEST VIRGINIA	**683,762**	**331,001**	**241,974**	**108,829**	**1,958**	**89,027**	**D**	**48.4**	**35.4**	**15.9**	**0.3**				**100.0**	**100.0**	**100.0**	**100.0**	**57.8**	**42.2**

Table G. — Vote for Governor: November 3, 1992, General Election

County	Total	Caperton (DEM)	Benedict (REP)	Pritt[1]	Plurality Total	Party	DEM	REP	Other	Rank DEM	Rank REP	Rank Other	Total	DEM	REP	Other
Barbour	6,830	3,805	2,699	326	1,106	D	55.7	39.5	4.8	24	26	35	1.0	1.0	1.1	0.7
Berkeley	18,912	9,969	8,605	338	1,364	D	52.7	45.5	1.8	32	13	49	2.9	2.7	3.6	0.7
Boone	9,273	6,543	2,069	661	4,474	D	70.6	22.3	7.1	3	52	26	1.4	1.8	0.9	1.4
Braxton	5,604	3,316	1,872	416	1,444	D	59.2	33.4	7.4	16	42	23	0.9	0.9	0.8	0.9
Brooke	9,917	6,322	3,190	405	3,132	D	63.7	32.2	4.1	6	44	37	1.5	1.7	1.3	0.8
Cabell	32,404	18,674	10,746	2,984	7,928	D	57.6	33.2	9.2	20	43	16	4.9	5.1	4.5	6.2
Calhoun	3,128	1,464	1,333	331	131	D	46.8	42.6	10.6	47	18	9	0.5	0.4	0.6	0.7
Clay	3,550	1,814	1,386	350	428	D	51.1	39.0	9.9	38	28	12	0.5	0.5	0.6	0.7
Doddridge	2,918	1,161	1,512	245	351	R	39.8	51.8	8.4	54	3	21	0.4	0.3	0.6	0.5
Fayette	15,100	8,908	4,395	1,797	4,513	D	59.0	29.1	11.9	17	47	4	2.3	2.4	1.8	3.7
Gilmer	3,076	1,554	1,250	272	304	D	50.5	40.6	8.8	39	25	19	0.5	0.4	0.5	0.6
Grant	4,148	1,356	2,739	53	1,383	R	32.7	66.0	1.3	55	1	51	0.6	0.4	1.1	0.1
Greenbrier	11,646	5,159	5,683	804	524	R	44.3	48.8	6.9	50	8	28	1.8	1.4	2.4	1.7
Hampshire	5,963	2,850	2,990	123	140	R	47.8	50.1	2.1	46	4	48	0.9	0.8	1.2	0.3
Hancock	14,047	8,700	4,927	420	3,773	D	61.9	35.1	3.0	11	38	45	2.1	2.4	2.0	0.9
Hardy	4,533	2,456	2,032	45	424	D	54.2	44.8	1.0	29	15	52	0.7	0.7	0.8	<.1
Harrison	29,314	18,335	8,195	2,784	10,140	D	62.5	28.0	9.5	8	50	15	4.5	5.0	3.4	5.7
Jackson	10,928	5,307	4,559	1,062	748	D	48.6	41.7	9.7	43	21	13	1.7	1.4	1.9	2.2
Jefferson	11,475	6,391	4,887	197	1,504	D	55.7	42.6	1.7	25	19	50	1.7	1.7	2.0	0.4
Kanawha	78,748	40,285	29,802	8,661	10,483	D	51.2	37.8	11.0	37	29	7	12.0	10.9	12.4	17.9
Lewis	6,447	4,009	2,175	263	1,834	D	62.2	33.7	4.1	10	41	38	1.0	1.1	0.9	0.5
Lincoln	7,706	4,158	2,857	691	1,301	D	54.0	37.1	9.0	30	32	18	1.2	1.1	1.2	1.4
Logan	15,220	10,460	3,378	1,382	7,082	D	68.7	22.2	9.1	4	53	17	2.3	2.8	1.4	2.8
McDowell	9,286	7,227	1,685	374	5,542	D	77.8	18.1	4.0	1	55	39	1.4	2.0	0.7	0.8
Marion	24,659	15,989	6,098	2,572	9,891	D	64.8	24.7	10.4	5	51	11	3.8	4.3	2.5	5.3
Marshall	14,478	8,299	5,459	720	2,840	D	57.3	37.7	5.0	21	30	34	2.2	2.3	2.3	1.5
Mason	10,878	6,040	3,445	1,393	2,595	D	55.5	31.7	12.8	26	45	2	1.7	1.6	1.4	2.9
Mercer	19,231	10,925	6,952	1,354	3,973	D	56.8	36.2	7.0	23	34	27	2.9	3.0	2.9	2.8
Mineral	10,560	5,278	5,241	41	37	D	50.0	49.6	0.4	40	5	54	1.6	1.4	2.2	<.1
Mingo	10,355	7,823	2,257	275	5,566	D	75.5	21.8	2.7	2	54	46	1.6	2.1	0.9	0.6
Monongalia	27,911	17,365	8,535	2,011	8,830	D	62.2	30.6	7.2	9	46	24	4.2	4.7	3.6	4.1
Monroe	5,293	2,590	2,456	247	134	D	48.9	46.4	4.7	41	10	36	0.8	0.7	1.0	0.5
Morgan	5,163	2,166	2,867	130	701	R	42.0	55.5	2.5	51	2	47	0.8	0.6	1.2	0.3
Nicholas	9,147	4,812	3,271	1,064	1,541	D	52.6	35.8	11.6	33	36	6	1.4	1.3	1.4	2.2
Ohio	20,121	12,148	7,196	777	4,952	D	60.4	35.8	3.9	12	35	40	3.1	3.3	3.0	1.6
Pendleton	3,477	1,834	1,610	33	224	D	52.7	46.3	0.9	31	11	53	0.5	0.5	0.7	<.1
Pleasants	3,264	1,580	1,481	203	99	D	48.4	45.4	6.2	45	14	30	0.5	0.4	0.6	0.4
Pocahontas	3,696	1,535	1,806	355	271	R	41.5	48.9	9.6	53	7	14	0.6	0.4	0.8	0.7
Preston	10,232	4,995	4,866	371	129	D	48.8	47.6	3.6	42	9	41	1.6	1.4	2.0	0.8
Putnam	16,932	7,567	7,538	1,827	29	D	44.7	44.5	10.8	49	16	8	2.6	2.1	3.1	3.8
Raleigh	23,605	12,840	8,281	2,484	4,559	D	54.4	35.1	10.5	28	37	10	3.6	3.5	3.4	5.1
Randolph	9,848	5,908	3,583	357	2,325	D	60.0	36.4	3.6	13	33	42	1.5	1.6	1.5	0.7
Ritchie	4,280	1,784	2,122	374	338	R	41.7	49.6	8.7	52	6	20	0.7	0.5	0.9	0.8
Roane	5,569	2,568	2,305	696	263	D	46.1	41.4	12.5	48	22	3	0.8	0.7	1.0	1.4
Summers	4,231	2,504	1,727	0	777	D	59.2	40.8	0.0	15	24	55	0.6	0.7	0.7	0.0
Taylor	6,074	3,477	2,275	322	1,202	D	57.2	37.5	5.3	22	31	33	0.9	0.9	0.9	0.7
Tucker	3,542	1,959	1,460	123	499	D	55.3	41.2	3.5	27	23	43	0.5	0.5	0.6	0.3
Tyler	4,111	2,108	1,735	268	373	D	51.3	42.2	6.5	36	20	29	0.6	0.6	0.7	0.6
Upshur	8,056	3,904	3,677	475	227	D	48.5	45.6	5.9	44	12	31	1.2	1.1	1.5	1.0
Wayne	15,312	8,959	5,256	1,097	3,703	D	58.5	34.3	7.2	18	39	25	2.3	2.4	2.2	2.3
Webster	3,496	2,081	1,005	410	1,076	D	59.5	28.7	11.7	14	49	5	0.5	0.6	0.4	0.8
Wetzel	7,359	4,622	2,489	248	2,133	D	62.8	33.8	3.4	7	40	44	1.1	1.3	1.0	0.5
Wirt	2,303	1,202	909	192	293	D	52.2	39.5	8.3	34	27	22	0.4	0.3	0.4	0.4
Wood	34,503	17,781	14,834	1,888	2,947	D	51.5	43.0	5.5	35	17	32	5.3	4.8	6.2	3.9
Wyoming	9,334	5,436	2,688	1,210	2,748	D	58.2	28.8	13.0	19	48	1	1.4	1.5	1.1	2.5
WEST VIRGINIA	**657,193**	**368,302**	**240,390**	**48,501**	**127,912**	**D**	**56.0**	**36.6**	**7.4**				**100.0**	**100.0**	**100.0**	**100.0**

[1] Write in candidate Pritt was the only other candidate (only three candidates on ballot).

Table H. — Vote for U.S. Representative in Congress: November 3, 1992, General Election

Congressional district and county	Total	Democrat (DEM)	Republican (REP)		Plurality Total	Party	Percent of total vote DEM	REP		Rank within district DEM	REP		Percent contribution to district vote Total	DEM	REP	
District 1	**172,924**	**172,924**	-	-	**172,924**	D	**100.0**	-	-				**100.0**	**100.0**	-	-
Barbour	4,714	4,714	-	-	4,714	D	100.0	-	-	13	-	-	2.7	2.7	-	-
Brooke	8,230	8,230	-	-	8,230	D	100.0	-	-	8	-	-	4.8	4.8	-	-
Doddridge	1,869	1,869	-	-	1,869	D	100.0	-	-	18	-	-	1.1	1.1	-	-
Grant	1,451	1,451	-	-	1,451	D	100.0	-	-	19	-	-	0.8	0.8	-	-
Hancock	10,752	10,752	-	-	10,752	D	100.0	-	-	7	-	-	6.2	6.2	-	-
Harrison	25,047	25,047	-	-	25,047	D	100.0	-	-	1	-	-	14.5	14.5	-	-
Marion	20,628	20,628	-	-	20,628	D	100.0	-	-	3	-	-	11.9	11.9	-	-
Marshall	11,580	11,580	-	-	11,580	D	100.0	-	-	6	-	-	6.7	6.7	-	-
Mineral	5,708	5,708	-	-	5,708	D	100.0	-	-	10	-	-	3.3	3.3	-	-
Monongalia	19,727	19,727	-	-	19,727	D	100.0	-	-	4	-	-	11.4	11.4	-	-
Ohio	14,178	14,178	-	-	14,178	D	100.0	-	-	5	-	-	8.2	8.2	-	-
Pleasants	2,481	2,481	-	-	2,481	D	100.0	-	-	16	-	-	1.4	1.4	-	-
Preston	6,364	6,364	-	-	6,364	D	100.0	-	-	9	-	-	3.7	3.7	-	-
Ritchie	2,793	2,793	-	-	2,793	D	100.0	-	-	15	-	-	1.6	1.6	-	-
Taylor	4,810	4,810	-	-	4,810	D	100.0	-	-	12	-	-	2.8	2.8	-	-
Tucker	2,353	2,353	-	-	2,353	D	100.0	-	-	17	-	-	1.4	1.4	-	-
Tyler	2,956	2,956	-	-	2,956	D	100.0	-	-	14	-	-	1.7	1.7	-	-
Wetzel	5,380	5,380	-	-	5,380	D	100.0	-	-	11	-	-	3.1	3.1	-	-
Wood	21,903	21,903	-	-	21,903	D	100.0	-	-	2	-	-	12.7	12.7	-	-
District 2	**203,090**	**143,988**	**59,102**	-	**84,886**	D	**70.9**	**29.1**	-				**100.0**	**100.0**	**100.0**	-
Berkeley	17,732	8,937	8,795	-	142	D	50.4	49.6	-	19	2	-	8.7	6.2	14.9	-
Braxton	5,116	4,405	711	-	3,694	D	86.1	13.9	-	1	20	-	2.5	3.1	1.2	-
Calhoun	2,793	2,212	581	-	1,631	D	79.2	20.8	-	4	17	-	1.4	1.5	1.0	-
Clay	3,247	2,516	731	-	1,785	D	77.5	22.5	-	8	13	-	1.6	1.7	1.2	-
Gilmer	2,865	2,240	625	-	1,615	D	78.2	21.8	-	5	16	-	1.4	1.6	1.1	-
Hampshire	5,079	2,803	2,276	-	527	D	55.2	44.8	-	18	3	-	2.5	1.9	3.9	-
Hardy	4,036	2,473	1,563	-	910	D	61.3	38.7	-	16	5	-	2.0	1.7	2.6	-
Jackson	9,920	7,230	2,690	-	4,540	D	72.9	27.1	-	12	9	-	4.9	5.0	4.6	-
Jefferson	10,553	5,947	4,606	-	1,341	D	56.4	43.6	-	17	4	-	5.2	4.1	7.8	-
Kanawha	71,888	54,222	17,666	-	36,556	D	75.4	24.6	-	11	10	-	35.4	37.7	29.9	-
Lewis	6,290	5,061	1,229	-	3,832	D	80.5	19.5	-	2	19	-	3.1	3.5	2.1	-
Mason	10,695	8,345	2,350	-	5,995	D	78.0	22.0	-	6	15	-	5.3	5.8	4.0	-
Morgan	4,152	1,792	2,360	-	568	R	43.2	56.8	-	20	1	-	2.0	1.2	4.0	-
Nicholas	7,980	6,411	1,569	-	4,842	D	80.3	19.7	-	3	18	-	3.9	4.5	2.7	-
Pendleton	2,971	1,933	1,038	-	895	D	65.1	34.9	-	15	6	-	1.5	1.3	1.8	-
Putnam	15,346	10,704	4,642	-	6,062	D	69.8	30.2	-	14	7	-	7.6	7.4	7.9	-
Randolph	8,152	6,155	1,997	-	4,158	D	75.5	24.5	-	10	11	-	4.0	4.3	3.4	-
Roane	5,451	4,198	1,253	-	2,945	D	77.0	23.0	-	9	12	-	2.7	2.9	2.1	-
Upshur	6,582	4,663	1,919	-	2,744	D	70.8	29.2	-	13	8	-	3.2	3.2	3.2	-
Wirt	2,242	1,741	501	-	1,240	D	77.7	22.3	-	7	14	-	1.1	1.2	0.8	-
District 3	**186,291**	**122,279**	**64,012**	-	**58,267**	D	**65.6**	**34.4**	-				**100.0**	**100.0**	**100.0**	-
Boone	8,264	6,516	1,748	-	4,768	D	78.8	21.2	-	4	13	-	4.4	5.3	2.7	-
Cabell	29,039	16,843	12,196	-	4,647	D	58.0	42.0	-	12	5	-	15.6	13.8	19.1	-
Fayette	13,821	9,604	4,217	-	5,387	D	69.5	30.5	-	7	10	-	7.4	7.9	6.6	-
Greenbrier	11,185	5,837	5,348	-	489	D	52.2	47.8	-	15	2	-	6.0	4.8	8.4	-
Lincoln	7,398	4,976	2,422	-	2,554	D	67.3	32.7	-	9	8	-	4.0	4.1	3.8	-
Logan	14,757	11,723	3,034	-	8,689	D	79.4	20.6	-	3	14	-	7.9	9.6	4.7	-
McDowell	9,099	7,360	1,739	-	5,621	D	80.9	19.1	-	2	15	-	4.9	6.0	2.7	-
Mercer	19,206	10,614	8,592	-	2,022	D	55.3	44.7	-	14	3	-	10.3	8.7	13.4	-
Mingo	9,524	7,823	1,701	-	6,122	D	82.1	17.9	-	1	16	-	5.1	6.4	2.7	-
Monroe	4,928	2,446	2,482	-	36	R	49.6	50.4	-	16	1	-	2.6	2.0	3.9	-
Pocahontas	3,465	1,936	1,529	-	407	D	55.9	44.1	-	13	4	-	1.9	1.6	2.4	-
Raleigh	24,398	15,208	9,190	-	6,018	D	62.3	37.7	-	10	7	-	13.1	12.4	14.4	-
Summers	4,522	2,644	1,878	-	766	D	58.5	41.5	-	11	6	-	2.4	2.2	2.9	-
Wayne	14,633	9,932	4,701	-	5,231	D	67.9	32.1	-	8	9	-	7.9	8.1	7.3	-
Webster	3,273	2,500	773	-	1,727	D	76.4	23.6	-	5	12	-	1.8	2.0	1.2	-
Wyoming	8,779	6,317	2,462	-	3,855	D	72.0	28.0	-	6	11	-	4.7	5.2	3.8	-
WEST VIRGINIA	**562,305**	**439,191**	**123,114**	-	**316,077**	D	**78.1**	**21.9**	-							

Table I. — Vote for Presidential Preference: May 12, 1992, Democratic Primary Election

County	Top candidates									Top three candidates (state vote)									
										Percent of total vote			Rank			Percent contribution to state vote			
	Total	Clinton	Brown	Tsongas	McDon-ald	Kerrey	LaRouche	Harkin	Other	Clinton	Brown	Tsongas	Clinton	Brown	Tsongas	Total	Clinton	Brown	Tsongas
Barbour	2,985	2,365	266	161	96	21	43	20	13	79.2	8.9	5.4	10	42	38	1.0	1.0	0.7	0.8
Berkeley	5,430	3,667	591	661	298	71	52	68	22	67.5	10.9	12.2	50	27	2	1.8	1.6	1.6	3.1
Boone	6,754	5,509	671	222	161	44	82	30	35	81.6	9.9	3.3	3	33	54	2.2	2.4	1.8	1.0
Braxton	3,681	2,932	328	161	141	34	44	23	18	79.7	8.9	4.4	8	43	45	1.2	1.3	0.9	0.8
Brooke	4,969	3,381	740	477	162	42	62	57	48	68.0	14.9	9.6	48	6	11	1.6	1.5	2.0	2.2
Cabell	13,109	9,013	2,408	911	284	147	115	99	132	68.8	18.4	6.9	47	1	27	4.3	4.0	6.6	4.3
Calhoun	1,913	1,418	229	100	83	18	27	16	22	74.1	12.0	5.2	30	19	40	0.6	0.6	0.6	0.5
Clay	2,212	1,765	147	103	100	23	21	31	22	79.8	6.6	4.7	7	52	43	0.7	0.8	0.4	0.5
Doddridge	698	506	77	43	29	7	12	10	14	72.5	11.0	6.2	37	26	37	0.2	0.2	0.2	0.2
Fayette	9,470	7,181	1,239	469	229	101	71	53	127	75.8	13.1	5.0	22	13	42	3.1	3.2	3.4	2.2
Gilmer	1,795	1,344	158	124	88	23	23	17	18	74.9	8.8	6.9	23	44	28	0.6	0.6	0.4	0.6
Grant	387	286	29	35	14	9	5	5	4	73.9	7.5	9.0	32	49	13	0.1	0.1	<.1	0.2
Greenbrier	5,930	4,253	600	525	225	70	137	64	56	71.7	10.1	8.9	42	31	14	1.9	1.9	1.6	2.5
Hampshire	2,693	1,869	210	245	174	43	80	33	39	69.4	7.8	9.1	46	47	12	0.9	0.8	0.6	1.2
Hancock	7,647	5,165	1,044	853	178	131	95	132	49	67.5	13.7	11.2	49	9	4	2.5	2.3	2.9	4.0
Hardy	2,504	1,830	160	221	164	36	37	38	18	73.1	6.4	8.8	35	53	15	0.8	0.8	0.4	1.0
Harrison	14,586	11,098	1,341	1,025	512	166	121	175	148	76.1	9.2	7.0	19	40	26	4.8	4.9	3.7	4.8
Jackson	4,378	3,224	750	190	76	26	28	64	20	73.6	17.1	4.3	34	2	46	1.4	1.4	2.1	0.9
Jefferson	4,100	2,479	471	518	453	86	35	48	10	60.5	11.5	12.6	55	23	1	1.3	1.1	1.3	2.4
Kanawha	34,072	25,353	4,760	2,415	655	254	256	201	178	74.4	14.0	7.1	27	8	25	11.1	11.1	13.0	11.4
Lewis	2,415	1,800	244	151	113	27	25	30	25	74.5	10.1	6.3	26	32	35	0.8	0.8	0.7	0.7
Lincoln	5,604	4,345	647	158	198	99	37	42	78	77.5	11.5	2.8	15	22	55	1.8	1.9	1.8	0.7
Logan	10,437	8,267	1,297	349	219	49	124	54	78	79.2	12.4	3.3	11	16	53	3.4	3.6	3.6	1.6
McDowell	6,736	5,700	347	343	144	32	39	21	110	84.6	5.2	5.1	1	55	41	2.2	2.5	1.0	1.6
Marion	13,798	10,324	1,579	979	451	119	120	126	100	74.8	11.4	7.1	24	24	24	4.5	4.5	4.3	4.6
Marshall	6,141	4,361	904	401	203	64	63	80	65	71.0	14.7	6.5	44	7	34	2.0	1.9	2.5	1.9
Mason	4,814	3,806	578	186	129	25	30	33	27	79.1	12.0	3.9	12	18	49	1.6	1.7	1.6	0.9
Mercer	8,385	6,229	753	829	223	117	108	94	32	74.3	9.0	9.9	28	41	8	2.7	2.7	2.1	3.9
Mineral	2,856	2,055	350	291	42	60	33	18	7	72.0	12.3	10.2	41	17	6	0.9	0.9	1.0	1.4
Mingo	8,281	6,739	655	280	259	91	118	51	88	81.4	7.9	3.4	4	46	52	2.7	3.0	1.8	1.3
Monongalia	11,138	7,506	1,719	1,098	399	149	71	132	64	67.4	15.4	9.9	51	5	9	3.6	3.3	4.7	5.2
Monroe	2,368	1,767	230	179	84	27	18	54	9	74.6	9.7	7.6	25	35	20	0.8	0.8	0.6	0.8
Morgan	1,201	852	118	118	59	19	10	11	14	70.9	9.8	9.8	45	34	10	0.4	0.4	0.3	0.6
Nicholas	4,991	3,836	523	308	141	39	51	37	56	76.9	10.5	6.2	17	28	36	1.6	1.7	1.4	1.4
Ohio	7,219	4,731	1,173	759	212	114	103	89	38	65.5	16.2	10.5	54	4	5	2.4	2.1	3.2	3.6
Pendleton	1,633	1,264	90	118	89	20	16	18	18	77.4	5.5	7.2	16	54	23	0.5	0.6	0.2	0.6
Pleasants	1,480	1,071	193	97	58	15	17	18	11	72.4	13.0	6.6	38	14	31	0.5	0.5	0.5	0.5
Pocahontas	1,714	1,263	164	134	62	16	28	15	32	73.7	9.6	7.8	33	37	19	0.6	0.6	0.4	0.6
Preston	3,536	2,572	340	281	173	40	46	43	41	72.7	9.6	7.9	36	36	18	1.2	1.1	0.9	1.3
Putnam	6,557	4,867	892	429	175	64	32	54	44	74.2	13.6	6.5	29	10	33	2.1	2.1	2.4	2.0
Raleigh	13,031	10,148	1,339	853	307	129	129	76	50	77.9	10.3	6.5	14	30	32	4.2	4.5	3.7	4.0
Randolph	5,873	4,229	668	404	237	77	120	70	68	72.0	11.4	6.9	40	25	29	1.9	1.9	1.8	1.9
Ritchie	1,207	926	113	65	56	15	10	15	7	76.7	9.4	5.4	18	39	39	0.4	0.4	0.3	0.3
Roane	2,135	1,693	249	80	51	17	10	16	19	79.3	11.7	3.7	9	20	50	0.7	0.7	0.7	0.4
Summers	2,856	2,171	296	207	73	45	31	18	15	76.0	10.4	7.2	20	29	22	0.9	1.0	0.8	1.0
Taylor	3,010	2,287	262	206	123	33	29	26	44	76.0	8.7	6.8	21	45	30	1.0	1.0	0.7	1.0
Tucker	1,718	1,272	132	149	100	15	23	17	10	74.0	7.7	8.7	31	48	16	0.6	0.6	0.4	0.7
Tyler	1,130	756	150	131	40	15	9	20	9	66.9	13.3	11.6	53	12	3	0.4	0.3	0.4	0.6
Upshur	2,319	1,675	301	190	70	18	29	17	19	72.2	13.0	8.2	39	15	17	0.8	0.7	0.8	0.9
Wayne	8,803	6,860	1,021	313	235	22	110	55	187	77.9	11.6	3.6	13	21	51	2.9	3.0	2.8	1.5
Webster	2,467	1,990	184	99	95	18	37	19	25	80.7	7.5	4.0	5	50	47	0.8	0.9	0.5	0.5
Wetzel	3,936	2,812	529	287	150	40	36	54	28	71.4	13.4	7.3	43	11	21	1.3	1.2	1.4	1.3
Wirt	1,014	812	97	46	29	8	6	9	7	80.1	9.6	4.5	6	38	44	0.3	0.4	0.3	0.2
Wood	10,230	6,846	1,672	1,039	267	120	63	121	102	66.9	16.3	10.2	52	3	7	3.3	3.0	4.6	4.9
Wyoming	6,520	5,345	477	255	244	42	64	37	56	82.0	7.3	3.9	2	51	48	2.1	2.3	1.3	1.2
WEST VIRGINIA	**306,866**	**227,815**	**36,505**	**21,271**	**9,632**	**3,152**	**3,141**	**2,774**	**2,576**	**74.2**	**11.9**	**6.9**				**100.0**	**100.0**	**100.0**	**100.0**

Table J. — Vote for Presidential Preference: May 12, 1992, Republican Primary Election

| County | Top candidates | | | | | Top four candidates (state vote) | | | | | | | | Percent contribution to state vote | | | | |
| | Total | Bush | Bu-chanan | Fellure | | Percent of total vote | | | | Rank | | | | Total | Bush | Bu-chanan | Fellure | |
						Bush	Bu-chanan	Fellure		Bush	Bu-chanan	Fellure						
Barbour	1,738	1,380	262	96	–	79.4	15.1	5.5	–	36	18	15	–	1.4	1.4	1.5	1.6	–
Berkeley	3,451	2,873	473	105	–	83.3	13.7	3.0	–	15	32	54	–	2.8	2.9	2.6	1.7	–
Boone	674	567	81	26	–	84.1	12.0	3.9	–	11	40	45	–	0.5	0.6	0.4	0.4	–
Braxton	612	518	63	31	–	84.6	10.3	5.1	–	8	49	24	–	0.5	0.5	0.3	0.5	–
Brooke	1,006	744	208	54	–	74.0	20.7	5.4	–	54	2	21	–	0.8	0.7	1.2	0.9	–
Cabell	6,105	4,887	896	322	–	80.0	14.7	5.3	–	33	20	22	–	4.9	4.9	5.0	5.3	–
Calhoun	547	444	70	33	–	81.2	12.8	6.0	–	30	36	11	–	0.4	0.4	0.4	0.5	–
Clay	589	481	66	42	–	81.7	11.2	7.1	–	27	44	2	–	0.5	0.5	0.4	0.7	–
Doddridge	1,540	1,293	178	69	–	84.0	11.6	4.5	–	12	41	34	–	1.2	1.3	1.0	1.1	–
Fayette	1,232	1,028	150	54	–	83.4	12.2	4.4	–	14	38	36	–	1.0	1.0	0.8	0.9	–
Gilmer	506	414	61	31	–	81.8	12.1	6.1	–	25	39	9	–	0.4	0.4	0.3	0.5	–
Grant	2,644	2,176	337	131	–	82.3	12.7	5.0	–	21	37	27	–	2.1	2.2	1.9	2.1	–
Greenbrier	1,789	1,507	197	85	–	84.2	11.0	4.8	–	9	47	31	–	1.4	1.5	1.1	1.4	–
Hampshire	789	645	126	18	–	81.7	16.0	2.3	–	26	16	55	–	0.6	0.6	0.7	0.3	–
Hancock	2,089	1,504	470	115	–	72.0	22.5	5.5	–	55	1	17	–	1.7	1.5	2.6	1.9	–
Hardy	593	518	47	28	–	87.4	7.9	4.7	–	3	53	32	–	0.5	0.5	0.3	0.5	–
Harrison	5,567	4,557	773	237	–	81.9	13.9	4.3	–	24	29	39	–	4.5	4.6	4.3	3.9	–
Jackson	3,506	2,704	603	199	–	77.1	17.2	5.7	–	49	9	13	–	2.8	2.7	3.3	3.3	–
Jefferson	1,433	1,128	243	62	–	78.7	17.0	4.3	–	41	11	38	–	1.2	1.1	1.3	1.0	–
Kanawha	14,960	12,360	1,984	616	–	82.6	13.3	4.1	–	17	35	41	–	12.0	12.4	11.0	10.1	–
Lewis	1,823	1,354	364	105	–	74.3	20.0	5.8	–	53	3	12	–	1.5	1.4	2.0	1.7	–
Lincoln	1,027	933	54	40	–	90.8	5.3	3.9	–	1	55	44	–	0.8	0.9	0.3	0.7	–
Logan	690	540	114	36	–	78.3	16.5	5.2	–	43	14	23	–	0.6	0.5	0.6	0.6	–
McDowell	409	323	66	20	–	79.0	16.1	4.9	–	38	15	29	–	0.3	0.3	0.4	0.3	–
Marion	3,168	2,438	556	174	–	77.0	17.6	5.5	–	50	7	18	–	2.6	2.4	3.1	2.9	–
Marshall	3,550	2,698	658	194	–	76.0	18.5	5.5	–	51	5	20	–	2.9	2.7	3.6	3.2	–
Mason	2,895	2,271	424	200	–	78.4	14.6	6.9	–	42	21	3	–	2.3	2.3	2.3	3.3	–
Mercer	2,274	1,874	326	74	–	82.4	14.3	3.3	–	20	25	52	–	1.8	1.9	1.8	1.2	–
Mineral	2,457	1,936	412	109	–	78.8	16.8	4.4	–	40	12	35	–	2.0	1.9	2.3	1.8	–
Mingo	584	502	50	32	–	86.0	8.6	5.5	–	6	52	19	–	0.5	0.5	0.3	0.5	–
Monongalia	4,141	3,239	693	209	–	78.2	16.7	5.0	–	44	13	25	–	3.3	3.2	3.8	3.4	–
Monroe	1,343	1,158	137	48	–	86.2	10.2	3.6	–	5	50	48	–	1.1	1.2	0.8	0.8	–
Morgan	1,889	1,532	282	75	–	81.1	14.9	4.0	–	31	19	43	–	1.5	1.5	1.6	1.2	–
Nicholas	1,474	1,163	215	96	–	78.9	14.6	6.5	–	39	22	8	–	1.2	1.2	1.2	1.6	–
Ohio	4,694	3,638	887	169	–	77.5	18.9	3.6	–	46	4	46	–	3.8	3.6	4.9	2.8	–
Pendleton	762	677	59	26	–	88.8	7.7	3.4	–	2	54	51	–	0.6	0.7	0.3	0.4	–
Pleasants	852	722	93	37	–	84.7	10.9	4.3	–	7	48	37	–	0.7	0.7	0.5	0.6	–
Pocahontas	878	724	127	27	–	82.5	14.5	3.1	–	19	23	53	–	0.7	0.7	0.7	0.4	–
Preston	3,631	2,882	510	239	–	79.4	14.0	6.6	–	37	28	7	–	2.9	2.9	2.8	3.9	–
Putnam	3,840	3,050	426	364	–	79.4	11.1	9.5	–	35	46	1	–	3.1	3.1	2.4	6.0	–
Raleigh	2,403	1,977	341	85	–	82.3	14.2	3.5	–	22	26	49	–	1.9	2.0	1.9	1.4	–
Randolph	1,274	1,051	170	53	–	82.5	13.3	4.2	–	18	34	40	–	1.0	1.1	0.9	0.9	–
Ritchie	2,130	1,738	285	107	–	81.6	13.4	5.0	–	29	33	26	–	1.7	1.7	1.6	1.8	–
Roane	1,695	1,365	235	95	–	80.5	13.9	5.6	–	32	30	14	–	1.4	1.4	1.3	1.6	–
Summers	501	435	48	18	–	86.8	9.6	3.6	–	4	51	47	–	0.4	0.4	0.3	0.3	–
Taylor	1,577	1,218	272	87	–	77.2	17.2	5.5	–	48	8	16	–	1.3	1.2	1.5	1.4	–
Tucker	770	637	106	27	–	82.7	13.8	3.5	–	16	31	50	–	0.6	0.6	0.6	0.4	–
Tyler	2,058	1,542	375	141	–	74.9	18.2	6.9	–	52	6	4	–	1.7	1.5	2.1	2.3	–
Upshur	3,429	2,736	483	210	–	79.8	14.1	6.1	–	34	27	10	–	2.8	2.7	2.7	3.4	–
Wayne	2,338	1,955	269	114	–	83.6	11.5	4.9	–	13	43	30	–	1.9	2.0	1.5	1.9	–
Webster	377	292	60	25	–	77.5	15.9	6.6	–	47	17	5	–	0.3	0.3	0.3	0.4	–
Wetzel	1,062	828	182	52	–	78.0	17.1	4.9	–	45	10	28	–	0.9	0.8	1.0	0.9	–
Wirt	728	596	84	48	–	81.9	11.5	6.6	–	23	42	6	–	0.6	0.6	0.5	0.8	–
Wood	9,108	7,437	1,309	362	–	81.7	14.4	4.0	–	28	24	42	–	7.3	7.4	7.2	5.9	–
Wyoming	956	805	107	44	–	84.2	11.2	4.6	–	10	45	33	–	0.8	0.8	0.6	0.7	–
WEST VIRGINIA	**124,157**	**99,994**	**18,067**	**6,096**	–	**80.5**	**14.6**	**4.9**	–					**100.0**	**100.0**	**100.0**	**100.0**	–

1992 Vote for President
Percent for Clinton (D), by County

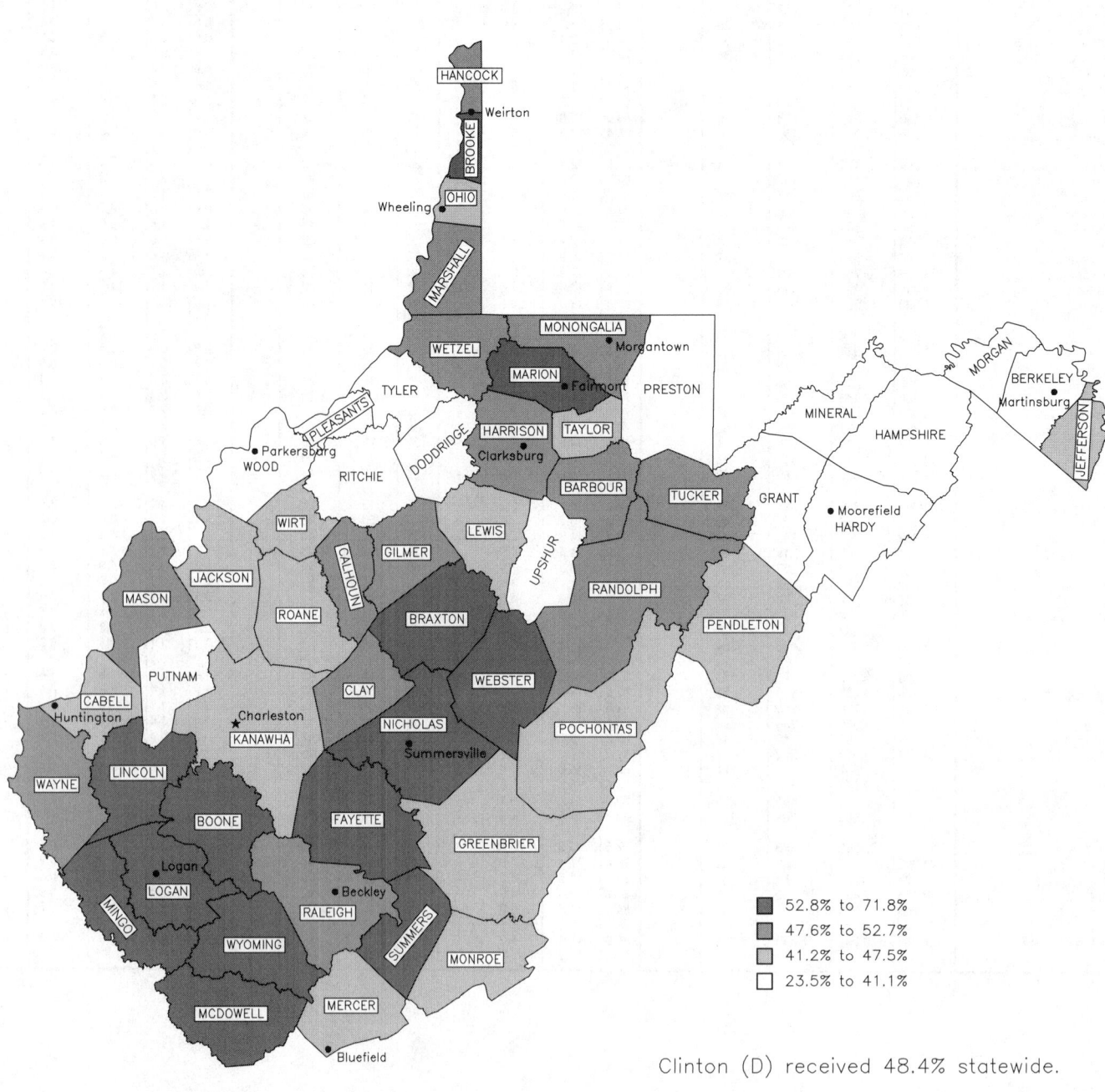

52.8% to 71.8%
47.6% to 52.7%
41.2% to 47.5%
23.5% to 41.1%

Clinton (D) received 48.4% statewide.

A framed county name indicates
a county carried by the winner.

990 West Virginia

1992 Vote for Governor
Percent for Caperton (D), by County

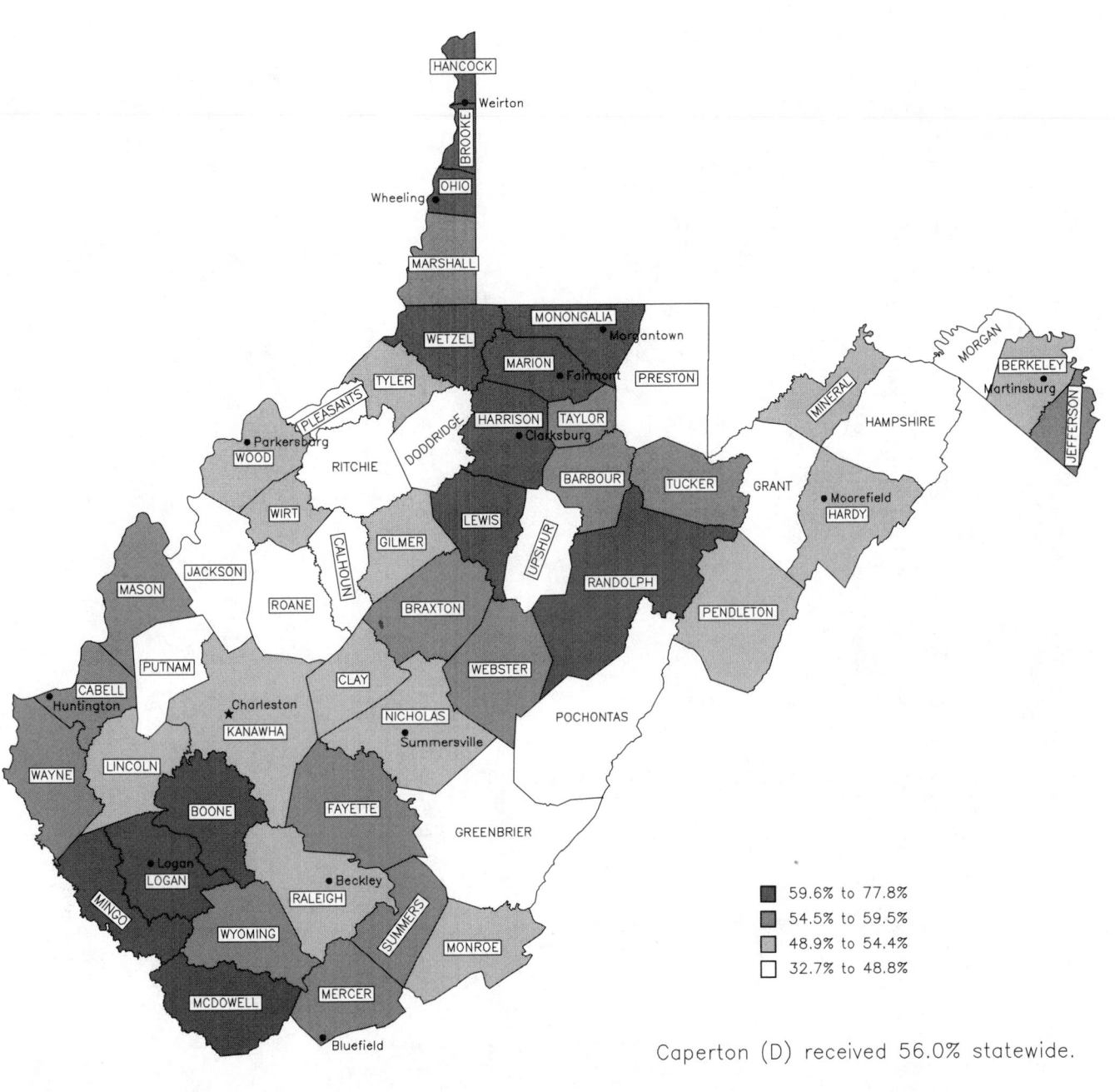

Legend:
- 59.6% to 77.8%
- 54.5% to 59.5%
- 48.9% to 54.4%
- 32.7% to 48.8%

Caperton (D) received 56.0% statewide.

A framed county name indicates a county carried by the winner.

West Virginia 991

WISCONSIN

Congressional Districts 9
   Average Population 543,530
State Senate Districts 33
   Average Population 148,235
State House Districts 99
   Average Population 49,412

Electoral College Votes...11
Counties 72
Voting Precincts 4,625

Alternative Registration Methods:[1]
   ....Deputized Registrars, Election day, Mail-in

Registration Deadline[1] (Days before Election).....................0

Voting Equipment Use (Counties)

Datavote Punch Card	0	Paper Ballot	27
Electronic	0	Other Punch Card	2
Lever Machine	0	Mixed Systems	43
Optical Scanner	0		

Party Control	DEM	REP	IND	VAC
1993 State Senate	16	17	0	0
1992 State Senate	19	14	0	0
1993 State House	51	45	0	3
1992 State House	58	41	0	0

Population Statistics 1990

Race/ Ethnicity	Total Population		Voting Age Population		Voting Age Population % of total population
	Number	%	Number	%	
Non-Hispanic					
White	4,464,677	91.3	3,349,908	93.0	75.0
Black	241,697	4.9	145,022	4.0	60.0
Asian/Pacific Islander	52,284	1.1	29,883	0.8	57.2
Native American	37,769	0.8	23,568	0.7	62.4
Other	2,148	<.1	554	<.1	25.8
All Hispanic	93,194	1.9	53,852	1.5	57.8
TOTAL	4,891,769	100.0	3,602,787	100.0	73.7

Estimated Voting Age Population 1992 (VAP) 3,669,000
Number of Registered Voters[1] ....N/A
   % of estimated VAP..N/A
Voter Turnout (Highest Office) 2,531,977
   % of VAP 69.0
   % of Registration ....N/A
Persons Not Voting—of Voting Age 1,137,023
   % of VAP 31.0
Persons Not Voting—of Registered[1] ....N/A
   % of Registration ....N/A
Straight Ticket Voting .... Yes, Exception

State Officials and Members of Congress

Governor:
Tommy Thompson (R) 1986, elected to a four-year term in 1990.

U.S. Senators:
Herbert Kohl (D) 1988, elected to a six-year term in 1988.
Russell D. Feingold (D) 1992, elected to a six-year term in 1992.

U.S. Representative in Congress:
(District, Name, Party, Date first elected)

1. Barca (D) 1993[2]
2. Klug (R) 1990
3. Gunderson (R) 1980
4. Kleczka (D) 1984
5. Barrett (D) 1992
6. Petri (R) 1979
7. Obey (D) 1969
8. Roth (R) 1978
9. Sensenbrenner (R) 1978

---

[1]No statewide voter registration requirement (registration required only for municipalities over 5,000 population). [2]Elected from May 4, 1993, special election to replace Les Aspin (D), who was appointed as U.S. Secretary of Defense.

Candidates: General Election, November 3, 1992

Candidate(s)	Total vote	Percent	Party	Status	First elected
President/Vice President					
Clinton/Gore	1,041,066	41.13%	Democrat	Challenger	1992
Bush/Quayle	930,855	36.78%	Republican	Incumbent	1988
Perot/Stockdale	544,479	21.51%	Independent	Challenger	
Marrou/Lord	2,877	0.11%	Libertarian	Challenger	
Gritz/Minett	2,311	0.09%	Independent	Challenger	
Daniels/Tupachache	1,883	0.07%	Labor-Farm	Challenger	
Phillips/Knight	1,772	0.07%	Independent	Challenger	
Brisben/Garson	1,211	0.05%	Independent	Challenger	
Hagelin/Tompkins	1,070	0.04%	Natural Law	Challenger	
Scattering (other)	961	0.04%	Write in	Challenger	
Fulani/Munoz	654	0.03%	Independent	Challenger	
LaRouche/Bevel	633	0.03%	Independent	Challenger	
Herer/Grimmer	547	0.02%	Independent	Challenger	
Hem/Roland	405	0.02%	Third Party	Challenger	
Warren/Reid	390	0.02%	Independent	Challenger	
U.S. Senator					
Russell Feingold	1,290,662	52.57%	Democrat	Challenger	1992
Robert Kasten, Jr.	1,129,599	46.01%	Republican	Incumbent	1980
Patrick Johnson	16,513	0.67%	Independent	Challenger	
William Bittner	9,147	0.37%	Libertarian	Challenger	
Mervin Hanson, Sr.	3,264	0.13%	Independent	Challenger	
Robert Kundert	2,747	0.11%	Independent	Challenger	
Joseph Selliken	2,733	0.11%	Independent	Challenger	
Scattering (other)	459	0.02%	Write in	Challenger	
Governor (No Contest)					
U.S. Representative in Congress					
District 1					
Les Aspin[1]	147,495	57.55%	Democrat	Incumbent	1970
Mark Neumann	104,352	40.72%	Republican	Challenger	
John Graf	4,391	1.71%	Independent	Challenger	
Scattering (other)	42	0.02%	Write in	Challenger	
District 2					
Scott Klug	183,366	62.60%	Republican	Incumbent	1990
Ada Deer	108,291	36.97%	Democrat	Challenger	
Joseph Schumacher	1,140	0.39%	Independent	Challenger	
Scattering (other)	101	0.03%	Write in	Challenger	
District 3					
Steven Gunderson	146,903	56.43%	Republican	Incumbent	1980
Paul Sacia	108,664	41.74%	Democrat	Challenger	
Jay Evenson	4,736	1.82%	Independent	Challenger	
Scattering (other)	32	0.01%	Write in	Challenger	
District 4					
Gerald Kleczka	173,482	65.76%	Democrat	Incumbent	1984
Joseph Cook	84,872	32.17%	Republican	Challenger	
Daniel Slak	2,803	1.06%	Independent	Challenger	
John Washburn	2,488	0.94%	Libertarian	Challenger	
Scattering (other)	158	0.06%	Write in	Challenger	
District 5					
Thomas Barrett	162,344	69.33%	Democrat	Challenger	1992
Donalda Hammersmith	71,085	30.36%	Republican	Challenger	
Scattering (other)	747	0.32%	Write in	Challenger	

[1]Resigned upon appointment as U.S. Secretary of Defense. Peter Barca (D) elected at May 4, 1993, special election to fill vacancy.

Candidate(s)	Total vote	Percent	Party	Status	First elected
U.S. Representative in Congress (cont)					
District 6					
Thomas Petri	143,875	52.87%	Republican	Incumbent	1979
Peggy Lautenschlager	128,232	47.12%	Democrat	Challenger	
Scattering (other)	30	0.01%	Write in	Challenger	
District 7					
David Obey	166,200	64.42%	Democrat	Incumbent	1969
Dale Vannes	91,772	35.57%	Republican	Challenger	
Scattering (other)	10	<.01%	Write in	Challenger	
District 8					
Toby Roth	191,704	70.08%	Republican	Incumbent	1978
Catherine Helms	81,792	29.90%	Democrat	Challenger	
Scattering (other)	36	0.01%	Write in	Challenger	
District 9					
F. James Sensenbrenner, Jr.	192,898	69.69%	Republican	Incumbent	1978
Ingrid Buxton	77,362	27.95%	Democrat	Challenger	
David Marlow	4,619	1.67%	Independent	Challenger	
Jeffrey Millikin	1,881	0.68%	Libertarian	Challenger	
Scattering (other)	27	<.01%	Write in	Challenger	

Candidates: April 7, 1992, Primary Election

Candidate	Total vote	Percent	Candidate	Total vote	Percent
Presidential Preference, Democratic			**Presidential Preference, Republican**		
Bill Clinton	287,356	37.19%	George Bush	364,507	75.58%
Jerry Brown	266,207	34.46%	Patrick Buchanan	78,516	16.28%
Paul Tsongas	168,619	21.82%	David Duke	12,867	2.67%
Uncommitted	15,487	2.00%	Scattering (other)	12,801	2.65%
Scattering (other)	13,650	1.77%	Uncommitted	8,725	1.81%
Eugene McCarthy	6,525	0.84%	Harold Stassen	3,819	0.79%
Tom Harkin	5,395	0.70%	Emmanuel Branch	1,013	0.21%
Larry Agran	3,193	0.41%			
Lyndon LaRouche, Jr.	3,120	0.40%			
Bob Kerrey	3,044	0.39%			

Voter Registration and Turnout, 1948-1992 Elections

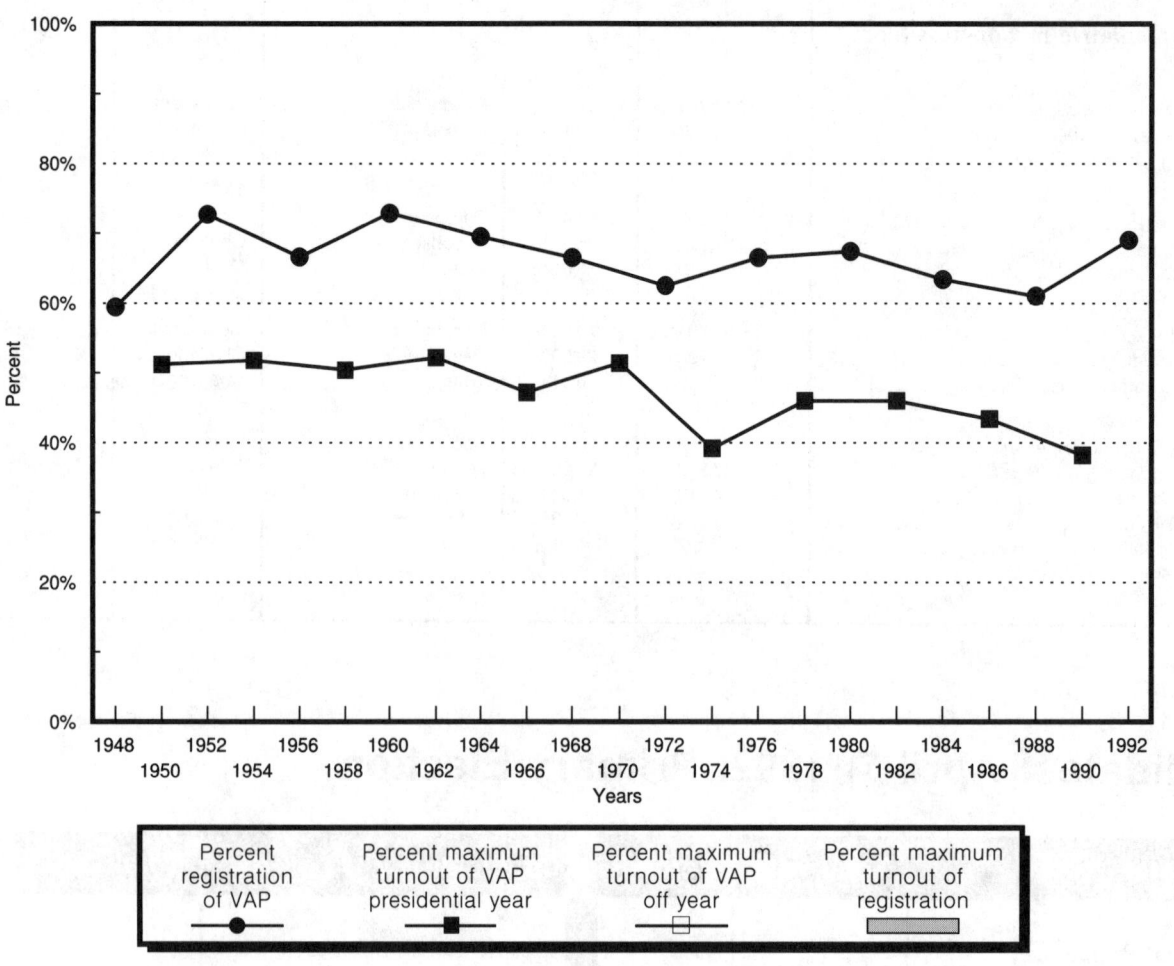

Year	Estimated Voting Age Population (VAP)	Voter registration (REG)[1]			Voter turnout											
						Highest office						Maximum vote				
		Total	Percent of VAP	Rank by percent of VAP	Actual	Total	Office	Percent total REG[1]	Rank by percent of REG[1]	Percent of VAP	Rank by percent of VAP	Total	Percent total REG[1]	Rank by percent of REG[1]	Percent total VAP	Rank by percent of VAP
1992........	3,669,000	-	-	-	-	2,531,114	P	-	-	69.0	4	2,531,114	-	-	69.0	4
1990........	3,616,000	-	-	-	-	1,379,727	G	-	-	38.2	29	1,379,727	-	-	38.2	31
1988........	3,593,000	-	-	-	-	2,191,608	P	-	-	61.0	5	2,191,608	-	-	61.0	7
1986........	3,522,000	-	-	-	-	1,526,960	G	-	-	43.4	15	1,526,960	-	-	43.4	18
1984........	3,487,000	-	-	-	-	2,211,689	P	-	-	63.4	4	2,211,689	-	-	63.4	6
1982........	3,437,000	-	-	-	-	1,580,344	G	-	-	46.0	19	1,580,344	-	-	46.0	20
1980........	3,375,000	-	-	-	-	2,273,221	P	-	-	67.4	3	2,273,221	-	-	67.4	4
1978........	3,263,000	-	-	-	-	1,500,996	G	-	-	46.0	12	1,500,996	-	-	46.0	14
1976[2]	3,163,000	-	-	-	-	2,104,175	P	-	-	66.5	4	2,104,175	-	-	66.5	4
1974........	3,059,000	-	-	-	-	1,199,495	S	-	-	39.2	33	1,199,495	-	-	39.2	34
1972........	2,965,000	-	-	-	-	1,852,890	P	-	-	62.5	13	1,852,890	-	-	62.5	18
1970........	2,615,000	-	-	-	-	1,343,160	G	-	-	51.4	20	1,343,160	-	-	51.4	24
1968........	2,543,000	-	-	-	-	1,691,538	P	-	-	66.5	18	1,691,538	-	-	66.5	18
1966........	2,481,000	-	-	-	-	1,170,173	G	-	-	47.2	33	1,170,173	-	-	47.2	33
1964........	2,434,000	-	-	-	-	1,691,815	P	-	-	69.5	17	1,691,815	-	-	69.5	19
1962........	2,426,000	-	-	-	-	1,265,900	G	-	-	52.2	23	1,265,900	-	-	52.2	26
1960........	2,372,000	-	-	-	-	1,729,082	P	-	-	72.9	15	1,729,082	-	-	72.9	16
1958........	2,387,000	-	-	-	-	1,202,219	G	-	-	50.4	27	1,202,219	-	-	50.4	28
1956........	2,328,000	-	-	-	-	1,550,558	P	-	-	66.6	25	1,550,558	-	-	66.6	26
1954........	2,237,000	-	-	-	-	1,158,666	G	-	-	51.8	21	1,158,666	-	-	51.8	22
1952........	2,212,000	-	-	-	-	1,607,370	P	-	-	72.7	16	1,607,370	-	-	72.7	20
1950........	2,222,000	-	-	-	-	1,138,148	G	-	-	51.2	20	1,138,148	-	-	51.2	23
1948........	2,148,000	-	-	-	-	1,276,800	P	-	-	59.4	23	1,276,800	-	-	59.4	25

[1]No statewide voter registration requirement (registration required only for municipalities over 5,000 population).   [2]Election day voter registration law enacted 1976.

WISCONSIN

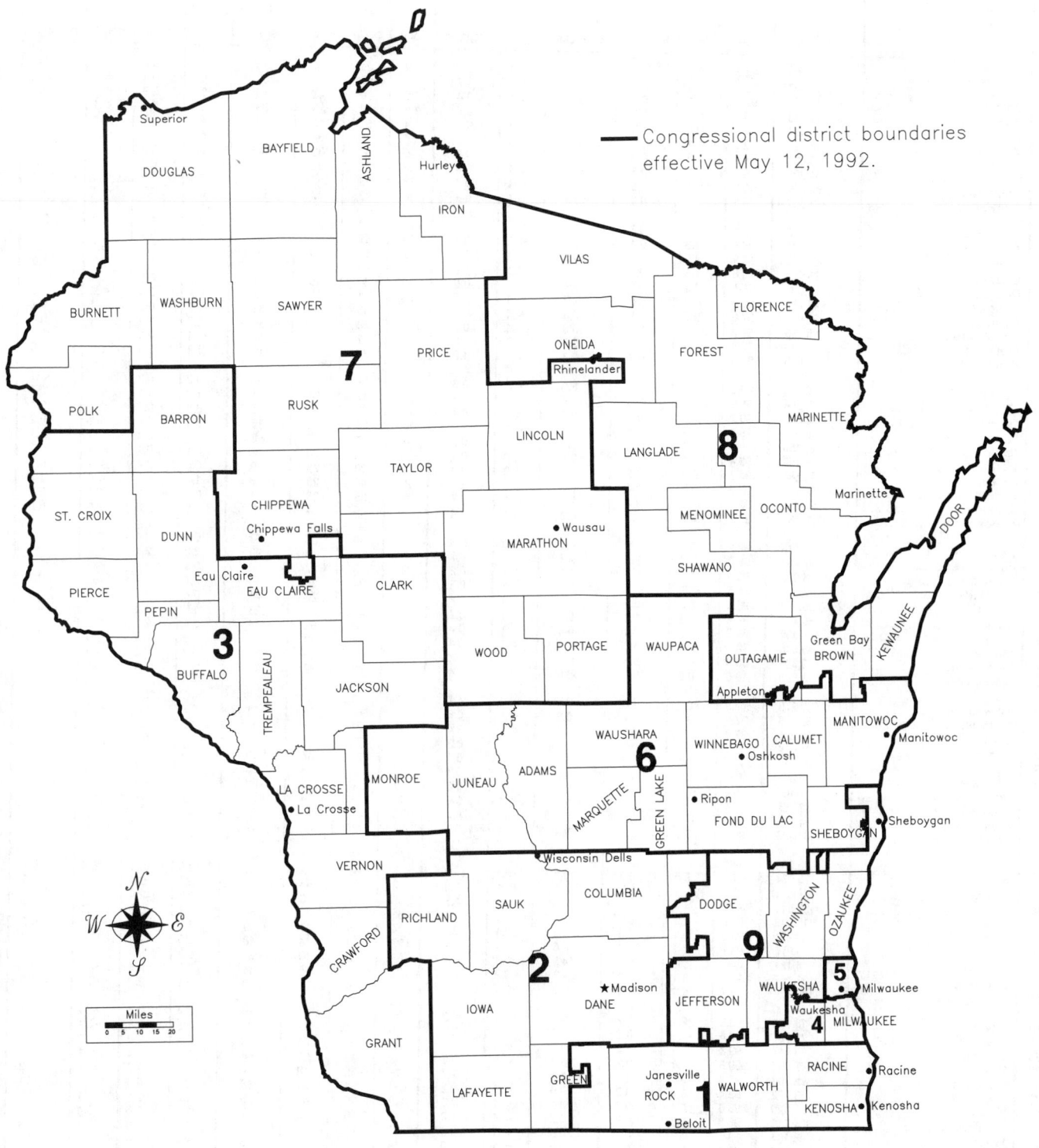

Congressional district boundaries effective May 12, 1992.

Wisconsin 997

Table A. — 1990 Population by Race and Ethnic Origin

State/ county code	County	Total persons	Percent of total persons — Non-Hispanic White	Non-Hisp. Black	Non-Hisp. Asian and Pacific Islander	Non-Hisp. Native American	Non-Hisp. Other	Hispanic	Rank Total	Rank Non-Hisp. White	Rank Non-Hisp. Black	Rank Hispanic	% contribution Total	% contribution Non-Hisp. White	% contribution Non-Hisp. Black	% contribution Hispanic
55 001	Adams	15,682	94.7	2.3	0.3	0.8	<.1	2.0	59	59	6	5	0.3	0.3	0.1	0.3
55 003	Ashland	16,307	90.1	<.1	0.3	8.9	<.1	0.7	56	67	52	30	0.3	0.3	<.1	0.1
55 005	Barron	40,750	98.8	<.1	0.2	0.5	<.1	0.4	30	20	48	45	0.8	0.9	<.1	0.2
55 007	Bayfield	14,008	90.5	0.2	0.2	8.8	<.1	0.4	63	66	29	53	0.3	0.3	<.1	<.1
55 009	Brown	194,594	95.5	0.5	1.3	1.9	0.0	0.8	4	57	12	22	4.0	4.2	0.4	1.6
55 011	Buffalo	13,584	99.3	<.1	0.2	0.2	0.0	0.3	65	7	66	62	0.3	0.3	<.1	<.1
55 013	Burnett	13,084	95.2	0.2	0.2	4.1	<.1	0.3	66	58	33	60	0.3	0.3	<.1	<.1
55 015	Calumet	34,291	98.6	<.1	0.5	0.4	<.1	0.4	36	27	51	42	0.7	0.8	<.1	0.2
55 017	Chippewa	52,360	98.8	<.1	0.5	0.3	<.1	0.4	23	18	59	59	1.1	1.2	<.1	0.2
55 019	Clark	31,647	99.1	<.1	0.1	0.3	<.1	0.4	39	13	47	52	0.6	0.7	<.1	0.1
55 021	Columbia	45,088	98.1	0.5	0.3	0.3	<.1	0.8	28	33	11	21	0.9	1.0	<.1	0.4
55 023	Crawford	15,940	98.8	0.3	0.4	0.1	<.1	0.4	58	19	21	43	0.3	0.4	<.1	<.1
55 025	Dane	367,085	92.9	2.8	2.3	0.3	<.1	1.2	2	63	5	10	7.5	7.6	4.3	6.2
55 027	Dodge	76,559	96.8	1.5	0.2	0.3	<.1	0.6	17	49	7	14	1.6	1.7	0.5	1.0
55 029	Door	25,690	98.4	0.1	0.2	0.7	<.1	0.5	43	30	46	33	0.5	0.6	<.1	0.2
55 031	Douglas	41,758	96.5	0.4	0.6	1.9	<.1	0.5	29	51	16	36	0.9	0.8	<.1	0.2
55 033	Dunn	35,909	97.0	0.5	1.7	0.3	<.1	0.5	34	48	14	36	0.7	0.8	<.1	0.2
55 035	Eau Claire	85,183	96.2	0.3	2.5	0.5	<.1	0.5	15	53	24	38	1.7	1.8	<.1	0.5
55 037	Florence	4,590	99.3	<.1	<.1	0.3	<.1	0.2	71	9	50	67	<.1	0.1	<.1	<.1
55 039	Fond du Lac	90,083	97.9	0.3	0.5	0.3	<.1	1.0	14	38	22	15	1.8	2.0	0.1	1.0
55 041	Forest	8,776	89.2	1.4	0.2	8.8	<.1	0.3	68	68	8	57	0.2	0.2	<.1	<.1
55 043	Grant	49,264	98.9	0.2	0.5	0.1	<.1	0.3	25	17	34	61	1.0	1.1	<.1	0.2
55 045	Green	30,339	99.2	0.2	0.2	0.2	<.1	0.4	40	12	56	46	0.6	0.7	<.1	0.2
55 047	Green Lake	18,651	98.1	0.1	0.6	0.2	<.1	1.0	52	34	43	16	0.4	0.4	<.1	<.1
55 049	Iowa	20,150	99.5	<.1	<.1	<.1	<.1	0.2	47	1	67	68	0.4	0.4	<.1	<.1
55 051	Iron	6,153	99.4	<.1	<.1	0.4	0.0	0.1	70	4	70	72	0.1	0.1	<.1	0.2
55 053	Jackson	16,588	94.7	0.3	0.2	4.0	0.0	0.9	55	60	25	19	1.4	1.5	<.1	1.2
55 055	Jefferson	67,783	97.3	0.3	0.4	0.3	<.1	1.7	21	44	23	8	0.4	0.5	<.1	0.2
55 057	Juneau	21,650	98.1	0.1	0.4	0.7	<.1	0.7	46	35	38	27	2.6	2.6	2.1	6.0
55 059	Kenosha	128,181	90.7	4.0	0.5	0.3	<.1	4.4	9	65	4	3	0.4	0.4	<.1	<.1
55 061	Kewaunee	18,878	99.2	0.1	0.1	0.3	0.0	0.3	51	10	39	63	0.4	0.4	<.1	<.1
55 063	La Crosse	97,904	96.0	0.4	2.6	0.3	<.1	0.7	12	54	15	29	2.0	2.1	0.2	0.7
55 065	Lafayette	16,076	99.5	<.1	<.1	0.1	<.1	0.2	57	2	57	69	0.3	0.4	<.1	<.1
55 067	Langlade	19,505	98.5	<.1	0.1	0.7	<.1	0.5	48	28	55	35	0.4	0.4	<.1	0.1
55 069	Lincoln	26,993	98.6	0.3	0.3	0.3	<.1	0.4	42	24	20	41	0.6	0.6	<.1	0.1
55 071	Manitowoc	80,421	97.4	0.1	1.3	0.4	<.1	0.7	16	42	36	23	1.6	1.8	<.1	0.5
55 073	Marathon	115,400	97.0	<.1	2.1	0.4	<.1	0.4	10	46	53	44	2.4	2.5	<.1	0.2
55 075	Marinette	40,548	99.1	<.1	0.2	0.4	<.1	0.4	31	14	69	47	0.8	0.9	<.1	0.2
55 077	Marquette	12,321	98.0	0.3	0.1	0.4	<.1	1.2	67	36	26	13	0.3	0.3	<.1	0.2
55 078	Menominee	3,890	10.6	0.0	0.0	88.0	0.0	1.4	72	72	72	11	<.1	<.1	0.0	<.1
55 079	Milwaukee	959,275	72.9	20.2	1.6	0.7	0.1	4.7	1	71	1	2	19.6	15.7	80.1	47.9
55 081	Monroe	36,633	97.8	0.4	0.4	0.8	<.1	0.6	33	40	18	31	0.7	0.8	<.1	0.3
55 083	Oconto	30,226	98.8	<.1	0.1	0.7	<.1	0.3	41	21	58	54	0.6	0.7	<.1	0.1
55 085	Oneida	31,679	98.7	0.2	0.2	0.7	<.1	0.3	38	22	32	64	0.6	0.7	<.1	<.1
55 087	Outagamie	140,510	96.4	0.1	1.3	1.4	<.1	0.7	6	52	37	28	2.9	3.0	<.1	1.1
55 089	Ozaukee	72,831	97.9	0.7	0.6	0.2	<.1	0.7	20	39	9	25	1.5	1.6	0.2	0.6
55 091	Pepin	7,107	99.3	<.1	0.1	0.3	<.1	0.3	69	6	68	65	0.1	0.2	<.1	<.1
55 093	Pierce	32,765	98.4	0.2	0.5	0.3	<.1	0.6	37	32	28	32	0.7	0.7	<.1	0.2
55 095	Polk	34,773	98.5	<.1	0.1	0.9	<.1	0.4	35	29	60	51	0.7	0.8	<.1	0.1
55 097	Portage	61,405	97.2	0.2	1.3	0.4	<.1	0.9	22	45	27	17	1.3	1.3	<.1	0.6
55 099	Price	15,600	98.9	<.1	0.1	0.5	<.1	0.4	60	16	65	50	0.3	0.3	<.1	<.1
55 101	Racine	175,034	84.4	9.5	0.6	0.3	<.1	5.2	5	69	2	1	3.6	3.3	6.9	9.7
55 103	Richland	17,521	99.2	<.1	0.2	0.2	<.1	0.3	54	11	54	58	0.4	0.4	<.1	<.1
55 105	Rock	139,510	93.0	4.7	0.7	0.3	<.1	1.3	8	62	3	12	2.9	2.9	2.7	1.9
55 107	Rusk	15,079	97.9	0.2	0.7	0.5	<.1	0.6	61	37	30	34	0.3	0.3	<.1	<.1
55 109	St. Croix	50,251	99.0	<.1	0.3	0.2	<.1	0.4	24	15	49	49	1.0	1.1	<.1	0.2
55 111	Sauk	46,975	98.7	0.1	0.2	0.6	<.1	0.4	26	23	44	40	1.0	1.0	<.1	0.2
55 113	Sawyer	14,181	84.1	0.1	0.1	14.9	<.1	0.7	62	70	40	24	0.3	0.3	<.1	0.1
55 115	Shawano	37,157	94.6	0.1	0.2	4.7	0.0	0.3	32	61	45	55	0.8	0.8	0.2	1.8
55 117	Sheboygan	103,877	95.7	0.4	1.9	0.3	<.1	1.6	11	56	17	9	2.1	2.2	0.2	1.8
55 119	Taylor	18,901	99.3	<.1	0.2	0.2	<.1	0.2	50	5	71	70	0.4	0.4	<.1	<.1
55 121	Trempealeau	25,263	99.4	<.1	0.2	0.1	0.0	0.2	45	3	63	71	0.5	0.6	<.1	0.1
55 123	Vernon	25,617	99.3	<.1	0.2	0.1	<.1	0.4	44	8	64	48	0.5	0.6	<.1	<.1
55 125	Vilas	17,707	90.8	<.1	0.2	8.6	<.1	0.3	53	64	61	56	0.4	0.4	<.1	<.1
55 127	Walworth	75,000	95.8	0.6	0.6	0.3	<.1	2.7	18	55	10	4	1.5	1.6	0.2	2.2
55 129	Washburn	13,772	98.4	0.2	0.2	0.9	<.1	0.2	64	31	31	66	0.3	0.3	<.1	<.1
55 131	Washington	95,328	98.6	0.1	0.3	0.2	<.1	0.7	13	26	41	26	1.9	2.1	<.1	0.7
55 133	Waukesha	304,715	96.8	0.3	0.9	0.2	<.1	1.8	3	50	19	7	6.2	6.6	0.4	5.8
55 135	Waupaca	46,104	98.6	<.1	0.2	0.3	<.1	0.9	27	25	62	18	0.9	1.0	<.1	0.4
55 137	Waushara	19,385	97.3	0.1	0.2	0.4	<.1	2.0	49	43	35	6	0.4	0.4	<.1	0.4

Table A. — 1990 Population by Race and Ethnic Origin (cont)

State/ county code	County	Total persons	Percent of total persons Non-Hispanic White	Black	Asian and Pacific Islander	Native American	Other	Hispanic	Rank Total	Percent of total persons Non-Hispanic White	Black	Hispanic	Percent contribution to state population Total	Non-Hispanic White	Black	Hispanic
55 139	Winnebago..............	140,320	97.0	0.5	1.2	0.5	<.1	0.8	7	47	13	20	2.9	3.0	0.3	1.2
55 141	Wood	73,605	97.8	0.1	0.9	0.6	<.1	0.5	19	41	42	37	1.5	1.6	<.1	0.4
55	**WISCONSIN**	**4,891,769**	**91.3**	**4.9**	**1.1**	**0.8**	**<.1**	**1.9**					**100.0**	**100.0**	**100.0**	**100.0**
	CONGRESSIONAL															
	District 1........................	543,530	90.3	5.3	0.6	0.3	<.1	3.4	5	8	2	2	11.1	11.0	12.0	20.0
	District 2........................	543,532	94.7	2.0	1.6	0.3	<.1	1.2	3	6	3	4	11.1	11.5	4.5	7.2
	District 3........................	543,533	97.7	0.2	1.1	0.4	<.1	0.5	2	1	8	8	11.1	11.9	0.5	2.8
	District 4........................	543,527	90.8	0.8	1.2	0.8	<.1	6.3	8	7	4	1	11.1	11.1	1.8	36.9
	District 5........................	543,530	60.2	34.9	1.7	0.5	0.1	2.6	6	9	1	3	11.1	7.3	78.4	15.4
	District 6........................	543,652	97.6	0.3	0.7	0.4	<.1	0.9	1	2	6	6	11.1	11.9	0.8	5.1
	District 7........................	543,529	96.9	0.1	0.9	1.5	<.1	0.5	7	4	9	9	11.1	11.8	0.3	2.8
	District 8........................	543,404	95.7	0.3	0.9	2.6	<.1	0.6	9	5	7	7	11.1	11.6	0.6	3.6
	District 9........................	543,532	97.5	0.4	0.8	0.2	<.1	1.0	4	3	5	5	11.1	11.9	0.9	6.1

Table B. — 1990 Voting Age Population (VAP) by Race and Ethnic Origin

County	Total Voting Age Population	Percent of total VAP						Rank				Percent contribution to state VAP				VAP percent of total population						
				Non-Hispanic					Percent of total VAP				Non-Hispanic					Non-Hispanic				
				Asian and Pacific Islander	Native American				Non-Hispanic										Asian and Pacific Islander	Native American		
		White	Black			Other	Hispanic	Total	White	Black	Hispanic	Total	White	Black	Hispanic	Total	White	Black			Other	Hispanic
Adams	12,378	94.2	2.7	0.3	0.9	0.0	1.9	55	62	5	5	0.3	0.3	0.2	0.4	78.9	78.5	94.6	74.5	89.1	0.0	77.3
Ashland	11,890	91.8	0.1	0.3	7.3	<.1	0.4	57	68	37	33	0.3	0.3	<.1	<.1	72.9	74.3	92.3	75.6	60.1	100.0	47.2
Barron	29,450	99.1	<.1	0.2	0.4	0.0	0.3	31	20	58	47	0.8	0.9	<.1	0.2	72.3	72.5	36.1	58.1	56.5	0.0	52.4
Bayfield	10,280	92.5	<.1	0.1	7.1	0.0	0.3	63	66	39	56	0.3	0.3	<.1	<.1	73.4	75.0	34.5	45.8	59.1	0.0	52.0
Brown	141,943	96.5	0.5	0.8	1.6	<.1	0.6	4	56	13	22	3.9	4.1	0.5	1.6	72.9	73.7	72.2	45.8	61.2	17.9	55.7
Buffalo	9,912	99.5	<.1	0.1	0.1	0.0	0.2	65	4	61	63	0.3	0.3	<.1	<.1	73.0	73.1	80.0	44.8	61.9	0.0	50.0
Burnett	9,811	96.3	0.1	<.1	3.4	<.1	0.2	66	58	34	68	0.3	0.3	<.1	<.1	75.0	75.8	50.0	37.5	62.0	100.0	37.2
Calumet	23,798	98.8	<.1	0.4	0.4	0.0	0.4	38	29	47	37	0.7	0.7	<.1	0.2	69.4	69.5	55.2	56.5	63.9	0.0	59.7
Chippewa	37,530	99.1	<.1	0.4	0.3	<.1	0.2	23	19	56	60	1.0	1.1	<.1	0.2	71.7	71.9	61.3	49.3	65.7	25.0	50.0
Clark	22,078	99.3	<.1	<.1	0.2	0.0	0.3	39	14	42	43	0.6	0.7	<.1	0.1	69.8	69.9	69.0	52.6	58.9	0.0	56.9
Columbia	33,211	98.2	0.6	0.2	0.3	<.1	0.6	28	38	9	20	0.9	1.0	0.1	0.4	73.7	73.8	90.6	56.3	72.4	33.3	58.1
Crawford	11,319	99.2	<.1	0.3	0.1	0.0	0.3	60	16	40	41	0.3	0.3	<.1	<.1	71.0	71.3	23.9	51.8	56.5	0.0	53.7
Dane	283,748	94.0	2.2	2.2	0.3	<.1	1.3	2	63	6	9	7.9	8.0	4.3	6.8	77.3	78.2	60.6	74.1	72.3	24.9	63.8
Dodge	56,109	96.6	1.9	0.2	0.3	<.1	1.0	18	55	7	12	1.6	1.6	0.7	1.1	73.3	73.1	97.6	58.9	71.8	20.0	63.4
Door	19,031	98.7	<.1	0.2	0.6	0.0	0.5	43	30	46	32	0.5	0.6	<.1	0.2	74.1	74.3	46.4	61.7	64.4	0.0	56.2
Douglas	31,077	97.3	0.3	0.4	1.6	<.1	0.3	29	53	16	40	0.9	0.9	<.1	0.2	74.4	75.0	62.1	48.3	63.3	25.0	52.2
Dunn	27,062	97.7	0.5	1.1	0.2	<.1	0.4	33	47	14	34	0.8	0.8	<.1	0.2	75.4	75.9	79.1	49.0	69.9	44.4	60.1
Eau Claire	64,088	97.5	0.2	1.5	0.4	<.1	0.4	15	49	26	35	1.8	1.9	<.1	0.5	75.2	76.2	57.0	44.7	59.6	47.8	60.4
Florence	3,368	99.3	<.1	<.1	0.4	0.0	0.2	71	10	51	66	<.1	<.1	<.1	<.1	73.4	73.4	50.0	50.0	85.7	0.0	54.5
Fond du Lac	65,514	98.2	0.3	0.3	0.3	<.1	0.8	14	39	21	17	1.8	1.9	0.1	1.0	72.7	73.0	70.9	51.3	75.3	55.0	58.6
Forest	6,395	92.1	1.4	0.2	6.1	<.1	0.3	68	67	8	53	0.2	0.2	<.1	<.1	72.9	75.2	72.0	85.7	49.9	66.7	56.7
Grant	36,088	98.9	0.2	0.5	0.2	<.1	0.3	24	26	27	45	1.0	1.1	<.1	0.2	73.3	73.3	81.6	71.0	78.1	28.6	66.9
Green	22,070	99.3	<.1	0.2	0.2	<.1	0.3	40	12	52	49	0.6	0.7	<.1	0.1	72.7	72.9	65.0	64.1	70.8	25.0	52.9
Green Lake	13,805	98.5	0.1	0.3	0.2	<.1	0.9	50	32	38	16	0.4	0.4	<.1	0.2	74.0	74.4	66.7	40.8	65.8	66.7	62.0
Iowa	14,389	99.6	<.1	<.1	0.1	<.1	0.2	48	3	60	67	0.4	0.4	<.1	<.1	71.4	71.5	85.7	52.6	85.0	40.0	52.1
Iron	4,842	99.5	<.1	<.1	0.3	0.0	0.1	70	5	66	71	0.1	0.1	<.1	<.1	78.7	78.7	100.0	100.0	60.0	0.0	87.5
Jackson	12,086	95.6	0.2	0.1	3.1	<.1	0.9	56	59	23	15	0.3	0.3	<.1	0.2	72.9	73.6	65.9	43.3	56.8	0.0	73.8
Jefferson	50,211	97.7	0.3	0.3	0.2	<.1	1.4	21	45	18	7	1.4	1.5	0.1	1.3	74.1	74.4	84.6	55.4	63.5	33.3	62.1
Juneau	15,736	98.4	0.1	0.3	0.7	0.0	0.5	46	36	31	29	0.4	0.5	<.1	0.1	72.7	72.9	71.4	64.5	65.4	0.0	52.6
Kenosha	93,848	92.8	3.0	0.5	0.3	<.1	3.4	9	65	4	3	2.6	2.6	2.0	5.8	73.2	74.9	54.9	68.1	70.2	19.4	56.4
Kewaunee	13,563	99.5	<.1	<.1	0.2	0.0	0.2	52	7	45	64	0.4	0.4	<.1	0.1	71.8	72.0	41.7	57.1	57.0	0.0	50.0
La Crosse	73,794	97.4	0.3	1.5	0.3	<.1	0.5	12	50	17	26	2.0	2.1	0.2	0.7	75.4	76.5	59.8	42.4	65.4	25.0	61.3
Lafayette	11,384	99.6	<.1	<.1	<.1	0.0	0.2	59	1	49	69	0.3	0.3	<.1	<.1	70.8	70.9	70.0	46.7	57.9	0.0	48.6
Langlade	14,302	99.0	<.1	<.1	0.6	<.1	0.4	49	24	65	36	0.4	0.4	<.1	0.1	73.3	73.6	30.8	45.5	57.7	14.3	52.9
Lincoln	19,722	99.2	<.1	0.2	0.2	<.1	0.3	42	15	50	54	0.5	0.6	<.1	<.1	73.1	73.5	15.2	52.6	51.7	16.7	44.1
Manitowoc	59,085	98.3	<.1	0.7	0.3	<.1	0.5	16	37	41	27	1.6	1.7	<.1	0.6	73.5	74.1	49.6	40.2	66.5	33.3	52.6
Marathon	82,947	98.2	<.1	1.1	0.3	<.1	0.3	10	41	54	44	2.3	2.4	<.1	0.5	71.9	72.8	50.6	38.5	59.3	20.0	52.6
Marinette	29,650	99.2	<.1	0.2	0.3	<.1	0.3	30	18	67	48	0.8	0.9	<.1	0.2	73.1	73.2	75.0	73.0	65.8	62.5	54.5
Marquette	9,296	98.5	0.2	0.2	0.3	0.0	0.9	67	35	28	14	0.3	0.3	<.1	0.2	75.4	75.8	48.4	77.8	66.7	0.0	55.7
Menominee	2,290	16.8	0.0	0.0	82.1	0.0	1.1	72	72	70	11	<.1	<.1	0.0	<.1	58.9	93.0	0.0	0.0	55.0	0.0	45.5
Milwaukee	712,973	78.3	16.2	1.3	0.6	<.1	3.6	1	71	1	2	19.8	16.7	79.7	47.6	74.3	79.9	59.7	61.3	65.0	24.4	57.4
Monroe	25,941	98.2	0.3	0.3	0.7	<.1	0.5	34	42	19	30	0.7	0.8	<.1	0.2	70.8	71.1	59.6	54.9	67.4	33.3	52.6
Oconto	21,995	99.0	<.1	<.1	0.7	0.0	0.3	41	23	68	50	0.6	0.6	<.1	0.1	72.8	72.9	22.2	42.4	69.7	0.0	57.0
Oneida	24,155	99.0	0.1	0.1	0.5	<.1	0.2	36	21	30	65	0.7	0.7	<.1	<.1	76.2	76.5	57.9	58.8	55.2	100.0	53.3
Outagamie	100,590	97.3	0.1	0.8	1.2	<.1	0.6	8	52	35	23	2.8	2.9	<.1	1.0	71.6	72.2	56.0	44.2	61.9	33.3	56.2
Ozaukee	53,146	98.2	0.6	0.5	0.2	<.1	0.5	19	43	10	25	1.5	1.6	0.2	0.5	73.0	73.2	68.7	59.0	77.6	28.6	56.5
Pepin	5,057	99.4	0.0	0.1	0.3	<.1	0.2	69	9	71	59	0.1	0.2	0.0	<.1	71.2	71.2	0.0	66.7	72.2	100.0	60.0
Pierce	23,917	98.5	0.3	0.5	0.2	<.1	0.5	37	33	20	28	0.7	0.7	<.1	0.2	73.0	73.1	83.5	66.9	64.6	33.3	62.2
Polk	24,845	98.9	<.1	0.1	0.7	0.0	0.2	35	28	62	58	0.7	0.7	<.1	0.1	71.4	71.7	50.0	53.2	56.9	0.0	47.3
Portage	45,661	97.7	0.2	1.0	0.3	<.1	0.7	22	46	25	18	1.3	1.3	<.1	0.6	74.4	74.8	63.2	61.7	64.0	44.4	56.1
Price	11,467	99.2	<.1	0.1	0.4	0.0	0.3	58	17	59	55	0.3	0.3	<.1	<.1	73.5	73.7	71.4	59.1	57.1	0.0	50.8
Racine	126,413	87.3	7.8	0.5	0.3	<.1	4.1	5	70	2	1	3.5	3.3	6.8	9.6	72.2	74.7	59.2	61.0	70.8	23.2	57.4
Richland	12,761	99.3	<.1	0.1	0.2	<.1	0.3	54	11	44	57	0.4	0.4	<.1	<.1	72.8	73.0	83.3	44.7	72.7	25.0	54.2
Rock	101,651	94.5	3.8	0.6	0.3	<.1	0.9	7	61	3	13	2.8	2.9	2.7	1.7	72.9	74.0	58.4	61.5	72.2	11.5	52.6
Rusk	10,919	98.2	0.2	0.6	0.5	<.1	0.5	61	40	24	31	0.3	0.3	<.1	<.1	72.4	72.6	83.9	56.6	67.9	100.0	58.8
St. Croix	35,134	99.3	<.1	0.2	0.2	<.1	0.3	25	13	48	51	1.0	1.0	<.1	0.2	69.9	70.1	50.0	41.9	58.3	25.0	49.5
Sauk	34,203	99.0	<.1	0.1	0.5	<.1	0.3	26	22	43	42	0.9	1.0	<.1	0.2	72.8	73.1	54.7	46.8	59.4	100.0	51.7
Sawyer	10,465	87.6	0.1	<.1	11.8	0.0	0.4	62	69	32	38	0.3	0.3	<.1	<.1	73.8	76.9	72.2	66.7	58.1	0.0	38.6
Shawano	27,171	95.6	<.1	0.1	4.0	0.0	0.2	32	60	55	61	0.8	0.8	<.1	0.1	73.1	73.9	33.3	55.1	62.0	0.0	48.1
Sheboygan	76,022	96.9	0.4	1.1	0.3	<.1	1.3	11	54	15	10	2.1	2.2	0.2	1.8	73.2	74.1	78.9	43.4	64.2	33.3	57.3
Taylor	13,191	99.4	0.0	0.2	0.2	<.1	0.2	53	8	72	62	0.4	0.4	0.0	<.1	69.8	69.9	0.0	50.0	66.7	50.0	69.0
Trempealeau	18,670	99.6	<.1	0.2	<.1	0.0	0.2	44	2	63	70	0.5	0.6	<.1	<.1	73.9	74.0	58.3	60.9	40.6	0.0	52.8
Vernon	18,590	99.5	<.1	<.1	0.1	<.1	0.3	45	6	69	46	0.5	0.6	<.1	0.1	72.6	72.7	25.0	35.7	71.4	100.0	56.1
Vilas	13,772	92.9	<.1	0.2	6.6	0.0	0.3	51	64	57	52	0.4	0.4	<.1	<.1	77.8	79.6	77.8	60.0	59.7	0.0	60.7
Walworth	57,021	96.5	0.6	0.5	0.2	<.1	2.1	17	57	11	4	1.6	1.6	0.2	2.2	76.0	76.6	77.9	64.6	67.9	43.3	59.6
Washburn	10,155	98.6	0.1	0.2	0.9	0.0	0.1	64	31	29	72	0.3	0.3	<.1	<.1	73.7	73.9	60.0	57.6	75.4	0.0	38.2
Washington	68,285	98.9	0.1	0.2	0.2	<.1	0.6	13	27	33	24	1.9	2.0	<.1	0.7	71.6	71.8	63.6	52.8	63.2	25.0	56.3
Waukesha	221,605	97.3	0.2	0.7	0.2	<.1	1.5	3	51	22	6	6.2	6.4	0.4	6.1	72.7	73.2	51.6	59.9	66.1	36.7	60.5
Waupaca	33,721	98.9	<.1	0.1	0.3	<.1	0.6	27	25	64	21	0.9	1.0	<.1	0.4	73.1	73.4	50.0	53.9	73.6	100.0	52.0
Waushara	14,589	98.0	0.1	0.2	0.3	<.1	1.4	47	44	36	8	0.4	0.4	<.1	0.4	75.3	75.8	51.7	56.1	67.6	100.0	53.8

Table B. — 1990 Voting Age Population (VAP) by Race and Ethnic Origin (cont)

County	Total Voting Age Population	Percent of total VAP — Non-Hispanic White	Black	Asian and Pacific Islander	Native American	Other	Hispanic	Rank — Percent of total VAP Total	Non-Hispanic White	Black	Hispanic	Percent contribution to state VAP Total	Non-Hispanic White	Black	Hispanic	VAP percent of total population Total	Non-Hispanic White	Black	Asian and Pacific Islander	Native American	Other	Hispanic
Winnebago	106,523	97.5	0.5	0.8	0.5	<.1	0.6	6	48	12	19	3.0	3.1	0.4	1.3	75.9	76.3	81.3	53.4	74.3	31.4	59.4
Wood	53,073	98.5	<.1	0.6	0.5	<.1	0.3	20	34	53	39	1.5	1.6	<.1	0.3	72.1	72.7	33.7	43.3	60.5	20.0	47.2
WISCONSIN	**3,602,787**	**93.0**	**4.0**	**0.8**	**0.7**	**<.1**	**1.5**					**100.0**	**100.0**	**100.0**	**100.0**	**73.7**	**75.0**	**60.0**	**57.2**	**62.4**	**25.8**	**57.8**
CONGRESSIONAL																						
District 1	397,289	92.3	4.3	0.5	0.3	<.1	2.7	6	8	2	2	11.0	10.9	11.7	19.7	73.1	74.7	58.6	63.2	70.3	21.0	56.9
District 2	412,393	95.4	1.6	1.6	0.3	<.1	1.0	1	6	3	4	11.4	11.7	4.7	7.9	75.9	76.4	62.3	73.3	70.4	26.0	63.1
District 3	398,432	98.3	0.2	0.7	0.4	<.1	0.4	4	1	8	8	11.1	11.7	0.5	2.9	73.3	73.8	61.7	46.2	60.3	35.2	59.4
District 4	408,049	92.9	0.7	1.0	0.6	<.1	4.8	2	7	4	1	11.3	11.3	1.9	36.2	75.1	76.8	62.8	58.4	63.8	32.2	56.7
District 5	397,983	67.5	28.4	1.5	0.4	<.1	2.2	5	9	1	3	11.0	8.0	78.0	16.0	73.2	82.1	59.7	63.7	67.4	22.4	60.0
District 6	400,441	98.0	0.4	0.5	0.4	<.1	0.7	3	2	6	6	11.1	11.7	1.0	5.2	73.7	74.0	79.1	49.9	71.5	36.5	58.6
District 7	395,676	97.7	0.1	0.6	1.3	<.1	0.3	9	4	9	9	11.0	11.5	0.3	2.5	72.8	73.4	53.3	45.6	60.2	28.9	51.1
District 8	396,350	96.7	0.3	0.5	2.1	<.1	0.5	7	5	7	7	11.0	11.4	0.7	3.5	72.9	73.7	67.0	46.2	59.1	27.0	55.3
District 9	396,174	98.0	0.4	0.6	0.2	<.1	0.8	8	3	5	5	11.0	11.6	1.1	6.2	72.9	73.3	71.0	51.1	65.3	31.4	58.4

Table C. — Voter Participation: November 3, 1992, General Election

County	Estimated Voting Age Population (VAP), 1992	Voter registration (REG)[1]				Voter turnout										Percent drop-off, by office[2]			
							Highest office			Maximum vote									
		Total	% contribution to state REG	% of 1992 VAP	Rank by % of 1992 VAP	Actual	Total	Office	% of 1992 VAP	Total	% contribution to state turnout	% of REG[1]	Rank by % of REG[1]	% of 1992 VAP	Rank by % 1992 VAP	President	Senator	Governor	Representative
Adams	12,929	-	-	-	-	-	8,048	P	62.2	8,048	0.3	-	-	62.2	71	0.0	6.4	-	9.6
Ashland	11,892	-	-	-	-	-	8,393	P	70.6	8,393	0.3	-	-	70.6	23	0.0	6.3	-	12.8
Barron	30,164	-	-	-	-	-	20,230	P	67.1	20,230	0.8	-	-	67.1	55	0.0	5.3	-	10.0
Bayfield	10,442	-	-	-	-	-	8,112	P	77.7	8,112	0.3	-	-	77.7	4	0.0	5.6	-	9.8
Brown	146,725	-	-	-	-	-	102,701	P	70.0	102,701	4.1	-	-	70.0	30	0.0	1.2	-	3.5
Buffalo	9,965	-	-	-	-	-	6,950	P	69.7	6,950	0.3	-	-	69.7	32	0.0	3.8	-	4.1
Burnett	10,060	-	-	-	-	-	7,436	P	73.9	7,436	0.3	-	-	73.9	11	0.0	6.9	-	8.7
Calumet	24,879	-	-	-	-	-	18,401	P	74.0	18,401	0.7	-	-	74.0	10	0.0	3.3	-	4.5
Chippewa	38,172	-	-	-	-	-	25,230	P	66.1	25,230	1.0	-	-	66.1	59	0.0	2.6	-	9.6
Clark	22,354	-	-	-	-	-	14,885	P	66.6	14,885	0.6	-	-	66.6	56	0.0	5.7	-	6.5
Columbia	34,001	-	-	-	-	-	23,984	P	70.5	23,984	0.9	-	-	70.5	24	0.0	2.2	-	1.5
Crawford	11,503	-	-	-	-	-	7,812	P	67.9	7,812	0.3	-	-	67.9	48	0.0	8.9	-	5.3
Dane	289,637	-	-	-	-	-	210,122	P	72.5	210,122	8.3	-	-	72.5	15	0.0	3.5	-	1.6
Dodge	57,159	-	-	-	-	-	35,709	P	62.5	35,709	1.4	-	-	62.5	70	0.0	0.3	-	4.4
Door	19,395	-	-	-	-	-	13,829	S	71.3	13,829	0.5	-	-	71.3	20	0.4	0.0	-	3.2
Douglas	30,946	-	-	-	-	-	22,253	P	71.9	22,253	0.9	-	-	71.9	17	0.0	5.7	-	18.5
Dunn	26,944	-	-	-	-	-	18,218	P	67.6	18,218	0.7	-	-	67.6	50	0.0	9.9	-	11.2
Eau Claire	64,432	-	-	-	-	-	47,076	P	73.1	47,076	1.9	-	-	73.1	14	0.0	2.4	-	5.2
Florence	3,485	-	-	-	-	-	2,646	P	75.9	2,646	0.1	-	-	75.9	7	0.0	10.0	-	5.7
Fond du Lac	66,711	-	-	-	-	-	45,176	C	67.7	45,176	1.8	-	-	67.7	49	1.5	1.0	-	0.0
Forest	6,425	-	-	-	-	-	4,368	P	68.0	4,368	0.2	-	-	68.0	47	0.0	7.3	-	11.7
Grant	35,640	-	-	-	-	-	23,157	P	65.0	23,157	0.9	-	-	65.0	64	0.0	5.5	-	10.8
Green	22,487	-	-	-	-	-	14,183	P	63.1	14,183	0.6	-	-	63.1	68	0.0	0.2	-	0.4
Green Lake	14,014	-	-	-	-	-	9,540	P	68.1	9,540	0.4	-	-	68.1	46	0.0	3.5	-	4.9
Iowa	14,688	-	-	-	-	-	10,151	P	69.1	10,151	0.4	-	-	69.1	40	0.0	4.9	-	4.1
Iron	4,850	-	-	-	-	-	3,891	P	80.2	3,891	0.2	-	-	80.2	2	0.0	7.2	-	14.9
Jackson	12,258	-	-	-	-	-	8,418	P	68.7	8,418	0.3	-	-	68.7	42	0.0	5.3	-	4.8
Jefferson	50,466	-	-	-	-	-	32,802	P	65.0	32,802	1.3	-	-	65.0	62	0.0	0.2	-	6.2
Juneau	16,088	-	-	-	-	-	10,993	P	68.3	10,993	0.4	-	-	68.3	44	0.0	5.4	-	10.5
Kenosha	95,507	-	-	-	-	-	61,837	P	64.7	61,837	2.4	-	-	64.7	65	0.0	4.5	-	6.7
Kewaunee	13,748	-	-	-	-	-	10,377	P	75.5	10,377	0.4	-	-	75.5	8	0.0	4.6	-	0.9
La Crosse	74,373	-	-	-	-	-	52,273	P	70.3	52,273	2.1	-	-	70.3	26	0.0	3.2	-	5.3
Lafayette	11,345	-	-	-	-	-	7,859	P	69.3	7,859	0.3	-	-	69.3	37	0.0	8.8	-	9.8
Langlade	14,411	-	-	-	-	-	10,042	P	69.7	10,042	0.4	-	-	69.7	33	0.0	3.9	-	5.6
Lincoln	20,176	-	-	-	-	-	13,304	P	65.9	13,304	0.5	-	-	65.9	61	0.0	1.4	-	5.1
Manitowoc	59,420	-	-	-	-	-	41,268	P	69.5	41,268	1.6	-	-	69.5	35	0.0	4.0	-	4.5
Marathon	85,209	-	-	-	-	-	57,378	P	67.3	57,378	2.3	-	-	67.3	52	0.0	1.7	-	4.4
Marinette	30,288	-	-	-	-	-	21,093	P	69.6	21,093	0.8	-	-	69.6	34	0.0	7.5	-	5.6
Marquette	9,497	-	-	-	-	-	6,720	P	70.8	6,720	0.3	-	-	70.8	22	0.0	6.2	-	6.8
Menominee	2,429	-	-	-	-	-	1,160	P	47.8	1,160	< .1	-	-	47.8	72	0.0	32.5	-	38.5
Milwaukee	716,406	-	-	-	-	-	465,496	P	65.0	465,496	18.4	-	-	65.0	63	0.0	2.2	-	7.5
Monroe	26,764	-	-	-	-	-	16,805	P	62.8	16,805	0.7	-	-	62.8	69	0.0	3.2	-	7.3
Oconto	22,603	-	-	-	-	-	16,073	P	71.1	16,073	0.6	-	-	71.1	21	0.0	8.7	-	8.5
Oneida	24,415	-	-	-	-	-	18,714	P	76.6	18,714	0.7	-	-	76.6	6	0.0	2.5	-	7.4
Outagamie	103,846	-	-	-	-	-	72,911	P	70.2	72,911	2.9	-	-	70.2	27	0.0	2.3	-	3.6
Ozaukee	54,825	-	-	-	-	-	43,011	S	78.5	43,011	1.7	-	-	78.5	3	0.2	0.0	-	2.8
Pepin	5,081	-	-	-	-	-	3,572	P	70.3	3,572	0.1	-	-	70.3	25	0.0	6.7	-	9.4
Pierce	24,088	-	-	-	-	-	17,272	P	71.7	17,272	0.7	-	-	71.7	19	0.0	5.8	-	8.8
Polk	25,755	-	-	-	-	-	18,071	P	70.2	18,071	0.7	-	-	70.2	28	0.0	5.4	-	6.5
Portage	45,883	-	-	-	-	-	33,716	P	73.5	33,716	1.3	-	-	73.5	12	0.0	4.3	-	9.6
Price	11,662	-	-	-	-	-	8,550	P	73.3	8,550	0.3	-	-	73.3	13	0.0	4.1	-	12.5
Racine	128,568	-	-	-	-	-	87,819	P	68.3	87,819	3.5	-	-	68.3	45	0.0	5.2	-	4.7
Richland	12,924	-	-	-	-	-	8,540	P	66.1	8,540	0.3	-	-	66.1	60	0.0	7.4	-	6.4
Rock	102,774	-	-	-	-	-	69,025	P	67.2	69,025	2.7	-	-	67.2	54	0.0	4.6	-	3.9
Rusk	11,025	-	-	-	-	-	7,967	P	72.3	7,967	0.3	-	-	72.3	16	0.0	4.2	-	7.4
St. Croix	37,382	-	-	-	-	-	25,676	P	68.7	25,676	1.0	-	-	68.7	41	0.0	3.5	-	6.5
Sauk	35,367	-	-	-	-	-	23,462	C	66.3	23,462	0.9	-	-	66.3	57	0.2	0.6	-	0.0
Sawyer	10,771	-	-	-	-	-	7,365	P	68.4	7,365	0.3	-	-	68.4	43	0.0	4.6	-	8.0
Shawano	27,897	-	-	-	-	-	17,952	P	64.4	17,952	0.7	-	-	64.4	66	0.0	5.4	-	7.8
Sheboygan	77,822	-	-	-	-	-	54,559	P	70.1	54,559	2.2	-	-	70.1	29	0.0	2.4	-	6.4
Taylor	13,514	-	-	-	-	-	9,359	P	69.3	9,359	0.4	-	-	69.3	38	0.0	4.7	-	6.6
Trempealeau	18,812	-	-	-	-	-	13,012	P	69.2	13,012	0.5	-	-	69.2	39	0.0	6.4	-	3.4
Vernon	18,903	-	-	-	-	-	12,716	P	67.3	12,716	0.5	-	-	67.3	53	0.0	3.7	-	4.6
Vilas	13,961	-	-	-	-	-	11,262	P	80.7	11,262	0.4	-	-	80.7	1	0.0	3.3	-	6.4
Walworth	57,510	-	-	-	-	-	36,796	P	64.0	36,796	1.5	-	-	64.0	67	0.0	0.3	-	0.9
Washburn	10,357	-	-	-	-	-	7,686	P	74.2	7,686	0.3	-	-	74.2	9	0.0	6.2	-	10.2
Washington	71,610	-	-	-	-	-	50,073	P	69.9	50,073	2.0	-	-	69.9	31	0.0	0.5	-	6.8
Waukesha	231,716	-	-	-	-	-	179,182	P	77.3	179,182	7.1	-	-	77.3	5	0.0	1.9	-	8.7
Waupaca	34,987	-	-	-	-	-	23,159	P	66.2	23,159	0.9	-	-	66.2	58	0.0	5.4	-	4.5
Waushara	14,895	-	-	-	-	-	10,329	P	69.3	10,329	0.4	-	-	69.3	36	0.0	5.3	-	4.2
Winnebago	107,779	-	-	-	-	-	77,386	P	71.8	77,386	3.1	-	-	71.8	18	0.0	3.1	-	3.0
Wood	53,984	-	-	-	-	-	36,436	P	67.5	36,436	1.4	-	-	67.5	51	0.0	0.8	-	2.3
WISCONSIN	3,669,000	-	-	-	-	-	2,531,977		69.0	2,531,977	100.0	-	-	69.0		0.0	3.0	-	5.7

[1]No statewide voter registration requirement (registration required only for municipalities over 5,000 population). [2]Percent drop-off is zero for any office used as highest office turnout.

1002 Wisconsin

Table E. — Vote for President: November 3, 1992, General Election

County	Total	Clinton (DEM)	Bush (REP)	Perot (IND)	Other	Plurality Total	Party	DEM	REP	IND	Other	Rank DEM	Rank REP	Rank IND	Total	DEM	REP	IND	DEM	REP
Adams	8,048	3,539	2,465	2,003	41	1,074	D	44.0	30.6	24.9	0.5	18	60	38	0.3	0.3	0.3	0.4	58.9	41.1
Ashland	8,393	4,213	2,372	1,746	62	1,841	D	50.2	28.3	20.8	0.7	5	68	63	0.3	0.4	0.3	0.3	64.0	36.0
Barron	20,230	8,063	6,572	5,479	116	1,491	D	39.9	32.5	27.1	0.6	33	47	13	0.8	0.8	0.7	1.0	55.1	44.9
Bayfield	8,112	3,873	2,393	1,786	60	1,480	D	47.7	29.5	22.0	0.7	7	64	57	0.3	0.4	0.3	0.3	61.8	38.2
Brown	102,701	37,513	42,352	22,395	441	4,839	R	36.5	41.2	21.8	0.4	52	11	59	4.1	3.6	4.5	4.1	47.0	53.0
Buffalo	6,950	2,996	2,029	1,889	36	967	D	43.1	29.2	27.2	0.5	23	66	9	0.3	0.3	0.2	0.3	59.6	40.4
Burnett	7,436	3,172	2,340	1,855	69	832	D	42.7	31.5	24.9	0.9	25	56	36	0.3	0.3	0.3	0.3	57.5	42.5
Calumet	18,401	5,701	7,541	5,055	104	1,840	R	31.0	41.0	27.5	0.6	66	13	6	0.7	0.5	0.8	0.9	43.1	56.9
Chippewa	25,230	10,487	8,215	6,408	120	2,272	D	41.6	32.6	25.4	0.5	28	45	31	1.0	1.0	0.9	1.2	56.1	43.9
Clark	14,885	5,540	4,977	4,284	84	563	D	37.2	33.4	28.8	0.6	49	41	2	0.6	0.5	0.5	0.8	52.7	47.3
Columbia	23,984	9,348	9,099	5,439	98	249	D	39.0	37.9	22.7	0.4	37	22	54	0.9	0.9	1.0	1.0	50.7	49.3
Crawford	7,812	3,540	2,390	1,797	85	1,150	D	45.3	30.6	23.0	1.1	10	61	51	0.3	0.3	0.3	0.3	59.7	40.3
Dane	210,122	114,724	61,957	31,874	1,567	52,767	D	54.6	29.5	15.2	0.7	3	65	72	8.3	11.0	6.7	5.9	64.9	35.1
Dodge	35,709	11,438	14,971	9,136	164	3,533	R	32.0	41.9	25.6	0.5	65	8	27	1.4	1.1	1.6	1.7	43.3	56.7
Door	13,777	4,735	5,468	3,506	68	733	R	34.4	39.7	25.4	0.5	59	17	29	0.5	0.5	0.6	0.6	46.4	53.6
Douglas	22,253	12,319	5,679	4,150	105	6,640	D	55.4	25.5	18.6	0.5	2	71	69	0.9	1.2	0.6	0.8	68.4	31.6
Dunn	18,218	7,965	5,283	4,809	161	2,682	D	43.7	29.0	26.4	0.9	20	67	17	0.7	0.8	0.6	0.9	60.1	39.9
Eau Claire	47,076	21,221	15,915	9,783	157	5,306	D	45.1	33.8	20.8	0.3	14	39	64	1.9	2.0	1.7	1.8	57.1	42.9
Florence	2,646	978	942	719	7	36	D	37.0	35.6	27.2	0.3	50	33	10	0.1	<.1	0.1	0.1	50.9	49.1
Fond du Lac	44,506	13,757	19,785	10,660	304	6,028	R	30.9	44.5	24.0	0.7	67	4	47	1.8	1.3	2.1	2.0	41.0	59.0
Forest	4,368	1,904	1,393	1,062	9	511	D	43.6	31.9	24.3	0.2	22	53	41	0.2	0.2	0.1	0.2	57.7	42.3
Grant	23,157	8,914	7,678	6,405	160	1,236	D	38.5	33.2	27.7	0.7	41	42	5	0.9	0.9	0.8	1.2	53.7	46.3
Green	14,183	5,467	4,887	3,735	94	580	D	38.5	34.5	26.3	0.7	39	36	18	0.6	0.5	0.5	0.7	52.8	47.2
Green Lake	9,540	2,772	3,897	2,827	44	1,070	R	29.1	40.8	29.6	0.5	68	14	1	0.4	0.3	0.4	0.5	41.6	58.4
Iowa	10,151	4,467	3,288	2,341	55	1,179	D	44.0	32.4	23.1	0.5	17	49	48	0.4	0.4	0.4	0.4	57.6	42.4
Iron	3,891	1,762	1,273	835	21	489	D	45.3	32.7	21.5	0.5	12	44	60	0.2	0.2	0.1	0.2	58.1	41.9
Jackson	8,418	3,681	2,644	2,040	53	1,037	D	43.7	31.4	24.2	0.6	19	57	45	0.3	0.4	0.3	0.4	58.2	41.8
Jefferson	32,802	11,593	13,072	7,960	177	1,479	R	35.3	39.9	24.3	0.5	56	16	44	1.3	1.1	1.4	1.5	47.0	53.0
Juneau	10,993	4,177	4,051	2,670	95	126	D	38.0	36.9	24.3	0.9	44	24	42	0.4	0.4	0.4	0.5	50.8	49.2
Kenosha	61,837	27,341	19,854	14,232	410	7,487	D	44.2	32.1	23.0	0.7	16	51	50	2.4	2.6	2.1	2.6	57.9	42.1
Kewaunee	10,377	4,050	3,570	2,700	57	480	D	39.0	34.4	26.0	0.5	36	37	23	0.4	0.4	0.4	0.5	53.1	46.9
La Crosse	52,273	22,838	18,891	10,224	320	3,947	D	43.7	36.1	19.6	0.6	21	30	67	2.1	2.2	2.0	1.9	54.7	45.3
Lafayette	7,859	3,143	2,582	2,079	55	561	D	40.0	32.9	26.5	0.7	32	43	16	0.3	0.3	0.3	0.4	54.9	45.1
Langlade	10,042	3,630	3,890	2,444	78	260	R	36.1	38.7	24.3	0.8	55	19	40	0.4	0.3	0.4	0.4	48.3	51.7
Lincoln	13,304	5,297	4,321	3,605	81	976	D	39.8	32.5	27.1	0.6	34	48	11	0.5	0.5	0.5	0.7	55.1	44.9
Manitowoc	41,268	15,903	14,008	11,179	178	1,895	D	38.5	33.9	27.1	0.4	40	38	12	1.6	1.5	1.5	2.1	53.2	46.8
Marathon	57,378	21,482	20,948	14,600	348	534	D	37.4	36.5	25.4	0.6	48	27	30	2.3	2.1	2.3	2.7	50.6	49.4
Marinette	21,093	7,626	7,984	5,412	71	358	R	36.2	37.9	25.7	0.3	54	23	26	0.8	0.7	0.9	1.0	48.9	51.1
Marquette	6,720	2,533	2,322	1,818	47	211	D	37.7	34.6	27.1	0.7	47	35	14	0.3	0.2	0.2	0.3	52.2	47.8
Menominee	1,160	691	244	221	4	447	D	59.6	21.0	19.1	0.3	1	72	68	<.1	<.1	<.1	<.1	73.9	26.1
Milwaukee	465,496	235,521	151,314	76,039	2,622	84,207	D	50.6	32.5	16.3	0.6	4	46	71	18.4	22.6	16.3	14.0	60.9	39.1
Monroe	16,805	6,427	6,118	4,183	77	309	D	38.2	36.4	24.9	0.5	43	29	37	0.7	0.6	0.7	0.8	51.2	48.8
Oconto	16,073	5,898	5,720	4,405	50	178	D	36.7	35.6	27.4	0.3	51	34	7	0.6	0.6	0.6	0.8	50.8	49.2
Oneida	18,714	7,160	6,725	4,782	47	435	D	38.3	35.9	25.6	0.3	42	32	28	0.7	0.7	0.7	0.9	51.6	48.4
Outagamie	72,911	23,735	30,370	18,479	327	6,635	R	32.6	41.7	25.3	0.4	63	9	32	2.9	2.3	3.3	3.4	43.9	56.1
Ozaukee	42,910	11,879	22,805	8,002	224	10,926	R	27.7	53.1	18.6	0.5	71	1	70	1.7	1.1	2.4	1.5	34.2	65.8
Pepin	3,572	1,673	1,098	781	20	575	D	46.8	30.7	21.9	0.6	8	59	58	0.1	0.2	0.1	0.1	60.4	39.6
Pierce	17,272	7,824	4,844	4,492	112	2,980	D	45.3	28.0	26.0	0.6	11	69	24	0.7	0.8	0.5	0.8	61.8	38.2
Polk	18,071	7,746	5,446	4,753	126	2,300	D	42.9	30.1	26.3	0.7	24	63	19	0.7	0.7	0.6	0.9	58.7	41.3
Portage	33,716	15,553	10,914	7,083	166	4,639	D	46.1	32.4	21.0	0.5	9	50	61	1.3	1.5	1.2	1.3	58.8	41.2
Price	8,550	3,575	2,654	2,286	35	921	D	41.8	31.0	26.7	0.4	27	58	15	0.3	0.3	0.3	0.4	57.4	42.6
Racine	87,819	34,875	32,310	20,227	407	2,565	D	39.7	36.8	23.0	0.5	35	26	48	3.5	3.3	3.5	3.7	51.9	48.1
Richland	8,540	3,458	3,144	1,899	39	314	D	40.5	36.8	22.2	0.5	29	25	56	0.3	0.3	0.3	0.3	52.4	47.6
Rock	69,025	31,154	21,942	15,700	229	9,212	D	45.1	31.8	22.7	0.3	13	54	52	2.7	3.0	2.4	2.9	58.7	41.3
Rusk	7,967	3,376	2,430	2,085	76	946	D	42.4	30.5	26.2	1.0	26	62	21	0.3	0.3	0.3	0.4	58.1	41.9
St. Croix	25,676	10,281	8,114	7,125	156	2,167	D	40.0	31.6	27.7	0.6	31	55	3	1.0	1.0	0.9	1.3	55.9	44.1
Sauk	23,422	9,128	8,886	5,280	128	242	D	39.0	37.9	22.5	0.5	38	21	55	0.9	0.9	1.0	1.0	50.7	49.3
Sawyer	7,365	2,796	2,658	1,861	50	138	D	38.0	36.1	25.3	0.7	45	31	34	0.3	0.3	0.3	0.3	51.3	48.7
Shawano	17,952	6,062	7,253	4,540	97	1,191	R	33.8	40.4	25.3	0.5	60	15	33	0.7	0.6	0.8	0.8	45.5	54.5
Sheboygan	54,559	20,568	22,526	11,295	170	1,958	R	37.7	41.3	20.7	0.3	46	10	65	2.2	2.0	2.4	2.1	47.7	52.3
Taylor	9,359	3,305	3,415	2,590	49	110	R	35.3	36.5	27.7	0.5	57	28	4	0.4	0.3	0.4	0.5	49.2	50.8
Trempealeau	13,012	6,218	3,577	3,160	57	2,641	D	47.8	27.5	24.3	0.4	6	70	43	0.5	0.6	0.4	0.6	63.5	36.5
Vernon	12,716	5,673	4,072	2,890	81	1,601	D	44.6	32.0	22.7	0.6	15	52	53	0.5	0.5	0.4	0.5	58.2	41.8
Vilas	11,262	3,764	4,616	2,827	55	852	R	33.4	41.0	25.1	0.5	61	12	35	0.4	0.4	0.5	0.5	44.9	55.1
Walworth	36,796	11,825	15,727	9,029	215	3,902	R	32.1	42.7	24.5	0.6	64	7	39	1.5	1.1	1.7	1.7	42.9	57.1
Washburn	7,686	3,080	2,586	1,978	42	494	D	40.1	33.6	25.7	0.5	30	40	25	0.3	0.3	0.3	0.4	54.4	45.6
Washington	50,073	13,339	22,739	13,045	950	9,400	R	26.6	45.4	26.1	1.9	72	3	22	2.0	1.3	2.4	2.4	37.0	63.0
Waukesha	179,182	50,270	91,461	36,622	829	41,191	R	28.1	51.0	20.4	0.5	70	2	66	7.1	4.8	9.8	6.7	35.5	64.5
Waupaca	23,159	6,666	10,252	6,088	153	3,586	R	28.8	44.3	26.3	0.7	69	5	20	0.9	0.6	1.1	1.1	39.4	60.6
Waushara	10,329	3,402	4,045	2,829	53	643	R	32.9	39.2	27.4	0.5	62	18	8	0.4	0.3	0.4	0.5	45.7	54.3
Winnebago	77,386	27,234	33,709	16,140	303	6,475	R	35.2	43.6	20.9	0.4	58	6	62	3.1	2.6	3.6	3.0	44.7	55.3
Wood	36,436	13,208	13,843	8,822	563	635	R	36.2	38.0	24.2	1.5	53	20	46	1.4	1.3	1.5	1.6	48.8	51.2
WISCONSIN	2,531,114	1,041,066	930,855	544,479	14,714	110,211	D	41.1	36.8	21.5	0.6				100.0	100.0	100.0	100.0	52.8	47.2

Table F. — Vote for U.S. Senator: November 3, 1992, General Election

County	Total	Feingold (DEM)	Kasten (REP)	Other	Plurality Total	Party	Percent of total vote DEM	REP	Other	Rank DEM	REP	Other	Percent contribution to state vote Total	DEM	REP	Other
Adams	7,529	3,979	3,491	59	488	D	52.8	46.4	0.8	20	47	63	0.3	0.3	0.3	0.2
Ashland	7,868	4,650	3,153	65	1,497	D	59.1	40.1	0.8	5	68	61	0.3	0.4	0.3	0.2
Barron	19,150	9,867	9,138	145	729	D	51.5	47.7	0.8	29	40	64	0.8	0.8	0.8	0.4
Bayfield	7,657	4,487	3,112	58	1,375	D	58.6	40.6	0.8	6	66	65	0.3	0.3	0.3	0.2
Brown	101,455	50,125	49,487	1,843	638	D	49.4	48.8	1.8	41	32	11	4.1	3.9	4.4	5.3
Buffalo	6,683	3,429	3,181	73	248	D	51.3	47.6	1.1	32	42	42	0.3	0.3	0.3	0.2
Burnett	6,924	3,627	3,052	245	575	D	52.4	44.1	3.5	24	57	1	0.3	0.3	0.3	0.7
Calumet	17,788	8,128	9,424	236	1,296	R	45.7	53.0	1.3	57	15	30	0.7	0.6	0.8	0.7
Chippewa	24,565	12,976	11,209	380	1,767	D	52.8	45.6	1.5	21	53	22	1.0	1.0	1.0	1.1
Clark	14,034	6,778	7,152	104	374	R	48.3	51.0	0.7	48	23	66	0.6	0.5	0.6	0.3
Columbia	23,447	13,000	10,183	264	2,817	D	55.4	43.4	1.1	13	59	39	1.0	1.0	0.9	0.8
Crawford	7,118	3,620	3,431	67	189	D	50.9	48.2	0.9	34	36	48	0.3	0.3	0.3	0.2
Dane	202,788	132,512	68,076	2,200	64,436	D	65.3	33.6	1.1	1	72	43	8.3	10.3	6.0	6.3
Dodge	35,616	15,904	19,025	687	3,121	R	44.7	53.4	1.9	61	12	7	1.5	1.2	1.7	2.0
Door	13,829	6,276	7,364	189	1,088	R	45.4	53.3	1.4	59	14	28	0.6	0.5	0.7	0.5
Douglas	20,990	13,502	7,083	405	6,419	D	64.3	33.7	1.9	2	71	8	0.9	1.0	0.6	1.2
Dunn	16,418	8,801	7,334	283	1,467	D	53.6	44.7	1.7	17	56	14	0.7	0.7	0.6	0.8
Eau Claire	45,944	25,846	19,495	603	6,351	D	56.3	42.4	1.3	11	62	31	1.9	2.0	1.7	1.7
Florence	2,382	1,038	1,324	20	286	R	43.6	55.6	0.8	64	6	59	<.1	<.1	0.1	<.1
Fond du Lac	44,710	20,583	23,425	702	2,842	R	46.0	52.4	1.6	56	18	20	1.8	1.6	2.1	2.0
Forest	4,050	2,120	1,915	15	205	D	52.3	47.3	0.4	25	45	72	0.2	0.2	0.2	<.1
Grant	21,892	9,664	12,034	194	2,370	R	44.1	55.0	0.9	62	11	54	0.9	0.7	1.1	0.6
Green	14,148	7,171	6,696	281	475	D	50.7	47.3	2.0	37	43	6	0.6	0.6	0.6	0.8
Green Lake	9,210	4,017	5,066	127	1,049	R	43.6	55.0	1.4	63	10	27	0.4	0.3	0.4	0.4
Iowa	9,652	5,169	4,413	70	756	D	53.6	45.7	0.7	18	52	67	0.4	0.4	0.4	0.2
Iron	3,609	1,912	1,666	31	246	D	53.0	46.2	0.9	19	49	58	0.1	0.1	0.1	<.1
Jackson	7,971	4,447	3,436	88	1,011	D	55.8	43.1	1.1	12	60	41	0.3	0.3	0.3	0.3
Jefferson	32,722	15,852	16,315	555	463	R	48.4	49.9	1.7	46	31	16	1.3	1.2	1.4	1.6
Juneau	10,395	4,955	5,355	85	400	R	47.7	51.5	0.8	52	21	62	0.4	0.4	0.5	0.2
Kenosha	59,080	31,920	25,413	1,747	6,507	D	54.0	43.0	3.0	15	61	3	2.4	2.5	2.2	5.0
Kewaunee	9,903	4,957	4,755	191	202	D	50.1	48.0	1.9	39	38	9	0.4	0.4	0.4	0.5
La Crosse	50,608	27,935	22,010	663	5,925	D	55.2	43.5	1.3	14	58	32	2.1	2.2	1.9	1.9
Lafayette	7,170	3,553	3,576	41	23	R	49.6	49.9	0.6	40	30	68	0.3	0.3	0.3	0.1
Langlade	9,647	4,193	5,370	84	1,177	R	43.5	55.7	0.9	66	5	56	0.4	0.3	0.5	0.2
Lincoln	13,115	6,742	6,159	214	583	D	51.4	47.0	1.6	30	46	17	0.5	0.5	0.5	0.6
Manitowoc	39,622	22,309	16,745	568	5,564	D	56.3	42.3	1.4	10	63	25	1.6	1.7	1.5	1.6
Marathon	56,374	27,308	28,237	829	929	R	48.4	50.1	1.5	47	28	23	2.3	2.1	2.5	2.4
Marinette	19,517	9,159	10,187	171	1,028	R	46.9	52.2	0.9	55	19	55	0.8	0.7	0.9	0.5
Marquette	6,305	3,196	3,049	60	147	D	50.7	48.4	1.0	36	34	47	0.3	0.2	0.3	0.2
Menominee	783	476	300	7	176	D	60.8	38.3	0.9	3	70	52	<.1	<.1	<.1	<.1
Milwaukee	455,301	273,748	175,676	5,877	98,072	D	60.1	38.6	1.3	4	69	33	18.5	21.2	15.6	16.9
Monroe	16,271	7,935	8,195	141	260	R	48.8	50.4	0.9	42	26	57	0.7	0.6	0.7	0.4
Oconto	14,678	7,151	7,391	136	240	R	48.7	50.4	0.9	43	27	50	0.6	0.6	0.7	0.4
Oneida	18,243	8,702	9,389	152	687	R	47.7	51.5	0.8	51	22	60	0.7	0.7	0.8	0.4
Outagamie	71,218	34,109	35,880	1,229	1,771	R	47.9	50.4	1.7	49	25	13	2.9	2.6	3.2	3.5
Ozaukee	43,011	16,825	25,563	623	8,738	R	39.1	59.4	1.4	72	1	24	1.8	1.3	2.3	1.8
Pepin	3,332	1,795	1,498	39	297	D	53.9	45.0	1.2	16	55	37	0.1	0.1	0.1	0.1
Pierce	16,269	8,481	7,462	326	1,019	D	52.1	45.9	2.0	27	51	5	0.7	0.7	0.7	0.9
Polk	17,099	9,031	7,752	316	1,279	D	52.8	45.3	1.8	22	54	10	0.7	0.7	0.7	0.9
Portage	32,275	18,750	13,190	335	5,560	D	58.1	40.9	1.0	7	65	44	1.3	1.5	1.2	1.0
Price	8,203	4,215	3,946	42	269	D	51.4	48.1	0.5	31	37	70	0.3	0.3	0.3	0.1
Racine	83,256	43,551	38,208	1,497	5,343	D	52.3	45.9	1.8	26	50	12	3.4	3.4	3.4	4.3
Richland	7,909	3,722	4,154	33	432	R	47.1	52.5	0.4	53	17	71	0.3	0.3	0.4	<.1
Rock	65,845	38,067	26,739	1,039	11,328	D	57.8	40.6	1.6	8	67	19	2.7	2.9	2.4	3.0
Rusk	7,633	3,948	3,612	73	336	D	51.7	47.3	1.0	28	44	45	0.3	0.3	0.3	0.2
St. Croix	24,788	12,065	11,873	850	192	D	48.7	47.9	3.4	44	39	2	1.0	0.9	1.1	2.4
Sauk	23,323	11,772	11,270	281	502	D	50.5	48.3	1.2	38	35	34	1.0	0.9	1.0	0.8
Sawyer	7,024	3,193	3,748	83	555	R	45.5	53.4	1.2	58	13	36	0.3	0.2	0.3	0.2
Shawano	16,977	7,059	9,830	88	2,771	R	41.6	57.9	0.5	70	3	69	0.7	0.5	0.9	0.3
Sheboygan	53,264	27,185	25,371	708	1,814	D	51.0	47.6	1.3	33	41	29	2.2	2.1	2.2	2.0
Taylor	8,918	4,191	4,644	83	453	R	47.0	52.1	0.9	54	20	49	0.4	0.3	0.4	0.2
Trempealeau	12,179	6,986	5,085	108	1,901	D	57.4	41.8	0.9	9	64	53	0.5	0.5	0.5	0.3
Vernon	12,242	6,433	5,662	147	771	D	52.5	46.3	1.2	23	48	35	0.5	0.5	0.5	0.4
Vilas	10,885	4,634	6,147	104	1,513	R	42.6	56.5	1.0	69	4	46	0.4	0.4	0.5	0.3
Walworth	36,688	16,552	19,318	818	2,766	R	45.1	52.7	2.2	60	16	4	1.5	1.3	1.7	2.3
Washburn	7,212	3,657	3,489	66	168	D	50.7	48.4	0.9	35	33	51	0.3	0.3	0.3	0.2
Washington	49,834	21,477	27,498	859	6,021	R	43.1	55.2	1.7	68	8	15	2.0	1.7	2.4	2.5
Waukesha	175,720	71,839	101,903	1,978	30,064	R	40.9	58.0	1.1	71	2	40	7.2	5.6	9.0	5.7
Waupaca	21,909	9,530	12,068	311	2,538	R	43.5	55.1	1.4	65	9	26	0.9	0.7	1.1	0.9
Waushara	9,783	4,247	5,424	112	1,177	R	43.4	55.4	1.1	67	7	38	0.4	0.3	0.5	0.3
Winnebago	75,006	36,372	37,440	1,194	1,068	R	48.5	49.9	1.6	45	29	18	3.1	2.8	3.3	3.4
Wood	36,161	17,257	18,338	566	1,081	R	47.7	50.7	1.6	50	24	21	1.5	1.3	1.6	1.6
WISCONSIN	2,455,124	1,290,662	1,129,599	34,863	161,063	D	52.6	46.0	1.4				100.0	100.0	100.0	100.0

Table H. — Vote for U.S. Representative in Congress: November 3, 1992, General Election

Congressional district and county	Total	Democrat (DEM)	Republican (REP)	Other	Plurality Total	Party	Percent of total vote DEM	REP	Other	Rank within district DEM	REP	Other	Percent contribution to district vote Total	DEM	REP	Other
District 1	**256,280**	**147,495**	**104,352**	**4,433**	**43,143**	**D**	**57.6**	**40.7**	**1.7**				**100.0**	**100.0**	**100.0**	**100.0**
Green (pt)	5,292	2,878	2,281	133	597	D	54.4	43.1	2.5	4	4	2	2.1	2.0	2.2	3.0
Jefferson (pt)	1,577	825	717	35	108	D	52.3	45.5	2.2	5	3	3	0.6	0.6	0.7	0.8
Kenosha......................	57,686	35,724	21,214	748	14,510	D	61.9	36.8	1.3	2	6	5	22.5	24.2	20.3	16.9
Racine........................	83,731	48,118	35,065	548	13,053	D	57.5	41.9	0.7	3	5	7	32.7	32.6	33.6	12.4
Rock...........................	66,320	41,132	22,854	2,334	18,278	D	62.0	34.5	3.5	1	7	1	25.9	27.9	21.9	52.7
Walworth.....................	36,468	16,454	19,428	586	2,974	R	45.1	53.3	1.6	7	2	4	14.2	11.2	18.6	13.2
Waukesha (pt)	5,206	2,364	2,793	49	429	R	45.4	53.6	0.9	6	1	6	2.0	1.6	2.7	1.1
District 2	**292,898**	**108,291**	**183,366**	**1,241**	**75,075**	**R**	**37.0**	**62.6**	**0.4**				**100.0**	**100.0**	**100.0**	**100.0**
Columbia....................	23,633	6,954	16,522	157	9,568	R	29.4	69.9	0.7	8	2	4	8.1	6.4	9.0	12.7
Dane...........................	206,750	81,689	124,275	786	42,586	R	39.5	60.1	0.4	1	9	6	70.6	75.4	67.8	63.3
Dodge (pt)..................	4,525	1,408	3,053	64	1,645	R	31.1	67.5	1.4	6	6	1	1.5	1.3	1.7	5.2
Green (pt)	8,840	2,510	6,267	63	3,757	R	28.4	70.9	0.7	9	1	3	3.0	2.3	3.4	5.1
Iowa...........................	9,733	3,117	6,597	19	3,480	R	32.0	67.8	0.2	4	5	7	3.3	2.9	3.6	1.5
Jefferson (pt)	875	300	564	11	264	R	34.3	64.5	1.3	3	7	2	0.3	0.3	0.3	0.9
Lafayette....................	7,090	2,237	4,847	6	2,610	R	31.6	68.4	<.1	5	4	9	2.4	2.1	2.6	0.5
Richland	7,990	2,890	5,087	13	2,197	R	36.2	63.7	0.2	2	8	8	2.7	2.7	2.8	1.0
Sauk	23,462	7,186	16,154	122	8,968	R	30.6	68.9	0.5	7	3	5	8.0	6.6	8.8	9.8
District 3	**260,335**	**108,664**	**146,903**	**4,768**	**38,239**	**R**	**41.7**	**56.4**	**1.8**				**100.0**	**100.0**	**100.0**	**100.0**
Barron.......................	18,211	8,029	10,069	113	2,040	R	44.1	55.3	0.6	6	11	15	7.0	7.4	6.9	2.4
Buffalo......................	6,667	3,467	3,106	94	361	D	52.0	46.6	1.4	3	15	8	2.6	3.2	2.1	2.0
Chippewa (pt)	335	183	152	0	31	D	54.6	45.4	0.0	2	16	17	0.1	0.2	0.1	0.0
Clark (pt)	7,787	2,808	4,905	74	2,097	R	36.1	63.0	1.0	15	3	13	3.0	2.6	3.3	1.6
Crawford....................	7,399	2,651	4,712	36	2,061	R	35.8	63.7	0.5	16	2	16	2.8	2.4	3.2	0.8
Dunn.........................	16,185	7,051	8,904	230	1,853	R	43.6	55.0	1.4	7	12	7	6.2	6.5	6.1	4.8
Eau Claire (pt)	44,207	18,199	24,784	1,224	6,585	R	41.2	56.1	2.8	11	9	2	17.0	16.7	16.9	25.7
Grant.........................	20,657	6,360	14,139	158	7,779	R	30.8	68.4	0.8	17	1	14	7.9	5.9	9.6	3.3
Jackson.....................	8,014	4,167	3,741	106	426	D	52.0	46.7	1.3	4	14	10	3.1	3.8	2.5	2.2
La Crosse	49,524	20,455	28,145	924	7,690	R	41.3	56.8	1.9	10	8	4	19.0	18.8	19.2	19.4
Monroe (pt)	5,504	2,175	3,247	82	1,072	R	39.5	59.0	1.5	13	4	6	2.1	2.0	2.2	1.7
Pepin.........................	3,236	1,578	1,613	45	35	R	48.8	49.8	1.4	5	13	9	1.2	1.5	1.1	0.9
Pierce	15,747	6,710	8,723	314	2,013	R	42.6	55.4	2.0	8	10	3	6.0	6.2	5.9	6.6
Polk (pt)	8,140	3,409	4,633	98	1,224	R	41.9	56.9	1.2	9	7	11	3.1	3.1	3.2	2.1
St. Croix	24,016	9,245	13,874	897	4,629	R	38.5	57.8	3.7	14	6	1	9.2	8.5	9.4	18.8
Trempealeau	12,569	7,213	5,128	228	2,085	D	57.4	40.8	1.8	1	17	5	4.8	6.6	3.5	4.8
Vernon	12,137	4,964	7,028	145	2,064	R	40.9	57.9	1.2	12	5	12	4.7	4.6	4.8	3.0
District 4	**263,803**	**173,482**	**84,872**	**5,449**	**88,610**	**D**	**65.8**	**32.2**	**2.1**				**100.0**	**100.0**	**100.0**	**100.0**
Milwaukee (pt)	196,495	137,914	54,225	4,356	83,689	D	70.2	27.6	2.2	1	2	1	74.5	79.5	63.9	79.9
Waukesha (pt)	67,308	35,568	30,647	1,093	4,921	D	52.8	45.5	1.6	2	1	2	25.5	20.5	36.1	20.1
District 5	**234,176**	**162,344**	**71,085**	**747**	**91,259**	**D**	**69.3**	**30.4**	**0.3**				**100.0**	**100.0**	**100.0**	**100.0**
Milwaukee (pt)	234,176	162,344	71,085	747	91,259	D	69.3	30.4	0.3	1	1	1	100.0	100.0	100.0	100.0
District 6	**272,137**	**128,232**	**143,875**	**30**	**15,643**	**R**	**47.1**	**52.9**	**<.1**				**100.0**	**100.0**	**100.0**	**100.0**
Adams........................	7,278	3,489	3,789	0	300	R	47.9	52.1	0.0	5	10	9	2.7	2.7	2.6	0.0
Brown (pt)..................	826	438	388	0	50	D	53.0	47.0	0.0	3	12	10	0.3	0.3	0.3	0.0
Calumet.....................	15,883	7,242	8,638	3	1,396	R	45.6	54.4	<.1	7	8	4	5.8	5.6	6.0	10.0
Fond du Lac (pt).........	44,793	21,565	23,227	1	1,662	R	48.1	51.9	<.1	4	11	8	16.5	16.8	16.1	3.3
Green Lake.................	9,077	3,913	5,164	0	1,251	R	43.1	56.9	0.0	11	4	11	3.3	3.1	3.6	0.0
Juneau.......................	9,839	3,410	6,427	2	3,017	R	34.7	65.3	<.1	14	1	2	3.6	2.7	4.5	6.7
Manitowoc (pt)	39,077	21,274	17,795	8	3,479	D	54.4	45.5	<.1	2	14	3	14.4	16.6	12.4	26.7
Marquette	6,266	2,811	3,455	0	644	R	44.9	55.1	0.0	9	6	12	2.3	2.2	2.4	0.0
Monroe (pt)	10,071	4,345	5,726	0	1,381	R	43.1	56.9	0.0	10	5	13	3.7	3.4	4.0	0.0
Outagamie (pt)	9,837	5,357	4,480	0	877	D	54.5	45.5	0.0	1	13	14	3.6	4.2	3.1	0.0
Sheboygan (pt)...........	12,102	4,985	7,115	2	2,130	R	41.2	58.8	<.1	13	2	5	4.4	3.9	4.9	6.7
Waupaca	22,124	9,932	12,191	1	2,259	R	44.9	55.1	<.1	8	7	7	8.1	7.7	8.5	3.3
Waushara	9,892	4,165	5,723	4	1,558	R	42.1	57.9	<.1	12	3	1	3.6	3.2	4.0	13.3
Winnebago	75,072	35,306	39,757	9	4,451	R	47.0	53.0	<.1	6	9	6	27.6	27.5	27.6	30.0
District 7	**257,982**	**166,200**	**91,772**	**10**	**74,428**	**D**	**64.4**	**35.6**	**<.1**				**100.0**	**100.0**	**100.0**	**100.0**
Ashland......................	7,320	5,334	1,986	0	3,348	D	72.9	27.1	0.0	3	17	8	2.8	3.2	2.2	0.0
Bayfield.....................	7,319	5,097	2,218	4	2,879	D	69.6	30.3	<.1	7	13	1	2.8	3.1	2.4	40.0
Burnett......................	6,788	4,442	2,345	1	2,097	D	65.4	34.5	<.1	12	8	2	2.6	2.7	2.6	10.0
Chippewa (pt)	22,483	15,936	6,547	0	9,389	D	70.9	29.1	0.0	5	15	9	8.7	9.6	7.1	0.0
Clark (pt)	6,130	3,931	2,199	0	1,732	D	64.1	35.9	0.0	14	6	10	2.4	2.4	2.4	0.0
Douglas.....................	18,135	13,660	4,475	0	9,185	D	75.3	24.7	0.0	1	19	11	7.0	8.2	4.9	0.0
Eau Claire (pt)	433	297	136	0	161	D	68.6	31.4	0.0	8	12	12	0.2	0.2	0.1	0.0
Iron	3,312	2,485	827	0	1,658	D	75.0	25.0	0.0	2	18	13	1.3	1.5	0.9	0.0
Lincoln......................	12,619	7,690	4,929	0	2,761	D	60.9	39.1	0.0	17	3	14	4.9	4.6	5.4	0.0
Marathon	54,844	29,945	24,899	0	5,046	D	54.6	45.4	0.0	19	1	15	21.3	18.0	27.1	0.0
Oneida.......................	6,455	4,650	1,804	1	2,846	D	72.0	27.9	<.1	4	16	3	2.5	2.8	2.0	10.0
Polk (pt)	8,759	5,754	3,005	0	2,749	D	65.7	34.3	0.0	10	10	16	3.4	3.5	3.3	0.0
Portage	30,495	20,579	9,915	1	10,664	D	67.5	32.5	<.1	9	11	7	11.8	12.4	10.8	10.0

Table H. — Vote for U.S. Representative in Congress: November 3, 1992, General Election (cont)

Congressional district and county	Total	Democrat (DEM)	Republican (REP)	Other	Plurality Total	Plurality Party	Percent of total vote DEM	REP	Other	Rank within district DEM	REP	Other	Percent contribution to district vote Total	DEM	REP	Other
District 7 (cont)																
Price	7,481	4,900	2,580	1	2,320	D	65.5	34.5	<.1	11	9	6	2.9	2.9	2.8	10.0
Rusk	7,379	5,146	2,232	1	2,914	D	69.7	30.2	<.1	6	14	5	2.9	3.1	2.4	10.0
Sawyer	6,774	3,718	3,055	1	663	D	54.9	45.1	<.1	18	2	4	2.6	2.2	3.3	10.0
Taylor	8,740	5,392	3,348	0	2,044	D	61.7	38.3	0.0	16	4	17	3.4	3.2	3.6	0.0
Washburn	6,905	4,272	2,633	0	1,639	D	61.9	38.1	0.0	15	5	18	2.7	2.6	2.9	0.0
Wood	35,611	22,972	12,639	0	10,333	D	64.5	35.5	0.0	13	7	19	13.8	13.8	13.8	0.0
District 8	273,532	81,792	191,704	36	109,912	R	29.9	70.1	<.1				100.0	100.0	100.0	100.0
Brown (pt)	98,249	33,968	64,268	13	30,300	R	34.6	65.4	<.1	2	14	5	35.9	41.5	33.5	36.1
Calumet (pt)	1,682	485	1,197	0	712	R	28.8	71.2	0.0	8	8	7	0.6	0.6	0.6	0.0
Door	13,391	3,736	9,655	0	5,919	R	27.9	72.1	0.0	10	6	8	4.9	4.6	5.0	0.0
Florence	2,495	703	1,792	0	1,089	R	28.2	71.8	0.0	9	7	9	0.9	0.9	0.9	0.0
Forest	3,858	1,277	2,580	1	1,303	R	33.1	66.9	<.1	3	13	2	1.4	1.6	1.3	2.8
Kewaunee	10,282	3,045	7,231	6	4,186	R	29.6	70.3	<.1	6	10	1	3.8	3.7	3.8	16.7
Langlade	9,483	2,212	7,271	0	5,059	R	23.3	76.7	0.0	15	1	10	3.5	2.7	3.8	0.0
Manitowoc (pt)	348	128	220	0	92	R	36.8	63.2	0.0	1	15	11	0.1	0.2	0.1	0.0
Marinette	19,911	4,938	14,973	0	10,035	R	24.8	75.2	0.0	13	3	12	7.3	6.0	7.8	0.0
Menominee	713	233	480	0	247	R	32.7	67.3	0.0	4	12	13	0.3	0.3	0.3	0.0
Oconto	14,701	4,502	10,199	0	5,697	R	30.6	69.4	0.0	5	11	14	5.4	5.5	5.3	0.0
Oneida (pt)	10,869	3,198	7,671	0	4,473	R	29.4	70.6	0.0	7	9	15	4.0	3.9	4.0	0.0
Outagamie (pt)	60,458	16,819	43,626	13	26,807	R	27.8	72.2	<.1	11	5	3	22.1	20.6	22.8	36.1
Shawano	16,553	3,924	12,628	1	8,704	R	23.7	76.3	<.1	14	2	6	6.1	4.8	6.6	2.8
Vilas	10,539	2,624	7,913	2	5,289	R	24.9	75.1	<.1	12	4	4	3.9	3.2	4.1	5.6
District 9	276,787	77,362	192,898	6,527	115,536	R	28.0	69.7	2.4				100.0	100.0	100.0	100.0
Dodge (pt)	29,602	9,111	19,507	984	10,396	R	30.8	65.9	3.3	4	5	1	10.7	11.8	10.1	15.1
Fond du Lac (pt)	383	119	256	8	137	R	31.1	66.8	2.1	3	4	5	0.1	0.2	0.1	0.1
Jefferson (pt)	28,317	8,996	18,441	880	9,445	R	31.8	65.1	3.1	2	6	2	10.2	11.6	9.6	13.5
Ozaukee	41,788	9,969	30,812	1,007	20,843	R	23.9	73.7	2.4	7	2	4	15.1	12.9	16.0	15.4
Sheboygan (pt)	38,953	14,318	23,877	758	9,559	R	36.8	61.3	1.9	1	7	6	14.1	18.5	12.4	11.6
Washington	46,674	12,625	32,842	1,207	20,217	R	27.0	70.4	2.6	5	3	3	16.9	16.3	17.0	18.5
Waukesha (pt)	91,070	22,224	67,163	1,683	44,939	R	24.4	73.7	1.8	6	1	7	32.9	28.7	34.8	25.8
WISCONSIN	2,387,930	1,153,862	1,210,827	23,241	56,965	R	48.3	50.7	1.0							

Table I. — Vote for Presidential Preference: April 7, 1992, Democratic Primary Election

County	Total	Clinton	Brown	Tsongas	Uncom-mitted	Scat-tering	McCarthy	Harkin	Other	Clinton	Brown	Tsongas	Clinton	Brown	Tsongas	Total	Clinton	Brown	Tsongas
										Percent of total vote			Rank			Percent contribution to state vote			
Adams	2,533	1,215	691	411	43	105	17	15	36	48.0	27.3	16.2	4	62	64	0.3	0.4	0.3	0.2
Ashland	3,394	1,343	1,348	434	56	78	38	27	70	39.6	39.7	12.8	37	5	72	0.4	0.5	0.5	0.3
Barron	4,740	2,005	1,386	1,001	67	109	54	51	67	42.3	29.2	21.1	30	51	25	0.6	0.7	0.5	0.6
Bayfield	2,940	902	1,227	480	68	124	75	24	40	30.7	41.7	16.3	70	1	62	0.4	0.3	0.5	0.3
Brown	31,983	11,687	12,394	6,436	534	213	226	196	297	36.5	38.8	20.1	55	7	31	4.1	4.1	4.7	3.8
Buffalo	1,886	815	579	355	17	44	20	24	32	43.2	30.7	18.8	24	40	48	0.2	0.3	0.2	0.2
Burnett	2,083	926	516	394	51	96	32	26	42	44.5	24.8	18.9	16	68	44	0.3	0.3	0.2	0.2
Calumet	5,226	1,818	1,956	1,107	79	126	27	56	57	34.8	37.4	21.2	61	10	24	0.7	0.6	0.7	0.7
Chippewa	6,833	2,629	2,242	1,534	165	90	44	46	83	38.5	32.8	22.4	46	31	20	0.9	0.9	0.8	0.9
Clark	4,562	1,910	1,397	905	61	147	37	32	73	41.9	30.6	19.8	31	41	33	0.6	0.7	0.5	0.5
Columbia	6,264	2,695	1,927	1,265	142	77	54	39	65	43.0	30.8	20.2	25	39	30	0.8	0.9	0.7	0.8
Crawford	2,772	1,274	672	478	55	88	29	127	49	46.0	24.2	17.2	8	69	59	0.4	0.4	0.3	0.3
Dane	78,061	25,918	28,131	18,377	1,964	1,150	841	607	1,073	33.2	36.0	23.5	66	16	10	10.1	9.0	10.6	10.9
Dodge	8,674	3,414	2,956	1,863	174	32	66	72	97	39.4	34.1	21.5	39	24	23	1.1	1.2	1.1	1.1
Door	3,971	1,508	1,292	961	95	3	37	36	39	38.0	32.5	24.2	49	34	7	0.5	0.5	0.5	0.6
Douglas	8,611	3,219	3,209	1,494	161	120	160	89	159	37.4	37.3	17.3	52	11	57	1.1	1.1	1.2	0.9
Dunn	5,032	1,962	1,713	982	97	122	43	44	69	39.0	34.0	19.5	43	25	38	0.7	0.7	0.6	0.6
Eau Claire	11,848	3,762	4,606	2,710	191	310	70	77	122	31.8	38.9	22.9	68	6	13	1.5	1.3	1.7	1.6
Florence	1,132	493	309	224	32	34	10	10	20	43.6	27.3	19.8	21	61	35	0.1	0.2	0.1	0.1
Fond du Lac	9,242	3,138	3,354	2,322	150	25	70	69	114	34.0	36.3	25.1	63	15	6	1.2	1.1	1.3	1.4
Forest	1,689	940	380	256	22	40	12	13	26	55.7	22.5	15.2	1	72	71	0.2	0.3	0.1	0.2
Grant	5,545	2,473	1,396	1,055	72	203	53	181	112	44.6	25.2	19.0	15	67	42	0.7	0.9	0.5	0.6
Green	3,234	1,443	869	728	72	0	34	35	53	44.6	26.9	22.5	14	65	18	0.4	0.5	0.3	0.4
Green Lake	2,082	868	627	402	42	93	14	7	29	41.7	30.1	19.3	33	46	40	0.3	0.3	0.2	0.2
Iowa	2,876	1,255	857	513	29	106	29	43	44	43.6	29.8	17.8	20	49	55	0.4	0.4	0.3	0.3
Iron	1,216	476	396	218	17	81	7	8	13	39.1	32.6	17.9	41	33	54	0.2	0.2	0.1	0.1
Jackson	2,267	974	620	513	26	65	17	27	25	43.0	27.3	22.6	26	60	16	0.3	0.3	0.2	0.3
Jefferson	7,836	2,990	2,735	1,711	192	1	60	71	76	38.2	34.9	21.8	48	22	21	1.0	1.0	1.0	1.0
Juneau	3,162	1,594	836	489	43	99	24	27	50	50.4	26.4	15.5	3	66	70	0.4	0.6	0.3	0.3
Kenosha	20,852	7,959	7,459	4,174	571	129	139	109	312	38.2	35.8	20.0	47	17	32	2.7	2.8	2.8	2.5
Kewaunee	4,101	1,809	1,342	656	70	102	40	25	57	44.1	32.7	16.0	17	32	69	0.5	0.6	0.5	0.4
La Crosse	14,777	5,351	4,887	3,513	289	301	119	160	157	36.2	33.1	23.8	58	30	9	1.9	1.9	1.8	2.1
Lafayette	2,614	1,341	608	421	30	73	33	56	52	51.3	23.3	16.1	2	71	66	0.3	0.5	0.2	0.2
Langlade	2,731	1,297	789	474	56	64	16	13	22	47.5	28.9	17.4	5	53	56	0.4	0.5	0.3	0.3
Lincoln	4,120	1,682	1,370	817	104	2	52	32	61	40.8	33.3	19.8	36	29	34	0.5	0.6	0.5	0.5
Manitowoc	14,178	5,351	4,807	3,251	197	231	104	59	178	37.7	33.9	22.9	50	26	12	1.8	1.9	1.8	1.9
Marathon	17,679	6,365	6,835	3,576	387	40	147	156	173	36.0	38.7	20.2	59	8	28	2.3	2.2	2.6	2.1
Marinette	6,099	2,614	1,834	1,198	112	147	59	48	87	42.9	30.1	19.6	28	47	37	0.8	0.9	0.7	0.7
Marquette	1,748	809	498	298	12	80	14	17	20	46.3	28.5	17.0	7	56	60	0.2	0.3	0.2	0.2
Menominee	306	126	88	69	3	12	4	1	3	41.2	28.8	22.5	35	54	17	<.1	<.1	<.1	<.1
Milwaukee	181,924	71,083	60,589	39,211	3,714	3,076	1,293	763	2,195	39.1	33.3	21.6	42	28	22	23.5	24.7	22.8	23.3
Monroe	5,117	2,237	1,410	1,078	93	118	57	44	80	43.7	27.6	21.1	19	58	26	0.7	0.8	0.5	0.6
Oconto	5,233	2,432	1,616	839	50	164	41	27	64	46.5	30.9	16.0	6	38	67	0.7	0.8	0.6	0.5
Oneida	5,180	1,947	1,418	1,342	74	248	57	36	58	37.6	27.4	25.9	51	59	4	0.7	0.7	0.5	0.8
Outagamie	20,531	6,457	8,184	4,647	337	427	162	118	199	31.5	39.9	22.6	69	4	15	2.7	2.2	3.1	2.8
Ozaukee	10,038	2,679	3,537	3,440	222	2	46	45	67	26.7	35.2	34.3	72	18	1	1.3	0.9	1.3	2.0
Pepin	1,150	498	341	187	26	26	22	21	29	43.3	29.7	16.3	23	50	63	0.1	0.2	0.1	0.1
Pierce	3,612	1,405	1,123	730	76	114	63	44	57	38.9	31.1	20.2	44	37	29	0.5	0.5	0.4	0.4
Polk	4,828	2,092	1,300	900	97	232	73	68	66	43.3	26.9	18.6	22	64	50	0.6	0.7	0.5	0.5
Portage	10,745	3,917	4,451	1,854	151	161	70	57	84	36.5	41.4	17.3	56	2	58	1.4	1.4	1.7	1.1
Price	2,525	1,057	766	479	31	112	28	24	28	41.9	30.3	19.0	32	44	43	0.3	0.4	0.3	0.3
Racine	25,079	8,333	10,031	5,275	581	122	206	181	350	33.2	40.0	21.0	65	3	27	3.2	2.9	3.8	3.1
Richland	2,615	1,194	816	419	31	50	34	34	37	45.7	31.2	16.0	9	36	68	0.3	0.4	0.3	0.2
Rock	18,026	8,163	5,111	3,303	356	617	147	125	204	45.3	28.4	18.3	11	57	52	2.3	2.8	1.9	2.0
Rusk	3,148	1,343	961	585	41	103	28	19	68	42.7	30.5	18.6	29	43	51	0.4	0.5	0.4	0.3
St. Croix	4,551	1,654	1,391	1,095	182	3	80	65	81	36.3	30.6	24.1	57	42	8	0.6	0.6	0.5	0.6
Sauk	6,143	2,637	1,988	1,146	144	71	54	40	63	42.9	32.4	18.7	27	35	49	0.8	0.9	0.7	0.7
Sawyer	1,784	702	628	298	17	79	28	13	19	39.3	35.2	16.7	40	19	61	0.2	0.2	0.2	0.2
Shawano	4,711	1,863	1,647	930	42	105	40	32	52	39.5	35.0	19.7	38	21	36	0.6	0.6	0.6	0.6
Sheboygan	15,996	5,438	5,909	3,630	376	350	84	73	136	34.0	36.9	22.7	62	13	14	2.1	1.9	2.2	2.2
Taylor	2,961	1,301	898	566	26	79	23	29	39	43.9	30.3	19.1	18	45	41	0.4	0.5	0.3	0.3
Trempealeau	3,967	1,787	1,140	749	33	110	46	42	60	45.0	28.7	18.9	12	55	47	0.5	0.6	0.4	0.4
Vernon	3,762	1,713	1,013	711	74	99	32	69	51	45.5	26.9	18.9	10	63	46	0.5	0.6	0.4	0.4
Vilas	2,892	1,035	701	958	46	92	22	5	33	35.8	24.2	33.1	60	70	2	0.4	0.4	0.3	0.6
Walworth	8,900	3,313	3,053	2,002	214	19	106	93	100	37.2	34.3	22.5	53	23	19	1.2	1.2	1.1	1.2
Washburn	2,264	933	678	413	44	101	33	25	37	41.2	29.9	18.2	34	48	53	0.3	0.3	0.3	0.2
Washington	11,691	3,716	4,344	3,008	342	19	85	72	105	31.8	37.2	25.7	67	12	5	1.5	1.3	1.6	1.8
Waukesha	44,041	12,122	16,605	12,713	952	809	269	180	391	27.5	37.7	28.9	71	9	3	5.7	4.2	6.2	7.5
Waupaca	5,047	1,850	1,700	954	73	209	127	74	60	36.7	33.7	18.9	54	27	45	0.7	0.6	0.6	0.6
Waushara	2,723	1,222	790	441	43	152	26	18	31	44.9	29.0	16.2	13	52	65	0.4	0.4	0.3	0.3
Winnebago	18,444	6,219	6,489	4,300	282	754	106	80	214	33.7	35.2	23.3	64	20	11	2.4	2.2	2.4	2.6
Wood	12,069	4,664	4,441	2,351	169	65	110	124	145	38.6	36.8	19.5	45	14	39	1.6	1.6	1.7	1.4
WISCONSIN	772,596	287,356	266,207	168,619	15,487	13,650	6,525	5,395	9,357	37.2	34.5	21.8				100.0	100.0	100.0	100.0

Table J. — Vote for Presidential Preference: April 7, 1992, Republican Primary Election

| County | Top candidates | | | | | Top four candidates (state vote) | | | | | | | | | | | | |
| | | | | | | Percent of total vote | | | | Rank | | | | Percent contribution to state vote | | | | |
	Total	Bush	Bu-chanan	Duke	Other	Bush	Bu-chanan	Duke	Other	Bush	Bu-chanan	Duke	Other	Total	Bush	Bu-chanan	Duke	Other
Adams	1,434	1,019	224	41	150	71.1	15.6	2.9	10.5	62	43	22	3	0.3	0.3	0.3	0.3	0.6
Ashland	1,921	1,465	307	52	97	76.3	16.0	2.7	5.0	29	36	28	52	0.4	0.4	0.4	0.4	0.4
Barron	3,103	2,304	538	53	208	74.3	17.3	1.7	6.7	39	27	68	23	0.6	0.6	0.7	0.4	0.8
Bayfield	1,495	1,075	287	25	108	71.9	19.2	1.7	7.2	55	15	69	16	0.3	0.3	0.4	0.2	0.4
Brown	21,587	15,872	4,256	469	990	73.5	19.7	2.2	4.6	45	10	52	58	4.5	4.4	5.4	3.6	3.8
Buffalo	1,153	842	188	42	81	73.0	16.3	3.6	7.0	48	33	6	19	0.2	0.2	0.2	0.3	0.3
Burnett	1,342	973	198	40	131	72.5	14.8	3.0	9.8	51	49	18	5	0.3	0.3	0.3	0.3	0.5
Calumet	3,948	2,902	752	84	210	73.5	19.0	2.1	5.3	46	16	53	47	0.8	0.8	1.0	0.7	0.8
Chippewa	3,424	2,444	705	80	195	71.4	20.6	2.3	5.7	59	5	46	41	0.7	0.7	0.9	0.6	0.7
Clark	2,531	1,667	589	79	196	65.9	23.3	3.1	7.7	72	1	11	14	0.5	0.5	0.8	0.6	0.7
Columbia	4,339	3,530	540	95	174	81.4	12.4	2.2	4.0	4	64	51	65	0.9	1.0	0.7	0.7	0.7
Crawford	1,733	1,315	264	41	113	75.9	15.2	2.4	6.5	32	46	44	27	0.4	0.4	0.3	0.3	0.4
Dane	30,858	23,954	4,027	815	2,062	77.6	13.1	2.6	6.7	18	62	33	24	6.4	6.6	5.1	6.3	7.8
Dodge	7,431	5,866	1,123	175	267	78.9	15.1	2.4	3.6	12	48	45	68	1.5	1.6	1.4	1.4	1.0
Door	3,382	2,655	493	91	143	78.5	14.6	2.7	4.2	15	50	29	64	0.7	0.7	0.6	0.7	0.5
Douglas	3,592	2,566	775	76	175	71.4	21.6	2.1	4.9	57	3	54	54	0.7	0.7	1.0	0.6	0.7
Dunn	2,994	2,114	592	72	216	70.6	19.8	2.4	7.2	64	8	43	17	0.6	0.6	0.8	0.6	0.8
Eau Claire	6,226	4,701	1,057	125	343	75.5	17.0	2.0	5.5	33	28	62	44	1.3	1.3	1.3	1.0	1.3
Florence	798	660	83	18	37	82.7	10.4	2.3	4.6	2	70	49	57	0.2	0.2	0.1	0.1	0.1
Fond du Lac	7,599	5,654	1,525	155	265	74.4	20.1	2.0	3.5	37	7	60	69	1.6	1.6	1.9	1.2	1.0
Forest	1,035	851	99	24	61	82.2	9.6	2.3	5.9	3	71	47	38	0.2	0.2	0.1	0.2	0.2
Grant	3,892	3,012	523	102	255	77.4	13.4	2.6	6.6	23	60	34	26	0.8	0.8	0.7	0.8	1.0
Green	2,136	1,686	295	64	91	78.9	13.8	3.0	4.3	13	57	16	63	0.4	0.5	0.4	0.5	0.3
Green Lake	2,345	1,607	380	48	310	68.5	16.2	2.0	13.2	71	35	59	1	0.5	0.4	0.5	0.4	1.2
Iowa	1,763	1,366	208	51	138	77.5	11.8	2.9	7.8	21	66	21	13	0.4	0.4	0.3	0.4	0.5
Iron	721	555	90	31	45	77.0	12.5	4.3	6.2	24	63	1	34	0.1	0.2	0.1	0.2	0.2
Jackson	1,344	955	259	44	86	71.1	19.3	3.3	6.4	63	14	10	33	0.3	0.3	0.3	0.3	0.3
Jefferson	6,419	4,803	997	159	460	74.8	15.5	2.5	7.2	34	44	40	18	1.3	1.3	1.3	1.2	1.7
Juneau	2,846	2,127	495	74	150	74.7	17.4	2.6	5.3	35	26	35	49	0.6	0.6	0.6	0.6	0.6
Kenosha	10,049	7,789	1,427	377	456	77.5	14.2	3.8	4.5	20	54	4	59	2.1	2.1	1.8	2.9	1.7
Kewaunee	2,604	1,875	482	88	159	72.0	18.5	3.4	6.1	54	20	8	36	0.5	0.5	0.6	0.7	0.6
La Crosse	10,048	7,626	1,661	204	557	75.9	16.5	2.0	5.5	31	30	61	43	2.1	2.1	2.1	1.6	2.1
Lafayette	1,923	1,522	258	50	93	79.1	13.4	2.6	4.8	10	61	36	55	0.4	0.4	0.3	0.4	0.4
Langlade	2,065	1,651	236	50	128	80.0	11.4	2.4	6.2	8	67	42	35	0.4	0.5	0.3	0.4	0.5
Lincoln	2,504	2,101	273	48	82	83.9	10.9	1.9	3.3	1	68	64	70	0.5	0.6	0.3	0.4	0.3
Manitowoc	8,136	5,796	1,695	237	408	71.2	20.8	2.9	5.0	60	4	19	53	1.7	1.6	2.2	1.8	1.5
Marathon	9,873	7,796	1,408	307	362	79.0	14.3	3.1	3.7	11	53	14	67	2.0	2.1	1.8	2.4	1.4
Marinette	4,695	3,474	792	128	301	74.0	16.9	2.7	6.4	44	29	27	32	1.0	1.0	1.0	1.0	1.1
Marquette	1,316	961	183	46	126	73.0	13.9	3.5	9.6	49	55	7	7	0.3	0.3	0.2	0.4	0.5
Menominee	134	94	25	4	11	70.1	18.7	3.0	8.2	67	18	17	11	<.1	<.1	<.1	<.1	<.1
Milwaukee	92,991	70,661	14,632	3,484	4,214	76.0	15.7	3.7	4.5	30	40	5	60	19.3	19.4	18.6	27.1	16.0
Monroe	4,099	3,197	567	101	234	78.0	13.8	2.5	5.7	17	56	41	40	0.9	0.9	0.7	0.8	0.9
Oconto	3,649	2,610	682	121	236	71.5	18.7	3.3	6.5	56	17	9	29	0.8	0.7	0.9	0.9	0.9
Oneida	3,246	2,492	340	98	316	76.8	10.5	3.0	9.7	25	69	15	6	0.7	0.7	0.4	0.8	1.2
Outagamie	15,065	11,661	2,398	223	783	77.4	15.9	1.5	5.2	22	37	71	50	3.1	3.2	3.1	1.7	3.0
Ozaukee	10,813	8,587	1,717	203	306	79.4	15.9	1.9	2.8	9	38	66	72	2.2	2.4	2.2	1.6	1.2
Pepin	638	438	143	16	41	68.7	22.4	2.5	6.4	70	2	39	30	0.1	0.1	0.2	0.1	0.2
Pierce	2,389	1,732	439	38	180	72.5	18.4	1.6	7.5	52	21	70	15	0.5	0.5	0.6	0.3	0.7
Polk	3,061	2,132	615	64	250	69.7	20.1	2.1	8.2	68	6	55	12	0.6	0.6	0.8	0.5	0.9
Portage	3,753	2,877	568	95	213	76.7	15.1	2.5	5.7	26	47	38	42	0.8	0.8	0.7	0.7	0.8
Price	1,418	1,058	231	38	91	74.6	16.3	2.7	6.4	36	34	32	31	0.3	0.3	0.3	0.3	0.3
Racine	14,754	10,637	2,654	460	1,003	72.1	18.0	3.1	6.8	53	24	12	22	3.1	2.9	3.4	3.6	3.8
Richland	2,006	1,567	291	52	96	78.1	14.5	2.6	4.8	16	51	37	56	0.4	0.4	0.4	0.4	0.4
Rock	10,712	8,191	1,449	334	738	76.5	13.5	3.1	6.9	27	59	13	20	2.2	2.2	1.8	2.6	2.8
Rusk	1,850	1,369	302	52	127	74.0	16.3	2.8	6.9	43	32	24	21	0.4	0.4	0.4	0.4	0.5
St. Croix	3,051	2,219	598	70	164	72.7	19.6	2.3	5.4	50	11	48	45	0.6	0.6	0.8	0.5	0.6
Sauk	4,827	3,873	597	100	257	80.2	12.4	2.1	5.3	7	65	56	46	1.0	1.1	0.8	0.8	1.0
Sawyer	1,317	910	237	37	133	69.1	18.0	2.8	10.1	69	23	25	4	0.3	0.2	0.3	0.3	0.5
Shawano	3,830	2,848	683	103	196	74.4	17.8	2.7	5.1	38	25	30	51	0.8	0.8	0.9	0.8	0.7
Sheboygan	10,859	8,418	1,775	199	467	77.5	16.3	1.8	4.3	19	31	67	62	2.3	2.3	2.3	1.5	1.8
Taylor	2,067	1,454	405	82	126	70.3	19.6	4.0	6.1	66	12	2	37	0.4	0.4	0.5	0.6	0.5
Trempealeau	2,033	1,551	291	59	132	76.3	14.3	2.9	6.5	28	52	20	28	0.4	0.4	0.4	0.5	0.5
Vernon	2,408	1,719	475	54	160	71.4	19.7	2.2	6.6	58	9	50	25	0.5	0.5	0.6	0.4	0.6
Vilas	2,464	1,990	235	94	145	80.8	9.5	3.8	5.9	5	72	3	39	0.5	0.5	0.3	0.7	0.6
Walworth	8,733	7,023	1,198	120	392	80.4	13.7	1.4	4.5	6	58	72	61	1.8	1.9	1.5	0.9	1.5
Washburn	1,413	997	255	38	123	70.6	18.0	2.7	8.7	65	22	31	9	0.3	0.3	0.3	0.3	0.5
Washington	11,545	8,545	2,233	329	438	74.0	19.3	2.8	3.8	42	13	23	66	2.4	2.3	2.8	2.6	1.7
Waukesha	40,937	30,379	7,607	783	2,168	74.2	18.6	1.9	5.3	40	19	65	48	8.5	8.3	9.7	6.1	8.2
Waupaca	4,666	3,414	733	96	423	73.2	15.7	2.1	9.1	47	42	58	8	1.0	0.9	0.9	0.7	1.6
Waushara	2,560	1,820	403	53	284	71.1	15.7	2.1	11.1	61	39	57	2	0.5	0.5	0.5	0.4	1.1
Winnebago	14,745	10,931	2,257	296	1,261	74.1	15.3	2.0	8.6	41	45	63	10	3.1	3.0	2.9	2.3	4.8
Wood	7,611	5,982	1,197	211	221	78.6	15.7	2.8	2.9	14	41	26	71	1.6	1.6	1.5	1.6	0.8
WISCONSIN	**482,248**	**364,507**	**78,516**	**12,867**	**26,358**	**75.6**	**16.3**	**2.7**	**5.5**					**100.0**	**100.0**	**100.0**	**100.0**	**100.0**

1992 Vote for President
Percent for Clinton (D), by County

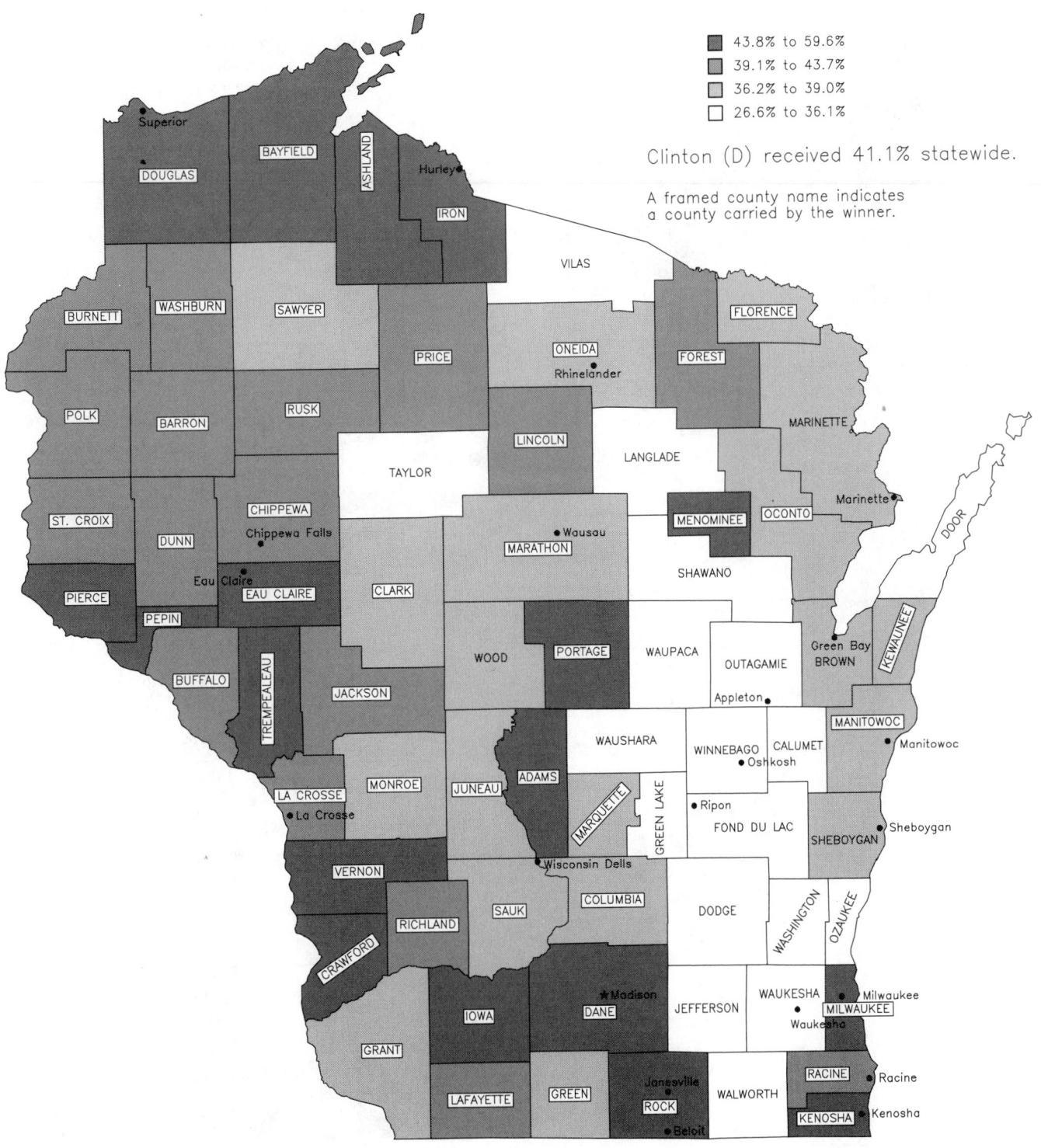

43.8% to 59.6%
39.1% to 43.7%
36.2% to 39.0%
26.6% to 36.1%

Clinton (D) received 41.1% statewide.

A framed county name indicates
a county carried by the winner.

Superior

DOUGLAS
BAYFIELD
ASHLAND
Hurley
IRON
VILAS
BURNETT
WASHBURN
SAWYER
FLORENCE
PRICE
ONEIDA
FOREST
POLK
BARRON
RUSK
Rhinelander
MARINETTE
LINCOLN
LANGLADE
ST. CROIX
TAYLOR
MARINETTE
CHIPPEWA
MENOMINEE
OCONTO
DUNN
Chippewa Falls
DOOR
Eau Claire
MARATHON
Wausau
SHAWANO
PIERCE
EAU CLAIRE
CLARK
PEPIN
Green Bay
BROWN
KEWAUNEE
BUFFALO
PORTAGE
WAUPACA
OUTAGAMIE
TREMPEALEAU
WOOD
Appleton
JACKSON
MANITOWOC
WAUSHARA
WINNEBAGO
CALUMET
Manitowoc
LA CROSSE
MONROE
JUNEAU
ADAMS
Oshkosh
La Crosse
MARQUETTE
Ripon
Sheboygan
GREEN LAKE
FOND DU LAC
SHEBOYGAN
VERNON
Wisconsin Dells
COLUMBIA
DODGE
WASHINGTON
OZAUKEE
RICHLAND
SAUK
CRAWFORD
Madison
WAUKESHA
Milwaukee
MILWAUKEE
IOWA
DANE
JEFFERSON
Waukesha
GRANT
Janesville
RACINE
Racine
LAFAYETTE
GREEN
ROCK
WALWORTH
KENOSHA
Kenosha
Beloit

1992 Vote for U.S. Senator
Percent for Feingold (D), by County

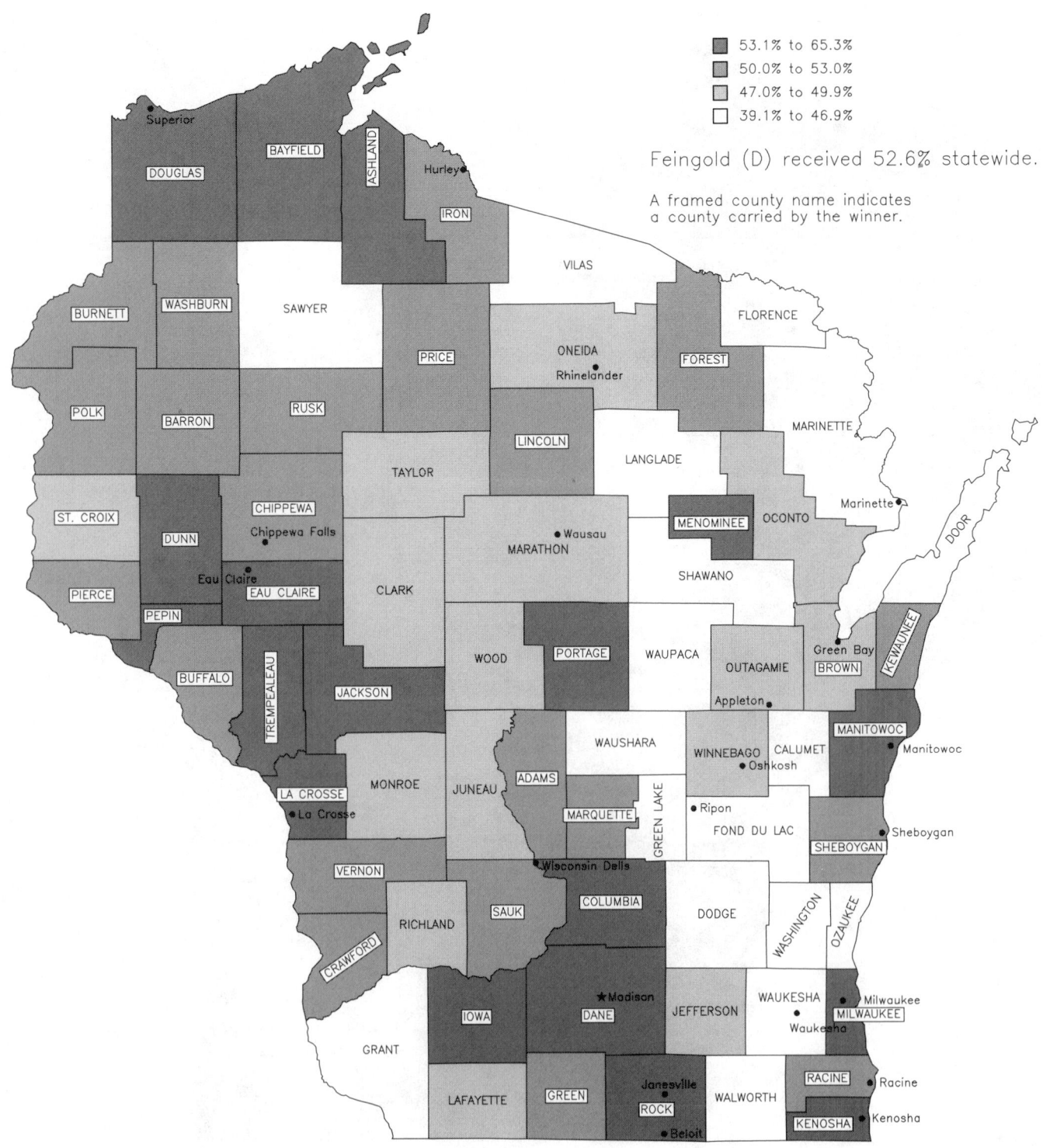

53.1% to 65.3%
50.0% to 53.0%
47.0% to 49.9%
39.1% to 46.9%

Feingold (D) received 52.6% statewide.

A framed county name indicates
a county carried by the winner.

Superior

DOUGLAS

BAYFIELD

ASHLAND

Hurley

IRON

VILAS

FLORENCE

BURNETT

WASHBURN

SAWYER

PRICE

ONEIDA

Rhinelander

FOREST

MARINETTE

POLK

BARRON

RUSK

LINCOLN

LANGLADE

Marinette

ST. CROIX

CHIPPEWA

Chippewa Falls

TAYLOR

CLARK

MENOMINEE

OCONTO

DOOR

DUNN

Eau Claire

EAU CLAIRE

MARATHON

Wausau

SHAWANO

PIERCE

PEPIN

WOOD

PORTAGE

WAUPACA

OUTAGAMIE

Green Bay

BROWN

KEWAUNEE

BUFFALO

TREMPEALEAU

JACKSON

Appleton

MANITOWOC

Manitowoc

WAUSHARA

WINNEBAGO

CALUMET

Oshkosh

LA CROSSE

MONROE

JUNEAU

ADAMS

MARQUETTE

GREEN LAKE

Ripon

FOND DU LAC

Sheboygan

La Crosse

SHEBOYGAN

VERNON

Wisconsin Dells

COLUMBIA

DODGE

WASHINGTON

OZAUKEE

CRAWFORD

RICHLAND

SAUK

★ Madison

DANE

JEFFERSON

WAUKESHA

Milwaukee

MILWAUKEE

IOWA

Waukesha

GRANT

LAFAYETTE

GREEN

Janesville

ROCK

WALWORTH

RACINE

Racine

KENOSHA

Kenosha

Beloit

Copyright © 1993 by Election Data Services, Inc.

1010 Wisconsin

WYOMING

Congressional Districts 1
    Average Population 453,588
State Senate Districts 30
    Average Population 15,120
State House Districts 60
    Average Population 7,560

Electoral College Votes..3
Counties 23
Voting Precincts 453

Alternative Registration Methods:
    .... None

Registration Deadline[1] (Days before Election)....................30

Voting Equipment Use (Counties)

Datavote Punch Card	0	Paper Ballot	1
Electronic	1	Other Punch Card	16
Lever Machine	2	Mixed Systems	3
Optical Scanner	0		

Party Control	DEM	REP	IND	VAC
1993 State Senate	10	20	0	0
1992 State Senate	10	20	0	0
1993 State House	19	41	0	0
1992 State House	22	42	0	0

Population Statistics 1990

Race/ Ethnicity	Total Population		Voting Age Population		Voting Age Population % of total population
	Number	%	Number	%	
Non-Hispanic					
White	412,711	91.0	293,133	92.2	71.0
Black	3,426	0.8	2,267	0.7	66.2
Asian/Pacific Islander	2,622	0.6	1,879	0.6	71.7
Native American	8,857	2.0	5,273	1.7	59.5
Other	221	<.1	125	<.1	56.6
All Hispanic	25,751	5.7	15,386	4.8	59.7
TOTAL	453,588	100.0	318,063	100.0	70.1

Estimated Voting Age Population 1992 (VAP) 322,000
Number of Registered Voters.................................... 234,260
    % of estimated VAP...................................... 72.8
Voter Turnout (Actual) 203,602
    % of VAP 63.2
    % of Registration 86.9
Persons Not Voting—of Voting Age 118,398
    % of VAP 36.8
Persons Not Voting—of Registered 30,658
    % of Registration 13.1
Straight Ticket Voting .... No

State Officials and Members of Congress

Governor:
Mike Sullivan (D) 1986, elected to a four-year term in 1990.

U.S. Senators:
Malcolm Wallop (R) 1976, elected to a six-year term in 1988.
Alan K. Simpson (R) 1978, elected to a six-year term in 1990.

U.S. Representative in Congress:
(District, Name, Party, Date first elected)

At-Large. Thomas (R) 1989

---

[1]Election day registration for primary election only.

Candidates: General Election, November 3, 1992

Candidate(s)	Total vote	Percent	Party	Status	First elected
President/Vice President					
Bush/Quayle	79,347	39.55%	Republican	Incumbent	1988
Clinton/Gore	68,160	33.98%	Democrat	Challenger	1992
Perot/Stockdale	51,263	25.55%	Independent	Challenger	
Marrou/Lord	844	0.42%	Libertarian	Challenger	
Write ins	733	0.37%	Write in	Challenger	
Fulani/Munoz	270	0.13%	Independent	Challenger	
U.S. Senator (No Contest)					
Governor (No Contest)					
U.S. Representative in Congress					
District At-Large					
Craig Thomas	113,882	57.81%	Republican	Incumbent	1989
Jon Herschler	77,418	39.30%	Democrat	Challenger	
Craig McCune	5,677	2.88%	Libertarian	Challenger	

Voter Registration and Turnout, 1948-1992 Elections

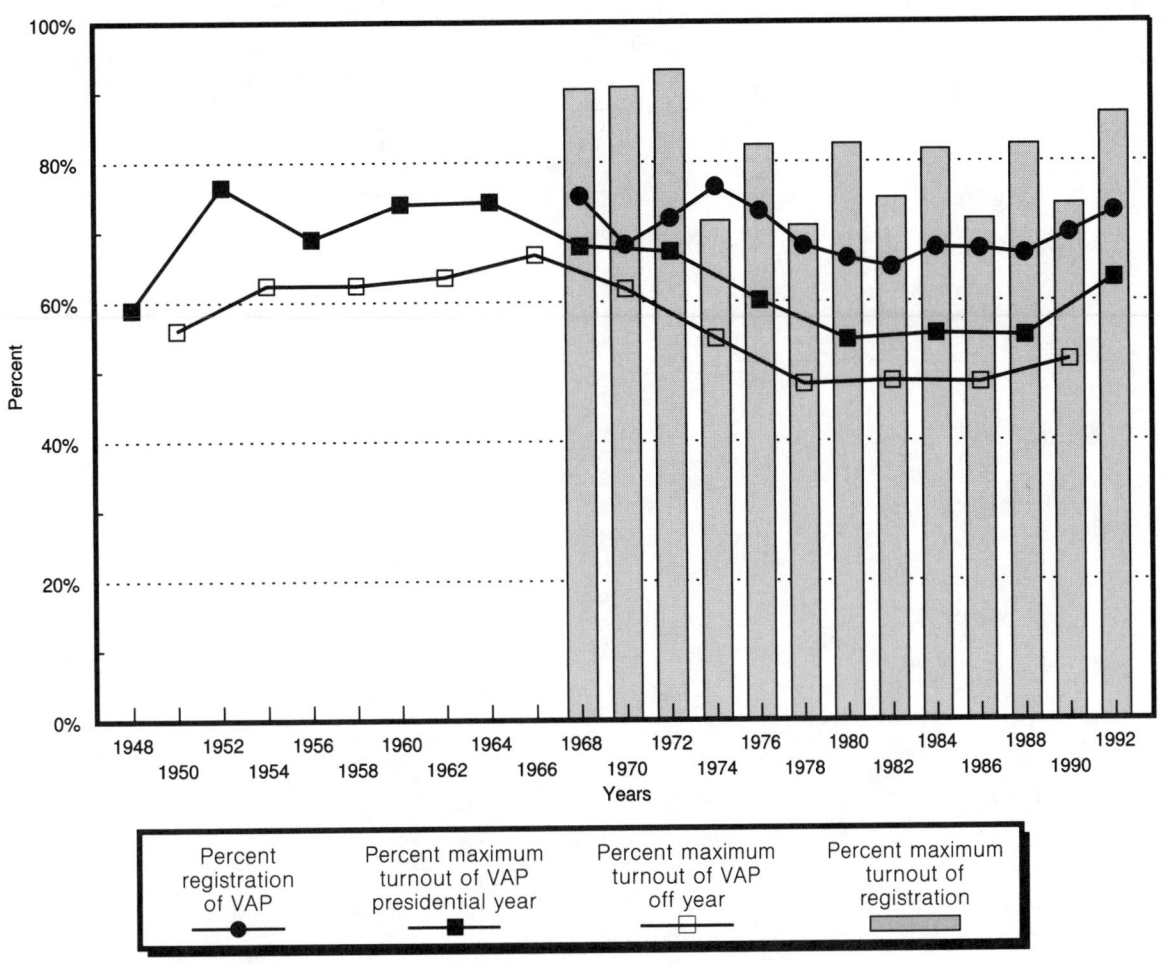

Percent registration of VAP	Percent maximum turnout of VAP presidential year	Percent maximum turnout of VAP off year	Percent maximum turnout of registration

Year	Estimated Voting Age Population (VAP)	Voter registration (REG)			Voter turnout										
						Highest office						Maximum vote			
		Total	Percent of VAP	Rank by percent of VAP	Actual	Total	Office	Percent total REG	Rank by percent of REG	Percent of VAP	Rank by percent of VAP	Total	Percent total REG	Rank by percent of REG	Percent total VAP	Rank by percent of VAP
1992	322,000	234,260	72.8	31	203,602	200,617	P	85.6	1	62.3	18	203,602	86.9	1	63.2	18
1990	319,000	222,331	69.7	21	164,309	160,109	G	72.0	5	50.2	10	164,309	73.9	5	51.5	11
1988	339,000	226,189	66.7	36	186,417	176,551	P	78.1	9	52.1	28	186,417	82.4	2	55.0	21
1986	349,000	235,292	67.4	28	168,615	164,720	G	70.0	7	47.2	10	168,615	71.7	5	48.3	10
1984	355,000	239,974	67.6	40	196,153	188,968	P	78.7	11	53.2	29	196,153	81.7	6	55.3	28
1982	355,000	230,074	64.8	32	172,065	168,555	G	73.3	3	47.5	12	172,065	74.8	4	48.5	12
1980	332,000	219,423	66.1	36	181,004	176,713	P	80.5	5	53.2	28	181,004	82.5	4	54.5	28
1978	296,000	200,951	67.9	27	142,299	137,567	G	68.5	4	46.5	10	142,299	70.8	4	48.1	9
1976	267,000	194,617	72.9	25	160,427	156,343	P	80.3	7	58.6	20	160,427	82.4	5	60.1	18
1974	242,000	185,000	76.4	12	132,271	128,386	G	69.4	6	53.1	4	132,271	71.5	4	54.7	4
1972	226,000	162,602	71.9	29	151,541	145,570	P	89.5	2	64.4	7	151,541	93.2	1	67.1	7
1970	198,000	134,875	68.1	33	122,354	120,486	S	89.3	1	60.9	4	122,354	90.7	1	61.8	5
1968	190,000	142,739	75.1	25	128,978	127,205	P	89.1	2	67.0	16	128,978	90.4	2	67.9	15
1966	184,000	-	-	-	-	122,689	S	-	-	66.7	1	122,689	-	-	66.7	1
1964	192,000	-	-	-	-	142,716	P	-	-	74.3	5	142,716	-	-	74.3	6
1962	193,000	-	-	-	122,494	119,372	S	-	-	61.9	7	122,494	-	-	63.5	5
1960	192,000	-	-	-	142,130	140,782	P	-	-	73.3	14	142,130	-	-	74.0	14
1958	183,000	-	-	-	-	114,157	S	-	-	62.4	6	114,157	-	-	62.4	7
1956	180,000	-	-	-	-	124,127	P	-	-	69.0	16	124,127	-	-	69.0	18
1954	180,000	-	-	-	-	112,252	S	-	-	62.4	6	112,252	-	-	62.4	6
1952	169,000	-	-	-	-	129,253	P	-	-	76.5	8	129,253	-	-	76.5	12
1950	173,000	-	-	-	-	96,959	G	-	-	56.0	13	96,959	-	-	56.0	15
1948	172,000	-	-	-	-	101,425	P	-	-	59.0	25	101,425	-	-	59.0	26

WYOMING

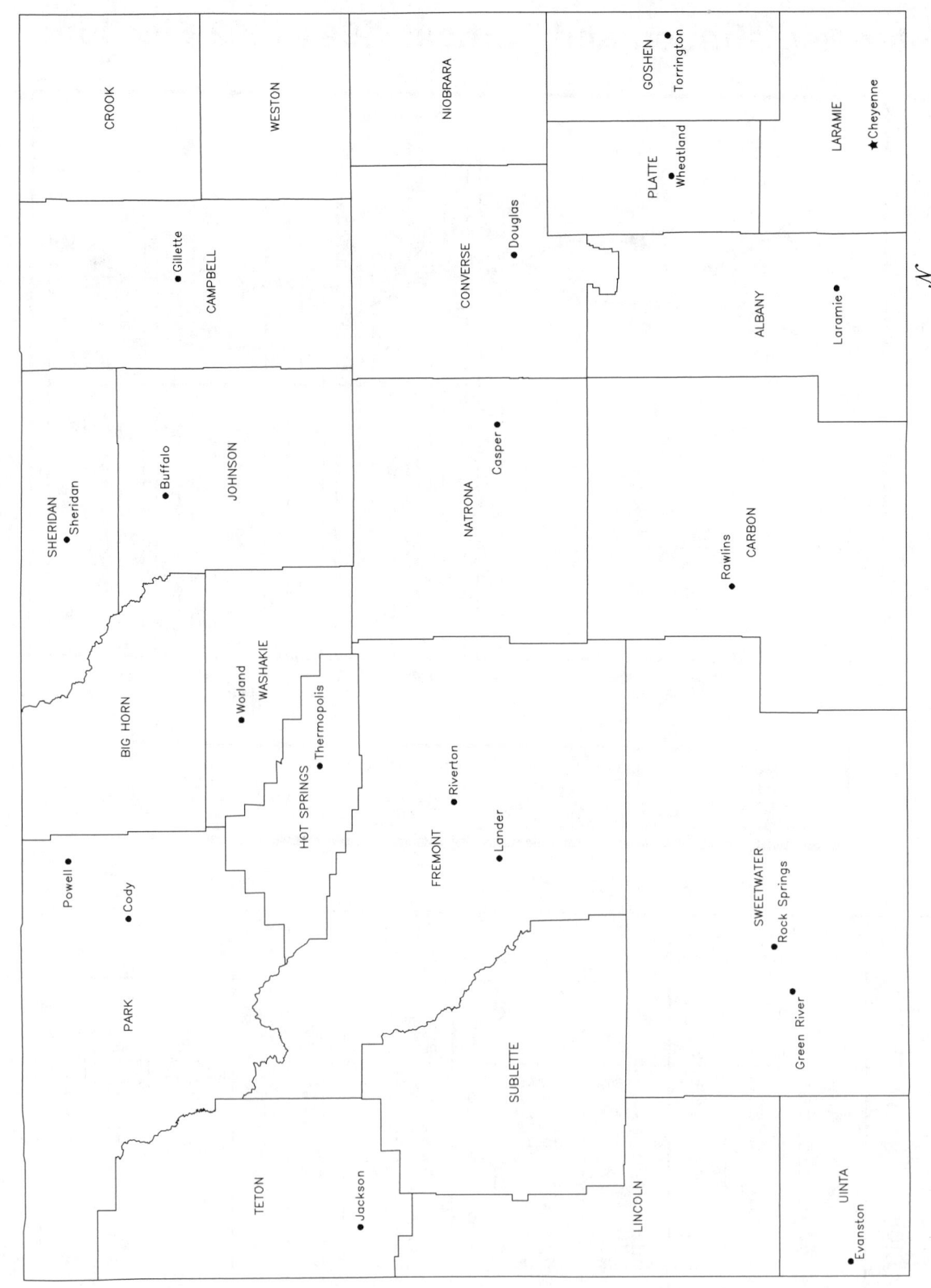

CROOK

WESTON

NIOBRARA

GOSHEN
Torrington •

PLATTE
Wheatland •

LARAMIE
★ Cheyenne

• Gillette
CAMPBELL

CONVERSE
• Douglas

ALBANY
Laramie •

SHERIDAN
• Sheridan

• Buffalo
JOHNSON

NATRONA
Casper •

CARBON
Rawlins •

BIG HORN

• Worland
WASHAKIE

• Thermopolis
HOT SPRINGS

FREMONT
Riverton •

Lander •

SWEETWATER
Rock Springs •

• Powell
• Cody

PARK

SUBLETTE

Green River •

TETON

• Jackson

LINCOLN

UINTA
• Evanston

Miles
0 5 10 15 20

U.S. Representative elected at large.

Copyright © 1993 by Election Data Services, Inc.

1014 Wyoming

Table A. — 1990 Population by Race and Ethnic Origin

State/ county code	County	Total persons	Percent of total persons — Non-Hispanic White	Black	Asian and Pacific Islander	Native American	Other	Hispanic	Rank — Percent of total persons Total	Non-Hispanic White	Black	Hispanic	Percent contribution to state population Total	Non-Hispanic White	Black	Hispanic
56 001	Albany	30,797	90.0	0.8	2.0	0.7	<.1	6.5	5	18	2	6	6.8	6.7	6.9	7.7
56 003	Big Horn	10,525	94.0	<.1	0.2	0.5	<.1	5.2	15	15	21	7	2.3	2.4	<.1	2.1
56 005	Campbell	29,370	95.6	0.1	0.3	1.0	<.1	3.0	6	10	14	14	6.5	6.8	1.0	3.4
56 007	Carbon	16,659	84.3	0.5	0.4	0.7	<.1	13.9	10	22	5	1	3.7	3.4	2.7	9.0
56 009	Converse	11,128	93.6	0.1	0.3	0.9	<.1	5.1	14	16	11	8	2.5	2.5	0.4	2.2
56 011	Crook	5,294	98.9	0.0	<.1	0.5	0.0	0.5	20	1	23	23	1.2	1.3	0.0	0.1
56 013	Fremont	33,662	78.0	0.1	0.3	17.5	<.1	4.0	4	23	12	11	7.4	6.4	1.3	5.2
56 015	Goshen	12,373	90.3	0.2	0.1	0.7	<.1	8.7	12	17	8	5	2.7	2.7	0.7	4.2
56 017	Hot Springs	4,809	96.2	0.3	<.1	2.1	0.0	1.4	22	9	6	19	1.1	1.1	0.4	0.3
56 019	Johnson	6,145	97.7	<.1	0.1	0.9	0.0	1.3	19	2	22	21	1.4	1.5	<.1	0.3
56 021	Laramie	73,142	85.3	2.9	1.0	0.6	0.1	10.0	1	21	1	2	16.1	15.1	61.7	28.4
56 023	Lincoln	12,625	97.2	<.1	0.3	0.5	<.1	2.0	11	6	18	15	2.8	3.0	0.3	1.0
56 025	Natrona	61,226	94.5	0.7	0.4	0.6	<.1	3.7	2	14	4	12	13.5	14.0	12.8	8.7
56 027	Niobrara	2,499	97.4	0.2	0.1	0.8	0.0	1.4	23	3	7	17	0.6	0.6	0.2	0.1
56 029	Park	23,178	95.4	<.1	0.4	0.5	0.0	3.6	8	11	17	13	5.1	5.4	0.6	3.2
56 031	Platte	8,145	94.6	<.1	0.1	0.2	0.0	5.0	17	13	20	9	1.8	1.9	<.1	1.6
56 033	Sheridan	23,562	96.7	0.1	0.4	0.8	<.1	1.9	7	8	10	16	5.2	5.5	1.0	1.7
56 035	Sublette	4,843	97.0	0.1	0.3	1.4	0.0	1.2	21	7	15	22	1.1	1.1	0.1	0.3
56 037	Sweetwater	38,823	88.9	0.7	0.6	0.7	<.1	8.9	3	20	3	4	8.6	8.4	8.2	13.5
56 039	Teton	11,172	97.2	0.2	0.4	0.8	<.1	1.4	13	5	9	18	2.5	2.6	0.5	0.6
56 041	Uinta	18,705	94.8	0.1	0.3	0.6	<.1	4.1	9	12	13	10	4.1	4.3	0.7	3.0
56 043	Washakie	8,388	89.3	<.1	0.4	0.6	<.1	9.5	16	19	16	3	1.8	1.8	0.2	3.1
56 045	Weston	6,518	97.3	<.1	0.2	1.2	0.0	1.3	18	4	19	20	1.4	1.5	<.1	0.3
56	WYOMING	453,588	91.0	0.8	0.6	2.0	<.1	5.7					100.0	100.0	100.0	100.0
	CONGRESSIONAL District At-Large	453,588	91.0	0.8	0.6	2.0	<.1	5.7								

Table B. — 1990 Voting Age Population (VAP) by Race and Ethnic Origin

County	Total Voting Age Population	Percent of total VAP — Non-Hispanic White	Black	Asian and Pacific Islander	Native American	Other	Hispanic	Rank Total	White	Black	Hispanic	Contrib to state VAP Total	White	Black	Hispanic	VAP % of total population Total	White	Black	Asian and Pacific Islander	Native American	Other	Hispanic
Albany	24,198	90.9	0.7	2.0	0.6	<.1	5.6	4	19	2	6	7.6	7.5	7.9	8.9	78.6	79.4	74.8	80.0	65.4	85.2	68.7
Big Horn	7,348	95.2	<.1	0.2	0.5	<.1	4.1	15	15	22	8	2.3	2.4	<.1	1.9	69.8	70.7	50.0	66.7	64.8	50.0	54.4
Campbell	18,894	96.2	0.1	0.3	0.9	<.1	2.5	6	10	14	14	5.9	6.2	0.8	3.0	64.3	64.8	55.9	67.9	57.6	40.0	53.2
Carbon	11,699	85.7	0.6	0.4	0.8	<.1	12.5	9	22	5	1	3.7	3.4	3.1	9.5	70.2	71.4	76.9	64.7	74.4	50.0	63.0
Converse	7,457	94.5	0.1	0.3	0.8	<.1	4.2	14	16	13	7	2.3	2.4	0.4	2.0	67.0	67.7	53.3	66.7	63.5	75.0	55.2
Crook	3,595	99.0	0.0	<.1	0.6	0.0	0.4	20	1	23	23	1.1	1.2	0.0	<.1	67.9	67.9	0.0	66.7	77.8	0.0	50.0
Fremont	23,108	81.9	0.1	0.3	14.5	<.1	3.2	5	23	11	11	7.3	6.5	1.3	4.7	68.6	72.0	66.7	70.6	56.8	80.0	54.6
Goshen	8,874	92.3	0.2	0.1	0.5	<.1	6.8	11	17	9	5	2.8	2.8	0.6	3.9	71.7	73.4	58.3	78.6	54.1	100.0	56.3
Hot Springs	3,554	97.2	<.1		1.5	0.0	0.9	21	8	7	21	1.1	1.2	0.4	0.2	73.2	73.6	100.0	28.6	58.2	0.0	56.4
Johnson	4,499	98.2	<.1	<.1	0.7	0.0	1.0	19	2	20	19	1.4	1.5	<.1	0.3	73.9	74.7	71.4	50.0	55.0	0.0	49.3
Laramie	52,767	87.0	2.6	1.0	0.6	<.1	8.7	1	21	1	2	16.6	15.7	61.4	29.7	72.1	73.6	65.9	70.6	67.4	48.4	62.6
Lincoln	7,816	97.3	<.1	0.3	0.4	0.0	1.9	13	7	17	15	2.5	2.6	0.3	1.0	61.9	62.0	66.7	75.0	51.7	0.0	58.7
Natrona	43,372	95.4	0.6	0.4	0.6	<.1	2.9	2	14	6	12	13.6	14.1	12.0	8.2	75.9	75.9	100.0	33.3	75.0	50.0	72.2
Niobrara	1,896	97.5	0.3	<.1	0.8	0.0	1.4	23	6	6	17	0.6	0.6	0.3	0.2	71.9	72.5	73.7	73.1	60.2	0.0	58.1
Park	16,669	96.2	<.1	0.5	0.4	0.0	2.9	8	11	15	13	5.2	5.5	0.6	3.1	71.1	71.1	<.1	90.0	65.0	0.0	57.9
Platte	5,795	95.6	<.1	0.2	0.2	0.0	4.0	17	12	21	9	1.8	1.9	<.1	1.5	73.2	73.6	82.9	67.0	69.7	100.0	59.0
Sheridan	17,258	97.1	0.2	0.4	0.8	<.1	0.9	7	3	10	22	5.4	5.7	1.3	1.7	71.8	72.4	100.0	38.5	52.9	0.0	54.4
Sublette	3,478	97.8	0.1	0.1	1.1	0.0	0.9	22	9	10	22	1.1	1.2	0.2	0.2	65.9	66.7	66.3	70.9	62.5	40.0	58.8
Sweetwater	25,603	89.9	0.7	0.7	0.7	<.1	8.0	3	20	3	3	8.0	7.9	8.2	13.3	75.8	76.0	41.2	76.1	70.9	100.0	65.8
Teton	8,463	97.5	<.1	0.4	0.7	<.1	1.2	12	4	16	18	2.7	2.8	0.3	0.7	60.2	60.7	28.0	52.5	65.8	71.4	50.6
Uinta	11,264	95.5	<.1	0.3	0.7	<.1	3.5	10	13	18	10	3.5	3.7	0.3	2.5	60.2	60.7	28.0	52.5	65.8	71.4	50.6
Washakie	5,873	91.0	0.1	0.4	0.5	0.1	7.9	16	18	12	4	1.8	1.8	0.3	3.0	70.0	71.3	100.0	76.5	60.4	75.0	57.8
Weston	4,583	97.5	<.1	0.2	1.2	0.0	1.0	18	5	19	20	1.4	1.5	<.1	0.3	70.3	70.5	66.7	100.0	72.2	0.0	53.0
WYOMING	318,063	92.2	0.7	0.6	1.7	<.1	4.8					100.0	100.0	100.0	100.0	70.1	71.0	66.2	71.7	59.5	56.6	59.7
CONGRESSIONAL District At-Large	318,063	92.2	0.7	0.6	1.7	<.1	4.8									70.1	71.0	66.2	71.7	59.5	56.6	59.7

Table C. — Voter Participation: November 3, 1992, General Election

County	Estimated Voting Age Population (VAP), 1992	Voter registration (REG) Total	% contribution to state REG	% of 1992 VAP	Rank by % of 1992 VAP	Voter turnout — Highest office Actual	Total	Office	% of 1992 VAP	Maximum vote Total	% contribution to state turnout	% of REG	Rank by % of REG	% of 1992 VAP	Rank by % 1992 VAP	Percent drop-off, by office President	Senator	Governor	Representative
Albany	23,674	15,082	6.4	63.7	21	12,932	12,867	P	54.4	12,932	6.4	85.7	17	54.6	22	0.5	-	-	1.6
Big Horn	7,292	5,889	2.5	80.8	8	4,843	4,762	P	65.3	4,843	2.4	82.2	22	66.4	12	1.7	-	-	6.3
Campbell	20,319	12,935	5.5	63.7	22	11,336	11,219	P	55.2	11,336	5.6	87.6	7	55.8	21	1.0	-	-	4.0
Carbon	11,385	8,107	3.5	71.2	17	6,868	6,678	P	58.7	6,868	3.4	84.7	19	60.3	18	2.8	-	-	3.2
Converse	7,343	5,554	2.4	75.6	12	4,828	4,777	C	65.1	4,828	2.4	86.9	15	65.7	14	1.6	-	-	1.1
Crook	3,637	3,148	1.3	86.6	3	2,698	2,683	P	73.8	2,698	1.3	85.7	18	74.2	3	0.6	-	-	1.6
Fremont	22,909	16,429	7.0	71.7	16	14,097	13,896	P	60.7	14,097	6.9	85.8	16	61.5	16	1.4	-	-	3.0
Goshen	9,139	6,317	2.7	69.1	18	5,547	5,318	P	58.2	5,547	2.7	87.8	5	60.7	17	4.1	-	-	6.4
Hot Springs	3,507	2,787	1.2	79.5	9	2,430	2,399	P	68.4	2,430	1.2	87.2	13	69.3	8	1.3	-	-	3.0
Johnson	4,520	3,656	1.6	80.9	7	3,188	3,146	P	69.6	3,188	1.6	87.2	12	70.5	7	1.3	-	-	4.1
Laramie	54,015	37,193	15.9	68.9	19	32,360	31,855	P	59.0	32,360	15.9	87.0	14	59.9	19	1.6	-	-	1.7
Lincoln	8,262	7,089	3.0	85.8	5	5,829	5,757	P	69.7	5,829	2.9	82.2	23	70.6	6	1.2	-	-	1.7
Natrona	42,513	31,732	13.5	74.6	15	27,938	27,400	P	64.5	27,938	13.7	88.0	4	65.7	15	1.9	-	-	7.4
Niobrara	1,875	1,591	0.7	84.9	6	1,333	1,300	P	69.3	1,333	0.7	83.8	20	71.1	5	2.5	-	-	5.0
Park	17,027	12,988	5.5	76.3	11	11,366	11,209	P	65.8	11,366	5.6	87.5	9	66.8	11	1.4	-	-	2.5
Platte	5,464	4,699	2.0	86.0	4	4,143	4,051	P	74.1	4,143	2.0	88.2	2	75.8	2	2.2	-	-	3.7
Sheridan	17,330	13,028	5.6	75.2	13	11,750	11,565	P	66.7	11,750	5.8	90.2	1	67.8	10	1.6	-	-	2.3
Sublette	3,590	3,185	1.4	88.7	2	2,623	2,582	C	71.9	2,623	1.3	82.4	21	73.1	4	1.9	-	-	1.6
Sweetwater	25,945	17,197	7.3	66.3	20	15,018	14,891	P	57.4	15,018	7.4	87.3	11	57.9	20	0.8	-	-	1.6
Teton	8,869	9,689	4.1	109.2	1	8,464	8,382	P	94.5	8,464	4.2	87.4	10	95.4	1	1.0	-	-	3.9
Uinta	12,893	7,932	3.4	61.5	23	6,959	6,905	P	53.6	6,959	3.4	87.7	6	54.0	23	0.8	-	-	1.6
Washakie	5,891	4,579	2.0	77.7	10	4,009	3,982	P	67.6	4,009	2.0	87.6	8	68.1	9	0.7	-	-	2.7
Weston	4,601	3,454	1.5	75.1	14	3,043	3,027	P	65.8	3,043	1.5	88.1	3	66.1	13	0.5	-	-	1.1
WYOMING	**322,000**	**234,260**	**100.0**	**72.8**		**203,602**	**200,651**		**62.3**	**203,602**	**100.0**	**86.9**		**63.2**		**1.5**	**-**	**-**	**3.3**

Table D. — Voter Registration by Political Party Affiliation: November 3, 1992, General Election

County	Total voter registration	Political party affiliation Democrat (DEM)	Republican (REP)	Independent (IND)	Plurality Total	Party	Percent of total registration DEM	REP	IND	Rank DEM	REP	IND	Percent contribution to state registration Total	DEM	REP	IND
Albany	15,082	6,370	6,013	2,681	357	D	42.3	39.9	17.8	4	22	2	6.4	7.7	4.8	10.4
Big Horn	5,889	1,104	4,276	509	3,172	R	18.7	72.6	8.6	19	7	12	2.5	1.3	3.4	2.0
Campbell	12,935	2,461	9,724	746	7,263	R	19.0	75.2	5.8	18	4	18	5.5	3.0	7.8	2.9
Carbon	8,107	3,888	3,258	958	630	D	48.0	40.2	11.8	2	21	6	3.5	4.7	2.6	3.7
Converse	5,554	1,460	3,759	335	2,299	R	26.3	67.7	6.0	13	10	17	2.4	1.8	3.0	1.3
Crook	3,148	631	2,297	220	1,666	R	20.0	73.0	7.0	17	5	15	1.3	0.8	1.8	0.9
Fremont	16,429	6,414	8,519	1,491	2,105	R	39.1	51.9	9.1	5	17	10	7.0	7.7	6.8	5.8
Goshen	6,317	2,255	3,822	239	1,567	R	35.7	60.5	3.8	9	12	23	2.7	2.7	3.0	0.9
Hot Springs	2,787	926	1,750	111	824	R	33.2	62.8	4.0	11	11	22	1.2	1.1	1.4	0.4
Johnson	3,656	503	2,907	241	2,404	R	13.8	79.6	6.6	22	3	16	1.6	0.6	2.3	0.9
Laramie	37,193	15,997	16,353	4,841	356	R	43.0	44.0	13.0	3	20	5	15.9	19.3	13.0	18.8
Lincoln	7,089	1,941	4,216	931	2,275	R	27.4	59.5	13.1	12	13	4	3.0	2.3	3.4	3.6
Natrona	31,732	11,347	16,651	3,718	5,304	R	35.8	52.5	11.7	8	16	7	13.5	13.7	13.3	14.5
Niobrara	1,591	204	1,301	86	1,097	R	12.8	81.8	5.4	23	1	19	0.7	0.2	1.0	0.3
Park	12,988	2,370	9,440	1,172	7,070	R	18.3	72.7	9.0	20	6	11	5.5	2.9	7.5	4.6
Platte	4,699	1,831	2,539	329	708	R	39.0	54.0	7.0	6	15	14	2.0	2.2	2.0	1.3
Sheridan	13,028	4,583	7,088	1,351	2,505	R	35.2	54.4	10.4	10	14	8	5.6	5.5	5.7	5.3
Sublette	3,185	456	2,579	147	2,123	R	14.3	81.0	4.6	21	2	20	1.4	0.5	2.1	0.6
Sweetwater	17,197	11,092	4,469	1,633	6,623	D	64.5	26.0	9.5	1	23	9	7.3	13.3	3.6	6.3
Teton	9,689	2,453	5,011	2,225	2,558	R	25.3	51.7	23.0	14	18	1	4.1	3.0	4.0	8.6
Uinta	7,932	2,864	3,785	1,279	921	R	36.1	47.7	16.1	7	19	3	3.4	3.4	3.0	5.0
Washakie	4,579	1,131	3,119	328	1,988	R	24.7	68.1	7.2	15	9	13	2.0	1.4	2.5	1.3
Weston	3,454	810	2,487	157	1,677	R	23.5	72.0	4.5	16	8	21	1.5	1.0	2.0	0.6
WYOMING[1]	**234,260**	**83,091**	**125,363**	**25,728**	**42,272**	**R**	**35.5**	**53.5**	**11.0**				**100.0**	**100.0**	**100.0**	**100.0**

[1]Total voter registration also includes 78 for Libertarian party.

Table E. — Vote for President: November 3, 1992, General Election

County		All candidates				Plurality		Percent of total vote				Rank			Percent contribution to state vote				Major party Percent of vote	
	Total	Clinton (DEM)	Bush (REP)	Perot (IND)	Other	Total	Party	DEM	REP	IND	Other	DEM	REP	IND	Total	DEM	REP	IND	DEM	REP
Albany	12,867	5,713	4,176	2,862	116	1,537	D	44.4	32.5	22.2	0.9	1	22	21	6.4	8.4	5.3	5.6	57.8	42.2
Big Horn	4,762	1,216	2,216	1,236	94	980	R	25.5	46.5	26.0	2.0	15	7	17	2.4	1.8	2.8	2.4	35.4	64.6
Campbell	11,219	2,709	5,315	3,133	62	2,182	R	24.1	47.4	27.9	0.6	18	5	4	5.6	4.0	6.7	6.1	33.8	66.2
Carbon	6,678	2,737	2,320	1,579	42	417	D	41.0	34.7	23.6	0.6	3	20	19	3.3	4.0	2.9	3.1	54.1	45.9
Converse	4,751	1,307	2,159	1,260	25	852	R	27.5	45.4	26.5	0.5	14	8	13	2.4	1.9	2.7	2.5	37.7	62.3
Crook	2,683	568	1,377	718	20	659	R	21.2	51.3	26.8	0.7	21	1	12	1.3	0.8	1.7	1.4	29.2	70.8
Fremont	13,896	4,765	5,387	3,594	150	622	R	34.3	38.8	25.9	1.1	9	17	18	6.9	7.0	6.8	7.0	46.9	53.1
Goshen	5,318	1,754	2,395	1,144	25	641	R	33.0	45.0	21.5	0.5	10	11	22	2.7	2.6	3.0	2.2	42.3	57.7
Hot Springs	2,399	740	978	652	29	238	R	30.8	40.8	27.2	1.2	11	14	10	1.2	1.1	1.2	1.3	43.1	56.9
Johnson	3,146	656	1,614	844	32	770	R	20.9	51.3	26.8	1.0	22	2	11	1.6	1.0	2.0	1.6	28.9	71.1
Laramie	31,855	12,177	12,890	6,607	181	713	R	38.2	40.5	20.7	0.6	4	15	23	15.9	17.9	16.2	12.9	48.6	51.4
Lincoln	5,757	1,430	2,595	1,495	237	1,100	R	24.8	45.1	26.0	4.1	16	10	16	2.9	2.1	3.3	2.9	35.5	64.5
Natrona	27,400	9,817	9,717	7,647	219	100	D	35.8	35.5	27.9	0.8	6	19	6	13.7	14.4	12.2	14.9	50.3	49.7
Niobrara	1,300	298	635	355	12	280	R	22.9	48.8	27.3	0.9	20	3	8	0.6	0.4	0.8	0.7	31.9	68.1
Park	11,209	2,771	5,218	3,145	75	2,073	R	24.7	46.6	28.1	0.7	17	6	3	5.6	4.1	6.6	6.1	34.7	65.3
Platte	4,051	1,398	1,668	956	29	270	R	34.5	41.2	23.6	0.7	8	13	20	2.0	2.1	2.1	1.9	45.6	54.4
Sheridan	11,565	4,139	4,303	3,035	88	164	R	35.8	37.2	26.2	0.8	7	18	14	5.8	6.1	5.4	5.9	49.0	51.0
Sublette	2,574	536	1,168	828	42	340	R	20.8	45.4	32.2	1.6	23	9	1	1.3	0.8	1.5	1.6	31.5	68.5
Sweetwater	14,891	6,417	4,476	3,879	119	1,941	D	43.1	30.1	26.0	0.8	2	23	15	7.4	9.4	5.6	7.6	58.9	41.1
Teton	8,382	3,120	2,854	2,340	68	266	D	37.2	34.0	27.9	0.8	5	21	5	4.2	4.6	3.6	4.6	52.2	47.8
Uinta	6,905	2,047	2,701	2,041	116	654	R	29.6	39.1	29.6	1.7	12	16	2	3.4	3.0	3.4	4.0	43.1	56.9
Washakie	3,982	1,118	1,720	1,084	60	602	R	28.1	43.2	27.2	1.5	13	12	9	2.0	1.6	2.2	2.1	39.4	60.6
Weston	3,027	727	1,465	829	6	636	R	24.0	48.4	27.4	0.2	19	4	7	1.5	1.1	1.8	1.6	33.2	66.8
WYOMING	**200,617**	**68,160**	**79,347**	**51,263**	**1,847**	**11,187**	**R**	**34.0**	**39.6**	**25.6**	**0.9**				**100.0**	**100.0**	**100.0**	**100.0**	**46.2**	**53.8**

Table H. — Vote for U.S. Representative in Congress: November 3, 1992, General Election

Congressional district and county					Plurality		Percent of total vote			Rank within district			Percent contribution to district vote			
	Total	Democrat (DEM)	Republican (REP)	Other	Total	Party	DEM	REP	Other	DEM	REP	Other	Total	DEM	REP	Other
District At-Large	**196,977**	**77,418**	**113,882**	**5,677**	**36,464**	**R**	**39.3**	**57.8**	**2.9**				**100.0**	**100.0**	**100.0**	**100.0**
Albany	12,726	6,050	6,322	354	272	R	47.5	49.7	2.8	3	21	13	6.5	7.8	5.6	6.2
Big Horn	4,537	1,368	3,036	133	1,668	R	30.2	66.9	2.9	18	7	10	2.3	1.8	2.7	2.3
Campbell	10,883	3,143	7,426	314	4,283	R	28.9	68.2	2.9	22	3	11	5.5	4.1	6.5	5.5
Carbon	6,648	3,253	3,245	150	8	D	48.9	48.8	2.3	2	22	18	3.4	4.2	2.8	2.6
Converse	4,777	1,835	2,852	90	1,017	R	38.4	59.7	1.9	8	15	23	2.4	2.4	2.5	1.6
Crook	2,655	673	1,902	80	1,229	R	25.3	71.6	3.0	23	1	7	1.3	0.9	1.7	1.4
Fremont	13,672	5,001	8,267	404	3,266	R	36.6	60.5	3.0	11	12	9	6.9	6.5	7.3	7.1
Goshen	5,192	1,651	3,425	116	1,774	R	31.8	66.0	2.2	14	9	19	2.6	2.1	3.0	2.0
Hot Springs	2,358	883	1,420	55	537	R	37.4	60.2	2.3	9	13	17	1.2	1.1	1.2	1.0
Johnson	3,057	897	2,057	103	1,160	R	29.3	67.3	3.4	20	5	3	1.6	1.2	1.8	1.8
Laramie	31,811	13,195	17,492	1,124	4,297	R	41.5	55.0	3.5	6	18	2	16.1	17.0	15.4	19.8
Lincoln	5,730	1,797	3,751	182	1,954	R	31.4	65.5	3.2	15	10	6	2.9	2.3	3.3	3.2
Natrona	25,857	11,318	13,842	697	2,524	R	43.8	53.5	2.7	5	19	14	13.1	14.6	12.2	12.3
Niobrara	1,267	383	859	25	476	R	30.2	67.8	2.0	17	4	22	0.6	0.5	0.8	0.4
Park	11,087	3,227	7,623	237	4,396	R	29.1	68.8	2.1	21	2	20	5.6	4.2	6.7	4.2
Platte	3,991	1,453	2,361	177	908	R	36.4	59.2	4.4	12	16	1	2.0	1.9	2.1	3.1
Sheridan	11,480	5,219	5,891	370	672	R	45.5	51.3	3.2	4	20	5	5.8	6.7	5.2	6.5
Sublette	2,582	792	1,704	86	912	R	30.7	66.0	3.3	16	8	4	1.3	1.0	1.5	1.5
Sweetwater	14,778	7,340	7,051	387	289	D	49.7	47.7	2.6	1	23	16	7.5	9.5	6.2	6.8
Teton	8,130	3,149	4,739	242	1,590	R	38.7	58.3	3.0	7	17	8	4.1	4.1	4.2	4.3
Uinta	6,847	2,538	4,117	192	1,579	R	37.1	60.1	2.8	10	14	12	3.5	3.3	3.6	3.4
Washakie	3,901	1,348	2,474	79	1,126	R	34.6	63.4	2.0	13	11	21	2.0	1.7	2.2	1.4
Weston	3,011	905	2,026	80	1,121	R	30.1	67.3	2.7	19	6	15	1.5	1.2	1.8	1.4
WYOMING	**196,977**	**77,418**	**113,882**	**5,677**	**36,464**	**R**	**39.3**	**57.8**	**2.9**							

1992 Vote for President
Percent for Bush (R), by County

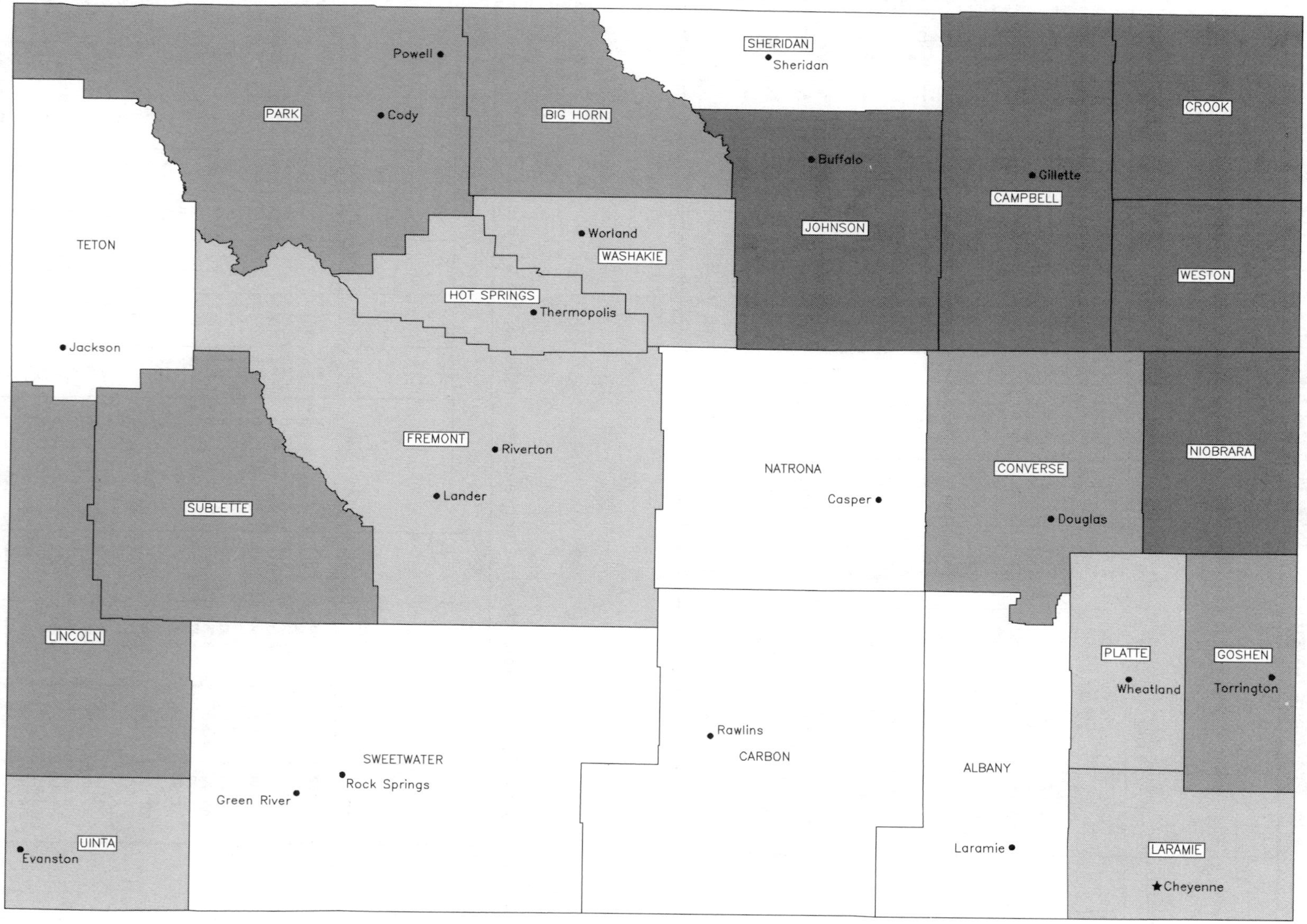

CROOK

WESTON

NIOBRARA

GOSHEN
• Torrington

LARAMIE
★ Cheyenne

• Gillette
CAMPBELL

CONVERSE
• Douglas

PLATTE
Wheatland

ALBANY
Laramie •

SHERIDAN
• Sheridan

• Buffalo
JOHNSON

NATRONA
Casper •

CARBON
Rawlins •

BIG HORN

WASHAKIE
• Worland

HOT SPRINGS
• Thermopolis

FREMONT
Riverton •

• Lander

PARK

Powell •
• Cody

SWEETWATER
• Rock Springs

TETON

Green River •

SUBLETTE

Jackson •

LINCOLN

UINTA
Evanston •

	47.3% to 51.4%
	43.4% to 47.2%
	37.4% to 43.3%
	30.2% to 37.3%

Bush (R) received 39.6% statewide.

A framed county name indicates
a county carried by the winner.

Copyright © 1993 by Election Data Services, Inc.

1018 Wyoming

DISTRICT OF COLUMBIA

Congressional Districts[1] 1
   Average Population 606,900
State Senate Districts[2]...N/A
   Average Population ....N/A
State House Districts[2]...N/A
   Average Population ....N/A

Electoral College Votes...3
Counties[3] 1
Voting Precincts 140

Alternative Registration Methods:
.... Agency-based, Mail-in, Motor-voter

Registration Deadline (Days before Election) 30

Population Statistics 1990

Race/ Ethnicity	Total Population		Voting Age Population		Voting Age Population % of total population
	Number	%	Number	%	
Non-Hispanic					
White	166,131	27.4	151,129	30.9	91.0
Black	395,213	65.1	302,334	61.7	76.5
Asian/Pacific Islander	10,734	1.8	9,246	1.9	86.1
Native American	1,252	0.2	1,055	0.2	84.3
Other	860	0.1	588	0.1	68.4
All Hispanic	32,710	5.4	25,456	5.2	77.8
TOTAL	606,900	100.0	489,808	100.0	80.7

Voting Equipment Use (Counties)

Datavote Punch Card	1	Paper Ballot	0
Electronic	0	Other Punch Card	0
Lever Machine	0	Mixed Systems	0
Optical Scanner	0		

Party Control	DEM	REP	IND	VAC
1993 State Senate	0	0	0	0
1992 State Senate	0	0	0	0
1993 State House	0	0	0	0
1992 State House	0	0	0	0

Estimated Voting Age Population 1992 (VAP) 459,000
Number of Registered Voters.................................... 340,953
   % of estimated VAP..................................... 74.3
Voter Turnout (Actual) 231,445
   % of VAP 50.4
   % of Registration 67.9
Persons Not Voting—of Voting Age 227,555
   % of VAP 49.6
Persons Not Voting—of Registered 109,508
   % of Registration 32.1
Straight Ticket Voting .... No

City Officials and Members of Congress

Mayor:
Sharon Pratt Kelly (D) 1990, elected to a four-year term in 1990.

U.S. Senators:
(N/A)

U.S. Delegate in Congress:
(District, Name, Party, Date first elected)

At-Large. Norton (D) 1990

---

[1]Elects one *delegate* to U.S. House of Representatives. [2]The District of Columbia has an eight-member city council to which members are elected on a non-partisan basis from single member districts (wards). [3]Although data is presented for the District of Columbia's eight wards, the Census Bureau considers the entire District a county equivalent for statistical purposes.

Candidates: General Election, November 3, 1992

Candidate(s)	Total vote	Percent	Party	Status	First elected
President/Vice President					
Clinton/Gore	192,619	84.64%	Democrat	Challenger	1992
Bush/Quayle	20,698	9.10%	Republican	Incumbent	1988
Perot/Stockdale	9,681	4.25%	Independent	Challenger	
Fulani/Munoz	1,459	0.64%	New Alliance	Challenger	
Daniels/Tupahache	1,186	0.52%	Independent	Challenger	
Write ins	676	0.30%	Write in	Challenger	
Marrou/Lord	467	0.21%	Libertarian	Challenger	
LaRouche/Bevel	260	0.11%	Independent	Challenger	
Hagelin/Tompkins	230	0.10%	Natural Law	Challenger	
Brisben/Garson	191	0.08%	Socialists	Challenger	
Warren/DeBates	105	0.05%	Socialist Workers	Challenger	
U.S. Senator (N/A)					
Mayor (No Contest)					
U.S. Delegate in Congress					
District At-Large					
Eleanor Holmes Norton	166,808	84.78%	Democrat	Incumbent	1990
Susan Emerson	20,108	10.22%	Republican	Challenger	
Susan Griffin	7,253	3.69%	Independent	Challenger	
Sam Manuel	1,840	0.94%	Independent	Challenger	
Write ins	745	0.38%	Write in	Challenger	

Candidates: May 5, 1992, Primary Election

Candidate	Total vote	Percent	Candidate	Total vote	Percent
Presidential Preference, Democratic			**Presidential Preference, Republican**		
Bill Clinton	45,716	75.85%	George Bush	4,265	81.47%
Paul E. Tsongas	6,452	10.42%	Patrick Buchanan	970	18.53%
Uncommitted	5,292	8.55%			
Edmund G. Brown	4,444	7.18%			

Voter Registration and Turnout, 1948-1992 Elections

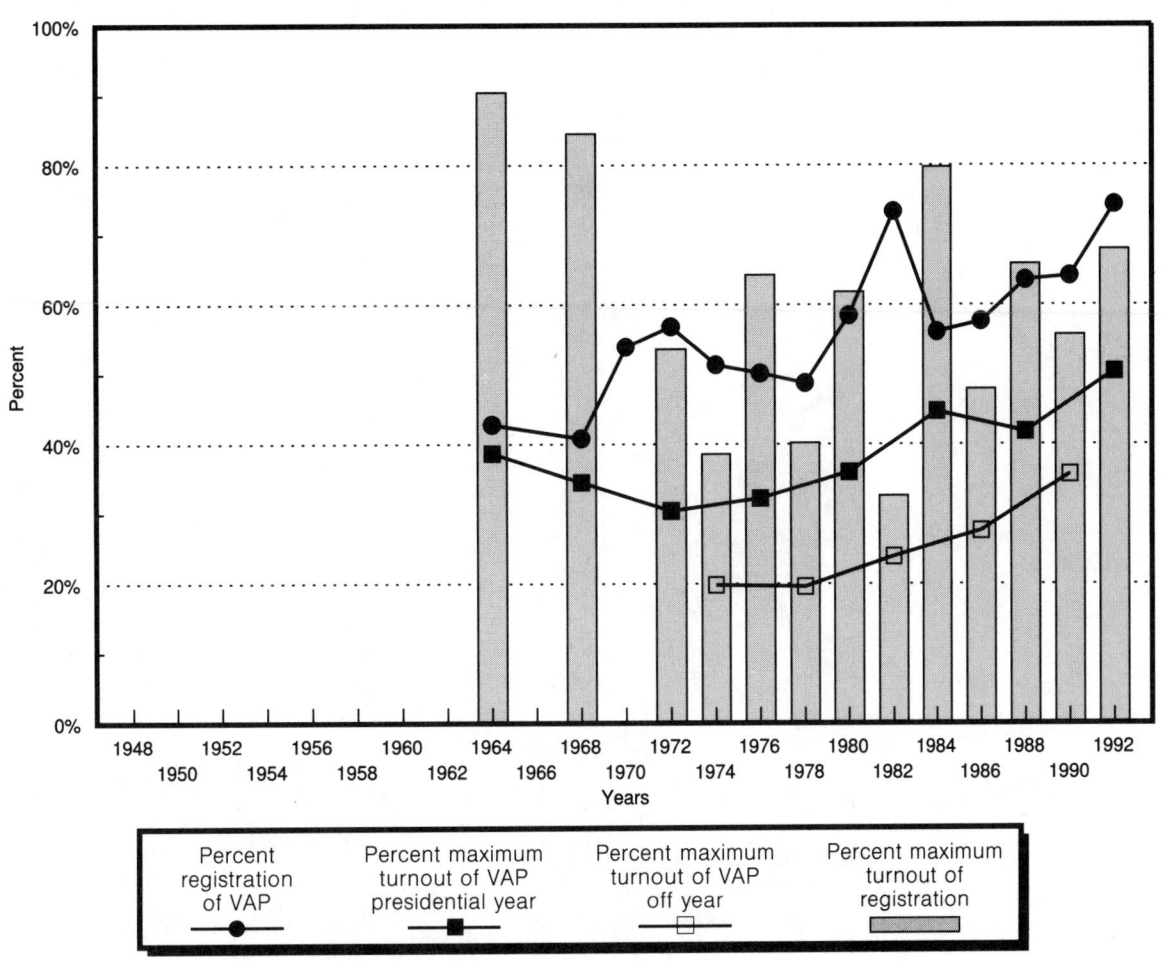

Percent registration of VAP ●

Percent maximum turnout of VAP presidential year ■

Percent maximum turnout of VAP off year □

Percent maximum turnout of registration ▨

Year	Estimated Voting Age Population (VAP)	Voter registration (REG)				Voter turnout											
							Highest office						Maximum vote				
		Total	Percent of VAP	Rank by percent of VAP	Actual	Total	Office	Percent total REG	Rank by percent of REG	Percent of VAP	Rank by percent of VAP	Total	Percent total REG	Rank by percent of REG	Percent total VAP	Rank by percent of VAP
1992	459,000	340,953	74.3	27	231,445	227,572	P	66.7	47	49.6	46	231,445	67.9	47	50.4	44
1990	481,000	308,105	64.1	34	171,677	169,066	M	54.9	30	35.1	36	171,677	55.7	32	35.7	36
1988	472,000	299,757	63.5	42	197,135	192,877	P	64.3	43	40.9	49	197,135	65.8	41	41.8	49
1986	486,000	280,175	57.6	46	134,158	131,802	M	47.0	41	27.1	48	134,158	47.9	38	27.6	49
1984	490,000	275,000	56.1	47	219,193	211,288	P	76.8	13	43.1	48	219,193	79.7	10	44.7	48
1982	492,000	360,648	73.3	17	-	117,623	M	32.6	48	23.9	50	117,623	32.6	48	23.9	50
1980	495,000	288,837	58.4	45	178,434	175,237	P	60.7	48	35.4	51	178,434	61.8	48	36.0	51
1978	515,000	250,750	48.7	49	-	100,861	M	40.2	45	19.6	48	100,861	40.2	45	19.6	48
1976	525,000	262,885	50.1	49	-	168,830	P	64.2	46	32.2	51	168,830	64.2	46	32.2	51
1974	531,000	272,608	51.3	48	-	105,183	M	38.6	44	19.8	51	105,183	38.6	44	19.8	51
1972	537,000	305,072	56.8	47	-	163,421	P	53.6	47	30.4	51	163,421	53.6	47	30.4	51
1970	483,000	260,234	53.9	46	-	-	-	-	-	-	-	-	-	-	-	-
1968	495,000	201,937	40.8	45	-	170,578	P	84.5	9	34.5	51	170,578	84.5	14	34.5	51
1966	506,000	-	-	-	-	-	-	-	-	-	-	-	-	-	-	-
1964	513,000	219,687	42.8	40	-	198,597	P	90.4	3	38.7	49	198,597	90.4	3	38.7	49
1962	527,000	-	-	-	-	-	-	-	-	-	-	-	-	-	-	-
1960	513,000	-	-	-	-	-	-	-	-	-	-	-	-	-	-	-
1958	520,000	-	-	-	-	-	-	-	-	-	-	-	-	-	-	-
1956	564,000	-	-	-	-	-	-	-	-	-	-	-	-	-	-	-
1954	563,000	-	-	-	-	-	-	-	-	-	-	-	-	-	-	-
1952	553,000	-	-	-	-	-	-	-	-	-	-	-	-	-	-	-
1950	573,000	-	-	-	-	-	-	-	-	-	-	-	-	-	-	-
1948	626,000	-	-	-	-	-	-	-	-	-	-	-	-	-	-	-

DISTRICT OF COLUMBIA

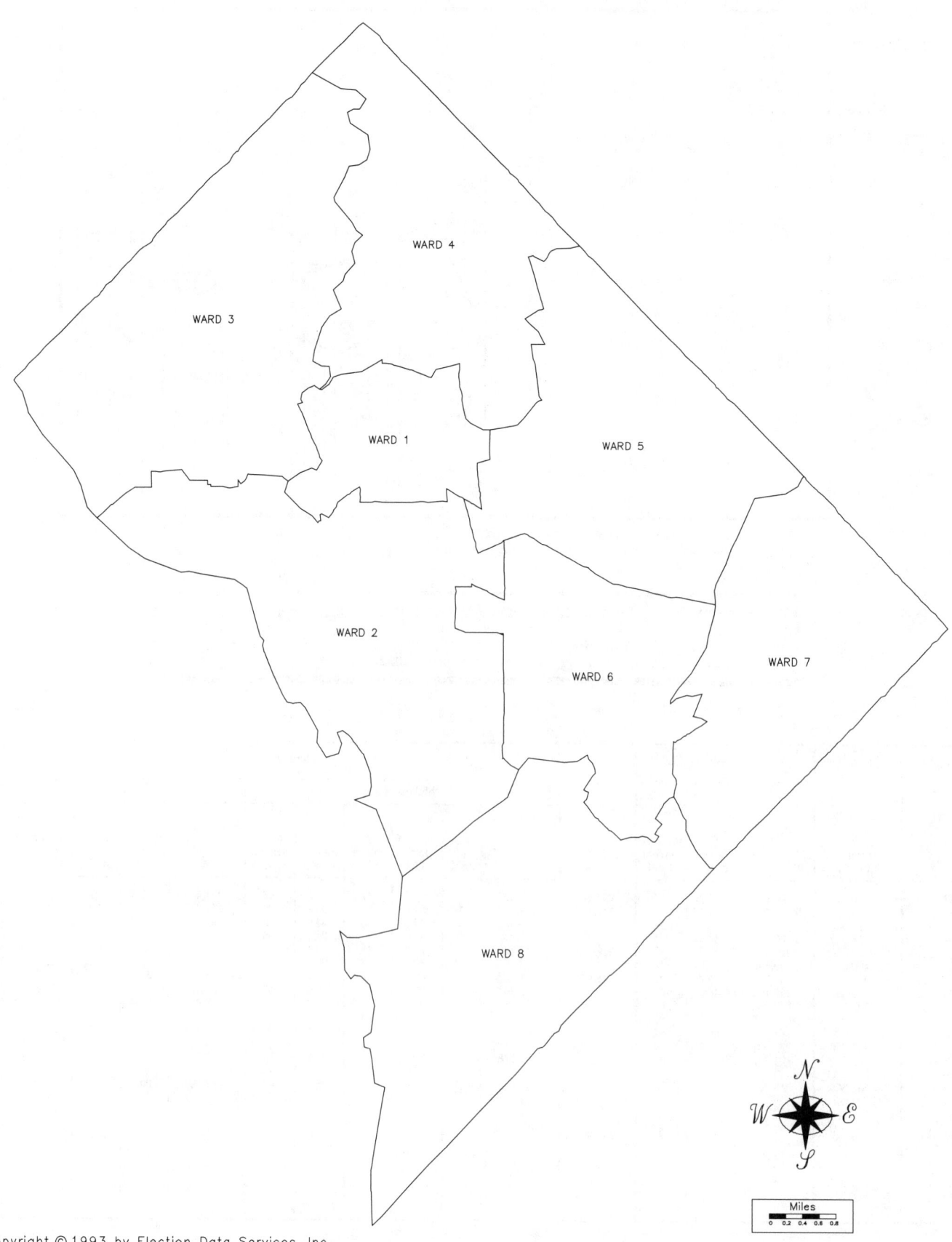

WARD 4

WARD 3

WARD 1

WARD 5

WARD 2

WARD 6

WARD 7

WARD 8

Miles
0 0.2 0.4 0.6 0.8

1022 District of Columbia

Table A. — 1990 Population by Race and Ethnic Origin

State/ county code	County	Total persons	Percent of total persons — Non-Hispanic White	Black	Asian and Pacific Islander	Native American	Other	Hispanic	Rank — Total	Non-Hispanic White	Black	Hispanic	Percent contribution to state population — Total	Non-Hispanic White	Black	Hispanic
11 001	Ward 1	79,641	24.9	55.0	2.0	0.2	0.3	17.6	1	4	6	1	13.1	11.9	11.1	42.8
11 001	Ward 2	78,743	53.0	34.6	4.7	0.3	0.2	7.3	2	2	7	2	13.0	25.1	6.9	17.6
11 001	Ward 3	77,774	83.3	5.7	4.1	0.1	0.2	6.6	4	1	8	3	12.8	39.0	1.1	15.6
11 001	Ward 4	78,425	10.5	83.5	0.7	0.3	0.2	4.8	3	5	4	4	12.9	5.0	16.6	11.4
11 001	Ward 5	75,054	8.2	89.2	0.6	0.2	0.1	1.7	5	6	3	6	12.4	3.7	16.9	3.9
11 001	Ward 6	72,273	25.6	71.4	0.9	0.2	<.1	1.8	7	3	5	5	11.9	11.1	13.1	4.0
11 001	Ward 7	72,769	2.3	96.6	0.1	0.2	<.1	0.8	6	8	1	8	12.0	1.0	17.8	1.7
11 001	Ward 8	72,221	7.2	90.5	0.7	0.2	<.1	1.4	8	7	2	7	11.9	3.1	16.5	3.1
11	**DISTRICT OF COLUMBIA**	**606,900**	**27.4**	**65.1**	**1.8**	**0.2**	**0.1**	**5.4**					**100.0**	**100.0**	**100.0**	**100.0**
	CONGRESSIONAL District At-Large	606,900	27.4	65.1	1.8	0.2	0.1	5.4								

Table B. — 1990 Voting Age Population (VAP) by Race and Ethnic Origin

County	Total Voting Age Population	Percent of total VAP — Non-Hispanic White	Black	Asian and Pacific Islander	Native American	Other	Hispanic	Rank — Total	Non-Hispanic White	Black	Hispanic	Percent contribution to state VAP — Total	Non-Hispanic White	Black	Hispanic	VAP percent of total population — Total	Non-Hispanic White	Black	Asian and Pacific Islander	Native American	Other	Hispanic
Ward 1	65,699	28.4	53.1	2.0	0.2	0.2	16.0	3	4	6	1	13.4	12.3	11.5	41.4	82.5	94.0	79.7	81.5	85.6	63.6	75.3
Ward 2	70,483	57.0	31.0	4.8	0.3	0.2	6.9	1	2	7	2	14.4	26.6	7.2	19.1	89.5	96.2	80.0	91.8	88.1	82.4	84.4
Ward 3	68,215	83.5	5.8	4.1	0.1	0.1	6.4	2	1	8	3	13.9	37.7	1.3	17.1	87.7	87.9	89.3	87.1	89.1	70.2	85.1
Ward 4	64,324	11.7	82.9	0.7	0.3	0.1	4.3	4	5	4	4	13.1	5.0	17.6	10.8	82.0	90.9	81.4	82.5	83.3	63.2	73.9
Ward 5	59,373	9.3	88.3	0.6	0.2	<.1	1.6	5	6	3	6	12.1	3.7	17.3	3.6	79.1	89.6	78.2	81.0	82.9	70.1	72.9
Ward 6	59,286	29.0	68.0	0.9	0.2	<.1	1.8	6	3	5	5	12.1	11.4	13.3	4.2	82.0	92.9	78.1	85.9	92.5	62.5	81.8
Ward 7	54,155	2.8	96.1	0.2	0.2	<.1	0.7	7	8	1	8	11.1	1.0	17.2	1.4	74.4	92.6	74.0	82.4	75.5	76.1	65.7
Ward 8	48,273	7.6	90.2	0.7	0.2	<.1	1.3	8	7	2	7	9.9	2.4	14.4	2.4	66.8	70.6	66.6	63.2	75.2	52.5	61.1
DISTRICT OF COLUMBIA	**489,808**	**30.9**	**61.7**	**1.9**	**0.2**	**0.1**	**5.2**					**100.0**	**100.0**	**100.0**	**100.0**	**80.7**	**91.0**	**76.5**	**86.1**	**84.3**	**68.4**	**77.8**
CONGRESSIONAL District At-Large	489,808	30.9	61.7	1.9	0.2	0.1	5.2									80.7	91.0	76.5	86.1	84.3	68.4	77.8

Table C. — Voter Participation: November 3, 1992, General Election

County	Estimated Voting Age Population (VAP), 1990	Voter registration (REG) Total	% contribution to state REG	% of 1992 VAP	Rank by % of 1992 VAP	Voter turnout — Highest office Actual	Total	Office	% of 1992 VAP	Maximum vote Total	% contribution to state turnout	% of REG	Rank by % of REG	% of 1992 VAP	Rank by % 1992 VAP	Percent drop-off, by office President	Senator	Governor	Representative
Ward 1	65,699	42,114	12.4	64.1	-	26,896	26,488	P	40.3	26,896	11.6	63.9	7	40.9	-	1.5	-	-	14.9
Ward 2	70,483	41,492	12.2	58.9	-	28,882	28,512	P	40.5	28,882	12.5	69.6	3	41.0	-	1.3	-	-	13.5
Ward 3	68,215	48,225	14.1	70.7	-	38,360	38,007	P	55.7	38,360	16.6	79.5	1	56.2	-	0.9	-	-	14.0
Ward 4	64,324	47,158	13.8	73.3	-	33,526	32,932	P	51.2	33,526	14.5	71.1	2	52.1	-	1.8	-	-	13.8
Ward 5	59,373	44,891	13.2	75.6	-	29,644	29,034	P	48.9	29,644	12.8	66.0	4	49.9	-	2.1	-	-	16.4
Ward 6	59,286	43,911	12.9	74.1	-	28,859	28,360	P	47.8	28,859	12.5	65.7	5	48.7	-	1.7	-	-	14.7
Ward 7	54,155	42,189	12.4	77.9	-	27,598	26,985	P	49.8	27,598	11.9	65.4	6	51.0	-	2.2	-	-	16.0
Ward 8	48,273	30,973	9.1	64.2	-	17,237	16,819	P	34.8	17,237	7.4	55.7	8	35.7	-	2.4	-	-	17.4
Federal Ballots	-	-	-	-	-	443	435	P	-	443	0.2	-	-	-	-	1.8	-	-	55.8
DISTRICT OF COLUMBIA	**459,000**	**340,953**	**100.0**	**74.3**	**-**	**231,445**	**227,572**		**49.6**	**231,445**	**100.0**	**67.9**		**50.4**		**1.7**	**-**	**-**	**15.0**

Table D. — Voter Registration by Political Party Affiliation: November 3, 1992, General Election

County	Total voter registration	Democrat (DEM)	Republican (REP)	Independent (IND)	Plurality Total	Party	Percent of total registration DEM	REP	IND	Rank DEM	REP	IND	Percent contribution to state registration Total	DEM	REP	IND
Ward 1	42,114	31,659	2,954	6,845	24,814	D	76.4	7.1	16.5	6	4	3	12.4	12.0	10.3	15.2
Ward 2	41,492	27,328	6,049	7,677	19,651	D	66.6	14.7	18.7	7	2	1	12.2	10.4	21.2	17.1
Ward 3	48,225	29,716	10,005	8,313	19,711	D	61.9	20.8	17.3	8	1	2	14.1	11.3	35.1	18.5
Ward 4	47,158	39,767	2,120	4,782	34,985	D	85.2	4.5	10.2	3	5	6	13.8	15.1	7.4	10.6
Ward 5	44,891	38,094	1,693	4,543	33,551	D	85.9	3.8	10.2	2	6	7	13.2	14.5	5.9	10.1
Ward 6	43,911	34,585	3,314	5,413	29,172	D	79.9	7.7	12.5	5	3	4	12.9	13.1	11.6	12.0
Ward 7	42,189	36,351	1,413	3,940	32,411	D	87.2	3.4	9.4	1	7	8	12.4	13.8	5.0	8.8
Ward 8	30,973	26,074	996	3,412	22,662	D	85.5	3.3	11.2	4	8	5	9.1	9.9	3.5	7.6
DISTRICT OF COLUMBIA[1]	**340,953**	**263,574**	**28,544**	**44,925**	**218,649**	**D**	**78.2**	**8.5**	**13.3**				**100.0**	**100.0**	**100.0**	**100.0**

[1]Total voter registration also includes 3,664 for Statehood party and 246 for other.

Table E. — Vote for President: November 3, 1992, General Election

County	All candidates Total	Clinton (DEM)	Bush (REP)	Perot (IND)	Other	Plurality Total	Party	Percent of total vote DEM	REP	IND	Other	Rank DEM	REP	IND	Percent contribution to state vote Total	DEM	REP	IND	Major party Percent of vote DEM	REP
Ward 1	26,488	22,832	1,892	1,112	652	20,940	D	86.2	7.1	4.2	2.5	5	4	4	11.6	11.9	9.1	11.5	92.3	7.7
Ward 2	28,512	22,143	4,157	1,692	520	17,986	D	77.7	14.6	5.9	1.8	7	2	2	12.5	11.5	20.1	17.5	84.2	15.8
Ward 3	38,007	26,906	8,001	2,606	494	18,905	D	70.8	21.1	6.9	1.3	8	1	1	16.7	14.0	38.7	26.9	77.1	22.9
Ward 4	32,932	29,457	1,650	1,068	757	27,807	D	89.4	5.0	3.2	2.3	4	5	5	14.5	15.3	8.0	11.0	94.7	5.3
Ward 5	29,034	26,243	1,352	814	625	24,891	D	90.4	4.7	2.8	2.2	3	6	6	12.8	13.6	6.5	8.4	95.1	4.9
Ward 6	28,360	24,329	2,115	1,294	622	22,214	D	85.8	7.5	4.6	2.2	6	3	3	12.5	12.6	10.2	13.4	92.0	8.0
Ward 7	26,985	24,882	924	638	541	23,958	D	92.2	3.4	2.4	2.0	1	7	8	11.9	12.9	4.5	6.6	96.4	3.6
Ward 8	16,819	15,484	546	431	358	14,938	D	92.1	3.2	2.6	2.1	2	8	7	7.4	8.0	2.6	4.5	96.6	3.4
Federal Ballots	435	343	61	26	5	282	D	78.9	14.0	6.0	1.1				0.2	0.2	0.3	0.3	84.9	15.1
DISTRICT OF COLUMBIA	**227,572**	**192,619**	**20,698**	**9,681**	**4,574**	**171,921**	**D**	**84.6**	**9.1**	**4.3**	**2.0**				**100.0**	**100.0**	**100.0**	**100.0**	**90.3**	**9.7**

Table H. — Vote for Delegate to the U.S. House of Representatives, November 3, 1992, General Election

Congressional district and county	Total	Democrat (DEM)	Republican (REP)	Other	Plurality Total	Plurality Party	Percent of total vote DEM	REP	Other	Rank within district DEM	REP	Other	Percent contribution to district vote Total	DEM	REP	Other
District At-Large	196,754	166,808	20,108	9,838	146,700	D	84.8	10.2	5.0				100.0	100.0	100.0	100.0
Ward 1	22,891	19,520	1,937	1,434	17,583	D	85.3	8.5	6.3	6	4	1	11.6	11.7	9.6	14.6
Ward 2	24,984	19,018	4,572	1,394	14,446	D	76.1	18.3	5.6	7	2	2	12.7	11.4	22.7	14.2
Ward 3	32,980	22,345	8,840	1,795	13,505	D	67.8	26.8	5.4	8	1	3	16.8	13.4	44.0	18.2
Ward 4	28,884	26,640	1,103	1,141	25,499	D	92.2	3.8	4.0	4	5	8	14.7	16.0	5.5	11.6
Ward 5	24,792	22,876	779	1,137	21,739	D	92.3	3.1	4.6	3	6	6	12.6	13.7	3.9	11.6
Ward 6	24,613	21,210	2,143	1,260	19,067	D	86.2	8.7	5.1	5	3	4	12.5	12.7	10.7	12.8
Ward 7	23,179	21,755	477	947	20,808	D	93.9	2.1	4.1	1	7	7	11.8	13.0	2.4	9.6
Ward 8	14,235	13,307	215	713	12,594	D	93.5	1.5	5.0	2	8	5	7.2	8.0	1.1	7.2
Federal Ballots	196	137	42	17	95	D	69.9	21.4	8.7				0.1	0.1	0.2	0.2
DISTRICT OF COLUMBIA	196,754	166,808	20,108	9,838	146,700	D	84.8	10.2	5.0							

Table I. — Vote for Presidential Preference: May 5, 1992, Democratic Primary Election

County	Total	Clinton	Tsongas	Uncommitted	Brown					Percent of total vote Clinton	Tsongas	Uncommitted	Rank Clinton	Tsongas	Uncommitted	Percent contribution to state vote Total	Clinton	Tsongas	Uncommitted
Ward 1	6,849	4,582	931	590	746	-	-	-	-	66.9	13.6	8.6	6	3	5	11.1	10.0	14.4	11.1
Ward 2	6,310	4,169	987	567	587	-	-	-	-	66.1	15.6	9.0	7	2	3	10.2	9.1	15.3	10.7
Ward 3	8,794	4,977	2,319	778	720	-	-	-	-	56.6	26.4	8.8	8	1	4	14.2	10.9	35.9	14.7
Ward 4	11,241	9,216	491	887	647	-	-	-	-	82.0	4.4	7.9	2	6	6	18.2	20.2	7.6	16.8
Ward 5	9,083	7,414	361	829	479	-	-	-	-	81.6	4.0	9.1	4	7	2	14.7	16.2	5.6	15.7
Ward 6	8,000	5,742	865	770	623	-	-	-	-	71.8	10.8	9.6	5	4	1	12.9	12.6	13.4	14.6
Ward 7	8,067	6,611	365	629	462	-	-	-	-	82.0	4.5	7.8	3	5	7	13.0	14.5	5.7	11.9
Ward 8	3,560	3,005	133	242	180	-	-	-	-	84.4	3.7	6.8	1	8	8	5.8	6.6	2.1	4.6
DISTRICT OF COLUMBIA	61,904	45,716	6,452	5,292	4,444	-	-	-	-	73.8	10.4	8.5				100.0	100.0	100.0	100.0

Table J. — Vote for Presidential Preference: May 5, 1992, Republican Primary Election

County	Total	Bush	Buchanan			Percent of total vote Bush	Buchanan			Rank Bush	Buchanan			Percent contribution to state vote Total	Bush	Buchanan		
Ward 1	484	390	94	-	-	80.6	19.4	-	-	5	4	-	-	9.2	9.1	9.7	-	-
Ward 2	1,095	889	206	-	-	81.2	18.8	-	-	3	6	-	-	20.9	20.8	21.2	-	-
Ward 3	2,279	1,875	404	-	-	82.3	17.7	-	-	1	8	-	-	43.5	44.0	41.6	-	-
Ward 4	365	300	65	-	-	82.2	17.8	-	-	2	7	-	-	7.0	7.0	6.7	-	-
Ward 5	256	202	54	-	-	78.9	21.1	-	-	7	2	-	-	4.9	4.7	5.6	-	-
Ward 6	508	412	96	-	-	81.1	18.9	-	-	4	5	-	-	9.7	9.7	9.9	-	-
Ward 7	204	164	40	-	-	80.4	19.6	-	-	6	3	-	-	3.9	3.8	4.1	-	-
Ward 8	44	33	11	-	-	75.0	25.0	-	-	8	1	-	-	0.8	0.8	1.1	-	-
DISTRICT OF COLUMBIA	5,235	4,265	970	-	-	81.5	18.5	-	-					100.0	100.0	100.0	-	-

1992 Vote for President
Percent for Clinton (D), by Ward

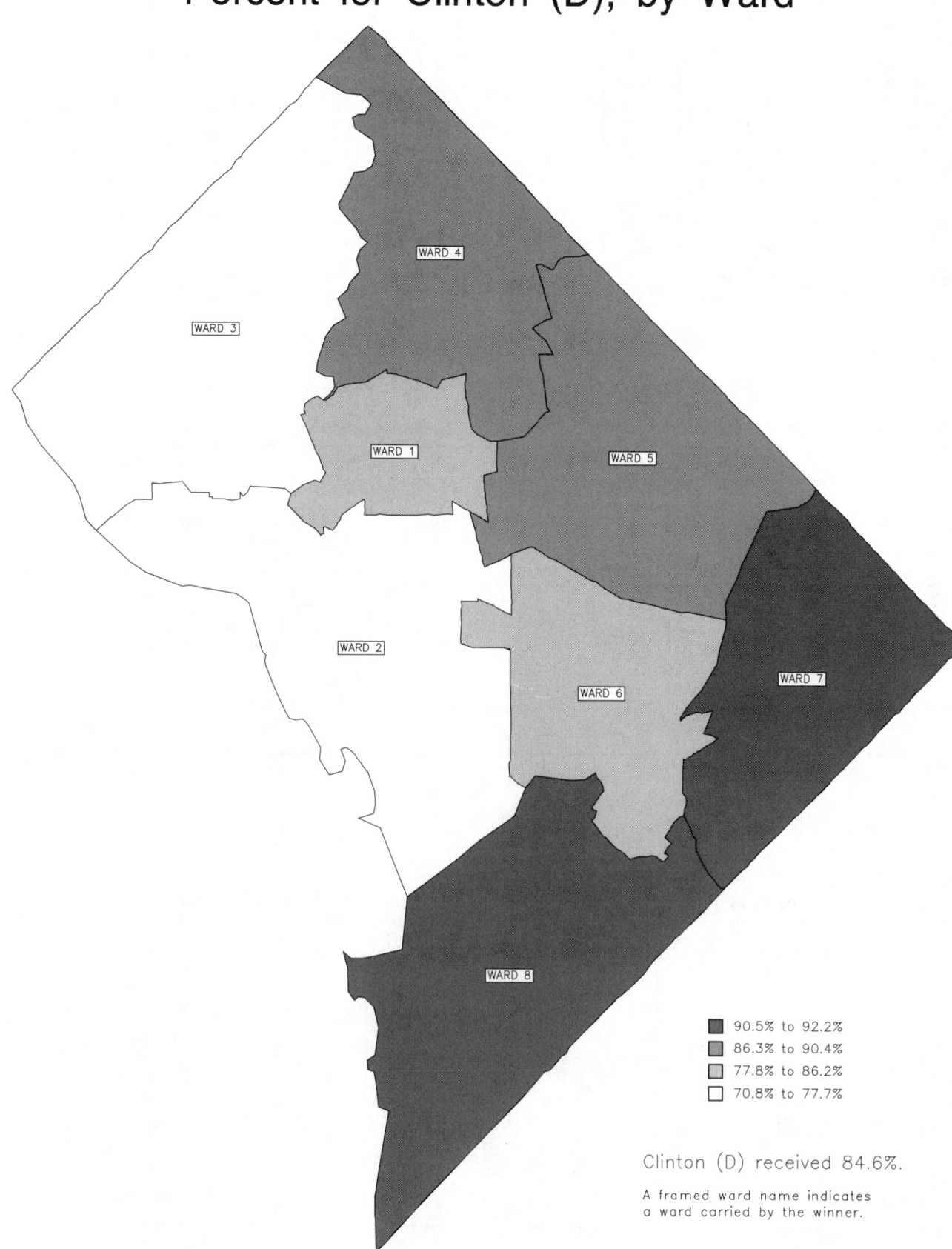

WARD 4

WARD 3

WARD 1

WARD 5

WARD 2

WARD 6

WARD 7

WARD 8

■ 90.5% to 92.2%
■ 86.3% to 90.4%
▫ 77.8% to 86.2%
□ 70.8% to 77.7%

Clinton (D) received 84.6%.

A framed ward name indicates
a ward carried by the winner.

1026 District of Columbia

NATIONWIDE COLOR MAPS

Voting Registration Methods, Number of Alternatives to In-Person Registration
Percent Non-Hispanic Black Population, 1990, by county
Percent Hispanic Population, 1990, by county
Counties covered by the Voting Rights Act
Type of Voting Equipment, by county
Percent Registered of Voting Age Population, 1992 General Election, by county
Percent Turnout of Voting Age Population, 1992 General Election, by county
Percent Turnout of Registered Voters, 1992 General Election, by county
Percent Registered of Voting Age Population, 1992 General Election, by state
Percent Turnout of Voting Age Population, 1992 General Election, by state
Percent Turnout of Registered Voters, 1992 General Election, by state
1992 Presidential Election Results, Winner by state
1992 Presidential Election Results, Winner by county
1992 Presidential Election Results for Bill Clinton, by county
1992 Presidential Election Results for George Bush, by county
1992 Presidential Election Results for H. Ross Perot, by county
1992 Congressional Election Results, Winner by Congressional District
1992 Election Results, Control of State Senate
1992 Election Results, Control of State House
1992 Gubernatorial Election Results

1992 Voter Registration Methods
Number of Alternatives to In-Person Registration

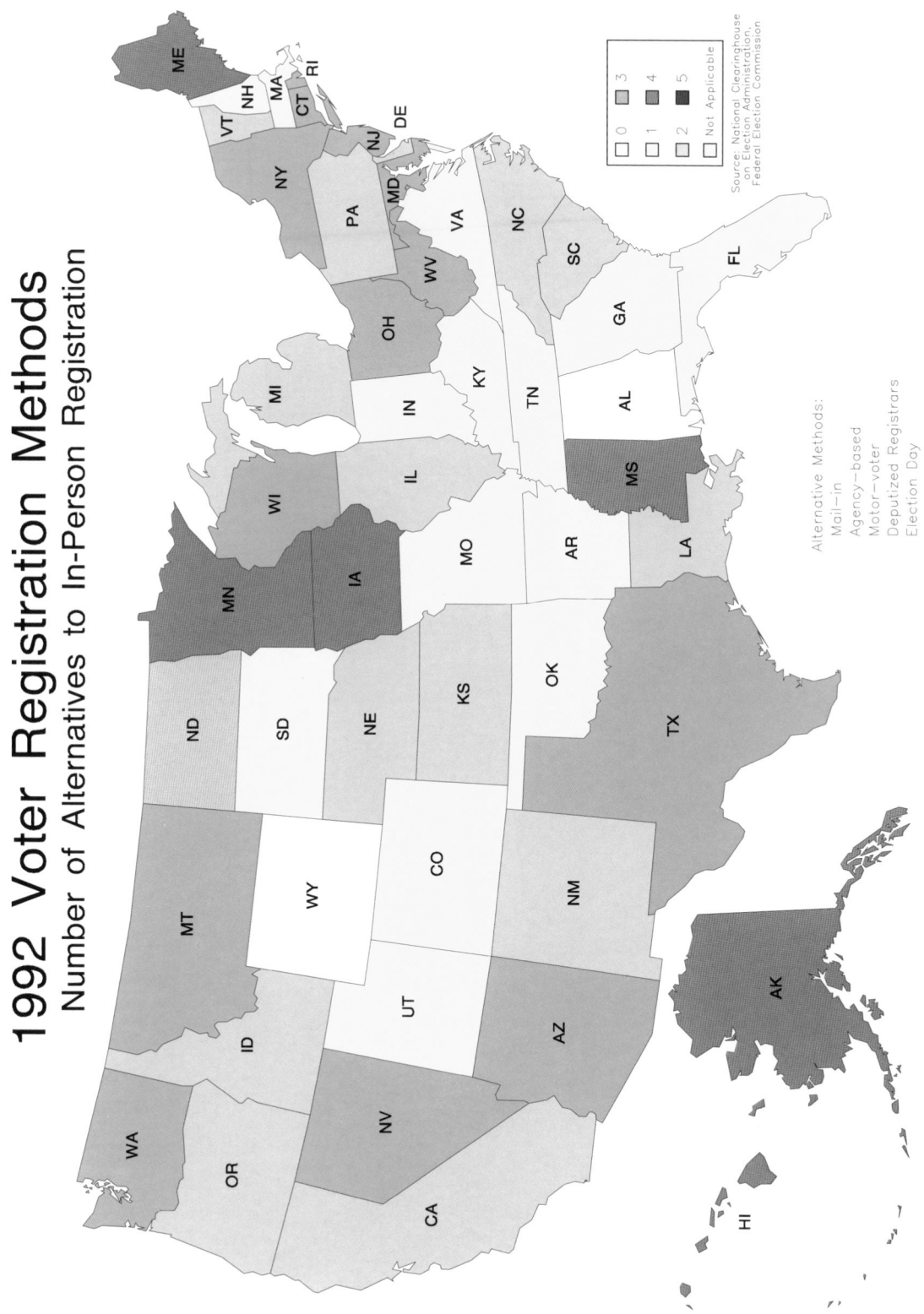

Alternative Methods:
Mail-in
Agency-based
Motor-voter
Deputized Registrars
Election Day

Source: National Clearinghouse
on Election Administration,
Federal Election Commission

3
4
5
Not Applicable

0
1
2

Percent Non-Hispanic

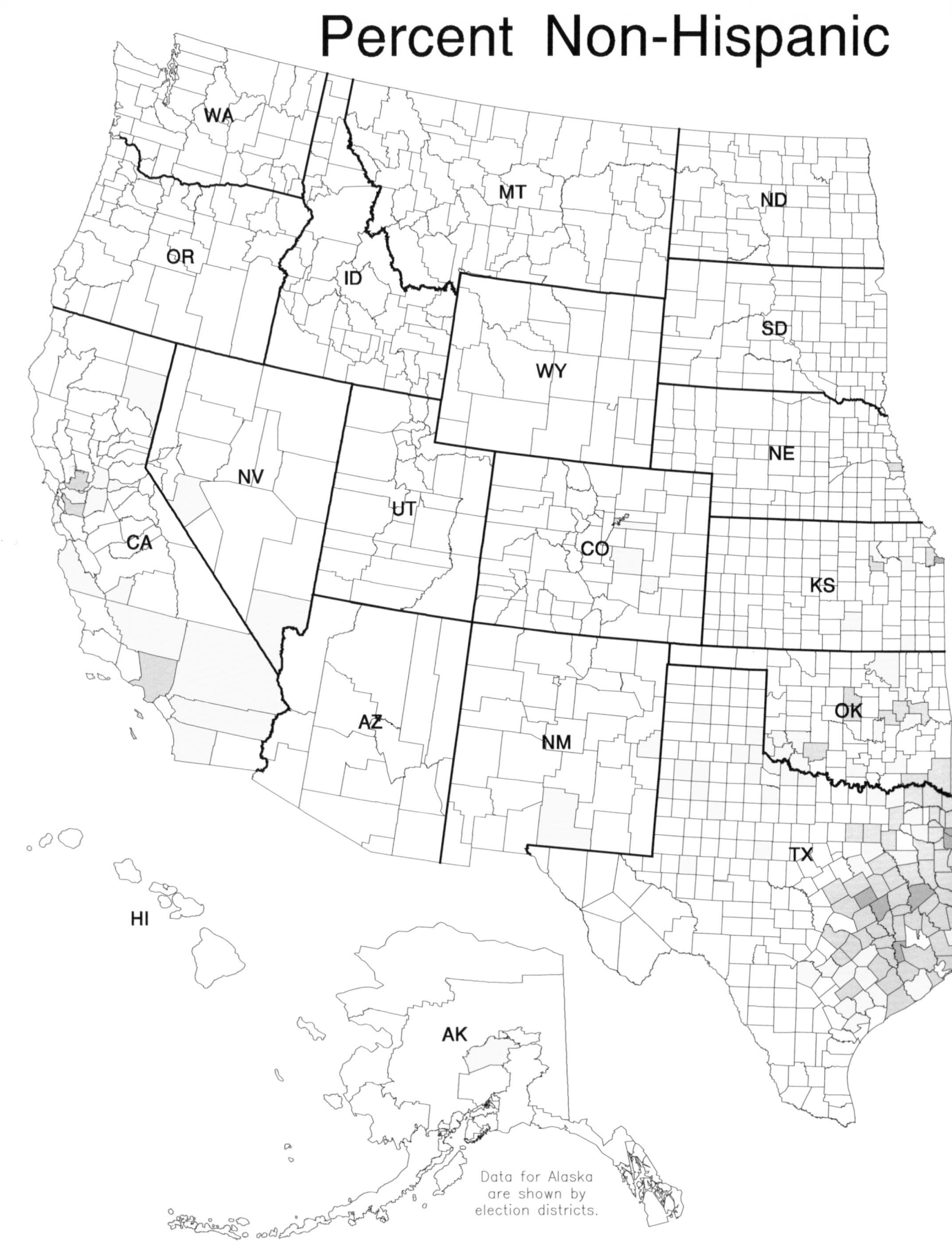

Data for Alaska are shown by election districts.

Black Population, 1990
By County

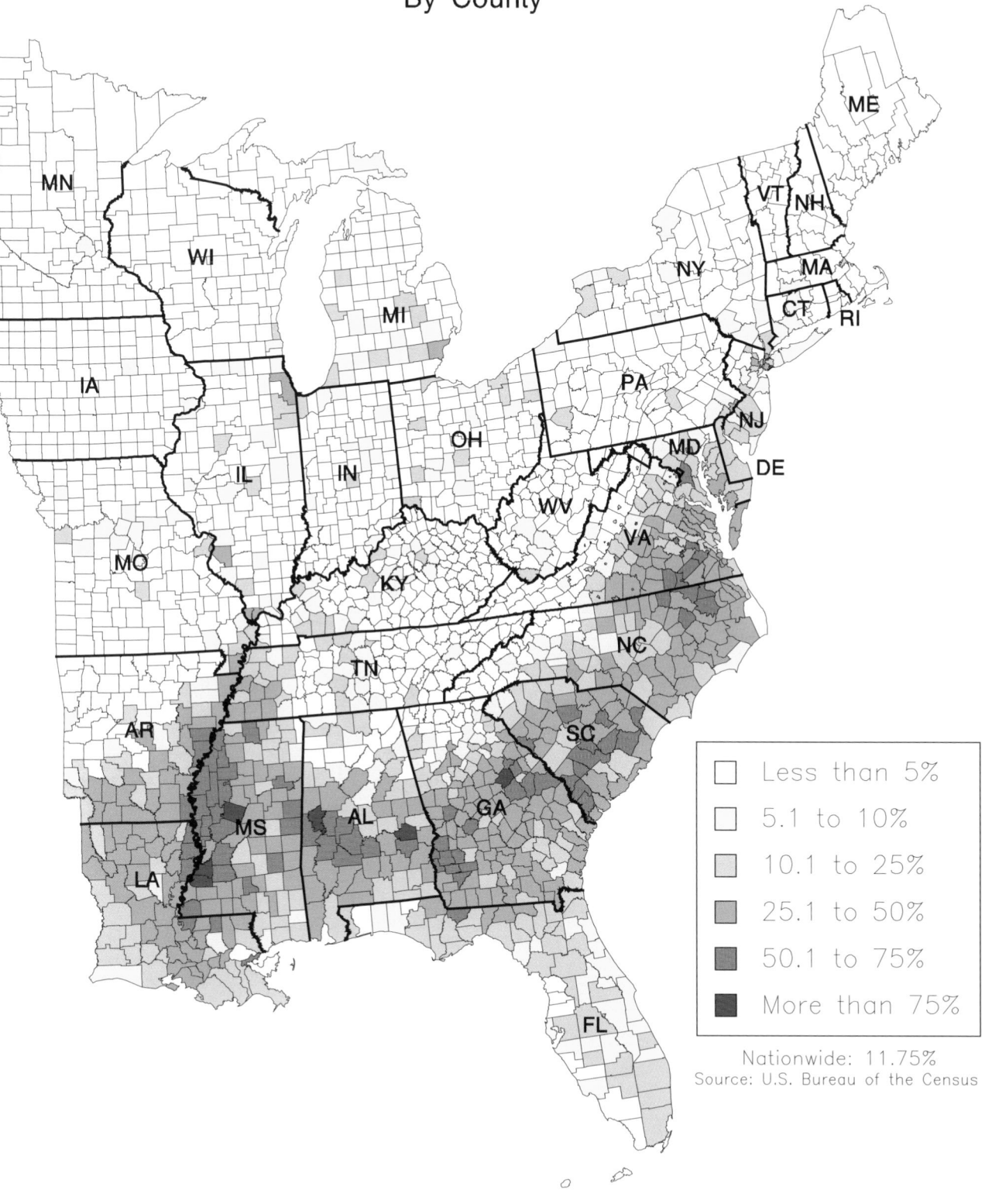

Legend:
- Less than 5%
- 5.1 to 10%
- 10.1 to 25%
- 25.1 to 50%
- 50.1 to 75%
- More than 75%

Nationwide: 11.75%
Source: U.S. Bureau of the Census

Percent   Hispanic

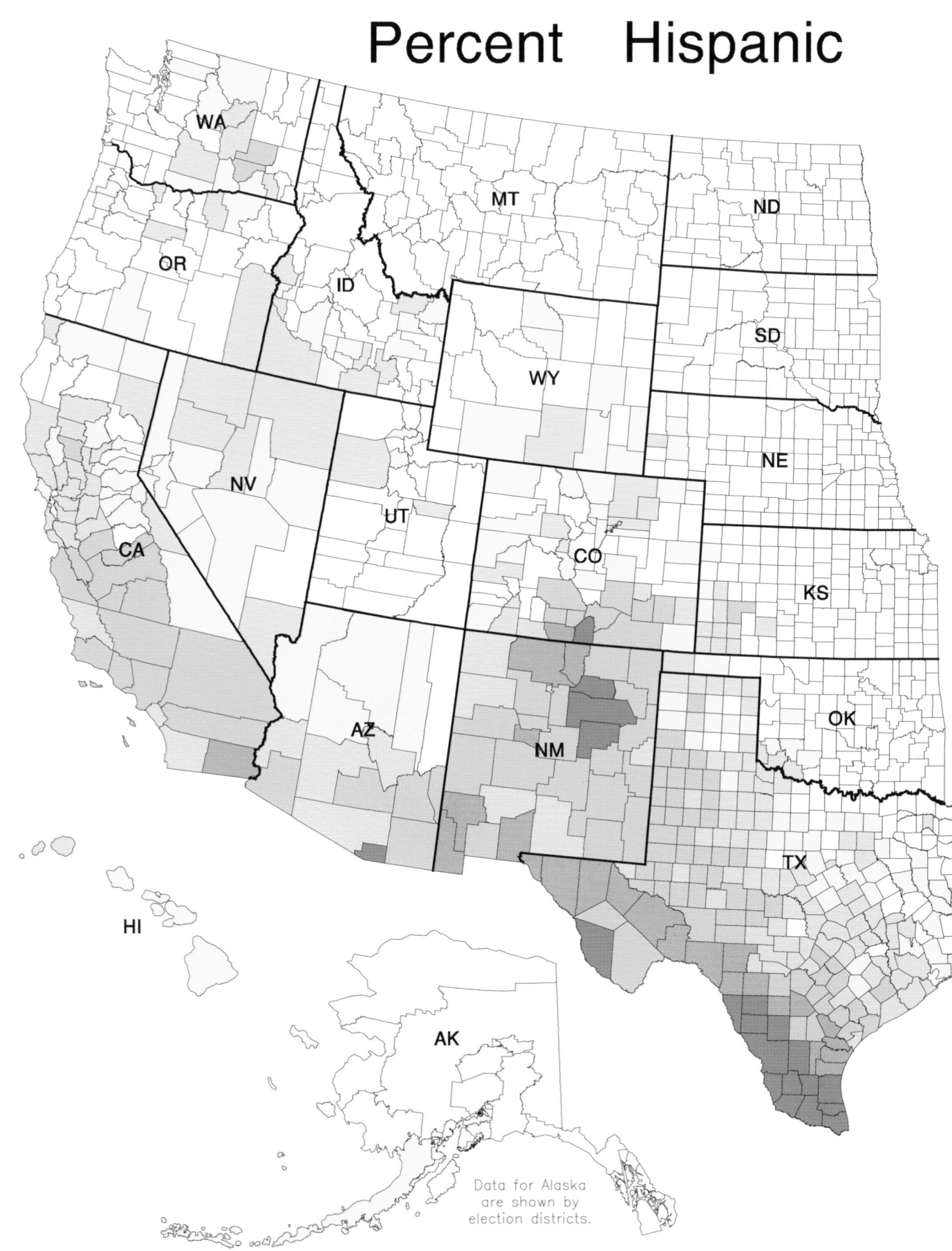

Data for Alaska
are shown by
election districts.

Population, 1990

By County

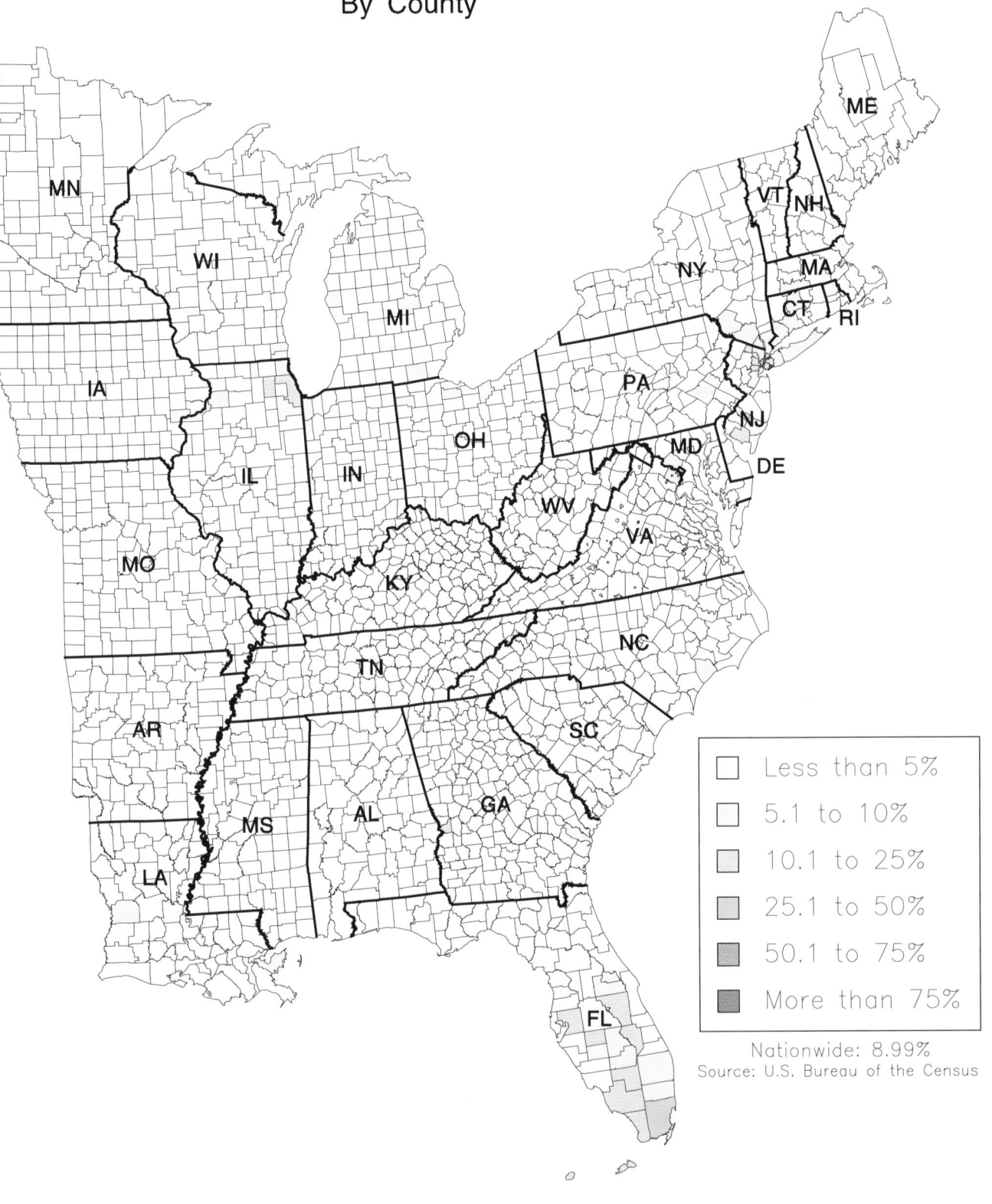

Legend:
- ☐ Less than 5%
- ☐ 5.1 to 10%
- ☐ 10.1 to 25%
- ☐ 25.1 to 50%
- ☐ 50.1 to 75%
- ☐ More than 75%

Nationwide: 8.99%
Source: U.S. Bureau of the Census

Counties Covered by

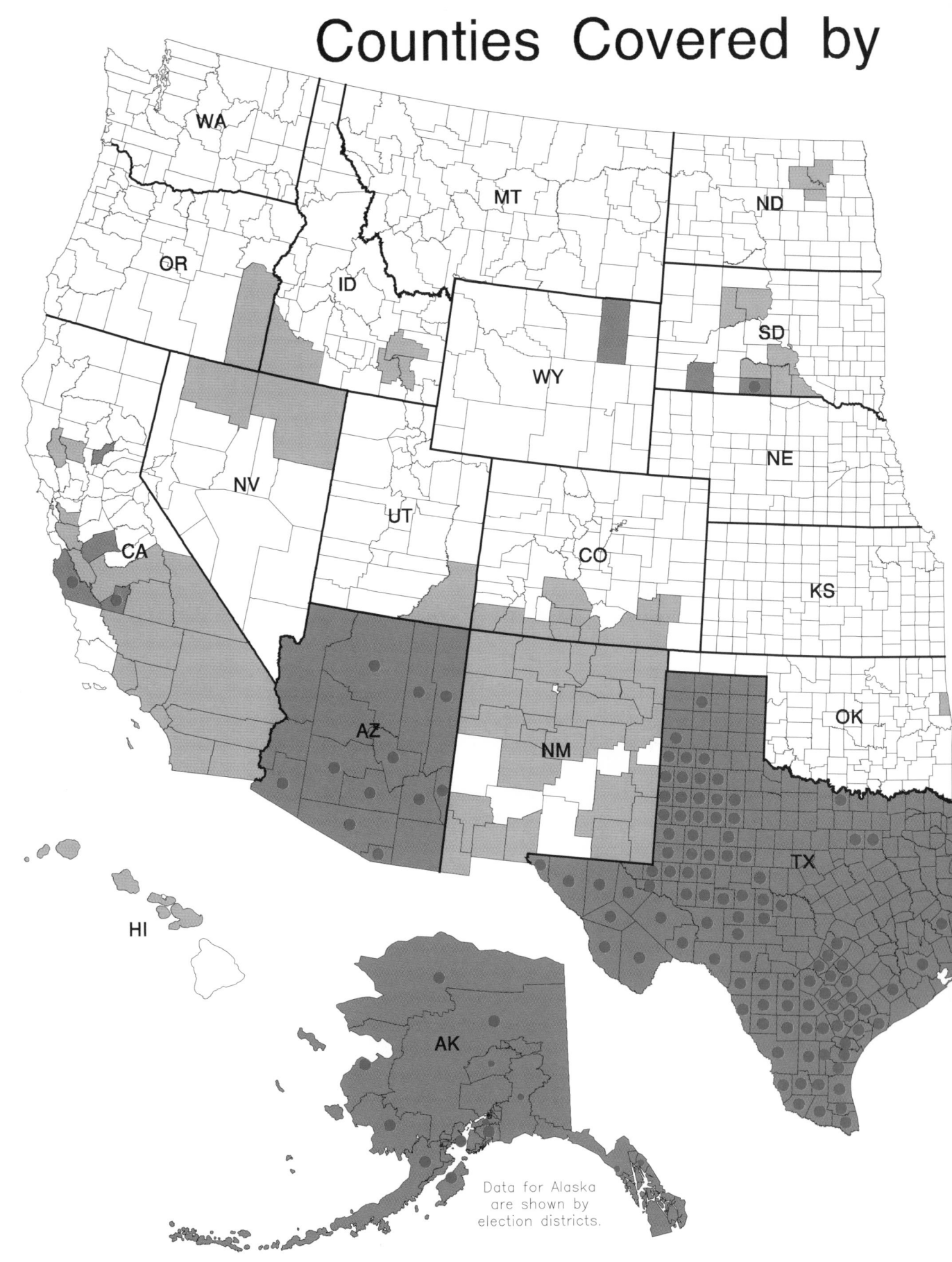

Data for Alaska are shown by election districts.

the Voting Rights Act

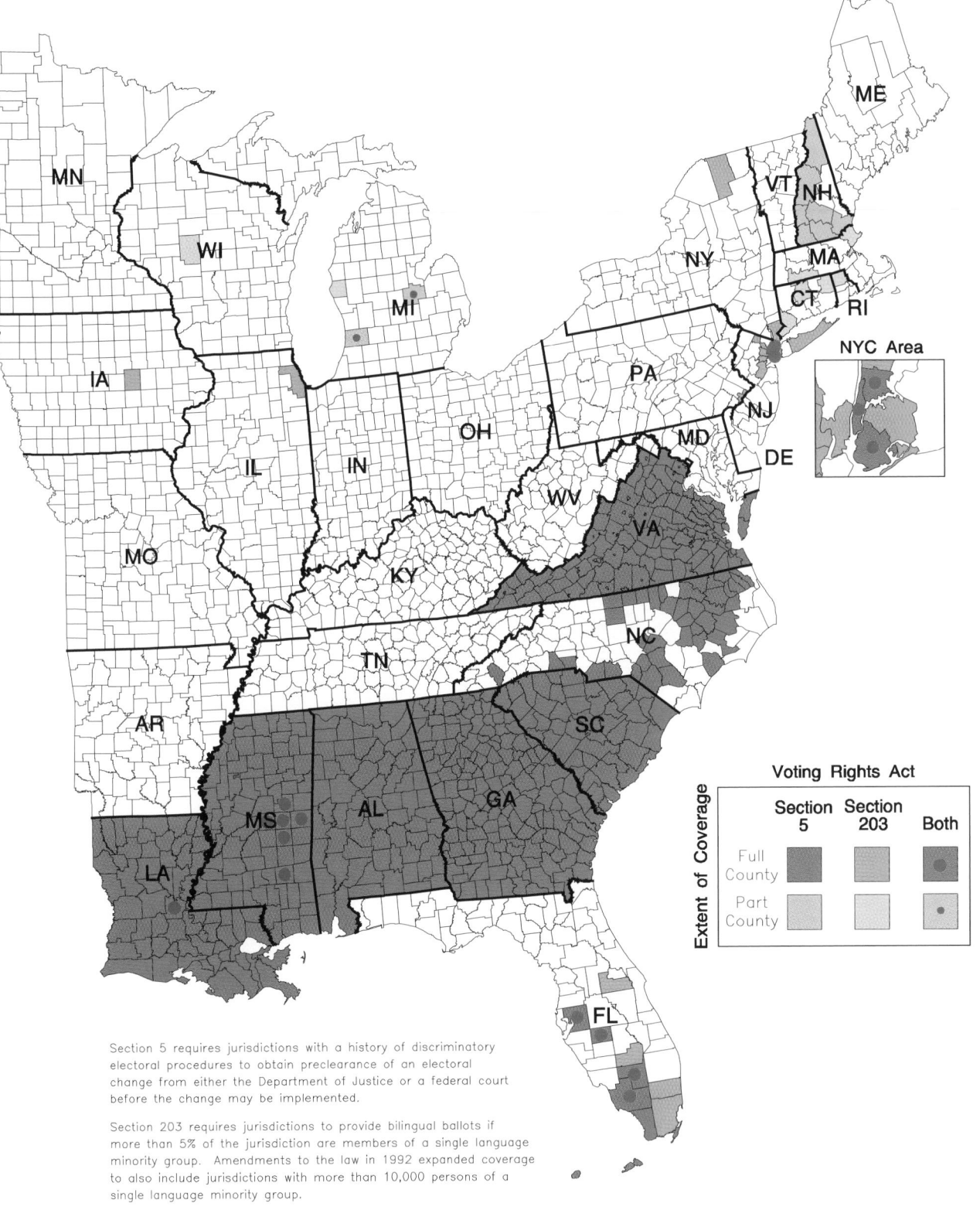

NYC Area

Voting Rights Act

Extent of Coverage

	Section 5	Section 203	Both
Full County			
Part County			

Section 5 requires jurisdictions with a history of discriminatory electoral procedures to obtain preclearance of an electoral change from either the Department of Justice or a federal court before the change may be implemented.

Section 203 requires jurisdictions to provide bilingual ballots if more than 5% of the jurisdiction are members of a single language minority group. Amendments to the law in 1992 expanded coverage to also include jurisdictions with more than 10,000 persons of a single language minority group.

Type of Voting

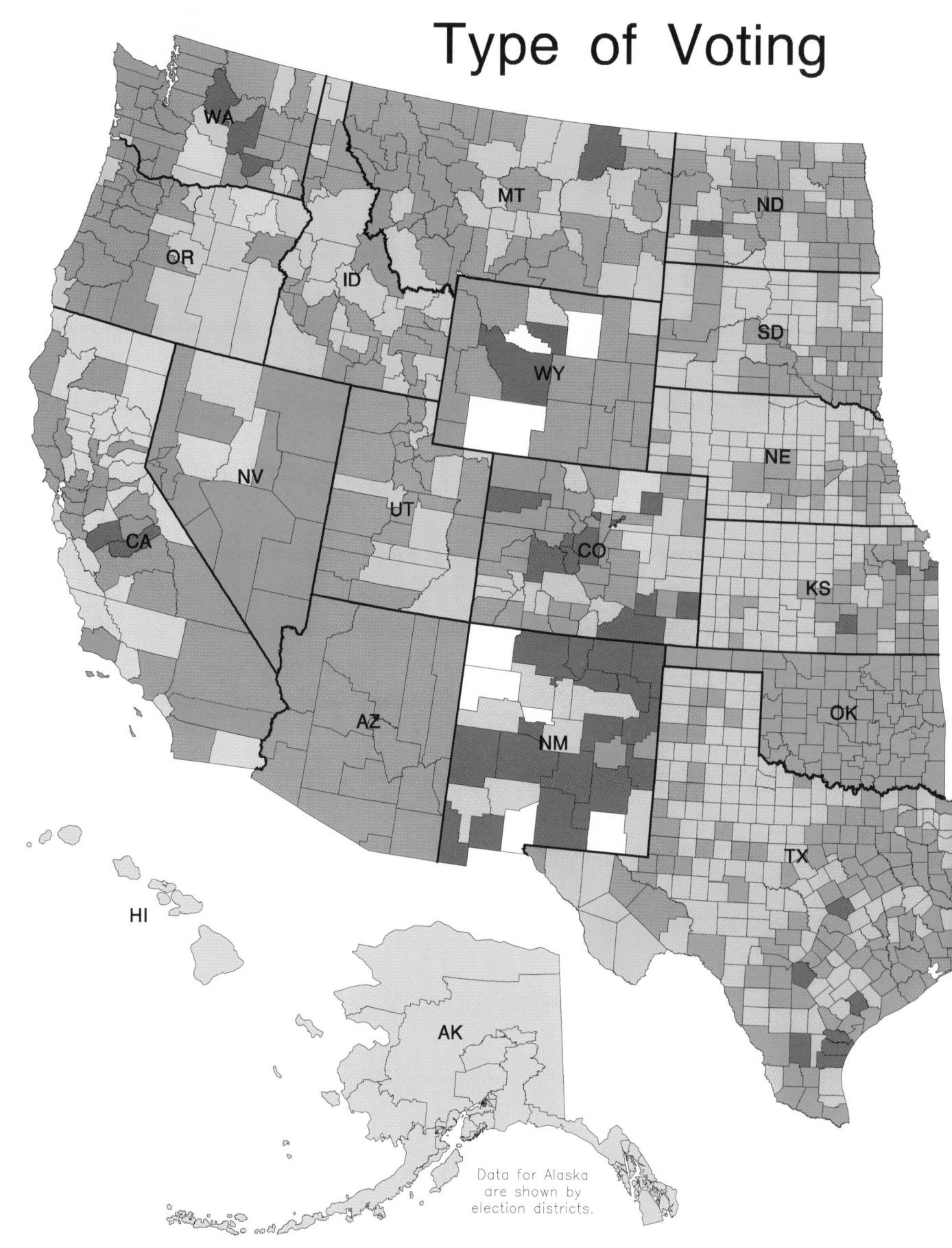

Equipment by County

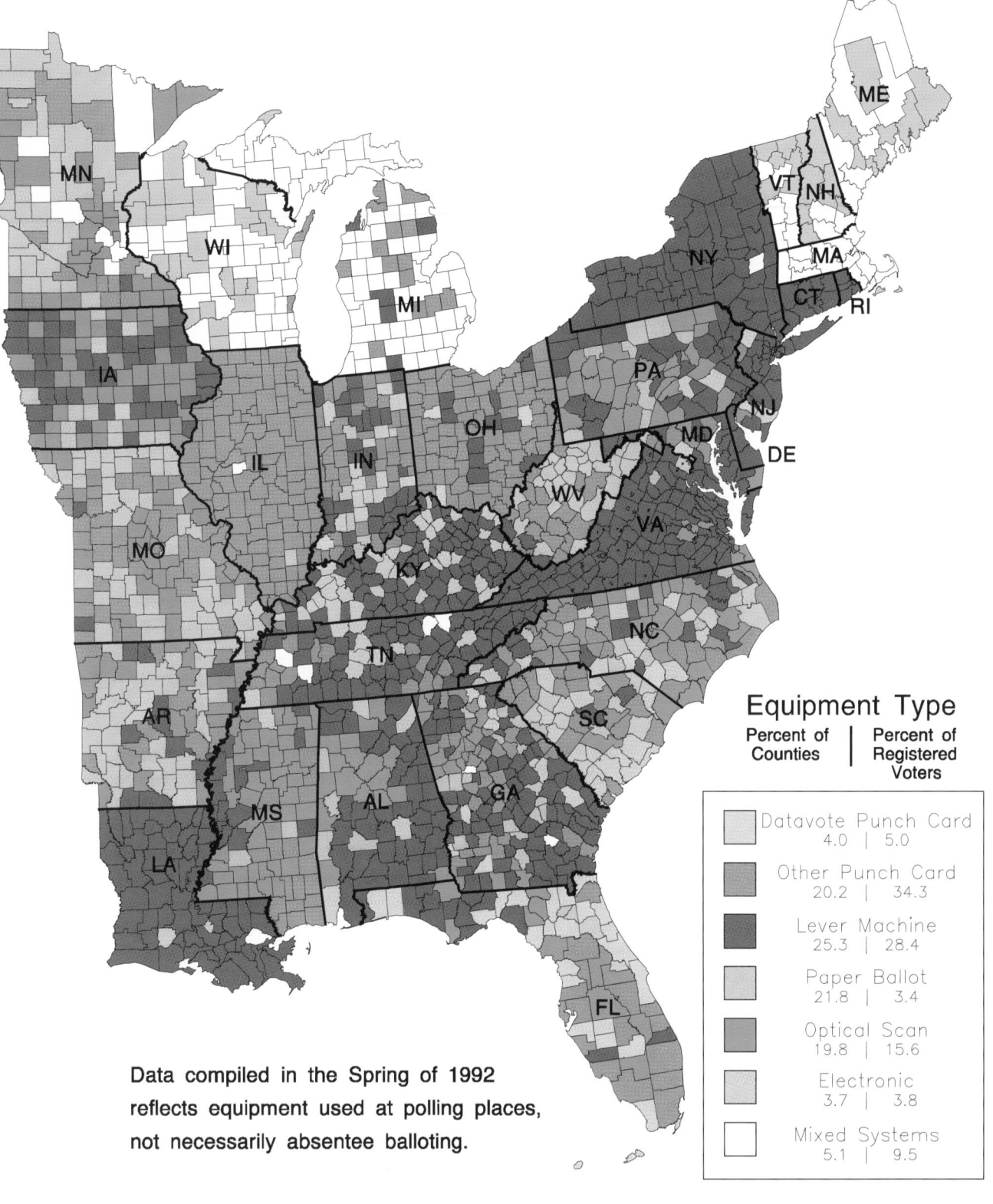

Equipment Type

Percent of Counties	Percent of Registered Voters

Datavote Punch Card
4.0 | 5.0

Other Punch Card
20.2 | 34.3

Lever Machine
25.3 | 28.4

Paper Ballot
21.8 | 3.4

Optical Scan
19.8 | 15.6

Electronic
3.7 | 3.8

Mixed Systems
5.1 | 9.5

Data compiled in the Spring of 1992 reflects equipment used at polling places, not necessarily absentee balloting.

Percent Registered of

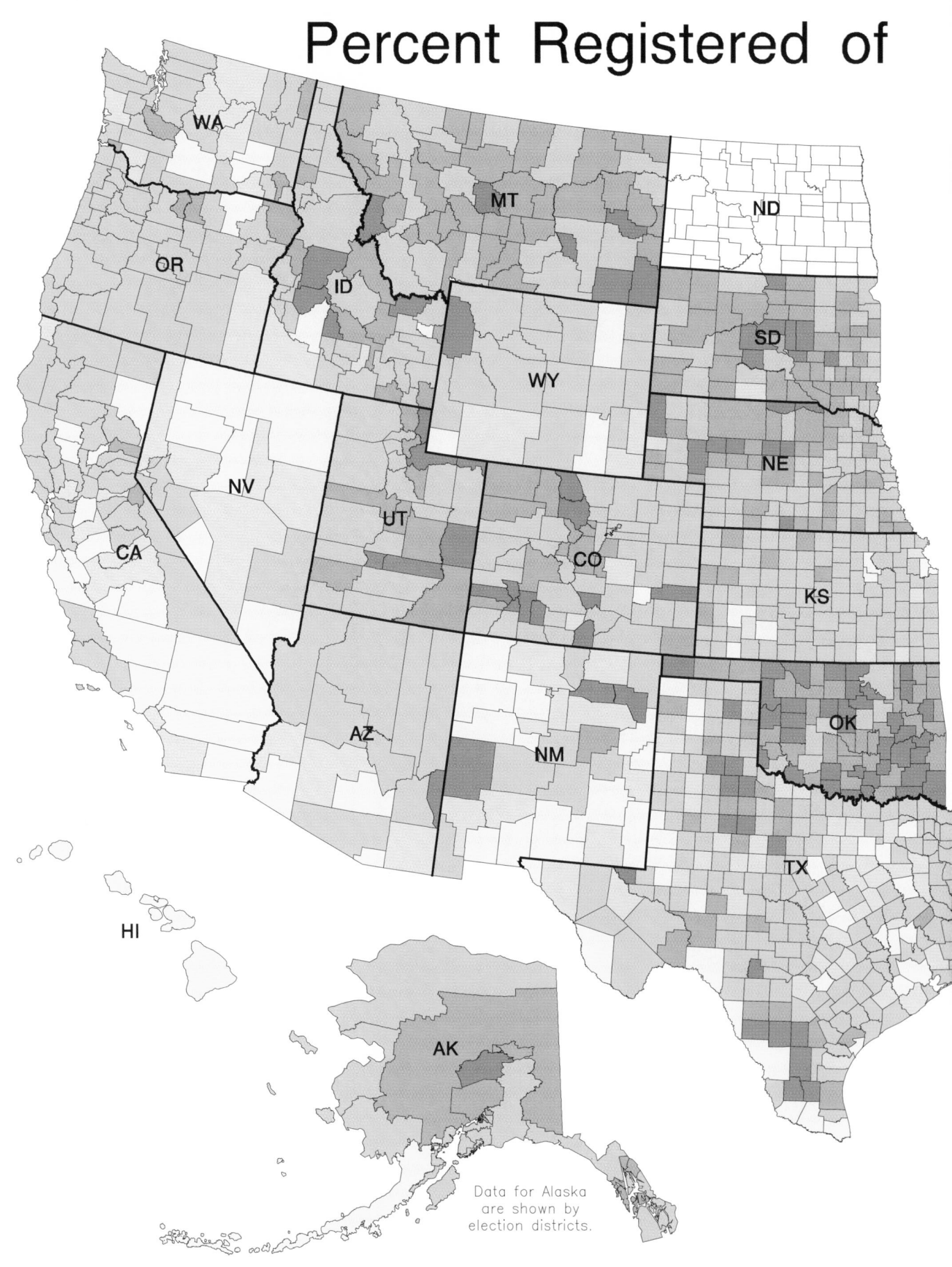

Voting Age Population

1992 General Election, By County

Legend:

- Less than 65%
- 65 to 70.9%
- 71 to 79.9%
- 80 to 89.9%
- 90 to 100%
- More than 100%
- No data available

Nationwide: 70.8%

This percentage may be overstated and may even exceed 100% if the roll of registered voters has not been recently updated, or if the VAP estimate is not accurate. See the chapter on using the data for a discussion of discrepancies in VAP and registration numbers.

Registration data by county were not available for Vermont at time of publication. North Dakota and Wisconsin have no statewide voter registration requirement.

Percent Turnout of

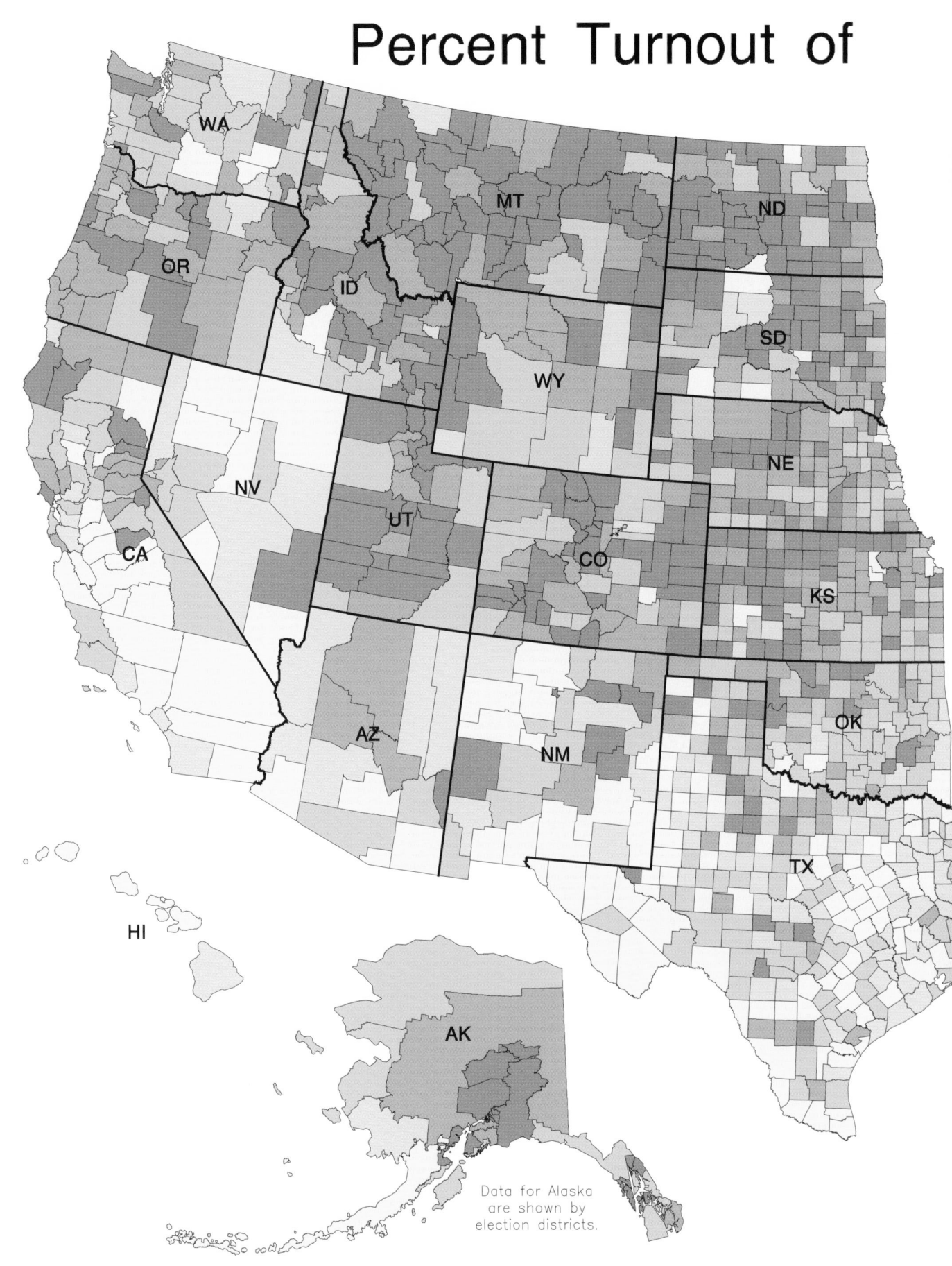

Voting Age Population

1992 General Election, By County

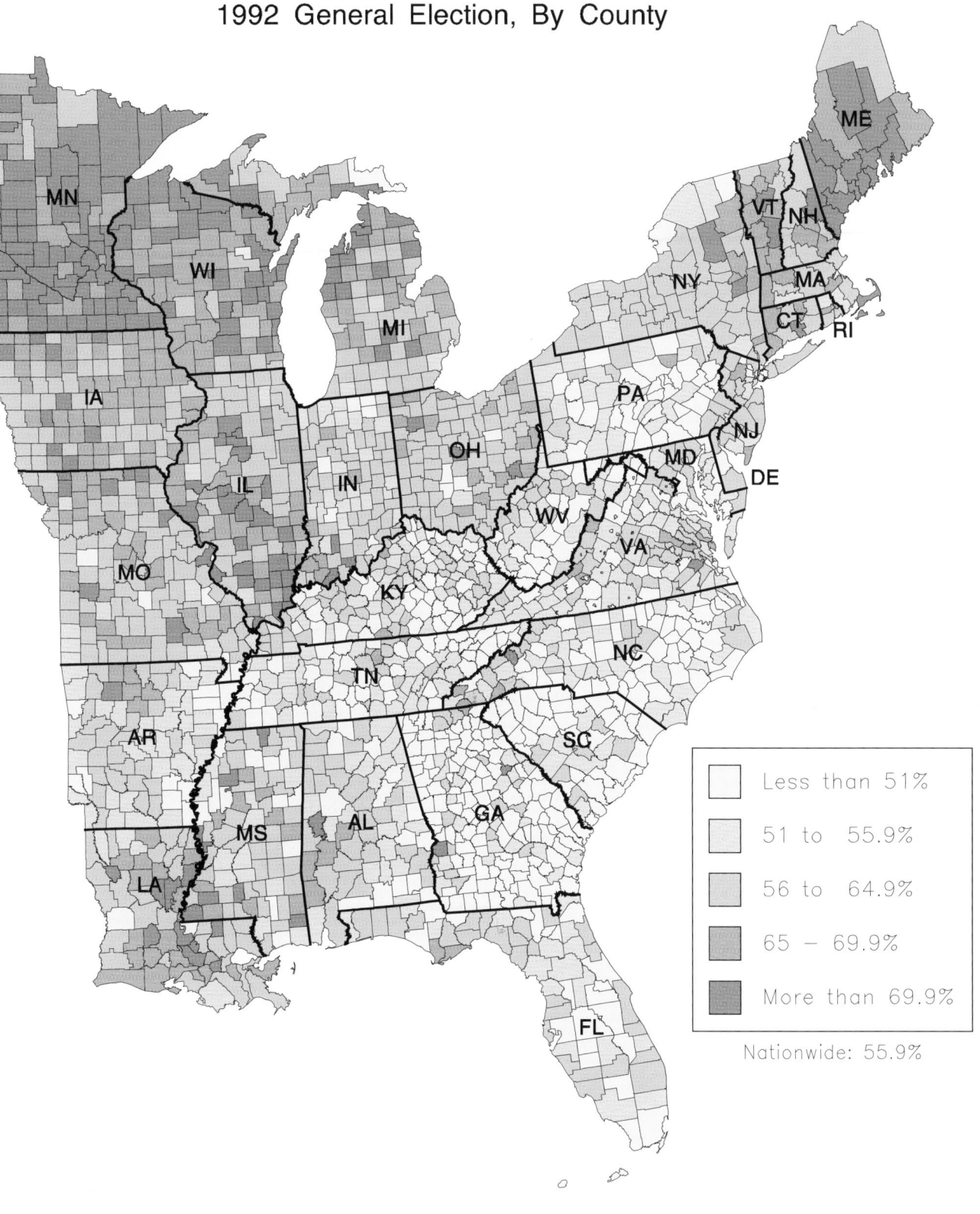

Legend:
- Less than 51%
- 51 to 55.9%
- 56 to 64.9%
- 65 – 69.9%
- More than 69.9%

Nationwide: 55.9%

Percent Turnout of

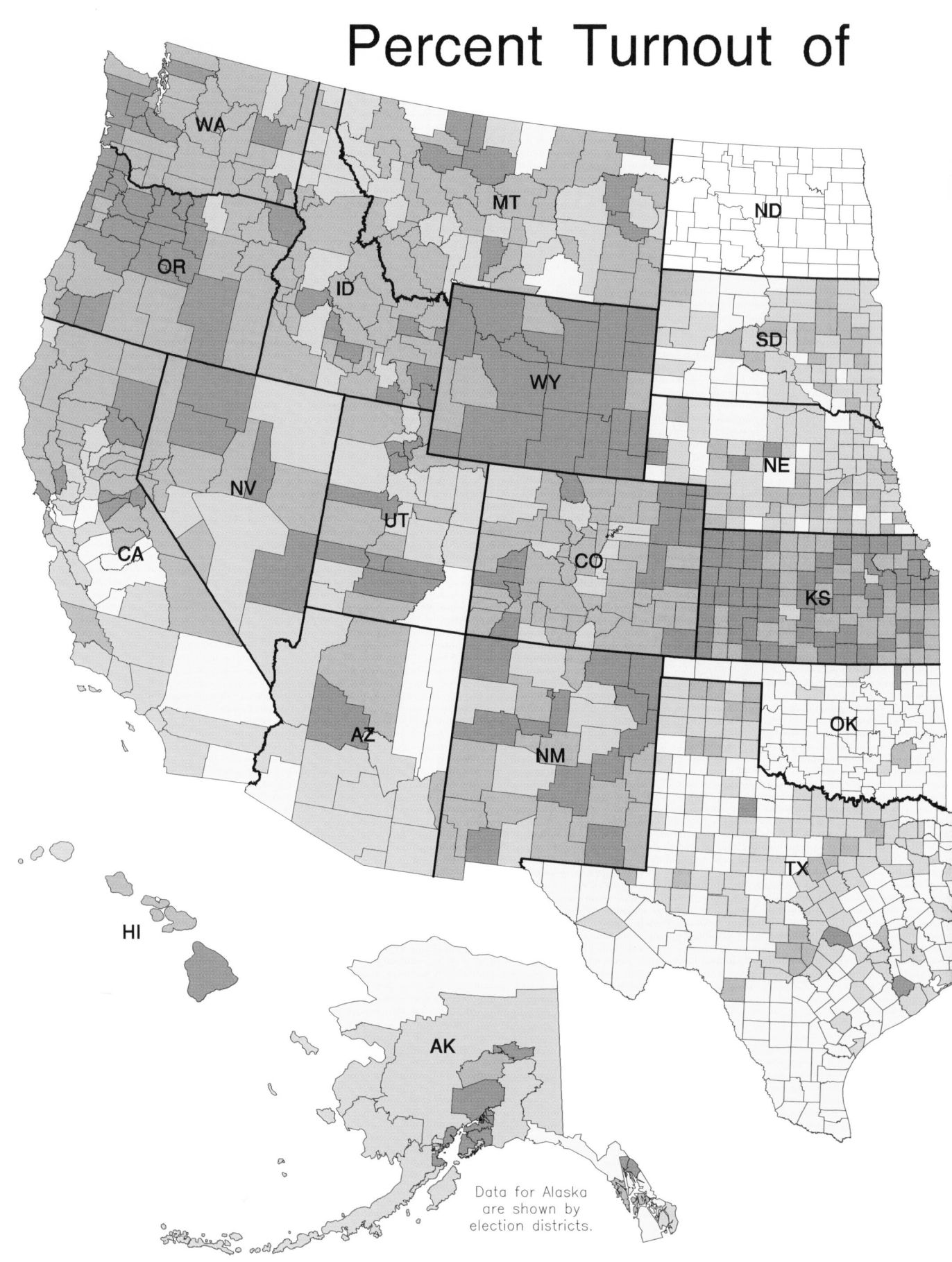

Data for Alaska
are shown by
election districts.

Registered Voters

1992 General Election, By County

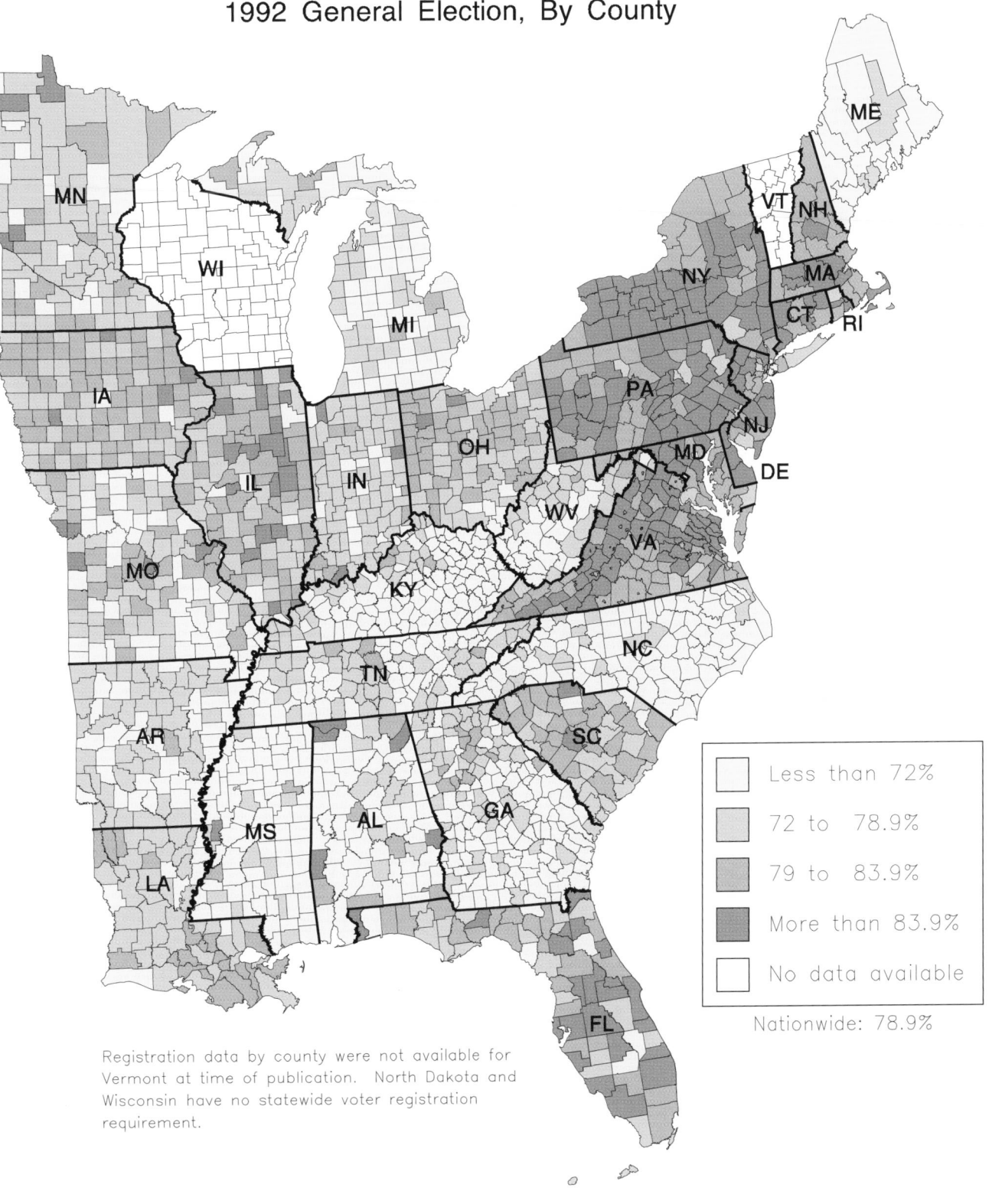

Less than 72%

72 to 78.9%

79 to 83.9%

More than 83.9%

No data available

Nationwide: 78.9%

Registration data by county were not available for Vermont at time of publication. North Dakota and Wisconsin have no statewide voter registration requirement.

Percent Registered of Voting Age Population

1992 General Election, by State

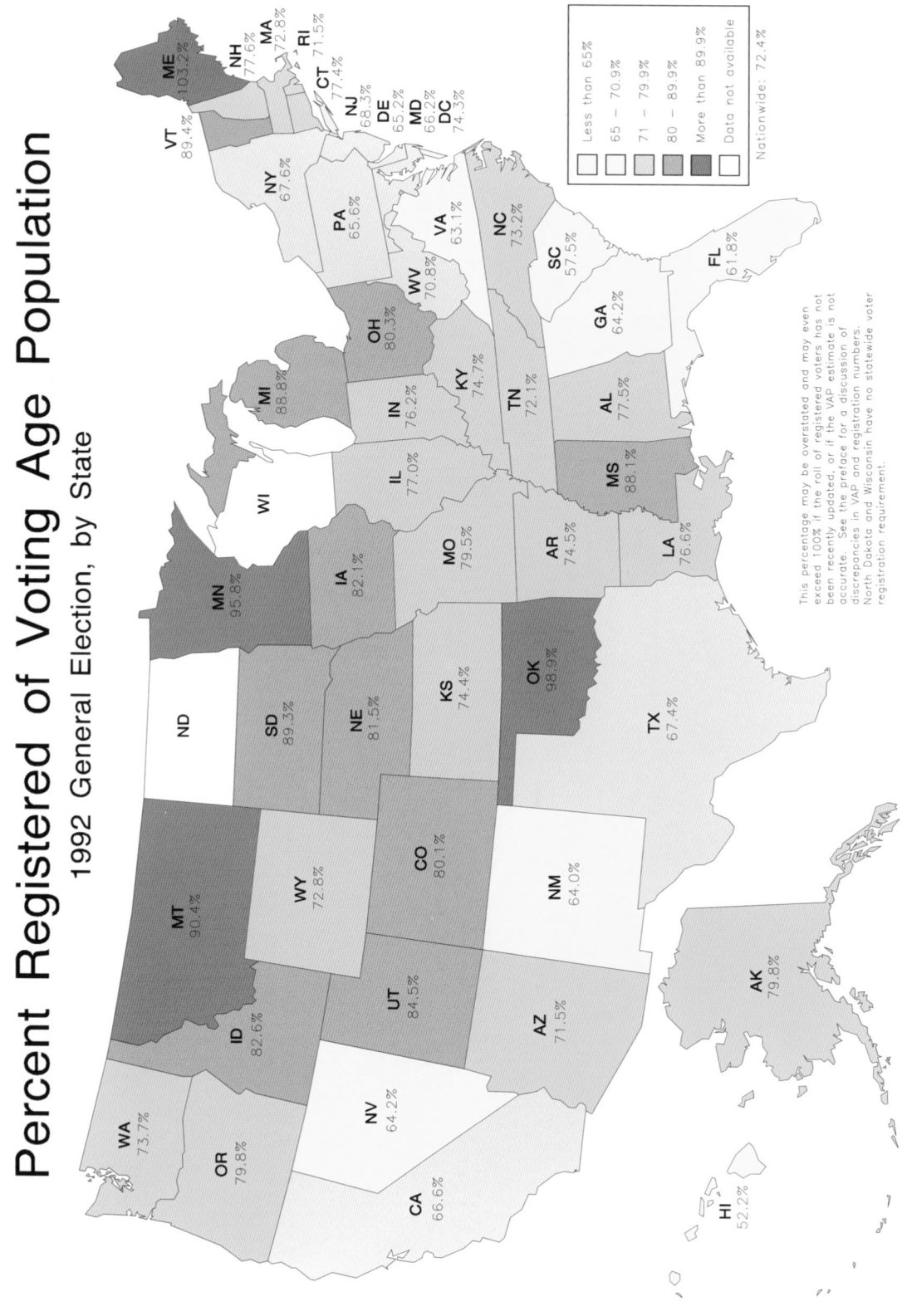

Legend:

- Less than 65%
- 65 – 70.9%
- 71 – 79.9%
- 80 – 89.9%
- More than 89.9%
- Data not available

Nationwide: 72.4%

This percentage may be overstated and may even exceed 100% if the roll of registered voters has not been recently updated, or if the VAP estimate is not accurate. See the preface for a discussion of discrepancies in VAP and registration numbers. North Dakota and Wisconsin have no statewide voter registration requirement.

State values:
- ME 103.2%
- NH 77.6%
- MA 72.8%
- RI 71.5%
- CT 77.4%
- VT 89.4%
- NY 67.6%
- PA 65.6%
- NJ 68.3%
- DE 65.2%
- MD 66.2%
- DC 74.3%
- VA 63.1%
- NC 73.2%
- SC 57.5%
- FL 61.8%
- WV 70.8%
- OH 80.3%
- MI 88.8%
- IN 76.2%
- KY 74.7%
- TN 72.1%
- AL 77.5%
- GA 64.2%
- IL 77.0%
- MS 88.1%
- WI (Data not available)
- MN 95.8%
- IA 82.1%
- MO 79.5%
- AR 74.5%
- LA 76.6%
- ND (Data not available)
- SD 89.3%
- NE 81.5%
- KS 74.4%
- OK 98.9%
- TX 67.4%
- MT 90.4%
- WY 72.8%
- CO 80.1%
- NM 64.0%
- ID 82.6%
- UT 84.5%
- AZ 71.5%
- WA 73.7%
- OR 79.8%
- NV 64.2%
- CA 66.6%
- AK 79.8%
- HI 52.2%

Percent Turnout of Voting Age Population

1992 General Election, by State

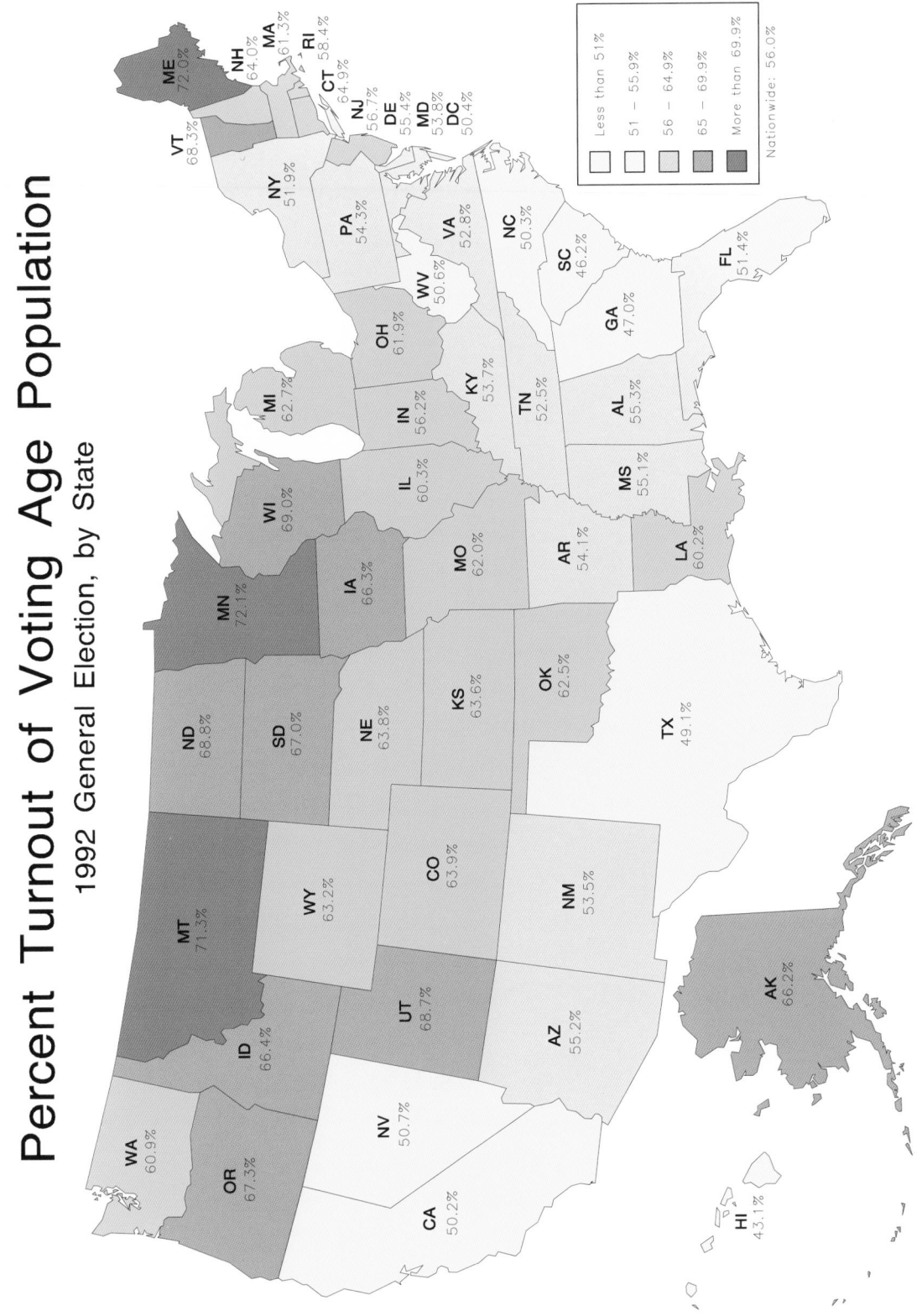

Legend:
- Less than 51%
- 51 - 55.9%
- 56 - 64.9%
- 65 - 69.9%
- More than 69.9%

Nationwide: 56.0%

ME 72.0%
NH 64.0%
MA 61.3%
RI 58.4%
CT 64.9%
NJ 56.7%
DE 55.4%
MD 53.8%
DC 50.4%
VT 68.3%
NY 51.9%
PA 54.3%
VA 52.8%
NC 50.3%
SC 46.2%
FL 51.4%
WV 50.6%
OH 61.9%
KY 53.7%
TN 52.5%
GA 47.0%
MI 62.7%
IN 56.2%
AL 55.3%
IL 60.3%
MO 62.0%
MS 55.1%
WI 69.0%
AR 54.1%
LA 60.2%
MN 72.1%
IA 66.3%
ND 68.8%
SD 67.0%
NE 63.8%
KS 63.6%
OK 62.5%
TX 49.1%
MT 71.3%
ID 66.4%
WY 63.2%
CO 63.9%
NM 53.5%
AK 66.2%
WA 60.9%
OR 67.3%
NV 50.7%
UT 68.7%
AZ 55.2%
CA 50.2%
HI 43.1%

Percent Turnout of Registered Voters

1992 General Election, by State

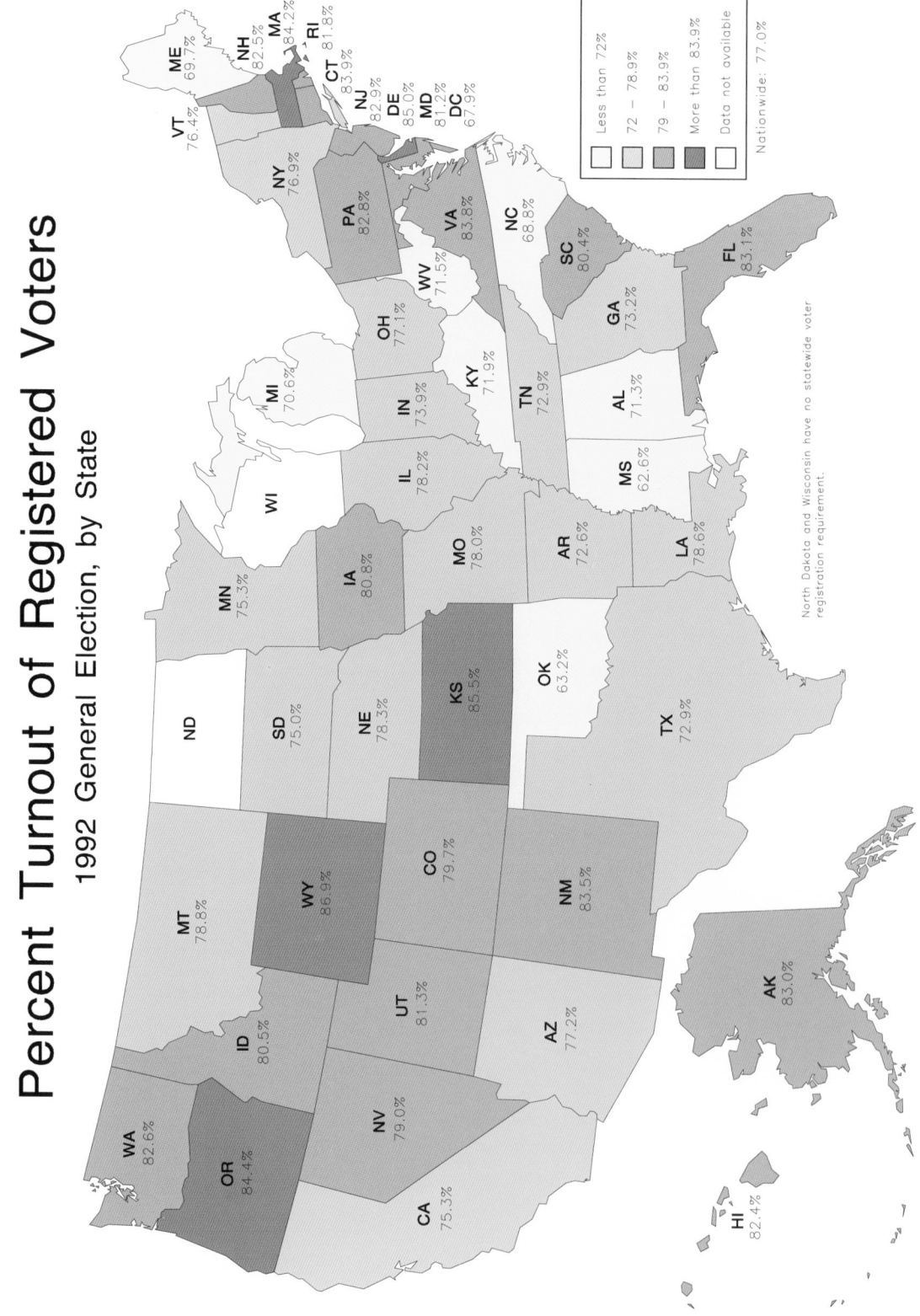

Legend:
- Less than 72%
- 72 – 78.9%
- 79 – 83.9%
- More than 83.9%
- Data not available

Nationwide: 77.0%

ME 69.7%
NH 82.5%
MA 84.2%
RI 81.8%
CT 83.9%
VT 76.4%
NY 76.9%
NJ 82.9%
DE 85.0%
MD 81.2%
DC 67.9%
PA 82.8%
VA 83.8%
NC 68.8%
SC 80.4%
FL 83.1%
WV 71.5%
OH 77.1%
GA 73.2%
MI 70.6%
IN 73.9%
KY 71.9%
TN 72.9%
AL 71.3%
WI
IL 78.2%
MS 62.6%
MN 75.3%
IA 80.8%
MO 78.0%
AR 72.6%
LA 78.6%
ND
SD 75.0%
NE 78.3%
KS 85.5%
OK 63.2%
TX 72.9%
MT 78.8%
WY 86.9%
CO 79.7%
NM 83.5%
AK 83.0%
ID 80.5%
UT 81.3%
AZ 77.2%
WA 82.6%
OR 84.4%
NV 79.0%
CA 75.3%
HI 82.4%

North Dakota and Wisconsin have no statewide voter registration requirement.

1992 Presidential Election Results
Winner by State

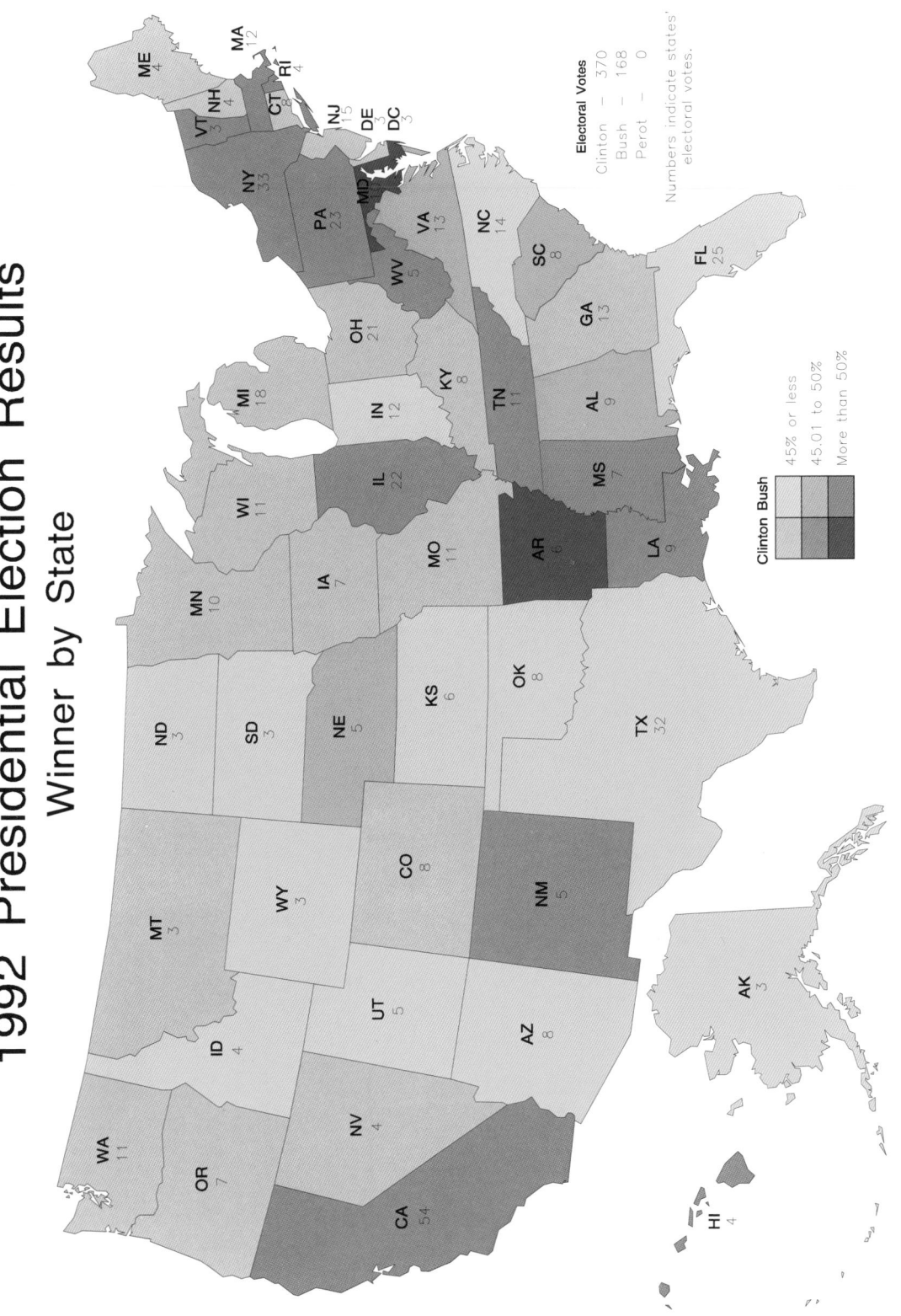

Electoral Votes

Clinton — 370
Bush — 168
Perot — 0

Numbers indicate states' electoral votes.

Clinton Bush

45% or less
45.01 to 50%
More than 50%

ME 4
MA 12
RI 4
NH 4
CT 8
VT 3
NJ 15
DE 3
DC 3
NY 33
PA 23
MD
VA 13
NC 14
SC 8
FL 25
WV 5
OH 21
GA 13
KY 8
TN 11
AL 9
MI 18
IN 12
IL 22
MS 7
WI 11
MO 11
AR 6
LA 9
MN 10
IA 7
ND 3
SD 3
NE 5
KS 6
OK 8
TX 32
CO 8
NM 5
WY 3
MT 3
UT 5
AZ 8
AK 3
ID 4
NV 4
WA 11
OR 7
CA 54
HI 4

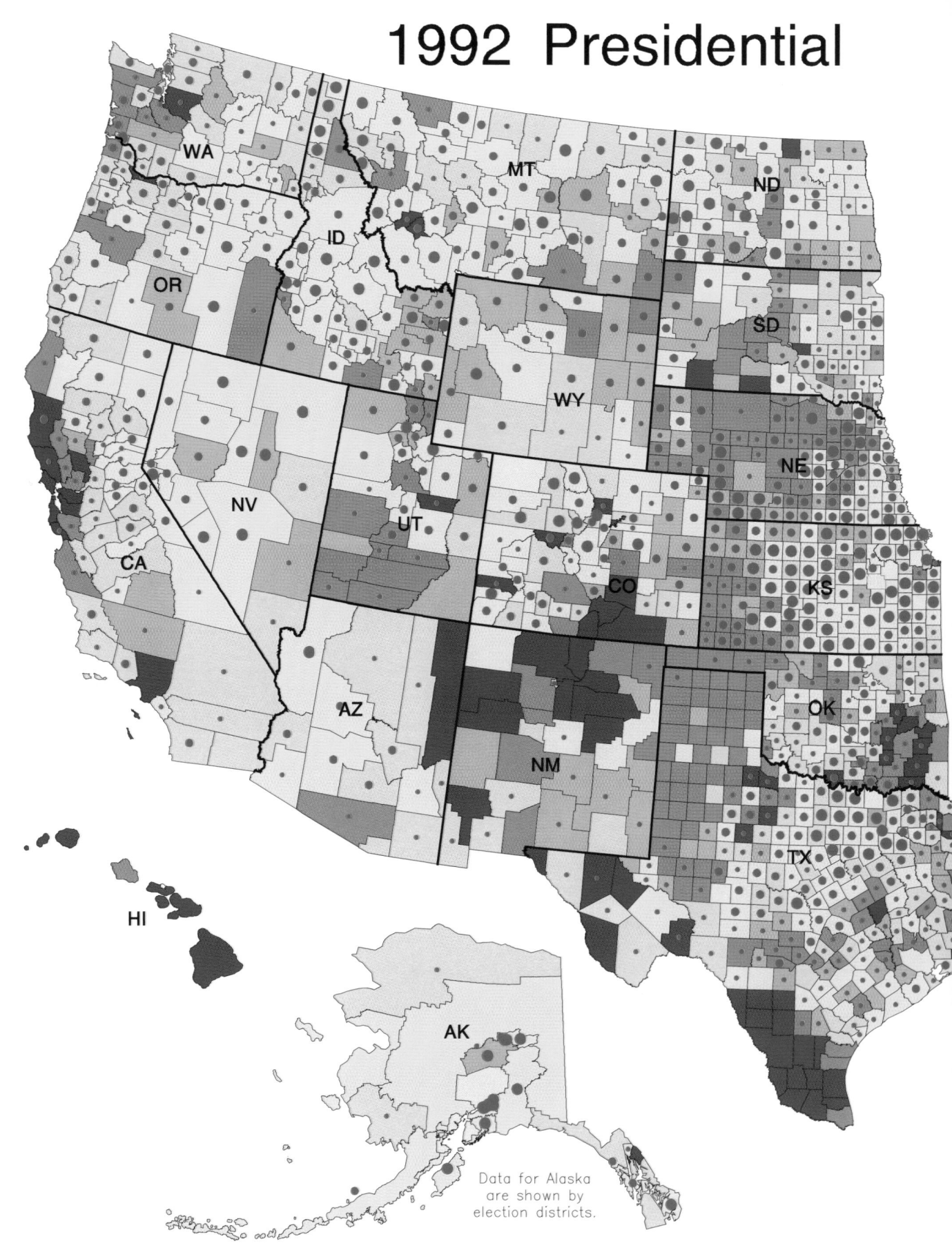

1992 Presidential

Data for Alaska are shown by election districts.

Election Results

Winner by County
With Results for H. Ross Perot

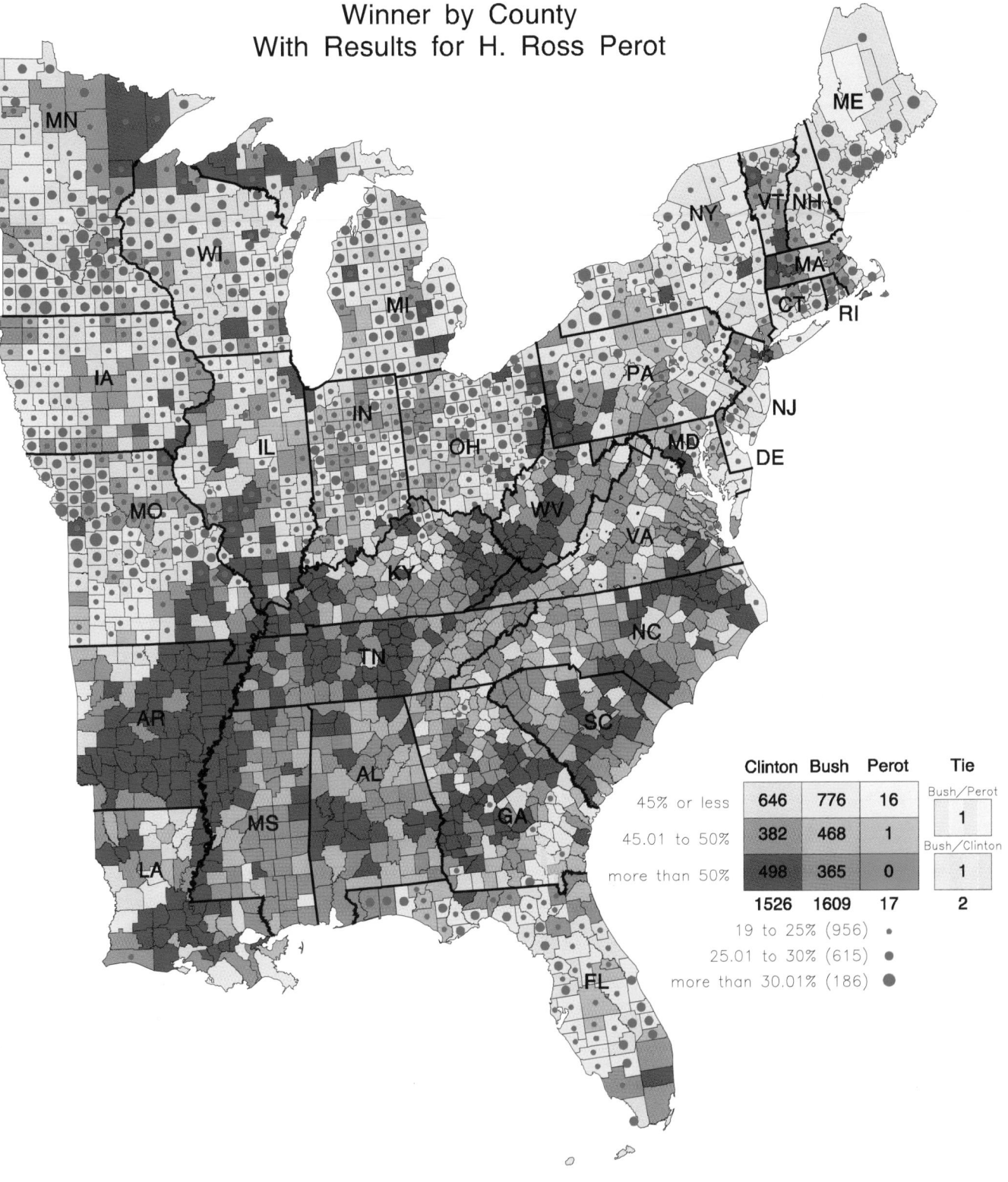

	Clinton	Bush	Perot	Tie	
				Bush/Perot	
45% or less	646	776	16	1	
				Bush/Clinton	
45.01 to 50%	382	468	1	1	
more than 50%	498	365	0		
	1526	1609	17	2	

19 to 25% (956) •
25.01 to 30% (615) •
more than 30.01% (186) •

1992 Presidential

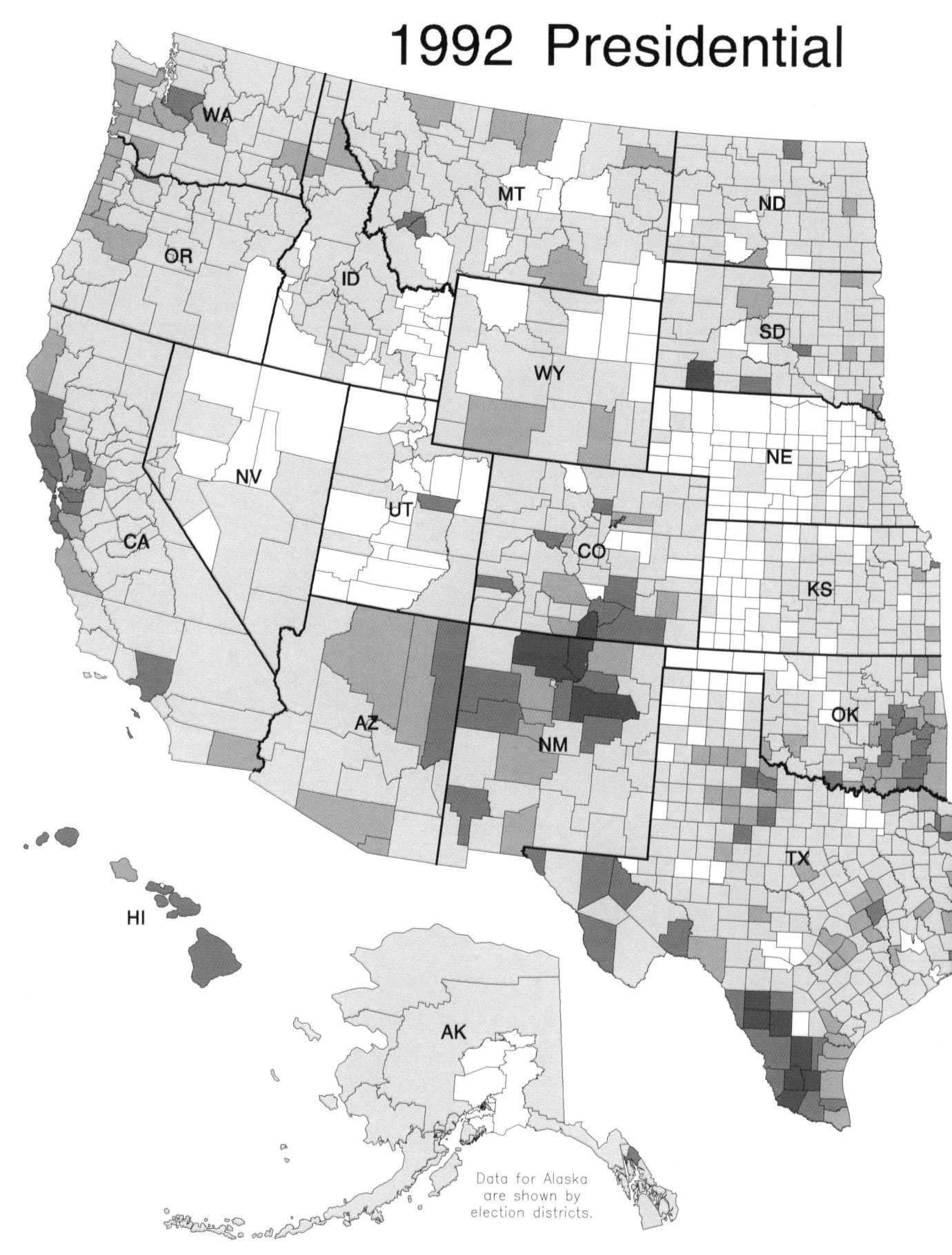

Election Results For
Bill Clinton (D)

By County

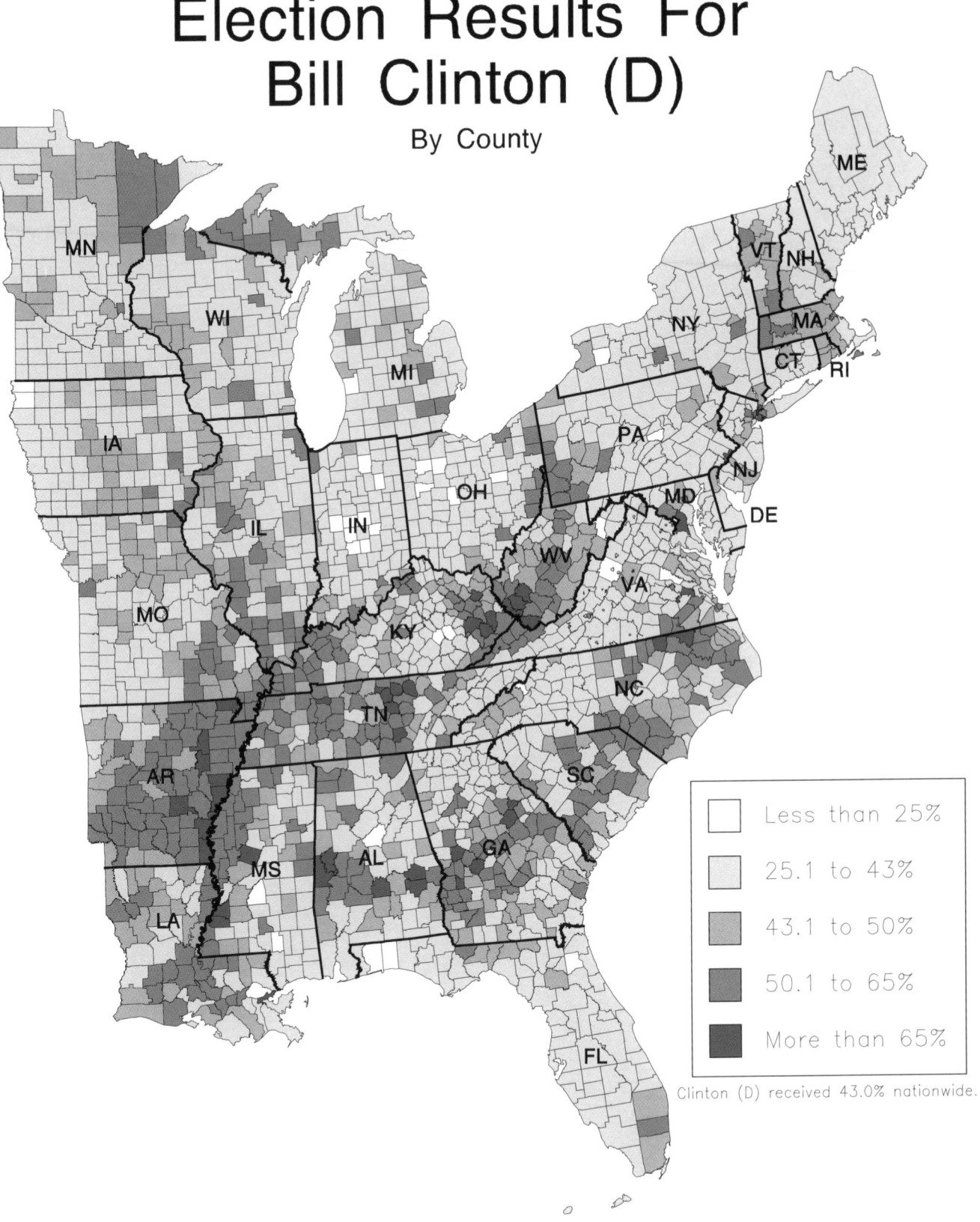

Less than 25%

25.1 to 43%

43.1 to 50%

50.1 to 65%

More than 65%

Clinton (D) received 43.0% nationwide.

1992 Presidential

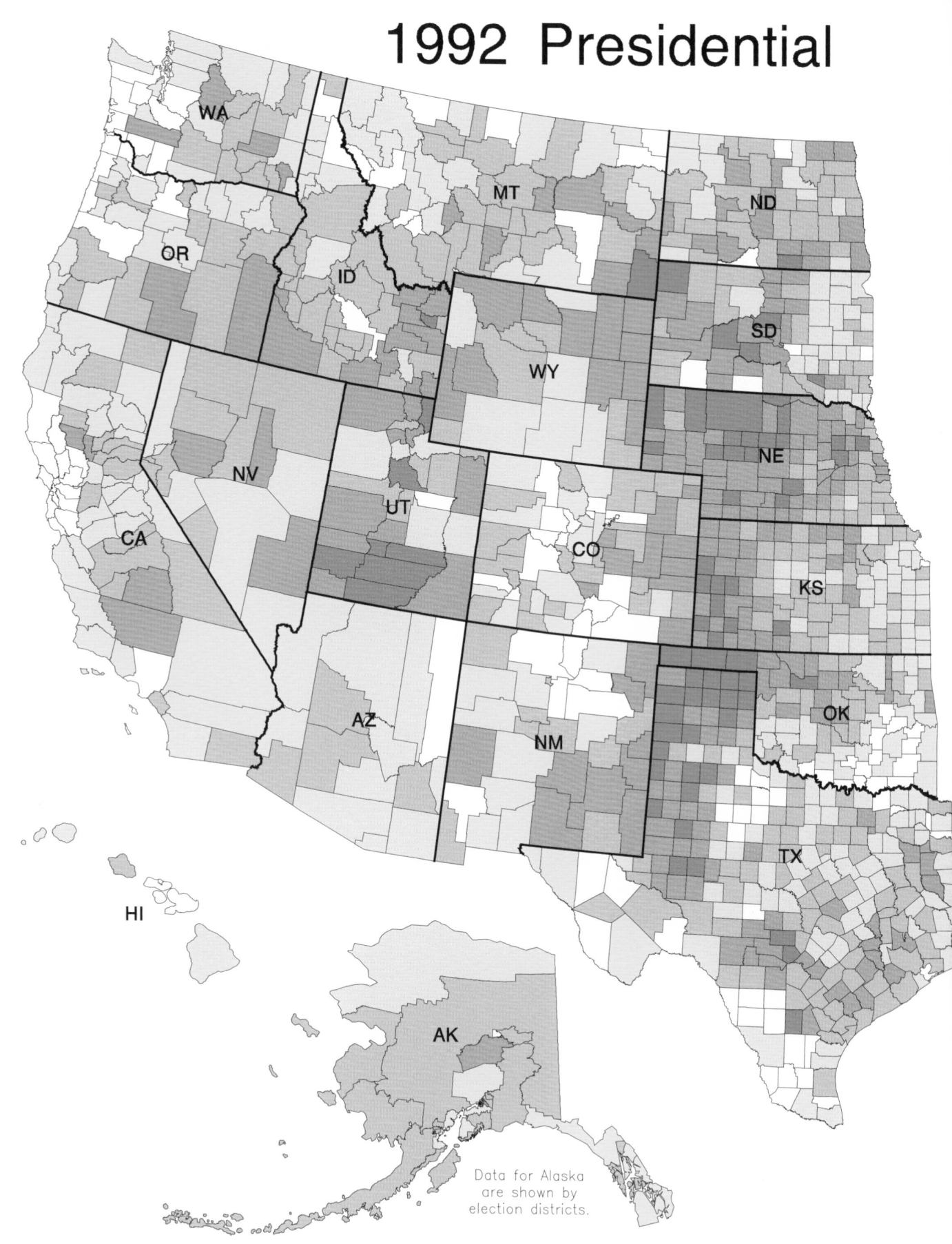

Data for Alaska
are shown by
election districts.

Election Results For George Bush (R)

By County

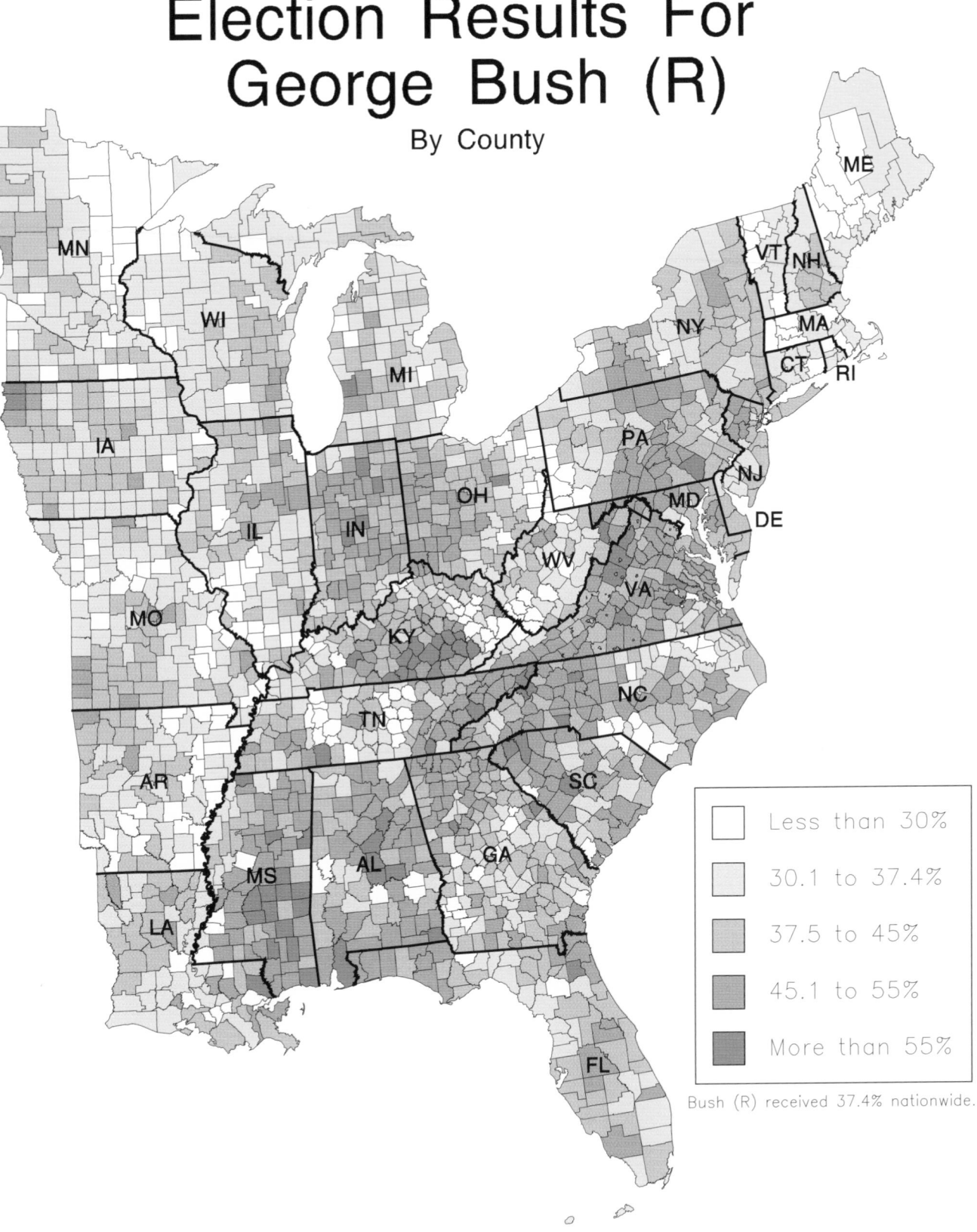

Less than 30%

30.1 to 37.4%

37.5 to 45%

45.1 to 55%

More than 55%

Bush (R) received 37.4% nationwide.

1992 Presidential

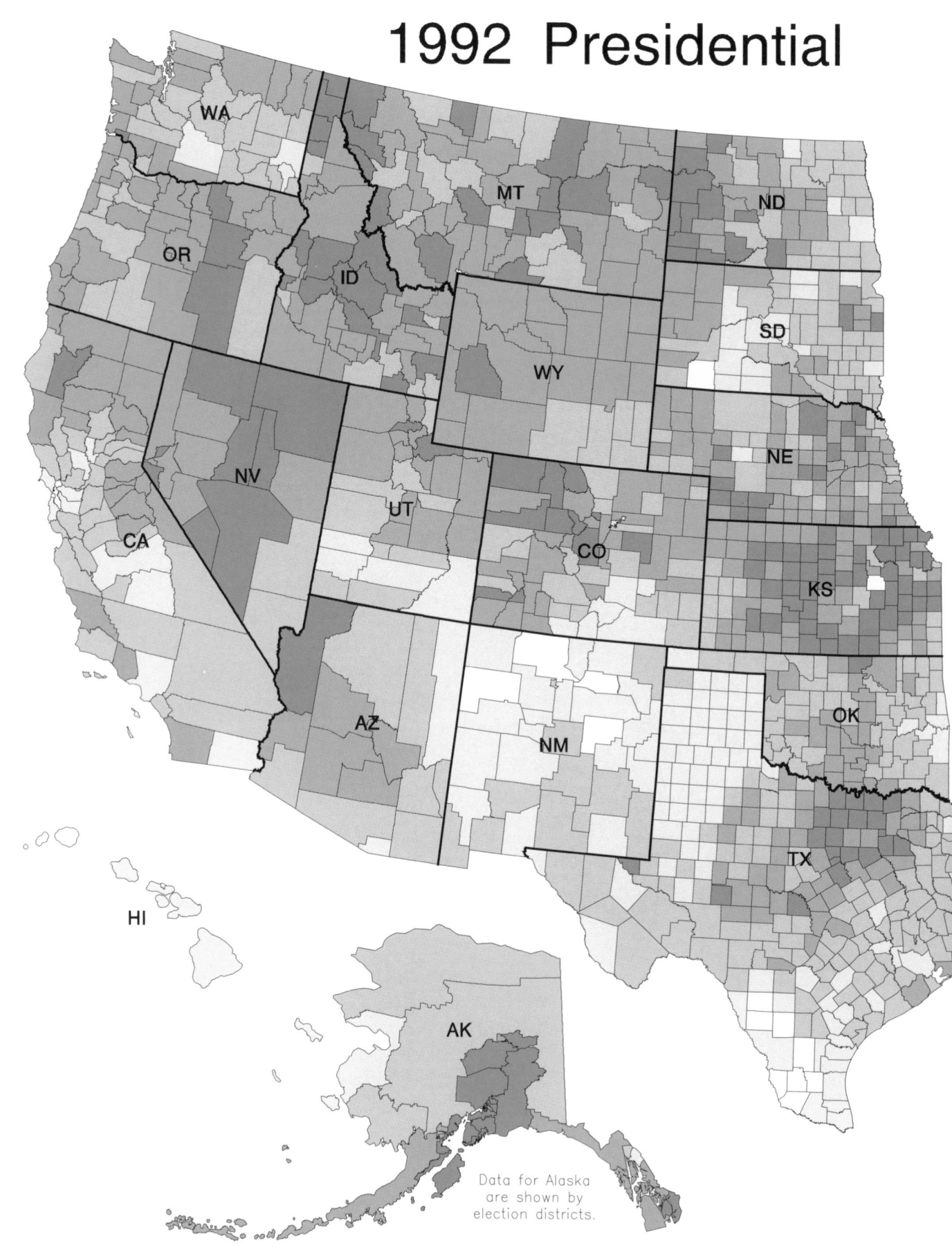

Data for Alaska
are shown by
election districts.

Election Results For
H. Ross Perot (I)
By County

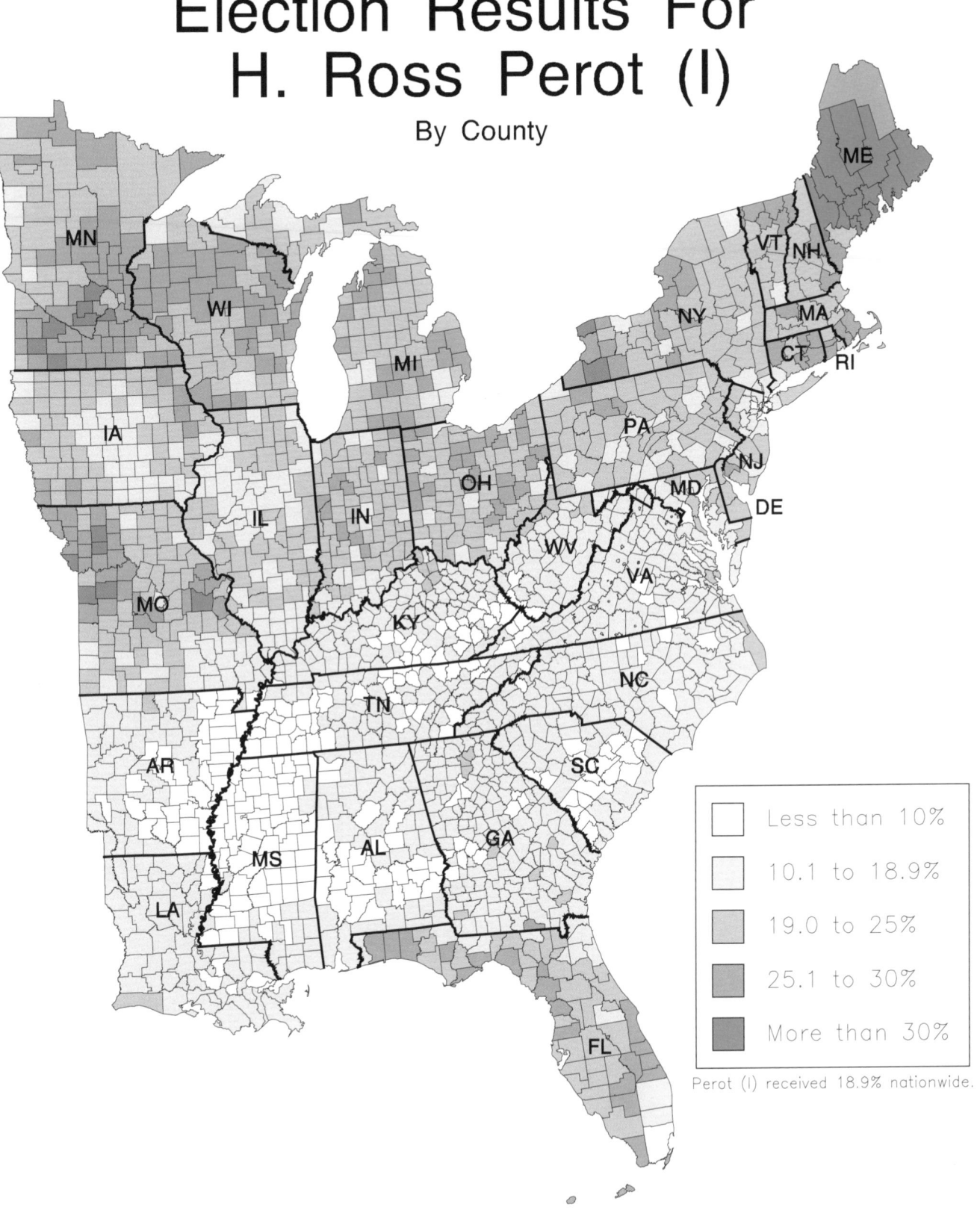

Legend:

- ☐ Less than 10%
- ☐ 10.1 to 18.9%
- ☐ 19.0 to 25%
- ☐ 25.1 to 30%
- ☐ More than 30%

Perot (I) received 18.9% nationwide.

1992 Congressional

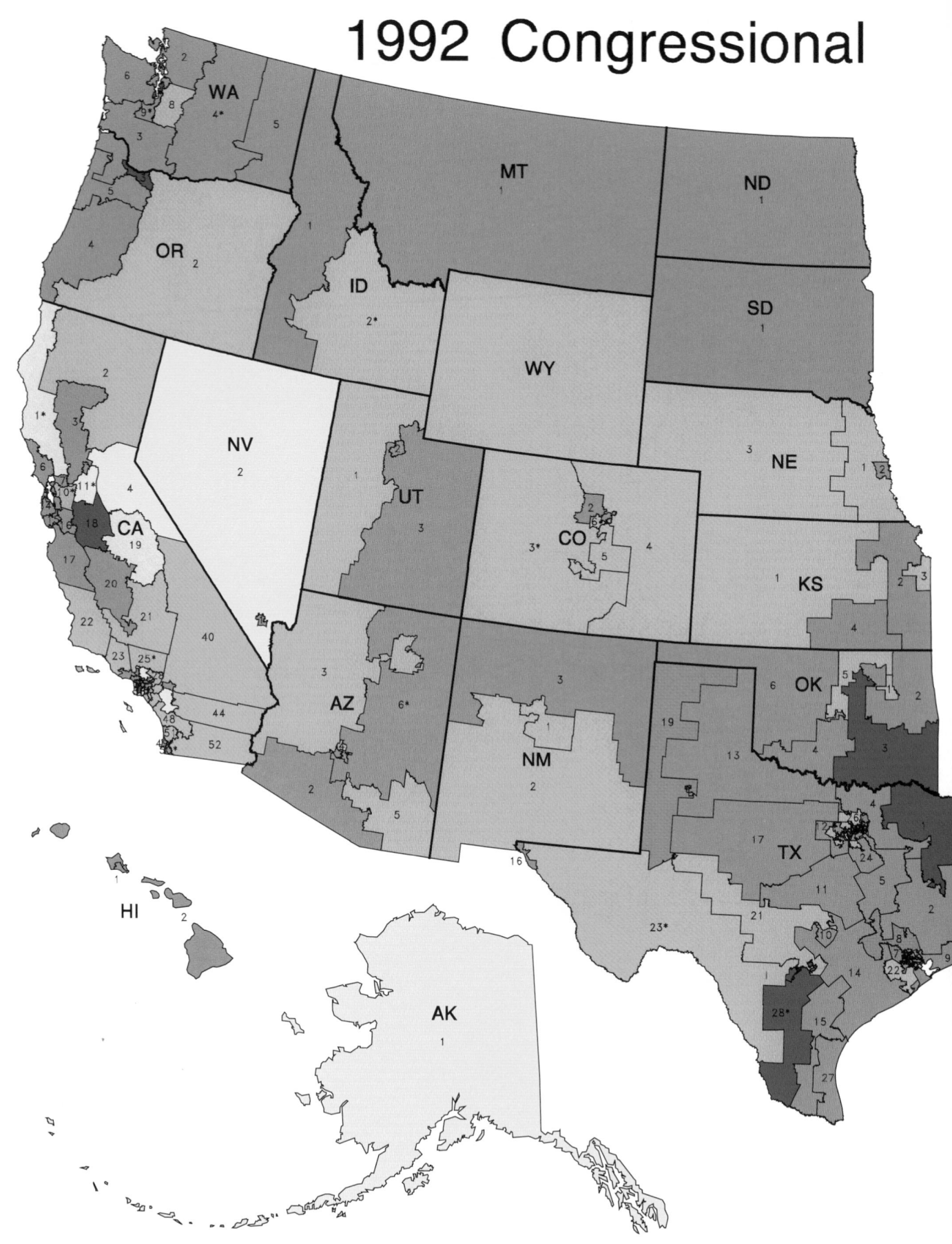

Election Results

Winner by Congressional District

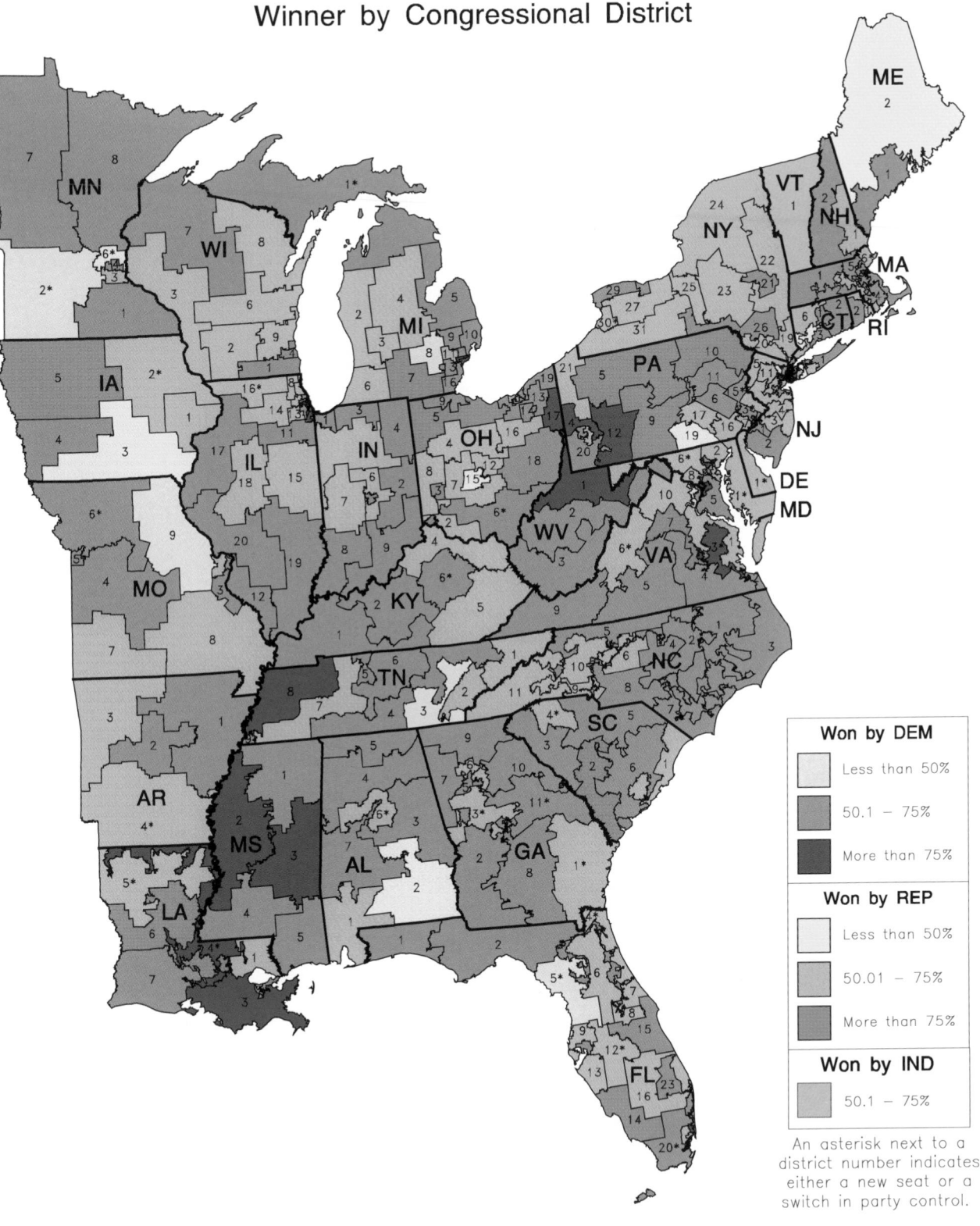

Won by DEM

	Less than 50%
	50.1 – 75%
	More than 75%

Won by REP

	Less than 50%
	50.01 – 75%
	More than 75%

Won by IND

| | 50.1 – 75% |

An asterisk next to a
district number indicates
either a new seat or a
switch in party control.

1992 Election Results
Control of State Senate

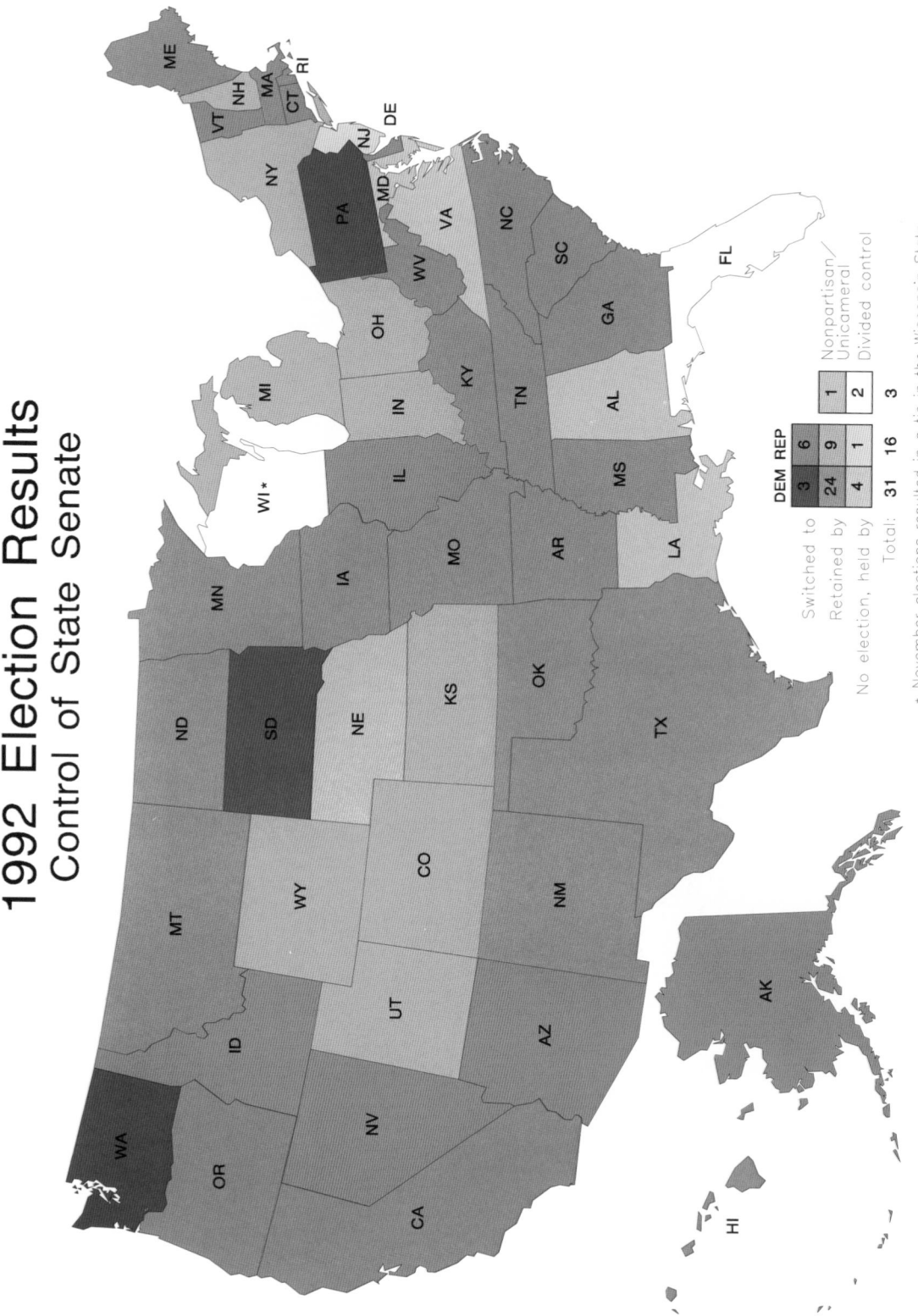

	DEM	REP
Switched to	3	6
Retained by	24	9
No election, held by	4	1
Total:	31	16

Nonpartisan/ Unicameral   1

Divided control   2

  3

* November elections resulted in a tie in the Wisconsin State Senate. Subsequent special elections to fill vacancies allowed Republicans to gain control of the chamber. As a result, Republicans control 17 State Senate chambers.

1992 Election Results
Control of State House

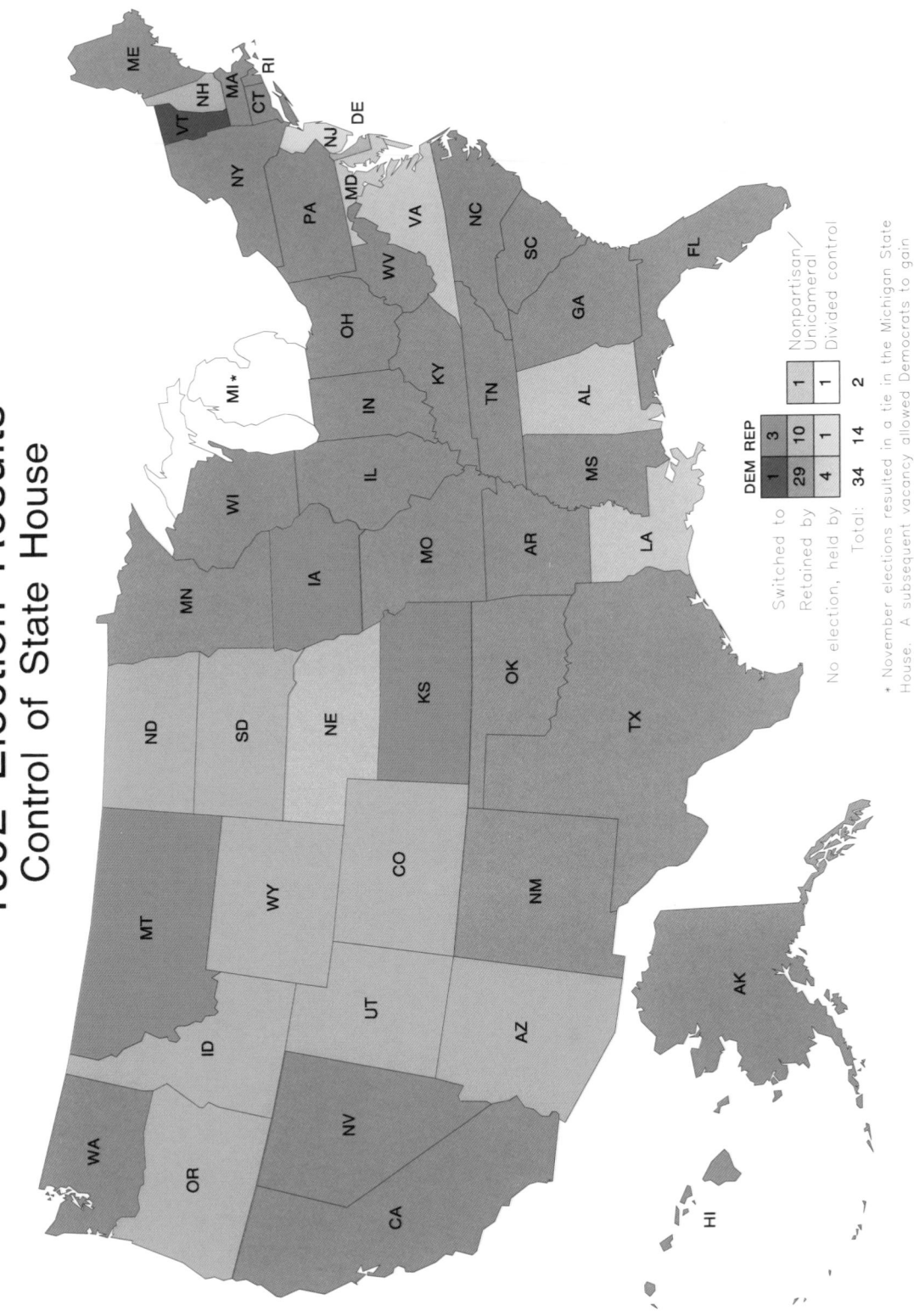

	DEM	REP
Switched to	1	3	1	Nonpartisan/ Unicameral
Retained by	29	10	1	Divided control
No election, held by	4	1		
Total:	34	14	2	

* November elections resulted in a tie in the Michigan State House. A subsequent vacancy allowed Democrats to gain control of the chamber. As a result, Democrats control 35 State House chambers.

1992 Gubernatorial Election Results

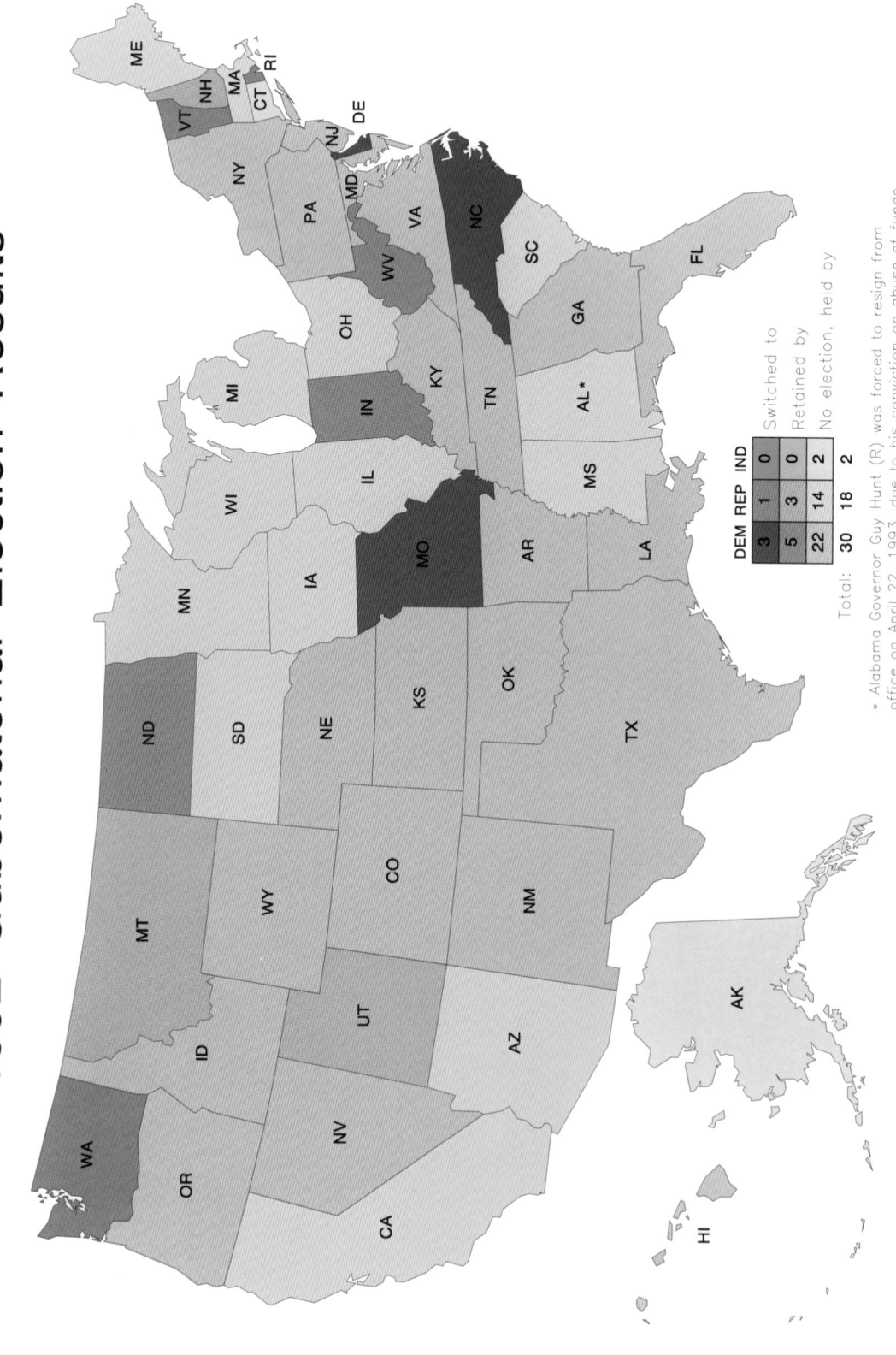

	DEM	REP	IND
	3	1	0	Switched to
	5	3	0	Retained by
	22	14	2	No election, held by
Total:	30	18	2	

* Alabama Governor Guy Hunt (R) was forced to resign from
office on April 22, 1993, due to his conviction on abuse of funds.
Democratic Lt. Governor Jim Folsom, Jr., was sworn in as governor,
thereby giving Democrats control of 31 gubernatorial seats as
compared to 17 for Republicans.